WHITAKER'S ALMANACK 1999

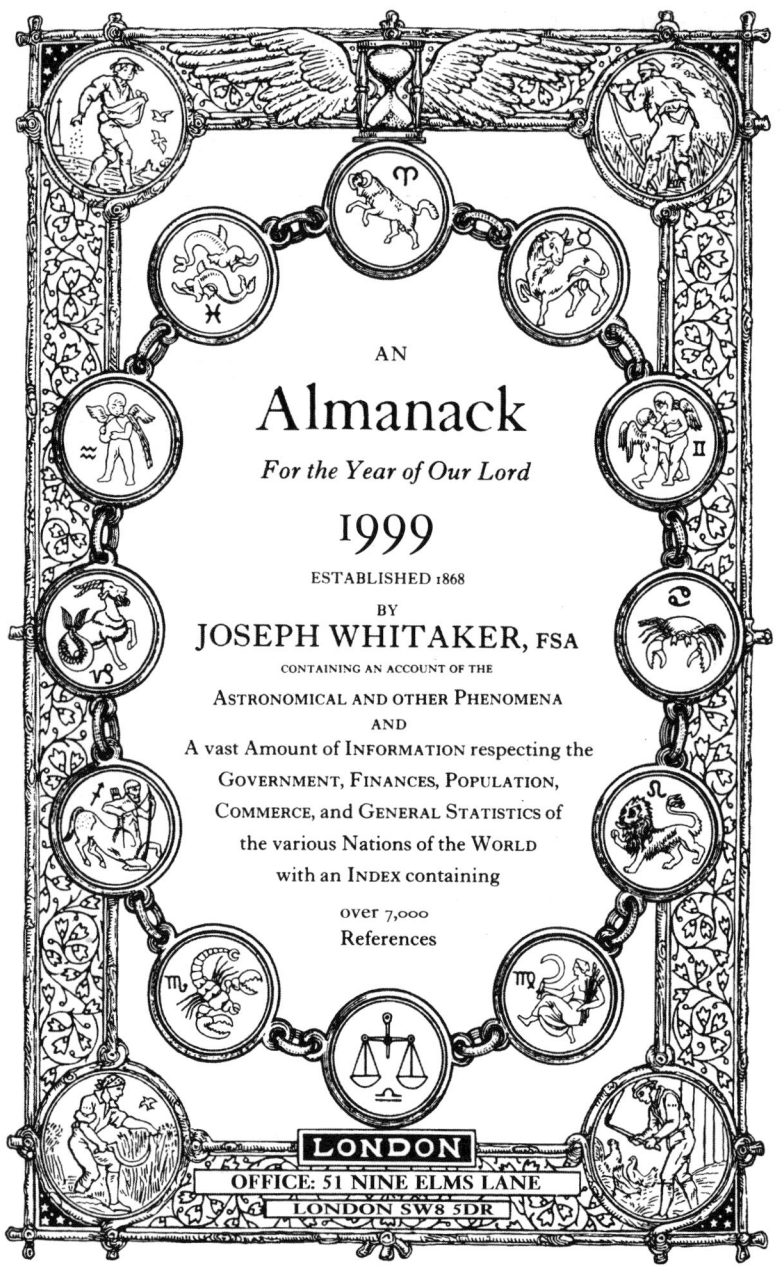

AN

Almanack

For the Year of Our Lord

1999

ESTABLISHED 1868

BY

JOSEPH WHITAKER, FSA

CONTAINING AN ACCOUNT OF THE

ASTRONOMICAL AND OTHER PHENOMENA

AND

A vast Amount of INFORMATION respecting the

GOVERNMENT, FINANCES, POPULATION,

COMMERCE, and GENERAL STATISTICS of

the various Nations of the WORLD

with an INDEX containing

over 7,000

References

LONDON

OFFICE: 51 NINE ELMS LANE
LONDON SW8 5DR

The traditional design of the title page for Whitaker's Almanack which has appeared in each edition since 1868

Whitaker's Almanack

1999

LONDON:
THE STATIONERY OFFICE

THE STATIONERY OFFICE LTD
51 Nine Elms Lane, London sw8 5DR

Whitaker's Almanack published annually since 1868
© 131st edition The Stationery Office Ltd 1998

Standard edition (1,280 pages)
Cloth covers
0 11 702240 3

Leather binding
0 11 702241 1

EDITORIAL CONSULTANTS
Sally Whitaker
Gyles Brandreth
Rupert Pennant-Rea

EDITORIAL STAFF
Hilary Marsden (*Editor*)
Bridie Macmahon; Neil Mackay (*Assistant Editors, UK*)
Daniel Carroll (*Assistant Editor, International*)
Surekha Davies (*Database Co-ordinator*)

Designed by Douglas Martin
Jacket designed by Bob Eames
Typeset by Page Bros (Norwich) Ltd
Printed and bound in Great Britain by
Clays Ltd, part of St Ives PLC, Bungay, Suffolk

Published by The Stationery Office and available from:
The Publications Centre
(mail, telephone and fax orders only)
PO Box 276, London sw8 5DT
General enquiries 0171-873 0011
Telephone orders 0171-873 9090
Fax orders 0171-873 8200

The Stationery Office Bookshops
123 Kingsway, London wc2b 6pq
0171-242 6393   Fax 0171-242 6394
16 Arthur Street, Belfast bt1 4gd
01232-238451   Fax 01232-235401
68–69 Bull Street, Birmingham b4 6ad
0121-236 9696   Fax 0121-236 9699
33 Wine Street, Bristol bs1 2bq
0117-926 4306   Fax 0117-929 4515
The Stationery Office Oriel Bookshop
The Friary, Cardiff cf1 4aa
01222-395548   Fax 01222-384347
71 Lothian Road, Edinburgh eh3 9az
0131-228 4181   Fax 0131-622 7017
9–21 Princess Street, Manchester m60 8as
0161-834 7201   Fax 0161-833 0634

The Stationery Office's Accredited Agents
(*see* Yellow Pages)

and through good booksellers

Contents

CONTENTS CONTINUED

Preface

TO THE 131ST ANNUAL VOLUME

The past year has seen dramatic progress towards a settlement in Northern Ireland, culminating in the historic peace agreement on Good Friday. The consequent moves towards self-government in Northern Ireland with the establishment of the new Northern Ireland assembly herald the similar developments which will take place in Scotland and Wales in the next few years as the Scottish parliament and Welsh assembly are set up. The progress of the legislation and the issues debated in the Westminster Parliament are recorded in the article on the year in Parliament, and developments to date are summarized in the Northern Ireland, Scotland and Wales parts of the Local Government section.

The environment has been of serious concern at both government and grass-roots level for some years. The international, European Union and UK initiatives to implement the Rio declaration are summarized in a new Environment section. The section on wildlife conservation has been expanded to add details of international and EU protection for endangered species and habitats to the existing information.

The nation's health is the subject of a new section of statistical data covering, for instance, the prevalence of drug-taking and the incidence of infectious diseases, as well as the Government's health strategy and targets.

The article about the National Health Service has been revised and expanded to include more information about NHS services, more statistical data and directories of the health authorities in the UK. In addition, new information and statistics about personal social services are included.

New information is included about religious observance in the UK and the existing information about faiths and the churches has been reorganized. The information on the royal households has also been reorganized, clarifying which positions are full-time permanent posts and which are purely honorary.

My thanks are due this year not only to the editorial team and our contributors but also to our new colleagues for ensuring that all ran as smoothly this year as in the past. I also wish to thank the many individuals and organizations who provide us with information or suggestions for further refinements to the contents of the Almanack.

51 NINE ELMS LANE
LONDON SW8 5DR
TEL: 0171-873 8442 (editorial office)
    0171-873 0011 (customer services)
E-MAIL: whitakers.almanack@theso.co.uk
WEB: http://www.whitakers-almanack.co.uk

HILARY MARSDEN
Editor
OCTOBER 1998

The Year 1999

CHRONOLOGICAL CYCLES AND ERAS

Dominical Letter	C
Epact	13
Golden Number (Lunar Cycle)	V
Julian Period	6712
Roman Indiction	7
Solar Cycle	20

	Beginning
Japanese year Heisei 11	1 January
Regnal year 48	6 February
Chinese year of the Rabbit	16 February
Hindu new year	18 March
Indian (Saka) year 1921	22 March
Sikh new year	14 April
Muslim year AH 1420	17 April
Jewish year AM 5760	11 September
Roman year 2752 AUC	

RELIGIOUS CALENDARS

Epiphany	6 January
Makara Sankranti	14 January
Vasant Panchami (Sarasvati-puja)	22 January
Presentation of Christ in the Temple	2 February
Mahashivaratri	14 February
Ash Wednesday	17 February
Holi	1 March
Chaitra (Hindu new year)	18 March
The Annunciation	25 March
Ramanavami	25 March
Maundy Thursday	1 April
Passover, first day	1 April
Good Friday	2 April
Easter Day (western churches)	4 April
Easter Day (Greek Orthodox)	11 April
Baisakhi Mela (Sikh new year)	14 April
Muslim new year	17 April
Rogation Sunday	9 May
Ascension Day	13 May
Feast of Weeks, first day	21 May
Pentecost (Whit Sunday)	23 May
Trinity Sunday	30 May
Corpus Christi	3 June
Martyrdom of Guru Arjan Dev Ji	17 June
Raksha-bandhan	26 August
Janmashtami	2 September
Jewish new year	11 September
Ganesh Chaturthi, first day	13 September
Yom Kippur (Day of Atonement)	20 September
Ganesh festival, last day	24 September
Feast of Tabernacles, first day	25 September
Durga-puja	10 October
Navaratri festival, first day	10 October
Sarasvati-puja	16 October
Dasara	19 October
All Saints' Day	1 November
Diwali (Hindu), first day	5 November
Diwali (Hindu), last day	10 November
Birthday of Guru Nanak Dev Ji	23 November
Advent Sunday	28 November
Chanucah, first day	4 December

CIVIL CALENDAR

Accession of Queen Elizabeth II	6 February
Duke of York's birthday	19 February
St David's Day	1 March
Commonwealth Day	8 March
Prince Edward's birthday	10 March
St Patrick's Day	17 March
Birthday of Queen Elizabeth II	21 April
St George's Day	23 April
Coronation of Queen Elizabeth II	2 June
Duke of Edinburgh's birthday	10 June
The Queen's Official Birthday	12 June
Queen Elizabeth the Queen Mother's birthday	4 August
Princess Royal's birthday	15 August
Princess Margaret's birthday	21 August
Lord Mayor's Day	13 November
Prince of Wales's birthday	14 November
Remembrance Sunday	14 November
Wedding Day of Queen Elizabeth II	20 November
St Andrew's Day	30 November

LEGAL CALENDAR

LAW TERMS

Hilary Term	11 January to 31 March
Easter Term	13 April to 28 May
Trinity Term	8 June to 30 July
Michaelmas Term	1 October to 21 December

QUARTER DAYS

England, Wales and Northern Ireland

Lady	25 March
Midsummer	24 June
Michaelmas	29 September
Christmas	25 December

TERM DAYS

Scotland

Candlemas	28 February
Whitsunday	28 May
Lammas	28 August
Martinmas	28 November
Removal Terms	28 May, 28 November

1999

JANUARY

Sunday		3	10	17	24	31
Monday		4	11	18	25	
Tuesday		5	12	19	26	
Wednesday		6	13	20	27	
Thursday		7	14	21	28	
Friday	1	8	15	22	29	
Saturday	2	9	16	23	30	

FEBRUARY

Sunday		7	14	21	28
Monday	1	8	15	22	
Tuesday	2	9	16	23	
Wednesday	3	10	17	24	
Thursday	4	11	18	25	
Friday	5	12	19	26	
Saturday	6	13	20	27	

MARCH

Sunday		7	14	21	28
Monday	1	8	15	22	29
Tuesday	2	9	16	23	30
Wednesday	3	10	17	24	31
Thursday	4	11	18	25	
Friday	5	12	19	26	
Saturday	6	13	20	27	

APRIL

Sunday		4	11	18	25
Monday		5	12	19	26
Tuesday		6	13	20	27
Wednesday		7	14	21	28
Thursday	1	8	15	22	29
Friday	2	9	16	23	30
Saturday	3	10	17	24	

MAY

Sunday		2	9	16	23	30
Monday		3	10	17	24	31
Tuesday		4	11	18	25	
Wednesday		5	12	19	26	
Thursday		6	13	20	27	
Friday		7	14	21	28	
Saturday	1	8	15	22	29	

JUNE

Sunday		6	13	20	27
Monday		7	14	21	28
Tuesday	1	8	15	22	29
Wednesday	2	9	16	23	30
Thursday	3	10	17	24	
Friday	4	11	18	25	
Saturday	5	12	19	26	

JULY

Sunday		4	11	18	25
Monday		5	12	19	26
Tuesday		6	13	20	27
Wednesday		7	14	21	28
Thursday	1	8	15	22	29
Friday	2	9	16	23	30
Saturday	3	10	17	24	31

AUGUST

Sunday	1	8	15	22	29
Monday	2	9	16	23	30
Tuesday	3	10	17	24	31
Wednesday	4	11	18	25	
Thursday	5	12	19	26	
Friday	6	13	20	27	
Saturday	7	14	21	28	

SEPTEMBER

Sunday		5	12	19	26
Monday		6	13	20	27
Tuesday		7	14	21	28
Wednesday	1	8	15	22	29
Thursday	2	9	16	23	30
Friday	3	10	17	24	
Saturday	4	11	18	25	

OCTOBER

Sunday		3	10	17	24	31
Monday		4	11	18	25	
Tuesday		5	12	19	26	
Wednesday		6	13	20	27	
Thursday		7	14	21	28	
Friday	1	8	15	22	29	
Saturday	2	9	16	23	30	

NOVEMBER

Sunday		7	14	21	28
Monday	1	8	15	22	29
Tuesday	2	9	16	23	30
Wednesday	3	10	17	24	
Thursday	4	11	18	25	
Friday	5	12	19	26	
Saturday	6	13	20	27	

DECEMBER

Sunday		5	12	19	26
Monday		6	13	20	27
Tuesday		7	14	21	28
Wednesday	1	8	15	22	29
Thursday	2	9	16	23	30
Friday	3	10	17	24	31
Saturday	4	11	18	25	

PUBLIC HOLIDAYS

	England and Wales	Scotland	Northern Ireland
New Year	†1 January	1, †4 January	†1 January
St Patrick's Day	—	—	17 March
*Good Friday	2 April	2 April	2 April
Easter Monday	5 April	—	5 April
Early May	†3 May	3 May	†3 May
Spring	31 May	†31 May	31 May
Battle of the Boyne	—	—	‡12 July
Summer	30 August	2 August	30 August
*Christmas	25, 26, 27, †28 December	25, 26, †27, †28 December	25, 26, 27, †28 December
New Year's Eve	†31 December	†31 December	†31 December

*In England, Wales and Northern Ireland, Christmas Day and Good Friday are common law holidays
In the Channel Islands, Liberation Day (9 May) is a bank and public holiday
†Subject to royal proclamation
‡Subject to proclamation by the Secretary of State for Northern Ireland

2000

JANUARY

Sunday		2	9	16	23	30
Monday		3	10	17	24	31
Tuesday		4	11	18	25
Wednesday		5	12	19	26
Thursday		6	13	20	27
Friday		7	14	21	28
Saturday	1	8	15	22	29

FEBRUARY

Sunday		6	13	20	27
Monday		7	14	21	28
Tuesday	1	8	15	22	29
Wednesday	2	9	16	23
Thursday	3	10	17	24
Friday	4	11	18	25
Saturday	5	12	19	26

MARCH

Sunday		5	12	19	26
Monday		6	13	20	27
Tuesday		7	14	21	28
Wednesday	1	8	15	22	29
Thursday	2	9	16	23	30
Friday	3	10	17	24	31
Saturday	4	11	18	25

APRIL

Sunday		2	9	16	23	30
Monday		3	10	17	24
Tuesday		4	11	18	25
Wednesday		5	12	19	26
Thursday		6	13	20	27
Friday		7	14	21	28
Saturday	1	8	15	22	29

MAY

Sunday		7	14	21	28
Monday	1	8	15	22	29
Tuesday	2	9	16	23	30
Wednesday	3	10	17	24	31
Thursday	4	11	18	25
Friday	5	12	19	26
Saturday	6	13	20	27

JUNE

Sunday		4	11	18	25
Monday		5	12	19	26
Tuesday		6	13	20	27
Wednesday		7	14	21	28
Thursday	1	8	15	22	29
Friday	2	9	16	23	30
Saturday	3	10	17	24

JULY

Sunday		2	9	16	23	30
Monday		3	10	17	24	31
Tuesday		4	11	18	25
Wednesday		5	12	19	26
Thursday		6	13	20	27
Friday		7	14	21	28
Saturday	1	8	15	22	29

AUGUST

Sunday		6	13	20	27
Monday		7	14	21	28
Tuesday	1	8	15	22	29
Wednesday	2	9	16	23	30
Thursday	3	10	17	24	31
Friday	4	11	18	25
Saturday	5	12	19	26

SEPTEMBER

Sunday		3	10	17	24
Monday		4	11	18	25
Tuesday		5	12	19	26
Wednesday		6	13	20	27
Thursday		7	14	21	28
Friday	1	8	15	22	29
Saturday	2	9	16	23	30

OCTOBER

Sunday	1	8	15	22	29
Monday	2	9	16	23	30
Tuesday	3	10	17	24	31
Wednesday	4	11	18	25
Thursday	5	12	19	26
Friday	6	13	20	27
Saturday	7	14	21	28

NOVEMBER

Sunday		5	12	19	26
Monday		6	13	20	27
Tuesday		7	14	21	28
Wednesday	1	8	15	22	29
Thursday	2	9	16	23	30
Friday	3	10	17	24
Saturday	4	11	18	25

DECEMBER

Sunday		3	10	17	24	31
Monday		4	11	18	25
Tuesday		5	12	19	26
Wednesday		6	13	20	27
Thursday		7	14	21	28
Friday	1	8	15	22	29
Saturday	2	9	16	23	30

PUBLIC HOLIDAYS

	England and Wales	Scotland	Northern Ireland
New Year	†3 January	3, †4 January	†3 January
St Patrick's Day	—	—	17 March
*Good Friday	21 April	21 April	21 April
Easter Monday	24 April	—	24 April
Early May	†1 May	1 May	†1 May
Spring	29 May	†29 May	29 May
Battle of the Boyne	—	—	‡12 July
Summer	28 August	7 August	28 August
*Christmas	25, 26 December	25, †26 December	25, 26 December

FORTHCOMING EVENTS 1999

This is the UN International Year for the Older Persons and the Arts Council Year for Architecture and Design
The European City of Culture is Weimar, Germany
* Provisional dates

8 January – 17 January	London International Boat Show Earls Court, London
23 January – 18 April	Monet in the 20th Century Exhibition Royal Academy of Arts, London
19 February – 6 June	J. E. Millais Exhibition National Portrait Gallery, London
7 March – 9 March	Liberal Democrat Party Spring Conference Harrogate International Centre
11 March – 14 March	Cruft's Dog Show National Exhibition Centre, Birmingham
18 March – 11 April	Ideal Home Exhibition Earls Court, London
25 March – 25 July	Arts of the Sikh Kingdoms Exhibition Victoria and Albert Museum, London
28 March – 30 March	London International Book Fair Olympia, London
23 April	World Book Day
*May – October	Chichester Festival Theatre season
15 May – 9 October	Pitlochry Festival Theatre season Tayside
19 May – 28 August	Glyndebourne Festival Opera season Lewes, E. Sussex
21 May – 6 June	Bath International Music Festival
27 May – 28 May	Chelsea Flower Show Royal Hospital, Chelsea, London
28 May – 6 June	Hay Festival of Literature Hay-on-Wye, Hereford
*June	York Mystery Plays York Minster
*7 June – 22 August	Royal Academy Summer Exhibition Piccadilly, London
11 June – 27 June	Aldeburgh Festival of Music and Arts Suffolk
12 June	Trooping the Colour Horse Guards Parade, London
2 July – 11 July	York Early Music Festival
3 July – 18 July	Cheltenham International Festival of Music
5 July – 8 July	The Royal Show Stoneleigh Park, Kenilworth, Warks
6 July – 11 July	Hampton Court Palace Flower Show East Molesey, Surrey
16 July – 11 September	Promenade Concerts season Royal Albert Hall, London
*16 July – 24 July	Welsh Proms 1999 St David's Hall, Cardiff
*16 July – 31 July	Buxton Festival Derbyshire
20 July – 1 August	Royal Tournament Earls Court, London
*27 July – 29 July	Wisley Flower Show RHS Garden, Wisley, Surrey
31 July – 7 August	Royal National Eisteddfod of Wales Anglesey

6 August – 28 August	Edinburgh Military Tattoo Edinburgh Castle
12 August – 13 August	Battle of the Flowers Jersey
15 August – 4 September	Edinburgh International Festival
21 August – 27 August	Three Choirs Festival Worcester
29 August – 30 August	Notting Hill Carnival Notting Hill, London
3 September – 7 November	Blackpool Illuminations
4 September	Braemar Royal Highland Gathering Aberdeenshire
11 September – 19 September	Southampton International Boat Show Western Esplanade, Southampton
13 September – 16 September	TUC Annual Congress Brighton
19 September – 23 September	Liberal Democrat Party Autumn Conference Edinburgh
27 September – 2 October	Labour Party Conference Bournemouth International Centre
5 October – 8 October	Conservative Party Conference Blackpool
*5 November – 22 November	London International Film Festival
7 November	London to Brighton Veteran Car Run
*7 November – 9 November	CBI Annual Conference Birmingham
11 November	Two-minute silence at 11 a.m.
13 November	Lord Mayor's Procession and Show City of London
17 November – 28 November	Huddersfield Contemporary Music Festival

SPORTS EVENTS

18 January – 31 January	Tennis: Australian Open Championships Melbourne, Australia
*6 February	Rugby Union: Scotland v. Wales Murrayfield, Edinburgh Rugby Union: Ireland v. France Lansdowne Road, Dublin
*20 February	Rugby Union: Wales v. Ireland Wembley Stadium, London Rugby Union: England v. Scotland Twickenham, London
5 March – 7 March	Athletics: World Indoor Championships Maebashi, Japan
*6 March	Rugby Union: Ireland v. England Lansdowne Road, Dublin Rugby Union: France v. Wales Parc des Princes, Paris
*20 March	Rugby Union: Scotland v. Ireland Murrayfield, Edinburgh Rugby Union: England v. France Twickenham, London
27 March – 28 March	World Cross-Country Championships Belfast
*3 April	Oxford and Cambridge Boat Race Putney to Mortlake, London

3 April – 11 April	World Curling Championships
	St John, New Brunswick, Canada
*10 April	Rugby Union: France v. Scotland
	Parc des Princes, Paris
	Rugby Union: Wales v. England
	Wembley Stadium, London
*17 April – 3 May	Snooker: World Professional
	Championships
	Crucible Theatre, Sheffield
18 April	Athletics: London Marathon
1 May	Rugby League: Challenge Cup final
6 May – 9 May	Badminton Horse Trial
	Badminton, Wilts
9 May	Football: Welsh FA Cup final
13 May – 16 May	Royal Windsor Horse Show
	Home Park, Windsor
15 May	Rugby Union: Tetley's Bitter Cup
	final
	Twickenham, London
17 May – 23 May	Badminton: World Championships
	Copenhagen, Denmark
22 May	Football: FA Cup final
	Wembley Stadium, London
*22 May	Rugby Union: County
	Championship finals
	Twickenham, London
24 May – 6 June	Tennis: French Open
	Championships
	Paris
29 May	Football: Scottish FA Cup final
	Hampden Park, Glasgow
31 May – 5 June	Golf: British Amateur
	Championship
	Royal County Down Golf Club and
	Kilkeel Golf Club
5 June – 11 June	TT Motorcycle Races
	Isle of Man
20 June	Cricket: World Cup final
	Lord's, London
21 June – 4 July	Lawn Tennis: All-England
	Championships
	Wimbledon, London
30 June – 4 July	Rowing: Henley Royal Regatta
	Henley-on-Thames, Oxon
1 July – 5 July	Cricket: 1st Test Match, England v.
	New Zealand
	Edgbaston, Birmingham
10 July – 24 July	Shooting: NRA Imperial Meeting
	Bisley Camp, Woking, Surrey
*11 July	British Formula 1 Grand Prix
	Silverstone, Northants
*12 July – 25 July	Yachting: Admiral's Cup
	Isle of Wight
15 July – 18 July	Golf: The Open
	Carnoustie
22 July – 26 July	Cricket: 2nd Test Match, England v.
	New Zealand
	Lord's, London
31 July –	Yachting: Cowes Week
7 August	Isle of Wight
1 August –	World Orienteering Championships
8 August	Inverness
5 August –	Cricket: 3rd Test Match, England v.
9 August	New Zealand
	Old Trafford, Manchester
*7 August	Yachting: Fastnet Race
	Isle of Wight

19 August –	Cricket: 4th Test Match, England v.
23 August	New Zealand
	The Oval, London
20 August –	Athletics: World Championships
29 August	Seville, Spain
22 August –	World Rowing Championships
29 August	St Catharine's, Canada
*24 August –	European Show Jumping
30 August	Championships
	Hickstead, Sussex
30 August –	Tennis: US Open Championships
12 September	New York, USA
*2 September –	Burghley Horse Trials
5 September	Burghley, Lincs
*5 September	Cricket: Natwest Trophy final
	Lord's, London
11 September –	Golf: Walker Cup
12 September	Nairn Golf Club
24 September –	Golf: Ryder Cup
26 September	Boston, USA
27 September –	Tennis: Grand Slam Cup
3 October	Munich, Germany
*29 September –	Horse of the Year Show
3 October	Wembley Arena, London
*6 November	Rugby Union: World Cup final
	Cardiff
29 November	Tennis: Davis Cup final

Horse-racing*	
18 March	Cheltenham Gold Cup
27 March	Lincoln Handicap
10 April	Grand National
	Aintree, Liverpool
1 May	Two Thousand Guineas
	Newmarket
2 May	One Thousand Guineas
	Newmarket
4 June	The Oaks
	Epsom
4 June	Coronation Cup
	Epsom
5 June	The Derby
	Epsom
15 June – 18 June	Royal Ascot
24 July	King George VI and Queen
	Elizabeth Diamond Stakes
	Ascot
8 September	St Leger
	Doncaster
2 October	Cambridgeshire Handicap
	Newmarket
16 October	Cesarewitch
	Newmarket

CENTENARIES OF 1999

1499	
23 November	Perkin Warbeck, pretender to the throne of Henry VII, died
1599	
22 March	Sir Anthony van Dyck, painter, born
25 April	Oliver Cromwell, Lord Protector 1653–8, born
1699	
21 April	Jean Racine, French playwright, died
1799	
19 March	Earl of Derby, Prime Minister 1852, 1858-9, 1866-8
18 May	Pierre de Beaumarchais, French author, died
14 December	George Washington, first President of the United States of America, died
1899	
7 January	Francis Poulenc, composer, born
17 January	Nevil Shute, novelist, born
29 January	Alfred Sisley, painter, died
27 February	Prof. Charles Best, Canadian physiologist who discovered insulin, born
22 April	Vladimir Nabokov, Russian-born novelist, born
23 April	Dame Ngaio Marsh, New Zealand crime novelist, born
29 April	'Duke' Ellington, American jazz pianist and composer, born
8 May	Friedrich von Hayek, Austrian-born political economist, born
10 May	Fred Astaire, American actor, singer and dancer, born
24 May	Suzanne Lenglen, French tennis player, born
3 June	Johann Strauss (the younger), Austrian composer, died
1 July	Charles Laughton, actor, born
13 August	Sir Alfred Hitchcock, film director and producer, born
16 August	Robert Bunsen, German chemist, died
24 August	Jorge Luis Borges, Argentinian novelist and poet, born
27 August	C. S. Forester, novelist and biographer, born
15 December	Harold Abrahams, athlete, born
16 December	Sir Noel Coward, actor and playwright, born
25 December	Humphrey Bogart, American actor, born

CENTENARIES OF 2000

1400	
14 February	Richard II, King 1377–99, killed
25 October	Geoffrey Chaucer, poet, died
1500	
29 May	Bartolomeu Diaz, Portuguese navigator who sailed around the Cape of Good Hope, died
1 November	Benvenuto Cellini, Italian sculptor and engraver, born
1600	
17 January	Pedro Caldéron de la Barca, Spanish playwright, born
19 November	Charles I, King 1625–49, born
1700	
1 May	John Dryden, poet, died
1800	
24 January	Sir Edwin Chadwick, social reformer, born
11 February	William Fox Talbot, photography pioneer, born
25 April	William Cowper, poet, died
9 May	John Brown, American slavery abolitionist, born
14 June	Battle of Marengo
25 October	Thomas, Lord Macaulay, historian, born
1900	
20 January	John Ruskin, author and art critic, died
24 January	Battle of Spion Kop, Boer War
22 February	Luis Buñuel, Spanish film director, born
27 February	Labour Party founded
28 February	Relief of Ladysmith, Boer War
2 March	Kurt Weill, German-born composer, born
2 March	Lord Cottesloe, soldier and philanthropist, born
5 April	Spencer Tracy, American actor, born
19 April	Richard Hughes, novelist, born
25 April	Gladwyn Jebb, diplomat, born
17 May	Relief of Mafeking, Boer War
28 May	Sir George Grove, musicologist, died
6 June	Arthur Askey, comedian, born
13 June	Boxer Rebellion broke out in China
25 June	Louis, Earl Mountbatten of Burma, born
2 July	Sir Tyrone Guthrie, theatre producer, born
4 July	Louis Armstrong, American trumpeter, born
10 July	Evelyn Laye, actress, born
4 August	Queen Elizabeth the Queen Mother born
25 August	Friedrich Nietzsche, philosopher, died
7 September	Joan Cross, opera singer, born
8 October	Sir Geoffrey Jellicoe, architect, born
16 October	Edward Ardizzone, illustrator, born
23 October	Douglas Jardine, cricketer, born
14 November	Aaron Copland, American composer, born
22 November	Sir Arthur Sullivan, composer, died
30 November	Oscar Wilde, novelist and playwright, died
16 December	Sir Victor Pritchett, author, born

Astronomy

The following pages give astronomical data for each month of the year 1999. There are four pages of data for each month. All data are given for 0h Greenwich Mean Time (GMT), i.e. at the midnight at the beginning of the day named. This applies also to data for the months when British Summer Time is in operation (for dates, *see* below).

The astronomical data are given in a form suitable for observation with the naked eye or with a small telescope. These data do not attempt to replace the *Astronomical Almanac* for professional astronomers.

A fuller explanation of how to use the astronomical data is given on pages 71–3.

CALENDAR FOR EACH MONTH

The calendar for each month shows dates of religious, civil and legal significance for the year 1999.

The days in bold type are the principal holy days and the festivals and greater holy days of the Church of England as set out in the calendar authorized for use from 1997. Observance of certain festivals and greater holy days is transferred if the day falls on a principal holy day. The calendar shows the date on which holy days and festivals are to be observed in 1999.

The days in small capitals are dates of significance in the calendars of non-Anglican denominations and non-Christian religions.

The days in italic type are dates of civil and legal significance. The royal anniversaries shown in italic type are the days on which the Union flag is to be flown.

The rest of the calendar comprises days of general interest and the dates of birth or death of well-known people.

Fuller explanations of the various calendars can be found under Time Measurement and Calendars (pages 81–9).

The zodiacal signs through which the Sun is passing during each month are illustrated. The date of transition from one sign to the next, to the nearest hour, is given under Astronomical Phenomena.

JULIAN DATE

The Julian date on 1999 January 0.0 is 2451178.5. To find the Julian date for any other date in 1999 (at 0h GMT), add the day-of-the-year number on the extreme right of the calendar for each month to the Julian date for January 0.0.

SEASONS

The seasons are defined astronomically as follows:

Spring from the vernal equinox to the summer solstice
Summer from the summer solstice to the autumnal equinox
Autumn from the autumnal equinox to the winter solstice
Winter from the winter solstice to the vernal equinox

The seasons in 1999 are:

Northern hemisphere

Vernal equinox	March 21d 02h GMT
Summer solstice	June 21d 20h GMT
Autumnal equinox	September 23d 12h GMT
Winter solstice	December 22d 08h GMT

Southern hemisphere

Autumnal equinox	March 20d 02h GMT
Winter solstice	June 21d 20h GMT
Vernal equinox	September 23d 12h GMT
Summer solstice	December 22d 08h GMT

The longest day of the year, measured from sunrise to sunset, is at the summer solstice. For the remainder of this century the longest day in the United Kingdom will fall each year on 21 June. *See also* page 81.

The shortest day of the year is at the winter solstice. For the remainder of this century the shortest day in the United Kingdom will fall on 22 December in 1999, and on 21 December in 2000. *See also* page 81.

The equinox is the point at which day and night are of equal length all over the world. *See also* page 81.

In popular parlance, the seasons in the northern hemisphere comprise the following months:

Spring	March, April, May
Summer	June, July, August
Autumn	September, October, November
Winter	December, January, February

BRITISH SUMMER TIME

British Summer Time is the legal time for general purposes during the period in which it is in operation (*see also* page 75). During this period, clocks are kept one hour ahead of Greenwich Mean Time. The hour of changeover is 01h Greenwich Mean Time. The duration of Summer Time in 1999 is from March 28 01h GMT to October 31 01h GMT.

TOTAL ECLIPSE OF THE SUN 1999

On 11 August 1999 the whole of the UK will, weather permitting, be able to see a partial eclipse of the Sun, with a total eclipse being visible in Southern Cornwall and Devon, and Alderney; for full details, *see* page 66. This is the first total eclipse to cross the UK since 1927 (apart from one grazing northern Shetland in 1954); the next will not be until 2090 for the mainland, 2081 for the Channel Islands.

Safety in viewing an eclipse is paramount, as the retina can be damaged if suitable eye protection or instruments are not used. A mylar viewer is recommended.

January 1999

FIRST MONTH, 31 DAYS. *Janus*, god of the portal, facing two ways, past and future

1	*Friday*	**Naming and Circumcision of Jesus.** *Bank Holiday in UK*	*week* 52 *day* 1
2	*Saturday*	Isaac Asimov b. 1920. David Bailey b. 1938	2
3	*Sunday*	**2nd S. of Christmas.** Clement Attlee b. 1883	*week* 1 *day* 3
4	*Monday*	*Bank Holiday in Scotland.* Albert Camus d. 1960	4
5	*Tuesday*	Twelfth Night. Frederic, Lord Leighton d. 1896	5
6	*Wednesday*	**The Epiphany.** Gustave Doré b. 1833	6
7	*Thursday*	Francis Poulenc b. 1899. Gerald Durrell b. 1925	7
8	*Friday*	Giotto d. 1337. Elvis Presley b. 1935	8
9	*Saturday*	Simone de Beauvoir b. 1908. Ruskin Spear d. 1990	9
10	*Sunday*	**Baptism of Christ. 1st S. of Epiphany.**	*week* 2 *day* 10
11	*Monday*	*Hilary Law Sittings begin.* Richmal Crompton d. 1969	11
12	*Tuesday*	Edmund Burke b. 1729. Nevil Shute d. 1960	12
13	*Wednesday*	Jan van Goyen b. 1596. James Joyce d. 1941	13
14	*Thursday*	Sir Cecil Beaton b. 1904. Humphrey Bogart d. 1957	14
15	*Friday*	British Museum opened 1759. Martin Luther King b. 1929	15
16	*Saturday*	Sir John Moore d. 1809. Laura Riding b. 1901	16
17	*Sunday*	**2nd S. of Epiphany.** Nevil Shute b. 1899	*week* 3 *day* 17
18	*Monday*	A. A. Milne b. 1882. Arthur Ransome b. 1884	18
19	*Tuesday*	Edgar Allen Poe b. 1809. Paul Cézanne b. 1839	19
20	*Wednesday*	Sir John Soane d. 1837. John Ruskin d. 1900	20
21	*Thursday*	Louis XVI of France executed 1793. George Orwell d. 1950	21
22	*Friday*	Francis Bacon b. 1561. Queen Victoria d. 1901	22
23	*Saturday*	Salvador Dali d. 1989. Brian Redhead d. 1994	23
24	*Sunday*	**3rd S. of Epiphany.** Charles James Fox b. 1749	*week* 4 *day* 24
25	*Monday*	**Conversion of Paul.** Robert Burns b. 1759	25
26	*Tuesday*	Gen. Gordon killed 1885. India declared a republic 1950	26
27	*Wednesday*	Kaiser Wilhelm II b. 1859. Giuseppe Verdi d. 1901	27
28	*Thursday*	Gen. Gordon b. 1833. W. B. Yeats d. 1939	28
29	*Friday*	Alfred Sisley d. 1899. Germaine Greer b. 1929	29
30	*Saturday*	Charles I executed 1649. Gandhi assassinated 1948	30
31	*Sunday*	**4th S. of Epiphany.** Samuel Goldwyn d. 1974	*week* 5 *day* 31

ASTRONOMICAL PHENOMENA

d	h	
3	13	Earth at perihelion (147 million km)
9	22	Mars in conjunction with Moon. Mars 3° S.
16	16	Mercury in conjunction with Moon. Mercury 4° S.
19	07	Venus in conjunction with Moon. Venus 2° S.
20	13	Sun's longitude 300° ≈
22	01	Jupiter in conjunction with Moon. Jupiter 2° N.
22	08	Neptune in conjunction
24	07	Saturn in conjunction with Moon. Saturn 2° N.

MINIMA OF ALGOL

d	h	d	h	d	h
2	16.1	14	03.4	25	14.7
5	12.9	17	00.2	28	11.5
8	09.7	19	21.0	31	08.3
11	06.6	22	17.9		

CONSTELLATIONS

The following constellations are near the meridian at

	d	h		d	h
December	1	24	January	16	21
December	16	23	February	1	20
January	1	22	February	15	19

Draco (below the Pole), Ursa Minor (below the Pole), Camelopardus, Perseus, Auriga, Taurus, Orion, Eridanus and Lepus

THE MOON

Phases, Apsides and Node	d	h	m
○ Full Moon	2	02	50
☾ Last Quarter	9	14	22
● New Moon	17	15	46
☽ First Quarter	24	19	15
○ Full Moon	31	16	07
Apogee (404,792 km)	11	11	44
Perigee (369,290 km)	26	21	34

Mean longitude of ascending node on January 1, 144°

THE SUN

s.d. 16'.3

Day	Right Ascension	Dec.	Equation of time	Rise 52°	Rise 56°	Transit	Set 52°	Set 56°	Sidereal time	Transit of First Point of Aries
	h m s	° ′	m s	h m	h m	h m	h m	h m	h m s	h m s
1	18 43 58	23 03	− 3 09	8 08	8 31	12 03	15 59	15 36	6 40 49	17 16 21
2	18 48 23	22 58	− 3 38	8 08	8 31	12 04	16 00	15 37	6 44 45	17 12 25
3	18 52 47	22 53	− 4 05	8 08	8 31	12 04	16 01	15 38	6 48 42	17 08 29
4	18 57 12	22 47	− 4 33	8 08	8 30	12 05	16 02	15 39	6 52 39	17 04 33
5	19 01 35	22 41	− 5 00	8 07	8 30	12 05	16 03	15 41	6 56 35	17 00 37
6	19 05 59	22 34	− 5 27	8 07	8 29	12 06	16 05	15 42	7 00 32	16 56 41
7	19 10 22	22 27	− 5 53	8 07	8 29	12 06	16 06	15 44	7 04 28	16 52 45
8	19 14 44	22 20	− 6 19	8 06	8 28	12 07	16 07	15 45	7 08 25	16 48 49
9	19 19 06	22 12	− 6 45	8 06	8 27	12 07	16 09	15 47	7 12 21	16 44 54
10	19 23 28	22 03	− 7 10	8 05	8 27	12 07	16 10	15 49	7 16 18	16 40 58
11	19 27 49	21 54	− 7 34	8 04	8 26	12 08	16 11	15 50	7 20 14	16 37 02
12	19 32 09	21 45	− 7 58	8 04	8 25	12 08	16 13	15 52	7 24 11	16 33 06
13	19 36 29	21 35	− 8 21	8 03	8 24	12 09	16 14	15 54	7 28 08	16 29 10
14	19 40 48	21 25	− 8 44	8 02	8 23	12 09	16 16	15 55	7 32 04	16 25 14
15	19 45 07	21 14	− 9 06	8 02	8 22	12 09	16 17	15 57	7 36 01	16 21 18
16	19 49 24	21 04	− 9 27	8 01	8 21	12 10	16 19	15 59	7 39 57	16 17 22
17	19 53 42	20 52	− 9 48	8 00	8 19	12 10	16 21	16 01	7 43 54	16 13 26
18	19 57 58	20 40	−10 08	7 59	8 18	12 10	16 22	16 03	7 47 50	16 09 30
19	20 02 14	20 28	−10 27	7 58	8 17	12 11	16 24	16 05	7 51 47	16 05 34
20	20 06 29	20 16	−10 46	7 57	8 16	12 11	16 26	16 07	7 55 44	16 01 39
21	20 10 44	20 03	−11 04	7 56	8 14	12 11	16 27	16 09	7 59 40	15 57 43
22	20 14 57	19 49	−11 21	7 54	8 13	12 11	16 29	16 11	8 03 37	15 53 47
23	20 19 10	19 36	−11 37	7 53	8 11	12 12	16 31	16 13	8 07 33	15 49 51
24	20 23 22	19 22	−11 53	7 52	8 10	12 12	16 33	16 15	8 11 30	15 45 55
25	20 27 33	19 07	−12 07	7 51	8 08	12 12	16 34	16 17	8 15 26	15 41 59
26	20 31 44	18 53	−12 21	7 49	8 06	12 12	16 36	16 19	8 19 23	15 38 03
27	20 35 54	18 38	−12 34	7 48	8 05	12 13	16 38	16 21	8 23 19	15 34 07
28	20 40 02	18 22	−12 46	7 47	8 03	12 13	16 40	16 23	8 27 16	15 30 11
29	20 44 10	18 06	−12 58	7 45	8 01	12 13	16 41	16 26	8 31 13	15 26 15
30	20 48 17	17 50	−13 08	7 44	7 59	12 13	16 43	16 28	8 35 09	15 22 19
31	20 52 24	17 34	−13 18	7 42	7 58	12 13	16 45	16 30	8 39 06	15 18 24

DURATION OF TWILIGHT (in minutes)

Latitude	52°	56°	52°	56°	52°	56°	52°	56°
	1 January		11 January		21 January		31 January	
Civil	41	47	40	45	38	43	37	41
Nautical	84	96	82	93	80	90	78	87
Astronomical	125	141	123	138	120	134	117	130

THE NIGHT SKY

Mercury is unsuitably placed for observation throughout the month.

Venus, magnitude − 3.9, is visible in the evenings but will only be seen for a short time after sunset, low above the south-western horizon. It is slowly moving out from the Sun but even by the end of the month it is not visible for much more than an hour after sunset. Shortly after sunset on the 19th, the thin crescent Moon, just over three days old, will be seen about 5° above and to the left of Venus.

Mars will be visible in the night sky throughout 1999. In January it is a morning object, its magnitude brightening during the month from +1.0 to +0.5. It will be seen crossing the meridian during morning twilight. Mars is moving eastwards in Virgo, passing 4° N. of Spica on the night of the 8th to 9th. The Moon, at Last Quarter, is near Mars on the mornings of the 9th and 10th.

Jupiter, magnitude − 2.2, is an evening object and after the end of twilight will be seen in the south-western quadrant of the sky. On the evening of the 21st, Jupiter will be seen about 4° above the thin crescent Moon, only four days old. Early in the month Jupiter moves from Aquarius into Pisces.

Saturn is visible in the south-western quadrant of the sky in the evenings, magnitude +0.4. On the evening of the 23rd the Moon, one day before First Quarter, is near the planet. Saturn is in the constellation of Pisces.

THE MOON

Day	RA h m	Dec. °	Hor. par. '	Semi-diam. '	Sun's co-long. °	PA of Bright Limb °	Phase %	Age d	Rise 52° h m	Rise 56° h m	Transit h m	Set 52° h m	Set 56° h m
1	5 39	+19.0	60.1	16.4	72	252	98	13.1	15 49	15 30	23 56	7 00	7 19
2	6 40	+19.6	59.7	16.3	84	208	100	14.1	16 51	16 32	—	8 01	8 21
3	7 41	+18.9	59.1	16.1	97	112	99	15.1	17 59	17 42	0 54	8 52	9 10
4	8 39	+17.0	58.3	15.9	109	108	95	16.1	19 09	18 55	1 51	9 33	9 48
5	9 35	+14.3	57.5	15.7	121	109	90	17.1	20 20	20 10	2 44	10 06	10 17
6	10 27	+10.9	56.7	15.4	133	111	83	18.1	21 29	21 23	3 33	10 34	10 42
7	11 16	+ 7.1	55.9	15.2	145	112	74	19.1	22 36	22 33	4 20	10 58	11 02
8	12 03	+ 3.1	55.2	15.0	157	112	65	20.1	23 42	23 43	5 04	11 20	11 21
9	12 49	− 1.0	54.7	14.9	169	112	56	21.1	—	—	5 47	11 41	11 39
10	13 34	− 4.9	54.4	14.8	182	112	46	22.1	0 46	0 50	6 29	12 03	11 57
11	14 20	− 8.7	54.2	14.8	194	110	37	23.1	1 50	1 57	7 12	12 26	12 17
12	15 06	−12.0	54.2	14.8	206	109	28	24.1	2 53	3 04	7 56	12 51	12 39
13	15 53	−14.9	54.3	14.8	218	106	20	25.1	3 55	4 10	8 41	13 21	13 06
14	16 42	−17.3	54.6	14.9	230	103	13	26.1	4 56	5 14	9 28	13 56	13 39
15	17 33	−18.8	55.1	15.0	242	100	7	27.1	5 55	6 14	10 18	14 39	14 19
16	18 25	−19.5	55.5	15.1	255	98	3	28.1	6 48	7 08	11 08	15 29	15 09
17	19 19	−19.3	56.1	15.3	267	103	1	29.1	7 36	7 55	12 00	16 27	16 09
18	20 13	−18.0	56.6	15.4	279	233	0	0.3	8 18	8 35	12 52	17 32	17 16
19	21 08	−15.8	57.1	15.6	291	251	2	1.3	8 54	9 07	13 44	18 42	18 30
20	22 01	−12.7	57.6	15.7	303	251	6	2.3	9 25	9 35	14 35	19 56	19 47
21	22 54	− 8.9	58.1	15.8	315	250	12	3.3	9 52	9 59	15 26	21 10	21 06
22	23 47	− 4.6	58.4	15.9	328	249	20	4.3	10 18	10 20	16 16	22 26	22 26
23	0 39	0.0	58.7	16.0	340	249	30	5.3	10 43	10 42	17 06	23 43	23 47
24	1 32	+ 4.7	59.0	16.1	352	249	41	6.3	11 10	11 04	17 58	—	—
25	2 26	+ 9.1	59.2	16.1	4	251	52	7.3	11 38	11 29	18 51	1 00	1 08
26	3 21	+13.0	59.3	16.2	16	254	64	8.3	12 11	11 58	19 46	2 17	2 29
27	4 19	+16.2	59.4	16.2	28	257	74	9.3	12 51	12 34	20 43	3 32	3 48
28	5 18	+18.4	59.2	16.1	41	262	84	10.3	13 38	13 19	21 41	4 43	5 02
29	6 18	+19.5	59.1	16.1	53	266	91	11.3	14 34	14 14	22 39	5 47	6 06
30	7 17	+19.3	58.8	16.0	65	270	97	12.3	15 38	15 19	23 36	6 41	7 00
31	8 16	+17.9	58.3	15.9	77	271	99	13.3	16 46	16 31	—	7 26	7 42

MERCURY

Day	RA h m	Dec. °	Diam. "	Phase %	Transit h m	5° high 52° h m	5° high 56° h m
1	17 22	−22.6	5	84	10 42	7 36	8 10
3	17 34	−23.0	5	86	10 47	7 43	8 19
5	17 47	−23.3	5	88	10 51	7 51	8 28
7	17 59	−23.6	5	90	10 56	7 58	8 36
9	18 12	−23.8	5	91	11 01	8 05	8 44
11	18 25	−24.0	5	92	11 06	8 12	8 50
13	18 39	−24.0	5	94	11 12	8 17	8 56
15	18 52	−24.0	5	95	11 17	8 22	9 01
17	19 06	−23.8	5	95	11 23	8 27	9 05
19	19 19	−23.6	5	96	11 29	8 30	9 08
21	19 33	−23.3	5	97	11 35	8 33	9 09
23	19 47	−22.9	5	98	11 41	8 36	9 10
25	20 01	−22.4	5	98	11 47	8 37	9 10
27	20 15	−21.8	5	99	11 53	8 38	9 09
29	20 29	−21.1	5	99	11 59	8 38	9 08
31	20 43	−20.3	5	100	12 05	15 33	15 05

VENUS

Day	RA h m	Dec. °	Diam. "	Phase %	Transit h m	5° high 52° h m	5° high 56° h m
1	19 50	−22.3	10	97	13 10	16 21	15 48
6	20 17	−21.2	10	96	13 17	16 37	16 08
11	20 43	−19.7	10	96	13 23	16 55	16 29
16	21 08	−18.1	11	95	13 29	17 13	16 50
21	21 33	−16.2	11	94	13 34	17 31	17 11
26	21 58	−14.1	11	94	13 39	17 50	17 33
31	22 22	−11.9	11	93	13 43	18 07	17 53

MARS

Day	RA h m	Dec. °	Diam. "	Phase %	Transit h m	5° high 52° h m	5° high 56° h m
1	13 11	− 5.4	6	91	6 29	1 31	1 39
6	13 20	− 6.3	6	90	6 19	1 25	1 34
11	13 29	− 7.2	7	90	6 08	1 19	1 29
16	13 37	− 8.0	7	90	5 57	1 13	1 23
21	13 46	− 8.8	7	90	5 46	1 06	1 17
26	13 54	− 9.5	8	90	5 34	0 58	1 10
31	14 01	−10.1	8	90	5 22	0 50	1 02

SUNRISE AND SUNSET

	London		Bristol		Birmingham		Manchester		Newcastle		Glasgow		Belfast	
	0°05'	51°30'	2°35'	51°28'	1°55'	52°28'	2°15'	53°28'	1°37'	54°59'	4°14'	55°52'	5°56'	54°35'
	h m	h m	h m	h m	h m	h m	h m	h m	h m	h m	h m	h m	h m	h m
1	8 06	16 02	8 16	16 12	8 18	16 04	8 25	16 00	8 31	15 49	8 47	15 53	8 46	16 08
2	8 06	16 03	8 16	16 13	8 18	16 05	8 25	16 01	8 31	15 50	8 47	15 55	8 46	16 09
3	8 06	16 04	8 16	16 14	8 18	16 06	8 25	16 02	8 31	15 51	8 47	15 56	8 46	16 11
4	8 06	16 05	8 15	16 15	8 18	16 07	8 24	16 03	8 30	15 52	8 46	15 57	8 45	16 12
5	8 05	16 06	8 15	16 16	8 17	16 09	8 24	16 05	8 30	15 54	8 46	15 59	8 45	16 13
6	8 05	16 07	8 15	16 18	8 17	16 10	8 24	16 06	8 30	15 55	8 45	16 00	8 44	16 15
7	8 05	16 09	8 14	16 19	8 17	16 11	8 23	16 07	8 29	15 56	8 45	16 02	8 44	16 16
8	8 04	16 10	8 14	16 20	8 16	16 13	8 23	16 09	8 28	15 58	8 44	16 03	8 43	16 17
9	8 04	16 11	8 13	16 21	8 16	16 14	8 22	16 10	8 28	15 59	8 43	16 05	8 43	16 19
10	8 03	16 13	8 13	16 23	8 15	16 15	8 21	16 12	8 27	16 01	8 43	16 06	8 42	16 21
11	8 03	16 14	8 12	16 24	8 14	16 17	8 21	16 13	8 26	16 03	8 42	16 08	8 41	16 22
12	8 02	16 15	8 12	16 26	8 14	16 18	8 20	16 15	8 25	16 04	8 41	16 10	8 40	16 24
13	8 01	16 17	8 11	16 27	8 13	16 20	8 19	16 16	8 25	16 06	8 40	16 11	8 40	16 25
14	8 00	16 18	8 10	16 29	8 12	16 21	8 18	16 18	8 24	16 08	8 39	16 13	8 39	16 27
15	8 00	16 20	8 09	16 30	8 11	16 23	8 17	16 20	8 23	16 09	8 38	16 15	8 38	16 29
16	7 59	16 22	8 09	16 32	8 10	16 25	8 16	16 21	8 22	16 11	8 37	16 17	8 37	16 31
17	7 58	16 23	8 08	16 33	8 09	16 26	8 15	16 23	8 20	16 13	8 36	16 19	8 36	16 32
18	7 57	16 25	8 07	16 35	8 08	16 28	8 14	16 25	8 19	16 15	8 34	16 21	8 34	16 34
19	7 56	16 26	8 06	16 37	8 07	16 30	8 13	16 26	8 18	16 17	8 33	16 23	8 33	16 36
20	7 55	16 28	8 05	16 38	8 06	16 31	8 12	16 28	8 17	16 19	8 32	16 25	8 32	16 38
21	7 54	16 30	8 04	16 40	8 05	16 33	8 11	16 30	8 15	16 20	8 30	16 27	8 31	16 40
22	7 53	16 31	8 03	16 42	8 04	16 35	8 10	16 32	8 14	16 22	8 29	16 29	8 29	16 42
23	7 52	16 33	8 01	16 43	8 03	16 37	8 08	16 34	8 13	16 24	8 27	16 31	8 28	16 44
24	7 50	16 35	8 00	16 45	8 02	16 38	8 07	16 36	8 11	16 26	8 26	16 33	8 27	16 45
25	7 49	16 37	7 59	16 47	8 00	16 40	8 06	16 37	8 10	16 28	8 24	16 35	8 25	16 47
26	7 48	16 38	7 58	16 48	7 59	16 42	8 04	16 39	8 08	16 30	8 23	16 37	8 24	16 49
27	7 47	16 40	7 56	16 50	7 57	16 44	8 03	16 41	8 07	16 32	8 21	16 39	8 22	16 51
28	7 45	16 42	7 55	16 52	7 56	16 46	8 01	16 43	8 05	16 34	8 19	16 41	8 20	16 53
29	7 44	16 44	7 54	16 54	7 55	16 47	8 00	16 45	8 03	16 36	8 18	16 43	8 19	16 55
30	7 42	16 45	7 52	16 56	7 53	16 49	7 58	16 47	8 02	16 38	8 16	16 45	8 17	16 57
31	7 41	16 47	7 51	16 57	7 52	16 51	7 56	16 49	8 00	16 41	8 14	16 47	8 15	16 59

JUPITER

Day	RA	Dec.	Transit	5° high	
				52°	56°
	h m	° '	h m	h m	h m
1	23 32.4	− 4 20	16 49	21 53	21 46
11	23 38.1	− 3 41	16 16	21 23	21 17
21	23 44.6	− 2 57	15 43	20 54	20 49
31	23 51.7	− 2 09	15 11	20 26	20 21

Diameters – equatorial 37" polar 34"

SATURN

Day	RA	Dec.	Transit	5° high	
				52°	56°
	h m	° '	h m	h m	h m
1	1 43.1	+ 7 57	18 59	1 10	1 13
11	1 43.5	+ 8 02	18 20	0 32	0 35
21	1 44.6	+ 8 12	17 42	23 51	23 54
31	1 46.4	+ 8 25	17 05	23 14	23 18

Diameters – equatorial 18" polar 16"
Rings – major axis 41" minor axis 10"

URANUS

Day	RA	Dec.	Transit	10° high	
				52°	56°
	h m	° '	h m	h m	h m
1	20 54.4	−18 05	14 11	17 08	16 34
11	20 56.5	−17 56	13 34	16 33	15 59
21	20 58.8	−17 47	12 57	15 57	15 24
31	21 01.2	−17 37	12 20	15 21	14 49

Diameter 4"

NEPTUNE

Day	RA	Dec.	Transit	10° high	
				52°	56°
	h m	° '	h m	h m	h m
1	20 12.8	−19 38	13 30	16 13	15 33
11	20 14.4	−19 33	12 52	15 36	14 56
21	20 15.9	−19 28	12 14	14 59	14 20
31	20 17.5	−19 23	11 37	14 22	13 43

Diameter 2"

 # February 1999

SECOND MONTH, 28 or 29 DAYS. *Februa*, Roman festival of Purification

1	*Monday*	Piet Mondrian d. 1944. Jo Richardson d. 1994	*week 5 day* 32
2	*Tuesday*	**Presentation of Christ in the Temple (Candlemas)**	33
3	*Wednesday*	Beau Nash d. 1762. Felix Mendelssohn b. 1809	34
4	*Thursday*	George Lillo b. 1693. Charles Lindbergh b. 1902	35
5	*Friday*	Sir Robert Peel b. 1788. John Boyd Dunlop b. 1840	36
6	*Saturday*	*Queen's Accession 1952.* Queen Anne b. 1665	37
7	*Sunday*	**2nd S. before Lent.** Charles Dickens b. 1812	*week 6 day* 38
8	*Monday*	Mary, Queen of Scots executed 1587. John Ruskin b. 1819	39
9	*Tuesday*	Edward Carson b. 1854. Brendan Behan b. 1923	40
10	*Wednesday*	Henry, Lord Darnley killed 1567. Harold Macmillan b. 1894	41
11	*Thursday*	Thomas Edison b. 1847. Mary Quant b. 1934	42
12	*Friday*	Charles Darwin b. 1809. Abraham Lincoln b. 1809	43
13	*Saturday*	Accession of William III and Mary II 1689	44
14	*Sunday*	**S. next before Lent.** St Valentine's Day	*week 7 day* 45
15	*Monday*	Graham Hill b. 1929. Norman Parkinson d. 1990	46
16	*Tuesday*	Shrove Tuesday. *Chinese Year of the Rabbit*	47
17	*Wednesday*	**Ash Wednesday.** Graham Sutherland d. 1980	48
18	*Thursday*	Mary I b. 1516. Michelangelo d. 1564	49
19	*Friday*	*Duke of York b. 1960.* Deng Xiaoping d. 1997	50
20	*Saturday*	Dame Marie Rambert b. 1888. Kurt Cobain b. 1967	51
21	*Sunday*	**1st S. of Lent.** Malcolm X assassinated 1965	*week 8 day* 52
22	*Monday*	Eric Gill b. 1882. Andy Warhol d. 1987	53
23	*Tuesday*	Samuel Pepys b. 1633. Sir Edward Elgar d. 1934	54
24	*Wednesday*	Wilhelm Grimm b. 1786. Joseph Rowntree d. 1925	55
25	*Thursday*	Sir Christopher Wren d. 1723. Pierre Renoir b. 1841	56
26	*Friday*	Frank Bridge b. 1879. Everton Weekes b. 1925	57
27	*Saturday*	John Evelyn d. 1706. Prof. Charles Best b. 1899	58
28	*Sunday*	**2nd S. of Lent.** Relief of Ladysmith 1900	*week 9 day* 59

ASTRONOMICAL PHENOMENA

d	h	
2	02	Uranus in conjunction
4	05	Mercury in superior conjunction
7	06	Mars in conjunction with Moon. Mars 3° S.
16	07	Annular eclipse of Sun (*see* page 66)
17	02	Mercury in conjunction with Moon. Mercury 0°.2 N.
18	08	Venus in conjunction with Moon. Venus 2° N.
18	17	Jupiter in conjunction with Moon. Jupiter 2° N.
19	03	Sun's longitude 330° ⋊
20	16	Saturn in conjunction with Moon. Saturn 3° N.
23	20	Jupiter in conjunction with Venus. Jupiter 0°.1 S.

MINIMA OF ALGOL

d	h	d	h	d	h
3	05.1	14	16.4	26	03.7
6	02.0	17	13.2		
8	22.8	20	10.1		
11	19.6	23	06.9		

CONSTELLATIONS

The following constellations are near the meridian at

	d	h		d	h
January	1	24	February	15	21
January	16	23	March	1	20
February	1	22	March	16	19

Draco (below the Pole), Camelopardus, Auriga, Taurus, Gemini, Orion, Canis Minor, Monoceros, Lepus, Canis Major and Puppis

THE MOON

Phases, Apsides and Node	d	h	m
☾ Last Quarter	8	11	58
● New Moon	16	06	39
☽ First Quarter	23	02	43
Apogee (404,346 km)	8	08	51
Perigee (368,685 km)	20	14	25

Mean longitude of ascending node on February 1, 143°

THE SUN

s.d. 16'.2

Day	Right Ascension	Dec. —	Equation of time	Rise 52°	Rise 56°	Transit	Set 52°	Set 56°	Sidereal time	Transit of First Point of Aries
	h m s	° '	m s	h m	h m	h m	h m	h m	h m s	h m s
1	20 56 29	17 17	−13 27	7 41	7 56	12 14	16 47	16 32	8 43 02	15 14 28
2	21 00 34	17 00	−13 35	7 39	7 54	12 14	16 49	16 34	8 46 59	15 10 32
3	21 04 38	16 43	−13 43	7 38	7 52	12 14	16 51	16 36	8 50 55	15 06 36
4	21 08 41	16 25	−13 49	7 36	7 50	12 14	16 53	16 39	8 54 52	15 02 40
5	21 12 43	16 07	−13 55	7 34	7 48	12 14	16 54	16 41	8 58 48	14 58 44
6	21 16 45	15 49	−14 00	7 33	7 46	12 14	16 56	16 43	9 02 45	14 54 48
7	21 20 45	15 31	−14 04	7 31	7 44	12 14	16 58	16 45	9 06 41	14 50 52
8	21 24 45	15 12	−14 07	7 29	7 42	12 14	17 00	16 47	9 10 38	14 46 56
9	21 28 44	14 53	−14 10	7 27	7 40	12 14	17 02	16 50	9 14 35	14 43 00
10	21 32 43	14 34	−14 12	7 25	7 37	12 14	17 04	16 52	9 18 31	14 39 04
11	21 36 40	14 14	−14 13	7 24	7 35	12 14	17 06	16 54	9 22 28	14 35 09
12	21 40 37	13 55	−14 13	7 22	7 33	12 14	17 07	16 56	9 26 24	14 31 13
13	21 44 33	13 35	−14 12	7 20	7 31	12 14	17 09	16 58	9 30 21	14 27 17
14	21 48 29	13 15	−14 11	7 18	7 29	12 14	17 11	17 01	9 34 17	14 23 21
15	21 52 23	12 54	−14 09	7 16	7 26	12 14	17 13	17 03	9 38 14	14 19 25
16	21 56 17	12 34	−14 07	7 14	7 24	12 14	17 15	17 05	9 42 10	14 15 29
17	22 00 10	12 13	−14 03	7 12	7 22	12 14	17 17	17 07	9 46 07	14 11 33
18	22 04 03	11 52	−13 59	7 10	7 19	12 14	17 19	17 09	9 50 04	14 07 37
19	22 07 54	11 31	−13 54	7 08	7 17	12 14	17 20	17 12	9 54 00	14 03 41
20	22 11 45	11 09	−13 49	7 06	7 15	12 14	17 22	17 14	9 57 57	13 59 45
21	22 15 36	10 48	−13 43	7 04	7 12	12 14	17 24	17 16	10 01 53	13 55 49
22	22 19 26	10 26	−13 36	7 02	7 10	12 14	17 26	17 18	10 05 50	13 51 54
23	22 23 15	10 04	−13 28	7 00	7 08	12 13	17 28	17 20	10 09 46	13 47 58
24	22 27 03	9 42	−13 20	6 58	7 05	12 13	17 30	17 22	10 13 43	13 44 02
25	22 30 51	9 20	−13 11	6 56	7 03	12 13	17 32	17 25	10 17 39	13 40 06
26	22 34 38	8 58	−13 02	6 53	7 00	12 13	17 33	17 27	10 21 36	13 36 10
27	22 38 25	8 36	−12 52	6 51	6 58	12 13	17 35	17 29	10 25 33	13 32 14
28	22 42 11	8 13	−12 42	6 49	6 55	12 13	17 37	17 31	10 29 29	13 28 18

DURATION OF TWILIGHT (in minutes)

Latitude	52°	56°	52°	56°	52°	56°	52°	56°
	1 February		11 February		21 February		28 February	
Civil	37	41	35	39	34	38	34	38
Nautical	77	86	75	83	74	81	73	81
Astronomical	117	130	114	126	113	125	112	124

THE NIGHT SKY

Mercury is unsuitably placed for observation for most of the month as it passes through superior conjunction on the 4th. For the last week of the month it may be glimpsed as an evening object, magnitude −1.1 to −0.7, low above the west-south-western horizon around the end of evening civil twilight. For observers in the northern hemisphere this is the most favourable evening apparition of the year.

Venus continues to be visible as a brilliant evening object, magnitude −3.9. Its rapid motion northwards in declination makes it visible for longer each night and by the end of February it is still visible low in the western sky two hours after sunset. Venus is moving out from the Sun while Jupiter is moving in towards the Sun, so that the two bodies are close to each other for several days around the 23rd to 24th. During the evening of the 23rd Jupiter will be seen only about 0°.1 to the left of Venus. The thin crescent Moon is near the planet on the evenings of the 17th and 18th.

Mars continues to be visible as a morning object, its magnitude brightening during February from +0.5 to −0.1. The Moon will be seen about 2° above the planet on the morning of the 7th. Mars moves from Virgo into Libra during the month.

Jupiter continues to be visible in the south-western sky in the early evening, magnitude −2.1. The thin crescent Moon may be detected about 3° below and to the left of Jupiter on the evening of the 18th.

Saturn, magnitude +0.5, continues to be visible in the south-western sky in the evenings. The crescent Moon, four days old, is near Saturn on the evening of the 20th.

Zodiacal Light. The evening cone may be observed in the western sky after the end of twilight from the 2nd to the 17th. This faint phenomenon is only visible under good conditions, in the absence of both moonlight and artificial lighting.

THE MOON

Day	RA	Dec.	Hor. par.	Semi-diam.	Sun's co-long.	PA of Bright Limb	Phase	Age	Rise 52°	Rise 56°	Transit	Set 52°	Set 56°
	h m	°	′	′	°	°	%	d	h m	h m	h m	h m	h m
1	9 12	+15.6	57.7	15.7	89	115	100	14.3	17 57	17 45	0 30	8 03	8 16
2	10 06	+12.4	57.1	15.6	101	108	98	15.3	19 08	19 00	1 22	8 33	8 43
3	10 57	+ 8.7	56.4	15.4	113	109	94	16.3	20 17	20 13	2 10	8 59	9 05
4	11 46	+ 4.7	55.8	15.2	126	110	88	17.3	21 25	21 24	2 56	9 23	9 25
5	12 33	+ 0.6	55.2	15.0	138	110	81	18.3	22 30	22 33	3 40	9 45	9 44
6	13 18	− 3.5	54.7	14.9	150	110	73	19.3	23 35	23 41	4 23	10 06	10 02
7	14 04	− 7.3	54.4	14.8	162	109	64	20.3	—	—	5 06	10 29	10 21
8	14 50	−10.9	54.2	14.8	174	107	55	21.3	0 38	0 48	5 50	10 53	10 42
9	15 37	−13.9	54.3	14.8	186	104	45	22.3	1 41	1 54	6 34	11 21	11 07
10	16 25	−16.5	54.5	14.8	198	101	36	23.3	2 42	2 59	7 20	11 53	11 36
11	17 15	−18.3	54.8	14.9	211	97	27	24.3	3 42	4 00	8 08	12 32	12 13
12	18 06	−19.3	55.3	15.1	223	93	19	25.3	4 37	4 57	8 58	13 18	12 58
13	18 59	−19.4	55.9	15.2	235	88	12	26.3	5 28	5 47	9 49	14 13	13 54
14	19 53	−18.6	56.6	15.4	247	83	6	27.3	6 13	6 30	10 42	15 15	14 58
15	20 48	−16.7	57.3	15.6	259	78	2	28.3	6 51	7 06	11 34	16 24	16 10
16	21 43	−13.8	58.0	15.8	272	69	0	29.3	7 25	7 36	12 27	17 38	17 28
17	22 37	−10.2	58.6	16.0	284	256	1	0.7	7 54	8 02	13 19	18 54	18 48
18	23 31	− 5.9	59.0	16.1	296	253	4	1.7	8 22	8 25	14 11	20 12	20 10
19	0 25	− 1.2	59.3	16.2	308	252	9	2.7	8 48	8 47	15 02	21 30	21 33
20	1 19	+ 3.5	59.4	16.2	320	252	17	3.7	9 14	9 10	15 54	22 49	22 56
21	2 13	+ 8.1	59.5	16.2	333	253	27	4.7	9 42	9 34	16 47	—	—
22	3 09	+12.2	59.4	16.2	345	256	37	5.7	10 14	10 01	17 42	0 07	0 18
23	4 06	+15.6	59.2	16.1	357	259	49	6.7	10 50	10 35	18 38	1 22	1 37
24	5 03	+18.0	58.9	16.1	9	263	60	7.7	11 34	11 16	19 34	2 34	2 52
25	6 02	+19.3	58.6	16.0	21	268	71	8.7	12 26	12 06	20 31	3 39	3 58
26	7 01	+19.4	58.2	15.9	33	274	80	9.7	13 25	13 07	21 27	4 35	4 54
27	7 58	+18.5	57.8	15.8	46	279	88	10.7	14 31	14 14	22 21	5 22	5 40
28	8 54	+16.4	57.4	15.6	58	284	94	11.7	15 40	15 26	23 13	6 01	6 15

MERCURY

Day	RA	Dec.	Diam.	Phase	Transit	5° high 52°	5° high 56°
	h m	°	″	%	h m	h m	h m
1	20 50	−19.9	5	100	12 08	15 39	15 13
3	21 04	−19.0	5	100	12 14	15 53	15 28
5	21 18	−17.9	5	100	12 20	16 06	15 44
7	21 32	−16.8	5	100	12 26	16 21	16 00
9	21 46	−15.6	5	99	12 33	16 35	16 16
11	21 59	−14.2	5	98	12 39	16 50	16 33
13	22 13	−12.8	5	97	12 44	17 05	16 50
15	22 27	−11.3	5	96	12 50	17 20	17 06
17	22 40	− 9.7	5	93	12 56	17 35	17 23
19	22 54	− 8.1	5	90	13 01	17 49	17 39
21	23 06	− 6.4	6	86	13 06	18 03	17 55
23	23 19	− 4.7	6	81	13 10	18 16	18 10
25	23 30	− 3.0	6	74	13 13	18 28	18 23
27	23 41	− 1.4	6	67	13 16	18 39	18 35
29	23 50	+ 0.1	7	58	13 17	18 47	18 45
31	23 58	+ 1.4	7	50	13 16	18 53	18 51

VENUS

Day	RA	Dec.	Diam.	Phase	Transit	5° high 52°	5° high 56°
	h m	°	″	%	h m	h m	h m
1	22 26	−11.4	11	93	13 44	18 11	17 57
6	22 50	− 9.0	11	92	13 47	18 28	18 17
11	23 13	− 6.6	11	91	13 51	18 45	18 37
16	23 35	− 4.0	11	90	13 53	19 02	18 56
21	23 58	− 1.4	12	89	13 56	19 19	19 14
26	0 20	+ 1.2	12	88	13 59	19 35	19 33
31	0 42	+ 3.8	12	87	14 01	19 51	19 51

MARS

Day	RA	Dec.	Diam.	Phase	Transit	5° high 52°	5° high 56°
1	14 03	−10.3	8	91	5 19	0 48	1 01
6	14 10	−10.9	8	91	5 07	0 39	0 52
11	14 17	−11.4	9	91	4 54	0 29	0 43
16	14 23	−11.9	9	91	4 40	0 18	0 33
21	14 28	−12.3	10	92	4 26	0 07	0 22
26	14 33	−12.7	10	92	4 10	23 51	0 09
31	14 36	−13.0	11	93	3 55	23 37	23 53

SUNRISE AND SUNSET

	London		Bristol		Birmingham		Manchester		Newcastle		Glasgow		Belfast	
	0°05′	51°30′	2°35′	51°28′	1°55′	52°28′	2°15′	53°28′	1°37′	54°59′	4°14′	55°52′	5°56′	54°35′
	h m	h m	h m	h m	h m	h m	h m	h m	h m	h m	h m	h m	h m	h m
1	7 39	16 49	7 49	16 59	7 50	16 53	7 55	16 51	7 58	16 43	8 12	16 50	8 14	17 01
2	7 38	16 51	7 48	17 01	7 48	16 55	7 53	16 53	7 56	16 45	8 10	16 52	8 12	17 04
3	7 36	16 53	7 46	17 03	7 47	16 57	7 51	16 55	7 54	16 47	8 08	16 54	8 10	17 06
4	7 35	16 54	7 45	17 05	7 45	16 59	7 50	16 57	7 53	16 49	8 06	16 56	8 08	17 08
5	7 33	16 56	7 43	17 06	7 43	17 01	7 48	16 59	7 51	16 51	8 04	16 58	8 06	17 10
6	7 31	16 58	7 41	17 08	7 42	17 03	7 46	17 01	7 49	16 53	8 02	17 00	8 05	17 12
7	7 30	17 00	7 40	17 10	7 40	17 04	7 44	17 03	7 47	16 55	8 00	17 03	8 03	17 14
8	7 28	17 02	7 38	17 12	7 38	17 06	7 42	17 05	7 45	16 57	7 58	17 05	8 01	17 16
9	7 26	17 04	7 36	17 14	7 36	17 08	7 40	17 07	7 43	16 59	7 56	17 07	7 59	17 18
10	7 24	17 05	7 34	17 15	7 34	17 10	7 39	17 09	7 41	17 02	7 54	17 09	7 57	17 20
11	7 23	17 07	7 32	17 17	7 32	17 12	7 37	17 11	7 39	17 04	7 52	17 11	7 55	17 22
12	7 21	17 09	7 31	17 19	7 31	17 14	7 35	17 13	7 36	17 06	7 50	17 14	7 53	17 24
13	7 19	17 11	7 29	17 21	7 29	17 16	7 33	17 15	7 34	17 08	7 47	17 16	7 50	17 26
14	7 17	17 13	7 27	17 23	7 27	17 18	7 31	17 17	7 32	17 10	7 45	17 18	7 48	17 28
15	7 15	17 15	7 25	17 25	7 25	17 20	7 29	17 19	7 30	17 12	7 43	17 20	7 46	17 30
16	7 13	17 16	7 23	17 26	7 23	17 22	7 26	17 21	7 28	17 14	7 41	17 22	7 44	17 32
17	7 11	17 18	7 21	17 28	7 21	17 23	7 24	17 22	7 26	17 16	7 38	17 24	7 42	17 35
18	7 09	17 20	7 19	17 30	7 19	17 25	7 22	17 24	7 23	17 18	7 36	17 27	7 40	17 37
19	7 07	17 22	7 17	17 32	7 17	17 27	7 20	17 26	7 21	17 20	7 34	17 29	7 37	17 39
20	7 05	17 24	7 15	17 34	7 15	17 29	7 18	17 28	7 19	17 23	7 31	17 31	7 35	17 41
21	7 03	17 25	7 13	17 36	7 13	17 31	7 16	17 30	7 17	17 25	7 29	17 33	7 33	17 43
22	7 01	17 27	7 11	17 37	7 10	17 33	7 14	17 32	7 14	17 27	7 27	17 35	7 31	17 45
23	6 59	17 29	7 09	17 39	7 08	17 35	7 11	17 34	7 12	17 29	7 24	17 37	7 28	17 47
24	6 57	17 31	7 07	17 41	7 06	17 37	7 09	17 36	7 10	17 31	7 22	17 40	7 26	17 49
25	6 55	17 33	7 05	17 43	7 04	17 38	7 07	17 38	7 07	17 33	7 19	17 42	7 24	17 51
26	6 53	17 34	7 03	17 44	7 02	17 40	7 05	17 40	7 05	17 35	7 17	17 44	7 21	17 53
27	6 51	17 36	7 01	17 46	7 00	17 42	7 02	17 42	7 02	17 37	7 14	17 46	7 19	17 55
28	6 49	17 38	6 59	17 48	6 57	17 44	7 00	17 44	7 00	17 39	7 12	17 48	7 17	17 57

JUPITER

Day	RA	Dec.		Transit	5° high	
					52°	56°
	h m	°	′	h m	h m	h m
1	23 52.5	− 2	04	15 07	20 24	20 19
11	0 00.2	− 1	13	14 36	19 57	19 52
21	0 08.3	− 0	19	14 05	19 30	19 27
31	0 16.7	+ 0	36	13 34	19 04	19 01

Diameters – equatorial 34″ polar 32″

SATURN

Day	RA	Dec.		Transit	5° high	
					52°	56°
	h m	°	′	h m	h m	h m
1	1 46.6	+ 8	26	17 01	23 11	23 14
11	1 49.1	+ 8	43	16 24	22 36	22 39
21	1 52.1	+ 9	02	15 48	22 01	22 05
31	1 55.6	+ 9	24	15 12	21 27	21 31

Diameters – equatorial 17″ polar 15″
Rings – major axis 39″ minor axis 10″

URANUS

Day	RA	Dec.		Transit	10° high	
					52°	56°
	h m	°	′	h m	h m	h m
1	21 01.4	−17	36	12 16	9 15	9 48
11	21 03.7	−17	26	11 39	8 37	9 09
21	21 06.0	−17	16	11 02	7 58	8 30
31	21 08.2	−17	07	10 25	7 20	7 51

Diameter 4″

NEPTUNE

Day	RA	Dec.		Transit	10° high	
					52°	56°
	h m	°	′	h m	h m	h m
1	20 17.7	−19	23	11 33	8 47	9 26
11	20 19.2	−19	18	10 55	8 09	8 47
21	20 20.7	−19	13	10 17	7 30	8 08
31	20 22.0	−19	08	9 39	6 51	7 29

Diameter 2″

 # March 1999

THIRD MONTH, 31 DAYS. *Mars*, Roman god of battle

1	*Monday*	St David's Day. David Niven b. 1910	*week* 9 *day* 60
2	*Tuesday*	Kurt Weill b. 1900. Archbishop Basil Hume b. 1923	61
3	*Wednesday*	Robert Adam d. 1792. Sir Henry Wood b. 1869	62
4	*Thursday*	Forth Railway Bridge opened 1890. Kenny Dalglish b. 1951	63
5	*Friday*	Flora Macdonald d. 1790. William Beveridge b. 1879	64
6	*Saturday*	Michelangelo b. 1474. Cyrano de Bergerac b. 1619	65
7	*Sunday*	**3rd S. of Lent.** Sir Edwin Landseer b. 1802	*week* 10 *day* 66
8	*Monday*	Commonwealth Day. Hector Berlioz d. 1869	67
9	*Tuesday*	Ernest Bevin b. 1881. Yuri Gagarin b. 1934	68
10	*Wednesday*	*Prince Edward b. 1964.* Jan Masaryk d. 1948	69
11	*Thursday*	Sir Alexander Fleming d. 1955. Haydn Wood d. 1959	70
12	*Friday*	Gabriele d'Annunzio b. 1864. Nijinsky b. 1890	71
13	*Saturday*	Joseph Priestley b. 1733. Uranus discovered 1781	72
14	*Sunday*	**4th S. of Lent.** Mothering Sunday	*week* 11 *day* 73
15	*Monday*	Lord Melbourne b. 1779. Sir Henry Bessemer d. 1898	74
16	*Tuesday*	Aubrey Beardsley d. 1898. William Beveridge d. 1963	75
17	*Wednesday*	St Patrick's Day. *Bank Holiday in Northern Ireland*	76
18	*Thursday*	HINDU NEW YEAR. Neville Chamberlain b. 1869	77
19	*Friday*	**St Joseph of Nazareth.** Dr Livingstone b. 1813	78
20	*Saturday*	Marshal Foch d. 1929. Brendan Behan d. 1964	79
21	*Sunday*	**5th S. of Lent.** Archbishop Cranmer executed 1556	*week* 12 *day* 80
22	*Monday*	Sir Anthony van Dyck b. 1599. Goethe d. 1832	81
23	*Tuesday*	Princess Eugenie of York b. 1990	82
24	*Wednesday*	Elizabeth I d. 1603. William Morris b. 1834	83
25	*Thursday*	**The Annunciation.** Treaty of Rome 1957	84
26	*Friday*	Sir John Vanbrugh d. 1726. Cecil Rhodes d. 1902	85
27	*Saturday*	James I d. 1625. James Callaghan b. 1912	86
28	*Sunday*	**Palm Sunday.** Eugene Ionesco d. 1994	*week* 13 *day* 87
29	*Monday*	Sir Edwin Lutyens b. 1869. John Major b. 1943	88
30	*Tuesday*	Beau Brummell d. 1840. Vincent van Gogh b. 1853	89
31	*Wednesday*	*Hilary Law Sittings end.* Eiffel Tower completed 1889	90

ASTRONOMICAL PHENOMENA

d	h	
3	13	Mercury at greatest elongation E.18°
7	04	Mars in conjunction with Moon. Mars 3° S.
10	09	Mercury at stationary point
13	22	Pluto at stationary point
18	01	Mercury in conjunction with Moon. Mercury 7° N.
18	13	Jupiter in conjunction with Moon. Jupiter 3° N.
18	14	Mars at stationary point
19	19	Mercury in inferior conjunction
20	02	Saturn in conjunction with Venus. Saturn 2° S.
20	04	Saturn in conjunction with Moon. Saturn 3° N.
20	05	Venus in conjunction with Moon. Venus 5° N.
21	02	Sun's longitude 0° ♈

MINIMA OF ALGOL

d	h	d	h	d	h
1	00.5	12	11.8	23	23.1
3	21.4	15	08.6	26	19.9
6	18.2	18	05.5	29	16.7
9	15.0	21	02.3		

CONSTELLATIONS

The following constellations are near the meridian at

d	h		d	h
February	1	24	March	16	21
February	15	23	April	1	20
March	1	22	April	15	19

Cepheus (below the Pole), Camelopardus, Lynx, Gemini, Cancer, Leo, Canis Minor, Hydra, Monoceros, Canis Major and Puppis

THE MOON

Phases, Apsides and Node	d	h	m
○ Full Moon	2	06	58
☾ Last Quarter	10	08	40
● New Moon	17	18	48
☽ First Quarter	24	10	18
○ Full Moon	31	22	49
Apogee (404,714 km)	8	05	05
Perigee (363,286 km)	20	00	07

Mean longitude of ascending node on March 1, 141°

THE SUN

s.d. 16'.1

Day	Right Ascension	Dec.	Equation of time	Rise 52°	Rise 56°	Transit	Set 52°	Set 56°	Sidereal time	Transit of First Point of Aries
	h m s	° '	m s	h m	h m	h m	h m	h m	h m s	h m s
1	22 45 56	− 7 50	−12 30	6 47	6 53	12 12	17 39	17 33	10 33 26	13 24 22
2	22 49 41	− 7 28	−12 19	6 45	6 50	12 12	17 41	17 35	10 37 22	13 20 26
3	22 53 26	− 7 05	−12 07	6 43	6 48	12 12	17 42	17 37	10 41 19	13 16 30
4	22 57 09	− 6 42	−11 54	6 40	6 45	12 12	17 44	17 39	10 45 15	13 12 34
5	23 00 53	− 6 19	−11 41	6 38	6 43	12 12	17 46	17 42	10 49 12	13 08 39
6	23 04 36	− 5 55	−11 28	6 36	6 40	12 11	17 48	17 44	10 53 08	13 04 43
7	23 08 19	− 5 32	−11 14	6 34	6 38	12 11	17 50	17 46	10 57 05	13 00 47
8	23 12 01	− 5 09	−10 59	6 31	6 35	12 11	17 51	17 48	11 01 02	12 56 51
9	23 15 43	− 4 46	−10 45	6 29	6 32	12 11	17 53	17 50	11 04 58	12 52 55
10	23 19 24	− 4 22	−10 30	6 27	6 30	12 10	17 55	17 52	11 08 55	12 48 59
11	23 23 06	− 3 59	−10 14	6 25	6 27	12 10	17 57	17 54	11 12 51	12 45 03
12	23 26 47	− 3 35	− 9 59	6 22	6 25	12 10	17 58	17 56	11 16 48	12 41 07
13	23 30 27	− 3 11	− 9 43	6 20	6 22	12 10	18 00	17 58	11 20 44	12 37 11
14	23 34 08	− 2 48	− 9 27	6 18	6 19	12 09	18 02	18 00	11 24 41	12 33 15
15	23 37 48	− 2 24	− 9 10	6 15	6 17	12 09	18 04	18 02	11 28 37	12 29 20
16	23 41 27	− 2 00	− 8 54	6 13	6 14	12 09	18 05	18 04	11 32 34	12 25 24
17	23 45 07	− 1 37	− 8 37	6 11	6 12	12 08	18 07	18 07	11 36 31	12 21 28
18	23 48 47	− 1 13	− 8 19	6 09	6 09	12 08	18 09	18 09	11 40 27	12 17 32
19	23 52 26	− 0 49	− 8 02	6 06	6 06	12 08	18 11	18 11	11 44 24	12 13 36
20	23 56 05	− 0 25	− 7 45	6 04	6 04	12 08	18 12	18 13	11 48 20	12 09 40
21	23 59 44	− 0 02	− 7 27	6 02	6 01	12 07	18 14	18 15	11 52 17	12 05 44
22	0 03 23	+ 0 22	− 7 09	5 59	5 58	12 07	18 16	18 17	11 56 13	12 01 48
23	0 07 01	+ 0 46	− 6 51	5 57	5 56	12 07	18 17	18 19	12 00 10	11 57 52
24	0 10 40	+ 1 09	− 6 33	5 55	5 53	12 06	18 19	18 21	12 04 06	11 53 56
25	0 14 18	+ 1 33	− 6 15	5 52	5 50	12 06	18 21	18 23	12 08 03	11 50 00
26	0 17 57	+ 1 57	− 5 57	5 50	5 48	12 06	18 23	18 25	12 11 59	11 46 05
27	0 21 35	+ 2 20	− 5 39	5 48	5 45	12 05	18 24	18 27	12 15 56	11 42 09
28	0 25 13	+ 2 44	− 5 21	5 45	5 43	12 05	18 26	18 29	12 19 53	11 38 13
29	0 28 52	+ 3 07	− 5 03	5 43	5 40	12 05	18 28	18 31	12 23 49	11 34 17
30	0 32 30	+ 3 30	− 4 44	5 41	5 37	12 05	18 29	18 33	12 27 46	11 30 21
31	0 36 09	+ 3 54	− 4 26	5 38	5 35	12 04	18 31	18 35	12 31 42	11 26 25

DURATION OF TWILIGHT (in minutes)

Latitude	52°	56°	52°	56°	52°	56°	52°	56°
	1 March		11 March		21 March		31 March	
Civil	34	38	34	37	34	37	34	38
Nautical	73	81	73	80	74	82	76	84
Astronomical	112	124	113	125	116	129	120	136

THE NIGHT SKY

Mercury reaches its greatest eastern elongation (18°) on the 3rd and continues to be visible low above the western horizon at the end of civil twilight in the evenings for the first week or ten days of the month. During this period its magnitude fades from −0.6 to +1.4. Thereafter it is too close to the Sun for observation, inferior conjunction occurring on the 19th. Mercury and Jupiter are within 5–6 degrees of each other during the first part of the month, Jupiter being much the brighter object, and also further from the Sun.

Venus, magnitude −4.0, is a magnificent object in the western sky in the evenings. On the evening of the 19th the thin crescent Moon, only two days old, will be seen about 9° below Venus.

Mars is now brightening considerably as it moves towards opposition next month, rising by 0.8 magnitudes and ending March with a magnitude of −1.0. The gibbous Moon will be seen about 2° above the planet on the morning of the 7th. Mars is in Libra and reaches its first stationary point on the 18th.

Jupiter, magnitude −2.1, is still visible for a short time in the south-western sky after sunset but only for the first two weeks of the month. Thereafter it is lost in the gathering twilight.

Saturn is still an evening object in the western sky but moving closer to the Sun and only visible for a short time after sunset. Its magnitude is +0.5. The thin crescent Moon, only two days old, is near the planet on the early evening of the 19th.

Zodiacal Light. The evening cone may be observed, stretching up from the western horizon along the ecliptic, after the end of twilight from the 4th to the 19th.

THE MOON

Day	RA h m	Dec. °	Hor. par.	Semi- diam.	Sun's co- long.	PA of Bright Limb	Phase %	Age d	Rise 52° h m	Rise 56° h m	Transit h m	Set 52° h m	Set 56° h m
1	9 48	+13.6	56.9	15.5	70	290	98	12.7	16 50	16 40	—	6 33	6 44
2	10 39	+10.0	56.4	15.4	82	314	100	13.7	17 59	17 53	0 02	7 01	7 08
3	11 28	+ 6.1	55.9	15.2	94	97	99	14.7	19 08	19 05	0 48	7 25	7 29
4	12 16	+ 2.0	55.4	15.1	106	104	97	15.7	20 15	20 16	1 33	7 47	7 48
5	13 02	− 2.1	54.9	15.0	118	106	93	16.7	21 20	21 25	2 17	8 09	8 06
6	13 48	− 6.1	54.5	14.9	131	106	87	17.7	22 24	22 33	3 00	8 31	8 25
7	14 34	− 9.7	54.3	14.8	143	104	80	18.7	23 28	23 40	3 44	8 55	8 45
8	15 21	−13.0	54.2	14.8	155	102	72	19.7	—	—	4 28	9 21	9 08
9	16 08	−15.7	54.2	14.8	167	99	63	20.7	0 30	0 45	5 13	9 51	9 35
10	16 57	−17.8	54.4	14.8	179	96	54	21.7	1 30	1 47	6 00	10 26	10 08
11	17 47	−19.1	54.8	14.9	191	92	44	22.7	2 26	2 45	6 48	11 08	10 49
12	18 39	−19.6	55.4	15.1	204	87	34	23.7	3 18	3 38	7 38	11 58	11 39
13	19 32	−19.1	56.1	15.3	216	83	25	24.7	4 05	4 23	8 29	12 57	12 38
14	20 26	−17.6	56.9	15.5	228	78	17	25.7	4 46	5 02	9 21	14 02	13 46
15	21 20	−15.1	57.7	15.7	240	73	10	26.7	5 21	5 34	10 13	15 14	15 02
16	22 15	−11.8	58.6	16.0	252	67	4	27.7	5 53	6 02	11 06	16 30	16 21
17	23 10	− 7.7	59.3	16.2	265	56	1	28.7	6 21	6 27	11 59	17 48	17 44
18	0 05	− 3.0	59.9	16.3	277	294	0	0.2	6 48	6 49	12 52	19 09	19 09
19	1 00	+ 1.9	60.2	16.4	289	261	2	1.2	7 15	7 12	13 45	20 30	20 35
20	1 56	+ 6.7	60.4	16.4	301	258	7	2.2	7 43	7 36	14 40	21 51	22 01
21	2 53	+11.2	60.2	16.4	313	258	14	3.2	8 14	8 03	15 35	23 10	23 24
22	3 51	+14.9	59.9	16.3	326	261	24	4.2	8 50	8 35	16 32	—	—
23	4 50	+17.6	59.5	16.2	338	265	34	5.2	9 32	9 14	17 30	0 25	0 43
24	5 49	+19.2	58.9	16.1	350	269	45	6.2	10 21	10 02	18 27	1 34	1 53
25	6 48	+19.6	58.4	15.9	2	274	56	7.2	11 19	10 59	19 23	2 33	2 52
26	7 45	+18.9	57.8	15.7	14	279	67	8.2	12 22	12 04	20 17	3 22	3 40
27	8 41	+17.1	57.2	15.6	27	284	77	9.2	13 29	13 15	21 08	4 03	4 18
28	9 34	+14.4	56.6	15.4	39	289	85	10.2	14 38	14 27	21 57	4 36	4 48
29	10 25	+11.1	56.1	15.3	51	293	92	11.2	15 47	15 39	22 44	5 04	5 13
30	11 14	+ 7.3	55.7	15.2	63	298	96	12.2	16 55	16 51	23 29	5 29	5 34
31	12 02	+ 3.3	55.2	15.1	75	310	99	13.2	18 02	18 02	—	5 51	5 53

MERCURY

Day	RA h m	Dec. °	Diam. "	Phase %	Transit h m	5° high 52° h m	5° high 56° h m
1	23 50	+ 0.1	7	58	13 17	18 47	18 45
3	23 58	+ 1.4	7	50	13 16	18 53	18 51
5	0 04	+ 2.6	8	41	13 14	18 56	18 55
7	0 08	+ 3.5	8	32	13 09	18 56	18 55
9	0 10	+ 4.2	9	23	13 03	18 52	18 52
11	0 10	+ 4.5	9	16	12 54	18 44	18 45
13	0 08	+ 4.6	10	10	12 44	18 33	18 33
15	0 04	+ 4.3	10	5	12 32	18 19	18 19
17	23 59	+ 3.7	11	2	12 19	18 02	18 02
19	23 53	+ 3.0	11	1	12 05	17 44	17 43
21	23 46	+ 2.0	11	1	11 50	6 15	6 17
23	23 40	+ 1.0	11	2	11 37	6 07	6 09
25	23 35	− 0.1	11	5	11 24	5 59	6 02
27	23 31	− 1.1	11	8	11 12	5 52	5 56
29	23 28	− 2.0	11	12	11 02	5 46	5 51
31	23 26	− 2.7	10	16	10 52	5 40	5 46

VENUS

Day	RA h m	Dec. °	Diam. "	Phase %	Transit h m	5° high 52° h m	5° high 56° h m
1	0 33	+ 2.8	12	88	14 00	19 44	19 44
6	0 56	+ 5.4	12	86	14 03	20 00	20 01
11	1 18	+ 7.9	12	85	14 06	20 16	20 19
16	1 41	+10.4	13	84	14 08	20 31	20 37
21	2 03	+12.7	13	83	14 11	20 47	20 54
26	2 26	+15.0	13	81	14 15	21 02	21 12
31	2 50	+17.1	13	80	14 19	21 17	21 29

MARS

Day	RA h m	Dec. °	Diam. "	Phase %	Transit h m	5° high 52° h m	5° high 56° h m
1	14 35	−12.9	10	93	4 01	23 43	0 01
6	14 38	−13.1	11	93	3 45	23 27	23 44
11	14 40	−13.3	11	94	3 27	23 11	23 27
16	14 42	−13.4	12	95	3 09	22 53	23 09
21	14 42	−13.5	13	96	2 49	22 33	22 49
26	14 40	−13.4	13	96	2 28	22 11	22 28
31	14 38	−13.3	14	97	2 06	21 48	22 04

SUNRISE AND SUNSET

	London		Bristol		Birmingham		Manchester		Newcastle		Glasgow		Belfast	
	0°05'	51°30'	2°35'	51°28'	1°55'	52°28'	2°15'	53°28'	1°37'	54°59'	4°14'	55°52'	5°56'	54°35'
	h m	h m	h m	h m	h m	h m	h m	h m	h m	h m	h m	h m	h m	h m
1	6 47	17 40	6 57	17 50	6 55	17 46	6 58	17 46	6 58	17 41	7 09	17 50	7 14	17 59
2	6 44	17 42	6 54	17 52	6 53	17 48	6 56	17 48	6 55	17 43	7 07	17 52	7 12	18 01
3	6 42	17 43	6 52	17 53	6 51	17 50	6 53	17 50	6 53	17 45	7 04	17 54	7 09	18 03
4	6 40	17 45	6 50	17 55	6 49	17 51	6 51	17 52	6 50	17 47	7 02	17 57	7 07	18 05
5	6 38	17 47	6 48	17 57	6 46	17 53	6 49	17 53	6 48	17 49	6 59	17 59	7 05	18 07
6	6 36	17 49	6 46	17 59	6 44	17 55	6 46	17 55	6 45	17 51	6 57	18 01	7 02	18 09
7	6 34	17 50	6 43	18 00	6 42	17 57	6 44	17 57	6 43	17 53	6 54	18 03	7 00	18 11
8	6 31	17 52	6 41	18 02	6 39	17 59	6 42	17 59	6 40	17 55	6 52	18 05	6 57	18 13
9	6 29	17 54	6 39	18 04	6 37	18 00	6 39	18 01	6 38	17 57	6 49	18 07	6 55	18 15
10	6 27	17 55	6 37	18 06	6 35	18 02	6 37	18 03	6 35	17 59	6 47	18 09	6 52	18 17
11	6 25	17 57	6 35	18 07	6 33	18 04	6 34	18 05	6 33	18 01	6 44	18 11	6 50	18 19
12	6 22	17 59	6 32	18 09	6 30	18 06	6 32	18 07	6 30	18 03	6 41	18 13	6 47	18 21
13	6 20	18 01	6 30	18 11	6 28	18 08	6 30	18 08	6 28	18 05	6 39	18 15	6 45	18 23
14	6 18	18 02	6 28	18 12	6 26	18 09	6 27	18 10	6 25	18 07	6 36	18 17	6 42	18 25
15	6 16	18 04	6 26	18 14	6 23	18 11	6 25	18 12	6 23	18 09	6 34	18 19	6 40	18 27
16	6 13	18 06	6 23	18 16	6 21	18 13	6 22	18 14	6 20	18 11	6 31	18 21	6 37	18 29
17	6 11	18 07	6 21	18 17	6 19	18 15	6 20	18 16	6 18	18 13	6 28	18 24	6 35	18 31
18	6 09	18 09	6 19	18 19	6 16	18 16	6 18	18 18	6 15	18 15	6 26	18 26	6 32	18 32
19	6 07	18 11	6 17	18 21	6 14	18 18	6 15	18 20	6 13	18 17	6 23	18 28	6 30	18 34
20	6 04	18 13	6 14	18 23	6 12	18 20	6 13	18 21	6 10	18 19	6 21	18 30	6 27	18 36
21	6 02	18 14	6 12	18 24	6 09	18 22	6 10	18 23	6 08	18 21	6 18	18 32	6 25	18 38
22	6 00	18 16	6 10	18 26	6 07	18 24	6 08	18 25	6 05	18 23	6 15	18 34	6 22	18 40
23	5 57	18 18	6 07	18 28	6 04	18 25	6 06	18 27	6 03	18 25	6 13	18 36	6 20	18 42
24	5 55	18 19	6 05	18 29	6 02	18 27	6 03	18 29	6 00	18 27	6 10	18 38	6 17	18 44
25	5 53	18 21	6 03	18 31	6 00	18 29	6 01	18 31	5 57	18 29	6 07	18 40	6 15	18 46
26	5 51	18 23	6 01	18 33	5 57	18 31	5 58	18 32	5 55	18 31	6 05	18 42	6 12	18 48
27	5 48	18 24	5 58	18 34	5 55	18 32	5 56	18 34	5 52	18 33	6 02	18 44	6 10	18 50
28	5 46	18 26	5 56	18 36	5 53	18 34	5 53	18 36	5 50	18 35	6 00	18 46	6 07	18 52
29	5 44	18 28	5 54	18 38	5 50	18 36	5 51	18 38	5 47	18 37	5 57	18 48	6 05	18 54
30	5 41	18 29	5 51	18 39	5 48	18 38	5 49	18 40	5 45	18 39	5 54	18 50	6 02	18 56
31	5 39	18 31	5 49	18 41	5 46	18 39	5 46	18 42	5 42	18 41	5 52	18 52	6 00	18 57

JUPITER

Day	RA	Dec.	Transit	5° high	
				52°	56°
	h m	° '	h m	h m	h m
1	0 15.0	+ 0 25	13 40	19 09	19 06
11	0 23.6	+ 1 22	13 09	18 43	18 41
21	0 32.4	+ 2 19	12 39	18 18	18 16
31	0 41.3	+ 3 16	12 08	17 52	17 51

Diameters – equatorial 33" polar 31"

SATURN

Day	RA	Dec.	Transit	5° high	
				52°	56°
	h m	° '	h m	h m	h m
1	1 54.9	+ 9 19	15 19	21 34	21 38
11	1 58.7	+ 9 42	14 44	21 00	21 05
21	2 02.9	+10 07	14 09	20 27	20 32
31	2 07.4	+10 32	13 34	19 55	20 00

Diameters – equatorial 16" polar 15"
Rings – major axis 38" minor axis 10"

URANUS

Day	RA	Dec.	Transit	10° high	
				52°	56°
	h m	° '	h m	h m	h m
1	21 07.8	−17 09	10 33	7 28	7 59
11	21 09.9	−17 00	9 55	6 49	7 20
21	21 11.8	−16 52	9 18	6 11	6 41
31	21 13.5	−16 44	8 40	5 32	6 02

Diameter 4"

NEPTUNE

Day	RA	Dec.	Transit	10° high	
				52°	56°
	h m	° '	h m	h m	h m
1	20 21.7	−19 09	9 47	6 59	7 37
11	20 23.0	−19 05	9 09	6 20	6 58
21	20 24.1	−19 02	8 30	5 42	6 19
31	20 25.0	−18 58	7 52	5 03	5 40

Diameter 2"

April 1999

FOURTH MONTH, 30 DAYS. *Aperire*, to open; Earth opens to receive seed

1	*Thursday*	**Maundy Thursday.** PASSOVER begins	*week* 13 *day* 91
2	*Friday*	**Good Friday.** *Public Holiday in the UK*	92
3	*Saturday*	Easter Eve. Graham Greene d. 1991	93
4	*Sunday*	**Easter Day** (Western churches)	*week* 14 *day* 94
5	*Monday*	*Bank Holiday in England, Wales and Northern Ireland*	95
6	*Tuesday*	Richard I d. 1199. Peary reached the North Pole 1909	96
7	*Wednesday*	William Wordsworth b. 1770. Henry Ford d. 1947	97
8	*Thursday*	Sir Adrian Boult b. 1889. Kurt Cobain d. 1994	98
9	*Friday*	Duke of Monmouth b. 1649. Frank Lloyd Wright d. 1959	99
10	*Saturday*	Gen. William Booth b. 1829. Chris Hani assassinated 1993	100
11	*Sunday*	**2nd S. of Easter.** EASTER DAY (Eastern Orthodox)	*week* 15 *day* 101
12	*Monday*	Alan Ayckbourn b. 1939. Bobby Moore b. 1941	102
13	*Tuesday*	*Easter Law Sittings begin.* Edict of Nantes 1598	103
14	*Wednesday*	SIKH NEW YEAR. Sir John Gielgud b. 1904	104
15	*Thursday*	Greta Garbo d. 1990. John Curry d. 1994	105
16	*Friday*	Mme Tussaud d. 1850. Sir Charles Chaplin b. 1889	106
17	*Saturday*	MUSLIM NEW YEAR. Benjamin Franklin d. 1790	107
18	*Sunday*	**3rd S. of Easter.** Judge Jeffreys d. 1689	*week* 16 *day* 108
19	*Monday*	Primrose Day. Lord Berners d. 1950	109
20	*Tuesday*	Adolf Hitler b. 1889. Bram Stoker d. 1912	110
21	*Wednesday*	*Queen Elizabeth II b. 1926.* Jean Racine d. 1699	111
22	*Thursday*	Kathleen Ferrier b. 1912. Yehudi Menuhin b. 1916	112
23	*Friday*	**St George.** Shakespeare d. 1616. Cervantes d. 1616	113
24	*Saturday*	Easter Rising, Dublin, began 1916	114
25	*Sunday*	**4th S. of Easter.** Oliver Cromwell b. 1599	*week* 17 *day* 115
26	*Monday*	**St Mark.** Eugène Delacroix b. 1798	116
27	*Tuesday*	Samuel Morse b. 1791. Dashiel Hammett b. 1894	117
28	*Wednesday*	Mutiny on the *Bounty*. Mussolini killed 1945	118
29	*Thursday*	Duke Ellington b. 1899. Easter Rising put down 1916	119
30	*Friday*	Mary II b. 1662. Adolf Hitler d. 1945	120

ASTRONOMICAL PHENOMENA

d	h	
1	06	Jupiter in conjunction
2	09	Mercury at stationary point
3	10	Mars in conjunction with Moon. Mars 3° S.
14	05	Mercury in conjunction with Moon. Mercury 1° N.
15	10	Jupiter in conjunction with Moon. Jupiter 3° N.
16	16	Mercury at greatest elongation W.28°
16	20	Saturn in conjunction with Moon. Saturn 3° N.
18	23	Venus in conjunction with Moon. Venus 7° N.
20	13	Sun's longitude 30° ♉
24	18	Mars at opposition
27	11	Saturn in conjunction
29	23	Mars in conjunction with Moon. Mars 4° S.

MINIMA OF ALGOL

d	h	d	h	d	h
1	13.6	13	00.8	24	12.1
4	10.4	15	21.7	27	08.9
7	07.2	18	18.5	30	05.8
10	04.0	21	15.3		

CONSTELLATIONS

The following constellations are near the meridian at

	d	h		d	h
March	1	24	April	15	21
March	16	23	May	1	20
April	1	22	May	16	19

Cepheus (below the Pole), Cassiopeia (below the Pole), Ursa Major, Leo Minor, Leo, Sextans, Hydra and Crater

THE MOON

Phases, Apsides and Node	d	h	m
☾ Last Quarter	9	02	51
● New Moon	16	04	22
☽ First Quarter	22	19	02
○ Full Moon	30	14	55
Apogee (405,568 km)	4	21	22
Perigee (358,904 km)	17	05	18

Mean longitude of ascending node on April 1, 140°

THE SUN

s.d. 16'.0

Day	Right Ascension	Dec. +	Equation of time	Rise 52°	Rise 56°	Transit	Set 52°	Set 56°	Sidereal time	Transit of First Point of Aries
	h m s	° '	m s	h m	h m	h m	h m	h m	h m s	h m s
1	0 39 47	4 17	− 4 08	5 36	5 32	12 04	18 33	18 37	12 35 39	11 22 29
2	0 43 26	4 40	− 3 50	5 34	5 29	12 04	18 35	18 39	12 39 35	11 18 33
3	0 47 04	5 03	− 3 32	5 32	5 27	12 03	18 36	18 41	12 43 32	11 14 37
4	0 50 43	5 26	− 3 15	5 29	5 24	12 03	18 38	18 43	12 47 28	11 10 41
5	0 54 22	5 49	− 2 57	5 27	5 22	12 03	18 40	18 45	12 51 25	11 06 45
6	0 58 01	6 12	− 2 40	5 25	5 19	12 03	18 41	18 47	12 55 22	11 02 50
7	1 01 41	6 35	− 2 23	5 22	5 16	12 02	18 43	18 49	12 59 18	10 58 54
8	1 05 20	6 57	− 2 06	5 20	5 14	12 02	18 45	18 51	13 03 15	10 54 58
9	1 09 00	7 20	− 1 49	5 18	5 11	12 02	18 47	18 54	13 07 11	10 51 02
10	1 12 40	7 42	− 1 33	5 16	5 09	12 01	18 48	18 56	13 11 08	10 47 06
11	1 16 21	8 04	− 1 17	5 13	5 06	12 01	18 50	18 58	13 15 04	10 43 10
12	1 20 02	8 26	− 1 01	5 11	5 03	12 01	18 52	19 00	13 19 01	10 39 14
13	1 23 43	8 48	− 0 45	5 09	5 01	12 01	18 53	19 02	13 22 57	10 35 18
14	1 27 24	9 10	− 0 30	5 07	4 58	12 00	18 55	19 04	13 26 54	10 31 22
15	1 31 06	9 32	− 0 15	5 05	4 56	12 00	18 57	19 06	13 30 51	10 27 26
16	1 34 48	9 53	− 0 01	5 02	4 53	12 00	18 59	19 08	13 34 47	10 23 30
17	1 38 30	10 14	+ 0 14	5 00	4 51	12 00	19 00	19 10	13 38 44	10 19 35
18	1 42 13	10 35	+ 0 27	4 58	4 48	11 59	19 02	19 12	13 42 40	10 15 39
19	1 45 56	10 56	+ 0 41	4 56	4 46	11 59	19 04	19 14	13 46 37	10 11 43
20	1 49 39	11 17	+ 0 54	4 54	4 43	11 59	19 05	19 16	13 50 33	10 07 47
21	1 53 23	11 38	+ 1 07	4 52	4 41	11 59	19 07	19 18	13 54 30	10 03 51
22	1 57 08	11 58	+ 1 19	4 49	4 38	11 59	19 09	19 20	13 58 26	9 59 55
23	2 00 52	12 18	+ 1 31	4 47	4 36	11 58	19 11	19 22	14 02 23	9 55 59
24	2 04 38	12 39	+ 1 42	4 45	4 34	11 58	19 12	19 24	14 06 19	9 52 03
25	2 08 23	12 58	+ 1 53	4 43	4 31	11 58	19 14	19 26	14 10 16	9 48 07
26	2 12 09	13 18	+ 2 03	4 41	4 29	11 58	19 16	19 28	14 14 13	9 44 11
27	2 15 56	13 37	+ 2 13	4 39	4 27	11 58	19 17	19 30	14 18 09	9 40 16
28	2 19 43	13 56	+ 2 23	4 37	4 24	11 58	19 19	19 32	14 22 06	9 36 20
29	2 23 30	14 15	+ 2 32	4 35	4 22	11 57	19 21	19 34	14 26 02	9 32 24
30	2 27 18	14 34	+ 2 40	4 33	4 20	11 57	19 22	19 36	14 29 59	9 28 28

DURATION OF TWILIGHT (in minutes)

Latitude	52°	56°	52°	56°	52°	56°	52°	56°
	1 April		11 April		21 April		30 April	
Civil	34	38	35	40	37	42	39	44
Nautical	76	85	79	90	84	96	89	105
Astronomical	121	137	128	148	138	167	152	200

THE NIGHT SKY

Mercury is unsuitably placed for observation throughout the month.

Venus continues to be visible as a magnificent object in the western sky in the evenings, magnitude −4.1. On the evening of the 18th the thin crescent Moon, less than three days old, will be seen near the planet. Venus passes 7° N. of Aldebaran on the evening of the 21st.

Mars reaches opposition on the 24th, and is thus visible throughout the hours of darkness, attaining a magnitude of −1.7. Because of the eccentricity of its orbit, closest approach to the Earth (87 million km) does not occur until May 1st. The gibbous Moon is near the planet during the night of the 2nd to 3rd: also the Full Moon is near during the night of the 29th to 30th. During April, Mars moves retrograde from Libra back into Virgo.

Jupiter passes through conjunction on the first day of the month and thus remains too close to the Sun for observation.

Saturn, magnitude +0.4, is disappearing into the lengthening evening twilight in the west, and is unlikely to be seen after the first few days of the month. Saturn passes through conjunction on the 27th.

THE MOON

Day	RA	Dec.	Hor. par.	Semi-diam.	Sun's co-long.	PA of Bright Limb	Phase	Age	Rise 52°	Rise 56°	Transit	Set 52°	Set 56°
	h m	°	′	′	°	°	%	d	h m	h m	h m	h m	h m
1	12 48	− 0.9	54.9	14.9	87	31	100	14.2	19 08	19 11	0 13	6 13	6 11
2	13 34	− 4.9	54.5	14.9	100	91	99	15.2	20 13	20 20	0 56	6 34	6 29
3	14 20	− 8.7	54.3	14.8	112	98	96	16.2	21 17	21 27	1 39	6 57	6 48
4	15 06	−12.2	54.1	14.7	124	98	91	17.2	22 19	22 33	2 23	7 22	7 10
5	15 53	−15.1	54.1	14.7	136	97	85	18.2	23 20	23 37	3 08	7 50	7 35
6	16 42	−17.4	54.1	14.8	148	94	78	19.2	—	—	3 54	8 23	8 05
7	17 31	−19.0	54.4	14.8	160	91	70	20.2	0 18	0 37	4 41	9 02	8 42
8	18 22	−19.7	54.8	14.9	173	87	61	21.2	1 11	1 31	5 30	9 48	9 28
9	19 14	−19.6	55.3	15.1	185	83	51	22.2	1 59	2 19	6 19	10 42	10 22
10	20 06	−18.4	56.0	15.3	197	78	41	23.2	2 41	2 59	7 10	11 43	11 25
11	20 59	−16.4	56.9	15.5	209	74	31	24.2	3 18	3 33	8 01	12 50	12 36
12	21 53	−13.4	57.8	15.7	221	70	22	25.2	3 50	4 02	8 52	14 03	13 52
13	22 46	− 9.6	58.7	16.0	234	66	14	26.2	4 19	4 27	9 44	15 19	15 13
14	23 41	− 5.1	59.6	16.2	246	62	7	27.2	4 46	4 50	10 36	16 39	16 37
15	0 36	− 0.3	60.4	16.4	258	54	2	28.2	5 13	5 12	11 30	18 01	18 04
16	1 32	+ 4.8	60.9	16.6	270	8	0	29.2	5 40	5 35	12 25	19 24	19 32
17	2 29	+ 9.5	61.1	16.6	283	274	1	0.8	6 10	6 01	13 21	20 47	21 00
18	3 29	+13.7	61.0	16.6	295	266	5	1.8	6 44	6 31	14 20	22 08	22 24
19	4 29	+17.0	60.6	16.5	307	267	12	2.8	7 25	7 08	15 20	23 22	23 41
20	5 31	+19.1	60.0	16.4	319	270	20	3.8	8 13	7 54	16 19	—	—
21	6 32	+19.9	59.3	16.2	331	275	31	4.8	9 10	8 50	17 17	0 27	0 47
22	7 31	+19.4	58.5	15.9	344	279	41	5.8	10 13	9 54	18 13	1 21	1 40
23	8 28	+17.8	57.7	15.7	356	284	52	6.8	11 20	11 04	19 06	2 05	2 22
24	9 22	+15.3	56.9	15.5	8	288	63	7.8	12 29	12 17	19 56	2 41	2 54
25	10 14	+12.1	56.3	15.3	20	291	73	8.8	13 38	13 29	20 43	3 10	3 20
26	11 03	+ 8.4	55.7	15.2	32	294	81	9.8	14 46	14 41	21 28	3 35	3 41
27	11 50	+ 4.4	55.2	15.0	45	297	88	10.8	15 52	15 51	22 11	3 57	4 00
28	12 36	+ 0.2	54.8	14.9	57	300	94	11.8	16 58	17 00	22 54	4 18	4 18
29	13 22	− 3.9	54.4	14.8	69	305	97	12.8	18 03	18 09	23 37	4 39	4 35
30	14 07	− 7.8	54.2	14.8	81	325	99	13.8	19 07	19 17	—	5 01	4 54

MERCURY

Day	RA	Dec.	Diam.	Phase	Transit	5° high 52°	5° high 56°
	h m	°	″	%	h m	h m	h m
1	23 26	− 3.0	10	18	10 48	5 38	5 44
3	23 26	− 3.5	10	22	10 41	5 33	5 39
5	23 28	− 3.8	10	26	10 36	5 29	5 35
7	23 31	− 4.0	9	30	10 31	5 25	5 31
9	23 35	− 3.9	9	34	10 27	5 21	5 28
11	23 40	− 3.8	9	38	10 25	5 17	5 24
13	23 46	− 3.5	8	41	10 23	5 14	5 20
15	23 53	− 3.0	8	44	10 22	5 10	5 16
17	0 00	− 2.5	8	47	10 21	5 07	5 12
19	0 08	− 1.8	8	50	10 22	5 03	5 08
21	0 17	− 1.0	7	53	10 22	5 00	5 04
23	0 26	− 0.2	7	56	10 24	4 56	5 00
25	0 35	+ 0.8	7	59	10 25	4 53	4 56
27	0 45	+ 1.8	7	62	10 28	4 50	4 52
29	0 56	+ 3.0	6	65	10 30	4 47	4 48
31	1 07	+ 4.2	6	68	10 34	4 44	4 44

VENUS

Day	RA	Dec.	Diam.	Phase	Transit	5° high 52°	5° high 56°
	h m	°	″	%	h m	h m	h m
1	2 54	+17.5	13	80	14 19	21 20	21 32
6	3 18	+19.4	14	78	14 23	21 35	21 49
11	3 42	+21.0	14	76	14 28	21 50	22 05
16	4 07	+22.5	15	75	14 33	22 03	22 21
21	4 32	+23.7	15	73	14 38	22 16	22 35
26	4 57	+24.7	16	71	14 43	22 27	22 47
31	5 22	+25.4	16	69	14 48	22 37	22 58

MARS

Day	RA	Dec.	Diam.	Phase	Transit	5° high 52°	5° high 56°
1	14 37	−13.2	14	98	2 01	21 43	21 59
6	14 33	−13.0	15	98	1 37	21 18	21 34
11	14 28	−12.7	15	99	1 13	20 51	21 06
16	14 22	−12.4	16	100	0 47	20 23	20 38
21	14 15	−11.9	16	100	0 20	19 54	20 08
26	14 07	−11.5	16	100	23 48	19 24	19 38
31	14 00	−11.1	16	100	23 21	18 54	19 08

SUNRISE AND SUNSET

	London		Bristol		Birmingham		Manchester		Newcastle		Glasgow		Belfast	
	0°05′	51°30′	2°35′	51°28′	1°55′	52°28′	2°15′	53°28′	1°37′	54°59′	4°14′	55°52′	5°56′	54°35′
	h m	h m	h m	h m	h m	h m	h m	h m	h m	h m	h m	h m	h m	h m
1	5 37	18 33	5 47	18 43	5 43	18 41	5 44	18 43	5 40	18 43	5 49	18 54	5 57	18 59
2	5 35	18 34	5 45	18 44	5 41	18 43	5 41	18 45	5 37	18 44	5 46	18 56	5 55	19 01
3	5 32	18 36	5 42	18 46	5 39	18 45	5 39	18 47	5 35	18 46	5 44	18 58	5 52	19 03
4	5 30	18 38	5 40	18 48	5 36	18 46	5 36	18 49	5 32	18 48	5 41	19 00	5 50	19 05
5	5 28	18 39	5 38	18 49	5 34	18 48	5 34	18 51	5 29	18 50	5 39	19 02	5 47	19 07
6	5 26	18 41	5 36	18 51	5 32	18 50	5 32	18 53	5 27	18 52	5 36	19 04	5 45	19 09
7	5 23	18 43	5 33	18 53	5 29	18 52	5 29	18 54	5 24	18 54	5 33	19 06	5 42	19 11
8	5 21	18 44	5 31	18 54	5 27	18 53	5 27	18 56	5 22	18 56	5 31	19 08	5 40	19 13
9	5 19	18 46	5 29	18 56	5 25	18 55	5 25	18 58	5 19	18 58	5 28	19 10	5 37	19 15
10	5 17	18 48	5 27	18 58	5 23	18 57	5 22	19 00	5 17	19 00	5 26	19 12	5 35	19 17
11	5 15	18 49	5 25	18 59	5 20	18 58	5 20	19 02	5 14	19 02	5 23	19 14	5 33	19 18
12	5 12	18 51	5 22	19 01	5 18	19 00	5 18	19 03	5 12	19 04	5 21	19 16	5 30	19 20
13	5 10	18 53	5 20	19 03	5 16	19 02	5 15	19 05	5 10	19 06	5 18	19 18	5 28	19 22
14	5 08	18 55	5 18	19 04	5 13	19 04	5 13	19 07	5 07	19 08	5 16	19 20	5 25	19 24
15	5 06	18 56	5 16	19 06	5 11	19 05	5 11	19 09	5 05	19 10	5 13	19 22	5 23	19 26
16	5 04	18 58	5 14	19 08	5 09	19 07	5 08	19 11	5 02	19 12	5 11	19 24	5 20	19 28
17	5 02	19 00	5 12	19 09	5 07	19 09	5 06	19 13	5 00	19 14	5 08	19 26	5 18	19 30
18	4 59	19 01	5 09	19 11	5 05	19 11	5 04	19 14	4 57	19 16	5 06	19 28	5 16	19 32
19	4 57	19 03	5 07	19 13	5 02	19 12	5 01	19 16	4 55	19 18	5 03	19 31	5 13	19 34
20	4 55	19 05	5 05	19 14	5 00	19 14	4 59	19 18	4 53	19 20	5 01	19 33	5 11	19 36
21	4 53	19 06	5 03	19 16	4 58	19 16	4 57	19 20	4 50	19 21	4 58	19 35	5 09	19 38
22	4 51	19 08	5 01	19 18	4 56	19 18	4 55	19 22	4 48	19 23	4 56	19 37	5 06	19 40
23	4 49	19 10	4 59	19 19	4 54	19 19	4 53	19 23	4 46	19 25	4 53	19 39	5 04	19 41
24	4 47	19 11	4 57	19 21	4 52	19 21	4 50	19 25	4 43	19 27	4 51	19 41	5 02	19 43
25	4 45	19 13	4 55	19 23	4 50	19 23	4 48	19 27	4 41	19 29	4 49	19 43	5 00	19 45
26	4 43	19 15	4 53	19 24	4 48	19 25	4 46	19 29	4 39	19 31	4 46	19 45	4 57	19 47
27	4 41	19 16	4 51	19 26	4 46	19 26	4 44	19 31	4 36	19 33	4 44	19 47	4 55	19 49
28	4 39	19 18	4 49	19 28	4 43	19 28	4 42	19 33	4 34	19 35	4 42	19 49	4 53	19 51
29	4 37	19 19	4 47	19 29	4 41	19 30	4 40	19 34	4 32	19 37	4 39	19 51	4 51	19 53
30	4 35	19 21	4 45	19 31	4 39	19 31	4 38	19 36	4 30	19 39	4 37	19 53	4 48	19 55

JUPITER

Day	RA	Dec.		Transit	5° high	
					52°	56°
	h m	°	′	h m	h m	h m
1	0 42.2	+ 3	21	12 05	6 21	6 21
11	0 51.1	+ 4	18	11 35	5 46	5 45
21	1 00.0	+ 5	13	11 04	5 11	5 10
31	1 08.7	+ 6	07	10 33	4 35	4 34

Diameters – equatorial 33″ polar 31″

SATURN

Day	RA	Dec.		Transit	5° high	
					52°	56°
	h m	°	′	h m	h m	h m
1	2 07.9	+10	35	13 30	19 51	19 57
11	2 12.6	+11	00	12 56	19 19	19 25
21	2 17.4	+11	26	12 21	18 47	18 53
31	2 22.3	+11	51	11 47	18 14	18 21

Diameters – equatorial 16″ polar 15″
Rings – major axis 37″ minor axis 11″

URANUS

Day	RA	Dec.		Transit	10° high	
					52°	56°
	h m	°	′	h m	h m	h m
1	21 13.7	−16	44	8 37	5 28	5 58
11	21 15.1	−16	38	7 59	4 50	5 19
21	21 16.3	−16	33	7 21	4 11	4 40
31	21 17.1	−16	29	6 42	3 32	4 01

Diameter 4″

NEPTUNE

Day	RA	Dec.		Transit	10° high	
					52°	56°
	h m	°	′	h m	h m	h m
1	20 25.1	−18	58	7 48	4 59	5 36
11	20 25.8	−18	56	7 10	4 20	4 57
21	20 26.2	−18	54	6 31	3 41	4 18
31	20 26.2	−18	53	5 52	3 02	3 39

Diameter 2″

May 1999

FIFTH MONTH, 31 DAYS. *Maia,* goddess of growth and increase

1	Saturday	**SS Philip and James.** Great Exhibition opened 1851	*week* 17 *day* 121
2	Sunday	**5th S. of Easter.** Leonardo da Vinci d. 1519	*week* 18 *day* 122
3	Monday	Bank Holiday in the UK. Festival of Britain opened 1951	123
4	Tuesday	Joseph Whitaker b. 1820. Sir Osbert Sitwell d. 1969	124
5	Wednesday	Napoleon Bonaparte d. 1821. Austin Reed d. 1954	125
6	Thursday	Tony Blair b. 1953. First four-minute mile 1954	126
7	Friday	Robert Browning b. 1812. Sir Huw Wheldon b. 1916	127
8	Saturday	John Stuart Mill d. 1873. Friedrich von Hayek b. 1899	128
9	Sunday	**6th S. of Easter.** Europe Day	*week* 19 *day* 129
10	Monday	Indian Mutiny began 1857. Fred Astaire b. 1899	130
11	Tuesday	Paul Nash b. 1889. Martha Graham b. 1894	131
12	Wednesday	John Masefield d. 1967. John Smith d. 1994	132
13	Thursday	**Ascension Day.** John Nash d. 1835	133
14	Friday	**St Matthias.** Thomas Gainsborough baptized 1727	134
15	Saturday	Joseph Whitaker d. 1895. James Mason b. 1909	135
16	Sunday	**7th S. of Easter.** 'Oscars' first presented 1929	*week* 20 *day* 136
17	Monday	Botticelli d. 1510. Relief of Mafeking 1900	137
18	Tuesday	Pierre de Beaumarchais d. 1799. Pope John Paul II b. 1920	138
19	Wednesday	Anne Boleyn executed 1536. Sir John Betjeman d. 1984	139
20	Thursday	John Stuart Mill b. 1806. First Chelsea Flower Show 1913	140
21	Friday	FEAST OF WEEKS begins. Lord Clark d. 1983	141
22	Saturday	Maria Edgeworth d. 1849. Blackwall Tunnel opened 1897	142
23	Sunday	**Pentecost (Whit Sunday).** Thomas Hood b. 1799	*week* 21 *day* 143
24	Monday	Queen Victoria b. 1819. Suzanne Lenglen b. 1899	144
25	Tuesday	Lord Beaverbrook b. 1879. Gustav Holst d. 1934	145
26	Wednesday	Samuel Pepys d. 1703. Queen Mary b. 1867	146
27	Thursday	John Calvin d. 1564. Jawaharlal Nehru d. 1964	147
28	Friday	*Easter Law Sittings end.* William Pitt (younger) b. 1759	148
29	Saturday	Constantinople captured by Turks 1453. Everest conquered 1953	149
30	Sunday	**Trinity Sunday.** Alexander Pope d. 1744	*week* 22 *day* 150
31	Monday	**Visit of Virgin Mary to Elizabeth.** *Bank Holiday in the UK*	151

ASTRONOMICAL PHENOMENA

d h
1 22 Jupiter in conjunction with Mercury. Jupiter 2° N.
7 01 Neptune at stationary point
13 07 Jupiter in conjunction with Moon. Jupiter 3° N.
13 16 Saturn in conjunction with Mercury. Saturn 0°.6 S.
14 12 Saturn in conjunction with Moon. Saturn 3° N.
14 15 Mercury in conjunction with Moon. Mercury 4° N.
18 14 Venus in conjunction with Moon. Venus 6° N.
21 12 Sun's longitude 60° II
21 22 Uranus at stationary point
25 18 Mercury in superior conjunction
26 15 Mars in conjunction with Moon. Mars 5° S.
31 00 Pluto at opposition

MINIMA OF ALGOL

Algol is inconveniently situated for observation during May.

CONSTELLATIONS
The following constellations are near the meridian at

	d	h		d	h
April	1	24	May	16	21
April	15	23	June	1	20
May	1	22	June	15	19

Cepheus (below the Pole), Cassiopeia (below the Pole), Ursa Minor, Ursa Major, Canes Venatici, Coma Berenices, Bootes, Leo, Virgo, Crater, Corvus and Hydra

THE MOON

Phases, Apsides and Node	d	h	m
☾ Last Quarter	8	17	29
● New Moon	15	12	05
☽ First Quarter	22	05	34
○ Full Moon	30	06	40
Apogee (406,265 km)	2	05	59
Perigee (357,095 km)	15	15	01
Apogee (406,404 km)	29	08	00

Mean longitude of ascending node on May 1, 138°

THE SUN   s.d. 15'.8

Day	Right Ascension	Dec. +	Equation of time	Rise 52°	Rise 56°	Transit	Set 52°	Set 56°	Sidereal time	Transit of First Point of Aries
	h m s	° '	m s	h m	h m	h m	h m	h m	h m s	h m s
1	2 31 07	14 52	+ 2 48	4 31	4 17	11 57	19 24	19 38	14 33 55	9 24 32
2	2 34 56	15 11	+ 2 56	4 29	4 15	11 57	19 26	19 40	14 37 52	9 20 36
3	2 38 46	15 29	+ 3 03	4 28	4 13	11 57	19 27	19 42	14 41 48	9 16 40
4	2 42 36	15 46	+ 3 09	4 26	4 11	11 57	19 29	19 44	14 45 45	9 12 44
5	2 46 27	16 04	+ 3 15	4 24	4 08	11 57	19 31	19 46	14 49 42	9 08 48
6	2 50 18	16 21	+ 3 20	4 22	4 06	11 57	19 32	19 48	14 53 38	9 04 52
7	2 54 10	16 38	+ 3 25	4 20	4 04	11 57	19 34	19 50	14 57 35	9 00 56
8	2 58 02	16 54	+ 3 29	4 18	4 02	11 56	19 36	19 52	15 01 31	8 57 01
9	3 01 55	17 11	+ 3 32	4 17	4 00	11 56	19 37	19 54	15 05 28	8 53 05
10	3 05 49	17 27	+ 3 35	4 15	3 58	11 56	19 39	19 56	15 09 24	8 49 09
11	3 09 43	17 42	+ 3 38	4 13	3 56	11 56	19 40	19 58	15 13 21	8 45 13
12	3 13 38	17 58	+ 3 39	4 12	3 54	11 56	19 42	20 00	15 17 17	8 41 17
13	3 17 34	18 13	+ 3 40	4 10	3 52	11 56	19 44	20 02	15 21 14	8 37 21
14	3 21 30	18 28	+ 3 41	4 08	3 50	11 56	19 45	20 04	15 25 11	8 33 25
15	3 25 26	18 42	+ 3 41	4 07	3 48	11 56	19 47	20 06	15 29 07	8 29 29
16	3 29 23	18 57	+ 3 40	4 05	3 46	11 56	19 48	20 08	15 33 04	8 25 33
17	3 33 21	19 11	+ 3 39	4 04	3 44	11 56	19 50	20 09	15 37 00	8 21 37
18	3 37 19	19 24	+ 3 37	4 02	3 43	11 56	19 51	20 11	15 40 57	8 17 41
19	3 41 18	19 37	+ 3 35	4 01	3 41	11 56	19 53	20 13	15 44 53	8 13 46
20	3 45 18	19 50	+ 3 32	4 00	3 39	11 56	19 54	20 15	15 48 50	8 09 50
21	3 49 18	20 03	+ 3 29	3 58	3 38	11 57	19 56	20 17	15 52 46	8 05 54
22	3 53 18	20 15	+ 3 25	3 57	3 36	11 57	19 57	20 18	15 56 43	8 01 58
23	3 57 19	20 27	+ 3 21	3 56	3 34	11 57	19 58	20 20	16 00 40	7 58 02
24	4 01 20	20 38	+ 3 16	3 55	3 33	11 57	20 00	20 22	16 04 36	7 54 06
25	4 05 22	20 50	+ 3 11	3 53	3 31	11 57	20 01	20 23	16 08 33	7 50 10
26	4 09 25	21 00	+ 3 05	3 52	3 30	11 57	20 02	20 25	16 12 29	7 46 14
27	4 13 27	21 11	+ 2 58	3 51	3 29	11 57	20 04	20 27	16 16 26	7 42 18
28	4 17 31	21 21	+ 2 52	3 50	3 27	11 57	20 05	20 28	16 20 22	7 38 22
29	4 21 35	21 31	+ 2 44	3 49	3 26	11 57	20 06	20 30	16 24 19	7 34 26
30	4 25 39	21 40	+ 2 37	3 48	3 25	11 57	20 07	20 31	16 28 15	7 30 31
31	4 29 44	21 49	+ 2 29	3 47	3 24	11 58	20 09	20 32	16 32 12	7 26 35

DURATION OF TWILIGHT (in minutes)

Latitude	52°	56°	52°	56°	52°	56°	52°	56°
	1 May		11 May		21 May		31 May	
Civil	39	45	41	49	44	53	46	57
Nautical	90	106	97	121	106	143	116	TAN
Astronomical	154	209	179	TAN	TAN	TAN	TAN	TAN

THE NIGHT SKY

Mercury is unsuitably placed for observation throughout the month, superior conjunction occurring on the 25th.

Venus, magnitude −4.2, is still a magnificent object, dominating the western sky in the evenings before setting to the north of west. At the end of the month Venus will be seen passing south of Castor and Pollux, the two bright stars in the constellation of Gemini.

Mars continues to be visible in the southern sky, though by the end of the month it is lost to view before midnight. It is still a conspicuous object, though during the month its magnitude fades from −1.6 to −1.1. The gibbous Moon is near the planet on the evening of the 26th. Mars is moving slowly retrograde in the constellation of Virgo.

Jupiter is too close to the Sun for observation for most of May. However, during the last few days of the month it may be glimpsed for a short time low above the eastern horizon before the morning twilight inhibits observation. Jupiter, magnitude −2.1, is in the constellation of Pisces.

Saturn is unsuitably placed for observation.

THE MOON

Day	RA h m	Dec. °	Hor. par. '	Semi- diam. '	Sun's co- long. °	PA of Bright Limb °	Phase %	Age d	Rise 52° h m	Rise 56° h m	Transit h m	Set 52° h m	Set 56° h m
1	14 54	−11.4	54.0	14.7	93	57	100	14.8	20 11	20 24	0 20	5 25	5 14
2	15 40	−14.5	54.0	14.7	105	85	98	15.8	21 13	21 29	1 05	5 51	5 37
3	16 28	−17.0	54.0	14.7	118	89	95	16.8	22 12	22 31	1 50	6 22	6 05
4	17 18	−18.8	54.1	14.7	130	89	90	17.8	23 07	23 27	2 37	6 59	6 40
5	18 08	−19.8	54.4	14.8	142	86	84	18.8	23 57	—	3 25	7 42	7 22
6	18 59	−19.9	54.8	14.9	154	82	76	19.8	—	0 17	4 14	8 32	8 12
7	19 51	−19.1	55.3	15.1	166	79	67	20.8	0 41	0 59	5 03	9 30	9 11
8	20 43	−17.4	55.9	15.2	179	75	58	21.8	1 18	1 35	5 53	10 33	10 18
9	21 35	−14.8	56.7	15.5	191	71	47	22.8	1 51	2 04	6 43	11 42	11 30
10	22 27	−11.3	57.6	15.7	203	68	37	23.8	2 20	2 30	7 33	12 55	12 47
11	23 19	− 7.2	58.6	16.0	215	66	27	24.8	2 47	2 52	8 23	14 11	14 07
12	0 12	− 2.5	59.5	16.2	228	63	17	25.8	3 12	3 14	9 14	15 30	15 30
13	1 07	+ 2.4	60.3	16.4	240	62	9	26.8	3 38	3 36	10 08	16 52	16 57
14	2 03	+ 7.4	61.0	16.6	252	58	4	27.8	4 06	3 59	11 03	18 16	18 25
15	3 02	+12.0	61.3	16.7	264	39	1	28.8	4 37	4 26	12 01	19 39	19 54
16	4 03	+15.8	61.4	16.7	276	293	1	0.5	5 15	5 00	13 02	21 00	21 18
17	5 06	+18.5	61.1	16.6	289	276	4	1.5	6 00	5 42	14 03	22 12	22 32
18	6 09	+19.9	60.5	16.5	301	276	9	2.5	6 55	6 34	15 05	23 14	23 34
19	7 11	+19.9	59.7	16.3	313	279	17	3.5	7 57	7 38	16 04	—	—
20	8 11	+18.7	58.8	16.0	325	283	27	4.5	9 06	8 48	17 00	0 03	0 21
21	9 08	+16.3	57.9	15.8	338	287	37	5.5	10 17	10 02	17 52	0 43	0 58
22	10 01	+13.2	57.0	15.5	350	290	48	6.5	11 27	11 17	18 41	1 15	1 26
23	10 51	+ 9.5	56.2	15.3	2	293	58	7.5	12 36	12 30	19 27	1 41	1 49
24	11 39	+ 5.5	55.5	15.1	14	295	68	8.5	13 44	13 41	20 10	2 04	2 09
25	12 26	+ 1.4	54.9	15.0	27	296	77	9.5	14 50	14 51	20 53	2 26	2 26
26	13 11	− 2.8	54.5	14.9	39	296	84	10.5	15 55	15 59	21 36	2 46	2 43
27	13 56	− 6.8	54.2	14.8	51	297	90	11.5	16 59	17 07	22 19	3 07	3 01
28	14 42	−10.5	54.0	14.7	63	298	95	12.5	18 03	18 15	23 03	3 30	3 20
29	15 29	−13.8	54.0	14.7	75	303	98	13.5	19 06	19 21	23 48	3 55	3 42
30	16 16	−16.5	54.0	14.7	87	337	100	14.5	20 06	20 24	—	4 24	4 08
31	17 05	−18.5	54.1	14.7	100	67	99	15.5	21 03	21 23	0 34	4 58	4 40

MERCURY

Day	RA h m	Dec. °	Diam. "	Phase %	Transit h m	5° high 52° h m	5° high 56° h m
1	1 07	+ 4.2	6	68	10 34	4 44	4 44
3	1 18	+ 5.4	6	71	10 37	4 41	4 40
5	1 30	+ 6.7	6	74	10 41	4 38	4 36
7	1 43	+ 8.1	6	77	10 46	4 36	4 32
9	1 55	+ 9.5	6	80	10 51	4 33	4 29
11	2 09	+11.0	6	83	10 57	4 32	4 26
13	2 23	+12.5	5	86	11 03	4 30	4 23
15	2 38	+14.0	5	89	11 10	4 29	4 20
17	2 53	+15.4	5	92	11 18	4 28	4 19
19	3 09	+16.9	5	95	11 26	4 29	4 17
21	3 26	+18.3	5	97	11 35	4 29	4 17
23	3 43	+19.7	5	99	11 45	4 31	4 17
25	4 01	+21.0	5	100	11 55	4 34	4 18
27	4 19	+22.1	5	100	12 06	19 36	19 53
29	4 38	+23.1	5	99	12 16	19 53	20 11
31	4 57	+23.9	5	96	12 27	20 08	20 28

VENUS

Day	RA h m	Dec. °	Diam. "	Phase %	Transit h m	5° high 52° h m	5° high 56° h m
1	5 22	+25.4	16	69	14 48	22 37	22 58
6	5 47	+25.8	17	67	14 54	22 44	23 06
11	6 11	+26.0	17	65	14 59	22 50	23 12
16	6 36	+25.8	18	63	15 03	22 53	23 15
21	7 00	+25.4	19	61	15 08	22 55	23 16
26	7 23	+24.8	20	58	15 11	22 53	23 13
31	7 46	+23.9	21	56	15 14	22 50	23 09

MARS

Day	RA h m	Dec. °	Diam. "	Phase %	Transit h m	5° high 52° h m	5° high 56° h m
1	14 00	−11.1	16	100	23 21	3 52	3 39
6	13 53	−10.6	16	99	22 54	3 28	3 15
11	13 46	−10.3	16	99	22 28	3 04	2 51
16	13 41	−10.0	16	98	22 03	2 40	2 28
21	13 36	− 9.8	15	97	21 39	2 17	2 05
26	13 33	− 9.7	15	96	21 16	1 55	1 43
31	13 31	− 9.7	14	94	20 55	1 33	1 21

SUNRISE AND SUNSET

	London		Bristol		Birmingham		Manchester		Newcastle		Glasgow		Belfast	
	0°05′	51°30′	2°35′	51°28′	1°55′	52°28′	2°15′	53°28′	1°37′	54°59′	4°14′	55°52′	5°56′	54°35′
	h m	h m	h m	h m	h m	h m	h m	h m	h m	h m	h m	h m	h m	h m
1	4 33	19 23	4 43	19 33	4 38	19 33	4 36	19 38	4 28	19 41	4 35	19 55	4 46	19 57
2	4 31	19 24	4 41	19 34	4 36	19 35	4 34	19 40	4 25	19 43	4 32	19 57	4 44	19 59
3	4 30	19 26	4 40	19 36	4 34	19 37	4 31	19 41	4 23	19 45	4 30	19 59	4 42	20 00
4	4 28	19 28	4 38	19 38	4 32	19 38	4 30	19 43	4 21	19 47	4 28	20 01	4 40	20 02
5	4 26	19 29	4 36	19 39	4 30	19 40	4 28	19 45	4 19	19 48	4 26	20 03	4 38	20 04
6	4 24	19 31	4 34	19 41	4 28	19 42	4 26	19 47	4 17	19 50	4 24	20 05	4 36	20 06
7	4 22	19 32	4 32	19 42	4 26	19 43	4 24	19 49	4 15	19 52	4 22	20 07	4 34	20 08
8	4 21	19 34	4 31	19 44	4 24	19 45	4 22	19 50	4 13	19 54	4 20	20 09	4 32	20 10
9	4 19	19 36	4 29	19 46	4 23	19 47	4 20	19 52	4 11	19 56	4 17	20 11	4 30	20 12
10	4 17	19 37	4 27	19 47	4 21	19 48	4 18	19 54	4 09	19 58	4 15	20 13	4 28	20 13
11	4 16	19 39	4 26	19 49	4 19	19 50	4 16	19 55	4 07	20 00	4 13	20 14	4 26	20 15
12	4 14	19 40	4 24	19 50	4 17	19 52	4 15	19 57	4 05	20 02	4 11	20 16	4 24	20 17
13	4 12	19 42	4 23	19 52	4 16	19 53	4 13	19 59	4 03	20 03	4 10	20 18	4 23	20 19
14	4 11	19 43	4 21	19 53	4 14	19 55	4 11	20 01	4 02	20 05	4 08	20 20	4 21	20 20
15	4 09	19 45	4 19	19 55	4 13	19 56	4 10	20 02	4 00	20 07	4 06	20 22	4 19	20 22
16	4 08	19 46	4 18	19 56	4 11	19 58	4 08	20 04	3 58	20 09	4 04	20 24	4 17	20 24
17	4 06	19 48	4 17	19 58	4 10	19 59	4 06	20 05	3 56	20 10	4 02	20 26	4 16	20 26
18	4 05	19 49	4 15	19 59	4 08	20 01	4 05	20 07	3 55	20 12	4 00	20 27	4 14	20 27
19	4 04	19 51	4 14	20 01	4 07	20 03	4 03	20 09	3 53	20 14	3 59	20 29	4 12	20 29
20	4 02	19 52	4 12	20 02	4 05	20 04	4 02	20 10	3 51	20 16	3 57	20 31	4 11	20 31
21	4 01	19 54	4 11	20 04	4 04	20 06	4 00	20 12	3 50	20 17	3 55	20 33	4 09	20 32
22	4 00	19 55	4 10	20 05	4 03	20 07	3 59	20 13	3 48	20 19	3 54	20 34	4 08	20 34
23	3 58	19 56	4 09	20 06	4 01	20 08	3 58	20 15	3 47	20 20	3 52	20 36	4 06	20 36
24	3 57	19 58	4 07	20 08	4 00	20 10	3 56	20 16	3 45	20 22	3 51	20 38	4 05	20 37
25	3 56	19 59	4 06	20 09	3 59	20 11	3 55	20 18	3 44	20 24	3 49	20 39	4 04	20 39
26	3 55	20 00	4 05	20 10	3 58	20 12	3 54	20 19	3 43	20 25	3 48	20 41	4 02	20 40
27	3 54	20 02	4 04	20 12	3 56	20 14	3 53	20 20	3 41	20 27	3 46	20 43	4 01	20 42
28	3 53	20 03	4 03	20 13	3 55	20 15	3 51	20 22	3 40	20 28	3 45	20 44	4 00	20 43
29	3 52	20 04	4 02	20 14	3 54	20 16	3 50	20 23	3 39	20 29	3 44	20 46	3 59	20 44
30	3 51	20 05	4 01	20 15	3 53	20 18	3 49	20 24	3 38	20 31	3 43	20 47	3 58	20 46
31	3 50	20 06	4 00	20 16	3 52	20 19	3 48	20 26	3 37	20 32	3 41	20 48	3 56	20 47

JUPITER

Day	RA	Dec.	Transit	5° high	
				52°	56°
	h m	° ′	h m	h m	h m
1	1 08.7	+ 6 07	10 33	4 35	4 34
11	1 17.3	+ 6 58	10 03	4 00	3 58
21	1 25.6	+ 7 47	9 32	3 25	3 22
31	1 33.5	+ 8 32	9 00	2 50	2 46

Diameters – equatorial 34″ polar 32″

SATURN

Day	RA	Dec.	Transit	5° high	
				52°	56°
	h m	° ′	h m	h m	h m
1	2 22.3	+11 51	11 47	5 19	5 13
11	2 27.3	+12 16	11 12	4 43	4 36
21	2 32.1	+12 39	10 38	4 06	3 59
31	2 36.8	+13 01	10 03	3 29	3 22

Diameters – equatorial 16″ polar 15″
Rings – major axis 37″ minor axis 12″

URANUS

Day	RA	Dec.	Transit	10° high	
				52°	56°
	h m	° ′	h m	h m	h m
1	21 17.1	−16 29	6 42	3 32	4 01
11	21 17.6	−16 27	6 03	2 53	3 22
21	21 17.8	−16 27	5 24	2 14	2 43
31	21 17.7	−16 28	4 45	1 34	2 04

Diameter 4″

NEPTUNE

Day	RA	Dec.	Transit	10° high	
				52°	56°
	h m	° ′	h m	h m	h m
1	20 26.5	−18 53	5 52	3 02	3 39
11	20 26.5	−18 53	5 12	2 22	2 59
21	20 26.3	−18 54	4 33	1 43	2 20
31	20 25.9	−18 55	3 53	1 03	1 41

Diameter 2″

 # June 1999

SIXTH MONTH, 30 DAYS. *Junius*, Roman *gens* (family)

1	Tuesday	John Masefield b. 1878. Marilyn Monroe b. 1926	week 22 day 152
2	Wednesday	Coronation Day 1953. Vita Sackville West d. 1962	153
3	Thursday	**Corpus Christi.** Johann Strauss (younger) d. 1899	154
4	Friday	Casanova d. 1798. Kaiser Wilhelm II d. 1941	155
5	Saturday	World Enviroment Day. Lord Kitchener d. 1916	156
6	Sunday	**1st S. after Trinity.** Pushkin b. 1799 (NS)	week 23 day 157
7	Monday	Beau Brummell b. 1778. Charles Rennie Mackintosh b. 1868	158
8	Tuesday	*Trinity Law Sittings begin.* Frank Lloyd Wright b. 1869	159
9	Wednesday	Charles Dickens d. 1870. Lord Beaverbrook d. 1964	160
10	Thursday	*Duke of Edinburgh b. 1921.* Judy Garland b. 1922	161
11	Friday	**St Barnabas.** Jackie Stewart b. 1939	162
12	Saturday	*Queen's Official Birthday.* Anne Frank b. 1929	163
13	Sunday	**2nd S. after Trinity.** Dorothy L. Sayers b. 1893	week 24 day 164
14	Monday	Steffi Graf b. 1969. Dame Peggy Ashcroft d. 1991	165
15	Tuesday	First non-stop transatlantic flight 1919	166
16	Wednesday	Duke of Marlborough d. 1722. Lord Alexander of Tunis d. 1969	167
17	Thursday	Edward I b. 1239. Sir Edward Burne-Jones d. 1898	168
18	Friday	Ethel Barrymore d. 1959. Jack Harkness d. 1994	169
19	Saturday	Lord Haig b. 1861. The Duchess of Windsor b. 1896	170
20	Sunday	**3rd S. after Trinity.** Errol Flynn b. 1909	week 25 day 171
21	Monday	Prince William of Wales b. 1982	172
22	Tuesday	Alexandra Rose Day. Fred Astaire d. 1987	173
23	Wednesday	The Duke of Windsor b. 1894. Sir Len Hutton b. 1916	174
24	Thursday	**John the Baptist.** Book of Common Prayer issued 1559	175
25	Friday	Earl Mountbatten of Burma b. 1900. George Orwell b. 1903	176
26	Saturday	Laurie Lee b. 1914. Ford Madox Ford d. 1939	177
27	Sunday	**4th S. after Trinity.** Charles Parnell b. 1846	week 26 day 178
28	Monday	Archduke Ferdinand assassinated 1914. Treaty of Versailles 1919	179
29	Tuesday	**SS Peter and Paul.** Peter Paul Rubens b. 1577	180
30	Wednesday	Tower Bridge opened 1894. Ruskin Spear b. 1911	181

ASTRONOMICAL PHENOMENA

d	h	
4	06	Mars at stationary point
10	02	Jupiter in conjunction with Moon. Jupiter 4° N.
11	03	Saturn in conjunction with Moon. Saturn 3° N.
11	12	Venus at greatest elongation E.45°
15	07	Mercury in conjunction with Moon. Mercury 4° N.
17	02	Venus in conjunction with Moon. Venus 2° N.
21	20	Sun's longitude 90° ♋
23	01	Mars in conjunction with Moon. Mars 6° S.
28	23	Mercury at greatest elongation E.26°

MINIMA OF ALGOL

Algol is inconveniently situated for observation during June.

CONSTELLATIONS

The following constellations are near the meridian at

d	h		d	h
May	1	24	June	15	21
May	16	23	July	1	20
June	1	22	July	16	19

Cassiopeia (below the Pole), Ursa Minor, Draco, Ursa Major, Canes Venatici, Bootes, Corona, Serpens, Virgo and Libra

THE MOON

Phases, Apsides and Node	d	h	m
☾ Last Quarter	7	04	20
● New Moon	13	19	03
☽ First Quarter	20	18	13
○ Full Moon	28	21	37
Perigee (358,185 km)	13	00	31
Apogee (405,882 km)	25	15	21

Mean longitude of ascending node on June 1, 136°

THE SUN   s.d. 15'.8

Day	Right Ascension	Dec. +	Equation of time	Rise 52°	Rise 56°	Transit	Set 52°	Set 56°	Sidereal time	Transit of First Point of Aries
	h m s	° '	m s	h m	h m	h m	h m	h m	h m s	h m s
1	4 33 49	21 58	+ 2 20	3 46	3 23	11 58	20 10	20 34	16 36 09	7 22 39
2	4 37 54	22 06	+ 2 11	3 46	3 21	11 58	20 11	20 35	16 40 05	7 18 43
3	4 42 00	22 14	+ 2 02	3 45	3 20	11 58	20 12	20 36	16 44 02	7 14 47
4	4 46 06	22 21	+ 1 52	3 44	3 20	11 58	20 13	20 38	16 47 58	7 10 51
5	4 50 13	22 28	+ 1 42	3 43	3 19	11 58	20 14	20 39	16 51 55	7 06 55
6	4 54 20	22 35	+ 1 31	3 43	3 18	11 59	20 15	20 40	16 55 51	7 02 59
7	4 58 27	22 41	+ 1 20	3 42	3 17	11 59	20 16	20 41	16 59 48	6 59 03
8	5 02 35	22 47	+ 1 09	3 42	3 16	11 59	20 17	20 42	17 03 44	6 55 07
9	5 06 43	22 52	+ 0 58	3 41	3 16	11 59	20 18	20 43	17 07 41	6 51 11
10	5 10 51	22 57	+ 0 46	3 41	3 15	11 59	20 18	20 44	17 11 38	6 47 15
11	5 15 00	23 02	+ 0 34	3 40	3 15	12 00	20 19	20 45	17 15 34	6 43 20
12	5 19 09	23 06	+ 0 22	3 40	3 14	12 00	20 20	20 46	17 19 31	6 39 24
13	5 23 18	23 10	+ 0 10	3 40	3 14	12 00	20 20	20 47	17 23 27	6 35 28
14	5 27 27	23 14	− 0 03	3 40	3 13	12 00	20 21	20 47	17 27 24	6 31 32
15	5 31 36	23 17	− 0 16	3 39	3 13	12 00	20 21	20 48	17 31 20	6 27 36
16	5 35 46	23 19	− 0 29	3 39	3 13	12 01	20 22	20 48	17 35 17	6 23 40
17	5 39 55	23 21	− 0 42	3 39	3 13	12 01	20 22	20 49	17 39 14	6 19 44
18	5 44 05	23 23	− 0 55	3 39	3 13	12 01	20 23	20 49	17 43 10	6 15 48
19	5 48 14	23 25	− 1 08	3 39	3 13	12 01	20 23	20 50	17 47 07	6 11 52
20	5 52 24	23 26	− 1 21	3 39	3 13	12 01	20 23	20 50	17 51 03	6 07 56
21	5 56 34	23 26	− 1 34	3 40	3 13	12 02	20 24	20 50	17 55 00	6 04 00
22	6 00 43	23 26	− 1 47	3 40	3 13	12 02	20 24	20 51	17 58 56	6 00 05
23	6 04 53	23 26	− 2 00	3 40	3 13	12 02	20 24	20 51	18 02 53	5 56 09
24	6 09 02	23 25	− 2 13	3 40	3 14	12 02	20 24	20 51	18 06 49	5 52 13
25	6 13 12	23 24	− 2 26	3 41	3 14	12 03	20 24	20 51	18 10 46	5 48 17
26	6 17 21	23 23	− 2 38	3 41	3 15	12 03	20 24	20 51	18 14 43	5 44 21
27	6 21 30	23 21	− 2 51	3 42	3 15	12 03	20 24	20 50	18 18 39	5 40 25
28	6 25 39	23 18	− 3 03	3 42	3 16	12 03	20 24	20 50	18 22 36	5 36 29
29	6 29 48	23 16	− 3 16	3 43	3 16	12 03	20 24	20 50	18 26 32	5 32 33
30	6 33 56	23 12	− 3 28	3 43	3 17	12 04	20 24	20 50	18 30 29	5 28 37

DURATION OF TWILIGHT (in minutes)

Latitude	52°	56°	52°	56°	52°	56°	52°	56°
	1 June		11 June		21 June		30 June	
Civil	47	58	48	61	49	63	49	62
Nautical	117	TAN	125	TAN	128	TAN	125	TAN
Astronomical	TAN	TAN	TAN	TAN	TAN	TAN	TAN	TAN

THE NIGHT SKY

Mercury is at greatest eastern elongation (26°) on the 28th and thus theoretically visible as an evening object. The long summer twilight will seriously hinder observation but under good conditions it may be possible to glimpse the planet during the third week of the month, very low above the west-north-western horizon at the end of evening civil twilight. Mercury will be about magnitude 0.

Venus continues to be visible as a magnificent object in the western skies in the evenings, magnitude −4.3. On the evening of the 16th the thin crescent Moon, only three days old, will be seen about 5° from the planet.

Mars is an evening object, visible in the south-western sky, its magnitude fading during the month from −1.0 to −0.4. On the evening of the 22nd the gibbous Moon will be seen approaching the planet. Mars reaches its second stationary point in Virgo on the 5th, resuming its direct motion.

Jupiter, magnitude −2.2, is a morning object, low in the eastern sky before dawn. The old crescent Moon will be seen about 5° below the planet on the morning of the 10th. During the month Jupiter moves eastwards from Pisces into Aries.

Saturn is not visible for the first three weeks of the month, then slowly begins to emerge from the long morning twilight and may be detected low above the east-north-eastern horizon before the sky gets too bright. The fact that in these latitudes even nautical twilight is continuous throughout the night means that it will not be an easy object to locate. Its magnitude is +0.4.

Twilight. Reference to the table above shows that astronomical twilight lasts all night for a period around the summer solstice (i.e. in June and July), even in southern England. Under these conditions the sky never gets completely dark as the Sun is always less than 18° below the horizon.

THE MOON

Day	RA h m	Dec. °	Hor. par. ′	Semi- diam. ′	Sun's co- long. °	PA of Bright Limb °	Phase %	Age d	Rise 52° h m	Rise 56° h m	Transit h m	Set 52° h m	Set 56° h m
1	17 56	−19.8	54.3	14.8	112	80	97	16.5	21 55	22 16	1 22	5 39	5 19
2	18 47	−20.2	54.6	14.9	124	80	93	17.5	22 41	23 01	2 11	6 27	6 06
3	19 38	−19.6	54.9	15.0	136	78	88	18.5	23 21	23 38	3 00	7 22	7 02
4	20 30	−18.1	55.4	15.1	148	75	81	19.5	23 55	—	3 49	8 23	8 06
5	21 21	−15.8	56.0	15.3	161	72	72	20.5	—	0 09	4 39	9 29	9 16
6	22 12	−12.6	56.7	15.4	173	70	63	21.5	0 24	0 35	5 27	10 39	10 29
7	23 03	− 8.7	57.5	15.7	185	67	52	22.5	0 51	0 58	6 16	11 52	11 46
8	23 55	− 4.3	58.3	15.9	197	66	41	23.5	1 15	1 19	7 05	13 07	13 06
9	0 47	+ 0.4	59.1	16.1	210	65	30	24.5	1 40	1 39	7 56	14 25	14 28
10	1 41	+ 5.3	59.9	16.3	222	65	20	25.5	2 05	2 01	8 48	15 46	15 53
11	2 37	+10.0	60.6	16.5	234	66	12	26.5	2 34	2 25	9 43	17 08	17 20
12	3 36	+14.2	61.1	16.6	246	66	5	27.5	3 07	2 54	10 42	18 30	18 46
13	4 37	+17.4	61.2	16.7	259	60	1	28.5	3 47	3 30	11 43	19 48	20 07
14	5 41	+19.5	61.1	16.6	271	321	0	0.2	4 37	4 17	12 45	20 57	21 17
15	6 44	+20.2	60.6	16.5	283	284	2	1.2	5 36	5 16	13 47	21 54	22 13
16	7 47	+19.5	59.9	16.3	295	283	7	2.2	6 44	6 25	14 46	22 40	22 56
17	8 47	+17.5	59.0	16.1	307	286	14	3.2	7 56	7 41	15 42	23 16	23 29
18	9 43	+14.6	58.1	15.8	320	289	23	4.2	9 10	8 58	16 34	23 45	23 55
19	10 36	+11.0	57.1	15.6	332	291	32	5.2	10 22	10 13	17 22	—	—
20	11 26	+ 6.9	56.3	15.3	344	293	42	6.2	11 31	11 27	18 08	0 10	0 16
21	12 13	+ 2.7	55.5	15.1	356	294	53	7.2	12 39	12 38	18 52	0 32	0 34
22	12 59	− 1.5	54.9	15.0	9	294	62	8.2	13 45	13 48	19 34	0 53	0 52
23	13 45	− 5.6	54.5	14.8	21	293	71	9.2	14 50	14 57	20 17	1 14	1 09
24	14 30	− 9.4	54.2	14.8	33	292	80	10.2	15 54	16 04	21 00	1 35	1 27
25	15 17	−12.8	54.0	14.7	45	291	87	11.2	16 57	17 11	21 45	1 59	1 48
26	16 04	−15.8	54.0	14.7	57	289	92	12.2	17 59	18 16	22 31	2 27	2 12
27	16 53	−18.1	54.1	14.7	70	288	97	13.2	18 58	19 17	23 19	2 59	2 41
28	17 43	−19.6	54.3	14.8	82	292	99	14.2	19 52	20 13	—	3 37	3 17
29	18 34	−20.2	54.6	14.9	94	17	100	15.2	20 40	21 01	0 08	4 23	4 02
30	19 26	−19.9	54.9	15.0	106	72	99	16.2	21 23	21 41	0 57	5 16	4 56

MERCURY

Day	RA h m	Dec. °	Diam. ″	Phase %	Transit h m	5° high 52° h m	5° high 56° h m
1	5 06	+24.3	5	95	12 33	20 16	20 36
3	5 24	+24.8	5	92	12 43	20 29	20 50
5	5 42	+25.2	5	88	12 53	20 41	21 02
7	6 00	+25.4	6	83	13 03	20 51	21 13
9	6 17	+25.4	6	79	13 11	21 00	21 21
11	6 33	+25.3	6	75	13 19	21 07	21 27
13	6 48	+25.0	6	70	13 27	21 12	21 32
15	7 03	+24.7	6	66	13 33	21 15	21 35
17	7 16	+24.2	6	62	13 39	21 17	21 36
19	7 29	+23.6	7	58	13 43	21 18	21 36
21	7 41	+22.9	7	54	13 47	21 17	21 34
23	7 52	+22.2	7	51	13 50	21 15	21 31
25	8 02	+21.5	8	47	13 52	21 12	21 28
27	8 11	+20.7	8	44	13 52	21 08	21 23
29	8 19	+19.9	8	40	13 52	21 03	21 17
31	8 26	+19.1	8	37	13 51	20 57	21 10

VENUS

Day	RA h m	Dec. °	Diam. ″	Phase %	Transit h m	5° high 52° h m	5° high 56° h m
1	7 50	+23.7	21	55	15 14	22 49	23 08
6	8 11	+22.5	22	53	15 16	22 43	23 00
11	8 32	+21.2	23	50	15 16	22 35	22 51
16	8 51	+19.8	25	47	15 15	22 26	22 39
21	9 09	+18.2	26	44	15 13	22 14	22 26
26	9 25	+16.5	28	41	15 10	22 01	22 12
31	9 40	+14.8	30	37	15 05	21 47	21 55

MARS

Day	RA h m	Dec. °	Diam. ″	Phase %	Transit h m	5° high 52° h m	5° high 56° h m
1	13 31	− 9.7	14	94	20 51	1 29	1 17
6	13 30	− 9.9	14	93	20 31	1 08	0 56
11	13 31	−10.1	13	92	20 12	0 48	0 35
16	13 33	−10.5	13	91	19 55	0 28	0 15
21	13 36	−10.9	12	90	19 38	0 09	23 52
26	13 40	−11.4	12	89	19 23	23 47	23 32
31	13 45	−12.0	11	89	19 08	23 28	23 14

SUNRISE AND SUNSET

	London 0°05' 51°30'		Bristol 2°35' 51°28'		Birmingham 1°55' 52°28'		Manchester 2°15' 53°28'		Newcastle 1°37' 54°59'		Glasgow 4°14' 55°52'		Belfast 5°56' 54°35'	
	h m	h m	h m	h m	h m	h m	h m	h m	h m	h m	h m	h m	h m	h m
1	3 49	20 08	3 59	20 17	3 52	20 20	3 47	20 27	3 36	20 34	3 40	20 50	3 55	20 48
2	3 48	20 09	3 59	20 18	3 51	20 21	3 46	20 28	3 35	20 35	3 39	20 51	3 54	20 50
3	3 48	20 10	3 58	20 19	3 50	20 22	3 46	20 29	3 34	20 36	3 38	20 52	3 54	20 51
4	3 47	20 11	3 57	20 20	3 49	20 23	3 45	20 30	3 33	20 37	3 37	20 54	3 53	20 52
5	3 46	20 12	3 57	20 21	3 48	20 24	3 44	20 31	3 32	20 38	3 37	20 55	3 52	20 53
6	3 46	20 13	3 56	20 22	3 48	20 25	3 43	20 32	3 31	20 39	3 36	20 56	3 51	20 54
7	3 45	20 13	3 55	20 23	3 47	20 26	3 43	20 33	3 31	20 40	3 35	20 57	3 50	20 55
8	3 45	20 14	3 55	20 24	3 47	20 27	3 42	20 34	3 30	20 41	3 34	20 58	3 50	20 56
9	3 44	20 15	3 54	20 25	3 46	20 28	3 42	20 35	3 29	20 42	3 34	20 59	3 49	20 57
10	3 44	20 16	3 54	20 26	3 46	20 29	3 41	20 36	3 29	20 43	3 33	21 00	3 49	20 58
11	3 44	20 17	3 54	20 26	3 45	20 29	3 41	20 37	3 28	20 44	3 33	21 01	3 48	20 59
12	3 43	20 17	3 53	20 27	3 45	20 30	3 40	20 37	3 28	20 45	3 32	21 02	3 48	20 59
13	3 43	20 18	3 53	20 28	3 45	20 31	3 40	20 38	3 28	20 46	3 32	21 02	3 48	21 00
14	3 43	20 18	3 53	20 28	3 45	20 31	3 40	20 39	3 27	20 46	3 31	21 03	3 47	21 01
15	3 43	20 19	3 53	20 29	3 44	20 32	3 40	20 39	3 27	20 47	3 31	21 04	3 47	21 01
16	3 43	20 20	3 53	20 29	3 44	20 32	3 40	20 40	3 27	20 47	3 31	21 04	3 47	21 02
17	3 43	20 20	3 53	20 30	3 44	20 33	3 39	20 40	3 27	20 48	3 31	21 05	3 47	21 02
18	3 42	20 20	3 53	20 30	3 44	20 33	3 39	20 41	3 27	20 48	3 31	21 05	3 47	21 03
19	3 43	20 21	3 53	20 30	3 44	20 34	3 39	20 41	3 27	20 49	3 31	21 06	3 47	21 03
20	3 43	20 21	3 53	20 31	3 44	20 34	3 40	20 41	3 27	20 49	3 31	21 06	3 47	21 04
21	3 43	20 21	3 53	20 31	3 45	20 34	3 40	20 42	3 27	20 49	3 31	21 06	3 47	21 04
22	3 43	20 21	3 53	20 31	3 45	20 34	3 40	20 42	3 27	20 50	3 31	21 06	3 47	21 04
23	3 43	20 22	3 53	20 31	3 45	20 34	3 40	20 42	3 28	20 50	3 31	21 07	3 48	21 04
24	3 44	20 22	3 54	20 31	3 45	20 35	3 41	20 42	3 28	20 50	3 32	21 07	3 48	21 04
25	3 44	20 22	3 54	20 31	3 46	20 35	3 41	20 42	3 28	20 50	3 32	21 07	3 48	21 04
26	3 44	20 22	3 55	20 31	3 46	20 35	3 41	20 42	3 29	20 50	3 33	21 06	3 49	21 04
27	3 45	20 22	3 55	20 31	3 47	20 34	3 42	20 42	3 29	20 49	3 33	21 06	3 49	21 04
28	3 45	20 21	3 55	20 31	3 47	20 34	3 42	20 42	3 30	20 49	3 34	21 06	3 50	21 04
29	3 46	20 21	3 56	20 31	3 48	20 34	3 43	20 42	3 30	20 49	3 34	21 06	3 50	21 04
30	3 46	20 21	3 57	20 31	3 48	20 34	3 44	20 41	3 31	20 49	3 35	21 05	3 51	21 03

JUPITER

Day	RA	Dec.	Transit	5° high 52°	56°
	h m	° '	h m	h m	h m
1	1 34.3	+ 8 37	8 57	2 46	2 42
11	1 41.8	+ 9 18	8 25	2 11	2 06
21	1 48.7	+ 9 55	7 53	1 35	1 30
31	1 54.9	+10 28	7 19	0 59	0 54

Diameters – equatorial 36" polar 34"

SATURN

Day	RA	Dec.	Transit	5° high 52°	56°
	h m	° '	h m	h m	h m
1	2 37.3	+13 03	10 00	3 26	3 18
11	2 41.8	+13 23	9 25	2 49	2 41
21	2 46.0	+13 41	8 50	2 12	2 04
31	2 49.8	+13 57	8 14	1 36	1 27

Diameters – equatorial 17" polar 15"
Rings – major axis 38" minor axis 13"

URANUS

Day	RA	Dec.	Transit	10° high 52°	56°
	h m	° '	h m	h m	h m
1	21 17.7	−16 28	4 41	1 30	2 00
11	21 17.2	−16 30	4 01	0 51	1 20
21	21 16.4	−16 34	3 21	0 11	0 41
31	21 15.4	−16 39	2 41	23 28	0 02

Diameter 4"

NEPTUNE

Day	RA	Dec.	Transit	10° high 52°	56°
	h m	° '	h m	h m	h m
1	20 25.8	−18 56	3 49	0 59	1 37
11	20 25.2	−18 58	3 09	0 20	0 57
21	20 24.4	−19 01	2 29	23 36	0 18
31	20 23.5	−19 04	1 49	22 56	23 34

Diameter 2"

July 1999

SEVENTH MONTH, 31 DAYS. *Julius* Caesar, formerly *Quintilis*, fifth month of Roman pre-Julian calendar

1	*Thursday*	Diana, Princess of Wales b. 1961	*week 26 day* 182
2	*Friday*	Archbishop Cranmer b. 1489. Joseph Chamberlain d. 1914	183
3	*Saturday*	**St Thomas.** Robert Adam b. 1728	184
4	*Sunday*	**5th S. after Trinity.** Independence Day, USA	*week 27 day* 185
5	*Monday*	Sir Harold Acton b. 1904. Georgette Heyer d. 1974	186
6	*Tuesday*	Henry II d. 1189. Edward VI d. 1553	187
7	*Wednesday*	Ernest Newman d. 1959. Dame Flora Robson d. 1984	188
8	*Thursday*	Joseph Chamberlain b. 1836. Percy Grainger b. 1882	189
9	*Friday*	Edward Heath b. 1916. David Hockney b. 1937	190
10	*Saturday*	John Calvin b. 1509. Evelyn Laye b. 1900	191
11	*Sunday*	**6th S. after Trinity.** Robert the Bruce b. 1274	*week 28 day* 192
12	*Monday*	*Bank Holiday in Northern Ireland.* Thoreau b. 1817	193
13	*Tuesday*	Sidney Webb b. 1859. Lord Clark b. 1903	194
14	*Wednesday*	Storming of the Bastille 1789. Ingmar Bergman b. 1918	195
15	*Thursday*	St Swithin's Day. Inigo Jones b. 1573	196
16	*Friday*	Sir Joshua Reynolds b. 1723. Ginger Rogers b. 1911	197
17	*Saturday*	Isaac Watts b. 1674. Sir Geoffrey Jellicoe d. 1996	198
18	*Sunday*	**7th S. after Trinity.** Jane Austen d. 1817	*week 29 day* 199
19	*Monday*	*Mary Rose* sank 1545. Edgar Degas b. 1834	200
20	*Tuesday*	Sir Edmund Hillary b. 1919. Calouste Gulbenkian d. 1955	201
21	*Wednesday*	Ernest Hemingway b. 1898. First men on the Moon 1969	202
22	*Thursday*	**Mary Magdalene.** Tate Gallery opened 1897	203
23	*Friday*	Raymond Chandler b. 1888. Jessica Mitford d. 1996	204
24	*Saturday*	Alexandre Dumas (père) b. 1802. Peter Sellers d. 1980	205
25	*Sunday*	**St James. 8th S. after Trinity**	*week 30 day* 206
26	*Monday*	Aldous Huxley b. 1894. Terry Scott d. 1994	207
27	*Tuesday*	Alexandre Dumas (fils) b. 1824. Ivy Compton-Burnett d. 1969	208
28	*Wednesday*	Thomas Cromwell executed 1540. Cyrano de Bergerac d. 1655	209
29	*Thursday*	Marriage of Prince Charles and Lady Diana Spencer 1981	210
30	*Friday*	*Trinity Law Sittings end.* Henry Moore b. 1898	211
31	*Saturday*	Franz Liszt d. 1886. Leonard Cheshire d. 1992	212

ASTRONOMICAL PHENOMENA

d	h	
6	22	Earth at aphelion (152 million km)
7	18	Jupiter in conjunction with Moon. Jupiter 4° N.
8	16	Saturn in conjunction with Moon. Saturn 3° N.
13	00	Mercury at stationary point
14	10	Mercury in conjunction with Moon. Mercury 3° S.
14	19	Venus at greatest brilliancy
16	01	Venus in conjunction with Moon. Venus 3° S.
21	03	Mars in conjunction with Moon. Mars 7° S.
23	07	Sun's longitude 120° ♌
26	10	Neptune at opposition
26	16	Mercury in inferior conjunction
28	11	Partial eclipse of Moon (*see* page 66)
30	02	Venus at stationary point

MINIMA OF ALGOL

d	h	d	h	d	h
2	07.7	13	18.9	25	06.2
5	04.5	16	15.7	28	03.0
8	01.3	19	12.5	30	23.8
10	22.1	22	09.3		

CONSTELLATIONS

The following constellations are near the meridian at

	d	h		d	h
June	1	24	July	16	21
June	15	23	August	1	20
July	1	22	August	16	19

Ursa Minor, Draco, Corona, Hercules, Lyra, Serpens, Ophiuchus, Libra, Scorpius and Sagittarius

THE MOON

Phases, Apsides and Node	d	h	m
☾ Last Quarter	6	11	57
● New Moon	13	02	24
☽ First Quarter	20	09	00
○ Full Moon	28	11	25
Perigee (361,762 km)	11	06	01
Apogee (404,959 km)	23	05	39

Mean longitude of ascending node on July 1, 135°

THE SUN   s.d. 15'.8

Day	Right Ascension	Dec. +	Equation of time	Rise 52°	Rise 56°	Transit	Set 52°	Set 56°	Sidereal time	Transit of First Point of Aries
	h m s	° '	m s	h m	h m	h m	h m	h m	h m s	h m s
1	6 38 05	23 09	− 3 39	3 44	3 18	12 04	20 23	20 49	18 34 25	5 24 41
2	6 42 13	23 05	− 3 51	3 45	3 19	12 04	20 23	20 49	18 38 22	5 20 45
3	6 46 21	23 01	− 4 02	3 45	3 20	12 04	20 22	20 48	18 42 18	5 16 50
4	6 50 28	22 56	− 4 13	3 46	3 21	12 04	20 22	20 47	18 46 15	5 12 54
5	6 54 36	22 51	− 4 24	3 47	3 22	12 04	20 22	20 47	18 50 12	5 08 58
6	6 58 43	22 45	− 4 35	3 48	3 23	12 05	20 21	20 46	18 54 08	5 05 02
7	7 02 49	22 39	− 4 45	3 49	3 24	12 05	20 20	20 45	18 58 05	5 01 06
8	7 06 56	22 33	− 4 54	3 50	3 25	12 05	20 20	20 44	19 02 01	4 57 10
9	7 11 02	22 26	− 5 04	3 51	3 26	12 05	20 19	20 43	19 05 58	4 53 14
10	7 15 07	22 19	− 5 13	3 52	3 27	12 05	20 18	20 43	19 09 54	4 49 18
11	7 19 12	22 11	− 5 22	3 53	3 29	12 05	20 17	20 41	19 13 51	4 45 22
12	7 23 17	22 03	− 5 30	3 54	3 30	12 06	20 17	20 40	19 17 47	4 41 26
13	7 27 22	21 55	− 5 38	3 55	3 31	12 06	20 16	20 39	19 21 44	4 37 30
14	7 31 25	21 47	− 5 45	3 56	3 33	12 06	20 15	20 38	19 25 41	4 33 35
15	7 35 29	21 38	− 5 52	3 57	3 34	12 06	20 14	20 37	19 29 37	4 29 39
16	7 39 32	21 28	− 5 58	3 58	3 36	12 06	20 13	20 35	19 33 34	4 25 43
17	7 43 34	21 18	− 6 04	4 00	3 37	12 06	20 12	20 34	19 37 30	4 21 47
18	7 47 36	21 08	− 6 09	4 01	3 39	12 06	20 11	20 33	19 41 27	4 17 51
19	7 51 37	20 58	− 6 14	4 02	3 40	12 06	20 09	20 31	19 45 23	4 13 55
20	7 55 38	20 47	− 6 18	4 04	3 42	12 06	20 08	20 30	19 49 20	4 09 59
21	7 59 38	20 36	− 6 21	4 05	3 43	12 06	20 07	20 28	19 53 16	4 06 03
22	8 03 37	20 24	− 6 24	4 06	3 45	12 06	20 06	20 27	19 57 13	4 02 07
23	8 07 36	20 12	− 6 27	4 08	3 47	12 06	20 04	20 25	20 01 10	3 58 11
24	8 11 35	20 00	− 6 29	4 09	3 48	12 06	20 03	20 23	20 05 06	3 54 15
25	8 15 32	19 48	− 6 30	4 11	3 50	12 07	20 02	20 22	20 09 03	3 50 20
26	8 19 30	19 35	− 6 30	4 12	3 52	12 07	20 00	20 20	20 12 59	3 46 24
27	8 23 26	19 22	− 6 30	4 13	3 54	12 07	19 59	20 18	20 16 56	3 42 28
28	8 27 22	19 08	− 6 30	4 15	3 56	12 06	19 57	20 16	20 20 52	3 38 32
29	8 31 18	18 54	− 6 29	4 16	3 57	12 06	19 56	20 14	20 24 49	3 34 36
30	8 35 12	18 40	− 6 27	4 18	3 59	12 06	19 54	20 12	20 28 45	3 30 40
31	8 39 06	18 26	− 6 24	4 19	4 01	12 06	19 52	20 10	20 32 42	3 26 44

DURATION OF TWILIGHT (in minutes)

Latitude	52°	56°	52°	56°	52°	56°	52°	56°
	1 July		11 July		21 July		31 July	
Civil	48	61	46	58	44	53	41	49
Nautical	124	TAN	116	TAN	107	144	98	122
Astronomical	TAN	TAN	TAN	TAN	TAN	TAN	180	TAN

THE NIGHT SKY

Mercury is unsuitably placed for observation throughout the month, inferior conjunction occurring on the 26th.

Venus, magnitude −4.5, attains its greatest brilliancy on the 14th. It is visible as a magnificent object in the western sky in the evenings but the period available for observation is shortening noticeably and it will be lost in the glare of sunset a few days before the end of July. On the evenings of the 15th and 16th the thin crescent Moon will be seen within a few degrees of Venus. Through a small telescope Venus exhibits marked changes during the month; its angular diameter increases from 30 to 45 arcseconds while the phase changes from 37 per cent to 16 per cent illuminated.

Mars continues to be visible as an evening object in the south-western sky, magnitude −0.2. The First Quarter Moon is near the planet on the evening of the 20th. Towards the end of the month Mars moves from Virgo into Libra.

Jupiter continues to be visible as a morning object in the south-eastern sky, magnitude −2.4.

Saturn, magnitude +0.4, is a morning object. By the end of the month it may be detected low above the eastern horizon shortly after midnight. On the morning of the 9th the crescent Moon, four days before New, is near Saturn.

Neptune is at opposition on the 26th, in Capricornus. It is not visible to the naked eye as its magnitude is +7.8.

THE MOON

Day	RA	Dec.	Hor. par.	Semi-diam.	Sun's co-long.	PA of Bright Limb	Phase	Age	Rise 52°	Rise 56°	Transit	Set 52°	Set 56°
	h m	°	'	'	°	°	%	d	h m	h m	h m	h m	h m
1	20 18	−18.7	55.3	15.1	118	75	96	17.2	21 58	22 14	1 47	6 16	5 58
2	21 10	−16.5	55.8	15.2	131	73	91	18.2	22 29	22 42	2 36	7 21	7 06
3	22 01	−13.5	56.3	15.3	143	71	84	19.2	22 56	23 05	3 25	8 29	8 18
4	22 52	− 9.9	56.9	15.5	155	69	76	20.2	23 21	23 26	4 13	9 41	9 33
5	23 42	− 5.6	57.5	15.7	167	68	66	21.2	23 45	23 46	5 02	10 54	10 51
6	0 33	− 1.0	58.2	15.9	179	67	56	22.2	—	—	5 50	12 09	12 10
7	1 25	+ 3.7	58.9	16.0	192	68	44	23.2	0 09	0 06	6 40	13 26	13 31
8	2 18	+ 8.3	59.5	16.2	204	69	33	24.2	0 35	0 28	7 32	14 45	14 55
9	3 14	+12.6	60.0	16.4	216	71	23	25.2	1 04	0 53	8 27	16 05	16 19
10	4 13	+16.2	60.4	16.5	228	74	14	26.2	1 40	1 24	9 25	17 23	17 41
11	5 14	+18.8	60.6	16.5	241	78	6	27.2	2 23	2 05	10 26	18 35	18 55
12	6 17	+20.1	60.5	16.5	253	80	2	28.2	3 17	2 57	11 28	19 38	19 59
13	7 20	+20.0	60.2	16.4	265	41	0	29.2	4 20	4 00	12 29	20 30	20 49
14	8 22	+18.5	59.7	16.3	277	287	1	0.9	5 32	5 14	13 27	21 12	21 27
15	9 20	+16.0	58.9	16.1	290	287	5	1.9	6 46	6 32	14 22	21 45	21 56
16	10 16	+12.5	58.1	15.8	302	289	11	2.9	8 00	7 50	15 13	22 12	22 20
17	11 08	+ 8.6	57.2	15.6	314	291	18	3.9	9 13	9 07	16 01	22 36	22 40
18	11 57	+ 4.3	56.3	15.4	326	292	27	4.9	10 23	10 21	16 47	22 58	22 58
19	12 45	0.0	55.6	15.1	339	292	37	5.9	11 31	11 33	17 30	23 19	23 15
20	13 31	− 4.2	55.0	15.0	351	291	46	6.9	12 37	12 43	18 14	23 40	23 33
21	14 17	− 8.2	54.5	14.9	3	290	56	7.9	13 42	13 51	18 57	—	23 53
22	15 03	−11.8	54.3	14.8	15	288	65	8.9	14 46	14 59	19 41	0 03	—
23	15 50	−14.9	54.1	14.8	28	285	74	9.9	15 48	16 04	20 27	0 29	0 16
24	16 38	−17.4	54.2	14.8	40	282	82	10.9	16 49	17 07	21 14	0 59	0 43
25	17 28	−19.2	54.4	14.8	52	278	89	11.9	17 45	18 05	22 02	1 35	1 16
26	18 19	−20.1	54.7	14.9	64	274	94	12.9	18 36	18 57	22 52	2 18	1 57
27	19 11	−20.1	55.0	15.0	76	271	98	13.9	19 21	19 40	23 42	3 08	2 48
28	20 03	−19.1	55.5	15.1	89	271	100	14.9	20 00	20 16	—	4 06	3 48
29	20 56	−17.2	56.0	15.2	101	73	100	15.9	20 33	20 46	0 32	5 11	4 55
30	21 48	−14.4	56.5	15.4	113	74	98	16.9	21 01	21 11	1 22	6 19	6 07
31	22 40	−10.8	57.0	15.5	125	72	93	17.9	21 27	21 33	2 11	7 31	7 22

MERCURY

Day	RA	Dec.	Diam.	Phase	Transit	5° high 52°	5° high 56°
	h m	°	"	%	h m	h m	h m
1	8 26	+19.1	8	37	13 51	20 57	21 10
3	8 32	+18.3	9	33	13 49	20 50	21 02
5	8 37	+17.6	9	30	13 46	20 43	20 54
7	8 41	+16.8	9	26	13 41	20 34	20 45
9	8 43	+16.2	10	23	13 35	20 25	20 35
11	8 44	+15.6	10	19	13 29	20 15	20 24
13	8 44	+15.0	11	16	13 20	20 04	20 13
15	8 43	+14.6	11	11	13 11	19 52	20 01
17	8 41	+14.3	11	9	13 00	19 40	19 49
19	8 37	+14.1	11	7	12 49	19 28	19 36
21	8 33	+14.1	11	4	12 36	19 15	19 23
23	8 28	+14.2	12	2	12 23	19 02	19 11
25	8 22	+14.4	12	1	12 10	18 50	18 59
27	8 16	+14.7	11	1	11 56	5 14	5 05
29	8 11	+15.0	11	2	11 43	4 59	4 50
31	8 06	+15.5	11	3	11 31	4 44	4 34

VENUS

Day	RA	Dec.	Diam.	Phase	Transit	5° high 52°	5° high 56°
	h m	°	"	%	h m	h m	h m
1	9 40	+14.8	30	37	15 05	21 47	21 55
6	9 53	+13.0	33	34	14 58	21 30	21 38
11	10 04	+11.3	35	30	14 49	21 12	21 18
16	10 13	+ 9.6	38	26	14 38	20 52	20 57
21	10 19	+ 8.0	41	23	14 24	20 30	20 33
26	10 22	+ 6.7	45	17	14 07	20 06	20 08
31	10 21	+ 5.5	48	12	13 46	19 40	19 41

MARS

Day	RA	Dec.	Diam.	Phase	Transit	5° high 52°	5° high 56°
1	13 45	−12.0	11	89	19 08	23 28	23 14
6	13 51	−12.7	11	88	18 55	23 11	22 55
11	13 58	−13.4	11	88	18 42	22 54	22 37
16	14 05	−14.1	10	87	18 30	22 37	22 19
21	14 13	−14.9	10	87	18 18	22 20	22 02
26	14 22	−15.7	10	86	18 08	22 04	21 44
31	14 32	−16.6	9	86	17 58	21 49	21 28

SUNRISE AND SUNSET

	London		Bristol		Birmingham		Manchester		Newcastle		Glasgow		Belfast	
	0°05'	51°30'	2°35'	51°28'	1°55'	52°28'	2°15'	53°28'	1°37'	54°59'	4°14'	55°52'	5°56'	54°35'
	h m	h m	h m	h m	h m	h m	h m	h m	h m	h m	h m	h m	h m	h m
1	3 47	20 21	3 57	20 31	3 49	20 34	3 44	20 41	3 32	20 48	3 36	21 05	3 52	21 03
2	3 48	20 20	3 58	20 30	3 50	20 33	3 45	20 41	3 33	20 48	3 37	21 05	3 53	21 02
3	3 48	20 20	3 59	20 30	3 50	20 33	3 46	20 40	3 33	20 47	3 38	21 04	3 53	21 02
4	3 49	20 20	3 59	20 29	3 51	20 32	3 47	20 40	3 34	20 47	3 38	21 03	3 54	21 01
5	3 50	20 19	4 00	20 29	3 52	20 32	3 47	20 39	3 35	20 46	3 39	21 03	3 55	21 01
6	3 51	20 19	4 01	20 28	3 53	20 31	3 48	20 38	3 36	20 45	3 40	21 02	3 56	21 00
7	3 52	20 18	4 02	20 28	3 54	20 31	3 49	20 38	3 37	20 45	3 42	21 01	3 57	20 59
8	3 53	20 17	4 03	20 27	3 55	20 30	3 50	20 37	3 38	20 44	3 43	21 00	3 58	20 59
9	3 54	20 17	4 04	20 27	3 56	20 29	3 51	20 36	3 39	20 43	3 44	20 59	3 59	20 58
10	3 55	20 16	4 05	20 26	3 57	20 28	3 52	20 35	3 41	20 42	3 45	20 59	4 00	20 57
11	3 56	20 15	4 06	20 25	3 58	20 28	3 54	20 35	3 42	20 41	3 46	20 57	4 02	20 56
12	3 57	20 14	4 07	20 24	3 59	20 27	3 55	20 34	3 43	20 40	3 48	20 56	4 03	20 55
13	3 58	20 14	4 08	20 23	4 00	20 26	3 56	20 33	3 44	20 39	3 49	20 55	4 04	20 54
14	3 59	20 13	4 09	20 22	4 01	20 25	3 57	20 32	3 46	20 38	3 50	20 54	4 05	20 53
15	4 00	20 12	4 10	20 21	4 03	20 24	3 58	20 31	3 47	20 37	3 52	20 53	4 07	20 52
16	4 01	20 11	4 11	20 20	4 04	20 23	4 00	20 29	3 48	20 36	3 53	20 52	4 08	20 50
17	4 03	20 10	4 13	20 19	4 05	20 22	4 01	20 28	3 50	20 34	3 55	20 50	4 10	20 49
18	4 04	20 09	4 14	20 18	4 06	20 21	4 02	20 27	3 51	20 33	3 56	20 49	4 11	20 48
19	4 05	20 07	4 15	20 17	4 08	20 19	4 04	20 26	3 53	20 32	3 58	20 47	4 12	20 47
20	4 06	20 06	4 16	20 16	4 09	20 18	4 05	20 24	3 54	20 30	4 00	20 46	4 14	20 45
21	4 08	20 05	4 18	20 15	4 10	20 17	4 07	20 23	3 56	20 29	4 01	20 44	4 15	20 44
22	4 09	20 04	4 19	20 14	4 12	20 16	4 08	20 22	3 57	20 27	4 03	20 43	4 17	20 42
23	4 10	20 02	4 20	20 12	4 13	20 14	4 10	20 20	3 59	20 26	4 05	20 41	4 19	20 41
24	4 12	20 01	4 22	20 11	4 15	20 13	4 11	20 19	4 01	20 24	4 06	20 39	4 20	20 39
25	4 13	20 00	4 23	20 10	4 16	20 11	4 13	20 17	4 02	20 22	4 08	20 38	4 22	20 38
26	4 14	19 58	4 25	20 08	4 18	20 10	4 14	20 16	4 04	20 21	4 10	20 36	4 23	20 36
27	4 16	19 57	4 26	20 07	4 19	20 08	4 16	20 14	4 06	20 19	4 11	20 34	4 25	20 34
28	4 17	19 55	4 27	20 05	4 21	20 07	4 17	20 13	4 07	20 17	4 13	20 32	4 27	20 33
29	4 19	19 54	4 29	20 04	4 22	20 05	4 19	20 11	4 09	20 16	4 15	20 31	4 28	20 31
30	4 20	19 52	4 30	20 02	4 24	20 04	4 21	20 09	4 11	20 14	4 17	20 29	4 30	20 29
31	4 22	19 51	4 32	20 01	4 25	20 02	4 22	20 08	4 13	20 12	4 19	20 27	4 32	20 27

JUPITER

Day	RA	Dec.	Transit	5° high	
				52°	56°
	h m	° '	h m	h m	h m
1	1 54.9	+10 28	7 19	0 59	0 54
11	2 00.4	+10 56	6 46	0 23	0 17
21	2 05.1	+11 19	6 11	23 42	23 36
31	2 08.7	+11 36	5 35	23 05	22 59

Diameters – equatorial 39" polar 37"

SATURN

Day	RA	Dec.	Transit	5° high	
				52°	56°
	h m	° '	h m	h m	h m
1	2 49.8	+13 57	8 14	1 36	1 27
11	2 53.2	+14 10	7 38	0 58	0 50
21	2 56.1	+14 21	7 02	0 21	0 12
31	2 58.5	+14 29	6 25	23 40	23 31

Diameters – equatorial 17" polar 16"
Rings – major axis 39" minor axis 14"

URANUS

Day	RA	Dec.	Transit	10° high	
				52°	56°
	h m	° '	h m	h m	h m
1	21 15.4	−16 39	2 41	23 28	0 02
11	21 14.2	−16 45	2 00	22 48	23 18
21	21 12.8	−16 52	1 19	22 08	22 39
31	21 11.2	−16 59	0 38	21 28	21 59

Diameter 4"

NEPTUNE

Day	RA	Dec.	Transit	10° high	
				52°	56°
	h m	° '	h m	h m	h m
1	20 23.5	−19 04	1 49	22 56	23 34
11	20 22.5	−19 07	1 08	22 17	22 55
21	20 21.4	−19 11	0 28	21 37	22 15
31	20 20.3	−19 15	23 44	20 57	21 35

Diameter 2"

August 1999

EIGHTH MONTH, 31 DAYS. Julius, Caesar *Augustus*, formerly *Sextilis*, sixth month of Roman pre-Julian calendar

1	Sunday	**9th S. after Trinity.** Queen Anne d. 1714	*week 31 day* 213
2	Monday	*Bank Holiday in Scotland.* William S. Burroughs d. 1997	214
3	Tuesday	Sir Joseph Paxton b. 1801. P. D. James b. 1920	215
4	Wednesday	*Queen Elizabeth the Queen Mother b. 1900*	216
5	Thursday	Neil Armstrong b. 1930. Marilyn Monroe d. 1962	217
6	Friday	**The Transfiguration.** Alfred, Lord Tennyson b. 1809	218
7	Saturday	Oliver Hardy d. 1957. Ossie Clark d. 1996	219
8	Sunday	**10th S. after Trinity.** Princess Beatrice of York b. 1988	*week 32 day* 220
9	Monday	John Dryden b. 1631. Philip Larkin b. 1922	221
10	Tuesday	Sir Charles Napier b. 1782. Charles Keene b. 1823	222
11	Wednesday	Enid Blyton b. 1897. Andrew Carnegie d. 1919	223
12	Thursday	George IV b. 1762. William Blake d. 1827	224
13	Friday	Sir Basil Spence b. 1907. Florence Nightingale d. 1910	225
14	Saturday	John Galsworthy b. 1867. J. B. Priestley d. 1984	226
15	Sunday	**Blessed Virgin Mary. 11th S. after Trinity.** *Princess Royal b. 1950*	*week 33 day* 227
16	Monday	Georgette Heyer b. 1902. Ted Hughes b. 1930	228
17	Tuesday	Davy Crockett b. 1786. Rudolf Hess d. 1987	229
18	Wednesday	Willie Rushton b. 1937. Sir Frederick Ashton d. 1988	230
19	Thursday	President Bill Clinton b. 1946. Sir Jacob Epstein d. 1959	231
20	Friday	Soviet invasion of Czechoslovakia 1968	232
21	Saturday	*Princess Margaret b. 1930.* William IV b. 1765	233
22	Sunday	**12th S. after Trinity.** Deng Xiaoping b. 1904	*week 34 day* 234
23	Monday	William Wallace executed 1305. Gene Kelly b. 1912	235
24	Tuesday	**St Bartholomew.** Aubrey Beardsley d. 1872	236
25	Wednesday	Ivan the Terrible b. 1530. Friedrich Nietzsche d. 1900	237
26	Thursday	Prince Albert b. 1819. Christopher Isherwood b. 1904	238
27	Friday	C. S. Forester b. 1899. Charles Le Corbusier d. 1965	239
28	Saturday	Goethe b. 1749. Leigh Hunt d. 1859	240
29	Sunday	**13th S. after Trinity.** Ingrid Bergman d. 1982	*week 35 day* 241
30	Monday	*Bank Holiday in England, Wales and Northern Ireland*	242
31	Tuesday	Diana, Princess of Wales d. 1997	243

ASTRONOMICAL PHENOMENA

d	h	
4	04	Jupiter in conjunction with Moon. Jupiter 4° N.
5	01	Saturn in conjunction with Moon. Saturn 3° N.
6	03	Mercury at stationary point
7	19	Uranus at opposition
10	03	Mercury in conjunction with Moon. Mercury 1° S.
11	11	Total eclipse of Sun (*see page 66*)
12	10	Venus in conjunction with Moon. Venus 9° S.
14	14	Mercury at greatest elongation W.19°
18	16	Mars in conjunction with Moon. Mars 7° S.
19	02	Pluto at stationary point
20	12	Venus in inferior conjunction
23	14	Sun's longitude 150° ♍
25	03	Jupiter at stationary point
27	21	Venus in conjunction with Mercury. Venus 10° S.
30	01	Saturn at stationary point
31	11	Jupiter in conjunction with Moon. Jupiter 4° N.

MINIMA OF ALGOL

d	h	d	h	d	h
2	20.6	14	07.8	25	19.1
5	17.4	17	04.6	28	15.9
8	14.2	20	01.4	31	12.7
11	11.0	22	22.2		

CONSTELLATIONS

The following constellations are near the meridian at

	d	h		d	h
July	1	24	August	16	21
July	16	23	September	1	20
August	1	22	September	15	19

Draco, Hercules, Lyra, Cygnus, Sagitta, Ophiuchus, Serpens, Aquila and Sagittarius

THE MOON

Phases, Apsides and Node

		d	h	m
☾	Last Quarter	4	17	27
●	New Moon	11	11	08
☽	First Quarter	19	01	47
○	Full Moon	26	23	48

		d	h	m
Perigee (366,679 km)		7	23	26
Apogee (404,301 km)		19	23	25

Mean longitude of ascending node on August 1, 133°

THE SUN

s.d. 15′.8

Day	Right Ascension	Dec. +	Equation of time	Rise 52°	Rise 56°	Transit	Set 52°	Set 56°	Sidereal time	Transit of First Point of Aries
	h m s	° ′	m s	h m	h m	h m	h m	h m	h m s	h m s
1	8 43 00	18 11	− 6 21	4 21	4 03	12 06	19 51	20 08	20 36 39	3 22 48
2	8 46 53	17 56	− 6 18	4 22	4 05	12 06	19 49	20 06	20 40 35	3 18 52
3	8 50 45	17 40	− 6 14	4 24	4 07	12 06	19 47	20 04	20 44 32	3 14 56
4	8 54 37	17 25	− 6 09	4 26	4 09	12 06	19 46	20 02	20 48 28	3 11 00
5	8 58 28	17 09	− 6 04	4 27	4 10	12 06	19 44	20 00	20 52 25	3 07 04
6	9 02 19	16 53	− 5 58	4 29	4 12	12 06	19 42	19 58	20 56 21	3 03 09
7	9 06 09	16 36	− 5 51	4 30	4 14	12 06	19 40	19 56	21 00 18	2 59 13
8	9 09 58	16 20	− 5 44	4 32	4 16	12 06	19 38	19 54	21 04 14	2 55 17
9	9 13 47	16 03	− 5 36	4 33	4 18	12 06	19 37	19 52	21 08 11	2 51 21
10	9 17 36	15 45	− 5 28	4 35	4 20	12 05	19 35	19 49	21 12 08	2 47 25
11	9 21 23	15 28	− 5 19	4 37	4 22	12 05	19 33	19 47	21 16 04	2 43 29
12	9 25 11	15 10	− 5 10	4 38	4 24	12 05	19 31	19 45	21 20 01	2 39 33
13	9 28 57	14 52	− 5 00	4 40	4 26	12 05	19 29	19 43	21 23 57	2 35 37
14	9 32 43	14 34	− 4 50	4 41	4 28	12 05	19 27	19 40	21 27 54	2 31 41
15	9 36 29	14 15	− 4 38	4 43	4 30	12 05	19 25	19 38	21 31 50	2 27 45
16	9 40 14	13 57	− 4 27	4 45	4 32	12 04	19 23	19 36	21 35 47	2 23 49
17	9 43 58	13 38	− 4 15	4 46	4 34	12 04	19 21	19 33	21 39 43	2 19 54
18	9 47 42	13 19	− 4 02	4 48	4 36	12 04	19 19	19 31	21 43 40	2 15 58
19	9 51 25	12 59	− 3 49	4 50	4 38	12 04	19 17	19 28	21 47 37	2 12 02
20	9 55 08	12 40	− 3 35	4 51	4 40	12 03	19 15	19 26	21 51 33	2 08 06
21	9 58 50	12 20	− 3 21	4 53	4 42	12 03	19 12	19 24	21 55 30	2 04 10
22	10 02 32	12 00	− 3 06	4 54	4 44	12 03	19 10	19 21	21 59 26	2 00 14
23	10 06 14	11 40	− 2 51	4 56	4 46	12 03	19 08	19 19	22 03 23	1 56 18
24	10 09 55	11 20	− 2 35	4 58	4 47	12 02	19 06	19 16	22 07 19	1 52 22
25	10 13 35	10 59	− 2 19	4 59	4 49	12 02	19 04	19 14	22 11 16	1 48 26
26	10 17 15	10 39	− 2 03	5 01	4 51	12 02	19 02	19 11	22 15 12	1 44 30
27	10 20 55	10 18	− 1 46	5 03	4 53	12 02	18 59	19 09	22 19 09	1 40 35
28	10 24 34	9 57	− 1 28	5 04	4 55	12 01	18 57	19 06	22 23 06	1 36 39
29	10 28 13	9 36	− 1 11	5 06	4 57	12 01	18 55	19 03	22 27 02	1 32 43
30	10 31 51	9 14	− 0 53	5 08	4 59	12 01	18 53	19 01	22 30 59	1 28 47
31	10 35 30	8 53	− 0 34	5 09	5 01	12 00	18 51	18 58	22 34 55	1 24 51

DURATION OF TWILIGHT (in minutes)

Latitude	52°	56°	52°	56°	52°	56°	52°	56°
	1 August		11 August		21 August		31 August	
Civil	41	48	39	45	37	42	35	40
Nautical	97	120	89	106	83	96	79	89
Astronomical	177	TAN	153	205	138	166	127	147

THE NIGHT SKY

Mercury becomes a morning object after the first ten days of the month, low above the east-north-eastern horizon at the beginning of morning civil twilight. It is visible for about a fortnight and during this time its magnitude brightens from +0.5 to −1.2.

Venus passes through inferior conjunction on the 20th and therefore remains too close to the Sun for observation for almost the whole of August. However for the last three or four days of the month it might be glimpsed low in the east for a few minutes before sunrise; its magnitude is −4.2.

Mars, magnitude +0.1, continues to be visible as an evening object in the south-western sky, in Libra. On the evening of the 18th the Moon, at First Quarter, will be seen about 6° above the planet.

Jupiter, magnitude −2.6, is still a splendid morning object in the south-eastern sky. The Moon, at Last Quarter, will be seen about 5° below and to the right of the planet during the early hours of the 4th. By the end of the month Jupiter may be detected low above the eastern horizon by about 21h. Jupiter has been moving eastwards in Aries but reaches its first stationary point on the 25th.

Saturn continues to be visible as a morning object, magnitude +0.3. By the end of the month the planet is visible low in the eastern sky by 22h. On the morning of the 5th, the Moon, at Last Quarter, will be seen about 4° below the planet. Saturn is in Aries and reaches its first stationary point on the last day of August.

Uranus is at opposition on the 7th, in Capricornus. Uranus is barely visible to the naked eye as its magnitude is +5.7, but it is readily located with only small optical aid.

Meteors. The maximum of the famous Perseid meteor shower occurs in the early hours of the 13th. Conditions are particularly favourable as there will be no interference by moonlight.

THE MOON

Day	RA	Dec.	Hor. par.	Semi- diam.	Sun's co- long.	PA of Bright Limb	Phase	Age	Rise 52°	Rise 56°	Transit	Set 52°	Set 56°
	h m	°	'	'	°	°	%	d	h m	h m	h m	h m	h m
1	23 31	− 6.7	57.5	15.7	137	70	87	18.9	21 51	21 53	3 00	8 44	8 39
2	0 21	− 2.2	57.9	15.8	150	70	79	19.9	22 14	22 13	3 48	9 58	9 58
3	1 13	+ 2.5	58.4	15.9	162	70	69	20.9	22 39	22 33	4 37	11 14	11 18
4	2 05	+ 7.2	58.8	16.0	174	71	58	21.9	23 07	22 57	5 28	12 31	12 39
5	2 59	+11.5	59.2	16.1	186	73	47	22.9	23 39	23 25	6 21	13 49	14 01
6	3 56	+15.2	59.5	16.2	198	77	36	23.9	—	—	7 16	15 05	15 22
7	4 55	+18.0	59.7	16.3	211	81	25	24.9	0 17	0 00	8 13	16 18	16 38
8	5 55	+19.7	59.8	16.3	223	86	16	25.9	1 05	0 45	9 13	17 24	17 44
9	6 57	+20.2	59.7	16.3	235	92	8	26.9	2 03	1 42	10 13	18 19	18 39
10	7 58	+19.3	59.4	16.2	247	97	3	27.9	3 09	2 50	11 12	19 05	19 22
11	8 57	+17.1	59.0	16.1	260	105	0	28.9	4 22	4 06	12 08	19 42	19 55
12	9 54	+14.0	58.4	15.9	272	280	0	0.5	5 37	5 25	13 01	20 12	20 21
13	10 48	+10.2	57.7	15.7	284	286	3	1.5	6 51	6 43	13 51	20 37	20 43
14	11 39	+ 6.0	57.0	15.5	296	288	8	2.5	8 04	8 00	14 38	21 00	21 02
15	12 27	+ 1.6	56.2	15.3	309	289	14	3.5	9 14	9 14	15 24	21 22	21 20
16	13 15	− 2.7	55.5	15.1	321	289	22	4.5	10 22	10 26	16 08	21 43	21 38
17	14 01	− 6.9	55.0	15.0	333	288	31	5.5	11 28	11 36	16 52	22 06	21 57
18	14 48	−10.6	54.6	14.9	345	286	40	6.5	12 33	12 44	17 36	22 31	22 18
19	15 35	−13.9	54.3	14.8	357	284	49	7.5	13 36	13 51	18 21	22 59	22 44
20	16 23	−16.7	54.2	14.8	10	280	59	8.5	14 37	14 55	19 07	23 32	23 14
21	17 12	−18.7	54.3	14.8	22	276	68	9.5	15 35	15 55	19 55	—	23 52
22	18 02	−19.9	54.6	14.9	34	272	77	10.5	16 28	16 49	20 44	0 12	—
23	18 54	−20.2	55.0	15.0	46	267	84	11.5	17 16	17 36	21 34	0 59	0 39
24	19 46	−19.5	55.5	15.1	58	262	91	12.5	17 57	18 15	22 24	1 54	1 35
25	20 39	−17.9	56.0	15.3	71	256	96	13.5	18 32	18 47	23 15	2 57	2 39
26	21 32	−15.4	56.6	15.4	83	248	99	14.5	19 03	19 14	—	4 04	3 50
27	22 24	−12.0	57.2	15.6	95	156	100	15.5	19 30	19 38	0 05	5 16	5 06
28	23 16	− 7.9	57.8	15.7	107	80	99	16.5	19 55	19 58	0 55	6 30	6 24
29	0 08	− 3.4	58.3	15.9	119	75	95	17.5	20 19	20 19	1 44	7 46	7 44
30	1 00	+ 1.4	58.7	16.0	132	73	89	18.5	20 44	20 39	2 34	9 03	9 06
31	1 53	+ 6.2	59.0	16.1	144	73	81	19.5	21 10	21 02	3 25	10 21	10 28

MERCURY

Day	RA	Dec.	Diam.	Phase	Transit	5° high 52°	5° high 56°
	h m	°	"	%	h m	h m	h m
1	8 04	+15.8	11	5	11 25	4 37	4 27
3	8 01	+16.3	10	8	11 15	4 23	4 13
5	8 00	+16.8	10	11	11 06	4 11	4 01
7	8 00	+17.3	9	16	10 58	4 01	3 50
9	8 02	+17.7	9	22	10 53	3 53	3 41
11	8 06	+18.1	8	28	10 50	3 48	3 35
13	8 12	+18.3	8	35	10 48	3 44	3 32
15	8 20	+18.5	7	43	10 48	3 44	3 31
17	8 30	+18.5	7	50	10 50	3 45	3 33
19	8 41	+18.3	7	58	10 54	3 50	3 37
21	8 53	+17.9	6	66	10 59	3 56	3 44
23	9 06	+17.4	6	74	11 04	4 05	3 54
25	9 21	+16.7	6	80	11 11	4 16	4 05
27	9 36	+15.8	6	86	11 18	4 28	4 18
29	9 51	+14.7	5	91	11 25	4 41	4 33
31	10 06	+13.5	5	94	11 33	4 55	4 48

VENUS

Day	RA	Dec.	Diam.	Phase	Transit	5° high 52°	5° high 56°
	h m	°	"	%	h m	h m	h m
1	10 21	+ 5.4	49	11	13 42	19 35	19 36
6	10 16	+ 4.6	52	7	13 17	19 06	19 07
11	10 08	+ 4.3	55	4	12 48	18 37	18 37
16	9 57	+ 4.4	57	2	12 18	18 07	18 07
21	9 45	+ 4.9	58	1	11 46	17 38	17 39
26	9 33	+ 5.7	57	1	11 15	17 11	17 13
31	9 24	+ 6.7	55	5	10 46	16 48	16 50

MARS

Day	RA	Dec.	Diam.	Phase	Transit	5° high 52°	5° high 56°
1	14 34	−16.7	9	86	17 56	21 46	21 24
6	14 44	−17.6	9	86	17 46	21 30	21 08
11	14 55	−18.4	9	86	17 37	21 16	20 51
16	15 06	−19.2	9	86	17 29	21 01	20 35
21	15 17	−20.0	8	86	17 21	20 47	20 20
26	15 30	−20.8	8	86	17 13	20 34	20 05
31	15 42	−21.5	8	86	17 06	20 21	19 50

SUNRISE AND SUNSET

	London		Bristol		Birmingham		Manchester		Newcastle		Glasgow		Belfast	
	0°05′	51°30′	2°35′	51°28′	1°55′	52°28′	2°15′	53°28′	1°37′	54°59′	4°14′	55°52′	5°56′	54°35′
	h m	h m	h m	h m	h m	h m	h m	h m	h m	h m	h m	h m	h m	h m
1	4 23	19 49	4 33	19 59	4 27	20 00	4 24	20 06	4 14	20 10	4 21	20 25	4 34	20 25
2	4 25	19 47	4 35	19 57	4 28	19 59	4 25	20 04	4 16	20 08	4 22	20 23	4 35	20 24
3	4 26	19 46	4 36	19 56	4 30	19 57	4 27	20 02	4 18	20 06	4 24	20 21	4 37	20 22
4	4 28	19 44	4 38	19 54	4 31	19 55	4 29	20 00	4 20	20 04	4 26	20 19	4 39	20 20
5	4 29	19 42	4 39	19 52	4 33	19 53	4 30	19 58	4 22	20 02	4 28	20 17	4 41	20 18
6	4 31	19 41	4 41	19 51	4 35	19 51	4 32	19 57	4 23	20 00	4 30	20 14	4 42	20 16
7	4 32	19 39	4 42	19 49	4 36	19 50	4 34	19 55	4 25	19 58	4 32	20 12	4 44	20 14
8	4 34	19 37	4 44	19 47	4 38	19 48	4 36	19 53	4 27	19 56	4 34	20 10	4 46	20 12
9	4 35	19 35	4 46	19 45	4 39	19 46	4 37	19 51	4 29	19 54	4 36	20 08	4 48	20 10
10	4 37	19 33	4 47	19 43	4 41	19 44	4 39	19 49	4 31	19 52	4 38	20 06	4 50	20 07
11	4 39	19 31	4 49	19 41	4 43	19 42	4 41	19 47	4 33	19 50	4 40	20 04	4 51	20 05
12	4 40	19 30	4 50	19 39	4 44	19 40	4 42	19 45	4 34	19 47	4 41	20 01	4 53	20 03
13	4 42	19 28	4 52	19 38	4 46	19 38	4 44	19 43	4 36	19 45	4 43	19 59	4 55	20 01
14	4 43	19 26	4 53	19 36	4 48	19 36	4 46	19 40	4 38	19 43	4 45	19 57	4 57	19 59
15	4 45	19 24	4 55	19 34	4 49	19 34	4 48	19 38	4 40	19 41	4 47	19 54	4 59	19 57
16	4 47	19 22	4 57	19 32	4 51	19 32	4 49	19 36	4 42	19 39	4 49	19 52	5 00	19 54
17	4 48	19 20	4 58	19 30	4 53	19 30	4 51	19 34	4 44	19 36	4 51	19 50	5 02	19 52
18	4 50	19 18	5 00	19 28	4 54	19 28	4 53	19 32	4 46	19 34	4 53	19 47	5 04	19 50
19	4 51	19 16	5 01	19 26	4 56	19 26	4 55	19 30	4 47	19 32	4 55	19 45	5 06	19 48
20	4 53	19 14	5 03	19 24	4 58	19 23	4 56	19 27	4 49	19 29	4 57	19 42	5 08	19 45
21	4 54	19 12	5 05	19 21	4 59	19 21	4 58	19 25	4 51	19 27	4 59	19 40	5 10	19 43
22	4 56	19 09	5 06	19 19	5 01	19 19	5 00	19 23	4 53	19 25	5 01	19 38	5 11	19 41
23	4 58	19 07	5 08	19 17	5 03	19 17	5 02	19 21	4 55	19 22	5 03	19 35	5 13	19 38
24	4 59	19 05	5 09	19 15	5 04	19 15	5 03	19 18	4 57	19 20	5 05	19 33	5 15	19 36
25	5 01	19 03	5 11	19 13	5 06	19 13	5 05	19 16	4 59	19 17	5 07	19 30	5 17	19 34
26	5 02	19 01	5 13	19 11	5 08	19 10	5 07	19 14	5 01	19 15	5 09	19 28	5 19	19 31
27	5 04	18 59	5 14	19 09	5 09	19 08	5 08	19 12	5 02	19 13	5 11	19 25	5 21	19 29
28	5 06	18 57	5 16	19 07	5 11	19 06	5 10	19 09	5 04	19 10	5 13	19 23	5 22	19 26
29	5 07	18 54	5 17	19 04	5 13	19 04	5 12	19 07	5 06	19 08	5 15	19 20	5 24	19 24
30	5 09	18 52	5 19	19 02	5 14	19 01	5 14	19 05	5 08	19 05	5 16	19 18	5 26	19 22
31	5 10	18 50	5 20	19 00	5 16	18 59	5 15	19 02	5 10	19 03	5 18	19 15	5 28	19 19

JUPITER

Day	RA	Dec.	Transit	5° high	
				52°	56°
	h m	° ′	h m	h m	h m
1	2 09.0	+11 37	5 32	23 02	22 55
11	2 11.4	+11 47	4 55	22 24	22 17
21	2 12.6	+11 51	4 16	21 45	21 39
31	2 12.6	+11 48	3 37	21 06	21 00

Diameters – equatorial 43″ polar 41″

SATURN

Day	RA	Dec.	Transit	5° high	
				52°	56°
	h m	° ′	h m	h m	h m
1	2 58.7	+14 29	6 21	23 36	23 27
11	3 00.4	+14 34	5 43	22 58	22 49
21	3 01.4	+14 36	5 05	22 19	22 10
31	3 01.8	+14 35	4 26	21 40	21 31

Diameters – equatorial 18″ polar 17″
Rings – major axis 42″ minor axis 15″

URANUS

Day	RA	Dec.	Transit	10° high	
				52°	56°
	h m	° ′	h m	h m	h m
1	21 11.1	−16 59	0 34	3 41	3 10
11	21 09.5	−17 06	23 49	2 59	2 28
21	21 07.9	−17 13	23 08	2 17	1 45
31	21 06.4	−17 20	22 28	1 35	1 03

Diameter 4″

NEPTUNE

Day	RA	Dec.	Transit	10° high	
				52°	56°
	h m	° ′	h m	h m	h m
1	20 20.2	−19 15	23 40	2 30	1 52
11	20 19.1	−19 19	22 59	1 49	1 11
21	20 18.0	−19 23	22 19	1 08	0 29
31	20 17.1	−19 26	21 39	0 28	23 44

Diameter 2″

September 1999

NINTH MONTH, 30 DAYS. *Septem* (seven), seventh month of Roman pre-Julian calendar

1	*Wednesday*	Engelbert Humperdinck b. 1854. Siegfried Sassoon d. 1967	*week* 35 *day* 244
2	*Thursday*	Thomas Telford d. 1834. J. R. R. Tolkien d. 1973	245
3	*Friday*	Oliver Cromwell d. 1658. Roy Castle d. 1994	246
4	*Saturday*	Anton Bruckner b. 1824. Georges Simenon d. 1989	247
5	*Sunday*	**14th S. after Trinity.** Pieter Brueghel (elder) d. 1569	*week* 36 *day* 248
6	*Monday*	The *Mayflower* sailed from Plymouth 1620	249
7	*Tuesday*	Elizabeth I b. 1533. Joan Cross b. 1900	250
8	*Wednesday*	Sir Peter Maxwell Davies b. 1934. Richard Strauss d. 1949	251
9	*Thursday*	End of soap rationing 1950. Mao Tse-tung d. 1976	252
10	*Friday*	Mary Wollstonecraft Godwin d. 1797. Arnold Palmer b. 1929	253
11	*Saturday*	JEWISH NEW YEAR. Jessica Mitford b. 1917	254
12	*Sunday*	**15th S. after Trinity.** Marshal von Blücher d. 1819	*week* 37 *day* 255
13	*Monday*	Gen. Wolfe d. 1759. Arnold Schönberg b. 1874	256
14	*Tuesday*	**Holy Cross Day.** Sir Peter Scott b. 1909	257
15	*Wednesday*	Prince Henry of Wales b. 1984. Battle of Britain Day	258
16	*Thursday*	Peter Darrell b. 1929. Maria Callas d. 1977	259
17	*Friday*	Sir Frederick Ashton b. 1904. Stirling Moss b. 1929	260
18	*Saturday*	Greta Garbo b. 1905. Sean O'Casey d. 1964	261
19	*Sunday*	**16th S. after Trinity.** Emil Zátopek b. 1922	*week* 38 *day* 262
20	*Monday*	YOM KIPPUR. Stevie Smith b. 1902	263
21	*Tuesday*	**St Matthew.** Gustav Holst b. 1874	264
22	*Wednesday*	Michael Faraday b. 1791. Irving Berlin d. 1989	265
23	*Thursday*	Wilkie Collins d. 1889. Sigmund Freud d. 1939	266
24	*Friday*	Scott Fitzgerald b. 1896. Dr Seuss d. 1991	267
25	*Saturday*	FEAST OF TABERNACLES begins. Johann Strauss (elder) d. 1849	268
26	*Sunday*	**17th S. after Trinity.** *Queen Mary* launched 1934	*week* 39 *day* 269
27	*Monday*	Adelina Patti d. 1919. Dame Gracie Fields d. 1979	270
28	*Tuesday*	Ellis Peters b. 1913. W. H. Auden d. 1973	271
29	*Wednesday*	**St Michael and All Angels.** Mrs Gaskell b. 1810	272
30	*Thursday*	Pierre Corneille d. 1684. Truman Capote b. 1924	273

ASTRONOMICAL PHENOMENA

d	h	
1	08	Saturn in conjunction with Moon. Saturn 3° N.
7	21	Venus in conjunction with Moon. Venus 8° S.
8	15	Mercury in superior conjunction
10	01	Mercury in conjunction with Moon. Mercury 1° S.
11	00	Venus at stationary point
16	12	Mars in conjunction with Moon. Mars 6° S.
23	12	Sun's longitude 180° ♎
26	14	Venus at greatest brilliancy
27	15	Jupiter in conjunction with Moon. Jupiter 4° N.
28	13	Saturn in conjunction with Moon. Saturn 3° N.

MINIMA OF ALGOL

d	h	d	h	d	h
3	09.5	14	20.7	26	08.0
6	06.3	17	17.5	29	04.8
9	03.1	20	14.3		
11	23.9	23	11.2		

CONSTELLATIONS

The following constellations are near the meridian at

	d	h		d	h
August	1	24	September	15	21
August	16	23	October	1	20
September	1	22	October	16	19

Draco, Cepheus, Lyra, Cygnus, Vulpecula, Sagitta, Delphinus, Equuleus, Aquila, Aquarius and Capricornus

THE MOON

Phases, Apsides and Node	d	h	m
☾ Last Quarter	2	22	17
● New Moon	9	22	02
☽ First Quarter	17	20	06
○ Full Moon	25	10	51
Perigee (369,783 km)	2	18	04
Apogee (404,431 km)	16	18	42
Perigee (366,227 km)	28	16	50

Mean longitude of ascending node on September 1, 132°

THE SUN   s.d. 15'.9

Day	Right Ascension	Dec.	Equation of time	Rise 52°	Rise 56°	Transit	Set 52°	Set 56°	Sidereal time	Transit of First Point of Aries
	h m s	° '	m s	h m	h m	h m	h m	h m	h m s	h m s
1	10 39 07	+ 8 31	− 0 16	5 11	5 03	12 00	18 48	18 56	22 38 52	1 20 55
2	10 42 45	+ 8 10	+ 0 03	5 12	5 05	12 00	18 46	18 53	22 42 48	1 16 59
3	10 46 22	+ 7 48	+ 0 22	5 14	5 07	11 59	18 44	18 51	22 46 45	1 13 03
4	10 49 59	+ 7 26	+ 0 42	5 16	5 09	11 59	18 41	18 48	22 50 41	1 09 07
5	10 53 36	+ 7 04	+ 1 02	5 17	5 11	11 59	18 39	18 45	22 54 38	1 05 11
6	10 57 13	+ 6 41	+ 1 22	5 19	5 13	11 58	18 37	18 43	22 58 34	1 01 15
7	11 00 49	+ 6 19	+ 1 42	5 21	5 15	11 58	18 35	18 40	23 02 31	0 57 20
8	11 04 26	+ 5 57	+ 2 02	5 22	5 17	11 58	18 32	18 38	23 06 28	0 53 24
9	11 08 02	+ 5 34	+ 2 23	5 24	5 19	11 57	18 30	18 35	23 10 24	0 49 28
10	11 11 37	+ 5 11	+ 2 43	5 25	5 21	11 57	18 28	18 32	23 14 21	0 45 32
11	11 15 13	+ 4 49	+ 3 04	5 27	5 23	11 57	18 25	18 30	23 18 17	0 41 36
12	11 18 49	+ 4 26	+ 3 25	5 29	5 25	11 56	18 23	18 27	23 22 14	0 37 40
13	11 22 24	+ 4 03	+ 3 46	5 30	5 27	11 56	18 21	18 24	23 26 10	0 33 44
14	11 26 00	+ 3 40	+ 4 07	5 32	5 28	11 56	18 18	18 22	23 30 07	0 29 48
15	11 29 35	+ 3 17	+ 4 29	5 34	5 30	11 55	18 16	18 19	23 34 03	0 25 52
16	11 33 10	+ 2 54	+ 4 50	5 35	5 32	11 55	18 14	18 16	23 38 00	0 21 56
17	11 36 45	+ 2 31	+ 5 11	5 37	5 34	11 55	18 11	18 14	23 41 57	0 18 00
18	11 40 20	+ 2 08	+ 5 33	5 39	5 36	11 54	18 09	18 11	23 45 53	0 14 05
19	11 43 56	+ 1 44	+ 5 54	5 40	5 38	11 54	18 07	18 08	23 49 50	0 10 09
20	11 47 31	+ 1 21	+ 6 16	5 42	5 40	11 54	18 04	18 06	23 53 46	0 06 13
21	11 51 06	+ 0 58	+ 6 37	5 43	5 42	11 53	18 02	18 03	23 57 43	{ 0 02 17 / 23 58 21
22	11 54 41	+ 0 35	+ 6 58	5 45	5 44	11 53	18 00	18 00	0 01 39	23 54 25
23	11 58 16	+ 0 11	+ 7 19	5 47	5 46	11 52	17 57	17 58	0 05 36	23 50 29
24	12 01 52	− 0 12	+ 7 41	5 48	5 48	11 52	17 55	17 55	0 09 32	23 46 33
25	12 05 27	− 0 35	+ 8 02	5 50	5 50	11 52	17 53	17 52	0 13 29	23 42 37
26	12 09 03	− 0 59	+ 8 22	5 52	5 52	11 51	17 50	17 50	0 17 26	23 38 41
27	12 12 39	− 1 22	+ 8 43	5 53	5 54	11 51	17 48	17 47	0 21 22	23 34 46
28	12 16 15	− 1 46	+ 9 04	5 55	5 56	11 51	17 46	17 44	0 25 19	23 30 50
29	12 19 51	− 2 09	+ 9 24	5 57	5 58	11 50	17 43	17 42	0 29 15	23 26 54
30	12 23 28	− 2 32	+ 9 44	5 58	6 00	11 50	17 41	17 39	0 33 12	23 22 58

DURATION OF TWILIGHT (in minutes)

Latitude	52°	56°	52°	56°	52°	56°	52°	56°
	1 September		11 September		21 September		30 September	
Civil	35	39	34	38	34	37	34	37
Nautical	79	89	76	84	74	82	73	80
Astronomical	127	146	120	135	115	129	113	126

THE NIGHT SKY

Mercury is unsuitably placed for observation throughout the month, superior conjunction occurring on the 8th.

Venus is emerging from the morning twilight and visible in the eastern sky before dawn. Venus attains its greatest brilliancy on the 26th with a magnitude of −4.6.

Mars, magnitude +0.4, is still visible in the south-western sky in the evenings. The Moon is about 6° from Mars on the evening of the 16th. Mars moves from Scorpius into Ophiuchus during September, passing 3° N. of Antares on the 17th.

Jupiter, magnitude −2.8, continues to be visible as a splendid object in the southern half of the sky as it moves towards opposition next month.

Saturn, magnitude +0.1, is still a morning object, in the constellation of Aries. The Moon is near the planet on the mornings of the 1st and the 28th.

Zodiacal Light. The morning cone may be seen reaching up from the eastern horizon along the ecliptic, before the beginning of morning twilight, from the 8th to the 23rd.

THE MOON

Day	RA	Dec.	Hor. par.	Semi-diam.	Sun's co-long.	PA of Bright Limb	Phase	Age	Rise 52°	Rise 56°	Transit	Set 52°	Set 56°
	h m	°	'	'	°	°	%	d	h m	h m	h m	h m	h m
1	2 47	+10.6	59.2	16.1	156	75	72	20.5	21 41	21 28	4 17	11 38	11 50
2	3 43	+14.5	59.3	16.1	168	78	61	21.5	22 17	22 00	5 11	12 55	13 11
3	4 40	+17.5	59.3	16.2	180	82	49	22.5	23 00	22 41	6 08	14 08	14 27
4	5 40	+19.5	59.2	16.1	193	87	38	23.5	23 53	23 33	7 05	15 15	15 36
5	6 40	+20.2	59.1	16.1	205	92	27	24.5	—	—	8 04	16 13	16 33
6	7 39	+19.7	58.9	16.0	217	98	18	25.5	0 55	0 35	9 02	17 01	17 19
7	8 38	+18.0	58.5	15.9	229	104	10	26.5	2 04	1 47	9 58	17 40	17 54
8	9 34	+15.2	58.1	15.8	241	110	4	27.5	3 17	3 03	10 51	18 12	18 22
9	10 28	+11.7	57.6	15.7	254	121	1	28.5	4 31	4 21	11 41	18 38	18 46
10	11 20	+ 7.6	57.1	15.5	266	221	0	0.1	5 44	5 38	12 30	19 02	19 06
11	12 10	+ 3.2	56.5	15.4	278	277	1	1.1	6 55	6 54	13 16	19 24	19 24
12	12 58	- 1.2	55.9	15.2	290	283	5	2.1	8 05	8 07	14 01	19 46	19 42
13	13 45	- 5.5	55.3	15.1	303	284	10	3.1	9 12	9 19	14 45	20 08	20 00
14	14 32	- 9.5	54.8	14.9	315	284	17	4.1	10 19	10 29	15 29	20 32	20 21
15	15 19	-13.0	54.5	14.8	327	282	24	5.1	11 23	11 37	16 14	20 58	20 44
16	16 06	-15.9	54.3	14.8	339	279	33	6.1	12 25	12 42	17 00	21 29	21 12
17	16 55	-18.2	54.2	14.8	352	276	42	7.1	13 25	13 44	17 47	22 06	21 46
18	17 45	-19.7	54.3	14.8	4	272	52	8.1	14 20	14 40	18 35	22 50	22 30
19	18 36	-20.3	54.6	14.9	16	267	61	9.1	15 09	15 30	19 24	23 41	23 20
20	19 27	-20.0	55.1	15.0	28	262	70	10.1	15 52	16 11	20 14	—	—
21	20 19	-18.7	55.7	15.2	40	257	79	11.1	16 30	16 46	21 04	0 40	0 21
22	21 12	-16.5	56.4	15.4	52	253	87	12.1	17 02	17 15	21 55	1 45	1 29
23	22 04	-13.4	57.2	15.6	65	247	93	13.1	17 31	17 40	22 45	2 55	2 43
24	22 57	- 9.5	57.9	15.8	77	240	97	14.1	17 56	18 02	23 35	4 09	4 01
25	23 49	- 5.0	58.6	16.0	89	216	100	15.1	18 21	18 22	—	5 26	5 22
26	0 42	- 0.1	59.2	16.1	101	98	99	16.1	18 46	18 43	0 26	6 44	6 45
27	1 36	+ 4.8	59.6	16.2	113	81	97	17.1	19 12	19 05	1 18	8 04	8 10
28	2 31	+ 9.5	59.8	16.3	125	79	91	18.1	19 41	19 30	2 11	9 24	9 35
29	3 28	+13.7	59.9	16.3	138	80	84	19.1	20 16	20 01	3 06	10 44	10 58
30	4 26	+17.1	59.7	16.3	150	83	74	20.1	20 58	20 39	4 03	12 00	12 18

MERCURY

Day	RA	Dec.	Diam.	Phase	Transit	5° high 52°	5° high 56°
	h m	°	"	%	h m	h m	h m
1	10 14	+12.8	5	96	11 36	5 03	4 55
3	10 29	+11.5	5	98	11 44	5 17	5 11
5	10 43	+10.0	5	99	11 50	5 32	5 27
7	10 58	+ 8.5	5	100	11 57	5 46	5 42
9	11 12	+ 7.0	5	100	12 03	18 04	18 06
11	11 26	+ 5.4	5	100	12 09	18 01	18 02
13	11 39	+ 3.8	5	99	12 14	17 59	17 58
15	11 52	+ 2.2	5	99	12 19	17 56	17 54
17	12 05	+ 0.6	5	98	12 24	17 52	17 49
19	12 17	- 0.9	5	97	12 28	17 48	17 44
21	12 29	- 2.5	5	96	12 33	17 45	17 39
23	12 41	- 4.0	5	95	12 37	17 41	17 33
25	12 53	- 5.5	5	93	12 40	17 36	17 28
27	13 04	- 6.9	5	92	12 44	17 32	17 22
29	13 16	- 8.3	5	91	12 47	17 28	17 16
31	13 27	- 9.7	5	90	12 51	17 23	17 10

VENUS

Day	RA	Dec.	Diam.	Phase	Transit	5° high 52°	5° high 56°
	h m	°	"	%	h m	h m	h m
1	9 22	+ 6.9	55	5	10 41	4 40	4 37
6	9 17	+ 7.8	52	9	10 17	4 10	4 07
11	9 16	+ 8.6	48	14	9 56	3 46	3 42
16	9 19	+ 9.2	45	18	9 40	3 26	3 21
21	9 25	+ 9.6	41	23	9 27	3 10	3 06
26	9 34	+ 9.8	38	27	9 16	2 59	2 55
31	9 46	+ 9.6	35	31	9 08	2 52	2 47

MARS

Day	RA	Dec.	Diam.	Phase	Transit	5° high 52°	5° high 56°
1	15 45	-21.7	8	86	17 05	20 19	19 47
6	15 58	-22.3	8	86	16 59	20 07	19 33
11	16 12	-23.0	8	86	16 53	19 55	19 20
16	16 26	-23.5	7	86	16 47	19 45	19 07
21	16 40	-24.0	7	86	16 42	19 35	18 56
26	16 55	-24.4	7	87	16 37	19 26	18 45
31	17 10	-24.8	7	87	16 32	19 19	18 36

SUNRISE AND SUNSET

	London		Bristol		Birmingham		Manchester		Newcastle		Glasgow		Belfast	
	0°05′	51°30′	2°35′	51°28′	1°55′	52°28′	2°15′	53°28′	1°37′	54°59′	4°14′	55°52′	5°56′	54°35′
	h m	h m	h m	h m	h m	h m	h m	h m	h m	h m	h m	h m	h m	h m
1	5 12	18 48	5 22	18 58	5 18	18 57	5 17	19 00	5 12	19 00	5 20	19 12	5 30	19 17
2	5 14	18 46	5 24	18 56	5 19	18 54	5 19	18 57	5 14	18 58	5 22	19 10	5 32	19 14
3	5 15	18 43	5 25	18 53	5 21	18 52	5 21	18 55	5 15	18 55	5 24	19 07	5 33	19 12
4	5 17	18 41	5 27	18 51	5 23	18 50	5 22	18 53	5 17	18 53	5 26	19 05	5 35	19 09
5	5 18	18 39	5 28	18 49	5 24	18 48	5 24	18 50	5 19	18 50	5 28	19 02	5 37	19 07
6	5 20	18 37	5 30	18 47	5 26	18 45	5 26	18 48	5 21	18 48	5 30	18 59	5 39	19 04
7	5 22	18 34	5 32	18 44	5 28	18 43	5 28	18 45	5 23	18 45	5 32	18 57	5 41	19 02
8	5 23	18 32	5 33	18 42	5 29	18 41	5 29	18 43	5 25	18 43	5 34	18 54	5 43	18 59
9	5 25	18 30	5 35	18 40	5 31	18 38	5 31	18 41	5 27	18 40	5 36	18 52	5 44	18 57
10	5 26	18 27	5 36	18 37	5 33	18 36	5 33	18 38	5 28	18 37	5 38	18 49	5 46	18 54
11	5 28	18 25	5 38	18 35	5 34	18 33	5 35	18 36	5 30	18 35	5 40	18 46	5 48	18 52
12	5 29	18 23	5 40	18 33	5 36	18 31	5 36	18 33	5 32	18 32	5 42	18 44	5 50	18 49
13	5 31	18 21	5 41	18 31	5 38	18 29	5 38	18 31	5 34	18 30	5 44	18 41	5 52	18 47
14	5 33	18 18	5 43	18 28	5 39	18 26	5 40	18 28	5 36	18 27	5 46	18 38	5 54	18 44
15	5 34	18 16	5 44	18 26	5 41	18 24	5 42	18 26	5 38	18 25	5 48	18 36	5 55	18 42
16	5 36	18 14	5 46	18 24	5 43	18 22	5 43	18 24	5 40	18 22	5 49	18 33	5 57	18 39
17	5 37	18 11	5 48	18 21	5 44	18 19	5 45	18 21	5 42	18 20	5 51	18 31	5 59	18 37
18	5 39	18 09	5 49	18 19	5 46	18 17	5 47	18 19	5 43	18 17	5 53	18 28	6 01	18 34
19	5 41	18 07	5 51	18 17	5 48	18 15	5 49	18 16	5 45	18 14	5 55	18 25	6 03	18 31
20	5 42	18 05	5 52	18 14	5 49	18 12	5 50	18 14	5 47	18 12	5 57	18 23	6 05	18 29
21	5 44	18 02	5 54	18 12	5 51	18 10	5 52	18 11	5 49	18 09	5 59	18 20	6 06	18 26
22	5 45	18 00	5 55	18 10	5 53	18 07	5 54	18 09	5 51	18 07	6 01	18 17	6 08	18 24
23	5 47	17 58	5 57	18 08	5 54	18 05	5 55	18 06	5 53	18 04	6 03	18 15	6 10	18 21
24	5 49	17 55	5 59	18 05	5 56	18 03	5 57	18 04	5 55	18 01	6 05	18 12	6 12	18 19
25	5 50	17 53	6 00	18 03	5 58	18 00	5 59	18 02	5 56	17 59	6 07	18 09	6 14	18 16
26	5 52	17 51	6 02	18 01	5 59	17 58	6 01	17 59	5 58	17 56	6 09	18 07	6 16	18 14
27	5 54	17 48	6 04	17 58	6 01	17 56	6 03	17 57	6 00	17 54	6 11	18 04	6 17	18 11
28	5 55	17 46	6 05	17 56	6 03	17 53	6 04	17 54	6 02	17 51	6 13	18 01	6 19	18 09
29	5 57	17 44	6 07	17 54	6 04	17 51	6 06	17 52	6 04	17 49	6 15	17 59	6 21	18 06
30	5 58	17 42	6 08	17 52	6 06	17 48	6 08	17 49	6 06	17 46	6 17	17 56	6 23	18 04

JUPITER

Day	RA	Dec.	Transit	5° high	
				52°	56°
	h m	° ′	h m	h m	h m
1	2 12.5	+11 48	3 33	21 02	20 56
11	2 11.0	+11 38	2 52	20 22	20 16
21	2 08.3	+11 22	2 10	19 41	19 35
31	2 04.6	+11 01	1 27	19 00	18 54

Diameters – equatorial 47″ polar 45″

SATURN

Day	RA	Dec.	Transit	5° high	
				52°	56°
	h m	° ′	h m	h m	h m
1	3 01.7	+14 35	4 22	21 36	21 27
11	3 01.3	+14 31	3 42	20 57	20 48
21	3 00.2	+14 24	3 02	20 17	20 08
31	2 58.4	+14 15	2 21	19 37	19 28

Diameters – equatorial 19″ polar 17″
Rings – major axis 44″ minor axis 16″

URANUS

Day	RA	Dec.	Transit	10° high	
				52°	56°
	h m	° ′	h m	h m	h m
1	21 06.3	−17 20	22 24	1 31	0 59
11	21 04.9	−17 26	21 43	0 50	0 18
21	21 03.8	−17 30	21 03	0 09	23 32
31	21 03.0	−17 34	20 22	23 24	22 51

Diameter 4″

NEPTUNE

Day	RA	Dec.	Transit	10° high	
				52°	56°
	h m	° ′	h m	h m	h m
1	20 17.0	−19 26	21 35	0 24	23 40
11	20 16.3	−19 29	20 54	23 39	23 00
21	20 15.7	−19 31	20 15	22 59	22 19
31	20 15.3	−19 32	19 35	22 19	21 39

Diameter 2″

 # October 1999

TENTH MONTH, 31 DAYS. *Octo* (eight), eighth month of Roman pre-Julian calendar

1	*Friday*	*Michaelmas Law Sittings begin.* Stanley Holloway b. 1890	*week* 39 *day*	274
2	*Saturday*	Mahatma Gandhi b. 1869. Graham Greene b. 1904		275
3	*Sunday*	**18th S. after Trinity.** Reunification of Germany 1990	*week* 40 *day*	276
4	*Monday*	Rembrandt d. 1669. *Sputnik I* launched 1957		277
5	*Tuesday*	Louis Lumière b. 1864. *R101* disaster 1930		278
6	*Wednesday*	Thor Heyerdahl b. 1914. Bette Davis d. 1989		279
7	*Thursday*	Edgar Allen Poe d. 1849. Mario Lanza d. 1959		280
8	*Friday*	Sir Geoffrey Jellicoe b. 1900. Kathleen Ferrier d. 1953		281
9	*Saturday*	Alfred Dreyfus b. 1859. John Lennon b. 1940		282
10	*Sunday*	**19th S. after Trinity.** Harold Pinter b. 1930	*week* 41 *day*	283
11	*Monday*	James Joule d. 1889. Boer War began 1899		284
12	*Tuesday*	Elizabeth Fry d. 1845. Edith Cavell executed 1915		285
13	*Wednesday*	Anatole France d. 1924. Margaret Thatcher b. 1925		286
14	*Thursday*	Dwight Eisenhower b. 1890. Cliff Richard b. 1940		287
15	*Friday*	Friedrich Nietzsche b. 1844. Sarah, Duchess of York b. 1959		288
16	*Saturday*	Oscar Wilde b. 1854. Edward Ardizzone b. 1900		289
17	*Sunday*	**20th S. after Trinity.** Frederic Chopin d. 1849	*week* 42 *day*	290
18	*Monday*	**St Luke.** Beau Nash b. 1674		291
19	*Tuesday*	Jonathan Swift d. 1745. Leigh Hunt b. 1784		292
20	*Wednesday*	Lord Palmerston b. 1784. Sir Anthony Quayle d. 1989		293
21	*Thursday*	Battle of Trafalgar 1805. Aberfan disaster 1966		294
22	*Friday*	Thomas Sheraton d. 1806. Pablo Casals d. 1973		295
23	*Saturday*	Dr W. G. Grace d. 1915. Pélé b. 1940		296
24	*Sunday*	**Last S. after Trinity.** Dame Sybil Thorndike b. 1882	*week* 43 *day*	297
25	*Monday*	Chaucer d. 1400. Lord Macauley b. 1800		298
26	*Tuesday*	Georges Danton b. 1759. Leon Trotsky b. 1879 (os)		299
27	*Wednesday*	Theodore Roosevelt b. 1858. Dylan Thomas b. 1914		300
28	*Thursday*	**SS Simon and Jude.** Capt. James Cook b. 1728		301
29	*Friday*	James Boswell b. 1740. Wall Street crash 1929		302
30	*Saturday*	Angelica Kauffmann b. 1741. Sir Barnes Wallis d. 1979		303
31	*Sunday*	**4th S. before Advent.** Hallowmass Eve	*week* 44 *day*	304

ASTRONOMICAL PHENOMENA

d	h	
5	20	Venus in conjunction with Moon. Venus 4° S.
11	08	Mercury in conjunction with Moon. Mercury 7° S.
14	01	Neptune at stationary point
15	13	Mars in conjunction with Moon. Mars 5° S.
23	06	Uranus at stationary point
23	19	Jupiter at opposition
23	21	Sun's longitude 210° ♏
24	19	Jupiter in conjunction with Moon. Jupiter 3° N.
24	22	Mercury at greatest elongation E.24°
25	19	Saturn in conjunction with Moon. Saturn 2° N.
31	00	Venus at greatest elongation W.46°

MINIMA OF ALGOL

d	h		d	h		d	h
2	01.6		13	12.8		25	00.1
4	22.4		16	09.6		27	20.9
7	19.2		19	06.5		30	17.7
10	16.0		22	03.3			

CONSTELLATIONS

The following constellations are near the meridian at

	d	h		d	h
September	1	24	October	16	21
September	15	23	November	1	20
October	1	22	November	15	19

Ursa Major (below the Pole), Cepheus, Cassiopeia, Cygnus, Lacerta, Andromeda, Pegasus, Capricornus, Aquarius and Piscis Austrinus

THE MOON

Phases, Apsides and Node	d	h	m
☾ Last Quarter	2	04	02
● New Moon	9	11	34
☽ First Quarter	17	15	00
○ Full Moon	24	21	02
☾ Last Quarter	31	12	04
Apogee (405,289 km)	14	13	54
Perigee (360,936 km)	26	13	05

Mean longitude of ascending node on October 1, 130°

THE SUN   s.d. 16′.1

Day	Right Ascension h m s	Dec. − ° ′	Equation of time m s	Rise 52° h m	Rise 56° h m	Transit h m	Set 52° h m	Set 56° h m	Sidereal time h m s	Transit of First Point of Aries h m s
1	12 27 05	2 56	+10 04	6 00	6 02	11 50	17 39	17 37	0 37 08	23 19 02
2	12 30 42	3 19	+10 23	6 02	6 04	11 49	17 36	17 34	0 41 05	23 15 06
3	12 34 19	3 42	+10 42	6 03	6 06	11 49	17 34	17 31	0 45 01	23 11 10
4	12 37 57	4 05	+11 01	6 05	6 08	11 49	17 32	17 29	0 48 58	23 07 14
5	12 41 35	4 28	+11 19	6 07	6 10	11 49	17 29	17 26	0 52 54	23 03 18
6	12 45 14	4 51	+11 37	6 08	6 12	11 48	17 27	17 24	0 56 51	22 59 22
7	12 48 52	5 15	+11 55	6 10	6 14	11 48	17 25	17 21	1 00 48	22 55 26
8	12 52 32	5 38	+12 12	6 12	6 16	11 48	17 23	17 18	1 04 44	22 51 31
9	12 56 11	6 00	+12 29	6 13	6 18	11 47	17 20	17 16	1 08 41	22 47 35
10	12 59 52	6 23	+12 46	6 15	6 20	11 47	17 18	17 13	1 12 37	22 43 39
11	13 03 32	6 46	+13 02	6 17	6 22	11 47	17 16	17 11	1 16 34	22 39 43
12	13 07 13	7 09	+13 17	6 19	6 24	11 47	17 11	17 08	1 20 30	22 35 47
13	13 10 55	7 31	+13 32	6 20	6 26	11 46	17 11	17 06	1 24 27	22 31 51
14	13 14 37	7 54	+13 47	6 22	6 28	11 46	17 09	17 03	1 28 23	22 27 55
15	13 18 19	8 16	+14 01	6 24	6 30	11 46	17 07	17 01	1 32 20	22 23 59
16	13 22 02	8 38	+14 14	6 26	6 32	11 46	17 05	16 58	1 36 17	22 20 03
17	13 25 46	9 00	+14·27	6 27	6 34	11 45	17 03	16 56	1 40 13	22 16 07
18	13 29 30	9 22	+14 39	6 29	6 36	11 45	17 01	16 53	1 44 10	22 12 11
19	13 33 15	9 44	+14 51	6 31	6 38	11 45	16 59	16 51	1 48 06	22 08 16
20	13 37 00	10 06	+15 02	6 33	6 41	11 45	16 56	16 48	1 52 03	22 04 20
21	13 40 46	10 27	+15 13	6 34	6 43	11 45	16 54	16 46	1 55 59	22 00 24
22	13 44 33	10 49	+15 23	6 36	6 45	11 45	16 52	16 43	1 59 56	21 56 28
23	13 48 20	11 10	+15 32	6 38	6 47	11 44	16 50	16 41	2 03 52	21 52 32
24	13 52 08	11 31	+15 41	6 40	6 49	11 44	16 48	16 39	2 07 49	21 48 36
25	13 55 57	11 52	+15 49	6 41	6 51	11 44	16 46	16 36	2 11 46	21 44 40
26	13 59 46	12 13	+15 56	6 43	6 53	11 44	16 44	16 34	2 15 42	21 40 44
27	14 03 36	12 33	+16 02	6 45	6 55	11 44	16 42	16 32	2 19 39	21 36 48
28	14 07 27	12 53	+16 08	6 47	6 57	11 44	16 40	16 29	2 23 35	21 32 52
29	14 11 19	13 14	+16 13	6 48	6 59	11 44	16 38	16 27	2 27 32	21 28 56
30	14 15 11	13 33	+16 17	6 50	7 02	11 44	16 36	16 25	2 31 28	21 25 01
31	14 19 04	13 53	+16 21	6 52	7 04	11 44	16 34	16 23	2 35 25	21 21 05

DURATION OF TWILIGHT (in minutes)

Latitude	52°	56°	52°	56°	52°	56°	52°	56°
	1 October		11 October		21 October		31 October	
Civil	34	37	34	37	34	38	36	40
Nautical	73	80	73	80	74	81	75	83
Astronomical	113	125	112	124	113	124	114	126

THE NIGHT SKY

Mercury is unsuitably placed for observation throughout October.

Venus, magnitude −4.5, is a magnificent morning object, visible in the eastern sky before 03h; by the end of the month it becomes visible low in the east almost four hours before sunrise. Venus passes 3° S. of Regulus on the 8th. On the mornings of October 5th and 6th the old crescent Moon is in the vicinity of the planet.

Mars, magnitude +0.6, continues to be visible in the south-western sky in the early part of the evening, though since it reaches a southern declination of 25° during the month it will only be seen at a very low altitude. The Moon, two days before First Quarter, will be seen about 5° from the planet on the evening of the

15th. Mars is now moving more rapidly eastwards, passing from Ophiuchus into Sagittarius during the month.

Jupiter, magnitude −2.9, is at opposition on the 23rd, and thus visible throughout the hours of darkness. During the night of the 24th to 25th the Full Moon is near the planet.

Saturn is now visible for the greater part of the night as it approaches opposition early in November. By the end of October it is visible in the eastern sky almost as soon as it gets dark. Its magnitude is −0.1. The Full Moon will be seen about 3° below Saturn on the evening of the 25th, shortly after the two bodies rise above the eastern horizon.

THE MOON

Day	RA h m	Dec. °	Hor. par. '	Semi-diam. '	Sun's co-long. °	PA of Bright Limb °	Phase %	Age d	Rise 52° h m	Rise 56° h m	Transit h m	Set 52° h m	Set 56° h m
1	5 26	+19.3	59.5	16.2	162	88	63	21.1	21 48	21 28	5 01	13 10	13 30
2	6 26	+20.4	59.1	16.1	174	93	52	22.1	22 47	22 27	5 59	14 10	14 31
3	7 26	+20.1	58.7	16.0	186	98	41	23.1	23 53	23 35	6 57	15 01	15 20
4	8 24	+18.6	58.2	15.9	199	103	30	24.1	—	—	7 52	15 41	15 57
5	9 20	+16.1	57.8	15.7	211	108	21	25.1	1 04	0 49	8 45	16 14	16 27
6	10 14	+12.8	57.3	15.6	223	113	13	26.1	2 17	2 05	9 36	16 42	16 50
7	11 05	+ 8.9	56.8	15.5	235	118	7	27.1	3 29	3 22	10 24	17 06	17 11
8	11 54	+ 4.6	56.3	15.3	247	125	2	28.1	4 40	4 37	11 10	17 28	17 29
9	12 42	+ 0.2	55.8	15.2	260	150	0	29.1	5 49	5 50	11 55	17 49	17 46
10	13 29	− 4.2	55.3	15.1	272	253	0	0.5	6 58	7 03	12 39	18 10	18 04
11	14 16	− 8.3	54.9	15.0	284	274	2	1.5	8 05	8 13	13 24	18 33	18 23
12	15 03	−12.1	54.5	14.9	296	277	6	2.5	9 11	9 23	14 08	18 58	18 45
13	15 51	−15.2	54.3	14.8	309	277	12	3.5	10 14	10 30	14 54	19 27	19 11
14	16 39	−17.8	54.1	14.7	321	274	18	4.5	11 15	11 34	15 40	20 02	19 42
15	17 29	−19.5	54.1	14.7	333	271	26	5.5	12 12	12 33	16 28	20 42	20 21
16	18 19	−20.4	54.3	14.8	345	267	35	6.5	13 03	13 24	17 16	21 29	21 08
17	19 10	−20.4	54.6	14.9	357	263	44	7.5	13 49	14 09	18 05	22 24	22 04
18	20 01	−19.5	55.1	15.0	9	259	54	8.5	14 28	14 46	18 54	23 26	23 08
19	20 52	−17.6	55.7	15.2	22	254	63	9.5	15 01	15 16	19 43	—	—
20	21 44	−14.9	56.5	15.4	34	250	73	10.5	15 30	15 42	20 33	0 33	0 19
21	22 35	−11.3	57.4	15.6	46	246	82	11.5	15 57	16 04	21 22	1 44	1 34
22	23 27	− 7.0	58.3	15.9	58	243	89	12.5	16 21	16 24	22 13	2 59	2 53
23	0 20	− 2.3	59.1	16.1	70	238	95	13.5	16 45	16 45	23 04	4 17	4 16
24	1 14	+ 2.8	59.9	16.3	82	227	99	14.5	17 11	17 06	23 57	5 37	5 41
25	2 09	+ 7.8	60.4	16.5	95	141	100	15.5	17 39	17 30	—	7 00	7 08
26	3 07	+12.4	60.7	16.5	107	91	98	16.5	18 12	17 58	0 53	8 23	8 35
27	4 07	+16.2	60.7	16.5	119	87	93	17.5	18 52	18 34	1 51	9 44	10 01
28	5 08	+19.0	60.5	16.5	131	89	86	18.5	19 40	19 20	2 51	11 00	11 20
29	6 10	+20.4	60.0	16.4	143	93	77	19.5	20 38	20 17	3 52	12 06	12 27
30	7 11	+20.5	59.4	16.2	155	98	67	20.5	21 44	21 24	4 51	13 00	13 21
31	8 11	+19.3	58.7	16.0	168	103	56	21.5	22 54	22 38	5 49	13 44	14 02

MERCURY

Day	RA h m	Dec. °	Diam. "	Phase %	Transit h m	5° high 52° h m	5° high 56° h m
1	13 27	− 9.7	5	90	12 51	17 23	17 10
3	13 38	−11.0	5	88	12 54	17 19	17 04
5	13 49	−12.3	5	87	12 57	17 14	16 58
7	14 00	−13.6	5	85	13 00	17 09	16 52
9	14 10	−14.7	5	84	13 03	17 05	16 46
11	14 21	−15.9	5	82	13 05	17 00	16 39
13	14 32	−16.9	6	80	13 08	16 55	16 33
15	14 42	−18.0	6	78	13 10	16 51	16 27
17	14 52	−18.9	6	75	13 12	16 46	16 20
19	15 02	−19.8	6	73	13 14	16 41	16 14
21	15 11	−20.6	6	70	13 15	16 37	16 08
23	15 20	−21.3	6	66	13 16	16 33	16 02
25	15 29	−21.9	7	62	13 17	16 28	15 56
27	15 36	−22.4	7	58	13 17	16 24	15 50
29	15 43	−22.8	7	53	13 15	16 19	15 44
31	15 49	−23.1	8	48	13 13	16 15	15 39

VENUS

Day	RA h m	Dec. °	Diam. "	Phase %	Transit h m	5° high 52° h m	5° high 56° h m
1	9 46	+ 9.6	35	31	9 08	2 52	2 47
6	10 00	+ 9.2	33	35	9 02	2 48	2 44
11	10 15	+ 8.6	31	38	8 58	2 47	2 43
16	10 31	+ 7.8	29	42	8 55	2 48	2 45
21	10 49	+ 6.7	27	45	8 53	2 51	2 49
26	11 07	+ 5.4	26	48	8 51	2 56	2 55
31	11 26	+ 4.0	24	51	8 51	3 03	3 03

MARS

Day	RA h m	Dec. °	Diam. "	Phase %	Transit h m	5° high 52° h m	5° high 56° h m
1	17 10	−24.8	7	87	16 32	19 19	18 36
6	17 25	−25.0	7	87	16 28	19 12	18 28
11	17 41	−25.2	7	87	16 24	19 07	18 22
16	17 57	−25.2	7	88	16 20	19 02	18 18
21	18 13	−25.2	6	88	16 16	18 59	18 15
26	18 29	−25.0	6	88	16 13	18 57	18 14
31	18 45	−24.7	6	89	16 09	18 57	18 15

SUNRISE AND SUNSET

	London		Bristol		Birmingham		Manchester		Newcastle		Glasgow		Belfast	
	0°05′	51°30′	2°35′	51°28′	1°55′	52°28′	2°15′	53°28′	1°37′	54°59′	4°14′	55°52′	5°56′	54°35′
	h m	h m	h m	h m	h m	h m	h m	h m	h m	h m	h m	h m	h m	h m
1	6 00	17 39	6 10	17 49	6 08	17 46	6 10	17 47	6 08	17 44	6 19	17 54	6 25	18 01
2	6 02	17 37	6 12	17 47	6 10	17 44	6 11	17 45	6 10	17 41	6 21	17 51	6 27	17 59
3	6 03	17 35	6 13	17 45	6 11	17 41	6 13	17 42	6 12	17 39	6 23	17 48	6 29	17 56
4	6 05	17 32	6 15	17 42	6 13	17 39	6 15	17 40	6 14	17 36	6 25	17 46	6 31	17 54
5	6 07	17 30	6 17	17 40	6 15	17 37	6 17	17 37	6 15	17 34	6 27	17 43	6 32	17 51
6	6 08	17 28	6 18	17 38	6 16	17 34	6 19	17 35	6 17	17 31	6 29	17 41	6 34	17 49
7	6 10	17 26	6 20	17 36	6 18	17 32	6 20	17 33	6 19	17 29	6 31	17 38	6 36	17 46
8	6 12	17 23	6 22	17 33	6 20	17 30	6 22	17 30	6 21	17 26	6 33	17 35	6 38	17 44
9	6 13	17 21	6 23	17 31	6 22	17 28	6 24	17 28	6 23	17 24	6 35	17 33	6 40	17 41
10	6 15	17 19	6 25	17 29	6 23	17 25	6 26	17 25	6 25	17 21	6 37	17 30	6 42	17 39
11	6 17	17 17	6 27	17 27	6 25	17 23	6 28	17 23	6 27	17 19	6 39	17 28	6 44	17 36
12	6 18	17 15	6 28	17 25	6 27	17 21	6 29	17 21	6 29	17 16	6 41	17 25	6 46	17 34
13	6 20	17 12	6 30	17 23	6 29	17 19	6 31	17 18	6 31	17 14	6 43	17 23	6 48	17 32
14	6 22	17 10	6 32	17 20	6 30	17 16	6 33	17 16	6 33	17 11	6 45	17 20	6 50	17 29
15	6 23	17 08	6 33	17 18	6 32	17 14	6 35	17 14	6 35	17 09	6 47	17 18	6 52	17 27
16	6 25	17 06	6 35	17 16	6 34	17 12	6 37	17 12	6 37	17 06	6 49	17 15	6 53	17 24
17	6 27	17 04	6 37	17 14	6 36	17 10	6 39	17 09	6 39	17 04	6 51	17 13	6 55	17 22
18	6 28	17 02	6 38	17 12	6 37	17 07	6 41	17 07	6 41	17 02	6 53	17 10	6 57	17 20
19	6 30	17 00	6 40	17 10	6 39	17 05	6 42	17 05	6 43	16 59	6 55	17 08	6 59	17 17
20	6 32	16 58	6 42	17 08	6 41	17 03	6 44	17 03	6 45	16 57	6 57	17 05	7 01	17 15
21	6 34	16 56	6 44	17 06	6 43	17 01	6 46	17 00	6 47	16 55	6 59	17 03	7 03	17 13
22	6 35	16 54	6 45	17 04	6 45	16 59	6 48	16 58	6 49	16 52	7 01	17 01	7 05	17 10
23	6 37	16 52	6 47	17 02	6 46	16 57	6 50	16 56	6 51	16 50	7 03	16 58	7 07	17 08
24	6 39	16 50	6 49	17 00	6 48	16 55	6 52	16 54	6 53	16 48	7 06	16 56	7 09	17 06
25	6 41	16 48	6 51	16 58	6 50	16 53	6 54	16 52	6 55	16 45	7 08	16 54	7 11	17 04
26	6 42	16 46	6 52	16 56	6 52	16 51	6 56	16 50	6 57	16 43	7 10	16 51	7 13	17 02
27	6 44	16 44	6 54	16 54	6 54	16 49	6 57	16 48	6 59	16 41	7 12	16 49	7 15	16 59
28	6 46	16 42	6 56	16 52	6 56	16 47	6 59	16 45	7 01	16 39	7 14	16 47	7 17	16 57
29	6 48	16 40	6 58	16 50	6 57	16 45	7 01	16 43	7 03	16 37	7 16	16 44	7 19	16 55
30	6 49	16 38	6 59	16 48	6 59	16 43	7 03	16 41	7 05	16 35	7 18	16 42	7 21	16 53
31	6 51	16 36	7 01	16 46	7 01	16 41	7 05	16 39	7 07	16 32	7 20	16 40	7 23	16 51

JUPITER

Day	RA	Dec.	Transit	5° high	
				52°	56°
	h m	° ′	h m	h m	h m
1	2 04.6	+11 01	1 27	7 50	7 56
11	2 00.0	+10 36	0 43	7 04	7 09
21	1 55.0	+10 08	23 55	6 17	6 22
31	1 49.9	+ 9 40	23 10	5 30	5 35

Diameters – equatorial 50″ polar 47″

SATURN

Day	RA	Dec.	Transit	5° high	
				52°	56°
	h m	° ′	h m	h m	h m
1	2 58.4	+14 15	2 21	19 37	19 28
11	2 56.1	+14 03	1 39	18 56	18 48
21	2 53.3	+13 50	0 57	18 15	18 07
31	2 50.3	+13 36	0 15	17 34	17 26

Diameters – equatorial 20″ polar 18″
Rings – major axis 46″ minor axis 16″

URANUS

Day	RA	Dec.	Transit	10° high	
				52°	56°
	h m	° ′	h m	h m	h m
1	21 03.0	−17 34	20 22	23 24	22 51
11	21 02.4	−17 36	19 43	22 44	22 11
21	21 02.1	−17 37	19 03	22 04	21 31
31	21 02.2	−17 36	18 24	21 25	20 52

Diameter 4″

NEPTUNE

Day	RA	Dec.	Transit	10° high	
				52°	56°
	h m	° ′	h m	h m	h m
1	20 15.3	−19 32	22 19	21 39	
11	20 15.1	−19 33	18 55	21 39	21 00
21	20 15.1	−19 33	18 16	21 00	20 20
31	20 15.4	−19 32	17 37	20 21	19 41

Diameter 2″

November 1999

ELEVENTH MONTH, 30 DAYS. *Novem* (nine), ninth month of Roman pre-Julian calendar

1	Monday	**All Saints' Day.** Benevenuto Cellini b. 1500	*week* 44 *day* 305
2	Tuesday	All Souls. George Bernard Shaw d. 1950	306
3	Wednesday	Karl Baedeker b. 1801. Henri Matisse d. 1954	307
4	Thursday	William III b. 1650. Yitzhak Rabin assassinated 1995	308
5	Friday	DIWALI begins. Robert Maxwell d. 1991	309
6	Saturday	John Philip Sousa b. 1854. Kate Greenaway d. 1901	310
7	Sunday	**3rd S. before Advent.** Steve McQueen d. 1980	*week* 45 *day* 311
8	Monday	Munich Putsch 1923. Edward Ardizzone d. 1979	312
9	Tuesday	Sir Giles Gilbert Scott b. 1880. Katherine Hepburn b. 1909	313
10	Wednesday	Johann von Schiller b. 1759. Sir Jacob Epstein b. 1880	314
11	Thursday	Armistice Day 1918. Dame Elizabeth Maconchy d. 1994	315
12	Friday	Mrs Elizabeth Gaskell b. 1865. Baroness Orczy d. 1947	316
13	Saturday	Archbishop of Canterbury b. 1935	317
14	Sunday	**2nd S. before Advent.** *Prince of Wales b. 1948*	*week* 46 *day* 318
15	Monday	William Pitt (the elder) b. 1708. Aneurin Bevan b. 1897	319
16	Tuesday	Opening of the Suez Canal 1869. Sir Oswald Mosley b. 1896	320
17	Wednesday	Eric Gill d. 1940. Martin Scorsese b. 1942	321
18	Thursday	Louis Daguerre b. 1789. Cab Calloway d. 1994	322
19	Friday	Indira Gandhi b. 1917. Sir Basil Spence d. 1976	323
20	Saturday	*Queen's Wedding Day.* Windsor Castle fire 1992	324
21	Sunday	**Christ the King. S. next before Advent**	*week* 47 *day* 325
22	Monday	George Eliot b. 1819. John Kennedy assassinated 1963	326
23	Tuesday	Thomas Tallis d. 1585. Roald Dahl d. 1990	327
24	Wednesday	Frances Hodgson Burnett b. 1849. Dodie Smith d. 1990	328
25	Thursday	Andrew Carnegie b. 1835. Imran Khan b. 1952	329
26	Friday	Eugene Ionesco b. 1912. Michael Bentine d. 1996	330
27	Saturday	Fanny Kemble b. 1809. Eugene O'Neill d. 1953	331
28	Sunday	**1st S. of Advent.** Ian Serraillier d. 1994	*week* 48 *day* 332
29	Monday	Louisa M. Alcott b. 1832. Giacomo Puccini d. 1924	333
30	Tuesday	**St Andrew.** Sir Philip Sydney b. 1554	334

ASTRONOMICAL PHENOMENA

d	h	
4	02	Venus in conjunction with Moon. Venus 3° S.
5	03	Mercury at stationary point
6	14	Saturn at opposition
9	10	Mercury in conjunction with Moon. Mercury 6° S.
13	15	Mars in conjunction with Moon. Mars 3° S.
15	22	Mercury in inferior conjunction (transits Sun)
21	01	Jupiter in conjunction with Moon. Jupiter 4° N.
22	03	Saturn in conjunction with Moon. Saturn 2° N.
22	18	Sun's longitude 240° ♐
25	04	Mercury at stationary point

MINIMA OF ALGOL

d	h	d	h	d	h
2	14.5	14	01.8	25	13.0
5	11.3	16	22.6	28	09.9
8	08.1	19	19.4		
11	05.0	22	16.2		

CONSTELLATIONS

The following constellations are near the meridian at

	d	h		d	h
October	1	24	November	15	21
October	16	23	December	1	20
November	1	22	December	16	19

Ursa Major (below the Pole), Cepheus, Cassiopeia, Andromeda, Pegasus, Pisces, Aquarius and Cetus

THE MOON

Phases, Apsides and Node	d	h	m
● New Moon	8	03	53
☽ First Quarter	16	09	03
○ Full Moon	23	07	04
☾ Last Quarter	29	23	19
Apogee (406,238 km)	11	05	41
Perigee (357,272 km)	23	22	01

Mean longitude of ascending node on November 1, 128°

THE SUN   s.d. 16'.2

Day	Right Ascension	Dec. −	Equation of time	Rise 52°	Rise 56°	Transit	Set 52°	Set 56°	Sidereal time	Transit of First Point of Aries
	h m s	° '	m s	h m	h m	h m	h m	h m	h m s	h m s
1	14 22 58	14 13	+16 23	6 54	7 06	11 44	16 33	16 21	2 39 21	21 17 09
2	14 26 53	14 32	+16 25	6 56	7 08	11 44	16 31	16 18	2 43 18	21 13 13
3	14 30 49	14 51	+16 26	6 58	7 10	11 44	16 29	16 16	2 47 15	21 09 17
4	14 34 45	15 10	+16 26	6 59	7 12	11 44	16 27	16 14	2 51 11	21 05 21
5	14 38 42	15 28	+16 26	7 01	7 14	11 44	16 25	16 12	2 55 08	21 01 25
6	14 42 40	15 47	+16 24	7 03	7 16	11 44	16 24	16 10	2 59 04	20 57 29
7	14 46 39	16 05	+16 22	7 05	7 19	11 44	16 22	16 08	3 03 01	20 53 33
8	14 50 39	16 22	+16 18	7 07	7 21	11 44	16 20	16 06	3 06 57	20 49 37
9	14 54 39	16 40	+16 14	7 08	7 23	11 44	16 19	16 04	3 10 54	20 45 41
10	14 58 41	16 57	+16 09	7 10	7 25	11 44	16 17	16 02	3 14 50	20 41 46
11	15 02 43	17 14	+16 04	7 12	7 27	11 44	16 15	16 00	3 18 47	20 37 50
12	15 06 46	17 31	+15 57	7 14	7 29	11 44	16 14	15 58	3 22 44	20 33 54
13	15 10 50	17 47	+15 50	7 15	7 31	11 44	16 12	15 56	3 26 40	20 29 58
14	15 14 55	18 03	+15 42	7 17	7 33	11 44	16 11	15 55	3 30 37	20 26 02
15	15 19 01	18 19	+15 32	7 19	7 35	11 45	16 10	15 53	3 34 33	20 22 06
16	15 23 07	18 34	+15 23	7 21	7 38	11 45	16 08	15 51	3 38 30	20 18 10
17	15 27 14	18 49	+15 12	7 22	7 40	11 45	16 07	15 50	3 42 26	20 14 14
18	15 31 23	19 04	+15 00	7 24	7 42	11 45	16 05	15 48	3 46 23	20 10 18
19	15 35 31	19 18	+14 48	7 26	7 44	11 45	16 04	15 46	3 50 19	20 06 22
20	15 39 41	19 32	+14 35	7 28	7 46	11 46	16 03	15 45	3 54 16	20 02 26
21	15 43 52	19 46	+14 21	7 29	7 48	11 46	16 02	15 43	3 58 13	19 58 31
22	15 48 03	19 59	+14 06	7 31	7 50	11 46	16 01	15 42	4 02 09	19 54 35
23	15 52 15	20 12	+13 51	7 33	7 52	11 46	16 00	15 41	4 06 06	19 50 39
24	15 56 28	20 24	+13 34	7 34	7 53	11 47	15 58	15 39	4 10 02	19 46 43
25	16 00 42	20 37	+13 17	7 36	7 55	11 47	15 58	15 38	4 13 59	19 42 47
26	16 04 56	20 48	+12 59	7 37	7 57	11 47	15 57	15 37	4 17 55	19 38 51
27	16 09 11	21 00	+12 40	7 39	7 59	11 47	15 56	15 36	4 21 52	19 34 55
28	16 13 27	21 11	+12 21	7 40	8 01	11 48	15 55	15 34	4 25 48	19 30 59
29	16 17 44	21 22	+12 01	7 42	8 03	11 48	15 54	15 33	4 29 45	19 27 03
30	16 22 02	21 32	+11 40	7 43	8 04	11 49	15 53	15 32	4 33 42	19 23 07

DURATION OF TWILIGHT (in minutes)

Latitude	52°	56°	52°	56°	52°	56°	52°	56°
	1 November		11 November		21 November		30 November	
Civil	36	40	37	41	38	43	39	45
Nautical	75	84	78	87	80	90	82	93
Astronomical	115	127	117	130	120	134	123	137

THE NIGHT SKY

Mercury is unsuitably placed for observation at first, inferior conjunction (and a transit across the face of the Sun) occurring on the 15th. During the last week of the month the planet is visible as a morning object, magnitude +1.0 to −0.5, low above the south-eastern horizon at the beginning of morning civil twilight. See page 66 for details of the transit.

Venus continues to be visible as a magnificent object, completely dominating the south-eastern sky for several hours before dawn, magnitude −4.3. On the morning of the 4th the old crescent Moon, four days before New, will be seen about 5° to the left of the planet. On the morning of the 29th Venus passes 5° N. of Spica.

Mars is still an evening object, low in the south-western sky in the early part of the evening, magnitude +0.8. The crescent Moon will be seen about 2° above the planet on the evening of the 13th. Towards the end of the month Mars moves from Sagittarius into Capricornus.

Jupiter, just past opposition, continues to be visible for the greater part of the night, magnitude −2.9. On the evening of the 20th the gibbous Moon will be seen passing 5° below the planet.

Saturn, magnitude −0.2, reaches opposition on the 6th and thus is visible throughout the hours of darkness. Saturn is in Aries. On the night of the 21st to 22nd the gibbous Moon will be seen passing 4° below the planet.

Meteors. Although the Leonids do not usually produce a brilliant display, there could be a sharp peak in the number of meteors seen within about an hour of midnight on the 17th to 18th; if so, it will be a noticeable display. The Moon, just past First Quarter, will not provide much interference as it will be low in the south-west, setting at half past midnight.

THE MOON

Day	RA h m	Dec. °	Hor. par. '	Semi-diam. '	Sun's co-long. °	PA of Bright Limb °	Phase %	Age d	Rise 52° h m	Rise 56° h m	Transit h m	Set 52° h m	Set 56° h m
1	9 08	+17.0	58.0	15.8	180	107	45	22.5	—	23 54	6 43	14 19	14 33
2	10 02	+13.8	57.4	15.6	192	111	34	23.5	0 07	—	7 34	14 48	14 58
3	10 53	+10.0	56.7	15.5	204	114	25	24.5	1 18	1 10	8 22	15 12	15 18
4	11 42	+ 5.8	56.2	15.3	216	117	16	25.5	2 29	2 25	9 08	15 34	15 36
5	12 30	+ 1.4	55.6	15.2	228	119	10	26.5	3 38	3 38	9 52	15 55	15 53
6	13 17	− 3.0	55.2	15.0	241	122	5	27.5	4 46	4 50	10 36	16 15	16 10
7	14 03	− 7.2	54.8	14.9	253	131	1	28.5	5 54	6 01	11 20	16 37	16 28
8	14 50	−11.1	54.5	14.8	265	177	0	29.5	7 00	7 11	12 04	17 01	16 49
9	15 37	−14.5	54.2	14.8	277	257	1	0.8	8 04	8 19	12 49	17 28	17 12
10	16 25	−17.3	54.1	14.7	289	268	3	1.8	9 07	9 25	13 36	18 00	17 41
11	17 14	−19.3	54.0	14.7	302	268	7	2.8	10 06	10 26	14 23	18 37	18 17
12	18 04	−20.5	54.0	14.7	314	266	13	3.8	10 59	11 21	15 11	19 22	19 00
13	18 55	−20.8	54.2	14.8	326	263	20	4.8	11 47	12 08	15 59	20 14	19 53
14	19 45	−20.2	54.5	14.8	338	259	28	5.8	12 27	12 47	16 47	21 12	20 53
15	20 36	−18.6	54.9	15.0	350	255	37	6.8	13 02	13 19	17 36	22 15	22 00
16	21 27	−16.2	55.5	15.1	3	252	46	7.8	13 32	13 45	18 24	23 23	23 11
17	22 17	−13.0	56.3	15.3	15	249	56	8.8	13 58	14 08	19 11	—	—
18	23 07	− 9.0	57.2	15.6	27	246	66	9.8	14 22	14 28	20 00	0 35	0 27
19	23 58	− 4.5	58.2	15.8	39	244	76	10.8	14 46	14 47	20 49	1 49	1 45
20	0 50	+ 0.4	59.1	16.1	51	243	85	11.8	15 10	15 07	21 41	3 06	3 07
21	1 44	+ 5.4	60.0	16.4	63	241	92	12.8	15 36	15 28	22 35	4 27	4 32
22	2 40	+10.3	60.8	16.6	75	237	97	13.8	16 06	15 54	23 32	5 50	6 00
23	3 39	+14.6	61.2	16.7	88	208	100	14.8	16 42	16 26	—	7 14	7 29
24	4 41	+18.0	61.4	16.7	100	104	99	15.8	17 27	17 07	0 33	8 36	8 55
25	5 45	+20.2	61.2	16.7	112	96	96	16.8	18 22	18 01	1 35	9 50	10 11
26	6 49	+20.9	60.7	16.5	124	98	89	17.8	19 27	19 07	2 38	10 53	11 14
27	7 52	+20.1	60.0	16.3	136	101	81	18.8	20 39	20 21	3 39	11 43	12 02
28	8 52	+18.0	59.1	16.1	148	106	71	19.8	21 53	21 39	4 37	12 22	12 37
29	9 48	+15.0	58.2	15.9	160	109	61	20.8	23 07	22 57	5 30	12 53	13 05
30	10 41	+11.2	57.4	15.6	173	112	50	21.8	—	—	6 20	13 19	13 27

MERCURY

Day	RA h m	Dec. °	Diam. "	Phase %	Transit h m	5° high 52° h m	5° high 56° h m
1	15 51	−23.1	8	45	13 11	16 12	15 37
3	15 55	−23.2	8	38	13 06	16 08	15 32
5	15 56	−23.0	8	31	12 59	16 02	15 27
7	15 55	−22.7	9	24	12 50	15 56	15 23
9	15 52	−22.1	9	16	12 38	15 50	15 18
11	15 46	−21.2	10	9	12 23	15 43	15 13
13	15 38	−20.2	10	3	12 07	15 35	15 08
15	15 28	−18.9	10	0	11 49	8 12	8 37
17	15 18	−17.6	10	1	11 31	7 45	8 07
19	15 08	−16.3	10	4	11 14	7 20	7 41
21	15 01	−15.3	9	11	11 00	7 00	7 18
23	14 57	−14.6	9	19	10 49	6 44	7 01
25	14 56	−14.2	8	29	10 40	6 33	6 50
27	14 57	−14.2	8	38	10 34	6 26	6 44
29	15 00	−14.4	7	47	10 30	6 24	6 42
31	15 06	−14.9	7	55	10 28	6 25	6 44

VENUS

Day	RA h m	Dec. °	Diam. "	Phase %	Transit h m	5° high 52° h m	5° high 56° h m
1	11 30	+ 3.7	24	51	8 50	3 04	3 05
6	11 49	+ 2.0	23	54	8 50	3 13	3 14
11	12 09	+ 0.3	22	56	8 51	3 22	3 25
16	12 30	− 1.5	21	58	8 51	3 32	3 37
21	12 50	− 3.5	20	61	8 52	3 43	3 50
26	13 12	− 5.4	19	63	8 54	3 55	4 03
31	13 33	− 7.4	18	65	8 56	4 08	4 18

MARS

Day	RA h m	Dec. °	Diam. "	Phase %	Transit h m	5° high 52° h m	5° high 56° h m
1	18 48	−24.7	6	89	16 08	18 57	18 15
6	19 04	−24.3	6	89	16 05	18 57	18 17
11	19 21	−23.8	6	89	16 01	18 58	18 21
16	19 37	−23.2	6	90	15 58	19 01	18 25
21	19 53	−22.5	6	90	15 54	19 03	18 30
26	20 09	−21.6	6	90	15 51	19 07	18 36
31	20 25	−20.7	6	91	15 47	19 10	18 42

SUNRISE AND SUNSET

	London		Bristol		Birmingham		Manchester		Newcastle		Glasgow		Belfast	
	0°05′	51°30′	2°35′	51°28′	1°55′	52°28′	2°15′	53°28′	1°37′	54°59′	4°14′	55°52′	5°56′	54°35′
	h m	h m	h m	h m	h m	h m	h m	h m	h m	h m	h m	h m	h m	h m
1	6 53	16 34	7 03	16 44	7 03	16 39	7 07	16 37	7 09	16 30	7 22	16 38	7 25	16 49
2	6 55	16 32	7 05	16 43	7 05	16 37	7 09	16 35	7 11	16 28	7 24	16 36	7 27	16 47
3	6 56	16 31	7 06	16 41	7 07	16 35	7 11	16 34	7 13	16 26	7 27	16 34	7 29	16 45
4	6 58	16 29	7 08	16 39	7 08	16 33	7 13	16 32	7 15	16 24	7 29	16 31	7 31	16 43
5	7 00	16 27	7 10	16 37	7 10	16 32	7 15	16 30	7 17	16 22	7 31	16 29	7 33	16 41
6	7 02	16 25	7 12	16 36	7 12	16 30	7 17	16 28	7 19	16 20	7 33	16 27	7 35	16 39
7	7 03	16 24	7 13	16 34	7 14	16 28	7 18	16 26	7 21	16 18	7 35	16 25	7 37	16 37
8	7 05	16 22	7 15	16 32	7 16	16 26	7 20	16 24	7 23	16 16	7 37	16 23	7 39	16 35
9	7 07	16 21	7 17	16 31	7 18	16 25	7 22	16 23	7 25	16 14	7 39	16 21	7 41	16 33
10	7 09	16 19	7 19	16 29	7 19	16 23	7 24	16 21	7 27	16 13	7 41	16 19	7 43	16 31
11	7 11	16 17	7 20	16 28	7 21	16 22	7 26	16 19	7 29	16 11	7 44	16 18	7 45	16 30
12	7 12	16 16	7 22	16 26	7 23	16 20	7 28	16 18	7 31	16 09	7 46	16 16	7 47	16 28
13	7 14	16 15	7 24	16 25	7 25	16 18	7 30	16 16	7 33	16 07	7 48	16 14	7 49	16 26
14	7 16	16 13	7 26	16 23	7 27	16 17	7 32	16 14	7 35	16 06	7 50	16 12	7 51	16 25
15	7 17	16 12	7 27	16 22	7 28	16 15	7 34	16 13	7 37	16 04	7 52	16 10	7 53	16 23
16	7 19	16 10	7 29	16 20	7 30	16 14	7 35	16 11	7 39	16 02	7 54	16 09	7 55	16 21
17	7 21	16 09	7 31	16 19	7 32	16 13	7 37	16 10	7 41	16 01	7 56	16 07	7 57	16 20
18	7 23	16 08	7 32	16 18	7 34	16 11	7 39	16 09	7 43	15 59	7 58	16 06	7 59	16 18
19	7 24	16 07	7 34	16 17	7 35	16 10	7 41	16 07	7 45	15 58	8 00	16 04	8 01	16 17
20	7 26	16 05	7 36	16 15	7 37	16 09	7 43	16 06	7 47	15 56	8 02	16 02	8 03	16 15
21	7 28	16 04	7 37	16 14	7 39	16 08	7 44	16 05	7 49	15 55	8 04	16 01	8 04	16 14
22	7 29	16 03	7 39	16 13	7 41	16 06	7 46	16 03	7 51	15 54	8 06	16 00	8 06	16 13
23	7 31	16 02	7 41	16 12	7 42	16 05	7 48	16 02	7 53	15 52	8 08	15 58	8 08	16 12
24	7 32	16 01	7 42	16 11	7 44	16 04	7 50	16 01	7 55	15 51	8 10	15 57	8 10	16 10
25	7 34	16 00	7 44	16 10	7 45	16 03	7 51	16 00	7 56	15 50	8 12	15 56	8 12	16 09
26	7 36	15 59	7 45	16 09	7 47	16 02	7 53	15 59	7 58	15 49	8 13	15 54	8 13	16 08
27	7 37	15 58	7 47	16 08	7 49	16 01	7 55	15 58	8 00	15 48	8 15	15 53	8 15	16 07
28	7 39	15 57	7 48	16 07	7 50	16 00	7 56	15 57	8 02	15 47	8 17	15 52	8 17	16 06
29	7 40	15 57	7 50	16 07	7 52	15 59	7 58	15 56	8 03	15 46	8 19	15 51	8 18	16 05
30	7 42	15 56	7 51	16 06	7 53	15 59	8 00	15 55	8 05	15 45	8 20	15 50	8 20	16 04

JUPITER

Day	RA	Dec.	Transit	5° high	
				52°	56°
	h m	° ′	h m	h m	h m
1	1 49.4	+ 9 38	23 06	5 26	5 30
11	1 44.5	+ 9 12	22 22	4 40	4 44
21	1 40.4	+ 8 51	21 38	3 54	3 58
31	1 37.3	+ 8 36	20 56	3 11	3 14

Diameters – equatorial 49″ polar 46″

SATURN

Day	RA	Dec.	Transit	5° high	
				52°	56°
	h m	° ′	h m	h m	h m
1	2 50.0	+13 35	0 11	6 47	6 55
11	2 46.8	+13 21	23 24	6 03	6 11
21	2 43.7	+13 08	22 41	5 20	5 27
31	2 40.8	+12 56	21 59	4 37	4 44

Diameters – equatorial 20″ polar 18″
Rings – major axis 46″ minor axis 15″

URANUS

Day	RA	Dec.	Transit	10° high	
				52°	56°
	h m	° ′	h m	h m	h m
1	21 02.3	−17 36	18 20	21 21	20 49
11	21 02.7	−17 34	17 41	20 43	20 10
21	21 03.5	−17 30	17 03	20 05	19 32
31	21 04.6	−17 25	16 24	19 27	18 55

Diameter 4″

NEPTUNE

Day	RA	Dec.	Transit	10° high	
				52°	56°
	h m	° ′	h m	h m	h m
1	20 15.5	−19 32	17 33	20 17	19 38
11	20 16.0	−19 31	16 54	19 39	18 59
21	20 16.7	−19 29	16 16	19 01	18 21
31	20 17.7	−19 26	15 38	18 23	17 43

Diameter 2″

December 1999

TWELFTH MONTH, 31 DAYS. *Decem* (ten), tenth month of Roman pre-Julian calendar

1	*Wednesday*	Henry I d. 1135. Woody Allen b. 1935	*week* 48 *day* 335
2	*Thursday*	John Brown executed 1859. Stephen Potter d. 1969	336
3	*Friday*	Robert Louis Stevenson d. 1894. Pierre Renoir d. 1919	337
4	*Saturday*	CHANUCAH begins. Frank Zappa d. 1993	338
5	*Sunday*	**2nd S. of Advent.** Walt Disney b. 1901	*week* 49 *day* 339
6	*Monday*	Henry VI b. 1421. Anthony Trollope d. 1882	340
7	*Tuesday*	Henry, Lord Darnley b. 1545. Capt Bligh d. 1817	341
8	*Wednesday*	Mary, Queen of Scots b. 1542. John Lennon killed 1980	342
9	*Thursday*	RAMADAN begins. John Milton b. 1608	343
10	*Friday*	Royal Academy founded 1768. Alfred Nobel d. 1896	344
11	*Saturday*	Alexander Solzhenitsyn b. 1918. Willie Rushton d. 1996	345
12	*Sunday*	**3rd S. of Advent.** John Osborne b. 1929	*week* 50 *day* 346
13	*Monday*	Dr Johnson d. 1784. Battle of the River Plate 1939	347
14	*Tuesday*	George Washington d. 1799. Andrei Sakharov d. 1989	348
15	*Wednesday*	Harold Abrahams b. 1899. Walt Disney d. 1966	349
16	*Thursday*	Jane Austen b. 1775. Sir Noel Coward b. 1899	350
17	*Friday*	Sir Humphrey Davy d. 1778. Elizabeth Garrett Anderson d. 1917	351
18	*Saturday*	Sir John Alcock b. 1919. Ben Travers d. 1980	352
19	*Sunday*	**4th S. of Advent.** Stella Gibbons d. 1989	*week* 51 *day* 353
20	*Monday*	Sir Robert Menzies b. 1894. John Steinbeck d. 1968	354
21	*Tuesday*	*Michaelmas Law Sittings end.* Joseph Stalin b. 1879	355
22	*Wednesday*	Dame Peggy Ashcroft b. 1907. Samuel Beckett d. 1989	356
23	*Thursday*	Richard Arkwright b. 1732. Ronnie Scott d. 1996	357
24	*Friday*	King John b. 1167. John Osborne d. 1994	358
25	*Saturday*	**Christmas Day.** Humphrey Bogart b. 1899	359
26	*Sunday*	**St Stephen. 1st S. of Christmas.** Boxing Day	*week* 52 *day* 360
27	*Monday*	**St John.** *Bank Holiday in the UK*	361
28	*Tuesday*	**Holy Innocents.** *Bank Holiday in the UK*	362
29	*Wednesday*	Thomas à Becket killed 1170. Christina Rossetti d. 1894	363
30	*Thursday*	Rudyard Kipling b. 1865. Richard Rodgers d. 1979	364
31	*Friday*	*Bank Holiday in the UK.* Henri Matisse b. 1869	365

ASTRONOMICAL PHENOMENA

d	h	
3	00	Pluto in conjunction
3	01	Mercury at greatest elongation W.20°
3	23	Venus in conjunction with Moon. Venus 3° S.
6	02	Mercury in conjunction with Moon. Mercury 3° S.
12	18	Mars in conjunction with Moon. Mars 0°.6 S.
18	08	Jupiter in conjunction with Moon. Jupiter 4° N.
19	11	Saturn in conjunction with Moon. Saturn 3° N.
20	15	Jupiter at stationary point
22	08	Sun's longitude 270° ♑

MINIMA OF ALGOL

d	h	d	h	d	h
1	06.7	12	17.9	24	05.2
4	03.5	15	14.8	27	02.0
7	00.3	18	11.6	29	22.9
9	21.1	21	08.4		

CONSTELLATIONS

The following constellations are near the meridian at

d	h		d	h
November	1	24	December	16	21
November	15	23	January	1	20
December	1	22	January	16	19

Ursa Major (below the Pole), Ursa Minor (below the Pole), Cassiopeia, Andromeda, Perseus, Triangulum, Aries, Taurus, Cetus and Eridanus

THE MOON

Phases, Apsides and Node	d	h	m
● New Moon	7	22	32
☽ First Quarter	16	00	50
○ Full Moon	22	17	31
☾ Last Quarter	29	14	04
Apogee (406,628 km)	8	11	20
Perigee (356,656 km)	22	11	01

Mean longitude of ascending node on December 1, 127°

THE SUN

s.d. 16'.3

Day	Right Ascension	Dec. −	Equation of time	Rise 52°	Rise 56°	Transit	Set 52°	Set 56°	Sidereal time	Transit of First Point of Aries
	h m s	° ′	m s	h m	h m	h m	h m	h m	h m s	h m s
1	16 26 20	21 42	+11 18	7 45	8 06	11 49	15 53	15 31	4 37 38	19 19 11
2	16 30 38	21 51	+10 56	7 46	8 08	11 49	15 52	15 30	4 41 35	19 15 16
3	16 34 58	22 00	+10 33	7 48	8 09	11 50	15 51	15 30	4 45 31	19 11 20
4	16 39 18	22 09	+10 10	7 49	8 11	11 50	15 51	15 29	4 49 28	19 07 24
5	16 43 39	22 17	+ 9 46	7 50	8 12	11 50	15 50	15 28	4 53 24	19 03 28
6	16 48 00	22 24	+ 9 21	7 52	8 14	11 51	15 50	15 28	4 57 21	18 59 32
7	16 52 22	22 32	+ 8 56	7 53	8 15	11 51	15 49	15 27	5 01 17	18 55 36
8	16 56 44	22 38	+ 8 30	7 54	8 17	11 52	15 49	15 27	5 05 14	18 51 40
9	17 01 07	22 45	+ 8 03	7 55	8 18	11 52	15 49	15 26	5 09 11	18 47 44
10	17 05 30	22 51	+ 7 37	7 56	8 19	11 53	15 49	15 26	5 13 07	18 43 48
11	17 09 54	22 56	+ 7 10	7 57	8 20	11 53	15 48	15 25	5 17 04	18 39 52
12	17 14 18	23 01	+ 6 42	7 58	8 22	11 54	15 48	15 25	5 21 00	18 35 56
13	17 18 43	23 06	+ 6 14	7 59	8 23	11 54	15 48	15 25	5 24 57	18 32 01
14	17 23 08	23 10	+ 5 46	8 00	8 24	11 54	15 48	15 25	5 28 53	18 28 05
15	17 27 33	23 14	+ 5 17	8 01	8 25	11 55	15 48	15 25	5 32 50	18 24 09
16	17 31 58	23 17	+ 4 48	8 02	8 26	11 55	15 49	15 25	5 36 46	18 20 13
17	17 36 24	23 20	+ 4 19	8 03	8 27	11 56	15 49	15 25	5 40 43	18 16 17
18	17 40 50	23 22	+ 3 50	8 04	8 27	11 56	15 49	15 25	5 44 40	18 12 21
19	17 45 15	23 24	+ 3 21	8 04	8 28	11 57	15 49	15 26	5 48 36	18 08 25
20	17 49 42	23 25	+ 2 51	8 05	8 29	11 57	15 50	15 26	5 52 33	18 04 29
21	17 54 08	23 26	+ 2 21	8 06	8 29	11 58	15 50	15 26	5 56 29	18 00 33
22	17 58 34	23 26	+ 1 52	8 06	8 30	11 58	15 51	15 27	6 00 26	17 56 37
23	18 03 00	23 26	+ 1 22	8 07	8 30	11 59	15 51	15 27	6 04 22	17 52 41
24	18 07 27	23 26	+ 0 52	8 07	8 31	11 59	15 52	15 28	6 08 19	17 48 46
25	18 11 53	23 25	+ 0 23	8 07	8 31	12 00	15 52	15 29	6 12 15	17 44 50
26	18 16 19	23 23	− 0 07	8 08	8 31	12 00	15 53	15 29	6 16 12	17 40 54
27	18 20 45	23 21	− 0 37	8 08	8 32	12 01	15 54	15 30	6 20 09	17 36 58
28	18 25 11	23 19	− 1 06	8 08	8 32	12 01	15 55	15 31	6 24 05	17 33 02
29	18 29 37	23 16	− 1 36	8 08	8 32	12 02	15 56	15 32	6 28 02	17 29 06
30	18 34 03	23 12	− 2 05	8 08	8 32	12 02	15 57	15 33	6 31 58	17 25 10
31	18 38 29	23 09	− 2 34	8 08	8 32	12 03	15 58	15 34	6 35 55	17 21 14

DURATION OF TWILIGHT (in minutes)

Latitude	52°	56°	52°	56°	52°	56°	52°	56°
	1 December		11 December		21 December		31 December	
Civil	40	45	41	47	41	47	41	47
Nautical	82	93	84	96	85	97	84	96
Astronomical	123	138	125	141	126	142	125	141

THE NIGHT SKY

Mercury continues to be visible in the mornings for the first half of the month, magnitude − 0.5. It may be glimpsed low above the south-eastern horizon at the beginning of morning twilight. This is the most suitable morning apparition of the year for observers in the northern hemisphere. On the morning of the 6th, the old crescent Moon, less than two days before New, may be detected about 3° to the left of the planet. For the remainder of the year Mercury is too close to the Sun for observation.

Venus, magnitude − 4.2, is still a brilliant object in the south-eastern sky in the early mornings. On the morning of the 4th the old crescent Moon will be seen about 5° to the left of the planet.

Mars, magnitude +1.0, continues to be visible low in the south-western sky in the early evenings. Although Mars has moved some 7°–8° nearer to the Sun during December, the period of time available for observation increases as the planet moves northward in declination. Shortly before the end of the year it moves from Capricornus into Aquarius. Before the crescent Moon sets on the evening of the 12th it will actually pass in front of the planet, though this will occur at a very low altitude (*see* page 67.)

Jupiter, magnitude − 2.7, continues to be visible as a brilliant object in the night sky, though by the end of the year it has sunk too low in the western sky to be visible after about 01h. On the night of the 17th to 18th the gibbous Moon passes 7° below the planet. Jupiter reaches its second stationary point on the 21st, in Aries, and then resumes its direct motion.

Saturn is an evening object, magnitude 0.0, visible from the end of evening twilight until the early hours of the morning. Jupiter has gradually been catching up with Saturn; the two bodies were 35° apart at the beginning of the year and only 15° at the end. Jupiter will pass Saturn at the end of May 2000; they will then be only about 15° from the Sun.

Meteors. The maximum of the well-known Geminid meteor shower occurs on the morning of the 14th. Conditions are favourable as the Moon sets several hours before midnight.

THE MOON

Day	RA h m	Dec. °	Hor. par. ′	Semi-diam. ′	Sun's co-long. °	PA of Bright Limb °	Phase %	Age d	Rise 52° h m	Rise 56° h m	Transit h m	Set 52° h m	Set 56° h m
1	11 32	+ 7.0	56.6	15.4	185	114	39	22.8	0 19	0 13	7 07	13 42	13 45
2	12 19	+ 2.6	55.9	15.2	197	115	30	23.8	1 29	1 27	7 52	14 02	14 02
3	13 06	− 1.8	55.3	15.1	209	116	21	24.8	2 37	2 39	8 35	14 22	14 19
4	13 52	− 6.1	54.8	14.9	221	116	14	25.8	3 44	3 50	9 19	14 43	14 36
5	14 38	−10.1	54.4	14.8	234	116	8	26.8	4 51	5 00	10 02	15 05	14 55
6	15 25	−13.6	54.2	14.8	246	117	4	27.8	5 56	6 09	10 47	15 31	15 16
7	16 12	−16.6	54.0	14.7	258	124	1	28.8	6 59	7 16	11 33	16 01	15 43
8	17 01	−18.9	53.9	14.7	270	196	0	0.1	8 00	8 19	12 19	16 36	16 16
9	17 51	−20.4	53.9	14.7	282	256	1	1.1	8 55	9 17	13 07	17 18	16 56
10	18 42	−20.9	54.0	14.7	294	261	4	2.1	9 45	10 07	13 56	18 07	17 46
11	19 32	−20.6	54.2	14.8	307	259	8	3.1	10 28	10 49	14 44	19 03	18 43
12	20 23	−19.3	54.5	14.9	319	256	14	4.1	11 05	11 23	15 32	20 05	19 47
13	21 13	−17.1	54.9	15.0	331	253	21	5.1	11 36	11 51	16 19	21 10	20 56
14	22 03	−14.2	55.5	15.1	343	251	30	6.1	12 03	12 14	17 06	22 18	22 09
15	22 52	−10.5	56.1	15.3	355	248	40	7.1	12 27	12 34	17 53	23 29	23 24
16	23 41	− 6.3	56.9	15.5	7	247	50	8.1	12 49	12 52	18 40	—	—
17	0 31	− 1.7	57.8	15.8	20	246	60	9.1	13 11	13 11	19 28	0 43	0 41
18	1 22	+ 3.2	58.8	16.0	32	246	71	10.1	13 35	13 30	20 19	1 59	2 02
19	2 15	+ 8.1	59.7	16.3	44	247	81	11.1	14 02	13 52	21 13	3 18	3 26
20	3 12	+12.6	60.5	16.5	56	248	89	12.1	14 33	14 19	22 11	4 40	4 52
21	4 11	+16.5	61.1	16.7	68	250	95	13.1	15 12	14 55	23 12	6 03	6 19
22	5 14	+19.3	61.4	16.7	80	246	99	14.1	16 02	15 41	—	7 22	7 42
23	6 19	+20.8	61.4	16.7	92	126	100	15.1	17 03	16 41	0 16	8 33	8 55
24	7 24	+20.7	61.1	16.6	105	102	98	16.1	18 14	17 54	1 19	9 32	9 52
25	8 28	+19.2	60.4	16.5	117	104	93	17.1	19 30	19 14	2 21	10 18	10 35
26	9 28	+16.4	59.6	16.2	129	107	85	18.1	20 48	20 36	3 19	10 54	11 07
27	10 24	+12.7	58.6	16.0	141	110	76	19.1	22 04	21 56	4 13	11 23	11 32
28	11 17	+ 8.5	57.6	15.7	153	112	66	20.1	23 16	23 13	5 02	11 47	11 52
29	12 06	+ 4.0	56.7	15.5	165	113	56	21.1	—	—	5 49	12 09	12 10
30	12 54	− 0.5	55.9	15.2	177	113	46	22.1	0 26	0 27	6 34	12 29	12 27
31	13 41	− 4.9	55.2	15.0	190	113	36	23.1	1 35	1 39	7 17	12 50	12 44

MERCURY

Day	RA h m	Dec. °	Diam. ″	Phase %	Transit h m	5° high 52° h m	5° high 56° h m
1	15 06	−14.9	7	55	10 28	6 25	6 44
3	15 13	−15.5	7	62	10 28	6 29	6 48
5	15 22	−16.2	6	68	10 29	6 34	6 55
7	15 31	−17.0	6	73	10 30	6 41	7 03
9	15 41	−17.8	6	77	10 33	6 49	7 13
11	15 52	−18.6	6	81	10 36	6 58	7 23
13	16 03	−19.4	6	84	10 39	7 08	7 34
15	16 15	−20.2	5	86	10 43	7 17	7 45
17	16 27	−20.9	5	88	10 47	7 27	7 57
19	16 40	−21.6	5	90	10 52	7 37	8 09
21	16 52	−22.2	5	92	10 57	7 47	8 21
23	17 05	−22.8	5	93	11 02	7 57	8 32
25	17 18	−23.3	5	94	11 07	8 06	8 43
27	17 31	−23.7	5	95	11 12	8 15	8 54
29	17 45	−24.0	5	96	11 18	8 24	9 03
31	17 58	−24.3	5	97	11 24	8 32	9 12

VENUS

Day	RA h m	Dec. °	Diam. ″	Phase %	Transit h m	5° high 52° h m	5° high 56° h m
1	13 33	− 7.4	18	65	8 56	4 08	4 18
6	13 55	− 9.4	17	67	8 58	4 21	4 33
11	14 18	−11.3	17	69	9 01	4 35	4 49
16	14 40	−13.2	16	70	9 04	4 50	5 06
21	15 04	−14.9	16	72	9 08	5 05	5 23
26	15 28	−16.6	15	74	9 12	5 20	5 41
31	15 52	−18.0	15	75	9 17	5 35	5 58

MARS

Day	RA h m	Dec. °	Diam. ″	Phase %	Transit h m	5° high 52° h m	5° high 56° h m
1	20 25	−20.7	6	91	15 47	19 10	18 42
6	20 41	−19.7	5	91	15 43	19 14	18 48
11	20 57	−18.7	5	91	15 39	19 18	18 54
16	21 12	−17.5	5	92	15 35	19 22	19 00
21	21 27	−16.3	5	92	15 30	19 26	19 06
26	21 43	−15.0	5	92	15 26	19 30	19 12
31	21 58	−13.6	5	93	15 21	19 34	19 18

SUNRISE AND SUNSET

	London		Bristol		Birmingham		Manchester		Newcastle		Glasgow		Belfast	
	0°05'	51°30'	2°35'	51°28'	1°55'	52°28'	2°15'	53°28'	1°37'	54°59'	4°14'	55°52'	5°56'	54°35'
	h m	h m	h m	h m	h m	h m	h m	h m	h m	h m	h m	h m	h m	h m
1	7 43	15 55	7 53	16 05	7 55	15 58	8 01	15 54	8 07	15 44	8 22	15 49	8 22	16 03
2	7 44	15 55	7 54	16 05	7 56	15 57	8 02	15 54	8 08	15 43	8 24	15 48	8 23	16 02
3	7 46	15 54	7 56	16 04	7 58	15 57	8 04	15 53	8 10	15 42	8 25	15 47	8 25	16 02
4	7 47	15 53	7 57	16 04	7 59	15 56	8 05	15 52	8 11	15 41	8 27	15 47	8 26	16 01
5	7 48	15 53	7 58	16 03	8 00	15 56	8 07	15 52	8 13	15 41	8 28	15 46	8 28	16 00
6	7 50	15 53	7 59	16 03	8 02	15 55	8 08	15 51	8 14	15 40	8 30	15 45	8 29	16 00
7	7 51	15 52	8 01	16 02	8 03	15 55	8 09	15 51	8 15	15 40	8 31	15 45	8 30	15 59
8	7 52	15 52	8 02	16 02	8 04	15 54	8 11	15 50	8 17	15 39	8 33	15 44	8 32	15 59
9	7 53	15 52	8 03	16 02	8 05	15 54	8 12	15 50	8 18	15 39	8 34	15 44	8 33	15 59
10	7 54	15 51	8 04	16 02	8 06	15 54	8 13	15 50	8 19	15 39	8 35	15 44	8 34	15 58
11	7 55	15 51	8 05	16 01	8 08	15 54	8 14	15 50	8 21	15 38	8 37	15 43	8 35	15 58
12	7 56	15 51	8 06	16 01	8 09	15 54	8 15	15 50	8 22	15 38	8 38	15 43	8 37	15 58
13	7 57	15 51	8 07	16 01	8 10	15 54	8 16	15 49	8 23	15 38	8 39	15 43	8 38	15 58
14	7 58	15 51	8 08	16 01	8 11	15 54	8 17	15 49	8 24	15 38	8 40	15 43	8 39	15 58
15	7 59	15 51	8 09	16 02	8 11	15 54	8 18	15 50	8 25	15 38	8 41	15 43	8 40	15 58
16	8 00	15 52	8 10	16 02	8 12	15 54	8 19	15 50	8 26	15 38	8 42	15 43	8 40	15 58
17	8 01	15 52	8 11	16 02	8 13	15 54	8 20	15 50	8 26	15 38	8 43	15 43	8 41	15 58
18	8 01	15 52	8 11	16 02	8 14	15 54	8 21	15 50	8 27	15 38	8 43	15 43	8 42	15 58
19	8 02	15 52	8 12	16 02	8 14	15 55	8 21	15 50	8 28	15 39	8 44	15 43	8 43	15 58
20	8 03	15 53	8 13	16 03	8 15	15 55	8 22	15 51	8 29	15 39	8 45	15 44	8 43	15 59
21	8 03	15 53	8 13	16 03	8 16	15 55	8 23	15 51	8 29	15 40	8 45	15 44	8 44	15 59
22	8 04	15 54	8 14	16 04	8 16	15 56	8 23	15 52	8 30	15 40	8 46	15 45	8 44	16 00
23	8 04	15 54	8 14	16 04	8 17	15 56	8 24	15 52	8 30	15 41	8 46	15 45	8 45	16 00
24	8 05	15 55	8 15	16 05	8 17	15 57	8 24	15 53	8 31	15 41	8 47	15 46	8 45	16 01
25	8 05	15 55	8 15	16 06	8 17	15 58	8 24	15 53	8 31	15 42	8 47	15 47	8 46	16 02
26	8 05	15 56	8 15	16 06	8 18	15 58	8 25	15 54	8 31	15 43	8 47	15 47	8 46	16 02
27	8 06	15 57	8 15	16 07	8 18	15 59	8 25	15 55	8 31	15 43	8 48	15 48	8 46	16 03
28	8 06	15 58	8 16	16 08	8 18	16 00	8 25	15 56	8 32	15 44	8 48	15 49	8 46	16 04
29	8 06	15 59	8 16	16 09	8 18	16 01	8 25	15 57	8 32	15 45	8 48	15 50	8 46	16 05
30	8 06	15 59	8 16	16 10	8 18	16 02	8 25	15 58	8 32	15 46	8 48	15 51	8 46	16 06
31	8 06	16 00	8 16	16 11	8 18	16 03	8 25	15 59	8 31	15 47	8 48	15 52	8 46	16 07

JUPITER

Day	RA	Dec.	Transit	5° high	
				52°	56°
	h m	° '	h m	h m	h m
1	1 37.3	+ 8 36	20 56	3 11	3 14
11	1 35.3	+ 8 28	20 15	2 29	2 32
21	1 34.6	+ 8 27	19 35	1 49	1 52
31	1 35.3	+ 8 34	18 56	1 11	1 14

Diameters – equatorial 45″ polar 42″

SATURN

Day	RA	Dec.	Transit	5° high	
				52°	56°
	h m	° '	h m	h m	h m
1	2 40.8	+12 56	21 59	4 37	4 44
11	2 38.4	+12 47	21 18	3 54	4 01
21	2 36.5	+12 40	20 36	3 12	3 19
31	2 35.2	+12 37	19 56	2 31	2 39

Diameters – equatorial 20″ polar 18″
Rings – major axis 45″ minor axis 15″

URANUS

Day	RA	Dec.	Transit	10° high	
				52°	56°
	h m	° '	h m	h m	h m
1	21 04.6	−17 25	16 24	19 27	18 55
11	21 06.0	−17 18	15 46	18 50	18 18
21	21 07.7	−17 11	15 09	18 14	17 42
31	21 09.6	−17 03	14 31	17 37	17 06

Diameter 4″

NEPTUNE

Day	RA	Dec.	Transit	10° high	
				52°	56°
	h m	° '	h m	h m	h m
1	20 17.7	−19 26	15 38	18 23	17 43
11	20 18.8	−19 22	14 59	17 45	17 06
21	20 20.1	−19 18	14 21	17 08	16 29
31	20 21.5	−19 14	13 43	16 30	15 52

Diameter 2″

RISING AND SETTING TIMES

TABLE 1. SEMI-DIURNAL ARCS (HOUR ANGLES AT RISING/SETTING)

Dec.	Latitude 0° h m	10° h m	20° h m	30° h m	40° h m	45° h m	50° h m	52° h m	54° h m	56° h m	58° h m	60° h m	Dec.
0°	6 00	6 00	6 00	6 00	6 00	6 00	6 00	6 00	6 00	6 00	6 00	6 00	0°
1°	6 00	6 01	6 01	6 02	6 03	6 04	6 05	6 05	6 06	6 06	6 06	6 07	1°
2°	6 00	6 01	6 03	6 05	6 07	6 08	6 10	6 10	6 11	6 12	6 13	6 14	2°
3°	6 00	6 02	6 04	6 07	6 10	6 12	6 14	6 15	6 17	6 18	6 19	6 21	3°
4°	6 00	6 03	6 06	6 09	6 13	6 16	6 19	6 21	6 22	6 24	6 26	6 28	4°
5°	6 00	6 04	6 07	6 12	6 17	6 20	6 24	6 26	6 28	6 30	6 32	6 35	5°
6°	6 00	6 04	6 09	6 14	6 20	6 24	6 29	6 31	6 33	6 36	6 39	6 42	6°
7°	6 00	6 05	6 10	6 16	6 24	6 28	6 34	6 36	6 39	6 42	6 45	6 49	7°
8°	6 00	6 06	6 12	6 19	6 27	6 32	6 39	6 41	6 45	6 48	6 52	6 56	8°
9°	6 00	6 06	6 13	6 21	6 31	6 36	6 44	6 47	6 50	6 54	6 59	7 04	9°
10°	6 00	6 07	6 15	6 23	6 34	6 41	6 49	6 52	6 56	7 01	7 06	7 11	10°
11°	6 00	6 08	6 16	6 26	6 38	6 45	6 54	6 58	7 02	7 07	7 12	7 19	11°
12°	6 00	6 09	6 18	6 28	6 41	6 49	6 59	7 03	7 08	7 13	7 20	7 26	12°
13°	6 00	6 09	6 19	6 31	6 45	6 53	7 04	7 09	7 14	7 20	7 27	7 34	13°
14°	6 00	6 10	6 21	6 33	6 48	6 58	7 09	7 14	7 20	7 27	7 34	7 42	14°
15°	6 00	6 11	6 22	6 36	6 52	7 02	7 14	7 20	7 27	7 34	7 42	7 51	15°
16°	6 00	6 12	6 24	6 38	6 56	7 07	7 20	7 26	7 33	7 41	7 49	7 59	16°
17°	6 00	6 12	6 26	6 41	6 59	7 11	7 25	7 32	7 40	7 48	7 57	8 08	17°
18°	6 00	6 13	6 27	6 43	7 03	7 16	7 31	7 38	7 46	7 55	8 05	8 17	18°
19°	6 00	6 14	6 29	6 46	7 07	7 21	7 37	7 45	7 53	8 03	8 14	8 26	19°
20°	6 00	6 15	6 30	6 49	7 11	7 25	7 43	7 51	8 00	8 11	8 22	8 36	20°
21°	6 00	6 16	6 32	6 51	7 15	7 30	7 49	7 58	8 08	8 19	8 32	8 47	21°
22°	6 00	6 16	6 34	6 54	7 19	7 35	7 55	8 05	8 15	8 27	8 41	8 58	22°
23°	6 00	6 17	6 36	6 57	7 23	7 40	8 02	8 12	8 23	8 36	8 51	9 09	23°
24°	6 00	6 18	6 37	7 00	7 28	7 46	8 08	8 19	8 31	8 45	9 02	9 22	24°
25°	6 00	6 19	6 39	7 02	7 32	7 51	8 15	8 27	8 40	8 55	9 13	9 35	25°
26°	6 00	6 20	6 41	7 05	7 37	7 57	8 22	8 35	8 49	9 05	9 25	9 51	26°
27°	6 00	6 21	6 43	7 08	7 41	8 03	8 30	8 43	8 58	9 16	9 39	10 08	27°
28°	6 00	6 22	6 45	7 12	7 46	8 08	8 37	8 52	9 08	9 28	9 53	10 28	28°
29°	6 00	6 22	6 47	7 15	7 51	8 15	8 45	9 01	9 19	9 41	10 10	10 55	29°
30°	6 00	6 23	6 49	7 18	7 56	8 21	8 54	9 11	9 30	9 55	10 30	12 00	30°
35°	6 00	6 28	6 59	7 35	8 24	8 58	9 46	10 15	10 58	12 00	12 00	12 00	35°
40°	6 00	6 34	7 11	7 56	8 59	9 48	12 00	12 00	12 00	12 00	12 00	12 00	40°
45°	6 00	6 41	7 25	8 21	9 48	12 00	12 00	12 00	12 00	12 00	12 00	12 00	45°
50°	6 00	6 49	7 43	8 54	12 00	12 00	12 00	12 00	12 00	12 00	12 00	12 00	50°
55°	6 00	6 58	8 05	9 42	12 00	12 00	12 00	12 00	12 00	12 00	12 00	12 00	55°
60°	6 00	7 11	8 36	12 00	12 00	12 00	12 00	12 00	12 00	12 00	12 00	12 00	60°
65°	6 00	7 29	9 25	12 00	12 00	12 00	12 00	12 00	12 00	12 00	12 00	12 00	65°
70°	6 00	7 56	12 00	12 00	12 00	12 00	12 00	12 00	12 00	12 00	12 00	12 00	70°
75°	6 00	8 45	12 00	12 00	12 00	12 00	12 00	12 00	12 00	12 00	12 00	12 00	75°
80°	6 00	12 00	12 00	12 00	12 00	12 00	12 00	12 00	12 00	12 00	12 00	12 00	80°

TABLE 2. CORRECTION FOR REFRACTION AND SEMI-DIAMETER

	m	m	m	m	m	m	m	m	m	m	m	m	
0°	3	3	4	4	4	5	5	5	6	6	6	7	0°
10°	3	3	4	4	4	5	5	6	6	6	7	7	10°
20°	4	4	4	4	5	5	6	7	7	8	8	9	20°
25°	4	4	4	4	5	6	7	8	8	9	11	13	25°
30°	4	4	4	5	6	7	8	9	11	14	21	—	30°

NB: Regarding Table 1. If latitude and declination are of the same sign, take out the respondent directly. If they are of opposite signs, subtract the respondent from 12h.
Example:

Lat.	Dec.	Semi-diurnal arc
+ 52°	+ 20°	7h 51m
+ 52°	− 20°	4h 09m

SUNRISE AND SUNSET

The local mean time of sunrise or sunset may be found by obtaining the hour angle from Table 1 and applying it to the time of transit. The hour angle is negative for sunrise and positive for sunset. A small correction to the hour angle, which always has the effect of increasing it numerically, is necessary to allow for the Sun's semi-diameter (16') and for refraction (34'); it is obtained from Table 2. The resulting local mean time may be converted into the standard time of the country by taking the difference between the longitude of the standard meridian of the country and that of the place, adding it to the local mean time if the place is west of the standard meridian, and subtracting it if the place is east.

Example – Required the New Zealand Mean Time (12h fast on GMT) of sunset on May 23 at Auckland, latitude 36° 50′ S. (or minus), longitude 11h 39m E. Taking the declination as $+20°.6$ (page 33), we find

	h	m
Tabular entry for Lat. 30° and Dec. 20°, opposite signs	+ 5	11
Proportional part for 6° 50′ of Lat.	–	15
Proportional part for 0°.6 of Dec.	–	2
Correction (Table 2)	+	4
Hour angle	4	58
Sun transits (page 33)	11	57
Longitudinal correction	+	21
New Zealand Mean Time	17	16

MOONRISE AND MOONSET

It is possible to calculate the times of moonrise and moonset using Table 1, though the method is more complicated because the apparent motion of the Moon is much more rapid and also more variable than that of the Sun.

The parallax of the Moon, about 57′, is near to the sum of the semi-diameter and refraction but has the opposite effect on these times. It is thus convenient to neglect all three quantities in the method outlined below.

TABLE 3. LONGITUDE CORRECTION

X	40m	45m	50m	55m	60m	65m	70m
A							
h	m	m	m	m	m	m	m
1	2	2	2	2	3	3	3
2	3	4	4	5	5	5	6
3	5	6	6	7	8	8	9
4	7	8	8	9	10	11	12
5	8	9	10	11	13	14	15
6	10	11	13	14	15	16	18
7	12	13	15	16	18	19	20
8	13	15	17	18	20	22	23
9	15	17	19	21	23	24	26
10	17	19	21	23	25	27	29
11	18	21	23	25	28	30	32
12	20	23	25	28	30	33	35
13	22	24	27	30	33	35	38
14	23	26	29	32	35	38	41
15	25	28	31	34	38	41	44
16	27	30	33	37	40	43	47
17	28	32	35	39	43	46	50
18	30	34	38	41	45	49	53
19	32	36	40	44	48	51	55
20	33	38	42	46	50	54	58
21	35	39	44	48	53	57	61
22	37	41	46	50	55	60	64
23	38	43	48	53	58	62	67
24	40	45	50	55	60	65	70

Notation

φ = latitude of observer
λ = longitude of observer (measured positively towards the west)
T_{-1} = time of transit of Moon on previous day
T_0 = time of transit of Moon on day in question
T_1 = time of transit of Moon on following day
δ_0 = approximate declination of Moon
δ_R = declination of Moon at moonrise
δ_S = declination of Moon at moonset
h_0 = approximate hour angle of Moon
h_R = hour angle of Moon at moonrise
h_S = hour angle of Moon at moonset
t_R = time of moonrise
t_S = time of moonset

Method

1. With arguments φ, δ_0 enter Table 1 on page 64 to determine h_0 where h_0 is negative for moonrise and positive for moonset.

2. Form approximate times from
   $t_R = T_0 + \lambda + h_0$
   $t_S = T_0 + \lambda + h_0$

3. Determine δ_R, δ_S for times t_R, t_S respectively.

4. Re-enter Table 1 on page 64 with
   (*a*) arguments φ, δ_R to determine h_R
   (*b*) arguments φ, δ_S to determine h_S

5. Form $t_R = T_0 + \lambda + h_R + AX$
   $t_S = T_0 + \lambda + h_S + AX$

   where $A = (\lambda + h)$

   and $X = (T_0 - T_{-1})$ if $(\lambda + h)$ is negative
   $X = (T_1 - T_0)$ if $(\lambda + h)$ is positive

   AX is the respondent in Table 3.

Example – To find the times of moonrise and moonset at Vancouver ($\varphi = +49°$, $\lambda = +8h\ 12m$) on 1999 March 16. The starting data (page 26) are

$T_{-1} = 10h\ 13m$
$T_0 = 11h\ 06m$
$T_1 = 11h\ 59m$
$\delta_0 = -10°$

1. $h_0 = 5h\ 13m$
2. Approximate values
   $t_R = 16d\ 11h\ 06m + 8h\ 12m + (-5h\ 13m)$
   $= 16d\ 14h\ 05m$
   $t_S = 16d\ 11h\ 06m + 8h\ 12m + (+5h\ 13m)$
   $= 17d\ 00h\ 31m$
3. $\delta_R = -9°.4$
   $\delta_S = -7°.6$
4. $h_R = -5h\ 16m$
   $h_S = +5h\ 24m$
5. $t_R = 16d\ 11h\ 06m + 8h\ 12m + (-5h\ 16m) + 7m$
   $= 16d\ 14h\ 09m$
   $t_S = 16d\ 11h\ 06m + 8h\ 12m + (+5h\ 24m) + 30m$
   $= 17d\ 01h\ 12m$

To get the LMT of the phenomenon the longitude is subtracted from the GMT thus:
Moonrise $= 16d\ 14h\ 09m - 8h\ 12m = 16d\ 05h\ 57m$
Moonset $= 17d\ 01h\ 12m - 8h\ 12m = 16d\ 17h\ 00m$

ECLIPSES AND OCCULTATIONS 1999

ECLIPSES

During 1999 there will be two eclipses of the Sun and one of the Moon. (Penumbral eclipses of the Moon are not mentioned in this section as they are too difficult to observe.)

1. An annular eclipse of the Sun on February 16 is visible as a partial eclipse from southern Africa, Madagascar, the Indian Ocean, Malaysia, Indonesia, the Philippines, the Southern Ocean, Australia and Antarctica. It begins at 03h 52m and ends at 09h 15m. The track of the annular phase crosses the Southern Ocean and the Indian Ocean before crossing Australia and ending in the Coral Sea. The annular phase begins at 04h 57m and ends at 08h 11m; the maximum duration is 1m 18s.

2. A partial eclipse of the Moon occurs on July 28 and is visible from the Americas, the Pacific Ocean, Australasia, eastern Asia, the Indian Ocean, and Antarctica. The eclipse begins at 10h 22m and ends at 12h 45m. At maximum, 40 per cent of the Moon is eclipsed.

3. A total eclipse of the Sun on August 11 is visible as a partial eclipse from eastern North America, Greenland, Iceland, the Atlantic Ocean, Europe, northern Africa, Asia and the Indian Ocean. It starts at 08h 26m and ends at 13h 40m. The path of totality starts in the Atlantic Ocean just south of Newfoundland, and crosses extreme south-west England, northern France, Germany, Austria, Hungary, Romania, northern Bulgaria, Turkey, northern Iraq, Iran, Pakistan and India. It ends in the Indian Ocean just east of India.

At Edinburgh the partial phase begins at 09h 06m and ends at 11h 34m, while at Greenwich the times are 09h 04m and 11h 40m respectively. At maximum eclipse, 85 per cent of the Sun is obscured as seen from Edinburgh and 97 per cent from Greenwich.

The path of totality across the British Isles covers Scilly Isles, southern Cornwall and Devon, and Alderney in the Channel Islands. From Land's End the partial phase begins at 08h 56m and ends at 11h 31m. Totality there lasts for about 2.1 minutes, centred on a mid-time of 10h 11.4m. The spectacle of a total eclipse being visible from mainland Britain is a rarity; the next one does not occur until 2090, and even then is visible only from southern Cornwall and with the Sun only about 6° high in the west.

TRANSIT

A near-grazing transit of Mercury across the northern edge of the Sun occurs on November 15, with a mid-time of about 21h 41m. The transit is visible from the Americas (except the north-east), the Pacific Ocean, extreme eastern Asia, Indonesia and Australasia. At ingress, the exterior contact occurs at about 21h 11m in North America, 21h 15m in Japan (at sunrise), and 21h 18m in New Zealand. At egress, the exterior contact occurs at 22h 10m, 22h 08m and 22h 04m respectively.

LUNAR OCCULTATIONS

Observations of the times of occultations are made by both amateur and professional astronomers. Such observations are later analysed to yield accurate positions of the Moon; this is one method of determining the difference between ephemeris time and universal time.

Many of the observations made by amateurs are obtained with the use of a stop-watch which is compared with a time-signal immediately after the observation. Thus an accuracy of about one-fifth of a second is obtainable,

though the observer's personal equation may amount to one-third or one-half of a second.

The list on page 67 includes most of the occultations visible under favourable conditions in the British Isles. No occultation is included unless the star is at least 10° above the horizon and the Sun sufficiently far below the horizon to permit the star to be seen with the naked eye or with a small telescope. The altitude limit is reduced from 10° to 2° for stars and planets brighter than magnitude 2.0 and such occultations are also predicted in daylight.

The column Phase shows (i) whether a disappearance (D) or reappearance (R) is to be observed; and (ii) whether it is at the dark limb (D) or bright limb (B). The column headed 'El. of Moon' gives the elongation of the Moon from the Sun, in degrees. The elongation increases from 0° at New Moon to 180° at Full Moon and on to 360° (or 0°) at New Moon again. Times and position angles (P), reckoned from the north point in the direction north, east, south, west, are given for Greenwich (lat. 51° 30', long. 0°) and Edinburgh (lat. 56° 00', long. 3° 12' west).

The coefficients a and b are the variations in the GMT for each degree of longitude (positive to the west) and latitude (positive to the north) respectively; they enable approximate times (to within about 1m generally) to be found for any point in the British Isles. If the point of observation is $\Delta\lambda$ degrees west and $\Delta\phi$ degrees north, the approximate time is found by adding $a.\Delta\lambda + b.\Delta\phi$ to the given GMT.

Example: the disappearance of ZC 692 on March 22 at Coventry, found from both Greenwich and Edinburgh.

	Greenwich	Edinburgh
	°	°
Longitude	0.0	+3.2
Long. of Coventry	+1.5	+1.5
$\Delta\lambda$	+1.5	−1.7
Latitude	+51.5	+56.0
Lat. of Coventry	+52.4	+52.4
$\Delta\phi$	+0.9	−3.6
	h m	h m
GMT	18 28.3	18 22.3
$a.\Delta\lambda$	− 2.0	+ 2.0
$b.\Delta\phi$	− 0.7	+ 0.7
	18 25.6	18 25.0

If the occultation is given for one station but not the other, the reason for the suppression is given by the following code:

N = star not occulted
A = star's altitude less than 10° (2° for bright stars and planets)
S = Sun not sufficiently below the horizon
G = occultation is of very short duration

In some cases the coefficients a and b are not given; this is because the occultation is so short that prediction for other places by means of these coefficients would not be reliable.

Observers may like to note that ZC 692 = *Aldebaran* (occulted on March 22, May 16 and July 10).

The other first-magnitude star (ZC1487 = Regulus) is occulted on April 24, July 15 and September 8.

LUNAR OCCULTATIONS 1999

Date		ZC No.	Mag.	Phase	El. of Moon	GREENWICH				EDINBURGH			
					°	UT	a	b	P	UT	a	b	P
						h m	m	m	°	h m	m	m	°
January	7	1644	4.1	R.D.	242	2 26.6	−1.4	0.6	279	2 25.0	−1.1	0.5	290
	23	210	6.6	D.D.	79	22 15.2	−0.3	−2.0	104	22 6.1	−0.4	−1.5	88
	25	462	5.9	D.D.	103	19 9.4	−1.1	1.6	38	19 15.4	−0.7	2.5	19
	26	608	6.0	D.D.	116	18 44.9	−1.1	1.6	54	18 49.8	−0.8	2.0	38
	26	626	6.4	D.D.	118	23 4.8	−0.9	−1.8	105	22 55.1	−0.9	−1.3	92
	27	635	3.9	D.D.	119	0 57.6	−0.3	−1.4	88	0 50.5	−0.4	−1.2	78
	28	814	5.3	D.D.	135	A				4 15.1	0.1	−1.0	69
	28	943	6.2	D.D.	144	22 11.5	−1.5	−2.9	142	21 58.3	−1.3	−1.2	122
	28	947	5.2	D.D.	145	23 3.4	G		21	N			
February	18	20	6.8	D.D.	33	18 28.8	G		149	18 6.6	−0.9	−2.4	114
	19	165	6.7	D.D.	46	19 38.7	−0.5	−1.0	74	19 33.5	−0.5	−0.7	59
	20	306	6.9	D.D.	61	21 19.7	−0.3	−0.4	51	21 17.8	−0.3	0.0	36
	21	444	6.2	D.D.	74	21 0.8	−0.6	−2.9	123	20 48.1	−0.7	−2.0	105
	23	741	5.7	D.D.	100	21 44.2	−0.9	−1.5	98	21 35.4	−1.0	−1.0	86
	28	1337	5.6	D.D.	153	1 58.4	−0.8	−1.5	94	1 49.5	−0.9	−1.3	88
	28	1336	5.2	D.D.	153	2 10.6	0.0	−3.1	161	1 57.2	−0.2	−2.7	152
March	20	405	4.4	D.D.	43	A				21 24.5	−0.1	−0.2	38
	21	526	6.9	D.D.	56	20 5.2	−0.8	1.4	21	N			
	22	692	1.1	D.D.	68	18 28.3	−1.3	−0.8	87	18 22.3	−1.2	−0.2	73
	22	692	1.1	R.B.	69	19 37.9	−1.0	−0.7	254	19 30.6	−0.9	−1.1	267
	23	871	6.9	D.D.	84	23 17.2	−0.6	0.1	37	23 16.9	G		22
	24	1038	6.8	D.D.	97	24 6.3	0.0	−1.9	115	23 57.7	−0.1	−1.8	108
	28	1425	6.9	D.D.	136	3 3.5	−0.1	−1.6	95	2 55.9	−0.2	−1.6	91
	30	1644	4.1	D.D.	160	4 12.7	−0.4	−1.1	61	4 6.2	−0.5	−1.1	55
April	22	1262	6.2	D.D.	92	23 38.9	−0.1	−1.8	115	23 30.2	−0.2	−1.8	110
	23	1375	5.6	D.D.	103	20 51.9	−1.0	−1.8	125	20 41.3	−1.1	−1.4	117
	24	1487	1.3	D.D.	115	21 21.5	−2.0	0.3	64	21 18.0	−2.1	1.1	53
	24	1487	1.3	R.B.	116	22 11.4	−0.4	−3.0	341	21 56.3	−0.1	−3.4	351
	26	1609	4.7	D.D.	129	1 39.4	−0.3	−1.8	105	1 30.1	−0.4	−1.8	102
May	16	692	1.1	D.D.	15	12 11.3	G		147	11 58.1	−1.5	−0.5	120
	16	692	1.1	R.D.	15	12 33.6	G		184	12 46.5	−0.8	−2.2	211
	21	1466	5.2	D.D.	87	23 25.2	0.0	−1.9	125	23 16.3	−0.1	−1.9	121
June	17	1415	6.2	D.D.	56	21 33.3	G		43	S			
	19	1645	6.6	D.D.	80	22 32.5	−0.6	−0.8	53	22 26.5	G		46
	20	1749	6.1	D.D.	92	23 12.8	G		178	22 59.6	−0.1	−2.7	171
	23	2072	6.7	D.D.	126	23 20.5	−1.2	−1.1	72	23 11.6	−1.2	−1.1	68
	25	2291	5.5	D.D.	147	21 50.7	−1.4	−0.8	131	21 44.0	−1.2	−0.4	128
July	10	692	1.1	D.B.	322	8 22.0	−1.8	−0.9	123	8 15.8	−1.3	0.2	105
	10	692	1.1	R.D.	322	9 9.5	−0.9	2.7	206	9 15.5	−1.0	1.6	225
	15	1487	1.3	D.D.	37	A				21 18.0	0.3	−1.9	138
	22	2247	5.6	D.D.	118	N				21 18.8	G		182
	25	2633	4.0	D.D.	150	20 55.9	−1.2	−0.3	140	S			
	25	2638	5.4	D.D.	151	21 49.0	−1.8	0.9	47	21 47.9	−1.6	1.0	41
	26	2797	3.0	D.D.	162	22 59.9	−1.7	−0.2	103	22 54.4	−1.4	0.0	98
September	8	1487	1.3	D.B.	344	15 53.6	0.3	−2.9	169	15 42.0	0.1	−2.6	163
	8	1487	1.3	R.D.	345	16 23.4	−0.5	−0.7	231	16 17.6	−0.5	−1.1	237
	21	3086	6.0	D.D.	136	21 54.7	−1.3	0.1	58	21 51.9	−1.1	0.3	49
	23	3237	4.4	D.D.	150	1 21.0	−0.7	−0.7	63	1 16.7	−0.5	−0.4	49
	27	364	4.3	R.D.	213	22 9.1	−0.7	1.4	269	22 13.4	−0.6	1.4	277
	29	508	4.3	R.D.	228	0 42.4	−0.4	2.7	202	0 51.5	−0.5	2.1	217
November	15	3115	6.3	D.D.	84	20 14.9	−1.3	−1.4	95	20 5.8	−1.1	−1.0	83
	16	3240	6.6	D.D.	95	19 21.3	−1.7	−0.5	91	19 14.9	−1.4	−0.2	81
	20	106	6.8	D.D.	134	0 21.7	−0.8	−0.8	72	0 16.6	−0.7	−0.4	57
	21	364	4.3	D.D.	157	17 33.3	−0.2	1.9	51	17 41.4	−0.1	1.9	44
	22	405	4.4	D.D.	162	2 21.5	−0.8	−1.0	77	2 15.7	−0.7	−0.6	63
December	12	Mars	0.9	D.D.	53	19 14.3	−0.4	−0.5	49	A			
	13	3190	3.0	D.D.	62	15 36.2	−1.7	0.5	87	15 33.9	−1.4	0.7	81
	13	3190	3.0	R.B.	63	16 54.0	−1.3	0.4	232	16 51.3	−1.2	0.2	241
	14	3327	6.8	D.D.	75	18 51.9	−1.7	−1.3	102	18 42.6	−1.4	−0.7	88
	15	3478	6.5	D.D.	88	21 46.9	−0.8	−1.4	85	21 39.5	−0.7	−1.0	70
	19	444	6.2	D.D.	138	18 12.3	−1.1	1.1	96	18 15.0	−0.8	1.4	86
	19	462	5.9	D.D.	141	23 42.7	−1.2	−1.5	100	23 34.1	−1.1	−0.8	84

MEAN PLACES OF STARS 1999.5

Name	Mag.	RA h m	Dec. ° '	Spectrum	Name	Mag.	RA h m	Dec. ° '	Spectrum
α And *Alpheratz*	2.1	0 08.4	+29 05	A0p	γ Corvi	2.6	12 15.8	−17 32	B8
β Cassiopeiae *Caph*	2.3	0 09.2	+59 09	F5	α Crucis	1.0	12 26.6	−63 06	B1
γ Pegasi *Algenib*	2.8	0 13.2	+15 11	B2	γ Crucis	1.6	12 31.1	−57 07	M3
β Mensae	2.9	0 25.7	−77 15	G0	γ Centauri	2.2	12 41.5	−48 57	A0
α Phoenicis	2.4	0 26.3	−42 19	K0	γ Virginis	2.7	12 41.6	− 1 27	F0
α Cassiopeiae *Schedar*	2.2	0 40.5	+56 32	K0	β Crucis	1.3	12 47.7	−59 41	B1
β Ceti *Diphda*	2.0	0 43.6	−17 59	K0	ε Ursae Majoris *Alioth*	1.8	12 54.0	+55 58	A0p
γ Cassiopeiae*	Var.	0 56.7	+60 43	B0p	α Canum Venaticorum	2.9	12 56.0	+38 19	A0p
β Andromedae *Mirach*	2.1	1 09.7	+35 37	M0	ζ Ursae Majoris *Mizar*	2.1	13 23.9	+54 56	A2p
δ Cassiopeiae	2.7	1 25.8	+60 14	A5	α Virginis *Spica*	1.0	13 25.2	−11 10	B2
α Eridani *Achernar*	0.5	1 37.7	−57 14	B5	ε Centauri	2.6	13 39.9	−53 28	B1
β Arietis *Sheratan*	2.6	1 54.6	+20 48	A5	η Ursae Majoris *Alkaid*	1.9	13 47.5	+49 19	B3
γ Andromedae *Almak*	2.3	2 03.9	+42 20	K0	β Centauri *Hadar*	0.6	14 03.8	−60 22	B1
α Arietis *Hamal*	2.0	2 07.1	+23 28	K2	θ Centauri	2.1	14 06.7	−36 22	K0
α Ursae Minoris *Polaris*	2.0	2 31.3	+89 16	F8	α Bootis *Arcturus*	0.0	14 15.6	+19 11	K0
β Persei *Algol**	Var.	3 08.1	+40 57	B8	α Centauri *Rigil Kent*	0.1	14 39.6	−60 50	G0
α Persei *Mirfak*	1.8	3 24.3	+49 52	F5	ε Bootis	2.4	14 45.0	+27 05	K0
η Tauri *Alcyone*	2.9	3 47.5	+24 06	B5p	β UMi *Kochab*	2.1	14 50.7	+74 09	K5
α Tauri *Aldebaran*	0.9	4 35.9	+16 31	K5	γ Ursae Minoris	3.1	15 20.7	+71 50	A2
β Orionis *Rigel*	0.1	5 14.5	− 8 12	B8p	α CrB *Alphecca*	2.2	15 34.7	+26 43	A0
α Aurigae *Capella*	0.1	5 16.7	+46 00	G0	β Trianguli Australis	3.0	15 55.1	−63 26	F0
γ Orionis *Bellatrix*	1.6	5 25.1	+ 6 21	B2	δ Scorpii	2.3	16 00.3	−22 37	B0
β Tauri *Elnath*	1.7	5 26.3	+28 36	B8	β Scorpii	2.6	16 05.4	−19 48	B1
δ Orionis	2.2	5 32.0	− 0 18	B0	α Scorpii *Antares*	1.0	16 29.4	−26 26	M0
α Leporis	2.6	5 32.7	−17 49	F0	α Trianguli Australis	1.9	16 48.6	−69 02	K2
ε Orionis	1.7	5 36.2	− 1 12	B0	ε Scorpii	2.3	16 50.1	−34 18	K0
ζ Orionis	1.8	5 40.7	− 1 57	B0	α Herculis†	Var.	17 14.6	+14 23	M3
κ Orionis	2.1	5 47.7	− 9 40	B0	λ Scorpii	1.6	17 33.6	−37 06	B2
α Orionis *Betelgeuse**	Var.	5 55.1	+ 7 24	M0	α Ophiuchi *Rasalhague*	2.1	17 34.9	+12 34	A5
β Aurigae *Menkalinan*	1.9	5 59.5	+44 57	A0p	θ Scorpii	1.9	17 37.3	−43 00	F0
β CMa *Mirzam*	2.0	6 22.7	−17 57	B1	κ Scorpii	2.4	17 42.5	−39 02	B2
α Carinae *Canopus*	−0.7	6 23.9	−52 42	F0	γ Draconis	2.2	17 56.6	+51 29	K5
γ Geminorum *Alhena*	1.9	6 37.7	+16 24	A0	ε Sgr *Kaus Australis*	1.9	18 24.1	−34 23	A0
α Canis Majoris *Sirius*	−1.5	6 45.1	−16 43	A0	α Lyrae *Vega*	0.0	18 36.9	+38 47	A0
ε Canis Majoris	1.5	6 58.6	−28 58	B1	σ Sagittarii	2.0	18 55.2	−26 18	B3
δ Canis Majoris	1.9	7 08.4	−26 24	F8p	β Cygni *Albireo*	3.1	19 30.7	+27 58	K0
α Geminorum *Castor*	1.6	7 34.6	+31 53	A0	α Aquilae *Altair*	0.8	19 50.8	+ 8 52	A5
α CMi *Procyon*	0.4	7 39.3	+ 5 14	F5	α Capricorni	3.8	20 18.0	−12 33	G5
β Geminorum *Pollux*	1.1	7 45.3	+28 02	K0	γ Cygni	2.2	20 22.2	+40 15	F8p
ζ Puppis	2.3	8 03.6	−40 00	Od	α Pavonis	1.9	20 25.6	−56 44	B3
γ Velorum	1.8	8 09.5	−47 20	Oap	α Cygni *Deneb*	1.3	20 41.4	+45 17	A2p
ε Carinae	1.9	8 22.5	−59 30	K0	α Cephei *Alderamin*	2.4	21 18.6	+62 35	A5
δ Velorum	2.0	8 44.7	−54 42	A0	ε Pegasi	2.4	21 44.2	+ 9 52	K0
λ Velorum *Suhail*	2.2	9 08.0	−43 26	K5	δ Capricorni	2.9	21 47.0	−16 08	A5
β Carinae	1.7	9 13.2	−69 43	A0	α Gruis	1.7	22 08.2	−46 58	B5
ι Carinae	2.2	9 17.1	−59 16	F0	δ Cephei†	3.7	22 29.2	+58 25	†
κ Velorum	2.6	9 22.1	−55 01	B3	β Gruis	2.1	22 42.6	−46 53	M3
α Hydrae *Alphard*	2.0	9 27.6	− 8 39	K2	α PsA *Fomalhaut*	1.2	22 57.6	−29 37	A3
α Leonis *Regulus*	1.3	10 08.3	+11 58	B8	β Pegasi *Scheat*	2.4	23 03.8	+28 05	M0
γ Leonis *Algeiba*	1.9	10 19.9	+19 51	K0	α Pegasi *Markab*	2.5	23 04.7	+15 12	A0
β Ursae Majoris *Merak*	2.4	11 01.8	+56 23	A0					
α Ursae Majoris *Dubhe*	1.8	11 03.7	+61 45	K0					
δ Leonis	2.6	11 14.1	+20 32	A3					
β Leonis *Denebola*	2.1	11 49.0	+14 34	A2					
γ Ursae Majoris *Phecda*	2.4	11 53.8	+53 42	A0					

*γ Cassiopeiae, 1998 mag. 2.5. β Persei, mag. 2.1 to 3.4.
α Orionis, mag. 0.1 to 1.2.
†α Herculis, mag. 3.1 to 3.9. δ Cephei, mag. 3.7 to 4.4,
spectrum F5 to G0.

The positions of heavenly bodies on the celestial sphere are defined by two co-ordinates, right ascension and declination, which are analogous to longitude and latitude on the surface of the Earth. If we imagine the plane of the terrestrial equator extended indefinitely, it will cut the celestial sphere in a great circle known as the celestial equator. Similarly the plane of the Earth's orbit, when extended, cuts in the great circle called the ecliptic. The two intersections of these circles are known as the First Point of Aries and the First Point of Libra. If from any star a perpendicular be drawn to the celestial equator, the length of this perpendicular is the star's declination. The arc, measured eastwards along the equator from the First Point of Aries to the foot of this perpendicular, is the right ascension. An alternative definition of right ascension is that it is the angle at the celestial pole (where the Earth's axis, if prolonged, would meet the sphere) between the great circles to the First Point of Aries and to the star.

The plane of the Earth's equator has a slow movement, so that our reference system for right ascension and declination is not fixed. The consequent alteration in these quantities from year to year is called precession. In right ascension it is an increase of about 3 seconds a year for equatorial stars, and larger or smaller changes in either direction for stars near the poles, depending on the right ascension of the star. In declination it varies between $+20''$ and $-20''$ according to the right ascension of the star.

A star or other body crosses the meridian when the sidereal time is equal to its right ascension. The altitude is then a maximum, and may be deduced by remembering that the altitude of the elevated pole is numerically equal to the latitude, while that of the equator at its intersection with the meridian is equal to the co-latitude, or complement of the latitude.

Thus in London (lat. 51° 30′) the meridian altitude of Sirius is found as follows:

	°	′
Altitude of equator	38	30
Declination south	16	43
Difference	21	47

The altitude of Capella (Dec. $+46°$ 00′) at lower transit is:

	°	′
Altitude of pole	51	30
Polar distance of star	44	00
Difference	7	30

The brightness of a heavenly body is denoted by its magnitude. Omitting the exceptionally bright stars Sirius and Canopus, the twenty brightest stars are of the first magnitude, while the faintest stars visible to the naked eye are of the sixth magnitude. The magnitude scale is a precise one, as a difference of five magnitudes represents a ratio of 100 to 1 in brightness. Typical second magnitude stars are Polaris and the stars in the belt of Orion. The scale is most easily fixed in memory by comparing the stars with Norton's *Star Atlas* (*see* page 71). The stars Sirius and Canopus and the planets Venus and Jupiter are so bright that their magnitudes are expressed by negative numbers. A small telescope will show stars down to the ninth or tenth magnitude, while stars fainter than the twentieth magnitude may be photographed by long exposures with the largest telescopes.

MEAN AND SIDEREAL TIME

Acceleration					Retardation			
h	m s	m s	s		h	m s	m s	s
1	0 10	0 00			1	0 10	0 00	
2	0 20	3 02	0		2	0 20	3 03	0
3	0 30	9 07	1		3	0 29	9 09	1
4	0 39	15 13	2		4	0 39	15 15	2
5	0 49	21 18	3		5	0 49	21 21	3
6	0 59	27 23	4		6	0 59	27 28	4
7	1 09	33 28	5		7	1 09	33 34	5
8	1 19	39 34	6		8	1 19	39 40	6
9	1 29	45 39	7		9	1 28	45 46	7
10	1 39	51 44	8		10	1 38	51 53	8
11	1 48	57 49	9		11	1 48	57 59	9
12	1 58	60 00	10		12	1 58	60 00	10
13	2 08				13	2 08		
14	2 18				14	2 18		
15	2 28				15	2 27		
16	2 38				16	2 37		
17	2 48				17	2 47		
18	2 57				18	2 57		
19	3 07				19	3 07		
20	3 17				20	3 17		
21	3 27				21	3 26		
22	3 37				22	3 36		
23	3 47				23	3 46		
24	3 57				24	3 56		

The length of a sidereal day in mean time is 23h 56m 04s.09. Hence 1h MT = 1h+9s.86 ST and 1h ST = 1h $-$9s.83 MT.

To convert an interval of mean time to the corresponding interval of sidereal time, enter the acceleration table with the given mean time (taking the hours and the minutes and seconds separately) and add the acceleration obtained to the given mean time. To convert an interval of sidereal time to the corresponding interval of mean time, take out the retardation for the given sidereal time and subtract.

The columns for the minutes and seconds of the argument are in the form known as critical tables. To use these tables, find in the appropriate left-hand column the two entries between which the given number of minutes and seconds lies; the quantity in the right-hand column between these two entries is the required acceleration or retardation. Thus the acceleration for 11m 26s (which lies between the entries 9m 07s and 15m 13s) is 2s. If the given number of minutes and seconds is a tabular entry, the required acceleration or retardation is the entry in the right-hand column above the given tabular entry, e.g. the retardation for 45m 46s is 7s.

Example – Convert 14h 27m 35s from ST to MT

	h	m	s
Given ST	14	27	35
Retardation for 14h		2	18
Retardation for 27m 35s			5
Corresponding MT	14	25	12

For further explanation, *see* pages 73–4.

ECLIPSES AND SHADOW TRANSITS OF JUPITER'S SATELLITES 1999

GMT	Sat.	Phen.
d h m		
JANUARY		
2 20 27	I	Sh.I
3 19 50	I	Ec.R
5 20 34	II	Ec.R
11 19 04	I	Sh.E
18 18 14	III	Ec.D
18 18 48	I	Sh.I
18 21 00	I	Sh.E
19 18 10	I	Ec.R
21 20 02	II	Sh.E
26 20 05	I	Ec.R
28 20 02	II	Sh.I
FEBRUARY		
3 19 21	I	Sh.E
5 19 29	III	Sh.E
10 19 04	I	Sh.I
11 18 24	I	Ec.R
JUNE		
27 01 49	I	Sh.I
29 01 10	III	Sh.I
JULY		
5 00 57	I	Ec.D
12 02 52	I	Ec.D
13 02 15	I	Sh.E
13 02 49	II	Ec.D
15 00 16	II	Sh.E
17 01 32	III	Ec.R
20 01 59	I	Sh.I
22 00 20	II	Sh.I
22 02 53	II	Sh.E
24 03 04	III	Ec.D
28 01 09	I	Ec.D
29 00 30	I	Sh.E
29 02 57	II	Sh.I
30 23 48	II	Ec.R
AUGUST		
3 23 39	III	Sh.E
4 03 03	I	Ec.D
5 00 15	I	Sh.I
5 02 24	I	Sh.E
6 23 50	II	Ec.D
7 02 22	II	Ec.R
11 01 16	III	Sh.I
11 03 38	III	Sh.E
12 02 08	I	Sh.I
12 23 26	I	Ec.D
13 22 46	I	Sh.E
14 02 25	II	Ec.D
16 00 02	II	Sh.E
19 04 02	I	Sh.I
20 01 20	I	Ec.D
20 22 30	I	Sh.I
21 00 40	I	Sh.E
21 21 32	III	Ec.R
23 00 07	II	Sh.I
23 02 38	II	Sh.E
27 03 14	I	Ec.D
28 00 24	I	Sh.I
28 02 34	I	Sh.E
28 21 43	I	Ec.D

GMT	Sat.	Phen.
AUGUST		
28 23 10	III	Ec.D
29 01 33	III	Ec.R
29 21 02	I	Sh.E
30 02 43	II	Sh.I
31 20 52	II	Ec.D
SEPTEMBER		
4 02 18	I	Sh.I
4 04 28	I	Sh.E
4 23 37	I	Ec.D
5 03 11	III	Ec.D
5 20 46	I	Sh.I
5 22 56	I	Sh.E
7 23 28	II	Ec.D
9 21 09	II	Sh.E
11 04 12	I	Sh.I
12 01 32	I	Ec.D
12 22 40	I	Sh.I
13 00 50	I	Sh.E
15 02 03	II	Ec.D
15 21 20	III	Sh.I
15 23 38	III	Sh.E
16 21 14	II	Sh.I
16 23 46	II	Sh.E
19 03 26	I	Ec.D
20 00 34	I	Sh.I
20 02 44	I	Sh.E
20 21 54	I	Ec.D
21 21 13	I	Sh.E
22 04 39	II	Ec.D
23 01 22	III	Sh.I
23 03 38	III	Sh.E
23 23 50	II	Sh.I
24 02 22	II	Sh.E
27 02 28	I	Sh.I
27 23 49	I	Ec.D
28 20 57	I	Sh.I
28 23 07	I	Sh.E
OCTOBER		
1 02 26	II	Sh.I
2 20 34	II	Ec.D
3 19 17	III	Ec.D
3 21 33	III	Ec.R
5 01 43	I	Ec.D
5 22 51	I	Sh.I
6 01 02	I	Sh.E
6 20 12	I	Ec.D
7 19 30	I	Sh.E
9 23 10	II	Ec.D
10 23 18	III	Ec.D
11 20 52	II	Sh.E
12 03 38	I	Ec.D
13 00 46	I	Sh.I
13 02 56	I	Sh.E
13 22 07	I	Ec.D
14 19 15	I	Sh.I
14 21 25	I	Sh.E
17 01 47	II	Ec.D
18 20 57	II	Sh.I
18 23 28	II	Sh.E
20 02 41	I	Sh.I
21 00 01	I	Ec.D
21 19 39	III	Sh.E
21 21 09	I	Sh.I

GMT	Sat.	Phen.
OCTOBER		
21 23 20	I	Sh.E
22 18 30	I	Ec.D
25 23 33	II	Sh.I
26 02 05	II	Sh.E
27 20 15	II	Ec.R
28 21 29	III	Sh.I
28 23 04	I	Sh.I
28 23 41	III	Sh.E
29 01 15	I	Sh.E
29 22 35	I	Ec.R
30 19 44	I	Sh.E
NOVEMBER		
2 02 09	II	Sh.I
3 22 53	II	Ec.R
5 01 00	I	Sh.I
5 01 31	III	Sh.E
5 17 58	II	Sh.E
6 00 30	I	Ec.R
6 19 28	I	Sh.I
6 21 39	I	Sh.E
7 18 58	I	Ec.R
8 17 37	III	Ec.R
11 01 31	II	Ec.R
12 18 04	II	Sh.I
12 20 34	II	Sh.E
13 21 24	I	Sh.I
13 23 34	I	Sh.E
14 20 53	I	Ec.R
15 18 03	I	Sh.E
15 19 27	III	Ec.D
15 21 38	III	Ec.R
19 20 40	II	Sh.I
19 23 10	II	Sh.E
20 23 19	I	Sh.I
21 17 28	II	Ec.R
21 22 48	I	Ec.R
22 17 48	I	Sh.I

GMT	Sat.	Phen.
NOVEMBER		
22 19 58	I	Sh.E
22 23 29	III	Ec.D
26 23 16	II	Sh.I
28 20 07	II	Ec.R
29 19 44	I	Sh.I
29 21 54	I	Sh.E
30 19 12	I	Ec.R
DECEMBER		
3 17 40	III	Sh.I
3 19 47	III	Sh.E
5 22 45	II	Ec.R
6 21 39	I	Sh.E
6 23 49	I	Sh.E
7 17 40	II	Sh.E
7 21 07	I	Ec.R
8 18 18	I	Sh.E
10 21 42	III	Sh.I
14 17 46	II	Sh.I
14 20 16	II	Sh.E
14 23 03	I	Ec.R
15 18 04	I	Sh.I
15 20 14	I	Sh.E
16 17 31	I	Ec.R
21 17 45	III	Ec.R
21 20 22	II	Sh.I
21 22 52	II	Sh.E
22 20 00	I	Sh.I
22 22 10	I	Sh.E
23 17 22	II	Ec.R
23 19 27	I	Ec.R
28 19 41	III	Ec.D
28 21 46	III	Ec.R
29 21 56	I	Sh.I
30 17 28	I	Ec.D
30 20 01	II	Ec.R
30 21 22	I	Ec.R
31 18 34	I	Sh.E

Jupiter's satellites transit across the disk from east to west, and pass behind the disk from west to east. The shadows that they cast also transit across the disk. With the exception at times of Satellite IV, the satellites also pass through the shadow of the planet, i.e. they are eclipsed. Just before opposition the satellite disappears in the shadow to the west of the planet and reappears from occultation on the east limb. Immediately after opposition the satellite is occulted at the west limb and reappears from eclipse to the east of the planet. At times approximately two to four months before and after opposition, both phases of eclipses of Satellite III may be seen. When Satellite IV is eclipsed, both phases may be seen.

The times given refer to the centre of the satellite. As the satellite is of considerable size, the immersion and emersion phases are not instantaneous. Even when the satellite enters or leaves the shadow along a radius of the shadow, the phase can last for several minutes. With Satellite IV, grazing phenomena can occur so that the light from the satellite may fade and brighten again without a complete eclipse taking place.

The list of phenomena gives most of the eclipses and shadow transits visible in the British Isles under favourable conditions.

Ec. = Eclipse	R. = Reappearance
Sh. = Shadow transit	I. = Ingress
D. = Disappearance	E. = Egress

EXPLANATION OF ASTRONOMICAL DATA

Positions of the heavenly bodies are given only to the degree of accuracy required by amateur astronomers for setting telescopes, or for plotting on celestial globes or star atlases. Where intermediate positions are required, linear interpolation may be employed.

Definitions of the terms used cannot be given here. They must be sought in astronomical literature and textbooks. Probably the best source for the amateur is Norton's *Star Atlas and Reference Handbook* (Longman, 18th edition, 1989; £26.99), which contains an introduction to observational astronomy, and a series of star maps for showing stars visible to the naked eye. Certain more extended ephemerides are available in the British Astronomical Association Handbook, an annual popular among amateur astronomers (Secretary: Burlington House, Piccadilly, London wiv 9AG).

A special feature has been made of the times when the various heavenly bodies are visible in the British Isles. Since two columns, calculated for latitudes 52° and 56°, are devoted to risings and settings, the range 50° to 58° can be covered by interpolation and extrapolation. The times given in these columns are Greenwich Mean Times for the meridian of Greenwich. An observer west of this meridian must add his/her longitude (in time) and vice versa.

In accordance with the usual convention in astronomy, + and − indicate respectively north and south latitudes or declinations.

All data are, unless otherwise stated, for 0h Greenwich Mean Time (GMT), i.e. at the midnight at the beginning of the day named. Allowance must be made for British Summer Time during the period that this is in operation (*see* pages 15 and 75).

PAGE ONE OF EACH MONTH

The calendar for each month is explained on page 15.

Under the heading Astronomical Phenomena will be found particulars of the more important conjunctions of the Sun, Moon and planets with each other, and also the dates of other astronomical phenomena of special interest.

Times of Minima of Algol are approximate times of the middle of the period of diminished light.

The Constellations listed each month are those that are near the meridian at the beginning of the month at 22h local mean time. Allowance must be made for British Summer Time if necessary. The fact that any star crosses the meridian 4m earlier each night or 2h earlier each month may be used, in conjunction with the lists given each month, to find what constellations are favourably placed at any moment. The table preceding the list of constellations may be extended indefinitely at the rate just quoted.

The principal phases of the Moon are the GMTs when the difference between the longitude of the Moon and that of the Sun is 0°, 90°, 180° or 270°. The times of perigee and apogee are those when the Moon is nearest to, and farthest from, the Earth, respectively. The nodes or points of intersection of the Moon's orbit and the ecliptic make a complete retrograde circuit of the ecliptic in about 19 years. From a knowledge of the longitude of the ascending node and the inclination, whose value does not vary much from 5°, the path of the Moon among the stars may be plotted on a celestial globe or star atlas.

PAGE TWO OF EACH MONTH

The Sun's semi-diameter, in arc, is given once a month.

The right ascension and declination (Dec.) is that of the true Sun. The right ascension of the mean Sun is obtained by applying the equation of time, with the sign given, to the right ascension of the true Sun, or, more easily, by applying 12h to the Sidereal Time. The direction in which the equation of time has to be applied in different problems is a frequent source of confusion and error. Apparent Solar Time is equal to the Mean Solar Time plus the Equation of Time. For example, at noon on August 8 the Equation of Time is − 5m 40s and thus at 12h Mean Time on that day the Apparent Time is 12h − 5m 40s = 11h 54m 20s.

The Greenwich Sidereal Time at 0h and the Transit of the First Point of Aries (which is really the mean time when the sidereal time is 0h) are used for converting mean time to sidereal time and vice versa.

The GMT of transit of the Sun at Greenwich may also be taken as the local mean time (LMT) of transit in any longitude. It is independent of latitude. The GMT of transit in any longitude is obtained by adding the longitude to the time given if west, and vice versa.

LIGHTING-UP TIME

The legal importance of sunrise and sunset is that the Road Vehicles Lighting Regulations 1989 (SI 1989 No. 1796) make the use of front and rear position lamps on vehicles compulsory during the period between sunset and sunrise. Headlamps on vehicles are required to be used during the hours of darkness on unlit roads or whenever visibility is seriously reduced. The hours of darkness are defined in these regulations as the period between half an hour after sunset and half an hour before sunrise.

In all laws and regulations 'sunset' refers to the local sunset, i.e. the time at which the Sun sets at the place in question. This common-sense interpretation has been upheld by legal tribunals. Thus the necessity for providing for different latitudes and longitudes, as already described, is evident.

SUNRISE AND SUNSET

The times of sunrise and sunset are those when the Sun's upper limb, as affected by refraction, is on the true horizon of an observer at sea-level. Assuming the mean refraction to be 34', and the Sun's semi-diameter to be 16', the time given is that when the true zenith distance of the Sun's centre is 90° + 34' + 16' or 90° 50', or, in other words, when the depression of the Sun's centre below the true horizon is 50'. The upper limb is then 34' below the true horizon, but is brought there by refraction. An observer on a ship might see the Sun for a minute or so longer, because of the dip of the horizon, while another viewing the sunset over hills or mountains would record an earlier time. Nevertheless, the moment when the true zenith distance of the Sun's centre is 90° 50' is a precise time dependent only on the latitude and longitude of the place, and independent of its altitude above sea-level, the contour of its horizon, the vagaries of refraction or the small seasonal change in the Sun's semi-diameter; this moment is suitable in every way as a definition of sunset (or sunrise) for all statutory purposes. (For further information, *see* footnote on page 72.)

TWILIGHT

Light reaches us before sunrise and continues to reach us for some time after sunset. The interval between darkness and sunrise or sunset and darkness is called twilight. Astronomically speaking, twilight is considered to begin or end when the Sun's centre is 18° below the horizon, as no light from the Sun can then reach the observer. As thus defined twilight may last several hours; in high latitudes at the summer solstice the depression of 18° is not reached, and twilight lasts from sunset to sunrise.

The need for some sub-division of twilight is met by dividing the gathering darkness into four stages.

(1) *Sunrise or Sunset*, defined as above
(2) *Civil twilight*, which begins or ends when the Sun's centre is 6° below the horizon. This marks the time when operations requiring daylight may commence or must cease. In England it varies from about 30 to 60 minutes after sunset and the same interval before sunrise
(3) *Nautical twilight*, which begins or ends when the Sun's centre is 12° below the horizon. This marks the time when it is, to all intents and purposes, completely dark
(4) *Astronomical twilight*, which begins or ends when the Sun's centre is 18° below the horizon. This marks theoretical perfect darkness. It is of little practical importance, especially if nautical twilight is tabulated

To assist observers the durations of civil, nautical and astronomical twilights are given at intervals of ten days. The beginning of a particular twilight is found by subtracting the duration from the time of sunrise, while the end is found by adding the duration to the time of sunset. Thus the beginning of astronomical twilight in latitude 52°, on the Greenwich meridian, on March 11 is found as 06h 25m − 113m = 04h 32m and similarly the end of civil twilight as 17h 57m + 34m = 18h 31m. The letters TAN (twilight all night) are printed when twilight lasts all night.

Under the heading The Night Sky will be found notes describing the position and visibility of the planets and other phenomena.

PAGE THREE OF EACH MONTH

The Moon moves so rapidly among the stars that its position is given only to the degree of accuracy that permits linear interpolation. The right ascension (RA) and declination (Dec.) are geocentric, i.e. for an imaginary observer at the centre of the Earth. To an observer on the surface of the Earth the position is always different, as the altitude is always less on account of parallax, which may reach 1°.

The lunar terminator is the line separating the bright from the dark part of the Moon's disk. Apart from irregularities of the lunar surface, the terminator is elliptical, because it is a circle seen in projection. It becomes the full circle forming the limb, or edge, of the Moon at New and Full Moon. The selenographic longitude of the terminator is measured from the mean centre of the visible disk, which may differ from the visible centre by as much as 8°, because of libration.

Instead of the longitude of the terminator the Sun's selenographic co-longitude (Sun's co-long.) is tabulated. It is numerically equal to the selenographic longitude of the morning terminator, measured eastwards from the mean centre of the disk. Thus its value is approximately 270° at New Moon, 360° at First Quarter, 90° at Full Moon and 180° at Last Quarter.

The Position Angle (PA) of the Bright Limb is the position angle of the midpoint of the illuminated limb, measured eastwards from the north point on the disk. The Phase column shows the percentage of the area of the Moon's disk illuminated; this is also the illuminated percentage of the diameter at right angles to the line of cusps. The terminator is a semi-ellipse whose major axis is the line of cusps, and whose semi-minor axis is determined by the tabulated percentage; from New Moon to Full Moon the east limb is dark, and vice versa.

The times given as moonrise and moonset are those when the upper limb of the Moon is on the horizon of an observer at sea-level. The Sun's horizontal parallax (Hor. par.) is about 9″, and is negligible when considering sunrise and sunset, but that of the Moon averages about 57′. Hence the computed time represents the moment when the true zenith distance of the Moon is 90° 50′ (as for the Sun) minus the horizontal parallax. The time required for the Sun or Moon to rise or set is about four minutes (except in high latitudes). *See also* page 65 and footnote below.

The GMT of transit of the Moon over the meridian of Greenwich is given; these times are independent of latitude but must be corrected for longitude. For places in the British Isles it suffices to add the longitude if west, and vice versa. For other places a further correction is necessary because of the rapid movement of the Moon relative to the stars. The entire correction is conveniently determined by first finding the west longitude λ of the place. If the place is in west longitude, λ is the ordinary west longitude; if the place is in east longitude λ is the complement to 24h (or 360°) of the longitude and will be greater than 12h (or 180°). The correction then consists of two positive portions, namely λ and the fraction $\lambda/24$ (or $\lambda°/360$) multiplied by the difference between consecutive transits. Thus for Sydney, New South Wales, the longitude is 10h 05m east, so λ=13h 55m and the fraction $\lambda/24$ is 0.58. The transit on the local date 1999 January 16 is found as follows:

	d	h	m
GMT of transit at Greenwich Jan.	16	11	08
λ		13	55
0.58×(11h 08m−10h 18m)			29
GMT of transit at Sydney		17	01	32
Corr. to NSW Standard Time			10	00
Local standard time of transit		17	11	32

As is evident, for any given place the quantities λ and the correction to local standard time may be combined permanently, being here 23h 55m.

Positions of Mercury are given for every second day, and those of Venus and Mars for every fifth day; they may be interpolated linearly. The diameter (Diam.) is given in seconds of arc. The phase is the illuminated percentage of the disk. In the case of the inner planets this approaches 100 at superior conjunction and 0 at inferior conjunction. When the phase is less than 50 the planet is crescent-shaped or horned; for greater phases it is gibbous. In the case of the exterior planet Mars, the phase approaches 100 at conjunction and opposition, and is a minimum at the quadratures.

Since the planets cannot be seen when on the horizon, the actual times of rising and setting are not given; instead, the time when the planet has an apparent altitude of 5° has

—————

SUNRISE, SUNSET AND MOONRISE, MOONSET

The tables have been constructed for the meridian of Greenwich, and for latitudes 52° and 56°. They give Greenwich Mean Time (GMT) throughout the year. To obtain the GMT of the phenomenon as seen from any other latitude and longitude in the British Isles, first interpolate or extrapolate for latitude by the usual rules of proportion. To the time thus found, the longitude (expressed in time) is to be added if west (as it usually is in Great Britain) or subtracted if east. If the longitude is expressed in degrees and minutes of arc, it must be converted to time at the rate of 1° = 4m and 15′ = 1m.

A method of calculating rise and set times for other places in the world is given on pages 64 and 65

been tabulated. If the time of transit is between 00h and 12h the time refers to an altitude of 5° above the eastern horizon; if between 12h and 24h, to the western horizon. The phenomenon tabulated is the one that occurs between sunset and sunrise. The times given may be interpolated for latitude and corrected for longitude, as in the case of the Sun and Moon.

The GMT at which the planet transits the Greenwich meridian is also given. The times of transit are to be corrected to local meridians in the usual way, as already described.

PAGE FOUR OF EACH MONTH

The GMTs of sunrise and sunset for seven cities, whose adopted positions in longitude (W.) and latitude (N.) are given immediately below the name, may be used not only for these phenomena, but also for lighting-up times (*see* page 71 for a fuller explanation).

The particulars for the four outer planets resemble those for the planets on Page Three of each month, except that, under Uranus and Neptune, times when the planet is 10° high instead of 5° high are given; this is because of the inferior brightness of these planets. The diameters given for the rings of Saturn are those of the major axis (in the plane of the planet's equator) and the minor axis respectively. The former has a small seasonal change due to the slightly varying distance of the Earth from Saturn, but the latter varies from zero when the Earth passes through the ring plane every 15 years to its maximum opening half-way between these periods. The rings were last open at their widest extent (and Saturn at its brightest) in 1988; this will occur again in 2002. The Earth passed through the ring plane in 1995–6 and will do so again in 2009.

TIME

From the earliest ages, the natural division of time into recurring periods of day and night has provided the practical time-scale for the everyday activities of the human race. Indeed, if any alternative means of time measurement is adopted, it must be capable of adjustment so as to remain in general agreement with the natural time-scale defined by the diurnal rotation of the Earth on its axis. Ideally the rotation should be measured against a fixed frame of reference; in practice it must be measured against the background provided by the celestial bodies. If the Sun is chosen as the reference point, we obtain Apparent Solar Time, which is the time indicated by a sundial. It is not a uniform time but is subject to variations which amount to as much as a quarter of an hour in each direction. Such wide variations cannot be tolerated in a practical time-scale, and this has led to the concept of Mean Solar Time in which all the days are exactly the same length and equal to the average length of the Apparent Solar Day.

The positions of the stars in the sky are specified in relation to a fictitious reference point in the sky known as the First Point of Aries (or the Vernal Equinox). It is therefore convenient to adopt this same reference point when considering the rotation of the Earth against the background of the stars. The time-scale so obtained is known as Apparent Sidereal Time.

GREENWICH MEAN TIME

The daily rotation of the Earth on its axis causes the Sun and the other heavenly bodies to appear to cross the sky from east to west. It is convenient to represent this relative motion as if the Sun really performed a daily circuit around

a fixed Earth. Noon in Apparent Solar Time may then be defined as the time at which the Sun transits across the observer's meridian. In Mean Solar Time, noon is similarly defined by the meridian transit of a fictitious Mean Sun moving uniformly in the sky with the same average speed as the true Sun. Mean Solar Time observed on the meridian of the transit circle telescope of the Old Royal Observatory at Greenwich is called Greenwich Mean Time (GMT). The mean solar day is divided into 24 hours and, for astronomical and other scientific purposes, these are numbered 0 to 23, commencing at midnight. Civil time is usually reckoned in two periods of 12 hours, designated a.m. (*ante meridiem*, i.e. before noon) and p.m. (*post meridiem*, i.e. after noon).

UNIVERSAL TIME

Before 1925 January 1, GMT was reckoned in 24 hours commencing at noon; since that date it has been reckoned from midnight. To avoid confusion in the use of the designation GMT before and after 1925, since 1928 astronomers have tended to use the term Universal Time (UT) or Weltzeit (WZ) to denote GMT measured from Greenwich Mean Midnight.

In precision work it is necessary to take account of small variations in Universal Time. These arise from small irregularities in the rotation of the Earth. Observed astronomical time is designated UT0. Observed time corrected for the effects of the motion of the poles (giving rise to a 'wandering' in longitude) is designated UT1. There is also a seasonal fluctuation in the rate of rotation of the Earth arising from meteorological causes, often called the annual fluctuation. UT1 corrected for this effect is designated UT2 and provides a time-scale free from short-period fluctuations. It is still subject to small secular and irregular changes.

APPARENT SOLAR TIME

As mentioned above, the time shown by a sundial is called Apparent Solar Time. It differs from Mean Solar Time by an amount known as the Equation of Time, which is the total effect of two causes which make the length of the apparent solar day non-uniform. One cause of variation is that the orbit of the Earth is not a circle but an ellipse, having the Sun at one focus. As a consequence, the angular speed of the Earth in its orbit is not constant; it is greatest at the beginning of January when the Earth is nearest the Sun.

The other cause is due to the obliquity of the ecliptic; the plane of the equator (which is at right angles to the axis of rotation of the Earth) does not coincide with the ecliptic (the plane defined by the apparent annual motion of the Sun around the celestial sphere) but is inclined to it at an angle of 23° 26'. As a result, the apparent solar day is shorter than average at the equinoxes and longer at the solstices. From the combined effects of the components due to obliquity and eccentricity, the equation of time reaches its maximum values in February (−14 minutes) and early November (+16 minutes). It has a zero value on four dates during the year, and it is only on these dates (approximately April 15, June 14, September 1, and December 25) that a sundial shows Mean Solar Time.

SIDEREAL TIME

A sidereal day is the duration of a complete rotation of the Earth with reference to the First Point of Aries. The term sidereal (or 'star') time is a little misleading since the time-scale so defined is not exactly the same as that which would be defined by successive transits of a selected star, as there is a small progressive motion between the stars and the First Point of Aries due to the precession of the Earth's axis. This makes the length of the sidereal day shorter than the true period of rotation by 0.008 seconds. Superimposed on this steady precessional motion are small oscillations (nutation), giving rise to fluctuations in apparent sidereal time amounting to as much as 1.2 seconds. It is therefore customary to employ Mean Sidereal Time, from which these fluctuations have been removed. The conversion of GMT to Greenwich sidereal time (GST) may be performed by adding the value of the GST at 0h on the day in question (Page Two of each month) to the GMT converted to sidereal time using the table on page 69.

Example – To find the GST at August 8d 02h 41m 11s GMT

	h	m	s
GST at 0h	21	05	12
GMT	2	41	11
Acceleration for 2h			20
Acceleration for 41m 11s			7
Sum = GST =	23	46	50

If the observer is not on the Greenwich meridian then his/her longitude, measured positively westwards from Greenwich, must be subtracted from the GST to obtain Local Sidereal Time (LST). Thus, in the above example, an observer 5h east of Greenwich, or 19h west, would find the LST as 4h 46m 50s.

EPHEMERIS TIME

An analysis of observations of the positions of the Sun, Moon and planets taken over an extended period is used in preparing ephemerides. (An ephemeris is a table giving the apparent position of a heavenly body at regular intervals of time, e.g. one day or ten days, and may be used to compare current observations with tabulated positions.) Discrepancies between the positions of heavenly bodies observed over a 300-year period and their predicted positions arose because the time-scale to which the observations were related was based on the assumption that the rate of rotation of the Earth is uniform. It is now known that this rate of rotation is variable. A revised time-scale, Ephemeris Time (ET), was devised to bring the ephemerides into agreement with the observations.

The second of ET is defined in terms of the annual motion of the Earth in its orbit around the Sun (1/31556925.9747 of the tropical year for 1900 January 0d 12h ET). The precise determination of ET from astronomical observations is a lengthy process as the requisite standard of accuracy can only be achieved by averaging over a number of years.

In 1976 the International Astronomical Union adopted a new dynamical time-scale for general use whose scale unit is the SI second (*see* Atomic Time). ET is now of little more than historical interest.

TERRESTRIAL DYNAMICAL TIME

The uniform time system used in computing the ephemerides of the solar system is Terrestrial Dynamical Time (TDT), which has replaced ET for this purpose. Except for the most rigorous astronomical calculations, it may be assumed to be the same as ET. During 1999 the estimated difference TDT – UT is about 64 seconds.

ATOMIC TIME

The fundamental standards of time and frequency must be defined in terms of a periodic motion adequately uniform, enduring and measurable. Progress has made it possible to use natural standards, such as atomic or molecular oscillations. Continuous oscillations are generated in an electrical circuit, the frequency of which is then compared or brought into coincidence with the frequency characteristic

of the absorption or emission by the atoms or molecules when they change between two selected energy levels. The National Physical Laboratory (NPL) routinely uses clocks of high stability produced by locking a quartz oscillator to the frequencies defined by caesium or hydrogen atoms.

International Atomic Time (TAI), established through international collaboration, is formed by combining the readings of many caesium clocks and was set close to the astronomically-based Universal Time (UT) near the beginning of 1958. It was formally recognized in 1971 and since 1988 January 1 has been maintained by the International Bureau of Weights and Measures (BIPM). The second markers are generated according to the International System (SI) definition adopted in 1967 at the 13th General Conference of Weights and Measures: 'The second is the duration of 9 192 631 770 periods of the radiation corresponding to the transition between the two hyperfine levels of the ground state of the caesium-133 atom.'

Civil time in almost all countries is now based on Coordinated Universal Time (UTC), which was adopted for scientific purposes on 1972 January 1. UTC differs from TAI by an integer number of seconds (determined from studies of the rate of rotation of the Earth) and was designed to make both atomic time and UT accessible with accuracies appropriate for most users. The UTC timescale is adjusted by the insertion (or, in principle, omission) of leap seconds in order to keep it within ± 0.9 s of UT. These leap seconds are introduced, when necessary, at the same instant throughout the world, either at the end of December or at the end of June. So, for example, the 22nd leap second occurs at 0h UTC on 1999 January 1. All leap seconds so far have been positive, with 61 seconds in the final minute of the UTC month. The time 23h 59m 60s UTC is followed one second later by 0h 0m 00s of the first day of the following month. Notices concerning the insertion of leap seconds are issued by the International Earth Rotation Service (IERS) at the Observatoire de Paris.

RADIO TIME-SIGNALS

UTC is made generally available through time-signals and standard frequency broadcasts such as MSF in the UK, CHU in Canada and WWV and WWVH in the USA. These are based on national time-scales that are maintained in close agreement with UTC and provide traceability to the national time-scale and to UTC. The markers of seconds in the UTC scale coincide with those of TAI.

To disseminate the national time-scale in the UK, special signals are broadcast on behalf of the National Physical Laboratory from the BT (British Telecom) radio station at Rugby (call-sign MSF). The signals are controlled from a caesium beam atomic frequency standard and consist of a precise frequency carrier of 60 kHz which is switched off, after being on for at least half a second, to mark every second. In part of the first second of each minute the carrier may be switched on and off to carry data at 100 bits/second. In the other seconds the carrier is always off for at least one tenth of a second at the start and then it carries an on-off code giving the British clock time and date, together with information identifying the start of the next minute. Changes to and from summer time are made following government announcements. Leap seconds are inserted as announced by the IERS and information provided by them on the difference between UTC and UT is also signalled. Other broadcast signals in the UK include the BBC six pips signal, the BT Timeline ('speaking clock'), the NPL Truetime service for computers, and a coded time-signal on the BBC 198 kHz transmitters which is used for timing in the electricity supply industry. From 1972 January 1 the six pips on the BBC have consisted of five short pips from second 55 to second 59 (six pips in the case of a leap second) followed by one lengthened pip, the start of which indicates the exact minute. From 1990 February 5 these signals have been controlled by the BBC with seconds markers referenced to the satellite-based US navigation system GPS (Global Positioning System) and time and day referenced to the MSF transmitter. Formerly they were generated by the Royal Greenwich Observatory. The BT Timeline is compared daily with the National Physical Laboratory caesium beam atomic frequency standard at the Rugby radio station. The NPL Truetime service is directly connected to the national time scale.

Accurate timing may also be obtained from the signals of international navigation systems such as the ground-based Omega, or the satellite-based American GPS or Russian GLONASS systems.

STANDARD TIME

Since 1880 the standard time in Britain has been Greenwich Mean Time (GMT); a statute that year enacted that the word 'time' when used in any legal document relating to Britain meant, unless otherwise specifically stated, the mean time of the Greenwich meridian. Greenwich was adopted as the universal meridian on 13 October 1884. A system of standard time by zones is used world-wide, standard time in each zone differing from that of the Greenwich meridian by an integral number of hours, either fast or slow. The large territories of the USA and Canada are divided into zones approximately 7.5° on either side of central meridians. (For time zones of countries of the world, *see* Index.)

Variations from the standard time of some countries occur during part of the year; they are decided annually and are usually referred to as Summer Time or Daylight Saving Time.

At the 180th meridian the time can be either 12 hours fast on Greenwich Mean Time or 12 hours slow, and a change of date occurs. The internationally-recognized date or calendar line is a modification of the 180th meridian, drawn so as to include islands of any one group on the same side of the line, or for political reasons. The line is indicated by joining up the following co-ordinates:

Lat.	Long.	Lat.	Long.
60° S.	180°	48° N.	180°
51° S.	180°	53° N.	170° E.
45° S.	172.5° W.	65.5° N. 169° W.	
15° S.	172.5° W.	75° N.	180°
5° S.	180°		

BRITISH SUMMER TIME

In 1916 an Act ordained that during a defined period of that year the legal time for general purposes in Great Britain should be one hour in advance of Greenwich Mean Time. The Summer Time Acts 1922 and 1925 defined the period during which Summer Time was to be in force, stabilizing practice until the Second World War.

During the war the duration of Summer Time was extended and in the years 1941 to 1945 and in 1947 Double Summer Time (two hours in advance of Greenwich Mean Time) was in force. After the war, Summer Time was extended each year in 1948–52 and 1961–4 by Order in Council.

Between 1968 October 27 and 1971 October 31 clocks were kept one hour ahead of Greenwich Mean Time throughout the year. This was known as British Standard Time.

The most recent legislation is the Summer Time Act 1972, which enacted that 'the period of summer time for the purposes of this Act is the period beginning at two o'clock,

Greenwich mean time, in the morning of the day after the third Saturday in March or, if that day is Easter Day, the day after the second Saturday in March, and ending at two o'clock, Greenwich mean time, in the morning of the day after the fourth Saturday in October.'

The duration of Summer Time can be varied by Order in Council and in recent years alterations have been made to bring the operation of Summer Time in Britain closer to similar provisions in other countries of the European Union; for instance, since 1981 the hour of changeover has been 01 h Greenwich Mean Time.

The duration of Summer Time in the next few years is:
1999   March 28 01h GMT to October 31 01h GMT
2000   March 26 01h GMT to October 29 01h GMT
2001   March 25 01h GMT to October 28 01h GMT

MEAN REFRACTION

Alt.	Ref.	Alt.	Ref.	Alt.	Ref.
° ′	′	° ′	′	° ′	′
1 20	21	3 12	13	7 54	6
1 30	20	3 34	12	9 27	5
1 41	19	4 00	11	11 39	4
1 52	18	4 30	10	15 00	3
2 05	17	5 06	9	20 42	2
2 19	16	5 50	8	32 20	1
2 35	15	6 44	7	62 17	0
2 52	14	7 54		90 00	
3 12					

The refraction table is in the form of a critical table (*see* page 69)

ASTRONOMICAL CONSTANTS

Solar parallax	8″.794
Astronomical unit	149597870 km
Precession for the year 1999	50″.291
Precession in right ascension	3s.075
Precession in declination	20″.043
Constant of nutation	9″.202
Constant of aberration	20″.496
Mean obliquity of ecliptic (1999)	23° 26′ 22″
Moon's equatorial hor. parallax	57′ 02″.70
Velocity of light in vacuo per second	299792.5 km
Solar motion per second	20.0 km
Equatorial radius of the Earth	6378.140 km
Polar radius of the Earth	6356.755 km
North galactic pole (IAU standard)	
	RA 12h 49m (1950.0). Dec. 27°.4 N.
Solar apex	RA 18h 06m Dec. + 30°

Length of year (in mean solar days)

Tropical	365.24219
Sidereal	365.25636
Anomalistic (perihelion to perihelion)	365.25964
Eclipse	346.6200

Length of month (mean values)

	d	h	m	s
New Moon to New	29	12	44	02.9
Sidereal	27	07	43	11.5
Anomalistic (perigee to perigee)	27	13	18	33.2

ELEMENTS OF THE SOLAR SYSTEM

Orb	Mean distance from Sun (Earth = 1) km 10^6	Sidereal period days	Synodic period days	Incl. of orbit to ecliptic ° ′	Diameter km	Mass (Earth = 1)	Period of rotation on axis days
Sun	—	—	—	—	1,392,530	332,946	25–35*
Mercury	0.39	58	88.0	116	7 00	4,879	0.0553	58.646
Venus	0.72	108	224.7	584	3 24	12,104	0.8150	243.019r
Earth	1.00	150	365.3	—	—	12,756e	1.0000	0.997
Mars	1.52	228	687.0	780	1 51	6,794e	0.1074	1.026
Jupiter	5.20	778	4,332.6	399	1 18	{142,984e / 133,708p}	317.89	{0.410e}
Saturn	9.54	1427	10,759.2	378	2 29	{120,536e / 108,728p}	95.18	{0.426e}
Uranus	19.18	2870	30,684.6	370	0 46	51,118e	14.54	0.718r
Neptune	30.06	4497	60,191.0	367	1 46	49,528e	17.15	0.671
Pluto	39.80	5954	91,708.2	367	17 09	2,302	0.002	6.387

e equatorial, p polar, r retrograde, * depending on latitude

THE SATELLITES

Name	Star mag.	Mean distance from primary km	Sidereal period of revolution d
EARTH			
I Moon	—	384,400	27.322
MARS			
I Phobos	12	9,378	0.319
II Deimos	13	23,459	1.262
JUPITER			
XVI Metis	17	127,960	0.295
XV Adrastea	19	128,980	0.298
V Amalthea	14	181,300	0.498
XIV Thebe	16	221,900	0.675
I Io	5	421,600	1.769
II Europa	5	670,900	3.551
III Ganymede	5	1,070,000	7.155
IV Callisto	6	1,883,000	16.689
XIII Leda	20	11,094,000	239
VI Himalia	15	11,480,000	251
X Lysithea	18	11,720,000	259
VII Elara	17	11,737,000	260
XII Ananke	19	21,200,000	631r
XI Carme	18	22,600,000	692r
VIII Pasiphae	17	23,500,000	735r
IX Sinope	18	23,700,000	758r
SATURN			
XVIII Pan	—	133,583	0.575
XV Atlas	18	137,670	0.602
XVI Prometheus	16	139,353	0.613
XVII Pandora	16	141,700	0.629
XI Epimetheus	15	151,422	0.694
X Janus	14	151,472	0.695
I Mimas	13	185,520	0.942
II Enceladus	12	238,020	1.370
III Tethys	10	294,660	1.888
XIII Telesto	19	294,660	1.888
XIV Calypso	19	294,660	1.888
IV Dione	10	377,400	2.737
XII Helene	18	377,400	2.737
V Rhea	10	527,040	4.518
VI Titan	8	1,221,830	15.945

Name	Star mag.	Mean distance from primary km	Sidereal period of revolution d
SATURN			
VII Hyperion	14	1,481,100	21.277
VIII Iapetus	11	3,561,300	79.330
IX Phoebe	16	12,952,000	550.48r
URANUS			
VI Cordelia	—	49,770	0.335
VII Ophelia	—	53,790	0.376
VIII Bianca	—	59,170	0.435
IX Cressida	—	61,780	0.464
X Desdemona	—	62,680	0.474
XI Juliet	—	64,350	0.493
XII Portia	—	66,090	0.513
XIII Rosalind	—	69,940	0.558
XIV Belinda	—	75,260	0.624
XV Puck	—	86,010	0.762
V Miranda	17	129,390	1.413
I Ariel	14	191,020	2.520
II Umbriel	15	266,300	4.144
III Titania	14	435,910	8.706
IV Oberon	14	583,520	13.463
S/1997U1	—	72,000,000	579
S/1997U2	—	122,000,000	1,289
NEPTUNE			
III Naiad	25	48,230	0.294
IV Thalassa	24	50,070	0.311
V Despina	23	52,530	0.335
VI Galatea	22	61,950	0.429
VII Larissa	22	73,550	0.555
VIII Proteus	20	117,650	1.122
I Triton	13	354,760	5.877
II Nereid	19	5,513,400	360.136
PLUTO			
I Charon	17	19,600	6.387

THE EARTH

The shape of the Earth is that of an oblate spheroid or solid of revolution whose meridian sections are ellipses not differing much from circles, whilst the sections at right angles are circles. The length of the equatorial axis is about 12,756 km, and that of the polar axis is 12,714 km. The mean density of the Earth is 5.5 times that of water, although that of the surface layer is less. The Earth and Moon revolve about their common centre of gravity in a lunar month; this centre in turn revolves round the Sun in a plane known as the ecliptic, that passes through the Sun's centre. The Earth's equator is inclined to this plane at an angle of 23.4°. This tilt is the cause of the seasons. In mid-latitudes, when the Sun is high above the Equator, not only does the high noon altitude make the days longer, but the Sun's rays fall more directly on the Earth's surface; these effects combine to produce summer. In equatorial regions the noon altitude is large throughout the year, and there is little variation in the length of the day. In higher latitudes the noon altitude is lower, and the days in summer are appreciably longer than those in winter.

The average velocity of the Earth in its orbit is 30 km a second. It makes a complete rotation on its axis in about 23h 56m of mean time, which is the sidereal day. Because of its annual revolution round the Sun, the rotation with respect to the Sun, or the solar day, is more than this by about four minutes (*see* page 73). The extremity of the axis of rotation, or the North Pole of the Earth, is not rigidly fixed, but wanders over an area roughly 20 metres in diameter.

TERRESTRIAL MAGNETISM

A magnetic compass points along the horizontal component of a magnetic line of force. These lines of force converge on the 'magnetic dip-poles', the places where a freely suspended magnetized needle would become vertical. Not only do these poles move with time, but their exact locations are ill-defined, particularly so in the case of the north dip-pole where the lines of force on the north side of it, instead of converging radially, tend to bunch into a channel. Although it is therefore unrealistic to attempt to specify the locations of the dip-poles exactly, the present approximate adopted positions are 79°.8 N., 106°.7 W. and 64°.6 S., 138°.5 E. The two magnetic dip-poles are thus not antipodal, the line joining them passing the centre of the Earth at a distance of about 1,250 km. The distances of the magnetic dip-poles from the north and south geographical poles are about 1,200 km and 2,800 km respectively.

There is also a 'magnetic equator', at all points of which the vertical component of the Earth's magnetic field is zero and a magnetized needle remains horizontal. This line runs between 2° and 10° north of the geographical equator in Asia and Africa, turns sharply south off the west African coast, and crosses South America through Brazil, Bolivia and Peru; it recrosses the geographical equator in mid-Pacific.

Reference has already been made to secular changes in the Earth's field. The following table indicates the changes in magnetic declination (or variation of the compass). Declination is the angle in the horizontal plane between the direction of true north and that in which a magnetic compass points. Similar, though much smaller, changes have occurred in 'dip' or magnetic inclination. Secular changes differ throughout the world. Although the London observations strongly suggest a cycle with a period of several hundred years, an exact repetition is unlikely.

London		Greenwich	
1580	11° 15' E.	1850	22° 24' W.
1622	5° 56' E.	1900	16° 29' W.
1665	1° 22' W.	1925	13° 10' W.
1730	13° 00' W.	1950	9° 07' W.
1773	21° 09' W.	1975	6° 39' W.

In order that up-to-date information on declination may be available, many governments publish magnetic charts on which there are lines (isogonic lines) passing through all places at which specified values of declination will be found at the date of the chart.

In the British Isles, isogonic lines now run approximately north-east to south-west. Though there are considerable local deviations due to geological causes, a rough value of magnetic declination may be obtained by assuming that at 50° N. on the meridian of Greenwich, the value in 1999 is 2° 46' west and allowing an increase of 15' for each degree of latitude northwards and one of 28' for each degree of longitude westwards. For example, at 53° N., 5° W., declination will be about 2° 46' + 45' + 140', i.e. 5° 51' west. The average annual change at the present time is about 11' decrease.

The number of magnetic observatories is about 200, irregularly distributed over the globe. There are three in Great Britain, run by the British Geological Survey: at Hartland, north Devon; at Eskdalemuir, Dumfriesshire; and at Lerwick, Shetland Islands. The following are some recent annual mean values of the magnetic elements for Hartland.

Year	Declination West ° '	Dip or inclination ° '	Horizontal force gauss	Vertical force gauss
1960	9 59	66 44	0.1871	0.4350
1965	9 30	66 34	0.1887	0.4354
1970	9 06	66 26	0.1903	0.4364
1975	8 32	66 17	0.1921	0.4373
1980	7 44	66 10	0.1933	0.4377
1985	6 56	66 08	0.1938	0.4380
1990	6 15	66 10	0.1939	0.4388
1995	5 33	66 07	0.1946	0.4395
1997	5 13	66 06	0.1948	0.4398

The normal world-wide terrestrial magnetic field corresponds approximately to that of a very strong small bar magnet near the centre of the Earth, but with appreciable smooth spatial departures. The origin and the slow secular change of the normal field are not fully understood but are generally ascribed to electric currents associated with fluid motions in the Earth's core. Superimposed on the normal field are local and regional anomalies whose magnitudes may in places approach that of the normal field; these are due to the influence of mineral deposits in the Earth's crust. A small proportion of the field is of external origin, mostly associated with electric currents in the ionosphere. The configuration of the external field and the ionization of the atmosphere depend on the incident particle and radiation flux from the Sun. There are, therefore, short-term and non-periodic as well as diurnal, 27-day, seasonal and 11-year periodic changes in the magnetic field, dependent upon the position of the Sun and the degree of solar activity.

MAGNETIC STORMS

Occasionally, sometimes with great suddenness, the Earth's magnetic field is subject for several hours to marked disturbance. During a severe storm in 1989 the declination at Lerwick changed by almost 8° in less than an hour. In many instances such disturbances are accompanied by widespread displays of aurorae, marked changes in the incidence of cosmic rays, an increase in the reception of 'noise' from the Sun at radio frequencies, and rapid changes in the ionosphere and induced electric currents within the Earth which adversely affect radio and telegraphic communications. The disturbances are caused by changes in the stream of ionized particles which emanates from the Sun and through which the Earth is continuously passing. Some of these changes are associated with visible eruptions on the Sun, usually in the region of sun-spots. There is a marked tendency for disturbances to recur after intervals of about 27 days, the apparent period of rotation of the Sun on its axis, which is consistent with the sources being located on particular areas of the Sun.

ARTIFICIAL SATELLITES

To consider the orbit of an artificial satellite, it is best to imagine that one is looking at the Earth from a distant point in space. The Earth would then be seen to be rotating about its axis inside the orbit described by the rapidly revolving satellite. The inclination of a satellite orbit to the Earth's equator (which generally remains almost constant throughout the satellite's lifetime) gives at once the maximum range of latitudes over which the satellite passes. Thus a satellite whose orbit has an inclination of 53° will pass overhead all latitudes between 53° S. and 53° N., but would never be seen in the zenith of any place nearer the poles than these latitudes. If we consider a particular place on the earth, whose latitude is less than the inclination of the satellite's orbit, then the Earth's rotation carries this place first under the northbound part of the orbit and then under the southbound portion of the orbit, these two occurrences being always less than 12 hours apart for satellites moving in direct orbits (i.e. to the east). (For satellites in retrograde orbits, the words 'northbound' and 'southbound' should be interchanged in the preceding statement.) As the value of the latitude of the observer increases and approaches the value of the inclination of the orbit, so this interval gets shorter until (when the latitude is equal to the inclination) only one overhead passage occurs each day.

Observation of Satellites

The regression of the orbit around the Earth causes alternate periods of visibility and invisibility, though this is of little concern to the radio or radar observer. To the visual observer the following cycle of events normally occurs (though the cycle may start in any position): invisibility, morning observations before dawn, invisibility, evening observations after dusk, invisibility, morning observations before dawn, and so on. With reasonably high satellites and for observers in high latitudes around the summer solstice, the evening observations follow the morning observations without interruption as sunlight passing over the polar regions can still illuminate satellites which are passing over temperate latitudes at local midnight. At the moment all satellites rely on sunlight to make them visible, though a satellite with a flashing light has been suggested for a future launching. The observer must be in darkness or twilight in order to make any useful observations. (For durations of twilight; and sunrise and sunset times, *see* Page Two of each month.)

Some of the satellites are visible to the naked eye and much interest has been aroused by the spectacle of a bright satellite disappearing into the Earth's shadow. The event is even more interesting telescopically as the disappearance occurs gradually as the satellite traverses the Earth's

penumbral shadow, and during the last few seconds before the eclipse is complete the satellite may change colour (in suitable atmospheric conditions) from yellow to red. This is because the last rays of sunlight are refracted through the denser layers of our atmosphere before striking the satellite.

Some satellites rotate about one or more axes so that a periodic variation in brightness is observed. This was particularly noticeable in several of the Soviet satellites.

Satellite research has provided some interesting results, including a revised value of the Earth's oblateness (1/298.2), and the discovery of the Van Allen radiation belts.

Launchings

Apart from their names, e.g. Cosmos 6 Rocket, the satellites are also classified according to their date of launch. Thus 1961 α refers to the first satellite launching of 1961. A number following the Greek letter indicated the relative brightness of the satellites put in orbit. From the beginning of 1963 the Greek letters were replaced by numbers and the numbers by roman letters e.g. 1963–01A. For all satellites successfully injected into orbit the following table gives the designation and names of the main objects, the launch date and some initial orbital data. These are the inclination to the equator (i), the nodal period of revolution (P), the eccentricity (e), and the perigee height.

Although most of the satellites launched are injected into orbits less than 1,000 km high, there are an increasing number of satellites in geostationary orbits, i.e. where the orbital inclination is zero, the eccentricity close to zero, and the period of revolution is 1436.1 minutes. Thus the satellite is permanently situated over the equator at one selected longitude at a mean height of 35,786 km. This geostationary band is crowded. In one case there are four television satellites (Astra 1A, Astra 1B, Astra 1C and Astra 1D) orbiting within a few tens of kilometres of each other. In the sky they appear to be separated by only a few arc minutes.

In 1997 a number of *Iridium* satellites have been launched into high inclination orbits (*see* table). These are owned by the mobile telephone company Cellnet. For visual observers, these satellites have an interesting characteristic, namely that the large solar panels they carry can, when in exactly the right orientation with respect to the Sun and the observer, give off a 'flare' in brightness which can on occasion attain a magnitude of -6, much brighter than Venus. The flare can be visible to the naked eye for nearly a minute.

ARTIFICIAL SATELLITE LAUNCHES 1997–8

Designation	Satellite	Launch date	i	P	e	Perigee height
1997–			°	m		km
021	China DHF3-2, rocket	May 11	0.2	1435.3	0.790	25759
022	Cosmos 2342, rocket, platform, rocket	May 14	62.7	717.1	0.733	505
023	Shuttle 84	May 15	51.6	92.3	0.044	384
024	Cosmos 2343, rocket	May 15	64.9	89.4	0.026	206
025	Comsat, rocket, rocket	May 20	19.6	667.5	0.722	1280
026	Telstar 5, rocket, platform, rocket	May 24	7.7	942.3	0.770	15107
027	Inmarsat 3F4, Insat2D, rocket	June 3	7.0	630.0	0.712	218
028	Cosmos 2344, rocket	June 6	63.2	130.1	0.235	1510
029	FY 2, CZ 3A, rocket	June 10	27.8	634.1	0.713	141
030	Iridium 14, 12, 10, 9, 13, 16, 11	June 18	86.4	94.9	0.061	502
031	Intelsat 802, rocket	June 25	0.1	1431.3	0.814	35610
032	Shuttle	June 30	28.5	90.4	0.032	300
033	Progress M35, rocket	July 5	51.6	90.2	0.030	264
034	Iridium 15, 17, 18, 20, 21, rocket	July 9	86.4	97.5	0.077	625
035	GPS Navstar, rocket, rocket	July 23	54.7	712.6	0.732	19875
036	Superbird C, rocket	July 28	25.3	1969.7	0.788	333
037	Orbview 2, rocket	August 1	98.2	99.0	0.000	707
038	Soyuz TM26, rocket	August 5	51.6	91.5	0.042	370
039	Shuttle 85, Christa Spas	August 7	57.0	90.0	0.029	280
040	Panamsat 6, rocket	August 8	0.0	1436.0	0.000	35773
041	Cosmos 2345, rocket, rocket	August 14	50.0	622.0	0.710	233
042	Agila 2, rocket	August 19	24.6	806.4	0.750	171
043	Iridium 26, 25, 24, 23, 22, rocket	August 21	86.7	95.7	0.066	544
044	SSTI Lewis, rocket	August 23	97.5	90.7	0.032	295
045	ACE, rocket	August 25		(unknown)		
046	Panamsat 5, rocket	August 28	14.5	804.4	0.749	8589
047	Forte, rocket	August 29	70.0	101.2	0.099	800
048	Iridium Sim2, Sim1, rocket	September 1	86.2	97.3	0.076	623
049	Hot Bird 3, Meteosat 7, rocket	September 2	7.0	631.2	0.713	213
050	GE 3, rocket	September 4	19.1	796.9	0.748	306
051	Iridium 29, 32, 33, 27, 28, 30, 31, rocket	September 14	86.5	95.0	0.061	506
052	Cosmos 2346, rocket	September 23	82.9	104.5	0.117	939
053	Intelsat 803	September 24	7.0	633.3	0.713	292
054	Molniya 1T, rocket, platform, rocket	September 24	62.7	735.9	0.737	445
055	Shuttle 86	September 26	51.6	91.7	0.044	384
056	Iridium 19, 37, 36, 35, 34, rocket	September 27	86.7	95.7	0.066	545
057	IRS 1D, rocket	September 29	98.5	96.8	0.072	381
058	Progress M36, rocket, Sputnik 40	October 5	51.6	92.2	0.044	383
059	Echostar 3, rocket	October 5	12.0	818.8	0.752	6571
060	Foton 11, rocket	October 9	62.7	90.4	0.031	219
061	Cassini, rocket	October 15		(Heliocentric orbit)		
062	Apstar 2R, rocket	October 16	0.1	1707.3	0.829	34276
063	Step M4, rocket	October 22	45.0	93.8	0.055	434
064	Lacrosse 3, rocket	October 24	57.0	98.0	0.081	665
065	DSCS III B13, rocket	October 25	0.0	1436.0	0.815	35789
066	Maqsat H, Maqsat B, YES, rocket	October 30	7.7	467.3	0.657	535
067	GPS Navstar, rocket, rocket	November 6	35.0	357.4	0.596	185
068	USA 134, rocket	November 8		(unknown)		
069	Iridium 43, 41, 40, 39, 38, rocket	November 9	86.5	97.5	0.077	627
070	Kupon, rocket, platform, rocket	November 12	0.0	1449.9	0.816	36035
071	Sirius 2, Indostar 1, rocket	November 12	0.1	1426.4	0.814	35420
072	Resurs F1M, rocket	November 18	82.2	89.1	0.021	209
073	Shuttle 87, Spartan 201	November 19	28.5	90.0	0.029	281
074	TRMM, Hikoboshi, Orihime, rocket	November 27	35.0	91.9	0.042	369
075	JCSAT 5, Equator S, rocket	December 2	4.0	630.7	0.713	220

Desig-nation	Satellite	Launch date	i	P	e	Perigee height
1997–			°	m		km
076	Astra 1G, Proton, platform, rocket	December 2	12.4	841.5	0.756	10320
077	Iridium 42, 44	December 8	86.2	97.4	0.076	627
078	Galaxy 8I, rocket	December 9	27.0	821.0	0.752	166
079	Cosmos 2347, rocket	December 9	65.0	92.8	0.047	406
080	Cosmos 2348, rocket	December 15	67.0	89.2	0.022	161
081	Progress M37, rocket	December 20	51.6	90.3	0.030	265
082	Iridium 45, 46, 47, 48, 49, rocket	December 20	86.5	97.4	0.076	625
083	Intelsat 804, rocket	December 22	7.0	630.3	0.713	266
084	Orbcomm F 5, 6, 7, 8, 9, 10, 11, 12, rocket, HAPS	December 23	45.0	101.2	0.100	816
085	Earlybird, rocket	December 24	97.2	94.3	0.057	480
086	Asiasat 3, rocket, platform, rocket	December 24	51.5	636.3	0.714	270
1998–						
001	Lunar Prospector, rocket	January 7		(Selenocentric orbit)		
002	Skynet 4D, rocket	January 10	23.6	654.8	0.719	1186
003	Shuttle 89	January 23	51.6	91.1	0.036	299
004	Soyuz TM27, rocket	January 29	51.6	89.9	0.028	256
005	US137 Capric, rocket	January 29		(Heliocentric orbit)		
006	Brasilsat B3, Inmarsat 3F5, platform, Spelda	February 4	7.0	631.2	0.713	212
007	GFO, Orbcomm G-1, Orbcomm G-2, Celestis 02, rocket	February 10	108.0	101.5	0.101	782
008	Globalstar FM1, FM2, FM3, FM4, rocket	February 14	52.0	110.5	0.150	1244
009	Cosmos 2349, rocket	February 17	70.4	89.4	0.023	212
010	Iridium 50, 56, 52, 53, 54, rocket	February 18	86.5	99.3	0.088	722
011	Kakehasha, rocket	February 21	30.1	106.3	0.129	249
012	Snoe, Teledisc-1, rocket	February 26	97.7	95.9	0.067	536
013	Hot Bird 4, rocket	February 27	7.0	627.8	0.712	183
014	Intelsat 806, rocket	February 28	23.8	627.8	0.712	189

Time Measurement and Calendars

MEASUREMENTS OF TIME

Measurements of time are based on the time taken by the earth to rotate on its axis (day); by the moon to revolve round the earth (month); and by the earth to revolve round the sun (year). From these, which are not commensurable, certain average or mean intervals have been adopted for ordinary use.

THE DAY

The day begins at midnight and is divided into 24 hours of 60 minutes, each of 60 seconds. The hours are counted from midnight up to 12 noon (when the sun crosses the meridian), and these hours are designated a.m. (*ante meridiem*); and again from noon up to 12 midnight, which hours are designated p.m. (*post meridiem*), except when the 24-hour reckoning is employed. The 24-hour reckoning ignores a.m. and p.m., numbering the hours 0 to 23 from midnight.

Colloquially the 24 hours are divided into day and night, day being the time while the sun is above the horizon (including the four stages of twilight defined on page 72). Day is subdivided into morning, the early part of daytime, ending at noon; afternoon, from noon to about 6 p.m.; and evening, which may be said to extend from 6 p.m. until midnight. Night, the dark period between day and day, begins at the close of astronomical twilight (*see* page 72) and extends beyond midnight to sunrise the next day.

The names of the days are derived from Old English translations or adaptations of the Roman titles.

Sunday	Sun	Sol
Monday	Moon	Luna
Tuesday	Tiw/Tyr (god of war)	Mars
Wednesday	Woden/Odin	Mercury
Thursday	Thor	Jupiter
Friday	Frigga/Freyja	
	(goddess of love)	Venus
Saturday	Saeternes	Saturn

THE MONTH

The month in the ordinary calendar is approximately the twelfth part of a year, but the lengths of the different months vary from 28 (or 29) days to 31.

THE YEAR

The equinoctial or tropical year is the time that the earth takes to revolve round the sun from equinox to equinox, i.e. 365.24219 mean solar days, or 365 days 5 hours 48 minutes and 45 seconds.

The calendar year usually consists of 365 days but a year containing 366 days is called bissextile (*see* Roman calendar, page 89) or leap year, one day being added to the month of February so that a date 'leaps over' a day of the week. In the Roman calendar the day that was repeated was the sixth day before the beginning of March, the equivalent of 24 February.

A year is a leap year if the date of the year is divisible by four without remainder, unless it is the last year of a century. The last year of a century is a leap year only if its number is divisible by 400 without remainder, e.g. the years 1800 and 1900 had only 365 days but the year 2000 will have 366 days.

THE SOLSTICE

A solstice is the point in the tropical year at which the sun attains its greatest distance, north or south, from the Equator. In the northern hemisphere the furthest point north of the Equator marks the summer solstice and the furthest point south the winter solstice.

The date of the solstice varies according to locality. For example, if the summer solstice falls on 21 June late in the day by Greenwich time, that day will be the longest of the year at Greenwich though it may be by only a second, but it will fall on 22 June, local date, in Japan, and so 22 June will be the longest day there. The date of the solstice is also affected by the length of the tropical year, which is 365 days 6 hours less about 11 minutes 15 seconds. If a solstice happens late on 21 June in one year, it will be nearly six hours later in the next (unless the next year is a leap year), i.e. early on 22 June, and that will be the longest day.

This delay of the solstice does not continue because the extra day in leap year brings it back a day in the calendar. However, because of the 11 minutes 15 seconds mentioned above, the additional day in leap year brings the solstice back too far by 45 minutes, and the time of the solstice in the calendar is earlier, in a four-year pattern, as the century progresses. The last year of a century is in most cases not a leap year, and the omission of the extra day puts the date of the solstice later by about six hours too much. Compensation for this is made by the fourth centennial year being a leap year. The solstice has become earlier in date throughout this century and, because the year 2000 is a leap year, the solstice will get earlier still throughout the 21st century.

The date of the winter solstice, the shortest day of the year, is affected by the same factors as the longest day.

At Greenwich the sun sets at its earliest by the clock about ten days before the shortest day. The daily change in the time of sunset is due in the first place to the sun's movement southwards at this time of the year, which diminishes the interval between the sun's transit and its setting. However, the daily decrease of the Equation of Time causes the time of apparent noon to be continuously later day by day, which to some extent counteracts the first effect. The rates of the change of these two quantities are not equal or uniform; their combination causes the date of earliest sunset to be 12 or 13 December at Greenwich. In more southerly latitudes the effect of the movement of the sun is less, and the change in the time of sunset depends on that of the Equation of Time to a greater degree, and the date of earliest sunset is earlier than it is at Greenwich, e.g. on the Equator it is about 1 November.

THE EQUINOX

The equinox is the point at which the sun crosses the Equator and day and night are of equal length all over the world. This occurs in March and September.

DOG DAYS

The days about the heliacal rising of the Dog Star, noted from ancient times as the hottest period of the year in the northern hemisphere, are called the Dog Days. Their incidence has been variously calculated as depending on the Greater or Lesser Dog Star (Sirius or Procyon) and their duration has been reckoned as from 30 to 54 days. A generally accepted period is from 3 July to 15 August.

CHRISTIAN CALENDAR

In the Christian chronological system the years are distinguished by cardinal numbers before or after the birth of Christ, the period being denoted by the letters BC (Before Christ) or, more rarely, AC (*Ante Christum*), and AD (*Anno Domini* – In the Year of Our Lord). The correlative dates of the epoch are the fourth year of the 194th Olympiad, the 753rd year from the foundation of Rome, AM 3761 (Jewish chronology), and the 4714th year of the Julian period. The actual date of the birth of Christ is somewhat uncertain.

The system was introduced into Italy in the sixth century. Though first used in France in the seventh century, it was not universally established there until about the eighth century. It has been said that the system was introduced into England by St Augustine (AD 596), but it was probably not generally used until some centuries later. It was ordered to be used by the Bishops at the Council of Chelsea (AD 816).

The Julian Calendar

In the Julian calendar (adopted by the Roman Empire in 45 BC, *see* page 89) all the centennial years were leap years, and for this reason towards the close of the 16th century there was a difference of ten days between the tropical and calendar years; the equinox fell on 11 March of the calendar, whereas at the time of the Council of Nicaea (AD 325), it had fallen on 21 March. In 1582 Pope Gregory ordained that 5 October should be called 15 October and that of the end-century years only the fourth should be a leap year (*see* page 81).

The Gregorian Calendar

The Gregorian calendar was adopted by Italy, France, Spain and Portugal in 1582, by Prussia, the Roman Catholic German states, Switzerland, Holland and Flanders on 1 January 1583, by Poland in 1586, Hungary in 1587, the Protestant German and Netherland states and Denmark in 1700, and by Great Britain and Dominions (including the North American colonies) in 1752, by the omission of eleven days (3 September being reckoned as 14 September). Sweden omitted the leap day in 1700 but observed leap days in 1704 and 1708, and reverted to the Julian calendar by having two leap days in 1712; the Gregorian calendar was adopted in 1753 by the omission of eleven days (18 February being reckoned as 1 March). Japan adopted the calendar in 1872, China in 1912, Bulgaria in 1915, Turkey and Soviet Russia in 1918, Yugoslavia and Romania in 1919, and Greece in 1923.

In the same year that the change was made in England from the Julian to the Gregorian calendar, the beginning of the new year was also changed from 25 March to 1 January (*see* page 86).

The Orthodox Churches

Some Orthodox Churches still use the Julian reckoning but the majority of Greek Orthodox Churches and the Romanian Orthodox Church have adopted a modified 'New Calendar', observing the Gregorian calendar for fixed feasts and the Julian for movable feasts.

The Orthodox Church year begins on 1 September. There are four fast periods and, in addition to Pascha (Easter), twelve great feasts, as well as numerous commemorations of the saints of the Old and New Testaments throughout the year.

The Dominical Letter

The dominical letter is one of the letters A–G which are used to denote the Sundays in successive years. If the first day of the year is a Sunday the letter is A; if the second, B; the third, C; and so on. A leap year requires two letters, the first for 1 January to 29 February, the second for 1 March to 31 December (*see* page 84).

Epiphany

The feast of the Epiphany, commemorating the manifestation of Christ, later associated with the offering of gifts by the Magi. The day was of great importance from the time of the Council of Nicaea (AD 325), as the primate of Alexandria was charged at every Epiphany feast with the announcement in a letter to the churches of the date of the forthcoming Easter. The day was also of importance in Britain as it influenced dates, ecclesiastical and lay, e.g. Plough Monday, when work was resumed in the fields, fell on the Monday in the first full week after Epiphany.

Lent

The Teutonic word *Lent*, which denotes the fast preceding Easter, originally meant no more than the spring season; but from Anglo-Saxon times at least it has been used as the equivalent of the more significant Latin term Quadragesima, meaning the 'forty days' or, more literally, the fortieth day. Ash Wednesday is the first day of Lent, which ends at midnight before Easter Day.

Palm Sunday

Palm Sunday, the Sunday before Easter and the beginning of Holy Week, commemorates the triumphal entry of Christ into Jerusalem and is celebrated in Britain (when palm is not available) by branches of willow gathered for use in the decoration of churches on that day.

Maundy Thursday

Maundy Thursday is the day before Good Friday, the name itself being a corruption of *dies mandati* (day of the mandate) when Christ washed the feet of the disciples and gave them the mandate to love one another.

Easter Day

Easter Day is the first Sunday after the full moon which happens on, or next after, the 21st day of March; if the full moon happens on a Sunday, Easter Day is the Sunday after.

This definition is contained in an Act of Parliament (24 Geo. II c. 23) and explanation is given in the preamble to the Act that the day of full moon depends on certain tables that have been prepared. These tables are summarized in the early pages of the Book of Common Prayer. The moon referred to is not the real moon of the heavens, but a hypothetical moon on whose 'full' the date of Easter depends, and the lunations of this 'calendar' moon consist of twenty-nine and thirty days alternately, with certain necessary modifications to make the date of its full agree as nearly as possible with that of the real moon, which is known as the Paschal Full Moon. At present, Easter falls on one of 35 days (22 March to 25 April).

A Fixed Easter

In 1928 the House of Commons agreed to a motion for the third reading of a bill proposing that Easter Day shall, in the calendar year next but one after the commencement of the Act and in all subsequent years, be the first Sunday after the second Saturday in April. Easter would thus fall on the second or third Sunday in April, i.e. between 9 and 15 April (inclusive). A clause in the Bill provided that before it shall come into operation, regard shall be had to any opinion expressed officially by the various Christian churches.

Efforts by the World Council of Churches to secure a unanimous choice of date for Easter by its member churches have so far been unsuccessful.

ROGATION DAYS

Rogation Days are the Monday, Tuesday and Wednesday preceding Ascension Day and from the fifth century were observed as public fasts with solemn processions and supplications. The processions were discontinued as religious observances at the Reformation, but survive in the ceremony known as 'beating the parish bounds'. Rogation Sunday is the Sunday before Ascension Day.

EMBER DAYS

The Ember Days at the four seasons are the Wednesday, Friday and Saturday (a) before the third Sunday in Advent,

(b) before the second Sunday in Lent, and (c) before the Sundays nearest to the festivals of St Peter and of St Michael and All Angels.

TRINITY SUNDAY

Trinity Sunday is eight weeks after Easter Day, on the Sunday following Pentecost (Whit Sunday). Subsequent Sundays are reckoned in the Book of Common Prayer calendar of the Church of England as 'after Trinity'.

Thomas Becket (1118–70) was consecrated Archbishop of Canterbury on the Sunday after Whit Sunday and his first act was to ordain that the day of his consecration should be held as a new festival in honour of the Holy Trinity. This observance spread from Canterbury throughout the whole of Christendom.

MOVABLE FEASTS TO THE YEAR 2031

Year	Ash Wednesday	Easter	Ascension	Pentecost (Whit Sunday)	Advent Sunday
1999	17 February	4 April	13 May	23 May	28 November
2000	8 March	23 April	1 June	11 June	3 December
2001	28 February	15 April	24 May	3 June	2 December
2002	13 February	31 March	9 May	19 May	1 December
2003	5 March	20 April	29 May	8 June	30 November
2004	25 February	11 April	20 May	30 May	28 November
2005	9 February	27 March	5 May	15 May	27 November
2006	1 March	16 April	25 May	4 June	3 December
2007	21 February	8 April	17 May	27 May	2 December
2008	6 February	23 March	1 May	11 May	30 November
2009	25 February	12 April	21 May	31 May	29 November
2010	17 February	4 April	13 May	23 May	28 November
2011	9 March	24 April	2 June	12 June	27 November
2012	22 February	8 April	17 May	27 May	2 December
2013	13 February	31 March	9 May	19 May	1 December
2014	5 March	20 April	29 May	8 June	30 November
2015	18 February	5 April	14 May	24 May	29 November
2016	10 February	27 March	5 May	15 May	27 November
2017	1 March	16 April	25 May	4 June	3 December
2018	14 February	1 April	10 May	20 May	2 December
2019	6 March	21 April	30 May	9 June	1 December
2020	26 February	12 April	21 May	31 May	29 November
2021	17 February	4 April	13 May	23 May	28 November
2022	2 March	17 April	26 May	5 June	27 November
2023	22 February	9 April	18 May	28 May	3 December
2024	14 February	31 March	9 May	19 May	1 December
2025	5 March	20 April	29 May	8 June	30 November
2026	18 February	5 April	14 May	24 May	29 November
2027	10 February	28 March	6 May	16 May	28 November
2028	1 March	16 April	25 May	4 June	3 December
2029	14 February	1 April	10 May	20 May	2 December
2030	6 March	21 April	30 May	9 June	1 December
2031	26 February	13 April	22 May	1 June	30 November

NOTES

Ash Wednesday (first day in Lent) can fall at earliest on 4 February and at latest on 10 March

Mothering Sunday (fourth Sunday in Lent) can fall at earliest on 1 March and at latest on 4 April

Easter Day can fall at earliest on 22 March and at latest on 25 April

Ascension Day is forty days after Easter Day and can fall at earliest on 30 April and at latest on 3 June

Pentecost (Whit Sunday) is seven weeks after Easter and can fall at earliest on 10 May and at latest on 13 June

Trinity Sunday is the Sunday after Whit Sunday

Corpus Christi falls on the Thursday after Trinity Sunday

Sundays after Pentecost – there are not less than 18 and not more than 23

Advent Sunday is the Sunday nearest to 30 November

EASTER DAYS AND DOMINICAL LETTERS 1500 to 2033

Dates up to and including 1752 are according to the Julian calendar

	1500–1599	1600–1699	1700–1799	1800–1899	1900–1999	2000–2033
March						
d 22	1573	1668	1761	1818		
e 23	1505/16	1600	1788	1845/56	1913	2008
f 24		1611/95	1706/99		1940	
g 25	1543/54	1627/38/49	1722/33/44	1883/94	1951	
A 26	1559/70/81/92	1654/65/76	1749/58/69/80	1815/26/37	1967/78/89	
b 27	1502/13/24/97	1608/87/92	1785/96	1842/53/64	1910/21/32	2005/16
c 28	1529/35/40	1619/24/30	1703/14/25	1869/75/80	1937/48	2027/32
d 29	1551/62	1635/46/57	1719/30/41/52	1807/12/91	1959/64/70	
e 30	1567/78/89	1651/62/73/84	1746/55/66/77	1823/34	1902/75/86/97	
f 31	1510/21/32/83/94	1605/16/78/89	1700/71/82/93	1839/50/61/72	1907/18/29/91	2002/13/24
April						
g 1	1526/37/48	1621/32	1711/16	1804/66/77/88	1923/34/45/56	2018/29
A 2	1553/64	1643/48	1727/38	1809/20/93/99	1961/72	
b 3	1575/80/86	1659/70/81		1825/31/36	1904/83/88/94	
c 4	1507/18/91	1602/13/75/86/97	1708/79/90	1847/58	1915/20/26/99	2010/21
d 5	1523/34/45/56	1607/18/29/40	1702/13/24/95	1801/63/74/85/96	1931/42/53	2015/26
e 6	1539/50/61/72	1634/45/56	1729/35/40/60	1806/17/28/90	1947/58/69/80	
f 7	1504/77/88	1667/72	1751/65/76	1822/33/44	1901/12/85/96	
g 8	1509/15/20/99	1604/10/83/94	1705/87/92/98	1849/55/60	1917/28	2007/12
A 9	1531/42	1615/26/37/99	1710/21/32	1871/82	1939/44/50	2023
b 10	1547/58/69	1631/42/53/64	1726/37/48/57	1803/14/87/98	1955/66/77	
c 11	1501/12/63/74/85/96	1658/69/80	1762/73/84	1819/30/41/52	1909/71/82/93	2004
d 12	1506/17/28	1601/12/91/96	1789	1846/57/68	1903/14/25/36/98	2009/20
e 13	1533/44	1623/28	1707/18	1800/73/79/84	1941/52	2031
f 14	1555/60/66	1639/50/61	1723/34/45/54	1805/11/16/95	1963/68/74	
g 15	1571/82/93	1655/66/77/88	1750/59/70/81	1827/38	1900/06/79/90	2001
A 16	1503/14/25/36/87/98	1609/20/82/93	1704/75/86/97	1843/54/65/76	1911/22/33/95	2006/17/28
b 17	1530/41/52	1625/36	1715/20	1808/70/81/92	1927/38/49/60	2022/33
c 18	1557/68	1647/52	1731/42/56	1802/13/24/97	1954/65/76	
d 19	1500/79/84/90	1663/74/85	1747/67/72/78	1829/35/40	1908/81/87/92	
e 20	1511/22/95	1606/17/79/90	1701/12/83/94	1851/62	1919/24/30	2003/14/25
f 21	1527/38/49	1622/33/44	1717/28	1867/78/89	1935/46/57	2019/30
g 22	1565/76	1660	1739/53/64	1810/21/32	1962/73/84	
A 23	1508	1671		1848	1905/16	2000
b 24	1519	1603/14/98	1709/91	1859		2011
c 25	1546	1641	1736	1886	1943	

HINDU CALENDAR

The Hindu calendar is a luni-solar calendar of twelve months, each containing 29 days, 12 hours. Each month is divided into a light fortnight (Shukla or Shuddha) and a dark fortnight (Krishna or Vadya) based on the waxing and waning of the moon. In most parts of India the month starts with the light fortnight, i.e. the day after the new moon, although in some regions it begins with the dark fortnight, i.e. the day after the full moon.

The new year begins in the month of Chaitra (March/April) and ends in the month of Phalgun (March). The twelve months, Chaitra, Vaishakh, Jyeshtha, Ashadh, Shravan, Bhadrapad, Ashvin, Kartik, Margashirsh, Paush, Magh and Phalgun, have Sanskrit names derived from twelve asterisms (constellations). There are regional variations to the names of the months but the Sanskrit names are understood throughout India.

Every lunar month must have a solar transit and is termed pure (shuddha). The lunar month without a solar transit is impure (mala) and called an intercalary month. An intercalary month occurs approximately every 32 lunar months, whenever the difference between the Hindu year of 360 lunar days (354 days 8 hours solar time) and the 365 days 6 hours of the solar year reaches the length of one Hindu lunar month (29 days 12 hours).

The leap month may be added at any point in the Hindu year. The name given to the month varies according to when it occurs but is taken from the month immediately following it. A leap month occurs in 1999–2000 (Jyeshtha).

The days of the week are called Raviwar (Sunday), Somawar (Monday), Mangalwar (Tuesday), Budhawar (Wednesday), Guruwar (Thursday), Shukrawar (Friday) and Shaniwar (Saturday). The names are derived from the Sanskrit names of the Sun, the Moon and five planets, Mars, Mercury, Jupiter, Venus and Saturn.

Most fasts and festivals are based on the lunar calendar but a few are determined by the apparent movement of the Sun, e.g. Sankranti and Pongal (in southern India), which are celebrated on 14/15 January to mark the start of the Sun's apparent journey northwards and a change of season.

Festivals celebrated throughout India are Chaitra (the New Year), Raksha-bandhan (the renewal of the kinship bond between brothers and sisters), Navaratri (a nine-night festival dedicated to the goddess Parvati), Dasara (the victory of Rama over the demon army), Diwali (a festival of lights), Makara Sankranti, Shivaratri (dedicated to Shiva), and Holi (a spring festival).

Regional festivals are Durga-puja (dedicated to the goddess Durga (Parvati)), Sarasvati-puja (dedicated to the goddess Sarasvati), Ganesh Chaturthi (worship of Ganesh on the fourth day (Chaturthi) of the light half of Bhadrapad), Ramanavami (the birth festival of the god Rama) and Janmashtami (the birth festival of the god Krishna).

The main festivals celebrated in Britain are Navaratri, Dasara, Durga-puja, Diwali, Holi, Sarasvati-puja, Ganesh Chaturthi, Raksha-bandhan, Ramanavami and Janmashtami.

For dates of the main festivals in 1999, *see* page 9.

JEWISH CALENDAR

The story of the Flood in the Book of Genesis indicates the use of a calendar of some kind and that the writers recognized thirty days as the length of a lunation. However, after the diaspora, Jewish communities were left in considerable doubt as to the times of fasts and festivals. This led to the formation of the Jewish calendar as used today. It is said that this was done in AD 358 by Rabbi Hillel II, though some assert that it did not happen until much later.

The calendar is luni-solar, and is based on the lengths of the lunation and of the tropical year as found by Hipparchus (*c*.120 BC), which differ little from those adopted at the present day. The year AM 5759 (1998–9) is the 2nd year of the 304th Metonic (Minor or Lunar) cycle of 19 years and the 19th year of the 206th Solar (or Major) cycle of 28 years since the Era of the Creation. Jews hold that the Creation occurred at the time of the autumnal equinox in the year known in the Christian calendar as 3760 BC (954 of the Julian period). The epoch or starting point of Jewish chronology corresponds to 7 October 3761 BC. At the beginning of each solar cycle, the Tekufah of Nisan (the vernal equinox) returns to the same day and to the same hour.

The hour is divided into 1080 minims, and the month between one new moon and the next is reckoned as 29 days, 12 hours, 793 minims. The normal calendar year, called a Regular Common year, consists of 12 months of 30 days and 29 days alternately. Since twelve months such as these comprise only 354 days, in order that each of them shall not diverge greatly from an average place in the solar year, a thirteenth month is occasionally added after the fifth month of the civil year (which commences on the first day of the month Tishri), or as the penultimate month of the ecclesiastical year (which commences on the first day of the month Nisan). The years when this happens are called Embolismic or leap years.

Of the 19 years that form a Metonic cycle, seven are leap years; they occur at places in the cycle indicated by the numbers 3, 6, 8, 11, 14, 17 and 19, these places being chosen so that the accumulated excesses of the solar years should be as small as possible.

A Jewish year is of one of the following six types:

Minimal Common	353 days
Regular Common	354 days
Full Common	355 days
Minimal Leap	383 days
Regular Leap	384 days
Full Leap	385 days.

The Regular year has alternate months of 30 and 29 days. In a Full year, whether common or leap, Marcheshvan, the second month of the civil year, has 30 days instead of 29; in Minimal years Kislev, the third month, has 29 instead of 30. The additional month in leap years is called Adar I and precedes the month called Adar in Common years. Adar II is called Adar Sheni in leap years, and the usual Adar festivals are kept in Adar Sheni. Adar I and Adar II always have 30 days, but neither this, nor the other variations mentioned, is allowed to change the number of days in the other months, which still follow the alternation of the normal twelve.

These are the main features of the Jewish calendar, which must be considered permanent because as a Jewish law it cannot be altered except by a great Sanhedrin.

The Jewish day begins between sunset and nightfall. The time used is that of the meridian of Jerusalem, which is 2h 21m in advance of Greenwich Mean Time. Rules for the beginning of sabbaths and festivals were laid down for the latitude of London in the 18th century and hours for nightfall are now fixed annually by the Chief Rabbi.

JEWISH CALENDAR 5759–60

AM 5759 (759) is a Full Common year of 12 months, 50 sabbaths and 355 days; AM 5760 (760) is a Full Leap year of 13 months, 55 sabbaths and 385 days.

Jewish Month	AM 5759	AM 5760
Tishri 1	21 September 1998	11 September 1999
Marcheshvan 1	21 October	11 October
Kislev 1	20 November	10 November
Tebet 1	20 December	10 December
Shebat 1	18 January 1999	8 January 2000
*Adar 1	17 February	7 February
†Adar II		8 March
Nisan 1	18 March	6 April
Iyar 1	17 April	6 May
Sivan 1	16 May	4 June
Tammuz 1	15 June	4 July
Ab 1	14 July	2 August
Elul 1	13 August	1 September

*Known as Adar Rishon in leap years
†Known as Adar Sheni in leap years

JEWISH FASTS AND FESTIVALS

For dates of principal festivals in 1999, *see* page 9

Tishri 1–2	Rosh Hashanah (New Year)
Tishri 3	*Fast of Gedaliah
Tishri 10	Yom Kippur (Day of Atonement)
Tishri 15–21	Succoth (Feast of Tabernacles)
Tishri 21	Hoshana Rabba
Tishri 22	Shemini Atseret (Solemn Assembly)
Tishri 23	Simchat Torah (Rejoicing of the Law)
Kislev 25	Chanucah (Dedication of the Temple) begins
Tebet 10	Fast of Tebet
†Adar 13	§Fast of Esther
†Adar 14	Purim
†Adar 15	Shushan Purim
Nisan 15–22	Pesach (Passover)
Sivan 6–7	Shavuot (Feast of Weeks)
Tammuz 17	*Fast of Tammuz
Ab 9	*Fast of Ab

*If these dates fall on the sabbath the fast is kept on the following day
†Adar Sheni in leap years
§This fast is observed on Adar 11 (or Adar Sheni 11 in leap years) if Adar 13 falls on a sabbath

THE MUSLIM CALENDAR

The Muslim era is dated from the *Hijrah*, or flight of the Prophet Muhammad from Mecca to Medina, the corresponding date of which in the Julian calendar is 16 July AD 622. The lunar *hijri* calendar is used principally in Iran, Egypt, Malaysia, Pakistan, Mauritania, various Arab states and certain parts of India. Iran uses the solar *hijri* calendar as well as the lunar *hijri* calendar. The dating system was adopted about AD 639, commencing with the first day of the month Muharram.

The lunar calendar consists of twelve months containing an alternate sequence of 30 and 29 days, with the intercalation of one day at the end of the twelfth month at stated intervals in each cycle of 30 years. The object of the intercalation is to reconcile the date of the first day of the month with the date of the actual new moon.

Some adherents still take the date of the evening of the first physical sighting of the crescent of the new moon as that of the first of the month. If cloud obscures the moon the present month may be extended to 30 days, after which the new month will begin automatically regardless of whether the moon has been seen. (Under religious law a month must have less than 31 days). This means that the beginning of a new month and the date of religious festivals can vary from the published calendars.

In each cycle of 30 years, 19 years are common and contain 354 days, and 11 years are intercalary (leap years) of 355 days, the latter being called *kabisah*. The mean length of the Hijrah years is 354 days 8 hours 48 minutes and the period of mean lunation is 29 days 12 hours 44 minutes.

To ascertain if a year is common or kabisah, divide it by 30: the quotient gives the number of completed cycles and the remainder shows the place of the year in the current cycle. If the remainder is 2, 5, 7, 10, 13, 16, 18, 21, 24, 26 or 29, the year is kabisah and consists of 355 days.

MUSLIM CALENDAR 1419–20

Hijrah year 1419 AH (remainder 9) is a common year; 1420 AH (remainder 10) is a kabisah year.

Month (length)	1419 AH	1420 AH
Muharram (30)	28 April 1998	17 April 1999
Safar (29)	28 May	17 May
Rabi' I (30)	26 June	15 June
Rabi' II (29)	26 July	15 July
Jumada I (30)	24 August	13 August
Jumada II (29)	23 September	12 September
Rajab (30)	22 October	11 October
Sha'ban (29)	21 November	10 November
Ramadân (30)	20 December	9 December
Shawwâl (29)	19 January 1999	8 January 2000
Dhû'l-Qa'da (30)	17 February	6 February
Dhû'l-Hijjah (29 or 30)	19 March	7 March

MUSLIM FESTIVALS

Ramadan is a month of fasting for all Muslims because it is the month in which the revelation of the *Qur'an* (Koran) began. During Ramadan Muslims abstain from food, drink and sexual pleasure from dawn until after sunset throughout the month.

The two major festivals are *Id al-Fitr* and *Id al-Adha*. Id al-Fitr marks the end of the Ramadan fast and is celebrated on the day after the sighting of the new moon of the following month. Id al-Adha, the festival of sacrifice (also known as the great festival), celebrates the submission of the Prophet Ibrahim (Abraham) to God. Id al-Adha falls on the tenth

day of Dhul-Hijjah, coinciding with the day when those on *hajj* (pilgrimage to Mecca) sacrifice animals.

Other days accorded special recognition are:

Muharram 1	New Year's Day
Muharram 10	Ashura (the day Prophet Noah left the Ark and Prophet Moses was saved from Pharaoh (Sunni), the death of the Prophet's grandson Husain (Shi'ite))
Rabi'u-l-Awwal (Rabi' I) 12	Mawlid al-Nabi (birthday of the Prophet Muhammad)
Rajab 27	Laylat al-Isra' wa'l-Mi'raj (The Night of Journey and Ascension)
Ramadân One of the odd-numbered nights in the last 10 of the month	Laylat al-Qadr (Night of Power)
Dhû'l-Hijjah 10	Id al-Adha (Festival of Sacrifice)

THE SIKH CALENDAR

The Sikh calendar is a lunar calendar of 365 days divided into 12 months. The length of the months varies between 29 and 32 days.

There are no prescribed feast days and no fasting periods. The main celebrations are Baisakhi Mela (the new year and the anniversary of the founding of the Khalsa), Diwali Mela (festival of light), Hola Mohalla Mela (a spring festival held in the Punjab), and the Gurpurbs (anniversaries associated with the ten Gurus).

For dates of the major celebrations in 1999, *see* page 9.

CIVIL AND LEGAL CALENDAR

THE HISTORICAL YEAR

Before 1752, two calendar systems were used in England. The civil or legal year began on 25 March and the historical year on 1 January. Thus the civil or legal date 24 March 1658 was the same day as the historical date 24 March 1659; a date in that portion of the year is written as 24 March 165⅞, the lower figure showing the historical year.

THE NEW YEAR

In England in the seventh century, and as late as the 13th, the year was reckoned from Christmas Day, but in the 12th century the Church in England began the year with the feast of the Annunciation of the Blessed Virgin ('Lady Day') on 25 March and this practice was adopted generally in the 14th century. The civil or legal year in the British Dominions (exclusive of Scotland) began with Lady Day until 1751. But in and since 1752 the civil year has begun with 1 January. New Year's Day in Scotland was changed from 25 March to 1 January in 1600.

Elsewhere in Europe, 1 January was adopted as the first day of the year by Venice in 1522, German states in 1544, Spain, Portugal, and the Roman Catholic Netherlands in 1556, Prussia, Denmark and Sweden in 1559, France in 1564, Lorraine in 1579, the Protestant Netherlands in 1583, Russia in 1725, and Tuscany in 1751.

REGNAL YEARS

Regnal years are the years of a sovereign's reign and each begins on the anniversary of his or her accession, e.g. regnal year 48 of the present Queen begins on 6 February 1999.

The system was used for dating Acts of Parliament until 1962. The Summer Time Act 1925, for example, is quoted as 15 and 16 Geo. V c. 64, because it became law in the parliamentary session which extended over part of both of these regnal years. Acts of a parliamentary session during which a sovereign died were usually given two year numbers, the regnal year of the deceased sovereign and the regnal year of his or her successor, e.g. those passed in 1952 were dated 16 Geo. VI and 1 Elizabeth II. Since 1962 Acts of Parliament have been dated by the calendar year.

QUARTER AND TERM DAYS

Holy days and saints days were the usual means in early times for setting the dates of future and recurrent appointments. The quarter days in England and Wales are the feast of the Nativity (25 December), the feast of the Annunciation (25 March), the feast of St John the Baptist (24 June) and the feast of St Michael and All Angels (29 September).

The term days in Scotland are Candlemas (the feast of the Purification), Whitsunday, Lammas (Loaf Mass), and Martinmas (St Martin's Day). These fell on 2 February, 15 May, 1 August and 11 November respectively. However, by the Term and Quarter Days (Scotland) Act 1990, the dates of the term days were changed to 28 February (Candlemas), 28 May (Whitsunday), 28 August (Lammas) and 28 November (Martinmas).

RED-LETTER DAYS

Red-letter days were originally the holy days and saints days indicated in early ecclesiastical calendars by letters printed in red ink. The days to be distinguished in this way were approved at the Council of Nicaea in AD 325.

These days still have a legal significance, as judges of the Queen's Bench Division wear scarlet robes on red-letter days falling during the law sittings. The days designated as red-letter days for this purpose are:

Holy and saints days (for dates, *see* pages 16, 20, etc.)
The Conversion of St Paul, the Purification, Ash Wednesday, the Annunciation, the Ascension, the feasts of St Mark, SS Philip and James, St Matthias, St Barnabas, St John the Baptist, St Peter, St Thomas, St James, St Luke, SS Simon and Jude, All Saints, St Andrew

Civil calendar (for dates, *see* page 9)
The anniversaries of The Queen's accession, The Queen's birthday and The Queen's coronation, The Queen's official birthday, the birthday of the Duke of Edinburgh, the birthday of Queen Elizabeth the Queen Mother, the birthday of the Prince of Wales, St David's Day and Lord Mayor's Day

PUBLIC HOLIDAYS

Public holidays are divided into two categories, common law and statutory. Common law holidays are holidays 'by habit and custom'; in England, Wales and Northern Ireland these are Good Friday and Christmas Day.

Statutory public holidays, known as bank holidays, were first established by the Bank Holidays Act 1871. They were, literally, days on which the banks (and other public institutions) were closed and financial obligations due on that day were payable the following day. The legislation currently governing public holidays in the UK, which is the Banking and Financial Dealings Act 1971 stipulates the days that are to be public holidays in England, Wales, Scotland and Northern Ireland.

Certain holidays (indicated by * below) are granted annually by royal proclamation, either throughout the UK or in any place in the UK. The public holidays are:

England and Wales
*New Year's Day
Easter Monday
*The first Monday in May
The last Monday in May
The last Monday in August
26 December, if it is not a Sunday
27 December when 25 or 26 December is a Sunday

Scotland
New Year's Day, or if it is a Sunday, 2 January
2 January, or if it is a Sunday, 3 January
Good Friday
The first Monday in May
*The last Monday in May
The first Monday in August
Christmas Day, or if it is a Sunday, 26 December
*Boxing Day – if Christmas Day falls on a Sunday, 26 December is given in lieu and an alternative day is given for Boxing Day

Northern Ireland
*New Year's Day
17 March, or if it is a Sunday, 18 March
Easter Monday
*The first Monday in May
The last Monday in May
*12 July, or if it is a Sunday, 13 July
The last Monday in August
26 December, if it is not a Sunday
27 December if 25 or 26 December is a Sunday

For dates of public holidays in 1999 and 2000, *see* pages 10–11.

CHRONOLOGICAL CYCLES AND ERAS

SOLAR (OR MAJOR) CYCLE

The solar cycle is a period of twenty-eight years in any corresponding year of which the days of the week recur on the same day of the month.

METONIC (LUNAR, OR MINOR) CYCLE

In 432 BC, Meton, an Athenian astronomer, found that 235 lunations are very nearly, though not exactly, equal in duration to 19 solar years and so after 19 years the phases of the Moon recur on the same days of the month (nearly). The dates of full moon in a cycle of 19 years were inscribed in figures of gold on public monuments in Athens, and the number showing the position of a year in the cycle is called the golden number of that year.

JULIAN PERIOD

The Julian period was proposed by Joseph Scaliger in 1582. The period is 7980 Julian years, and its first year coincides with the year 4713 BC. The figure of 7980 is the product of the number of years in the solar cycle, the Metonic cycle and the cycle of the Roman indiction (28 × 19 × 15).

ROMAN INDICTION

The Roman indiction is a period of fifteen years, instituted for fiscal purposes about AD 300.

EPACT

The epact is the age of the calendar Moon, diminished by one day, on 1 January, in the ecclesiastical lunar calendar.

CHINESE CALENDAR

A lunar calendar was the sole calendar in use in China until 1911, when the government adopted the new (Gregorian) calendar for official and most business activities. The Chinese tend to follow both calendars, the lunar calendar playing an important part in personal life, e.g. birth celebrations, festivals, marriages; and in rural villages the lunar calendar dictates the cycle of activities, denoting the change of weather and farming activities.

The lunar calendar is used in Hong Kong, Singapore, Malaysia, Tibet and elsewhere in south-east Asia. The calendar has a cycle of 60 years. The new year begins at the first new moon after the sun enters the sign of Aquarius, i.e. the new year falls between 21 January and 19 February in the Gregorian calendar.

Each year in the Chinese calendar is associated with one of 12 animals: the rat, the ox, the tiger, the rabbit, the dragon, the snake, the horse, the goat or sheep, the monkey, the chicken or rooster, the dog, and the pig.

The date of the Chinese new year and the astrological sign for the years 1999–2003 are:

1999	16 February	Rabbit
2000	5 February	Dragon
2001	—	Snake
2002	—	Horse
2003	—	Goat or Sheep

COPTIC CALENDAR

In the Coptic calendar, which is used in parts of Egypt and Ethiopia, the year is made up of 12 months of 30 days each, followed, in general, by five complementary days. Every fourth year is an intercalary or leap year and in these years there are six complementary days. The intercalary year of the Coptic calendar immediately precedes the leap year of the Julian calendar. The era is that of Diocletian or the Martyrs, the origin of which is fixed at 29 August AD 284 (Julian date).

INDIAN ERAS

In addition to the Muslim reckoning, other eras are used in India. The Saka era of southern India, dating from 3 March AD 78, was declared the national calendar of the Republic of India with effect from 22 March 1957, to be used concurrently with the Gregorian calendar. As revised, the year of the new Saka era begins at the spring equinox, with five successive months of 31 days and seven of 30 days in ordinary years, and six months of each length in leap years. The year AD 1999 is 1921 of the revised Saka era.

The year AD 1999 corresponds to the following years in other eras:

Year 2056 of the Vikram Samvat era
Year 1406 of the Bengali San era
Year 1175 of the Kollam era
Vedanga Jyotisa year 5 of the five-yearly cycle (384th cycle of Paitamah Siddhanta)
Year 6000 of the Kaliyuga era
Year 2543 of the Buddha Nirvana era

JAPANESE CALENDAR

The Japanese calendar is essentially the same as the Gregorian calendar, the years, months and weeks being of the same length and beginning on the same days as those of the Gregorian calendar. The numeration of the years is different, based on a system of epochs or periods each of which begins at the accession of an Emperor or other important occurrence. The method is not unlike the British system of regnal years, except that each year of a period closes on 31 December. The Japanese chronology begins about AD 650 and the three latest epochs are defined by the reigns of Emperors, whose actual names are not necessarily used:

Epoch

Taishō	1 August 1912 to 25 December 1926
Shōwa	26 December 1926 to 7 January 1989
Heisei	8 January 1989

The year Heisei 11 begins on 1 January 1999.

The months are known as First Month, Second Month, etc., First Month being equivalent to January. The days of the week are Nichiyōbi (Sun-day), Getsuyōbi (Moon-day), Kayōbi (Fire-day), Suiyōbi (Water-day), Mokuyōbi (Wood-day), Kinyōbi (Metal-day), Doyōbi (Earth-day).

THE MASONIC YEAR

Two dates are quoted in warrants, dispensations, etc., issued by the United Grand Lodge of England, those for the current year being expressed as *Anno Domini* 1999 – *Anno Lucis* 5999. This *Anno Lucis* (year of light) is based on the Book of Genesis 1:3, the 4000-year difference being derived, in modified form, from *Ussher's Notation*, published in 1654, which places the Creation of the World in 4004 BC.

OLYMPIADS

Ancient Greek chronology was reckoned in Olympiads, cycles of four years corresponding with the periodic Olympic Games held on the plain of Olympia in Elis once every four years. The intervening years were the first, second, etc., of the Olympiad, which received the name of the victor at the Games. The first recorded Olympiad is that of Choroebus, 776 BC.

ZOROASTRIAN CALENDAR

Zoroastrians, followers of the Iranian prophet Zarathushtra (known to the Greeks as Zoroaster) are mostly to be found in Iran and in India, where they are known as Parsees.

The Zoroastrian era dates from the coronation of the last Zoroastrian Sasanian king in AD 631. The Zoroastrian calendar is divided into twelve months, each comprising 30 days, followed by five holy days of the Gathas at the end of each year to make the year consist of 365 days.

In order to synchronize the calendar with the solar year of 365 days, an extra month was intercalated once every 120 years. However, this intercalation ceased in the 12th century and the New Year, which had fallen in the spring, slipped back to August. Because intercalation ceased at different times in Iran and India, there was one month's difference between the calendar followed in Iran (Kadmi calendar) and by the Parsees (Shenshai calendar). In 1906 a group of Zoroastrians decided to bring the calendar back in line with the seasons again and restore the New Year to 21 March each year (Fasli calendar).

The Shenshai calendar (New Year in August) is mainly used by Parsees. The Fasli calendar (New Year, 21 March) is mainly used by Zoroastrians living in Iran, in the Indian subcontinent, or away from Iran.

THE ROMAN CALENDAR

Roman historians adopted as an epoch the foundation of Rome, which is believed to have happened in the year 753 BC. The ordinal number of the years in Roman reckoning is followed by the letters AUC (*ab urbe condita*), so that the year 1999 is 2752 AUC (MMDCCLII). The calendar that we know has developed from one said to have been established by Romulus using a year of 304 days divided into ten months, beginning with March. To this Numa added January and February, making the year consist of 12 months of 30 and 29 days alternately, with an additional day so that the total was 355. It is also said that Numa ordered an intercalary month of 22 or 23 days in alternate years, making 90 days in eight years, to be inserted after 23 February.

However, there is some doubt as to the origination and the details of the intercalation in the Roman calendar. It is certain that some scheme of this kind was inaugurated and not fully carried out, for in the year 46 BC Julius Caesar found that the calendar had been allowed to fall into some confusion. He sought the help of the Egyptian astronomer Sosigenes, which led to the construction and adoption (45 BC) of the Julian calendar, and, by a slight alteration, to the Gregorian calendar now in use. The year 46 BC was made to consist of 445 days and is called the Year of Confusion.

In the Roman (Julian) calendar the days of the month were counted backwards from three fixed points, or days, and an intervening day was said to be so many days before the next coming point, the first and last being counted. These three points were the Kalends, the Nones, and the Ides. Their positions in the months and the method of counting from them will be seen in the table below. The year containing 366 days was called *bissextillis annus*, as it had a doubled sixth day (*bissextus dies*) before the March Kalends on 24 February – *ante diem sextum Kalendas Martias*, or a.d. VI Kal. Mart.

Present days of the month	March, May, July, October have thirty-one days	January, August, December have thirty-one days	April, June, September, November have thirty days	February has twenty-eight days, and in leap year twenty-nine
1	Kalendis	Kalendis	Kalendis	Kalendis
2	VI	IV ⎫	IV ⎫	IV ⎫
3	V ⎫	III ⎬ Nonas	III ⎬ Nonas	III ⎬ Nonas
4	IV ⎬ Nonas	pridie Nonas	pridie Nonas	pridie Nonas
5	III ⎭	Nonis	Nonis	Nonis
6	pridie Nonas	VIII ⎫	VIII ⎫	VIII ⎫
7	Nonis	VII ⎪	VII ⎪	VII ⎪
8	VIII ⎫	VI ⎬ ante	VI ⎬ ante	VI ⎬ ante
9	VII ⎪	V ⎭ Idus	V ⎭ Idus	V ⎭ Idus
10	VI ⎬ ante	IV	IV	IV
11	V ⎭ Idus	III	III	III
12	IV	pridie Idus	pridie Idus	pridie Idus
13	III	Idibus	Idibus	Idibus
14	pridie Idus	XIX	XVIII	XVI
15	Idibus	XVIII	XVII	XV
16	XVII	XVII	XVI	XIV
17	XVI	XVI	XV	XIII
18	XV	XV	XIV	XII
19	XIV	XIV	XIII	XI
20	XIII	XIII	XII ante Kalendas	X ante Kalendas
21	XII	XII ante Kalendas	XI (of the month	IX Martias
22	XI ante Kalendas	XI (of the month	X following)	VIII
23	X (of the month	X following)	IX	VII
24	IX following)	IX	VIII	*VI
25	VIII	VIII	VII	V
26	VII	VII	VI	IV
27	VI	VI	V	III
28	V	V	IV	pridie Kalendas
29	IV	IV	III	Martias
30	III	III	pridie Kalendas	
31	pridie Kalendas (Aprilis, Iunias, Sextilis, Novembris)	pridie Kalendas (Februarias, Septembris, Ianuarias)	(Maias, Quinctilis, Octobris, Decembris)	* (repeated in leap year)

Calendar for Any Year 1780–2040

To select the correct calendar for any year between 1780 and 2040, consult the index below
* leap year

1780 N*	1813 K	1846 I	1879 G	1912 D*	1945 C	1978 A	2011 M
1781 C	1814 M	1847 K	1880 J*	1913 G	1946 E	1979 C	2012 B*
1782 E	1815 A	1848 N*	1881 M	1914 I	1947 G	1980 F*	2013 E
1783 G	1816 D*	1849 C	1882 A	1915 K	1948 J*	1981 I	2014 G
1784 J*	1817 G	1850 E	1883 C	1916 N*	1949 M	1982 K	2015 I
1785 M	1818 I	1851 G	1884 F*	1917 C	1950 A	1983 M	2016 L*
1786 A	1819 K	1852 J*	1885 I	1918 E	1951 C	1984 B*	2017 A
1787 C	1820 N*	1853 M	1886 K	1919 G	1952 F*	1985 E	2018 C
1788 F*	1821 C	1854 A	1887 M	1920 J*	1953 I	1986 G	2019 E
1789 I	1822 E	1855 C	1888 B*	1921 M	1954 K	1987 I	2020 H*
1790 K	1823 G	1856 F*	1889 E	1922 A	1955 M	1988 L*	2021 K
1791 M	1824 J*	1857 I	1890 G	1923 C	1956 B*	1989 A	2022 M
1792 B*	1825 M	1858 K	1891 I	1924 F*	1957 E	1990 C	2023 A
1793 E	1826 A	1859 M	1892 L*	1925 I	1958 G	1991 E	2024 D*
1794 G	1827 C	1860 B*	1893 A	1926 K	1959 I	1992 H*	2025 G
1795 I	1828 F*	1861 E	1894 C	1927 M	1960 L*	1993 K	2026 I
1796 L*	1829 I	1862 G	1895 E	1928 B*	1961 A	1994 M	2027 K
1797 A	1830 K	1863 I	1896 H*	1929 E	1962 C	1995 A	2028 N*
1798 C	1831 M	1864 L*	1897 K	1930 G	1963 E	1996 D*	2029 C
1799 E	1832 B*	1865 A	1898 M	1931 I	1964 H*	1997 G	2030 E
1800 G	1833 E	1866 C	1899 A	1932 L*	1965 K	1998 I	2031 G
1801 I	1834 G	1867 E	1900 C	1933 A	1966 M	1999 K	2032 J*
1802 K	1835 I	1868 H*	1901 E	1934 C	1967 A	2000 N*	2033 M
1803 M	1836 L*	1869 K	1902 G	1935 E	1968 D*	2001 C	2034 A
1804 B*	1837 A	1870 M	1903 I	1936 H*	1969 G	2002 E	2035 C
1805 E	1838 C	1871 A	1904 L*	1937 K	1970 I	2003 G	2036 D*
1806 G	1839 E	1872 D*	1905 A	1938 M	1971 K	2004 J*	2037 I
1807 I	1840 H*	1873 G	1906 C	1939 A	1972 N*	2005 M	2038 K
1808 L*	1841 K	1874 I	1907 E	1940 D*	1973 C	2006 A	2039 M
1809 A	1842 M	1875 K	1908 H*	1941 G	1974 E	2007 C	2040 B*
1810 C	1843 A	1876 N*	1909 K	1942 I	1975 G	2008 F*	
1811 E	1844 D*	1877 C	1910 M	1943 K	1976 J*	2009 I	
1812 H*	1845 G	1878 E	1911 A	1944 N*	1977 M	2010 K	

A

January
- Sun. 1 8 15 22 29
- Mon. 2 9 16 23 30
- Tue. 3 10 17 24 31
- Wed. 4 11 18 25
- Thur. 5 12 19 26
- Fri. 6 13 20 27
- Sat. 7 14 21 28

February
- Sun. 5 12 19 26
- Mon. 6 13 20 27
- Tue. 7 14 21 28
- Wed. 1 8 15 22
- Thur. 2 9 16 23
- Fri. 3 10 17 24
- Sat. 4 11 18 25

March
- Sun. 5 12 19 26
- Mon. 6 13 20 27
- Tue. 7 14 21 28
- Wed. 1 8 15 22 29
- Thur. 2 9 16 23 30
- Fri. 3 10 17 24 31
- Sat. 4 11 18 25

April
- Sun. 2 9 16 23 30
- Mon. 3 10 17 24
- Tue. 4 11 18 25
- Wed. 5 12 19 26
- Thur. 6 13 20 27
- Fri. 7 14 21 28
- Sat. 1 8 15 22 29

May
- Sun. 7 14 21 28
- Mon. 1 8 15 22 29
- Tue. 2 9 16 23 30
- Wed. 3 10 17 24 31
- Thur. 4 11 18 25
- Fri. 5 12 19 26
- Sat. 6 13 20 27

June
- Sun. 4 11 18 25
- Mon. 5 12 19 26
- Tue. 6 13 20 27
- Wed. 7 14 21 28
- Thur. 1 8 15 22 29
- Fri. 2 9 16 23 30
- Sat. 3 10 17 24

July
- Sun. 2 9 16 23 30
- Mon. 3 10 17 24 31
- Tue. 4 11 18 25
- Wed. 5 12 19 26
- Thur. 6 13 20 27
- Fri. 7 14 21 28
- Sat. 1 8 15 22 29

August
- Sun. 6 13 20 27
- Mon. 7 14 21 28
- Tue. 1 8 15 22 29
- Wed. 2 9 16 23 30
- Thur. 3 10 17 24 31
- Fri. 4 11 18 25
- Sat. 5 12 19 26

September
- Sun. 3 10 17 24
- Mon. 4 11 18 25
- Tue. 5 12 19 26
- Wed. 6 13 20 27
- Thur. 7 14 21 28
- Fri. 1 8 15 22 29
- Sat. 2 9 16 23 30

October
- Sun. 1 8 15 22 29
- Mon. 2 9 16 23 30
- Tue. 3 10 17 24 31
- Wed. 4 11 18 25
- Thur. 5 12 19 26
- Fri. 6 13 20 27
- Sat. 7 14 21 28

November
- Sun. 5 12 19 26
- Mon. 6 13 20 27
- Tue. 7 14 21 28
- Wed. 1 8 15 22 29
- Thur. 2 9 16 23 30
- Fri. 3 10 17 24
- Sat. 4 11 18 25

December
- Sun. 3 10 17 24 31
- Mon. 4 11 18 25
- Tue. 5 12 19 26
- Wed. 6 13 20 27
- Thur. 7 14 21 28
- Fri. 1 8 15 22 29
- Sat. 2 9 16 23 30

Easter Days

March 26	1815, 1826, 1837, 1967, 1978, 1989
April 2	1809, 1893, 1899, 1961
April 9	1871, 1882, 1939, 1950, 2023, 2034
April 16	1786, 1797, 1843, 1854, 1865, 1911, 1922, 1933, 1995, 2006, 2017
April 23	1905

B (LEAP YEAR)

January
- Sun. 1 8 15 22 29
- Mon. 2 9 16 23 30
- Tue. 3 10 17 24 31
- Wed. 4 11 18 25
- Thur. 5 12 19 26
- Fri. 6 13 20 27
- Sat. 7 14 21 28

February
- Sun. 5 12 19 26
- Mon. 6 13 20 27
- Tue. 7 14 21 28
- Wed. 1 8 15 22 29
- Thur. 2 9 16 23
- Fri. 3 10 17 24
- Sat. 4 11 18 25

March
- Sun. 4 11 18 25
- Mon. 5 12 19 26
- Tue. 6 13 20 27
- Wed. 7 14 21 28
- Thur. 1 8 15 22 29
- Fri. 2 9 16 23 30
- Sat. 3 10 17 24 31

April
- Sun. 1 8 15 22 29
- Mon. 2 9 16 23 30
- Tue. 3 10 17 24
- Wed. 4 11 18 25
- Thur. 5 12 19 26
- Fri. 6 13 20 27
- Sat. 7 14 21 28

May
- Sun. 6 13 20 27
- Mon. 7 14 21 28
- Tue. 1 8 15 22 29
- Wed. 2 9 16 23 30
- Thur. 3 10 17 24 31
- Fri. 4 11 18 25
- Sat. 5 12 19 26

June
- Sun. 3 10 17 24
- Mon. 4 11 18 25
- Tue. 5 12 19 26
- Wed. 6 13 20 27
- Thur. 7 14 21 28
- Fri. 1 8 15 22 29
- Sat. 2 9 16 23 30

July
- Sun. 1 8 15 22 29
- Mon. 2 9 16 23 30
- Tue. 3 10 17 24 31
- Wed. 4 11 18 25
- Thur. 5 12 19 26
- Fri. 6 13 20 27
- Sat. 7 14 21 28

August
- Sun. 5 12 19 26
- Mon. 6 13 20 27
- Tue. 7 14 21 28
- Wed. 1 8 15 22 29
- Thur. 2 9 16 23 30
- Fri. 3 10 17 24 31
- Sat. 4 11 18 25

September
- Sun. 2 9 16 23 30
- Mon. 3 10 17 24
- Tue. 4 11 18 25
- Wed. 5 12 19 26
- Thur. 6 13 20 27
- Fri. 7 14 21 28
- Sat. 1 8 15 22 29

October
- Sun. 7 14 21 28
- Mon. 1 8 15 22 29
- Tue. 2 9 16 23 30
- Wed. 3 10 17 24 31
- Thur. 4 11 18 25
- Fri. 5 12 19 26
- Sat. 6 13 20 27

November
- Sun. 4 11 18 25
- Mon. 5 12 19 26
- Tue. 6 13 20 27
- Wed. 7 14 21 28
- Thur. 1 8 15 22 29
- Fri. 2 9 16 23 30
- Sat. 3 10 17 24

December
- Sun. 2 9 16 23 30
- Mon. 3 10 17 24 31
- Tue. 4 11 18 25
- Wed. 5 12 19 26
- Thur. 6 13 20 27
- Fri. 7 14 21 28
- Sat. 1 8 15 22 29

Easter Days

April 1	1804, 1888, 1956, 2040
April 8	1792, 1860, 1928, 2012
April 22	1832, 1984

C

	January	February	March
Sun.	7 14 21 28	4 11 18 25	4 11 18 25
Mon.	1 8 15 22 29	5 12 19 26	5 12 19 26
Tue.	2 9 16 23 30	6 13 20 27	6 13 20 27
Wed.	3 10 17 24 31	7 14 21 28	7 14 21 28
Thur.	4 11 18 25	1 8 15 22	1 8 15 22 29
Fri.	5 12 19 26	2 9 16 23	2 9 16 23 30
Sat.	6 13 20 27	3 10 17 24	3 10 17 24 31

	April	May	June
Sun.	1 8 15 22 29	6 13 20 27	3 10 17 24
Mon.	2 9 16 23 30	7 14 21 28	4 11 18 25
Tue.	3 10 17 24	1 8 15 22 29	5 12 19 26
Wed.	4 11 18 25	2 9 16 23 30	6 13 20 27
Thur.	5 12 19 26	3 10 17 24 31	7 14 21 28
Fri.	6 13 20 27	4 11 18 25	1 8 15 22 29
Sat.	7 14 21 28	5 12 19 26	2 9 16 23 30

	July	August	September
Sun.	1 8 15 22 29	5 12 19 26	2 9 16 23 30
Mon.	2 9 16 23 30	6 13 20 27	3 10 17 24
Tue.	3 10 17 24 31	7 14 21 28	4 11 18 25
Wed.	4 11 18 25	1 8 15 22 29	5 12 19 26
Thur.	5 12 19 26	2 9 16 23 30	6 13 20 27
Fri.	6 13 20 27	3 10 17 24 31	7 14 21 28
Sat.	7 14 21 28	4 11 18 25	1 8 15 22 29

	October	November	December
Sun.	7 14 21 28	4 11 18 25	2 9 16 23 30
Mon.	1 8 15 22 29	5 12 19 26	3 10 17 24 31
Tue.	2 9 16 23 30	6 13 20 27	4 11 18 25
Wed.	3 10 17 24 31	7 14 21 28	5 12 19 26
Thur.	4 11 18 25	1 8 15 22 29	6 13 20 27
Fri.	5 12 19 26	2 9 16 23 30	7 14 21 28
Sat.	6 13 20 27	3 10 17 24	1 8 15 22 29

EASTER DAYS

March 25	1883, 1894, 1951, 2035
April 1	1866, 1877, 1923, 1934, 1945, 2018, 2029
April 8	1787, 1798, 1849, 1855, 1917, 2007
April 15	1781, 1827, 1838, 1900, 1906, 1979, 1990, 2001
April 22	1810, 1821, 1962, 1973

E

	January	February	March
Sun.	6 13 20 27	3 10 17 24	3 10 17 24 31
Mon.	7 14 21 28	4 11 18 25	4 11 18 25
Tue.	1 8 15 22 29	5 12 19 26	5 12 19 26
Wed.	2 9 16 23 30	6 13 20 27	6 13 20 27
Thur.	3 10 17 24 31	7 14 21 28	7 14 21 28
Fri.	4 11 18 25	1 8 15 22	1 8 15 22 29
Sat.	5 12 19 26	2 9 16 23	2 9 16 23 30

	April	May	June
Sun.	7 14 21 28	5 12 19 26	2 9 16 23 30
Mon.	1 8 15 22 29	6 13 20 27	3 10 17 24
Tue.	2 9 16 23 30	7 14 21 28	4 11 18 25
Wed.	3 10 17 24	1 8 15 22 29	5 12 19 26
Thur.	4 11 18 25	2 9 16 23 30	6 13 20 27
Fri.	5 12 19 26	3 10 17 24 31	7 14 21 28
Sat.	6 13 20 27	4 11 18 25	1 8 15 22 29

	July	August	September
Sun.	7 14 21 28	4 11 18 25	1 8 15 22 29
Mon.	1 8 15 22 29	5 12 19 26	2 9 16 23 30
Tue.	2 9 16 23 30	6 13 20 27	3 10 17 24
Wed.	3 10 17 24 31	7 14 21 28	4 11 18 25
Thur.	4 11 18 25	1 8 15 22 29	5 12 19 26
Fri.	5 12 19 26	2 9 16 23 30	6 13 20 27
Sat.	6 13 20 27	3 10 17 24 31	7 14 21 28

	October	November	December
Sun.	6 13 20 27	3 10 17 24	1 8 15 22 29
Mon.	7 14 21 28	4 11 18 25	2 9 16 23 30
Tue.	1 8 15 22 29	5 12 19 26	3 10 17 24 31
Wed.	2 9 16 23 30	6 13 20 27	4 11 18 25
Thur.	3 10 17 24 31	7 14 21 28	5 12 19 26
Fri.	4 11 18 25	1 8 15 22 29	6 13 20 27
Sat.	5 12 19 26	2 9 16 23 30	7 14 21 28

EASTER DAYS

March 24	1799
March 31	1782, 1793, 1839, 1850, 1861, 1907
	1918, 1929, 1991, 2002, 2013
April 7	1822, 1833, 1901, 1985
April 14	1805, 1811, 1895, 1963, 1974
April 21	1867, 1878, 1889, 1935, 1946, 1957, 2019, 2030

D (LEAP YEAR)

	January	February	March
Sun.	7 14 21 28	4 11 18 25	3 10 17 24 31
Mon.	1 8 15 22 29	5 12 19 26	4 11 18 25
Tue.	2 9 16 23 30	6 13 20 27	5 12 19 26
Wed.	3 10 17 24 31	7 14 21 28	6 13 20 27
Thur.	4 11 18 25	1 8 15 22 29	7 14 21 28
Fri.	5 12 19 26	2 9 16 23	1 8 15 22 29
Sat.	6 13 20 27	3 10 17 24	2 9 16 23 30

	April	May	June
Sun.	7 14 21 28	5 12 19 26	2 9 16 23 30
Mon.	1 8 15 22 29	6 13 20 27	3 10 17 24
Tue.	2 9 16 23 30	7 14 21 28	4 11 18 25
Wed.	3 10 17 24	1 8 15 22 29	5 12 19 26
Thur.	4 11 18 25	2 9 16 23 30	6 13 20 27
Fri.	5 12 19 26	3 10 17 24 31	7 14 21 28
Sat.	6 13 20 27	4 11 18 25	1 8 15 22 29

	July	August	September
Sun.	7 14 21 28	4 11 18 25	1 8 15 22 29
Mon.	1 8 15 22 29	5 12 19 26	2 9 16 23 30
Tue.	2 9 16 23 30	6 13 20 27	3 10 17 24
Wed.	3 10 17 24 31	7 14 21 28	4 11 18 25
Thur.	4 11 18 25	1 8 15 22 29	5 12 19 26
Fri.	5 12 19 26	2 9 16 23 30	6 13 20 27
Sat.	6 13 20 27	3 10 17 24 31	7 14 21 28

	October	November	December
Sun.	6 13 20 27	3 10 17 24	1 8 15 22 29
Mon.	7 14 21 28	4 11 18 25	2 9 16 23 30
Tue.	1 8 15 22 29	5 12 19 26	3 10 17 24 31
Wed.	2 9 16 23 30	6 13 20 27	4 11 18 25
Thur.	3 10 17 24 31	7 14 21 28	5 12 19 26
Fri.	4 11 18 25	1 8 15 22 29	6 13 20 27
Sat.	5 12 19 26	2 9 16 23 30	7 14 21 28

EASTER DAYS

March 24	1940
March 31	1872, 2024
April 7	1844, 1912, 1996
April 14	1816, 1968

F (LEAP YEAR)

	January	February	March
Sun.	6 13 20 27	3 10 17 24	2 9 16 23 30
Mon.	7 14 21 28	4 11 18 25	3 10 17 24 31
Tue.	1 8 15 22 29	5 12 19 26	4 11 18 25
Wed.	2 9 16 23 30	6 13 20 27	5 12 19 26
Thur.	3 10 17 24 31	7 14 21 28	6 13 20 27
Fri.	4 11 18 25	1 8 15 22 29	7 14 21 28
Sat.	5 12 19 26	2 9 16 23	1 8 15 22 29

	April	May	June
Sun.	6 13 20 27	4 11 18 25	1 8 15 22 29
Mon.	7 14 21 28	5 12 19 26	2 9 16 23 30
Tue.	1 8 15 22 29	6 13 20 27	3 10 17 24
Wed.	2 9 16 23 30	7 14 21 28	4 11 18 25
Thur.	3 10 17 24	1 8 15 22 29	5 12 19 26
Fri.	4 11 18 25	2 9 16 23 30	6 13 20 27
Sat.	5 12 19 26	3 10 17 24 31	7 14 21 28

	July	August	September
Sun.	6 13 20 27	3 10 17 24 31	7 14 21 28
Mon.	7 14 21 28	4 11 18 25	1 8 15 22 29
Tue.	1 8 15 22 29	5 12 19 26	2 9 16 23 30
Wed.	2 9 16 23 30	6 13 20 27	3 10 17 24
Thur.	3 10 17 24 31	7 14 21 28	4 11 18 25
Fri.	4 11 18 25	1 8 15 22 29	5 12 19 26
Sat.	5 12 19 26	2 9 16 23 30	6 13 20 27

	October	November	December
Sun.	5 12 19 26	2 9 16 23 30	7 14 21 28
Mon.	6 13 20 27	3 10 17 24	1 8 15 22 29
Tue.	7 14 21 28	4 11 18 25	2 9 16 23 30
Wed.	1 8 15 22 29	5 12 19 26	3 10 17 24 31
Thur.	2 9 16 23 30	6 13 20 27	4 11 18 25
Fri.	3 10 17 24 31	7 14 21 28	5 12 19 26
Sat.	4 11 18 25	1 8 15 22 29	6 13 20 27

EASTER DAYS

March 23	1788, 1856, 2008
April 6	1828, 1980
April 13	1884, 1952, 2036
April 20	1924

G

	January	February	March
Sun.	5 12 19 26	2 9 16 23	2 9 16 23 30
Mon.	6 13 20 27	3 10 17 24	3 10 17 24 31
Tue.	7 14 21 28	4 11 18 25	4 11 18 25
Wed.	1 8 15 22 29	5 12 19 26	5 12 19 26
Thur.	2 9 16 23 30	6 13 20 27	6 13 20 27
Fri.	3 10 17 24 31	7 14 21 28	7 14 21 28
Sat.	4 11 18 25	1 8 15 22	1 8 15 22 29

	April	May	June
Sun.	6 13 20 27	4 11 18 25	1 8 15 22 29
Mon.	7 14 21 28	5 12 19 26	2 9 16 23 30
Tue.	1 8 15 22 29	6 13 20 27	3 10 17 24
Wed.	2 9 16 23 30	7 14 21 28	4 11 18 25
Thur.	3 10 17 24	1 8 15 22 29	5 12 19 26
Fri.	4 11 18 25	2 9 16 23 30	6 13 20 27
Sat.	5 12 19 26	3 10 17 24 31	7 14 21 28

	July	August	September
Sun.	6 13 20 27	3 10 17 24 31	7 14 21 28
Mon.	7 14 21 28	4 11 18 25	1 8 15 22 29
Tue.	1 8 15 22 29	5 12 19 26	2 9 16 23 30
Wed.	2 9 16 23 30	6 13 20 27	3 10 17 24
Thur.	3 10 17 24 31	7 14 21 28	4 11 18 25
Fri.	4 11 18 25	1 8 15 22 29	5 12 19 26
Sat.	5 12 19 26	2 9 16 23 30	6 13 20 27

	October	November	December
Sun.	5 12 19 26	2 9 16 23 30	7 14 21 28
Mon.	6 13 20 27	3 10 17 24	1 8 15 22 29
Tue.	7 14 21 28	4 11 18 25	2 9 16 23 30
Wed.	1 8 15 22 29	5 12 19 26	3 10 17 24 31
Thur.	2 9 16 23 30	6 13 20 27	4 11 18 25
Fri.	3 10 17 24 31	7 14 21 28	5 12 19 26
Sat.	4 11 18 25	1 8 15 22 29	6 13 20 27

EASTER DAYS

March 23	1845, 1913
March 30	1823, 1834, 1902, 1975, 1986, 1997
April 6	1806, 1817, 1890, 1947, 1958, 1969
April 13	1800, 1873, 1879, 1941, 2031
April 20	1783, 1794, 1851, 1862, 1919, 1930, 2003, 2014, 2025

I

	January	February	March
Sun.	4 11 18 25	1 8 15 22	1 8 15 22 29
Mon.	5 12 19 26	2 9 16 23	2 9 16 23 30
Tue.	6 13 20 27	3 10 17 24	3 10 17 24 31
Wed.	7 14 21 28	4 11 18 25	4 11 18 25
Thur.	1 8 15 22 29	5 12 19 26	5 12 19 26
Fri.	2 9 16 23 30	6 13 20 27	6 13 20 27
Sat.	3 10 17 24 31	7 14 21 28	7 14 21 28

	April	May	June
Sun.	5 12 19 26	3 10 17 24 31	7 14 21 28
Mon.	6 13 20 27	4 11 18 25	1 8 15 22 29
Tue.	7 14 21 28	5 12 19 26	2 9 16 23 30
Wed.	1 8 15 22 29	6 13 20 27	3 10 17 24
Thur.	2 9 16 23 30	7 14 21 28	4 11 18 25
Fri.	3 10 17 24	1 8 15 22 29	5 12 19 26
Sat.	4 11 18 25	2 9 16 23 30	6 13 20 27

	July	August	September
Sun.	5 12 19 26	2 9 16 23 30	6 13 20 27
Mon.	6 13 20 27	3 10 17 24 31	7 14 21 28
Tue.	7 14 21 28	4 11 18 25	1 8 15 22 29
Wed.	1 8 15 22 29	5 12 19 26	2 9 16 23 30
Thur.	2 9 16 23 30	6 13 20 27	3 10 17 24
Fri.	3 10 17 24 31	7 14 21 28	4 11 18 25
Sat.	4 11 18 25	1 8 15 22 29	5 12 19 26

	October	November	December
Sun.	4 11 18 25	1 8 15 22 29	6 13 20 27
Mon.	5 12 19 26	2 9 16 23 30	7 14 21 28
Tue.	6 13 20 27	3 10 17 24	1 8 15 22 29
Wed.	7 14 21 28	4 11 18 25	2 9 16 23 30
Thur.	1 8 15 22 29	5 12 19 26	3 10 17 24 31
Fri.	2 9 16 23 30	6 13 20 27	4 11 18 25
Sat.	3 10 17 24 31	7 14 21 28	5 12 19 26

EASTER DAYS

March 22	1818
March 29	1807, 1891, 1959, 1970
April 5	1795, 1801, 1863, 1874, 1885, 1931, 1942, 1953, 2015, 2026, 2037
April 12	1789, 1846, 1857, 1903, 1914, 1925, 1998, 2009
April 19	1829, 1835, 1981, 1987

H (LEAP YEAR)

	January	February	March
Sun.	5 12 19 26	2 9 16 23	1 8 15 22 29
Mon.	6 13 20 27	3 10 17 24	2 9 16 23 30
Tue.	7 14 21 28	4 11 18 25	3 10 17 24 31
Wed.	1 8 15 22 29	5 12 19 26	4 11 18 25
Thur.	2 9 16 23 30	6 13 20 27	5 12 19 26
Fri.	3 10 17 24 31	7 14 21 28	6 13 20 27
Sat.	4 11 18 25	1 8 15 22 29	7 14 21 28

	April	May	June
Sun.	5 12 19 26	3 10 17 24 31	7 14 21 28
Mon.	6 13 20 27	4 11 18 25	1 8 15 22 29
Tue.	7 14 21 28	5 12 19 26	2 9 16 23 30
Wed.	1 8 15 22 29	6 13 20 27	3 10 17 24
Thur.	2 9 16 23 30	7 14 21 28	4 11 18 25
Fri.	3 10 17 24	1 8 15 22 29	5 12 19 26
Sat.	4 11 18 25	2 9 16 23 30	6 13 20 27

	July	August	September
Sun.	5 12 19 26	2 9 16 23 30	6 13 20 27
Mon.	6 13 20 27	3 10 17 24 31	7 14 21 28
Tue.	7 14 21 28	4 11 18 25	1 8 15 22 29
Wed.	1 8 15 22 29	5 12 19 26	2 9 16 23 30
Thur.	2 9 16 23 30	6 13 20 27	3 10 17 24
Fri.	3 10 17 24 31	7. 14 21 28	4 11 18 25
Sat.	4 11 18 25	1 8 15 22 29	5 12 19 26

	October	November	December
Sun.	4 11 18 25	1 8 15 22 29	6 13 20 27
Mon.	5 12 19 26	2 9 16 23 30	7 14 21 28
Tue.	6 13 20 27	3 10 17 24	1 8 15 22 29
Wed.	7 14 21 28	4 11 18 25	2 9 16 23 30
Thur.	1 8 15 22 29	5 12 19 26	3 10 17 24 31
Fri.	2 9 16 23 30	6 13 20 27	4 11 18 25
Sat.	3 10 17 24 31	7 14 21 28	5 12 19 26

EASTER DAYS

March 29	1812, 1964
April 5	1896
April 12	1868, 1936, 2020
April 19	1840, 1908, 1992

J (LEAP YEAR)

	January	February	March
Sun.	4 11 18 25	1 8 15 22 29	7 14 21 28
Mon.	5 12 19 26	2 9 16 23	1 8 15 22 29
Tue.	6 13 20 27	3 10 17 24	2 9 16 23 30
Wed.	7 14 21 28	4 11 18 25	3 10 17 24 31
Thur.	1 8 15 22 29	5 12 19 26	4 11 18 25
Fri.	2 9 16 23 30	6 13 20 27	5 12 19 26
Sat.	3 10 17 24 31	7 14 21 28	6 13 20 27

	April	May	June
Sun.	4 11 18 25	2 9 16 23 30	6 13 20 27
Mon.	5 12 19 26	3 10 17 24 31	7 14 21 28
Tue.	6 13 20 27	4 11 18 25	1 8 15 22 29
Wed.	7 14 21 28	5 12 19 26	2 9 16 23 30
Thur.	1 8 15 22 29	6 13 20 27	3 10 17 24
Fri.	2 9 16 23 30	7 14 21 28	4 11 18 25
Sat.	3 10 17 24	1 8 15 22 29	5 12 19 26

	July	August	September
Sun.	4 11 18 25	1 8 15 22 29	5 12 19 26
Mon.	5 12 19 26	2 9 16 23 30	6 13 20 27
Tue.	6 13 20 27	3 10 17 24 31	7 14 21 28
Wed.	7 14 21 28	4 11 18 25	1 8 15 22 29
Thur.	1 8 15 22 29	5 12 19 26	2 9 16 23 30
Fri.	2 9 16 23 30	6 13 20 27	3 10 17 24
Sat.	3 10 17 24 31	7 14 21 28	4 11 18 25

	October	November	December
Sun.	3 10 17 24 31	7 14 21 28	5 12 19 26
Mon.	4 11 18 25	1 8 15 22 29	6 13 20 27
Tue.	5 12 19 26	2 9 16 23 30	7 14 21 28
Wed.	6 13 20 27	3 10 17 24	1 8 15 22 29
Thur.	7 14 21 28	4 11 18 25	2 9 16 23 30
Fri.	1 8 15 22 29	5 12 19 26	3 10 17 24 31
Sat.	2 9 16 23 30	6 13 20 27	4 11 18 25

EASTER DAYS

March 28	1880, 1948, 2032
April 4	1920
April 11	1784, 1852, 2004
April 18	1824, 1976

K

	January	February	March
Sun.	3 10 17 24 31	7 14 21 28	7 14 21 28
Mon.	4 11 18 25	1 8 15 22	1 8 15 22 29
Tue.	5 12 19 26	2 9 16 23	2 9 16 23 30
Wed.	6 13 20 27	3 10 17 24	3 10 17 24 31
Thur.	7 14 21 28	4 11 18 25	4 11 18 25
Fri.	1 8 15 22 29	5 12 19 26	5 12 19 26
Sat.	2 9 16 23 30	6 13 20 27	6 13 20 27
	April	May	June
Sun.	4 11 18 25	2 9 16 23 30	6 13 20 27
Mon.	5 12 19 26	3 10 17 24 31	7 14 21 28
Tue.	6 13 20 27	4 11 18 25	1 8 15 22 29
Wed.	7 14 21 28	5 12 19 26	2 9 16 23 30
Thur.	1 8 15 22 29	6 13 20 27	3 10 17 24
Fri.	2 9 16 23 30	7 14 21 28	4 11 18 25
Sat.	3 10 17 24	1 8 15 22 29	5 12 19 26
	July	August	September
Sun.	4 11 18 25	1 8 15 22 29	5 12 19 26
Mon.	5 12 19 26	2 9 16 23 30	6 13 20 27
Tue.	6 13 20 27	3 10 17 24 31	7 14 21 28
Wed.	7 14 21 28	4 11 18 25	1 8 15 22 29
Thur.	1 8 15 22 29	5 12 19 26	2 9 16 23 30
Fri.	2 9 16 23 30	6 13 20 27	3 10 17 24
Sat.	3 10 17 24 31	7 14 21 28	4 11 18 25
	October	November	December
Sun.	3 10 17 24 31	7 14 21 28	5 12 19 26
Mon.	4 11 18 25	1 8 15 22 29	6 13 20 27
Tue.	5 12 19 26	2 9 16 23 30	7 14 21 28
Wed.	6 13 20 27	3 10 17 24	1 8 15 22 29
Thur.	7 14 21 28	4 11 18 25	2 9 16 23 30
Fri.	1 8 15 22 29	5 12 19 26	3 10 17 24 31
Sat.	2 9 16 23 30	6 13 20 27	4 11 18 25

EASTER DAYS

March 28	1869, 1875, 1937, 2027
April 4	1790, 1847, 1858, 1915, 1926, 1999, 2010, 2021
April 11	1819, 1830, 1841, 1909, 1971, 1982, 1993
April 18	1802, 1813, 1897, 1954, 1965
April 25	1886, 1943, 2038

M

	January	February	March
Sun.	2 9 16 23 30	6 13 20 27	6 13 20 27
Mon.	3 10 17 24 31	7 14 21 28	7 14 21 28
Tue.	4 11 18 25	1 8 15 22	1 8 15 22 29
Wed.	5 12 19 26	2 9 16 23	2 9 16 23 30
Thur.	6 13 20 27	3 10 17 24	3 10 17 24 31
Fri.	7 14 21 28	4 11 18 25	4 11 18 25
Sat.	1 8 15 22 29	5 12 19 26	5 12 19 26
	April	May	June
Sun.	3 10 17 24	1 8 15 22 29	5 12 19 26
Mon.	4 11 18 25	2 9 16 23 30	6 13 20 27
Tue.	5 12 19 26	3 10 17 24 31	7 14 21 28
Wed.	6 13 20 27	4 11 18 25	1 8 15 22 29
Thur.	7 14 21 28	5 12 19 26	2 9 16 23 30
Fri.	1 8 15 22 29	6 13 20 27	3 10 17 24
Sat.	2 9 16 23 30	7 14 21 28	4 11 18 25
	July	August	September
Sun.	3 10 17 24 31	7 14 21 28	4 11 18 25
Mon.	4 11 18 25	1 8 15 22 29	5 12 19 26
Tue.	5 12 19 26	2 9 16 23 30	6 13 20 27
Wed.	6 13 20 27	3 10 17 24 31	7 14 21 28
Thur.	7 14 21 28	4 11 18 25	1 8 15 22 29
Fri.	1 8 15 22 29	5 12 19 26	2 9 16 23 30
Sat.	2 9 16 23 30	6 13 20 27	3 10 17 24
	October	November	December
Sun.	2 9 16 23 30	6 13 20 27	4 11 18 25
Mon.	3 10 17 24 31	7 14 21 28	5 12 19 26
Tue.	4 11 18 25	1 8 15 22 29	6 13 20 27
Wed.	5 12 19 26	2 9 16 23 30	7 14 21 28
Thur.	6 13 20 27	3 10 17 24	1 8 15 22 29
Fri.	7 14 21 28	4 11 18 25	2 9 16 23 30
Sat.	1 8 15 22 29	5 12 19 26	3 10 17 24 31

EASTER DAYS

March 27	1785, 1842, 1853, 1910, 1921, 2005
April 3	1825, 1831, 1983, 1994
April 10	1803, 1814, 1887, 1898, 1955, 1966, 1977, 2039
April 17	1870, 1881, 1927, 1938, 1949, 2022, 2033
April 24	1791, 1859, 2011

L (LEAP YEAR)

	January	February	March
Sun.	3 10 17 24 31	7 14 21 28	6 13 20 27
Mon.	4 11 18 25	1 8 15 22 29	7 14 21 28
Tue.	5 12 19 26	2 9 16 23	1 8 15 22 29
Wed.	6 13 20 27	3 10 17 24	2 9 16 23 30
Thur.	7 14 21 28	4 11 18 25	3 10 17 24 31
Fri.	1 8 15 22 29	5 12 19 26	4 11 18 25
Sat.	2 9 16 23 30	6 13 20 27	5 12 19 26
	April	May	June
Sun.	3 10 17 24	1 8 15 22 29	5 12 19 26
Mon.	4 11 18 25	2 9 16 23 30	6 13 20 27
Tue.	5 12 19 26	3 10 17 24 31	7 14 21 28
Wed.	6 13 20 27	4 11 18 25	1 8 15 22 29
Thur.	7 14 21 28	5 12 19 26	2 9 16 23 30
Fri.	1 8 15 22 29	6 13 20 27	3 10 17 24
Sat.	2 9 16 23 30	7 14 21 28	4 11 18 25
	July	August	September
Sun.	3 10 17 24 31	7 14 21 28	4 11 18 25
Mon.	4 11 18 25	1 8 15 22 29	5 12 19 26
Tue.	5 12 19 26	2 9 16 23 30	6 13 20 27
Wed.	6 13 20 27	3 10 17 24 31	7 14 21 28
Thur.	7 14 21 28	4 11 18 25	1 8 15 22 29
Fri.	1 8 15 22 29	5 12 19 26	2 9 16 23 30
Sat.	2 9 16 23 30	6 13 20 27	3 10 17 24
	October	November	December
Sun.	2 9 16 23 30	6 13 20 27	4 11 18 25
Mon.	3 10 17 24 31	7 14 21 28	5 12 19 26
Tue.	4 11 18 25	1 8 15 22 29	6 13 20 27
Wed.	5 12 19 26	2 9 16 23 30	7 14 21 28
Thur.	6 13 20 27	3 10 17 24	1 8 15 22 29
Fri.	7 14 21 28	4 11 18 25	2 9 16 23 30
Sat.	1 8 15 22 29	5 12 19 26	3 10 17 24 31

EASTER DAYS

March 27	1796, 1864, 1932, 2016
April 3	1836, 1904, 1988
April 17	1808, 1892, 1960

N (LEAP YEAR)

	January	February	March
Sun.	2 9 16 23 30	6 13 20 27	5 12 19 26
Mon.	3 10 17 24 31	7 14 21 28	6 13 20 27
Tue.	4 11 18 25	1 8 15 22 29	7 14 21 28
Wed.	5 12 19 26	2 9 16 23	1 8 15 22 29
Thur.	6 13 20 27	3 10 17 24	2 9 16 23 30
Fri.	7 14 21 28	4 11 18 25	3 10 17 24 31
Sat.	1 8 15 22 29	5 12 19 26	4 11 18 25
	April	May	June
Sun.	2 9 16 23 30	7 14 21 28	4 11 18 25
Mon.	3 10 17 24	1 8 15 22 29	5 12 19 26
Tue.	4 11 18 25	2 9 16 23 30	6 13 20 27
Wed.	5 12 19 26	3 10 17 24 31	7 14 21 28
Thur.	6 13 20 27	4 11 18 25	1 8 15 22 29
Fri.	7 14 21 28	5 12 19 26	2 9 16 23 30
Sat.	1 8 15 22 29	6 13 20 27	3 10 17 24
	July	August	September
Sun.	2 9 16 23 30	6 13 20 27	3 10 17 24
Mon.	3 10 17 24 31	7 14 21 28	4 11 18 25
Tue.	4 11 18 25	1 8 15 22 29	5 12 19 26
Wed.	5 12 19 26	2 9 16 23 30	6 13 20 27
Thur.	6 13 20 27	3 10 17 24 31	7 14 21 28
Fri.	7 14 21 28	4 11 18 25	1 8 15 22 29
Sat.	1 8 15 22 29	5 12 19 26	2 9 16 23 30
	October	November	December
Sun.	1 8 15 22 29	5 12 19 26	3 10 17 24 31
Mon.	2 9 16 23 30	6 13 20 27	4 11 18 25
Tue.	3 10 17 24 31	7 14 21 28	5 12 19 26
Wed.	4 11 18 25	1 8 15 22 29	6 13 20 27
Thur.	5 12 19 26	2 9 16 23 30	7 14 21 28
Fri.	6 13 20 27	3 10 17 24	1 8 15 22 29
Sat.	7 14 21 28	4 11 18 25	2 9 16 23 30

EASTER DAYS

March 26	1780
April 2	1820, 1972
April 9	1944
April 16	2028
April 23	1848, 1916, 2000

GEOLOGICAL TIME

The earth is thought to have come into existence approximately 4,600 million years ago, but for nearly half this time, the Archean era, it was uninhabited. Life is generally believed to have emerged in the succeeding Proterozoic era. The Archean and the Proterozoic eras are often together referred to as the Precambrian.

Although primitive forms of life, e.g. algae and bacteria, existed during the Proterozoic era, it is not until the strata of Palaeozoic rocks is reached that abundant fossilized remains appear.

Since the Precambrian, there have been three great geological eras:

PALAEOZOIC ('ancient life')
*c.*570–*c.*245 million years ago

Cambrian – Mainly sandstones, slate and shales; limestones in Scotland. Shelled fossils and invertebrates, e.g. trilobites and brachiopods appear
Ordovician – Mainly shales and mudstones, e.g. in north Wales; limestones in Scotland. First fishes
Silurian – Shales, mudstones and some limestones, found mostly in Wales and southern Scotland
Devonian – Old red sandstone, shale, limestone and slate, e.g. in south Wales and the West Country
Carboniferous – Coal-bearing rocks, millstone grit, limestone and shale. First traces of land-living life
Permian – Marls, sandstones and clays. First reptile fossils

There were two great phases of mountain building in the Palaeozoic era: the Caledonian, characterized in Britain by NE–SW lines of hills and valleys; and the later Hercynian, widespread in west Germany and adjacent areas, and in Britain exemplified in E.–W. lines of hills and valleys.

The end of the Palaeozoic era was marked by the extensive glaciations of the Permian period in the southern continents and the decline of amphibians. It was succeeded by an era of warm conditions.

MESOZOIC ('middle forms of life')
*c.*245–*c.*65 million years ago

Triassic – Mostly sandstone, e.g. in the West Midlands
Jurassic – Mainly limestones and clays, typically displayed in the Jura mountains, and in England in a NE–SW belt from Lincolnshire and the Wash to the Severn and the Dorset coast
Cretaceous – Mainly chalk, clay and sands, e.g. in Kent and Sussex

Giant reptiles were dominant during the Mesozoic era, but it was at this time that marsupial mammals first appeared, as well as *Archaeopteryx lithographica*, the earliest known species of bird. Coniferous trees and flowering plants also developed during the era and, with the birds and the mammals, were the main species to survive into the Cenozoic era. The giant reptiles became extinct.

CENOZOIC ('recent life')
from *c.*65 million years ago

Palaeocene ⎫ The emergence of new forms of life, includ-
Eocene   ⎬ ing existing species
Oligocene – Fossils of a few still existing species
Miocene – Fossil remains show a balance of existing and extinct species
Pliocene – Fossil remains show a majority of still existing species
Pleistocene – The majority of remains are those of still existing species

Holocene – The present, post-glacial period. Existing species only, except for a few exterminated by man

In the last 25 million years, from the Miocene through the Pliocene periods, the Alpine-Himalayan and the circum-Pacific phases of mountain building reached their climax. During the Pleistocene period ice-sheets repeatedly locked up masses of water as land ice; its weight depressed the land, but the locking-up of the water lowered the sea-level by 100–200 metres. The glaciations and interglacials of the Ice Age are difficult to date and classify, but recent scientific opinion considers the Pleistocene period to have begun approximately 1.64 million years ago. The last glacial retreat, merging into the Holocene period, was 10,000 years ago.

HUMAN DEVELOPMENT

Any consideration of the history of mankind must start with the fact that all members of the human race belong to one species of animal, i.e. *Homo sapiens*, the definition of a species being in biological terms that all its members can interbreed. As a species of mammal it is possible to group man with other similar types, known as the primates. Amongst these is found a sub-group, the apes, which includes, in addition to man, the chimpanzees, gorillas, orang-utans and gibbons. All lack a tail, have shoulder blades at the back, and a Y-shaped chewing pattern on the surface of their molars, as well as showing the more general primate characteristics of four incisors, a thumb which is able to touch the fingers of the same hand, and finger and toe nails instead of claws. The factors available to scientific study suggest that human beings have chimpanzees and gorillas as their nearest relatives in the animal world. However, there remains the possibility that there once lived creatures, now extinct, which were closer to modern man than the chimpanzees and gorillas, and which shared with modern man the characteristics of having flat faces (i.e. the absence of a pronounced muzzle), being bipedal, and possessing large brains.

There are two broad groups of extinct apes recognized by specialists. The ramapithecines, the remains of which, mainly jaw fragments, have been found in east Africa, Asia, and Turkey. They lived about 14 to 8 million years ago, and from the evidence of their teeth it seems they chewed more in the manner of modern man than the other presently living apes. The second group, the australo-pithecines, have left more numerous remains amongst which sub-groups may be detected, although the geographic spread is limited to south and east Africa. Living between 5 and 1.5 million years ago, they were closer relatives of modern man to the extent that they walked upright, did not have an extensive muzzle and had similar types of pre-molars. The first australopithecine remains were recognized at Taung in South Africa in 1924 and subsequent discoveries include those at the Olduvai Gorge in Tanzania. The most impressive discovery was made at Hadar, Ethiopia, in 1974 when about half a skeleton, known as 'Lucy', was found.

Also in east Africa, between 2 million and 1.5 million years ago, lived a hominid group which not only walked upright, had a flat face, and a large brain case, but also made simple pebble and flake stone tools. On present evidence these habilines seem to have been the first people to make tools, however crude. This facility is related to the larger brain size and human beings are the only animals to make implements to be used in other processes. These early pebble tool users, because of their distinctive

GEOLOGICAL TIME

Era	Period	Epoch	Date began*	Evolutionary stages
Cenozoic	Quaternary	Holocene	0.01	Man
Cenozoic	Quaternary	Pleistocene	1.64	Man
Cenozoic	Tertiary	Pliocene	5.2	
Cenozoic	Tertiary	Miocene	23.3	
Cenozoic	Tertiary	Oligocene	35.4	
Cenozoic	Tertiary	Eocene	56.5	
Cenozoic	Tertiary	Palaeocene	65.0	
Mesozoic	Cretaceous		145.6	
Mesozoic	Jurassic		208.0	First birds
Mesozoic	Triassic		245.0	First mammals
Palaeozoic	Permian		290.0	First reptiles
Palaeozoic	Carboniferous		362.5	First amphibians and insects
Palaeozoic	Devonian		408.5	
Palaeozoic	Silurian		439.0	
Palaeozoic	Ordovician		510.0	First fishes
Palaeozoic	Cambrian		570.0	First invertebrates
Precambrian			4,600.0	First primitive life forms, e.g. algae and bacteria

*millions of years ago

characteristics, have been grouped as a separate sub-species, now extinct, of the genus *Homo* and are known as *Homo habilis*.

The use of fire, again a human characteristic, is associated with another group of extinct hominids whose remains, about a million years old, are found in south and east Africa, China, Indonesia, north Africa and Europe. Mastery of the techniques of making fire probably helped the colonization of the colder northern areas and in this respect the site of Vertesszollos in Hungary is of particular importance. *Homo erectus* is the name given to this group of fossils and it includes a number of famous individual discoveries, e.g. Solo Man, Heidelberg Man, and especially Peking Man who lived at the cave site at Choukoutien which has yielded evidence of fire and burnt bone.

The well-known group Neanderthal Man, or *Homo sapiens neandertalensis*, is an extinct form of modern man who lived between about 100,000 and 40,000 years ago, thus spanning the last Ice Age. Indeed, its ability to adapt to the cold climate on the edge of the ice-sheets is one of its characteristic features, the remains being found only in Europe, Asia and the Middle East. Complete neanderthal skeletons were found during excavations at Tabun in Israel, together with evidence of tool-making and the use of fire. Distinguished by very large brains, it seems that neanderthal man was the first to develop recognizable social customs, especially deliberate burial rites. Why the neanderthalers became extinct is not clear but it may be connected with the climatic changes at the end of the Ice Ages, which would have seriously affected their food supplies; possibly they became too specialized for their own good.

The Swanscombe skull is the only known human fossil remains found in England. Some specialists see Swanscombe Man (or, more probably, woman) as a neanderthaler. Others group these remains together with the Steinheim skull from Germany, seeing both as a separate sub-species. There is too little evidence as yet on which to form a final judgement.

Modern Man, *Homo sapiens sapiens*, the surviving sub-species of *Homo sapiens*, had evolved to our present physical condition and had colonized much of the world by about 30,000 years ago. There are many previously distinguished individual specimens, e.g. Cromagnon Man, which may now be grouped together as *Homo sapiens sapiens*. It was modern man who spread to the American continent by crossing the landbridge between Siberia and Alaska and thence moved south through North America and into South America. Equally it is modern man who over the last 30,000 years has been responsible for the major developments in technology, art and civilization generally.

One of the problems for those studying fossil man is the lack in many cases of sufficient quantities of fossil bone for analysis. It is important that theories should be tested against evidence, rather than the evidence being made to fit the theory. The Piltdown hoax is a well-known example of 'fossils' being forged to fit what was seen in some quarters as the correct theory of man's evolution.

CULTURAL DEVELOPMENT

The Eurocentric bias of early archaeologists meant that the search for a starting point for the development and transmission of cultural ideas, especially by migration, trade and warfare, concentrated unduly on Europe and the Near East. The Three Age system, whereby pre-history was divided into a Stone Age, a Bronze Age and an Iron Age, was devised by Christian Thomsen, curator of the National Museum of Denmark in the early 19th century, to facilitate the classification of the museum's collections.

The descriptive adjectives referred to the materials from which the implements and weapons were made and came to be regarded as the dominant features of the societies to which they related. The refinement of the Three Age system once dominated archaeological thought and remains a generally accepted concept in the popular mind. However, it is now seen by archaeologists as an inadequate model for human development.

Common sense suggests that there were no complete breaks between one so-called Age and another, any more than contemporaries would have regarded 1485 as a complete break between medieval and modern English history. Nor can the Three Age system be applied universally. In some areas it is necessary to insert a Copper Age, while in Africa south of the Sahara there would seem to be no Bronze Age at all; in Australia, Old Stone Age societies survived, while in South America, New Stone Age communities existed into modern times. The civilizations in other parts of the world clearly invalidate a Eurocentric theory of human development.

The concept of the 'Neolithic revolution', associated with the domestication of plants and animals, was a development of particular importance in the human cultural pattern. It reflected change from the primitive hunter/gatherer economies to a more settled agricultural way of life and therefore, so the argument goes, made possible the development of urban civilization. However, it can no longer be argued that this 'revolution' took place only in one area from which all development stemmed. Though it appears that the cultivation of wheat and barley was first undertaken, together with the domestication of cattle and goats/sheep in the Fertile Crescent (the area bounded by the rivers Tigris and Euphrates), there is evidence that rice was first deliberately planted and pigs domesticated in south-east Asia, maize first cultivated in Central America and llamas first domesticated in South America. It has been recognized in recent years that cultural changes can take place independently of each other in different parts of the world at different rates and different times. There is no need for a general diffusionist theory.

Although scholars will continue to study the particular societies which interest them, it may be possible to obtain a reliable chronological framework, in absolute terms of years, against which the cultural development of any particular area may be set. The development and refinement of radio-carbon dating and other scientific methods of producing absolute chronologies is enabling the cross-referencing of societies to be undertaken. As the techniques of dating become more rigorous in application and the number of scientifically obtained dates increases, the attainment of an absolute chronology for prehistoric societies throughout the world comes closer to being achieved.

Tidal Tables

CONSTANTS

The constant tidal difference may be used in conjunction with the time of high water at a standard port shown in the predictions data (pages 98–103) to find the time of high water at any of the ports or places listed below.

These tidal differences are very approximate and should be used only as a guide to the time of high water at the places below. More precise local data should be obtained for navigational and other nautical purposes.

All data allow high water time to be found in Greenwich Mean Time; this applies also to data for the months when British Summer Time is in operation and the hour's time difference should be allowed for. Ports marked * are in a different time zone and the standard time zone difference also needs to be added/subtracted to give local time.

EXAMPLE

Required time of high water at Stranraer at 2 January 1999
Appropriate time of high water at Greenock

Afternoon tide 2 January	1227 hrs
Tidal difference	−0020 hrs
High water at Stranraer	1207 hrs

The columns headed 'Springs' and 'Neaps' show the height, in metres, of the tide above datum for mean high water springs and mean high water neaps respectively.

Port	Diff. h m	Springs m	Neaps m
Aberdeen	Leith −1 19	4.3	3.4
*Antwerp (Prosperpolder)	London +0 50	5.8	4.8
Ardrossan	Greenock −0 15	3.2	2.6
Avonmouth	London −6 45	13.2	9.8
Ayr	Greenock −0 25	3.0	2.5
Barrow (Docks)	Liverpool 0 00	9.3	7.1
Belfast	London −2 47	3.5	3.0
Blackpool	Liverpool −0 10	8.9	7.0
*Boulogne	London −2 44	8.9	7.2
*Calais	London −2 04	7.2	5.9
*Cherbourg	London −6 00	6.4	5.0
Cobh	Liverpool −5 55	4.2	3.2
Cowes	London −2 38	4.2	3.5
Dartmouth	London +4 25	4.9	3.8
*Dieppe	London −3 03	9.3	7.3
Douglas, IOM	Liverpool −0 04	6.9	5.4
Dover	London −2 52	6.7	5.3
Dublin	London −2 05	4.1	3.4
Dun Laoghaire	London −2 10	4.1	3.4
*Dunkirk	London −1 54	6.0	4.9
Fishguard	Liverpool −4 01	4.8	3.4
Fleetwood	Liverpool 0 00	9.2	7.3
*Flushing	London −0 15	4.7	3.9
Folkestone	London −3 04	7.1	5.7
Galway	Liverpool −6 08	5.1	3.9
Glasgow	Greenock +0 26	4.7	4.0
Harwich	London −2 06	4.0	3.4
*Le Havre	London −3 55	7.9	6.6
Heysham	Liverpool +0 05	9.4	7.4
Holyhead	Liverpool −0 50	5.6	4.4
*Hook of Holland	London −0 01	2.1	1.7
Hull (Albert Dock)	London −7 40	7.5	5.8
Immingham	London −8 00	7.3	5.8
Larne	London −2 40	2.8	2.5
Lerwick	Leith −3 48	2.2	1.6
Londonderry	London −5 37	2.7	2.1
Lowestoft	London −4 25	2.4	2.1
Margate	London −1 53	4.8	3.9
Milford Haven	Liverpool −5 08	7.0	5.2
Morecambe	Liverpool +0 07	9.5	7.4
Newhaven	London −2 46	6.7	5.1
Oban	Greenock +5 43	4.0	2.9
*Ostend	London −1 32	5.1	4.2
Plymouth (Devonport)	London +4 05	5.5	4.4
Portland	London +5 09	2.1	1.4
Portsmouth	London −2 38	4.7	3.8
Ramsgate	London −2 32	5.2	4.1
Richmond Lock	London +1 00	4.9	3.7
Rosslare Harbour	Liverpool −5 24	1.9	1.4
Rosyth	Leith +0 09	5.8	4.7
*Rotterdam	London +1 45	2.0	1.7
St Helier	London +4 48	11.0	8.1
St Malo	London +4 27	12.2	9.2
St Peter Port	London +4 54	9.3	7.0
Scrabster	Leith −6 06	5.0	4.0
Sheerness	London −1 19	5.8	4.7
Shoreham	London −2 44	6.3	4.9
Southampton (1st high water)	London −2 54	4.5	3.7
Spurn Head	London −8 25	6.9	5.5
Stornoway	Liverpool −4 16	4.8	3.7
Stranraer	Greenock −0 20	3.0	2.4
Stromness	Leith −5 26	3.6	2.7
Swansea	London −7 35	9.5	7.2
Tees (River Entrance)	Leith +1 09	5.5	4.3
Tilbury	London −0 49	6.4	5.4
Tobermory	Liverpool −5 11	4.4	3.3
Tyne River (North Shields)	London −1030	5.0	3.9
Ullapool	Leith −7 40	5.2	3.9
Walton-on-the-Naze	London −2 10	4.2	3.4
Wick	Leith −3 26	3.5	2.8
*Zeebrugge	London −0 55	4.8	3.9

PREDICTIONS

The data on pages 98–103 are daily predictions of the time and height of high water at London Bridge, Liverpool, Greenock and Leith. The time of the data is Greenwich Mean Time; this applies also to data for the months when British Summer Time is in operation and the hour's time difference should be allowed for. The datum of predictions for each port shows the difference of height, in metres from Ordnance data (Newlyn).

The tidal information for London Bridge, Liverpool, Greenock and Leith is reproduced with the permission of the UK Hydrographic Office and the Controller of HMSO. Crown copyright reserved.

JANUARY 1999 *High water* GMT

		London Bridge *Datum of predictions 3.20 m below				Liverpool *Datum of predictions 4.93 m below				Greenock *Datum of predictions 1.62 m below				Leith *Datum of predictions 2.90 m below			
		hr	ht m	hr	ht m	hr	ht m	hr	ht m	hr	ht m	hr	ht m	hr	ht m	hr	ht m
1	Friday	00 29	6.9	12 51	7.0	10 17	9.5	22 43	9.6	11 41	3.6	——	—	01 19	5.6	13 47	5.6
2	Saturday	01 21	7.1	13 43	7.3	11 06	9.8	23 31	9.7	00 13	3.5	12 27	3.7	02 11	5.7	14 35	5.7
3	Sunday	02 10	7.2	14 33	7.4	11 52	9.8	——	—	01 04	3.5	13 11	3.8	03 00	5.8	15 22	5.8
4	Monday	02 55	7.2	15 21	7.4	00 17	9.6	12 37	9.8	01 52	3.5	13 53	3.9	03 49	5.7	16 08	5.7
5	Tuesday	03 39	7.1	16 06	7.3	01 02	9.4	13 20	9.6	02 37	3.5	14 34	3.9	04 36	5.6	16 55	5.6
6	Wednesday	04 19	6.9	16 49	7.1	01 45	9.2	14 02	9.3	03 20	3.4	15 15	3.9	05 23	5.4	17 42	5.4
7	Thursday	04 56	6.7	17 30	6.8	02 26	8.8	14 43	8.9	04 01	3.4	15 56	3.8	06 09	5.2	18 29	5.1
8	Friday	05 32	6.5	18 10	6.5	03 08	8.4	15 25	8.5	04 43	3.3	16 38	3.6	06 55	4.9	19 17	4.9
9	Saturday	06 11	6.3	18 52	6.2	03 53	7.9	16 12	8.0	05 28	3.1	17 22	3.4	07 43	4.7	20 09	4.7
10	Sunday	06 57	6.0	19 42	5.9	04 46	7.5	17 10	7.6	06 16	3.0	18 10	3.2	08 35	4.5	21 04	4.6
11	Monday	07 57	5.7	20 42	5.8	05 53	7.3	18 20	7.4	07 09	2.9	19 04	3.1	09 30	4.5	22 04	4.5
12	Tuesday	09 11	5.6	21 49	5.8	07 07	7.4	19 33	7.5	08 18	2.9	20 08	3.0	10 30	4.5	23 09	4.5
13	Wednesday	10 24	5.7	22 51	6.0	08 11	7.7	20 34	7.8	09 43	3.0	21 29	2.9	11 34	4.6	——	—
14	Thursday	11 25	6.0	23 47	6.3	09 02	8.1	21 24	8.1	10 41	3.1	22 36	3.0	00 12	4.6	12 32	4.8
15	Friday	——	—	12 19	6.3	09 47	8.5	22 06	8.5	11 25	3.3	23 23	3.1	01 04	4.8	13 20	5.0
16	Saturday	00 37	6.5	13 06	6.5	10 26	8.9	22 45	8.7	——	—	12 02	3.4	01 47	5.0	14 01	5.2
17	Sunday	01 22	6.7	13 49	6.7	11 04	9.1	23 23	8.9	00 03	3.1	12 36	3.4	02 26	5.2	14 39	5.3
18	Monday	02 03	6.8	14 29	6.8	11 42	9.3	——	—	00 42	3.2	13 08	3.5	03 03	5.3	15 16	5.4
19	Tuesday	02 42	6.9	15 09	6.9	00 01	9.1	12 20	9.4	01 21	3.2	13 43	3.5	03 40	5.4	15 51	5.5
20	Wednesday	03 19	6.9	15 48	7.0	00 41	9.1	13 00	9.5	02 02	3.2	14 20	3.6	04 17	5.4	16 27	5.5
21	Thursday	03 56	6.9	16 29	7.0	01 21	9.2	13 41	9.5	02 43	3.2	14 59	3.6	04 56	5.4	17 05	5.5
22	Friday	04 35	6.9	17 11	6.9	02 03	9.1	14 24	9.4	03 24	3.3	15 38	3.6	05 38	5.3	17 48	5.4
23	Saturday	05 16	6.8	17 56	6.8	02 47	8.9	15 10	9.1	04 05	3.2	16 20	3.5	06 25	5.2	18 35	5.3
24	Sunday	06 01	6.7	18 45	6.5	03 35	8.6	16 02	8.8	04 49	3.2	17 07	3.3	07 16	5.1	19 29	5.1
25	Monday	06 52	6.4	19 41	6.3	04 32	8.2	17 03	8.4	05 38	3.1	18 01	3.2	08 14	4.9	20 33	4.9
26	Tuesday	07 54	6.2	20 49	6.1	05 40	7.9	18 14	8.2	06 35	3.0	19 10	3.0	09 21	4.8	21 48	4.9
27	Wednesday	09 11	6.1	22 03	6.1	06 57	7.9	19 31	8.2	07 48	2.9	20 52	3.0	10 34	4.8	23 04	4.9
28	Thursday	10 29	6.2	23 11	6.3	08 12	8.2	20 43	8.5	09 28	3.0	22 14	3.1	11 44	5.0		
29	Friday	11 38	6.5	——	—	09 15	8.7	21 43	8.9	10 35	3.2	23 15	3.2	00 14	5.1	12 46	5.2
30	Saturday	00 12	6.6	12 39	6.8	10 08	9.2	22 35	9.3	11 28	3.4	——	—	01 14	5.3	13 39	5.4
31	Sunday	01 06	6.9	13 32	7.1	10 56	9.5	23 21	9.5	00 08	3.3	12 15	3.6	02 06	5.5	14 27	5.6

FEBRUARY 1999 *High water* GMT

		London Bridge				Liverpool				Greenock				Leith			
1	Monday	01 55	7.1	14 21	7.3	11 40	9.7	——	—	00 58	3.4	12 59	3.7	02 52	5.6	15 11	5.7
2	Tuesday	02 40	7.1	15 07	7.3	00 04	9.5	12 22	9.7	01 43	3.4	13 40	3.7	03 35	5.6	15 54	5.7
3	Wednesday	03 22	7.0	15 48	7.2	00 45	9.4	13 01	9.6	02 24	3.4	14 19	3.8	04 17	5.5	16 35	5.6
4	Thursday	03 58	6.9	16 26	7.0	01 22	9.2	13 38	9.4	03 00	3.3	14 56	3.8	04 57	5.4	17 15	5.4
5	Friday	04 31	6.8	16 59	6.8	01 57	9.0	14 13	9.1	03 35	3.3	15 32	3.7	05 36	5.2	17 54	5.2
6	Saturday	05 03	6.7	17 33	6.7	02 33	8.7	14 49	8.7	04 10	3.3	16 09	3.6	06 16	5.0	18 34	5.0
7	Sunday	05 38	6.5	18 09	6.5	03 10	8.3	15 28	8.3	04 47	3.2	16 47	3.4	06 58	4.8	19 18	4.8
8	Monday	06 19	6.3	18 51	6.3	03 52	7.8	16 14	7.8	05 28	3.1	17 29	3.2	07 43	4.6	20 08	4.5
9	Tuesday	07 06	6.0	19 40	6.0	04 46	7.4	17 12	7.3	06 14	2.9	18 17	3.0	08 34	4.4	21 05	4.4
10	Wednesday	08 03	5.7	20 39	5.8	05 56	7.1	18 27	7.1	07 08	2.8	19 13	2.8	09 32	4.3	22 11	4.3
11	Thursday	09 13	5.6	21 51	5.9	07 19	7.3	19 50	7.3	08 21	2.8	20 23	2.8	10 38	4.3	23 25	4.4
12	Friday	10 35	5.7	23 05	6.0	08 28	7.7	20 54	7.7	09 59	2.9	21 50	2.8	11 49	4.5	——	—
13	Saturday	11 44	6.0	——	—	09 20	8.2	21 43	8.2	10 55	3.1	22 57	2.9	00 31	4.6	12 50	4.8
14	Sunday	00 06	6.3	12 40	6.4	10 04	8.7	22 25	8.6	11 36	3.2	23 43	3.0	01 22	4.9	13 37	5.1
15	Monday	00 58	6.6	13 27	6.7	10 44	9.1	23 05	9.0	——	—	12 11	3.3	02 03	5.1	14 17	5.3
16	Tuesday	01 43	6.8	14 10	7.0	11 23	9.4	23 44	9.2	00 24	3.1	12 47	3.4	02 42	5.4	14 54	5.5
17	Wednesday	02 25	6.9	14 52	7.1	——	—	12 02	9.6	01 05	3.2	13 25	3.5	03 19	5.5	15 30	5.7
18	Thursday	03 04	7.0	15 32	7.2	00 23	9.4	12 43	9.8	01 45	3.2	14 03	3.6	03 56	5.6	16 07	5.7
19	Friday	03 42	7.1	16 12	7.2	01 04	9.5	13 24	9.8	02 24	3.3	14 42	3.6	04 35	5.6	16 46	5.7
20	Saturday	04 20	7.1	16 53	7.1	01 45	9.5	14 07	9.7	03 02	3.3	15 22	3.6	05 17	5.5	17 29	5.6
21	Sunday	05 00	7.1	17 36	6.9	02 28	9.3	14 51	9.4	03 41	3.3	16 02	3.5	06 03	5.4	18 16	5.5
22	Monday	05 43	6.9	18 21	6.6	03 13	8.9	15 40	8.9	04 22	3.3	16 46	3.4	06 51	5.1	19 09	5.2
23	Tuesday	06 31	6.6	19 12	6.2	04 05	8.3	16 38	8.3	05 07	3.2	17 36	3.2	07 48	4.9	20 14	4.9
24	Wednesday	07 29	6.2	20 19	5.9	05 12	7.8	17 52	7.8	05 59	3.0	18 39	2.9	08 56	4.7	21 32	4.7
25	Thursday	08 50	5.9	21 42	5.8	06 36	7.6	19 19	7.8	07 06	2.9	20 41	2.8	10 13	4.6	22 54	4.7
26	Friday	10 18	6.0	22 55	6.0	08 00	7.9	20 36	8.2	09 07	2.9	22 11	2.9	11 31	4.8		
27	Saturday	11 28	6.1	23 57	6.4	09 06	8.4	21 35	8.6	10 22	3.1	23 10	3.1	00 10	4.9	12 39	5.0
28	Sunday	——	—	12 27	6.8	09 58	9.0	22 24	9.0	11 15	3.3	——	—	01 11	5.2	13 33	5.3

MARCH 1999   *High water*   GMT

	LONDON BRIDGE *Datum of predictions 3.20 m below*				LIVERPOOL *Datum of predictions 4.93 m below*				GREENOCK *Datum of predictions 1.62 m below*				LEITH *Datum of predictions 2.90 m below*			
	hr m	ht	hr m	ht	hr m	ht	hr m	ht	hr m	ht	hr m	ht	hr m	ht	hr m	ht
1 Monday	00 51	6.8	13 20	7.1	10 43	9.4	23 07	9.3	00 00	3.2	12 01	3.5	01 59	5.3	14 18	5.5
2 Tuesday	01 40	7.0	14 07	7.3	11 24	9.6	23 46	9.4	00 46	3.3	12 43	3.5	02 40	5.5	14 58	5.6
3 Wednesday	02 24	7.1	14 49	7.2	—	—	12 02	9.6	01 27	3.3	13 23	3.6	03 18	5.5	15 36	5.6
4 Thursday	03 02	7.0	15 27	7.1	00 22	9.3	12 38	9.5	02 03	3.3	13 59	3.6	03 54	5.5	16 12	5.5
5 Friday	03 36	6.9	15 59	6.9	00 56	9.2	13 11	9.3	02 34	3.3	14 33	3.6	04 29	5.4	16 46	5.4
6 Saturday	04 05	6.8	16 28	6.8	01 28	9.1	13 43	9.1	03 04	3.3	15 06	3.6	05 03	5.2	17 21	5.2
7 Sunday	04 35	6.7	16 59	6.7	02 00	8.8	14 17	8.8	03 35	3.2	15 40	3.5	05 39	5.0	17 57	5.0
8 Monday	05 09	6.6	17 34	6.6	02 34	8.5	14 53	8.4	04 08	3.2	16 15	3.4	06 17	4.8	18 37	4.8
9 Tuesday	05 48	6.5	18 13	6.4	03 12	8.1	15 34	7.9	04 45	3.1	16 55	3.2	06 59	4.6	19 23	4.5
10 Wednesday	06 31	6.2	18 58	6.1	03 58	7.6	16 25	7.3	05 27	2.9	17 40	3.0	07 45	4.4	20 15	4.3
11 Thursday	07 22	5.9	19 52	5.9	04 58	7.2	17 33	7.0	06 19	2.7	18 36	2.8	08 41	4.2	21 19	4.2
12 Friday	08 24	5.6	20 58	5.7	06 18	7.0	18 57	7.0	07 25	2.6	19 43	2.7	09 46	4.2	22 34	4.2
13 Saturday	09 40	5.6	22 19	5.8	07 44	7.3	20 18	7.4	08 51	2.7	21 07	2.7	11 02	4.3	23 51	4.5
14 Sunday	11 06	5.9	23 32	6.1	08 47	7.9	21 14	8.0	10 13	2.9	22 27	2.8	—	—	12 12	4.6
15 Monday	—	—	12 10	6.3	09 35	8.5	21 59	8.6	11 02	3.1	23 19	3.0	00 49	4.8	13 06	5.0
16 Tuesday	00 29	6.5	13 01	6.8	10 18	9.1	22 40	9.1	11 42	3.2	—	—	01 35	5.1	13 49	5.3
17 Wednesday	01 18	6.8	13 47	7.1	10 59	9.5	23 21	9.4	00 02	3.1	12 22	3.4	02 15	5.4	14 27	5.6
18 Thursday	02 01	7.0	14 30	7.3	11 40	9.8	—	—	00 44	3.2	13 03	3.5	02 53	5.6	15 05	5.8
19 Friday	02 42	7.2	15 11	7.4	00 01	9.7	12 22	10.0	01 24	3.3	13 44	3.6	03 32	5.8	15 44	5.9
20 Saturday	03 22	7.3	15 52	7.4	00 43	9.8	13 05	10.0	02 02	3.4	14 25	3.6	04 13	5.8	16 26	5.9
21 Sunday	04 03	7.4	16 34	7.3	01 25	9.7	13 48	9.8	02 40	3.4	15 05	3.6	04 56	5.6	17 11	5.8
22 Monday	04 45	7.3	17 15	7.0	02 08	9.4	14 33	9.4	03 17	3.5	15 46	3.6	05 41	5.4	18 01	5.5
23 Tuesday	05 28	7.1	17 59	6.7	02 54	9.0	15 22	8.8	03 57	3.4	16 30	3.4	06 31	5.2	18 56	5.2
24 Wednesday	06 16	6.7	18 48	6.2	03 45	8.4	16 21	8.1	04 41	3.2	17 20	3.1	07 27	4.8	20 03	4.8
25 Thursday	07 15	6.2	19 55	5.8	04 52	7.8	17 39	7.6	05 34	3.0	18 26	2.8	08 36	4.6	21 21	4.6
26 Friday	08 40	5.9	21 25	5.7	06 20	7.5	19 08	7.5	06 40	2.9	20 41	2.7	09 55	4.5	22 43	4.6
27 Saturday	10 07	6.0	22 37	5.9	07 44	7.7	20 22	7.9	08 45	2.8	22 02	2.9	11 16	4.7	—	—
28 Sunday	11 13	6.4	23 37	6.4	08 48	8.3	21 19	8.4	10 03	3.0	22 57	3.0	00 00	4.8	12 25	4.9
29 Monday	—	—	12 10	6.8	09 40	8.8	22 06	8.8	10 56	3.2	23 44	3.2	00 59	5.1	13 18	5.1
30 Tuesday	00 31	6.7	13 01	7.1	10 24	9.1	22 46	9.1	11 41	3.4	—	—	01 44	5.2	14 01	5.3
31 Wednesday	01 19	7.0	13 47	7.2	11 03	9.3	23 23	9.2	00 26	3.2	12 23	3.4	02 22	5.3	14 39	5.4

APRIL 1999   *High water*   GMT

	LONDON BRIDGE				LIVERPOOL				GREENOCK				LEITH			
1 Thursday	02 02	7.0	14 27	7.2	11 39	9.3	23 56	9.2	01 04	3.2	13 00	3.4	02 56	5.4	15 14	5.4
2 Friday	02 40	7.0	15 01	7.0	—	—	12 12	9.3	01 36	3.2	13 35	3.4	03 28	5.4	15 47	5.4
3 Saturday	03 12	6.8	15 30	6.8	00 27	9.1	12 44	9.1	02 05	3.2	14 07	3.4	04 00	5.3	16 20	5.3
4 Sunday	03 40	6.7	15 57	6.8	00 58	9.0	13 15	8.9	02 33	3.2	14 39	3.4	04 33	5.2	16 53	5.2
5 Monday	04 10	6.7	16 28	6.8	01 30	8.9	13 48	8.7	03 02	3.3	15 12	3.3	05 07	5.1	17 29	5.0
6 Tuesday	04 43	6.6	17 02	6.7	02 03	8.6	14 23	8.4	03 33	3.2	15 48	3.2	05 43	4.9	18 07	4.8
7 Wednesday	05 21	6.5	17 41	6.5	02 39	8.2	15 02	7.9	04 08	3.1	16 27	3.1	06 22	4.7	18 49	4.6
8 Thursday	06 04	6.3	18 25	6.3	03 21	7.8	15 50	7.4	04 47	2.9	17 12	2.9	07 05	4.5	19 39	4.4
9 Friday	06 53	6.0	19 16	6.0	04 16	7.4	16 53	7.0	05 37	2.8	18 07	2.7	07 58	4.3	20 39	4.2
10 Saturday	07 52	5.8	20 18	5.8	05 29	7.1	18 11	7.0	06 42	2.6	19 14	2.6	09 02	4.2	21 49	4.2
11 Sunday	09 02	5.7	21 34	5.8	06 52	7.3	19 32	7.3	08 00	2.6	20 32	2.7	10 16	4.3	23 05	4.4
12 Monday	10 24	6.0	22 51	6.1	08 04	7.8	20 36	8.0	09 23	2.8	21 51	2.8	11 30	4.5	—	—
13 Tuesday	11 34	6.4	23 53	6.4	08 59	8.5	21 26	8.6	10 22	3.0	22 49	3.0	00 10	4.8	12 28	4.9
14 Wednesday	—	—	12 30	6.8	09 46	9.1	22 11	9.2	11 10	3.2	23 35	3.1	01 02	5.2	13 15	5.3
15 Thursday	00 46	6.8	13 19	7.1	10 31	9.6	22 54	9.6	11 54	3.4	—	—	01 45	5.5	13 58	5.6
16 Friday	01 33	7.1	14 05	7.4	11 15	9.9	23 37	9.8	00 18	3.2	12 39	3.5	02 26	5.7	14 39	5.8
17 Saturday	02 18	7.3	14 48	7.5	11 59	10.1	—	—	01 00	3.4	13 24	3.6	03 08	5.8	15 22	6.0
18 Sunday	03 02	7.5	15 31	7.5	00 20	9.9	12 45	10.0	01 40	3.5	14 08	3.6	03 50	5.8	16 08	5.9
19 Monday	03 46	7.5	16 14	7.3	01 05	9.8	13 31	9.8	02 19	3.5	14 51	3.6	04 35	5.7	16 56	5.8
20 Tuesday	04 31	7.4	16 57	7.1	01 50	9.5	14 18	9.3	02 58	3.6	15 34	3.6	05 22	5.5	17 49	5.5
21 Wednesday	05 17	7.2	17 41	6.7	02 38	9.0	15 09	8.7	03 38	3.5	16 21	3.3	06 13	5.2	18 47	5.2
22 Thursday	06 07	6.8	18 30	6.3	03 31	8.4	16 08	8.1	04 23	3.3	17 16	3.0	07 12	4.9	19 53	4.8
23 Friday	07 08	6.3	19 38	5.9	04 37	7.9	17 24	7.6	05 16	3.1	18 30	2.8	08 21	4.6	21 06	4.6
24 Saturday	08 30	6.0	21 03	5.8	06 00	7.6	18 47	7.5	06 23	2.9	20 25	2.7	09 36	4.6	22 22	4.6
25 Sunday	09 47	6.1	22 12	6.0	07 18	7.7	19 56	7.8	08 09	2.9	21 39	2.9	10 52	4.6	23 35	4.8
26 Monday	10 49	6.5	23 11	6.3	08 21	8.1	20 52	8.3	09 35	3.0	22 33	3.0	11 59	4.8	—	—
27 Tuesday	11 45	6.8	—	—	09 13	8.5	21 39	8.6	10 29	3.2	23 18	3.1	00 33	4.9	12 53	5.0
28 Wednesday	00 04	6.7	12 35	7.0	09 58	8.8	22 19	8.8	11 15	3.2	23 58	3.1	01 19	5.1	13 37	5.1
29 Thursday	00 53	6.9	13 20	7.1	10 37	9.0	22 55	9.0	11 56	3.3	—	—	01 57	5.2	14 15	5.2
30 Friday	01 37	6.9	14 00	7.1	11 13	9.0	23 27	9.0	00 34	3.2	12 34	3.2	02 30	5.2	14 50	5.3

MAY 1999 *High water* GMT

		LONDON BRIDGE *Datum of predictions 3.20 m below				LIVERPOOL *Datum of predictions 4.93 m below				GREENOCK *Datum of predictions 1.62 m below				LEITH *Datum of predictions 2.90 m below			
		hr	ht m	hr	ht m	hr	ht m	hr	ht m	hr	ht m	hr	ht m	hr	ht m	hr	ht m
1	Saturday	02 15	6.9	14 34	6.9	11 45	9.0	23 59	9.0	01 08	3.2	13 08	3.2	03 02	5.3	15 23	5.3
2	Sunday	02 48	6.7	15 02	6.8	—	—	12 17	8.9	01 37	3.2	13 40	3.2	03 34	5.2	15 56	5.2
3	Monday	03 18	6.6	15 30	6.7	00 30	8.9	12 49	8.8	02 05	3.2	14 12	3.2	04 06	5.2	16 30	5.1
4	Tuesday	03 48	6.6	16 01	6.7	01 03	8.8	13 23	8.6	02 33	3.3	14 46	3.2	04 40	5.1	17 05	5.0
5	Wednesday	04 22	6.6	16 36	6.7	01 37	8.6	13 58	8.4	03 04	3.2	15 24	3.1	05 15	4.9	17 43	4.8
6	Thursday	05 00	6.5	17 15	6.6	02 14	8.4	14 38	8.1	03 38	3.2	16 04	3.0	05 53	4.8	18 24	4.7
7	Friday	05 43	6.4	17 58	6.3	02 55	8.0	15 24	7.7	04 16	3.0	16 51	2.9	06 34	4.6	19 11	4.5
8	Saturday	06 32	6.2	18 49	6.1	03 47	7.7	16 22	7.4	05 03	2.8	17 45	2.8	07 24	4.4	20 07	4.4
9	Sunday	07 28	6.0	19 48	5.9	04 52	7.5	17 32	7.2	06 04	2.7	18 49	2.7	08 25	4.3	21 13	4.4
10	Monday	08 35	6.0	20 58	5.9	06 06	7.5	18 47	7.5	07 19	2.7	19 59	2.7	09 35	4.4	22 24	4.5
11	Tuesday	09 48	6.1	22 11	6.1	07 18	7.9	19 54	8.0	08 37	2.8	21 12	2.8	10 46	4.6	23 30	4.8
12	Wednesday	10 58	6.5	23 16	6.5	08 19	8.5	20 50	8.6	09 44	3.0	22 15	3.0	11 49	4.9	—	—
13	Thursday	11 57	6.8	—	—	09 13	9.1	21 40	9.2	10 38	3.2	23 07	3.1	00 26	5.2	12 42	5.3
14	Friday	00 13	6.8	12 50	7.1	10 03	9.6	22 27	9.6	11 27	3.4	23 53	3.3	01 15	5.5	13 29	5.6
15	Saturday	01 05	7.1	13 39	7.4	10 51	9.9	23 13	9.8	—	—	12 15	3.5	02 00	5.7	14 15	5.8
16	Sunday	01 55	7.4	14 26	7.4	11 38	10.0	23 59	9.9	00 37	3.4	13 04	3.5	02 44	5.8	15 03	5.9
17	Monday	02 43	7.5	15 12	7.4	—	—	12 26	9.9	01 20	3.5	13 52	3.5	03 30	5.8	15 52	5.9
18	Tuesday	03 30	7.6	15 56	7.3	00 46	9.8	13 15	9.7	02 01	3.6	14 39	3.5	04 17	5.7	16 44	5.8
19	Wednesday	04 18	7.5	16 41	7.1	01 35	9.5	14 05	9.3	02 43	3.6	15 27	3.4	05 06	5.5	17 38	5.5
20	Thursday	05 07	7.3	17 27	6.8	02 24	9.1	14 56	8.8	03 25	3.6	16 18	3.2	05 59	5.2	18 35	5.2
21	Friday	05 59	6.9	18 16	6.4	03 17	8.6	15 53	8.2	04 11	3.5	17 14	3.1	06 58	5.0	19 37	4.9
22	Saturday	06 57	6.5	19 18	6.1	04 18	8.1	16 59	7.7	05 03	3.3	18 21	2.9	08 02	4.8	20 41	4.7
23	Sunday	08 08	6.3	20 32	5.9	05 29	7.8	18 12	7.5	06 05	3.1	19 44	2.8	09 10	4.6	21 48	4.6
24	Monday	09 17	6.2	21 38	6.0	06 40	7.7	19 19	7.6	07 23	3.0	21 00	2.8	10 17	4.6	22 55	4.6
25	Tuesday	10 17	6.4	22 37	6.2	07 44	7.9	20 17	7.9	08 51	3.0	21 57	2.9	11 22	4.7	23 55	4.8
26	Wednesday	11 12	6.6	23 31	6.4	08 39	8.2	21 05	8.3	09 54	3.0	22 44	3.0	—	—	12 19	4.8
27	Thursday	—	—	12 03	6.8	09 26	8.4	21 47	8.5	10 43	3.1	23 26	3.1	00 45	4.9	13 07	4.9
28	Friday	00 22	6.6	12 49	6.9	10 08	8.6	22 25	8.7	11 26	3.1	—	—	01 27	5.0	13 48	5.0
29	Saturday	01 08	6.7	13 30	6.9	10 45	8.7	22 59	8.8	00 05	3.1	12 05	3.1	02 03	5.1	14 25	5.1
30	Sunday	01 48	6.7	14 05	6.8	11 20	8.7	23 32	8.9	00 40	3.2	12 40	3.1	02 37	5.2	15 00	5.1
31	Monday	02 24	6.7	14 37	6.8	11 53	8.7	—	—	01 11	3.2	13 12	3.1	03 10	5.2	15 34	5.1

JUNE 1999 *High water* GMT

		LONDON BRIDGE				LIVERPOOL				GREENOCK				LEITH			
1	Tuesday	02 57	6.6	15 08	6.7	00 06	8.9	12 27	8.6	01 40	3.2	13 46	3.1	03 44	5.2	16 09	5.1
2	Wednesday	03 30	6.6	15 40	6.7	00 40	8.8	13 02	8.6	02 09	3.3	14 23	3.1	04 18	5.1	16 45	5.0
3	Thursday	04 05	6.6	16 16	6.7	01 16	8.7	13 39	8.4	02 41	3.3	15 03	3.0	04 53	5.0	17 22	4.9
4	Friday	04 44	6.5	16 54	6.6	01 54	8.6	14 19	8.3	03 16	3.2	15 46	3.0	05 30	4.9	18 02	4.8
5	Saturday	05 26	6.5	17 37	6.4	02 36	8.4	15 04	8.0	03 55	3.1	16 33	2.9	06 11	4.8	18 48	4.7
6	Sunday	06 14	6.4	18 26	6.3	03 25	8.1	15 56	7.8	04 38	3.0	17 25	2.8	06 58	4.7	19 40	4.6
7	Monday	07 08	6.2	19 22	6.1	04 23	8.0	16 59	7.7	05 33	2.9	18 22	2.8	07 54	4.6	20 41	4.6
8	Tuesday	08 10	6.2	20 27	6.1	05 30	7.9	18 08	7.8	06 41	2.8	19 25	2.8	08 58	4.6	21 47	4.7
9	Wednesday	09 18	6.3	21 36	6.2	06 37	8.2	19 15	8.1	07 56	2.9	20 32	2.8	10 07	4.7	22 53	4.9
10	Thursday	10 25	6.5	22 42	6.5	07 42	8.5	20 17	8.6	09 09	3.0	21 41	2.9	11 12	4.9	23 54	5.1
11	Friday	11 27	6.8	23 43	6.8	08 42	9.0	21 13	9.1	10 11	3.2	22 40	3.1	—	—	12 12	5.2
12	Saturday	—	—	12 24	7.0	09 38	9.4	22 04	9.5	11 05	3.3	23 31	3.3	00 48	5.4	13 06	5.5
13	Sunday	00 41	7.0	13 17	7.2	10 31	9.6	22 53	9.7	11 57	3.4	—	—	01 38	5.6	13 57	5.7
14	Monday	01 35	7.3	14 06	7.3	11 21	9.8	23 42	9.8	00 18	3.4	12 49	3.4	02 25	5.7	14 48	5.8
15	Tuesday	02 26	7.4	14 54	7.4	—	—	12 12	9.7	01 04	3.5	13 41	3.4	03 13	5.7	15 39	5.8
16	Wednesday	03 16	7.5	15 40	7.3	00 31	9.7	13 02	9.6	01 48	3.6	14 31	3.4	04 02	5.7	16 31	5.7
17	Thursday	04 06	7.5	16 26	7.1	01 20	9.5	13 51	9.3	02 31	3.7	15 21	3.3	04 52	5.6	17 24	5.5
18	Friday	04 54	7.3	17 11	6.9	02 08	9.3	14 39	8.9	03 14	3.7	16 10	3.2	05 45	5.4	18 18	5.3
19	Saturday	05 44	7.0	17 57	6.6	02 58	8.9	15 29	8.4	03 58	3.6	17 01	3.1	06 40	5.1	19 13	5.0
20	Sunday	06 35	6.7	18 47	6.3	03 50	8.4	16 23	7.9	04 46	3.4	17 54	3.0	07 37	4.9	20 08	4.8
21	Monday	07 33	6.4	19 48	6.1	04 48	8.0	17 25	7.6	05 39	3.2	18 51	2.9	08 35	4.7	21 05	4.6
22	Tuesday	08 36	6.2	20 54	6.0	05 53	7.7	18 31	7.5	06 37	3.1	19 54	2.8	09 35	4.6	22 04	4.5
23	Wednesday	09 36	6.1	21 56	6.0	06 58	7.6	19 33	7.6	07 45	2.9	21 05	2.8	10 37	4.6	23 06	4.6
24	Thursday	10 32	6.2	22 53	6.1	07 59	7.8	20 27	7.9	09 02	2.9	22 04	2.9	11 38	4.6	—	—
25	Friday	11 24	6.4	23 47	6.3	08 51	8.0	21 14	8.2	10 06	2.9	22 53	3.0	00 03	4.7	12 34	4.7
26	Saturday	—	—	12 14	6.6	09 38	8.2	21 56	8.5	10 55	3.0	23 36	3.1	00 53	4.8	13 20	4.9
27	Sunday	00 36	6.5	12 58	6.7	10 19	8.4	22 34	8.7	11 37	3.0	—	—	01 35	5.0	14 01	5.0
28	Monday	01 21	6.6	13 38	6.8	10 57	8.5	23 10	8.8	00 14	3.2	12 14	3.0	02 12	5.1	14 38	5.1
29	Tuesday	02 02	6.6	14 15	6.8	11 32	8.6	23 45	8.9	00 49	3.2	12 48	3.0	02 48	5.2	15 13	5.1
30	Wednesday	02 39	6.7	14 50	6.8	—	—	12 08	8.6	01 18	3.2	13 24	3.0	03 24	5.2	15 49	5.2

JULY 1999 *High water* GMT

		London Bridge				Liverpool				Greenock				Leith			
		*Datum of predictions 3.20 m below				*Datum of predictions 4.93 m below				*Datum of predictions 1.62 m below				*Datum of predictions 2.90 m below			
		hr	ht m	hr	ht m	hr	ht m	hr	ht m	hr	ht m	hr	ht m	hr	ht m	hr	ht m
1	Thursday	03 15	6.6	15 25	6.7	00 21	8.9	12 45	8.6	01 49	3.3	14 04	3.0	03 59	5.2	16 25	5.1
2	Friday	03 51	6.6	16 01	6.7	00 59	8.9	13 23	8.6	02 22	3.3	14 46	3.0	04 34	5.2	17 02	5.1
3	Saturday	04 30	6.7	16 38	6.6	01 38	8.8	14 03	8.6	02 58	3.3	15 28	3.0	05 10	5.1	17 42	5.0
4	Sunday	05 11	6.6	17 19	6.6	02 19	8.8	14 45	8.5	03 37	3.2	16 13	3.0	05 50	5.1	18 26	5.0
5	Monday	05 57	6.6	18 04	6.5	03 05	8.6	15 33	8.3	04 19	3.2	17 00	2.9	06 35	5.0	19 15	4.9
6	Tuesday	06 47	6.4	18 56	6.4	03 57	8.5	16 28	8.1	05 07	3.1	17 51	2.9	07 26	4.9	20 11	4.8
7	Wednesday	07 44	6.3	19 56	6.3	04 57	8.3	17 32	8.0	06 04	3.0	18 46	2.9	08 25	4.8	21 14	4.8
8	Thursday	08 48	6.2	21 04	6.2	06 03	8.3	18 41	8.1	07 14	2.9	19 50	2.8	09 33	4.8	22 21	4.9
9	Friday	09 56	6.3	22 13	6.3	07 12	8.4	19 49	8.4	08 36	2.9	21 07	2.9	10 43	4.9	23 27	5.0
10	Saturday	11 01	6.5	23 20	6.6	08 19	8.7	20 52	8.8	09 49	3.1	22 17	3.0	11 50	5.1	—	—
11	Sunday	—	—	12 02	6.8	09 21	9.0	21 48	9.2	10 51	3.2	23 14	3.2	00 27	5.2	12 51	5.4
12	Monday	00 22	6.9	12 58	7.0	10 17	9.3	22 39	9.5	11 46	3.3	—	—	01 21	5.4	13 46	5.6
13	Tuesday	01 20	7.1	13 50	7.2	11 09	9.5	23 29	9.7	00 04	3.4	12 41	3.3	02 11	5.6	14 38	5.7
14	Wednesday	02 13	7.4	14 38	7.3	11 59	9.6	—	—	00 51	3.5	13 33	3.3	02 59	5.7	15 28	5.8
15	Thursday	03 03	7.4	15 25	7.2	00 16	9.7	12 47	9.5	01 36	3.6	14 23	3.3	03 48	5.7	16 17	5.7
16	Friday	03 51	7.4	16 09	7.2	01 03	9.6	13 33	9.3	02 18	3.7	15 09	3.3	04 36	5.6	17 05	5.5
17	Saturday	04 37	7.3	16 50	7.0	01 48	9.4	14 16	9.0	03 00	3.7	15 52	3.2	05 25	5.5	17 53	5.3
18	Sunday	05 21	7.1	17 30	6.8	02 31	9.1	14 58	8.6	03 41	3.6	16 34	3.2	06 14	5.3	18 41	5.1
19	Monday	06 03	6.7	18 10	6.5	03 14	8.7	15 41	8.2	04 23	3.5	17 17	3.1	07 03	5.0	19 29	4.8
20	Tuesday	06 47	6.4	18 54	6.2	04 00	8.2	16 30	7.7	05 07	3.3	18 02	3.0	07 54	4.8	20 18	4.6
21	Wednesday	07 36	6.1	19 48	6.0	04 53	7.7	17 29	7.4	05 54	3.1	18 50	2.9	08 47	4.6	21 11	4.5
22	Thursday	08 34	5.9	20 55	5.8	05 58	7.4	18 39	7.3	06 46	2.9	19 47	2.8	09 45	4.5	22 09	4.4
23	Friday	09 37	5.8	22 05	5.8	07 10	7.4	19 46	7.5	07 48	2.8	21 07	2.8	10 49	4.4	23 12	4.5
24	Saturday	10 39	6.0	23 09	5.9	08 15	7.5	20 42	7.9	09 08	2.8	22 19	2.9	11 55	4.5	—	—
25	Sunday	11 35	6.2	—	—	09 09	7.9	21 30	8.3	10 23	2.8	23 09	3.0	00 14	4.6	12 51	4.7
26	Monday	00 05	6.2	12 27	6.5	09 55	8.2	22 12	8.6	11 13	2.9	23 51	3.1	01 06	4.8	13 37	4.9
27	Tuesday	00 55	6.5	13 13	6.7	10 36	8.4	22 50	8.9	11 53	2.9	—	—	01 48	5.0	14 15	5.1
28	Wednesday	01 39	6.7	13 55	6.8	11 14	8.6	23 27	9.0	00 26	3.2	12 30	3.0	02 27	5.2	14 52	5.2
29	Thursday	02 20	6.8	14 34	6.8	11 51	8.7	—	—	00 58	3.3	13 07	3.0	03 03	5.3	15 28	5.3
30	Friday	02 59	6.8	15 11	6.8	00 03	9.1	12 28	8.8	01 29	3.3	13 47	3.0	03 39	5.4	16 04	5.3
31	Saturday	03 36	6.8	15 46	6.8	00 41	9.2	13 06	8.9	02 04	3.3	14 27	3.1	04 14	5.4	16 41	5.3

AUGUST 1999 *High water* GMT

		London Bridge				Liverpool				Greenock				Leith			
1	Sunday	04 14	6.8	16 22	6.8	01 20	9.2	13 44	8.9	02 41	3.4	15 08	3.1	04 49	5.4	17 20	5.3
2	Monday	04 54	6.8	17 00	6.8	02 01	9.2	14 25	8.8	03 19	3.4	15 49	3.1	05 28	5.4	18 03	5.2
3	Tuesday	05 36	6.7	17 42	6.7	02 44	9.0	15 09	8.6	03 59	3.3	16 31	3.1	06 12	5.3	18 50	5.1
4	Wednesday	06 22	6.5	18 29	6.5	03 32	8.8	16 00	8.4	04 42	3.2	17 16	3.0	07 01	5.1	19 43	4.9
5	Thursday	07 14	6.3	19 25	6.3	04 28	8.4	17 00	8.0	05 32	3.1	18 07	2.9	07 58	5.0	20 44	4.8
6	Friday	08 17	6.1	20 33	6.1	05 34	8.1	18 13	7.9	06 35	2.9	19 07	2.9	09 08	4.8	21 54	4.8
7	Saturday	09 29	6.0	21 51	6.1	06 49	8.1	19 30	8.1	08 06	2.8	20 34	2.9	10 25	4.9	23 06	4.9
8	Sunday	10 41	6.2	23 05	6.3	08 05	8.3	20 40	8.5	09 40	2.9	22 01	3.0	11 39	5.0	—	—
9	Monday	11 46	6.5	—	—	09 12	8.7	21 39	9.0	10 47	3.1	23 01	3.2	00 13	5.1	12 45	5.2
10	Tuesday	00 11	6.7	12 43	6.8	10 09	9.1	22 30	9.4	11 43	3.2	23 52	3.4	01 11	5.4	13 40	5.5
11	Wednesday	01 09	7.1	13 35	7.1	10 59	9.4	23 17	9.7	—	—	12 35	3.1	02 01	5.6	14 29	5.6
12	Thursday	02 01	7.4	14 23	7.2	11 46	9.5	—	—	00 38	3.5	13 24	3.3	02 47	5.7	15 14	5.7
13	Friday	02 49	7.4	15 07	7.2	00 01	9.7	12 29	9.4	01 22	3.6	14 09	3.3	03 32	5.8	15 58	5.7
14	Saturday	03 33	7.4	15 47	7.1	00 43	9.7	13 09	9.2	02 02	3.7	14 49	3.3	04 16	5.7	16 41	5.5
15	Sunday	04 14	7.2	16 24	7.0	01 22	9.5	13 47	9.0	02 41	3.7	15 25	3.3	04 59	5.6	17 23	5.3
16	Monday	04 52	7.0	16 58	6.8	02 00	9.1	14 23	8.7	03 18	3.6	16 00	3.3	05 41	5.4	18 04	5.1
17	Tuesday	05 26	6.7	17 32	6.6	02 36	8.8	14 58	8.4	03 54	3.6	16 37	3.2	06 24	5.1	18 46	4.9
18	Wednesday	06 00	6.5	18 09	6.4	03 15	8.3	15 40	7.9	04 32	3.4	17 16	3.1	07 08	4.9	19 31	4.7
19	Thursday	06 39	6.2	18 53	6.1	03 59	7.8	16 28	7.5	05 13	3.2	17 59	3.0	07 57	4.6	20 20	4.5
20	Friday	07 25	5.9	19 48	5.7	04 54	7.3	17 33	7.2	06 00	3.0	18 49	2.8	08 52	4.4	21 15	4.4
21	Saturday	08 24	5.7	20 58	5.5	06 08	7.0	18 56	7.2	06 56	2.8	19 52	2.8	09 56	4.3	22 18	4.4
22	Sunday	09 40	5.7	22 23	5.6	07 35	7.1	20 09	7.6	08 07	2.7	21 33	2.8	11 08	4.3	23 28	4.5
23	Monday	10 55	5.9	23 33	6.0	08 41	7.5	21 04	8.1	09 44	2.7	22 40	3.0	—	—	12 18	4.6
24	Tuesday	11 55	6.3	—	—	09 31	8.0	21 49	8.6	10 52	2.9	23 24	3.1	00 32	4.7	13 09	4.8
25	Wednesday	00 28	6.4	12 47	6.6	10 14	8.4	22 28	8.9	11 35	3.0	—	—	01 20	5.0	13 50	5.1
26	Thursday	01 15	6.7	13 32	6.8	10 52	8.7	23 05	9.2	00 00	3.2	12 13	3.1	02 01	5.3	14 27	5.3
27	Friday	01 58	6.9	14 13	6.9	11 29	8.9	23 42	9.4	00 34	3.3	12 49	3.1	02 38	5.5	15 03	5.5
28	Saturday	02 38	7.0	14 51	6.9	—	—	12 06	9.1	01 08	3.4	13 27	3.2	03 14	5.6	15 40	5.6
29	Sunday	03 16	7.1	15 26	7.0	00 19	9.5	12 44	9.2	01 44	3.5	14 06	3.3	03 49	5.7	16 17	5.6
30	Monday	03 54	7.1	16 02	7.0	00 59	9.6	13 23	9.2	02 21	3.5	14 44	3.3	04 26	5.7	16 57	5.6
31	Tuesday	04 32	7.0	16 39	7.0	01 40	9.5	14 03	9.1	03 00	3.5	15 22	3.3	05 06	5.6	17 39	5.4

SEPTEMBER 1999   *High water*   GMT

		London Bridge *Datum of predictions 3.20 m below				Liverpool *Datum of predictions 4.93 m below				Greenock *Datum of predictions 1.62 m below				Leith *Datum of predictions 2.90 m below			
		hr	ht m	hr	ht m	hr	ht m	hr	ht m	hr	ht m	hr	ht m	hr	ht m	hr	ht m
1	Wednesday	05 13	6.9	17 20	6.9	02 23	9.3	14 46	8.9	03 39	3.5	16 01	3.3	05 51	5.5	18 26	5.2
2	Thursday	05 56	6.6	18 06	6.7	03 10	8.9	15 35	8.5	04 20	3.3	16 43	3.2	06 41	5.3	19 18	5.0
3	Friday	06 44	6.3	18 59	6.3	04 05	8.4	16 35	8.0	05 07	3.1	17 33	3.1	07 40	5.0	20 20	4.8
4	Saturday	07 45	5.9	20 09	5.9	05 14	7.9	17 52	7.7	06 07	2.9	18 33	3.0	08 53	4.8	21 34	4.7
5	Sunday	09 07	5.7	21 38	5.9	06 38	7.7	19 19	7.8	07 52	2.8	20 06	2.9	10 15	4.8	22 52	4.8
6	Monday	10 27	5.9	22 57	6.2	08 01	8.0	20 33	8.3	09 43	2.9	21 50	3.1	11 35	4.9	—	—
7	Tuesday	11 32	6.3	—	—	09 07	8.5	21 30	8.9	10 46	3.1	22 49	3.3	00 04	5.1	12 41	5.2
8	Wednesday	00 01	6.7	12 29	6.8	10 00	9.0	22 18	9.4	11 37	3.3	23 38	3.5	01 03	5.3	13 34	5.4
9	Thursday	00 57	7.1	13 19	7.1	10 46	9.3	23 01	9.6	—	—	12 24	3.3	01 50	5.5	14 17	5.6
10	Friday	01 46	7.4	14 04	7.2	11 27	9.4	23 41	9.7	00 22	3.6	13 08	3.4	02 33	5.7	14 57	5.6
11	Saturday	02 31	7.4	14 46	7.2	—	—	12 06	9.4	01 04	3.6	13 47	3.4	03 13	5.7	15 36	5.6
12	Sunday	03 11	7.3	15 23	7.1	00 19	9.6	12 42	9.3	01 42	3.7	14 21	3.4	03 52	5.7	16 13	5.5
13	Monday	03 47	7.1	15 56	6.9	00 54	9.4	13 15	9.1	02 17	3.7	14 52	3.4	04 30	5.5	16 49	5.4
14	Tuesday	04 18	6.9	16 26	6.8	01 27	9.1	13 48	8.8	02 51	3.6	15 24	3.4	05 07	5.4	17 26	5.2
15	Wednesday	04 47	6.7	16 58	6.7	02 01	8.8	14 21	8.5	03 25	3.5	15 57	3.3	05 45	5.1	18 04	5.0
16	Thursday	05 19	6.6	17 34	6.5	02 36	8.3	14 58	8.1	04 00	3.4	16 33	3.2	06 26	4.9	18 46	4.7
17	Friday	05 55	6.4	18 15	6.2	03 17	7.8	15 42	7.7	04 38	3.2	17 14	3.1	07 12	4.6	19 33	4.5
18	Saturday	06 38	6.1	19 03	5.8	04 07	7.3	16 39	7.2	05 23	3.0	18 03	2.9	08 05	4.4	20 27	4.4
19	Sunday	07 29	5.8	20 04	5.5	05 14	6.9	17 57	7.0	06 19	2.8	19 04	2.8	09 06	4.2	21 29	4.3
20	Monday	08 36	5.6	21 23	5.5	06 45	6.9	19 28	7.3	07 29	2.7	20 24	2.8	10 18	4.3	22 41	4.4
21	Tuesday	10 07	5.7	22 54	5.8	08 09	7.3	20 32	7.9	08 58	2.7	21 59	3.0	11 35	4.5	23 52	4.7
22	Wednesday	11 20	6.0	23 56	6.3	09 03	7.9	21 19	8.5	10 24	2.9	22 49	3.2	—	—	12 34	4.8
23	Thursday	—	—	12 15	6.5	09 46	8.4	22 00	9.0	11 10	3.1	23 28	3.3	00 46	5.0	13 19	5.1
24	Friday	00 45	6.7	13 03	6.8	10 24	8.9	22 38	9.4	11 49	3.2	—	—	01 30	5.3	13 58	5.4
25	Saturday	01 30	7.0	13 45	7.0	11 01	9.2	23 16	9.6	00 04	3.4	12 26	3.3	02 08	5.6	14 36	5.6
26	Sunday	02 11	7.2	14 24	7.1	11 39	9.4	23 55	9.8	00 42	3.5	13 04	3.4	02 45	5.8	15 13	5.8
27	Monday	02 51	7.2	15 02	7.2	—	—	12 19	9.6	01 22	3.6	13 41	3.4	03 22	5.9	15 52	5.8
28	Tuesday	03 30	7.2	15 41	7.2	00 36	9.8	13 00	9.5	02 01	3.6	14 18	3.5	04 02	5.9	16 33	5.7
29	Wednesday	04 10	7.2	16 21	7.2	01 19	9.7	13 42	9.4	02 41	3.7	14 56	3.5	04 46	5.8	17 16	5.6
30	Thursday	04 50	7.0	17 03	7.1	02 04	9.4	14 26	9.0	03 20	3.6	15 35	3.5	05 33	5.6	18 04	5.3

OCTOBER 1999   *High water*   GMT

		London Bridge				Liverpool				Greenock				Leith			
1	Friday	05 32	6.7	17 49	6.7	02 52	8.9	15 16	8.5	04 02	3.4	16 17	3.4	06 26	5.3	18 57	5.1
2	Saturday	06 18	6.2	18 43	6.3	03 49	8.2	16 17	8.0	04 50	3.2	17 06	3.3	07 29	5.0	20 02	4.8
3	Sunday	07 18	5.8	19 58	5.9	05 02	7.7	17 39	7.6	05 53	2.9	18 08	3.1	08 45	4.8	21 20	4.7
4	Monday	08 51	5.6	21 32	5.9	06 33	7.6	19 09	7.8	08 04	2.8	19 48	3.0	10 07	4.7	22 40	4.8
5	Tuesday	10 11	5.9	22 44	6.3	07 53	7.9	20 19	8.3	09 39	3.0	21 33	3.2	11 26	4.9	23 51	5.1
6	Wednesday	11 13	6.3	23 44	6.8	08 53	8.5	21 14	8.8	10 35	3.2	22 31	3.4	—	—	12 30	5.2
7	Thursday	—	—	12 08	6.8	09 43	8.9	22 00	9.3	11 23	3.4	23 18	3.5	00 48	5.3	13 20	5.4
8	Friday	00 37	7.2	12 58	7.1	10 26	9.2	22 41	9.5	—	—	12 05	3.4	01 35	5.5	14 00	5.5
9	Saturday	01 25	7.4	13 42	7.2	11 04	9.3	23 19	9.5	00 01	3.6	12 45	3.4	02 14	5.6	14 36	5.6
10	Sunday	02 08	7.4	14 22	7.2	11 39	9.3	23 53	9.4	00 41	3.6	13 19	3.4	02 51	5.6	15 10	5.6
11	Monday	02 46	7.2	14 58	7.0	—	—	12 11	9.2	01 17	3.6	13 50	3.4	03 27	5.6	15 44	5.5
12	Tuesday	03 17	7.0	15 28	6.8	00 25	9.2	12 43	9.1	01 51	3.6	14 20	3.5	04 02	5.5	16 17	5.4
13	Wednesday	03 44	6.8	15 57	6.7	00 57	9.0	13 15	8.9	02 23	3.6	14 50	3.5	04 36	5.3	16 52	5.2
14	Thursday	04 11	6.7	16 28	6.6	01 29	8.7	13 48	8.6	02 56	3.5	15 21	3.5	05 13	5.1	17 28	5.0
15	Friday	04 43	6.7	17 04	6.5	02 05	8.4	14 24	8.3	03 31	3.4	15 56	3.4	05 52	4.9	18 07	4.8
16	Saturday	05 19	6.5	17 45	6.3	02 44	7.9	15 06	7.9	04 09	3.3	16 35	3.2	06 36	4.7	18 51	4.6
17	Sunday	06 01	6.2	18 31	6.0	03 31	7.4	15 57	7.4	04 54	3.1	17 23	3.1	07 26	4.5	19 43	4.4
18	Monday	06 49	5.9	19 27	5.7	04 32	7.0	17 06	7.1	05 49	2.9	18 23	2.9	08 24	4.3	20 45	4.4
19	Tuesday	07 49	5.7	20 35	5.6	05 52	6.9	18 31	7.2	06 58	2.8	19 35	2.9	09 32	4.3	21 56	4.4
20	Wednesday	09 08	5.6	22 01	5.8	07 20	7.2	19 46	7.7	08 19	2.8	20 59	3.0	10 46	4.5	23 07	4.7
21	Thursday	10 33	5.9	23 13	6.2	08 23	7.8	20 40	8.4	09 41	3.0	22 04	3.2	11 51	4.8	—	—
22	Friday	11 35	6.3	—	—	09 10	8.5	21 25	9.0	10 36	3.2	22 51	3.3	00 06	5.0	12 42	5.2
23	Saturday	00 09	6.7	12 26	6.7	09 51	9.0	22 07	9.5	11 19	3.3	23 34	3.5	00 55	5.3	13 26	5.5
24	Sunday	00 57	7.0	13 12	7.0	10 32	9.4	22 49	9.8	11 59	3.4	—	—	01 37	5.6	14 06	5.7
25	Monday	01 42	7.2	13 55	7.2	11 12	9.7	23 31	10.0	00 16	3.6	12 38	3.5	02 17	5.9	14 46	5.9
26	Tuesday	02 24	7.3	14 38	7.4	11 54	9.8	—	—	00 59	3.7	13 17	3.6	02 58	6.0	15 27	5.9
27	Wednesday	03 06	7.3	15 21	7.4	00 15	10.0	12 38	9.8	01 42	3.7	13 56	3.7	03 42	6.0	16 10	5.8
28	Thursday	03 48	7.3	16 05	7.4	01 01	9.8	13 23	9.6	02 25	3.7	14 35	3.8	04 29	5.9	16 56	5.7
29	Friday	04 31	7.1	16 51	7.2	01 49	9.4	14 11	9.2	03 07	3.6	15 15	3.7	05 19	5.7	17 45	5.4
30	Saturday	05 14	6.7	17 39	6.9	02 39	8.9	15 02	8.7	03 52	3.5	15 59	3.6	06 16	5.4	18 41	5.1
31	Sunday	06 01	6.3	18 36	6.4	03 38	8.3	16 04	8.1	04 45	3.2	16 49	3.4	07 20	5.0	19 49	4.9

NOVEMBER 1999   *High water*   GMT

Day	London Bridge *Datum of predictions 3.20 m below* hr	ht m	hr	ht m	Liverpool *Datum of predictions 4.93 m below* hr	ht m	hr	ht m	Greenock *Datum of predictions 1.62 m below* hr	ht m	hr	ht m	Leith *Datum of predictions 2.90 m below* hr	ht m	hr	ht m
1 Monday	07 00	5.9	19 51	6.0	04 51	7.7	17 23	7.8	05 56	3.0	17 52	3.2	08 33	4.8	21 04	4.8
2 Tuesday	08 32	5.7	21 14	6.1	06 16	7.6	18 46	7.8	07 54	2.9	19 23	3.1	09 50	4.8	22 20	4.8
3 Wednesday	09 47	5.9	22 21	6.4	07 30	7.9	19 54	8.2	09 17	3.1	21 03	3.2	11 04	4.9	23 28	5.0
4 Thursday	10 47	6.3	23 19	6.7	08 29	8.3	20 49	8.6	10 12	3.3	22 04	3.4	—	—	12 07	5.1
5 Friday	11 41	6.7	—	—	09 18	8.7	21 36	9.0	10 58	3.4	22 53	3.5	00 25	5.2	12 56	5.3
6 Saturday	00 11	7.0	12 32	7.0	10 00	9.0	22 17	9.2	11 39	3.5	23 36	3.5	01 13	5.4	13 37	5.4
7 Sunday	00 59	7.2	13 17	7.1	10 38	9.2	22 54	9.2	—	—	12 16	3.5	01 53	5.4	14 12	5.4
8 Monday	01 41	7.2	13 57	7.0	11 12	9.2	23 27	9.2	00 15	3.5	12 50	3.5	02 30	5.5	14 45	5.5
9 Tuesday	02 18	7.0	14 33	6.9	11 44	9.2	23 58	9.0	00 52	3.5	13 22	3.5	03 04	5.5	15 17	5.4
10 Wednesday	02 48	6.9	15 04	6.7	—	—	12 15	9.1	01 25	3.5	13 51	3.6	03 38	5.4	15 50	5.4
11 Thursday	03 14	6.8	15 33	6.6	00 30	8.9	12 48	8.9	01 57	3.4	14 21	3.6	04 12	5.3	16 23	5.3
12 Friday	03 42	6.7	16 05	6.6	01 04	8.7	13 22	8.8	02 31	3.4	14 52	3.6	04 48	5.1	16 59	5.1
13 Saturday	04 14	6.7	16 41	6.5	01 40	8.4	13 58	8.5	03 07	3.4	15 26	3.5	05 26	5.0	17 36	4.9
14 Sunday	04 50	6.6	17 21	6.4	02 18	8.1	14 38	8.2	03 46	3.3	16 04	3.4	06 08	4.8	18 17	4.8
15 Monday	05 31	6.4	18 07	6.2	03 03	7.7	15 26	7.8	04 31	3.1	16 48	3.2	06 55	4.6	19 06	4.6
16 Tuesday	06 18	6.1	19 00	6.0	03 58	7.3	16 27	7.5	05 24	3.0	17 43	3.0	07 48	4.5	20 04	4.5
17 Wednesday	07 14	5.9	20 02	5.9	05 07	7.2	17 39	7.5	06 28	2.9	18 51	3.0	08 51	4.4	21 12	4.5
18 Thursday	08 22	5.8	21 14	6.0	06 24	7.3	18 51	7.8	07 39	2.9	20 05	3.0	09 59	4.6	22 21	4.7
19 Friday	09 40	5.9	22 26	6.3	07 33	7.8	19 54	8.4	08 52	3.0	21 17	3.2	11 06	4.8	23 24	5.0
20 Saturday	10 48	6.3	23 29	6.6	08 29	8.5	20 48	9.0	09 56	3.2	22 15	3.3	—	—	12 04	5.2
21 Sunday	11 47	6.6	—	—	09 18	9.0	21 36	9.5	10 47	3.3	23 05	3.5	00 18	5.3	12 54	5.5
22 Monday	00 23	7.0	12 40	7.0	10 03	9.5	22 23	9.8	11 32	3.5	23 52	3.6	01 06	5.6	13 39	5.7
23 Tuesday	01 13	7.2	13 29	7.2	10 48	9.8	23 10	10.0	—	—	12 14	3.6	01 52	5.8	14 22	5.9
24 Wednesday	02 00	7.3	14 17	7.4	11 34	10.0	23 58	10.0	00 39	3.7	12 57	3.8	02 37	6.0	15 05	5.9
25 Thursday	02 45	7.4	15 04	7.5	—	—	12 20	9.9	01 26	3.7	13 38	3.8	03 25	6.0	15 51	5.9
26 Friday	03 30	7.3	15 52	7.5	00 46	9.8	13 09	9.7	02 13	3.7	14 20	3.9	04 15	5.9	16 39	5.7
27 Saturday	04 15	7.1	16 41	7.3	01 37	9.5	13 58	9.4	03 00	3.6	15 03	3.9	05 08	5.7	17 30	5.5
28 Sunday	05 00	6.8	17 31	7.0	02 28	9.0	14 51	9.0	03 49	3.5	15 48	3.8	06 05	5.4	18 28	5.2
29 Monday	05 47	6.5	18 27	6.7	03 25	8.5	15 48	8.5	04 44	3.3	16 38	3.6	07 07	5.1	19 32	5.0
30 Tuesday	06 44	6.1	19 32	6.3	04 29	8.0	16 56	8.1	05 51	3.1	17 37	3.4	08 12	4.9	20 41	4.9

DECEMBER 1999   *High water*   GMT

Day	London Bridge hr	ht m	hr	ht m	Liverpool hr	ht m	hr	ht m	Greenock hr	ht m	hr	ht m	Leith hr	ht m	hr	ht m
1 Wednesday	08 01	5.9	20 45	6.2	05 43	7.7	18 10	7.9	07 14	3.0	18 47	3.3	09 20	4.8	21 49	4.9
2 Thursday	09 13	6.0	21 49	6.3	06 54	7.7	19 18	8.0	08 36	3.1	20 14	3.2	10 27	4.8	22 55	4.9
3 Friday	10 14	6.2	22 46	6.5	07 56	8.0	20 17	8.3	09 37	3.2	21 28	3.3	11 31	4.9	23 55	5.0
4 Saturday	11 10	6.4	23 39	6.7	08 47	8.4	21 07	8.5	10 26	3.3	22 23	3.4	—	—	12 24	5.0
5 Sunday	—	—	12 01	6.7	09 32	8.7	21 51	8.8	11 09	3.4	23 09	3.4	00 46	5.1	13 09	5.2
6 Monday	00 28	6.8	12 49	6.8	10 11	8.9	22 29	8.9	11 48	3.5	23 51	3.4	01 30	5.2	13 48	5.3
7 Tuesday	01 11	6.9	13 32	6.8	10 47	9.0	23 04	8.9	—	—	12 24	3.5	02 09	5.3	14 22	5.3
8 Wednesday	01 49	6.9	14 10	6.8	11 20	9.1	23 37	8.9	00 28	3.3	12 58	3.5	02 45	5.3	14 55	5.3
9 Thursday	02 21	6.8	14 43	6.7	11 53	9.1	—	—	01 02	3.3	13 29	3.5	03 19	5.3	15 28	5.3
10 Friday	02 50	6.7	15 15	6.6	00 10	8.8	12 27	9.0	01 35	3.3	13 58	3.6	03 53	5.2	16 02	5.3
11 Saturday	03 20	6.7	15 47	6.6	00 45	8.7	13 02	8.9	02 10	3.3	14 30	3.6	04 28	5.2	16 36	5.2
12 Sunday	03 52	6.6	16 23	6.6	01 21	8.6	13 39	8.7	02 47	3.3	15 04	3.6	05 05	5.1	17 12	5.1
13 Monday	04 29	6.6	17 03	6.5	01 59	8.4	14 18	8.5	03 27	3.2	15 41	3.4	05 44	4.9	17 50	4.9
14 Tuesday	05 09	6.5	17 47	6.4	02 41	8.1	15 02	8.3	04 11	3.1	16 22	3.3	06 28	4.8	18 35	4.8
15 Wednesday	05 54	6.3	18 37	6.3	03 29	7.9	15 54	8.1	04 59	3.0	17 10	3.2	07 17	4.7	19 26	4.7
16 Thursday	06 45	6.1	19 33	6.2	04 28	7.6	16 56	7.9	05 54	3.0	18 07	3.1	08 13	4.6	20 27	4.7
17 Friday	07 46	6.0	20 37	6.2	05 36	7.6	18 04	8.0	06 54	2.9	19 14	3.1	09 16	4.7	21 34	4.7
18 Saturday	08 55	6.1	21 45	6.3	06 45	7.8	19 10	8.3	08 02	3.0	20 30	3.1	10 23	4.8	22 41	4.9
19 Sunday	10 05	6.3	22 52	6.5	07 50	8.3	20 13	8.8	09 12	3.1	21 40	3.2	11 26	5.0	23 44	5.2
20 Monday	11 11	6.5	23 52	6.8	08 48	8.9	21 10	9.2	10 15	3.3	22 39	3.4	—	—	12 23	5.3
21 Tuesday	—	—	12 11	6.8	09 40	9.4	22 03	9.6	11 07	3.4	23 33	3.5	00 40	5.4	13 14	5.6
22 Wednesday	00 47	7.0	13 07	7.1	10 30	9.7	22 55	9.9	11 55	3.6	—	—	01 32	5.7	14 02	5.7
23 Thursday	01 38	7.2	14 00	7.4	11 18	9.9	23 45	9.9	00 24	3.6	12 41	3.7	02 23	5.9	14 48	5.8
24 Friday	02 27	7.3	14 50	7.5	—	—	12 07	10.0	01 16	3.6	13 25	3.8	03 13	6.0	15 35	5.9
25 Saturday	03 14	7.3	15 40	7.5	00 35	9.8	12 57	9.9	02 06	3.6	14 09	3.9	04 04	5.9	16 25	5.8
26 Sunday	04 00	7.2	16 29	7.4	01 25	9.6	13 46	9.7	02 55	3.6	14 53	3.9	04 56	5.7	17 16	5.6
27 Monday	04 45	7.0	17 18	7.2	02 14	9.2	14 34	9.3	03 45	3.5	15 37	3.8	05 50	5.5	18 11	5.4
28 Tuesday	05 31	6.7	18 08	6.9	03 04	8.8	15 25	8.9	04 34	3.4	16 24	3.8	06 45	5.2	19 08	5.2
29 Wednesday	06 18	6.4	19 01	6.5	03 57	8.3	16 19	8.4	05 26	3.2	17 14	3.6	07 42	5.0	20 08	5.0
30 Thursday	07 15	6.1	20 02	6.2	04 56	7.8	17 21	8.0	06 22	3.1	18 09	3.4	08 40	4.8	21 10	4.8
31 Friday	08 24	5.9	21 06	6.1	06 04	7.6	18 30	7.7	07 25	3.0	19 10	3.2	09 40	4.7	22 12	4.7

World Geographical Statistics

THE EARTH

The shape of the Earth is that of an oblate spheroid or solid of revolution whose meridian sections are ellipses, whilst the sections at right angles are circles.

DIMENSIONS

Equatorial diameter = 12,756.27 km (7,926.38 miles)
Polar diameter = 12,713.50 km (7,899.80 miles)
Equatorial circumference = 40,075.01 km (24,901.46 miles)
Polar circumference = 40,007.86 km (24,859.73 miles)

The equatorial circumference is divided into 360 degrees of longitude, which is measured in degrees, minutes and seconds east or west of the Greenwich meridian (0°) to 180°, the meridian 180° E. coinciding with 180° W. This was internationally ratified in 1884.

Distance north and south of the Equator is measured in degrees, minutes and seconds of latitude. The Equator is 0°, the North Pole is 90° N. and the South Pole is 90° S. The Tropics lie at 23° 26′ N. (Tropic of Cancer) and 23° 26′ S. (Tropic of Capricorn). The Arctic Circle lies at 66° 34′ N. and the Antarctic Circle at 66° 34′ S. (NB The Tropics and the Arctic and Antarctic circles are affected by the slow decrease in obliquity, of about 0.5 arcseconds per century. The effect of this is that the Arctic and Antarctic circles are currently moving towards their respective poles by about 14 metres per century, while the Tropics move towards the Equator by the same amount.

AREA, ETC.

The surface area of the Earth is 510,069,120 km^2 (196,938,800 miles^2), of which the water area is 70.92 per cent and the land area is 29.08 per cent.

The velocity of a given point on the Earth's surface at the Equator is 1,669.79 km per hour (1,037.56 m.p.h.). The Earth's mean velocity in its orbit around the Sun is 107,229 km per hour (66,629 m.p.h.). The Earth's mean distance from the Sun is 149,597,870 km (92,955,807 miles).

Source: Royal Greenwich Observatory

OCEANS

AREA

	km^2	miles^2
Pacific	166,240,000	64,186,300
Atlantic	86,550,000	33,420,000
Indian	73,427,000	28,350,500
Arctic	13,223,700	5,105,700

The division by the Equator of the Pacific into the North and South Pacific and the Atlantic into the North and South Atlantic makes a total of six oceans.

GREATEST DEPTHS

Greatest depth location	metres	feet
Mariana Trench, Pacific	10,924	35,840
Puerto Rico Trench, Atlantic	9,220	30,249
Java (Sunda) Trench, Indian	7,725	25,344
Eurasian Basin, Arctic	5,450	17,880

SEAS

AREA

	km^2	miles^2
South China	2,974,600	1,148,500
Caribbean	2,515,900	971,400
Mediterranean	2,509,900	969,100
Bering	2,226,100	873,000
Gulf of Mexico	1,507,600	582,100
Okhotsk	1,392,000	537,500
Japan	1,015,000	391,100
Hudson Bay	730,100	281,900
East China	664,600	256,600
Andaman	564,880	218,100
Black Sea	507,900	196,100
Red Sea	453,000	174,900
North Sea	427,100	164,900
Baltic Sea	382,000	147,500
Yellow Sea	294,000	113,500
Persian/Arabian Gulf	230,000	88,800

GREATEST DEPTHS

	Maximum depth metres	feet
Caribbean	9,220	30,250
East China	7,507	24,629
South China	7,258	23,812
Mediterranean	5,150	16,896
Andaman	4,267	14,000
Bering	3,936	12,913
Gulf of Mexico	3,504	11,496
Okhotsk	3,365	11,040
Japan	3,053	10,016
Red Sea	2,266	7,434
Black Sea	2,212	7,257
North Sea	439	1,440
Hudson Bay	111	364
Baltic Sea	90	295
Yellow Sea	73	240
Persian Gulf	73	240

THE CONTINENTS

There are six geographic continents, although America is often divided politically into North and Central America, and South America.

AFRICA is surrounded by sea except for the narrow isthmus of Suez in the north-east, through which is cut the Suez Canal. Its extreme longitudes are 17° 20′ W. at Cape Verde, Senegal, and 51° 24′ E. at Ras Hafun, Somalia. The extreme latitudes are 37° 20′ N. at Cape Blanc, Tunisia, and 34° 50′ S. at Cape Agulhas, South Africa, about 4,400 miles apart. The Equator passes through the middle of the continent.

NORTH AMERICA, including Mexico, is surrounded by ocean except in the south, where the isthmian states of CENTRAL AMERICA link North America with South America. Its extreme longitudes are 168° 5′ W. at Cape Prince of Wales, Alaska, and 55° 40′ W. at Cape Charles,

Newfoundland. The extreme continental latitudes are the tip of the Boothia peninsula, NW Territories, Canada (71° 51' N.) and 14° 22' N. at Ocós in the south of Mexico.

SOUTH AMERICA lies mostly in the southern hemisphere; the Equator passes through the north of the continent. It is surrounded by ocean except where it is joined to Central America in the north by the narrow isthmus through which is cut the Panama Canal. Its extreme longitudes are 34° 47' W. at Cape Branco in Brazil and 81° 20' W. at Punta Pariña, Peru. The extreme continental latitudes are 12° 25' N. at Punta Gallinas, Colombia, and 53° 54' S. at the southernmost tip of the Brunswick peninsula, Chile. Cape Horn, on Cape Island, Chile, lies at 55° 59' S.

ANTARCTICA lies almost entirely within the Antarctic Circle (66° 34' S.) and is the largest of the world's glaciated areas. The continent has an area of 5.4 million square miles, 99 per cent of which is permanently ice-covered. The ice amounts to some 7.2 million cubic miles and represents more than 90 per cent of the world's fresh water. The environment is too hostile for unsupported human habitation. See also pages 786–7

ASIA is the largest continent and occupies 30 per cent of the world's land surface. The extreme longitudes are 26° 05' E. at Baba Buran, Turkey and 169° 40' W. at Mys Dežneva (East Cape), Russia, a distance of about 6,000 miles. Its extreme northern latitude is 77° 45' N. at Cape Čeljuskin, Russia, and it extends over 5,000 miles south to about 1° 15' N. of the Equator.

AUSTRALIA is the smallest of the continents and lies in the southern hemisphere. It is entirely surrounded by ocean. Its extreme longitudes are 113° 11' E. at Steep Point and 153° 11' E. at Cape Byron. The extreme latitudes are 10° 42' S. at Cape York and 39° S. at South East Point, Tasmania.

EUROPE, including European Russia, is the smallest continent in the northern hemisphere. Its extreme latitudes are 71° 11' N. at North Cape in Norway, and 36° 23' N. at Cape Matapan in southern Greece, a distance of about 2,400 miles. Its breadth from Cabo Carvoeiro in Portugal (9° 34' W.) in the west to the Kara River, north of the Urals (66° 30' E.) in the east is about 3,300 miles. The division between Europe and Asia is generally regarded as the watershed of the Ural Mountains; down the Ural river to Gur'yev, Kazakhstan; across the Caspian Sea to Apsheronskiy Poluostrov, near Baku; along the watershed of the Caucasus Mountains to Anapa and thence across the Black Sea to the Bosporus in Turkey; across the Sea of Marmara to Çanakkale Boğazi (Dardanelles).

	Area km²	miles²
Asia	43,998,000	16,988,000
*America	41,918,000	16,185,000
Africa	29,800,000	11,506,000
Antarctica	13,980,000	5,400,000
†Europe	9,699,000	3,745,000
Australia	7,618,493	2,941,526

*North and Central America has an area of 24,255,000 km² (9,365,000 miles²)

†Includes 5,571,000 km² (2,151,000 miles²) of former USSR territory, including the Baltic states, Belarus, Moldova, the Ukraine, that part of Russia west of the Ural Mountains and Kazakhstan west of the Ural river. European Turkey (24,378 km²/9,412 miles²) comprises territory to the west and north of the Bosporus and the Dardanelles

GLACIATED AREAS

It is estimated that 15,915,000 km² (6,145,000 miles²) or 10.73 per cent of the world's land surface is permanently covered with ice.

	Area km²	miles²
South Polar regions	13,830,000	5,340,000
North Polar regions (incl. Greenland or Kalaallit Nunaat)	1,965,000	758,500
Alaska-Canada	58,800	22,700
Asia	37,800	14,600
South America	11,900	4,600
Europe	10,700	4,128
New Zealand	1,015	391
Africa	238	92

The largest glacier is the 515 km/320 mile-long Lambert-Fisher Ice Passage, Antarctica.

PENINSULAS

	Area km²	miles²
Arabian	3,250,000	1,250,000
Southern Indian	2,072,000	800,000
Alaskan	1,500,000	580,000
Labradorian	1,300,000	500,000
Scandinavian	800,300	309,000
Iberian	584,000	225,500

LARGEST ISLANDS

Island, and Ocean	Area km²	miles²
Greenland (Kalaallit Nunaat), Arctic	2,175,500	840,000
New Guinea, Pacific	821,030	317,000
Borneo, Pacific	725,450	280,100
Madagascar, Indian	587,040	226,658
Baffin Island, Arctic	507,451	195,928
Sumatra, Indian	427,350	165,000
Honshu, Pacific	227,413	87,805
*Great Britain, Atlantic	218,077	84,200
Victoria Island, Arctic	217,292	83,897
Ellesmere Island, Arctic	196,236	75,767
Sulawesi (Celebes), Indian	189,036	72,987
South Island, NZ, Pacific	151,213	58,384
Java, Indian	126,650	48,900
North Island, NZ, (Pacific)	115,777	44,702
Cuba, Atlantic	110,862	42,804
Newfoundland, Atlantic	108,855	42,030
Luzon, Pacific	105,880	40,880
Iceland, Atlantic	102,817	39,698
Mindanao, Pacific	95,247	36,775
Ireland, Atlantic	82,462	31,839

*Mainland only

LARGEST DESERTS

	Area (approx.)	
	km²	miles²
The Sahara, N. Africa	8,400,000	3,250,000
Australian Desert	1,550,000	600,000
Arabian Desert	1,200,000	470,000
The Gobi, Mongolia/China	1,040,000	400,000
Kalahari Desert, Botswana/		
Namibia/S. Africa	520,000	200,000
Takla Makan, Mongolia/		
China	320,000	125,000
Sonoran Desert, USA/		
Mexico	310,000	120,000
*Kara Kum, Turkmenistan	310,000	120,000
Namib Desert, Namibia	285,000	110,000
Thar Desert, India/Pakistan	260,000	100,000
Somali Desert, Somalia	260,000	100,000
Atacama Desert, Chile	180,000	70,000
Dasht-e Lut, Iran	52,000	20,000
Mojave Desert, USA	38,850	15,000

*Together with the Kyzyl Kum known as the Turkestan Desert

DEEPEST DEPRESSIONS

	Maximum depth below sea level	
	metres	feet
Dead Sea, Jordan/Israel	395	1,296
Turfan Depression, Sinkiang, China	153	505
Qattara Depression, Egypt	132	436
Mangyshlak peninsula, Kazakhstan	131	433
Danakil Depression, Ethiopia	116	383
Death Valley, California, USA	86	282
Salton Sink, California, USA	71	235
W. of Ustyurt plateau, Kazakhstan	70	230
Prikaspiyskaya Nizmennost',		
Russia/Kazakhstan	67	220
Lake Sarykamysh, Uzbekistan/		
Turkmenistan	45	148
El Faiyûm, Egypt	44	147
Valdies peninsula, Lago Enriquillo,		
Dominican Republic	40	131

The world's largest exposed depression is the Prikaspiys-kaya Nizmennost' covering the hinterland of the northern third of the Caspian Sea, which is itself 28 m (92 ft) below sea level.

Western Antarctica and Central Greenland largely comprise crypto-depressions under ice burdens. The Antarctic Wilkes subglacial basin has a bedrock 2,341 m (7,680 ft) below sea-level. In Greenland (lat. 73° N., long. 39° W.) the bedrock is 365 m (1,197 ft) below sea-level.

More than a quarter of the area of The Netherlands lies marginally below sea-level, an area of more than 10,000 km²/3,860 miles².

LONGEST MOUNTAIN RANGES

Range, and location	Length	
	km	miles
Cordillera de Los Andes, W. South		
America	7,200	4,500
Rocky Mountains, W. North America	4,800	3,000
Himalaya-Karakoram-Hindu Kush, S.		
Central Asia	3,800	2,400
Great Dividing Range, E. Australia	3,600	2,250
Trans-Antarctic Mts, Antarctica	3,500	2,200
Atlantic Coast Range, E. Brazil	3,000	1,900
West Sumatran-Javan Range,		
Indonesia	2,900	1,800
Aleutian Range, Alaska and NW		
Pacific	2,650	1,650
Tien Shan, S. Central Asia	2,250	1,400
Central New Guinea Range, Irian		
Jaya/Papua New Guinea	2,000	1,250

HIGHEST MOUNTAINS

The world's 8,000-metre mountains (with six subsidiary peaks) are all in the Himalaya-Karakoram-Hindu Kush range.

Mountain	Height	
	metres	feet
Mt Everest*	8,848	29,028
K2 (Chogori)†	8,607	28,238
Kangchenjunga	8,597	28,208
Lhotse	8,511	27,923
Makalu I	8,481	27,824
Lhotse Shar (II)	8,383	27,504
Dhaulagiri I	8,171	26,810
Manaslu I (Kutang I)	8,156	26,760
Cho Oyu	8,153	26,750
Nanga Parbat (Diamir)	8,125	26,660
Annapurna I	8,091	26,546
Gasherbrum I (Hidden Peak)	8,068	26,470
Broad Peak I	8,046	26,400
Shisham Pangma (Gosainthan)	8,046	26,400
Gasherbrum II	8,034	26,360
Makalu South-East	8,010	26,280
Broad Peak Central	8,000	26,246

*Named after Sir George Everest (1790–1866), Surveyor-General of India 1830–43, in 1863. He pronounced his name Eve-rest
†Formerly Godwin-Austin

The culminating summits in the other major mountain ranges are:

Mountain, by range or country	Height	
	metres	feet
Pik Pobedy, Tien Shan	7,439	24,406
Cerro Aconcagua, Cordillera de Los		
Andes	6,960	22,834
Mt McKinley (S. Peak), Alaska Range	6,194	20,320
Kilimanjaro (Kibo), Tanzania	5,894	19,340
Hkakabo Razi, Myanmar	5,881	19,296
El'brus, (W. Peak), Caucasus	5,642	18,510
Citlaltépetl (Orizaba), Sierra Madre		
Oriental, Mexico	5,610	18,405
Vinson Massif, E. Antarctica	4,900	16,073

Mountain, by range or country	Height metres	feet
Puncak Jaya, Central New Guinea Range	4,884	16,023
Mt Blanc, Alps	4,807	15,771
Klyuchevskaya Sopka, Kamchatka peninsula, Russia	4,750	15,584
Ras Dashan, Ethiopian Highlands	4,620	15,158
Zard Kūh, Zagros Mts, Iran	4,547	14,921
Mt Kirkpatrick, Trans Antarctic	4,529	14,860
Mt Belukha, Altai Mts, Russia/ Kazakhstan	4,505	14,783
Mt Elbert, Rocky Mountains	4,400	14,433
Mt Rainier, Cascade Range, N. America	4,392	14,410
Nevado de Colima, Sierra Madre Occidental, Mexico	4,268	14,003
Jebel Toubkal, Atlas Mts, N. Africa	4,165	13,665
Kinabalu, Crocker Range, Borneo	4,101	13,455
Kerinci, West Sumatran-Javan Range, Indonesia	3,800	12,467
Jabal an Nabī Shu'ayb, N. Tihāmat, Yemen	3,760	12,336
Mt Cook (Aorangi), Southern Alps, New Zealand	3,754	12,315
Teotepec, Sierra Madre del Sur, Mexico	3,703	12,149
Thaban Ntlenyana, Drakensberg, South Africa	3,482	11,425
Pico de Bandeira, Atlantic Coast Range	2,890	9,482
Shishaldin, Aleutian Range	2,861	9,387
Kosciusko, Great Dividing Range	2,228	7,310

HIGHEST VOLCANOES

Volcano (last major eruption), and location	Height metres	feet
Ojos del Salado (1981), Andes, Argentina	6,895	22,588
Llullaillaco (1877), Andes, Argentina/Chile	6,723	22,057
San Pedro (1960), Andes, Chile	6,199	20,325
Guallatiri (1960, 1993), Andes, Chile	6,060	19,882
Láscar (1995), Andes, Chile	5,990	19,652
Cotopaxi (1940, 1975), Andes, Ecuador	5,897	19,347
Tupungatito (1986), Andes, Chile	5,640	18,504
Popocatépetl (1996), Mexico	5,465	17,930
Nevado del Ruiz (1985, 1991), Colombia	5,400	17,716
Sangay (1996), Andes, Ecuador	5,230	17,159
Guagua Pichincha (1993), Andes, Ecuador	4,784	15,696
Purace (1977), Colombia	4,756	15,601
Klyuchevskaya Sopka (1997), Kamchatka peninsula, Russia	4,750	15,584
Galeras (1993), Colombia	4,275	14,028
Nevado de Colima (1991, 1994), Mexico	4,268	14,003
Mauna Loa (1984, 1987), Hawaii Is.	4,170	13,680
Cameroon (1982), Cameroon	4,095	13,435
Acatenango (1972), Guatemala	3,960	12,992
Fuego (1987, 1991), Guatemala	3,835	12,582
Kerinci (1970, 1987), Sumatra, Indonesia	3,800	12,467

Volcano (last major eruption), and location	Height metres	feet
Erebus (1995), Ross Island, Antarctica	3,794	12,450
Tacana (1986, 1988), Guatemala	3,780	12,400
Fuji (1708), Honshu, Japan	3,775	12,388
Santa Maria (1902, 1993), Guatemala	3,768	12,362
Rindjani (1966), Lombok, Indonesia	3,726	12,224
Semeru (1995, 1997), Java, Indonesia	3,675	12,060
Nyiragongo (1994), Dem. Rep. of Congo	3,475	11,400
Koryakskaya (1957), Kamchatka, Russia	3,456	11,339
Irazú (1965, 1992), Costa Rica	3,432	11,260
Slamet (1989), Java, Indonesia	3,428	11,247
Spurr (1953), Alaska, USA	3,374	11,069
Mt Etna (1169, 1669, 1993, 1996, 1997), Sicily, Italy	3,350	10,990
Turrialba (1866, 1992), Costa Rica	3,339	10,956
Raung (1993, 1997), Java, Indonesia	3,322	10,932
Sheveluch (1964, 1997), Kamchatka, Russia	3,283	10,771
Agung (1964), Bali, Indonesia	3,142	10,308
Llaima (1995), Chile	3,128	10,239
Redoubt (1990), Alaska, USA	3,108	10,197
Tjareme (1938), Java, Indonesia	3,078	10,098
On-Take (1980, 1991), Honshu, Japan	3,063	10,049
Nyamuragira (1994), Dem. Rep. of Congo	3,056	10,028
Iliamna (1953, 1978), Alaska, USA	3,052	10,016

OTHER NOTABLE VOLCANOES

	Height metres	feet
Tambora (1815), Sumbawa, Indonesia	2,850	9,353
Mt St Helens (1980, 1986, 1991), Washington State, USA	2,549	8,363
Beerenberg (1985), Jan Mayen Island	2,546	8,347
Pinatubo (1991, 1995), Philippines	1,598	5,249
Hekla (1981, 1991), Iceland	1,501	4,920
Mt Pelée (1902), Martinique	1,397	4,583
Mt Unzen (1792, 1991, 1996), Kyushu, Japan	1,360	4,462
Vesuvius (AD 79, 1631, 1944), Italy	1,280	4,198
Kilauea (1996, 1997), Hawaii, USA	1,249	4,009
Soufrière (1979, 1997), St Vincent	1,234	4,048
Soufrière Hills (1997), Montserrat	942	3,091
Stromboli (1996, 1997), Lipari Is., Italy	926	3,038
Krakatau (1883, 1995), Sunda Strait, Indonesia	813	2,667
Santoriní (Thíra) (1628 BC, 1950), Aegean Sea, Greece	566	1,857
Vulcano (Monte Aria) (1988), Lipari Is., Italy	499	1,637
Tristan da Cunha (1961), South Atlantic	243	800
Surtsey (1963–7), off Iceland	173	568

LARGEST LAKES

The areas of some of these lakes are subject to seasonal variation.

	Area km²	miles²	Length km	miles
Caspian Sea, Iran/ Azerbaijan/Russia/ Turkmenistan/ Kazakhstan	371,000	143,000	1,171	728
*Michigan–Huron, USA/Canada	117,610	45,300	1,010	627
Superior, Canada/ USA	82,100	31,700	563	350
Victoria, Uganda/ Tanzania/Kenya	69,500	26,828	362	225
Aral Sea, Kazakhstan/ Uzbekistan	40,000	15,444	134	217
Tanganyika, Dem. Rep. of Congo/ Tanzania/Zambia/ Burundi	32,900	12,665	725	450
Great Bear, Canada	31,328	12,096	309	192
†Baykal (Baikal), Russia	30,500	11,776	620	385
Malawi (Nyasa), Tanzania/Malawi/ Mozambique	29,600	11,430	580	360
Great Slave, Canada	28,570	11,031	480	298
Erie, Canada/USA	25,670	9,910	388	241
Winnipeg, Canada	24,390	9,417	428	266
Ontario, Canada/USA	19,010	7,340	310	193
Ladozhskoye (Ladoga), Russia	17,700	6,835	193	120
Balkhash, Kazakhstan	17,400	6,718	482	299

*Lakes Michigan and Huron are regarded as lobes of the same lake. The Michigan lobe has an area of 57,750 km² (22,300 miles²) and the Huron lobe an area of 59,570 km² (23,000 miles²)

†World's deepest lake (1,940 m/6,365 ft)

UNITED KINGDOM, BY COUNTRY

Lough Neagh, Northern Ireland	381.73	147.39	28.90	18.00
Loch Lomond, Scotland	71.12	27.46	36.44	22.64
Windermere, England	14.74	5.69	16.90	10.50
Lake Vyrnwy, Wales (artificial)	4.53	1.75	7.56	4.70
Llyn Tegid (Bala), Wales (natural)	4.38	1.69	5.80	3.65

LONGEST RIVERS

River, source and outflow	Length km	miles
Nile (Bahr-el-Nil), R. Luvironza, Burundi – E. Mediterranean Sea	6,670	4,145
Amazon (Amazonas), Lago Villafro, Peru – S. Atlantic Ocean	6,448	4,007
Mississippi-Missouri-Red Rock, Montana – Gulf of Mexico	5,970	3,710
Yenisey-Angara, W. Mongolia – Kara Sea	5,540	3,442

River, source and outflow	Length km	miles
Yangtze-Kiang (Chang Jiang), Kunlun Mts, W. China – Yellow Sea	5,530	3,436
Huang He (Yellow River), Bayan Har Shan range, central China – Yellow Sea	5,463	3,395
Ob'-Irtysh, W. Mongolia – Kara Sea	5,410	3,362
Río de la Plata-Paraná, R. Paranáiba, central Brazil – S. Atlantic Ocean	4,880	3,032
Zaïre (Congo), R. Lualaba, Dem. Rep. of Congo-Zambia – S. Atlantic Ocean	4,700	2,920
Lena-Kirenga, R. Kirenga, W. of Lake Baykal – Arctic Ocean	4,400	2,734
Mekong, Lants'ang, Tibet – South China Sea	4,350	2,702
Amur-Argun, R. Argun, Khingan Mts, N. China – Sea of Okhotsk	4,345	2,700
Mackenzie-Peace, Tatlatui Lake, British Columbia – Beaufort Sea	4,240	2,635
Niger, Loma Mts, Guinea – Gulf of Guinea, E. Atlantic Ocean	4,181	2,600
Murray-Darling, SE Queensland – Lake Alexandrina, S. Australia	3,717	2,310
Volga, Valdai plateau – Caspian Sea	3,530	2,193
Zambezi, NW Zambia – S. Indian Ocean	2,736	1,700

OTHER NOTABLE RIVERS

St Lawrence, Minnesota, USA – Gulf of St Lawrence	3,130	1,945
Ganges-Brahmaputra, R. Matsang, SW Tibet – Bay of Bengal	2,900	1,800
Indus, R. Sengge, SW Tibet – N. Arabian Sea	2,880	1,790
Danube (Donau), Black Forest, SW Germany – Black Sea	2,856	1,775
Tigris-Euphrates, R. Murat, E. Turkey – Persian Gulf	2,800	1,740
Irrawaddy, R. Mali Hka, Myanmar – Andaman Sea	2,151	1,337
Don, SE of Novomoskovsk – Sea of Azov	1,969	1,224

BRITISH ISLES

Shannon, Co. Cavan, Rep. of Ireland – Atlantic Ocean	386	240
Severn, Powys, Wales – Bristol Channel	354	220
Thames, Gloucestershire, England – North Sea	346	215
Tay, Perthshire, Scotland – North Sea	188	117
Clyde, Lanarkshire, Scotland – Firth of Clyde	158	98½
Tweed, Peeblesshire, Scotland – North Sea	155	96½
Bann (Upper and Lower), Co. Down, N. Ireland – Atlantic Ocean	122	76

GREATEST WATERFALLS – BY HEIGHT

Waterfall, river and location	Total drop		Greatest single leap	
	metres	feet	metres	feet
Angel, Carrao, Venezuela	979	3,212	807	2,648
Tugela, Tugela, Natal, S. Africa	947	3,110	410	1,350
Utigård, Jostedal Glacier, Norway	800	2,625	600	1,970
Mongefossen, Monge, Norway	774	2,540	—	—
Yosemite, Yosemite Creek, USA	739	2,425	435	1,430
Østre Mardøla Foss, Mardals, Norway	656	2,154	296	974
Tyssestrengane, Tysso, Norway	646	2,120	289	948
Cuquenán, Arabopó, Venezuela	610	2,000	—	—
Sutherland, Arthur, NZ	580	1,904	248	815
*Kjellfossen (Kile), Naeröfjord, Norway	561	1,841	149	490

*Volume often so low the fall atomizes into a 'bridal veil'

BRITISH ISLES, BY COUNTRY

Eas a' Chuàl Aluinn, Glas Bheinn, Sutherland, Scotland	200	658		
Powerscourt Falls, Dargle, Co. Wicklow, Rep. of Ireland	106	350		
Pistyll-y-Llyn, Powys/ Dyfed border, Wales	c.73	230– 240		(cascades)
Pistyll Rhyadr, Clwyd/ Powys border, Wales	71.5	235		(single leap)
Caldron Snout, R. Tees, Cumbria/Durham, England	61	200		(cascades)

GREATEST WATERFALLS – BY VOLUME

Waterfall, river and location	Mean annual flow	
	m³/sec	galls/sec
Boyoma (Stanley), R. Lualaba, Dem. Rep. of Congo	c.17,000	c.3,750,000
Khône, Mekong, Laos	11,500	2,530,000
Niagara (Horseshoe), R. Niagara/Lake Erie–Lake Ontario	5,640	1,260,000
Paulo Afonso, R. São Francisco, Brazil	2,800	625,000
Urubupunga, Alto Paraná, Brazil	2,800	625,000
Cataratas del Iguazú, R. Iguaçu, Brazil/Argentina	1,725	380,000
Patos-Maribando, Rio Grande, Brazil	1,500	330,000
Victoria (Mosi-oa-tunya), R. Zambezi, Zambia/ Zimbabwe	1,100	242,000
Churchill, R. Churchill, Canada	975	215,000
Kaieteur, R. Potaro, Guyana	660	145,000

TALLEST DAMS

	metres	feet
*Rogun, R. Vakhsh, Tajikistan	335	1,098
Nurek, R. Vakhsh, Tajikistan	300	984
Grande Dixence, Switzerland	285	935
*Longtan, R. Hangshui, China	285	935
Inguri, Georgia	272	892
Chicoasén, Mexico	261	856
Tehri, R. Bhagivathi, India	261	856

*Under construction

The world's most massive dam is the Syncrude Tailings dam in Alberta, Canada, which will have a volume of 540 million cubic metres/706 million cubic yards.

The Three Gorges Chang Jiang (Yangtze) Dam, China, with a crest length of 1,983 m/6,505 ft, is due for completion in 2009.

The Yacyretá-Apipe dam across the River Paraná, Argentina-Paraguay, is being completed to a length of 69,600 m/43.24 miles.

TALLEST INHABITED BUILDINGS

Building and city	Height	
	metres	feet
Chongqing Tower, China	457	1,499
Petronas Towers I and II, Kuala Lumpur, Malaysia	451.9	1,482
Sears Tower, Chicago[1]	443	1,454
Jin Mao, Shanghai, China (1998)	420	1,378
One World Trade Center Tower, New York[2]	417	1,368
Plaza Rakyat, Kuala Lumpur, Malaysia	382	1,254
Empire State Building, New York[3]	381	1,250
Central Plaza, Hong Kong	373	1,227
T & C Tower, Kaohsiung, Taiwan	347	1,140
Amoco Building, Chicago	346	1,136
John Hancock Center, Chicago	343	1,127
Shun Hing Square, Shenzhen, China	325	1,066
Sky Central Plaza, Guangzhou, China	321	1,056
Chicago Beach Tower, Dubai	320	1,050
Baiyoke Tower, Bangkok, Thailand	320	1,050
Chrysler Building, New York	319	1,046
Bank of China, Hong Kong[4]	315	1,033
Nation's Bank Tower, Atlanta, USA	312	1,023

1. With TV antennae, 520 m/1,707 ft
2. With TV antennae, 521.2 m/1,710 ft; Two World Trade Center Tower, 415 m/1,362 ft
3. With TV tower (added 1950–1), 430.9 m/1,414 ft
4. With steel mast, 368.5 m/1,209 ft

TALLEST STRUCTURES

Structure and location	Height	
	metres	feet
*Warszawa Radio Mast, Konstantynow, Poland	646	2,120
KTHI-TV Mast, Blanchard, North Dakota (guyed)	629	2,063
CN Tower, Metro Centre, Toronto, Canada	555	1,822
Ostankino Tower, Moscow	537	1,762

*Collapsed during renovation, August 1991

LONGEST BRIDGES – BY SPAN

Bridge and location	Length	
	metres	feet

SUSPENSION SPANS

Bridge and location	metres	feet
*Akashi-Kaikyo, Shikoku, Japan (1998)	1,990	6,529
Store Baelt East Bridge, Denmark	1,624	5,328
Humber Estuary, Humberside, England	1,410	4,626
*Jiangyin (Yangtze), China (1999)	1,385	4,488
Verrazano Narrows, Brooklyn–Staten I,		
USA	1,298	4,260
Golden Gate, San Francisco Bay, USA	1,280	4,200
Hoga Kustan, Sweden	1,210	3,970
Mackinac Straits, Michigan, USA	1,158	3,800
Minami Bisan-Seto, Japan	1,100	3,609
Bosporus I, Istanbul, Turkey	1,089	3,576
Bosporus II, Istanbul, Turkey	1,074	3,524
George Washington, Hudson River, New		
York City, USA	1,067	3,500
Kurushima III, Japan	1,030	3,379
Ponte 25 de Abril (Tagus), Lisbon,		
Portugal	1,013	3,323
Firth of Forth (road), nr Edinburgh,		
Scotland	1,006	3,300
Kita Bisan-Seto, Japan	990	3,248
Severn River, Severn Estuary, England	988	3,240

*Under construction

The main span of the 5.15 km/3.2 mile long Second Severn bridging, opened in 1996, is 456 m/1,496 ft.

CANTILEVER SPANS

	metres	feet
Pont de Québec (rail-road), St Lawrence,		
Canada	548.6	1,800
Ravenswood, W. Virginia, USA	525.1	1,723
Firth of Forth (rail), nr Edinburgh,		
Scotland	521.2	1,710
Nanko, Osaka, Japan	510.0	1,673
Commodore Barry, Chester,		
Pennsylvania, USA	494.3	1,622
Greater New Orleans, Louisiana, USA	480.0	1,575
Howrah (rail-road), Calcutta, India	457.2	1,500

STEEL ARCH SPANS

	metres	feet
New River Gorge, Fayetteville, W.		
Virginia, USA	518.0	1,700
Bayonne (Kill van Kull), Bayonne, NJ –		
Staten I, USA	503.5	1,652
Sydney Harbour, Sydney, Australia	502.9	1,650

The 'floating' bridging at Evergreen, Seattle, Washington State, USA, is 3,839 m/12,596 ft long.

The longest stretch of bridgings of any kind is that carrying the Interstate 55 and Interstate 10 highways at Manchac, Louisiana, on twin concrete trestles over 55.21 km/34.31 miles.

LONGEST VEHICULAR TUNNELS

Tunnel and location	Length	
	km	miles
*Seikan (rail), Tsugaru Channel, Japan	53.90	33.49
*Channel Tunnel, Cheriton, Kent –		
Sangatte, Calais	49.94	31.03
Moscow metro, Belyaevo – Bittsevsky,		
Moscow, Russia	37.90	23.50
Northern line tube, East Finchley –		
Morden, London	27.84	17.30
Oshimizu (rail), Honshū, Japan	22.17	13.78
Simplon II (rail), Brigue, Switzerland –		
Iselle, Italy	19.82	12.31
Simplon I (rail), Brigue, Switzerland –		
Iselle, Italy	19.80	12.30
*Shin-Kanmon (rail), Kanmon Strait,		
Japan	18.68	11.61
Great Appennine (rail), Vernio, Italy	18.49	11.49
St Gotthard (road), Göschenen –		
Airolo, Switzerland	16.32	10.14
Rokko (rail), Ōsaka – Kōbe, Japan	16.09	10.00

*Sub-aqueous

The longest non-vehicular tunnelling in the world is the Delaware Aqueduct in New York State, USA, constructed in 1937–44 to a length of 168.9 km/105 miles.

BRITAIN – RAIL TUNNELS

	miles	yards
Severn, Bristol – Newport	4	484
Totley, Manchester – Sheffield	3	950
Standedge, Manchester – Huddersfield	3	66
Sodbury, Swindon – Bristol	2	924
Disley, Stockport – Sheffield	2	346
Ffestiniog, Llandudno – Blaenau		
Ffestiniog	2	338
Bramhope, Leeds – Harrogate	2	241
Cowburn, Manchester – Sheffield	2	182

The longest road tunnel in Britain is the Mersey Road Tunnel, 2 miles 228 yards long. The longest canal tunnel, at Standedge, W. Yorks, is 3 miles 330 yards long; it was closed in 1944 but is currently being restored.

LONGEST SHIP CANALS

Canal (opening date)	Length		Min. depth	
	km	miles	metres	feet
White Sea-Baltic				
(formerly				
Stalin) (1933)				
Canalized river; canal				
51.5 km/32 miles	227	141.00	5.0	16.5
*Suez (1869)				
Links Red and				
Mediterranean Seas	162	100.60	12.9	42.3
V. I. Lenin Volga-Don				
(1952)				
Links Black and				
Caspian Seas	100	62.20	n/a	n/a

Canal (opening date)	Length		Min. depth	
	km	miles	metres	feet
Kiel (or North Sea) (1895) Links North and Baltic Seas	98	60.90	13.7	45.0
*Houston (1940) Links inland city with sea	91	56.70	10.4	34.0
Alphonse XIII (1926) Gives Seville access to sea	85	53.00	7.6	25.0
Panama (1914) Links Pacific Ocean and Caribbean Sea; lake chain, 78.9 km/49 miles dug	82	50.71	12.5	41.0
Manchester Ship (1894) Links city with Irish Channel	64	39.70	8.5	28.0
Welland (1932) Circumvents Niagara Falls and Rapids	43	26.70	8.8	29.0
Brussels (Rupel Sea) (1922) Renders Brussels an inland port	32	19.80	6.4	21.0

*Has no locks

The first section of China's Grand Canal, running 1,782 km/1,107 miles from Beijing to Hangzhou, was opened AD 610 and completed in 1283. Today it is limited to 2,000 tonne vessels.

The St Lawrence Seaway comprises Beauharnois, Welland and Welland Bypass and Seaway 54–59 canals, and allows access to Duluth, Minnesota, USA via the Great Lakes from the Atlantic end of Canada's Gulf of St Lawrence, a distance of 3,769 km/2,342 miles.

LARGEST CITIES OF THE WORLD

In most cases figures refer to urban agglomerations (Ψ seaport)

	Population
Mexico City, Mexico	15,047,685
Cairo, Egypt	13,000,000
Ψ Bombay/Mumbai, India	12,596,243
Tokyo, Japan	11,927,457
Ψ Calcutta, India	11,021,918
Ψ Buenos Aires, Argentina	10,686,163
Seoul, South Korea	10,412,000
São Paulo, Brazil	9,842,059
Paris, France	9,319,367
Ψ Jakarta, Indonesia	9,160,500
Moscow, Russia	8,600,000
Manila, Philippines	8,594,150
Delhi, India	8,419,084
Ψ Shanghai, China	8,205,598
Bogotá, Colombia	8,000,000
Istanbul, Turkey	7,784,100
Ψ New York, USA	7,380,906
Beijing, China	7,362,426
Ψ Karachi, Pakistan	7,183,000
Washington DC, USA	7,051,495

The United Kingdom

The United Kingdom comprises Great Britain (England, Wales and Scotland) and Northern Ireland. The Isle of Man and the Channel Islands are Crown dependencies with their own legislative systems, and not a part of the United Kingdom.

AREA AS AT 31 MARCH 1981

	Land miles^2	km^2	*Inland water miles^2	km^2	Total miles^2	km^2
United Kingdom	93,006	240,883	1,242	3,218	94,248	244,101
England	50,058	129,652	293	758	50,351	130,410
Wales	7,965	20,628	50	130	8,015	20,758
Scotland	29,767	77,097	653	1,692	30,420	78,789
†Northern Ireland	5,225	13,532	249	628	5,467	14,160
Isle of Man	221	572	—	—	221	572
Channel Islands	75	194	—	—	75	194

*Excluding tidal water
†Excluding certain tidal waters that are parts of statutory areas in Northern Ireland

POPULATION

The first official census of population in England, Wales and Scotland was taken in 1801 and a census has been taken every ten years since, except in 1941 when there was no census because of war. The last official census in the United Kingdom was taken on 21 April 1991 and the next is due in April 2001.

The first official census of population in Ireland was taken in 1841. However, all figures given below refer only to the area which is now Northern Ireland. Figures for Northern Ireland in 1921 and 1931 are estimates based on the censuses taken in 1926 and 1937 respectively.

Estimates of the population of England before 1801, calculated from the number of baptisms, burials and marriages, are:

1570	4,160,221	1670	5,773,646
1600	4,811,718	1700	6,045,008
1630	5,600,517	1750	6,517,035

	United Kingdom			England and Wales			Scotland			Northern Ireland		
Thousands	Total	Male	Female	Total	Male	Female	Total	Male	Female	Total	Male	Female
CENSUS RESULTS 1801–1991												
1801	—	—	—	8,893	4,255	4,638	1,608	739	869	—	—	—
1811	13,368	6,368	7,000	10,165	4,874	5,291	1,806	826	980	—	—	—
1821	15,472	7,498	7,974	12,000	5,850	6,150	2,092	983	1,109	—	—	—
1831	17,835	8,647	9,188	13,897	6,771	7,126	2,364	1,114	1,250	—	—	—
1841	20,183	9,819	10,364	15,914	7,778	8,137	2,620	1,242	1,378	1,649	800	849
1851	22,259	10,855	11,404	17,928	8,781	9,146	2,889	1,376	1,513	1,443	698	745
1861	24,525	11,894	12,631	20,066	9,776	10,290	3,062	1,450	1,612	1,396	668	728
1871	27,431	13,309	14,122	22,712	11,059	11,653	3,360	1,603	1,757	1,359	647	712
1881	31,015	15,060	15,955	25,974	12,640	13,335	3,736	1,799	1,936	1,305	621	684
1891	34,264	16,593	17,671	29,003	14,060	14,942	4,026	1,943	2,083	1,236	590	646
1901	38,237	18,492	19,745	32,528	15,729	16,799	4,472	2,174	2,298	1,237	590	647
1911	42,082	20,357	21,725	36,070	17,446	18,625	4,761	2,309	2,452	1,251	603	648
1921	44,027	21,033	22,994	37,887	18,075	19,811	4,882	2,348	2,535	1,258	610	648
1931	46,038	22,060	23,978	39,952	19,133	20,819	4,843	2,326	2,517	1,243	601	642
1951	50,225	24,118	26,107	43,758	21,016	22,742	5,096	2,434	2,662	1,371	668	703
1961	52,709	25,481	27,228	46,105	22,304	23,801	5,179	2,483	2,697	1,425	694	731
1971	55,515	26,952	28,562	48,750	23,683	25,067	5,229	2,515	2,714	1,536	755	781
1981	55,848	27,104	28,742	49,155	23,873	25,281	5,131	2,466	2,664	*1,533	750	783
1991	56,467	27,344	29,123	49,890	24,182	25,707	4,999	2,392	2,607	1,578	769	809
†RESIDENT POPULATION: PROJECTIONS (MID-YEAR)												
2001	59,618	29,377	30,241	52,818	26,062	26,756	5,106	2,484	2,622	1,694	830	864
2011	60,929	30,206	30,723	54,151	26,881	27,269	5,059	2,476	2,583	1,720	848	872
2021	62,244	30,916	31,328	55,526	27,614	27,913	4,993	2,449	2,544	1,724	853	871

*Figures include 44,500 non-enumerated persons
† Projections are 1996 based

Source: The Stationery Office – *Annual Abstract 1998*; ONS – Census reports (Crown copyright)

ISLANDS: Census Results 1901–91

	Isle of Man Total	Male	Female	Jersey Total	Male	Female	*Guernsey Total	Male	Female
1901	54,752	25,496	29,256	52,576	23,940	28,636	40,446	19,652	20,794
1911	52,016	23,937	28,079	51,898	24,014	27,884	41,858	20,661	21,197
1921	60,284	27,329	32,955	49,701	22,438	27,263	38,315	18,246	20,069
1931	49,308	22,443	26,865	50,462	23,424	27,038	40,643	19,659	20,984
1951	55,123	25,749	29,464	57,296	27,282	30,014	43,652	21,221	22,431
1961	48,151	22,060	26,091	57,200	27,200	30,000	45,068	21,671	23,397
1971	56,289	26,461	29,828	72,532	35,423	37,109	51,458	24,792	26,666
1981	64,679	30,901	33,778	77,000	37,000	40,000	53,313	25,701	27,612
1991	69,788	33,693	36,095	84,082	40,862	43,220	58,867	28,297	30,570

* Population of Guernsey, Herm, Jethou and Lithou. Figures for 1901–71 record all persons present on census night; census figures for 1981 and 1991 record all persons resident in the islands on census night
Source: 1991 Census

RESIDENT POPULATION

MID-YEAR ESTIMATE

	1986	1996
United Kingdom	56,852,000	58,801,000
England	47,342,000	49,089,000
Wales	2,820,000	2,921,000
Scotland	5,123,000	5,128,000
Northern Ireland	1,567,000	1,663,000

Source: The Stationery Office – *Annual Abstract of Statistics 1998* (Crown copyright)

BY AGE AND SEX 1996

Males	Under 16	65 and over
United Kingdom	6,205,000	3,768,000
England	5,158,000	3,167,000
Wales	308,000	207,000
Scotland	526,000	309,000
Northern Ireland	212,000	85,000

Females	Under 16	60 and over
United Kingdom	5,893,000	6,900,000
England	4,894,000	5,755,000
Wales	293,000	375,000
Scotland	503,000	606,000
Northern Ireland	203,000	164,000

Source: The Stationery Office – *Annual Abstract of Statistics 1998* (Crown copyright)

BY ETHNIC GROUP (1991 CENSUS (GREAT BRITAIN))

Ethnic group	Estimated population	Percentage
Caribbean	500,000	16.6
African	212,000	7
Other black	178,000	5.9
Indian	840,000	27.9
Pakistani	477,000	15.8
Bangladeshi	163,000	5.4
Chinese	157,000	5.2
Other Asian	198,000	6.6
Other	290,000	9.6
Total ethnic minority groups	3,015,000	100
White	51,874,000	—
All ethnic groups	54,889,000	—

Source: The Stationery Office – *Population Trends* 72 (Crown copyright)

AVERAGE DENSITY *Persons per hectare*

	1981	1991
England	3.55	3.61
Wales	1.34	1.36
Scotland	0.66	0.65
Northern Ireland	1.12	1.11

Sources: ONS – Census reports (Crown copyright)

IMMIGRATION 1996
Acceptances for settlement in the UK by nationality

Region	Number of persons
Europe: total	7,500
European Economic Area	130
Remainder of Europe	7,370
Americas: total	8,470
USA	4.030
Canada	970
Africa: total	12,970
Asia: total	27,880
Indian sub-continent	13,590
Middle East	4,790
Oceania: total	3,520
British Overseas Citizens	620
Stateless	780
Total	61,730

Source: The Stationery Office – *Annual Abstract of Statistics 1998* (Crown copyright)

LIVE BIRTHS AND BIRTH RATES 1996

	Live births	Birth rate*
United Kingdom	733,000	12.5
England and Wales	649,000	12.5
Scotland	59,000	11.6
Northern Ireland	25,000	14.8

*Live births per 1,000 population
Source: The Stationery Office – *Annual Abstract of Statistics 1998* (Crown copyright)

LEGAL ABORTIONS 1996

Age group	England and Wales	Scotland
Under 16	3,645	323
16–19	28,790	2,355
20–34	113,895	7,966
35–44	21,145	1,290
45 and over	428	27
Age not stated	13	—
Total	179,877	

Source: The Stationery Office – *Annual Abstract of Statistics 1998*
(Crown copyright)

BIRTHS OUTSIDE MARRIAGE (UK)

Age group	1981	1996
Under 20	30,000	45,000
20–24	33,000	80,000
25–29	16,000	69,000
Over 30	13,000	66,000
Total	91,000	260,000

Source: The Stationery Office – *Annual Abstract of Statistics 1998*
(Crown copyright)

MARRIAGE AND DIVORCE 1995

	Marriages	Divorces
United Kingdom	322,251p	170,283
England and Wales	283,012p	155,499
Scotland	30,663	12,249
Northern Ireland	8,576	2,535

p provisional
Source: The Stationery Office – *Annual Abstract of Statistics 1998*
(Crown copyright)

DEATHS AND DEATH RATES 1996

Males	Deaths	Death rate*
United Kingdom	305,323	10.6
England and Wales	268,682	10.6p
Scotland	29,223	11.8
Northern Ireland	7,418	9.1
Females		
United Kingdom	330,701	11.1
England and Wales	291,453	11.1p
Scotland	31,448	11.9
Northern Ireland	7,800	9.2

* Deaths per 1,000 population
p provisional
Sources: The Stationery Office – *Annual Abstract of Statistics 1998*;
ONS; General Register Office for Scotland; *Annual Report of the
Registrar-General for Northern Ireland 1995* (Crown copyright)

INFANT MORTALITY 1996p
Deaths of infants under 1 year of age per 1,000 live births

	Number
United Kingdom	6.1
England and Wales	6.1
Scotland	6.2
Northern Ireland	5.8

p provisional
Source: The Stationery Office – *Annual Abstract of Statistics 1998*
(Crown copyright)

EXPECTATION OF LIFE LIFE TABLES 1994–96 (INTERIM FIGURES)

	England and Wales		Scotland		Northern Ireland	
Age	Male	Female	Male	Female	Male	Female
0	74.4	79.6	72.1	77.6	73.3	78.7
5	70.0	75.1	67.7	73.2	68.9	74.2
10	65.0	70.1	62.7	68.2	63.9	69.3
15	60.1	65.2	57.8	63.2	59.0	64.3
20	55.2	60.3	53.1	58.3	54.3	59.4
25	50.5	55.3	48.3	53.4	49.6	54.5
30	45.7	50.4	43.6	48.6	44.8	49.6
35	40.9	45.6	38.9	43.7	40.0	44.7
40	36.2	40.7	34.2	38.9	35.3	39.9
45	31.5	36.0	29.6	34.2	30.6	35.1
50	26.9	31.3	25.2	29.6	26.1	30.5
55	22.6	26.8	21.0	25.2	21.7	26.0
60	18.5	22.5	17.2	21.0	17.7	21.7
65	14.8	18.4	13.7	17.2	14.2	17.8
70	11.6	14.7	10.8	13.7	11.0	14.0
75	8.9	11.4	8.3	10.6	8.3	10.8
80	6.6	8.6	6.2	7.9	6.0	7.9
85	4.9	6.3	4.6	5.7	4.2	5.6

Source: The Stationery Office – *Annual Abstract of Statistics 1998* (Crown copyright)

DEATHS ANALYSED BY CAUSE 1996

	England & Wales	Scotland	N. Ireland
TOTAL DEATHS	563,007	60,671	15,218
Infectious and parasitic diseases	3,662	493	54
Neoplasms	140,120	15,419	3,715
Malignant neoplasm of stomach	6,778	699	200
Malignant neoplasm of trachea, bronchus and lung	30,972	4,126	816
Malignant neoplasm of breast	12,298	1,200	309
Malignant neoplasm of uterus	1,309	105	28
Malignant neoplasm of cervix	1,329	138	45
Benign and unspecified neoplasms	1,673	194	60
Leukaemia	3,472	319	92
Endocrine, nutritional and metabolic diseases and immunity disorders	7,551	722	81
Diabetes mellitus	6,027	526	49
Nutritional deficiencies	71	16	—
Other metabolic and immunity disorders	1,060	140	28
Diseases of blood and blood-forming organs	1,992	180	22
Anaemias	725	76	11
Mental disorders	9,354	1,595	100
Diseases of the nervous system and sense organs	9,809	852	236
Meningitis	247	14	7
Diseases of the circulatory system	238,855	26,728	6,633
Rheumatic heart disease	1,694	154	29
Hypertensive disease	3,023	281	75
Ischaemic heart disease	129,680	14,650	3,856
Diseases of pulmonary circulation and other forms of heart disease	26,322	3,063	655
Cerebrovascular disease	60,031	7,130	1,653
Diseases of the respiratory system	89,216	7,863	2,749
Influenza	182	45	6
Pneumonia	54,502	4,158	1,817
Bronchitis, emphysema	4,275	348	137
Asthma	1,356	122	31
Diseases of the digestive system	19,958	2,440	483
Ulcer of stomach and duodenum	4,108	344	102
Appendicitis	103	9	—
Hernia of the abdominal cavity and other intestinal obstruction	1,977	196	52
Chronic liver disease and cirrhosis	3,756	723	88
Diseases of the genitourinary system	6,788	839	254
Nephritis, nephrotic syndrome and nephrosis	3,068	549	168
Hyperplasia of prostate	236	11	3
Complications of pregnancy, childbirth and the puerperium	47	6	1
Abortion	6	—	—
Diseases of the skin and subcutaneous tissue	1,089	75	29
Diseases of the musculo-skeletal system	3,540	252	35
Congenital anomalies	1,238	192	72
Certain conditions originating in the perinatal period	151	181	68
Birth trauma, hypoxia, birth asphyxia and other respiratory conditions	116	94	28
Signs, symptoms and ill-defined conditions	10,842	337	88
Sudden infant death syndrome	337	43	15
Deaths from injury and poisoning	16,120	2,497	598
All accidents	10,438	1,497	402
Motor vehicle accidents	3,217	363	121
Suicide and self-inflicted injury	3,455	596	124
All other external causes	2,227	404	72

Source; The Stationery Office – *Annual Abstract of Statistics 1998* (Crown copyright)

The National Flag

The national flag of the United Kingdom is the Union Flag, generally known as the Union Jack.

The Union Flag is a combination of the cross of St George, patron saint of England, the cross of St Andrew, patron saint of Scotland, and a cross similar to that of St Patrick, patron saint of Ireland.

Cross of St George: cross Gules in a field Argent (red cross on a white ground)

Cross of St Andrew: saltire Argent in a field Azure (white diagonal cross on a blue ground)

Cross of St Patrick: saltire Gules in a field Argent (red diagonal cross on a white ground)

The Union Flag was first introduced in 1606 after the union of the kingdoms of England and Scotland under one sovereign. The cross of St Patrick was added in 1801 after the union of Great Britain and Ireland.

FLYING THE UNION FLAG

The correct orientation of the Union Flag when flying is with the broader diagonal band of white uppermost in the hoist (i.e. near the pole) and the narrower diagonal band of white uppermost in the fly (i.e. furthest from the pole).

It is the practice to fly the Union Flag daily on some customs houses. In all other cases, flags are flown on government buildings by command of The Queen.

Days for hoisting the Union Flag are notified to the Department for Culture, Media and Sport by The Queen's command and communicated by the department to the other government departments. On the days appointed, the Union Flag is flown on government buildings in the United Kingdom from 8 a.m. to sunset.

DAYS FOR FLYING FLAGS

The Queen's Accession	6 February
Birthday of The Duke of York	19 February
*St David's Day (in Wales only)	1 March
Commonwealth Day (1999)	8 March
Birthday of The Prince Edward	10 March
Birthday of The Queen	21 April
*St George's Day (in England only)	23 April
†Europe Day	9 May
Coronation Day	2 June
Birthday of The Duke of Edinburgh	10 June
The Queen's Official Birthday (1999)	12 June
Birthday of Queen Elizabeth the Queen Mother	4 August
Birthday of The Princess Royal	15 August
Birthday of The Princess Margaret	21 August
Remembrance Sunday (1999)	14 November
Birthday of The Prince of Wales	14 November
The Queen's Wedding Day	20 November
*St Andrew's Day (in Scotland only)	30 November
‡The opening of Parliament by The Queen	
‡The prorogation of Parliament by The Queen	

*Where a building has two or more flagstaffs, the appropriate national flag may be flown in addition to the Union Flag, but not in a superior position
†The Union Flag should fly alongside the European flag. On government buildings that have only one flagpole, the Union Flag should take precedence
‡Flags are flown whether or not The Queen performs the ceremony in person. Flags are flown only in the Greater London area

FLAGS AT HALF-MAST

Flags are flown at half-mast (i.e. two-thirds up between the top and bottom of the flagstaff) on the following occasions:

(a) From the announcement of the death up to the funeral of the Sovereign, except on Proclamation Day, when flags are hoisted right up from 11 a.m. to sunset

(b) The funerals of members of the royal family, subject to special commands from The Queen in each case

(c) The funerals of foreign rulers, subject to special commands from The Queen in each case

(d) The funerals of prime ministers and ex-prime ministers of the UK, subject to special commands from The Queen in each case

(e) Other occasions by special command of The Queen

On occasions when days for flying flags coincide with days for flying flags at half-mast, the following rules are observed. Flags are flown:

(a) although a member of the royal family, or a near relative of the royal family, may be lying dead, unless special commands be received from The Queen to the contrary

(b) although it may be the day of the funeral of a foreign ruler

If the body of a very distinguished subject is lying at a government office, the flag may fly at half-mast on that office until the body has left (provided it is a day on which the flag would fly) and then the flag is to be hoisted right up. On all other government buildings the flag will fly as usual.

THE ROYAL STANDARD

The Royal Standard is hoisted only when The Queen is actually present in the building, and never when Her Majesty is passing in procession.

The Royal Family

THE SOVEREIGN

ELIZABETH II, by the Grace of God, of the United Kingdom of Great Britain and Northern Ireland and of her other Realms and Territories Queen, Head of the Commonwealth, Defender of the Faith

Her Majesty Elizabeth Alexandra Mary of Windsor, elder daughter of King George VI and of HM Queen Elizabeth the Queen Mother
Born 21 April 1926, at 17 Bruton Street, London W1
Ascended the throne 6 February 1952
Crowned 2 June 1953, at Westminster Abbey
Married 20 November 1947, in Westminster Abbey, HRH The Duke of Edinburgh
Official residences: Buckingham Palace, London SW1A 1AA; Windsor Castle, Berks; Palace of Holyroodhouse, Edinburgh
Private residences: Sandringham, Norfolk; Balmoral Castle, Aberdeenshire

HUSBAND OF THE QUEEN

HRH The PRINCE PHILIP, DUKE OF EDINBURGH, KG, KT, OM, GBE, AC, QSO, PC, Ranger of Windsor Park
Born 10 June 1921, son of Prince and Princess Andrew of Greece and Denmark (*see* page 128), naturalized a British subject 1947, created Duke of Edinburgh, Earl of Merioneth and Baron Greenwich 1947

CHILDREN OF THE QUEEN

HRH The PRINCE OF WALES (Prince Charles Philip Arthur George), KG, KT, GCB and Great Master of the Order of the Bath, AK, QSO, PC, ADC(P)
Born 14 November 1948, created Prince of Wales and Earl of Chester 1958, succeeded as Duke of Cornwall, Duke of Rothesay, Earl of Carrick and Baron Renfrew, Lord of the Isles and Prince and Great Steward of Scotland 1952
Married 29 July 1981 Lady Diana Frances Spencer (Diana, Princess of Wales (1961–97), youngest daughter of the 8th Earl Spencer and the Hon. Mrs Shand Kydd), marriage dissolved 1996
Issue:
(1) HRH Prince William of Wales (Prince William Arthur Philip Louis), born 21 June 1982
(2) HRH Prince Henry of Wales (Prince Henry Charles Albert David), *born* 15 September 1984
Residences of the Prince of Wales: St James's Palace, London SW1A 1BS; Highgrove, Doughton, Tetbury, Glos GL8 8TN

HRH The PRINCESS ROYAL (Princess Anne Elizabeth Alice Louise), KG, GCVO
Born 15 August 1950, declared The Princess Royal 1987
Married (1) 14 November 1973 Captain Mark Anthony Peter Phillips, CVO (*born* 22 September 1948); marriage dissolved 1992; (2) 12 December 1992 Captain Timothy James Hamilton Laurence, MVO, RN (*born* 1 March 1955)
Issue:

(1) Peter Mark Andrew Phillips, *born* 15 November 1977
(2) Zara Anne Elizabeth Phillips, *born* 15 May 1981
Residence: Gatcombe Park, Minchinhampton, Glos

HRH The DUKE OF YORK (Prince Andrew Albert Christian Edward), CVO, ADC(P)
Born 19 February 1960, created Duke of York, Earl of Inverness and Baron Killyleagh 1986
Married 23 July 1986 Sarah Margaret Ferguson, now Sarah, Duchess of York (*born* 15 October 1959, younger daughter of Major Ronald Ferguson and Mrs Hector Barrantes), marriage dissolved 1996
Issue:
(1) HRH Princess Beatrice of York (Princess Beatrice Elizabeth Mary), *born* 8 August 1988
(2) HRH Princess Eugenie of York (Princess Eugenie Victoria Helena), *born* 23 March 1990
Residences: Buckingham Palace, London SW1A 1AA; Sunninghill Park, Ascot, Berks

HRH The PRINCE EDWARD (Prince Edward Antony Richard Louis), CVO
Born 10 March 1964
Residence: Buckingham Palace, London SW1A 1AA

SISTER OF THE QUEEN

HRH The PRINCESS MARGARET, COUNTESS OF SNOWDON, CI, GCVO, Royal Victorian Chain, Dame Grand Cross of the Order of St John of Jerusalem
Born 21 August 1930, younger daughter of King George VI and HM Queen Elizabeth the Queen Mother
Married 6 May 1960 Antony Charles Robert Armstrong-Jones, GCVO (*born* 7 March 1930, created Earl of Snowdon 1961, Constable of Caernarvon Castle); marriage dissolved 1978
Issue:
(1) David Albert Charles, Viscount Linley, *born* 3 November 1961, *married* 8 October 1993 the Hon. Serena Stanhope
(2) Lady Sarah Chatto (Sarah Frances Elizabeth), *born* 1 May 1964, *married* 14 July 1994 Daniel Chatto, and has issue, Samuel David Benedict Chatto, *born* 28 July 1996
Residence: Kensington Palace, London W8 4PU

MOTHER OF THE QUEEN

HM QUEEN ELIZABETH THE QUEEN MOTHER (Elizabeth Angela Marguerite), Lady of the Garter, Lady of the Thistle, CI, GCVO, GBE, Dame Grand Cross of the Order of St John, Royal Victorian Chain, Lord Warden and Admiral of the Cinque Ports and Constable of Dover Castle
Born 4 August 1900, youngest daughter of the 14th Earl of Strathmore and Kinghorne
Married 26 April 1923 (as Lady Elizabeth Bowes-Lyon) Prince Albert, Duke of York, afterwards King George VI (*see* page 127)
Residences: Clarence House, St James's Palace, London SW1A 1BA; Royal Lodge, Windsor Great Park, Berks; Castle of Mey, Caithness

AUNT OF THE QUEEN

HRH PRINCESS ALICE, DUCHESS OF GLOUCESTER (Alice Christabel), GCB, CI, GCVO, GBE, Grand Cordon of Al Kamal
Born 25 December 1901, third daughter of the 7th Duke of Buccleuch and Queensberry
Married 6 November 1935 (as Lady Alice Montagu-Douglas-Scott) Prince Henry, Duke of Gloucester, third son of King George V (*see* page 127)
Residence: Kensington Palace, London W8 4PU

COUSINS OF THE QUEEN

HRH THE DUKE OF GLOUCESTER (Prince Richard Alexander Walter George), KG, GCVO, Grand Prior of the Order of St John of Jerusalem
Born 26 August 1944
Married 8 July 1972 Birgitte Eva van Deurs, now HRH The Duchess of Gloucester, GCVO (*born* 20 June 1946, daughter of Asger Henriksen and Vivian van Deurs)
Issue:
(1)   Earl of Ulster (Alexander Patrick Gregers Richard), *born* 24 October 1974
(2)   Lady Davina Windsor (Davina Elizabeth Alice Benedikte), *born* 19 November 1977
(3)   Lady Rose Windsor (Rose Victoria Birgitte Louise), *born* 1 March 1980
Residence: Kensington Palace, London W8 4PU

HRH THE DUKE OF KENT (Prince Edward George Nicholas Paul Patrick), KG, GCMG, GCVO, ADC(P)
Born 9 October 1935
Married 8 June 1961 Katharine Lucy Mary Worsley, now HRH The Duchess of Kent, GCVO (*born* 22 February 1933, daughter of Sir William Worsley, Bt.)
Issue:
(1)   Earl of St Andrews (George Philip Nicholas), *born* 26 June 1962, *married* 9 January 1988 Sylvana Tomaselli, and has issue, Edward Edmund Maximilian George, Baron Downpatrick, *born* 2 December 1988; Lady Marina Charlotte Alexandra Katharine Windsor, *born* 30 September 1992; Lady Amelia Sophia Theodora Mary Margaret Windsor, *born* 24 August 1995
(2)   Lady Helen Taylor (Helen Marina Lucy), *born* 28 April 1964, *married* 18 July 1992 Timothy Taylor, and has issue, Columbus George Donald Taylor, *born* 6 August 1994; Cassius Edward Taylor, *born* 26 December 1996
(3)   Lord Nicholas Windsor (Nicholas Charles Edward Jonathan), *born* 25 July 1970

HRH PRINCESS ALEXANDRA, THE HON. LADY OGILVY (Princess Alexandra Helen Elizabeth Olga Christabel), GCVO
Born 25 December 1936
Married 24 April 1963 The Rt. Hon. Sir Angus Ogilvy, KCVO (*born* 14 September 1928, second son of 12th Earl of Airlie)
Issue:
(1)   James Robert Bruce Ogilvy, *born* 29 February 1964, *married* 30 July 1988 Julia Rawlinson, and has issue, Flora Alexandra Ogilvy, *born* 15 December 1994; Alexander Charles Ogilvy, *born* 12 November 1996

(2)   Marina Victoria Alexandra, Mrs Mowatt, *born* 31 July 1966, *married* 2 February 1990 Paul Mowatt (marriage dissolved 1997), and has issue, Zenouska May Mowatt, *born* 26 May 1990; Christian Alexander Mowatt, *born* 4 June 1993
Residence: Thatched House Lodge, Richmond Park, Surrey

HRH PRINCE MICHAEL OF KENT (Prince Michael George Charles Franklin), KCVO
Born 4 July 1942
Married 30 June 1978 Baroness Marie-Christine Agnes Hedwig Ida von Reibnitz, now HRH Princess Michael of Kent (*born* 15 January 1945, daughter of Baron Gunther von Reibnitz)
Issue:
(1)   Lord Frederick Windsor (Frederick Michael George David Louis), *born* 6 April 1979
(2)   Lady Gabriella Windsor (Gabriella Marina Alexandra Ophelia), *born* 23 April 1981
Residences: Kensington Palace, London W8 4PU; Nether Lypiatt Manor, Stroud, Glos.

ORDER OF SUCCESSION

1   HRH The Prince of Wales
2   HRH Prince William of Wales
3   HRH Prince Henry of Wales
4   HRH The Duke of York
5   HRH Princess Beatrice of York
6   HRH Princess Eugenie of York
7   HRH The Prince Edward
8   HRH The Princess Royal
9   Peter Phillips
10   Zara Phillips
11   HRH The Princess Margaret, Countess of Snowdon
12   Viscount Linley
13   Lady Sarah Chatto
14   Samuel Chatto
15   HRH The Duke of Gloucester
16   Earl of Ulster
17   Lady Davina Windsor
18   Lady Rose Windsor
19   HRH The Duke of Kent
20   Baron Downpatrick
21   Lady Marina Charlotte Windsor
22   Lady Amelia Windsor
23   Lord Nicholas Windsor
24   Lady Helen Taylor
25   Columbus Taylor
26   Cassius Taylor
27   Lord Frederick Windsor
28   Lady Gabriella Windsor
29   HRH Princess Alexandra, the Hon. Lady Ogilvy
30   James Ogilvy
31   Alexander Ogilvy
32   Flora Ogilvy
33   Marina, Mrs Paul Mowatt
34   Christian Mowatt
35   Zenouska Mowatt
36   The Earl of Harewood

The Earl of St Andrews and HRH Prince Michael of Kent lost the right of succession to the throne through marriage to a Roman Catholic. Their children remain in succession provided that they are in communion with the Church of England

Royal Households

Office: Buckingham Palace, London SW1A 1AA
Tel: 0171-930 4832
Web: http://www.royal.gov.uk

The Lord Chamberlain is the most senior member of The Queen's Household and under him come the heads of the six departments: the Private Secretary, the Keeper of the Privy Purse, the Comptroller of the Lord Chamberlain's Office, the Master of the Household, the Crown Equerry, and the Director of the Royal Collection. Positions in these departments are full-time salaried posts.

There are also a number of honorary or now largely ceremonial appointments which carry no remuneration or a small honorarium. In the following list, most honorary appointments have been placed at the end; however, where this is not the case, such appointments are indicated by an asterisk.

GREAT OFFICERS OF STATE
Lord Chamberlain, The Lord Camoys, GCVO, PC
Lord Steward, The Viscount Ridley, KG, GCVO, TD
Master of the Horse, The Lord Somerleyton, KCVO

LADIES-IN-WAITING AND EQUERRIES
Mistress of the Robes, The Duchess of Grafton, GCVO
Ladies of the Bedchamber, The Countess of Airlie, DCVO; The Lady Farnham, CVO
Women of the Bedchamber, Hon. Mary Morrison, DCVO; Lady Susan Hussey, DCVO; Lady Dugdale, DCVO; The Lady Elton, CVO; Mrs Christian Adams (temp.)
Equerries, Lt.-Col. Sir Guy Acland, Bt., MVO; Sqn. Ldr. S. Brailsford

THE PRIVATE SECRETARY'S OFFICE
Buckingham Palace, London SW1A 1AA
Private Secretary to The Queen, The Rt Hon. Sir Robert Fellowes, GCB, GCVO (until Feb. 1999); Sir Robin Janvrin, KCVO, CB (from Feb. 1999)
Deputy Private Secretary, Sir Robin Janvrin, KCVO, CB (until Feb. 1999); Mrs M. Francis (from Feb. 1999)
Communications Secretary, S. Lewis
Assistant Private Secretary, Mrs M. Francis (until Feb. 1999)
Special Assistant to the Private Secretary, A. Dent
Chief Clerk, Mrs G. Middleburgh
Secretary to the Private Secretary, Miss E. Ash

PRESS OFFICE
Press Secretary, G. Crawford, LVO
Deputy Press Secretary, Miss P. Russell-Smith
Assistant Press Secretaries, R. Arbiter, LVO; D. Tuck

THE QUEEN'S ARCHIVES
Round Tower, Windsor Castle, Berks
Keeper of The Queen's Archives, The Rt Hon. Sir Robert Fellowes, GCB, GCVO
Assistant Keeper, O. Everett, CVO
Registrar, Lady de Bellaigue, MVO

THE PRIVY PURSE AND TREASURER'S OFFICE
Buckingham Palace, London SW1A 1AA
Keeper of the Privy Purse and Treasurer to The Queen, Sir Michael Peat, KCVO
Director of Property Services, J. Tiltman, LVO

Director of Royal Travel, Air Cdre the Hon. T. Elworthy
Director of Finance, Property Services and Royal Travel, S. Cawley
Deputy Keeper of the Privy Purse and Deputy Treasurer, J. Parsons, CVO
Chief Accountant and Paymaster, I. McGregor
Personnel Officer, Miss P. Lloyd
Land Agent, Sandringham, M. O'Lone, FRICS
Resident Factor, Balmoral, P. Ord, FRICS

THE LORD CHAMBERLAIN'S OFFICE
Buckingham Palace, London SW1A 1AA
Comptroller, Lt.-Col. W. H. M. Ross, CVO, OBE
Assistant Comptroller, Lt.-Col. A. Mather, CVO, OBE
Secretary, J. Spencer, MVO
Assistant Secretary, Miss A. Krysztofiak
State Invitations Assistant, J. O. Hope
Marshal of the Diplomatic Corps, Vice-Adm. Sir James Weatherall, KBE
Vice-Marshal, P. Astley, LVO

CENTRAL CHANCERY OF THE ORDERS OF KNIGHTHOOD
St James's Palace, London SW1A 1BS
Secretary, Lt.-Col. A. Mather, CVO, OBE
Assistant Secretary, Miss R. Wells, MVO

MASTER OF THE HOUSEHOLD'S DEPARTMENT
Buckingham Palace, London SW1A 1AA
Master of the Household, Maj.-Gen. Sir Simon Cooper, KCVO
Deputy Master of the Household, Lt.-Col. Sir Guy Acland, Bt., MVO
Assistants to the Master of the Household, M. T. Parker, MVO; A. Jarman; A. Smith
Chief Clerk, M. C. W. N. Jephson, LVO
Chief Housekeeper, Miss H. Colebrook, MVO
Palace Steward, P. S. Croasdale, RVM
Royal Chef, L. Mann, RVM
Superintendent, Windsor Castle, Maj. M. Davidson, MBE, BEM
Superintendent, The Palace of Holyroodhouse, Lt.-Col. D. Anderson, OBE

ROYAL MEWS DEPARTMENT
Buckingham Palace, London SW1W 0QH
Crown Equerry, Lt.-Col. S. Gilbart-Denham, CVO
Superintendent, Royal Mews, Buckingham Palace, Maj. I. Kelly

THE ROYAL COLLECTION
St James's Palace, London SW1A 1BS
Director of Royal Collection and Surveyor of The Queen's Works of Art, H. Roberts, CVO, FSA
Surveyor of The Queen's Pictures, C. Lloyd, LVO
Librarian, The Royal Library, Windsor Castle, O. Everett, CVO
Deputy Surveyor of The Queen's Works of Art, J. Marsden
Director of Media Affairs, R. Arbiter, LVO
Curator of the Print Room, The Hon. Mrs Roberts, LVO
Financial Director, M. Stevens
Financial Controller, Mrs G. Johnson
Administrator and Assistant to The Surveyors, D. Rankin-Hunt, MVO, TD
Senior Picture Restorer, Miss V. Pemberton-Pigott, MVO
Chief Restorer, Old Master Drawings, A. Donnithorne
Senior Furniture Restorer, E. Fancourt, MVO, RVM
Armourer, J. Jackson, RVM
Chief Binder, R. Day, MVO, RVM

ROYAL COLLECTION ENTERPRISES LTD
Managing Director, M. E. K. Hewlett, LVO

ECCLESIASTICAL HOUSEHOLD

Clerk of the Closet, The Bishop of Derby
Deputy Clerk of the Closet, Revd W. Booth
Chaplains and Extra Chaplains to The Queen: approx. 30–40
Dean of the Chapels Royal, The Bishop of London
Sub-Dean of the Chapels Royal, Revd W. Booth
Organist, Choirmaster and Composer, R. J. Popplewell, MVO, FRCO, FRCM
Domestic Chaplain, Buckingham Palace, Revd W. Booth
Domestic Chaplain, Windsor Castle, The Dean of Windsor
Domestic Chaplain, Sandringham, Revd Canon G. R. Hall

MEDICAL HOUSEHOLD

Head of the Medical Household and Physician to The Queen, R. Thompson, DM, FRCP
Serjeant Surgeon, B. T. Jackson, FRCS
Apothecary to The Queen and to the Household, N. R. Southward, CVO
Apothecary to the Household at Windsor, J. Holliday
Apothecary to the Household at Sandringham, I. K. Campbell, D.O bst., FRCGP
Coroner of The Queen's Household, J. Burton, CBE

OTHER HONORARY/CEREMONIAL APPOINTMENTS

Lord High Almoner, The Bishop of Wakefield
Master of The Queen's Music, M. Williamson, CBE, AO
Poet Laureate, Ted Hughes, OM, OBE
Keeper of the Royal Philatelic Collection, C. Goodwyn
Bargemaster, R. Crouch
Swan Warden, Prof. C. Perrins, LVO
Swan Marker, D. Barber

POLITICAL (GOVERNMENT WHIPS)
(*see also* page 277)

Captain, Honourable Corps of Gentlemen-at-Arms (Chief Whip in the Lords), The Lord Carter, PC
Captain, Queen's Bodyguard of the Yeomen of the Guard (Deputy Chief Whip in the Lords), The Lord McIntosh of Haringey
Lords-in-Waiting, The Lord Hoyle; The Lord Hunt of King's Heath
Baronesses-in-Waiting, The Baroness Farrington of Ribbleton; The Baroness Ramsay of Cartvale; The Baroness Amos
Treasurer of the Household (Deputy Chief Whip in the Commons), K. Bradley, MP
Comptroller of the Household, T. McAvoy, MP
Vice-Chamberlain, G. Allen, MP

ARMED FORCES

Gold Sticks, Maj.-Gen. Lord Michael Fitzalan-Howard, GCVO, CB, CBE, MC; Gen. Sir Desmond Fitzpatrick, GCB, GCVO, DSO, MBE, MC
Vice-Admiral of the United Kingdom, Adm. Sir Nicholas Hunt, GCB, LVO
Rear-Admiral of the United Kingdom, Adm. Sir John Black
First and Principal Naval Aide-de-Camp, Adm. Sir Michael Boyce, KCB, OBE
Flag Aide-de-Camp, Adm. Sir John Brigstocke, KCB
Aides-de-Camp-General, Gen. Sir Charles Guthrie, GCB, LVO, OBE; Gen. Sir Jeremy Mackenzie, GCB, OBE
Air Aides-de-Camp, Air Chief Marshal Sir Richard Johns, GCB, CBE, LVO; Air Chief Marshal Sir John Allison, KCB, CBE

Gentleman Usher to the Sword of State, Adm. Sir Michael Layard, KCB, CBE
Constable and Governor of Windsor Castle, Gen. Sir Patrick Palmer, KBE
Governor of Edinburgh Castle, Maj.-Gen. M. J. Strudwick, CBE

BODYGUARDS

THE HONOURABLE CORPS OF GENTLEMEN-AT-ARMS
Captain, The Lord Carter, PC
Lieutenant, Lt.-Col. R. Mayfield, DSO
Clerk of the Cheque and Adjutant, Col. D. Fanshawe, OBE; *Gentlemen of the Corps*: 27

THE QUEEN'S BODY GUARD OF THE YEOMEN OF THE GUARD
Captain, The Lord McIntosh of Haringey
Lieutenant, Col. G. W. Tufnell
Clerk of the Cheque and Adjutant, Col. S. Longsdon
Yeomen of the Guard: 81

THE QUEEN'S HOUSEHOLD IN SCOTLAND

Hereditary Lord High Constable of Scotland, The Earl of Erroll
Hereditary Master of the Household in Scotland, The Duke of Argyll
Lord Lyon King of Arms, Sir Malcolm Innes of Edingight, KCVO, WS
Hereditary Banner-Bearer for Scotland, The Earl of Dundee
Hereditary Bearer of the National Flag of Scotland, The Earl of Lauderdale
Hereditary Keeper of the Palace of Holyroodhouse, The Duke of Hamilton and Brandon
Historiographer, Prof. T. C. Smout, CBE, FBA, FRSE, FSAScot.
Botanist, Prof. D. Henderson, CBE, FRSE
Painter and Limner, vacant
Sculptor in Ordinary, Prof. Sir Eduardo Paolozzi, CBE, RA
Astronomer, Prof. J. Brown, Ph.D., FRSE
Heralds and Pursuivants, see page 282

ECCLESIASTICAL HOUSEHOLD

Dean of the Chapel Royal, Very Revd J. Harkness, CB, OBE
Dean of the Order of the Thistle, Very Revd G. I. Macmillan
Chaplains in Ordinary: 10
Domestic Chaplain, Balmoral, Revd R. P. Sloan

MEDICAL HOUSEHOLD

Physicians in Scotland, P. Brunt, OBE, MD, FRCP; A. Toft, CBE, FRCPE
Surgeons in Scotland, J. Engeset, FRCS; I. Macintyre
Apothecary to the Household at Balmoral, D. J. A. Glass
Apothecary to the Household at the Palace of Holyroodhouse, Dr J. Cormack, MD, FRCPE, FRCGP

*ROYAL COMPANY OF ARCHERS (QUEEN'S BODYGUARD FOR SCOTLAND)

Captain-General and Gold Stick for Scotland, Maj. Sir Hew Hamilton-Dalrymple, Bt., KCVO
Adjutant, Maj. the Hon. Sir Lachlan Maclean, Bt.
President of the Council and Silver Stick for Scotland, The Duke of Buccleuch and Queensberry, KT, VRD
Secretary, Capt. J. D. B. Younger
Treasurer, J. M. Haldane of Gleneagles
Members on the active list: c.400

HOUSEHOLD OF THE PRINCE PHILIP, DUKE OF EDINBURGH

Office: Buckingham Palace, London SW1A 1AA
Tel: 0171-930 4832

Treasurer, Sir Brian McGrath, KCVO
Private Secretary, Brig. M. G. Hunt-Davis, CVO, CBE
Equerry, Lt.-Cdr. R. Tarran
Temporary Equerries, Capt. P. Wise; Lt.-Col. P. Denning; Capt. S. Courtauld
Chief Clerk and Accountant, G. D. Partington

HOUSEHOLD OF QUEEN ELIZABETH THE QUEEN MOTHER

Office: Clarence House, St James's Palace, London SW1A 1BA
Tel: 0171-930 3141

Lord Chamberlain, The Earl of Crawford and Balcarres, KT, PC
Private Secretary, Comptroller and Equerry, Capt. Sir Alastair Aird, GCVO
Assistant Private Secretary and Equerry, Maj. R. Seymour, CVO
Treasurer and Extra Equerry, Hon. N. Assheton
Treasurer Emeritus and Equerry, Maj. Sir Ralph Anstruther, Bt., GCVO, MC
Equerry, Capt. W. de Rouet (temp.)
Apothecary to the Household, Dr N. Southward, CVO
Surgeon-Apothecary to the Household (Royal Lodge, Windsor), J. Holliday
Ladies of the Bedchamber, The Lady Grimthorpe, DCVO; The Countess of Scarbrough
Women of the Bedchamber, Dame Frances Campbell-Preston, DCVO; Lady Angela Oswald, LVO; The Hon. Mrs Rhodes; Mrs Michael Gordon-Lennox
Clerk Comptroller, A. Kirkpatrick-Smith
Information Officer, Mrs R. Murphy, LVO
Clerks, Miss F. Fletcher, LVO; Mrs W. Stevens

HOUSEHOLD OF THE PRINCE OF WALES

Office: St James's Palace, London SW1A 1BS
Tel: 0171-930 4832

Private Secretary and Treasurer, S. M. J. Lamport
Deputy Private Secretary, M. Bolland
Assistant Private Secretaries, J. Skan; N. S. Archer; Ms E. Buchanan
Press Secretary, Miss S. Henney
Deputy Press Secretary, Mrs C. Harris
Equerry, Lt. Cdr. J. Lavery, RN
Secretary to the Duchy of Cornwall and Keeper of the Records, W. R. A. Ross

HOUSEHOLD OF THE DUKE OF YORK

Office: Buckingham Palace, London SW1A 1AA
Tel: 0171-930 4832

Private Secretary, Treasurer and Extra Equerry, Capt. R. N. Blair, LVO, RN

Comptroller and Assistant Private Secretary, Cdr. C. Manley, OBE
Equerry, Capt. R. L. Gerrard-Wright

HOUSEHOLD OF THE PRINCE EDWARD

Office: Buckingham Palace, London SW1A 1AA
Tel: 0171-930 4832

Private Secretary, Lt.-Col. S. G. O'Dwyer, LVO
Clerk, Mrs L. Sharp

HOUSEHOLD OF THE PRINCESS ROYAL

Office: Buckingham Palace, London SW1A 1AA
Tel: 0171-930 4832

Private Secretary, R. McGuigan
Assistant Private Secretary, Mrs S. Gee
Ladies-in-Waiting, Lady Carew Pole, LVO; Mrs Andrew Feilden, LVO; The Hon. Mrs Legge-Bourke, LVO; Mrs William Nunneley, LVO; Mrs Timothy Holderness-Roddam; Mrs Charles Ritchie; Mrs David Bowes Lyon

HOUSEHOLD OF THE PRINCESS MARGARET, COUNTESS OF SNOWDON

Office: Kensington Palace, London W8 4PU
Tel: 0171-930 3141

Private Secretary, The Viscount Ullswater, PC
Treasurer, Maj. The Lord Napier and Ettrick, KCVO
Lady-in-Waiting, The Hon. Mrs Whitehead, LVO

HOUSEHOLD OF THE DUKE AND DUCHESS OF GLOUCESTER

Office: Kensington Palace, London W8 4PU
Tel: 0171-937 6374

Private Secretary, Comptroller and Equerry, Maj. N. M. L. Barne, LVO
Assistant Private Secretary to the Duchess of Gloucester, Miss S. Marland, LVO
Ladies-in-Waiting, Mrs Michael Wigley, CVO; Mrs Euan McCorquodale, LVO; Mrs Howard Page, LVO

HOUSEHOLD OF PRINCESS ALICE, DUCHESS OF GLOUCESTER

Office: Kensington Palace, London W8 4PU
Tel: 0171-937 6374

Private Secretary, Comptroller and Equerry, Maj. N. M. L. Barne, LVO
Ladies-in-Waiting, Dame Jean Maxwell-Scott, DCVO; Mrs Michael Harvey, LVO

HOUSEHOLD OF THE DUKE AND DUCHESS OF KENT

Office: York House, St James's Palace, London SW1 1BQ
Tel: 0171-930 4872

Private Secretary, N. C. Adamson, OBE
Temporary Equerry, Capt. D. Hampshire
Ladies-in-Waiting, Mrs Fiona Henderson, CVO; Mrs Colin Marsh, LVO; Mrs Julian Tomkins; Mrs Peter Troughton; Mrs Richard Beckett

HOUSEHOLD OF PRINCE AND PRINCESS MICHAEL OF KENT

Office: Kensington Palace, London W8 4PU
Tel: 0171-938 3519

Personal Secretaries, Miss C. Jenkins, Miss K. Garrod
Ladies-in-Waiting, The Hon. Mrs Sanders; Miss A. Frost; Mrs J. Fellowes

HOUSEHOLD OF PRINCESS ALEXANDRA, THE HON. LADY OGILVY

Office: Buckingham Palace, London SW1A 1AA
Tel: 0171-930 1860

Comptroller and Private Secretary, Capt. N. Blair, LVO, RN
Lady-in-Waiting, Lady Mary Mumford, DCVO

Royal Salutes

ENGLAND
A salute of 62 guns is fired on the wharf at the Tower of London on the following occasions:
(a) the anniversaries of the birth, accession and coronation of the Sovereign
(b) the anniversary of the birth of HM Queen Elizabeth the Queen Mother
(c) the anniversary of the birth of HRH Prince Philip, Duke of Edinburgh
A salute of 41 guns only is fired on extraordinary and triumphal occasions, e.g. on the occasion of the Sovereign opening, proroguing or dissolving Parliament in person, or when passing through London in procession, except when otherwise ordered.
A salute of 41 guns is fired from the two saluting stations in London (the Tower of London and Hyde Park) on the occasion of the birth of a royal infant.
Constable of the Royal Palace and Fortress of London, Field Marshal the Lord Inge, GCB
Lieutenant of the Tower of London, Lt.-Gen. Sir Anthony Denison-Smith, KBE
Resident Governor and Keeper of the Jewel House, Maj.-Gen. G. Field, CB, OBE

Master Gunner of St James's Park, Field Marshal the Lord Vincent of Coleshill, GBE, KCB, DSO
Master Gunner within the Tower, Col. S. Lalor

SCOTLAND
Royal salutes are authorized at Edinburgh Castle and Stirling Castle, although in practice Edinburgh Castle is the only operating saluting station in Scotland.
A salute of 21 guns is fired on the following occasions:
(a) the anniversaries of the birth, accession and coronation of the Sovereign
(b) the anniversary of the birth of HM Queen Elizabeth the Queen Mother
(c) the anniversary of the birth of HRH Prince Philip, Duke of Edinburgh
A salute of 21 guns is fired in Edinburgh on the occasion of the opening of the General Assembly of the Church of Scotland.
A salute of 21 guns may also be fired in Edinburgh on the arrival of HM The Queen, HM Queen Elizabeth the Queen Mother, or a member of the royal family who is a Royal Highness on an official visit.

Royal Finances

FUNDING

THE CIVIL LIST

The Civil List dates back to the late 17th century. It was originally used by the sovereign to supplement hereditary revenues for paying the salaries of judges, ambassadors and other government officers as well as the expenses of the royal household. In 1760 on the accession of George III it was decided that the Civil List would be provided by Parliament to cover all relevant expenditure in return for the King surrendering the hereditary revenues of the Crown. At that time Parliament undertook to pay the salaries of judges, ambassadors, etc. In 1831 Parliament agreed also to meet the costs of the royal palaces in return for a reduction in the Civil List. Each sovereign has agreed to continue this arrangement.

The Civil List paid to The Queen is charged on the Consolidated Fund. Until 1972, the amount of money allocated annually under the Civil List was set for the duration of a reign. The system was then altered to a fixed annual payment for ten years but from 1975 high inflation made an annual review necessary. The system of payments reverted to the practice of a fixed annual payment for ten years from 1 January 1991.

The Civil List Acts provide for other members of the royal family to receive parliamentary annuities from government funds to meet the expenses of carrying out their official duties. Since 1975 The Queen has reimbursed the Treasury for the annuities paid to the Duke of Gloucester, the Duke of Kent and Princess Alexandra. Since 1993 The Queen has reimbursed all the annuities except those paid to herself, Queen Elizabeth the Queen Mother and the Duke of Edinburgh.

The Prince of Wales does not receive a parliamentary annuity. He derives his income from the revenues of the Duchy of Cornwall and these monies meet the official and private expenses of the Prince of Wales and his family.

The annual payments for the years 1991–2000 are:

The Queen	£7,900,000
Queen Elizabeth the Queen Mother	643,000
The Duke of Edinburgh	359,000
*The Duke of York	249,000
*The Prince Edward	96,000
*The Princess Royal	228,000
*The Princess Margaret, Countess of Snowdon	219,000
*Princess Alice, Duchess of Gloucester	87,000
*The Duke of Gloucester	175,000
*The Duke of Kent	236,000
*Princess Alexandra	225,000
	10,417,000
*Refunded to the Treasury	1,515,000
Total	8,902,000

GRANTS-IN-AID

Several government departments provide grants-in-aid to the royal household to meet various official expenses. Property Services grant-in-aid is provided by the Department for Culture, Media and Sport to pay for the upkeep of English occupied royal palaces which are used as offices, for official or ceremonial purposes and to which there is public access. Royal Travel grant-in-aid is provided by the Department of the Environment, Transport and the Regions to meet the cost of official royal travel by air and rail, using mainly

aircraft from 32 (The Royal) Squadron, chartered commercial aircraft for major overseas state visits and the Royal Train. From 1 April 1998 Communications and Information grant-in-aid has been provided by the Central Office of Information to meet the cost of media and information services.

In July 1998 it was announced that control of the budget for overseas royal visits would be transferred from the Foreign and Commonwealth Office to the royal household.

Grant-in-aid for 1998–9 is:

Property Services	£15,800,000
Royal Travel	16,400,000
Communications and Information	471,000

THE PRIVY PURSE

The funds received by the Privy Purse pay for official expenses incurred by The Queen as head of state and for some of The Queen's private expenditure. The revenues of the Duchy of Lancaster are the principal source of income for the Privy Purse. The revenues of the Duchy were retained by George III in 1760 when the hereditary revenues were surrendered in exchange for the Civil List.

PERSONAL INCOME

The Queen's personal income derives mostly from investments, and is used to meet private expenditure.

DEPARTMENTAL VOTES

Items of expenditure connected with the official duties of the royal family which fall directly on votes of government departments include:

Ministry of Defence – equerries

Foreign and Commonwealth Office – Marshal of the Diplomatic Corps; costs (other than travel costs) associated with overseas visits at the request of government departments

HM Treasury – Central Chancery of the Orders of Knighthood

The Post Office – postal services

TAXATION

The sovereign is not legally liable to pay income tax, capital gains tax or inheritance tax. After income tax was reintroduced in 1842, some income tax was paid voluntarily by the sovereign but over a long period these payments were phased out. In 1992 The Queen offered to pay tax on a voluntary basis from 6 April 1993, and the Prince of Wales to pay tax on a voluntary basis on his income from the Duchy of Cornwall. (He was already taxed in all other respects.)

The main provisions for The Queen and the Prince of Wales to pay tax, set out in a Memorandum of Understanding on Royal Taxation presented to Parliament on 11 February 1993, are that The Queen will pay income tax and capital gains tax in respect of her private income and assets, and on the proportion of the income and capital gains of the Privy Purse used for private purposes. Inheritance tax will be paid on The Queen's assets, except for those which pass to the next sovereign, whether automatically or by gift or bequest. The Prince of Wales will pay income tax on income from the Duchy of Cornwall used for private purposes.

The Prince of Wales has confirmed that he intends to pay tax on the same basis following his accession to the throne.

Other members of the royal family are subject to tax as for any taxpayer.

Military Ranks and Titles

THE QUEEN

Lord High Admiral of the United Kingdom

Colonel-in-Chief
The Life Guards; The Blues and Royals (Royal Horse Guards and 1st Dragoons); The Royal Scots Dragoon Guards (Carabiniers and Greys); The Queen's Royal Lancers; Royal Tank Regiment; Corps of Royal Engineers; Grenadier Guards; Coldstream Guards; Scots Guards; Irish Guards; Welsh Guards; The Royal Welch Fusiliers; The Queen's Lancashire Regiment; The Argyll and Sutherland Highlanders (Princess Louise's); The Royal Green Jackets; Adjutant General's Corps; The Royal Mercian and Lancastrian Yeomanry; The Governor General's Horse Guards (of Canada); The King's Own Calgary Regiment; Canadian Forces Military Engineers Branch; Royal 22e Regiment (of Canada); Governor-General's Foot Guards (of Canada); The Canadian Grenadier Guards; Le Regiment de la Chaudiere (of Canada); 2nd Bn Royal New Brunswick Regiment (North Shore); The 48th Highlanders of Canada; The Argyll and Sutherland Highlanders of Canada (Princess Louise's); The Calgary Highlanders; Royal Australian Engineers; Royal Australian Infantry Corps; Royal Australian Army Ordnance Corps; Royal Australian Army Nursing Corps; The Corps of Royal New Zealand Engineers; Royal New Zealand Infantry Regiment; Royal Malta Artillery; The Malawi Rifles

Affiliated Colonel-in-Chief
The Queen's Gurkha Engineers

Captain-General
Royal Regiment of Artillery; The Honourable Artillery Company; Combined Cadet Force Association; Royal Regiment of Canadian Artillery; Royal Regiment of Australian Artillery; Royal Regiment of New Zealand Artillery; Royal New Zealand Armoured Corps

Patron
Royal Army Chaplains' Department

Air Commodore-in-Chief
Royal Auxiliary Air Force; Royal Air Force Regiment; Air Reserve (of Canada); Royal Australian Air Force Reserve; Territorial Air Force (of New Zealand)

Commandant-in-Chief
Royal Air Force College, Cranwell

Hon. Air Commodore
RAF Marham

HRH THE PRINCE PHILIP, DUKE OF EDINBURGH

Admiral of the Fleet
Field Marshal
Marshal of the Royal Air Force
Admiral of the Fleet, Royal Australian Navy
Field Marshal, Australian Military Forces
Marshal of the Royal Australian Air Force
Admiral of the Fleet, Royal New Zealand Navy

Field Marshal, New Zealand Army
Marshal of the Royal New Zealand Air Force
Captain-General, Royal Marines

Admiral
Royal Canadian Sea Cadets

Colonel-in-Chief
The Royal Gloucestershire, Berkshire and Wiltshire Regiment; The Highlanders (Seaforth, Gordons and Camerons); Corps of Royal Electrical and Mechanical Engineers; Intelligence Corps; Army Cadet Force Association; The Royal Canadian Regiment; The Royal Hamilton Light Infantry (Wentworth Regiment) (of Canada); The Cameron Highlanders of Ottawa; The Queen's Own Cameron Highlanders of Canada; The Seaforth Highlanders of Canada; The Royal Canadian Army Cadets; The Royal Corps of Australian Electrical and Mechanical Engineers; The Australian Cadet Corps

Deputy Colonel-in-Chief
The Queen's Royal Hussars (Queen's Own and Royal Irish)

Colonel
Grenadier Guards

Hon. Colonel
City of Edinburgh Universities Officers' Training Corps; The Trinidad and Tobago Regiment

Air Commodore-in-Chief
Air Training Corps; Royal Canadian Air Cadets

Hon. Air Commodore
RAF Kinloss

HM QUEEN ELIZABETH THE QUEEN MOTHER

Colonel-in-Chief
1st The Queen's Dragoon Guards; The Queen's Royal Hussars (Queen's Own and Royal Irish); 9th/12th Royal Lancers (Prince of Wales's); The King's Regiment; The Royal Anglian Regiment; The Light Infantry; The Black Watch (Royal Highland Regiment); Royal Army Medical Corps; The Black Watch (Royal Highland Regiment) of Canada; The Toronto Scottish Regiment; Canadian Forces Medical Services; Royal Australian Army Medical Corps; Royal New Zealand Army Medical Corps

Hon. Colonel
The Royal Yeomanry; The London Scottish; Inns of Court and City Yeomanry; The King's Own Yorkshire Yeomanry (Light Infantry)

Commandant-in-Chief
Women in the Royal Navy; Women, Royal Air Force; Royal Air Force Central Flying School

HRH THE PRINCE OF WALES

Captain, Royal Navy
Group Captain, Royal Air Force

Colonel-in-Chief
The Royal Dragoon Guards; The 22nd (Cheshire) Regiment; The Royal Regiment of Wales (24th/41st Foot); The Parachute Regiment; The Royal Gurkha Rifles; Army Air Corps; The Royal Canadian Dragoons; Lord Strathcona's Horse (Royal Canadians); Royal Regiment of Canada; Royal Winnipeg Rifles; Air Reserve Group of Air Command (of Canada); Royal Australian Armoured Corps; The Royal Pacific Islands Regiment

Deputy Colonel-in-Chief
The Highlanders (Seaforth, Gordons and Camerons)

Colonel
Welsh Guards

Air Commodore-in-Chief
Royal New Zealand Air Force

Hon. Air Commodore
RAF Valley

HRH THE DUKE OF YORK

Lieutenant-Commander, Royal Navy

Admiral
Sea Cadet Corps

Colonel-in-Chief
The Staffordshire Regiment (The Prince of Wales's); The Royal Irish Regiment (27th (Inniskilling), 83rd, 87th and The Ulster Defence Regiment); Royal New Zealand Army Logistic Regiment; The Queen's York Rangers (First Americans)

Hon. Air Commodore
RAF Lossiemouth

HRH THE PRINCESS ROYAL

Rear Admiral
Chief Commandant for Women in the Royal Navy

Colonel-in-Chief
The Household Cavalry; The King's Royal Hussars; Royal Corps of Signals; The Royal Scots (The Royal Regiment); The Worcestershire and Sherwood Foresters Regiment (29th/45th Foot); The Royal Logistic Corps; 8th Canadian Hussars (Princess Louise's); Canadian Forces Communications and Electronics Branch; The Grey and Simcoe Foresters; The Royal Regina Rifle Regiment; Royal Australian Corps of Signals; Royal New Zealand Corps of Signals; Royal New Zealand Nursing Corps

Affiliated Colonel-in-Chief
The Queen's Gurkha Signals; The Queen's Own Gurkha Transport Regiment

Hon. Colonel
University of London Officers' Training Corps

Hon. Air Commodore
RAF Lyneham; University of London Air Squadron

HRH THE PRINCESS MARGARET, COUNTESS OF SNOWDON

Colonel-in-Chief
The Light Dragoons; The Royal Highland Fusiliers (Princess Margaret's Own Glasgow and Ayrshire Regiment); Queen Alexandra's Royal Army Nursing Corps; The Highland Fusiliers of Canada; The Princess Louise Fusiliers (of Canada); The Bermuda Regiment

Deputy Colonel-in-Chief
The Royal Anglian Regiment

Hon. Air Commodore
RAF Coningsby

HRH PRINCESS ALICE, DUCHESS OF GLOUCESTER

Air Chief Marshal

Colonel-in-Chief
The King's Own Scottish Borderers; Royal Australian Corps of Transport

Deputy Colonel-in-Chief
The King's Royal Hussars; The Royal Anglian Regiment

Air Chief Commandant
Women, Royal Air Force

HRH THE DUKE OF GLOUCESTER

Hon. Air Marshal

Deputy Colonel-in-Chief
The Royal Gloucestershire, Berkshire and Wiltshire Regiment; The Royal Logistic Corps

Hon. Colonel
Royal Monmouthshire Royal Engineers (Militia)

Hon. Air Commodore
RAF Odiham

HRH THE DUCHESS OF GLOUCESTER

Colonel-in-Chief
Royal Australian Army Educational Corps; Royal New Zealand Army Educational Corps

Deputy Colonel-in-Chief
Adjutant-General's Corps

HRH THE DUKE OF KENT

Field Marshal
Hon. Air Chief Marshal

Colonel-in-Chief
The Royal Regiment of Fusiliers; The Devonshire and Dorset Regiment; The Lorne Scots (Peel, Dufferin and Hamilton Regiment)

Deputy Colonel-in-Chief
The Royal Scots Dragoon Guards (Carabiniers and Greys)

Colonel
Scots Guards

Hon. Air Commodore
RAF Leuchars

HRH THE DUCHESS OF KENT

Hon. Major-General

Colonel-in-Chief
The Prince of Wales's Own Regiment of Yorkshire

Deputy Colonel-in-Chief
The Royal Dragoon Guards; Adjutant-General's Corps; The Royal Logistic Corps

HRH PRINCE MICHAEL OF KENT

Major (retd), The Royal Hussars (Prince of Wales's Own)

Hon. Commodore
Royal Naval Reserve

HRH PRINCESS ALEXANDRA, THE HON. LADY OGILVY

Patron
Queen Alexandra's Royal Naval Nursing Service

Colonel-in-Chief
The King's Own Royal Border Regiment; The Queen's Own Rifles of Canada; The Canadian Scottish Regiment (Princess Mary's)

Deputy Colonel-in-Chief
The Queen's Royal Lancers; The Light Infantry

Deputy Hon. Colonel
The Royal Yeomanry; The King's Own Yorkshire Yeomanry (Light Infantry)

Patron and Air Chief Commandant
Princess Mary's Royal Air Force Nursing Service

The House of Windsor

King George V assumed by royal proclamation (17 July 1917) for his House and family, as well as for all descendants in the male line of Queen Victoria who are subjects of these realms, the name of Windsor.

KING GEORGE V (George Frederick Ernest Albert), second son of King Edward VII, *born* 3 June 1865; *married* 6 July 1893 HSH Princess Victoria Mary Augusta Louise Olga Pauline Claudine Agnes of Teck (Queen Mary, *born* 26 May 1867; *died* 24 March 1953); *succeeded* to the throne 6 May 1910; *died* 20 January 1936. *Issue:*

1. HRH PRINCE EDWARD Albert Christian George Andrew Patrick David, *born* 23 June 1894, *succeeded* to the throne as King Edward VIII, 20 January 1936; *abdicated* 11 December 1936; created *Duke of Windsor* 1937; *married* 3 June 1937, Mrs Wallis Warfield (Her Grace The Duchess of Windsor, *born* 19 June 1896; *died* 24 April 1986), *died* 28 May 1972

2. HRH PRINCE ALBERT Frederick Arthur George, *born* 14 December 1895, *created* Duke of York 1920; *married* 26 April 1923, Lady Elizabeth Bowes-Lyon, youngest daughter of the 14th Earl of Strathmore and Kinghorne (HM Queen Elizabeth the Queen Mother, *see* page 117), *succeeded* to the throne as King George VI, 11 December 1936; *died* 6 February 1952, having had issue (*see* page 117)

3. HRH PRINCESS (Victoria Alexandra Alice) MARY, *born* 25 April 1897, *created* Princess Royal 1932; *married* 28 February 1922, Viscount Lascelles, later the 6th Earl of Harewood (1882–1947), *died* 28 March 1965. *Issue:*
   (1) George Henry Hubert Lascelles, 7th Earl of Harewood, KBE, *born* 7 February 1923; *married* (1) 1949, Maria (Marion) Stein (marriage dissolved 1967); *issue*, (*a*) David Henry George, Viscount Lascelles, *born* 1950; (*b*) James Edward, *born* 1953; (*c*)

(Robert) Jeremy Hugh, *born* 1955; (2) 1967, Mrs Patricia Tuckwell; *issue*, (*d*) Mark Hubert, *born* 1964
   (2) Gerald David Lascelles (1924–98), *married* (1) 1952, Miss Angela Dowding (marriage dissolved 1978); *issue*, (*a*) Henry Ulick, *born* 1953; (2) 1978, Mrs Elizabeth Colvin; *issue*, (*b*) Martin David, *born* 1962

4. HRH PRINCE HENRY William Frederick Albert, *born* 31 March 1900, *created* Duke of Gloucester, Earl of Ulster and Baron Culloden 1928, *married* 6 November 1935, Lady Alice Christabel Montagu-Douglas-Scott, daughter of the 7th Duke of Buccleuch (HRH Princess Alice, Duchess of Gloucester, *see* page 118); *died* 10 June 1974. *Issue:*
   (1) HRH Prince William Henry Andrew Frederick, *born* 18 December 1941; *accidentally killed* 28 August 1972
   (2) HRH Prince Richard Alexander Walter George (HRH The Duke of Gloucester), *see* page 118

5. HRH PRINCE GEORGE Edward Alexander Edmund, *born* 20 December 1902, *created* Duke of Kent, Earl of St Andrews and Baron Downpatrick 1934, *married* 29 November 1934, HRH Princess Marina of Greece and Denmark (*born* 30 November OS, 1906; *died* 27 August 1968); *killed on active service*, 25 August 1942. *Issue:*
   (1) HRH Prince Edward George Nicholas Paul Patrick (HRH The Duke of Kent), *see* page 118
   (2) HRH Princess Alexandra Helen Elizabeth Olga Christabel (HRH Princess Alexandra, the Hon. Lady Ogilvy), *see* page 118
   (3) HRH Prince Michael George Charles Franklin (HRH Prince Michael of Kent), *see* page 118

6. HRH PRINCE JOHN Charles Francis, *born* 12 July 1905; *died* 18 January 1919

Descendants of Queen Victoria

QUEEN VICTORIA (Alexandrina Victoria), *born* 24 May 1819; *succeeded* to the throne 20 June 1837; *married* 10 February 1840 (Francis) Albert Augustus Charles Emmanuel, Duke of Saxony, Prince of Saxe-Coburg and Gotha (HRH Albert, Prince Consort, *born* 26 August 1819, *died* 14 December 1861); *died* 22 January 1901. *Issue:*

1. HRH PRINCESS VICTORIA Adelaide Mary Louisa (Princess Royal) (1840–1901), *m.* 1858, Friedrich III (1831–88), German Emperor March–June 1888. *Issue:*
   (1) HIM Wilhelm II (1859–1941), German Emperor 1888–1918, *m.* (1) 1881 Princess Augusta Victoria of Schleswig-Holstein-Sonderburg-Augustenburg (1858–1921); (2) 1922 Princess Hermine of Reuss (1887–1947). *Issue:*
      (*a*) Prince Wilhelm (1882–1951), *Crown Prince* 1888–1918, *m.* 1905 Duchess Cecilie of Mecklenburg-Schwerin; *issue:* Prince Wilhelm (1906–40); Prince Louis Ferdinand (1907–94), *m.* 1938 Grand Duchess Kira (*see* page 128); Prince Hubertus (1909–50); Prince Friedrich Georg (1911–66); Princess Alexandrine Irene (1915–80); Princess Cecilie (1917–75)
      (*b*) Prince Eitel-Friedrich (1883–1942), *m.* 1906 Duchess Sophie of Oldenburg (marriage dissolved 1926)
      (*c*) Prince Adalbert (1884–1948), *m.* 1914 Duchess Adelheid of Saxe-Meiningen; *issue:* Princess Victoria Marina (1917–81); Prince Wilhelm Victor (1919–89)
      (*d*) Prince August Wilhelm (1887–1949), *m.* 1908 Princess Alexandra of Schleswig-Holstein-Sonderburg-Glücksburg (marriage dissolved 1920); *issue:* Prince Alexander (1912–85)
      (*e*) Prince Oskar (1888–1958), *m.* 1914 Countess von Ruppin; *issue:* Prince Oskar (1915–39); Prince Burchard (1917–88); Princess Herzeleide (1918–89); Prince Wilhelm-Karl (*b.* 1922)

(*f*) Prince Joachim (1890–1920), *m.* 1916 Princess Marie of Anhalt; *issue:* Prince (Karl) Franz Joseph (1916–75), and has issue
   (*g*) Princess Viktoria Luise (1892–1980), *m.* 1913 Ernst, Duke of Brunswick 1913–18 (1887–1953); *issue:* Prince Ernst (1914–87); Prince Georg (*b.* 1915), *m.* 1946 Princess Sophie of Greece (*see* page 128) and has issue (two sons, one daughter); Princess Frederika (1917–81), *m.* 1938 Paul I, King of the Hellenes (*see* page 128); Prince Christian (1919–81); Prince Welf Heinrich (*b.* 1923)
   (2) Princess Charlotte (1860–1919), *m.* 1878 Bernhard, Duke of Saxe-Meiningen 1914 (1851–1914). *Issue:*
      Princess Feodora (1879–1945), *m.* 1898 Prince Heinrich XXX of Reuss
   (3) Prince Heinrich (1862–1929), *m.* 1888 Princess Irene of Hesse (*see* page 128). *Issue:*
      (*a*) Prince Waldemar (1889–1945), *m.* Princess Calixta Agnes of Lippe
      (*b*) Prince Sigismund (1896–1978), *m.* 1919 Princess Charlotte of Saxe-Altenburg; *issue:* Princess Barbara (1920–94); Prince Alfred (*b.* 1924)
      (*c*) Prince Heinrich (1900–4)
   (4) Prince Sigismund (1864–6)
   (5) Princess Victoria (1866–1929), *m.* (1) 1890, Prince Adolf of Schaumburg-Lippe (1859–1916); (2) 1927 Alexander Zubkov
   (6) Prince Waldemar (1868–79)
   (7) Princess Sophie (1870–1932), *m.* 1889 Constantine I (1868–1923), King of the Hellenes 1913–17, 1920–3. *Issue:*
      (*a*) George II (1890–1947), King of the Hellenes 1923–4 and 1935–47, *m.* 1921 Princess Elisabeth of Roumania (marriage dissolved 1935) (*see* page 128)

(b) Alexander I (1893–1920), King of the Hellenes 1917–20, m. 1919 Aspasia Manos; issue: Princess Alexandra (1921–93), m. 1944 King Petar II of Yugoslavia (see below)
(c) Princess Helena (1896–1982), m. 1921 King Carol of Roumania (see below), (marriage dissolved 1928)
(d) Paul I (1901–64), King of the Hellenes 1947–64, m. 1938 Princess Frederika of Brunswick (see page 127); issue: King Constantine II (b. 1940), m. 1964 Princess Anne-Marie of Denmark (see page 129), and has issue (three sons, two daughters); Princess Sophie (b. 1938), m. 1962 Juan Carlos I of Spain (see page 129); Princess Irene (b. 1942)
(e) Princess Irene (1904–74), m. 1939 4th Duke of Aosta; issue: Prince Amedeo, 5th Duke of Aosta (b. 1943)
(f) Princess Katherine (Lady Katherine Brandram) (b. 1913), m. 1947 Major R. C. A. Brandram, MC, TD; issue: R. Paul G. A. Brandram (b. 1948)
(8) Princess Margarethe (1872–1954), m. 1893 Prince Friedrich Karl of Hesse (1868–1940). Issue:
    (a) Prince Friedrich Wilhelm (1893–1916)
    (b) Prince Maximilian (1894–1914)
    (c) Prince Philipp (1896–1980), m. 1925 Princess Mafalda of Italy; issue: Prince Moritz (b. 1926); Prince Heinrich (b. 1927); Prince Otto (b. 1937); Princess Elisabeth (b. 1940)
    (d) Prince Wolfgang (1896–1989), m. (1) 1924 Princess Marie Alexandra of Baden; (2) 1948 Ottilie Möller
    (e) Prince Richard (1901–69)
    (f) Prince Christoph (1901–43), m. 1930 Princess Sophie of Greece (see below) and has issue (two sons, three daughters)

2. HRH Prince Albert Edward (HM King Edward VII), b. 9 November 1841, m. 1863 HRH Princess Alexandra of Denmark (1844–1925), succeeded to the throne 22 January 1901, d. 6 May 1910. Issue:
(1) Albert Victor, Duke of Clarence and Avondale (1864–92)
(2) George (HM King George V) (see page 127)
(3) Louise (1867–1931) Princess Royal 1905–31, m. 1889 1st Duke of Fife (1849–1912). Issue:
    (a) Princess Alexandra, Duchess of Fife (1891–1959), m. 1913 Prince Arthur of Connaught (see page 129)
    (b) Princess Maud (1893–1945), m. 1923 11th Earl of Southesk (1893–1992); issue: The Duke of Fife (b. 1929)
(4) Victoria (1868–1935)
(5) Maud (1869–1938), m. 1896 Prince Carl of Denmark (1872–1957), later King Haakon VII of Norway 1905–57. Issue:
    (a) Olav V (1903–91), King of Norway 1957–91, m. 1929 Princess Märtha of Sweden (1901–54); issue: Princess Ragnhild (b. 1930); Princess Astrid (b. 1932); Harald V, King of Norway (b. 1937)
(6) Alexander (6–7 April 1871)

3. HRH Princess Alice Maud Mary (1843–78), m. 1862 Prince Ludwig (1837–92), Grand Duke of Hesse 1877–92. Issue:
(1) Victoria (1863–1950), m. 1884 Admiral of the Fleet Prince Louis of Battenberg (1854–1921), cr. 1st Marquess of Milford Haven 1917. Issue:
    (a) Alice (1885–1969), m. 1903 Prince Andrew of Greece (1882–1944); issue: Princess Margarita (1905–81), m. 1931 Prince Gottfried of Hohenlohe-Langenburg (see below); Princess Theodora (1906–69), m. Prince Berthold of Baden (1906–63) and has issue (two sons, one daughter); Princess Cecilie (1911–37), m. George, Grand Duke of Hesse (see below); Princess Sophie (b. 1914), m. (1) 1930 Prince Christoph of Hesse (see above); (2) 1946 Prince Georg of Hanover (see page 127); Prince Philip, Duke of Edinburgh (b. 1921) (see page 117)
    (b) Louise (1889–1965), m. 1923 Gustaf VI Adolf (1882–1973), King of Sweden 1950–73
    (c) George, 2nd Marquess of Milford Haven (1892–1938), m. 1916 Countess Nadejda, daughter of Grand Duke Michael of Russia; issue: Lady Tatiana (1917–88); David Michael, 3rd Marquess (1919–70)
    (d) Louis, 1st Earl Mountbatten of Burma (1900–79), m. 1922 Edwina Ashley, daughter of Lord Mount Temple; issue: Patricia, Countess Mountbatten of Burma (b. 1924), Pamela (b. 1929)
(2) Elizabeth (1864–1918), m. 1884 Grand Duke Sergius of Russia (1857–1905)
(3) Irene (1866–1953), m. 1888 Prince Heinrich of Prussia (see page 127)

(4) Ernst Ludwig (1868–1937), Grand Duke of Hesse 1892–1918, m. (1) 1894 Princess Victoria Melita of Saxe-Coburg (see below) (marriage dissolved 1901); (2) 1905 Princess Eleonore of Solms-Hohensolmslich. Issue:
    (a) Princess Elizabeth (1895–1903)
    (b) George, Hereditary Grand Duke of Hesse (1906–37), m. Princess Cecilie of Greece (see above), and had issue, two sons, accidentally killed with parents 1937
    (c) Ludwig, Prince of Hesse (1908–68), m. 1937 Margaret, daughter of 1st Lord Geddes
(5) Frederick William (1870–3)
(6) Alix (Tsaritsa of Russia) (1872–1918), m. 1894 Nicholas II (1868–1918) Tsar of All the Russias 1894–1917, assassinated 16 July 1918. Issue:
    (a) Grand Duchess Olga (1895–1918)
    (b) Grand Duchess Tatiana (1897–1918)
    (c) Grand Duchess Marie (1899–1918)
    (d) Grand Duchess Anastasia (1901–18)
    (e) Alexis, Tsarevich of Russia (1904–18)
(7) Marie (1874–8)

4. HRH Prince Alfred Ernest Albert, Duke of Edinburgh, Admiral of the Fleet (1844–1900), m. 1874 Grand Duchess Marie Alexandrovna of Russia (1853–1920); succeeded as Duke of Saxe-Coburg and Gotha 22 August 1893. Issue:
(1) Alfred, Prince of Saxe-Coburg (1874–99)
(2) Marie (1875–1938), m. 1893 Ferdinand (1865–1927), King of Roumania 1914–27. Issue:
    (a) Carol II (1893–1953), King of Roumania 1930–40, m. (2) 1921 Princess Helena of Greece (see above) (marriage dissolved 1928); issue: Michael (b. 1921), King of Roumania 1927–30, 1940–7, m. 1948 Princess Anne of Bourbon-Parma, and has issue (five daughters)
    (b) Elisabeth (1894–1956), m. 1921 George II, King of the Hellenes (see page 127)
    (c) Marie (1900–61), m. 1922 Alexander (1888–1934), King of Yugoslavia 1921–34; issue: Petar II (1923–70), King of Yugoslavia 1934–45, m. 1944 Princess Alexandra of Greece (see above) and has issue (Crown Prince Alexander, b. 1945); Prince Tomislav (b. 1928), m. (1) 1957 Princess Margarita of Baden (daughter of Princess Theodora of Greece and Prince Berthold of Baden, see above); (2) 1982 Linda Bonney; and has issue (three sons, one daughter); Prince Andrej (1929–90), m. (1) 1956 Princess Christina of Hesse (daughter of Prince Christoph of Hesse and Princess Sophie of Greece, see above); (2) 1963 Princess Kira-Melita of Leiningen (see below); and has issue (three sons, two daughters)
    (d) Prince Nicolas (1903–78)
    (e) Princess Ileana (1909–91), m. (1) 1931 Archduke Anton of Austria; (2) 1954 Dr Stefan Issarescu; issue: Archduke Stefan (b. 1932); Archduchess Maria Ileana (1933–59); Archduchess Alexandra (b. 1935); Archduke Dominic (b. 1937); Archduchess Maria Magdalena (b. 1939); Archduchess Elisabeth (b. 1942)
    (f) Prince Mircea (1913–16)
(3) Victoria Melita (1876–1936), m. (1) 1894 Grand Duke Ernst Ludwig of Hesse (see above) (marriage dissolved 1901); (2) 1905 the Grand Duke Kirill of Russia (1876–1938). Issue:
    (a) Marie Kirillovna (1907–51), m. 1925 Prince Friedrich Karl of Leiningen; issue: Prince Emich (1926–91); Prince Karl (1928–90); Princess Kira-Melita (b. 1930), m. Prince Andrej of Yugoslavia (see above); Princess Margarita (b. 1932); Princess Mechtilde (b. 1936); Prince Friedrich (b. 1938)
    (b) Kira Kirillovna (1909–67), m. 1938 Prince Louis Ferdinand of Prussia (see page 127); issue: Prince Friedrich Wilhelm (b. 1939); Prince Michael (b. 1940); Princess Marie (b. 1942); Princess Kira (b. 1943); Prince Louis Ferdinand (1944–77); Prince Christian (b. 1946); Princess Xenia (1949–92)
    (c) Vladimir Kirillovich (1917–92), m. 1948 Princess Leonida Bagration-Mukhransky; issue: Grand Duchess Maria (b. 1953), and has issue
(4) Alexandra (1878–1942), m. 1896 Ernst, Prince of Hohenlohe Langenburg. Issue:
    (a) Gottfried (1897–1960), m. 1931 Princess Margarita of Greece (see above); issue: Prince Kraft (b. 1935), Princess Beatrice (1936–97), Prince Georg Andreas (b. 1938), Prince Ruprecht (1944–76); Prince Albrecht (1944–92)

(*b*) Maria (1899–1967), *m.* 1916 Prince Friedrich of Schleswig-Holstein-Sonderburg-Glücksburg; *issue:* Prince Peter (1922–80); Princess Marie (*b.* 1927)
(*c*) Princess Alexandra (1901–63)
(*d*) Princess Irma (1902–86)
(5) Princess Beatrice (1884–1966), *m.* 1909 Alfonso of Orleans, Infante of Spain. *Issue:*
(*a*) Prince Alvaro (*b.* 1910), *m.* 1937 Carla Parodi-Delfino; *issue:* Doña Gerarda (*b.* 1939); Don Alonso (1941–75); Doña Beatriz (*b.* 1943); Don Alvaro (*b.* 1947)
(*b*) Prince Alonso (1912–36)
(*c*) Prince Ataulfo (1913–74)

5. HRH Princess Helena Augusta Victoria (1846–1923), *m.* 1866 Prince Christian of Schleswig-Holstein-Sonderburg-Augustenburg (1831–1917). *Issue:*
(1) Prince Christian Victor (1867–1900)
(2) Prince Albert (1869–1931), Duke of Schleswig-Holstein 1921–31
(3) Princess Helena (1870–1948)
(4) Princess Marie Louise (1872–1956), *m.* 1891 Prince Aribert of Anhalt (marriage dissolved 1900)
(5) Prince Harold (12–20 May 1876)

6. HRH Princess Louise Caroline Alberta (1848–1939), *m.* 1871 the Marquess of Lorne, afterwards 9th Duke of Argyll (1845–1914); without issue

7. HRH Prince Arthur William Patrick Albert, Duke of Connaught, *Field Marshal* (1850–1942), *m.* 1879 Princess Louisa of Prussia (1860–1917). *Issue:*
(1) Margaret (1882–1920), *m.* 1905 Crown Prince Gustaf Adolf (1882–1973), afterwards King of Sweden 1950–73. *Issue:*
(*a*) Gustaf Adolf, Duke of Västerbotten (1906–47), *m.* 1932 Princess Sibylla of Saxe-Coburg-Gotha (*see* below); *issue:* Princess Margaretha (*b.* 1934); Princess Birgitta (*b.* 1937); Princess Désirée (*b.* 1938); Princess Christina (*b.* 1943); Carl XVI Gustaf, King of Sweden (*b.* 1946)
(*b*) Count Sigvard Bernadotte (*b.* 1907), *m.; issue:* Count Michael (*b.* 1944)
(*c*) Princess Ingrid (Queen Mother of Denmark) (*b.* 1910), *m.* 1935 Frederick IX (1899–1972), King of Denmark 1947–72; *issue:* Margrethe II, Queen of Denmark (*b.* 1940); Princess Benedikte (*b.* 1946); Princess Anne-Marie (*b.* 1946), *m.* 1964 Constantine II of Greece (*see* page 128)
(*d*) Prince Bertil, Duke of Halland (1912–97), *m.* 1976 Mrs Lilian Craig
(*e*) Count Carl Bernadotte (*b.* 1916), *m.* (1) 1946 Mrs Kerstin Johnson; (2) 1988 Countess Gunnila Bussler

(2) Arthur (1883–1938), *m.* 1913 HH the Duchess of Fife (*see* page 128). *Issue:*
Alastair Arthur, 2nd Duke of Connaught (1914–43)
(3) (Victoria) Patricia (1886–1974), *m.* 1919 Adm. Hon. Sir Alexander Ramsay. *Issue:*
Alexander Ramsay of Mar (*b.* 1919), *m.* 1956 Hon. Flora Fraser (Lady Saltoun)

8. HRH Prince Leopold George Duncan Albert, Duke of Albany (1853–84), *m.* 1882 Princess Helena of Waldeck (1861–1922). *Issue:*
(1) Alice (1883–1981), *m.* 1904 Prince Alexander of Teck (1874–1957), *cr.* 1st Earl of Athlone 1917. *Issue:*
(*a*) Lady May (1906–94), *m.* 1931 Sir Henry Abel-Smith, KCMG, KCVO, DSO; *issue:* Anne (*b.* 1932); Richard (*b.* 1933); Elizabeth (*b.* 1936)
(*b*) Rupert, Viscount Trematon (1907–28)
(*c*) Prince Maurice (March–September 1910)
(2) Charles Edward (1884–1954), Duke of Albany 1884 until title suspended 1917, Duke of Saxe-Coburg-Gotha 1900–18, *m.* 1905 Princess Victoria Adelheid of Schleswig-Holstein-Sonderburg-Glücksburg. *Issue:*
(*a*) Prince Johann Leopold (1906–72), and has issue
(*b*) Princess Sibylla (1908–72), *m.* 1932 Prince Gustav Adolf of Sweden (*see* above)
(*c*) Prince Dietmar Hubertus (1909–43)
(*d*) Princess Caroline (1912–83), and has issue
(*e*) Prince Friedrich Josias (*b.* 1918), and has issue

9. HRH Princess Beatrice Mary Victoria Feodore (1857–1944), *m.* 1885 Prince Henry of Battenberg (1858–96). *Issue:*
(1) Alexander, 1st Marquess of Carisbrooke (1886–1960), *m.* 1917 Lady Irene Denison. *Issue:*
Lady Iris Mountbatten (1920–82), *m.; issue:* Robin A. Bryan (*b.* 1957)
(2) Victoria Eugénie (1887–1969), *m.* 1906 Alfonso XIII (1886–1941) King of Spain 1886–1931. *Issue:*
(*a*) Prince Alfonso (1907–38)
(*b*) Prince Jaime (1908–75), and has issue
(*c*) Princess Beatrice (*b.* 1909), and has issue
(*d*) Princess Maria (1911–96), and has issue
(*e*) Prince Juan (1913–93), Count of Barcelona; *issue:* Princess Maria (*b.* 1936); Juan Carlos I, King of Spain (*b.* 1938), *m.* 1962 Princess Sophie of Greece (*see* page 128) and has issue (one son, two daughters); Princess Margarita (*b.* 1939)
(*f*) Prince Gonzalo (1914–34)
(3) Major Lord Leopold Mountbatten (1889–1922)
(4) Maurice (1891–1914), died of wounds received in action

Kings and Queens

ENGLISH KINGS AND QUEENS 927 to 1603

HOUSES OF CERDIC AND DENMARK

Reign
927–939 ÆTHELSTAN
Son of Edward the Elder, by Ecgwynn, and grandson of Alfred
Acceded to Wessex and Mercia *c.*924, established direct rule over Northumbria 927, effectively creating the Kingdom of England
Reigned 15 years
939–946 EDMUND I
Born 921, son of Edward the Elder, by Eadgifu
Married (1) Ælfgifu (2) Æthelflæd
Killed aged 25, *reigned* 6 years
946–955 EADRED
Son of Edward the Elder, by Eadgifu
Reigned 9 years
955–959 EADWIG
Born before 943, son of Edmund and Ælfgifu

Married Ælfgifu
Reigned 3 years
959–975 EDGAR I
Born 943, son of Edmund and Ælfgifu
Married (1) Æthelflæd (2) Wulfthryth (3) Ælfthryth
Died aged 32, *reigned* 15 years
975–978 EDWARD I (the Martyr)
*Born c.*962, son of Edgar and Æthelflæd
Assassinated aged *c.*16, *reigned* 2 years
978–1016 ÆTHELRED (the Unready)
*Born c.*968/969, son of Edgar and Ælfthryth
Married (1) Ælfgifu (2) Emma, daughter of Richard I, count of Normandy
1013–14 dispossessed of kingdom by Swegn Forkbeard (king of Denmark 987–1014)
Died aged *c.*47, *reigned* 38 years
1016 EDMUND II (Ironside)
Born before 993, son of Æthelred and Ælfgifu
Married Ealdgyth
Died aged over 23, *reigned* 7 months (April–November)
1016–1035 CNUT (Canute)
*Born c.*995, son of Swegn Forkbeard, king of Denmark, and Gunhild

Married (1) Ælfgifu (2) Emma, widow of
Æthelred the Unready
Gained submission of West Saxons 1015,
Northumbrians 1016, Mercia 1016, king of all
England after Edmund's death
King of Denmark 1019–35, king of Norway
1028–35
Died aged *c*.40, *reigned* 19 years

1035–1040   HAROLD I (Harefoot)
Born c.1016/17, son of Cnut and Ælfgifu
Married Ælfgifu
1035 recognized as regent for himself and his
brother Harthacnut; 1037 recognized as king
Died aged *c*.23, *reigned* 4 years

1040–1042   HARTHACNUT
Born c.1018, son of Cnut and Emma
Titular king of Denmark from 1028
Acknowledged king of England 1035–7 with
Harold I as regent; effective king after Harold's
death
Died aged *c*.24, *reigned* 2 years

1042–1066   EDWARD II (the Confessor)
Born between 1002 and 1005, son of Æthelred the
Unready and Emma
Married Eadgyth, daughter of Godwine, earl of
Wessex
Died aged over 60, *reigned* 23 years

1066   HAROLD II (Godwinesson)
Born c.1020, son of Godwine, earl of Wessex, and
Gytha
Married (1) Eadgyth (2) Ealdgyth
Killed in battle aged *c*.46, *reigned* 10 months
(January–October)

THE HOUSE OF NORMANDY

1066–1087   WILLIAM I (the Conqueror)
Born 1027/8, son of Robert I, duke of Normandy;
obtained the Crown by conquest
Married Matilda, daughter of Baldwin, count of
Flanders
Died aged *c*.60, *reigned* 20 years

1087–1100   WILLIAM II (Rufus)
Born between 1056 and 1060, third son of
William I; succeeded his father in England only
Killed aged *c*.40, *reigned* 12 years

1100–1135   HENRY I (Beauclerk)
Born 1068, fourth son of William I
Married (1) Edith or Matilda, daughter of
Malcolm III of Scotland (2) Adela, daughter of
Godfrey, count of Louvain
Died aged 67, *reigned* 35 years

1135–1154   STEPHEN
Born not later than 1100, third son of Adela,
daughter of William I, and Stephen, count of Blois
Married Matilda, daughter of Eustace, count of
Boulogne
1141 (February–November) held captive by
adherents of Matilda, daughter of Henry I, who
contested the crown until 1153
Died aged over 53, *reigned* 18 years

THE HOUSE OF ANJOU (PLANTAGENETS)

1154–1189   HENRY II (Curtmantle)
Born 1133, son of Matilda, daughter of Henry I,
and Geoffrey, count of Anjou
Married Eleanor, daughter of William, duke of
Aquitaine, and divorced queen of Louis VII of
France
Died aged 56, *reigned* 34 years

1189–1199   RICHARD I (Coeur de Lion)
Born 1157, third son of Henry II
Married Berengaria, daughter of Sancho VI, king of
Navarre
Died aged 42, *reigned* 9 years

1199–1216   JOHN (Lackland)
Born 1167, fifth son of Henry II

Married (1) Isabella or Avisa, daughter of William,
earl of Gloucester (divorced) (2) Isabella, daughter
of Aymer, count of Angoulême
Died aged 48, *reigned* 17 years

1216–1272   HENRY III
Born 1207, son of John and Isabella of Angoulême
Married Eleanor, daughter of Raymond, count of
Provence
Died aged 65, *reigned* 56 years

1272–1307   EDWARD I (Longshanks)
Born 1239, eldest son of Henry III
Married (1) Eleanor, daughter of Ferdinand III,
king of Castile (2) Margaret, daughter of Philip III
of France
Died aged 68, *reigned* 34 years

1307–1327   EDWARD II
Born 1284, eldest surviving son of Edward I and
Eleanor
Married Isabella, daughter of Philip IV of France
Deposed January 1327, *killed* September 1327 aged
43, *reigned* 19 years

1327–1377   EDWARD III
Born 1312, eldest son of Edward II
Married Philippa, daughter of William, count of
Hainault
Died aged 64, *reigned* 50 years

1377–1399   RICHARD II
Born 1367, son of Edward (the Black Prince), eldest
son of Edward III
Married (1) Anne, daughter of Emperor Charles IV
(2) Isabelle, daughter of Charles VI of France
Deposed September 1399, *killed* February 1400 aged
33, *reigned* 22 years

THE HOUSE OF LANCASTER

1399–1413   HENRY IV
Born 1366, son of John of Gaunt, fourth son of
Edward III, and Blanche, daughter of Henry, duke
of Lancaster
Married (1) Mary, daughter of Humphrey, earl of
Hereford (2) Joan, daughter of Charles, king of
Navarre, and widow of John, duke of Brittany
Died aged *c.* 47, *reigned* 13 years

1413–1422   HENRY V
Born 1387, eldest surviving son of Henry IV and
Mary
Married Catherine, daughter of Charles VI of
France
Died aged 34, *reigned* 9 years

1422–1471   HENRY VI
Born 1421, son of Henry V
Married Margaret, daughter of René, duke of
Anjou and count of Provence
Deposed March 1461, *restored* October 1470
Deposed April 1471, *killed* May 1471 aged 49, *reigned*
39 years

THE HOUSE OF YORK

1461–1483   EDWARD IV
Born 1442, eldest son of Richard of York (grandson
of Edmund, fifth son of Edward III, and son of
Anne, great-granddaughter of Lionel, third son of
Edward III)
Married Elizabeth Woodville, daughter of Richard,
Lord Rivers, and widow of Sir John Grey
Acceded March 1461, *deposed* October 1470, *restored*
April 1471
Died aged 40, *reigned* 21 years

1483   EDWARD V
Born 1470, eldest son of Edward IV
Deposed June 1483, *died* probably July–September
1483, aged 12, *reigned* 2 months (April–June)

1483–1485   RICHARD III
Born 1452, fourth son of Richard of York
Married Anne Neville, daughter of Richard, earl of
Warwick, and widow of Edward, Prince of Wales,
son of Henry VI
Killed in battle aged 32, *reigned* 2 years

THE HOUSE OF TUDOR

1485–1509   HENRY VII
Born 1457, son of Margaret Beaufort (great-granddaughter of John of Gaunt, fourth son of Edward III) and Edmund Tudor, earl of Richmond
Married Elizabeth, daughter of Edward IV
Died aged 52, *reigned* 23 years

1509–1547   HENRY VIII
Born 1491, second son of Henry VII
Married (1) Catherine, daughter of Ferdinand II, king of Aragon, and widow of his elder brother Arthur (divorced) (2) Anne, daughter of Sir Thomas Boleyn (executed) (3) Jane, daughter of Sir John Seymour (died in childbirth) (4) Anne, daughter of John, duke of Cleves (divorced) (5) Catherine Howard, niece of the Duke of Norfolk (executed) (6) Catherine, daughter of Sir Thomas Parr and widow of Lord Latimer
Died aged 55, *reigned* 37 years

1547–1553   EDWARD VI
Born 1537, son of Henry VIII and Jane Seymour
Died aged 15, *reigned* 6 years

1553   JANE
Born 1537, daughter of Frances (daughter of Mary Tudor, the younger daughter of Henry VII) and Henry Grey, duke of Suffolk
Married Lord Guildford Dudley, son of the Duke of Northumberland
Deposed July 1553, *executed* February 1554 aged 16, *reigned* 14 days

1553–1558   MARY I
Born 1516, daughter of Henry VIII and Catherine of Aragon
Married Philip II of Spain
Died aged 42, *reigned* 5 years

1558–1603   ELIZABETH I
Born 1533, daughter of Henry VIII and Anne Boleyn
Died aged 69, *reigned* 44 years

BRITISH KINGS AND QUEENS   SINCE 1603

THE HOUSE OF STUART

Reign
1603–1625   JAMES I (VI OF SCOTLAND)
Born 1566, son of Mary, queen of Scots (granddaughter of Margaret Tudor, elder daughter of Henry VII), and Henry Stewart, Lord Darnley
Married Anne, daughter of Frederick II of Denmark
Died aged 58, *reigned* 22 years
(*see also* page 133)

1625–1649   CHARLES I
Born 1600, second son of James I
Married Henrietta Maria, daughter of Henry IV of France
Executed 1649 aged 48, *reigned* 23 years

COMMONWEALTH DECLARED 19 May 1649
1649–53 Government by a council of state
1653–8 Oliver Cromwell, *Lord Protector*
1658–9 Richard Cromwell, *Lord Protector*

1660–1685   CHARLES II
Born 1630, eldest son of Charles I
Married Catherine, daughter of John IV of Portugal
Died aged 54, *reigned* 24 years

1685–1688   JAMES II (VII of Scotland)
Born 1633, second son of Charles I
Married (1) Lady Anne Hyde, daughter of Edward, earl of Clarendon (2) Mary, daughter of Alphonso, duke of Modena
Reign ended with flight from kingdom December 1688
Died 1701 aged 67, *reigned* 3 years

INTERREGNUM 11 December 1688 to 12 February 1689

1689–1702   WILLIAM III
Born 1650, son of William II, prince of Orange, and Mary Stuart, daughter of Charles I
Married Mary, elder daughter of James II
Died aged 51, *reigned* 13 years

and
1689–1694   MARY II
Born 1662, elder daughter of James II and Anne
Died aged 32, *reigned* 5 years

1702–1714   ANNE
Born 1665, younger daughter of James II and Anne
Married Prince George of Denmark, son of Frederick III of Denmark
Died aged 49, *reigned* 12 years

THE HOUSE OF HANOVER

1714–1727   GEORGE I (Elector of Hanover)
Born 1660, son of Sophia (daughter of Frederick, elector palatine, and Elizabeth Stuart, daughter of James I) and Ernest Augustus, elector of Hanover
Married Sophia Dorothea, daughter of George William, duke of Lüneburg-Celle
Died aged 67, *reigned* 12 years

1727–1760   GEORGE II
Born 1683, son of George I
Married Caroline, daughter of John Frederick, margrave of Brandenburg-Anspach
Died aged 76, *reigned* 33 years

1760–1820   GEORGE III
Born 1738, son of Frederick, eldest son of George II
Married Charlotte, daughter of Charles Louis, duke of Mecklenburg-Strelitz
Died aged 81, *reigned* 59 years

REGENCY 1811–20
Prince of Wales regent owing to the insanity of George III

1820–1830   GEORGE IV
Born 1762, eldest son of George III
Married Caroline, daughter of Charles, duke of Brunswick-Wolfenbüttel
Died aged 67, *reigned* 10 years

1830–1837   WILLIAM IV
Born 1765, third son of George III
Married Adelaide, daughter of George, duke of Saxe-Meiningen
Died aged 71, *reigned* 7 years

1837–1901   VICTORIA
Born 1819, daughter of Edward, fourth son of George III
Married Prince Albert of Saxe-Coburg and Gotha
Died aged 81, *reigned* 63 years

THE HOUSE OF SAXE-COBURG AND GOTHA

1901–1910   EDWARD VII
Born 1841, eldest son of Victoria and Albert
Married Alexandra, daughter of Christian IX of Denmark
Died aged 68, *reigned* 9 years

THE HOUSE OF WINDSOR

1910–1936   GEORGE V
Born 1865, second son of Edward VII
Married Victoria Mary, daughter of Francis, duke of Teck
Died aged 70, *reigned* 25 years

1936   EDWARD VIII
Born 1894, eldest son of George V
Married (1937) Mrs Wallis Warfield
Abdicated 1936, *died* 1972 aged 77, *reigned* 10 months (20 January to 11 December)

1936–1952   GEORGE VI
Born 1895, second son of George V
Married Lady Elizabeth Bowes-Lyon, daughter of 14th Earl of Strathmore and Kinghorne (*see also* page 117)
Died aged 56, *reigned* 15 years

1952–   ELIZABETH II
       Born 1926, elder daughter of George VI
       Married Philip, son of Prince Andrew of Greece
       (*see also* page 117)
       WHOM GOD PRESERVE

KINGS AND QUEENS OF SCOTS 1016 TO 1603

Reign
1016–1034   MALCOLM II
       *Born c.*954, son of Kenneth II
       Acceded to Alba 1005, secured Lothian *c.*1016,
       obtained Strathclyde for his grandson Duncan
       *c.*1016, thus reigning over an area approximately
       the same as that governed by later rulers of
       Scotland
       Died aged *c.*80, *reigned* 18 years

THE HOUSE OF ATHOLL

1034–1040   DUNCAN I
       Son of Bethoc, daughter of Malcolm II, and
       Crinan, mormaer of Atholl
       Married a cousin of Siward, earl of Northumbria
       Reigned 5 years
1040–1057   MACBETH
       *Born c.*1005, son of a daughter of Malcolm II and
       Finlaec, mormaer of Moray
       Married Gruoch, granddaughter of Kenneth III
       Killed aged *c.*52, *reigned* 17 years
1057–1058   LULACH
       *Born c.*1032, son of Gillacomgan, mormaer of
       Moray, and Gruoch (and stepson of Macbeth)
       Died aged *c.*26, *reigned* 7 months (August–March)
1058–1093   MALCOLM III (Canmore)
       *Born c.*1031, elder son of Duncan I
       Married (1) Ingiborg (2) Margaret (St Margaret),
       granddaughter of Edmund II of England
       Killed in battle aged *c.*62, *reigned* 35 years
1093–1097   DONALD III BÁN
       *Born c.*1033, second son of Duncan I
       Deposed May 1094, *restored* November 1094, *deposed*
       October 1097, *reigned* 3 years
1094   DUNCAN II
       *Born c.*1060, elder son of Malcolm III and Ingiborg
       Married Octreda of Dunbar
       Killed aged *c.*34, *reigned* 6 months
       (May–November)
1097–1107   EDGAR
       *Born c.*1074, second son of Malcolm III and
       Margaret
       Died aged *c.*32, *reigned* 9 years
1107–1124   ALEXANDER I (The Fierce)
       *Born c.*1077, fifth son of Malcolm III and Margaret
       Married Sybilla, illegitimate daughter of Henry I
       of England
       Died aged *c.*47, *reigned* 17 years
1124–1153   DAVID I (The Saint)
       *Born c.*1085, sixth son of Malcolm III and Margaret
       Married Matilda, daughter of Waltheof, earl of
       Huntingdon
       Died aged *c.*68, *reigned* 29 years
1153–1165   MALCOLM IV (The Maiden)
       *Born c.*1141, son of Henry, earl of Huntingdon,
       second son of David I
       Died aged *c.*24, *reigned* 12 years
1165–1214   WILLIAM I (The Lion)
       *Born c.*1142, brother of Malcolm IV
       Married Ermengarde, daughter of Richard,
       viscount of Beaumont
       Died aged *c.*72, *reigned* 49 years
1214–1249   ALEXANDER II
       Born 1198, son of William I
       Married (1) Joan, daughter of John, king of
       England (2) Marie, daughter of Ingelram de Coucy
       Died aged 50, *reigned* 34 years

1249–1286   ALEXANDER III
       Born 1241, son of Alexander II and Marie
       Married (1) Margaret, daughter of Henry III of
       England (2) Yolande, daughter of the Count of
       Dreux
       Killed accidentally aged 44, *reigned* 36 years
1286–1290   MARGARET (The Maid of Norway)
       Born 1283, daughter of Margaret (daughter of
       Alexander III) and Eric II of Norway
       Died aged 7, *reigned* 4 years

       FIRST INTERREGNUM 1290–2
       Throne disputed by 13 competitors. Crown
       awarded to John Balliol by adjudication of Edward
       I of England

THE HOUSE OF BALLIOL

1292–1296   JOHN (Balliol)
       *Born c.*1250, son of Dervorguilla, great-great-
       granddaughter of David I, and John de Balliol
       Married Isabella, daughter of John, earl of Surrey
       Abdicated 1296, *died* 1313 aged *c.*63, *reigned* 3 years

       SECOND INTERREGNUM 1296–1306
       Edward I of England declared John Balliol to have
       forfeited the throne for contumacy in 1296 and
       took the government of Scotland into his own
       hands

THE HOUSE OF BRUCE

1306–1329   ROBERT I (Bruce)
       Born 1274, son of Robert Bruce and Marjorie,
       countess of Carrick, and great-grandson of the
       second daughter of David, earl of Huntingdon,
       brother of William I
       Married (1) Isabella, daughter of Donald, earl of
       Mar (2) Elizabeth, daughter of Richard, earl of
       Ulster
       Died aged 54, *reigned* 23 years
1329–1371   DAVID II
       Born 1324, son of Robert I and Elizabeth
       Married (1) Joanna, daughter of Edward II of
       England (2) Margaret Drummond, widow of Sir
       John Logie (divorced)
       Died aged 46, *reigned* 41 years

       1332 Edward Balliol, son of John Balliol, crowned
       King of Scots September, expelled December
       1333–6 Edward Balliol restored as King of Scots

THE HOUSE OF STEWART

1371–1390   ROBERT II (Stewart)
       Born 1316, son of Marjorie (daughter of Robert I)
       and Walter, High Steward of Scotland
       Married (1) Elizabeth, daughter of Sir Robert Mure
       of Rowallan (2) Euphemia, daughter of Hugh, earl
       of Ross
       Died aged 74, *reigned* 19 years
1390–1406   ROBERT III
       *Born c.*1337, son of Robert II and Elizabeth
       Married Annabella, daughter of Sir John
       Drummond of Stobhall
       Died aged *c.*69, *reigned* 16 years
1406–1437   JAMES I
       Born 1394, son of Robert III
       Married Joan Beaufort, daughter of John, earl of
       Somerset
       Assassinated aged 42, *reigned* 30 years
1437–1460   JAMES II
       Born 1430, son of James I
       Married Mary, daughter of Arnold, duke of
       Gueldres
       Killed accidentally aged 29, *reigned* 23 years
1460–1488   JAMES III
       Born 1452, son of James II
       Married Margaret, daughter of Christian I of
       Denmark
       Assassinated aged 36, *reigned* 27 years

1488–1513	JAMES IV
	Born 1473, son of James III
	Married Margaret Tudor, daughter of Henry VII of England
	Killed in battle aged 40, *reigned* 25 years
1513–1542	JAMES V
	Born 1512, son of James IV
	Married (1) Madeleine, daughter of Francis I of France (2) Mary of Lorraine, daughter of the Duc de Guise
	Died aged 30, *reigned* 29 years
1542–1567	MARY
	Born 1542, daughter of James V and Mary
	Married (1) the Dauphin, afterwards Francis II of France (2) Henry Stewart, Lord Darnley (3) James Hepburn, earl of Bothwell
	Abdicated 1567, prisoner in England from 1568, *executed* 1587, *reigned* 24 years
1567–1625	JAMES VI (and I of England)
	Born 1566, son of Mary, queen of Scots, and Henry, Lord Darnley
	Acceded 1567 to the Scottish throne, *reigned* 58 years
	Succeeded 1603 to the English throne, so joining the English and Scottish crowns in one person. The two kingdoms remained distinct until 1707 when the parliaments of the kingdoms became conjoined
	For British Kings and Queens since 1603, *see* pages 131–2

WELSH SOVEREIGNS AND PRINCES

Wales was ruled by sovereign princes from the earliest times until the death of Llywelyn in 1282. The first English Prince of Wales was the son of Edward I, who was born in Caernarvon town on 25 April 1284. According to a discredited legend, he was presented to the Welsh chieftains as their prince, in fulfilment of a promise that they should have a prince who 'could not speak a word of English' and should be native born. This son, who afterwards became Edward II, was created 'Prince of Wales and Earl of Chester' at the Lincoln Parliament on 7 February 1301.

The title Prince of Wales is borne after individual conferment and is not inherited at birth, though some Princes have been declared and styled Prince of Wales but never formally so created (*s.*). The title was conferred on Prince Charles by The Queen on 26 July 1958. He was invested at Caernarvon on 1 July 1969.

INDEPENDENT PRINCES AD 844 TO 1282

844–878	Rhodri the Great
878–916	Anarawd, son of Rhodri
916–950	Hywel Dda, the Good
950–979	Iago ab Idwal (or Ieuaf)
979–985	Hywel ab Ieuaf, the Bad
985–986	Cadwallon, his brother
986–999	Maredudd ab Owain ap Hywel Dda
999–1008	Cynan ap Hywel ab Ieuaf
1018–1023	Llywelyn ap Seisyll
1023–1039	Iago ab Idwal ap Meurig
1039–1063	Gruffydd ap Llywelyn ap Seisyll
1063–1075	Bleddyn ap Cynfyn
1075–1081	Trahaern ap Caradog
1081–1137	Gruffydd ap Cynan ab Iago
1137–1170	Owain Gwynedd
1170–1194	Dafydd ab Owain Gwynedd
1194–1240	Llywelyn Fawr, the Great
1240–1246	Dafydd ap Llywelyn
1246–1282	Llywelyn ap Gruffydd ap Llywelyn

ENGLISH PRINCES SINCE 1301

1301	Edward (Edward II)
1343	Edward the Black Prince, s. of Edward III
1376	Richard (Richard II), s. of the Black Prince
1399	Henry of Monmouth (Henry V)
1454	Edward of Westminster, son of Henry VI

1471	Edward of Westminster (Edward V)
1483	Edward, son of Richard III (d. 1484)
1489	Arthur Tudor, son of Henry VII
1504	Henry Tudor (Henry VIII)
1610	Henry Stuart, son of James I (d. 1612)
1616	Charles Stuart (Charles I)
c.1638 (s.)	Charles Stuart (Charles II)
1688 (s.)	James Francis Edward Stuart (The Old Pretender), son of James II (d. 1766)
1714	George Augustus (George II)
1729	Frederick Lewis, s. of George II (d. 1751)
1751	George William Frederick (George III)
1762	George Augustus Frederick (George IV)
1841	Albert Edward (Edward VII)
1901	George (George V)
1910	Edward (Edward VIII)
1958	Charles Philip Arthur George

PRINCESSES ROYAL

The style Princess Royal is conferred at the Sovereign's discretion on his or her eldest daughter. It is an honorary title, held for life, and cannot be inherited or passed on. It was first conferred on Princess Mary, daughter of Charles I, in approximately 1642.

c.1642	Princess Mary (1631–60), daughter of Charles I
1727	Princess Anne (1709–59), daughter of George II
1766	Princess Charlotte (1766–1828), daughter of George III
1840	Princess Victoria (1840–1901), daughter of Victoria
1905	Princess Louise (1867–1931), daughter of Edward VII
1932	Princess Mary (1897–1965), daughter of George V
1987	Princess Anne (b. 1950), daughter of Elizabeth II

Precedence

The Sovereign
The Prince Philip, Duke of
  Edinburgh
The Prince of Wales
The Sovereign's younger sons
The Sovereign's grandsons
The Sovereign's cousins
Archbishop of Canterbury
Lord High Chancellor
Archbishop of York
The Prime Minister
Lord President of the Council
Speaker of the House of Commons
Lord Privy Seal
Ambassadors and High
  Commissioners
Lord Great Chamberlain
Earl Marshal
Lord Steward of the Household
Lord Chamberlain of the Household
Master of the Horse
Dukes, according to their patent of
  creation:
  (1) of England
  (2) of Scotland
  (3) of Great Britain
  (4) of Ireland
  (5) those created since the Union
Ministers and Envoys
Eldest sons of Dukes of Blood Royal
Marquesses, according to their
  patent of creation:
  (1) of England
  (2) of Scotland
  (3) of Great Britain
  (4) of Ireland
  (5) those created since the Union
Dukes' eldest sons
Earls, according to their patent of
  creation:
  (1) of England
  (2) of Scotland
  (3) of Great Britain
  (4) of Ireland
  (5) those created since the Union
Younger sons of Dukes of Blood
  Royal
Marquesses' eldest sons
Dukes' younger sons
Viscounts, according to their patent
  of creation:
  (1) of England
  (2) of Scotland
  (3) of Great Britain
  (4) of Ireland
  (5) those created since the Union
Earls' eldest sons
Marquesses' younger sons
Bishops of London, Durham and
  Winchester

Other English Diocesan Bishops,
  according to seniority of
  consecration
Suffragan Bishops, according to
  seniority of consecration
Secretaries of State, if of the degree
  of a Baron
Barons, according to their patent of
  creation:
  (1) of England
  (2) of Scotland
  (3) of Great Britain
  (4) of Ireland
  (5) those created since the Union
Treasurer of the Household
Comptroller of the Household
Vice-Chamberlain of the Household
Secretaries of State under the degree
  of Baron
Viscounts' eldest sons
Earls' younger sons
Barons' eldest sons
Knights of the Garter
Privy Counsellors
Chancellor of the Exchequer
Chancellor of the Duchy of
  Lancaster
Lord Chief Justice of England
Master of the Rolls
President of the Family Division
Vice-Chancellor
Lords Justices of Appeal
Judges of the High Court
Viscounts' younger sons
Barons' younger sons
Sons of Life Peers
Baronets, according to date of patent
Knights of the Thistle
Knights Grand Cross of the Bath
Members of the Order of Merit
Knights Grand Commanders of the
  Star of India
Knights Grand Cross of St Michael
  and St George
Knights Grand Commanders of the
  Indian Empire
Knights Grand Cross of the Royal
  Victorian Order
Knights Grand Cross of the British
  Empire
Companions of Honour
Knights Commanders of the Bath
Knights Commanders of the Star of
  India
Knights Commanders of St Michael
  and St George
Knights Commanders of the Indian
  Empire
Knights Commanders of the Royal
  Victorian Order
Knights Commanders of the British
  Empire
Knights Bachelor
Vice-Chancellor of the County
  Palatine of Lancaster

Official Referees of the Supreme
  Court
Circuit judges and judges of the
  Mayor's and City of London
  Court
Companions of the Bath
Companions of the Star of India
Companions of St Michael and St
  George
Companions of the Indian Empire
Commanders of the Royal Victorian
  Order
Commanders of the British Empire
Companions of the Distinguished
  Service Order
Lieutenants of the Royal Victorian
  Order
Officers of the British Empire
Companions of the Imperial Service
  Order
Eldest sons of younger sons of Peers
Baronets' eldest sons
Eldest sons of Knights, in the same
  order as their fathers
Members of the Royal Victorian
  Order
Members of the British Empire
Younger sons of the younger sons of
  Peers
Baronets' younger sons
Younger sons of Knights, in the same
  order as their fathers
Naval, Military, Air, and other
  Esquires by office

WOMEN

Women take the same rank as their
husbands or as their brothers; but the
daughter of a peer marrying a commoner retains her title as Lady or
Honourable. Daughters of peers rank
next immediately after the wives of
their elder brothers, and before their
younger brothers' wives. Daughters
of peers marrying peers of lower
degree take the same order of precedence as that of their husbands; thus
the daughter of a Duke marrying a
Baron becomes of the rank of
Baroness only, while her sisters
married to commoners retain their
rank and take precedence of the
Baroness. Merely official rank on the
husband's part does not give any
similar precedence to the wife.

Peeresses in their own right take
the same precedence as peers of the
same rank, i.e. from their date of
creation.

Forms of address

It is only possible to cover here the forms of address for peers, baronets and knights, their wife and children, and Privy Counsellors. Greater detail should be sought in one of the publications devoted to the subject.

Both formal and social forms of address are given where usage differs; nowadays, the social form is generally preferred to the formal, which increasingly is used only for official documents and on very formal occasions.

F— represents forename
S— represents surname

Baron – *Envelope (formal)*, The Right Hon. Lord __; *(social)*, The Lord __. *Letter (formal)*, My Lord; *(social)*, Dear Lord __. *Spoken*, Lord __ .

Baron's Wife – *Envelope (formal)*, The Right Hon. Lady __; *(social)*, The Lady __. *Letter (formal)*, My Lady; *(social)*, Dear Lady __. *Spoken*, Lady __.

Baron's Children – *Envelope*, The Hon. F— S—. *Letter*, Dear Mr/Miss/Mrs S—. *Spoken*, Mr/Miss/Mrs S—.

Baroness in own right – *Envelope*, may be addressed in same way as a Baron's wife or, if she prefers *(formal)*, The Right Hon. the Baroness __; *(social)*, The Baroness __. Otherwise as for a Baron's wife.

Baronet – *Envelope*, Sir F— S—, Bt. *Letter (formal)*, Dear Sir; *(social)*, Dear Sir F—. *Spoken*, Sir F—.

Baronet's Wife – *Envelope*, Lady S—. *Letter (formal)*, Dear Madam; *(social)*, Dear Lady S—. *Spoken*, Lady S—.

Countess in own right – As for an Earl's wife.

Courtesy Titles – The heir apparent to a Duke, Marquess or Earl uses the highest of his father's other titles as a courtesy title. (For list, *see* pages 165–6.) The holder of a courtesy title is not styled The Most Hon. or The Right Hon., and in correspondence 'The' is omitted before the title. The heir apparent to a Scottish title may use the title 'Master' (*see* below).

Dame – *Envelope*, Dame F— S—, followed by appropriate post-nominal letters. *Letter (formal)*, Dear Madam; *(social)*, Dear Dame F—. *Spoken*, Dame F—.

Duke – *Envelope (formal)*, His Grace the Duke of __; *(social)*, The Duke of __. *Letter (formal)*, My Lord Duke; *(social)*, Dear Duke. *Spoken (formal)*, Your Grace; *(social)*, Duke.

Duke's Wife – *Envelope (formal)*, Her Grace the Duchess of __; *(social)*, The Duchess of __. *Letter (formal)*, Dear Madam; *(social)*, Dear Duchess. *Spoken*, Duchess.

Duke's Eldest Son – *see* Courtesy titles.

Duke's Younger Sons – *Envelope*, Lord F— S—. *Letter (formal)*, My Lord; *(social)*, Dear Lord F—. *Spoken (formal)*, My Lord; *(social)*, Lord F—.

Duke's Daughter – *Envelope*, Lady F— S—. *Letter (formal)*, Dear Madam; *(social)*, Dear Lady F—. *Spoken*, Lady F— .

Earl – *Envelope (formal)*, The Right Hon. the Earl (of) __; *(social)*, The Earl (of) __. *Letter (formal)*, My Lord; *(social)*, Dear Lord __. *Spoken (formal)*, My Lord; *(social)*, Lord __.

Earl's Wife – *Envelope (formal)*, The Right Hon. the Countess (of) __; *(social)*, The Countess (of) __. *Letter (formal)*, Madam; *(social)*, Lady __. *Spoken (formal)*, Madam; *(social)*, Lady __.

Earl's Children – *Eldest son, see* Courtesy titles. *Younger sons*, The Hon. F— S— (for forms of address, *see* Baron's children). *Daughters*, Lady F— S— (for forms of address, *see* Duke's daughter).

Knight (Bachelor) – *Envelope*, Sir F— S—. *Letter (formal)*, Dear Sir; *(social)*, Dear Sir F—. *Spoken*, Sir F—.

Knight (Orders of Chivalry) – *Envelope*, Sir F— S—, followed by appropriate post-nominal letters. Otherwise as for Knight Bachelor.

Knight's Wife – As for Baronet's wife.

Life Peer – As for Baron/Baroness in own right.

Life Peer's Wife – As for Baron's wife.

Life Peer's Children – As for Baron's children.

Marquess – *Envelope (formal)*, The Most Hon. the Marquess of __; *(social)*, The Marquess of __. *Letter (formal)*, My Lord; *(social)*, Dear Lord __. *Spoken (formal)*, My Lord; *(social)*, Lord __.

Marquess's Wife – *Envelope (formal)*, The Most Hon. the Marchioness of __; *(social)*, The Marchioness of __. *Letter (formal)*, Madam; *(social)*, Dear Lady __. *Spoken*, Lady __.

Marquess's Children – *Eldest son, see* Courtesy titles. *Younger sons*, Lord F— S— (for forms of address, *see* Duke's younger sons). *Daughters*, Lady F— S— (for forms of address, *see* Duke's daughter).

Master – The title is used by the heir apparent to a Scottish peerage, though usually the heir apparent to a Duke, Marquess or Earl uses his courtesy title rather than 'Master'. *Envelope*, The Master of __. *Letter (formal)*, Dear Sir; *(social)*, Dear Master of __. *Spoken (formal)*, Master, or Sir; *(social)*, Master, or Mr S—.

Master's Wife – Addressed as for the wife of the appropriate peerage style, otherwise as Mrs S—.

Privy Counsellor – *Envelope*, The Right (or Rt.) Hon. F— S—. *Letter*, Dear Mr/Miss/Mrs S—. *Spoken*, Mr/Miss/Mrs S—. It is incorrect to use the letters PC after the name in conjunction with the prefix The Right Hon., unless the Privy Counsellor is a peer below the rank of Marquess and so is styled The Right Hon. because of his rank. In this case only, the post-nominal letters may be used in conjunction with the prefix The Right Hon.

Viscount – *Envelope (formal)*, The Right Hon. the Viscount __; *(social)*, The Viscount __. *Letter (formal)*, My Lord; *(social)*, Dear Lord __. *Spoken*, Lord __.

Viscount's Wife – *Envelope (formal)*, The Right Hon. the Viscountess __; *(social)*, The Viscountess __. *Letter (formal)*, Madam; *(social)*, Dear Lady __. *Spoken*, Lady __.

Viscount's Children – As for Baron's children.

The Peerage

and Members of the House of Lords

The rules which govern the creation and succession of peerages are extremely complicated. There are, technically, five separate peerages, the Peerage of England, of Scotland, of Ireland, of Great Britain, and of the United Kingdom. The Peerage of Great Britain dates from 1707 when an Act of Union combined the two kingdoms of England and Scotland and separate peerages were discontinued. The Peerage of the United Kingdom dates from 1801 when Great Britain and Ireland were combined under an Act of Union. Some Scottish peers have received additional peerages of Great Britain or of the United Kingdom since 1707, and some Irish peers additional peerages of the United Kingdom since 1801.

The Peerage of Ireland was not entirely discontinued from 1801 but holders of Irish peerages, whether predating or created subsequent to the Union of 1801, are not entitled to sit in the House of Lords if they have no additional English, Scottish, Great Britain or United Kingdom peerage. However, they are eligible for election to the House of Commons and to vote in parliamentary elections, which other peers are not. An Irish peer holding a peerage of a lower grade which enables him to sit in the House of Lords is introduced there by the title which enables him to sit, though for all other purposes he is known by his higher title.

In the Peerage of Scotland there is no rank of Baron; the equivalent rank is Lord of Parliament, abbreviated to 'Lord' (the female equivalent is 'Lady'). All peers of England, Scotland, Great Britain or the United Kingdom who are 21 years or over, and of British, Irish or Commonwealth nationality are entitled to sit in the House of Lords.

No fees for dignities have been payable since 1937. The House of Lords surrendered the ancient right of peers to be tried for treason or felony by their peers in 1948.

Hereditary Women Peers

Most hereditary peerages pass on death to the nearest male heir, but there are exceptions, and several are held by women (*see* pages 144 and 156).

A woman peer in her own right retains her title after marriage, and if her husband's rank is the superior she is designated by the two titles jointly, the inferior one second. Her hereditary claim still holds good in spite of any marriage whether higher or lower. No rank held by a woman can confer any title or even precedence upon her husband but the rank of a hereditary woman peer in her own right is inherited by her eldest son (or in some cases daughter).

Since the Peerage Act 1963, hereditary women peers in their own right have been entitled to sit in the House of Lords, subject to the same qualifications as men.

Life Peers

Since 1876 non-hereditary or life peerages have been conferred on certain eminent judges to enable the judicial functions of the House of Lords to be carried out. These Lords are known as Lords of Appeal or law lords and, to date, such appointments have all been male.

Since 1958 life peerages have been conferred upon distinguished men and women from all walks of life, giving them seats in the House of Lords in the degree of Baron or Baroness. They are addressed in the same way as heredi-

tary Lords and Barons, and their children have similar courtesy titles.

Peerages Extinct Since the Last Edition

Marquessates: Ormonde (*cr.*1825)
Viscountcies: Tonypandy (*cr.*1983)
Baronies: Morrison (*cr.*1945)
Life Peerages: Boyd-Carpenter (*cr.*1972);Cudlipp (*cr.*1974); Dainton (*cr.*1986); Denington (*cr.*1978); Donaldson of Kingsbridge (*cr.*1967); Granville of Eye (*cr.* 1967); Howell (*cr.*1992); Kings Norton (*cr.*1965); Kissin (*cr.*1974); Lestor of Eccles (*cr.*1997); Llewelyn-Davies of Hastoe (*cr.*1967); McGregor of Durris (*cr.*1978); Mellish (*cr.*1985); Rayner (*cr.*1983); Smith (*cr.*1978); Wallace of Campsie (*cr.*1974); Wilson of Langside (*cr.*1969); Wyatt of Weeford (*cr.*1987)

Disclaimer of Peerages

The Peerage Act 1963 enables peers to disclaim their peerages for life. Peers alive in 1963 could disclaim within twelve months after the passing of the Act (31 July 1963); a person subsequently succeeding to a peerage may disclaim within 12 months (one month if an MP) after the date of succession, or of reaching 21, if later. The disclaimer is irrevocable but does not affect the descent of the peerage after the disclaimant's death, and children of a disclaimed peer may, if they wish, retain their precedence and any courtesy titles and styles borne as children of a peer. The disclaimer permits the disclaimant to sit in the House of Commons if elected as an MP.

The following peerages are currently disclaimed:

Earldoms: Durham (1970); Selkirk (1994)
Viscountcies: Camrose (1995); Hailsham (1963); Stansgate (1963)
Baronies: Altrincham (1963); Merthyr (1977); Reith (1972); Sanderson of Ayot (1971); Silkin (1972)

Peers Who Are Minors (i.e. under 21 years of age)

Earls: Craven (*b.*1989)
Barons: Elphinstone (*b.*1980)

Contractions and Symbols

s.   Scottish title
I.   Irish title
*   The peer holds also an Imperial title, specified after the name by Engl., Brit. or UK
°   there is no 'of' in the title
b.   born
s.   succeeded
m.   married
w.   widower or widow
M. minor
†   heir not ascertained at time of going to press

Hereditary Peers

ROYAL DUKES

Style, His Royal Highness The Duke of ___
Style of address (formal) May it please your Royal Highness; *(informal)* Sir

Created	Title, order of succession, name, etc.	Heir
1947	*Edinburgh* (1st), The Prince Philip, Duke of Edinburgh, *(see* page 117)	The Prince of Wales
1337	*Cornwall,* Charles, Prince of Wales, *s.* 1952 *(see* page 117)	‡
1398	*Rothesay,* Charles, Prince of Wales, *s.* 1952 *(see* page 117)	‡
1986	*York* (1st), The Prince Andrew, Duke of York *(see* page 117)	None
1928	*Gloucester* (2nd), Prince Richard, Duke of Gloucester, *s.* 1974 *(see* page 118)	Earl of Ulster *(see* page 118)
1934	*Kent* (2nd), Prince Edward, Duke of Kent, *s.* 1942 *(see* page 118)	Earl of St Andrews *(see* page 118)

‡ The title is not hereditary but is held by the Sovereign's eldest son from the moment of his birth or the Sovereign's accession

DUKES

Coronet, Eight strawberry leaves
Style, His Grace the Duke of ___
Wife's style, Her Grace the Duchess of ___
Eldest son's style, Takes his father's second title as a courtesy title
Younger sons' style, 'Lord' before forename and family name
Daughters' style, 'Lady' before forename and family name
For forms of address, *see* page 135

Created	Title, order of succession, name, etc.	Heir
1868 I.*	*Abercorn* (5th), James Hamilton (6th *Brit. Marq., Abercorn,* 1790; 14th *Scott. Earl, Abercorn,* 1606), *b.* 1934, *s.* 1979, *m.*	Marquess of Hamilton, *b.* 1969
1701 s.*	*Argyll* (12th), Ian Campbell (5th *UK Duke, Argyll,* 1892), *b.* 1937, *s.* 1973, *m.*	Marquess of Lorne, *b.* 1968
1703 s.	*Atholl* (11th), John Murray, *b.* 1929, *s.* 1996, *m.*	Marquess of Tullibardine, *b.* 1960
1682	*Beaufort* (11th), David Robert Somerset, *b.* 1928, *s.* 1984, *w.*	Marquess of Worcester, *b.* 1952
1694	*Bedford* (13th), John Robert Russell, *b.* 1917, *s.* 1953, *m.*	Marquess of Tavistock, *b.* 1940
1663 s.*	*Buccleuch* (9th) and *Queensberry* (11th) (s. 1684), Walter Francis John Montagu Douglas Scott, KT, VRD (8th *Engl. Earl, Doncaster,* 1662), *b.* 1923, *s.* 1973, *m.*	Earl of Dalkeith, *b.* 1954
1694	*Devonshire* (11th), Andrew Robert Buxton Cavendish, KG, MC, PC, *b.* 1920, *s.* 1950, *m.*	Marquess of Hartington CBE, *b.* 1944
1900	*Fife* (3rd), James George Alexander Bannerman Carnegie (12th *Scott. Earl, Southesk,* 1633, *s.* 1992), *b.* 1929, *s.* 1959. *(see* page 128)	Earl of Southesk, *b.* 1961
1675	*Grafton* (11th), Hugh Denis Charles FitzRoy, KG, *b.* 1919, *s.* 1970, *m.*	Earl of Euston, *b.* 1947
1643 s.*	*Hamilton* (15th) and *Brandon* (12th) *(Brit.* 1711), Angus Alan Douglas Douglas-Hamilton, *b.* 1938, *s.* 1973. *Premier Peer of Scotland*	Marquess of Douglas and Clydesdale, *b.* 1978
1766 I.*	*Leinster* (8th), Gerald FitzGerald (8th *Brit. Visct., Leinster,* 1747), *b.* 1914, *s.* 1976, *m. Premier Duke and Marquess of Ireland*	Marquess of Kildare, *b.* 1948
1719	*Manchester* (12th), Angus Charles Drogo Montagu, *b.* 1938, *s.* 1985, *m.*	Viscount Mandeville, *b.* 1962
1702	*Marlborough* (11th), John George Vanderbilt Henry Spencer-Churchill, *b.* 1926, *s.* 1972, *m.*	Marquess of Blandford, *b.* 1955
1707 s.*	*Montrose* (8th), James Graham (6th *Brit. Earl, Graham,* 1722), *b.* 1935, *s.* 1992, *m.*	Marquess of Graham, *b.* 1973
1483	*Norfolk* (17th), Miles Francis Stapleton Fitzalan-Howard, KG, GCVO, CB, CBE, MC (12th *Engl. Baron, Beaumont,* 1309, *s.* 1971; 4th *UK Baron Howard of Glossop,* 1869, *s.* 1972), *b.* 1915, *s.* 1975, *m. Premier Duke and Earl Marshal*	Earl of Arundel and Surrey, *b.* 1956
1766	*Northumberland* (12th), Ralph George Algernon Percy, *b.* 1956, *s.* 1995, *m.*	Earl Percy, *b.* 1984
1675	*Richmond* (10th) and *Gordon* (5th) (*UK* 1876), Charles Henry Gordon Lennox (10th *Scott. Duke, Lennox,* 1675), *b.* 1929, *s.* 1989, *m.*	Earl of March and Kinrara, *b.* 1955
1707 s.*	*Roxburghe* (10th), Guy David Innes-Ker (5th *UK Earl, Innes,* 1837), *b.* 1954, *s.* 1974, *m. Premier Baronet of Scotland*	Marquess of Bowmont and Cessford, *b.* 1981

Created	Title, order of succession, name, etc.	Heir
1703	*Rutland* (10th), Charles John Robert Manners, CBE, *b.* 1919, *s.* 1940, *m.*	Marquess of Granby, *b.* 1959
1684	*St Albans* (14th), Murray de Vere Beauclerk, *b.* 1939, *s.* 1988, *m.*	Earl of Burford, *b.* 1965
1547	*Somerset* (19th), John Michael Edward Seymour, *b.* 1952, *s.* 1984, *m.*	Lord Seymour, *b.* 1982
1833	*Sutherland* (6th), John Sutherland Egerton, TD (5th *UK Earl, Ellesmere,* 1846, *s.* 1944), *b.* 1915, *s.* 1963, *m.*	Francis R. E., *b.* 1940
1814	*Wellington* (8th), Arthur Valerian Wellesley, KG, LVO, OBE, MC (9th *Irish Earl, Mornington,* 1760), *b.* 1915, *s.* 1972, *m.*	Marquess of Douro, *b.* 1945
1874	*Westminster* (6th), Gerald Cavendish Grosvenor, OBE, *b.* 1951, *s.* 1979, *m.*	Earl Grosvenor, *b.* 1991

MARQUESSES

Coronet, Four strawberry leaves alternating with four silver balls
Style, The Most Hon. the Marquess (of) ___ . In Scotland the spelling 'Marquis' is preferred for pre-Union creations
Wife's style, The Most Hon. the Marchioness (of) ___
Eldest son's style, Takes his father's second title as a courtesy title
Younger sons' style, 'Lord' before forename and family name
Daughters' style, 'Lady' before forename and family name
For forms of address, *see* page 135

Created	Title, order of succession, name, etc.	Heir
1916	*Aberdeen and Temair* (6th), Alastair Ninian John Gordon (12th *Scott. Earl, Aberdeen,* 1682), *b.* 1920, *s.* 1984, *m.*	Earl of Haddo, *b.* 1955
1876	*Abergavenny* (5th), John Henry Guy Nevill, KG, OBE, *b.* 1914, *s.* 1954, *m.*	Christopher G. C. N., *b.* 1955
1821	*Ailesbury* (8th), Michael Sidney Cedric Brudenell-Bruce, *b.* 1926, *s.* 1974.	Earl of Cardigan, *b.* 1952
1831	*Ailsa* (8th), Archibald Angus Charles Kennedy (20th *Scott. Earl, Cassillis,* 1509), *b.* 1956, *s.* 1994.	Lord David Kennedy, *b.* 1958
1815	*Anglesey* (7th), George Charles Henry Victor Paget, *b.* 1922, *s.* 1947, *m.*	Earl of Uxbridge, *b.* 1950
1789	*Bath* (7th), Alexander George Thynn, *b.* 1932, *s.* 1992, *m.*	Viscount Weymouth, *b.* 1974
1826	*Bristol* (7th), (Frederick William) John Augustus Hervey, *b.* 1954, *s.* 1985.	Lord Frederick W. A. H., *b.* 1979
1796	*Bute* (7th), John Colum Crichton-Stuart (12th *Scott. Earl, Dumfries,* 1633), *b.* 1958, *s.* 1993, *m.*	Earl of Dumfries, *b.* 1989
1812	°*Camden* (6th), David George Edward Henry Pratt, *b.* 1930, *s.* 1983.	Earl of Brecknock, *b.* 1965
1815	*Cholmondeley* (7th), David George Philip Cholmondeley (11th *Irish Visct., Cholmondeley,* 1661), *b.* 1960, *s.* 1990. *Lord Great Chamberlain*	Charles G. C., *b.* 1959
1816 I.*	°*Conyngham* (7th), Frederick William Henry Francis Conyngham (7th *UK Baron, Minster,* 1821), *b.* 1924, *s.* 1974, *m.*	Earl of Mount Charles, *b.* 1951
1791 I.*	*Donegall* (7th), Dermot Richard Claud Chichester, LVO (7th *Brit. Baron, Fisherwick,* 1790; 6th *Brit. Baron, Templemore,* 1831, *s.* 1953), *b.* 1916, *s.* 1975, *m.*	Earl of Belfast, *b.* 1952
1789 I.*	*Downshire* (8th), (Arthur) Robin Ian Hill (8th *Brit. Earl, Hillsborough,* 1772), *b.* 1929, *s.* 1989, *m.*	Earl of Hillsborough, *b.* 1959
1801 I.*	*Ely* (8th), Charles John Tottenham (8th *UK Baron, Loftus,* 1801), *b.* 1913, *s.* 1969, *m.*	Viscount Loftus, *b.* 1943
1801	*Exeter* (8th), (William) Michael Anthony Cecil, *b.* 1935, *s.* 1988, *m.*	Lord Burghley, *b.* 1970
1800 I.*	*Headfort* (6th), Thomas Geoffrey Charles Michael Taylour (4th *UK Baron, Kenlis,* 1831), *b.* 1932, *s.* 1960, *m.*	Earl of Bective, *b.* 1959
1793	*Hertford* (9th), Henry Jocelyn Seymour (10th *Irish Baron, Conway,* 1712), *b.* 1958, *s.* 1997, *m.*	Earl of Yarmouth, *b.* 1993
1599 S.*	*Huntly* (13th), Granville Charles Gomer Gordon (5th *UK Baron, Meldrum,* 1815), *b.* 1944, *s.* 1987, *m. Premier Marquess of Scotland*	Earl of Aboyne, *b.* 1973
1784	*Lansdowne* (8th), George John Charles Mercer Nairne Petty-Fitzmaurice, PC (8th *Irish Earl, Kerry,* 1723), *b.* 1912, *s.* 1944, *m.*	Earl of Shelburne, *b.* 1941
1902	*Linlithgow* (4th), Adrian John Charles Hope (10th *Scott. Earl, Hopetoun,* 1703), *b.* 1946, *s.* 1987, *m.*	Earl of Hopetoun, *b.* 1969
1816 I.*	*Londonderry* (9th), Alexander Charles Robert Vane-Tempest-Stewart (6th *UK Earl, Vane,* 1823), *b.* 1937, *s.* 1955, *m.*	Viscount Castlereagh, *b.* 1972
1701 S.*	*Lothian* (12th), Peter Francis Walter Kerr, KCVO (6th *UK Baron, Kerr,* 1821), *b.* 1922, *s.* 1940, *m.*	Earl of Ancram PC, MP, *b.* 1945
1917	*Milford Haven* (4th), George Ivar Louis Mountbatten, *b.* 1961, *s.* 1970, *m.*	Earl of Medina, *b.* 1991
1838	*Normanby* (5th), Constantine Edmund Walter Phipps (9th *Irish Baron, Mulgrave,* 1767), *b.* 1954, *s.* 1994, *m.*	Lord Justin C. P., *b.* 1958

Created	Title, order of succession, name, etc.	Heir
1812	*Northampton* (7th), Spencer Douglas David Compton, *b.* 1946, *s.* 1978, *m.*	Earl Compton, *b.* 1973
1682 s.	*Queensberry* (12th), David Harrington Angus Douglas, *b.* 1929, *s.* 1954.	Viscount Drumlanrig, *b.* 1967
1926	*Reading* (4th), Simon Charles Henry Rufus Isaacs, *b.* 1942, *s.* 1980, *m.*	Viscount Erleigh, *b.* 1986
1789	*Salisbury* (6th), Robert Edward Peter Cecil, *b.* 1916, *s.* 1972, *m.*	Viscount Cranborne PC, *b.* 1946 (see also Baron Cecil, page 148)
1800 I.*	*Sligo* (11th), Jeremy Ulick Browne (11th *UK Baron, Monteagle*, 1806), *b.* 1939, *s.* 1991, *m.*	Sebastian U. B., *b.* 1964
1787	°*Townshend* (7th), George John Patrick Dominic Townshend, *b.* 1916, *s.* 1921, *w.*	Viscount Raynham, *b.* 1945
1694 s.*	°*Tweeddale* (13th), Edward Douglas John Hay (4th *UK Baron Tweeddale*, 1881), *b.* 1947, *s.* 1979.	Lord Charles D. M. H., *b.* 1947
1789 I.*	*Waterford* (8th), John Hubert de la Poer Beresford (8th *Brit. Baron Tyrone*, 1786), *b.* 1933, *s.* 1934, *m.*	Earl of Tyrone, *b.* 1958
1551	*Winchester* (18th), Nigel George Paulet, *b.* 1941, *s.* 1968, *m.* Premier Marquess of England	Earl of Wiltshire, *b.* 1969
1892	*Zetland* (4th), Lawrence Mark Dundas (6th *UK Earl, Zetland*, 1838; 7th *Brit. Baron Dundas*, 1794), *b.* 1937, *s.* 1989, *m.*	Earl of Ronaldshay, *b.* 1965

EARLS

Coronet, Eight silver balls on stalks alternating with eight gold strawberry leaves
Style, The Right Hon. the Earl (of) —
Wife's style, The Right Hon. the Countess (of) —
Eldest son's style, Takes his father's second title as a courtesy title
Younger sons' style, 'The Hon.' before forename and family name
Daughters' style, 'Lady' before forename and family name
For forms of address, *see* page 135

Created	Title, order of succession, name, etc.	Heir
1639 s.	*Airlie* (13th), David George Coke Patrick Ogilvy, KT, GCVO, PC, Royal Victorian Chain, *b.* 1926, *s.* 1968, *m.*	Lord Ogilvy, *b.* 1958
1696	*Albemarle* (10th), Rufus Arnold Alexis Keppel, *b.* 1965, *s.* 1979.	Crispian W. J. K., *b.* 1948
1952	°*Alexander of Tunis* (2nd), Shane William Desmond Alexander, *b.* 1935, *s.* 1969, *m.*	Hon. Brian J. A., *b.* 1939
1662 s.	*Annandale and Hartfell* (11th), Patrick Andrew Wentworth Hope Johnstone, *b.* 1941, claim established 1985, *m.*	Lord Johnstone, *b.* 1971
1789 I.	°*Annesley* (10th), Patrick Annesley, *b.* 1924, *s.* 1979, *m.*	Hon. Philip H. A., *b.* 1927
1785 I.	*Antrim* (9th), Alexander Randal Mark McDonnell, *b.* 1935, *s.* 1977, *m.* Viscount Dunluce	Hon. Randal A. St J. M., *b.* 1967
1762 I.*	*Arran* (9th), Arthur Desmond Colquhoun Gore (5th *UK Baron Sudley*, 1884), *b.* 1938, *s.* 1983, *m.*	Paul A. G. CMG, CVO, *b.* 1921
1955	°*Attlee* (3rd), John Richard Attlee, *b.* 1956, *s.* 1991, *m.*	None
1714	*Aylesford* (11th), Charles Ian Finch-Knightley, *b.* 1918, *s.* 1958, *w.*	Lord Guernsey, *b.* 1947
1937	°*Baldwin of Bewdley* (4th), Edward Alfred Alexander Baldwin, *b.* 1938, *s.* 1976, *m.*	Viscount Corvedale, *b.* 1973
1922	*Balfour* (4th), Gerald Arthur James Balfour, *b.* 1925, *s.* 1968, *m.*	Eustace A. G. B., *b.* 1921
1772	°*Bathurst* (8th), Henry Allen John Bathurst, *b.* 1927, *s.* 1943, *m.*	Lord Apsley, *b.* 1961
1919	°*Beatty* (3rd), David Beatty, *b.* 1946, *s.* 1972, *m.*	Viscount Borodale, *b.* 1973
1797 I.	*Belmore* (8th), John Armar Lowry-Corry, *b.* 1951, *s.* 1960, *m.*	Viscount Corry, *b.* 1985
1739 I.*	*Bessborough* (11th), Arthur Mountifort Longfield Ponsonby (8th *UK Baron Duncannon*, 1834), *b.* 1912, *s.* 1993, *m.*	Hon. Myles F. L. P., *b.* 1941
1815	*Bradford* (7th), Richard Thomas Orlando Bridgeman, *b.* 1947, *s.* 1981, *m.*	Viscount Newport, *b.* 1980
1469 s.*	*Buchan* (17th), Malcolm Harry Erskine (8th *UK Baron Erskine*, 1806), *b.* 1930, *s.* 1984, *m.*	Lord Cardross, *b.* 1960
1746	*Buckinghamshire* (10th), (George) Miles Hobart-Hampden, *b.* 1944, *s.* 1983, *m.*	Sir John Hobart, Bt., *b.* 1945
1800	°*Cadogan* (8th), Charles Gerald John Cadogan, *b.* 1937, *s.* 1997, *m.*	Viscount Chelsea, *b.* 1966
1878	°*Cairns* (6th), Simon Dallas Cairns, CBE, *b.* 1939, *s.* 1989, *m.*	Viscount Garmoyle, *b.* 1965
1455 s.	*Caithness* (20th), Malcolm Ian Sinclair, PC, *b.* 1948, *s.* 1965, *w.*	Lord Berriedale, *b.* 1981
1800 I.	*Caledon* (7th), Nicholas James Alexander, *b.* 1955, *s.* 1980, *m.*	Viscount Alexander, *b.* 1990
1661	*Carlisle* (13th), George William Beaumont Howard (13th *Scott. Baron Ruthven of Freeland*, 1651), *b.* 1949, *s.* 1994.	Hon. Philip C. W. H., *b.* 1963

Created	Title, order of succession, name, etc.	Heir
1793	*Carnarvon* (7th), Henry George Reginald Molyneux Herbert, KCVO, KBE, *b.* 1924, *s.* 1987, *m.*	Lord Porchester, *b.* 1956
1748 I.*	*Carrick* (10th), David James Theobald Somerset Butler (4th *UK Baron Butler*, 1912), *b.* 1953, *s.* 1992, *m.*	Viscount Ikerrin, *b.* 1975
1800 I.	°*Castle Stewart* (8th), Arthur Patrick Avondale Stuart, *b.* 1928, *s.* 1961, *m.*	Viscount Stuart, *b.* 1953
1814	°*Cathcart* (6th), Alan Cathcart, CB, DSO, MC (15th *Scott. Baron Cathcart*, 1447), *b.* 1919, *s.* 1927, *m.*	Lord Greenock, *b.* 1952
1647 I.	*Cavan.* The 12th Earl died in 1988. Heir had not established his claim to the title at the time of going to press	Roger C. *Lambart, b.* 1944
1827	°*Cawdor* (7th), Colin Robert Vaughan Campbell, *b.* 1962, *s.* 1993, *m.*	Hon. Frederick W. *C., b.* 1965
1801	*Chichester* (9th), John Nicholas Pelham, *b.* 1944, *s.* 1944, *m.*	Richard A. H. *P., b.* 1952
1803 I.*	*Clancarty* (9th), Nicholas Power Richard Le Poer Trench (8th *UK Visct. Clancarty*, 1823), *b.* 1952, *s.* 1995.	None
1776 I.*	*Clanwilliam* (7th), John Herbert Meade (5th *UK Baron Clanwilliam*, 1828), *b.* 1919, *s.* 1989, *m.*	Lord Gillford, *b.* 1960
1776	*Clarendon* (7th), George Frederick Laurence Hyde Villiers, *b.* 1933, *s.* 1955, *m.*	Lord Hyde, *b.* 1976
1620 I.*	*Cork* (14th) and *Orrery* (14th) (I. 1660), John William Boyle, DSC (10th *Brit. Baron Boyle of Marston*, 1711), *b.* 1916, *s.* 1995, *m.*	Hon. John R. *B., b.* 1945
1850	*Cottenham* (8th), Kenelm Charles Everard Digby Pepys, *b.* 1948, *s.* 1968, *m.*	Viscount Crowhurst, *b.* 1983
1762 I.*	*Courtown* (9th), James Patrick Montagu Burgoyne Winthrop Stopford (8th *Brit. Baron Saltersford*, 1796), *b.* 1954, *s.* 1975, *m.*	Viscount Stopford, *b.* 1988
1697	*Coventry* (11th), George William Coventry, *b.* 1934, *s.* 1940, *m.*	Hon. Francis H. *C., b.* 1912
1857	°*Cowley* (7th), Garret Graham Wellesley, *b.* 1934, *s.* 1975, *m.*	Viscount Dangan, *b.* 1965
1892	*Cranbrook* (5th), Gathorne Gathorne-Hardy, *b.* 1933, *s.* 1978, *m.*	Lord Medway, *b.* 1968
1801	*Craven* (9th), Benjamin Robert Joseph Craven, *b.* 1989, *s.* 1990, *M.*	Rupert J. E. *C., b.* 1926
1398 S.*	*Crawford* (29th) and *Balcarres* (12th) (s. 1651), Robert Alexander Lindsay, KT, PC (5th *UK Baron, Wigan*, 1826; *Baron Balniel* (life peerage), 1974), *b.* 1927, *s.* 1975, *m. Premier Earl on Union Roll*	Lord Balniel, *b.* 1958
1861	*Cromartie* (5th), John Ruaridh Blunt Grant Mackenzie, *b.* 1948, *s.* 1989, *m.*	Viscount Tarbat, *b.* 1987
1901	*Cromer* (4th), Evelyn Rowland Esmond Baring, *b.* 1946, *s.* 1991, *m.*	Viscount Errington, *b.* 1994
1633 S.*	*Dalhousie* (16th), Simon Ramsay, KT, GCVO, GBE, MC (4th *UK Baron Ramsay*, 1875), *b.* 1914, *s.* 1950, *w.*	Lord Ramsay, *b.* 1948
1725 I.	*Darnley* (11th), Adam Ivo Stuart Bligh (20th *Engl. Baron Clifton of Leighton Bromswold*, 1608), *b.* 1941, *s.* 1980, *m.*	Lord Clifton, *b.* 1968
1711	*Dartmouth* (10th), William Legge, *b.* 1949, *s.* 1997.	Hon. Rupert *L., b.* 1951
1761	°*De La Warr* (11th), William Herbrand Sackville, *b.* 1948, *s.* 1988, *m.*	Lord Buckhurst, *b.* 1979
1622	*Denbigh* (12th) and *Desmond* (11th) (I. 1622), Alexander Stephen Rudolph Feilding, *b.* 1970, *s.* 1995, *m.*	William D. *F., b.* 1939
1485	*Derby* (19th), Edward Richard William Stanley, *b.* 1962, *s.* 1994, *m.*	Hon. Peter H. C. *S., b.* 1964
1553	*Devon* (17th), Charles Christopher Courtenay, *b.* 1916, *s.* 1935, *m.*	Lord Courtenay, *b.* 1942
1800 I.*	*Donoughmore* (8th), Richard Michael John Hely-Hutchinson (8th *UK Visct. Hutchinson*, 1821), *b.* 1927, *s.* 1981, *m.*	Viscount Suirdale, *b.* 1952
1661 I.*	*Drogheda* (12th), Henry Dermot Ponsonby Moore (3rd *UK Baron Moore*, 1954), *b.* 1937, *s.* 1989, *m.*	Viscount Moore, *b.* 1983
1837	*Ducie* (7th), David Leslie Moreton, *b.* 1951, *s.* 1991, *m.*	Lord Moreton, *b.* 1981
1860	*Dudley* (4th), William Humble David Ward, *b.* 1920, *s.* 1969, *m.*	Viscount Ednam, *b.* 1947
1660 S.*	*Dundee* (12th), Alexander Henry Scrymgeour (2nd *UK Baron Glassary*, 1954), *b.* 1949, *s.* 1983, *m.*	Lord Scrymgeour, *b.* 1982
1669 S.	*Dundonald* (15th), Iain Alexander Douglas Blair Cochrane, *b.* 1961, *s.* 1986, *m.*	Lord Cochrane, *b.* 1991
1686 S.	*Dunmore* (12th), Malcolm Kenneth Murray, *b.* 1946, *s.* 1995, *m.*	Hon. Geoffrey C. *M., b.* 1949
1822 I.	*Dunraven and Mount-Earl* (7th), Thady Windham Thomas Wyndham-Quin, *b.* 1939, *s.* 1965, *m.*	None
1833	*Durham.* Disclaimed for life 1970. (*Antony Claud Frederick Lambton, b.*1922, *s.*1970, *m.*)	Hon. Edward R. *L.* (Baron Durham), *b.* 1961
1837	*Effingham* (7th), David Mowbray Algernon Howard (17th *Engl. Baron Howard of Effingham*, 1554), *b.* 1939, *s.* 1996, *m.*	Lord Howard of Effingham, *b.* 1971
1507 S.*	*Eglinton* (18th) and *Winton* (9th) (s. 1600), Archibald George Montgomerie (6th *UK Earl Winton*, 1859), *b.* 1939, *s.* 1966, *m.*	Lord Montgomerie, *b.* 1966
1733 I.*	*Egmont* (11th), Frederick George Moore Perceval (9th *Brit. Baron Lovel and Holland*, 1762), *b.* 1914, *s.* 1932, *m.*	Viscount Perceval, *b.* 1934
1821	*Eldon* (5th), John Joseph Nicholas Scott, *b.* 1937, *s.* 1976, *m.*	Viscount Encombe, *b.* 1962
1633 S.*	*Elgin* (11th) and *Kincardine* (15th) (s. 1647), Andrew Douglas Alexander Thomas Bruce, KT (4th *UK Baron, Elgin*, 1849), *b.* 1924, *s.* 1968, *m.*	Lord Bruce, *b.* 1961

Created	Title, order of succession, name, etc.	Heir
1789 I.*	*Enniskillen* (7th), Andrew John Galbraith Cole (5th *UK Baron, Grinstead*, 1815), *b.* 1942, *s.* 1989, *m.*	Arthur G. C., *b.* 1920
1789 I.*	*Erne* (6th), Henry George Victor John Crichton (3rd *UK Baron, Fermanagh*, 1876), *b.* 1937, *s.* 1940, *m.*	Viscount Crichton, *b.* 1971
1452 S.	*Erroll* (24th), Merlin Sereld Victor Gilbert Hay, *b.* 1948, *s.* 1978, *m.* Hereditary Lord High Constable and Knight Marischal of Scotland	Lord Hay, *b.* 1984
1661	*Essex* (10th), Robert Edward de Vere Capell, *b.* 1920, *s.* 1981, *m.*	Viscount Malden, *b.* 1944
1711	°*Ferrers* (13th), Robert Washington Shirley, PC, *b.* 1929, *s.* 1954, *m.*	Viscount Tamworth, *b.* 1952
1789	°*Fortescue* (8th), Charles Hugh Richard Fortescue, *b.* 1951, *s.* 1993, *m.*	Hon. Martin D. F., *b.* 1924
1841	*Gainsborough* (5th), Anthony Gerard Edward Noel, *b.* 1923, *s.* 1927, *m.*	Viscount Campden, *b.* 1950
1623 S.*	*Galloway* (13th), Randolph Keith Reginald Stewart (6th *Brit. Baron Stewart of Garlies*, 1796), *b.* 1928, *s.* 1978, *m.*	Andrew C. S., *b.* 1949
1703 S.*	*Glasgow* (10th), Patrick Robin Archibald Boyle (4th *UK Baron, Fairlie*, 1897), *b.* 1939, *s.* 1984, *m.*	Viscount of Kelburn, *b.* 1978
1806 I.*	*Gosford* (7th), Charles David Nicholas Alexander John Sparrow Acheson (5th *UK Baron, Worlingham*, 1835), *b.* 1942, *s.* 1966, *m.*	Hon. Patrick B. V. M. A., *b.* 1915
1945	*Gowrie* (2nd), Alexander Patric Greysteil Hore-Ruthven, PC (3rd *UK Baron Ruthven of Gowrie*, 1919), *b.* 1939, *s.* 1955, *m.*	Viscount Ruthven of Canberra, *b.* 1964
1684 I.*	*Granard* (10th), Peter Arthur Edward Hastings Forbes (5th *UK Baron, Granard*, 1806), *b.* 1957, *s.* 1992, *m.*	Viscount Forbes, *b.* 1981
1833	°*Granville* (6th), Granville George Fergus Leveson-Gower, *b.* 1959, *s.* 1996, *m.*	Hon. Niall J. L.-G., *b.* 1963
1806	°*Grey* (6th), Richard Fleming George Charles Grey, *b.* 1939, *s.* 1963, *m.*	Philip K. G., *b.* 1940
1752	*Guilford* (9th), Edward Francis North, *b.* 1933, *s.* 1949, *w.*	Lord North, *b.* 1971
1619 S.	*Haddington* (13th), John George Baillie-Hamilton, *b.* 1941, *s.* 1986, *m.*	Lord Binning, *b.* 1985
1919	°*Haig* (2nd), George Alexander Eugene Douglas Haig, OBE, *b.* 1918, *s.* 1928, *m.*	Viscount Dawick, *b.* 1961
1944	*Halifax* (3rd), Charles Edward Peter Neil Wood (5th *UK Visct., Halifax*, 1866), *b.* 1944, *s.* 1980, *m.*	Lord Irwin, *b.* 1977
1898	*Halsbury* (3rd), John Anthony Hardinge Giffard, FRS, FEng, *b.* 1908, *s.* 1943, *w.*	Adam E. G., *b.* 1934
1754	*Hardwicke* (10th), Joseph Philip Sebastian Yorke, *b.* 1971, *s.* 1974.	Richard C. J. Y., *b.* 1916
1812	*Harewood* (7th), George Henry Hubert Lascelles, KBE, *b.* 1923, *s.* 1947, *m.* (*see also* page 127)	Viscount Lascelles, *b.* 1950 (*see also* page 127)
1742	*Harrington* (11th), William Henry Leicester Stanhope (8th *Brit. Visct. Stanhope of Mahon*, 1717), *b.* 1922, *s.* 1929, *m.*	Viscount Petersham, *b.* 1945
1809	*Harrowby* (7th), Dudley Danvers Granville Coutts Ryder, TD, *b.* 1922, *s.* 1987, *m.*	Viscount Sandon, *b.* 1951
1605 S.	*Home* (15th), David Alexander Cospatrick Douglas-Home, CVO, *b.* 1943, *s.* 1995, *m.*	Lord Dunglass, *b.* 1987
1821	°*Howe* (7th), Frederick Richard Penn Curzon, *b.* 1951, *s.* 1984, *m.*	Viscount Curzon, *b.* 1994
1529	*Huntingdon* (16th), William Edward Robin Hood Hastings Bass, *b.* 1948, *s.* 1990, *m.*	Hon. Simon A. R. H. H. B., *b.* 1950
1885	*Iddesleigh* (4th), Stafford Henry Northcote, *b.* 1932, *s.* 1970, *m.*	Viscount St Cyres, *b.* 1957
1756	*Ilchester* (9th), Maurice Vivian de Touffreville Fox-Strangways, *b.* 1920, *s.* 1970, *m.*	Hon. Raymond G. F.-S., *b.* 1921
1929	*Inchcape* (4th), (Kenneth) Peter (Lyle) Mackay, *b.* 1943, *s.* 1994, *m.*	Viscount Glenapp, *b.* 1979
1919	*Iveagh* (4th), Arthur Edward Rory Guinness, *b.* 1969, *s.* 1992.	Hon. Rory M. B. G., *b.* 1974
1925	°*Jellicoe* (2nd), George Patrick John Rushworth Jellicoe, KBE, DSO, MC, PC, FRS, *b.* 1918, *s.* 1935, *m.*	Viscount Brocas, *b.* 1950
1697	*Jersey* (10th), (George Francis) William Villiers (13th *Irish Visct., Grandison*, 1620), *b.* 1976, *s.* 1998.	Hon. Jamie C. V., *b.* 1994
1822 I.	*Kilmorey* (6th), Richard Francis Needham, Kt, PC, *b.* 1942, *s.* 1977, *m.*	Viscount Newry and Morne, *b.* 1966
1866	*Kimberley* (4th), John Wodehouse, *b.* 1924, *s.* 1941, *m.*	Lord Wodehouse, *b.* 1951
1768 I.	*Kingston* (11th), Barclay Robert Edwin King-Tenison, *b.* 1943, *s.* 1948, *m.*	Viscount Kingsborough, *b.* 1969
1633 S.*	*Kinnoull* (15th), Arthur William George Patrick Hay (9th *Brit. Baron Hay of Pedwardine*, 1711), *b.* 1935, *s.* 1938, *m.*	Viscount Dupplin, *b.* 1962
1677 S.*	*Kintore* (13th), Michael Canning William John Keith (3rd *UK Visct. Stonehaven*, 1938), *b.* 1939, *s.* 1989, *m.*	Lord Inverurie, *b.* 1976
1914	°*Kitchener of Khartoum* (3rd), Henry Herbert Kitchener, TD, *b.* 1919, *s.* 1937.	None
1756 I.	*Lanesborough* (9th), Denis Anthony Brian Butler, TD, *b.* 1918, *s.* 1950, *m.*	None
1624 S.	*Lauderdale* (17th), Patrick Francis Maitland, *b.* 1911, *s.* 1968, *m.*	Viscount Maitland, *b.* 1937
1837	*Leicester* (7th), Edward Douglas Coke, *b.* 1936, *s.* 1994, *m.*	Viscount Coke, *b.* 1965
1641 S.	*Leven* (14th) and *Melville* (13th) (s. 1690), Alexander Robert Leslie Melville, *b.* 1924, *s.* 1947, *m.*	Lord Balgonie, *b.* 1954
1831	*Lichfield* (5th), Thomas Patrick John Anson, *b.* 1939, *s.* 1960.	Viscount Anson, *b.* 1978

Created	Title, order of succession, name, etc.	Heir
1803 I.*	*Limerick* (6th), Patrick Edmund Pery, KBE (6th *UK Baron Foxford*, 1815), *b.* 1930, *s.* 1967, *m.*	Viscount Glentworth, *b.* 1963
1572	*Lincoln* (18th), Edward Horace Fiennes-Clinton, *b.* 1913, *s.* 1988, *m.*	Hon. Edward G. *F.-C.*, *b.* 1943
1633 S.	*Lindsay* (16th), James Randolph Lindesay-Bethune, *b.* 1955, *s.* 1989, *m.*	Viscount Garnock, *b.* 1990
1626	*Lindsey* (14th) and *Abingdon* (9th) (1682), Richard Henry Rupert Bertie, *b.* 1931, *s.* 1963, *m.*	Lord Norreys, *b.* 1958
1776 I.	*Lisburne* (8th), John David Malet Vaughan, *b.* 1918, *s.* 1965, *m.*	Viscount Vaughan, *b.* 1945
1822 I.*	*Listowel* (6th), Francis Michael Hare (4th *UK Baron Hare*, 1869), *b.* 1964, *s.* 1997, *m.*	Hon. Timothy P. *H.*, *b.* 1966
1905	*Liverpool* (5th), Edward Peter Bertram Savile Foljambe, *b.* 1944, *s.* 1969, *m.*	Viscount Hawkesbury, *b.* 1972
1945	°*Lloyd George of Dwyfor* (3rd), Owen Lloyd George, *b.* 1924, *s.* 1968, *m.*	Viscount Gwynedd, *b.* 1951
1785 I.*	*Longford* (7th), Francis Aungier Pakenham, KG, PC (6th *UK Baron, Silchester*, 1821; 1st *UK Baron Pakenham*, 1945), *b.* 1905, *s.* 1961, *m.*	Thomas F. D. *P.*, *b.* 1933
1807	*Lonsdale* (7th), James Hugh William Lowther, *b.* 1922, *s.* 1953, *m.*	Viscount Lowther, *b.* 1949
1838	*Lovelace* (5th), Peter Axel William Locke King (12th *Brit. Baron King*, 1725), *b.* 1951, *s.* 1964, *m.*	None
1795 I.*	*Lucan* (7th), Richard John Bingham (3rd *UK Baron Bingham*, 1934), *b.* 1934, *s.* 1964, *m.*	Lord Bingham, *b.* 1967
1880	*Lytton* (5th), John Peter Michael Scawen Lytton (18th *Engl. Baron, Wentworth*, 1529), *b.* 1950, *s.* 1985, *m.*	Viscount Knebworth, *b.* 1989
1721	*Macclesfield* (9th), Richard Timothy George Mansfield Parker, *b.* 1943, *s.* 1992, *m.*	Hon. J. David G. *P.*, *b.* 1945
1800	*Malmesbury* (6th), William James Harris, TD, *b.* 1907, *s.* 1950, *w.*	Viscount FitzHarris, *b.* 1946
1776 & 1792	*Mansfield and Mansfield* (8th), William David Mungo James Murray (14th *Scott. Visct. Stormont*, 1621), *b.* 1930, *s.* 1971, *m.*	Viscount Stormont, *b.* 1956
1565 S.	*Mar* (14th) and *Kellie* (16th) (S. 1616), James Thorne Erskine, *b.* 1949, *s.* 1994, *m.*	Hon. Alexander D. *E.*, *b.* 1952
1785 I.	*Mayo* (10th), Terence Patrick Bourke, *b.* 1929, *s.* 1962.	Lord Naas, *b.* 1953
1627 I.*	*Meath* (14th), Anthony Windham Normand Brabazon (5th *UK Baron, Chaworth*, 1831), *b.* 1910, *s.* 1949, *m.*	Lord Ardee, *b.* 1941
1766 I.	*Mexborough* (8th), John Christopher George Savile, *b.* 1931, *s.* 1980, *m.*	Viscount Pollington, *b.* 1959
1813	*Minto* (6th), Gilbert Edward George Lariston Elliot-Murray-Kynynmound, OBE, *b.* 1928, *s.* 1975, *m.*	Viscount Melgund, *b.* 1953
1562 S.*	*Moray* (20th), Douglas John Moray Stuart (12th *Brit. Baron Stuart of Castle Stuart*, 1796), *b.* 1928, *s.* 1974, *m.*	Lord Doune, *b.* 1966
1815	*Morley* (6th), John St Aubyn Parker, KCVO, *b.* 1923, *s.* 1962, *m.*	Viscount Boringdon, *b.* 1956
1458 S.	*Morton* (22nd), John Charles Sholto Douglas, *b.* 1927, *s.* 1976, *m.*	Lord Aberdour, *b.* 1952
1789	*Mount Edgcumbe* (8th), Robert Charles Edgcumbe, *b.* 1939, *s.* 1982.	Piers V. *E.*, *b.* 1946
1831	*Munster* (7th), Anthony Charles FitzClarence, *b.* 1926, *s.* 1983, *m.*	None
1805	°*Nelson* (9th), Peter John Horatio Nelson, *b.* 1941, *s.* 1981, *m.*	Viscount Merton, *b.* 1971
1660 S.	*Newburgh* (12th), Don Filippo Giambattista Camillo Francesco Aldo Maria Rospigliosi, *b.* 1942, *s.* 1986, *m.*	Princess Donna Benedetta F. M. *R.*, *b.* 1974
1827 I.	*Norbury* (6th), Noel Terence Graham-Toler, *b.* 1939, *s.* 1955, *m.*	Viscount Glandine, *b.* 1967
1806 I.*	*Normanton* (6th), Shaun James Christian Welbore Ellis Agar (9th *Brit. Baron, Mendip*, 1794; 4th *UK Baron, Somerton*, 1873), *b.* 1945, *s.* 1967, *m.*	Viscount Somerton, *b.* 1982
1647 S.	*Northesk* (14th), David John MacRae Carnegie, *b.* 1954, *s.* 1994, *m.*	Lord Rosehill, *b.* 1980
1801	*Onslow* (7th), Michael William Coplestone Dillon Onslow, *b.* 1938, *s.* 1971, *m.*	Viscount Cranley, *b.* 1967
1696 S.	*Orkney* (9th), (Oliver) Peter St John, *b.* 1938, *s.* 1998, *m.*	Viscount Kirkwall, *b.* 1969
1328 I.	*Ormonde* and *Ossory*. The 8th Marquess of Ormonde died in 1997, when the marquessate became extinct. The heir to his earldoms had not established his claim at the time of going to press	Viscount Mountgarret, *b.* 1936 (*see* page 146)
1925	*Oxford and Asquith* (2nd), Julian Edward George Asquith, KCMG, *b.* 1916, *s.* 1928, *w.*	Viscount Asquith OBE, *b.* 1952
1929	°*Peel* (3rd), William James Robert Peel (4th *UK Visct. Peel*, 1895), *b.* 1947, *s.* 1969, *m.*	Viscount Clanfield, *b.* 1976
1551	*Pembroke* (17th) and *Montgomery* (14th) (1605), Henry George Charles Alexander Herbert, *b.* 1939, *s.* 1969.	Lord Herbert, *b.* 1978
1605 S.	*Perth* (17th), John David Drummond, PC, *b.* 1907, *s.* 1951, *w.*	Viscount Strathallan, *b.* 1935
1905	*Plymouth* (3rd), Other Robert Ivor Windsor-Clive (15th *Engl. Baron, Windsor*, 1529), *b.* 1923, *s.* 1943, *m.*	Viscount Windsor, *b.* 1951
1785 I.	*Portarlington* (7th), George Lionel Yuill Seymour Dawson-Damer, *b.* 1938, *s.* 1959, *m.*	Viscount Carlow, *b.* 1965
1689	*Portland* (12th), Count Timothy Charles Robert Noel Bentinck, *b.* 1953, *s.* 1997, *m.*	Viscount Woodstock, *b.* 1984
1743	*Portsmouth* (10th), Quentin Gerard Carew Wallop, *b.* 1954, *s.* 1984, *m.*	Viscount Lymington, *b.* 1981
1804	*Powis* (8th), John George Herbert (9th *Irish Baron, Clive*, 1762), *b.* 1952, *s.* 1993, *m.*	Viscount Clive, *b.* 1979

Created	Title, order of succession, name, etc.	Heir
1765	*Radnor* (8th), Jacob Pleydell-Bouverie, *b.* 1927, *s.* 1968, *m.*	Viscount Folkestone, *b.* 1955
1831 I.*	*Ranfurly* (7th), Gerald Françoys Needham Knox (8th *UK Baron, Ranfurly*, 1826), *b.* 1929, *s.* 1988, *m.*	Edward J. K., *b.* 1957
1771 I.	*Roden* (10th), Robert John Jocelyn, *b.* 1938, *s.* 1993, *m.*	Viscount Jocelyn, *b.* 1989
1801	*Romney* (7th), Michael Henry Marsham, *b.* 1910, *s.* 1975, *m.*	Julian C. M., *b.* 1948
1703 s.*	*Rosebery* (7th), Neil Archibald Primrose (3rd *UK Earl Midlothian*, 1911), *b.* 1929, *s.* 1974, *m.*	Lord Dalmeny, *b.* 1967
1806 I.	*Rosse* (7th), William Brendan Parsons, *b.* 1936, *s.* 1979, *m.*	Lord Oxmantown, *b.* 1969
1801	*Rosslyn* (7th), Peter St Clair-Erskine, *b.* 1958, *s.* 1977, *m.*	Lord Loughborough, *b.* 1986
1457 s.	*Rothes* (21st), Ian Lionel Malcolm Leslie, *b.* 1932, *s.* 1975, *m.*	Lord Leslie, *b.* 1958
1861	°*Russell* (5th), Conrad Sebastian Robert Russell, FBA, *b.* 1937, *s.* 1987, *m.*	Viscount Amberley, *b.* 1968
1915	°*St Aldwyn* (3rd), Michael Henry Hicks Beach, *b.* 1950, *s.* 1992, *m.*	Hon. David S. H. B., *b.* 1955
1815	*St Germans* (10th), Peregrine Nicholas Eliot, *b.* 1941, *s.* 1988.	Lord Eliot, *b.* 1966
1660	*Sandwich* (11th), John Edward Hollister Montagu, *b.* 1943, *s.* 1995, *m.*	Viscount Hinchingbrooke, *b.* 1969
1690	*Scarbrough* (12th), Richard Aldred Lumley (13th *Irish Visct. Lumley*, 1628), *b.* 1932, *s.* 1969, *m.*	Viscount Lumley, *b.* 1973
1701 s.	*Seafield* (13th), Ian Derek Francis Ogilvie-Grant, *b.* 1939, *s.* 1969, *m.*	Viscount Reidhaven, *b.* 1963
1882	*Selborne* (4th), John Roundell Palmer, KBE, FRS, *b.* 1940, *s.* 1971, *m.*	Viscount Wolmer, *b.* 1971
1646 s.	*Selkirk*. Disclaimed for life 1994. (*see* Lord Selkirk of Douglas, page 161)	Hon. John A. *Douglas-Hamilton*, *b.* 1978
1672	*Shaftesbury* (10th), Anthony Ashley-Cooper, *b.* 1938, *s.* 1961, *m.*	Lord Ashley, *b.* 1977
1756 I.*	*Shannon* (9th), Richard Bentinck Boyle (8th *Brit. Baron Carleton*, 1786), *b.* 1924, *s.* 1963.	Viscount Boyle, *b.* 1960
1442	*Shrewsbury and Waterford* (22nd) (I. 1446), Charles Henry John Benedict Crofton Chetwynd Chetwynd-Talbot (7th *Engl. Earl Talbot*, 1784), *b.* 1952, *s.* 1980, *m.* Premier Earl of England and Ireland	Viscount Ingestre, *b.* 1978
1961	*Snowdon* (1st), Antony Charles Robert Armstrong-Jones, GCVO, *b.* 1930, *m.* (*see also* page 117)	Viscount Linley, *b.* 1961 (*see also* page 117)
1765	°*Spencer* (9th), Charles Edward Maurice Spencer, *b.* 1964, *s.* 1992.	Viscount Althorp, *b.* 1994
1703 s.*	*Stair* (14th), John David James Dalrymple (7th *UK Baron, Oxenfoord*, 1841), *b.* 1961, *s.* 1996.	Hon. David H. D., *b.* 1963
1984	*Stockton* (2nd), Alexander Daniel Alan Macmillan, *b.* 1943, *s.* 1986, *m.*	Viscount Macmillan of Ovenden, *b.* 1974
1821	*Stradbroke* (6th), Robert Keith Rous, *b.* 1937, *s.* 1983, *m.*	Viscount Dunwich, *b.* 1961
1847	*Strafford* (8th), Thomas Edmund Byng, *b.* 1936, *s.* 1984, *m.*	Viscount Enfield, *b.* 1964
1606 s.*	*Strathmore and Kinghorne* (18th), Michael Fergus Bowes Lyon (16th *Scott. Earl, Strathmore*, 1677; 18th *Scott. Earl, Kinghorne*, 1606; 5th *UK Earl, Strathmore and Kinghorne*, 1937), *b.* 1957, *s.* 1987, *m.*	Lord Glamis, *b.* 1986
1603	*Suffolk* (21st) and *Berkshire* (14th) (1626), Michael John James George Robert Howard, *b.* 1935, *s.* 1941, *m.*	Viscount Andover, *b.* 1974
1955	*Swinton* (2nd), David Yarburgh Cunliffe-Lister, *b.* 1937, *s.* 1972, *m.*	Hon. Nicholas J. C.-L., *b.* 1939
1714	*Tankerville* (10th), Peter Grey Bennet, *b.* 1956, *s.* 1980.	Revd the Hon. George A. G. B., *b.* 1925
1822	°*Temple of Stowe* (8th), (Walter) Grenville Algernon Temple-Gore-Langton, *b.* 1924, *s.* 1988, *m.*	Lord Langton, *b.* 1955
1815	*Verulam* (7th), John Duncan Grimston (11th *Irish Visct. Grimston*, 1719; 16th *Scott. Baron Forrester of Corstorphine*, 1633), *b.* 1951, *s.* 1973, *m.*	Viscount Grimston, *b.* 1978
1729	°*Waldegrave* (13th), James Sherbrooke Waldegrave, *b.* 1940, *s.* 1995, *m.*	Viscount Chewton, *b.* 1986
1759	*Warwick* (9th) and *Brooke* (9th) (*Brit.* 1746), Guy David Greville, *b.* 1957, *s.* 1996, *m.*	Lord Brooke, *b.* 1982
1633 s.*	*Wemyss* (12th) and *March* (8th) (s. 1697), Francis David Charteris, KT (5th *UK Baron Wemyss*, 1821), *b.* 1912, *s.* 1937, *m.*	Lord Neidpath, *b.* 1948
1621 I.	*Westmeath* (13th), William Anthony Nugent, *b.* 1928, *s.* 1971, *m.*	Hon. Sean C. W. N., *b.* 1965
1624	*Westmorland* (16th), Anthony David Francis Henry Fane, *b.* 1951, *s.* 1993, *m.*	Hon. Harry St C. F., *b.* 1953
1876	*Wharncliffe* (5th), Richard Alan Montagu Stuart Wortley, *b.* 1953, *s.* 1987, *m.*	Viscount Carlton, *b.* 1980
1801	*Wilton* (7th), Seymour William Arthur John Egerton, *b.* 1921, *s.* 1927, *m.*	Baron Ebury, *b.* 1934 (*see* page 149)
1628	*Winchilsea* (16th) and *Nottingham* (11th) (1681), Christopher Denys Stormont Finch Hatton, *b.* 1936, *s.* 1950, *m.*	Viscount Maidstone, *b.* 1967
1766 I.	°*Winterton* (8th), (Donald) David Turnour, *b.* 1943, *s.* 1991, *m.*	Robert C. T., *b.* 1950
1956	*Woolton* (3rd), Simon Frederick Marquis, *b.* 1958, *s.* 1969, *m.*	None
1837	*Yarborough* (8th), Charles John Pelham, *b.* 1963, *s.* 1991, *m.*	Lord Worsley, *b.* 1990

COUNTESSES IN THEIR OWN RIGHT

Style, The Right Hon. the Countess (of) __
Husband, Untitled
Children's style, As for children of an Earl
For forms of address, *see* page 135

Created	Title, order of succession, name, etc.	Heir
1643 s.	*Dysart* (11th in line), Rosamund Agnes Greaves, *b.* 1914, *s.* 1975.	Lady Katherine *Grant of Rothiemurchus, b.* 1918
1633 s.	*Loudoun* (13th in line), Barbara Huddleston Abney-Hastings, *b.* 1919, *s.* 1960, *m.*	Lord Mauchline, *b.* 1942
c.1115 s.	*Mar* (31st in line), Margaret of Mar, *b.* 1940, *s.* 1975, *m. Premier Earldom of Scotland*	Mistress of Mar, *b.* 1963
1947	°*Mountbatten of Burma* (2nd in line), Patricia Edwina Victoria Knatchbull, CBE, *b.* 1924, *s.* 1979, *m.*	Lord Romsey, *b.* 1947 (*see also* page 148)
c.1235 s.	*Sutherland* (24th in line), Elizabeth Millicent Sutherland, *b.* 1921, *s.* 1963, *m.*	Lord Strathnaver, *b.* 1947

VISCOUNTS

Coronet, Sixteen silver balls
Style, The Right Hon. the Viscount __
Wife's style, The Right Hon. the Viscountess __
Children's style, 'The Hon.' before forename and family name
In Scotland, the heir apparent to a Viscount may be styled 'The Master of __ (title of peer)'
For forms of address, *see* page 135

Created	Title, order of succession, name, etc.	Heir
1945	*Addison* (4th), William Matthew Wand Addison, *b.* 1945, *s.* 1992, *m.*	Hon. Paul W. *A., b.* 1973
1946	*Alanbrooke* (3rd), Alan Victor Harold Brooke, *b.* 1932, *s.* 1972.	None
1919	*Allenby* (3rd), Lt.-Col. Michael Jaffray Hynman Allenby, *b.* 1931, *s.* 1984, *m.*	Hon. Henry J. H. *A., b.* 1968
1911	*Allendale* (3rd), Wentworth Hubert Charles Beaumont, *b.* 1922, *s.* 1956.	Hon. Wentworth P. I. *B., b.* 1948
1642 s.	*of Arbuthnott* (16th), John Campbell Arbuthnott, KT, CBE, DSC, FRSE, *b.* 1924, *s.* 1966, *m.*	Master of Arbuthnott, *b.* 1950
1751 I.	*Ashbrook* (11th), Michael Llowarch Warburton Flower, *b.* 1935, *s.* 1995, *m.*	Hon. Rowland F. W. *F., b.* 1975
1917	*Astor* (4th), William Waldorf Astor, *b.* 1951, *s.* 1966, *m.*	Hon. William W. *A., b.* 1979
1781 I.	*Bangor* (8th), William Maxwell David Ward, *b.* 1948, *s.* 1993, *m.*	Hon. E. Nicholas *W., b.* 1953
1925	*Bearsted* (5th), Nicholas Alan Samuel, *b.* 1950, *s.* 1996, *m.*	Hon. Harry R. *S., b.* 1988
1963	*Blakenham* (2nd), Michael John Hare, *b.* 1938, *s.* 1982, *m.*	Hon. Caspar J. *H., b.* 1972
1935	*Bledisloe* (3rd), Christopher Hiley Ludlow Bathurst, QC, *b.* 1934, *s.* 1979.	Hon. Rupert E. L. *B., b.* 1964
1712	*Bolingbroke* (7th) and *St John* (8th) (1716), Kenneth Oliver Musgrave St John, *b.* 1927, *s.* 1974.	Hon. Henry F. *St J., b.* 1957
1960	*Boyd of Merton* (2nd), Simon Donald Rupert Neville Lennox-Boyd, *b.* 1939, *s.* 1983, *m.*	Hon. Benjamin A. *L.-B., b.* 1964
1717 I.*	*Boyne* (11th), Gustavus Michael Stucley Hamilton-Russell (5th UK *Baron Brancepeth,* 1866), *b.* 1965, *s.* 1995, *m.*	Hon. Richard G. *H.-R.* DSO, LVO, *b.* 1909
1929	*Brentford* (4th), Crispin William Joynson-Hicks, *b.* 1933, *s.* 1983, *m.*	Hon. Paul W. *J.-H., b.* 1971
1929	*Bridgeman* (3rd), Robin John Orlando Bridgeman, *b.* 1930, *s.* 1982, *m.*	Hon. William O. C. *B., b.* 1968
1868	*Bridport* (4th), Alexander Nelson Hood (7th *Duke, Brontë in Sicily,* 1799; 6th *Irish Baron Bridport,* 1794), *b.* 1948, *s.* 1969, *m.*	Hon. Peregrine A. N. *H., b.* 1974
1952	*Brookeborough* (3rd), Alan Henry Brooke, *b.* 1952, *s.* 1987, *m.*	Hon. Christopher A. *B., b.* 1954
1933	*Buckmaster* (3rd), Martin Stanley Buckmaster, OBE, *b.* 1921, *s.* 1974.	Hon. Colin J. *B., b.* 1923
1939	*Caldecote* (2nd), Robert Andrew Inskip, KBE, DSC, FEng, *b.* 1917, *s.* 1947, *m.*	Hon. Piers J. H. *I., b.* 1947
1941	*Camrose.* Disclaimed for life 1995. (*see* Baron Hartwell, page 159)	Hon. Adrian M. *Berry, b.* 1937

Created	Title, order of succession, name, etc.	Heir
1954	*Chandos* (3rd), Thomas Orlando Lyttelton, *b.* 1953, *s.* 1980, *m.*	Hon. Oliver A. *L.*, *b.* 1986
1665 I.	*Charlemont* (14th), John Day Caulfeild (18th *Irish Baron Caulfeild of Charlemont*, 1620), *b.* 1934, *s.* 1985, *m.*	Hon. John D. *C.*, *b.* 1966
1921	*Chelmsford* (3rd), Frederic Jan Thesiger, *b.* 1931, *s.* 1970, *m.*	Hon. Frederic C. P. *T.*, *b.* 1962
1717 I.	*Chetwynd* (10th), Adam Richard John Casson Chetwynd, *b.* 1935, *s.* 1965, *m.*	Hon. Adam D. *C.*, *b.* 1969
1911	*Chilston* (4th), Alastair George Akers-Douglas, *b.* 1946, *s.* 1982, *m.*	Hon. Oliver I. *A.-D.*, *b.* 1973
1902	*Churchill* (3rd), Victor George Spencer (5th *UK Baron Churchill*, 1815), *b.* 1934, *s.* 1973.	None to Viscountcy. To Barony, Richard H. R. *S.*, *b.* 1926
1718	*Cobham* (11th), John William Leonard Lyttelton (8th *Irish Baron Westcote*, 1776), *b.* 1943, *s.* 1977, *m.*	Hon. Christopher C. *L.*, *b.* 1947
1902	*Colville of Culross* (4th), John Mark Alexander Colville, QC (13th *Scott. Baron Colville of Culross*, 1604), *b.* 1933, *s.* 1945, *m.*	Master of Colville, *b.* 1959
1826	*Combermere* (5th), Michael Wellington Stapleton-Cotton, *b.* 1929, *s.* 1969, *m.*	Hon. Thomas R. W. *S.-C.*, *b.* 1969
1917	*Cowdray* (4th), Michael Orlando Weetman Pearson (4th *UK Baron Cowdray*, 1910), *b.* 1944, *s.* 1995, *m.*	Hon. Charles A. *P.*, *b.* 1956
1927	*Craigavon* (3rd), Janric Fraser Craig, *b.* 1944, *s.* 1974.	None
1886	*Cross* (3rd), Assheton Henry Cross, *b.* 1920, *s.* 1932.	None
1943	*Daventry* (3rd), Francis Humphrey Maurice FitzRoy Newdegate, *b.* 1921, *s.* 1986, *m.*	Hon. James E. *F. N.*, *b.* 1960
1937	*Davidson* (2nd), John Andrew Davidson, *b.* 1928, *s.* 1970, *m.*	Hon. Malcolm W. M. *D.*, *b.* 1934
1956	*De L'Isle* (2nd), Philip John Algernon Sidney, MBE (7th *UK Baron De L'Isle and Dudley*, 1835), *b.* 1945, *s.* 1991, *m.*	Hon. Philip W. E. *S.*, *b.* 1985
1776 I.	*De Vesci* (7th), Thomas Eustace Vesey (8th *Irish Baron Knapton*, 1750), *b.* 1955, *s.* 1983, *m.*	Hon. Oliver I. *V.*, *b.* 1991
1917	*Devonport* (3rd), Terence Kearley, *b.* 1944, *s.* 1973.	Chester D. H. *K.*, *b.* 1932
1964	*Dilhorne* (2nd), John Mervyn Manningham-Buller, *b.* 1932, *s.* 1980, *m.*	Hon. James E. *M.-B.*, *b.* 1956
1622 I.	*Dillon* (22nd), Henry Benedict Charles Dillon, *b.* 1973, *s.* 1982.	Hon. Richard A. L. *D.*, *b.* 1948
1785 I.	*Doneraile* (10th), Richard Allen St Leger, *b.* 1946, *s.* 1983, *m.*	Hon. Nathaniel W. R. St J. *St L.*, *b.* 1971
1680 I.*	*Downe* (11th), John Christian George Dawnay (4th *UK Baron Dawnay*, 1897), *b.* 1935, *s.* 1965, *m.*	Hon. Richard H. *D.*, *b.* 1967
1959	*Dunrossil* (2nd), John William Morrison, CMG, *b.* 1926, *s.* 1961, *m.*	Hon. Andrew W. R. *M.*, *b.* 1953
1964	*Eccles* (1st), David McAdam Eccles, CH, KCVO, PC, *b.* 1904, *m.*	Hon. John D. *E.* CBE, *b.* 1931
1897	*Esher* (4th), Lionel Gordon Baliol Brett, CBE, *b.* 1913, *s.* 1963, *m.*	Hon. Christopher L. B. *B.*, *b.* 1936
1816	*Exmouth* (10th), Paul Edward Pellew, *b.* 1940, *s.* 1970, *m.*	Hon. Edward F. *P.*, *b.* 1978
1620 S.	*Falkland* (15th), Lucius Edward William Plantagenet Cary, *b.* 1935, *s.* 1984, *m. Premier Scottish Viscount on the Roll*	Master of Falkland, *b.* 1963
1720	*Falmouth* (9th), George Hugh Boscawen (26th *Engl. Baron Le Despencer*, 1264), *b.* 1919, *s.* 1962, *m.*	Hon. Evelyn A. H. *B.*, *b.* 1955
1720 I.*	*Gage* (8th), (Henry) Nicolas Gage (7th *Brit. Baron Gage*, 1790), *b.* 1934, *s.* 1993, *m.*	Hon. Henry W. *G.*, *b.* 1975
1727 I.	*Galway* (12th), George Rupert Monckton-Arundell, *b.* 1922, *s.* 1980, *m.*	Hon. J. Philip *M.-A.*, *b.* 1952
1478 I.*	*Gormanston* (17th), Jenico Nicholas Dudley Preston (5th *UK Baron Gormanston*, 1868), *b.* 1939, *s.* 1940, *w. Premier Viscount of Ireland*	Hon. Jenico F. T. *P.*, *b.* 1974
1816 I.	*Gort* (9th), Foley Robert Standish Prendergast Vereker, *b.* 1951, *s.* 1995, *m.*	Hon. Nicholas L. P. *V.*, *b.* 1954
1900	*Goschen* (4th), Giles John Harry Goschen, *b.* 1965, *s.* 1977, *m.*	None
1849	*Gough* (5th), Shane Hugh Maryon Gough, *b.* 1941, *s.* 1951.	None
1937	*Greenwood* (2nd), David Henry Hamar Greenwood, *b.* 1914, *s.* 1948.	Hon. Michael G. H. *G.*, *b.* 1923
1929	*Hailsham.* Disclaimed for life 1963. (*see* Lord Hailsham of St Marylebone, page 159)	Rt. Hon. Douglas M. *Hogg* QC, MP, *b.* 1945
1891	*Hambleden* (4th), William Herbert Smith, *b.* 1930, *s.* 1948, *m.*	Hon. William H. B. *S.*, *b.* 1955
1884	*Hampden* (6th), Anthony David Brand, *b.* 1937, *s.* 1975, *m.*	Hon. Francis A. *B.*, *b.* 1970
1936	*Hanworth* (3rd), David Stephen Geoffrey Pollock, *b.* 1946, *s.* 1996, *m.*	Hon. Richard C. S. *P.*, *b.* 1951
1791 I.	*Harberton* (10th), Thomas de Vautort Pomeroy, *b.* 1910, *s.* 1980, *m.*	Hon. Robert W. *P.*, *b.* 1916
1846	*Hardinge* (6th), Charles Henry Nicholas Hardinge, *b.* 1956, *s.* 1984, *m.*	Hon. Andrew H. *H.*, *b.* 1960
1791 I.	*Hawarden* (9th), (Robert) Connan Wyndham Leslie Maude, *b.* 1961, *s.* 1991, *m.*	Hon. Thomas P. C. *M.*, *b.* 1964
1960	*Head* (2nd), Richard Antony Head, *b.* 1937, *s.* 1983, *m.*	Hon. Henry J. *H.*, *b.* 1980
1550	*Hereford* (18th), Robert Milo Leicester Devereux, *b.* 1932, *s.* 1952. *Premier Viscount of England*	Hon. Charles R. de B. *D.*, *b.* 1975
1842	*Hill* (8th), Antony Rowland Clegg-Hill, *b.* 1931, *s.* 1974, *m.*	Peter D. R. C. *C.-H.*, *b.* 1945
1796	*Hood* (7th), Alexander Lambert Hood (7th *Irish Baron, Hood*, 1782), *b.* 1914, *s.* 1981, *m.*	Hon. Henry L. A. *H.*, *b.* 1958
1956	*Ingleby* (2nd), Martin Raymond Peake, *b.* 1926, *s.* 1966, *w.*	None
1945	*Kemsley* (2nd), (Geoffrey) Lionel Berry, *b.* 1909, *s.* 1968, *m.*	Richard G. *B.*, *b.* 1951

Created	Title, order of succession, name, etc.	Heir
1911	*Knollys* (3rd), David Francis Dudley Knollys, *b*. 1931, *s*. 1966, *m*.	Hon. Patrick N. M. *K.*, *b*. 1962
1895	*Knutsford* (6th), Michael Holland-Hibbert, *b*. 1926, *s*. 1986, *m*.	Hon. Henry T. *H.-H.*, *b*. 1959
1945	*Lambert* (3rd), Michael John Lambert, *b*. 1912, *s*. 1989, *m*.	None
1954	*Leathers* (3rd), Christopher Graeme Leathers, *b*. 1941, *s*. 1996, *m*.	Hon. James F. *L.*, *b*. 1969
1922	*Leverhulme* (3rd), Philip William Bryce Lever, KG,TD, *b*. 1915, *s*. 1949, *w*.	None
1781 I.	*Lifford* (9th), (Edward) James Wingfield Hewitt, *b*. 1949, *s*. 1987, *m*.	Hon. James T. W. *H.*, *b*. 1979
1921	*Long* (4th), Richard Gerard Long, CBE, *b*. 1929, *s*. 1967, *m*.	Hon. James R. *L.*, *b*. 1960
1957	*Mackintosh of Halifax* (3rd), (John) Clive Mackintosh, *b*. 1958, *s*. 1980, *m*.	Hon. Thomas H. G. *M.*, *b*. 1985
1955	*Malvern* (3rd), Ashley Kevin Godfrey Huggins, *b*. 1949, *s*. 1978.	Hon. M. James *H.*, *b*. 1928
1945	*Marchwood* (3rd), David George Staveley Penny, *b*. 1936, *s*. 1979, *w*.	Hon. Peter G. W. *P.*, *b*. 1965
1942	*Margesson* (2nd), Francis Vere Hampden Margesson, *b*. 1922, *s*. 1965, *m*.	Capt. Hon. Richard F. D. *M.*, *b*. 1960
1660 I.*	*Massereene* (14th) and *Ferrard* (7th) (1797), John David Clotworthy Whyte-Melville Foster Skeffington (7th *UK Baron, Oriel*, 1821), *b*. 1940, *s*. 1992, *m*.	Hon. Charles J. C. W.-M. F. *S.*, *b*. 1973
1802	*Melville* (9th), Robert David Ross Dundas, *b*. 1937, *s*. 1971, *m*.	Hon. Robert H. K. *D.*, *b*. 1984
1916	*Mersey* (4th), Richard Maurice Clive Bigham (13th *Scott. Lord Nairne*, 1681, *s*. 1995), *b*. 1934, *s*. 1979, *m*.	Hon. Edward J. H. *B.*, *b*. 1966
1717 I.*	*Midleton* (12th), Alan Henry Brodrick (9th *Brit. Baron Brodrick of Peper Harow*, 1796), *b*. 1949, *s*. 1988, *m*.	Hon. Ashley R. *B.*, *b*. 1980
1962	*Mills* (3rd), Christopher Philip Roger Mills, *b*. 1956, *s*. 1988, *m*.	None
1716 I.	*Molesworth* (11th), Richard Gosset Molesworth, *b*. 1907, *s*. 1961, *w*.	Hon. Robert B. K. *M.*, *b*. 1959
1801 I.*	*Monck* (7th), Charles Stanley Monck (4th *UK Baron, Monck*, 1866), *b*. 1953, *s*. 1982 (does not use title)	Hon. George S. *M.*, *b*. 1957
1957	*Monckton of Brenchley* (2nd), Maj.-Gen. Gilbert Walter Riversdale Monckton, CB, OBE, MC, *b*. 1915, *s*. 1965, *m*.	Hon. Christopher W. *M.*, *b*. 1952
1946	*Montgomery of Alamein* (2nd), David Bernard Montgomery, CBE, *b*. 1928, *s*. 1976, *m*.	Hon. Henry D. *M.*, *b*. 1954
1550 I.*	*Mountgarret* (17th), Richard Henry Piers Butler (4th *UK Baron Mountgarret*, 1911), *b*. 1936, *s*. 1966, *m*.	Hon. Piers J. R. *B.*, *b*. 1961
1952	*Norwich* (2nd), John Julius Cooper, CVO, *b*. 1929, *s*. 1954, *m*.	Hon. Jason C. D. B. *C.*, *b*. 1959
1651 S.	*of Oxfuird* (13th), George Hubbard Makgill, CBE, *b*. 1934, *s*. 1986, *m*.	Master of Oxfuird, *b*. 1969
1873	*Portman* (9th), Edward Henry Berkeley Portman, *b*. 1934, *s*. 1967, *m*.	Hon. Christopher E. B. *P.*, *b*. 1958
1743 I.*	*Powerscourt* (10th), Mervyn Niall Wingfield (4th *UK Baron Powerscourt*, 1885), *b*. 1935, *s*. 1973, *m*.	Hon. Mervyn A. *W.*, *b*. 1963
1900	*Ridley* (4th), Matthew White Ridley, KG, GCVO, TD, *b*. 1925, *s*. 1964, *m*. Lord Steward	Hon. Matthew W. *R.*, *b*. 1958
1960	*Rochdale* (2nd), St John Durival Kemp, *b*. 1938, *s*. 1993, *m*.	Hon. Jonathan H. D. *K.*, *b*. 1961
1919	*Rothermere* (3rd), Vere Harold Esmond Harmsworth, *b*. 1925, *s*. 1978, *m*.	Hon. H. Jonathan E. V. *H.*, *b*. 1967
1937	*Runciman of Doxford* (3rd), Walter Garrison Runciman (Garry), CBE, FBA (4th *UK Baron, Runciman*, 1933), *b*. 1934, *s*. 1989, *m*.	Hon. David W. *R.*, *b*. 1967
1918	*St Davids* (3rd), Colwyn Jestyn John Philipps (20th *Engl. Baron Strange of Knokin*, 1299; 8th *Engl. Baron, Hungerford*, 1426; *Baron De Moleyns*, 1445), *b*. 1939, *s*. 1991, *m*.	Hon. Rhodri C. *P.*, *b*. 1966
1801	*St Vincent* (7th), Ronald George James Jervis, *b*. 1905, *s*. 1940, *m*.	Hon. Edward R. J. *J.*, *b*. 1951
1937	*Samuel* (3rd), David Herbert Samuel, OBE, PH.D., *b*. 1922, *s*. 1978, *m*.	Hon. Dan J. *S.*, *b*. 1925
1911	*Scarsdale* (3rd), Francis John Nathaniel Curzon (7th *Brit. Baron Scarsdale*, 1761), *b*. 1924, *s*. 1977, *m*.	Hon. Peter G. N. *C.*, *b*. 1949
1905	*Selby* (5th), Edward Thomas William Gully, *b*. 1967, *s*. 1997, *m*.	Hon. Christopher R. T. *G.*, *b*. 1993
1805	*Sidmouth* (7th), John Tonge Anthony Pellew Addington, *b*. 1914, *s*. 1976, *m*.	Hon. Jeremy F. *A.*, *b*. 1947
1940	*Simon* (3rd), Jan David Simon, *b*. 1940, *s*. 1993, *m*.	None
1960	*Slim* (2nd), John Douglas Slim, OBE, *b*. 1927, *s*. 1970, *m*.	Hon. Mark W. R. *S.*, *b*. 1960
1954	*Soulbury* (2nd), James Herwald Ramsbotham, *b*. 1915, *s*. 1971, *w*.	Hon. Sir Peter E. *R.* GCMG, GCVO, *b*. 1919
1776 I.	*Southwell* (7th), Pyers Anthony Joseph Southwell, *b*. 1930, *s*. 1960, *m*.	Hon. Richard A. P. *S.*, *b*. 1956
1942	*Stansgate*. Disclaimed for life 1963. (*Rt. Hon. Anthony Neil Wedgwood Benn*, MP, *b*.1925, *s*.1960, *m*.)	Stephen M. W. *B.*, *b*. 1951
1959	*Stuart of Findhorn* (2nd), David Randolph Moray Stuart, *b*. 1924, *s*. 1971, *m*.	Hon. J. Dominic *S.*, *b*. 1948
1957	*Tenby* (3rd), William Lloyd George, *b*. 1927, *s*. 1983, *m*.	Hon. Timothy H. G. *L. G.*, *b*. 1962
1952	*Thurso* (3rd), John Archibald Sinclair, *b*. 1953, *s*. 1995, *m*.	Hon. James A. R. *S.*, *b*. 1984
1721	*Torrington* (11th), Timothy Howard St George Byng, *b*. 1943, *s*. 1961, *m*.	John L. *B.* MC, *b*. 1919
1936	*Trenchard* (3rd), Hugh Trenchard, *b*. 1951, *s*. 1987, *m*.	Hon. Alexander T. *T.*, *b*. 1978
1921	*Ullswater* (2nd), Nicholas James Christopher Lowther, PC, *b*. 1942, *s*. 1949, *m*.	Hon. Benjamin J. *L.*, *b*. 1975

Created	Title, order of succession, name, etc.	Heir
1621 I.	*Valentia* (15th), Richard John Dighton Annesley, *b.* 1929, *s.* 1983, *m.*	Hon. Francis W. D. *A.*, *b.* 1959
1952	*Waverley* (3rd), John Desmond Forbes Anderson, *b.* 1949, *s.* 1990.	None
1938	*Weir* (3rd), William Kenneth James Weir, *b.* 1933, *s.* 1975, *m.*	Hon. James W. H. *W.*, *b.* 1965
1983	*Whitelaw* (1st), William Stephen Ian Whitelaw, KT, CH, MC, PC, *b.* 1918.	None
1918	*Wimborne* (4th), Ivor Mervyn Vigors Guest (5th *UK Baron Wimborne*, 1880), *b.* 1968, *s.* 1993.	Hon. Julian J. *G.*, *b.* 1945
1923	*Younger of Leckie* (4th), George Kenneth Hotson Younger, KT, KCVO, TD, PC (*Baron Younger of Prestwick* (life peerage), 1992), *b.* 1931, *s.* 1997, *m.*	Hon. James E. G. *Y.*, *b.* 1955

BARONS/LORDS

Coronet, Six silver balls
Style, The Right Hon. the Lord __. In the Peerage of Scotland there is no rank of Baron; the equivalent rank is Lord of Parliament (*see* page 136) and Scottish peers should always be styled 'Lord', never 'Baron'
Wife's style, The Right Hon. the Lady __
Children's style, 'The Hon.' before forename and family name
In Scotland, the heir apparent to a Lord may be styled 'The Master of __ (title of peer)'
For forms of address, *see* page 135

Created	Title, order of succession, name, etc.	Heir
1911	*Aberconway* (3rd), Charles Melville McLaren, *b.* 1913, *s.* 1953, *m.*	Hon. H. Charles *M.*, *b.* 1948
1873	*Aberdare* (4th), Morys George Lyndhurst Bruce, KBE, PC, *b.* 1919, *s.* 1957, *m.*	Hon. Alastair J. L. *B.*, *b.* 1947
1835	*Abinger* (8th), James Richard Scarlett, *b.* 1914, *s.* 1943, *m.*	Hon. James H. *S.*, *b.* 1959
1869	*Acton* (4th), Richard Gerald Lyon-Dalberg-Acton, *b.* 1941, *s.* 1989, *m.*	Hon. John C. F. H. *L.-D.-A.*, *b.* 1966
1887	*Addington* (6th), Dominic Bryce Hubbard, *b.* 1963, *s.* 1982.	Hon. Michael W. L. *H.*, *b.* 1965
1896	*Aldenham* (6th) and *Hunsdon of Hunsdon* (4th) (1923), Vicary Tyser Gibbs, *b.* 1948, *s.* 1986, *m.*	Hon. Humphrey W. F. *G.*, *b.* 1989
1962	*Aldington* (1st), Toby Austin Richard William Low, KCMG, CBE, DSO, TD, PC, *b.* 1914.	Hon. Charles H. S. *L.*, *b.* 1948
1945	*Altrincham*. Disclaimed for life 1963. (*John Edward Poynder Grigg*, *b.* 1924, *s.* 1955, *m.*)	Hon. Anthony U. D. D. *G.*, *b.* 1934
1929	*Alvingham* (2nd), Maj.-Gen. Robert Guy Eardley Yerburgh, CBE, *b.* 1926, *s.* 1955, *m.*	Capt. Hon. Robert R. G. *Y.*, *b.* 1956
1892	*Amherst of Hackney* (4th), William Hugh Amherst Cecil, *b.* 1940, *s.* 1980, *m.*	Hon. H. William A. *C.*, *b.* 1968
1881	*Ampthill* (4th), Geoffrey Denis Erskine Russell, CBE, PC, *b.* 1921, *s.* 1973.	Hon. David W. E. *R.*, *b.* 1947
1947	*Amwell* (3rd), Keith Norman Montague, *b.* 1943, *s.* 1990, *m.*	Hon. Ian K. *M.*, *b.* 1973
1863	*Annaly* (6th), Luke Richard White, *b.* 1954, *s.* 1990, *m.*	Hon. Luke H. *W.*, *b.* 1990
1885	*Ashbourne* (4th), Edward Barry Greynville Gibson, *b.* 1933, *s.* 1983, *m.*	Hon. Edward C. d'O. *G.*, *b.* 1967
1835	*Ashburton* (7th), John Francis Harcourt Baring, KG, KCVO, *b.* 1928, *s.* 1991, *m.*	Hon. Mark F. R. *B.*, *b.* 1958
1892	*Ashcombe* (4th), Henry Edward Cubitt, *b.* 1924, *s.* 1962, *m.*	Mark E. *C.*, *b.* 1964
1911	*Ashton of Hyde* (3rd), Thomas John Ashton, TD, *b.* 1926, *s.* 1983, *m.*	Hon. Thomas H. *A.*, *b.* 1958
1800 I.	*Ashtown* (7th), Nigel Clive Crosby Trench, KCMG, *b.* 1916, *s.* 1990, *m.*	Hon. Roderick N. G. *T.*, *b.* 1944
1956	*Astor of Hever* (3rd), John Jacob Astor, *b.* 1946, *s.* 1984, *m.*	Hon. Charles G. J. *A.*, *b.* 1990
1789 I.*	*Auckland* (10th), Robert Ian Burnard Eden (10th *Brit. Baron Auckland*, 1793), *b.* 1962, *s.* 1997, *m.*	Hon. Ronald J. *E.*, *b.* 1931
1313	*Audley*. The 25th Lord Audley died in July 1997, leaving three co-heiresses	
1900	*Avebury* (4th), Eric Reginald Lubbock, *b.* 1928, *s.* 1971, *m.*	Hon. Lyulph A. J. *L.*, *b.* 1954
1718 I.	*Aylmer* (13th), Michael Anthony Aylmer, *b.* 1923, *s.* 1982, *m.*	Hon. A. Julian *A.*, *b.* 1951
1929	*Baden-Powell* (3rd), Robert Crause Baden-Powell, *b.* 1936, *s.* 1962, *m.*	Hon. David M. *B.-P.*, *b.* 1940
1780	*Bagot* (9th), Heneage Charles Bagot, *b.* 1914, *s.* 1979, *m.*	Hon. C. H. Shaun *B.*, *b.* 1944
1953	*Baillieu* (3rd), James William Latham Baillieu, *b.* 1950, *s.* 1973, *m.*	Hon. Robert L. *B.*, *b.* 1979
1607 S.	*Balfour of Burleigh* (8th), Robert Bruce, FRSE, *b.* 1927, *s.* 1967, *m.*	Hon. Victoria *B.*, *b.* 1973
1945	*Balfour of Inchrye* (2nd), Ian Balfour, *b.* 1924, *s.* 1988, *m.*	None
1924	*Banbury of Southam* (3rd), Charles William Banbury, *b.* 1953, *s.* 1981, *m.*	None
1698	*Barnard* (11th), Harry John Neville Vane, TD, *b.* 1923, *s.* 1964.	Hon. Henry F. C. *V.*, *b.* 1959
1887	*Basing* (5th), Neil Lutley Sclater-Booth, *b.* 1939, *s.* 1983, *m.*	Hon. Stuart W. *S.-B.*, *b.* 1969
1917	*Beaverbrook* (3rd), Maxwell William Humphrey Aitken, *b.* 1951, *s.* 1985, *m.*	Hon. Maxwell F. *A.*, *b.* 1977

Created	Title, order of succession, name, etc.	Heir
1647 s.	*Belhaven and Stenton* (13th), Robert Anthony Carmichael Hamilton, *b.* 1927, *s.* 1961, *m.*	Master of Belhaven, *b.* 1953
1848 i.	*Bellew* (7th), James Bryan Bellew, *b.* 1920, *s.* 1981, *m.*	Hon. Bryan E. *B.*, *b.* 1943
1856	*Belper* (4th), (Alexander) Ronald George Strutt, *b.* 1912, *s.* 1956.	Hon. Richard H. *S.*, *b.* 1941
1938	*Belstead* (2nd), John Julian Ganzoni, PC, *b.* 1932, *s.* 1958.	None
1421	*Berkeley* (18th), Anthony Fitzhardinge Gueterbock, OBE, *b.* 1939, *s.* 1992, *m.*	Hon. Thomas F. *G.*, *b.* 1969
1922	*Bethell* (4th), Nicholas William Bethell, *b.* 1938, *s.* 1967, *m.*	Hon. James N. *B.*, *b.* 1967
1938	*Bicester* (3rd), Angus Edward Vivian Smith, *b.* 1932, *s.* 1968.	Hugh C. V. *S.*, *b.* 1934
1903	*Biddulph* (5th), (Anthony) Nicholas Colin Maitland Biddulph, *b.* 1959, *s.* 1988, *m.*	Hon. William I. R. *M. B.*, *b.* 1963
1938	*Birdwood* (3rd), Mark William Ogilvie Birdwood, *b.* 1938, *s.* 1962, *m.*	None
1958	*Birkett* (2nd), Michael Birkett, *b.* 1929, *s.* 1962, *m.*	Hon. Thomas *B.*, *b.* 1982
1907	*Blyth* (4th), Anthony Audley Rupert Blyth, *b.* 1931, *s.* 1977, *m.*	Hon. Riley A. J. *B.*, *b.* 1955
1797	*Bolton* (7th), Richard William Algar Orde-Powlett, *b.* 1929, *s.* 1963, *m.*	Hon. Harry A. N. *O.-P.*, *b.* 1954
1452 s.	*Borthwick* (24th), John Hugh Borthwick, *b.* 1940, *s.* 1997, *m.*	Hon. James H. A. *B. of Glengelt*, *b.* 1940
1922	*Borwick* (4th), James Hugh Myles Borwick, MC, *b.* 1917, *s.* 1961, *m.*	Hon. Robin S. *B.*, *b.* 1927
1761	*Boston* (10th), Timothy George Frank Boteler Irby, *b.* 1939, *s.* 1978, *m.*	Hon. George W. E. B. *I.*, *b.* 1971
1942	*Brabazon of Tara* (3rd), Ivon Anthony Moore-Brabazon, *b.* 1946, *s.* 1974, *m.*	Hon. Benjamin R. *M.-B.*, *b.* 1983
1880	*Brabourne* (7th), John Ulick Knatchbull, CBE, *b.* 1924, *s.* 1943, *m.*	Lord Romsey, *b.* 1947 (*see* page 144)
1925	*Bradbury* (3rd), John Bradbury, *b.* 1940, *s.* 1994, *m.*	Hon. John *B.*, *b.* 1973
1962	*Brain* (2nd), Christopher Langdon Brain, *b.* 1926, *s.* 1966, *m.*	Hon. Michael C. *B.* DM, FRCP, *b.* 1928
1938	*Brassey of Apethorpe* (3rd), David Henry Brassey, OBE, *b.* 1932, *s.* 1967, *m.*	Hon. Edward *B.*, *b.* 1964
1788	*Braybrooke* (10th), Robin Henry Charles Neville, *b.* 1932, *s.* 1990, *m.*	George *N.*, *b.* 1943
1957	*Bridges* (2nd), Thomas Edward Bridges, GCMG, *b.* 1927, *s.* 1969, *m.*	Hon. Mark T. *B.*, *b.* 1954
1945	*Broadbridge* (3rd), Peter Hewett Broadbridge, *b.* 1938, *s.* 1972, *m.*	Martin H. *B.*, *b.* 1929
1933	*Brocket* (3rd), Charles Ronald George Nall-Cain, *b.* 1952, *s.* 1967, *m.*	Hon. Alexander C. C. *N.-C.*, *b.* 1984
1860	*Brougham and Vaux* (5th), Michael John Brougham, CBE, *b.* 1938, *s.* 1967.	Hon. Charles W. *B.*, *b.* 1971
1945	*Broughshane* (3rd), (William) Kensington Davison, DSO, DFC, *b.* 1914, *s.* 1995.	None
1776	*Brownlow* (7th), Edward John Peregrine Cust, *b.* 1936, *s.* 1978, *m.*	Hon. Peregrine E. Q. *C.*, *b.* 1974
1942	*Bruntisfield* (2nd), John Robert Warrender, OBE, MC, TD, *b.* 1921, *s.* 1993, *m.*	Hon. Michael J. V. *W.*, *b.* 1949
1950	*Burden* (3rd), Andrew Philip Burden, *b.* 1959, *s.* 1995.	Hon. Fraser W. E. *B.*, *b.* 1964
1529	*Burgh* (7th), Alexander Peter Willoughby Leith, *b.* 1935, *s.* 1959, *m.*	Hon. A. Gregory D. *L.*, *b.* 1958
1903	*Burnham* (6th), Hugh John Frederick Lawson, *b.* 1931, *s.* 1993, *m.*	Hon. Harry F. A. *L.*, *b.* 1968
1897	*Burton* (3rd), Michael Evan Victor Baillie, *b.* 1924, *s.* 1962, *m.*	Hon. Evan M. R. *B.*, *b.* 1949
1643	*Byron* (13th), Robert James Byron, *b.* 1950, *s.* 1989, *m.*	Hon. Charles R. G. *B.*, *b.* 1990
1937	*Cadman* (3rd), John Anthony Cadman, *b.* 1938, *s.* 1966, *m.*	Hon. Nicholas A. J. *C.*, *b.* 1977
1945	*Calverley* (3rd), Charles Rodney Muff, *b.* 1946, *s.* 1971, *m.*	Hon. Jonathan E. *M.*, *b.* 1975
1383	*Camoys* (7th), (Ralph) Thomas Campion George Sherman Stonor, GCVO, PC, *b.* 1940, *s.* 1976, *m. Lord Chamberlain*	Hon. R. William R. T. *S.*, *b.* 1974
1715 i.	*Carbery* (11th), Peter Ralfe Harrington Evans-Freke, *b.* 1920, *s.* 1970, *m.*	Hon. Michael P. *E.-F.*, *b.* 1942
1834 i.*	*Carew* (7th), Patrick Thomas Conolly-Carew (7th *UK Baron, Carew,* 1838), *b.* 1938, *s.* 1994, *m.*	Hon. William P. *C.-C.*, *b.* 1973
1916	*Carnock* (4th), David Henry Arthur Nicolson, *b.* 1920, *s.* 1982.	Nigel *N.* MBE, *b.* 1917
1796 i.*	*Carrington* (6th), Peter Alexander Rupert Carington, KG, GCMG, CH, MC, PC (6th *Brit. Baron Carrington,* 1797), *b.* 1919, *s.* 1938, *m.*	Hon. Rupert F. J. *C.*, *b.* 1948
1812 i.	*Castlemaine* (8th), Roland Thomas John Handcock, MBE, *b.* 1943, *s.* 1973, *m.*	Hon. Ronan M. E. *H.*, *b.* 1989
1936	*Catto* (2nd), Stephen Gordon Catto, *b.* 1923, *s.* 1959, *m.*	Hon. Innes G. *C.*, *b.* 1950
1918	*Cawley* (3rd), Frederick Lee Cawley, *b.* 1913, *s.* 1954, *m.*	Hon. John F. *C.*, *b.* 1946
1603	*Cecil.* A subsidiary title of the Marquess of Salisbury. His heir Viscount Cranborne, PC, was given a Writ in Acceleration in this title to enable him to sit in the House of Lords whilst his father is still alive (*see also* page 139)	
1937	*Chatfield* (2nd), Ernle David Lewis Chatfield, *b.* 1917, *s.* 1967, *m.*	None
1858	*Chesham* (6th), Nicholas Charles Cavendish, *b.* 1941, *s.* 1989, *m.*	Hon. Charles G. C. *C.*, *b.* 1974
1945	*Chetwode* (2nd), Philip Chetwode, *b.* 1937, *s.* 1950, *m.*	Hon. Roger *C.*, *b.* 1968
1945	*Chorley* (2nd), Roger Richard Edward Chorley, *b.* 1930, *s.* 1978, *m.*	Hon. Nicholas R. D. *C.*, *b.* 1966
1858	*Churston* (5th), John Francis Yarde-Buller, *b.* 1934, *s.* 1991, *m.*	Hon. Benjamin A. *Y.-B.*, *b.* 1974
1946	*Citrine* (2nd), Norman Arthur Citrine, *b.* 1914, *s.* 1983, *w.*	Hon. Ronald E. *C.*, *b.* 1919
1800 i.	*Clanmorris* (8th), Simon John Ward Bingham, *b.* 1937, *s.* 1988, *m.*	Robert D. de B. *B.*, *b.* 1942
1672	*Clifford of Chudleigh* (14th), Thomas Hugh Clifford, *b.* 1948, *s.* 1988, *m.*	Hon. Alexander T. H. *C.*, *b.* 1985
1299	*Clinton* (22nd), Gerard Nevile Mark Fane Trefusis, *b.* 1934, *title called out of abeyance* 1965, *m.*	Hon. Charles P. R. F. *T.*, *b.* 1962

Created	Title, order of succession, name, etc.	Heir
1955	*Clitheroe* (2nd), Ralph John Assheton, *b.* 1929, *s.* 1984, *m.*	Hon. Ralph C. *A.*, *b.* 1962
1919	*Clwyd* (3rd), (John) Anthony Roberts, *b.* 1935, *s.* 1987, *m.*	Hon. J. Murray *R.*, *b.* 1971
1948	*Clydesmuir* (3rd), David Ronald Colville, *b.* 1949, *s.* 1996, *m.*	Hon. Richard *C.*, *b.* 1980
1960	*Cobbold* (2nd), David Antony Fromanteel Lytton Cobbold, *b.* 1937, *s.* 1987, *m.*	Hon. Henry F. *L. C.*, *b.* 1962
1919	*Cochrane of Cults* (4th), (Ralph Henry) Vere Cochrane, *b.* 1926, *s.* 1990, *m.*	Hon. Thomas H. V. *C.*, *b.* 1957
1954	*Coleraine* (2nd), (James) Martin (Bonar) Law, *b.* 1931, *s.* 1980, *w.*	Hon. James P. B. *L.*, *b.* 1975
1873	*Coleridge* (5th), William Duke Coleridge, *b.* 1937, *s.* 1984, *m.*	Hon. James D. *C.*, *b.* 1967
1946	*Colgrain* (3rd), David Colin Campbell, *b.* 1920, *s.* 1973, *m.*	Hon. Alastair C. L. *C.*, *b.* 1951
1917	*Colwyn* (3rd), (Ian) Anthony Hamilton-Smith, CBE, *b.* 1942, *s.* 1966, *m.*	Hon. Craig P. *H.-S.*, *b.* 1968
1956	*Colyton* (2nd), Alisdair John Munro Hopkinson, *b.* 1958, *s.* 1996, *m.*	Hon. James P. M. *H.*, *b.* 1983
1841	*Congleton* (8th), Christopher Patrick Parnell, *b.* 1930, *s.* 1967, *m.*	Hon. John P. C. *P.*, *b.* 1959
1927	*Cornwallis* (3rd), Fiennes Neil Wykeham Cornwallis, OBE, *b.* 1921, *s.* 1982, *m.*	Hon. F. W. Jeremy *C.*, *b.* 1946
1874	*Cottesloe* (5th), Cdr. John Tapling Fremantle, *b.* 1927, *s.* 1994, *m.*	Hon. Thomas F. H. *F.*, *b.* 1966
1929	*Craigmyle* (4th), Thomas Columba Shaw, *b.* 1960, *s.* 1998, *m.*	Hon. Alexander F. *S.*, *b.* 1988
1899	*Cranworth* (3rd), Philip Bertram Gurdon, *b.* 1940, *s.* 1964, *m.*	Hon. Sacha W. R. *G.*, *b.* 1970
1959	*Crathorne* (2nd), Charles James Dugdale, *b.* 1939, *s.* 1977, *m.*	Hon. Thomas A. J. *D.*, *b.* 1977
1892	*Crawshaw* (5th), David Gerald Brooks, *b.* 1934, *s.* 1997, *m.*	Hon. John P. *B.*, *b.* 1938
1940	*Croft* (3rd), Bernard William Henry Page Croft, *b.* 1949, *s.* 1997, *w.*	None
1797 I.	*Crofton* (7th), Guy Patrick Gilbert Crofton, *b.* 1951, *s.* 1989, *m.*	Hon. E. Harry P. *C.*, *b.* 1988
1375	*Cromwell* (7th), Godfrey John Bewicke-Copley, *b.* 1960, *s.* 1982, *m.*	Hon. Thomas D. *B.-C.*, *b.* 1964
1947	*Crook* (2nd), Douglas Edwin Crook, *b.* 1926, *s.* 1989, *m.*	Hon. Robert D. E. *C.*, *b.* 1955
1920	*Cullen of Ashbourne* (2nd), Charles Borlase Marsham Cokayne, MBE, *b.* 1912, *s.* 1932, *w.*	Hon. Edmund W. M. *C.*, *b.* 1916
1914	*Cunliffe* (3rd), Roger Cunliffe, *b.* 1932, *s.* 1963, *m.*	Hon. Henry *C.*, *b.* 1962
1927	*Daresbury* (4th), Peter Gilbert Greenall, *b.* 1953, *s.* 1996, *m.*	Hon. Thomas E. *G.*, *b.* 1984
1924	*Darling* (2nd), Robert Charles Henry Darling, *b.* 1919, *s.* 1936, *m.*	Hon. R. Julian H. *D.*, *b.* 1944
1946	*Darwen* (3rd), Roger Michael Davies, *b.* 1938, *s.* 1988, *m.*	Hon. Paul *D.*, *b.* 1962
1932	*Davies* (3rd), David Davies, *b.* 1940, *s.* 1944, *m.*	Hon. David D. *D.*, *b.* 1975
1299	*de Clifford* (27th), John Edward Southwell Russell, *b.* 1928, *s.* 1982, *m.*	Hon. William S. *R.*, *b.* 1930
1851	*De Freyne* (7th), Francis Arthur John French, *b.* 1927, *s.* 1935, *m.*	Hon. Fulke C. A. J. *F.*, *b.* 1957
1838	*de Mauley* (6th), Gerald John Ponsonby, *b.* 1921, *s.* 1962, *m.*	Hon. Col. Thomas M. *P.* TD, *b.* 1930
1887	*De Ramsey* (4th), John Ailwyn Fellowes, *b.* 1942, *s.* 1993, *m.*	Hon. Freddie J. *F.*, *b.* 1978
1264	*de Ros* (28th), Peter Trevor Maxwell, *b.* 1958, *s.* 1983, *m. Premier Baron of England*	Hon. Finbar J. *M.*, *b.* 1988
1831	*de Saumarez* (7th), Eric Douglas Saumarez, *b.* 1956, *s.* 1991, *m.*	Hon. Victor T. *S.*, *b.* 1956
1910	*de Villiers* (3rd), Arthur Percy de Villiers, *b.* 1911, *s.* 1934.	Hon. Alexander C. *de V.*, *b.* 1940
1812 I.	*Decies* (7th), Marcus Hugh Tristram de la Poer Beresford, *b.* 1948, *s.* 1992, *m.*	Hon. Robert M. D. *de la P. B.*, *b.* 1988
1821	*Delamere* (5th), Hugh George Cholmondeley, *b.* 1934, *s.* 1979, *m.*	Hon. Thomas P. G. *C.*, *b.* 1968
1937	*Denham* (2nd), Bertram Stanley Mitford Bowyer, KBE, PC, *b.* 1927, *s.* 1948, *m.*	Hon. Richard G. G. *B.*, *b.* 1959
1834	*Denman* (5th), Charles Spencer Denman, CBE, MC, TD, *b.* 1916, *s.* 1971, *w.*	Hon. Richard T. S. *D.*, *b.* 1946
1885	*Deramore* (6th), Richard Arthur de Yarburgh-Bateson, *b.* 1911, *s.* 1964, *m.*	None
1881	*Derwent* (5th), Robin Evelyn Leo Vanden-Bempde-Johnstone, LVO, *b.* 1930, *s.* 1986, *m.*	Hon. Francis P. H. *V.-B.-J.*, *b.* 1965
1930	*Dickinson* (2nd), Richard Clavering Hyett Dickinson, *b.* 1926, *s.* 1943, *m.*	Hon. Martin H. *D.*, *b.* 1961
1620 I.*	*Digby* (12th), Edward Henry Kenelm Digby (6th *Brit. Baron Digby*, 1765), *b.* 1924, *s.* 1964, *m.*	Hon. Henry N. K. *D.*, *b.* 1954
1615	*Dormer* (17th), Geoffrey Henry Dormer, *b.* 1920, *s.* 1995, *m.*	Hon. William R. *D.*, *b.* 1960
1943	*Dowding* (3rd), Piers Hugh Tremenheere Dowding, *b.* 1948, *s.* 1992.	Hon. Mark D. J. *D.*, *b.* 1949
1800 I.	*Dufferin and Clandeboye.* The 10th Baron died in 1991. Heir had not established his claim to the title at the time of going to press	Sir John Blackwood, Bt., *b.* 1944
1929	*Dulverton* (3rd), (Gilbert) Michael Hamilton Wills, *b.* 1944, *s.* 1992, *m.*	Hon. Robert A. H. *W.*, *b.* 1983
1800 I.	*Dunalley* (7th), Henry Francis Cornelius Prittie, *b.* 1948, *s.* 1992, *m.*	Hon. Joel H. *P.*, *b.* 1981
1324 I.	*Dunboyne* (28th), Patrick Theobald Tower Butler, VRD, *b.* 1917, *s.* 1945, *m.*	Hon. John F. *B.*, *b.* 1951
1892	*Dunleath* (6th), Brian Henry Mulholland, *b.* 1950, *s.* 1997, *m.*	Hon. Andrew H. *M.*, *b.* 1981
1439 I.	*Dunsany* (19th), Randal Arthur Henry Plunkett, *b.* 1906, *s.* 1957, *m.*	Hon. Edward J. C. *P.*, *b.* 1939
1780	*Dynevor* (9th), Richard Charles Uryan Rhys, *b.* 1935, *s.* 1962.	Hon. Hugo G. U. *R.*, *b.* 1966
1857	*Ebury* (6th), Francis Egerton Grosvenor, *b.* 1934, *s.* 1957, *m.*	Hon. Julian F. M. *G.*, *b.* 1959
1963	*Egremont* (2nd) and *Leconfield* (7th) (1859), John Max Henry Scawen Wyndham, *b.* 1948, *s.* 1972, *m.*	Hon. George R. V. *W.*, *b.* 1983
1643	*Elibank* (14th), Alan D'Ardis Erskine-Murray, *b.* 1923, *s.* 1973, *w.*	Master of Elibank, *b.* 1964

Created	Title, order of succession, name, etc.	Heir
1802	*Ellenborough* (8th), Richard Edward Cecil Law, *b.* 1926, *s.* 1945, *m.*	Maj. Hon. Rupert E. H. *L.*, *b.* 1955
1509 s.*	*Elphinstone* (19th), Alexander Mountstuart Elphinstone (5th *UK Baron, Elphinstone*, 1885), *b.* 1980, *s.* 1994, *M.*	Hon. Angus J. *E.*, *b.* 1982
1934	*Elton* (2nd), Rodney Elton, TD, *b.* 1930, *s.* 1973, *m.*	Hon. Edward P. *E.*, *b.* 1966
1964	*Erroll of Hale* (1st), Frederick James Erroll, TD, PC, *b.* 1914, *m.*	None
1627 s.	*Fairfax of Cameron* (14th), Nicholas John Albert Fairfax, *b.* 1956, *s.* 1964, *m.*	Hon. Edward N. T. *F.*, *b.* 1984
1961	*Fairhaven* (3rd), Ailwyn Henry George Broughton, *b.* 1936, *s.* 1973, *m.*	Maj. Hon. James H. A. *B.*, *b.* 1963
1916	*Faringdon* (3rd), Charles Michael Henderson, *b.* 1937, *s.* 1977, *m.*	Hon. James H. *H.*, *b.* 1961
1756 I.	*Farnham* (12th), Barry Owen Somerset Maxwell, *b.* 1931, *s.* 1957, *m.*	Hon. Simon K. *M.*, *b.* 1933
1856 I.	*Fermoy* (6th), Patrick Maurice Burke Roche, *b.* 1967, *s.* 1984, *m.*	Hon. E. Hugh B. *R.*, *b.* 1972
1826	*Feversham* (6th), Charles Antony Peter Duncombe, *b.* 1945, *s.* 1963, *m.*	Hon. Jasper O. S. *D.*, *b.* 1968
1798 I.	*ffrench* (8th), Robuck John Peter Charles Mario ffrench, *b.* 1956, *s.* 1986, *m.*	Hon. John C. M. J. F. *ff.*, *b.* 1928
1909	*Fisher* (3rd), John Vavasseur Fisher, DSC, *b.* 1921, *s.* 1955, *m.*	Hon. Patrick V. *F.*, *b.* 1953
1295	*Fitzwalter* (21st), (Fitzwalter) Brook Plumptre, *b.* 1914, *title called out of abeyance* 1953, *m.*	Hon. Julian B. *P.*, *b.* 1952
1776	*Foley* (8th), Adrian Gerald Foley, *b.* 1923, *s.* 1927, *m.*	Hon. Thomas H. *F.*, *b.* 1961
1445 s.	*Forbes* (22nd), Nigel Ivan Forbes, KBE, *b.* 1918, *s.* 1953, *m. Premier Lord of Scotland*	Master of Forbes, *b.* 1946
1821	*Forester* (8th), (George Cecil) Brooke Weld-Forester, *b.* 1938, *s.* 1977, *m.*	Hon. C. R. George *W.-F.*, *b.* 1975
1922	*Forres* (4th), Alastair Stephen Grant Williamson, *b.* 1946, *s.* 1978, *m.*	Hon. George A. M. *W.*, *b.* 1972
1917	*Forteviot* (4th), John James Evelyn Dewar, *b.* 1938, *s.* 1993, *m.*	Hon. Alexander J. E. *D.*, *b.* 1971
1951	*Freyberg* (3rd), Valerian Bernard Freyberg, *b.* 1970, *s.* 1993.	None
1917	*Gainford* (3rd), Joseph Edward Pease, *b.* 1921, *s.* 1971, *m.*	Hon. George *P.*, *b.* 1926
1818 I.	*Garvagh* (5th), (Alexander Leopold Ivor) George Canning, *b.* 1920, *s.* 1956, *m.*	Hon. Spencer G. S. de R. *C.*, *b.* 1953
1942	*Geddes* (3rd), Euan Michael Ross Geddes, *b.* 1937, *s.* 1975, *m.*	Hon. James G. N. *G.*, *b.* 1969
1876	*Gerard* (5th), Anthony Robert Hugo Gerard, *b.* 1949, *s.* 1992, *m.*	Hon. Rupert B. C. *G.*, *b.* 1981
1824	*Gifford* (6th), Anthony Maurice Gifford, QC, *b.* 1940, *s.* 1961, *m.*	Hon. Thomas A. *G.*, *b.* 1967
1917	*Gisborough* (3rd), Thomas Richard John Long Chaloner, *b.* 1927, *s.* 1951, *m.*	Hon. T. Peregrine L. *C.*, *b.* 1961
1960	*Gladwyn* (2nd), Miles Alvery Gladwyn Jebb, *b.* 1930, *s.* 1996.	None
1899	*Glanusk* (5th), Christopher Russell Bailey, *b.* 1942, *s.* 1997, *m.*	Hon. Charles H. *B.*, *b.* 1976
1918	*Glenarthur* (4th), Simon Mark Arthur, *b.* 1944, *s.* 1976, *m.*	Hon. Edward A. *A.*, *b.* 1973
1911	*Glenconner* (3rd), Colin Christopher Paget Tennant, *b.* 1926, *s.* 1983, *m.*	Hon. Cody *T.*, *b.* 1994
1964	*Glendevon* (2nd), Julian John Somerset Hope, *b.* 1950, *s.* 1996.	Hon. Jonathan C. *H.*, *b.* 1952
1922	*Glendyne* (3rd), Robert Nivison, *b.* 1926, *s.* 1967, *m.*	Hon. John *N.*, *b.* 1960
1939	*Glentoran* (3rd), (Thomas) Robin (Valerian) Dixon, CBE, *b.* 1935, *s.* 1995, *m.*	Hon. Daniel G. *D.*, *b.* 1959
1909	*Gorell* (4th), Timothy John Radcliffe Barnes, *b.* 1927, *s.* 1963, *m.*	Hon. Ronald A. H. *B.*, *b.* 1931
1953	*Grantchester* (3rd), Christopher John Suenson-Taylor, *b.* 1951, *s.* 1995, *m.*	Hon. Jesse D. *S.-T.*, *b.* 1977
1782	*Grantley* (8th), Richard William Brinsley Norton, *b.* 1956, *s.* 1995.	Hon. Francis J. H. *N.*, *b.* 1960
1794 I.	*Graves* (9th), Evelyn Paget Graves, *b.* 1926, *s.* 1994, *m.*	Hon. Timothy E. *G.*, *b.* 1960
1445 s.	*Gray* (22nd), Angus Diarmid Ian Campbell-Gray, *b.* 1931, *s.* 1946, *m.*	Master of Gray, *b.* 1964
1950	*Greenhill* (3rd), Malcolm Greenhill, *b.* 1924, *s.* 1989.	None
1927	*Greenway* (4th), Ambrose Charles Drexel Greenway, *b.* 1941, *s.* 1975, *m.*	Hon. Mervyn S. K. *G.*, *b.* 1942
1902	*Grenfell* (3rd), Julian Pascoe Francis St Leger Grenfell, *b.* 1935, *s.* 1976, *m.*	Francis P. J. *G.*, *b.* 1938
1944	*Gretton* (4th), John Lysander Gretton, *b.* 1975, *s.* 1989.	None
1397	*Grey of Codnor* (6th), Richard Henry Cornwall-Legh, *b.* 1936, *s.* 1996, *m.*	Hon. Richard S. C. *C.-L.*, *b.* 1976
1955	*Gridley* (3rd), Richard David Arnold Gridley, *b.* 1956, *s.* 1996, *m.*	Hon. Carl R. *G.*, *b.* 1981
1964	*Grimston of Westbury* (2nd), Robert Walter Sigismund Grimston, *b.* 1925, *s.* 1979, *m.*	Hon. Robert J. S. *G.*, *b.* 1951
1886	*Grimthorpe* (4th), Christopher John Beckett, OBE, *b.* 1915, *s.* 1963, *m.*	Hon. Edward J. *B.*, *b.* 1954
1945	*Hacking* (3rd), Douglas David Hacking, *b.* 1938, *s.* 1971, *m.*	Hon. Douglas F. *H.*, *b.* 1968
1950	*Haden-Guest* (5th), Christopher Haden-Guest, *b.* 1948, *s.* 1996, *m.*	Hon. Nicholas *H.-G.*, *b.* 1951
1886	*Hamilton of Dalzell* (4th), James Leslie Hamilton, *b.* 1938, *s.* 1990, *m.*	Hon. Gavin G. *H.*, *b.* 1968
1874	*Hampton* (6th), Richard Humphrey Russell Pakington, *b.* 1925, *s.* 1974, *m.*	Hon. John H. A. *P.*, *b.* 1964
1939	*Hankey* (3rd), Donald Robin Alers Hankey, *b.* 1938, *s.* 1996, *m.*	Hon. Alexander M. A. *H.*, *b.* 1947
1958	*Harding of Petherton* (2nd), John Charles Harding, *b.* 1928, *s.* 1989, *m.*	Hon. William A. J. *H.*, *b.* 1969
1910	*Hardinge of Penshurst* (4th), Julian Alexander Hardinge, *b.* 1945, *s.* 1997.	Hon. Hugh F. *H.*, *b.* 1948
1876	*Harlech* (6th), Francis David Ormsby-Gore, *b.* 1954, *s.* 1985, *m.*	Hon. Jasset D. C. *O.-G.*, *b.* 1986
1939	*Harmsworth* (3rd), Thomas Harold Raymond Harmsworth, *b.* 1939, *s.* 1990, *m.*	Hon. Dominic M. E. *H.*, *b.* 1973

Created	Title, order of succession, name, etc.	Heir
1815	*Harris* (8th), Anthony Harris, *b.* 1942, *s.* 1996, *m.*	Ronald G. T. *H.*, *b.* 1911
1954	*Harvey of Tasburgh* (2nd), Peter Charles Oliver Harvey, *b.* 1921, *s.* 1968, *w.*	Charles J. G. *H.*, *b.* 1951
1295	*Hastings* (22nd), Edward Delaval Henry Astley, *b.* 1912, *s.* 1956, *m.*	Hon. Delaval T. H. *A.*, *b.* 1960
1835	*Hatherton* (8th), Edward Charles Littleton, *b.* 1950, *s.* 1985, *m.*	Hon. Thomas E. *L.*, *b.* 1977
1776	*Hawke* (11th), Edward George Hawke, TD, *b.* 1950, *s.* 1992, *m.*	None
1927	*Hayter* (3rd), George Charles Hayter Chubb, KCVO, CBE, *b.* 1911, *s.* 1967, *m.*	Hon. G. William M. *C.*, *b.* 1943
1945	*Hazlerigg* (2nd), Arthur Grey Hazlerigg, MC, TD, *b.* 1910, *s.* 1949, *w.*	Hon. Arthur G. *H.*, *b.* 1951
1943	*Hemingford* (3rd), (Dennis) Nicholas Herbert, *b.* 1934, *s.* 1982, *m.*	Hon. Christopher D. C. *H.*, *b.* 1973
1906	*Hemphill* (5th), Peter Patrick Fitzroy Martyn Martyn-Hemphill, *b.* 1928, *s.* 1957, *m.*	Hon. Charles A. M. *M.-H.*, *b.* 1954
1799 I.*	*Henley* (8th), Oliver Michael Robert Eden (6th *UK Baron Northington*, 1885), *b.* 1953, *s.* 1977, *m.*	Hon. John W. O. *E.*, *b.* 1988
1800 I.*	*Henniker* (8th), John Patrick Edward Chandos Henniker-Major, KCMG, CVO, MC (4th *UK Baron Hartismere*, 1866), *b.* 1916, *s.* 1980, *m.*	Hon. Mark I. P. C. *H.-M.*, *b.* 1947
1886	*Herschell* (3rd), Rognvald Richard Farrer Herschell, *b.* 1923, *s.* 1929, *m.*	None
1935	*Hesketh* (3rd), Thomas Alexander Fermor-Hesketh, KBE, PC, *b.* 1950, *s.* 1955, *m.*	Hon. Frederick H. *F.-H.*, *b.* 1988
1828	*Heytesbury* (6th), Francis William Holmes à Court, *b.* 1931, *s.* 1971, *m.*	Hon. James W. H. *à. C.*, *b.* 1967
1886	*Hindlip* (6th), Charles Henry Allsopp, *b.* 1940, *s.* 1993, *m.*	Hon. Henry W. *A.*, *b.* 1973
1950	*Hives* (3rd), Matthew Peter Hives, *b.* 1971, *s.* 1997.	Hon. Michael B. *H.*, *b.* 1926
1912	*Hollenden* (3rd), Gordon Hope Hope-Morley, *b.* 1914, *s.* 1977, *m.*	Hon. Ian H. *H.-M.*, *b.* 1946
1897	*HolmPatrick* (4th), Hans James David Hamilton, *b.* 1955, *s.* 1991, *m.*	Hon. Ion H. J. *H.*, *b.* 1956
1797 I.	*Hotham* (8th), Henry Durand Hotham, *b.* 1940, *s.* 1967, *m.*	Hon. William B. *H.*, *b.* 1972
1881	*Hothfield* (6th), Anthony Charles Sackville Tufton, *b.* 1939, *s.* 1991, *m.*	Hon. William S. *T.*, *b.* 1977
1597	*Howard de Walden* (9th), John Osmael Scott-Ellis, TD (5th *UK Baron Seaford*, 1826), *b.* 1912, *s.* 1946, *m.*	To Barony of Howard de Walden, four co-heiresses. To Barony of Seaford, Colin H. F. *Ellis*, *b.* 1946
1930	*Howard of Penrith* (2nd), Francis Philip Howard, *b.* 1905, *s.* 1939, *m.*	Hon. Philip E. *H.*, *b.* 1945
1960	*Howick of Glendale* (2nd), Charles Evelyn Baring, *b.* 1937, *s.* 1973, *m.*	Hon. David E. C. *B.*, *b.* 1975
1796 I.	*Huntingfield* (7th), Joshua Charles Vanneck, *b.* 1954, *s.* 1994, *m.*	Hon. Gerard C. A. *V.*, *b.* 1985
1866	*Hylton* (5th), Raymond Hervey Jolliffe, *b.* 1932, *s.* 1967, *m.*	Hon. William H. M. *J.*, *b.* 1967
1933	*Iliffe* (3rd), Robert Peter Richard Iliffe, *b.* 1944, *s.* 1996, *m.*	Hon. Edward R. *I.*, *b.* 1968
1543 I.	*Inchiquin* (18th), Conor Myles John O'Brien, *b.* 1943, *s.* 1982, *m.*	Murrough R. *O.*, *b.* 1910
1962	*Inchyra* (2nd), Robert Charles Reneke Hoyer Millar, *b.* 1935, *s.* 1989, *m.*	Hon. C. James C. H. *M.*, *b.* 1962
1964	*Inglewood* (2nd), (William) Richard Fletcher-Vane, *b.* 1951, *s.* 1989, *m.*	Hon. Henry W. F. *F.-V.*, *b.* 1990
1919	*Inverforth* (4th), Andrew Peter Weir, *b.* 1966, *s.* 1982.	Hon. John V. *W.*, *b.* 1935
1941	*Ironside* (2nd), Edmund Oslac Ironside, *b.* 1924, *s.* 1959, *m.*	Hon. Charles E. G. *I.*, *b.* 1956
1952	*Jeffreys* (3rd), Christopher Henry Mark Jeffreys, *b.* 1957, *s.* 1986, *m.*	Hon. Arthur M. H. *J.*, *b.* 1989
1906	*Joicey* (5th), James Michael Joicey, *b.* 1953, *s.* 1993, *m.*	Hon. William J. *J.*, *b.* 1990
1937	*Kenilworth* (4th), (John) Randle Siddeley, *b.* 1954, *s.* 1981, *m.*	Hon. William R. J. *S.*, *b.* 1992
1935	*Kennet* (2nd), Wayland Hilton Young, *b.* 1923, *s.* 1960, *m.*	Hon. W. A. Thoby *Y.*, *b.* 1957
1776 I.*	*Kensington* (8th), Hugh Ivor Edwardes (5th *UK Baron Kensington*, 1886), *b.* 1933, *s.* 1981, *m.*	Hon. W. Owen A. *E.*, *b.* 1964
1951	*Kenswood* (2nd), John Michael Howard Whitfield, *b.* 1930, *s.* 1963, *m.*	Hon. Michael C. *W.*, *b.* 1955
1788	*Kenyon* (6th), Lloyd Tyrell-Kenyon, *b.* 1947, *s.* 1993, *m.*	Hon. Lloyd N. *T.-K.*, *b.* 1972
1947	*Kershaw* (4th), Edward John Kershaw, *b.* 1936, *s.* 1962, *m.*	Hon. John C. E. *K.*, *b.* 1971
1943	*Keyes* (2nd), Roger George Bowlby Keyes, *b.* 1919, *s.* 1945, *m.*	Hon. Charles W. P. *K.*, *b.* 1951
1909	*Kilbracken* (3rd), John Raymond Godley, DSC, *b.* 1920, *s.* 1950.	Hon. Christopher J. *G.*, *b.* 1945
1900	*Killanin* (3rd), Michael Morris, MBE, TD, *b.* 1914, *s.* 1927, *m.*	Hon. G. Redmond F. *M.*, *b.* 1947
1943	*Killearn* (3rd), Victor Miles George Aldous Lampson, *b.* 1941, *s.* 1996, *m.*	Hon. Miles H. M. *L.*, *b.* 1977
1789 I.	*Kilmaine* (7th), John David Henry Browne, *b.* 1948, *s.* 1978, *m.*	Hon. John F. S. *B.*, *b.* 1983
1831	*Kilmarnock* (7th), Alastair Ivor Gilbert Boyd, *b.* 1927, *s.* 1975, *m.*	Hon. Robin J. *B.*, *b.* 1941
1941	*Kindersley* (3rd), Robert Hugh Molesworth Kindersley, *b.* 1929, *s.* 1976, *m.*	Hon. Rupert J. M. *K.*, *b.* 1955
1223 I.	*Kingsale* (35th), John de Courcy, *b.* 1941, *s.* 1969. *Premier Baron of Ireland*	Nevinson R. *de C.*, *b.* 1920
1902	*Kinross* (5th), Christopher Patrick Balfour, *b.* 1949, *s.* 1985, *m.*	Hon. Alan I. *B.*, *b.* 1978
1951	*Kirkwood* (3rd), David Harvie Kirkwood, PH.D., *b.* 1931, *s.* 1970, *m.*	Hon. James S. *K.*, *b.* 1937
1800 I.	*Langford* (9th), Col. Geoffrey Alexander Rowley-Conwy, OBE, *b.* 1912, *s.* 1953, *m.*	Hon. Owain G. *R.-C.*, *b.* 1958
1942	*Latham* (2nd), Dominic Charles Latham, *b.* 1954, *s.* 1970.	Anthony M. *L.*, *b.* 1954
1431	*Latymer* (8th), Hugo Nevill Money-Coutts, *b.* 1926, *s.* 1987, *m.*	Hon. Crispin J. A. N. *M.-C.*, *b.* 1955
1869	*Lawrence* (5th), David John Downer Lawrence, *b.* 1937, *s.* 1968.	None
1947	*Layton* (3rd), Geoffrey Michael Layton, *b.* 1947, *s.* 1989, *m.*	Hon. David *L.* MBE, *b.* 1914
1839	*Leigh* (5th), John Piers Leigh, *b.* 1935, *s.* 1979, *m.*	Hon. Christopher D. P. *L.*, *b.* 1960

Created	Title, order of succession, name, etc.	Heir
1962	*Leighton of St Mellons* (2nd), (John) Leighton Seager, *b.* 1922, *s.* 1963, *m.*	Hon. Robert W. H. L. S., *b.* 1955
1797	*Lilford* (7th), George Vernon Powys, *b.* 1931, *s.* 1949, *m.*	Hon. Mark V. P., *b.* 1975
1945	*Lindsay of Birker* (3rd), James Francis Lindsay, *b.* 1945, *s.* 1994, *m.*	Alexander S. L., *b.* 1940
1758 I.	*Lisle* (8th), Patrick James Lysaght, *b.* 1931, *s.* 1998.	Hon. John N. G. L., *b.* 1960
1850	*Londesborough* (9th), Richard John Denison, *b.* 1959, *s.* 1968, *m.*	Hon. James F. D., *b.* 1990
1541 I.	*Louth* (16th), Otway Michael James Oliver Plunkett, *b.* 1929, *s.* 1950, *m.*	Hon. Jonathan O. P., *b.* 1952
1458 S.*	*Lovat* (16th), Simon Fraser (5th *UK Baron, Lovat,* 1837), *b.* 1977, *s.* 1995	Hon. Jack F., *b.* 1984
1663	*Lucas* (11th) and *Dingwall* (8th) (s. 1609), Ralph Matthew Palmer, *b.* 1951, *s.* 1991, *m.*	Hon. Lewis E. P., *b.* 1987
1946	*Lucas of Chilworth* (2nd), Michael William George Lucas, *b.* 1926, *s.* 1967, *m.*	Hon. Simon W. L., *b.* 1957
1929	*Luke* (3rd), Arthur Charles St John Lawson-Johnston, *b.* 1933, *s.* 1996, *m.*	Hon. Ian J. St J. L.-J., *b.* 1963
1914	*Lyell* (3rd), Charles Lyell, *b.* 1939, *s.* 1943.	None
1859	*Lyveden* (6th), Ronald Cecil Vernon, *b.* 1915, *s.* 1973, *m.*	Hon. Jack L. V., *b.* 1938
1959	*MacAndrew* (3rd), Christopher Anthony Colin MacAndrew, *b.* 1945, *s.* 1989, *m.*	Hon. Oliver C. J. M., *b.* 1983
1776 I.	*Macdonald* (8th), Godfrey James Macdonald of Macdonald, *b.* 1947, *s.* 1970, *m.*	Hon. Godfrey E. H. T. M., *b.* 1982
1949	*Macdonald of Gwaenysgor* (2nd), Gordon Ramsay Macdonald, *b.* 1915, *s.* 1966, *m.*	None
1937	*McGowan* (3rd), Harry Duncan Cory McGowan, *b.* 1938, *s.* 1966, *m.*	Hon. Harry J. C. M., *b.* 1971
1922	*Maclay* (3rd), Joseph Paton Maclay, *b.* 1942, *s.* 1969, *m.*	Hon. Joseph P. M., *b.* 1977
1955	*McNair* (3rd), Duncan James McNair, *b.* 1947, *s.* 1989, *m.*	Hon. Thomas J. M., *b.* 1990
1951	*Macpherson of Drumochter* (2nd), (James) Gordon Macpherson, *b.* 1924, *s.* 1965, *m.*	Hon. James A. M., *b.* 1979
1937	*Mancroft* (3rd), Benjamin Lloyd Stormont Mancroft, *b.* 1957, *s.* 1987, *m.*	None
1807	*Manners* (5th), John Robert Cecil Manners, *b.* 1923, *s.* 1972, *m.*	Hon. John H. R. M., *b.* 1956
1922	*Manton* (3rd), Joseph Rupert Eric Robert Watson, *b.* 1924, *s.* 1968, *m.*	Maj. Hon. Miles R. M. W., *b.* 1958
1908	*Marchamley* (4th), William Francis Whiteley, *b.* 1968, *s.* 1994.	None
1964	*Margadale* (2nd), James Ian Morrison, TD, *b.* 1930, *s.* 1996, *m.*	Hon. Alastair J. M., *b.* 1958
1961	*Marks of Broughton* (2nd), Michael Marks, *b.* 1920, *s.* 1964, *m.*	Hon. Simon R. M., *b.* 1950
1964	*Martonmere* (2nd), John Stephen Robinson, *b.* 1963, *s.* 1989.	David A. R., *b.* 1965
1776 I.	*Massy* (9th), Hugh Hamon John Somerset Massy, *b.* 1921, *s.* 1958, *m.*	Hon. David H. S. M., *b.* 1947
1935	*May* (3rd), Michael St John May, *b.* 1931, *s.* 1950, *m.*	Hon. Jasper B. St J. M., *b.* 1965
1928	*Melchett* (4th), Peter Robert Henry Mond, *b.* 1948, *s.* 1973.	None
1925	*Merrivale* (3rd), Jack Henry Edmond Duke, *b.* 1917, *s.* 1951, *m.*	Hon. Derek J. P. D., *b.* 1948
1911	*Merthyr.* Disclaimed for life 1977. (*Trevor Oswin Lewis, Bt,* CBE, *b.*1935, *s.*1977, *m.*)	David T. L., *b.* 1977
1919	*Meston* (3rd), James Meston, *b.* 1950, *s.* 1984, *m.*	Hon. Thomas J. D. M., *b.* 1977
1838	*Methuen* (7th), Robert Alexander Holt Methuen, *b.* 1931, *s.* 1994, *m.*	Christopher P. M. C. Methuen-Campbell., *b.* 1928
1711	*Middleton* (12th), (Digby) Michael Godfrey John Willoughby, MC, *b.* 1921, *s.* 1970, *m.*	Hon. Michael C. J. W., *b.* 1948
1939	*Milford* (3rd), Hugo John Laurence Philipps, *b.* 1929, *s.* 1993, *m.*	Hon. Guy W. P., *b.* 1961
1933	*Milne* (2nd), George Douglass Milne, TD, *b.* 1909, *s.* 1948, *m.*	Hon. George A. M., *b.* 1941
1951	*Milner of Leeds* (2nd), Arthur James Michael Milner, AE, *b.* 1923, *s.* 1967, *m.*	Hon. Richard J. M., *b.* 1959
1947	*Milverton* (2nd), Revd Fraser Arthur Richard Richards, *b.* 1930, *s.* 1978, *m.*	Hon. Michael H. R., *b.* 1936
1873	*Moncreiff* (5th), Harry Robert Wellwood Moncreiff, *b.* 1915, *s.* 1942, *w.*	Hon. Rhoderick H. W. M., *b.* 1954
1884	*Monk Bretton* (3rd), John Charles Dodson, *b.* 1924, *s.* 1933, *m.*	Hon. Christopher M. D., *b.* 1958
1885	*Monkswell* (5th), Gerard Collier, *b.* 1947, *s.* 1984, *m.*	Hon. James A. C., *b.* 1977
1728	*Monson* (11th), John Monson, *b.* 1932, *s.* 1958, *m.*	Hon. Nicholas J. M., *b.* 1955
1885	*Montagu of Beaulieu* (3rd), Edward John Barrington Douglas-Scott-Montagu, *b.* 1926, *s.* 1929, *m.*	Hon. Ralph D.-S.-M., *b.* 1961
1839	*Monteagle of Brandon* (6th), Gerald Spring Rice, *b.* 1926, *s.* 1946, *m.*	Hon. Charles J. S. R., *b.* 1953
1943	*Moran* (2nd), (Richard) John (McMoran) Wilson, KCMG, *b.* 1924, *s.* 1977, *m.*	Hon. James M. W., *b.* 1952
1918	*Morris* (3rd), Michael David Morris, *b.* 1937, *s.* 1975, *m.*	Hon. Thomas A. S. M., *b.* 1982
1950	*Morris of Kenwood* (2nd), Philip Geoffrey Morris, *b.* 1928, *s.* 1954, *m.*	Hon. Jonathan D. M., *b.* 1968
1831	*Mostyn* (5th), Roger Edward Lloyd Lloyd-Mostyn, MC, *b.* 1920, *s.* 1965, *m.*	Hon. Llewellyn R. L. L.-M., *b.* 1948
1933	*Mottistone* (4th), David Peter Seely, CBE, *b.* 1920, *s.* 1966, *m.*	Hon. Peter J. P. S., *b.* 1949
1945	*Mountevans* (3rd), Edward Patrick Broke Evans, *b.* 1943, *s.* 1974, *m.*	Hon. Jeffrey de C. R. E., *b.* 1948
1283	*Mowbray* (26th), *Segrave* (27th) (1283) and *Stourton* (23rd) (1448), Charles Edward Stourton, CBE, *b.* 1923, *s.* 1965, *w.*	Hon. Edward W. S. S., *b.* 1953

Created	Title, order of succession, name, etc.	Heir
1932	*Moyne* (3rd), Jonathan Bryan Guinness, *b.* 1930, *s.* 1992, *m.*	Hon. Jasper J. R. G., *b.* 1954
1929	*Moynihan* (4th), Colin Berkeley Moynihan, *b.* 1955, *s.* 1997, *m.*	Hon. Nicholas E. B. M., *b.* 1994
1781 I.	*Muskerry* (9th), Robert Fitzmaurice Deane, *b.* 1948, *s.* 1988, *m.*	Hon. Jonathan F. D., *b.* 1986
1627 s.	*Napier* (14th) and *Ettrick* (5th) (*UK* 1872), Francis Nigel Napier, KCVO, *b.* 1930, *s.* 1954, *m.*	Master of Napier, *b.* 1962
1868	*Napier of Magdala* (6th), Robert Alan Napier, *b.* 1940, *s.* 1987, *m.*	Hon. James R. N., *b.* 1966
1940	*Nathan* (2nd), Roger Carol Michael Nathan, *b.* 1922, *s.* 1963, *m.*	Hon. Rupert H. B. N., *b.* 1957
1960	*Nelson of Stafford* (3rd), Henry Roy George Nelson, *b.* 1943, *s.* 1995, *m.*	Hon. Alistair W. H. N., *b.* 1973
1959	*Netherthorpe* (3rd), James Frederick Turner, *b.* 1964, *s.* 1982, *m.*	Hon. Andrew J. E. T., *b.* 1993
1946	*Newall* (2nd), Francis Storer Eaton Newall, *b.* 1930, *s.* 1963, *m.*	Hon. Richard H. E. N., *b.* 1961
1776 I.	*Newborough* (7th), Robert Charles Michael Vaughan Wynn, DSC, *b.* 1917, *s.* 1965, *m.*	Hon. Robert V. W., *b.* 1949
1892	*Newton* (5th), Richard Thomas Legh, *b.* 1950, *s.* 1992, *m.*	Hon. Piers R. L., *b.* 1979
1930	*Noel-Buxton* (3rd), Martin Connal Noel-Buxton, *b.* 1940, *s.* 1980, *m.*	Hon. Charles C. N.-B., *b.* 1975
1957	*Norrie* (2nd), (George) Willoughby Moke Norrie, *b.* 1936, *s.* 1977, *m.*	Hon. Mark W. J. N., *b.* 1972
1884	*Northbourne* (5th), Christopher George Walter James, *b.* 1926, *s.* 1982, *m.*	Hon. Charles W. H. J., *b.* 1960
1866	*Northbrook* (6th), Francis Thomas Baring, *b.* 1954, *s.* 1990, *m.*	None
1878	*Norton* (8th), James Nigel Arden Adderley, *b.* 1947, *s.* 1993, *m.*	Hon. Edward J. A. A., *b.* 1982
1906	*Nunburnholme* (5th), Charles Thomas Wilson, *b.* 1935, *s.* 1998.	Hon. Stephen C. W., *b.* 1973
	Oaksey. See *Trevethin and Oaksey*	
1950	*Ogmore* (2nd), Gwilym Rees Rees-Williams, *b.* 1931, *s.* 1976, *m.*	Hon. Morgan R.-W., *b.* 1937
1870	*O'Hagan* (4th), Charles Towneley Strachey, *b.* 1945, *s.* 1961.	Hon. Richard T. S., *b.* 1950
1868	*O'Neill* (4th), Raymond Arthur Clanaboy O'Neill, TD, *b.* 1933, *s.* 1944, *m.*	Hon. Shane S. C. O'N., *b.* 1965
1836 I.*	*Oranmore and Browne* (4th), Dominick Geoffrey Edward Browne (2nd *UK Baron, Mereworth*, 1926), *b.* 1901, *s.* 1927, *m.*	Hon. Dominick G. T. B., *b.* 1929
1933	*Palmer* (4th), Adrian Bailie Nottage Palmer, *b.* 1951, *s.* 1990, *m.*	Hon. Hugo B. R. P., *b.* 1980
1914	*Parmoor* (4th), (Frederick Alfred) Milo Cripps, *b.* 1929, *s.* 1977.	Michael L. S. C., *b.* 1942
1937	*Pender* (3rd), John Willoughby Denison-Pender, *b.* 1933, *s.* 1965, *m.*	Hon. Henry J. R. D.-P., *b.* 1968
1866	*Penrhyn* (6th), Malcolm Frank Douglas-Pennant, DSO, MBE, *b.* 1908, *s.* 1967, *m.*	Hon. Nigel D.-P., *b.* 1909
1603	*Petre* (18th), John Patrick Lionel Petre, *b.* 1942, *s.* 1989, *m.*	Hon. Dominic W. P., *b.* 1966
1918	*Phillimore* (5th), Francis Stephen Phillimore, *b.* 1944, *s.* 1994, *m.*	Hon. Tristan A. S. P., *b.* 1977
1945	*Piercy* (3rd), James William Piercy, *b.* 1946, *s.* 1981.	Hon. Mark E. P. P., *b.* 1953
1827	*Plunket* (8th), Robin Rathmore Plunket, *b.* 1925, *s.* 1975, *m.*	Hon. Shaun A. F. S. P., *b.* 1931
1831	*Poltimore* (7th), Mark Coplestone Bampfylde, *b.* 1957, *s.* 1978, *m.*	Hon. Henry A. W. B., *b.* 1985
1690 s.	*Polwarth* (10th), Henry Alexander Hepburne-Scott, TD, *b.* 1916, *s.* 1944, *m.*	Master of Polwarth, *b.* 1947
1930	*Ponsonby of Shulbrede* (4th), Frederick Matthew Thomas Ponsonby, *b.* 1958, *s.* 1990.	None
1958	*Poole* (2nd), David Charles Poole, *b.* 1945, *s.* 1993, *m.*	Hon. Oliver J. P., *b.* 1972
1852	*Raglan* (5th), FitzRoy John Somerset, *b.* 1927, *s.* 1964.	Hon. Geoffrey S., *b.* 1932
1932	*Rankeillour* (4th), Peter St Thomas More Henry Hope, *b.* 1935, *s.* 1967.	Michael R. H., *b.* 1940
1953	*Rathcavan* (3rd), Hugh Detmar Torrens O'Neill, *b.* 1939, *s.* 1994, *m.*	Hon. François H. N. O'N., *b.* 1984
1916	*Rathcreedan* (3rd), Christopher John Norton, *b.* 1949, *s.* 1990, *m.*	Hon. Adam G. N., *b.* 1952
1868 I.	*Rathdonnell* (5th), Thomas Benjamin McClintock-Bunbury, *b.* 1938, *s.* 1959, *m.*	Hon. William L. M.-B., *b.* 1966
1911	*Ravensdale* (3rd), Nicholas Mosley, MC, *b.* 1923, *s.* 1966, *m.*	Hon. Shaun N. M., *b.* 1949
1821	*Ravensworth* (8th), Arthur Waller Liddell, *b.* 1924, *s.* 1950, *m.*	Hon. Thomas A. H. L., *b.* 1954
1821	*Rayleigh* (6th), John Gerald Strutt, *b.* 1960, *s.* 1988, *m.*	Hon. John F. S., *b.* 1993
1937	*Rea* (3rd), John Nicolas Rea, MD, *b.* 1928, *s.* 1981, *m.*	Hon. Matthew J. R., *b.* 1956
1628 s.	*Reay* (14th), Hugh William Mackay, *b.* 1937, *s.* 1963, *m.*	Master of Reay, *b.* 1965
1902	*Redesdale* (6th), Rupert Bertram Mitford, *b.* 1967, *s.* 1991.	None
1940	*Reith.* Disclaimed for life 1972. (*Christopher John Reith*, *b.*1928, *s.*1971, *m.*)	Hon. James H. J. R., *b.* 1971
1928	*Remnant* (3rd), James Wogan Remnant, CVO, *b.* 1930, *s.* 1967, *m.*	Hon. Philip J. R., *b.* 1954
1806 I.	*Rendlesham* (8th), Charles Anthony Hugh Thellusson, *b.* 1915, *s.* 1943, *w.*	Hon. Charles W. B. T., *b.* 1954
1933	*Rennell* (3rd), (John Adrian) Tremayne Rodd, *b.* 1935, *s.* 1978, *m.*	Hon. James R. D. T. R., *b.* 1978
1964	*Renwick* (2nd), Harry Andrew Renwick, *b.* 1935, *s.* 1973, *m.*	Hon. Robert J. R., *b.* 1966
1885	*Revelstoke* (5th), John Baring, *b.* 1934, *s.* 1994.	Hon. James C. B., *b.* 1938
1905	*Ritchie of Dundee* (5th), (Harold) Malcolm Ritchie, *b.* 1919, *s.* 1978, *m.*	Hon. C. Rupert R. R., *b.* 1958
1935	*Riverdale* (3rd), Anthony Robert Balfour, *b.* 1960, *s.* 1998.	Hon. David R. B., *b.* 1938
1961	*Robertson of Oakridge* (2nd), William Ronald Robertson, *b.* 1930, *s.* 1974, *m.*	Hon. William B. E. R., *b.* 1975
1938	*Roborough* (3rd), Henry Massey Lopes, *b.* 1940, *s.* 1992, *m.*	Hon. Massey J. H. L., *b.* 1969
1931	*Rochester* (2nd), Foster Charles Lowry Lamb, *b.* 1916, *s.* 1955, *m.*	Hon. David C. L., *b.* 1944
1934	*Rockley* (3rd), James Hugh Cecil, *b.* 1934, *s.* 1976, *m.*	Hon. Anthony R. C., *b.* 1961
1782	*Rodney* (10th), George Brydges Rodney, *b.* 1953, *s.* 1992, *m.*	Nicholas S. H. R., *b.* 1947

Created	Title, order of succession, name, etc.	Heir
1651 s.*	*Rollo* (14th), David Eric Howard Rollo (5th *UK Baron Dunning*, 1869), b. 1943, s. 1997, m.	Master of Rollo, b. 1972
1959	*Rootes* (3rd), Nicholas Geoffrey Rootes, b. 1951, s. 1992, m.	William B. R., b. 1944
1796 I.*	*Rossmore* (7th), William Warner Westenra (6th *UK Baron, Rossmore*, 1838), b. 1931, s. 1958, m.	Hon. Benedict W. W., b. 1983
1939	*Rotherwick* (3rd), (Herbert) Robin Cayzer, b. 1954, s. 1996, m.	Hon. H. Robin C., b. 1989
1885	*Rothschild* (4th), (Nathaniel Charles) Jacob Rothschild, GBE, b. 1936, s. 1990, m.	Hon. Nathaniel P. V. J. R., b. 1971
1911	*Rowallan* (4th), John Polson Cameron Corbett, b. 1947, s. 1993	Hon. Jason W. P. C. C., b. 1972
1947	*Rugby* (3rd), Robert Charles Maffey, b. 1951, s. 1990, m.	Hon. Timothy J. H. M., b. 1975
1919	*Russell of Liverpool* (3rd), Simon Gordon Jared Russell, b. 1952, s. 1981, m.	Hon. Edward C. S. R., b. 1985
1876	*Sackville* (6th), Lionel Bertrand Sackville-West, b. 1913, s. 1965, m.	Hugh R. I. S.-W., MC, b. 1919
1964	*St Helens* (2nd), Richard Francis Hughes-Young, b. 1945, s. 1980, m.	Hon. Henry T. H.-Y., b. 1986
1559	*St John of Bletso* (21st), Anthony Tudor St John, b. 1957, s. 1978, m.	Hon. Oliver B. St J., b. 1995
1887	*St Levan* (4th), John Francis Arthur St Aubyn, DSC, b. 1919, s. 1978, m.	Hon. O. Piers St A. MC, b. 1920
1885	*St Oswald* (5th), Derek Edward Anthony Winn, b. 1919, s. 1984, m.	Hon. Charles R. A. W., b. 1959
1960	*Sanderson of Ayot.* Disclaimed for life 1971. (*Alan Lindsay Sanderson*, b. 1931, s. 1971, m.)	Hon. Michael S., b. 1959
1945	*Sandford* (2nd), Revd John Cyril Edmondson, DSC, b. 1920, s. 1959, m.	Hon. James J. M. E., b. 1949
1871	*Sandhurst* (5th), (John Edward) Terence Mansfield, DFC, b. 1920, s. 1964, m.	Hon. Guy R. J. M., b. 1949
1802	*Sandys* (7th), Richard Michael Oliver Hill, b. 1931, s. 1961, m.	The Marquess of Downshire (*see* page 138)
1888	*Savile* (3rd), George Halifax Lumley-Savile, b. 1919, s. 1931.	Hon. Henry L. T. L.-S., b. 1923
1447	*Saye and Sele* (21st), Nathaniel Thomas Allen Fiennes, b. 1920, s. 1968, m.	Hon. Richard I. F., b. 1959
1932	*Selsdon* (3rd), Malcolm McEacharn Mitchell-Thomson, b. 1937, s. 1963, m.	Hon. Callum M. M. M.-T., b. 1969
1489 s.	*Sempill* (21st), James William Stuart Whitemore Sempill, b. 1949, s. 1995, m.	Master of Sempill, b. 1979
1916	*Shaughnessy* (3rd), William Graham Shaughnessy, b. 1922, s. 1938, m.	Hon. Michael J. S., b. 1946
1946	*Shepherd* (2nd), Malcolm Newton Shepherd, PC, b. 1918, s. 1954, w.	Hon. Graeme G. S., b. 1949
1964	*Sherfield* (2nd), Christopher James Makins, b. 1942, s. 1996, m.	Hon. Dwight W. M., b. 1951
1902	*Shuttleworth* (5th), Charles Geoffrey Nicholas Kay-Shuttleworth, b. 1948, s. 1975, m.	Hon. Thomas E. K.-S., b. 1976
1950	*Silkin.* Disclaimed for life 1972. (*Arthur Silkin*, b. 1916, s. 1972, m.)	Hon. Christopher L. S., b. 1947
1963	*Silsoe* (2nd), David Malcolm Trustram Eve, QC, b. 1930, s. 1976, m.	Hon. Simon R. T. E., b. 1966
1947	*Simon of Wythenshawe* (2nd), Roger Simon, b. 1913, s. 1960, m.	Hon. Matthew S., b. 1955
1449 s.	*Sinclair* (17th), Charles Murray Kennedy St Clair, CVO, b. 1914, s. 1957, m.	Master of Sinclair, b. 1968
1957	*Sinclair of Cleeve* (3rd), John Lawrence Robert Sinclair, b. 1953, s. 1985.	None
1919	*Sinha* (5th), Anindo Kumar Sinha, b. 1930, s. 1992.	Hon. Arup K. S., b. 1966
1828	*Skelmersdale* (7th), Roger Bootle-Wilbraham, b. 1945, s. 1973, m.	Hon. Andrew B.-W., b. 1977
1916	*Somerleyton* (3rd), Savile William Francis Crossley, KCVO, b. 1928, s. 1959, m. Master of the Horse	Hon. Hugh F. S. C., b. 1971
1784	*Somers* (9th), Philip Sebastian Somers Cocks, b. 1948, s. 1995.	Alan B. C., b. 1930
1780	*Southampton* (6th), Charles James FitzRoy, b. 1928, s. 1989, m.	Hon. Edward C. F., b. 1955
1959	*Spens* (3rd), Patrick Michael Rex Spens, b. 1942, s. 1984, m.	Hon. Patrick N. G. S., b. 1968
1640	*Stafford* (15th), Francis Melfort William Fitzherbert, b. 1954, s. 1986, m.	Hon. Benjamin J. B. F., b. 1983
1938	*Stamp* (4th), Trevor Charles Bosworth Stamp, MD, FRCP, b. 1935, s. 1987, m.	Hon. Nicholas C. T. S., b. 1978
1839	*Stanley of Alderley* (8th) and *Sheffield* (8th) (I. 1738), Thomas Henry Oliver Stanley (7th *UK Baron, Eddisbury*, 1848), b. 1927, s. 1971, m.	Hon. Richard O. S., b. 1956
1318	*Strabolgi* (11th), David Montague de Burgh Kenworthy, b. 1914, s. 1953, m.	Andrew D. W. K., b. 1967
1954	*Strang* (2nd), Colin Strang, b. 1922, s. 1978, m.	None
1955	*Strathalmond* (3rd), William Roberton Fraser, b. 1947, s. 1976, m.	Hon. William G. F., b. 1976
1936	*Strathcarron* (2nd), David William Anthony Blyth Macpherson, b. 1924, s. 1937, m.	Hon. Ian D. P. M., b. 1949
1955	*Strathclyde* (2nd), Thomas Galloway Dunlop du Roy de Blicquy Galbraith, PC, b. 1960, s. 1985, m.	Hon. Charles W. du R. de B. G., b. 1962
1900	*Strathcona and Mount Royal* (4th), Donald Euan Palmer Howard, b. 1923, s. 1959, m.	Hon. D. Alexander S. H., b. 1961
1836	*Stratheden* (6th) and *Campbell* (6th) (1841), Donald Campbell, b. 1934, s. 1987, m.	Hon. David A. C., b. 1963
1884	*Strathspey* (6th), James Patrick Trevor Grant of Grant, b. 1943, s. 1992, m.	Hon. Michael P. F. G., b. 1953

Created	*Title, order of succession, name, etc.*	*Heir*
1838	*Sudeley* (7th), Merlin Charles Sainthill Hanbury-Tracy, *b.* 1939, *s.* 1941.	D. Andrew J. *H.-T.*, *b.* 1928
1786	*Suffield* (11th), Anthony Philip Harbord-Hamond, MC, *b.* 1922, *s.* 1951, *m.*	Hon. Charles A. A. *H.-H.*, *b.* 1953
1893	*Swansea* (4th), John Hussey Hamilton Vivian, *b.* 1925, *s.* 1934, *m.*	Hon. Richard A. H. *V.*, *b.* 1957
1907	*Swaythling* (5th), Charles Edgar Samuel Montagu, *b.* 1954, *s.* 1998, *m.*	Hon. Anthony T. S. *M.*, *b.* 1931
1919	*Swinfen* (3rd), Roger Mynors Swinfen Eady, *b.* 1938, *s.* 1977, *m.*	Hon. Charles R. P. S. *E.*, *b.* 1971
1935	*Sysonby* (3rd), John Frederick Ponsonby, *b.* 1945, *s.* 1956.	None
1831 I.	*Talbot of Malahide* (10th), Reginald John Richard Arundell, *b.* 1931, *s.* 1987, *m.*	Hon. Richard J. T. *A.*, *b.* 1957
1946	*Tedder* (3rd), Robin John Tedder, *b.* 1955, *s.* 1994, *m.*	Hon. Benjamin J. *T.*, *b.* 1985
1884	*Tennyson* (5th), Cdr. Mark Aubrey Tennyson, DSC, *b.* 1920, *s.* 1991, *m.*	Lt-Cdr. James A. *T.* DSC, *b.* 1913
1918	*Terrington* (5th), (Christopher) Montague Woodhouse, DSO, OBE, *b.* 1917, *s.* 1998, *w.*	Hon. Christopher R. J. *W.*, *b.* 1946
1940	*Teviot* (2nd), Charles John Kerr, *b.* 1934, *s.* 1968, *m.*	Hon. Charles R. *K.*, *b.* 1971
1616	*Teynham* (20th), John Christopher Ingham Roper-Curzon, *b.* 1928, *s.* 1972, *m.*	Hon. David J. H. I. *R.-C.*, *b.* 1965
1964	*Thomson of Fleet* (2nd), Kenneth Roy Thomson, *b.* 1923, *s.* 1976, *m.*	Hon. David K. R. *T.*, *b.* 1957
1792	*Thurlow* (8th), Francis Edward Hovell-Thurlow-Cumming-Bruce, KCMG, *b.* 1912, *s.* 1971, *w.*	Hon. Roualeyn R. *H.-T.-C.-B.*, *b.* 1952
1876	*Tollemache* (5th), Timothy John Edward Tollemache, *b.* 1939, *s.* 1975, *m.*	Hon. Edward J. H. *T.*, *b.* 1976
1564 S.	*Torphichen* (15th), James Andrew Douglas Sandilands, *b.* 1946, *s.* 1975, *m.*	Douglas R. A. *S.*, *b.* 1926
1947	*Trefgarne* (2nd), David Garro Trefgarne, PC, *b.* 1941, *s.* 1960, *m.*	Hon. George G. *T.*, *b.* 1970
1921	*Trevethin* (4th) and *Oaksey* (2nd) (1947), John Geoffrey Tristram Lawrence, OBE, *b.* 1929, *s.* 1971, *m.*	Hon. Patrick J. T. *L.*, *b.* 1960
1880	*Trevor* (5th), Marke Charles Hill-Trevor, *b.* 1970, *s.* 1997, *m.*	Hon. Iain R. *H.-T.*, *b.* 1971
1461 I.	*Trimlestown* (21st), Raymond Charles Barnewall, *b.* 1930, *s.* 1997.	None
1940	*Tryon* (3rd), Anthony George Merrik Tryon, *b.* 1940, *s.* 1976.	Hon. Charles G. B. *T.*, *b.* 1976
1935	*Tweedsmuir* (3rd), William de l'Aigle Buchan, *b.* 1916, *s.* 1996, *m.*	Hon. John W. H. de l'A. *B.*, *b.* 1950
1523	*Vaux of Harrowden* (10th), John Hugh Philip Gilbey, *b.* 1915, *s.* 1977, *m.*	Hon. Anthony W. *G.*, *b.* 1940
1800 I.	*Ventry* (8th), Andrew Wesley Daubeny de Moleyns, *b.* 1943, *s.* 1987, *m.*	Hon. Francis W. D. *de M.*, *b.* 1965
1762	*Vernon* (10th), John Lawrance Vernon, *b.* 1923, *s.* 1963, *m.*	Col. William R. D. *Vernon-Harcourt* OBE, *b.* 1909
1922	*Vestey* (3rd), Samuel George Armstrong Vestey, *b.* 1941, *s.* 1954, *m.*	Hon. William G. *V.*, *b.* 1983
1841	*Vivian* (6th), Nicholas Crespigny Laurence Vivian, *b.* 1935, *s.* 1991, *m.*	Hon. Charles H. C. *V.*, *b.* 1966
1934	*Wakehurst* (3rd), (John) Christopher Loder, *b.* 1925, *s.* 1970, *m.*	Hon. Timothy W. *L.*, *b.* 1958
1723	*Walpole* (10th), Robert Horatio Walpole (8th *Brit. Baron Walpole of Wolterton*, 1756), *b.* 1938, *s.* 1989, *m.*	Hon. Jonathan R. H. *W.*, *b.* 1967
1780	*Walsingham* (9th), John de Grey, MC, *b.* 1925, *s.* 1965, *m.*	Hon. Robert *de G.*, *b.* 1969
1936	*Wardington* (2nd), Christopher Henry Beaumont Pease, *b.* 1924, *s.* 1950, *m.*	Hon. William S. *P.*, *b.* 1925
1792 I.	*Waterpark* (7th), Frederick Caryll Philip Cavendish, *b.* 1926, *s.* 1948, *m.*	Hon. Roderick A. *C.*, *b.* 1959
1942	*Wedgwood* (4th), Piers Anthony Weymouth Wedgwood, *b.* 1954, *s.* 1970, *m.*	John *W.* CBE, MD, FRCP, *b.* 1919
1861	*Westbury* (5th), David Alan Bethell, CBE, MC, *b.* 1922, *s.* 1961, *m.*	Hon. Richard N. *B.* MBE, *b.* 1950
1944	*Westwood* (3rd), (William) Gavin Westwood, *b.* 1944, *s.* 1991, *m.*	Hon. W. Fergus *W.*, *b.* 1972
1935	*Wigram* (2nd), (George) Neville (Clive) Wigram, MC, *b.* 1915, *s.* 1960, *w.*	Maj. Hon. Andrew F. C. *W.* MVO, *b.* 1949
1491	*Willoughby de Broke* (21st), Leopold David Verney, *b.* 1938, *s.* 1986, *m.*	Hon. Rupert G. *V.*, *b.* 1966
1946	*Wilson* (2nd), Patrick Maitland Wilson, *b.* 1915, *s.* 1964, *w.*	None
1937	*Windlesham* (3rd), David James George Hennessy, CVO, PC, *b.* 1932, *s.* 1962, *w.*	Hon. James R. *H.*, *b.* 1968
1951	*Wise* (2nd), John Clayton Wise, *b.* 1923, *s.* 1968, *m.*	Hon. Christopher J. C. *W.* PH.D., *b.* 1949
1869	*Wolverton* (7th), Christopher Richard Glyn, *b.* 1938, *s.* 1988.	Hon. Andrew J. *G.*, *b.* 1943
1928	*Wraxall* (2nd), George Richard Lawley Gibbs, *b.* 1928, *s.* 1931.	Hon. Sir Eustace H. B. *G.* KCVO, CMG, *b.* 1929
1915	*Wrenbury* (3rd), Revd John Burton Buckley, *b.* 1927, *s.* 1940, *m.*	Hon. William E. *B.*, *b.* 1966
1838	*Wrottesley* (6th), Clifton Hugh Lancelot de Verdon Wrottesley, *b.* 1968, *s.* 1977.	Hon. Stephen J. *W.*, *b.* 1955
1919	*Wyfold* (3rd), Hermon Robert Fleming Hermon-Hodge, ERD, *b.* 1915, *s.* 1942.	None
1829	*Wynford* (8th), Robert Samuel Best, MBE, *b.* 1917, *s.* 1943, *m.*	Hon. John P. R. *B.*, *b.* 1950
1308	*Zouche* (18th), James Assheton Frankland, *b.* 1943, *s.* 1965, *m.*	Hon. William T. A. *F.*, *b.* 1984

BARONESSES/LADIES IN THEIR OWN RIGHT

Style, The Right Hon. the Lady ___ , *or* The Right Hon. the Baroness ___ , according to her preference. Either style may be used, except in the case of Scottish titles (indicated by s.), which are not baronies (*see* page 136) and whose holders are always addressed as Lady
Husband, Untitled
Children's style, As for children of a Baron
For forms of address, *see* page 135

Created	Title, order of succession, name, etc.	Heir
1455	*Berners* (16th in line), Pamela Vivien Kirkham, *b.* 1929, *title called out of abeyance* 1995, *m.*	Hon. Rupert W. T. *K.*, *b.* 1953
1529	*Braye* (8th in line), Mary Penelope Aubrey-Fletcher, *b.* 1941, *s.* 1985, *m.*	Two co-heiresses
1321	*Dacre* (27th in line), Rachel Leila Douglas-Home, *b.* 1929, *title called out of abeyance* 1970, *w.*	Hon. James T. A. *D.-H.*, *b.* 1952
1332	*Darcy de Knayth* (18th in line), Davina Marcia Ingrams, DBE, *b.* 1938, *s.* 1943, *w.*	Hon. Caspar D. *I.*, *b.* 1962
1439	*Dudley* (14th in line), Barbara Amy Felicity Hamilton, *b.* 1907, *s.* 1972, *m.*	Hon. Jim A. H. *Wallace, b.* 1930
1490 s.	*Herries of Terregles* (14th in line), Anne Elizabeth Fitzalan-Howard, *b.* 1938, *s.* 1975, *m.*	Lady Mary *Mumford* CVO, *b.* 1940
1602 s.	*Kinloss* (12th in line), Beatrice Mary Grenville Freeman-Grenville, *b.* 1922, *s.* 1944, *m.*	Master of Kinloss, *b.* 1953
1445 s.	*Saltoun* (20th in line), Flora Marjory Fraser, *b.* 1930, *s.* 1979, *m.*	Hon. Katharine I. M. I. *F.*, *b.* 1957
1628	*Strange* (16th in line), (Jean) Cherry Drummond of Megginch, *b.* 1928, *title called out of abeyance* 1986, *m.*	Hon. Adam H. *D. of M.*, *b.* 1953
1544/5	*Wharton* (11th in line), Myrtle Olive Felix Robertson, *b.* 1934, *title called out of abeyance* 1990, *m.*	Hon. Myles C. D. *R.*, *b.* 1964
1313	*Willoughby de Eresby* (27th in line), (Nancy) Jane Marie Heathcote-Drummond-Willoughby, *b.* 1934, *s.* 1983.	Two co-heiresses

Life Peers

New Life Peerages *1 September 1997 to 31 August 1998*
New Year's Honours (30 December 1997): Sir Robin Butler, GCB, CVO; Sir Ronald Dearing, CB; Paul Hamlyn, CBE; Rt. Revd David Sheppard
Queen's Birthday Honours (13 June 1998): Sir Terence Burns, GCB; Sir David English (died 11 June 1998); Sir Herbert Laming, CBE; Sir Colin Marshall; Revd Kathleen Richardson, OBE
Working Peers (20 June 1998): Nazir Ahmed; Waheed Alli; William Bach; Sir Tim Bell; Melvyn Bragg; David Brookman; Peta Buscombe; Anthony Christopher, CBE; Anthony Clarke, CBE; Tim Clements-Jones, CBE; Christine Crawley, MEP; David Evans; Mary Goudie; Toby Harris; Christopher Haskins; Rt. Hon. Norman Lamont; Brian Mackenzie, OBE; Sue Miller; Philip Norton; Andrew Phillips, OBE; Tom Sawyer; Margaret Sharp; Glenys Thornton; John Tomlinson, MEP; Manzila Uddin; Norman Warner; Paul White
New Minister (August 1998): Angus Macdonald*
*Title not gazetted at time of going to press

CREATED UNDER THE APPELLATE JURISDICTION ACT 1876 (AS AMENDED)

BARONS

Created
1986   *Ackner*, Desmond James Conrad Ackner, PC, *b.* 1920, *m.*
1981   *Brandon of Oakbrook*, Henry Vivian Brandon, MC, PC, *b.* 1920, *m.*
1980   *Bridge of Harwich*, Nigel Cyprian Bridge, PC, *b.* 1917, *m.*
1982   *Brightman*, John Anson Brightman, PC, *b.* 1911, *m.*
1991   *Browne-Wilkinson*, Nicolas Christopher Henry Browne-Wilkinson, PC, *b.* 1930, *m.* Lord of Appeal in Ordinary
1996   *Clyde*, James John Clyde, *b.* 1932, *m.* Lord of Appeal in Ordinary
1957   *Denning*, Alfred Thompson Denning, OM, PC, *b.* 1899, *w.*
1986   *Goff of Chieveley*, Robert Lionel Archibald Goff, PC, *b.* 1926, *m.*
1985   *Griffiths*, (William) Hugh Griffiths, MC, PC, *b.* 1923, *m.*
1995   *Hoffmann*, Leonard Hubert Hoffmann, PC, *b.* 1934, *m.* Lord of Appeal in Ordinary
1997   *Hutton*, (James) Brian (Edward) Hutton, PC, *b.* 1931, *m.* Lord of Appeal in Ordinary
1988   *Jauncey of Tullichettle*, Charles Eliot Jauncey, PC, *b.* 1925, *m.*
1977   *Keith of Kinkel*, Henry Shanks Keith, GBE, PC, *b.* 1922, *m.*
1979   *Lane*, Geoffrey Dawson Lane, AFC, PC, *b.* 1918, *m.*
1993   *Lloyd of Berwick*, Anthony John Leslie Lloyd, PC, *b.* 1929, *m.* Lord of Appeal in Ordinary
1992   *Mustill*, Michael John Mustill, PC, *b.* 1931, *m.*
1994   *Nicholls of Birkenhead*, Donald James Nicholls, PC, *b.* 1933, *m.* Lord of Appeal in Ordinary
1994   *Nolan*, Michael Patrick Nolan, PC, *b.* 1928, *m.*
1986   *Oliver of Aylmerton*, Peter Raymond Oliver, PC, *b.* 1921, *m.*
1997   *Saville of Newdigate*, Mark Oliver Saville, PC, *b.* 1936, *m.* Lord of Appeal in Ordinary

1977   *Scarman*, Leslie George Scarman, OBE, PC, *b.* 1911, *m.*
1992   *Slynn of Hadley*, Gordon Slynn, PC, *b.* 1930, *m.* Lord of Appeal in Ordinary
1995   *Steyn*, Johan van Zyl Steyn, PC, *b.* 1932, *m.* Lord of Appeal in Ordinary
1982   *Templeman*, Sydney William Templeman, MBE, PC, *b.* 1920, *m.*
1964   *Wilberforce*, Richard Orme Wilberforce, CMG, OBE, PC, *b.* 1907, *m.*
1992   *Woolf*, Harry Kenneth Woolf, PC, *b.* 1933, *m.* Master of the Rolls

CREATED UNDER THE LIFE PEERAGES ACT 1958

BARONS

Created
1998   *Ahmed*, Nazir Ahmed.
1996   *Alderdice*, John Thomas Alderdice, *b.* 1955, *m.*
1988   *Alexander of Weedon*, Robert Scott Alexander, QC, *b.* 1936, *m.*
1976   *Allen of Abbeydale*, Philip Allen, GCB, *b.* 1912, *m.*
1998   *Alli*, Waheed Alli.
1961   *Alport*, Cuthbert James McCall Alport, TD, PC, *b.* 1912, *w.*
1997   *Alton of Liverpool*, David Patrick Paul Alton, *b.* 1951, *m.*
1965   *Annan*, Noël Gilroy Annan, OBE, *b.* 1916, *m.*
1992   *Archer of Sandwell*, Peter Kingsley Archer, PC, QC, *b.* 1926, *m.*
1992   *Archer of Weston-super-Mare*, Jeffrey Howard Archer, *b.* 1940, *m.*
1988   *Armstrong of Ilminster*, Robert Temple Armstrong, GCB, CVO, *b.* 1927, *m.*
1992   *Ashley of Stoke*, Jack Ashley, CH, PC, *b.* 1922, *m.*
1993   *Attenborough*, Richard Samuel Attenborough, CBE, *b.* 1923, *m.*
1998   *Bach*, William Stephen Goulden Bach.
1997   *Bagri*, Raj Kumar Bagri, CBE, *b.* 1930, *m.*
1997   *Baker of Dorking*, Kenneth Wilfred Baker, CH, PC, *b.* 1934, *m.*
1974   *Balniel*, The Earl of Crawford and Balcarres (*see* page 140)
1974   *Barber*, Anthony Perrinott Lysberg Barber, TD, PC, *b.* 1920, *m.*
1992   *Barber of Tewkesbury*, Derek Coates Barber, *b.* 1918, *m.*
1983   *Barnett*, Joel Barnett, PC, *b.* 1923, *m.*
1997   *Bassam of Brighton*, (John) Steven Bassam, *b.* 1953.
1982   *Bauer*, Prof. Peter Thomas Bauer, D.SC., FBA, *b.* 1915.
1967   *Beaumont of Whitley*, Revd Timothy Wentworth Beaumont, *b.* 1928, *m.*
1998   *Bell*, Timothy John Leigh Bell, *b.* 1941, *m.*
1979   *Bellwin*, Irwin Norman Bellow, *b.* 1923, *m.*
1981   *Beloff*, Max Beloff, FBA, *b.* 1913, *m.*
1997   *Biffen*, (William) John Biffen, PC, *b.* 1930, *m.*
1996   *Bingham of Cornhill*, Thomas Henry Bingham, PC, *b.* 1933, *m. Lord Chief Justice of England*
1997   *Blackwell*, Norman Roy Blackwell, *b.* 1952, *m.*
1971   *Blake*, Robert Norman William Blake, FBA, *b.* 1916, *w.*

1994   *Blaker*, Peter Allan Renshaw Blaker, KCMG, PC, *b.* 1922, *m.*

1978   *Blease*, William John Blease, *b.* 1914, *m.*

1995   *Blyth of Rowington*, James Blyth, *b.* 1940, *m.*

1980   *Boardman*, Thomas Gray Boardman, MC, TD, *b.* 1919, *m.*

1996   *Borrie*, Gordon Johnson Borrie, QC, *b.* 1931, *m.*

1976   *Boston of Faversham*, Terence George Boston, QC, *b.* 1930, *m.*

1996   *Bowness*, Peter Spencer Bowness, CBE, *b.* 1943, *m.*

1998   *Bragg*, Melvyn Bragg, *b.* 1939, *m.*

1992   *Braine of Wheatley*, Bernard Richard Braine, PC, *b.* 1914, *w.*

1987   *Bramall*, Edwin Noel Westby Bramall, KG, GCB, OBE, MC, *b.* 1923, *m. Field Marshal*

1976   *Briggs*, Asa Briggs, FBA, *b.* 1921, *m.*

1997   *Brooke of Alverthorpe*, Clive Brooke, *b.* 1942, *m.*

1975   *Brookes*, Raymond Percival Brookes, *b.* 1909, *m.*

1998   *Brookman*, David Keith Brookman, *b.* 1937, *m.*

1979   *Brooks of Tremorfa*, John Edward Brooks, *b.* 1927, *m.*

1974   *Bruce of Donington*, Donald William Trevor Bruce, *b.* 1912, *m.*

1976   *Bullock*, Alan Louis Charles Bullock, FBA, *b.* 1914, *m.*

1997   *Burlison*, Thomas Henry Burlison, *b.* 1936, *m.*

1998   *Burns*, Terence Burns, GCB, *b.* 1944, *m.*

1998   *Butler of Brockwell*, (Frederick Edward) Robin Butler, GCB, CVO, *b.* 1938, *m.*

1988   *Butterfield*, (William) John (Hughes) Butterfield, OBE, DM, FRCP, *b.* 1920, *m.*

1985   *Butterworth*, John Blackstock Butterworth, CBE, *b.* 1918, *m.*

1978   *Buxton of Alsa*, Aubrey Leland Oakes Buxton, KCVO, MC, *b.* 1918, *m.*

1987   *Callaghan of Cardiff*, (Leonard) James Callaghan, KG, PC, *b.* 1912, *m.*

1984   *Cameron of Lochbroom*, Kenneth John Cameron, PC, *b.* 1931, *m.*

1981   *Campbell of Alloway*, Alan Robertson Campbell, QC, *b.* 1917, *m.*

1974   *Campbell of Croy*, Gordon Thomas Calthrop Campbell, MC, PC, *b.* 1921, *m.*

1987   *Carlisle of Bucklow*, Mark Carlisle, QC, PC, *b.* 1929, *m.*

1983   *Carmichael of Kelvingrove*, Neil George Carmichael, *b.* 1921.

1975   *Carr of Hadley*, (Leonard) Robert Carr, PC, *b.* 1916, *m.*

1987   *Carter*, Denis Victor Carter, PC, *b.* 1932, *m.*

1977   *Carver*, (Richard) Michael (Power) Carver, GCB, CBE, DSO, MC, *b.* 1915, *m. Field Marshal*

1990   *Cavendish of Furness*, (Richard) Hugh Cavendish, *b.* 1941, *m.*

1982   *Cayzer*, (William) Nicholas Cayzer, *b.* 1910, *w.*

1996   *Chadlington*, Peter Selwyn Gummer, *b.* 1942, *m.*

1964   *Chalfont*, (Alun) Arthur Gwynne Jones, OBE, MC, PC, *b.* 1919, *m.*

1985   *Chapple*, Francis (Frank) Joseph Chapple, *b.* 1921, *w.*

1978   *Charteris of Amisfield*, Martin Michael Charles Charteris, GCB, GCVO, OBE, PC, Royal Victorian Chain , *b.* 1913, *m.*

1987   *Chilver*, (Amos) Henry Chilver, FRS, FEng., *b.* 1926, *m.*

1977   *Chitnis*, Pratap Chidamber Chitnis, *b.* 1936, *m.*

1998   *Christopher*, Anthony Martin Grosvenor Christopher, CBE, *b.* 1925, *m.*

1992   *Clark of Kempston*, William Gibson Haig Clark, PC, *b.* 1917, *m.*

1998   *Clarke of Hampstead*, Anthony James Clarke, CBE.

1979   *Cledwyn of Penrhos*, Cledwyn Hughes, CH, PC, *b.* 1916, *m.*

1998   *Clement-Jones*, Timothy Francis Clement-Jones, CBE.

1990   *Clinton-Davis*, Stanley Clinton Clinton-Davis, PC, *b.* 1928, *m.*

1978   *Cockfield*, (Francis) Arthur Cockfield, PC, *b.* 1916, *w.*

1987   *Cocks of Hartcliffe*, Michael Francis Lovell Cocks, PC, *b.* 1929, *m.*

1980   *Coggan*, Rt. Revd (Frederick) Donald Coggan, PC, Royal Victorian Chain, *b.* 1909, *m.*

1981   *Constantine of Stanmore*, Theodore Constantine, CBE, AE, *b.* 1910, *w.*

1992   *Cooke of Islandreagh*, Victor Alexander Cooke, OBE, *b.* 1920, *m.*

1996   *Cooke of Thorndon*, Robin Brunskill Cooke, KBE, PC, ph.D., *b.* 1926, *m.*

1997   *Cope of Berkeley*, John Ambrose Cope, PC, *b.* 1937, *m.*

1997   *Cowdrey of Tonbridge*, (Michael) Colin Cowdrey, CBE, *b.* 1932, *m.*

1991   *Craig of Radley*, David Brownrigg Craig, GCB, OBE, *b.* 1929, *m. Marshal of the Royal Air Force*

1987   *Crickhowell*, (Roger) Nicholas Edwards, PC, *b.* 1934, *m.*

1978   *Croham*, Douglas Albert Vivian Allen, GCB, *b.* 1917, *w.*

1995   *Cuckney*, John Graham Cuckney, *b.* 1925, *m.*

1996   *Currie of Marylebone*, David Anthony Currie, *b.* 1946, *m.*

1979   *Dacre of Glanton*, Hugh Redwald Trevor-Roper, *b.* 1914, *w.*

1993   *Dahrendorf*, Ralf Dahrendorf, KBE, ph.D., D.phil., FBA, *b.* 1929, *m.*

1997   *Davies of Coity*, (David) Garfield Davies, CBE, *b.* 1935, *m.*

1997   *Davies of Oldham*, Bryan Davies, *b.* 1939, *m.*

1983   *Dean of Beswick*, Joseph Jabez Dean, *b.* 1922.

1993   *Dean of Harptree*, (Arthur) Paul Dean, PC, *b.* 1924, *m.*

1998   *Dearing*, Ronald Ernest Dearing, CB, *b.* 1930, *m.*

1986   *Deedes*, William Francis Deedes, MC, PC, *b.* 1913, *m.*

1991   *Desai*, Prof. Meghnad Jagdishchandra Desai, ph.D., *b.* 1940, *m.*

1997   *Dholakia*, Navnit Dholakia, OBE, *b.* 1937, *m.*

1970   *Diamond*, John Diamond, PC, *b.* 1907, *m.*

1997   *Dixon*, Donald Dixon, PC, *b.* 1929, *m.*

1993   *Dixon-Smith*, Robert William Dixon-Smith, *b.* 1934, *m.*

1988   *Donaldson of Lymington*, John Francis Donaldson, PC, *b.* 1920, *m.*

1985   *Donoughue*, Bernard Donoughue, D.phil., *b.* 1934.

1987   *Dormand of Easington*, John Donkin Dormand, *b.* 1919, *m.*

1994   *Dubs*, Alfred Dubs, *b.* 1932, *m.*

1995   *Eames*, Robert Henry Alexander Eames, ph.D., *b.* 1937, *m.*

1992   *Eatwell*, John Leonard Eatwell, *b.* 1945, *m.*

1983   *Eden of Winton*, John Benedict Eden, PC, *b.* 1925, *m.*

1992   *Elis-Thomas*, Dafydd Elis Elis-Thomas, *b.* 1946, *m.*

1985   *Elliott of Morpeth*, Robert William Elliott, *b.* 1920, *m.*

1981   *Elystan-Morgan*, Dafydd Elystan Elystan-Morgan, *b.* 1932, *m.*

1980   *Emslie*, George Carlyle Emslie, MBE, PC, FRSE, *b.* 1919, *m.*

1997 *Evans of Parkside*, John Evans, *b*. 1930, *m*.

1998 *Evans of Watford*, David Charles Evans.

1992 *Ewing of Kirkford*, Harry Ewing, *b*. 1931, *m*.

1983 *Ezra*, Derek Ezra, MBE, *b*. 1919, *m*.

1997 *Falconer of Thoroton*, Charles Leslie Falconer, QC, *b*. 1951, *m*.

1983 *Fanshawe of Richmond*, Anthony Henry Fanshawe Royle, KCMG, *b*. 1927, *m*.

1996 *Feldman*, Basil Feldman, *b*. 1926, *m*.

1983 *Fitt*, Gerard Fitt, *b*. 1926, *w*.

1979 *Flowers*, Brian Hilton Flowers, FRS, *b*. 1924, *m*.

1967 *Foot*, John Mackintosh Foot, *b*. 1909, *m*.

1982 *Forte*, Charles Forte, *b*. 1908, *m*.

1989 *Fraser of Carmyllie*, Peter Lovat Fraser, PC, QC, *b*. 1945, *m*.

1997 *Freeman*, Roger Norman Freeman, PC, *b*. 1942, *m*.

1982 *Gallacher*, John Gallacher, *b*. 1920, *m*.

1997 *Garel-Jones*, (William Armand Thomas) Tristan Garel-Jones, PC, *b*. 1941, *m*.

1992 *Geraint*, Geraint Wyn Howells, *b*. 1925, *m*.

1975 *Gibson*, (Richard) Patrick (Tallentyre) Gibson, *b*. 1916, *m*.

1979 *Gibson-Watt*, (James) David Gibson-Watt, MC, PC, *b*. 1918, *m*.

1997 *Gilbert*, John William Gilbert, PC, PH.D., *b*. 1927, *m*.

1996 *Gillmore of Thamesfield*, David Howe Gillmore, GCMG, *b*. 1934, *m*.

1992 *Gilmour of Craigmillar*, Ian Hedworth John Little Gilmour, PC, *b*. 1926, *m*.

1994 *Gladwin of Clee*, Derek Oliver Gladwin, CBE, *b*. 1930, *m*.

1977 *Glenamara*, Edward Watson Short, CH, PC, *b*. 1912, *m*.

1997 *Goodhart*, William Howard Goodhart, QC, *b*. 1933, *m*.

1997 *Gordon of Strathblane*, James Stuart Gordon, CBE, *b*. 1936, *m*.

1976 *Grade*, Lew Grade, *b*. 1906, *m*.

1983 *Graham of Edmonton*, (Thomas) Edward Graham, *b*. 1925, *m*.

1983 *Gray of Contin*, James (Hamish) Hector Northey Gray, PC, *b*. 1927, *m*.

1974 *Greene of Harrow Weald*, Sidney Francis Greene, CBE, *b*. 1910, *m*.

1974 *Greenhill of Harrow*, Denis Arthur Greenhill, GCMG, OBE, *b*. 1913, *m*.

1975 *Gregson*, John Gregson, *b*. 1924.

1968 *Grey of Naunton*, Ralph Francis Alnwick Grey, GCMG, GCVO, OBE, *b*. 1910, *w*.

1991 *Griffiths of Fforestfach*, Brian Griffiths, *b*. 1941, *m*.

1995 *Habgood*, Rt. Revd John Stapylton Habgood, PC, PH.D., *b*. 1927, *m*.

1970 *Hailsham of St Marylebone*, Quintin McGarel Hogg, KG, CH, PC, FRS, *b*. 1907, *m*.

1994 *Hambro*, Charles Eric Alexander Hambro, *b*. 1930, *m*.

1998 *Hamlyn*, Paul Bertrand Hamlyn, CBE, *b*. 1926, *m*.

1998 *Hanningfield*, Paul Edward Winston White

1983 *Hanson*, James Edward Hanson, *b*. 1922, *m*.

1997 *Hardie*, Andrew Rutherford Hardie, QC, PC, *b*. 1946, *m*. *Lord Advocate*

1997 *Hardy of Wath*, Peter Hardy, *b*. 1931, *m*.

1974 *Harmar-Nicholls*, Harmar Harmar-Nicholls, *b*. 1912, *m*.

1974 *Harris of Greenwich*, John Henry Harris, PC, *b*. 1930, *m*.

1998 *Harris of Haringey*, (Jonathan) Toby Harris, *b*. 1953, *m*.

1979 *Harris of High Cross*, Ralph Harris, *b*. 1924, *m*.

1996 *Harris of Peckham*, Philip Charles Harris, *b*. 1942, *m*.

1968 *Hartwell*, (William) Michael Berry, MBE, TD, *b*. 1911, *w*.

1993 *Haskel*, Simon Haskel, *b*. 1934, *m*.

1998 *Haskins*, Christopher Robin Haskins, *b*. 1937, *m*.

1990 *Haslam*, Robert Haslam, *b*. 1923, *m*.

1997 *Hattersley*, Roy Sidney George Hattersley, PC, *b*. 1932, *m*.

1992 *Hayhoe*, Bernard John (Barney) Hayhoe, *b*. 1925, *m*.

1992 *Healey*, Denis Winston Healey, CH, MBE, PC, *b*. 1917, *m*.

1984 *Henderson of Brompton*, Peter Gordon Henderson, KCB, *b*. 1922, *m*.

1997 *Higgins*, Terence Langley Higgins, KBE, PC, *b*. 1928, *m*.

1979 *Hill-Norton*, Peter John Hill-Norton, GCB, *b*. 1915, *m*. *Admiral of the Fleet*

1997 *Hogg of Cumbernauld*, Norman Hogg, *b*. 1938, *m*.

1979 *Holderness*, Richard Frederick Wood, PC, *b*. 1920, *m*.

1991 *Hollick*, Clive Richard Hollick, *b*. 1945, *m*.

1990 *Holme of Cheltenham*, Richard Gordon Holme, CBE, *b*. 1936, *m*.

1979 *Hooson*, (Hugh) Emlyn Hooson, QC, *b*. 1925, *m*.

1995 *Hope of Craighead*, (James Arthur) David Hope, PC, *b*. 1938, *m*. *Lord of Appeal in Ordinary*

1992 *Howe of Aberavon*, (Richard Edward) Geoffrey Howe, CH, PC, QC, *b*. 1926, *m*.

1997 *Howell of Guildford*, David Arthur Russell Howell, PC, *b*. 1936, *m*.

1978 *Howie of Troon*, William Howie, *b*. 1924, *m*.

1997 *Hoyle*, (Eric) Douglas Harvey Hoyle, *b*. 1930, *w*.

1961 *Hughes*, William Hughes, CBE, PC, *b*. 1911, *w*.

1997 *Hughes of Woodside*, Robert Hughes, *b*. 1932, *m*.

1966 *Hunt*, (Henry Cecil) John Hunt, KG, CBE, DSO, *b*. 1910, *m*.

1997 *Hunt of Kings Heath*, Philip Alexander Hunt, OBE, *b*. 1949, *m*.

1980 *Hunt of Tanworth*, John Joseph Benedict Hunt, GCB, *b*. 1919, *m*.

1997 *Hunt of Wirral*, David James Fletcher Hunt, MBE, PC, *b*. 1942, *m*.

1997 *Hurd of Westwell*, Douglas Richard Hurd, CH, CBE, PC, *b*. 1930, *m*.

1996 *Hussey of North Bradley*, Marmaduke James Hussey, *b*. 1923, *m*.

1978 *Hutchinson of Lullington*, Jeremy Nicolas Hutchinson, QC, *b*. 1915, *m*.

1997 *Inge*, Peter Anthony Inge, GCB, *b*. 1935, *m*. *Field Marshal*

1982 *Ingrow*, John Aked Taylor, OBE, TD, *b*. 1917, *m*.

1987 *Irvine of Lairg*, Alexander Andrew Mackay Irvine, PC, QC, *b*. 1940, *m*. *Lord High Chancellor*

1997 *Islwyn*, Royston John (Roy) Hughes, *b*. 1925, *m*.

1997 *Jacobs*, (David) Anthony Jacobs, *b*. 1931, *m*.

1988 *Jakobovits*, Immanuel Jakobovits, *b*. 1921, *m*.

1997 *Janner of Braunstone*, Greville Ewan Janner, QC, *b*. 1928, *w*.

1987 *Jenkin of Roding*, (Charles) Patrick (Fleeming) Jenkin, PC, *b*. 1926, *m*.

1987 *Jenkins of Hillhead*, Roy Harris Jenkins, OM, PC, *b*. 1920, *m*.

1981 *Jenkins of Putney*, Hugh Gater Jenkins, *b*. 1908, *w*.

1987 *Johnston of Rockport*, Charles Collier Johnston, TD, *b*. 1915, *m*.

1997 *Jopling*, (Thomas) Michael Jopling, PC, *b*. 1930, *m*.

1991 *Judd*, Frank Ashcroft Judd, *b*. 1935, *m*.

1980 *Keith of Castleacre*, Kenneth Alexander Keith, *b*. 1916, *m*.

1997 *Kelvedon*, (Henry) Paul Guinness Channon, PC, *b*. 1935, *m*.

1996   *Kilpatrick of Kincraig*, Robert Kilpatrick, CBE, *b.* 1926, *m.*
1985   *Kimball*, Marcus Richard Kimball, *b.* 1928, *m.*
1983   *King of Wartnaby*, John Leonard King, *b.* 1918, *m.*
1993   *Kingsdown*, Robert (Robin) Leigh-Pemberton, KG, PC, *b.* 1927, *m.*
1994   *Kingsland*, Christopher James Prout, TD, PC, QC, *b.* 1942.
1975   *Kirkhill*, John Farquharson Smith, *b.* 1930, *m.*
1987   *Knights*, Philip Douglas Knights, CBE, QPM, *b.* 1920, *m.*
1991   *Laing of Dunphail*, Hector Laing, *b.* 1923, *m.*
1998   *Laming*, (William) Herbert Laming, CBE, *b.* 1936, *m.*
1998   *Lamont of Lerwick*, Norman Stewart Hughson Lamont, PC, *b.* 1942, *m.*
1990   *Lane of Horsell*, Peter Stewart Lane, *b.* 1925, *w.*
1997   *Lang of Monkton*, Ian Bruce Lang, PC, *b.* 1940, *m.*
1992   *Lawson of Blaby*, Nigel Lawson, PC, *b.* 1932, *m.*
1993   *Lester of Herne Hill*, Anthony Paul Lester, QC, *b.* 1936, *m.*
1997   *Levene of Portsoken*, Peter Keith Levene, KBE, *b.* 1941, *m.*
1997   *Levy*, Michael Abraham Levy, *b.* 1944, *m.*
1982   *Lewin*, Terence Thornton Lewin, KG, GCB, LVO, DSC, *b.* 1920, *m. Admiral of the Fleet*
1989   *Lewis of Newnham*, Jack Lewis, FRS, *b.* 1928, *m.*
1997   *Lloyd-Webber*, Andrew Lloyd Webber, *b.* 1948, *m.*
1997   *Lofthouse of Pontefract*, Geoffrey Lofthouse, *b.* 1925, *w.*
1974   *Lovell-Davis*, Peter Lovell Lovell-Davis, *b.* 1924, *m.*
1979   *Lowry*, Robert Lynd Erskine Lowry, PC, PC (NI), *b.* 1919, *m.*
1984   *McAlpine of West Green*, (Robert) Alistair McAlpine, *b.* 1942, *m.*
1988   *Macaulay of Bragar*, Donald Macaulay, QC, *b.* 1933, *m.*
1975   *McCarthy*, William Edward John McCarthy, D.phil., *b.* 1925, *m.*
1976   *McCluskey*, John Herbert McCluskey, *b.* 1929, *m.*
1989   *McColl of Dulwich*, Ian McColl, CBE, FRCS, FRCSE, *b.* 1933, *m.*
1995   *McConnell*, Robert William Brian McConnell, PC (NI), *b.* 1922, *m.*
1991   *Macfarlane of Bearsden*, Norman Somerville Macfarlane, KT, FRSE, *b.* 1926, *m.*
1982   *McIntosh of Haringey*, Andrew Robert McIntosh, *b.* 1933, *m.*
1991   *Mackay of Ardbrecknish*, John Jackson Mackay, PC, *b.* 1938, *m.*
1979   *Mackay of Clashfern*, James Peter Hymers Mackay, KT, PC, FRSE, *b.* 1927, *m.*
1995   *Mackay of Drumadoon*, Donald Sage Mackay, *b.* 1946, *m.*
1998   *Mackenzie of Framwellgate*, Brian Mackenzie, OBE.
1988   *Mackenzie-Stuart*, Alexander John Mackenzie Stuart, *b.* 1924, *m.*
1974   *Mackie of Benshie*, George Yull Mackie, CBE, DSO, DFC, *b.* 1919, *m.*
1996   *MacLaurin*, Ian Charter MacLaurin, *b.* 1937, *m.*
1982   *MacLehose of Beoch*, (Crawford) Murray MacLehose, KT, GBE, KCMG, KCVO, *b.* 1917, *m.*
1995   *McNally*, Tom McNally, *b.* 1943, *m.*
1991   *Marlesford*, Mark Shuldham Schreiber, *b.* 1931, *m.*
1981   *Marsh*, Richard William Marsh, PC, *b.* 1928, *m.*
1998   *Marshall of Knightsbridge*, Colin Marsh Marshall, *b.* 1933, *m.*
1987   *Mason of Barnsley*, Roy Mason, PC, *b.* 1924, *m.*
1997   *Mayhew of Twysden*, Patrick Barnabas Burke Mayhew, QC, PC, *b.* 1929, *m.*

1993   *Menuhin*, Yehudi Menuhin, OM, KBE, *b.* 1916, *m.*
1992   *Merlyn-Rees*, Merlyn Merlyn-Rees, PC, *b.* 1920, *m.*
1978   *Mishcon*, Victor Mishcon, *b.* 1915, *m.*
1981   *Molloy*, William John Molloy, *b.* 1918
1997   *Molyneaux of Killead*, James Henry Molyneaux, KBE, PC, *b.* 1920
1997   *Monro of Langholm*, Hector Seymour Peter Monro, AE, PC, *b.* 1922, *m.*
1997   *Montague of Oxford*, Michael Jacob Montague, CBE, *b.* 1932.
1992   *Moore of Lower Marsh*, John Edward Michael Moore, PC, *b.* 1937, *m.*
1986   *Moore of Wolvercote*, Philip Brian Cecil Moore, GCB, GCVO, CMG, PC, *b.* 1921, *m.*
1990   *Morris of Castle Morris*, Brian Robert Morris, D.phil., *b.* 1930, *m.*
1997   *Morris of Manchester*, Alfred Morris, PC, *b.* 1928, *m.*
1971   *Moyola*, James Dawson Chichester-Clark, PC (NI), *b.* 1923, *m.*
1985   *Murray of Epping Forest*, Lionel Murray, OBE, PC, *b.* 1922, *m.*
1979   *Murton of Lindisfarne*, (Henry) Oscar Murton, OBE, TD, PC, *b.* 1914, *m.*
1997   *Naseby*, Michael Wolfgang Laurence Morris, PC, *b.* 1936, *m.*
1997   *Neill of Bladen*, (Francis) Patrick Neill, QC, *b.* 1926, *m.*
1997   *Newby*, Richard Mark Newby, OBE, *b.* 1953, *m.*
1997   *Newton of Braintree*, Antony Harold Newton, OBE, PC, *b.* 1937, *m.*
1994   *Nickson*, David Wigley Nickson, KBE, FRSE, *b.* 1929, *m.*
1975   *Northfield*, (William) Donald Chapman, *b.* 1923.
1998   *Norton of Louth*, Philip Norton.
1997   *Onslow of Woking*, Cranley Gordon Douglas Onslow, KCMG, PC, *b.* 1926, *m.*
1976   *Oram*, Albert Edward Oram, *b.* 1913, *m.*
1997   *Orme*, Stanley Orme, PC, *b.* 1923, *m.*
1971   *Orr-Ewing*, (Charles) Ian Orr-Ewing, OBE, *b.* 1912, *m.*
1992   *Owen*, David Anthony Llewellyn Owen, CH, PC, *b.* 1938, *m.*
1991   *Palumbo*, Peter Garth Palumbo, *b.* 1935, *m.*
1992   *Parkinson*, Cecil Edward Parkinson, PC, *b.* 1931, *m.*
1975   *Parry*, Gordon Samuel David Parry, *b.* 1925, *m.*
1997   *Patten*, John Haggitt Charles Patten, PC, *b.* 1945, *m.*
1996   *Paul*, Swraj Paul, *b.* 1931, *m.*
1990   *Pearson of Rannoch*, Malcolm Everard MacLaren Pearson, *b.* 1942, *m.*
1979   *Perry of Walton*, Walter Laing Macdonald Perry, OBE, FRS, FRSE, *b.* 1921, *m.*
1987   *Peston*, Maurice Harry Peston, *b.* 1931, *m.*
1983   *Peyton of Yeovil*, John Wynne William Peyton, PC, *b.* 1919, *m.*
1994   *Phillips of Ellesmere*, Prof. David Chilton Phillips, KBE, FRS, *b.* 1924, *m.*
1998   *Phillips of Sudbury*, Andrew Wyndham Phillips, OBE.
1996   *Pilkington of Oxenford*, Revd Canon Peter Pilkington, *b.* 1933, *w.*
1992   *Plant of Highfield*, Prof. Raymond Plant, PH.D., *b.* 1945, *m.*
1959   *Plowden*, Edwin Noel Plowden, GBE, KCB, *b.* 1907, *m.*
1987   *Plumb*, (Charles) Henry Plumb, MEP, *b.* 1925, *m.*
1981   *Plummer of St Marylebone*, (Arthur) Desmond (Herne) Plummer, TD, *b.* 1914, *m.*
1990   *Porter of Luddenham*, George Porter, OM, FRS, *b.* 1920, *m.*
1992   *Prentice*, Reginald Ernest Prentice, PC, *b.* 1923, *m.*
1987   *Prior*, James Michael Leathes Prior, PC, *b.* 1927, *m.*

1982 *Prys-Davies*, Gwilym Prys Prys-Davies, *b.* 1923, *m.*

1997 *Puttnam*, David Terence Puttnam, CBE, *b.* 1941, *m.*

1987 *Pym*, Francis Leslie Pym, MC, PC, *b.* 1922, *m.*

1982 *Quinton*, Anthony Meredith Quinton, FBA, *b.* 1925, *m.*

1994 *Quirk*, Prof. (Charles) Randolph Quirk, CBE, FBA, *b.* 1920, *m.*

1997 *Randall of St Budeaux*, Stuart Jeffrey Randall, *b.* 1938, *m.*

1978 *Rawlinson of Ewell*, Peter Anthony Grayson Rawlinson, PC, QC, *b.* 1919, *m.*

1976 *Rayne*, Max Rayne, *b.* 1918, *m.*

1997 *Razzall*, (Edward) Timothy Razzall, CBE, *b.* 1943, *m.*

1987 *Rees*, Peter Wynford Innes Rees, PC, QC, *b.* 1926, *m.*

1988 *Rees-Mogg*, William Rees-Mogg, *b.* 1928, *m.*

1991 *Renfrew of Kaimsthorn*, (Andrew) Colin Renfrew, FBA, *b.* 1937, *m.*

1979 *Renton*, David Lockhart-Mure Renton, KBE, TD, PC, QC, *b.* 1908, *w.*

1997 *Renton of Mount Harry*, (Ronald) Timothy Renton, PC, *b.* 1932, *m.*

1997 *Renwick of Clifton*, Robin William Renwick, KCMG, *b.* 1937, *m.*

1990 *Richard*, Ivor Seward Richard, PC, QC, *b.* 1932, *m.*

1979 *Richardson*, John Samuel Richardson, LVO, MD, FRCP, *b.* 1910, *w.*

1983 *Richardson of Duntisbourne*, Gordon William Humphreys Richardson, KG, MBE, TD, PC, *b.* 1915, *m.*

1992 *Rix*, Brian Norman Roger Rix, CBE, *b.* 1924, *m.*

1961 *Robens of Woldingham*, Alfred Robens, PC, *b.* 1910, *m.*

1997 *Roberts of Conwy*, (Ieuan) Wyn (Pritchard) Roberts, PC, *b.* 1930, *m.*

1992 *Rodger of Earlsferry*, Alan Ferguson Rodger, PC, QC, FBA, *b.* 1944.

1992 *Rodgers of Quarry Bank*, William Thomas Rodgers, PC, *b.* 1928, *m.*

1996 *Rogers of Riverside*, Richard George Rogers, RA, RIBA, *b.* 1933, *m.*

1977 *Roll of Ipsden*, Eric Roll, KCMG, CB, *b.* 1907, *w.*

1991 *Runcie*, Rt Revd Robert Alexander Kennedy Runcie, MC, PC, Royal Victorian Chain, *b.* 1921, *m.*

1997 *Russell-Johnston*, (David) Russell Russell-Johnston, *b.* 1932, *m.*

1975 *Ryder of Eaton Hastings*, Sydney Thomas Franklin (Don) Ryder, *b.* 1916, *m.*

1997 *Ryder of Wensum*, Richard Andrew Ryder, OBE, PC, *b.* 1949, *m.*

1996 *Saatchi*, Maurice Saatchi, *b.* 1946, *m.*

1962 *Sainsbury*, Alan John Sainsbury, *b.* 1902, *w.*

1989 *Sainsbury of Preston Candover*, John Davan Sainsbury, KG, *b.* 1927, *m.*

1997 *Sainsbury of Turville*, David John Sainsbury, *b.* 1940, *m.*

1987 *St John of Fawsley*, Norman Antony Francis St John-Stevas, PC, *b.* 1929.

1997 *Sandberg*, Michael Graham Ruddock Sandberg, CBE, *b.* 1927, *m.*

1985 *Sanderson of Bowden*, Charles Russell Sanderson, *b.* 1933, *m.*

1998 *Sawyer*, Lawrence (Tom) Sawyer.

1979 *Scanlon*, Hugh Parr Scanlon, *b.* 1913, *m.*

1978 *Sefton of Garston*, William Henry Sefton, *b.* 1915, *m.*

1997 *Selkirk of Douglas*, James Alexander Douglas-Hamilton, PC, QC, *b.* 1942, *m.*

1996 *Sewel*, John Buttifant Sewel, CBE.

1994 *Shaw of Northstead*, Michael Norman Shaw, *b.* 1920, *m.*

1959 *Shawcross*, Hartley William Shawcross, GBE, PC, QC, *b.* 1902, *m.*

1994 *Sheppard of Didgemere*, Allan John George Sheppard, KCVO, *b.* 1932, *m.*

1998 *Sheppard of Liverpool*, David Stuart Sheppard, *b.* 1929, *m.*

1997 *Shore of Stepney*, Peter David Shore, PC, *b.* 1924, *m.*

1980 *Sieff of Brimpton*, Marcus Joseph Sieff, OBE, *b.* 1913, *w.*

1971 *Simon of Glaisdale*, Jocelyn Edward Salis Simon, PC, *b.* 1911, *m.*

1997 *Simon of Highbury*, David Alec Gwyn Simon, CBE, *b.* 1939, *m.*

1997 *Simpson of Dunkeld*, George Simpson, *b.* 1942, *m.*

1991 *Skidelsky*, Robert Jacob Alexander Skidelsky, D.Phil., *b.* 1939, *m.*

1997 *Smith of Clifton*, Trevor Arthur Smith, *b.* 1937, *m.*

1965 *Soper*, Revd Donald Oliver Soper, PH.D., *b.* 1903, *m.*

1990 *Soulsby of Swaffham Prior*, Ernest Jackson Lawson Soulsby, PH.D., *b.* 1926, *m.*

1983 *Stallard*, Albert William Stallard, *b.* 1921, *m.*

1997 *Steel of Aikwood*, David Martin Scott Steel, KBE, PC, *b.* 1938, *m.*

1991 *Sterling of Plaistow*, Jeffrey Maurice Sterling, CBE, *b.* 1934, *m.*

1987 *Stevens of Ludgate*, David Robert Stevens, *b.* 1936, *m.*

1992 *Stewartby*, (Bernard Harold) Ian (Halley) Stewart, RD, PC, FBA, FRSE, *b.* 1935, *m.*

1981 *Stodart of Leaston*, James Anthony Stodart, PC, *b.* 1916, *w.*

1983 *Stoddart of Swindon*, David Leonard Stoddart, *b.* 1926, *m.*

1969 *Stokes*, Donald Gresham Stokes, TD, FEng., *b.* 1914, *w.*

1997 *Stone of Blackheath*, Andrew Zelig Stone, *b.* 1942, *m.*

1971 *Tanlaw*, Simon Brooke Mackay, *b.* 1934, *m.*

1996 *Taverne*, Dick Taverne, QC, *b.* 1928, *m.*

1978 *Taylor of Blackburn*, Thomas Taylor, CBE, *b.* 1929, *m.*

1968 *Taylor of Gryfe*, Thomas Johnston Taylor, FRSE, *b.* 1912, *m.*

1996 *Taylor of Warwick*, John David Beckett Taylor, *b.* 1952, *m.*

1992 *Tebbit*, Norman Beresford Tebbit, CH, PC, *b.* 1931, *m.*

1996 *Thomas of Gresford*, Donald Martin Thomas, OBE, QC, *b.* 1937, *m.*

1987 *Thomas of Gwydir*, Peter John Mitchell Thomas, PC, QC, *b.* 1920, *w.*

1997 *Thomas of Macclesfield*, Terence James Thomas, CBE, *b.* 1937, *m.*

1981 *Thomas of Swynnerton*, Hugh Swynnerton Thomas, *b.* 1931, *m.*

1977 *Thomson of Monifieth*, George Morgan Thomson, KT, PC, *b.* 1921, *m.*

1990 *Tombs*, Francis Leonard Tombs, FEng., *b.* 1924, *m.*

1998 *Tomlinson*, John Edward Tomlinson, MEP, *b.* 1939.

1994 *Tope*, Graham Norman Tope, CBE, *b.* 1943, *m.*

1981 *Tordoff*, Geoffrey Johnson Tordoff, *b.* 1928, *m.*

1993 *Tugendhat*, Christopher Samuel Tugendhat, *b.* 1937, *m.*

1990 *Varley*, Eric Graham Varley, PC, *b.* 1932, *m.*

1996 *Vincent of Coleshill*, Richard Frederick Vincent, GBE, KCB, DSO, *b.* 1931, *m.* (Field Marshal)

1985 *Vinson*, Nigel Vinson, LVO, *b.* 1931, *m.*

1990	*Waddington*, David Charles Waddington, GCVO, PC, QC, *b.* 1929, *m.*
1990	*Wade of Chorlton*, (William) Oulton Wade, *b.* 1932, *m.*
1992	*Wakeham*, John Wakeham, PC, *b.* 1932, *m.*
1997	*Walker of Doncaster*, Harold Walker, PC, *b.* 1927, *m.*
1992	*Walker of Worcester*, Peter Edward Walker, MBE, PC, *b.* 1932, *m.*
1974	*Wallace of Coslany*, George Douglas Wallace, *b.* 1906, *m.*
1995	*Wallace of Saltaire*, William John Lawrence Wallace, PH.D., *b.* 1941, *m.*
1989	*Walton of Detchant*, John Nicholas Walton, TD, FRCP, *b.* 1922, *m.*
1998	*Warner*, Norman Reginald Warner, *b.* 1940, *m.*
1997	*Watson of Invergowrie*, Michael Goodall Watson, *b.* 1949, *m.*
1992	*Weatherill*, (Bruce) Bernard Weatherill, PC, *b.* 1920, *m.*
1977	*Wedderburn of Charlton*, (Kenneth) William Wedderburn, FBA, QC, *b.* 1927, *m.*
1976	*Weidenfeld*, (Arthur) George Weidenfeld, *b.* 1919, *m.*
1980	*Weinstock*, Arnold Weinstock, *b.* 1924, *m.*
1978	*Whaddon*, (John) Derek Page, *b.* 1927, *m.*
1996	*Whitty*, John Lawrence (Larry) Whitty, *b.* 1943, *m.*
1974	*Wigoder*, Basil Thomas Wigoder, QC, *b.* 1921, *m.*
1985	*Williams of Elvel*, Charles Cuthbert Powell Williams, CBE, *b.* 1933, *m.*
1992	*Williams of Mostyn*, Gareth Wyn Williams, QC, *b.* 1941, *m.*
1992	*Wilson of Tillyorn*, David Clive Wilson, GCMG, PH.D., *b.* 1935, *m.*
1995	*Winston*, Robert Maurice Lipson Winston, FRCOG, *b.* 1940, *m.*
1985	*Wolfson*, Leonard Gordon Wolfson, *b.* 1927, *m.*
1991	*Wolfson of Sunningdale*, David Wolfson, *b.* 1935, *m.*
1994	*Wright of Richmond*, Patrick Richard Henry Wright, GCMG, *b.* 1931, *m.*
1978	*Young of Dartington*, Michael Young, PH.D., *b.* 1915, *m.*
1984	*Young of Graffham*, David Ivor Young, PC, *b.* 1932, *m.*
1992	*Younger of Prestwick*, The Viscount Younger of Leckie. (*see* page 147)

BARONESSES

Created

1997	*Amos*, Valerie Ann Amos, *b.* 1954.
1996	*Anelay of St Johns*, Joyce Anne Anelay, DBE, *b.* 1947, *m.*
1987	*Blackstone*, Tessa Ann Vosper Blackstone, PH.D., *b.* 1942.
1987	*Blatch*, Emily May Blatch, CBE, PC, *b.* 1937, *m.*
1990	*Brigstocke*, Heather Renwick Brigstocke, *b.* 1929, *w.*
1964	*Brooke of Ystradfellte*, Barbara Muriel Brooke, DBE, *b.* 1908, *w.*
1998	*Buscombe*, Peta Jane Buscombe.
1996	*Byford*, Hazel Byford, DBE, *b.* 1941, *m.*
1982	*Carnegy of Lour*, Elizabeth Patricia Carnegy of Lour, *b.* 1925.
1990	*Castle of Blackburn*, Barbara Anne Castle, PC, *b.* 1910, *w.*
1992	*Chalker of Wallasey*, Lynda Chalker, PC, *b.* 1942, *m.*
1982	*Cox*, Caroline Anne Cox, *b.* 1937, *m.*
1998	*Crawley*, Christine Mary Crawley, MEP, *b.* 1950, *m.*
1990	*Cumberlege*, Julia Frances Cumberlege, CBE, *b.* 1943, *m.*

1978	*David*, Nora Ratcliff David, *b.* 1913, *w.*
1993	*Dean of Thornton-le-Fylde*, Brenda Dean, PC, *b.* 1943, *m.*
1974	*Delacourt-Smith of Alteryn*, Margaret Rosalind Delacourt-Smith, *b.* 1916, *m.*
1991	*Denton of Wakefield*, Jean Denton, CBE, *b.* 1935.
1990	*Dunn*, Lydia Selina Dunn, DBE, *b.* 1940, *m.*
1990	*Eccles of Moulton*, Diana Catherine Eccles, *b.* 1933, *m.*
1972	*Elles*, Diana Louie Elles, *b.* 1921, *m.*
1997	*Emerton*, Audrey Caroline Emerton, DBE, *b.* 1935.
1974	*Falkender*, Marcia Matilda Falkender, CBE, *b.* 1932.
1994	*Farrington of Ribbleton*, Josephine Farrington, *b.* 1940, *m.*
1974	*Fisher of Rednal*, Doris Mary Gertrude Fisher, *b.* 1919, *m.*
1990	*Flather*, Shreela Flather, *m.*
1997	*Fookes*, Janet Evelyn Fookes, DBE, *b.* 1936.
1981	*Gardner of Parkes*, (Rachel) Trixie (Anne) Gardner, *b.* 1927, *m.*
1998	*Goudie*, Mary Teresa Goudie, *m.*
1993	*Gould of Potternewton*, Joyce Brenda Gould, *b.* 1932, *m.*
1991	*Hamwee*, Sally Rachel Hamwee, *b.* 1947.
1996	*Hayman*, Helene Valerie Hayman, *b.* 1949, *m.*
1991	*Hilton of Eggardon*, Jennifer Hilton, QPM, *b.* 1936.
1995	*Hogg*, Sarah Elizabeth Mary Hogg, *b.* 1946, *m.*
1990	*Hollis of Heigham*, Patricia Lesley Hollis, D.PHIL., *b.* 1941, *m.*
1985	*Hooper*, Gloria Dorothy Hooper, *b.* 1939.
1965	*Hylton-Foster*, Audrey Pellew Hylton-Foster, DBE, *b.* 1908, *w.*
1991	*James of Holland Park*, Phyllis Dorothy White (P. D. James), OBE, *b.* 1920, *w.*
1992	*Jay of Paddington*, Margaret Ann Jay, PC, *b.* 1939. *Lord Privy Seal*
1979	*Jeger*, Lena May Jeger, *b.* 1915, *w.*
1997	*Kennedy of the Shaws*, Helena Ann Kennedy, QC, *b.* 1950, *m.*
1997	*Knight of Collingtree*, (Joan Christabel) Jill Knight, DBE, *b.* 1923, *w.*
1997	*Linklater of Butterstone*, Veronica Linklater, *b.* 1943, *m.*
1996	*Lloyd of Highbury*, Prof. June Kathleen Lloyd, DBE, FRCP, FRCPE, FRCGP, *b.* 1928.
1978	*Lockwood*, Betty Lockwood, *b.* 1924, *w.*
1997	*Ludford*, Sarah Ann Ludford, *b.* 1951.
1979	*McFarlane of Llandaff*, Jean Kennedy McFarlane, *b.* 1926.
1971	*Macleod of Borve*, Evelyn Hester Macleod, *b.* 1915, *w.*
1997	*Maddock*, Diana Margaret Maddock, *b.* 1945, *m.*
1991	*Mallalieu*, Ann Mallalieu, QC, *b.* 1945, *m.*
1970	*Masham of Ilton*, Susan Lilian Primrose Cunliffe-Lister, *b.* 1935, *m.* (*Countess of Swinton*)
1998	*Miller of Chilthorne Domer*, Susan Elizabeth Miller.
1993	*Miller of Hendon*, Doreen Miller, MBE, *b.* 1933, *m.*
1997	*Nicholson of Winterbourne*, Emma Harriet Nicholson, *b.* 1941, *m.*
1982	*Nicol*, Olive Mary Wendy Nicol, *b.* 1923, *m.*
1991	*O'Cathain*, Detta O'Cathain, OBE, *b.* 1938, *m.*
1989	*Oppenheim-Barnes*, Sally Oppenheim-Barnes, PC, *b.* 1930, *m.*
1990	*Park of Monmouth*, Daphne Margaret Sybil Désirée Park, CMG, DBE, *b.* 1921.
1991	*Perry of Southwark*, Pauline Perry, *b.* 1931, *m.*
1974	*Pike*, (Irene) Mervyn (Parnicott) Pike, DBE, *b.* 1918.
1997	*Pitkeathley*, Jill Elizabeth Pitkeathley, OBE, *b.* 1940.

1981	*Platt of Writtle*, Beryl Catherine Platt, CBE, FEng., b. 1923, m.
1996	*Ramsay of Cartvale*, Margaret Mildred (Meta) Ramsay, b. 1936.
1994	*Rawlings*, Patricia Elizabeth Rawlings, b. 1939.
1997	*Rendell of Babergh*, Ruth Barbara Rendell, CBE, b. 1930, m.
1998	*Richardson of Calow*, Kathleen Margaret Richardson, OBE, b. 1938, m.
1974	*Robson of Kiddington*, Inga-Stina Robson, b. 1919, w.
1979	*Ryder of Warsaw*, Margaret Susan Cheshire (Sue Ryder), CMG, OBE, b. 1923, w.
1997	*Scotland of Asthal*, Patricia Janet Scotland, QC, m.
1991	*Seccombe*, Joan Anna Dalziel Seccombe, DBE, b. 1930, m.
1967	*Serota*, Beatrice Serota, DBE, b. 1919, m.
1998	*Sharp of Guildford*, Margaret Lucy Sharp, m.
1973	*Sharples*, Pamela Sharples, b. 1923, m.
1995	*Smith of Gilmorehill*, Elizabeth Margaret Smith, b. 1940, w.
1996	*Symons of Vernham Dean*, Elizabeth Conway Symons, b. 1951.
1992	*Thatcher*, Margaret Hilda Thatcher, KG, OM, PC, FRS, b. 1925, m.
1994	*Thomas of Walliswood*, Susan Petronella Thomas, OBE, b. 1935, m.
1998	*Thornton*, (Dorothea) Glenys Thornton.
1980	*Trumpington*, Jean Alys Barker, PC, b. 1922, w.
1985	*Turner of Camden*, Muriel Winifred Turner, b. 1927, m.
1998	*Uddin*, Manzila Pola Uddin.
1985	*Warnock*, Helen Mary Warnock, DBE, b. 1924, w.
1970	*White*, Eirene Lloyd White, b. 1909, w.
1996	*Wilcox*, Judith Ann Wilcox, w.
1993	*Williams of Crosby*, Shirley Vivien Teresa Brittain Williams, PC, b. 1930, m.
1971	*Young*, Janet Mary Young, PC, b. 1926, m.
1997	*Young of Old Scone*, Barbara Scott Young, b. 1948.

Lords Spiritual

The Lords Spiritual are the Archbishops of Canterbury and York and 24 diocesan bishops of the Church of England. The Bishops of London, Durham and Winchester always have seats in the House of Lords; the other 21 seats are filled by the remaining diocesan bishops in order of seniority. The Bishop of Sodor and Man and the Bishop of Gibraltar are not eligible to sit in the House of Lords.

ARCHBISHOPS

Style, The Most Revd and Right Hon. the Lord Archbishop of __
Addressed as Archbishop, *or* Your Grace

Introduced to House of Lords
1991 *Canterbury* (103rd), George Leonard Carey, PC, PH.D., *b.* 1935, *m., cons.* 1987, *trans.* 1991
1990 *York* (96th), David Michael Hope, KCVO, PC, D.Phil., *b.* 1940, *cons.* 1985, *elected* 1985, *trans.* 1991, 1995

BISHOPS

Style, The Right Revd the Lord Bishop of __
Addressed as My Lord
elected date of election as diocesan bishop

Introduced to House of Lords
1996 *London* (132nd), Richard John Carew Chartres, *b.* 1947, *m., cons.* 1992
1994 *Durham* (93rd), (Anthony) Michael (Arnold) Turnbull, *b.* 1935, *m., cons.* 1988, *elected* 1988, *trans.* 1994
1996 *Winchester* (96th), Michael Charles Scott-Joynt, *b.* 1943, *m., cons.* 1987
1979 *Chichester* (102nd), Eric Waldram Kemp, DD, *b.* 1915, *m., cons.* 1974, *elected* 1974
1984 *Ripon* (11th), David Nigel de Lorentz Young, *b.* 1931, *m., cons.* 1977, *elected* 1977
1989 *Lichfield* (97th), Keith Norman Sutton, *b.* 1934, *m., cons.* 1978, *elected* 1984
1990 *Exeter* (69th), (Geoffrey) Hewlett Thompson, *b.* 1929, *m., cons.* 1974, *elected* 1985
1990 *Bristol* (54th), Barry Rogerson, *b.* 1936, *m., cons.* 1979, *elected* 1985
1991 *Norwich* (70th), Peter John Nott, *b.* 1933, *m., cons.* 1977, *elected* 1985
1993 *Lincoln* (70th), Robert Maynard Hardy, *b.* 1936, *m., cons.* 1980, *elected* 1986
1993 *Oxford* (41st), Richard Douglas Harries, *b.* 1936, *m., cons.* 1987, *elected* 1987
1994 *Birmingham* (7th), Mark Santer, *b.* 1936, *w., cons.* 1981, *elected* 1987
1995 *Southwell* (9th), Patrick Burnet Harris, *b.* 1934, *m., cons.* 1973, *elected* 1988
1995 *Blackburn* (7th), Alan David Chesters, *b.* 1937, *m., cons.* 1989, *elected* 1989
1996 *Carlisle* (65th), Ian Harland, *b.* 1932, *m., cons.* 1985, *elected* 1989
1996 *Ely* (67th), Stephen Whitefield Sykes, *b.* 1939, *m., cons.* 1990, *elected* 1990

1996 *Hereford* (103rd), John Keith Oliver, *b.* 1935, *m., cons.* 1990, *elected* 1990
1996 *Leicester* (5th), Thomas Frederick Butler, *b.* 1940, *m., cons.* 1985, *elected* 1991

Bishops awaiting seats, in order of seniority
  Bath and Wells (77th), James Lawton Thompson, *b.* 1936, *m., cons.* 1978, *elected* 1991
  Wakefield (11th), Nigel Simeon McCulloch, *b.* 1942, *m., cons.* 1986, *elected* 1992
  Bradford (8th), David James Smith, *b.* 1935, *m., cons.* 1987, *elected* 1992
  Manchester (10th), Christopher John Mayfield, *b.* 1935, *m., cons.* 1985, *elected* 1993
  Salisbury (77th), David Staffurth Stancliffe, *b.* 1942, *m., cons.* 1993, *elected* 1993
  Gloucester (39th), David Edward Bentley, *b.* 1935, *m., cons.* 1986, *elected* 1993
  Rochester (106th), Michael James Nazir-Ali, PH.D., *b.* 1949, *m., cons.* 1984, *elected* 1995
  Guildford (8th), John Warren Gladwin, *b.* 1942, *m., cons.* 1994, *elected* 1994
  Portsmouth (8th), Kenneth William Stevenson, *b.* 1949, *m., cons.* 1995, *elected* 1995
  Derby (6th), Jonathan Sansbury Bailey, *b.* 1940, *m., cons.* 1992, *elected* 1995
  St Albans (9th), Christopher William Herbert, *b.* 1944, *m., cons.* 1995, *elected* 1995
  Chelmsford (8th), John Freeman Perry, *b.* 1935, *m., cons.* 1989, *elected* 1996
  Peterborough (37th), Ian Cundy, *b.* 1945, *m., cons.* 1992, *elected* 1996
  Chester (40th), Peter Robert Forster, PH.D., *b.* 1950, *cons.* 1996, *elected* 1996
  St Edmundsbury and Ipswich (9th), (John Hubert) Richard Lewis, *b.* 1943, *m., cons.* 1992, *elected* 1997
  Worcester (112th), Peter Stephen Maurice Selby, *b.* 1941, *cons.* 1984, *elected* 1997
  Newcastle (11th), (John) Martin Wharton, *b.* 1944, *m., cons.* 1992, *elected* 1997
  Sheffield (6th), John Nicholls, *b.* 1943, *m., cons.* 1990, *elected* 1997
  Truro (14th), William Ind, *b.* 1942, *m., cons.* 1987, *elected* 1997
  Coventry (8th), Colin J. Bennetts, *b.* 1940, *m., cons.* 1994, *elected* 1997
  Liverpool (7th), James Jones, *b.* 1948, *m., cons.* 1994, *elected* 1998

*In September 1998 the Bishop of Leicester will become the Bishop of Southwark; he will retain his seat in the House of Lords

COURTESY TITLES

From this list it will be seen that, for example, the Marquess of Blandford is heir to the Dukedom of Marlborough, and Viscount Amberley to the Earldom of Russell. Titles of second heirs are also given, and the courtesy title of the father of a second heir is indicated by *; e.g. Earl of Burlington, eldest son of *Marquess of Hartington
For forms of address, *see* page 135

MARQUESSES

*Blandford – *Marlborough, D.*
Bowmont and Cessford – *Roxburghe, D.*
Douglas and Clydesdale – *Hamilton, D.*
*Douro – *Wellington, D.*
Graham – *Montrose, D.*
Granby – *Rutland, D.*
Hamilton – *Abercorn, D.*
*Hartington – *Devonshire, D.*
*Kildare – *Leinster, D.*
Lorne – *Argyll, D.*
*Tavistock – *Bedford, D.*
Tullibardine – *Atholl, D.*
*Worcester – *Beaufort, D.*

EARLS

Aboyne – *Huntly, M.*
Altamont – *Sligo, M.*
Ancram – *Lothian, M.*
Arundel and Surrey – *Norfolk, D.*
*Bective – *Headfort, M.*
*Belfast – *Donegall, M.*
Brecknock – *Camden, M.*
Burford – *St Albans, D.*
Burlington – *Hartington, M.*
*Cardigan – *Ailesbury, M.*
Compton – *Northampton, M.*
*Dalkeith – *Buccleuch, D.*
Dumfries – *Bute, M.*
*Euston – *Grafton, D.*
Glamorgan – *Worcester, M.*
Grosvenor – *Westminster, D.*
*Haddo – *Aberdeen and Temair, M.*
Hillsborough – *Downshire, M.*
Hopetoun – *Linlithgow, M.*
March and Kinrara – *Richmond, D.*
*Mount Charles – *Conyngham, M.*
Mornington – *Douro, M.*
Percy – *Northumberland, D.*
Ronaldshay – *Zetland, M.*
*St Andrews – *Kent, D.*
*Shelburne – *Lansdowne, M.*
*Southesk – *Fife, D.*
Sunderland – *Blandford, M.*
*Tyrone – *Waterford, M.*

Ulster – *Gloucester, D.*
*Uxbridge – *Anglesey, M.*
Wiltshire – *Winchester, M.*
Yarmouth – *Hertford, M.*

VISCOUNTS

Althorp – *Spencer, E.*
Amberley – *Russell, E.*
Andover – *Suffolk and Berkshire, E.*
Anson – *Lichfield, E.*
Asquith – *Oxford and Asquith, E.*
Boringdon – *Morley, E.*
Borodale – *Beatty, E.*
Boyle – *Shannon, E.*
Brocas – *Jellicoe, E.*
Calne and Calstone – *Shelburne, E.*
Campden – *Gainsborough, E.*
Carlow – *Portarlington, E.*
Carlton – *Wharncliffe, E.*
Castlereagh – *Londonderry, M.*
Chelsea – *Cadogan, E.*
Chewton – *Waldegrave, E.*
Chichester – *Belfast, E.*
Clanfield – *Peel, E.*
Clive – *Powis, E.*
Coke – *Leicester, E.*
Corry – *Belmore, E.*
Corvedale – *Baldwin of Bewdley, E.*
Cranborne – *Salisbury, M.*
Cranley – *Onslow, E.*
Crichton – *Erne, E.*
Crowhurst – *Cottenham, E.*
Curzon – *Howe, E.*
Dangan – *Cowley, E.*
Dawick – *Haig, E.*
Drumlanrig – *Queensberry, M.*
Dunwich – *Stradbroke, E.*
Dupplin – *Kinnoull, E.*
Ebrington – *Fortescue, E.*
Ednam – *Dudley, E.*
Emlyn – *Cawdor, E.*
Encombe – *Eldon, E.*
Enfield – *Strafford, E.*
Erleigh – *Reading, M.*
Errington – *Cromer, E.*
FitzHarris – *Malmesbury, E.*
Folkestone – *Radnor, E.*
Forbes – *Granard, E.*
Garmoyle – *Cairns, E.*
Garnock – *Lindsay, E.*
Glandine – *Norbury, E.*

Glenapp – *Inchcape, E.*
Glentworth – *Limerick, E.*
Grimstone – *Verulam, E.*
Gwynedd – *Lloyd George of Dwyfor, E.*
Hawkesbury – *Liverpool, E.*
Hinchingbrooke – *Sandwich, E.*
Ikerrin – *Carrick, E.*
Ingestre – *Shrewsbury, E.*
Ipswich – *Euston, E.*
Jocelyn – *Roden, E.*
Kelburn – *Glasgow, E.*
Kilwarlin – *Hillsborough, E.*
Kingsborough – *Kingston, E.*
Kirkwall – *Orkney, E.*
Knebworth – *Lytton, E.*
Lascelles – *Harewood, E.*
Linley – *Snowdon, E.*
Loftus – *Ely, M.*
Lowther – *Lonsdale, E.*
Lumley – *Scarbrough, E.*
Lymington – *Portsmouth, E.*
Macmillan of Ovenden – *Stockton, E.*
Maidstone – *Winchilsea and Nottingham, E.*
Maitland – *Lauderdale, E.*
Malden – *Essex, E.*
Mandeville – *Manchester, D.*
Medina – *Milford Haven, M.*
Melgund – *Minto, E.*
Merton – *Nelson, E.*
Moore – *Drogheda, E.*
Newport – *Bradford, E.*
Newry and Mourne – *Kilmorey, E.*
Parker – *Macclesfield, E.*
Perceval – *Egmont, E.*
Petersham – *Harrington, E.*
Pollington – *Mexborough, E.*
Raynham – *Townshend, M.*
Reidhaven – *Seafield, E.*
Ruthven of Canberra – *Gowrie, E.*
St Cyres – *Iddesleigh, E.*
Sandon – *Harrowby, E.*
Savernake – *Cardigan, E.*
Slane – *Mount Charles, E.*
Somerton – *Normanton, E.*
Stopford – *Courtown, E.*
Stormont – *Mansfield, E.*
Strathallan – *Perth, E.*
Stuart – *Castle Stewart, E.*
Suirdale – *Donoughmore, E.*
Tamworth – *Ferrers, E.*
Tarbat – *Cromartie, E.*

Vaughan – *Lisburne, E.*
Weymouth – *Bath, M.*
Windsor – *Plymouth, E.*
Wolmer – *Selborne, E.*
Woodstock – *Portland, E.*

BARONS (LORD ___)

Aberdour – *Morton, E.*
Apsley – *Bathurst, E.*
Ardee – *Meath, E.*
Ashley – *Shaftesbury, E.*
Balgonie – *Leven and Melville, E.*
Balniel – *Crawford and Balcarres, E.*
Berriedale – *Caithness, E.*
Bingham – *Lucan, E.*
Binning – *Haddington, E.*
Brooke – *Warwick, E.*
Bruce – *Elgin, E.*
Buckhurst – *De La Warr, E.*
Burghley – *Exeter, M.*
Cardross – *Buchan, E.*
Carnegie – *Southesk, E.*
Clifton – *Darnley, E.*
Cochrane – *Dundonald, E.*
Courtenay – *Devon, E.*
Dalmeny – *Rosebery, E.*
Doune – *Moray, E.*
Downpatrick – *St Andrews, E.*
Dunglass – *Home, E.*
Eliot – *St Germans, E.*
Eskdail – *Dalkeith, E.*
Formartine – *Haddo, E.*
Gillford – *Clanwilliam, E.*
Glamis – *Strathmore, E.*
Greenock – *Cathcart, E.*
Guernsey – *Aylesford, E.*
Hay – *Erroll, E.*
Herbert – *Pembroke, E.*
Howard of Effingham – *Effingham, E.*
Howland – *Tavistock, M.*
Hyde – *Clarendon, E.*
Inverurie – *Kintore, E.*
Irwin – *Halifax, E.*
Johnstone – *Annandale and Hartfell, E.*
Kenlis – *Bective, E.*
Langton – *Temple of Stowe, E.*
La Poer – *Tyrone, E.*
Leslie – *Rothes, E.*
Loughborough – *Rosslyn, E.*
Maltravers – *Arundel and Surrey, E.*
Mauchline – *Loudoun, C.*
Medway – *Cranbrook, E.*
Montgomerie – *Eglinton and Winton, E.*
Moreton – *Ducie, E.*
Naas – *Mayo, E.*

Neidpath – *Wemyss and March, E.*
Norreys – *Lindsey and Abingdon, E.*
North – *Guilford, E.*

Ogilvy – *Airlie, E.*
Oxmantown – *Rosse, E.*
Paget de Beaudesert – **Uxbridge, E.*
Porchester – *Carnarvon, E.*

Ramsay – *Dalhousie, E.*
Romsey – *Mountbatten of Burma, C.*
Rosehill – *Northesk, E.*
Scrymgeour – *Dundee, E.*

Seymour – *Somerset, D.*
Strathnaver – *Sutherland, C.*
Wodehouse – *Kimberley, E.*
Worsley – *Yarborough, E.*

PEERS' SURNAMES WHICH DIFFER FROM THEIR TITLES

The following symbols indicate the rank of the peer holding each title:

B. Baron/Lord or Baroness/Lady
C. Countess
D. Duke
E. Earl
M. Marquess
V. Viscount
* Life Peer

Abney-Hastings – *Loudoun, C.*
Acheson – *Gosford, E.*
Adderley – *Norton, B.*
Addington – *Sidmouth, V.*
Agar – *Normanton, E.*
Aitken – *Beaverbrook, B.*
Akers-Douglas – *Chilston, V.*
Alexander – *A. of Tunis, E.*
Alexander – *A. of Weedon, B.**
Alexander – *Caledon, E.*
Allen – *A. of Abbeydale, B.**
Allen – *Croham, B.**
Allsopp – *Hindlip, B.*
Alton – *A. of Liverpool, B.**
Anderson – *Waverley, V.*
Anelay – *A. of St Johns, B.**
Annesley – *Valentia, V.*
Anson – *Lichfield, E.*
Arbuthnott – *of Arbuthnott, V.*
Archer – *A. of Sandwell, B.**
Archer – *A. of Weston-super-Mare, B.**
Armstrong – *A. of Ilminster, B.**
Armstrong-Jones – *Snowdon, E.*
Arthur – *Glenarthur, B.*
Arundell – *Talbot of Malahide, B.*
Ashley – *A. of Stoke, B.**
Ashley-Cooper – *Shaftesbury, E.*
Ashton – *A. of Hyde, B.*
Asquith – *Oxford and Asquith, E.*
Assheton – *Clitheroe, B.*
Astley – *Hastings, B.*
Astor – *A. of Hever, B.*
Aubrey-Fletcher – *Braye, B.*
Bailey – *Glanusk, B.*
Baillie – *Burton, B.*
Baillie-Hamilton – *Haddington, E.*
Baker – *B. of Dorking, B.**
Balcarres – *Balniel, B.**
Baldwin – *B. of Bewdley, E.*
Balfour – *B. of Inchrye, B.*
Balfour – *Kinross, B.*
Balfour – *Riverdale, B.*

Bampfylde – *Poltimore, B.*
Banbury – *B. of Southam, B.*
Barber – *B. of Tewkesbury, B.**
Baring – *Ashburton, B.*
Baring – *Cromer, E.*
Baring – *Howick of Glendale, B.*
Baring – *Northbrook, B.*
Baring – *Revelstoke, B.*
Barker – *Trumpington, B.**
Barnes – *Gorell, B.*
Barnewall – *Trimlestown, B.*
Bassam – *B. of Brighton, B.**
Bathurst – *Bledisloe, V.*
Beauclerk – *St Albans, D.*
Beaumont – *Allendale, V.*
Beaumont – *B. of Whitley, B.**
Beckett – *Grimthorpe, B.*
Bellow – *Bellwin, B.**
Benn – *Stansgate, V.*
Bennet – *Tankerville, E.*
Bentinck – *Portland, E.*
Beresford – *Waterford, M.*
Berry – *Hartwell, B.**
Berry – *Kemsley, V.*
Bertie – *Lindsey, E.*
Best – *Wynford, B.*
Bethell – *Westbury, B.*
Bewicke-Copley – *Cromwell, B.*
Bigham – *Mersey, V.*
Bingham – *B. of Cornhill, B.**
Bingham – *Clanmorris, B.*
Bingham – *Lucan, E.*
Bligh – *Darnley, E.*
Blyth – *B. of Rowington, B.**
Bootle-Wilbraham – *Skelmersdale, B.*
Boscawen – *Falmouth, V.*
Boston – *B. of Faversham, B.**
Bourke – *Mayo, E.*
Bowes Lyon – *Strathmore and Kinghorne, E.*
Bowyer – *Denham, B.*
Boyd – *Kilmarnock, B.*
Boyle – *Cork and Orrery, E.*
Boyle – *Glasgow, E.*
Boyle – *Shannon, E.*
Brabazon – *Meath, E.*
Braine – *B. of Wheatley, B.**
Brand – *Hampden, V.*
Brandon – *B. of Oakbrook, B.**
Brassey – *B. of Apethorpe, B.**
Brett – *Esher, V.*
Bridge – *B. of Harwich, B.**
Bridgeman – *Bradford, E.*
Brodrick – *Midleton, V.*
Brooke – *Alanbrooke, V.*
Brooke – *B. of Alverthorpe, B.**
Brooke – *B. of Ystradfellte, B.**
Brooke – *Brookeborough, V.*
Brooks – *B. of Tremorfa, B.**

Brooks – *Crawshaw, B.*
Brougham – *B. and Vaux, B.*
Broughton – *Fairhaven, B.*
Browne – *Kilmaine, B.*
Browne – *Oranmore and Browne, B.*
Browne – *Sligo, M.*
Bruce – *Aberdare, B.*
Bruce – *Balfour of Burleigh, B.*
Bruce – *B. of Donington, B.**
Bruce – *Elgin and Kincardine, E.*
Brudenell-Bruce – *Ailesbury, M.*
Buchan – *Tweedsmuir, B.*
Buckley – *Wrenbury, B.*
Butler – *B. of Brockwell, B.**
Butler – *Carrick, E.*
Butler – *Dunboyne, B.*
Butler – *Lanesborough, E.*
Butler – *Mountgarret, V.*
Buxton – *B. of Alsa, B.**
Byng – *Strafford, E.*
Byng – *Torrington, V.*
Callaghan – *C. of Cardiff, B.**
Cameron – *C. of Lochbroom, B.**
Campbell – *Argyll, D.*
Campbell – *C. of Alloway, B.**
Campbell – *C. of Croy, B.**
Campbell – *Cawdor, E.*
Campbell – *Colgrain, B.*
Campbell – *Stratheden and Campbell, B.*
Campbell-Gray – *Gray, B.*
Canning – *Garvagh, B.*
Capell – *Essex, E.*
Carington – *Carrington, B.*
Carlisle – *C. of Bucklow, B.**
Carmichael – *C. of Kelvingrove, B.**
Carnegie – *Fife, D.*
Carnegie – *Northesk, E.*
Carr – *C. of Hadley, B.**
Cary – *Falkland, V.*
Castle – *C. of Blackburn, B.**
Caulfeild – *Charlemont, V.*
Cavendish – *C. of Furness, B.**
Cavendish – *Chesham, B.*
Cavendish – *Devonshire, D.*
Cavendish – *Waterpark, B.*
Cayzer – *Rotherwick, B.*
Cecil – *Amherst of Hackney, B.*
Cecil – *Exeter, M.*
Cecil – *Rockley, B.*
Cecil – *Salisbury, M.*
Chalker – *C. of Wallasey, B.**
Chaloner – *Gisborough, B.*
Channon – *Kelvedon, B.**
Chapman – *Northfield, B.**
Charteris – *C. of Amisfield, B.**

Charteris – *Wemyss and March, E.*
Cheshire – *Ryder of Warsaw, B.**
Chetwynd-Talbot – *Shrewsbury and Waterford, E.*
Chichester – *Donegall, M.*
Chichester-Clark – *Moyola, B.**
Child Villiers – *Jersey, E.*
Cholmondeley – *Delamere, B.*
Chubb – *Hayter, B.*
Clark – *C. of Kempston, B.**
Clarke – *C. of Hampstead, B.**
Clegg-Hill – *Hill, V.*
Clifford – *C. of Chudleigh, B.*
Cochrane – *C. of Cults, B.*
Cochrane – *Dundonald, E.*
Cocks – *C. of Hartcliffe, B.**
Cocks – *Somers, B.*
Cokayne – *Cullen of Ashbourne, B.*
Coke – *Leicester, E.*
Cole – *Enniskillen, E.*
Collier – *Monkswell, B.*
Colville – *Clydesmuir, B.*
Colville – *C. of Culross, V.*
Compton – *Northampton, M.*
Conolly-Carew – *Carew, E.*
Constantine – *C. of Stanmore, B.**
Cooke – *C. of Islandreagh, B.**
Cooke – *C. of Thorndon, B.**
Cooper – *Norwich, V.*
Cope – *C. of Berkeley, B.**
Corbett – *Rowallan, B.*
Cornwall-Legh – *Grey of Codnor, B.*
Courtenay – *Devon, E.*
Cowdrey – *C. of Tonbridge, B.**
Craig – *C. of Radley, B.**
Craig – *Craigavon, V.*
Crichton – *Erne, E.*
Crichton-Stuart – *Bute, M.*
Cripps – *Parmoor, B.*
Crossley – *Somerleyton, B.*
Cubitt – *Ashcombe, B.*
Cunliffe-Lister – *Masham of Ilton, B.**
Cunliffe-Lister – *Swinton, E.*
Currie – *C. of Marylebone, B.**
Curzon – *Howe, E.*
Curzon – *Scarsdale, V.*
Cust – *Brownlow, B.*
Dalrymple – *Stair, E.*
Daubeny de Moleyns – *Ventry, B.*
Davies – *D. of Coity, B.**
Davies – *D. of Oldham, B.**

Irvine – *I. of Lairg, B.* *
Isaacs – *Reading, M.*
James – *J. of Holland Park, B.* *
James – *Northbourne, B.*
Janner – *J. of Braunstone, B.* *
Jauncey – *J. of Tullichettle, W.* *
Jay – *J. of Paddington, B.* *
Jebb – *Gladwyn, B.*
Jenkin – *J. of Roding, B.* *
Jenkins – *J. of Hillhead, B.* *
Jenkins – *J. of Putney, B.* *
Jervis – *St Vincent, V.*
Jocelyn – *Roden, E.*
Johnston – *J. of Rockport, B.* *
Jolliffe – *Hylton, B.*
Joynson-Hicks – *Brentford, V.*
Kay-Shuttleworth – *Shuttleworth, B.*
Kearley – *Devonport, V.*
Keith – *K. of Castleacre, B.* *
Keith – *K. of Kinkel, B.* *
Keith – *Kintore, E.*
Kemp – *Rochdale, V.*
Kennedy – *Ailsa, M.*
Kennedy – *K. of the Shaws, B.* *
Kenworthy – *Strabolgi, B.*
Keppel – *Albemarle, E.*
Kerr – *Lothian, M.*
Kerr – *Teviot, B.*
Kilpatrick – *K. of Kincraig, B.* *
King – *K. of Wartnaby, B.* *
King – *Lovelace, E.*
King-Tenison – *Kingston, E.*
Kirkham – *Berners, B.*
Kitchener – *K. of Khartoum, E.*
Knatchbull – *Brabourne, B.*
Knatchbull – *Mountbatten of Burma, C.*
Knight – *K. of Collingtree, B.* *
Knox – *Ranfurly, E.*
Laing – *L. of Dunphail, B.* *
Lamb – *Rochester, B.*
Lambton – *Durham, E.*
Lamont – *L. of Lerwick, B.* *
Lampson – *Killearn, B.*
Lane – *L. of Horsell, B.* *
Lang – *L. of Monkton, B.* *
Lascelles – *Harewood, E.*
Law – *Coleraine, B.*
Law – *Ellenborough, B.*
Lawrence – *Trevethin and Oaksey, B.*
Lawson – *Burnham, B.*
Lawson – *L. of Blaby, B.* *
Lawson-Johnston – *Luke, B.*
Leckie – *Younger of Prestwick, B.* *
Legge – *Dartmouth, E.*
Legh – *Newton, B.*
Leigh-Pemberton – *Kingsdown, B.* *
Leith – *Burgh, B.*
Lennox-Boyd – *Boyd of Merton, V.*
Le Poer Trench – *Clancarty, E.*
Leslie – *Rothes, E.*
Leslie Melville – *Leven, E.*
Lester – *L. of Herne Hill, B.* *
Levene – *L. of Portsoken, B.* *
Lever – *Leverhulme, V.*

Leveson-Gower – *Granville, E.*
Lewis – *L. of Newnham, B.* *
Lewis, Bt – *Merthyr, B.*
Liddell – *Ravensworth, B.*
Lindesay-Bethune – *Lindsay, E.*
Lindsay – *Crawford, E.*
Lindsay – *L. of Birker, B.*
Linklater – *L. of Butterstone, B.* *
Littleton – *Hatherton, B.*
Lloyd – *L. of Berwick, B.* *
Lloyd – *L. of Highbury, B.* *
Lloyd George – *L. G. of Dwyfor, E.*
Lloyd George – *Tenby, V.*
Lloyd-Mostyn – *Mostyn, B.*
Loder – *Wakehurst, B.*
Lofthouse – *L. of Pontefract, B.* *
Lopes – *Roborough, B.*
Lour – *Carnegy of Lour, B.* *
Low – *Aldington, B.*
Lowry-Corry – *Belmore, E.*
Lowther – *Lonsdale, E.*
Lowther – *Ullswater, V.*
Lubbock – *Avebury, B.*
Lucas – *L. of Chilworth, B.*
Lumley – *Scarbrough, E.*
Lumley-Savile – *Savile, B.*
Lyon-Dalberg-Acton – *Acton, B.*
Lysaght – *Lisle, B.*
Lyttelton – *Chandos, V.*
Lyttelton – *Cobham, V.*
Lytton Cobbold – *Cobbold, B.*
McAlpine – *M. of West Green, B.* *
Macaulay – *M. of Bragar, B.* *
McClintock-Bunbury – *Rathdonnell, B.*
McColl – *M. of Dulwich, B.* *
Macdonald – *M. of Gwaenysgor, B.*
McDonnell – *Antrim, E.*
Macfarlane – *M. of Bearsden, B.* *
McFarlane – *M. of Llandaff, B.* *
McIntosh – *M. of Haringey, B.* *
Mackay – *Inchcape, E.*
Mackay – *M. of Ardbrecknish, B.* *
Mackay – *M. of Clashfern, B.* *
Mackay – *M. of Drumadoon, B.* *
Mackay – *Reay, B.*
Mackay – *Tanlaw, B.* *
Mackenzie – *Cromartie, E.*
Mackenzie – *M. of Framwellgate, B.* *
Mackie – *M. of Benshie, B.* *
Mackintosh – *M. of Halifax, V.*
McLaren – *Aberconway, B.*
MacLehose – *M. of Beoch, B.* *
Macleod – *M. of Borve, B.* *
Macmillan – *Stockton, E.*
Macpherson – *M. of Drumochter, B.*

Macpherson – *Strathcarron, B.*
Maffey – *Rugby, B.*
Maitland – *Lauderdale, E.*
Maitland Biddulph – *Biddulph, B.*
Makgill – *of Oxfuird, V.*
Makins – *Sherfield, B.*
Manners – *Rutland, D.*
Manningham-Buller – *Dilhorne, V.*
Mansfield – *Sandhurst, B.*
Marks – *M. of Broughton, B.*
Marquis – *Woolton, E.*
Marshall – *M. of Knightsbridge, B.* *
Marsham – *Romney, E.*
Martyn-Hemphill – *Hemphill, B.*
Mason – *M. of Barnsley, B.* *
Maude – *Hawarden, V.*
Maxwell – *de Ros, B.*
Maxwell – *Farnham, B.*
Mayhew – *M. of Twysden, B.* *
Meade – *Clanwilliam, E.*
Mercer Nairne Petty-Fitzmaurice – *Lansdowne, M.*
Millar – *Inchyra, B.*
Miller – *M. of Chilthorne Domer, B.* *
Miller – *M. of Hendon, B.* *
Milner – *M. of Leeds, B.*
Mitchell-Thomson – *Selsdon, B.*
Mitford – *Redesdale, B.*
Molyneaux – *M. of Killead, B.* *
Monckton – *M. of Brenchley, V.*
Monckton-Arundell – *Galway, V.*
Mond – *Melchett, B.*
Money-Coutts – *Latymer, B.*
Monro – *M. of Langholm, B.* *
Montagu – *Manchester, D.*
Montagu – *Sandwich, E.*
Montagu – *Swaythling, B.*
Montagu Douglas Scott – *Buccleuch, D.*
Montagu Scot Wortley – *Wharncliffe, E.*
Montague – *Amwell, B.*
Montague – *M. of Oxford, B.* *
Montgomerie – *Eglinton, E.*
Montgomery – *M. of Alamein, V.*
Moore – *Drogheda, E.*
Moore – *M. of Lower Marsh, B.* *
Moore – *M. of Wolvercote, B.* *
Moore-Brabazon – *Brabazon of Tara, B.*
Moreton – *Ducie, E.*
Morris – *Killanin, B.*
Morris – *M. of Castle Morris, B.* *
Morris – *M. of Kenwood, B.*
Morris – *M. of Manchester, B.* *
Morris – *Naseby, B.* *
Morrison – *Dunrossil, V.*
Morrison – *Margadale, B.*

Mosley – *Ravensdale, B.*
Mountbatten – *Milford Haven, M.*
Muff – *Calverley, B.*
Mulholland – *Dunleath, B.*
Murray – *Atholl, D.*
Murray – *Dunmore, E.*
Murray – *Mansfield and Mansfield, E.*
Murray – *M. of Epping Forest, B.* *
Murton – *M. of Lindisfarne, B.* *
Nall-Cain – *Brocket, B.*
Napier – *N. and Ettrick, B.*
Napier – *N. of Magdala, B.*
Needham – *Kilmorey, E.*
Neill – *N. of Bladen, B.* *
Nelson – *N. of Stafford, B.*
Nevill – *Abergavenny, M.*
Neville – *Braybrooke, B.*
Newton – *N. of Braintree, B.*
Nicholls – *N. of Birkenhead, B.* *
Nicholson – *N. of Winterbourne, B.* *
Nicolson – *Carnock, B.*
Nivison – *Glendyne, B.*
Noel – *Gainsborough, E.*
North – *Guilford, E.*
Northcote – *Iddesleigh, E.*
Norton – *Grantley, B.*
Norton – *N. of Louth, B.* *
Norton – *Rathcreedan, B.*
Nugent – *Westmeath, E.*
O'Brien – *Inchiquin, B.*
Ogilvie-Grant – *Seafield, E.*
Ogilvy – *Airlie, E.*
Oliver – *O. of Aylmerton, B.* *
O'Neill – *Rathcavan, B.*
Onslow – *O. of Woking, B.* *
Orde-Powlett – *Bolton, B.*
Ormsby-Gore – *Harlech, B.*
Page – *Whaddon, B.*
Paget – *Anglesey, M.*
Pakenham – *Longford, E.*
Pakington – *Hampton, B.*
Palmer – *Lucas and Dingwall, B.*
Palmer – *Selborne, E.*
Park – *P. of Monmouth, B.* *
Parker – *Macclesfield, E.*
Parker – *Morley, E.*
Parnell – *Congleton, B.*
Parsons – *Rosse, E.*
Paulet – *Winchester, M.*
Peake – *Ingleby, V.*
Pearson – *Cowdray, V.*
Pearson – *P. of Rannoch, B.* *
Pease – *Gainford, B.*
Pease – *Wardington, B.*
Pelham – *Chichester, E.*
Pelham – *Yarborough, E.*
Pellew – *Exmouth, V.*
Penny – *Marchwood, V.*
Pepys – *Cottenham, E.*
Perceval – *Egmont, E.*
Percy – *Northumberland, D.*
Perry – *P. of Southwark, B.* *
Perry – *P. of Walton, B.* *
Pery – *Limerick, E.*
Peyton – *P. of Yeovil, B.* *
Philipps – *Milford, B.*

Philipps – *St Davids, V.*
Phillips – *P. of Ellesmere, B.**
Phillips – *P. of Sudbury, B.**
Phipps – *Normanby, M.*
Pilkington – *P. of Oxenford, B.**
Plant – *P. of Highfield, B.**
Platt – *P. of Writtle, B.**
Pleydell-Bouverie – *Radnor, E.*
Plummer – *P. of St Marylebone, B.**
Plumptre – *Fitzwalter, B.*
Plunkett – *Dunsany, B.*
Plunkett – *Louth, B.*
Pollock – *Hanworth, V.*
Pomeroy – *Harberton, V.*
Ponsonby – *Bessborough, E.*
Ponsonby – *de Mauley, B.*
Ponsonby – *P. of Shulbrede, B.*
Ponsonby – *Sysonby, B.*
Porter – *P. of Luddenham, B.**
Powys – *Lilford, B.*
Pratt – *Camden, M.*
Preston – *Gormanston, V.*
Primrose – *Rosebery, E.*
Prittie – *Dunalley, B.*
Prout – *Kingsland, B.**
Ramsay – *Dalhousie, E.*
Ramsay – *R. of Cartvale, B.**
Ramsbotham – *Soulbury, V.*
Randall – *R. of St Budeaux, B.**
Rawlinson – *R. of Ewell, B.**
Rees-Williams – *Ogmore, B.*
Rendell – *R. of Babergh, B.**
Renfrew – *R. of Kaimsthorn, B.**
Renton – *R. of Mount Harry, B.**
Renwick – *R. of Clifton, B.**
Rhys – *Dynevor, B.*
Richards – *Milverton, B.*
Richardson – *R. of Calow, B.**
Richardson – *R. of Duntisbourne, B.**
Ritchie – *R. of Dundee, B.*
Robens – *R. of Woldingham, B.**
Roberts – *Clwyd, B.*
Roberts – *R. of Conwy, B.**
Robertson – *R. of Oakridge, B.*
Robertson – *Wharton, B.*
Robinson – *Martonmere, B.*
Robson – *R. of Kiddington, B.**
Roche – *Fermoy, B.*
Rodd – *Rennell, B.*
Rodger – *R. of Earlsferry, B.**
Rodgers – *R. of Quarry Bank, B.**
Rogers – *R. of Riverside, B.**
Roll – *R. of Ipsden, B.**
Roper-Curzon – *Teynham, B.*
Rospigliosi – *Newburgh, E.*
Rous – *Stradbroke, E.*
Rowley-Conwy – *Langford, B.*
Royle – *Fanshawe of Richmond, B.**
Runciman (Garry) – *Runciman of Doxford, V.*
Russell – *Ampthill, B.*
Russell – *Bedford, D.*

Russell – *de Clifford, B.*
Russell – *R. of Liverpool, B.*
Ryder – *Harrowby, E.*
Ryder – *R. of Eaton Hastings, B.**
Ryder – *R. of Warsaw, B.**
Ryder – *R. of Wensum, B.**
Sackville – *De La Warr, E.*
Sackville-West – *Sackville, B.*
Sainsbury – *S. of Preston Candover, B.**
Sainsbury – *S. of Turville, B.**
St Aubyn – *St Levan, B.*
St Clair – *Sinclair, B.*
St Clair-Erskine – *Rosslyn, E.*
St John – *Bolingbroke, V.*
St John – *Orkney, E.*
St John – *St. J. of Bletso, B.*
St John-Stevas – *St J. of Fawsley, B.**
St Leger – *Doneraile, V.*
Samuel – *Bearsted, V.*
Sanderson – *S. of Ayot, B.*
Sanderson – *S. of Bowden, B.**
Sandilands – *Torphichen, B.*
Saumarez – *de Saumarez, B.*
Savile – *Mexborough, E.*
Saville – *S. of Newdigate, W.**
Scarlett – *Abinger, B.*
Schreiber – *Marlesford, B.**
Sclater-Booth – *Basing, B.*
Scotland – *S. of Asthal, B.**
Scott – *Eldon, E.*
Scott-Ellis – *Howard de Walden, B.*
Scrymgeour – *Dundee, E.*
Seager – *Leighton of St Mellons, B.*
Seely – *Mottistone, B.*
Sefton – *S. of Garston, B.**
Seymour – *Hertford, M.*
Seymour – *Somerset, D.*
Sharp – *S. of Guildford, B.**
Shaw – *Craigmyle, B.*
Shaw – *S. of Northstead, B.**
Sheppard – *S. of Didgemere, B.**
Sheppard – *S. of Liverpool, B.**
Shirley – *Ferrers, E.*
Shore – *S. of Stepney, B.**
Short – *Glenamara, B.**
Siddeley – *Kenilworth, B.*
Sidney – *De L'Isle, V.*
Sieff – *S. of Brimpton, B.**
Simon – *S. of Glaisdale, B.**
Simon – *S. of Highbury, B.**
Simon – *S. of Wythenshawe, B.*
Simpson – *S. of Dunkeld, B.**
Sinclair – *Caithness, E.*
Sinclair – *S. of Cleeve, B.*
Sinclair – *Thurso, V.*
Skeffington – *Massereene, V.*
Slynn – *S. of Hadley, B.**
Smith – *Bicester, B.*
Smith – *Hambleden, V.*
Smith – *Kirkhill, B.**
Smith – *S. of Clifton, B.**
Smith – *S. of Gilmorehill, B.**
Somerset – *Beaufort, D.*
Somerset – *Raglan, B.*
Soulsby – *S. of Swaffham Prior, B.**
Spencer – *Churchill, V.*

Spencer-Churchill – *Marlborough, D.*
Spring Rice – *Monteagle of Brandon, B.*
Stanhope – *Harrington, E.*
Stanley – *Derby, E.*
Stanley – *S. of Alderley and Sheffield, B.*
Stapleton-Cotton – *Combermere, V.*
Steel – *S. of Aikwood, B.**
Sterling – *S. of Plaistow, B.**
Stevens – *S. of Ludgate, B.**
Stewart – *Galloway, E.*
Stewart – *Stewartby, B.**
Stodart – *S. of Leaston, B.**
Stoddart – *S. of Swindon, B.**
Stone – *S. of Blackheath, B.**
Stonor – *Camoys, B.*
Stopford – *Courtown, E.*
Stourton – *Mowbray, B.*
Strachey – *O'Hagan, B.*
Strutt – *Belper, B.*
Strutt – *Rayleigh, B.*
Stuart – *Castle Stewart, E.*
Stuart – *Mackenzie-Stuart, B.**
Stuart – *Moray, E.*
Stuart – *S. of Findhorn, V.*
Suenson-Taylor – *Grantchester, B.*
Symons – *S. of Vernham Dean, B.**
Taylor – *Ingrow, B.**
Taylor – *T. of Blackburn, B.**
Taylor – *T. of Gryfe, B.**
Taylor – *T. of Warwick, B.**
Taylour – *Headfort, M.*
Temple-Gore-Langton – *Temple of Stowe, E.*
Tennant – *Glenconner, B.*
Thellusson – *Rendlesham, B.*
Thesiger – *Chelmsford, V.*
Thomas – *T. of Gresford, B.**
Thomas – *T. of Gwydir, B.**
Thomas – *T. of Macclesfield, B.**
Thomas – *T. of Swynnerton, B.**
Thomas – *T. of Walliswood, B.**
Thomson – *T. of Fleet, B.*
Thomson – *T. of Monifieth, B.**
Thynn – *Bath, M.*
Tottenham – *Ely, M.*
Trefusis – *Clinton, B.*
Trench – *Ashtown, B.*
Trevor-Roper – *Dacre of Glanton, B.**
Tufton – *Hothfield, B.*
Turner – *Netherthorpe, B.*
Turner – *T. of Camden, B.**
Turnour – *Winterton, E.*
Tyrell-Kenyon – *Kenyon, B.*
Vanden-Bempde-Johnstone – *Derwent, B.*
Vane – *Barnard, B.*
Vane-Tempest-Stewart – *Londonderry, M.*
Vanneck – *Huntingfield, B.*
Vaughan – *Lisburne, E.*
Vereker – *Gort, V.*

Verney – *Willoughby de Broke, B.*
Vernon – *Lyveden, B.*
Vesey – *De Vesci, V.*
Villiers – *Clarendon, E.*
Vincent – *V. of Coleshill, B.**
Vivian – *Swansea, B.*
Wade – *W. of Chorlton, B.**
Walker – *W. of Doncaster, B.**
Walker – *W. of Worcester, B.**
Wallace – *W. of Coslany, B.**
Wallace – *W. of Saltaire, B.**
Wallop – *Portsmouth, E.*
Walton – *W. of Detchant, B.**
Ward – *Bangor, V.*
Ward – *Dudley, E.*
Warrender – *Bruntisfield, B.*
Watson – *Manton, B.*
Watson – *W. of Invergowrie, B.**
Webber – *Lloyd-Webber, B.**
Wedderburn – *W. of Charlton, B.**
Weir – *Inverforth, B.*
Weld-Forester – *Forester, B.*
Wellesley – *Cowley, E.*
Wellesley – *Wellington, D.*
Westenra – *Rossmore, B.*
White – *Annaly, B.*
White – *Hanningfield, B.**
White – *James of Holland Park, B.**
Whiteley – *Marchamley, B.*
Whitfield – *Kenswood, B.*
Williams – *W. of Crosby, B.**
Williams – *W. of Elvel, B.**
Williams – *W. of Mostyn, B.**
Williamson – *Forres, B.*
Willoughby – *Middleton, B.*
Wills – *Dulverton, B.*
Wilson – *Moran, B.*
Wilson – *Nunburnholme, B.*
Wilson – *W. of Tillyorn, B.**
Windsor – *Gloucester, D.*
Windsor – *Kent, D.*
Windsor-Clive – *Plymouth, E.*
Wingfield – *Powerscourt, V.*
Winn – *St Oswald, B.*
Wodehouse – *Kimberley, E.*
Wolfson – *W. of Sunningdale, B.**
Wood – *Halifax, E.*
Wood – *Holderness, B.**
Woodhouse – *Terrington, B.*
Wright – *W. of Richmond, B.**
Wyndham – *Egremont and Leconfield, B.*
Wyndham-Quin – *Dunraven and Mount-Earl, E.*
Wynn – *Newborough, B.*
Yarde-Buller – *Churston, B.*
Yerburgh – *Alvingham, B.*
Yorke – *Hardwicke, E.*
Young – *Kennet, B.*
Young – *Y. of Dartington, B.**
Young – *Y. of Graffham, B.**
Young – *Y. of Old Scone, B.**
Younger – *Y. of Leckie, V.*

Orders of Chivalry

THE MOST NOBLE ORDER OF THE GARTER (1348)

KG

Ribbon, Blue
Motto, Honi soit qui mal y pense
  (*Shame on him who thinks evil of it*)
The number of Knights Companions is limited to 24

SOVEREIGN OF THE ORDER
The Queen

LADIES OF THE ORDER
HM Queen Elizabeth the Queen
  Mother, 1936
HRH The Princess Royal, 1994

ROYAL KNIGHTS
HRH The Prince Philip, Duke of
  Edinburgh, 1947
HRH The Prince of Wales, 1958
HRH The Duke of Kent, 1985
HRH The Duke of Gloucester, 1997

EXTRA KNIGHTS COMPANIONS AND LADIES
HRH Princess Juliana of the
  Netherlands, 1958
HRH The Grand Duke of
  Luxembourg, 1972
HM The Queen of Denmark, 1979
HM The King of Sweden, 1983
HM The King of Spain, 1988
HM The Queen of the Netherlands,
  1989
HIM The Emperor of Japan, 1998

KNIGHTS AND LADY COMPANIONS
The Earl of Longford, 1971
The Marquess of Abergavenny, 1974
The Duke of Grafton, 1976
The Lord Hunt, 1979
The Duke of Norfolk, 1983
The Lord Lewin, 1983
The Lord Richardson of
  Duntisbourne, 1983
The Lord Carrington, 1985
The Lord Callaghan of Cardiff, 1987
The Viscount Leverhulme, 1988
The Lord Hailsham of St
  Marylebone, 1988
The Duke of Wellington, 1990
Field Marshal the Lord Bramall, 1990
Sir Edward Heath, 1992
The Viscount Ridley, 1992
The Lord Sainsbury of Preston
  Candover, 1992
The Lord Ashburton, 1994

The Lord Kingsdown, 1994
Sir Ninian Stephen, 1994
The Baroness Thatcher, 1995
Sir Edmund Hillary, 1995
The Duke of Devonshire, 1996
Sir Timothy Colman, 1996

Prelate, The Bishop of Winchester
Chancellor, The Lord Carrington, KG,
  GCMG, CH, MC
Register, The Dean of Windsor
Garter King of Arms, P. Gwynn-Jones,
  CVO
Gentleman Usher of the Black Rod, Gen.
  Sir Edward Jones, KCB, CBE
Secretary, D. H. B. Chesshyre, LVO

THE MOST ANCIENT AND MOST NOBLE ORDER OF THE THISTLE (REVIVED 1687)

KT

Ribbon, Green
Motto, Nemo me impune lacessit (*No
  one provokes me with impunity*)
The number of Knights is limited to 16

SOVEREIGN OF THE ORDER
The Queen

LADY OF THE THISTLE
HM Queen Elizabeth the Queen
  Mother, 1937

ROYAL KNIGHTS
HRH The Prince Philip, Duke of
  Edinburgh, 1952
HRH The Prince of Wales, Duke of
  Rothesay, 1977

KNIGHTS
The Earl of Wemyss and March, 1966
The Earl of Dalhousie, 1971
Sir Donald Cameron of Lochiel, 1973
The Duke of Buccleuch and
  Queensberry, 1978
The Earl of Elgin and Kincardine,
  1981
The Lord Thomson of Monifieth,
  1981
The Lord MacLehose of Beoch, 1983
The Earl of Airlie, 1985
Capt. Sir Iain Tennant, 1986
The Viscount Whitelaw, 1990
The Viscount Younger of Leckie,
  1995
The Viscount of Arbuthnott, 1996
The Earl of Crawford and Balcarres,
  1996
Lady Fraser, 1996

The Lord Macfarlane of Bearsden,
  1996
The Lord Mackay of Clashfern, 1997

Chancellor, The Duke of Buccleuch
  and Queensberry, KT, VRD
Dean, The Very Revd G. I. Macmillan
Secretary and Lord Lyon King of Arms, Sir
  Malcolm Innes of Edingight, KCVO,
  WS
Usher of the Green Rod, Rear-Adm. C. H.
  Layman, CB, DSO, LVO

THE MOST HONOURABLE ORDER OF THE BATH (1725)

GCB *Military*   GCB *Civil*

GCB   Knight (or Dame) Grand
      Cross
KCB   Knight Commander
DCB   Dame Commander
CB   Companion
Ribbon, Crimson
Motto, Tria juncta in uno (*Three joined
  in one*)

Remodelled 1815, and enlarged many
times since. The Order is divided into
civil and military divisions. Women
became eligible for the Order from 1
January 1971

THE SOVEREIGN

GREAT MASTER AND FIRST OR
PRINCIPAL KNIGHT GRAND
CROSS
HRH The Prince of Wales, KG, KT,
  GCB

Dean of the Order, The Dean of
  Westminster
Bath King of Arms, Air Chief Marshal
  Sir David Evans, GCB, CBE
Registrar and Secretary, Rear-Adm.
  D. E. Macey, CB
Genealogist, P. Gwynn-Jones, CVO
Gentleman Usher of the Scarlet Rod, Air
  Vice-Marshal Sir Richard Peirse,
  KCVO, CB
Deputy Secretary, The Secretary of the
  Central Chancery of the Orders of
  Knighthood
Chancery, Central Chancery of the
  Orders of Knighthood, St James's
  Palace, London SW1A 1BH

THE ORDER OF MERIT
(1902)

OM *Military*   OM *Civil*

OM

Ribbon, Blue and crimson

This Order is designed as a special distinction for eminent men and women without conferring a knighthood upon them. The Order is limited in numbers to 24, with the addition of foreign honorary members. Membership is of two kinds, military and civil, the badge of the former having crossed swords, and the latter oak leaves

THE SOVEREIGN

HRH The Prince Philip, Duke of
  Edinburgh, 1968
Sir George Edwards, 1971
Sir Alan Hodgkin, 1973
Revd Prof. Owen Chadwick, KBE,
  1983
Sir Andrew Huxley, 1983
Frederick Sanger, 1986
The Lord Menuhin, 1987
Prof. Sir Ernst Gombrich, 1988
Dr Max Perutz, 1988
Dame Cicely Saunders, 1989
The Lord Porter of Luddenham,
  1989
The Baroness Thatcher, 1990
Dame Joan Sutherland, 1991
Prof. Francis Crick, 1991
Dame Ninette de Valois, 1992
Sir Michael Atiyah, 1992
Lucian Freud, 1993
The Lord Jenkins of Hillhead, 1993
Sir Aaron Klug, 1995
Sir John Gielgud, 1996
The Lord Denning, 1997
Sir Norman Foster, 1997
Sir Denis Rooke, 1997
Ted Hughes, 1998
Honorary Member, Nelson Mandela,
  1995

Secretary and Registrar, Sir Edward
  Ford, GCVO, KCB, ERD
Chancery, Central Chancery of the
  Orders of Knighthood, St James's
  Palace, London SW1A 1BH

THE MOST EXALTED ORDER OF THE STAR OF INDIA (1861)

GCSI   Knight Grand Commander
KCSI   Knight Commander
CSI   Companion

Ribbon, Light blue, with white edges
Motto, Heaven's Light our Guide

THE SOVEREIGN

Registrar, The Secretary of the
  Central Chancery of the Orders of
  Knighthood
No conferments have been made
  since 1947

THE MOST DISTINGUISHED ORDER OF ST MICHAEL AND ST GEORGE (1818)

GCMG   KCMG

GCMG   Knight (or Dame) Grand
          Cross
KCMG   Knight Commander
DCMG   Dame Commander
CMG   Companion

Ribbon, Saxon blue, with scarlet centre
Motto, Auspicium melioris aevi
  (*Token of a better age*)

THE SOVEREIGN

GRAND MASTER
HRH The Duke of Kent, KG, GCMG,
  GCVO, ADC

Prelate, The Rt. Revd Simon
  Barrington-Ward
Chancellor, Sir Antony Acland, GCMG,
  GCVO
Secretary, The Permanent Under-
  Secretary of State at the Foreign
  and Commonwealth Office and
  Head of the Diplomatic Service
Registrar, Sir John Graham, Bt., GCMG
King of Arms, Sir Ewen Fergusson,
  GCMG, GCVO
Gentleman Usher of the Blue Rod, Sir
  John Margetson, KCMG
Dean, The Dean of St Paul's
Deputy Secretary, The Secretary of the
  Central Chancery of the Orders of
  Knighthood
Chancery, Central Chancery of the
  Orders of Knighthood, St James's
  Palace, London SW1A 1BH

THE MOST EMINENT ORDER OF THE INDIAN EMPIRE (1868)

GCIE   Knight Grand Commander
KCIE   Knight Commander
CIE   Companion

Ribbon, Imperial purple
Motto, Imperatricis auspiciis (*Under
  the auspices of the Empress*)

THE SOVEREIGN

Registrar, The Secretary of the
  Central Chancery of the Orders of
  Knighthood
No conferments have been made
  since 1947

THE IMPERIAL ORDER OF THE CROWN OF INDIA
(1877) FOR LADIES

CI

Badge, the royal cipher in jewels
  within an oval, surmounted by an
  heraldic crown and attached to a
  bow of light blue watered ribbon,
  edged white
The honour does not confer any rank
  or title upon the recipient
No conferments have been made
  since 1947

HM The Queen, 1947
HM Queen Elizabeth the Queen
  Mother, 1931
HRH The Princess Margaret,
  Countess of Snowdon, 1947
HRH Princess Alice, Duchess of
  Gloucester, 1937

THE ROYAL VICTORIAN ORDER (1896)

GCVO   KCVO

GCVO   Knight or Dame Grand
          Cross
KCVO   Knight Commander
DCVO   Dame Commander
CVO   Commander
LVO   Lieutenant
MVO   Member

Ribbon, Blue, with red and white edges
Motto, Victoria

THE SOVEREIGN
GRAND MASTER
HM Queen Elizabeth the Queen
  Mother

Chancellor, The Lord Chamberlain
Secretary, The Keeper of the Privy
  Purse
Registrar, The Secretary of the
  Central Chancery of the Orders of
  Knighthood
Chaplain, The Chaplain of the
  Queen's Chapel of the Savoy
Hon. Genealogist, D. H. B. Chesshyre,
  LVO

THE MOST EXCELLENT ORDER OF THE BRITISH EMPIRE (1917)

GBE   KBE

The Order was divided into military and civil divisions in December 1918

GBE   Knight or Dame Grand Cross
KBE   Knight Commander
DBE   Dame Commander
CBE   Commander
OBE   Officer
MBE   Member

Ribbon, Rose pink edged with pearl grey with vertical pearl stripe in centre (military division); without vertical pearl stripe (civil division)
Motto, For God and the Empire

THE SOVEREIGN

GRAND MASTER
HRH The Prince Philip, Duke of Edinburgh, KG, KT, OM, GBE, PC

Prelate, The Bishop of London
King of Arms, Air Chief Marshal Sir Patrick Hine, GCB, GBE
Registrar, The Secretary of the Central Chancery of the Orders of Knighthood
Secretary, The Secretary of the Cabinet and Head of the Home Civil Service
Dean, The Dean of St Paul's
Gentleman Usher of the Purple Rod, Sir Robin Gillett, Bt., GBE, RD
Chancery, Central Chancery of the Orders of Knighthood, St James's Palace, London SW1A 1BH

ORDER OF THE COMPANIONS OF HONOUR (1917)

CH

Ribbon, Carmine, with gold edges
This Order consists of one class only and carries with it no title. The number of awards is limited to 65 (excluding honorary members)

Anthony, Rt. Hon. John, 1981
Ashley of Stoke, The Lord, 1975
Astor, Hon. David, 1993
Attenborough, Sir David, 1995
Baker, Dame Janet, 1993

Baker of Dorking, The Lord, 1992
Brenner, Sydney, 1986
Brook, Peter, 1998
Brooke, Rt. Hon. Peter, 1992
Carrington, The Lord, 1983
Casson, Sir Hugh, 1984
Cledwyn of Penrhos, The Lord, 1976
de Valois, Dame Ninette, 1981
Doll, Prof. Sir Richard, 1995
Eccles, The Viscount, 1984
Fraser, Rt. Hon. Malcolm, 1977
Freud, Lucian, 1983
Gielgud, Sir John, 1977
Glenamara, The Lord, 1976
Gorton, Rt. Hon. Sir John, 1971
Guinness, Sir Alec, 1994
Hailsham of St Marylebone, The Lord, 1974
Hawking, Prof. Stephen, 1989
Healey, The Lord, 1979
Heseltine, Rt. Hon. Michael, 1997
Hobsbawm, Prof. Eric, 1998
Hockney, David, 1997
Howe of Aberavon, The Lord, 1996
Hurd of Westwell, The Lord, 1995
Jones, James, 1977
King, Rt. Hon. Tom, 1992
Lange, Rt. Hon. David, 1989
Lasdun, Sir Denys, 1995
Milstein, César, 1994
Owen, The Lord, 1994
Patten, Rt. Hon. Christopher, 1998
Perutz, Dr Max, 1975
Powell, Anthony, 1987
Powell, Sir Philip, 1984
Runciman, Sir Steven, 1984
Rylands, George, 1987
Sanger, Frederick, 1981
Sisson, Charles, 1993
Smith, Sir John, 1993
Somare, Rt. Hon. Sir Michael, 1978
Talboys, Rt. Hon. Sir Brian, 1981
Tebbit, The Lord, 1987
Trudeau, Rt. Hon. Pierre, 1984
Whitelaw, The Viscount, 1974
Widdowson, Dr Elsie, 1993
Honorary Members, Lee Kuan Yew, 1970; Dr Joseph Luns, 1971

Secretary and Registrar, The Secretary of the Central Chancery of the Orders of Knighthood

THE DISTINGUISHED SERVICE ORDER (1886)

DSO

Ribbon, Red, with blue edges
Bestowed in recognition of especial services in action of commissioned officers in the Navy, Army and Royal Air Force and (since 1942) Mercantile Marine. The members are

Companions only. A Bar may be awarded for any additional act of service

THE IMPERIAL SERVICE ORDER (1902)

ISO
Ribbon, Crimson, with blue centre

Appointment as Companion of this Order is open to members of the Civil Services whose eligibility is determined by the grade they hold. The Order consists of The Sovereign and Companions to a number not exceeding 1,900, of whom 1,300 may belong to the Home Civil Services and 600 to Overseas Civil Services. The Prime Minister announced in March 1993 that he would make no further recommendations for appointments to the Order.

Secretary, The Secretary of the Cabinet and Head of the Home Civil Service
Registrar, The Secretary of the Central Chancery of the Orders of Knighthood, St James's Palace, London SW1A 1BH

THE ROYAL VICTORIAN CHAIN (1902)

It confers no precedence on its holders

HM THE QUEEN
HM Queen Elizabeth the Queen Mother, 1937

HRH Princess Juliana of the Netherlands, 1950
HM The King of Thailand, 1960
HM The King of Jordan, 1966
HM King Zahir Shah of Afghanistan, 1971
HM The Queen of Denmark, 1974
HM The King of Nepal, 1975
HM The King of Sweden, 1975
The Lord Coggan, 1980
HM The Queen of the Netherlands, 1982
Gen. Antonio Eanes, 1985
HM The King of Spain, 1986
HM The King of Saudi Arabia, 1987
HRH The Princess Margaret, Countess of Snowdon, 1990
The Lord Runcie, 1991
The Lord Charteris of Amisfield, 1992
HE Richard von Weizsäcker, 1992
HM The King of Norway, 1994
The Earl of Airlie, 1997

Baronetage and Knightage

BARONETS

Style, 'Sir' before forename and surname, followed by 'Bt.'
Wife's style, 'Lady' followed by surname
For forms of address, *see* page 135

There are five different creations of baronetcies: Baronets of England (creations dating from 1611); Baronets of Ireland (creations dating from 1619); Baronets of Scotland or Nova Scotia (creations dating from 1625); Baronets of Great Britain (creations after the Act of Union 1707 which combined the kingdoms of England and Scotland); and Baronets of the United Kingdom (creations after the union of Great Britain and Ireland in 1801).

Badge of Baronets of the United Kingdom

Badge of Baronets of Nova Scotia

Badge of Ulster

The patent of creation limits the destination of a baronetcy, usually to male descendants of the first baronet, although special remainders allow the baronetcy to pass, if the male issue of sons fail, to the male issue of daughters of the first baronet. In the case of baronetcies of Scotland or Nova Scotia, a special remainder of 'heirs male and of tailzie' allows the baronetcy to descend to heirs general, including women. There are four existing Scottish baronets with such a remainder.

The Official Roll of Baronets is kept at the Home Office by the Registrar of the Baronetage. Anyone who considers that he is entitled to be entered on the Roll may petition the Crown through the Home Secretary. Every person succeeding to a baronetcy must exhibit proofs of succession to the Home Secretary. A person whose name is not entered on the Official Roll will not be addressed or mentioned by the title of baronet in any official document, nor will he be accorded precedence as a baronet.

BARONETCIES EXTINCT SINCE THE LAST EDITION
Bethune (*cr.* 1683); Holland (*cr.* 1917); Platt (*cr.* 1958); Roll (*cr.* 1921)

Registrar of the Baronetage, Miss C. E. C. Sinclair
Assistant Registrar, Mrs F. G. Bright
Office, Home Office, 50 Queen Anne's Gate, London SW1H 9AT. Tel: 0171-273 3498

KNIGHTS

Style, 'Sir' before forename and surname, followed by appropriate post-nominal initials if a Knight Grand Cross, Knight Grand Commander or Knight Commander
Wife's style, 'Lady' followed by surname

For forms of address, *see* page 135
The prefix 'Sir' is not used by knights who are clerics of the Church of England, who do not receive the accolade. Their wives are entitled to precedence as the wife of a knight but not to the style of 'Lady'.

ORDERS OF KNIGHTHOOD
Knight Grand Cross, Knight Grand Commander, and Knight Commander are the higher classes of the Orders of Chivalry (*see* pages 170–2). Honorary knighthoods of these Orders may be conferred on men who are citizens of countries of which The Queen is not head of state. As a rule, the prefix 'Sir' is not used by honorary knights.

KNIGHTS BACHELOR

The Knights Bachelor do not constitute a Royal Order, but comprise the surviving representation of the ancient State Orders of Knighthood. The Register of Knights Bachelor, instituted by James I in the 17th century, lapsed, and in 1908 a voluntary association under the title of The Society of Knights (now The Imperial Society of Knights Bachelor by Royal Command) was formed with the primary objects of continuing the various registers dating from 1257 and obtaining the uniform registration of every created Knight Bachelor. In 1926 a design for a badge to be worn by Knights Bachelor was approved and adopted; in 1974 a neck badge and miniature were added.
Knight Principal, Sir Conrad Swan, KCVO
Chairman of Council, The Lord Lane of Horsell
Prelate, Rt. Revd and Rt. Hon. The Bishop of London
Hon. Registrar, Sir Robert Balchin
Hon. Treasurer, Sir Douglas Morpeth, TD
Clerk to the Council, R. M. Esden
Office, 21 Old Buildings, Lincoln's Inn, London WC2A 3UJ

LIST OF BARONETS AND KNIGHTS
Revised to 31 August 1998

Peers are not included in this list

†	Not registered on the Official Roll of the Baronetage at the time of going to press
( )	The date of creation of the baronetcy is given in parenthesis
I	Baronet of Ireland
NS	Baronet of Nova Scotia
S	Baronet of Scotland

If a baronet or knight has a double barrelled or hyphenated surname, he is listed under the final element of the name
A full entry in italic type indicates that the recipient of a knighthood died during the year in which the honour was conferred. The name is included for purposes of record

Abal, Sir Tei, Kt., CBE
Abbott, Sir Albert Francis, Kt., CBE
Abbott, *Adm.* Sir Peter Charles, KCB
Abdy, Sir Valentine Robert Duff, Bt.
  (1850)
Abel, Sir Seselo (Cecil) Charles
  Geoffrey, Kt., OBE
Abeles, Sir (Emil Herbert) Peter, Kt.
Abercromby, Sir Ian George, Bt.
  (s. 1636)
Abraham, Sir Edward Penley, Kt.,
  CBE, FRS
Acheson, *Prof.* Sir (Ernest) Donald,
  KBE
Ackers, Sir James George, Kt.
Ackroyd, Sir Timothy Robert
  Whyte, Bt. (1956)
Acland, Sir Antony Arthur, GCMG,
  GCVO
Acland, *Lt.-Col.* Sir (Christopher)
  Guy (Dyke), Bt., MVO (1890)
Acland, Sir John Dyke, Bt. (1644)
Acland, *Maj.-Gen.* Sir John Hugh
  Bevil, KCB, CBE
Adam, Sir Christopher Eric Forbes,
  Bt. (1917)
Adams, Sir Philip George Doyne,
  KCMG
Adams, Sir William James, KCMG
Adamson, Sir (William Owen)
  Campbell, Kt.
Adrien, *Hon.* Sir Maurice Latour-, Kt.
Adye, Sir John Anthony, KCMG
Agnew, Sir Crispin Hamlyn, Bt.
  (s. 1629)
Agnew, Sir John Keith, Bt. (1895)
Aiken, *Air Chief Marshal* Sir John
  Alexander Carlisle, KCB
Ainsworth, Sir (Thomas) David, Bt.
  (1916)
Aird, *Capt.* Sir Alastair Sturgis, GCVO
Aird, Sir (George) John, Bt. (1901)
Airey, Sir Lawrence, KCB
Airy, *Maj.-Gen.* Sir Christopher John,
  KCVO, CBE
Aitchison, Sir Charles Walter de
  Lancey, Bt. (1938)
Akehurst, *Gen.* Sir John Bryan, KCB,
  CBE
Albu, Sir George, Bt. (1912)
Alcock, *Air Chief Marshal* Sir (Robert
  James) Michael, GCB, KBE
Aldous, *Rt. Hon.* Sir William, Kt.
Alexander, Sir Charles Gundry, Bt.
  (1945)
Alexander, Sir Claud Hagart-, Bt.
  (1886)
Alexander, Sir Douglas, Bt. (1921)
Alexander, Sir (John) Lindsay, Kt.
Alexander, *Prof.* Sir Kenneth John
  Wilson, Kt.
Alexander, Sir Michael O'Donal
  Bjarne, GCMG
†Alexander, Sir Patrick Desmond
  William Cable-, Bt. (1809)
Allan, Sir Anthony James Allan
  Havelock-, Bt. (1858)
Allen, *Prof.* Sir Geoffrey, Kt., Ph.D.,
  FRS
Allen, Sir John Derek, Kt., CBE

Allen, *Hon.* Sir Peter Austin Philip
  Jermyn, Kt.
Allen, Sir William Guilford, Kt.
Allen, Sir (William) Kenneth
  (Gwynne), Kt.
Alleyne, Sir George Allanmoore
  Ogarren, Kt.
Alleyne, *Revd* Sir John Olpherts
  Campbell, Bt. (1769)
Alliance, Sir David, Kt., CBE
Allinson, Sir (Walter) Leonard, KCVO,
  CMG
Alliott, *Hon.* Sir John Downes, Kt.
Allison, *Air Chief Marshal* Sir John
  Shakespeare, KCB, CBE
Alment, Sir (Edward) Anthony John,
  Kt.
Althaus, Sir Nigel Frederick, Kt.
Ambo, *Rt. Revd* George, KBE
Amet, *Hon.* Sir Arnold Karibone, Kt.
Amies, Sir (Edwin) Hardy, KCVO
Amory, Sir Ian Heathcoat, Bt. (1874)
Anderson, Sir John Anthony, KBE
Anderson, *Maj.-Gen.* Sir John
  Evelyn, KBE
Anderson, Sir John Muir, Kt., CMG
Anderson, *Hon.* Sir Kevin Victor, Kt.
Anderson, Sir Leith Reinsford
  Steven, Kt., CBE
Anderson, *Vice-Adm.* Sir Neil
  Dudley, KBE, CB
Anderson, *Prof.* Sir (William)
  Ferguson, Kt., OBE
Anderton, Sir (Cyril) James, Kt., CBE,
  QPM
Andrew, Sir Robert John, KCB
Andrews, Sir Derek Henry, KCB, CBE
Andrews, *Hon.* Sir Dormer George,
  Kt.
Angus, Sir Michael Richardson, Kt.
Annesley, Sir Hugh Norman, Kt.,
  QPM
Anson, *Vice-Adm.* Sir Edward
  Rosebery, KCB
Anson, Sir John, KCB
Anson, *Rear-Adm.* Sir Peter, Bt., CB
  (1831)
Anstey, *Brig.* Sir John, Kt., CBE, TD
Anstruther, *Maj.* Sir Ralph Hugo, Bt.,
  GCVO, MC (s. 1694)
Antico, Sir Tristan Venus, Kt.
Antrobus, Sir Charles James, GCMG,
  OBE
Antrobus, Sir Edward Philip, Bt.
  (1815)
Appleyard, Sir Leonard Vincent,
  KCMG
Appleyard, Sir Raymond Kenelm,
  KBE
Arbuthnot, Sir Keith Robert Charles,
  Bt. (1823)
Arbuthnot, Sir William Reierson, Bt.
  (1964)
Arbuthnott, *Prof.* Sir John Peebles,
  Kt., Ph.D., FRSE
Archdale, *Capt.* Sir Edward Folmer,
  Bt., DSC, RN (1928)
Archer, *Gen.* Sir (Arthur) John, KCB,
  OBE
Arculus, Sir Ronald, KCMG, KCVO

Armitage, *Air Chief Marshal* Sir
  Michael John, KCB, CBE
Armour, *Prof.* Sir James, Kt., CBE
†Armstrong, Sir Christopher John
  Edmund Stuart, Bt., MBE (1841)
Armytage, Sir John Martin, Bt.
  (1738)
Arnold, *Rt. Hon.* Sir John Lewis, Kt.
Arnold, Sir Malcolm Henry, Kt., CBE
Arnold, Sir Thomas Richard, Kt.
Arnott, Sir Alexander John Maxwell,
  Bt. (1896)
Arnott, *Prof.* Sir (William) Melville,
  Kt., TD, MD
Arrindell, Sir Clement Athelston,
  GCMG, GCVO, QC
Arthur, *Lt.-Gen.* Sir (John) Norman
  Stewart, KCB
Arthur, Sir Stephen John, Bt. (1841)
Ash, *Prof.* Sir Eric Albert, Kt., CBE, FRS,
  FENG.
Ashburnham, Sir Denny Reginald,
  Bt. (1661)
Ashe, Sir Derick Rosslyn, KCMG
Ashley, Sir Bernard Albert, Kt.
Ashmore, *Admiral of the Fleet* Sir
  Edward Beckwith, GCB, DSC
Ashmore, *Vice-Adm.* Sir Peter
  William Beckwith, KCB, KCVO, DSC
Ashworth, Sir Herbert, Kt.
Aske, *Revd* Sir Conan, Bt. (1922)
Askew, Sir Bryan, Kt.
Asscher, *Prof.* (Adolf) William, Kt.,
  MD, FRCP
Astill, *Hon.* Sir Michael John, Kt.
Aston, Sir Harold George, Kt., CBE
Aston, *Hon.* Sir William John, KCMG
Astor, *Hon.* Sir John Jacob, Kt., MBE
Astwood, *Hon.* Sir James Rufus, KBE
Atcherley, Sir Harold Winter, Kt.
Atiyah, Sir Michael Francis, Kt., OM,
  Ph.D., FRS
Atkins, *Rt. Hon.* Sir Robert James, Kt.
Atkinson, *Air Marshal* Sir David
  William, KBE
Atkinson, Sir Frederick John, KCB
Atkinson, Sir John Alexander, KCB,
  DFC
Atkinson, Sir Robert, Kt., DSC, FENG.
Atopare, Sir Sailas, GCMG
Attenborough, Sir David Frederick,
  Kt., CH, CVO, CBE, FRS
Atwell, Sir John William, Kt., CBE,
  FRSE, FENG.
Atwill, Sir (Milton) John (Napier),
  Kt.
Audland, Sir Christopher John,
  KCMG
Audley, Sir George Bernard, Kt.
Augier, *Prof.* Sir Fitz-Roy Richard,
  Kt.
Auld, *Rt. Hon.* Sir Robin Ernest, Kt.
†Austin, Sir Anthony Leonard, Bt.
  (1894)
Austin, *Vice-Adm.* Sir Peter Murray,
  KCB
Austin, *Air Marshal* Sir Roger Mark,
  KCB, AFC
Axford, Sir William Ian, Kt.
Ayckbourn, Sir Alan, Kt., CBE

Aykroyd, Sir James Alexander
Frederic, Bt. (1929)
Aykroyd, Sir William Miles, Bt., MC
(1920)
Aylmer, Sir Richard John, Bt. (I.
1622)
Bacha, Sir Bhinod, Kt., CMG
Backhouse, Sir Jonathan Roger, Bt.
(1901)
Bacon, Sir Nicholas Hickman
Ponsonby, Bt. *Premier Baronet of
England* (1611 and 1627)
Bacon, Sir Sidney Charles, Kt., CB,
FENG.
Baddeley, Sir John Wolsey
Beresford, Bt. (1922)
Baddiley, *Prof.* Sir James, Kt., PH.D.,
D.SC., FRS, FRSE
Badge, Sir Peter Gilmour Noto, Kt.
Badger, Sir Geoffrey Malcolm, Kt.
Baer, Sir Jack Mervyn Frank, Kt.
Bagge, Sir (John) Jeremy Picton, Bt.
(1867)
Bagnall, *Air Marshal* Sir Anthony
John Crowther, KCB, OBE
Bagnall, *Field Marshal* Sir Nigel
Thomas, GCB, CVO, MC
Bailey, Sir Alan Marshall, KCB
Bailey, Sir Brian Harry, Kt., OBE
Bailey, Sir Derrick Thomas Louis,
Bt., DFC (1919)
Bailey, Sir John Bilsland, KCB
Bailey, Sir Richard John, Kt., CBE
Bailey, Sir Stanley Ernest, Kt., CBE,
QPM
Bailhache, Sir Philip Martin, Kt.
Baillie, Sir Gawaine George Hope,
Bt. (1823)
Baines, *Prof.* Sir George Grenfell-,
Kt., OBE
Baird, Sir David Charles, Bt. (1809)
†Baird, Sir James Andrew Gardiner,
Bt. (s. 1695)
Baird, *Lt.-Gen.* Sir James Parlane,
KBE, MD
Baird, *Vice-Adm.* Sir Thomas Henry
Eustace, KCB
Bairsto, *Air Marshal* Sir Peter
Edward, KBE, CB
Baker, Sir Bryan William, Kt.
Baker, Sir Robert George Humphrey
Sherston-, Bt. (1796)
Baker, *Hon.* Sir (Thomas) Scott
(Gillespie), Kt.
Balchin, Sir Robert George
Alexander, Kt.
Balcombe, *Rt. Hon.* Sir (Alfred) John,
Kt.
Balderstone, Sir James Schofield, Kt.
Baldwin, *Prof.* Sir Jack Edward, Kt.,
FRS
Baldwin, Sir Peter Robert, KCB
Ball, *Air Marshal* Sir Alfred Henry
Wynne, KCB, DSO, DFC
Ball, Sir Charles Irwin, Bt. (1911)
Ball, Sir Christopher John Elinger,
Kt.
Ball, *Prof.* Sir Robert James, Kt., PH.D.
Bamford, Sir Anthony Paul, Kt.

Banham, Sir John Michael
Middlecott, Kt.
Bannerman, Sir David Gordon, Bt.,
OBE (S. 1682)
Bannister, Sir Roger Gilbert, Kt., CBE,
DM, FRCP
Barber, Sir (Thomas) David, Bt.
(1960)
Barbour, *Very Revd* Sir Robert
Alexander Stewart, KCVO, MC
Barclay, Sir Colville Herbert
Sanford, Bt. (s. 1668)
Barclay, Sir Peter Maurice, Kt., CBE
Barder, Sir Brian Leon, KCMG
Barker, Sir Alwyn Bowman, Kt., CMG
Barker, Sir Colin, Kt.
Barker, *Hon.* Sir (Richard) Ian, Kt.
Barlow, Sir Christopher Hilaro, Bt.
(1803)
Barlow, Sir Frank, Kt., CBE
Barlow, Sir (George) William, Kt.,
FENG.
Barlow, Sir John Kemp, Bt. (1907)
Barlow, Sir Thomas Erasmus, Bt.,
DSC (1902)
Barnard, Sir Joseph Brian, Kt.
Barnes, Sir (James) David (Francis),
Kt., CBE
Barnes, Sir Kenneth, KCB
Barnewall, Sir Reginald Robert, Bt.
(I. 1623)
Baron, Sir Thomas, Kt., CBE
Barraclough, *Air Chief Marshal* Sir
John, KCB, CBE, DFC, AFC
Barraclough, Sir Kenneth James
Priestley, Kt., CBE, TD
Barran, Sir David Haven, Kt.
Barran, Sir John Napoleon Ruthven,
Bt. (1895)
Barratt, Sir Lawrence Arthur, Kt.
Barratt, Sir Richard Stanley, Kt., CBE,
QPM
Barrett, *Lt.-Gen.* Sir David William
Scott-, KBE, MC
Barrett, Sir Stephen Jeremy, KCMG
Barrington, Sir Alexander
(Fitzwilliam Croker), Bt. (1831)
Barrington, Sir Nicholas John, KCMG,
CVO
Barron, Sir Donald James, Kt.
Barrow, *Capt.* Sir Richard John
Uniacke, Bt. (1835)
Barrowclough, Sir Anthony Richard,
Kt., QC
Barry, Sir (Lawrence) Edward
(Anthony Tress), Bt. (1899)
†Bartlett, Sir Andrew Alan, Bt. (1913)
Barttelot, *Col.* Sir Brian Walter de
Stopham, Bt., OBE (1875)
Batchelor, Sir Ivor Ralph Campbell,
Kt., CBE
Bate, Sir David Lindsay, KBE
Bate, Sir (Walter) Edwin, Kt., OBE
Bateman, Sir Cecil Joseph, KBE
Bateman, Sir Geoffrey Hirst, Kt.,
FRCS
Bates, Sir Geoffrey Voltelin, Bt., MC
(1880)
Bates, Sir Malcolm Rowland, Kt.
Batho, Sir Peter Ghislain, Bt. (1928)

Bathurst, *Admiral of the Fleet* Sir
(David) Benjamin, GCB
Bathurst, Sir Frederick John Charles
Gordon Hervey-, Bt. (1818)
Bathurst, Sir Maurice Edward, Kt.,
CMG, CBE, QC
Batten, Sir John Charles, KCVO
Battersby, *Prof.* Sir Alan Rushton,
Kt., FRS
Battishill, Sir Anthony Michael
William, GCB
Batty, Sir William Bradshaw, Kt., TD
Baxendell, Sir Peter Brian, Kt., CBE,
FENG.
Bayliss, Sir Richard Ian Samuel,
KCVO, MD, FRCP
Bayne, Sir Nicholas Peter, KCMG
Baynes, Sir John Christopher
Malcolm, Bt. (1801)
†Bazley, Sir Thomas John Sebastian,
Bt. (1869)
Beach, *Gen.* Sir (William Gerald)
Hugh, GBE, KCB, MC
Beale, *Lt.-Gen.* Sir Peter John, KBE,
FRCP
Beament, Sir James William
Longman, Kt., SC.D., FRS
Beattie, *Hon.* Sir Alexander Craig, Kt.
Beattie, *Hon.* Sir David Stuart, GCMG,
GCVO
Beauchamp, Sir Christopher
Radstock Proctor-, Bt. (1745)
Beaumont, *Capt.* the Hon. Sir
(Edward) Nicholas (Canning),
KCVO
Beaumont, Sir George (Howland
Francis), Bt. (1661)
Beaumont, Sir Richard Ashton,
KCMG, OBE
Beavis, *Air Chief Marshal* Sir Michael
Gordon, KCB, CBE, AFC
Becher, Sir William Fane Wrixon,
Bt., MC (1831)
Beck, Sir Edgar Charles, Kt., CBE,
FENG.
Beck, Sir Edgar Philip, Kt.
Beckett, *Capt.* Sir (Martyn) Gervase,
Bt., MC (1921)
Beckett, Sir Terence Norman, KBE,
FENG.
Bedingfeld, *Capt.* Sir Edmund
George Felix Paston-, Bt. (1661)
Bedser, Sir Alec Victor, Kt., CBE
Beecham, Sir Jeremy Hugh, Kt.
Beecham, Sir John Stratford Roland,
Bt. (1914)
Beeley, Sir Harold, KCMG, CBE
Beetham, *Marshal of the Royal Air Force*
Sir Michael James, GCB, CBE, DFC,
AFC
Beevor, Sir Thomas Agnew, Bt.
(1784)
Beith, Sir John Greville Stanley,
KCMG
Belch, Sir Alexander Ross, Kt., CBE,
FRSE
Beldam, *Rt. Hon.* Sir (Alexander) Roy
(Asplan), Kt.
Belich, Sir James, Kt.
Bell, Sir Brian Ernest, KBE

Bell, Sir (George) Raymond, KCMG, CB

Bell, Sir John Lowthian, Bt. (1885)

Bell, *Hon.* Sir Rodger, Kt.

Bell, Sir (William) Ewart, KCB

Bell, Sir William Hollin Dayrell Morrison-, Bt. (1905)

Bellew, Sir Henry Charles Gratton-, Bt. (1838)

Bellinger, Sir Robert Ian, GBE

Bellingham, Sir Noel Peter Roger, Bt. (1796)

Bengough, *Col.* Sir Piers, KCVO, OBE

Benn, Sir (James) Jonathan, Bt. (1914)

Bennett, Sir Charles Moihi Te Arawaka, Kt., DSO

Bennett, *Air Vice-Marshal* Sir Erik Peter, KBE, CB

Bennett, *Rt. Hon.* Sir Frederic Mackarness, Kt.

Bennett, Sir Hubert, Kt.

Bennett, *Hon.* Sir Hugh Peter Derwyn, Kt.

Bennett, Sir John Mokonuiarangi, Kt.

Bennett, *Gen.* Sir Phillip Harvey, KBE, DSO

Bennett, Sir Reginald Frederick Brittain, Kt., VRD

Bennett, Sir Richard Rodney, Kt., CBE

Bennett, Sir Ronald Wilfrid Murdoch, Bt. (1929)

Benson, Sir Christopher John, Kt.

Benyon, Sir William Richard, Kt.

Beresford, Sir (Alexander) Paul, Kt., MP

Berger, *Vice-Adm.* Sir Peter Egerton Capel, KCB, LVO, DSC

Berghuser, *Hon.* Sir Eric, Kt., MBE

Berman, Sir Franklin Delow, KCMG

Bernard, Sir Dallas Edmund, Bt. (1954)

Berney, Sir Julian Reedham Stuart, Bt. (1620)

Berridge, *Prof.* Sir Michael John, Kt., FRS

Berrill, Sir Kenneth Ernest, GBE, KCB

Berriman, Sir David, Kt.

Berry, *Prof.* Sir Colin Leonard, Kt., FRCPath.

Berry, *Prof.* Sir Michael Victor, Kt., FRS

Berthon, *Vice-Adm.* Sir Stephen Ferrier, KCB

Berthoud, Sir Martin Seymour, KCVO, CMG

Best, Sir Richard Radford, KCVO, CBE

Bethune, *Hon.* Sir (Walter) Angus, Kt.

Bett, Sir Michael, Kt., CBE

Bevan, Sir Martyn Evan Evans, Bt. (1958)

Bevan, Sir Timothy Hugh, Kt.

Beveridge, Sir Gordon Smith Grieve, Kt., FRSE, FEng., FRSA

Beverley, *Lt.-Gen.* Sir Henry York La Roche, KCB, OBE, RM

Bibby, Sir Derek James, Bt., MC (1959)

Bick, *Hon.* Sir Martin James Moore-, Kt.

Bickersteth, *Rt. Revd* John Monier, KCVO

Biddulph, Sir Ian D'Olier, Bt. (1664)

Bide, Sir Austin Ernest, Kt.

Bidwell, Sir Hugh Charles Philip, GBE

Biggam, Sir Robin Adair, Kt.

Biggs, *Vice-Adm.* Sir Geoffrey William Roger, KCB

Biggs, Sir Norman Paris, Kt.

Bilas, Sir Angmai Simon, Kt., OBE

Billière, *Gen.* Sir Peter Edgar de la Cour de la, KCB, KBE, DSO, MC

Bingham, *Hon.* Sir Eardley Max, Kt., QC

Birch, Sir John Allan, KCVO, CMG

Birch, Sir Roger, Kt., CBE, QPM

Bird, Sir Richard Geoffrey Chapman, Bt. (1922)

Birkin, Sir John Christian William, Bt. (1905)

Birkin, Sir (John) Derek, Kt., TD

Birkmyre, Sir Archibald, Bt. (1921)

Birley, Sir Derek Sydney, Kt.

Birrell, Sir James Drake, Kt.

Birt, Sir John, Kt.

Birtwistle, Sir Harrison, Kt.

Bishop, Sir Frederick Arthur, Kt., CB, CVO

Bishop, Sir George Sidney, Kt., CB, OBE

Bishop, Sir Michael David, Kt., CBE

Bisson, *Rt. Hon.* Sir Gordon Ellis, Kt.

Black, *Prof.* Sir Douglas Andrew Kilgour, Kt., MD, FRCP

Black, Sir James Whyte, Kt., FRCP, FRS

Black, *Adm.* Sir (John) Jeremy, GBE, KCB, DSO

Black, Sir Robert Brown, GCMG, OBE

Black, Sir Robert David, Bt. (1922)

Blackburne, *Hon.* Sir William Anthony, Kt.

Blacker, *Gen.* Sir (Anthony Stephen) Jeremy, KCB, CBE

Blacker, *Gen.* Sir Cecil Hugh, GCB, OBE, MC

Blackett, Sir Hugh Francis, Bt. (1673)

Blacklock, *Surgeon Capt. Prof.* Sir Norman James, KCVO, OBE

Blackman, Sir Frank Milton, KCVO, OBE

Blackwell, Sir Basil Davenport, Kt., FEng.

Blackwood, Sir John Francis, Bt. (1814)

Blair, Sir Alastair Campbell, KCVO, TD, WS

Blair, *Lt.-Gen.* Sir Chandos, KCVO, OBE, MC

Blair, Sir Edward Thomas Hunter, Bt. (1786)

Blake, Sir Alfred Lapthorn, KCVO, MC

Blake, Sir Francis Michael, Bt. (1907)

Blake, Sir Peter James, KBE

Blake, Sir (Thomas) Richard (Valentine), Bt. (I. 1622)

Blaker, Sir John, Bt. (1919)

Blakiston, Sir Ferguson Arthur James, Bt. (1763)

Blanch, Sir Malcolm, KCVO

Bland, Sir (Francis) Christopher (Buchan), Kt.

Bland, Sir Henry Armand, Kt., CBE

Bland, *Lt.-Col.* Sir Simon Claud Michael, KCVO

Blatherwick, Sir David Elliott Spiby, KCMG, OBE

Blelloch, Sir John Nial Henderson, KCB

Blennerhassett, Sir (Marmaduke) Adrian Francis William, Bt. (1809)

Blewitt, *Maj.* Sir Shane Gabriel Basil, GCVO

Blofeld, *Hon.* Sir John Christopher Calthorpe, Kt.

Blois, Sir Charles Nicholas Gervase, Bt. (1686)

Blomefield, Sir Thomas Charles Peregrine, Bt. (1807)

Bloomfield, Sir Kenneth Percy, KCB

Blosse, *Capt.* Sir Richard Hely Lynch-, Bt. (1622)

Blount, Sir Walter Edward Alpin, Bt., DSC (1642)

Blundell, Sir Thomas Leon, Kt., FRS

Blunden, Sir George, Kt.

†Blunden, Sir Philip Overington, Bt. (I. 1766)

Blunt, Sir David Richard Reginald Harvey, Bt. (1720)

Blyth, Sir Charles (Chay), Kt., CBE, BEM

Boardman, *Prof.* Sir John, Kt., FSA, FBA

Bodmer, Sir Walter Fred, Kt., PH.D., FRS

Body, Sir Richard Bernard Frank Stewart, Kt., MP

Boevey, Sir Thomas Michael Blake Crawley-, Bt. (1784)

Bogan, Sir Nagora, KBE

Bogarde, Sir Dirk (Derek Niven van den Bogaerde), Kt.

Boileau, Sir Guy (Francis), Bt. (1838)

Boles, Sir Jeremy John Fortescue, Bt. (1922)

Boles, Sir John Dennis, Kt., MBE

Bolland, Sir Edwin, KCMG

Bollers, *Hon.* Sir Harold Brodie Smith, Kt.

Bolton, Sir Frederic Bernard, Kt., MC

Bona, Sir Kina, KBE

Bonallack, Sir Michael Francis, Kt., OBE

Bond, Sir Kenneth Raymond Boyden, Kt.

Bond, *Prof.* Sir Michael Richard, Kt., FRCP sych., FRCPGlas., FRCSE

Bondi, *Prof.* Sir Hermann, KCB, FRS

Bonfield, Sir Peter Leahy, Kt., CBE, FEng.

Bonham, *Maj.* Sir Antony Lionel Thomas, Bt. (1852)

Bonington, Sir Christian John Storey, Kt., CBE

Bonsall, Sir Arthur Wilfred, KCMG, CBE

Bonsor, Sir Nicholas Cosmo, Bt. (1925)

Boolell, Sir Satcam, Kt.

Boord, Sir Nicolas John Charles, Bt. (1896)

Boorman, *Lt.-Gen.* Sir Derek, KCB

Booth, Sir Christopher Charles, Kt., MD, FRCP

Booth, Hon. Sir David Alwyn Gore-, KCMG, KCVO

Booth, Sir Douglas Allen, Bt. (1916)

Booth, Sir Gordon, KCMG, CVO

Booth, Sir Josslyn Henry Robert Gore-, Bt. (I. 1760)

Booth, Sir Michael Addison John Wheeler-, KCB

Boothby, Sir Brooke Charles, Bt. (1660)

Boreel, Sir Francis David, Bt. (1645)

Boreham, *Hon.* Sir Leslie Kenneth Edward, Kt.

Bornu, The Waziri of, KCMG, CBE

Borthwick, Sir John Thomas, Bt., MBE (1908)

Bossom, *Hon.* Sir Clive, Bt. (1953)

Boswall, Sir (Thomas) Alford Houstoun-, Bt. (1836)

Boswell, *Lt.-Gen.* Sir Alexander Crawford Simpson, KCB, CBE

Bosworth, Sir Neville Bruce Alfred, Kt., CBE

Bottomley, Sir James Reginald Alfred, KCMG

Boughey, Sir John George Fletcher, Bt. (1798)

Boulton, Sir Clifford John, GCB

Boulton, Sir (Harold Hugh) Christian, Bt. (1905)

Boulton, Sir William Whytehead, Bt., CBE, TD (1944)

Bourn, Sir John Bryant, KCB

Bourne, Sir (John) Wilfrid, KCB

Bovell, *Hon.* Sir (William) Stewart, Kt.

Bowater, Sir Euan David Vansittart, Bt. (1939)

Bowater, Sir (John) Vansittart, Bt. (1914)

Bowden, Sir Andrew, Kt., MBE

Bowden, Sir Frank, Bt. (1915)

Bowen, Sir Geoffrey Fraser, Kt.

Bowen, Sir Mark Edward Mortimer, Bt. (1921)

Bowett, *Prof.* Sir Derek William, Kt., CBE, QC, FBA

†Bowlby, Sir Richard Peregrine Longstaff, Bt. (1923)

Bowman, Sir Jeffery Haverstock, Kt.

Bowman, Sir Paul Humphrey Armytage, Bt. (1884)

Bowmar, Sir Charles Erskine, Kt.

Bowness, Sir Alan, Kt., CBE

Boyce, *Adm.* Sir Michael Cecil, KCB, OBE

Boyce, Sir Robert Charles Leslie, Bt. (1952)

Boyd, Sir Alexander Walter, Bt. (1916)

Boyd, Sir John Dixon Iklé, KCMG

Boyd, The Hon. Sir Mark Alexander Lennox-, Kt.

Boyd, *Prof.* Sir Robert Lewis Fullarton, Kt., CBE, D.SC., FRS

Boyes, Sir Brian Gerald Barratt-, KBE

Boyle, Sir Stephen Gurney, Bt. (1904)

Boynton, Sir John Keyworth, Kt., MC

Boys, *Rt. Hon.* Sir Michael Hardie, GCMG

Boyson, *Rt. Hon.* Sir Rhodes, Kt.

Brabham, Sir John Arthur, Kt., OBE

Bradbeer, Sir John Derek Richardson, Kt., OBE, TD

Bradbury, *Surgeon Vice-Adm.* Sir Eric Blackburn, KBE, CB

Bradford, Sir Edward Alexander Slade, Bt. (1902)

Bradman, Sir Donald George, Kt.

Bradshaw, Sir Kenneth Anthony, KCB

Bradshaw, *Lt.-Gen.* Sir Richard Phillip, KBE

Brain, Sir (Henry) Norman, KBE, CMG

Braithwaite, Sir (Joseph) Franklin Madders, Kt.

Braithwaite, *Rt. Hon.* Sir Nicholas Alexander, Kt., OBE

Braithwaite, Sir Rodric Quentin, GCMG

Bramall, Sir (Ernest) Ashley, Kt.

Bramley, *Prof.* Sir Paul Anthony, Kt.

Branigan, Sir Patrick Francis, Kt., QC

Bray, Sir Theodor Charles, Kt., CBE

Brennan, *Hon.* Sir (Francis) Gerard, KBE

Brett, Sir Charles Edward Bainbridge, Kt., CBE

Brickwood, Sir Basil Greame, Bt. (1927)

Bridges, *Hon.* Sir Phillip Rodney, Kt., CMG

Brierley, Sir Ronald Alfred, Kt.

Bright, Sir Graham Frank James, Kt.

Bright, Sir Keith, Kt.

Brigstocke, *Adm.* Sir John Richard, KCB

Brinckman, Sir Theodore George Roderick, Bt. (1831)

†Brisco, Sir Campbell Howard, Bt. (1782)

Briscoe, Sir John Geoffrey James, Bt. (1910)

Brise, Sir John Archibald Ruggles-, Bt., CB, OBE, TD (1935)

Bristow, *Hon.* Sir Peter Henry Rowley, Kt.

Brittan, *Rt. Hon.* Sir Leon, Kt., QC

Brittan, Sir Samuel, Kt.

Britton, Sir Edward Louis, Kt., CBE

Broackes, Sir Nigel, Kt.

†Broadbent, Sir Andrew George, Bt. (1893)

Brocklebank, Sir Aubrey Thomas, Bt. (1885)

Brockman, *Vice-Adm.* Sir Ronald Vernon, KCB, CSI, CIE, CVO, CBE

Brodie, Sir Benjamin David Ross, Bt. (1834)

Broers, *Prof.* Sir Alec Nigel, Kt., PH.D., FRS

Bromhead, Sir John Desmond Gonville, Bt. (1806)

Bromley, Sir Michael Roger, KBE

Bromley, Sir Rupert Charles, Bt. (1757)

Bromley, Sir Thomas Eardley, KCMG

Brook, Sir Robin, Kt., CMG, OBE

†Brooke, Sir Alistair Weston, Bt. (1919)

Brooke, Sir Francis George Windham, Bt. (1903)

Brooke, *Rt. Hon.* Sir Henry, Kt.

Brooke, Sir (Richard) David Christopher, Bt. (1662)

Brookes, Sir Wilfred Deakin, Kt., CBE, DSO

Brooksbank, Sir (Edward) Nicholas, Bt. (1919)

Broom, *Air Marshal* Sir Ivor Gordon, KCB, CBE, DSO, DFC, AFC

Broomfield, Sir Nigel Hugh Robert Allen, KCMG

†Broughton, Sir David Delves, Bt. (1661)

Broun, Sir William Windsor, Bt. (s. 1686)

Brown, Sir Allen Stanley, Kt., CBE

Brown, Sir (Austen) Patrick, KCB

Brown, *Adm.* Sir Brian Thomas, KCB, CBE

Brown, Sir (Cyril) Maxwell Palmer, KCB, CMG

Brown, *Vice-Adm.* Sir David Worthington, KCB

Brown, Sir Derrick Holden-, Kt.

Brown, Sir Douglas Denison, Kt.

Brown, *Hon.* Sir Douglas Dunlop, Kt.

Brown, Sir George Francis Richmond, Bt. (1863)

Brown, Sir George Noel, Kt.

Brown, Sir John Douglas Keith, Kt.

Brown, Sir John Gilbert Newton, Kt., CBE

Brown, Sir Mervyn, KCMG, OBE

Brown, Sir Peter Randolph, Kt.

Brown, *Hon.* Sir Ralph Kilner, Kt., OBE, TD

Brown, Sir Robert Crichton-, KCMG, CBE, TD

Brown, *Rt. Hon.* Sir Simon Denis, Kt.

Brown, *Rt. Hon.* Sir Stephen, Kt.

Brown, Sir Thomas, Kt.

Brown, Sir William Brian Piggott-, Bt. (1903)

Browne, Sir (Edmund) John (Phillip), Kt., FEng.

Brownrigg, Sir Nicholas (Gawen), Bt. (1816)

Browse, *Prof.* Sir Norman Leslie, Kt., MD, FRCS

Bruce, Sir (Francis) Michael Ian, Bt. (s. 1628)

Bruce, Sir Hervey James Hugh, Bt. (1804)

Bruce, *Rt. Hon.* Sir (James) Roualeyn Hovell-Thurlow-Cumming-, Kt.

Brunner, Sir John Henry Kilian, Bt. (1895)

Brunton, Sir (Edward Francis) Lauder, Bt. (1908)

Brunton, Sir Gordon Charles, Kt.

Bryan, Sir Arthur, Kt.

Bryan, Sir Paul Elmore Oliver, Kt., DSO, MC

Bryce, *Hon.* Sir (William) Gordon, Kt., CBE

Bryson, *Adm.* Sir Lindsay Sutherland, KCB, FEng.

Buchan, Sir John, Kt., CMG

Buchanan, Sir Andrew George, Bt. (1878)

Buchanan, Sir Charles Alexander James Leith-, Bt. (1775)

Buchanan, *Prof.* Sir Colin Douglas, Kt., CBE

Buchanan, *Vice-Adm.* Sir Peter William, KBE

Buchanan, Sir (Ranald) Dennis, Kt., MBE

Buchanan, Sir Robert Wilson (Robin), Kt.

Buck, Sir (Philip) Antony (Fyson), Kt., QC

Buckland, Sir Ross, Kt.

Buckley, *Rt. Hon.* Sir Denys Burton, Kt., MBE

Buckley, Sir John William, Kt.

Buckley, *Lt.-Cdr.* Sir (Peter) Richard, KCVO

Buckley, *Hon.* Sir Roger John, Kt.

Budd, Sir Alan Peter, Kt.

Bulkeley, Sir Richard Thomas Williams-, Bt. (1661)

Bull, Sir George Jeffrey, Kt.

Bull, Sir Simeon George, Bt. (1922)

Bullard, Sir Julian Leonard, GCMG

Bullus, Sir Eric Edward, Kt.

Bulmer, Sir William Peter, Kt.

Bultin, Sir Bato, Kt., MBE

Bunbury, Sir Michael William, Bt. (1681)

Bunbury, Sir (Richard David) Michael Richardson-, Bt. (I. 1787)

Bunch, Sir Austin Wyeth, Kt., CBE

Bunyard, Sir Robert Sidney, Kt., CBE, QPM

Burbidge, Sir Herbert Dudley, Bt. (1916)

Burdett, Sir Savile Aylmer, Bt. (1665)

Burgen, Sir Arnold Stanley Vincent, Kt., FRS

Burgess, *Gen.* Sir Edward Arthur, KCB, OBE

Burgess, Sir (Joseph) Stuart, Kt., CBE, ph.D., FRSC

Burgh, Sir John Charles, KCMG, CB

Burke, Sir James Stanley Gilbert, Bt. (I. 1797)

Burke, Sir (Thomas) Kerry, Kt.

Burley, Sir Victor George, Kt., CBE

Burman, Sir (John) Charles, Kt.

Burnet, Sir James William Alexander (Sir Alastair Burnet), Kt.

Burnett, *Air Chief Marshal* Sir Brian Kenyon, GCB, DFC, AFC

Burnett, Sir David Humphery, Bt., MBE, TD (1913)

Burnett, Sir John Harrison, Kt.

Burnett, Sir Walter John, Kt.

Burney, Sir Cecil Denniston, Bt. (1921)

Burns, Sir (Robert) Andrew, KCMG

Burrell, Sir John Raymond, Bt. (1774)

Burrenchobay, Sir Dayendranath, KBE, CMG, CVO

Burrows, Sir Bernard Alexander Brocas, GCMG

Burston, Sir Samuel Gerald Wood, Kt., OBE

Burt, *Hon.* Sir Francis Theodore Page, KCMG

Burton, Sir Carlisle Archibald, Kt., OBE

Burton, Sir George Vernon Kennedy, Kt., CBE

Burton, Sir Michael St Edmund, KCVO, CMG

Bush, *Adm.* Sir John Fitzroy Duyland, GCB, DSC

Butler, *Rt. Hon.* Sir Adam Courtauld, Kt.

Butler, *Hon.* Sir Arlington Griffith, KCMG

Butler, Sir Clifford Charles, Kt., ph.D., FRS

Butler, Sir Michael Dacres, GCMG

Butler, Sir (Reginald) Michael (Thomas), Bt. (1922)

Butler, *Hon.* Sir Richard Clive, Kt.

†Butler, Sir Richard Pierce, Bt. (1628)

Butt, Sir (Alfred) Kenneth Dudley, Bt. (1929)

Butter, *Maj.* Sir David Henry, KCVO, MC

Butterfield, *Hon.* Sir Alexander Neil Logie, Kt.

Buxton, Sir Jocelyn Charles Roden, Bt. (1840)

Buxton, *Rt. Hon.* Sir Richard Joseph, Kt.

Buzzard, Sir Anthony Farquhar, Bt. (1929)

Byatt, Sir Hugh Campbell, KCVO, CMG

Byers, Sir Maurice Hearne, Kt., CBE, QC

Byford, Sir Lawrence, Kt., CBE, QPM

Cable, Sir James Eric, KCVO, CMG

Cadbury, Sir (George) Adrian (Hayhurst), Kt.

Cadbury, Sir (Nicholas) Dominic, Kt.

Cadogan, *Prof.* Sir John Ivan George, Kt., CBE, FRS, FRSE

Cahn, Sir Albert Jonas, Bt. (1934)

Cain, Sir Henry Edney Conrad, Kt.

Caine, Sir Michael Harris, Kt.

Caines, Sir John, KCB

Cairncross, Sir Alexander Kirkland, KCMG

Calcutt, Sir David Charles, Kt., QC

Calderwood, Sir Robert, Kt.

Caldwell, *Surgeon Vice-Adm.* Sir (Eric) Dick, KBE, CB

Callard, Sir Eric John, Kt., FEng.

Callaway, *Prof.* Sir Frank Adams, Kt., CMG, OBE

Calman, *Prof.* Sir Kenneth Charles, KCB, MD, FRCP, FRCS, FRSE

Calne, *Prof.* Sir Roy Yorke, Kt., FRS

Calthorpe, Sir Euan Hamilton Anstruther-Gough-, Bt. (1929)

Cameron of Lochiel, Sir Donald Hamish, KT, CVO, TD

Cameron, Sir (Eustace) John, Kt., CBE

Campbell, Sir Alan Hugh, GCMG

Campbell, *Prof.* Sir Colin Murray, Kt.

Campbell, *Prof.* Sir Donald, Kt., CBE, FRCS, FRCPGlas.

Campbell, Sir Ian Tofts, Kt., CBE, VRD

Campbell, Sir Ilay Mark, Bt. (1808)

Campbell, Sir James Alexander Moffat Bain, Bt. (s. 1668)

Campbell, Sir Lachlan Philip Kemeys, Bt. (1815)

Campbell, Sir Matthew, KBE, CB, FRSE

Campbell, Sir Niall Alexander Hamilton, Bt. (1831)

Campbell, Sir Robin Auchinbreck, Bt. (s. 1628)

Campbell, Sir Thomas Cockburn-, Bt. (1821)

Campbell, *Hon.* Sir Walter Benjamin, Kt.

Campbell, *Hon.* Sir William Anthony, Kt.

†Carden, Sir Christopher Robert, Bt. (1887)

Carden, Sir John Craven, Bt. (I. 1787)

Carew, Sir Rivers Verain, Bt. (1661)

Carey, Sir Peter Willoughby, GCB

Carlisle, Sir James Beethoven, GCMG

Carlisle, Sir John Michael, Kt.

Carlisle, Sir Kenneth Melville, Kt.

Carmichael, Sir David Peter William Gibson-Craig-, Bt. (s. 1702 and 1831)

Carnac, *Revd Canon* Sir (Thomas) Nicholas Rivett-, Bt. (1836)

Carnegie, *Lt.-Gen.* Sir Robin Macdonald, KCB, OBE

Carnegie, Sir Roderick Howard, Kt.

Carnwath, Sir Robert John Anderson, Kt., CVO

Caro, Sir Anthony Alfred, Kt., CBE

Carpenter, *Lt.-Gen.* the Hon. Sir Thomas Patrick John Boyd-, KBE

Carr, Sir (Albert) Raymond (Maillard), Kt.

Carrick, *Hon.* Sir John Leslie, KCMG

Carrick, Sir Roger John, KCMG, LVO

Carsberg, *Prof.* Sir Bryan Victor, Kt.

Carswell, *Rt. Hon.* Sir Robert Douglas, Kt.

Carter, Sir Charles Frederick, Kt., FBA

Carter, *Prof.* Sir David Craig, Kt., FRCSE, FRCSG las., FRCPE

Carter, Sir John, Kt., QC

Carter, Sir John Alexander, Kt.

Carter, Sir John Gordon Thomas, Kt.

Carter, Sir Philip David, Kt., CBE

Carter, Sir Richard Henry Alwyn, Kt.

Carter, Sir William Oscar, Kt.

Cartland, Sir George Barrington, Kt., CMG

Cartledge, Sir Bryan George, KCMG

Cary, Sir Roger Hugh, Bt. (1955)

Casey, *Rt. Hon.* Sir Maurice Eugene, Kt.

Cash, Sir Gerald Christopher, GCMG, GCVO, OBE

Cass, Sir Geoffrey Arthur, Kt.

Cassel, Sir Harold Felix, Bt., TD, QC (1920)

Cassels, Sir John Seton, Kt., CB

Cassels, *Adm.* Sir Simon Alastair Cassillis, KCB, CBE

Cassidi, *Adm.* Sir (Arthur) Desmond, GCB

Casson, Sir Hugh Maxwell, CH, KCVO, PPRA, FRIBA

Cater, Sir Jack, KBE

Catford, Sir (John) Robin, KCVO, CBE

Catherwood, Sir (Henry) Frederick (Ross), Kt.

Catling, Sir Richard Charles, Kt., CMG, OBE

Cato, *Hon.* Sir Arnott Samuel, KCMG

Cave, Sir Charles Edward Coleridge, Bt. (1896)

Cave, Sir (Charles) Philip Haddon-, KBE, CMG

Cave, Sir Robert Cave-Browne-, Bt. (1641)

Cawley, Sir Charles Mills, Kt., CBE, ph.D.

Cayley, Sir Digby William David, Bt. (1661)

Cayzer, Sir James Arthur, Bt. (1904)

Cazalet, *Hon.* Sir Edward Stephen, Kt.

Cazalet, Sir Peter Grenville, Kt.

Cecil, *Rear-Adm.* Sir (Oswald) Nigel Amherst, KBE, CB

Chacksfield, *Air Vice-Marshal* Sir Bernard Albert, KBE, CB

Chadwick, *Revd Prof.* Henry, KBE

Chadwick, *Rt. Hon.* Sir John Murray, Kt., ED

Chadwick, Sir Joshua Kenneth Burton, Bt. (1935)

Chadwick, *Revd Prof.* (William) Owen, OM, KBE, FBA

Chalstrey, Sir (Leonard) John, Kt., MD, FRCS

Chan, *Rt. Hon.* Sir Julius, GCMG, KBE

Chance, Sir (George) Jeremy ffolliott, Bt. (1900)

Chandler, Sir Colin Michael, Kt.

Chandler, Sir Geoffrey, Kt., CBE

Chaney, *Hon.* Sir Frederick Charles, KBE, AFC

Chantler, *Prof.* Sir Cyril, Kt., MD, FRCP

Chaplin, Sir Malcolm Hilbery, Kt., CBE

Chapman, Sir David Robert Macgowan, Bt. (1958)

Chapman, Sir George Alan, Kt.

Chapman, Sir Sidney Brookes, Kt., MP

Chapple, *Field Marshal* Sir John Lyon, GCB, CBE

Charles, *Hon.* Sir Arthur William Hessin, Kt

Charles, Sir George Frederick Lawrence, KCMG, CBE

Charlton, Sir Robert (Bobby), Kt., CBE

Charnley, Sir (William) John, Kt., CB, FEng.

Chataway, *Rt. Hon.* Sir Christopher, Kt.

Chatfield, Sir John Freeman, Kt., CBE

Chaytor, Sir George Reginald, Bt. (1831)

Checketts, *Sqn. Ldr.* Sir David John, KCVO

Checkland, Sir Michael, Kt.

Cheetham, Sir Nicolas John Alexander, KCMG

Cheshire, *Air Chief Marshal* Sir John Anthony, KBE, CB

Chessells, Sir Arthur David (Tim), Kt.

Chesterman, Sir (Dudley) Ross, Kt., ph.D.

Chesterton, Sir Oliver Sidney, Kt., MC

Chetwood, Sir Clifford Jack, Kt.

Chetwynd, Sir Arthur Ralph Talbot, Bt. (1795)

Cheung, Sir Oswald Victor, Kt., CBE

Cheyne, Sir Joseph Lister Watson, Bt., OBE (1908)

Chichester, Sir (Edward) John, Bt. (1641)

Chilcot, Sir John Anthony, GCB

Child, Sir (Coles John) Jeremy, Bt. (1919)

Chilton, *Brig.* Sir Frederick Oliver, Kt., CBE, DSO

Chilwell, *Hon.* Sir Muir Fitzherbert, Kt.

Chinn, Sir Trevor Edwin, Kt., CVO

Chipperfield, Sir Geoffrey Howes, KCB

Chitty, Sir Thomas Willes, Bt. (1924)

Cholmeley, Sir Montague John, Bt. (1806)

Christie, Sir George William Langham, Kt.

Christie, Sir William, Kt., MBE

Christopherson, Sir Derman Guy, Kt., OBE, D.phil., FRS, FEng.

Chung, Sir Sze-yuen, GBE, FEng.

Clapham, Sir Michael John Sinclair, KBE

Clark, Sir Francis Drake, Bt. (1886)

Clark, Sir John Allen, Kt.

Clark, Sir John Stewart-, Bt., MEP (1918)

Clark, Sir Jonathan George, Bt. (1917)

Clark, Sir Robert Anthony, Kt., DSC

Clark, Sir Robin Chichester-, Kt.

Clark, Sir Terence Joseph, KBE, CMG, CVO

Clark, Sir Thomas Edwin, Kt.

Clarke, *Hon.* Sir Anthony Peter, Kt.

Clarke, Sir Arthur Charles, Kt., CBE

Clarke, Sir (Charles Mansfield) Tobias, Bt. (1831)

Clarke, *Prof.* Sir Cyril Astley, KBE, MD, SC.D., FRS, FRCP

Clarke, Sir Ellis Emmanuel Innocent, GCMG

Clarke, Sir Jonathan Dennis, Kt.

Clarke, *Maj.* Sir Peter Cecil, KCVO

Clarke, Sir Robert Cyril, Kt.

Clarke, Sir Rupert William John, Bt., MBE (1882)

Clay, Sir Richard Henry, Bt. (1841)

Clayton, Sir David Robert, Bt. (1732)

Cleaver, Sir Anthony Brian, Kt.

Cleminson, Sir James Arnold Stacey, KBE, MC

Clerk, Sir John Dutton, Bt., CBE, VRD (s. 1679)

Clerke, Sir John Edward Longueville, Bt. (1660)

Clifford, Sir Roger Joseph, Bt. (1887)

Clothier, Sir Cecil Montacute, KCB, QC

Clucas, Sir Kenneth Henry, KCB

Clutterbuck, *Vice-Adm.* Sir David Granville, KBE, CB

Coates, Sir Anthony Robert Milnes, Bt. (1911)

Coates, Sir David Frederick Charlton, Bt. (1921)

Coats, Sir Alastair Francis Stuart, Bt. (1905)

Coats, Sir William David, Kt.

Cobban, Sir James Macdonald, Kt., CBE, TD

Cobham, Sir Michael John, Kt., CBE

Cochrane, Sir (Henry) Marc (Sursock), Bt. (1903)

Cockburn, Sir John Elliot, Bt. (s. 1671)

Cockcroft, Sir Wilfred Halliday, Kt., D.phil.

Cockerell, Sir Christopher Sydney, Kt., CBE, FRS

Cockram, Sir John, Kt.

Cockshaw, Sir Alan, Kt., FEng.

Codrington, Sir Simon Francis Bethell, Bt. (1876)

Codrington, Sir William Alexander, Bt. (1721)

Coghill, Sir Egerton James Nevill Tobias, Bt. (1778)

Coghlin, *Hon.* Sir Patrick, Kt.

Cohen, Sir Edward, Kt.

Cohen, Sir Ivor Harold, Kt., CBE, TD

Cohen, *Prof.* Sir Philip, Kt., ph.D, FRS

Cohen, Sir Stephen Harry Waley-, Bt. (1961)

Coldstream, Sir George Phillips, KCB, KCVO, QC

Cole, Sir (Alexander) Colin, KCB, KCVO, TD

Cole, Sir (Robert) William, Kt.

Coleman, Sir Timothy, KG

Coles, Sir (Arthur) John, GCMG

Colfox, Sir (William) John, Bt. (1939)

Collett, Sir Christopher, GBE

Collett, Sir Ian Seymour, Bt. (1934)

Collins, *Hon.* Sir Andrew David, Kt.

Collins, Sir Arthur James Robert, KCVO

Collins, Sir Bryan Thomas Alfred, Kt., OBE, QFSM
Collins, Sir John Alexander, Kt.
Collyear, Sir John Gowen, Kt., FEng.
Colman, *Hon.* Sir Anthony David, Kt.
Colman, Sir Michael Jeremiah, Bt. (1907)
Colquhoun of Luss, Sir Ivar Iain, Bt. (1786)
Colt, Sir Edward William Dutton, Bt. (1694)
Colthurst, Sir Richard La Touche, Bt. (1744)
Coltman, Sir (Arthur) Leycester Scott, KBE, CMG
Colvin, Sir Howard Montagu, Kt., CVO, CBE, FBA
Compston, *Vice-Adm.* Sir Peter Maxwell, KCB
Compton, *Rt. Hon.* Sir John George Melvin, KCMG
Conant, Sir John Ernest Michael, Bt. (1954)
Condon, Sir Paul Leslie, Kt., QPM
Connell, *Hon.* Sir Michael Bryan, Kt.
Conran, Sir Terence Orby, Kt.
Cons, *Hon.* Sir Derek, Kt.
Constable, Sir Frederic Strickland-, Bt. (1641)
Constantinou, Sir Georkios, Kt., OBE
Cook, *Prof.* Sir Alan Hugh, Kt.
Cook, Sir Christopher Wymondham Rayner Herbert, Bt. (1886)
Cooke, Sir Charles Fletcher-, Kt., QC
Cooke, *Lt.-Col.* Sir David William Perceval, Bt. (1661)
Cooke, Sir Howard Felix Hanlan, GCMG, GCVO
Cooksey, Sir David James Scott, Kt.
Cooley, Sir Alan Sydenham, Kt., CBE
Cooper, *Hon.* Sir Frank, GCB, CMG
Cooper, Sir (Frederick Howard) Michael Craig-, Kt., CBE, TD
Cooper, *Gen.* Sir George Leslie Conroy, GCB, MC
Cooper, Sir Louis Jacques Blom-, Kt., QC
Cooper, Sir Patrick Graham Astley, Bt. (1821)
Cooper, Sir Richard Powell, Bt. (1905)
Cooper, Sir Robert George, Kt., CBE
Cooper, *Maj.-Gen.* Sir Simon Christie, KCVO
Cooper, Sir William Daniel Charles, Bt. (1863)
Coote, Sir Christopher John, Bt., *Premier Baronet of Ireland* (I. 1621)
Copas, *Most Revd* Virgil, KBE, DD
Copisarow, Sir Alcon Charles, Kt.
Corbett, *Maj.-Gen.* Sir Robert John Swan, KCVO, CB
Corby, Sir (Frederick) Brian, Kt.
Corfield, *Rt. Hon.* Sir Frederick Vernon, Kt., QC
Corfield, Sir Kenneth George, Kt., FEng.
Cork, Sir Roger William, Kt.
Corley, Sir Kenneth Sholl Ferrand, Kt.

Cormack, Sir Magnus Cameron, KBE
Cormack, Sir Patrick Thomas, Kt., MP
Corness, Sir Colin Ross, Kt.
Cornford, Sir (Edward) Clifford, KCB, FEng.
Cornforth, Sir John Warcup, Kt., CBE, D.Phil., FRS
Corry, Sir William James, Bt. (1885)
Cortazzi, Sir (Henry Arthur) Hugh, GCMG
Cory, Sir (Clinton Charles) Donald, Bt. (1919)
Cossons, Sir Neil, Kt., OBE
Cotter, *Lt.-Col.* Sir Delaval James Alfred, Bt., DSO (I. 1763)
Cotterell, Sir John Henry Geers, Bt. (1805)
Cotton, Sir John Richard, KCMG, OBE
Cotton, *Hon.* Sir Robert Carrington, KCMG
Cottrell, Sir Alan Howard, Kt., Ph.D., FRS, FEng.
†Cotts, Sir Richard Crichton Mitchell, Bt. (1921)
Couper, Sir (Robert) Nicholas (Oliver), Bt. (1841)
Court, *Hon.* Sir Charles Walter Michael, KCMG, OBE
Cousins, *Air Marshal* Sir David, KCB, AFC
Coutts, Sir David Burdett Money-, KCVO
Couzens, Sir Kenneth Edward, KCB
Covacevich, Sir (Anthony) Thomas, Kt., DFC
Cowan, *Lt.-Gen.* Sir Samuel, KCB, CBE
Coward, *Vice-Adm.* Sir John Francis, KCB, DSO
Cowen, *Rt. Hon. Prof.* Sir Zelman, GCMG, GCVO, QC
Cowie, Sir Thomas (Tom), Kt., OBE
Cowperthwaite, Sir John James, KBE, CMG
Cox, Sir Alan George, Kt., CBE
Cox, *Prof.* Sir David Roxbee, Kt., FRS
Cox, Sir Geoffrey Sandford, Kt., CBE
Cox, *Vice-Adm.* Sir John Michael Holland, KCB
Cradock, *Rt. Hon.* Sir Percy, GCMG
Craig, Sir (Albert) James (Macqueen), GCMG
Craufurd, Sir Robert James, Bt. (1781)
Craven, Sir John Anthony, Kt.
Craven, *Air Marshal* Sir Robert Edward, KBE, CB, DFC
Crawford, *Prof.* Sir Frederick William, Kt., FEng.
Crawford, Sir (Robert) Stewart, GCMG, CVO
Crawford, *Vice-Adm.* Sir William Godfrey, KBE, CB, DSC
Creagh, *Maj.-Gen.* Sir (Kilner) Rupert Brazier-, KBE, CB, DSO
Cresswell, *Hon.* Sir Peter John, Kt.
Crill, Sir Peter Leslie, KBE
Cripps, Sir Cyril Humphrey, Kt.
Crisp, Sir (John) Peter, Bt. (1913)

Critchett, Sir Ian (George Lorraine), Bt. (1908)
Critchley, Sir Julian Michael Gordon, Kt.
Croft, Sir Owen Glendower, Bt. (1671)
Croft, Sir Thomas Stephen Hutton, Bt. (1818)
†Crofton, Sir Hugh Denis, Bt. (1801)
Crofton, *Prof.* Sir John Wenman, Kt.
Crofton, Sir Malby Sturges, Bt. (1838)
Croker, Sir Walter Russell, KBE
Crookenden, *Lt.-Gen.* Sir Napier, KCB, DSO, OBE
Cross, *Air Chief Marshal* Sir Kenneth Brian Boyd, KCB, CBE, DSO, DFC
Crossland, *Prof.* Sir Bernard, Kt., CBE, FEng.
Crossland, Sir Leonard, Kt.
Crossley, Sir Nicholas John, Bt. (1909)
Cruthers, Sir James Winter, Kt.
Cubbon, Sir Brian Crossland, GCB
Cubitt, Sir Hugh Guy, Kt., CBE
Cullen, Sir (Edward) John, Kt., FEng.
Cumming, Sir William Gordon Gordon-, Bt. (1804)
Cuninghame, Sir John Christopher Foggo Montgomery-, Bt. (NS 1672)
†Cuninghame, Sir William Henry Fairlie-, Bt. (S. 1630)
Cunliffe, Sir David Ellis, Bt. (1759)
Cunningham, *Lt.-Gen.* Sir Hugh Patrick, KBE
Cunynghame, Sir Andrew David Francis, Bt. (S. 1702)
†Currie, Sir Donald Scott, Bt. (1847)
Currie, Sir Neil Smith, Kt., CBE
Curtis, Sir Barry John, Kt.
Curtis, Sir (Edward) Leo, Kt.
Curtis, *Hon.* Sir Richard Herbert, Kt.
Curtis, Sir William Peter, Bt. (1802)
Curtiss, *Air Marshal* Sir John Bagot, KCB, KBE
Curwen, Sir Christopher Keith, KCMG
Cuschieri, *Prof.* Sir Alfred, Kt.
Cutler, Sir (Arthur) Roden, VC, KCMG, KCVO, CBE
Cutler, Sir Charles Benjamin, KBE, ED
Dacie, *Prof.* Sir John Vivian, Kt., MD, FRS
Dain, Sir David John Michael, KCVO
Dale, Sir William Leonard, KCMG
Dalrymple, *Maj.* Sir Hew Fleetwood Hamilton-, Bt., KCVO (S. 1697)
Dalton, Sir Alan Nugent Goring, Kt., CBE
Dalton, *Vice-Adm.* Sir Geoffrey Thomas James Oliver, KCB
Daly, *Lt.-Gen.* Sir Thomas Joseph, KBE, CB, DSO
Dalyell, Sir Tam (Thomas), Bt., MP (NS 1685)
Daniel, Sir Goronwy Hopkin, KCVO, CB, D.Phil.
Daniel, Sir John Sagar, Kt., D.Sc.
Daniell, Sir Peter Averell, Kt., TD

Darby, Sir Peter Howard, Kt., CBE, QFSM

Darell, Sir Jeffrey Lionel, Bt., MC (1795)

Dargie, Sir William Alexander, Kt., CBE

Dark, Sir Anthony Michael Beaumont-, Kt.

Darling, Sir Clifford, GCVO

Darling, *Gen.* Sir Kenneth Thomas, GBE, KCB, DSO

Darvall, Sir (Charles) Roger, Kt., CBE

Dashwood, Sir Francis John Vernon Hereward, Bt., *Premier Baronet of Great Britain* (1707)

Dashwood, Sir Richard James, Bt. (1684)

Daunt, Sir Timothy Lewis Achilles, KCMG

Davey, *Hon.* Sir David Herbert Penry-, Kt.

David, Sir Jean Marc, Kt., CBE, QC

David, *His Hon.* Sir Robin (Robert) Daniel George, Kt., QC

Davidson, Sir Robert James, Kt., FEng.

Davie, Sir John Ferguson-, Bt. (1847)

Davies, *Hon.* Sir (Alfred William) Michael, Kt.

Davies, Sir Alun Talfan, Kt., QC

Davies, Sir (Charles) Noel, Kt.

Davies, *Prof.* Sir David Evan Naughton, Kt., CBE, FRS, FEng.

Davies, Sir David Henry, Kt.

Davies, *Hon.* Sir (David Herbert) Mervyn, Kt., MC, TD

Davies, *Prof.* Sir Graeme John, Kt., FEng.

Davies, *Vice-Adm.* Sir Lancelot Richard Bell, KBE

Davies, Sir Peter Maxwell, Kt., CBE

Davies, Sir Victor Caddy, Kt., OBE

Davis, Sir Charles Sigmund, Kt., CB

Davis, Sir Colin Rex, Kt., CBE

Davis, Sir (Ernest) Howard, Kt., CMG, OBE

Davis, Sir John Gilbert, Bt. (1946)

Davis, Sir Peter John, Kt.

Davis, Sir Rupert Charles Hart-, Kt.

Davis, *Hon.* Sir Thomas Robert Alexander Harries, KBE

Davison, *Rt. Hon.* Sir Ronald Keith, GBE, KCMG

Davson, Sir Christopher Michael Edward, Bt. (1927)

Dawbarn, Sir Simon Yelverton, KCVO, CMG

Dawson, *Hon.* Sir Daryl Michael, KBE, CB

Dawson, Sir Hugh Michael Trevor, Bt. (1920)

Dawtry, Sir Alan (Graham), Kt., CBE, TD

Day, Sir Derek Malcolm, KCMG

Day, Sir (Judson) Graham, Kt.

Day, Sir Michael John, Kt., OBE

Day, Sir Robin, Kt.

Day, Sir Simon James, Kt.

Deakin, Sir (Frederick) William (Dampier), Kt., DSO

Deane, *Hon.* Sir William Patrick, KBE

Dear, Sir Geoffrey James, Kt., QPM

de Bellaigue, Sir Geoffrey, GCVO

Debenham, Sir Gilbert Ridley, Bt. (1931)

de Deney, Sir Geoffrey Ivor, KCVO

de Hoghton, Sir (Richard) Bernard (Cuthbert), Bt. (1611)

De la Bère, Sir Cameron, Bt. (1953)

de la Rue, Sir Andrew George Ilay, Bt. (1898)

Dellow, Sir John Albert, Kt., CBE

de Montmorency, Sir Arnold Geoffroy, Bt. (I. 1631)

Denholm, Sir John Ferguson (Ian), Kt., CBE

Denman, Sir (George) Roy, KCB, CMG

Denny, Sir Anthony Coningham de Waltham, Bt. (I. 1782)

Denny, Sir Charles Alistair Maurice, Bt. (1913)

Dent, Sir John, Kt., CBE, FEng.

Dent, Sir Robin John, KCVO

Denton, *Prof.* Sir Eric James, Kt., CBE, FRS

Derbyshire, Sir Andrew George, Kt.

Derham, Sir Peter John, Kt.

de Trafford, Sir Dermot Humphrey, Bt. (1841)

Devesi, Sir Baddeley, GCMG, GCVO

De Ville, Sir Harold Godfrey Oscar, Kt., CBE

Devitt, Sir James Hugh Thomas, Bt. (1916)

de Waal, Sir (Constant Henrik) Henry, KCB, QC

Dewey, Sir Anthony Hugh, Bt. (1917)

Dewhurst, *Prof.* Sir (Christopher) John, Kt.

d'Eyncourt, Sir Mark Gervais Tennyson-, Bt. (1930)

Dhenin, *Air Marshal* Sir Geoffrey Howard, KBE, AFC, GM, MD

Dhrangadhra, HH the Maharaja Raj Saheb of, KCIE

Dibela, *Hon.* Sir Kingsford, GCMG

Dick, *Maj.-Gen.* Sir Iain Charles Mackay-, KCVO, MBE

Dickenson, Sir Aubrey Fiennes Trotman-, Kt.

Dickinson, Sir Harold Herbert, Kt.

Dickinson, Sir Samuel Benson, Kt.

Dilbertson, Sir Geoffrey, Kt., CBE

Dilke, Sir Charles John Wentworth, Bt. (1862)

Dillon, *Rt. Hon.* Sir (George) Brian (Hugh), Kt.

Dixon, Sir Ian Leonard, Kt., CBE

Dixon, Sir Jonathan Mark, Bt. (1919)

Djanogly, Sir Harry Ari Simon, Kt., CBE

Dobbs, *Capt.* Sir Richard Arthur Frederick, KCVO

Dobson, *Vice-Adm.* Sir David Stuart, KBE

Dobson, *Gen.* Sir Patrick John Howard-, GCB

Dodds, Sir Ralph Jordan, Bt. (1964)

Dodson, Sir Derek Sherborne Lindsell, KCMG, MC

Dodsworth, Sir John Christopher Smith-, Bt. (1784)

Doll, *Prof.* Sir (William) Richard (Shaboe), Kt., CH, OBE, FRS, DM, MD, D.SC.

Dollery, Sir Colin Terence, Kt.

Donald, Sir Alan Ewen, KCMG

Donald, *Air Marshal* Sir John George, KBE

Donne, *Hon.* Sir Gaven John, KBE

Donne, Sir John Christopher, Kt.

Dookun, Sir Dewoonarain, Kt.

Dorey, Sir Graham Martyn, Kt.

Dorman, Sir Philip Henry Keppel, Bt. (1923)

Dougherty, *Maj.-Gen.* Sir Ivan Noel, Kt., CBE, DSO, ED

Doughty, Sir William Roland, Kt.

Douglas, Sir (Edward) Sholto, Kt.

Douglas, *Hon.* Sir Roger Owen, Kt.

Douglas, *Rt. Hon.* Sir William Randolph, KCMG

Dover, *Prof.* Sir Kenneth James, Kt., D.Litt., FBA, FRSE

Dowell, Sir Anthony James, Kt., CBE

Down, Sir Alastair Frederick, Kt., OBE, MC, TD

Downes, Sir Edward Thomas, Kt., CBE

Downey, Sir Gordon Stanley, KCB

Downs, Sir Diarmuid, Kt., CBE, FEng.

Downward, Sir William Atkinson, Kt.

Dowson, Sir Philip Manning, Kt., CBE, PRA

Doyle, Sir Reginald Derek Henry, Kt., CBE

D'Oyly, Sir Nigel Hadley Miller, Bt. (1663)

Drake, *Hon.* Sir (Frederick) Maurice, Kt., DFC

Dreyer, *Adm.* Sir Desmond Parry, GCB, CBE, DSC

Drinkwater, Sir John Muir, Kt., QC

Driver, Sir Antony Victor, Kt.

Driver, Sir Eric William, Kt.

Drummond, Sir John Richard Gray, Kt., CBE

Drury, Sir (Victor William) Michael, Kt., OBE

Dryden, Sir John Stephen Gyles, Bt. (1733 and 1795)

du Cann, *Rt. Hon.* Sir Edward Dillon Lott, KBE

†Duckworth, Sir Edward Richard Dyce, Bt. (1909)

du Cros, Sir Claude Philip Arthur Mallet, Bt. (1916)

Duff, *Rt. Hon.* Sir (Arthur) Antony, GCMG, CVO, DSO, DSC

Duffell, *Lt.-Gen.* Sir Peter Royson, KCB, CBE, MC

Duffus, *Hon.* Sir William Algernon Holwell, Kt.

Duffy, Sir (Albert) (Edward) Patrick, Kt., ph.D.

Dugdale, Sir William Stratford, Bt., MC (1936)

Dunbar, Sir Archibald Ranulph, Bt. (s. 1700)

Dunbar, Sir David Hope-, Bt. (s. 1664)

Dunbar, Sir Drummond Cospatrick Ninian, Bt., MC (s. 1698)

Dunbar, Sir James Michael, Bt. (s. 1694)

†Dunbar of Hempriggs, Sir Richard Francis, Bt. (s. 1706)

Duncan, Sir James Blair, Kt.

Duncombe, Sir Philip Digby Pauncefort-, Bt. (1859)

Dunham, Sir Kingsley Charles, Kt., PH.D., FRS, FRSE, FEng.

Dunlop, Sir Thomas, Bt. (1916)

Dunlop, Sir William Norman Gough, Kt.

Dunn, *Air Marshal* Sir Eric Clive, KBE, CB, BEM

Dunn, *Air Marshal* Sir Patrick Hunter, KBE, CB, DFC

Dunn, *Rt. Hon.* Sir Robin Horace Walford, Kt., MC

Dunne, Sir Thomas Raymond, KCVO

Dunnett, Sir Alastair MacTavish, Kt.

Dunning, Sir Simon William Patrick, Bt. (1930)

Dunphie, *Maj.-Gen.* Sir Charles Anderson Lane, Kt., CB, CBE, DSO

Dunstan, *Lt.-Gen.* Sir Donald Beaumont, KBE, CB

Dunt, *Vice-Adm.* Sir John Hugh, KCB

†Duntze, Sir Daniel Evans, Bt. (1774)

Dupre, Sir Tumun, Kt., MBE

Dupree, Sir Peter, Bt. (1921)

Durand, Sir Edward Alan Christopher David Percy, Bt. (1892)

Durant, Sir (Robert) Anthony (Bevis), Kt.

Durham, Sir Kenneth, Kt.

Durie, Sir Alexander Charles, Kt., CBE

Durkin, *Air Marshal* Sir Herbert, KBE, CB

Durrant, Sir William Alexander Estridge, Bt. (1784)

Duthie, *Prof.* Sir Herbert Livingston, Kt.

Duthie, Sir Robert Grieve (Robin), Kt., CBE

Dyer, *Prof.* Sir (Henry) Peter (Francis) Swinnerton-, Bt., KBE, FRS (1678)

Dyke, Sir David William Hart, Bt. (1677)

Dyson, *Hon.* Sir John Anthony, Kt.

Eady, *Hon.* Sir David, Kt.

Earle, Sir (Hardman) George (Algernon), Bt. (1869)

East, Sir (Lewis) Ronald, Kt., CBE

Easton, Sir Robert William Simpson, Kt., CBE

Eaton, *Adm.* Sir Kenneth John, GBE, KCB

Eberle, *Adm.* Sir James Henry Fuller, GCB

Ebrahim, Sir (Mahomed) Currimbhoy, Bt. (1910)

Echlin, Sir Norman David Fenton, Bt. (I. 1721)

Eckersley, Sir Donald Payze, Kt., OBE

Edge, *Capt.* Sir (Philip) Malcolm, KCVO

†Edge, Sir William, Bt. (1937)

Edmonstone, Sir Archibald Bruce Charles, Bt. (1774)

Edwardes, Sir Michael Owen, Kt.

Edwards, Sir Christopher John Churchill, Bt. (1866)

Edwards, Sir George Robert, Kt., OM, CBE, FRS, FEng.

Edwards, Sir (John) Clive (Leighton), Bt. (1921)

Edwards, Sir Llewellyn Roy, Kt.

Edwards, *Prof.* Sir Samuel Frederick, Kt., FRS

Egan, Sir John Leopold, Kt.

Egerton, Sir John Alfred Roy, Kt.

Egerton, Sir (Philip) John (Caledon) Grey-, Bt. (1617)

Egerton, Sir Stephen Loftus, KCMG

Eggleston, *Hon.* Sir Richard Moulton, Kt.

Eichelbaum, *Rt. Hon.* Sir Thomas, GBE

Eliott of Stobs, Sir Charles Joseph Alexander, Bt. (s. 1666)

Ellerton, Sir Geoffrey James, Kt., CMG, MBE

Elliot, Sir Gerald Henry, Kt.

Elliott, Sir Clive Christopher Hugh, Bt. (1917)

Elliott, Sir David Murray, KCMG, CB

Elliott, *Prof.* Sir John Huxtable, Kt., FBA

Elliott, Sir Randal Forbes, KBE

Elliott, *Prof.* Sir Roger James, Kt., FRS

Elliott, Sir Ronald Stuart, Kt.

Ellis, Sir Ronald, Kt., FEng.

Ellison, *Col.* Sir Ralph Harry Carr-, Kt., TD

Elphinstone, Sir John, Bt. (s. 1701)

Elphinstone, Sir John Howard Main, Bt. (1816)

Elton, Sir Arnold, Kt., CBE

Elton, Sir Charles Abraham Grierson, Bt. (1717)

Elwes, Sir Jeremy Vernon, Kt., CBE

Elwood, Sir Brian George Conway, Kt., CBE

Elworthy, Sir Peter Herbert, Kt.

Elyan, Sir (Isadore) Victor, Kt.

Emery, *Rt. Hon.* Sir Peter Frank Hannibal, Kt., MP

Engineer, Sir Noshirwan Phirozshah, Kt.

Engle, Sir George Lawrence Jose, KCB, QC

English, Sir Terence Alexander Hawthorne, KBE, FRCS

Epstein, *Prof.* Sir (Michael) Anthony, Kt., CBE, FRS

Ereaut, Sir (Herbert) Frank Cobbold, Kt.

Errington, *Col.* Sir Geoffrey Frederick, Bt., OBE (1963)

Errington, Sir Lancelot, KCB

Erskine, Sir (Thomas) David, Bt. (1821)

Esmonde, Sir Thomas Francis Grattan, Bt. (I. 1629)

Espie, Sir Frank Fletcher, Kt., OBE

Esplen, Sir John Graham, Bt. (1921)

Eustace, Sir Joseph Lambert, GCMG, GCVO

Evans, Sir Anthony Adney, Bt. (1920)

Evans, *Rt. Hon.* Sir Anthony Howell Meurig, Kt., RD

Evans, *Air Chief Marshal* Sir David George, GCB, CBE

Evans, *Air Chief Marshal* Sir David Parry-, GCB, CBE

Evans, *Hon.* Sir Haydn Tudor, Kt.

Evans, *Prof.* Sir John Grimley, Kt., FRCP

Evans, Sir Richard Harry, Kt., CBE

Evans, Sir Richard Mark, KCMG, KCVO

Evans, Sir Robert, Kt., CBE, FEng.

Evans, Sir (William) Vincent (John), GCMG, MBE, QC

Eveleigh, *Rt. Hon.* Sir Edward Walter, Kt., ERD

Everard, Sir Robin Charles, Bt. (1911)

Everson, Sir Frederick Charles, KCMG

Every, Sir Henry John Michael, Bt. (1641)

Ewans, Sir Martin Kenneth, KCMG

†Ewart, Sir William Michael, Bt. (1887)

Ewbank, *Hon.* Sir Anthony Bruce, Kt.

Ewin, Sir (David) Ernest Thomas Floyd, Kt., OBE, LVO

Ewing, Sir Ronald Archibald Orr-, Bt. (1886)

Eyre, Sir Graham Newman, Kt., QC

Eyre, *Maj.-Gen.* Sir James Ainsworth Campden Gabriel, KCVO, CBE

Eyre, Sir Reginald Edwin, Kt.

Eyre, Sir Richard Charles Hastings, Kt., CBE

Faber, Sir Richard Stanley, KCVO, CMG

Fadahunsi, Sir Joseph Odeleye, KCMG

Fagge, Sir John William Frederick, Bt. (1660)

Fairbairn, Sir (James) Brooke, Bt. (1869)

Fairclough, Sir John Whitaker, Kt., FEng.

Fairgrieve, Sir (Thomas) Russell, Kt., CBE, TD

Fairhall, *Hon.* Sir Allen, KBE

Fairweather, Sir Patrick Stanislaus, KCMG

Falconer, *Hon.* Sir Douglas William, Kt., MBE

†Falkiner, Sir Benjamin Simon Patrick, Bt. (I. 1778)

Fall, Sir Brian James Proetel, GCVO, KCMG

Falle, Sir Samuel, KCMG, KCVO, DSC

Fang, *Prof.* Sir Harry, Kt., CBE

Fareed, Sir Djamil Sheik, Kt.

Farmer, Sir Thomas, Kt., CBE

Farndale, *Gen.* Sir Martin Baker, KCB

Farquhar, Sir Michael Fitzroy
Henry, Bt. (1796)

Farquharson, *Rt. Hon.* Sir Donald
Henry, Kt.

Farquharson, Sir James Robbie, KBE

Farrer, Sir (Charles) Matthew, GCVO

Farrington, Sir Henry Francis
Colden, Bt. (1818)

Fat, Sir (Maxime) Edouard (Lim
Man) Lim, Kt.

Faulkner, Sir (James) Dennis
(Compton), Kt., CBE, VRD

Fawcus, Sir (Robert) Peter, KBE, CMG

Fawkes, Sir Randol Francis, Kt.

Fay, Sir (Humphrey) Michael
Gerard, Kt.

Fayrer, Sir John Lang Macpherson,
Bt. (1896)

Fearn, Sir (Patrick) Robin, KCMG

Feilden, Sir Bernard Melchior, Kt.,
CBE

Feilden, Sir Henry Wemyss, Bt.,
(1846)

Fell, Sir David, KCB

Fellowes, *Rt. Hon.* Sir Robert, GCB,
GCVO

Fenn, Sir Nicholas Maxted, GCMG

Fennell, *Hon.* Sir (John) Desmond
Augustine, Kt., OBE

Fennessy, Sir Edward, Kt., CBE

Ferguson, Sir Ian Edward Johnson-,
Bt. (1906)

Fergusson of Kilkerran, Sir Charles,
Bt. (s. 1703)

Fergusson, Sir Ewan Alastair John,
GCMG, GCVO

Fergusson, Sir James Herbert
Hamilton Colyer-, Bt. (1866)

Feroze, Sir Rustam Moolan, Kt., FRCS

Ferris, *Hon.* Sir Francis Mursell, Kt.,
TD

ffolkes, Sir Robert Francis
Alexander, Bt, OBE (1774)

Field, Sir Malcolm David, Kt.

Fielding, Sir Colin Cunningham, Kt.,
CB

Fielding, Sir Leslie, KCMG

Fieldsend, *Hon.* Sir John Charles
Rowell, KBE

Fiennes, Sir Ranulph Twisleton-
Wykeham-, Bt., OBE (1916)

Figg, Sir Leonard Clifford William,
KCMG

Figgis, Sir Anthony St John Howard,
KCVO, CMG

Figures, Sir Colin Frederick, KCMG,
OBE

Fingland, Sir Stanley James Gunn,
KCMG

Finlay, Sir David Ronald James Bell,
Bt. (1964)

Finney, Sir Thomas, Kt., OBE

Firth, *Prof.* Sir Raymond William,
Kt., ph.D., FBA

Fish, Sir Hugh, Kt., CBE

Fisher, Sir George Read, Kt., CMG

Fisher, *Hon.* Sir Henry Arthur Pears,
Kt.

Fison, Sir (Richard) Guy, Bt., DSC
(1905)

†Fitzgerald, *Revd* (Sir) Daniel
Patrick, Bt. (1903)

FitzGerald, Sir George Peter
Maurice, Bt., MC (*The Knight of
Kerry*) (1880)

FitzHerbert, Sir Richard Ranulph,
Bt. (1784)

Fitzpatrick, *Gen.* Sir (Geoffrey
Richard) Desmond, GCB, GCVO,
DSO, MBE, MC

Fitzpatrick, *Air Marshal* Sir John
Bernard, KBE, CB

Flanagan, Sir James Bernard, Kt., CBE

Fletcher, Sir Henry Egerton
Aubrey-, Bt. (1782)

Fletcher, Sir James Muir Cameron,
Kt.

Fletcher, Sir Leslie, Kt., DSC

Fletcher, *Air Chief Marshal* Sir Peter
Carteret, KCB, OBE, DFC, AFC

Floissac, Sir Vincent Frederick,
Kt., CMG, OBE, QC

Floyd, Sir Giles Henry Charles, Bt.
(1816)

Foley, *Lt.-Gen.* Sir John Paul, KCB,
OBE, MC

Foley, Sir (Thomas John) Noel, Kt.,
CBE

Follett, *Prof.* Sir Brian Keith, Kt., FRS

Foot, Sir Geoffrey James, Kt.

Foots, Sir James William, Kt.

Forbes, *Hon.* Sir Alastair Granville,
Kt.

Forbes, *Maj.* Sir Hamish Stewart, Bt.,
MBE, MC (1823)

Forbes of Craigievar, Sir John
Alexander Cumnock, Bt. (s. 1630)

Forbes, *Vice-Adm.* Sir John Morrison,
KCB

Forbes, *Hon.* Sir Thayne John, Kt.

†Forbes of Pitsligo, Sir William
Daniel Stuart-, Bt. (s. 1626)

Ford, Sir Andrew Russell, Bt. (1929)

Ford, Sir David Robert, KBE, LVO, OBE

Ford, *Maj.* Sir Edward William
Spencer, GCVO, KCB, ERD

Ford, *Air Marshal* Sir Geoffrey
Harold, KBE, CB, FEng.

Ford, *Prof.* Sir Hugh, Kt., FRS, FEng.

Ford, Sir James Anson St Clair-, Bt.
(1793)

Ford, Sir John Archibald, KCMG, MC

Ford, Sir Richard Brinsley, Kt., CBE

Ford, *Gen.* Sir Robert Cyril, GCB, CBE

Foreman, Sir Philip Frank, Kt., CBE,
FEng.

Forman, Sir John Denis, Kt., OBE

Forrest, *Prof.* Sir (Andrew) Patrick
(McEwen), Kt.

Forrest, *Rear-Adm.* Sir Ronald
Stephen, KCVO

Forster, Sir Archibald William, Kt.,
FEng.

Forster, Sir Oliver Grantham, KCMG,
LVO

Forsyth, *Rt. Hon.* Sir Michael Bruce,
Kt.

Forte, *Hon.* Sir Rocco John Vincent,
Kt.

Forwood, Sir Dudley Richard, Bt.
(1895)

Foster, *Prof.* Sir Christopher David,
Kt.

Foster, Sir John Gregory, Bt. (1930)

Foster, Sir Norman Robert, Kt., OM

Foster, Sir Robert Sidney, GCMG,
KCVO

Foulis, Sir Ian Primrose Liston-, Bt.
(s. 1634)

Foulkes, Sir Nigel Gordon, Kt.

Fountain, *Hon.* Sir Cyril Stanley
Smith, Kt.

Fowden, Sir Leslie, Kt., FRS

Fowke, Sir David Frederick
Gustavus, Bt. (1814)

Fowler, Sir (Edward) Michael
Coulson, Kt.

Fowler, *Rt. Hon.* Sir (Peter) Norman,
Kt., MP

Fox, Sir (Henry) Murray, GBE

Fox, *Rt. Hon.* Sir (John) Marcus, Kt.,
MBE

Fox, *Rt. Hon.* Sir Michael John, Kt.

Fox, Sir Paul Leonard, Kt., CBE

France, Sir Christopher Walter, GCB

France, Sir Joseph Nathaniel, KCMG,
CBE

Francis, Sir Horace William
Alexander, Kt., CBE, FEng.

Frank, Sir Douglas George Horace,
Kt., QC

Frank, Sir Robert Andrew, Bt. (1920)

Frankel, Sir Otto Herzberg, Kt., D.SC.,
FRS

Franklin, Sir Michael David Milroy,
KCB, CMG

Franks, Sir Arthur Temple, KCMG

Fraser, Sir Angus McKay, KCB, TD

Fraser, Sir Charles Annand, KCVO

Fraser, *Gen.* Sir David William, GCB,
OBE

Fraser, *Air Marshal Revd* Sir (Henry)
Paterson, KBE, CB, AFC

Fraser, Sir Iain Michael Duncan, Bt.
(1943)

Fraser, Sir Ian, Kt., DSO, OBE

Fraser, Sir Ian James, Kt., CBE, MC

Fraser, Sir (James) Campbell, Kt.

Fraser, Sir William Kerr, GCB

Frederick, Sir Charles Boscawen, Bt.
(1723)

Freeland, Sir John Redvers, KCMG

Freeman, Sir James Robin, Bt. (1945)

Freer, *Air Chief Marshal* Sir Robert
William George, GBE, KCB

Freeth, *Hon.* Sir Gordon, KBE

French, *Hon.* Sir Christopher James
Saunders, Kt.

Frere, *Vice-Adm.* Sir Richard Tobias,
KCB

Fretwell, Sir (Major) John (Emsley),
GCMG

Freud, Sir Clement Raphael, Kt.

Froggatt, Sir Leslie Trevor, Kt.

Froggatt, Sir Peter, Kt.

Frossard, Sir Charles Keith, KBE

Frost, Sir David Paradine, Kt., OBE

Frost, Sir Terence Ernest Manitou, Kt., RA

Frost, *Hon.* Sir (Thomas) Sydney, Kt.

Fry, Sir Peter Derek, Kt.

Fry, *Hon.* Sir William Gordon, Kt.

Fuchs, Sir Vivian Ernest, Kt., Ph.D.

†Fuller, Sir James Henry Fleetwood, Bt. (1910)

Fuller, *Hon.* Sir John Bryan Munro, Kt.

Fung, *Hon.* Sir Kenneth Ping-Fan, Kt., CBE

Furness, Sir Stephen Roberts, Bt. (1913)

Gadsden, Sir Peter Drury Haggerston, GBE, FEng.

Gage, *Hon.* Sir William Marcus, Kt.

Gainsford, Sir Ian Derek, Kt., DDS

Gaius, *Rt. Revd* Saimon, KBE

Gallwey, Sir Philip Frankland Payne-, Bt. (1812)

Gam, *Rt. Revd* Sir Getake, KBE

Gamble, Sir David Hugh Norman, Bt. (1897)

Gambon, Sir Michael John, Kt., CBE

Garden, *Air Marshal* Sir Timothy, KCB

Gardiner, Sir George Arthur, Kt.

Gardiner, Sir John Eliot, Kt., CBE

Gardner, Sir Edward Lucas, Kt., QC

†Gardner, Sir Robert Henry Bruce-, Bt. (1945)

Garland, *Hon.* Sir Patrick Neville, Kt.

Garland, *Hon.* Sir Ransley Victor, KBE

Garlick, Sir John, KCB

Garner, Sir Anthony Stuart, Kt.

Garnett, *Vice-Adm.* Sir Ian David Graham, KCB

Garnier, *Rear-Adm.* Sir John, KCVO, CBE

Garrett, Sir Anthony Peter, Kt., CBE

Garrick, Sir Ronald, Kt., CBE, FEng.

Garrioch, Sir (William) Henry, Kt.

Garrod, *Lt.-Gen.* Sir (John) Martin Carruthers, KCB, OBE

Garthwaite, Sir (William) Mark (Charles), Bt. (1919)

Gaskell, Sir Richard Kennedy Harvey, Kt.

Gatehouse, *Hon.* Sir Robert Alexander, Kt.

Geno, Sir Makena Viora, KBE

George, Sir Arthur Thomas, Kt.

George, *Prof.* Sir Charles Frederick, MD, FRCP

George, Sir Richard William, Kt., CVO

Gerken, *Vice-Adm.* Sir Robert William Frank, KCB, CBE

Gery, Sir Robert Lucian Wade-, KCMG, KCVO

Gethin, Sir Richard Joseph St Lawrence, Bt. (I. 1665)

Getty, Sir (John) Paul, KBE

Ghurburrun, Sir Rabindrah, Kt.

Gibb, Sir Francis Ross (Frank), Kt., CBE, FEng.

Gibbings, Sir Peter Walter, Kt.

Gibbons, Sir (John) David, KBE

Gibbons, Sir William Edward Doran, Bt. (1752)

Gibbs, *Hon.* Sir Eustace Hubert Beilby, KCVO, CMG

Gibbs, *Rt. Hon.* Sir Harry Talbot, GCMG, KBE

Gibbs, *Lt.-Col.* Sir Peter Evan Wyldbore, KCVO

Gibbs, Sir Roger Geoffrey, Kt.

Gibbs, *Field Marshal* Sir Roland Christopher, GCB, CBE, DSO, MC

†Gibson, Revd Sir Christopher Herbert, Bt. (1931)

Gibson, *Revd* Sir David, Bt. (1926)

Gibson, *Vice-Adm.* Sir Donald Cameron Ernest Forbes, KCB, DSC

Gibson, *Rt. Hon.* Sir Peter Leslie, Kt.

Gibson, *Rt. Hon.* Sir Ralph Brian, Kt.

Giddings, *Air Marshal* Sir (Kenneth Charles) Michael, KCB, OBE, DFC, AFC

Gielgud, Sir (Arthur) John, Kt., OM, CH

Giffard, Sir (Charles) Sydney (Rycroft), KCMG

Gilbert, *Air Chief Marshal* Sir Joseph Alfred, KCB

Gilbert, Sir Martin John, Kt., CBE

†Gilbey, Sir Walter Gavin, Bt. (1893)

Giles, *Rear-Adm.* Sir Morgan Charles Morgan-, Kt., DSO, OBE, GM

Gill, Sir Anthony Keith, Kt., FEng.

Gillam, Sir Patrick John, Kt.

Gillett, Sir Robin Danvers Penrose, Bt., GBE, RD (1959)

Gilmour, *Col.* Sir Allan Macdonald, KCVO, OBE, MC

Gilmour, Sir John Edward, Bt., DSO, TD (1897)

Gina, Sir Lloyd Maepeza, KBE

Gingell, *Air Chief Marshal* Sir John, GBE, KCB, KCVO

Girolami, Sir Paul, Kt.

Girvan, *Hon.* Sir (Frederick) Paul, Kt.

Gladstone, Sir (Erskine) William, Bt. (1846)

Glasspole, Sir Florizel Augustus, GCMG, GCVO

Glen, Sir Alexander Richard, KBE, DSC

Glenn, Sir (Joseph Robert) Archibald, Kt., OBE

Glidewell, *Rt. Hon.* Sir Iain Derek Laing, Kt.

Glock, Sir William Frederick, Kt., CBE

Glover, *Gen.* Sir James Malcolm, KCB, MBE

Glover, Sir Victor Joseph Patrick, Kt.

Glyn, Sir Richard Lindsay, Bt. (1759 and 1800)

Goavea, Sir Sinaka Vakai, KBE

Godber, Sir George Edward, GCB, DM

Goff, Sir Robert (William) Davis-, Bt. (1905)

Gold, Sir Arthur Abraham, Kt., CBE

Gold, Sir Joseph, Kt.

Goldberg, *Prof.* Sir Abraham, Kt., MD, D.SC., FRCP

Goldberg, *Prof.* Sir David Paul Brandes, Kt.

Goldman, Sir Samuel, KCB

Gombrich, *Prof.* Sir Ernst Hans Josef, Kt., OM, CBE, Ph.D., FBA, FSA

Gooch, Sir (Richard) John Sherlock, Bt. (1746)

Gooch, Sir Trevor Sherlock (Sir Peter), Bt. (1866)

Good, Sir John Kennedy-, KBE

Goodall, Sir (Arthur) David Saunders, GCMG

Goodenough, Sir Anthony Michael, KCMG

Goodenough, Sir William McLernon, Bt. (1943)

Goodhart, Sir Philip Carter, Kt.

Goodhart, Sir Robert Anthony Gordon, Bt. (1911)

Goodhew, Sir Victor Henry, Kt.

Goodison, Sir Alan Clowes, KCMG

Goodison, Sir Nicholas Proctor, Kt.

Goodlad, *Rt. Hon.* Sir Alastair Robertson, KCMG, MP

Goodman, Sir Patrick Ledger, Kt., CBE

Goodson, Sir Mark Weston Lassam, Bt. (1922)

Goodwin, Sir Matthew Dean, Kt., CBE

Goold, Sir George Leonard, Bt. (1801)

Gordon, Sir Alexander John, Kt., CBE

Gordon, Sir Andrew Cosmo Lewis Duff-, Bt. (1813)

Gordon, Sir Charles Addison Somerville Snowden, KCB

Gordon, Sir Keith Lyndell, Kt., CMG

Gordon, Sir (Lionel) Eldred (Peter) Smith-, Bt. (1838)

Gordon, Sir Robert James, Bt. (s. 1706)

Gordon, Sir Sidney Samuel, Kt., CBE

Gordon Lennox, Lord Nicholas Charles, KCMG, KCVO

†Gore, Sir Nigel Hugh St George, Bt. (I. 1622)

Gorham, Sir Richard Masters, Kt., CBE, DFC

Goring, Sir William Burton Nigel, Bt. (1627)

Gorman, Sir John Reginald, Kt., CVO, CBE, MC

Gorst, Sir John Michael, Kt.

Gorton, *Rt. Hon.* Sir John Grey, GCMG, CH

Goschen, Sir Edward Christian, Bt., DSO (1916)

Gosling, Sir (Frederick) Donald, Kt.

Goswell, Sir Brian Lawrence, Kt.

Goulden, Sir (Peter) John, KCMG

Goulding, Sir (Ernest) Irvine, Kt.

Goulding, Sir Marrack Irvine, KCMG

Goulding, Sir (William) Lingard Walter, Bt. (1904)

Gourlay, *Gen.* Sir (Basil) Ian (Spencer), KCB, OBE, MC, RM

Gourlay, Sir Simon Alexander, Kt.

Govan, Sir Lawrence Herbert, Kt.

Gow, *Gen.* Sir (James) Michael, GCB

Gowans, Sir James Learmonth, Kt., CBE, FRCP, FRS
Graaff, Sir de Villiers, Bt., MBE (1911)
Grabham, Sir Anthony Henry, Kt.
Graham, Sir Alexander Michael, GBE
Graham, Sir James Bellingham, Bt. (1662)
Graham, Sir James Fergus Surtees, Bt. (1783)
Graham, Sir James Thompson, Kt., CMG
Graham, Sir John Alexander Noble, Bt., GCMG (1906)
Graham, Sir John Moodie, Bt. (1964)
Graham, Sir Norman William, Kt., CB
Graham, Sir Peter, KCB, QC
Graham, Sir Peter Alfred, Kt., OBE
Graham, Lt.-Gen. Sir Peter Walter, KCB, CBE
†Graham, Sir Ralph Stuart, Bt. (1629)
Graham, Hon. Sir Samuel Horatio, Kt., CMG, OBE
Grandy, Marshal of the Royal Air Force Sir John, GCB, GCVO, KBE, DSO
Grant, Sir Archibald, Bt. (s. 1705)
Grant, Sir Clifford, Kt.
Grant, Sir (John) Anthony, Kt.
Grant, Sir (Matthew) Alistair, Kt.
Grant, Sir Patrick Alexander Benedict, Bt. (s. 1688)
Gray, Sir John Archibald Browne, Kt., SC.D., FRS
Gray, Sir John Walton David, KBE, CMG
Gray, Lt.-Gen. Sir Michael Stuart, KCB, OBE
Gray, Sir Robert McDowall (Robin), Kt.
Gray, Sir William Hume, Bt. (1917)
Gray, Sir William Stevenson, Kt.
Graydon, Air Chief Marshal Sir Michael James, GCB, CBE
Grayson, Sir Jeremy Brian Vincent Harrington, Bt. (1922)
Green, Sir Allan David, KCB, QC
Green, Sir Andrew Fleming, KCMG
Green, Hon. Sir Guy Stephen Montague, KBE
Green, Sir Kenneth, Kt.
Green, Sir Owen Whitley, Kt.
†Green, Sir Stephen Lycett, Bt., TD (1886)
Greenaway, Sir John Michael Burdick, Bt. (1933)
Greenbury, Sir Richard, Kt.
Greene, Sir (John) Brian Massy-, Kt.
Greengross, Sir Alan David, Kt.
Greening, Rear-Adm. Sir Paul Woollven, GCVO
Greenstock, Sir Jeremy Quentin, KCMG
Greenwell, Sir Edward Bernard, Bt. (1906)
Gregson, Sir Peter Lewis, GCB
Greig, Sir (Henry Louis) Carron, KCVO, CBE
Grenside, Sir John Peter, Kt., CBE
Grey, Sir Anthony Dysart, Bt. (1814)

Grierson, Sir Michael John Bewes, Bt. (s. 1685)
Grierson, Sir Ronald Hugh, Kt.
Griffin, Maj. Sir (Arthur) John (Stewart), KCVO
Griffin, Sir (Charles) David, Kt., CBE
Griffiths, Sir Eldon Wylie, Kt.
Griffiths, Sir John Norton-, Bt. (1922)
Grimwade, Sir Andrew Sheppard, Kt., CBE
Grindrod, Most Revd John Basil Rowland, KBE
Grinstead, Sir Stanley Gordon, Kt.
Grose, Vice-Adm. Sir Alan, KBE
Grossart, Sir Angus McFarlane McLeod, Kt., CBE
Grotrian, Sir Philip Christian Brent, Bt. (1934)
Grove, Sir Charles Gerald, Bt. (1874)
Grove, Sir Edmund Frank, KCVO
Grugeon, Sir John Drury, Kt.
Grylls, Sir (William) Michael (John), Kt.
Guinness, Sir Alec, Kt., CH, CBE
Guinness, Sir Howard Christian Sheldon, Kt., VRD
Guinness, Sir Kenelm Ernest Lee, Bt. (1867)
Guise, Sir John Grant, Bt. (1783)
Gull, Sir Rupert William Cameron, Bt. (1872)
Gumbs, Sir Emile Rudolph, Kt.
Gunn, Prof. Sir John Currie, Kt., CBE
Gunn, Sir Robert Norman, Kt.
Gunn, Sir William Archer, KBE, CMG
†Gunning, Sir Charles Theodore, Bt. (1778)
Gunston, Sir John Wellesley, Bt. (1938)
Gurdon, Prof. Sir John Bertrand, Kt., D.phil., FRS
Guthrie, Gen. Sir Charles Ronald Llewelyn, GCB, LVO, OBE
Guthrie, Sir Malcolm Connop, Bt. (1936)
Guy, Gen. Sir Roland Kelvin, GCB, CBE, DSO
Habakkuk, Sir John Hrothgar, Kt., FBA
Hadfield, Sir Ronald, Kt., QPM
Hadlee, Sir Richard John, Kt., MBE
Hadley, Sir Leonard Albert, Kt.
Hague, Prof. Sir Douglas Chalmers, Kt., CBE
Halberg, Sir Murray Gordon, Kt., MBE
Hale, Prof. Sir John Rigby, Kt.
Hall, Sir Arnold Alexander, Kt., FRS, FEng.
Hall, Sir Basil Brodribb, KCB, MC, TD
Hall, Air Marshal Sir Donald Percy, KCB, CBE, AFC
Hall, Sir Douglas Basil, Bt., KCMG (s. 1687)
Hall, Sir Ernest, Kt., OBE
Hall, Sir (Frederick) John (Frank), Bt. (1923)
Hall, Sir John, Kt.
Hall, Sir John Bernard, Bt. (1919)

Hall, Sir Peter Edward, KBE, CMG
Hall, Prof. Sir Peter Geoffrey, Kt., FBA
Hall, Sir Peter Reginald Frederick, Kt., CBE
Hall, Sir Robert de Zouche, KCMG
Hall, Brig. Sir William Henry, KBE, DSO, ED
Halliday, Vice-Adm. Sir Roy William, KBE, DSC
Halpern, Sir Ralph Mark, Kt.
Halsey, Revd Sir John Walter Brooke, Bt. (1920)
Halstead, Sir Ronald, Kt., CBE
Ham, Sir David Kenneth Rowe-, GBE
Hambling, Sir (Herbert) Hugh, Bt. (1924)
Hamburger, Sir Sidney Cyril, Kt., CBE
Hamer, Hon. Sir Rupert James, KCMG, ED
Hamill, Sir Patrick, Kt., QPM
Hamilton, Rt. Hon. Sir Archibald Gavin, Kt., MP
Hamilton, Sir Edward Sydney, Bt. (1776 and 1819)
Hamilton, Sir James Arnot, KCB, MBE, FEng.
Hamilton, Sir Malcolm William Bruce Stirling-, Bt. (s. 1673)
Hamilton, Sir Michael Aubrey, Kt.
Hamilton, Sir (Robert Charles) Richard Caradoc, Bt. (s. 1646)
Hammett, Hon. Sir Clifford James, Kt.
Hammick, Sir Stephen George, Bt. (1834)
Hampel, Sir Ronald Claus, Kt.
Hampshire, Sir Stuart Newton, Kt., FBA
Hampson, Sir Stuart, Kt.
Hampton, Sir (Leslie) Geoffrey, Kt.
Hancock, Sir David John Stowell, KCB
Hancock, Air Marshal Sir Valston Eldridge, KBE, CB, DFC
Hand, Most Revd Geoffrey David, KBE
Handley, Sir David John Davenport-, Kt., OBE
Hanham, Sir Michael William, Bt., DFC (1667)
Hanley, Rt. Hon. Sir Jeremy James, KCMG
Hanley, Sir Michael Bowen, KCB
Hanmer, Sir John Wyndham Edward, Bt. (1774)
Hann, Sir James, Kt., CBE
Hannam, Sir John Gordon, Kt.
Hannay, Sir David Hugh Alexander, GCMG
Hanson, Sir (Charles) Rupert (Patrick), Bt. (1918)
Hanson, Sir John Gilbert, KCMG, CBE
Hardcastle, Sir Alan John, Kt.
Hardie, Sir Douglas Fleming, Kt., CBE
Harding, Sir Christopher George Francis, Kt.
Harding, Sir George William, KCMG, CVO

Harding, *Marshal of the Royal Air Force* Sir Peter Robin, GCB

Harding, Sir Roy Pollard, Kt., CBE

Hardman, Sir Henry, KCB

Hardy, Sir David William, Kt.

Hardy, Sir James Gilbert, Kt., OBE

Hardy, Sir Richard Charles Chandos, Bt. (1876)

Hare, Sir David, Kt., FRSL

Hare, Sir Philip Leigh, Bt. (1818)

Harford, Sir (John) Timothy, Bt. (1934)

Hargroves, *Brig.* Sir Robert Louis, Kt., CBE

Harington, *Gen.* Sir Charles Henry Pepys, GCB, CBE, DSO, MC

Harington, Sir Nicholas John, Bt. (1611)

Harland, *Air Marshal* Sir Reginald Edward Wynyard, KBE, CB

Harley, *Gen.* Sir Alexander George Hamilton, KBE, CB

Harman, *Gen.* Sir Jack Wentworth, GCB, OBE, MC

Harman, *Hon.* Sir Jeremiah LeRoy, Kt.

Harman, Sir John Andrew, Kt.

Harmsworth, Sir Hildebrand Harold, Bt. (1922)

Harpham, Sir William, KBE, CMG

Harris, *Prof.* Sir Alan James, Kt., CBE, FEng.

Harris, *Prof.* Sir Henry, Kt., FRCP, FRCpath., FRS

Harris, *Lt.-Gen.* Sir Ian Cecil, KBE, CB, DSO

Harris, Sir Jack Wolfred Ashford, Bt. (1932)

Harris, *Air Marshal* Sir John Hulme, KCB, CBE

Harris, Sir William Gordon, KBE, CB, FEng.

Harrison, Sir David, Kt., CBE, FEng.

Harrison, *Prof.* Sir Donald Frederick Norris, Kt., FRCS

Harrison, Sir Ernest Thomas, Kt., OBE

Harrison, Sir Francis Alexander Lyle, Kt., MBE, QC

Harrison, *Surgeon Vice-Adm.* Sir John Albert Bews, KBE

Harrison, *Hon.* Sir (John) Richard, Kt., ED

Harrison, *Hon.* Sir Michael Guy Vicat, Kt.

Harrison, Sir Michael James Harwood, Bt. (1961)

Harrison, *Prof.* Sir Richard John, Kt., FRS

Harrison, Sir (Robert) Colin, Bt. (1922)

Harrison, Sir Terence, Kt., FEng

Harrop, Sir Peter John, KCB

Hart, Sir Graham Allan, KCB

Hart, *Hon.* Sir Michael Christopher Campbell, Kt.

Hartopp, *Lt. Cdr* Sir Kenneth Alston Cradock-, Bt., MBE, DSC (1796)

Hartwell, Sir (Francis) Anthony Charles Peter, Bt. (1805)

Harvey, Sir Charles Richard Musgrave, Bt. (1933)

Harvie, Sir John Smith, Kt., CBE

Haselhurst, Sir Alan Gordon Barraclough, Kt., MP

Haskard, Sir Cosmo Dugal Patrick Thomas, KCMG, MBE

Haslam, *Hon.* Sir Alec Leslie, Kt.

Haslam, *Rear-Adm.* Sir David William, KBE, CB

Hassett, *Gen.* Sir Francis George, KBE, CB, DSO, LVO

Hastings, Sir Stephen Lewis Edmonstone, Kt., MC

Hatty, *Hon.* Sir Cyril James, Kt.

Haughton, Sir James, Kt., CBE, QPM

Havelock, Sir Wilfrid Bowen, Kt.

Hawkins, Sir Arthur Ernest, Kt.

†Hawkins, Sir Howard Caesar, Bt. (1778)

Hawkins, Sir Paul Lancelot, Kt., TD

Hawley, Sir Donald Frederick, KCMG, MBE

†Hawley, Sir Henry Nicholas, Bt. (1795)

Haworth, Sir Philip, Bt. (1911)

Hawthorne, *Prof.* Sir William Rede, Kt., CBE, SC.D., FRS, FEng.

Hay, Sir David Osborne, Kt., CBE, DSO

Hay, Sir David Russell, Kt., CBE, FRCP, MD

Hay, Sir Hamish Grenfell, Kt.

Hay, Sir James Brian Dalrymple-, Bt. (1798)

Hay, Sir John Erroll Audley, Bt. (s. 1663)

†Hay, Sir Ronald Frederick Hamilton, Bt. (s. 1703)

Haydon, Sir Walter Robert, KCMG

Hayes, Sir Brian, Kt., CBE, QPM

Hayes, Sir Brian David, GCB

Hayes, *Vice-Adm.* Sir John Osier Chattock, KCB, OBE

Hayr, *Air Marshal* Sir Kenneth William, KCB, KBE, AFC

Hayward, Sir Anthony William Byrd, Kt.

Hayward, Sir Jack Arnold, Kt., OBE

Haywood, Sir Harold, KCVO, OBE

Head, Sir Francis David Somerville, Bt. (1838)

Healey, Sir Charles Edward Chadwyck-, Bt. (1919)

Heap, Sir Peter William, KCMG

Hearne, Sir Graham James, Kt., CBE

Heath, *Rt. Hon.* Sir Edward Richard George, KG, MBE, MP

Heath, Sir Mark Evelyn, KCVO, CMG

Heathcote, *Brig.* Sir Gilbert Simon, Bt., CBE (1733)

Heathcote, Sir Michael Perryman, Bt. (1733)

Heatley, Sir Peter, Kt., CBE

Heaton, Sir Yvo Robert Henniker-, Bt. (1912)

Heiser, Sir Terence Michael, GCB

Hellaby, Sir (Frederick Reed) Alan, Kt.

Henderson, Sir Denys Hartley, Kt.

Henderson, Sir (John) Nicholas, GCMG, KCVO

Henderson, Sir William MacGregor, Kt., D.SC., FRS

Henley, Sir Douglas Owen, KCB

Henley, *Rear-Adm.* Sir Joseph Charles Cameron, KCVO, CB

Hennessy, Sir James Patrick Ivan, KBE, CMG

†Henniker, Sir Adrian Chandos, Bt. (1813)

Henry, Sir Denis Aynsley, Kt., OBE, QC

Henry, *Rt. Hon.* Sir Denis Robert Maurice, Kt.

Henry, *Hon.* Sir Geoffrey Arama, KBE

Henry, Sir Patrick Denis, Bt. (1923)

Henry, *Hon.* Sir Trevor Ernest, Kt.

Hepburn, Sir John Alastair Trant Kidd Buchan-, Bt. (1815)

Herbecq, Sir John Edward, KCB

Herbert, *Adm.* Sir Peter Geoffrey Marshall, KCB, OBE

Hermon, Sir John Charles, Kt., OBE, QPM

Heron, Sir Conrad Frederick, KCB, OBE

Heron, Sir Michael Gilbert, Kt.

Hervey, Sir Roger Blaise Ramsay, KCVO, CMG

Heseltine, *Rt. Hon.* Sir William Frederick Payne, GCB, GCVO

Hetherington, Sir Arthur Ford, Kt., DSC, FEng.

Hetherington, Sir Thomas Chalmers, KCB, CBE, TD, QC

Hewetson, Sir Christopher Raynor, Kt., TD

Hewett, Sir Peter John Smithson, Bt., MM (1813)

Hewitt, Sir (Cyrus) Lenox (Simson), Kt., OBE

Hewitt, Sir Nicholas Charles Joseph, Bt. (1921)

Heygate, Sir Richard John Gage, Bt. (1831)

Heyman, Sir Horace William, Kt.

Heywood, Sir Peter, Bt. (1838)

Hezlet, *Vice-Adm.* Sir Arthur Richard, KBE, DSO, DSC

Hibbert, Sir Jack, KCB

Hibbert, Sir Reginald Alfred, GCMG

Hickey, Sir Justin, Kt.

Hickman, Sir (Richard) Glenn, Bt. (1903)

Hicks, Sir Robert, Kt.

Hidden, *Hon.* Sir Anthony Brian, Kt.

Hielscher, Sir Leo Arthur, Kt.

Higgins, *Hon.* Sir Malachy Joseph, Kt.

Higginson, Sir Gordon Robert, Kt., ph.D., FEng.

Hill, Sir Alexander Rodger Erskine-, Bt. (1945)

Hill, Sir Arthur Alfred, Kt., CBE

Hill, Sir Brian John, Kt.

Hill, Sir James Frederick, Bt. (1917)

Hill, Sir John McGregor, Kt., ph.D., FEng.

Hill, Sir John Maxwell, Kt., CBE, DFC

†Hill, Sir John Rowley, Bt. (I. 1779)

Hill, *Vice-Adm.* Sir Robert Charles Finch, KBE, FEng.

Hill, Sir (Stanley) James (Allen), Kt.

Hillary, Sir Edmund, KG, KBE

Hillhouse, Sir (Robert) Russell, KCB

Hills, Sir Graham John, Kt.

Hine, *Air Chief Marshal* Sir Patrick Bardon, GCB, GBE

Hines, Sir Colin Joseph, Kt., OBE

Hirsch, *Prof.* Sir Peter Bernhard, Kt., Ph.D., FRS

Hirst, *Rt. Hon.* Sir David Cozens-Hardy, Kt.

Hirst, Sir Michael William, Kt.

Hoare, Sir Peter Richard David, Bt. (1786)

Hoare, Sir Timothy Edward Charles, Bt., OBE (I. 1784)

Hobart, Sir John Vere, Bt. (1914)

Hobbs, *Maj.-Gen.* Sir Michael Frederick, KCVO, CBE

Hobday, Sir Gordon Ivan, Kt.

Hobhouse, Sir Charles John Spinney, Bt. (1812)

Hobhouse, *Rt. Hon.* Sir John Stewart, Kt.

Hockaday, Sir Arthur Patrick, KCB, CMG

Hockley, *Gen.* Sir Anthony Heritage Farrar-, GBE, KCB, DSO, MC

Hoddinott, Sir John Charles, Kt., CBE, QPM

†Hodge, Sir Andrew Rowland, Bt. (1921)

Hodge, Sir James William, KCVO, CMG

Hodge, Sir Julian Stephen Alfred, Kt.

Hodges, *Air Chief Marshal* Sir Lewis MacDonald, KCB, CBE, DSO, DFC

Hodgkin, *Prof.* Sir Alan Lloyd, OM, KBE, FRS, SC.D.

Hodgkin, Sir Gordon Howard Eliot, Kt., CBE

Hodgkinson, *Air Chief Marshal* Sir (William) Derek, KCB, CBE, DFC, AFC

Hodgson, Sir Maurice Arthur Eric, Kt., FEng.

Hodgson, *Hon.* Sir (Walter) Derek (Thornley), Kt.

Hodson, Sir Michael Robin Adderley, Bt. (I. 1789)

Hoffenberg, *Prof.* Sir Raymond, KBE

Hogg, Sir Christopher Anthony, Kt.

Hogg, Sir Edward William Lindsay-, Bt. (1905)

Hogg, *Vice-Adm.* Sir Ian Leslie Trower, KCB, DSC

Hogg, Sir John Nicholson, Kt., TD

Hogg, Sir Michael David, Bt. (1846)

Holcroft, Sir Peter George Culcheth, Bt. (1921)

Holden, Sir Edward, Bt. (1893)

Holden, Sir John David, Bt. (1919)

Holder, Sir John Henry, Bt. (1898)

Holder, *Air Marshal* Sir Paul Davie, KBE, CB, DSO, DFC, Ph.D.

Holdgate, Sir Martin Wyatt, Kt., CB, Ph.D.

Holland, *Hon.* Sir Alan Douglas, Kt.

Holland, *Hon.* Sir Christopher John, Kt.

Holland, Sir Clifton Vaughan, Kt.

Holland, Sir Geoffrey, KCB

Holland, Sir Kenneth Lawrence, Kt., CBE, QFSM

Holland, Sir Philip Welsby, Kt.

Holliday, *Prof.* Sir Frederick George Thomas, Kt., CBE, FRSE

Hollings, *Hon.* Sir (Alfred) Kenneth, Kt., MC

Hollis, *Hon.* Sir Anthony Barnard, Kt.

Hollom, Sir Jasper Quintus, KBE

Holloway, *Hon.* Sir Barry Blyth, KBE

Holm, Sir Carl Henry, Kt., OBE

Holm, Sir Ian (Ian Holm Cuthbert), Kt., CBE

Holman, *Hon.* Sir (Edward) James, Kt.

Holmes, *Prof.* Sir Frank Wakefield, Kt.

Holmes, Sir Peter Fenwick, Kt., MC

Holroyd, *Air Marshal* Sir Frank Martyn, KBE, CB, FEng.

Holt, *Prof.* Sir James Clarke, Kt.

Holt, Sir Michael, Kt., CBE

Home, Sir William Dundas, Bt. (S. 1671)

Honeycombe, *Prof.* Sir Robert William Kerr, Kt., FRS, FEng.

Honywood, Sir Filmer Courtenay William, Bt. (1660)

Hood, Sir Harold Joseph, Bt., TD (1922)

Hookway, Sir Harry Thurston, Kt.

Hooper, *Hon.* Sir Anthony, Kt.

Hope, Sir (Charles) Peter, KCMG, TD

Hope, Sir Colin Frederick Newton, Kt.

Hope, *Rt. Revd and Rt. Hon.* David Michael, KCVO

Hope, Sir John Carl Alexander, Bt. (S. 1628)

Hopkin, Sir (William Aylsham) Bryan, Kt., CBE

Hopkins, Sir Anthony Philip, Kt., CBE

Hopkins, Sir Michael John, Kt., CBE, RA, RIBA

Hopwood, *Prof.* Sir David Alan, Kt., FRS

Hordern, *Rt. Hon.* Sir Peter Maudslay, Kt.

Horlick, *Vice-Adm.* Sir Edwin John, KBE, FEng.

Horlick, Sir James Cunliffe William, Bt. (1914)

Horlock, *Prof.* Sir John Harold, Kt., FRS, FEng.

Hornby, Sir Derek Peter, Kt.

Hornby, Sir Simon Michael, Kt.

Horne, Sir Alan Gray Antony, Bt. (1929)

Horsfall, Sir John Musgrave, Bt., MC, TD (1909)

Horsley, *Air Marshal* Sir (Beresford) Peter (Torrington), KCB, CBE, LVO, AFC

†Hort, Sir Andrew Edwin Fenton, Bt. (1767)

Horton, Sir Robert Baynes, Kt.

Hosker, Sir Gerald Albery, KCB, QC

Hoskyns, Sir Benedict Leigh, Bt. (1676)

Hoskyns, Sir John Austin Hungerford Leigh, Kt.

Hotung, Sir Joseph Edward, Kt.

Houghton, Sir John Theodore, Kt., CBE, FRS

†Houldsworth, Sir Richard Thomas Reginald, Bt. (1887)

Hounsfield, Sir Godfrey Newbold, Kt., CBE

Hourston, Sir Gordon Minto, Kt.

House, *Lt.-Gen.* Sir David George, GCB, KCVO, CBE, MC

Houssemayne du Boulay, Sir Roger William, KCVO, CBE

Howard, Sir (Hamilton) Edward de Coucey, Bt., GBE (1955)

Howard, *Prof.* Sir Michael Eliot, Kt., CBE, MC

Howard, *Maj.-Gen.* Lord Michael Fitzalan-, GCVO, CB, CBE, MC

Howard, Sir Walter Stewart, Kt., MBE

Howell, Sir Ralph Frederic, Kt.

Howells, Sir Eric Waldo Benjamin, Kt., CBE

Howlett, *Gen.* Sir Geoffrey Hugh Whitby, KBE, MC

Hoyle, *Prof.* Sir Fred, Kt., FRS

Hoyos, *Hon.* Sir Fabriciano Alexander, Kt.

Huddleston, Most Revd (Ernest Urban) Trevor, KCMG

Hudson, *Lt.-Gen.* Sir Peter, KCB, CBE

Huggins, *Hon.* Sir Alan Armstrong, Kt.

Hughes, *Hon.* Sir Anthony Philip Gilson, Kt.

Hughes, Sir David Collingwood, Bt. (1773)

Hughes, *Prof.* Sir Edward Stuart Reginald, Kt., CBE

Hughes, Sir Jack William, Kt.

Hughes, Sir Trevor Denby Lloyd-, Kt.

Hughes, Sir Trevor Poulton, KCB

Hugo, *Lt.-Col.* Sir John Mandeville, KCVO, OBE

Hull, *Prof.* Sir David, Kt.

Hulse, Sir Edward Jeremy Westrow, Bt. (1739)

Hume, Sir Alan Blyth, Kt., CB

Humphreys, Sir (Raymond Evelyn) Myles, Kt.

Hunn, Sir Jack Kent, Kt., CMG

Hunt, Sir John Leonard, Kt.

Hunt, *Adm.* Sir Nicholas John Streynsham, GCB, LVO

Hunt, Sir Rex Masterman, Kt., CMG

Hunt, Sir Robert Frederick, Kt., CBE, FEng.

Hunter, *Hon.* Sir Alexander Albert, KBE

Hunter, Sir Alistair John, KCMG

Hunter, Sir Ian Bruce Hope, Kt., MBE

Hunter, *Prof.* Sir Laurence Colvin, Kt., CBE, FRSE

Hurn, Sir (Francis) Roger, Kt.

Hurrell, Sir Anthony Gerald, KCVO, CMG

Hurst, Sir Geoffrey Charles, Kt., MBE

Husbands, Sir Clifford Straugh, GCMG

Hutchinson, *Hon.* Sir Ross, Kt., DFC

Hutchison, *Lt.-Cdr.* Sir (George) Ian Clark, Kt., RN

Hutchison, *Rt. Hon.* Sir Michael, Kt.

Hutchison, Sir Peter Craft, Bt. (1956)

Hutchison, Sir Robert, Bt. (1939)

Huxley, *Prof.* Sir Andrew Fielding, Kt., OM, FRS

Huxtable, *Gen.* Sir Charles Richard, KCB, CBE

Hyatali, *Hon.* Sir Isaac Emanuel, Kt.

Hyslop, Sir Robert John (Robin) Maxwell-, Kt.

Ibbs, Sir (John) Robin, KBE

Imbert, Sir Peter Michael, Kt., QPM

Imray, Sir Colin Henry, KBE, CMG

Ingham, Sir Bernard, Kt.

Ingilby, Sir Thomas Colvin William, Bt. (1866)

Inglis, Sir Brian Scott, Kt.

Inglis of Glencorse, Sir Roderick John, Bt. (s. 1703)

Ingram, Sir James Herbert Charles, Bt. (1893)

Ingram, Sir John Henderson, Kt., CBE

Inkin, Sir Geoffrey David, Kt., OBE

†Innes, Sir David Charles Kenneth Gordon, Bt. (NS 1686)

Innes of Edingight, Sir Malcolm Rognvald, KCVO

Innes, Sir Peter Alexander Berowald, Bt. (s. 1628)

Inniss, *Hon.* Sir Clifford de Lisle, Kt.

Irvine, Sir Donald Hamilton, Kt., CBE, MD, FRCGP

Irving, *Prof.* Sir Miles Horsfall, Kt., MD, FRCS, FRCSE

Isaacs, Sir Jeremy Israel, Kt.

Isham, Sir Ian Vere Gyles, Bt. (1627)

Jack, *Hon.* Sir Alieu Sulayman, Kt.

Jack, Sir David, Kt., CBE, FRS, FRSE

Jack, Sir David Emmanuel, GCMG, MBE

Jackson, *Air Chief Marshal* Sir Brendan James, GCB

Jackson, Sir (John) Edward, KCMG

Jackson, *Lt.-Gen.* Sir Michael David, KCB, CBE

Jackson, Sir Michael Roland, Bt. (1902)

Jackson, Sir Nicholas Fane St George, Bt. (1913)

Jackson, Sir Robert, Bt. (1815)

Jackson, *Gen.* Sir William Godfrey Fothergill, GBE, KCB, MC

Jackson, Sir William Thomas, Bt. (1869)

Jacob, Sir Isaac Hai, Kt., QC

Jacob, *Hon.* Sir Robert Raphael Hayim (Robin), Kt.

Jacobi, Sir Derek George, Kt., CBE

Jacobi, *Dr* Sir James Edward, Kt., OBE

Jacobs, *Hon.* Sir Kenneth Sydney, KBE

Jacobs, Sir Piers, KBE

Jacobs, Sir Wilfred Ebenezer, GCMG, GCVO, OBE, QC

Jacomb, Sir Martin Wakefield, Kt.

Jaffray, Sir William Otho, Bt. (1892)

James, Sir Cynlais Morgan, KCMG

James, Sir Gerard Bowes Kingston, Bt. (1823)

James, Sir John Nigel Courtenay, KCVO, CBE

James, Sir Robert Vidal Rhodes, Kt.

James, Sir Stanislaus Anthony, GCMG, OBE

Jamieson, *Air Marshal* Sir David Ewan, KBE, CB

Jansen, Sir Ross Malcolm, KBE

Janvrin, Sir Robin Berry, KCVO, CB

Jardine of Applegirth, Sir Alexander Maule, Bt. (s. 1672)

Jardine, Sir Andrew Colin Douglas, Bt. (1916)

Jardine, *Maj.* Sir (Andrew) Rupert (John) Buchanan-, Bt., MC (1885)

Jarman, *Prof.* Sir Brian, Kt., OBE

Jarratt, Sir Alexander Anthony, Kt., CB

Jawara, *Hon.* Sir Dawda Kairaba, Kt.

Jay, Sir Antony Rupert, Kt., CVO

Jeewoolall, Sir Ramesh, Kt.

Jefferson, Sir George Rowland, Kt., CBE, FEng.

Jefferson, Sir Mervyn Stewart Dunnington-, Bt. (1958)

Jeffreys, *Prof.* Sir Alec John, Kt., FRS

Jeffries, *Hon.* Sir John Francis, Kt.

Jehangir, Sir Hirji, Bt. (1908)

Jejeebhoy, Sir Rustom, Bt. (1857)

Jenkins, Sir Brian Garton, GBE

Jenkins, Sir Elgar Spencer, Kt., OBE

Jenkins, Sir Michael Nicholas Howard, Kt., OBE

Jenkins, Sir Michael Romilly Heald, KCMG

Jenkinson, Sir John Banks, Bt. (1661)

†Jenks, Sir Maurice Arthur Brian, Bt. (1932)

Jennings, Sir John Southwood, Kt., CBE, FRSE

Jennings, *Prof.* Sir Robert Yewdall, Kt., QC

Jephcott, Sir (John) Anthony, Bt. (1962)

Jessel, Sir Charles John, Bt. (1883)

Jewkes, Sir Gordon Wesley, KCMG

Joel, *Hon.* Sir Asher Alexander, KBE

John, Sir Elton Hercules (Reginald Kenneth Dwight), Kt., CBE

Johns, *Air Chief Marshal* Sir Richard Edward, GCB, CBE, LVO

Johnson, *Rt. Hon.* Sir David Powell Croom-, Kt., DSC, VRD

Johnson, *Gen.* Sir Garry Dene, KCB, OBE, MC

Johnson, Sir John Rodney, KCMG

†Johnson, Sir Patrick Eliot, Bt. (1818)

Johnson, Sir Peter Colpoys Paley, Bt. (1755)

Johnson, *Hon.* Sir Robert Lionel, Kt.

Johnson, Sir Vassel Godfrey, Kt., CBE

Johnston, Sir John Baines, GCMG, KCVO

Johnston, *Lt.-Col.* Sir John Frederick Dame, GCVO, MC

Johnston, *Lt.-Gen.* Sir Maurice Robert, KCB, OBE

Johnston, Sir Thomas Alexander, Bt. (s. 1626)

Johnston, Sir William Robert Patrick Knox- (Sir Robin), Kt., CBE, RD

Johnstone, Sir (George) Richard Douglas, Bt. (s. 1700)

Johnstone, Sir (John) Raymond, Kt., CBE

Jolliffe, Sir Anthony Stuart, GBE

Jones, Sir (Charles) Edward Webb, KCB, CBE

Jones, Sir Christopher Lawrence-, Bt. (1831)

Jones, Sir David Akers-, KBE, CMG

Jones, *Air Marshal* Sir Edward Gordon, KCB, CBE, DSO, DFC

Jones, Sir Ewart Ray Herbert, Kt., D.SC., PH.D., FRS

Jones, Sir Gordon Pearce, Kt.

Jones, Sir Harry Ernest, Kt., CBE

Jones, Sir (John) Derek Alun-, Kt.

Jones, Sir John Henry Harvey-, Kt., MBE

Jones, Sir John Prichard-, Bt. (1910)

Jones, Sir Keith Stephen, Kt.

Jones, *Hon.* Sir Kenneth George Illtyd, Kt.

Jones, Sir (Owen) Trevor, Kt.

Jones, Sir (Peter) Hugh (Jefferd) Lloyd-, Kt.

Jones, Sir Richard Anthony Lloyd, KCB

Jones, Sir Robert Edward, Kt.

Jones, Sir Simon Warley Frederick Benton, Bt. (1919)

Jones, Sir (Thomas) Philip, Kt., CB

Jones, Sir (William) Emrys, Kt.

Jones, *Hon.* Sir William Lloyd Mars-, Kt., MBE

Jones, Sir Wynn Normington Hugh-, Kt., LVO

†Joseph, *Hon.* Sir James Samuel, Bt. (1943)

Jowitt, *Hon.* Sir Edwin Frank, Kt.

Joyce, *Lt.-Gen.* Sir Robert John Hayman-, KCB, CBE

Judge, *Rt. Hon.* Sir Igor, Kt.

Judge, Sir Paul Rupert, Kt.

Jugnauth, *Rt. Hon.* Sir Anerood, KCMG, QC

Jungius, *Vice-Adm.* Sir James George, KBE

Jupp, *Hon.* Sir Kenneth Graham, Kt., MC

Kaberry, *Hon.* Sir Christopher Donald, Bt. (1960)

Kalms, Sir (Harold) Stanley, Kt.

Kalo, Sir Kwamala, Kt., MBE

Kan Yuet-Keung, Sir, GBE

Kapi, Sir Mari, Kt., CBE

Kaputin, Sir John Rumet, KBE, CMG

Katsina, The Emir of, KBE, CMG

Katz, Sir Bernard, Kt., FRS

Kausimae, Sir David Nanau, KBE

Kavali, Sir Thomas, Kt., OBE
Kawharu, *Prof.* Sir Ian Hugh, Kt.
Kay, *Prof.* Sir Andrew Watt, Kt.
Kay, *Hon.* Sir John William, Kt.
Kay, *Hon.* Sir Maurice Ralph, Kt.
Kaye, Sir Emmanuel, Kt., CBE
Kaye, Sir John Phillip Lister Lister-, Bt. (1812)
Kaye, Sir Paul Henry Gordon, Bt. (1923)
Keane, Sir Richard Michael, Bt. (1801)
Keeble, Sir (Herbert Ben) Curtis, GCMG
Keene, *Hon.* Sir David Wolfe, Kt.
Keith, *Prof.* Sir James, KBE
Kellett, Sir Stanley Charles, Bt. (1801)
Kelly, Sir David Robert Corbett, Kt., CBE
Kelly, *Rt. Hon.* Sir (John William) Basil, Kt.
Kelly, Sir William Theodore, Kt., OBE
Kemball, *Air Marshal* Sir (Richard) John, KCB, CBE
Kemp, Sir (Edward) Peter, KCB
Kenilorea, *Rt. Hon.* Sir Peter, KBE
Kennard, *Lt.-Col.* Sir George Arnold Ford, Bt. (1891)
Kennaway, Sir John Lawrence, Bt. (1791)
Kennedy, Sir Clyde David Allen, Kt.
Kennedy, Sir Francis, KCMG, CBE
Kennedy, *Hon.* Sir Ian Alexander, Kt.
Kennedy, Sir Ludovic Henry Coverley, Kt.
†Kennedy, Sir Michael Edward, Bt., (1836)
Kennedy, *Rt. Hon.* Sir Paul Joseph Morrow, Kt.
Kennedy, *Air Chief Marshal* Sir Thomas Lawrie, GCB, AFC
Kenny, Sir Anthony John Patrick, Kt., D.Phil., D.Litt., FBA
Kenny, *Gen.* Sir Brian Leslie Graham, GCB, CBE
Kent, Sir Harold Simcox, GCB, QC
Kenyon, Sir George Henry, Kt.
Kermode, Sir (John) Frank, Kt., FBA
Kermode, Sir Ronald Graham Quale, KBE
Kerr, *Hon.* Sir Brian Francis, Kt.
Kerr, *Adm.* Sir John Beverley, GCB
Kerr, Sir John Olav, KCMG
Kerr, *Rt. Hon.* Sir Michael Robert Emanuel, Kt.
Kerruish, Sir (Henry) Charles, Kt., OBE
Kerry, Sir Michael James, KCB, QC
Kershaw, Sir (John) Anthony, Kt., MC
Keswick, Sir John Chippendale Lindley, Kt.
Kidd, Sir Robert Hill, KBE, CB
Kikau, *Ratu* Sir Jone Latianara, KBE
Killen, *Hon.* Denis James, KCMG
Killick, Sir John Edward, GCMG
Kimber, Sir Charles Dixon, Bt. (1904)

King, Sir John Christopher, Bt. (1888)
King, *Vice-Adm.* Sir Norman Ross Dutton, KBE
King, Sir Richard Brian Meredith, KCB, MC
King, Sir Wayne Alexander, Bt. (1815)
Kingman, *Prof.* Sir John Frank Charles, Kt., FRS
Kingsland, Sir Richard, Kt., CBE, DFC
Kingsley, Sir Patrick Graham Toler, KCVO
Kinloch, Sir David, Bt. (s. 1686)
Kinloch, Sir David Oliphant, Bt. (1873)
Kipalan, Sir Albert, Kt.
Kirby, *Hon.* Sir Richard Clarence, Kt.
Kirkham, Sir Graham, Kt.
Kirkpatrick, Sir Ivone Elliott, Bt. (s. 1685)
Kirkwood, *Hon.* Sir Andrew Tristram Hammett, Kt.
Kirwan, Sir (Archibald) Laurence Patrick, KCMG, TD
Kitcatt, Sir Peter Julian, Kt., CB
Kitson, *Gen.* Sir Frank Edward, GBE, KCB, MC
Kitson, Sir Timothy Peter Geoffrey, Kt.
Kleinwort, Sir Richard Drake, Bt. (1909)
Klug, Sir Aaron, Kt., OM
Kneller, Sir Alister Arthur, Kt.
Knight, Sir Arthur William, Kt.
Knight, Sir Harold Murray, KBE, DSC
Knight, *Air Chief Marshal* Sir Michael William Patrick, KCB, AFC
Knill, *Prof.* Sir John Lawrence, Kt., FEng.
†Knill, Sir Thomas John Pugin Bartholomew, Bt. (1893)
Knott, Sir John Laurence, Kt., CBE
Knowles, Sir Charles Francis, Bt. (1765)
Knowles, Sir Durward Randolph, Kt., OBE
Knowles, Sir Leonard Joseph, Kt., CBE
Knowles, Sir Richard Marchant, Kt.
Knox, Sir Bryce Muir, KCVO, MC, TD
Knox, Sir David Laidlaw, Kt.
Knox, *Hon.* Sir John Leonard, Kt.
Knox, *Hon.* Sir William Edward, Kt.
Koraea, Sir Thomas, Kt.
Kornberg, *Prof.* Sir Hans Leo, Kt., D.SC, SC.D., Ph.D., FRS
Korowi, Sir Wiwa, GCMG
Kroto, *Prof.* Sir Harold Walter, Kt., FRS
Kulukundis, Sir Elias George (Eddie), Kt., OBE
Kurongku, *Most Revd* Peter, KBE
Labouchere, Sir George Peter, GBE, KCMG
Lacon, Sir Edmund Vere, Bt. (1818)
Lacy, Sir Hugh Maurice Pierce, Bt. (1921)
Lacy, Sir John Trend, Kt., CBE
Laddie, *Hon.* Sir Hugh Ian Lang, Kt.

Laidlaw, Sir Christophor Charles Fraser, Kt.
Laing, Sir (John) Martin (Kirby), Kt., CBE
Laing, Sir (John) Maurice, Kt.
Laing, Sir (William) Kirby, Kt., FEng.
Laird, Sir Gavin Harry, Kt., CBE
Lake, Sir (Atwell) Graham, Bt. (1711)
Laker, Sir Frederick Alfred, Kt.
Lakin, Sir Michael, Bt. (1909)
Laking, Sir George Robert, KCMG
Lamb, Sir Albert (Larry), Kt.
Lamb, Sir Albert Thomas, KBE, CMG, DFC
Lambert, Sir Anthony Edward, KCMG
Lambert, Sir John Henry, KCVO, CMG
†Lambert, Sir Peter John Biddulph, Bt. (1711)
Lampl, Sir Frank William, Kt.
Landale, Sir David William Neil, KCVO
Landau, Sir Dennis Marcus, Kt.
Lane, Sir David William Stennis Stuart, Kt.
Lang, *Lt.-Gen.* Sir Derek Boileau, KCB, DSO, MC
Langham, Sir James Michael, Bt. (1660)
Langlands, Sir Robert Alan, Kt.
Langley, *Hon.* Sir Gordon Julian Hugh, Kt.
Langley, *Maj.-Gen.* Sir Henry Desmond Allen, KCVO, MBE
†Langrishe, Sir James Hercules, Bt. (I. 1777)
Lankester, Sir Timothy Patrick, KCB
Lapun, *Hon.* Sir Paul, Kt.
Larcom, Sir (Charles) Christopher Royde, Bt. (1868)
Large, Sir Andrew McLeod Brooks, Kt.
Large, Sir Peter, Kt., CBE
Larmour, Sir Edward Noel, KCMG
Lasdun, Sir Denys Louis, Kt., CH, CBE, FRIBA
Latey, *Rt. Hon.* Sir John Brinsmead, Kt., MBE
Latham, *Hon.* Sir David Nicholas Ramsey, Kt.
Latham, Sir Michael Anthony, Kt.
Latham, Sir Richard Thomas Paul, Bt. (1919)
Latimer, Sir (Courtenay) Robert, Kt., CBE
Latimer, Sir Graham Stanley, KBE
Lauder, Sir Piers Robert Dick-, Bt. (s. 1690)
Laughton, Sir Anthony Seymour, Kt.
Laurantus, Sir Nicholas, Kt., MBE
Laurence, Sir Peter Harold, KCMG, MC
Laurie, Sir Robert Bayley Emilius, Bt. (1834)
Lauterpacht, Sir Elihu, Kt., CBE, QC
Lauti, *Rt. Hon.* Sir Toaripi, GCMG
Lavan, *Hon.* Sir John Martin, Kt.
Law, *Adm.* Sir Horace Rochfort, GCB, OBE, DSC
Lawes, Sir (John) Michael Bennet, Bt. (1882)

Lawler, Sir Peter James, Kt., OBE

Lawrence, Sir David Roland Walter, Bt. (1906)

Lawrence, Sir Guy Kempton, Kt., DSO, OBE, DFC

Lawrence, Sir Ivan John, Kt., QC

Lawrence, Sir John Patrick Grosvenor, Kt., CBE

Lawrence, Sir John Waldemar, Bt., OBE (1858)

Lawrence, Sir William Fettiplace, Bt. (1867)

Laws, *Hon.* Sir John Grant McKenzie, Kt.

Lawson, Sir Christopher Donald, Kt.

Lawson, *Col.* Sir John Charles Arthur Digby, Bt., DSO, MC (1900)

Lawson, Sir John Philip Howard-, Bt. (1841)

Lawson, *Gen.* Sir Richard George, KCB, DSO, OBE

Lawton, *Prof.* Sir Frank Ewart, Kt.

Lawton, *Rt. Hon.* Sir Frederick Horace, Kt.

Layard, *Adm.* Sir Michael Henry Gordon, KCB, CBE

Layfield, Sir Frank Henry Burland Willoughby, Kt., QC

Lea, *Vice-Adm.* Sir John Stuart Crosbie, KBE

Lea, Sir Thomas William, Bt. (1892)

Leach, *Admiral of the Fleet* Sir Henry Conyers, GCB

Leahy, Sir Daniel Joseph, Kt.

Leahy, Sir John Henry Gladstone, KCMG

Learmont, *Gen.* Sir John Hartley, KCB, CBE

Leask, *Lt.-Gen.* Sir Henry Lowther Ewart Clark, KCB, DSO, OBE

Leather, Sir Edwin Hartley Cameron, KCMG, KCVO

Leaver, Sir Christopher, GBE

Le Bailly, *Vice-Adm.* Sir Louis Edward Stewart Holland, KBE, CB

Le Cheminant, *Air Chief Marshal* Sir Peter de Lacey, GBE, KCB, DFC

Lechmere, Sir Berwick Hungerford, Bt. (1818)

Lee, Sir Arthur James, KBE, MC

Lee, *Air Chief Marshal* Sir David John Pryer, GBE, CB

Lee, *Brig.* Sir Leonard Henry, Kt., CBE

Lee, Sir Quo-wei, Kt., CBE

Leeds, Sir Christopher Anthony, Bt. (1812)

Lees, Sir David Bryan, Kt.

Lees, Sir Thomas Edward, Bt. (1897)

Lees, Sir Thomas Harcourt Ivor, Bt. (1804)

Lees, Sir (William) Antony Clare, Bt. (1937)

Leese, Sir John Henry Vernon, Bt. (1908)

Le Fanu, *Maj.* Sir (George) Victor (Sheridan), KCVO

le Fleming, Sir David Kelland, Bt. (1705)

Legard, Sir Charles Thomas, Bt. (1660)

Legg, Sir Thomas Stuart, KCB, QC

Leggatt, *Rt. Hon.* Sir Andrew Peter, Kt.

Leggatt, Sir Hugh Frank John, Kt.

Leggett, Sir Clarence Arthur Campbell, Kt., MBE

Leigh, Sir Geoffrey Norman, Kt.

Leigh, Sir Richard Henry, Bt. (1918)

Leighton, Sir Michael John Bryan, Bt. (1693)

Leitch, Sir George, KCB, OBE

Leith, Sir Andrew George Forbes-, Bt. (1923)

Le Marchant, Sir Francis Arthur, Bt. (1841)

Lemon, Sir (Richard) Dawnay, Kt., CBE

Leng, *Gen.* Sir Peter John Hall, KCB, MBE, MC

Lennard, *Revd* Sir Hugh Dacre Barrett-, Bt. (1801)

Leon, Sir John Ronald, Bt. (1911)

Leonard, *Rt. Revd and Rt. Hon.* Graham Douglas, KCVO

Leonard, *Hon.* Sir (Hamilton) John, Kt.

Lepping, Sir George Geria Dennis, GCMG, MBE

Le Quesne, Sir (Charles) Martin, KCMG

Le Quesne, Sir (John) Godfray, Kt., QC

Leslie, Sir Colin Alan Bettridge, Kt.

Leslie, Sir John Norman Ide, Bt. (1876)

†Leslie, Sir (Percy) Theodore, Bt. (s. 1625)

Leslie, Sir Peter Evelyn, Kt.

Lester, Sir James Theodore, Kt.

Lethbridge, Sir Thomas Periam Hector Noel, Bt. (1804)

Lever, Sir Paul, KCMG

Lever, Sir (Tresham) Christopher Arthur Lindsay, Bt. (1911)

Levey, Sir Michael Vincent, Kt., LVO

Levine, Sir Montague Bernard, Kt.

Levinge, Sir Richard George Robin, Bt. (I. 1704)

Lewando, Sir Jan Alfred, Kt., CBE

Lewinton, Sir Christopher, Kt.

Lewis, Sir David Courtenay Mansel, KCVO

Lewthwaite, *Brig.* Sir Rainald Gilfrid, Bt., CVO, OBE, MC (1927)

Ley, Sir Ian Francis, Bt. (1905)

Leyland, Sir Philip Vyvyan Naylor-, Bt. (1895)

Lickiss, Sir Michael Gillam, Kt.

Lidderdale, Sir David William Shuckburgh, KCB

Liggins, *Prof.* Sir Graham Collingwood, Kt., CBE, FRS

Lightman, *Hon.* Sir Gavin Anthony, Kt.

Lighton, Sir Thomas Hamilton, Bt. (I. 1791)

Lim, Sir Han-Hoe, Kt., CBE

Limon, Sir Donald William, KCB

Linacre, Sir (John) Gordon (Seymour), Kt., CBE, AFC, DFM

Lindop, Sir Norman, Kt.

Lindsay, Sir James Harvey Kincaid Stewart, Kt.

Lindsay, *Hon.* Sir John Edmund Frederic, Kt.

Lindsay, Sir Ronald Alexander, Bt., (1962)

Lipworth, Sir (Maurice) Sydney, Kt.

Lithgow, Sir William James, Bt. (1925)

Little, *Most Revd* Thomas Francis, KBE

Littler, Sir (James) Geoffrey, KCB

Livesay, *Adm.* Sir Michael Howard, KCB

Llewellyn, Sir Henry Morton, Bt., CBE (1922)

Llewelyn, Sir John Michael Dillwyn-Venables-, Bt. (1890)

Lloyd, *Prof.* Sir Geoffrey Ernest Richard, Kt., FBA

Lloyd, Sir Ian Stewart, Kt.

Lloyd, Sir Nicholas Markley, Kt.

Lloyd, *Rt. Hon.* Sir Peter Robert Cable, Kt., MP

Lloyd, Sir Richard Ernest Butler, Bt. (1960)

Lloyd, *Hon.* Sir Timothy Andrew Wigram, Kt.

Loader, Sir Leslie Thomas, Kt., CBE

Loane, *Most Revd* Marcus Lawrence, KBE

Lobo, Sir Rogerio Hyndman, Kt., CBE

Lock, *Cdr.* Sir (John) Duncan, Kt.

Lockhart, Sir Simon John Edward Francis Sinclair-, Bt. (s. 1636)

Loder, Sir Giles Rolls, Bt. (1887)

Logan, Sir Donald Arthur, KCMG

Logan, Sir Raymond Douglas, Kt.

Lokoloko, Sir Tore, GCMG, GCVO, OBE

Lombe, *Hon.* Sir Edward Christopher Evans-, Kt.

Longmore, *Hon.* Sir Andrew Centlivres, Kt.

Loram, *Vice-Adm.* Sir David Anning, KCB, CVO

Lorimer, Sir (Thomas) Desmond, Kt.

Los, *Hon.* Sir Kubulan, Kt., CBE

Lovell, Sir (Alfred Charles) Bernard, Kt., OBE, FRS

Lovelock, Sir Douglas Arthur, KCB

Loveridge, Sir John Warren, Kt.

Lovill, Sir John Roger, Kt., CBE

Low, Sir Alan Roberts, Kt.

Low, Sir James Richard Morrison-, Bt. (1908)

Lowe, *Air Chief Marshal* Sir Douglas Charles, GCB, DFC, AFC

Lowe, Sir Thomas William Gordon, Bt. (1918)

Lowry, Sir John Patrick, Kt., CBE

Lowson, Sir Ian Patrick, Bt. (1951)

Lowther, *Maj.* Sir Charles Douglas, Bt. (1824)

Lowther, Sir John Luke, KCVO, CBE

Loyd, Sir Francis Alfred, KCMG, OBE

Loyd, Sir Julian St John, KCVO

Lu, Sir Tseng Chi, Kt.

Lucas, Sir Cyril Edward, Kt., CMG, FRS

Lucas, Sir Thomas Edward, Bt. (1887)

Luce, *Rt. Hon.* Sir Richard Napier, Kt.

Lucy, Sir Edmund John William Hugh Cameron-Ramsay-Fairfax, Bt. (1836)

Luddington, Sir Donald Collin Cumyn, KBE, CMG, CVO

Lumsden, Sir David James, Kt.

Lus, *Hon.* Sir Pita, Kt., OBE

Lush, *Hon.* Sir George Hermann, Kt.

Lushington, Sir John Richard Castleman, Bt. (1791)

Luttrell, *Col.* Sir Geoffrey Walter Fownes, KCVO, MC

Lyell, *Rt. Hon.* Sir Nicholas Walter, Kt., QC, MP

Lygo, *Adm.* Sir Raymond Derek, KCB

Lyle, Sir Gavin Archibald, Bt. (1929)

Lyons, Sir Edward Houghton, Kt.

Lyons, Sir James Reginald, Kt.

Lyons, Sir John, Kt.

McAdam, Sir Ian William James, Kt., OBE

McAlpine, Sir William Hepburn, Bt. (1918)

Macara, Sir Alexander Wiseman, Kt., FRCP, FRCGP

†Macara, Sir Hugh Kenneth, Bt. (1911)

Macartney, Sir John Barrington, Bt. (I. 1799)

McAvoy, Sir (Francis) Joseph, Kt., CBE

McCaffrey, Sir Thomas Daniel, Kt.

McCall, Sir (Charles) Patrick Home, Kt., MBE, TD

McCallum, Sir Donald Murdo, Kt., CBE, FEng.

McCamley, Sir Graham Edward, Kt., MBE

McCarthy, *Rt. Hon.* Sir Thaddeus Pearcey, KBE

McCartney, Sir (James) Paul, Kt., MBE

McClellan, *Col.* Sir Herbert Gerard Thomas, Kt., CBE, TD

McClintock, Sir Eric Paul, Kt.

McColl, Sir Colin Hugh Verel, KCMG

McCollum, *Rt. Hon.* Sir William, Kt.

McConnell, Sir Robert Shean, Bt. (1900)

McCorkell, *Col.* Sir Michael William, KCVO, OBE, TD

McCowan, *Rt. Hon.* Sir Anthony James Denys, Kt.

McCowan, Sir Hew Cargill, Bt. (1934)

McCrea, *Prof.* Sir William Hunter, Kt., FRS

McCrindle, Sir Robert Arthur, Kt.

McCullough, *Hon.* Sir (Iain) Charles (Robert), Kt.

MacDermott, *Rt. Hon.* Sir John Clarke, Kt.

McDermott, Sir (Lawrence) Emmet, KBE

MacDonald, *Gen.* Sir Arthur Leslie, KBE, CB

Macdonald of Sleat, Sir Ian Godfrey Bosville, Bt. (s. 1625)

Macdonald, Sir Kenneth Carmichael, KCB

Macdonald, *Vice-Adm.* Sir Roderick Douglas, KBE

McDonald, Sir Tom, Kt., OBE

MacDougall, Sir (George) Donald (Alastair), Kt., CBE, FBA

McDowell, Sir Eric Wallace, Kt., CBE

McDowell, Sir Henry McLorinan, KBE

Mace, *Lt.-Gen.* Sir John Airth, KBE, CB

McEwen, Sir John Roderick Hugh, Bt. (1953)

McFarland, Sir John Talbot, Bt. (1914)

Macfarlane, Sir (David) Neil, Kt.

Macfarlane, Sir George Gray, Kt., CB, FEng.

McFarlane, Sir Ian, Kt.

McGeoch, *Vice-Adm.* Sir Ian Lachlan Mackay, KCB, DSO, DSC

McGrath, Sir Brian Henry, KCVO

Macgregor, Sir Edwin Robert, Bt. (1828)

MacGregor of MacGregor, Sir Gregor, Bt. (1795)

McGregor, Sir Ian Alexander, Kt., CBE, FRS

McGrigor, *Capt.* Sir Charles Edward, Bt. (1831)

McIntosh, *Vice-Adm.* Sir Ian Stewart, KBE, CB, DSO, DSC

McIntosh, Sir Malcolm Kenneth, Kt., PH.D.

McIntosh, Sir Ronald Robert Duncan, KCB

McIntyre, Sir Donald Conroy, Kt., CBE

McIntyre, Sir Meredith Alister, Kt.

MacKay, *Prof.* Sir Donald Iain, Kt., FRSE

McKay, Sir John Andrew, Kt., CBE

Mackechnie, Sir Alistair John, Kt.

McKee, *Maj.* Sir (William) Cecil, Kt., ERD

McKellen, Sir Ian Murray, Kt., CBE

McKenzie, Sir Alexander, KBE

Mackenzie, Sir Alexander Alwyne Henry Charles Brinton Muir-, Bt. (1805)

†Mackenzie, Sir (James William) Guy, Bt. (1890)

Mackenzie, *Gen.* Sir Jeremy John George, GCB, OBE

†Mackenzie, Sir Peter Douglas, Bt. (s. 1673)

†Mackenzie, Sir Roderick McQuhae, Bt. (s. 1703)

McKenzie, Sir Roy Allan, KBE

Mackeson, Sir Rupert Henry, Bt. (1954)

MacKinlay, Sir Bruce, Kt., CBE

McKinnon, Sir James, Kt.

McKinnon, *Hon.* Sir Stuart Neil, Kt.

Mackintosh, Sir Cameron Anthony, Kt.

Macklin, Sir Bruce Roy, Kt., OBE

†Mackworth, Sir Digby John, Bt. (1776)

McLaren, Sir Robin John Taylor, KCMG

†Maclean of Dunconnell, Sir Charles Edward, Bt. (1957)

Maclean, Sir Donald Og Grant, Kt.

McLean, Sir Francis Charles, Kt., CBE

MacLean, *Vice-Adm.* Sir Hector Charles Donald, KBE, CB, DSC

Maclean, Sir Lachlan Hector Charles, Bt. (NS 1631)

Maclean, Sir Robert Alexander, KBE

McLennan, Sir Ian Munro, KCMG, KBE

McLeod, Sir Charles Henry, Bt. (1925)

McLeod, Sir Ian George, Kt.

MacLeod, Sir (John) Maxwell Norman, Bt. (1924)

Macleod, Sir (Nathaniel William) Hamish, KBE

McLintock, Sir Michael William, Bt. (1934)

Maclure, Sir John Robert Spencer, Bt. (1898)

McMahon, Sir Brian Patrick, Bt. (1817)

McMahon, Sir Christopher William, Kt.

Macmillan, Sir (Alexander McGregor) Graham, Kt.

MacMillan, *Lt.-Gen.* Sir John Richard Alexander, KCB, CBE

McMullin, *Rt. Hon.* Sir Duncan Wallace, Kt.

Macnaghten, Sir Patrick Alexander, Bt. (1836)

McNamara, *Air Chief Marshal* Sir Neville Patrick, KBE

Macnaughton, *Prof.* Sir Malcolm Campbell, Kt.

McNee, Sir David Blackstock, Kt., QPM

McNulty, Sir (Robert William) Roy, Kt., CBE

MacPhail, Sir Bruce Dugald, Kt.

Macpherson, Sir Ronald Thomas Steward (Tommy), CBE, MC, TD

Macpherson of Cluny, *Hon.* Sir William Alan, Kt., TD

McQuarrie, Sir Albert, Kt.

MacRae, Sir (Alastair) Christopher (Donald Summerhayes), KCMG

Macrae, *Col.* Sir Robert Andrew Scarth, KCVO, MBE

Macready, Sir Nevil John Wilfrid, Bt. (1923)

Mactaggart, Sir John Auld, Bt. (1938)

Macwhinnie, Sir Gordon Menzies, Kt., CBE

McWilliam, Sir Michael Douglas, KCMG

McWilliams, Sir Francis, GBE, FEng.

Madden, *Adm.* Sir Charles Edward, Bt., GCB (1919)

Maddocks, Sir Kenneth Phipson, KCMG, KCVO

Maddox, Sir John Royden, Kt.

Madel, Sir (William) David, Kt., MP

Madigan, Sir Russel Tullie, Kt., OBE

Magnus, Sir Laurence Henry Philip, Bt. (1917)

Maguire, *Air Marshal* Sir Harold John, KCB, DSO, OBE

Mahon, Sir (John) Denis, Kt., CBE

Mahon, Sir William Walter, Bt. (1819)

Maiden, Sir Colin James, Kt., D.phil.

Main, Sir Peter Tester, Kt., ERD

Maini, Sir Amar Nath, Kt., CBE

Maino, Sir Charles, KBE

†Maitland, Sir Charles Alexander, Bt. (1818)

Maitland, Sir Donald James Dundas, GCMG, OBE

Makins, Sir Paul Vivian, Bt. (1903)

Malcolm, Sir James William Thomas Alexander, Bt. (s. 1665)

Malet, Sir Harry Douglas St Lo, Bt. (1791)

Mallaby, Sir Christopher Leslie George, GCMG, GCVO

Mallick, *Prof.* Sir Netar Prakash, Kt., FRCP, FRCPed

†Mallinson, Sir William James, Bt. (1935)

Malone, *Hon.* Sir Denis Eustace Gilbert, Kt.

Malpas, Sir Robert, Kt., CBE, FEng

Mamo, Sir Anthony Joseph, Kt., OBE

Mance, *Hon.* Sir Jonathan Hugh, Kt.

Manchester, Sir William Maxwell, KBE

Mander, Sir Charles Marcus, Bt. (1911)

Manduell, Sir John, Kt., CBE

Mann, *Rt. Revd* Michael Ashley, KCVO

Mann, Sir Rupert Edward, Bt. (1905)

Mansel, Sir Philip, Bt. (1622)

Mansfield, *Vice-Adm.* Sir (Edward) Gerard (Napier), KBE, CVO

Mansfield, *Prof.* Sir Peter, Kt., FRS

Mansfield, Sir Philip (Robert Aked), KCMG

Mantell, *Rt. Hon.* Sir Charles Barrie Knight, Kt.

Manton, Sir Edwin Alfred Grenville, Kt.

Manuella, Sir Tulaga, GCMG, MBE

Manzie, Sir (Andrew) Gordon, KCB

Mara, *Rt. Hon. Ratu* Sir Kamisese Kapaiwai Tuimacilai, GCMG, KBE

Margetson, Sir John William Denys, KCMG

Marjoribanks, Sir James Alexander Milne, KCMG

Mark, Sir Robert, GBE

Markham, Sir Charles John, Bt. (1911)

Marking, Sir Henry Ernest, KCVO, CBE, MC

Marling, Sir Charles William Somerset, Bt. (1882)

Marr, Sir Leslie Lynn, Bt. (1919)

Marriner, Sir Neville, Kt., CBE

Marriott, Sir Hugh Cavendish Smith-, Bt. (1774)

Marriott, Sir John Brook, KCVO

†Marsden, Sir Simon Neville Llewelyn, Bt. (1924)

Marshall, Sir Arthur Gregory George, Kt., OBE

Marshall, Sir Denis Alfred, Kt.

Marshall, *Prof.* Sir (Oshley) Roy, Kt., CBE

Marshall, Sir Peter Harold Reginald, KCMG

Marshall, Sir Robert Braithwaite, KCB, MBE

Marshall, Sir (Robert) Michael, Kt.

Martell, *Vice-Adm.* Sir Hugh Colenso, KBE, CB

Martin, Sir George Henry, Kt., CBE

Martin, *Vice-Adm.* Sir John Edward Ludgate, KCB, DSC

Martin, *Prof.* Sir (John) Leslie, Kt., ph.D.

Martin, *Prof.* Sir Laurence Woodward, Kt.

Martin, Sir (Robert) Bruce, Kt., QC

Marychurch, Sir Peter Harvey, KCMG

Masefield, Sir Charles Beech Gordon, Kt.

Masefield, Sir Peter Gordon, Kt.

Masire, Sir Ketumile, GCMG

Mason, *Hon.* Sir Anthony Frank, KBE

Mason, Sir (Basil) John, Kt., CB, D.SC., FRS

Mason, *Prof.* Sir David Kean, Kt., CBE

Mason, Sir Frederick Cecil, KCVO, CMG

Mason, Sir Gordon Charles, Kt., OBE

Mason, Sir John Charles Moir, KCMG

Mason, Sir John Peter, Kt., CBE

Mason, *Prof.* Sir Ronald, KCB, FRS

Matane, Sir Paulias Nguna, Kt., CMG, OBE

Mather, Sir (David) Carol (Macdonell), Kt., MC

Mather, Sir William Loris, Kt., CVO, OBE, MC, TD

Mathers, Sir Robert William, Kt.

Matheson of Matheson, Sir Fergus John, Bt. (1882)

Matheson, Sir (James Adam) Louis, KBE, CMG, FEng

Matthews, Sir Peter Alec, Kt.

Matthews, Sir Peter Jack, Kt., CVO, OBE, QPM

Matthews, Sir Stanley, Kt., CBE

Maud, The Hon. Sir Humphrey John Hamilton, KCMG

Mawhinney, *Rt. Hon.* Sir Brian Stanley, Kt., MP

Maxwell, Sir Michael Eustace George, Bt. (s. 1681)

Maxwell, Sir Nigel Mellor Heron-, Bt. (s. 1683)

May, *Rt. Hon.* Sir Anthony Tristram Kenneth, Kt.

May, Sir Kenneth Spencer, Kt., CBE

May, *Prof.* Sir Robert McCredie, Kt., FRS

Maynard, *Hon.* Sir Clement Travelyan, Kt.

Mayne, *Very Revd* Michael Clement Otway, KCVO

Meadow, *Prof.* Sir (Samuel) Roy, Kt., FRCP, FRCPE

Medlycott, Sir Mervyn Tregonwell, Bt. (1808)

Megarry, *Rt. Hon.* Sir Robert Edgar, Kt., FBA

Meinertzhagen, Sir Peter, Kt., CMG

Melhuish, Sir Michael Ramsay, KBE, CMG

Mellon, Sir James, KCMG

Melville, Sir Harry Work, KCB, ph.D., D.SC., FRS

Melville, Sir Leslie Galfreid, KBE

Melville, Sir Ronald Henry, KCB

Mensforth, Sir Eric, Kt., CBE, F.ENG.

Menter, Sir James Woodham, Kt., ph.D., SC.D., FRS

Menteth, Sir James Wallace Stuart-, Bt. (1838)

Menzies, Sir Peter Thomson, Kt.

Meyer, Sir Anthony John Charles, Bt. (1910)

Meyer, Sir Christopher John Rome, KCMG

Meyjes, Sir Richard Anthony, Kt.

Meyrick, Sir David John Charlton, Bt. (1880)

Meyrick, Sir George Christopher Cadafael Tapps-Gervis-, Bt. (1791)

Miakwe, *Hon.* Sir Akepa, KBE

Michael, Sir Peter Colin, Kt., CBE

Middleton, Sir Lawrence Monck, Bt. (1662)

Middleton, Sir Peter Edward, GCB

Miers, Sir (Henry) David Alastair Capel, KBE, CMG

Milbank, Sir Anthony Frederick, Bt. (1882)

Milburn, Sir Anthony Rupert, Bt. (1905)

Mildmay, Sir Walter John Hugh St John-, Bt. (1772)

Miles, Sir Peter Tremayne, KCVO

Miles, Sir William Napier Maurice, Bt. (1859)

Millais, Sir Geoffrey Richard Everett, Bt. (1885)

Millar, Sir Oliver Nicholas, GCVO, FBA

Millard, Sir Guy Elwin, KCMG, CVO

Miller, Sir Donald John, Kt., FRSE, FEng.

Miller, Sir Harry Holmes, Bt. (1705)

Miller, Sir Hilary Duppa (Hal), Kt.

Miller, *Lt.-Col.* Sir John Mansel, GCVO, DSO, MC

Miller, Sir (Oswald) Bernard, Kt.

Miller, Sir Peter North, Kt.

Miller, Sir Ronald Andrew Baird, Kt., CBE

Miller of Glenlee, Sir Stephen William Macdonald, Bt. (1788)

Millett, *Rt. Hon.* Sir Peter Julian, Kt.

Millichip, Sir Frederick Albert (Bert), Kt.

Mills, *Vice-Adm.* Sir Charles Piercy, KCB, CBE, DSC

Mills, Sir Frank, KCVO, CMG

Nelson, *Hon.* Sir Robert Franklyn, Kt.
Nelson, *Air Marshal* Sir (Sidney)
    Richard (Carlyle), KCB, OBE, MD
Nepean, *Lt.-Col.* Sir Evan Yorke, Bt.
    (1802)
Neuberger, *Hon.* Sir David Edmond,
    Kt.
Neubert, Sir Michael John, Kt.
Neville, Sir Roger Albert Gartside,
    Kt., VRD
New, *Maj.-Gen.* Sir Laurence
    Anthony Wallis, Kt., CB, CBE
Newall, Sir Paul Henry, Kt., TD
Newington, Sir Michael John, KCMG
Newman, Sir Francis Hugh Cecil, Bt.
    (1912)
Newman, Sir Geoffrey Robert, Bt.
    (1836)
Newman, *Hon.* Sir George Michael,
    Kt.
Newman, Sir Kenneth Leslie, GBE,
    QPM
Newman, *Vice-Adm.* Sir Roy
    Thomas, KCB
Newman, *Col.* Sir Stuart Richard, Kt.,
    CBE, TD
Newsam, Sir Peter Anthony, Kt.
Newton, Sir (Charles) Wilfred, Kt.,
    CBE
Newton, Sir (Harry) Michael (Rex),
    Bt. (1900)
Newton, Sir Kenneth Garnar, Bt.,
    OBE, TD (1924)
Ngata, Sir Henare Kohere, KBE
Nichol, Sir Duncan Kirkbride, Kt.,
    CBE
Nicholas, Sir David, Kt., CBE
Nicholas, Sir John William, KCVO,
    CMG
Nicholls, *Air Marshal* Sir John
    Moreton, KCB, CBE, DFC, AFC
Nichols, Sir Richard Everard, Kt.
Nicholson, Sir Bryan Hubert, Kt.
†Nicholson, Sir Charles Christian,
    Bt. (1912)
Nicholson, *Hon.* Sir David Eric, Kt.
Nicholson, *Rt. Hon.* Sir Michael, Kt.
Nicholson, Sir Paul Douglas, Kt.
Nicholson, Sir Robin Buchanan, Kt.,
    ph.D., FRS, FEng.
Nicoll, Sir William, KCMG
Nightingale, Sir Charles Manners
    Gamaliel, Bt. (1628)
Nightingale, Sir John Cyprian, Kt.,
    CBE, BEM, QPM
Nimmo, *Hon.* Sir John Angus, Kt.,
    CBE
Nixon, *Maj.* Sir Cecil Dominic
    Henry Joseph, Bt., MC (1906)
Nixon, Sir Edwin Ronald, Kt., CBE
Noble, Sir David Brunel, Bt. (1902)
Noble, Sir Iain Andrew, Bt., OBE
    (1923)
Noble, Sir (Thomas Alexander)
    Fraser, Kt., MBE
Nombri, Sir Joseph Karl, Kt., ISO, BEM
Norman, Sir Arthur Gordon, KBE,
    DFC
Norman, Sir Mark Annesley, Bt.
    (1915)

Norman, Sir Robert Henry, Kt., OBE
Norman, Sir Ronald, Kt., OBE
Norrington, Sir Roger Arthur
    Carver, Kt., CBE
Norris, *Air Chief Marshal* Sir
    Christopher Neil Foxley-, GCB,
    DSO, OBE
Norris, Sir Eric George, KCMG
North, Sir Peter Machin, Kt., CBE, QC,
    DCL, FBA
North, Sir Thomas Lindsay, Kt.
North, Sir (William) Jonathan
    (Frederick), Bt. (1920)
Norton, *Vice-Adm. Hon.* Sir Nicholas
    John Hill-, KCB
Norwood, Sir Walter Neville, Kt.
Nossal, Sir Gustav Joseph Victor,
    Kt., CBE
Nott, *Rt. Hon.* Sir John William
    Frederic, KCB
Nourse, *Rt. Hon.* Sir Martin Charles,
    Kt.
Nugent, Sir John Edwin Lavallin, Bt.
    (I. 1795)
Nugent, *Maj.* Sir Peter Walter James,
    Bt. (1831)
Nugent, Sir Robin George Colborne,
    Bt. (1806)
Nursaw, Sir James, KCB, QC
Nuttall, Sir Nicholas Keith
    Lillington, Bt. (1922)
Nutting, *Rt. Hon.* Sir (Harold)
    Anthony, Bt. (1903)
Oakeley, Sir John Digby Atholl, Bt.
    (1790)
Oakes, Sir Christopher, Bt. (1939)
Oakshott, Hon. Sir Anthony
    Hendrie, Bt. (1959)
Oates, Sir Thomas, Kt., CMG, OBE
Obolensky, *Prof.* Sir Dimitri, Kt.
O'Brien, Sir Frederick William
    Fitzgerald, Kt.
O'Brien, Sir Richard, Kt., DSO, MC
O'Brien, Sir Timothy John, Bt.
    (1849)
O'Brien, *Adm.* Sir William Donough,
    KCB, DSC
O'Connell, Sir Maurice James
    Donagh MacCarthy, Bt. (1869)
O'Connor, *Rt. Hon.* Sir Patrick
    McCarthy, Kt.
O'Dea, Sir Patrick Jerad, KCVO
Odell, Sir Stanley John, Kt.
Odgers, Sir Graeme David William,
    Kt.
Ogden, Sir (Edward) Michael, Kt., QC
Ogilvy, *Rt. Hon.* Sir Angus James
    Bruce, KCVO
Ogilvy, Sir Francis Gilbert Arthur,
    Bt. (s. 1626)
Ognall, *Hon.* Sir Harry Henry, Kt.
Ohlson, Sir Brian Eric Christopher,
    Bt. (1920)
Okeover, *Capt.* Sir Peter Ralph
    Leopold Walker-, Bt. (1886)
Olewale, *Hon.* Sir Niwia Ebia, Kt.
Oliphant, Sir Mark (Marcus
    Laurence Elwin), KBE, FRS
O'Loghlen, Sir Colman Michael, Bt.
    (1838)

Olver, Sir Stephen John Linley, KBE,
    CMG
O'Neil, *Hon.* Sir Desmond Henry, Kt.
Ongley, *Hon.* Sir Joseph Augustine,
    Kt.
Onslow, Sir John Roger Wilmot, Bt.
    (1797)
Oppenheim, Sir Duncan Morris, Kt.
Oppenheimer, Sir Michael Bernard
    Grenville, Bt. (1921)
Orde, Sir John Alexander
    Campbell-, Bt. (1790)
O'Regan, *Dr* Sir Stephen Gerard
    (Tipene), Kt.
Orlebar, Sir Michael Keith Orlebar
    Simpson-, KCMG
Orr, Sir David Alexander, Kt., MC
Osborn, Sir John Holbrook, Kt.
Osborn, Sir Richard Henry Danvers,
    Bt. (1662)
Osborne, Sir Peter George, Bt.
    (I. 1629)
Osifelo, Sir Frederick Aubarua, Kt.,
    MBE
Osmond, Sir Douglas, Kt., CBE
Osmond, Sir (Stanley) Paul, Kt., CB
O'Sullevan, Sir Peter John, Kt., CBE
Oswald, *Admiral of the Fleet* Sir (John)
    Julian Robertson, GCB
Oswald, Sir (William Richard)
    Michael, KCVO
Otton, Sir Geoffrey John, KCB
Otton, *Rt. Hon.* Sir Philip Howard, Kt.
Oulton, Sir Antony Derek Maxwell,
    GCB, QC
Ouseley, Sir Herman George, Kt.
Outram, Sir Alan James, Bt. (1858)
Overall, Sir John Wallace, Kt., CBE,
    MC
Owen, Sir Geoffrey, Kt.
Owen, Sir Hugh Bernard Pilkington,
    Bt. (1813)
Owen, Sir Hugo Dudley Cunliffe-,
    Bt. (1920)
Owen, *Hon.* Sir John Arthur Dalziel,
    Kt.
Owo, The Olowo of, Kt.
Oxburgh, *Prof.* Sir Ernest Ronald,
    KBE, ph.D., FRS
Oxford, Sir Kenneth Gordon, Kt.,
    CBE, QPM
Packard, *Lt.-Gen.* Sir (Charles)
    Douglas, KBE, CB, DSO
Page, Sir (Arthur) John, Kt.
Page, Sir Frederick William, Kt., CBE,
    FEng.
Page, Sir John Joseph Joffre, Kt., OBE
Paget, Sir Julian Tolver, Bt., CVO
    (1871)
Paget, Sir Richard Herbert, Bt.
    (1886)
Pain, *Lt.-Gen.* Sir (Horace) Rollo
    (Squarey), KCB, MC
Pain, *Hon.* Sir Peter Richard, Kt.
Paine, Sir Christopher Hammon, Kt.,
    FRCP, FRCR
Palin, *Air Chief Marshal* Sir Roger
    Hewlett, KCB, OBE
Palliser, *Rt. Hon.* Sir (Arthur)
    Michael, GCMG

Palmer, Sir Derek James, Kt.
Palmer, Sir (Charles) Mark, Bt. (1886)
Palmer, *Gen.* Sir (Charles) Patrick (Ralph), KBE
Palmer, Sir Geoffrey Christopher John, Bt. (1660)
Palmer, *Rt. Hon.* Sir Geoffrey Winston Russell, KCMG
Palmer, Sir John Chance, Kt.
Palmer, Sir John Edward Somerset, Bt. (1791)
Palmer, *Maj.-Gen.* Sir (Joseph) Michael, KCVO
Palmer, Sir Reginald Oswald, GCMG, MBE
Pantlin, Sir Dick Hurst, Kt., CBE
Paolozzi, Sir Eduardo Luigi, Kt., CBE, RA
Parbo, Sir Arvi Hillar, Kt.
Parish, Sir David Elmer Woodbine, Kt., CBE
Park, *Hon.* Sir Andrew Edward Wilson, Kt.
Park, *Hon.* Sir Hugh Eames, Kt.
Parker, Sir (Arthur) Douglas Dodds-, Kt.
Parker, Sir Eric Wilson, Kt.
Parker, *Hon.* Sir Jonathan Frederic, Kt.
Parker, Sir Peter, KBE, LVO
Parker, Sir Richard (William) Hyde, Bt. (1681)
Parker, *Rt. Hon.* Sir Roger Jocelyn, Kt.
Parker, *Vice-Adm.* Sir (Wilfred) John, KBE, CB, DSC
Parker, Sir William Peter Brian, Bt. (1844)
Parkes, Sir Edward Walter, Kt., FEng
Parkinson, Sir Nicholas Fancourt, Kt.
Parsons, Sir (John) Michael, Kt.
Parsons, Sir Richard Edmund (Clement Fownes), KCMG
Partridge, Sir Michael John Anthony, KCB
Pascoe, *Gen.* Sir Robert Alan, KCB, MBE
Pasley, Sir John Malcolm Sabine, Bt. (1794)
Patel, *Prof.* Sir Narendra Babubhai, Kt.
Paterson, Sir Dennis Craig, Kt.
Paterson, Sir John Valentine Jardine, Kt.
Patnick, Sir (Cyril) Irvine, Kt., OBE
Paton, Sir (Thomas) Angus (Lyall), Kt., CMG, FRS, FEng.
Pattie, *Rt. Hon.* Sir Geoffrey Edwin, Kt.
Pattinson, Sir (William) Derek, Kt.
Pattison, *Prof.* Sir John Ridley, Kt., DM, FRCPath.
Pattullo, Sir (David) Bruce, Kt., CBE
Paul, Sir John Warburton, GCMG, OBE, MC
Paul, *Air Marshal* Sir Ronald Ian Stuart-, KBE
Payne, Sir Norman John, Kt., CBE, FEng.

Peach, Sir Leonard Harry, Kt.
Peacock, *Prof.* Sir Alan Turner, Kt., DSC
Pearce, Sir Austin William, Kt., CBE, ph.D., FEng.
Pearce, Sir (Daniel Norton) Idris, Kt., CBE, TD
Pearce, Sir Eric Herbert, Kt., OBE
Pearse, Sir Brian Gerald, Kt.
Pearson, Sir Francis Nicholas Fraser, Bt. (1964)
Pearson, *Gen.* Sir Thomas Cecil Hook, KCB, CBE, DSO
Peart, *Prof.* Sir William Stanley, Kt., MD, FRS
Pease, Sir (Alfred) Vincent, Bt. (1882)
Pease, Sir Richard Thorn, Bt. (1920)
Peat, Sir Gerrard Charles, KCVO
Peat, Sir Michael Charles Gerrard, KCVO
Peck, Sir Edward Heywood, GCMG
Peckham, *Prof.* Sir Michael John, Kt., FRCP, FRCPGlas., FRCR, FRCPath.
Pedder, *Air Marshal* Sir Ian Maurice, KCB, OBE, DFC
Peek, *Vice-Adm.* Sir Richard Innes, KBE, CB, DSC
Peek, Sir William Grenville, Bt. (1874)
Peel, Sir John Harold, KCVO
Peel, Sir (William) John, Kt.
Peirse, Sir Henry Grant de la Poer Beresford-, Bt. (1814)
Peirse, *Air Vice-Marshal* Sir Richard Charles Fairfax, KCVO, CB
Pelgen, Sir Harry Friedrich, Kt., MBE
Peliza, Sir Robert John, KBE, ED
Pelly, Sir Richard John, Bt. (1840)
Pemberton, Sir Francis Wingate William, Kt., CBE
Penrose, *Prof.* Sir Roger, Kt., FRS
Pereira, Sir (Herbert) Charles, Kt., D.SC., FRS
Perring, Sir John Raymond, Bt. (1963)
Perris, Sir David (Arthur), Kt., MBE
Perry, Sir David Howard, KCB
Perry, Sir (David) Norman, Kt., MBE
Perry, Sir Michael Sydney, Kt., CBE
Pestell, Sir John Richard, KCVO
Peterkin, Sir Neville, Kt.
Peters, *Prof.* Sir David Keith, Kt., FRCP
Petersen, Sir Jeffrey Charles, KCMG
Petersen, Sir Johannes Bjelke-, KCMG
Peterson, Sir Christopher Matthew, Kt., CBE, TD
†Petit, Sir Jehangir, Bt. (1890)
Peto, Sir Henry George Morton, Bt. (1855)
Peto, Sir Michael Henry Basil, Bt. (1927)
Petrie, Sir Peter Charles, Bt., CMG (1918)
Pettigrew, Sir Russell Hilton, Kt.
Pettit, Sir Daniel Eric Arthur, Kt.
Pettitt, Sir Dennis, Kt.
Philips, *Prof.* Sir Cyril Henry, Kt.
Phillips, Sir Fred Albert, Kt., CVO

Phillips, Sir (Gerald) Hayden, KCB
Phillips, Sir Henry Ellis Isidore, Kt., CMG, MBE
Phillips, Sir Horace, KCMG
Phillips, *Hon.* Sir Nicholas Addison, Kt.
Phillips, Sir Peter John, Kt., OBE
Phillips, Sir Robin Francis, Bt. (1912)
Pickard, Sir (John) Michael, Kt.
Pickering, Sir Edward Davies, Kt.
Pickthorn, Sir James Francis Mann, Bt. (1959)
Pidgeon, Sir John Allan Stewart, Kt.
†Piers, Sir James Desmond, Bt. (I. 1661)
Pigot, Sir George Hugh, Bt. (1764)
Pigott, Sir Berkeley Henry Sebastian, Bt. (1808)
Pike, *Lt.-Gen.* Sir Hew William Royston, KCB, DSO, MBE
Pike, Sir Michael Edmund, KCVO, CMG
Pike, Sir Philip Ernest Housden, Kt., QC
Pilditch, Sir Richard Edward, Bt. (1929)
Pile, Sir Frederick Devereux, Bt., MC (1900)
Pilkington, Sir Antony Richard, Kt.
Pilkington, Sir Thomas Henry Milborne-Swinnerton-, Bt. (s. 1635)
Pill, *Rt. Hon.* Sir Malcolm Thomas, Kt.
Pillar, *Adm.* Sir William Thomas, GBE, KCB
Pindling, *Rt. Hon.* Sir Lynden Oscar, KCMG
Pinker, Sir George Douglas, KCVO
Pinsent, Sir Christopher Roy, Bt. (1938)
Pippard, *Prof.* Sir (Alfred) Brian, Kt., FRS
Pirie, *Gp Capt* Sir Gordon Hamish, Kt., CVO, CBE
Pitakaka, Sir Moses Puibangara, GCMG
Pitcher, Sir Desmond Henry, Kt.
Pitman, Sir Brian Ivor, Kt.
Pitoi, Sir Sere, Kt., CBE
Pitt, Sir Harry Raymond, Kt., ph.D., FRS
Pitts, Sir Cyril Alfred, Kt.
Plastow, Sir David Arnold Stuart, Kt.
Platt, Sir Harold Grant, Kt.
Platt, *Prof.* Hon. Sir Peter, Bt. (1959)
Playfair, Sir Edward Wilder, KCB
Pliatzky, Sir Leo, KCB
Plowman, *Hon.* Sir John Robin, Kt., CBE
Plumb, *Prof.* Sir John Harold, Kt.
Pohai, Sir Timothy, Kt., MBE
Pole, Sir (John) Richard (Walter Reginald) Carew, Bt. (1628)
Pole, Sir Peter Van Notten, Bt. (1791)
Polkinghorne, *Revd Canon* John Charlton, KBE, FRS
Pollen, Sir John Michael Hungerford, Bt. (1795)

Rhodes, Sir Peregrine Alexander, KCMG

Rice, *Maj.-Gen.* Sir Desmond Hind Garrett, KCVO, CBE

Rice, Sir Timothy Miles Bindon, Kt.

Richard, Sir Cliff, Kt., OBE

Richards, Sir Brian Mansel, Kt., CBE, PH.D.

Richards, Sir (Francis) Brooks, KCMG, DSC

Richards, *Lt.-Gen.* Sir John Charles Chisholm, KCB, KCVO, RM

Richards, Sir Rex Edward, Kt., D.SC., FRS

Richards, *Hon.* Sir Stephen Price, Kt.

Richardson, Sir Anthony Lewis, Bt. (1924)

Richardson, *Rt. Hon.* Sir Ivor Lloyd Morgan, Kt.

Richardson, Sir (John) Eric, Kt., CBE

Richardson, Sir Michael John de Rougemont, Kt.

Richardson, *Lt.-Gen.* Sir Robert Francis, KCB, CVO, CBE

Richardson, Sir Simon Alaisdair Stewart-, Bt. (s. 1630)

Richmond, Sir John Frederick, Bt. (1929)

Richmond, *Prof.* Sir Mark Henry, Kt., FRS

Ricketts, Sir Robert Cornwallis Gerald St Leger, Bt. (1828)

Riddell, Sir John Charles Buchanan, Bt., CVO (s. 1628)

Ridley, Sir Adam (Nicholas), Kt.

Ridsdale, Sir Julian Errington, Kt., CBE

Rifkind, *Rt. Hon.* Sir Malcolm Leslie, KCMG, QC

Rigby, *Lt.-Col.* Sir (Hugh) John (Macbeth), Bt. (1929)

Riley, Sir Ralph, Kt., FRS

Rimer, *Hon.* Sir Colin Percy Farquharson, Kt.

Ringadoo, *Hon.* Sir Veerasamy, GCMG

Ripley, Sir Hugh, Bt. (1880)

Risk, Sir Thomas Neilson, Kt.

Ritako, Sir Thomas Baha, Kt., MBE

Rix, *Hon.* Sir Bernard Anthony, Kt.

Rix, Sir John, Kt., MBE, FEng.

Roberts, *Hon.* Sir Denys Tudor Emil, KBE, QC

Roberts, Sir Derek Harry, Kt., CBE, FRS, FEng.

Roberts, Sir (Edward Fergus) Sidney, Kt., CBE

Roberts, *Prof.* Sir Gareth Gwyn, Kt., FRS

Roberts, Sir Gilbert Howland Rookehurst, Bt. (1809)

Roberts, Sir Gordon James, Kt., CBE

Roberts, Sir Samuel, Bt. (1919)

Roberts, Sir Stephen James Leake, Kt.

Roberts, Sir William James Denby, Bt. (1909)

Robertson, Sir John Fraser, KCMG, CBE

Robertson, Sir Lewis, Kt., CBE, FRSE

Robertson, *Prof.* Sir Rutherford Ness, Kt., CMG

Robins, Sir Ralph Harry, Kt., FEng.

Robinson, Sir Albert Edward Phineas, Kt.

†Robinson, Sir Christopher Philipse, Bt. (1854)

Robinson, Sir Dominick Christopher Lynch-, Bt. (1920)

Robinson, Sir John James Michael Laud, Bt. (1660)

Robinson, Sir Wilfred Henry Frederick, Bt. (1908)

Robotham, *Hon.* Sir Lascelles Lister, Kt.

Robson, *Prof.* Sir James Gordon, Kt., CBE

Robson, Sir John Adam, KCMG

Roch, *Rt. Hon.* Sir John Ormond, Kt.

Roche, Sir David O'Grady, Bt. (1838)

Rodgers, Sir (Andrew) Piers (Wingate Aikin-Sneath), Bt. (1964)

Rodrigues, Sir Alberto Maria, Kt., CBE, ED

Roe, *Air Chief Marshal* Sir Rex David, GCB, AFC

Rogers, Sir Frank Jarvis, Kt.

Rogers, *Air Chief Marshal* Sir John Robson, KCB, CBE

Rooke, Sir Denis Eric, Kt., OM, CBE, FRS, FEng.

Ropner, Sir John Bruce Woollacott, Bt. (1952)

Ropner, Sir Robert Douglas, Bt. (1904)

Roscoe, Sir Robert Bell, KBE

Rose, *Rt. Hon.* Sir Christopher Dudley Roger, Kt.

Rose, Sir Clive Martin, GCMG

Rose, Sir David Lancaster, Bt. (1874)

Rose, *Gen.* Sir (Hugh) Michael, KCB, CBE, DSO, QGM

Rose, Sir Julian Day, Bt. (1872 and 1909)

Rosier, *Air Chief Marshal* Sir Frederick Ernest, GCB, CBE, DSO

Ross, Sir (James) Keith, Bt., RD, FRCS (1960)

Ross, *Lt.-Gen.* Sir Robert Jeremy, KCB, OBE

Rosser, Sir Melvyn Wynne, Kt.

Rossi, Sir Hugh Alexis Louis, Kt.

Rotblat, *Prof.* Joseph, KCMG, CBE, FRS

Roth, *Prof.* Sir Martin, Kt., MD, FRCP

Rothschild, Sir Evelyn Robert Adrian de, Kt.

Rougier, *Hon.* Sir Richard George, Kt.

Rous, *Lt.-Gen.* Hon. Sir William Edward, KCB, OBE

Rowell, Sir John Joseph, Kt., CBE

Rowland, *Air Marshal* Sir James Anthony, KBE, DFC, AFC

Rowland, Sir (John) David, Kt.

Rowlands, *Air Marshal* Sir John Samuel, GC, KBE

Rowley, Sir Charles Robert, Bt. (1836) †(1786)

Roxburgh, *Vice-Adm.* Sir John Charles Young, KCB, CBE, DSO, DSC

Royden, Sir Christopher John, Bt. (1905)

Rudd, Sir (Anthony) Nigel (Russell), Kt.

Rumbold, Sir Henry John Sebastian, Bt. (1779)

Rumbold, Sir Jack Seddon, Kt.

Runchorelal, Sir (Udayan) Chinubhai Madhowlal, Bt. (1913)

Runciman, *Hon.* Sir James Cochran Stevenson (Sir Steven), Kt., CH

Rusby, *Vice-Adm.* Sir Cameron, KCB, LVO

†Russell, Sir (Arthur) Mervyn, Bt. (1812)

Russell, Sir Charles Dominic, Bt. (1916)

Russell, *Hon.* Sir David Sturrock West-, Kt.

Russell, Sir George, Kt., CBE

Russell, *Prof.* Sir Peter Edward Lionel, Kt., D.Litt., FBA

Russell, Sir (Robert) Mark, KCMG

Russell, *Rt. Hon.* Sir (Thomas) Patrick, Kt.

Rutter, Sir Frank William Eden, KBE

Rutter, *Prof.* Sir Michael Llewellyn, Kt., CBE, MD, FRS

Ryan, Sir Derek Gerald, Bt. (1919)

Rycroft, Sir Richard Newton, Bt. (1784)

Ryrie, Sir William Sinclair, KCB

Sabola, *Hon.* Sir Joaquim Claudino Gonsalves-, Kt.

Sachs, *Hon.* Sir Michael Alexander Geddes, Kt.

Sainsbury, Sir Robert James, Kt.

Sainsbury, *Rt. Hon.* Sir Timothy Alan Davan, Kt.

†St Aubyn, Sir William Molesworth-, Bt. (1689)

†St George, Sir John Avenel Bligh, Bt. (I. 1766)

St Johnston, Sir Kerry, Kt.

Sainty, Sir John Christopher, KCB

Sakzewski, Sir Albert, Kt.

Salisbury, Sir Robert William, Kt.

Salt, Sir Patrick MacDonnell, Bt. (1869)

Salt, Sir (Thomas) Michael John, Bt. (1899)

Sampson, Sir Colin, Kt., CBE, QPM

Samuel, Sir John Michael Glen, Bt. (1898)

Samuelson, Sir (Bernard) Michael (Francis), Bt. (1884)

Samuelson, Sir Sydney Wylie, Kt., CBE

Sanders, Sir John Reynolds Mayhew-, Kt.

Sanders, Sir Robert Tait, KBE, CMG

Sanderson, Sir Frank Linton, Bt. (1920)

Sarei, Sir Alexis Holyweek, Kt., CBE

Sarell, Sir Roderick Francis Gisbert, KCMG, KCVO

Saunders, *Hon.* Sir John Anthony Holt, Kt., CBE, DSO, MC

Saunders, Sir Peter, Kt.
Sauzier, Sir (André) Guy, Kt., CBE, ED
Savage, Sir Ernest Walter, Kt.
Savile, Sir James Wilson Vincent, Kt., OBE
Say, *Rt. Revd* Richard David, KCVO
Schiemann, *Rt. Hon.* Sir Konrad Hermann Theodor, Kt.
Scholey, Sir David Gerald, Kt., CBE
Scholey, Sir Robert, Kt., CBE, FEng.
Scholtens, Sir James Henry, KCVO
Schubert, Sir Sydney, Kt.
Scipio, Sir Hudson Rupert, Kt.
Scoon, Sir Paul, GCMG, GCVO, OBE
Scott, Sir Anthony Percy, Bt. (1913)
Scott, Sir (Charles) Peter, KBE, CMG
Scott, Sir David Aubrey, GCMG
Scott, Sir Dominic James Maxwell-, Bt. (1642)
Scott, Sir Ian Dixon, KCMG, KCVO, CIE
Scott, Sir James Jervoise, Bt. (1962)
Scott, Sir Kenneth Bertram Adam, KCVO, CMG
Scott, Sir Michael, KCVO, CMG
Scott, *Rt. Hon.* Sir Nicholas Paul, KBE
Scott, Sir Oliver Christopher Anderson, Bt. (1909)
Scott, *Prof.* Sir Philip John, KBE
Scott, *Rt. Hon.* Sir Richard Rashleigh Folliott, Kt.
Scott, Sir Robert David Hillyer, Kt.
Scott, Sir Walter John, Bt. (1907)
Scott, *Rear-Adm.* Sir (William) David (Stewart), KBE, CB
Scowen, Sir Eric Frank, Kt., MD, D.SC., LLD, FRCP, FRCS
Scrivenor, Sir Thomas Vaisey, Kt., CMG
Seale, Sir John Henry, Bt. (1838)
Seaman, Sir Keith Douglas, KCVO, OBE
Sebastian, Sir Cuthbert Montraville, GCMG, OBE
†Sebright, Sir Peter Giles Vivian, Bt. (1626)
Seccombe, Sir (William) Vernon Stephen, Kt.
Secombe, Sir Harry Donald, Kt., CBE
Seconde, Sir Reginald Louis, KCMG, CVO
Sedley, *Hon.* Sir Stephen John, Kt.
Seely, Sir Nigel Edward, Bt. (1896)
Seeto, Sir Ling James, Kt., MBE
Seeyave, Sir Rene Sow Choung, Kt., CBE
Seligman, Sir Peter Wendel, Kt., CBE
Sergeant, Sir Patrick, Kt.
Series, Sir (Joseph Michel) Emile, Kt., CBE
Serpell, Sir David Radford, KCB, CMG, OBE
Seton, Sir Iain Bruce, Bt. (s. 1663)
†Seton, Sir James Christall, Bt. (s. 1683)
Severne, *Air Vice-Marshal* Sir John de Milt, KCVO, OBE, AFC
Seymour, *Cdr.* Sir Michael Culme-, Bt., RN (1809)

Shackleton, *Prof.* Sir Nicholas John, Kt., PH.D., FRS
Shakerley, Sir Geoffrey Adam, Bt. (1838)
Shakespeare, Sir Thomas William, Bt. (1942)
Sharp, Sir Adrian, Bt. (1922)
Sharp, Sir George, Kt., OBE
Sharp, Sir Kenneth Johnston, Kt., TD
Sharp, Sir Leslie, Kt., QPM
Sharp, Sir Richard Lyall, KCVO, CB
†Sharp, Sir Samuel Christopher Reginald, Bt. (1920)
Sharpe, *Hon.* Sir John Henry, Kt., CBE
Sharples, Sir James, Kt., QPM
Shattock, Sir Gordon, Kt.
Shaw, Sir Brian Piers, Kt.
Shaw, Sir (Charles) Barry, Kt., CB, QC
Shaw, Sir (George) Neville Bowan-, Kt.
Shaw, *Prof.* Sir John Calman, Kt., CBE, FRSE
Shaw, Sir (John) Giles (Dunkerley), Kt.
Shaw, Sir John Michael Robert Best-, Bt. (1665)
Shaw, Sir Neil McGowan, Kt.
Shaw, Sir Robert, Bt. (1821)
Shaw, Sir Roy, Kt.
Shaw, Sir Run Run, Kt., CBE
Sheehy, Sir Patrick, Kt.
Sheen, *Hon.* Sir Barry Cross, Kt.
Sheffield, Sir Reginald Adrian Berkeley, Bt. (1755)
Shehadie, Sir Nicholas Michael, Kt., OBE
Sheil, *Hon.* Sir John, Kt.
Sheldon, *Hon.* Sir (John) Gervase (Kensington), Kt.
Shelley, Sir John Richard, Bt. (1611)
Shelton, Sir William Jeremy Masefield, Kt.
Shepheard, Sir Peter Faulkner, Kt., CBE
Shepherd, Sir Colin Ryley, Kt.
Shepperd, Sir Alfred Joseph, Kt.
Sherlock, Sir Philip Manderson, KBE
Sherman, Sir Alfred, Kt.
Sherman, Sir Louis, Kt., OBE
Shields, Sir Neil Stanley, Kt., MC
Shields, *Prof.* Sir Robert, Kt., MD
Shiffner, Sir Henry David, Bt. (1818)
Shillington, Sir (Robert Edward) Graham, Kt., CBE
Shinwell, Sir (Maurice) Adrian, Kt.
Shock, Sir Maurice, Kt.
Short, Sir Apenera Pera, KBE
Short, *Brig.* Sir Noel Edward Vivian, Kt., MBE, MC
Shuckburgh, Sir Rupert Charles Gerald, Bt. (1660)
Siaguru, Sir Anthony Michael, KBE
Siddall, Sir Norman, Kt., CBE, FEng.
Sidey, *Air Marshal* Sir Ernest Shaw, KBE, CB, MD
Sie, Sir Banja Tejan-, GCMG
Simeon, Sir John Edmund Barrington, Bt. (1815)
Simmons, *Air Marshal* Sir Michael George, KCB, AFC

Simmons, Sir Stanley Clifford, Kt., FRCS, FRCOG
Simms, Sir Neville Ian, Kt., FEng.
Simon, Sir David Alec Gwyn, Kt., CBE
Simonet, Sir Louis Marcel Pierre, Kt., CBE
Simpson, *Hon.* Sir Alfred Henry, Kt.
Simpson, *Lt.-Gen.* Sir Roderick Alexander Cordy-, KBE, CB
Simpson, Sir William James, Kt.
Sims, Sir Roger Edward, Kt.
Sinclair, Sir Clive Marles, Kt.
Sinclair, Sir George Evelyn, Kt., CMG, OBE
Sinclair, Sir Ian McTaggart, KCMG, QC
Sinclair, *Air Vice-Marshal* Sir Laurence Frank, GC, KCB, CBE, DSO
Sinclair, Sir Patrick Robert Richard, Bt. (s. 1704)
Sinden, Sir Donald Alfred, Kt., CBE
Singer, *Prof.* Sir Hans Wolfgang, Kt.
Singer, *Hon.* Sir Jan Peter, Kt.
Singh, *Hon.* Sir Vijay Raghubir, Kt.
Sitwell, Sir (Sacheverell) Reresby, Bt. (1808)
Skeet, Sir Trevor Herbert Harry, Kt.
Skeggs, Sir Clifford George, Kt.
Skehel, Sir John James, Kt., FRS
Skingsley, *Air Chief Marshal* Sir Anthony Gerald, GBE, KCB
Skinner, Sir (Thomas) Keith (Hewitt), Bt. (1912)
Skipwith, Sir Patrick Alexander d'Estoteville, Bt. (1622)
Skyrme, Sir (William) Thomas (Charles), KCVO, CB, CBE, TD
Slack, Sir William Willatt, KCVO, FRCS
Slade, Sir Benjamin Julian Alfred, Bt. (1831)
Slade, *Rt. Hon.* Sir Christopher John, Kt.
Slaney, *Prof.* Sir Geoffrey, KBE
Slater, *Adm.* Sir John (Jock) Cunningham Kirkwood, GCB, LVO
Sleight, Sir Richard, Bt. (1920)
Sloan, Sir Andrew Kirkpatrick, Kt., QPM
Sloman, Sir Albert Edward, Kt., CBE
Smart, *Prof.* Sir George Algernon, Kt., MD, FRCP
Smart, Sir Jack, Kt., CBE
Smedley, *Hon.* Sir (Frank) Brian, Kt.
Smedley, Sir Harold, KCMG, MBE
Smiley, *Lt.-Col.* Sir John Philip, Bt. (1903)
Smith, Sir Alan, Kt., CBE, DFC
Smith, Sir Alexander Mair, Kt., PH.D.
Smith, Sir Andrew Colin Hugh-, Kt.
Smith, *Lt.-Gen.* Sir Anthony Arthur Denison-, KBE
Smith, Sir Charles Bracewell-, Bt. (1947)
Smith, Sir Christopher Sydney Winwood, Bt. (1809)
Smith, *Prof.* Sir Colin Stansfield, Kt., CBE
Smith, Sir Cyril, Kt., MBE

Smith, *Prof.* Sir David Cecil, Kt., FRS

Smith, *Air Chief Marshal* Sir David Harcourt-, GBE, KCB, DFC

Smith, Sir David Iser, KCVO

Smith, Sir Douglas Boucher, KCB

Smith, Sir Dudley (Gordon), Kt.

Smith, *Maj.-Gen.* Sir (Francis) Brian Wyldbore-, Kt., CB, DSO, OBE

Smith, *Prof.* Sir Francis Graham-, Kt., FRS

Smith, Sir Geoffrey Johnson, Kt., MP

Smith, Sir John Alfred, Kt., QPM

Smith, *Prof.* Sir John Cyril, Kt., CBE, QC, FBA

Smith, Sir John Hamilton-Spencer-, Bt. (1804)

Smith, Sir John Jonah Walker-, Bt. (1960)

Smith, Sir John Lindsay Eric, Kt., CH, CBE

Smith, Sir John Rathbone Vassar-, Bt. (1917)

Smith, Sir Joseph William Grenville, Kt., MD, FRCP

Smith, Sir Leslie Edward George, Kt.

Smith, *Maj.-Gen.* Sir Michael Edward Carleton-, Kt., CBE

Smith, Sir Michael John Llewellyn, KCVO, CMG

Smith, *Rt. Hon.* Sir Murray Stuart-, Kt.

Smith, Sir (Norman) Brian, Kt., CBE, Ph.D.

†Smith, Sir Peter Frank Graham Newson-, Bt. (1944)

Smith, Sir Raymond Horace, KBE

Smith, Sir Robert Courtney, Kt., CBE

Smith, Sir Robert Hill, Bt. (1945)

Smith, *Prof.* Sir Roland, Kt.

Smith, *Air Marshal* Sir Roy David Austen-, KBE, CB, CVO, DFC

Smith, *Gen.* Sir Rupert Anthony, KCB, DSO, OBE, QGM

Smith, Sir (Thomas) Gilbert, Bt. (1897)

Smith, Sir (William) Antony (John) Reardon-, Bt. (1920)

Smith, Sir (William) Richard Prince-, Bt. (1911)

Smithers, Sir Peter Henry Berry Otway, Kt., VRD, D.Phil.

Smyth, Sir Thomas Weyland Bowyer-, Bt. (1661)

Smyth, Sir Timothy John, Bt. (1955)

Soakimori, Sir Frederick Pa-Nukuanca, KBE, CPM

Soame, Sir Charles John Buckworth-Herne-, Bt. (1697)

Sobers, Sir Garfield St Auburn, Kt.

Solomon, Sir Harry, Kt.

Somare, *Rt. Hon.* Sir Michael Thomas, GCMG, CH

Somers, *Rt. Hon.* Sir Edward Jonathan, Kt.

Somerville, *Brig.* Sir John Nicholas, Kt., CBE

Somerville, Sir Quentin Charles Somerville Agnew-, Bt. (1957)

Soutar, *Air Marshal* Sir Charles John Williamson, KBE

South, Sir Arthur, Kt.

Southby, Sir John Richard Bilbe, Bt. (1937)

Southern, Sir Richard William, Kt., FBA

Southern, Sir Robert, Kt., CBE

Southey, Sir Robert John, Kt., CMG

Southgate, Sir Colin Grieve, Kt.

Southgate, Sir William David, Kt.

Southward, Sir Leonard Bingley, Kt., OBE

Southwood, *Prof.* Sir (Thomas) Richard (Edmund), Kt., FRS

Southworth, Sir Frederick, Kt., QC

Souyave, *Hon.* Sir (Louis) Georges, Kt.

Sowrey, *Air Marshal* Sir Frederick Beresford, KCB, CBE, AFC

Sparkes, Sir Robert Lyndley, Kt.

Sparrow, Sir John, Kt.

Spearman, Sir Alexander Young Richard Mainwaring, Bt. (1840)

Spedding, *Prof.* Sir Colin Raymond William, Kt., CBE

Spedding, Sir David Rolland, KCMG, CVO, OBE

Speed, Sir (Herbert) Keith, Kt., RD

Speed, Sir Robert William Arney, Kt., CB, QC

Speelman, Sir Cornelis Jacob, Bt. (1686)

Speight, *Hon.* Sir Graham Davies, Kt.

Speir, Sir Rupert Malise, Kt.

Spencer, Sir Derek Harold, Kt., QC

Spicer, Sir James Wilton, Kt.

Spicer, Sir Nicholas Adrian Albert, Bt., MB (1906)

Spicer, Sir (William) Michael Hardy, Kt., MP

Spiers, Sir Donald Maurice, Kt., CB, TD

Spooner, Sir James Douglas, Kt.

Spotswood, *Marshal of the Royal Air Force* Sir Denis Frank, GCB, CBE, DSO, DFC

Spratt, *Col.* Sir Greville Douglas, GBE, TD

Spring, Sir Dryden Thomas, Kt.

Spry, *Hon.* Sir John Farley, Kt.

Squire, *Air Marshal* Sir Peter Ted, KCB, DFC, AFC

Stabb, *Hon.* Sir William Walter, Kt., QC

Stainton, Sir (John) Ross, Kt., CBE

Stakis, Sir Reo Argiros, Kt.

Stamer, Sir (Lovelace) Anthony, Bt. (1809)

Stanbridge, *Air Vice-Marshal* Sir Brian Gerald Tivy, KCVO, CBE, AFC

Stanier, Sir Beville Douglas, Bt. (1917)

Stanier, *Field Marshal* Sir John Wilfred, GCB, MBE

Stanley, *Rt. Hon.* Sir John Paul, Kt., MP

†Staples, Sir Thomas, Bt. (I. 1628)

Stark, Sir Andrew Alexander Steel, KCMG, CVO

Starkey, Sir John Philip, Bt. (1935)

Starrit, Sir James, KCVO

Statham, Sir Norman, KCMG, CVO

Staughton, *Rt. Hon.* Sir Christopher Stephen Thomas Jonathan Thayer, Kt.

Staveley, Sir John Malfroy, KBE, MC

Stear, *Air Chief Marshal* Sir Michael James Douglas, KCB, CBE

Steel, Sir David Edward Charles, Kt., DSO, MC, TD

Steel, *Hon.* Sir David William, Kt.

Steel, *Maj.* Sir (Fiennes) Michael Strang, Bt. (1938)

Steele, Sir (Philip John) Rupert, Kt.

Steere, Sir Ernest Henry Lee-, KBE

Stephen, *Rt. Hon.* Sir Ninian Martin, KG, GCMG, GCVO, KBE

Stephens, Sir (Edwin) Barrie, Kt.

Stephenson, Sir Henry Upton, Bt. (1936)

Stephenson, *Rt. Hon.* Sir John Frederick Eustace, Kt.

Sternberg, Sir Sigmund, Kt.

Stevens, Sir Jocelyn Edward Greville, Kt., CVO

Stevens, Sir Laurence Houghton, Kt., CBE

Stevenson, Sir Henry Dennistoun (Sir Dennis), Kt., CBE

Stevenson, *Vice-Adm.* Sir (Hugh) David, KBE

Stevenson, Sir Simpson, Kt.

Stewart, Sir Alan, KBE

Stewart, Sir Alan d'Arcy, Bt. (I. 1623)

Stewart, Sir David James Henderson-, Bt. (1957)

Stewart, Sir David John Christopher, Bt. (1803)

Stewart, Sir Edward Jackson, Kt.

Stewart, *Prof.* Sir Frederick Henry, Kt., Ph.D., FRS, FRSE

Stewart, Sir Houston Mark Shaw-, Bt., MC, TD (S. 1667)

Stewart, Sir James Douglas, Kt.

Stewart, Sir James Moray, KCB

Stewart, Sir (John) Simon (Watson), Bt. (1920)

Stewart, Sir Robertson Huntly, Kt., CBE

Stewart, Sir Robin Alastair, Bt. (1960)

Stewart, Sir Ronald Compton, Bt. (1937)

Stewart, *Prof.* Sir William Duncan Paterson, Kt., FRS, FRSE

Stibbon, *Gen.* Sir John James, KCB, OBE

Stirling, Sir Alexander John Dickson, KBE, CMG

Stirling, Sir Angus Duncan Aeneas, Kt.

Stockdale, Sir Arthur Noel, Kt.

Stockdale, Sir Thomas Minshull, Bt. (1960)

Stoddart, *Wg Cdr.* Sir Kenneth Maxwell, KCVO, AE

Stoker, *Prof.* Sir Michael George Parke, Kt., CBE, FRCP, FRS, FRSE

Stokes, Sir John Heydon Romaine, Kt.

Stones, Sir William Frederick, Kt., OBE

Stonhouse, *Revd* Sir Michael Philip, Bt. (1628)
Stonor, *Air Marshal* Sir Thomas Henry, KCB
Stoppard, Sir Thomas, Kt., CBE
Storey, *Hon.* Sir Richard, Bt., CBE (1960)
Stormonth Darling, Sir James Carlisle, Kt., CBE, MC, TD
Stott, Sir Adrian George Ellingham, Bt. (1920)
Stoute, Sir Michael Ronald, Kt.
Stow, Sir Christopher Philipson-, Bt., DFC (1907)
Stowe, Sir Kenneth Ronald, GCB, CVO
Stracey, Sir John Simon, Bt. (1818)
Strachan, Sir Curtis Victor, Kt., CVO
Strachey, Sir Charles, Bt. (1801)
Straker, Sir Michael Ian Bowstead, Kt., CBE
Strawson, *Prof.* Sir Peter Frederick, Kt., FBA
Street, *Hon.* Sir Laurence Whistler, KCMG
Streeton, Sir Terence George, KBE, CMG
Stringer, Sir Donald Edgar, Kt., CBE
Strong, Sir Roy Colin, Kt., PH.D., FSA
Stronge, Sir James Anselan Maxwell, Bt. (1803)
Stroud, *Prof.* Sir (Charles) Eric, Kt., FRCP
Strutt, Sir Nigel Edward, Kt., TD
Stuart, Sir James Keith, Kt.
Stuart, Sir Kenneth Lamonte, Kt.
†Stuart, Sir Phillip Luttrell, Bt. (1660)
Stubblefield, Sir (Cyril) James, Kt., D.SC., FRS
Stubbs, Sir James Wilfrid, KCVO, TD
Stubbs, Sir William Hamilton, Kt., PH.D.
Stucley, *Lt.* Sir Hugh George Coplestone Bampfylde, Bt. (1859)
Studd, Sir Edward Fairfax, Bt. (1929)
Studd, Sir Peter Malden, GBE, KCVO
Studholme, Sir Henry William, Bt. (1956)
Stuttaford, Sir William Royden, Kt., CBE
Style, *Lt.-Cdr.* Sir Godfrey William, Kt., CBE, DSC, RN
†Style, Sir William Frederick, Bt. (1627)
Suffield, Sir (Henry John) Lester, Kt.
Sugden, Sir Arthur, Kt.
Sullivan, *Hon.* Sir Jeremy Mirth, Kt.
Sullivan, Sir Richard Arthur, Bt. (1804)
Sumner, *Hon.* Sir Christopher John, Kt.
Sutherland, Sir John Brewer, Bt. (1921)
Sutherland, Sir Maurice, Kt.
Sutherland, *Prof.* Sir Stewart Ross, Kt., FBA
Sutherland, Sir William George MacKenzie, Kt.
Suttie, Sir James Edward Grant-, Bt. (s. 1702)

Sutton, Sir Frederick Walter, Kt., OBE
Sutton, *Air Marshal* Sir John Matthias Dobson, KCB
Sutton, Sir Richard Lexington, Bt. (1772)
Swaffield, Sir James Chesebrough, Kt., CBE, RD
Swaine, Sir John Joseph, Kt., CBE
Swan, Sir Conrad Marshall John Fisher, KCVO, PH.D.
Swan, Sir John William David, KBE
Swann, Sir Michael Christopher, Bt., TD (1906)
Swanwick, Sir Graham Russell, Kt., MBE
Swartz, *Hon.* Sir Reginald William Colin, KBE, ED
Sweetnam, Sir (David) Rodney, KCVO, CBE, FRCS
Swinburn, *Lt.-Gen.* Sir Richard Hull, KCB
Swinson, Sir John Henry Alan, Kt., OBE
Swinton, *Maj.-Gen.* Sir John, KCVO, OBE
Swire, Sir Adrian Christopher, Kt.
Swire, Sir John Anthony, Kt., CBE
Swynnerton, Sir Roger John Massy, Kt., CMG, OBE, MC
Sykes, Sir Francis John Badcock, Bt. (1781)
Sykes, Sir Hugh Ridley, Kt.
Sykes, Sir John Charles Anthony le Gallais, Bt. (1921)
Sykes, *Prof.* Sir (Malcolm) Keith, Kt.
Sykes, Sir Richard, Kt.
Sykes, Sir Tatton Christopher Mark, Bt. (1783)
Symington, *Prof.* Sir Thomas, Kt., MD, FRSE
Symons, *Vice-Adm.* Sir Patrick Jeremy, KBE
Synge, Sir Robert Carson, Bt. (1801)
Tait, *Adm.* Sir (Allan) Gordon, KCB, DSC
Tait, Sir Peter, KBE
Talbot, *Hon.* Sir Hilary Gwynne, Kt.
Talboys, *Rt. Hon.* Sir Brian Edward, CH, KCB
Tancred, Sir Henry Lawson-, Bt. (1662)
Tangaroa, *Hon.* Sir Tangaroa, Kt., MBE
Tange, Sir Arthur Harold, Kt., CBE
Tapsell, Sir Peter Hannay Bailey, Kt., MP
Tate, Sir (Henry) Saxon, Bt. (1898)
Tavaiqia, *Ratu* Sir Josaia, KBE
Tavare, Sir John, Kt., CBE
Taylor, *Lt.-Gen.* Sir Allan Macnab, KBE, MC
Taylor, Sir (Arthur) Godfrey, Kt.
Taylor, Sir Cyril Julian Hebden, Kt.
Taylor, Sir Edward Macmillan (Teddy), Kt., MP
Taylor, *Rt. Revd* John Bernard, KCVO
Taylor, Sir John Lang, KCMG
Taylor, Sir Nicholas Richard Stuart, Bt. (1917)

Taylor, *Prof.* Sir William, Kt., CBE
Teagle, *Vice-Adm.* Sir Somerford Francis, KBE
Tebbit, Sir Donald Claude, GCMG
Telford, Sir Robert, Kt., CBE, FENG.
Temple, Sir Ernest Sanderson, Kt., MBE, QC
Temple, Sir Rawden John Afamado, Kt., CBE, QC
Temple, *Maj.* Sir Richard Anthony Purbeck, Bt., MC (1876)
Templeton, Sir John Marks, Kt.
Tenison, Sir Richard Hanbury-, KCVO
Tennant, Sir Anthony John, Kt.
Tennant, *Capt.* Sir Iain Mark, KT
Teo, Sir Fiatau Penitala, GCMG, GCVO, ISO, MBE
Terry, *Air Marshal* Sir Colin George, KBE, CB
Terry, Sir Michael Edward Stanley Imbert-, Bt. (1917)
Terry, *Air Chief Marshal* Sir Peter David George, GCB, AFC
Tetley, Sir Herbert, KBE, CB
Tett, Sir Hugh Charles, Kt.
Thatcher, Sir Denis, Bt., MBE, TD (1990)
Thesiger, Sir Wilfred Patrick, KBE, DSO
Thomas, Sir Derek Morison David, KCMG
Thomas, Sir Frederick William, Kt.
Thomas, Sir (Godfrey) Michael (David), Bt. (1694)
Thomas, Sir Jeremy Cashel, KCMG
Thomas, Sir (John) Alan, Kt.
Thomas, Sir John Maldwyn, Kt.
Thomas, *Prof.* Sir John Meurig, Kt., FRS
Thomas, Sir Keith Vivian, Kt.
Thomas, Sir Robert Evan, Kt.
Thomas, *Hon.* Sir Roger John Laugharne, Kt.
Thomas, *Hon.* Sir Swinton Barclay, Kt.
Thomas, Sir William James Cooper, Bt., TD (1919)
Thomas, Sir (William) Michael (Marsh), Bt. (1918)
Thomas, *Adm.* Sir (William) Richard Scott, KCB, KCVO, OBE
Thompson, Sir Christopher Peile, Bt. (1890)
Thompson, Sir Clive Malcolm, Kt.
Thompson, Sir Donald, Kt.
Thompson, Sir Gilbert Williamson, Kt., OBE
Thompson, *Surgeon Vice-Adm.* Sir Godfrey James Milton-, KBE
Thompson, Sir (Humphrey) Simon Meysey-, Bt. (1874)
Thompson, *Prof.* Sir Michael Warwick, Kt., D.SC
Thompson, Sir Paul Anthony, Bt. (1963)
Thompson, Sir Peter Anthony, Kt.
Thompson, Sir Richard Hilton Marler, Bt. (1963)

Thompson, Sir (Thomas) Lionel Tennyson, Bt. (1806)

Thomson, Sir Adam, Kt., CBE

Thomson, Sir (Frederick Douglas) David, Bt. (1929)

Thomson, Sir John Adam, GCMG

Thomson, Sir John (Ian) Sutherland, KBE, CMG

Thomson, Sir Mark Wilfrid Home, Bt. (1925)

Thomson, Sir Thomas James, Kt., CBE, FRCP

Thorn, Sir John Samuel, Kt., OBE

Thorne, *Maj.-Gen.* Sir David Calthrop, KBE, CVO

Thorne, Sir Neil Gordon, Kt., OBE, TD

Thorne, Sir Peter Francis, KCVO, CBE

Thornton, Sir (George) Malcolm, Kt.

Thornton, *Lt.-Gen.* Sir Leonard Whitmore, KCB, CBE

Thornton, Sir Peter Eustace, KCB

Thornton, Sir Richard Eustace, KCVO, OBE

Thorold, Sir Anthony Henry, Bt., OBE, DSC (1642)

Thorpe, *Hon.* Sir Mathew Alexander, Kt.

Thouron, Sir John Rupert Hunt, KBE

Thwaites, Sir Bryan, Kt., ph.D.

Thwin, Sir U, Kt.

Tibbits, *Capt.* Sir David Stanley, Kt., DSC

Tickell, Sir Crispin Charles Cervantes, GCMG, KCVO

Tidbury, Sir Charles Henderson, Kt.

Tikaram, Sir Moti, KBE

Tims, Sir Michael David, KCVO

Tindle, Sir Ray Stanley, Kt., CBE

Tippet, *Vice-Adm.* Sir Anthony Sanders, KCB

†Tipping, Sir David Gwynne Evans-, Bt. (1913)

Tirvengadum, Sir Harry Krishnan, Kt.

Titman, Sir John Edward Powis, KCVO

Tod, *Air Marshal* Sir John Hunter Hunter-, KBE, CB

Tod, *Vice-Adm.* Sir Jonathan James Richard, KCB, CBE

Todd, *Prof.* Sir David, Kt., CBE

Todd, Sir Ian Pelham, KBE, FRCS

Todd, *Hon.* Sir (Reginald Stephen) Garfield, Kt.

Tollemache, Sir Lyonel Humphry John, Bt. (1793)

Tololo, Sir Alkan, KBE

Tomkins, Sir Alfred George, Kt., CBE

Tomkins, Sir Edward Emile, GCMG, CVO

Tomkys, Sir (William) Roger, KCMG

Tomlinson, *Prof.* Sir Bernard Evans, Kt., CBE

Tooley, Sir John, Kt.

Tooth, Sir (Hugh) John Lucas-, Bt. (1920)

ToRobert, Sir Henry Thomas, KBE

Tory, Sir Geofroy William, KCMG

Touche, Sir Anthony George, Bt. (1920)

Touche, Sir Rodney Gordon, Bt. (1962)

Toulson, *Hon.* Sir Roger Grenfell, Kt.

Tovey, Sir Brian John Maynard, KCMG

ToVue, Sir Ronald, Kt., OBE

Towneley, Sir Simon Peter Edmund Cosmo William, KCVO

Townsend, Sir Cyril David, Kt.

Townsend, *Rear-Adm.* Sir Leslie William, KCVO, CBE

Townsing, Sir Kenneth Joseph, Kt., CMG

Traill, Sir Alan Towers, GBE

Trant, *Gen.* Sir Richard Brooking, KCB

Travers, Sir Thomas à'Beckett, Kt.

Treacher, *Adm.* Sir John Devereux, KCB

Trehane, Sir (Walter) Richard, Kt.

Treitel, *Prof.* Sir Guenter Heinz, Kt., FBA, QC

Trelawny, Sir John Barry Salusbury-, Bt. (1628)

Trench, Sir Peter Edward, Kt., CBE, TD

Trescowthick, Sir Donald Henry, KBE

†Trevelyan, Sir Edward (Norman), Bt. (1662)

Trevelyan, Sir Geoffrey Washington, Bt. (1874)

Trewby, *Vice-Adm.* Sir (George Francis) Allan, KCB, FEng.

Trezise, Sir Kenneth Bruce, Kt., OBE

Trippier, Sir David Austin, Kt., RD

Tritton, Sir Anthony John Ernest, Bt. (1905)

Trollope, Sir Anthony Simon, Bt. (1642)

Trotman, Sir Alexander, Kt.

Trotter, Sir Neville Guthrie, Kt.

Trotter, Sir Ronald Ramsay, Kt.

Troubridge, Sir Thomas Richard, Bt. (1799)

Troup, *Vice-Adm.* Sir (John) Anthony (Rose), KCB, DSC

Trowbridge, *Rear-Adm.* Sir Richard John, KCVO

Truscott, Sir George James Irving, Bt. (1909)

Tuck, Sir Bruce Adolph Reginald, Bt. (1910)

Tucker, *Hon.* Sir Richard Howard, Kt.

Tuckey, *Hon.* Sir Simon Lane, Kt.

Tuita, Sir Mariano Kelesimalefo, Kt., OBE

Tuite, Sir Christopher Hugh, Bt., ph.D. (1622)

Tuivaga, Sir Timoci Uluiburotu, Kt.

Tuke, Sir Anthony Favill, Kt.

Tumim, *His Hon.* Sir Stephen, Kt.

Tupper, Sir Charles Hibbert, Bt. (1888)

Turbott, Sir Ian Graham, Kt., CMG, CVO

Turing, Sir John Dermot, Bt. (s. 1638)

Turnberg, *Prof.* Sir Leslie Arnold, Kt., MD, FRCP

Turnbull, Sir Andrew, KCB, CVO

Turnbull, Sir Richard Gordon, GCMG

Turner, Sir Colin William Carstairs, Kt., CBE, DFC

Turner, *Hon.* Sir Michael John, Kt.

Turnquest, Sir Orville Alton, GCMG, QC

Tuti, *Revd* Dudley, KBE

Tweedie, *Prof.* Sir David Philip, Kt.

Tyree, Sir (Alfred) William, Kt., OBE

Tyrwhitt, Sir Reginald Thomas Newman, Bt. (1919)

Udoma, *Hon.* Sir (Egbert) Udo, Kt.

Unsworth, *Hon.* Sir Edgar Ignatius Godfrey, Kt., CMG

Unwin, Sir (James) Brian, KCB

Ure, Sir John Burns, KCMG, LVO

Urquhart, Sir Brian Edward, KCMG, MBE

Urwick, Sir Alan Bedford, KCVO, CMG

Usher, Sir Leonard Gray, KBE

Usher, Sir (William) John Tevenar, Bt. (1899)

Ustinov, Sir Peter Alexander, Kt., CBE

Utting, Sir William Benjamin, Kt., CB

Vai, Sir Mea, Kt., CBE, ISO

Vallance, Sir Iain David Thomas, Kt.

Vallat, Sir Francis Aimé, GBE, KCMG, QC

Vallings, *Vice-Adm.* Sir George Montague Francis, KCB

Vanderfelt, Sir Robin Victor, KBE

Vane, Sir John Robert, Kt., D.phil., D.SC., FRS

Vanneck, *Air Cdre* Hon. Sir Peter Beckford Rutgers, GBE, CB, AFC

van Straubenzee, Sir William Radcliffe, Kt., MBE

Vasquez, Sir Alfred Joseph, Kt., CBE, QC

Vaughan, Sir Gerard Folliott, Kt. , FRCP

†Vavasour, Sir Eric Michael Joseph Marmaduke, Bt. (1828)

Veale, Sir Alan John Ralph, Kt., FEng.

Verco, Sir Walter John George, KCVO

†Verney, Sir John Sebastian, Bt. (1946)

Verney, *Hon.* Sir Lawrence John, Kt., TD

Verney, Sir Ralph Bruce, Bt., KBE (1818)

Vernon, Sir James, Kt., CBE

Vernon, Sir Nigel John Douglas, Bt. (1914)

Vernon, Sir (William) Michael, Kt.

Vesey, Sir (Nathaniel) Henry (Peniston), Kt., CBE

Vestey, Sir (John) Derek, Bt. (1921)

Vial, Sir Kenneth Harold, Kt., CBE

Vick, Sir (Francis) Arthur, Kt., OBE, ph.D.

Vickers, *Lt.-Gen.* Sir Richard Maurice Hilton, KCB, LVO, OBE

Victoria, Sir (Joseph Aloysius) Donatus, Kt., CBE

Vincent, Sir William Percy Maxwell, Bt. (1936)

Vinelott, *Hon.* Sir John Evelyn, Kt.

Vines, Sir William Joshua, Kt., CMG

†Vyvyan, Sir Ralph Ferrers Alexander, Bt. (1645)

Waddell, Sir Alexander Nicol Anton, KCMG, DSC

Waddell, Sir James Henderson, Kt., CB

Wade, *Prof.* Sir Henry William Rawson, Kt., QC, FBA

Wade, *Air Chief Marshal* Sir Ruthven Lowry, KCB, DFC

Waine, *Rt. Revd* John, KCVO

Waite, *Rt. Hon.* Sir John Douglas, Kt.

Wake, Sir Hereward, Bt., MC (1621)

Wakefield, Sir (Edward) Humphry (Tyrell), Bt. (1962)

Wakefield, Sir Norman Edward, Kt.

Wakefield, Sir Peter George Arthur, KBE, CMG

Wakeford, *Air Marshal* Sir Richard Gordon, KCB, OBE, LVO, AFC

Wakeley, Sir John Cecil Nicholson, Bt., FRCS (1952)

†Wakeman, Sir Edward Offley Bertram, Bt. (1828)

Walford, Sir Christopher Rupert, Kt.

Walker, *Revd* Alan Edgar, Kt., OBE

Walker, *Gen.* Sir Antony Kenneth Frederick, KCB

Walker, Sir Baldwin Patrick, Bt. (1856)

Walker, Sir (Charles) Michael, GCMG

Walker, Sir Colin John Shedlock, Kt., OBE

Walker, Sir David Alan, Kt.

Walker, Sir Gervas George, Kt.

Walker, Sir Harold Berners, KCMG

Walker, *Maj.* Sir Hugh Ronald, Bt. (1906)

Walker, Sir James Graham, Kt., MBE

Walker, Sir James Heron, Bt. (1868)

Walker, *Air Marshal* Sir John Robert, KCB, CBE, AFC

Walker, *Gen.* Sir Michael John Dawson, KCB, CMG, CBE

Walker, Sir Michael Leolin Forestier-, Bt. (1835)

Walker, Sir Miles Rawstron, Kt., CBE

Walker, Sir Patrick Jeremy, KCB

Walker, *Rt. Hon.* Sir Robert, Kt.

Walker, Sir Rodney Myerscough, Kt.

Walker, *Hon.* Sir Timothy Edward, Kt.

Walker, *Gen.* Sir Walter Colyear, KCB, CBE, DSO

Wall, Sir (John) Stephen, KCMG, LVO

Wall, *Hon.* Sir Nicholas Peter Rathbone, Kt.

Wall, Sir Robert William, Kt., OBE

Wallace, *Lt.-Gen.* Sir Christopher Brooke Quentin, KBE

Wallace, Sir Ian James, Kt., CBE

Waller, *Hon.* Sir (George) Mark, Kt.

Waller, *Rt. Hon.* Sir George Stanley, Kt., OBE

Waller, Sir Robert William, Bt. (I. 1780)

Walley, Sir John, KBE, CB

Wallis, Sir Peter Gordon, KCVO

Wallis, Sir Timothy William, Kt.

Walmsley, *Vice-Adm.* Sir Robert, KCB

Walsh, Sir Alan, Kt., D.SC., FRS

Walsh, *Prof.* Sir John Patrick, KBE

†Walsham, Sir Timothy John, Bt. (1831)

Walters, *Prof.* Sir Alan Arthur, Kt.

Walters, Sir Dennis Murray, Kt., MBE

Walters, Sir Frederick Donald, Kt.

Walters, Sir Peter Ingram, Kt.

Walters, Sir Roger Talbot, KBE, FRIBA

Walton, Sir John Robert, Kt.

Wan, Sir Wamp, Kt., MBE

Wanstall, *Hon.* Sir Charles Gray, Kt.

Ward, *Rt. Hon.* Sir Alan Hylton, Kt.

Ward, Sir John Devereux, Kt., CBE

Ward, Sir Joseph James Laffey, Bt. (1911)

Ward, *Maj.-Gen.* Sir Philip John Newling, KCVO, CBE

Ward, Sir Timothy James, Kt.

Wardale, Sir Geoffrey Charles, KCB

Wardlaw, Sir Henry (John), Bt. (S. 1631)

Waring, Sir (Alfred) Holburt, Bt. (1935)

Warmington, Sir David Marshall, Bt. (1908)

Warner, Sir (Edward Courtenay) Henry, Bt. (1910)

Warner, Sir Edward Redston, KCMG, OBE

Warner, *Prof.* Sir Frederick Edward, Kt., FRS, FEng.

Warner, Sir Gerald Chierici, KCMG

Warner, *Hon.* Sir Jean-Pierre Frank Eugene, Kt.

Warren, Sir (Frederick) Miles, KBE

Warren, Sir Kenneth Robin, Kt.

†Warren, Sir Michael Blackley, Bt. (1784)

Wass, Sir Douglas William Gretton, GCB

Waterhouse, *Hon.* Sir Ronald Gough, Kt.

Waterlow, Sir Christopher Rupert, Bt. (1873)

Waterlow, Sir (James) Gerard, Bt. (1930)

Waters, *Gen.* Sir (Charles) John, GCB, CBE

Waters, Sir (Thomas) Neil (Morris), Kt.

Wates, Sir Christopher Stephen, Kt.

Watkins, *Rt. Hon.* Sir Tasker, VC, GBE

Watson, Sir Bruce Dunstan, Kt.

Watson, *Prof.* Sir David John, Kt., PH.D.

Watson, Sir Duncan Amos, Kt., CBE

Watson, Sir (James) Andrew, Bt. (1866)

Watson, Sir John Forbes Inglefield-, Bt. (1895)

Watson, Sir Michael Milne-, Bt., CBE (1937)

Watson, Sir (Noel) Duncan, KCMG

Watson, *Vice-Adm.* Sir Philip Alexander, KBE, LVO

Watson, Sir Ronald Matthew, Kt., CBE

Watt, *Surgeon Vice-Adm.* Sir James, KBE, FRCS

Watt, Sir James Harvie-, Bt. (1945)

Watts, Sir Arthur Desmond, KCMG

Watts, *Lt.-Gen.* Sir John Peter Barry Condliffe, KBE, CB, MC

Wauchope, Sir Roger (Hamilton) Don-, Bt. (S. 1667)

Way, Sir Richard George Kitchener, KCB, CBE

Weatherall, *Prof.* Sir David John, Kt., FRS

Weatherall, *Vice-Adm.* Sir James Lamb, KBE

Weatherstone, Sir Dennis, KBE

Weaver, Sir Tobias Rushton, Kt., CB

Webb, Sir Thomas Langley, Kt.

Webster, *Very Revd* Alan Brunskill, KCVO

Webster, *Vice-Adm.* Sir John Morrison, KCB

Webster, *Hon.* Sir Peter Edlin, Kt.

Wedderburn, Sir Andrew John Alexander Ogilvy-, Bt. (1803)

Wedgwood, Sir (Hugo) Martin, Bt. (1942)

Weekes, Sir Everton DeCourcey, KCMG, OBE

Weinberg, Sir Mark Aubrey, Kt.

Weir, Sir Michael Scott, KCMG

Weir, Sir Roderick Bignell, Kt.

Welby, Sir (Richard) Bruno Gregory, Bt. (1801)

Welch, Sir John Reader, Bt. (1957)

Weldon, Sir Anthony William, Bt. (I. 1723)

Weller, Sir Arthur Burton, Kt., CBE

Wellings, Sir Jack Alfred, Kt., CBE

†Wells, Sir Christopher Charles, Bt. (1944)

Wells, Sir John Julius, Kt.

Wells, Sir William Henry Weston, Kt., FRICS

Westbrook, Sir Neil Gowanloch, Kt., CBE

Westerman, Sir (Wilfred) Alan, Kt., CBE

Weston, Sir Michael Charles Swift, KCMG, CVO

Weston, Sir (Philip) John, KCMG

Whalen, Sir Geoffrey Henry, Kt., CBE

Wheeler, Sir Harry Anthony, Kt., OBE

Wheeler, *Air Chief Marshal* Sir (Henry) Neil (George), GCB, CBE, DSO, DFC, AFC

Wheeler, *Rt. Hon.* Sir John Daniel, Kt.

Wheeler, Sir John Hieron, Bt. (1920)

Wheeler, *Gen.* Sir Roger Neil, GCB, CBE

Wheler, Sir Edward Woodford, Bt. (1660)

Whent, Sir Gerald Arthur, Kt., CBE

Whishaw, Sir Charles Percival Law, Kt.

Whitaker, *Maj.* Sir James Herbert Ingham, Bt., OBE (1936)

White, Sir Christopher Robert Meadows, Bt. (1937)

White, *Hon.* Sir Christopher Stuart Stuart-, Kt.

White, Sir David Harry, Kt.

White, Sir Frank John, Kt.

White, Sir George Stanley James, Bt. (1904)

White, *Wg Cdr.* Sir Henry Arthur Dalrymple-, Bt., DFC (1926)

White, *Adm.* Sir Hugo Moresby, GCB, CBE

White, *Hon.* Sir John Charles, Kt., MBE

White, Sir John Woolmer, Bt. (1922)

White, Sir Lynton Stuart, Kt., MBE, TD

White, Sir Nicholas Peter Archibald, Bt. (1802)

White, *Adm.* Sir Peter, GBE

Whitehead, Sir John Stainton, GCMG, CVO

Whitehead, Sir Rowland John Rathbone, Bt. (1889)

Whiteley, Sir Hugo Baldwin Huntington-, Bt. (1918)

Whiteley, *Gen.* Sir Peter John Frederick, GCB, OBE, RM

Whitfield, Sir William, Kt., CBE

Whitford, *Hon.* Sir John Norman Keates, Kt.

Whitmore, Sir Clive Anthony, GCB, CVO

Whitmore, Sir John Henry Douglas, Bt. (1954)

Whitney, Sir Raymond William, Kt., OBE, MP

Whittome, Sir (Leslie) Alan, Kt.

Wickerson, Sir John Michael, Kt.

Wicks, Sir James Albert, Kt.

Wicks, Sir Nigel Leonard, KCB, CVO, CBE

†Wigan, Sir Michael Iain, Bt. (1898)

Wiggin, Sir Alfred William (Jerry), Kt., TD

†Wiggin, Sir Charles Rupert John, Bt. (1892)

Wigram, *Revd Canon* Sir Clifford Woolmore, Bt. (1805)

Wilbraham, Sir Richard Baker, Bt. (1776)

Wilford, Sir (Kenneth) Michael, GCMG

Wilkes, *Gen.* Sir Michael John, KCB, CBE

Wilkins, Sir Graham John, Kt.

Wilkinson, Sir (David) Graham (Brook) Bt. (1941)

Wilkinson, *Prof.* Sir Denys Haigh, Kt., FRS

Wilkinson, Sir Peter Allix, KCMG, DSO, OBE

Wilkinson, Sir Philip William, Kt.

Willcocks, Sir David Valentine, Kt., CBE, MC

Williams, Sir Alastair Edgcumbe James Dudley-, Bt. (1964)

Williams, Sir Alwyn, Kt., PH.D., FRS, FRSE

Williams, Sir Arthur Dennis Pitt, Kt.

Williams, Sir (Arthur) Gareth Ludovic Emrys Rhys, Bt. (1918)

Williams, *Prof.* Sir Bruce Rodda, KBE

Williams, Sir Daniel Charles, GCMG, QC

Williams, *Adm.* Sir David, GCB

Williams, *Prof.* Sir David Glyndwr Tudor, Kt.

Williams, Sir David Innes, Kt.

Williams, *Hon.* Sir Denys Ambrose, KCMG

Williams, Sir Donald Mark, Bt. (1866)

Williams, *Prof.* Sir (Edward) Dillwyn, Kt., FRCP

Williams, *Hon.* Sir Edward Stratten, KCMG, KBE

Williams, *Prof.* Sir Glanmor, Kt., CBE, FBA

Williams, Sir Henry Sydney, Kt., OBE

Williams, Sir John Robert, KCMG

Williams, Sir (Lawrence) Hugh, Bt. (1798)

Williams, Sir Leonard, KBE, CB

Williams, Sir Osmond, Bt., MC (1909)

Williams, Sir Peter Michael, Kt.

Williams, *Prof.* Sir Robert Evan Owen, Kt., MD, FRCP

Williams, Sir (Robert) Philip Nathaniel, Bt. (1915)

Williams, Sir Robin Philip, Bt. (1953)

Williams, Sir (William) Maxwell (Harries), Kt.

Williamson, Sir David Francis, GCMG, CB

Williamson, *Marshal of the Royal Air Force* Sir Keith Alec, GCB, AFC

Williamson, Sir (Nicholas Frederick) Hedworth, Bt. (1642)

Willink, Sir Charles William, Bt. (1957)

Willis, *Hon.* Sir Eric Archibald, KBE, CMG

Willis, *Vice-Adm.* Sir (Guido) James, KBE

Willis, *Air Chief Marshal* Sir John Frederick, GBE, KCB

Willison, *Lt.-Gen.* Sir David John, KCB, OBE, MC

Willison, Sir John Alexander, Kt., OBE

†Wills, Sir David James Vernon, Bt. (1923)

Wills, Sir David Seton, Bt. (1904)

Wills, Sir (Hugh) David Hamilton, Kt., CBE, TD

Wills, Sir John Vernon, Bt., KCVO, TD (1923)

Wilmot, Sir Henry Robert, Bt. (1759)

Wilmot, Sir Michael John Assheton Eardley-, Bt. (1821)

Wilsey, *Gen.* Sir John Finlay Willasey, GCB, CBE

Wilson, *Lt.-Gen.* Sir (Alexander) James, KBE, MC

Wilson, Sir Anthony, Kt.

Wilson, *Vice-Adm.* Sir Barry Nigel, KCB

Wilson, *Lt.-Col.* Sir Blair Aubyn Stewart-, KCVO

Wilson, Sir Charles Haynes, Kt.

Wilson, *Prof.* Sir Colin Alexander St John, Kt., RA, FRIBA

Wilson, Sir David, Bt. (1920)

Wilson, Sir David Mackenzie, Kt.

Wilson, Sir Geoffrey Masterman, KCB, CMG

Wilson, Sir James William Douglas, Bt. (1906)

Wilson, Sir John Foster, Kt., CBE

Wilson, *Brig.* Sir Mathew John Anthony, Bt., OBE, MC (1874)

Wilson, *Hon.* Sir Nicholas Allan Roy, Kt.

Wilson, Sir Patrick Michael Ernest David McNair-, Kt.

Wilson, Sir Reginald Holmes, Kt.

Wilson, Sir Richard Thomas James, KCB

Wilson, Sir Robert, Kt., CBE

Wilson, Sir Robert Donald, KBE

Wilson, *Rt. Revd* Roger Plumpton, KCVO, DD

Wilson, Sir Roland, KBE

Wilson, *Air Chief Marshal* Sir (Ronald) Andrew (Fellowes), KCB, AFC

Wilson, *Hon.* Sir Ronald Darling, KBE, CMG

Wilton, Sir (Arthur) John, KCMG, KCVO, MC

Wingate, *Capt.* Sir Miles Buckley, KCVO

Winnington, Sir Francis Salwey William, Bt. (1755)

Winskill, *Air Cdre* Sir Archibald Little, KCVO, CBE, DFC

Winterbottom, Sir Walter, Kt., CBE

Wiseman, Sir John William, Bt. (1628)

Wolfendale, *Prof.* Sir Arnold Whittaker, Kt., FRS

Wolfson, Sir Brian Gordon, Kt.

Wolseley, Sir Charles Garnet Richard Mark, Bt. (1628)

†Wolseley, Sir James Douglas, Bt. (I. 1745)

Wolstenholme, Sir Gordon Ethelbert Ward, Kt., OBE

Wombwell, Sir George Philip Frederick, Bt. (1778)

Womersley, Sir Peter John Walter, Bt. (1945)

Woo, Sir Leo Joseph, Kt.

Wood, Sir Alan Marshall Muir, Kt., FRS, FEng.

Wood, Sir Andrew Marley, KCMG

Wood, Sir Anthony John Page, Bt. (1837)

Wood, Sir David Basil Hill-, Bt. (1921)

Wood, Sir Frederick Ambrose Stuart, Kt.

Wood, Sir Ian Clark, Kt., CBE

Wood, *Prof.* Sir John Crossley, Kt., CBE

The Military Knights of Windsor

The Military Knights of Windsor take part in all ceremonies of the Noble Order of the Garter and attend Sunday morning service in St George's Chapel, Windsor Castle, as representatives of the Knights of the Garter. The Knights receive a small stipend in addition to their army pensions and quarters in Windsor Castle.

The Knights of Windsor were originally founded in 1348 after the wars in France to assist English knights, who, having been prisoners in the hands of the French, had become impoverished by the payment of heavy ransoms. When Edward III founded the Order of the Garter later the same year, he incorporated the Knights of Windsor and the College of St George into its foundation and raised the number of Knights to 26 to correspond with the number of the Knights of the Garter. Known later as the Alms Knights or Poor Knights of Windsor, their establishment was

reduced under the will of Henry VIII to 13 and statutes were drawn up by Elizabeth I.

In 1833, William IV changed their designation to The Military Knights and granted them their present uniform which consists of a scarlet tail-coat with white cross sword-belt, crimson sash and cocked hat with plume. The badges are the Shield of St George and the Star of the Order of the Garter.

Governor, Maj.-Gen. Peter Downward, CB, DSO, DFC
Military Knights, Brig. A. L. Atkinson, OBE; Brig. J. F. Lindner, OBE, MC; Maj. W. L. Thompson, MVO, MBE, DCM; Maj. J. C. Cowley, OBE, DCM; Maj. G. R. Mitchell, MBE, BEM; Lt.-Col. R. L. C. Tamplin; Maj. P. H. Bolton, MBE; Brig. T. W. Hackworth, OBE; Maj. R. J. Moore; Lt.-Col. R. R. Giles; Maj. R. J. de M. Gainher; Maj. A. H. Clarkson
Supernumerary, Brig. A. C. Tyler, CBE, MC

The Order of St John

THE MOST VENERABLE ORDER OF THE HOSPITAL OF ST JOHN OF JERUSALEM (1888)

GCStJ   Bailiff/Dame Grand Cross
KStJ   Knight of Justice/Grace
DStJ   Dame of Justice/Grace
ChStJ   Chaplain
CStJ   Commander
OStJ   Officer
SBStJ   Serving Brother
SSStJ   Serving Sister
EsqStJ   Esquire

Mottoes, Pro Fide *and* Pro Utilitate Hominum

The Order of St John, founded in the early 12th century in Jerusalem, was a religious order with a particular duty to care for the sick. In Britain the Order was dissolved by Henry VIII in 1540 but the British branch was revived in the early 19th century. The branch was not accepted by the Grand Magistracy of the Order in Rome but its search for a role in the tradition of the Hospitallers led to the founding of the St John Ambulance Association in 1877 and later the St John Ambulance Brigade; in 1882 the St

John Ophthalmic Hospital was founded in Jerusalem. A royal charter was granted in 1888 establishing the British Order of St John as a British Order of Chivalry with the Sovereign as its head.

Admission to the Order is conferred in recognition of service, usually in St John Ambulance. Membership does not confer any rank, style, title or precedence on a recipient.

SOVEREIGN HEAD OF THE ORDER
HM The Queen

GRAND PRIOR
HRH The Duke of Gloucester, KG, GCVO

Lord Prior, The Lord Vestey
Prelate, The Rt. Revd M. A. Mann, KCVO
Chancellor, Prof. A. R. Mellows, TD
Bailiff of Egle, The Lord Remnant
Headquarters, St John's Gate, Clerkenwell, London ECIM 4DA. Tel: 0171-253 6644

Dames Grand Cross and Dames Commanders

Style, 'Dame' before forename and surname, followed by appropriate post-nominal initials. Where such an award is made to a lady already in enjoyment of a higher title, the appropriate initials follow her name
Husband, Untitled
For forms of address, *see* page 135

Dame Grand Cross and Dame Commander are the higher classes for women of the Order of the Bath, the Order of St Michael and St George, the Royal Victorian Order, and the

Order of the British Empire. Dames Grand Cross rank after the wives of Baronets and before the wives of Knights Grand Cross. Dames Commanders rank after the wives of Knights Grand Cross and before the wives of Knights Commanders.

Honorary Dames Commanders may be conferred on women who are citizens of countries of which The Queen is not head of state.

LIST OF DAMES   *Revised to 31 August 1998*

Women peers in their own right and life peers are not included in this list. Female members of the royal family are not included in this list; details of the orders they hold are given on pages 117–8

If a dame has a double barrelled or hyphenated surname, she is listed under the final element of the name
A full entry in italic type indicates that the recipient of an honour died during the year in which the honour was conferred. The name is included for the purposes of record

Abaijah, Dame Josephine, DBE
Abel Smith, Lady, DCVO
Abergavenny, The Marchioness of, DCVO
Airlie, The Countess of, DCVO
Albemarle, The Countess of, DBE
Anderson, *Brig.* Hon. Dame Mary Mackenzie (Mrs Pihl), DBE
Anglesey, The Marchioness of, DBE
Anson, Lady (Elizabeth Audrey), DBE
Anstee, Dame Margaret Joan, DCMG
Arden, *Hon.* Dame Mary Howarth (Mrs Mance), DBE
Baker, Dame Janet Abbott (Mrs Shelley), CH, DBE
Ballin, Dame Reubina Ann, DBE
Barnes, Dame (Alice) Josephine (Mary Taylor), DBE, FRCP, FRCS
Barrow, Dame Jocelyn Anita (Mrs Downer), DBE
Barstow, Dame Josephine Clare (Mrs Anderson), DBE
Basset, Lady Elizabeth, DCVO
Bean, Dame Majorie Louise, DBE
Beaurepaire, Dame Beryl Edith, DBE
Beer, *Prof.* Dame Gillian Patricia Kempster, DBE, FBA
Bergquist, *Prof.* Dame Patricia Rose, DBE
Berry, Dame Alice Miriam, DBE
Blaize, Dame Venetia Ursula, DBE
Blaxland, Dame Helen Frances, DBE
Booth, *Hon.* Dame Margaret Myfanwy Wood, DBE
Bottomley, Dame Bessie Ellen, DBE
Bowman, Dame (Mary) Elaine Kellett-, DBE
Bowtell, Dame Ann Elizabeth, DCB

Boyd, Dame Vivienne Myra, DBE
Bracewell, *Hon.* Dame Joyanne Winifred (Mrs Copeland), DBE
Brain, Dame Margaret Anne (Mrs Wheeler), DBE
Brazill, Dame Josephine (Sister Mary Philippa), DBE
Bridges, Dame Mary Patricia, DBE
Brown, Dame Gillian Gerda, DCVO, CMG
Browne, Lady Moyra Blanche Madeleine, DBE
Bryans, Dame Anne Margaret, DBE
Buttfield, Dame Nancy Eileen, DBE
Bynoe, Dame Hilda Louisa, DBE
Caldicott, Dame Fiona, DBE, FRCP, FRCPsych.
Cartland, Dame Barbara Hamilton, DBE
Cartwright, Dame Silvia Rose, DBE
Casey, Dame Stella Katherine, DBE
Charles, Dame (Mary) Eugenia, DBE
Chesterton, Dame Elizabeth Ursula, DBE
Clark, *Prof.* Dame (Margaret) June, DBE, PH.D.
Clay, Dame Marie Mildred, DBE
Clayton, Dame Barbara Evelyn (Mrs Klyne), DBE
Cleland, Dame Rachel, DBE
Coll, Dame Elizabeth Anne Loosemore Esteve-, DBE
Collarbone, Dame Patricia, DBE
Corsar, The Hon. Dame Mary Drummond, DBE
Coulshed, Dame (Mary) Frances, DBE, TD
Daws, Dame Joyce Margaretta, DBE
Dell, Dame Miriam Patricia, DBE
Dench, Dame Judith Olivia (Mrs Williams), DBE
de Valois, Dame Ninette, OM, CH, DBE
Digby, Lady, DBE
Donaldson, Dame (Dorothy) Mary (Lady Donaldson of Lymington), GBE
Drake, *Brig.* Dame Jean Elizabeth Rivett-, DBE
Dugdale, Kathryn, Lady, DCVO
Dumont, Dame Ivy Leona, DCMG
Dyche, Dame Rachael Mary, DBE
Ebsworth, *Hon.* Dame Ann Marian, DBE

Engel, Dame Pauline Frances (Sister Pauline Engel), DBE
Evison, Dame Helen June Patricia, DBE
Fenner, Dame Peggy Edith, DBE
Fitton, Dame Doris Alice (Mrs Mason), DBE
Fort, Dame Maeve Geraldine, DCMG
Fraser, Dame Dorothy Rita, DBE
Friend, Dame Phyllis Muriel, DBE
Fritchie, Dame Irene Tordoff (Dame Rennie Fritchie), DBE
Frost, Dame Phyllis Irene, DBE
Fry, Dame Margaret Louise, DBE
Gallagher, Dame Monica Josephine, DBE
Gardiner, Dame Helen Louisa, DBE, MVO
Giles, *Air Comdt.* Dame Pauline (Mrs Parsons), DBE, RRC
Goodman, Dame Barbara, DBE
Gordon, Dame Minita Elmira, GCMG, GCVO
Gow, Dame Jane Elizabeth (Mrs Whiteley), DBE
Grafton, The Duchess of, GCVO
Green, Dame Mary Georgina, DBE
Grey, Dame Beryl Elizabeth (Mrs Svenson), DBE
Grimthorpe, The Lady, DCVO
Guilfoyle, Dame Margaret Georgina Constance, DBE
Guthardt, *Revd Dr* Dame Phyllis Myra, DBE
Haig, Dame Mary Alison Glen-, DBE
Hale, *Hon.* Dame Brenda Marjorie (Mrs Farrand), DBE
Harper, Dame Elizabeth Margaret Way, DBE
Heilbron, *Hon.* Dame Rose, DBE
Henderson, Dame Louise Etiennette Sidonie, DBE
Henrison, Dame Anne Elizabeth Rosina, DBE
Herbison, Dame Jean Marjory, DBE, CMG
Hercus, *Hon.* Dame (Margaret) Ann, DCMG
Hetet, Dame Rangimarie, DBE
Higgins, *Prof.* Dame Rosalyn, DBE, QC
Hill, *Air Cdre* Dame Felicity Barbara, DBE
Hiller, Dame Wendy (Mrs Gow), DBE

Hine, Dame Deirdre Joan, DBE, FRCP

Hird, Dame Thora (Mrs Scott), DBE

Hogg, *Hon.* Dame Mary Claire (Mrs Koops), DBE

Howard, Dame (Rosemary) Christian, DBE

Hunter, Dame Pamela, DBE

Hurley, *Prof.* Dame Rosalinde (Mrs Gortvai), DBE

Hussey, Lady Susan Katharine (Lady Hussey of North Bradley), DCVO

Imison, Dame Tamsyn, DBE

Isaacs, Dame Albertha Madeline, DBE

James, Dame Naomi Christine (Mrs Haythorne), DBE

Jenkins, Dame (Mary) Jennifer (Lady Jenkins of Hillhead), DBE

Jones, Dame Gwyneth (Mrs Haberfeld-Jones), DBE

Jones, Dame (Lilian) Pauline Neville-, DCMG

Kekedo, Dame Mary, DBE, BEM

Kekedo, Dame Rosalina Violet, DBE

Kelleher, Dame Joan, DBE

Kelly, Dame Lorna May Boreland, DBE

Kershaw, Dame Janet Elizabeth Murray (Dame Betty), DBE

Kettlewell, *Comdt.* Dame Marion Mildred, DBE

Kilroy, Dame Alix Hester Marie (Lady Meynell), DBE

Kirby, Dame Georgina Kamiria, DBE

Kirk, Dame (Lucy) Ruth, DBE

Kramer, *Prof.* Dame Leonie Judith, DBE

Laine, Dame Cleo (Clementine) Dinah (Mrs Dankworth), DBE

Lamb, Dame Dawn Ruth, DBE

Lewis, Dame Edna Leofrida (Lady Lewis), DBE

Lister, Dame Unity Viola, DBE

Litchfield, Dame Ruby Beatrice, DBE

Lott, Dame Felicity Ann Emwhyla (Mrs Woolf), DBE

Lowrey, *Air Comdt.* Dame Alice, DBE, RRC

Lympany, Dame Moura, DBE

Lynn, Dame Vera (Mrs Lewis), DBE

Mackinnon, Dame (Una) Patricia, DBE

Macknight, Dame Ella Annie Noble, DBE, MD

McLaren, Dame Anne Laura, DBE, FRCOG, FRS

Macmillan of Ovenden, Katharine, Viscountess, DBE

Major, Dame Malvina Lorraine (Mrs Fleming), DBE

Mann, Dame Ida Caroline, DBE, D.SC., FRCS

Markova, Dame Alicia, DBE

Martin, Rosamund Mary Holland-, Lady, DBE

Masters, Dame Sheila Valerie (Mrs Noakes), DBE

Metcalf, Dame Helen, DBE

Metge, *Dr* Dame (Alice) Joan, DBE

Middleton, Dame Elaine Madoline, DCMG, MBE

Miller, Dame Mabel Flora Hobart, DBE

Miller, Dame Mary Elizabeth Hedley-, DCVO, CB

Mills, Dame Barbara Jean Lyon, DBE, QC

Mitchell, Dame Mona, DCVO

Mitchell, *Hon.* Dame Roma Flinders, DBE

Mitchell, Dame Wendy, DBE

Morrison, *Hon.* Dame Mary Anne, DCVO

Mueller, Dame Anne Elisabeth, DCB

Muldoon, Thea Dale, Lady, DBE, QSO

Mumford, Lady Mary Katharine, DCVO

Munro, Dame Alison, DBE

Murdoch, Dame Elisabeth Joy, DBE

Murdoch, Dame (Jean) Iris (Mrs Bayley), DBE

Murray, Dame (Alice) Rosemary, DBE, D.Phil.

Ogilvie, Dame Bridget Margaret, DBE, ph.D., D.SC.

Oliver, Dame Gillian Frances, DBE

Ollerenshaw, Dame Kathleen Mary, DBE, D.Phil.

Oxenbury, Dame Shirley Anne, DBE

Park, Dame Merle Florence (Mrs Bloch), DBE

Paterson, Dame Betty Fraser Ross, DBE

Peake, *Air Cdre* Dame Felicity Hyde, DBE, AE

Penhaligon, Dame Annette (Mrs Egerton), DBE

Plowden, The Lady, DBE

Poole, Dame Avril Anne Barker, DBE

Porter, Dame Shirley (Lady Porter), DBE

Prendergast, Dame Simone Ruth, DBE

Prentice, Dame Winifred Eva, DBE

Preston, Dame Frances Olivia Campbell-, DCVO

Price, Dame Margaret Berenice, DBE

Purves, Dame Daphne Helen, DBE

Pyke, Lady, DBE

Quinn, Dame Sheila Margaret Imelda, DBE

Railton, Dame Ruth (Mrs King), DBE

Rankin, Lady Jean Margaret Florence, DCVO

Raven, Dame Kathleen Annie (Mrs Ingram), DBE

Restieaux, *Dr* Dame Norma Jean, DBE

Riddelsdell, Dame Mildred, DCB, CBE

Ridley, Dame (Mildred) Betty, DBE

Ridsdale, Dame Victoire Evelyn Patricia (Lady Ridsdale), DBE

Rigg, Dame Diana, DBE

Rimington, Dame Stella, DCB

Robertson, *Cmdt.* Dame Nancy Margaret, DBE

Roe, Dame Raigh Edith, DBE

Rue, Dame (Elsie) Rosemary, DBE

Rumbold, *Rt. Hon.* Dame Angela Claire Rosemary, DBE

Runciman of Doxford, The Viscountess, DBE

Salas, Dame Margaret Laurence, DBE

Salmond, *Prof.* Dame Mary Anne, DBE

Saunders, Dame Cicely Mary Strode, OM, DBE, FRCP

Sawyer, *Hon.* Dame Joan Augusta, DBE

Schwarzkopf, Dame Elisabeth Friederike Marie Olga Legge-, DBE

Scott, Dame Catherine Campbell, DBE

Scott, Dame Jean Mary Monica Maxwell-, DCVO

Scott, Dame (Catherine) Margaret (Mary Denton), DBE

Shenfield, Dame Barbara Estelle, DBE

Sherlock, *Prof.* Dame Sheila Patricia Violet, DBE, MD, FRCP

Sibley, Dame Antoinette (Mrs Corbett), DBE

Sloss, *Rt. Hon.* Dame (Ann) Elizabeth (Oldfield) Butler-, DBE

Smieton, Dame Mary Guillan, DBE

Smith, *Hon.* Dame Janet Hilary (Mrs Mathieson), DBE

Smith, Dame Margaret Natalie (Maggie) (Mrs Cross), DBE

Smith, Dame Margot, DBE

Snagge, Dame Nancy Marion, DBE

Soames, Mary, Lady, DBE

Spark, Dame Muriel Sarah, DBE

Steel, *Hon.* Dame (Anne) Heather (Mrs Beattie), DBE

Stephens, *Air Cmdt.* Dame Anne, DBE

Stewart, Dame Muriel Acadia, DBE

Strachan, Dame Valerie Patricia Marie, DCB

Sutherland, Dame Joan (Mrs Bonynge), OM, DBE

Sutherland, Dame Veronica Evelyn, DBE, CMG

Szaszy, Dame Miraka Petricevich, DBE

Taylor, Dame Jean Elizabeth, DCVO

Te Atairangikaahu, Te Arikinui, Dame, DBE

Te Kanawa, Dame Kiri Janette (Mrs Park), DBE

Thorneycroft, Carla, Lady, DBE

Tinson, Dame Sue, DBE

Tizard, Dame Catherine Anne, GCMG, GCVO, DBE

Tokiel, Dame Rosa, DBE

Uatioa, Dame Mere, DBE

Uprichard, Dame Mary Elizabeth, DBE

Uvarov, Dame Olga, DBE

Varley, Dame Joan Fleetwood, DBE

Wagner, Dame Gillian Mary Millicent (Lady Wagner), DBE

Wall, (Alice) Anne, (Mrs Michael Wall), DCVO

Wallace, Dame (Georgina Catriona Pamela) Augusta, DBE

Warburton, Dame Anne Marion, DCVO, CMG

Warwick, Dame Margaret Elizabeth Harvey Turner-, DBE, FRCP, FRCPEd.

Waterhouse, Dame Rachel Elizabeth, DBE, ph.D.

Weir, Dame Gillian Constance (Mrs Phelps), DBE

Weston, Dame Margaret Kate, DBE

Williamson, Dame (Elsie) Marjorie, DBE, ph.D.

Winstone, Dame Dorothy Gertrude, DBE, CMG

Wong Yick-ming, Dame Rosanna, DBE

Decorations and Medals

PRINCIPAL DECORATIONS AND MEDALS
In order of precedence

Victoria Cross (VC), 1856 (*see* page 209)
George Cross (GC), 1940 (*see* pages 209–210)

British Orders of Knighthood, etc.
Baronet's Badge
Knight Bachelor's Badge

Decorations
Conspicuous Gallantry Cross (CGC), 1995
Royal Red Cross Class I (RRC), 1883
Distinguished Service Cross (DSC), 1914. For all ranks for actions at sea
Military Cross (MC), December 1914. For all ranks for actions on land
Distinguished Flying Cross (DFC), 1918. For all ranks for acts of gallantry when flying in active operations against the enemy
Air Force Cross (AFC), 1918. For all ranks for acts of courage when flying, although not in active operations against the enemy
Royal Red Cross Class II (ARRC)
Order of British India
Kaisar-i-Hind Medal
Order of St John

Medals for Gallantry and Distinguished Conduct
Union of South Africa Queen's Medal for Bravery, in Gold
Distinguished Conduct Medal (DCM), 1854
Conspicuous Gallantry Medal (CGM), 1874
Conspicuous Gallantry Medal (Flying)
George Medal (GM), 1940
Queen's Police Medal for Gallantry
Queen's Fire Service Medal for Gallantry
Royal West African Frontier Force Distinguished Conduct Medal
King's African Rifles Distinguished Conduct Medal
Indian Distinguished Service Medal
Union of South Africa Queen's Medal for Bravery, in Silver
Distinguished Service Medal (DSM), 1914
Military Medal (MM), 1916
Distinguished Flying Medal (DFM), 1918
Air Force Medal (AFM)
Constabulary Medal (Ireland)
Medal for Saving Life at Sea
Sea Gallantry Medal
Indian Order of Merit (Civil)
Indian Police Medal for Gallantry
Ceylon Police Medal for Gallantry
Sierra Leone Police Medal for Gallantry
Sierra Leone Fire Brigades Medal for Gallantry
Colonial Police Medal for Gallantry (CPM)
Queen's Gallantry Medal, 1974
Royal Victorian Medal (RVM), Gold, Silver and Bronze
British Empire Medal (BEM), (formerly the Medal of the Order of the British Empire, for Meritorious Service; also includes the Medal of the Order awarded before 29 December 1922)
Canada Medal
Queen's Police (QPM) and Queen's Fire Service Medals (QFSM) for Distinguished Service
Queen's Medal for Chiefs

War Medals and Stars (in order of date)
Polar Medals (in order of date)
Police Medals for Valuable Service
Jubilee, Coronation and Durbar Medals
King George V, King George VI and Queen Elizabeth II Long and Faithful Service Medals

Efficiency and Long Service Decorations and Medals
Medal for Meritorious Service
Accumulated Campaign Service Medal
The Medal for Long Service and Good Conduct (Military)
Naval Long Service and Good Conduct Medal
Royal Marines Meritorious Service Medal
Royal Air Force Meritorious Service Medal
Royal Air Force Long Service and Good Conduct Medal
Medal for Long Service and Good Conduct (Ulster Defence Regiment)
Police Long Service and Good Conduct Medal
Fire Brigade Long Service and Good Conduct Medal
Colonial Police and Fire Brigades Long Service Medals
Colonial Prison Service Medal
Hong Kong Disciplined Services Medal
Army Emergency Reserve Decoration (ERD), 1952
Volunteer Officers' Decoration (VD)
Volunteer Long Service Medal
Volunteer Officers' Decoration for India and the Colonies
Volunteer Long Service Medal for India and the Colonies
Colonial Auxiliary Forces Officers' Decoration
Colonial Auxiliary Forces Long Service Medal
Medal for Good Shooting (Naval)
Militia Long Service Medal
Imperial Yeomanry Long Service Medal
Territorial Decoration (TD), 1908
Efficiency Decoration (ED)
Territorial Efficiency Medal
Efficiency Medal
Special Reserve Long Service and Good Conduct Medal
Decoration for Officers, Royal Navy Reserve (RD), 1910
Decoration for Officers, RNVR (VRD)
Royal Naval Reserve Long Service and Good Conduct Medal
RNVR Long Service and Good Conduct Medal
Royal Naval Auxiliary Sick Berth Reserve Long Service and Good Conduct Medal
Royal Fleet Reserve Long Service and Good Conduct Medal
Royal Naval Wireless Auxiliary Reserve Long Service and Good Conduct Medal
Air Efficiency Award (AE), 1942
Ulster Defence Regiment Medal
Northern Ireland Home Service Medal
The Queen's Medal. For champion shots in the RN, RM, RNZN, Army, RAF
Cadet Forces Medal, 1950
Coastguard Auxiliary Service Long Service Medal (formerly Coast Life Saving Corps Long Service Medal)
Special Constabulary Long Service Medal
Royal Observer Corps Medal
Civil Defence Long Service Medal
Ambulance Service (Emergency Duties) Long Service and Good Conduct Medal
Rhodesia Medal
Royal Ulster Constabulary Service Medal
Service Medal of the Order of St John
Badge of the Order of the League of Mercy
Voluntary Medical Service Medal, 1932

Women's Voluntary Service Medal
Colonial Special Constabulary Medal

FOREIGN ORDERS, DECORATIONS AND MEDALS (in order of date)

THE VICTORIA CROSS (1856)
FOR CONSPICUOUS BRAVERY

VC

Ribbon, Crimson, for all Services (until 1918 it was blue for the Royal Navy)

Instituted on 29 January 1856, the Victoria Cross was awarded retrospectively to 1854, the first being held by Lt. C. D. Lucas, RN, for bravery in the Baltic Sea on 21 June 1854 (gazetted 24 February 1857). The first 62 Crosses were presented by Queen Victoria in Hyde Park, London, on 26 June 1857.

The Victoria Cross is worn before all other decorations, on the left breast, and consists of a cross-pattée of bronze, one and a half inches in diameter, with the Royal Crown surmounted by a lion in the centre, and beneath there is the inscription *For Valour*. Holders of the VC receive a tax-free annuity of £1,300, irrespective of need or other conditions. In 1911, the right to receive the Cross was extended to Indian soldiers, and in 1920 to matrons, sisters and nurses, and the staff of the Nursing Services and other services pertaining to hospitals and nursing, and to civilians of either sex regularly or temporarily under the orders, direction or supervision of the naval, military, or air forces of the Crown.

SURVIVING RECIPIENTS OF THE VICTORIA CROSS
as at 31 August 1998

Agansing Rai, *Capt.*, MM (5th Royal Gurkha Rifles)
   1944 *World War*
Ali Haidar, *Jemadar* (13th Frontier Force Rifles)
   1945 *World War*
Annand, *Capt.* R. W. (Durham Light Infantry)
   1940 *World War*
Bhan Bhagta Gurung, *Havildar* (2nd Gurkha Rifles)
   1945 *World War*
Bhandari Ram, *Capt.* (10th Baluch Regiment)
   1944 *World War*
Chapman, *Sgt.* E. T., BEM (Monmouthshire Regiment)
   1945 *World War*
Cruickshank, *Flt. Lt.* J. A. (RAFVR)
   1944 *World War*
Cutler, *Capt.* Sir Roden, AK, KCMG, KCVO, CBE (Australian Military Forces, 2/5th Field Artillery)
   1941 *World War*
Fraser, *Lt.-Cdr.* I. E., DSC (RNR)
   1945 *World War*
Gaje Ghale, *Capt.* (5th Royal Gurkha Rifles)
   1943 *World War*
Ganju Lama, *Capt.*, MM (7th Gurkha Rifles)
   1944 *World War*
Gardner, *Capt.* P. J., MC (Royal Tank Regiment)
   1941 *World War*
Gould, *Lt.* T. W. (RN)
   1942 *World War*

Jamieson, *Maj.* D. A., CVO (Royal Norfolk Regiment)
   1944 *World War*
Kenna, *Pte.* E. (Australian Military Forces, 2/4th (NSW))
   1945 *World War*
Kenneally, *Guardsman* J. P. (Irish Guards)
   1943 *World War*
Lachhiman Gurung, *Havildar* (8th Gurkha Rifles)
   1945 *World War*
Merritt, *Lt.-Col.* C. C. I., CD (South Saskatchewan Regiment)
   1942 *World War*
Norton, *Capt.* G. R., MM (South African Forces, Kaffrarian Rifles)
   1944 *World War*
Payne, *WO* K., DSC (USA) (Australian Army Training Team)
   1969 *Vietnam*
Porteous, *Col.* P. A. (Royal Regiment of Artillery)
   1942 *World War*
Rambahadur Limbu, *Capt.*, MVO (10th Princess Mary's Gurkha Rifles)
   1965 *Sarawak*
Reid, *Flt. Lt.* W. (RAFVR)
   1943 *World War*
Smith, *Sgt.* E. A., CD (Seaforth Highlanders of Canada)
   1944 *World War*
Speakman-Pitts, *Sgt.* W. (Black Watch)
   1951 *Korea*
Tulbahadur Pun, *Lt.* (6th Gurkha Rifles)
   1944 *World War*
Umrao Singh, *Sub Major* (Royal Indian Artillery)
   1944 *World War*
Watkins, *Maj. Rt. Hon.* Sir Tasker, GBE (Welch Regiment)
   1944 *World War*
Wilson, *Lt.-Col.* E. C. T. (East Surrey Regiment)
   1940 *World War*

THE GEORGE CROSS (1940)
FOR GALLANTRY

GC

Ribbon, Dark blue, threaded through a bar adorned with laurel leaves
Instituted 24 September 1940 (with amendments, 3 November 1942)

The George Cross is worn before all other decorations (except the VC) on the left breast (when worn by a woman it may be worn on the left shoulder from a ribbon of the same width and colour fashioned into a bow). It consists of a plain silver cross with four equal limbs, the cross having in the centre a circular medallion bearing a design showing St George and the Dragon. The inscription *For Gallantry* appears round the medallion and in the angle of each limb of the cross is the Royal cypher 'G VI' forming a circle concentric with the medallion. The reverse is plain and bears the name of the recipient and the date of the award. The cross is suspended by a ring from a bar adorned with laurel leaves on dark blue ribbon one and a half inches wide.

The cross is intended primarily for civilians; awards to the fighting services are confined to actions for which purely military honours are not normally granted. It is awarded only for acts of the greatest heroism or of the most conspicuous courage in circumstances of extreme danger. From 1 April 1965, holders of the Cross have received a tax-free annuity, which is now £1,300.

The royal warrant which ordained that the grant of the Empire Gallantry Medal should cease authorized holders of that medal to return it to the Central Chancery of the Orders of Knighthood and to receive in exchange the George Cross. A similar provision applied to posthumous awards of the Empire Gallantry Medal made after the outbreak of war in 1939. In October 1971 all surviving holders of the Albert Medal and the Edward Medal exchanged those decorations for the George Cross.

SURVIVING RECIPIENTS OF THE GEORGE CROSS
as at 31 August 1998

If the recipient originally received the Empire Gallantry Medal (EGM), the Albert Medal (AM) or the Edward Medal (EM), this is indicated by the initials in parenthesis.

Archer, *Col.* B. S. T., GC, OBE, ERD, 1941
Baker, J. T., GC (EM), 1929
Bamford, J., GC, 1952
Beaton, J., GC, CVO, 1974
Bridge, *Lt.-Cdr.* J., GC, GM and bar, 1944
Butson, *Lt.-Col.* A. R. C., GC, CD, MD (AM), 1948
Bywater, R. A. S., GC, GM, 1944
Errington, H., GC, 1941
Farrow, K., GC (AM), 1948
Flintoff, H. H., GC (EM), 1944
Gledhill, A. J., GC, 1967
Gregson, J. S., GC (AM), 1943
Hawkins, E., GC (AM), 1943
Johnson, *WO1* (*SSM*) B., GC, 1990
Kinne, D. G., GC, 1954
Lowe, A. R., GC (AM), 1949
Lynch, J., GC, BEM (AM), 1948
Malta, GC, 1942
Manwaring, T. G., GC (EM), 1949
Moore, R. V., GC, CBE, 1940
Moss, B., GC, 1940
Naughton, F., GC (EGM), 1937
Pearson, Miss J. D. M., GC (EGM), 1940
Pratt, M. K., GC, 1978
Purves, Mrs M., GC (AM), 1949
Raweng, Awang anak, GC, 1951
Riley, G., GC (AM), 1944
Rowlands, *Air Marshal* Sir John, GC, KBE, 1943
Sinclair, *Air Vice-Marshal* Sir Laurence, GC, KCB, CBE, DSO, 1941
Stevens, H. W., GC, 1958
Stronach, *Capt.* G. P., GC, 1943
Styles, *Lt.-Col.* S. G., GC, 1972
Taylor, *Lt.-Cdr.* W. H., GC, MBE, 1941
Walker, C., GC, 1972
Walker, C. H., GC (AM), 1942
Walton, E. W. K., GC (AM), DSO, 1948
Wilcox, C., GC (EM), 1949
Wiltshire, S. N., GC (EGM), 1930
Wooding, E. A., GC (AM), 1945

Chiefs of Clans and Names in Scotland

Only chiefs of whole Names or Clans are included, except certain special instances (marked *) who, though not chiefs of a whole name, were or are for some reason (e.g. the Macdonald forfeiture) independent. Under decision (*Campbell-Gray*, 1950) that a bearer of a 'double or triple-barrelled' surname cannot be held chief of a part of such, several others cannot be included in the list at present.

The Royal House: HM The Queen

Agnew: Sir Crispin Agnew of Lochnaw, Bt., QC, 6 Palmerston Road, Edinburgh EH9 1TN

Anstruther: Sir Ralph Anstruther of that Ilk, Bt., GCVO, MC, Balcaskie, Pittenweem, Fife KY10 2RD

Arbuthnott: The Viscount of Arbuthnott, KT, CBE, DSC, Arbuthnott House, Laurencekirk, Kincardineshire AB30 1PA

Barclay: Peter C. Barclay of Towie Barclay and of that Ilk, 28A Gordon Place, London W8 4JE

Borthwick: The Lord Borthwick, Crookston, Heriot, Midlothian EH38 5YS

Boyd: The Lord Kilmarnock, 194 Regent's Park Road, London NW1 8XP

Boyle: The Earl of Glasgow, Kelburn, Fairlie, Ayrshire KA29 0BE

Brodie: Ninian Brodie of Brodie, Brodie Castle, Forres, Morayshire IV36 0TE

Bruce: The Earl of Elgin and Kincardine, KT, Broomhall, Dunfermline, Fife KY11 3DU

Buchan: David S. Buchan of Auchmacoy, Auchmacoy House, Ellon, Aberdeenshire

Burnett: J. C. A. Burnett of Leys, Crathes Castle, Banchory, Kincardineshire

Cameron: Sir Donald Cameron of Lochiel, KT, CVO, TD, Achnacarry, Spean Bridge, Inverness-shire

Campbell: The Duke of Argyll, Inveraray, Argyll PA32 8XF

Carmichael: Richard J. Carmichael of Carmichael, Carmichael, Thankerton, Biggar, Lanarkshire

Carnegie: The Duke of Fife, Elsick House, Stonehaven, Kincardineshire AB3 2NT

Cathcart: Maj.-Gen. The Earl Cathcart, CB, DSO, MC, Moor Hatches, West Amesbury, Salisbury SP4 7BH

Charteris: The Earl of Wemyss and March, KT, Gosford House, Longniddry, East Lothian EH32 0PX

Clan Chattan: M. K. Mackintosh of Clan Chattan, Maxwell Park, Gwelo, Zimbabwe

Chisholm: Hamish Chisholm of Chisholm (*The Chisholm*), Elmpine, Beck Row, Bury St Edmunds, Suffolk

Cochrane: The Earl of Dundonald, Lochnell Castle, Ledaig, Argyllshire

Colquhoun: Sir Ivar Colquhoun of Luss, Bt., Camstraddan, Luss, Dunbartonshire G83 8NX

Cranstoun: David A. S. Cranstoun of that Ilk, Corehouse, Lanark

Crichton: vacant

Cumming: Sir William Cumming of Altyre, Bt., Altyre, Forres, Moray

Darroch: Capt. Duncan Darroch of Gourock, The Red House, Branksome Park Road, Camberley, Surrey

Davidson: Alister G. Davidson of Davidston, 21 Winscombe Street, Takapuna, Auckland, New Zealand

Dewar: Kenneth Dewar of that Ilk and Vogrie, The Dower House, Grayshott, nr Hindhead, Surrey

Drummond: The Earl of Perth, PC, Stobhall, Perth PH2 6DR

Dunbar: Sir James Dunbar of Mochrum, Bt., Bld 848 C.2, 66877 Flugplatz, Ramstein, Germany

Dundas: David D. Dundas of Dundas, 8 Derna Road, Kenwyn 7700, South Africa

Durie: Raymond V. D. Durie of Durie, Court House, Pewsey, Wilts

Eliott: Mrs Margaret Eliott of Redheugh, Redheugh, Newcastleton, Roxburghshire

Erskine: The Earl of Mar and Kellie, Erskine House, Kirk Wynd, Alloa, Clackmannan FK10 4JF

Farquharson: Capt. A. Farquharson of Invercauld, MC, Invercauld, Braemar, Aberdeenshire AB35 5TT

Fergusson: Sir Charles Fergusson of Kilkerran, Bt., Kilkerran, Maybole, Ayrshire

Forbes: The Lord Forbes, KBE, Balforbes, Alford, Aberdeenshire AB33 8DR

Forsyth: Alistair Forsyth of that Ilk, Ethie Castle, by Arbroath, Angus DD11 5SP

Fraser: The Lady Saltoun, Inverey House, Aberdeenshire AB35 5YB

*Fraser (of Lovat): The Lord Lovat, Beaufort Lodge, Beauly, Inverness-shire IV4 7AZ

Gayre: R. Gayre of Gayre and Nigg, Minard Castle, Minard, Inveraray, Argyll PA32 8YB

Gordon: The Marquess of Huntly, Aboyne Castle, Aberdeenshire AB34 5JP

Graham: The Duke of Montrose, Buchanan Auld House, Drymen, Stirlingshire

Grant: The Lord Strathspey, The House of Lords, London SW1A 0PW

Grierson: Sir Michael Grierson of Lag, Bt., 40C Palace Road, London SW2 3NJ

Haig: The Earl Haig, OBE, Bemersyde, Melrose, Roxburghshire TD6 9DP

Haldane: Martin Haldane of Gleneagles, Gleneagles, Auchterarder, Perthshire

Hannay: Ramsey Hannay of Kirkdale and of that Ilk, Cardoness House, Gatehouse-of-Fleet, Kirkcudbrightshire

Hay: The Earl of Erroll, Woodbury Hall, Sandy, Beds

Henderson: John Henderson of Fordell, 7 Owen Street, Toowoomba, Queensland, Australia

Hunter: Pauline Hunter of Hunterston, Plovers Ridge, Lon Cecrist, Treaddur Bay, Holyhead, Gwynedd

Irvine of Drum: David C. Irvine of Drum, 20 Enville Road, Bowden, Altrincham, Cheshire WA14 2PQ

Jardine: Sir Alexander Jardine of Applegirth, Bt., Ash House, Thwaites, Millom, Cumbria LA18 5HY

Johnstone: The Earl of Annandale and Hartfell, Raehills, Lockerbie, Dumfriesshire

Keith: The Earl of Kintore, The Stables, Keith Hall, Inverurie, Aberdeenshire AB51 0LD

Kennedy: The Marquess of Ailsa, Cassillis House, Maybole, Ayrshire

Kerr: The Marquess of Lothian, KCVO, Ferniehurst Castle, Jedburgh, Roxburghshire TN8 6NX

Kincaid: Mrs Heather V. Kincaid of Kincaid, 4 Watling Street, Leintwardine, Craven Arms, Shropshire

Lamont: Peter N. Lamont of that Ilk, St Patrick's College, Manly, NSW 2095, Australia

Leask: Madam Leask of Leask, 1 Vincent Road, Sheringham, Norfolk

Lennox: Edward J. H. Lennox of that Ilk, Pools Farm, Downton on the Rock, Ludlow, Shropshire

LESLIE: The Earl of Rothes, Tanglewood, West Tytherley, Salisbury, Wilts SP5 1LX

LINDSAY: The Earl of Crawford and Balcarres, KT, PC, Balcarres, Colinsburgh, Fife

LOCKHART: Angus H. Lockhart of the Lee, Newholme, Dunsyre, Lanark

LUMSDEN: Gillem Lumsden of that Ilk and Blanerne, Stapely Howe, Hoe Benham, Newbury, Berks

MACALESTER: William St J. S. McAlester of Loup and Kennox, 2 Avon Road East, Christchurch, Dorset

MCBAIN: J. H. McBain of McBain, 7025 North Finger Rock Place, Tucson, Arizona, USA

MACDONALD: The Lord Macdonald (*The Macdonald of Macdonald*), Kinloch Lodge, Sleat, Isle of Skye

*MACDONALD OF CLANRANALD: Ranald A. Macdonald of Clanranald, Mornish House, Killin, Perthshire FK21 8TX

*MACDONALD OF SLEAT (CLAN HUSTEAIN): Sir Ian Macdonald of Sleat, Bt., Thorpe Hall, Rudston, Driffield, N. Humberside YO25 0JE

*MACDONELL OF GLENGARRY: Air Cdre Aeneas R. MacDonell of Glengarry, CB, DFC, Elonbank, Castle Street, Fortrose, Ross-shire IV10 8TH

MACDOUGALL: vacant

MACDOWALL: Fergus D. H. Macdowall of Garthland, 9170 Ardmore Drive, North Saanich, British Columbia, Canada

MACGREGOR: Brig. Sir Gregor MacGregor of MacGregor, Bt., Bannatyne, Newtyle, Blairgowrie, Perthshire PH12 8TR

MACINTYRE: James W. MacIntyre of Glenoe, 15301 Pine Orchard Drive, Apartment 3H, Silver Spring, Maryland, USA

MACKAY: The Lord Reay, House of Lords, London SW1

MACKENZIE: The Earl of Cromartie, Castle Leod, Strathpeffer, Ross-shire IV14 9AA

MACKINNON: Madam Anne Mackinnon of Mackinnon, 16 Purleigh Road, Bridgwater, Somerset

MACKINTOSH: *The Mackintosh of Mackintosh*, Moy Hall, Inverness IV13 7YQ

MACLACHLAN: vacant

MACLAREN: Donald MacLaren of MacLaren and Achleskine, Achleskine, Kirkton, Balquidder, Lochearnhead

MACLEAN: The Hon. Sir Lachlan Maclean of Duart, Bt., Arngask House, Glenfarg, Perthshire PH2 9QA

MACLENNAN: vacant

MACLEOD: John MacLeod of MacLeod, Dunvegan Castle, Isle of Skye

MACMILLAN: George MacMillan of MacMillan, Finlaystone, Langbank, Renfrewshire

MACNAB: J. C. Macnab of Macnab (*The Macnab*), Leuchars Castle Farmhouse, Leuchars, Fife KY16 0EY

MACNAGHTEN: Sir Patrick Macnaghten of Macnaghten and Dundarave, Bt., Dundarave, Bushmills, Co. Antrim

MACNEACAIL: Iain Macneacail of Macneacail and Scorrybreac, 12 Fox Street, Ballina, NSW, Australia

MACNEIL OF BARRA: Ian R. Macneil of Barra (*The Macneil of Barra*), 95/6 Grange Loan, Edinburgh

MACPHERSON: The Hon. Sir William Macpherson of Cluny, TD, Newtown Castle, Blairgowrie, Perthshire

MCTAVISH: E. S. Dugald McTavish of Dunardry

MACTHOMAS: Andrew P. C. MacThomas of Finegand, c/o Roslin Cottage, Pitmedden, Aberdeenshire AB41 7NY

MAITLAND: The Earl of Lauderdale, 12 St Vincent Street, Edinburgh

MAKGILL: The Viscount of Oxfuird, Hill House, St Mary Bourne, Andover, Hants SP11 6BG

MALCOLM (MACCALLUM): Robin N. L. Malcolm of Poltalloch, Duntrune Castle, Lochgilphead, Argyll

MAR: The Countess of Mar, St Michael's Farm, Great Witley, Worcs WR6 6JB

MARJORIBANKS: Andrew Marjoribanks of that Ilk, 10 Newark Street, Greenock

MATHESON: Maj. Sir Fergus Matheson of Matheson, Bt., Old Rectory, Hedenham, Bungay, Suffolk NR35 2LD

MENZIES: David R. Menzies of Menzies, Wester Auchnagallin Farmhouse, Braes of Castle Grant, Grantown on Spey PH26 3PL

MOFFAT: Madam Moffat of that Ilk, St Jasual, Bullocks Farm Lane, Wheeler End Common, High Wycombe

MONCREIFFE: vacant

MONTGOMERIE: The Earl of Eglinton and Winton, Balhomie, Cargill, Perth PH2 6DS

MORRISON: Dr Iain M. Morrison of Ruchdi, Magnolia Cottage, The Street, Walberton, Sussex

MUNRO: Hector W. Munro of Foulis, Foulis Castle, Evanton, Ross-shire IV16 9UX

MURRAY: The Duke of Atholl, Blair Castle, Blair Atholl, Perthshire

NESBITT (or NISBET): Robert Nesbitt of that Ilk, Upper Roundhurst Farm, Roundhurst, Haslemere, Surrey

NICOLSON: The Lord Carnock, 90 Whitehall Court, London SW1A 2EL

OGILVY: The Earl of Airlie, KT, GCVO, PC, Cortachy Castle, Kirriemuir, Angus

RAMSAY: The Earl of Dalhousie, KT, GCVO, GBE, MC, Brechin Castle, Brechin, Angus DD7 6SH

RATTRAY: James S. Rattray of Rattray, Craighall, Rattray, Perthshire

ROBERTSON: Alexander G. H. Robertson of Struan (*Struan-Robertson*), The Breach Farm, Goudhurst Road, Cranbrook, Kent

ROLLO: The Lord Rollo, Pitcairns, Dunning, Perthshire

ROSE: Miss Elizabeth Rose of Kilravock, Kilravock Castle, Croy, Inverness

ROSS: David C. Ross of that Ilk, Shandwick, Perth Road, Stanley, Perthshire

RUTHVEN: The Earl of Gowrie, PC, Castlemartin, Kilcullen, Co. Kildare, Republic of Ireland

SCOTT: The Duke of Buccleuch and Queensberry, KT, VRD, Bowhill, Selkirk

SCRYMGEOUR: The Earl of Dundee, Birkhill, Cupar, Fife

SEMPILL: The Lord Sempill, 3 Vanburgh Street, Edinburgh

SHAW: John Shaw of Tordarroch, Newhall, Balblair, by Conon Bridge, Ross-shire

SINCLAIR: The Earl of Caithness, Churchill, Chipping Norton, Oxford OX7 5UX

SKENE: Danus Skene of Skene, Nether Pitlour, Strathmiglo, Fife

STIRLING: Fraser J. Stirling of Cader, 44A Oakley Street, London SW3 5HA

STRANGE: Maj. Timothy Strange of Balcaskie, Little Holme, Porton Road, Amesbury, Wilts

SUTHERLAND: The Countess of Sutherland, House of Tongue, Brora, Sutherland

SWINTON: John Swinton of that Ilk, 123 Superior Avenue SW, Calgary, Alberta, Canada

TROTTER: Alexander Trotter of Mortonhall, Charterhall, Duns, Berwickshire

URQUHART: Kenneth T. Urquhart of Urquhart, 507 Jefferson Park Avenue, Jefferson, New Orleans, Louisiana 70121, USA

WALLACE: Ian F. Wallace of that Ilk, 5 Lennox Street, Edinburgh EH4 1QB

WEDDERBURN OF THAT ILK: The Master of Dundee, Birkhill, Cupar, Fife

WEMYSS: David Wemyss of that Ilk, Invermay, Forteviot, Perthshire

The Privy Council

The Sovereign in Council, or Privy Council, was the chief source of executive power until the system of Cabinet government developed in the 18th century. Now the Privy Council's main functions are to advise the Sovereign and to exercise its own statutory responsibilities independent of the Sovereign in Council (*see also* page 216).

Membership of the Privy Council is automatic upon appointment to certain government and judicial positions in the United Kingdom, e.g. Cabinet ministers must be Privy Counsellors and are sworn in on first assuming office. Membership is also accorded by The Queen to eminent people in the UK and independent countries of the Commonwealth of which Her Majesty is Queen, on the recommendation of the British Prime Minister. Membership of the Council is retained for life, except for very occasional removals.

The administrative functions of the Privy Council are carried out by the Privy Council Office (*see* page 334) under the direction of the President of the Council, who is always a member of the Cabinet.

President of the Council, The Rt. Hon. Margaret Beckett, MP
Clerk of the Council, N. H. Nicholls, CBE

MEMBERS *as at 31 August 1998*

HRH The Duke of Edinburgh, 1951
HRH The Prince of Wales, 1977

Aberdare, Lord, 1974
Ackner, Lord, 1980
Airlie, Earl of, 1984
Aldington, Lord, 1954
Aldous, Sir William, 1995
Alebua, Ezekiel, 1988
Alison, Michael, 1981
Alport, Lord, 1960
Ampthill, Lord, 1995
Ancram, Michael, 1996
Anthony, Douglas, 1971
Arbuthnot, James, 1998
Archer of Sandwell, Lord, 1977
Arnold, Sir John, 1979
Arthur, Hon. Owen, 1995
Ashdown, Paddy, 1989
Ashley of Stoke, Lord, 1979
Atkins, Sir Robert, 1995
Auld, Sir Robin, 1995
Baker of Dorking, Lord, 1984
Balcombe, Sir John, 1985
Barber, Lord, 1963

Barnett, Lord, 1975
Beckett, Margaret, 1993
Beith, Alan, 1992
Beldam, Sir Roy, 1989
Belstead, Lord, 1983
Benn, Anthony, 1964
Bennett, Sir Frederic, 1985
Biffen, Lord, 1979
Bingham of Cornhill, Lord, 1986
Birch, William, 1992
Bird, Vere, 1982
Bisson, Sir Gordon, 1987
Blair, Anthony, 1994
Blaker, Lord, 1983
Blanchard, Peter, 1998
Blatch, Baroness, 1993
Blunkett, David, 1997
Bolger, James, 1991
Booth, Albert, 1976
Boothroyd, Betty, 1992
Boscawen, Hon. Robert, 1992
Bottomley, Virginia, 1992
Boyson, Sir Rhodes, 1987
Braine of Wheatley, Lord, 1985
Brandon of Oakbrook, Lord, 1978
Brathwaite, Sir Nicholas, 1991
Bridge of Harwich, Lord, 1975
Brightman, Lord, 1979
Brittan, Sir Leon, 1981
Brooke, Sir Henry, 1996
Brooke, Peter, 1988
Brown, Gordon, 1996
Brown, Nicholas, 1997
Brown, Sir Simon, 1992
Brown, Sir Stephen, 1983
Browne-Wilkinson, Lord, 1983
Buckley, Sir Denys, 1970
Butler, Sir Adam, 1984
Butler-Sloss, Dame Elizabeth, 1988
Buxton, Sir Richard, 1997
Byers, Stephen, 1998
Caithness, Earl of, 1990
Callaghan of Cardiff, Lord, 1964
Cameron of Lochbroom, Lord, 1984
Camoys, Lord, 1997
Campbell of Croy, Lord, 1970
Canterbury, The Archbishop of, 1991
Carlisle of Bucklow, Lord, 1979
Carr of Hadley, Lord, 1963
Carrington, Lord, 1959
Carswell, Sir Robert, 1993
Carter, Lord, 1997
Casey, Sir Maurice, 1986
Castle of Blackburn, Baroness, 1964
Chadwick, Sir John, 1997
Chalfont, Lord, 1964
Chalker of Wallasey, Baroness, 1987
Chan, Sir Julius, 1981
Charteris of Amisfield, Lord, 1972
Chataway, Sir Christopher, 1970
Clark, Alan, 1991
Clark, David, 1997
Clark, Helen, 1990

Clark of Kempston, Lord, 1990
Clarke, Kenneth, 1984
Clarke, Thomas, 1997
Cledwyn of Penrhos, Lord, 1966
Clinton-Davis, Lord, 1998
Clyde, Lord, 1996
Cockfield, Lord, 1982
Cocks of Hartcliffe, Lord, 1976
Coggan, Lord, 1961
Colman, Fraser, 1986
Compton, Sir John, 1983
Concannon, John, 1978
Cook, Robin, 1996
Cooke of Thorndon, Lord, 1977
Cooper, Sir Frank, 1983
Cope of Berkeley, Lord, 1988
Corfield, Sir Frederick, 1970
Cowen, Sir Zelman, 1981
Cradock, Sir Percy, 1993
Cranborne, Viscount, 1994
Crawford and Balcarres, Earl of, 1972
Crickhowell, Lord, 1979
Croom-Johnson, Sir David, 1984
Cullen, *Hon.* Lord, 1997
Cumming-Bruce, Sir Roualeyn, 1977
Cunningham, Jack, 1993
Curry, David, 1996
Darling, Alistair, 1997
Davies, Denzil, 1978
Davies, Ronald, 1997
Davis, David, 1997
Davison, Sir Ronald, 1978
Dean of Harptree, Lord, 1991
Dean of Thornton-le-Fylde, Baroness, 1998
Deedes, Lord, 1962
Dell, Edmund, 1970
Denham, Lord, 1981
Denning, Lord, 1948
Devonshire, Duke of, 1964
Dewar, Donald, 1996
Diamond, Lord, 1965
Dillon, Sir Brian, 1982
Dixon, Lord, 1996
Dobson, Frank, 1997
Donaldson of Lymington, Lord, 1979
Dorrell, Stephen, 1994
Douglas, Sir William, 1977
du Cann, Sir Edward, 1964
Duff, Sir Antony, 1980
Dunn, Sir Robin, 1980
East, Paul, 1998
Eccles, Viscount, 1951
Eden of Winton, Lord, 1972
Eggar, Timothy, 1995
Eichelbaum, Sir Thomas, 1989
Emery, Sir Peter, 1993
Emslie, Lord, 1972
Erroll of Hale, Lord, 1960
Esquivel, Manuel, 1986
Evans, Sir Anthony, 1992
Eveleigh, Sir Edward, 1977
Farquharson, Sir Donald, 1989

Prentice, Lord, 1966
Prescott, John, 1994
Price, George, 1982
Prior, Lord, 1970
Puapua, Sir Tomasi, 1982
Purchas, Sir Francis, 1982
Pym, Lord, 1970
Raison, Sir Timothy, 1982
Ramsden, James, 1963
Rawlinson of Ewell, Lord, 1964
Redwood, John, 1993
Rees, Lord, 1983
Reid, John, 1998
Renton, Lord, 1962
Renton of Mount Harry, Lord, 1989
Richard, Lord, 1993
Richardson, Sir Ivor, 1978
Richardson of Duntisbourne, Lord, 1976
Rifkind, Sir Malcolm, 1986
Robens of Woldingham, Lord, 1951
Roberts of Conwy, Lord, 1991
Robertson, George, 1997
Roch, Sir John, 1993
Rodger of Earlsferry, Lord, 1992
Rodgers of Quarry Bank, Lord, 1975
Rose, Sir Christopher, 1992
Ross, *Hon.* Lord, 1985
Rumbold, Dame Angela, 1991
Runcie, Lord, 1980
Russell, Sir Patrick, 1987
Ryder of Wensum, Lord, 1990
Sainsbury, Sir Timothy, 1992
St John of Fawsley, Lord, 1979
Sandiford, Erskine, 1989
Saville of Newdigate, Lord, 1994
Scarman, Lord, 1973
Schiemann, Sir Konrad, 1995
Scott, Sir Nicholas, 1989
Scott, Sir Richard, 1991
Seaga, Edward, 1981

Selkirk of Douglas, Lord, 1996
Shawcross, Lord, 1946
Shearer, Hugh, 1969
Sheldon, Robert, 1977
Shephard, Gillian, 1992
Shepherd, Lord, 1965
Shipley, Jennifer, 1998
Shore of Stepney, Lord, 1967
Short, Clare, 1997
Simmonds, Kennedy, 1984
Simon of Glaisdale, Lord, 1961
Sinclair, Ian, 1977
Slade, Sir Christopher, 1982
Slynn of Hadley, Lord, 1992
Smith, Andrew, 1997
Smith, Christopher, 1997
Smith, Sir Geoffrey Johnson, 1996
Somare, Sir Michael, 1977
Somers, Sir Edward, 1981
Stanley, Sir John, 1984
Staughton, Sir Christopher, 1988
Steel of Aikwood, Lord, 1977
Stephen, Sir Ninian, 1979
Stephenson, Sir John, 1971
Stewartby, Lord, 1989
Steyn, Lord, 1992
Stodart of Leaston, Lord, 1974
Stott, Lord, 1964
Strang, Gavin, 1997
Strathclyde, Lord, 1995
Straw, Jack, 1997
Stuart-Smith, Sir Murray, 1988
Talboys, Sir Brian, 1977
Taylor, Ann, 1997
Tebbit, Lord, 1981
Templeman, Lord, 1978
Thatcher, Baroness, 1970
Thomas, Edmund, 1996
Thomas, Sir Swinton, 1994
Thomas of Gwydir, Lord, 1964
Thomson, David, 1981

Thomson of Monifieth, Lord, 1966
Thorpe, Jeremy, 1967
Thorpe, Sir Matthew, 1995
Tipping, Andrew, 1998
Tizard, Robert, 1986
Trefgarne, Lord, 1989
Trimble, David, 1997
Trumpington, Baroness, 1992
Ullswater, Viscount, 1994
Varley, Lord, 1974
Waddington, Lord, 1987
Waite, Sir John, 1993
Wakeham, Lord, 1983
Waldegrave, William, 1990
Walker of Doncaster, Lord, 1979
Walker of Worcester, Lord, 1970
Walker, Sir Robert, 1997
Waller, Sir George, 1976
Waller, Sir Mark, 1996
Ward, Sir Alan, 1995
Watkins, Sir Tasker, 1980
Weatherill, Lord, 1980
Wheeler, Sir John, 1993
Whitelaw, Viscount, 1967
Widdecombe, Ann, 1997
Wigley, Dafydd, 1997
Wilberforce, Lord, 1964
Williams, Alan, 1977
Williams of Crosby, Baroness, 1974
Windlesham, Lord, 1973
Wingti, Paias, 1987
Withers, Reginald, 1977
Woodhouse, Sir Owen, 1974
Woolf, Lord, 1986
Wylie, *Hon.* Lord, 1970
York, The Archbishop of, 1991
Young, Baroness, 1981
Young, Sir George, 1993
Young of Graffham, Lord, 1984
Younger of Leckie, Viscount, 1979
Zacca, Edward, 1992

The Privy Council of Northern Ireland

The Privy Council of Northern Ireland had responsibilities in Northern Ireland similar to those of the Privy Council in Great Britain until the Northern Ireland Act 1974 instituted direct rule and a UK Cabinet minister became responsible for the functions previously exercised by the Northern Ireland government.

Membership of the Privy Council of Northern Ireland is retained for life. The postnominal initials PC (NI)

are used to differentiate its members from those of the Privy Council.

MEMBERS *as at 31 August 1998*

Bailie, Robin, 1971
Bleakley, David, 1971
Bradford, Roy, 1969
Craig, William, 1963
Dobson, John, 1969
Kelly, Sir Basil, 1969

Kirk, Herbert, 1962
Long, William, 1966
Lowry, The Lord, 1971
McConnell, The Lord, 1964
McIvor, Basil, 1971
Morgan, William, 1961
Moyola, The Lord, 1966
Neill, Sir Ivan, 1950
Porter, Sir Robert, 1969
Taylor, John, MP, 1970
West, Henry, 1960

Parliament

The United Kingdom constitution is not contained in any single document but has evolved in the course of time, formed partly by statute, partly by common law and partly by convention. A constitutional monarchy, the United Kingdom is governed by Ministers of the Crown in the name of the Sovereign, who is head both of the state and of the government.

The organs of government are the legislature (Parliament), the executive and the judiciary. The executive consists of HM Government (Cabinet and other Ministers) (*see* pages 276–7), government departments (*see* pages 278–353), local authorities (*see* Local Government), and public corporations operating nationalized industries or social or cultural services (*see* pages 278–353). The judiciary (*see* Law Courts and Offices) pronounces on the law, both written and unwritten, interprets statutes and is responsible for the enforcement of the law; the judiciary is independent of both the legislature and the executive.

THE MONARCHY

The Sovereign personifies the state and is, in law, an integral part of the legislature, head of the executive, head of the judiciary, commander-in-chief of all armed forces of the Crown and 'Supreme Governor' of the Church of England. The seat of the monarchy is in the United Kingdom. In the Channel Islands and the Isle of Man, which are Crown dependencies, the Sovereign is represented by a Lieutenant-Governor. In the member states of the Commonwealth of which the Sovereign is head of state, her representative is a Governor-General; in UK dependencies the Sovereign is usually represented by a Governor, who is responsible to the British Government.

Although in practice the powers of the monarchy are now very limited, restricted mainly to the advisory and ceremonial, there are important acts of government which require the participation of the Sovereign. These include summoning, proroguing and dissolving Parliament, giving royal assent to bills passed by Parliament, appointing important office-holders, e.g. government ministers, judges, bishops and governors, conferring peerages, knighthoods and other honours, and granting pardon to a person wrongly convicted of a crime. The Sovereign appoints the Prime Minister; by convention this office is held by the leader of the political party which enjoys, or can secure, a majority of votes in the House of Commons. In international affairs the Sovereign as head of state has the power to declare war and make peace, to recognize foreign states and governments, to conclude treaties and to annex or cede territory. However, as the Sovereign entrusts executive power to Ministers of the Crown and acts on the advice of her Ministers, which she cannot ignore, royal prerogative powers are in practice exercised by Ministers, who are responsible to Parliament.

Ministerial responsibility does not diminish the Sovereign's importance to the smooth working of government. She holds meetings of the Privy Council (*see* below), gives audiences to her Ministers and other officials at home and overseas, receives accounts of Cabinet decisions, reads dispatches and signs state papers; she must be informed and consulted on every aspect of national life; and she must show complete impartiality.

COUNSELLORS OF STATE

In the event of the Sovereign's absence abroad, it is necessary to appoint Counsellors of State under letters patent to carry out the chief functions of the Monarch, including the holding of Privy Councils and giving royal assent to acts passed by Parliament. The normal procedure is to appoint as Counsellors three or four members of the royal family among those remaining in the UK.

In the event of the Sovereign on accession being under the age of 18 years, or at any time unavailable or incapacitated by infirmity of mind or body for the performance of the royal functions, provision is made for a regency.

THE PRIVY COUNCIL

The Sovereign in Council, or Privy Council, was the chief source of executive power until the system of Cabinet government developed. Nowadays its main function is to advise the Sovereign to approve Orders in Council and to advise on the issue of royal proclamations. The Council's own statutory responsibilities (independent of the powers of the Sovereign in Council) include powers of supervision over the registering bodies for the medical and allied professions. A full Council is summoned only on the death of the Sovereign or when the Sovereign announces his or her intention to marry. (For full list of Counsellors, *see* pages 213–5.)

There are a number of advisory Privy Council committees, whose meetings the Sovereign does not attend. Some are prerogative committees, such as those dealing with legislative matters submitted by the legislatures of the Channel Islands and the Isle of Man or with applications for charters of incorporation; and some are provided for by statute, e.g. those for the universities of Oxford and Cambridge and the Scottish universities.

The Judicial Committee of the Privy Council is the final court of appeal from courts of the UK dependencies, courts of independent Commonwealth countries which have retained the right of appeal, courts of the Channel Islands and the Isle of Man, some professional and disciplinary committees, and church sources. The Committee is composed of Privy Counsellors who hold, or have held, high judicial office, although usually only three or five hear each case.

Administrative work is carried out by the Privy Council Office under the direction of the President of the Council, a Cabinet Minister.

PARLIAMENT

Parliament is the supreme law-making authority and can legislate for the UK as a whole or for any parts of it separately (the Channel Islands and the Isle of Man are Crown dependencies and not part of the UK). The main functions of Parliament are to pass laws, to provide (by

autldformattinglll

voting taxation) the means of carrying on the work of government and to scrutinize government policy and administration, particularly proposals for expenditure. International treaties and agreements are by custom presented to Parliament before ratification.

Parliament emerged during the late 13th and early 14th centuries. The officers of the King's household and the King's judges were the nucleus of early Parliaments, joined by such ecclesiastical and lay magnates as the King might summon to form a prototype 'House of Lords', and occasionally by the knights of the shires, burgesses and proctors of the lower clergy. By the end of Edward III's reign a 'House of Commons' was beginning to appear; the first known Speaker was elected in 1377.

Parliamentary procedure is based on custom and precedent, partly formulated in the Standing Orders of both Houses of Parliament, and each House has the right to control its own internal proceedings and to commit for contempt. The system of debate in the two Houses is similar; when a motion has been moved, the Speaker proposes the question as the subject of a debate. Members speak from wherever they have been sitting. Questions are decided by a vote on a simple majority. Draft legislation is introduced, in either House, as a bill. Bills can be introduced by a Government Minister or a private Member, but in practice the majority of bills which become law are introduced by the Government. To become law, a bill must be passed by each House (for parliamentary stages, *see* Bill, page 221) and then sent to the Sovereign for the royal assent, after which it becomes an Act of Parliament.

Proceedings of both Houses are public, except on extremely rare occasions. The minutes (called Votes and Proceedings in the Commons, and Minutes of Proceedings in the Lords) and the speeches (The Official Report of Parliamentary Debates, *Hansard*) are published daily. Proceedings are also recorded for transmission on radio and television and stored in the Parliamentary Recording Unit before transfer to the National Sound Archive. Television cameras have been allowed into the House of Lords since 1985 and into the House of Commons since 1989; committee meetings may also be televised.

By the Parliament Act of 1911, the maximum duration of a Parliament is five years (if not previously dissolved), the term being reckoned from the date given on the writs for the new Parliament. The maximum life has been prolonged by legislation in such rare circumstances as the two world wars (31 January 1911 to 25 November 1918; 26 November 1935 to 15 June 1945). Dissolution and writs for a general election are ordered by the Sovereign on the advice of the Prime Minister. The life of a Parliament is divided into sessions, usually of one year in length, beginning and ending most often in October or November.

DEVOLUTION

The Northern Ireland Assembly elected in June 1998 is due to be formally established by legislation in early 1999; it will have legislative authority in the fields currently administered by the Northern Ireland departments. The Welsh Assembly due to be elected in May 1999 will have power to make secondary legislation in the areas where executive functions have been transferred to it. The Scottish Parliament due to be elected in 1999 will have legislative power over all devolved matters, i.e. matters not reserved to Westminster or otherwise outside its powers. For further details, *see* Local Government section.

THE HOUSE OF LORDS
London SW1A 0PW
Tel 0171-219 3000
Information Office: 0171-219 3107
E-mail: HLINFO@parliament.uk
Web site: http://www.parliament.uk

The House of Lords consists of the Lords Spiritual and Temporal. The Lords Spiritual are the Archbishops of Canterbury and York, the Bishops of London, Durham and Winchester, and the 21 senior diocesan bishops of the Church of England. The Lords Temporal currently consist of all hereditary peers of England, Scotland, Great Britain and the UK who have not disclaimed their peerages, life peers created under the Life Peerages Act 1958, and those Lords of Appeal in Ordinary created life peers under the Appellate Jurisdiction Act 1876, as amended (law lords). The Government is planning to introduce legislation removing the right of hereditary peers to sit in the House of Lords.

Disclaimants of a hereditary peerage lose their right to sit in the House of Lords but gain the right to vote at parliamentary elections and to offer themselves for election to the House of Commons (*see also* page 136). Those peers disqualified from sitting in the House include:

– aliens, i.e. any peer who is not a British citizen, a Commonwealth citizen (under the British Nationality Act 1981) or a citizen of the Republic of Ireland
– peers under the age of 21
– undischarged bankrupts or, in Scotland, those whose estate is sequestered
– peers convicted of treason

Peers who do not wish to attend sittings of the House of Lords may apply for leave of absence for the duration of a Parliament.

Until the beginning of this century the House of Lords had considerable power, being able to veto any bill submitted to it by the House of Commons, but those powers were greatly reduced by the Parliament Acts of 1911 and 1949 (*see* page 221).

Combined with its legislative role, the House of Lords has judicial powers as the ultimate Court of Appeal for courts in Great Britain and Northern Ireland, except for criminal cases in Scotland. These powers are exercised by the Lord Chancellor and the law lords.

Members of the House of Lords are unpaid. However, they are entitled to reimbursement of travelling expenses on parliamentary business within the UK and certain other expenses incurred for the purpose of attendance at sittings of the House, within a maximum for each day of £78 for overnight subsistence, £34.50 for day subsistence and incidental travel, and £33.50 for secretarial costs, postage and certain additional expenses.

COMPOSITION *as at 1 July 1998*

Archbishops and Bishops, 26
Peers by succession, 750 (16 women)
Hereditary peers of first creation (including the Prince of Wales), 9
Life peers under the Appellate Jurisdiction Act 1876, 26
Life peers under the Life Peerages Act 1958, 458 (80 women)
Total 1,269
Of whom:
Peers without writs of summons, 69 (3 minors)
Peers on leave of absence from the House, 66

STATE OF PARTIES *as at 1 July 1998* *

More than half of the members of the House of Lords take the whip of one of the three main political parties. The other members sit on the cross-benches as independents, support other parties or have declared no political affiliation.

Conservative, 471
Labour, 158
Liberal Democrats, 66
Cross-bench, 323
Other (including Lords Spiritual), 117
* Excluding peers without writs of summons and peers on leave of absence from the House

OFFICERS

The House is presided over by the Lord Chancellor, who is *ex officio* Speaker of the House. A panel of deputy Speakers is appointed by Royal Commission. The first deputy Speaker is the Chairman of Committees, appointed at the beginning of each session, a salaried officer of the House who takes the chair in committee of the whole House and in some select committees. He is assisted by a panel of deputy chairmen, headed by the salaried Principal Deputy Chairman of Committees, who is also chairman of the European Communities Committee of the House.

The permanent officers include the Clerk of the Parliaments, who is in charge of the administrative and procedural staff collectively known as the Parliament Office; the Gentleman Usher of the Black Rod, who is also Serjeant-at-Arms in attendance upon the Lord Chancellor and is responsible for security and for accommodation and services in the House of Lords; and the Yeoman Usher who is Deputy Serjeant-at-Arms and assists Black Rod in his duties.

Speaker (£148,850), The Lord Irvine of Lairg, PC, QC
 Private Secretary, Ms E. Hutchinson
Chairman of Committees (£53,264), The Lord Boston of Faversham, QC
Principal Deputy Chairman of Committees (£49,052), The Lord Tordoff

DEPARTMENT OF THE CLERK OF THE PARLIAMENTS

Clerk of the Parliaments (£116,045), J. M. Davies
Clerk Assistant and Clerk of Legislation (£70,220–£105,740), P. D. G. Hayter, LVO
Reading Clerk and Principal Finance Officer (£58,590–£94,330), M. G. Pownall
Counsel to Chairman of Committees (£58,590–£94,330), D. Rippengal, CB, QC; Sir James Nursaw, KCB, QC: Dr C. S. Kerse
Principal Clerks (£53,450–£89,090), J. A. Vallance White, CB (*Judicial Office and Fourth Clerk at the Table*); B. P. Keith (*Clerk of the Journals*); (£48,420–£79,230) D. R. Beamish (*Committees and Overseas Office*); R. H. Walters, D.Phil. (*Establishment Officer*); Dr F. P. Tudor (*Private Bills*); E. C. Ollard (*Public Bills*); A. Makower; T. V. Mohan (*Select Committees*)
Senior Clerks (£30,431–£46,108), Mrs M. E. Ollard; E. J. J. Wells; S. P. Burton (*seconded as Secretary to the Leader of the House and Chief Whip*); Mrs M. B. Bloor; T. E. Radice; Dr D. Rolt; D. J. Batt; I. Smyth
Clerks (£15,862–£27,564), Dr C. A. Mylne; Miss L. J. Mouland; J. A. Vaughan
Clerk of the Records (£43,910–£70,430), D. J. Johnson, FSA
Deputy Clerk of the Records (£34,462–£55,915), S. K. Ellison
Librarian (£48,420–£79,230), D. L. Jones
Deputy Librarian (£34,462–£55,915), P. G. Davis, PH.D.
Senior Library Clerk (£30,431–£46,108), Miss J. L. Victory, PH.D.
Examiners of Petitions for Private Bills, Dr F. P. Tudor; W. A. Proctor

Editor, Official Report (*Hansard*), (£43,910–£70,430), Mrs M. E. Villiers
Deputy Editor, Official Report (£34,462–£55,915), G. R. Goodbarne

DEPARTMENT OF THE GENTLEMAN USHER OF THE BLACK ROD

Gentleman Usher of the Black Rod and Serjeant-at-Arms (£58,590–£94,330), Gen. Sir Edward Jones, KCB, CBE
Yeoman Usher of the Black Rod and Deputy Serjeant-at-Arms (£30,431–£46,108), Air Vice-Marshal D. R. Hawkins, CB, MBE

SELECT COMMITTEES

The main House of Lords select committees, as at 8 June 1998, are as follows:

European Communities – Sub-committees:
 A (*Economic and Financial Affairs, Trade and External Relations*) – *Chair,* The Lord Barnett, PC; *Clerk,* Dr F. P. Tudor
 B (*Energy, Industry and Transport*) – *Chair,* The Lord Geddes; *Clerk,* Ms K. Ball
 C (*Environment, Transport and Consumer Protection*) – *Chair,* The Baroness Hilton of Eggardon, QPM; *Clerk,* T. Radice
 D (*Agriculture, Fisheries and Food*) – *Chair,* The Lord Reay; *Clerk,* A. Mackersie
 E (*Law and Institutions*) – *Chair,* The Lord Hoffmann, PC; *Clerk,* T. Radice
 F (*Social Affairs, Education and Home Affairs*) – *Chair,* The Lord Wallace of Saltaire, PH.D.; *Clerk,* Ms M. Bloor
Science and Technology – *Chair,* The Lord Phillips of Ellesmere, KBE, FRS; *Clerk,* A. Makower
Delegated Powers and Deregulation – *Chair,* The Lord Alexander of Weedon, QC; *Clerk,* Dr F. P. Tudor

THE HOUSE OF COMMONS

London SW1A 0AA
Tel 0171-219 3000
Information Office: 0171-219 4272
Forthcoming business: 0171-219 5532
E-mail: hcinfo@parliament.uk
Web site: http://www.parliament.uk

The members of the House of Commons are elected by universal adult suffrage. For electoral purposes, the United Kingdom is divided into constituencies, each of which returns one member to the House of Commons, the member being the candidate who obtains the largest number of votes cast in the constituency. To ensure equitable representation, the four Boundary Commissions (*see* page 285) keep constituency boundaries under review and recommend any redistribution of seats which may seem necessary because of population movements, etc. The number of seats was raised to 640 in 1945, reduced to 625 in 1948, and subsequently rose to 630 in 1955, 635 in 1970, 650 in 1983, 651 in 1992 and 659 in 1997. Of the present 659 seats, there are 529 for England, 40 for Wales, 72 for Scotland and 18 for Northern Ireland. The number of Scottish MPs at Westminster is to be cut by about 12 by 2007.

ELECTIONS

Elections are by secret ballot, each elector casting one vote; voting is not compulsory. For entitlement to vote in parliamentary elections, *see* Legal Notes section. When a seat becomes vacant between general elections, a by-election is held.

British subjects and citizens of the Irish Republic can stand for election as Members of Parliament (MPs) provided they are 21 or over and not subject to disqualification. Those disqualified from sitting in the House include:

– undischarged bankrupts
– people sentenced to more than one year's imprisonment
– clergy of the Church of England, Church of Scotland, Church of Ireland and Roman Catholic Church
– members of the House of Lords
– holders of certain offices listed in the House of Commons Disqualification Act 1975, e.g. members of the judiciary, Civil Service, regular armed forces, police forces, some local government officers and some members of public corporations and government commissions

A candidate does not require any party backing but his or her nomination for election must be supported by the signatures of ten people registered in the constituency. A candidate must also deposit with the returning officer £500, which is forfeit if the candidate does not receive more than 5 per cent of the votes cast. All election expenses at a general election, except the candidate's personal expenses, are subject to a statutory limit of £4,965, plus 4.2 pence for each elector in a borough constituency or 5.6 pence for each elector in a county constituency.

See pages 226–33 for an alphabetical list of MPs, pages 236–68 for the results of the last general election, and page 233 for the results of by-elections since the general election.

STATE OF PARTIES *as at 31 July 1998*

Conservative, 162 (14 women)
Labour, 418 (101 women)
Liberal Democrats, 46 (3 women)
Plaid Cymru, 4
Scottish Nationalist, 6 (2 women)
Sinn Fein, 2
Social Democratic and Labour, 3
Ulster Democratic Unionist, 2
Ulster Unionist, 10
United Kingdom Unionist, 1
Independent, 1
The Speaker and three Deputy Speakers, 4 (1 woman)
Total, 659 (121 women)
Government majority, 181

BUSINESS

The week's business of the House is outlined each Thursday by the Leader of the House, after consultation between the Chief Government Whip and the Chief Opposition Whip. A quarter to a third of the time will be taken up by the Government's legislative programme and the rest by other business. As a rule, bills likely to raise political controversy are introduced in the Commons before going on to the Lords, and the Commons claims exclusive control in respect of national taxation and expenditure. Bills such as the Finance Bill, which imposes taxation, and the Consolidated Fund Bills, which authorize expenditure, must begin in the Commons. A bill of which the financial provisions are subsidiary may begin in the Lords; and the Commons may waive its rights in regard to Lords' amendments affecting finance.

The Commons has a public register of MPs' financial and certain other interests; this is published annually as a House of Commons paper. Members must also disclose any relevant financial interest or benefit in a matter before the House when taking part in a debate, in certain other proceedings of the House, or in consultations with other MPs, with Ministers or with civil servants.

MEMBERS' PAY AND ALLOWANCES

Since 1911 members of the House of Commons have received salary payments; facilities for free travel were introduced in 1924. Salary rates since 1911 are as follows:

1911	£400 p.a.	1982 June	£14,510 p.a.
1931	360	1983 June	15,308
1934	380	1984 Jan	16,106
1935	400	1985 Jan	16,904
1937	600	1986 Jan	17,702
1946	1,000	1987 Jan	18,500
1954	1,250	1988 Jan	22,548
1957	1,750	1989 Jan	24,107
1964	3,250	1990 Jan	26,701
1972 Jan	4,500	1991 Jan	28,970
1975 June	5,750	1992 Jan	30,854
1976 June	6,062	1994 Jan	31,687
1977 July	6,270	1995 Jan	33,189
1978 June	6,897	1996 Jan	34,085
1979 June	9,450	1996 July	43,000
1980 June	11,750	1997 April	43,860
1981 June	13,950	1998 April	45,066

In 1969 MPs were granted an allowance for secretarial and research expenses, now known as the Office Costs Allowance. From April 1998 the allowance is £49,232 a year.

Since 1972 MPs have been able to claim reimbursement for the additional cost of staying overnight away from their main residence while on parliamentary business; this is known as the Additional Costs Allowance and from April 1998 is £12,717 a year.

Since 1980 each MP in receipt of the Office Costs Allowance has been able to contribute sums to an approved pension scheme for the provision of a pension, or other benefits, for or in respect of persons whose salary is met by him/her from the Office Costs Allowance.

MEMBERS' PENSIONS

Pension arrangements for MPs were first introduced in 1964. The arrangements currently provide a pension of one-fiftieth of salary for each year of pensionable service with a maximum of two-thirds of salary at age 65. Pension is payable normally at age 65, for men and women, or on later retirement. Pensions may be paid earlier, e.g. on retirement due to ill health. The widow/widower of a former MP receives a pension of five-eighths of the late MP's pension. Pensions are index-linked. Members currently contribute 6 per cent of salary to the pension fund; there is an Exchequer contribution, currently slightly more than the amount contributed by MPs.

The House of Commons Members' Fund provides for annual or lump sum grants to ex-MPs, their widows or widowers, and children whose incomes are below certain limits. Alternatively, payments of £2,325.72 a year to ex-MPs with at least ten years' service and who left the House of Commons before October 1964, and £1,454.16 a year to their widows or widowers are made as of right. Members contribute £24 a year and the Exchequer £215,000 a year to the fund.

OFFICERS AND OFFICIALS

The House of Commons is presided over by the Speaker, who has considerable powers to maintain order in the House. A deputy Speaker, called the Chairman of Ways and Means, and two Deputy Chairmen may preside over sittings of the House of Commons; they are elected by the House, and, like the Speaker, neither speak nor vote other than in their official capacity.

The staff of the House are employed by a Commission chaired by the Speaker. The heads of the six House of Commons departments are permanent officers of the House, not MPs. The Clerk of the House is the principal adviser to the Speaker on the privileges and procedures of the House, the conduct of the business of the House, and committees. The Serjeant-at-Arms is responsible for security, ceremonial, and for accommodation in the Commons part of the Palace of Westminster.

Speaker (£106,716), The Rt. Hon. Betty Boothroyd, MP (West Bromwich West)
Chairman of Ways and Means (£77,047), Sir Alan Haselhurst, MP (Saffron Walden)
First Deputy Chairman of Ways and Means (£73,173), Michael Martin, MP (Glasgow Springburn)
Second Deputy Chairman of Ways and Means (£73,173), Michael Lord, MP (Suffolk Central and Ipswich North)

OFFICES OF THE SPEAKER AND CHAIRMAN OF WAYS AND MEANS

Speaker's Secretary (£43,910–£70,430), N. Bevan, CB
Chaplain to the Speaker, Revd Canon R. Wright
Secretary to the Chairman of Ways and Means,   (£29,533 –£44,678), Ms L. M. Gardner

DEPARTMENT OF THE CLERK OF THE HOUSE

Clerk of the House of Commons (£116,045), W. R. McKay, CB
Clerk Assistant (£64,140–£99,880), G. Cubie
Clerk of Committees (£64,140–£99,880), C. B. Winnifrith, CB
Clerk of Legislation (£64,140–£99,880), R. B. Sands
Principal Clerks (£58,590–£94,330)
    Journals, A. J. Hastings
    Table Office, D. G. Millar
    Domestic Committees, M. R. Jack, PH.D.
Principal Clerks (£48,420–£79,230)
    Overseas Office, R. W. G. Wilson
    Bills, W. A. Proctor
    Select Committees, Ms H. E. Irwin; Mrs J. Sharpe; F. A. Cranmer
    Delegated Legislation, R. J. Rogers
Deputy Principal Clerks (£43,910–£70,430), Ms A. Barry; C. R. M. Ward, PH.D.; D. W. N. Doig; A. Sandall; D. L. Natzler; E. P. Silk; L. C. Laurence Smyth; S. J. Patrick; D. J. Gerhold; C. J. Poyser; D. F. Harrison; S. J. Priestley; A. H. Doherty; P. A. Evans; R. I. S. Phillips; R. G. James, PH.D.; Ms P. A. Helme; D. R. Lloyd; B. M. Hutton; J. S. Benger, D.phil.; Ms E. C. Samson; N. P. Walker; M. D. Hamlyn; Mrs E. J. Flood; P. C. Seaward, D.phil.
Senior Clerks (£29,533–£44,678), C. G. Lee; C. D. Stanton; A. Y. A. Azad; C. A. Shaw; Ms L. M. Gardner; K. J. Brown; F. J. Reid; M. Hennessy; G. R. Devine; P. G. Moon; M. Clark; Mrs J. N. St J. Mulley; T. W. P. Healey; Mrs S. A. R. Davies; J. D. Whatley; K. C. Fox; J. D. W. Rhys; Ms J. A. Long; Ms J. J. Eldred (*acting*); S. T. Fiander (*acting*); D. H. Griffiths (*acting*)
Examiners of Petitions for Private Bills, W. A. Proctor; Dr F. P. Tudor
Registrar of Members' Interests (£58,590–£94,330), R. J. Willoughby (*seconded to Speaker's Office*)
Taxing Officer, W. A. Proctor

Vote Office

Deliverer of the Vote (£43,910–£70,430), H. C. Foster
Deputy Deliverers of the Vote (£29,533–£44,678), J. F. Collins (*Distribution*); O. B. T. Sweeney (*Parliamentary*); F. W. Hallett (*Production*)

Speaker's Counsel

Speaker's Counsel (£58,590–£94,330), J. Mason, CB

Speaker's Counsel (European legislation) (£58,590–£94,330), J. E. G. Vaux
Speaker's Assistant Counsel (£43,910–£70,430), A. Akbar; J. R. Mallinson

DEPARTMENT OF THE SERJEANT-AT-ARMS

Serjeant-at-Arms (£58,590–£94,330), P. N. W. Jennings
Deputy Serjeant-at-Arms (£43,910–£70,430), M. J. A. Cummins
Assistant Serjeant-at-Arms (£33,447–£54,170), P. A. J. Wright
Deputy Assistant Serjeants-at-Arms (£29,533–£44,678), J. M. Robertson; M. Harvey

DEPARTMENT OF THE LIBRARY

Librarian (£58,590–£94,330), Miss J. B. Tanfield
Directors (£43,910–£79,230), Miss P. Baines; K. G. Cuninghame; Mrs J. Wainwright; R. Clements; R. Ware, D.phil.
Heads of Sections (£33,447–£54,170), C. Pond, PH.D.; Mrs C. Andrews; Mrs J. Lourie; C. Barclay; Mrs J. Fiddick; Mrs C. Gillie; R. Twigger; Mrs G. Allen; R. Cracknell
Senior Library Clerks (£29,533–£44,678), Ms F. Poole; T. Edmonds; Ms O. Gay; Miss E. McInnes; Dr D. Gore; B. Winetrobe; Miss M. Baber; Ms A. Walker; Mrs H. Holden; Mrs P. Carling; Miss J. Seaton; Ms K. Greener; Ms P. Strickland; Miss V. Miller; M. P. Hillyard; Ms J. Roll; Ms W. Wilson; S. Wise; E. Wood; P. Bowers, PH.D.; T. Dodd; A. Seely; Mrs J. Hough; G. Danby, PH.D.; Miss P. Hughes, PH.D.; B. Morgan; Ms K. Wright; Miss L. Conway; C. Blair, PH.D.

DEPARTMENT OF FINANCE AND ADMINISTRATION

Director of Finance and Administration (£58,590–£94,330), A. Walker
Accountant (£48,420–£79,230), A. Marskell
Head of Establishments Office (£48,420–£79,230), B. Wilson

DEPARTMENT OF THE OFFICIAL REPORT

Editor (£48,420–£79,230), I. Church
Deputy Editors (£39,830–£62,570), P. Walker; W. G. Garland; Miss L. Sutherland

SELECT COMMITTEES

The more important committees, as at August 1998, are:

DEPARTMENTAL COMMITTEES
Agriculture – *Chair*, Peter Luff, MP; *Clerk*, Ms L. M. Gardner
Culture, Media and Sport – *Chair*, Rt. Hon. Gerald Kaufman, MP; *Clerk*, C. G. Lee
Defence – *Chair*, Bruce George, MP; *Clerks*, P. A. Evans; Ms S. McGlashan
Education and Employment – *Clerks*, M. D. Hamlyn; K. C. Fox
    Sub-committees: Education – *Chair*, vacant; *Clerk*, M. D. Hamlyn; *Employment* – *Chair*, Derek Foster, MP; *Clerk*, T. W. P. Healey
Environment, Transport and the Regions – *Chairs*, Andrew Bennett, MP; Gwyneth Dunwoody, MP; *Clerk*, D. F. Harrison
    Sub-committees: Environment – *Chair*, Andrew Bennett, MP; *Clerk*, H. A. Yardley; *Transport* – *Chair*, Gwyneth Dunwoody, MP; *Clerk*, G. R. Devine
Foreign Affairs – *Chair*, Donald Anderson, MP; *Clerks*, E. P. Silk; M. P. Atkins
Health – *Chair*, David Hinchliffe, MP; *Clerks*, J. S. Benger, D.phil.; J. D. Whatley
Home Affairs – *Chair*, Chris Mullin, MP; *Clerks*, C. J. Poyser; T. Goldsmith

International Development – Chair, Bowen Wells, MP; *Clerk,* A. Y. A. Azad

Northern Ireland – Chair, Rt. Hon. Peter Brooke, CH, MP; *Clerk,* C. R. M. Ward

Science and Technology – Chair, Dr Michael Clark, MP; *Clerk,* Mrs J. N. St J. Mulley

Scottish Affairs – Chair, David Marshall, MP; *Clerk,* F. A. Cranmer

Social Security – Chair, Archy Kirkwood, MP; *Clerk,* L. C. Laurence Smyth

Trade and Industry – Chair, Martin O'Neill, MP; *Clerk,* Ms A. Barry

Treasury – Chair, Giles Radice, MP; *Clerks,* Mrs J. Sharpe; Ms J. A. Long

  Treasury departments and agencies sub-committee: Chair, rotating chairmanship; *Clerk,* Ms J. A. Long

Welsh Affairs – Chair, Martyn Jones, MP; *Clerk,* Ms P. A. Helme

NON-DEPARTMENTAL COMMITTEES

Deregulation – Chair, Peter Pike, MP; *Clerk,* J. D. W. Rhys

Environmental Audit – Chair, John Horam, MP; *Clerk,* F. J. Reid

European Legislation – Chair, James Hood, MP; *Clerk,* Mrs E. J. Flood

Modernization – Chair, Rt. Hon. Margaret Beckett, MP; *Clerks,* C. B. Winnifrith, CB; A. Sandall

Procedure – Chair, Nicholas Winterton, MP; *Clerks,* Ms E. C. Samson; H. A. Yardley

Public Accounts – Chair, Rt. Hon. David Davis, MP; *Clerk,* K. J. Brown

Public Administration – Chair, Rhodri Morgan, MP; *Clerk,* Dr P. C. Seaward

Standards and Privileges – Chair, Rt. Hon. Robert Sheldon, MP; *Clerks,* A. Sandall; Mrs S. A. R. Davies

PARLIAMENTARY INFORMATION

The following is a short glossary of aspects of the work of Parliament. Unless otherwise stated, references are to House of Commons procedures.

BILL – Proposed legislation is termed a bill. The stages of a public bill (for private bills, *see* page 222) in the House of Commons are as follows:

First Reading: There is no debate at this stage, which nowadays merely constitutes an order to have the bill printed

Second Reading: The debate on the principles of the bill

Committee Stage: The detailed examination of a bill, clause by clause. In most cases this takes place in a standing committee, or the whole House may act as a committee. A special standing committee may take evidence before embarking on detailed scrutiny of the bill. Very rarely, a bill may be examined by a select committee (*see* page 222)

Report Stage: Detailed review of a bill as amended in committee

Third Reading: Final debate on a bill

Public bills go through the same stages in the House of Lords, except that in almost all cases the committee stage is taken in committee of the whole House.

A bill may start in either House, and has to pass through both Houses to become law. Both Houses have to agree the same text of a bill, so that the amendments made by the second House are then considered in the originating House, and if not agreed, sent back or themselves amended, until agreement is reached.

CHILTERN HUNDREDS – A legal fiction, a nominal office of profit under the Crown, the acceptance of which requires an MP to vacate his seat. The Manor of Northstead is similar. These are the only means by which an MP may resign.

CONSOLIDATED FUND BILL – A bill to authorize issue of money to maintain Government services. The bill is dealt with without debate.

EARLY DAY MOTION – A motion put on the notice paper by an MP without in general the real prospect of its being debated. Such motions are expressions of back-bench opinion.

FATHER OF THE HOUSE – The Member whose continuous service in the House of Commons is the longest. The present Father of the House is the Rt. Hon. Sir Edward Heath, KG, MBE, MP, elected first in 1950.

HOURS OF MEETING – The House of Commons meets Monday, Tuesday and Thursday at 2.30 p.m., and on Wednesday and Friday at 9.30 a.m.; there are ten Fridays without sittings in each session. The House of Lords normally meets at 2.30 p.m. Monday to Wednesday and at 3 p.m. on Thursday. In the latter part of the session, the House of Lords sometimes sits on Fridays at 11 a.m.

LEADER OF THE OPPOSITION – In 1937 the office of Leader of the Opposition was recognized and a salary was assigned to the post. Since April 1998 the salary has been £101,579 (including parliamentary salary of £45,066). The present Leader of the Opposition is the Rt. Hon. William Hague, MP.

THE LORD CHANCELLOR – The Lord High Chancellor of Great Britain is (*ex officio*) the Speaker of the House of Lords. Unlike the Speaker of the House of Commons, he is a member of the Government, takes part in debates and votes in divisions. He has none of the powers to maintain order that the Speaker in the Commons has, these powers being exercised in the Lords by the House as a whole. The Lord Chancellor sits in the Lords on one of the Woolsacks, couches covered with red cloth and stuffed with wool. If he wishes to address the House in any way except formally as Speaker, he leaves the Woolsack.

NORTHERN IRELAND GRAND COMMITTEE – The Northern Ireland Grand Committee consists of all MPs representing constituencies in Northern Ireland, together with not more than 25 other MPs nominated by the Committee of Selection. The business of the committee includes questions, short debates, ministerial statements, bills, legislative proposals and other matters relating exclusively to Northern Ireland, and delegated legislation.

The Northern Ireland Affairs Committee is one of the departmental select committees, empowered to examine the expenditure, administration and policy of the Northern Ireland Office and the administration and expenditure of the Crown Solicitor's Office.

OPPOSITION DAY – A day on which the topic for debate is chosen by the Opposition. There are 20 such days in a normal session. On 17 days, subjects are chosen by the Leader of the Opposition; on the remaining three days by the leader of the next largest opposition party.

PARLIAMENT ACTS 1911 AND 1949 – Under these Acts, bills may become law without the consent of the Lords, though the House of Lords has the power to delay a public bill for 13 months from its first second reading in the House of Commons.

PRIME MINISTER'S QUESTIONS – The Prime Minister answers questions from 3.00 to 3.30 p.m. on Wednesdays.

PRIVATE BILL – A bill promoted by a body or an individual to give powers additional to, or in conflict with, the general law, and to which a special procedure applies to enable people affected to object.

PRIVATE MEMBER'S BILL – A public bill promoted by a Member who is not a member of the Government.

PRIVATE NOTICE QUESTION – A question adjudged of urgent importance on submission to the Speaker (in the Lords, the Leader of the House), answered at the end of oral questions, usually at 3.30 p.m.

PRIVILEGE – The following are covered by the privilege of Parliament:
(i) freedom from interference in going to, attending at, and going from, Parliament
(ii) freedom of speech in parliamentary proceedings
(iii) the printing and publishing of anything relating to the proceedings of the two Houses is subject to privilege
(iv) each House is the guardian of its dignity and may punish any insult to the House as a whole

QUESTION TIME – Oral questions are answered by Ministers in the Commons from 2.30 to 3.30 p.m. every day except Friday. They are also taken at the start of the Lords sittings, with a daily limit of four oral questions.

ROYAL ASSENT – The royal assent is signified by letters patent to such bills and measures as have passed both Houses of Parliament (or bills which have been passed under the Parliament Acts 1911 and 1949). The Sovereign has not given royal assent in person since 1854. On occasion, for instance in the prorogation of Parliament, royal assent may be pronounced to the two Houses by Lords Commissioners. More usually royal assent is notified to each House sitting separately in accordance with the Royal Assent Act 1967. The old French formulae for royal assent are then endorsed on the acts by the Clerk of the Parliaments.

The power to withhold assent resides with the Sovereign but has not been exercised in the UK since 1707, in the reign of Queen Anne.

SCOTTISH GRAND COMMITTEE – Established in its present form in 1957, the committee consists of all 72 MPs representing Scottish constituencies, with a quorum of ten. The functions of the committee are to consider the principle of all public bills relating exclusively to Scotland (constituting in effect the bill's second reading); to consider the Scottish estimates on not less than six days a session; and to consider matters relating exclusively to Scotland on not more than six days a session. From the beginning of the 1994–5 session, the committee's powers were enhanced to allow oral questions, short debates, ministerial statements, and consideration of appropriate statutory instruments. The committee can meet on appointed days at specified places in Scotland.

The Scottish Affairs Committee, one of the departmental select committees, is empowered to examine the expenditure, administration and policy of the Scottish Office, and the expenditure and administration of the Lord Advocate's Office.

SELECT COMMITTEES – Consisting usually of ten to 15 members of all parties, select committees are a means used by both Houses in order to investigate certain matters.

Most select committees in the House of Commons are now tied to departments: each committee investigates subjects within a government department's remit. There are other House of Commons select committees dealing with public accounts (i.e. the spending by the Government

of money voted by Parliament) and European legislation, and also domestic committees dealing, for example, with privilege and procedure. Major select committees usually take evidence in public; their evidence and reports are published by The Stationery Office. House of Commons select committees are reconstituted after a general election. For main committees, *see* pages 220–1.

The principal select committee in the House of Lords is that on the European Communities, which has, at present, six sub-committees dealing with all areas of Community policy. The House of Lords also has a select committee on science and technology, which appoints sub-committees to deal with specific subjects, and a select committee on delegated powers and deregulation. For committees, *see* page 218. In addition, *ad hoc* select committees have been set up from time to time to investigate specific subjects, e.g. overseas trade, murder and life imprisonment. There are also some joint committees of the two Houses, e.g. the committees on statutory instruments and on parliamentary privilege.

THE SPEAKER – The Speaker of the House of Commons is the spokesman and president of the Chamber. He or she is elected by the House at the beginning of each Parliament or when the previous Speaker retires or dies. The Speaker neither speaks in debates nor votes in divisions except when the voting is equal.

VACANT SEATS – When a vacancy occurs in the House of Commons during a session of Parliament, the writ for the by-election is moved by a Whip of the party to which the member whose seat has been vacated belonged. If the House is in recess, the Speaker can issue a warrant for a writ, should two members certify to him that a seat is vacant.

WELSH GRAND COMMITTEE – First appointed in the 1959–60 session, the committee consists of all 40 MPs representing Welsh constituencies plus not more than five other members nominated by the Committee of Selection. The functions of the committee are to consider the principle of all public bills referred to it (constituting in effect the second reading of such a bill); and to consider matters relating exclusively to Wales. Since 1996 the business of the committee may also include questions, ministerial statements and short debates. Since June 1996 members of the committee have been permitted to speak in Welsh.

The Welsh Affairs Committee, one of the departmental select committees, is empowered to examine the expenditure, administration and policy of the Welsh Office.

WHIPS – In order to secure the attendance of Members of a particular party in Parliament on all occasions, and particularly on the occasion of an important vote, Whips (originally known as 'Whippers-in') are appointed. The written appeal or circular letter issued by them is also known as a 'whip', its urgency being denoted by the number of times it is underlined. Failure to respond to a three-line whip, headed 'Most important', is tantamount in the Commons to secession (at any rate temporarily) from the party. Whips are officially recognized by Parliament and are provided with office accommodation in both Houses. In both Houses, Government and some Opposition Whips receive salaries from public funds.

PARLIAMENTARY EDUCATION UNIT – Norman Shaw Building (North), London SW1A 2TT. Tel: 0171-219 2105
E-mail: edunit@parliament.uk

GOVERNMENT OFFICE

The Government is the body of Ministers responsible for the administration of national affairs, determining policy and introducing into Parliament any legislation necessary to give effect to government policy. The majority of Ministers are members of the House of Commons but members of the House of Lords or of neither House may also hold ministerial responsibility. The Lord Chancellor is always a member of the House of Lords. The Prime Minister is, by current convention, always a member of the House of Commons.

THE PRIME MINISTER

The office of Prime Minister, which had been in existence for nearly 200 years, was officially recognized in 1905 and its holder was granted a place in the table of precedence. The Prime Minister, by tradition also First Lord of the Treasury and Minister for the Civil Service, is appointed by the Sovereign and is usually the leader of the party which enjoys, or can secure, a majority in the House of Commons. Other Ministers are appointed by the Sovereign on the recommendation of the Prime Minister, who also allocates functions amongst Ministers and has the power to obtain their resignation or dismissal individually.

The Prime Minister informs the Sovereign of state and political matters, advises on the dissolution of Parliament, and makes recommendations for important Crown appointments, the award of honours, etc.

As the chairman of Cabinet meetings and leader of a political party, the Prime Minister is responsible for translating party policy into government activity. As leader of the Government, the Prime Minister is responsible to Parliament and to the electorate for the policies and their implementation.

The Prime Minister also represents the nation in international affairs, e.g. summit conferences.

THE CABINET

The Cabinet developed during the 18th century as an inner committee of the Privy Council, which was the chief source of executive power until that time. The Cabinet is composed of about 20 Ministers chosen by the Prime Minister, usually the heads of government departments (generally known as Secretaries of State unless they have a special title, e.g. Chancellor of the Exchequer), the leaders of the two Houses of Parliament, and the holders of various traditional offices.

The Cabinet's functions are the final determination of policy, control of government and co-ordination of government departments. The exercise of its functions is dependent upon enjoying majority support in the House of Commons. Cabinet meetings are held in private, taking place once or twice a week during parliamentary sittings and less often during a recess. Proceedings are confidential, the members being bound by their oath as Privy Counsellors not to disclose information about the proceedings.

The convention of collective responsibility means that the Cabinet acts unanimously even when Cabinet Ministers do not all agree on a subject. The policies of departmental Ministers must be consistent with the policies of the Government as a whole, and once the Government's policy has been decided, each Minister is expected to support it or resign.

The convention of ministerial responsibility holds a Minister, as the political head of his or her department, accountable to Parliament for the department's work. Departmental Ministers usually decide all matters within their responsibility, although on matters of political importance they normally consult their colleagues collectively. A decision by a departmental Minister is binding on the Government as a whole.

POLITICAL PARTIES

Before the reign of William and Mary the principal officers of state were chosen by and were responsible to the Sovereign alone and not to Parliament or the nation at large. Such officers acted sometimes in concert with one another but more often independently, and the fall of one did not, of necessity, involve that of others, although all were liable to be dismissed at any moment.

In 1693 the Earl of Sunderland recommended to William III the advisability of selecting a ministry from the political party which enjoyed a majority in the House of Commons and the first united ministry was drawn in 1696 from the Whigs, to which party the King owed its throne. This group became known as the Junto and was regarded with suspicion as a novelty in the political life of the nation, being a small section meeting in secret apart from the main body of Ministers. It may be regarded as the forerunner of the Cabinet and in course of time it led to the establishment of the principle of joint responsibility of Ministers, so that internal disagreement caused a change of personnel or resignation of the whole body of Ministers.

The accession of George I, who was unfamiliar with the English language, led to a disinclination on the part of the Sovereign to preside at meetings of his Ministers and caused the appearance of a Prime Minister, a position first acquired by Robert Walpole in 1721 and retained by him without interruption for 20 years and 326 days.

DEVELOPMENT OF PARTIES

In 1828 the Whigs became known as Liberals, a name originally given to it by its opponents to imply laxity of principles, but gradually accepted by the party to indicate its claim to be pioneers and champions of political reform and progressive legislation. In 1861 a Liberal Registration Association was founded and Liberal Associations became widespread. In 1877 a National Liberal Federation was formed, with headquarters in London. The Liberal Party was in power for long periods during the second half of the 19th century and for several years during the first quarter of the 20th century, but after a split in the party the numbers elected were small from 1931. In 1988, a majority of the Liberals agreed on a merger with the Social Democratic Party under the title Social and Liberal Democrats; since 1989 they have been known as the Liberal Democrats. A minority continue separately as the Liberal Party.

Soon after the change from Whig to Liberal the Tory Party became known as Conservative, a name believed to have been invented by John Wilson Croker in 1830 and to have been generally adopted about the time of the passing of the Reform Act of 1832 to indicate that the preservation of national institutions was the leading principle of the party. After the Home Rule crisis of 1886 the dissentient Liberals entered into a compact with the Conservatives, under which the latter undertook not to contest their seats, but a separate Liberal Unionist organization was maintained until 1912, when it was united with the Conservatives.

Labour candidates for Parliament made their first appearance at the general election of 1892, when there were 27 standing as Labour or Liberal-Labour. In 1900 the

Labour Representation Committee was set up in order to establish a distinct Labour group in Parliament, with its own whips, its own policy, and a readiness to co-operate with any party which might be engaged in promoting legislation in the direct interest of labour. In 1906 the LRC became known as the Labour Party.

The Council for Social Democracy was announced by four former Labour Cabinet Ministers in January 1981 and on 26 March 1981 the Social Democratic Party was launched. Later that year the SDP and the Liberal Party formed an electoral alliance. In 1988 a majority of the SDP agreed on a merger with the Liberal Party (*see* above) but a minority continued as a separate party under the SDP title. In 1990 it was decided to wind up the party organization and its three sitting MPs were known as independent social democrats. None were returned at the 1992 general election.

Plaid Cymru was founded in 1926 to provide an independent political voice for Wales and to campaign for self-government in Wales.

The Scottish National Party was founded in 1934 to campaign for independence for Scotland.

The Social Democratic and Labour Party was founded in 1970, emerging from the civil rights movement of the 1960s, with the aim of promoting reform, reconciliation and partnership across the sectarian divide in Northern Ireland and of opposing violence from any quarter.

The Ulster Democratic Unionist Party was founded in 1971 to resist moves by the Ulster Unionist Party which were considered a threat to the Union. Its aim is to maintain Northern Ireland as an integral part of the UK.

The Ulster Unionist Council first met formally in 1905. Its objectives are to maintain Northern Ireland as an integral part of the UK and to promote the aims of the Ulster Unionist Party.

GOVERNMENT AND OPPOSITION

The government of the day is formed by the party which wins the largest number of seats in the House of Commons at a general election, or which has the support of a majority of members in the House of Commons. By tradition, the leader of the majority party is asked by the Sovereign to form a government, while the largest minority party becomes the official Opposition with its own leader and a 'Shadow Cabinet'. Leaders of the Government and Opposition sit on the front benches of the Commons with their supporters (the back-benchers) sitting behind them.

FINANCIAL SUPPORT

Financial support to Opposition parties was introduced in 1975 and is commonly known as Short Money, after Edward Short, the Leader of the House at that time, who introduced the scheme. For 1998–9 financial support is:

Conservative	£1,112,885.74
Liberal Democrats	419,559.87
Plaid Cymru	23,921.74
SNP	52,070.47
SDLP	20,925.09
Democratic Unionists	13,103.96
Ulster Unionsts	53,660.30

The parties included here are those with MPs sitting in the House of Commons in the present Parliament. Addresses of other political parties may be found in the Societies and Institutions section.

CONSERVATIVE AND UNIONIST PARTY

Central Office, 32 Smith Square, London SW1P 3HH
Tel 0171-222 9000; fax 0171-233 0701
E-mail: ccoffice@conservative-party.org.uk
Web: http://www.tory.org.uk

Chairman, Rt. Hon. Michael Ancram, QC, MP
Deputy Chairman and Chief Executive, Archie Norman, MP
Vice-Chairmen, The Baroness Buscombe; Andrew Lansley, CBE, MP; Hon. David Prior, MP; Tim Yeo, MP
Treasurer, M. Ashcroft

SHADOW CABINET *as at 3 August 1998*
Leader of the Opposition, Rt. Hon. William Hague, MP
Deputy Leader, Rt. Hon. Peter Lilley, MP
Agriculture, Fisheries and Food, Tim Yeo, MP
Constitutional Affairs, Dr Liam Fox, MP
Culture, Media and Sport, Peter Ainsworth, MP
Defence, John Maples, MP
Education and Employment, David Willetts, MP
Environment, Transport and the Regions, Rt. Hon. Gillian Shephard, MP
Foreign and Commonwealth Affairs, Rt. Hon. Michael Howard, QC, MP
Health, Rt. Hon. Ann Widdecombe, MP
Home Affairs, Rt. Hon. Sir Norman Fowler, MP
International Development, Gary Streeter, MP
Leader of the House of Commons and Chancellor of the Duchy of Lancaster, Rt. Hon. Sir George Young, Bt., MP
Leader of the House of Lords, Viscount Cranborne, PC
Northern Ireland, Rt. Hon. Andrew Mackay, MP
Social Security, Iain Duncan-Smith, MP
Trade and Industry, Rt. Hon. John Redwood, MP
Treasury, Rt. Hon. Francis Maude, MP
Chief Secretary to the Treasury, Rt. Hon. David Heathcoat-Amory, MP

CHIEF WHIPS
House of Lords, The Lord Strathclyde, PC
House of Commons, James Arbuthnot, MP (*Chief Whip*); Patrick McLoughlin, MP (*Deputy Chief Whip*)

SCOTTISH CONSERVATIVE AND UNIONIST CENTRAL OFFICE

Suite 1/1, 14 Links Place, Leith, Edinburgh EH6 7EZ
Tel 0131-555 2900
E-mail: SCUCO@Scottish.tory.org.uk

Chairman, R. Robertson
Deputy Chairman, Mrs K. Donald
Hon. Treasurer, W. Y. Hughes, CBE
Head of Campaigns and Operations, D. Canzini

LABOUR PARTY

Millbank Tower, Millbank, London SW1P 4GT
Tel 0171-802 1000; fax 0171-802 1234
E-mail: labour-party@geo2.poptel.org.uk
Web: http://www.labour.org.uk

Parliamentary Party Leader, Rt. Hon. Anthony Blair, MP
Deputy Party Leader, Rt. Hon. John Prescott, MP
Leader in the Lords, The Lord Richard, PC, QC
Chair, R. Rosser
Vice-Chair, Rt. Hon. Clare Short, MP
Treasurer, Ms M. Prosser
General Secretary, Ms M. McDonagh
General Secretary, Scottish Labour Party, A. Rowley

LIBERAL DEMOCRATS
4 Cowley Street, London SW1P 3NB
Tel 0171-222 7999; fax 0171-799 2170
E-mail: libdems@cix.co.uk
Web: http://www.libdems.org.uk

President, Rt. Hon. Robert Maclennan, MP
Hon. Treasurer, The Lord Razzall, CBE
Chief Executive, Ms E. Pamplin
Parliamentary Party Leader, Rt. Hon. Paddy Ashdown, MP
Leader in the Lords, The Lord Rodgers of Quarry Bank, PC

LIBERAL DEMOCRAT SPOKESMEN *as at June 1998*
Deputy Leader, Home and Legal Affairs, Alan Beith, MP
Agriculture and Rural Affairs, Charles Kennedy, MP
Culture, Media and Sport, Constitution, Rt. Hon. Robert
   Maclennan, MP
Education and Employment, Don Foster, MP
Environment and Transport, Matthew Taylor, MP
Foreign Affairs, Defence and Europe, Menzies Campbell, MP
Health, Simon Hughes, MP
Local Government and Housing, Paul Burstow, MP
Social Security and Welfare, David Rendel, MP
Trade and Industry, David Chidgey, MP
Treasury, Malcolm Bruce, MP
Women, Jackie Ballard, MP
Young People, Lembit Opik, MP
Northern Ireland, The Lord Holme of Cheltenham
Scotland, Jim Wallace, MP
Wales, Richard Livsey, MP

LIBERAL DEMOCRAT WHIPS
House of Lords, The Lord Harris of Greenwich, PC
House of Commons, Paul Tyler, MP (*Chief Whip*); Andrew
   Stunell, MP (*Deputy Whip*)

LIBERAL DEMOCRATS WALES
Bay View House, 102 Bute Street, Cardiff CF1 6AD
Tel 01222-313400; fax 01222-313401
E-mail: ldwales@cix.co.uk

Party President, A. Carlile, QC
Party Leader, Richard Livsey, CBE, MP
Chairman, C. Davies
Treasurer, N. Howells
Secretary, Ms K. Lloyd
Administrative Officer, Ms H. Northmore

SCOTTISH LIBERAL DEMOCRATS
4 Clifton Terrace, Edinburgh EH12 5DR
Tel 0131-337 2314; fax 0131-337 3566
E-mail: scotlibdem@cix.co.uk
Web: http://www.scotlibdems.org.uk

Party President, R. Thomson
Party Leader, Jim Wallace, MP
Convener, S. Gallagher
Treasurer, D. R. Sullivan
Chief Executive, W. Rennie

PLAID CYMRU
18 Park Grove, Cardiff CF1 3BN
Tel 01222-646000; fax 01222-646001
E-mail: post@plaidcymru.org
Web: http://www.plaidcymru.org

Party President, Dafydd Wigley, MP
Chairman, M. Phillips
Hon. Treasurer, O. Williams
Chief Executive/General Secretary, K. Davies

SCOTTISH NATIONAL PARTY
6 North Charlotte Street, Edinburgh EH2 4JH
Tel 0131-226 3661; fax 0131-225 9597
Web: http://www.snp.org.uk

Parliamentary Party Leader, Margaret Ewing, MP
Chief Whip, Andrew Welsh, MP
National Convener, Alex Salmond, MP
Senior Vice-Convener, Dr A. Macartney, MEP
National Treasurer, K. MacAskill
National Secretary, C. Campbell

NORTHERN IRELAND

SOCIAL DEMOCRATIC AND LABOUR PARTY
121 Ormeau Road, Belfast BT7 1SH
Tel 01232-247700; fax 01232-236699
E-mail: sdlp@indigo.ie
Web: http://www.indigo.ie/sdlp

Parliamentary Party Leader, John Hume, MP, MEP
Deputy Leader, Seamus Mallon, MP
Chief Whip, Eddie McGrady, MP
Chairman, J. Stephenson
Hon. Treasurer, J. Lennon
General Secretary, Mrs G. Cosgrove

ULSTER DEMOCRATIC UNIONIST PARTY
91 Dundela Avenue, Belfast BT4 3BU
Tel 01232-471155; fax 01232-471797
E-mail: info@dup.org.uk
Web: http://www.dup.org.uk

Parliamentary Party Leader, I. Paisley, MP, MEP
Deputy Leader, Peter Robinson, MP
Chairman, W. J. McClure
Hon. Treasurer, G. Campbell
Party Secretary, N. Dodds

ULSTER UNIONIST PARTY
3 Glengall Street, Belfast BT12 5AE
Tel 01232-324601; fax 01232-246738
E-mail: uup@uup.org
Web: http://www.uup.org

Party Leader, Rt. Hon. David Trimble, MP
Chief Whip, Revd Martin Smyth, MP

ULSTER UNIONIST COUNCIL
President, J. Cunningham
Chairman, D. Rogan
Hon. Treasurer, J. Allen, OBE
Party Secretary, J. Wilson

MEMBERS OF PARLIAMENT as at 1 August 1998

For abbreviations, *see* page 235
* Member of last Parliament
† Former Member of Parliament
An entire entry in italic indicates that the MP was elected at the general election but has died since; the name is included for the purposes of record

*Abbott, Ms Diane J. (*b.* 1953) *Lab., Hackney North and Stoke Newington*, maj. 15,627

Adams, Gerard (Gerry) (*b.* 1948) *SF, Belfast West*, maj. 7,909

*Adams, Mrs K. Irene (*b.* 1948) *Lab., Paisley North*, maj. 12,814

*Ainger, Nicholas R. (*b.* 1949) *Lab., Carmarthen West and Pembrokeshire South*, maj. 9,621

*Ainsworth, Peter M. (*b.* 1956) *C., Surrey East*, maj. 15,093

*Ainsworth, Robert W. (*b.* 1952) *Lab., Coventry North East*, maj. 22,569

Alexander, Douglas G. (*b.* 1967) *Lab., Paisley South*, maj. 2,731

Allan, Richard B. (*b.* 1966) *LD, Sheffield Hallam*, maj. 8,271

*Allen, Graham W. (*b.* 1953) *Lab., Nottingham North*, maj. 18,801

*Amess, David A. A. (*b.* 1952) *C., Southend West*, maj. 2,615

*Ancram, Rt. Hon. Michael A. F. J. K. (Earl of Ancram) (*b.* 1945) *C., Devizes*, maj. 9,782

*Anderson, Donald (*b.* 1939) *Lab., Swansea East*, maj. 25,569

*Anderson, Mrs Janet (*b.* 1949) *Lab., Rossendale and Darwen*, maj. 10,949

*Arbuthnot, Rt. Hon. James N. (*b.* 1952) *C., Hampshire North East*, maj. 14,398

*Armstrong, Miss Hilary J. (*b.* 1945) *Lab., Durham North West*, maj. 24,754

*Ashdown, Rt. Hon. J. J. D. (Paddy) (*b.* 1941) *LD, Yeovil*, maj. 11,403

*Ashton, Joseph W. (*b.* 1933) *Lab., Bassetlaw*, maj. 17,460

Atherton, Ms Candice K. (*b.* 1955) *Lab., Falmouth and Camborne*, maj. 2,688

Atkins, Ms Charlotte (*b.* 1950) *Lab., Staffordshire Moorlands*, maj. 10,049

*Atkinson, David A. (*b.* 1940) *C., Bournemouth East*, maj. 4,346

*Atkinson, Peter L. (*b.* 1943) *C., Hexham*, maj. 222

*Austin-Walker, John E. (*b.* 1944) *Lab., Erith and Thamesmead*, maj. 17,424

Baker, Norman J. (*b.* 1957) *LD, Lewes*, maj. 1,300

*Baldry, Antony B. (*b.* 1950) *C., Banbury*, maj. 4,737

Ballard, Mrs Jacqueline M. (*b.* 1953) *LD, Taunton*, maj. 2,443

*Banks, Anthony L. (*b.* 1943) *Lab., West Ham*, maj. 19,494

*Barnes, Harold (*b.* 1936) *Lab., Derbyshire North East*, maj. 18,321

*Barron, Kevin J. (*b.* 1946) *Lab., Rother Valley*, maj. 23,485

*Battle, John D. (*b.* 1951) *Lab., Leeds West*, maj. 19,771

*Bayley, Hugh (*b.* 1952) *Lab., City of York*, maj. 20,523

Beard, C. Nigel (*b.* 1936) *Lab., Bexleyheath and Crayford*, maj. 3,415

*Beckett, Rt. Hon. Margaret M. (*b.* 1943) *Lab., Derby South*, maj. 16,106

Begg, Ms Anne (*b.* 1955) *Lab., Aberdeen South*, maj. 3,365

*Beggs, Roy (*b.* 1936) *UUP, Antrim East*, maj. 6,389

*Beith, Rt. Hon. Alan J. (*b.* 1943) *LD, Berwick upon Tweed*, maj. 8,042

Bell, Martin, OBE (*b.* 1938) *Ind., Tatton*, maj. 11,077

*Bell, Stuart (*b.* 1938) *Lab., Middlesbrough*, maj. 25,018

*Benn, Rt. Hon. Anthony N. W. (*b.* 1925) *Lab., Chesterfield*, maj. 5,775

*Bennett, Andrew F. (*b.* 1939) *Lab., Denton and Reddish*, maj. 20,311

*Benton, Joseph E. (*b.* 1933) *Lab., Bootle*, maj. 28,421

Bercow, John S. (*b.* 1963) *C., Buckingham*, maj. 12,386

*Beresford, Sir Paul (*b.* 1946) *C., Mole Valley*, maj. 10,221

*Bermingham, Gerald E. (*b.* 1940) *Lab., St Helens South*, maj. 23,739

*Berry, Roger L., D.Phil. (*b.* 1948) *Lab., Kingswood*, maj. 14,253

Best, Harold (*b.* 1939) *Lab., Leeds North West*, maj. 3,844

*Betts, Clive J. C. (*b.* 1950) *Lab., Sheffield Attercliffe*, maj. 21,818

Blackman, Ms Elizabeth M. (*b.* 1949) *Lab., Erewash*, maj. 9,135

*Blair, Rt. Hon. Anthony C. L. (*b.* 1953) *Lab., Sedgefield*, maj. 25,143

Blears, Hazel A. (*b.* 1956) *Lab., Salford*, maj. 17,069

Blizzard, Robert J. (*b.* 1950) *Lab., Waveney*, maj. 12,453

*Blunkett, Rt. Hon. David (*b.* 1947) *Lab., Sheffield Brightside*, maj. 19,954

Blunt, Crispin J. R. (*b.* 1960) *C., Reigate*, maj. 7,741

*Boateng, Paul Y. (*b.* 1951) *Lab., Brent South*, maj. 19,691

*Body, Sir Richard (*b.* 1927) *C., Boston and Skegness*, maj. 647

*Boothroyd, Rt. Hon. Betty (*b.* 1929) *The Speaker, West Bromwich West*, maj. 15,423

Borrow, David S. (*b.* 1952) *Lab., Ribble South*, maj. 5,084

*Boswell, Timothy E. (*b.* 1942) *C., Daventry*, maj. 7,378

*Bottomley, Peter J. (*b.* 1944) *C., Worthing West*, maj. 7,713

*Bottomley, Rt. Hon. Virginia H. B. M. (*b.* 1948) *C., Surrey South West*, maj. 2,694

*Bradley, Keith J. C. (*b.* 1950) *Lab., Manchester Withington*, maj. 18,581

Bradley, Peter C. S. (*b.* 1953) *Lab., Wrekin, The*, maj. 3,025

Bradshaw, Benjamin P. J. (*b.* 1960) *Lab., Exeter*, maj. 11,705

Brady, Graham (*b.* 1967) *C., Altrincham and Sale West*, maj. 1,505

Brake, Thomas A. (*b.* 1962) *LD, Carshalton and Wallington*, maj. 2,267

Brand, Dr Peter (*b.* 1947) *LD, Isle of Wight*, maj. 6,406

*Brazier, Julian W. H., TD (*b.* 1953) *C., Canterbury*, maj. 3,964

Breed, Colin E. (*b.* 1947) *LD, Cornwall South East*, maj. 6,480

Brinton, Ms Helen R. (*b.* 1954) *Lab., Peterborough*, maj. 7,323

*Brooke, Rt. Hon. Peter L., CH (*b.* 1934) *C., Cities of London and Westminster*, maj. 4,881

*Brown, Rt. Hon. J. Gordon, PH.D. (*b.* 1951) *Lab., Dunfermline East*, maj. 18,751

*Brown, Nicholas H. (*b.* 1950) *Lab., Newcastle upon Tyne East and Wallsend*, maj. 23,811

Brown, Russell L. (*b.* 1951) *Lab., Dumfries*, maj. 9,643

Browne, Desmond (*b.* 1952) *Lab., Kilmarnock and Loudoun*, maj. 7,256

*Browning, Mrs Angela F. (*b.* 1946) *C., Tiverton and Honiton*, maj. 1,653

*Bruce, Ian C. (*b.* 1947) *C., Dorset South*, maj. 77

*Bruce, Malcolm G. (*b.* 1944) *LD, Gordon*, maj. 6,997

Buck, Ms Karen P. (*b.* 1958) *Lab., Regent's Park and Kensington North*, maj. 14,657

*Burden, Richard H. (*b.* 1954) *Lab., Birmingham Northfield*, maj. 11,443

Burgon, Colin (*b.* 1948) *Lab., Elmet*, maj. 8,779

Burnett, John P. A. (*b.* 1945) *LD, Devon West and Torridge*, maj. 1,957

*Burns, Simon H. M. (*b.* 1952) *C., Chelmsford West*, maj. 6,691

Burstow, Paul K. (*b.* 1962) *LD, Sutton and Cheam*, maj. 2,097

Butler, Ms Christine M. (*b.* 1943) *Lab., Castle Point*, maj. 1,116

*Donohoe, Brian H. (*b.* 1948) *Lab., Cunninghame South,* maj. 14,869

Doran, Frank (*b.* 1949) *Lab., Aberdeen Central,* maj. 10,801

*Dorrell, Rt. Hon. Stephen J. (*b.* 1952) *C., Charnwood,* maj. 5,900

*Dowd, James P. (*b.* 1951) *Lab., Lewisham West,* maj. 14,337

Drew, David E. (*b.* 1952) *Lab. Co-op., Stroud,* maj. 2,910

Drown, Ms Julia K. (*b.* 1962) *Lab., Swindon South,* maj. 5,645

*Duncan, Alan J. C. (*b.* 1957) *C., Rutland and Melton,* maj. 8,836

*Duncan Smith, G. Iain (*b.* 1954) *C., Chingford and Woodford Green,* maj. 5,714

*Dunwoody, Hon. Mrs Gwyneth P. (*b.* 1930) *Lab., Crewe and Nantwich,* maj. 15,798

*Eagle, Ms Angela (*b.* 1961) *Lab., Wallasey,* maj. 19,074

Eagle, Ms Maria (*b.* 1961) *Lab., Liverpool Garston,* maj. 18,417

Edwards, Huw W. E. (*b.* 1953) *Lab., Monmouth,* maj. 4,178

Efford, Clive S. (*b.* 1958) *Lab., Eltham,* maj. 10,182

Ellman, Ms Louise J. (*b.* 1945) *Lab. Co-op., Liverpool Riverside,* maj. 21,799

*Emery, Rt. Hon. Sir Peter (*b.* 1926) *C., Devon East,* maj. 7,489

*Ennis, Jeffrey (*b.* 1952) *Lab., Barnsley East and Mexborough,* maj. 26,763

*Etherington, William (*b.* 1941) *Lab., Sunderland North,* maj. 19,697

*Evans, Nigel M. (*b.* 1957) *C., Ribble Valley,* maj. 6,640

*Ewing, Mrs Margaret A. (*b.* 1945) *SNP, Moray,* maj. 5,566

*Faber, David J. C. (*b.* 1961) *C., Westbury,* maj. 6,068

*Fabricant, Michael L. D. (*b.* 1950) *C., Lichfield,* maj. 238

Fallon, Michael C (*b.* 1952) *C., Sevenoaks,* maj. 10,461

*Fatchett, Derek J. (*b.* 1945) *Lab., Leeds Central,* maj. 20,689

Fearn, Ronald C., OBE (*b.* 1931) *LD, Southport,* maj. 6,160

*Field, Rt. Hon. Frank (*b.* 1942) *Lab., Birkenhead,* maj. 21,843

*Fisher, Mark (*b.* 1944) *Lab., Stoke-on-Trent Central,* maj. 19,924

Fitzpatrick, James (*b.* 1952) *Lab., Poplar and Canning Town,* maj. 18,915

Fitzsimons, Ms Lorna (*b.* 1967) *Lab., Rochdale,* maj. 4,545

*Flight, Howard E. (*b.* 1948) *C., Arundel and South Downs,* maj. 14,035

Flint, Ms Caroline L. (*b.* 1961) *Lab., Don Valley,* maj. 14,659

*Flynn, Paul P. (*b.* 1935) *Lab., Newport West,* maj. 14,537

Follett, Ms D. Barbara (*b.* 1942) *Lab., Stevenage,* maj. 11,582

*Forsythe, Clifford (*b.* 1929) *UUP, Antrim South,* maj. 16,611

*Forth, Rt. Hon. Eric (*b.* 1944) *C., Bromley and Chislehurst,* maj. 11,118

*Foster, Rt. Hon. Derek (*b.* 1937) *Lab., Bishop Auckland,* maj. 21,064

*Foster, Donald M. E. (*b.* 1947) *LD, Bath,* maj. 9,319

Foster, Michael J. (*b.* 1946) *Lab., Hastings and Rye,* maj. 2,560

Foster, Michael J. (*b.* 1963) *Lab., Worcester,* maj. 7,425

*Foulkes, George (*b.* 1942) *Lab. Co-op., Carrick, Cumnock and Doon Valley,* maj. 21,062

*Fowler, Rt. Hon. Sir Norman (*b.* 1938) *C., Sutton Coldfield,* maj. 14,885

*Fox, Dr Liam (*b.* 1961) *C., Woodspring,* maj. 7,734

Fraser, Christopher J. (*b.* 1962) *C., Dorset Mid and Poole North,* maj. 681

*Fyfe, Ms Maria (*b.* 1938) *Lab., Glasgow Maryhill,* maj. 14,264

*Galbraith, Samuel L. (*b.* 1945) *Lab., Strathkelvin and Bearsden,* maj. 16,292

*Gale, Roger J. (*b.* 1943) *C., Thanet North,* maj. 2,766

*Galloway, George (*b.* 1954) *Lab., Glasgow Kelvin,* maj. 9,665

*Gapes, Michael J. (*b.* 1952) *Lab. Co-op., Ilford South,* maj. 14,200

Gardiner, Barry S. (*b.* 1957) *Lab., Brent North,* maj. 4,019

*Garnier, Edward H., QC (*b.* 1952) *C., Harborough,* maj. 6,524

George, Andrew H. (*b.* 1958) *LD, St Ives,* maj. 7,170

*George, Bruce T. (*b.* 1942) *Lab., Walsall South,* maj. 11,312

*Gerrard, Neil F. (*b.* 1942) *Lab., Walthamstow,* maj. 17,149

Gibb, Nicholas J. (*b.* 1960) *C., Bognor Regis and Littlehampton,* maj. 7,321

Gibson, Dr Ian (*b.* 1938) *Lab., Norwich North,* maj. 9,470

*Gill, Christopher J. F., RD (*b.* 1936) *C., Ludlow,* maj. 5,909

*Gillan, Mrs Cheryl E. K. (*b.* 1952) *C., Chesham and Amersham,* maj. 13,859

Gilroy, Mrs Linda (*b.* 1949) *Lab. Co-op., Plymouth Sutton,* maj. 9,440

*Godman, Norman A., PH.D. (*b.* 1938) *Lab., Greenock and Inverclyde,* maj. 13,040

*Godsiff, Roger D. (*b.* 1946) *Lab., Birmingham Sparkbrook and Small Heath,* maj. 19,526

Goggins, Paul G. (*b.* 1953) *Lab., Wythenshawe and Sale East,* maj. 15,019

*Golding, Mrs Llinos (*b.* 1933) *Lab., Newcastle under Lyme,* maj. 17,206

*Goodlad, Rt. Hon. Sir Alastair, KCMG (*b.* 1943) *C., Eddisbury,* maj. 1,185

Gordon, Mrs Eileen (*b.* 1946) *Lab., Romford,* maj. 649

*Gorman, Mrs Teresa E. (*b.* 1931) *C., Billericay,* maj. 1,356

Gorrie, Donald C. E. (*b.* 1933) *LD, Edinburgh West,* maj. 7,253

*Graham, Thomas (*b.* 1944) *Lab., Renfrewshire West,* maj. 7,979

*Grant, Bernard A. M. (*b.* 1944) *Lab., Tottenham,* maj. 20,200

Gray, James W. (*b.* 1954) *C., Wiltshire North,* maj. 3,475

Green, Damian H. (*b.* 1956) *C., Ashford,* maj. 5,355

*Greenway, John R. (*b.* 1946) *C., Ryedale,* maj. 5,058

Grieve, Dominic C. R. (*b.* 1956) *C., Beaconsfield,* maj. 13,987

Griffiths, Ms Jane P. (*b.* 1954) *Lab., Reading East,* maj. 3,795

*Griffiths, Nigel (*b.* 1955) *Lab., Edinburgh South,* maj. 11,452

*Griffiths, Winston J. (*b.* 1943) *Lab., Bridgend,* maj. 15,248

*Grocott, Bruce J. (*b.* 1940) *Lab., Telford,* maj. 11,290

Grogan, John T. (*b.* 1961) *Lab., Selby,* maj. 3,836

*Gummer, Rt. Hon. John S. (*b.* 1939) *C., Suffolk Coastal,* maj. 3,254

*Gunnell, W. John (*b.* 1933) *Lab., Morley and Rothwell,* maj. 14,750

*Hague, Rt. Hon. William J. (*b.* 1961) *C., Richmond,* maj. 10,051

*Hain, Peter G. (*b.* 1950) *Lab., Neath,* maj. 26,741

*Hall, Michael T. (*b.* 1952) *Lab., Weaver Vale,* maj. 13,448

Hall, Patrick (*b.* 1951) *Lab., Bedford,* maj. 8,300

*Hamilton, Rt. Hon. Sir Archibald (*b.* 1941) *C., Epsom and Ewell,* maj. 11,525

Hamilton, Fabian (*b.* 1955) *Lab., Leeds North East,* maj. 6,959

Hammond, Philip (*b.* 1955) *C., Runnymede and Weybridge,* maj. 9,875

Hancock, Michael T., CBE (*b.* 1946) *LD, Portsmouth South,* maj. 4,327

*Hanson, David G. (*b.* 1957) *Lab., Delyn,* maj. 11,693

*Harman, Rt. Hon. Harriet (*b.* 1950) *Lab., Camberwell and Peckham,* maj. 16,351

Harris, Dr Evan (*b.* 1965) *LD, Oxford West and Abingdon,* maj. 6,285

*Harvey, Nicholas B. (*b.* 1961) *LD, Devon North,* maj. 6,181

*Haselhurst, Sir Alan (*b.* 1937) *C., Saffron Walden,* maj. 10,573

*Hawkins, Nicholas J. (*b.* 1957) *C., Surrey Heath,* maj. 16,287

Hayes, John H. (*b.* 1958) *C., South Holland and the Deepings,* maj. 7,991

Heal, Mrs Sylvia L. (*b.* 1942) *Lab. Co-op., Halesowen and Rowley Regis,* maj. 10,337

*Heald, Oliver (*b.* 1954) *C., Hertfordshire North East,* maj. 3,088

Healey, John (*b.* 1960) *Lab., Wentworth,* maj. 23,959

Heath, David W. St J. (*b.* 1954) *LD, Somerton and Frome,* maj. 130

*Heath, Rt. Hon. Sir Edward, KG, MBE (*b.* 1916) *C., Old Bexley and Sidcup,* maj. 3,569

*Heathcoat-Amory, Rt. Hon. David P. (*b.* 1949) *C., Wells,* maj. 528

*Henderson, Douglas J. (*b.* 1949) *Lab., Newcastle upon Tyne North,* maj. 19,332

Henderson, Ivan J. (*b.* 1958) *Lab., Harwich,* maj. 1,216

Hepburn, Stephen (*b.* 1959) *Lab., Jarrow,* maj. 21,933

*Heppell, John B. (*b.* 1948) *Lab., Nottingham East,* maj. 15,419

*Heseltine, Rt. Hon. Michael R. D., CH (*b.* 1933) *C., Henley,* maj. 11,167

Hesford, Stephen (*b.* 1957) *Lab., Wirral West,* maj. 2,738

Hewitt, Ms Patricia H. (*b.* 1948) *Lab., Leicester West,* maj. 12,864

*Hill, T. Keith (*b.* 1943) *Lab., Streatham,* maj. 18,423

*Hinchliffe, David M. (*b.* 1948) *Lab., Wakefield,* maj. 14,604

*Hodge, Mrs Margaret E., MBE (*b.* 1944) *Lab., Barking,* maj. 15,896

*Hoey, Ms Catharine (Kate) L. (*b.* 1946) *Lab., Vauxhall,* maj. 18,660

*Hogg, Rt. Hon. Douglas M., QC (*b.* 1945) *C., Sleaford and North Hykeham,* maj. 5,123

*Home Robertson, John D. (*b.* 1948) *Lab., East Lothian,* maj. 14,221

*Hood, James (*b.* 1948) *Lab., Clydesdale,* maj. 13,809

*Hoon, Geoffrey W. (*b.* 1953) *Lab., Ashfield,* maj. 22,728

Hope, Philip I. (*b.* 1955) *Lab. Co-op., Corby,* maj. 11,860

Hopkins, Kelvin P. (*b.* 1941) *Lab., Luton North,* maj. 9,626

*Horam, John R. (*b.* 1939) *C., Orpington,* maj. 2,952

*Howard, Rt. Hon. Michael, QC (*b.* 1941) *C., Folkestone and Hythe,* maj. 6,332

*Howarth, Alan T., CBE (*b.* 1944) *Lab., Newport East,* maj. 13,523

*Howarth, George E. (*b.* 1949) *Lab., Knowsley North and Sefton East,* maj. 26,147

Howarth, J. Gerald D. (*b.* 1947) *C., Aldershot,* maj. 6,621

*Howells, Kim S., PH.D. (*b.* 1946) *Lab., Pontypridd,* maj. 23,129

Hoyle, Lindsay H. (*b.* 1957) *Lab., Chorley,* maj. 9,870

*Hughes, Ms Beverley J. (*b.* 1950) *Lab., Stretford and Urmston,* maj. 13,640

*Hughes, Kevin M. (*b.* 1952) *Lab., Doncaster North,* maj. 21,937

*Hughes, Simon H. W. (*b.* 1951) *LD, Southwark North and Bermondsey,* maj. 3,387

Humble, Mrs Jovanka (Joan) (*b.* 1951) *Lab., Blackpool North and Fleetwood,* maj. 8,946

*Hume, John, MEP (*b.* 1937) *SDLP, Foyle,* maj. 13,664

*Hunter, Andrew R. F. (*b.* 1943) *C., Basingstoke,* maj. 2,397

Hurst, Alan A. (*b.* 1945) *Lab., Braintree,* maj. 1,451

*Hutton, John M. P. (*b.* 1955) *Lab., Barrow and Furness,* maj. 14,497

Iddon, Brian (*b.* 1940) *Lab., Bolton South East,* maj. 21,311

*Illsley, Eric E. (*b.* 1955) *Lab., Barnsley Central,* maj. 24,501

*Ingram, Adam P. (*b.* 1947) *Lab., East Kilbride,* maj. 17,384

*Jack, Rt. Hon. J. Michael (*b.* 1946) *C., Fylde,* maj. 8,963

*Jackson, Ms Glenda M., CBE (*b.* 1936) *Lab., Hampstead and Highgate,* maj. 13,284

*Jackson, Mrs Helen M. (*b.* 1939) *Lab., Sheffield Hillsborough,* maj. 16,451

*Jackson, Robert V. (*b.* 1946) *C., Wantage,* maj. 6,039

*Jamieson, David C. (*b.* 1947) *Lab., Plymouth Devonport,* maj. 19,067

*Jenkin, Hon. Bernard C. (*b.* 1959) *C., Essex North,* maj. 5,476

*Jenkins, Brian D. (*b.* 1942) *Lab., Tamworth,* maj. 7,496

Johnson, Alan A. (*b.* 1950) *Lab., Hull West and Hessle,* maj. 15,525

Johnson, Ms Melanie J. (*b.* 1955) *Lab., Welwyn Hatfield,* maj. 5,595

*Johnson Smith, Rt. Hon. Sir Geoffrey (*b.* 1924) *C., Wealden,* maj. 14,204

Jones, Ms Fiona E. A. (*b.* 1957) *Lab., Newark,* maj. 3,016

Jones, Ms Helen M. (*b.* 1954) *Lab., Warrington North,* maj. 19,527

*Jones, Ieuan W. (*b.* 1949) *PC, Ynys Môn,* maj. 2,481

Jones, Ms Jennifer G. (*b.* 1948) *Lab., Wolverhampton South West,* maj. 5,118

*Jones, Jonathan O. (*b.* 1954) *Lab. Co-op., Cardiff Central,* maj. 7,923

*Jones, Ms Lynne M., PH.D. (*b.* 1951) *Lab., Birmingham Selly Oak,* maj. 14,088

*Jones, Martyn D. (*b.* 1947) *Lab., Clwyd South,* maj. 13,810

*Jones, Nigel D. (*b.* 1948) *LD, Cheltenham,* maj. 6,645

*Jones, S. Barry (*b.* 1938) *Lab., Alyn and Deeside,* maj. 16,403

*Jowell, Ms Tessa J. H. D. (*b.* 1947) *Lab., Dulwich and West Norwood,* maj. 16,769

*Kaufman, Rt. Hon. Gerald B. (*b.* 1930) *Lab., Manchester Gorton,* maj. 17,342

Keeble, Ms Sally C. (*b.* 1951) *Lab., Northampton North,* maj. 10,000

*Keen, D. Alan (*b.* 1937) *Lab. Co-op., Feltham and Heston,* maj. 15,273

*Keen, Mrs Ann L. (*b.* 1948) *Lab., Brentford and Isleworth,* maj. 14,424

Keetch, Paul S. (*b.* 1961) *LD, Hereford,* maj. 6,648

Kelly, Ms Ruth M. (*b.* 1968) *Lab., Bolton West,* maj. 7,072

Kemp, Fraser (*b.* 1958) *Lab., Houghton and Washington East,* maj. 26,555

*Kennedy, Charles P. (*b.* 1959) *LD, Ross, Skye and Inverness West,* maj. 4,019

*Kennedy, Mrs Jane E. (*b.* 1958) *Lab., Liverpool Wavertree,* maj. 19,701

*Key, S. Robert (*b.* 1945) *C., Salisbury,* maj. 6,276

*Khabra, Piara S. (*b.* 1924) *Lab., Ealing Southall,* maj. 21,423

Kidney, David N. (*b.* 1955) *Lab., Stafford,* maj. 4,314

*Kilfoyle, Peter (*b.* 1946) *Lab., Liverpool Walton,* maj. 27,038

King, Andrew (*b.* 1948) *Lab., Rugby and Kenilworth,* maj. 495

King, Ms Oona T. (*b.* 1967) *Lab., Bethnal Green and Bow,* maj. 11,285

*King, Rt. Hon. Thomas J., CH (*b.* 1933) *C., Bridgwater,* maj. 1,796

Kingham, Ms Teresa J. (*b.* 1963) *Lab., Gloucester,* maj. 8,259

Kirkbride, Miss Julie (*b.* 1960) *C., Bromsgrove,* maj. 4,895

*Kirkwood, Archibald J. (*b.* 1946) *LD, Roxburgh and Berwickshire,* maj. 7,906

Kumar, Dr Ashok (*b.* 1956) *Lab., Middlesbrough South and Cleveland East,* maj. 10,607

Ladyman, Dr Stephen J. (*b.* 1952) *Lab., Thanet South,* maj. 2,878

Laing, Mrs Eleanor F. (*b.* 1958) *C., Epping Forest,* maj. 5,252

Lait, Ms Jacqueline A. H. (*b.* 1947) *C., Beckenham,* maj. 1,227

Lansley, Andrew D. (*b.* 1956) *C., Cambridgeshire South,* maj. 8,712

Lawrence, Mrs Jacqueline R. (*b.* 1948) *Lab., Preseli Pembrokeshire,* maj. 8,736

Laxton, Robert (*b.* 1944) *Lab., Derby North,* maj. 10,615

*Leigh, Edward J. E. (*b.* 1950) *C., Gainsborough,* maj. 6,826

*Lepper, David (*b.* 1945) *Lab. Co-op., Brighton Pavilion,* maj. 13,181

Leslie, Christopher M. (*b.* 1972) *Lab., Shipley,* maj. 2,996

Letwin, Oliver (*b.* 1956) *C., Dorset West,* maj. 1,840

Levitt, Tom (*b.* 1954) *Lab., High Peak,* maj. 8,791

Lewis, Ivan (*b.* 1967) *Lab., Bury South,* maj. 12,433

Lewis, Dr Julian M. (*b.* 1951) *C., New Forest East,* maj. 5,215

*Lewis, Terence (*b.* 1935) *Lab., Worsley,* maj. 17,741

*Liddell, Mrs Helen (*b.* 1950) *Lab., Airdrie and Shotts,* maj. 15,412

*Lidington, David R., PH.D. (*b.* 1956) *C., Aylesbury,* maj. 8,419

*Lilley, Rt. Hon. Peter B. (*b.* 1943) *C., Hitchin and Harpenden,* maj. 6,671

Linton, J. Martin (*b.* 1944) *Lab., Battersea,* maj. 5,360

*Livingstone, Kenneth R. (*b.* 1945) *Lab., Brent East,* maj. 15,882

Livsey, Richard A. L., CBE (*b.* 1935) *LD, Brecon and Radnorshire,* maj. 5,097

*Lloyd, Anthony J. (*b.* 1950) *Lab., Manchester Central,* maj. 19,682

*Lloyd, Rt. Hon. Sir Peter (*b.* 1937) *C., Fareham,* maj. 10,358

*Llwyd, Elfyn (*b.* 1951) *PC, Meirionnydd nant Conwy,* maj. 6,805

Lock, David A. (*b.* 1960) *Lab., Wyre Forest,* maj. 6,946

*Lord, Michael N. (*b.* 1938) *C., Suffolk Central and Ipswich North,* maj. 3,538

Loughton, Timothy P. (*b.* 1962) *C., Worthing East and Shoreham,* maj. 5,098

Love, Andrew (*b.* 1949) *Lab. Co-op., Edmonton,* maj. 13,472

*Luff, Peter J. (*b.* 1955) *C., Worcestershire Mid,* maj. 9,412

*Lyell, Rt. Hon. Sir Nicholas, QC (*b.* 1938) *C., Bedfordshire North East,* maj. 5,883

*McAllion, John (*b.* 1948) *Lab., Dundee East,* maj. 9,961

*McAvoy, Thomas M. (*b.* 1943) *Lab. Co-op., Glasgow Rutherglen,* maj. 15,007

McCabe, Stephen J. (*b.* 1955) *Lab., Birmingham Hall Green,* maj. 8,420

McCafferty, Ms Christine (*b.* 1945) *Lab., Calder Valley,* maj. 6,255

*McCartney, Ian (*b.* 1951) *Lab., Makerfield,* maj. 26,177

*McCartney, Robert L., QC(NI) (*b.* 1936) *UKU, Down North,* maj. 1,449

McDonagh, Ms Siobhain A. (*b.* 1960) *Lab., Mitcham and Morden,* maj. 13,741

*Macdonald, Calum A., PH.D. (*b.* 1956) *Lab., Western Isles,* maj. 3,576

McDonnell, John M. (*b.* 1951) *Lab., Hayes and Harlington,* maj. 14,291

*McFall, John (*b.* 1944) *Lab. Co-op., Dumbarton,* maj. 10,883

*McGrady, Edward K. (*b.* 1935) *SDLP, Down South,* maj. 9,933

*MacGregor, Rt. Hon. John R. R., OBE (*b.* 1937) *C., Norfolk South,* maj. 7,378

McGuinness, Martin (*b.* 1950) *SF, Ulster Mid,* maj. 1,883

McGuire, Mrs Anne (*b.* 1949) *Lab., Stirling,* maj. 6,411

McIntosh, Miss Anne C. B., MEP (*b.* 1954) *C., Vale of York,* maj. 9,721

McIsaac, Ms Shona (*b.* 1960) *Lab., Cleethorpes,* maj. 9,176

*Mackay, Rt. Hon. Andrew J. (*b.* 1949) *C., Bracknell,* maj. 10,387

McKenna, Ms Rosemary (*b.* 1941) *Lab., Cumbernauld and Kilsyth,* maj. 11,128

*MacKinlay, Andrew S. (*b.* 1949) *Lab., Thurrock,* maj. 17,256

*Maclean, Rt. Hon. David J. (*b.* 1953) *C., Penrith and the Border,* maj. 10,233

*McLeish, Henry B. (*b.* 1948) *Lab., Fife Central,* maj. 13,713

*Maclennan, Rt. Hon. Robert A. R. (*b.* 1936) *LD, Caithness, Sutherland and Easter Ross,* maj. 2,259

*McLoughlin, Patrick A. (*b.* 1957) *C., Derbyshire West,* maj. 4,885

*McNamara, J. Kevin (*b.* 1934) *Lab., Hull North,* maj. 19,705

McNulty, Anthony J. (*b.* 1958) *Lab., Harrow East,* maj. 9,738

*MacShane, Denis, PH.D. (*b.* 1948) *Lab., Rotherham,* maj. 21,469

MacTaggart, Ms Fiona M. (*b.* 1953) *Lab., Slough,* maj. 13,071

McWalter, Tony (*b.* 1945) *Lab. Co-op., Hemel Hempstead,* maj. 3,636

*McWilliam, John D. (*b.* 1941) *Lab., Blaydon,* maj. 16,605

*Madel, Sir David (*b.* 1938) *C., Bedfordshire South West,* maj. 132

*Maginnis, Kenneth (*b.* 1938) *UUP, Fermanagh and South Tyrone,* maj. 13,688

*Mahon, Mrs Alice (*b.* 1937) *Lab., Halifax,* maj. 11,212

*Major, Rt. Hon. John (*b.* 1943) *C., Huntingdon,* maj. 18,140

Malins, Humfrey J., CBE (*b.* 1945) *C., Woking,* maj. 5,678

Mallaber, Ms C. Judith (*b.* 1951) *Lab., Amber Valley,* maj. 11,613

*Mallon, Seamus (*b.* 1936) *SDLP, Newry and Armagh,* maj. 4,889

*Mandelson, Rt. Hon. Peter B. (*b.* 1953) *Lab., Hartlepool,* maj. 17,508

Maples, John C. (*b.* 1943) *C., Stratford-upon-Avon,* maj. 14,106

*Marek, John, PH.D. (*b.* 1940) *Lab., Wrexham,* maj. 11,762

Marsden, Gordon (*b.* 1953) *Lab., Blackpool South,* maj. 11,616

Marsden, Paul W. B. (*b.* 1968) *Lab., Shrewsbury and Atcham,* maj. 1,670

*Marshall, David, PH.D. (*b.* 1941) *Lab., Glasgow Shettleston,* maj. 15,868

*Marshall, James, PH.D. (*b.* 1941) *Lab., Leicester South,* maj. 16,493

Marshall-Andrews, Robert G., QC (*b.* 1944) *Lab., Medway,* maj. 5,354

*Martin, Michael J. (*b.* 1945) *Lab., Glasgow Springburn,* maj. 17,326

*Martlew, Eric A. (*b.* 1949) *Lab., Carlisle,* maj. 12,390

*Mates, Michael J. (*b.* 1934) *C., Hampshire East,* maj. 11,590

Maude, Rt. Hon. Francis A. A. (*b.* 1953) *C., Horsham,* maj. 14,862

*Mawhinney, Rt. Hon. Sir Brian, PH.D. (*b.* 1940) *C., Cambridgeshire North West,* maj. 7,754

*Maxton, John A. (*b.* 1936) *Lab., Glasgow Cathcart,* maj. 12,245

May, Mrs Theresa M. (*b.* 1956) *C., Maidenhead,* maj. 11,981

*Meacher, Rt. Hon. Michael H. (*b.* 1939) *Lab., Oldham West and Royton,* maj. 16,201

*Meale, J. Alan (*b.* 1949) *Lab., Mansfield,* maj. 20,518

Merron, Ms Gillian J. (*b.* 1959) *Lab., Lincoln,* maj. 11,130

*Michael, Alun E. (*b.* 1943) *Lab. Co-op., Cardiff South and Penarth,* maj. 13,881

*Michie, Mrs J. Ray (*b.* 1934) *LD, Argyll and Bute,* maj. 6,081

*Michie, William (*b.* 1935) *Lab., Sheffield Heeley,* maj. 17,078

*Milburn, Alan (*b.* 1958) *Lab., Darlington,* maj. 16,025

*Miller, Andrew P. (*b.* 1949) *Lab., Ellesmere Port and Neston,* maj. 16,036

*Mitchell, Austin V., D.PHIL. (*b.* 1934) *Lab., Great Grimsby,* maj. 16,244

Moffatt, Mrs Laura J. (*b.* 1954) *Lab., Crawley,* maj. 11,707

*Moonie, Dr Lewis G. (*b.* 1947) *Lab. Co-op., Kirkcaldy,* maj. 10,710

Moore, Michael K. (*b.* 1965) *LD, Tweeddale, Ettrick and Lauderdale,* maj. 1,489

Moran, Ms Margaret (*b.* 1955) *Lab., Luton South,* maj. 11,319

Morgan, Alastair N. (*b.* 1945) *SNP, Galloway and Upper Nithsdale,* maj. 5,624

*Morgan, H. Rhodri (*b.* 1939) *Lab., Cardiff West,* maj. 15,628

Morgan, Ms Julie (*b.* 1944) *Lab., Cardiff North,* maj. 8,126

*Morley, Elliot A. (*b.* 1952) *Lab., Scunthorpe,* maj. 14,173

*Morris, Ms Estelle, QC (*b.* 1952) *Lab., Birmingham Yardley,* maj. 5,315

*Morris, Rt. Hon. John, QC (*b.* 1931) *Lab., Aberavon,* maj. 21,571

*Moss, Malcolm D. (*b.* 1943) *C., Cambridgeshire North East,* maj. 5,101

Singh, Marsha (*b.* 1954) *Lab., Bradford West*, maj. 3,877

*Skinner, Dennis E. (*b.* 1932) *Lab., Bolsover*, maj. 27,149

*Smith, Rt. Hon. Andrew D. (*b.* 1951) *Lab., Oxford East*, maj. 16,665

Smith, Ms Angela E. (*b.* 1959) *Lab. Co-op., Basildon*, maj. 13,280

*Smith, Rt. Hon. Christopher R., ph.d. (*b.* 1951) *Lab., Islington South and Finsbury*, maj. 14,563

Smith, Ms Geraldine (*b.* 1961) *Lab., Morecambe and Lunesdale*, maj. 5,965

Smith, Ms Jacqueline J. (*b.* 1962) *Lab., Redditch*, maj. 6,125

Smith, John W. P. (*b.* 1951) *Lab., Vale of Glamorgan*, maj. 10,532

*Smith, Llewellyn T. (*b.* 1944) *Lab., Blaenau Gwent*, maj. 28,035

Smith, Sir Robert, Bt. (*b.* 1958) *LD, Aberdeenshire West and Kincardine*, maj. 2,662

*Smyth, Revd W. Martin (*b.* 1931) *UUP, Belfast South*, maj. 4,600

*Snape, Peter C. (*b.* 1942) *Lab., West Bromwich East*, maj. 13,584

*Soames, Hon. A. Nicholas W. (*b.* 1948) *C., Sussex Mid*, maj. 6,854

*Soley, Clive S. (*b.* 1939) *Lab., Ealing Acton and Shepherd's Bush*, maj. 15,647

Southworth, Ms Helen M. (*b.* 1956) *Lab., Warrington South*, maj. 10,807

*Spellar, John F. (*b.* 1947) *Lab., Warley*, maj. 15,451

Spelman, Mrs Caroline A. (*b.* 1958) *C., Meriden*, maj. 582

*Spicer, Sir Michael (*b.* 1943) *C., Worcestershire West*, maj. 3,846

*Spring, Richard J. G. (*b.* 1946) *C., Suffolk West*, maj. 1,867

*Squire, Ms Rachel A. (*b.* 1954) *Lab., Dunfermline West*, maj. 12,354

St Aubyn, Nicholas F. (*b.* 1955) *C., Guildford*, maj. 4,791

*Stanley, Rt. Hon. Sir John (*b.* 1942) *C., Tonbridge and Malling*, maj. 10,230

Starkey, Mrs Phyllis M. (*b.* 1947) *Lab., Milton Keynes South West*, maj. 10,292

*Steen, Sir Anthony (*b.* 1939) *C., Totnes*, maj. 877

*Steinberg, Gerald N. (*b.* 1945) *Lab., City of Durham*, maj. 22,504

*Stevenson, George W. (*b.* 1938) *Lab., Stoke-on-Trent South*, maj. 18,303

Stewart, David J. (*b.* 1956) *Lab., Inverness East, Nairn and Lochaber*, maj. 2,339

Stewart, Ian (*b.* 1950) *Lab., Eccles*, maj. 21,916

Stinchcombe, Paul D. (*b.* 1962) *Lab., Wellingborough*, maj. 187

Stoate, Howard G. A. (*b.* 1954) *Lab., Dartford*, maj. 4,328

Stott, Roger, cbe (*b.* 1943) *Lab., Wigan*, maj. 22,643

*Strang, Rt. Hon. Gavin S., ph.d. (*b.* 1943) *Lab., Edinburgh East and Musselburgh*, maj. 14,530

*Straw, Rt. Hon. J. W. (Jack) (*b.* 1946) *Lab., Blackburn*, maj. 14,451

*Streeter, Gary N. (*b.* 1955) *C., Devon South West*, maj. 7,433

Stringer, Graham E. (*b.* 1950) *Lab., Manchester Blackley*, maj. 19,588

Stuart, Mrs Gisela G. (*b.* 1955) *Lab., Birmingham Edgbaston*, maj. 4,842

Stunell, Andrew (*b.* 1942) *LD, Hazel Grove*, maj. 11,814

*Sutcliffe, Gerard (*b.* 1953) *Lab., Bradford South*, maj. 12,936

Swayne, Desmond A. (*b.* 1956) *C., New Forest West*, maj. 11,332

Swinney, John R. (*b.* 1964) *SNP, Tayside North*, maj. 4,160

Syms, Robert A. R. (*b.* 1956) *C., Poole*, maj. 5,298

*Tapsell, Sir Peter (*b.* 1930) *C., Louth and Horncastle*, maj. 6,900

Taylor, Ms Dari J. (*b.* 1944) *Lab., Stockton South*, maj. 11,585

Taylor, David L. (*b.* 1946) *Lab., Leicestershire North West*, maj. 13,219

*Taylor, Sir Edward (Teddy) (*b.* 1937) *C., Rochford and Southend East*, maj. 4,225

*Taylor, Ian C., mbe (*b.* 1945) *C., Esher and Walton*, maj. 14,528

*Taylor, Rt. Hon. John D. (*b.* 1937) *UUP, Strangford*, maj. 5,852

*Taylor, John M. (*b.* 1941) *C., Solihull*, maj. 11,397

*Taylor, Matthew O. J. (*b.* 1963) *LD, Truro and St Austell*, maj. 12,501

*Taylor, Rt. Hon. W. Ann (*b.* 1947) *Lab., Dewsbury*, maj. 8,323

*Temple-Morris, Peter (*b.* 1938) *Lab., Leominster*, maj. 8,835

Thomas, Gareth (*b.* 1954) *Lab., Clwyd West*, maj. 1,848

Thomas, Gareth R. (*b.* 1967) *Lab., Harrow West*, maj. 1,240

Thompson, William J. (*b.* 1939) *UUP, Tyrone West*, maj. 1,161

*Timms, Stephen C. (*b.* 1955) *Lab., East Ham*, maj. 19,358

*Tipping, S. P. (Paddy) (*b.* 1949) *Lab., Sherwood*, maj. 16,812

Todd, Mark W. (*b.* 1954) *Lab., Derbyshire South*, maj. 13,967

Tonge, Dr Jennifer L. (*b.* 1941) *LD, Richmond Park*, maj. 2,951

*Touhig, J. Donnelly (Don) (*b.* 1947) *Lab. Co-op., Islwyn*, maj. 23,931

*Townend, John E. (*b.* 1934) *C., Yorkshire East*, maj. 3,337

*Tredinnick, David A. S. (*b.* 1950) *C., Bosworth*, maj. 1,027

*Trend, Hon. Michael St J., cbe (*b.* 1952) *C., Windsor*, maj. 9,917

*Trickett, Jon H. (*b.* 1950) *Lab., Hemsworth*, maj. 23,992

*Trimble, Rt. Hon. W. David (*b.* 1944) *UUP, Upper Bann*, maj. 9,252

Truswell, Paul A. (*b.* 1955) *Lab., Pudsey*, maj. 6,207

*Turner, Dennis (*b.* 1942) *Lab. Co-op., Wolverhampton South East*, maj. 15,182

Turner, Desmond S. (*b.* 1939) *Lab., Brighton Kemptown*, maj. 3,534

Turner, Dr George (*b.* 1940) *Lab., Norfolk North West*, maj. 1,339

Twigg, J. Derek (*b.* 1959) *Lab., Halton*, maj. 23,650

Twigg, Stephen (*b.* 1966) *Lab., Enfield Southgate*, maj. 1,433

*Tyler, Paul A., cbe (*b.* 1941) *LD, Cornwall North*, maj. 13,933

Tyrie, Andrew G. (*b.* 1957) *C., Chichester*, maj. 9,734

*Vaz, N. Keith A. S. (*b.* 1956) *Lab., Leicester East*, maj. 18,422

*Viggers, Peter J. (*b.* 1938) *C., Gosport*, maj. 6,258

Vis, R. J. (Rudi) (*b.* 1941) *Lab., Finchley and Golders Green*, maj. 3,189

*Walker, A. Cecil (*b.* 1924) *UUP, Belfast North*, maj. 13,024

*Wallace, James R. (*b.* 1954) *LD, Orkney and Shetland*, maj. 6,968

*Walley, Ms Joan L. (*b.* 1949) *Lab., Stoke-on-Trent North*, maj. 17,392

Walter, Robert J. (*b.* 1948) *C., Dorset North*, maj. 2,746

Ward, Ms Claire M. (*b.* 1972) *Lab., Watford*, maj. 5,792

*Wardle, Charles F. (*b.* 1939) *C., Bexhill and Battle*, maj. 11,100

*Wareing, Robert N. (*b.* 1930) *Lab., Liverpool West Derby*, maj. 25,965

*Waterson, Nigel C. (*b.* 1950) *C., Eastbourne*, maj. 1,994

Watts, David L. (*b.* 1951) *Lab., St Helens North*, maj. 23,417

Webb, Prof. Steven J. (*b.* 1965) *LD, Northavon*, maj. 2,137

*Wells, Bowen (*b.* 1935) *C., Hertford and Stortford*, maj. 6,885

*Welsh, Andrew P. (*b.* 1944) *SNP, Angus*, maj. 10,189

White, Brian A. R. (*b.* 1957) *Lab., Milton Keynes North East*, maj. 240

Whitehead, Alan P. V. (*b.* 1950) *Lab., Southampton Test*, maj. 13,684

*Whitney, Sir Raymond, obe (*b.* 1930) *C., Wycombe*, maj. 2,370

*Whittingdale, John F. L., obe (*b.* 1959) *C., Maldon and Chelmsford East*, maj. 10,039

*Wicks, Malcolm H. (*b.* 1947) *Lab., Croydon North,* maj. 18,398

*Widdecombe, Rt. Hon. Ann N. (*b.* 1947) *C., Maidstone and the Weald,* maj. 9,603

*Wigley, Rt. Hon. Dafydd (*b.* 1943) *PC, Caernarfon,* maj. 7,949

*Wilkinson, John A. D. (*b.* 1940) *C., Ruislip-Northwood,* maj. 7,794

*Willetts, David L. (*b.* 1956) *C., Havant,* maj. 3,729

*Williams, Rt. Hon. Alan J. (*b.* 1930) *Lab., Swansea West,* maj. 14,459

*Williams, Dr Alan W. (*b.* 1945) *Lab., Carmarthen East and Dinefwr,* maj. 3,450

Williams, Mrs Betty H. (*b.* 1944) *Lab., Conwy,* maj. 1,596

Willis, G. Philip (*b.* 1941) *LD, Harrogate and Knaresborough,* maj. 6,236

Wills, Michael D. (*b.* 1952) *Lab., Swindon North,* maj. 7,688

*Wilshire, David (*b.* 1943) *C., Spelthorne,* maj. 3,473

*Wilson, Brian D. H. (*b.* 1948) *Lab., Cunninghame North,* maj. 11,039

*Winnick, David J. (*b.* 1933) *Lab., Walsall North,* maj. 12,588

*Winterton, Mrs J. Ann (*b.* 1941) *C., Congleton,* maj. 6,130

*Winterton, Nicholas R. (*b.* 1938) *C., Macclesfield,* maj. 8,654

Winterton, Ms Rosalie (*b.* 1958) *Lab., Doncaster Central,* maj. 17,856

*Wise, Mrs Audrey (*b.* 1935) *Lab., Preston,* maj. 18,680

Wood, Michael R. (*b.* 1946) *Lab., Batley and Spen,* maj. 6,141

Woodward, Shaun A. (*b.* 1958) *C., Witney,* maj. 7,028

Woolas, Philip J. (*b.* 1959) *Lab., Oldham East and Saddleworth,* maj. 3,389

*Worthington, Anthony (*b.* 1941) *Lab., Clydebank and Milngavie,* maj. 13,320

*Wray, James (*b.* 1938) *Lab., Glasgow Bailieston,* maj. 14,840

Wright, Anthony D. (*b.* 1954) *Lab., Great Yarmouth,* maj. 8,668

*Wright, Anthony W., D.phil. (*b.* 1948) *Lab., Cannock Chase,* maj. 14,478

Wyatt, Derek M. (*b.* 1949) *Lab., Sittingbourne and Sheppey,* maj. 1,929

*Yeo, Timothy S. K. (*b.* 1945) *C., Suffolk South,* maj. 4,175

*Young, Rt. Hon. Sir George, Bt. (*b.* 1941) *C., Hampshire North West,* maj. 11551

BY-ELECTIONS SINCE THE GENERAL ELECTION

UXBRIDGE
(31 July 1997)
*E.*57,733 *T.*55.2%

J. Randall, *C.*	16,288
A. Slaughter, *Lab.*	12,522
K. Kerr, *LD*	1,792
'Lord Sutch', *Loony*	396
Ms J. Leonard, *Soc.*	259
Ms F. Taylor, *BNP*	205
I. Anderson, *Nat. Dem.*	157
J. McCauley, *NF*	110
H. Middleton, *Original Lib. Party*	69
J. Feisenberger, *UK Ind.*	39
R. Carroll, *Emerald Rainbow Islands Dream Ticket*	30
C. majority	3,766

PAISLEY SOUTH
(6 November 1997)
E. 54,040 *T.*42%

D. Alexander, *Lab.*	10,346
I. Blackford, *SNP*	7,615
Ms E. McCartin, *LD*	2,582
Ms S. Laidlaw, *C.*	1,643
J. Deighan, *ProLife*	578
F. Curran, *Soc. All. Fighting Corruption*	306
C. McLauchlan, *Scottish Ind. Lab.*	155
C. Herriot, *Soc. Lab.*	153
K. Blair, *NLP*	57
Lab. majority	2,731

BECKENHAM
(20 November 1997)
*E.*72,807 *T.*43.7%

Ms J. Lait, *C.*	13,162
R. Hughes, *Lab.*	11,935
Ms R. Vetterlein, *LD*	5,864
P. Rimmer, *Lib.*	330
J. McAuley, *NF*	267
L. Mead, *New Britain Ref.*	237
T. Campion, *Social Foundation*	69
J. Small, *NLP*	44
C. majority	1,227

WINCHESTER
(20 November 1997)
*E.*78,884 *T.* 68.7%

M. Oaten, *LD*	37,006
G. Malone, *C.*	15,450
P. Davies, *Lab.*	944
R. Page, *Ref./UK Ind. Alliance*	521
'Lord' Sutch, *Loony*	316
R. Huggett, *Literal Dem.*	59
Ms R. Barry, *NLP*	48
R. Everest, *European C.*	40
LD majority	21,556

General Election statistics

PRINCIPAL PARTIES IN PARLIAMENT since 1970

	1970	1974 Feb.	1974 Oct.	1979	1983	1987	1992	1997
Conservative	330*	296	276	339	397	375	336	165
Labour	287	301	319	268	209	229	270	418
Liberal/LD	6	14	13	11	17	17	20	46
Social Democrat	—	1	—	—	6	5	—	—
Independent	5†	1	1	2	—	—	—	1
Plaid Cymru	—	2	3	2	2	3	4	4
Scottish Nationalist	1	7	11	2	2	3	3	6
Democratic Unionist	—	—	—	3	3	3	3	2
SDLP	—	1	1	1	1	3	4	3
Sinn Fein	—	—	—	—	1	1	—	2
Ulster Popular Unionist	—	—	—	—	1	1	1	—
Ulster Unionist‡	*	11	10	6	10	9	9	10
UK Unionist	—	—	—	—	—	—	—	1
The Speaker	1	1	1	1	1	1	1	1
Total	630	635	635	635	650	650	651	659

* Including 8 Ulster Unionists
† Comprising: Independent Labour 1, Independent Unity 1, Protestant Unity 1, Republican Labour 1, Unity 1
‡ Comprises:
    1974 (February) United Ulster Unionist Council 11
    1974 (October) United Ulster Unionist 10
    1979 Ulster Unionist 5, United Ulster Unionist 1
    1983 Official Unionist 10

PARLIAMENTS since 1970

		Duration		
Assembled	*Dissolved*	*yr*	*m.*	*d.*
29 June 1970	8 February 1974	3	7	10
6 March 1974	20 September 1974	0	6	14
22 October 1974	7 April 1979	4	5	16
9 May 1979	13 May 1983	4	0	4
15 June 1983	18 May 1987	3	11	3
17 June 1987	16 March 1992	4	8	28
27 April 1992	8 April 1997	4	11	12
7 May 1997				

MAJORITIES IN THE COMMONS since 1970

Year	*Party*	*Maj.*
1970	Conservative	31
1974 *Feb.*	No majority	
1974 *Oct.*	Labour	5
1979	Conservative	43
1983	Conservative	144
1987	Conservative	102
1992	Conservative	21
1997	Labour	178

VOTES CAST 1992 and 1997

	1992	1997
Conservative	14,089,722	9,600,940
Labour	11,567,764	13,517,911
Liberal Democrats	6,027,552	5,243,440
Scottish Nationalist	629,564	622,260
Plaid Cymru	154,390	161,030
N. Ireland parties	740,859	780,920
Others	401,239	1,361,701
Total	33,619,090	31,287,702

DISTRIBUTION OF SEATS BY COUNTRY 1997

	England	Wales	Scotland	N. Ireland
Conservative	165	—	—	—
Labour	328	34	56	—
Lib. Dem.	34	2	10	—
SNP	—	—	6	—
Plaid Cymru	—	4	—	—
Other	2*	—	—	18

* Includes the Speaker

SIZE OF ELECTORATE 1997

England	36,806,557
Wales	2,222,533
Scotland	3,984,406
Northern Ireland	1,190,198
Total	44,203,694

PARLIAMENTARY CONSTITUENCIES AS AT 1 MAY 1997

The results of voting in each parliamentary division at the general election of 1 May 1997 are given below. The majority in the 1992 general election, and any by-election between 1987 and 1992, is given below the 1992 result where the constituency covers the same area as in 1992. Where the boundaries of a constituency have changed since 1992, a notional result for 1992 is given.

Symbols

E.	Total number of electors in the constituency at the 1997 general election
T.	Turnout of electors at the 1997 general election
*	Member of the last Parliament in unchanged constituency
†	Member of the last Parliament in different constituency or one affected by boundary changes

Abbreviations

All.	Alliance Party (NI)
C.	Conservative
DUP	Democratic Unionist Party
Green	Green Party
Ind.	Independent
Lab.	Labour
Lab. Co-op.	Labour Co-operative
LD	Liberal Democrat
PC	Plaid Cymru
SDLP	Social Democratic and Labour Party
SF	Sinn Fein
SNP	Scottish National Party
UKU	United Kingdom Unionist
UUP	Ulster Unionist Party
ACA	Anti-Child Abuse
ACC	Anti-Corruption Candidate
Albion	Albion Party
Alt.	Alternative
ANP	All Night Party
Anti-maj.	Independent Anti-majority Democracy
AS	Anti-sleaze
Barts	Independent Save Barts Candidate
BDP	British Democratic Party
Beanus	Space Age Superhero from Planet Beanus
Beaut.	Independently Beautiful Party
Bert.	Berties Party
BFAIR	British Freedom and Individual Rights
BHMBCM	Black Haired Medium Build Caucasian Male
BHR	British Home Rule
B. Ind.	Beaconsfield Independent: Unity Through Electoral Reform
BIPF	British Isles People First Party
BNP	British National Party
Bypass	Newbury Bypass Stop Construction Now
Byro	Lord Byro versus the Scallywag Tories
Care	Care in the Community
CASC	Conservatives Against the Single Currency
CFSS	Country Field and Shooting Sports
Ch. D.	Christian Democrat
Ch. Nat.	Christian Nationalist
Choice	People's Choice
Ch. P.	Christian Party
Ch. U.	Christian Unity
Comm. L.	Communist League
Comm. P.	Communist Party of Britain
Constit.	Constitutionalist
Consult.	Independent Democracy Means Consulting the People
CRP	Community Representative Party
CSSPP	Common Sense Sick of Politicians Party
Cvty	Conservatory
D. Nat.	Democratic Nationalist
Dream	Rainbow Dream Ticket Party
Dynamic	First Dynamic Party
EDP	English Democratic Party
Embryo	Anti-Abortion Euthanasia Embryo Experiments
EUP	European Unity Party
Fair	Building a Fair Society
FDP	Fancy Dress Party
Fellowship	Fellowship Party for Peace and Justice
FEP	Full Employment Party
FP	Freedom Party
Glow	Glow Bowling Party
GRLNSP	Green Referendum Lawless Naturally Street Party
Heart	Heart 106.2 Alien Party
Hemp	Hemp Coalition
HR	Human Rights '97
Hum.	Humanist Party
IAC	Independent Anti-Corruption in Government/TGWU
Ind. AFE	Independent Against a Federal Europe
Ind. BB	Independent Back to Basics
Ind. CRP	Independent Conservative Referendum Party
Ind. Dean	Independent Royal Forest of Dean
Ind. Dem.	Independent Democrat
Ind. ECR	Independent English Conservative and Referendum
Ind. F.	Independent Forester
Ind. Green	Independent Green: Your Children's Future
Ind. Hum.	English Independent Humanist Party
Ind. Is.	Island Independent
Ind. JRP	Justice and Renewal Independent Party
Ind. No	Independent No to Europe
IZB	Islam Zinda Baad Platform
JP	Justice Party
Juice	Juice Party
KBF	Keep Britain Free and Independent Party
Lab. Change	Labour Time for Change Candidate
LC	Loyal Conservative
LCP	Legalize Cannabis Party
LGR	Local Government Reform
Lib.	Liberal
Loc.	Local
Logic	Logic Party Truth Only Allowed
Loony	Monster Raving Loony Party
Mal	Mal Voice of the People Party
Miss M.	Miss Moneypenny's Glamorous One Party
MK	Mebyon Kernow
Mongolian	Mongolian Barbeque Great Place to Party
MRAC	Multi-racial Anti-Corruption Alliance
Nat. Dem.	National Democrat
New Way	New Millennium New Way Hemp Candidate
NF	National Front
NIFT	Former Captain NI Football Team
NIP	Northern Ireland Party
NI Women	Northern Ireland Women's Coalition
NLP	Natural Law Party
NLPC	New Labour Party Candidate
None	None of the Above Parties
NPC	Non-party Conservative
Pacifist	Pacifist for Peace, Justice, Co-operation, Environment
PAYR	Protecting All Your Rights Locally Effectively
Pf	Pathfinders
PLP	People's Labour Party
Plymouth	Plymouth First Group
PP	People's Party
PPP	People's Party Party
ProLife	ProLife Alliance
PUP	Progressive Unionist Party
RA	Residents Association
Rain. Is.	Rainbow Connection Your Island Candidate
Rain. Ref.	Rainbow Referendum
R. Alt.	Radical Alternative
Ref.	Referendum Party
Ren. Dem.	Renaissance Democrat
Rep. GB	Republican Party of Great Britain
Rights	Charter for Basic Rights
Ronnie	Ronnie the Rhino Party
Route 66	Route 66 Party Posse Party
Scrapit	Scrapit Stop Avon Ring Road Now
SCU	Scottish Conservative Unofficial
SEP	Socialist Equality Party
SFDC	Stratford First Democratic Conservative
SG	Sub-genus Party
Shields	Pro Interests of South Shields People
SIP	Sheffield Independent Party
SLI	Scottish Labour Independent
Slough	People in Slough Shunning Useless Politicians
SLU	Scottish Labour Unofficial
Soc.	Socialist Party
Soc. Dem.	Social Democrat
Soc. Lab.	Socialist Labour Party
SPGB	Socialist Party of Great Britain
Spts All.	Sportsman's Alliance: Anything but Mellor
SSA	Scottish Socialist Alliance
Stan	Happiness Stan's Freedom to Party Party
Teddy	Teddy Bear Alliance Party
Top	Top Choice Liberal Democrat
21st Cent.	21st Century Independent Foresters
UA	Universal Alliance
UK Ind.	UK Independence Party
UKPP	UK Pensioners Party
WCCC	West Cheshire College in Crisis Party
Wessex	Wessex Regionalist
WP	Workers' Party
WRP	Workers' Revolutionary Party

ENGLAND

ALDERSHOT
E.76,189   T. 71.07%
G. Howarth, *C.* — 23,119
A. Collett, *LD* — 16,498
T. Bridgeman, *Lab.* — 13,057
J. Howe, *UK Ind.* — 794
A. Pendragon, *Ind.* — 361
Dr D. Stevens, *BNP* — 322
C. majority 6,621
(Boundary change: notional C.)

ALDRIDGE-BROWNHILLS
E.62,441   T. 74.26%
*R. Shepherd, *C.* — 21,856
J. Toth, *Lab.* — 19,330
Ms C. Downie, *LD* — 5,184
C. majority 2,526
(April 1992, C. maj. 11,024)

ALTRINCHAM AND SALE WEST
E.70,625   T. 73.32%
G. Brady, *C.* — 22,348
Ms J. Baugh, *Lab.* — 20,843
M. Ramsbottom, *LD* — 6,535
A. Landes, *Ref.* — 1,348
J. Stephens, *ProLife* — 313
Dr R. Mrozinski, *UK Ind.* — 270
J. Renwick, *NLP* — 125
C. majority 1,505
(Boundary change: notional C.)

AMBER VALLEY
E.72,005   T. 76.07%
Ms J. Mallaber, *Lab.* — 29,943
†P. Oppenheim, *C.* — 18,330
R. Shelley, *LD* — 4,219
Mrs I. McGibbon, *Ref.* — 2,283
Lab. majority 11,613
(Boundary change: notional C.)

ARUNDEL AND SOUTH DOWNS
E.67,641   T. 75.90%
H. Flight, *C.* — 27,251
J. Goss, *LD* — 13,216
R. Black, *Lab.* — 9,376
J. Herbert, *UK Ind.* — 1,494
C. majority 14,035
(Boundary change: notional C.)

ASHFIELD
E.72,269   T. 70.02%
†G. Hoon, *Lab.* — 32,979
M. Simmonds, *C.* — 10,251
W. Smith, *LD* — 4,882
M. Betts, *Ref.* — 1,896
S. Belshaw, *BNP* — 595
Lab. majority 22,728
(Boundary change: notional Lab.)

ASHFORD
E.74,149   T. 74.57%
D. Green, *C.* — 22,899
J. Ennals, *Lab.* — 17,544
J. Williams, *LD* — 10,901
C. Cruden, *Ref.* — 3,201
R. Boden, *Green* — 660
S. Tyrell, *NLP* — 89
C. majority 5,355
(April 1992, C. maj. 17,359)

ASHTON UNDER LYNE
E.72,206   T. 65.48%
†Rt. Hon. R. Sheldon, *Lab.* — 31,919
R. Mayson, *C.* — 8,954
T. Pickstone, *LD* — 4,603
Mrs L. Clapham, *Ref.* — 1,346
Prince Cymbal, *Loony* — 458
Lab. majority 22,965
(Boundary change: notional Lab.)

AYLESBURY
E.79,047   T. 72.81%
†D. Lidington, *C.* — 25,426
Ms S. Bowles, *LD* — 17,007
R. Langridge, *Lab.* — 12,759
M. John, *Ref.* — 2,196
L. Sheaff, *NLP* — 166
C. majority 8,419
(Boundary change: notional C.)

BANBURY
E.77,456   T. 75.46%
†A. Baldry, *C.* — 25,076
Ms H. Peperell, *Lab.* — 20,339
Mrs C. Bearder, *LD* — 9,761
J. Ager, *Ref.* — 2,245
Ms B. Cotton, *Green* — 530
Mrs L. King, *UK Ind.* — 364
I. Pearson, *NLP* — 131
C. majority 4,737
(Boundary change: notional C.)

BARKING
E.53,682   T. 61.41%
†Mrs M. Hodge, *Lab.* — 21,698
K. Langford, *C.* — 5,802
M. Marsh, *LD* — 3,128
C. Taylor, *Ref.* — 1,283
M. Tolman, *BNP* — 894
D. Mearns, *ProLife* — 159
Lab. majority 15,896
(Boundary change: notional Lab.)

BARNSLEY CENTRAL
E.61,133   T. 59.68%
†E. Illsley, *Lab.* — 28,090
S. Gutteridge, *C.* — 3,589
D. Finlay, *LD* — 3,481
J. Walsh, *Ref.* — 1,325
Lab. majority 24,501
(Boundary change: notional Lab.)

BARNSLEY EAST AND MEXBOROUGH
E.67,840   T. 63.88%
†J. Ennis, *Lab.* — 31,699
Miss J. Ellison, *C.* — 4,936
D. Willis, *LD* — 4,489
K. Capstick, *Soc. Lab.* — 1,213
A. Miles, *Ref.* — 797
Ms J. Hyland, *SEP* — 201
Lab. majority 26,763
(Boundary change: notional Lab.)

BARNSLEY WEST AND PENISTONE
E.64,894   T. 65.04%
*M. Clapham, *Lab.* — 25,017
P. Watkins, *C.* — 7,750
Mrs W. Knight, *LD* — 7,613
Mrs J. Miles, *Ref.* — 1,828
Lab. majority 17,267
(April 1992, Lab. maj. 14,504)

BARROW AND FURNESS
E.66,960   T. 72.03%
*J. Hutton, *Lab.* — 27,630
R. Hunt, *C.* — 13,133
Mrs A. Metcalfe, *LD* — 4,264
J. Hamzeian, *PLP* — 1,995
D. Mitchell, *Ref.* — 1,208
Lab. majority 14,497
(April 1992, Lab. maj. 3,578)

BASILDON
E.73,989   T. 71.74%
Ms A. Smith, *Lab. Co-op.* — 29,646
J. Baron, *C.* — 16,366
Ms L. Granshaw, *LD* — 4,608
C. Robinson, *Ref.* — 2,462
Lab. Co-op. majority 13,280
(Boundary change: notional C.)

BASINGSTOKE
E.77,035   T. 74.16%
†A. Hunter, *C.* — 24,751
N. Lickley, *Lab.* — 22,354
M. Rimmer, *LD* — 9,714
E. Selim, *Ind.* — 310
C. majority 2,397
(Boundary change: notional C.)

BASSETLAW
E.68,101   T. 70.37%
†J. Ashton, *Lab.* — 29,298
M. Cleasby, *C.* — 11,838
M. Kerrigan, *LD* — 4,950
R. Graham, *Ref.* — 1,838
Lab. majority 17,460
(Boundary change: notional Lab.)

BATH
E.70,815   T. 76.24%
†D. Foster, *LD* — 26,169
Ms A. McNair, *C.* — 16,850
T. Bush, *Lab.* — 8,828
A. Cook, *Ref.* — 1,192
R. Scrase, *Green* — 580
P. Sandell, *UK Ind.* — 315
N. Pullen, *NLP* — 55
LD majority 9,319
(Boundary change: notional LD)

BATLEY AND SPEN
E.64,209   T. 73.14%
M. Wood, *Lab.* — 23,213
†Mrs E. Peacock, *C.* — 17,072
Mrs K. Pinnock, *LD* — 4,133
E. Wood, *Ref.* — 1,691
R. Smith, *BNP* — 472
C. Lord, *Green* — 384
Lab. majority 6,141
(Boundary change: notional C.)

BATTERSEA
E.66,928   T. 70.82%
M. Linton, *Lab.* — 24,047
†J. Bowis, *C.* — 18,687
Ms P. Keaveney, *LD* — 3,482
M. Slater, *Ref.* — 804
R. Banks, *UK Ind.* — 250
J. Marshall, *Dream* — 127
Lab. majority 5,360
(Boundary change: notional C.)

BEACONSFIELD
*E.*68,959 *T.* 72.80%
D. Grieve, *C.*	24,709
P. Mapp, *LD*	10,722
A. Hudson, *Lab.*	10,063
H. Lloyd, *Ref.*	2,197
C. Story, *CASC*	1,434
C. Cooke, *UK Ind.*	451
Ms G. Duval, *ProLife*	286
T. Dyball, *NLP*	193
R. Matthews, *B. Ind.*	146

C. majority 13,987
(Boundary change: notional C.)

BECKENHAM
*E.*72,807 *T.* 74.65%
†P. Merchant, *C.*	23,084
R. Hughes, *Lab.*	18,131
Ms R. Vetterlein, *LD*	9,858
L. Mead, *Ref.*	1,663
P. Rimmer, *Lib.*	720
C. Pratt, *UK Ind.*	506
J. Mcauley, *NF*	388

C. majority 4,953
(Boundary change: notional C.)
See also page 233

BEDFORD
*E.*66,560 *T.* 73.53%
P. Hall, *Lab.*	24,774
R. Blackman, *C.*	16,474
C. Noyce, *LD*	6,044
P. Conquest, *Ref.*	1,503
Ms P. Saunders, *NLP*	149

Lab. majority 8,300
(Boundary change: notional C.)

BEDFORDSHIRE MID
*E.*66,979 *T.* 78.41%
J. Sayeed, *C.*	24,176
N. Mallett, *Lab.*	17,086
T. Hill, *LD*	8,823
Mrs S. Marler, *Ref.*	2,257
M. Lorys, *NLP*	174

C. majority 7,090
(Boundary change: notional C.)

BEDFORDSHIRE NORTH EAST
*E.*64,743 *T.* 77.83%
†Rt. Hon. Sir N. Lyell, *C.*	22,311
J. Lehal, *Lab.*	16,428
P. Bristow, *LD*	7,179
J. Taylor, *Ref.*	2,490
L. Foley, *Ind. C.*	1,842
B. Bence, *NLP*	138

C. majority 5,883
(Boundary change: notional C.)

BEDFORDSHIRE SOUTH WEST
*E.*69,781 *T.* 75.76%
†Sir D. Madel, *C.*	21,534
A. Date, *Lab.*	21,402
S. Owen, *LD*	7,559
Ms R. Hill, *Ref.*	1,761
T. Wise, *UK Ind.*	446
A. Le Carpentier, *NLP*	162

C. majority 132
(Boundary change: notional C.)

BERWICK-UPON-TWEED
*E.*56,428 *T.* 74.08%
*A. Beith, *LD*	19,007
P. Brannen, *Lab.*	10,965

N. Herbert, *C.*	10,056
N. Lambton, *Ref.*	1,423
I. Dodds, *UK Ind.*	352

LD majority 8,042
(April 1992, LD maj. 5,043)

BETHNAL GREEN AND BOW
*E.*73,008 *T.* 61.20%
Ms O. King, *Lab.*	20,697
K. Choudhury, *C.*	9,412
S. N. Islam, *LD*	5,361
D. King, *BNP*	3,350
T. Milson, *Lib.*	2,963
S. Osman, *Real Lab.*	1,117
S. Petter, *Green*	812
M. Abdullah, *Ref.*	557
A. Hamid, *Soc. Lab.*	413

Lab. majority 11,285
(Boundary change: notional Lab.)

BEVERLEY AND HOLDERNESS
*E.*71,916 *T.* 73.62%
†J. Cran, *C.*	21,629
N. O'Neill, *Lab.*	20,818
J. Melling, *LD*	9,689
D. Barley, *UK Ind.*	695
S. Withers, *NLP*	111

C. majority 811
(Boundary change: notional C.)

BEXHILL AND BATTLE
*E.*65,584 *T.* 74.70%
†C. Wardle, *C.*	23,570
Mrs K. Field, *LD*	12,470
R. Beckwith, *Lab.*	8,866
Mrs V. Thompson, *Ref.*	3,302
J. Pankhurst, *UK Ind.*	786

C. majority 11,100
(Boundary change: notional C.)

BEXLEYHEATH AND CRAYFORD
*E.*63,334 *T.* 76.14%
N. Beard, *Lab.*	21,942
†D. Evennett, *C.*	18,527
Mrs F. Montford, *LD*	5,391
B. Thomas, *Ref.*	1,551
Ms P. Smith, *BNP*	429
W. Jenner, *UK Ind.*	383

Lab. majority 3,415
(Boundary change: notional C.)

BILLERICAY
*E.*76,550 *T.* 72.40%
†Mrs T. Gorman, *C.*	22,033
P. Richards, *Lab.*	20,677
G. Williams, *LD*	8,763
B. Hughes, *LC*	3,377
J. Buchanan, *ProLife*	570

C. majority 1,356
(Boundary change: notional C.)

BIRKENHEAD
*E.*59,782 *T.* 65.78%
*F. Field, *Lab.*	27,825
J. Crosby, *C.*	5,982
R. Wood, *LD*	3,548
M. Cullen, *Soc. Lab.*	1,168
R. Evans, *Ref.*	800

Lab. majority 21,843
(April 1992, Lab. maj. 17,613)

BIRMINGHAM EDGBASTON
*E.*70,204 *T.* 69.03%
Mrs G. Stuart, *Lab.*	23,554

A. Marshall, *C.*	18,712
J. Gallagher, *LD*	4,691
J. Oakton, *Ref.*	1,065
D. Campbell, *BDP*	443

Lab. majority 4,842
(Boundary change: notional C.)

BIRMINGHAM ERDINGTON
*E.*66,380 *T.* 60.87%
†R. Corbett, *Lab.*	23,764
A. Tompkins, *C.*	11,107
I. Garrett, *LD*	4,112
G. Cable, *Ref.*	1,424

Lab. majority 12,657
(Boundary change: notional Lab.)

BIRMINGHAM HALL GREEN
*E.*58,767 *T.* 71.16%
S. McCabe, *Lab.*	22,372
*A. Hargreaves, *C.*	13,952
A. Dow, *LD*	4,034
P. Bennett, *Ref.*	1,461

Lab. majority 8,420
(April 1992, C. maj. 3,665)

BIRMINGHAM HODGE HILL
*E.*56,066 *T.* 60.91%
*T. Davis, *Lab.*	22,398
E. Grant, *C.*	8,198
H. Thomas, *LD*	2,891
P. Johnson, *UK Ind.*	660

Lab. majority 14,200
(April 1992, Lab. maj. 7,068)

BIRMINGHAM LADYWOOD
*E.*70,013 *T.* 54.24%
†Ms C. Short, *Lab.*	28,134
S. Vara, *C.*	5,052
S. S. Marwa, *LD*	3,020
Mrs R. Gurney, *Ref.*	1,086
A. Carmichael, *Nat. Dem.*	685

Lab. majority 23,082
(Boundary change: notional Lab.)

BIRMINGHAM NORTHFIELD
*E.*56,842 *T.* 68.34%
†R. Burden, *Lab.*	22,316
A. Blumenthal, *C.*	10,873
M. Ashall, *LD*	4,078
D. Gent, *Ref.*	1,243
K. Axon, *BNP*	337

Lab. majority 11,443
(Boundary change: notional Lab.)

BIRMINGHAM PERRY BARR
*E.*71,031 *T.* 64.60%
†J. Rooker, *Lab.*	28,921
A. Dunnett, *C.*	9,964
R. Hassall, *LD*	4,523
S. Mahmood, *Ref.*	843
A. Baxter, *Lib.*	718
L. Windridge, *BNP*	544
A. S. Panesar, *Fourth Party*	374

Lab. majority 18,957
(Boundary change: notional Lab.)

BIRMINGHAM SELLY OAK
*E.*72,049 *T.* 70.16%
*Dr L. Jones, *Lab.*	28,121
G. Greene, *C.*	14,033
D. Osborne, *LD*	6,121
L. Marshall, *Ref.*	1,520
Dr G. Gardner, *ProLife*	417

P. Sherriff-Knowles, *Loony*   253
H. Meads, *NLP*   85
Lab. majority 14,088
(April 1992, Lab. maj. 2,060)

BIRMINGHAM SPARKBROOK AND SMALL HEATH
*E.*73,130   *T.* 57.11%
†R. Godsiff, *Lab.*   26,841
K. Hardeman, *C.*   7,315
R. Harmer, *LD*   3,889
A. Clawley, *Green*   959
R. Dooley, *Ref.*   737
P. Patel, *Fourth Party*   538
R. M. Syed, *PAYR*   513
Ms S. Bi, *Ind.*   490
C. Wren, *Soc. Lab.*   483
Lab. majority 19,526
(Boundary change: notional Lab.)

BIRMINGHAM YARDLEY
*E.*53,058   *T.* 71.22%
*Ms E. Morris, *Lab.*   17,778
J. Hemming, *LD*   12,463
Mrs A. Jobson, *C.*   6,736
D. Livingston, *Ref.*   646
A. Ware, *UK Ind.*   164
Lab. majority 5,315
(April 1992, Lab. maj. 162)

BISHOP AUCKLAND
*E.*66,754   *T.* 68.88%
†Rt. Hon. D. Foster, *Lab.* 30,359
Mrs J. Fergus, *C.*   9,295
L. Ashworth, *LD*   4,223
D. Blacker, *Ref.*   2,104
Lab. majority 21,064
(Boundary change: notional Lab.)

BLABY
*E.*70,471   *T.* 76.05%
†A. Robathan, *C.*   24,564
R. Willmott, *Lab.*   18,090
G. Welsh, *LD*   8,001
R. Harrison, *Ref.*   2,018
J. Peacock, *BNP*   523
T. Stokes, *Ind.*   397
C. majority 6,474
(Boundary change: notional C.)

BLACKBURN
*E.*73,058   *T.* 65.01%
*J. Straw, *Lab.*   26,141
Ms S. Sidhu, *C.*   11,690
S. Fenn, *LD*   4,990
D. Bradshaw, *Ref.*   1,892
Mrs T. Wingfield, *Nat. Dem.* 671
Mrs H. Drummond, *Soc. Lab.*   637
R. Field, *Green*   608
Mrs M. Carmichael-Grimshaw,
   KBF   506
W. Batchelor, *CSSPP*   362
Lab. majority 14,451
(April 1992, Lab. maj. 6,027)

BLACKPOOL NORTH AND FLEETWOOD
*E.*74,989   *T.* 71.67%
Mrs J. Humble, *Lab.*   28,051
†H. Elletson, *C.*   19,105
Mrs B. Hill, *LD*   4,600
Ms K. Stacey, *Ref.*   1,704
J. Ellis, *BNP*   288

Lab. majority 8,946
(Boundary change: notional C.)

BLACKPOOL SOUTH
*E.*75,720   *T.* 67.80%
G. Marsden, *Lab.*   29,282
R. Booth, *C.*   17,666
Mrs D. Holt, *LD*   4,392
Lab. majority 11,616
(Boundary change: notional C.)

BLAYDON
*E.*64,699   *T.* 70.98%
*J. McWilliam, *Lab.*   27,535
P. Maughan, *LD*   10,930
M. Watson, *C.*   6,048
R. Rook, *Ind. Lab.*   1,412
Lab. majority 16,605
(April 1992, Lab. maj. 13,343)

BLYTH VALLEY
*E.*61,761   *T.* 68.78%
*R. Campbell, *Lab.*   27,276
A. Lamb, *LD*   9,540
Mrs B. Musgrave, *C.*   5,666
Lab. majority 17,736
(April 1992, Lab. maj. 8,044)

BOGNOR REGIS AND LITTLEHAMPTON
*E.*66,480   *T.* 69.86%
N. Gibb, *C.*   20,537
R. Nash, *Lab.*   13,216
Dr J. Walsh, *LD*   11,153
G. Stride, *UK Ind.*   1,537
C. majority 7,321
(Boundary change: notional C.)

BOLSOVER
*E.*66,476   *T.* 71.32%
†D. Skinner, *Lab.*   35,073
R. Harwood, *C.*   7,924
I. Cox, *LD*   4,417
Lab. majority 27,149
(Boundary change: notional Lab.)

BOLTON NORTH EAST
*E.*67,930   *T.* 72.44%
D. Crausby, *Lab.*   27,621
R. Wilson, *C.*   14,952
Dr E. Critchley, *LD*   4,862
D. Staniforth, *Ref.*   1,096
W. Kelly, *Soc. Lab.*   676
Lab. majority 12,669
(Boundary change: notional Lab.)

BOLTON SOUTH EAST
*E.*66,459   *T.* 65.23%
B. Iddon, *Lab.*   29,856
P. Carter, *C.*   8,545
F. Harasiwka, *LD*   3,805
W. Pickering, *Ref.*   973
L. Walch, *NLP*   170
Lab. majority 21,311
(Boundary change: notional Lab.)

BOLTON WEST
*E.*63,535   *T.* 77.37%
Ms R. Kelly, *Lab.*   24,342
†T. Sackville, *C.*   17,270
Mrs B. Ronson, *LD*   5,309
Mrs D. Kelly, *Soc. Lab.*   1,374
Mrs G. Frankl-Slater, *Ref.*   865

Lab. majority 7,072
(Boundary change: notional C.)

BOOTLE
*E.*57,284   *T.* 66.73%
†J. Benton, *Lab.*   31,668
R. Mathews, *C.*   3,247
K. Reid, *LD*   2,191
J. Elliott, *Ref.*   571
P. Glover, *Soc.*   420
S. Cohen, *NLP*   126
Lab. majority 28,421
(Boundary change: notional Lab.)

BOSTON AND SKEGNESS
*E.*67,623   *T.* 68.87%
†Sir R. Body, *C.*   19,750
P. McCauley, *Lab.*   19,103
J. Dodsworth, *LD*   7,721
C. majority 647
(Boundary change: notional C.)

BOSWORTH
*E.*68,113   *T.* 76.57%
†D. Tredinnick, *C.*   21,189
A. Furlong, *Lab.*   20,162
J. Ellis, *LD*   9,281
S. Halborg, *Ref.*   1,521
C. majority 1,027
(Boundary change: notional C.)

BOURNEMOUTH EAST
*E.*61,862   *T.* 70.20%
†D. Atkinson, *C.*   17,997
D. Eyre, *LD*   13,651
Mrs J. Stevens, *Lab.*   9,181
A. Musgrave-Scott, *Ref.*   1,808
K. Benney, *UK Ind.*   791
C. majority 4,346
(Boundary change: notional C.)

BOURNEMOUTH WEST
*E.*62,028   *T.* 66.22%
†J. Butterfill, *C.*   17,115
Ms J. Dover, *LD*   11,405
D. Gritt, *Lab.*   10,093
R. Mills, *Ref.*   1,910
Mrs L. Tooley, *UK Ind.*   281
J. Morse, *BNP*   165
A. Springham, *NLP*   103
C. majority 5,710
(Boundary change: notional C.)

BRACKNELL
*E.*79,292   *T.* 74.52%
†A. Mackay, *C.*   27,983
Ms A. Snelgrove, *Lab.*   17,596
A. Hilliar, *LD*   9,122
J. Tompkins, *New Lab.*   1,909
W. Cairns, *Ref.*   1,636
L. Boxall, *UK Ind.*   569
Ms D. Roberts, *ProLife*   276
C. majority 10,387
(Boundary change: notional C.)

BRADFORD NORTH
*E.*66,228   *T.* 63.26%
*T. Rooney, *Lab.*   23,493
R. Skinner, *C.*   10,723
T. Browne, *LD*   6,083
H. Wheatley, *Ref.*   1,227
W. Beckett, *Loony*   369

Lab. majority 12,770
(April 1992, Lab. maj. 7,664)

BRADFORD SOUTH
*E.*68,391 *T.* 65.88%
*G. Sutcliffe, *Lab.*   25,558
Mrs A. Hawkesworth, *C.*   12,622
A. Wilson-Fletcher, *LD*   5,093
Mrs M. Kershaw, *Ref.*   1,785
Lab. majority 12,936
(April 1992, Lab. maj. 4,902)
(June 1994, Lab. maj. 9,664)

BRADFORD WEST
*E.*71,961 *T.* 63.32%
M. Singh, *Lab.*   18,932
M. Riaz, *C.*   15,055
Mrs H. Wright, *LD*   6,737
A. Khan, *Soc. Lab.*   1,551
C. Royston, *Ref.*   1,348
J. Robinson, *Green*   861
G. Osborn, *BNP*   839
S. Shah, *Soc.*   245
Lab. majority 3,877
(April 1992, Lab. maj. 9,502)

BRAINTREE
*E.*72,772 *T.* 76.37%
A. Hurst, *Lab.*   23,729
†Rt. Hon. A. Newton, *C.*   22,278
T. Ellis, *LD*   6,418
N. Westcott, *Ref.*   2,165
J. Abbott, *Green*   712
M. Nolan, *New Way*   274
Lab. majority 1,451
(Boundary change: notional C.)

BRENT EAST
*E.*53,548 *T.* 65.87%
†K. Livingstone, *Lab.*   23,748
M. Francois, *C.*   7,866
I. Hunter, *LD*   2,751
S. Keable, *Soc. Lab.*   466
A. Shanks, *ProLife*   218
Ms C. Warrilo, *Dream*   120
D. Jenkins, *NLP*   103
Lab. majority 15,882
(Boundary change: notional Lab.)

BRENT NORTH
*E.*54,149 *T.* 70.50%
B. Gardiner, *Lab.*   19,343
†Rt. Hon. Sir R. Boyson, *C.*   15,324
P. Lorber, *LD*   3,104
A. Davids, *NLP*   204
G. Clark, *Dream*   199
Lab. majority 4,019
(Boundary change: notional C.)

BRENT SOUTH
*E.*53,505 *T.* 64.48%
†P. Boateng, *Lab.*   25,180
S. Jackson, *C.*   5,489
J. Brazil, *LD*   2,670
Ms J. Phythian, *Ref.*   497
D. Edler, *Green*   389
C. Howard, *Dream*   175
Ms A. Mahaldar, *NLP*   98
Lab. majority 19,691
(Boundary change: notional Lab.)

BRENTFORD AND ISLEWORTH
*E.*79,058 *T.* 71.00%
Mrs A. Keen, *Lab.*   32,249
†N. Deva, *C.*   17,825
Dr G. Hartwell, *LD*   4,613
J. Bradley, *Green*   687
Mrs B. Simmerson, *UK Ind.*   614
M. Ahmed, *NLP*   147
Lab. majority 14,424
(Boundary change: notional C.)

BRENTWOOD AND ONGAR
*E.*66,005 *T.* 76.85%
†E. Pickles, *C.*   23,031
Mrs E. Bottomley, *LD*   13,341
M. Young, *Lab.*   11,231
Mrs A. Kilmartin, *Ref.*   2,658
Capt. D. Mills, *UK Ind.*   465
C. majority 9,690
(Boundary change: notional C.)

BRIDGWATER
*E.*73,038 *T.* 74.79%
*Rt. Hon. T. King, *C.*   20,174
M. Hoban, *LD*   18,378
R. Lavers, *Lab.*   13,519
Ms F. Evens, *Ref.*   2,551
C. majority 1,796
(April 1992, C. maj. 9,716)

BRIGG AND GOOLE
*E.*63,648 *T.* 73.53%
I. Cawsey, *Lab.*   23,493
D. Stewart, *C.*   17,104
Mrs M.-R. Hardy, *LD*   4,692
D. Rigby, *Ref.*   1,513
Lab. majority 6,389
(Boundary change: notional C.)

BRIGHTON KEMPTOWN
*E.*65,147 *T.* 70.81%
D. Turner, *Lab.*   21,479
†Sir A. Bowden, *C.*   17,945
C. Gray, *LD*   4,478
D. Inman, *Ref.*   1,526
Ms H. Williams, *Soc. Lab.*   316
J. Bowler, *NLP*   172
Ms L. Newman, *Loony*   123
R. Darlow, *Dream*   93
Lab. majority 3,534
(Boundary change: notional C.)

BRIGHTON PAVILION
*E.*66,431 *T.* 73.69%
D. Lepper, *Lab. Co-op.*   26,737
†Sir D. Spencer, *C.*   13,556
K. Blanshard, *LD*   4,644
P. Stocken, *Ref.*   1,304
P. West, *Green*   1,249
R. Huggett, *Ind. C.*   1,098
F. Stevens, *UK Ind.*   179
R. Dobbs, *SG*   125
A. Card, *Dream*   59
Lab. Co-op. majority 13,181
(Boundary change: notional C.)

BRISTOL EAST
*E.*68,990 *T.* 69.87%
†Ms J. Corston, *Lab.*   27,418
E. Vaizey, *C.*   11,259
P. Tyzack, *LD*   7,121
G. Philp, *Ref.*   1,479
P. Williams, *Soc. Lab.*   766

J. McLaggan, *NLP*   158
Lab. majority 16,159
(Boundary change: notional Lab.)

BRISTOL NORTH WEST
*E.*75,009 *T.* 73.65%
D. Naysmith, *Lab. Co-op.*   27,575
†M. Stern, *C.*   16,193
I. Parry, *LD*   7,263
C. Horton, *Ind. Lab.*   1,718
J. Quintanilla, *Ref.*   1,609
G. Shorter, *Soc. Lab.*   482
S. Parnell, *BNP*   265
T. Leighton, *NLP*   140
Lab. Co-op. majority 11,382
(Boundary change: notional Lab.
Co-op.)

BRISTOL SOUTH
*E.*72,393 *T.* 68.87%
†Ms D. Primarolo, *Lab.*   29,890
M. Roe, *C.*   10,562
S. Williams, *LD*   6,691
D. Guy, *Ref.*   1,486
J. Boxall, *Green*   722
I. Marshall, *Soc.*   355
Louis Taylor, *Glow*   153
Lab. majority 19,328
(Boundary change: notional Lab.)

BRISTOL WEST
*E.*84,870 *T.* 73.81%
Ms V. Davey, *Lab.*   22,068
†Rt. Hon. W. Waldegrave, *C.*   20,575
C. Boney, *LD*   17,551
Lady M. Beauchamp, *Ref.*   1,304
J. Quinnell, *Green*   852
R. Nurse, *Soc. Lab.*   244
J. Brierley, *NLP*   47
Lab. majority 1,493
(Boundary change: notional C.)

BROMLEY AND CHISLEHURST
*E.*71,104 *T.* 74.17%
†Rt. Hon. E. Forth, *C.*   24,428
R. Yeldham, *Lab.*   13,310
Dr P. Booth, *LD*   12,530
R. Bryant, *UK Ind.*   1,176
Ms F. Speed, *Green*   640
M. Stoneman, *NF*   369
G. Aitman, *Lib.*   285
C. majority 11,118
(Boundary change: notional C.)

BROMSGROVE
*E.*67,744 *T.* 77.07%
Miss J. Kirkbride, *C.*   24,620
P. McDonald, *Lab.*   19,725
Mrs J. Davy, *LD*   6,200
Mrs D. Winsor, *Ref.*   1,411
Mrs G. Wetton, *UK Ind.*   251
C. majority 4,895
(Boundary change: notional C.)

BROXBOURNE
*E.*66,720 *T.* 70.41%
†Mrs M. Roe, *C.*   22,952
B. Coleman, *Lab.*   16,299
Mrs J. Davies, *LD*   5,310
D. Millward, *Ref.*   1,633
D. Bruce, *BNP*   610
B. Cheetham, *Third Way*   172

C. majority 6,653
(Boundary change: notional C.)

BROXTOWE
*E.*74,144   *T.* 78.41%
N. Palmer, *Lab.* 27,343
†Sir J. Lester, *C.* 21,768
T. Miller, *LD* 6,934
R. Tucker, *Ref.* 2,092
Lab. majority 5,575
(Boundary change: notional C.)

BUCKINGHAM
*E.*62,945   *T.* 78.48%
J. Bercow, *C.* 24,594
R. Lehmann, *Lab.* 12,208
N. Stuart, *LD* 12,175
Dr G. Clements, *NLP* 421
C. majority 12,386
(Boundary change: notional C.)

BURNLEY
*E.*67,582   *T.* 66.95%
*P. Pike, *Lab.* 26,210
W. Wiggin, *C.* 9,148
G. Birtwistle, *LD* 7,877
R. Oakley, *Ref.* 2,010
Lab. majority 17,062
(April 1992, Lab. maj. 11,491)

BURTON
*E.*72,601   *T.* 75.08%
Ms J. Dean, *Lab.* 27,810
†Sir I. Lawrence, *C.* 21,480
D. Fletcher, *LD* 4,617
K. Sharp, *Nat. Dem.* 604
Lab. majority 6,330
(Boundary change: notional C.)

BURY NORTH
*E.*70,515   *T.* 78.07%
D. Chaytor, *Lab.* 28,523
*A. Burt, *C.* 20,657
N. Kenyon, *LD* 4,536
R. Hallewell, *Ref.* 1,337
Lab. majority 7,866
(April 1992, C. maj. 4,764)

BURY SOUTH
*E.*66,568   *T.* 75.60%
I. Lewis, *Lab.* 28,658
†D. Sumberg, *C.* 16,225
V. D'Albert, *LD* 4,227
B. Slater, *Ref.* 1,216
Lab. majority 12,433
(Boundary change: notional C.)

BURY ST EDMUNDS
*E.*74,017   *T.* 75.02%
D. Ruffley, *C.* 21,290
M. Ereira-Guyer, *Lab.* 20,922
D. Cooper, *LD* 10,102
I. McWhirter, *Ref.* 2,939
Mrs J. Lillis, *NLP* 272
C. majority 368
(Boundary change: notional C.)

CALDER VALLEY
*E.*74,901   *T.* 75.39%
Ms C. McCafferty, *Lab.* 26,050
*Sir D. Thompson, *C.* 19,795
S. Pearson, *LD* 8,322
A. Mellor, *Ref.* 1,380
Ms V. Smith, *Green* 488

C. Jackson, *BNP* 431
Lab. majority 6,255
(April 1992, C. maj. 4,878)

CAMBERWELL AND PECKHAM
*E.*50,214   *T.* 56.71%
†Ms H. Harman, *Lab.* 19,734
K. Humphreys, *C.* 3,383
N. Williams, *LD* 3,198
N. China, *Ref.* 692
Ms A. Ruddock, *Soc. Lab.* 685
G. Williams, *Lib.* 443
Ms J. Barker, *Soc.* 233
C. Eames, *WRP* 106
Lab. majority 16,351
(Boundary change: notional Lab.)

CAMBRIDGE
*E.*71,669   *T.* 71.63%
*A. Campbell, *Lab.* 27,436
D. Platt, *C.* 13,299
G. Heathcock, *LD* 8,287
W. Burrows, *Ref.* 1,262
Ms M. Wright, *Green* 654
Ms A. Johnstone, *ProLife* 191
R. Athow, *WRP* 107
Ms P. Gladwin, *NLP* 103
Lab. majority 14,137
(April 1992, Lab. maj. 580)

CAMBRIDGESHIRE NORTH EAST
*E.*76,056   *T.* 72.87%
†M. Moss, *C.* 23,855
Mrs V. Bucknor, *Lab.* 18,754
A. Nash, *LD* 9,070
M. Bacon, *Ref.* 2,636
C. Bennett, *Soc. Lab.* 851
L. Leighton, *NLP* 259
C. majority 5,101
(Boundary change: notional C.)

CAMBRIDGESHIRE NORTH WEST
*E.*65,791   *T.* 74.20%
†Rt. Hon. Dr B. Mawhinney, *C.* 23,488
L. Steptoe, *Lab.* 15,734
Mrs B. McCoy, *LD* 7,388
A.Watt, *Ref.* 1,939
W. Wyatt, *UK Ind.* 269
C. majority 7,754
(Boundary change: notional C.)

CAMBRIDGESHIRE SOUTH
*E.*69,850   *T.* 76.85%
A. Lansley, *C.* 22,572
J. Quinlan, *LD* 13,860
A. Gray, *Lab.* 13,485
R. Page, *Ref.* 3,300
D. Norman, *UK Ind.* 298
F. Chalmers, *NLP* 168
C. majority 8,712
(Boundary change: notional C.)

CAMBRIDGESHIRE SOUTH EAST
*E.*75,666   *T.* 75.08%
†J. Paice, *C.* 24,397
R. Collinson, *Lab.* 15,048
Ms S. Brinton, *LD* 14,246
J. Howlett, *Ref.* 2,838
K. Lam, *Fair* 167
P. While, *NLP* 111
C. majority 9,349
(Boundary change: notional C.)

CANNOCK CHASE
*E.*72,362   *T.* 72.37%
†Dr A. Wright, *Lab.* 28,705
J. Backhouse, *C.* 14,227
R. Kirby, *LD* 4,537
P. Froggatt, *Ref.* 1,663
W. Hurley, *New Lab.* 1,615
M. Conroy, *Soc. Lab.* 1,120
M. Hartshorn, *Loony* 499
Lab. majority 14,478
(Boundary change: notional Lab.)

CANTERBURY
*E.*74,548   *T.* 72.58%
†J. Brazier, *C.* 20,913
Ms C. Hall, *Lab.* 16,949
M. Vye, *LD* 12,854
J. Osborne, *Ref.* 2,460
G. Meaden, *Green* 588
J. Moore, *UK Ind.* 281
A. Pringle, *NLP* 64
C. majority 3,964
(Boundary change: notional C.)

CARLISLE
*E.*59,917   *T.* 72.78%
†E. Martlew, *Lab.* 25,031
R. Lawrence, *C.* 12,641
C. Mayho, *LD* 4,576
A. Fraser, *Ref.* 1,233
W. Stevens, *NLP* 126
Lab. majority 12,390
(Boundary change: notional Lab.)

CARSHALTON AND WALLINGTON
*E.*66,038   *T.* 73.33%
T. Brake, *LD* 18,490
*N. Forman, *C.* 16,223
A. Theobald, *Lab.* 11,565
J. Storey, *Ref.* 1,289
P. Hickson, *Green* 377
G. Ritchie, *BNP* 261
L. Povey, *UK Ind.* 218
LD majority 2,267
(April 1992, C. maj. 9,943)

CASTLE POINT
*E.*67,146   *T.* 72.34%
Ms C. Butler, *Lab.* 20,605
*Dr R. Spink, *C.* 19,489
D. Baker, *LD* 4,477
H. Maulkin, *Ref.* 2,700
Miss L. Kendall, *Consult.* 1,301
Lab. majority 1,116
(April 1992, C. maj. 16,830)

CHARNWOOD
*E.*72,692   *T.* 77.28%
†Rt. Hon. S. Dorrell, *C.* 26,110
D. Knaggs, *Lab.* 20,210
R. Wilson, *LD* 7,224
H. Meechan, *Ref.* 2,104
M. Palmer, *BNP* 525
C. majority 5,900
(Boundary change: notional C.)

CHATHAM AND AYLESFORD
*E.*69,172   *T.* 71.07%
J. Shaw, *Lab.* 21,191
R. Knox-Johnston, *C.* 18,401
R. Murray, *LD* 7,389
K. Riddle, *Ref.* 1,538
A. Harding, *UK Ind.* 493

T. Martel, *NLP* 149
Lab. majority 2,790
(Boundary change: notional C.)

CHEADLE
E.67,627   T. 77.58%
†S. Day, *C.* 22,944
Mrs P. Calton, *LD* 19,755
P. Diggett, *Lab.* 8,253
P. Brook, *Ref.* 1,511
C. majority 3,189
(Boundary change: notional C.)

CHELMSFORD WEST
E.76,086   T. 76.99%
†S. Burns, *C.* 23,781
M. Bracken, *LD* 17,090
Dr R. Chad, *Lab.* 15,436
T. Smith, *Ref.* 1,536
G. Rumens, *Green* 411
M. Levin, *UK Ind.* 323
C. majority 6,691
(Boundary change: notional C.)

CHELTENHAM
E.67,950   T. 74.03%
†N. Jones, *LD* 24,877
J. Todman, *C.* 18,232
B. Leach, *Lab.* 5,100
Mrs A. Powell, *Ref.* 1,065
K. Hanks, *Loony* 375
G. Cook, *UK Ind.* 302
Ms A. Harriss, *ProLife* 245
Ms S. Brighouse, *NLP* 107
LD majority 6,645
(Boundary change: notional LD)

CHESHAM AND AMERSHAM
E.69,244   T. 75.38%
†Mrs C. Gillan, *C.* 26,298
M. Brand, *LD* 12,439
P. Farrelly, *Lab.* 10,240
P. Andrews, *Ref.* 2,528
C. Shilson, *UK Ind.* 618
H. Godfrey, *NLP* 74
C. majority 13,859
(Boundary change: notional C.)

CHESTER, CITY OF
E.71,730   T. 78.43%
Ms C. Russell, *Lab.* 29,806
†G. Brandreth, *C.* 19,253
D. Simpson, *LD* 5,353
R. Mullen, *Ref.* 1,487
I. Sanderson, *Loony* 204
J. Gerrard, *WCCC* 154
Lab. majority 10,553
(Boundary change: notional C.)

CHESTERFIELD
E.72,472   T. 70.91%
*Rt. Hon. A. Benn, *Lab.* 26,105
A. Rogers, *LD* 20,330
M. Potter, *C.* 4,752
N. Scarth, *Ind. OAP* 202
Lab. majority 5,775
(April 1992, Lab. maj. 6,414)

CHICHESTER
E.74,489   T. 74.88%
A. Tyrie, *C.* 25,895
Prof. P. Gardiner, *LD* 16,161
C. Smith, *Lab.* 9,605

D. Denny, *Ref.* 3,318
J. Rix, *UK Ind.* 800
C. majority 9,734
(Boundary change: notional C.)

CHINGFORD AND WOODFORD GREEN
E.62,904   T. 70.66%
†I. Duncan Smith, *C.* 21,109
T. Hutchinson, *Lab.* 15,395
G. Seeff, *LD* 6,885
A. Gould, *BNP* 1,059
C. majority 5,714
(Boundary change: notional C.)

CHIPPING BARNET
E.69,049   T. 71.78%
†Sir S. Chapman, *C.* 21,317
G. Cooke, *Lab.* 20,282
S. Hooker, *LD* 6,121
V. Ribekow, *Ref.* 1,190
B. Miskin, *Loony* 253
B. Scallan, *ProLife* 243
Ms D. Dirksen, *NLP* 159
C. majority 1,035
(Boundary change: notional C.)

CHORLEY
E.74,387   T. 77.58%
L. Hoyle, *Lab.* 30,607
†D. Dover, *C.* 20,737
S. Jones, *LD* 4,900
A. Heaton, *Ref.* 1,319
P. Leadbetter, *NLP* 143
Lab. majority 9,870
(Boundary change: notional C.)

CHRISTCHURCH
E.71,488   T. 78.61%
C. Chope, *C.* 26,095
†Mrs D. Maddock, *LD* 23,930
C. Mannan, *Lab.* 3,884
R. Spencer, *Ref.* 1,684
R. Dickinson, *UK Ind.* 606
C. majority 2,165
(Boundary change: notional C.)

CITIES OF LONDON AND WESTMINSTER
E.69,047   T. 58.16%
†Rt. Hon. P. Brooke, *C.* 18,981
Ms K. Green, *Lab.* 14,100
M. Dumigan, *LD* 4,933
Sir A. Walters, *Ref.* 1,161
Ms P. Wharton, *Barts* 266
C. Merton, *UK Ind.* 215
R. Johnson, *NLP* 176
N. Walsh, *Loony* 138
G. Webster, *Hemp* 112
J. Sadowitz, *Dream* 73
C. majority 4,881
(Boundary change: notional C.)

CLEETHORPES
E.68,763   T. 73.40%
Ms S. McIsaac, *Lab.* 26,058
†M. Brown, *C.* 16,882
K. Melton, *LD* 5,746
J. Berry, *Ref.* 1,787
Lab. majority 9,176
(Boundary change: notional C.)

COLCHESTER
E.74,743   T.69.58%
R. Russell, *LD* 17,886
S. Shakespeare, *C.* 16,305
R. Green, *Lab.* 15,891
J. Hazell, *Ref.* 1,776
Ms L. Basker, *NLP* 148
LD majority 1,581
(Boundary change: notional C.)

COLNE VALLEY
E.73,338   T.76.92%
Ms K. Mountford, *Lab.* 23,285
*G. Riddick, *C.* 18,445
N. Priestley, *LD* 12,755
A. Brooke, *Soc. Lab.* 759
A. Cooper, *Green* 493
J. Nunn, *UK Ind.* 478
Ms M. Staniforth, *Loony* 196
Lab. majority 4,840
(April 1992, C. maj. 7,225)

CONGLETON
E.68,873   T.77.56%
†Mrs A. Winterton, *C.* 22,012
Mrs J. Walmsley, *LD* 15,882
Ms H. Scholey, *Lab.* 14,714
J. Lockett, *UK Ind.* 811
C. majority 6,130
(Boundary change: notional C.)

COPELAND
E.54,263   T.76.19%
*Rt. Hon. Dr J. Cunningham,
  Lab. 24,025
A. Cumpsty, *C.* 12,081
R. Putnam, *LD* 3,814
C. Johnston, *Ref.* 1,036
G. Hanratty, *ProLife* 389
Lab. majority 11,944
(April 1992, Lab. maj. 2,439)

CORBY
E.69,252   T.77.91%
P. Hope, *Lab. Co-op.* 29,888
*W. Powell, *C.* 18,028
I. Hankinson, *LD* 4,045
S. Riley-Smith, *Ref.* 1,356
I. Gillman, *UK Ind.* 507
Ms J. Bence, *NLP* 133
Lab. Co-op. majority 11,860
(April 1992, C. maj. 342)

CORNWALL NORTH
E.80,076   T.73.16%
*P. Tyler, *LD* 31,186
N. Linacre, *C.* 17,253
Ms A. Lindo, *Lab.* 5,523
Ms F. Odam, *Ref.* 3,636
J. Bolitho, *MK* 645
R. Winfield, *Lib.* 186
N. Cresswell, *NLP* 152
LD majority 13,933
(April 1992, LD maj. 1,921)

CORNWALL SOUTH EAST
E.75,825   T.75.74%
C. Breed, *LD* 27,044
W. Lightfoot, *C.* 20,564
Mrs D. Kirk, *Lab.* 7,358
J. Wonnacott, *UK Ind.* 1,428
P. Dunbar, *MK* 573
W. Weights, *Lib* 268

Ms M. Hartley, *NLP* 197
LD majority 6,480
(April 1992, C. maj. 7,704)

COTSWOLD
*E.*67,333 *T.*75.92%
†G. Clifton-Brown, *C.* 23,698
D. Gayler, *LD* 11,733
D. Elwell, *Lab.* 11,608
R. Lowe, *Ref.* 3,393
Ms V. Michael, *Green* 560
H. Brighouse, *NLP* 129
C. majority 11,965
(Boundary change: notional C.)

COVENTRY NORTH EAST
*E.*74,274 *T.*64.74%
†R. Ainsworth, *Lab.* 31,856
M. Burnett, *C.* 9,287
G. Sewards, *LD* 3,866
N. Brown, *Lib.* 1,181
R. Hurrell, *Ref.* 1,125
H. Khamis, *Soc. Lab.* 597
C. Sidwell, *Dream* 173
Lab. majority 22,569
(Boundary change: notional Lab.)

COVENTRY NORTH WEST
*E.*76,439 *T.*71.07%
†G. Robinson, *Lab.* 30,901
P. Bartlett, *C.* 14,300
Dr N. Penlington, *LD* 5,690
D. Butler, *Ref.* 1,269
D. Spencer, *Soc. Lab.* 940
R. Wheway, *Lib.* 687
P. Mills, *ProLife* 359
L. Francis, *Dream* 176
Lab. majority 16,601
(Boundary change: notional Lab.)

COVENTRY SOUTH
*E.*71,826 *T.*69.79%
†J. Cunningham, *Lab.* 25,511
P. Ivey, *C.* 14,558
G. MacDonald, *LD* 4,617
D. Nellist, *Soc.* 3,262
P. Garratt, *Ref.* 943
R. Jenking, *Lib.* 725
J. Astbury, *BNP* 328
Ms A.-M. Bradshaw, *Dream* 180
Lab. majority 10,953
(Boundary change: notional C.)

CRAWLEY
*E.*69,040 *T.*73.03%
Mrs L. Moffatt, *Lab.* 27,750
Miss J. Crabb, *C.* 16,043
H. de Souza, *LD* 4,141
R. Walters, *Ref.* 1,931
E. Saunders, *UK Ind.* 322
A. Kahn, *JP* 230
Lab. majority 11,707
(Boundary change: notional C.)

CREWE AND NANTWICH
*E.*68,694 *T.*73.67%
†Mrs G. Dunwoody, *Lab.* 29,460
M. Loveridge, *C.* 13,662
D. Cannon, *LD* 5,940
P. Astbury, *Ref.* 1,543
Lab. majority 15,798
(Boundary change: notional Lab.)

CROSBY
*E.*57,190 *T.*77.18%
Ms C. Curtis-Tansley, *Lab.* 22,549
†Sir M. Thornton, *C.* 15,367
P. McVey, *LD* 5,080
J. Gauld, *Ref.* 813
J. Marks, *Lib.* 233
W. Hite, *NLP* 99
Lab. majority 7,182
(Boundary change: notional C.)

CROYDON CENTRAL
*E.*80,152 *T.*69.62%
G. Davies, *Lab.* 25,432
†D. Congdon, *C.* 21,535
G. Schlich, *LD* 6,061
C. Cook, *Ref.* 1,886
M.-S. Barnsley, *Green* 595
J. Woollcott, *UK Ind.* 290
Lab. majority 3,897
(Boundary change: notional C.)

CROYDON NORTH
*E.*77,063 *T.*68.21%
†M. Wicks, *Lab.* 32,672
I. Martin, *C.* 14,274
M. Morris, *LD* 4,066
R. Billis, *Ref.* 1,155
J. Feisenberger, *UK Ind.* 396
Lab. majority 18,398
(Boundary change: notional C.)

CROYDON SOUTH
*E.*73,787 *T.*73.45%
†R. Ottaway, *C.* 25,649
C. Burling, *Lab.* 13,719
S. Gauge, *LD* 11,441
A. Barber, *Ref.* 2,631
P. Ferguson, *BNP* 354
A. Harker, *UK Ind.* 309
M. Samuel, *Choice* 96
C. majority 11,930
(Boundary change: notional C.)

DAGENHAM
*E.*58,573 *T.*61.74%
†Mrs J. Church, *Lab.* 23,759
J. Fairrie, *C.* 6,705
T. Dobrashian, *LD* 2,704
S. Kraft, *Ref.* 1,411
W. Binding, *BNP* 900
R. Dawson, *Ind.* 349
M. Hipperson, *Nat. Dem.* 183
Ms K. Goble, *ProLife* 152
Lab. majority 17,054
(Boundary change: notional Lab.)

DARLINGTON
*E.*65,140 *T.*73.95%
*A. Milburn, *Lab.* 29,658
P. Scrope, *C.* 13,633
L. Boxell, *LD* 3,483
M. Blakey, *Ref.* 1,399
Lab. majority 16,025
(April 1992, Lab. maj. 2,798)

DARTFORD
*E.*69,726 *T.*74.57%
H. Stoate, *Lab.* 25,278
†R. Dunn, *C.* 20,950
Mrs D. Webb, *LD* 4,827
P. McHale, *BNP* 428
P. Homden, *FDP* 287

J. Pollitt, *Ch. D.* 228
Lab. majority 4,328
(Boundary change: notional C.)

DAVENTRY
*E.*80,151 *T.*77.04%
†T. Boswell, *C.* 28,615
K. Ritchie, *Lab.* 21,237
J. Gordon, *LD* 9,233
Mrs B. Russocki, *Ref.* 2,018
B. Mahoney, *UK Ind.* 443
R. France, *NLP* 204
C. majority 7,378
(Boundary change: notional C.)

DENTON AND REDDISH
*E.*68,866 *T.*66.92%
†A. Bennett, *Lab.* 30,137
Ms B. Nutt, *C.* 9,826
I. Donaldson, *LD* 6,121
Lab. majority 20,311
(Boundary change: notional Lab.)

DERBY NORTH
*E.*76,116 *T.*73.76%
R. Laxton, *Lab.* 29,844
*Rt. Hon. G. Knight, *C.* 19,229
R. Charlesworth, *LD* 5,059
P. Reynolds, *Ref.* 1,816
J. Waters, *ProLife* 195
Lab. majority 10,615
(April 1992, C. maj. 4,453)

DERBY SOUTH
*E.*76,386 *T.*67.84%
†Rt. Hon. Mrs M. Beckett, *Lab.* 29,154
J. Arain, *C.* 13,048
J. Beckett, *LD* 7,438
J. Browne, *Ref.* 1,862
R. Evans, *Nat. Dem.* 317
Lab. majority 16,106
(Boundary change: notional Lab.)

DERBYSHIRE NORTH EAST
*E.*71,653 *T.*72.54%
*H. Barnes, *Lab.* 31,425
S. Elliott, *C.* 13,104
S. Hardy, *LD* 7,450
Lab. majority 18,321
(April 1992, Lab. maj. 6,270)

DERBYSHIRE SOUTH
*E.*76,672 *T.*78.21%
M. Todd, *Lab.* 32,709
†Mrs E. Currie, *C.* 18,742
R. Renold, *LD* 5,408
R. North, *Ref.* 2,491
Dr I. Crompton, *UK Ind.* 617
Lab. majority 13,967
(Boundary change: notional C.)

DERBYSHIRE WEST
*E.*72,716 *T.*78.23%
†P. McLoughlin, *C.* 23,945
S. Clamp, *Lab.* 19,060
C. Seeley, *LD* 9,940
J. Gouriet, *Ref.* 2,499
G. Meynell, *Ind. Green* 593
H. Price, *UK Ind.* 484
N. Delves, *Loony* 281
M. Kyslun, *Ind. BB* 81

C. *majority* 4,885
(Boundary change: notional C.)

DEVIZES
*E.*80,383   *T.*74.69%

†Rt. Hon. M. Ancram, *C.*	25,710
A. Vickers, *LD*	15,928
F. Jeffrey, *Lab.*	14,551
J. Goldsmith, *Ref.*	3,021
S. Oram, *UK Ind.*	622
S. Haysom, *NLP*	204

C. *majority* 9,782
(Boundary change: notional C.)

DEVON EAST
*E.*69,094   *T.*76.06%

†Rt. Hon. Sir P. Emery, *C.*	22,797
Miss R. Trethewey, *LD*	15,308
A. Siantonas, *Lab.*	9,292
W. Dixon, *Ref.*	3,200
G. Halliwell, *Lib.*	1,363
C. Giffard, *UK Ind.*	459
G. Needs, *Nat. Dem.*	131

C. *majority* 7,489
(Boundary change: notional C.)

DEVON NORTH
*E.*70,350   *T.*77.94%

†N. Harvey, *LD*	27,824
R. Ashworth, *C.*	21,643
Mrs E. Brenton, *Lab.*	5,367

LD *majority* 6,181
(Boundary change: notional LD)

DEVON SOUTH WEST
*E.*69,293   *T.*76.22%

†G. Streeter, *C.*	22,695
C. Mavin, *Lab.*	15,262
K. Baldry, *LD*	12,542
R. Sadler, *Ref.*	1,668
Mrs H. King, *UK Ind.*	491
J. Hyde, *NLP*	159

C. *majority* 7,433
(Boundary change: notional C.)

DEVON WEST AND TORRIDGE
*E.*75,919   *T.*77.91%

J. Burnett, *LD*	24,744
I. Liddell-Grainger, *C.*	22,787
D. Brenton, *Lab.*	7,319
R. Lea, *Ref.*	1,946
M. Jackson, *UK Ind.*	1,841
M. Pithouse, *Lib.*	508

LD *majority* 1,957
(Boundary change: notional C.)

DEWSBURY
*E.*61,523   *T.*70.01%

†Mrs A. Taylor, *Lab.*	21,286
Dr P. McCormick, *C.*	12,963
K. Hill, *LD*	4,422
Ms F. Taylor, *BNP*	2,232
Ms W. Goff, *Ref.*	1,019
D. Daniel, *Ind. Lab.*	770
I. McCourtie, *Green*	383

Lab. *majority* 8,323
(Boundary change: notional Lab.)

DONCASTER CENTRAL
*E.*67,965   *T.*63.92%

Ms R. Winterton, *Lab.*	26,961
D. Turtle, *C.*	9,105
S. Tarry, *LD*	4,091

M. Cliff, *Ref.*	1,273
M. Kenny, *Soc. Lab.*	854
J. Redden, *ProLife*	697
P. Davies, *UK Ind.*	462

Lab. *majority* 17,856
(April 1992, Lab. maj. 10,682)

DONCASTER NORTH
*E.*63,019   *T.*63.30%

†K. Hughes, *Lab.*	27,843
P. Kennerley, *C.*	5,906
M. Cook, *LD*	3,369
R. Thornton, *Ref.*	1,589
M. Swan, *AS Lab.*	1,181

Lab. *majority* 21,937
(Boundary change: notional Lab.)

DON VALLEY
*E.*65,643   *T.*66.35%

Ms C. Flint, *Lab.*	25,376
Mrs C. Gledhill, *C.*	10,717
P. Johnston, *LD*	4,238
P. Davis, *Ref.*	1,379
N. Ball, *Soc. Lab.*	1,024
S. Platt, *Green*	493
Ms C. Johnson, *ProLife*	330

Lab. *majority* 14,659
(Boundary change: notional Lab.)

DORSET MID AND POOLE NORTH
*E.*67,049   *T.*75.67%

C. Fraser, *C.*	20,632
A. Leaman, *LD*	19,951
D. Collis, *Lab.*	8,014
D. Nabarro, *Ref.*	2,136

C. *majority* 681
(Boundary change: notional C.)

DORSET NORTH
*E.*68,923   *T.*76.30%

R. Walter, *C.*	23,294
Mrs P. Yates, *LD*	20,548
J. Fitzmaurice, *Lab.*	5,380
Mrs M. Evans, *Ref.*	2,564
Revd D. Wheeler, *UK Ind.*	801

C. *majority* 2,746
(Boundary change: notional C.)

DORSET SOUTH
*E.*66,318   *T.*74.16%

†I. Bruce, *C.*	17,755
J. Knight, *Lab.*	17,678
M. Plummer, *LD*	9,936
P. McAndrew, *Ref.*	2,791
Capt. M. Shakesby, *UK Ind.*	861
G. Napper, *NLP*	161

C. *majority* 77
(Boundary change: notional C.)

DORSET WEST
*E.*70,369   *T.*76.10%

O. Letwin, *C.*	22,036
R. Legg, *LD*	20,196
R. Bygraves, *Lab.*	9,491
P. Jenkins, *UK Ind.*	1,590
M. Griffiths, *NLP*	239

C. *majority* 1,840
(Boundary change: notional C.)

DOVER
*E.*68,669   *T.*78.93%

G. Prosser, *Lab.*	29,535
†D. Shaw, *C.*	17,796

M. Corney, *LD*	4,302
Mrs S. Anderson, *Ref.*	2,124
C. Hyde, *UK Ind.*	443

Lab. *majority* 11,739
(Boundary change: notional C.)

DUDLEY NORTH
*E.*68,835   *T.*69.45%

R. Cranston, *Lab.*	24,471
C. MacNamara, *C.*	15,014
G. Lewis, *LD*	3,939
M. Atherton, *Soc. Lab.*	2,155
S. Bavester, *Ref.*	1,201
G. Cartwright, *NF*	559
S. Darby, *Nat. Dem.*	469

Lab. *majority* 9,457
(Boundary change: notional Lab.)

DUDLEY SOUTH
*E.*66,731   *T.*71.78%

†I. Pearson, *Lab.*	27,124
M. Simpson, *C.*	14,097
R. Burt, *LD*	5,214
C. Birch, *Ref.*	1,467

Lab. *majority* 13,027
(Boundary change: notional Lab.)

DULWICH AND WEST NORWOOD
*E.*69,655   *T.*65.49%

†Ms T. Jowell, *Lab.*	27,807
R. Gough, *C.*	11,038
Mrs S. Kramer, *LD*	4,916
B. Coles, *Ref.*	897
Dr A. Goldie, *Lib.*	587
D. Goodman, *Dream*	173
E. Pike, *UK Ind.*	159
Capt. Rizz, *Rizz Party*	38

Lab. *majority* 16,769
(Boundary change: notional Lab.)

DURHAM NORTH
*E.*67,891   *T.*69.48%

†G. Radice, *Lab.*	33,142
M. Hardy, *C.*	6,843
B. Moore, *LD*	5,225
I. Parkin, *Ref.*	1,958

Lab. *majority* 26,299
(Boundary change: notional Lab.)

DURHAM NORTH WEST
*E.*67,156   *T.*68.97%

†Miss H. Armstrong, *Lab.*	31,855
Mrs L. St J. Howe, *C.*	7,101
A. Gillings, *LD*	4,991
R. Atkinson, *Ref.*	2,372

Lab. *majority* 24,754
(Boundary change: notional Lab.)

DURHAM, CITY OF
*E.*69,340   *T.*70.86%

*G. Steinberg, *Lab.*	31,102
R. Chalk, *C.*	8,598
Dr N. Martin, *LD*	7,499
Ms M. Robson, *Ref.*	1,723
P. Kember, *NLP*	213

Lab. *majority* 22,504
(April 1992, Lab. maj. 15,058)

EALING ACTON AND SHEPHERD'S BUSH
*E.*72,078   *T.*66.68%

†C. Soley, *Lab.*	28,052
Mrs B. Yerolemou, *C.*	12,405

A. Mitchell, *LD*	5,163
C. Winn, *Ref.*	637
J. Gilbert, *Soc. Lab.*	635
J. Gomm, *UK Ind.*	385
P. Danon, *ProLife*	265
C. Beasley, *Glow*	209
W. Edwards, *Ch. P.*	163
K. Turner, *NLP*	150

Lab. majority 15,647
(Boundary change: notional Lab.)

EALING NORTH
*E.*78,144   *T.*71.31%

S. Pound, *Lab.*	29,904
†H. Greenway, *C.*	20,744
A. Gupta, *LD*	3,887
G. Slysz, *UK Ind.*	689
Ms A. Siebe, *Green*	502

Lab. majority 9,160
(Boundary change: notional C.)

EALING SOUTHALL
*E.*81,704   *T.*66.88%

†P. Khabra, *Lab.*	32,791
J. Penrose, *C.*	11,368
Ms N. Thomson, *LD*	5,687
H. Brar, *Soc. Lab.*	2,107
N. Goodwin, *Green*	934
B. Cherry, *Ref.*	854
Ms K. Klepacka, *ProLife*	473
Dr R. Mead, *UK Ind.*	428

Lab. majority 21,423
(Boundary change: notional Lab.)

EASINGTON
*E.*62,518   *T.*67.01%

*J. Cummings, *Lab.*	33,600
J. Hollands, *C.*	3,588
J. Heppell, *LD*	3,025
R. Pulfrey, *Ref.*	1,179
S. Colborn, *SPGB*	503

Lab. majority 30,012
(April 1992, Lab. maj. 26,390)

EASTBOURNE
*E.*72,347   *T.*72.80%

†N. Waterson, *C.*	22,183
C. Berry, *LD*	20,189
D. Lines, *Lab.*	6,576
T. Lowe, *Ref.*	2,724
Mrs T. Williamson, *Lib.*	741
J. Dawkins, *UK Ind.*	254

C. majority 1,994
(Boundary change: notional C.)

EAST HAM
*E.*65,591   *T.*60.81%

†S. Timms, *Lab.*	25,779
Miss A. Bray, *C.*	6,421
I. Khan, *Soc. Lab.*	2,697
M. Sole, *LD*	2,599
C. Smith, *BNP*	1,258
Mrs J. McCann, *Ref.*	845
G. Hardy, *Nat. Dem.*	290

Lab. majority 19,358
(Boundary change: notional Lab.)

EASTLEIGH
*E.*72,155   *T.*76.91%

†D. Chidgey, *LD*	19,453
S. Reid, *C.*	18,699
A. Lloyd, *Lab.*	14,883
V. Eldridge, *Ref.*	2,013

P. Robinson, *UK Ind.*	446

LD majority 754
(Boundary change: notional C.)

ECCLES
*E.*69,645   *T.*65.60%

I. Stewart, *Lab.*	30,468
G. Barker, *C.*	8,552
R. Boyd, *LD*	4,905
J. De Roeck, *Ref.*	1,765

Lab. majority 21,916
(Boundary change: notional Lab.)

EDDISBURY
*E.*65,256   *T.*75.78%

†Rt. Hon. A. Goodlad, *C.*	21,027
Ms M. Hanson, *Lab.*	19,842
D. Reaper, *LD*	6,540
Ms N. Napier, *Ref.*	2,041

C. majority 1,185
(Boundary change: notional C.)

EDMONTON
*E.*63,718   *T.*70.37%

A. Love, *Lab. Co-op.*	27,029
*Dr I. Twinn, *C.*	13,557
A. Wiseman, *LD*	2,847
J. Wright, *Ref.*	708
B. Cowd, *BNP*	437
Mrs P. Weald, *UK Ind.*	260

Lab. Co-op. majority 13,472
(April 1992, C. maj. 593)

ELLESMERE PORT AND NESTON
*E.*67,573   *T.*77.79%

†A. Miller, *Lab.*	31,310
Mrs L. Turnbull, *C.*	15,274
Ms J. Pemberton, *LD*	4,673
C. Rodden, *Ref.*	1,305

Lab. majority 16,036
(Boundary change: notional Lab.)

ELMET
*E.*70,423   *T.*76.81%

C. Burgon, *Lab.*	28,348
*S. Batiste, *C.*	19,569
B. Jennings, *LD*	4,691
C. Zawadski, *Ref.*	1,487

Lab. majority 8,779
(April 1992, C. maj. 3,261)

ELTHAM
*E.*57,358   *T.*75.71%

C. Efford, *Lab.*	23,710
C. Blackwood, *C.*	13,528
Ms A. Taylor, *LD*	3,701
M. Clark, *Ref.*	1,414
H. Middleton, *Lib.*	584
W. Hitches, *BNP*	491

Lab. majority 10,182
(Boundary change: notional C.)

ENFIELD NORTH
*E.*67,680   *T.*70.43%

Ms J. Ryan, *Lab.*	24,148
M. Field, *C.*	17,326
M. Hopkins, *LD*	4,264
R. Ellingham, *Ref.*	857
Ms J. Griffin, *BNP*	590
Mrs J. O'Ware, *UK Ind.*	484

Lab. majority 6,822
(April 1992, C. maj. 9,430)

ENFIELD SOUTHGATE
*E.*65,796   *T.*70.72%

S. Twigg, *Lab.*	20,570
†Rt. Hon. M. Portillo, *C.*	19,137
J. Browne, *LD*	4,966
N. Luard, *Ref.*	1,342
A. Storkey, *Ch. D.*	289
A. Malakouna, *Mal*	229

Lab. majority 1,433
(Boundary change: notional C.)

EPPING FOREST
*E.*72,795   *T.*72.82%

Mrs E. Laing, *C.*	24,117
S. Murray, *Lab.*	18,865
S. Robinson, *LD*	7,074
J. Berry, *Ref.*	2,208
P. Henderson, *BNP*	743

C. majority 5,252
(Boundary change: notional C.)

EPSOM AND EWELL
*E.*73,222   *T.*74.00%

†Rt. Hon. Sir A. Hamilton, *C.*	24,717
P. Woodford, *Lab.*	13,192
J. Vincent, *LD*	12,380
C. Macdonald, *Ref.*	2,355
H. Green, *UK Ind.*	544
H. Charlton, *Green*	527
Ms K. Weeks, *ProLife*	466

C. majority 11,525
(Boundary change: notional C.)

EREWASH
*E.*77,402   *T.*77.95%

Ms E. Blackman, *Lab.*	31,196
†Mrs A. Knight, *C.*	22,061
Dr M. Garnett, *LD*	5,181
S. Stagg, *Ref.*	1,404
M. Simmons, *Soc. Lab.*	496

Lab. majority 9,135
(Boundary change: notional C.)

ERITH AND THAMESMEAD
*E.*62,887   *T.*66.13%

†J. Austin-Walker, *Lab.*	25,812
N. Zahawi, *C.*	8,388
A. Grigg, *LD*	5,001
J. Flunder, *Ref.*	1,394
V. Dooley, *BNP*	718
M. Jackson, *UK Ind.*	274

Lab. majority 17,424
(Boundary change: notional Lab.)

ESHER AND WALTON
*E.*72,382   *T.*74.14%

†I. Taylor, *C.*	26,747
Ms J. Reay, *Lab.*	12,219
G. Miles, *LD*	10,937
A. Cruickshank, *Ref.*	2,904
B. Collignon, *UK Ind.*	558
Ms S. Kay, *Dream*	302

C. majority 14,528
(Boundary change: notional C.)

ESSEX NORTH
*E.*68,008   *T.*75.30%

†B. Jenkin, *C.*	22,480
T. Young, *Lab.*	17,004
A. Phillips, *LD*	10,028
R. Lord, *UK Ind.*	1,202
Ms S. Ransome, *Green*	495

C. majority 5,476
(Boundary change: notional C.)

EXETER
E.79,154   T.78.16%
B. Bradshaw, *Lab.*	29,398
Dr A. Rogers, *C.*	17,693
D. Brewer, *LD*	11,148
D. Morrish, *Lib.*	2,062
P. Edwards, *Green*	643
Mrs C. Haynes, *UK Ind.*	638
J. Meakin, *UKPP*	282

Lab. majority 11,705
(Boundary change: notional C.)

FALMOUTH AND CAMBORNE
E.71,383   T.75.13%
Ms C. Atherton, *Lab.*	18,151
*S. Coe, *C.*	15,463
Mrs T. Jones, *LD*	13,512
P. de Savary, *Ref.*	3,534
J. Geach, *Ind. Lab.*	1,691
P. Holmes, *Lib.*	527
R. Smith, *UK Ind.*	355
Ms R. Lewarne, *MK*	238
G. Glitter, *Loony*	161

Lab. majority 2,688
(April 1992, C. maj. 3,267)

FAREHAM
E.68,787   T.75.85%
†Rt. Hon. Sir P. Lloyd, *C.*	24,436
M. Pryor, *Lab.*	14,078
Mrs G. Hill, *LD*	10,234
D. Markham, *Ref.*	2,914
W. O'Brien, *Ind. No*	515

C. majority 10,358
(Boundary change: notional C.)

FAVERSHAM AND KENT MID
E.67,490   T.73.50%
†A. Rowe, *C.*	22,016
A. Stewart, *Lab.*	17,843
B. Parmenter, *LD*	6,138
R. Birley, *Ref.*	2,073
N. Davidson, *Loony*	511
M. Cunningham, *UK Ind.*	431
D. Currer, *Green*	380
Ms C. Morgan, *GRLNSP*	115
N. Pollard, *NLP*	99

C. majority 4,173
(Boundary change: notional C.)

FELTHAM AND HESTON
E.71,093   T.65.58%
†A. Keen, *Lab. Co-op.*	27,836
P. Ground, *C.*	12,563
C. Penning, *LD*	4,264
R. Stubbs, *Ref.*	1,099
R. Church, *BNP*	682
D. Fawcett, *NLP*	177

Lab. Co-op. majority 15,273
(Boundary change: notional Lab. Co-op.)

FINCHLEY AND GOLDERS GREEN
E.72,225   T.69.65%
R. Vis, *Lab.*	23,180
†J. Marshall, *C.*	19,991
J. Davies, *LD*	5,670
G. Shaw, *Ref.*	684
A. Gunstock, *Green*	576
D. Barraclough, *UK Ind.*	205

Lab. majority 3,189
(Boundary change: notional C.)

FOLKESTONE AND HYTHE
E.71,153   T.73.15%
†Rt. Hon. M. Howard, *C.*	20,313
D. Laws, *LD*	13,981
P. Doherty, *Lab.*	12,939
J. Aspinall, *Ref.*	4,188
J. Baker, *UK Ind.*	378
E. Segal, *Soc.*	182
R. Saint, *CFSS*	69

C. majority 6,332
(Boundary change: notional C.)

FOREST OF DEAN
E.63,465   T.79.07%
Ms D. Organ, *Lab.*	24,203
†P. Marland, *C.*	17,860
Dr A. Lynch, *LD*	6,165
J. Hopkins, *Ref.*	1,624
G. Morgan, *Ind. Dean*	218
C. Palmer, *21st Cent.*	80
S. Porter, *Ind. F.*	34

Lab. majority 6,343
(Boundary change: notional Lab.)

FYLDE
E.71,385   T.72.94%
†Rt. Hon. M. Jack, *C.*	25,443
J. Garrett, *Lab.*	16,480
W. Greene, *LD*	7,609
D. Britton, *Ref.*	2,372
T. Kerwin, *NLP*	163

C. majority 8,963
(Boundary change: notional C.)

GAINSBOROUGH
E.64,106   T.74.56%
†E. Leigh, *C.*	20,593
P. Taylor, *Lab.*	13,767
N. Taylor, *LD*	13,436

C. majority 6,826
(Boundary change: notional C.)

GATESHEAD EAST AND WASHINGTON WEST
E.64,114   T.67.19%
†Miss J. Quin, *Lab.*	31,047
Miss J. Burns, *C.*	6,097
A. Ord, *LD*	4,622
M. Daley, *Ref.*	1,315

Lab. majority 24,950
(Boundary change: notional Lab.)

GEDLING
E.68,820   T.75.80%
V. Coaker, *Lab.*	24,390
*A. Mitchell, *C.*	20,588
R. Poynter, *LD*	5,180
J. Connor, *Ref.*	2,006

Lab. majority 3,802
(April 1992, C. maj. 10,637)

GILLINGHAM
E.70,389   T.72.00%
P. Clark, *Lab.*	20,187
†J. Couchman, *C.*	18,207
R. Sayer, *LD*	9,649
G. Cann, *Ref.*	1,492
C. MacKinlay, *UK Ind.*	590
D. Robinson, *Loony*	305
C. Jury, *BNP*	195

Ms G. Duguay, *NLP*	58

Lab. majority 1,980
(Boundary change: notional C.)

GLOUCESTER
E.78,682   T.73.61%
Ms T. Kingham, *Lab.*	28,943
†D. French, *C.*	20,684
P. Munisamy, *LD*	6,069
A. Reid, *Ref.*	1,482
A. Harris, *UK Ind.*	455
Ms M. Hamilton, *NLP*	281

Lab. majority 8,259
(Boundary change: notional C.)

GOSPORT
E.68,830   T.70.25%
*P. Viggers, *C.*	21,085
I. Gray, *Lab.*	14,827
S. Hogg, *LD*	9,479
A. Blowers, *Ref.*	2,538
P. Ettie, *Ind.*	426

C. majority 6,258
(April 1992, C. maj. 16,318)

GRANTHAM AND STAMFORD
E.72,310   T.73.25%
†Q. Davies, *C.*	22,672
P. Denning, *Lab.*	19,980
J. Sellick, *LD*	6,612
Ms M. Swain, *Ref.*	2,721
M. Charlesworth, *UK Ind.*	556
Ms R. Clark, *ProLife*	314
I. Harper, *NLP*	115

C. majority 2,692
(Boundary change: notional C.)

GRAVESHAM
E.69,234   T.76.92%
C. Pond, *Lab.*	26,460
†J. Arnold, *C.*	20,681
Dr M. Canet, *LD*	4,128
Mrs P. Curtis, *Ref.*	1,441
A. Leyshon, *Ind.*	414
D. Palmer, *NLP*	129

Lab. majority 5,779
(Boundary change: notional C.)

GREAT GRIMSBY
E.65,043   T.66.26%
*A. Mitchell, *Lab.*	25,765
D. Godson, *C.*	9,521
A. De Freitas, *LD*	7,810

Lab. majority 16,244
(April 1992, Lab. maj. 7,504)

GREAT YARMOUTH
E.68,625   T.71.23%
A. Wright, *Lab.*	26,084
*M. Carttiss, *C.*	17,416
D. Wood, *LD*	5,381

Lab. majority 8,668
(April 1992, C. maj. 5,309)

GREENWICH AND WOOLWICH
E.61,352   T.65.85%
†N. Raynsford, *Lab.*	25,630
M. Mitchell, *C.*	7,502
Mrs C. Luxton, *LD*	5,049
D. Ellison, *Ref.*	1,670
R. Mallone, *Fellowship*	428
D. Martin-Eagle, *Constit.*	124

Lab. majority 18,128
(Boundary change: notional Lab.)

GUILDFORD
E.75,541   T.75.40%
N. St Aubyn, *C.*   24,230
Mrs M. Sharp, *LD*   19,439
J. Burns, *Lab.*   9,945
J. Gore, *Ref.*   2,650
R. McWhirter, *UK Ind.*   400
J. Morris, *Pacifist*   294
C. majority 4,791
(Boundary change: notional C.)

HACKNEY NORTH AND STOKE
NEWINGTON
E.62,045   T.52.95%
*Ms D. Abbott, *Lab.*   21,110
M. Lavender, *C.*   5,483
D. Taylor, *LD*   3,806
Yen Chit Chong, *Green*   1,395
B. Maxwell, *Ref.*   544
D. Tolson, *None*   368
Miss L. Lovebucket, *Rain. Ref.* 146
Lab. majority 15,627
(April 1992, Lab. maj. 10,727)

HACKNEY SOUTH AND
SHOREDITCH
E.61,728   T.54.67%
†B. Sedgemore, *Lab.*   20,048
M. Pantling, *LD*   5,068
C. O'Leary, *C.*   4,494
T. Betts, *New Lab.*   2,436
R. Franklin, *Ref.*   613
G. Callow, *BNP*   531
M. Goldman, *Comm. P.*   298
Ms M. Goldberg, *NLP*   145
W. Rogers, *WRP*   113
Lab. majority 14,980
(Boundary change: notional Lab.)

HALESOWEN AND ROWLEY REGIS
E.66,245   T.73.61%
Mrs S. Heal, *Lab.*   26,366
J. Kennedy, *C.*   16,029
Ms E. Todd, *LD*   4,169
P. White, *Ref.*   1,244
Ms K. Meeds, *Nat. Dem.*   592
T. Weller, *Green*   361
Lab. majority 10,337
(Boundary change: notional C.)

HALIFAX
E.71,701   T.70.51%
*Mrs A. Mahon, *Lab.*   27,465
R. Light, *C.*   16,253
E. Waller, *LD*   6,059
Mrs C. Whitaker, *UK Ind.*   779
Lab. majority 11,212
(April 1992, Lab. maj. 478)

HALTEMPRICE AND HOWDEN
E.65,602   T.75.53%
†Rt. Hon. D. Davis, *C.*   21,809
Ms D. Wallis, *LD*   14,295
G. McManus, *Lab.*   11,701
T. Pearson, *Ref.*   1,370
G. Bloom, *UK Ind.*   301
B. Stevens, *NLP*   74
C. majority 7,514
(Boundary change: notional C.)

HALTON
E.64,987   T.68.38%
D. Twigg, *Lab.*   31,497
P. Balmer, *C.*   7,847
Ms J. Jones, *LD*   3,263
R. Atkins, *Ref.*   1,036
D. Proffitt, *Lib.*   600
J. Alley, *Rep. GB*   196
Lab. majority 23,650
(Boundary change: notional Lab.)

HAMMERSMITH AND FULHAM
E.78,637   T.68.70%
I. Coleman, *Lab.*   25,262
†M. Carrington, *C.*   21,420
Ms A. Sugden, *LD*   4,728
Mrs M. Bremner, *Ref.*   1,023
W. Johnson-Smith, *New Lab.*   695
Ms E. Streeter, *Green*   562
G. Roberts, *UK Ind.*   183
A. Phillips, *NLP*   79
A. Elston, *Care*   74
Lab. majority 3,842
(Boundary change: notional C.)

HAMPSHIRE EAST
E.76,604   T.75.88%
†M. Mates, *C.*   27,927
R. Booker, *LD*   16,337
R. Hoyle, *Lab.*   9,945
J. Hayter, *Ref.*   2,757
I. Foster, *Green*   649
S. Coles, *UK Ind.*   513
C. majority 11,590
(Boundary change: notional C.)

HAMPSHIRE NORTH EAST
E.69,111   T.73.95%
†J. Arbuthnot, *C.*   26,017
I. Mann, *LD*   11,619
P. Dare, *Lab.*   8,203
D. Rees, *Ref.*   2,420
K. Jessavala, *Ind.*   2,400
C. Berry, *UK Ind.*   452
C. majority 14,398
(Boundary change: notional C.)

HAMPSHIRE NORTH WEST
E.73,222   T.74.66%
†Rt. Hon. Sir G. Young, Bt., *C.*
                                              24,730
C. Fleming, *LD*   13,179
M. Mumford, *Lab.*   12,900
Mrs P. Callaghan, *Ref.*   1,533
T. Rolt, *UK Ind.*   1,383
W. Baxter, *Green*   486
H. Anscomb, *Bypass*   231
R. Dodd, *Ind.*   225
C. majority 11,551
(Boundary change: notional C.)

HAMPSTEAD AND HIGHGATE
E.64,889   T.67.86%
†Ms G. Jackson, *Lab.*   25,275
Miss E. Gibson, *C.*   11,991
Mrs B. Fox, *LD*   5,481
Ms M. Siddique, *Ref.*   667
J. Leslie, *NLP*   147
R. Carroll, *Dream*   141
Miss P. Prince, *UK Ind.*   123
R. J. Harris, *Hum.*   105
Capt. Rizz, *Rizz Party*   101

Lab. majority 13,284
(Boundary change: notional Lab.)

HARBOROUGH
E.70,424   T.75.27%
†E. Garnier, *C.*   22,170
M. Cox, *LD*   15,646
N. Holden, *Lab.*   13,332
N. Wright, *Ref.*   1,859
C. majority 6,524
(Boundary change: notional C.)

HARLOW
E.64,072   T.74.62%
W. Rammell, *Lab.*   25,861
†J. Hayes, *C.*   15,347
Ms L. Spenceley, *LD*   4,523
M. Wells, *Ref.*   1,422
G. Batten, *UK Ind.*   340
J. Bowles, *BNP*   319
Lab. majority 10,514
(Boundary change: notional C.)

HARROGATE AND KNARESBOROUGH
E.65,155   T.73.14%
P. Willis, *LD*   24,558
†Rt. Hon. N. Lamont, *C.*   18,322
Ms B. Boyce, *Lab.*   4,159
J. Blackburn, *LC*   614
LD majority 6,236
(Boundary change: notional C.)

HARROW EAST
E.79,846   T.71.37%
A. McNulty, *Lab.*   29,927
†H. Dykes, *C.*   20,189
B. Sharma, *LD*   4,697
B. Casey, *Ref.*   1,537
A. Scholefield, *UK Ind.*   464
A. Planton, *NLP*   171
Lab. majority 9,738
(Boundary change: notional C.)

HARROW WEST
E.72,005   T.72.92%
G. Thomas, *Lab.*   21,811
*R. Hughes, *C.*   20,571
Mrs P. Nandhra, *LD*   8,127
H. Crossman, *Ref.*   1,997
Lab. majority 1,240
(Boundary change: notional C.)

HARTLEPOOL
E.67,712   T.65.65%
*P. Mandelson, *Lab.*   26,997
M. Horsley, *C.*   9,489
R. Clark, *LD*   6,248
Miss M. Henderson, *Ref.*   1,718
Lab. majority 17,508
(April 1992, Lab. maj. 8,782)

HARWICH
E.75,775   T.70.62%
I. Henderson, *Lab.*   20,740
†I. Sproat, *C.*   19,524
Mrs A. Elvin, *LD*   7,037
J. Titford, *Ref.*   4,923
R. Knight, *CRP*   1,290
Lab. majority 1,216
(Boundary change: notional C.)

HASTINGS AND RYE
E.70,388   T.69.71%
M. Foster, *Lab.*   16,867

*Mrs J. Lait, *C.* 14,307
M. Palmer, *LD* 13,717
C. McGovern, *Ref.* 2,511
Ms J. Amstad, *Lib.* 1,046
W. Andrews, *UK Ind.* 472
D. Howell, *Loony* 149
Lab. majority 2,560
(April 1992, C. maj. 6,634)

HAVANT
*E.*68,420　*T.*70.63%
†D. Willetts, *C.* 19,204
Ms L. Armstrong, *Lab.* 15,475
M. Kooner, *LD* 10,806
A. Green, *Ref.* 2,395
M. Atwal, *BIPF* 442
C. majority 3,729
(Boundary change: notional C.)

HAYES AND HARLINGTON
*E.*56,829　*T.*72.31%
J. McDonnell, *Lab.* 25,458
A. Retter, *C.* 11,167
A. Little, *LD* 3,049
F. Page, *Ref.* 778
J. Hutchins, *NF* 504
D. Farrow, *ANP* 135
Lab. majority 14,291
(Boundary change: notional C.)

HAZEL GROVE
*E.*63,694　*T.*77.46%
A. Stunell, *LD* 26,883
B. Murphy, *C.* 15,069
J. Lewis, *Lab.* 5,882
J. Stanyer, *Ref.* 1,055
G. Black, *UK Ind.* 268
D. Firkin-Flood, *Ind. Hum.* 183
LD majority 11,814
(April 1992, C. maj. 929)

HEMEL HEMPSTEAD
*E.*71,468　*T.*77.09%
A. McWalter, *Lab. Co-op.* 25,175
†R. Jones, *C.* 21,539
Mrs P. Lindsley, *LD* 6,789
P. Such, *Ref.* 1,327
Ms D. Harding, *NLP* 262
Lab. Co-op. majority 3,636
(Boundary change: notional C.)

HEMSWORTH
*E.*66,964　*T.*67.91%
†J. Trickett, *Lab.* 32,088
N. Hazell, *C.* 8,096
Ms J. Kirby, *LD* 4,033
D. Irvine, *Ref.* 1,260
Lab. majority 23,992
(Boundary change: notional Lab.)

HENDON
*E.*76,195　*T.*65.67%
A. Dismore, *Lab.* 24,683
†Sir J. Gorst, *C.* 18,528
W. Casey, *LD* 5,427
S. Rabbow, *Ref.* 978
B. Wright, *UK Ind.* 267
Ms S. Taylor, *WRP* 153
Lab. majority 6,155
(Boundary change: notional C.)

HENLEY
*E.*66,424　*T.*77.60%
†Rt. Hon. M. Heseltine, *C.* 23,908
T. Horton, *LD* 12,741
D. Enright, *Lab.* 11,700
S. Sainsbury, *Ref.* 2,299
Mrs S. Miles, *Green* 514
N. Barlow, *NLP* 221
T. Hibbert, *Whig Party* 160
C. majority 11,167
(Boundary change: notional C.)

HEREFORD
*E.*69,864　*T.*75.22%
P. Keetch, *LD* 25,198
†Sir C. Shepherd, *C.* 18,550
C. Chappell, *Lab.* 6,596
C. Easton, *Ref.* 2,209
LD majority 6,648
(Boundary change: notional C.)

HERTFORD AND STORTFORD
*E.*71,759　*T.*76.03%
†B. Wells, *C.* 24,027
S. Speller, *Lab.* 17,142
M. Wood, *LD* 9,679
H. Page Croft, *Ref.* 2,105
B. Smalley, *UK Ind.* 1,223
M. Franey, *ProLife* 259
D. Molloy, *Logic* 126
C. majority 6,885
(Boundary change: notional C.)

HERTFORDSHIRE NORTH EAST
*E.*67,161　*T.*77.42%
†O. Heald, *C.* 21,712
I. Gibbons, *Lab.* 18,624
S. Jarvis, *LD* 9,493
J. Grose, *Ref.* 2,166
C. majority 3,088
(Boundary change: notional C.)

HERTFORDSHIRE SOUTH WEST
*E.*71,671　*T.*77.31%
†R. Page, *C.* 25,462
M. Wilson, *Lab.* 15,441
Mrs A. Shaw, *LD* 12,381
T. Millward, *Ref.* 1,853
C. Adamson, *NLP* 274
C. majority 10,021
(Boundary change: notional C.)

HERTSMERE
*E.*68,011　*T.*74.03%
†J. Clappison, *C.* 22,305
Ms E. Kelly, *Lab.* 19,230
Mrs A. Gray, *LD* 6,466
J. Marlow, *Ref.* 1,703
R. Saunders, *UK Ind.* 453
N. Kahn, *NLP* 191
C. majority 3,075
(Boundary change: notional C.)

HEXHAM
*E.*58,914　*T.*77.52%
*P. Atkinson, *C.* 17,701
I. McMinn, *Lab.* 17,479
Dr P. Carr, *LD* 7,959
R. Waddell, *Ref.* 1,362
D. Lott, *UK Ind.* 1,170
C. majority 222
(April 1992, C. maj. 13,438)

HEYWOOD AND MIDDLETON
*E.*73,898　*T.*68.41%
J. Dobbin, *Lab. Co-op.* 29,179
S. Grigg, *C.* 11,637
D. Clayton, *LD* 7,908
Mrs C. West, *Ref.* 1,076
P. Burke, *Lib.* 750
Lab. Co-op. majority 17,542
(Boundary change: notional Lab.
Co-op.)

HIGH PEAK
*E.*72,315　*T.*79.03%
T. Levitt, *Lab.* 29,052
†C. Hendry, *C.* 20,261
Mrs S. Barber, *LD* 6,420
C. Hanson-Orr, *Ref.* 1,420
Lab. majority 8,791
(Boundary change: notional C.)

HITCHIN AND HARPENDEN
*E.*67,219　*T.*77.99%
†Rt. Hon. P. Lilley, *C.* 24,038
Ms R. Sanderson, *Lab.* 17,367
C. White, *LD* 10,515
D. Cooke, *NLP* 290
J. Horton, *Soc.* 217
C. majority 6,671
(Boundary change: notional C.)

HOLBORN AND ST PANCRAS
*E.*63,037　*T.*60.28%
†F. Dobson, *Lab.* 24,707
J. Smith, *C.* 6,804
Ms J. McGuinness, *LD* 4,750
Mrs J. Carr, *Ref.* 790
T. Bedding, *NLP* 191
S. Smith, *JP* 173
Ms B. Conway, *WRP* 171
M. Rosenthal, *Dream* 157
P. Rice-Evans, *EUP* 140
B. Quintavalle, *ProLife* 114
Lab. majority 17,903
(Boundary change: notional Lab.)

HORNCHURCH
*E.*60,775　*T.*72.30%
J. Cryer, *Lab.* 22,066
*R. Squire, *C.* 16,386
R. Martins, *LD* 3,446
R. Khilkoff-Boulding, *Ref.* 1,595
Miss J. Trueman, *Third Way* 259
J. Sowerby, *ProLife* 189
Lab. majority 5,680
(April 1992, C. maj. 9,165)

HORNSEY AND WOOD GREEN
*E.*74,537　*T.*69.08%
*Mrs B. Roche, *Lab.* 31,792
Mrs H. Hart, *C.* 11,293
Ms L. Featherstone, *LD* 5,794
Ms H. Jago, *Green* 1,214
Ms R. Miller, *Ref.* 808
P. Sikorski, *Soc. Lab.* 586
Lab. majority 20,499
(April 1992, Lab. maj. 5,177)

HORSHAM
*E.*75,432　*T.*75.78%
Rt. Hon. F. Maude, *C.* 29,015
Mrs M. Millson, *LD* 14,153
Ms M. Walsh, *Lab.* 10,691
R. Grant, *Ref.* 2,281

H. Miller, *UK Ind.* 819
M. Corbould, *FEP* 206
C. majority 14,862
(Boundary change: notional C.)

HOUGHTON AND WASHINGTON
EAST
E.67,343   T.62.10%
F. Kemp, *Lab.* 31,946
P. Booth, *C.* 5,391
K. Miller, *LD* 3,209
J. Joseph, *Ref.* 1,277
Lab. majority 26,555
(Boundary change: notional Lab.)

HOVE
E.69,016   T.69.72%
I. Caplin, *Lab.* 21,458
R. Guy, *C.* 17,499
T. Pearce, *LD* 4,645
S. Field, *Ref.* 1,931
J. Furness, *Ind. C.* 1,735
P. Mulligan, *Green* 644
J. Vause, *UK Ind.* 209
Lab. majority 3,959
(April 1992, C. maj. 12,268)

HUDDERSFIELD
E.65,824   T.67.69%
*B. Sheerman, *Lab. Co-op.* 25,171
W. Forrow, *C.* 9,323
G. Beever, *LD* 7,642
P. McNulty, *Ref.* 1,480
J. Phillips, *Green* 938
Lab. Co-op. majority 15,848
(April 1992, *Lab. majority* 7,258)

HULL EAST
E.68,733   T.58.90%
*Rt. Hon. J. Prescott, *Lab.* 28,870
A. West, *C.* 5,552
J. Wastling, *LD* 3,965
G. Rogers, *Ref.* 1,788
Ms M. Nolan, *ProLife* 190
D. Whitley, *NLP* 121
Lab. majority 23,318
(April 1992, Lab. maj. 18,719)

HULL NORTH
E.68,106   T.56.96%
*K. McNamara, *Lab.* 25,542
D. Lee, *C.* 5,837
D. Nolan, *LD* 5,667
A. Scott, *Ref.* 1,533
T. Brotheridge, *NLP* 215
Lab. majority 19,705
(April 1992, Lab. maj. 15,384)

HULL WEST AND HESSLE
E.65,840   T.58.25%
A. Johnson, *Lab.* 22,520
R. Tress, *LD* 6,995
C. Moore, *C.* 6,933
R. Bate, *Ref.* 1,596
B. Franklin, *NLP* 310
Lab. majority 15,525
(Boundary change: notional Lab.)

HUNTINGDON
E.76,094   T.74.86%
†Rt. Hon. J. Major, *C.* 31,501
J. Reece, *Lab.* 13,361
M. Owen, *LD* 8,390

D. Bellamy, *Ref.* 3,114
C. Coyne, *UK Ind.* 331
Ms V. Hufford, *Ch. D.* 177
D. Robertson, *Ind.* 89
C. majority 18,140
(Boundary change: notional C.)

HYNDBURN
E.66,806   T.72.26%
†G. Pope, *Lab.* 26,831
P. Britcliffe, *C.* 15,383
L. Jones, *LD* 4,141
P. Congdon, *Ref.* 1,627
J. Brown, *IAC* 290
Lab. majority 11,448
(Boundary change: notional Lab.)

ILFORD NORTH
E.68,218   T.71.60%
Ms L. Perham, *Lab.* 23,135
†V. Bendall, *C.* 19,911
A. Dean, *LD* 5,049
P. Wilson, *BNP* 750
Lab. majority 3,224
(Boundary change: notional C.)

ILFORD SOUTH
E.72,104   T.69.37%
†M. Gapes, *Lab. Co-op.* 29,273
Sir N. Thorne, *C.* 15,073
Ms A. Khan, *LD* 3,152
D. Hodges, *Ref.* 1,073
B. Ramsey, *Soc. Lab.* 868
A. Owens, *BNP* 580
Lab. Co-op. majority 14,200
(Boundary change: notional C.)

IPSWICH
E.66,947   T.72.24%
†J. Cann, *Lab.* 25,484
S. Castle, *C.* 15,045
N. Roberts, *LD* 5,881
T. Agnew, *Ref.* 1,637
W. Vinyard, *UK Ind.* 208
E. Kaplan, *NLP* 107
Lab. majority 10,439
(Boundary change: notional Lab.)

ISLE OF WIGHT
E.101,680   T.71.95%
Dr P. Brand, *LD* 31,274
A. Turner, *C.* 24,868
Ms D. Gardiner, *Lab.* 9,646
T. Bristow, *Ref.* 4,734
M. Turner, *UK Ind.* 1,072
H. Rees, *Ind. Is.* 848
P. Scivier, *Green* 544
C. Daly, *NLP* 87
J. Eveleigh, *Rain. Is.* 86
LD majority 6,406
(April 1992, C. maj. 1,827)

ISLINGTON NORTH
E.57,385   T.62.49%
*J. Corbyn, *Lab.* 24,834
J. Kempton, *LD* 4,879
S. Fawthrop, *C.* 4,631
C. Ashby, *Green* 1,516
Lab. majority 19,955
(April 1992, Lab. maj. 12,784)

ISLINGTON SOUTH AND FINSBURY
E.55,468   T.63.67%
†C. Smith, *Lab.* 22,079
Ms S. Ludford, *LD* 7,516
D. Berens, *C.* 4,587
Miss J. Bryett, *Ref.* 741
A. Laws, *ACA* 171
M. Creese, *NLP* 121
E. Basarik, *Ind.* 101
Lab. majority 14,563
(Boundary change: notional Lab.)

JARROW
E.63,828   T.68.84%
S. Hepburn, *Lab.* 28,497
M. Allatt, *C.* 6,564
T. Stone, *LD* 4,865
A. LeBlond, *Ind. Lab.* 2,538
P. Mailer, *Ref.* 1,034
J. Bissett, *SPGB* 444
Lab. majority 21,933
(Boundary change: notional Lab.)

KEIGHLEY
E.67,231   T.76.57%
Mrs A. Cryer, *Lab.* 26,039
*G. Waller, *C.* 18,907
M. Doyle, *LD* 5,064
C. Carpenter, *Ref.* 1,470
Lab. majority 7,132
(April 1992, C. maj. 3,596)

KENSINGTON AND CHELSEA
E.67,786   T.54.71%
Rt. Hon. A. Clark, *C.* 19,887
R. Atkinson, *Lab.* 10,368
R. Woodthorpe Browne, *LD* 5,668
Ms A. Ellis-Jones, *UK Ind.* 540
E. Bear, *Teddy* 218
G. Oliver, *UKPP* 176
Ms S. Hamza, *NLP* 122
P. Sullivan, *Dream* 65
P. Parliament, *Heart* 44
C. majority 9,519
(Boundary change: notional C.)

KETTERING
E.75,153   T.75.79%
P. Sawford, *Lab.* 24,650
†Rt. Hon. R. Freeman, *C.* 24,461
R. Aron, *LD* 6,098
A. Smith, *Ref.* 1,551
Mrs R. le Carpentier, *NLP* 197
Lab. majority 189
(Boundary change: notional C.)

KINGSTON AND SURBITON
E.73,879   T.75.35%
E. Davey, *LD* 20,411
†R. Tracey, *C.* 20,355
Ms S. Griffin, *Lab.* 12,811
Mrs G. Tchiprout, *Ref.* 1,470
Ms P. Burns, *UK Ind.* 418
C. Port, *Dream* 100
M. Leighton, *NLP* 100
LD majority 56
(Boundary change: notional C.)

KINGSWOOD
E.77,026   T.77.75%
†Dr R. Berry, *Lab.* 32,181
J. Howard, *C.* 17,928
Mrs J. Pinkerton, *LD* 7,672

Ms A. Reather, *Ref.* 1,463
P. Hart, *BNP* 290
A. Harding, *NLP* 238
A. Nicolson, *Scrapit* 115
Lab. majority 14,253
(Boundary change: notional C.)

KNOWSLEY NORTH AND SEFTON EAST
*E.*70,918   *T.*70.09%
†G. Howarth, *Lab.* 34,747
C. Doran, *C.* 8,600
D. Bamber, *LD* 5,499
C. Jones, *Soc. Lab.* 857
Lab. majority 26,147
(Boundary change: notional Lab.)

KNOWSLEY SOUTH
*E.*70,532   *T.*67.47%
†E. O'Hara, *Lab.* 36,695
G. Robertson, *C.* 5,987
C. Mainey, *LD* 3,954
A. Wright, *Ref.* 954
Lab. majority 30,708
(Boundary change: notional Lab.)

LANCASHIRE WEST
*E.*73,175   *T.*74.79%
†C. Pickthall, *Lab.* 33,022
C. Varley, *C.* 15,903
A. Wood, *LD* 3,938
M. Carter, *Ref.* 1,025
J. Collins, *NLP* 449
D. Hill, *Home Rule* 392
Lab. majority 17,119
(Boundary change: notional Lab.)

LANCASTER AND WYRE
*E.*78,168   *T.*75.30%
H. Dawson, *Lab.* 25,173
†K. Mans, *C.* 23,878
J. Humberstone, *LD* 6,802
Mrs V. Ivell, *Ref.* 1,516
J. Barry, *Green* 795
Dr J. Whittaker, *UK Ind.* 698
Lab. majority 1,295
(Boundary change: notional C.)

LEEDS CENTRAL
*E.*67,664   *T.*54.70%
†D. Fatchett, *Lab.* 25,766
E. Wild, *C.* 5,077
D. Freeman, *LD* 4,164
P. Myers, *Ref.* 1,042
D. Rix, *Soc. Lab.* 656
C. Hill, *Soc.* 304
Lab. majority 20,689
(Boundary change: notional Lab.)

LEEDS EAST
*E.*56,963   *T.*62.83%
*G. Mudie, *Lab.* 24,151
J. Emsley, *C.* 6,685
Mrs M. Kirk, *LD* 3,689
L. Parish, *Ref.* 1,267
Lab. majority 17,466
(April 1992, Lab. maj. 12,697)

LEEDS NORTH EAST
*E.*63,185   *T.*72.03%
F. Hamilton, *Lab.* 22,368
*T. Kirkhope, *C.* 15,409
Dr W. Winlow, *LD* 6,318

I. Rose, *Ref.* 946
Ms J. Egan, *Soc. Lab.* 468
Lab. majority 6,959
(April 1992, C. maj. 4,244)

LEEDS NORTH WEST
*E.*69,972   *T.*70.57%
H. Best, *Lab.* 19,694
*Dr K. Hampson, *C.* 15,850
Mrs B. Pearce, *LD* 11,689
S. Emmett, *Ref.* 1,325
R. Lamb, *Soc. Lab.* 335
R. Toone, *ProLife* 251
D. Duffy, *Ronnie* 232
Lab. majority 3,844
(April 1992, C. maj. 7,671)

LEEDS WEST
*E.*63,965   *T.*62.88%
*J. Battle, *Lab.* 26,819
J. Whelan, *C.* 7,048
N. Amor, *LD* 3,622
W. Finley, *Ref.* 1,210
D. Blackburn, *Green* 896
N. Nowosielski, *Lib.* 625
Lab. majority 19,771
(April 1992, Lab. maj. 13,828)

LEICESTER EAST
*E.*64,012   *T.*69.37%
*K. Vaz, *Lab.* 29,083
S. Milton, *C.* 10,661
J. Matabudul, *LD* 3,105
P. Iwaniw, *Ref.* 1,015
S. Sidhu, *Soc. Lab.* 436
N. Slack, *Glow* 102
Lab. majority 18,422
(April 1992, Lab. maj. 11,316)

LEICESTER SOUTH
*E.*71,750   *T.*67.06%
*J. Marshall, *Lab.* 27,914
C. Heaton-Harris, *C.* 11,421
B. Coles, *LD* 6,654
J. Hancock, *Ref.* 1,184
J. Dooher, *Soc. Lab.* 634
K. Sills, *Nat. Dem.* 307
Lab. majority 16,493
(April 1992, Lab. maj. 9,440)

LEICESTER WEST
*E.*64,570   *T.*63.36%
Ms P. Hewitt, *Lab.* 22,580
R. Thomas, *C.* 9,716
M. Jones, *LD* 5,795
W. Shooter, *Ref.* 970
G. Forse, *Green* 586
D. Roberts, *Soc. Lab.* 452
Ms J. Nicholls, *Soc.* 327
A. Belshaw, *BNP* 302
C. Potter, *Nat. Dem.* 186
Lab. majority 12,864
(April 1992, Lab. maj. 3,978)

LEICESTERSHIRE NORTH WEST
*E.*65,069   *T.*79.95%
D. Taylor, *Lab.* 29,332
R. Goodwill, *C.* 16,113
S. Heptinstall, *LD* 4,492
M. Abney-Hastings, *Ref.* 2,088
Lab. majority 13,219
(Boundary change: notional C.)

LEIGH
*E.*69,908   *T.*65.69%
†L. Cunliffe, *Lab.* 31,652
E. Young, *C.* 7,156
P. Hough, *LD* 5,163
R. Constable, *Ref.* 1,949
Lab. majority 24,496
(Boundary change: notional Lab.)

LEOMINSTER
*E.*65,993   *T.*76.60%
†P. Temple-Morris, *C.* 22,888
T. James, *LD* 14,053
R. Westwood, *Lab.* 8,831
A. Parkin, *Ref.* 2,815
Ms F. Norman, *Green* 1,086
R. Chamings, *UK Ind.* 588
J. Haycock, *BNP* 292
C. majority 8,835
(Boundary change: notional C.)

LEWES
*E.*64,340   *T.*76.42%
N. Baker, *LD* 21,250
†T. Rathbone, *C.* 19,950
Dr M. Patton, *Lab.* 5,232
Mrs L. Butler, *Ref.* 2,481
J. Harvey, *UK Ind.* 256
LD majority 1,300
(Boundary change: notional C.)

LEWISHAM DEPTFORD
*E.*58,141   *T.*57.87%
†Mrs J. Ruddock, *Lab.* 23,827
Mrs I. Kimm, *C.* 4,949
K. Appiah, *LD* 3,004
J. Mulrenan, *Soc. Lab.* 996
Ms S. Shepherd, *Ref.* 868
Lab. majority 18,878
(Boundary change: notional Lab.)

LEWISHAM EAST
*E.*56,333   *T.*66.41%
†Ms B. Prentice, *Lab.* 21,821
P. Hollobone, *C.* 9,694
D. Buxton, *LD* 4,178
S. Drury, *Ref.* 910
R. Croucher, *NF* 431
P. White, *Lib.* 277
Capt. Rizz, *Dream* 97
Lab. majority 12,127
(Boundary change: notional Lab.)

LEWISHAM WEST
*E.*58,659   *T.*64.00%
*J. Dowd, *Lab.* 23,273
Mrs C. Whelan, *C.* 8,936
Miss K. McGrath, *LD* 3,672
A. Leese, *Ref.* 1,098
N. Long, *Soc. Lab.* 398
Ms E. Oram, *Lib.* 167
Lab. majority 14,337
(April 1992, Lab. maj. 1,809)

LEYTON AND WANSTEAD
*E.*62,176   *T.*63.24%
†H. Cohen, *Lab.* 23,922
R. Vaudry, *C.* 8,736
C. Anglin, *LD* 5,920
S. Duffy, *ProLife* 488
A. Mian, *Ind.* 256
Lab. majority 15,186
(Boundary change: notional Lab.)

LICHFIELD
E.62,720   T.77.48%
†M. Fabricant, *C.*   20,853
Ms S. Woodward, *Lab.*   20,615
Dr P. Bennion, *LD*   5,473
G. Seward, *Ref.*   1,652
C. majority 238
(Boundary change: notional C.)

LINCOLN
E.65,485   T.71.08%
Ms G. Merron, *Lab.*   25,563
A. Brown, *C.*   14,433
Ms L. Gabriel, *LD*   5,048
J. Ivory, *Ref.*   1,329
A. Myers, *NLP*   175
Lab. majority 11,130
(Boundary change: notional Lab.)

LIVERPOOL GARSTON
E.66,755   T.65.14%
Ms M. Eagle, *Lab.*   26,667
Ms F. Clucas, *LD*   8,250
N. Gordon-Johnson, *C.*   6,819
F. Dunne, *Ref.*   833
G. Copeland, *Lib.*   666
J. Parsons, *NLP*   127
S. Nolan, *SEP*   120
Lab. majority 18,417
(Boundary change: notional Lab.)

LIVERPOOL RIVERSIDE
E.73,429   T.51.93%
Ms L. Ellman, *Lab. Co-op.*   26,858
Ms B. Fraenkel, *LD*   5,059
D. Sparrow, *C.*   3,635
Ms C. Wilson, *Soc.*   776
D. Green, *Lib.*   594
G. Skelly, *Ref.*   586
Ms H. Neilson, *ProLife*   277
D. Braid, *MRAC*   179
G. Gay, *NLP*   171
Lab. Co-op. majority 21,799
(Boundary change: notional Lab.
Co-op.)

LIVERPOOL WALTON
E.67,527   T.59.54%
*P. Kilfoyle, *Lab.*   31,516
R. Roberts, *LD*   4,478
M. Kotecha, *C.*   2,551
C. Grundy, *Ref.*   620
Ms L. Mahmood, *Soc.*   444
Ms H. Williams, *Lib.*   352
Ms V. Mearns, *ProLife*   246
Lab. majority 27,038
(April 1992, Lab. maj. 28,299)

LIVERPOOL WAVERTREE
E.73,063   T.62.85%
†Ms J. Kennedy, *Lab.*   29,592
R. Kemp, *LD*   9,891
C. Malthouse, *C.*   4,944
P. Worthington, *Ref.*   576
K. McCullough, *Lib.*   391
Ms R. Kingsley, *ProLife*   346
Ms C. Corkhill, *WRP*   178
Lab. majority 19,701
(Boundary change: notional Lab.)

LIVERPOOL WEST DERBY
E.68,682   T.61.38%
†R. Wareing, *Lab.*   30,002

S. Radford, *Lib.*   4,037
Ms A. Hines, *LD*   3,805
N. Morgan, *C.*   3,656
P. Forrest, *Ref.*   657
Lab. majority 25,965
(Boundary change: notional Lab.)

LOUGHBOROUGH
E.68,945   T.75.95%
A. Reed, *Lab.*   25,448
K. Andrew, *C.*   19,736
Ms D. Brass, *LD*   6,190
R. Gupta, *Ref.*   991
Lab. majority 5,712
(Boundary change: notional C.)

LOUTH AND HORNCASTLE
E.68,824   T.72.58%
†Sir P. Tapsell, *C.*   21,699
J. Hough, *Lab.*   14,799
Mrs F. Martin, *LD*   12,207
Ms R. Robinson, *Green*   1,248
C. majority 6,900
(Boundary change: notional C.)

LUDLOW
E.61,267   T.75.55%
†C. Gill, *C.*   19,633
I. Huffer, *LD*   13,724
Ms N. O'Kane, *Lab.*   11,745
T. Andrewes, *Green*   798
E. Freeman-Keel, *UK Ind.*   385
C. majority 5,909
(Boundary change: notional C.)

LUTON NORTH
E.64,618   T.73.25%
K. Hopkins, *Lab.*   25,860
D. Senior, *C.*   16,234
Mrs K. Newbound, *LD*   4,299
C. Brown, *UK Ind.*   689
A. Custance, *NLP*   250
Lab. majority 9,626
(Boundary change: notional C.)

LUTON SOUTH
E.68,395   T.70.45%
Ms M. Moran, *Lab.*   26,428
†Sir G. Bright, *C.*   15,109
K. Fitchett, *LD*   4,610
C. Jacobs, *Ref.*   1,205
C. Lawman, *UK Ind.*   390
M. Scheimann, *Green*   356
Ms C. Perrin, *NLP*   86
Lab. majority 11,319
(Boundary change: notional C.)

MACCLESFIELD
E.72,049   T.75.22%
†N. Winterton, *C.*   26,888
Ms J. Jackson, *Lab.*   18,234
M. Flynn, *LD*   9,075
C. majority 8,654
(Boundary change: notional C.)

MAIDENHEAD
E.67,302   T.75.61%
Mrs T. May, *C.*   25,344
A. Ketteringham, *LD*   13,363
Ms D. Robson, *Lab.*   9,205
C. Taverner, *Ref.*   1,638
D. Munkley, *Lib.*   896
N. Spiers, *UK Ind.*   277

K. Ardley, *Glow*   166
C. majority 11,981
(Boundary change: notional C.)

MAIDSTONE AND THE WEALD
E.72,466   T.73.98%
†Rt. Hon. Miss A. Widdecombe,
  C.   23,657
J. Morgan, *Lab.*   14,054
Mrs J. Nelson, *LD*   11,986
Ms S. Hopkins, *Ref.*   1,998
Ms M. Cleator, *Soc. Lab.*   979
Ms P. Kemp, *Green*   480
Mrs R. Owen, *UK Ind.*   339
J. Oldbury, *NLP*   115
C. majority 9,603
(Boundary change: notional C.)

MAKERFIELD
E.67,358   T.66.83%
†I. McCartney, *Lab.*   33,119
M. Winstanley, *C.*   6,942
B. Hubbard, *LD*   3,743
A. Seed, *Ref.*   1,210
Lab. majority 26,177
(Boundary change: notional Lab.)

MALDON AND CHELMSFORD EAST
E.66,184   T.76.13%
†J. Whittingdale, *C.*   24,524
K. Freeman, *Lab.*   14,485
G. Pooley, *LD*   9,758
L. Overy-Owen, *UK Ind.*   935
Ms E. Burgess, *Green*   685
C. majority 10,039
(Boundary change: notional C.)

MANCHESTER BLACKLEY
E.62,227   T.57.46%
G. Stringer, *Lab.*   25,042
S. Barclay, *C.*   5,454
S. Wheale, *LD*   3,937
P. Stanyer, *Ref.*   1,323
Lab. majority 19,588
(Boundary change: notional Lab.)

MANCHESTER CENTRAL
E.63,815   T.52.55%
†A. Lloyd, *Lab.*   23,803
Ms A. Firth, *LD*   4,121
S. McIlwaine, *C.*   3,964
F. Rafferty, *Soc. Lab.*   810
J. Maxwell, *Ref.*   742
T. Rigby, *Comm L.*   97
Lab. majority 19,682
(Boundary change: notional Lab.)

MANCHESTER GORTON
E.64,349   T.56.43%
†Rt. Hon. G. Kaufman, *Lab.*   23,704
Dr J. Pearcey, *LD*   6,362
G. Senior, *C.*   4,249
K. Hartley, *Ref.*   812
Dr S. Fitz-Gibbon, *Green*   683
T. Wongsam, *Soc. Lab.*   501
Lab. majority 17,342
(Boundary change: notional Lab.)

MANCHESTER WITHINGTON
E.66,116   T.66.59%
†K. Bradley, *Lab.*   27,103
J. Smith, *C.*   8,522
Dr Y. Zalzala, *LD*   6,000

M. Sheppard, *Ref.*   1,079
S. Caldwell, *ProLife*   614
Ms J. White, *Soc.*   376
S. Kingston, *Dream*   181
M. Gaskell, *NLP*   152
Lab. majority 18,581
(Boundary change: notional Lab.)

MANSFIELD
E.67,057   T.70.72%
*A. Meale, *Lab.*   30,556
T. Frost, *C.*   10,038
P. Smith, *LD*   5,244
W. Bogusz, *Ref.*   1,588
Lab. majority 20,518
(April 1992, Lab. maj. 11,724)

MEDWAY
E.61,736   T.72.47%
R. Marshall-Andrews, *Lab.*   21,858
*Dame P. Fenner, *C.*   16,504
R. Roberts, *LD*   4,555
J. Main, *Ref.*   1,420
Mrs S. Radlett, *UK Ind.*   405
Lab. majority 5,354
(April 1992, C. maj. 8,786)

MERIDEN
E.76,287   T.71.73%
Mrs C. Spelman, *C.*   22,997
B. Seymour-Smith, *Lab.*   22,415
A. Dupont, *LD*   7,098
P. Gilbert, *Ref.*   2,208
C. majority 582
(April 1992, C. maj. 14,699)

MIDDLESBROUGH
E.70,931   T.64.99%
†S. Bell, *Lab.*   32,925
L. Benham, *C.*   7,907
Miss A. Charlesworth, *LD*   3,934
R. Edwards, *Ref.*   1,331
Lab. majority 25,018
(Boundary change: notional Lab.)

MIDDLESBROUGH SOUTH AND
CLEVELAND EAST
E.70,481   T.76.03%
Dr A. Kumar, *Lab.*   29,319
†M. Bates, *C.*   18,712
H. Garrett, *LD*   4,004
R. Batchelor, *Ref.*   1,552
Lab. majority 10,607
(Boundary change: notional C.)

MILTON KEYNES NORTH EAST
E.70,395   T.72.78%
B. White, *Lab.*   20,201
†P. Butler, *C.*   19,961
G. Mabbutt, *LD*   8,907
M. Phillips, *Ref.*   1,492
A. Francis, *Green*   576
M. Simson, *NLP*   99
Lab. majority 240
(Boundary change: notional C.)

MILTON KEYNES SOUTH WEST
E.71,070   T.71.42%
Mrs P. Starkey, *Lab.*   27,298
*B. Legg, *C.*   17,006
P. Jones, *LD*   6,065
H. Kelly, *NLP*   389

Lab. majority 10,292
(April 1992, C. maj. 4,687)

MITCHAM AND MORDEN
E.65,385   T.73.33%
Ms S. McDonagh, *Lab.*   27,984
*Rt. Hon. Dame A. Rumbold, *C.*
  14,243
N. Harris, *LD*   3,632
P. Isaacs, *Ref.*   810
Ms L. Miller, *BNP*   521
T. Walsh, *Green*   415
K. Vasan, *Ind.*   144
J. Barrett, *UK Ind.*   117
N. Dixon, *ACC*   80
Lab. majority 13,741
(April 1992, C. maj. 1,734)

MOLE VALLEY
E.69,140   T.78.86%
†Sir P. Beresford, *C.*   26,178
S. Cooksey, *LD*   15,957
C. Payne, *Lab.*   8,057
N. Taber, *Ref.*   2,424
R. Burley, *Ind. CRP*   1,276
Capt. I. Cameron, *UK Ind.*   435
Ms J. Thomas, *NLP*   197
C. majority 10,221
(Boundary change: notional C.)

MORECAMBE AND LUNESDALE
E.68,013   T.72.41%
Ms G. Smith, *Lab.*   24,061
†Sir M. Lennox-Boyd, *C.*   18,096
Mrs J. Greenwell, *LD*   5,614
I. Ogilvie, *Ref.*   1,313
D. Walne, *NLP*   165
Lab. majority 5,965
(Boundary change: notional C.)

MORLEY AND ROTHWELL
E.68,385   T.67.12%
†J. Gunnell, *Lab.*   26,836
A. Barraclough, *C.*   12,086
M. Galdas, *LD*   5,087
D. Mitchell-Innes, *Ref.*   1,359
R. Wood, *BNP*   381
Ms P. Sammon, *ProLife*   148
Lab. majority 14,750
(Boundary change: notional Lab.)

NEW FOREST EAST
E.65,717   T.74.64%
Dr J. Lewis, *C.*   21,053
G. Dawson, *LD*   15,838
A. Goodfellow, *Lab.*   12,161
C. majority 5,215
(Boundary change: notional C.)

NEW FOREST WEST
E.66,522   T.74.79%
D. Swayne, *C.*   25,149
R. Hale, *LD*   13,817
D. Griffiths, *Lab.*   7,092
Mrs M. Elliott, *Ref.*   2,150
M. Holmes, *UK Ind.*   1,542
C. majority 11,332
(Boundary change: notional C.)

NEWARK
E.69,763   T.74.50%
Ms F. Jones, *Lab.*   23,496
*R. Alexander, *C.*   20,480

P. Harris, *LD*   5,960
G. Creedy, *Ref.*   2,035
Lab. majority 3,016
(April 1992, C. maj. 8,229)

NEWBURY
E.73,680   T.76.65%
†D. Rendel, *LD*   29,887
R. Benyon, *C.*   21,370
P. Hannon, *Lab.*   3,107
E. Snook, *Ref.*   992
Ms R. Stark, *Green*   644
R. Tubb, *UK Ind.*   302
Ms K. Howse, *Soc. Lab.*   174
LD majority 8,517
(Boundary change: notional C.)

NEWCASTLE-UNDER-LYME
E.66,686   T.73.67%
*Mrs L. Golding, *Lab.*   27,743
M. Hayes, *C.*   10,537
Dr R. Studd, *LD*   6,858
Ms K. Suttle, *Ref.*   1,510
S. Mountford, *Lib.*   1,399
Ms B. Bell, *Soc. Lab.*   1,082
Lab. majority 17,206
(April 1992, Lab. maj. 9,839)

NEWCASTLE UPON TYNE CENTRAL
E.69,781   T.66.05%
†J. Cousins, *Lab.*   27,272
B. Newmark, *C.*   10,792
Ms R. Berry, *LD*   6,911
C. Coxon, *Ref.*   1,113
Lab. majority 16,480
(Boundary change: notional Lab.)

NEWCASTLE UPON TYNE EAST AND
WALLSEND
E.63,272   T.65.73%
†N. Brown, *Lab.*   29,607
J. Middleton, *C.*   5,796
G. Morgan, *LD*   4,415
P. Cossins, *Ref.*   966
Ms B. Carpenter, *Soc. Lab.*   642
M. Levy, *Comm. P.*   163
Lab. majority 23,811
(Boundary change: notional Lab.)

NEWCASTLE UPON TYNE NORTH
E.65,357   T.69.20%
*D. Henderson, *Lab.*   28,125
G. White, *C.*   8,793
P. Allen, *LD*   6,578
Mrs D. Chipchase, *Ref.*   1,733
Lab. majority 19,332
(April 1992, Lab. maj. 8,946)

NORFOLK MID
E.75,311   T.76.29%
K. Simpson, *C.*   22,739
D. Zeichner, *Lab.*   21,403
Mrs S. Frary, *LD*   8,617
N. Holder, *Ref.*   3,229
A. Park, *Green*   1,254
B. Parker, *NLP*   215
C. majority 1,336
(Boundary change: notional C.)

NORFOLK NORTH
E.77,113   T.76.27%
D. Prior, *C.*   21,456
N. Lamb, *LD*   20,163

M. Cullingham, *Lab.* 14,736
J. Allen, *Ref.* 2,458
C. majority 1,293
(April 1992, C. maj. 12,545)

NORFOLK NORTH WEST
*E.*77,083 *T.*74.72%
Dr G. Turner, *Lab.* 25,250
*H. Bellingham, *C.* 23,911
Ms E. Knowles, *LD* 5,513
R. Percival, *Ref.* 2,923
Lab. majority 1,339
(April 1992, C. maj. 11,564)

NORFOLK SOUTH
*E.*79,239 *T.*78.37%
†Rt. Hon. J. MacGregor, *C.* 24,935
Mrs B. Hacker, *LD* 17,557
Ms J. Ross, *Lab.* 16,188
Mrs P. Bateson, *Ref.* 2,533
Mrs S. Ross-Wagenknecht, *Green* 484
A. Boddy, *UK Ind.* 400
C. majority 7,378
(Boundary change: notional C.)

NORFOLK SOUTH WEST
*E.*80,236 *T.*73.28%
†Rt. Hon. Mrs G. Shephard, *C.* 24,694
A. Heffernan, *Lab.* 22,230
D. Buckton, *LD* 8,178
R. Hoare, *Ref.* 3,694
C. majority 2,464
(Boundary change: notional C.)

NORMANTON
*E.*62,980 *T.*68.28%
†W. O'Brien, *Lab.* 26,046
Miss F. Bulmer, *C.* 10,153
D. Ridgway, *LD* 5,347
K. Shuttleworth, *Ref.* 1,458
Lab. majority 15,893
(Boundary change: notional Lab.)

NORTHAMPTON NORTH
*E.*73,664 *T.*70.18%
Ms S. Keeble, *Lab.* 27,247
†A. Marlow, *C.* 17,247
Ms L. Dunbar, *LD* 6,579
D. Torbica, *UK Ind.* 464
B. Spivack, *NLP* 161
Lab. majority 10,000
(Boundary change: notional C.)

NORTHAMPTON SOUTH
*E.*79,384 *T.*71.94%
A. Clarke, *Lab.* 24,214
†Rt. Hon. M. Morris, *C.* 23,470
A. Worgan, *LD* 6,316
C. Petrie, *Ref.* 1,405
D. Clark, *UK Ind.* 1,159
G. Woollcombe, *NLP* 541
Lab. majority 744
(Boundary change: notional C.)

NORTHAVON
*E.*78,943 *T.*79.21%
Prof. S. Webb, *LD* 26,500
†Rt. Hon. Sir J. Cope, *C.* 24,363
R. Stone, *Lab.* 9,767
J. Parfitt, *Ref.* 1,900
LD majority 2,137
(Boundary change: notional C.)

NORWICH NORTH
*E.*72,521 *T.*75.92%
Dr I. Gibson, *Lab.* 27,346
Dr R. Kinghorn, *C.* 17,876
P. Young, *LD* 6,951
A. Bailey-Smith, *Ref.* 1,777
H. Marks, *LCP* 512
J. Hood, *Soc. Lab.* 495
Mrs D. Mills, *NLP* 100
Lab. majority 9,470
(Boundary change: notional C.)

NORWICH SOUTH
*E.*70,009 *T.*72.56%
C. Clarke, *Lab.* 26,267
B. Khanbhai, *C.* 12,028
A. Aalders-Dunthorne, *LD* 9,457
Dr D. Holdsworth, *Ref.* 1,464
H. Marks, *LCP* 765
A. Holmes, *Green* 736
B. Parsons, *NLP* 84
Lab. majority 14,239
(Boundary change: notional Lab.)

NOTTINGHAM EAST
*E.*65,581 *T.*60.60%
*J. Heppell, *Lab.* 24,755
A. Raca, *C.* 9,336
K. Mulloy, *LD* 4,008
B. Brown, *Ref.* 1,645
Lab. majority 15,419
(April 1992, Lab. maj. 7,680)

NOTTINGHAM NORTH
*E.*65,698 *T.*63.02%
*G. Allen, *Lab.* 27,203
Ms G. Shaw, *C.* 8,402
Ms R. Oliver, *LD* 3,301
J. Neal, *Ref.* 1,858
A. Belfield, *Soc.* 637
Lab. majority 18,801
(April 1992, Lab. maj. 10,743)

NOTTINGHAM SOUTH
*E.*72,418 *T.*67.00%
*A. Simpson, *Lab.* 26,825
B. Kirsch, *C.* 13,461
G. Long, *LD* 6,265
K. Thompson, *Ref.* 1,523
Ms S. Edwards, *Nat. Dem.* 446
Lab. majority 13,364
(April 1992, Lab. maj. 3,181)

NUNEATON
*E.*72,032 *T.*74.29%
*W. Olner, *Lab.* 30,080
R. Blunt, *C.* 16,540
R. Cockings, *LD* 4,732
R. English, *Ref.* 1,533
D. Bray, *Loc. Ind.* 390
P. Everitt, *UK Ind.* 238
Lab. majority 13,540
(April 1992, Lab. maj. 1,631)

OLD BEXLEY AND SIDCUP
*E.*68,044 *T.*75.53%
†Rt. Hon. Sir E. Heath, *C.* 21,608
R. Justham, *Lab.* 18,039
I. King, *LD* 8,284
B. Reading, *Ref.* 2,457
C. Bullen, *UK Ind.* 489

Ms V. Tyndall, *BNP* 415
R. Stephens, *NLP* 99
C. majority 3,569
(Boundary change: notional C.)

OLDHAM EAST AND SADDLEWORTH
*E.*73,189 *T.*73.92%
P. Woolas, *Lab.* 22,546
†C. Davies, *LD* 19,157
J. Hudson, *C.* 10,666
D. Findlay, *Ref.* 1,116
J. Smith, *Soc. Lab.* 470
I. Dalling, *NLP* 146
Lab. majority 3,389
(Boundary change: notional C.)

OLDHAM WEST AND ROYTON
*E.*69,203 *T.*66.09%
†M. Meacher, *Lab.* 26,894
J. Lord, *C.* 10,693
H. Cohen, *LD* 5,434
G. Choudhury, *Soc. Lab.* 1,311
P. Etherden, *Ref.* 1,157
Mrs S. Dalling, *NLP* 249
Lab. majority 16,201
(Boundary change: notional Lab.)

ORPINGTON
*E.*78,749 *T.*76.40%
†J. Horam, *C.* 24,417
C. Maines, *LD* 21,465
Ms S. Polydorou, *Lab.* 10,753
D. Clark, *Ref.* 2,316
J. Carver, *UK Ind.* 526
R. Almond, *Lib.* 494
N. Wilton, *ProLife* 191
C. majority 2,952
(Boundary change: notional C.)

OXFORD EAST
*E.*69,339 *T.*69.05%
†A. Smith, *Lab.* 27,205
J. Djanogly, *C.* 10,540
G. Kershaw, *LD* 7,038
M. Young, *Ref.* 1,391
C. Simmons, *Green* 975
W. Harper-Jones, *Embryo* 318
Dr P. Gardner, *UK Ind.* 234
J. Thompson, *NLP* 108
P. Mylvaganam, *Anti-maj.* 68
Lab. majority 16,665
(Boundary change: notional Lab.)

OXFORD WEST AND ABINGDON
*E.*79,329 *T.*77.14%
Dr E. Harris, *LD* 26,268
L. Harris, *C.* 19,983
Ms S. Brown, *Lab.* 12,361
Mrs G. Eustace, *Ref.* 1,258
Dr M. Woodin, *Green* 691
R. Buckton, *UK Ind.* 258
Mrs L. Hodge, *ProLife* 238
Ms A.-M. Wilson, *NLP* 91
J. Rose, *LGR* 48
LD majority 6,285
(Boundary change: notional C.)

PENDLE
*E.*63,049 *T.*74.60%
*G. Prentice, *Lab.* 25,059
J. Midgeley, *C.* 14,235
A. Greaves, *LD* 5,460

D. Hockney, *Ref.* 2,281
Lab. majority 10,824
(April 1992, Lab. maj. 2,113)

PENRITH AND THE BORDER
*E.*66,496   *T.*73.63%
†Rt. Hon. D. Maclean, *C.* 23,300
G. Walker, *LD* 13,067
Mrs M. Meling, *Lab.* 10,576
C. Pope, *Ref.* 2,018
C. majority 10,233
(Boundary change: notional C.)

PETERBOROUGH
*E.*65,926   *T.*73.46%
Ms H. Brinton, *Lab.* 24,365
Mrs J. Foster, *C.* 17,042
D. Howarth, *LD* 5,170
P. Slater, *Ref.* 924
C. Brettell, *NLP* 334
J. Linskey, *UK Ind.* 317
S. Goldspink, *ProLife* 275
Lab. majority 7,323
(Boundary change: notional C.)

PLYMOUTH DEVONPORT
*E.*74,483   *T.*69.76%
†D. Jamieson, *Lab.* 31,629
A. Johnson, *C.* 12,562
R. Copus, *LD* 5,570
C. Norsworthy, *Ref.* 1,486
Mrs C. Farrand, *UK Ind.* 478
S. Ebbs, *Nat. Dem.* 238
Lab. majority 19,067
(Boundary change: notional Lab.)

PLYMOUTH SUTTON
*E.*70,666   *T.*67.43%
Mrs L. Gilroy, *Lab. Co-op.* 23,881
A. Crisp, *C.* 14,441
S. Melia, *LD* 6,613
T. Hanbury, *Ref.* 1,654
R. Bullock, *UK Ind.* 499
K. Kelway, *Plymouth* 396
F. Lyons, *NLP* 168
Lab. Co-op. majority 9,440
(Boundary change: notional C.)

PONTEFRACT AND CASTLEFORD
*E.*62,350   *T.*66.39%
Ms Y. Cooper, *Lab.* 31,339
A. Flook, *C.* 5,614
W. Paxton, *LD* 3,042
R. Wood, *Ref.* 1,401
Lab. majority 25,725
(April 1992, Lab. maj. 23,495)

POOLE
*E.*66,078   *T.*70.84%
R. Syms, *C.* 19,726
A. Tetlow, *LD* 14,428
H. White, *Lab.* 10,100
J. Riddington, *Ref.* 1,932
P. Tyler, *UK Ind.* 487
Mrs J. Rosta, *NLP* 137
C. majority 5,298
(Boundary change: notional C.)

POPLAR AND CANNING TOWN
*E.*67,172   *T.*58.46%
J. Fitzpatrick, *Lab.* 24,807
B. Steinberg, *C.* 5,892
Ms J. Ludlow, *LD* 4,072

J. Tyndall, *BNP* 2,849
I. Hare, *Ref.* 1,091
Ms J. Joseph, *Soc. Lab.* 557
Lab. majority 18,915
(Boundary change: notional Lab.)

PORTSMOUTH NORTH
*E.*64,539   *T.*70.14%
S. Rapson, *Lab.* 21,339
†P. Griffiths, *C.* 17,016
S. Sollitt, *LD* 4,788
S. Evelegh, *Ref.* 1,757
P. Coe, *UK Ind.* 298
C. Bex, *Wessex* 72
Lab. majority 4,323
(Boundary change: notional C.)

PORTSMOUTH SOUTH
*E.*80,514   *T.*64.21%
M. Hancock, *LD* 20,421
*D. Martin, *C.* 16,094
A. Burnett, *Lab.* 13,086
C. Trim, *Ref.* 1,629
J. Thompson, *Lib.* 184
Mrs J. Evans, *UK Ind.* 141
W. Treend, *NLP* 140
LD majority 4,327
(April 1992, C. maj. 242)

PRESTON
*E.*72,933   *T.*65.92%
†Mrs A. Wise, *Lab.* 29,220
P. Gray, *C.* 10,540
W. Chadwick, *LD* 7,045
J. C. Porter, *Ref.* 924
J. Ashforth, *NLP* 345
Lab. majority 18,680
(Boundary change: notional Lab.)

PUDSEY
*E.*70,922   *T.*74.35%
P. Truswell, *Lab.* 25,370
P. Bone, *C.* 19,163
Dr J. Brown, *LD* 7,375
D. Crabtree, *Ref.* 823
Lab. majority 6,207
(April 1992, C. maj. 8,972)

PUTNEY
*E.*60,176   *T.*73.11%
A. Colman, *Lab.* 20,084
*Rt. Hon. D. Mellor, *C.* 17,108
R. Pyne, *LD* 4,739
Sir J. Goldsmith, *Ref.* 1,518
W. Jamieson, *UK Ind.* 233
L. Beige, *Stan* 101
M. Yardley, *Spts All.* 90
J. Small, *NLP* 66
Ms A. Poole, *Beaut.* 49
D. Vanbraam, *Ren. Dem.* 7
Lab. majority 2,976
(April 1992, C. maj. 7,526)

RAYLEIGH
*E.*68,737   *T.*74.65%
†Dr M. Clark, *C.* 25,516
R. Ellis, *Lab.* 14,832
S. Cumberland, *LD* 10,137
A. Farmer, *Lib.* 829
C. majority 10,684
(Boundary change: notional C.)

READING EAST
*E.*71,586   *T.*70.15%
Ms J. Griffiths, *Lab.* 21,461
†J. Watts, *C.* 17,666
R. Samuel, *LD* 9,307
D. Harmer, *Ref.* 1,042
J. Buckley, *NLP* 254
Miss A. Thornton, *UK Ind.* 252
Ms B. Packer, *BNP* 238
Lab. majority 3,795
(Boundary change: notional C.)

READING WEST
*E.*69,073   *T.*70.05%
M. Salter, *Lab.* 21,841
N. Bennett, *C.* 18,844
Mrs D. Tomlin, *LD* 6,153
S. Brown, *Ref.* 976
I. Dell, *BNP* 320
D. Black, *UK Ind.* 255
Lab. majority 2,997
(Boundary change: notional C.)

REDCAR
*E.*68,965   *T.*70.99%
†Dr M. Mowlam, *Lab.* 32,972
A. Isaacs, *C.* 11,308
Ms J. Benbow, *LD* 4,679
Lab. majority 21,664
(Boundary change: notional Lab.)

REDDITCH
*E.*60,841   *T.*73.55%
Ms J. Smith, *Lab.* 22,280
Miss A. McIntyre, *C.* 16,155
M. Hall, *LD* 4,935
R. Cox, *Ref.* 1,151
P. Davis, *NLP* 227
Lab. majority 6,125
(Boundary change: notional C.)

REGENT'S PARK AND KENSINGTON
NORTH
*E.*73,752   *T.*64.19%
Ms K. Buck, *Lab.* 28,367
P. McGuinness, *C.* 13,710
Miss E. Gasson, *LD* 4,041
Ms S. Dangoor, *Ref.* 867
J. Hinde, *NLP* 192
Ms D. Sadowitz, *Dream* 167
Lab. majority 14,657
(Boundary change: notional Lab.)

REIGATE
*E.*64,750   *T.*74.40%
C. Blunt, *C.* 21,123
A. Howard, *Lab.* 13,382
P. Samuel, *LD* 9,615
†Sir G. Gardiner, *Ref.* 3,352
R. Higgs, *Ind.* 412
S. Smith, *UK Ind.* 290
C. majority 7,741
(Boundary change: notional C.)

RIBBLE SOUTH
*E.*71,670   *T.*77.06%
D. Borrow, *Lab.* 25,856
†Rt. Hon. R. Atkins, *C.* 20,772
T. Farron, *LD* 5,879
G. Adams, *Ref.* 1,475
N. Ashton, *Lib.* 1,127
Ms B. Leadbetter, *NLP* 122

Lab. majority 5,084
(Boundary change: notional C.)

RIBBLE VALLEY
*E.*72,664   *T.*78.75%
†N. Evans, *C.*   26,702
M. Carr, *LD*   20,062
M. Johnstone, *Lab.*   9,013
J. Parkinson, *Ref.*   1,297
Miss N. Holmes, *NLP*   147
C. majority 6,640
(Boundary change: notional C.)

RICHMOND (Yorks)
*E.*65,058   *T.*73.38%
†Rt. Hon. W. Hague, *C.*   23,326
S. Merritt, *Lab.*   13,275
Mrs J. Harvey, *LD*   8,773
A. Bentley, *Ref.*   2,367
C. majority 10,051
(Boundary change: notional C.)

RICHMOND PARK
*E.*71,572   *T.*79.43%
Dr J. Tonge, *LD*   25,393
†Rt. Hon. J. Hanley, *C.*   22,442
Ms S. Jenkins, *Lab.*   7,172
J. Pugh, *Ref.*   1,467
D. Beaupre, *Loony*   204
B. D'Arcy, *NLP*   102
P. Davies, *Dream*   73
LD majority 2,951
(Boundary change: notional C.)

ROCHDALE
*E.*68,529   *T.*70.16%
Ms L. Fitzsimons, *Lab.*   23,758
†Miss E. Lynne, *LD*   19,213
M. Turnberg, *C.*   4,237
G. Bergin, *BNP*   653
S. Mohammed, *IZB*   221
Lab. majority 4,545
(Boundary change: notional LD)

ROCHFORD AND SOUTHEND EAST
*E.*72,848   *T.*63.97%
†Sir E. Taylor, *C.*   22,683
N. Smith, *Lab.*   18,458
Ms P. Smith, *LD*   4,387
B. Lynch, *Lib.*   1,070
C. majority 4,225
(Boundary change: notional C.)

ROMFORD
*E.*59,611   *T.*70.66%
Mrs E. Gordon, *Lab.*   18,187
†Sir M. Neubert, *C.*   17,538
N. Meyer, *LD*   3,341
S. Ward, *Ref.*   1,431
T. Hurlstone, *Lib.*   1,100
M. Carey, *BNP*   522
Lab. majority 649
(Boundary change: notional C.)

ROMSEY
*E.*67,306   *T.*76.99%
†M. Colvin, *C.*   23,834
M. Cooper, *LD*   15,249
Ms J. Ford, *Lab.*   9,623
Dr A. Sked, *UK Ind.*   1,824
M. Wigley, *Ref.*   1,291
C. majority 8,585
(Boundary change: notional C.)

ROSSENDALE AND DARWEN
*E.*69,749   *T.*73.42%
†Mrs J. Anderson, *Lab.*   27,470
Mrs P. Buzzard, *C.*   16,521
B. Dunning, *LD*   5,435
R. Newstead, *Ref.*   1,108
A. Wearden, *BNP*   674
Lab. majority 10,949
(Boundary change: notional Lab.)

ROTHER VALLEY
*E.*68,622   *T.*67.26%
*K. Barron, *Lab.*   31,184
S. Stanbury, *C.*   7,699
S. Burgess, *LD*   5,342
S. Cook, *Ref.*   1,932
Lab. majority 23,485
(April 1992, Lab. maj. 17,222)

ROTHERHAM
*E.*59,895   *T.*62.86%
*D. MacShane, *Lab.*   26,852
S. Gordon, *C.*   5,383
D. Wildgoose, *LD*   3,919
R. Hollibone, *Ref.*   1,132
A. Neal, *ProLife*   364
Lab. majority 21,469
(April 1992, Lab. maj. 17,561)

RUGBY AND KENILWORTH
*E.*79,384   *T.*77.10%
A. King, *Lab.*   26,356
†J. Pawsey, *C.*   25,861
J. Roodhouse, *LD*   8,737
M. Twite, *NLP*   251
Lab. majority 495
(Boundary change: notional C.)

RUISLIP-NORTHWOOD
*E.*60,393   *T.*74.24%
†J. Wilkinson, *C.*   22,526
P. Barker, *Lab.*   14,732
C. Edwards, *LD*   7,279
Ms C. Griffin, *NLP*   296
C. majority 7,794
(Boundary change: notional C.)

RUNNYMEDE AND WEYBRIDGE
*E.*72,177   *T.*71.44%
P. Hammond, *C.*   25,051
I. Peacock, *Lab.*   15,176
G. Taylor, *LD*   8,397
P. Rolt, *Ref.*   2,150
S. Slater, *UK Ind.*   625
J. Sleeman, *NLP*   162
C. majority 9,875
(Boundary change: notional C.)

RUSHCLIFFE
*E.*78,735   *T.*78.89%
*Rt. Hon. K. Clarke, *C.*   27,558
Ms J. Pettit, *Lab.*   22,503
S. Boote, *LD*   8,851
Miss S. Chadd, *Ref.*   2,682
J. Moore, *UK Ind.*   403
Ms A. Maszwska, *NLP*   115
C. majority 5,055
(April 1992, C. maj. 19,766)

RUTLAND AND MELTON
*E.*70,150   *T.*75.02%
†A. Duncan, *C.*   24,107
J. Meads, *Lab.*   15,271

K. Lee, *LD*   10,112
R. King, *Ref.*   2,317
J. Abbott, *UK Ind.*   823
C. majority 8,836
(Boundary change: notional C.)

RYEDALE
*E.*65,215   *T.*74.80%
†J. Greenway, *C.*   21,351
J. Orrell, *LD*   16,293
Ms A. Hiles, *Lab.*   8,762
J. Mackfall, *Ref.*   1,460
S. Feaster, *UK Ind.*   917
C. majority 5,058
(Boundary change: notional C.)

SAFFRON WALDEN
*E.*74,097   *T.*76.99%
†Sir A. Haselhurst, *C.*   25,871
M. Caton, *LD*   15,298
M. Fincken, *Lab.*   12,275
R. Glover, *Ref.*   2,308
I. Evans, *UK Ind.*   658
B. Tyler, *Ind.*   486
C. Edwards, *NLP*   154
C. majority 10,573
(Boundary change: notional C.)

ST ALBANS
*E.*65,560   *T.*77.49%
K. Pollard, *Lab.*   21,338
D. Rutley, *C.*   16,879
A. Rowlands, *LD*   10,692
J. Warrilow, *Ref.*   1,619
Ms S. Craigen, *Dream*   166
I. Docker, *NLP*   111
Lab. majority 4,459
(Boundary change: notional C.)

ST HELENS NORTH
*E.*71,380   *T.*68.97%
D. Watts, *Lab.*   31,953
P. Walker, *C.*   8,536
J. Beirne, *LD*   6,270
D. Johnson, *Ref.*   1,276
R. Waugh, *Soc. Lab.*   832
R. Rudin, *UK Ind.*   363
Lab. majority 23,417
(April 1992, Lab. maj. 16,244)

ST HELENS SOUTH
*E.*66,526   *T.*66.53%
†G. Bermingham, *Lab.*   30,367
Ms M. Russell, *C.*   6,628
B. Spencer, *LD*   5,919
W. Holdaway, *Ref.*   1,165
Ms H. Jump, *NLP*   179
Lab. majority 23,739
(Boundary change: notional Lab.)

ST IVES
*E.*71,680   *T.*75.20%
A. George, *LD*   23,966
W. Rogers, *C.*   16,796
C. Fegan, *Lab.*   8,184
M. Faulkner, *Ref.*   3,714
Mrs P. Garnier, *UK Ind.*   567
G. Stephens, *Lib.*   425
K. Lippiatt, *R. Alt.*   178
W. Hitchins, *BHMBCM*   71
LD majority 7,170
(April 1992, C. maj. 1,645)

SALFORD
E.58,610   T.56.51%

Ms H. Blears, *Lab.*		22,848
E. Bishop, *C.*		5,779
N. Owen, *LD*		3,407
R. Cumpsty, *Ref.*		926
Ms S. Herman, *NLP*		162
Lab. majority 17,069		
(Boundary change: notional Lab.)		

SALISBURY
E.78,973   T.73.75%

*R. Key, *C.*		25,012
Ms Y. Emmerson-Peirce, *LD*		18,736
R. Rogers, *Lab.*		10,242
N. Farage, *UK Ind.*		3,332
H. Soutar, *Green*		623
W. Holmes, *Ind.*		184
Mrs S. Haysom, *NLP*		110
C. majority 6,276		
(April 1992, C. maj. 8,973)		

SCARBOROUGH AND WHITBY
E.75,862   T.71.61%

L. Quinn, *Lab.*		24,791
*J. Sykes, *C.*		19,667
M. Allinson, *LD*		7,672
Ms S. Murray, *Ref.*		2,191
Lab. majority 5,124		
(April 1992, C. maj. 11,734)		

SCUNTHORPE
E.60,393   T.68.84%

†E. Morley, *Lab.*		25,107
M. Fisher, *C.*		10,934
G. Smith, *LD*		3,497
P. Smith, *Ref.*		1,637
B. Hopper, *Soc. Lab.*		399
Lab. majority 14,173		
(Boundary change: notional Lab.)		

SEDGEFIELD
E.64,923   T.72.57%

†Rt. Hon. A. Blair, *Lab.*		33,526
Mrs E. Pitman, *C.*		8,383
R. Beadle, *LD*		3,050
Miss M. Hall, *Ref.*		1,683
B. Gibson, *Soc. Lab.*		474
Lab. majority 25,143		
(Boundary change: notional Lab.)		

SELBY
E.75,141   T.74.95%

J. Grogan, *Lab.*		25,838
K. Hind, *C.*		22,002
E. Batty, *LD*		6,778
D. Walker, *Ref.*		1,162
P. Spence, *UK Ind.*		536
Lab. majority 3,836		
(Boundary change: notional C.)		

SEVENOAKS
E.66,474   T.75.44%

M. Fallon, *C.*		22,776
J. Hayes, *Lab.*		12,315
R. Walshe, *LD*		12,086
N. Large, *Ref.*		2,138
Ms M. Lawrence, *Green*		443
M. Ellis, *PF*		244
A. Hankey, *NLP*		147
C. majority 10,461		
(Boundary change: notional C.)		

SHEFFIELD ATTERCLIFFE
E.68,548   T.64.65%

*C. Betts, *Lab.*		28,937
B. Doyle, *C.*		7,119
Mrs G. Smith, *LD*		6,973
J. Brown, *Ref.*		1,289
Lab. majority 21,818		
(April 1992, Lab. maj. 15,480)		

SHEFFIELD BRIGHTSIDE
E.58,930   T.57.47%

*D. Blunkett, *Lab.*		24,901
F. Butler, *LD*		4,947
C. Buckwell, *C.*		2,850
B. Farnsworth, *Ref.*		624
P. Davidson, *Soc. Lab.*		482
R. Scott, *NLP*		61
Lab. majority 19,954		
(April 1992, Lab. maj. 22,681)		

SHEFFIELD CENTRAL
E.68,667   T.53.04%

†R. Caborn, *Lab.*		23,179
A. Qadar, *LD*		6,273
M. Hess, *C.*		4,341
A. D'Agorne, *Green*		954
A. Brownlow, *Ref.*		863
K. Douglas, *Soc.*		466
Ms M. Aitken, *ProLife*		280
M. Driver, *WRP*		63
Lab. majority 16,906		
(Boundary change: notional Lab.)		

SHEFFIELD HALLAM
E.62,834   T.72.38%

R. Allan, *LD*		23,345
†Sir I. Patnick, *C.*		15,074
S. Conquest, *Lab.*		6,147
I. Davidson, *Ref.*		788
P. Booler, *SIP*		125
LD majority 8,271		
(Boundary change: notional C.)		

SHEFFIELD HEELEY
E.66,599   T.64.96%

*W. Michie, *Lab.*		26,274
R. Davison, *LD*		9,196
J. Harthman, *C.*		6,767
D. Mawson, *Ref.*		1,029
Lab. majority 17,078		
(April 1992, Lab. maj. 14,954)		

SHEFFIELD HILLSBOROUGH
E.74,642   T.71.04%

*Mrs H. Jackson, *Lab.*		30,150
A. Dunworth, *LD*		13,699
D. Nuttall, *C.*		7,707
J. Rusling, *Ref.*		1,468
Lab. majority 16,451		
(April 1992, Lab. maj. 7,068)		

SHERWOOD
E.74,788   T.75.59%

*P. Tipping, *Lab.*		33,071
R. Spencer, *C.*		16,259
B. Moult, *LD*		4,889
L. Slack, *Ref.*		1,882
P. Ballard, *BNP*		432
Lab. majority 16,812		
(April 1992, Lab. maj. 2,910)		

SHIPLEY
E.69,281   T.76.32%

C. Leslie, *Lab.*		22,962
*Rt. Hon. Sir M. Fox, *C.*		19,966
J. Cole, *LD*		7,984
Dr S. Ellams, *Ref.*		1,960
Lab. majority 2,996		
(April 1992, C. maj. 12,382)		

SHREWSBURY AND ATCHAM
E.73,542   T.75.25%

P. Marsden, *Lab.*		20,484
*D. Conway, *C.*		18,814
Mrs A. Woolland, *LD*		13,838
D. Barker, *Ref.*		1,346
D. Rowlands, *UK Ind.*		477
A. Dignan, *CFSS*		257
A. Williams, *PPP*		128
Lab. majority 1,670		
(April 1992, C. maj. 10,965)		

SHROPSHIRE NORTH
E.70,852   T.72.71%

O. Paterson, *C.*		20,730
I. Lucas, *Lab.*		18,535
J. Stevens, *LD*		10,489
D. Allen, *Ref.*		1,764
C. majority 2,195		
(Boundary change: notional C.)		

SITTINGBOURNE AND SHEPPEY
E.63,850   T.72.30%

D. Wyatt, *Lab.*		18,723
†Sir R. Moate, *C.*		16,794
R. Truelove, *LD*		8,447
P. Moull, *Ref.*		1,082
C. Driver, *Loony*		644
N. Risi, *UK Ind.*		472
Lab. majority 1,929		
(Boundary change: notional C.)		

SKIPTON AND RIPON
E.72,042   T.75.44%

†Rt. Hon. D. Curry, *C.*		25,294
T. Mould, *LD*		13,674
R. Marchant, *Lab.*		12,171
Mrs N. Holdsworth, *Ref.*		3,212
C. majority 11,620		
(Boundary change: notional C.)		

SLEAFORD AND NORTH HYKEHAM
E.71,486   T.74.39%

†Rt. Hon. D. Hogg, *C.*		23,358
S. Harriss, *Lab.*		18,235
J. Marriott, *LD*		8,063
P. Clery, *Ref.*		2,942
R. Overton, *Ind.*		578
C. majority 5,123		
(Boundary change: notional C.)		

SLOUGH
E.70,283   T.67.91%

Ms F. MacTaggart, *Lab.*		27,029
Mrs P. Buscombe, *C.*		13,958
C. Bushill, *LD*		3,509
Ms A. Bradshaw, *Lib.*		1,835
T. Sharkey, *Ref.*		1,124
P. Whitmore, *Slough*		277
Lab. majority 13,071		
(Boundary change: notional Lab.)		

SOLIHULL
E.78,898   T.74.66%
†J. Taylor, *C.* — 26,299
M. Southcombe, *LD* — 14,902
Ms R. Harris, *Lab.* — 14,334
M. Nattrass, *Ref.* — 2,748
J. Caffery, *ProLife* — 623
C. majority 11,397
(Boundary change: notional C.)

SOMERTON AND FROME
E.73,988   T.77.58%
D. Heath, *LD* — 22,684
†M. Robinson, *C.* — 22,554
R. Ashford, *Lab.* — 9,385
R. Rodwell, *Ref.* — 2,449
R. Gadd, *UK Ind.* — 331
LD majority 130
(Boundary change: notional C.)

SOUTHAMPTON ITCHEN
E.76,869   T.70.06%
†J. Denham, *Lab.* — 29,498
P. Fleet, *C.* — 15,289
D. Harrison, *LD* — 6,289
J. Clegg, *Ref.* — 1,660
K. Rose, *Soc. Lab.* — 628
C. Hoar, *UK Ind.* — 172
G. Marsh, *Soc.* — 113
Ms R. Barry, *NLP* — 110
F. McDermott, *ProLife* — 99
Lab. majority 14,209
(Boundary change: notional Lab.)

SOUTHAMPTON TEST
E.72,983   T.71.85%
A. Whitehead, *Lab.* — 28,396
†Sir J. Hill, *C.* — 14,712
A. Dowden, *LD* — 7,171
P. Day, *Ref.* — 1,397
H. Marks, *LCP* — 388
A. McCabe, *UK Ind.* — 219
P. Taylor, *Glow* — 81
J. Sinel, *NLP* — 77
Lab. majority 13,684
(Boundary change: notional Lab.)

SOUTHEND WEST
E.66,493   T.69.95%
†D. Amess, *C.* — 18,029
Mrs N. Stimson, *LD* — 15,414
A. Harley, *Lab.* — 10,600
C. Webster, *Ref.* — 1,734
B. Lee, *UK Ind.* — 636
P. Warburton, *NLP* — 101
C. majority 2,615
(April 1992, C. maj. 11,902)

SOUTH HOLLAND AND THE DEEPINGS
E.69,642   T.71.98%
J. Hayes, *C.* — 24,691
J. Lewis, *Lab.* — 16,700
P. Millen, *LD* — 7,836
G. Erwood, *NPC* — 902
C. majority 7,991
(Boundary change: notional C.)

SOUTHPORT
E.70,194   T.72.08%
R. Fearn, *LD* — 24,346
*M. Banks, *C.* — 18,186
Ms S. Norman, *Lab.* — 6,125

F. Buckle, *Ref.* — 1,368
Ms S. Ashton, *Lib.* — 386
E. Lines, *NLP* — 93
M. Middleton, *Nat. Dem.* — 92
LD majority 6,160
(April 1992, C. maj. 3,063)

SOUTH SHIELDS
E.62,261   T.62.60%
†Dr D. Clark, *Lab.* — 27,834
M. Hoban, *C.* — 5,681
D. Ord, *LD* — 3,429
A. Loraine, *Ref.* — 1,660
I. Wilburn, *Shields* — 374
Lab. majority 22,153
(Boundary change: notional Lab.)

SOUTHWARK NORTH AND BERMONDSEY
E.65,598   T.62.19%
†S. Hughes, *LD* — 19,831
J. Fraser, *Lab.* — 16,444
G. Shapps, *C.* — 2,835
M. Davidson, *BNP* — 713
W. Newton, *Ref.* — 545
I. Grant, *Comm L.* — 175
J. Munday, *Lib.* — 157
Ms I. Yngvison, *Nat. Dem.* — 95
LD majority 3,387
(Boundary change: notional LD)

SPELTHORNE
E.70,562   T.73.58%
*D. Wilshire, *C.* — 23,306
K. Dibble, *Lab.* — 19,833
E. Glynn, *LD* — 6,821
B. Coleman, *Ref.* — 1,495
J. Fowler, *UK Ind.* — 462
C. majority 3,473
(April 1992, C. maj. 19,843)

STAFFORD
E.67,555   T.76.64%
D. Kidney, *Lab.* — 24,606
D. Cameron, *C.* — 20,292
Mrs P. Hornby, *LD* — 5,480
S. Culley, *Ref.* — 1,146
A. May, *Loony* — 248
Lab. majority 4,314
(Boundary change: notional C.)

STAFFORDSHIRE MOORLANDS
E.66,095   T.77.34%
Ms C. Atkins, *Lab.* — 26,686
Dr A. Ashworth, *C.* — 16,637
Mrs C. Jebb, *LD* — 6,191
D. Stanworth, *Ref.* — 1,603
Lab. majority 10,049
(Boundary change: notional Lab.)

STAFFORDSHIRE SOUTH
E.68,896   T.74.19%
†Sir P. Cormack, *C.* — 25,568
Ms J. LeMaistre, *Lab.* — 17,747
Mrs J. Calder, *LD* — 5,797
P. Carnell, *Ref.* — 2,002
C. majority 7,821
(Boundary change: notional C.)

STALYBRIDGE AND HYDE
E.65,468   T.65.80%
†T. Pendry, *Lab.* — 25,363
N. de Bois, *C.* — 10,557

M. Cross, *LD* — 5,169
R. Clapham, *Ref.* — 1,992
Lab. majority 14,806
(Boundary change: notional Lab.)

STEVENAGE
E.66,889   T.76.82%
Ms B. Follett, *Lab.* — 28,440
†T. Wood, *C.* — 16,858
A. Wilcock, *LD* — 4,588
J. Coburn, *Ref.* — 1,194
D. Bundy, *ProLife* — 196
A. Calcraft, *NLP* — 110
Lab. majority 11,582
(Boundary change: notional C.)

STOCKPORT
E.65,232   T.71.54%
†Ms A. Coffey, *Lab.* — 29,338
S. Fitzsimmons, *C.* — 10,426
Mrs S. Roberts, *LD* — 4,951
W. Morley-Scott, *Ref.* — 1,280
G. Southern, *Soc. Lab.* — 255
C. Newitt, *Loony* — 213
C. Dronfield, *Ind.* — 206
Lab. majority 18,912
(Boundary change: notional Lab.)

STOCKTON NORTH
E.64,380   T.69.08%
†F. Cook, *Lab.* — 29,726
B. Johnston, *C.* — 8,369
Mrs S. Fletcher, *LD* — 4,816
K. McConnell, *Ref.* — 1,563
Lab. majority 21,357
(Boundary change: notional Lab.)

STOCKTON SOUTH
E.68,470   T.76.12%
Ms D. Taylor, *Lab.* — 28,790
†T. Devlin, *C.* — 17,205
P. Monck, *LD* — 4,721
J. Horner, *Ref.* — 1,400
Lab. majority 11,585
(Boundary change: notional C.)

STOKE-ON-TRENT CENTRAL
E.64,113   T.62.77%
*M. Fisher, *Lab.* — 26,662
N. Jones, *C.* — 6,738
E. Fordham, *LD* — 4,809
P. Stanyer, *Ref.* — 1,071
M. Coleman, *BNP* — 606
Ms F. Oborski, *Lib.* — 359
Lab. majority 19,924
(April 1992, Lab. maj. 13,420)

STOKE-ON-TRENT NORTH
E.59,030   T.65.50%
†Ms J. Walley, *Lab.* — 25,190
C. Day, *C.* — 7,798
H. Jebb, *LD* — 4,141
Ms J. Tobin, *Ref.* — 1,537
Lab. majority 17,392
(Boundary change: notional Lab.)

STOKE-ON-TRENT SOUTH
E.69,968   T.66.08%
*G. Stevenson, *Lab.* — 28,645
Mrs S. Scott, *C.* — 10,342
P. Barnett, *LD* — 4,710
R. Adams, *Ref.* — 1,103
Mrs A. Micklem, *Lib.* — 580

S. Batkin, *BNP* — 568
B. Lawrence, *Nat. Dem.* — 288
Lab. majority 18,303
(April 1992, Lab. maj. 6,909)

STONE
*E.*68,242   *T.*77.77%
†W. Cash, *C.* — 24,859
J. Wakefield, *Lab.* — 21,041
B. Stamp, *LD* — 6,392
Ms A. Winfield, *Lib.* — 545
Ms D. Grice, *NLP* — 237
C. majority 3,818
(Boundary change: notional C.)

STOURBRIDGE
*E.*64,966   *T.*76.50%
Ms D. Shipley, *Lab.* — 23,452
†W. Hawksley, *C.* — 17,807
C. Bramall, *LD* — 7,123
P. Quick, *Ref.* — 1,319
Lab. majority 5,645
(Boundary change: notional C.)

STRATFORD-ON-AVON
*E.*81,434   *T.*76.26%
J. Maples, *C.* — 29,967
Dr S. Juned, *LD* — 15,861
S. Stacey, *Lab.* — 12,754
A. Hilton, *Ref.* — 2,064
J. Spilsbury, *UK Ind.* — 556
J. Brewster, *NLP* — 307
S. Marcus, *SFDC* — 306
Ms S. Miller, *ProLife* — 284
C. majority 14,106
(Boundary change: notional C.)

STREATHAM
*E.*74,509   *T.*60.24%
†K. Hill, *Lab.* — 28,181
E. Noad, *C.* — 9,758
R. O'Brien, *LD* — 6,082
J. Wall, *Ref.* — 864
Lab. majority 18,423
(Boundary change: notional Lab.)

STRETFORD AND URMSTON
*E.*69,913   *T.*69.65%
Ms B. Hughes, *Lab.* — 28,480
J. Gregory, *C.* — 14,840
J. Bridges, *LD* — 3,978
Ms C. Dore, *Ref.* — 1,397
Lab. majority 13,640
(Boundary change: notional Lab.)

STROUD
*E.*77,494   *T.*80.45%
D. Drew, *Lab. Co-op.* — 26,170
†R. Knapman, *C.* — 23,260
P. Hodgkinson, *LD* — 9,502
J. Marjoram, *Green* — 3,415
Lab. Co-op. majority 2,910
(Boundary change: notional C.)

SUFFOLK CENTRAL AND IPSWICH NORTH
*E.*70,222   *T.*75.22%
†M. Lord, *C.* — 22,493
Ms C. Jones, *Lab.* — 18,955
Dr M. Goldspink, *LD* — 10,886
Ms S. Bennell, *Ind.* — 489
C. majority 3,538
(Boundary change: notional C.)

SUFFOLK COASTAL
*E.*74,219   *T.*75.80%
†Rt. Hon. J. Gummer, *C.* — 21,696
M. Campbell, *Lab.* — 18,442
Ms A. Jones, *LD* — 12,036
S. Caulfield, *Ref.* — 3,416
A. Slade, *Green* — 514
Ms F. Kaplan, *NLP* — 152
C. majority 3,254
(Boundary change: notional C.)

SUFFOLK SOUTH
*E.*67,323   *T.*77.20%
†T. Yeo, *C.* — 19,402
P. Bishop, *Lab.* — 15,227
Mrs K. Pollard, *LD* — 14,395
C. de Chair, *Ref.* — 2,740
Mrs A. Holland, *NLP* — 211
C. majority 4,175
(Boundary change: notional C.)

SUFFOLK WEST
*E.*68,638   *T.*71.51%
†R. Spring, *C.* — 20,081
M. Jefferys, *Lab.* — 18,214
A. Graves, *LD* — 6,892
J. Carver, *Ref.* — 3,724
A. Shearer, *NLP* — 171
C. majority 1,867
(Boundary change: notional C.)

SUNDERLAND NORTH
*E.*64,711   *T.*59.05%
†W. Etherington, *Lab.* — 26,067
A. Selous, *C.* — 6,370
G. Pryke, *LD* — 3,973
M. Nicholson, *Ref.* — 1,394
K. Newby, *Loony* — 409
Lab. majority 19,697
(Boundary change: notional Lab.)

SUNDERLAND SOUTH
*E.*67,937   *T.*58.77%
†C. Mullin, *Lab.* — 27,174
T. Schofield, *C.* — 7,536
J. Lennox, *LD* — 4,606
M. Wilkinson, *UK Ind.* — 609
Lab. majority 19,638
(Boundary change: notional Lab.)

SURREY EAST
*E.*72,852   *T.*75.02%
†P. Ainsworth, *C.* — 27,389
Ms B. Ford, *LD* — 12,296
D. Ross, *Lab.* — 11,573
M. Sydney, *Ref.* — 2,656
A. Stone, *UK Ind.* — 569
Ms S. Bartrum, *NLP* — 173
C. majority 15,093
(Boundary change: notional C.)

SURREY HEATH
*E.*73,813   *T.*74.14%
†N. Hawkins, *C.* — 28,231
D. Newman, *LD* — 11,944
Ms S. Jones, *Lab.* — 11,511
J. Gale, *Ref.* — 2,385
R. Squire, *UK Ind.* — 653
C. majority 16,287
(Boundary change: notional C.)

SURREY SOUTH WEST
*E.*72,350   *T.*78.03%
*Rt. Hon. Mrs V. Bottomley, *C.* — 25,165
N. Sherlock, *LD* — 22,471
Ms M. Leicester, *Lab.* — 5,333
Mrs J. Clementson, *Ref.* — 2,830
J. Kirby, *UK Ind.* — 401
Ms J. Quintavalle, *ProLife* — 258
C. majority 2,694
(April 1992, C. maj. 14,975)

SUSSEX MID
*E.*68,784   *T.*77.73%
†N. Soames, *C.* — 23,231
Mrs M. Collins, *LD* — 16,377
M. Hamilton, *Lab.* — 9,969
T. Large, *Ref.* — 3,146
J. Barnett, *UK Ind.* — 606
E. Tudway, *Ind. JRP* — 134
C. majority 6,854
(Boundary change: notional C.)

SUTTON AND CHEAM
*E.*62,785   *T.*75.01%
P. Burstow, *LD* — 19,919
*Lady O. Maitland, *C.* — 17,822
M. Allison, *Lab.* — 7,280
P. Atkinson, *Ref.* — 1,784
S. McKie, *UK Ind.* — 191
Ms D. Wright, *NLP* — 96
LD majority 2,097
(April 1992, C. maj. 10,756)

SUTTON COLDFIELD
*E.*71,864   *T.*72.92%
*Rt. Hon. Sir N. Fowler, *C.* — 27,373
A. York, *Lab.* — 12,488
J. Whorwood, *LD* — 10,139
D. Hope, *Ref.* — 2,401
C. majority 14,885
(April 1992, C. maj. 26,036)

SWINDON NORTH
*E.*65,535   *T.*73.66%
M. Wills, *Lab.* — 24,029
G. Opperman, *C.* — 16,341
M. Evemy, *LD* — 6,237
Ms G. Goldsmith, *Ref.* — 1,533
A. Fiskin, *NLP* — 130
Lab. majority 7,688
(Boundary change: notional Lab.)

SWINDON SOUTH
*E.*70,207   *T.*72.87%
Ms J. Drown, *Lab.* — 23,943
†S. Coombs, *C.* — 18,298
S. Pajak, *LD* — 7,371
D. Mackintosh, *Ref.* — 1,273
R. Charman, *Route 66* — 181
K. Buscombe, *NLP* — 96
Lab. majority 5,645
(Boundary change: notional C.)

TAMWORTH
*E.*67,205   *T.*74.18%
†B. Jenkins, *Lab.* — 25,808
Lady A. Lightbown, *C.* — 18,312
Mrs J. Pinkett, *LD* — 4,025
Mrs D. Livesey, *Ref.* — 1,163
C. Lamb, *UK Ind.* — 369
Ms C. Twelvetrees, *Lib.* — 177

Lab. majority 7,496
(Boundary change: notional C.)

TATTON
*E.*63,822 *T.*76.45%
M. Bell, *Ind.* — 29,354
†N. Hamilton, *C.* — 18,277
S. Hill, *Ind.* — 295
S. Kinsey, *Ind.* — 187
B. Penhaul, *Miss M.* — 128
J. Muir, *Albion* — 126
M. Kennedy, *NLP* — 123
D. Bishop, *Byro* — 116
R. Nicholas, *Ind.* — 113
J. Price, *Juice* — 73
Ind. majority 11,077
(Boundary change: notional C.)

TAUNTON
*E.*79,783 *T.*76.47%
Mrs J. Ballard, *LD* — 26,064
*D. Nicholson, *C.* — 23,621
Ms E. Lisgo, *Lab.* — 8,248
B. Ahern, *Ref.* — 2,760
L. Andrews, *BNP* — 318
LD majority 2,443
(April 1992, C. maj. 3,336)

TEIGNBRIDGE
*E.*81,667 *T.*77.08%
†P. Nicholls, *C.* — 24,679
R. Younger-Ross, *LD* — 24,398
Ms S. Dann, *Lab.* — 11,311
S. Stokes, *UK Ind.* — 1,601
N. Banwell, *Green* — 817
Mrs L. Golding, *Dream* — 139
C. majority 281
(Boundary change: notional C.)

TELFORD
*E.*56,558 *T.*65.62%
†B. Grocott, *Lab.* — 21,456
B. Gentry, *C.* — 10,166
N. Green, *LD* — 4,371
C. Morris, *Ref.* — 1,119
Lab. majority 11,290
(Boundary change: notional Lab.)

TEWKESBURY
*E.*68,208 *T.*76.46%
L. Robertson, *C.* — 23,859
J. Sewell, *LD* — 14,625
K. Tustin, *Lab.* — 13,665
C. majority 9,234
(Boundary change: notional C.)

THANET NORTH
*E.*71,112 *T.*68.84%
*R. Gale, *C.* — 21,586
Ms I. Johnston, *Lab.* — 18,820
P. Kendrick, *LD* — 5,576
M. Chambers, *Ref.* — 2,535
Ms J. Haines, *UK Ind.* — 438
C. majority 2,766
(April 1992, C. maj. 18,210)

THANET SOUTH
*E.*62,792 *T.*71.65%
Dr S. Ladyman, *Lab.* — 20,777
†Rt. Hon. J. Aitken, *C.* — 17,899
Ms B. Hewett-Silk, *LD* — 5,263
C. Crook, *UK Ind.* — 631
D. Wheatley, *Green* — 418

Lab. majority 2,878
(Boundary change: notional C.)

THURROCK
*E.*71,600 *T.*65.94%
*A. MacKinlay, *Lab.* — 29,896
A. Rosindell, *C.* — 12,640
J. White, *LD* — 3,843
P. Compobassi, *UK Ind.* — 833
Lab. majority 17,256
(April 1992, Lab. maj. 1,172)

TIVERTON AND HONITON
*E.*75,744 *T.*78.06%
†Mrs A. Browning, *C.* — 24,438
Dr J. Barnard, *LD* — 22,785
J. King, *Lab.* — 7,598
S. Lowings, *Ref.* — 2,952
Mrs J. Roach, *Lib.* — 635
Ms E. McIvor, *Green* — 485
D. Charles, *Nat. Dem.* — 236
C. majority 1,653
(Boundary change: notional C.)

TONBRIDGE AND MALLING
*E.*64,798 *T.*75.97%
†Rt. Hon. Sir J. Stanley, *C.* — 23,640
Mrs B. Withstandley, *Lab.* — 13,410
K. Brown, *LD* — 9,467
J. Scrivenor, *Ref.* — 2,005
Mrs B. Bullen, *UK Ind.* — 502
G. Valente, *NLP* — 205
C. majority 10,230
(Boundary change: notional C.)

TOOTING
*E.*66,653 *T.*69.17%
*T. Cox, *Lab.* — 27,516
J. Hutchings, *C.* — 12,505
S. James, *LD* — 4,320
Mrs A. Husband, *Ref.* — 829
J. Rattray, *Green* — 527
P. Boddington, *BFAIR* — 161
J. Koene, *Rights* — 94
D. Bailey-Bond, *Dream* — 83
P. Miller, *NLP* — 70
Lab. majority 15,011
(April 1992, Lab. maj. 4,107)

TORBAY
*E.*72,258 *T.*73.79%
A. Sanders, *LD* — 21,094
*R. Allason, *C.* — 21,082
M. Morey, *Lab.* — 7,923
G. Booth, *UK Ind.* — 1,962
B. Cowling, *Lib.* — 1,161
P. Wild, *Dream* — 100
LD majority 12
(April 1992, C. maj. 5,787)

TOTNES
*E.*70,473 *T.*76.30%
†Sir A. Steen, *C.* — 19,637
R. Chave, *LD* — 18,760
V. Ellery, *Lab.* — 8,796
Ms P. Cook, *Ref.* — 2,552
C. Venmore, *Loc. C.* — 2,369
H. Thomas, *UK Ind.* — 999
A. Pratt, *Green* — 548
J. Golding, *Dream* — 108
C. majority 877
(Boundary change: notional C.)

TOTTENHAM
*E.*66,173 *T.*56.98%
*B. Grant, *Lab.* — 26,121
A. Scantlebury, *C.* — 5,921
N. Hughes, *LD* — 4,064
P. Budge, *Green* — 1,059
Ms E. Tay, *ProLife* — 210
C. Anglin, *WRP* — 181
Ms T. Kent, *SEP* — 148
Lab. majority 20,200
(April 1992, Lab. maj. 11,968)

TRURO AND ST AUSTELL
*E.*76,824 *T.*73.87%
*M. Taylor, *LD* — 27,502
N. Badcock, *C.* — 15,001
M. Dooley, *Lab.* — 8,697
C. Hearn, *Ref.* — 3,682
A. Haithwaite, *UK Ind.* — 576
Mrs D. Robinson, *Green* — 482
D. Hicks, *MK* — 450
Mrs L. Yelland, *PP* — 240
P. Boland, *NLP* — 117
LD majority 12,501
(April 1992, LD maj. 7,570)

TUNBRIDGE WELLS
*E.*65,259 *T.*74.10%
A. Norman, *C.* — 21,853
A. Clayton, *LD* — 14,347
P. Warner, *Lab.* — 9,879
T. Macpherson, *Ref.* — 1,858
M. Anderson Smart, *UK Ind.* — 264
P. Levy, *NLP* — 153
C. majority 7,506
(Boundary change: notional C.)

TWICKENHAM
*E.*73,281 *T.*79.34%
Dr V. Cable, *LD* — 26,237
†T. Jessel, *C.* — 21,956
Ms E. Tutchell, *Lab.* — 9,065
Miss J. Harrison, *Ind. ECR* — 589
T. Haggar, *Dream* — 155
A. Hardy, *NLP* — 142
LD majority 4,281
(Boundary change: notional C.)

TYNE BRIDGE
*E.*61,058 *T.*57.08%
†D. Clelland, *Lab.* — 26,767
A. Lee, *C.* — 3,861
Mrs M. Wallace, *LD* — 2,785
G. Oswald, *Ref.* — 919
Ms E. Brunskill, *Soc.* — 518
Lab. majority 22,906
(Boundary change: notional Lab.)

TYNEMOUTH
*E.*66,341 *T.*77.11%
A. Campbell, *Lab.* — 28,318
M. Callanan, *C.* — 17,045
A. Duffield, *LD* — 4,509
C. Rook, *Ref.* — 819
Dr F. Rogers, *UK Ind.* — 462
Lab. majority 11,273
(Boundary change: notional C.)

TYNESIDE NORTH
*E.*66,449 *T.*67.90%
†S. Byers, *Lab.* — 32,810
M. McIntyre, *C.* — 6,167
T. Mulvenna, *LD* — 4,762

M. Rollings, *Ref.* 1,382
Lab. majority 26,643
(Boundary change: notional Lab.)

UPMINSTER
E.57,149   T.72.30%
K. Darvill, *Lab.* 19,085
†Sir N. Bonsor, *C.* 16,315
Mrs P. Peskett, *LD* 3,919
T. Murray, *Ref.* 2,000
Lab. majority 2,770
(Boundary change: notional C.)

UXBRIDGE
E.57,497   T.72.26%
†Sir M. Shersby, *C.* 18,095
D. Williams, *Lab.* 17,371
Dr A. Malyan, *LD* 4,528
G. Aird, *Ref.* 1,153
Ms J. Leonard, *Soc.* 398
C. majority 724
(Boundary change: notional C.)
See also page 233

VALE OF YORK
E.70,077   T.76.01%
Miss A. McIntosh, *C.* 23,815
M. Carter, *Lab.* 14,094
C. Hall, *LD* 12,656
C. Fairclough, *Ref.* 2,503
A. Pelton, *Soc. Dem.* 197
C. majority 9,721
(Boundary change: notional C.)

VAUXHALL
E.70,402   T.55.49%
†Ms K. Hoey, *Lab.* 24,920
K. Kerr, *LD* 6,260
R. Bacon, *C.* 5,942
I. Driver, *Soc. Lab.* 983
S. Collins, *Green* 864
R. Headicar, *SPGB* 97
Lab. majority 18,660
(Boundary change: notional Lab.)

WAKEFIELD
E.73,210   T.68.96%
†D. Hinchliffe, *Lab.* 28,977
J. Peacock, *C.* 14,373
D. Dale, *LD* 5,656
S. Shires, *Ref.* 1,480
Lab. majority 14,604
(Boundary change: notional Lab.)

WALLASEY
E.63,714   T.73.52%
*Ms A. Eagle, *Lab.* 30,264
Mrs P. Wilcock, *C.* 11,190
P. Reisdorf, *LD* 3,899
R. Hayes, *Ref.* 1,490
Lab. majority 19,074
(April 1992, Lab. maj. 3,809)

WALSALL NORTH
E.67,587   T.64.07%
*D. Winnick, *Lab.* 24,517
M. Bird, *C.* 11,929
Ms T. O'Brien, *LD* 4,050
D. Bennett, *Ref.* 1,430
M. Pitt, *Ind.* 911
A. Humphries, *NF* 465
Lab. majority 12,588
(April 1992, Lab. maj. 3,824)

WALSALL SOUTH
E.64,221   T.67.33%
*B. George, *Lab.* 25,024
L. Leek, *C.* 13,712
H. Harris, *LD* 2,698
Dr T. Dent, *Ref.* 1,662
Mrs L. Meads, *NLP* 144
Lab. majority 11,312
(April 1992, Lab. maj. 3,178)

WALTHAMSTOW
E.63,818   T.62.76%
†N. Gerrard, *Lab.* 25,287
Mrs J. Andrew, *C.* 8,138
Dr J. Jackson, *LD* 5,491
Revd G. Hargreaves, *Ref.* 1,139
Lab. majority 17,149
(Boundary change: notional Lab.)

WANSBECK
E.62,998   T.71.70%
D. Murphy, *Lab.* 29,569
A. Thompson, *LD* 7,202
P. Green, *C.* 6,299
P. Gompertz, *Ref.* 1,146
Dr N. Best, *Green* 956
Lab. majority 22,367
(April 1992, Lab. maj. 18,174)

WANSDYKE
E.69,032   T.79.27%
D. Norris, *Lab.* 24,117
M. Prisk, *C.* 19,318
J. Manning, *LD* 9,205
K. Clinton, *Ref.* 1,327
T. Hunt, *UK Ind.* 438
P. House, *Loony* 225
Ms S. Lincoln, *NLP* 92
Lab. majority 4,799
(Boundary change: notional C.)

WANTAGE
E.71,657   T.78.23%
*R. Jackson, *C.* 22,311
Ms C. Wilson, *Lab.* 16,272
Ms J. Riley, *LD* 14,822
S. Rising, *Ref.* 1,549
Ms M. Kennet, *Green* 640
Count N. Tolstoy-Miloslausky,
    UK Ind. 465
C. majority 6,039
(April 1992, C. maj. 16,473)

WARLEY
E.59,758   T.65.08%
†J. Spellar, *Lab.* 24,813
C. Pincher, *C.* 9,362
J. Pursehouse, *LD* 3,777
K. Gamre, *Ref.* 941
Lab. majority 15,451
(Boundary change: notional Lab.)

WARRINGTON NORTH
E.72,694   T.70.50%
Ms H. Jones, *Lab.* 31,827
Ms R. Lacey, *C.* 12,300
I. Greenhalgh, *LD* 5,308
Dr A. Smith, *Ref.* 1,816
Lab. majority 19,527
(Boundary change: notional Lab.)

WARRINGTON SOUTH
E.72,262   T.76.23%
Ms H. Southworth, *Lab.* 28,721
C. Grayling, *C.* 17,914
P. Walker, *LD* 7,199
G. Kelly, *Ref.* 1,082
S. Ross, *NLP* 166
Lab. majority 10,807
(Boundary change: notional C.)

WARWICK AND LEAMINGTON
E.79,374   T.75.71%
J. Plaskitt, *Lab.* 26,747
†Sir D. Smith, *C.* 23,349
N. Hicks, *LD* 7,133
Mrs V. Davis, *Ref.* 1,484
P. Baptie, *Green* 764
G. Warwick, *UK Ind.* 306
M. Gibbs, *EDP* 183
R. McCarthy, *NLP* 125
Lab. majority 3,398
(Boundary change: notional C.)

WARWICKSHIRE NORTH
E.72,602   T.74.71%
†M. O'Brien, *Lab.* 31,669
S. Hammond, *C.* 16,902
W. Powell, *LD* 4,040
R. Mole, *Ref.* 917
C. Cooke, *UK Ind.* 533
I. Moorecroft, *Bert.* 178
Lab. majority 14,767
(Boundary change: notional Lab.)

WATFORD
E.74,015   T.74.63%
Ms C. Ward, *Lab.* 25,019
R. Gordon, *C.* 19,227
A. Canning, *LD* 9,272
Dr P. Roe, *Ref.* 1,484
L. Davis, *NLP* 234
Lab. majority 5,792
(Boundary change: notional C.)

WAVENEY
E.75,266   T.75.21%
R. Blizzard, *Lab.* 31,846
†D. Porter, *C.* 19,393
C. Thomas, *LD* 5,054
N. Clark, *Ind.* 318
Lab. majority 12,453
(Boundary change: notional C.)

WEALDEN
E.79,519   T.74.32%
†Rt. Hon. Sir G. Johnson Smith,
    C. 29,417
M. Skinner, *LD* 15,213
N. Levine, *Lab.* 10,185
B. Taplin, *Ref.* 3,527
Mrs M. English, *UK Ind.* 569
P. Cragg, *NLP* 188
C. majority 14,204
(Boundary change: notional C.)

WEAVER VALE
E.66,011   T.73.17%
†M. Hall, *Lab.* 27,244
J. Byrne, *C.* 13,796
T. Griffiths, *LD* 5,949
R. Cockfield, *Ref.* 1,312
Lab. majority 13,448
(Boundary change: notional Lab.)

WELLINGBOROUGH
*E.*74,955   *T.*75.10%
P. Stinchcombe, *Lab.*   24,854
*Sir P. Fry, *C.*   24,667
P. Smith, *LD*   5,279
A. Ellwood, *UK Ind.*   1,192
Ms A. Lowrys, *NLP*   297
Lab. majority 187
(April 1992, C. maj. 11,816)

WELLS
*E.*72,178   *T.*78.11%
*Rt. Hon. D. Heathcoat-Amory,
     C.   22,208
Dr P. Gold, *LD*   21,680
M. Eavis, *Lab.*   10,204
Mrs P. Phelps, *Ref.*   2,196
Ms L. Royse, *NLP*   92
C. majority 528
(April 1992, C. maj. 6,649)

WELWYN HATFIELD
*E.*67,395   *T.*78.59%
Ms M. Johnson, *Lab.*   24,936
†D. Evans, *C.*   19,341
R. Schwartz, *LD*   7,161
E. Cox, *RA*   1,263
Ms H. Harold, *ProLife*   267
Lab. majority 5,595
(Boundary change: notional C.)

WENTWORTH
*E.*63,951   *T.*65.33%
J. Healey, *Lab.*   30,225
K. Hamer, *C.*   6,266
J. Charters, *LD*   3,867
A. Battley, *Ref.*   1,423
Lab. majority 23,959
(April 1992, Lab. maj. 22,449)

WEST BROMWICH EAST
*E.*63,401   *T.*65.44%
†P. Snape, *Lab.*   23,710
B. Matsell, *C.*   10,126 ·
M. Smith, *LD*   6,179
G. Mulley, *Ref.*   1,472
Lab. majority 13,584
(Boundary change: notional Lab.)

WEST BROMWICH WEST
*E.*67,496   *T.*54.37%
†Rt. Hon. Miss B. Boothroyd,
     Speaker   23,969
R. Silvester, *Lab. Change*   8,546
S. Edwards, *Nat. Dem.*   4,181
Speaker majority 15,423
(Boundary change: notional Lab.)

WESTBURY
*E.*74,301   *T.*76.38%
†D. Faber, *C.*   23,037
J. Miller, *LD*   16,969
K. Small, *Lab.*   11,969
G. Hawkins, *Lib.*   1,956
N. Hawkings-Byass, *Ref.*   1,909
R. Westbury, *UK Ind.*   771
C. Haysom, *NLP*   140
C. majority 6,068
(Boundary change: notional C.)

WEST HAM
*E.*57,058   *T.*58.99%
†A. Banks, *Lab.*   24,531

M. MacGregor, *C.*   5,037
Ms S. McDonough, *LD*   2,479
K. Francis, *BNP*   1,198
T. Jug, *Loony*   300
J. Rainbow, *Dream*   116
Lab. majority 19,494
(Boundary change: notional Lab.)

WESTMORLAND AND LONSDALE
*E.*68,389   *T.*74.29%
T. Collins, *C.*   21,470
S. Collins, *LD*   16,949
J. Harding, *Lab.*   10,459
M. Smith, *Ref.*   1,931
C. majority 4,521
(Boundary change: notional C.)

WESTON-SUPER-MARE
*E.*72,445   *T.*73.68%
B. Cotter, *LD*   21,407
Mrs M. Daly, *C.*   20,133
D. Kraft, *Lab.*   9,557
T. Sewell, *Ref.*   2,280
LD majority 1,274
(Boundary change: notional C.)

WIGAN
*E.*64,689   *T.*67.74%
†R. Stott, *Lab.*   30,043
M. Loveday, *C.*   7,400
T. Beswick, *LD*   4,390
A. Bradborne, *Ref.*   1,450
C. Maile, *Green*   442
W. Ayliffe, *NLP*   94
Lab. majority 22,643
(Boundary change: notional Lab.)

WILTSHIRE NORTH
*E.*77,237   *T.*75.11%
J. Gray, *C.*   25,390
S. Cordon, *LD*   21,915
N. Knowles, *Lab.*   8,261
Ms M. Purves, *Ref.*   1,774
A. Wood, *UK Ind.*   410
Ms J. Forsyth, *NLP*   263
C. majority 3,475
(Boundary change: notional C.)

WIMBLEDON
*E.*64,070   *T.*75.47%
R. Casale, *Lab.*   20,674
*Dr C. Goodson-Wickes, *C.*   17,694
Ms A. Willott, *LD*   8,014
H. Abid, *Ref.*   993
R. Thacker, *Green*   474
Ms S. Davies, *ProLife*   346
M. Kirby, *Mongolian*   112
G. Stacey, *Dream*   47
Lab. majority 2,980
(April 1992, C. maj. 14,761)

WINCHESTER
*E.*78,884   *T.*78.66%
M. Oaten, *LD*   26,100
†G. Malone, *C.*   26,098
P. Davies, *Lab.*   6,528
P. Strand, *Ref.*   1,598
R. Huggett, *Top*   640
D. Rumsey, *UK Ind.*   476
J. Browne, *Ind. AFE*   307
P. Stockton, *Loony*   307
LD majority 2
(Boundary change: notional C.)
See also page 233

WINDSOR
*E.*69,132   *T.*73.46%
†M. Trend, *C.*   24,476
C. Fox, *LD*   14,559
Mrs A. Williams, *Lab.*   9,287
J. McDermott, *Ref.*   1,676
P. Bradshaw, *Lib.*   388
Mrs E. Bigg, *UK Ind.*   302
Mr R. Parr, *Dynamic*   93
C. majority 9,917
(Boundary change: notional C.)

WIRRAL SOUTH
*E.*59,372   *T.*81.01%
†B. Chapman, *Lab.*   24,499
L. Byrom, *C.*   17,495
P. Gilchrist, *LD*   5,018
D. Wilcox, *Ref.*   768
Ms J. Nielsen, *ProLife*   264
G. Mead, *NLP*   51
Lab. majority 7,004
(Boundary change: notional C.)

WIRRAL WEST
*E.*60,908   *T.*76.98%
S. Hesford, *Lab.*   21,035
*Rt. Hon. D. Hunt, *C.*   18,297
J. Thornton, *LD*   5,945
D. Wharton, *Ref.*   1,613
Lab. majority 2,738
(April 1992, C. maj. 11,064)

WITNEY
*E.*73,520   *T.*76.72%
S. Woodward, *C.*   24,282
A. Hollingsworth, *Lab.*   17,254
Mrs A. Lawrence, *LD*   11,202
G. Brown, *Ref.*   2,262
M. Montgomery, *UK Ind.*   765
Ms S. Chapple-Perrie, *Green*   636
C. majority 7,028
(Boundary change: notional C.)

WOKING
*E.*70,053   *T.*72.68%
H. Malins, *C.*   19,553
P. Goldenberg, *LD*   13,875
Ms K. Hanson, *Lab.*   10,695
H. Bell, *Ind. C.*   3,933
C. Skeate, *Ref.*   2,209
M. Harvey, *UK Ind.*   512
Miss D. Sleeman, *NLP*   137
C. majority 5,678
(Boundary change: notional C.)

WOKINGHAM
*E.*66,161   *T.*75.74%
†Rt. Hon. J. Redwood, *C.*   25,086
Dr R. Longton, *LD*   15,721
Ms P. Colling, *Lab.*   8,424
P. Owen, *Loony*   877
C. majority 9,365
(Boundary change: notional C.)

WOLVERHAMPTON NORTH EAST
*E.*61,642   *T.*67.17%
K. Purchase, *Lab. Co-op.*   24,534
D. Harvey, *C.*   11,547
B. Niblett, *LD*   2,214
C. Hallmark, *Lib.*   1,560
A. Muchall, *Ref.*   1,192
M. Wingfield, *Nat. Dem.*   356
Lab. Co-op. majority 12,987

WOLVERHAMPTON SOUTH EAST
E.54,291   T.64.15%
*D. Turner, *Lab. Co-op.*		22,202
W. Hanbury, *C.*		7,020
R. Whitehouse, *LD*		3,292
T. Stevenson-Platt, *Ref.*		980
N. Worth, *Soc. Lab.*		689
K. Bullman, *Lib.*		647

Lab. Co-op. majority 15,182
(April 1992, Lab. maj. 10,240)

WOLVERHAMPTON SOUTH WEST
E.67,482   T.72.49%
Ms J. Jones, *Lab.*		24,657
*N. Budgen, *C.*		19,539
M. Green, *LD*		4,012
M. Hyde, *Lib.*		713

Lab. majority 5,118
(April 1992, C. maj. 4,966)

WOODSPRING
E.69,964   T.78.51%
†Dr L. Fox, *C.*		24,425
Mrs N. Kirsen, *LD*		16,691
Ms D. Sander, *Lab.*		11,377
R. Hughes, *Ref.*		1,614
Dr R. Lawson, *Green*		667
A. Glover, *Ind.*		101
M. Mears, *NLP*		52

C. majority 7,734
(Boundary change: notional C.)

WORCESTER
E.69,234   T.74.56%
M. Foster, *Lab.*		25,848
N. Bourne, *C.*		18,423
P. Chandler, *LD*		6,462
Mrs P. Wood, *UK Ind.*		886

Lab. majority 7,425
(Boundary change: notional C.)

WORCESTERSHIRE MID
E.68,381   T.74.32%
†P. Luff, *C.*		24,092
Mrs D. Smith, *Lab.*		14,680
D. Barwick, *LD*		9,458
T. Watson, *Ref.*		1,780
D. Ingles, *UK Ind.*		646
A. Dyer, *NLP*		163

C. majority 9,412
(Boundary change: notional C.)

WORCESTERSHIRE WEST
E.64,712   T.76.25%
†Sir M. Spicer, *C.*		22,223
M. Hadley, *LD*		18,377

N. Stone, *Lab.*		7,738
Ms S. Cameron, *Green*		1,006

C. majority 3,846
(Boundary change: notional C.)

WORKINGTON
E.65,766   T.75.08%
†D. Campbell-Savours, *Lab.*		31,717
R. Blunden, *C.*		12,061
P. Roberts, *LD*		3,967
G. Donnan, *Ref.*		1,412
C. Austin, *UA*		217

Lab. majority 19,656
(Boundary change: notional Lab.)

WORSLEY
E.68,978   T.67.82%
†T. Lewis, *Lab.*		29,083
D. Garrido, *C.*		11,342
R. Bleakley, *LD*		6,356

Lab. majority 17,741
(Boundary change: notional Lab.)

WORTHING EAST AND SHOREHAM
E.70,771   T.72.87%
T. Loughton, *C.*		20,864
M. King, *LD*		15,766
M. Williams, *Lab.*		12,335
J. McCulloch, *Ref.*		1,683
Mrs R. Jarvis, *UK Ind.*		921

C. majority 5,098
(Boundary change: notional C.)

WORTHING WEST
E.71,329   T.72.12%
†P. Bottomley, *C.*		23,733
C. Hare, *LD*		16,020
J. Adams, *Lab.*		8,347
N. John, *Ref.*		2,313
T. Cross, *UK Ind.*		1,029

C. majority 7,713
(Boundary change: notional C.)

WREKIN, THE
E.59,126   T.76.56%
P. Bradley, *Lab.*		21,243
P. Bruinvels, *C.*		18,218
I. Jenkins, *LD*		5,807

Lab. majority 3,025
(Boundary change: notional C.)

WYCOMBE
E.73,589   T.71.10%
†Sir R. Whitney, *C.*		20,890
C. Bryant, *Lab.*		18,520
P. Bensilum, *LD*		9,678
A. Fulford, *Ref.*		2,394
J. Laker, *Green*		716
M. Heath, *NLP*		121

C. majority 2,370
(Boundary change: notional C.)

WYRE FOREST
E.73,063   T.75.35%
D. Lock, *Lab.*		26,843
†A. Coombs, *C.*		19,897
D. Cropp, *LD*		4,377
W. Till, *Ref.*		1,956
C. Harvey, *Lib.*		1,670
J. Millington, *UK Ind.*		312

Lab. majority 6,946
(Boundary change: notional C.)

WYTHENSHAWE AND SALE EAST
E.71,986   T.63.25%
P. Goggins, *Lab.*		26,448
P. Fleming, *C.*		11,429
Ms V. Tucker, *LD*		5,639
B. Stanyer, *Ref.*		1,060
J. Flannery, *Soc. Lab.*		957

Lab. majority 15,019
(Boundary change: notional Lab.)

YEOVIL
E.74,165   T.72.88%
†Rt. Hon. J. D. D. Ashdown, *LD*		26,349
N. Cambrook, *C.*		14,946
P. Conway, *Lab.*		8,053
J. Beveridge, *Ref.*		3,574
D. Taylor, *Green*		728
J. Archer, *Musician*		306
C. Hudson, *Dream*		97

LD majority 11,403
(Boundary change: notional LD)

YORK, CITY OF
E.79,383   T.73.50%
*H. Bayley, *Lab.*		34,956
S. Mallett, *C.*		14,433
A. Waller, *LD*		6,537
J. Sheppard, *Ref.*		1,083
M. Hill, *Green*		880
E. Wegener, *UK Ind.*		319
A. Lightfoot, *Ch. Nat.*		137

Lab. majority 20,523
(April 1992, Lab. maj. 6,342)

YORKSHIRE EAST
E.69,409   T.70.55%
†J. Townend, *C.*		20,904
I. Male, *Lab.*		17,567
D. Leadley, *LD*		9,070
R. Allerston, *Soc. Dem.*		1,049
M. Cooper, *Nat. Dem.*		381

C. majority 3,337
(Boundary change: notional C.)

WALES

ABERAVON
E.50,025   T.71.89%
*Rt. Hon. J. Morris, *Lab.*		25,650
R. McConville, *LD*		4,079
P. Harper, *C.*		2,835
P. Cockwell, *PC*		2,088
P. David, *Ref.*		970
Capt. Beany, *Beanus*		341

Lab. majority 21,571
(April 1992, Lab. maj. 21,310)

ALYN AND DEESIDE
E.58,091   T.72.21%
†B. Jones, *Lab.*		25,955
T. Roberts, *C.*		9,552
Mrs E. Burnham, *LD*		4,076
M. Jones, *Ref.*		1,627

Mrs S. Hills, *PC*		738

Lab. majority 16,403
(Boundary change: notional Lab.)

BLAENAU GWENT
E.54,800   T.72.32%
*L. Smith, *Lab.*		31,493
Mrs G. Layton, *LD*		3,458
Mrs M. Williams, *C.*		2,607

J. Criddle, *PC* 2,072
Lab. majority 28,035
(April 1992, Lab. maj. 30,067)

BRECON AND RADNORSHIRE
*E.*52,142   *T.*82.24%
R. Livsey, *LD* 17,516
*J. Evans, *C.* 12,419
C. Mann, *Lab.* 11,424
Ms E. Phillips, *Ref.* 900
S. Cornelius, *PC* 622
LD majority 5,097
(April 1992, C. maj. 130)

BRIDGEND
*E.*59,721   *T.*72.44%
*W. Griffiths, *Lab.* 25,115
D. Davies, *C.* 9,867
A. McKinlay, *LD* 4,968
T. Greaves, *Ref.* 1,662
D. Watkins, *PC* 1,649
Lab. majority 15,248
(April 1992, Lab. maj. 7,326)

CAERNARFON
*E.*46,815   *T.*72.65%
*D. Wigley, *PC* 17,616
E. Williams, *Lab.* 9,667
E. Williams, *C.* 4,230
Ms M. McQueen, *LD* 1,686
C. Collins, *Ref.* 811
PC majority 7,949
(April 1992, PC maj. 14,476)

CAERPHILLY
*E.*64,621   *T.*70.05%
*R. Davies, *Lab.* 30,697
R. Harris, *C.* 4,858
L. Whittle, *PC* 4,383
A. Ferguson, *LD* 3,724
M. Morgan, *Ref.* 1,337
Mrs C. Williams, *ProLife* 270
Lab. majority 25,839
(April 1992, Lab. maj. 22,672)

CARDIFF CENTRAL
*E.*60,354   *T.*70.01%
*J. Owen Jones, *Lab. Co-op.* 18,464
Mrs J. Randerson, *LD* 10,541
D. Melding, *C.* 8,470
T. Burns, *Soc. Lab.* 2,230
W. Vernon, *PC* 1,504
N. Lloyd, *Ref.* 760
C. James, *Loony* 204
A. Hobbs, *NLP* 80
Lab. Co-op. majority 7,923
(April 1992, Lab. maj. 3,465)

CARDIFF NORTH
*E.*60,430   *T.*80.24%
Ms J. Morgan, *Lab.* 24,460
*G. Jones, *C.* 16,334
R. Rowland, *LD* 5,294
Dr C. Palfrey, *PC* 1,201
E. Litchfield, *Ref.* 1,199
Lab. majority 8,126
(April 1992, C. maj. 2,969)

CARDIFF SOUTH AND PENARTH
*E.*61,838   *T.*68.57%
*A. Michael, *Lab. Co-op.* 22,647
Mrs C. Roberts, *C.* 8,766
Dr S. Wakefield, *LD* 3,964

J. Foreman, *New Lab.* 3,942
D. Haswell, *PC* 1,356
P. Morgan, *Ref.* 1,211
M. Shepherd, *Soc.* 344
Ms B. Caves, *NLP* 170
Lab. Co-op. majority 13,881
(April 1992, Lab. maj. 10,425)

CARDIFF WEST
*E.*58,198   *T.*69.21%
†R. Morgan, *Lab.* 24,297
S. Hoare, *C.* 8,669
Ms J. Gasson, *LD* 4,366
Ms G. Carr, *PC* 1,949
T. Johns, *Ref.* 996
Lab. majority 15,628
(Boundary change: notional Lab.)

CARMARTHEN EAST AND DINEFWR
*E.*53,079   *T.*78.62%
†Dr A. Wynne Williams, *Lab.* 17,907
R. Thomas, *PC* 14,457
E. Hayward, *C.* 5,022
Mrs J. Hughes, *LD* 3,150
I. Humphreys-Evans, *Ref.* 1,196
Lab. majority 3,450
(Boundary change: notional Lab.)

CARMARTHEN WEST AND
PEMBROKESHIRE SOUTH
*E.*55,724   *T.*76.52%
†N. Ainger, *Lab.* 20,956
O. J. Williams, *C.* 11,335
R. Llewellyn, *PC* 5,402
K. Evans, *LD* 3,516
Mrs J. Poirrier, *Ref.* 1,432
Lab. majority 9,621
(Boundary change: notional Lab.)

CEREDIGION
*E.*54,378   *T.*73.90%
†C. Dafis, *PC* 16,728
R. Harris, *Lab.* 9,767
D. Davies, *LD* 6,616
Dr F. Aubel, *C.* 5,983
J. Leaney, *Ref.* 1,092
PC majority 6,961
(Boundary change: notional PC)

CLWYD SOUTH
*E.*53,495   *T.*73.62%
†M. Jones, *Lab.* 22,901
B. Johnson, *C.* 9,091
A. Chadwick, *LD* 3,684
G. Williams, *PC* 2,500
A. Lewis, *Ref.* 1,207
Lab. majority 13,810
(Boundary change: notional Lab.)

CLWYD WEST
*E.*53,467   *T.*75.29%
G. Thomas, *Lab.* 14,918
†R. Richards, *C.* 13,070
E. Williams, *PC* 5,421
G. Williams, *LD* 5,151
Ms H. Collins, *Ref.* 1,114
D. Neal, *Cvty* 583
Lab. majority 1,848
(Boundary change: notional C.)

CONWY
*E.*55,092   *T.*75.44%
Mrs B. Williams, *Lab.* 14,561

R. Roberts, *LD* 12,965
D. Jones, *C.* 10,085
R. Davies, *PC* 2,844
A. Barham, *Ref.* 760
R. Bradley, *Alt. LD* 250
D. Hughes, *NLP* 95
Lab. majority 1,596
(April 1992, C. maj. 995)

CYNON VALLEY
*E.*48,286   *T.*69.22%
*Mrs A. Clwyd, *Lab.* 23,307
A. Davies, *PC* 3,552
H. Price, *LD* 3,459
A. Smith, *C.* 2,262
G. John, *Ref.* 844
Lab. majority 19,755
(April 1992, Lab. maj. 21,364)

DELYN
*E.*53,693   *T.*74.02%
†D. Hanson, *Lab.* 22,300
Mrs K. Lumley, *C.* 10,607
P. Lloyd, *LD* 4,160
A. Drake, *PC* 1,558
Ms E. Soutter, *Ref.* 1,117
Lab. majority 11,693
(Boundary change: notional Lab.)

GOWER
*E.*57,691   *T.*75.12%
M. Caton, *Lab.* 23,313
A. Cairns, *C.* 10,306
H. Evans, *LD* 5,624
E. Williams, *PC* 2,226
R. Lewis, *Ref.* 1,745
A. Popham, *FP* 122
Lab. majority 13,007
(April 1992, Lab. maj. 7,018)

ISLWYN
*E.*50,540   *T.*72.03%
*D. Touhig, *Lab. Co-op.* 26,995
C. Worker, *LD* 3,064
R. Walters, *C.* 2,864
D. Jones, *PC* 2,272
Mrs S. Monaghan, *Ref.* 1,209
Lab. Co-op. majority 23,931
(April 1992, Lab. maj. 24,728)
(Feb. 1995, Lab. maj. 13,097)

LLANELLI
*E.*58,323   *T.*70.66%
†Rt. Hon. D. Davies, *Lab.* 23,851
M. Phillips, *PC* 7,812
A. Hayes, *C.* 5,003
N. Burree, *LD* 3,788
J. Willock, *Soc. Lab.* 757
Lab. majority 16,039
(Boundary change: notional Lab.)

MEIRIONNYDD NANT CONWY
*E.*32,345   *T.*75.98%
*E. Llwyd, *PC* 12,465
H. Rees, *Lab.* 5,660
J. Quin, *C.* 3,922
Mrs B. Feeley, *LD* 1,719
P. Hodge, *Ref.* 809
PC majority 6,805
(April 1992, PC maj. 4,613)

MERTHYR TYDFIL AND RHYMNEY
*E.*56,507   *T.*69.27%

*T. Rowlands, *Lab.* 30,012
D. Anstey, *LD* 2,926
J. Morgan, *C.* 2,508
A. Cox, *PC* 2,344
A. Cowdell, *Old Lab.* 691
R. Hutchings, *Ref.* 660
Lab. majority 27,086
(April 1992, Lab. maj. 26,713)

MONMOUTH
E.60,703   T.80.76%
H. Edwards, *Lab.* 23,404
*R. Evans, *C.* 19,226
M. Williams, *LD* 4,689
N. Warry, *Ref.* 1,190
A. Cotton, *PC* 516
Lab. majority 4,178
(April 1992, C. maj. 3,204)

MONTGOMERYSHIRE
E.42,618   T.74.91%
L. Opik, *LD* 14,647
G. Davies, *C.* 8,344
Ms A. Davies, *Lab.* 6,109
Ms H. M. Jones, *PC* 1,608
J. Bufton, *Ref.* 879
Ms S. Walker, *Green* 338
LD majority 6,303
(April 1992, LD maj. 5,209)

NEATH
E.55,525   T.74.28%
*P. Hain, *Lab.* 30,324
D. Evans, *C.* 3,583
T. Jones, *PC* 3,344
F. Little, *LD* 2,597
P. Morris, *Ref.* 975
H. Marks, *LCP* 420
Lab. majority 26,741
(April 1992, Lab. maj. 23,975)

NEWPORT EAST
E.50,997   T.73.06%
†A. Howarth, *Lab.* 21,481
D. Evans, *C.* 7,958
A. Cameron, *LD* 3,880
A. Scargill, *Soc. Lab.* 1,951
G. Davis, *Ref.* 1,267
C. Holland, *PC* 721
Lab. majority 13,523
(April 1992, Lab. maj. 9,899)

NEWPORT WEST
E.53,914   T.74.57%
*P. Flynn, *Lab.* 24,331
P. Clarke, *C.* 9,794
S. Wilson, *LD* 3,907
C. Thompsett, *Ref.* 1,199
H. Jackson, *PC* 648
H. Moelwyn Hughes, *UK Ind.* 323

Lab. majority 14,537
(April 1992, Lab. maj. 7,779)

OGMORE
E.52,078   T.73.10%
*Sir R. Powell, *Lab.* 28,163
D. Unwin, *C.* 3,716
Ms K. Williams, *LD* 3,510
J. Rogers, *PC* 2,679
Lab. majority 24,447
(April 1992, Lab. maj. 23,827)

PONTYPRIDD
E.64,185   T.71.44%
*Dr K. Howells, *Lab.* 29,290
N. Howells, *LD* 6,161
J. Cowen, *C.* 5,910
O. Llewelyn, *PC* 2,977
J. Wood, *Ref.* 874
P. Skelly, *Soc. Lab.* 380
R. Griffiths, *Comm. P.* 178
A. Moore, *NLP* 85
Lab. majority 23,129
(April 1992, Lab. maj. 19,797)

PRESELI PEMBROKESHIRE
E.54,088   T.78.40%
Mrs J. Lawrence, *Lab.* 20,477
R. Buckland, *C.* 11,741
J. Clarke, *LD* 5,527
A. Lloyd Jones, *PC* 2,683
D. Berry, *Ref.* 1,574
Ms M. Scott Cato, *Green* 401
Lab. majority 8,736
(Boundary change: notional C.)

RHONDDA
E.57,105   T.71.46%
*A. Rogers, *Lab.* 30,381
Ms L. Wood, *PC* 5,450
Dr R. Berman, *LD* 2,307
S. Whiting, *C.* 1,551
S. Gardiner, *Ref.* 658
K. Jakeway, *Green* 460
Lab. majority 24,931
(April 1992, Lab. maj. 28,816)

SWANSEA EAST
E.57,373   T.67.41%
*D. Anderson, *Lab.* 29,151
Ms C. Dibble, *C.* 3,582
E. Jones, *LD* 3,440
Ms M. Pooley, *PC* 1,308
Ms C. Maggs, *Ref.* 904
R. Job, *Soc.* 289
Lab. majority 25,569
(April 1992, Lab. maj. 23,482)

SWANSEA WEST
E.58,703   T.68.94%

*Rt. Hon. A. Williams, *Lab.* 22,748
A. Baker, *C.* 8,289
J. Newbury, *LD* 5,872
D. Lloyd, *PC* 2,675
D. Proctor, *Soc. Lab.* 885
Lab. majority 14,459
(April 1992, Lab. maj. 9,478)

TORFAEN
E.60,343   T.71.67%
*P. Murphy, *Lab.* 29,863
N. Parish, *C.* 5,327
Ms J. Gray, *LD* 5,249
Ms D. Holler, *Ref.* 1,245
R. Gough, *PC* 1,042
R. Coghill, *Green* 519
Lab. majority 24,536
(April 1992, Lab. maj. 20,754)

VALE OF CLWYD
E.52,418   T.74.65%
C. Ruane, *Lab.* 20,617
D. Edwards, *C.* 11,662
D. Munford, *LD* 3,425
Ms G. Kensler, *PC* 2,301
S. Vickers, *Ref.* 834
S. Cooke, *UK Ind.* 293
Lab. majority 8,955
(Boundary change: notional C.)

VALE OF GLAMORGAN
E.67,213   T.80.21%
J. Smith, *Lab.* 29,054
†W. Sweeney, *C.* 18,522
Mrs S. Campbell, *LD* 4,945
Ms M. Corp, *PC* 1,393
Lab. majority 10,532
(Boundary change: notional C.)

WREXHAM
E.50,741   T.71.78%
Dr J. Marek, *Lab.* 20,450
S. Andrew, *C.* 8,688
A. Thomas, *LD* 4,833
J. Cronk, *Ref.* 1,195
K. Plant, *PC* 1,170
N. Low, *NLP* 86
Lab. majority 11,762
(Boundary change: notional Lab.)

YNYS MÔN
E.52,952   T.75.41%
*I. Wyn Jones, *PC* 15,756
O. Edwards, *Lab.* 13,275
G. Owen, *C.* 8,569
D. Burnham, *LD* 1,537
H. Gray Morris, *Ref.* 793
PC majority 2,481
(April 1992, PC maj. 1,106)

SCOTLAND

ABERDEEN CENTRAL
E.54,257   T.65.64%
F. Doran, *Lab.* 17,745
Mrs J. Wisely, *C.* 6,944
B. Topping, *SNP* 5,767
J. Brown, *LD* 4,714
J. Farquharson, *Ref.* 446

Lab. majority 10,801
(Boundary change: notional Lab.)

ABERDEEN NORTH
E.54,302   T.70.74%
M. Savidge, *Lab.* 18,389
B. Adam, *SNP* 8,379
J. Gifford, *C.* 5,763

M. Rumbles, *LD* 5,421
A. Mackenzie, *Ref.* 463
Lab. majority 10,010
(Boundary change: notional Lab.)

ABERDEEN SOUTH
E.60,490   T.72.84%
Ms A. Begg, *Lab.* 15,541

N. Stephen, *LD* 12,176
†R. Robertson, *C.* 11,621
J. Towers, *SNP* 4,299
R. Wharton, *Ref.* 425
Lab. majority 3,365
(Boundary change: notional C.)

**ABERDEENSHIRE WEST AND
KINCARDINE**
*E.*59,123   *T.*73.05%
Sir R. Smith, *LD* 17,742
†G. Kynoch, *C.* 15,080
Ms J. Mowatt, *SNP* 5,639
Ms Q. Khan, *Lab.* 3,923
S. Ball, *Ref.* 805
LD majority 2,662
(Boundary change: notional C.)

AIRDRIE AND SHOTTS
*E.*57,673   *T.*71.40%
†Mrs H. Liddell, *Lab.* 25,460
K. Robertson, *SNP* 10,048
Dr N. Brook, *C.* 3,660
R. Wolseley, *LD* 1,719
C. Semple, *Ref.* 294
Lab. majority 15,412
(Boundary change: notional Lab.)

ANGUS
*E.*59,708   *T.*72.14%
†A. Welsh, *SNP* 20,792
S. Leslie, *C.* 10,603
Ms C. Taylor, *Lab.* 6,733
Dr R. Speirs, *LD* 4,065
B. Taylor, *Ref.* 883
SNP majority 10,189
(Boundary change: notional SNP)

ARGYLL AND BUTE
*E.*49,451   *T.*72.23%
*Mrs R. Michie, *LD* 14,359
Prof. N. MacCormick, *SNP* 8,278
R. Leishman, *C.* 6,774
A. Syed, *Lab.* 5,596
M. Stewart, *Ref.* 713
LD majority 6,081
(April 1992, LD maj. 2,622)

AYR
*E.*55,829   *T.*80.17%
Mrs S. Osborne, *Lab.* 21,679
†P. Gallie, *C.* 15,136
I. Blackford, *SNP* 5,625
Miss C. Hamblen, *LD* 2,116
J. Enos, *Ref.* 200
Lab. majority 6,543
(Boundary change: notional Lab.)

BANFF AND BUCHAN
*E.*58,493   *T.*68.69%
†A. Salmond, *SNP* 22,409
W. Frain-Bell, *C.* 9,564
Ms M. Harris, *Lab.* 4,747
N. Fletcher, *LD* 2,398
A. Buchan, *Ref.* 1,060
SNP majority 12,845
(Boundary change: notional SNP)

**CAITHNESS, SUTHERLAND AND
EASTER ROSS**
*E.*41,566   *T.*70.18%
†R. Maclennan, *LD* 10,381
J. Hendry, *Lab.* 8,122

E. Harper, *SNP* 6,710
T. Miers, *C.* 3,148
Ms C. Ryder, *Ref.* 369
J. Martin, *Green* 230
M. Carr, *UK Ind.* 212
LD majority 2,259
(Boundary change: notional LD)

**CARRICK, CUMNOCK AND DOON
VALLEY**
*E.*65,593   *T.*74.96%
†G. Foulkes, *Lab. Co-op.* 29,398
A. Marshall, *C.* 8,336
Mrs C. Hutchison, *SNP* 8,190
D. Young, *LD* 2,613
J. Higgins, *Ref.* 634
Lab. Co-op. majority 21,062
(Boundary change: notional Lab. Co-op.)

CLYDEBANK AND MILNGAVIE
*E.*52,092   *T.*75.03%
†A. Worthington, *Lab.* 21,583
J. Yuill, *SNP* 8,263
Ms N. Morgan, *C.* 4,885
K. Moody, *LD* 4,086
I. Sanderson, *Ref.* 269
Lab. majority 13,320
(Boundary change: notional Lab.)

CLYDESDALE
*E.*63,428   *T.*71.60%
*J. Hood, *Lab.* 23,859
A. Doig, *SNP* 10,050
M. Izatt, *C.* 7,396
Mrs S. Grieve, *LD* 3,796
K. Smith, *BNP* 311
Lab. majority 13,809
(April 1992, Lab. maj. 10,187)

COATBRIDGE AND CHRYSTON
*E.*52,024   *T.*72.30%
†T. Clarke, *Lab.* 25,697
B. Nugent, *SNP* 6,402
A. Wauchope, *C.* 3,216
Mrs M. Daly, *LD* 2,048
B. Bowsley, *Ref.* 249
Lab. majority 19,295
(Boundary change: notional Lab.)

CUMBERNAULD AND KILSYTH
*E.*48,032   *T.*75.00%
Ms R. McKenna, *Lab.* 21,141
C. Barrie, *SNP* 10,013
I. Sewell, *C.* 2,441
J. Biggam, *LD* 1,368
Ms J Kara, *ProLife* 609
K. McEwan, *SSA* 345
Ms P. Cook, *Ref.* 107
Lab. majority 11,128
(April 1992, Lab. maj. 9,215)

CUNNINGHAME NORTH
*E.*55,526   *T.*74.07%
*B. Wilson, *Lab.* 20,686
Mrs M. Mitchell, *C.* 9,647
Ms K. Nicoll, *SNP* 7,584
Ms K. Freel, *LD* 2,271
Ms L. McDaid, *Soc. Lab.* 501
I. Winton, *Ref.* 440
Lab. majority 11,039
(April 1992, Lab. maj. 2,939)

CUNNINGHAME SOUTH
*E.*49,543   *T.*71.54%
*B. Donohoe, *Lab.* 22,233
Mrs M. Burgess, *SNP* 7,364
Mrs P. Paterson, *C.* 3,571
E. Watson, *LD* 1,604
K. Edwin, *Soc. Lab.* 494
A. Martlew, *Ref.* 178
Lab. majority 14,869
(April 1992, Lab. maj. 10,680)

DUMBARTON
*E.*56,229   *T.*73.39%
*J. McFall, *Lab. Co-op.* 20,470
W. Mackechnie, *SNP* 9,587
P. Ramsay, *C.* 7,283
A. Reid, *LD* 3,144
L. Robertson, *SSA* 283
G. Dempster, *Ref.* 255
D. Lancaster, *UK Ind.* 242
Lab. Co-op. majority 10,883
(April 1992, Lab. maj. 6,129)

DUMFRIES
*E.*62,759   *T.*78.92%
R. Brown, *Lab.* 23,528
S. Stevenson, *C.* 13,885
R. Higgins, *SNP* 5,977
N. Wallace, *LD* 5,487
D. Parker, *Ref.* 533
Ms E. Hunter, *NLP* 117
Lab. majority 9,643
(Boundary change: notional C.)

DUNDEE EAST
*E.*58,388   *T.*69.41%
†J. McAllion, *Lab.* 20,718
Ms S. Robison, *SNP* 10,757
B. Mackie, *C.* 6,397
Dr G. Saluja, *LD* 1,677
E. Galloway, *Ref.* 601
H. Duke, *SSA* 232
Ms E. MacKenzie, *NLP* 146
Lab. majority 9,961
(Boundary change: notional Lab.)

DUNDEE WEST
*E.*57,346   *T.*67.67%
†E. Ross, *Lab.* 20,875
J. Dorward, *SNP* 9,016
N. Powrie, *C.* 5,105
Dr E. Dick, *LD* 2,972
Ms M. Ward, *SSA* 428
J. MacMillan, *Ref.* 411
Lab. majority 11,859
(Boundary change: notional Lab.)

DUNFERMLINE EAST
*E.*52,072   *T.*70.25%
†Rt. Hon. G. Brown, *Lab.* 24,441
J. Ramage, *SNP* 5,690
I. Mitchell, *C.* 3,656
J. Tolson, *LD* 2,164
T. Dunsmore, *Ref.* 632
Lab. majority 18,751
(Boundary change: notional Lab.)

DUNFERMLINE WEST
*E.*52,467   *T.*69.44%
†Ms R. Squire, *Lab.* 19,338
J. Lloyd, *SNP* 6,984
Mrs E. Harris, *LD* 4,963
K. Newton, *C.* 4,606

J. Bain, *Ref.* 543
Lab. majority 12,354
(Boundary change: notional Lab.)

EAST KILBRIDE
*E.*65,229   *T.*74.81%
†A. Ingram, *Lab.* 27,584
G. Gebbie, *SNP* 10,200
C. Herbertson, *C.* 5,863
Mrs K. Philbrick, *LD* 3,527
J. Deighan, *ProLife* 1,170
Ms J. Gray, *Ref.* 306
E. Gilmour, *NLP* 146
Lab. majority 17,384
(Boundary change: notional Lab.)

EAST LOTHIAN
*E.*57,441   *T.*75.61%
†J. Home Robertson, *Lab.* 22,881
M. Fraser, *C.* 8,660
D. McCarthy, *SNP* 6,825
Ms A. MacAskill, *LD* 4,575
N. Nash, *Ref.* 491
Lab. majority 14,221
(Boundary change: notional Lab.)

EASTWOOD
*E.*66,697   *T.*78.32%
J. Murphy, *Lab.* 20,766
P. Cullen, *C.* 17,530
D. Yates, *SNP* 6,826
Dr C. Mason, *LD* 6,110
D. Miller, *Ref.* 497
Dr M. Tayan, *ProLife* 393
D. McPherson, *UK Ind.* 113
Lab. majority 3,236
(Boundary change: notional C.)

EDINBURGH CENTRAL
*E.*63,695   *T.*67.09%
†A. Darling, *Lab.* 20,125
M. Scott-Hayward, *C.* 9,055
Ms F. Hyslop, *SNP* 6,750
Ms K. Utting, *LD* 5,605
Ms L. Hendry, *Green* 607
A. Skinner, *Ref.* 495
M. Benson, *Ind. Dem.* 98
Lab. majority 11,070
(Boundary change: notional Lab.)

EDINBURGH EAST AND
MUSSELBURGH
*E.*59,648   *T.*70.61%
†Dr G. Strang, *Lab.* 22,564
D. White, *SNP* 8,034
K. Ward, *C.* 6,483
Dr C. MacKellar, *LD* 4,511
J. Sibbet, *Ref.* 526
Lab. majority 14,530
(Boundary change: notional Lab.)

EDINBURGH NORTH AND LEITH
*E.*61,617   *T.*66.45%
†M. Chisholm, *Lab.* 19,209
Ms A. Dana, *SNP* 8,231
E. Stewart, *C.* 7,312
Ms H. Campbell, *LD* 5,335
A. Graham, *Ref.* 441
G. Brown, *SSA* 320
P. Douglas-Reid, *NLP* 97
Lab. majority 10,978
(Boundary change: notional Lab.)

EDINBURGH PENTLANDS
*E.*59,635   *T.*76.70%
Ms L. Clark, *Lab.* 19,675
†Rt. Hon. M. Rifkind, *C.* 14,813
S. Gibb, *SNP* 5,952
Dr J. Dawe, *LD* 4,575
M. McDonald, *Ref.* 422
R. Harper, *Green* 224
A. McConnachie, *UK Ind.* 81
Lab. majority 4,862
(Boundary change: notional C.)

EDINBURGH SOUTH
*E.*62,467   *T.*71.78%
†N. Griffiths, *Lab.* 20,993
Miss E. Smith, *C.* 9,541
M. Pringle, *LD* 7,911
Dr J. Hargreaves, *SNP* 5,791
I. McLean, *Ref.* 504
B. Dunn, *NLP* 98
Lab. majority 11,452
(Boundary change: notional Lab.)

EDINBURGH WEST
*E.*61,133   *T.*77.91%
D. Gorrie, *LD* 20,578
†Rt. Hon. Lord J. Douglas-
Hamilton, *C.* 13,325
Ms L. Hinds, *Lab.* 8,948
G. Sutherland, *SNP* 4,210
Dr S. Elphick, *Ref.* 277
P. Coombes, *Lib.* 263
A. Jack, *AS* 30
LD majority 7,253
(Boundary change: notional C.)

FALKIRK EAST
*E.*56,792   *T.*73.24%
†M. Connarty, *Lab.* 23,344
K. Brown, *SNP* 9,959
M. Nicol, *C.* 5,813
R. Spillane, *LD* 2,153
S. Mowbray, *Ref.* 326
Lab. majority 13,385
(Boundary change: notional Lab.)

FALKIRK WEST
*E.*52,850   *T.*72.60%
†D. Canavan, *Lab.* 22,772
D. Alexander, *SNP* 8,989
Mrs C. Buchanan, *C.* 4,639
D. Houston, *LD* 1,970
Lab. majority 13,783
(Boundary change: notional Lab.)

FIFE CENTRAL
*E.*58,315   *T.*69.90%
†H. McLeish, *Lab.* 23,912
Mrs P. Marwick, *SNP* 10,199
J. Rees-Mogg, *C.* 3,669
R. Laird, *LD* 2,610
J. Scrymgeour-Wedderburn, *Ref.* 375
Lab. majority 13,713
(Boundary change: notional Lab.)

FIFE NORTH EAST
*E.*58,794   *T.*71.16%
*M. Campbell, *LD* 21,432
A. Bruce, *C.* 11,076
C. Welsh, *SNP* 4,545
C. Milne, *Lab.* 4,301
W. Stewart, *Ref.* 485

LD majority 10,356
(Boundary change: notional LD)

GALLOWAY AND UPPER NITHSDALE
*E.*52,751   *T.*79.65%
A. Morgan, *SNP* 18,449
†Rt. Hon. I. Lang, *C.* 12,825
Ms K. Clark, *Lab.* 6,861
J. McKerchar, *LD* 2,700
R. Wood, *Ind.* 566
A. Kennedy, *Ref.* 428
J. Smith, *UK Ind.* 189
SNP majority 5,624
(Boundary change: notional C.)

GLASGOW ANNIESLAND
*E.*52,955   *T.*63.98%
†Rt. Hon. D. Dewar, *Lab.* 20,951
Dr W. Wilson, *SNP* 5,797
A. Brocklehurst, *C.* 3,881
C. McGinty, *LD* 2,453
A. Majid, *ProLife* 374
W. Bonnar, *SSA* 229
A. Milligan, *UK Ind.* 86
Ms G. McKay, *Ref.* 84
T. Pringle, *NLP* 24
Lab. majority 15,154
(Boundary change: notional Lab.)

GLASGOW BAILLIESTON
*E.*51,152   *T.*62.27%
†J. Wray, *Lab.* 20,925
Mrs P. Thomson, *SNP* 6,085
M. Kelly, *C.* 2,468
Ms S. Rainger, *LD* 1,217
J. McVicar, *SSA* 970
J. McClafferty, *Ref.* 188
Lab. majority 14,840
(Boundary change: notional Lab.)

GLASGOW CATHCART
*E.*49,312   *T.*69.17%
†J. Maxton, *Lab.* 19,158
Ms M. Whitehead, *SNP* 6,913
A. Muir, *C.* 4,248
C. Dick, *LD* 2,302
Ms Z. Indyk, *ProLife* 687
R. Stevenson, *SSA* 458
S. Haldane, *Ref.* 344
Lab. majority 12,245
(Boundary change: notional Lab.)

GLASGOW GOVAN
*E.*49,836   *T.*64.70%
M. Sarwar, *Lab.* 14,216
Ms N. Sturgeon, *SNP* 11,302
W. Thomas, *C.* 2,839
R. Stewart, *LD* 1,915
A. McCombes, *SSA* 755
P. Paton, *SLU* 325
I. Badar, *SLI* 319
Z. J. Abbasi, *SCU* 221
K. MacDonald, *Ref.* 201
J. White, *BNP* 149
Lab. majority 2,914
(Boundary change: notional Lab.)

GLASGOW KELVIN
*E.*57,438   *T.*56.85%
†G. Galloway, *Lab.* 16,643
Ms S. White, *SNP* 6,978
Ms E. Buchanan, *LD* 4,629
D. McPhie, *C.* 3,539

A. Green, *SSA* — 386
R. Grigor, *Ref.* — 282
V. Vanni, *SPGB* — 102
G. Stidolph, *NLP* — 95
Lab. majority 9,665
(Boundary change: notional Lab.)

GLASGOW MARYHILL
*E.*52,523 *T.*56.59%
†Ms M. Fyfe, *Lab.* — 19,301
J. Wailes, *SNP* — 5,037
Ms E. Attwooll, *LD* — 2,119
S. Baldwin, *C.* — 1,747
Ms L. Blair, *NLP* — 651
Ms A. Baker, *SSA* — 409
J. Hanif, *ProLife* — 344
R. Paterson, *Ref.* — 77
S. Johnstone, *SEP* — 36
Lab. majority 14,264
(Boundary change: notional Lab.)

GLASGOW POLLOK
*E.*49,284 *T.*66.56%
†I. Davidson, *Lab. Co-op.* — 19,653
D. Logan, *SNP* — 5,862
T. Sheridan, *SSA* — 3,639
E. Hamilton, *C.* — 1,979
D. Jago, *LD* — 1,137
Ms M. Gott, *ProLife* — 380
D. Haldane, *Ref.* — 152
Lab. Co-op. majority 13,791
(Boundary change: notional Lab. Co-op.)

GLASGOW RUTHERGLEN
*E.*50,646 *T.*70.14%
†T. McAvoy, *Lab. Co-op.* — 20,430
I. Gray, *SNP* — 5,423
R. Brown, *LD* — 5,167
D. Campbell Bannerman, *C.* — 3,288
G. Easton, *Ind. Lab.* — 812
Ms R. Kane, *SSA* — 251
Ms J. Kerr, *Ref.* — 150
Lab. Co-op. majority 15,007
(Boundary change: notional Lab. Co-op.)

GLASGOW SHETTLESTON
*E.*47,990 *T.*55.87%
†D. Marshall, *Lab.* — 19,616
H. Hanif, *SNP* — 3,748
C. Simpson, *C.* — 1,484
Ms K. Hiles, *LD* — 1,061
Ms C. McVicar, *SSA* — 482
R. Currie, *BNP* — 191
T. Montguire, *Ref.* — 151
J. Graham, *WRP* — 80
Lab. majority 15,868
(Boundary change: notional Lab.)

GLASGOW SPRINGBURN
*E.*53,473 *T.*59.05%
†M. Martin, *Lab.* — 22,534
J. Brady, *SNP* — 5,208
M.Holdsworth, *C.* — 1,893
J. Alexander, *LD* — 1,349
J. Lawson, *SSA* — 407
A. Keating, *Ref.* — 186
Lab. majority 17,326
(Boundary change: notional Lab.)

GORDON
*E.*58,767 *T.*71.89%
†M. Bruce, *LD* — 17,999
J. Porter, *C.* — 11,002
R. Lochhead, *SNP* — 8,435
Ms L. Kirkhill, *Lab.* — 4,350
F. Pidcock, *Ref.* — 459
LD majority 6,997
(Boundary change: notional C.)

GREENOCK AND INVERCLYDE
*E.*48,818 *T.*71.05%
†Dr N. Godman, *Lab.* — 19,480
B. Goodall, *SNP* — 6,440
R. Ackland, *LD* — 4,791
H. Swire, *C.* — 3,976
Lab. majority 13,040
(Boundary change: notional Lab.)

HAMILTON NORTH AND BELLSHILL
*E.*53,607 *T.*70.88%
†Dr J. Reid, *Lab.* — 24,322
M. Matheson, *SNP* — 7,255
G. McIntosh, *C.* — 3,944
K. Legg, *LD* — 1,924
R. Conn, *Ref.* — 554
Lab. majority 17,067
(Boundary change: notional Lab.)

HAMILTON SOUTH
*E.*46,562 *T.*71.07%
†G. Robertson, *Lab.* — 21,709
I. Black, *SNP* — 5,831
R. Kilgour, *C.* — 2,858
R. Pitts, *LD* — 1,693
C. Gunn, *ProLife* — 684
S. Brown, *Ref.* — 316
Lab. majority 15,878
(Boundary change: notional Lab.)

INVERNESS EAST, NAIRN AND LOCHABER
*E.*65,701 *T.*72.71%
D. Stewart, *Lab.* — 16,187
F. Ewing, *SNP* — 13,848
S. Gallagher, *LD* — 8,364
Mrs M. Scanlon, *C.* — 8,355
Ms W. Wall, *Ref.* — 436
M. Falconer, *Green* — 354
D. Hart, *Ch. U.* — 224
Lab. majority 2,339
(Boundary change: notional LD)

KILMARNOCK AND LOUDOUN
*E.*61,376 *T.*77.24%
D. Browne, *Lab.* — 23,621
A. Neil, *SNP* — 16,365
D. Taylor, *C.* — 5,125
J. Stewart, *LD* — 1,891
W. Sneddon, *Ref.* — 284
W. Gilmour, *NLP* — 123
Lab. majority 7,256
(April 1992, Lab. maj. 6,979)

KIRKCALDY
*E.*52,186 *T.*67.02%
†L. Moonie, *Lab. Co-op.* — 18,730
S. Hosie, *SNP* — 8,020
Miss C. Black, *C.* — 4,779
J. Mainland, *LD* — 3,031
V. Baxter, *Ref.* — 413

Lab. Co-op. majority 10,710
(Boundary change: notional Lab. Co-op.)

LINLITHGOW
*E.*53,706 *T.*73.84%
†T. Dalyell, *Lab.* — 21,469
K. MacAskill, *SNP* — 10,631
T. Kerr, *C.* — 4,964
A. Duncan, *LD* — 2,331
K. Plomer, *Ref.* — 259
Lab. majority 10,838
(Boundary change: notional Lab.)

LIVINGSTON
*E.*60,296 *T.*71.04%
†Rt. Hon. R. Cook, *Lab.* — 23,510
P. Johnston, *SNP* — 11,763
H. Craigie Halkett, *C.* — 4,028
E. Hawthorn, *LD* — 2,876
Ms H. Campbell, *Ref.* — 444
M. Culbert, *SPGB* — 213
Lab. majority 11,747
(Boundary change: notional Lab.)

MIDLOTHIAN
*E.*47,552 *T.*74.13%
†E. Clarke, *Lab.* — 18,861
L. Millar, *SNP* — 8,991
Miss A. Harper, *C.* — 3,842
R. Pinnock, *LD* — 3,235
K. Docking, *Ref.* — 320
Lab. majority 9,870
(Boundary change: notional Lab.)

MORAY
*E.*58,302 *T.*68.21%
†Mrs M. Ewing, *SNP* — 16,529
A. Findlay, *C.* — 10,963
L. Macdonald, *Lab.* — 7,886
Ms D. Storr, *LD* — 3,548
P. Mieklejohn, *Ref.* — 840
SNP majority 5,566
(Boundary change: notional SNP)

MOTHERWELL AND WISHAW
*E.*52,252 *T.*70.08%
F. Roy, *Lab.* — 21,020
J. McGuigan, *SNP* — 8,229
S. Dickson, *C.* — 4,024
A. Mackie, *LD* — 2,331
C. Herriot, *Soc. Lab.* — 797
T. Russell, *Ref.* — 218
Lab. majority 12,791
(Boundary change: notional Lab.)

OCHIL
*E.*56,572 *T.*77.40%
†M. O'Neill, *Lab.* — 19,707
G. Reid, *SNP* — 15,055
A. Hogarth, *C.* — 6,383
Mrs A. Watters, *LD* — 2,262
D. White, *Ref.* — 210
I. McDonald, *D. Nat.* — 104
M. Sullivan, *NLP* — 65
Lab. majority 4,652
(Boundary change: notional Lab.)

ORKNEY AND SHETLAND
*E.*32,291 *T.*64.00%
*J. Wallace, *LD* — 10,743
J. Paton, *Lab.* — 3,775
W. Ross, *SNP* — 2,624

e

H. Vere Anderson, *C.*	2,527
F. Adamson, *Ref.*	820
Ms C. Wharton, *NLP*	116
A. Robertson, *Ind.*	60

LD majority 6,968
(April 1992, LD maj. 5,033)

PAISLEY NORTH
*E.*49,725   *T.*68.65%

†Mrs I. Adams, *Lab.*	20,295
I. Mackay, *SNP*	7,481
K. Brookes, *C.*	3,267
A. Jelfs, *LD*	2,365
R. Graham, *ProLife*	531
E. Mathew, *Ref.*	196

Lab. majority 12,814
(Boundary change: notional Lab.)

PAISLEY SOUTH
*E.*54,040   *T.*69.12%

†G. McMaster, *Lab. Co-op.*	21,482
W. Martin, *SNP*	8,732
Ms E. McCartin, *LD*	3,500
R. Reid, *C.*	3,237
J. Lardner, *Ref.*	254
S. Clerkin, *SSA*	146

Lab. Co-op. majority 12,750
(Boundary change: notional Lab. Co-op.)
See also page 233

PERTH
*E.*60,313   *T.*73.87%

†Ms R. Cunningham, *SNP*	16,209
J. Godfrey, *C.*	13,068
D. Alexander, *Lab.*	11,036
C. Brodie, *LD*	3,583
R. MacAuley, *Ref.*	366
M. Henderson, *UK Ind.*	289

SNP majority 3,141
(Boundary change: notional C.)

RENFREWSHIRE WEST
*E.*52,348   *T.*76.00%

†T. Graham, *Lab.*	18,525
C. Campbell, *SNP*	10,546
C. Cormack, *C.*	7,387
B. MacPherson, *LD*	3,045
S. Lindsay, *Ref.*	283

Lab. majority 7,979
(Boundary change: notional Lab.)

ROSS, SKYE AND INVERNESS WEST
*E.*55,639   *T.*71.81%

†C. Kennedy, *LD*	15,472
D. Munro, *Lab.*	11,453
Mrs M. Paterson, *SNP*	7,821
Miss M. Macleod, *C.*	4,368
L. Durance, *Ref.*	535
A. Hopkins, *Green*	306

LD majority 4,019
(Boundary change: notional LD)

ROXBURGH AND BERWICKSHIRE
*E.*47,259   *T.*73.91%

†A. Kirkwood, *LD*	16,243
D. Younger, *C.*	8,337
Ms H. Eadie, *Lab.*	5,226
M. Balfour, *SNP*	3,959
J. Curtis, *Ref.*	922
P. Neilson, *UK Ind.*	202
D. Lucas, *NLP*	42

LD majority 7,906
(Boundary change: notional LD)

STIRLING
*E.*52,491   *T.*81.84%

Mrs A. McGuire, *Lab.*	20,382
†Rt. Hon. M. Forsyth, *C.*	13,971
E. Dow, *SNP*	5,752
A. Tough, *LD*	2,675
W. McMurdo, *UK Ind.*	154
Ms E. Olsen, *Value Party*	24

Lab. majority 6,411
(Boundary change: notional C.)

STRATHKELVIN AND BEARSDEN
*E.*62,974   *T.*78.94%

†S. Galbraith, *Lab.*	26,278
D. Sharpe, *C.*	9,986
G. McCormick, *SNP*	8,111
J. Morrison, *LD*	4,843
D. Wilson, *Ref.*	339
Ms J. Fisher, *NLP*	155

Lab. majority 16,292
(Boundary change: notional Lab.)

TAYSIDE NORTH
*E.*61,398   *T.*74.25%

J. Swinney, *SNP*	20,447
†W. Walker, *C.*	16,287
I. McFatridge, *Lab.*	5,141
P. Regent, *LD*	3,716

SNP majority 4,160
(Boundary change: notional C.)

TWEEDDALE, ETTRICK AND LAUDERDALE
*E.*50,891   *T.*76.64%

M. Moore, *LD*	12,178
K. Geddes, *Lab.*	10,689
A. Jack, *C.*	8,623
I. Goldie, *SNP*	6,671
C. Mowbray, *Ref.*	406
J. Hein, *Lib.*	387
D. Paterson, *NLP*	47

LD majority 1,489
(Boundary change: notional LD)

WESTERN ISLES
*E.*22,983   *T.*70.08%

*C. Macdonald, *Lab.*	8,955
Dr A. Lorne Gillies, *SNP*	5,379
J. McGrigor, *C.*	1,071
N. Mitchison, *LD*	495
R. Lionel, *Ref.*	206

Lab. majority 3,576
(April 1992, Lab. maj. 1,703)

NORTHERN IRELAND

ANTRIM EAST
*E.*58,963   *T.*58.26%

†R. Beggs, *UUP*	13,318
S. Neeson, *All.*	6,929
J. McKee, *DUP*	6,682
T. Dick, *C.*	2,334
W. Donaldson, *PUP*	1,757
D. O'Connor, *SDLP*	1,576
R. Mason, *Ind.*	1,145
Ms C. McAuley, *SF*	543
Ms M. McCann, *NLP*	69

UUP majority 6,389
(Boundary change: notional UUP)

ANTRIM NORTH
*E.*72,411   *T.*63.78%

*Revd I. Paisley, *DUP*	21,495
J. Leslie, *UUP*	10,921
S. Farren, *SDLP*	7,333
J. McCarry, *SF*	2,896
Dr D. Alderdice, *All.*	2,845
Ms B. Hinds, *NI Women*	580
J. Wright, *NLP*	116

DUP majority 10,574
(April 1992, DUP maj. 14,936)

ANTRIM SOUTH
*E.*69,414   *T.*57.91%

†C. Forsythe, *UUP*	23,108
D. McClelland, *SDLP*	6,497
D. Ford, *All.*	4,668
H. Smyth, *PUP*	3,490
H. Cushinan, *SF*	2,229
Ms B. Briggs, *NLP*	203

UUP majority 16,611
(Boundary change: notional UUP)

BELFAST EAST
*E.*61,744   *T.*63.21%

†P. Robinson, *DUP*	16,640
R. Empey, *UUP*	9,886
J. Hendron, *All.*	9,288
Miss S. Dines, *C.*	928
D. Corr, *SF*	810
Mrs P. Lewsley, *SDLP*	629
D. Dougan, *NIFT*	541
J. Bell, *WP*	237
D. Collins, *NLP*	70

DUP majority 6,754
(Boundary change: notional DUP)

BELFAST NORTH
*E.*64,577   *T.*64.19%

†C. Walker, *UUP*	21,478
A. Maginness, *SDLP*	8,454
G. Kelly, *SF*	8,375
T. Campbell, *All.*	2,221
P. Emerson, *Green*	539
P. Treanor, *WP*	297
Ms A. Gribben, *NLP*	88

UUP majority 13,024
(Boundary change: notional UUP)

BELFAST SOUTH
*E.*63,439   *T.*62.24%

†Revd M. Smyth, *UUP*	14,201
Dr A. McDonnell, *SDLP*	9,601
D. Ervine, *PUP*	5,687
S. McBride, *All.*	5,112
S. Hayes, *SF*	2,019
Ms A. Campbell, *NI Women*	1,204
Miss M. Boal, *C.*	962
N. Cusack, *Ind. Lab.*	292

P. Lynn, *WP*   286
J. Anderson, *NLP*   120
UUP majority 4,600
(Boundary change: notional UUP)

BELFAST WEST
*E.*61,785   *T.*74.27%
G. Adams, *SF*   25,662
†Dr J. Hendron, *SDLP*   17,753
F. Parkinson, *UUP*   1,556
J. Lowry, *WP*   721
L. Kennedy, *HR*   102
Ms M. Daly, *NLP*   91
SF majority 7,909
(Boundary change: notional SDLP)

DOWN NORTH
*E.*63,010   *T.*58.03%
†R. McCartney, *UKU*   12,817
A. McFarland, *UUP*   11,368
Sir O. Napier, *All.*   7,554
L. Fee, *C.*   1,810
Miss M. Farrell, *SDLP*   1,602
Ms J. Morrice, *NI Women*   1,240
T. Mullins, *NLP*   108
R. Mooney, *NIP*   67
UKU majority 1,449
(Boundary change: notional Popular
Unionist)

DOWN SOUTH
*E.*69,855   *T.*70.84%
†E. McGrady, *SDLP*   26,181
D. Nesbitt, *UUP*   16,248
M. Murphy, *SF*   5,127
J. Crozier, *All.*   1,711
Ms R. McKeon, *NLP*   219
SDLP majority 9,933
(Boundary change: notional SDLP)

FERMANAGH AND SOUTH TYRONE
*E.*64,600   *T.*74.75%
†K. Maginnis, *UUP*   24,862
G. McHugh, *SF*   11,174
T. Gallagher, *SDLP*   11,060
S. Farry, *All.*   977
S. Gillan, *NLP*   217
UUP majority 13,688
(Boundary change: notional UUP)

FOYLE
*E.*67,620   *T.*70.71%
†J. Hume, *SDLP*   25,109
M. McLaughlin, *SF*   11,445
W. Hay, *DUP*   10,290
Mrs H.-M. Bell, *All.*   817
D. Brennan, *NLP*   154
SDLP majority 13,664
(Boundary change: notional SDLP)

LAGAN VALLEY
*E.*71,225   *T.*62.21%
J. Donaldson, *UUP*   24,560
S. Close, *All.*   7,635
E. Poots, *DUP*   6,005
Ms D. Kelly, *SDLP*   3,436
S. Sexton, *C.*   1,212
Ms S. Ramsey, *SF*   1,110
Ms F. McCarthy, *WP*   203
H. Finlay, *NLP*   149
UUP majority 16,925
(Boundary change: notional UUP)

LONDONDERRY EAST
*E.*58,831   *T.*64.77%
†W. Ross, *UUP*   13,558
G. Campbell, *DUP*   9,764
A. Doherty, *SDLP*   8,273
M. O'Kane, *SF*   3,463
Ms Y. Boyle, *All.*   2,427
J. Holmes, *C.*   436
Ms C. Gallen, *NLP*   100
I. Anderson, *Nat. Dem.*   81
UUP majority 3,794
(Boundary change: notional UUP)

NEWRY AND ARMAGH
*E.*70,652   *T.*75.40%
†S. Mallon, *SDLP*   22,904
D. Kennedy, *UUP*   18,015
P. McNamee, *SF*   11,218
P. Whitcroft, *All.*   1,015
D. Evans, *NLP*   123
SDLP majority 4,889
(Boundary change: notional SDLP)

STRANGFORD
*E.*69,980   *T.*59.47%
†Rt. Hon. J. Taylor, *UUP*   18,431
Mrs I. Robinson, *DUP*   12,579
K. McCarthy, *All.*   5,467
P. O'Reilly, *SDLP*   2,775
G. Chalk, *C.*   1,743
G. O Fachtna, *SF*   503
Mrs S. Mullins, *NLP*   121
UUP majority 5,852
(Boundary change: notional UUP)

TYRONE WEST
*E.*58,168   *T.*79.55%
W. Thompson, *UUP*   16,003
J. Byrne, *SDLP*   14,842
P. Doherty, *SF*   14,280
Ms A. Gormley, *All.*   829
T. Owens, *WP*   230
R. Johnstone, *NLP*   91
UUP majority 1,161
(Boundary change: notional DUP)

ULSTER MID
*E.*58,836   *T.*86.12%
M. McGuinness, *SF*   20,294
†Revd W. McCrea, *DUP*   18,411
D. Haughey, *SDLP*   11,205
E. Bogues, *All.*   460
Mrs M. Donnelly, *WP*   238
Ms M. Murray, *NLP*   61
SF majority 1,883
(Boundary change: notional DUP)

UPPER BANN
*E.*70,398   *T.*67.88%
*D. Trimble, *UUP*   20,836
Ms B. Rodgers, *SDLP*   11,584
Ms B. O'Hagan, *SF*   5,773
M. Carrick, *DUP*   5,482
Dr W. Ramsay, *All.*   3,017
T. French, *WP*   554
B. Price, *C.*   433
J. Lyons, *NLP*   108
UUP majority 9,252
(Boundary change: notional UUP)

European Parliament

European Parliament elections take place at five-yearly intervals. In mainland Britain MEPs have so far been elected in all constituencies on a first-past-the-post basis; in Northern Ireland three MEPs are elected by the single transferable vote system of proportional representation. From 1979 to 1994 the number of seats held by the UK in the European Parliament was 81. At the June 1994 election the number of seats increased to 87 (England 71, Wales 5, Scotland 8, Northern Ireland 3).

At the European Parliament elections to be held on 10 June 1999, all British MEPs will be elected under a 'closed-list' regional system of proportional representation, with England being divided into nine regions and Scotland and Wales each constituting a region. Parties will submit a list of candidates for each region in their own order of preference. Voters will vote for a party rather than a candidate, and seats will then be allocated in proportion to each party's vote. Candidates further up the party's list will therefore have a better chance of being elected. Each region will return the following number of members: East Midlands, 6; Eastern, 8; London, 10; North-East, 4; North-West, 10; South-East, 11; South-West, 7; West Midlands, 8; Yorkshire and the Humber, 7; Wales, 5; Scotland 8.

British subjects and citizens of the Irish Republic are eligible for election to the European Parliament provided they are 21 or over and not subject to disqualification. Since 1994, nationals of member states of the European Union have had the right to vote in elections to the European Parliament in the UK.

MEPs receive a salary from the parliaments or governments of their respective member states, set at the level of the national parliamentary salary and subject to national taxation rules (for salary of British MPs, *see* page 219).

UK MEMBERS AS AT END JULY 1998

*Denotes membership of the last European Parliament

*Adam, Gordon J., PH.D. (*b.* 1934), *Lab., Northumbria,* maj. 66,158
*Balfe, Richard A. (*b.* 1944), *Lab., London South Inner,* maj. 59,220
*Barton, Roger (*b.* 1945), *Lab., Sheffield,* maj. 50,288
Billingham, Mrs Angela T. (*b.* 1939), *Lab., Northamptonshire and Blaby,* maj. 26,085
*Bowe, David R. (*b.* 1955), *Lab., Cleveland and Richmond,* maj. 57,568
*Cassidy, Bryan M. D. (*b.* 1934), *C., Dorset and Devon East,* maj. 2,264
Chichester, Giles B. (*b.* 1946), *C., Devon and Plymouth East,* maj. 700
*Coates, Kenneth S. (*b.* 1930), *European United Left/Nordic Green Left Group, Nottinghamshire North and Chesterfield,* maj. 76,260
*Collins, Kenneth D. (*b.* 1939), *Lab., Strathclyde East,* maj. 52,340
Corbett, Richard (*b.* 1955), *Lab., Merseyside West,* maj. 18,704
Corrie, John A. (*b.* 1935), *C., Worcestershire and Warwickshire South,* maj. 1,204
*Crampton, Peter D. (*b.* 1932), *Lab., Humberside,* maj. 40,618
*Crawley, The Baroness (Christine) (*b.* 1950), *Lab., Birmingham East,* maj. 55,120
Cunningham, Thomas A. (Tony) (*b.* 1952), *Lab., Cumbria and Lancashire North,* maj. 22,988

*David, Wayne (*b.* 1957), *Lab., South Wales Central,* maj. 86,082
*Donnelly, Alan J. (*b.* 1957), *Lab., Tyne and Wear,* maj. 88,380
Donnelly, Brendan P. (*b.* 1950), *C., Sussex South and Crawley,* maj. 1,746
*Elles, James E. M. (*b.* 1949), *C., Buckinghamshire and Oxfordshire East,* maj. 30,665
*Elliott, Michael N. (*b.* 1932), *Lab., London West,* maj. 42,275
Evans, Robert J. E. (*b.* 1956), *Lab., London North West,* maj. 17,442
*Ewing, Mrs Winifred M. (*b.* 1929), *SNP, Highlands and Islands,* maj. 54,916
*Falconer, Alexander (*b.* 1940), *Lab., Scotland Mid and Fife,* maj. 31,413
*Ford, J. Glyn (*b.* 1950), *Lab., Greater Manchester East,* maj. 55,986
*Green, Mrs Pauline (*b.* 1948), *Lab., London North,* maj. 48,348
Hallam, David J. A. (*b.* 1948), *Lab., Herefordshire and Shropshire,* maj. 1,850
Hardstaff, Mrs Veronica M. (*b.* 1941), *Lab., Lincolnshire and Humberside South,* maj. 13,745
*Harrison, Lyndon H. A. (*b.* 1947), *Lab., Cheshire West and Wirral,* maj. 47,176
Hendrick, Mark P. (*b.* 1958), *Lab., Lancashire Central,* maj. 12,191
*Hindley, Michael J. (*b.* 1947), *Lab., Lancashire South,* maj. 41,404
Howitt, Richard (*b.* 1961), *Lab., Essex South,* maj. 21,367
*Hughes, Stephen S. (*b.* 1952), *Lab., Durham,* maj. 111,638
*Hume, John, MP (*b.* 1937), *SDLP, Northern Ireland,* polled 161,992 votes
*Jackson, Mrs Caroline F., D.PHIL. (*b.* 1946), *C., Wiltshire North and Bath,* maj. 8,787
*Kellett-Bowman, Edward T. (*b.* 1931), *C., Itchen, Test and Avon,* maj. 6,903
Kerr, Hugh (*b.* 1944), *Green, Essex West and Hertfordshire East,* maj. 3,067
Kinnock, Mrs Glenys E. (*b.* 1944), *Lab., South Wales East,* maj. 120,247
*Lomas, Alfred (*b.* 1928), *Lab., London North East,* maj. 57,085
Macartney, W. J. Allan, PH.D. (*b.* 1941), *SNP, Scotland North East,* maj. 31,227
McAvan, Ms Linda (*b.* 1962), *Lab., Yorkshire South,* maj. 40,224
McCarthy, Ms Arlene (*b.* 1960), *Lab., Peak District,* maj. 49,307
*McGowan, Michael (*b.* 1940), *Lab., Leeds,* maj. 53,082
*McIntosh, Miss Anne C. B., MP (*b.* 1954), *C., Essex North and Suffolk South,* maj. 3,633
*McMahon, Hugh R. (*b.* 1938), *Lab., Strathclyde West,* maj. 25,023
*McMillan-Scott, Edward H. C. (*b.* 1949), *C., Yorkshire North,* maj. 7,072
McNally, Mrs Eryl M. (*b.* 1942), *Lab., Bedfordshire and Milton Keynes,* maj. 33,209
*Martin, David W. (*b.* 1954), *Lab., Lothians,* maj. 37,207
Mather, Graham C. S. (*b.* 1954), *C., Hampshire North and Oxford,* maj. 9,194
*Megahy, Thomas (*b.* 1929), *Lab., Yorkshire South West,* maj. 59,562
Miller, Bill (*b.* 1954), *Lab., Glasgow,* maj. 43,158
*Moorhouse, C. James O. (*b.* 1924), *C., London South and Surrey East,* maj. 8,739

Morgan, Ms Eluned (*b.* 1967), *Lab., Wales Mid and West,* maj. 29,234

*Morris, Revd David R. (*b.* 1930), *Lab., South Wales West,* maj. 84,970

Murphy, Simon F., ᴘʜ.ᴅ . (*b.* 1962), *Lab., Midlands West,* maj. 54,823

Needle, Clive (*b.* 1956), *Lab., Norfolk,* maj. 26,287

*Newens, A. Stanley (*b.* 1930), *Lab., London Central,* maj. 25,059

*Newman, Edward (*b.* 1953), *Lab., Greater Manchester Central,* maj. 42,445

*Nicholson, James F. (*b.* 1945), *UUUP, Northern Ireland,* polled 133,459 votes

*Oddy, Ms Christine M. (*b.* 1955), *Lab., Coventry and Warwickshire North,* maj. 43,901

*Paisley, Revd Ian R. K., ᴍᴘ (*b.* 1926), *DUP, Northern Ireland,* polled 163,246 votes

Perry, Roy J. (*b.* 1943), *C., Wight and Hampshire South,* maj. 5,101

*Plumb, The Lord (*b.* 1925), *C., Cotswolds,* maj. 4,268

*Pollack, Ms Anita J. (*b.* 1946), *Lab., London South West,* maj. 30,975

Provan, James L. C. (*b.* 1936), *C., South Downs West,* maj. 21,067

*Read, Ms I. M. (Mel) (*b.* 1939), *Lab., Nottingham and Leicestershire North West,* maj. 39,668

*Seal, Barry H., ᴘʜ.ᴅ. (*b.* 1937), *Lab., Yorkshire West,* maj. 48,197

*Simpson, Brian (*b.* 1953), *Lab., Cheshire East,* maj. 39,279

Skinner, Peter W. (*b.* 1959), *Lab., Kent West,* maj. 16,777

*Smith, Alexander (*b.* 1943), *Lab., Scotland South,* maj. 45,155

*Spencer, Thomas N. B. (*b.* 1948), *C., Surrey,* maj. 27,018

Spiers, Shaun M. (*b.* 1962), *Lab., London South East,* maj. 8,022

*Stevens, John C. C. (*b.* 1955), *C., Thames Valley,* maj. 758

*Stewart-Clark, Sir John, Bt. (*b.* 1929), *C., Sussex East and Kent South,* maj. 6,212

Sturdy, Robert W. (*b.* 1944), *C., Cambridgeshire,* maj. 3,942

Tappin, Michael (*b.* 1946), *Lab., Staffordshire West and Congleton,* maj. 40,277

Teverson, Robin (*b.* 1952), *LD, Cornwall and Plymouth West,* maj. 29,498

Thomas, David E. (*b.* 1955), *Lab., Suffolk and Norfolk South West,* maj. 12,535

*Titley, Gary (*b.* 1950), *Lab., Greater Manchester West,* maj. 58,635

* Tomlinson, The Lord (John) (*b.* 1939), *Lab., Birmingham West,* maj. 39,350

*Tongue, Ms Carole (*b.* 1955), *Lab., London East,* maj. 57,389

Truscott, Peter, ᴘʜ.ᴅ. (*b.* 1959), *Lab., Hertfordshire,* maj. 10,304

Waddington, Mrs Susan A. (*b.* 1944), *Lab., Leicester,* maj. 20,284

Watson, Graham R. (*b.* 1956), *LD, Somerset and Devon North,* maj. 22,509

Watts, Mark F. (*b.* 1964), *Lab., Kent East,* maj. 635

*White, Ian (*b.* 1947), *Lab., Bristol,* maj. 29,955

Whitehead, Phillip (*b.* 1937), *Lab., Staffordshire East and Derby,* maj. 72,196

*Wilson, A. Joseph (*b.* 1937), *Lab., Wales North,* maj. 15,242

*Wynn, Terence (*b.* 1946), *Lab., Merseyside East and Wigan,* maj. 74,087

UK CONSTITUENCIES ᴀs ᴀᴛ 9 Jᴜɴᴇ 1994

Abbreviations	
Anti Fed.	UK Independence Anti-Federal
Anti Fed. C.	Official Anti-Federalist Conservative
Beanus	Eurobean from Planet Beanus
C. Non Fed.	Conservative Non-Federal Party
Capital P.	Restoration of Capital Punishment
Comm.	Communist
Comm. YBG	Communist Y Blaid Gomiwyddol
Const. NI	Constitutional Independence for N. Ireland
Corr.	Corrective Party
CPP	Christian People's Party
ICP	International Communist Party
ICP4	International Communist Party (4th International)
Ind. AES	Independent Anti-European Superstate
Ind. Out	Independent Out of Europe
Judo	European People's Party Judo Christian Alliance
Loony C	Raving Loony Commonsense
Loony CP	Monster Raving Loony Christian Party
Loony X	Monster Raving Loony Project X Party
MCCARTHY	Make Criminals Concerned About Our Response To Hostility and Yobbishness
MK	Mebyon Kernow
NCSA	Network Against Child Support Agency

Neeps	North East Ethnic Party, The Neeps
Rainbow	Rainbow Connection – Oui-Say-Non-Party
Sportsman	Sportsman Against Common Market Bureaucracy
UUUP	United Ulster Unionist Party

For other abbreviations, *see* page 235

ENGLAND

Bᴇᴅꜰᴏʀᴅsʜɪʀᴇ ᴀɴᴅ Mɪʟᴛᴏɴ Kᴇʏɴᴇs
E. 525,524   *T.* 38.74%

E. McNally, *Lab.*	94,837
Mrs E. Currie, *C.*	61,628
Ms M. Howes, *LD*	27,994
A. Sked, *UK Independence*	7,485
A. Francis, *Green*	6,804
A. Howes, *New Britain*	3,878
L. Sheaff, *NLP*	939
Lab. majority	33,209
(Boundary change since June 1989)

Bɪʀᴍɪɴɢʜᴀᴍ Eᴀsᴛ
E. 520,782   *T.* 29.77%

*Mrs C. Crawley, *Lab.*	90,291
A. Turner, *C.*	35,171
Ms C. Cane, *LD*	19,455
P. Simpson, *Green*	6,268
R. Cook, *Soc.*	1,969
M. Brierley, *NLP*	1,885
Lab. majority	55,120
(June 1989, Lab. maj. 46,948)

Bɪʀᴍɪɴɢʜᴀᴍ Wᴇsᴛ
E. 509,948   *T.* 28.49%

*J. Tomlinson, *Lab.*	77,957
D. Harman, *C.*	38,607
N. McGeorge, *LD*	14,603
Dr B. Juby, *Anti Fed.*	5,237
M. Abbott, *Green*	4,367
A. Carmichael, *NF*	3,727
H. Meads, *NLP*	789
Lab. majority	39,350
(June 1989, Lab. maj. 30,860)

Bʀɪsᴛᴏʟ
E. 503,218   *T.* 40.91%

*I. White, *Lab.*	90,790
The Earl of Stockton, *C.*	60,835
J. Barnard, *LD*	40,394
J. Boxall, *Green*	7,163
T. Whittingham, *UK Independence*	5,798
T. Dyball, *NLP*	876
Lab. majority	29,955
(Boundary change since June 1989)

Bᴜᴄᴋɪɴɢʜᴀᴍsʜɪʀᴇ ᴀɴᴅ Oxꜰᴏʀᴅsʜɪʀᴇ Eᴀsᴛ
E. 487,692   *T.* 37.31%

*J. Elles, *C.*	77,037
D. Enright, *Lab.*	46,372
Ms S. Bowles, *LD*	42,836
L. Roach, *Green*	8,433
Ms A. Micklem, *Lib.*	5,111
Dr G. Clements, *NLP*	2,156
C. majority	30,665
(Boundary change since June 1989)

CAMBRIDGESHIRE
E. 495,383   T. 35.91%

R. Sturdy, *C.*	66,921
Ms M. Johnson, *Lab.*	62,979
A. Duff, *LD*	36,114
Ms M. Wright, *Green*	5,756
P. Wiggin, *Lib.*	4,051
F. Chalmers, *NLP*	2,077
C. majority	3,942

(Boundary change since June 1989)

CHESHIRE EAST
E. 502,726   T. 32.46%

*B. Simpson, *Lab.*	87,586
P. Slater, *C.*	48,307
P. Harris, *LD*	20,552
D. Wild, *Green*	3,671
P. Dixon, *Loony CP*	1,600
P. Leadbetter, *NLP*	1,488
Lab. majority	39,279

(Boundary change since June 1989)

CHESHIRE WEST AND WIRRAL
E. 538,571   T. 36.78%

*L. Harrison, *Lab.*	106,160
D. Senior, *C.*	58,984
I. Mottershaw, *LD*	20,746
D. Carson, *British Home Rule*	6,167
M. Money, *Green*	5,096
A. Wilmot, *NLP*	929
Lab. majority	47,176

(Boundary change since June 1989)

CLEVELAND AND RICHMOND
E. 499,580   T. 35.26%

*D. Bowe, *Lab.*	103,355
R. Goodwill, *C.*	45,787
B. Moore, *LD*	21,574
G. Parr, *Green*	4,375
R. Scott, *NLP*	1,068
Lab. majority	57,568

(Boundary change since June 1989)

CORNWALL AND PLYMOUTH WEST
E. 484,697   T. 44.92%

R. Teverson, *LD*	91,113
*C. Beazley, *C.*	61,615
Mrs D. Kirk, *Lab.*	42,907
Mrs P. Garnier, *UK Independence*	
	6,466
P. Holmes, *Lib.*	6,414
Ms K. Westbrook, *Green*	4,372
Dr L. Jenkin, *MK*	3,315
F. Lyons, *NLP*	921
M. Fitzgerald, *Subsidiarity*	606
LD majority	29,498

(Boundary change since June 1989)

COTSWOLDS
E. 497,588   T. 39.27%

*The Lord Plumb, *C.*	67,484
Ms T. Kingham, *Lab.*	63,216
J. Thomson, *LD*	44,269
M. Rendell, *New Britain*	11,044
D. McCanlis, *Green*	8,254
H. Brighouse, *NLP*	1,151
C. majority	4,268

(Boundary change since June 1989)

COVENTRY AND WARWICKSHIRE NORTH
E. 523,448   T. 32.54%

*Ms C. Oddy, *Lab.*	89,500

Ms J. Crabb, *C.*	45,599
G. Sewards, *LD*	17,453
R. Meacham, *Free Trade*	9,432
P. Baptie, *Green*	4,360
R. Wheway, *Lib.*	2,885
R. France, *NLP*	1,098
Lab. majority	43,901

(Boundary change since June 1989)

CUMBRIA AND LANCASHIRE NORTH
E. 498,557   T. 40.78%

A. Cunningham, *Lab.*	97,599
*The Lord Inglewood, *C.*	74,611
R. Putnam, *LD*	24,233
R. Frost, *Green*	5,344
I. Docker, *NLP*	1,500
Lab. majority	22,988

(Boundary change since June 1989)

DEVON AND PLYMOUTH EAST
E. 524,320   T. 45.07%

G. Chichester, *C.*	74,953
A. Sanders, *LD*	74,253
Ms L. Gilroy, *Lab.*	47,596
D. Morrish, *Lib.*	14,621
P. Edwards, *Green*	11,172
R. Huggett, *Literal Democrat*	10,203
J. Everard, *Ind.*	2,629
A. Pringle, *NLP*	908
C. majority	700

(Boundary change since June 1989)

DORSET AND DEVON EAST
E. 531,842   T. 41.21%

*B. Cassidy, *C.*	81,551
P. Goldenberg, *LD*	79,287
A. Gardner, *Lab.*	34,856
M. Floyd, *UK Independence*	10,548
Mrs K. Bradbury, *Green*	8,642
I. Mortimer, *C. Non Fed.*	3,229
M. Griffiths, *NLP*	1,048
C. majority	2,264

(Boundary change since June 1989)

DURHAM
E. 532,051   T. 35.62%

*S. Hughes, *Lab.*	136,671
P. Bradbourn, *C.*	25,033
Dr N. Martin, *LD*	20,935
S. Hope, *Green*	5,670
C. Adamson, *NLP*	1,198
Lab. majority	111,638

(June 1989, Lab. maj. 86,848)

ESSEX NORTH AND SUFFOLK SOUTH
E. 497,098   T. 41.33%

*Ms A. McIntosh, *C.*	68,311
C. Pearson, *Lab.*	64,678
S. Mole, *LD*	52,536
S. de Chair, *Ind. AES*	12,409
J. Abbott, *Green*	6,641
N. Pullen, *NLP*	884
C. majority	3,633

(Boundary change since June 1989)

ESSEX SOUTH
E. 487,221   T. 33.08%

R. Howitt, *Lab.*	71,883
L. Stanbrook, *C.*	50,516
G. Williams, *LD*	26,132
B. Lynch, *Lib.*	6,780
G. Rumens, *Green*	4,691

M. Heath, *NLP*	1,177
Lab. majority	21,367

(Boundary change since June 1989)

ESSEX WEST AND HERTFORDSHIRE EAST
E. 504,095   T. 36.39%

H. Kerr, *Lab.*	66,379
*Ms P. Rawlings, *C.*	63,312
Ms G. James, *LD*	35,695
B. Smalley, *Britain*	10,277
Ms F. Mawson, *Green*	5,632
P. Carter, *Sportsman*	1,127
L. Davis, *NLP*	1,026
Lab. majority	3,067

(Boundary change since June 1989)

GREATER MANCHESTER CENTRAL
E. 481,779   T. 29.11%

*E. Newman, *Lab.*	74,935
Mrs S. Mason, *C.*	32,490
J. Begg, *LD*	22,988
B. Candeland, *Green*	4,952
P. Burke, *Lib.*	3,862
P. Stanley, *NLP*	1,017
Lab. majority	42,445

(Boundary change since June 1989)

GREATER MANCHESTER EAST
E. 501,125   T. 27.17%

*G. Ford, *Lab.*	82,289
J. Pinniger, *C.*	26,303
A. Riley, *LD*	20,545
T. Clarke, *Green*	5,823
W. Stevens, *NLP*	1,183
Lab. majority	55,986

(Boundary change since June 1989)

GREATER MANCHESTER WEST
E. 512,618   T. 29.70%

*G. Titley, *Lab.*	94,129
D. Newns, *C.*	35,494
F. Harasiwka, *LD*	13,650
R. Jackson, *Green*	3,950
G. Harrison, *MCCARTHY*	3,693
T. Brotheridge, *NLP*	1,316
Lab. majority	58,635

(Boundary change since June 1989)

HAMPSHIRE NORTH AND OXFORD
E. 525,982   T. 38.31%

G. Mather, *C.*	72,209
Ms J. Hawkins, *LD*	63,015
J. Tanner, *Lab.*	48,525
D. Wilkinson, *UK Independence*	8,377
Dr M. Woodin, *Green*	7,310
H. Godfrey, *NLP*	1,027
R. Boston, *Boston Tea Party*	1,018
C. majority	9,194

(Boundary change since June 1989)

HEREFORDSHIRE AND SHROPSHIRE
E. 536,470   T. 38.69%

D. Hallam, *Lab.*	76,120
*Sir C. Prout, *C.*	74,270
J. Gallagher, *LD*	44,130
Ms F. Norman, *Green*	11,578
T. Mercer, *NLP*	1,480
Lab. majority	1,850

(Boundary change since June 1989)

HERTFORDSHIRE
E. 522,338   *T.* 40.11%

Dr P. Truscott, *Lab.*	81,821
P. Jenkinson, *C.*	71,517
D. Griffiths, *LD*	38,995
Ms L. Howitt, *Green*	7,741
M. Biggs, *New Britain*	6,555
J. McAuley, *NF*	1,755
D. Lucas, *NLP*	734
J. Laine, *Century*	369
Lab. majority	10,304

(Boundary change since June 1989)

HUMBERSIDE
E. 519,013   *T.* 32.38%

*P. Crampton, *Lab.*	87,296
D. Stewart, *C.*	46,678
Ms D. Wallis, *LD*	28,818
Ms S. Mummery, *Green*	4,170
Ms A. Miszewska, *NLP*	1,100
Lab. majority	40,618

(Boundary change since June 1989)

ITCHEN, TEST AND AVON
E. 550,406   *T.* 41.83%

*E. Kellett-Bowman, *C.*	81,456
A. Barron, *LD*	74,553
E. Read, *Lab.*	52,416
N. Farage, *UK Independence*	12,423
Ms F. Hulbert, *Green*	7,998
A. Miller-Smith, *NLP*	1,368
C. majority	6,903

(Boundary change since June 1989)

KENT EAST
E. 499,662   *T.* 40.34%

M. Watts, *Lab.*	69,641
*C. Jackson, *C.*	69,006
J. Macdonald, *LD*	44,549
C. Bullen, *UK Independence*	9,414
S. Dawe, *Green*	7,196
C. Beckley, *NLP*	1,746
Lab. majority	635

(Boundary change since June 1989)

KENT WEST
E. 505,658   *T.* 37.33%

P. Skinner, *Lab.*	77,346
*B. Patterson, *C.*	60,569
J. Daly, *LD*	33,869
C. Mackinlay, *UK Independence*	9,750
Ms P. Kemp, *Green*	5,651
J. Bowler, *NLP*	1,598
Lab. majority	16,777

(Boundary change since June 1989)

LANCASHIRE CENTRAL
E. 505,224   *T.* 33.23%

M. Hendrick, *Lab.*	73,420
*M. Welsh, *C.*	61,229
Ms J. Ross-Mills, *LD*	20,578
D. Hill, *Home Rule*	6,751
C. Maile, *Green*	4,169
Ms J. Ayliffe, *NLP*	1,727
Lab. majority	12,191

(Boundary change since June 1989)

LANCASHIRE SOUTH
E. 514,840   *T.* 33.14%

*M. Hindley, *Lab.*	92,598
R. Topham, *C.*	51,194
J. Ault, *LD*	17,008
J. Gaffney, *Green*	4,774

Mrs E. Rokas, *Ind.*	3,439
J. Renwick, *NLP*	1,605
Lab. majority	41,404

(Boundary change since June 1989)

LEEDS
E. 521,989   *T.* 30.03%

*M. McGowan, *Lab.*	89,160
N. Carmichael, *C.*	36,078
Ms J. Harvey, *LD*	17,575
M. Meadowcroft, *Lib.*	6,617
Ms C. Nash, *Green*	6,283
Ms S. Hayward, *NLP*	1,018
Lab. majority	53,082

(June 1989, Lab. maj. 42,518)

LEICESTER
E. 515,343   *T.* 37.63%

Ms S. Waddington, *Lab.*	87,048
A. Marshall, *C.*	66,764
M. Jones, *LD*	28,890
G. Forse, *Green*	8,941
Ms P. Saunders, *NLP*	2,283
Lab. majority	20,284

(Boundary change since June 1989)

LINCOLNSHIRE AND HUMBERSIDE SOUTH
E. 539,981   *T.* 36.34%

Mrs V. Hardstaff, *Lab.*	83,172
*W. Newton Dunn, *C.*	69,427
K. Melton, *LD*	27,241
Ms R. Robinson, *Green*	8,563
E. Wheeler, *Lib.*	3,434
I. Selby, *NCSA*	2,973
H. Kelly, *NLP*	1,429
Lab. majority	13,745

(Boundary change since June 1989)

LONDON CENTRAL
E. 494,610   *T.* 32.57%

*S. Newens, *Lab.*	75,711
A. Elliott, *C.*	50,652
Ms S. Ludford, *LD*	20,176
Ms N. Kortvelyessy, *Green*	7,043
H. Le Fanu, *UK Independence*	4,157
C. Slapper, *Soc.*	1,593
Ms S. Hamza, *NLP*	1,215
G. Weiss, *Rainbow*	547
Lab. majority	25,059

(June 1989, Lab. maj. 11,542)

LONDON EAST
E. 511,523   *T.* 33.38%

*Ms C. Tongue, *Lab.*	98,759
Ms V. Taylor, *C.*	41,370
K. Montgomery, *LD*	15,566
G. Batten, *UK Independence*	5,974
J. Baguley, *Green*	4,337
O. Tillett, *Third Way Independence*	3,484
N. Kahn, *NLP*	1,272
Lab. majority	57,389

(June 1989, Lab. maj. 27,385)

LONDON NORTH
E. 541,269   *T.* 34.00%

*Mrs P. Green, *Lab.*	102,059
M. Keegan, *C.*	53,711
I. Mann, *LD*	15,739
Ms H. Jago, *Green*	5,666
I. Booth, *UK Independence*	5,099
G. Sabrizi, *Judo*	880

J. Hinde, *NLP*	856
Lab. majority	48,348

(June 1989, Lab. maj. 5,837)

LONDON NORTH EAST
E. 486,016   *T.* 26.60%

*A. Lomas, *Lab.*	80,256
S. Gordon, *C.*	23,171
K. Appiah, *LD*	10,242
Ms J. Lambert, *Green*	8,386
E. Murat, *Lib.*	2,573
P. Compobassi, *UK Independence*	2,015
R. Archer, *NLP*	1,111
M. Fischer, *Comm. GB*	869
A. Hyland, *ICP4*	679
Lab. majority	57,085

(June 1989, Lab. maj. 47,767)

LONDON NORTH WEST
E. 481,272   *T.* 35.13%

R. Evans, *Lab.*	80,192
*The Lord Bethell, *C.*	62,750
Ms H. Leighter, *LD*	18,998
D. Johnson, *Green*	4,743
Ms A. Murphy, *Comm. GB*	858
Ms T. Sullivan, *NLP*	807
C. Palmer, *Century*	740
Lab. majority	17,442

(June 1989, C. maj. 7,400)

LONDON SOUTH AND SURREY EAST
E. 486,358   *T.* 34.38%

*J. Moorhouse, *C.*	64,813
Ms G. Rolles, *Lab.*	56,074
M. Reinisch, *LD*	32,059
J. Cornford, *Green*	7,046
J. Major, *Loony X*	3,339
A. Reeve, *Capital P.*	2,983
P. Levy, *NLP*	887
C. majority	8,739

(Boundary change since June 1989)

LONDON SOUTH EAST
E. 493,178   *T.* 35.38%

S. Spiers, *Lab.*	71,505
*P. Price, *C.*	63,483
J. Fryer, *LD*	25,271
I. Mouland, *Green*	6,399
R. Almond, *Lib.*	3,881
K. Lowne, *NF*	2,926
J. Small, *NLP*	1,025
Lab. majority	8,022

(Boundary change since June 1989)

LONDON SOUTH INNER
E. 510,609   *T.* 27.30%

*R. Balfe, *Lab.*	85,079
A. Boff, *C.*	25,856
A. Graves, *LD*	20,708
S. Collins, *Green*	6,570
M. Leighton, *NLP*	1,179
Lab. majority	59,220

(Boundary change since June 1989)

LONDON SOUTH WEST
E. 479,246   *T.* 34.35%

*Ms A. Pollack, *Lab.*	81,850
Prof. P. Treleaven, *C.*	50,875
G. Blanchard, *LD*	18,667
T. Walsh, *Green*	5,460
A. Scholefield, *UK Independence*	4,912
C. Hopewell, *Capital P.*	1,840
M. Simson, *NLP*	625

J. Quanjer, *Spirit of Europe* 377
Lab. majority 30,975
(Boundary change since June 1989)

LONDON WEST
E. 505,791 T. 36.02%
*M. Elliott, *Lab.* 94,562
R. Guy, *C.* 52,287
W. Mallinson, *LD* 21,561
J. Bradley, *Green* 6,134
G. Roberts, *UK Independence* 4,583
W. Binding, *NF* 1,963
R. Johnson, *NLP* 1,105
Lab. majority 42,275
(June 1989, Lab. maj. 14,808)

MERSEYSIDE EAST AND WIGAN
E. 518,196 T. 24.66%
*T. Wynn, *Lab.* 91,986
C. Manson, *C.* 17,899
Ms F. Clucas, *LD* 8,874
J. Melia, *Lib.* 4,765
L. Brown, *Green* 3,280
G. Hutchard, *NLP* 1,009
Lab. majority 74,087
(June 1989, Lab. maj. 76,867)

MERSEYSIDE WEST
E. 515,909 T. 26.18%
*K. Stewart, *Lab.* 78,819
C. Varley, *C.* 27,008
D. Bamber, *LD* 19,097
S. Radford, *Lib.* 4,714
Ms L. Lever, *Green* 4,573
J. Collins, *NLP* 852
Lab. majority 51,811
(June 1989, Lab. maj. 49,817)
See also page 275

MIDLANDS WEST
E. 533,742 T. 31.28%
S. Murphy, *Lab.* 99,242
M. Simpson, *C.* 44,419
G. Baldauf-Good, *LD* 12,195
M. Hyde, *Lib.* 5,050
C. Mattingly, *Green* 4,390
J. Oldbury, *NLP* 1,641
Lab. majority 54,823
(June 1989, Lab. maj. 42,364)

NORFOLK
E. 513,553 T. 44.25%
C. Needle, *Lab.* 102,711
*P. Howell, *C.* 76,424
P. Burall, *LD* 39,107
A. Holmes, *Green* 7,938
B. Parsons, *NLP* 1,075
Lab. majority 26,287
(Boundary change since June 1989)

NORTHAMPTONSHIRE AND BLABY
E. 524,916 T. 39.37%
Mrs A. Billingham, *Lab.* 95,317
*A. Simpson, *C.* 69,232
K. Scudder, *LD* 27,616
Ms A. Bryant, *Green* 9,121
I. Whitaker, *Ind.* 4,397
B. Spivack, *NLP* 972
Lab. majority 26,085
(Boundary change since June 1989)

NORTHUMBRIA
E. 516,680 T. 33.65%
*G. Adam, *Lab.* 103,087
J. Flack, *C.* 36,929
L. Opik, *LD* 20,195
D. Lott, *UK Independence* 7,210
J. Hartshorne, *Green* 5,714
L. Walch, *NLP* 740
Lab. majority 66,158
(June 1989, Lab. maj. 60,040)

NOTTINGHAM AND
LEICESTERSHIRE NORTH WEST
E. 507,915 T. 37.68%
*Ms M. Read, *Lab.* 95,344
M. Brandon-Bravo, *C.* 55,676
A. Wood, *LD* 23,836
Ms S. Blount, *Green* 7,035
J. Downes, *UK Independence* 5,849
P. Walton, *Ind. Out* 2,710
Mrs J. Christou, *NLP* 927
Lab. majority 39,668
(Boundary change since June 1989)

NOTTINGHAMSHIRE NORTH AND
CHESTERFIELD
E. 490,330 T. 36.95%
*K. Coates, *Lab.* 114,353
D. Hazell, *C.* 38,093
Ms S. Pearce, *LD* 21,936
G. Jones, *Green* 5,159
Ms S. Lincoln, *NLP* 1,632
Lab. majority 76,260
(Boundary change since June 1989)

PEAK DISTRICT
E. 511,357 T. 39.02%
Ms A. McCarthy, *Lab.* 105,853
R. Fletcher, *C.* 56,546
Ms S. Barber, *LD* 29,979
M. Shipley, *Green* 5,598
D. Collins, *NLP* 1,533
Lab. majority 49,307
(Boundary change since June 1989)

SHEFFIELD
E. 476,530 T. 27.50%
*R. Barton, *Lab.* 76,397
Ms S. Anginotti, *LD* 26,109
Ms K. Twitchen, *C.* 22,374
B. New, *Green* 4,742
M. England, *Comm.* 834
R. Hurford, *NLP* 577
Lab. majority 50,288
(Boundary change since June 1989)

SOMERSET AND DEVON NORTH
E. 517,349 T. 47.09%
G. Watson, *LD* 106,187
*Mrs M. Daly, *C.* 83,678
J. Pilgrim, *Lab.* 34,540
D. Taylor, *Green* 10,870
G. Livings, *New Britain* 7,165
M. Lucas, *NLP* 1,200
LD majority 22,509
(Boundary change since June 1989)

SOUTH DOWNS WEST
E. 486,793 T. 39.45%
J. Provan, *C.* 83,813
Dr J. Walsh, *LD* 62,746
Ms L. Armstrong, *Lab.* 32,344
E. Paine, *Green* 7,703

W. Weights, *Lib.* 3,630
P. Kember, *NLP* 1,794
C. majority 21,067
(Boundary change since June 1989)

STAFFORDSHIRE EAST AND DERBY
E. 519,553 T. 35.46%
P. Whitehead, *Lab.* 102,393
Ms J. Evans, *C.* 50,197
Ms D. Brass, *LD* 17,469
I. Crompton, *UK Independence* 6,993
R. Clarke, *Green* 4,272
R. Jones, *NF* 2,098
Ms D. Grice, *NLP* 793
Lab. majority 72,196
(Boundary change since June 1989)

STAFFORDSHIRE WEST AND
CONGLETON
E. 502,395 T. 31.60%
M. Tappin, *Lab.* 84,337
A. Brown, *C.* 44,060
J. Stevens, *LD* 24,430
D. Hoppe, *Green* 4,533
D. Lines, *NLP* 1,403
Lab. majority 40,277
(Boundary change since June 1989)

SUFFOLK AND NORFOLK SOUTH
WEST
E. 477,668 T. 38.38%
D. Thomas, *Lab.* 74,304
*A. Turner, *C.* 61,769
R. Atkins, *LD* 37,975
A. Slade, *Green* 7,760
E. Kaplan, *NLP* 1,530
Lab. majority 12,535
(Boundary change since June 1989)

SURREY
E. 514,130 T. 37.51%
*T. Spencer, *C.* 83,405
Mrs S. Thomas, *LD* 56,387
Ms F. Wolf, *Lab.* 30,894
Mrs S. Porter, *UK Independence* 7,717
H. Charlton, *Green* 7,198
J. Walker, *Ind. Britain in Europe* 4,627
Mrs J. Thomas, *NLP* 2,638
C. majority 27,018
(Boundary change since June 1989)

SUSSEX EAST AND KENT SOUTH
E. 513,550 T. 41.90%
*Sir J. Stewart-Clark, *C.* 83,141
D. Bellotti, *LD* 76,929
N. Palmer, *Lab.* 35,273
A. Burgess, *UK Independence* 9,058
Ms R. Addison, *Green* 7,439
Ms T. Williamson, *Lib.* 2,558
P. Cragg, *NLP* 765
C. majority 6,212
(Boundary change since June 1989)

SUSSEX SOUTH AND CRAWLEY
E. 492,413 T. 37.64%
B. Donnelly, *C.* 62,860
Ms J. Edmond Smith, *Lab.* 61,114
J. Williams, *LD* 41,410
Ms P. Beever, *Green* 9,348
D. Horner, *Ind. Euro-Sceptic* 7,106
N. Furness, *Anti Fed. C.* 2,618
A. Hankey, *NLP* 901

C. majority 1,746
(Boundary change since June 1989)

THAMES VALLEY
E. 543,685   *T.* 34.80%
*J. Stevens, *C.* 70,485
J. Howarth, *Lab.* 69,727
N. Bathurst, *LD* 33,187
P. Unsworth, *Green* 6,120
J. Clark, *Lib.* 5,381
P. Owen, *Loony C* 2,859
M. Grenville, *NLP* 1,453
C. majority 758
(June 1989, C. maj. 26,491)

TYNE AND WEAR
E. 516,436   *T.* 28.02%
*A. Donnelly, *Lab.* 107,604
I. Liddell-Grainger, *C.* 19,224
P. Maughan, *LD* 8,706
G. Edwards, *Green* 4,375
Ms W. Lundgren, *Lib.* 4,164
A. Fisken, *NLP* 650
Lab. majority 88,380
(June 1989, Lab. maj. 95,780)

WIGHT AND HAMPSHIRE SOUTH
E. 488,398   *T.* 37.16%
R. Perry, *C.* 63,306
M. Hancock, *LD* 58,205
Ms S. Fry, *Lab.* 40,442
J. Browne, *Ind.* 12,140
P. Fuller, *Green* 6,697
W. Treend, *NLP* 722
C. majority 5,101
(Boundary change since June 1989)

WILTSHIRE NORTH AND BATH
E. 496,591   *T.* 41.46%
*Mrs C. Jackson, *C.* 71,872
Ms J. Matthew, *LD* 63,085
Ms J. Norris, *Lab.* 50,489
P. Cullen, *Lib.* 6,760
M. Davidson, *Green* 5,974
T. Hedges, *UK Independence* 5,842
D. Cooke, *NLP* 1,148
Dr J. Day, *CPP* 725
C. majority 8,787
(Boundary change since June 1989)

WORCESTERSHIRE AND
WARWICKSHIRE SOUTH
E. 551,162   *T.* 37.98%
J. Corrie, *C.* 73,573
Ms G. Gschaider, *Lab.* 72,369
P. Larner, *LD* 44,168
Ms J. Alty, *Green* 9,273
C. Hards, *National Independence* 8,447
J. Brewster, *NLP* 1,510
C. majority 1,204
(Boundary change since June 1989)

YORKSHIRE NORTH
E. 475,686   *T.* 38.70%
*E. McMillan-Scott, *C.* 70,036
B. Regan, *Lab.* 62,964
M. Pitts, *LD* 43,171
Dr R. Richardson, *Green* 7,036
S. Withers, *NLP* 891
C. majority 7,072
(Boundary change since June 1989)

YORKSHIRE SOUTH
E. 523,401   *T.* 28.64%
*N. West, *Lab.* 109,004
J. Howard, *C.* 20,695
Ms C. Roderick, *LD* 11,798
P. Davies, *UK Independence* 3,948
J. Waters, *Green* 3,775
N. Broome, *NLP* 681
Lab. majority 88,309
(June 1989, Lab. maj. 91,784)
See also page 275

YORKSHIRE SOUTH WEST
E. 547,469   *T.* 29.03%
*T. Megahy, *Lab.* 94,025
Mrs C. Adamson, *C.* 34,463
D. Ridgway, *LD* 21,595
A. Cooper, *Green* 7,163
G. Mead, *NLP* 1,674
Lab. majority 59,562
(Boundary change since June 1989)

YORKSHIRE WEST
E. 490,078   *T.* 34.61%
*B. Seal, *Lab.* 90,652
R. Booth, *C.* 42,455
C. Bidwell, *LD* 20,452
R. Pearson, *New Britain* 8,027
C. Harris, *Green* 7,154
D. Whitley, *NLP* 894
Lab. majority 48,197
(Boundary change since June 1989)

WALES

SOUTH WALES CENTRAL
E. 477,182   *T.* 39.40%
*W. David, *Lab.* 115,396
Ms L. Verity, *C.* 29,314
G. Llywelyn, *PC* 18,857
J. Dixon, *LD* 18,471
C. von Ruhland, *Green* 4,002
R. Griffiths, *Comm. YBG* 1,073
G. Duguay, *NLP* 889
Lab. majority 86,082
(Boundary change since June 1989)

SOUTH WALES EAST
E. 454,794   *T.* 43.07%
Mrs G. Kinnock, *Lab.* 144,907
Mrs R. Blomfield-Smith, *C.* 24,660
C. Woolgrove, *LD* 9,963
C. Mann, *PC* 9,550
R. Coghill, *Green* 4,509
Ms S. Williams, *Welsh Soc.* 1,270
Dr R. Brussatis, *NLP* 1,027
Lab. majority 120,247
(Boundary change since June 1989)

SOUTH WALES WEST
E. 395,131   *T.* 39.92%
*Revd D. Morris, *Lab.* 104,263
R. Buckland, *C.* 19,293
J. Bushell, *LD* 15,499
Ms C. Adams, *PC* 12,364
Ms J. Evans, *Green* 4,114
Ms H. Evans, *NLP* 1,112
Capt. Beany, *Beanus* 1,106
Lab. majority 84,970
(Boundary change since June 1989)

WALES MID AND WEST
E. 401,529   *T.* 48.00%
Ms E. Morgan, *Lab.* 78,092
M. Phillips, *PC* 48,858
P. Bone, *C.* 31,606
Ms J. Hughes, *LD* 23,719
D. Rowlands, *UK Independence* 5,536
Dr C. Busby, *Green* 3,938
T. Griffith-Jones, *NLP* 988
Lab. majority 29,234
(Boundary change since June 1989)

WALES NORTH
E. 475,829   *T.* 45.34%
*J. Wilson, *Lab.* 88,091
D. Wigley, *PC* 72,849
G. Mon Hughes, *C.* 33,450
Ms R. Parry, *LD* 14,828
P. Adams, *Green* 2,850
D. Hughes, *NLP* 2,065
M. Cooksey, *Ind.* 1,623
Lab. majority 15,242
(Boundary change since June 1989)

SCOTLAND

GLASGOW
E. 463,364   *T.* 34.46%
W. Miller, *Lab.* 83,953
T. Chalmers, *SNP* 40,795
T. Sheridan, *SML* 12,113
R. Wilkinson, *C.* 10,888
J. Money, *LD* 7,291
P. O'Brien, *Green* 2,252
J. Fleming, *Soc.* 1,125
M. Wilkinson, *NLP* 868
C. Marsden, *ICP* 381
Lab. majority 43,158
(June 1989, Lab. maj. 59,232)

HIGHLANDS AND ISLANDS
E. 328,104   *T.* 39.09%
*Mrs W. Ewing, *SNP* 74,872
M. Macmillan, *Lab.* 19,956
M. Tennant, *C.* 15,767
H. Morrison, *LD* 12,919
Dr E. Scott, *Green* 3,140
M. Carr, *UK Independence* 1,096
Ms M. Gilmour, *NLP* 522
SNP majority 54,916
(June 1989, SNP maj. 44,695)

LOTHIANS
E. 520,943   *T.* 38.69%
*D. Martin, *Lab.* 90,531
K. Brown, *SNP* 53,324
Dr P. McNally, *C.* 33,526
Ms H. Campbell, *LD* 17,883
R. Harper, *Green* 5,149
J. McGregor, *Soc.* 637
M. Siebert, *NLP* 500
Lab. majority 37,207
(June 1989, Lab. maj. 38,826)

SCOTLAND MID AND FIFE
E. 546,060   *T.* 38.25%
*A. Falconer, *Lab.* 95,667
R. Douglas, *SNP* 64,254
P. Page, *C.* 28,192

Ms H. Lyall, *LD*	17,192	B. Cooklin, *C.*	13,915	Miss M. Boal, *C.*	5,583
M. Johnston, *Green*	3,015	R. Stewart, *LD*	6,383	J. Lowry, *WP*	2,543
T. Pringle, *NLP*	532	A. Whitelaw, *Green*	1,874	N. Cusack, *Ind. Lab.*	2,464
Lab. majority	31,413	D. Gilmour, *NLP*	787	J. Anderson, *NLP*	1,418
(June 1989, Lab. maj. 52,157)		*Lab. majority*	52,340	Mrs J. Campion, *Peace Coalition*	1,088

SCOTLAND NORTH EAST
E. 575,748   *T.* 37.72%

(June 1989, Lab. maj. 60,317)

A. Macartney, *SNP*	92,892
*H. McCubbin, *Lab.*	61,665
Dr R. Harris, *C.*	40,372
S. Horner, *LD*	18,008
K. Farnsworth, *Green*	2,569
Ms M. Ward, *Comm. GB*	689
L. Mair, *Neeps*	584
D. Paterson, *NLP*	371
SNP majority	31,227

(June 1989, Lab. maj. 2,613)

STRATHCLYDE WEST
E. 489,129   *T.* 40.05%

*H. McMahon, *Lab.*	86,957
C. Campbell, *SNP*	61,934
J. Godfrey, *C.*	28,414
D. Herbison, *LD*	14,772
Ms K. Allan, *Green*	2,886
Ms S. Gilmour, *NLP*	918
Lab. majority	25,023

(June 1989, Lab. maj. 39,591)

D. Kerr, *Independence for Ulster*	571
Ms S. Thompson, *NLP*	454
M. Kennedy, *NLP*	419
R. Mooney, *Const. NI*	400

BY-ELECTIONS SINCE 9 JUNE 1994

MERSEYSIDE WEST
(12 December 1996)
E. 515,549   *T.* 11.4%

R. Corbett, *Lab.*	31,484
J. Myers, *C.*	12,780
K. J. C. Reid, *LD*	8,829
S. R. Radford, *Lib.*	4,050
S. Darby, *Nat. Dem.*	718
J. D. Collins, *NLP*	680
Lab. majority	18,704

SCOTLAND SOUTH
E. 500,643   *T.* 40.14%

*A. Smith, *Lab.*	90,750
A. Hutton, *C.*	45,595
Mrs C. Creech, *SNP*	45,032
D. Millar, *LD*	13,363
J. Hein, *Lib.*	3,249
Ms L. Hendry, *Green*	2,429
G. Gay, *NLP*	539
Lab. majority	45,155

(June 1989, Lab. maj. 15,693)

STRATHCLYDE EAST
E. 492,618   *T.* 37.26%

*K. Collins, *Lab.*	106,476
I. Hamilton, *SNP*	54,136

NORTHERN IRELAND

Northern Ireland forms a three-member seat with a single transferable vote system
E. 1,150,304   *T.* 48.67%

*Revd I. Paisley, *DUP*	163,246
*J. Hume, *SDLP*	161,992
*J. Nicholson, *UUUP*	133,459
Mrs M. Clark-Glass, *All.*	23,157
T. Hartley, *SF*	21,273
Ms D. McGuinness, *SF*	17,195
F. Molloy, *SF*	16,747
Revd H. Ross, *Ulster Independence*	7,858

YORKSHIRE SOUTH
(7 May 1998)
E. 221,741   *T.* 28.29%

Ms L. McAvan, *Lab.*	62,275
Ms D. P. Wallis, *LD*	22,051
R. Goodwill, *C.*	21,085
P. Davis, *UK Ind.*	13,830
Lab. majority	40,224

COMMONWEALTH PARLIAMENTARY ASSOCIATION (1911)

The Commonwealth Parliamentary Association consists of 141 branches in the national, state, provincial or territorial parliaments in the countries of the Commonwealth. Conferences and general assemblies are held every year in different countries of the Commonwealth.

President (1998–9), Hon. Hector McClean, MP, Speaker of the House of Representatives, Trinidad and Tobago

Chairman of the Executive Committee (1996–), Hon. Billie Miller, MP (Barbados)

Secretary-General, A. R. Donahoe, QC, Suite 700, Westminster House, 7 Millbank, London SWIP 3JA

UNITED KINGDOM BRANCH

Hon. Presidents, The Lord Chancellor; Madam Speaker
Chairman of Branch, Rt. Hon. Tony Blair, MP
Chairman of Executive Committee, Donald Anderson, MP

Secretary, A. Pearson, Westminster Hall, Houses of Parliament, London, SWIA OAA

THE INTER-PARLIAMENTARY UNION (1889)

The Union exists to facilitate personal contact between members of all parliaments in the promotion of representative institutions, peace and international co-operation.

Secretary-General, A. Johnsson, Place du Petit-Saconnex, BP 99, 1211 Geneva 19, Switzerland

BRITISH GROUP
Palace of Westminster, London SWIA OAA

Hon. Presidents, The Lord Chancellor; Madam Speaker
President, Rt. Hon. Tony Blair, MP
Chairman, David Marshall, MP
Secretary, D. Ramsay

The Government

Prime Minister, First Lord of the Treasury and Minister for the Civil Service
The Rt. Hon. Anthony (Tony) Blair, MP, since May 1997
Deputy Prime Minister and Secretary of State for the Environment, Transport and the Regions
The Rt. Hon. John Prescott, MP, since May 1997
Chancellor of the Exchequer
The Rt. Hon. Gordon Brown, MP, since May 1997
Secretary of State for Foreign and Commonwealth Affairs
The Rt. Hon. Robin Cook, MP, since May 1997
Lord Chancellor
The Lord Irvine of Lairg, PC, QC, since May 1997
Secretary of State for the Home Department
The Rt. Hon. Jack Straw, MP, since May 1997
Secretary of State for Education and Employment
The Rt. Hon. David Blunkett, MP, since May 1997
President of the Council and Leader of the House of Commons
The Rt. Hon. Margaret Beckett, MP, since July 1998
Minister for the Cabinet Office and Chancellor of the Duchy of Lancaster
The Rt. Hon. Dr Jack Cunningham, MP, since July 1998
Secretary of State for Scotland
The Rt. Hon. Donald Dewar, MP, since May 1997
Secretary of State for Defence
The Rt. Hon. George Robertson, MP, since May 1997
Secretary of State for Health
The Rt. Hon. Frank Dobson, MP, since May 1997
Parliamentary Secretary to the Treasury (Chief Whip)
The Rt. Hon. Ann Taylor, MP
Secretary of State for Culture, Media and Sport
The Rt. Hon. Chris Smith, MP, since May 1997
Secretary of State for Northern Ireland
The Rt. Hon. Dr Marjorie (Mo) Mowlam, MP, since May 1997
Secretary of State for Wales
The Rt. Hon. Ron Davies, MP, since May 1997
Secretary of State for International Development
The Rt. Hon. Clare Short, MP, since May 1997
Secretary of State for Social Security
The Rt. Hon. Alistair Darling, MP, since July 1998
Minister of Agriculture, Fisheries and Food
The Rt. Hon. Nick Brown, MP, since July 1998
Leader of the House of Lords and Minister for Women
The Baroness Jay of Paddington*, since July 1998
Secretary of State for Trade and Industry
The Rt. Hon. Peter Mandelson, MP, since July 1998
Chief Secretary to the Treasury
The Rt. Hon. Stephen Byers, MP, since July 1998

The Minister of State at the Department of the Environment, Transport and the Regions with responsibility for Transport, and the Government Chief Whip in the House of Lords will attend Cabinet meetings although they are not members of the Cabinet.
* Appointed as Lord Privy Seal

LAW OFFICERS

Attorney-General
The Rt. Hon. John Morris, QC, MP, since May 1997
Lord Advocate
The Lord Hardie, PC, QC, since May 1997
Solicitor-General
Ross Cranston, MP, since July 1998
Solicitor-General for Scotland
Colin Boyd, QC

MINISTERS OF STATE

Agriculture, Fisheries and Food
Jeff Rooker, MP (*Food Safety*)
Cabinet Office
The Lord Falconer of Thoroton, QC
Defence
Doug Henderson, MP (*Armed Forces*)
The Lord Gilbert, PC, PH.D. (*Defence Procurement*)
Education and Employment
The Rt. Hon. Andrew Smith, MP (*Welfare to Work, Equal Opportunities*)
Estelle Morris, MP (*School Standards*)
The Baroness Blackstone, PH.D.
Environment, Transport and the Regions
The Rt. Hon. Dr John Reid, MP (*Transport*)
The Rt. Hon. Michael Meacher, MP (*Environment*)
Hilary Armstrong, MP (*Local Government, Housing*)
Richard Caborn, MP (*Regions, Regeneration, Planning*)
Foreign and Commonwealth Office
Joyce Quin, MP (*Minister for Europe*)
Derek Fatchett, MP
Tony Lloyd, MP
Health
Alan Milburn, MP (*NHS Structure and Resources*)
Tessa Jowell, MP (*Public Health, Women's Issues*)
Home Office
Alun Michael, MP (*Criminal and Police Policy*)
The Lord Williams of Mostyn, QC (*Constitution, Prisons, Probation*)
Lord Chancellor's Department
Geoff Hoon, MP
Northern Ireland Office
Paul Murphy, MP (*Political Development, Finance, Personnel, Information*)
Adam Ingram, MP (*Security, Criminal Justice, Economic Development*)
Scottish Office
Helen Liddell, MP (*Education, Women's Issues, Co-ordination and Presentation of Policy*)
Henry McLeish, MP (*Home Affairs, Devolution, Local Government*)
Social Security
John Denham, MP
Trade and Industry
John Battle, MP (*Energy, Industry, Environment*)
Ian McCartney, MP (*Employment Relations*)
Brian Wilson, MP (*Trade*)
The Lord Simon of Highbury, CBE (*Trade and Competitiveness in Europe*)†

Treasury
Geoffrey Robinson, MP (*Paymaster-General*)
Dawn Primarolo, MP (*Financial Secretary*)
Patricia Hewitt, MP (*Economic Secretary*)
The Lord Simon of Highbury, CBE (*Trade and Competitiveness in Europe*)†
† Joint DTI/Treasury minister

UNDER-SECRETARIES OF STATE

Agriculture, Fisheries and Food
Elliot Morley, MP (*Fisheries, Countryside*)
The Lord Donoughue, D.phil. (*Farming, Food Industry*)
Cabinet Office
Peter Kilfoyle, MP
Culture, Media and Sport
Alan Howarth, MP (*Arts*)
Tony Banks, MP (*Sport*)
Janet Anderson, MP (*Tourism, Film, Broadcasting*)
Defence
John Spellar, MP
Education and Employment
Margaret Hodge, MP (*Employment, Equal Opportunities*)
Charles Clarke, MP (*Schools*)
George Mudie, MP (*Lifelong Learning*)
Environment, Transport and the Regions
Nick Raynsford, MP (*London, Construction*)
Glenda Jackson, MP (*Transport in London*)
The Lord Whitty (*Roads*)
Alan Meale, MP (*Environment, Wildlife, Health and Safety Executive, Regeneration, the Regions*)
Foreign and Commonwealth Office
The Baroness Symons of Vernham Dean
Health
Paul Boateng, MP (*Social Care, Mental Health*)
The Baroness Hayman (*NHS Development, Cancer, Emergency Services*)
Home Office
George Howarth, MP (*Prisons, Probation, Fire and Emergency Planning, Drugs, Elections, Gambling, Data Protection*)
Michael O'Brien, MP (*Immigration, Nationality*)
Kate Hoey, MP (*Metropolitan Police, Women's Issues, International Co-operation*)
International Development
George Foulkes, MP
Northern Ireland Office
John McFall, MP (*Education, Training and Employment, Health, Community Relations*)
The Lord Dubs (*Environment, Agriculture*)
Scottish Office
Dr Calum MacDonald, MP (*Housing, Transport, European Affairs*)
Sam Galbraith, MP (*Health, Arts*)
The Lord Sewel, CBE (*Agriculture, Environment, Fisheries*)
Gus Macdonald‡ (*Business and Industry*)

Social Security
The Baroness Hollis of Heigham, D.phil. (*Child Benefit, Child Support, War Pensions*)
Angela Eagle, MP (*Income-related Benefits, International and Green Issues*)
Stephen Timms, MP (*Disability and Sickness Benefits, National Insurance Contributions, Devolution, Independent Living Fund*)
Trade and Industry
Dr Kim Howells, MP (*Competition, Consumer Affairs*)
Barbara Roche, MP (*Small Firms, Regional Policy*)
The Lord Sainsbury of Turville (*Science*)
Welsh Office
Peter Hain, MP
Jon Owen Jones, MP
‡ Not an MP; will receive a life peerage to enable him to sit in the House of Lords

GOVERNMENT WHIPS

HOUSE OF LORDS

Captain of the Honourable Corps of Gentlemen-at-Arms (Chief Whip)
The Lord Carter, PC
Captain of The Queen's Bodyguard of the Yeoman of the Guard (Deputy Chief Whip)
The Lord McIntosh of Haringey
Lords-in-Waiting
The Lord Hoyle; The Lord Hunt of King's Heath
Baronesses-in-Waiting
The Baroness Farrington of Ribbleton; The Baroness Ramsay of Cartvale; The Baroness Amos

HOUSE OF COMMONS

Parliamentary Secretary to the Treasury (Chief Whip)
The Rt. Hon. Ann Taylor, MP
Treasurer of HM Household (Deputy Chief Whip)
Keith Bradley, MP
Comptroller of HM Household
Thomas McAvoy, MP
Vice-Chamberlain of HM Household
Graham Allen, MP
Lords Commissioners
Robert Ainsworth, MP; James Dowd, MP; Clive Betts, MP; David Jamieson, MP; Jane Kennedy, MP
Assistant Whips
David Clelland, MP; Kevin Hughes, MP; Anne McGuire, MP; David Hanson, MP; Michael Hall, MP; Keith Hill, MP; G regory Pope, MP

Government Departments and Public Offices

For changes notified after 31 August, *see* Stop-press

This section covers central government departments, executive agencies, regulatory bodies, other statutory independent organizations, and bodies which are government-financed or whose head is appointed by a government minister.

THE CIVIL SERVICE

Under the Next Steps programme, launched in 1988, many semi-autonomous executive agencies have been established with the aim of improving the performance of the Civil Service. Executive agencies operate within a framework set by the responsible minister which specifies policies, objectives and available resources. All executive agencies are set annual performance targets by their minister. Each agency has a chief executive, who is responsible for the day-to-day operations of the agency and who is accountable to the minister for the use of resources and for meeting the agency's targets. The minister accounts to Parliament for the work of the agency. Nearly 60 per cent of civil servants now work in executive agencies. Customs and Excise, the Inland Revenue, the Crown Prosecution Service and the Serious Fraud Office, which employ a further 17 per cent of civil servants, also operate on 'Next Steps' lines. In January 1998 there were about 468,180 permanent civil servants.

The Senior Civil Service was created in April 1996 and comprises about 3,000 staff from Permanent Secretary to the former Grade 5 level, including all agency chief executives. All government departments and executive agencies are now responsible for their own pay and grading systems for civil servants outside the Senior Civil Service. In practice the grades of the former Open structure are still in use in some organizations. The Open structure represented the following:

Grade	Title
1	Permanent Secretary
1A	Second Permanent Secretary
2	Deputy Secretary
3	Under-Secretary
4	Chief Scientific Officer B, Professional and Technology Directing A
5	Assistant Secretary, Deputy Chief Scientific Officer, Professional and Technology Directing B
6	Senior Principal, Senior Principal Scientific Officer, Professional and Technology Superintending Grade
7	Principal, Principal Scientific Officer, Principal Professional and Technology Officer

SALARIES 1998–9

MINISTERIAL SALARIES from 1 April 1998

Ministers who are Members of the House of Commons receive a parliamentary salary (£45,066) in addition to their ministerial salary.

*Prime Minister	£102,750
*Cabinet minister (Commons)	£61,650
*†Cabinet minister (Lords)	£80,107
Minister of State (Commons)	£31,981
Minister of State (Lords)	£53,264
Parliamentary Under-Secretary (Commons)	£24,273
Parliamentary Under-Secretary (Lords)	£44,832

* These ministers have decided not to take the full salaries provided for them for the financial year 1998–9. They will instead draw the following ministerial salaries: Prime Minister, £60,167; Cabinet minister (Commons), £45,201; Cabinet minister (Lords), £60,495

† Except the Lord Chancellor, who receives a salary of £148,850

SPECIAL ADVISERS' SALARIES from 1 April 1998

Special advisers are paid out of public funds; their salaries are negotiated individually, but are usually in the range £24,836 to £74,954.

CIVIL SERVICE SALARIES from 1 December 1998

Senior Civil Service (SCS)

Secretary of the Cabinet and Head of the Home Civil Service	£95,720–£164,310
Permanent Secretary	£95,720–£164,310
Band 9	£85,080–£120,490
Band 8	£77,840–£113,680
Band 7	£71,250–£107,300
Band 6	£65,080–£101,350
Band 5	£59,450–£95,720
Band 4	£54,230–£90,400
Band 3	£49,130–£80,400
Band 2	£44,560–£71,470
Band 1	£40,420–£63,490

Staff are placed in pay bands according to their level of responsibility and taking account of other factors such as experience and marketability. Movement within and between bands is based on performance. A recruitment and retention allowance of up to £3,000 may be paid in certain circumstances shown for bands 1 to 9.

Other Civil Servants

Following the delegation of responsibility for pay and grading to government departments and agencies from 1 April 1996, it is no longer possible to show the pay rates for staff outside the Senior Civil Service. Individual departments and agencies now have their own pay systems in operation.

ADJUDICATOR'S OFFICE

Haymarket House, 28 Haymarket, London SW1Y 4SP
Tel 0171-930 2292; fax 0171-930 2298

The Adjudicator's Office opened in 1993 and investigates complaints about the way the Inland Revenue (including the Valuation Office Agency), Customs and Excise, the Contributions Agency and the Contributions Unit of the Social Security Agency in Northern Ireland have handled an individual's affairs.

The Adjudicator, Ms E. Filkin
Head of Office, M. Savage

ADVISORY, CONCILIATION AND ARBITRATION SERVICE

Brandon House, 180 Borough High Street, London
SE1 1LW
Tel 0171-210 3613; fax 0171-210 3708

The Advisory, Conciliation and Arbitration Service (ACAS) was set up under the Employment Protection Act 1975 (the provisions now being found in the Trade Union and Labour Relations (Consolidation) Act 1992). ACAS is directed by a Council consisting of a full-time chairman and part-time employer, trade union and independent members, all appointed by the Secretary of State for Trade and Industry. The functions of the Service are to promote the improvement of industrial relations in general, to provide facilities for conciliation, mediation and arbitration as means of avoiding and resolving industrial disputes, and to provide advisory and information services on industrial relations matters to employers, employees and their representatives.

ACAS has regional offices in Birmingham, Bristol, Cardiff, Fleet, Glasgow, Leeds, Liverpool, London, Manchester, Newcastle upon Tyne and Nottingham.

Chairman, J. Hougham, CBE
Chief Conciliator (G4), D. Evans

MINISTRY OF AGRICULTURE, FISHERIES AND FOOD

Nobel House, 17 Smith Square, London SW1P 3JR
Tel 0171-238 6000; fax 0171-238 6591
E-mail: helpline@inf.maff.gov.uk
Web: http://www.maff.gov.uk/maffhome.htm

The Ministry of Agriculture, Fisheries and Food is responsible for government policies on agriculture, horticulture and fisheries in England and for policies relating to the safety and quality of food in the UK as a whole, including composition, labelling, additives, contaminants and new production processes. In association with the agriculture departments of the Scottish, Welsh and Northern Ireland Offices and with the Intervention Board (*see* page 315–16), the Ministry is responsible for negotiations in the EU on the common agricultural and fisheries policies, and for single European market questions relating to its responsibilities. Its remit also includes international agricultural and food trade policy.

The Ministry exercises responsibilities for the protection and enhancement of the countryside and the marine environment, for flood defence and for other rural issues. It is the licensing authority for veterinary medicines and the registration authority for pesticides. It administers policies relating to the control of animal, plant and fish diseases. It provides scientific, technical and professional services and advice to farmers, growers and ancillary industries, and it commissions research to assist in the formulation and assessment of policy and to underpin applied research and development work done by industry. Responsibility for food safety and standards will be transferred to the new Food Standards Agency, expected to be in operation by mid 1999.

Minister of Agriculture, Fisheries and Food, The Rt. Hon. Nick Brown, MP
Principal Private Secretary (SCS), D. North
Private Secretary, A. K. R. Slade

Minister of State, Jeff Rooker, MP (*Food Safety*)
Private Secretary, Mrs K. Lepper
Parliamentary Private Secretary, R. Burden, MP
Parliamentary Secretaries, Elliot Morley, MP (*Fisheries, the Countryside*); The Lord Donoughue, D.Phil. (*Farming, the Food Industry*)
Private Secretary to Mr Morley, C. Porro
Private Secretary to Lord Donoughue, Dr P. Grimley
Parliamentary Clerk, M. Stickings
Permanent Secretary (SCS), R. J. Packer
Private Secretary, Mrs J. Milne

ESTABLISHMENT DEPARTMENT

Director of Establishments (SCS), R. A. Saunderson

ESTABLISHMENTS (GENERAL) AND OFFICE SERVICES DIVISION
Head of Division (G6), Dr J. A. Bailey

WELFARE BRANCH
Whitehall Place (West Block), London SW1A 2HH
Tel 0171-238 6000
Chief Welfare Officer (SEO), D. J. Jones

PERSONNEL MANAGEMENT AND DEVELOPMENT DIVISION
Head of Division (SCS), T. J. Osmond

DEPARTMENTAL HEALTH AND SAFETY UNIT
Spur 6, C Block, Government Buildings, Epsom Road, Guildford GU1 2LD
Tel 01483-403120/403753
Head of Unit (G7), C. R. Bradburn

TRAINING AND DEVELOPMENT BRANCH
Principal (G7), J. M. Cowley

BUILDING AND ESTATE MANAGEMENT
Eastbury House, 30–34 Albert Embankment,
London SE1 7TL
Tel 0171-238 6000
Head of Division (SCS), J. A. S. Nickson

INFORMATION TECHNOLOGY DIRECTORATE

Room 755, St Christopher House, Southwark Street, London SE1 0UD
Tel 0171-921 1886
Director (SCS), A. G. Matthews
Head of Strategies (G6), P. Barber
Head of Applications (G6), D. D. Brown
Head of Infrastructure (G6), S. Soper

INFORMATION DIVISION

Tel 0171-238 6000; helpline 0645-335577
Chief Information Officer (SCS), G. Blakeway
Chief Press Officer (G7), M. Smith
Chief Publicity Officer (G7), N. Wagstaffe
Principal Librarian (G7), P. McShane

FINANCE DEPARTMENT

3–8 Whitehall Place (West Block), London SW1A 2HH
Tel 0171-238 6000
Principal Finance Officer (SCS), P. Elliott

FINANCIAL POLICY DIVISION
Head of Division (SCS), B. J. Harding

FINANCIAL MANAGEMENT DIVISION
Head of Division (SCS), J. M. Lowi

PROCUREMENT AND CONTRACTS DIVISION
Director of Audit (SCS), D. V. Fisher

CAP SCHEMES MANAGEMENT
Head of Division (SCS), L. G. Mitchell

MARKET TESTING AND PROCUREMENT ADVICE
Director (SCS), D. B. Rabey

RESOURCE MANAGEMENT STRATEGY UNIT
Head of Division (SCS), Mrs J. Flint

LEGAL DEPARTMENT
55 Whitehall, London SW1A 2EY
Tel 0171-238 6000

Legal Adviser and Solicitor (SCS), Miss K. M. S. Morton
Principal Assistant Solicitors (SCS), D. J. Pearson; Ms C. A.
  Crisham

LEGAL DIVISIONS

Assistant Solicitor, Division A1 (SCS), P. Davis
Assistant Solicitor, Division A2 (SCS), P. Kent
Assistant Solicitor, Division A3 (SCS), C. Gregory
Assistant Solicitor, Division A4 (SCS), C. Allen
Assistant Solicitor, Division A5 (SCS), Mrs C. A. Davis
Assistant Solicitor, Division B1 (SCS), Dr G. Davis
Assistant Solicitor, Division B2 (SCS), Ms S. B. Spence
Assistant Solicitor, Division B3 (SCS), A. I. Corbett
Assistant Solicitor, Division B4 (SCS), Mrs F. C. Nash

INVESTIGATION UNIT
Chief Investigation Officer, Miss J. Panting

ECONOMICS AND STATISTICS
Under-Secretary (SCS), D. Thompson

DIVISIONS

*Senior Economic Adviser, Economics and Statistics (Farm
  Business) (SCS)*, H. Fearn
*Senior Economic Adviser, Economics (International and Food)
  (SCS)*, N. Atkinson
Senior Economic Adviser, Economics (Resource Use) (SCS), J. P.
  Muriel

STATISTICS DIVISION
Foss House, Kingspool, 1–2 Peasholme Green, York
YO1 2PX
Tel 01904-455328

Chief Statistician (Commodities and Food) (SCS), S. Platt
Chief Statistician (Census and Surveys) (SCS), P. F. Helm

CHIEF SCIENTIST'S GROUP
St Christopher House, 80–112 Southwark Street,
London SE1 OUD
Tel 0171-928 3666

Chief Scientist (SCS), Dr D. W. F. Shannon

DIVISIONS

Head, Agriculture and Food Technology (SCS),
  Dr J. C. Sherlock
Head, Food and Veterinary Science Division (SCS),
  Dr K. J. MacOwan
Head, Environment, Fisheries and International Science (SCS),
  Dr M. Parker
Head, Research Policy Co-ordination (SCS), A. R. Burne

FISHERIES DEPARTMENT
Fisheries Secretary (SCS), S. Wentworth

DIVISIONS

Head, Fisheries I (SCS), A. Kuyk
Head, Fisheries II (SCS), C. I. Llewellyn
Head, Fisheries III (SCS), J. E. Robbs
Head, Fisheries IV (G6), B. S. Edwards
Chief Inspector, Sea Fisheries Inspectorate (G6), S. G. Ellson

AGRICULTURAL COMMODITIES, TRADE AND FOOD PRODUCTION
Deputy Secretary (SCS), Ms V. K. Timms

EUROPEAN UNION AND LIVESTOCK GROUP
Under-Secretary (SCS), D. P. Hunter

DIVISIONS

Head, European Union (SCS), A. J. Lebrecht
Head, Beef and Sheep (SCS), J. R. Cowan
Head, Milk, Pigs, Eggs and Poultry (SCS), P. P. Nash
Head, Livestock Schemes (G6), Ms L. Cornish

ARABLE CROPS AND HORTICULTURE
Under-Secretary (SCS), vacant

DIVISIONS

Head, Cereals and Set-Aside (SCS), R. A. Hathaway
Head, Sugar, Tobacco, Oilseeds and Protein (SCS), H. B. Brown
Head, Horticulture and Potatoes (SCS), G. W. Noble

PLANT VARIETY RIGHTS OFFICE AND SEEDS DIVISION
White House Lane, Huntingdon Road, Cambridge
CB3 OLF
Tel 01223-277151

Head of Office (SCS), D. A. Boreham

FOOD, DRINK AND MARKETING POLICY
Under-Secretary (SCS), N. Thornton

DIVISIONS

Head, Food and Drinks Industry (SCS), Miss C. J. Rabagliati
Head, International Relations and Export Promotion (SCS),
  D. V. Orchard
Head, Trade Policy and Tropical Foods (SCS), Miss
  S. E. Brown
Head, Market Task Force (SCS), vacant
Head, Devolution Unit (SCS), Miss V. A. Smith

REGIONAL SERVICES AND DEFENCE GROUP
Under-Secretary (SCS), Mrs K. J. A. Brown
Head, Agricultural Resources and Better Regulation (SCS), Mrs
  A. M. Blackburn
*Head, Plant Health, and Plant Health and Seeds Inspectorate
  (SCS)*, A. J. Perrins
Head, Flood and Coastal Protection (SCS), Dr J. Park

REGIONAL ORGANIZATION
Head, Regional Support Unit (G7), D. Putley

Regional Service Centres

ANGLIA REGION, Block B, Government Buildings,
  Brooklands Avenue, Cambridge CB2 2DR. Tel: 01223-
  462727. *Regional Director (G6)*, M. Edwards
EAST MIDLANDS REGION, Block 7, Government
  Buildings, Chalfont Drive, Nottingham NG8 3SN. Tel:
  0115-929 1191. *Regional Director (G6)*, G. Norbury
NORTH-EAST REGION, Government Buildings, Crosby
  Road, Northallerton, N. Yorks DL6 1AD. Tel: 01609-
  773751. *Regional Director (G6)*, P. Watson
NORTHERN REGION, Eden Bridge House, Lowther
  Street, Carlisle, Cumbria CA3 8DX. Tel: 01228-23400.
  Regional Director (SCS), I. G. Pearson
NORTH MERCIA REGION, Electra Way, Crewe Business
  Park, Crewe, Cheshire CW1 6GL. Tel: 01270-
  754000. *Regional Director (G6)*, F. Whitehouse
SOUTH-EAST REGION, Block A, Government Buildings,
  Coley Park, Reading, Berks RG1 6DT. Tel: 01734-
  581222. *Regional Director (G6)*, Mrs V. Silvester

SOUTH MERCIA REGION, Block C, Government Buildings, Whittington Road, Worcester WR5 2LQ. Tel: 01905-763355. *Regional Director (G6)*, B. Davies
SOUTH-WEST REGION, Clyst House, Winslade Park, Clyst St Mary, Exeter EX5 1DY. Tel: 01392-447400. *Regional Director (G6)*, M. R. W. Highman
WESSEX REGION, Block 3, Government Buildings, Burghill Road, Westbury-on-Trym, Bristol BS10 6NJ. Tel: 01272-591000. *Regional Director (G6)*, Mrs A. J. L. Ould

FOOD SAFETY AND ENVIRONMENT GROUP
Deputy Secretary (SCS), R. J. D. Carden, CB

ENVIRONMENT GROUP
Under-Secretary (SCS), D. J. Coates
Head, Conservation and Rural Development (SCS), Ms J. Allfrey
Head, Conservation Management Division (SCS), P. M. Boyling
Head, Environmental Protection (SCS), D. E. Jones

FOOD SAFETY AND STANDARDS GROUP
Under-Secretary (SCS), G. Podger

DIVISIONS
Head, Additives and Novel Foods (SCS), Dr J. R. Bell
Head, Food Contaminants (SCS), Dr R. Burt
Head, Food Labelling and Standards (SCS), G. F. Meekings
Head, Radiological Safety and Nutrition (SCS), Dr M. G. Segal
Head, Food Hygiene (SCS), R. J. Harding
Head, Meat Hygiene I (SCS), R. C. McIvor
Head, Meat Hygiene II (SCS), C. J. Lawson
Head, Food Standards Agency Division (SCS), Miss E. J. Wordley

ANIMAL HEALTH GROUP
Government Buildings, Hook Rise South, Tolworth, Surbiton, Surrey KT6 7NF
Tel 0181-330 4411

Under-Secretary (SCS), B. H. B. Dickinson

DIVISIONS
Head, Animal Health (BSE and International Trade) (SCS), T. E. D. Eddy
Head, Animal Health (Disease Control) (SCS), T. D. Rossington
Head, Services (G6), R. Gurd
Head, Animal Welfare (SCS), C. J. Ryder

CHIEF VETERINARY OFFICER'S GROUP
Government Buildings, Hook Rise South, Tolworth, Surbiton, Surrey KT6 7NF
Tel 0181-330 8057

Chief Veterinary Officer (SCS), J. M. Scudamore
Assistant Chief Veterinary Officer (SCS), R. J. G. Cawthorne

DIVISIONS
Head, Veterinary International Trade Team (SCS), R. A. Bell
Head, Veterinary Notifiable Disease Team (Exotic Diseases and BSE) (SCS), Dr D. Matthews
Head, Veterinary Notifiable Disease Team (Endemic Animal Diseases and Zoonoses) (SCS), Dr D. Reynolds
Head, Welfare Team (SCS), A. T. Turnbull

VETERINARY FIELD SERVICE
Government Buildings, Hook Rise South, Tolworth, Surbiton, Surrey KT15 3NB
Tel 0181-330 4411

Director of Veterinary Field Services (SCS), M. J. Atkinson

EXECUTIVE AGENCIES

CENTRAL SCIENCE LABORATORY
Sand Hutton, York YO4 1LZ
Tel 01904-462000; fax 01904-462111

The agency provides MAFF with technical support and policy advice on the protection and quality of the food supply and on related environmental issues.
Chief Executive (G3), Prof. P. I. Stanley
Research Directors (G5), Prof. A. R. Hardy (*Agriculture and Environment*); Dr M. Parker (*Food*)

CENTRE FOR ENVIRONMENT, FISHERIES AND AQUACULTURE SCIENCE
Pakefield Road, Lowestoft, Suffolk NR33 0HT
Tel 01502-562244; fax: 01502-513865

The Agency, established in April 1997, provides research and consultancy services in fisheries science and management, aquaculture, fish health and hygiene, environmental impact assessment, and environmental quality assessment.
Chief Executive, Dr P. Greig-Smith

FARMING AND RURAL CONSERVATION AGENCY
Nobel House, 17 Smith Square, London SW1P 3JR
Tel 0171-238 5432; fax 0171-238 5588

The Agency, established in April 1997, is responsible jointly to MAFF and the Welsh Office. It assists the Government in the design, development and implementation of policies on the integration of farming and conservation, environmental protection and the rural economy. This includes agri-environment schemes such as Environmentally Sensitive Areas, Countryside Stewardship and access schemes, land use and tenure, milk hygiene inspections and wildlife management.
Chief Executive (SCS), Miss S. Nason

INTERVENTION BOARD
— *see* page 315–16

MEAT HYGIENE SERVICE
Foss House, Kingspool, 1–2 Peasholme Green, York YO1 7PX
Tel 01904-455655; fax 01904-455502

The Agency was launched in April 1995. It protects public health and animal welfare through veterinary supervision and meat inspection in licensed fresh meat establishments.
Chief Executive (G4), J. McNeill

PESTICIDES SAFETY DIRECTORATE
Mallard House, Kingspool, 3 Peasholme Green, York YO1 7PX
Tel 01904-640500; fax 01904-455733

The Pesticides Safety Directorate is responsible for the evaluation and approval of pesticides and the development of policies relating to them, in order to protect consumers, users and the environment.
Chief Executive (G4), G. K. Bruce
Director (Policy) (G5), J. A. Bainton
Director (Approvals) (G5), Dr A. D. Martin

VETERINARY LABORATORIES AGENCY
Woodham Lane, New Haw, Addlestone, Surrey KT15 3NB
Tel 01932-341111; fax 01932-347046

The Veterinary Laboratories Agency provides scientific and technical expertise in animal and public health.
Chief Executive (G3), Dr T. W. A. Little
Director of Research (G4), Dr J. A. Morris
Director of Laboratory Services (G5), Dr S. Edwards
Director of Surveillance (G5), J. W. Harkness
Director of Finance (G6), I. Grattidge
Laboratory Secretary (G6), C. Edwards

VETERINARY MEDICINES DIRECTORATE
Woodham Lane, New Haw, Addlestone, Surrey KT15 3NB
Tel 01932-336911; fax 01932-336618

The Veterinary Medicines Directorate is responsible for all aspects of the authorization and control of veterinary medicines, including post-authorization surveillance of residues in meat and animal products, and the provision of policy advice to ministers.

Chief Executive and Director of Veterinary Medicines (G4), Dr J. M. Rutter
Director (Policy) (G5), R. Anderson
Director (Licensing) (G5), S. Dean
Secretary and Head of Business Unit (G6), J. FitzGerald
Licensing Manager, Pharmaceuticals and Feed Additives (G6), J. P. O'Brien
Licensing Manager, Immunologicals (G6) (acting), Dr D. Fawthrop

COLLEGE OF ARMS OR HERALDS COLLEGE
Queen Victoria Street, London EC4V 4BT
Tel 0171-248 2762

The Sovereign's Officers of Arms (Kings, Heralds and Pursuivants of Arms) were first incorporated by Richard III. The powers vested in the Crown in the Earl Marshal (the Duke of Norfolk) with regard to state ceremonial are largely exercised through the College. The College is also the official repository of the arms and pedigrees of English, Welsh, Northern Irish and Commonwealth (except Canadian) families and their descendants, and its records include official copies of the records of Ulster King of Arms, the originals of which remain in Dublin. The 13 officers of the College specialize in genealogical and heraldic work for their respective clients.

Arms have been and still are granted by letters patent from the Kings of Arms. A right to arms can only be established by the registration in the official records of the College of Arms of a pedigree showing direct male line descent from an ancestor already appearing therein as being entitled to arms, or by making application through the College of Arms for a grant of arms. Grants are made to corporations as well as to individuals.

The College of Arms is open Monday–Friday 10–4.

Earl Marshal, The Duke of Norfolk, KG, GCVO, CB, CBE, MC

KINGS OF ARMS
Garter, P. L. Gwynn-Jones, CVO, FSA
Clarenceux (and Registrar), D. H. B. Chesshyre, LVO, FSA
Norroy and Ulster, T. Woodcock, LVO, FSA

HERALDS
Richmond (and Earl Marshal's Secretary), P. L. Dickinson
York, H. E. Paston-Bedingfeld
Chester, T. H. S. Duke

PURSUIVANTS
Bluemantle, R. J. B. Noel
Portcullis, W. G. Hunt, TD
Rouge Croix, D. V. White

COURT OF THE LORD LYON
HM New Register House, Edinburgh EH1 3YT
Tel 0131-556 7255; fax 0131-557 2148

The Court of the Lord Lyon is the Scottish Court of Chivalry (including the genealogical jurisdiction of the *Ri-Sennachie* of Scotland's Celtic Kings). The Lord Lyon King of Arms has jurisdiction, subject to appeal to the Court of Session and the House of Lords, in questions of heraldry and the right to bear arms. The Court also administers the Scottish Public Register of All Arms and Bearings and the Public Register of All Genealogies. Pedigrees are established by decrees of Lyon Court and by letters patent. As Royal Commissioner in Armory, the Lord Lyon grants patents of arms (which constitute the grantee and heirs noble in the Noblesse of Scotland) to 'virtuous and well-deserving' Scotsmen and to petitioners (personal or corporate) in The Queen's overseas realms of Scottish connection, and issues birthbrieves.

Lord Lyon King of Arms, Sir Malcolm Innes of Edingight, KCVO, WS

HERALDS
Albany, J. A. Spens, RD, WS
Rothesay, Sir Crispin Agnew of Lochnaw, Bt., QC
Ross, C. J. Burnett, FSA scot

PURSUIVANTS
Kintyre, J. C. G. George, FSA scot
Unicorn, Alastair Campbell of Airds, FSA scot
Carrick, Mrs C. G. W. Roads, MVO, FSA scot

Lyon Clerk and Keeper of Records, Mrs C. G. W. Roads, MVO, FSA scot
Procurator-Fiscal, D. F. Murby, WS
Herald Painter, Mrs J. Phillips
Macer, A. M. Clark

ARTS COUNCILS

The Arts Council of Great Britain was established as an independent body in 1946 to be the principal channel for the Government's support of the arts. In 1994 the Scottish and Welsh Arts Councils became autonomous and the Arts Council of Great Britain became the Arts Council of England.

The Arts Councils are responsible for the distribution of the proceeds of the National Lottery allocated to the arts (*see* page 610).

ARTS COUNCIL OF ENGLAND
14 Great Peter Street, London SW1P 3NQ
Tel 0171-333 0100; fax 0171-973 6590

The Arts Council of England's objectives are to develop and improve the understanding and practice of the arts and to increase their accessibility to the public. The Council funds the major arts organizations in England and the ten Regional Arts Boards. It is funded by the Department for Culture, Media and Sport but operates at 'arm's length' from Government as regards artistic decision-making, although it is expected to account for such decisions to the Government and the public. The Council also provides advice, information and help to artists and arts organizations. Its members are unpaid.

The Council distributes an annual grant from the Department for Culture, Media and Sport; the grant for 1998–9 is £184.6 million.

In July 1998 the Government published a discussion document including a proposal to merge the Arts Council of England and the Crafts Council.

Chairman, G. Robinson
Members, D. Anderson; D. Brierley, CBE; Ms D. Bull; Prof. C. Frayling; A. Gormley; A. Kapoor; Prof. J. MacGregor; Prof. A. Motion; Ms P. Skene; Ms H. Strong
Chief Executive, P. Hewitt

REGIONAL ARTS BOARDS

EASTERN ARTS BOARD, Cherry Hinton Hall, Cherry
Hinton Road, Cambridge CB1 4DW. Tel: 01223-215355.
Chair, S. Timperley
EAST MIDLANDS ARTS BOARD, Mountfields House,
Epinal Way, Loughborough, Leics LE11 0QE. Tel: 01509-
218292. *Chair*, Prof. R. Cowell
LONDON ARTS BOARD, Elme House, 133 Long Acre,
London WC2E 9AF. Tel: 0171-240 1313. *Chair*, T.
Phillips
NORTHERN ARTS BOARD, 9–10 Osborne Terrace,
Newcastle upon Tyne NE2 1NZ. Tel: 0191-281 6334.
Chair, G. Loggie
NORTH-WEST ARTS BOARD, Manchester House, 22
Bridge Street, Manchester M3 3AB. Tel: 0161-834 6644.
Chair, Prof. B. Cox, CBE
SOUTH-EAST ARTS BOARD, Union House, Eridge Road,
Tunbridge Wells, Kent TN4 8HF. Tel: 01892-507200.
Chair, R. Reed
SOUTHERN ARTS BOARD, 13 St Clement Street,
Winchester SO23 9DQ. Tel: 01962-855099. *Chair*, D.
Astor
SOUTH-WEST ARTS BOARD, Bradninch Place, Gandy
Street, Exeter EX4 3LS. Tel: 01392-218188. *Chair*, D.
Brierley, CBE
WEST MIDLANDS ARTS BOARD, 82 Granville Street,
Birmingham B1 2LH. Tel: 0121-631 3121. *Chair*, R.
Natkiel
YORKSHIRE AND HUMBERSIDE ARTS BOARD, 21 Bond
Street, Dewsbury, W. Yorks WF13 1AX. Tel: 01924-
455555. *Chair*, C. Price

SCOTTISH ARTS COUNCIL

12 Manor Place, Edinburgh EH3 7DD
Tel 0131-226 6051; fax 0131-225 9833

The Scottish Arts Council funds arts organizations in
Scotland and is funded directly by the Scottish Office. The
grant for 1998–9 is £26.9 million.
Chairman, M. Linklater
Members, Ms S. Ainsley; H. Buchanan; R. Chester; W.
English; J. Faulds; K. Geddes; P. Iles; R. Love; Ms M.
Marshall; Dr Ann Matheson; Ms J. Richardson; W.
Speirs; Prof. E. Spiller; Ms J. Urquart
Director, Ms S. Reid
Lottery Director, D. Bonnar

ARTS COUNCIL OF WALES

9 Museum Place, Cardiff CF1 3NX
Tel 01222-376500; fax 01222-221447

The Arts Council of Wales funds arts organizations in
Wales and is funded directly by the Welsh Office. The
grant for 1998–9 is £14.189 million.
Chairman, Sir Richard Lloyd Jones, KCB
Members, Ms E. Bennet; Ms J. Davidson; R. Davies; Ms A.
Davis; K. Evans; Ms K. Gass; G. Jenkins; D. Johnston;
G. S. Jones; L. Jones; G. Lewis; A. Lloyd; C. Lyddon;
D. Richards; A. Roberts; Ms C. Thomas; Ms M.
Vincentelli
Chief Executive, Ms J. Weston

ARTS COUNCIL OF NORTHERN IRELAND

MacNeice House, 77 Malone Road, Belfast BT9 6AQ
Tel 01232-385200; fax 01232-661715

The Arts Council of Northern Ireland disburses govern-
ment funds in support of the arts in Northern Ireland. It is
funded by the Department of Education for Northern
Ireland, and the grant for 1998–9 is £6.67 million.
Chairman, Prof. B. Walker
Vice-Chairman, vacant

Members, M. Bradley; W. Burns; S. Burnside; F. Cobain;
P. Donnelly; Dr Tess Hurson; Mrs R. McMullan; Ms
M. O'Neill; G. Patterson; Ms C. Poulter; Ms I.
Sandford; A. Shortt; Dr B. Walker
Chief Executive, B. Ferran

ART GALLERIES, ETC

ROYAL FINE ART COMMISSION

7 St James's Square, London SW1Y 4JU
Tel 0171-839 6537; fax 0171-839 8475

Established in 1924, the Commission is an autonomous
authority on the aesthetic implications of any project or
development, primarily but not exclusively architectural,
which affects the visual environment.

In July 1998 the Government published a discussion
document including a proposal to reform or abolish the
Commission.
Chairman, The Lord St John of Fawsley, PC, FRSL
Commissioners, Miss S. Andreae; Prof. R. D. Carter, CBE;
E. Cullinan, CBE, RA; D. H. Fraser, RA; E. Hollinghurst;
Sir Michael Hopkins, CBE, RA; S. A. Lipton; Prof.
Margaret MacKeith, PH.D.; H. T. Moggridge, OBE; G.
Morrison; Mrs J. Nutting; T. Osborne, FRICS; I. Ritchie;
Sir Colin Stansfield Smith, CBE; Prof. J. R. Steer, FSA;
Miss W. Taylor, CBE; Dr G. Worsley
Secretary, F. Golding

ROYAL FINE ART COMMISSION FOR SCOTLAND

Bakehouse Close, 146 Canongate, Edinburgh EH8 8DD
Tel 0131-556 6699; fax 0131-556 6633

The Commission was established in 1927 and advises
ministers and local authorities on the visual impact and
quality of design of construction projects. It is an indepen-
dent body and gives its opinions impartially.
Chairman, The Lord Cameron of Lochbroom, PC, FRSE
Commissioners, Prof. G. Benson; W. A. Cadell; Mrs
K. Dalyell; Ms J. Malvenan; R. G. Maund; M. Murray;
D. Page; B. Rae; R. Russell; M. Turnbull; A. Wright
Secretary, C. Prosser

NATIONAL GALLERY

Trafalgar Square, London WC2N 5DN
Tel 0171-839 3321; fax 0171-747 2403

The National Gallery, which houses a permanent collection of western painting from the 13th to the 20th century,
was founded in 1824, following a parliamentary grant of
£60,000 for the purchase and exhibition of the Angerstein
collection of pictures. The present site was first occupied
in 1838; an extension to the north of the building with a
public entrance in Orange Street was opened in 1975, and
the Sainsbury wing was opened in 1991. Total government
grant-in-aid for 1998–9 is £18.6 million.

BOARD OF TRUSTEES
Chairman, P. Hughes, CBE
Trustees, Lady Bingham; Sir Mark Richmond, SC.D., FRS; A.
Bennett; Lady Monck; Mrs P. Ridley; Sir Ewen
Fergusson, GCMG, GCVO; R. Gavron, CBE; C. Le Brun;
The Hon. R. G. H. Seitz; Dr D. Landau; Sir Colin
Southgate

OFFICERS
Director, R. N. MacGregor
Keeper, Dr N. Penny
Senior Curator, vacant
Chief Restorer, M. H. Wyld, CBE

Head of Exhibitions, M. J. Wilson
Scientific Adviser, Dr A. Roy
Director of Administration, J. MacAuslan
Head of Press and Public Relations, Miss J. Liddiard

NATIONAL PORTRAIT GALLERY
St Martin's Place, London wc2h 0he
Tel 0171-306 0055; fax 0171-306 0058

A grant was made in 1856 to form a gallery of the portraits of the most eminent persons in British history. The present building was opened in 1896 and an extension in 1933. There are four outstations displaying portraits in appropriate settings: Montacute House, Gawthorpe Hall, Beningbrough Hall and Bodelwyddan Castle. Total government grant-in-aid for 1998–9 is £4.697 million.

Board of Trustees
Chairman, H. Keswick
Trustees, The Lord President of the Council (*ex officio*); The President of the Royal Academy of Arts (*ex officio*); J. Roberts, cbe, d.phil.; The Lord Morris of Castle Morris, d.phil.; Prof. N. Lynton; J. Tusa; Sir Antony Acland, gcmg, gcvo; Mrs J. E. Benson, lvo, obe; Lady Tumim, obe; Sir David Scholey, cbe; Mrs C. Tomalin; Baroness Willoughby de Eresby; M. Hastings; Prof. The Earl Russell, fba; T. Phillips, ra
Director (*G3*), C. Saumarez Smith, ph.d.

TATE GALLERY
Millbank, London sw1p 4rg
Tel 0171-887 8000; fax 0171-887 8007

The Tate Gallery comprises the national collections of British painting and 20th-century painting and sculpture. The Gallery was opened in 1897, the cost of erection (£80,000) being defrayed by Sir Henry Tate, who also contributed the nucleus of the present collection. The Turner wing was opened in 1910, galleries to contain the collection of modern foreign painting in 1926, and a new sculpture hall in 1937. In 1979 a further extension was built, and the Clore Gallery, for the Turner collection, was opened in 1987. The Tate Gallery Liverpool opened in 1988 and the Tate Gallery St Ives in 1993. The new Tate Gallery of Modern Art at Bankside is due to open in 2000, with the Millbank gallery then being devoted to British art. Total government grant-in-aid for 1998–9 is £18.218 million.

Board of Trustees
Chairman, D. Verey
Trustees, Prof. Dawn Ades; The Hon. Mrs J. de Botton; Sir Richard Carew Pole; Prof. M. Craig-Martin; P. Doig; Sir Christopher Mallaby, gcmg, gcvo; Sir Mark Richmond; Mrs P. Ridley, obe; W. Woodrow

Officers
Director, N. Serota
Director of Public and Regional Services, S. Nairne
Director of Collections, J. Lewison
Director, Tate Gallery of Modern Art, L. Nittve
Director, Tate Gallery of British Art, S. Deuchar
Curator, Tate Gallery Liverpool, L. Biggs
Curator, Tate Gallery St Ives, M. Tooby

WALLACE COLLECTION
Hertford House, Manchester Square, London w1m 6bn
Tel 0171-935 0687; fax 0171-224 2155

The Wallace Collection was bequeathed to the nation by the widow of Sir Richard Wallace, Bt. in 1897, and Hertford House was subsequently acquired by the Government.

Total government grant-in-aid for 1998–9 is £1.816 million.
Director, Miss R. J. Savill
Head of Administration, A. W. Houldershaw

NATIONAL GALLERIES OF SCOTLAND
The Mound, Edinburgh eh2 2el
Tel 0131-624 6200; fax 0131-343 3250

The National Galleries of Scotland comprise the National Gallery of Scotland, the Scottish National Portrait Gallery and the Scottish National Gallery of Modern Art. There are also outstations at Paxton House, Berwickshire, and Duff House, Banffshire. Total government grant-in-aid for 1998–9 is £7.460 million.

Trustees
Chairman of the Trustees, The Countess of Airlie, cvo
Trustees, E. Hagman; Dr M. Shea; Mrs A. McCurley; Prof. J. R. Harper, cbe; Prof. Christina Lodder; J. H. Blair; Ms V. Atkinson; Lord Gordon of Strathblane, cbe; G. Weaver; Prof. I. Whyte

Officers
Director (*G4*), T. Clifford
Keeper of Conservation (*G6*), J. P. Dick, obe
Head of Press and Information (*G7*), Mrs A. M. Wagener
Keeper of Education (*G7*), M. Cassin
Registrar (*G7*), Miss A. Buddle
Secretary (*G6*), Ms S. Edwards
Buildings (*G7*), R. Galbraith
Keeper, National Gallery of Scotland (*G6*), M. Clarke
Keeper, Scottish National Portrait Gallery (*G6*), J. Holloway
   Curator of Photography, Miss S. F. Stevenson
Keeper, Scottish National Gallery of Modern Art (*G6*), R. Calvocoressi

UK ATOMIC ENERGY AUTHORITY
Harwell, Didcot, Oxon ox11 0ra
Tel 01235-820220; fax 01235-436401

The UKAEA was established by the Atomic Energy Authority Act 1954 and took over responsibility for the research and development of the civil nuclear power programme. The Authority's commercial arm, AEA Technology plc, was privatized in 1996. UKAEA is responsible for the safe management and decommissioning of its radioactive plant and for maximizing the income from its still-operating active facilities, buildings and land on its six sites. UKAEA also undertakes special nuclear tasks for the Government, including the UK's contribution to the international fusion programme.
Chairman, Adm. Sir Kenneth Eaton
Chief Executive, Dr J. McKeown

AUDIT COMMISSIONS

AUDIT COMMISSION FOR LOCAL AUTHORITIES AND THE NATIONAL HEALTH SERVICE IN ENGLAND AND WALES
1 Vincent Square, London sw1p 2pn
Tel 0171-828 1212; fax 0171-976 6187

The Audit Commission was set up in 1983 with responsibility for the external audit of local authorities. This remit was extended from 1990 to include the audit of the National Health Service bodies in England and Wales.

The Commission appoints the auditors, who may be from the District Audit Service or from a private firm of accountants. The Commission is also responsible for promoting value for money in the services provided by local authorities and health bodies.

The Commission has 15–17 members who, though appointed by the Secretary of State for the Environment, Transport and the Regions in consultation with the Secretaries of State for Wales and for Health, are responsible to Parliament.

Chairman, R. Brooke
Deputy Chairman, J. Orme
Controller of Audit, A. Foster
Chief Executive of District Audit Service, D. Prince

ACCOUNTS COMMISSION FOR SCOTLAND

18 George Street, Edinburgh EH2 2QU
Tel 0131-477 1234; fax 0131-477 4567

The Commission was set up in 1975. It is responsible for securing the audit of the accounts of Scottish local authorities and certain joint boards and joint committees, and for value-for-money audits of authorities. In 1995 it assumed responsibility for securing the audit of National Health Service bodies in Scotland. The Commission is required to deal with reports made by the Controller of Audit on items of account contrary to law; on incorrect accounting; and on losses due to misconduct, negligence and failure to carry out statutory duties.

Members are appointed by the Secretary of State for Scotland.

Chairman, Prof. J. P. Percy, CBE
Controller of Audit, R. W. Black
Secretary, W. F. Magee

ASSEMBLY OMBUDSMAN FOR NORTHERN IRELAND

— *see* Parliamentary Ombudsman for Northern Ireland

THE BANK OF ENGLAND

Threadneedle Street, London EC2R 8AH
Tel 0171-601 4444; fax 0171-601 4771

The Bank of England was incorporated in 1694 under royal charter. It is the banker of the Government and manages the note issue. Since May 1997 it has been operationally independent and its new Monetary Policy Committee has had responsibility for setting short-term interest rates to meet the Government's inflation target. As the central reserve bank of the country, the Bank keeps the accounts of British banks, who maintain with it a proportion of their cash resources, and of most overseas central banks. The Bank is divided into two divisions, Monetary Stability and Financial Stability. Its responsibility for banking supervision has been transferred to the Financial Services Authority. (*See also* pages 634–5).

Governor, E. A. J. George
Deputy Governors, D. Clementi; M. A. King
Directors, C. J. Allsopp; R. Bailie, OBE; A. R. F. Buxton; Sir David Cooksey; H. J. Davies; G. Hawker; Mrs F. A. Heaton; Sir John Keswick; Sir David Lees; Dame Sheila Masters, DBE; Ms S. McKechnie, OBE; W. Morris; J. Neill, CBE, PH.D.; N. I. Simms; Sir Colin Southgate; J. Stretton
Monetary Policy Committee, The Governor; the Deputy Governors; I. Plenderleith; Prof. C. Goodhart; Dr D. Julius; Sir Alan Budd; Prof. W. Buiter; J. Vickers

Advisers to the Governor, Sir Peter Petrie; L. Berkowitz; M. Foster; D. Brearley
Chief Cashier and Deputy Director, Banking and Market Services, G. E. A. Kentfield
Chief Registrar, G. P. Sparkes
General Manager, Printing Works, A. W. Jarvis
Secretary, P. D. Rodgers
The Auditor, K. Butler

BOUNDARY COMMISSIONS

The Commissions are constituted under the Parliamentary Constituencies Act 1986. The Speaker of the House of Commons is *ex officio* chairman of all four commissions in the UK. Each of the four commissions is required by law to keep the parliamentary constituencies in their part of the UK under review. The latest review was completed in 1995 and its proposals took effect at the 1997 general election. The next review is due to be completed between 2002 and 2006.

ENGLAND
1 Drummond Gate, London SW1V 2QQ
Tel 0171-533 5177; fax 0171-533 5176
Deputy Chairman, The Hon. Mr Justice Harrison
Joint Secretaries, R. Farrance; S. Limpkin

WALES
1 Drummond Gate, London SW1V 2QQ
Tel 0171-533 5172; fax 0171-533 5176
Deputy Chairman, The Hon. Mr Justice Kay
Joint Secretaries, R. Farrance; S. Limpkin

SCOTLAND
Saughton House, Edinburgh EH1 3XD
Tel 0131-244 2196/2188; fax 0131-244 2195
Deputy Chairman, The Hon. Lady Cosgrove
Secretary, vacant

NORTHERN IRELAND
REL Division, 11 Millbank, London SW1P 4QE
Tel 0171-210 6569
Deputy Chairman, The Hon. Mr Justice Pringle
Secretary, Ms C. Marson

BRITISH BROADCASTING CORPORATION

Broadcasting House, Portland Place, London W1A 1AA
Tel 0171-580 4468; fax 0171-637 1630
Television Centre, Wood Lane, London W12 7RJ
Tel 0181-743 8000; fax 0181-749 7520

The BBC was incorporated under royal charter as successor to the British Broadcasting Company Ltd, whose licence expired in 1926. The current charter came into force on 1 May 1996 and extends to 31 December 2006. The chairman, vice-chairman and other governors are appointed by The Queen-in-Council. The BBC is financed by revenue from receiving licences for the home services and by grant-in-aid from Parliament for the World Service (radio). In 1996 the BBC was restructured into six divisions: Production, Broadcast, News, Worldwide, Resources, and Corporate Centre.

For services, *see* Broadcasting section.

BOARD OF GOVERNORS

Chairman (£66,000), Sir Christopher Bland
Vice-Chairman (£17,000), The Baroness Young of Old
Scone
National Governors (*each* £17,000), Sir Kenneth Bloomfield,
KCB (*N. Ireland*); R. S. Jones, OBE (*Wales*); N. Drummond
(*Scotland*)
Chairman, English National Forum (£13,000), R. Sondhi
Governors (*each* £8,000), W. B. Jordan, CBE; Mrs J. Cohen;
Sir David Scholey, CBE; Sir Richard Eyre, CBE; A. White,
CBE; Dame Pauline Neville-Jones, DCMG; A. Young

BOARD OF MANAGEMENT

EXECUTIVE COMMITTEE
Director-General (£354,000), Sir John Birt
Chief Executives, R. Neil (*BBC Production*); W. Wyatt (*BBC
Broadcast*); T. Hall (*BBC News*); R. Lynch (*BBC Resources
Ltd*); R. Gavin (*BBC Worldwide*)
Managing Director, S. Younger (*World Service*)
Directors, Ms M. Salmon (*Personnel*); Ms P. Hodgson (*Policy
and Planning*); J. Smith (*Finance*); C. Browne (*Corporate
Affairs*)

OTHER BOARD OF MANAGEMENT MEMBERS
Directors, A. Yentob (*Television*); M. Bannister (*Radio*); Ms
J. Drabble (*Education*); M. Byford (*Regional Broadcasting*)

OTHER SENIOR STAFF

The Secretary, C. Graham
Director, Continuous News, Ms J. Abramsky
Controller, BBC1, P. Salmon
Controller, BBC2, M. Thompson
Controller, Radio 1, A. Parfitt
Controller, Radio 2, J. Moir
Controller, Radio 3, R. Wright
Controller, Radio 4, J. Boyle
Controller, Radio 5 Live, R. Mosey
Controller, BBC Proms and Millennium Programmes,
N. Kenyon
Controller, BBC Scotland, J. McCormick
Controller, BBC Wales, G. Talfan Davies
Controller, BBC N. Ireland, P. Loughrey
Controller, English Regions, N. Chapman

THE BRITISH COUNCIL
10 Spring Gardens, London SW1A 2BN
Tel 0171-930 8466; fax 0171-839 6347
Bridgewater House, 58 Whitworth Street, Manchester
M15 4AA
Tel 0161-957 7755; fax 0161-957 7762
Arts Division: 11 Portland Place, London W1N 4EJ
Tel 0171-389 3001; fax 0171-389 3199

The British Council was established in 1934, incorporated
by royal charter in 1940 and granted a supplemental
charter in 1993. It is an independent, non-political
organization which promotes Britain abroad. It is the UK's
international network for education, culture and development services. The Council is represented in 230 towns
and cities in 109 countries and runs 209 libraries, 95
teaching centres and 29 resource centres around the world.
   Total income in 1997–8, including Foreign and Commonwealth Office grants and contracted money, was
£412.662 million.
Chairman, The Baroness Kennedy of The Shaws, QC
Deputy Chairman, The Lord Chorley
Director-General, Dr D. Drewery

BRITISH FILM COMMISSION
70 Baker Street, London W1M 1DJ
Tel 0171-224 5000; fax 0171-224 1013

The British Film Commission was set up in 1991 and is
funded by the Department for Culture, Media and Sport.
The Commission promotes the UK as an international
production centre, encourages the use of locations, facilities, services and personnel, and provides, at no charge to
the enquirer, comprehensive advice and information
relating to the practical aspects of filming in the UK.
   In July 1998 the Government published a discussion
document including a proposal to establish a new film body
which would incorporate the work currently undertaken
by the Commision.
Commissioner and Chief Executive, S. Norris

BRITISH FILM INSTITUTE
21 Stephen Street, London W1P 2LN
Tel 0171-255 1444; fax 0171-436 7950

The British Film Institute was first set up in 1933 and is
now established by royal charter. It is the UK national
agency with responsibility for encouraging the arts of film
and television and conserving them in the national interest.
BFI divisions include the National Film and Television
Archive, the National Cinema Centre (comprising the
National Film Theatre and the London Film Festival) and
BFI Films, which deals with distribution and film sales.
The BFI also supports a network of regional film theatres
and the BFI National Library contains the world's largest
collection of material relating to film and television. Total
government funding for 1998–9 is £15.1 million.
   In July 1998 the Government published a discussion
document including a proposal to establish a new film body
which would incorporate the work currently undertaken
by the Institute.
Chairman, A. Parker
Deputy Chairman, Ms J. Bakewell
Director, J. Woodward

BRITISH PHARMACOPOEIA COMMISSION
Market Towers, 1 Nine Elms Lane, London SW8 5NQ
Tel 0171-273 0561; fax 0171-273 0566

The British Pharmacopoeia Commission sets standards for
medicinal products used in human and veterinary medicines and is responsible for publication of the British
Pharmacopoeia (a publicly available statement of the
standard that a product must meet throughout its shelf-
life), the British Pharmacopoeia (Veterinary) and the
selection of British Approved Names. It has 13 members
who are appointed by the Secretary of State for Health, the
Minister for Agriculture, Fisheries and Food, the Secretaries of State for Scotland and Wales, and the relevant
Northern Ireland departments.
Chairman, Prof. D. Calam, OBE, D.Phil.
Vice-Chairman, Prof. J. A. Goldsmith
Secretary and Scientific Director, Dr R. C. Hutton

BRITISH RAILWAYS BOARD
Whittles House, 14 Pentonville Road, London NI 9HF
Tel 0171-904 5000; fax 0171-904 5040

The British Railways Board came into being in 1963 under the terms of the Transport Act 1962. Under the Railways Act 1993, the activities of the Board have been restructured and largely transferred to the private sector. Its residual responsibilities include disposing of surplus land and advising the Government on rail policy issues.

The Government announced in July 1998 that British Rail's residual functions would be taken over by a new strategic rail authority.

Chairman and Chief Executive (part-time) (£76,000), J. K. Welsby, CBE
Vice-Chairman, J. J. Jerram, CBE
Executive Member, A. P. Watkinson
Non-executive Members (part-time), A. D. Begg; J. D. Hughes; Miss K. T. Kantor; R. J. Kennedy; N. J. Wakefield
Secretary, P. Trewin

BRITISH STANDARDS INSTITUTION (BSI)
389 Chiswick High Road, London w4 4AL
Tel 0181-996 9000; fax 0181-996 7344

The British Standards Institution is the recognized authority in the UK for the preparation and publication of national standards for industrial and consumer products. About 90 per cent of its standards work is now internationally linked. British Standards are issued for voluntary adoption, though in a number of cases compliance with a British Standard is required by legislation. Industrial and consumer products certified as complying with the relevant British Standard may carry the Institution's certification trade mark, known as the 'Kitemark'.

Chairman, V. E. Thomas, CBE
Chief Executive, K. Tozzi

BRITISH TOURIST AUTHORITY
Thames Tower, Black's Road, London w6 9EL
Tel 0181-846 9000; fax 0181-563 0302

Established under the Development of Tourism Act 1969, the British Tourist Authority has specific responsibility for promoting tourism to Great Britain from overseas. It also has a general responsibility for the promotion and development of tourism and tourist facilities within Great Britain as a whole, and for advising the Secretary of State for Culture, Media and Sport on tourism matters.

Chairman (part-time), D. Quarmby
Chief Executive, A. Sell

BRITISH WATERWAYS
Willow Grange, Church Road, Watford, Herts wd1 3QA
Tel 01923-226422; fax 01923-201400

British Waterways is the navigation authority for over 2,000 miles of canals and rivers in England, Scotland and Wales. It is responsible to the Secretary of State for the Environment, Transport and the Regions. Its responsibilities include maintaining the waterways and structures on and around them; looking after wildlife and the waterway environment; and ensuring that canals and rivers are safe and enjoyable places to visit.

Chairman (part-time), B. Henderson, CBE
Members (part-time), D. H. R. Yorke; Sir Neil Cossons; Ms J. Elvey; Ms J. Lewis-Jones; Ms C. Dobson; P. King; P. Soulsby; C. Christie
Chief Executive, D. Fletcher
Director of Corporate Services, R. J. Duffy

BROADCASTING STANDARDS COMMISSION
7 The Sanctuary, London swip 3js
Tel 0171-233 0544; fax 0171-233 0397

The Commission was established in April 1997 under the Broadcasting Act 1996. It is an independent organization representing the interests of the consumer, and its remit covers all television and radio broadcasting. The Commission considers the portrayal of violence and sexual conduct and matters of taste and decency. It also provides redress for people who believe they have been unfairly treated or subjected to unwarranted infringement of privacy. The Commission conducts research into standards and fairness in broadcasting and produces codes of practice, and it considers and adjudicates on complaints. Members of the Commission are appointed by the Secretary of State for Culture, Media and Sport. The appointments are part-time.

Chair (£45,210), The Lady Howe of Aberavon
Deputy Chairmen (£34,000–£36,000), Ms J. Leighton; Mrs S. Warner
Commissioners (each £14,450), Ms D. Barr; Ms R. Bevan; D. Boulton; Dame Fiona Caldicott, DBE; S. Heppel, CB; R. Kernohan, OBE; the Very Revd J. Lang; Ms S. Lloyd; Ms S. O'Sullivan; M. Parris; Ms S. Wyn Thomas
Director, S. Whittle

THE BROADS AUTHORITY
Thomas Harvey House, 18 Colegate, Norwich NR3 1BQ
Tel 01603-610734; fax 01603-765710

The Broads Authority is a special statutory authority set up under the Norfolk and Suffolk Broads Act 1988. The functions of the Authority are to conserve and enhance the natural beauty of the Broads; to promote the enjoyment of the Broads by the public; and to protect the interests of navigation. The Authority comprises 35 members, appointed by the local authorities in the area covered, environmental conservation bodies, the Environment Agency, and the Great Yarmouth Port Authority.

Chairman, The Viscountess Knollys
Chief Executive, Prof. M. A. Clark, OBE

THE CABINET OFFICE
70 Whitehall, London SW1A 2AS
Tel 0171-270 3000
*Horse Guards Road, London SW1P 3AL
Tel 0171-270 1234
Web: http://www.open.gov.uk.cabinetoffice

The Cabinet Office comprises the Secretariat, who support Ministers collectively in the conduct of Cabinet business; and units responsible for the progress and development of the Better Government, Better Regulation, Citizen's Charter and Next Steps programmes, policy on open government, Senior Civil Service and public appointments, market testing and efficiency in the Civil Service, and Civil Service recruitment. The Cabinet Office supports the Prime Minister in his capacity as Minister for the Civil Service, with responsibility for day-to-day supervision delegated to the Chancellor of the Duchy of Lancaster. The former Office of Public Service was merged with the Cabinet Office in July 1998 in order to integrate more closely the formulation and the implementation of policies.

In July 1998 the Prime Minister announced plans to set up a Performance and Innovation Unit, a Centre for Management and Policy Studies (incorporating a re-shaped Civil Service College), and a Management Board for the Civil Service within the Cabinet Office.

Prime Minister and Minister for the Civil Service,
  The Rt. Hon. Tony Blair, MP
Minister for the Cabinet Office and Chancellor of the Duchy of
  Lancaster, The Rt. Hon. Dr Jack Cunningham, MP
  Principal Private Secretary, Dr M. Taylor
  Private Secretary, Ms B. Feeny
Minister of State, The Lord Falconer of Thoroton, QC
Parliamentary Under-Secretary, Peter Kilfoyle, MP
  Private Secretary, Dr C. Brake
Secretary of the Cabinet and Head of the Home Civil Service, Sir
  Richard Wilson, KCB
  Private Secretary, Ms J. A. Polley
Second Permanent Secretary, R. Mountfield, CB
  Private Secretary, Ms D. Crewe
Parliamentary Clerk, S. Brown
Press Secretary, B. Sutlieff
Head of the Government Information and Communication
  Service, M. Granatt
Chief Scientific Adviser, Sir Robert May, FRS

PRIME MINISTER'S OFFICE
10 Downing Street, London SW1A 2AA
Tel 0171-270 3000; fax 0171-925 0918
Web: http://www.number-10.gov.uk

Principal Private Secretary, J. E. Holmes, CMG
Chief of Staff, J. Powell
Private Secretaries, J. J. Heywood (*Economic Affairs*); R. Read
  (*Parliamentary Affairs*); A. Lapsley (*Home Affairs*); P.
  Barton (*Assistant on Overseas Affairs*); Ms C. Hawley
  (*Assistant on Home Affairs*)
Diary Secretary, Ms K. Garvey
Special Assistant for Presentation and Planning, Ms A. Hunter
Assistant to Mrs Blair, Ms F. Millar
Political Secretary, Ms S. Morgan
Head of Policy Unit, D. Miliband
Policy Unit, G. Mulgan; R. Liddle; D. Scott; Ms E. Lloyd; P.
  Hyman; J. Purnell; P. McFadden; R. Hill; G. Norris; Ms
  S. White; A. Adonis
Parliamentary Private Secretaries, B. Grocott, MP; Ms A.
  Coffey, MP

Chief Press Secretary, A. Campbell
Deputy Press Secretary, G. Smith
Special Advisers, Press Office, Ms H. Coffman; L. Price
Strategic Communications Unit, A. Evans; P. Bassett; D.
  Bradshaw; J. Humphreys; Ms S. Kenny; A. Silverman
Secretary for Appointments, and Ecclesiastical Secretary to the
  Lord Chancellor, J. Holroyd, CB
Parliamentary Clerk, Mrs H. Murray

SECRETARIAT
Economic and Domestic Secretariat, W. Rickett; J. Elvidge
Defence and Overseas Affairs Secretariat, M. Pakenham, CMG;
  D. Fisher
Joint Intelligence Organization, J. Alpass; R. Gozny
European Secretariat, B. Bender, CB; M. Donnelly

Constitution Secretariat, Q. Thomas

*CITIZEN'S CHARTER UNIT
Tel 0171-270 1826

Director, J. Rees
Deputy Director, Mrs G. Craig

CENTRAL IT UNIT
53 Parliament Street, London SW1A 2NG
Tel 0171-238 2015

Director, D. Cooke

*EFFICIENCY AND EFFECTIVENESS GROUP
Tel 0171-270 0257

Director, J. R. C. Oughton
Head of Next Steps Project Team, Dr J. G. Fuller

*CIVIL SERVICE EMPLOYER GROUP
Director, J. Barker
Development and Equal Opportunities Division, Ms A.
  Schofield
Fast Stream and European Staffing Division, Ms J. Lemprière
International Public Service Unit, C. J. Parry
Personnel Management and Conditions of Service Division, Ms
  E. Goodison
Top Management Programme, Ms H. Dudley (*Course Director*)
Civil Service Pensions Division, D. G. Pain

*OFFICE OF THE COMMISSIONER FOR PUBLIC
APPOINTMENTS (OCPA)
Tel 0171-270 5792

The role of the Commissioner for Public Appointments (CPA) is to monitor, regulate and approve departmental appointment procedures for ministerial appointments to advisory and executive non-departmental public bodies, public corporations, nationalized industries, regulators and NHS bodies. The Commissioner is appointed by Order-in-Council.

Commissioner, Sir Leonard Peach
Head of Office, J. Barron

*OFFICE OF THE CIVIL SERVICE COMMISSIONERS
(OCSC)
Tel 0171-270 5081; fax 0171-270 5967

First Commissioner, Sir Michael Bett, CBE
Commissioners (part-time), D. J. Burr; Ms S. Forbes; Ms J. A.
  Hunt; H. J. F. McLean, CBE; Sir Leonard Peach; J.
  Shrigley; K. Singh; C. Stevens; Ms
Secretary to the Commissioners and Head of the Office, J. Barron

GOVERNMENT INFORMATION AND COMMUNICATION
SERVICE DEVELOPMENT CENTRE
Ashley House, 2 Monck Street, London SW1P 2BQ
Tel 0171-270 1234

Director, C. Skinner

*BETTER REGULATION UNIT
Director, M. Stanley

*SENIOR CIVIL SERVICE GROUP
Director, B. M. Fox, CB
Deputy Director, S. Mitha

*MACHINERY OF GOVERNMENT AND STANDARDS
GROUP
Director, D. A. Wilkinson
Queen's Printer, Mrs C. Tullo

CEREMONIAL BRANCH
Ashley House, 2 Monck Street, London SW1P 2BQ
Tel 0171-270 1234
Honours Nomination Unit: Tel 0171-276 2775
Ceremonial Officer, A. J. Merifield, CB

ESTABLISHMENT OFFICER'S GROUP
Queen Anne's Chambers, 28 Broadway, London SW1H 9JS
Tel 0171-270 3000

Principal Establishment and Finance Officer, Mrs N. A.
    Oppenheimer
Deputy Establishment Officer, Miss E. Chennells
Senior Finance Officer, K. Tolladay

EXECUTIVE AGENCIES

THE BUYING AGENCY
Royal Liver Building, Pier Head, Liverpool L3 1PE
Tel 0151-227 4262; fax 0151-227 3315
The Agency provides a professional purchasing service to
government departments and other public bodies.
Chief Executive (G5), S. P. Sage

CCTA (CENTRAL COMPUTER AND
TELECOMMUNICATIONS AGENCY)
Rosebery Court, St Andrew's Business Park, Norwich
NR7 OHS
Tel 01603-704567; fax 01603-704817
Steel House, 11 Tothill Street, London SW1H 9NF
Tel 0171-273 6565; fax 0171-273 6555
CCTA's objective is to develop, maintain and make
available expertise about information technology which
public sector organizations can draw on in order to operate
more effectively and efficiently.
Chief Executive, R. Assirati

CENTRAL OFFICE OF INFORMATION
— *see* below

CIVIL SERVICE COLLEGE
Sunningdale Park, Ascot, Berks SL5 OQE
Tel 01344-634000; fax 01344-634781
11 Belgrave Road, London SW1V 1RB
Tel 0171-834 6644; fax 01344-634451
199 Cathedral Street, Glasgow G4 OQU
Tel 0141-553 6021; fax 0141-553 6171
The College provides training in management and pro-
fessional skills for the public and private sectors.
Chief Executive (G3), R. Bayley
Business Executives (G5/G6), M. N. Barnes; R. Behrens;
    G. W. Llewellyn; Ms L. Oliver (*Non-Executive Director*);
    P. Tebby; M. Timmis; Dr A. Wyatt

GOVERNMENT CAR AND DESPATCH AGENCY
46 Ponton Road, London SW8 5AX
Tel 0171-217 3839; fax 0171-217 3840

*Unless otherwise stated, this is the address and telephone number for
divisions of the Cabinet Office

The Agency provides secure transport and document
transfers between government departments.
Chief Executive, N. Matheson

PROPERTY ADVISERS TO THE CIVIL ESTATE
6th Floor, Trevelyan House, Great Peter Street, London
SW1P 2BY
Tel 0171-271 2626; fax 0171-271 2622
The Agency co-ordinates government activity on the civil
estate, and provides general property guidance and sup-
port to government departments.
Chief Executive, J. C. Locke, FRICS

CENTRAL ADJUDICATION SERVICES
Quarry House, Quarry Hill, Leeds LS2 7UB
Tel 0113-232 4000; fax 0113-232 4841
New Court, 48 Carey Street, London WC2A 2LS
Tel 0171-412 1504; fax 0171-412 1220

The Chief Adjudication Officer and Chief Child Support
Officer are independent statutory authorities under the
Social Security Act 1975 (as amended) and the Child
Support Act 1991. They are appointed by the Secretary of
State for Social Security to give advice to adjudication
officers dealing with claims for social security cash benefits
and to child support officers, and to keep under review the
operation of the systems of adjudication. They report
annually to the Secretary of State on adjudication standards.
Chief Adjudication Officer, and Chief Child Support Officer,
    E. W. Hazlewood

CENTRAL OFFICE OF INFORMATION
Hercules Road, London SE1 7DU
Tel 0171-928 2345; fax 0171-928 5037

The Central Office of Information (COI) is an executive
agency which offers consultancy, procurement and project
management services to central government for publicity.
Though the majority of COI's work is for government
departments in the UK, it also procures a range of publicity
materials for overseas consumption. Administrative responsibility for the COI rests with the Chancellor of the
Duchy of Lancaster within the Cabinet Office.
Chief Executive (G3), A. Douglas
    Senior Personal Secretary, Ms L. Sheasgreen

MANAGEMENT BOARD
Members, K. Williamson; R. Smith; P. Buchanan; I.
    Hamilton; R. Haslam; Ms S. Whetton; M. Reid
Secretary, Ms L. Sheasgreen

DIRECTORS
Director, New Business (G6), Ms S. Whetton
Director, Marketing Communications (G6), P. Buchanan
Director, Films, Radio and Events (G6), I. Hamilton
Director, Publications (G6), M. Reid
Director, Central Services (G5), K. Williamson
Director, Regional Network (G6), R. Haslam

NETWORK OFFICES
EASTERN, Three Crowns House, 72–80 Hills Road,
    Cambridge CB2 1LL. *Network Director (G7)*, P. Powell
MIDLANDS EAST, 1st Floor, Severns House, 20 Middle
    Pavement, Nottingham NG1 7DW. *Network Director (G7)*,
    P. Smith

MIDLANDS WEST, Five Ways House, Islington Row Middleway, Edgbaston, Birmingham B15 1SH. *Network Director* (*G6*), B. Garner
NORTH-EAST, Wellbar House, Gallowgate, Newcastle upon Tyne NE1 4TB. *Network Director* (*G7*), Ms L. Taylor
NORTH-WEST, Sunley Tower, Piccadilly Plaza, Manchester M1 4BD. *Network Director* (*G7*), Mrs E. Jones
SOUTH-EAST, Hercules Road, London SE1 7DU. *Network Director* (*G6*), Ms V. Burdon
SOUTH-WEST, The Pithay, Bristol BS1 2NF. *Network Director* (*G7*), P. Whitbread
YORKSHIRE AND HUMBERSIDE, City House, New Station Street, Leeds LS1 4JG. *Network Director* (*G7*), Ms W. Miller

---

CERTIFICATION OFFICE FOR TRADE UNIONS AND EMPLOYERS' ASSOCIATIONS
180 Borough High Street, London SE1 1LW
Tel 0171-210 3734/5; fax 0171-210 3612

The Certification Office is an independent statutory authority. The Certification Officer is appointed by the Secretary of State for Trade and Industry and is responsible for receiving and scrutinizing annual returns from trade unions and employers' associations; for investigating allegations of financial irregularities in the affairs of a trade union or employers' association; for dealing with complaints concerning trade union elections; for ensuring observance of statutory requirements governing political funds and trade union mergers; and for certifying the independence of trade unions.
Certification Officer, E. G. Whybrew
Assistant Certification Officer, G. S. Osborne

SCOTLAND
58 Frederick Street, Edinburgh EH2 1LN
Tel 0131-226 3224; fax 0131-200 1300
Assistant Certification Officer for Scotland, J. L. J. Craig

CHARITY COMMISSION
St Alban's House, 57–60 Haymarket, London SW1Y 4QX
Tel 0171-210 4556; fax 0171-210 4545
2nd Floor, 20 King's Parade, Queen's Dock, Liverpool L3 4DQ
Tel 0151-703 1500; fax 0151-703 1557
Woodfield House, Tangier, Taunton, Somerset TA1 4BL
Tel 01823-345000; fax 01823-345008

The Charity Commission is established under the Charities Act 1993 with the general function of promoting the effective use of charitable resources in England and Wales. The Commission gives information and advice to charity trustees to make the administration of their charity more effective; investigates misconduct and the abuse of charitable assets, and takes or recommends remedial action; and maintains a public register of charities. The Commission does not have at its disposal any funds with which to make grants to organizations or individuals.

At the end of 1997 there were 184,000 registered charities.
Chief Commissioner (*G3*), R. Fries
Legal Commissioner (*G3*), M. Carpenter
Commissioners (*part-time*) (*G4*), J. Bonds; Ms J. Warburton; Ms J. Unwin
Heads of Legal Sections (*G5*), J. A. Dutton; G. S. Goodchild; K. M. Dibble; S. Slack

Executive Director (*G4*), Ms L. Berry
Head of Policy Division (*G5*), R. Carter
Establishment Officer (*G5*), Ms C. Stewart
Information Systems Controller (*G5*), Ms G. Cruickshank

The offices responsible for charities in Scotland and Northern Ireland are:
SCOTLAND – Scottish Charities Office, Crown Office, 25 Chambers Street, Edinburgh EH1 1LA. Tel: 0131-226 2626
NORTHERN IRELAND – Department of Health and Social Services, Charities Branch, Annexe 3, Castle Buildings, Stormont Estate, Belfast BT4 3RA. Tel: 01232-522780

CHIEF ADJUDICATION OFFICER AND CHIEF CHILD SUPPORT OFFICER
— *see* Central Adjudication Services

CHILD SUPPORT AGENCY
— *see* page 345

CHURCH COMMISSIONERS
1 Millbank, London SW1P 3JZ
Tel 0171-222 7010; fax 0171-233 0171

The Church Commissioners were established in 1948 by the amalgamation of Queen Anne's Bounty (established 1704) and the Ecclesiastical Commissioners (established 1836). They are responsible for the management of most of the Church of England's assets, the income from which is predominantly used to pay, house and pension the clergy. The Commissioners own 131,970 acres of agricultural land, a number of residential estates in central London, and commercial property in Great Britain. They also carry out administrative duties in connection with pastoral reorganization and redundant churches.

The Commissioners are: the Archbishops of Canterbury and of York; four bishops, three clergy and four lay persons elected by the respective houses of the General Synod; two deans or provosts elected by all the deans and provosts; three persons nominated by The Queen; three persons nominated by the Archbishops of Canterbury and York; three persons nominated by the Archbishops after consultation with others including the lord mayors of London and York and the vice-chancellors of the universities of Oxford and Cambridge; the First Lord of the Treasury; the Lord President of the Council; the Home Secretary; the Lord Chancellor; the Secretary of State for Culture, Media and Sport; and the Speaker of the House of Commons.

INCOME AND EXPENDITURE
for year ended 31 December 1997

	£ million
Total income	143.7
Net income	135.3
Investments	80.0
Property	43.2
Interest from loans, etc.	20.5
Total expenditure	131.5
Clergy stipends	24.8
Clergy and widows' pensions	82.1
Episcopal and cathedral housing	2.6
Financial provision for resigning clergy	2.4
Commissioners' administration of central church functions	4.7
Episcopal administration and payments to Chapters	10.6

Church buildings	0.8
Administration costs of other bodies	2.6
Surplus for year	3.8

CHURCH ESTATES COMMISSIONERS
First, Sir Michael Colman, Bt.
Second, S. Bell, MP
Third, Mrs M. H. Laird

OFFICERS
Secretary, H. H. Hughes
Deputy Secretary (Finance and Investment), C. W. Daws
Official Solicitor, N. I. Johnson
Assistant Secretaries:
    The Accountant, G. C. Baines
    Management Accountant, B. J. Hardy
    Chief Surveyor, A. C. Brown
    Computer Manager, J. W. Ferguson
    Bishoprics Secretary, E. G. Peacock
    Investments Manager, A. S. Hardy
    Pastoral, Houses and Redundant Churches, M. D. Elengorn
    Senior Architect, J. A. Taylor

CIVIL AVIATION AUTHORITY
CAA House, 45–59 Kingsway, London WC2B 6TE
Tel 0171-379 7311; fax: 0171-240 1153

The CAA is responsible for the economic regulation of UK airlines and for the safety regulation of UK civil aviation by the certification of airlines and aircraft and by licensing aerodromes, flight crew and aircraft engineers. Through its subsidiary company, National Air Traffic Services Ltd (NATS), it is also responsible for the provision of air traffic control and telecommunications services. The Government announced in June 1998 that it planned to sell 51 per cent of NATS to the private sector.

The CAA advises the Government on aviation issues, represents consumer interests, conducts economic and scientific research, produces statistical data, and provides specialist services and other training and consultancy services to clients world-wide.
Chairman (part-time), Sir Malcolm Field
Secretary, R. J. Britton

THE COAL AUTHORITY
200 Lichfield Lane, Mansfield, Notts NG18 4RG
Tel 01623-427162; fax: 01623-622072

The Coal Authority was established under the Coal Industry Act 1994 to manage certain functions previously undertaken by British Coal, including ownership of unworked coal. It is responsible for licensing coal mining operations and for providing information on coal reserves and past and future coal mining. It settles subsidence claims not falling on coal mining operators. It deals with the management and disposal of property, and with surface hazards such as abandoned coal mine shafts.
Chairman, Sir David White
Chief Executive, K. J. Fergusson

COMMONWEALTH DEVELOPMENT CORPORATION
1 Bessborough Gardens, London SW1V 2JQ
Tel 0171-828 4488; fax 0171-828 6505

The Commonwealth Development Corporation (CDC) assists overseas countries in the development of their economies. Its sponsoring department is the Department for International Development. Its main activity is providing long-term finance, as loans and risk capital, for financially viable and developmentally sound business enterprises. CDC's area of operations includes UK overseas territories and, with ministerial approval, Commonwealth or other developing countries. At present, CDC is authorized to operate in more than 60 countries and territories. Its investments at the end of 1997 were £1,560 million.

The Government announced in June 1998 that it planned to sell its majority stake in CDC.
Chairman (part-time), The Earl Cairns, CBE
Deputy Chairman (part-time), Sir William Ryrie, KCB
Chief Executive, Dr R. Reynolds

COMMONWEALTH SECRETARIAT
— see Index

COMMONWEALTH WAR GRAVES COMMISSION
2 Marlow Road, Maidenhead, Berks SL6 7DX
Tel 01628-634221; fax 01628-771208

The Commonwealth War Graves Commission (formerly Imperial War Graves Commission) was founded by royal charter in 1917. It is responsible for the commemoration of 1,695,098 members of the forces of the Commonwealth who fell in the two world wars. More than one million graves are maintained in 23,216 burial grounds throughout the world. Over three-quarters of a million men and women who have no known grave or who were cremated are commemorated by name on memorials built by the Commission.

The funds of the Commission are derived from the six participating governments, i.e. the UK, Canada, Australia, India, New Zealand and South Africa.
President, HRH The Duke of Kent, KG, GCMG, GCVO, ADC
Chairman, The Secretary of State for Defence in the UK
Vice-Chairman, Adm. Sir John Kerr, GCB
Members, The High Commissioners in London for Canada, New Zealand, India, South Africa and Australia; The Viscount Ridley, KG, GCVO, TD; Prof. R. J. O'Neill, AO; Mrs L. Golding, MP; J. Wilkinson, MP; Sir John Gray, KBE, CMG; P. D. Orchard-Lisle, CBE, TD; Air Chief Marshal Sir Michael Stear, KCB, CBE; Gen. Sir John Wilsey, GCB, CBE
Director-General and Secretary to the Commission, D. Kennedy, CMG
Deputy Director-General, R. J. Dalley
Legal Adviser and Solicitor, G. C. Reddie
Directors, D. R. Parker (*Personnel*); A. Coombe (*Works*); R. D. Wilson (*Finance*); D. C. Parker (*Horticulture*); L. J. Hanna (*Information and Secretariat*)

IMPERIAL WAR GRAVES ENDOWMENT FUND
Trustees, The Lord Remnant, CVO (*Chairman*); A. C. Barker; Adm. Sir John Kerr, GCB
Secretary to the Trustees, R. D. Wilson

COUNTRYSIDE COMMISSION
John Dower House, Crescent Place, Cheltenham, Glos
GL50 3RA
Tel 01242-521381; fax 01242-584270

The Countryside Commission was set up in 1968 and is an independent agency which promotes the conservation and enhancement of landscape beauty in England. It encourages the provision and improvement of facilities in the countryside, and works to secure access for open air recreation. The Commission is funded by an annual grant from the Department of the Environment, Transport and the Regions, and members of the Commission are appointed by the Secretary of State. The Government announced in March 1998 that the Countryside Commission would merge with the Rural Development Commission in April 1999.
Chairman, R. Simmonds, CBE
Commissioners, D. Barker, MBE; the Rt. Revd Bishop of Blackburn; The Lord Denham, KBE; Dr Victoria Edwards, FRICS; Dr Susan Owens; W. Rogers-Coltman, OBE; R. Swarbrick, CBE; D. Woodhall, CBE
Chief Executive (G3), R. G. Wakeford
Directors (G5), R. Clarke (*Programmes*); M. Taylor (*Resources*)
Head of Strategic Affairs (G7), D. E. Coleman
Head, Farms and Woodlands Branch (G7), R. Lloyd
Head, National Heritage Unit (G7), P. Walshe
Head, Sustainable Leisure Branch (G7), R. Roberts
Head, Planning for Sustainable Development Branch (G7), J. Worth
Head, Local Identity Branch (G7), T. Robinson
Head, Countryside Around Towns Branch (G7), Dr M. Rawson
Head, Information Services (G7), J. Huntley
Head, Resources Management (G7), V. Ellis
Regional Officers (G7), Dr M. Carroll (*Eastern*); T. Allen (*Midlands*); K. Buchanan (*North-East*); Dr Liz Newton (*North-West*); Ms M. Spain (*South-East*); N. Holliday (*South-West*); Dr S. A. Bucknall (*Yorkshire and Humber*)

COUNTRYSIDE COUNCIL FOR WALES/ CYNGOR CEFN GWLAD CYMRU
Plas Penrhos, Ffordd Penrhos, Bangor LL57 2LQ
Tel 01248-385500; fax 01248-385505

The Countryside Council for Wales is the Government's statutory adviser on wildlife, countryside and maritime conservation matters in Wales, and it is the executive authority for the conservation of habitats and wildlife. It promotes the protection of the Welsh landscape and encourages opportunities for public access and enjoyment of the countryside. It provides grant aid to local authorities, voluntary organizations and individuals to pursue countryside management. It is funded by the Welsh Office and accountable to the Secretary of State for Wales, who appoints its members.
Chairman, E. M. W. Griffith, CBE
Chief Executive, P. E. Loveluck, CBE
Senior Director and Chief Scientist, Dr M. E. Smith
Director, Countryside Policy, Dr J. Taylor
Director, Conservation, Dr D. Parker

COVENT GARDEN MARKET AUTHORITY
Covent House, New Covent Garden Market, London
SW8 5NX
Tel 0171-720 2211; fax 0171-622 5307

The Covent Garden Market Authority is constituted under the Covent Garden Market Acts 1961 to 1977, the members being appointed by the Minister of Agriculture, Fisheries and Food. The Authority owns and operates the 56-acre New Covent Garden Markets (fruit, vegetables, flowers) which have been trading since 1974.
Chairman (part-time), L. Mills, CBE
General Manager, Dr P. M. Liggins
Secretary, C. Farey

CRIMINAL CASES REVIEW COMMISSION
Alpha Tower, Suffolk Street Queensway, Birmingham B1 1TT
Tel 0121-633 1800; fax 0121-633 1823

The Criminal Cases Review Commission is an independent body set up under the Criminal Appeal Act 1995. It is a non-departmental public body reporting to Parliament via the Home Secretary. It is responsible for investigating suspected miscarriages of justice in England, Wales and Northern Ireland, and deciding whether or not to refer cases back to an appeal court. Membership of the Commission is by royal appointment; the senior executive staff are appointed by the Commission.
A commission to investigate alleged miscarriages of justice in Scotland is to be established by 1 April 1999.
Chairman, Sir Frederick Crawford, FENG.
Members, B. Capon; L. Elks; A. Foster; Ms J. Gort; Ms F. King; J. Knox; D. Kyle; J. Leckey; Prof. L. Leigh; J. MacKeith; K. Singh; B. Skitt; E. Weiss
Chief Executive, Ms G. Stacey
Director of Finance and Personnel, D. Robson
Legal Advisers, J. Wagstaff; M. Aspinall
Police Adviser, R. Barrington

CRIMINAL INJURIES COMPENSATION AUTHORITY AND BOARD
Morley House, 26–30 Holborn Viaduct, London EC1A 2JQ
Tel 0171-842 6800; fax 0171-436 0804
Tay House, 300 Bath Street, Glasgow G2 4JR
Tel 0141-331 2726; 0141-331 2287

All applications for compensation for personal injury arising from crimes of violence in England, Scotland and Wales are dealt with at the above locations. (Separate arrangements apply in Northern Ireland.) Applications received up to 31 March 1996 were assessed on the basis of common law damages under the 1990 compensation scheme by the Criminal Injuries Compensation Board (CICB), which also hears appeals. Applications received on or after 1 April 1996 are assessed under a tariff-based scheme by the Criminal Injuries Compensation Authority (CICA); there is a separate avenue of appeal to the Criminal Injuries Compensation Appeals Panel (CICAP). In 1996–7 total compensation paid was £209,208,500.
Chairman of the Criminal Injuries Compensation Board (part-time) (£35,306), The Lord Carlisle of Bucklow, PC, QC
Chief Executive of the Board and of the Criminal Injuries Compensation Authority, P. G. Spurgeon

Head of Legal Services, Mrs A. M. Johnstone
Operations Manager, E. McKeown
Chairman of the Criminal Injuries Compensation Appeals Panel, M. Lewer, QC
Secretary to the Panel, Miss V. Jenson

CROFTERS COMMISSION
4–6 Castle Wynd, Inverness IV2 3EQ
Tel 01463-663450; fax 01463-711820

The Crofters Commission was established in 1955. It advises the Secretary of State for Scotland on all matters relating to crofting. It controls the letting, subletting and, in certain circumstances, the assignation or enlargement of crofts; the removal of land from crofting tenure; and the regulation of common grazings. It delivers schemes to develop crofts and crofting townships and for the improvement of crofters' livestock.
Chairman, I. MacAskill
Secretary (G6), M. Grantham

CROWN ESTATE
16 Carlton House Terrace, London SW1Y 5AH
Tel 0171-210 4377; fax 0171-930 8202

The land revenues of the Crown in England and Wales have been collected on the public account since 1760, when George III surrendered them to Parliament and received a fixed annual payment or Civil List. At the time of the surrender the gross revenues amounted to about £89,000 and the net return to about £11,000. The land revenues in Ireland have been carried to the Consolidated Fund since 1820; from 1923, as regards the Republic of Ireland, they have been collected and administered by the Irish Government. The land revenues in Scotland were transferred to the predecessors of the Crown Estate Commissioners in 1833.

In the year ended 31 March 1998, the gross revenue from the Crown Estate totalled £160.1 million and £113.2 million was paid to the Exchequer as surplus revenue.
First Commissioner and Chairman (part-time), Sir Denys Henderson
Second Commissioner and Chief Executive, C. K. Howes, CB, CVO
Commissioners (part-time), Sir John James, KCVO, CBE; I. Grant; J. H. M. Norris, CBE; The Lord De Ramsey; Mrs H. Chapman, CBE, FRICS
Commissioner and Deputy Chief Executive, D. E. G. Griffiths
Legal Adviser, D. Harris
Director of Urban Estates, N. Borrett
Urban Estates Managers, M. W. Dillon; A. Bickmore; R. Wyatt
Development and Investment Manager, L. Colgan
Agricultural Estates Manager, C. Bourchier
Marine Estates Manager, F. G. Parrish
Information Systems Manager, D. Kingston-Smith
Valuation and Investment Analysis Manager, P. Shearmur
Internal Audit Manager, J. E. Ford
Finance Manager, J. G. Lelliott
Personnel and Office Services Manager, R. H. Blake
Public Relations and Press Officer, Mrs G. Coates

SCOTLAND
10 Charlotte Square, Edinburgh EH2 4BR
Tel 0131-226 7241; fax 0131-220 1366

Crown Estate Receiver for Scotland, M. J. Gravestock

WINDSOR ESTATE
The Great Park, Windsor, Berks SL4 2HT
Tel 01753-860222; fax 01753-859617
Deputy Ranger and Surveyor, P. Everrett

CROWN PROSECUTION SERVICE
— *see* pages 363–4

DEPARTMENT FOR CULTURE, MEDIA AND SPORT
2–4 Cockspur Street, London SW1Y 5DH
Tel 0171-211 6200; fax 0171-211 6032
E-mail: enquiries@culture.gov.uk
Web: http://www.culture.gov.uk

The Department for Culture, Media and Sport was established in July 1997 and is responsible for government policy relating to the arts, broadcasting, the press, museums and galleries, libraries, sport and recreation, historic buildings and ancient monuments, tourism, and the music industry. It funds the Arts Councils and other arts bodies, is responsible for policy on the National Lottery and the Millennium, and sponsors the Millennium Commission.
Secretary of State for Culture, Media and Sport, The Rt. Hon. Chris Smith, MP
 Private Secretary, T. Dyer
 Special Advisers, J. Eccles; J. Newbigin
 Parliamentary Private Secretary, Ms F. Mactaggart, MP
Parliamentary Under-Secretaries, Alan Howarth, MP (*Arts*); Tony Banks, MP (*Sport*); Janet Anderson, MP (*Tourism, Film and Broadcasting*)
 Private Secretaries, M. McGann; S. Green; D. Tambling
Parliamentary Clerk, T. English
Permanent Secretary (SCS), R. Young
 Private Secretary, J. Priestland

LIBRARIES, GALLERIES AND MUSEUMS GROUP
Head of Group (SCS), Miss S. Booth, CBE
Head of Libraries and Information Division (SCS), N. Mackay
Head of British Library Project and IT Strategy Unit (A(U)), E. D'Silva
Head of Museums and Galleries Division (SCS), H. Corner
Director, Government Art Collection (SCS), Ms P. Johnson
Head of Cultural Property Unit (A(L)), M. Helston

SPORT, TOURISM, NATIONAL LOTTERY CHARITIES BOARD AND MILLENNIUM GROUP
Head of Group (SCS), D. Chesterton
Head of Sport and Recreation Division (SCS), S. Broadley
Head of Tourism Division (SCS), Ms B. Phillips
Head of National Lottery Charities Board Division (A(L)), Mrs V. Molloy
Head of Millennium Unit (A(L)), Miss C. Pillman

ARTS, BUILDING AND CREATIVE INDUSTRIES GROUP
Head of Group (SCS), L. P. Wright
Head of Arts Division (SCS), Ms M. Leech
Head of Buildings, Monuments and Sites Division (SCS), N. Pittman
Head of Creative Industries Unit (A(L)), D. Fawcett

BROADCASTING AND MEDIA GROUP
Head of Group (SCS), N. J. Kroll
Head of Broadcasting Policy Division (SCS), vacant
Head of Media Division (SCS), Ms J. Evans

FINANCE, LOTTERY AND PERSONNEL GROUP
Director (SCS), A. Ramsay
Head of Finance Division (SCS), Ms A. Stewart
Head of National Lottery Division (SCS), A. McLellan

Head of Personnel and Central Services Division (SCS), Ms R. Siemaszko

STRATEGY AND COMMUNICATIONS
Head of Strategy and Communications (SCS), P. Bolt

EXECUTIVE AGENCY

ROYAL PARKS AGENCY
The Old Police House, Hyde Park, London W2 2UH
Tel 0171-298 2000; fax 0171-298 2005

The Agency is responsible for maintaining and developing the royal parks.
Chief Executive (G5), D. Welch

BOARD OF CUSTOMS AND EXCISE
*New King's Beam House, 22 Upper Ground, London SE1 9PJ
Tel 0171-620 1313
Web: http://www.open.gov.uk/customs/c&ehome/htm

Commissioners of Customs were first appointed in 1671 and housed by the King in London. The Excise Department was formerly under the Inland Revenue Department and was amalgamated with the Customs Department in 1909.

HM Customs and Excise is responsible for collecting and administering customs and excise duties and VAT, and advises the Chancellor of the Exchequer on any matters connected with them. The Department is also responsible for preventing and detecting the evasion of revenue laws and for enforcing a range of prohibitions and restrictions on the importation of certain classes of goods. In addition, the Department undertakes certain agency work on behalf of other departments, including the compilation of UK overseas trade statistics from customs import and export documents.

THE BOARD
Chairman (G1), Dame Valerie Strachan, DCB
 Private Secretaries, Ms J. Mellon; L. Allen
Deputy Chairman, A. W. Russell, CB
Commissioners (G3), A. C. Sawyer; P. R. H. Allen; A. R. Rawsthorne; D. J. Howard; A. Paynter; M. R. Brown; R. N. McAfee; M. W. Norgrove
Head of Board's Secretariat, J. Bone

PUBLIC RELATIONS OFFICE
Tel 0171-865 5665
Head of Public Relations, Ms L. J. Sinclair

INFORMATION SYSTEMS DIRECTORATE
Alexander House, 21 Victoria Avenue, Southend-on-Sea SS99 1AA
Tel 01702-348944
Director, A. Paynter

CUSTOMS POLICY DIRECTORATE
Director, A. R. Rawsthorne

EXCISE AND CENTRAL POLICY DIRECTORATE
Director, D. J. Howard

VAT POLICY DIRECTORATE
Director, M. R. Brown

PERSONNEL AND FINANCE DIRECTORATE
Director, P. R. H. Allen

---
*Unless otherwise stated, this is the address and telephone number of directorates of the Board

CENTRAL OPERATIONS DIRECTORATE
Director, R. N. McAfee

Tariff and Statistical Office
Portcullis House, 27 Victoria Avenue, Southend-on-Sea SS2 6AL
Tel 01702-348944
Controller, M. McDowall

Accounting Services Division
Alexander House, 21 Victoria Avenue, Southend-on-Sea SS99 1AA
Tel 01702-348944
Accountant and Comptroller-General, D. Robinson

OPERATIONS (COMPLIANCE) DIRECTORATE
Director, M. W. Norgrove

OPERATIONS (PREVENTION) DIRECTORATE
Director, A. C. Sawyer

National Investigation Service
Custom House, Lower Thames Street, London EC3R 6EE
Tel 0171-283 5353
Chief Investigation Officer, R. Kellaway

SOLICITOR'S OFFICE
Solicitor, D. Pickup
Deputy Solicitor, G. Fotherby

COLLECTORS OF HM CUSTOMS AND EXCISE (G5)
Anglia, M. Hill
Central England, D. Garlick
Eastern England, A. Durrant
London Airports, M. Peach
London Central, J. Maclean
Northern England, H. Peden
Northern Ireland, T. W. Logan
North-west England, A. Allen
Scotland, C. Arnott
South-east England, W. I. Stuttle
South London and Thames, J. Hendry
Southern England, H. Burnard
Thames Valley, J. Barnard
Wales, the West and Borders, B. Flavill

OFFICE OF THE DATA PROTECTION COMMISSIONER
Wycliffe House, Water Lane, Wilmslow, Cheshire SK9 5AF
Tel 01625-545745; fax 01625-524510

The Office of the Data Protection Registrar was created by the Data Protection Act 1984; the Registrar was renamed the Data Protection Commissioner under the Data Protection Act 1998, which implemented the EU Data Protection Directive (95/46/EC) in the UK. It is the Commissioner's duty to compile and maintain the register of data users and computer bureaux and to provide facilities for members of the public to examine the register; to promote observance of data protection principles; to consider complaints made by data subjects; to disseminate information about the Data Protection Act; to encourage the production of codes of practice by trade associations and other bodies; to guide data users in complying with data protection principles; and to co-operate with other parties to the Council of Europe Convention and act as UK authority for the purposes of Article 13 of the Convention.
Commissioner, Mrs E. France

DEER COMMISSION FOR SCOTLAND
Knowsley, 82 Fairfield Road, Inverness IV3 5LH
Tel 01463-231751; fax 01463-712931

The Deer Commission for Scotland has the general functions of furthering the conservation and control of deer in Scotland. It has the statutory duty, with powers, to prevent damage to agriculture, forestry and the habitat by deer. It is funded by the Scottish Office.
Chairman (part-time), P. Gordon-Duff-Pennington, OBE
Director, A. Rinning
Technical Director, R. W. Youngson

MINISTRY OF DEFENCE
— *see* pages 384–7

DESIGN COUNCIL
34 Bow Street, London WC2E 7DL
Tel 0171-420 5200; fax 0171-420 5300

The Design Council is incorporated by royal charter and is a registered charity. It works with government, industry and academia to generate information and practical tools for uptake in industry and education which demonstrate the contribution, value and effectiveness of design. Its sponsoring department is the Department of Trade and Industry.
Chairman, J. Sorrell, CBE
Chief Executive, A. Summers

THE DUCHY OF CORNWALL
10 Buckingham Gate, London SW1E 6LA
Tel 0171-834 7346; fax 0171-931 9541

The Duchy of Cornwall was created by Edward III in 1337 for the support of his eldest son Edward, later known as the Black Prince. It is the oldest of the English duchies. The duchy is acquired by inheritance by the sovereign's eldest son either at birth or on the accession of his parent to the throne, whichever is the later. The primary purpose of the estate remains to provide an income for the Prince of Wales. The estate is mainly agricultural, consisting of 129,000 acres in 24 counties mainly in the south-west of England. The duchy also has some residential property, a number of shops and offices, and a Stock Exchange portfolio. Prince Charles is the 24th Duke of Cornwall.

THE PRINCE'S COUNCIL
Chairman, HRH The Prince of Wales, KG, KT, GCB
Lord Warden of the Stannaries, The Earl Peel
Receiver-General, The Earl Cairns, CBE
Attorney-General to the Prince of Wales, N. Underhill, QC
Secretary and Keeper of the Records, W. R. A. Ross
Other members, Earl of Shelburne; J. E. Pugsley; A. M. J. Galsworthy; C. Howes, CB; W. N. Hood, CBE; S. Lamport

OTHER OFFICERS
Auditors, I. Brindle; R. Hughes
Sheriff (1998–9), P. R. Thompson

THE DUCHY OF LANCASTER
Lancaster Place, Strand, London WC2E 7ED
Tel 0171-836 8277; fax 0171-836 3098

The estates and jurisdiction known as the Duchy of Lancaster have belonged to the reigning monarch since 1399 when John of Gaunt's son came to the throne as Henry IV. As the Lancaster Inheritance it goes back as far as 1265 when Henry III granted his youngest son Edmund lands and possessions following the Baron's war. In 1267 Henry gave Edmund the County, Honor and Castle of Lancaster and created him the first Earl of Lancaster. In 1351 Edward III created Lancaster a County Palatine.

The Chancellor of the Duchy of Lancaster is responsible for the administration of the Duchy, the appointment of justices of the peace in Lancashire, Greater Manchester and Merseyside and ecclesiastical patronage in the Duchy gift.
Chancellor of the Duchy of Lancaster (and Minister for the Cabinet Office), The Rt. Hon. Dr Jack Cunningham, MP (*see also* page 288)
Attorney-General, R. G. B. McCombe, QC
Receiver-General, Sir Michael Peat, KCVO
Clerk of the Council, M. K. Ridley, CVO
Chief Clerk, Col. F. N. J. Davies

ECGD (EXPORT CREDITS GUARANTEE DEPARTMENT)
PO Box 2200, 2 Exchange Tower, Harbour Exchange Square, London E14 9GS
Tel 0171-512 7000; fax 0171-512 7649

ECGD (Export Credits Guarantee Department), the UK's official export credit insurer, is a government department responsible to the Secretary of State for Trade and Industry and functions under the Export and Investment Guarantees Act 1991. This enables ECGD to facilitate UK exports by making available export credit insurance to firms engaged in selling overseas and to guarantee repayment to banks providing finance for capital goods. The Act also empowers ECGD to insure UK companies investing overseas against political risks such as war, expropriation and restrictions on remittances.
Chief Executive, H. V. B. Brown
Group Directors (G3), V. P. Lunn-Rockliffe (*Asset Management*); J. R. Weiss (*Underwriting*); T. M. Jaffray (*Resource Management*)

DIVISIONS
Director, Finance (G5), R. J. Healey
Director, Central Services (G5), P. J. Callaghan
Directors, Underwriting Divisions (G5), G. G. W. Welsh (*Division 1*); J. C. W. Croall (*Division 2*); M. D. Pentecost (*Division 3*); Mrs M. E. Maddox (*Division 4*); S. R. Dodgson (*Division 5*); C. J. Leeds (*Division 6*)
Director, Office of the General Counsel (G5), R. G. Elden
Director, International Debt (G5), A. J. T. Steele
Director, Claims (G5), R. F. Lethbridge
Director, Treasury and Export Finance (G5), J. S. Snowdon
Director, Risk Management (G5), P. J. Radford
Director, External Relations (G5), R. Gotts
Director, IT Services (G6), E. J. Walsby
Director, Internal Audit (G6), G. Cassell
Director, Operational Research (G6), Ms R. Kaufman

EXPORT GUARANTEES ADVISORY COUNCIL
Chairman, D. H. A. Harrison
Other Members, Ms E. Airey; Dr A. K. Banerji; R. F. T.
Binyon; S. J. Doughty; M. S. Jaskel; Ms L. Knox;
G. W. Lynch, OBE; P. J. Mason; R. H. Maudslay

DEPARTMENT FOR EDUCATION AND EMPLOYMENT

Sanctuary Buildings, Great Smith Street, London
SW1P 3BT
Tel 0171-925 5000; fax 0171-925 6000
E-mail: info@dfee.gov.uk
Web: http://www.dfee.gov.uk
Caxton House, Tothill Street, London SW1H 9NF
Tel 0171-273 3000; fax 0171-273 5124
Moorfoot, Sheffield S1 4PQ
Tel 0114-275 3275; fax 0114-259 4724
Mowden Hall, Staindrop Road, Darlington DL3 9BG
Tel 01325-460155

The Department for Education and Employment was
formed in July 1995, bringing together the functions of the
former Department for Education with the training and
labour market functions of the former Employment
Department Group. It includes an executive agency, the
Employment Service. The Department aims to support
economic growth and improve the nation's competitive-
ness and quality of life by raising standards of educational
achievement and skill and by promoting an efficient and
flexible labour market. In April 1998 it took over from the
Department of Health responsibility for day care, includ-
ing the regulation of nurseries and childminders.
Secretary of State for Education and Employment, The Rt. Hon.
David Blunkett, MP
Principal Private Secretary, M. Wardle
Special Advisers, C. Ryan; T. Bently; H. Benn; Ms L.
Barclay
Parliamentary Private Secretary, Ms J. Corston, MP
Minister of State, The Rt. Hon. Andrew Smith, MP (*Welfare
to Work, Equal Opportunities*)
Private Secretary, Ms K. Driver
Parliamentary Private Secretary, Ms J. Ryan, MP
Minister of State, Estelle Morris, MP (*School Standards*)
Private Secretary, Ms C. Maye
Minister in the Lords, The Baroness Blackstone, PH.D.
Private Secretary, M. Boo
Parliamentary Private Secretary, T. McNulty, MP
Parliamentary Under-Secretaries of State, Margaret Hodge,
MP (*Employment and Equal Opportunities*); Charles Clarke,
MP (*Schools*) George Mudie, MP (*Lifelong Learning*)
Private Secretaries, Ms G. Magliocco; D. McGrath; Ms L.
Welsh
Permanent Secretary, M. Bichard
Private Secretary, H. Nicholson-Lailey

EMPLOYMENT, LIFELONG LEARNING AND INTERNATIONAL DIRECTORATE
Director-General, N. Stuart

INTERNATIONAL
Director, C. Tucker, CB
Heads of Divisions, Miss E. Hodkinson (*EC Education and
Training*); Ms W. Harris (*European Union*); Ms E.
Trewartha (*European Social Fund*); B. Shaw (*International
Relations*)

SKILLS AND LIFELONG LEARNING
Director, D. Grover

Heads of Divisions, J. Temple (*Skills Unit*); Mrs F. Everiss
(*Individual Learning*); vacant (*Learning at Work*); Dr J.
Pugh (*University for Industry*)
EMPLOYMENT POLICY
Director, M. J. Richardson
Heads of Divisions, M. Neale (*New Deal Policy*); C. Barnham
(*Employment and Benefits Policy*); E. Galvin (*Employment
and Training Programmes*); B. Wells (*Economy and Labour
Market*)

EQUAL OPPORTUNITIES, TECHNOLOGY AND OVERSEAS
LABOUR
Director, B. Niven
Heads of Divisions, Ms S. Trundle (*Childcare Unit*); Ms J.
Eastabrook (*Sex and Race Equality*); Miss D. Fordham
(*Disability Policy*); R. Ritzema (*Education and Training
Technology*); N. Atkinson (*Overseas Labour Service*)

FINANCE AND ANALYTICAL SERVICES DIRECTORATE
Director-General, P. Shaw

FINANCE
Heads of Divisions, D. Sandeman (*Expenditure*); S. Burt
(*Private Finance*); Mrs C. Hunter (*Programmes*); R. Wye
(*Efficiency*); P. Connor (*Financial Accounting*); N. Thirtle
(*Internal Audit*)

ANALYTICAL SERVICES
Director, D. Allnutt
Heads of Divisions, M. Britton (*Qualifications, Pupil
Assessment and International*); J. Elliott (*Youth and Further
Education*); D. Thompson (*Higher Education*); B. Butcher
(*Employability and Adult Learning*); R. Bartholomew
(*Equal Opportunities and Research Programmes*); Ms A.
Brown (*Schools, Teachers and Resources*)

FURTHER AND HIGHER EDUCATION AND YOUTH TRAINING DIRECTORATE
Director-General, R. Dawe

QUALIFICATIONS AND OCCUPATIONAL STANDARDS
Director, R. Hull
Heads of Divisions, M. Waring (*School and College
Qualifications*); J. West (*Qualifications for Work*)

FURTHER EDUCATION AND YOUTH TRAINING
Director, D. Forrester
Heads of Divisions, Ms C. Tyler (*16-19 Policy*); Mrs L.
Ammon, CBE (*Choice and Careers*); J. Stanyer (*Further
Education Support Unit*); A. Shaw (*Further Education*); A.
Davies (*Training for Young People*); Ms B. Evans (*16-19
Student Support*)

HIGHER EDUCATION
Director, A. C. Clark
Heads of Divisions, Mrs I. Wilde (*Higher Education Funding*);
N. Flint (*Student Support 1*); A. Clarke (*Student Support 2*);
T. Fellowes (*Higher Education and Employment*)

LEGAL ADVISER'S OFFICE
Legal Adviser, F. Croft
Heads of Divisions, F. Clarke; S. Harker; C. House; N.
Lambert

OPERATIONS DIRECTORATE
Director, J. Hedger, CB
Heads of Divisions, P. Houten (*TECs and Careers Service
Operational Policy*); P. Lauener (*Resources and Budget
Management*); Mrs P. Jones (*Financial Control, Operations*);
Ms S. Orr (*Quality and Performance Improvement*); H.
Sharp (*Regional Development and Government Offices*); J.
Fuller (*National Training Organizations*)

PERSONNEL AND SUPPORT SERVICES DIRECTORATE
Director, Mrs H. Douglas
Heads of Divisions, R. Hinchcliffe (*Information Systems*); Ms C. Johnson (*Personnel*); S. Green (*Procurement and Contracting*); J. Gordon (*Training and Development*); L. Webb (*Facilities Management*); T. Jeffery (*Corporate Change and Senior Staff*); B. Hillon (*Senior Equal Opportunities Adviser*)

SCHOOLS DIRECTORATE
Director-General, D. Normington
Heads of Division, S. Kershaw (*Education Bill*); S. Edwards (*Schools Communication*)

SCHOOLS ORGANIZATION AND BUILDINGS
Director, P. Makeham
Heads of Divisions, S. Marston (*Schools Framework*); A. Cranston (*Organization of School Places*); R. Jacobs (*Specialist Schools and School Governance*); K. Beeton (*Schools Capital and Buildings*); M. Hipkins (*Under-Fives Policy*); M. Patel (*Architects and Buildings*)

SCHOOL CURRICULUM, FUNDING, AND TEACHERS
Director, N. J. Sanders, CB
Heads of Divisions, A. Wye (*School Recurrent Funding and LEA Finance*); Ms A. Jackson (*School Teachers' Pay and Pensions*); Ms C. Bienkowska (*Teacher Supply, Training and Qualifications*); I. Berry (*Curriculum and Assessment*)

PUPILS, PARENTS AND YOUTH
Director, R. Smith
Heads of Divisions, Miss C. Macready (*Admissions and Information for Parents*); R. Green (*Special Educational Needs*); P. Cohen (*Discipline and Attendance*); G. Holley (*Youth Service and Preparation for Adulthood*); M. Phipps (*Pupil Welfare and Opportunities*); Ms S. Johnson (*Pupil Motivation and Community Links*)

SCHOOL STANDARDS AND EFFECTIVENESS UNIT
Head of Unit, Prof. M. Barber
Heads of Divisions, S. Adamson (*Standards*); Ms S. Scales (*School Effectiveness*)

STRATEGY AND COMMUNICATIONS DIRECTORATE

Director, P. Wanless
Heads of Divisions, Ms J. Simpson (*Head of News*); T. Cook (*Media Relations*); J. Ross (*Publicity*); R. Harrison (*Strategy and Board Secretariat*); J. Dewsbury (*Briefing*); C. Wells (*Millennium Project*)

EXECUTIVE AGENCY

THE EMPLOYMENT SERVICE
Caxton House, Tothill Street, London SW1H 9NA
Tel 0171-273 6060; fax 0171-273 6099

The aims of the Employment Service are to contribute to high levels of employment and growth by helping all people without a job to find work and by helping employers to fill their vacancies, and to help individuals lead rewarding working lives.
Chief Executive, L. Lewis
Director of Jobcentre Services, J. Turner
Director of Human Resources, K. White
Director of Policy and Process Design, R. Foster
Director of Finance, Planning and Research, P. Collis
Non-executive Directors, R. Dykes; Ms L. de Groot
Regional Directors, M. Groves (*East Midlands and Eastern*); S. Holt (*London and South-East*); P. Robson (*Northern*); J. Roberts (*North-West*); K. Pascoe (*South-West*); S. McIntyre (*West Midlands*); R. Lasko (*Yorkshire and Humberside*)
Director for Scotland, A. R. Brown
Director for Wales, Mrs S. Keyse

OFFICE OF ELECTRICITY REGULATION
Hagley House, Hagley Road, Birmingham B16 8QG
Tel 0121-456 2100; fax 0121-456 4664
SCOTLAND: Regent Court, 70 West Regent Street, Glasgow G2 2QZ
Tel 0141-331 2678; fax 0141-331 2777

The Office of Electricity Regulation (OFFER) was set up under the Electricity Act 1989 and is headed by the Director-General of Electricity Supply. It is the independent regulatory body for the electricity supply industry in England, Scotland and Wales. Its functions are to promote competition in the generation and supply of electricity; to ensure that all reasonable demands for electricity are satisfied; to protect customers' interests in relation to prices, security of supply and quality of services; and to promote the efficient use of electricity.

The Government has announced its intention of establishing an Energy Regulator, with responsibility for both electricity and gas, by 1999.
Director-General of Electricity Supply, Prof. S. C. Littlechild (*until the appointment of the new regulator*)
Deputy Director-General, C. P. Carter
Deputy Director-General for Scotland, D. Wilson
Director of Regulation and Business Affairs, J. Saunders
Director of Supply Competition, A. J. Boorman
Director of Consumer Affairs, Dr D. P. Hauser
Technical Director, Dr B. Wharmby
Director of Public Affairs, Miss J. D. Luke
Director of Administration, H. P. Jones
Legal Adviser, D. R. B. Bevan
Chief Examiner, J. D. Cooper

OFFICE FOR THE REGULATION OF ELECTRICITY AND GAS
Brookmount Buildings, 42 Fountain Street, Belfast BT1 5EE
Tel 01232-311575 (*Electricity*); 01232-314212 (*Gas*); fax 01232-311740

The Office for the Regulation of Electricity and Gas (OFREG) is the combined regulatory body for the electricity and gas supply industries in Northern Ireland.
Director-General of Electricity Supply and Director-General of Gas for Northern Ireland, D. B. McIldoon
Deputy Director-General of Electricity and Gas, C. H. Coulthard

ENGLISH HERITAGE
— *see* Historic Buildings and Monuments Commission for England

ENGLISH NATURE
Northminster House, Peterborough PE1 1UA
Tel 01733-455000; fax 01733-568834

English Nature (the Nature Conservancy Council for England) was established in 1991 and is responsible for advising the Secretary of State for the Environment, Transport and the Regions on nature conservation in England. It promotes, directly and through others, the conservation of England's wildlife and natural features. It selects, establishes and manages National Nature Reserves and identifies and notifies Sites of Special Scientific Interest. It provides advice and information about nature conservation, and supports and conducts research relevant to these functions. Through the Joint Nature Conservation Committee (*see* page 329), it works with its sister organizations in Scotland and Wales on UK and international nature conservation issues.

Chairman, The Baroness Young of Old Scone
Chief Executive, Dr D. R. Langslow
Directors, Dr K. L. Duff; Miss C. E. M. Wood; Ms S. Collins

ENGLISH PARTNERSHIPS
16–18 Old Queen Street, London SW1H 9HP
Tel 0171-976 7070; fax 0171-976 7740

English Partnerships, in statute the Urban Regeneration Agency, came into operation in 1994. Its task is to regenerate derelict, vacant and under-used land and buildings throughout England. Its aim is to deliver regeneration, economic development, job creation and environmental improvement. It works in partnership with the public, private and voluntary sectors. Its sponsoring department is the Department of the Environment, Transport and the Regions.

English Partnerships' regional responsibilities will transfer to the new regional development agencies in April 1999, and the Government has announced plans for English Partnerships to merge with the Commission for the New Towns (*see* page 496) by 1 April 2000.

Chairman, Sir Alan Cockshaw, FEng.
Deputy Chairman, Sir Idris Pearce, CBE, TD
Chief Executive, A. Dunnett

DEPARTMENT OF THE ENVIRONMENT, TRANSPORT AND THE REGIONS
Eland House, Bressenden Place, London SW1E 5DU
Great Minster House, 76 Marsham Street, London SW1P 4DR
Ashdown House, 123 Victoria Street, London SW1E 6DE
Tel 0171-890 3000
Web: http://www.detr.gov.uk

The Department of the Environment, Transport and the Regions (DETR) was formed in June 1997 by the merger of the Department of the Environment and the Department of Transport. It is responsible for policies relating to the environment, housing, transport services, rural affairs, planning, local government, regional development, regeneration, the construction industry and health and safety.

The Department's ministers are based at Eland House.

Deputy Prime Minister and Secretary of State for the Environment, Transport and the Regions, The Rt. Hon. John Prescott, MP
Private Secretary, P. Unwin
Special Advisers, J. Irvin; Ms J. Hammell
Parliamentary Private Secretary, A. Meale, MP
Minister for Transport, The Rt. Hon. Dr John Reid, MP
Private Secretary, P. Kirk
Minister for the Environment, The Rt. Hon. Michael Meacher, MP
Private Secretary, Mrs T. Vokes
Parliamentary Private Secretary, T. Rooney, MP
Minister of State, Hilary Armstrong, MP (*Local Government, Housing*)
Private Secretary, A. J. Redpath
Special Adviser, D. Murphy
Parliamentary Private Secretary, K. Hill, MP

Minister of State, Richard Caborn, MP (*Regions, Regeneration, Planning*)
Private Secretary, C. T. Wood
Special Adviser, P. Hackett
Parliamentary Private Secretary, B. Chapman, MP
Parliamentary Under-Secretaries of State, Nick Raynsford, MP (*London, Construction*); Glenda Jackson, CBE, MP (*Transport in London*); The Lord Whitty (*Roads*); Alan Meale, MP (*Environment, Wildlife, Health and Safety Executive, Regeneration and the Regions*)
Private Secretaries, Ms K. Willison; Ms S. Bolt; L. Sambrook; R. O'Donnell
Parliamentary Clerk, Ms P. Gaunt
Permanent Secretary (*SCS*), Sir Richard Mottram, KCB
Private Secretary, Mrs S. Bishop

DIRECTORATE OF COMMUNICATION*
Director (*SCS*), S. Dugdale
Deputy Directors (*SCS*), K. Kerslake (*Publicity*); D. Plews (*Press*)

ENVIRONMENT PROTECTION GROUP†
Director-General (*SCS*), Miss D. A. Nichols

ENERGY, ENVIRONMENT AND WASTE DIRECTORATE
Director (*SCS*), P. Ward
Heads of Divisions (*SCS*), L. Packer (*Energy Efficiency Policy and Sponsorship*); D. Vincent (*Energy Environment Market Innovation*); H. Cleary (*Environment and Business 1–3*); B. Ryder (*Environment and Business 4–5*); Ms L. Simcock (*Waste Policy*); D. Prior (*Joint Environmental Markets Unit*)

ENVIRONMENT AND INTERNATIONAL DIRECTORATE
Director (*SCS*), Dr D. J. Fisk
Heads of Divisions (*SCS*), Dr P. Hinchcliffe (*Chemicals and Biotechnology*); Dr S. Brown (*Radioactive Substances*); P. F. Unwin (*Global Atmosphere*); Dr B. Hackland (*Air and Environment Quality 1–5*); M. Williams (*Air and Environment Quality 6–8*); Ms S. McCabe (*Environment Protection International*)

ENVIRONMENT PROTECTION STRATEGY DIRECTORATE
Director (*SCS*), B. H. Leonard
Heads of Divisions (*SCS*), Mrs H. C. Hillier (*EP Statistics and Information Management*); B. Glicksman (*Environment Agency Sponsorship and Navigation*); J. Stevens (*European Environment*); R. Wilson (*Environment Protection Economics*); J. Adams (*Sustainable Development Unit*); A. Ring (*EPSDU Special Projects*)

WATER AND LAND DIRECTORATE
Director (*SCS*), A. H. Davis
Heads of Divisions (*SCS*), M. Rouse (*Drinking Water Inspectorate*); A. Simcock (*Land and Liabilities*); S. Hoggan (*Water Quality*); A. Wells (*Water Supply and Regulation*)

FINANCE GROUP†
Director and Principal Finance Officer (*SCS*), J. Ballard
Heads of Divisions (*SCS*), R. Bennett (*Finance Programmes*); I. McBrayne (*Finance Sponsorship and Programme*); R. Anderson (*Finance Departmental Administration*); A. Beard (*Finance Accounting Services, Resource Accounting and Budgeting*); M. Haselip (*Internal Audit*)

HOUSING, CONSTRUCTION, REGENERATION AND COUNTRYSIDE GROUP*
Director-General (*SCS*), Mrs M. McDonald, CB

HOUSING, PRIVATE POLICY AND ANALYSIS
Director (*SCS*), M. Gahagan

Heads of Divisons (*SCS*), Mrs J. Littlewood (*Housing and Urban Monitoring and Analysis*); M. Hughes (*Housing Data and Statistics*); S. Aldridge (*Housing and Urban Economics*); Ms B. Campbell (*Housing Policy and Home Ownership*); M. Faulkner (*Housing Private Rented Sector*); C. Braun (*Housing Renewal Policy*)

HOUSING, SOCIAL POLICY AND RESOURCES
Director (*SCS*), Mrs D. S. Phillips
Heads of Divisions (*SCS*), Mrs H. Chipping (*Local Authority Housing Finance*); R. J. Dinwiddy (*Housing Associations and Private Finance*); A. Allberry (*Homelessness and Housing Management*)

CONSTRUCTION DIRECTORATE
Director (*SCS*), J. Hobson
Heads of Divisions (*SCS*), J. P. Channing (*Construction Industry Sponsorship*); J. Stambollouian (*Construction Innovation and Research Management*); R. Wood (*Construction Export Promotion and Materials Sponsorship*); P. Everall (*Building Regulations*); H. Neuberger (*Construction Market Intelligence*)

WILDLIFE AND COUNTRYSIDE DIRECTORATE
Director (*SCS*), Ms S. Lambert
Heads of Divisions (*SCS*), R. M. Pritchard (*European Wildlife*); R. Hepworth (*Global Wildlife*); Ms D. Kahn (*Rural Development*); Ms S. Carter (*Countryside*)

REGENERATION DIRECTORATE
Director (*SCS*), P. Evans
Heads of Divisions (*SCS*), J. Roberts; W. Chapman; Ms L. Derrick

LEGAL GROUP*
Director-General (*SCS*), D. Hogg

COUNTRYSIDE, PLANNING AND TRANSPORT
Director (*SCS*), Ms S. Unerman
Heads of Divisions (*SCS*), N. Lefton (*Countryside and Wildlife*); Ms G. Hedley-Dent (*Planning*); R. Lines (*Highways*); N. Thomas (*Road Traffic*); A. Jones (*Aviation*); C. Ingram (*Marine*); D. Aries (*Railways*)

ENVIRONMENT, HOUSING AND LOCAL GOVERNMENT
Director (*SCS*), A. Roberts
Heads of Divisions (*SCS*), J. Comber (*Environment (National)*); Ms C. Cooper (*Local Government (Finance)*); Ms P. Conlon (*Local Government (General)*); Ms D. Phillips (*Housing Private Sector*); K. Baublys (*Housing Public Sector*); Ms S. Headley (*Special Projects*); I. Day (*Commercial and Establishments*); M. Devine (*Health and Safety Sponsorship*)

ENVIRONMENT (INTERNATIONAL AND EC)
Director (*SCS*), P. Szell
Head of Division (*SCS*), A. McGlone

LOCAL AND REGIONAL GOVERNMENT GROUP*
Director-General (*SCS*), P. Wood

LOCAL GOVERNMENT DIRECTORATE
Director (*SCS*), A. Whetnall
Heads of Divisions (*SCS*), P. Rowsell (*Local Government Sponsorship*); J. R. Footitt (*Local Government Competition and Quality*)

LOCAL GOVERNMENT FINANCE POLICY DIRECTORATE
Director (*SCS*), M. Lambirth

Heads of Divisions (*SCS*), R. J. Gibson (*Local Government Grant Distribution*); Mrs P. Penneck (*Local Government Finance Statistics*); Dr C. Myerscough (*Local Government Capital Finance*); N. Dorling (*Local Government Taxation*); I. Scotter (*Local Government Revenue Expenditure*)

GOVERNMENT OFFICES AND REGIONAL POLICY DIRECTORATE
Director (*SCS*), Miss L. Bell
Heads of Divisions (*SCS*), M. Coulshed; M. Ross; Mrs J. Scoones (*Government Offices Central Unit*)

REGIONAL OFFICES
— *see* pages 304–5

PLANNING, ROADS AND LOCAL TRANSPORT‡
Director-General (*SCS*), C. J. S. Brearley, CB

MOBILITY UNIT
Head of Unit (*SCS*), Miss E. A. Frye, OBE

FREIGHT DISTRIBUTION AND LOGISTICS
Director (*SCS*), B. Wadsworth
Heads of Divisions (*SCS*), Ms A. Moss (*Road Haulage*); R. Butchart (*Transport Statistics Freight*); Ms M. Carleton (*Traffic Area Network Unit*)

PLANNING DIRECTORATE
Director (*SCS*), J. Jacobs
Heads of Divisions (*SCS*), vacant (*Plans and Policies*); R. Jones (*Development Control Policy*); M. R. Ash (*Planning and Compensation*); J. Zetter (*Environmental Assessment, Internet and Research*); A. M. Oliver (*Planning and Land Use Statistics*); L. Hicks (*Minerals and Waste*); J. M. Leigh-Pollitt (*Land and Property*)

NATIONAL ROADS POLICY DIRECTORATE
Director (*SCS*), H. Wenban-Smith
Heads of Divisions (*SCS*), T. Worsley (*Highways, Economics and Traffic Appraisal*); N. McDonald (*Highways Policy and Programmes*); Mrs C. M. Dixon (*Tolling and Private Finance*); R. Donachie (*Transport Statistics*)

URBAN AND LOCAL TRANSPORT
Director (*SCS*), R. Bird
Heads of Divisions (*SCS*), E. C. Neve (*Buses and Taxis*); P. McCarthy (*Local Transport Policy*); A. S. D. Whybrow (*Traffic Policy*); M. F. Talbot (*Driver Information and Traffic Management*); M. Walsh (*Local Transport and General*); P. Capell (*Transport Statistics: Personal Travel*)

ROAD AND VEHICLE SAFETY
Director (*SCS*), J. Plowman
Heads of Divisions (*SCS*), M. Fendick (*Vehicle Standards and Engineering*); R. Peal (*Road Safety*); I. Todd (*Licensing and Roadworthiness Policy*); Dr Patricia Diamond, OBE (*Chief Medical Adviser*)

RAILWAYS, AVIATION AND SHIPPING GROUP‡
Director-General (*SCS*), D. Rowlands

RAILWAYS
Director (*SCS*), R. J. Griffins
Heads of Divisions (*SCS*), M. Fuhr (*Channel Tunnel and Rail Link*); P. Cox (*Railways Economics and Finance*); P. Thomas (*Railways International and General*); B. Linnard (*Railways Sponsorship*); S. Connolly (*Railways National Audit Office*)

---

* Based at Eland House
† Based at Ashdown House
‡ Based at Great Minster House

AVIATION
Director (SCS), A. J. Goldman, CB
Heads of Divisions (SCS), M. Fawcett (*Airports Policy*); Ms
M. J. Clare (*CAA*); M. C. Mann (*Economics, Aviation,
Maritime and International*); Ms E. Duthie (*Aviation
Environmental*); M. Smethers (*Multilateral*); A. T. Baker
(*International Aviation*); N. Starling (*International Aviation
Negotiations*)

AIR ACCIDENTS INVESTIGATION BRANCH
Defence Evaluation and Research Agency, Farnborough,
Hants GU14 6TD
Tel 01252-510300

Chief Inspector of Air Accidents, K. P. R. Smart, CBE
Deputy Chief Inspector, R. McKinlay

SHIPPING AND PORTS
Director (SCS), R. E. Clarke
Heads of Divisions (SCS), D. Cooke (*Shipping Policy 1*);
G. D. Rowe (*Shipping Policy 2*); J. F. Wall (*Shipping Policy
3*); C. Young (*Radioactive Materials Transport*); S. Reeves
(*Ports*); D. Lord (*Director, Transport Security*); W. Gillan
(*Deputy Director, Transport Security*)

MARINE ACCIDENTS INVESTIGATION BRANCH
5–7 Brunswick Place, Southampton SO1 2AN
Tel 01703-395500

Chief Inspector of Marine Accidents, Rear-Adm. J. Lang
Deputy Chief Inspector, S. Harwood

STRATEGY AND CORPORATE SERVICES
GROUP*
Director-General (SCS), R. S. Dudding
Heads of Divisions (SCS), I. Heawood (*Information
Management*); I. Harris (*Working Environment*); P. Walton
(*Corporate, Business and Agencies*); A. Murray (*Driver,
Vehicle and Operator Project*); G. Jones (*Procurement, Policy
and Advice*); J. O'Callaghan (*IT Services*); A. Apling
(*Science and Technology Policy*)

PERSONNEL AND CHANGE MANAGEMENT
Director (SCS), Ms J. Cotton
Heads of Divisions (SCS), M. Bailey (*Personnel Support*); G.
Kemp (*Personnel Advice and Support*); E. Gibbons (*Group
Facing Teams*); K. Arnold (*Pay and Industrial Relations*); B.
Meakins (*Change Management, Development and Training*)

TRANSPORT STRATEGY DIRECTORATE
Director (SCS), A. Burchell
Heads of Divisions (SCS), D. McMillan (*Integrated Transport
1*); Ms B. Hill (*Integrated Transport 2*); D. Instone
(*Transport and Environment*); I. Jordan (*Europe, Transport
and General*)

STRATEGY AND ECONOMIC DIRECTORATE
Director (SCS), C. Riley
Head of Division (SCS), M. Hurst (*Central Economics and
Policy*)

EXECUTIVE AGENCIES

DRIVER AND VEHICLE LICENSING AGENCY
Longview Road, Morriston, Swansea SA6 7JL
Tel 01792-772151 (*drivers*); 01792-772134 (*vehicles*)

The Agency issues driving licences, registers and licenses
vehicles, and collects excise duty.
Chief Executive, Dr S. J. Ford

DRIVING STANDARDS AGENCY
Stanley House, Talbot Street, Nottingham NG1 5GU
Tel 0115-947 4222; fax 0115-955 7334

The Agency's role is to carry out driving tests and approve
driving instructors.
Chief Executive, B. L. Herdan

HIGHWAYS AGENCY
St Christopher House, Southwark Street, London SE1 0TE
Tel 0645-556575

The Agency is responsible for the operation, management
and maintenance of the motorway and trunk road network
and for road construction and improvement.
Chief Executive, L. J. Haynes

MARITIME AND COASTGUARD AGENCY
Spring Place, 105 Commercial Road, Southampton
SO15 1EG
Tel 01703-329100

The Agency was formed in April 1998 by the merger of the
Coastguard Agency and the Marine Safety Agency. Its role
is to develop, promote and enforce high standards of
marine safety; to minimize loss of life amongst seafarers
and coastal users; and to minimize pollution from ships of
the sea and coastline.
Chief Executive, M. Storey
Chief Coastguard, J. Astbury

PLANNING INSPECTORATE
Tollgate House, Houlton Street, Bristol BS2 9DJ
Tel 0117-987 8000

The Inspectorate is responsible for casework involving
planning, housing, roads, environmental and related legislation. It is a joint executive agency of the Department of
the Environment, Transport and the Regions and the
Welsh Office.
Chief Executive and Chief Planning Inspector, C. Shepley

QUEEN ELIZABETH II CONFERENCE CENTRE
Broad Sanctuary, London SW1P 3EE
Tel 0171-222 5000; fax 0171-798 4200

The Centre provides conference and banqueting facilities
for both private sector and government use.
Chief Executive, M. C. Buck

VEHICLE CERTIFICATION AGENCY
1 Eastgate Office Centre, Eastgate Road, Bristol BS5 6XX
Tel 0117-951 5151; fax 0117-952 4103

The Agency tests and certificates vehicles to UK and
international standards.
Chief Executive, D. W. Harvey

VEHICLE INSPECTORATE
Berkeley House, Croydon Street, Bristol BS5 0DA
Tel 0117-954 3200; fax 0117-954 3212

The Agency carries out annual testing and inspection of
heavy goods and other vehicles and administers the MOT
testing scheme.
Chief Executive, R. J. Oliver

TRAFFIC AREA OFFICES AND
COMMISSIONERS
Senior Traffic Commissioner, Brig. M. W. Betts

Eastern, G. Simms
North-Eastern and North-Western, K. R. Waterworth
Scottish, Brig. M. W. Betts
South-Eastern and Metropolitan, Brig. M. H. Turner
Western, C. Heaps
West Midlands and S. Wales, J. M. C. Pugh

TRAFFIC DIRECTOR FOR LONDON
College House, Great Peter Street, London SW1P 3LN
Tel 0171-222 4545; fax 0171-976 8640

The Traffic Director for London is a non-departmental
public body which is independent from the Department of

* Based at Eland House
† Based at Ashdown House
‡ Based at Great Minster House

the Environment, Transport and the Regions but is responsible to the Secretary of State and to Parliament. Its role is to co-ordinate the Priority (Red) Route Network in London and monitor its operation.
Traffic Director for London, D. Turner

THE ENVIRONMENT AGENCY
25th Floor, Millbank Tower, 21–24 Millbank, London SW1P 4XL
Tel 0171-863 8600; fax 0171-863 8650
Rio House, Waterside Drive, Aztec West, Almondsbury, Bristol BS12 4UD
Tel 01454-624400; fax 01454-624409

The Environment Agency was established in April 1996 under the Environment Act 1995 and is a non-departmental public body sponsored by the Department of the Environment, Transport and the Regions, MAFF and the Welsh Office. The Agency is responsible for pollution prevention and control in England and Wales, and for the management and use of water resources, including flood defences, fisheries and navigation. It has head offices in London and Bristol and eight regional offices.

THE BOARD
Chairman, The Lord De Ramsey
Members, C. Beardwood; E. Gallagher; Sir Richard George; N. Haigh, OBE; C. Hampson, CBE; Sir John Harman; Prof. Jacqueline McGlade; G. Manning, OBE; Mrs K. Morgan; Dr A. Powell; Prof. D. Ritchie; T. Rodgers; G. Wardell; Mrs J. Wykes

THE EXECUTIVE
Chief Executive, E. Gallagher
Director of Finance, N. Reader
Director of Personnel, G. Duncan
Director of Environmental Protection, Dr P. Leinster
Director of Water Management, G. Mance
Director of Operations, A. Robertson
Director of Corporate Affairs, M. Wilson
Director of Legal Services, R. Navarro
Chief Scientist, J. Pentreath

ROYAL COMMISSION ON ENVIRONMENTAL POLLUTION
Steel House, 11 Tothill Street, London SW1H 9NF
Tel 0171-273 6635

The Commission was set up in 1970 to advise on national and international matters concerning the pollution of the environment.
Chairman, Prof. Sir Thomas Blundell
Members, Sir Geoffrey Allen, FRS; Revd Prof. M. C. Banner; Prof. G. S. Boulton, FRS, FRSE; Prof. C. E. D. Chilvers; Prof. R. Clift, OBE, FEng.; Dr P. Doyle, CBE, FRSE; J. Flemming; Sir Martin Holdgate, CB; Prof. R. Macrory; Prof. M. G. Marmot, PH.D.; Prof. J. G. Morris, CBE, FRS; Dr Penelope A. Rowlatt; The Earl of Selborne, KBE, FRS
Secretary, D. R. Lewis

EQUAL OPPORTUNITIES COMMISSION
Overseas House, Quay Street, Manchester M3 3HN
Tel 0161-833 9244; fax 0161-835 1657

Press Office, 36 Broadway, London SW1H 0XH. Tel: 0171-222 1110
Other Offices, Stock Exchange House, 7 Nelson Mandela

Place, Glasgow G2 1QW. Tel: 0141-248 5833; Windsor House, Windsor Place, Cardiff. Tel: 01222-343552

The Commission was set up in 1975 as a result of the passing of the Sex Discrimination Act. It works towards the elimination of discrimination on the grounds of sex or marital status and to promote equality of opportunity between men and women generally. It is responsible to the Department for Education and Employment.
Chairwoman, Ms K. Bahl, CBE
Deputy Chairwomen, Mrs E. Hodder; Ms G. James
Members, P. Smith; Ms M. Berg; R. Grayson; Dr J. Stringer; Prof. T. Rees; R. Penn; Ms J. Rubin; Dr A. Wright; Prof. M. Schofield
Chief Executive (acting), F. Spencer

EQUAL OPPORTUNITIES COMMISSION FOR NORTHERN IRELAND
Chamber of Commerce House, 22 Great Victoria Street, Belfast BT2 7BA
Tel 01232-242752; fax 01232-331047
Chair and Chief Executive, Mrs J. Smyth, CBE

OFFICE OF FAIR TRADING
Field House, Bream's Buildings, London EC4A 1PR
Tel 0171-211 8000; fax 0171-211 8800

The Office of Fair Trading is a non-ministerial government department headed by the Director-General of Fair Trading. It keeps commercial activities in the UK under review and seeks to protect consumers against unfair trading practices. The Director-General's consumer protection duties under the Fair Trading Act 1973, together with his responsibilities under the Consumer Credit Act 1974, the Estate Agents Act 1979, the Control of Misleading Advertisements Regulations 1988, and the Unfair Terms in Consumer Contracts Regulations 1994, are administered by the Office's Consumer Affairs Division. The Competition Policy Division is concerned with monopolies and mergers (under the Fair Trading Act 1973), and the Director-General's other responsibilities for competition matters, including those under the Restrictive Trade Practices Act 1976, the Resale Prices Act 1976, the Competition Act 1980, the Financial Services Act 1986 and the Broadcasting Act 1990. The Office is the UK competent authority on the application of the European Commission's competition rules, and also liaises with the Commission on consumer protection initiatives.
Director-General, J. Bridgeman

CONSUMER AFFAIRS DIVISION
Director (G3), Miss C. Banks
Assistant Directors (G5), R. Watson; M. Graham

COMPETITION POLICY DIVISION
Director (G3), Mrs M. J. Bloom
Assistant Directors (G5), A. J. White; H. L. Emden; E. L. Whitehorn; S. Wood; P. Bamford

LEGAL DIVISION
Director (G3), Miss P. Edwards
Assistant Directors (G5), M. A. Khan; S. Brindley
Establishment and Finance Officer (G5), Mrs R. Heyhoe
Chief Information Officer (G6), D. Hill

FOREIGN AND COMMONWEALTH OFFICE
Downing Street, London SW1A 2AL
Tel 0171-270 3000
Web: http://www.fco.gov.uk

The Foreign and Commonwealth Office provides, mainly through diplomatic missions, the means of communication between the British Government and other governments and international governmental organizations for the discussion and negotiation of all matters falling within the field of international relations. It is responsible for alerting the British Government to the implications of developments overseas; for protecting British interests overseas; for protecting British citizens abroad; for explaining British policies to, and cultivating friendly relations with, governments overseas; and for the discharge of British responsibilities to the UK overseas territories.

Secretary of State for Foreign and Commonwealth Affairs, The Rt. Hon. Robin Cook, MP
  Principal Private Secretary, J. Grant
  Private Secretaries, T. Barrow; A. Patrick
  Special Advisers, A. Hood; D. Clark
  Parliamentary Private Secretary, K. Purchase, MP
Minister for Europe, Joyce Quin, MP
  Private Secretary, N. Hopton
Minister of State, Derek Fatchett, MP
  Private Secretary, F. Baker
Minister of State, Tony Lloyd, MP
  Private Secretary, Ms P. Phillips
  Parliamentary Private Secretary to the Ministers of State, D. MacShane, MP
Parliamentary Under-Secretary of State, The Baroness Symons of Vernham Dean
Parliamentary Relations Department, E. Jenkinson (*Head*); P. Bromley (*Deputy Head and Parliamentary Clerk*)
Permanent Under-Secretary of State and Head of the Diplomatic Service, Sir John Kerr, KCMG
  Private Secretary, D. Frost
Deputy Under-Secretaries, J. R. Young, CMG (*Chief Clerk*); C. Budd (*Economic Director*); E. Jones Parry (*Political Director*); J. Shepherd (*Trade and Investment*); vacant (*Security/Intelligence*); Sir Franklin Berman, KCMG, QC (*Legal Adviser*)
Directors, J. R. de Fonblanque (*Europe*); J. Rollo, CMG (*Chief Economic Adviser*); R. H. Smith (*International Security*); R. Dales (*Africa and Commonwealth*); P. J. Westmacott (*Americas*); H. N. H. Synnott (*Southern Asia*); D. Hall (*Overseas Trade*); D. Plumbly, CMG (*Middle East and North Africa*); P. Ricketts (*Deputy Political Director*); R. Dibble (*General Services*); P. Nixon (*International Crime and Terrorism*); R. Dalton (*Personnel and Security*); M. Arthur (*Resources and Chief Inspector*); E. Clay (*Public Services*); T. Brenton (*Global Issues*); N. Sheinwald (*European Union*)
Director of Protocol and HM Vice-Marshal of the Diplomatic Corps, P. S. Astley, LVO

HEADS OF DEPARTMENTS

Allowances Review Team, M. Legg
Aviation and Maritime Department, N. Ling
British Diplomatic Spouses Association, Mrs E. Nixon
Central European Department, H. Pearce
Change Management Unit, Dr J. Hughes
China/Hong Kong Department, D. Warren
Commonwealth Co-ordination Department, C. Bright
Commonwealth Foreign and Security Policy Unit, Ms A. Pringle
Conference Unit, M. Dalton
Consular Division, D. Taylor

Counter Terrorism Policy Department, V. Fean
Cultural Relations Department, Ms A. Lewis
Diplomatic Service Language Centre, Dr Vanessa Davies
Drugs and International Crime, M. Raven
Eastern Department, P. Thomas
Eastern Adriatic Department, T. Phillips
Economic Advisers Department, J. Rollo, CMG
Economic Relations Department, N. Westcott
Engineering Services, N. Stickells
Environment, Science and Energy Department, J. Ashton
Equatorial Africa Department, Ms A. Grant
European Union Department (External), R. Stagg
European Union Department (Internal), S. Gass
Far Eastern and Pacific Department, vacant
Financial Compliance Unit, M. Purvis
Financial Policy, M. Brown
General Services Management Department, Ms J. Link
Government Hospitality Fund, Col. T. Earl
Home Estates Department, S. Attwood
Honours Unit, R. M. Sands
Human Rights Policy Unit, R. P. Nash
Information Department, P. J. Dun
Information Systems Department, P. McDermott, MVO
Internal Audit, R. Elias
Investment in Britain Bureau, A. Fraser
†*Joint Export Promotion Directorate,* D. Hall
Latin America and Caribbean Department, H. Hogger
Library and Records Department, J. Thompson
Management Consultancy and Inspection Department, M. Aron
Medical and Welfare, Ms E. Kennedy
Middle East Department, E. Chaplin
Migration and Visa Department, R. White
National Audit Office, J. Pearce
Near East and North Africa Department, P. W. Ford
News Department, K. Darroch
Non-Proliferation Department, P. Hare
North America Department, P. J. Priestley
North-East Asia and Pacific Department, D. Coates
OSCE and Council of Europe Department, S. N. Evans, OBE
Overseas Estates Department, M. H. R. Bertram, CBE
Overseas Territories Department, J. White
Permanent Under-Secretary's Department, D. Martin
Personnel Policy Unit, Ms P. Major
Personnel – Senior Management, Ms D. Holt
Personnel Services Department, R. Fell
Policy Planning, Miss A. M. Leslie
PROSPER, C. J. Edgerton, OBE
Protocol Department, R. S. Gorham (*First Assistant Marshal of the Diplomatic Corps*)
Purchasing Directorate, M. Gower
Republic of Ireland Department, G. Ferguson
Research Analysts, S. Jack
Resource and Planning Department, R. Kinchen
Royal Matters Unit, B. England
Security, T. Duggin
Security Policy, vacant
South Asian Department, C. Elmes
South-East Asian Department, N. J. Cox
Southern Africa Department, C. Wilton
Southern European Department, D. Reddaway
Support Services Department, M. Carr
Training, Ms C. Dharawarkar

---

* Joint Foreign and Commonwealth Office/Department for International Development department
† Joint Foreign and Commonwealth Office/Department of Trade and Industry directorate

United Nations Department, Ms R. M. Marsden
Western European Department, A. Layden
Whitley Council, P. May

EXECUTIVE AGENCY

WILTON PARK CONFERENCE CENTRE
Wiston House, Steyning, W. Sussex BN44 3DZ
Tel 01903-815020; fax 01903-816373

The Centre organizes international affairs conferences and is hired out to government departments and commercial users.
Chief Executive and Director, C. B. Jennings

CORPS OF QUEEN'S MESSENGERS
Support Services Department, Foreign and Commonwealth Office, London SW1A 2AH
Tel 0171-270 2779

Superintendent of the Corps of Queen's Messengers, B. Garside
Queen's Messengers, P. Allen; Maj. J. E. A. Andre; Maj.
A. N. D. Bols; Lt.-Cdr. K. E. Brown; Lt.-Col. W. P. A.
Bush; Lt.-Col. M. B. de S. Clayton; Maj.
P. C. H. Dening-Smitherman; Sqn. Ldr. J. S. Frizzell;
Capt. N. C. E. Gardner; Maj. D. A. Griffiths; Maj. K. J.
Rowbottom; Maj. M. R. Senior; Cdr. K. M. C. Simmons,
AFC; Maj. P. M. O. Springfield; Maj. J. S. Steele

FOREIGN COMPENSATION COMMISSION
Room 03, 4 Central Buildings, Matthew Parker Street,
London SW1H 9NL
Tel 0171-210 0400; fax 0171-210 0401

The Commission was set up by the Foreign Compensation Act 1950 primarily to distribute, under Orders in Council, funds received from other governments in accordance with agreements to pay compensation for expropriated British property and other losses sustained by British nationals.
Chairman (£83,586), A. W. E. Wheeler, CBE
Secretary, A. N. Grant

FORESTRY COMMISSION
231 Corstorphine Road, Edinburgh EH12 7AT
Tel 0131-334 0303; fax 0131-334 3047

The Forestry Commission is the government department responsible for forestry policy in Great Britain. It reports directly to forestry ministers (i.e. the Secretary of State for Scotland, who takes the lead role, the Minister of Agriculture, Fisheries and Food and the Secretary of State for Wales), to whom it is responsible for advice on forestry policy and for the implementation of that policy.

The Commission's principal objectives are to protect Britain's forests and woodlands; expand Britain's forest area; enhance the economic value of the forest resources; conserve and improve the biodiversity, landscape and cultural heritage of forests and woodlands; develop opportunities for woodland recreation; and increase public understanding of and community participation in forestry. Forest Enterprise, a trading body operating as an executive agency of the Commission, manages its forestry estate on a multi-use basis.

Chairman (*part-time*) (£36,965), Sir Peter Hutchison, Bt.,
    CBE
Director-General and Deputy Chairman (G2), D. J. Bills
Head of the Forestry Authority (G3), D. L. Foot, CB
Secretary to the Commissioners (G5), F. Strong

FOREST ENTERPRISE, 231 Corstorphine Road, Edinburgh
EH12 7AT. Tel: 0131-334 0303. *Chief Executive*, Dr B.
McIntosh

REGISTRY OF FRIENDLY SOCIETIES
Victory House, 30–34 Kingsway, London WC2B 6ES
Tel 0171-663 5000

The Registry of Friendly Societies is a government department serving three statutory bodies, the Building Societies Commission, the Friendly Societies Commission, and the Central Office of the Registry of Friendly Societies (together with the Assistant Registrar of Friendly Societies for Scotland).

The Building Societies Commission was established by the Building Societies Act 1986. The Commission is responsible for the supervision of building societies and administers the system of regulation. It also advises the Treasury and other government departments on matters relating to building societies.

The Friendly Societies Commission was established by the Friendly Societies Act 1992. Its responsibilities for the supervision of friendly societies parallel those of the Building Societies Commission for building societies.

The Central Office of the Registry of Friendly Societies provides a public registry for mutual organizations registered under the Building Societies Act 1986, Friendly Societies Acts 1974 and 1992, and the Industrial and Provident Societies Act 1965. It is responsible for the supervision of credit unions, and advises the Government on issues affecting them.

The Registry of Friendly Societies will be subsumed into the Financial Services Authority (*see* page 634) in January 1999.

BUILDING SOCIETIES COMMISSION
Chairman, G. E. Fitchew
Deputy Chairman, M. Owen
Commissioners, J. M. Palmer; *F. E. Worsley;
    *F. G. Sunderland; *N. Fox Bassett; *Sir James Birrell;
    *Ms C. Sergeant
* part-time

FRIENDLY SOCIETIES COMMISSION
Chairman, *M. Roberts
Commissioners, F. da Rocha; *B. Richardson; *J. A. Geddes;
    *Ms S. Brown; *Ms P. Triggs
* part-time

CENTRAL OFFICE OF THE REGISTRY
Chief Registrar, G. E. Fitchew
Assistant Registrars, A. J. Perrett; Ms S. Eden; E. Engstrom;
    N. Fawcett

BUILDING SOCIETIES COMMISSION STAFF
Grade 3, M. Owen
Grade 4, J. M. Palmer
Grade 5, W. Champion; E. Engstrom
Grade 6, N. F. Digance; A. G. Tebbutt

FRIENDLY SOCIETIES COMMISSION STAFF
Grade 6, F. da Rocha

CENTRAL SERVICES STAFF
Legal Adviser (G4), A. J. Perrett
Establishment and Finance Officer (G5), J. Stevens
Legal Staff (G5), A. D. Preston; Ms P. Henderson; *(G6)*, Ms
   S. Bagga

REGISTRY OF FRIENDLY SOCIETIES, SCOTLAND
58 Frederick Street, Edinburgh EH2 1NB
Tel 0131-226 3224
Assistant Registrar (G5), J. L. J. Craig, WS

GAMING BOARD FOR GREAT BRITAIN
Berkshire House, 168–173 High Holborn, London
WC1V 7AA
Tel 0171-306 6200; fax 0171-306 6266

The Board was established in 1968 and is responsible to the
Home Secretary. It is the regulatory body for casinos, bingo
clubs, gaming machines and the larger society and all local
authority lotteries in Great Britain. Its functions are to
ensure that those involved in organizing gaming and
lotteries are fit and proper to do so and to keep gaming free
from criminal infiltration; to ensure that gaming and
lotteries are run fairly and in accordance with the law; and
to advise the Home Secretary on developments in gaming
and lotteries.
Chairman (part-time) (£37,105), P. Dean, CBE
Secretary, T. Kavanagh

OFFICE OF GAS SUPPLY
Stockley House, 130 Wilton Road, London SW1V 1LQ
Tel 0171-828 0898; fax 0171-932 1600

The Office of Gas Supply (Ofgas) was set up under the Gas
Act 1986 and is headed by the Director-General of Gas
Supply. It is the independent regulatory body for the gas
industry in England, Scotland and Wales. Its functions are
to promote competition in the gas industry and to protect
customers' interests in relation to prices, security of supply
and quality of services.
   The Government has announced its intention of estab-
lishing an Energy Regulator, with responsibility for both
gas and electricity, by 1999.
Director-General, vacant
Chief Economic Adviser, Dr Eileen Marshall, CBE
Legal Adviser, W. Sprigge
Director, Public Affairs, C. Webb
Director, Administration, R. Field

GOVERNMENT ACTUARY'S DEPARTMENT
22 Kingsway, London WC2B 6LE
Tel 0171-211 2600; fax 0171-211 2640

The Government Actuary provides a consulting service to
government departments, the public sector, and overseas
governments. The actuaries advise on social security
schemes and superannuation arrangements in the public
sector at home and abroad, on population and other
statistical studies, and on government supervision of
insurance companies, friendly societies and pension funds.
Government Actuary, C. D. Daykin, CB
Directing Actuaries, D. G. Ballantine; T. W. Hewitson; A. G.
   Young

Chief Actuaries, E. I. Battersby; Ms W. M. Beaver; A. J.
   Chamberlain; Ms C. Cresswell; A. I. Johnston; D. Lewis;
   J. C. A. Rathbone

GOVERNMENT HOSPITALITY FUND
8 Cleveland Row, London SW1A 1DH
Tel 0171-210 4282; fax 0171-930 1148

The Government Hospitality Fund was instituted in 1908
for the purpose of organizing official hospitality on a
regular basis with a view to the promotion of international
goodwill. It is responsible to the Foreign and Commonwealth Office.
Minister in Charge, The Baroness Symons of Vernham
   Dean
Secretary, Col. T. Earl

GOVERNMENT OFFICES FOR THE
REGIONS

The Government Offices for the Regions were established
in April 1994. The regional directors are accountable to the
Secretary of State for the Environment, Transport and the
Regions, the Secretary of State for Trade and Industry, and
the Secretary of State for Education and Employment. The
offices' role is to promote a coherent approach to competitiveness, sustainable economic development and regeneration using public and private resources.
Central Unit, 1st Floor, Eland House, Bressenden Place,
London SW1E 5DU
Tel 0171-890 5157; fax 0171-890 5019

Director (G3), Miss L. Bell
Head of Unit (G5), Mrs J. Scoones

EASTERN
Secretariat: Building A, Westbrook Centre, Milton Road,
Cambridge CB4 1YG
Tel 01223-346700; fax 01223-461941

Regional Director (G3), A. Riddell
Directors (G5), C. Dunabin (*Housing, Environment and
   Regeneration*); Ms C. Bowdler (*Planning and Transport*);
   M. Oldham (*Economic Development*); J. Street (*Skills and
   Enterprise*)

EAST MIDLANDS
Secretariat: The Belgrave Centre, Stanley Place, Talbot
Street, Nottingham NG1 5GG
Tel 0115-971 2755; fax 0115-971 2404

Regional Director (G3), D. Morrison
Directors (G5), Dr S. Kennett (*Environment and Transport*);
   M. Briggs (*Competitiveness, Trade and Industry*); P.
   Mucklow (*Skills and Enterprise*)

LONDON
Secretariat: 10th Floor, Riverwalk House, 157–161
Millbank, London SW1P 4RR
Tel 0171-217 3456; fax 0171-217 3450
Director of Office (G2), Miss E. C. Turton, CB

Directors (G3), J. A. Owen *(Skills, Education and Regeneration);* S. Lord *(Planning, Transport and Corporate Strategy);* R. Allan *(New London Governance); (G5),* B. Glickman *(Skills and Education);* Mrs J. Bridges *(Planning);* Ms A. Munro *(Transport);* K. Timmins *(London North-West/Industry);* Ms H. Ghosh *(London East);* S. Gooding *(London Underground);* P. Sanders *(Transport for London);* A. Melville *(London Transport);* Ms E. Meek *(GLA); (G6),* A. Weeden *(Transport Task Force);* Ms C. Lyons *(Corporate Strategy);* J. Sienkiewicz *(London Development Unit);* R. Wragg *(Operations and Business Management);* N. Robinson *(Trade and Business Development);* P. Fiddeman *(London South);* B. Mann *(Home Office/GOL Liaison)*

MERSEYSIDE
Secretariat: Cunard Building, Pier Head, Liverpool L3 9TN
Tel 0151-224 6300; fax 0151-224 6470

Regional Director (SCS), Ms M. Neville-Rolfe
Directors (SCS), P. Holme *(Skills and Enterprise, Education, Competitiveness and Innovation);* P. Styche *(Regeneration, Transport, Planning and Investment);* Ms K. Himsworth *(European Policy and Implementation)*

NORTH-EAST
Secretariat: Wellbar House, Gallowgate, Newcastle upon Tyne NE1 4TD
Tel 0191-201 3300; fax 0191-202 3744

Regional Director (G3), Dr R. Dobbie
Directors (G5), J. Darlington *(Planning, Environment and Transport);* Miss D. Caudle *(Regeneration and Housing);* A. Dell *(Competitiveness, Industry and Europe);* S. Geary *(Education Skills and Business Development); (G6),* Mrs D. Pearce *(Strategy and Resources)*

NORTH-WEST
Secretariat: 20th Floor, Sunley Tower, Piccadilly Plaza, Manchester M1 4BE
Tel 0161-952 4000; fax 0161-952 4099

Regional Director (G3), Ms M. Neville-Rolfe
Directors, (G5), Dr B. Isherwood *(Regeneration);* D. Higham *(Competitiveness);* Ms I. Hughes *(Infrastructure and Planning);* D. Duff *(Skills and Enterprise); (G6),* D. Stewart *(Europe (Regeneration))*

SOUTH-EAST
Secretariat: 2nd Floor, Bridge House, 1 Walnut Tree Close, Guildford, Surrey GU1 4GA
Tel 01483-882481; fax 01483-882259

Regional Director (G3), D. Saunders
Directors (G5), Ms L. Robinson *(Hants/IOW);* N. Wilson *(Berks/Oxon/Bucks);* J. Vaughan *(Kent);* D. Andrews *(Surrey/E. and W. Sussex);* Mrs A. Baker *(Regional Strategy Team)*

SOUTH-WEST
Secretariat: 4th Floor, The Pithay, Bristol BS1 2PB
Tel 0117-900 1708; fax 0117-900 1900

Regional Director (G3), Ms J. Henderson
Directors (G5), S. McQuillin *(Devon and Cornwall);* M. Quinn *(Environment and Transport);* T. Shearer *(Education, Trade and Industry);* G. Nevitte *(Strategy and Resources)*

WEST MIDLANDS
Secretariat: 6th Floor, 77 Paradise Circus, Queensway, Birmingham B1 2DT
Tel 0121-212 5000; fax 0121-212 5456

Regional Director (G3), D. Ritchie

Directors (G4), Dr H. M. Sutton *(Trade, Industrial Development and Europe); (G5),* Mrs P. Holland *(Housing and Regeneration);* P. Langley *(Planning, Transport and Environment);* D. Way *(Education, Skills and Enterprise); (G6),* D. Mahoney *(Strategy and Resource Management)*

YORKSHIRE AND HUMBERSIDE
Secretariat: PO Box 213, City House, New Station Street, Leeds LS1 4US
Tel 0113-280 0600; fax 0113-244 4898

Regional Director (G3), J. Walker
Directors (G4), G. Dyche *(Strategy and Europe); (G5),* J. Jarvis *(Planning and Transport);* D. Stewart *(Regeneration);* S. Perryman *(Business, Enterprise and Skills); (G6),* M. Doxey *(Personnel and Resources)*

DEPARTMENT OF HEALTH
Richmond House, 79 Whitehall, London SW1A 2NS
Tel 0171-972 2000
Web: http://www.open.gov.uk/doh/dhhome.htm

The Department of Health is responsible for the provision of the National Health Service in England and for social care, including oversight of personal social services run by local authorities in England for children (except day care, which is now the responsibility of the DfEE), the elderly, the infirm, the handicapped and other persons in need. It is responsible for health promotion and has functions relating to public and environmental health, food safety and nutrition. The Department is also responsible for the ambulance and emergency first aid services, under the Civil Defence Act 1948. The Department represents the UK at the European Union and other international organizations including the World Health Organization. It also supports UK-based healthcare and pharmaceutical industries.

Responsibility for food safety will be transferred to the new Food Standards Agency, expected to be in operation by mid 1999.

Secretary of State for Health, The Rt. Hon. Frank Dobson, MP
    Principal Private Secretary, C. Kenny
    Private Secretaries, H. Rogers; F. Anderson
    Special Advisers, J. McCrea; S. Stevens
    Parliamentary Private Secretary, H. Bayley, MP
Minister of State, Alan Milburn, MP *(NHS Structure and Resources)*
    Private Secretary, S. Roughton
    Parliamentary Private Secretary, Ms H. Blears, MP
Minister of State, Tessa Jowell, MP *(Public Health, Women's Issues)*
    Private Secretary, Ms K. Jarvie
    Parliamentary Private Secretary, J. Ennis, MP
Parliamentary Under-Secretaries of State, Paul Boateng, MP *(Social Care, Mental Health);* The Baroness Hayman *(NHS Development, Cancer, Emergency Services)*
    Private Secretaries, J. Marron; W. Connon
Parliamentary Clerk, J. Fowles
Permanent Secretary (SCS), C. Kelly
    Private Secretary, Mrs H. Steele
Chief Medical Officer (SCS), Prof. L. Donaldson, FRCSED., FRCP
Chief Executive, NHS Executive (SCS), Sir Alan Langlands
Deputy Chief Medical Officer (SCS), Dr J. S. Metters, CB

REGIONAL CHAIRMEN'S MEETING
Chairman, The Secretary of State for Health

Members, Alan Milburn, MP (*Minister of State*); Tessa Jowell, MP (*Minister of State*); Paul Boateng, MP (*Parliamentary Under-Secretary*); The Baroness Hayman (*Parliamentary Under-Secretary*); Prof. L. Donaldson, FRCSEd., FRCP (*Chief Medical Officer*); Sir Alan Langlands (*Chief Executive, NHS Executive*); C. Kelly (*Permanent Secretary*); Mrs Y. Moores; C. Wilkinson; Mrs Z. Manzoor, CBE; P. Hammersley; Mrs R. Varley; Miss J. Trotter, OBE; I. Mills; W. Wells; Prof. A. Breckenridge, CBE; A. D. M. Liddell, CBE

DEPARTMENTAL RESOURCES AND SERVICES GROUP
Head of Group (SCS), Ms A. Perkins

STATISTICS DIVISION
Director of Statistics (SCS), Mrs R. J. Butler
Chief Statisticians (SCS), R. K. Willmer; G. J. O. Phillpotts

PERSONNEL SERVICES
Director of Personnel (SCS), D. J. Clark
Heads of Branches (SCS), C. Muir; I. Forsyth; S. Redmond

INFORMATION SERVICES DIVISION
Head of Division (SCS), Dr A. A. Holt
Heads of Branches, Mrs L. Wishart; C. Horsey; M. Rainsford; Mrs J. Dainty; M. Smith; R. Long; P. G. Cobb

RESOURCE MANAGEMENT AND FINANCE
Head of Division (SCS), A. B. Barton
Heads of Branches, P. Kendall; B. Burleigh; J. Stopes-Roe; A. McNeil

ECONOMICS AND OPERATIONAL RESEARCH DIVISION (HEALTH)
Chief Economic Adviser (SCS), C. H. Smee, CB
Heads of Branches, Dr S. Harding; J. W. Hurst; Dr G. Royston; A. Hare; D. Franklin

PRESS AND PUBLICITY DIVISION
Director of Press and Publicity, Miss R. Christopherson, CB (*until the end of 1998*)
Deputy Directors, P. Aylett (*News*); W. Roberts (*Publicity*)

POLICY MANAGEMENT UNIT
Head of Branch, Mrs F. Goldhill

SOLICITOR'S OFFICE
Solicitor (SCS), M. Morgan
Director of Legal Services (SCS), Mrs G. S. Kerrigan

PUBLIC HEALTH POLICY GROUP

PROTECTION OF HEALTH DIVISION
Head of Division (SCS), Dr Eileen Rubery, CB
Heads of Branches, Dr E. Smales; A. Smith; J. Walden

JOINT FOOD SAFETY AND STANDARDS DIVISION
Head of Division (SCS), G. Podger
Heads of Branches, Dr R. Skinner; Ms P. Stewart

HEALTH PROMOTION DIVISION
Head of Division (SCS), D. P. Walden
Principal Medical Officer (SCS), Dr D. McInnes
Heads of Branches (SCS), Miss A. Mithani; Dr D. McInnes; R. Kornicki; M. Fry

SOCIAL CARE GROUP
Chief Social Services Inspector, Ms D. Platt
Head of Social Care Policy, T. R. H. Luce, CB
Deputy Chief Inspectors, D. Gilroy; Ms A. Nottage
Heads of Branches (SCS), N. F. Duncan; S. Mitchell; N. Boyd; J. Kennedy; Mrs E. Johnson; S. Hiller
Assistant Chief Inspector (HQ), J. Cleary

Assistant Chief Inspectors (Regions), S. Allard; J. Cypher; B. Riddell; A. Jones; D. G. Lambert, CBE; Mrs P. K. Hall; C. P. Brearley; J. Fraser; Mrs L. Hoare; Ms J. Owen

NURSING GROUP
Chief Nursing Officer / Director of Nursing (SCS), Mrs Y. Moores
Assistant Chief Nursing Officers (SCS), Mrs P. Cantrill; Mrs G. Stephens; D. Moore

RESEARCH AND DEVELOPMENT DIVISION
Director of Research and Development, Prof. J. D. Swales
Deputy Director of Research and Development (SCS), Dr C. Henshall
Heads of Branches (SCS), Dr P. Greenaway; J. Ennis; Mrs J. Griffin; Ms A. Kauder

NHS EXECUTIVE
Quarry House, Quarry Hill, Leeds LS2 7UE
Tel 0113-254 5000

Chief Executive, Sir Alan Langlands
Director of Human Resources, H. Taylor
Director of Finance and Performance, C. Reeves
Medical Director, Dr G. Winyard
Chief Nursing Officer, Mrs Y. Moores
Director of Research and Development, Prof. J. D. Swales
Director of Planning and Performance Management, A. D. M. Liddell, CBE

CORPORATE AFFAIRS
Head of Corporate Affairs (SCS), M. Staniforth

HUMAN RESOURCES
Deputy Director of Human Resources (SCS), M. Deegan

INFORMATION MANAGEMENT
Head of Information Management (SCS), F. Burns

PLANNING DIRECTORATE
Director (SCS), A. D. M. Liddell, CBE
Chief Economic Adviser, C. Smee, CB
Head of Planning, L. Bradley
Head of Communications, Mrs H. McCallum
Director of Statistics, Mrs R. Butler

HEALTH SERVICES DIRECTORATE
Director (SCS), Dr G. Winyard
Deputy Director (SCS), Dr S. Adam
Heads of Branches, M. Brown; Mrs L. Wolstenholme; Ms J. McKessack; Ms G. Fletcher-Cooke; L. Percival; Dr G. Radford; Mrs Z. Muth

PRIMARY CARE DIVISION
Head of Division, A. McKeon
Fraud Supremo, J. Gee
Chief Dental Officer, J. R. Wild
Chief Pharmaceutical Officer, B. H. Hartley
Heads of Branches, G. Denham (*Dental and Optical Services*); J. Thompson (*Pharmacy and Prescribing*); Miss H. Gwynn (*White Paper Implementation Team*); M. Farrar (*General Medical Services*)

FINANCE AND PERFORMANCE DIRECTORATE
Director (SCS), C. L. Reeves
Deputy Directors, P. Garland; R. Douglas
Heads of Branches, B. McCarthy; J. Lawler; Dr S. Peck; M. Sturges; A. Angilley; M. A. Harris, CBE; J. Thomlinson; P. Coates; J. Havelock; J. Copeland

REGIONAL OFFICES
– *see* page 479

ADVISORY COMMITTEES

Advisory Committee on the Microbiological Safety of Food, Room 502A, Skipton House, 80 London Road, London SE1 6LH. Tel: 0171-972 5045. *Chairman*, Prof. D. Georgala, CBE, ph.d.

Clinical Standards Advisory Group, Wellington House, 133–155 Waterloo Road, London SE1 8UG. Tel: 0171-972 4926. *Chairman*, Prof. M. Harris

Committee on the Safety of Medicines, Market Towers, 1 Nine Elms Lane, London SW8 5NQ. Tel: 0171-273 0451. *Chairman*, Prof. A. M. Breckenridge, CBE, FRCP, FRCPEd., FRSE (from Jan. 1999)

Medicines Commission, Market Towers, 1 Nine Elms Lane, London SW8 5NQ. Tel: 0171-273 0652. *Chairman*, Prof. D. H. Lawson, CBE, FRCPEd., FRCP(Glas.)

EXECUTIVE AGENCIES

Medicines Control Agency
Market Towers, 1 Nine Elms Lane, London SW8 5NQ
Tel 0171-273 0000; fax 0171-273 0353
The Agency controls medicines through licensing, monitoring and inspection, and enforces safety standards.
Chief Executive, Dr K. H. Jones, CB

Medical Devices Agency
Hannibal House, Elephant and Castle, London SE1 6TQ
Tel 0171-972 8000; fax 0171-972 8108
The Agency safeguards the performance, quality and safety of medical devices.
Chief Executive, A. Kent

NHS Estates
1 Trevelyan Square, Boar Lane, Leeds LS1 6AE
Tel 0113-254 7000; fax 0113-254 7299
NHS Estates provides advice and support in the area of healthcare estate functions to the NHS and the healthcare industry.
Chief Executive, Mrs K. Priestley

NHS Pensions
Hesketh House, 200–220 Broadway, Fleetwood, Lancs FY7 8LG
Tel 01253-774774; fax 01253-774860
NHS Pensions administers the NHS occupational pension scheme.
Chief Executive, A. F. Cowan

NHS Supplies
Premier House, 60 Caversham Road, Reading, Berks RG1 7EB
Tel 0118-980 8600; fax 0118-980 8650
NHS Supplies procures goods and services for the NHS.
Chief Executive, T. Hunt, CBE

SPECIAL HOSPITALS

Ashworth Hospital, Parkbourn, Maghull, Merseyside L31 1HW. Tel: 0151-473 0303. *Director of Care Services and Nursing*, K. M. Barron

Broadmoor Hospital, Crowthorne, Berks RG45 7EG. Tel: 01344-773111. *Chief Executive*, Dr J. Hollyman

Rampton Hospital, Retford, Notts DN22 0PD. Tel: 01777-248321. *Chief Executive*, Mrs S. Foley

HEALTH AND SAFETY COMMISSION
Rose Court, 2 Southwark Bridge, London SE1 9HS
Tel 0171-717 6000; fax 0171-717 6717

The Health and Safety Commission was created under the Health and Safety at Work etc. Act 1974, with duties to reform health and safety law, to propose new regulations, and generally to promote the protection of people at work and of the public from hazards arising from industrial and commercial activity, including major industrial accidents and the transportation of hazardous materials. The members of the Commission are appointed by the Secretary of State for the Environment, Transport and the Regions. The Commission is made up of representatives of employers, trades unions and local authorities, and has a full-time chairman.
Chairman, F. J. Davies, CBE
Members, R. Symons, CBE; A. Grant; Ms A. Gibson; Dr M. McKiernan; Ms J. Edmond-Smith; D. Coulston; R. Turney; G. Brumwell; Ms M. Burns
Secretary, T. A. Gates

HEALTH AND SAFETY EXECUTIVE
Rose Court, 2 Southwark Bridge, London SE1 9HS
Tel 0171-717 6000; fax 0171-717 6717

The Health and Safety Executive is the Health and Safety Commission's major instrument. Through its inspectorates it enforces health and safety law in the majority of industrial premises. The Executive advises the Commission in its major task of laying down safety standards through regulations and practical guidance for many industrial processes. The Executive is also the licensing authority for nuclear installations and the reporting officer on the severity of nuclear incidents in Britain. In November 1997 the Executive took over responsibility for the Channel Tunnel Safety Authority.
Director-General, Miss J. H. Bacon, CB
Deputy Director-General, D. C. T. Eves, CB (*HM Chief Inspector of Factories*)
Director, Field Operations Directorate, Dr A. Ellis
Director, Nuclear Safety, Dr L. G. Williams (*HM Chief Inspector of Nuclear Installations*)
Director, Science and Technology, Dr J. McQuaid, CB
Director, Safety Policy, C. Norris
Director, Health Directorate, Dr P. J. Graham
Director, Resources and Planning, R. Hillier
Director, Offshore Safety, A. Sefton

HIGHLANDS AND ISLANDS ENTERPRISE
Bridge House, 20 Bridge Street, Inverness IV1 1QR
Tel 01463-234171; fax 01463-244241

Highlands and Islands Enterprise (HIE) was set up under the Enterprise and New Towns (Scotland) Act 1991. Its role is to design, direct and deliver enterprise development, training, environmental and social projects and services. HIE is made up of a strategic core body and ten Local Enterprise Companies (LECs) to which many of its individual functions are delegated.
Chairman, vacant
Chief Executive, I. A. Robertson, CBE

HISTORIC BUILDINGS AND MONUMENTS COMMISSION FOR ENGLAND (ENGLISH HERITAGE)
23 Savile Row, London W1X 1AB
Tel 0171-973 3000; fax 0171-973 3001

Under the National Heritage Act 1983, the duties of the Commission are to secure the preservation of ancient monuments and historic buildings; to promote the preservation and enhancement of conservation areas; and to promote the public's enjoyment of, and advance their knowledge of, ancient monuments and historic buildings and their preservation. The Commission is funded by the Department for Culture, Media and Sport.

In July 1998 the Government published a discussion document including a proposal to merge English Heritage and the Royal Commission on the Historical Monuments of England.

Chairman, Sir Jocelyn Stevens, CVO
Commissioners, HRH The Duke of Gloucester, KG, GCVO; The Lord Cavendish of Furness; Ms B. Cherry; Mrs C. Lycett-Green; J. Seymour; A. Fane; Lady Gass; Prof. E. Fernie, CBE; Ms K. McLeod; Prof. R. Morris, FSA; Miss S. Underwood
Chief Executive, Ms P. Alexander

HISTORIC BUILDINGS COUNCIL FOR SCOTLAND
Longmore House, Salisbury Place, Edinburgh EH9 1SH
Tel 0131-668 8600; fax 0131-668 8749

The Historic Buildings Council for Scotland is the advisory body to the Secretary of State for Scotland on matters related to buildings of special architectural or historical interest and in particular to proposals for awards by him of grants for the repair of buildings of outstanding architectural or historical interest or lying within outstanding conservation areas.

Chairman, Sir Raymond Johnstone, CBE
Members, R. Cairns; Sir Ilay Campbell, Bt.; Mrs A. Dundas-Bekker; M. Ellington; Dr J. Frew; J. Hunter Blair; I. Hutchison, OBE; K. Martin; Revd C. Robertson; Mrs P. Robertson; Ms F. Sinclair
Secretary, Ms S. Adams

HISTORIC BUILDINGS COUNCIL FOR WALES
Crown Building, Cathays Park, Cardiff CF1 3NQ
Tel 01222-500200; fax 01222-826375

The Council's function is to advise the Secretary of State for Wales on the built heritage through Cadw: Welsh Historic Monuments (*see* page 353), which is an executive agency within the Welsh Office.

Chairman, T. Lloyd, FSA
Members, R. Haslam; Dr P. Morgan; Mrs S. Furse; Dr S. Unwin; Dr E. Wiliam; Miss E. Evans
Secretary, R. W. Hughes

HISTORIC ROYAL PALACES
Hampton Court Palace, East Molesey, Surrey KT8 9AU
Tel 0181-781 9752; fax 0181-781 9754

Historic Royal Palaces was formerly an executive agency of the Department for Culture, Media and Sport; it became a non-departmental public body on 1 April 1998 and now has charitable trust status. The Secretary of State for Culture, Media and Sport is still accountable to Parliament for the care and presentation of the palaces, which are owned by the Sovereign in right of the Crown. The chairman of the trustees is appointed by The Queen on the advice of the Secretary of State.

Historic Royal Palaces is responsible for the Tower of London, Hampton Court Palace, Kensington Palace State Apartments and the Royal Ceremonial Dress Collection, Kew Palace with Queen Charlotte's Cottage, and the Banqueting House, Whitehall. Government grant-in-aid for 1998–9 is £3.5 million.

TRUSTEES
Chairman, The Earl of Airlie, KT, GCVO, PC
Appointed by The Queen, The Lord Camoys, GCVO, PC; Sir Michael Peat, KCVO; H. Roberts, CVO, FSA
Appointed by the Secretary of State, M. Herbert; Ms A. Heylin; S. Jones; Ms J. Sharman
Ex officio, Field Marshal the Lord Inge, GCB (*Constable of the Tower of London*)

OFFICERS
Chief Executive, D. C. Beeton, CBE
Director of Finance, Ms A. McLeish
Director of Human Resources, M. Bridger
Surveyor of the Fabric, R. Davidson
Curator, Historic Royal Palaces, Dr E. Impey
Director, Palaces Group, R. Evans, FRICS
Resident Governor, HM Tower of London, Maj.-Gen. G. Field, CB, OBE

ROYAL COMMISSION ON THE HISTORICAL MONUMENTS OF ENGLAND
National Monuments Record Centre, Kemble Drive, Swindon SN2 2GZ
Tel 01793-414700; fax 01793-414707
London Search Room: 55 Blandford Street, London W1H 3AF
Tel 0171-208 8200; fax 0171-224 5333

The Royal Commission on the Historical Monuments of England was established in 1908. It is the national body of architectural and archaeological survey and record and manages England's public archive of heritage information, the National Monuments Record. It is funded by the Department for Culture, Media and Sport.

In July 1998 the Government published a discussion document including a proposal to merge the Commission and English Heritage.

Chairman, The Lord Faringdon
Commissioners, Prof. R. Bradley, FSA; D. J. Keene, PH.D.; R. D. H. Gem, PH.D., FSA; T. R. M. Longman; R. A. Yorke; Miss A. Riches, FSA; Dr M. Airs, FSA; Prof. M. Fulford, PH.D., FSA; Dr M. Palmer, FSA; Miss A. Arrowsmith; P. Addyman, FSA; Prof. E. Fernie, CBE, FSA, FRSE; Ms H. Maclagan; Dr W. Sudbury
Secretary, T. G. Hassall, FSA

ROYAL COMMISSION ON THE ANCIENT AND HISTORICAL MONUMENTS OF SCOTLAND
John Sinclair House, 16 Bernard Terrace, Edinburgh EH8 9NX
Tel 0131-662 1456; fax 0131-662 1477

The Royal Commission was established in 1908 and is appointed to provide for the survey and recording of ancient and historical monuments connected with the culture, civilization and conditions of life of the people in Scotland from the earliest times. It is funded by the Scottish Office. The Commission compiles and maintains the National Monuments Record of Scotland as the national record of the archaeological and historical environment. The National Monuments Record is open for reference Monday–Thursday 9.30–4.30, Friday 9.30–4.
Chairman, Sir William Fraser, GCB, FRSE
Commissioners, Prof. J. M. Coles, ph.D., FBA; Prof. Rosemary Cramp, CBE, FSA; Prof. T. C. Smout, CBE, FRSE, FBA; Dr Deborah Howard, FSA; Prof. R. A. Paxton, FRSE; Dr Barbara Crawford, FSA, FSA scot.; Miss A. Riches; J. Simpson, FSA scot.; Ms M. Mackay, ph.D.
Secretary, R. J. Mercer, FSA, FRSE

ROYAL COMMISSION ON THE ANCIENT AND HISTORICAL MONUMENTS OF WALES
Crown Building, Plas Crug, Aberystwyth SY23 1NJ
Tel 01970-621200; fax 01970-627701

The Royal Commission was established in 1908 and is currently empowered by a royal warrant of 1992 to survey, record, publish and maintain a database of ancient and historical and maritime sites and structures, and landscapes in Wales. The Commission is funded by the Welsh Office and is also responsible for the National Monuments Record of Wales, which is open daily for public reference, for the supply of archaeological information to the Ordnance Survey, for the co-ordination of archaeological aerial photography in Wales, and for sponsorship of the regional Sites and Monuments Records.
Chairman, Prof. J. B. Smith
Commissioners, Prof. R. A. Griffiths, ph.D., D.Litt.; D. Gruffyd Jones; Prof. G. B. D. Jones, D.Phil., FSA; Mrs A. Nicol; Prof. P. Sims-Williams, FBA; Prof. G. J. Wainwright, MBE, ph.D., FSA; E. Wiliam, ph.D., FSA
Secretary, P. R. White, FSA

ANCIENT MONUMENTS BOARD FOR SCOTLAND
Longmore House, Salisbury Place, Edinburgh EH9 1SH
Tel 0131-668 8764; fax 0131-668 8765

The Ancient Monuments Board for Scotland advises the Secretary of State for Scotland on the exercise of his functions, under the Ancient Monuments and Archaeological Areas Act 1979, of providing protection for monuments of national importance.
Chairman, Prof. M. Lynch, ph.D., FRSE, PSA scot.

Members, A. Wright, FRSA; Mrs K. Dalyell, FSA scot.; P. Clarke, FSA; Ms A. Ritchie, OBE, ph.D., FSA, FSA scot.; Prof. C. D. Morris, FRSE, FSA, FSA scot.; R. J. Mercer, FRSE, FSA, FSA scot.; W. D. H. Sellar, FSA scot.; B. Mackie; Miss L. M. Thoms, FSA scot.; J. Higgitt, FSA; Ms C. Swanson, ph.D., FSA scot.; M. Baughan; Ms J. Cannizzo, ph.D.; S. Peake, ph.D.; M. Taylor
Secretary, R. A. J. Dalziel
Assessor, D. J. Breeze, ph. D., FRSE, FSA, FSA scot.

ANCIENT MONUMENTS BOARD FOR WALES
Crown Building, Cathays Park, Cardiff CF1 3NQ
Tel 01222-500200; fax 01222-826375

The Ancient Monuments Board for Wales advises the Secretary of State for Wales on his statutory functions in respect of ancient monuments.
Chairman, Prof. R. R. Davies, CBE, D.Phil., FBA
Members, R. G. Keen; Mrs F. M. Lynch Llewellyn, FSA; Prof. W. H. Manning, ph.D., FSA; Prof. J. B. Smith; Prof. W. E. Davies, ph.D., FBA; M. J. Garner
Secretary, Mrs J. Booker

HOME-GROWN CEREALS AUTHORITY
Caledonia House, 223 Pentonville Road, London N1 9NG
Tel 0171-520 3914; fax 0171-520 3918

Set up under the Cereals Marketing Act 1965, the Authority consists of seven members representing UK cereal growers, seven representing dealers in, or processors of, grain and two independent members. The Authority's functions are to improve the production and marketing of UK-grown cereals and oilseeds through a research and development programme, to provide a market information service, and to promote UK cereals in export markets.
Chairman (part-time) (£19,750), A. Pike
Chief Executive, A. J. Williams

HOME OFFICE
50 Queen Anne's Gate, London SW1H 9AT
Tel 0171-273 4000; fax 0171-273 2190
E-mail: gen.ho@gtnet.gov.uk
Web: http://www.homeoffice.gov.uk

The Home Office deals with those internal affairs in England and Wales which have not been assigned to other government departments. The Home Secretary is particularly concerned with the administration of justice; criminal law; the treatment of offenders, including probation and the prison service; the police; immigration and nationality; passport policy matters; community relations; certain public safety matters; and fire and civil emergencies services. The Home Secretary personally is the link between The Queen and the public, and exercises certain powers on her behalf, including that of the royal pardon.

Other subjects dealt with include electoral arrangements; ceremonial and formal business connected with honours; scrutiny of local authority by-laws; granting of licences for scientific procedures involving animals; cremations, burials and exhumations; firearms; dangerous drugs and poisons; general policy on laws relating to shops, liquor licensing, gaming and marriage; theatre and cinema licensing; and race relations policy.

The Home Secretary is also the link between the UK government and the governments of the Channel Islands and the Isle of Man.

Secretary of State for the Home Department, The Rt. Hon. Jack Straw, MP
  Principal Private Secretary (SCS), K. D. Sutton
  Private Secretaries, Ms C. Sumner; Ms I. Hopton; D. Redhouse
  Special Advisers, Lord Warner; E. Owen
  Parliamentary Private Secretary, P. Tipping, MP
Minister of State, Alun Michael, MP (*Criminal and Police Policy*)
  Parliamentary Private Secretary, C. Pickthall, MP
Minister of State, The Lord Williams of Mostyn, QC (*Constitution, Prisons, Probation*)
  Parliamentary Private Secretary, B. Jenkins, MP
  Private Secretary to the Ministers of State, A. Smith
Parliamentary Under-Secretaries of State, George Howarth, MP (*Prisons, Probation, Fire and Emergency Planning, Drugs, Elections, Gambling, Data Protection*); Michael O'Brien, MP (*Immigration and Nationality*); Kate Hoey, MP (*Metropolitan Police, Women's Issues, International Co-operation*)
  Private Secretaries, Miss C. McCombie; J. Payne
Parliamentary Clerk, Ms A. Scott
Permanent Under-Secretary of State (SCS), D. B. Omand
  Private Secretary, Miss A. Rutherford
Chief Medical Officer (at Department of Health), Prof. L. Donaldson, FRCSEd., FRCP

COMMUNICATION DIRECTORATE
Director (SCS), B. Butler
Deputy Head of Communication (Head of News) (SCS), vacant
Head of Publicity and Corporate Services (SCS), Miss A. Nash
Assistant Director, News (G6), B. McBride
Assistant Director and Head of Information Services Group (G7), P. Griffiths

CONSTITUTIONAL AND COMMUNITY POLICY DIRECTORATE
Director (SCS), Miss C. Sinclair
Heads of Units (SCS), Mrs G. Catto; R. Evans; M. Gillespie; S. B. Hickson

ANIMALS (SCIENTIFIC PROCEDURES) INSPECTORATE
Chief Inspector (SCS), Dr J. Richmond
Superintendent Inspector (SCS), Dr J. Anderson
Inspectors (G6), Dr R. Curtis; Dr V. Navaratnam; Dr C. Wilkins

GAMING BOARD FOR GREAT BRITAIN
— *see* page 304

CORPORATE DEVELOPMENT DIRECTORATE
Director (SCS), Dr D. Pepper
Heads of Units (SCS), Mrs S. Atkins; T. Edwards; Ms E. Sparrow; S. Wharton
Senior Principals (G6), Mrs C. Burrows; T. Lewis; D. Rigby; S. Thornton

CORPORATE RESOURCES DIRECTORATE
Grenadier House, 99–105 Horseferry Road, London SW1P 2DD
Tel 0171-273 4000
Clive House, Petty France, London SW1H 9HD
Tel 0171-273 4000
Director (SCS), Miss P. Drew
Head of Unit (SCS), Dr M. Allnutt

Senior Principals (G6), T. Cobley; R. Creedon; A. Ford; J. G. Jones; Ms E. Moody

CRIMINAL POLICY DIRECTORATE
Directors (SCS), J. Halliday, CB; W. Fittall; J. Lyon
Heads of Units (SCS), M. Boyle; R. Childs; I. Chisholm; J. Duke-Evans; E. Grant; A. Harding; P. Honour; Ms H. Jackson; H. Marriage; Miss C. Stewart
Senior Principals (G6), Mrs A. Johnstone; A. Macfarlane; Ms L. Rogerson

CENTRAL DRUGS PREVENTION UNIT
Horseferry House, Dean Ryle Street, London SW1P 2AW
Tel 0171-273 4000
Head of Unit (G6), Ms L. Rogerson

HOME OFFICE CRIME PREVENTION COLLEGE
The Hawkhills, Easingwold, York YO6 3EG
Tel 01347-825060
Director, J. Acton

HM INSPECTORATE OF PROBATION
Chief Inspector (SCS), G. W. Smith, CBE
Assistant Chief Inspector (G6), G. Childs

FIRE AND EMERGENCY PLANNING DIRECTORATE
Horseferry House, Dean Ryle Street, London SW1P 2AW
Tel 0171-273 4000
50 Queen Anne's Gate, London SW1H 9AT
Tel 0171-273 4000
Director (SCS), Mrs S. Street
Heads of Units (SCS), E. Guy; Mrs V. Harris; Miss S. Paul; Dr D. Peace

HM FIRE SERVICE INSPECTORATE
HM Chief Inspector, G. Meldrum, CBE, QFSM
HM Territorial Inspectors, A. R. Currie, OBE, QFSM; P. Morphew, QFSM; A. Rule, QFSM
Lay Inspector, vacant
HM Inspectors, W. Ambalino; R. A. M. Baillie, QFSM; D. Berry; G. P. Bowles; S. D. Christian; D. Kent; C. Moseley; R. Pearce; E. G. Pearn, QFSM; K. Phillips; M. Robinson; R. M. Simpson, OBE; A. C. Wells, QFSM; D. Wright
Principal (G7), Miss G. Kirton

EMERGENCY PLANNING COLLEGE
The Hawkhills, Easingwold, Yorks YO6 3EG
Tel 01347-821406

IMMIGRATION AND NATIONALITY DIRECTORATE, AND EU AND INTERNATIONAL UNIT
Lunar House, 40 Wellesley Road, Croydon, Surrey CR9 2BY
Tel 0181-686 0333
Apollo House, 36 Wellesley Road, Croydon, Surrey CR9 3RR
Tel 0181-686 0333
50 Queen Anne's Gate, London SW1H 9AT
Tel 0171-273 4000
India Buildings, 3rd Floor, Water Street, Liverpool L2 0QN
Tel 0151-237 5200
Director-General (SCS), T. E. H. Walker, CB
Deputy Directors-General (SCS), M. J. Eland (*Policy*); Miss K. Collins (*Operations*)
Heads of Directorates (SCS), J. Acton; Miss V. M. Dews; Mrs E. C. L. Pallett; J. Potts; A. Walmsley; R. M. Whalley; R. G. Yates

Senior Principals (G6), Ms C. Checksfield; P. Dawson; B. Downie; M. Rumble

IMMIGRATION SERVICE
Director (Ports) (SCS), T. Farrage
Deputy Director (G6), V. Hogg
Director (Enforcement) (SCS), I. Boon
Deputy Director (G6), C. Harbin

EU AND INTERNATIONAL UNIT
Head of Unit (SCS), P. Edwards

LEGAL ADVISERS'S BRANCH
Legal Adviser (SCS), Miss J. Wheldon, CB
Deputy Legal Advisers (SCS), Mrs S. A. Evans; T. Middleton
Assistant Legal Advisers (SCS), R. J. Clayton; J. R. O'Meara; R. Green; S. A. Parker

ORGANIZED AND INTERNATIONAL CRIME DIRECTORATE
Director (SCS), J. Warne

PLANNING AND FINANCE DIRECTORATE
50 Queen Anne's Gate, London SW1H 9AT
Tel 0171-273 4000
Horseferry House, Dean Ryle Street, London SW1P 2AW
Tel 0171-273 4000

Director (SCS), R. Fulton
Heads of Units (SCS), C. Harnett; A. Mortimer
Senior Principals (G6), P. Dare; P. Davies; T. Williams

POLICE POLICY DIRECTORATE
Director (SCS), S. Boys Smith
Heads of Units (SCS), N. Benger; Ms L. Lockyer; Miss D. Loudon
Senior Principals (G6), R. Ginman; Dr G. Laycock

NATIONAL DIRECTORATE OF POLICE TRAINING
National Director of Police Training, P. Hermitage, QPM

Corporate Services
Senior Principal (G6), P. Curwen

POLICE STAFF COLLEGE
Bramshill House, Bramshill, Hook, Hants RG27 0JW
Tel 0125-126 2931
Head of Higher Training, I. McDonald

HENDON DATA CENTRE
Aerodrome Road, Colindale, London NW9 5LN
Tel 0181-200 2424

Head of Unit (G6), J. Ladley

POLICE SCIENTIFIC DEVELOPMENT BRANCH
Sandridge, St Albans, Herts AL4 9HQ
Tel 01727-865051

Director (SCS), B. R. Coleman, OBE
Chief Scientist/Deputy Director (G6), Dr P. Young

Langhurst House, Langhurstwood Road, Nr Horsham, W. Sussex RH12 4WX
Tel 01403-255451
Head of Unit Langhurst (G6), Dr G. Thomas

HM INSPECTORATE OF CONSTABULARY
HM Chief Inspector of Constabulary (SCS), D. J. O'Dowd, CBE, QPM
HM Inspectors (SCS), D. Crompton, CBE, QPM; K. Povey, QPM; C. Smith, CBE, CVO, QPM; P. J. Winship, CBE, QPM; J. A. Stevens, QPM
Lay Inspector, P. T. G. Hobbs
Senior Principal (G6), L. Davidoff

METROPOLITAN POLICE COMMITTEE AND SECRETARIAT
Clive House, Petty France, London SW1H 9HD
Tel 0171-273 4000

Head of Secretariat (SCS), R. Halward

RESEARCH AND STATISTICS DIRECTORATE
Director (SCS), C. Nuttall
Heads of Units (SCS), C. Lewis; D. Moxon; A. Norbury; P. Ward
Senior Principals (G6), G. Barclay; Ms M. Colledge; Mrs P. Dowdeswell; Dr S. Field; Ms M. FitzGerald; P. Goldblatt; J. Graham; Mrs C. Lehman; Mrs P. Mayhew, OBE; Ms J. Vennard; R. Walmsley

STRATEGY UNIT
Head of Unit (SCS), R. Weatherill

HM INSPECTORATE OF PRISONS
HM Chief Inspector, Gen. Sir David Ramsbotham, GCB, CBE
HM Deputy Chief Inspector, C. Allen
HM Inspectors (Governor 1), R. Jacques; G. Hughes

PRISONS OMBUDSMAN
— *see* page 334

PAROLE BOARD FOR ENGLAND AND WALES
— *see* pages 332

HM PRISON SERVICE
— *see* pages 379 – 81

FIRE SERVICE COLLEGE
Moreton-in-Marsh, Glos GL56 0RH
Tel 01608-650831

An executive agency of the Home Office.
Chief Executive and Commandant, T. Glossop, QFSM
College Secretary, Miss R. Jones

UK PASSPORT AGENCY
Clive House, Petty France, London SW1H 9HD
Tel 0171-799 2728

An executive agency of the Home Office.
Chief Executive (SCS), D. Gatenby
Deputy Chief Executive and Director of Operations (G6), K. J. Sheehan
Director of Systems (G6), J. Davies

HORSERACE TOTALISATOR BOARD
74 Upper Richmond Road, London SW15 2SU
Tel 0181-874 6411; fax 0181-874 6107

The Horserace Totalisator Board was established by the Betting, Gaming and Lotteries Act 1963. Its function is to operate totalisators on approved racecourses in Great Britain, and it also provides on- and off-course cash and credit offices. Under the Horserace Totalisator and Betting Levy Board Act 1972, it is further empowered to offer bets at starting price (or other bets at fixed odds) on any sporting event. The chairman and members of the Board are appointed by the Home Secretary.

The Government announced in June 1998 that it would require the Board to enter into partnerships with the private sector.
Chairman (£75,000), P. I. Jones
Chief Executive, W. J. Heaton

HOUSING CORPORATION
149 Tottenham Court Road, London WIP OBN
Tel 0171-393 2000; fax 0171-393 2111

Established by Parliament in 1964, the Housing Corporation regulates, funds and promotes the proper performance of registered social landlords, which are non-profit making bodies run by voluntary committees. There are over 2,200 registered social landlords, most of which are housing associations, and they now provide homes for more than 1.5 million people. Under the Housing Act 1996, the Corporation's regulatory role was widened to embrace new types of landlords, in particular local housing companies. The Corporation is funded by the Department of the Environment, Transport and the Regions.
Chairman, The Baroness Dean of Thornton-le-Fylde, PC
Deputy Chairman, E. Armitage
Chief Executive, A. Mayer

HUMAN FERTILIZATION AND EMBRYOLOGY AUTHORITY
Paxton House, 30 Artillery Lane, London EI 7LS
Tel 0171-377 5077; fax 0171-377 1871

The Human Fertilization and Embryology Authority (HFEA) was established under the Human Fertilization and Embryology Act 1990. Its function is to license persons carrying out any of the following activities: the creation or use of embryos outside the body in the provision of infertility treatment services; the use of donated gametes in infertility treatment; the storage of gametes or embryos; and research on human embryos. It maintains a confidential database of all such treatments and of egg and sperm donors, and provides information to patients, clinics and the public. The HFEA also keeps under review information about embryos and, when requested to do so, gives advice to the Secretary of State for Health.
Chairman, Mrs R. Deech
Deputy Chairman, Mrs J. Denton
Members, Dr G. Bahadur; Prof. D. Barlow; Prof. Ruth Chambers; Mrs M. E. Coath; Ms E. Forgan; Prof. Christine Gosden; D. Greggains; Prof. A. Grubb; Prof. M. Johnson; R. Jones; Prof. S. Lewis; Dr B. Lieberman; Dr Anne McLaren; The Rt. Revd Bishop of Rochester; Dr Joan Stringer; Prof. A. Templeton; Prof. the Revd A. Thiselton; Julia, Lady Tugendhat; J. Williams
Chief Executive, Mrs S. McCarthy

HUMAN GENETICS ADVISORY COMMISSION
Room 12, Albany House, 94–98 Petty France, London SWIH 9ST
Tel 0171-271 2131; fax 0171-271 2028

The Human Genetics Advisory Commission was established in December 1996. It is an advisory body with the remit of taking a broad view of developments in human genetics and advising ministers on ways to build public confidence in the application of the new science. Members of the Commission are appointed by the Secretary of State for Trade and Industry and the Secretary of State for Health.
Chairman, Prof. Sir Colin Campbell

Members, Prof. C. Aitken, CBE; Dr Michaela Aldred; Prof. M. Bobrow; Mrs D. Littlejohn, CBE; Prof. N. Nevin; Dr Onora O'Neill; Dr G. Poste, FRS; Revd Dr J. Polkinghorne, KBE, FRS; Ms M. Stuart
Head of Secretariat, Dr Amanda Goldin

INDEPENDENT COMMISSION FOR POLICE COMPLAINTS FOR NORTHERN IRELAND
Chamber of Commerce House, 22 Great Victoria Street, Belfast BT2 7LP
Tel 01232-244821; fax 01232-248563

The Independent Commission for Police Complaints was established under the Police (Northern Ireland) Order 1987. It has powers to supervise the investigation of certain categories of serious complaints, can direct that disciplinary charges be brought, and has oversight of the informal resolution procedure for less serious complaints.

Subject to legislation currently before Parliament, the Commission will be replaced in March 1999 by a Police Ombudsman.
Chairman, P. A. Donnelly
Chief Executive, B. McClelland

INDEPENDENT COMMISSION ON POLICING FOR NORTHERN IRELAND
67 Tufton Street, London SWIP 3QS
Tel 0171-210 2625; fax 0171-210 2628
3/F Interpoint, 20–24 York Street, Belfast BT15 IAQ
Tel 01232-258848; fax 01232-258843

The Commission was set up following the Belfast Agreement of April 1998. Its remit is to inquire into policing in Northern Ireland and put forward proposals for future policing structures and arrangements, including means of encouraging widespread community support for those arrangements. The Commission will report to the Secretary of State for Northern Ireland by summer 1999.
Chairman, The Rt. Hon. C. F. Patten, CH
Members, Dr M. Hayes; Dr G. Lynch; The Hon. Ms K. O'Toole; Prof. C. Shearing; Sir John Smith, QPM; P. Smith, QC; Mrs L. Woods
Secretary, R. N. Peirce

INDEPENDENT HOUSING OMBUDSMAN
Norman House, 105–109 Strand, London WC2R OAA
Tel 0171-836 3630; fax 0171-836 3900

The Independent Housing Ombudsman was established in April 1997 under the Housing Act 1996. The Ombudsman deals with complaints against registered social landlords (not including local authorities).
Ombudsman, R. Jefferies
Chair of Board, Ms P. Brown
General Manager, L. Greenberg

INDEPENDENT INTERNATIONAL COMMISSION ON DECOMMISSIONING
Dublin Castle, Block M, Ship Street, Dublin 2
Tel 00 353 1-478 0111; fax 00 353 1-478 0600
Rosepark House, Upper Newtownards Road, Belfast
BT4 3NR
Tel 01232-488600; fax 01232-488601

The Commission was established by agreement between the British and Irish governments in August 1997. Its objective is to facilitate the decommissioning of illegally-held firearms and explosives in accordance with the relevant legislation in both jurisdictions. Its members are appointed jointly by the two governments; staff are appointed by the Commission. All are drawn from countries other than the UK and the Republic of Ireland.
Chairman, Gen. J. de Chastelain (Canada)
Members, Brig. T. Nieminen (Finland); Ambassador D. C. Johnson (USA)
Chief of Staff, C. E. Garrard (Canada)

INDEPENDENT REVIEW SERVICE FOR THE SOCIAL FUND
4th Floor, Centre City Podium, 5 Hill Street,
Birmingham B5 4UB
Tel 0121-606 2100; fax 0121-606 2180

The Social Fund Commissioner is appointed by the Secretary of State for Social Security. The Commissioner appoints Social Fund Inspectors, who provide an independent review of decisions made by Social Fund Officers in the Benefits Agency of the Department of Social Security.
Social Fund Commissioner, J. Scampion

INDEPENDENT TELEVISION COMMISSION
33 Foley Street, London WIP 7LB
Tel 0171-255 3000; fax 0171-306 7800

The Independent Television Commission replaced the Independent Broadcasting Authority in 1991. The Commission is responsible for licensing and regulating all commercially funded television services broadcast from the UK. Members are appointed by the Secretary of State for Culture, Media and Sport.
Chairman (£65,580), Sir Robin Biggam
Deputy Chairman (£16,830), Earl of Dalkeith
Members (*part-time*) (£12,630), Dr J. Beynon, FENG.; Ms J. Goffe; Dr M. Moloney; J. Ranelagh; Dr M. Shea, CVO; Sir Michael Checkland; A. Balls, CB; W. Roddick
Chief Executive (£140,000), P. Rogers
Secretary, M. Redley

INDUSTRIAL INJURIES ADVISORY COUNCIL
6th Floor, The Adelphi, 1–11 John Adam Street, London
WC2N 6HT
Tel 0171-962 8066; fax 0171-712 2255

The Industrial Injuries Advisory Council is a statutory body under the Social Security Administration Act 1992 which considers and advises the Secretary of State for Social Security on regulations and other questions relating to industrial injuries benefits or their administration.
Chairman, Prof. A. J. Newman Taylor, OBE, FRCP
Secretary, A. Packer

BOARD OF INLAND REVENUE
Somerset House, Strand, London WC2R ILB
Tel 0171-438 6622

The Board of Inland Revenue was constituted under the Inland Revenue Board Act 1849. The Board administers and collects direct taxes – income tax, corporation tax, capital gains tax, inheritance tax, stamp duty, and petroleum revenue tax – and advises the Chancellor of the Exchequer on policy questions involving them. The Department's Valuation Office is an executive agency responsible for valuing property for tax purposes.
The Inland Revenue and the Contributions Agency of the Department of Social Security are to merge in April 1999.

THE BOARD
Chairman (*G1*), N. Montagu, CB
  Private Secretary, Ms C. Lunney
Deputy Chairmen (*G2*), S. C. T. Matheson, CB; G. H. Bush, CB
Director-General (*G2*), T. J. Flesher

DIVISIONS
Director, Human Resources Division (*G3*), J. Gant
Director, Business and Management Services Division (*G3*), J. Yard
Head, Strategy and Planning Division, P. Wardle
Principal Finance Officer (*G3*), R. R. Martin
Director, Business Operations Division (*G3*), D. A. Smith
Director, Statistics and Economics Division (*G3*), R. G. Ward
Director, Company Tax Division, Financial Institutions Division and Business Management Unit (*G3*), M. F. Cayley
Director, Customer Service Division (*G3*), T. Evans
Director, International Division (*G3*), I. Spence
Director, Business Profits Division and Compliance Division (*G3*), E. J. Gribbon
Director, Personal Tax Division (*G3*), E. McGivern, CB
Director, Capital and Valuation Division, and Savings and Investment Division (*G3*), B. A. Mace

EXECUTIVE OFFICES

ACCOUNTS OFFICE (CUMBERNAULD), St Mungo's Road, Cumbernauld, Glasgow G70 5TR. *Director,* A. Geddes, OBE
ACCOUNTS OFFICE (SHIPLEY), Shipley, Bradford, W. Yorks BD98 8AA. *Director,* R. J. Warner
CAPITAL TAXES OFFICE, Ferrers House, PO Box 38, Castle Meadow Road, Nottingham NG2 1BB. *Director,* E. McKeegan
CAPITAL TAXES OFFICE (SCOTLAND), Mulberry House, 16 Picardy Place, Edinburgh EH1 3NB. *Registrar,* Mrs J. Templeton
COMMUNICATIONS UNITS, North-West Wing, Bush House, London WC2B 4PP. *Head of External Communications Unit,* P. Whyatt; *Head of Internal Communications Unit,* Mrs S. M. Walton
ENFORCEMENT OFFICE, Durrington Bridge House, Barrington Road, Worthing, W. Sussex BN12 4SE. *Director,* Mrs S. F. Walsh

FINANCIAL ACCOUNTING OFFICE, South Block, Barrington Road, Worthing, W. Sussex BN12 4XH. *Director,* J. D. Easey

FINANCIAL INTERMEDIARIES AND CLAIMS OFFICE, St John's House, Merton Road, Bootle L26 9BB; Fitz Roy House, PO Box 46, Castle Meadow, Nottingham NG2 1BD. *Director,* S. W. Jones

INTERNAL AUDIT OFFICE, North-West Wing, Bush House, London WC2B 4PP. *Director,* N. R. Buckley

OIL TAXATION OFFICE, Melbourne House, Aldwych, London WC2B 4LL. *Director,* R. C. Mountain

PENSION SCHEME OFFICE, Yorke House, PO Box 62, Castle Meadow Road, Nottingham NG2 1BG. *Director,* S. J. McManus

SOLICITOR'S OFFICE, East Wing, Somerset House, London WC2R 1LB. *Solicitor (G2),* B. E. Cleave, CB

SOLICITOR'S OFFICE (SCOTLAND), Clarendon House, 114–116 George Street, Edinburgh EH2 4LH. *Solicitor,* I. K. Laing

SPECIAL COMPLIANCE OFFICE, Angel Court, 199 Borough High Street, London SE1 1HZ. *Director,* F. J. Brannigan

STAMP OFFICE, South-West Wing, Bush House, Strand, London WC2B 4QN. *Director,* K. S. Hodgson, OBE

TRAINING OFFICE, Lawress Hall, Riseholme Park, Lincoln LN2 2BJ. *Director,* T. Kuczys

REGIONAL EXECUTIVE OFFICES

INLAND REVENUE EAST, Churchgate, New Road, Peterborough PE1 1TD. *Director,* M. J. Hodgson

INLAND REVENUE LARGE BUSINESS OFFICE, New Court, Carey Street, London WC2A 2JE. *Director,* Mrs M. E. Williams

INLAND REVENUE LONDON, New Court, Carey Street, London WC2A 2JE. *Director,* J. F. Carling

INLAND REVENUE NORTH, 100 Russell Street, Middlesbrough TS1 2RZ. *Director,* R. I. Ford

INLAND REVENUE NORTH-WEST, The Triad, Stanley Road, Bootle, Merseyside L75 2DD. *Director,* G. W. Lunn

INLAND REVENUE SOUTH-EAST, Dukes Court, Dukes Street, Woking GU21 5XR. *Director,* D. L. S. Bean

INLAND REVENUE SOUTH-WEST, 3rd Floor, Longbrook House, New North Road, Exeter EX4 4UA. *Director,* R. S. Hurcombe

INLAND REVENUE SOUTH YORKSHIRE, Concept House, 5 Young Street, Sheffield S1 4LF. *Director,* A. C. Sleeman

INLAND REVENUE WALES AND MIDLANDS, 1st Floor, Phase II Building, Tŷ Glas Avenue, Llanishen, Cardiff CF4 5TS; 550 Streetsbrook Road, Solihull, West Midlands B91 1QU. *Director,* M. W. Kirk

INLAND REVENUE SCOTLAND, Clarendon House, 114–116 George Street, Edinburgh EH2 4LH. *Director,* I. S. Gerrie

INLAND REVENUE NORTHERN IRELAND, Dorchester House, 52–58 Great Victoria Street, Belfast BT2 7QE. *Director,* R. S. T. Ewing

VALUATION OFFICE AGENCY
New Court, 48 Carey Street, London WC2A 2JE
Tel 0171-324 1183/1057; fax 0171-324 1073
Meldrum House, 15 Drumsheugh Gardens, Edinburgh EH3 7UN
Tel 0131-225 4938; fax 0131-220 4384

Chief Executive, M. A. Johns
Chief Valuer, Scotland, A. Ainslie

ADJUDICATOR'S OFFICE
— see page 278

INTELLIGENCE SERVICES TRIBUNAL
PO Box 4823, London SW1A 9XD
Tel 0171-273 4383

The Intelligence Services Act 1994 established a tribunal of three senior members of the legal profession, independent of the Government and appointed by The Queen, to investigate complaints from any person about anything which they believe the Secret Intelligence Service or the Government Communications Headquarters has done to them or to their property.

President, The Rt. Hon. Lord Justice Simon Brown
Vice-President, Sheriff J. McInnes, QC
Member, Sir Richard Gaskell
Secretary, E. R. Wilson

INTERCEPTION COMMISSIONER
c/o PO Box 12376, London SW1P 1XU
Tel 0171-273 4096

The Commissioner is appointed by the Prime Minister. He keeps under review the issue by the Home Secretary, the Foreign Secretary, and the Secretaries of State for Scotland and for Northern Ireland, of warrants under the Interception of Communications Act 1985 and safeguards made in respect of intercepted material obtained through the use of such warrants. He is also required to give all such assistance as the Interception of Communications Tribunal may require to enable it to carry out its functions, and to submit an annual report to the Prime Minister with respect to the carrying out of his functions.

Commissioner, The Lord Nolan, PC
Private Secretary, E. R. Wilson

INTERCEPTION OF COMMUNICATIONS TRIBUNAL
PO Box 12376, London SW1P 1XU
Tel 0171-273 4096

Under the Interception of Communications Act 1985, the Tribunal is required to investigate complaints from any person who believes that communications sent to or by them have been intercepted in the course of their transmission by post or by means of a public telecommunications system. The Tribunal comprises senior members of the legal profession, who are appointed by The Queen.

President, The Hon. Mr Justice Macpherson of Cluny
Vice-President, Sir David Calcutt, QC
Members, P. Scott, QC; R. Seabrook, QC; W. Carmichael
Secretary, E. R. Wilson

DEPARTMENT FOR INTERNATIONAL DEVELOPMENT
94 Victoria Street, London SW1E 5JL
Tel 0171-917 7000; fax 0171-917 0016
Web: http://www.dfid.gov.uk
Abercrombie House, Eaglesham Road, East Kilbride, Glasgow G75 8EA
Tel 01355-844000; fax 01355-844099

The Department for International Development (DFID) was established in May 1997 from the former Overseas

Development Administration of the Foreign and Commonwealth Office. It takes the lead on British policy towards developing countries. It also manages the development assistance budget, including financial aid and technical assistance (specialist staff abroad and training facilities in the UK), whether provided directly to developing countries or through the various multilateral aid organizations, including the EU, the World Bank and the UN agencies.

Secretary of State for International Development, The Rt. Hon. Clare Short, MP
  Private Secretary, A. Smith
  Special Advisers, D. Harris; D. Mepham
  Parliamentary Private Secretary, D. Turner, MP
Parliamentary Under-Secretary, George Foulkes, MP
Permanent Secretary (*SCS*), J. M. M. Vereker
  Private Secretary, J. Gordon

PROGRAMMES

Director-General (*SCS*), B. R. Ireton
Head of Conflict and Humanitarian Affairs Department (*SCS*)
  (*acting*), Dr M. Kapila

AFRICA
Director (*SCS*), P. D. M. Freeman
Heads of Departments (*SCS*), Mrs B. M. Kelly, CBE (*Africa, Greater Horn and Co-ordination*); S. Ray (*West and North Africa*); D. Fish (*Nairobi*); J. R. Drummond (*Harare*); J. H. S. Chard (*Pretoria*)

ASIA
Director (*SCS*), S. Unsworth
Heads of Departments (*SCS*), C. Myhill (*East Asia and Pacific*); R. Graham-Harrison (*India*); Ms M. H. Vowles (*Western Asia*); A. K. C. Wood (*South-East Asia*); K. L. Sparkhall (*Bangladesh*)

EASTERN EUROPE AND WESTERN HEMISPHERE
Director (*SCS*), J. Kerby
Heads of Departments (*SCS*), A. Coverdale (*Eastern Europe and Central Asia*); J. S. Laing (*Central and South-Eastern Europe*); B. P. Thomson (*Caribbean*)
Heads of Departments, D. R. Curran (*Latin America, Caribbean and Atlantic*); J. D. Moye (*EBRD Unit*)

ECONOMICS AND GOVERNANCE
Director, and Chief Economic Adviser (*SCS*), J. Goudie
Chief Statistician (*SCS*), A. B. Williams
Head of Asia, Latin America and Oceans Economics, P. J. Ackroyd
Head of African Economics Department (*SCS*), M. G. Foster
Head of International Economics Department (*SCS*), P. D. Grant
Senior Small Enterprise Development Adviser, D. L. Wright
Senior Economic Advisers, Ms R. L. Turner; P. L. Owen; P. J. Dearden; P. J. Landymore; E. Hawthorn; F. C. Clift; J. L. Hoy
Head of Government Institutions Advisory Department (*SCS*), R. J. Wilson
Senior Government and Institutions Advisers, Dr G. W. Glentworth; D. W. Baker; Mrs A. Newsum; S. Sharples; J. G. Clarke
Criminal Justice Adviser, vacant

HUMAN RESOURCE DEVELOPMENT
Director, and Chief Health and Population Adviser (*SCS*), Dr D. N. Nabarro
Senior Health and Population Advisers, J. N. Lambert; T. Martineau; S. Tyson; R. N. Grose; Ms C. M. Sergeant
Chief Social Development Adviser, Dr R. Eyben
Senior Social Development Adviser, Ms P. M. Holden
Chief Education Adviser (*SCS*), Ms M. A. Harrison

Senior Education Advisers, Dr C. Treffgarne; M. E. Seath; M. D. Francis; R. T. Allsop; Dr D. B. Pennycuick; S. E. Packer; Dr K. M. Lillis; Dr G. R. H. Jones
Senior Technical Education Adviser, C. Lewis

PRODUCTIVE CAPACITY AND ENVIRONMENT
Director, and Chief Natural Resources Adviser (*SCS*), A. J. Bennett, CMG
Head of Environment Policy Department (*SCS*), D. P. Turner
Head of Natural Resources Policy and Advisory Department, and Deputy Chief Natural Resources Adviser (*SCS*), J. M. Scott
Head of Natural Resources Research Department (*SCS*), Dr J. Tarbit, OBE
Senior Natural Resources Advisers, Ms F. Proctor; R. C. Fox; M. J. Wilson; A. J. Tainsh; J. R. F. Hansell; Dr B. E. Grimwood; J. A. Harvey; A. Hall
Natural Resources Systems Programme Manager, J. C. Barrett
Senior Environment and Research Adviser, Ms L. C. Brown
Senior Fisheries Adviser, R. W. Beales
Senior Forestry Advisers, J. M. Hudson; I. A. Napier
Senior Animal Health Advisers, G. G. Freeland; Ms L. M. Bell
Chief Engineering Adviser (*SCS*), J. W. Hodges
Senior Engineering Advisers, B. Dolton; C. I. Ellis; P. J. Davies; D. F. Gillett; P. W. D. H. Roberts; M. F. Sergeant; R. J. Cadwallader; C. J. Hunt
Senior Water Resources Adviser, A. Wray
Senior Architectural and Physical Planning Adviser, M. W. Parkes
Senior Electrical and Mechanical Adviser, R. P. Jones
Senior Renewable Energy and Research Adviser, A. Gilchrist
Industrial Training Adviser, D. G. Marr

RESOURCES

Director-General (*SCS*), R. G. Manning
Heads of Departments (*SCS*), M. J. Dinham (*Personnel*); D. Sands-Smith (*Procurement, Appointments and NGO*); R. Calvert (*Information*); G. M. Stegmann (*Aid Policy and Resources*); A. D. Davis (*Information Systems*); R. A. Elias (*Internal Audit Unit*); C. P. Raleigh (*Evaluation*)
Head of Department, R. Plumb (*Overseas Pensions*)

INTERNATIONAL DEVELOPMENT AFFAIRS
Director (*SCS*), J. A. L. Faint
Heads of Departments (*SCS*), M. Lowcock (*European Union*); D. J. Batt (*International Economic Policy*); G. Toulmin (*United Nations and Commonwealth*); M. E. Cund (*International Financial Institutions*)

INTERVENTION BOARD
PO Box 69, Reading RG1 3YD
Tel 0118-958 3626; fax 0118-953 1370

The Intervention Board was established as a government department in 1972 and became an executive agency in 1990. The Board is responsible for the implementation of European Union regulations covering the market support arrangements of the Common Agricultural Policy. Members are appointed by and are responsible to the Minister of Agriculture, Fisheries and Food and the Secretaries of State for Scotland, Wales and Northern Ireland.

Chairman, I. Kent
Chief Executive (*G3*), G. Trevelyan

HEADS OF DIVISIONS
External Trade Division (*G5*), J. P. Bradbury
Internal Market Division (*G5*), H. MacKinnon
Corporate Services Division (*G5*), Mrs A. Parker
Finance Division (*G5*), G. R. R. Jenkins
Legal Division (*G5*), J. F. McCleary

Chief Accountant (G6), R. Bryant
Procurement and Supply (G6), P. J. Offer
Information Systems (G7), T. G. Lamberstock
Internal Market Operations (G6), J. A. Sutton

LAND AUTHORITY FOR WALES
— *see* Welsh Development Agency

LAND REGISTRIES

HM LAND REGISTRY
Lincoln's Inn Fields, London WC2A 3PH
Tel 0171-917 8888; fax 0171-955 0110

The registration of title to land was first introduced in England and Wales by the Land Registry Act 1862; HM Land Registry operates today under the Land Registration Acts 1925 to 1988. The object of registering title to land is to create and maintain a register of landowners whose title is guaranteed by the state and so to simplify the transfer, mortgage and other dealings with real property. Registration on sale is now compulsory throughout England and Wales. The register has been open to inspection by the public since 1990.

HM Land Registry is an executive agency administered under the Lord Chancellor by the Chief Land Registrar.

HEADQUARTERS OFFICE
Chief Land Registrar and Chief Executive, Dr S. J. Hill
Solicitor to Land Registry, C. J. West
Director of Corporate Services, E. G. Beardsall
Senior Land Registrar, J. V. Timothy
Director of Operations, G. N. French
Director of Information Technology, P. J. Smith
Director of Management Services, P. R. Laker
Land Registrar, M. L. Wood
Deputy Establishment Officer, J. Hodder
Controller of Operations Development, P. Norman
Head of Legal Practice, P. Morris
Head of Survey and Plans Practice, M. K. Brown

COMPUTER SERVICES DIVISION
Burrington Way, Plymouth PL5 3LP
Tel 01752-635600
Head of IT Services Division, P. A. Maycock
Head of IT Development Division, R. T. Davis
Head of National Land Information Service (*NLIS*), R. J. Smith
Head of IT Management Services, K. Deards

LAND CHARGES AND AGRICULTURAL CREDITS DEPARTMENT
Burrington Way, Plymouth PL5 3LP
Tel 01752-635600
Superintendent of Land Charges, J. Hughes

DISTRICT LAND REGISTRIES
BIRKENHEAD – Old Market House, Hamilton Street, Birkenhead L41 5FL. Tel: 0151-473 1110. *District Land Registrar*, M. G. Garwood
COVENTRY – Leigh Court, Torrington Avenue, Coventry CV4 9XZ. Tel: 01203-860860. *District Land Registrar*, S. P. Kelway
CROYDON – Sunley House, Bedford Park, Croydon CR9 3LE. Tel: 0181-781 9100. *District Land Registrar*, D. M. J. Moss
DURHAM (BOLDON HOUSE) – Boldon House, Wheatlands Way, Pity Me, Durham DH1 5GJ. Tel: 0191-301 2345. *District Land Registrar*, R. B. Fearnley

DURHAM (SOUTHFIELD HOUSE) – Southfield House, Southfield Way, Durham DH1 5TR. Tel: 0191-301 3500. *District Land Registrar*, P. J. Timothy
GLOUCESTER – Twyver House, Bruton Way, Gloucester GL1 1DQ. Tel: 01452-511111. *District Land Registrar*, W. W. Budden
HARROW – Lyon House, Lyon Road, Harrow, Middx HA1 2EU. Tel: 0181-235 1181. *District Land Registrar*, C. Tate
KINGSTON UPON HULL – Earle House, Portland Street, Hull HU2 8JN. Tel: 01482-223244. *District Land Registrar*, S. R. Coveney
LEICESTER – Westbridge Place, Leicester LE3 5DR. Tel: 0116-265 4000. *District Land Registrar*, Mrs J. A. Goodfellow
LYTHAM – Birkenhead House, East Beach, Lytham, Lancs FY8 5AB. Tel: 01253-849849. *District Land Registrar*, J. G. Cooper
NOTTINGHAM (EAST) – Robins Wood Road, Nottingham NG8 3RQ. Tel: 0115-906 5353. *District Land Registrar*, vacant
NOTTINGHAM (WEST) – Chalfont Drive, Nottingham NG8 3RN. Tel: 0115-935 1166. *District Land Registrar*, Ms A. M. Goss
PETERBOROUGH – Touthill Close, City Road, Peterborough PE1 1XN. Tel: 01733-288288. *District Land Registrar*, C. W. Martin
PLYMOUTH – Plumer House, Tailyour Road, Crownhill, Plymouth PL6 5HY. Tel: 01752-636000. *District Land Registrar*, A. J. Pain
PORTSMOUTH – St Andrews Court, St Michael's Road, Portsmouth PO1 2JH. Tel: 01705-768888. *District Land Registrar*, S. R. Sehrawat
STEVENAGE – Brickdale House, Swingate, Stevenage, Herts SG1 1XG. Tel: 01438-788888. *District Land Registrar*, vacant
SWANSEA – Tŷ Bryn Glas, High Street, Swansea SA1 1PW. Tel: 01792-458877. *District Land Registrar*, T. M. Lewis
TELFORD – Parkside Court, Hall Park Way, Telford TF3 4LR. Tel: 01952-290355. *District Land Registrar*, A. M. Lewis
TUNBRIDGE WELLS – Curtis House, Hawkenbury, Tunbridge Wells, Kent TN2 5AQ. Tel: 01892-510015. *District Land Registrar*, G. R. Tooke
WALES – Tŷ Cwm Tave, Phoenix Way, Llansamlet, Swansea SA7 9FQ. Tel: 01792-355000. *District Land Registrar*, G. A. Hughes
WEYMOUTH – Melcombe Court, 1 Cumberland Drive, Weymouth, Dorset DT4 9TT. Tel: 01305-363636. *District Land Registrar*, Mrs P. M. Reeson
YORK – James House, James Street, York YO1 3YZ. Tel: 01904-450000. *District Land Registrar*, Mrs R. F. Lovel

REGISTERS OF SCOTLAND (EXECUTIVE AGENCY)
Meadowbank House, 153 London Road, Edinburgh EH8 7AU
Tel 0131-659 6111; fax 0131-479 3688

The Registers of Scotland is an executive agency of the Scottish Office. The Registers consist of: General Register of Sasines and Land Register of Scotland; Register of Deeds in the Books of Council and Session; Register of Protests; Register of Judgments; Register of Service of Heirs; Register of the Great Seal; Register of the Quarter Seal; Register of the Prince's Seal; Register of Crown Grants; Register of Sheriffs' Commissions; Register of the Cachet Seal; Register of Inhibitions and Adjudications; Register of Entails; Register of Hornings.

The General Register of Sasines and the Land Register of Scotland form the chief security in Scotland of the rights of land and other heritable (or real) property.

Chief Executive and Keeper of the Registers of Scotland, A. W. Ramage

Deputy Keeper, A. G. Rennie

Managing Director, F. Manson

Directors, Ms M. Cameron (*Non-Executive Director*); Miss J. Kyle (*Human Resources*); Ms A. Rooney (*Finance and Planning*); M. Traynor (*Business Development and Marketing*); B. J. Corr (*IT*); I. A. Davis (*Legal Services*); D. McCallum (*Production*)

LAW COMMISSION

Conquest House, 37–38 John Street, London WC1N 2BQ
Tel 0171-453 1220; fax 0171-453 1297

The Law Commission was set up in 1965, under the Law Commissions Act 1965, to make proposals to the Government for the examination of the law in England and Wales and for its revision where it is unsuited for modern requirements, obscure, or otherwise unsatisfactory. It recommends to the Lord Chancellor programmes for the examination of different branches of the law and suggests whether the examination should be carried out by the Commission itself or by some other body. The Commission is also responsible for the preparation of Consolidation and Statute Law (Repeals) Bills.

Chairman, The Hon. Mrs Justice Arden, DBE

Commissioners, C. Harpum; A. S. Burrows; Miss D. Faber; S. Silber, QC

Secretary, M. W. Sayers

SCOTTISH LAW COMMISSION

140 Causewayside, Edinburgh EH9 1PR
Tel 0131-668 2131; fax 0131-662 4900

The Commission keeps the law in Scotland under review and makes proposals for its development and reform. It is responsible to the Scottish Courts Administration (*see* page 365).

Chairman (part-time), The Hon. Lord Gill

Commissioners (full-time), Dr E. M. Clive; N. R. Whitty; (*part-time*) Prof. K. G. C. Reid; P. S. Hodge, QC

Secretary, J. G. S. MacLean

LAW OFFICERS' DEPARTMENTS

Legal Secretariat to the Law Officers, Attorney-General's Chambers, 9 Buckingham Gate, London SW1E 6JP
Tel 0171-828 7155; fax 0171-233 7194
Attorney-General's Chambers, Royal Courts of Justice, Belfast BT1 3JY
Tel 01232-235111; fax 01232-546049

The Law Officers of the Crown for England and Wales are the Attorney-General and the Solicitor-General. The Attorney-General, assisted by the Solicitor-General, is the chief legal adviser to the Government and is also ultimately responsible for all Crown litigation. He has overall responsibility for the work of the Law Officers' Departments (the Treasury Solicitor's Department, the Crown Prosecution Service, the Serious Fraud Office and the Legal Secretariat to the Law Officers). He has a specific statutory duty to superintend the discharge of their duties by the Director of Public Prosecutions (who heads the Crown Prosecution Service) and the Director of the Serious Fraud Office. The Director of Public Prosecutions for Northern Ireland is also responsible to the Attorney-General for the performance of his functions. The Attorney-General has additional responsibilities in relation to aspects of the civil and criminal law.

Attorney-General (*£65,509), The Rt. Hon. John Morris, QC, MP

  Private Secretary, Ms D. Hermer

  Parliamentary Private Secretary, K. Vaz, MP

Solicitor-General (*£53,716), Ross Cranston, MP

  Private Secretary, Ms D. Hermer

Legal Secretary (G2), D. Seymour

Deputy Legal Secretary (G3), S. J. Wooler

* In addition to a parliamentary salary of £45,066

LEGAL AID BOARD

85 Gray's Inn Road, London WC1X 8AA
Tel 0171-813 1000

The Legal Aid Board has the general function of ensuring that advice, assistance, mediation and representation are available to those who need them within the framework of the Legal Aid Act 1988. In 1989 the Board took over from the Law Society responsibility for administering legal aid. The Board is a non-departmental government body whose members are appointed by the Lord Chancellor.

Chairman, Sir Tim Chessells

Deputy Chairman, H. Hodge

Members, S. Orchard (*Chief Executive*); Ms D. Charnock; Ms J. Dunkley; P. Ely; B. Harvey; P. Hollingworth; Ms D. Payne; J. Shearer; D. Sinker

SCOTTISH LEGAL AID BOARD

44 Drumsheugh Gardens, Edinburgh EH3 7SW
Tel 0131-226 7061; fax 0131-220 4878

The Scottish Legal Aid Board was set up under the Legal Aid (Scotland) Act 1986. It is responsible for ensuring that advice, assistance and representation are available in accordance with the Act. The Board is a non-departmental government body whose members are appointed by the Secretary of State for Scotland.

Chairman, Mrs J. Couper

Members, B. C. Adair; Mrs K. Blair; Prof. P. H. Grinyer; Sheriff A. Jessop; N. Kuenssberg; D. O'Carroll; Mrs Y. Osman; Ms M. Scanlan; R. Scott; M. C. Thomson, QC; A. F. Wylie, QC

Chief Executive, R. Scott

OFFICE OF THE LEGAL SERVICES OMBUDSMAN

22 Oxford Court, Oxford Street, Manchester M2 3WQ
Tel 0161-236 9532; fax 0161-236 2651

The Legal Services Ombudsman is appointed by the Lord Chancellor under the Courts and Legal Services Act 1990 to oversee the handling of complaints against solicitors, barristers, licensed conveyancers and legal executives by their professional bodies. A complainant must first complain to the relevant professional body before raising the matter with the Ombudsman. The Ombudsman is independent of the legal profession and his services are free of charge.

Legal Services Ombudsman, Ms A. Abraham
Secretary, S. Murray

OFFICE OF THE SCOTTISH LEGAL SERVICES
OMBUDSMAN
2 Greenside Lane, Edinburgh EH1 3AH
Tel 0131-556 5574; fax 0131-556 1519
Scottish Legal Services Ombudsman, G. S. Watson

LIBRARIES

LIBRARY AND INFORMATION COMMISSION
2 Sheraton Street, London W1V 4BH
Tel 0171-411 0059; fax 0171-411 0057

The Commission is an independent body set up by the then Secretary of State for National Heritage in 1995 to advise the Government and others on library and information matters, notably in the areas of research strategy and international links. It also aims to promote co-operation and co-ordination between different types of information services.

In July 1998 the Government published a discussion document including a proposal to merge the Library and Information Commission and the Museums and Galleries Commission.

Chairman, M. Evans, CBE
Commissioners, E. Arram; Sir Charles Chadwyck-Healey; Prof. M. Collier; Prof. Judith Elkin; Ms G. Kempster; Dr B. Lang; D. Law; Dr R. McKee; Dr Sandra Ward; M. Wood
Chief Executive, Ms M. Haines

THE BRITISH LIBRARY
96 Euston Road, London NW1 2DB
Tel 0171-412 7000

The British Library was established in 1973. It is the UK's national library and occupies a key position in the library and information network. The Library aims to serve scholarship, research, industry, commerce and all other major users of information. Its services are based on collections which include over 18 million volumes, 1 million discs, and 55,000 hours of tape recordings. By 1999 the Library will be based at two sites: London (St Pancras and Colindale) and Boston Spa, W. Yorks. The British Library's new purpose-built accommodation at St Pancras was opened by The Queen in June 1998 and will be fully operational by the middle of 1999. Government grant-in-aid to the British Library in 1998–9 is £80.450 million; the British Library St Pancras Project receives £349,000. The Library's sponsoring department is the Department for Culture, Media and Sport.

Access to the reading rooms at St Pancras is limited to holders of a British Library Reader's Pass; information about eligibility is available from the Reader Admissions Office. The exhibition galleries and public areas are open to all, free of charge.

Opening hours of services vary; some services may close for one week each year. Specific information should be checked by telephone.

In July 1998 the Government published a discussion document including a proposal to transfer the British Library's research function to the Library and Information Commission.

BRITISH LIBRARY BOARD
96 Euston Road, London NW1 2DB
Tel 0171-412 7262

Chairman, Dr J. M. Ashworth
Chief Executive and Deputy Chairman, Dr B. Lang
Deputy Chief Executive, D. Russon
Director-General, Collections and Services, D. Bradbury
Part-time Members, The Hon. E. Adeane, CVO; Sir Matthew Farrer, GCVO; Mrs P. M. Lively, OBE; Prof. M. Anderson, FBA, FRSE; A. Bloom; Sir Peter Hordern; C. G. R. Leach; B. Naylor; J. Ritblat; P. Scherer

BRITISH LIBRARY, BOSTON SPA
Boston Spa, Wetherby, W. Yorks LS23 7BQ
Tel 01937-546000

BIBLIOGRAPHIC SERVICES AND DOCUMENT SUPPLY, *Director* (G5), M. Smith
NATIONAL BIBLIOGRAPHIC SERVICE. Tel: 01937-546585. *Director* (G6), R. Smith
London Unit, 96 Euston Road, London NW1 2DB. Tel: 0171-412 7077
ACQUISITIONS PROCESSING AND CATALOGUING, *Director* (G5), S. Ede
INFORMATION SYSTEMS. Tel: 01937-546879. *Director* (G5), J. R. Mahoney

BRITISH LIBRARY, ST PANCRAS
96 Euston Road, London NW1 2DB
Tel 0171-412 7000

PLANNING AND RESOURCES. Tel: 0171-412 7132. *Director* (G5), D. Gesua

PUBLIC AFFAIRS. *Director* (G5), Ms J. Carr
Press and Public Relations. Tel: 0171-412 7111. *Head* (G7), M. Jackson
Exhibitions Service, Education Service and Visitor Services. Tel: 0171-412 7332

READER SERVICES AND COLLECTION DEVELOPMENT. *Director* (G5), M. J. Crump
Reader Admissions. Tel: 0171-412 7677
Reader Services. Tel: 0171-412 7676
West European Collections, Slavonic and East European Collections, English Language Collections. Tel: 0171-412 7676
Newspaper Library, Colindale Avenue, London NW9 5HE. Tel: 0171-412 7353

COLLECTIONS AND PRESERVATION. *Director* (G5), Dr M. Foot
Preservation Service (National Preservation Office). Tel: 0171-412 7612

SPECIAL COLLECTIONS. Tel: 0171-412 7513. *Director* (G5), Dr A. Prochaska
Oriental and India Office Collections. Tel: 0171-412 7873
Western Manuscripts. Tel: 0171-412 7513 (opens Jan. 1999)
Map Library. Tel: 0171-412 7700
Music Library. Tel: 0171-412 7635
Philatelic Collections. Tel: 0171-412 7729
National Sound Archive. Tel: 0171-412 7440

SCIENCE REFERENCE AND INFORMATION SERVICE, 25 Southampton Buildings, London WC2A 1AW. Tel: 0171-412 7494; 9 Kean Street, London WC2B 4AT. Tel: 0171-412 7288. Moves to St Pancras early summer 1999. *Director*, A. Gomersall
Social Policy Information Service. Tel: 0171-412 7536

RESEARCH AND INNOVATION CENTRE. Tel: 0171-412 7055. *Director*, N. Macartney

NATIONAL LIBRARY OF SCOTLAND
George IV Bridge, Edinburgh EH1 1EW
Tel 0131-226 4531; fax 0131-622 4803

The Library, which was founded as the Advocates' Library in 1682, became the National Library of Scotland in 1925. It is funded by the Scottish Office. It contains about six million books and pamphlets, 18,000 current periodicals, 230 newspaper titles and 100,000 manuscripts. It has an unrivalled Scottish collection.

The Reading Room is for reference and research which cannot conveniently be pursued elsewhere. Admission is by ticket issued to an approved applicant. Opening hours: Reading Room, weekdays, 9.30–8.30 (Wednesday, 10–8.30); Saturday 9.30–1. Map Library, weekdays, 9.30–5 (Wednesday, 10–5); Saturday 9.30–1. Exhibition, weekdays, 10–5; Saturday 10–5; Sunday 2–5. Scottish Science Library, weekdays, 9.30–5 (Wednesday, 10–8.30).

Chairman of the Trustees, The Earl of Crawford and Balcarres, PC
Librarian and Secretary to the Trustees (*G4*), I. D. McGowan
Secretary of the Library (*G6*), M. C. Graham
Keeper of Printed Books (*G6*), Ms A. Matheson, OBE, Ph.D.
Keeper of Manuscripts (*G6*), I. C. Cunningham
Director of Public Services (*G6*), A. M. Marchbank, Ph.D.

NATIONAL LIBRARY OF WALES/ LLYFRGELL GENEDLAETHOL CYMRU
Aberystwyth SY23 3BU
Tel 01970-632800; fax 01970-615709

The National Library of Wales was founded by royal charter in 1907, and is funded by the Welsh Office. It contains about four million printed books, 40,000 manuscripts, four million deeds and documents, numerous maps, prints and drawings, and a sound and moving image collection. It specializes in manuscripts and books relating to Wales and the Celtic peoples. It is the repository for pre-1858 Welsh probate records, manorial records and tithe documents, and certain legal records. Readers' room open weekdays, 9.30–6 (Saturday 9.30–5); closed first week of October. Admission by reader's ticket.

President, Dr R. Brinley Jones
Librarian (*G4*), A. M. W. Green
Heads of Departments (*G6*), M. W. Mainwaring (*Administration and Technical Services*); G. Jenkins (*Manuscripts and Records*); Dr W. R. M. Griffiths (*Printed Books*); Dr D. H. Owen (*Pictures and Maps*)

LIGHTHOUSE AUTHORITIES

CORPORATION OF TRINITY HOUSE
Trinity House, Tower Hill, London EC3N 4DH
Tel 0171-480 6601; fax 0171-480 7662

Trinity House, the first general lighthouse and pilotage authority in the kingdom, was granted its first charter by Henry VIII in 1514. The Corporation is the general lighthouse authority for England, Wales and the Channel Islands and maintains 72 lighthouses, 13 major floating aids to navigation (e.g. light vessels) and more than 420 buoys. The last four manned lighthouses will be automated by November 1998. The Corporation also has certain statutory jurisdiction over aids to navigation maintained by local harbour authorities and is responsible for dealing with wrecks dangerous to navigation, except those occurring within port limits or wrecks of HM ships.

The Trinity House Lighthouse Service is maintained out of the General Lighthouse Fund which is provided from light dues levied on ships calling at ports of the UK and the Republic of Ireland. The Corporation is also a deep-sea pilotage authority and a charitable organization.

The affairs of the Corporation are controlled by a board of Elder Brethren and the Secretary. A separate board, which comprises Elder Brethren, senior staff and outside representatives, currently controls the Lighthouse Service. The Elder Brethren also act as nautical assessors in marine cases in the Admiralty Division of the High Court of Justice.

ELDER BRETHREN
Master, HRH The Prince Philip, Duke of Edinburgh, KG, KT
Deputy Master, Rear-Adm. P. B. Rowe, CBE, LVO
Elder Brethren, Capt. D. J. Orr; Capt. N. M. Turner, RD; HRH The Prince of Wales, KG, KT; HRH The Duke of York, CVO, ADC; Capt. Sir David Tibbits, DSC, RN; Capt. D. A. G. Dickens; Capt. J. E. Bury; Capt. J. A. N. Bezant, DSC, RD, RNR (retd.); Capt. D. J. Cloke; Capt. Sir Miles Wingate, KCVO; The Rt. Hon. Sir Edward Heath, KG, MBE, MP; Capt. I. R. C. Saunders; Capt. P. F. Mason, CBE; Capt. T. Woodfield, OBE; The Lord Simon of Glaisdale, PC; Admiral of the Fleet the Lord Lewin, KG, GCB, LVO, DSC; Capt. D. T. Smith, RN; Cdr. Sir Robin Gillett, Bt., GBE, RD, RNR; Capt. Sir Malcolm Edge, KCVO; The Lord Cuckney; The Lord Carrington, KG, GCMG, CH, MC, PC; Sir Brian Shaw; The Lord Mackay of Clashfern, KT, PC; Sir Adrian Swire; Capt. P. H. King; The Lord Sterling of Plaistow, CBE, RNR; Cdr. M. J. Rivett-Carnac, RN; Capt. C. M. C. Stewart; Adm. Sir Jock Slater, GCB, LVO, ADC; Capt. J. R. Burton-Hall, RD; Capt. I. Gibb; Cdre P. J. Melson, CBE, RN

OFFICERS
Secretary, R. F. Dobb
Director of Finance, K. W. Clark
Director of Engineering, M. G. B. Wannell
Director of Administration, D. I. Brewer
Human Resources and Communication Manager, N. J. Cutmore
Navigation Manager, Mrs K. Hossain
Legal and Insurance Manager, J. D. Price
Head of Management Services, S. J. W. Dunning
Deputy Director of Engineering, P. N. Hyde
Senior Inspector of Shipping, J. R. Dunnett
Media and Communication Officer, H. L. Cooper

NORTHERN LIGHTHOUSE BOARD
84 George Street, Edinburgh EH2 3DA
Tel 0131-473 3100; fax 0131-220 2093

The Lighthouse Board is the general lighthouse authority for Scotland and the Isle of Man. The present board owes its origin to an Act of Parliament passed in 1786. At present the Commissioners operate under the Merchant Shipping Act 1894 and are 19 in number.

The Commissioners control 84 major automatic lighthouses, 116 minor lights and many lighted and unlighted buoys. They have a fleet of two motor vessels.

COMMISSIONERS
The Lord Advocate; the Solicitor-General for Scotland; the Lord Provosts of Edinburgh, Glasgow and Aberdeen; the Provost of Inverness; the Convener of Argyll and Bute Council; the Sheriffs-Principal of North Strathclyde, Tayside, Central and Fife, Grampian, Highlands and Islands, South Strathclyde, Dumfries and Galloway, Lothians and Borders, and Glasgow and Strathkelvin; A. J. Struthers; W. F. Hay, CBE; Capt. D. M. Cowell; Adm. Sir Michael Livesay, KCB; The Lord Maclay

OFFICERS
Chief Executive, Capt. J. B. Taylor, RN
Director of Finance, D. Gorman
Director of Engineering, W. Paterson
Director of Operations and Navigational Requirements,
  P. J. Christmas

LOCAL COMMISSIONERS

COMMISSION FOR LOCAL ADMINISTRATION IN ENGLAND
21 Queen Anne's Gate, London SW1H 9BU
Tel 0171-915 3210; fax 0171-233 0396
Local Commissioners (local government ombudsmen) are responsible for investigating complaints from members of the public against local authorities (but not town and parish councils); police authorities; the Commission for New Towns (housing functions); education appeal committees and certain other authorities. The Commissioners are appointed by the Crown on the recommendation of the Secretary of State for the Environment, Transport and the Regions.

Certain types of action are excluded from investigation, including personnel matters and commercial transactions unless they relate to the purchase or sale of land. Complaints can be sent direct to the Local Government Ombudsman or through a councillor, although the Local Government Ombudsman will not consider a complaint unless the council has had an opportunity to investigate and reply to a complainant.

A free leaflet *Complaint about the council? How to complain to the Local Government Ombudsman* is available from the Commission's office.
Chairman and Chief Executive of the Commission and Local Commissioner (£112,011), E. B. C. Osmotherly, CB
Vice-Chairman and Local Commissioner (£84,586), Mrs P. A. Thomas
Local Commissioner (£83,586), J. R. White
Member (*ex officio*), The Parliamentary Commissioner for Administration
Deputy Chief Executive and Secretary (£57,340), N. J. Karney

COMMISSION FOR LOCAL ADMINISTRATION IN WALES
Derwen House, Court Road, Bridgend CF31 1BN
Tel 01656-661325; fax 01656-658317
The Local Commissioner for Wales has similar powers to the Local Commissioners in England. The Commissioner is appointed by the Crown on the recommendation of the Secretary of State for Wales. A free leaflet *Your Local Ombudsman in Wales* is available from the Commission's office.
Local Commissioner, E. R. Moseley
Secretary, D. Bowen
Member (*ex officio*), The Parliamentary Commissioner for Administration

COMMISSIONER FOR LOCAL ADMINISTRATION IN SCOTLAND
23 Walker Street, Edinburgh EH3 7HX
Tel 0131-225 5300; fax 0131-225 9495
The Local Commissioner for Scotland has similar powers to the Local Commissioners in England, and is appointed by the Crown on the recommendation of the Secretary of State for Scotland.
Local Commissioner, F. C. Marks, OBE
Deputy Commissioner and Secretary, Ms J. H. Renton

LONDON REGIONAL TRANSPORT
55 Broadway, London SW1H 0BD
Tel 0171-222 5600

Subject to the financial objectives and principles approved by the Secretary of State for the Environment, Transport and the Regions, London Regional Transport has a general duty to provide or secure the provision of public transport services for Greater London.
Chairman (*part-time non-executive*) (*acting*), B. Appleton
Chief Executive, D. Tunnicliffe, CBE
Member, and Managing Director of London Transport Buses, C. Hodson, CBE
Member, and Managing Director of London Underground Ltd, vacant

LORD ADVOCATE'S DEPARTMENT
2 Carlton Gardens, London SW1Y 5AA
Tel 0171-210 1050; fax 0171-210 1025

The Law Officers for Scotland are the Lord Advocate and the Solicitor-General for Scotland. The Lord Advocate's Department is responsible for drafting Scottish legislation, for providing legal advice to other departments on Scottish questions and for assistance to the Law Officers for Scotland in certain of their legal duties.
Lord Advocate (£80,219), The Lord Hardie, PC, QC
  Private Secretary, J. A. Gibbons
Solicitor-General for Scotland (£68,648), Colin Boyd, QC
  Private Secretary, J. A. Gibbons
Legal Secretary and First Scottish Parliamentary Counsel (*SCS*), J. C. McCluskie, QC
Assistant Legal Secretaries and Scottish Parliamentary Counsel (*SCS*), G. M. Clark; G. Kowalski; P. J. Layden, TD; C. A. M. Wilson
Assistant Legal Secretary and Depute Scottish Parliamentary Counsel (*SCS*), J. D. Harkness

LORD CHANCELLOR'S DEPARTMENT
Selborne House, 54–60 Victoria Street, London SW1E 6QW
Tel 0171-210 8500
E-mail: enquiries.lcdhq@gtnet.gov.uk
Web: http://www.open.gov.uk/lcd

The Lord Chancellor appoints Justices of the Peace (except in the Duchy of Lancaster) and advises the Crown on the appointment of most members of the higher judiciary. He is responsible for promoting general reforms in the civil law, for the procedure of the civil courts and for legal aid. He is a member of the Cabinet. He also has ministerial responsibility for magistrates' courts, which are administered locally. Administration of the Supreme Court and county courts in England and Wales was taken over by the Court Service, an executive agency of the department, in April 1995.

The Lord Chancellor is also responsible for ensuring that letters patent and other formal documents are passed in the proper form under the Great Seal of the Realm, of which he is the custodian. The work in connection with this is carried out under his direction in the Office of the Clerk of the Crown in Chancery.

The Lord Chancellor is also the senior Lord of Appeal in Ordinary and speaker of the House of Lords.
Lord Chancellor (£148,850), The Lord Irvine of Lairg, PC, QC
  Principal Private Secretary, Ms J. Rowe
  Special Adviser, G. Hart
  Parliamentary Private Secretaries, A. Wright, MP; D. Lock, MP
Minister of State, Geoff Hoon, MP
  Private Secretary, J. Freeman
Permanent Secretary (*SCS*), Sir Hayden Phillips, KCB
  Private Secretary, Ms L. Sullivan

CROWN OFFICE
House of Lords, London SW1A 0PW
Tel 0171-219 4713

Clerk of the Crown in Chancery (*SCS*), Sir Hayden Phillips, KCB
Deputy Clerk of the Crown in Chancery (*SCS*), vacant
Clerk of the Chamber, C. I. P. Denyer

JUDICIAL APPOINTMENTS GROUP
Tel 0171-210 8926

Head of Group (*SCS*), M. Huebner, CB
Heads of Divisions (*SCS*), D. E. Staff (*Policy and Conditions of Service*); Mrs M. Pigott (*Circuit Bench*); Miss J. Killick (*Circuit Bench*); E. Adams (*District Bench and Tribunals*); R. Venne (*Magistrates' Appointments*)

Judicial Studies Board
9th Floor, Millbank Tower, London SW1P 4QW
Tel 0171-925 4762

Secretary (*SCS*), D. Hill

POLICY GROUP
Tel 0171-210 8719

Director-General (*SCS*), I. M. Burns, CB
Heads of Divisions (*SCS*), P. G. Harris (*Legal Aid*); M. Ormerod (*Criminal Policy*); D. Gladwell (*Civil Justice*); R. Sams (*Law Reform and Tribunals*); W. Arnold (*Family Policy*); A. Cogbill (*Civil Justice and Legal Aid Reform*); vacant (*Special Projects*); Ms M. Morse (*Community Legal Services*); Ms A. Finlay (*ECHR Incorporation Team*); D. A. Hill (*Modernization of Justice and Legal Services Development*)
Head of Secretariat and Agency Monitoring Unit (*SCS*), Ms A. Jones

LEGAL ADVISER'S GROUP
Tel 0171-210 0711

Legal Adviser (*SCS*), P. Jenkins
Heads of Divisions (*SCS*), M. H. Collon (*Legal Advice and Litigation*); A. Wallace (*International and Common Law Services*); M. Kron (*Drafting Services*)

COMMUNICATIONS GROUP
Tel 0171-210 8672

Director of Communications (*SCS*), A. Percival, LVO

CORPORATE SERVICES GROUP
Tel 0171-210 8503

Director of Corporate Services and Principal Establishment and Finance Officer (*SCS*), Mrs E. Grimsey
Heads of Divisions (*SCS*), Mrs S. Anderson (*Personnel Management*); Mrs S. Webber (*Personnel Management*); S. Smith (*Finance*); K. Cregeen (*Facilities and Support Services*); A. Rummins (*Internal Assurance*); K. Garrett (*Statutory Publications Office*)

MAGISTRATES' COURTS GROUP
Tel 0171-210 8809

Director (*SCS*), L. C. Oates
Heads of Divisions (*SCS*), Mrs S. Field (*Magistrates' Courts*); P. White (*LIBRA Project and Magistrates' Courts IT*)

ECCLESIASTICAL PATRONAGE
10 Downing Street, London SW1A 2AA
Tel 0171-930 4433

Secretary for Ecclesiastical Patronage, J. H. Holroyd, CB
Assistant Secretary for Ecclesiastical Patronage, N. C. Wheeler

MAGISTRATES' COURTS' SERVICE INSPECTORATE
Southside, 105 Victoria Street, London SW1E 6QJ
Tel 0171-210 1655

Chief Inspector (*SCS*), C. Chivers
Senior Inspectors (*SCS*), Ms J. Eeles; D. Gear; C. Monson; Ms S. Steel

LORD CHANCELLOR'S ADVISORY COMMITTEE ON STATUTE LAW
67 Tufton Street, London SW1P 3QS
Tel 0171-210 2600

The Advisory Committee advises the Lord Chancellor on all matters relating to the revision, modernization and publication of the statute book.
Chairman, The Lord Chancellor
Deputy Chairman, Sir Thomas Legg, KCB, QC
Members, C. Jenkins, CB, QC; J. C. McCluskie, QC; R. Brodie, CB; R. H. H White; G. Gray; J. M. Davies; Sir Donald Limon, KCB; The Hon. Mrs Justice Arden, DBE; The Hon. Lord Gill; A. H. Hammond, CB; Mrs E. Grimsey; P. Macdonald, CBE; C. Carey; K. Garrett
Secretary, vacant

EXECUTIVE AGENCIES

THE COURT SERVICE
Southside, 105 Victoria Street, London SW1E 6QT
Tel 0171-210 1775

The Court Service provides administrative support to the Supreme Court of England and Wales, county courts and a number of tribunals.
Chief Executive (*SCS*), I. Magee
Director of Civil and Family Operations (*SCS*), P. L. Jacob
Director of Criminal Operations (*SCS*), N. J. Smedley
Director of Tribunals (*SCS*), P. Stockton

Resources and Support Services Directorate
Director (*SCS*), C. W. V. Everett
SCS, K. Pogson (*Resources and Planning*); Miss B. Kenny (*Personnel and Training*); A. Shaw (*Accommodation and Procurement*); I. Hyams (*Information Services*)

Royal Courts of Justice
Strand, London WC2A 2LL
Tel 0171-936 6000
Administrator, G. E. Calvett

For Supreme Court departments and offices and circuit administrators, *see* Law Courts and Offices section

HM LAND REGISTRY
— *see* page 316

PUBLIC RECORD OFFICE
— *see* page 336

PUBLIC TRUST OFFICE
— *see* page 335

LORD GREAT CHAMBERLAIN'S OFFICE
House of Lords, London SW1A OPW
Tel 0171-219 3100; fax 0171-219 2500

The Lord Great Chamberlain is a Great Officer of State, the office being hereditary since the grant of Henry I to the family of De Vere, Earls of Oxford. It is now a joint hereditary office between the Cholmondeley and Carington families. The Lord Great Chamberlain is responsible for the royal apartments of the Palace of Westminster, i.e. The Queen's Robing Room, the Royal Gallery and, in conjunction with the Lord Chancellor and the Speaker, Westminster Hall. The Lord Great Chamberlain has particular responsibility for the internal administrative arrangements within the House of Lords for State Openings of Parliament.
Lord Great Chamberlain, The Marquess of Cholmondeley
Secretary to the Lord Great Chamberlain, Gen. Sir Edward Jones, KCB, CBE
Clerks to the Lord Great Chamberlain, Miss C. J. Bostock; Miss R. M. Wilkinson

LORD PRIVY SEAL'S OFFICE
Privy Council Office, 68 Whitehall, London SW1A 2AT
Tel 0171-270 3000

The Lord Privy Seal is a member of the Cabinet and Leader of the House of Lords. She has no departmental portfolio, but is a member of a number of domestic and economic Cabinet committees. She is responsible to the Prime Minister for the organization of government business in the House and has a responsibility to the House itself to advise it on procedural matters and other difficulties which arise.
Lord Privy Seal, Leader of the House of Lords and Minister for Women, The Baroness Jay of Paddington, PC
Principal Private Secretary, Ms L. Bainsfair
Private Secretary (House of Lords), S. Burton

LOTTERY, OFFICE OF THE NATIONAL
— *see* page 328

OFFICE OF MANPOWER ECONOMICS
Oxford House, 76 Oxford Street, London W1N 9FD
Tel 0171-467 7244; fax 0171-467 7248

The Office of Manpower Economics was set up in 1971. It is an independent non-statutory organization which is responsible for servicing independent review bodies which advise on the pay of various public service groups (*see* Review Bodies, pages 337–8), the Pharmacists Review Panel and the Police Negotiating Board. The Office is also responsible for servicing *ad hoc* bodies of inquiry and for undertaking research into pay and associated matters as requested by the Government.
OME Director, M. J. Horsman
Director, Statistics, Office Services and Police Secretariat, G. S. Charles
Director, Armed Forces and Teachers' Secretariats, G. McGregor
Director, Health Secretariat, and OME Deputy Director, Miss S. M. Haird
Director, Senior Salaries Secretariat, Mrs C. Haworth
Press Liaison Officer, M. C. Cahill

MENTAL HEALTH ACT COMMISSION
Maid Marian House, 56 Hounds Gate, Nottingham
NG1 6BG
Tel 0115-943 7100; fax 0115-943 7101

The Mental Health Act Commission was established in 1983. Its functions are to keep under review the operation of the Mental Health Act 1983; to visit and meet patients detained under the Act; to investigate complaints falling within the Commission's remit; to operate the consent to treatment safeguards in the Mental Health Act; to publish a biennial report on its activities; to monitor the implementation of the Code of Practice; and to advise ministers. Commissioners are appointed by the Secretary of State for Health.
Chairman, The Viscountess Runciman of Doxford, OBE
Vice-Chairman, Prof. R. Williams
Chief Executive (G6), W. Bingley

MILLENNIUM COMMISSION
Portland House, Stag Place, London SW1E 5EZ
Tel 0171-880 2001; fax 0171-880 2000

The Millennium Commission was established in February 1994 and is funded by the Department for Culture, Media and Sport. It is an independent body which distributes money from National Lottery proceeds to projects to mark the millennium.
Chairman, The Rt. Hon. Chris Smith, MP
Members, Dr D. Clarke; Prof. Heather Couper, FRAS; Earl of Dalkeith; The Lord Glentoran, CBE; Sir John Hall; The Rt. Hon. M. Heseltine, MP; S. Jenkins; The Baroness Scotland of Asthal, QC
Director, M. O'Connor

MONOPOLIES AND MERGERS COMMISSION
New Court, 48 Carey Street, London WC2A 2JT
Tel 0171-324 1467; fax 0171-324 1400

The Commission was established in 1948 as the Monopolies and Restrictive Practices Commission and became the Monopolies and Mergers Commission under the Fair Trading Act 1973. Its role is to investigate and report on matters which are referred to it by the Secretary of State for Trade and Industry or the Director-General of Fair Trading or, in the case of privatized industries, by the appropriate regulator. Its decisions are determined by the criteria set out in the legislation covering the different types of reference. The main types of reference which can be made are: monopolies; mergers; newspaper mergers; general, involving general practices in an industry; restrictive labour practices; competition, involving anti-competitive practices of individual firms; public sector audits; privatized industries; and Channel 3 (ITV) networking arrangements between holders of regional Channel 3 licences. References may be made under the Fair Trading Act 1973, the Competition Act 1980, the Broadcasting Act or other relevant statutes.
The Commission consists of about 35 members, including a full-time chairman and three part-time deputy chairmen, all appointed by the Secretary of State for Trade and Industry. Each inquiry is conducted on behalf of the

Commission by a group of four to six members who are appointed by the chairman.

The Government has announced plans to reform competition law and replace the Commission with a Competition Commission, subject to parliamentary approval.

Chairman (£120,000), D. Morris, ph.D.

Deputy Chairmen (£51,000–£68,000), P. G. Corbett, CBE; Ms D. Kingsmill

Members (£14,731/*£9,821 each), H. Aldous; Prof. J. Beatson; R. Bertram; Mrs S. Brown; Prof. M. Cave; *A. T. Clothier; R. H. F. Croft, CB; C. Darke; *R. O. Davies; *N. H. Finney, OBE; *Sir Archibald Forster; Prof. P. Geroski; *Sir Ronald Halstead, CBE; D. B. Hammond; *Ms J. C. Hanratty; C. Henderson, CB; *Ms P. A. Hodgson, CBE; D. J. Jenkins, MBE; R. Lyons; P. MacKay, CB; *Ms K. M. H. Mortimer; *R. J. Munson; *Prof. D. M. G. Newberry, FBA; Dr Gill Owen; Prof. J. F. Pickering; M. R. Prosser; A. Pryor, CB; R. Rawlinson; Prof. Judith Rees; *T. S. Richmond, MBE; J. Rickford; Dr Ann Robinson; *J. K. Roe; Ms H. Shovelton; *G. H. Stacy, CBE; D. Start; Prof. A. Steele

Secretary, Miss P. Boys

* Reserve members

MUSEUMS

MUSEUMS AND GALLERIES COMMISSION
16 Queen Anne's Gate, London SW1H 9AA
Tel 0171-233 4200; fax 0171-233 3686

Established in 1931 as the Standing Commission on Museums and Galleries, the Commission was renamed in 1981. Its sponsor department is the Department for Culture, Media and Sport. The Commission advises the Government, including the Department of Education for Northern Ireland, the Scottish Education Department and the Welsh Office, on museum affairs. Commissioners are appointed by the Prime Minister.

The Commission's executive functions include providing the services of the Museums Security Adviser; allocating grants to the seven Area Museum Councils in England; funding and monitoring the work of the Museum Documentation Association; and administering grant schemes for non-national museums. The Commission administers the arrangements for government indemnities and the acceptance of works of art in lieu of inheritance tax, and its Conservation Unit advises on conservation and environmental standards. A registration scheme for museums in the UK is operated by the Commission.

In July 1998 the Government published a discussion document including a proposal to merge the Museums and Galleries Commission and the Library and Information Commission.

Chairman, J. Joll

Members, Prof. P. Bateson, FRS (*Vice-Chairman*); The Baroness Brigstocke; Prof. R. Buchanan; Ms R. Butler; Penelope, Viscountess Cobham; R. Foster; L. Grossman; R. Hiscox; Adm. Sir John Kerr, GCB; Dr I. McKenzie Smith, RSA; A. Warhurst, CBE; Mrs C. Wilson

Director and Secretary, T. Mason

THE BRITISH MUSEUM
Great Russell Street, London WC1B 3DG
Tel 0171-636 1555; fax 0171-323 8614

The British Museum houses the national collection of antiquities, ethnography, coins and paper money, medals, and prints and drawings. The British Museum may be said to date from 1753, when Parliament approved the holding of a public lottery to raise funds for the purchase of the collections of Sir Hans Sloane and the Harleian manuscripts, and for their proper housing and maintenance. The building (Montagu House) was opened in 1759. The present buildings were erected between 1823 and the present day, and the original collection has increased to its present dimensions by gifts and purchases. Total government grant-in-aid for 1998–9 is £32.921 million.

BOARD OF TRUSTEES

Appointed by the Sovereign, HRH The Duke of Gloucester, KG, GCVO

Appointed by the Prime Minister, N. Barber; Prof. Gillian Beer, FBA; Sir John Boyd; E. J. P. Browne, FE ng.; Sir Matthew Farrer, GCVO; Sir Michael Hopkins, CBE, RA, RIBA; Sir Joseph Hotung; Prof. M. Kemp, FBA; S. Keswick; Hon. Mrs M. Marten, OBE; Sir John Morgan, KCMG; The Rt. Hon. Sir Timothy Raison; Sir Martin Rees, FRS; Prof. Sir Gunter Treitel, DCL, FBA, QC

Nominated by the Learned Societies, Prof. Jean Thomas, CBE (*Royal Society*); A. Jones, RA (*Royal Academy*); Sir Claus Moser, KCB, CBE, FBA (*British Academy*); The Lord Renfrew of Kaimsthorn, FBA, FSA (*Society of Antiquaries*)

Appointed by the Trustees of the British Museum, G. C. Greene, CBE (*Chairman*); Sir David Attenborough, CH, CVO, CBE, FRS; Prof. Rosemary Cramp, CBE, FSA; The Lord Egremont; Dr Jennifer Montagu, FBA

OFFICERS

Director, Dr R. G. W. Anderson, FRSC, FSA
Director of Finance and Resources, A. B. Blackstock
Secretary, Mrs C. Nihoul Parker
Head of Public Services, G. A. L. House
Head of Press and Public Relations, A. E. Hamilton
Head of Design, Miss M. Hall, OBE
Head of Education, J. F. Reeve
Head of Administration, C. E. I. Jones
Head of Building Development and Planning, K. T. Stannard
Head of Building Management, T. R. A. Giles
Head of Finance, Miss S. E. Davies
Head of Personnel and Office Services, Miss B. A. Hughes

KEEPERS

Keeper of Prints and Drawings, A. V. Griffiths
Keeper of Coins and Medals, Dr A. M. Burnett
Keeper of Egyptian Antiquities, W. V. Davies
Keeper of Western Asiatic Antiquities, Dr J. E. Curtis
Keeper of Greek and Roman Antiquities, Dr D. J. R. Williams
Keeper of Medieval and Later Antiquities, J. Cherry
Keeper of Prehistoric and Romano-British Antiquities, Dr T. M. Potter
Keeper of Japanese Antiquities, V. T. Harris
Keeper of Oriental Antiquities, R. J. Knox
Keeper of Ethnography, B. J. Mack
Keeper of Scientific Research, Dr S. G. E. Bowman
Keeper of Conservation, W. A. Oddy

NATURAL HISTORY MUSEUM
Cromwell Road, London SW7 5BD
Tel 0171-938 9123

The Natural History Museum originates from the natural history departments of the British Museum, which grew extensively during the 19th century; in 1860 the natural history collection was moved from Bloomsbury to a new location. Part of the site of the 1862 International Exhibition in South Kensington was acquired for the new museum, and the Museum opened to the public in 1881. In 1963 the Natural History Museum became completely independent with its own board of trustees. The Walter

Rothschild Zoological Museum, Tring, bequeathed by the second Lord Rothschild, has formed part of the Museum since 1938. The Geological Museum merged with the Natural History Museum in 1985. Total government grant-in-aid for 1998–9 is £26.96 million.

BOARD OF TRUSTEES

Appointed by the Prime Minister: Sir Robert May, FRS (*Chairman*); Mrs J. M. d'Abo; Sir Denys Henderson; Sir Crispin Tickell, GCMG, KCVO; Prof. Sir Ronald Oxburgh, FRS; Dame Anne McLaren, DBE, FRS; Sir Richard Sykes; Miss J. Mayhew

Appointed by the Secretary of State for Culture, Media and Sport, Prof. C. Leaver, FRS

Appointed by the Trustees of the Natural History Museum, Prof. Sir Brian Follett, FRS; The Lord Palumbo; Prof. K. O'Nions, FRS

SENIOR STAFF

Director, N. R. Chalmers, PH.D.
Director of Science, Prof. P. Henderson, D.Phil.
Policy and Planning Co-ordinator, Ms N. Donlon
Science Policy Co-ordinator, J. Jackson
Head of Development and Marketing, Ms T. Burman
Keeper of Zoology, P. Rainbow
Director, Tring Zoological Museum, Mrs T. Wild
Keeper of Entomology, R. Vane-Wright
Keeper of Botany, S. Blackmore, PH.D.
Keeper of Palaeontology, Prof. S. K. Donaldson
Keeper of Mineralogy, Dr A. Fleet
Head of Finance, N. Greenwood
Head of Human Resources, Mrs J. Rowe
Head of Library and Information Services, R. Lester
Head of Education and Exhibitions (G5), Dr G. Clarke
Head of Visitor Services, Mrs W. B. Gullick
Head of Estates, G. Pellow

THE SCIENCE MUSEUM

Exhibition Road, London SW7 2DD
Tel 0171-938 8000; fax 0171-938 8112

The Science Museum, part of the National Museum of Science and Industry, houses the national collections of science, technology, industry and medicine. The Museum began as the science collection of the South Kensington Museum and first opened in 1857. In 1883 it acquired the collections of the Patent Museum and in 1909 the science collections were transferred to the new Science Museum, leaving the art collections with the Victoria and Albert Museum.

Some of the Museum's commercial aircraft, agricultural machinery, and road and rail transport collections are at Wroughton, Wilts. The National Museum of Science and Industry also incorporates the National Railway Museum, York and the National Museum of Photography, Film and Television, Bradford.

Total government grant-in-aid for 1998–9 is £21.281 million.

BOARD OF TRUSTEES

Chairman, Sir Peter Williams, CBE, PH.D., FEng.
Members, HRH The Duke of Kent, KG, GCMG, GCVO, ADC; Dr M. Archer; G. Dyke; Dr A. Grocock; Mrs A. Higham, OBE; Mrs J. Kennedy, OBE; Dame Bridget Ogilvie, DBE; The Lord Puttnam, CBE; Sir Michael Quinlan, GCB; D. E. Rayner, CBE; Sir Christopher Wates

OFFICERS

Director, Sir Neil Cossons, OBE, FSA
Assistant Director and Head of Resource Management Division, J. J. Defries
Head of Personnel and Legal Services, C. Gosling

Head of Finance, Ms A. Caine
Head of Information Systems, S. Gordon
Head of Estates, J. Bevin
Assistant Director and Head of Collections Division (acting), Dr D. A. Robinson
Head of Physical Sciences and Engineering Group (acting), Dr A. Q. Morton
Head of Life and Communications Technologies Group, Dr R. F. Bud
Head of Collections Management Group, Dr S. Keene
Assistant Director and Head of Public Affairs Division, C. M. Pemberton
Head of Corporate Relations, F. Kirk
Head of Commercial Development, M. Sullivan
Head of Marketing and Communications, H. Roderick
Head of Wellcome Wing Commercial and Access, B. Jones
Assistant Director, Wellcome Wing Project Director and Head of Science Communication Division, Prof. J. R. Durant
Head of Education and Programmes, Dr R. Jackson
Head of Exhibition and Wellcome Wing Content, Dr G. Farmelo
Head of Design, T. Molloy
Head of National Railway Museum, A. Scott
Head of National Museum of Photography, Film and Television, Ms A. Nevill

VICTORIA AND ALBERT MUSEUM

Cromwell Road, London SW7 2RL
Tel 0171-938 8500

The Victoria and Albert Museum is the national museum of fine and applied art and design. It descends directly from the Museum of Manufactures, which opened in Marlborough House in 1852 after the Great Exhibition of 1851. The Museum was moved in 1857 to become part of the South Kensington Museum. It was renamed the Victoria and Albert Museum in 1899. It also houses the National Art Library and Print Room.

The Museum administers three branch museums: the National Museum of Childhood in Bethnal Green, the Theatre Museum in Covent Garden, and the Wellington Museum at Apsley House. The museum in Bethnal Green was opened in 1872 and the building is the most important surviving example of the type of glass and iron construction used by Paxton for the Great Exhibition. Total government grant-in-aid for 1998–9 is £29.127 million.

BOARD OF TRUSTEES

Chairman, vacant
Deputy Chairman, J. Scott, CBE, FSA
Members, Miss N. Campbell; Penelope, Viscountess Cobham; Lady Copisarow; R. Fitch, CBE; Prof. C. Frayling, PH.D.; Sir Terence Heiser, GCB; Mrs A. Heseltine; A. Irby III; A. Snow; Prof. J. Steer, FSA, DLitt.; A. Wheatley; Prof. C. White, CVO, FBA
Secretary to the Board of Trustees, P. A. Wilson

OFFICERS

Director, Dr A. C. N. Borg, CBE, FSA
Assistant Directors, T. J. Stevens (*Collections*); J. W. Close (*Administration*)
Head of Buildings and Estate, R. P. Whitehouse
Chief Curator, Ceramics and Glass, Dr O. Watson
Head of Conservation, Dr J. Ashley-Smith
Head of Education, D. Anderson
Chief Curator, Far Eastern, Miss R. Kerr
Head of Finance and Central Services, Miss R. M. Sykes
Chief Curator, Furniture and Woodwork, C. Wilk
Chief Curator, Indian and South-East Asian, Dr D. Swallow
Head of Information Systems Services, A. Cooper
Head of Major Projects, Mrs G. F. Miles

Chief Curator, Metalwork, Silver and Jewellery,
Mrs P. Glanville
Chief Librarian, National Art Library, J. F. van den Wateren
Head of Personnel, Mrs G. Henchley
Chief Curator, Prints, Drawings and Paintings,
Miss S. B. Lambert
Head of Public Services, R. Cole-Hamilton
Head of Records and Collections Services, A. Seal
Head of Research, P. Greenhalgh
Head of Safety and Security, R. Bland
Chief Curator, Sculpture, Dr P. E. D. Williamson
Chief Curator, Textiles and Dress, Mrs V. D. Mendes
Managing Director, V. and A. Enterprises Ltd, M. Cass
Director of Development, Ms C. Morley
Head of National Museum of Childhood (acting), Dr S.
Laurence
Head of Theatre Museum, Miss M. Benton
Head of Wellington Museum, Miss A. Robinson

MUSEUM OF LONDON
London Wall, London EC2Y 5HN
Tel 0171-600 3699; fax 0171-600 1058

The Museum of London illustrates the history of London
from prehistoric times to the present day. It opened in 1976
and is based on the amalgamation of the former Guildhall
Museum and London Museum. The Museum is controlled by a Board of Governors, appointed (nine each) by
the Government and the Corporation of London. The
Museum is currently funded jointly by the Department for
Culture, Media and Sport and the Corporation of London,
each contributing £4.210 million in 1998–9.
Chairman of Board of Governors, P. Revell-Smith, CBE
Director, Dr S. Thurley

COMMONWEALTH INSTITUTE
Kensington High Street, London W8 6NQ
Tel 0171-603 4535; fax 0171-602 7374

The Commonwealth Institute is the UK centre responsible for promoting the Commonwealth in Britain through
exhibitions, educational programmes, publications, resources and information. The Institute houses an Education Centre, a Commonwealth Resource Centre (CRC)
and Literature Library, and a Conference and Events
Centre.
  The Institute is an independent statutory body funded
by the British government with contributions from other
Commonwealth governments. It is controlled by a board of
governors which includes the high commissioners of all
Commonwealth countries represented in London. Total
government grant-in-aid for 1998–9 is £600,000.
Director-General, D. French
Administrative and Commercial Director, P. Kennedy
Head of CRC, Ms K. Peters

IMPERIAL WAR MUSEUM
Lambeth Road, London SE1 6HZ
Tel 0171-416 5000; fax 0171-416 5374

The Museum, founded in 1917, illustrates and records all
aspects of the two world wars and other military operations
involving Britain and the Commonwealth since 1914. It
was opened in its present home, formerly Bethlem
Hospital or Bedlam, in 1936. The Museum also administers HMS *Belfast* in the Pool of London, Duxford Airfield
near Cambridge and the Cabinet War Rooms in Westminster.
  Total government grant-in-aid for 1998–9 is £10.573
million.

NATIONAL MARITIME MUSEUM
Greenwich, London SE10 9NF
Tel 0181-858 4422; fax 0181-312 6632

Established by Act of Parliament in 1934, the National
Maritime Museum illustrates the maritime history of
Great Britain in the widest sense, underlining the importance of the sea and its influence on the nation's power,
wealth, culture, technology and institutions. The Museum
is in three groups of buildings in Greenwich Park – the
main building, the Queen's House (built by Inigo Jones,
1616–35) and the Old Royal Observatory (including
Wren's Flamsteed House). Total government grant-in-
aid for 1998–9 is £10.184 million.
Director, R. L. Ormond

NATIONAL ARMY MUSEUM
Royal Hospital Road, London SW3 4HT
Tel 0171-730 0717; fax 0171-823 6573

The National Army Museum covers the history of five
centuries of the British Army. It was established by royal
charter in 1960. Total government grant-in-aid for
1998–9 is £3.2 million.
Director, I. G. Robertson
Assistant Directors, D. K. Smurthwaite; A. J. Guy;
Maj. P. R. Bateman

ROYAL AIR FORCE MUSEUM
Grahame Park Way, London NW9 5LL
Tel 0181-205 2266; fax 0181-200 1751

Situated on the former airfield at RAF Hendon, the
Museum illustrates the development of aviation from
before the Wright brothers to the present-day RAF. Total
government grant-in-aid for 1998–9, including funding
for the aerospace museum at Cosford, is £4.86 million.
Director, Dr M. A. Fopp
Assistant Directors, H. Hall; J. Hutchinson; A. Wright
Senior Keeper, P. Elliott

NATIONAL MUSEUMS AND GALLERIES
ON MERSEYSIDE
PO Box 33, 127 Dale Street, Liverpool L69 3LA
Tel 0151-207 0001; fax 0151-478 4190

The Board of Trustees of the National Museums and
Galleries on Merseyside is responsible for the Liverpool
Museum, the Merseyside Maritime Museum (incorporat-
ing HM Customs and Excise National Museum), the
Museum of Liverpool Life, the Lady Lever Art Gallery,

326   Government Departments and Public Offices

the Walker Art Gallery and Sudley House, and the Conservation Centre. Total government grant-in-aid for 1998–9 is £12.696 million.
Chairman of the Board of Trustees, D. McDonnell
Director, R. Foster
Keeper of Art Galleries, J. Treuherz
Keeper of Conservation, A. Durham
Keeper, Liverpool Museum, Ms L. Knowles
Keeper, Merseyside Maritime Museum and Museum of Liverpool Life, M. Stammers

NATIONAL MUSEUMS AND GALLERIES OF WALES/AMGUEDDFEYDD AC ORIELAU CENEDLAETHOL CYMRU
Cathays Park, Cardiff CF1 3NP
Tel 01222-573500; fax 01222-577010

The National Museums and Galleries of Wales comprise the National Museum and Gallery, the Museum of Welsh Life, the Roman Legionary Museum, Turner House Art Gallery, the Welsh Slate Museum, the Segontium Roman Museum and the Museum of the Welsh Woollen Industry. Total funding from the Welsh Office for 1998–9 is £12.427 million.
President, M. C. T. Prichard, CBE
Vice-President, A. Thomas

OFFICERS
Director, C. Ford, CBE
Assistant Directors, T. Arnold (*Resource Management*); C. Thomas (*Public Services*); A. Southall (*Museums Development*); I. Fell (*Education and Interpretation*); Dr E. Williams (*Collections and Research*)
Keeper of Geology, M. G. Bassett, PH. D.
Keeper of Bio-diversity and Systematic Diversity, Dr P. G. Oliver
Keeper of Art, D. Alston
Keeper of Archaeology, R. Brewer
Keeper, Museum of Welsh Life, J. Williams-Davies
Officer in Charge, Roman Legionary Museum (*acting*), D. Dollery
Keeper in Charge, Turner House Art Gallery, D. Alston
Keeper in Charge, Welsh Slate Museum, D. Roberts, PH.D.
Officer in Charge, Segontium Roman Museum, R. J. Brewer
Officer in Charge, Museum of the Welsh Woollen Industry, J. Williams-Davies

NATIONAL MUSEUMS OF SCOTLAND
Chambers Street, Edinburgh EH1 1JF
Tel 0131-225 7534; fax 0131-220 4819

The National Museums of Scotland comprise the Royal Museum of Scotland, the Scottish United Services Museum, the Scottish Agricultural Museum, the Museum of Flight, Shambellie House Museum of Costume and (from 1 December 1998) the Museum of Scotland. Total funding from the Scottish Office for 1998–9 is £16.9 million.

BOARD OF TRUSTEES
Chairman, R. Smith, FSA SCOT.
Members, Countess of Dalkeith; Prof. T. Devine; Dr L. Glasser, MBE, FRSE; S. G. Gordon, CBE; Sir Alistair Grant, FRSE; Dr V. van Heyingen, FRSE; G. Johnston, OBE, TD; Prof. P. H. Jones; Prof. A. Manning, OBE; Prof. J. Murray; Sir William Purves, CBE, DSO; Dr A. Ritchie, OBE; The Countess of Rosebery; Sir John Thomson

OFFICERS
Director, M. Jones, FSA, FSA SCOT., FRSA
Depute Director (Resources) and Project Director, Museum of Scotland, I. Hooper, FSA SCOT.

Depute Director (Collections) and Keeper of History and Applied Art, Miss D. Idiens, FRSA, FSA SCOT.
Development Director, C. McCallum
Keeper of Archaeology, D. V. Clarke, PH. D., FSA, FSA SCOT.
Keeper of Geology and Zoology, M. Shaw, D.PHIL.
Keeper of Social and Technological History, G. Sprott
Head of Public Affairs, Ms M. Bryden
Head of Museum Services, S. R. Elson, FSA SCOT.
Head of Administration, A. G. Young
Campaign Director, Museum of Scotland, S. Brock, PH.D., FRSA
Keeper, Scottish United Services Museum, S. C. Wood
Curator, Scottish Agricultural Museum, G. Sprott
Curator, Museum of Flight, A. Smith
Keeper, Shambellie House Museum of Costume, Miss N. Tarrant

NATIONAL AUDIT OFFICE
157–197 Buckingham Palace Road, London SW1W 9SP
Tel 0171-798 7000; fax 0171-828 3774
22 Melville Street, Edinburgh EH3 7NS
Tel 0131-244 2736; fax 0131-244 2721
Audit House, 23–24 Park Place, Cardiff CF1 3BA
Tel 01222-378661; fax 01222-388415

The National Audit Office came into existence under the National Audit Act 1983 to replace and continue the work of the former Exchequer and Audit Department. The Act reinforced the Office's total financial and operational independence from the Government and brought its head, the Comptroller and Auditor-General, into a closer relationship with Parliament as an officer of the House of Commons.

The National Audit Office provides independent information, advice and assurance to Parliament and the public about all aspects of the financial operations of government departments and many other bodies receiving public funds. It does this by examining and certifying the accounts of these organizations and by regularly publishing reports to Parliament on the results of its value for money investigations of the economy, efficiency and effectiveness with which public resources have been used. The National Audit Office is also the auditor by agreement of the accounts of certain international and other organizations. In addition, the Office authorizes the issue of public funds to government departments.
Comptroller and Auditor-General, Sir John Bourn, KCB
  Private Secretary, F. Grogan
Deputy Comptroller and Auditor-General, R. N. Le Marechal, CB
Assistant Auditors-General, T. Burr; J. A. Higgins; L. H. Hughes, CB; J. Marshall; Miss C. Mawhood; M. C. Pfleger
Directors, Mrs C. Allen; Miss J. Angus; J. Ashcroft; Ms G. Body; A. Burchell; P. Cannon; J. Cavanagh; D. Clarke; J. Colman; M. Daynes; S. Doughty; R. Eales; A. Fiander; R. Frith; N. Gale; Mrs A. Hands; K. Hawkeswell; J. Jones; J. Jones; Ms W. Kenway-Smith; Mrs P. Leahy; J. McEwen; R. Maggs; G. Miller; R. Parker; B. Payne; J. Pearce; Ms M. Radford; J. Rickleton; M. Reeves; A. Roberts; J. Robertson; M. Sinclair; B. Skeen; N. Sloan; Mrs P. Smith; I. Summers; R. Swan; Miss J. Wheeler; M. Whitehouse; D. Woodward; P. Woodward

NATIONAL CONSUMER COUNCIL
20 Grosvenor Gardens, London SW1W 0DH
Tel 0171-730 3469; fax 0171-730 0191

The National Consumer Council was set up by the Government in 1975 to give an independent voice to consumers in the UK. Its job is to advocate the consumer interest to decision-makers in national and local government, industry and regulatory bodies, business and the professions. It does this through a combination of research and campaigning. It is largely funded by grant-in-aid from the Department of Trade and Industry.
Chairman, D. Hatch, CBE
Vice-Chairman, Mrs D. Hutton, CBE
Director, Ms R. Evans

NATIONAL CRIMINAL INTELLIGENCE SERVICE
— *see* Police section

NATIONAL DEBT OFFICE
— *see* National Investment and Loans Office

NATIONAL ENDOWMENT FOR SCIENCE, TECHNOLOGY AND THE ARTS
Department of Culture, Media and Sport, 2–4 Cockspur Street, London SW1Y 5DH
Tel 0171-211 2850; fax 0171-211 2875

The National Endowment for Science, Technology and the Arts (NESTA) was established under the National Lottery Act 1998 with a £200 million endowment from the proceeds of the National Lottery. Its aims are to help talented individuals; to enable innovative ideas to be successfully commercially exploited; and to promote public knowledge of science, technology and the arts.
Chairman, The Lord Puttnam, CBE
Trustees, Dame Bridget Ogilvie, DBE; Prof. Sir Martin Rees, FRS; Dr C. Evans, OBE; Ms C. Vorderman; D. Wardell; F. Matarasso; C. Gillinson; Ms G. McIntosh; Ms C. McKeever; Ms J. Kirkpatrick
Chief Executive (acting), J. Newton

NATIONAL HERITAGE MEMORIAL FUND
7 Holbein Place, London SW1W 0NR
Tel 0171-591 6000; fax 0171-591 6001

The National Heritage Memorial Fund is an independent body established in 1980 as a memorial to those who have died for the UK. The Fund is empowered by the National Heritage Act 1980 to give financial assistance towards the cost of acquiring, maintaining or preserving land, buildings, works of art and other objects of outstanding interest which are also of importance to the national heritage. The Fund is administered by 13 trustees who are appointed by the Prime Minister.

The National Lottery Act 1993 designated the Fund as distributor of the heritage share of proceeds from the National Lottery. As a result, the Fund now operates two funds: the Heritage Memorial Fund and the Heritage Lottery Fund. The Heritage Memorial Fund receives an annual grant from the Department for Culture, Media and Sport (£2 million in 1998–9).

Chairman, Dr E. Anderson
Trustees, R. Boas; Sir Richard Carew Pole, Bt.; W. L. Evans; Sir Alistair Grant; Mrs C. Hubbard; J. Keegan; Ms P. Lankester; Prof. P. J. Newbould; Ms S. Palmer; Mrs C. Porteous; Ms M. A. Sieghart; Dame Sue Tinson, DBE
Director, Ms A. Case

NATIONAL INSURANCE JOINT AUTHORITY
The Adelphi, 1–11 John Adam Street, London WC2N 6HT
Tel 0171-962 8523; fax 0171-962 8647

The Authority's function is to co-ordinate the operation of social security legislation in Great Britain and Northern Ireland, including the necessary financial adjustments between the two National Insurance Funds.
Members, The Secretary of State for Social Security; the Head of the Department of Health and Social Services for Northern Ireland
Secretary, M. Driver

NATIONAL INVESTMENT AND LOANS OFFICE
1 King Charles Street, London SW1A 2AP
Tel 0171-270 3861; fax 0171-270 3860

The National Investment and Loans Office is a non-ministerial government department which was set up in 1980 by the merger of the National Debt Office and the Public Works Loan Board. The Office provides the staff and administrative support for the National Debt Commissioners, the Public Works Loan Commissioners and the Office of HM Paymaster-General. The National Debt Office is responsible for managing the investment portfolios of certain public funds and the management of some residual operations relating to the national debt. The function of the Public Works Loan Board is to make loans from the National Loans Fund to local authorities and certain other statutory bodies, primarily for capital purposes.

The Office of HM Paymaster-General has continuously existed in its present form since 1836; the Paymaster-General has responsibilities assigned from time to time by the Prime Minister and is currently a Treasury minister. The Assistant Paymaster-General is responsible for the banking and financial information services provided to the Government and public sector bodies by the Office of HM Paymaster-General.
Director, I. H. Peattie
Establishment Officer, A. G. Ladd

NATIONAL DEBT OFFICE
Comptroller-General, I. H. Peattie

PUBLIC WORKS LOAN BOARD
Chairman, A. D. Loehnis, CMG
Deputy Chairman, Miss V. J. Di Palma, OBE
Other Commissioners, L. B. Woodhall; Dame Sheila Masters, DBE; Mrs R. V. Hale; R. Burton; J. A. Parkes, CBE; J. Andrews; B. Tanner, CBE; T. Fellowes; Mrs R. Terry
Secretary, I. H. Peattie
Assistant Secretary, Miss L. M. Ashcroft

OFFICE OF HM PAYMASTER-GENERAL
Paymaster-General, Geoffrey Robinson, MP
Assistant Paymaster-General, I. H. Peattie

Deputy Paymaster-General, L. Palmer
BANKING OPERATIONS, National Investment and Loans
Office, Sutherland House, Russell Way, Crawley, W.
Sussex RH10 1UH. *Banking Manager*, P. Harris

OFFICE OF THE NATIONAL LOTTERY
2 Monck Street, London SW1P 2BQ
Tel 0171-227 2000; fax 0171-227 2005

The Office of the National Lottery (OFLOT) was
established as a non-ministerial government department
under the National Lottery Act 1993 and is headed by the
Director-General of the National Lottery. The Director-
General regulates the National Lottery operations and
licenses games promoted as part of the Lottery. The
Director-General will be replaced by a five-member
National Lottery Commission in spring 1999.
Director-General, J. Stoker
Deputy Director-General, K. Jones

For details of National Lottery operations, *see* National
Lottery section

NATIONAL LOTTERY CHARITIES BOARD
St Vincent House, 16 Suffolk Street, London SW1Y 4NL
Tel 0171-747 5299; fax 0171-747 5347

The Board is the independent body set up under the
National Lottery Act 1993 to distribute funds from the
Lottery to support charitable, benevolent and philan-
thropic organizations. The chairman and members are
appointed by the Secretary of State for Culture, Media and
Sport. The Board's main aim is to help meet the needs of
those at greatest disadvantage in society and to improve the
quality of life in the community through grants pro-
grammes in the UK and an international grants programme
for UK-based agencies working abroad.
Chairman, The Hon. D. Sieff
Deputy Chairman, Sir Adam Ridley
Members, Mrs T. Baring; A. Bhatia, OBE; S. Burkeman; Mrs
J. Churchman, OBE; Mrs A. Clark; I. Clarke; Ms S.
Clarke, CBE; Ms P. de Lima; Ms K. Hampton; A.
Higgins, OBE; T. Jones, OBE; Ms A. Jordan; Ms
J. Kaufmann, OBE; W. B. Kirkpatrick, OBE; Mrs B.
Lowndes; Ms M. McWilliams; W. G. Morrison, CBE; W.
Osborne; R. Partington; J. Simpson, OBE; N. Stewart,
OBE; Prof. Sir Eric Stroud, FRCP; Mrs E. Watkins
Chief Executive, T. Hornsby

NATIONAL PHYSICAL LABORATORY
Queens Road, Teddington, Middx TW11 0LW
Tel 0181-977 3222; fax 0181-943 6458

The Laboratory is the UK's national standards laboratory.
It develops, maintains and disseminates national measurement standards for physical quantities such as mass, length,
time, temperature, voltage, force and pressure. It also
conducts underpinning research on engineering materials
and information technology and disseminates good measurement practice. It is government-owned but contrac-
tor-operated.
Managing Director, Dr J. Rae
Director of Marketing and Communications, D. C. Richardson

NATIONAL RADIOLOGICAL PROTECTION BOARD
Chilton, Didcot, Oxon OX11 0RQ
Tel 01235-831600; fax 01235-833891

The National Radiological Protection Board is an independent statutory body created by the Radiological
Protection Act 1970. It is the national point of authoritative
reference on radiological protection for both ionizing and
non-ionizing radiations, and has issued recommendations
on limiting human exposure to electromagnetic fields and
radiation from a range of sources, including X-rays, the
Sun and power generators. Its sponsoring department is the
Department of Health.
Chairman, vacant
Director, Prof. R. H. Clarke

NATIONAL SAVINGS
Charles House, 375 Kensington High Street, London
W14 8SD
Tel 0171-605 9300; fax 0171-605 9438

National Savings was established as a government depart-
ment in 1969. It became an executive agency of the
Treasury in July 1996 and is responsible for the adminis-
tration of a wide range of schemes for personal savers. The
Government is currently considering bids for outsourcing
to a private company most of the work undertaken by
National Savings.
Chief Executive, P. Bareau
Deputy Chief Executive and Contracting Director, K. Chivers
Operational Services Director, D. H. Monaghan
Personnel Director, D. S. Speedie
Finance Director, V. Raimondo
Commercial Director, C. Moxey
Funding Director, M. Corcoran

For details of schemes, *see* National Savings section

OFFICE FOR NATIONAL STATISTICS
1 Drummond Gate, London SW1V 2QQ
Tel 0171-533 6363; fax 0171-533 5719

The Office for National Statistics was created in April 1996
by the merger of the Central Statistical Office and the
Office of Population, Censuses and Surveys. It is an
executive agency of the Treasury and is responsible for
preparing and interpreting key economic statistics for
government policy; collecting and publishing business
statistics; publishing annual and monthly statistical digests;
providing researchers, analysts and other customers with a
statistical service; administration of the marriage laws and
local registration of births, marriages and deaths in
England and Wales; provision of population estimates and
projections and statistics on health and other demographic
matters in England and Wales; population censuses in
England and Wales; surveys for government departments
and public bodies; and promoting these functions within
the UK, the European Union and internationally to
provide a statistical service to meet European Union and
international requirements.
    The Office for National Statistics is also responsible for
establishing and maintaining a central database of key

economic and social statistics produced to common classifications, definitions and standards.
Chief Executive, Prof. T. Holt
Directors (G3), J. Calder (*Survey and Statistical Services*); J. Fox (*Census, Population and Health*); J. Kidgell (*Macro-Economic Statistics*); D. Roberts (*Administration and Registration*); M. Pepper (*Business Statistics*); (*acting*) J. Pullinger (*Socio-Economic Statistics*)
Principal Establishment Officer (G5), E. Williams
Principal Finance Officer (G5), P. Murphy
Head of Information (G6), I. Scott
Parliamentary Clerk, L. Land

FAMILY RECORDS CENTRE, 1 Myddelton Street, London ECIR IUW. Tel: 0181-392 5300. Open Mon., Wed., Fri. 9 a.m.-5 p.m.; Tues. 10 a.m.-7 p.m.; Thurs. 9 a.m.-7 p.m.; Sat. 9.30 a.m.-5 p.m.

JOINT NATURE CONSERVATION COMMITTEE
Monkstone House, City Road, Peterborough PEI IJY
Tel 01733-562626; fax 01733-555948

The Committee was established under the Environmental Protection Act 1990. It advises the Government and others on UK and international nature conservation issues and disseminates knowledge on these subjects. It establishes common standards for the monitoring of nature conservation and research, and provides guidance to English Nature, Scottish Natural Heritage, the Countryside Council for Wales and the Department of the Environment for Northern Ireland.
Chairman, Sir Angus Stirling
Chief Officer, vacant
Director, Dr M. A. Vincent

NEW OPPORTUNITIES FUND
Dacre House, Dacre Street, London SWIH ODH
Tel 0171-222 3084; fax 0171-222 3085

The New Opportunities Fund was established under the National Lottery Act 1998 and is responsible for distributing funds allocated from the proceeds of the National Lottery to health, education and environment projects within initiatives determined by the Government.
Chair of the Board, The Baroness Pitkeathley
Members of the Board, Ms J. Barrow; Prof. E. Bolton; Ms N. Clarke; Ms M. Letts; Prof. A. Patmore, CBE; D. Mackie; D. Campbell; Ms J. Hutt
Chief Executive (acting), S. Dunmore

NOLAN COMMITTEE (FORMER)
— *see* Committee on Standards in Public Life, page 345

NORTHERN IRELAND AUDIT OFFICE
106 University Street, Belfast BT7 IEU
Tel 01232-251000; fax 01232-251106

The primary aim of the Northern Ireland Audit Office is to provide independent assurance, information and advice to Parliament on the proper accounting for Northern Ireland departmental and certain other public expenditure, revenue, assets and liabilities; on regularity and propriety; and

on the economy, efficiency and effectiveness of the use of resources.
Comptroller and Auditor-General for Northern Ireland, J. M. Dowdall

NORTHERN IRELAND OFFICE
11 Millbank, London SWIP 4QE
Tel 0171-210 3000
Parliament Buildings, Stormont, Belfast BT4 3SS
Tel 01232-520700; fax 01232-528478
Web: http://www.nics.gov.uk/centgov/nio/nio.htm

The Northern Ireland Office was established in 1972, when the Northern Ireland (Temporary Provisions) Act transferred the legislative and executive powers of the Northern Ireland Parliament and Government to the UK Parliament and a Secretary of State.
The Northern Ireland Office is responsible primarily for security issues, law and order and prisons, and for matters relating to the political and constitutional future of the province. It also deals with international issues as they affect Northern Ireland, including the Anglo-Irish Agreement. The Northern Ireland departments are responsible for the administration of social, industrial and economic policies.
The names of most civil servants are not listed for security reasons.
Secretary of State for Northern Ireland, The Rt. Hon. Dr Marjorie (Mo) Mowlam, MP
  Special Advisers, N. Warner; Ms A. Healy
  Parliamentary Private Secretaries, H. Jackson, MP; S. Timms, MP
Minister of State, Paul Murphy, MP (*Political Development, Finance, Personnel, Information*)
  Parliamentary Private Secretary, M. Gapes, MP
Minister of State, Adam Ingram, MP (*Security, Criminal Justice, Economic Development*)
  Parliamentary Private Secretary, T. Colman, MP
Parliamentary Under-Secretaries of State, The Lord Dubs (*Environment, Agriculture*); John McFall, MP (*Education, Training and Employment, Health, Community Relations*)
Permanent Under-Secretary of State (SCS), J. Pilling, CB
Second Permanent Under-Secretary of State, Head of the Northern Ireland Civil Service, J. Semple, CB

LONDON
SCS, (Political Director)
SCS, (Associate Political Director); (International and Planning); (Constitutional and Political); (Rights and European); (Personnel and Office Services)
SCS, (Director of Information Services)

BELFAST
SCS, (Political Director)
SCS, (Associate Political Director); (Security); (Criminal Justice); (Political); (Personnel and Finance)

NORTHERN IRELAND INFORMATION SERVICE
Parliament Buildings, Stormont, Belfast BT4 3ST
Tel 01232-520700

Director of Communications

EXECUTIVE AGENCIES
COMPENSATION AGENCY, Royston House, Upper Queen Street, Belfast BTI 6FD. Tel: 01232-2499444
FORENSIC SCIENCE AGENCY, Seapark, 151 Belfast Road, Carrickfergus, Co. Antrim BT38 8PL. Tel: 01232-365744
NORTHERN IRELAND PRISON SERVICE, *see* page 382

DEPARTMENT OF AGRICULTURE FOR NORTHERN IRELAND
Dundonald House, Upper Newtownards Road, Belfast BT4 3SB
Tel 01232-520100; fax 01232-525015

Parliamentary Under-Secretary of State, The Lord Dubs
Permanent Secretary (SCS)
Under-Secretaries (SCS), (Central Services and Rural Development); (Food, Farm and Environmental Policy); (Veterinary); (Science); (Agri-Food Development)

EXECUTIVE AGENCIES

INTERVENTION BOARD
— *see* pages 315–16
RIVERS AGENCY, 4 Hospital Road, Belfast BT8 8JP. Tel: 01232-253355

DEPARTMENT OF ECONOMIC DEVELOPMENT NORTHERN IRELAND
Netherleigh, Massey Avenue, Belfast BT4 2JP
Tel 01232-529900; fax 01232-529550

Minister of State, Adam Ingram, MP
Permanent Secretary (SCS)
Under-Secretaries (SCS), (Resources Group); (Regulatory Services Group)

INDUSTRIAL DEVELOPMENT BOARD, IDB House, 64 Chichester Street, Belfast BT1 4JX. Tel: 01232-233233

EXECUTIVE AGENCIES

INDUSTRIAL RESEARCH AND TECHNOLOGY UNIT, 17 Antrim Road, Lisburn BT28 3AL. Tel: 01846-623000
TRAINING AND EMPLOYMENT AGENCY (NORTHERN IRELAND), Adelaide Street, Belfast BT2 8FD. Tel: 01232-257777

DEPARTMENT OF EDUCATION FOR NORTHERN IRELAND
Rathgael House, Balloo Road, Bangor, Co. Down BT19 7PR
Tel 01247-279279; fax 01247-279100

Parliamentary Under-Secretary of State, John McFall, MP
Permanent Secretary (SCS)
Deputy Secretaries (SCS), (Schools); (Finance and Corporate Services)
Chief Inspector (SCS), (Education and Training Inspectorate)

DEPARTMENT OF THE ENVIRONMENT FOR NORTHERN IRELAND
Clarence Court, 10–18 Adelaide Street, Belfast BT2 8GB
Tel 01232-540540

Parliamentary Under-Secretary of State, The Lord Dubs
Permanent Secretary (SCS)
Under-Secretaries (SCS), (Personnel, Finance, Housing and Local Government); (Rural and Urban Affairs); (Roads, Water and Transport); (Planning, Works and Environment)

EXECUTIVE AGENCIES

CONSTRUCTION SERVICE, Churchill House, Victoria Square, Belfast BT1 4QW. Tel: 01232-250284
DRIVER AND VEHICLE LICENSING AGENCY (NORTHERN IRELAND), County Hall, Castlerock Road, Coleraine, Co. Londonderry BT51 3HS. Tel: 01265-41200
DRIVER AND VEHICLE TESTING AGENCY (NORTHERN IRELAND), Balmoral Road, Belfast BT12 6QL. Tel: 01232-681831

ENVIRONMENT AND HERITAGE SERVICE, Commonwealth House, Castle Street, Belfast BT1 1GU. Tel: 01232-251477
LAND REGISTERS OF NORTHERN IRELAND, Lincoln Building, 27–45 Great Victoria Street, Belfast BT2 7SL. Tel: 01232-251515
ORDNANCE SURVEY OF NORTHERN IRELAND, Colby House, Stranmillis Court, Belfast BT9 5BJ. Tel: 01232-255755
PLANNING SERVICE, Clarence Court, 10–18 Adelaide Street, Belfast BT2 8GB. Tel: 01232-540540
PUBLIC RECORD OFFICE (NORTHERN IRELAND) – *see* page 337
RATE COLLECTION AGENCY (NORTHERN IRELAND), Oxford House, 49–55 Chichester Street, Belfast BT1 4HH. Tel: 01232-252252
ROADS SERVICE, Clarence Court, 10–18 Adelaide Street, Belfast BT2 8GB. Tel: 01232-540540
WATER SERVICE, Northland House, 3 Frederick Street, Belfast BT1 2NR. Tel: 01232-244711

ADVISORY BODIES

HISTORIC BUILDINGS COUNCIL FOR NORTHERN IRELAND, c/o Environment and Heritage Service, Historic Monuments and Buildings, Commonwealth House, Castle Street, Belfast BT1 1GU. Tel: 01232-251477
COUNCIL FOR NATURE CONSERVATION AND THE COUNTRYSIDE, c/o Environment and Heritage Service, Commonwealth House, Castle Street, Belfast BT1 1GU. Tel: 01232-251477

DEPARTMENT OF FINANCE AND PERSONNEL
Parliament Buildings, Stormont, Belfast BT4 3SG
Tel 01232-520400

Minister of State, Paul Murphy, MP
Permanent Secretary (SCS)
Under-Secretaries (SCS), (Supply Group); (Resources Control and Professional Services Group); (Central Personnel Group); (Government Purchasing Service)

NORTHERN IRELAND CIVIL SERVICE (NICS)
Parliament Buildings, Stormont, Belfast BT4 3TT
Tel 01232-520700

Head of Civil Service (SCS), J. Semple, CB
Under-Secretaries (SCS), (Central Secretariat); (Legal Services); (Office of the Legislative Council)

GENERAL REGISTER OFFICE (NORTHERN IRELAND), Oxford House, 49–65 Chichester Street, Belfast BT1 4HL. Tel: 01232-252000. *Registrar-General* (G6)

EXECUTIVE AGENCIES

BUSINESS DEVELOPMENT SERVICE, Craigantlet Buildings, Stoney Road, Belfast BT4 3SX. Tel: 01232-520400
GOVERNMENT PURCHASING AGENCY, Rosepark House, Upper Newtownards Road, Belfast BT4 3NR. Tel: 01232-520400
NORTHERN IRELAND STATISTICS AND RESEARCH AGENCY, The Arches Centre, 11–13 Bloomfield Avenue, Belfast BT5 5HD. Tel: 01232-526093
VALUATION AND LANDS AGENCY, Queen's Court, 56–66 Upper Queen Street, Belfast BT4 6FD. Tel: 01232-250700

DEPARTMENT OF HEALTH AND SOCIAL SERVICES NORTHERN IRELAND
Castle Buildings, Stormont, Belfast BT4 3PP
Tel 01232-520000; fax 01232-520572

Parliamentary Under-Secretary of State, John McFall, MP
Permanent Secretary (*SCS*)
Chief Medical Officer (*SCS*)
Under-Secretaries (*SCS*), (Health and Social Services Executive); (Health and Social Policy); (Medical and Allied Services); (Central Management and Social Security Policy Group)

HEALTH AND SOCIAL SERVICES BOARDS
— *see* page 480

EXECUTIVE AGENCIES

NORTHERN IRELAND CHILD SUPPORT AGENCY, Great Northern Tower, 17 Great Victoria Street, Belfast BT2 7AD. Tel: 01232-339000
NORTHERN IRELAND HEALTH AND SOCIAL SERVICES ESTATES AGENCY, Stoney Road, Dundonald, Belfast BT16 1US. Tel: 01232-520025
NORTHERN IRELAND SOCIAL SECURITY AGENCY, Castle Buildings, Stormont, Belfast BT4 3SJ. Tel: 01232-520520

OCCUPATIONAL PENSIONS REGULATORY AUTHORITY
Invicta House, Trafalgar Place, Brighton BN1 4DW
Tel 01273-627600; fax 01273-627688

The Occupational Pensions Regulatory Authority (OPRA) was set up under the Pensions Act 1995 and became fully operational on 6 April 1997. It is the independent, statutory regulator of occupational pension schemes in the UK.
Chairman, J. Hayes, CBE
Chief Executive, Ms C. Johnston

OMBUDSMEN
— *see* Local Commissioners *and* Parliamentary Commissioner. For non-statutory Ombudsmen, *see* Index

ORDNANCE SURVEY
Romsey Road, Maybush, Southampton SO16 4GU
Tel 01703-792000; fax 01703-792452

Ordnance Survey is the national mapping agency for Britain. It is a government department funded by parliamentary vote, and reports to the Secretary of State for the Environment, Transport and the Regions.
Director-General and Chief Executive, Prof. D. Rhind

PARADES COMMISSION
12th Floor, Windsor House, 6–12 Bedford Street, Belfast BT2 7EL
Tel 01232-895900; fax 01232-322988

The Parades Commission was set up under the Public Processions (Northern Ireland) Act 1998. Its function is to encourage and facilitate local accommodation on contentious parades; where this is not possible, the Commission is empowered to make legal determinations about such parades, which may include imposing conditions on aspects of the notified parade.

The chairman and members are appointed by the Secretary of State for Northern Ireland; the membership must, as far as is practicable, be representative of the community in Northern Ireland.
Chairman, A. Graham
Members, D. Hewitt, CBE; Mrs R. A. McCormick; A. Canavan; F. Guckian, CBE; W. Martin; Dr Barbara Erwin
Secretary (*G5*), R. Buchanan

OFFICE OF THE PARLIAMENTARY COMMISSIONER FOR ADMINISTRATION AND HEALTH SERVICE COMMISSIONER
Millbank Tower, Millbank, London SW1P 4QP
Parliamentary Commissioner: Tel 0171-217 4163; fax 0171-276 4160; *Health Service Commissioner:* Tel 0171-217 4051; fax 0171-217 4000

The Parliamentary Commissioner for Administration (the Parliamentary Ombudsman) is independent of Government and is an officer of Parliament. He is responsible for investigating complaints referred to him by MPs from members of the public who claim to have sustained injustice in consequence of maladministration by or on behalf of government departments and certain non-departmental public bodies. Certain types of action by government departments or bodies are excluded from investigation. The Parliamentary Commissioner is also responsible for investigating complaints, referred by MPs, alleging that access to official information has been wrongly refused under the Code of Practice on Access to Government Information 1994.

The Health Service Commissioners (the Health Service Ombudsmen) for England, for Scotland and for Wales are responsible for investigating complaints against National Health Service authorities and trusts that are not dealt with by those authorities to the satisfaction of the complainant. Complaints can be referred direct by the member of the public who claims to have sustained injustice or hardship in consequence of the failure in a service provided by a relevant body, failure of that body to provide a service or in consequence of any other action by that body. The Ombudsmens' jurisdiction now covers complaints about family doctors, dentists, pharmacists and opticians, and complaints about actions resulting from clinical judgment. The Health Service Ombudsmen are also responsible for investigating complaints that information has been wrongly refused under the Code of Practice on Openness in the National Health Service 1995. The three offices are presently held by the Parliamentary Commissioner.
Parliamentary Commissioner and Health Service Commissioner (*G1*), M. S. Buckley
Deputy Parliamentary Commissioners (*G3*), J. E. Avery, CB; J. Tate
Deputy Health Service Commissioner (*G3*), Miss M. I. Nisbet
Directors, Parliamentary Commissioner (*G5*), N. Cleary; D. J. Coffey; Mrs S. P. Maunsell; G. Monk; A. Watson
Directors, Health Service Commissioners (*G5*), Miss H. Bainbridge; N. J. Jordan; D. R. G. Pinchin; R. Tyrrell
Finance and Establishment Officer (*G5*), T. G. Hull

PARLIAMENTARY COMMISSIONER FOR STANDARDS
House of Commons, London SW1A OAA
Tel 0171-219 0320

Following recommendations of the Committee on Standards in Public Life (the Nolan Committee) the House of Commons agreed to the appointment of an independent Parliamentary Commissioner for Standards with effect from November 1995. The Commissioner has responsibility for maintaining and monitoring the operation of the Register of Members' Interests; advising Members of Parliament and the select committee on standards and privileges, on the interpretation of the rules on disclosure and advocacy, and on other questions of propriety; and receiving and, if he thinks fit, investigating complaints about the conduct of MPs.
Parliamentary Commissioner for Standards, Sir Gordon
   Downey, KCB (*until November 1998*)

PARLIAMENTARY COUNSEL
36 Whitehall, London SW1A 2AY
Tel 0171-210 6637; fax 0171-210 6632

Parliamentary Counsel draft all government bills (i.e. primary legislation) except those relating exclusively to Scotland, the latter being drafted by the Lord Advocate's Department. They also advise on all aspects of parliamentary procedure in connection with such bills and draft government amendments to them as well as any motions (including financial resolutions) necessary to secure their introduction into, and passage through, Parliament.
First Counsel (SCS), J. C. Jenkins, CB, QC
Counsel (SCS), D. W. Saunders, CB; E. G. Caldwell, CB;
   E. G. Bowman, CB; G. B. Sellers, CB; E. R. Sutherland, CB;
   P. F. A. Knowles, CB; S. C. Laws, CB; R. S. Parker, CB;
   Miss C. E. Johnston; P. J. Davies

PARLIAMENTARY OMBUDSMAN FOR NORTHERN IRELAND AND NORTHERN IRELAND COMMISSIONER FOR COMPLAINTS
Progressive House, 33 Wellington Place, Belfast BT1 6HN
Tel 01232-233821; fax 01232-234912

The Ombudsman is appointed under legislation with powers to investigate complaints by people claiming to have sustained injustice in consequence of maladministration arising from action taken by a Northern Ireland government department, or any other public body within his remit. Staff are presently seconded from the Northern Ireland Civil Service.
Ombudsman, G. Burns, MBE
Deputy Ombudsman, J. MacQuarrie
Directors, C. O'Hare; R. Doherty; H. Mallon

PAROLE BOARD FOR ENGLAND AND WALES
Abell House, John Islip Street, London SW1P 4LH
Tel 0171-217 5314; 0171-217 5793

The Board was constituted under the Criminal Justice Act 1967 and continued under the Criminal Justice Act 1991. It is an executive non-departmental public body and its duty is to advise the Home Secretary with respect to matters referred to it by him which are connected with the early release or recall of prisoners. Its functions include giving directions concerning the release on licence of prisoners serving discretionary life sentences and of certain prisoners serving long-term determinate sentences.
Chairman, Ms U. Prashar, CBE
Vice-Chairman, The Hon. Mr Justice Tucker
Chief Executive, M. S. Todd

PAROLE BOARD FOR SCOTLAND
Saughton House, Broomhouse Drive, Edinburgh EH11 3XD
Tel 0131-244 8755; fax 0131-244 6974

The Board directs and advises the Secretary of State for Scotland on the release of prisoners on licence, and related matters.
Chairman, I. McNee
Vice-Chairmen, Sheriff G. Shiach; Ms J. Freeman
Secretary, H. P. Boyle

PASSENGER RAIL FRANCHISING, OFFICE OF
— see Transport section

PATENT OFFICE
Cardiff Road, Newport NP9 1RH
Tel 0645-500505; fax 01633-814444

The Patent Office is an executive agency of the Department of Trade and Industry. The duties of the Patent Office are to administer the Patent Acts, the Registered Designs Act and the Trade Marks Act, and to deal with questions relating to the Copyright, Designs and Patents Act 1988. The Search and Advisory Service carries out commercial searches through patent information. In 1996 the Office granted 7,132 patents and registered 9,293 designs and 29,196 trade marks.
Comptroller-General, P. R. S. Hartnack
Director, Intellectual Property Policy Directorate, G. Jenkins
Director, Patents and Designs, R. J. Marchant
Director and Assistant Registrar of Trade Marks, P. Lawrence
*Director, Administration and Resources and Secretary to the
   Patent Office,* C. Octon
Director, Copyright, J. Startup
Director, Finance, J. Thompson

HM PAYMASTER-GENERAL
— see National Investment and Loans Office

PENSIONS COMPENSATION BOARD
5th Floor, 11 Belgrave Road, London SW1V 1RB
Tel 0171-828 9794; fax 0171-931 7239

The Pensions Compensation Board was established under the Pensions Act 1995 and is funded by a levy paid by all eligible occupational pension schemes. Its function is to compensate occupational pension schemes for losses due to dishonesty where the employer is solvent.
Chairman, Dr J. T. Farrand, QC
Secretary, M. Lydon

OFFICE OF THE PENSIONS OMBUDSMAN
6th Floor, 11 Belgrave Road, London SW1V 1RB
Tel 0171-834 9144; fax 0171-821 0065

The Pensions Ombudsman is appointed under the Pension Schemes Act 1993 as amended by the Pensions Act 1995. He investigates and decides complaints and disputes concerning occupational pension schemes. Complaints concerning personal pensions would normally be dealt with only if outside the jurisdiction of the Personal Investment Authority. The Ombudsman is completely independent and there is no charge for bringing a complaint or dispute to him.
Pensions Ombudsman, Dr J. T. Farrand, QC

POLICE COMPLAINTS AUTHORITY
10 Great George Street, London SW1P 3AE
Tel 0171-273 6450; fax 0171-273 6401

The Police Complaints Authority was established under the Police and Criminal Evidence Act 1984 to provide an independent system for dealing with serious complaints by members of the public against police officers in England and Wales. It is funded by the Home Office. The authority has powers to supervise the investigation of certain categories of serious complaints and certain statutory functions in relation to the disciplinary aspects of complaints. It does not deal with police operational matters; these are usually dealt with by the Chief Constable of the relevant force.
Chairman, P. Moorhouse
Deputy Chairman, J. Cartwright
Members, Mrs L. Allan; I. Bynoe; Ms J. Dobry; J. Elliott; M. Meacher; Miss M. Mian; Mrs C. Mitchell; A. Potts; Mrs M. Scorer; Ms L. Whyte; A. Williams

INDEPENDENT COMMISSION FOR POLICE COMPLAINTS FOR NORTHERN IRELAND
— *see* page 312

POLITICAL HONOURS SCRUTINY COMMITTEE
Cabinet Office, Ashley House, 2 Monck Street, London SW1P 2BQ
Tel 0171-276 2770; fax 0171-276 2766

The function of the Political Honours Scrutiny Committee (a committee of Privy Councillors) was set out in an Order in Council in 1991 and amended by Orders in Council in 1994, 1997 and 1998. The Prime Minister submits certain particulars to the Committee about persons proposed to be recommended for honour for their political services. The Committee, after such enquiry as they think fit, report to the Prime Minister whether, so far as they believe, the persons whose names are submitted to them are fit and proper persons to be recommended.
Chairman, The Lord Pym, MC, PC
Members, The Lord Thomson of Monifieth, KT, PC; The Baroness Dean of Thornton-le-Fylde, PC
Secretary, A. J. Merifield, CB

PORT OF LONDON AUTHORITY
Devon House, 58 – 60 St Katharine's Way, London E1 9LB
Tel 0171-265 2656; fax 0171-265 2699

The Port of London Authority is a public trust constituted under the Port of London Act 1908 and subsequent legislation. It is the governing body for the Port of London, covering the tidal portion of the River Thames from Teddington to the seaward limit. The Board comprises a chairman and up to seven but not less than four non-executive members appointed by the Secretary of State for the Environment, Transport and the Regions, and up to four but not less than one executive members appointed by the Board.
Chairman, Sir Brian Shaw
Vice-Chairman, J. H. Kelly, CBE
Chief Executive, D. Jeffery
Secretary, G. E. Ennals

THE POST OFFICE
148 Old Street, London EC1V 9HQ
Tel 0171-490 2888

Crown services for the carriage of government dispatches were set up in about 1516. The conveyance of public correspondence began in 1635 and the mail service was made a parliamentary responsibility with the setting up of a Post Office in 1657. Telegraphs came under Post Office control in 1870 and the Post Office Telephone Service began in 1880. The National Girobank service of the Post Office began in 1968. The Post Office ceased to be a government department in 1969 when responsibility for the running of the postal, telecommunications, giro and remittance services was transferred to a public authority called The Post Office. The 1981 British Telecommunications Act separated the functions of the Post Office, making it solely responsible for postal services and Girobank. Girobank was privatized in 1990. The Government is conducting a review of the Post Office with a view to greater involvement of the private sector in its operations; the results of the review are expected in autumn 1998.

The chairman, chief executive and members of the Post Office Board are appointed by the Secretary of State for Trade and Industry but responsibility for the running of the Post Office as a whole rests with the Board in its corporate capacity.

334   Government Departments and Public Offices

FINANCIAL RESULTS £m	1996–7	1997–8
Post Office Group		
Turnover	6,370	6,759
Profit before tax	577	651
Royal Mail		
Turnover	5,019	5,411
Profit before tax	463	496
Parcelforce		
Turnover	457	465
Profit (loss) before tax	(21)	(14)
Post Office Counters		
Turnover	1,161	1,130
Profit before tax	34	33

POST OFFICE BOARD
Chairman, Dr N. Bain
Chief Executive, J. Roberts, CBE
Members, R. Close (*Managing Director, Finance*); J. Cope (*Managing Director, Strategy and Personnel*)
Secretary, R. Adams

For postal services, *see* pages 515–17

PRIME MINISTER'S OFFICE
— *see* page 288

PRISONS OMBUDSMAN FOR ENGLAND AND WALES
Ashley House, 2 Monck Street, London SW1P 2BQ
Tel 0171-276 2876; fax 0171-276 2860

The post of Prisons Ombudsman was instituted in 1994. The Ombudsman is appointed by the Home Secretary and is an independent point of appeal for prisoners' grievances about their lives in prison, including disciplinary issues. The Ombudsman cannot investigate grievances relating to issues which are the subject of litigation or criminal proceedings, decisions taken by ministers, or actions of bodies outside the prison service.
Prisons Ombudsman, Sir Peter Woodhead, KCB

For Scotland, *see* Scottish Prisons Complaints Commission

PRIVY COUNCIL OFFICE
Whitehall, London SW1A 2AT
Tel 0171-270 0472; fax 0171-270 0109

The Office is responsible for the arrangements leading to the making of all royal proclamations and Orders in Council; for certain formalities connected with ministerial changes; for considering applications for the granting (or amendment) of royal charters; for the scrutiny and approval of by-laws and statutes of chartered bodies; and for the appointment of high sheriffs and many Crown and Privy Council appointments to governing bodies.
President of the Council (and Leader of the House of Commons), The Rt. Hon. Margaret Beckett, MP
Private Secretary, Ms V. A. Scarborough
Clerk of the Council (G3), N. H. Nicholls, CBE
Deputy Clerk of the Council (G5), R. P. Bulling
Senior Clerks, Miss M. A. McCullagh; Mrs P. J. Birleson
Registrar, J. A. C. Watherston

CENTRAL DRUGS CO-ORDINATION UNIT
Government Offices, Great George Street, London SW1P 3AL
Tel 0171-270 5776; fax 0171-270 5857
UK Anti-Drugs Co-ordinator, K. Hellawell
Deputy Anti-Drugs Co-ordinator, M. Trace
Director of Unit, Ms L. Rogerson

PROCURATOR FISCAL SERVICE
— *see* pages 366–7

PUBLIC HEALTH LABORATORY SERVICE
61 Colindale Avenue, London NW9 5DF
Tel 0181-200 1295; fax 0181-200 8130

The Public Health Laboratory Service comprises nine groups of laboratories, the Central Public Health Laboratory and the Communicable Disease Surveillance Centre. The PHLS provides diagnostic microbiological services to hospitals, and has reference facilities that are available nationally. It collates information on the incidence of infection, and when necessary it institutes special inquiries into outbreaks and the epidemiology of infectious disease. It also undertakes bacteriological surveillance of the quality of food and water for local authorities and others.
Chairman (£15,125), Prof. Sir Leslie Turnberg, MD
Deputy Chairman, R. Tabor
Director, Dr Diana Walford, FRCP, FRCPath.
Deputy Directors, Prof. B. I. Duerden, MD, FRCPath. (*Programmes*); K. M. Saunders (*Corporate Planning and Resources*)
Board Secretary, K. M. Saunders

CENTRAL PUBLIC HEALTH LABORATORY
Colindale Avenue, London NW9 5HT
Director, Prof. S. P. Borriello

COMMUNICABLE DISEASES SURVEILLANCE CENTRE
Colindale Avenue, NW9 5EQ
Director, Dr C. L. R. Bartlett

PHLS GROUPS OF LABORATORIES AND GROUP DIRECTORS
East, Dr P. M. B. White
Midlands, Dr R. E. Warren
North, Dr N. F. Lightfoot
North-West, Dr P. Morgan-Capner
South-West, Dr K. A. V. Cartwright
Thames, Dr R. Gross
Trent, Dr P. J. Wilkinson
Wessex, Dr S. A. Rousseau
Wales, Dr A. J. Howard

OTHER SPECIAL LABORATORIES AND UNITS
ANAEROBE REFERENCE UNIT, Public Health Laboratory, Cardiff. *Head,* Prof. B. I. Duerden, MD, FRCPath.
ANTIVIRAL SUSCEPTIBILITY REFERENCE UNIT, Public Health Laboratory, Birmingham. *Head,* Dr D. P. Pillay
CRYPTOSPRORIDIUM REFERENCE UNIT, Public Health Laboratory, Rhyl. *Head,* Dr D. Casemore
FOOD MICROBIOLOGY RESEARCH UNIT, Public Health Laboratory, Exeter. *Head,* Prof. T. J. Humphrey
GENITO-URINARY INFECTIONS REFERENCE LABORATORY, Public Health Laboratory, Bristol. *Head,* Dr A. J. Herring
LEPTOSPIRA REFERENCE LABORATORY, Public Health Laboratory, Hereford. *Director,* Dr T. J. Coleman
LYME DISEASE REFERENCE UNIT, Public Health Laboratory, Southampton. *Head,* Dr S. O'Connell

MALARIA REFERENCE LABORATORY, London School of Hygiene and Tropical Medicine, London WC1E 7HT. *Directors,* Prof. D. J. Bradley, DM; Dr D. C. Warhurst, FRCPath.

MENINGOCOCCAL REFERENCE LABORATORY, Public Health Laboratory, Manchester. *Director,* Dr B. A. Oppenheim

MYCOBACTERIUM REFERENCE UNIT, Public Health Laboratory, Dulwich, London. *Director,* Dr F. Drobniewski

MYCOLOGY REFERENCE LABORATORY, Public Health Laboratory, Bristol. *Head,* Dr D. Warnock; University of Leeds. *Head,* Prof. E. G. V. Evans

PARASITOLOGY REFERENCE LABORATORY, Hospital for Tropical Diseases, London. *Director,* Dr P. L. Chiodini

TOXOPLASMA REFERENCE LABORATORY, Public Health Laboratory, Swansea. *Head,* D. H. M. Joynson

WATER AND ENVIRONMENTAL MICROBIOLOGY RESEARCH UNIT, Public Health Laboratory, Nottingham. *Head,* Dr J. V. Lee

---

REGISTRAR OF PUBLIC LENDING RIGHT
Bayheath House, Prince Regent Street, Stockton-on-Tees TS18 1DF
Tel 01642-604699; fax 01642-615641

Under the Public Lending Right system, in operation since 1983, payment is made from public funds to authors whose books are lent out from public libraries. Payment is made once a year and the amount each author receives is proportionate to the number of times (established from a sample) that each registered book has been lent out during the previous year. The Registrar of PLR, who is appointed by the Secretary of State for Culture, Media and Sport, compiles the register of authors and books. Only living authors resident in the UK or Germany are eligible to apply. (The term 'author' covers writers, illustrators, translators, and some editors/compilers.)

A payment of 2.07 pence was made in 1997–8 for each estimated loan of a registered book, up to a top limit of £6,000 for the books of any one registered author; the money for loans above this level is used to augment the remaining PLR payments. In February 1998, the sum of £4.251 million was made available for distribution to 17,512 registered authors and assignees as the annual payment of PLR.

Registrar, Dr J. G. Parker
Chairman of Advisory Committee, M. Holroyd

PUBLIC RECORD OFFICE
— *see* page 336

PUBLIC TRUST OFFICE
Stewart House, 24 Kingsway, London WC2B 6JX
Tel 0171-664 7000; fax 0171-664 7705
COURT FUNDS OFFICE, 22 Kingsway, London WC2B 6LE
Tel 0171-936 6000

The Public Trust Office became an executive agency of the Lord Chancellor's Department in 1994. The chief executive of the agency holds the statutory titles of Public Trustee and Accountant-General of the Supreme Court.

The Public Trustee is a trust corporation created to undertake the business of executorship and trusteeship; she can act as executor or administrator of the estate of a deceased person, or as trustee of a will or settlement. The Public Trustee is also responsible for the performance of all the administrative, but not the judicial, tasks required of the Court of Protection under Part VII of the Mental Health Act 1983, relating to the management and administration of the property and affairs of persons suffering from mental disorder. The Public Trustee also acts as Receiver when so directed by the Court, usually where there is no other person willing or able so to act.

The Accountant-General of the Supreme Court, through the Court Funds Office, is responsible for the investment and accounting of funds in court for persons under a disability, monies in court subject to litigation and statutory deposits.

Chief Executive (Public Trustee and Accountant-General), Ms J. C. Lomas
Assistant Public Trustee, Mrs S. Hutcheson
Investment Manager, H. Stevenson
Chief Property Adviser, A. Nightingale

MENTAL HEALTH SECTOR
Director of Mental Health, Mrs H. M. Bratton
Principal of Receivership Division, D. Adams
Principal of Protection Division, P. L. Hales

TRUSTS AND FUNDS SECTOR
Director of Trusts and Funds, F. J. Eddy
Divisional Manager, Court Funds Office, P. MacDermott
Divisional Manager, Trust Division, M. Munt
Finance Officer, M. Guntrip

PLANNING AND PAY POLICY
Head of Human Resources and Planning, Mrs N. M. Hunt

PUBLIC WORKS LOAN BOARD
— *see* National Investment and Loans Office

COMMISSION FOR RACIAL EQUALITY
Elliot House, 10–12 Allington Street, London SW1E 5EH
Tel 0171-828 7022; fax 0171-630 7605

The Commission was established in 1977, under the Race Relations Act 1976, to work towards the elimination of discrimination and promote equality of opportunity and good relations between different racial groups. It is funded by the Home Office.

Chairman, Sir Herman Ouseley
Deputy Chairman, H. Harris
Commissioners, R. Purkiss; Dr R. Chandran; M. Hastings; Dr M. Jogee; Ms J. Mellor; Mrs B. Cluff; Dame Simone Prendergast, DBE; M. Amran; S. Malik; C. Moraes; Ms C. Short; Dr J. Singh; R. Singh
Executive Director, D. Sharma

THE RADIO AUTHORITY
Holbrook House, 14 Great Queen Street, London WC2B 5DG
Tel 0171-430 2724; fax 0171-405 7062

The Radio Authority was established in 1991 under the Broadcasting Act 1990. It is the regulator and licensing authority for all independent radio services. Members of the Authority are appointed by the Secretary of State for Culture, Media and Sport; senior executive staff are appointed by the Authority.

Chairman, Sir Peter Gibbings
Deputy Chairman, M. Moriarty, CB
Members, M. Reupke; Lady Sheil; A. Reid; Mrs H. Tennant

Chief Executive, A. Stoller
Deputy Chief Executive, D. Vick
Secretary to the Authority and Head of Legal Affairs, Ms E. Salomon

---

OFFICE OF THE RAIL REGULATOR
1 Waterhouse Square, 138–142 Holborn, London
ECIN 2ST
Tel 0171-282 2000; fax 0171-282 2040

The Office of the Rail Regulator was set up under the Railways Act 1993. It is headed by the Rail Regulator, who is independent of ministerial control. The Regulator's main functions are the licensing of operators of railway assets; the approval of agreements for access by those operators to track, stations and light maintenance depots; the enforcement of domestic competition law; and consumer protection. The Regulator also sponsors a network of Rail Users' Consultative Committees, which represent the interests of passengers.

The Government announced in July 1998 that the consumer protection function of the Rail Regulator would be taken over by a new Strategic Rail Authority.
Rail Regulator, J. A. Swift, QC
Director, Economic Regulation Group, C. W. Bolt
Director, Railway Network Group, C. J. F. Brown
Director, Passenger Services Group, J. A. Rhodes
Chief Legal Adviser, M. R. Brocklehurst
Director, Resources and RUCC Sponsorship, P. D. Murphy
Director, Communications, K. R. Webb

RECORD OFFICES

ADVISORY COUNCIL ON PUBLIC RECORDS
Secretariat: Public Record Office, Kew, Richmond, Surrey
TW9 4DU
Tel 0181-876 3444 ext. 2351; fax 0181-392 5295

Council members are appointed by the Lord Chancellor, under the Public Records Act 1958, to advise him on matters concerning public records in general and, in particular, on those aspects of the work of the Public Record Office which affect members of the public who make use of it.
Chairman, The Master of the Rolls
Secretary, T. R. Padfield

THE PUBLIC RECORD OFFICE
Kew, Richmond, Surrey TW9 4DU
Tel 0181-876 3444; fax 0181-878 8905

The Public Record Office, originally established in 1838 under the Master of the Rolls, was placed under the direction of the Lord Chancellor in 1958; it became an executive agency in 1992. The Lord Chancellor appoints a Keeper of Public Records, whose duties are to co-ordinate and supervise the selection of records of government departments and the law courts for permanent preservation, to safeguard the records and to make them available to the public. There is a separate record office for Scotland, now called the National Archives of Scotland (*see* page 337).

The Office holds records of central government dating from the Domesday Book (1086) to the present. Under the Public Records Act 1967 they are normally open to inspection when 30 years old, and are then available,

without charge, in the reading rooms (Monday, Wednesday, Friday, Saturday, 9.30–5; Tuesday 10–7; Thursday 9.30–7).
Keeper of Public Records (G3), Mrs S. Tyacke, CB
Director, Public Services Division (G5), Dr E. Hallam Smith
Director, Government, Corporate and Information Services Division (G5), Dr D. Simpson

---

HOUSE OF LORDS RECORD OFFICE
House of Lords, London SW1A 0PW
Tel 0171-219 3074; fax 0171-219 2570

Since 1497, the records of Parliament have been kept within the Palace of Westminster. They are in the custody of the Clerk of the Parliaments. In 1946 a record department was established to supervise their preservation and their availability to the public. The search room of the office is open to the public Monday–Friday, 9.30–5 (Tuesday to 8, by appointment).

Some three million documents are preserved, including Acts of Parliament from 1497, journals of the House of Lords from 1510, minutes and committee proceedings from 1610, and papers laid before Parliament from 1531. Amongst the records are the Petition of Right, the Death Warrant of Charles I, the Declaration of Breda, and the Bill of Rights. The House of Lords Record Office also has charge of the journals of the House of Commons (from 1547), and other surviving records of the Commons (from 1572), including documents relating to private bill legislation from 1818. Among other documents are the records of the Lord Great Chamberlain, the political papers of certain members of the two Houses, and documents relating to Parliament acquired on behalf of the nation. A permanent exhibition was established in the Royal Gallery in 1979.
Clerk of the Records (£43,910–£70,430), D. J. Johnson, FSA
Deputy Clerk of the Records (£34,462–£55,915), S. K. Ellison
Assistant Clerk of the Records (£30,431–£46,108), D. L. Prior

---

ROYAL COMMISSION ON HISTORICAL MANUSCRIPTS
Quality House, Quality Court, Chancery Lane, London
WC2A 1HP
Tel 0171-242 1198; fax 0171-831 3550

The Commission was set up by royal warrant in 1869 to enquire and report on collections of papers of value for the study of history which were in private hands. In 1959 a new warrant enlarged these terms of reference to include all historical records, wherever situated, outside the Public Records and gave it added responsibilities as a central co-ordinating body to promote, assist and advise on their proper preservation and storage. The Commission is sponsored by the Department for Culture, Media and Sport.

The Commission also maintains the National Register of Archives (NRA), which contains over 41,000 unpublished lists and catalogues of manuscript collections describing the holdings of local record offices, national and university libraries, specialist repositories and others in the UK and overseas. The NRA can be searched using computerized indices which are available in the Commission's search room.

The Commission also administers the Manorial and Tithe Documents Rules on behalf of the Master of the Rolls.
Chairman, The Lord Bingham of Cornhill, PC

Commissioners, Sir Patrick Cormack, FSA, MP;
D. G. Vaisey, CBE, FSA; The Lord Egremont and
Leconfield; Sir Matthew Farrer, GCVO; Sir John Sainty,
KCB, FSA; Prof. R. H. Campbell, OBE, Ph.D.; Very Revd
H. E. C. Stapleton, FSA; Sir Keith Thomas, PBA; Mrs
C. M. Short; The Earl of Scarbrough; Mrs A. Dundas-
Bekker; G. E. Aylmer, D.Phil, FBA; Mrs S. J. Davies, Ph.D.;
Mrs A. Prochaska, Ph.D.; Prof. H. C. G. Matthew, D.Phil,
FBA
Secretary, C. J. Kitching, Ph.D., FSA

SCOTTISH RECORDS ADVISORY COUNCIL
HM General Register House, Edinburgh EH1 3YY
Tel 0131-535 1314; fax 0131-535 1360

The Council was established under the Public Records
(Scotland) Act 1937. Its members are appointed by the
Secretary of State for Scotland and it may submit proposals
or make representations to the Secretary of State, the Lord
Justice General or the Lord President of the Court of
Session on questions relating to the public records of
Scotland.
Chairman, Prof. Anne Crowther
Secretary, D. M. Abbott

NATIONAL ARCHIVES OF SCOTLAND
HM General Register House, Edinburgh EH1 3YY
Tel 0131-535 1314; fax 0131-535 1360

The history of the national archives of Scotland can be
traced back to the 13th century. The National Archives of
Scotland (formerly the Scottish Record Office) is an
executive agency of the Scottish Office and keeps the
administrative records of pre-Union Scotland, the registers of central and local courts of law, the public registers of
property rights and legal documents, and many collections
of local and church records and private archives. Certain
groups of records, mainly the modern records of government departments in Scotland, the Scottish railway
records, the plans collection, and private archives of an
industrial or commercial nature, are preserved in the
branch repository at the West Register House in Charlotte
Square. The search rooms in both buildings are open
Monday–Friday, 9–4.45. A permanent exhibition at the
West Register House and changing exhibitions at the
General Register House are open to the public on weekdays, 10–4. The National Register of Archives (Scotland)
is based in the West Register House.
Keeper of the Records of Scotland, P. M. Cadell
Deputy Keeper, Dr P. D. Anderson

PUBLIC RECORD OFFICE (NORTHERN
IRELAND)
66 Balmoral Avenue, Belfast BT9 6NY
Tel 01232-251318; fax 01232-255999

The Public Record Office (Northern Ireland) is responsible for identifying and preserving Northern Ireland's
archival heritage and making it available to the public. It is
an executive agency of the Department of the Environment for Northern Ireland. The search room is open on
weekdays, 9.15–4.15 (Thursday, 9.15–8.45).
Chief Executive, Dr A. P. W. Malcomson

CORPORATION OF LONDON RECORDS
OFFICE
Guildhall, London EC2P 2EJ
Tel 0171-332 1251; fax 0171-710 8682

The Corporation of London Records Office contains the
municipal archives of the City of London which are
regarded as the most complete collection of ancient

municipal records in existence. The collection includes
charters of William the Conqueror, Henry II, and later
kings and queens to 1957; ancient custumals: Liber Horn,
Dunthorne, Custumarum, Ordinacionum, Memoran-
dorum and Albus, Liber de Antiquis Legibus, and collections of statutes; continuous series of judicial rolls and
books from 1252 and Council minutes from 1275; records
of the Old Bailey and Guildhall sessions from 1603;
financial records from the 16th century; the records of
London Bridge from the 12th century; and numerous
subsidiary series and miscellanea of historical interest.
The Readers' Room is open Monday–Friday, 9.30–4.45.
Keeper of the City Records, The City Secretary
City Archivist, J. R. Sewell
Deputy City Archivist, Mrs J. M. Bankes

RESEARCH COUNCILS
— *see* pages 704–10

REVIEW BODIES

The secretariat for these bodies is provided by the Office of
Manpower Economics (*see* page 322)

ARMED FORCES PAY
The Review Body on Armed Forces Pay was appointed in
1971 to advise the Prime Minister on the pay and
allowances of members of naval, military and air forces of
the Crown and of any women's service administered by the
Defence Council.
Chairman, Sir Gordon Hourston
Members, Mrs K. Coleman, OBE; J. C. L. Cox, CBE;
J. Crosby; Vice-Adm. Sir Toby Frere, KCB; The Lord
Gladwin of Clee, CBE; Prof. D. Greenaway; Ms G.
Haskins

DOCTORS' AND DENTISTS'
REMUNERATION
The Review Body on Doctors' and Dentists' Remuner-
ation was set up in 1971 to advise the Prime Minister on the
remuneration of doctors and dentists taking any part in the
National Health Service.
Chairman, C. B. Gough
Members, Mrs M. Alderson; Prof. N. Bourne; Miss C. Hui;
R. Jackson; C. King, CBE; Prof. Sheila McLean;
D. Penton

NURSING STAFF, MIDWIVES, HEALTH
VISITORS AND PROFESSIONS ALLIED TO
MEDICINE
The Review Body for nursing staff, midwives, health
visitors and professions allied to medicine was set up in
1983 to advise the Prime Minister on the remuneration of
nursing staff, midwives and health visitors employed in the
National Health Service; and also of physiotherapists,
radiographers, remedial gymnasts, occupational thera-
pists, orthoptists, chiropodists, dietitians and related
grades employed in the National Health Service.
Chairman, Prof. C. Booth
Members, J. Bartlett; Mrs S. Gleig; Miss A. Mackie, OBE; M.
Malone-Lee, CB; K. Miles; C. Monks, OBE; Prof. G. Raab

SCHOOL TEACHERS
The School Teachers' Review Body (STRB) was set up
under the School Teachers' Pay and Conditions Act 1991.
It is required to examine and report on such matters
relating to the statutory conditions of employment of

school teachers in England and Wales as may be referred to it by the Secretary of State for Education and Employment.
Chairman, A. R. Vineall
Members, Mrs B. Amey; P. Gedling; M. Harding; V. Harris; Miss J. Langdon; C. Lyddon; Mrs P. Sloane

SENIOR SALARIES
The Senior Salaries Review Body (formerly the Top Salaries Review Body) was set up in 1971 to advise the Prime Minister on the remuneration of the judiciary, senior civil servants and senior officers of the armed forces. In 1993 its remit was extended to cover the pay, pensions and allowances of MPs, ministers and others whose pay is determined by a Ministerial and Other Salaries Order, and the allowances of peers.
Chairman, Sir Michael Perry, CBE
Members, The Hon. M. Beloff, QC; D. Clayman; Prof. S. Dawson; Mrs R. Day; Sir Terry Heiser, GCB; Sir Gordon Hourston; Sir Sydney Lipworth, QC; Miss P. Mann, OBE; M. Sheldon, CBE; Prof. Sir David Williams, QC

ROYAL BOTANIC GARDEN EDINBURGH
20A Inverleith Row, Edinburgh EH3 5LR
Tel 0131-552 7171; fax 0131-248 2901

The Royal Botanic Garden Edinburgh (RBGE) originated as the Physic Garden, established in 1670 beside the Palace of Holyroodhouse. The Garden moved to its present 28-hectare site at Inverleith, Edinburgh, in 1821. There are also three specialist gardens: Younger Botanic Garden Benmore, near Dunoon, Argyllshire; Logan Botanic Garden, near Stranraer, Wigtownshire; and Dawyck Botanic Garden, near Stobo, Peeblesshire. Since 1986, RBGE has been administered by a board of trustees established under the National Heritage (Scotland) Act 1985. It receives an annual grant from the Scottish Office.
RBGE is an international centre for scientific research on plant diversity and for education and conservation. It has an extensive library and a herbarium with over two million dried plant specimens. Public opening hours: Edinburgh site, daily (except Christmas Day and New Year's Day) November–January 9.30–4; February and October 9.30–5; March and September 9.30–6; April–August 9.30–7; specialist gardens, 1 March–31 October 9.30–6. Admission free to Edinburgh site; admission charge to specialist gardens.
Chairman of the Board of Trustees, Prof. M. Wilkins, FRSE
Regius Keeper, vacant

ROYAL BOTANIC GARDENS KEW
Richmond, Surrey TW9 3AB
Tel 0181-332 5000; fax 0181-332 5197
Wakehurst Place, Ardingly, nr Haywards Heath, W. Sussex RH17 6TN
Tel 01444-894066; fax 01444-894069

The Royal Botanic Gardens (RBG) Kew were originally laid out as a private garden for Kew House for George III's mother, Princess Augusta, in 1759. They were much enlarged in the 19th century, notably by the inclusion of the grounds of the former Richmond Lodge. In 1965 the garden at Wakehurst Place was acquired; it is owned by the National Trust and managed by RBG Kew. Under the National Heritage Act 1983 a board of trustees was set up to administer the gardens, which in 1984 became an

independent body supported by grant-in-aid from the Ministry of Agriculture, Fisheries and Food.
The functions of RBG Kew are to carry out research into plant sciences, to disseminate knowledge about plants and to provide the public with the opportunity to gain knowledge and enjoyment from the gardens' collections. There are extensive national reference collections of living and preserved plants and a comprehensive library and archive. The main emphasis is on plant conservation and bio-diversity.
The gardens are open daily (except Christmas Day and New Year's Day) from 9.30 a.m. (Wakehurst, 10 a.m.). The closing hour varies from 4 p.m. in mid-winter to 6 p.m. on weekdays and 7.30 p.m. on Sundays and Bank Holidays in mid-summer. Admission, 1997, £5.00; concessionary schemes available. Glasshouses (Kew only), 9.30–4.30 (winter); 9.30–5.30 (summer). No dogs except guide-dogs for the blind.

BOARD OF TRUSTEES
Chairman, The Viscount Blakenham
Members, The Earl of Selborne, KBE, FRS (*Queen's Trustee*); R. P. Bauman; Sir Jeffery Bowman; Prof. H. Dickinson; Miss A. Ford; S. de Grey; Lady Lennox-Boyd; Prof. M. Crawley; Prof. J. S. Parker; Prof. C. Payne, OBE; Miss M. Black
Director, Prof. Sir Ghillean Prance, FRS

ROYAL COMMISSION FOR THE EXHIBITION OF 1851
Sherfield Building, Imperial College of Science, Technology and Medicine, London SW7 2AZ
Tel 0171-594 8790; fax 0171-594 8794

The Royal Commission was incorporated by supplemental charter as a permanent commission after winding up the affairs of the Great Exhibition of 1851. Its object is to promote scientific and artistic education by means of funds derived from its Kensington estate, purchased with the surplus left over from the Great Exhibition.
President, HRH The Prince Philip, Duke of Edinburgh, KG, KT, PC
Chairman, Board of Management, Sir Denis Rooke, OM, CBE, FRS, FEng.
Secretary to Commissioners, J. P. W. Middleton, CB

THE ROYAL MINT
Llantrisant, Pontyclun CF72 8YT
Tel 01443-623000

The prime responsibility of the Royal Mint is the provision of United Kingdom coinage, but it actively competes in world markets for a share of the available circulating coin business and, based on the last ten years, two-thirds of the 18,000 tonnes of coins produced annually is exported. The Mint also manufactures special proof and uncirculated quality coins in gold, silver and other metals; military and civil decorations and medals; commemorative and prize medals; and royal and official seals.
The Royal Mint became an executive agency of the Treasury in 1990. The Government announced in June 1998 that it would require the Royal Mint to enter into partnerships with the private sector.
Master of the Mint, The Chancellor of the Exchequer (*ex officio*)
Deputy Master and Comptroller, R. de L. Holmes

ROYAL NATIONAL THEATRE BOARD
South Bank, London, SE1 9PX
Tel 0171-452 3333; fax 0171-452 3344

The chairman and members of the Board of the Royal National Theatre are appointed by the Secretary of State for Culture, Media and Sport.
Chairman, Sir Christopher Hogg
Members, Ms J. Bakewell; The Hon. P. Benson; Gabrielle Lady Greenbury; Sir David Hancock, KCB; G. Hutchings; Ms K. Jones; Ms S. MacGregor, OBE; Sir Ian McKellen; M. Oliver; Sir Tom Stoppard, CBE; P. Wiegand
Company Secretary, Mrs M. McGregor
Director, T. Nunn, CBE

RURAL DEVELOPMENT COMMISSION
141 Castle Street, Salisbury, Wilts. SP1 3TP
Tel 01722-336255; fax 01722-332769

The Rural Development Commission is the government agency for economic and social development in rural England. The Commission advises the Government and undertakes activities aimed at stimulating job creation and the provision of essential services in the countryside. Its sponsoring department is the Department of the Environment, Transport and the Regions. The Government announced in March 1998 that the Rural Development Commission would merge with the Countryside Commission in April 1999 and its rural regeneration work would be transferred to the new regional development agencies.
Chairman, M. Middleton, CBE
Chief Executive, J. Edwards

SCOTTISH COURTS ADMINISTRATION
— *see* page 365

SCOTTISH ENTERPRISE
120 Bothwell Street, Glasgow G2 7JP
Tel 0141-248 2700; fax 0141-221 3217

Scottish Enterprise was established in 1991 and its purpose is to create jobs and prosperity for the people of Scotland. It is funded largely by the Scottish Office and is responsible to the Secretary of State for Scotland. Working in partnership with the private and public sectors, Scottish Enterprise aims to further the development of Scotland's economy, to enhance the skills of the Scottish workforce and to promote Scotland's international competitiveness. Through Locate in Scotland (*see* page 341), Scottish Enterprise is also concerned with attracting firms to Scotland.
Chairman (£30,948), Sir Ian Wood, CBE
Chief Executive, C. Beveridge, CBE

SCOTTISH ENVIRONMENT PROTECTION AGENCY
Erskine Court, The Castle Business Park, Stirling FK9 4TR
Tel 01786-457700; fax 01786-446885

The Scottish Environment Protection Agency came into being on 1 April 1996 under the Environment Act 1995. It is responsible for pollution prevention and control in Scotland, and for the management and use of water resources. It has regional offices in East Kilbride, Riccarton and Dingwall, and 18 local offices throughout Scotland. It receives funding from the Scottish Office.

THE BOARD
Chairman, Prof. W. Turmeau, CBE
Members, A. Buchan; G. Gordon, OBE; D. Hughes Hallett, FRICS; A. Hewat, OBE; Prof. C. Johnston; C. McChord; Ms A. Magee; A. Paton; Ms J. Shaw

THE EXECUTIVE
Chief Executive, A. Paton
Director of Corporate Services, W. Halcrow
Director of Environmental Strategy, Ms P. Henton
Director, North Region, Prof. D. Mackay
Director, East Region (acting), Dr T. Leatherland
Director, West Region, J. Beveridge

SCOTTISH HOMES
Thistle House, 91 Haymarket Terrace, Edinburgh EH12 5HE
Tel 0131-313 0044; fax 0131-313 2680

Scottish Homes, the national housing agency for Scotland, aims to improve the quality and variety of housing available in Scotland by working in partnership with the public and private sectors. The agency is a major funder of new and improved housing provided by housing associations and private developers. It is currently transferring its own rented houses to alternative landlords. It is also involved in housing research. Board members are appointed by the Secretary of State for Scotland.
Chairman, J. Ward, CBE
Chief Executive, P. McKinlay, CBE

SCOTTISH NATURAL HERITAGE
12 Hope Terrace, Edinburgh EH9 2AS
Tel 0131-447 4784; fax 0131-446 2277

Scottish Natural Heritage was established in 1992 under the Natural Heritage (Scotland) Act 1991. It provides advice on nature conservation to all those whose activities affect wildlife, landforms and features of geological interest in Scotland, and seeks to develop and improve facilities for the enjoyment and understanding of the Scottish countryside. It is funded by the Scottish Office.
Chairman, M. Magnusson, KBE
Chief Executive, R. Crofts
Chief Scientific Adviser, M. B. Usher
Directors of Operations, J. Thomson (*West*); I. Jardine (*East*); J. Watson (*North*)
Director of Corporate Services, L. Montgomery

SCOTTISH OFFICE
*Dover House, Whitehall, London, SW1A 2AU
Tel 0171-270 3000; fax 0171-270 6730
St Andrew's House, Edinburgh EH1 3DG
Tel 0131-556 8400; fax 0131-244 8240
E-mail: ceu@isdoi.scotoff.gov.uk
Web: http://www.scotland.gov.uk

The Secretary of State for Scotland is responsible in Scotland for a wide range of statutory functions which in England and Wales are the responsibility of a number of departmental ministers. He also works closely with ministers in charge of Great Britain departments on topics of special significance to Scotland within their fields of responsibility. His statutory functions are administered by five main departments collectively known as the Scottish Office. The departments are: the Scottish Office Agriculture, Environment and Fisheries Department; the Scottish Office Development Department; the Scottish Office Education and Industry Department; the Scottish Office Department of Health; and the Scottish Office Home Department.

In addition there are a number of other Scottish departments for which the Secretary of State has some degree of responsibility; these include the Scottish Courts Administration, the General Register Office, the National Archives of Scotland (formerly the Scottish Record Office) and the Department of the Registers of Scotland. The Secretary of State also bears ministerial responsibility for the activities in Scotland of several statutory bodies, such as the Forestry Commission, whose functions extend throughout Great Britain.

The directly-elected Scottish Parliament which is to be established in 1999 will assume legislative powers in many of the areas of responsibility of the Scottish Office.

Secretary of State for Scotland, The Rt. Hon. Donald Dewar, MP
  Private Secretary (SCS), K. A. L. Thomson
  Special Advisers, M. Elder; Ms W. Alexander; D. Whitton
  Parliamentary Private Secretary, Ms A. McGuire, MP
Minister of State, Helen Liddell, MP (*Education, Women's Issues, the Co-ordination and Presentation of Policy*)
  Private Secretary, Miss S. Davidson
Minister of State, Henry McLeish, MP (*Home Affairs, Devolution, Local Government*)
  Private Secretary, M. Kellet
Parliamentary Under-Secretaries of State, Dr Calum MacDonald, MP (*Housing, Transport, European Affairs*); Sam Galbraith, MP (*Health, the Arts*); The Lord Sewel, CBE (*Agriculture, the Environment, Fisheries*); Gus Macdonald† (*Business and Industry*)
  Private Secretaries, G. Owenson; Ms R. Sunderland; Miss J. Campbell
Parliamentary Clerk, I. Campbell
Permanent Under-Secretary of State, A. M. Russell
  Private Secretary, Miss S. Morrell

† Not an MP; will receive a life peerage to enable him to sit in the House of Lords

*LIAISON DIVISION
Head of Division (SCS),* E. W. Ferguson

*MANAGEMENT GROUP SUPPORT STAFF
Head of Group,* M. Grant

PERSONNEL GROUP
16 Waterloo Place, Edinburgh EH1 3DN
Tel 0131-556 8400

Principal Establishment Officer (SCS), C. C. MacDonald
Head of Personnel (SCS), D. F. Middleton

FINANCE DIVISION
Victoria Quay, Edinburgh EH6 6QQ
Tel 0131-556 8400

Principal Finance Officer (SCS), Dr P. S. Collings
Assistant Secretaries (SCS), M. T. S. Batho; J. G. Henderson; D. G. N. Reid; W. T. Tait
Head of Accountancy Services Unit, I. M. Smith
Assistant Director of Finance Strategy, I. A. McLeod

SOLICITOR'S OFFICE
For the Scottish departments and certain UK services, including HM Treasury, in Scotland

Solicitor (SCS), R. Brodie, CB
Deputy Solicitor (SCS), R. M. Henderson

Divisional Solicitors (SCS), J. L. Jamieson, CBE; R. Bland (*seconded to Scottish Law Commission*); G. C. Duke; I. H. Harvie; H. F. Macdiarmid; J. G. S. Maclean; N. Raven; Mrs L. A. Towers

DIRECTORATE OF ADMINISTRATIVE SERVICES
Victoria Quay, Edinburgh EH6 6QQ
Tel 0131-556 8400

Director of Administrative Services (SCS), A. M. Brown
Chief Estates Officer, J. A. Andrew

Saughton House, Broomhouse Drive, Edinburgh EH11 3DX
Head of Information Technology (SCS), Ms M. McGinn
Director of Telecommunications, K. Henderson, OBE

James Craig Walk, Edinburgh EH1 3BA
Head of Purchasing and Supplies (SCS), N. Bowd

CONSTITUTION GROUP
Pentland House, 47 Robb's Loan, Edinburgh EH14 1TY
Tel 0131-556 8400

Head of Constitution Group (SCS), R. S. B. Gordon
Constitutional Policy (SCS), J. A. Ewing
Referendum and Implementation (SCS), P. E. Grice
Functions and Whitehall Negotiations (SCS), I. N. Walford
Legal Support to Constitution Group, J. L. Jamieson, CBE

SCOTTISH OFFICE INFORMATION DIRECTORATE
For the Scottish departments and certain UK services in Scotland

Director (SCS), R. Williams
Deputy Director, W. A. McNeill

SCOTTISH OFFICE AGRICULTURE, ENVIRONMENT AND FISHERIES DEPARTMENT
Pentland House, 47 Robb's Loan, Edinburgh EH14 1TY
Tel 0131-556 8400

Secretary (SCS), J. S. Graham
Under-Secretaries (SCS), T. A. Cameron (*Agriculture*); S. F. Hampson (*Environment*)
Fisheries Secretary (SCS), I. W. Gordon
Assistant Secretaries (SCS), I. R. Anderson; D. A. Brew; D. R. Dickson; Ms I. M. Low; A. J. Rushworth; Dr P. Rycroft; G. M. D. Thomson; I. M. Whitelaw; J. R. Wildgoose
Chief Agricultural Officer (SCS), W. A. Macgregor
Deputy Chief Agricultural Officer (SCS), J. I. Woodrow
Assistant Chief Agricultural Officers, J. Henderson; A. Robb; A. J. Robertson
Chief Agricultural Economist, D. J. Greig
Chief Food and Dairy Officer, S. D. Rooke
Principal Surveyor, vacant
Senior Principal Scientific Officers, Mrs L. A. D. Turl; Dr R. Waterhouse

FISHERIES RESEARCH SERVICES
Marine Laboratory, PO Box 101, Victoria Road, Torry, Aberdeen AB9 8DB
Tel 01224-876544

Director of Fisheries Research for Scotland (SCS), Prof. A. D. Hawkins, PH.D., FRSE
Deputy Director (SCS), J. Davies

Freshwater Fisheries Laboratory
Faskally, Pitlochry, Perthshire PH6 5LB
Tel 01796-472060

Senior Principal Scientific Officers, Dr R. M. Cook; Dr J. M. Davies; Dr A. E. Ellis; Dr A. L. S. Munro; R. G. J. Shelton; Dr P. A. Stewart; Dr C. S. Wardle
Inspector of Salmon and Freshwater Fisheries for Scotland, D. A. Dunkley

ENVIRONMENTAL AFFAIRS GROUP
Under-Secretary (SCS), S. F. Hampson
Assistant Secretaries (SCS), J. D. Calder; J. N. Randall; J. A.
  Rennie
Chief Water Engineer, P. Wright
Ecological Adviser, Dr J. Miles

EXECUTIVE AGENCIES

INTERVENTION BOARD
— *see* pages 315–16

SCOTTISH AGRICULTURAL SCIENCE AGENCY
East Craig, Edinburgh EH12 8NJ
Tel 0131-244 8890; fax 0131-244 8988

The Agency provides scientific information and advice on
agricultural and horticultural crops and the environment,
and has various statutory and regulatory functions.
Director, Dr R. K. M. Hay
Deputy Director, S. R. Cooper
Senior Principal Scientific Officer, W. J. Rennie

SCOTTISH FISHERIES PROTECTION AGENCY
Pentland House, 47 Robb's Loan, Edinburgh EH14 ITY
Tel 0131-556 8400; fax 0131-244 6086

The Agency enforces fisheries law and regulations in
Scottish waters and ports.
Chief Executive, Capt. P. Du Vivier, RN
Director of Corporate Strategy and Resources, J. B. Roddin
Director of Operational Enforcement, R. J. Walker
Marine Superintendent, Capt. W. A. Brown

SCOTTISH OFFICE DEVELOPMENT DEPARTMENT
Victoria Quay, Edinburgh EH6 6QQ
Tel 0131-556 8400

Secretary (SCS), K. MacKenzie
Under-Secretaries (SCS), D. J. Belfall; J. S. B. Martin
Assistant Secretaries (SCS), M. T. Affolter; A. M. Burnside;
  E. C. Davidson; J. D. Gallacher; R. A. Grant; D. S.
  Henderson; Mrs D. Mellon; W. J. R. McQueen; C.
  Smith; R. Tait
Senior Economic Adviser (SCS), C. L. Wood

PROFESSIONAL STAFF
*Director of Construction and Building Control Group and Chief
  Architect (SCS)*, J. E. Gibbons, PH.D., FSA SCOT.
*Deputy Director of Construction and Building Control Group and
  Deputy Chief Architect (SCS)*, Dr J. P. Cornish
*Deputy Director of Construction and Building Control Group and
  Chief Quantity Surveyor (SCS)*, A. J. Wyllie
Chief Planner (SCS), A. Mackenzie, CBE
Chief Statistician (SCS), C. R. MacLean

INQUIRY REPORTERS
Robert Stevenson House, 2 Greenside Lane, Edinburgh
EH1 3AG
Tel 0131-244 5680
Chief Reporter (SCS), R. M. Hickman
Deputy Chief Reporter (SCS), J. M. McCulloch

NATIONAL ROADS DIRECTORATE
Victoria Quay, Edinburgh EH6 6QQ
Tel 0131-556 8400
Director of Roads (SCS), J. Innes
Deputy Chief Engineers (SCS), J. A. Howison (*Roads*);
  N. B. MacKenzie (*Bridges*)

EXECUTIVE AGENCY

HISTORIC SCOTLAND
Longmore House, Salisbury Place, Edinburgh EH9 1SH
Tel 0131-668 8600; fax 0131-668 8699

The agency's role is to protect Scotland's historic monu-
ments, buildings and lands, and to promote public under-
standing and enjoyment of them.
Chief Executive (G3), G. N. Munro
Directors (G5), F. J. Lawrie; I. Maxwell; B. Naylor; B.
  O'Neil; L. Wilson
Chief Inspector of Ancient Monuments, Dr D. J. Breeze
Chief Inspector, Historic Buildings, J. R. Hume, OBE

SCOTTISH OFFICE EDUCATION AND INDUSTRY DEPARTMENT
Victoria Quay, Edinburgh EH6 6QQ
Tel 0131-556 8400

Secretary (SCS), G. R. Wilson, CB
Under-Secretaries (SCS), D. J. Crawley; E. J. Weeple
Assistant Secretaries (SCS), G. F. Dickson; A. W. Fraser; R.
  N. Irvine; J. W. L. Lonie; S. Y. MacDonald; A. K.
  MacLeod; Mrs R. Menlowe; Ms J. Morgan; C. M.
  Reeves; D. A. Stewart
Chief Statistician (SCS), C. R. MacLean

HM INSPECTORS OF SCHOOLS
Senior Chief Inspector (SCS), D. A. Osler
Depute Senior Chief Inspectors (SCS), F. Crawford;
  G. H. C. Donaldson
Chief Inspectors (SCS), P. Banks; J. Boyes; Miss
  K. M. Fairweather; D. E. Kelso; J. J. McDonald;
  A. S. McGlynn; H. M. Stalker
There are 79 Grade 6 Inspectors

INDUSTRIAL EXPANSION
Meridian Court, 5 Cadogan Street, Glasgow G2 6AT
Tel 0141-248 2855
Under-Secretary (SCS), G. Robson
Industrial Adviser, D. Blair
Scientific Adviser, Prof. D. J. Tedford
Assistant Secretaries (SCS), W. Malone; J. K. Mason; Dr J.
  Rigg

LOCATE IN SCOTLAND
120 Bothwell Street, Glasgow G2 7JP
Tel 0141-248 2700
Director (SCS), M. Togneri

SCOTTISH TRADE INTERNATIONAL
120 Bothwell Street, Glasgow G2 7JP
Tel 0141-248 2700
Director, D. Taylor

EXECUTIVE AGENCIES

STUDENT AWARDS AGENCY FOR SCOTLAND
Gyleview House, 3 Redheughs Rigg, Edinburgh EH12 9HH
Tel 0131-476 8212; fax 0131-244 5887
Chief Executive, K. MacRae

SCOTTISH OFFICE PENSIONS AGENCY
St Margaret's House, 151 London Road, Edinburgh
EH8 7TG
Tel 0131-556 8400; fax 0131-244 3334

The Agency is responsible for the pension arrangements of
some 300,000 people, mainly NHS and teaching services
employees and pensioners.
Chief Executive, R. Garden
Directors, G. Mowat (*Policy*); A. M. Small (*Operations*); M. J.
  McDermott (*Resources and Customer Services*)

SCOTTISH OFFICE DEPARTMENT OF HEALTH
St Andrew's House, Edinburgh EH1 3DG
Tel 0131-556 8400

NATIONAL HEALTH SERVICE IN SCOTLAND
MANAGEMENT EXECUTIVE
Chief Executive (SCS), G. R. Scaife
Director of Purchasing (SCS), Dr K. J. Woods
Director of Primary Care (SCS), Mrs A. Robson
Director of Finance (SCS), P. Brady
Director of Human Resources (SCS), G. Marr
Director of Nursing, Miss A. Jarvie
Medical Director (SCS), Dr A. B. Young, FRCPE
Director of Trusts (SCS), P. Wilson
Director of Information Services, NHS, C. B. Knox
Director of Estates, H. R. McCallum
Chief Pharmacist (SCS), W. Scott
Chief Scientist, Prof. G. R. D. Catto
Chief Dental Officer, T. R. Watkins

PUBLIC HEALTH POLICY UNIT
Head of Unit and Chief Medical Officer (SCS), Prof. Sir David
  Carter, FRCSE, FRCSGlas., FRCPE
Deputy Chief Medical Officer (SCS), Dr A. B. Young, FRCPE
Head of Group (SCS), Mrs N. Munro
Assistant Secretary (SCS), J. T. Brown
Principal Medical Officers, Dr J. B. Louden (*part-time*); Dr A.
  MacDonald (*part-time*); Dr R. Skinner; Dr E. Sowler
Senior Medical Officers, Dr Angela Anderson; Dr
  P. W. Brooks; Dr K. G. Brotherston; Dr D. Campbell; Dr
  D. Colin-Thome (*part-time*); Dr J. Cumming; Dr B.
  Davis; Dr D. J. Ewing; Dr G. R. Foster; Dr A. Keel; Dr
  Patricia Madden; Dr H. Whyte

STATE HOSPITAL
Carstairs Junction, Lanark ML11 8RP
Tel 01555-840293

Chairman, D. N. James
General Manager, R. Manson

COMMON SERVICES AGENCY
Trinity Park House, South Trinity Road, Edinburgh
EH5 3SE
Tel 0131-552 6255

Chairman, G. Scaife
General Manager, Dr F. Gibb

HEALTH BOARDS
— *see* pages 479–80

SCOTTISH OFFICE HOME DEPARTMENT
Saughton House, Broomhouse Drive, Edinburgh EH11 3XD
Tel 0131-556 8400

Secretary (SCS), J. Hamill, CB
Under-Secretaries (SCS), N. G. Campbell; D. Macniven, TD;
  Mrs G. M. Stewart
Assistant Secretaries (SCS), C. Baxter; Mrs M. H. Brannan;
  Mrs M. B. Gunn; R. S. T. MacEwen
Chief Research Officer, Dr C. P. A. Levein
Senior Principal Research Officer, Mrs A. Millar

SOCIAL WORK SERVICES GROUP
James Craig Walk, Edinburgh EH1 3BA
Tel 0131-556 8400

Under-Secretary (SCS), N. G. Campbell
Assistant Secretaries (SCS), G. A. Anderson; Dr J. M.
  Francis; G. A. McHugh; Mrs V. M. Macniven
Chief Inspector of Social Work Services, A. Skinner
Assistant Chief Inspectors, Mrs G. Ottley; D. Pia;
  I. C. Robertson

OTHER APPOINTMENTS
HM Chief Inspector of Constabulary, W. Taylor, QPM
HM Chief Inspector of Prisons, C. Fairweather, OBE
Commandant, Scottish Police College, H. I. Watson, OBE, QPM
HM Chief Inspector of Fire Services, N. Morrison, CBE, QFSM
Commandant, Scottish Fire Service Training School, D. Grant,
  QFSM

MENTAL WELFARE COMMISSION FOR SCOTLAND
K Floor, Argyle House, 3 Lady Lawson Street, Edinburgh
EH3 9SH
Tel 0131-222 6111

Chairman, Sir William Reid, KCB
Vice-Chairman, Mrs N. Bennie
Commissioners (part-time), C. Campbell, QC; Mrs F. Cotter;
  W. Gent; Dr P. Jauhar; Dr Shainool Jiwa; Dr
  Elizabeth McCall-Smith; D. J. Macdonald; C. McKay;
  Dr Linda Pollock; A. Robb; Dr Margaret Thomas;
  Ms M. Whoriskey
Director, Dr J. A. T. Dyer

COUNSEL TO THE SECRETARY OF STATE FOR SCOTLAND UNDER THE PRIVATE LEGISLATION PROCEDURE (SCOTLAND) ACT 1936
50 Frederick Street, Edinburgh EH2 1EN
Tel 0131-226 6499

Senior Counsel, G. S. Douglas, QC
Junior Counsel, N. M. P. Morrison

EXECUTIVE AGENCIES

NATIONAL ARCHIVES OF SCOTLAND
— *see* page 337

REGISTERS OF SCOTLAND
— *see* pages 316–17

SCOTTISH COURT SERVICE
— *see* page 365

SCOTTISH PRISON SERVICE
— *see* pages 381–2

GENERAL REGISTER OFFICE
New Register House, Edinburgh EH1 3YT
Tel 0131-334 0380; fax 0131-314 4400

The General Register Office for Scotland is an associated
department of the Scottish Office. It is the office of the
Registrar-General for Scotland, who has responsibility for
civil registration and the taking of censuses in Scotland and
has in his custody the following records: the statutory
registers of births, deaths, still births, adoptions, marriages
and divorces; the old parish registers (recording births,
deaths and marriages, etc., before civil registration began in
1855); and records of censuses of the population in
Scotland. Hours of public access: Monday–Friday 9–4.30.
Registrar-General, J. Meldrum
Deputy Registrar-General, B. V. Philp
Senior Principal (G6), D. A. Orr
Principals (G7), D. B. L. Brownlee; R. C. Lawson;
  F. D. Garvie
Statisticians (G7), G. Compton; G. W. L. Jackson;
  F. G. Thomas

SCOTTISH PRISONS COMPLAINTS COMMISSION
Government Buildings, Broomhouse Drive, Edinburgh
EH11 3XD
Tel 0131-244 8423; fax 0131-244 8430

The Commission was established in 1994. It is an independent body to which prisoners in Scottish prisons can make application in relation to any matter where they have failed to obtain satisfaction from the Prison Service's internal grievance procedures. Clinical judgments made by medical officers, matters which are the subject of legal proceedings and matters relating to sentence, conviction and parole decision-making are excluded from the Commission's jurisdiction. The Commissioner is appointed by the Secretary of State for Scotland.
Commissioner, Dr J. McManus

SEA FISH INDUSTRY AUTHORITY
18 Logie Mill, Logie Green Road, Edinburgh EH7 4HG
Tel 0131-558 3331; fax 0131-558 1442

Established under the Fisheries Act 1981, the Authority is required to promote the efficiency of the sea fish industry. It carries out research relating to the industry and gives advice on related matters. It provides training, promotes the marketing, consumption and export of sea fish and sea fish products, and may provide financial assistance for the improvement of fishing vessels in respect of essential safety equipment. It is responsible to the Ministry of Agriculture, Fisheries and Food.
Chairman, E. Davey
Chief Executive, A. C. Fairbairn

THE SECURITY AND INTELLIGENCE SERVICES

Under the Intelligence Services Act 1994, the Intelligence and Security Committee of Parliamentarians was established to oversee the work of GCHQ, MI5 and MI6. The Act also established the Intelligence Services Tribunal (*see* page 314), which hears complaints made against GCHQ and MI6. The Security Service Tribunal and Commissioner (*see* below) investigate complaints about MI5.

DEFENCE INTELLIGENCE STAFF
— *see* Defence section

GOVERNMENT COMMUNICATIONS HEADQUARTERS (GCHQ)
Priors Road, Cheltenham, Glos GL52 5AJ
Tel 01242-221491; fax 01242-226816
GCHQ produces signals intelligence in support of the Government's security, defence and economic policies. It also provides advice and assistance to government departments and the armed forces on the security of their communications and information technology systems. It was placed on a statutory footing by the Intelligence Services Act 1994 and is headed by a director who is directly accountable to the Foreign Secretary.
Director, F. N. Richards, CVO, CMG

THE SECRET INTELLIGENCE SERVICE (MI6)
Vauxhall Cross, PO Box 1300, London SE1 1BD
The Secret Intelligence Service produces secret intelligence in support of the Government's security, defence, foreign and economic policies. It was placed on a statutory footing by the Intelligence Services Act 1994 and is headed by a director-general who is directly accountable to the Foreign Secretary.
Director-General, Sir David Spedding, KCMG, CVO, OBE

THE SECURITY SERVICE (MI5)
Thames House, PO Box 3255, London SW1P 1AE
Tel 0171-930 9000
The function of the Security Service is the protection of national security, in particular against threats from espionage, terrorism, sabotage and the proliferation of weapons of mass destruction, from the activities of agents of foreign powers, and from actions intended to overthrow or undermine parliamentary democracy by political, industrial or violent means. It is also the Service's function to safeguard the economic well-being of the UK against threats posed by the actions or intentions of persons outside the British Islands. Under the Security Service Act 1996, the Service's role was extended to support the police and customs in the prevention and detection of serious crime.
The Security Service was placed on a statutory footing by the Security Service Act 1989 and is headed by a director-general who is directly accountable to the Home Secretary.
Director-General, S. Lander

SECURITY SERVICE COMMISSIONER
c/o PO Box 18, London SE1 0TZ
Tel 0171-273 4095

The Commissioner is appointed by the Prime Minister. He keeps under review the issue of warrants by the Home Secretary under the Intelligence Services Act 1994, and is required to help the Security Service Tribunal by investigating complaints which allege interference with property and by offering all such assistance in discharging its functions as it may require. He is also required to submit an annual report on the discharge of his functions to the Prime Minister.
Commissioner, The Rt. Hon. Lord Justice Stuart-Smith
Private Secretary, E. R. Wilson

SECURITY SERVICE TRIBUNAL
PO Box 18, London SE1 0TZ
Tel 0171-273 4095

The Security Service Act 1989 established a tribunal of three to five senior members of the legal profession, independent of the Government and appointed by The Queen, to investigate complaints from any person about anything which they believe the Security Service has done to them or to their property.
President, The Rt. Hon. Lord Justice Simon Brown
Vice-President, Sheriff J. McInnes, QC
Member, Sir Richard Gaskell
Secretary, E. R. Wilson

SERIOUS FRAUD OFFICE
Elm House, 10–16 Elm Street, London WC1X 0BJ
Tel 0171-239 7272; fax 0171-837 1689

The Serious Fraud Office works under the superintendence of the Attorney-General. Its remit is to investigate and prosecute serious and complex fraud. (Other fraud cases are currently handled by the fraud divisions of the Crown Prosecution Service.) The scope of its powers covers England, Wales and Northern Ireland. The staff includes lawyers, accountants and other support staff; investigating teams work closely with the police.
Director, Mrs R. Wright

DEPARTMENT OF SOCIAL SECURITY
Richmond House, 79 Whitehall, London SW1A 2NS
Tel 0171-238 0800

The Department of Social Security is responsible for the payment of benefits and the collection of contributions under the National Insurance and Industrial Injuries schemes, and for the payment of child benefit, one-parent benefit, income support and family credit. It administers the Social Fund, and is responsible for assessing the means of applicants for legal aid. It is also responsible for the payment of war pensions and the operation of the child maintenance system.
Secretary of State for Social Security, The Rt. Hon. Alistair Darling, MP
  Principal Private Secretary, R. Clark
  Special Advisers, J. McTernan; A. Maugham
  Parliamentary Private Secretary, Ms A. Coffey, MP
Minister of State, John Denham, MP
  Private Secretary, D. Higlett
Parliamentary Under-Secretaries of State, The Baroness Hollis of Heigham, D.Phil. (*Family Policy, Child Benefit, Child Support, War Pensions*); Angela Eagle, MP (*Income-related Benefits, International and Green Issues*); Stephen Timms, MP (*Disability and Sickness Benefits, National Insurance Contributions, Devolution, Independent Living Fund*)
  Private Secretaries, B. Stayte; D. Topping; Ms V. Hutchinson; Ms H. McCarthy; R. Sanguinaza; Ms L. Wright
Permanent Secretary (G1), Dame Ann Bowtell, DCB (*until April 1999*)
  Private Secretary, C. Jackson

CORPORATE MANAGEMENT GROUP
Director (G2), J. Tross

PERSONNEL AND HQ SUPPORT SERVICES DIRECTORATE
Director, S. Hewitt
Section Heads (G5), T. Perl; (G7), R. Yeats; B. Glew; J. Elliott

ANALYTICAL SERVICES DIVISION
The Adelphi, 1–11 John Adam Street, London WC2N 6HT
Tel 0171-962 8000

Director (G3), D. Stanton
Chief Statistician (G5), N. Dyson
Senior Economic Advisers (G5), J. Ball; G. Harris; R. D'Souza
Deputy Chief Scientific Officer (G5), D. Barnbrook
Chief Research Officers (G5), Ms S. Duncan; S. Rice

FINANCE DIVISION
Grade 3, S. Lord

INFORMATION DIRECTORATE
Director of Information (G4), M. Sixsmith
Deputy Head of Information (G6), J. Bretherton
Chief Press Officer (G7), Ms S. Lewis
Chief Publicity Officer (G7), Ms A. Martin

SOCIAL SECURITY POLICY GROUP
Head of Policy Group (G2), P. R. C. Gray
Policy Directors (G3), M. L. Whippman, CB; Miss M. Peirson, CB; D. Brereton; U. Brennan
Head of Women's Unit (G3), Ms F. Reynolds, CBE
Policy Managers (G5), Mrs A. Lingwood; D. Jackson; B. O'Gorman; M. Street; J. Groombridge; Mrs C. Rookes; B. Calderwood; D. Allsop, CBE; C. Evans; J. Hughes; P. Cleasby; P. Morgan; Mrs L. Richards; Ms J. Shersby; (G6), B. Layton; I. Williams; P. Barrett; J. Griffiths-Chayes; K. Sadler; N. Ward

SOLICITOR'S OFFICE
Solicitor (G2), Mrs M. A. Morgan, CB

SOLICITOR'S DIVISION A
New Court, 48 Carey Street, London WC2A 2LS
Tel 0171-412 1466
Principal Assistant Solicitor (G3), J. A. Catlin
Assistant Solicitors (G5), J. M. Swainson; Mrs G. Massiah; Mrs F. A. Logan; C. Cooper; H. Connell; P. Milledge

SOLICITOR'S DIVISION B
New Court, 48 Carey Street, London WC2A 2LS
Tel 0171-412 1528
Solicitor (G2), Mrs M. A. Morgan, CB
Assistant Solicitors (G5), R. G. S. Aitken; Ms S. Edwards; S. Cooper

SOLICITOR'S DIVISION C
New Court, 48 Carey Street, London WC2A 2LS
Tel 0171-412 1342
Principal Assistant Solicitor (G3), Mrs G. S. Kerrigan
Assistant Solicitors (G5), R. J. Dormer; Miss M. E. Trefgarne; Mrs S. Walker; G. Aitkin

BENEFITS FRAUD INSPECTORATE
Berkeley House, 12A North Park Road, Harrogate HG1 5QA
Tel 01423-832922
Director-General (G3), I. Stewart

EXECUTIVE AGENCIES
BENEFITS AGENCY
Quarry House, Quarry Hill, Leeds LS2 7UA
Tel 0113-232 4000

The Agency administers claims for and payments of social security benefits.
Chief Executive, P. Mathison
  Private Secretary, R. Baldwin
Directors, J. Codling (*Finance*); M. Fisher (*Personnel and Communications*); S. Heminsley (*Strategic and Planning*); A. Cleveland (*Operations Support*); N. Haighton, G. McCorkell (*Projects*)

Medical Policy
Principal Medical Officers, Dr M. Aylward; Dr P. Dewis; Dr P. Sawney; Dr A. Braidwood; Dr P. Stidolph

CHILD SUPPORT AGENCY
DSS Long Benton, Benton Park Road, Newcastle upon
Tyne NE98 1YX
Tel 0191-213 5000

The Agency was set up in April 1993. It is responsible for
the administration of the Child Support Act and for the
assessment, collection and enforcement of maintenance
payments for all new cases.
Chief Executive, Ms F. Boardman
Directors, M. Davison; C. Peters; M. Isaacs; T. Read

CONTRIBUTIONS AGENCY
DSS Longbenton, Benton Park Road, Newcastle upon
Tyne NE98 1YX
Tel 0191-213 5000

The Agency collects and records National Insurance
contributions, maintains individual records, and provides
an advisory service on National Insurance matters. The
Contributions Agency and the Board of Inland Revenue
are to merge in April 1999.
Chief Executive (G3), G. Bertram
Management Board, T. Lord; D. Slater; B. Woodley; A.
   Fisher
Non-Executive Members, S. Banyard; C. Dodgson

INFORMATION TECHNOLOGY SERVICES AGENCY
4th Floor, Verulam Point, Station Way, St Albans, Herts
AL1 5HE
Tel 01727-815835; fax 01727-833740

The Agency maintains and oversees policies on informa-
tion technology strategy, procurement, technical stan-
dards and security.
Chief Executive (acting), P. Sharkey
Directors, J. Thomas; J. Brewood; G. Brown; B. Barnes; B.
   Gormley; J. Delamere; C. Nicholls
Non-Executive Directors, K. Pfotzer; K. Bogg

WAR PENSIONS AGENCY
Norcross, Blackpool, Lancs FY5 3WP
Tel 01253-856123

The Agency administers the payment of war disablement
and war widows' pensions and provides welfare services
and support to war disablement pensioners, war widows
and their dependants and carers.
Chief Executive, G. Hextall

Central Advisory Committee on War Pensions
6th Floor, The Adelphi, 1–11 John Adam Street, London
WC2N 6HT
Tel 0171-962 8062
Secretary, C. Pike

ADVISORY BODIES

NATIONAL DISABILITY COUNCIL, Level 4, Caxton
   House, Tothill Street, London SW1H 9NA. Tel: 0171-273
   5636. *Chairman*, D. Grayson, OBE; *Secretary*, R. Timm
SOCIAL SECURITY ADVISORY COMMITTEE, New Court,
   Carey Street, London WC2A 2LS. Tel 0171-412 1508.
   Chairman, Lt.-Gen. Sir Thomas Boyd-Carpenter, KBE;
   Secretary, Ms G. Saunders

SPORTS COUNCIL
— *see* United Kingdom Sports Council

OFFICE FOR STANDARDS IN EDUCATION (OFSTED)
Alexandra House, 33 Kingsway, London WC2B 6SE
Tel 0171-421 6574; fax 0171-421 6522

A non-ministerial government department established in
1992 to keep the Secretary of State and the public informed
about the standards and management of schools in England, and to establish and monitor an independent inspection system for maintained schools in England. *See also* page
425.
HM Chief Inspector, C. Woodhead
Directors of Inspection, A. J. Rose, CBE; M. J. Tomlinson, CBE

TEAM MANAGERS
Planning and Resources, Miss J. M. Phillips, CBE
Personnel Management, C. Payne
Contracts, C. Bramley
Communications, Media and Public Relations, J. Lawson
Information Systems, vacant
Administrative Support and Estates Management, K. Francis
Training and Assessment of Independent Inspectors, B.
   McCafferty
Inspection Quality, Monitoring and Development, P. Matthews
LEA Reviews, Reorganization Proposals, D. Singleton
School Improvement, Ms E. Passmore
Nursery and Primary, K. Lloyd
Secondary and Independent, C. Gould
Post-Compulsory, D. West
Special Educational Needs, C. Marshall
Research, Analysis and International, Ms C. Agambar
Teacher Education and Training, D. Taylor
Nursery Education Scheme, D. Bradley
Specialist Advisers, N. Bufton; B. Ponchaud; A. Dobson; M.
   Ive; P. Smith; Ms J. Mills; G. Clay; P. Jones; J. Hertrich;
   Ms B. Wintersgill; S. Harrison
There are about 200 HM Inspectors

COMMITTEE ON STANDARDS IN PUBLIC LIFE
Horse Guards Road, London SW1P 3AL
Tel 0171-270 5875; fax 0171-270 5874

The Committee on Standards in Public Life (formerly
known as the Nolan Committee, now known as the Neill
Committee) was set up in October 1994. It is a standing
body whose chairman and members are appointed by the
Prime Minister; three members are nominated by the
leaders of the three main political parties. The committee's
remit is to examine current concerns about standards of
conduct of all holders of public office, including arrangements relating to financial and commercial activities, and
to make recommendations as to any changes in present
arrangements which might be required to ensure the
highest standards of propriety in public life. In November
1997 the committee's remit was widened to review issues
in relation to the funding of political parties, and to make
recommendations as to any changes in present arrangements. The committee does not investigate individual
allegations of misconduct.
Chairman, The Lord Neill of Bladen, QC
Members, Sir Clifford Boulton, GCB; Sir Anthony Cleaver;
   The Lord Goodhart, QC; Ms F. Heaton; Prof. A. King;
   The Rt. Hon. J. MacGregor, OBE, MP; The Lord Shore
   of Stepney, PC; Sir William Utting, CB; Ms D. Warwick
Secretary (SCS), R. Horsman

OFFICE OF TELECOMMUNICATIONS
50 Ludgate Hill, London EC4M 7JJ
Tel 0171-634 8700; fax 0171- 634 8943

The Office of Telecommunications (Oftel) is a non-ministerial government department responsible for supervising telecommunications activities and broadcast transmission in the UK. Its principal functions are to ensure that holders of telecommunications licences comply with their licence conditions; to maintain and promote effective competition in telecommunications; and to promote the interests of purchasers and other users of telecommunication services and apparatus in respect of prices, quality and variety.

The Director-General has powers to deal with anti-competitive practices and monopolies. He also has a duty to consider all reasonable complaints and representations about telecommunication apparatus and services.

Director-General, D. Edmonds
Deputy Director-General, Miss A. Lambert
Director of Network Competition, Mrs A. Taylor
Director of Consumer Affairs, Mrs V. Peters
Director of Licensing Policy, Ms S. Chambers
Director of Competition and Fair Trading, Mrs J. Whittles
Technical Director, P. Walker
Economic Director, A. Bell
Legal Director, D. H. M. Ingham
Administration Director, D. Smith
Director of Communications, N. Gammage
Director of Convergence and International Affairs, J. Niblett

TOURIST BOARDS
(For British Tourist Authority, *see* page 287)

The English Tourist Board, the Scottish Tourist Board, the Wales Tourist Board and the Northern Ireland Tourist Board are responsible for developing and marketing the tourist industry in their respective countries. The Boards' main objectives are to promote holidays and to encourage the provision and improvement of tourist amenities.

In July 1998 the Government published a discussion document including a proposal to reform the structure and workings of the English Tourist Board.

ENGLISH TOURIST BOARD, Thames Tower, Black's Road, London W6 9EL. Tel: 0181-846 9000. *Chief Executive*, T. Bartlett
SCOTTISH TOURIST BOARD, 23 Ravelston Terrace, Edinburgh EH4 3EU. Tel: 0131-332 2433; Thistle House, Beechwood Park North, Inverness IV2 3ED. Tel: 01463-716996. *Chief Executive*, T. Buncle
WALES TOURIST BOARD, Brunel House, 2 Fitzalan Road, Cardiff CF2 1UY. Tel: 01222-499909. *Chief Executive*, J. French
NORTHERN IRELAND TOURIST BOARD, St Anne's Court, 59 North Street, Belfast BT1 1NB. Tel: 01232-231221. *Chief Executive*, I. Henderson

DEPARTMENT OF TRADE AND INDUSTRY
1 Victoria Street, London SW1H 0ET
Tel 0171-215 5000; fax 0171-222 2629
Web: http://www.dti.gov.uk

The Department is responsible for international trade policy, including the promotion of UK trade interests in the European Union, GATT, OECD, UNCTAD and other international organizations; the promotion of UK exports and assistance to exporters; policy in relation to industry and commerce, including industrial relations policy; policy towards small firms; regional industrial assistance; legislation and policy in relation to the Post Office; competition policy and consumer protection; the development of national policies in relation to all forms of energy and the development of new sources of energy, including international aspects of energy policy; policy on science and technology research and development; space policy; standards, quality and design; and company legislation.

Secretary of State for Trade and Industry, The Rt. Hon. Peter Mandelson, MP
   Principal Private Secretary, A. Phillipson
   Private Secretaries, B. Coates; J. Fiennes
Minister of State, John Battle, MP (*Energy, Industry, Environment*)
   Senior Private Secretary, R. Riley
   Parliamentary Private Secretary, Ms A. Campbell, MP
Minister of State, Ian McCartney, MP (*Employment Relations*)
   Private Secretary, Ms R. Hill
   Parliamentary Private Secretary, F. Doran, MP
Minister of State, Brian Wilson, MP (*Trade*)
   Private Secretary, U. Marthaler
Minister of State, The Lord Simon of Highbury, CBE (*Trade and Competitiveness in Europe*) (*joint DTI/Treasury minister*)
   Private Secretary, J. Mitchell
Parliamentary Under-Secretaries of State, Dr Kim Howells, MP (*Competition and Consumer Affairs*); Barbara Roche, MP (*Small Firms and Regional Policy*); The Lord Sainsbury of Turville (*Science*)
   Private Secretaries, Ms D. Parr; Ms P. Ciniewicz
British Overseas Trade Board Chairman, M. Laing, CBE
   Private Secretary, M. Shute
Parliamentary Clerk, T. Williams
Permanent Secretary, M. Scholar, CB
   Private Secretary, R. Collins
Chief Scientific Adviser and Head of Office of Science and Technology, Sir Robert May, FRS
   Private Secretary, R. Clay
Directors-General, Sir John Cadogan, CBE, FRS (*Director-General of the Research Councils*); A. Hutton, CB (*Trade Policy*); T. Harris, CMG (*Export Promotion*); D. Durie, CMG (*Regional and Small and Medium Enterprises*); B. Hilton, CB (*Corporate and Consumer Affairs*); D. Nissen (*The Solicitor*); Ms A. Walker (*Energy*); J. Spencer (*Resources and Services*); A. Macdonald, CB (*Industry*)

DIVISIONAL ORGANIZATION

‡BRITISH NATIONAL SPACE CENTRE
Director-General (*SCS*), D. R. Davis
Deputy Director-General (*SCS*), D. Leadbeater
Directors (*SCS*), A. Cooper; Dr P. Murdin; Dr D. Lumley

BUSINESS LINK DIRECTORATE
Director of Business Link (*SCS*), P. Waller
Directors (*SCS*), J. Reid; P. Bentley; Mrs P. Jackson; T. Evans

COMPETITIVENESS UNIT
Director of Competitiveness Unit (*SCS*), D. Evans
Directors (*SCS*), S. Haddrill; T. Soane; J. Reynolds

‡CHEMICALS AND BIOTECHNOLOGY DIRECTORATE
Director of Chemicals and Biotechnology (*SCS*), M. Baker
Directors (*SCS*), Ms G. Alliston; Dr E. A. M. Baker

COAL DIRECTORATE
Director (SCS), M. Atkinson

COMMUNICATIONS DIRECTORATE
Director of Information (SCS), Dr S. Sklaroff
Director of News (SCS), M. Ricketts
Director of Publicity (SCS), Miss P. R. A. Freedman

‡COMMUNICATIONS AND INFORMATION INDUSTRIES
DIRECTORATE
Director of Communications and Information Industries (SCS),
  W. MacIntyre
Directors (SCS), R. King; N. McMillan, CMG; N. Worman;
  S. Pride

COMPANY LAW AND INVESTIGATIONS DIRECTORATE
Director of Company Law and Investigations (SCS), R. Rogers
Directors (SCS), N. D. Peace; D. E. Love

CONSUMER AFFAIRS AND COMPETITION POLICY
DIRECTORATE
Director of Consumer Affairs and Competition Policy (SCS), P.
  Salvidge
Directors (SCS), P. Mason; Miss D. Gane; Dr A. Eggington;
  G. Boon; A. Brimelow; M. Higson

CONSUMER GOODS, BUSINESS AND POSTAL SERVICES
DIRECTORATE
Director of Consumer Goods, Business and Postal Services (SCS),
  M. Baker
Directors (SCS), B. Hopson; Ms J. Britton

ECONOMICS AND STATISTICS DIRECTORATE
Chief Economic Adviser (SCS), D. R. Coates
Directors (SCS), K. Warwick; Ms J. Dougharty; M.
  Bradbury

ELECTRICITY DIRECTORATE
Director of Electricity (SCS), J. Green

EMPLOYMENT RELATIONS DIRECTORATE
Director of Industrial Relations (SCS), Ms H. Leiser
Directors (SCS), Dr E. Baker; R. Niblett; A. Wright; Mrs
  Z. Hornstein; Ms N. Carter; K. Masson

ENERGY POLICY AND ANALYSIS UNIT
Director of Energy Policy and Analysis (SCS), M. Keay
Directors (SCS), E. Evans; G. C. White

ENERGY TECHNOLOGIES DIRECTORATE
Director (SCS), G. Bevan

‡ENGINEERING INDUSTRIES DIRECTORATE
Director of Engineering Industries (SCS), M. O'Shea
Directors (SCS), J. Neilson; M. Ralph; R. Kingcombe; H.
  Brown; J. Grewe; R. Poole; A. Vinall; Ms A. Wilks

ENGINEERING INSPECTORATE
Director of Engineering Inspectorate (SCS), Dr P. Fenwick

‡ENVIRONMENT DIRECTORATE
Director of Environment (SCS), Dr C. Hicks
Director (SCS), D. Prior

‡ESTATES AND FACILITIES MANAGEMENT
DIRECTORATE
Director (SCS), M. Coolican

EUROPE DIRECTORATE
Kingsgate House, 66–74 Victoria Street, London
SW1E 6SW

Director (SCS), B. Stow

EXPORT CONTROL AND NON-PROLIFERATION
DIRECTORATE
Kingsgate House, 66–74 Victoria Street, London
SW1E 6SW

Director of Export Control and Non-Proliferation (SCS), Dr R.
  Heathcote
Directors (SCS), A. J. Mantle, J. Neve

EXPORT PROMOTION DIRECTORATES
Kingsgate House, 66–74 Victoria Street, London
SW1E 6SW

Director, Markets and Sectors (SCS), M. Gibson
Directors (SCS), M. Mowlam (*The Americas*); M. Cohen
  (*Asia Pacific*); K. Levinson (*Central and Eastern Europe*); S.
  Lyle Smythe (*Business in Europe*); S. Khanna (*Middle
  East, Near East and North Africa*); N. McInnes (*Sub-
  Saharan Africa and South Asia*); A. Sparkes (*Sectors,
  Services and Outward Investment*)

EXPORT SERVICES DIRECTORATE
Kingsgate House, 66–74 Victoria Street, London
SW1E 6SW

Director (SCS), A. Reynolds

FINANCE AND RESOURCE MANAGEMENT DIRECTORATE
Director of Finance and Resource Management (SCS), J.
  Phillips
Directors (SCS), E. Hosker; K. Hills; N. Nandra

IMPORT POLICY DIRECTORATE
Kingsgate House, 66–74 Victoria Street, London
SW1E 6SW

Director (SCS), A. Berry

‡INDUSTRY ECONOMICS AND STATISTICS
DIRECTORATE
Director (SCS), Dr N. Owen

‡INFORMATION MANAGEMENT AND TECHNOLOGY
DIRECTORATE
Director (SCS), R. Wheeler

INFRASTRUCTURE AND ENERGY PROJECTS
DIRECTORATE
Director of Infrastructure and Energy Projects (SCS), M.
  Stanley
Directors (SCS), G. Atkinson; Dr K. Forrest; B. Gallagher; J.
  Campbell

‡INNOVATION UNIT
Director (SCS), Dr A. Keddie

INSURANCE DIRECTORATE
Director of Insurance (SCS), G. Dart
Directors (SCS), R. Allen; K. Long; J. Whitlock; P. Casey

‡INTERNAL AUDIT
Director of Internal Audit (SCS), A. C. Elkington

INTERNATIONAL ECONOMICS DIRECTORATE
Kingsgate House, 66–74 Victoria Street, London
SW1E 6SW

Director (SCS), C. Moir

INVEST IN BRITAIN BUREAU
Chief Executive (SCS), A. Fraser

JOINT EXPORT PROMOTION DIRECTORATE
(FCO/DTI)
Kingsgate House, 66–74 Victoria Street, London
SW1E 6SW

Director-General of Export Promotion (SCS), T. Harris, CMG
Director, JEPD (SCS), D. Hall

LEGAL RESOURCE MANAGEMENT AND BUSINESS LAW
UNIT
10 Victoria Street, London SW1H 0NN

---

‡ At 151 Buckingham Palace Road, London SW1W 9SS

The Solicitor and Director-General (SCS), D. Nissen
Director (SCS), P. Burke

LEGAL SERVICES DIRECTORATE A
10 Victoria Street, London SWIH ONN

Director of Legal A (SCS), J. Stanley
Legal Directors (SCS), J. Roberts; Miss N. O'Flynn;
  S. Hyett; Miss G. Richmond

LEGAL SERVICES DIRECTORATE B
10 Victoria Street, London SWIH ONN

Director of Legal B (SCS), P. Bovey
Legal Directors (SCS), R. Baker; T. Susman; B. Welch; R.
  Perkins; Ms C. Croft; Ms S. Hardy

LEGAL SERVICES DIRECTORATE C
10 Victoria Street, London SWIH ONN

Director of Legal C (SCS), Ms A. Brett-Holt
Legal Directors (SCS), R. Perkins; R. Green; M. Bucknill; C.
  Raikes; A. Woods; C. Osborne

LEGAL SERVICES DIRECTORATE D
10 Victoria Street, London SWIH ONN

Director of Legal D (SCS), Mrs T. Dunstan
Directors (SCS), S. Milligan; S. Clements

MANAGEMENT BEST PRACTICE
Director of Management Best Practice, Dr K. Poulter
Deputy Director (SCS), Dr I. Harrison

NEW ISSUES AND DEVELOPING COUNTRIES
Kingsgate House, 66–74 Victoria Street, London
SWIE 6SW

Director (SCS), C. Bridge

NUCLEAR INDUSTRIES DIRECTORATE
Director of Nuclear Industries (SCS), N. Hirst
Directors (SCS), Dr M. Draper; Dr E. Drage; I. Downing; S.
  Bowen

**OFFICE OF SCIENCE AND TECHNOLOGY: SCIENCE AND
ENGINEERING BASE DIRECTORATE**
Albany House, 84–86 Petty France, London SWIH 9ST
Director, Science and Engineering Base (SCS), A. Quigley
Directors (SCS), Ms F. Price; Dr K. Root

**OFFICE OF SCIENCE AND TECHNOLOGY:
TRANSDEPARTMENTAL SCIENCE AND TECHNOLOGY
DIRECTORATE**
Albany House, 84–86 Petty France, London SWIH 9ST
Director, Transdepartmental Science and Technology (SCS), Ms
  H. Williams
Directors (SCS), R. Wright; S. Spivey; Mrs P. Sellers; Ms J.
  Donaldson

OIL AND GAS DIRECTORATE
1 Victoria Street, London SWIH OET

Director of Oil and Gas (SCS), G. Dart
Directors (SCS), J. R. V. Brooks, CBE; D. Saunders

Atholl House, 86–88 Guild Street, Aberdeen AB9 1DR
Tel 01224-254059

Director of Oil and Gas (SCS), S. Toole

REGIONAL ASSISTANCE DIRECTORATE
Director of Regional Assistance (SCS), D. Miner
Director (SCS), S. Robins

REGIONAL EUROPEAN FUNDS DIRECTORATE
Director (SCS), Ms R. Anderson

REGIONAL POLICY DIRECTORATE
Director (SCS), D. Smith

SENIOR STAFF MANAGEMENT
Director (SCS), Ms K. Elliott

**SMALL AND MEDIUM-SIZED ENTERPRISES (SME)
POLICY DIRECTORATE**
St Mary's House, Level 2, c/o Moorfoot, Sheffield S1 4PQ
Director (SCS), J. Thompson

**SMALL AND MEDIUM-SIZED ENTERPRISES (SME)
TECHNOLOGY DIRECTORATE**
Director (SCS), R. Allpress

STAFF PAY AND CONDITIONS
Director (SCS), C. Johnston

STAFF PERSONNEL OPERATIONS
Director (SCS), I. Cameron

STAFF POLICY AND DEVELOPMENT UNIT
Director (SCS), Ms B. Habberjam

‡TECHNOLOGY AND STANDARDS DIRECTORATE
Director of Technology and Standards (SCS), R. Foster
Directors (SCS), J. M. Barber; G. C. Riggs; J. Hobday; G.
  McGregor; D. Reed

TRADE POLICY DIRECTORATE
Kingsgate House, 66–74 Victoria Street, London
SWIE 6SW

Director (SCS), J. Hunt

UTILITIES REVIEW TEAM
Director of Utilities Review Team (SCS), Dr C. Bell
Director (SCS), R. Bent

BRITISH OVERSEAS TRADE BOARD
Kingsgate House, 66–74 Victoria Street, London SWIE
6SW
Tel 0171-215 5000

President, The Secretary of State for Trade and Industry
Chairman, M. Laing, CBE
Vice-Chairman, HRH The Duke of Kent, KG, GCMG, GCVO
Members, A. Buxton; A. Turner; P. Godwin, CBE; R.
  Burman, CBE; T. Harris, CMG; Sir Gilbert Thompson,
  OBE; Sir Clive Thompson; R. Turner, OBE; V. Wark; V.
  Brown; J. Shepherd, CMG; D. Hall; C. Robinson; A.
  Summers
Secretary, Dr D. Walker

REGIONAL OFFICES
— see pages 304–5

EXECUTIVE AGENCIES

COMPANIES HOUSE
Companies House, Crown Way, Cardiff CF4 3UZ
Tel 01222-380801; fax 01222-380900
London Search Room, 55–71 City Road, London EC1Y 1BB
Tel 0171-253 9393; fax 0171-490 1147
37 Castle Terrace, Edinburgh EH1 2EB
Tel 0131-535 5800; fax 0131-535 5820

Companies House incorporates companies, registers company documents and provides company information.
Registrar of Companies for England and Wales, J. Holden
Registrar for Scotland, J. Henderson

EMPLOYMENT TRIBUNALS SERVICE
19–29 Woburn Place, London WC1H OLU
Tel 0171-273 8666; fax 0171-273 8670

The Service became an executive agency in April 1997 and brought together the administrative support for the industrial tribunals and the Employment Appeal Tribunal.
Chief Executive, I. Jones

---

‡ At 151 Buckingham Palace Road, London SW1W 9SS

THE INSOLVENCY SERVICE
PO Box 203, 21 Bloomsbury Street, London WC1B 3QW
Tel 0171-637 1110; fax 0171-636 4709

The Service administers and investigates the affairs of bankrupts and companies in compulsory liquidation; deals with the disqualification of directors in all corporate failures; regulates insolvency practitioners and their professional bodies; provides banking and investment services for bankruptcy and liquidation estates; and advises ministers on insolvency policy issues.
Inspector-General and Chief Executive, P. R. Joyce
Deputy Inspectors-General, D. J. Flynn; L. T. Cramp

NATIONAL WEIGHTS AND MEASURES LABORATORY
Stanton Avenue, Teddington, Middx TW11 0JZ
Tel 0181-943 7272; fax 0181-943 7270

The Laboratory administers weights and measures legislation, carries out type examination, calibration and testing, and runs courses on metrological topics.
Chief Executive, Dr S. Bennett

PATENT OFFICE
— *see* page 332

RADIOCOMMUNICATIONS AGENCY
New King's Beam House, 22 Upper Ground, London SE1 9SA
Tel 0171-211 0211; fax 0171-211 0507

The Agency is responsible for the management of the radio spectrum used for civilian purposes within the UK. It also represents UK radio interests internationally.
Chief Executive, D. Hendon

THE TREASURY
Parliament Street, London SW1P 3AG
Tel 0171-270 3000
Web: http://www.hm-treasury.gov.uk

The Office of the Lord High Treasurer has been continuously in commission for well over 200 years. The Lord High Commissioners of HM Treasury are the First Lord of the Treasury (who is also the Prime Minister), the Chancellor of the Exchequer and five junior Lords (who are government whips in the House of Commons). This Board of Commissioners is assisted at present by the Chief Secretary, a Parliamentary Secretary who is also the government Chief Whip, a Financial Secretary, an Economic Secretary, the Paymaster-General, and the Permanent Secretary.

The Prime Minister is not primarily concerned in the day-to-day aspects of Treasury business; the management of the Treasury devolves upon the Chancellor of the Exchequer and the other Treasury ministers.

The Chief Secretary is responsible for the planning and control of public expenditure; value for money in the public services; comprehensive spending reviews; public sector pay; strategic oversight of the financial system and financial services; devolution; and export credit.

The Paymaster-General's responsibilities include enterprise and growth; welfare-to-work issues; competition and deregulation policy; review of corporation tax; Treasury interest in small firms; and government procurement policy and practice. The Paymaster-General's Office is part of the National Investment and Loans Office (*see* pages 327–8).

The Financial Secretary has responsibility for parliamentary financial business; oversight of the Inland Revenue, Customs and Excise and the Valuation Office Agency; Inland Revenue taxes (excluding the windfall levy); Customs and Excise duties and taxes; charities; and the environment, including energy efficiency.

The Economic Secretary has responsibility for the financial system and financial services; Economic and Monetary Union; foreign exchange reserves management; debt management policy; international issues; parliamentary questions; low pay and the minimum wage; women's issues; economic briefing; the Royal Mint; National Savings; the Office for National Statistics; the National Investment and Loans Office; and the Government Actuary's Department.

The Minister for Trade and Competitiveness in Europe deals with *ad hoc* projects and is chairman of an interdepartmental task force and a member of the Economic and European Cabinet committees.

All Treasury ministers are concerned in tax matters.
Prime Minister and First Lord of the Treasury, The Rt. Hon. Tony Blair, MP
Chancellor of the Exchequer, The Rt. Hon. Gordon Brown, MP
  Principal Private Secretary, T. Scholar
  Private Secretary, vacant
  Special Advisers, E. Balls; C. Whelan; E. Miliband; A. Maugham
  Parliamentary Private Secretary, D. Touhig, MP
Chief Secretary to the Treasury, The Rt. Hon. Stephen Byers, MP
  Private Secretary, P. Schofield
Paymaster-General, Geoffrey Robinson, MP
  Private Secretary, S. Field
  Parliamentary Private Secretary, I. Pearson, MP
Financial Secretary to the Treasury, Dawn Primarolo, MP
  Private Secretary, Ms P. Murray
  Parliamentary Private Secretary, A. Johnson, MP
Economic Secretary, Patricia Hewitt, MP
  Private Secretary, Ms A. King
Minister of State, The Lord Simon of Highbury, CBE (*Trade and Competitiveness in Europe*) (*joint Treasury/DTI minister*)
Parliamentary Secretary to the Treasury and Government Chief Whip (*£45,201), The Rt. Hon. Ann Taylor, MP
  Private Secretary, M. Maclean
Treasurer of HM Household and Deputy Chief Whip (*£31,981), Keith Bradley, MP
Comptroller of HM Household (*£20,580), Thomas McAvoy, MP
Vice-Chamberlain of HM Household (*20,580), Graham Allen, MP
Lord Commissioners of the Treasury (*£20,580), Robert Ainsworth, MP; James Dowd, MP; Clive Betts, MP; David Jamieson, MP; Jane Kennedy, MP
Assistant Whips (*£20,580), David Clelland, MP; Kevin Hughes, MP; Greg Pope, MP; Anne McGuire, MP; David Hanson, MP; Michael Hall, MP; Keith Hill, MP
Parliamentary Clerk, D. S. Martin
Permanent Secretary to the Treasury, Sir Andrew Turnbull, KCB, CVO
  Private Secretary, Ms S. Riach
Head of Government Accountancy Service and Chief Accountancy Adviser to the Treasury, A. Likierman

---

* In addition to a parliamentary salary of £45,066

DIRECTORATES

Leader, Ministerial Support Team (SCS), T. Scholar
Leader, Communications Team (SCS), P. Curwen
Leader, Strategy Team (SCS), Dr R. Kosmin

MACROECONOMIC POLICY AND PROSPECTS
Director, and Head of the Government Economic Service (SCS), A. O'Donnell
Deputy Directors (SCS), J. Grice; J. S. Cunliffe
Team Leaders (SCS), M. Bradbury; Ms M. Dawes; D. Deaton; C. M. Kelly; Ms S. Killen; A. Kilpatrick

INTERNATIONAL FINANCE
Director (SCS), Sir Nigel Wicks, KCB, CVO, CBE
Deputy Directors (SCS), P. McIntyre; D. L. C. Peretz, CB
Team Leaders (SCS), S. Brooks; A. Gibbs; N. J. Ilett; Ms S. Owen; M. Richardson

BUDGET AND PUBLIC FINANCES
Director (SCS), E. J. W. Gieve
Deputy Directors (SCS), Ms S. Chakrabarti; C. J. Mowl
Team Leaders (SCS), N. M. Hansford; P. Kane; S. N. Matthews; A. W. Ritchie; D. Savage; Ms C. Slocock; P. Wynn Owen

SPENDING
Director (SCS), R. P. Culpin, CB, CVO
Deputy Directors (SCS), †N. Glass; N. Macpherson; Miss G. M. Noble; P. N. Sedgwick
Team Leaders (SCS), P. Brook; J. Halligan; N. Holgate; A. Hudson; S. Judge; Ms G. Maklouf; J. Moore; M. Parkinson; I. V. W. Taylor; Ms R. Thompson; Ms S. Thomson; Ms S. Walker

FINANCIAL MANAGEMENT, REPORTING AND AUDIT
Director (Chief Accountancy Adviser) (SCS), A. Likierman
Deputy Director (SCS), †J. E. Mortimer
Team Leaders (SCS), J. Breckenbridge; C. Butler; Mrs R. M. Dunn; Dr R. Kosmin; Ms A. M. Jones; D. Loweth; D. Slaughter

FINANCE, REGULATION AND INDUSTRY
Director (SCS), S. Robson, CB
Deputy Directors (SCS), H. J. Bush; R. Fellgett; B. Rigby; M. Roberts
Team Leaders (SCS), R. Allen; M. Burt; P. Casey; J. Colling; Mrs P. C. Diggle; C. Farthing; D. Griffiths; J. May; C. R. Pickering; D. Roe; A. Sharples; Ms C. Speck; J. Whitlock; T. Wilson

PERSONNEL AND SUPPORT
Director (SCS), Ms M. O'Mara
Team Leaders (SCS), I. Cooper; J. Dodds; D. Rayson
† Combined deputy director and head of team

EXECUTIVE AGENCIES

NATIONAL SAVINGS
— *see* page 328

OFFICE FOR NATIONAL STATISTICS
— *see* pages 328–9

ROYAL MINT
— *see* page 338

UNITED KINGDOM DEBT MANAGEMENT OFFICE
1st Floor, Cheapside House, 138 Cheapside, London EC2V 6BB
Tel 0171-862 6500; fax 0171 862 6509

The UK Debt Management Office was launched as an executive agency of the Treasury in April 1998 after the transfer from the Bank of England to the Treasury of responsibility for debt management, the sale of gilts and oversight of the gilts market. It will in due course take over responsibility for the management of the Exchequer's daily cash flow.
Chief Executive, M. L. Williams

THE TREASURY SOLICITOR
DEPARTMENT OF HM PROCURATOR-GENERAL AND TREASURY SOLICITOR
Queen Anne's Chambers, 28 Broadway, London SW1H 9JS
Tel 0171-210 3000; fax 0171-210 3004

The Treasury Solicitor's Department provides legal services for many government departments. Those without their own lawyers are provided with legal advice, and both they and other departments are provided with litigation services. The Treasury Solicitor is also the Queen's Proctor, and is responsible for collecting Bona Vacantia on behalf of the Crown. The Department became an executive agency in April 1996.
HM Procurator-General and Treasury Solicitor (SCS), A. H. Hammond, CB
Deputy Treasury Solicitor (SCS), A. M. Inglese

CENTRAL ADVISORY DIVISION
SCS, Mrs I. G. Letwin

LITIGATION DIVISION
SCS, D. Brummell; Mrs D. Babar; A. D. Lawton; A. Leithead; B. McKay; P. R. Messer; Ms L. Nicoll; Mrs J. B. C. Oliver; D. Palmer; S. Parkinson; R. J. Phillips; A. J. Sandal

QUEEN'S PROCTOR DIVISION
Queen's Proctor (SCS), A. H. Hammond, CB
Assistant Queen's Proctor (SCS), Mrs D. Babar

RESOURCES AND SERVICES DIVISION
Principal Establishment and Finance Officer and Security Officer (SCS), J. P. Burnett
Deputy Establishment Officer (G7), Ms H. Donnelly
Finance Officer (G7), C. A. Woolley
Information Systems Manager (G7), M. Gabbidon
Business Support Manager (SEO), E. Blishen

BONA VACANTIA DIVISION
SCS, R. A. D. Jackson

EUROPEAN DIVISION
SCS, J. E. Collins; A. Ridout; M. C. P. Thomas

CULTURE, MEDIA AND SPORT DIVISION
SCS, C. P. J. Muttukumaru

CABINET OFFICE DIVISION
SCS, M. C. L. Carpenter

MINISTRY OF DEFENCE ADVISORY DIVISION
Metropole Building, Northumberland Avenue, London WC2N 5BL
Tel 0171-218 4691
SCS, Mrs V. Collett; M. Hemming; D. Macrae

DEPARTMENT FOR EDUCATION AND EMPLOYMENT ADVISORY DIVISION
Caxton House, Tothill Street, London SW1H 9NF
Tel 0171-273 3000
SCS, F. D. W. Clarke; F. L. Croft; S. T. Harker; C. House; N. A. D. Lambert

HM TREASURY ADVISORY DIVISION
Treasury Chambers, Parliament Street, London SW1P 3AG
Tel 0171-270 3000
SCS, M. A. Blythe; J. R. J. Braggins; Ms R. Ford; J. Jones; R. Ricks; Miss J. V. Stokes

CONSTITUTIONAL REFORM DIVISION
70 Whitehall, London SW1A 2AS
Tel 0171-270 6093
SCS, Miss R. A. Jeffreys

GOVERNMENT PROPERTY LAWYERS
Riverside Chambers, Castle Street, Taunton, Somerset
TA1 4AP
Tel 01823-345200; fax 01823-345202

An executive agency of the Treasury Solicitor's Department.
Chief Executive (G3), P. Horner
Group Directors (G5), D. Ager; M. Benmayor; A. M. Scarfe
Director of Lands Advisory (G5), R. C. Paddock

COUNCIL ON TRIBUNALS
7th Floor, 22 Kingsway, London WC2B 6LE
Tel 0171-936 7045; fax 0171-936 7044

The Council on Tribunals is an independent body that operates under the Tribunals and Inquiries Act 1992. It consists of 16 members appointed by the Lord Chancellor and the Lord Advocate; one member is appointed to represent the interests of people in Wales. The Scottish Committee of the Council generally considers Scottish tribunals and matters relating only to Scotland.

The Council advises on and keeps under review the constitution and working of administrative tribunals, and considers and reports on administrative procedures relating to statutory inquiries. Some 70 tribunals are currently under the Council's supervision. It is consulted by and advises government departments on a wide range of subjects relating to adjudicative procedures.
Chairman, The Lord Archer of Sandwell, PC, QC
Members, The Parliamentary Commissioner for
   Administration (*ex officio*); R. J. Elliot, WS (*Chairman of the Scottish Committee*); S. M. D. Brown; S. R. Davie, CB; J. H. Eames; Mrs A. Galbraith; ; Mrs S. R. Howdle; I. J. Irvine; R. H. Jones, CVO; S. Jones, CBE; Dr C. A. Kaplan; Prof. T. M. Partington; I. D. Penman, CB; D. G. Readings; P. A. A. Waring
Secretary, A. Twort

SCOTTISH COMMITTEE OF THE COUNCIL ON TRIBUNALS
44 Palmerston Place, Edinburgh EH12 5BJ
Tel 0131-220 1236; fax 0131-225 4271
Chairman, R. J. Elliot, WS
Members, The Parliamentary Commissioner for
   Administration; Mrs H. Sheerin, OBE; Ms M. Burns; Mrs A. Middleton; I. D. Penman, CB; Mrs P. Y. Berry, MBE; I. J. Irvine
Secretary, Mrs E. M. MacRae

TRIBUNALS
— *see* pages 369–72

UNITED KINGDOM SPORTS COUNCIL
Walkden House, 10 Melton Street, London NW1 2EB
Tel 0171-380 8000; fax 0171-380 8010

The UK Sports Council replaced the former Great Britain Sports Council on 1 January 1997. It promotes the development of sport and fosters the provision of facilities for sport and recreation at a UK level. It co-ordinates support to sports which compete internationally as the UK,

works to combat drug misuse, deals with international relations and major events, and undertakes development work on the planned UK Sports Institute. Funding for 1998–9 from the Department for Culture, Media and Sport is £11.6 million.

The Government announced in July 1998 that responsibility for distributing the funds allocated to sport from the proceeds of the National Lottery would be transferred from the English, Welsh, Scottish and Northern Ireland Sports Councils to the UK Sports Council.
Chairman, Sir Rodney Walker
Chief Executive, D. Chesterton

UNRELATED LIVE TRANSPLANT
REGULATORY AUTHORITY
Department of Health, c/o Room 311, Wellington House, 133–155 Waterloo Road, London SE1 8UG
Tel 0171-972 4812; fax 0171-972 4852

The Unrelated Live Transplant Regulatory Authority (ULTRA) is a statutory body established in 1990. In every case where the transplant of an organ within the definition of the Human Organ Transplants Act 1989 is proposed between a living donor and a recipient who are not genetically related, the proposal must be referred to ULTRA. Applications must be made by registered medical practitioners.

The Authority comprises a chairman and ten members appointed by the Secretary of State for Health. The secretariat is provided by Department of Health officials.
Chairman, Prof. M. Bobrow, CBE
Members, Mrs J. H. Callman; Dr J. F. Douglas; Dr H. Draper; Dr P. A. Dyer; Lady Eccles; Miss P. M. Franklin; A. Hooker; S. G. Macpherson; Prof. N. P. Mallick; Prof. J. R. Salaman
Administrative Secretary, W. Kent
Medical Secretary, Dr P. Doyle

WALES YOUTH AGENCY
Leslie Court, Lon-y-Llyn, Caerphilly CF83 1BQ
Tel 01222-880088; fax 01222-880824

The Wales Youth Agency is an independent organization funded by the Welsh Office. Its functions include the encouragement and development of the partnership between statutory and voluntary agencies relating to young people; the promotion of staff development and training; and the extension of marketing and information services in the relevant fields. The board of directors is appointed by the Secretary of State for Wales; directors do not receive a salary.
Chairman of the Board of Directors, R. Noble
Vice-Chairman of the Board of Directors, Dr H. Williamson
Executive Director, B. Williams

OFFICE OF WATER SERVICES
Centre City Tower, 7 Hill Street, Birmingham B5 4UA
Tel 0121-625 1300; fax 0121-625 1400

The Office of Water Services (Ofwat) was set up under the Water Act 1989 and is a non-ministerial government department headed by the Director-General of Water Services. It is the independent economic regulator of the water and sewerage companies in England and Wales.

Ofwat's main duties are to ensure that the companies can finance and carry out the functions specified in the Water Industry Act 1991 and to protect the interests of water customers. There are ten regional customer service committees which are concerned solely with the interests of water customers. Representation of customer interests at national level is the responsibility of the Ofwat National Customer Council (ONCC).

Director-General of Water Services, I. C. R. Byatt
Chairman, Ofwat National Customer Council, Ms S. Reiter

WELSH DEVELOPMENT AGENCY
Principality House, The Friary, Cardiff CF1 4AE
Tel 0345-775577/66; fax 01443-845589

The Agency was established under the Welsh Development Agency Act 1975. Its remit is to help further the regeneration of the economy and improve the environment in Wales. The Agency's main activities include site assembly, provision of premises, encouraging investment by the private sector in property development, grant-aiding land reclamation, stimulating quality urban and rural development, promoting Wales as a location for inward investment, helping to boost the growth, profitability and competitiveness of indigenous Welsh companies, and providing investment capital for industry. Its sponsoring department is the Welsh Office.

Under the Government of Wales Act 1998, the Land Authority for Wales and the Development Board for Rural Wales have merged with the Welsh Development Agency.

Chairman, D. Rowe-Beddoe
Deputy Chairman, R. Lewis, OBE
Chief Executive, W. B. Willott, CB

WELSH OFFICE
*Gwydyr House, Whitehall, London SW1A 2ER
Tel 0171-270 3000
Cathays Park, Cardiff CF1 3NQ
Tel 01222-825111
E-mail: webmaster@wales.gov.uk
Web: http://www.wales.gov.uk

The Welsh Office has responsibility in Wales for ministerial functions relating to health and personal social services; education, except for terms and conditions of service and student awards; training; the Welsh language, arts and culture; the implementation of the Citizen's Charter in Wales; local government; housing; water and sewerage; environmental protection; sport; agriculture and fisheries; forestry; land use, including town and country planning and countryside and nature conservation; new towns; non-departmental public bodies and appointments in Wales; ancient monuments and historic buildings and the Welsh Arts Council; roads; tourism; financial assistance to industry; the Strategic Development Scheme in Wales and the Programme for the Valleys; the operation of the European Regional Development Fund in Wales and other European Union matters; civil emergencies; and all financial aspects of these matters, including Welsh rate support grant.

The directly-elected Welsh Assembly which is to be established in 1999 will take over the budget of the Welsh Office and will be serviced by Welsh Office civil servants.

Secretary of State for Wales, The Rt. Hon. Ron Davies, MP*
Private Secretary, Dr J. E. Milligan*
Special Advisers, J. Adams; H. Roberts

Parliamentary Private Secretary, N. Ainger, MP
Parliamentary Under-Secretaries, Peter Hain, MP; Jon Owen Jones, MP
Private Secretaries, S. George; Ms J. Cole
Parliamentary Clerk, A. Green*
Permanent Secretary (G1), Mrs R. Lomax
Private Secretary, G. Haggaty

LEGAL GROUP
Legal Adviser (G3), D. G. Lambert
Deputy Legal Adviser (G5), J. H. Turnbull

INFORMATION DIVISION
Director of Information (G5), C. P. Wilson
Head of Publicity (G7), W. J. Edwards
Chief Press Officer (G7), D. Clifford

ESTABLISHMENT GROUP
Principal Establishment Officer (G3), S. H. Martin
Heads of Divisions (G5), Mrs B. Wilson; Dr A. G. Thornton; Ms K. Cassidy
Chief Statistician (G5), W. R. L. Alldritt
Head of Health Statistics and Analysis Unit (G6), P. Demery

FINANCE GROUP
Principal Finance Officer (G3), D. T. Richards
Head of Division (G5), L. A. Pavelin
Senior Economic Adviser (G5), M. G. Phelps
Head of Internal Audit (G6), D. A. McNeill

ECONOMIC AFFAIRS
Deputy Secretary (G2), J. D. Shortridge

AGRICULTURE DEPARTMENT
Head of Department (G3), L. K. Walford
Heads of Divisions (G5), Mrs A. M. Jackson; H. D. Brodie

ECONOMIC DEVELOPMENT GROUP
Head of Group (G3), M. J. Cochlin
Heads of Divisions (G5), A. D. Lansdown; L. Conway; P. Fullerton

INDUSTRY AND TRAINING DEPARTMENT
Director (G3), D. W. Jones
Industrial Director (G4), vacant
Heads of Divisions (G5), R. Keveren; N. E. Thomas; W. G. Davies; (G6), Dr R. J. Loveland

SOCIAL POLICY
Deputy Secretary (G2), J. W. Lloyd, CB

EDUCATION DEPARTMENT
Head of Department (G3), R. J. Davies
Heads of Divisions (G5)†, R. Thomas; D. R. Adams; J. Howells; Mrs E. A. Taylor

OFFICE OF HM CHIEF INSPECTOR FOR SCHOOLS IN WALES
Chief Inspector (G4)†, Miss S. Lewis
Staff Inspectors (G5)†, M. G. Haines; C. Abbott
There are 45 Grade 6 Inspectors.
Head of Administration (G7), Mrs S. Howells

LOCAL GOVERNMENT GROUP
Head of Group (G3), B. J. Mitchell
Heads of Divisions (G5), D. A. Pritchard; Ms H. F. O. Thomas; M. J. Shanahan
Chief Inspector, Social Services Inspectorate (Wales) (G5), D. G. Evans
Deputy Chief Inspectors, R. Tebboth; R. C. Woodward; Mrs P. E. White

HEALTH DEPARTMENT
Director (G3), P. R. Gregory

Heads of Divisions (G5), D. H. Jones; A. C. Wood;
B. Wilcox; R. C. Williams; Dr J. Blamire

HEALTH PROFESSIONAL GROUP
Chief Medical Officer (G3), Dr R. Hall
Principal Medical Officers (G4), Dr B. Fuge; Dr J. K.
Richmond
Senior Medical Officers (G5), Dr J. Ludlow; Dr H. N.
Williams; Dr D. Salter
Medical Adviser (part-time), vacant
Chief Dental Officer (G5), P. Langmaid
Chief Scientific Adviser (G5), Dr J. A. V. Pritchard
Deputy Scientific Adviser (G6), Dr E. O. Crawley
Chief Pharmaceutical Adviser (G5), Miss C. W. Howells
Chief Environmental Health Adviser (G5), R. Alexander
Deputy Environmental Health Adviser (G6), D. Worthington

NURSING DIVISION
Chief Nursing Officer, Miss M. P. Bull, CBE
Nursing Officers, P. Johnson; M. F. Tonkin; Mrs H. Wood;
Mrs R. Johnson

TRANSPORT, PLANNING AND ENVIRONMENT GROUP
Head of Group (G3), G. C. G. Craig
Director of Highways (G4), K. J. Thomas
Heads of Divisions (G5), J. R. Rees *(Roads Construction)*;
G. A. Thomas *(Transport Policy)*; *(G6)*, R. J. Shaw
(Network Management); B. H. Hawker, OBE *(Roads Major
Projects)*
Grade 7, R. H. Powell; I. P. Davies; R. K. Cones; K. J. A.
Tengy; T. J. Collins; S. C. Shouler; M. J. Gilbert; T. C.
Dorken; M. J. A. Parker; I. A. Grindulis; A. D. Perry; Dr
M. C. Dunn

HEALTH AUTHORITIES
– see page 480

EXECUTIVE AGENCIES

CADW: WELSH HISTORIC MONUMENTS
Crown Building, Cathays Park, Cardiff CF1 3NQ
Tel 01222-500200; fax 01222-826375

Cadw supports the preservation, conservation, apprecia-
tion and enjoyment of the built heritage in Wales.
Chief Executive, T. Cassidy
Director of Policy and Administration, R. W. Hughes
Conservation Architect, J. D. Hogg
*Principal Inspector of Ancient Monuments and Historic
Buildings*, J. R. Avent
Inspectors of Ancient Monuments and Historic Buildings,
A. D. McLees; Dr S. E. Rees; R. C. Turner; M. J. Yates

FARMING AND RURAL CONSERVATION AGENCY
— see page 281

INTERVENTION BOARD
— see pages 315–16

PLANNING INSPECTORATE
Cathays Park, Cardiff CF1 3NQ
Tel 01222-825670; fax 01222-825150

A joint executive agency of the Department of the
Environment, Transport and the Regions and the Welsh
Office (*see* page 300).
Chief Executive and Chief Planning Inspector (G3), C. Shepley
Director (G5), R. Davies

WOMEN'S NATIONAL COMMISSION
5th Floor, The Adelphi, 1–11 John Adam Street, London
WC2N 6HT
Tel 0171-712 2443; fax 0171-962 8171

The Women's National Commission is an independent
advisory committee to the Government. Its remit is to
ensure that the informed opinions of women are given their
due weight in the deliberations of the Government and in
public debate on matters of public interest including those
of special interest to women. The Commission's sponsoring department is the Department for Social Security.
Government Co-Chairman, The Baroness Symons of
Vernham Dean
Elected Co-Chairman, Miss V. Evans, CBE
Secretary, Ms J. Bailey

CIVIL SERVICE STAFF

BY MAIN DEPARTMENTS *as at 1 April 1997*

	Total	Of whom in agencies
Agriculture, Fisheries and Food	9,092	3,443
Cabinet Office	2,569	1,542
Customs and Excise	23,071	—
Defence	100,206	62,415
Education and Employment	33,662	29,181
Environment	3,687	681
Foreign Office	5,574	35
Health	4,695	1,013
HM Prison Service	37,704	37,704
Home Office	12,165	2,807
Inland Revenue	54,029	4,301
Lord Chancellor's Department	10,625	9,749
National Heritage	1,004	666
Northern Ireland Office	204	—
Scottish Departments	12,910	7,955
Social Security	93,055	90,372
Trade and Industry	8,398	3,897
Transport	11,154	9,494
Treasury	888	—
Welsh Office	2,180	179
Other departments	48,467	20,100
TOTAL	475,339	285,534

Source: The Stationery Office *– Civil Service Yearbook 1998*

† Based at Tŷ Glas Road, Llanishen, Cardiff CF4 5LE. Tel: 01222-761456

Law Courts and Offices

THE JUDICIAL COMMITTEE OF THE PRIVY COUNCIL

The Judicial Committee of the Privy Council is primarily the final court of appeal for the United Kingdom dependent territories and those independent Commonwealth countries which have retained the avenue of appeal upon achieving independence (Antigua and Barbuda, The Bahamas, Barbados, Belize, Brunei, Dominica, The Gambia, Jamaica, Kiribati, Mauritius, New Zealand, St Christopher and Nevis, St Lucia, St Vincent and the Grenadines, Trinidad and Tobago, and Tuvalu). The Committee also hears appeals from the Channel Islands and the Isle of Man and the disciplinary and health committees of the medical and allied professions. It has a limited jurisdiction to hear appeals under the Pastoral Measure 1983. In 1997 the Judicial Committee heard 69 appeals and 82 petitions for special leave to appeal.

The members of the Judicial Committee include the Lord Chancellor, the Lords of Appeal in Ordinary (*see* page 355), other Privy Counsellors who hold or have held high judicial office and certain judges from the Commonwealth.

PRIVY COUNCIL OFFICE (JUDICIAL COMMITTEE), Downing Street, London SW1A 2AJ. Tel: 0171-270 0483. *Registrar of the Privy Council*, J. A. C. Watherston; *Chief Clerk*, F. G. Hart

The Judicature of England and Wales

The legal system of England and Wales is separate from those of Scotland and Northern Ireland and differs from them in law, judicial procedure and court structure, although there is a common distinction between civil law (disputes between individuals) and criminal law (acts harmful to the community).

The supreme judicial authority for England and Wales is the House of Lords, which is the ultimate Court of Appeal from all courts in Great Britain and Northern Ireland (except criminal courts in Scotland) for all cases except those concerning the interpretation and application of European Community law, including preliminary rulings requested by British courts and tribunals, which are decided by the European Court of Justice (*see* page 778). (At the time of going to press, legislation was before Parliament under which the European Convention on Human Rights would be incorporated into British law; until the legislation comes into force, an applicant must, when all remedies available at national level have been exhausted, petition the European Commission of Human Rights to investigate an alleged violation of the Convention.) As a Court of Appeal the House of Lords consists of the Lord Chancellor and the Lords of Appeal in Ordinary (law lords).

SUPREME COURT OF JUDICATURE

The Supreme Court of Judicature comprises the Court of Appeal, the High Court of Justice and the Crown Court. The High Court of Justice is the superior civil court and is divided into three divisions. The Chancery Division is concerned mainly with equity, bankruptcy and contentious probate business. The Queen's Bench Division deals with commercial and maritime law, serious personal injury and medical negligence cases, cases involving a breach of contract and professional negligence actions. The Family Division deals with matters relating to family law. Sittings are held at the Royal Courts of Justice in London or at 126 district registries outside the capital. High Court judges sit alone to hear cases at first instance. Appeals from lower courts are heard by two or three judges, or by single judges of the appropriate division. The Restrictive Practices Court, set up under the Restrictive Trade Practices Act 1956, and the Technology and Construction Court, which deals with cases which require expert evidence on technical and other issues concerning mainly the construction industry, defective products, property valuations, and landlord and tenant disputes, are also part of the High Court. Appeals from the High Court are heard in the Court of Appeal (Civil Division), presided over by the Master of the Rolls, and may go on to the House of Lords.

CRIMINAL CASES

In criminal matters the decision to prosecute in the majority of cases rests with the Crown Prosecution Service, the independent prosecuting body in England and Wales (*see* pages 363–4). The Service is headed by the Director of Public Prosecutions, who works under the superintendence of the Attorney-General. Certain categories of offence continue to require the Attorney-General's consent for prosecution.

The Crown Court sits in about 90 centres, divided into six circuits, and is presided over by High Court judges, full-time circuit judges, and part-time recorders and assistant recorders, sitting with a jury in all trials which are contested. There were 395 assistant recorders at 30 June 1998. The Crown Court deals with trials of the more serious criminal offences, the sentencing of offenders committed for sentence by magistrates' courts (when the magistrates consider their own power of sentence inadequate), and appeals from magistrates' courts. Magistrates usually sit with a circuit judge or recorder to deal with appeals and committals for sentence. Appeals from the Crown Court, either against sentence or conviction, are made to the Court of Appeal (Criminal Division), presided over by the Lord Chief Justice. A further appeal from the Court of Appeal to the House of Lords can be brought if a point of law of general public importance is considered to be involved.

Minor criminal offences (summary offences) are dealt with in magistrates' courts, which usually consist of three unpaid lay magistrates (justices of the peace) sitting without a jury, who are advised on points of law and procedure by a legally-qualified clerk to the justices. There were 30,361 justices of the peace at 1 January 1998. In busier courts a full-time, salaried and legally-qualified stipendiary magistrate presides alone. Cases involving people under 18 are heard in youth courts, specially constituted magistrates' courts which sit apart from other courts. Preliminary proceedings in a serious case to decide whether there is evidence to justify committal for trial in the Crown Court are also dealt with in the magistrates' courts. Appeals from magistrates' courts against sentence or conviction are made to the Crown Court. Appeals upon a point of law are made to the High Court, and may go on to the House of Lords.

CIVIL CASES

Most minor civil cases are dealt with by the county courts, of which there are about 270 (details may be found in the local telephone directory). Cases are heard by circuit judges or district judges. There were 342 district judges at 31 May 1998. For cases involving small claims there are special simplified procedures. Where there are financial limits on county court jurisdiction, claims which exceed those limits may be tried in the county courts with the consent of the parties, or in certain circumstances on transfer from the High Court. Outside London, bankruptcy proceedings can be heard in designated county courts. Magistrates' courts can deal with certain classes of civil case and committees of magistrates license public houses, clubs and betting shops. For the implementation of the Children Act 1989, a new structure of hearing centres was set up in 1991 for family proceedings cases, involving magistrates' courts (family proceedings courts), divorce county courts, family hearing centres and care centres. Appeals in family matters heard in the family proceedings courts go to the Family Division of the High Court; affiliation appeals and appeals from decisions of the licensing committees of magistrates go to the Crown Court. Appeals from county courts are heard in the Court of Appeal (Civil Division), and may go on to the House of Lords.

CORONERS' COURTS

Coroners' courts investigate violent and unnatural deaths or sudden deaths where the cause is unknown. Cases may be brought before a local coroner (a senior lawyer or doctor) by doctors, the police, various public authorities or members of the public. Where a death is sudden and the cause is unknown, the coroner may order a post-mortem examination to determine the cause of death rather than hold an inquest in court.

Judicial appointments are made by The Queen; the most senior appointments are made on the advice of the Prime Minister and other appointments on the advice of the Lord Chancellor.

Under the provisions of the Criminal Appeal Act 1995, a Commission was set up to direct and supervise investigations into possible miscarriages of justice and to refer cases to the courts on the grounds of conviction and sentence (*see* page 292); these functions were formerly the responsibility of the Home Secretary.

For late changes to this section, *see* Stop-Press

THE HOUSE OF LORDS
AS FINAL COURT OF APPEAL

The Lord High Chancellor (£148,850)
The Rt. Hon. the Lord Irvine of Lairg, *born* 1940, *apptd* 1997

LORDS OF APPEAL IN ORDINARY (each £138,889)
Style, The Rt. Hon. Lord —

Rt. Hon. Lord Browne-Wilkinson, *born* 1930, *apptd* 1991
Rt. Hon. Lord Slynn of Hadley, *born* 1930, *apptd* 1992

Rt. Hon. Lord Lloyd of Berwick, *born* 1929, *apptd* 1993
Rt. Hon. Lord Nicholls of Birkenhead, *born* 1933, *apptd* 1994
Rt. Hon. Lord Steyn, *born* 1932, *apptd* 1995
Rt. Hon. Lord Hoffman, *born* 1934, *apptd* 1995
Rt. Hon. Lord Hope of Craighead, *born* 1938, *apptd* 1996
Rt. Hon. Lord Clyde, *born* 1932, *apptd* 1996
Rt. Hon. Lord Hutton, *born* 1931, *apptd* 1997
Rt. Hon. Lord Saville of Newdigate, *born* 1936, *apptd* 1997
*Rt. Hon. Sir John Hobhouse, *born* 1932, *apptd* 1998
*Rt. Hon. Sir Peter Millett, *born* 1932, *apptd* 1998

Registrar, The Clerk of the Parliaments (*see* page 218)
* To receive a life peerage

SUPREME COURT OF JUDICATURE

COURT OF APPEAL

The Master of the Rolls (£138,889), The Rt. Hon. Lord Woolf, *born* 1933, *apptd* 1996
Secretary, Mrs L. Grace
Clerk, Ms J. Jones

LORDS JUSTICES OF APPEAL (each £132,017)
Style, The Rt. Hon. Lord/Lady Justice [surname]

Rt. Hon. Sir Martin Nourse, *born* 1932, *apptd* 1985
Rt. Hon. Dame Elizabeth Butler-Sloss, DBE, *born* 1933, *apptd* 1988
Rt. Hon. Sir Murray Stuart-Smith, *born* 1927, *apptd* 1988
Rt. Hon. Sir Roy Beldam, *born* 1925, *apptd* 1989
Rt. Hon. Sir Paul Kennedy, *born* 1935, *apptd* 1992
Rt. Hon. Sir David Hirst, *born* 1925, *apptd* 1992
Rt. Hon. Sir Simon Brown, *born* 1937, *apptd* 1992
Rt. Hon. Sir Anthony Evans, *born* 1934, *apptd* 1992
Rt. Hon. Sir Christopher Rose, *born* 1937, *apptd* 1992
Rt. Hon. Sir John Roch, *born* 1934, *apptd* 1993
Rt. Hon. Sir Peter Gibson, *born* 1934, *apptd* 1993
Rt. Hon. Sir Denis Henry, *born* 1931, *apptd* 1993
Rt. Hon. Sir Swinton Thomas, *born* 1931, *apptd* 1994
Rt. Hon. Sir Andrew Morritt, cvo, *born* 1938, *apptd* 1994
Rt. Hon. Sir Philip Otton, *born* 1933, *apptd* 1995
Rt. Hon. Sir Robin Auld, *born* 1937, *apptd* 1995
Rt. Hon. Sir Malcolm Pill, *born* 1938, *apptd* 1995
Rt. Hon. Sir William Aldous, *born* 1936, *apptd* 1995
Rt. Hon. Sir Alan Ward, *born* 1938, *apptd* 1995
Rt. Hon. Sir Michael Hutchison, *born* 1933, *apptd* 1995
Rt. Hon. Sir Konrad Schiemann, *born* 1937, *apptd* 1995
Rt. Hon. Sir Nicholas Phillips, *born* 1938, *apptd* 1995
Rt. Hon. Sir Mathew Thorpe, *born* 1938, *apptd* 1995
Rt. Hon. Sir Mark Potter, *born* 1937, *apptd* 1996
Rt. Hon. Sir Henry Brooke, *born* 1936, *apptd* 1996
Rt. Hon. Sir Igor Judge, *born* 1941, *apptd* 1996
Rt. Hon. Sir Mark Waller, *born* 1940, *apptd* 1996
Rt. Hon. Sir John Mummery, *born* 1938, *apptd* 1996
Rt. Hon. Sir Charles Mantell, *born* 1937, *apptd* 1997
Rt. Hon. Sir John Chadwick, ED, *born* 1941, *apptd* 1997
Rt. Hon. Sir Robert Walker, *born* 1938, *apptd* 1997
Rt. Hon. Sir Richard Buxton, *born* 1938, *apptd* 1997
Rt. Hon. Sir Anthony May, *born* 1940, *apptd* 1997

Ex officio Judges, The Lord High Chancellor; the Lord Chief Justice of England; the Master of the Rolls; the President of the Family Division; and the Vice-Chancellor

COURT OF APPEAL (CRIMINAL DIVISION)
Vice-President, The Rt. Hon. Lord Justice Rose
Judges, The Lord Chief Justice of England; the Master of the Rolls; Lords Justices of Appeal; and Judges of the High Court of Justice

COURTS-MARTIAL APPEAL COURT

Judges, The Lord Chief Justice of England; the Master of the Rolls; Lords Justices of Appeal; and Judges of the High Court of Justice

HIGH COURT OF JUSTICE

CHANCERY DIVISION

President, The Lord High Chancellor
The Vice-Chancellor (£132,017), The Rt. Hon. Sir Richard Scott, *born* 1934, *apptd* 1994
  Clerk, W. Northfield, BEM

JUDGES (each £117,752)
Style, The Hon. Mr/Mrs Justice [surname]

Hon. Sir Donald Rattee, *born* 1937, *apptd* 1989
Hon. Sir Francis Ferris, TD, *born* 1932, *apptd* 1990
Hon. Sir Jonathan Parker, *born* 1937, *apptd* 1991
Hon. Sir John Lindsay, *born* 1935, *apptd* 1992
Hon. Dame Mary Arden, DBE, *born* 1947, *apptd* 1993
Hon. Sir Edward Evans-Lombe, *born* 1937, *apptd* 1993
Hon. Sir Robin Jacob, *born* 1941, *apptd* 1993
Hon. Sir William Blackburne, *born* 1944, *apptd* 1993
Hon. Sir Gavin Lightman, *born* 1939, *apptd* 1994
Hon. Sir Robert Carnwath, *born* 1945, *apptd* 1994
Hon. Sir Colin Rimer, *born* 1944, *apptd* 1994
Hon. Sir Hugh Laddie, *born* 1946, *apptd* 1995
Hon. Sir Timothy Lloyd, *born* 1946, *apptd* 1996
Hon. Sir David Neuberger, *born* 1948, *apptd* 1996
Hon. Sir Andrew Park, *born* 1939, *apptd* 1997
Hon. Sir Nicholas Pumfrey, *born* 1951, *apptd* 1997
Hon. Sir Michael Hart, *born* 1948, *apptd* 1998

HIGH COURT OF JUSTICE IN BANKRUPTCY

Judges, The Vice-Chancellor and judges of the Chancery Division of the High Court

COMPANIES COURT

Judges, The Vice Chancellor and judges of the Chancery Division of the High Court

PATENT COURT (APPELLATE SECTION)

Judge, The Hon. Mr Justice Jacob

QUEEN'S BENCH DIVISION

The Lord Chief Justice of England (£148,502) The Rt. Hon. the Lord Bingham of Cornhill, *born* 1933, *apptd* 1996
  Private Secretary, E. Adams
  Clerk, J. Bond
Vice-President, The Rt. Hon. Lord Justice Kennedy

JUDGES (EACH £117,752)
Style, The Hon. Mr/Mrs Justice [surname]

Hon. Sir Oliver Popplewell, *born* 1927, *apptd* 1983
Hon. Sir Richard Tucker, *born* 1930, *apptd* 1985
Hon. Sir Patrick Garland, *born* 1929, *apptd* 1985
Hon. Sir Michael Turner, *born* 1931, *apptd* 1985
Hon. Sir John Alliott, *born* 1932, *apptd* 1986
Hon. Sir Harry Ognall, *born* 1934, *apptd* 1986
Hon. Sir John Owen, *born* 1925, *apptd* 1986
Hon. Sir Humphrey Potts, *born* 1931, *apptd* 1986
Hon. Sir Richard Rougier, *born* 1932, *apptd* 1986
Hon. Sir Ian Kennedy, *born* 1930, *apptd* 1986
Hon. Sir Stuart McKinnon, *born* 1938, *apptd* 1988
Hon. Sir Scott Baker, *born* 1937, *apptd* 1988
Hon. Sir Edwin Jowitt, *born* 1929, *apptd* 1988
Hon. Sir Douglas Brown, *born* 1931, *apptd* 1996
Hon. Sir Michael Morland, *born* 1929, *apptd* 1989
Hon. Sir Roger Buckley, *born* 1939, *apptd* 1989

Hon. Sir Anthony Hidden, *born* 1936, *apptd* 1989
Hon. Sir Michael Wright, *born* 1932, *apptd* 1990
Hon. Sir John Blofeld, *born* 1932, *apptd* 1990
Hon. Sir Peter Cresswell, *born* 1944, *apptd* 1991
Hon. Sir John Laws, *born* 1945, *apptd* 1992
Hon. Dame Ann Ebsworth, DBE, *born* 1937, *apptd* 1992
Hon. Sir Simon Tuckey, *born* 1941, *apptd* 1992
Hon. Sir David Latham, *born* 1942, *apptd* 1992
Hon. Sir Christopher Holland, *born* 1937, *apptd* 1992
Hon. Sir John Kay, *born* 1943, *apptd* 1992
Hon. Sir Richard Curtis, *born* 1933, *apptd* 1992
Hon. Sir Stephen Sedley, *born* 1939, *apptd* 1992
Hon. Dame Janet Smith, DBE, *born* 1940, *apptd* 1992
Hon. Sir Anthony Colman, *born* 1938, *apptd* 1992
Hon. Sir Anthony Clarke, *born* 1943, *apptd* 1993
Hon. Sir John Dyson, *born* 1943, *apptd* 1993
Hon. Sir Thayne Forbes, *born* 1938, *apptd* 1993
Hon. Sir Michael Sachs, *born* 1932, *apptd* 1993
Hon. Sir Stephen Mitchell, *born* 1941, *apptd* 1993
Hon. Sir Rodger Bell, *born* 1939, *apptd* 1993
Hon. Sir Michael Harrison, *born* 1939, *apptd* 1993
Hon. Sir Bernard Rix, *born* 1944, *apptd* 1993
Hon. Dame Heather Steel, DBE, *born* 1940, *apptd* 1993
Hon. Sir William Gage, *born* 1938, *apptd* 1993
Hon. Sir Jonathan Mance, *born* 1943, *apptd* 1993
Hon. Sir Andrew Longmore, *born* 1944, *apptd* 1993
Hon. Sir Thomas Morison, *born* 1939, *apptd* 1993
Hon. Sir David Keene, *born* 1941, *apptd* 1994
Hon. Sir Andrew Collins, *born* 1942, *apptd* 1994
Hon. Sir Maurice Kay, *born* 1942, *apptd* 1995
Hon. Sir Brian Smedley, *born* 1934, *apptd* 1995
Hon. Sir Anthony Hooper, *born* 1937, *apptd* 1995
Hon. Sir Alexander Butterfield, *born* 1942, *apptd* 1995
Hon. Sir George Newman, *born* 1941, *apptd* 1995
Hon. Sir David Poole, *born* 1938, *apptd* 1995
Hon. Sir Martin Moore-Bick, *born* 1946, *apptd* 1995
Hon. Sir Gordon Langley, *born* 1943, *apptd* 1995
Hon. Sir Roger Thomas, *born* 1947, *apptd* 1996
Hon. Sir Robert Nelson, *born* 1942, *apptd* 1996
Hon. Sir Roger Toulson, *born* 1946, *apptd* 1996
Hon. Sir Michael Astill, *born* 1938, *apptd* 1996
Hon. Sir Alan Moses, *born* 1945, *apptd* 1996
Hon. Sir Timothy Walker, *born* 1946, *apptd* 1996
Hon. Sir David Eady, *born* 1943, *apptd* 1997
Hon. Sir Jeremy Sullivan, *born* 1945, *apptd* 1997
Hon. Sir David Penry-Davey, *born* 1942, *apptd* 1997
Hon. Sir Stephen Richards, *born* 1950, *apptd* 1997
Hon. Sir David Steel, *born* 1943, *apptd* 1998

FAMILY DIVISION

President (£132,017) The Rt. Hon. Sir Stephen Brown, *born* 1924, *apptd* 1988
  Secretary, Mrs S. Leung
  Clerk, Mrs S. Bell

JUDGES (each £117,752)
Style, The Hon. Mr/Mrs Justice [surname]

Hon. Sir Edward Cazalet, *born* 1936, *apptd* 1988
Hon. Sir Robert Johnson, *born* 1933, *apptd* 1989
Hon. Dame Joyanne Bracewell, DBE, *born* 1934, *apptd* 1990
Hon. Sir Michael Connell, *born* 1939, *apptd* 1991
Hon. Sir Peter Singer, *born* 1944, *apptd* 1993
Hon. Sir Nicholas Wilson, *born* 1945, *apptd* 1993
Hon. Sir Nicholas Wall, *born* 1945, *apptd* 1993
Hon. Sir Andrew Kirkwood, *born* 1944, *apptd* 1993
Hon. Sir Christopher Stuart-White, *born* 1933, *apptd* 1993
Hon. Dame Brenda Hale, DBE, *born* 1945, *apptd* 1994
Hon. Sir Hugh Bennett, *born* 1943, *apptd* 1995
Hon. Sir Edward Holman, *born* 1947, *apptd* 1995

Hon. Dame Mary Hogg, DBE, born 1947, *apptd* 1995
Hon. Sir Christopher Sumner, *born* 1939, *apptd* 1996
Hon. Sir Anthony Hughes, *born* 1948, *apptd* 1997
Hon. Sir Arthur Charles, *born* 1948, *apptd* 1998

RESTRICTIVE PRACTICES COURT
Room 410, Thomas More Building, Royal Courts of
Justice, Strand, London WC2A 2LL
Tel 0171-936 6727

President, The Hon. Mr Justice Buckley
Judges, The Hon. Mr Justice Ferris; The Hon. Mr Justice
   Lightman
Lay Members, B. M. Currie; Sir Lewis Robertson, CBE;
   R. Garrick, CBE; S. J. Ahearne; J. A. Graham; Mrs D. H.
   Hatfield; J. A. Scott; B. D. Colgate; J. A. C. King
Clerk of the Court, M. Buckley

TECHNOLOGY AND CONSTRUCTION COURT
St Dunstan's House, 133–137 Fetter Lane, London
EC4A 1HD
Tel 0171-936 7427

JUDGES (each £96,214)
The Hon. Mr Justice Dyson (*Presiding Judge*)
His Hon. Judge Bowsher, QC
His Hon. Judge Hicks, QC
His Hon. Judge Havery, QC
His Hon. Judge Lloyd, QC
His Hon. Judge Newman, QC
His Hon. Judge Thornton, QC
His Hon. Judge Wilcox
His Hon. Judge Toulmin, CMG, QC

Court Manager, Miss B. Joy

LORD CHANCELLOR'S DEPARTMENT
— *see* Government Departments and Public Offices

SUPREME COURT DEPARTMENTS AND OFFICES
Royal Courts of Justice, London WC2A 2LL
Tel 0171-936 6000

DIRECTOR'S OFFICE
Director, G. E. Calvett
Group Manager and Deputy Director, J. Selch
Group Manager, Family Proceedings and Probate Service, R. P.
   Knight
Finance and Performance Officer, K. T. Fairweather

ADMIRALTY AND COMMERCIAL REGISTRY AND
MARSHAL'S OFFICE
Registrar (£70,820), P. Miller
Admiralty Marshal and Court Manager, A. Ferrigno

BANKRUPTCY DEPARTMENT
Chief Registrar (£84,752), M. C. B. Buckley
Bankruptcy Registrars (£70,820), W. S. James;
   J. A. Simmonds; P. J. S. Rawson; S. Baister; G. W. Jaques
Court Manager, M. A. Brown

CENTRAL OFFICE OF THE SUPREME COURT
*Senior Master of the Supreme Court (QBD), and Queen's
   Remembrancer* (£84,752), R. L. Turner

Masters of the Supreme Court (QBD) (£70,820), D. L.
   Prebble; G. H. Hodgson; J. Trench; M. Tennant; P.
   Miller; N. O. G. Murray; I. H. Foster; G. H. Rose; P. G.
   A. Eyre; H. J. Leslie; J. G. G. Ungley
Senior Court Manager, P. Emery

CHANCERY DIVISION
Senior Court Manager, P. Emery

CHANCERY CHAMBERS
Chief Master of the Supreme Court (£84,752), vacant
Masters of the Supreme Court (£70,820), G. A. Barratt; J. I.
   Winegarten; J. A. Moncaster, R. A. Bowman; N. W.
   Bragge
Court Manager, G. Robinson
Conveyancing Counsel of the Supreme Court, W. D. Ainger;
   H. M. Harrod; A. C. Taussig

COMPANIES COURT
Registrar (£70,820), M. Buckley
Court Manager, M. A. Brown

COURT OF APPEAL CIVIL DIVISION
Registrar (£84,752), vacant
Deputy Registrar, I. M. Joseph
Court Manager, Miss H. M. Goddard

COURT OF APPEAL CRIMINAL DIVISION
Registrar (£84,752), M. McKenzie, QC
Deputy Registrar, Mrs L. G. Knapman
Chief Clerk, M. Bishop

COURTS-MARTIAL APPEALS OFFICE
Registrar (£84,752), M. McKenzie, QC
Chief Clerk, M. Bishop

CROWN OFFICE OF THE SUPREME COURT
Master of the Crown Office, and Queen's Coroner and Attorney
   (£84,752), M. McKenzie, QC
Head of Crown Office, Mrs L. G. Knapman
Chief Clerk, M. Bishop

EXAMINERS OF THE COURT
Empowered to take examination of witnesses in all
Divisions of the High Court
R. G. Wood; Mrs G. M. Kenne; R. M. Planterose; Miss
   V. E. I. Selvaratnam

RESTRICTIVE PRACTICES COURT
Clerk of the Court, M. Buckley
Court Manager, M. A. Brown

SUPREME COURT TAXING OFFICE
Chief Master (£84,752), P. T. Hurst
Masters of the Supreme Court (£70,820), M. Ellis; T. H.
   Seager Berry; C. C. Wright; P. A. Rogers; G. N. Pollard;
   J. E. O'Hare; C. D. N. Campbell
Court Manager, Mrs H. Oakey

COURT OF PROTECTION
Stewart House, 24 Kingsway, London WC2B 6HD
Tel 0171-664 7000
Master (£84,752), D. A. Lush

ELECTION PETITIONS OFFICE
Room E218, Royal Courts of Justice, Strand, London
WC2A 2LL
Tel 0171-936 6131

The office accepts petitions and deals with all matters
relating to the questioning of parliamentary, European

Parliament and local government elections, and with applications for relief under the Representation of the People legislation.

Prescribed Officer, R. L. Turner
Chief Clerk, Miss J. L. Waine

OFFICE OF THE LORD CHANCELLOR'S VISITORS
Stewart House, 24 Kingsway, London WC2B 6HD
Tel 0171-664 7317

Legal Visitor, A. R. Tyrrell
Medical Visitors, K. Khan; W. B. Sprey; E. Mateu; S. E. Mahapatra; A. Bailey; A. Kaeser

OFFICIAL RECEIVERS' DEPARTMENT
21 Bloomsbury Street, London WC1B 3SS
Tel 0171-323 3090

Senior Official Receiver, M. C. A. Osborne
Official Receivers, M. J. Pugh; L. T. Cramp; J. Norris

OFFICIAL SOLICITOR'S DEPARTMENT
81 Chancery Lane, London WC2B 6HD
Tel 0171-911 7105

Official Solicitor to the Supreme Court, P. M. Harris
Deputy Official Solicitor, H. J. Baker
Chief Clerk, R. Lancaster

PRINCIPAL REGISTRY (FAMILY DIVISION)
First Avenue House, 42–49 High Holborn, London WC1V 6HA
Tel 0171-936 6000

Senior District Judge (£84,752), G. B. N. A. Angel
District Judges (£70,820), B. P. F. Kenworthy-Browne; Mrs K. T. Moorhouse; M. J. Segal; R. Conn; Miss I. M. Plumstead; G. J. Maple; Miss H. C. Bradley; K. J. White; A. R. S. Bassett-Cross; N. A. Grove; M. C. Berry; Miss S. M. Bowman; C. Million; P. Waller; Miss P. Cushing; R. Harper; G. C. Brasse; Miss D. C. Redgrave
Group Manager, Family Proceedings and Probate Service, R. P. Knight

District Probate Registrars

Birmingham and Stoke-on-Trent, C. Marsh
Brighton and Maidstone, P. Ellwood
Bristol, Exeter and Bodmin, R. H. P. Joyce
Ipswich, Norwich and Peterborough, D. N. Mee
Leeds, Lincoln and Sheffield, A. P. Dawson
Liverpool, Lancaster and Chester, C. Fox
Llandaff, Bangor, Carmarthen and Gloucester, R. F. Yeldam
Manchester and Nottingham, M. A. Moran
Newcastle, Carlisle, York and Middlesbrough, P. Sanderson
Oxford, R. R. Da Costa
Winchester, A. K. Biggs

OFFICE OF THE JUDGE ADVOCATE OF THE FLEET
c/o Group Manager's Office, The Court Service, Concorde House, 10–12 London Road, Maidstone ME16 8QA
Tel 01622-200120

Judge Advocate of the Fleet (£88,077), His Hon. Judge Sessions

OFFICE OF THE JUDGE ADVOCATE-GENERAL OF THE FORCES
(Joint Service for the Army and the Royal Air Force)
22 Kingsway, London WC2B 6LE
Tel 0171-218 8079

Judge Advocate-General (£96,214), His Hon. Judge J. W. Rant, CB, QC
Vice-Judge Advocate-General (£84,752), E. G. Moelwyn-Hughes
Judge Advocates (£70,820), D. M. Berkson; M. A. Hunter; J. P. Camp; Miss S. E. Woollam; R. C. C. Seymour; I. H. Pearson; R. G. Chapple; J. F. T. Bayliss

HIGH COURT AND CROWN COURT CENTRES

First-tier centres deal with both civil and criminal cases and are served by High Court and circuit judges. Second-tier centres deal with criminal cases only and are served by High Court and circuit judges. Third-tier centres deal with criminal cases only and are served only by circuit judges.

MIDLAND AND OXFORD CIRCUIT

First-tier – Birmingham, Lincoln, Nottingham, Oxford, Stafford, Warwick
Second-tier – Leicester, Northampton, Shrewsbury, Worcester
Third-tier – Coventry, Derby, Grimsby, Hereford, Peterborough, Stoke-on-Trent, Wolverhampton
Circuit Administrator, P. Handcock, The Priory Courts, 6th Floor, 33 Bull Street, Birmingham B4 6DS. Tel: 0121-681 3000
Group Managers: Birmingham Group, K. Dickerson; *Coventry Group*, Mrs D. Ponsonby; *Lincoln Group*, A. Phillips; *Northampton Group*, S. Smith; *Nottingham Group*, Mrs E. A. Folman; *Stafford Group*, D. Bennett

NORTH-EASTERN CIRCUIT

First-tier – Leeds, Newcastle upon Tyne, Sheffield, Teesside
Second-tier – Bradford, York
Third-tier – Doncaster, Durham, Kingston-upon-Hull
Circuit Administrator, P. J. Farmer, 17th Floor, West Riding House, Albion Street, Leeds LS1 5AA. Tel: 0113-251 1200
Group Managers: Bradford Group, F. Taylor; *Leeds Group*, P. M. Norris; *Newcastle upon Tyne Group*, K. Budgen; *Sheffield Group*, G. Bingham, OBE; *Teesside Group*, Miss E. Yates

NORTHERN CIRCUIT

First-tier – Carlisle, Liverpool, Manchester (Crown Square), Preston
Third-tier – Barrow-in-Furness, Bolton, Burnley, Lancaster; Manchester (Minshull Street)
Circuit Administrator, R. A. Vincent, 15 Quay Street, Manchester M60 9FD. Tel: 0161-833 1005
Group Managers: Liverpool Group, Mrs J. Roche; *Manchester Central Group*, Mrs C. A. Mayer; *Outer Manchester Group*, Mrs B. Handcock; *Preston Group*, B. Wilson

SOUTH-EASTERN CIRCUIT

First-tier – Chelmsford, Croydon, Lewes, Norwich
Second-tier – Ipswich, London (Central Criminal Court), Luton, Maidstone, Reading, St Albans
Third-tier – Aylesbury, Basildon, Bury St Edmunds, Cambridge, Canterbury, Chichester, Guildford, Hove, King's Lynn, London (Croydon, Harrow, Inner London Sessions House, Isleworth, Knightsbridge, Middlesex Guildhall, Snaresbrook, Southwark, Wood Green, Woolwich)
Circuit Administrator, R. J. Clark, New Cavendish House, 18 Maltravers Street, London WC2R 3EU. Tel: 0171-936 7234
Provincial Administrator, J. Powell, Steeple House, Church Lane, Chelmsford CMI INH. Tel: 01245-257425
Group Managers: Chelmsford Group, M. Littlewood; *Maidstone Group*, Mrs H. Hartwell; *Kingston Group*, Miss S. Proudlock; *Lewes Group*, B. Macbeth; *London Group (Civil)*, D. Marsh; *London Group (Crime)*, G. F. Addicott; *Luton Group*, M. McIver

The High Court in Greater London sits at the Royal Courts of Justice.

WALES AND CHESTER CIRCUIT

First-tier – Caernarfon, Cardiff, Chester, Mold, Swansea
Second-tier – Carmarthen, Merthyr Tydfil, Newport, Welshpool
Third-tier – Dolgellau, Haverfordwest, Knutsford, Warrington
Circuit Administrator, P. Risk, Churchill House, Churchill Way, Cardiff CF1 4HH. Tel: 01222-396925
Group Managers: Cardiff Group, G. Pickett; *Chester Group*, G. Kenney; *Swansea Group*, Mrs D. Thomas

WESTERN CIRCUIT

First-tier – Bristol, Exeter, Truro, Winchester
Second-tier – Dorchester, Gloucester, Plymouth, Weymouth
Third-tier – Barnstaple, Bournemouth, Newport (IOW), Portsmouth, Salisbury, Southampton, Swindon, Taunton
Circuit Administrator, D. Ryan, Bridge House, Clifton, Bristol BS8 4BN. Tel: 0117-974 3763
Group Managers: Bristol Group, N. Jeffery; *Exeter Group*, D. Gentry; *Winchester Group*, A. Davison

CIRCUIT JUDGES

Senior Circuit Judges, each £96,214
Circuit Judges at the Central Criminal Court, London (Old Bailey Judges), each £96,214
Circuit Judges, each £88,077
Style, His/Her Hon. Judge [surname]
Senior Presiding Judge, The Rt. Hon. Lord Justice Judge

MIDLAND AND OXFORD CIRCUIT

Presiding Judges, The Hon. Mr Justice Jowitt; The Hon. Mr Justice Astill *(from Jan. 1999)*

F. A. Allan; Miss C. Alton; B. J. Appleby, QC; D. P. Bennett; R. S. A. Benson; J. G. Boggis, QC; R. W. A. Bray; D. W. Brunning; N. B. Cameron Coles, QC; J. J. Cavell; F. A. Chapman; P. N. R. Clark; M. F. Coates; R. R. B. Cole; T. G. E. Corrie; P. F. Crane; *P. J. Crawford, QC *(Recorder of Birmingham)*; Mrs P. A. Deeley; M. de Mille; T. M. Dillon, QC; C. H. Durman; B. A. Farrer, QC; Miss E. N. Fisher; J. E. Fletcher; A. C. Geddes; R. J. H. Gibbs, QC; J. Hall; V. E. Hall; D. R. D. Hamilton; S. T. Hammond; G. C. W. Harris, QC; M. J. Heath; Miss E. J. Hindley, QC; C. R. Hodson; J. R. Hopkin;

Mrs H. M. Hughes; R. H. Hutchinson; R. A. G. Inglis; R. P. V. Jenkins; A. W. P. King; M. K. Lee, QC; D. L. McCarthy; A. W. McCreath; A. G. MacDuff, QC; D. D. McEvoy, QC; J. V. Machin; M. H. Mander; L. Marshall; K. Matthewman, QC; W. D. Matthews; H. R. Mayor, QC; N. J. Mitchell; P. R. Morrell; J. I. Morris; M. D. Mott; A. J. D. Nicholl; R. T. N. Orme; R. C. C. O'Rorke; J. F. F. Orrell; D. S. Perrett, QC; C. J. Pitchers; R. F. D. Pollard; D. P. Pugsley; J. R. Pyke; R. J. Rubery; J. A. O. Shand; D. P. Stanley; P. J. Stretton; G. C. Styler; H. C. Tayler, QC; A. B. Taylor; J. J. Teare; R. S. W. F. Tonking; J. J. Wait; J. C. Warner; H. Wilson; J. W. Wilson

NORTH-EASTERN CIRCUIT

Presiding Judges, The Hon. Mr Justice Hooper; The Hon. Mr Justice Bennett *(from Jan. 1999)*

J. R. S. Adams; J. Altman; P. M. Baker, QC; T. W. Barber; J. E. Barry; G. N. Barr Young; R. Bartfield; C. O. J. Behrens; D. R. Bentley, QC; P. H. Bowers; A. N. J. Briggs; D. M. A. Bryant; J. W. M. Bullimore; B. Bush; M. C. Carr; M. L. Cartlidge; P. J. Charlesworth; P. J. Cockroft; G. J. K. Coles, QC; J. Crabtree; M. T. Cracknell; W. H. R. Crawford, QC; Mrs J. Davies; I. J. Dobkin; E. J. Faulks; P. J. Fox, QC; A. N. Fricker, QC; M. S. Garner; A. R. Goldsack, QC; R. A. Grant; S. P. Grenfell; S. J. Gullick; G. F. R. Harkins; P. J. M. Heppel, QC; *T. D. T. Hodson *(Recorder of Newcastle upon Tyne)*; P. M. L. Hoffman; D. P. Hunt; R. Hunt; A. E. Hutchinson, QC; N. H. Jones, QC; G. H. Kamil; T. D. Kent-Jones, TD; G. M. Lightfoot; R. P. Lowden; A. G. McCallum; C. I. McGonigal; M. K. Mettyear; R. J. Moore; A. L. Myerson, QC; D. A. Orde; Miss H. E. Paling; J. Prophet; P. E. Robertshaw; R. M. Scott; A. Simpson; L. Spittle; Mrs L. Sutcliffe; J. A. Swanson; M. J. Taylor; R. C. Taylor; J. D. G. Walford; M. Walker; P. H. C. Walker; *B. Walsh, QC; C. T. Walton; G. Whitburn, QC; J. S. Wolstenholme; D. R. Wood

NORTHERN CIRCUIT

Presiding Judge, The Hon. Mr Justice Forbes; The Hon. Mr Justice Douglas Brown

M. P. Allweis; H. H. Andrew, QC; J. F. Appleton; S. W. Baker; A. W. Bell; R. C. W. Bennett; Miss I. Bernstein; M. S. Blackburn; C. Bloom, QC; R. Brown; J. K. Burke, QC; I. B. Campbell; F. B. Carter, QC; B. I. Caulfield; D. Clark; *D. C. Clarke, QC (Recorder of Liverpool)*; G. M. Clifton; I. W. Crompton; *R. E. Davies, QC *(Recorder of Manchester)*; Miss A. E. Downey; B. R. Duckworth; S. B. Duncan; Miss D. B. Eaglestone; T. K. Earnshaw; G. A. Ensor; D. M. Evans, QC; J. D. Fawcus; P. S. Fish; J. R. B. Geake; D. S. Gee; W. George; J. A. D. Gilliland, QC; J. A. Hammond; M. Hedley; T. B. Hegarty, QC; M. J. Henshell; F. R. B. Holloway; R. C. Holman; N. J. G. Howarth; G. W. Humphries; C. E. F. James; P. M. Kershaw, QC *(Commercial Circuit Judge)*; H. L. Lachs; P. M. Lakin; B. W. Lewis; R. J. D. Livesey, QC; *R. Lockett; D. Lynch; D. I. Mackay; J. B. Macmillan; D. G. Maddison; B. C. Maddocks; C. J. Mahon; J. A. Morgan; W. P. Morris; T. J. Mort; F. D. Owen, TD; J. A. Phillips; J. C. Phipps; D. A. Pirie; A. J. Proctor; J. H. Roberts; Miss G. D. Ruaux; H. S. Singer; E. Slinger; A. C. Smith; W. P. Smith; Miss E. M. Steel; D. R. Swift; C. B. Tetlow; J. P. Townend; I. J. C. Trigger; P. W. G. Urquhart; K. H. P. Wilkinson; B. Woodward

SOUTH-EASTERN CIRCUIT

Presiding Judges, The Hon. Mr Justice Gage; The Hon. Mr Justice Moses *(from Jan. 1999)*

J. R. D. Adams; M. F. Addison; A. R. L. Ansell;
M. G. Anthony; S. A. Anwyl, QC; M. F. Baker, QC;
M. J. D. Baker; A. F. Balston; G. S. Barham;
C. J. A. Barnett, QC; W. E. Barnett, QC; R. A. Barratt, QC;
K. Bassingthwaighte; *G. A. Bathurst Norman;
P. J. L. Beaumont, QC; N. E. Beddard; Mrs C. V. Bevington;
M. G. Binning; J. E. Bishop; B. M. B. Black; H. O. Blacksell,
QC; J. G. Boal, QC; A. V. Bradbury; P. N. Brandt;
L. J. Bromley, QC; R. G. Brown; J. M. Bull, QC;
*N. M. Butter, QC; H. J. Byrt, QC; C. V. Callman;
J. Q. Campbell; B. E. Capstick, QC; M. J. Carroll;
B. E. F. Catlin; *B. L. Charles, QC; P. C. L. Clark;
P. C. Clegg; Miss S. Coates; S. H. Colgan; P. H. Collins;
C. C. Colston, QC; S. S. Coltart; Viscount Colville of
Culross, QC; J. S. Colyer, QC; C. D. Compston;
T. A. C. Coningsby, QC; J. G. Connor; R. D. Connor;
M. J. Cook; R. A. Cooke; M. R. Coombe; P. E. Copley;
Dr E. Cotran; P. R. Cowell; R. C. Cox; M. L. S. Cripps;
J. F. Crocker; D. L. Croft, QC; H. M. Crush; D. M. Cryan;
P. Curl; G. L. Davies; I. H. Davies, TD; W. L. M. Davies, QC;
M. Dean, QC; W. N. Denison, QC (*Common Serjeant*);
J. E. Devaux; M. N. Devonshire, TD; P. H. Downes;
W. H. Dunn, QC; A. H. Durrant; C. M. Edwards; D. F. Elfer,
QC; D. R. Ellis; R. C. Elly; C. Elwen; F. P. L. Evans;
S. J. Evans; J. D. Farnworth; P. Fingret; J. J. Finney;
P. E. J. Focke, QC; P. Ford; J. J. Fordham; G. C. F. Forrester;
Ms D. A. Freedman; R. Gee; L. Gerber; C. A. H. Gibson;
Miss A. F. Goddard, QC; S. A. Goldstein; M. B. Goodman;
C. G. M. Gordon; J. B. Gosschalk; M. Graham, QC;
B. S. Green, QC; P. B. Greenwood; D. J. Griffiths;
G. D. Grigson; R. B. Groves, TD, VRD; N. T. Hague, QC;
A. B. R. Hallgarten, QC; Miss G. Hallon; J. Hamilton;
Miss S. Hamilton, QC; C. R. H. Hardy;
B. Hargrove, OBE; M. F. Harris; R. G. Hawkins, QC;
J. M. Haworth; R. J. Haworth; R. M. Hayward;
A. N. Hitching; D. Holden; J. F. Holt;
A. C. W. Hordern, QC; K. A. D. Hornby; M. Hucker;
Sir David Hughes-Morgan, Bt., CB, CBE; J. G. Hull, QC;
M. J. Hyam (*Recorder of London*); D. A. Inman; A. B. Issard-
Davies; Dr P. J. E. Jackson; T. J. C. Joseph; S. S. Katkhuda;
M. Kennedy, QC; A. M. Kenny; T. R. King; B. J. Knight, QC;
L. G. Krikler; L. H. C. Lait; P. St J. H. Langan, QC;
Capt. J. B. R. Langdon, RN; P. H. Latham; R. Laurie;
T. Lawrence; D. M. Levy, QC; C. C. D. Lindsay, QC;
S. H. Lloyd; F. R. Lockhart; D. B. Lowe;
Mrs C. M. Ludlow; Capt. S. Lyons; R. J. McGregor-
Johnson; K. M. McHale; K. A. Machin, QC;
R. G. McKinnon; W. N. McKinnon; K. C. Macrae;
T. Maher; F. J. M. Marr-Johnson; D. N. N. Martineau;
N. A. Medawar, QC; D. B. Meier; D. J. Mellor;
G. D. Mercer; D. Q. Miller; Miss A. E. Mitchell;
F. I. Mitchell; H. M. Morgan; D. Morton Jack; R. T. Moss;
Miss M. J. S. Mowat; J. I. Murchie; T. M. E. Nash;
M. H. D. Neligan; Mrs M. F. Norrie; Brig. A. P. Norris,
OBE; P. W. O'Brien; M. A. Oppenheimer; D. C. J. Paget, QC;
D. A. Paiba; D. J. Parry; Mrs N. Pearce; Prof. D. S. Pearl;
Miss V. A. Pearlman; B. P. Pearson; J. R. Peppitt, QC;
N. A. J. Philpot; T. D. Pillay; D. C. Pitman; J. R. Platt;
P. B. Pollock; T. G. Pontius; W. D. C. Poulton;
H. C. Pownall; S. Pratt; R. J. C. V. Prendergast;
J. E. Previté, QC; B. H. Pryor, QC; J. E. Pullinger;
D. W. Radford; J. W. Rant, CB, QC; E. V. P. Reece;
M. P. Reynolds; G. K. Rice; M. S. Rich, QC; N. P. Riddell;
G. Rivlin, QC; S. D. Robbins; D. A. H. Rodwell, QC;
J. W. Rogers, QC; G. H. Rooke, TD, QC; W. M. Rose;
P. C. R. Rountree; J. H. Rucker; T. R. G. Ryland;
J. E. A. Samuels, QC; R. B. Sanders; A. R. G. Scott-Gall;
J. S. Sennitt; J. L. Sessions; J. D. Sheerin; D. R. A. Sich;
A. G. Simmons; K. T. Simpson; P. R. Simpson;
M. Singh, QC; J. K. E. Slack, TD; S. P. Sleeman;

C. M. Smith, QC; S. A. R. Smith; R. J. Southan; S. B. Spence;
W. F. C. Thomas; P. J. Thompson; A. G. Y. Thorpe;
A. H. Tibber; C. H. Tilling; J. K. Toulmin, CMG, QC;
C. J. M. Tyrer; Mrs A. P. Uziell-Hamilton; J. E. van der
Werff; A. O. R. Vick, QC; T. L. Viljoen;
Miss M. S. Viner, CBE, QC; R. Wakefield; R. Walker;
S. P. Walker; D. B. Watling, QC; V. B. Watts;
C. S. Welchman; A. F. Wilkie, QC; S. R. Wilkinson;
R. J. Winstanley; E. G. Wrintmore; K. H. Zucker, QC

WALES AND CHESTER CIRCUIT

Presiding Judges, The Hon. Mr Justice Maurice Kay; The
Hon. Mr Justice Connell; The Hon. Mr Justice
Thomas

K. E. Barnett; M. R. Burr; S. P. Clarke; T. R. Crowther, QC;
J. T. Curran; Miss J. M. P. Daley; G. H. M. Daniel;
D. T. A. Davies; J. B. S. Diehl, QC; R. T. Dutton;
D. E. H. Edwards; G. O. Edwards, QC; The Lord Elystan-
Morgan; D. R. Evans, QC; M. R. Furness; J. W. Gaskell;
*M. Gibbon, QC; D. R. Halbert; D. J. Hale;
Miss J. E. Hayward; P. J. Jacobs; G. J. Jones; H. D. H. Jones;
G. E. Kilfoil; C. G. Masterman; D. G. Morgan;
D. G. Morris; D. C. Morton; T. H. Moseley, QC;
P. J. Price, QC; E. J. Prosser, QC; J. M. T. Rogers, QC;
S. M. Stephens, QC; H. V. Williams, QC

WESTERN CIRCUIT

Presiding Judges, The Hon. Mr Justice Butterfield; The
Hon. Mr Justice Toulson

P. R. Barclay; P. T. S. Batterbury; J. F. Beashel; R. H. Bond;
Miss J. A. M. Bonvin; C. L. Boothman; M. J. L. Brodrick;
J. M. J. Burford, QC; R. D. H. Bursell, QC; M. G. Cotterill;
G. W. A. Cottle; K. C. Cutler; P. M. Darlow;
S. C. Darwall Smith; Mrs S. P. Darwall Smith;
Mrs L. H. Davies; *M. Dyer; J. D. Foley; D. L. Griffiths;
J. D. Griggs; Mrs C. M. A. Hagen; P. J. C. R. Hooton;
G. B. Hutton; R. E. Jack, QC; A. G. H. Jones;
T. N. Mackean; Miss S. M. D. McKinney; I. S. McKintosh;
J. G. McNaught; T. J. Milligan; J. Neligan; E. G. Neville;
S. K. O'Malley; S. K. Overend; R. Price; R. C. Pryor, QC;
J. N. P. Rudd; A. Rutherford; Miss A. O. H. Sander;
D. H. D. Selwood; R. M. Shawcross; D. A. Smith, QC;
W. E. M. Taylor; P. M. Thomas; A. A. R. Thompson, QC;
D. K. Ticehurst, QC; H. J. M. Tucker, QC;
D. M. Webster, QC; J. H. Weeks, QC; J. S. Wiggs;
J. A. J. Wigmore; J. C. Willis

RECORDERS (each £420 per day)

F. A. Abbott; R. D. I. Adam; P. C. Ader; R. J. P. Aikens, QC;
J. F. Akast; D. J. Ake; R. Akenhead, QC;
I. D. G. Alexander, QC; C. D. Allan, QC; C. J. Alldis;
J. H. Allen, QC; D. M. Altaras; A. J. Anderson, QC;
W. P. Andreae-Jones, QC; Mrs E. H. Andrew;
P. J. Andrews, QC; R. A. Anelay, QC;
Miss L. E. Appleby, QC; J. F. A. Archer, QC; The Lord
Archer of Sandwell, PC, QC; E. K. Armitage, QC;
P. J. B. Armstrong; G. K. Arran; E. G. Aspley;
N. J. Atkinson, QC; D. J. M. Aubrey, QC; D. S. Aubrey;
M. G. Austin-Smith, QC; M. J. S. Axtell; W. S. Aylen, QC;
P. D. Babb; J. F. Badenoch, QC; Miss P. H. Badley;
E. H. Bailey; A. B. Baillie; N. R. J. Baker, QC; Miss A. Ball,
QC; C. G. Ball, QC; A. Barker, QC; B. J. Barker, QC;
D. Barker, QC; G. E. Barling, QC; D. N. Barnard;
H. J. Barnes; T. P. Barnes, QC; A. J. Barnett; D. A. Bartlett;
G. R. Bartlett, QC; J. C. T. Barton, QC; D. C. Bate, QC;
S. D. Batten; P. D. Batty, QC; J. J. Baughan, QC;
R. A. Bayliss; D. M. Bean; J. Beatson; C. H. Beaumont;
R. V. M. E. Behar; R. W. Belben; J. K. Benson; P. C. Benson;
R. A. Benson, QC; H. L. Bentham, QC; D. M. Berkson;

C. R. Berry; M. Bethel, QC; J. P. V. Bevan;
Mrs M. O. Bickford-Smith; N. Bidder; I. G. Bing;
P. V. Birkett, QC; M. I. Birnbaum; W. J. Birtles;
P. W. Birts, QC; B. G. D. Blair, QC; W. J. L. Blair, QC;
J. A. Blair-Gould; A. N. H. Blake; P. E. Bleasdale; R. H. L.
Blomfield, TD; D. J. Blunt, QC; O. S. P. Blunt, QC;
D. R. L. Bodey, QC; G. T. K. Boney, QC; J. J. Boothby;
D. J. Boulton; S. N. Bourne-Arton, QC; Ms M. R. Bowron;
W. Boyce; S. C. Boyd, QC; J. J. Boyle; D. L. Bradshaw;
W. T. S. Braithwaite, QC; N. D. Bratza, QC; G. B. Breen;
D. J. Brennan, QC; M. L. Brent, QC; G. J. B. G. Brice, QC;
A. J. Brigden; D. R. Bright; R. P. Brittain; R. A. Britton;
J. Bromley-Davenport; L. F. M. Brown; S. C. Brown, QC;
D. J. M. Browne, QC; J. N. Browne; A. J. N. Brunner, QC;
R. V. Bryan; Miss B. M. Bucknall, QC; A. Bueno, QC;
J. E. Bullen; P. E. Bullock; J. P. Burke, QC;
H. W. Burnett, QC; R. H. Burns; S. J. Burnton, QC;
G. Burrell, QC; M. J. Burton, QC; K. Bush; A. J. Butcher, QC;
Miss J. Butler; C. W. Byers; D. W. Caddick; D. Calvert-
Smith; R. Camden Pratt, QC; Miss S. M. C. Cameron, QC;
A. N. Campbell, QC; J. M. Caplan, QC; G. M. C. Carey, QC;
A. C. Carlile, QC, MP; H. B. H. Carlisle, QC; The Lord
Carlisle of Bucklow, PC, QC; J. J. Carter-Manning, QC;
R. Carus, QC; Mrs J. R. Case; P. D. Cattan;
Miss M. T. Catterson; R. M. Challinor;
N. M. Chambers, QC; Miss D. C. Champion;
V. R. Chapman; J. M. Cherry, QC; C. F. Chruszcz, QC;
A. V. Chubb; C. H. Clark, QC; C. S. C. S. Clarke, QC;
P. W. Clarke; P. R. J. Clarkson, QC; T. Clayson;
A. S. L. Cleary; W. Clegg, QC; P. Clements; T. A. Clover;
W. P. Coates; D. J. Cocks, QC; J. J. Coffey, QC;
T. A. Coghlan, QC; J. L. Cohen; L. F. R. Cohen, QC;
W. J. Coker, QC; J. R. Cole; A. J. S. Coleman; N. J. Coleman;
P. J. D. Coleridge, QC; A. R. Collender, QC;
P. N. Collier, QC; J. M. Collins; M. G. Collins, QC; I. Collis;
Ms M. Colton; Mrs J. R. Comyns; A. D. Conrad;
C. S. Cook; J. L. Cooke; N. O. Cooke;
K. B. Coonan; A. E. M. Cooper; Miss B. P. Cooper, QC;
P. J. Cooper, QC; C. J. Cornwall; P. J. Cosgrove, QC;
Miss D. R. Cotton, QC; J. S. Coward, QC; T. G. Cowling;
Mrs L. M. Cox, QC; C. Crampin, QC; R. F. Cranston, QC;
L. S. Crawford; N. Crichton; D. I. Crigman, QC;
C. A. Critchlow; D. R. Crome; S. R. Crookenden, QC;
Mrs J. Crowley; J. D. Crowley, QC; T. S. Culver;
Miss E. A. M. Curnow, QC; P. D. Curran;
J. W. O. Curtis, QC; M. J. Curwen; A. J. G. Dalziel;
Mrs P. M. T. Dangor; A. M. Darroch; C. P. M. Davidson;
A. M. Davies; A. R. M. Davies; H. Davies; J. T. L. Davies;
Miss N. V. Davies, QC; R. L. Davies, QC; N. A. L. Davis, QC;
W. E. Davis; A. W. Dawson; D. H. Day, QC; P. G. Dedman;
C. F. Dehn, QC; P. A. de la Piquerie; M. A. de Navarro, QC;
R. L. Denyer, QC; H. A. D. de Silva; P. N. Digney;
C. E. Dines; A. D. Dinkin, QC; D. R. Dobbin; P. Dodgson;
R. A. M. Doggett; Ms B. Dohmann, QC;
D. T. Donaldson, QC; A. M. Donne, QC; A. F. S. Donovan;
A. K. Dooley; J. Dowse; J. R. Duggan; P. R. Dunkels, QC;
J. D. Durham Hall, QC; H. W. P. Eccles, QC;
C. N. Edelman, QC; A. H. Edwards;
Miss S. M. Edwards, QC; A. J. C. Edwards-Stuart, QC;
G. Elias, QC; E. A. Elliott; J. A. Elvidge;
R. M. Englehart, QC; D. A. Evans, QC; D. H. Evans, QC;
F. W. H. Evans, QC; G. J. Evans; G. W. R. Evans, QC;
M. Evans, QC; M. J. Evans; M. A. Everall, QC; Miss D.
Faber; T. M. Faber; R. B. Farley, QC; P. M. Farmer, QC;
D. J. Farrer, QC; P. E. Feinberg, QC; R. Fernyhough, QC;
M. C. Field; J. E. Finestein; J. E. P. Finnigan; D. T. Fish;
D. P. Fisher, QC; G. D. Flather, CBE, QC; N. M. Ford, QC;
R. A. Fordham, QC; B. C. Forster; M. D. P. Fortune;
D. R. Foskett, QC; I. H. Foster; J. R. Foster, QC;
Miss R. M. Foster; D. P. Friedman, QC;

C. J. E. Gardner, QC; P. R. Garlick, QC; C. R. Garside, QC;
R. C. Gaskell; S. A. G. L. Gault; A. H. Gee, QC;
I. W. Geering, QC; D. S. Geey; C. R. George, QC; S. M.
Gerlis; D. C. Gerrey; J. S. Gibbons, QC; A. J. Gilbart, QC;
F. H. S. Gilbert, QC; N. J. Gilchrist; K. Gillance;
N. B. D. Gilmour, QC; L. Giovene; A. T. Glass, QC; M. G. J.
Gledhill; H. B. Globe, QC; Miss E. Gloster, QC;
H. K. Goddard; H. A. Godfrey, QC;
Ms L. S. Godfrey, QC; J. J. Goldberg, QC; J. B. Goldring, QC;
P. H. Goldsmith, QC; L. C. Goldstone, QC;
A. J. J. Gompertz, QC; Miss R. M. Goode; J. R. W. Goss;
T. J. C. Goudie, QC; A. A. Goymer; G. Gozem;
A. S. Grabiner, QC; C. A. St J. Gray, QC; H. Green, QC; Miss
J. E. G. Greenberg, QC; A. E. Greenwood;
J. C. Greenwood; J. G. Grenfell, QC; R. D. Grey, QC;
D. E. Griffith-Jones; R. H. Griffith-Jones;
J. P. G. Griffiths, QC; M. G. Grills; M. S. E. Grime, QC;
P. Grobel; P. H. Gross, QC; M. A. W. Grundy; B. P.
Gulbenkian; A. S. Hacking, QC; J. W. Haines; N. J. Hall;
S. J. Hall; J. P. N. Hallam; Miss H. C. Hallett, QC;
G. M. Hamilton, TD, QC; I. M. Hamilton; P. L. Hamlin;
J. L. Hand, QC; Miss R. S. A. Hare, QC; G. T. Harrap; M. K.
Harington; P. J. Harrington, QC; D. M. Harris, QC;
R. D. Harrison; R. M. Harrison, QC; H. M. Harrod;
J. M. Harrow; C. P. Hart-Leverton, QC; B. Harvey;
J. G. Harvey; M. L. T. Harvey, QC; D. W. Hatton, QC;
A. M. D. Havelock-Allan, QC; The Hon. P. N. Havers, QC;
T. S. A. Hawkesworth, QC; W. G. Hawkesworth;
R. W. P. Hay; Prof. D. J. Hayton; R. Hayward-Smith, QC;
A. T. Hedworth, QC; R. A. Henderson, QC;
R. H. Q. Henriques, QC; R. C. Herman; M. S. Heslop QC;
T. Hewitt; G. R. Hickinbottom; B. J. Higgs, QC;
J. W. Hillyer; A. J. H. Hilton, QC; J. W. Hirst, QC;
W. T. J. Hirst; J. D. Hitchen; S. A. Hockman, QC;
H. E. G. Hodge, OBE; A. J. C. Hoggett, QC; T. V. Holroyde,
QC; R. M. Hone; A. D. Hope; S. Hopkins;
M. A. P. Hopmeier; M. Horowitz, QC; Miss R. Horwood-
Smart; C. P. Hotten, QC; B. F. Houlder, QC;
M. N. Howard, QC; C. I. Howells; M. J. Hubbard, QC; D. L.
Hughes; Miss J. C. A. Hughes, QC; P. T. Hughes, QC;
R. P. Hughes; T. M. Hughes, QC; L. D. Hull;
Capt. D. R. Humphrey, RN; W. G. B. Hungerford;
D. R. N. Hunt, QC; P. J. Hunt, QC; I. G. A. Hunter, QC;
M. A. Hunter; M. Hussain, QC; J. G. K. Hyland;
P. R. Isaacs; S. L. Isaacs, QC; S. Jack; D. G. A. Jackson;
M. R. Jackson; R. M. Jackson, QC; I. E. Jacob;
N. F. B. Jarman; J. M. Jarvis, QC; J. R. Jarvis;
A. H. Jeffreys; D. A. Jeffreys, QC; J. D. Jenkins, QC;
D. B. Johnson, QC; Miss A. M. Jolles; D. A. F. Jones;
D. L. Jones; N. G. Jones; P. H. F. Jones; S. E. Jones, QC;
T. G. Jones; W. J. Jones; W. H. Joss; H. M. Joy;
P. S. L. Joyce, QC; R. W. S. Juckes; M. L. Kallipetis, QC;
Miss L. N. R. Kamill; I. G. F. Karsten, QC; R. G. Kaye, QC;
C. B. Kealy; K. R. Keen, QC; Mrs S. M. Keen;
B. R. Keith, QC; C. J. B. Kemp; D. Kennett Brown;
D. M. Kerr; L. D. Kershen, QC; M. I. Khan;
G. M. Khayat, QC; C. A. Kinch; T. R. A. King, QC;
W. M. Kingston; R. C. Klevan; M. S. Knott;
Miss P. E. Knowles; C. Knox; Miss J. C. M. Korner, QC;
S. E. Kramer, QC; Miss L. J. Kushner, QC; P. E. Kyte, QC;
N. R. W. Lambert; D. A. Landau; D. G. Lane, QC;
T. J. Langdale; B. F. J. Langstaff, QC; D. H. Latham;
R. B. Latham, QC; S. W. Lawler, QC; Sir Ivan Lawrence, QC;
Miss E. A. Lawson, QC; M. H. Lawson, QC; G. S. Lawson-
Rogers, QC; P. L. O. Leaver, QC; D. Lederman, QC;
B. W. T. Leech; I. Leeming, QC; C. H. de V. Leigh, QC;
H. B. G. Lett; B. L. Lever; B. H. Leveson, QC;
A. E. Levy, QC; M. E. Lewer, QC; J. A. Lewis;
K. M. J. Lewison, QC; S. J. Linehan, QC; G. W. Little;
B. J. E. Livesey, QC; C. G. Llewellyn-Jones, QC;

C. J. Lockhart-Mummery, QC; A. J. C. Lodge, QC;
T. Longbotham; D. C. Lovell-Pank, QC; A. C. Lowcock;
G. W. Lowe; J. A. M. Lowen; Rt. Hon. Sir Nicholas Lyell,
QC, MP; A. P. Lyon; E. Lyons, QC; P. G. McCahill, QC;
R. G. B. McCombe, QC; A. G. McDowall; K. M. P. Macgill;
R. D. Machell, QC; B. M. McIntyre; C. C. Mackay, QC;
D. L. Mackie; N. A. McKittrick; I. A. B. McLaren, QC;
I. McLeod; N. R. B. Macleod, QC; A. G. Mainds;
A. H. R. Maitland; A. R. Malcolm; H. J. Malins;
M. E. Mann, QC; The Hon. R. G. J. Mansfield;
A. C. B. Markham-David; R. L. Marks; J. W. Marrin, QC; A.
L. Marriott, QC; G. M. Marriott; A. S. Marron, QC;
P. Marsh; R. G. Marshall-Andrews, QC; G. C. Marson;
H. R. A. Martineau; S. A. Maskrey, QC; C. P. Mather;
D. Matheson, QC; P. R. Matthews; Mrs S. P. Matthews;
P. B. Mauleverer, QC; R. B. Mawrey, QC; J. F. M. Maxwell;
R. Maxwell, QC; Mrs P. R. May; G. M. Mercer;
N. F. Merriman, QC; The Lord Meston, QC;
C. S. J. Metcalf; J. T. Milford, QC; K. S. H. Miller;
R. A. Miller; S. M. Miller, QC; C. J. Millington;
J. B. M. Milmo, QC; D. C. Milne, QC; C. J. M. Miskin, QC;
Miss C. M. Miskin; A. P. Mitchell; C. R. Mitchell;
D. C. Mitchell; J. R. Mitchell; J. E. Mitting, QC; F. R. Moat;
E. G. Moelwyn-Hughes; C. R. D. Moger, QC;
Mrs J. P. Moir; D. R. P. Mole, QC; M. G. C. Moorhouse;
A. G. Moran, QC; D. W. Morgan; P. B. Morgan;
A. P. Morris, QC; C. Morris-Coole; H. A. C. Morrison, OBE;
G. E. Morrow, QC; C. J. Moss, QC; P. C. Mott, QC;
R. W. Moxon-Browne, QC; J. H. Muir; F. J. Muller, QC; A.
H. Munday, QC; G. S. Murdoch, QC; I. P. Murphy, QC;
M. J. A. Murphy, QC; N. O. G. Murray; N. J. Mylne, QC;
H. G. Narayan; A. R. H. Newman, QC; A. I. Niblett;
G. Nice, QC; C. A. A. Nicholls, QC; C. V. Nicholls, QC;
A. S. T. E. Nicol; A. E. R. Noble; B. Nolan, QC;
M. C. Norman; J. M. Norris; P. H. Norris; G. Nuttall;
J. G. Nutting, QC; D. P. O'Brien, QC; Mrs
F. M. Oldham, QC; S. Oliver-Jones, QC; R. W. Onions;
C. P. L. Openshaw, QC; M. N. O'Sullivan;
D. B. W. Ouseley, QC; R. M. Owen, QC; T. W. Owen;
N. D. Padfield, QC; S. R. Page; A. O. Palmer, QC;
A. W. Palmer, QC; D. P. Pannick, QC; A. D. W. Pardoe, QC;
S. A. B. Parish; G. C. Parkins; G. E. Parkinson;
M. P. Parroy, QC; E. O. Parry; N. S. K. Pascoe, QC;
A. Patience, QC; Miss A. E. H. Pauffley, QC; J. G. Paulusz;
W. E. Pawlak; R. J. Pearse Wheatley;
The Hon. I. J. C. Peddie, QC; J. V. Pegden; J. Perry, QC;
M. Pert, QC; N. M. Peters, QC; D. J. Phillips, QC;
W. B. Phillips; M. A. Pickering, QC; J. K. Pickup;
C. J. Pitchford, QC; The Hon. B. M. D. Pitt;
Miss E. F. Platt, QC; R. Platts; J. R. Playford, QC; R. O.
Plender, QC; Miss J. C. Plumptre; Miss I. M. Plumstead; S.
D. Popat; A. R. Porten, QC; L. R. Portnoy; J. R. L.
Posnansky, QC; Mrs R. M. Poulet, QC; S. R. Powles, QC;
T. W. Preston, QC; D. Price; G. A. L. Price, QC;
J. A. Price, QC; J. C. Price; N. P. L. Price, QC; F. S. K.
Privett; H. W. Prosser; A. P. Pugh, QC; G. V. Pugh, QC;
G. F. Pulman, QC; C. P. B. Purchas, QC; R. M. Purchas, QC;
N. R. Purnell, QC; P. O. Purnell, QC; Q. C. W. Querelle;
D. A. Radcliffe; Mrs N. P. Radford, QC;
Ms A. J. Rafferty, QC; T. W. H. Raggatt, QC; Miss E. A.
Ralphs; A. D. Rawley, QC; J. E. Rayner James, QC;
P. R. Raynor, QC; L. F. Read, QC; J. H. Reddihough;
A. R. F. Redgrave, QC; D. W. Rees; G. W. Rees; P. Rees;
C. E. Reese, QC; J. R. Reid, QC; P. C. Reid; D. J. Rennie;
R. E. Rhodes, QC; D. W. Richards; D. J. Richardson;
T. Rigby; S. V. Riordan, QC; G. Risius;
Miss J. H. Ritchie, QC; M. W. Roach; J. M. Roberts;
J. M. G. Roberts, QC; T. D. Roberts; A. J. Robertson;
V. Robinson, QC; D. E. H. Robson, QC; G. W. Roddick, QC;
Miss M. B. Roddy; Miss D. J. Rodgers; P. F. G. Rook, QC;
J. G. Ross; J. G. Ross Martyn; P. C. Rouch; J. J. Rowe, QC;
R. J. Royce, QC; M. W. Rudland; P. E. B. M. Rueff;
A. A. Rumbelow, QC; N. J. Rumfitt, QC; R. J. Rundell;
J. R. T. Rylance; C. R. A. Sallon, QC; C. N. Salmon;
D. A. Salter; A. T. Sander; G. R. Sankey, QC; N. L. Sarony;
J. H. B. Saunders, QC; M. P. Sayers, QC; Ms Z. P. Smith;
Miss P. Scriven, QC; R. J. Seabrook, QC; C. Seagroatt, QC;
M. R. Selfe; W. P. L. Sellick; O. M. Sells, QC; D. Serota, QC;
R. W. Seymour, QC; A. J. Seys-Llewellyn; A. R. F. Sharp;
P. P. Shears; S. J. Sher, QC; Miss J. Shipley;
J. M. Shorrock, QC; S. R. Silber, QC; Miss M. A. Simmons,
QC; P. F. Singer, QC; Miss E. A. Slade, QC; J. C. N. Slater, QC;
A. C. Smith, QC; A. T. Smith, QC; P. W. Smith, QC;
R. D. H. Smith, QC; R. S. Smith, QC; Ms Z. P. Smith;
C. J. Smyth; S. M. Solley, QC; E. Somerset Jones, QC;
R. C. Southwell, QC; R. C. E. Southwell; M. H. Spence, QC;
Sir Derek Spencer, QC; J. Spencer, QC; M. G. Spencer, QC;
R. G. Spencer; S. M. Spencer, QC; R. V. Spencer Bernard;
D. P. Spens, QC; R. W. Spon-Smith; D. Steer, QC;
M. T. Steiger, QC; Mrs L. J. Stern, QC; A. W. Stevenson, TD;
J. S. H. Stewart, QC; N. A. Stewart; R. M. Stewart, QC;
W. R. Stewart Smith; A. C. Steynor; G. J. C. Still;
D. A. Stockdale, QC; Mrs D. M. Stocken;
D. M. A. Stokes, QC; M. G. T. Stokes, QC; J. B. Storey, QC;
P. L. Storr; T. M. F. Stow, QC; D. M. A. Strachan, QC;
M. Stuart-Moore, QC; F. R. C. Such; A. B. Suckling, QC;
Ms L. E. Sullivan, QC; D. M. Sumner;
J. P. C. Sumption, QC; M. A. Supperstone, QC; P. J. Susman;
R. P. Sutton, QC; N. H. Sweeney; Miss C. J. Swift, QC;
M. R. Swift, QC; Miss H. H. Swindells, QC;
C. J. M. Symons, QC; J. P. Tabor, QC; J. A. Tackaberry, QC;
P. J. Talbot, QC; R. K. K. Talbot; R. B. Tansey, QC; J. B. C.
Tanzer; G. F. Tattersall, QC; E. T. H. Teague;
N. J. M. Teare, QC; R. H. Tedd, QC; A. D. Temple, QC;
V. B. A. Temple, QC; M. H. Tennant; D. O. Thomas, QC;
P. A. Thomas; R. L. Thomas, QC; R. M. Thomas;
R. U. Thomas, QC; Miss S. M. Thomas; C. F. J. Thompson;
A. R. Thornhill, QC; P. R. Thornton, QC; A. C. Tickle;
J. Tiley; M. B. Tillett, QC; J. W. Tinnion;
R. N. Titheridge, QC; S. M. Tomlinson, QC;
P. J. H. Towler; J. B. S. Townend, QC; C. M. Treacy, QC;
H. B. Trethowan; A. D. H. Trollope, QC;
M. G. Tugendhat, QC; H. W. Turcan; D. A. Turner, QC;
P. A. Twigg, QC; A. R. Tyrrell, QC; J. F. Uff, QC;
N. E. Underhill, QC; J. G. G. Ungley; N. P. Valios, QC;
N. C. van der Bijl; D. A. J. Vaughan, QC; M. J. D. Vere-
Hodge, QC; C. J. Vosper; J. P. Wadsworth, QC; S. P. Waine;
Miss A. P. Wakefield; R. M. Wakerley, QC; Mrs
E. A. Walker; R. A. Walker, QC; R. J. Walker, QC;
Sir Jonah Walker-Smith, Bt.; T. M. Walsh; J. J. Wardlow;
J. Warren, QC; N. J. Warren; D. E. B. Waters; Miss
B. J. Watson; Sir James Watson, Bt.; B. J. Waylen;
A. R. Webb; R. S. Webb, QC; A. S. Webster, QC;
P. Weitzman, QC; C. H. Whitby, QC; G. B. N. White;
W. J. M. White; D. R. B. Whitehouse, QC; R. P. Whitehurst;
P. G. Whiteman, QC; P. J. M. Whiteman, TD;
A. Whitfield, QC; C. T. Wide, QC; R. Wigglesworth;
A. D. F. Wilcken; N. V. M. Wilkinson; Miss E. Willers;
G. H. G. Williams, QC; Miss J. A. Williams;
J. G. Williams, QC; J. L. Williams, QC; M. J. Williams;
W. L. Williams, QC; The Lord Williams of Mostyn, QC;
Miss H. E. Williamson, QC; S. W. Williamson, QC;
A. J. D. Wilson, QC; A. M. Wilson, QC; I. K. R. Wilson;
C. Wilson-Smith, QC; G. W. Wingate-Saul, QC; Miss S. E.
Wollam; H. Wolton, QC; N. A. Wood; R. L. J. Wood, QC;
W. R. Wood; L. G. Woodley, QC; Miss S. Woodley;
J. T. Woods; W. C. Woodward, QC; A. P. L. Woolman;
T. H. Workman; Miss A. M. Worrall, QC; D. Worsley;
P. F. Worsley, QC; J. J. Wright; M. P. Yelton;
D. E. M. Young, QC

STIPENDIARY MAGISTRATES

Provincial (each £70,820)

Cheshire, P. K. Dodd, OBE, *apptd* 1991
Derbyshire, M. J. Friel, *apptd* 1997; Mrs J. H. Alderson, *apptd* 1997
Devon, P. H. Wassall, *apptd* 1994
East and West Sussex, P. C. Tain, *apptd* 1992
Essex, K. A. Gray, *apptd* 1995
Greater Manchester, A. Berg, *apptd* 1994; C. R. Darnton, *apptd* 1994
Hampshire, T. G. Cowling, *apptd* 1989
Humberside, N. H. White, *apptd* 1985
Lancashire/Merseyside, J. Finestein, *apptd* 1992
Leicestershire, D. M. Meredith, *apptd* 1995
Merseyside, D. R. G. Tapp, *apptd* 1992; P. S. Ward, *apptd* 1994; P. J. Firth, *apptd* 1994
Middlesex, N. A. McKittrick, *apptd* 1989; S. N. Day, *apptd* 1991; C. S. Wiles, *apptd* 1996
Mid Glamorgan, Miss P. J. Watkins, *apptd* 1995
Norfolk, N. P. Heley, *apptd* 1994
North-East London, G. E. Cawdron, *apptd* 1993
Nottinghamshire, P. F. Nuttall, *apptd* 1991; M. L. R. Harris, *apptd* 1991
Shropshire, P. H. R. Browning, *apptd* 1994
South Glamorgan, G. R. Watkins, *apptd* 1993
South Wales and Gwent, D. V. Manning-Davies, *apptd* 1996
South Yorkshire, C. R. Browne, *apptd* 1992; W. D. Thomas, *apptd* 1989; M. A. Rosenberg, *apptd* 1993; P. H. F. Jones, *apptd* 1995; Mrs S. E. Driver, *apptd* 1995
Staffordshire, P. G. G. Richards, *apptd* 1991
West Midlands, W. M. Probert, *apptd* 1983; B. Morgan, *apptd* 1989; I. Gillespie, *apptd* 1991; M. F. James, *apptd* 1991; C. M. McColl, *apptd* 1994
West Yorkshire, Mrs P. A. Hewitt, *apptd* 1990; G. A. K. Hodgson, *apptd* 1993; N. R. Cadbury, *apptd* 1997

Metropolitan

Chief Metropolitan Stipendiary Magistrate and Chairman of Magistrates' Courts Committee for Inner London Area (£88,077), G. E. Parkinson, *apptd* 1997 (*Bow Street*)

Magistrates (each £70,820)
Bow Street, The Chief Magistrate; R. D. Bartle, *apptd* 1972; C. L. Pratt, *apptd* 1990; H. N. Evans, *apptd* 1994
Camberwell Green, C. P. M. Davidson, *apptd* 1984; B. Loosley, *apptd* 1989; H. Gott, *apptd* 1992; Miss E. Roscoe, *apptd* 1994; R. House, *apptd* 1995; Miss C. S. R. Tubbs, *apptd* 1996
Clerkenwell, M. A. Johnstone, *apptd* 1980; I. M. Baker, *apptd* 1990
Greenwich, D. A. Cooper, *apptd* 1991; M. Kelly, *apptd* 1992; P. S. Wallis, *apptd* 1993; H. C. F. Riddle, *apptd* 1995
Highbury Corner, Miss D. Quick, *apptd* 1986; A. T. Evans, *apptd* 1990; Mrs L. Morgan, *apptd* 1995; P. A. M. Clark, *apptd* 1996; Miss D. Lachhar, *apptd* 1996
Horseferry Road, A. R. Davies, *apptd* 1985; G. Breen, *apptd* 1986; T. Workman, *apptd* 1986; Mrs K. R. Keating, *apptd* 1987; G. Wicks, *apptd* 1987; Mrs E. Rees, *apptd* 1994
Inner London and City Family Proceedings Court, N. Crichton, *apptd* 1987
Marylebone, D. Kennett Brown, *apptd* 1982; K. Maitland-Davies, *apptd* 1984; A. C. Baldwin, *apptd* 1990; Ms G. Babington-Browne, *apptd* 1991
South-Western, C. D. Voelcker, *apptd* 1982; A. W. Ormerod, *apptd* 1988; Miss D. Wickham, *apptd* 1989

Thames, Mrs J. Comyns, *apptd* 1982; I. G. Bing, *apptd* 1989; W. A. Kennedy, *apptd* 1991; S. E. Dawson, *apptd* 1984
Tower Bridge, C. S. F. Black, *apptd* 1993; M. Read, *apptd* 1993; S. Somjee, *apptd* 1995
West London Magistrates' Court, Miss A. Jennings, *apptd* 1972; T. English, *apptd* 1986; J. Philips, *apptd* 1989; D. L. Thomas, *apptd* 1990; D. Simpson, *apptd* 1993; J. Coleman, *apptd* 1995

Magistrates' Courts Committee for the Inner London Area
65 Romney Street, London SW1P 3RD
Tel 0171-799 3332
Justices' Chief Executive and Clerk to the Committee (£82,116), Miss C. Glenn
Justices' Clerk (Training) (£46,722), Miss C. Lewis

CROWN PROSECUTION SERVICE
50 Ludgate Hill, London EC4M 7EX
Tel 0171-273 8000

The Crown Prosecution Service (CPS) is responsible for the independent review and conduct of criminal proceedings instituted by police forces in England and Wales, with the exception of cases conducted by the Serious Fraud Office (*see* page 344) and certain minor offences.

The Service is headed by the Director of Public Prosecutions (DPP), who works under the superintendence of the Attorney-General, and a chief executive. The Service currently comprises a headquarters office and 14 areas covering England and Wales, with each area supervised by a Chief Crown Prosecutor. It is in the process of being decentralized, with 42 areas being created to correspond to the police areas in England and Wales.

For salary information, *see* page 278

Director of Public Prosecutions (SCS), Dame Barbara Mills, DBE, QC (*successor to be appointed in autumn 1998*)
Chief Executive (SCS), M. E. Addison
Director of Casework Evaluation (SCS), C. Newell
Director of Casework Services (SCS), G. Duff

CPS AREAS

CPS Anglia, Queen's House, 58 Victoria Street, St Albans AL1 3HZ. Tel: 01727-818100. *Chief Crown Prosecutor* (SCS), R. J. Chronnell
CPS Central Casework, 50 Ludgate Hill, London EC4M 7EX. Tel: 0171-273 8000. *Chief Crown Prosecutor* (SCS), Miss D. Sharpling
CPS East Midlands, 2 King Edward Court, King Edward Street, Nottingham NG1 1EL. Tel: 0115-948 0480. *Chief Crown Prosecutor* (SCS), B. T. McArdle
CPS Humber, Greenfield House, Scotland Street, Sheffield S3 7DQ. Tel: 0114-291 2164. *Chief Crown Prosecutor* (SCS), D. Adams, CBE
CPS London, Portland House, Stag Place, London SW1E 5BH. Tel: 0171-915 5700. *Chief Crown Prosecutor* (SCS), G. D. Etherington
CPS Mersey/Lancashire, 7th Floor (South), Royal Liver Building, Pier Head, Liverpool L3 1HN. Tel: 0151-236 7575. *Chief Crown Prosecutor* (SCS), G. Brown
CPS Midlands, 14th Floor, Colmore Gate, 2 Colmore Row, Birmingham B3 2QA. Tel: 0121-629 7202. *Chief Crown Prosecutor* (SCS), D. Blundell

CPS North, 1st Floor, Benton House, 136 Sandyford Road, Newcastle upon Tyne NE2 1QE. Tel: 0191-201 2390. *Chief Crown Prosecutor (SCS)*, M. Graham
CPS North-West, PO Box 237, 8th Floor, Sunlight House, Quay Street, Manchester M60 3PS. Tel: 0161-908 2771. *Chief Crown Prosecutor (SCS)*, A. R. Taylor
CPS Severn /Thames, Artillery House, Heritage Way, Droitwich, Worcester WR9 8YB. Tel: 01905-795477. *Chief Crown Prosecutor (SCS)*, N. Franklin
CPS South-East, 1 Onslow Street, Guildford, Surrey GU1 4YA. Tel: 01483-882600. *Chief Crown Prosecutor (SCS)*, C. Nicholls
CPS South-West, 8 Kew Court, Pynes Hill, Rydon Lane, Exeter EX2 5SS. Tel: 01392-422555. *Chief Crown Prosecutor (SCS)*, P. Boeuf
CPS Wales, Tudor House, 16 Cathedral Road, Cardiff CF1 9LJ. Tel: 01222-783000. *Chief Crown Prosecutor (SCS)*, R. A. Prickett
CPS Yorkshire, 6th Floor, Ryedale Building, 60 Piccadilly, York YO1 1NS. Tel: 01904-610726. *Chief Crown Prosecutor (SCS)*, D. V. Dickenson

The Scottish Judicature

Scotland has a legal system separate from and differing greatly from the English legal system in enacted law, judicial procedure and the structure of courts.

In Scotland the system of public prosecution is headed by the Lord Advocate and is independent of the police, who have no say in the decision to prosecute. The Lord Advocate, discharging his functions through the Crown Office in Edinburgh, is responsible for prosecutions in the High Court, sheriff courts and district courts. Prosecutions in the High Court are prepared by the Crown Office and conducted in court by one of the law officers, by an advocate-depute, or by a solicitor advocate. In the inferior courts the decision to prosecute is made and prosecution is preferred by procurators fiscal, who are lawyers and full-time civil servants subject to the directions of the Crown Office. A permanent legally-qualified civil servant known as the Crown Agent is responsible for the running of the Crown Office and the organization of the Procurator Fiscal Service, of which he is the head.

Scotland is divided into six sheriffdoms, each with a full-time sheriff principal. The sheriffdoms are further divided into sheriff court districts, each of which has a legally-qualified resident sheriff or sheriffs, who are the judges of the court.

In criminal cases sheriffs principal and sheriffs have the same powers; sitting with a jury of 15 members, they may try more serious cases on indictment, or, sitting alone, may try lesser cases under summary procedure. Minor summary offences are dealt with in district courts which are administered by the district and the islands local government authorities and presided over by lay justices of the peace (of whom there are about 4,000) and, in Glasgow only, by stipendiary magistrates. Juvenile offenders (children under 16) may be brought before an informal children's hearing comprising three local lay people. The superior criminal court is the High Court of Justiciary which is both a trial and an appeal court. Cases on indictment are tried by a High Court judge, sitting with a jury of 15, in Edinburgh and on circuit in other towns. Appeals from the lower courts against conviction or sentence are heard also by the High Court, which sits as

an appeal court only in Edinburgh. There is no further appeal to the House of Lords in criminal cases.

In civil cases the jurisdiction of the sheriff court extends to most kinds of action. Appeal against decisions of the sheriff may be made to the sheriff principal and thence to the Court of Session, or direct to the Court of Session, which sits only in Edinburgh. The Court of Session is divided into the Inner and the Outer House. The Outer House is a court of first instance in which cases are heard by judges sitting singly, sometimes with a jury of 12. The Inner House, itself subdivided into two divisions of equal status, is mainly an appeal court. Appeals may be made to the Inner House from the Outer House as well as from the sheriff court. An appeal may be made from the Inner House to the House of Lords.

The judges of the Court of Session are the same as those of the High Court of Justiciary, the Lord President of the Court of Session also holding the office of Lord Justice General in the High Court. Senators of the College of Justice are Lords Commissioners of Justiciary as well as judges of the Court of Session. On appointment, a Senator takes a judicial title, which is retained for life. Although styled 'The Hon./Rt. Hon. Lord —', the Senator is not a peer.

The office of coroner does not exist in Scotland. The local procurator fiscal inquires privately into sudden or suspicious deaths and may report findings to the Crown Agent. In some cases a fatal accident inquiry may be held before the sheriff.

COURT OF SESSION and HIGH COURT OF JUSTICIARY

The Lord President and Lord Justice General (£138,889)
  The Rt. Hon. the Lord Rodger of Earlsferry, *born* 1944, *apptd* 1996
  Secretary, A. Maxwell

INNER HOUSE

Lords of Session (each £132,017)

FIRST DIVISION
The Lord President
Hon. Lord Sutherland (Ranald Sutherland), *born* 1932, *apptd* 1985
Hon. Lord Prosser (William Prosser), *born* 1934, *apptd* 1986
Hon. Lord Caplan (Philip Caplan), *born* 1929, *apptd* 1989

SECOND DIVISION
Lord Justice Clerk (£132,017), The Rt. Hon. Lord Cullen (William Cullen), *born* 1935, *apptd* 1997
Rt. Hon. The Lord McCluskey, *born* 1929, *apptd* 1984
Hon. Lord Kirkwood (Ian Kirkwood), *born* 1932, *apptd* 1987
Hon. Lord Coulsfield (John Cameron), *born* 1934, *apptd* 1987

OUTER HOUSE
Lords of Session (each £117,752)

Hon. Lord Milligan (James Milligan), *born* 1934, *apptd* 1988
Rt. Hon. The Lord Cameron of Lochbroom, *born* 1931, *apptd* 1989
Hon. Lord Marnoch (Michael Bruce), *born* 1938, *apptd* 1990
Hon. Lord MacLean (Ranald MacLean), *born* 1938, *apptd* 1990
Hon. Lord Penrose (George Penrose), *born* 1938, *apptd* 1990

Hon. Lord Osborne (Kenneth Osborne), *born* 1937, *apptd* 1990

Hon. Lord Abernethy (Alistair Cameron), *born* 1938, *apptd* 1992

Hon. Lord Johnston (Alan Johnston), *born* 1942, *apptd* 1994
Hon. Lord Gill (Brian Gill), *born* 1942, *apptd* 1994
Hon. Lord Hamilton (Arthur Hamilton), *born* 1942, *apptd* 1995

Hon. Lord Dawson (Thomas Dawson), *born* 1948, *apptd* 1995

Hon. Lord Macfadyen (Donald Macfadyen), *born* 1945, *apptd* 1995

Hon. Lady Cosgrove (Hazel Aronson), *born* 1946, *apptd* 1996

Hon. Lord Nimmo Smith (William Nimmo Smith), *born* 1942, *apptd* 1996

Hon. Lord Philip (Alexander Philip), *born* 1942, *apptd* 1996
Hon. Lord Kingarth (Derek Emslie), *born* 1949, *apptd* 1997
Hon. Lord Bonomy (Iain Bonomy), *born* 1946, *apptd* 1997
Hon. Lord Eassie (Ronald Mackay), *born* 1945, *apptd* 1997

COURT OF SESSION AND HIGH COURT OF JUSTICIARY
Parliament House, Parliament Square, Edinburgh EH1 1RQ
Tel 0131-225 2595

Principal Clerk of Session and Justiciary (£30,991–£51,608), J. L. Anderson
Deputy Principal Clerk of Justiciary and Administration (£27,172–£42,023), T. Fyffe
Deputy Principal Clerk of Session and Principal Extractor (£27,172–£42,023), G. McKeand
Deputy Principal Clerk (Keeper of the Rolls) (£27,172–£42,023), R. Cockburn
Depute Clerks of Session and Justiciary (£20,741–£27,216), N. J. Dowie; I. F. Smith; T. Higgins; T. B. Cruickshank; Q. A. Oliver; F. Shannly; A. S. Moffat; D. J. Shand; G. G. Ellis; W. Dunn; A. M. Finlayson; C. C. Armstrong; G. M. Prentice; R. Jenkins; J. O. McLean; M. Weir; R. M. Sinclair; E. G. Appelbe; B. Watson; D. W. Cullen; D. J. Cullum; I. D. Martin; N. McGinley; J. Lynn; E. Dickson

SCOTTISH COURTS ADMINISTRATION
Hayweight House, 23 Lauriston Street, Edinburgh EH3 9DQ
Tel 0131-229 9200

The Scottish Courts Administration is responsible to the Secretary of State for Scotland for the performance of the Scottish Court Service and central administration pertaining to the judiciary in the Supreme and Sheriff Courts; and to the Lord Advocate for certain aspects of court procedures, jurisdiction and legislation, law reform and other matters.
Director (G2), J. Hamill, CB
Deputy Director (*Legal Policy*) (*Assistant Solicitor*) (G5), P. M. Beaton
Deputy Director (*Resources and Liaison*) (G5), D. Stewart

SCOTTISH COURT SERVICE
Hayweight House, 23 Lauriston Street, Edinburgh EH3 9DQ
Tel 0131-229 9200

The Scottish Court Service became an executive agency within the Scottish Courts Administration in 1995. It is responsible to the Secretary of State for Scotland for the provision of staff, court houses and associated services for the Supreme and Sheriff Courts.
Chief Executive, M. Ewart

SHERIFF COURT OF CHANCERY
27 Chambers Street, Edinburgh EH1 1LB
Tel 0131-225 2525

The Court deals with service of heirs and completion of title in relation to heritable property.
Sheriff of Chancery, C. G. B. Nicholson, QC

HM COMMISSARY OFFICE
27 Chambers Street, Edinburgh EH1 1LB
Tel 0131-225 2525

The Office is responsible for issuing confirmation, a legal document entitling a person to execute a deceased person's will, and other related matters.
Commissary Clerk, J. M. Ross

SCOTTISH LAND COURT
1 Grosvenor Crescent, Edinburgh EH12 5ER
Tel 0131-225 3595

The court deals with disputes relating to agricultural and crofting land in Scotland.
Chairman (£96,214), The Hon. Lord McGhie (James McGhie), QC
Members, D. J. Houston; D. M. Macdonald; J. Kinloch (*part-time*)
Principal Clerk, K. H. R. Graham, WS

SHERIFFDOMS

SALARIES

Sheriff Principal	£96,214
Sheriff	£88,077
Regional Sheriff Clerk/Area Director	£30,991–£59,000
Sheriff Clerk	£12,206–£42,023

*Floating Sheriff

GRAMPIAN, HIGHLANDS AND ISLANDS
Sheriff Principal, D. J. Risk
Area Director North, J. Robertson

SHERIFFS AND SHERIFF CLERKS
Aberdeen and Stonehaven, D. Kelbie; L. A. S. Jessop; A. Pollock; Mrs A. M. Cowan; C. J. Harris, QC *Sheriff Clerks*, Mrs E. Laing (*Aberdeen*); B. McBride (*Stonehaven*)
Peterhead and Banff, K. A. McLernan; *Sheriff Clerk*, A. Hempseed (*Peterhead*); *Sheriff Clerk Depute*, Mrs F. L. MacPherson (*Banff*)
Elgin, N. McPartlin; *Sheriff Clerk*, M. McBey
Inverness, Lochmaddy, Portree, Stornoway, Dingwall, Tain, Wick and Dornoch, W. J. Fulton; D. Booker-Milburn; J. O. A. Fraser; I. A. Cameron; *G. K. Buchanan; *Sheriff Clerks*, J. Robertson (*Inverness*); W. Cochrane (*Dingwall*); *Sheriff Clerks Depute*, Miss M. Campbell (*Lochmaddy and Portree*); Mrs M. Macdonald (*Stornoway*); L. MacLachlan (*Tain*); Mrs J. McEwan (*Wick*); K. Kerr (*Dornoch*)
Kirkwall and Lerwick, C. S. Mackenzie; *Sheriff Clerks Depute*, P. Cushen (*Kirkwall*); M. Flanagan (*Lerwick*)
Fort William, C. G. McKay (also *Oban*); *Sheriff Clerk Depute*, D. Hood

TAYSIDE, CENTRAL AND FIFE
Sheriff Principal, J. J. Maguire, QC
Area Director East, M. Bonar (*from Dec. 1998*)

SHERIFFS AND SHERIFF CLERKS
Arbroath and Forfar, K. A. Veal; *C. N. R. Stein; *Sheriff Clerks*, M. Herbertson (*Arbroath*); S. Munro (*Forfar*)
Dundee, R. A. Davidson; A. L. Stewart, QC; *J. P. Scott; G. J. Evans (also *Cupar*); *Sheriff Clerk*, J. S. Doig (*until late 1998*)
Perth, J. F. Wheatley, QC; J. C. McInnes, QC; *Mrs P. M. M. Bowman; *Sheriff Clerk*, J. Murphy
Falkirk, A. V. Sheehan; A. J. Murphy; *Sheriff Clerk*, D. Forrester
Stirling, The Hon. R. E. G. Younger; *Sheriff Clerk*, J. Clark
Alloa, W. M. Reid; *Sheriff Clerk*, R. G. McKeand
Cupar, G. J. Evans (also *Dundee*); *Sheriff Clerk*, R. Hughes
Dunfermline, J. S. Forbes; C. W. Palmer; *Sheriff Clerk*, W. McCulloch
Kirkcaldy, F. J. Keane; Mrs L. G. Patrick; *I. D. Dunbar; *Sheriff Clerk*, W. Jones

LOTHIAN AND BORDERS

Sheriff Principal, C. G. B. Nicholson, QC
Area Director East, M. Bonar (*from Dec. 1998*)

SHERIFFS AND SHERIFF CLERKS
Edinburgh, R. G. Craik, QC (also *Peebles*); R. J. D. Scott (also *Peebles*); Miss I. A. Poole; A. M. Bell; J. M. S. Horsburgh, QC; G. W. S. Presslie (also *Haddington*); J. A. Farrell; *A. Lothian; I. D. Macphail, QC; C. N. Stoddart; A. B. Wilkinson, QC; Mrs D. J. B. Robertson; N. M. P. Morrison, QC; *Miss M. M. Stephen; Mrs M. L. E. Jarvie, QC; *Sheriff Clerk*, M. Bonar
Peebles, R. G. Craik, QC (also *Edinburgh*); R. J. D. Scott (also *Edinburgh*); Sheriff *Clerk Depute*, R. McArthur
Linlithgow, H. R. MacLean; G. R. Fleming; *K. A. Ross; *Sheriff Clerk*, R. D. Sinclair
Haddington, G. W. S. Presslie (also *Edinburgh*); *Sheriff Clerk*, J. O'Donnell
Jedburgh and Duns, J. V. Paterson; *Sheriff Clerk*, I. W. Williamson
Selkirk, J. V. Paterson; *Sheriff Clerk Depute*, L. McFarlane

NORTH STRATHCLYDE

Sheriff Principal, R. C. Hay, CBE
Area Director West, I. Scott

SHERIFFS AND SHERIFF CLERKS
Oban, C. G. McKay (also *Fort William*); *Sheriff Clerk Depute*, G. Whitelaw
Dumbarton, J. T. Fitzsimons; T. Scott; S. W. H. Fraser; *Sheriff Clerk*, P. Corcoran
Paisley, R. G. Smith; J. Spy; C. K. Higgins; N. Douglas; *D. J. Pender; *W. Dunlop (also *Campbeltown*); *Sheriff Clerk (acting)*, R. McMillan
Greenock, J. Herald (also *Rothesay*); Sir Stephen Young; *Sheriff Clerk*, J. Tannahill
Kilmarnock, T. M. Croan; D. B. Smith; T. F. Russell; *Sheriff Clerk*, G. Waddell
Dunoon, A. W. Noble; *Sheriff Clerk Depute*, Mrs C. Carson
Campbeltown, *W. Dunlop (also *Paisley*); *Sheriff Clerk Depute*, P. G. Hay
Rothesay, J. Herald (also *Greenock*); *Sheriff Clerk Depute*, Mrs C. K. McCormick

GLASGOW AND STRATHKELVIN

Sheriff Principal, E. F. Bowen, QC
Area Director West, I. Scott

SHERIFFS AND SHERIFF CLERKS
Glasgow, B. Kearney; G. H. Gordon, CBE, Ph.D., QC; B. A. Lockhart; I. G. Pirie; Mrs A. L. A. Duncan;

A. C. Henry; J. K. Mitchell; A. G. Johnston; J. P. Murphy; Miss S. A. O. Raeburn, QC; D. Convery; J. McGowan; B. A. Kerr, QC; Mrs C. M. A. F. Gimblett; I. A. S. Peebles, QC; C. W. McFarlane, QC; K. M. Maciver; H. Matthews, QC; J. D. Lowe, CB; J. A. Baird; Miss R. E. A. Rae, QC; T. A. K. Drummond, QC; *Sheriff Clerk*, D. Nicoll

SOUTH STRATHCLYDE, DUMFRIES AND GALLOWAY

Sheriff Principal, G. L. Cox, QC
Area Director West, I. Scott

SHERIFFS AND SHERIFF CLERKS
Hamilton, L. Cameron; A. C. MacPherson; W. F. Lunny; D. C. Russell; V. J. Canavan (also *Airdrie*); W. E. Gibson; H. Stirling; J. H. Stewart; *H. S. Neilson; *Sheriff Clerk*, P. Feeney
Lanark, J. D. Allan; *Sheriff Clerk*, A. Whyte
Ayr, N. Gow, QC; R. G. McEwan, QC; *C. B. Miller; *Sheriff Clerk*, Miss C. D. Cockburn
Stranraer and Kirkcudbright, J. R. Smith (also *Dumfries*); *Sheriff Clerks*, W. McIntosh (*Stranraer*); B. Lindsay (*Kirkcudbright*)
Dumfries, K. G. Barr; M. J. Fletcher; J. R. Smith (also *Stranraer and Kirkcudbright*); *Sheriff Clerk*, P. McGonigle
Airdrie, V. J. Canavan (also *Hamilton*); R. H. Dickson; I. C. Simpson; *J. C. Morris, QC; *Sheriff Clerk*, K. Carter

STIPENDIARY MAGISTRATES

GLASGOW
R. Hamilton, *apptd* 1984; J. B. C. Nisbet, *apptd* 1984; R. B. Christie, *apptd* 1985; Mrs J. A. M. MacLean, *apptd* 1990

PROCURATOR FISCAL SERVICE

CROWN OFFICE
25 Chambers Street, Edinburgh EH1 1LA
Tel 0131-226 2626

Crown Agent (£76,710–£112,040), A. C. Normand
Deputy Crown Agent (£53,450–£89,090), F. R. Crowe (*from Jan. 1999*)

PROCURATORS FISCAL

SALARIES

Regional Procurator Fiscal – grade 3	£58,590–£94,330
Regional Procurator Fiscal – grade 4	£53,450–£89,090
Procurator Fiscal – upper level	£39,830–£62,570
Procurator Fiscal – lower level	£36,000–£42,000

GRAMPIAN, HIGHLANDS AND ISLANDS REGION
Regional Procurator Fiscal, L. A. Higson (*Aberdeen*)
Procurators Fiscal, E. K. Barbour (*Stonehaven*); A. J. M. Colley (*Banff*); Miss A. Thom (*Peterhead*) (*interim*); J. F. MacKay (*Elgin*); A. N. Perry (*Wick*); J. Bamber (*Portree, Lochmaddy*); F. Redman (*Stornoway*); G. Napier (*Inverness*); R. W. Urquhart (*Kirkwall, Lerwick*); Mrs A. Neizer (*Fort William*); A. N. MacDonald (*Dingwall, Tain*)

TAYSIDE, CENTRAL AND FIFE REGION
Regional Procurator Fiscal, B. K. Heywood (*Dundee*)

Procurators Fiscal, I. C. Walker (*Forfar*); I. A. McLeod (*Perth*); J. J. Miller (*Falkirk*); C. Ritchie (*Stirling and Alloa*); E. B. Russell (*Cupar*); R. G. Stott (*Dunfermline*); Miss E. C. Munro (*Kirkcaldy*)

LOTHIAN AND BORDERS REGION
Regional Procurator Fiscal, N. McFadyen (*from Jan. 1999*) (*Edinburgh*)
Procurators Fiscal, Miss L. M. Ruxton (*Linlithgow*); A. J. P. Reith (*Haddington*); A. R. G. Fraser (*Duns, Jedburgh*); D. MacNeill (*Selkirk*)

NORTH STRATHCLYDE REGION
Regional Procurator Fiscal, J. D. Friel (*Paisley*)
Procurators Fiscal, I. Henderson (*Campbeltown*); C. C. Donnelly (*Dumbarton*); W. S. Carnegie (*Greenock*); D. L. Webster (*Dunoon*); J. G. MacGlennan (*Kilmarnock*); B. R. Maguire (*Oban*)

GLASGOW AND STRATHKELVIN REGION
Regional Procurator Fiscal, A. D. Vannet (*Glasgow*)

SOUTH STRATHCLYDE, DUMFRIES AND GALLOWAY REGION
Regional Procurator Fiscal, vacant (*Hamilton*)
Procurators Fiscal, S. R. Houston (*Lanark*); J. T. O'Donnell (*Ayr*); F. R. Crowe (*Stranraer*) (*interim*); D. J. Howdle (*Dumfries, Stranraer, Kirkcudbright*); D. Spiers (*Airdrie*)

Northern Ireland Judicature

In Northern Ireland the legal system and the structure of courts closely resemble those of England and Wales; there are, however, often differences in enacted law.

The Supreme Court of Judicature of Northern Ireland comprises the Court of Appeal, the High Court of Justice and the Crown Court. The practice and procedure of these courts is similar to that in England. The superior civil court is the High Court of Justice, from which an appeal lies to the Northern Ireland Court of Appeal; the House of Lords is the final civil appeal court.

The Crown Court, served by High Court and county court judges, deals with criminal trials on indictment. Cases are heard before a judge and, except those involving offences specified under emergency legislation, a jury. Appeals from the Crown Court against conviction or sentence are heard by the Northern Ireland Court of Appeal; the House of Lords is the final court of appeal.

The decision to prosecute in cases tried on indictment and in summary cases of a serious nature rests in Northern Ireland with the Director of Public Prosecutions, who is responsible to the Attorney-General. Minor summary offences are prosecuted by the police.

Minor criminal offences are dealt with in magistrates' courts by a legally qualified resident magistrate and, where an offender is under 17, by juvenile courts each consisting of a resident magistrate and two lay members specially qualified to deal with juveniles (at least one of whom must be a woman). In July 1998 there were 919 justices of the peace in Northern Ireland. Appeals from magistrates' courts are heard by the county court, or by the Court of Appeal on a point of law or an issue as to jurisdiction.

Magistrates' courts in Northern Ireland can deal with certain classes of civil case but most minor civil cases are dealt with in county courts. Judgments of all civil courts are enforceable through a centralized procedure administered by the Enforcement of Judgments Office.

SUPREME COURT OF JUDICATURE
The Royal Courts of Justice, Belfast BT1 3JF
Tel 01232-235111

Lord Chief Justice of Northern Ireland (£138,889)
 The Rt. Hon. Sir Robert Carswell, *born* 1934, *apptd* 1997
 Principal Secretary, G. W. Johnston

LORDS JUSTICES OF APPEAL (each £132,017)
Style, The Rt. Hon. Lord Justice [surname]
Rt. Hon. Sir John MacDermott, *born* 1927, *apptd* 1987
Rt. Hon. Sir Michael Nicholson, *born* 1933, *apptd* 1995
Rt. Hon. Sir William McCollum, *born* 1933, *apptd* 1997

PUISNE JUDGES (each £117,752)
Style, The Hon. Mr Justice [surname]
Hon. Sir Anthony Campbell, *born* 1936, *apptd* 1988
Hon. Sir John Sheil, *born* 1938, *apptd* 1989
Hon. Sir Brian Kerr, *born* 1948, *apptd* 1993
Hon. Sir John Pringle, *born* 1929, *apptd* 1993
Hon. Sir Malachy Higgins, *born* 1944, *apptd* 1993
Hon. Sir Paul Girvan, *born* 1948, *apptd* 1995
Hon. Sir Patrick Coghlin, *born* 1945, *apptd* 1997

MASTERS OF THE SUPREME COURT (each £70,820)
Master, Queen's Bench and Appeals and Clerk of the Crown, J. W. Wilson, QC
Master, High Court, Mrs D. M. Kennedy
Master, Office of Care and Protection, F. B. Hall
Master, Chancery Office, R. A. Ellison
Master, Bankruptcy and Companies Office, C. W. G. Redpath
Master, Probate and Matrimonial Office, N. Lockie
Master, Taxing Office, J. C. Napier

OFFICIAL SOLICITOR
Official Solicitor to the Supreme Court of Northern Ireland, vacant

COUNTY COURTS

Judges (each £88,077–£96,214)
Style, His Hon. Judge [surname]
Judge Curran, QC; Judge McKee, QC; Judge Gibson, QC; Judge Petrie, QC; Judge Smyth, QC; Judge Markey, QC; Judge McKay, QC; Judge Martin, QC (*Chief Social Security and Child Support Commissioner*); Judge Brady, QC; Judge Rodgers; Judge Foote, QC

RECORDERS (each £96,214)
Belfast, Judge Hart, QC
Londonderry, Judge Burgess

MAGISTRATES' COURTS

RESIDENT MAGISTRATES (each £70,820)
There are 17 resident magistrates in Northern Ireland.

CROWN SOLICITOR'S OFFICE
PO Box 410, Royal Courts of Justice, Belfast BT1 3JY
Tel 01232-542555

Crown Solicitor, N. P. Roberts

DEPARTMENT OF THE DIRECTOR OF
PUBLIC PROSECUTIONS
Royal Courts of Justice, Belfast BT1 3NX
Tel 01232-542444

Director of Public Prosecutions, A. Fraser, CB, QC
Deputy Director of Public Prosecutions, vacant

NORTHERN IRELAND COURT SERVICE
Windsor House, Bedford Street, Belfast BT2 7LT
Tel 01232-328594

Director (G3)

Crime Statistics

ENGLAND AND WALES

NOTIFIABLE OFFENCES RECORDED 1996

Violence against the person	239,300
Sexual offences	31,400
Burglary	1,164,600
Robbery	74,000
Theft and handling stolen goods	2,383,900
Fraud and forgery	136,200
Criminal damage	951,300
Other offences	55,800
Total offences	5,036,600

Source: The Stationery Office – *Annual Abstract of Statistics 1998*

CRIMINAL JUSTICE STATISTICS 1996

Number of arrests	1,750,000
Notifiable offences cleared up	1,288,000
Clear-up rate	26%
*Number of offenders cautioned	286,200
Defendants proceeded against at magistrates' courts	1,919,500
Defendants found guilty at magistrates' courts	1,368,900
Defendants tried at Crown Courts	85,900
Defendants found guilty at Crown Courts	72,100
Defendants sentenced at Crown Courts after summary conviction	4,600
Total offenders found guilty at both courts	1,441,000
*Total offenders found guilty or cautioned	1,727,200

*Excludes motoring offences

OFFENDERS SENTENCED BY TYPE OF SENTENCE OR ORDER 1996

Absolute discharge	20,100
Conditional discharge	104,800
Fine	1,075,500
Probation order	50,900
Supervision order	10,900
Community service order	45,900
Attendance sentence order	7,500
Combination order	17,300
Curfew order	200
Young offender institution	20,600
Imprisonment:	
Suspended	3,400
Unsuspended	64,000
Otherwise dealt with	19,400
All sentences or orders: total	1,440,600

AVERAGE LENGTH OF SENTENCE 1996 *in months*

	Males aged 21 and over	Females aged 21 and over
Magistrates' courts	2.7	2.3
Crown court	24.0	20.0

Source: The Stationery Office – *Criminal Statistics England and Wales 1996*

SCOTLAND

CRIMES AND OFFENCES RECORDED 1996

Non-sexual crimes of violence against the person	21,500
Crimes involving indecency	5,700
Crimes involving dishonesty	295,400
Fire-raising, vandalism, etc.	89,000
Other crimes	40,300
Miscellaneous offences	146,100
Motor vehicle offences	305,900
Total crimes and offences	903,900*

Source: The Stationery Office – *Annual Abstract of Statistics 1998*

CRIMINAL JUSTICE STATISTICS 1996

Number of persons proceeded against	177,168
Persons with charge proved	156,707

PERSONS WITH CHARGE PROVED BY MAIN PENALTY 1996

Absolute discharge	1,008
Remit to children's hearing	193
Admonition or caution	15,859
Compensation order	1,415
Fine	105,384
Probation	6,435
Community service order	5,711
Insanity or hospital order	159
Detention of child	45
Young offender institution	4,744
Prison	12,134
All penalties: total	153,087

Source: The Scottish Office

Tribunals

AGRICULTURAL LAND TRIBUNALS

c/o Rural and Marine Environment Division, Ministry of Agriculture, Fisheries and Food, Nobel House, 17 Smith Square, London SW1P 3JR
Tel 0171-238 6991

Agricultural Land Tribunals settle disputes and other issues between agricultural landlords and tenants, and drainage disputes between neighbours.

There are seven tribunals covering England and one covering Wales. For each tribunal the Lord Chancellor appoints a chairman and one or more deputies (barristers or solicitors of at least seven years standing). The Lord Chancellor also appoints lay members to three statutory panels: the 'landowners' panel, the 'farmers' panel and the 'drainage' panel.

Each tribunal is an independent statutory body with jurisdiction only within its own area. A separate tribunal is constituted for each case, and consists of a chairman (who may be the chairman or one of the deputy chairmen) and two lay members nominated by the chairman.
Chairmen (England) (£253 a day), W. D. Greenwood;
K. J. Fisher; P. A. de la Piquerie; C. H. Beaumont; His Hon. Judge Lee; G. L. Newsom; His Hon. Judge Robert Taylor
Chairman (Wales) (£253 a day), W. J. Owen

COMMONS COMMISSIONERS

Room 818, Tollgate House, Houlton Street, Bristol BS2 9DJ
Tel 0117-987 8928

The Commons Commissioners are responsible for deciding disputes arising under the Commons Registration Act 1965 and the Common Land (Rectification of Registers) Act 1989. They also enquire into the ownership of unclaimed common land. Commissioners are appointed by the Lord Chancellor.
Chief Commons Commissioner (part-time) (£34,720), D. M. Burton
Commissioner, I. L. R. Romer
Clerk, Miss S. Hargreaves

COPYRIGHT TRIBUNAL

25 Southampton Buildings, London WC2A 1AY
Tel 0171-438 4776

The Copyright Tribunal, which replaced the Performing Right Tribunal, resolves disputes over copyright licences, principally where there is collective licensing.

The chairman and two deputy chairmen are appointed by the Lord Chancellor. Up to eight ordinary members are appointed by the Secretary of State for Trade and Industry.
Chairman (£316 a day), C. P. Tootal
Secretary, Miss J. E. M. Durdin

DATA PROTECTION TRIBUNAL

c/o The Home Office, Queen Anne's Gate, London SW1H 9AT
Tel 0171-273 3492

The Data Protection Tribunal determines appeals against decisions of the Data Protection Registrar (now Commissioner) (*see* page 294). The chairman and two deputy chairmen are appointed by the Lord Chancellor and must be legally qualified. Lay members are appointed by the Home Secretary to represent the interests of data users or data subjects.

A tribunal consists of a legally-qualified chairman sitting with equal numbers of the lay members appointed to represent the interests of data users and data subjects.
Chairman (£370 a day), J. A. C. Spokes, QC
Secretary, D. Anderson

EMPLOYMENT TRIBUNALS

CENTRAL OFFICE (ENGLAND AND WALES)
19–29 Woburn Place, London WC1H 0LU
Tel 0171-273 8666

Employment Tribunals for England and Wales sit in 11 regions. The tribunals deal with matters of employment law, redundancy, dismissal, contract disputes, sexual, racial and disability discrimination, and related areas of dispute which may arise in the workplace. A central registration unit records all applications and maintains a public register at Southgate Street, Bury St Edmunds, Suffolk IP33 2AQ. The tribunals are funded by the Department of Trade and Industry; administrative support is provided by the Employment Tribunal Service (*see* pages 348–9).

Chairmen, who may be full-time or part-time, are legally qualified. They are appointed by the Lord Chancellor. Tribunal members are nominated by specified employer and employee groups and appointed by the Secretary of State for Trade and Industry.
President, His Hon. Judge Prophet

CENTRAL OFFICE (SCOTLAND)
Eagle Building, 215 Bothwell Street, Glasgow G2 7TS
Tel 0141-204 0730

Tribunals in Scotland have the same remit as those in England and Wales. Chairmen are appointed by the Lord President of the Court of Session and lay members by the Secretary of State for Trade and Industry.
President (£96,214), Mrs D. Littlejohn, CBE

EMPLOYMENT APPEAL TRIBUNAL

Central Office, Audit House, 58 Victoria Embankment, London EC4Y 0DS
Tel 0171-273 1041
Divisional Office, 52 Melville Street, Edinburgh EH3 7HF
Tel 0131-225 3963

The Employment Appeal Tribunal hears appeals on a question of law arising from any decision of an employment tribunal. A tribunal consists of a high court judge and two lay members, one from each side of industry. They are appointed by The Queen on the recommendation of the Lord Chancellor and the Secretary of State for Trade and Industry. Administrative support is provided by the Employment Tribunal Service (*see* pages 348–9).

President, The Hon. Mr Justice Morison
Scottish Chairman, The Hon. Lord Johnston
Registrar, Miss V. J. Selio

IMMIGRATION APPELLATE AUTHORITIES

Taylor House, 88 Rosebery Avenue, London EC1R 4QU
Tel 0171-862 4200

The Immigration Appeal Adjudicators hear appeals from immigration decisions concerning the need for, and refusal of, leave to enter or remain in the UK, refusals to grant asylum, decisions to make deportation orders and directions to remove persons subject to immigration control from the UK. The Immigration Appeal Tribunal hears appeals direct from decisions to make deportation orders in matters concerning conduct contrary to the public good and refusals to grant asylum. Its principal jurisdiction is, however, the hearing of appeals from adjudicators by the party (Home Office or individual) who is aggrieved by the decision. Appeals are subject to leave being granted by the tribunal.

An adjudicator sits alone. The tribunal sits in divisions of three, normally a legally qualified member and two lay members. Members of the tribunal and adjudicators are appointed by the Lord Chancellor.

IMMIGRATION APPEAL TRIBUNAL
President, His Hon. Judge Pearl
Vice-Presidents, Mrs J. Chatwani; A. F. Hatt; M. Rapinet; A. O'Brien-Quinn

IMMIGRATION APPEAL ADJUDICATORS
Chief Adjudicator, His Hon. Judge Dunn, QC
Deputy Chief Adjudicator, J. Latter

INDEPENDENT TRIBUNAL SERVICE

Whittington House, 19–30 Alfred Place, London WC1E 7LW
Tel 0171-814 6500

The service is the judicial authority which exercises judicial and administrative control over the independent social security and child support appeal tribunals, medical and disability appeal tribunals, and vaccine damage tribunals.

President, His Hon. Judge Michael Harris
Chief Executive, vacant

INDUSTRIAL TRIBUNALS AND THE FAIR EMPLOYMENT TRIBUNAL (NORTHERN IRELAND)

Long Bridge House, 20–24 Waring Street, Belfast BT1 2EB
Tel 01232-327666

The industrial tribunal system in Northern Ireland was set up in 1965 and has a similar remit to the employment tribunals in the rest of the UK. There is also in Northern Ireland a Fair Employment Tribunal, which hears and determines individual cases of alleged religious or political discrimination in employment. Employers can appeal to the Fair Employment Tribunal if they consider the directions of the Fair Employment Commission to be

unreasonable, inappropriate or unnecessary, and the Fair Employment Commission can make application to the Tribunal for the enforcement of undertakings or directions with which an employer has not complied.

The president, vice-president and part-time chairmen of the Fair Employment Tribunal are appointed by the Lord Chancellor. The full-time chairman and the part-time chairmen of the industrial tribunals and the panel members to both the industrial tribunals and the Fair Employment Tribunal are appointed by the Department of Economic Development Northern Ireland.

President of the Industrial Tribunals and the Fair Employment Tribunal (£88,077), J. Maguire, CBE
Vice-President of the Industrial Tribunals and the Fair Employment Tribunal, Mrs M. P. Price
Secretary, Mrs P. McVeigh

LANDS TRIBUNAL

48–49 Chancery Lane, London WC2A 1JR
Tel 0171-936 7200

The Lands Tribunal is an independent judicial body which determines questions relating to the valuation of land, rating appeals from valuation tribunals, the discharge or modification of restrictive covenants, and compulsory purchase compensation. The tribunal may also arbitrate under references by consent. The president and members are appointed by the Lord Chancellor.

President, vacant
Members (£84,752), M. St J. Hopper, FRICS; P. H. Clarke, FRICS; N. J. Rose, FRICS; P. R. Francis
Member (part-time), His Hon. Judge Rich, QC
Members (part-time) (£400 a day), J. C. Hill, TD; A. P. Musto, FRICS
Registrar, C. A. McMullan

LANDS TRIBUNAL FOR SCOTLAND

1 Grosvenor Crescent, Edinburgh EH12 5ER
Tel 0131-225 7996

The Lands Tribunal for Scotland has the same remit as the tribunal for England and Wales but also covers questions relating to tenants' rights. The president is appointed by the Lord President of the Court of Session.

President, The Hon. Lord McGhie, QC
Members (£84,752), A. R. MacLeary, FRICS; J. Devine, FRICS
Members (part-time), Sheriff A. C. Henry; R. A. Edwards, CBE, WS
Clerk, N. M. Tainsh

MENTAL HEALTH REVIEW TRIBUNALS

The Mental Health Review Tribunals are independent judicial bodies which review the cases of patients compulsorily detained under the provisions of the Mental Health Act 1983. They have the power to discharge the patient, to recommend leave of absence, delayed discharge, transfer to another hospital or that a guardianship order be made, to reclassify both restricted and unrestricted patients, and to recommend consideration of a supervision application. There are eight tribunals in England, each headed by a regional chairman who is appointed by the Lord Chancellor on a part-time basis. Each tribunal is made up of at least three members, and must include a lawyer, who acts as president (£239 a day), a medical member (£226 a day) and a lay member (£97 a day).

The Mental Health Review Tribunals' secretariat is based in five regional offices:

LIVERPOOL, 3rd Floor, Cressington House, 249 St Mary's Road, Garston, Liverpool L19 0NF. Tel: 0151-494 0095. *Clerk*, Mrs B. Foot

LONDON (NORTH), Spur 3, Block 1, Government Buildings, Honeypot Lane, Stanmore, Middx HA7 1AY. Tel: 0171-972 3734. *Clerk*, Ms K. Vale

LONDON (SOUTH), Block 3, Crown Offices, Kingston Bypass Road, Surbiton, Surrey KT6 5QN. Tel: 0181-268 4520. *Clerk*, C. Lilly

NOTTINGHAM, Spur A, Block 5, Government Buildings, Chalfont Drive, Western Boulevard, Nottingham NG8 3RZ. Tel: 0115-929 4222. *Clerk*, M. Chapman

WALES, 4th Floor, Crown Buildings, Cathays Park, Cardiff CF1 3NQ. Tel: 01222-825328. *Clerk*, Mrs C. Thomas

NATIONAL HEALTH SERVICE TRIBUNAL

The NHS Tribunal considers representations that the continued inclusion of a doctor, dentist, pharmacist or optician on a health authority's list would be prejudicial to the efficiency of the service concerned. The tribunal sits when required, about eight times a year, and usually in London. The chairman is appointed by the Lord Chancellor and members by the Secretary of State for Health.
Chairman, A. Whitfield, QC
Deputy Chairmen, Miss E. Platt, QC; Dr R. N. Ough
Clerk, I. D. Keith, East Hookers, Twineham, nr Haywards Heath, W. Sussex RH17 5NN. Tel: 01444-881345

NATIONAL HEALTH SERVICE TRIBUNAL (SCOTLAND)
Clerk: 66 Queen Street, Edinburgh EH2 4NE
Tel 0131-226 4771

The tribunal considers representations that the continued inclusion of a registered doctor, dentist, optometrist or pharmacist on a health board's list would be prejudicial to the continuing efficiency of the service concerned.

The tribunal meets when required and is composed of a chairman, one lay member, and one practitioner member drawn from a representative professional panel. The chairman is appointed by the Lord President of the Court of Session, and the lay member and the members of the professional panel are appointed by the Secretary of State for Scotland.
Chairman, M. G. Thomson, QC
Lay member, J. D. M. Robertson
Clerk to the Tribunal, D. G. Brash, WS

PENSIONS APPEAL TRIBUNALS

CENTRAL OFFICE (ENGLAND AND WALES)
48–49 Chancery Lane, London WC2A 1JR
Tel 0171-936 7032/3/4

The Pensions Appeal Tribunals are responsible for hearing appeals from ex-servicemen or women and widows who have had their claims for a war pension rejected by the Secretary of State for Social Security. The Entitlement Appeal Tribunals hear appeals in cases where the Secretary of State has refused to grant a war pension. The Assessment Appeal Tribunals hear appeals against the

Secretary of State's assessment of the degree of disablement caused by an accepted condition. The tribunal members are appointed by the Lord Chancellor.
President (£70,820), Dr H. M. G. Concannon
Secretary, Miss N. Collins

PENSIONS APPEAL TRIBUNALS FOR SCOTLAND
20 Walker Street, Edinburgh EH3 7HS
Tel 0131-220 1404
President (£285 a day), C. N. McEachran, QC

OFFICE OF THE SOCIAL SECURITY AND CHILD SUPPORT COMMISSIONERS
5th Floor, Newspaper House, 8–16 Great New Street, London EC4A 3BN
Tel 0171-353 5145
23 Melville Street, Edinburgh EH3 7PW
Tel 0131-225 2201

The Social Security Commissioners are the final statutory authority to decide appeals relating to entitlement to social security benefits. The Child Support Commissioners are the final statutory authority to decide appeals relating to child support. Appeals may be made in relation to both matters only on a point of law. The Commissioners' jurisdiction covers England, Wales and Scotland. There are 17 commissioners; they are all qualified lawyers.
Chief Social Security Commissioner and Chief Child Support Commissioner, His Hon. Judge Machin, QC
Secretary, S. Hill (*London*); E. Barschtschyk (*Edinburgh*)

OFFICE OF THE SOCIAL SECURITY AND CHILD SUPPORT COMMISSIONERS FOR NORTHERN IRELAND
Lancashire House, 5 Linenhall Street, Belfast BT2 8AA
Tel 01232-332344

The role of Northern Ireland Social Security and Child Support Commissioners is similar to that of the Commissioners in Great Britain. There are two commissioners for Northern Ireland.
Chief Commissioner, His Hon. Judge Martin, QC
Registrar of Appeals, W. D. Pollock

THE SOLICITORS' DISCIPLINARY TRIBUNAL
50–52 Chancery Lane, London WC2A 1SX
Tel 0171-242 0219

The Solicitors' Disciplinary Tribunal is an independent statutory body whose members are appointed by the Master of the Rolls. The tribunal considers applications made to it alleging either professional misconduct and/or a breach of the statutory rules by which solicitors are bound against an individually named solicitor, former solicitor, registered foreign lawyer, or solicitor's clerk. The president and solicitor members do not receive remuneration.
President, G. B. Marsh
Clerk, Mrs S. C. Elson

THE SCOTTISH SOLICITORS' DISCIPLINE TRIBUNAL
22 Rutland Square, Edinburgh EH1 2BB
Tel 0131-229 5860

The Scottish Solicitors' Discipline Tribunal is an independent statutory body with a panel of 18 members, ten of whom are solicitors; members are appointed by the Lord President of the Court of Session. Its principal function is to consider complaints of misconduct against solicitors in Scotland.
Chairman, J. W. Laughland
Clerk, J. M. Barton, WS

SPECIAL COMMISSIONERS OF INCOME TAX
15–19 Bedford Avenue, London WC1B 3AS
Tel 0171-631 4242

The Special Commissioners are an independent body appointed by the Lord Chancellor to hear complex appeals against decisions of the Board of Inland Revenue and its officials. In addition to the Presiding Special Commissioner there are two full-time and 13 deputy special commissioners; all are legally qualified.
Presiding Special Commissioner, His Hon. Stephen Oliver, QC
Special Commissioners (£84,752), T. H. K. Everett;
     D. A. Shirley
Clerk, R. P. Lester

SPECIAL IMMIGRATION APPEALS COMMISSION
Taylor House, 88 Rosebery Avenue, London EC1R 4QU
Tel 0171-862 4200

The Commission was set up under the Special Immigration Appeals Commission Act 1998. Its main function is to consider appeals against orders for deportations in cases which involve, in the main, considerations of national security. Members are appointed by the Lord Chancellor.
Chairman, The Hon. Mr Justice Potts
Secretary, Ms P. Dews

TRAFFIC COMMISSIONERS
c/o Scottish Traffic Area, Argyle House, 3 Lady Lawson Street, Edinburgh EH3 9SE
Tel 0131-529 8500

The Traffic Commissioners are responsible for licensing operators of heavy goods and public service vehicles. They also have responsibility for appeals relating to the licensing of operators and for disciplinary cases involving the conduct of drivers of these vehicles. There are six Commissioners in the eight traffic areas covering Britain. Each Traffic Commissioner constitutes a tribunal for the purposes of the Tribunals and Inquiries Act 1971. For Traffic Area Offices and Commissioners, *see* page 300.
Senior Traffic Commissioner (£56,520), M. Betts

TRANSPORT TRIBUNAL
48–49 Chancery Lane, London WC2A 1JR
Tel 0171-936 7493

The Transport Tribunal hears appeals against decisions made by Traffic Commissioners at public inquiries. The tribunal consists of a legally-qualified president, two legal members who may sit as chairman, and five lay members. The president and legal members are appointed by the Lord Chancellor and the lay members by the Secretary of State for the Environment, Transport and the Regions.
President (part-time), H. B. H. Carlisle, QC
Legal member (part-time) (£290 a day), His Hon. Judge Brodrick
Lay members (£232 a day), T. W. Hall; J. W. Whitworth; Miss E. B. Haran; P. Rogers
Secretary, P. J. Fisher

VALUATION TRIBUNALS
c/o Warwickshire Valuation Tribunal, 2nd Floor, Walton House, 11 Parade, Leamington Spa, Warks CV32 4DG
Tel 01926-421875

The Valuation Tribunals hear appeals concerning the council tax, non-domestic rating and land drainage rates in England and Wales, and have residual jurisdiction to hear appeals concerning the community charge, the pre-1990 rating list, disabled rating and mixed hereditaments. There are 56 tribunals in England and eight in Wales; those in England are funded by the Department of the Environment, Transport and the Regions and those in Wales by the Welsh Office. A separate tribunal is constituted for each hearing, and normally consists of a chairman and two other members. Members are appointed by the local authorities and serve on a voluntary basis. A National Association of Valuation Tribunals considers all matters affecting valuations tribunals in England, and the Council of Wales Valuation Tribunals performs the same function in Wales.
President, National Association of Valuation Tribunals, P. Wood
Secretary, National Committee of Valuation Tribunals, B. P. Massen
President, Council of Wales Valuation Tribunals, P. J. Law

VAT AND DUTIES TRIBUNALS
15–19 Bedford Avenue, London WC1B 3AS
Tel 0171-631 4242

VAT and Duties Tribunals are administered by the Lord Chancellor in England and Wales, and by the Secretary of State in Scotland. They are independent, and decide disputes between taxpayers and Customs and Excise. In England and Wales, the president and chairmen are appointed by the Lord Chancellor and members by the Treasury. Chairmen in Scotland are appointed by the Lord President of the Court of Session.
President, His Hon. Stephen Oliver, QC
Vice-President, England and Wales (£84,752), A. W. Simpson
Vice-President, Scotland (£84,752), T. G. Coutts, QC
Vice-President, Northern Ireland (£84,752), His Hon. Judge McKee, QC
Registrar, R. P. Lester

TRIBUNAL CENTRES
EDINBURGH, 44 Palmerston Place, Edinburgh EH12 5BJ.
     Tel: 0131-226 3551
LONDON (including Belfast), 15–19 Bedford Avenue,
     London WC1B 3AS. Tel: 0171-631 4242
MANCHESTER, Warwickgate House, Warwick Road, Old
     Trafford, Manchester M16 0GP. Tel: 0161-872 6471

The Police Service

There are 52 police forces in the United Kingdom, each responsible for policing in its area. Most forces' area is conterminous with one or more local authority areas. Policing in London is carried out by the Metropolitan Police and the City of London Police; in Northern Ireland by the Royal Ulster Constabulary; and by the Isle of Man, States of Jersey, and Guernsey forces in their respective islands and bailiwicks. National services include the National Criminal Intelligence Service and the National Missing Persons Bureau and the National Crime Squad.

Police authorities are responsible for maintaining an effective and efficient police force in their areas. The authorities of English and Welsh forces comprise local councillors, magistrates and independent members. In Scotland, there are six joint police boards made up of local councillors; the other two police authorities are councils. In London the authority for the Metropolitan Police is the Home Secretary, advised by the Metropolitan Police Committee; for the City of London Police the authority is a committee of the Corporation of London and includes councillors and magistrates. In Northern Ireland the Secretary of State appoints the police authority.

Police authorities are financed by central and local government grants and a precept on the council tax. Subject to the approval of the Home Secretary and to regulations, they appoint the chief constable. In England and Wales they are responsible for publishing annual policing plans and annual reports, setting local objectives and a budget, and levying the precept. The police authorities in Scotland are responsible for setting a budget, providing the resources necessary to police the area adequately, appointing officers of the rank of Assistant Chief Constable and above, and determining the number of officers and civilian staff in the force. The structure and responsibilities of the police authority in Northern Ireland are under review.

The Home Secretary and the Secretaries of State for Scotland and Northern Ireland are responsible for the organization, administration and operation of the police service. They make regulations covering matters such as police ranks, discipline, hours of duty, and pay and allowances. All police forces are subject to inspection by HM Inspectors of Constabulary, who report to the respective Secretary of State. In Scotland, a review of the structure of police forces began in April 1998. In Northern Ireland a commission on policing was established by the Belfast Agreement in April 1998. It will make recommendations to the Secretary of State by summer 1999.

COMPLAINTS

The investigation and resolution of a serious complaint against a police officer in England and Wales is subject to the scrutiny of the Police Complaints Authority. An officer who is disciplined by his chief constable, whether as a result of a complaint or not, may appeal to the Home Secretary. In Scotland, chief constables are obliged to investigate a complaint against one of their officers; if there is a suggestion of criminal activity, the complaint is investigated by an independent public prosecutor. In Northern Ireland complaints are investigated by the Independent Commission for Police Complaints, which will be replaced by the Police Ombudsman in spring 1999.

BASIC RATES OF PAY *since 1 September 1997*

Chief Constable	
No fixed term	£68,325–£101,241
Fixed term appointment	£71,745–£106,182
Assistant Chief Constable-designate	80% of their Chief Constable's pay
Assistant Chief Constable	
No fixed term	£57,012–£65,445
Fixed term appointment	£59,865–£68,718
Superintendent	£41,484–£51,495
Chief Inspector	£33,189–£35,499
Inspector	£30,498–£32,295
Sergeant	£23,583–£27,504
Constable	£15,438–£24,432

Metropolitan Police

Metropolitan Commissioner	£133,212
Deputy Commissioner	£95,739–£108,183
Assistant Commissioner	£86,574–£95,316
Commander	£57,012–£68,718

The rank of Chief Superintendent was abolished in April 1995. Existing appointments continue and receive the higher ranges of the pay scale for Superintendents
1998 pay negotiations still in progress at time of going to press

THE SPECIAL CONSTABULARY

Each police force has its own special constabulary, made up of volunteers who work in their spare time. Special Constables have full police powers within their force and adjoining force areas, and assist regular officers with routine policing duties.

NATIONAL CRIME SQUAD

The National Crime Squad (NCS) was established on 1 April 1998, replacing the six regional crime squads in England and Wales. It investigates organized and serious crime occurring across police force boundaries and abroad. It also supports police forces investigating serious crime. The squad is accountable to the National Crime Squad Service Authority.
Headquarters: PO Box 2500, London
  SW1V 2WF. Tel: 0171-238 2500
Director General, Roy Penrose, OBE, QPM

NATIONAL CRIMINAL INTELLIGENCE SERVICE

The National Criminal Intelligence Service (NCIS) provides intelligence about serious and organized crime to law enforcement, government and other relevant agencies nationally and internationally. Previously run by the Home Office, on 1 April 1998 NCIS was placed on a statutory footing. It is accountable to the NCIS Service Authority.
Headquarters: PO Box 8000, London
  SE11 5EN. Tel: 0171-238 8000
Strength, 564
Director-General, J. Abbott, QPM
Deputy Director-General (Director (Intelligence)),
  R. Gaspar
Director, International Division, N. Bailly
Director, UK Division, V. Harvey
Director, Resources Division, J. Bamfield

NCS and NCIS Service Authorities

The Service Authorities are responsible for ensuring the effective operation of the National Crime Squad and NCIS, and direct policy; they fulfil a similar role to a police authority. The chairman and nine other core members serve on both authorities.

Headquarters: PO Box 2600, London SW1V 2WG. Tel: 0171-238 2600
Chairman, Rt. Hon. Sir John Wheeler
Clerk, T. Simmons
Treasurer, B. Harty

National Missing Persons Bureau

The Police National Missing Persons Bureau (PNMPB) acts as a central clearing house of information, receiving reports about vulnerable missing persons that are still outstanding after 28 days and details of unidentified persons or remains within 48 hours of being found from all forces in England and Wales. Reports are also received from Scottish police forces, the RUC, and foreign police forces via Interpol.

Headquarters: New Scotland Yard, Broadway, London SW1H 0BG. Tel: 0171-230 1212
Director, C. J. Coombes

Police Information Technology Organization

The Police Information Technology Organization (PITO) became a non-departmental public body on 1 April 1998. It develops and manages the delivery of national police information technology services, such as the Police National Computer, co-ordinates the development of local information technology systems where common standards and systems are needed, and provides a procurement service.

Headquarters: Horseferry House, Dean Ryle Street, London SW1P 2AW. Tel: 0181-358 5367
Chairman, Sir Trefor Morris
Chief Executive, Miss J. MacNaughton

Forensic Science Service

The Forensic Science Service (FSS) provides forensic science support to the police forces in England and Wales for the investigation of scenes of crime, scientific analysis of material, and interpretation of scientific results. The FSS is organized into serious crime, volume crime, drugs and specialist services, supported by intelligence and consultancy services. Laboratories are located at Birmingham, Chepstow, Chorley, Huntingdon, London and Wetherby.

Headquarters: Priory House, Gooch Street North, Birmingham B5 6QQ. Tel: 0121-607 6800
Chief Executive, Dr J. Thompson

POLICE FORCES AND AUTHORITIES

Strength: actual strength of force as at mid 1998
Chair: chairman/convener of the police authority/police committee/joint police board

ENGLAND

Avon and Somerset Constabulary, *HQ,* PO Box 37, Valley Road, Portishead, Bristol BS20 8QJ. Tel: 01275-818181. *Strength,* 2,980; *Chief Constable,* S. Pilkington, QPM; *Chair,* I. Hoddell

Bedfordshire Police, *HQ,* Woburn Road, Kempston, Bedford MK43 9AX. Tel: 01234-841212. *Strength,* 1,095; *Chief Constable,* M. O'Byrne, QPM; *Chair,* A. P. Hendry, CBE

Cambridgeshire Constabulary, *HQ,* Hinchingbrooke Park, Huntingdon, Cambs PE18 8NP. Tel: 01480-456111. *Strength,* 1,296; *Chief Constable,* D. G. Gunn, QPM; *Chair,* J. Reynolds

Cheshire Constabulary, *HQ,* Nuns Road, Chester CH1 2PP. Tel: 01244-350000. *Strength,* 2,070; *Chief Constable,* N. Burgess, QPM; *Chair,* R. Nichols

Cleveland Police, *HQ,* PO Box 70, Ladgate Lane, Middlesbrough TS8 9EH. Tel: 01642-326326. *Strength,* 1,509; *Chief Constable,* B. D. D. Shaw, QPM; *Chair,* K. Walker

Cumbria Constabulary, *HQ,* Carleton Hall, Penrith, Cumbria CA10 2AU. Tel: 01768-891999. *Strength,* 1,154; *Chief Constable,* C. Phillips, QPM; *Chair,* R. Watson

Derbyshire Constabulary, *HQ,* Butterley Hall, Ripley, Derbyshire DE5 3RS. Tel: 01773-570100. *Strength,* 1,767; *Chief Constable,* J. F. Newing, QPM; *Chair,* K. Wilkinson

Devon and Cornwall Constabulary, *HQ,* Middlemoor, Exeter EX2 7HQ. Tel: 0990-777444. *Strength,* 2,997; *Chief Constable,* J. S. Evans, QPM; *Chair,* O. May

Dorset Police Force, *HQ,* Winfrith, Dorchester, Dorset DT2 8DZ. Tel: 01929-462727. *Strength,* 1,305; *Chief Constable,* D. W. Aldous, QPM; *Chair,* P. I. Jones

Durham Constabulary, *HQ,* Aykley Heads, Durham DH1 5TT. Tel: 0191-386 4929. *Strength,* 1,533; *Chief Constable,* G. Hedges; *Chair,* A. Barker

Essex Police, *HQ,* PO Box 2, Springfield, Chelmsford CM2 6DA. Tel: 01245-491491. *Strength,* 2,990; *Chief Constable,* D. F. Stevens; *Chair,* E. A. Peel

Gloucestershire Constabulary, *HQ,* Holland House, Lansdown Road, Cheltenham, Glos GL51 6QH. Tel: 01242-521321. *Strength,* 1,121; *Chief Constable,* A. J. P. Butler, QPM; *Chair,* Brig. M. A. Browne, CBE

Greater Manchester Police, *HQ,* PO Box 22 (S. West PDO), Chester House, Boyer Street, Manchester M16 0RE. Tel: 0161-872 5050. *Strength,* 6,958; *Chief Constable,* D. Wilmot, QPM; *Chair,* S. Murphy

Hampshire Constabulary, *HQ,* West Hill, Winchester, Hants SO22 5DB. Tel: 01962-841500. *Strength,* 3,490; *Chief Constable,* Sir John. Hoddinott, Kt., CBE, QPM; *Chair,* M. J. Clark

Hertfordshire Constabulary, *HQ,* Stanborough Road, Welwyn Garden City, Herts AL8 6XF. Tel: 01707-354200. *Strength,* 1,741; *Chief Constable,* P. Sharpe, QPM; *Chair,* P. Holland

Humberside Police, *HQ,* Queens Gardens, Kingston upon Hull HU1 3DJ. Tel: 01482-326111. *Strength,* 2,024; *Chief Constable,* D. A. Leonard, QPM; *Chair,* F. Bovill

Kent Constabulary, *HQ,* Sutton Road, Maidstone, Kent ME15 9BZ. Tel: 01622-690690. *Strength,* 3,235; *Chief Constable,* J. D.Phillips, QPM; *Chair,* Mrs P. F. Stubbs

Lancashire Constabulary, *HQ,* PO Box 77, Hutton, Preston, Lancs PR4 5SB. Tel: 01772-614444. *Strength,* 3,347; *Chief Constable,* Mrs P. A. Clare, QPM; *Chair,* Dr R. B. Henig

Leicestershire Constabulary, *HQ,* St Johns, Narborough, Leicester LE9 5BX. Tel: 0116-222 2222. *Strength,* 1,993; *Chief Constable,* D. J. Wyrko, QPM; *Chair,* vacant

Lincolnshire Police, *HQ,* PO Box 999, Lincoln LN5 7PH. Tel: 01522-532222. *Strength,* 1,190; *Chief Constable,* R. Childs, QPM; *Chair,* M. D. Kennedy

Merseyside Police, *HQ,* PO Box 59, Canning Place, Liverpool L69 1JD. Tel: 0151-709 6010. *Strength,* 4,360; *Chief Constable,* Sir James Sharples, QPM; *Chair,* Ms C. Gustafason

Norfolk Constabulary, *HQ,* Martineau Lane, Norwich NR1 2DJ. Tel: 01603-768769. *Strength,* 1,425; *Chief Constable,* K. R. Williams, QPM; *Chair,* B. J. Landale

NORTHAMPTONSHIRE POLICE, *HQ,* Wootton Hall, Northampton NN4 0JQ. Tel: 01604-700700. *Strength,* 1,170; *Chief Constable,* C. Fox, QPM; *Chair,* Dr M. Dickie

NORTHUMBRIA POLICE, *HQ,* Ponteland, Newcastle upon Tyne NE20 0BL. Tel: 01661-872555. *Strength,* 3,846; *Chief Constable,* C. STRACHAN, QPM; *Chair,* G. Gill

NORTH YORKSHIRE POLICE, *HQ,* Newby Wiske Hall, Newby Wiske, Northallerton, N. Yorks DL7 9HA. Tel: 01609-783131. *Strength,* 1,369; *Chief Constable,* D. R. Kenworthy, QPM; *Chair,* Mrs A. F. Harris

NOTTINGHAMSHIRE POLICE, *HQ,* Sherwood Lodge, Arnold, Nottingham NG5 8PP. Tel: 0115-967 0999. *Strength,* 2,352; *Chief Constable,* C. F. Bailey, QPM; *Chair,* R. A. Hassett

SOUTH YORKSHIRE POLICE, *HQ,* Snig Hill, Sheffield S3 8LY. Tel: 0114-220 2020. *Strength,* 3,180; *Chief Constable,* M. Hedges; *Chair,* C. Swindells

STAFFORDSHIRE POLICE, *HQ,* Cannock Road, Stafford ST17 0QG. Tel: 01785-257717. *Strength,* 2,292; *Chief Constable,* J. W. Giffard, QPM; *Chair,* J. T. Meir

SUFFOLK CONSTABULARY, *HQ,* Martlesham Heath, Ipswich IP5 3QS. Tel: 01473-613500. *Strength,* 1,177; *Chief Constable,* P. J. Scott-Lee, QPM; *Chair,* M. N. Smith

SURREY POLICE, *HQ,* Mount Browne, Sandy Lane, Guildford, Surrey GU3 1HG. Tel: 01483-571212. *Strength,* 2,451; *Chief Constable,* I. Blair; *Chair,* A. Peirce

SUSSEX POLICE, *HQ,* Malling House, Church Lane, Lewes, E. Sussex BN7 2DZ. Tel: 01273-475432. *Strength,* 3,089; *Chief Constable,* P. Whitehouse, QPM; *Chair,* K. Bodfish

THAMES VALLEY POLICE, *HQ,* Oxford Road, Kidlington, Oxon OX5 2NX. Tel: 01865-846000. *Strength,* 3,864; *Chief Constable,* C. Pollard, QPM; *Chair,* Mrs D. J. Priestley, OBE

WARWICKSHIRE CONSTABULARY, *HQ,* PO Box 4, Leek Wootton, Warwick CV35 7QB. Tel: 01926-415000. *Strength,* 940; *Chief Constable,* A. Timpson; *Chair,* C. Cleaver

WEST MERCIA CONSTABULARY, *HQ,* Hindlip Hall, PO Box 55, Hindlip, Worcester WR3 8SP. Tel: 01905-723000. *Strength,* 2,016; *Chief Constable,* D. C. Blakey, CBE, QPM; *Chair,* D. B. Watkins

WEST MIDLANDS POLICE, *HQ,* PO Box 52, Lloyd House, Colmore Circus, Queensway, Birmingham B4 6NQ. Tel: 0121-626 5000. *Strength,* 7,205; *Chief Constable,* E. Crew, QPM; *Chair,* R. Jones

WEST YORKSHIRE POLICE, *HQ,* PO Box 9, Laburnum Road, Wakefield, W. Yorks WF1 3QP. Tel: 01924-375222. *Strength,* 5,167; *Chief Constable,* G. Moore, QPM; *Chair,* N. Taggart

WILTSHIRE CONSTABULARY, *HQ,* London Road, Devizes, Wilts SN10 2DN. Tel: 01380-722341. *Strength,* 1,196; *Chief Constable,* Miss E. Neville, QPM, Ph.D.; *Chair,* H. A. Woolnough

WALES

DYFED-POWYS POLICE, *HQ,* PO Box 99, Llangunnor, Carmarthen SA31 2PF. Tel: 01267-222020. *Strength,* 1,002; *Chief Constable,* R. White, CBE, QPM; *Chair,* Ms M. Roberts

GWENT CONSTABULARY, *HQ,* Croesyceiliog, Cwmbran NP44 2XJ. Tel: 01633-838111. *Strength,* 1,241; *Chief Constable,* F. J. Wilkinson; *Chair,* D. Turnbull

NORTH WALES POLICE, *HQ,* Glan-y-don, Colwyn Bay, Conwy LL29 8AW. Tel: 01492-517171. *Strength,* 1,401; *Chief Constable,* M. J. Argent, QPM; *Chair,* C. M. Ley

SOUTH WALES POLICE, *HQ,* Cowbridge Road, Bridgend CF31 3SU. Tel: 01656-655555. *Strength,* 3,055; *Chief Constable,* A. T. Burden, QPM; *Chair,* B. P. Murray

SCOTLAND

CENTRAL SCOTLAND POLICE, *HQ,* Randolphfield, Stirling FK8 2HD. Tel: 01786-456000. *Strength,* 702; *Chief Constable,* W. J. M. Wilson, QPM; *Convener,* Mrs J. Burness

DUMFRIES AND GALLOWAY CONSTABULARY, *HQ,* Cornwall Mount, Dumfries DG1 1PZ. Tel: 01387-252112. *Strength,* 436; *Chief Constable,* W. Rae, QPM; *Chair,* K. Cameron

FIFE CONSTABULARY, *HQ,* Detroit Road, Glenrothes, Fife KY6 2RJ. Tel: 01592-418888. *Strength,* 840; *Chief Constable,* J. P. Hamilton, QPM; *Chair,* A. Keddie

GRAMPIAN POLICE, *HQ,* Queen Street, Aberdeen AB10 1ZA. Tel: 01224-386000. *Strength,* 1,176; *Chief Constable,* A. G. Brown, QPM; *Chair,* P. Chalmers

LOTHIAN AND BORDERS POLICE, *HQ,* Fettes Avenue, Edinburgh EH4 1RB. Tel: 0131-311 3131. *Strength,* 2,590; *Chief Constable,* R. Cameron, QPM; *Convenor,* E. Drummond

NORTHERN CONSTABULARY, *HQ,* Old Perth Road, Inverness IV2 3SY. Tel: 01463-715555. *Strength,* 654; *Chief Constable,* W. A. Robertson, QPM; *Chair,* Maj. N. Graham

STRATHCLYDE POLICE, *HQ,* 173 Pitt Street, Glasgow G2 4JS. Tel: 0141-532 2000. *Strength,* 7,178; *Chief Constable,* J. Orr, OBE, QPM; *Chair,* W. Timoney

TAYSIDE POLICE, *HQ,* PO Box 59, West Bell Street, Dundee DD1 9JU. Tel: 01382-223200. *Strength,* 1,143; *Chief Constable,* W. A. Spence, QPM; *Chair,* A. Shand

NORTHERN IRELAND

ROYAL ULSTER CONSTABULARY, *HQ,* Brooklyn, Knock Road, Belfast BT5 6LD. Tel: 01232-650222. *Strength,* 8,450; *Chief Constable,* R. Flanagan, OBE; *Chair,* P. Armstrong

ISLANDS

ISLAND POLICE FORCE, *HQ,* Hospital Lane, St Peter Port, Guernsey GY1 2QN. Tel: 01481-725111. *Strength,* 146; *Chief Officer,* M. H. Wyeth; *President, States Committee for Home Affairs,* M. W. Torode

STATES OF JERSEY POLICE, *HQ,* Rouge Bouillon, PO Box 789, St Helier, Jersey JE4 8ZD. Tel: 01534-612612. *Strength,* 240; *Chief Officer,* R. H. Le Breton; *President, Defence Committee,* M. Wavell

ISLE OF MAN CONSTABULARY, *HQ,* Glencrutchery Road, Douglas, Isle of Man IM2 4RG. Tel: 01624-631212. *Strength,* 213; *Chief Constable,* R. E. N. Oake, QPM; *Chairman, Police Committee,* Hon. A. R. Bell

---

METROPOLITAN POLICE SERVICE
New Scotland Yard, Broadway, London SW1H 0BG
Tel 0171-230 1212

Establishment, 26,902

Commissioner, Sir Paul Condon, QPM
Deputy Commissioner, J. Stevens, QPM
Receiver, P. Fletcher
Chair, Sir John Quinton

OPERATIONAL AREAS
Assistant Commissioners, A. J. Speed, QPM (*Central*); A. Dunn, QPM (*North-East*); P. A. Manning, QPM (*North-West*); W. I. R. Johnston, QPM (*South-East*); D. F. O'Connor, QPM (*South-West*)
Deputy Assistant Commissioner, D. Flanders, QPM; J. Townsend, QPM; J. Stichbury; A. S. Trotter; B. Wilding; M. Todd

Commanders, D. M. T. Kendrick, QPM; T. D. Laidlaw, LVO, QPM; A. L. Rowe, QPM; M. Briggs, QPM; M. R. Campbell; W. I. Griffiths, BEM, QPM; S. C. Pilkington; D. A. Ray, QPM; R. Gaspar; D. Gilbertson; P. Tomkins; R. Currie, QPM ; C. A. Howlett; Mrs S. E. Becks

SPECIALIST OPERATIONS DEPARTMENT
Assistant Commissioner, D. C. Veness, QPM
Deputy Assistant Commissioner, A. G. Fry, QPM
Commanders, R. C. Marsh, CVO, QPM; B. G. Moss, QPM; J. G. D. Grieve, QPM; N. G. Mulvihill, QPM

COMPLAINTS INVESTIGATION BUREAU
Commander, I. G. Quinn, QPM

INSPECTORATE
Commander, B. J. Luckhurst, QPM

OTHER DEPARTMENTS
Director, Strategic Co-ordination, Commander T. C. Lloyd
Director, Personnel, Mrs P. Woods
Director, Consultancy and Information Services, Mrs S. Merchant
Director, Public Affairs, R. Fedorcio
Solicitor, D. Hamilton
Director, Technology, N. Boothman
Director, Property Services, T. G. Lawrence

CITY OF LONDON POLICE
26 Old Jewry, London EC2R 8DJ
Tel 0171-601 2222

Strength, 824
The City of London Police is responsible for policing the City of London. Though small, the area includes one of the most important financial centres in the world and the force has particular expertise in areas such as fraud investigation as well as the areas required of any police force.
    The force has a wholly elected police authority, the police committee of the Corporation of London, which appoints the Commissioner.
Commissioner (£95,316), P. Nove, QPM
Assistant Commissioner (acting) (£76,254), J. Davison
Commander (acting) (£66,393), J. Kitchen
Chairman of Police Committee, L. St J. T. Jackson

BRITISH TRANSPORT POLICE
15 Tavistock Place, London WC1H 9SJ
Tel 0171-388 7541

Strength (March 1998), 2,095
British Transport Police is the national police force for the railways in England, Wales and Scotland, including the London Underground system and the Docklands Light Railway. The Chief Constable reports to the British Transport Police Committee. The members of the Committee are appointed by the British Railways Board and include representatives of Railtrack and London Underground Ltd as well as independent members.
Chief Constable, D. J. Williams, QPM
Deputy Chief Constable, A. Parker, QPM

MINISTRY OF DEFENCE POLICE
MDP Wethersfield, Braintree, Essex CM7 4AZ
Tel 01371-854000

Strength (March 1998), 3,856
The Ministry of Defence Police is an agency of the Ministry of Defence. It is a national civilian police force whose officers are appointed by the Secretary of State for Defence. It is responsible for the policing of all military land, stations and establishments in the United Kingdom. The agency also has certain responsibilities for the civilian Ministry of Defence Guard Service.
Chief Constable, W. E. E. Boreham, OBE
Deputy Chief Constable, A. V. Comben
Head of Secretariat, P. A. Crowther

ROYAL PARKS CONSTABULARY
The Old Police House, Hyde Park, London W2 2UH
Tel 0171-298 2000

Strength (June 1998), 166
The Royal Parks Constabulary is maintained by the Royal Parks Agency, an executive agency of the Department of National Heritage, and is responsible for the policing of eight royal parks in and around London. These comprise an area in excess of 6,300 acres. Officers of the force are appointed under the Parks Regulations Act 1872 as amended.
Chief Officer, W. Ross, OBE
Deputy Chief Officer, A. McLean

UK ATOMIC ENERGY AUTHORITY CONSTABULARY
Building E6, Culham Science Centre, Abingdon, Oxon OX14 3DB
Tel 01235-463760

Strength (June 1998), 490
The Constabulary is responsible for policing UK Atomic Energy Authority and British Nuclear Fuels PLC establishments and for escorting nuclear material between establishments. The Chief Constable is responsible, through the Atomic Energy Authority Police Authority, to the President of the Board of Trade.
Chief Constable, W. F. Pryke
Assistant Chief Constable (acting), J. S. Thomas

STAFF ASSOCIATIONS

Police officers are not permitted to join a trade union or to take strike action. All ranks have their own staff associations.
ASSOCIATION OF CHIEF POLICE OFFICERS OF ENGLAND, WALES AND NORTHERN IRELAND, 7th Floor, 25 Victoria Street, London SW1H 0EX. Tel: 0171-227 3434. Represents Chief Constables, Deputy and Assistant Chief Constables in England, Wales and Northern Ireland; officers of the rank of Commander and above in the Metropolitan and City of London Police and senior civilian members of these forces. *General Secretary,* Miss M. C. E. Barton

THE POLICE SUPERINTENDENTS' ASSOCIATION OF ENGLAND AND WALES, 67A Reading Road, Pangbourne, Reading RG8 7JD. Tel: 0118-984 4005. Represents officers of the rank of Superintendent. *Secretary,* Chief Supt. D. C. Parkinson

THE POLICE FEDERATION OF ENGLAND AND WALES, 15–17 Langley Road, Surbiton, Surrey KT6 6LP. Tel: 0181-399 2224. Represents officers up to and including the rank of Chief Inspector. *General Secretary,* J. Moseley

ASSOCIATION OF CHIEF POLICE OFFICERS IN SCOTLAND, Police Headquarters, Fettes Avenue, Edinburgh EH4 1RB. Tel: 0131-311 3051. Represents the Chief Constables, Deputy and Assistant Chief Constables of the Scottish police forces. *Hon. Secretary,* H. R. Cameron, QPM

THE ASSOCIATION OF SCOTTISH POLICE SUPERINTENDENTS, Secretariat, 173 Pitt Street, Glasgow G2 4JS. Tel: 0141-221 5796. Represents officers of the rank of Superintendent. *President,* Chief Supt. S. Davidson

THE SCOTTISH POLICE FEDERATION, 5 Woodside Place, Glasgow G3 7QF. Tel: 0141-332 5234. Represents officers up to and including the rank of Chief Inspector. *General Secretary,* D. J. Keil, QPM

THE SUPERINTENDENTS' ASSOCIATION OF NORTHERN IRELAND, RUC Training Centre, Garnerville Road, Belfast BT4 2NX. Tel: 01232-700660. Represents Superintendents and Chief Superintendents in the RUC. *Hon. Secretary,* Supt. W. T. Brown

THE POLICE FEDERATION FOR NORTHERN IRELAND, Royal Ulster Constabulary, Garnerville, Garnerville Road, Belfast BT4 2NX. Tel: 01232-760831. Represents officers up to and including the rank of Chief Inspector. *Secretary,* D. A. McClurg

POLICE STRENGTHS 1998

	Male	*Female*	*Total*
ENGLAND AND WALES p			
Total officers	107,028	19,828	126,856
Ethnic minority officers	1,957	526	2,483
Special constables	12,483	6,680	19,163
Civilians	22,502	34,260	56,762
SCOTLAND*			
Officers	12,752	2,036	14,788
Special constables	1,336	450	1,786
Civilians	1,861	3,316	5,177
NORTHERN IRELAND			
Officers	7,529	921	8,450
Special constables	829	451	1,280
Civilians	1,212	2,328	3,540

p provisional
* Figures for Scotland as at 31 March 1997
Sources: Home Office; Scottish Office; RUC

The Prison Service

The prison services in the United Kingdom are the responsibility of the Home Secretary, the Secretary of State for Scotland and the Secretary of State for Northern Ireland. The chief executives of the Prison Service, the Scottish Prison Service and the Northern Ireland Prison Service are responsible for the day-to-day running of the system.

There are 135 prison establishments in England and Wales, 20 in Scotland and four in Northern Ireland. Convicted prisoners are classified according to their perceived security risk and are housed in establishments appropriate to that level of security. There are no open prisons in Northern Ireland. Female prisoners are housed in women's establishments or in separate wings of mixed prisons. Remand prisoners are, where possible, housed separately from convicted prisoners. Offenders under the age of 21 are usually detained in a young offenders' institution, which may be a separate establishment or part of a prison.

Seven prisons are now run by the private sector, and in England and Wales all escort services have been contracted out to private companies. Four prisons are being built and financed under the Private Finance Initiative and will also be run by private contractors.

There are independent prison inspectorates in England and Wales (*see* page 311) and Scotland (*see* page 342) which report annually to the Secretary of State on prison conditions and the treatment of prisoners. HM Chief Inspector of Prisons for England and Wales also performs an inspectorate role for prisons in Northern Ireland. Every prison establishment also has an independent board of visitors or visiting committee made up of local volunteers appointed by the Secretary of State. Any prisoner whose complaint is not satisfied by the internal complaints procedures may complain to the Prisons Ombudsman for England and Wales (*see* page 334) or the Scottish Prisons Complaints Commission (*see* page 343). There is no Prisons Ombudsman for Northern Ireland, but complaints by prisoners regarding maladministration may be made to the Parliamentary Commissioner for Administration (*see* page 331).

The Home Secretary is currently conducting a review into the organization of and links between the prison and probation services in England and Wales.

Average Prison Population 1997–8 (UK)

	Remand	Sentenced	Other
England and Wales*			
Male	11,532	46,360	547
Female	599	2,052	25
Total	12,131	48,412	572
Scotland			
Male	n/a	n/a	—
Female	n/a	n/a	—
Total	927	5,133	—
N. Ireland			
Male	359	1,190	10
Female	9	21	—
Total	368	1,211	10
UK Total	13,426	54,756	582

* 1997 figures

The prison population for 2005 in England and Wales is projected to reach 82,800 if current trends continue

Sources: Home Office – *Statistical Bulletin 5/98*; Scottish Prison Service – *Annual Report and Accounts 1997–8*; Northern Ireland Prison Service – *Annual Report 1997–8*

Sentenced Prison Population by Sex and Offence (England and Wales) as at June 1997

	Male	Female
Violence against the person	9,836	387
Sexual offences	3,973	9
Burglary	7,642	96
Robbery	6,069	154
Theft, handling, fraud and forgery	5,068	453
Drugs offences	6,309	675
Other offences	5,242	193
Offence not known	2,599	100
Total	46,739	2,066

Source: Home Office – *Statistical Bulletin 5/98*

Average Sentenced Population by Length of Sentence 1996 (England and Wales)

	Adults	Young Offenders
Up to 18 months	8,199	2,930
18 months–4 years	10,320	2,606
Over 4 years	17,644	1,164
Total	36,162	6,700

Source: HMSO – *Annual Abstract of Statistics 1998*

Average Daily Sentenced Population by Length of Sentence 1997–8 (Scotland)

	Adults	Young Offenders
Less than 4 years	2,141	574
4 years or over (including life)	2,218	200
Total	4,359	774

Source: Scottish Prison Service – *Annual Report and Accounts 1997–8*

Prison Suicides 1997–8 (England and Wales)

Adults	66
Young offenders	9
Total	75

Source: HM Prison Service – *Annual Report and Accounts 1997–8*

Average Number of Prison Service Staff 1997–8 (Great Britain)

	England and Wales	Scotland
No. of prison service staff	39,553	4,791

Sources: HM Prison Service – *Annual Report and Accounts 1997–8*; Scottish Prison Service – *Annual Report and Accounts 1997–8*

Operating Costs of Prison Service in England and Wales 1997–8

	£ million
Staff costs	935.9
Other operating costs	752.8
Operating income	(16.4)
Net operating costs before notional charge on capital employed	1,672.3
Charge on capital employed	231.3
Net operating costs	1,903.6
Average net operating costs per prisoner per annum	18,700

Source: HM Prison Service – *Annual Report and Accounts 1997–8*

OPERATING COSTS OF SCOTTISH PRISON SERVICE
1997–8

	£
Total income	1,598,000
Total expenditure	172,071,000
Staff costs	110,874,000
Running costs	47,675,000
Other current expenditure	13,522,000
Operating deficit	(170,473,000)
Interest on capital	(23,199,000)
Interest payable and similar charges	(15,000)
Interest receivable	145,000
Deficit for financial year	(193,542,000)
Average annual cost per prisoner per place	26,170

Source: Scottish Prison Service – Annual Report and Accounts 1997–8

OPERATING COSTS OF NORTHERN IRELAND PRISON
SERVICE 1997–8

	£
Custodial	120,159,080
Non-custodial	5,967,549
Headquarters	7,600,935
Total	133,727,565
Average annual cost per prisoner place	75,297

Source: Northern Ireland Prison Service

THE PRISON SERVICES

HM PRISON SERVICE

Cleland House, Page Street, London SW1P 4LN
Tel 0171-217 6000

SALARIES 1997–8

Governor 1	£49,058–£50,703
Governor 2	£44,298–£45,615
Governor 3	£38,256–£39,300
Governor 4	£31,479–£33,756
Governor 5	£27,761–£30,236

For civil service salaries, see page 278

THE PRISONS BOARD

Director-General (SCS), R. R. Tilt
  Private Secretary, R. Hughes
  Staff Officer, J. Heavens
Director of Security and Deputy Director-General (SCS),
  A. J. Pearson
Director of Personnel (SCS), B. Clark
Director of Finance (SCS), J. Le Vay
Directors of Operations (SCS), A. Papps (North); A. Walker
  (South)
Director of Dispersals (SCS), P. Wheatley
Director of Regimes (SCS), M. Narey
Director of Health Care (SCS), Dr M. Longfield
Director of Service Delivery (Quantum), J. Powls
Non-Executive Members, Sir Duncan Nichol, CBE; Mrs R.
  Thomson, CBE; Mrs P. A. Clare, QPM
Board Secretary, N. Newcomen

Chaplain-General and Archdeacon of the Prison Service,
  Ven. D. Fleming
Senior Roman Catholic Chaplain, Mgr J. Branson

AREA MANAGERS (SCS)

Directorate of Operations (North)
East Midlands, M. Egan; Mercia, D. Curtis; Mersey and
  Manchester, A. Fitzpatrick; North-East, R. Mitchell; North-
  West, D. I. Lockwood; Yorkshire, J. Staples

Directorate of Operations (South)
Central, J. Dring; Kent, T. Murtagh, OBE; London North and
  East Anglia, I. Ward; London South, P. J. Kitteridge, CBE;
  South Coast, J. Perriss; Wales and the West, J. May

PRISON ESTABLISHMENTS

CNA Average number of in use certified normal
  accommodation places 1997–8
Prisoners/Young Offenders Average number of prisoners/
  young offenders 1997–8

ACKLINGTON, Morpeth, Northumberland NE65 9XF. CNA,
  662. Prisoners, 654. Governor, I. Woods
ALBANY, Newport, Isle of Wight PO30 5RS. CNA, 436.
  Prisoners, 429. Governor, I. Murray
ALDINGTON, Ashford, Kent TN25 7BQ. CNA, 145. Prisoners,
  137. Governor, L. Cruttenden
ALTCOURSE (private prison), Higher Lane, Fazakerley,
  Liverpool L9 7LH. CNA, 450. Prisoners, 478. Director, W.
  MacGowan
ASHWELL, Oakham, Leics LE15 7LF. CNA, 444. Prisoners, 453.
  Governor, C. Bushell
*‡ASKHAM GRANGE, Askham Richard, York YO2 3PT. CNA,
  130. Prisoners and Young Offenders, 127. Governor,
  H. E. Crew
‡AYLESBURY, Bierton Road, Aylesbury, Bucks HP20 1EH.
  CNA, 318. Young Offenders, 311. Governor, N. Pascoe
BEDFORD, St Loyes Street, Bedford MK40 1HG. CNA, 343.
  Prisoners, 381. Governor, vacant
BELMARSH, Western Way, Thamesmead, London SE28 0EB.
  CNA, 823. Prisoners, 865. Governor, W. S. Duff
BIRMINGHAM, Winson Green Road, Birmingham B18 4AS.
  CNA, 719. Prisoners, 1,040. Governor, G. Gregory-Smith
BLAKENHURST (private prison), Hewell Lane, Redditch,
  Worcs B97 6QS. CNA, 647. Prisoners, 803. Director,
  P. Siddons
BLANTYRE HOUSE, Goudhurst, Cranbrook, Kent TN17 2NH.
  CNA, 120. Prisoners, 120. Governor, E. McLennan-Murray
BLUNDESTON, Lowestoft, Suffolk NR32 5BG. CNA, 417.
  Prisoners, 402. Governor, S. Robinson
†‡BRINSFORD, New Road, Featherstone, Wolverhampton
  WV10 7PY. CNA, 477. Young Offenders, 521. Governor, C.
  Davidson
BRISTOL, Cambridge Road, Bristol BS7 8PS. CNA, 487.
  Prisoners, 583. Governor, N. Wall
BRIXTON, PO Box 369, Jebb Avenue, London SW2 5XF.
  CNA, 492. Prisoners, 598. Governor, M. O'Sullivan
*†‡BROCKHILL, Redditch, Worcs B97 6RD. CNA, 159.
  Prisoners and Young Offenders, 129. Governor, N. Croft
BUCKLEY HALL (private prison), Buckley Farm Lane,
  Rochdale, Lancs OL12 9DP. CNA, 350. Prisoners, 374.
  Director, S. Mitson
BULLINGDON, PO Box 50, Bicester, Oxon OX6 0PR. CNA,
  655. Prisoners, 687. Governor, J. Cann
*‡BULLWOOD HALL, High Road, Hockley, Essex SS5 4TE.
  CNA, 131. Prisoners and Young Offenders, 131. Governor,
  Mrs C. H. Cawley
CAMP HILL, Newport, Isle of Wight PO30 5PB. CNA, 467.
  Prisoners, 502. Governor, W. Preston
CANTERBURY, 46 Longport, Canterbury CT1 1PJ. CNA, 165.
  Prisoners, 268. Governor, Ms J. Galbally
†‡CARDIFF, Knox Road, Cardiff CF2 1UG. CNA, 527.
  Prisoners and Young Offenders, 710. Governor, J. Thomas-
  Ferrand
‡CASTINGTON, Morpeth, Northumberland NE65 9XG.
  CNA, 320. Young Offenders, 316. Governor, M. Lees
CHANNINGS WOOD, Denbury, Newton Abbott, Devon
  TQ12 6DW. CNA, 482. Prisoners, 605. Governor, R. Mullen

†‡CHELMSFORD, 200 Springfield Road, Chelmsford, Essex CM2 6LQ. *CNA*, 448. *Prisoners and Young Offenders*, 469. *Governor*, Ms A. Gomme

COLDINGLEY, Bisley, Woking, Surrey GU24 9EX. *CNA*, 298. *Prisoners*, 296. *Governor*, E. R. Butt

*COOKHAM WOOD, Rochester, Kent MEI 3LU. *CNA*, 120. *Prisoners*, 147. *Governor*, Miss C. Kershaw

DARTMOOR, Princetown, Yelverton, Devon PL20 6RR. *CNA*, 620. *Prisoners*, 627. *Governor*, J. Lawrence

‡DEERBOLT, Bowes Road, Barnard Castle, Co. Durham DL12 9BG. *CNA*, 435. *Young Offenders*, 418. *Governor*, P. Atkinson

†‡DONCASTER (private prison), Off North Bridge, Marshgate, Doncaster DN5 8UX. *CNA*, 771. *Prisoners and Young Offenders*, 1,066. *Director*, H. Jones

†‡DORCHESTER, North Square, Dorchester DT1 IJD. *CNA*, 147. *Prisoners and Young Offenders*, 230. *Governor*, Mrs D. Calvert

‡DOVER, The Citadel, Western Heights, Dover CT17 9DR. *CNA*, 316. *Young Offenders*, 304. *Governor*, B. Pollett

DOWNVIEW, Sutton Lane, Sutton, Surrey SM2 5PD. *CNA*, 327. *Prisoners*, 337. *Governor*, C. Lambert

*‡DRAKE HALL, Eccleshall, Staffs ST21 6LQ. *CNA*, 281. *Prisoners and Young Offenders*, 267. *Governor*, P. Tidball

*DURHAM, Old Elvet, Durham DH1 3HU. *CNA*, 663. *Prisoners*, 932. *Governor*, N. Clifford

*‡EAST SUTTON PARK, Sutton Valence, Maidstone, Kent ME17 3DN. *CNA*, 94. *Prisoners and Young Offenders*, 96. *Governor (acting)*, Miss P. Nearney

*†‡EASTWOOD PARK, Falfield, Wotton-under-Edge, Glos GL12 8DB. *CNA*, 175. *Prisoners and Young Offenders*, 157. *Governor*, P. Winkley

ELMLEY, Church Road, Eastchurch, Sheerness, Kent ME12 4AY. *CNA*, 740. *Prisoners*, 843. *Governor*, A. Smith

ERLESTOKE HOUSE, Devizes, Wilts SN10 5TU. *CNA*, 310. *Prisoners*, 307. *Governor*, M. Cook

EVERTHORPE, Brough, E. Yorks HU15 IRB. *CNA*, 433. *Prisoners*, 460. *Governor*, P. Midgley

†‡EXETER, New North Road, Exeter EX4 4EX. *CNA*, 266. *Prisoners and Young Offenders*, 458. *Governor*, N. Evans

FEATHERSTONE, New Road, Wolverhampton WV10 7PU. *CNA*, 599. *Prisoners*, 596. *Governor*, C. Scott

†‡FELTHAM, Bedfont Road, Feltham, Middx TW13 4ND. *CNA*, 849. *Prisoners and Young Offenders*, 894. *Governor*, C. Welsh

FORD, Arundel, W. Sussex BN18 0BX. *CNA*, 481. *Prisoners*, 448. *Governor*, R. S. Brandon

*‡FOSTON HALL, Foston, Derbys DE65 5DN. *CNA*, 142. *Prisoners and Young Offenders*, 123. *Governor*, Ms P. Scriven

FRANKLAND, Brasside, Durham DH1 5YD. *CNA*, 447. *Prisoners*, 448. *Governor*, I. Woods

FULL SUTTON, Full Sutton, York YO41 1PS. *CNA*, 481. *Prisoners*, 500. *Governor*, R. Tasker

GARTH, Ulnes Walton Lane, Leyland, Preston PR5 3NE. *CNA*, 603. *Prisoners*, 617. *Governor*, W. Rose-Quirie

GARTREE, Gallow Field Road, Market Harborough, Leics LE16 7RP. *CNA*, 364. *Prisoners*, 363. *Governor*, R. J. Perry

†‡GLEN PARVA, Tigers Road, Wigston, Leicester LE8 4TN. *CNA*, 720. *Young Offenders*, 872. *Governor*, B. Payling

†‡GLOUCESTER, Barrack Square, Gloucester GL1 2JN. *CNA*, 220. *Prisoners and Young Offenders*, 282. *Governor*, R. Dempsey

GRENDON/SPRING HILL, HMP Grendon, Grendon Underwood, Aylesbury, Bucks HP18 0TL. *CNA*, 454. *Prisoners*, 430. *Governor*, T. C. Newell

‡GUYS MARSH, Shaftesbury, Dorset SP7 0AH. *CNA*, 360. *Prisoners and Young Offenders*, 370. *Governor*, D. Godfrey

HASLAR, 2 Dolphin Way, Gosport, Hants PO12 2AW. *CNA*, 158. *Prisoners*, 141. *Governor*, I. Truffet

‡HATFIELD, Thorne Road, Hatfield, Doncaster DN7 6EL. *CNA*, 180. *Young Offenders*, 151. *Governor*, Ms C. Davies

HAVERIGG, Millom, Cumbria LA18 4NA. *CNA*, 530. *Prisoners*, 550. *Governor*, G. Brunskill

HEWELL GRANGE, Redditch, Worcs B97 6QQ. *CNA*, 203. *Prisoners*, 193. *Governor*, D. W. Bamber

HIGH DOWN, Sutton Lane, Sutton, Surrey SM2 5PJ. *CNA*, 649. *Prisoners*, 696. *Governor*, D. Wilson

*HIGHPOINT, Stradishall, Newmarket, Suffolk CB8 9YG. *CNA*, 679. *Prisoners*, 695. *Governor*, R. Woolford

†‡HINDLEY, Gibson Street, Bickershaw, Wigan, Lancs WN2 5TH. *CNA*, 528. *Prisoners and Young Offenders*, 522. *Governor*, C. Sheffield

‡HOLLESLEY BAY COLONY, Woodbridge, Suffolk IP12 3JW. *CNA*, 458. *Prisoners and Young Offenders*, 424. *Governor*, J. Forster

*†‡HOLLOWAY, Parkhurst Road, London N7 0NU. *CNA*, 517. *Prisoners and Young Offenders*, 521. *Governor*, M. Sheldrick

HOLME HOUSE, Holme House Road, Stockton-on-Tees TS18 2QU. *CNA*, 918. *Prisoners*, 894. *Governor*, D. Roberts

†‡HULL, Hedon Road, Hull HU9 5LS. *CNA*, 522. *Prisoners and Young Offenders*, 508. *Governor*, M. Newell

‡HUNTERCOMBE, Huntercombe Place, Nuffield, Henley-on-Thames RG9 5SB. *CNA*, 256. *Young Offenders*, 260. *Governor*, P. Manwaring

KINGSTON, 122 Milton Road, Portsmouth PO3 6AS. *CNA*, 129. *Prisoners*, 116. *Governor*, S. McLean

KIRKHAM, Freckleton Road, Preston PR4 2RN. *CNA*, 702. *Prisoners*, 658. *Governor*, A. F. Jennings, OBE

KIRKLEVINGTON GRANGE, Yarm, Cleveland TS15 9PA. *CNA*, 177. *Prisoners*, 174. *Governor*, Ms S. Anthony

LANCASTER, The Castle, Lancaster LA1 1YL. *CNA*, 218. *Prisoners*, 216. *Governor*, D. G. McNaughton

†‡LANCASTER FARMS, Far Moor Lane, Stone Row Head, off Quernmore Road, Lancaster LA1 3QZ. *CNA*, 496. *Prisoners and Young Offenders*, 502. *Governor*, D. Thomas

LATCHMERE HOUSE, Church Road, Ham Common, Richmond, Surrey TW10 5HH. *CNA*, 192. *Prisoners*, 179. *Governor*, T. Hinchliffe

LEEDS, Armley, Leeds LS12 2TJ. *CNA*, 907. *Prisoners*, 1,008. *Governor*, R. Daly

LEICESTER, Welford Road, Leicester LE2 7AJ. *CNA*, 215. *Prisoners*, 346. *Governor*, Ms M. Bartlett

†‡LEWES, Brighton Road, Lewes, E. Sussex BN7 1EA. *CNA*, 485. *Prisoners and Young Offenders*, 482. *Governor*, J. F. Dixon

LEYHILL, Wotton-under-Edge, Glos GL12 8BT. *CNA*, 410. *Prisoners*, 390. *Governor*, D. T. Williams

LINCOLN, Greetwell Road, Lincoln LN2 4BD. *CNA*, 434. *Prisoners*, 625. *Governor*, B. McCourt

LINDHOLME, Bawtry Road, Hatfield Woodhouse, Doncaster DN7 6EE. *CNA*, 682. *Prisoners*, 679. *Governor*, A. Holman

LITTLEHEY, Perry, Huntingdon PE18 0SR. *CNA*, 624. *Prisoners*, 640. *Governor*, C. Morris

LIVERPOOL, 68 Hornby Road, Liverpool L9 3DF. *CNA*, 1,216. *Prisoners*, 1,460. *Governor*, W. Abbott

LONG LARTIN, South Littleton, Evesham, Worcs WR11 5TZ. *CNA*, 379. *Prisoners*, 381. *Governor*, J. Mullen

LOWDHAM GRANGE (private prison), Lowdham, Notts NG14 7TA. *CNA*, 175. *Prisoners*, 175. *Director*, A. Reid

---

* Women's establishment or establishment with units for women
† Remand Centre or establishment with units for remand prisoners
‡ Young Offender Institution or establishment with units for young offenders

††Low Newton, Brasside, Durham DH1 5SD. *CNA*, 199. *Prisoners and Young Offenders*, 298. *Governor*, M. Kirby

Maidstone, 36 County Road, Maidstone ME14 1UZ. *CNA*, 541. *Prisoners*, 558. *Governor*, M. Conway

Manchester, Southall Street, Manchester M60 9AH. *CNA*, 883. *Prisoners*, 1,056. *Governor*, J. Smith

‡Moorland, Bawtry Road, Hatfield Woodhouse, Doncaster DN7 6BW. *CNA*, 650. *Prisoners and Young Offenders*, 674. *Governor*, D. J. Waplington, OBE

Morton Hall, Swinderby, Lincoln LN6 9PS. *CNA*, 203. *Prisoners*, 200. *Governor*, M. Murphy

The Mount, Molyneaux Avenue, Bovingdon, Hemel Hempstead HP3 0NZ. *CNA*, 588. *Prisoners*, 620. *Governor*, P. Wailen

*††New Hall, Dial Wood, Flockton, Wakefield WF4 4AX. *CNA*, 313. *Prisoners and Young Offenders*, 331. *Governor*, M. Goodwin

††Northallerton, 15a East Road, Northallerton, N. Yorks DL6 1NW. *CNA*, 152. *Prisoners and Young Offenders*, 271. *Governor*, D. P. G. Appleton

North Sea Camp, Freiston, Boston, Lincs PE22 0QX. *CNA*, 213. *Prisoners*, 199. *Governor*, M. A. Lewis

††Norwich, Mousehold, Norwich NR1 4LU. *CNA*, 570. *Prisoners and Young Offenders*, 722. *Governor*, M. Spurr

Nottingham, Perry Road, Sherwood, Nottingham NG5 3AG. *CNA*, 388. *Prisoners*, 389. *Governor*, P. J. Bennett

‡Onley, Willoughby, Rugby CV23 8AP. *CNA*, 583. *Young Offenders*, 578. *Governor*, J. N. Brooke

††Parc (private prison), Heol Hopcyn John, Bridgend CF35 6AR. *CNA*, 470. *Prisoners and Young Offenders*, 411. *Director*, R. Dixon

Parkhurst, Newport, Isle of Wight PO30 5NX. *CNA*, 365. *Prisoners*, 353. *Governor*, D. M. Morrison

Pentonville, Caledonian Road, London N7 8TT. *CNA*, 740. *Prisoners*, 934. *Governor*, R. Duncan

‡Portland, Easton, Portland, Dorset DT5 1DL. *CNA*, 526. *Young Offenders*, 549. *Governor*, Miss S. F. McCormick

‡Prescoed, 47 Maryport Street, Usk, Gwent NP5 1XP. *CNA*, see Usk. *Prisoners and Young Offenders*, see Usk. *Governor*, R. J. Comber

Preston, 2 Ribbleton Lane, Preston PR1 5AB. *CNA*, 398. *Prisoners*, 354. *Governor*, R. J. Crouch

Ranby, Ranby, Retford, Notts DN22 8EU. *CNA*, 519. *Prisoners*, 561. *Governor*, J. Slater

††Reading, Forbury Road, Reading RG1 3HY. *CNA*, 203. *Prisoners and Young Offenders*, 228. *Governor*, R. Fielder

*Risley, Risley, Warrington WA3 6BP. *CNA*, 851. *Prisoners*, 872. *Governor*, J. Harrison

††Rochester, 1 Fort Road, Rochester, Kent ME1 3QS. *CNA*, 432. *Prisoners and Young Offenders*, 401. *Governor*, R. A. Chapman

*Send, Ripley Road, Send, Woking, Surrey GU23 7LJ. *CNA*, 224. *Prisoners*, 219. *Governor*, S. Guy-Gibbons

Shepton Mallet, Cornhill, Shepton Mallet, Somerset BA4 5LU. *CNA*, 159. *Prisoners*, 213. *Governor*, R. Bennett

Shrewsbury, The Dana, Shrewsbury SY1 2HR. *CNA*, 180. *Prisoners*, 324. *Governor*, K. Beaumont

Spring Hill, see Grendon

Stafford, 54 Gaol Road, Stafford ST16 3AW. *CNA*, 568. *Prisoners*, 622. *Governor*, P. Wright

Standford Hill, Church Road, Eastchurch, Isle of Sheppey, Kent ME12 4AA. *CNA*, 384. *Prisoners*, 336. *Governor*, K. Naisbitt

Stocken, Stocken Hall Road, Stretton, nr Oakham, Leics LE15 7RD. *CNA*, 436. *Prisoners*, 458. *Governor*, R. Curtis

‡Stoke Heath, Stoke Heath, Market Drayton, Shropshire TF9 2JL. *CNA*, 455. *Young Offenders*, 448. *Governor*, J. Alldridge

*‡Styal, Wilmslow, Cheshire SK9 4HR. *CNA*, 271. *Prisoners and Young Offenders*, 272. *Governor*, Ms M. Moulden

Sudbury, Ashbourne, Derbys DE6 5HW. *CNA*, 511. *Prisoners*, 492. *Governor*, P. E. Salter

Swaleside, Brabazon Road, Eastchurch, Isle of Sheppey, Kent ME12 4AX. *CNA*, 572. *Prisoners*, 593. *Governor*, J. Podmore

†Swansea, 200 Oystermouth Road, Swansea SA1 3SR. *CNA*, 260. *Prisoners*, 334. *Governor*, G. Deighton

‡Swinfen Hall, Lichfield, Staffs WS14 9QS. *CNA*, 203. *Young Offenders*, 201. *Governor*, Ms J. P. Francis

‡Thorn Cross, Arley Road, Appleton Thorn, Warrington WA4 4RL. *CNA*, 316. *Young Offenders*, 221. *Governor*, I. Windebank

Usk, 47 Maryport Street, Usk, Gwent NP5 1XP. *CNA* (*Usk and Prescoed*), 243. *Prisoners* (*Usk and Prescoed*), 281. *Governor*, R. J. Comber

The Verne, Portland, Dorset DT5 1EQ. *CNA*, 552. *Prisoners*, 571. *Governor*, T. M. Turner

Wakefield, 5 Love Lane, Wakefield WF2 9AG. *CNA*, 531. *Prisoners*, 608. *Governor*, D. Shaw

Wandsworth, Heathfield Road, London SW18 3HS. *CNA*, 810. *Prisoners*, 881. *Governor*, M. Knight

Wayland, Griston, Thetford, Norfolk IP25 6RL. *CNA*, 620. *Prisoners*, 644. *Governor* (*acting*), R. Orton

Wealstun, Wetherby, W. Yorks LS23 7AZ. *CNA*, 599. *Prisoners*, 591. *Governor*, S. Tasker

Weare, Portland Dock, Castletown, Portland, Dorset DT5 1PZ. *CNA*, 365. *Prisoners*, 284. *Governor*, P. O'Sullivan

Wellingborough, Millers Park, Doddington Road, Wellingborough, Northants NN8 2NH. *CNA*, 354. *Prisoners*, 321. *Governor*, E. Willetts

‡Werrington, Werrington, Stoke-on-Trent ST9 0DX. *CNA*, 153. *Young Offenders*, 155. *Governor*, S. Habgood

‡Wetherby, York Road, Wetherby, W. Yorks LS22 5ED. *CNA*, 320. *Young Offenders*, 285. *Governor*, D. Hall

Whatton, 14 Cromwell Road, Nottingham NG13 9FQ. *CNA*, 231. *Prisoners*, 228. *Governor*, D. Walmesley

Whitemoor, Longhill Road, March, Cambs PE15 0PR. *CNA*, 521. *Prisoners*, 522. *Governor*, T. Williams

*Winchester, Romsey Road, Winchester SO22 5DF. *CNA*, 463. *Prisoners*, 606. *Governor*, R. J. Gaines

The Wolds (private prison), Everthorpe, Brough, E. Yorks HU15 2JZ. *CNA*, 360. *Prisoners*, 400. *Director*, Ms A. Rose-Quirie

††Woodhill, Tattenhoe Street, Milton Keynes MK4 4DA. *CNA*, 616. *Prisoners and Young Offenders*, 688. *Governor*, Mrs M. Boon

Wormwood Scrubs, PO Box 757, Du Cane Road, London W12 0AE. *CNA*, 1,171. *Prisoners*, 1,333. *Governor*, S. Moore

Wymott, Ulnes Walton Lane, Leyland, Preston PR5 3LW. *CNA*, 809. *Prisoners*, 797. *Governor*, R. Doughty

SCOTTISH PRISON SERVICE

Calton House, 5 Redheughs Rigg, Edinburgh EH12 9HW
Tel 0131-556 8400

Salaries 1997–8

Senior managers in the Scottish Prison Service, including governors and deputy governors of prisons, are paid across three pay bands in the range £24,200–£53,625.

Chief Executive of Scottish Prison Service (*SCS*), E. W. Frizzell
Director of Custody, J. Durno
Director, Human Resources, Ms A. Mitchell
Director, Finance and Information Systems, W. Pretswell
Director, Strategy and Corporate Affairs, Ms J. Hutchison
Deputy Director, Regime Services and Supplies, J. McNeill
Deputy Director, Estates and Buildings, B. Paterson
Area Director, South and West, P. Withers
Area Director, North and East, P. Russell
Head of Training, Scottish Prison Service College, J. Matthews

PRISON ESTABLISHMENTS

Prisoners/ Young Offenders Average number of prisoners/ young offenders 1997–8

*ABERDEEN, Craiginches, Aberdeen AB9 2HN. *Prisoners,* 201. *Governor,* I. Gunn

BARLINNIE, Barlinnie, Glasgow G33 2QX. *Prisoners,* 1,208. *Governor,* R. L. Houchin

CASTLE HUNTLY, Castle Huntly, Longforgan, nr Dundee DD2 5HL. *Prisoners,* 107. *Governor,* K. Rennie

*‡CORNTON VALE, Cornton Road, Stirling FK9 5NY. *Prisoners and Young Offenders,* 166. *Governor,* Mrs K. Donegan

*‡DUMFRIES, Terregles Street, Dumfries DG2 9AX. *Young Offenders,* 147. *Governor,* G. Taylor

DUNGAVEL, Dungavel House, Strathaven, Lanarkshire ML10 6RF. *Prisoners,* 100. *Governor,* T. Pitt

EDINBURGH, 33 Stenhouse Road, Edinburgh EH1 3LN. *Prisoners,* 728. *Governor,* A. Spencer

FRIARTON, Friarton, Perth PH2 8DW. *Prisoners,* 60. *Governor,* E. A. Gordon

‡GLENOCHIL, King O'Muir Road, Tullibody, Clackmannanshire FK10 3AD. *Prisoners and Young Offenders,* 584. *Governor,* L. McBain

GREENOCK, Gateside, Greenock PA16 9AH. *Prisoners,* 242. *Governor,* R. MacCowan

*INVERNESS, Porterfield, Inverness IV2 3HH. *Prisoners,* 140. *Governor,* H. Ross

LONGRIGGEND, Longriggend, nr Airdrie, Lanarkshire ML6 7TL. *Prisoners,* 151. *Governor,* Ms R. Kite

LOW MOSS, Low Moss, Bishopbriggs, Glasgow G64 2QB. *Prisoners,* 362. *Governor,* W. Middleton

NATIONAL INDUCTION UNIT, Shotts ML7 4LE. *Prisoners,* 46. *Governor,* J. Gerrie

NORANSIDE, Noranside, Fern, by Forfar, Angus DD8 3QY. *Prisoners,* 118. *Governor,* A. MacDonald

PENNINGHAME, Penninghame, Newton Stewart DG8 6RG. *Prisoners,* 60. *Governor,* S. Swan

PERTH, 3 Edinburgh Road, Perth PH2 8AT. *Prisoners,* 472. *Governor,* M. Duffy

PETERHEAD, Salthouse Head, Peterhead, Aberdeenshire AB4 6YY. *Prisoners,* 221. *Governor,* W. Rattray; *Governor, Peterhead Unit,* B. McConnell

‡POLMONT, Brightons, Falkirk, Stirlingshire FK2 0AB. *Young Offenders,* 473. *Governor,* D. Gunn

SHOTTS, Shotts ML7 4LF. *Prisoners,* 471. *Governor,* W. McKinlay; *Governor, Shotts Unit,* A. MacVicar

NORTHERN IRELAND PRISON SERVICE

Dundonald House, Upper Newtownards Road, Belfast BT4 3SU

Tel 01232-520700

§SALARIES 1997–8

Governor 1	£50,530
Governor 2	£45,627
Governor 3	£39,404
Governor 4	£32,423–£33,887
Governor 5	£28,568–£30,419

§A Northern Ireland allowance is also payable

PRISON ESTABLISHMENTS

Prisoners/ Young Offenders Average number of prisoners/ young offenders 1997–8

‡HYDEBANK WOOD, Hospital Road, Belfast BT 8 8NA. *Young Offenders,* 159

*‡MAGHABERRY, Old Road, Ballinderry Upper, Lisburn, Co. Antrim BT28 2PT. *Prisoners and Young Offenders,* 512

MAGILLIGAN, Point Road, Magilligan, Co. Londonderry BT49 0LR. *Prisoners,* 371

MAZE, Halftown Road, Maze, Lisburn, Co. Antrim BT27 5RF. *Prisoners,* 547

---

*   Women's establishment or establishment with units for women
†   Remand Centre or establishment with units for remand prisoners
‡   Young Offender Institution or establishment with units for young offenders

Defence

The armed forces of the United Kingdom comprise the Royal Navy, the Army and the Royal Air Force. The Queen is commander-in-chief of all the armed forces. The Ministry of Defence, headed by a Secretary of State, provides the support structure for the armed forces. Within the Ministry of Defence, the Defence Council has overall responsibility for running the armed forces. The Chief of Staff of each service reports through the Chief of the Defence Staff to the Secretary of State on matters relating to the running of his service. The Chief of Staff also chairs the executive committee of the appropriate service board, which manages the service in accordance with centrally determined objectives and budgets. The military-civilian Central Staffs, headed by the Vice-Chief of the Defence Staff and the Second Permanent Under-Secretary of State, are responsible for policy, operational requirements, commitments, financial management, resource planning and civilian personnel management. The Procurement Executive is responsible for purchasing equipment. The Defence Scientific Staff and the Defence Intelligence Staff also form part of the Ministry of Defence; names of the latter are not listed for security reasons.

A permanent Joint Headquarters for the conduct of joint operations was set up at Northwood in 1996. The Joint Headquarters connects the policy and strategic functions of the MoD Head Office with the conduct of operations and is intended to strengthen the policy/executive division. A Joint Rapid Deployment Force was established in August 1996.

Britain pursues its defence and security policies through its membership of NATO (to which most of its armed forces are committed), the Western European Union, the European Union, the Organization for Security and Co-operation in Europe and the UN (*see* International Organizations section).

In July 1998 the Government published the results of a review of Britain's defence needs and the role of the armed forces, including plans to enhance joint capabilities, create a new post of Chief of Defence Logistics (*see* below) and turn the Procurement Executive into a defence agency by April 1999 (for details, *see* White Papers section).

ARMED FORCES STRENGTHS *as at 1 January 1998*

All Services	210,587
Men	195,091
Women	15,496
Royal Naval Services	44,468
Men	41,236
Women	3,232
Army	110,055
Men	102,808
Women	7,247
Royal Air Force	56,064
Men	51,047
Women	5,017

Source: Ministry of Defence

DEPLOYMENT OF UK PERSONNEL

Service personnel in UK *as at 1 July 1997*	171,600
England	142,600
Wales	3,300
Scotland	13,900
N. Ireland	11,500

Service personnel overseas *as at 1 April 1998*	43,444
Royal Naval Services	5,221
Army	29,810
Royal Air Force	8,413

Forces overseas were deployed in Continental Europe, Gibraltar, Cyprus and elsewhere in the Mediterranean, the Near East, the Gulf, the Far East and other locations.

There were also 4,007 locally entered army personnel as at 1 April 1998, of whom 1,983 were deployed in the UK, 367 in Gibraltar, 1,556 in the Far East and 101 in other areas.

At 1 August 1997 there were 11,646 US forces based in the UK (9,570 Air Force, 1,700 Navy and 376 Army).

Sources: The Stationery Office: *UK Defence Statistics 1998; The Military Balance 1997–8* (OUP)

NUCLEAR FORCES

Britain's nuclear forces comprise three ballistic missile submarines carrying Trident missiles and equipped with nuclear warheads. The fourth and final Trident submarine is due to be launched in late 1998. All nuclear free-fall bombs have now been taken out of service.

ARMS CONTROL

The 1990 Conventional Armed Forces in Europe Treaty (the CFE Treaty), which is currently being revised, commits all NATO and former Warsaw Pact members to limiting five major classes of conventional weapons. In 1968 Britain signed the Nuclear Non-Proliferation Treaty, which was indefinitely and unconditionally extended in 1995. In September 1996 it signed a Comprehensive Nuclear Test Ban Treaty. Britain was a party to the 1972 Biological and Toxin Weapons Convention, which provides for a world-wide ban on biological weapons, and the 1993 Chemical Weapons Convention, which came into force in April 1997 and provides for a world-wide ban on chemical weapons. In December 1997 Britain signed the Ottawa Convention, which provides for an immediate ban on the use, production and transfer of anti-personnel land-mines; the convention enters into force on 1 March 1999. Britain ratified the convention on 31 July 1998 and announced a complete ban on the use of anti-personnel land-mines by British forces.

DEFENCE CUTS

DEFENCE BUDGET

	£ million
1996–7 outturn	22,345
1997–8 estimated outturn	21,840
1998–9 plans	22,240
1999–2000 plans	22,295
2000–1 plans	22,830
2001–2 plans	22,987

The Government estimated in July 1998 that defence expenditure as a percentage of GDP would fall from 2.7 per cent to 2.4 per cent by 2001–2.

Sources: The Stationery Office: *Financial Statement and Budget Report March 1998;* Ministry of Defence: *The Strategic Defence Review*

SERVICE PERSONNEL
1 April

	Royal Navy	Army	RAF	All Services
1975 strength	76,200	167,100	95,000	338,400
1990 strength	63,200	152,800	89,700	305,700
1998 strength	44,500	109,800	55,800	210,100

Source: The Stationery Office: *UK Defence Statistics 1998*

CIVILIAN PERSONNEL
1 April

1975 level	316,700
1990 level	172,300
1998 level	119,100

Source: The Stationery Office: *UK Defence Statistics 1998*

MINISTRY OF DEFENCE
Main Building, Whitehall, London SW1A 2HB
Tel 0171-218 9000
Public Enquiry Office: Tel 0171-218 6645
Web http://www.mod.uk.

For ministerial and civil service salaries, *see* page 278
For Services salaries, *see* pages 391–2
Officers promoted in an acting capacity to a more senior
rank are listed under the more senior rank. Promotion to
five-star rank is no longer usual in peacetime.
For changes after 31 August 1998, *see* Stop-press

Secretary of State for Defence, The Rt. Hon. George
 Robertson, MP
  Private Secretary (SCS), T. C. McKane
  Special Advisers, A. McGowan; B. Gray
  Parliamentary Private Secretary, Ms S. Heal, MP
Minister of State for the Armed Forces, The Rt. Hon. Doug
 Henderson, MP
  Private Secretary (SCS), D. King
Minister of State for Defence Procurement, The Lord Gilbert,
 PC, ph.D.
  Private Secretary (SCS), R. D. Keen
Parliamentary Under-Secretary of State, John Spellar, MP
  Private Secretary (SCS), Dr S. Cholerton
Permanent Under-Secretary of State (SCS), K. R. Tebbit
Chief of the Defence Staff, Gen. Sir Charles Guthrie, GCB,
 LVO, OBE, ADC *(Gen.)*

THE DEFENCE COUNCIL
The Defence Council is responsible for running the
Armed Forces. It is chaired by the Secretary of State for
Defence and consists of: the Ministers of State; the
Parliamentary Under-Secretary of State; the Chief of the
Defence Staff; the Permanent Under-Secretary of State;
the Chief of the Naval Staff; the Chief of the General Staff;
the Chief of the Air Staff; the Vice-Chief of the Defence
Staff; the Chief Scientific Adviser; the Chief of Defence
Procurement; and the Second Permanent Under-Secre-
tary of State.

CHIEFS OF STAFF

CHIEF OF THE NAVAL STAFF
Chief of the Naval Staff and First Sea Lord, Adm. Sir Michael
 Boyce, KCB, OBE, ADC
Asst Chief of the Naval Staff, Rear-Adm. J. Band
Secretariat (Naval Staff) (SCS), C. Verey

CHIEF OF THE GENERAL STAFF
Chief of the General Staff, Gen. Sir Roger Wheeler, GCB, CBE,
 ADC *(Gen.)*
Asst Chief of the General Staff, Maj.-Gen. M. A. Willcocks, CB

Director-General, Development and Doctrine, Maj.-Gen. A. D.
 Pigott, CBE

CHIEF OF THE AIR STAFF
Chief of the Air Staff, Air Chief Marshal Sir Richard Johns,
 GCB, CBE, LVO, ADC
Asst Chief of the Air Staff, Air Vice-Marshal G. E. Stirrup,
 AFC
Secretariat (Air Staff) (SCS), M. J. D. Fuller
British-American Community Relations Co-ordinator, Air
 Marshal Sir John Kemball, KCB, CBE, RAF (retd)
Chief Executive, National Air Traffic Services (SCS),
 D. J. McLauchlan
Director, Airspace Policy, Air Vice-Marshal R. D. Elder, CBE

CENTRAL STAFFS

Vice-Chief of the Defence Staff, Adm. Sir Peter Abbott, KCB
Second Permanent Under-Secretary of State (SCS), R. T.
 Jackling, CB, CBE
Deputy CDS (Systems), Lt.-Gen. E. F. G. Burton, OBE
Asst CDS, Operational Requirements (Sea Systems), Rear-Adm.
 R. T. R. Phillips, CB
Asst CDS, Operational Requirements (Land Systems), Maj.-
 Gen. P. J. Russell-Jones, OBE
Asst CDS, Operational Requirements (Air Systems), Air Vice-
 Marshal S. M. Nicholl, CBE, AFC
Deputy CDS (Programmes and Personnel), Air Marshal Sir
 Peter Squire, KCB, DFC, AFC
Asst CDS (Programmes), Maj.-Gen. J. P. Kiszely, MC
Asst Under-Secretary of State (Service Personnel Policy) (SCS),
 Miss P. M. Aldred
Defence Housing Executive (SCS), C. J. I. James
Surgeon-General, Air Marshal J. A. Baird, QHP
*Chief Executive, Defence Medical Training Organization, and
 Chief Executive, Defence Secondary Care Agency,* Maj.-Gen.
 C. G. Callow, OBE, QHP
*Deputy Under-Secretary of State (Resources, Programmes and
 Finance) (SCS),* C. V. Balmer
Asst Under-Secretary of State (Programmes) (SCS), D. J.
 Seammen
Asst Under-Secretary of State (Systems) (SCS), T. A. Woolley
Asst Under-Secretary of State (Financial Management) (SCS),
 D. G. Jones
Asst Under-Secretary of State (General Finance) (SCS), D. C. R.
 Heyhoe
Defence Services Secretary, Rear-Adm. R. B. Lees
Deputy CDS (Commitments), Air Marshal J. R. Day, OBE
Asst CDS (Operations), Rear-Adm. S. Moore
Asst Under-Secretary of State (Home and Overseas) (SCS), E. V.
 Buckley
Chief of Defence Logistics, Gen. Sir Samuel Cowan, KCB, CBE
Chief of Staff to the Chief of Defence Logistics, Air Vice-
 Marshal I. Brackenbury, OBE
Asst CDS (Logistics), Maj.-Gen. G. A. Ewer, CBE
Director of Policy (SCS), R. P. Hatfield, CBE
Asst CDS (Policy), Maj.-Gen. C. F. Drewry, CBE
Deputy Under-Secretary of State (Civilian Management (SCS),
 J. Howe
Director-General, Management and Organization (SCS), N. K.
 J. Witney
*Asst Under-Secretary of State, Civilian Management
 (Personnel) (SCS),* B. A. E. Taylor
Chief Constable, MOD Police, W. E. E. Boreham, OBE
Asst Under-Secretary of State (Security and Support) (SCS), A.
 G. Rucker
Legal Adviser (SCS), M. J. Hemming
*Director-General, Information and Communications Services
 (SCS),* A. C. Sleigh

Defence Estate Organization (*SCS*), B. L. Hirst
Commandant, Joint Services Command and Staff College, Maj.-Gen. T. J. Granville-Chapman, CBE

DEFENCE INFORMATION STAFF

Director, Information Strategy and News (*SCS*), Ms O. Muirhead
Director, Internal Communications and Media Training (*SCS*), A. Boardman
Director, Public Relations (*Navy*), Cdre B. Leighton
Director, Public Relations (*Army*), Brig. R. D. S. Gordon, CBE
Director, Public Relations (*RAF*), Air Cdre G. L. McRobbie

DEFENCE INTELLIGENCE STAFF

Old War Office Building, Whitehall, London SW1A 2EU
Tel 0171-218 6645; fax 0171-218 1562

Chief of Defence Intelligence
Deputy Chief of Defence Intelligence
Director-General, Intelligence and Geographic Resources

DEFENCE SCIENTIFIC STAFF

Chief Scientific Adviser (*SCS*), Prof. Sir David Davies, KBE
Chief Scientist (*SCS*), G. H. B. Jordan
Deputy Chief Scientists (*Scrutiny and Analysis*) (*SCS*), M. J. Earwicker; P. M. Sutcliffe
Asst Chief Scientific Adviser (*Nuclear*) (*SCS*), P. W. Roper
Nuclear Weapon Safety Adviser (*SCS*), Dr A. Ferguson

SECOND SEA LORD/COMMANDER-IN-CHIEF NAVAL HOME COMMAND

Second Sea Lord and C.-in-C. Naval Home Command, Adm. Sir John Brigstocke, KCB
Director-General, Naval Personnel (*Strategy and Plans*) *and Chief of Staff to Second Sea Lord and C.-in-C. Naval Home Command*, Rear-Adm. P. A. Dunt
Asst Under-Secretary of State (*Naval Personnel*) (*SCS*), B. Miller
Flag Officer Training and Recruiting and Chief Executive, Naval Recruiting and Training Agency, Rear-Adm. J. Chadwick
Naval Secretary and Chief Executive, Naval Manning Agency, Rear-Adm. F. M. Malbon (until Jan. 1999)
Director-General, Naval Medical Services, Surgeon Rear-Adm. M. P. W. H. Paine, QHS, FRCS
Director-General, Naval Chaplaincy Services, Revd Dr C. Stewart

NAVAL SUPPORT COMMAND

Chief of Fleet Support, Vice-Adm. Sir John Dunt, KCB
Director-General, Fleet Support (*Operations and Plans*), Rear-Adm. B. B. Perowne
Asst Under-Secretary of State (*Fleet Support*) (*SCS*), D. J. Gould
Chief Executive, Ships Support Agency (*SCS*), J. Coles
Chief Executive, Naval Bases and Supply Agency, and Chief Naval Engineering Officer, Rear-Adm. J. A. Trewby
Director-General, Aircraft (*Navy*), Rear-Adm. J. A. Burch
Flag Officer Scotland, N. England and N. Ireland, Rear-Adm. A. M. Gregory, OBE

COMMANDER-IN-CHIEF FLEET

C.-in-C. Fleet, Adm. N. R. Essenhigh
Deputy Commander Fleet, Vice-Adm. J. J. Blackham (until Jan. 1999); Vice-Adm. F. M. Malbon (from Jan. 1999)
Chief of Staff (*Operations*) *and Flag Officer Submarines*, Rear-Adm. R. P. Stevens, OBE
Flag Officer Surface Flotilla, Rear-Adm. P. M. Franklyn, MVO
Flag Officer Sea Training, Rear-Adm. R. J. Lippiett, MBE

Commander, UK Task Group/Commander, Anti-Submarine Warfare Strike Force, Rear-Adm. I. A. Forbes
Flag Officer Naval Aviation, Rear-Adm. I. R. Henderson
Commandant-General, Royal Marines, Maj.-Gen. R. H. G. Fulton

QUARTERMASTER-GENERAL'S DEPARTMENT

Quartermaster-General, Lt.-Gen. S. C. Grant, CB
Chief of Staff, Maj.-Gen. K. O'Donoghue, CBE
Asst Under-Secretary (*Quartermaster*) (*SCS*), N. H. R. Evans
Director of Contracts (*Army*) (*SCS*), P. D. Batt
Director-General, Logistic Support (*Army*), Maj.-Gen. A. W. Lyons, CBE
Director-General, Equipment Support (*Army*), Maj.-Gen. P. V. R. Besgrove, CBE

ADJUTANT-GENERAL'S DEPARTMENT

Adjutant-General, Gen. Sir Alexander Harley, KBE, CB
Chief of Staff, Maj.-Gen. R. A. Oliver, OBE
Head, Command Secretariat (*SCS*), M. E. McLoughlin
Director-General, Army Training and Recruiting and Chief Executive, Army Training and Recruiting Agency, Maj.-Gen. C. L. Elliott, MBE
Chaplain-General, Revd Dr V. Dobbin, MBE, QHC
Director-General, Army Medical Services, Maj.-Gen. W. R. Short, QHP
Director, Army Legal Services, Maj.-Gen. G. Risius
Military Secretary and Chief Executive, Army Personnel Centre, Maj.-Gen. D. L. Burden, CB, CBE
Commandant, Royal Military Academy, Sandhurst, Maj.-Gen. A. G. Denaro, CBE
Commandant, Royal Military College of Science, Maj.-Gen. A. S. H. Irwin, CBE

COMMANDER-IN-CHIEF LAND COMMAND

C.-in-C., Land Command, Gen. Sir Michael Walker, KCB, CMG, CBE, ADC (*Gen.*)
Deputy C.-in-C., Land Command, and Inspector-General, Territorial Army, Maj.-Gen. J. D. Stokoe (until March 1999)
Chief of Staff, HQ Land Command, Maj.-Gen. P. C. C. Trousdell
Deputy Chief of Staff, HQ Land Command, Maj.-Gen. P. A. Chambers, MBE

HQ STRIKE COMMAND

Air Officer Commanding-in-Chief, Air Chief Marshal Sir John Allison, KCB, CBE, ADC
Chief of Staff and Deputy C.-in-C., Air Marshal T. I. Jenner, CB
Senior Air Staff Officer and Air Officer Commanding, No. 38 Group, Air Vice-Marshal P. O. Sturley, MBE
Air Officer Logistics and Communications Information Systems, Air Vice-Marshal P. J. Scott
Air Officer Administration, Air Vice-Marshal A. J. Burton
Head, Command Secretariat (*SCS*), C. J. Wright
Air Officer Commanding, No. 1 Group, Air Vice-Marshal J. H. Thompson
Air Officer Commanding, No. 11/18 Group, Air Vice-Marshal B. K. Burridge, CBE

HQ LOGISTICS COMMAND

Air Officer Commanding-in-Chief, Air Member for Logistics and Chief Engineer (*RAF*), Air Marshal Sir Colin Terry, KBE, CB
Chief of Staff (*Air Officer Commanding Directly Administered Units*), Air Vice-Marshal M. D. Pledger, OBE, AFC

Command Secretary (SCS), H. Griffiths
Air Officer Communications Information Systems and Support Services, Air Vice-Marshal B. C. McCandless, CBE
Director-General, Support Management (RAF), Air Vice-Marshal P. W. Henderson, MBE
Chief Executive, RAF Maintenance Group Agency, Cdre K. J. M. Proctor

HQ PERSONNEL AND TRAINING COMMAND

Air Member for Personnel and Air Officer Commanding-in-Chief, Air Marshal Sir Anthony Bagnall, KCB, OBE
Chief of Staff, Air Vice-Marshal R. A. Wright, AFC
Chief Executive, Training Group Defence Agency, Air Vice-Marshal A. J. Stables, CBE
Commandant, RAF College, Cranwell, Air Vice-Marshal T. W. Rimmer, OBE
Air Secretary and Chief Executive, RAF Personnel Management Agency, Air Vice-Marshal I. M. Stewart, AFC
Director-General, Medical Services (RAF), Air Vice-Marshal C. J. Sharples, QHP
Director, Legal Services (RAF), Air Vice-Marshal J. Weeden
Chaplain-in-Chief (RAF), Revd A. P. Bishop, QHC
Command Secretary (SCS), L. D. Kyle

PROCUREMENT EXECUTIVE

EXECUTIVE

Chief of Defence Procurement, Vice-Adm. Sir Robert Walmsley, KCB
Deputy Chief of Defence Procurement (Operations), and Master-General of the Ordnance, Lt.-Gen. Sir Robert Hayman-Joyce, KCB, CBE
Deputy Chief of Defence Procurement (Support) (SCS), J. F. Howe, CB, OBE

BUSINESS UNITS

Principal Directors of Contracts (SCS), P. A. Gerard (Navy); A. V. Carey (Ordnance); J. A. Harford (Air)
Director-General, Commercial (SCS), A. T. Phipps
Director-General (Resources) (SCS), S. Webb
Director-General, Technical Services, and President of the Ordnance Board, Air Vice-Marshal P. J. O'Reilly
Chief, Strategic Systems Executive, and Director-General, Submarines (SCS), G. N. Beaven
Director-General, Surface Ships, and Controller of the Navy, Rear-Adm. P. Spencer
Director-General, Land Systems, Maj.-Gen. D. J. M. Jenkins, CBE
Director-General, Command Information Systems (SCS), A. W. McClelland
Director-General, Air Systems 1, and Controller, Aircraft, Air Vice-Marshal P. C. Norriss, CB, AFC
Director-General, Air Systems 2 (SCS), I. Fauset
Director-General, Weapons and Electronic Systems (SCS), J. Allen
Head of Defence Export Services (SCS), C. B. G. Masefield
Asst Under-Secretary (Export Policy and Finance) (SCS), Dr A. M. Fox
Military Deputy to Head of DES, Rear-Adm. J. F. T. G. Salt, CB (retd)
Director-General, Saudi Armed Forces Projects, Air Vice-Marshal C. R. Spink, CBE
Director-General, Marketing (SCS), D. J. Bowen

DEFENCE AGENCIES

ARMED FORCES PERSONNEL ADMINSTRATION AGENCY, Building 182, RAF Innsworth, Gloucester GL3 1HW. Tel: 01452-712612 ext. 7347. *Chief Executive*, Air Cdre C. G. Winsland, OBE

ARMY BASE REPAIR ORGANIZATION, Monxton Road, Andover, Hants SP11 8HT. Tel: 01264-383295. *Chief Executive*, J. R. Drew, CBE

ARMY BASE STORAGE AND DISTRIBUTION AGENCY, Monxton Road, Andover, Hants SP11 8HT. Tel: 01264-383332. *Chief Executive*, Brig. P. D. Foxton

ARMY PERSONNEL CENTRE, Kentigern House, 65 Brown Street, Glasgow G2 8EX. Tel: 0141-248 7890. *Chief Executive*, Maj.-Gen. D. L. Burden, CB, CBE

ARMY TECHNICAL SUPPORT AGENCY, Room 60/1, HQ QMG, Monxton Road, Andover, Hants SP11 8HT. Tel: 01264-383161. *Chief Executive*, Brig. A. D. Ball, CBE

ARMY TRAINING AND RECRUITING AGENCY, Trenchard Lines, Upavon, Pewsey, Wilts SN9 6BE. Tel: 01980-615024. *Chief Executive*, Maj.-Gen. C. L. Elliott, MBE

DEFENCE ANALYTICAL SERVICES AGENCY, Northumberland House, Northumberland Avenue, London WC2N 5BP. Tel: 0171-218 0729. *Chief Executive*, P. Altobell

DEFENCE ANIMAL CENTRE, Welby Lane, Melton Mowbray, Leics LE13 0SL. Tel: 01664-411811, ext. 8628. *Chief Executive*, Col. Julia Kneale, MBE

DEFENCE BILLS AGENCY, Room 410, Mersey House, Drury Lane, Liverpool L2 7PX. Tel: 0151-242 2234. *Chief Executive*, I. S. Elrick

DEFENCE CLOTHING AND TEXTILES AGENCY, Skimmingdish Lane, Caversfield, Oxon OX6 9TS. Tel: 01869-875501. *Chief Executive*, Brig. M. J. Roycroft

DEFENCE CODIFICATION AGENCY, Kentigern House, 65 Brown Street, Glasgow G2 8EX. Tel: 0141-224 2066. *Chief Executive*, K. A. Bradshaw

DEFENCE COMMUNICATION SERVICES AGENCY, Building 111, Basil Hill Barracks, Park Lane, Corsham, Wilts SN13 9NR. Tel: 01225-814886. *Chief Executive*, Maj.-Gen. A. J. Raper, CBE

DEFENCE DENTAL AGENCY, RAF Halton, Aylesbury, Bucks HP22 5PG. Tel: 01296-623535, ext. 6851. *Chief Executive*, Air Vice-Marshal I. G. McIntyre, QHDS

DEFENCE ESTATE ORGANIZATION, St George's House, Blakemore Drive, Sutton Coldfield, W. Midlands B95 7RL. Tel: 0121-311 2140. *Chief Executive*, I. Andrews, CBE

DEFENCE EVALUATION AND RESEARCH AGENCY, Ively Road, Farnborough, Hants GU14 0LX. Tel: 01252-392000. *Chief Executive*, J. A. R. Chisholm

DEFENCE INTELLIGENCE AND SECURITY CENTRE, Chicksands, Shefford, Beds SG17 5PR. Tel: 01462-752125. *Chief Executive*, Brig. C. G. Holtom

DEFENCE MEDICAL TRAINING ORGANIZATION, Brunel House, 42 The Hard, Portsmouth PO1 3DS. Tel: 01705-822341. *Chief Executive*, Maj.-Gen. C. G. Callow, OBE, QHP

DEFENCE POSTAL AND COURIER SERVICE AGENCY, Inglis Barracks, Mill Hill, London NW7 1PX. Tel: 0181-818 6417. *Director and Chief Executive*, Brig. T. M. Brown, OBE

DEFENCE SECONDARY CARE AGENCY, Room 564, St Giles Court, 1–13 St Giles High Street, London WC2H 8LD. Tel: 0171-305 6190. *Chief Executive*, Maj.-Gen. C. G. Callow, OBE, QHP

DEFENCE TRANSPORT AND MOVEMENTS EXECUTIVE, Monxton Road, Andover, Hants SP11 8HT. Tel: 01264-382537. *Chief Executive*, Brig. R. E. Ratazzi, CBE

DEFENCE VETTING AGENCY, Room 4/54, Metropole Building, Northumberland Avenue, London WC2N 5BL. Tel: 0171-807 0435. *Chief Executive*, M. P. B. G. Wilson

DISPOSAL SALES AGENCY, 7th Floor, 6 Hercules Road, London SE1 7DJ. Tel: 0171-261 8853. *Chief Executive*, M. Westgate

JOINT AIR RECONNAISSANCE INTELLIGENCE CENTRE, RAF Brampton, Huntingdon, Cambs PE18 8QL. Tel: 01480-52151. *Chief Executive*, Gp Capt S. J. Lloyd

LOGISTICS INFORMATION SYSTEMS AGENCY, Monxton Road, Andover, Hants SP11 8HT. Tel: 01264-382025. *Chief Executive,* Brig. P. A. Flanagan

MEDICAL SUPPLIES AGENCY, Drummond Barracks, Ludgershall, Andover, Hants SP11 9RU. Tel: 01980-608606. *Chief Executive,* B. Nimick

METEOROLOGICAL OFFICE, London Road, Bracknell, Berks RG12 2SZ. Tel: 01344-420242. *Chief Executive,* P. D. Ewins, CB, FENG.

MILITARY SURVEY, Elmwood Avenue, Feltham, Middx TW13 7AH. Tel: 0181-818 2181. *Chief Executive,* Brig. P. R. Wildman, OBE

MINISTRY OF DEFENCE POLICE, Wethersfield, Braintree, Essex CM7 4AZ. Tel: 01371-854000. *Chief Executive,* Chief Constable W. E. E. Boreham, OBE

NAVAL AIRCRAFT REPAIR ORGANIZATION, Fareham Road, Gosport, Hants PO13 0AA. Tel: 01705-544910. *Chief Executive,* S. R. Hill

NAVAL BASES AND SUPPLY AGENCY, Room 8, C Block, Ensleigh, Bath BA1 5AB. Tel: 01225-467707. *Chief Executive,* Rear-Adm. J. A. Trewby

NAVAL MANNING AGENCY, Victory Building, HM Naval Base, Portsmouth PO1 3LS. Tel: 01705-727340. *Chief Executive,* Rear-Adm. F. M. Malbon (until Jan. 1999)

NAVAL RECRUITING AND TRAINING AGENCY, Victory Building, HM Naval Base, Portsmouth PO1 3LS. Tel: 01705-727602. *Chief Executive,* Rear-Adm. J. Chadwick

PAY AND PERSONNEL AGENCY, Warminster Road, Bath BA1 5AA. Tel: 01225-828105. *Chief Executive,* M. A. Rowe

RAF LOGISTICS SUPPORT SERVICES, H105, RAF Wyton, PO Box 70, Huntingdon, Cambs PE17 2PY. Tel: 01480-52451, ext. 6604. *Chief Executive,* Air Cdre I. Sloss

RAF MAINTENANCE GROUP AGENCY, RAF Brampton, Huntingdon, Cambs PE18 8QL. Tel: 01480-52151, ext. 6302. *Chief Executive,* Air Cdre K. J. M. Proctor

RAF PERSONNEL MANAGEMENT AGENCY, RAF Innsworth, Gloucester GL3 1EZ. Tel: 01452-712612, ext. 7810. *Chief Executive,* Air Vice-Marshal I. M. Stewart, AFC

RAF SIGNALS ENGINEERING ESTABLISHMENT, RAF Henlow, Beds SG16 6DN. Tel: 01462-851515, ext. 7625. *Chief Executive,* Air Cdre G. Jones, MBE

SERVICE CHILDREN'S EDUCATION, HQ SCE, Building 5, Wegberg Military Complex, BFPO 40. Tel: 00-49 2161-908 2295. *Chief Executive,* D. G. Wadsworth

SHIPS SUPPORT AGENCY, B Block, Foxhill, Bath BA1 5AB. Tel: 01225-883935. *Chief Executive,* J. Coles

SPECIALIST PROCUREMENT SERVICES, MOD Abbey Wood #185, Bristol BS34 8JH. Tel: 0117-913 2721. *Chief Executive,* N. J. Bennett

TRAINING GROUP DEFENCE AGENCY, RAF Innsworth, Gloucester GL3 1EZ. Tel: 01452-712612, ext. 5344. *Chief Executive,* Air Vice-Marshal A. J. Stables, CBE

UNITED KINGDOM HYDROGRAPHIC OFFICE, Admiralty Way, Taunton, Somerset TA1 2DN. Tel: 01823-337900. *Chief Executive, and Hydrographer of the Royal Navy,* Rear-Adm. J. P. Clarke, CB, LVO, MBE

The Royal Navy

LORD HIGH ADMIRAL OF THE UNITED KINGDOM
HM THE QUEEN

ADMIRALS OF THE FLEET

HRH The Prince Philip, Duke of Edinburgh, KG, KT, OM, GBE, AC, QSO, PC, *apptd* 1953
The Lord Hill-Norton, GCB, *apptd* 1971
Sir Michael Pollock, GCB, LVO, DSC, *apptd* 1974
Sir Edward Ashmore, GCB, DSC, *apptd* 1977
The Lord Lewin, KG, GCB, LVO, DSC, apptd 1979

Sir Henry Leach, GCB, *apptd* 1982
Sir Julian Oswald, GCB, *apptd* 1993
Sir Benjamin Bathurst, GCB, *apptd* 1995

ADMIRALS

Boyce, Sir Michael, KCB, OBE, ADC (*Chief of the Naval Staff and First Sea Lord*)
Abbott, Sir Peter, KCB (*Vice-Chief of the Defence Staff*)
Brigstocke, Sir John, KCB, ADC (*C.-in-C. Naval Home Command and Second Sea Lord*)
Essenhigh, N. R. (*C.-in-C. Fleet, C.-in-C. Eastern Atlantic Area and Commander Allied Forces North-Western Europe*)

VICE-ADMIRALS

Dunt, Sir John, KCB (*Chief of Fleet Support*)
Garnett, Sir Ian, KCB (*Chief of Joint Operations*)
Haddacks, P. K. (*UK Military Rep. at NATO HQ*)
Blackham, J. J. (*Deputy Commander Fleet* until Jan. 1999)
Blackburn, D. A. J., LVO (*Chief of Staff to Commander, Allied Naval Forces Southern Europe*)
West, A. W. J., DSC
McAnally, J. H. S., LVO (*Commandant, Royal College of Defence Studies*)
Malbon, F. M. (*Deputy Commander Fleet*) (from Jan. 1999)

REAR-ADMIRALS

Trewby, J. A. (*Chief Executive, Naval Bases and Supply Agency, and Chief Naval Engineering Officer*)
Clarke, J. P., CB, LVO, MBE (*Hydrographer of the Navy and Chief Executive, UK Hydrographic Office*)
Franklyn, P. M., MVO (*Flag Officer Surface Flotilla*)
Perowne, J. F., OBE (*Dep. SACLANT*)
Lees, R. B. (*Defence Services Secretary*)
Spencer, P. (*Director-General, Surface Ships, and Controller of the Navy*)
Malbon, F. M. (*Naval Secretary and Chief Executive, Naval Manning Agency*) (until Jan. 1999)
Phillips, R. T. R., CB (*Asst CDS Operational Requirements (Sea Systems)*)
Ross, A. B., CBE (*Asst Director Operations Divn International Military Staff*)
Perowne, B. B. (*Director-General, Fleet Support (Operations and Plans)*)
Forbes, I. A. (*Commander, UK Task Group/Commander, Anti-Submarine Warfare Strike Force*)
Gough, A. B. (*Asst CDS (Policy and Requirements) to Supreme Allied Commander Europe*)
Paine, M. P. W. H., QHS, FRCS (*Director-General, Naval Medical Services*)
Band, J. (*Asst Chief of Naval Staff*)
Lippiett, R. J., MBE (*Flag Officer Sea Training*)
Gregory, A. M., OBE (*Flag Officer Scotland, N. England and N. Ireland*)
Moore, S. (*Asst CDS (Operations)*)
Dunt, P. A. (*Director-General, Naval Personnel (Strategy and Plans) and Chief of Staff to Second Sea Lord and C.-in-C. Naval Home Command*)
Burch, J. A. (*Director-General, Aircraft (Navy)*)
Rickard, H. W. (*Senior Directing Staff (Naval), Royal College of Defence Studies*)
Stevens, R. P., OBE (*Chief of Staff (Operations), Flag Officer Submarines, COMSUBEASTLANT and COMSUBNORTHWEST*)
Henderson, I. R. (*Flag Officer Naval Aviation*)
Chadwick, J. (*Flag Officer Training and Recruiting and Chief Executive, Naval Recruiting and Training Agency*)

Enquiries regarding records of serving officers should be directed to The Naval Secretary, Room 161, Victory Building, HM Naval Base, Portsmouth, Hants PO1 3LS.

HM FLEET *as at 1 April 1998*

SUBMARINES

Trident	Vanguard, Victorious, Vigilant
Fleet	Sceptre, Sovereign, Spartan, Splendid, Superb, Talent, Tireless, Torbay, Trafalgar, Trenchant, Triumph, Turbulent

ANTI-SUBMARINE
WARFARE CARRIERS	Ark Royal, Illustrious, Invincible
ASSAULT SHIPS	Fearless, Intrepid
LANDING PLATFORM HELICOPTER	Ocean

DESTROYERS
Type 42	Birmingham, Cardiff, Edinburgh, Exeter, Glasgow, Gloucester, Liverpool, Manchester, Newcastle, Nottingham, Southampton, York

FRIGATES
Type 23	Argyll, Grafton, Iron Duke, Lancaster, Marlborough, Monmouth, Montrose, Norfolk, Northumberland, Richmond, Somerset, Sutherland, Westminster
Type 22	Beaver, Boxer, Brave, Campbeltown, Chatham, Cornwall, Coventry, Cumberland, London, Sheffield

OFFSHORE PATROL
Castle Class	Dumbarton Castle, Leeds Castle
Island Class	Alderney, Anglesey, Guernsey, Lindisfarne, Orkney, Shetland

MINEHUNTERS
Hunt Class	Atherstone, Berkeley, Bicester, Brecon, Brocklesby, Cattistock, Chiddingfold, Cottesmore, Dulverton, Hurworth, Ledbury, Middleton, Quorn
Sandown Class	Bridport, Cromer, Inverness, Penzance, Sandown, Walney

PATROL CRAFT
River Class	Arun, Blackwater, Orwell, Spey
Coastal Training Craft*	Archer, Biter, Blazer, Charger, Dasher, Example, Exploit, Explorer, Express, Puncher, Pursuer, Raider, Smiter, Tracker
Gibralter Search and Rescue Craft	Ranger, Trumpeter
ICE PATROL SHIP	Endurance
SURVEY SHIPS	Beagle, Bulldog, Gleaner, Herald, Roebuck, Scott

SOLD/DECOMMISSIONED
1997–8	Britannia, Hecla, Itchen, Loyal Chancellor, Loyal Watcher, Peacock, Plover, Starling

* Operated by the University Royal Naval Units

OTHER PARTS OF THE NAVAL SERVICE

ROYAL MARINES

The Royal Marines were formed in 1664 and are part of the Naval Service. Their primary purpose is to conduct amphibious and land warfare. The principal operational units are 3 Commando Brigade Royal Marines, an amphibious all-arms brigade trained to operate in arduous environments, which is a core element of the UK's Joint Rapid Reaction Force; Comacchio Group Royal Marines, which is responsible for the security of nuclear weapon facilities; and Special Boat Service Royal Marines, the maritime special forces. The Royal Marines also provide detachments for warships and land-based naval parties as required. The Royal Marines Band Service provides military musical support for the Naval Service. The headquarters of the Royal Marines is at Portsmouth, along with the Royal Marines School of Music, and principal bases are at Plymouth, Arbroath, Poole, Taunton and Chivenor. The Corps of Royal Marines is about 6,500 strong.

Commandant-General, Royal Marines, Maj.-Gen. R. H. G. Fulton

ROYAL MARINES RESERVE (RMR)

The Royal Marines Reserve is a commando-trained volunteer force with the principal role, when mobilized, of supporting the Royal Marines. There are RMR centres in London, Glasgow, Bristol, Liverpool and Newcastle. The current strength of the RMR is about 1,000.

Director, RMR, Lt.-Col. A. W. MacCormick

ROYAL FLEET AUXILIARY (RFA)

The Royal Fleet Auxiliary supplies ships of the fleet with fuel, food, water, spares and ammunition while at sea. Its ships are manned by merchant seamen. In April 1997 there were 22 ships in the RFA.

FLEET AIR ARM

The Fleet Air Arm was established in 1937 and operates aircraft (including helicopters) for the Royal Navy. In April 1997 there were 203 aircraft in the Fleet Air Arm.

ROYAL NAVAL RESERVE (RNR)

The Royal Naval Reserve is an integral part of the Naval Service. It comprises up to 3,500 men and women nationwide who volunteer to train in their spare time to enable the Royal Navy to meet its operational commitments, at sea and ashore, in crisis or war. Under the Strategic Defence Review, the strength of the RNR will be increased by 350.

Director, Naval Reserves, Capt N. R. Hodgson, RN

QUEEN ALEXANDRA'S ROYAL NAVAL NURSING SERVICE

The first nursing sisters were appointed to naval hospitals in 1884 and the Queen Alexandra's Royal Naval Nursing Service (QARNNS) gained its current title in 1902. Nursing ratings were introduced in 1960 and men were integrated into the Service in 1982; both men and women serve as officers and ratings. Female medical assistants were introduced in 1987.

Patron, HRH Princess Alexandra, the Hon. Lady Ogilvy, GCVO

Matron-in-Chief, Capt. P. M. Hambling, QHNS

The Army

THE QUEEN

FIELD MARSHALS

HRH The Prince Philip, Duke of Edinburgh, KG, KT, OM, GBE, AC, QSO, PC, *apptd* 1953

The Lord Carver, GCB, CBE, DSO, MC, *apptd* 1973

Sir Roland Gibbs, GCB, CBE, DSO, MC, *apptd* 1979

The Lord Bramall, KG, GCB, OBE, MC, *apptd* 1982

Sir John Stanier, GCB, MBE, *apptd* 1985

Sir Nigel Bagnall, GCB, CVO, MC, *apptd* 1988

The Lord Vincent of Coleshill, GBE, KCB, DSO (Col. Cmdt. RA), *apptd* 1991

Sir John Chapple, GCB, CBE, *apptd* 1992

HRH The Duke of Kent, KG, GCMG, GCVO, ADC, *apptd* 1993

The Lord Inge, GCB (Col. Green Howards, Col. Cmdt. APTC), *apptd* 1994

GENERALS

Guthrie, Sir Charles, GCB, LVO, OBE, ADC (*Gen.*) (*Chief of the Defence Staff*)

Mackenzie, Sir Jeremy, GCB, OBE, ADC (*Gen.*), Col. Cmdt. AG Corps, Col. The Highlanders

Wheeler, Sir Roger, GCB, CBE, ADC (*Gen.*), Col. Cmdt. Int. Corps, Col. R. Irish (*Chief of the General Staff*)

Walker, Sir Michael, KCB, CMG, CBE, ADC (*Gen.*), Col. Cmdt. The Queen's Division, Col. Cmdt. AAC (*C.-in-C., Land*)

Harley, Sir Alexander, KBE, CB (*Adjutant-General*)

Smith, Sir Rupert, KCB, DSO, OBE, QGM, Col. Cmdt. Parachute Regiment, Col. Cmdt. REME (*D. SACEUR*)

Cowan, Sir Samuel, KCB, CBE, Col. Cmdt. Bde of Gurkhas (*Chief of Defence Logistics*)

LIEUTENANT-GENERALS

Hayman-Joyce, Sir Robert, KCB, CBE, Col. Cmdt. RAC (*Deputy Chief of Defence Procurement (Operations), and Master-General of the Ordnance*)

Pike, Sir Hew, KCB, DSO, MBE (*GOC Northern Ireland*)

Grant, S. C., CB, Col. QLR, Col. Cmdt. King's Division, Col. Cmdt. RE (*Quartermaster-General*)

Wallace, Sir Christopher, KBE, Col. Cmdt. RGJ, Col Cmdt. LI (*Commander Permanent Joint HQ*)

Jackson, Sir Michael, KCB, CBE (*Commander ACE Rapid Reaction Corps*)

Burton, E. F. G., OBE, Col. Cmdt. RA (*Deputy CDS (Systems)*)

Deverell, J. F., OBE, Col. LI, Col. Cmdt. SASC (*Deputy Commander (Operations) SFOR*)

MAJOR-GENERALS

Burden, D. L., CB, CBE (*Military Secretary and Chief Executive, Army Personnel Centre*)

Cordingley, P. A. J., DSO (*Senior British Loan Service Officer, Oman*)

Willcocks, M. A., CB (*Asst Chief of the General Staff*)

Pigott, A. D., CBE, Coi. The Queen's Gurkha Engineers, Col. Cmdt. RE (*Director-General, Development and Doctrine*)

McAfee, R. W. M., Col. Cmdt. RTR (*Commander Multinational Divn Central (Airmobile)*)

Vyvyan, C. G. C., CB, CBE, Col. Cmdt. RGJ (*Head of British Defence Staff, Washington*)

White, M. S., CB, CBE, Col. Cmdt. RLC

Jenkins, D. J. M., CBE, Col. Cmdt. REME (*Director-General, Land Systems*)

Granville-Chapman, T. J., CBE (*Commandant, Joint Services Command and Staff College*)

Drewienkiewicz, K. J., CB, Col. Cmdt. RE (*Senior Army Member, Royal College of Defence Studies*)

Oliver, R. A., OBE (*Chief of Staff to Adjutant-General*)

Sulivan, T. J., CBE (*GOC HQ 4 Divn*)

Drewry, C. F., CBE (*Asst CDS (Policy)*)

Elliott, C. L., MBE (*Director-General, Army Training and Recruiting and Chief Executive, Army Training and Recruiting Agency*)

Kiszely, J. P., MC (*Asst CDS (Programmes)*)

O'Donoghue, K., CBE (*Chief of Staff, HQ Quartermaster-General*)

Ewer, G. A., CBE (*Asst CDS (Logistics)*)

Short, W. R., QHP (*Director-General, Army Medical Services*)

Callow, C. G., OBE, QHP (*Chief Executive, Defence Medical Training Organization, and Chief Executive, Defence Secondary Care Agency*)

Denaro, A. G., CBE (*Commandant, RMAS*)

Irwin, A. S. H., CBE (*Commandant, RMCS*)

Trousdell, P. C. C., Col. The Queen's Own Gurkha Transport Regiment (*Chief of Staff, HQ Land Command*)

Besgrove, P. V. R., CBE (*Director-General, Equipment Support (Army)*)

Farrar-Hockley, C. D., MC (*GOC HQ 2 Divn*)

Searby, R. V. (*GOC HQ 5 Divn*)

Russell-Jones, P. J., OBE (*Asst CDS, Operational Requirements (Land Systems)*)

Risius, G. (*Director, Army Legal Services*)

Chambers, P. A., MBE (*Deputy Chief of Staff, HQ Land Command*)

Stokoe, J. D., Col. Cmdt R SIGNALS (*Deputy C.-in-C., Land Command, and Inspector-General, Territorial Army until March 1999*)

Reith, J. G., CBE (*Commander Allied Command Europe Mobile Force*)

Ramsay, A. I., CBE, DSO, Col. Cmdt. RHF (*Commander British Forces Cyprus*)

Webb-Carter, E. J., OBE

Pringle, A. R. D., CBE (*Chief of Staff to Chief of Joint Operations*)

Strudwick, M. J., CBE, Col. Cmdt. The Scottish Division (*GOC Scotland*)

Milne, J. (*Director Support, HQ Allied Land Forces Central Europe*)

Raper, A. J., CBE (*Chief Executive, Defence Communications Services Agency*)

Ridgway, A. P., CBE (*Chief of Staff HQ ACE Rapid Reaction Corps*)

Truluck, A. E. G., CBE (*Executive Assistant to the Chief of Staff Supreme HQ Allied Powers Europe*)

Currie, A. P. N. (*Military Assistant to the High Representative in Sarajevo*)

Lyons, A. W., CBE (*Director-General, Logistic Support (Army)*)

Watt, C. R., CBE (*GOC 1 (UK) Armd Divn*)

CONSTITUTION OF THE ARMY

The regular forces include the following arms, branches and corps. They are listed in accordance with the order of precedence within the British Army. All enquiries with regard to records of officers and soldiers should be directed to Relations with the Public, Army Personnel Office, Kentigern House, 65 Brown Street, Glasgow G2 8EX. Tel: 0141-224 3508/3509/3510.

THE ARMS

HOUSEHOLD CAVALRY – The Household Cavalry Regiment (The Life Guards and The Blues and Royals)

ROYAL ARMOURED CORPS – Cavalry Regiments: 1st The Queen's Dragoon Guards; The Royal Scots Dragoon Guards (Carabiniers and Greys); The Royal Dragoon Guards; The Queen's Royal Hussars (The Queen's Own and Royal Irish); 9th/12th Royal Lancers (Prince of Wales's); The King's Royal Hussars; The Light Dragoons; The Queen's Royal Lancers; Royal Tank Regiment, comprising two regular regiments

ARTILLERY – Royal Regiment of Artillery

ENGINEERS – Corps of Royal Engineers

SIGNALS – Royal Corps of Signals

THE INFANTRY

The Foot Guards and regiments of Infantry of the Line are grouped in divisions as follows:

GUARDS DIVISION – Grenadier, Coldstream, Scots, Irish and Welsh Guards. *Divisional Office,* HQ Infantry, Imber Road, Warminster, Wilts. *Training Centre,* Infantry Training Centre, Vimy Barracks, Catterick, N. Yorks

SCOTTISH DIVISION – The Royal Scots (The Royal Regiment); The Royal Highland Fusiliers (Princess Margaret's Own Glasgow and Ayrshire Regiment); The King's Own Scottish Borderers; The Black Watch (Royal Highland Regiment); The Highlanders (Seaforth, Gordons and Camerons); The Argyll and Sutherland Highlanders (Princess Louise's). *Divisional Office,* HQ Infantry, Imber Road, Warminster, Wilts. *Training Centre,* Infantry Training Centre, Vimy Barracks, Catterick, N. Yorks

QUEEN'S DIVISION – The Princess of Wales's Royal Regiment (Queen's and Royal Hampshire's); The Royal Regiment of Fusiliers; The Royal Anglian Regiment. *Divisional Office,* HQ Infantry, Imber Road, Warminster, Wilts. *Training Centre,* Infantry Training Centre, Vimy Barracks, Catterick, N. Yorks

KING'S DIVISION – The King's Own Royal Border Regiment; The King's Regiment; The Prince of Wales's Own Regiment of Yorkshire; The Green Howards (Alexandra, Princess of Wales's Own Yorkshire Regiment); The Queen's Lancashire Regiment; The Duke of Wellington's Regiment (West Riding). *Divisional Office,* HQ Infantry, Imber Road, Warminster, Wilts. *Training Centre,* Infantry Training Centre, Vimy Barracks, Catterick, N. Yorks

THE ROYAL IRISH REGIMENT (one regular service and six home service battalions) – 27th (Inniskilling), 83rd, 87th and the Ulster Defence Regiment. *Regimental HQ and Training Centre,* St Patrick's Barracks, BFPO 808

PRINCE OF WALES'S DIVISION – The Devonshire and Dorset Regiment; The Cheshire Regiment; The Royal Welch Fusiliers; The Royal Regiment of Wales (24th/41st Foot); The Royal Gloucestershire, Berkshire and Wiltshire Regiment; The Worcestershire and Sherwood Foresters Regiment (29th/45th Foot); The Staffordshire Regiment (The Prince of Wales's). *Divisional Office,* HQ Infantry, Imber Road, Warminster, Wilts. *Training Centre,* Infantry Training Centre, Vimy Barracks, Catterick, N. Yorks

LIGHT DIVISION – The Light Infantry; The Royal Green Jackets. *Divisional Office,* HQ Infantry, Imber Road, Warminster, Wilts. *Training Centre,* Infantry Training Centre, Vimy Barracks, Catterick, N. Yorks

BRIGADE OF GURKHAS – The Royal Gurkha Rifles; The Queen's Gurkha Engineers; Queen's Gurkha Signals; The Queen's Own Gurkha Transport Regiment. *Regimental HQ and Training Centre,* Queen Elizabeth Barracks, Church Crookham, Fleet, Aldershot, Hants

THE PARACHUTE REGIMENT (three regular battalions) – *Regimental HQ,* Browning Barracks, Aldershot, Hants.

Training Centre, Infantry Training Centre, Vimy Barracks, Catterick, N. Yorks

SPECIAL AIR SERVICE REGIMENT – *Regimental HQ and Training Centre,* Stirling Lines, Hereford

ARMY AIR CORPS – *Regimental HQ and Training Centre,* Middle Wallop, Stockbridge, Hants

SERVICES/ARMS*

Royal Army Chaplains' Department – *Regimental HQ,* HQ AG, Upavon, Pewsey, Wilts. *Training Centre,* Netheravon House, Netheravon, Wilts SP4 9NF (until end 1998); Amport House, Amport, Andover, Hants (from end 1998)

The Royal Logistic Corps – *Regimental HQ,* Blackdown Barracks, Deepcut, Camberley, Surrey. *Training Centre,* Princess Royal Barracks, Deepcut, Camberley, Surrey

Royal Army Medical Corps – *Regimental HQ,* Keogh Barracks, Ash Vale, Aldershot, Hants. *Training Centre,* Defence Medical Services Training Centre, Keogh Barracks, Ash Vale, Aldershot, Hants

Corps of Royal Electrical and Mechanical Engineers – *Regimental HQ and Training Centre,* Hazebrouck Barracks, Isaac Newton Road, Arborfield, Reading, Berks

Adjutant-General's Corps – *Corps HQ and Training Centre,* Worthy Down, Winchester, Hants

Royal Army Veterinary Corps – *Regimental HQ,* Keogh Barracks, Ash Vale, Aldershot, Hants. *Training Centre,* Defence Animal Centre, Welby Lane Camp, Melton Mowbray, Leics

Small Arms School Corps – *Corps HQ and Training Centre,* School of Infantry, Imber Road, Warminster, Wilts

Royal Army Dental Corps – *Regimental HQ,* Keogh Barracks, Ash Vale, Aldershot, Hants. *Training Centre,* Defence Dental Agency Training Establishment, Evelyn Wood Road, Aldershot, Hants

*Intelligence Corps – *Corps HQ and Training Centre,* Chicksands, Shefford, Beds

Army Physical Training Corps – *Regimental HQ and Depot,* Queen's Avenue, Aldershot, Hants

General Service Corps

Queen Alexandra's Royal Army Nursing Corps – *Regimental HQ,* Keogh Barracks, Ash Vale, Aldershot, Hants. *Training Centre,* Health Studies Division, Royal Defence Medical College, Vulcan Block, HMS Dolphin, Gosport, Hants

Corps of Army Music – *Corps HQ and Training Centre,* Army School of Music, Kneller Hall, Kneller Road, Twickenham, Middx

ARMY EQUIPMENT HOLDINGS *as at July 1998*

Tanks	483
Armoured combat vehicles or ACV lookalikes	6,000
Artillery pieces	371
Landing craft	
Large	2
Medium	6
Assorted personnel landing craft	many
Helicopters	222

THE TERRITORIAL ARMY (TA)

The Territorial Army is designed to be a General Reserve to the Army. It exists to reinforce the regular Army as and when required, with individuals, sub-units or units either in the UK or overseas, and to provide the framework and basis for regeneration and reconstitution in times of national emergency. The TA also provides an essential link between the military and civilian communities. Its

peacetime establishment is currently 59,000, but is to be cut to 40,000 under the Strategic Defence Review.
Inspector-General, Maj.-Gen. J. D. Stokoe (until March 1998)

QUEEN ALEXANDRA'S ROYAL ARMY NURSING CORPS

The Queen Alexandra's Royal Army Nursing Corps (QARANC) was founded in 1902 as Queen Alexandra's Imperial Military Nursing Service (QAIMNS) and gained its present title in 1949. The QARANC has trained nurses for the register since 1950 and also trains and employs health care assistants. Qualified Registered General Nurses are recruited. Since 1992 men have been eligible to join the QARANC. Members of the Corps serve in military hospitals in the UK and abroad and in MOD hospital units in the UK.

Colonel-in-Chief, HRH The Princess Margaret, Countess of Snowdon, GCVO, CI
Matron-in-Chief (Army) and Director, Army Nursing Services, Brig. J. Arigho, QHNS

The Royal Air Force

THE QUEEN

MARSHALS OF THE ROYAL AIR FORCE

HRH The Prince Philip, Duke of Edinburgh, KG, KT, OM, GBE, AC, QSO, PC, *apptd* 1953
Sir John Grandy, GCB, GCVO, KBE, DSO, *apptd* 1971
Sir Denis Spotswood, GCB, CBE, DSO, DFC, *apptd* 1974
Sir Michael Beetham, GCB, CBE, DFC, AFC, *apptd* 1982
Sir Keith Williamson, GCB, AFC, *apptd* 1985
The Lord Craig of Radley, GCB, OBE, *apptd* 1988

AIR CHIEF MARSHALS

Johns, Sir Richard, GCB, CBE, LVO, ADC (*Chief of the Air Staff*)
Allison, Sir John, KCB, CBE, ADC (*Air Officer Commanding-in-Chief, HQ Strike Command, and Commander Allied Air Forces NW Europe*)
Cheshire, Sir John, KBE, CB (*C.-in-C. Allied Forces NW Europe*)

AIR MARSHALS

Squire, Sir Peter, KCB, DFC, AFC (*Deputy CDS (Programmes and Personnel)*)
Bagnall, Sir Anthony, KCB, OBE (*Air Member for Personnel and Air Officer C.-in-C., HQ Personnel and Training Command*)
Baird, J. A., QHP (*Surgeon-General*)
Day, J. R., OBE (*Deputy CDS (Commitments)*)
Terry, Sir Colin, KBE, CB (*Air Officer C.-in-C., HQ Logistics Command, Air Member for Logistics and Chief Engineer (RAF)*)
Coville, C. C. C., CB (*Deputy C.-in-C. Allied Forces Central Europe*)
Jenner, T. I., CB (*Chief of Staff and Deputy C.-in-C., HQ Strike Command*)

AIR VICE-MARSHALS

Norriss, P. C., CB, AFC (*Director-General, Air Systems 1, and Controller, Aircraft*)
Feesey, J. D. L., AFC (*Deputy Commander ICAOC 4, Messtetten*)
Goodall, R. H., CBE, AFC
Stables, A. J., CBE (*Chief Executive, Training Group Defence Agency*)

French, J. C., CBE (*Director-General, Intelligence and Geographical Resources*)
McCandless, B. C., CBE (*Air Officer Communications Information Systems and Support Services*)
Elder, R. D., CBE (*Director, Airspace Policy, Joint Air Navigation Services Council*)
Spink, C. R., CBE (*Director-General, Saudi Armed Forces Projects*)
Thompson, J. H. (*AOC No. 1 Group*)
O'Reilly, P. J. (*Director-General, Technical Services (Procurement Executive), and President of the Ordnance Board*)
Stewart, I. M., AFC (*Air Secretary and Chief Executive, RAF Personnel Management Agency*)
Weeden, J. (*Director, Legal Services (RAF)*)
Pledger, M. D., OBE, AFC (*Chief of Staff, HQ Logistics Command (Air Officer Commanding Directly Administered Units)*)
Stirrup, G. E., AFC (*Asst Chief of Air Staff*)
Wright, R. A., AFC (*Chief of Staff, HQ Personnel and Training Command*)
McIntyre, I. G., QHDS (*Chief Executive, Defence Dental Agency*)
Sharples, C. J., QHP (*Director-General, Medical Services (RAF)*)
Filbey, K. D., CBE (*Senior Directing Staff (Air), Royal College of Defence Studies*)
Sturley, P. O., MBE (*Senior Air Staff Officer, HQ Strike Command, and AOC No. 38 Group*)
Brackenbury, I., OBE (*Chief of Staff to Chief of Defence Logistics*)
Henderson, P. W., MBE (*Director-General, Support Management, HQ Logistics Command*)
Burridge, B. K., CBE (*AOC No. 11/18 Group*)
Nicholl, S. M., CBE, AFC (*Asst CDS Operational Requirements (Air Systems)*)
Niven, D. M., CBE (*Leader, Joint Helicopter Command Study Team*)
Scott, P. J. (*Air Officer Logistics and Communications Information Systems, HQ Strike Command*)
Burton, A. J. (*Air Officer Administration, HQ Strike Command*)
Rimmer, T. W., OBE (*Commandant, RAF College, Cranwell*)

CONSTITUTION OF THE ROYAL AIR FORCE

The RAF consists of three commands: Strike Command, Personnel and Training Command and Logistics Command. Strike Command is responsible for all the RAF's front-line forces. Its roles include strike/attack, air defence, reconnaissance, maritime patrol, strategic air transport, air-to-air refuelling, search and rescue, and aeromedical facilities. Personnel and Training Command is responsible for personnel administration and training in the RAF. Logistics Command is responsible for all logistics, engineering and materiel support.

Enquiries regarding records of serving officers should be directed to the RAF Personnel Management Agency (*see* Defence Agencies, above).

RAF EQUIPMENT *as at 1 July 1998*

AIRCRAFT

Tornado ADV	107
Tornado	IDS 142
Harrier	70
Jaguar	54
Canberra	7
Nimrod	28
VC10	24
Tristar	9
Hercules	55
BAe 125	6
BAe 146	3
Sentry	7
Hawk	98
Bulldog	115
Domenie	10
Islander	2
Jetstream	11
Tucano	73

HELICOPTERS

Chinook	34
Puma	41
Sea King	25
Wessex	15
Gazelle	1

ROYAL AUXILIARY AIR FORCE (RAUXAF)

Formed in 1924, the Auxiliary Air Force received the prefix 'Royal' in 1947 in recognition of its war record. The RAuxAF amalgamated with the Royal Air Force Volunteer Reserve in April 1997. The RAuxAF supports the RAF in many roles, including maritime air operations, air and ground defence of airfields, air movements, aeromedical evacuation, intelligence and public relations. In August 1998 there were 1,732 reservists; under the Strategic Defence Review, an additional 270 reserve posts will be created.

Air Commodore-in-Chief, HM The Queen
Controller of Reserve Forces (RAF), Air Cdre C. Davison, MBE

PRINCESS MARY'S ROYAL AIR FORCE NURSING SERVICE

The Princess Mary's Royal Air Force Nursing Service (PMRAFNS) offers commissions to Registered General Nurses (RGN) with a minimum of two years experience after obtaining RGN and normally with a second qualification. RGNs with no additional experience or qualification are recruited as non-commissioned officers in the grade of Staff Nurse.

Air Chief Commandant, HRH Princess Alexandra, the Hon. Lady Ogilvy, GCVO
Matron-in-Chief, Gp Capt R. H. Williams, QHNS

SERVICE SALARIES

The following rates of pay apply from 1 December 1998. Annual salaries are derived from daily rates in whole pence and rounded to the nearest £.

The pay rates shown are for Army personnel. The rates apply also to personnel of equivalent rank and pay band in the other services (*see* page 394 for table of relative ranks).

OFFICERS' SALARIES

MAIN SCALE

Rank	Daily	Annual	Rank	Daily	Annual
Second Lieutenant	£41.58	£15,177	Lieutenant-Colonel *contd*		
Lieutenant			After 4 years in the rank or with 21 years' service	£131.99	£48,176
On appointment	54.98	20,068	After 6 years in the rank or with 23 years' service	135.29	49,381
After 1 year in the rank	56.42	20,593			
After 2 years in the rank	57.86	21,119	After 8 years in the rank or with 25 years' service	138.59	50,585
After 3 years in the rank	59.30	21,645			
After 4 years in the rank	60.74	22,170	Colonel		
Captain			On appointment	145.74	53,195
On appointment	70.09	25,583	After 2 years in the rank	149.58	54,597
After 1 year in the rank	71.99	26,276	After 4 years in the rank	153.42	55,998
After 2 years in the rank	73.89	26,970	After 6 years in the rank	157.26	57,400
After 3 years in the rank	75.79	27,663	After 8 years in the rank	161.10	58,802
After 4 years in the rank	77.69	28,357	Brigadier	178.88	65,291
After 5 years in the rank	79.59	29,050	Major-General		
After 6 years in the rank	81.49	29,744	Range 1	190.35	69,478
Major			Range 2	194.56	71,014
On appointment	88.88	32,441	Range 3	200.24	73,088
After 1 year in the rank	91.08	33,244	Lieutenant-General		
After 2 years in the rank	93.28	34,047	Range 4	216.93	79,179
After 3 years in the rank	95.48	34,850	Range 5	230.88	84,271
After 4 years in the rank	97.68	35,653	General		
After 5 years in the rank	99.88	36,456	Range 6	290.68	106,098
After 6 years in the rank	102.08	37,259	Range 7	304.28	111,062
After 7 years in the rank	104.28	38,062	Range 8	368.64	134,554
After 8 years in the rank	106.48	38,865			
Special List Lieutenant-Colonel	122.93	44,869			

Field Marshal – appointments to this rank will not usually be made in peacetime. The salary for existing holders of the rank is equivalent to the salary of a range 8 General

Rank	Daily	Annual
Lieutenant-Colonel		
On appointment with less than 19 years' service	125.39	45,767
After 2 years in the rank or with 19 years' service	128.69	46,972

SALARIES OF OFFICERS COMMISSIONED FROM THE RANKS (LIEUTENANTS AND CAPTAINS ONLY)

YEARS OF COMMISSIONED SERVICE	YEARS OF NON-COMMISSIONED SERVICE FROM AGE 18					
	Less than 12 years		12 years but less than 15 years		15 years or more	
	Daily	Annual	Daily	Annual	Daily	Annual
On commissioning	£77.32	£28,222	£81.32	£29,682	£85.30	£31,135
After 1 year's service	79.32	28,952	83.31	30,408	86.62	31,616
After 2 years' service	81.32	29,682	85.30	31,135	87.91	32,087
After 3 years' service	83.31	30,408	86.62	31,616	89.19	32,554
After 4 years' service	85.30	31,135	87.91	32,087	90.48	32,025
After 5 years' service	86.62	31,616	89.19	32,554	91.77	33,496
After 6 years' service	87.91	32,087	90.48	33,025	93.05	33,963
After 8 years' service	89.19	32,554	91.77	33,496	94.34	34,434
After 10 years' service	90.48	33,025	93.05	33,963	94.34	34,434
After 12 years' service	91.77	33,496	94.34	34,434	94.34	34,434
After 14 years' service	93.05	33,963	94.34	34,434	94.34	34,434
After 16 years' service	94.34	34,434	94.34	34,434	94.34	34,434

SOLDIERS' SALARIES

The pay structure below officer level is divided into pay bands. Jobs at each rank are allocated to bands according to their score in the job evaluation system. Length of service is from age 18.

Scale A: committed to serve for less than 6 years, or those with less than 9 years' service who are serving on Open Engagement

Scale B: committed to serve for 6 years but less than 9 years

Scale C: committed to serve for 9 years or more, or those with more than 9 years' service who are serving on Open Engagement

Daily rates of pay effective from 1 December 1998 are:

RANK — SCALE A

	Band 1	Band 2	Band 3
Private			
Class 4	£26.10	£ —	£ —
Class 3	29.37	34.09	39.33
Class 2	32.83	37.59	42.83
Class 1	35.70	40.45	45.68
Lance Corporal			
Class 3	35.70	40.45	45.68
Class 2	38.00	42.75	48.40
Class 1	40.88	45.63	51.27
Corporal			
Class 2	43.72	48.45	54.10
Class 1	46.94	51.65	57.29

	Band 4	Band 5	Band 6	Band 7
Sergeant	£51.62	£56.75	£62.35	£ —
Staff Sergeant	54.58	59.70	65.33	72.10
Warrant Officer				
Class 2	58.36	63.50	70.41	77.33
Class 1	62.23	67.36	74.37	81.27

SCALE B

	Band 1	Band 2	Band 3
Private			
Class 4	£26.40	£ —	£ —
Class 3	29.67	34.39	39.63
Class 2	33.13	37.89	43.13
Class 1	36.00	40.75	45.98

SCALE B

	Band 1	Band 2	Band 3
Lance Corporal			
Class 3	£36.00	£40.75	£45.98
Class 2	38.30	43.05	48.70
Class 1	41.18	45.93	51.57
Corporal			
Class 2	44.02	48.75	54.40
Class 1	47.24	51.95	57.59

	Band 4	Band 5	Band 6	Band 7
Sergeant	£51.92	£57.05	£62.65	£ —
Staff Sergeant	54.88	60.00	65.63	72.40
Warrant Officer				
Class 2	58.66	63.80	70.71	77.63
Class 1	62.53	67.66	74.67	81.57

SCALE C

	Band 1	Band 2	Band 3
Private			
Class 4	£26.85	£ —	£ —
Class 3	30.12	34.84	40.08
Class 2	33.58	38.34	43.58
Class 1	36.45	41.20	46.43
Lance Corporal			
Class 3	36.45	41.20	46.43
Class 2	38.75	43.50	49.15
Class 1	41.63	46.38	52.02
Corporal			
Class 2	44.47	49.20	54.85
Class 1	47.69	52.40	58.04

	Band 4	Band 5	Band 6	Band 7
Sergeant	£52.37	£57.50	£63.10	£ —
Staff Sergeant	55.33	60.45	66.08	72.85
Warrant Officer				
Class 2	59.11	64.25	71.16	78.08
Class 1	62.98	68.11	75.12	82.02

RELATIVE RANK – ARMED FORCES

	Royal Navy		*Army*		*Royal Air Force*
1	Admiral of the Fleet	1	Field Marshal	1	Marshal of the RAF
2	Admiral (Adm.)	2	General (Gen.)	2	Air Chief Marshal
3	Vice-Admiral (Vice-Adm.)	3	Lieutenant-General (Lt.-Gen.)	3	Air Marshal
4	Rear-Admiral (Rear-Adm.)	4	Major-General (Maj.-Gen.)	4	Air Vice-Marshal
5	Commodore (Cdre)	5	Brigadier (Brig.)	5	Air Commodore (Air Cdre)
6	Captain (Capt.)	6	Colonel (Col.)	6	Group Captain (Gp Capt)
7	Commander (Cdr.)	7	Lieutenant-Colonel (Lt.-Col.)	7	Wing Commander (Wg Cdr.)
8	Lieutenant-Commander (Lt.-Cdr.)	8	Major (Maj.)	8	Squadron Leader (Sqn. Ldr.)
9	Lieutenant (Lt.)	9	Captain (Capt.)	9	Flight Lieutenant (Flt. Lt.)
10	Sub-Lieutenant (Sub-Lt.)	10	Lieutenant (Lt.)	10	Flying Officer (FO)
11	Acting Sub-Lieutenant (Acting Sub-Lt.)	11	Second Lieutenant (2nd Lt.)	11	Pilot Officer (PO)

SERVICE RETIRED PAY on compulsory retirement

Those who leave the services having served at least five years, but not long enough to qualify for the appropriate immediate pension, now qualify for a preserved pension and terminal grant, both of which are payable at age 60. The tax-free resettlement grants shown below are payable on release to those who qualify for a preserved pension and who have completed nine years service from age 21 (officers) or 12 years from age 18 (other ranks).

The annual rates for army personnel are given. The rates apply also to personnel of equivalent rank in the other services, including the nursing services.

OFFICERS

Applicable to officers who give full pay service on the active list on or after 30 November 1998. Senior officers (*) can elect to receive a pension calculated as a percentage of their pensionable earnings.

Capt. and below	Major	Lt.-Col.	Colonel	Brigadier	Major-General*	Lieutenant-General*	General*	
16	£ 8,477	£10,161	£13,387	£ —	£ —	£ —	£ —	£ —
17	8,871	10,644	14,006	—	—	—	—	—
18	9,264	11,126	14,626	17,000	—	—	—	—
19	9,658	11,609	15,245	17,720	—	—	—	—
20	10,051	12,092	15,864	18,440	—	—	—	—
21	10,445	12,575	16,483	19,160	—	—	—	—
22	10,839	13,057	17,103	19,880	22,961	—	—	—
23	11,232	13,540	17,722	20,600	23,686	—	—	—
24	11,626	14,023	18,341	21,320	24,412	26,652	—	—
25	12,019	14,505	18,961	22,039	25,137	27,445	—	—
26	12,413	14,988	19,580	22,759	25,862	28,238	—	—
27	12,807	15,471	20,199	23,479	26,588	29,031	33,280	—
28	13,200	15,954	20,818	24,199	27,313	29,824	34,189	—
29	13,594	16,436	21,438	24,919	28,039	30,617	35,098	—
30	13,988	16,919	22,057	25,639	28,764	31,410	36,007	47,836
31	14,381	17,402	22,676	26,359	29,490	32,203	36,916	49,043
32	14,775	17,885	23,295	27,079	30,215	32,996	37,825	50,250
33	15,168	18,367	23,915	27,799	30,941	33,789	38,734	51,457
34	15,562	18,850	24,534	28,519	31,666	34,572	39,637	52,661

Field Marshal – active list half pay at the rate of £67,277 a year

WARRANT OFFICERS, NCOs AND PRIVATES

Applicable to soldiers who give full pay service on or after 30 November 1998

No. of years reckonable service	Below Corporal	Corporal	Sergeant	Staff Sergeant	Warrant Officer Class II	Warrant Officer Class I
22	£4,931	£6,264	£ 6,938	£ 7,897	£ 8,164	£ 9,025
23	5,103	6,483	7,180	8,173	8,453	9,349
24	5,275	6,701	7,422	8,448	8,743	9,674
25	5,447	6,920	7,664	8,724	9,032	9,998
26	5,620	7,138	7,907	9,000	9,321	10,323
27	5,792	7,357	8,149	9,275	9,610	10,647
28	5,964	7,576	8,391	9,551	9,900	10,971
29	6,136	7,794	8,633	9,827	10,189	11,296
30	6,308	8,013	8,875	10,102	10,478	11,620
31	6,480	8,231	9,117	10,378	10,767	11,945
32	6,652	8,450	9,359	10,654	11,057	12,269
33	6,824	8,669	9,601	10,929	11,346	12,593
34	6,997	8,887	9,844	11,205	11,635	12,918
35	7,169	9,106	10,086	11,481	11,924	13,242
36	7,341	9,324	10,328	11,756	12,214	13,567
37	7,513	9,543	10,570	12,032	12,503	13,891

RESETTLEMENT GRANTS

Terminal grants are in each case three times the rate of retired pay or pension. There are special rates of retired pay for certain other ranks not shown above. Lower rates are payable in cases of voluntary retirement.

A gratuity of £2,880 is payable for officers with short service commissions for each year completed. Resettlement grants are: officers £9,915; non-commissioned ranks £6,526.

Religion in the UK

There are two established, i.e. state, churches in the United Kingdom: the Church of England and the Church of Scotland. There are no established churches in Wales or Northern Ireland, though the Church in Wales, the Scottish Episcopal Church and the Church of Ireland are members of the Anglican Communion.

About 65 per cent of the population of the UK (38.1 million people) would call itself broadly Christian (in the Trinitarian sense), with 45 per cent (26.1 million) identifying with Anglican churches, 10 per cent (5.7 million) with the Roman Catholic Church, 4 per cent (2.6 million) with Presbyterian Churches, 2 per cent (1.3 million) with the Methodist Churches and 4 per cent (2.6 million) with other Christian churches; but only about 8.7 per cent of the population of Great Britain (3.98 million people) regularly attends a Christian church. Church attendance in Northern Ireland is estimated at 30–35 per cent of the population.

About 2 per cent of the population (1.3 million people) is affiliated to non-Trinitarian churches, e.g. Jehovah's Witnesses, the Church of Jesus Christ of Latter-Day Saints (Mormons), the Church of Christ, Scientist and the Unitarian churches.

A further 5 per cent of the population (3.25 million people) are adherents of other faiths, including Hinduism, Islam, Judaism and Sikhism.

About 28 per cent of the population is non-religious.

ADHERENTS TO RELIGIONS IN UK *(millions)*

	1975	1985	1995
Christian (Trinitarian)	40.2	39.1	38.1
Non-Trinitarian	0.7	1.0	1.3
Hindu	0.3	0.4	0.4
Jew	0.4	0.3	0.3
Muslim	0.4	0.9	1.2
Sikh	0.2	0.3	0.6
Other	0.1	0.3	0.3
Total	42.3	42.3	42.2

PERCENTAGE OF UK POPULATION ADHERING TO RELIGIONS

	1975	1985	1995
Christian (Trinitarian)	72	69	65
Non-Trinitarian	1	2	2
Non-Christian religions	3	3	5
All religions	76	74	72

Source: Christian Research/Paternoster Publishing – *UK Christian Handbook Religious Trends No. 1 1998–9;* figures in text are for 1995

INTER-CHURCH AND INTER-FAITH CO-OPERATION

The main umbrella body for the Christian churches in the UK is the Council of Churches for Britain and Ireland (formerly the British Council of Churches). There are also ecumenical bodies in each of the constituent countries of the UK: Churches Together in England, Action of Churches Together in Scotland, CYTUN (Churches Together in Wales), and the Irish Council of Churches. The Free Churches' Council comprises most of the Free Churches in England and Wales, and the Evangelical Alliance represents evangelical Christians.

The Inter Faith Network for the United Kingdom promotes co-operation between faiths, and the Council of Christians and Jews works to improve relations between the two religions. The Council of Churches for Britain and Ireland also has a Commission on Inter Faith Relations.

ACTION OF CHURCHES TOGETHER IN SCOTLAND, Scottish Churches House, Kirk Street, Dunblane, Perthshire FK15 0AJ. Tel: 01786-825844. *General Secretary,* Revd M. Craig

CHURCHES TOGETHER IN ENGLAND, Inter-Church House, 35–41 Lower Marsh, London SE1 7RL. Tel: 0171-620 4444. *Administration Officer,* Ms J. Lampard

COUNCIL OF CHRISTIANS AND JEWS, Drayton House, 30 Gordon Street, London WC1H 0AN. Tel: 0171-388 3322. *Executive Director,* P. Mendel

COUNCIL OF CHURCHES FOR BRITAIN AND IRELAND, Inter-Church House, 35–41 Lower Marsh, London SE1 7RL. Tel: 0171-620 4444. *General Secretary,* Revd J. Reardon

CYTUN (CHURCHES TOGETHER IN WALES) - Tŷ John Penri, 11 St Helen's Road, Swansea SA1 4AL. Tel: 01792-460876. *General Secretary,* Revd N. A. Davies

EVANGELICAL ALLIANCE, Whitefield House, 186 Kennington Park Road, London SE11 4BT. Tel: 0171-207 2100. *General Director,* Revd J. Edwards

FREE CHURCHES' COUNCIL, 27 Tavistock Square, London WC1H 9HH. Tel: 0171-387 8413. *General Secretary,* Revd G. H. Roper

INTER FAITH NETWORK FOR THE UNITED KINGDOM, 5–7 Tavistock Place, London WC1H 9SN. Tel: 0171-388 0008. *Director,* B. Pearce

IRISH COUNCIL OF CHURCHES, Inter-Church Centre, 48 Elmwood Avenue, Belfast BT9 6AZ. Tel: 01232-663145. *General Secretary,* Dr R. D. Stevens

Christianity

In the first millennium of the Christian era the faith was slowly formulated. Between AD 325 and 787 there were seven Oecumenical Councils at which bishops from the entire Christian world assembled to resolve various doctrinal disputes which had arisen. The estrangement between East and West began after Constantine moved the centre of the Roman Empire from Rome to Constantinople, and it gained momentum after the temporal administration was divided. Linguistic and cultural differences between Greek East and Latin West served to encourage separate ecclesiastical developments which became pronounced in the tenth and early 11th centuries.

The administration of the church was divided between five ancient patriarchates: Rome and all the West, Constantinople (the imperial city – the 'New Rome'), Jerusalem and all Palestine, Antioch and all the East, and Alexandria and all Africa. Of these, only Rome was in the Latin West and after the Great Schism in 1054, Rome developed a structure of authority centralized on one source, the Papacy, while the Orthodox East maintained the style of localized administration.

Papal authority over the doctrine and jurisdiction of the Church in western Europe was unrivalled after the split with the Eastern Orthodox Church until the Protestant Reformation in the 16th century.

CHRISTIANITY IN BRITAIN

A Church of England already existed when Pope Gregory sent Augustine to evangelize the English in AD 596. Conflicts between Church and State during the Middle Ages culminated in the Act of Supremacy in 1534. This repudiated papal supremacy and declared Henry VIII to be the supreme head of the Church in England. Since 1559 the English monarch has been termed the Supreme Governor of the Church of England.

In 1560 the jurisdiction of the Roman Catholic Church in Scotland was abolished and the first assembly of the

Church of Scotland ratified the Confession of Faith, drawn up by a committee including John Knox. In 1592 Parliament passed an Act guaranteeing the liberties of the Church and its presbyterian government. James VI (James I of England) and later Stuart monarchs attempted to restore episcopacy, but a presbyterian church was finally restored in 1690 and secured by the Act of Settlement (1690) and the Act of Union (1707).

PORVOO DECLARATION

The Porvoo Declaration was drawn up by representatives of the British and Irish Anglican churches and the Nordic and Baltic Lutheran churches and was approved by the General Synod of the Church of England in July 1995. Churches that approve the Declaration regard baptized members of each other's churches as members of their own, and allow free interchange of episcopally ordained ministers within the rules of each church.

For Christian churches in the UK, *see* pages 400–22

Non-Christian Religions

BUDDHISM

Buddhism originated in northern India, in the teachings of Siddharta Gautama, who was born near Kapilavastu about 560 BC. After a long spiritual quest he experienced enlightenment beneath a tree at the place now known as Bodhgaya, and began missionary work.

Fundamental to Buddhism is the concept that there is no such thing as a permanent soul or self; when someone dies, consciousness is the only one of the elements of which they were composed which is lost. All the other elements regroup in a new body and carry with them the consequences of the conduct of the earlier life (known as the law of *karma*). This cycle of death and rebirth is broken only when the state of *nirvana* has been reached. Buddhism steers a middle path between belief in personal immortality and belief in death as the final end.

The Four Noble Truths of Buddhism (*dukkha*, suffering; *tanha*, a thirst or desire for continued existence which causes dukkha; *nirvana*, the final liberation from desire and ignorance; and *ariya*, the path to nirvana) are all held to be universal and to sum up the *dhamma* or true nature of life. Necessary qualities to promote spiritual development are *sila* (morality), *samadhi* (meditation) and *panna* (wisdom).

There are two main schools of Buddhism: *Theravada* Buddhism, the earliest extant school, which is more traditional, and *Mahayana* Buddhism, which began to develop about 100 years after the Buddha's death and is more liberal; it teaches that all people may attain Buddahood. Important schools which have developed within Mahayana Buddhism are *Zen* Buddhism, *Nichiren* Buddhism and Pure Land Buddhism or *Amidism*. There are also distinctive Tibetan forms of Buddhism. Buddhism began to establish itself in the West in the early 20th century.

The scripture of Theravada Buddhism is the *Pali Canon*, which dates from the first century BC. Mahayana Buddhism uses a Sanskrit version of the Pali Canon but also has many other works of scripture.

There is no set time for Buddhist worship, which may take place in a temple or in the home. Worship centres around *paritta* (chanting), acts of devotion centering on the image of the Buddha, and, where possible, offerings to a relic of the Buddha. Buddhist festivals vary according to local traditions and within Theravada and Mahayana Buddhism. For religious purposes Buddhists use solar and lunar calendars, the New Year being celebrated in April. Other festivals mark events in the life of the Buddha.

There is no supreme governing authority in Buddhism. In the United Kingdom communities representing all schools of Buddhism have developed and operate independently. The Buddhist Society was established in 1924; it runs courses and lectures, and publishes books about Buddhism. It represents no one school of Buddhism.

There are estimated to be at least 300 million Buddhists world-wide, and more than 500 groups and centres, an estimated 25,000 adherents and up to 20 temples or monasteries in the UK.

THE BUDDHIST SOCIETY, 58 Eccleston Square, London SW1V 1PH. Tel: 0171-834 5858. *General Secretary,* R. C. Maddox

HINDUISM

Hinduism has no historical founder but had become highly developed in India by about 1200 BC. Its adherents originally called themselves Aryans; Muslim invaders first called the Aryans 'Hindus' (derived from 'Sindhu', the name of the river Indus) in the eighth century.

Hinduism's evolution has become complex and it embraces many different religious beliefs, mythologies and practices. Most Hindus hold that *satya* (truthfulness), *ahimsa* (non-violence), honesty, physical labour and tolerance of other faiths are essential for good living. They believe in one supreme spirit (*Brahman*), and in the transmigration of *atman* (the soul). Most Hindus accept the doctrine of *karma* (consequences of actions), the concept of *samsara* (successive lives) and the possibility of all atmans achieving *moksha* (liberation from samsara) through *jnana* (knowledge), *yoga* (meditation), *karma* (work or action) and *bhakti* (devotion).

Most Hindus offer worship to *murtis* (images or statues) representing different aspects of Brahman, and follow their *dharma* (religious and social duty) according to the traditions of their *varna* (social class), *ashrama* (stage in life), *jati* (caste) and *kula* (family).

Hinduism's sacred texts are divided into *shruti* ('heard' or divinely inspired), including the *Vedas*, or *smriti* ('remembered' tradition), including the *Ramayana*, the *Mahabharata*, the *Puranas* (ancient myths), and the sacred law books. Most Hindus recognize the authority of the *Vedas*, the oldest holy books, and accept the philosophical teachings of the *Upanishads*, the *Vedanta Sutras* and the *Bhagavad-Gita*.

Brahman is formless, limitless and all-pervading, and is represented in worship by murtis which may be male or female and in the form of a human, animal or bird. Brahma, Vishnu and Shiva are the most important gods worshipped by Hindus; their respective consorts are Saraswati, Lakshmi and Durga or Parvati, also known as Shakti. There are held to have been ten *avatars* (incarnations) of Vishnu, of whom the most important are Rama and Krishna. Other popular gods are Ganesha, Hanuman and Subrahmanyam. All gods are seen as aspects of the supreme God, not as competing deities.

Orthodox Hindus revere all gods and goddesses equally, but there are many sects, including the Hare-Krishna movement (ISKCon), the Arya Samaj, the Swami Narayan Hindu mission and the Satya Sai-Baba movement, in which worship is concentrated on one deity to the exclusion of others. In some sects a human *guru* (spiritual teacher) is revered more than the deity, while in other sects the guru is seen as the source of spiritual guidance.

Hinduism does not have a centrally-trained and ordained priesthood. The pronouncements of the *shankaracharyas* (heads of monasteries) of Shringeri, Puri,

Dwarka and Badrinath are heeded by the orthodox but may be ignored by the various sects.

The commonest form of worship is a *puja*, in which offerings of red and yellow powders, rice grains, water, flowers, food, fruit, incense and light are made to the *murti* (image) of a deity. Puja may be done either in a home shrine or a *mandir* (temple). Many British Hindus celebrate life-cycle rituals with Sanskrit mantras for naming a baby, the sacred thread (an initiation ceremony), marriage and cremation. For details of the Hindu calendar, main festivals etc, *see* pages 84–5.

The largest communities of Hindus in Britain are in Leicester, London, Birmingham and Bradford, and developed as a result of immigration from India, eastern Africa and Sri Lanka.

There are an estimated 800 million Hindus world-wide; there are about 360,000 adherents and over 150 temples in the UK.

ARYA PRATINIDHI SABHA (UK) AND ARYA SAMAJ
   LONDON, 69A Argyle Road, London WI3 0LY. Tel: 0181-
   991 1732. *President*, Prof. S. N. Bharadwaj
BHARATIYA VIDYA BHAVAN, Institute of Indian Art and
   Culture, 4A Castletown Road, London WI4 9HQ. Tel:
   0171-381 4608. *Executive Director*, Dr M. N.
   Nandakumara
INTERNATIONAL SOCIETY FOR KRISHNA
   CONSCIOUSNESS (ISKCon), Bhaktivedanta Manor,
   Dharam Marg, Hilfield Lane, Aldenham, Watford, Herts
   WD2 8EZ. Tel: 01923-857244. *Governing Body*
   Commissioner, P. Latai
NATIONAL COUNCIL OF HINDU TEMPLES (UK),
   Bhaktivedanta Manor, Dharam Marg, Hilfield Lane,
   Aldenham, Watford WD2 8EZ. Tel: 01923-856269.
   Secretary, V. Aery
SWAMINARAYAN HINDU MISSION, 105–119 Brentfield
   Road, London NWI0 8JB. Tel: 0181-965 2651. *Head of*
   Mission, Pujya Atmaswarup Swami
VISHWA HINDU PARISHAD (UK), 48 Wharfedale
   Gardens, Thornton Heath, Surrey CR7 6LB. Tel: 0181-
   684 9716. *General Secretary*, K. Ruparelia

ISLAM

Islam (which means 'peace arising from submission to the will of Allah' in Arabic) is a monotheistic religion which was taught in Arabia by the Prophet Muhammad, who was born in Mecca (Makkah) in AD 570. Islam spread to Egypt, North Africa, Spain and the borders of China in the century following the prophet's death, and is now the predominant religion in Indonesia, the Near and Middle East, northern and parts of western Africa, Pakistan, Bangladesh, Malaysia and some of the former Soviet republics. There are also large Muslim communities in other countries.

For Muslims (adherents of Islam), God (*Allah*) is one and holds absolute power. His commands were revealed to mankind through the prophets, who include Abraham, Moses and Jesus, but his message was gradually corrupted until revealed finally and in perfect form to Muhammad through the angel *Jibril* (Gabriel) over a period of 23 years. This last, incorruptible message has been recorded in the *Qur'an* (Koran), which contains 114 divisions called *surahs*, each made up of *ayahs*, and is held to be the essence of all previous scriptures. The *Ahadith* are the records of the Prophet Muhammad's deeds and sayings (the *Sunnah*) as recounted by his immediate followers. A culture and a system of law and theology gradually developed to form a distinctive Islamic civilization. Islam makes no distinction between sacred and worldly affairs and provides rules for

every aspect of human life. The *Shari'ah* is the sacred law of Islam based upon prescriptions derived from the Qur'an and the Sunnah of the Prophet.

The 'five pillars of Islam' are *shahadah* (a declaration of faith in the oneness and supremacy of Allah and the messengership of Muhammad); *salat* (formal prayer, to be performed five times a day facing the *Ka'bah* (sacred house) in the holy city of Mecca); *zakat* (welfare due); *sawm* (fasting during the month of Ramadan); and *hajj* (pilgrimage to Mecca); some Muslims would add *jihad* (striving for the cause of good and resistance to evil).

Two main groups developed among Muslims. *Sunni* Muslims accept the legitimacy of Muhammad's first four *caliphs* (successors as head of the Muslim community) and of the authority of the Muslim community as a whole. About 90 per cent of Muslims are Sunni Muslims. *Shi'ites* recognize only Muhammad's son-in-law Ali as his rightful successor and the *Imams* (descendants of Ali, not to be confused with *imams* (prayer leaders or religious teachers)) as the principal legitimate religious authority. The largest group within Shi'ism is *Twelver Shi'ism*, which has been the official school of law and theology in Iran since the 16th century; other subsects include the *Ismailis* and the *Druze*, the latter being an offshoot of the Ismailis and differing considerably from the main body of Muslims.

There is no organized priesthood, but learned men such as *ulama*, *imams* and *ayatollahs* are accorded great respect. The *Sufis* are the mystics of Islam. Mosques are centres for worship and teaching and also for social and welfare activities. For details of the Muslim calendar and festivals, *see* page 86.

Islam was first known in western Europe in the eighth century AD when 800 years of Muslim rule began in Spain. Later, Islam spread to eastern Europe. More recently, Muslims came to Europe from Africa, the Middle East and Asia in the late 19th century. Both the Sunni and Shi'ah traditions are represented in Britain, but the majority of Muslims in Britain adhere to Sunni Islam.

The largest communities are in London, Liverpool, Manchester, Birmingham, Bradford, Cardiff, Edinburgh and Glasgow. There is no central organization, but the Islamic Cultural Centre, which is the London Central Mosque, and the Imams and Mosques Council are influential bodies; there are many other Muslim organizations in Britain.

There are about 1,000 million Muslims world-wide, with more than one million adherents and about 900 mosques in Britain.

IMAMS AND MOSQUES COUNCIL, 20–22 Creffield Road,
   London W5 3RP. Tel: 0181-992 6636. *Director of the Council*
   and Principal of the Muslim College, Dr M. A. Z. Badawi
ISLAMIC CULTURAL CENTRE, 146 Park Road, London
   NW8 7RG. Tel: 0171-724 3363. *Director*, H. Al-Majed
MUSLIM WORLD LEAGUE, 46 Goodge Street, London WIP
   IFJ. Tel: 0171-636 7568. *Director*, U. A. Baidulmaal
UNION OF MUSLIM ORGANIZATIONS OF THE UK AND
   EIRE, 109 Campden Hill Road, London W8 7TL. Tel:
   0171-229 0538. *Geneal Secretary*, Dr S. A. Pasha

JUDAISM

Judaism is the oldest monotheistic faith. The primary authority of Judaism is the Hebrew Bible or *Tanakh*, which records how the descendants of Abraham were led by Moses out of their slavery in Egypt to Mount Sinai where God's law (*Torah*) was revealed to them as the chosen people. The *Talmud*, which consists of commentaries on the *Mishnah* (the first text of rabbinical Judaism), is also held to be authoritative, and may be divided into two main categories: the *halakah* (dealing with legal and ritual matters) and the *Aggadah* (dealing with theological and ethical matters not directly concerned with the regulation of conduct). The *Midrash* comprises rabbinic writings containing biblical interpretations in the spirit of the Aggadah. The *halakah* has become a source of division; Orthodox Jews regard Jewish law as derived from God and therefore unalterable; Reform and Liberal Jews seek to interpret it in the light of contemporary considerations; and Conservative Jews aim to maintain most of the traditional rituals but to allow changes in accordance with tradition. Reconstructionist Judaism, a 20th-century movement, regards Judaism as a culture rather than a theological system and accepts all forms of Jewish practice.

The family is the basic unit of Jewish ritual, with the synagogue playing an important role as the centre for public worship and religious study. A synagogue is led by a group of laymen who are elected to office. The Rabbi is primarily a teacher and spiritual guide. The Sabbath is the central religious observance. For details of the Jewish calendar, fasts and festivals, *see* page 85. Most British Jews are descendants of either the *Ashkenazim* of central and eastern Europe or the *Sephardim* of Spain and Portugal.

The Chief Rabbi of the United Hebrew Congregations of the Commonwealth is appointed by a Chief Rabbinate Conference, and is the rabbinical authority of the Orthodox sector of the Ashkenazi Jewish community. His authority is not recognized by the Reform Synagogues of Great Britain (the largest progressive group), the Union of Liberal and Progressive Synagogues, the Union of Orthodox Hebrew Congregations, the Federation of Synagogues, the Sephardi community, or the Assembly of Masorti Synagogues. He is, however, generally recognized both outside the Jewish community and within it as the public religious representative of the totality of British Jewry.

The *Beth Din* (Court of Judgment) is the rabbinic court. The *Dayanim* (Assessors) adjudicate in disputes over matters of Jewish law and tradition; they also oversee dietary law administration. The Chief Rabbi is President of the *Beth Din* of the United Synagogue.

The Board of Deputies of British Jews, established in 1760, is the representative body of British Jewry. The basis of representation is mainly synagogal, but communal organizations are also represented. It watches over the interests of British Jewry, acts as a voice of the community and seeks to counter anti-Jewish discrimination and anti-Semitic activities.

There are over 12.5 million Jews world-wide; in Great Britain and Ireland there are an estimated 285,000 adherents and about 365 synagogues. Of these, 191 congregations and about 150 rabbis and ministers are under the jurisdiction of the Chief Rabbi; 99 orthodox congregations have a more independent status; and 75 congregations do not recognize the authority of the Chief Rabbi.

CHIEF RABBINATE, 735 High Road, London NI2 OUS. Tel: 0181-343 6301. *Chief Rabbi*, Dr Jonathan Sacks; *Executive Director*, Mrs S. Weinberg

BETH DIN (COURT OF THE CHIEF RABBI), 735 High Road, London NI2 OUS. Tel: 0181-343 6280. *Registrar*, vacant; *Dayanim*, Rabbi C. Ehrentreu; Rabbi I. Binstock; Rabbi C. D. Kaplin; Rabbi M. Gelley

BOARD OF DEPUTIES OF BRITISH JEWS, Commonwealth House, 1–19 New Oxford Street, London WCIA INF. Tel: 0171-543 5400. *President*, E. Tabachnik, QC; *Director-General*, N. A. Nagler

ASSEMBLY OF MASORTI SYNAGOGUES, 1097 Finchley Road, London NWII OPU. Tel: 0181-201 8772. *Director*, H. Freedman

FEDERATION OF SYNAGOGUES, 65 Watford Way, London NW4 3AQ. Tel: 0181-202 2263. *Administrator*, G. Coleman

REFORM SYNAGOGUES OF GREAT BRITAIN, The Sternberg Centre for Judaism, 80 East End Road,

London N3 2SY. Tel: 0181-349 4731. *Chief Executive*, Rabbi T. Bayfield

SPANISH AND PORTUGUESE JEWS' CONGREGATION, 2 Ashworth Road, London W9 IJY. Tel: 0171-289 2573. *Chief Administrator and Secretary*, H. Miller

UNION OF LIBERAL AND PROGRESSIVE SYNAGOGUES, The Montagu Centre, 21 Maple Street, London WIP 6DS. Tel: 0171-580 1663. *Director*, Rabbi Dr C. H. Middleburgh

UNION OF ORTHODOX HEBREW CONGREGATIONS, 140 Stamford Hill, London NI6 6QT. Tel: 0181-802 6226.

UNITED SYNAGOGUE HEAD OFFICE, 735 High Road, London NI2 OUS. Tel: 0181-343 8989. *Chief Executive*, vacant

SIKHISM

The Sikh religion dates from the birth of Guru Nanak in the Punjab in 1469. 'Guru' means teacher but in Sikh tradition has come to represent the divine presence of God giving inner spiritual guidance. Nanak's role as the human vessel of the divine guru was passed on to nine successors, the last of whom (Guru Gobind Singh) died in 1708. The immortal guru is now held to reside in the sacred scripture, *Guru Granth Sahib*, and so to be present in all Sikh gatherings.

Guru Nanak taught that there is one God and that different religions are like different roads leading to the same destination. He condemned religious conflict, ritualism and caste prejudices. The fifth Guru, Guru Arjan Dev, largely compiled the Sikh Holy Book, a collection of hymns (*gurbani*) known as the *Adi Granth*. It includes the writings of the first five Gurus and the ninth Guru, and selected writings of Hindu and Muslim saints whose views are in accord with the Gurus' teachings. Guru Arjan Dev also built the Golden Temple at Amritsar, the centre of Sikhism. The tenth Guru, Guru Gobind Singh, passed on the guruship to the sacred scripture, Guru Granth Sahib. He also founded the *Khalsa*, an order intended to fight against tyranny and injustice. Male initiates to the order added 'Singh' to their given names and women added 'Kaur'. Guru Gobind Singh also made five symbols obligatory: *kaccha* (a special undergarment), *kara* (a steel bangle), *kirpan* (a small sword), *kesh* (long unshorn hair, and consequently the wearing of a turban), and *kangha* (a comb). These practices are still compulsory for those Sikhs who are initiated into the Khalsa (the *Amritdharis*). Those who do not seek initiation are known as *Sehajdharis*.

There are no professional priests in Sikhism; anyone with a reasonable proficiency in the Punjabi language can conduct a service. Worship can be offered individually or communally, and in a private house or a *gurdwara* (temple). Sikhs are forbidden to eat meat prepared by ritual slaughter; they are also asked to abstain from smoking, alcohol and other intoxicants. Such abstention is compulsory for the *Amritdharis*. For details of the Sikh calendar and main celebrations, *see* page 86.

There are about 20 million Sikhs world-wide and about 400,000 adherents and 250 gurdwaras in Great Britain. The largest communities are in London, Bradford, Leeds, Huddersfield, Birmingham, Coventry and Wolverhampton. Every gurdwara manages its own affairs and there is no central body in the UK. The Sikh Missionary Society provides an information service.

SIKH MISSIONARY SOCIETY UK, 10 Featherstone Road, Southall, Middx UB2 5AA. Tel: 0181-574 1902. *Hon. General Secretary*, M. Singh

WORLD SIKH FOUNDATION, 33 Wargrave Road, South Harrow, Middx HA2 8LL. Tel: 0181-864 9228. *Secretary*, Mrs H. Bharara

The Churches

For changes notified after 31 August, *see* Stop-press

The Church of England

The Church of England is the established (i.e. state) church in England and the mother church of the Anglican Communion. The Thirty-Nine Articles, a set of doctrinal statements which, together with the Book of Common Prayer of 1662 and the Ordinal, define the position of the Church of England, were adopted in their final form in 1571 and include the emphasis on personal faith and the authority of the scriptures common to the Protestant Reformation throughout Europe.

THE ANGLICAN COMMUNION

The Anglican Communion consists of 38 independent provincial or national Christian churches throughout the world, many of which are in Commonwealth countries and originated from missionary activity by the Church of England. There is no single world authority linking the Communion, but all recognize the leadership of the Archbishop of Canterbury and have strong ecclesiastical and historical links with the Church of England. Every ten years all the bishops in the Communion meet at the Lambeth Conference, convened by the Archbishop of Canterbury. The Conference has no policy-making authority but is an important forum for the discussion of issues of common concern. The Anglican Consultative Council was set up in 1968 to function between conferences and the meeting of the Primates every two years.

There are about 70 million Anglicans and 800 archbishops and bishops world-wide.

STRUCTURE

The Church of England is divided into the two provinces of Canterbury and York, each under an archbishop. The two provinces are subdivided into 44 dioceses. Decisions on matters concerning the Church of England are made by the General Synod, established in 1970. It also discusses and expresses opinion on any other matter of religious or public interest. The General Synod has 574 members in total, divided between three houses: the House of Bishops, the House of Clergy and the House of Laity. It is presided over jointly by the Archbishops of Canterbury and York and normally meets twice a year. The Synod has the power, delegated by Parliament, to frame statute law (known as a Measure) on any matter concerning the Church of England. A Measure must be laid before both Houses of Parliament, who may accept or reject it but cannot amend it. Once accepted the Measure is submitted for royal assent and then has the full force of law. There are a number of committees, boards and councils answerable to the Synod, which deal with, or advise on, a wide range of matters. In addition to the General Synod, there are synods of clergy and laity at diocesan level.

Changes to the national structures of the Church of England were recommended in a report accepted by the General Synod in November 1995. The National Institutions Measure was subsequently approved by the Synod and Parliament. An Archbishops' Council has been created and will begin work in January 1999. The Council will oversee the work of all the central institutions of the Church and will report frequently to the General Synod. The Archbishops' Council comprises six appointed members – the Archbishops of Canterbury and York, the prolocutors of the Convocations of Canterbury and York, the chairman and vice-chairman of the House of Laity – and two bishops, two clergy and two lay members each elected by their respective Houses of the General Synod.

GENERAL SYNOD OF THE CHURCH OF ENGLAND, Church House, Great Smith Street, London SW1P 3NZ. Tel: 0171-222 9011. *Secretary-General*, P. Mawer
HOUSE OF BISHOPS: *Chairman*, The Archbishop of Canterbury; *Vice-Chairman*, The Archbishop of York
HOUSE OF CLERGY: *Chairmen (alternating)*, Canon J. Stanley; Canon H. Wilcox
HOUSE OF LAITY: *Chairman*, Dr Christina Baxter; *Vice-Chairman*, Dr P. Giddings

THE ORDINATION OF WOMEN

The canon making it possible for women to be ordained to the priesthood was promulged in the General Synod in February 1994 and the first 32 women priests were ordained on 12 March 1994. The Priests (Ordination of Women) Measure 1993 contains provisions safeguarding the position of bishops and parishes who are opposed to the priestly ministry of women. The General Synod agreed to the appointment of up to three 'provincial episcopal visitors' to work with those who are unable to accept the ministry of bishops ordaining women priests. The provincial episcopal visitors, who are suffragan bishops in the newly created sees of Ebbsfleet and Richborough (Province of Canterbury) and Beverley (Province of York) are allowed to carry out confirmations and ordinations in parishes opposed to women priests, as long as they have the permission of the diocesan bishop.

MEMBERSHIP

In 1996 the Church of England had an electoral roll membership of 1.3 million, of whom up to 1 million regularly attended Sunday services. There are (1997 figures) two archbishops, 107 diocesan, suffragan and (stipendiary) assistant bishops, 8,984 other male and 919 female full-time stipendiary clergy, and over 16,000 churches and places of worship. (The Diocese in Europe is not included in these figures.)

STIPENDIARY CLERGY 1997 AND ELECTORAL ROLL MEMBERSHIP 1996

| | Clergy | | Membership |
	Male	Female	
Bath and Wells	228	23	42,700
Birmingham	177	28	19,300
Blackburn	239	10	37,400
Bradford	113	9	12,700
Bristol	135	19	19,000
Canterbury	162	12	21,000
Carlisle	153	12	24,900
Chelmsford	387	36	50,800
Chester	275	17	48,600
Chichester	341	7	58,200
Coventry	133	16	17,700
Derby	185	15	20,100
Durham	215	26	27,400
Ely	139	22	20,900
Exeter	259	9	33,900

	Clergy		Membership
	Male	Female	
Gloucester	153	15	26,300
Guildford	182	25	30,600
Hereford	103	14	18,900
Leicester	152	18	16,100
Lichfield	335	38	52,200
Lincoln	194	33	31,300
Liverpool	221	35	32,500
London	509	44	52,500
Manchester	293	31	38,000
Newcastle	149	10	17,500
Norwich	186	14	25,900
Oxford	391	56	60,600
Peterborough	145	16	19,500
Portsmouth	106	10	18,000
Ripon	140	22	19,300
Rochester	212	22	31,300
St Albans	258	40	43,100
St Edmundsbury and Ipswich	161	14	25,300
Salisbury	223	16	45,900
Sheffield	181	20	20,700
Sodor and Man	22	0	2,800
Southwark	333	59	45,400
Southwell	170	28	18,700
Truro	119	4	17,600
Wakefield	156	16	23,200
Winchester	234	13	42,100
Worcester	144	17	22,440
York	262	28	38,200
TOTAL	8,875	919	1,290,500

STIPENDS 1998–9

Archbishop of Canterbury	£51,020
Archbishop of York	£44,700
Bishop of London	£41,660
Other diocesan bishops	£27,660
Suffragan bishops	£22,740
Deans and provosts	£22,740
Residentiary canons	£18,600
Incumbents and clergy of similar status	£15,220*

*national average, provisional estimate

CANTERBURY

103RD ARCHBISHOP AND PRIMATE OF ALL ENGLAND
Most Revd and Rt. Hon. George L. Carey, PH.D., *cons.* 1987, *trans.* 1991, *apptd* 1991; Lambeth Palace, London SE1 7JU. *Signs* George Cantuar:

BISHOPS SUFFRAGAN
Dover, Rt. Revd J. Richard A. Llewellin, *cons.* 1985, *apptd* 1992; Upway, St Martin's Hill, Canterbury, Kent CT1 1PR
Maidstone, Rt. Revd Gavin H. Reid, *cons.* 1992, *apptd* 1992; Bishop's House, Pett Lane, Charing, Ashford, Kent TN27 0DL
Ebbsfleet, Rt. Revd Michael A. Houghton, *apptd* 1998 (provincial episcopal visitor); c/o Bishop of Richborough (*see* address below)
Richborough, Rt. Revd Edwin Barnes, *cons.* 1995, *apptd* 1995 (provincial episcopal visitor); 14 Hall Place Gardens, St Albans, Herts AL1 3SP

DEAN
Very Revd John Arthur Simpson, *apptd* 1986

CANONS RESIDENTIARY
P. Brett, *apptd* 1983; R. H. C. Symon, *apptd* 1994; Dr M. Chandler, *apptd* 1995; Ven. J. Pritchard, *apptd* 1996

Organist, D. Flood, FRCO, *apptd* 1988

ARCHDEACONS
Canterbury, Ven. J. Pritchard, *apptd* 1996
Maidstone, Ven. P. Evans, *apptd* 1989

Vicar-General of Province and Diocese, Chancellor S. Cameron, QC
Commissary-General, His Hon. Judge Richard Walker
Joint Registrars of the Province, F. E. Robson, OBE; B. J. T. Hanson, CBE
Diocesan Registrar and Legal Adviser, R. H. B. Sturt
Diocesan Secretary, D. Kemp, Diocesan House, Lady Wootton's Green, Canterbury CT1 1NQ. Tel: 01227-459401

YORK

96TH ARCHBISHOP AND PRIMATE OF ENGLAND
Most Revd and Rt. Hon. David M. Hope, KCVO, D.Phil., LLD, *cons.* 1985, *trans.* 1995, *apptd* 1995; Bishopthorpe, York YO23 2GE. *Signs* David Ebor:

BISHOPS SUFFRAGAN
Hull, Rt. Revd Richard M. C. Frith, *cons.* 1998, *apptd* 1998; Hullen House, Woodfield Lane, Hessle, Hull HU13 0ES
Selby, Rt. Revd Humphrey V. Taylor, *cons.* 1991, *apptd* 1991; 10 Precentor's Court, York YO1 2ES
Whitby, Rt. Revd Gordon Bates, *cons.* 1983, *apptd* 1983; 60 West Green, Stokesley, Middlesbrough TS9 5BD
Beverley, Rt. Revd John Gaisford, *cons.* 1994, *apptd* 1994 (provincial episcopal visitor); 3 North Lane, Roundhay, Leeds LS8 2QJ

DEAN
Very Revd Raymond Furnell, *apptd* 1994

CANONS RESIDENTIARY
J. Toy, PH.D., *apptd* 1983; R. Metcalfe, *apptd* 1988; P. J. Ferguson, *apptd* 1995; E. R. Norman, PH.D., DD, *apptd* 1995
Organist, P. Moore, FRCO, *apptd* 1983

ARCHDEACONS
Cleveland, Ven. C. J. Hawthorn, *apptd* 1991
East Riding, Ven. P. R. W. Harrison, *apptd* 1998
York, Ven. G. B. Austin, *apptd* 1988

Official Principal and Auditor of the Chancery Court, Sir John Owen, QC
Chancellor of the Diocese, His Hon. Judge Coningsby, QC, *apptd* 1977
Vicar-General of the Province and Official Principal of the Consistory Court, His Hon. Judge Coningsby, QC
Registrar and Legal Secretary, L. P. M. Lennox
Diocesan Secretary, C. Sheppard, Church House, Ogleforth, York YO1 7JE. Tel: 01904-611696

LONDON (Province of Canterbury)

132ND BISHOP
Rt. Revd and Rt. Hon Richard J. C. Chartres; The Old Deanery, Dean's Court, London EC4V 5AA. *Signs* Richard Londin:

AREA BISHOPS
Edmonton, Rt. Revd Brian J. Masters, *cons.* 1982, *apptd* 1984; 1 Regent's Park Terrace, London NW1 7EE
Kensington, Rt. Revd Michael Colclough, *cons.* 1996, *apptd* 1996; 19 Campden Hill Square, London W8 7JY
Stepney, Rt. Revd Dr John M. Sentamu, *cons.* 1996, *apptd* 1996; 63 Coborn Road, London E3 2DB

Willesden, Rt. Revd Graham G. Dow, *cons.* 1992, *apptd* 1992; 173 Willesden Lane, London NW6 7YN

BISHOP SUFFRAGAN
Fulham, Rt. Revd John Broadhurst, *cons.* 1996, *apptd* 1996; 26 Canonbury Park South, London N1 2FN

DEAN OF ST PAUL'S
Very Revd John H. Moses, PH.D., *apptd* 1996

CANONS RESIDENTIARY
Ven. G. Cassidy, *apptd* 1987; R. J. Halliburton, *apptd* 1990; M. J. Saward, *apptd* 1991; S. J. Oliver, *apptd* 1997
Registrar and Receiver of St Paul's, Brig. R. W. Acworth, CBE
Organist, J. Scott, FRCO, *apptd* 1990

ARCHDEACONS
Charing Cross, Ven. Dr W. Jacob, *apptd* 1996
Hackney, Ven. C. Young, *apptd* 1992
Hampstead, Ven. P. Wheatley, *apptd* 1995
London, Ven. G. Cassidy, *apptd* 1987
Middlesex, Ven. M. Colmer, *apptd* 1996
Northolt, Ven. P. Broadbent, *apptd* 1995

Chancellor, Miss S. Cameron, QC, *apptd* 1992
Registrar and Legal Secretary, P. C. E. Morris
Diocesan Secretary, C. J. A. Smith, 36 Causton Street, London SW1P 4AU. Tel: 0171-932 1100

DURHAM (Province of York)

92ND BISHOP
Rt. Revd A. Michael A. Turnbull, *cons.* 1988, *apptd* 1994; Auckland Castle, Bishop Auckland DL14 7NR. *Signs* Michael Dunelm:

BISHOP SUFFRAGAN
Jarrow, Rt. Revd Alan Smithson, *cons.* 1990, *apptd* 1990; The Old Vicarage, Hallgarth, Pittington, Durham DH6 1AB

DEAN
Very Revd John R. Arnold, *apptd* 1989

CANONS RESIDENTIARY
D. W. Brown, *apptd* 1990; T. Willmott, *apptd* 1997; M. Kitchen, *apptd* 1997; D. J. Whittington, *apptd* 1998; N. Stock, *apptd* 1998
Organist, J. B. Lancelot, FRCO, *apptd* 1985

ARCHDEACONS
Auckland, Ven. G. G. Gibson, *apptd* 1993
Durham, Ven. T. Willmott, *apptd* 1997
Sunderland, Ven. F. White, *apptd* 1997

Chancellor, His Hon. Judge Bursell, QC, *apptd* 1989
Registrar and Legal Secretary, A. N. Fairclough
Diocesan Secretary, W. Hurworth, Auckland Castle, Bishop Auckland, Co. Durham DL14 7QJ. Tel: 01388-604515

WINCHESTER (Canterbury)

96TH BISHOP
Rt. Revd Michael C. Scott-Joynt, *cons.* 1987, *trans.* 1995, *apptd* 1995; Wolvesey, Winchester SO23 9ND. *Signs* Michael Winton:

BISHOPS SUFFRAGAN
Basingstoke, Rt. Revd D. Geoffrey Rowell, *cons.* 1994, *apptd* 1994; Bishopswood End, Kingswood Rise, Four Marks, Alton, Hants GU34 5BD

Southampton, Rt. Revd Jonathan M. Gledhill, *cons.* 1996, *apptd* 1996; Ham House, The Crescent, Romsey SO51 7NG

DEAN
Very Revd Michael Till, *apptd* 1996

Dean of Jersey (A Peculiar), Very Revd John Seaford, *apptd* 1993
Dean of Guernsey (A Peculiar), Very Revd Marc Trickey, *apptd* 1995

CANONS RESIDENTIARY
A. K. Walker, *apptd* 1987; P. B. Morgan, *apptd* 1994; C. Stewart, *apptd* 1997; Ven. J. A. Guille, *apptd* 1998 (from Jan. 1999)
Organist, D. Hill, FRCO, *apptd* 1988

ARCHDEACONS
Basingstoke, Ven. J. A. Guille, *apptd* 1998 (from Jan. 1999)
Winchester, Ven. A. G. Clarkson, *apptd* 1984

Chancellor, C. Clark, *apptd* 1993
Registrar and Legal Secretary, P. M. White
Diocesan Secretary, R. Anderton, Church House, 9 The Close, Winchester, Hants SO23 9LS. Tel: 01962-844644

BATH AND WELLS (Canterbury)

76TH BISHOP
Rt. Revd James L. Thompson, *cons.* 1978, *apptd* 1991; The Palace, Wells BA5 2PD. *Signs* James Bath Wells

BISHOP SUFFRAGAN
Taunton, Rt. Revd Andrew John Radford, *cons.* Dec. 1998, *apptd* 1998; Sherford Farm House, Sherford, Taunton TA1 3RF

DEAN
Very Revd Richard Lewis, *apptd* 1990

CANONS RESIDENTIARY
P. de N. Lucas, *apptd* 1988; R. Acworth, *apptd* 1993; P. G. Walker, *apptd* 1994; M. W. Matthews, *apptd* 1997
Organist, M. Archer, *apptd* 1996

ARCHDEACONS
Bath, Ven. R. J. S. Evens, *apptd* 1996
Taunton, Ven. R. M. C. Frith, *apptd* 1992
Wells, Ven. R. Acworth, *apptd* 1993

Chancellor, T. Briden, *apptd* 1993
Registrar and Legal Secretary, T. Berry
Diocesan Secretary, N. Denison, The Old Deanery, Wells, Somerset BA5 2UG. Tel: 01749-670777

BIRMINGHAM (Canterbury)

7TH BISHOP
Rt. Revd Mark Santer, *cons.* 1981, *apptd* 1987; Bishop's Croft, Harborne, Birmingham B17 0BG. *Signs* Mark Birmingham

BISHOP SUFFRAGAN
Aston, Rt. Revd John Austin, *cons.* 1992, *apptd* 1992; Strensham House, 8 Strensham Hill, Moseley, Birmingham B13 8AG

PROVOST
Very Revd Peter A. Berry, *apptd* 1986

CANONS RESIDENTIARY
Ven. C. J. G. Barton, *apptd* 1990; Revd D. Lee, *apptd* 1996;
Revd G. O'Neill, *apptd* 1997

Organist, M. Huxley, FRCO, *apptd* 1986

ARCHDEACONS
Aston, Ven. C. J. G. Barton, *apptd* 1990
Birmingham, Ven. J. F. Duncan, *apptd* 1985

Chancellor, His Hon. Judge Aglionby, *apptd* 1970
Registrar and Legal Secretary, H. Carslake
Diocesan Secretary, J. Drennan, 175 Harborne Park Road,
Harborne, Birmingham B17 0BH. Tel: 0121-427 5141

BLACKBURN (York)

7TH BISHOP
Rt. Revd Alan D. Chesters, *cons.* 1989, *apptd* 1989; Bishop's
House, Ribchester Road, Blackburn BB1 9EF. *Signs* Alan
Blackburn

BISHOPS SUFFRAGAN
Burnley, Rt. Revd Martyn W. Jarrett, *cons.* 1994, *apptd* 1994;
Dean House, 449 Padiham Road, Burnley BB12 6TE
Lancaster, Rt. Revd Stephen Pedley, *cons.* 1998, *apptd* 1997;
The Vicarage, Shireshead, Forton, Preston PR3 0AE

PROVOST
Very Revd David Frayne, *apptd* 1992

CANONS RESIDENTIARY
D. M. Galilee, *apptd* 1995; A. D. Hindley, *apptd* 1996; P. J.
Ballard, *apptd* 1998

Organist, R. Tanner, *apptd* 1998

ARCHDEACONS
Blackburn, Ven. F. J. Marsh, *apptd* 1996
Lancaster, Ven. R. S. Ladds, *apptd* 1997

Chancellor, J. W. M. Bullimore, *apptd* 1990
Registrar and Legal Secretary, T. A. Hoyle
Diocesan Secretary, Revd M. J. Wedgeworth, Diocesan
Office, Cathedral Close, Blackburn BB1 5AA. Tel: 01254-
54421

BRADFORD (York)

8TH BISHOP
Rt. Revd David J. Smith, cons. 1987, *apptd* 1992; Bishopscroft,
Ashwell Road, Heaton, Bradford BD9 4AU. *Signs* David
Bradford

PROVOST
Very Revd John S. Richardson, *apptd* 1990

CANONS RESIDENTIARY
C. G. Lewis, *apptd* 1993; G. Smith, *apptd* 1996

Organist, A. Horsey, FRCO, *apptd* 1986

ARCHDEACONS
Bradford, Ven. D. H. Shreeve, *apptd* 1984
Craven, Ven. M. L. Grundy, *apptd* 1994

Chancellor, D. M. Savill, QC, *apptd* 1976
Registrar and Legal Secretary, J. G. H. Mackrell
Diocesan Secretary, M. Halliday, Cathedral Hall, Stott Hill,
Bradford BD1 4ET. Tel: 01274-725958

BRISTOL (Canterbury)

54TH BISHOP
Rt. Revd Barry Rogerson, *cons.* 1979, *apptd* 1985; Bishop's
House, Clifton Hill, Bristol BS8 1BW. *Signs* Barry Bristol

BISHOP SUFFRAGAN
Swindon, Rt. Revd Michael Doe, *cons.* 1994, *apptd* 1994;
Mark House, Field Rise, Old Town, Swindon SN1 4HP

DEAN
Very Revd Robert W. Grimley, *apptd* 1997

CANONS RESIDENTIARY
J. L. Simpson, *apptd* 1989; P. F. Johnson, *apptd* 1990; D. R.
Holt, *apptd* 1998

Organist, vacant

ARCHDEACONS
Bristol, Ven. D. J. Banfield, *apptd* 1990
Swindon, Ven. A. F. Hawker, *apptd* 1998

Chancellor, Sir David Calcutt, QC, *apptd* 1971
Registrar and Legal Secretary, T. Berry
Diocesan Secretary, Mrs L. Farrall, Diocesan Church House,
23 Great George Street, Bristol, Avon BS1 5QZ. Tel:
0117-921 4411

CARLISLE (York)

65TH BISHOP
Rt. Revd Ian Harland, *cons.* 1985, *apptd* 1989; Rose Castle,
Dalston, Carlisle CA5 7BZ. *Signs* Ian Carliol:

BISHOP SUFFRAGAN
Penrith, Rt. Revd Richard Garrard, *cons.* 1994, *apptd* 1994;
Holm Croft, Castle Road, Kendal, Cumbria LA9 7AU

DEAN
Very Revd Graeme P. Knowles, apptd 1998

CANONS RESIDENTIARY
R. A. Chapman, *apptd* 1978; Ven. D. C. Turnbull, *apptd* 1993;
D. W. V. Weston, *apptd* 1994; C. Hill, *apptd* 1996

Organist, J. Suter, FRCO, *apptd* 1991

ARCHDEACONS
Carlisle, Ven. D. C. Turnbull, *apptd* 1993
West Cumberland, Ven. A. N. Davis, *apptd* 1996
Westmorland and Furness, Ven. D. T. I. Jenkins, *apptd* 1995

Chancellor, His Hon. Judge Aglionby, *apptd* 1991
Registrar and Legal Secretary, Mrs S. Holmes
Diocesan Secretary, Canon C. Hill, Church House, West
Walls, Carlisle CA3 8UE. Tel: 01228-522573

CHELMSFORD (Canterbury)

8TH BISHOP
Rt. Revd John F. Perry, *cons.* 1989, *apptd* 1996;
Bishopscourt, Margaretting, Ingatestone CM4 0HD. *Signs*
John Chelmsford

BISHOPS SUFFRAGAN
Barking, Rt. Revd Roger F. Sainsbury, *cons.* 1991, *apptd*
1991; 110 Capel Road, Forest Gate, London E7 0JS
Bradwell, Rt. Revd Laurence Green, *cons.* 1993, *apptd* 1993;
The Vicarage, Orsett Road, Horndon-on-the-Hill,
Stanford-le-Hope, Essex SS17 8NS

Colchester, Rt. Revd Edward Holland, *cons.* 1986, *apptd* 1995; 1 Fitzwalter Road, Lexden, Colchester CO3 3SS

PROVOST
Very Revd Peter S. M. Judd, *apptd* 1997

CANONS RESIDENTIARY
T. Thompson, *apptd* 1988; B. P. Thompson, *apptd* 1988; D. Knight, *apptd* 1991

Organist, Dr G. Elliott, PH.D., FRCO, *apptd* 1981

ARCHDEACONS
Colchester, Ven. M. W. Wallace, *apptd* 1997
Harlow, Ven. P. F. Taylor, *apptd* 1996
Southend, Ven. D. Jennings, *apptd* 1992
West Ham, Ven. M. J. Fox, *apptd* 1996

Chancellor, Miss S. M. Cameron, QC, *apptd* 1970
Registrar and Legal Secretary, B. Hood
Diocesan Secretary, D.Phillips, 53 New Street, Chelmsford, Essex CMI IAT. Tel: 01245-266731

CHESTER (York)

40TH BISHOP
Rt. Revd Peter R. Forster, PH.D., *cons.* 1996, *apptd* 1996; Bishop's House, Chester CHI 2JD. *Signs* Peter Cestr:

BISHOPS SUFFRAGAN
Birkenhead, Rt. Revd Michael L. Langrish, *cons.* 1993, *apptd* 1993; Bishop's Lodge, 67 Bidston Road, Oxton, Birkenhead L43 6TR
Stockport, Rt. Revd Geoffrey M. Turner, *cons.* 1994, *apptd* 1994; Bishop's Lodge, Back Lane, Dunham Town, Altrincham, Cheshire WA14 4SG

DEAN
Very Revd Dr Stephen S. Smalley, *apptd* 1986

CANONS RESIDENTIARY
R. M. Rees, *apptd* 1990; O. A. Conway, *apptd* 1991; Dr T. J. Dennis, *apptd* 1994; J. W. S. Newcome, *apptd* 1994

Organist and Director of Music, D. G. Poulter, FRCO, *apptd* 1997

ARCHDEACONS
Chester, Ven. C. Hewetson, *apptd* 1994
Macclesfield, Ven. R. J. Gillings, *apptd* 1994

Chancellor, D. G. P. Turner, *apptd* 1998
Registrar and Legal Secretary, A. K. McAllester
Diocesan Secretary, S. P. A. Marriott, Diocesan House, Raymond Street, Chester CHI 4PN. Tel: 01244-379222

CHICHESTER (Canterbury)

102ND BISHOP
Rt. Revd Eric W. Kemp, DD, *cons.* 1974, *apptd* 1974; The Palace, Chichester PO19 IPY. *Signs* Eric Cicestr:

BISHOPS SUFFRAGAN
Horsham, Rt. Revd Lindsay G. Urwin, *cons.* 1993, *apptd* 1993; Bishop's House, 21 Guildford Road, Horsham, W. Sussex RH12 ILU
Lewes, Rt. Revd Wallace P. Benn, *cons.* 1997, *apptd* 1997; 16A Prideaux Road, Eastbourne, E. Sussex BN21 2NB

DEAN
Very Revd John D. Treadgold, LVO, *apptd* 1989

CANONS RESIDENTIARY
R. T. Greenacre, *apptd* 1975; F. J. Hawkins, *apptd* 1981; P. G. Atkinson, *apptd* 1997

Organist, A. J. Thurlow, FRCO, *apptd* 1980

ARCHDEACONS
Chichester, Ven. M. Brotherton, *apptd* 1991
Horsham, Ven. W. C. L. Filby, *apptd* 1983
Lewes and Hastings, Ven. N. S. Reade, *apptd* 1997

Chancellor, His Hon. Judge Q. T. Edwards, QC, *apptd* 1978
Registrar and Legal Secretary, C. L. Hodgetts
Diocesan Secretary, J. Prichard, Diocesan Church House, 211 New Church Road, Hove, E. Sussex BN3 4ED. Tel: 01273-421021

COVENTRY (Canterbury)

8TH BISHOP
Rt. Revd Colin J. Bennetts; *cons.* 1994, *apptd* 1997; The Bishop's House, 23 Davenport Road, Coventry CV5 6PW. *Signs* Colin Coventry

BISHOP SUFFRAGAN
Warwick, Rt. Revd Anthony M. Priddis, *cons.* 1996, *apptd* 1996; 139 Kenilworth Road, Coventry CV4 7AF

PROVOST
Very Revd John F. Petty, *apptd* 1987

CANONS RESIDENTIARY
V. Faull, *apptd* 1994; J. C. Burch, *apptd* 1995; A. White, *apptd* 1998

Director of Music, R. Jeffcoat, *apptd* 1997

ARCHDEACONS
Coventry, Ven. H. I. L. Russell, *apptd* 1989
Warwick, Ven. M. J. J. Paget-Wilkes, *apptd* 1990

Chancellor, Sir William Gage, *apptd* 1980
Registrar and Legal Secretary, D. J. Dumbleton
Diocesan Secretary, Mrs I. Chapman, Church House, Palmerston Road, Coventry CV5 6FJ. Tel: 01203-674328

DERBY (Canterbury)

6TH BISHOP
Rt. Revd Jonathan S. Bailey, cons. 1992, *apptd* 1995; Derby Church House, Full Street, Derby DEI 3DR. *Signs* Jonathan Derby

BISHOP SUFFRAGAN
Repton, vacant

PROVOST
Very Revd Michael F. Perham, *apptd* 1998

CANONS RESIDENTIARY
G. A. Chesterman, *apptd* 1989; Ven. I. Gatford, *apptd* 1992; G. O. Marshall, *apptd* 1992; D. C. Truby, *apptd* 1998

Organist, P. Gould, *apptd* 1982

ARCHDEACONS
Chesterfield, Ven. D. C. Garnett, *apptd* 1996
Derby, Ven. I. Gatford, *apptd* 1992

Chancellor, J. W. M. Bullimore, *apptd* 1981
Registrar and Legal Secretary, J. S. Battie
Diocesan Secretary, R. J. Carey, Derby Church House, Full Street, Derby DEI 3DR. Tel: 01332-382233

ELY (Canterbury)

67TH BISHOP
Rt. Revd Stephen W. Sykes, *cons.* 1990, *apptd* 1990; The Bishop's House, Ely, Cambs CB7 4DW. *Signs* Stephen Ely

BISHOP SUFFRAGAN
Huntingdon, Rt. Revd John R. Flack, *cons.* 1997, *apptd* 1996; 14 Lynn Road, Ely, Cambs CB6 1DA

DEAN
Very Revd Michael Higgins, apptd 1991

CANONS RESIDENTIARY
D. J. Green, *apptd* 1980; J. Inge, *apptd* 1996
Organist, P. Trepte, FRCO, *apptd* 1991

ARCHDEACONS
Ely, Ven. J. Watson, *apptd* 1993
Huntingdon, Ven. J. Beer, *apptd* 1997
Wisbech, Ven. J. Rone, *apptd* 1995

Chancellor, W. Gage, QC
Joint Registrars, W. H. Godfrey; P. F. B. Beesley (*Legal Secretary*)
Diocesan Secretary, Dr M. Lavis, Bishop Woodford House, Barton Road, Ely, Cambs CB7 4DX. Tel: 01353-663579

EXETER (Canterbury)

69TH BISHOP
Rt. Revd G. Hewlett Thompson, *cons.* 1974, *apptd* 1985; The Palace, Exeter EX1 1HY. *Signs* Hewlett Exon:

BISHOPS SUFFRAGAN
Crediton, Rt. Revd Richard S. Hawkins, *cons.* 1988, *apptd* 1996; 10 The Close, Exeter EX1 1EZ
Plymouth, Rt. Revd John H. Garton, *cons.* 1996, *apptd* 1996; 31 Riverside Walk, Tamerton Foliot, Plymouth PL5 4AQ

DEAN
Very Revd Keith B. Jones, *apptd* 1996

CANONS RESIDENTIARY
A. C. Mawson, *apptd* 1979; K. C. Parry, *apptd* 1991
Organist, L. A. Nethsingha, FRCO, *apptd* 1973

ARCHDEACONS
Barnstaple, Ven. T. Lloyd, *apptd* 1989
Exeter, Ven. A. F. Tremlett, *apptd* 1994
Plymouth, Ven. R. G. Ellis, *apptd* 1982
Totnes, Preb. R. T. Gilpin, *apptd* 1996

Chancellor, Sir David Calcutt, QC, *apptd* 1971
Registrar and Legal Secretary, R. K. Wheeler
Diocesan Secretary, M. Beedell, Diocesan House, Palace Gate, Exeter, Devon EX1 1HX. Tel: 01392-72686

GIBRALTAR IN EUROPE (Canterbury)

BISHOP
Rt. Revd John Hind, *cons.* 1991, *apptd* 1993; 14 Tufton Street, London SW1P 3QZ

BISHOP SUFFRAGAN
In Europe Rt. Revd Henry Scriven, *cons.* 1995, *apptd* 1994; 14 Tufton Street, London SW1P 3QZ

Dean, Cathedral Church of the Holy Trinity, Gibraltar, Very Revd W. G. Reid

Chancellor, Pro-Cathedral of St Paul, Valletta, Malta, Canon A. Woods
Chancellor, Pro-Cathedral of the Holy Trinity, Brussels, Belgium, Canon N. Walker

ARCHDEACONS
Eastern, Ven. S. J. B. Peake
North-West Europe, Ven. G. G. Allen
France, Ven. M. Draper, OBE
Gibraltar, Ven. K. Robinson
Italy, Ven. W. E. Edebohls
Scandinavia and Germany, Ven. D. Ratcliff
Switzerland, Ven. P. J. Hawker, OBE

Chancellor, Sir David Calcutt, QC
Registrar and Legal Secretary, J. G. Underwood
Diocesan Secretary, A. C. Mumford, 14 Tufton Street, London SW1P 3QZ. Tel: 0171-976 8001

GLOUCESTER (Canterbury)

39TH BISHOP
Rt. Revd David Bentley, *cons.* 1986, *apptd* 1993; Bishopscourt, Gloucester GL1 2BQ. *Signs* David Gloucestr

BISHOP SUFFRAGAN
Tewkesbury, Rt. Revd John S. Went, *cons.* 1995, *apptd* 1995; Green Acre, Hempsted, Gloucester GL2 6LG

DEAN
Very Revd Nicholas A. S. Bury, *apptd* 1997

CANONS RESIDENTIARY
R. D. M. Grey, *apptd* 1982; N. Chatfield, *apptd* 1992; N. Heavisides, *apptd* 1993; C. H. Morgan, *apptd* 1996
Organist, D. Briggs, FRCO, *apptd* 1994

ARCHDEACONS
Cheltenham, Ven. H. S. Ringrose, *apptd* 1998
Gloucester, Ven. C. J. H. Wagstaff, *apptd* 1982

Chancellor and Vicar-General, Ms D. J. Rodgers, *apptd* 1990
Registrar and Legal Secretary, C. G. Peak
Diocesan Secretary, M. Williams, Church House, College Green, Gloucester GL1 2LY. Tel: 01452-410022

GUILDFORD (Canterbury)

8TH BISHOP
Rt. Revd John W. Gladwin, *cons.* 1994, *apptd* 1994; Willow Grange, Woking Road, Guildford GU4 7QS. *Signs* John Guildford

BISHOP SUFFRAGAN
Dorking, Rt. Revd Ian Brackley, *cons.* 1996, *apptd* 1995; Dayspring, 13 Pilgrims Way, Guildford GU4 8AD

DEAN
Very Revd Alexander G. Wedderspoon, *apptd* 1987

CANONS RESIDENTIARY
J. Schofield, *apptd* 1995; Dr Maureen Palmer, *apptd* 1996
Organist, A. Millington, FRCO, *apptd* 1982

ARCHDEACONS
Dorking, Ven. M. Wilson, *apptd* 1995
Surrey, Ven. R. Reiss, *apptd* 1995

Chancellor, His Hon. Judge Goodman
Registrar and Legal Secretary, P. F. B. Beesley

Diocesan Secretary, Mrs K. Ingate, Diocesan House, Quarry Street, Guildford GU1 3XG. Tel: 01483-571826

HEREFORD (Canterbury)

103RD BISHOP
Rt. Revd John Oliver, *cons.* 1990, *apptd* 1990; The Palace, Hereford HR4 9BN. *Signs* John Hereford

BISHOP SUFFRAGAN
Ludlow, Rt. Revd Dr John Saxbee, *cons.* 1994, *apptd* 1994; Bishop's House, Halford, Craven Arms, Shropshire SY7 9BT

DEAN
Very Revd Robert A. Willis, *apptd* 1992

CANONS RESIDENTIARY
P. Iles, *apptd* 1983; J. Tiller, *apptd* 1984; J. Butterworth, *apptd* 1994

Organist, Dr R. Massey, FRCO, *apptd* 1974

ARCHDEACONS
Hereford, Ven. M. W. Hooper, *apptd* 1997
Ludlow, Rt. Revd J. C. Saxbee, *apptd* 1992

Chancellor, J. M. Henty
Joint Registrars and Legal Secretaries, V. T. Jordan; P. F. B. Beesley
Diocesan Secretary, Miss S. Green, The Palace, Hereford HR4 9BL. Tel: 01432-353863

LEICESTER (Canterbury)

BISHOP
vacant; Bishop's Lodge, 10 Springfield Road, Leicester LE2 3BD. *Signs:* — Leicester

STIPENDIARY ASSISTANT BISHOP
Rt. Revd William Down, *cons.* 1990, *apptd* 1995

PROVOST
Very Revd Derek Hole, *apptd* 1992

CANONS RESIDENTIARY
M. T. H. Banks, *apptd* 1988; M. Wilson, *apptd* 1988

Organist, J. T. Gregory, *apptd* 1994

ARCHDEACONS
Leicester, Ven. M. Edson, *apptd* 1994
Loughborough, Ven. I. Stanes, *apptd* 1992

Chancellor, N. Seed, *apptd* 1989
Registrars and Legal Secretaries, P. C. E. Morris; R. H. Bloor
Diocesan Secretary, vacant; Church House, 3–5 St Martin's East, Leicester LE1 5FX. Tel: 0116-262 7445

LICHFIELD (Canterbury)

97TH BISHOP
Rt. Revd Keith N. Sutton, *cons.* 1978, *apptd* 1984; Bishop's House, The Close, Lichfield WS13 7LG. *Signs* Keith Lichfield

BISHOPS SUFFRAGAN
Shrewsbury, Rt. Revd David M. Hallatt, *cons.* 1994, *apptd* 1994; 68 London Road, Shrewsbury SY2 6PG

Stafford, Rt. Revd Christopher J. Hill, *cons.* 1996, *apptd* 1996; Ash Garth, Broughton Crescent, Barlaston, Staffs ST12 9DD
Wolverhampton, Rt. Revd Michael G. Bourke, *cons.* 1993, *apptd* 1993; 61 Richmond Road, Wolverhampton WV3 9JH

DEAN
Very Revd Tom Wright, *apptd* 1993

CANONS RESIDENTIARY
A. N. Barnard, *apptd* 1977; C. W. Taylor, *apptd* 1995; Ven. G. Frost, *apptd* 1998

Organist, A. Lumsden, *apptd* 1992

ARCHDEACONS
Lichfield, Ven. G. Frost, *apptd* 1998
Salop, Ven . J. B. Hall, *apptd* 1998
Stoke-on-Trent, Ven. A. G. C. Smith, *apptd* 1997
Walsall, Ven. A. G. Sadler, *apptd* 1997

Chancellor, His Hon. Judge Shand
Registrar and Legal Secretary, J. P. Thorneycroft
Diocesan Secretary, D. R. Taylor, St Mary's House, The Close, Lichfield, Staffs WS13 7LD. Tel: 01543-306030

LINCOLN (Canterbury)

70TH BISHOP
Rt. Revd Robert M. Hardy, *cons.* 1980, *apptd* 1987; Bishop's House, Eastgate, Lincoln LN2 1QQ. *Signs* Robert Lincoln

BISHOPS SUFFRAGAN
Grantham, Rt. Revd Alastair L. J. Redfern, *cons.* 1997, *apptd* 1997; Fairacre, 234 Barronby Road, Grantham, Lincs NG31 8NP
Grimsby, Rt. Revd David Tustin, *cons.* 1979, *apptd* 1979; Bishop's House, Church Lane, Irby-upon-Humber, Grimsby DN37 7JR

DEAN
Very Revd Alexander F. Knight, *apptd* 1998

CANONS RESIDENTIARY
B. R. Davis, *apptd* 1977; A. J. Stokes, *apptd* 1992; V. White, *apptd* 1994

Organist, C. S. Walsh, FRCO, *apptd* 1988

ARCHDEACONS
Lincoln, Ven. A. Hawes, *apptd* 1995
Lindsey, vacant
Stow, Ven. R. J. Wells, *apptd* 1989

Chancellor, His Hon. Judge Goodman, *apptd* 1971
Registrar and Legal Secretary, D. M. Wellman
Diocesan Secretary, P. Hamlyn Williams, The Old Palace, Lincoln LN2 1PU. Tel: 01522-529241

LIVERPOOL (York)

7TH BISHOP
Rt. Revd James Jones, *cons.* 1994, *apptd* 1998; Bishop's Lodge, Woolton Park, Liverpool L25 6DT. *Signs* James Liverpool

BISHOP SUFFRAGAN
Warrington, Rt. Revd John Packer, *cons.* 1996, *apptd* 1996; 34 Central Avenue, Eccleston Park, Prescot, Merseyside L34 2QP

DEAN
Very Revd Rhys D. C. Walters, OBE, *apptd* 1983

CANONS RESIDENTIARY
D. J. Hutton, *apptd* 1983; M. C. Boyling, *apptd* 1994; N. T. Vincent, *apptd* 1995
Organist, Prof. I. Tracey, *apptd* 1980

ARCHDEACONS
Liverpool, Ven. R. L. Metcalf, *apptd* 1994
Warrington, Ven. C. D. S. Woodhouse, *apptd* 1981

Chancellor, R. G. Hamilton
Registrar and Legal Secretary, R. H. Arden
Diocesan Secretary, K. Cawdron, Church House, 1 Hanover Street, Liverpool L1 3DW. Tel: 0151-709 9722

MANCHESTER (York)

10TH BISHOP
Rt. Revd Christopher J. Mayfield, *cons.* 1985, *apptd* 1993; Bishopscourt, Bury New Road, Manchester M7 4LE. *Signs* Christopher Manchester

BISHOPS SUFFRAGAN
Bolton, Rt. Revd David Bonser, *cons.* 1991, *apptd* 1991; 4 Sandfield Drive, Lostock, Bolton BL6 4DU
Hulme, Rt. Revd Colin J. F. Scott, *cons.* 1984, *apptd* 1984 (retires 31 Dec. 1998); 1 Raynham Avenue, Didsbury, Manchester M20 0BW
Middleton, Rt. Revd Stephen Venner, *cons.* 1994, *apptd* 1994; The Hollies, Manchester Road, Rochdale OL11 3QY

DEAN
Very Revd Kenneth Riley, *apptd* 1993

CANONS RESIDENTIARY
J. R. Atherton, PH.D., *apptd* 1984; A. E. Radcliffe, *apptd* 1991; P. Denby, *apptd* 1995
Organist, C. Stokes, *apptd* 1992

ARCHDEACONS
Bolton, Ven. L. M. Davies, *apptd* 1992
Manchester, vacant
Rochdale, Ven. J. M. M. Dalby, *apptd* 1991

Chancellor, J. Holden, *apptd* 1997
Registrar and Legal Secretary, M. Darlington
Diocesan Secretary, Mrs J. Park, Diocesan Church House, 90 Deansgate, Manchester M3 2GH. Tel: 0161-833 9521

NEWCASTLE (York)

11TH BISHOP
Rt. Revd J. Martin Wharton, *cons.* 1992, *apptd* 1997; Bishop's House, 29 Moor Road South, Gosforth, Newcastle upon Tyne NE3 1PA. *Signs* Martin Newcastle

STIPENDIARY ASSISTANT BISHOP
Rt. Revd Kenneth Gill, *cons.* 1972, *apptd* 1980

PROVOST
Very Revd Nicholas G. Coulton, *apptd* 1990

CANONS RESIDENTIARY
R. Langley, *apptd* 1985; P. R. Strange, *apptd* 1986; Ven. P. Elliott, *apptd* 1993
Organist, T. G. Hone, FRCO, *apptd* 1987

ARCHDEACONS
Lindisfarne, Ven. M. E. Bowering, *apptd* 1987
Northumberland, Ven. P. Elliott, *apptd* 1993

Chancellor, Prof. D. McClean, *apptd* 1998

Registrar and Legal Secretary, Mrs B. J. Lowdon
Diocesan Secretary, P. Davies, Church House, Grainger Park Road, Newcastle upon Tyne NE4 8SX. Tel: 0191-273 0120

NORWICH (Canterbury)

70TH BISHOP
Rt. Revd Peter J. Nott, *cons.* 1977, *apptd* 1985; Bishop's House, Norwich NR3 1SB. *Signs* Peter Norvic:

BISHOPS SUFFRAGAN
Lynn, vacant
Thetford, Rt. Revd Hugo F. de Waal, *cons.* 1992, *apptd* 1992; Rectory Meadow, Bramerton, Norwich NR14 7DW

DEAN
Very Revd Stephen Platten, *apptd* 1995

CANONS RESIDENTIARY
J. M. Haselock, *apptd* 1998; Ven. C. J. Offer, *apptd* 1994; R. J. Hanmer, *apptd* 1994
Organist, D. Dunnett, *apptd* 1996

ARCHDEACONS
Lynn, Ven. A. C. Foottit, *apptd* 1987
Norfolk, Ven. A. M. Handley, *apptd* 1993
Norwich, Ven. C. J. Offer, *apptd* 1994

Chancellor, The Hon. Mr Justice Blofeld, *apptd* 1998
Registrar and Legal Secretary, J. W. F. Herring
Diocesan Secretary, D. Adeney, Diocesan House, 109 Dereham Road, Easton, Norwich, Norfolk NR9 5ES. Tel: 01603-880853

OXFORD (Canterbury)

41ST BISHOP
Rt. Revd Richard D. Harries, *cons.* 1987, *apptd* 1987; Diocesan Church House, North Hinksey, Oxford OX2 0NB. *Signs* Richard Oxon:

AREA BISHOPS
Buckingham, Rt. Revd Michael A. Hill *cons.* 1998, *apptd* 1998; 28 Church Street, Great Missenden, Bucks HP16 0AZ
Dorchester, Rt. Revd Anthony J. Russell, *cons.* 1988, *apptd* 1988; Holmby House, Sibford Ferris, Banbury, Oxon OX15 5RG
Reading, Rt. Revd Edward W. M. (Dominic) Walker, *cons.* 1997, *apptd* 1997; Bishop's House, Tidmarsh Lane, Tidmarsh, Reading RG8 8HA

DEAN OF CHRIST CHURCH
Very Revd John H. Drury, *apptd* 1991

CANONS RESIDENTIARY
O. M. T. O'Donovan, D.PHIL., *apptd* 1982; J. M. Pierce, *apptd* 1987; J. S. K. Ward, *apptd* 1991; R. Jeffery, *apptd* 1996; Prof. J. Webster, *apptd* 1996; Prof. H. M. R. E. Mayr-Harting, *apptd* 1997; Ven. J. A. Morrison, *apptd* 1998
Organist, S. Darlington, FRCO, *apptd* 1985

ARCHDEACONS
Berkshire, Ven. N. A. Russell, *apptd* 1998
Buckingham, Ven. D. Goldie, *apptd* 1998
Oxford, Ven. J. A. Morrison, *apptd* 1998

Chancellor, P. T. S. Boydell, QC, *apptd* 1958
Registrar and Legal Secretary, Dr F. E. Robson
Diocesan Secretary, R. Pearce, Diocesan Church House, North Hinksey, Oxford OX2 0NB. Tel: 01865-244566

PETERBOROUGH (Canterbury)

37TH BISHOP
Rt. Revd Ian P. M. Cundy, *cons.* 1992, *apptd* 1996; The
Palace, Peterborough PEI IYA. *Signs* Ian Petriburg:

BISHOP SUFFRAGAN
Brixworth, Rt. Revd Paul E. Barber, *cons.* 1989, *apptd* 1989; 4
The Avenue, Dallington, Northampton NNI 4RZ

DEAN
Very Revd Michael Bunker, *apptd* 1992

CANONS RESIDENTIARY
T. R. Christie, *apptd* 1980; J. Higham, *apptd* 1983; P. A.
Spence, *apptd* 1998

Organist, C. S. Gower, FRCO, *apptd* 1977

ARCHDEACONS
Northampton, Ven. M. R. Chapman, *apptd* 1991
Oakham, Ven. B. Fernyhough, *apptd* 1977

Chancellor, T. A. C. Coningsby, QC, *apptd* 1989
Registrar and Legal Secretary, R. Hemingray
Diocesan Secretary, Revd Canon R. J. Cattle, The Palace,
Peterborough, Cambs PEI IYB. Tel: 01733-64448

PORTSMOUTH (Canterbury)

8TH BISHOP
Rt. Revd Dr Kenneth W. Stevenson, *cons.* 1995, *apptd* 1995;
Bishopsgrove, 26 Osborn Road, Fareham, Hants PO16
7DQ. *Signs* Kenneth Portsmouth

PROVOST
Very Revd Michael L. Yorke, *apptd* 1994

CANONS RESIDENTIARY
D. T. Isaac, *apptd* 1990; Jane B. Hedges, *apptd* 1993; G. Kirk,
apptd 1998

Organist, D. J. C. Price, *apptd* 1996

ARCHDEACONS
Isle of Wight, Ven. K. M. L. H. Banting, *apptd* 1996
Portsmouth, vacant

Chancellor, His Hon. Judge Aglionby, *apptd* 1978
Registrar and Legal Secretary, Miss H. A. G. Tyler
Diocesan Secretary, M. F. Jordan, Cathedral House, St
Thomas's Street, Portsmouth, Hants PO1 2HA. Tel:
01705-825731

RIPON (York)

11TH BISHOP
Rt. Revd David N. de L. Young, *cons.* 1977, *apptd* 1977;
Bishop Mount, Ripon HG4 5DP. *Signs* David Ripon

BISHOP SUFFRAGAN
Knaresborough, Rt. Revd Frank V. Weston, *cons.* 1997, *apptd*
1997; 16 Shaftesbury Avenue, Roundhay, Leeds LS8 IDT

DEAN
Very Revd John Methuen, *apptd* 1995

CANONS RESIDENTIARY
M. R. Glanville-Smith, *apptd* 1990; K. Punshon, *apptd* 1996;
J. Bell, *apptd* 1997

Organist, K. Beaumont, FRCO, *apptd* 1994

ARCHDEACONS
Leeds, Ven. J. M. Oliver, *apptd* 1992
Richmond, Ven. K. Good, *apptd* 1993

Chancellor, His Hon. Judge Grenfell, *apptd* 1992
Registrar and Legal Secretary, J. R. Balmforth
Diocesan Secretary, P. M. Arundel, Diocesan Office, St
Mary's Street, Leeds LS9 7DP. Tel: 0113-248 7487

ROCHESTER (Canterbury)

106TH BISHOP
Rt. Revd Dr Michael Nazir-Ali, *cons.* 1984, *apptd* 1994;
Bishopscourt, Rochester MEI ITS. *Signs* Michael Roffen:

BISHOP SUFFRAGAN
Tonbridge, Rt. Revd Brian A. Smith, *cons.* 1993, *apptd* 1993;
Bishop's Lodge, 48 St Botolph's Road, Sevenoaks TN13
3AG

DEAN
Very Revd Edward F. Shotter, *apptd* 1990

CANONS RESIDENTIARY
E. R. Turner, *apptd* 1981; J. M. Armson, *apptd* 1989; N. L.
Warren, *apptd* 1989; C. J. Meyrick, *apptd* 1998

Organist, R. Sayer, FRCO, *apptd* 1995

ARCHDEACONS
Bromley, Ven. G. Norman, *apptd* 1994
Rochester, Ven. N. L. Warren, *apptd* 1989
Tonbridge, Ven. Judith Rose, *apptd* 1996

Chancellor, His Hon. Judge Goodman, *apptd* 1971
Registrar and Legal Secretary, M. Thatcher
Diocesan Secretary, P. Law, St Nicholas Church, Boley Hill,
Rochester MEI ISL. Tel: 01634-830333

ST ALBANS (Canterbury)

9TH BISHOP
Rt. Revd Christopher W. Herbert, *cons.* 1995, *apptd* 1995;
Abbey Gate House, St Albans AL3 4HD. *Signs* Christopher
St Albans

BISHOPS SUFFRAGAN
Bedford, Rt. Revd John H. Richardson, *cons.* 1994, *apptd*
1994; 168 Kimbolton Road, Bedford MK41 8DN
Hertford, Rt. Revd Robin J. N. Smith, *cons.* 1990, *apptd* 1990;
Hertford House, Abbey Mill Lane, St Albans AL3 4HE

DEAN
Very Revd Christopher Lewis, *apptd* 1993

CANONS RESIDENTIARY
C. Garner, *apptd* 1984; G. R. S. Ritson, *apptd* 1987;
M. Sansom, *apptd* 1988; C. R. J. Foster, *apptd* 1994

Organist, A. Lucas, *apptd* 1998

ARCHDEACONS
Bedford, Ven. M. L. Lesiter, *apptd* 1993
Hertford, Ven. T. P. Jones, *apptd* 1997
St Albans, Ven. R. I. Cheetham, *apptd* 1998 (from March
1999)

Chancellor, His Hon. Judge Bursell, QC, *apptd* 1992
Registrar and Legal Secretary, D. N. Cheetham
Diocesan Secretary, L. Nicholls, Holywell Lodge, 41
Holywell Hill, St Albans ALI IHE. Tel: 01727-854532

ST EDMUNDSBURY AND IPSWICH
(Canterbury)

9TH BISHOP
Rt. Revd J. H. Richard Lewis, *cons.* 1992, *apptd* 1997;
Bishop's House, 4 Park Road, Ipswich IP1 3ST. *Signs*
Richard St Edmundsbury and Ipswich

BISHOP SUFFRAGAN
Dunwich, Rt. Revd Timothy J. Stevens, *cons.* 1995, *apptd*
1995; The Old Vicarage, Stowupland, Stowmarket
IP14 4BQ

PROVOST
Very Revd J. Atwell, *apptd* 1995

CANONS RESIDENTIARY
A. M. Shaw, *apptd* 1989; M. E. Mingins, *apptd* 1993

Organist, J. Thomas, *apptd* 1997

ARCHDEACONS
Ipswich, Ven. T. A. Gibson, *apptd* 1987
Sudbury, Ven. J. Cox, *apptd* 1995
Suffolk, Ven. G. Arrand, *apptd* 1994

Chancellor, The Hon. Mr Justice Blofeld, *apptd* 1974
Registrar and Legal Secretary, J. Hall
Diocesan Secretary, N. Edgell, 13–15 Tower Street, Ipswich
IP1 3BG. Tel: 01473-211028

SALISBURY (Canterbury)

77TH BISHOP
Rt. Revd David S. Stancliffe, *cons.* 1993, *apptd* 1993; South
Canonry, The Close, Salisbury SP1 2ER. *Signs* David
Sarum

BISHOPS SUFFRAGAN
Ramsbury, vacant
Sherborne, Rt. Revd John D. G. Kirkham, *cons.* 1976, *apptd*
1976; Little Bailie, Sturminster Marshall, Wimborne
BH21 4AD

DEAN
Very Revd Derek Watson, *apptd* 1996

CANONS RESIDENTIARY
D. J. C. Davies, *apptd* 1985; D. M. K. Durston, *apptd* 1992;
June Osborne, *apptd* 1995

Organist, S. R. A. Lole, *apptd* 1997

ARCHDEACONS
Dorset, Ven. G. E. Walton, *apptd* 1982
Sherborne, Ven. P. C. Wheatley, *apptd* 1991
Wilts, Ven. B. J. Hopkinson, *apptd* 1986 (Sarum), 1998
(Wilts)

Chancellor, His Hon. Judge Wiggs, *apptd* 1997
Registrar and Legal Secretary, A. Johnson
Diocesan Secretary, Revd Karen Curnock, Church House,
Crane Street, Salisbury SP1 2QB. Tel: 01722-411922

SHEFFIELD (York)

6TH BISHOP
Rt. Revd John (Jack) Nicholls, *cons.* 1990, *apptd* 1997;
Bishopscroft, Snaithing Lane, Sheffield S10 3LG. *Signs*
Jack Sheffield

BISHOP SUFFRAGAN
Doncaster, Rt. Revd Michael F. Gear, *cons.* 1993, *apptd* 1993;
Bishops Lodge, Hooton Roberts, Rotherham S65 4PF

PROVOST
Very Revd Michael Sadgrove, *apptd* 1995

CANONS RESIDENTIARY
T. M. Page, *apptd* 1982; Ven. S. R. Lowe, *apptd* 1988;
C. M. Smith, *apptd* 1991; Jane E. M. Sinclair, *apptd* 1993

Organist, N. Taylor, *apptd* 1997

ARCHDEACONS
Doncaster, Ven. B. L. Holdridge, *apptd* 1994
Sheffield, Ven. S. R. Lowe, *apptd* 1988

Chancellor, Prof. J. D. McClean, *apptd* 1992
Registrar and Legal Secretary, Mrs M. Myers
Diocesan Secretary, C. A. Beck, FCIS, Diocesan Church
House, 95–99 Effingham Street, Rotherham S65 1BL.
Tel: 01709-511116

SODOR AND MAN (York)

79TH BISHOP
Rt. Revd Noel D. Jones, CB, *cons.* 1989, *apptd* 1989; The
Bishop's House, Quarterbridge Road, Douglas, Isle of
Man IM2 3RF. *Signs* Noel Sodor and Man

CANONS
B. H. Kelly, *apptd* 1980; F. H. Bird, *apptd* 1993; D. Whitworth,
apptd 1996; P. Robinson, *apptd* 1998

ARCHDEACON
Isle of Man, Ven. B. H. Partington, *apptd* 1996

Vicar-General and Chancellor, Ms C. Faulds
Registrar and Legal Secretary, C. J. Callow
Diocesan Secretary, The Hon. C. Murphy, c/o 26 The
Fountains, Ramsey, Isle of Man IM8 2AR. Tel: 01624-
816545

SOUTHWARK (Canterbury)

9TH BISHOP
Rt. Revd Thomas F. Butler, PH.D, LLD, *cons.* 1985, *apptd*
1998; Bishop's House, 38 Tooting Bec Gardens, London
SW16 1QZ. *Signs* Thomas Southwark

AREA BISHOPS
Croydon, Rt. Revd Dr Wilfred D. Wood, DD, *cons.* 1985, *apptd*
1985; St Matthew's House, George Street, Croydon CR0
1PE
Kingston upon Thames, Rt Revd Peter B. Price, *cons.* 1997,
apptd 1998; *Kingston Episcopal Area Office*, Whitelands
College, West Hill, London SW15 3SN
Woolwich, Rt. Revd Colin O. Buchanan, *cons.* 1985, *apptd*
1996; 37 South Road, Forest Hill, London SE23 2UJ

PROVOST
Very Revd Colin B. Slee, *apptd* 1994

CANONS RESIDENTIARY
D. Painter, *apptd* 1991; R. White, *apptd* 1991; Helen Cunliffe,
apptd 1995; J. John, *apptd* 1997; B. Saunders, *apptd* 1997

Organist, P. Wright, FRCO, *apptd* 1989

ARCHDEACONS
Croydon, Ven. V. A. Davies, *apptd* 1994
Lambeth, Ven. C. R. B. Bird, *apptd* 1988
Lewisham, Ven. D. J. Atkinson, *apptd* 1996
Reigate, Ven. M. Baddeley, *apptd* 1996

Southwark, Ven. D. L. Bartles-Smith, *apptd* 1985
Wandsworth, Ven. D. Gerrard, *apptd* 1989

Chancellor, C. George, QC
Registrar and Legal Secretary, P. Morris
Diocesan Secretary, S. Parton, Trinity House, 4 Chapel
Court, Borough High Street, London SE1 1HW. Tel: 0171-
403 8686

SOUTHWELL (York)

9TH BISHOP
Rt. Revd Patrick B. Harris, *cons.* 1973, *apptd* 1988; Bishop's
Manor, Southwell NG25 0JR. *Signs* Patrick Southwell

BISHOP SUFFRAGAN
Sherwood, Rt. Revd Alan W. Morgan, *cons.* 1989, *apptd* 1989;
Sherwood House, High Oakham Road, Mansfield
NG18 5AJ

PROVOST
Very Revd David Leaning, *apptd* 1991

CANONS RESIDENTIARY
I. G. Collins, *apptd* 1985; G. A. Hendy *apptd* 1997
Organist, P. Hale, *apptd* 1989

ARCHDEACONS
Newark, Ven. D. C. Hawtin, *apptd* 1992
Nottingham, Ven. G. Ogilvie, *apptd* 1996

Chancellor, J. Shand, *apptd* 1981
Registrar and Legal Secretary, C. C. Hodson
Diocesan Secretary, B. Noake, Dunham House, Westgate,
Southwell, Notts NG25 0JL. Tel: 01636-814331

TRURO (Canterbury)

14TH BISHOP
Rt. Revd William Ind, *cons.* 1987, *apptd* 1997; Lis Escop, Truro
TR3 6QQ. *Signs* William Truro

BISHOP SUFFRAGAN
St Germans, Rt. Revd Graham R. James, *cons.* 1993, *apptd*
1993; 32 Falmouth Road, Truro TR1 2HX

DEAN
Very Revd Michael A. Moxon, LVO, *apptd* 1998

CANONS RESIDENTIARY
P. R. Gay, *apptd* 1994; K. P. Mellor, *apptd* 1994; P. D.
Goodridge, *apptd* 1996
Organist, A. Nethsingha, FRCO, *apptd* 1994

ARCHDEACONS
Cornwall, Ven. J. T. McCabe, *apptd* 1996
Bodmin, Ven. R. D. C. Whiteman, *apptd* 1989

Chancellor, T. Briden, *apptd* 1998
Registrar and Legal Secretary, M. J. Follett
Diocesan Secretary, B. C. Laite, Diocesan House, Kenwyn,
Truro TR1 3DU. Tel: 01872-274351

WAKEFIELD (York)

11TH BISHOP
Rt. Revd Nigel S. McCulloch, *cons.* 1986, *apptd* 1992;
Bishop's Lodge, Woodthorpe Lane, Wakefield WF2 6JL.
Signs Nigel Wakefield

BISHOP SUFFRAGAN
Pontefract, Rt. Revd David James, *cons.* 1998, *apptd* 1998;
Pontefract House, 181A Manygates Lane, Wakefield
WF2 7DR

PROVOST
Very Revd George P. Nairn-Briggs, *apptd* 1997

CANONS RESIDENTIARY
R. Capper, *apptd* 1997; R. Gage, *apptd* 1997; I. Gaskell, *apptd*
1998; J. Holmes, *apptd* 1998

Organist, J. Bielby, FRCO, *apptd* 1972

ARCHDEACONS
Halifax, Ven. R. Inwood, *apptd* 1995
Pontefract, Ven. A. Robinson, *apptd* 1997

Chancellor, P. Collier, QC, *apptd* 1992
Registrar and Legal Secretary, L. Box
Diocesan Secretary, W. J. B. Smith, Church House, 1 South
Parade, Wakefield WF1 1LP. Tel: 01924-371802

WORCESTER (Canterbury)

112TH BISHOP
Rt. Revd Dr Peter S. M. Selby, *cons.* 1984, *apptd* 1997; The
Bishop's House, Hartlebury Castle, Kidderminster DY11
7XX. *Signs* Peter Wigorn:

BISHOP SUFFRAGAN
Dudley, Rt. Revd Dr Rupert Hoare, *cons.* 1993, *apptd* 1993;
The Bishop's House, Brooklands, Halesowen Road,
Cradley Heath B64 7JF

DEAN
Very Revd Peter J. Marshall, *apptd* 1997

CANONS RESIDENTIARY
Ven. F. Bentley, *apptd* 1984; D. G. Thomas, *apptd* 1987;
I. M. MacKenzie, *apptd* 1989

Organist, A. Lucas, *apptd* 1996

ARCHDEACONS
Dudley, Ven. J. Gathercole, *apptd* 1987
Worcester, Ven. F. Bentley, *apptd* 1984

Deputy Chancellor, C. Nynors, *apptd* 1998
Registrar and Legal Secretary, M. Huskinson
Diocesan Secretary, J. Stanbury (until 31 Dec. 1998), The
Old Palace, Deansway, Worcester WR1 2JE. Tel: 01905-
20537

ROYAL PECULIARS

WESTMINSTER
The Collegiate Church of St Peter

Dean, Very Revd Dr A. W. Carr, *apptd* 1997
Sub Dean and Archdeacon, A. E. Harvey, *apptd* 1987
Canons of Westminster, A. E. Harvey, *apptd* 1982; D. H. Hutt,
apptd 1995; M. J. Middleton, *apptd* 1997; R. Wright, *apptd*
1998
Chapter Clerk and Receiver-General, vacant
Organist, vacant
Registrar, S. J. Holmes, MVO, 20 Dean's Yard, London
SW1P 3PA
Legal Secretary, C. L. Hodgetts

WINDSOR
The Queen's Free Chapel of St George within Her Castle of Windsor

Dean, Very Revd D. J. Conner, *apptd* 1998
Canons Residentiary, J. A. White, *apptd* 1982; L. F. P. Gunner, *apptd* 1996; B. P. Thompson, PH.D., *apptd* 1998; J. A. Ovenden, *apptd* 1998
Chapter Clerk, Lt.-Col. N. J. Newman, *apptd* 1990, Chapter Office, The Cloisters, Windsor Castle, Windsor, Berks SL4 1NJ
Organist, J. Rees-Williams, FRCO, *apptd* 1991

Other Anglican Churches

THE CHURCH IN WALES

The Anglican Church was the established church in Wales from the 16th century until 1920, when the estrangement of the majority of Welsh people from Anglicanism resulted in disestablishment. Since then the Church in Wales has been an autonomous province consisting of six sees. The bishops are elected by an electoral college comprising elected lay and clerical members, who also elect one of the diocesan bishops as Archbishop of Wales.

The legislative body of the Church in Wales is the Governing Body, which has 365 members divided between the three orders of bishops, clergy and laity. Its President is the Archbishop of Wales and it meets twice annually. Its decisions are binding upon all members of the Church. The Church's property and finances are the responsibility of the Representative Body. There are about 96,000 members of the Church in Wales, with about 700 stipendiary clergy and 1,142 parishes.

THE GOVERNING BODY OF THE CHURCH IN WALES, 39 Cathedral Road, Cardiff CF1 9XF. Tel: 01222-231638. *Secretary-General,* J. W. D. McIntyre

10TH ARCHBISHOP OF WALES, Most Revd Alwyn R. Jones (Bishop of St Asaph), *elected* 1991

BISHOPS
Bangor (79*th*), Rt. Revd Dr Barry C. Morgan, *b.* 1947, *cons.* 1993, *elected* 1992; Tŷ'r Esgob, Bangor LL57 2SS. *Signs* Barry Bangor. *Stipendiary clergy,* 65
Llandaff (101*st*), Rt. Revd Roy T. Davies, *b.* 1934, *cons.* 1985, *elected* 1985; Llys Esgob, The Cathedral Green, Llandaff, Cardiff CF5 2YE. *Signs* Roy Landav. *Stipendiary clergy*, 167
Monmouth (8*th*), Rt. Revd Rowan D. Williams, *b* 1950, *cons.* 1992, *elected* 1992; Bishopstow, Stow Hill, Newport NP9 4EA. *Signs* Rowan Monmouth. *Stipendiary clergy,* 120
St Asaph (74*th*), Most Revd Alwyn R. Jones, *b.* 1934, *cons.* 1982, *elected* 1982; Esgobty, St Asaph, Clwyd LL17 0TW. *Signs* Alwyn Cambrensis. *Stipendiary clergy,* 112
St David's (126*th*), Rt. Revd D. Huw Jones, *b.* 1934, *cons.* 1993, *elected* 1995; Llys Esgob, Abergwili, Carmarthen SA31 2JG. *Signs* Huw St Davids. *Stipendiary clergy,* 138
Swansea and Brecon (7*th*), Rt. Revd Dewi M. Bridges, *b.* 1933, *cons.* 1988, *elected* 1988 (retires 30 Nov. 1998); Ely Tower, Brecon, Powys LD3 9DE. *Signs* Dewi Swansea Brecon. *Stipendiary clergy,* 100

The stipend of a diocesan bishop of the Church in Wales is £26,674 a year from 1998

THE SCOTTISH EPISCOPAL CHURCH

The Scottish Episcopal Church was founded after the Act of Settlement (1690) established the presbyterian nature of the Church of Scotland. The Scottish Episcopal Church is in full communion with the Church of England but is autonomous. The governing authority is the General Synod, an elected body of 180 members which meets once a year. The diocesan bishop who convenes and presides at meetings of the General Synod is called the Primus and is elected by his fellow bishops.

There are 54,382 members of the Scottish Episcopal Church, of whom 33,795 are communicants. There are seven bishops, 210 stipendiary clergy, and 320 churches and places of worship.

THE GENERAL SYNOD OF THE SCOTTISH EPISCOPAL CHURCH, 21 Grosvenor Crescent, Edinburgh EH12 5EE. Tel: 0131-225 6357. *Secretary-General,* J. F. Stuart

PRIMUS OF THE SCOTTISH EPISCOPAL CHURCH, Most Revd Richard F. Holloway (Bishop of Edinburgh), *elected* 1992

BISHOPS
Aberdeen and Orkney, A. Bruce Cameron, *b.* 1941, *cons.* 1992, *elected* 1992. *Clergy,* 19
Argyll and the Isles, Douglas M. Cameron, *b.* 1935, *cons.* 1993, *elected* 1992. *Clergy,* 9
Brechin, Neville Chamberlain, *b.* 1939, *cons.* 1997, *elected* 1997. *Clergy,* 19
Edinburgh, Richard F. Holloway, *b.* 1933, *cons.* 1986, *elected* 1986. *Clergy,* 53
Glasgow and Galloway, vacant. *Clergy,* 48
Moray, Ross and Caithness, Gregor Macgregor, *b.* 1933, *cons.* 1994, *elected* 1994. *Clergy,* 13
St Andrews, Dunkeld and Dunblane, Michael H. G. Henley, *b.* 1938, *cons.* 1995, *elected* 1995. *Clergy,* 30

The minimum stipend of a diocesan bishop of the Scottish Episcopal Church was £21,510 in 1998 (i.e. 1.5 × the minimum clergy stipend of £14,340)

THE CHURCH OF IRELAND

The Anglican Church was the established church in Ireland from the 16th century but never secured the allegiance of a majority of the Irish and was disestablished in 1871. The Church in Ireland is divided into the provinces of Armagh and Dublin, each under an archbishop. The provinces are subdivided into 12 dioceses.

The legislative body is the General Synod, which has 660 members in total, divided between the House of Bishops and the House of Representatives. The Archbishop of Armagh is elected by the House of Bishops; other episcopal elections are made by an electoral college.

There are about 375,000 members of the Church of Ireland, with two archbishops, ten bishops, about 600 clergy and about 1,000 churches and places of worship.

CENTRAL OFFICE, Church of Ireland House, Church Avenue, Rathmines, Dublin 6. Tel: 00-353-1-4978422. *Chief Officer and Secretary of the Representative Church Body,* R. H. Sherwood; *Assistant Secretary of the General Synod,* V. F. Beatty

PROVINCE OF ARMAGH

ARCHBISHOP OF ARMAGH AND PRIMATE OF ALL IRELAND, Most Revd Robert H. A. Eames, ph.D., *b.* 1937, *cons.* 1975, *trans.* 1986. *Clergy*, 51

BISHOPS
Clogher, Brian D. A. Hannon, *b.* 1936, *cons.* 1986, *apptd* 1986. *Clergy*, 32
Connor, James E. Moore, *b.* 1933, *cons.* 1995, *apptd.* 1995. *Clergy*, 106
Derry and Raphoe, James Mehaffey, ph.D., *b.* 1931, *cons.* 1980, *apptd* 1980. *Clergy*, 50
Down and Dromore, Harold C. Miller, *b.* 1950, *cons.* 1997, *apptd* 1997. *Clergy*, 109
Kilmore, Elphin and Ardagh, Michael H. G. Mayes, *b.* 1941, *cons.* 1993, *apptd* 1993. *Clergy*, 24
Tuam, Killala and Achonry, Richard C. A. Henderson, *b.* 1957, *cons.* 1998, *apptd* 1998. *Clergy*, 12

PROVINCE OF DUBLIN

ARCHBISHOP OF DUBLIN, BISHOP OF GLENDALOUGH, AND PRIMATE OF IRELAND, Most Revd Walton N. F. Empey, *b.* 1934, *cons.* 1981, *trans.* 1985, 1996. *Clergy*, 90

BISHOPS
Cashel and Ossory, John R. W. Neill, *b.* 1945, *cons.* 1986, *trans.* 1997. *Clergy*, 37
Cork, Cloyne and Ross, Robert A. Warke, *b.* 1930, *cons.* 1988, *apptd* 1988. *Clergy*, 28
Limerick and Killaloe, Edward F. Darling, *b.* 1933, *cons.* 1985, *apptd* 1985. *Clergy*, 23
Meath and Kildare, (Most Revd) Robert L. Clarke, ph.D., *b.* 1949, *cons.* 1996, *apptd* 1996. *Clergy*, 23

OVERSEAS

PRIMATES

PRIMATE AND PRESIDING BISHOP OF AOTEAROA, NEW ZEALAND AND POLYNESIA, Rt. Revd John Paterson (Bishop of Auckland), *cons.* 1995, *apptd* 1998
PRIMATE OF AUSTRALIA, Most Revd Keith Rayner (Archbishop of Melbourne), *cons.* 1969, *apptd* 1991
PRIMATE OF BRAZIL, Most Revd Glauco Soares de Lima (Bishop of São Paulo), *cons.* 1989, *apptd* 1994
ARCHBISHOP OF THE PROVINCE OF BURUNDI, Most Revd Samuel Ndayisenga (Bishop of Buye), *apptd* 1998
ARCHBISHOP AND PRIMATE OF CANADA, Most Revd Michael G. Peers, *cons.* 1977, *elected* 1986
ARCHBISHOP OF THE PROVINCE OF CENTRAL AFRICA, Most Revd Walter P. K. Makhulu (Bishop of Botswana), *cons.* 1979, *apptd* 1980
PRIMATE OF THE CENTRAL REGION OF AMERICA, Most Revd Cornelius J. Wilson (Bishop of Costa Rica)
ARCHBISHOP OF THE PROVINCE OF CONGO, Most Revd Byankya Njojo (Bishop of Boga), *cons.* 1980, *apptd* 1992
ARCHBISHOP OF THE PROVINCE OF THE INDIAN OCEAN, Most Revd Remi Rabenirina (Bishop of Antananarivo), *cons.* 1984, *apptd* 1995
PRIMATE OF JAPAN , Rt. Revd John M. Takeda (Bishop of Tokyo), *cons.* 1988, *apptd* 1998
PRESIDENT -BISHOP OF JERUSALEM AND THE MIDDLE EAST, Rt. Revd Ghais A. Malik (Bishop of Egypt), *cons.* 1984, *apptd* 1996
ARCHBISHOP OF THE PROVINCE OF KENYA, Most Revd Dr David Gitari (Bishop of Nairobi), *cons.* 1975, *apptd* 1996
ARCHBISHOP OF THE PROVINCE OF KOREA, Most Revd Bundo C. H. Kim (Bishop of Pusan), *cons.* 1988, *apptd* 1995

ARCHBISHOP OF THE PROVINCE OF MELANESIA, Most Revd Ellison L. Pogo (Bishop of Central Melanesia), *cons.* 1981, *apptd* 1994
ARCHBISHOP OF MEXICO, Most Revd José G. Saucedo (Bishop of Cuernavaca), *cons.* 1958, *elected* 1995
ARCHBISHOP OF THE PROVINCE OF MYANMAR, Most Revd Andrew Mya Han (Bishop of Yangon), *cons.* 1988, *apptd* 1988
ARCHBISHOP OF THE PROVINCE OF NIGERIA, Most Revd Joseph Adetiloye (Bishop of Lagos), *apptd* 1991
ARCHBISHOP OF PAPUA NEW GUINEA, Most Revd James Ayong (Bishop of Aipo Rongo), *cons.* 1995, *elected* 1996
PRIME BISHOP OF THE PHILIPPINES, Most Revd Ignacio C. Soliba, *cons.* 1990, *apptd* 1997
ARCHBISHOP OF THE PROVINCE OF RWANDA, Most Revd Kolini Mboni (Bishop of Kigali)
METROPOLITAN OF THE PROVINCE OF SOUTHERN AFRICA, Most Revd Winston H. N. Ndungane *(*Archbishop of Cape Town), *cons.* 1991, *trans.* 1996
PRESIDING BISHOP OF THE SOUTHERN CONE OF AMERICA, Rt. Revd Maurice Sinclair (Bishop of Northern Argentina), *cons.* 1990
ARCHBISHOP OF THE PROVINCE OF THE SUDAN, Most Revd Benjamin W. Yugusuk (Bishop of Juba)
ARCHBISHOP OF THE PROVINCE OF TANZANIA, Most Revd Donald Mtetemela (Bishop of Ruaha), *cons.* 1982, *apptd* 1998
ARCHBISHOP OF THE PROVINCE OF UGANDA, Most Revd Livingstone Mpalanyi-Nkoyoyo (Bishop of Kampala)
PRESIDING BISHOP AND PRIMATE OF THE USA, Most Revd Frank T. Griswold III, *cons.* 1985, *apptd* 1997
ARCHBISHOP OF THE PROVINCE OF WEST AFRICA, Most Revd Robert Okine (Bishop of Koforidua), *cons.* 1981, *apptd* 1993
ARCHBISHOP OF THE PROVINCE OF THE WEST INDIES, Most Revd Orland Lindsay (Bishop of North-Eastern Caribbean and Aruba), *cons.* 1970, *apptd* 1986

OTHER CHURCHES AND EXTRA-PROVINCIAL DIOCESES

ANGLICAN CHURCH OF BERMUDA, Rt. Revd Ewen Ratteray, *apptd* 1996
EPISCOPAL CHURCH OF CUBA, Rt. Revd Jorge Perera Hurtado, *apptd* 1995
HONG KONG AND MACAO, Rt. Revd Peter Kwong
KUCHING, Rt. Revd Made Katib, *apptd* 1995
LUSITANIAN CHURCH (*Portuguese Episcopal Church*), Rt. Revd Fernando da Luz Soares, *apptd* 1971
SPANISH REFORMED EPISCOPAL CHURCH, Rt. Revd Carlos Lozano Lopez, *apptd* 1995

The Church of Scotland

The Church of Scotland is the established (i.e. state) church of Scotland. The Church is Reformed and evangelical in doctrine, and presbyterian in constitution, i.e. based on a hierarchy of councils of ministers and elders and, since 1990, of members of a diaconate. At local level the kirk session consists of the parish minister and ruling elders. At district level the presbyteries, of which there are 47, consist of all the ministers in the district, one ruling elder from each congregation, and those members of the diaconate who qualify for membership. The General Assembly is the supreme authority, and is presided over by a Moderator chosen annually by the Assembly. The Sovereign, if not present in person, is represented by a Lord High Commissioner who is appointed each year by the Crown.

The Church of Scotland has about 700,000 members, 1,200 ministers and 1,600 churches. There are about 100 ministers and other personnel working overseas.

Lord High Commissioner (1998), The Lord Hogg of
    Cumbernauld
Moderator of the General Assembly (1998), The Rt. Revd Prof.
    A. Main, TD, Ph.D.
Principal Clerk, Revd F. A. J. Macdonald
Depute Clerk, Revd M. A. MacLean
Procurator, A. Dunlop, QC
Law Agent and Solicitor of the Church, Mrs J. S. Wilson
Parliamentary Agent, I. McCulloch (*London*)
General Treasurer, D. F. Ross
CHURCH OFFICE, 121 George Street, Edinburgh EH2 4YN.
    Tel: 0131-225 5722

PRESBYTERIES AND CLERKS

Edinburgh, Revd W. P. Graham
West Lothian, Revd D. Shaw
Lothian, J. D. McCulloch

Melrose and Peebles, Revd J. H. Brown
Duns, Revd A. C. D. Cartwright
Jedburgh, Revd A. D. Reid

Annandale and Eskdale, Revd C. B. Haston
Dumfries and Kirkcudbright, Revd G. M. A. Savage
Wigtown and Stranraer, Revd D. Dutton

Ayr, Revd J. Crichton
Irvine and Kilmarnock, Revd C. G. F. Brockie
Ardrossan, Revd D. Broster

Lanark, Revd I. D. Cunningham
Paisley, Revd D. Kay
Greenock, Revd D. Mill
Glasgow, Revd A. Cunningham
Hamilton, Revd J. H. Wilson
Dumbarton, Revd D. P. Munro

South Argyll, M. A. J. Gossip
Dunoon, Revd R. Samuel
Lorn and Mull, Revd W. Hogg

Falkirk, Revd D. E. McClements
Stirling, Revd B. W. Dunsmore

Dunfermline, Revd W. E. Farquhar
Kirkcaldy, Revd B. L. Tomlinson
St Andrews, Revd J. W. Patterson

Dunkeld and Meigle, Revd A. B. Reid
Perth, Revd M. Ward
Dundee, Revd J. A. Roy
Angus, Revd M. I. G. Rooney

Aberdeen, Revd A. Douglas
Kincardine and Deeside, Revd J. W. S. Brown
Gordon, Revd I. U. Thomson
Buchan, Revd R. Neilson
Moray, Revd D. J. Ferguson

Abernethy, Revd J. A. I. MacEwan
Inverness, Revd A. S. Younger
Lochaber, Revd A. Ramsay

Ross, Revd R. M. MacKinnon
Sutherland, Revd J. L. Goskirk
Caithness, Revd M. G. Mappin
Lochcarron / Skye, Revd A. I. Macarthur
Uist, Revd A. P. J. Varwell
Lewis, Revd T. S. Sinclair

Orkney (*Finstown*), Revd T. Hunt
Shetland (*Lerwick*), Revd N. R. Whyte
England (*London*), Revd W. A. Cairns

Europe (*Portugal*), Revd J. W. McLeod

The minimum stipend of a minister in the Church of Scotland in 1998 was £16,093

The Roman Catholic Church

The Roman Catholic Church is one world-wide Christian Church acknowledging as its head the Bishop of Rome, known as the Pope (Father). The Pope is held to be the successor of St Peter and thus invested with the power which was entrusted to St Peter by Jesus Christ. A direct line of succession is therefore claimed from the earliest Christian communities. With the fall of the Roman Empire the Pope also became an important political leader. His temporal power is now limited to the 107 acres of the Vatican City State.

The Pope exercises spiritual authority over the Church with the advice and assistance of the Sacred College of Cardinals, the supreme council of the Church. He is also advised about the concerns of the Church locally by his ambassadors, who liaise with the Bishops' Conference in each country.

In addition to advising the Pope, those members of the Sacred College of Cardinals who are under the age of 80 also elect a successor following the death of a Pope. The assembly of the Cardinals at the Vatican for the election of a new Pope is known as the Conclave in which, in complete seclusion, the Cardinals elect by a secret ballot; a two-thirds majority is necessary before the vote can be accepted as final. When a Cardinal receives the necessary votes, the Dean of the Sacred College formally asks him if he will accept election and the name by which he wishes to be known. On his acceptance of the office the Conclave is dissolved and the First Cardinal Deacon announces the election to the assembled crowd in St Peter's Square. On the first Sunday or Holyday following the election, the new Pope assumes the pontificate at High Mass in St Peter's Square. A new pontificate is dated from the assumption of the pontificate.

The number of cardinals was fixed at 70 by Pope Sixtus V in 1586, but has been steadily increased since the pontificate of John XXIII and at the end of June 1998 stood at 166, plus two cardinals created 'in pectore' (their names being kept secret by the Pope for fear of persecution; they are thought to be Chinese).

The Roman Catholic Church universally and the Vatican City State are run by the Curia, which is made up of the Secretariat of State, the Sacred Council for the Public Affairs of the Church, and various congregations, secretariats and tribunals assisted by commissions and offices. The congregations are permanent commissions for conducting the affairs of the Church and are made up of cardinals, one of whom occupies the office of prefect. Below the Secretariat of State and the congregations are the secretariats and tribunals, all of which are headed by cardinals. (The Curial cardinals are analogous to ministers in charge of government departments.)

The Vatican State has its own diplomatic service, with representatives known as nuncios. Papal nuncios with full diplomatic recognition are given precedence over all other ambassadors to the country to which they are appointed; where precedence is not recognized the Papal representative is known as a pro-nuncio. Where the representation is only to the local churches and not to the government of a country, the Papal representative is known as an apostolic delegate. The Roman Catholic Church has an estimated 890.9 million adherents world-wide.

SOVEREIGN PONTIFF

His Holiness Pope John Paul II (Karol Wojtyla), *born* Wadowice, Poland, 18 May 1920; *ordained priest* 1946; *appointed Archbishop* of Krakow 1964; *created Cardinal* 1967; *assumed pontificate* 16 October 1978

SECRETARIAT OF STATE

Secretary of State, HE Cardinal Angelo Sodano
First Section (General Affairs), Mgr G. Re (Archbishop of Vescovio)
Second Section (Relations with other states), Mgr J. L. Tauran (Archbishop of Telepte)

BISHOPS' CONFERENCE

The Roman Catholic Church in England and Wales is governed by the Bishops' Conference, membership of which includes the Diocesan Bishops, the Apostolic Exarch of the Ukrainians, the Bishop of the Forces and the Auxiliary Bishops. The Conference is headed by the President (Cardinal Basil Hume, Archbishop of Westminster) and Vice-President. There are five departments, each with an episcopal chairman: the Department for Christian Life and Worship (the Archbishop of Southwark), the Department for Mission and Unity (the Bishop of Arundel and Brighton), the Department for Catholic Education and Formation (the Bishop of Leeds), the Department for Christian Responsibility and Citizenship (the Bishop of Plymouth), and the Department for International Affairs.

The Bishops' Standing Committee, made up of all the Archbishops and the chairman of each of the above departments, has general responsibility for continuity and policy between the plenary sessions of the Conference. It prepares the Conference agenda and implements its decisions. It is serviced by a General Secretariat. There are also agencies and consultative bodies affiliated to the Conference.

The Bishops' Conference of Scotland has as its president Archbishop Winning of Glasgow and is the permanently constituted assembly of the Bishops of Scotland. To promote its work, the Conference establishes various agencies which have an advisory function in relation to the Conference. The more important of these agencies are called Commissions and each one has a Bishop President who, with the other members of the Commissions, are appointed by the Conference.

The Irish Episcopal Conference has as its acting president Archbishop Connell of Dublin. Its membership comprises all the Archbishops and Bishops of Ireland and it appoints various Commissions to assist it in its work. There are three types of Commissions: (a) those made up of lay and clerical members chosen for their skills and experience, and staffed by full-time expert secretariats; (b) Commissions whose members are selected from existing institutions and whose services are supplied on a part-time basis; and (c) Commissions of Bishops only.

The Roman Catholic Church in Britain and Ireland has an estimated 8,992,000 members, 11 archbishops, 67 bishops, 11,260 priests, and 8,588 churches and chapels open to the public.

Bishops' Conferences secretariats:

ENGLAND AND WALES, 39 Eccleston Square, London SW1V 1PD. Tel: 0171-630 8220. *General Secretary*, The Rt. Revd Arthur Roche

SCOTLAND, Candida Casa, 8 Corsehill Road, Ayr, Scotland KA7 2ST. Tel: 01292-256750. *General Secretary*, The Rt. Revd Maurice Taylor (Bishop of Galloway)

IRELAND, Iona, 65 Newry Road, Dundalk, Co. Louth. *Executive Secretary*, Revd Hugh G. Connelly

---

GREAT BRITAIN

APOSTOLIC NUNCIO TO GREAT BRITAIN
The Most Revd Pablo Puente, 54 Parkside, London SW19 5NE. Tel: 0181-946 1410

ENGLAND AND WALES

THE MOST REVD ARCHBISHOPS
Westminster, HE Cardinal Basil Hume, *cons.* 1976
  Auxiliaries, Vincent Nichols, *cons.* 1992; James J. O'Brien, *cons.* 1977; Patrick O'Donoghue, *cons.* 1993
  Clergy, 789
  Archbishop's Residence, Archbishop's House, Ambrosden Avenue, London SW1P 1QJ. Tel: 0171-834 4717
Birmingham, Maurice Couve de Murville, *cons.* 1982, *apptd* 1982
  Auxiliaries, Philip Pargeter, *cons.* 1989
  Clergy, 490
  Diocesan Curia, Cathedral House, St Chad's Queensway, Birmingham B4 6EX. Tel: 0121-236 5535
Cardiff, John A. Ward, *cons.* 1981, *apptd* 1983
  Clergy, 137
  Diocesan Curia, Archbishop's House, 41–43 Cathedral Road, Cardiff CF1 9HD. Tel: 01222-220411
Liverpool, Patrick Kelly, *cons.* 1984, *apptd* 1996
  Auxiliary, Vincent Malone, *cons.* 1989
  Clergy, 533
  Diocesan Curia, 152 Brownlow Hill, Liverpool L3 5RQ. Tel: 0151-709 4801
Southwark, Michael Bowen, *cons.* 1970, *apptd* 1977
  Auxiliaries, Charles Henderson, *cons.* 1972; Howard Tripp, *cons.* 1980; John Jukes, *cons.* 1980
  Clergy, 516
  Diocesan Curia, Archbishop's House, 150 St George's Road, London SE1 6HX. Tel: 0171-928 5592

THE RT. REVD BISHOPS
Arundel and Brighton, Cormac Murphy-O'Connor, *cons.* 1977. *Clergy*, 313. *Diocesan Curia*, Bishop's House, The Upper Drive, Hove, E. Sussex BN3 6NE. Tel: 01273-506387
Brentwood, Thomas McMahon, *cons.* 1980, *apptd* 1980. *Clergy*, 174. *Bishop's Office*, Cathedral House, Ingrave Road, Brentwood, Essex CM15 8AT. Tel: 01277-232266
Clifton, Mervyn Alexander, *cons.* 1972, *apptd* 1975. *Clergy*, 251. *Diocesan Curia*, Egerton Road, Bishopston, Bristol BS7 8HU. Tel: 0117-924 1378
East Anglia, Peter Smith, *cons.* 1995, *apptd* 1995. *Clergy*, 173. *Diocesan Curia*, The White House, 21 Upgate, Poringland, Norwich NR14 7SH. Tel: 01508-492202
Hallam, John Rawsthorne, *cons.* 1981, *apptd* 1997. *Clergy*, 89. *Bishop's Residence*, 'Quarters', Carsick Hill Way, Sheffield S10 3LT. Tel: 0114-230 9101
Hexham and Newcastle, Michael Ambrose Griffiths, *cons.* 1992. *Clergy*, 259. *Diocesan Curia*, Bishop's House, East Denton Hall, 800 West Road, Newcastle upon Tyne NE5 2BJ. Tel: 0191-228 0003
Lancaster, John Brewer, *cons.* 1971, *apptd* 1985. *Clergy*, 256. *Bishop's Residence*, Bishop's House, Cannon Hill, Lancaster LA1 5NG. Tel: 01524-32231
Leeds, David Konstant, *cons.* 1977, *apptd* 1985. *Clergy*, 253. *Diocesan Curia*, 7 St Marks Avenue, Leeds LS2 9BN. Tel: 0113-244 4788

Menevia (*Wales*), Daniel Mullins, *cons.* 1970, *apptd* 1987.
Clergy, 61. *Diocesan Curia*, 115 Walter Road, Swansea
SA1 5RE. Tel: 01792-644017
Middlesbrough, John Crowley, *cons.* 1986, *apptd* 1992. *Clergy*,
187. *Diocesan Curia*, 50A The Avenue, Linthorpe,
Middlesbrough, Cleveland TS5 6QT. Tel: 01642-850505
Northampton, Patrick Leo McCartie, *cons.* 1977, *apptd* 1990.
Clergy, 154. *Diocesan Curia*, Bishop's House, Marriott
Street, Northampton NN2 6AW. Tel: 01604-715635
Nottingham, James McGuinness, *cons.* 1972, *apptd* 1975.
Clergy, 217. *Diocesan Curia*, Willson House, Derby Road,
Nottingham NG1 5AW. Tel: 0115-953 9800
Plymouth, Christopher Budd, *cons.* 1986. *Clergy*, 143. *Diocesan
Curia*, Vescourt, Hartley Road, Plymouth PL3 5LR. Tel:
01752-772950
Portsmouth, F. Crispian Hollis, *cons.* 1987, *apptd* 1989. *Clergy*,
268. *Bishop's Residence*, Bishop's House, Edinburgh Road,
Portsmouth, Hants PO1 3HG. Tel: 01705-820894
Salford, Terence J. Brain, *cons.* 1994, *apptd* 1997. *Clergy*, 394.
Diocesan Curia, Cathedral House, 250 Chapel Street,
Salford M3 5LL. Tel: 0161-834 9052
Shrewsbury, Brian Noble, *cons.* 1995, *apptd* 1995. *Clergy* 196.
Diocesan Curia, 2 Park Road South, Birkenhead,
Merseyside L43 4UX. Tel: 0151-652 9855
Wrexham (*Wales*), Edwin Regan, *apptd* 1994. *Clergy*, 86.
Diocesan Curia, Bishop's House, Sontley Road,
Wrexham, Clwyd LL13 7EW. Tel: 01978-262726

SCOTLAND

THE MOST REVD ARCHBISHOPS
St Andrews and Edinburgh, Keith Patrick O'Brien, *cons.* 1985
Clergy, 201
Diocesan Curia, 106 Whitehouse Loan, Edinburgh
EH9 1BD. Tel: 0131-452 8244
Glasgow, HE Cardinal Thomas Winning, *cons.* 1971, *apptd*
1974
Clergy, 303
Diocesan Curia, 196 Clyde Street, Glasgow G1 4JY. Tel:
0141-226 5898

THE RT. REVD BISHOPS
Aberdeen, Mario Conti, *cons.* 1977. *Clergy*, 58. *Bishop's
Residence*, 156 King's Gate, Aberdeen AB2 6BR. Tel:
01224-319154
Argyll and the Isles, vacant. *Clergy*, 32. *Diocesan Curia*, St
Mary's, Belford Road, Fort William, Inverness-shire
PH33 6BT. Tel: 01397-706046
Dunkeld, Vincent Logan, *cons.* 1981. *Clergy*, 55. *Diocesan
Curia*, 26 Roseangle, Dundee DD1 4LR. Tel: 01382-25453
Galloway, Maurice Taylor, *cons.* 1981. *Clergy*, 66. *Diocesan
Curia*, 8 Corsehill Road, Ayr KA7 2ST. Tel: 01292-266750
Motherwell, Joseph Devine, *cons.* 1977, *apptd* 1983.
Clergy, 180. *Diocesan Curia*, Coursington Road,
Motherwell ML1 1PW. Tel: 01698-269114
Paisley, John A. Mone, *cons.* 1984, *apptd* 1988. *Clergy*, 95.
Diocesan Curia, Cathedral House, 8 East Buchanan
Street, Paisley, Renfrewshire PA1 1HS. Tel: 0141-889
3601

IRELAND

There is one hierarchy for the whole of Ireland. Several of
the dioceses have territory partly in the Republic of
Ireland and partly in Northern Ireland.

APOSTOLIC NUNCIO TO IRELAND
Most Revd Giovanni Ceirano (titular Archbishop of
Tigimma), 183 Navan Road, Dublin 7. Tel: 00 353 1-
380577

THE MOST REVD ARCHBISHOPS
Armagh, HE Cardinal Sean Brady, *cons.* 1993, *apptd* 1996
Auxiliary, Gerard Clifford, *cons.* 1991
Clergy, 183
Diocesan Curia, Ara Coeli, Armagh BT61 7QY. Tel: 01861-
522045
Cashel, Dermot Clifford, *cons.* 1986
Clergy, 136
Archbishop's Residence, Archbishop's House, Thurles, Co.
Tipperary. Tel: 00 353 504-21512
Dublin, Desmond Connell, *cons.* 1988, *apptd* 1988
Auxiliaries, James Moriarty, *cons.* 1992; Eamonn Walsh,
cons. 1990; Fiachra O'Ceallaigh, *cons* 1994; James
Kavanagh, *cons.* 1996
Clergy, 994
Archbishop's Residence, Archbishop's House, Drumcondra,
Dublin 9. Tel: 00 353 1-8373732
Tuam, Michael Neary, *cons.* 1992
Clergy, 180
Archbishop's Residence, Archbishop's House, Tuam, Co.
Galway. Tel: 00 353 93-24166

THE MOST REVD BISHOPS
Achonry, Thomas Flynn, *cons.* 1975. *Clergy*, 62. *Bishop's
Residence*, Bishop's House, Ballaghadaderreen, Co.
Roscommon. Tel: 00 353 907-60021
Ardagh and Clonmacnois, Colm O'Reilly, *cons.* 1983.
Clergy, 100. *Diocesan Office*, Bishop's House, St Michael's,
Longford, Co. Longford. Tel: 00 353 43-46432
Clogher, Joseph Duffy, *cons.* 1979. *Clergy*, 108. *Bishop's
Residence*, Bishop's House, Monaghan. Tel: 00 353 47-
81019
Clonfert, Joseph Kirby, *cons.* 1988. *Clergy*, 71. *Bishop's
Residence*, St Brendan's, Coorheen, Loughrea, Co.
Galway. Tel: 00 353 91-41560
Cloyne, John Magee, *cons.* 1987. *Clergy*, 158. *Diocesan Centre*,
Cobh, Co. Cork. Tel: 00 353 21-811430
Cork and Ross, John Buckley, *cons.* 1984, *apptd* 1998. *Clergy*,
338. *Diocesan Office*, Bishop's House, Redemption Road,
Cork. Tel: 00 353 21-301717
Derry, Seamus Hegarty, *cons.* 1984, *apptd* 1994. *Clergy*, 157.
Bishop's Residence, Bishop's House, St Eugene's
Cathedral, Derry BT48 9AP. Tel: 01504-262302
Auxiliary, Francis Lagan, *cons.* 1988
Down and Connor, Patrick J. Walsh, *cons.* 1991. *Clergy*, 248.
Bishop's Residence, Lisbreen, 73 Somerton Road, Belfast,
Co. Antrim BT15 4DE. Tel: 01232-776185
Auxiliaries, Anthony Farquhar, *cons.* 1983; Michael
Dallat, *cons.* 1994
Dromore, Francis Brooks, *cons.* 1976. *Clergy*, 78. *Bishop's
Residence*, Bishop's House, Violet Hill, Newry, Co. Down
BT35 6PN. Tel: 01693-62444
Elphin, Christopher Jones, *cons.* 1994. *Clergy*, 101. *Bishop's
Residence*, St Mary's, Sligo. Tel: 00 353 71-62670
Ferns, Brendon Comiskey, *cons.* 1980. *Clergy*, 161. *Bishop's
Office*, Bishop's House, Summerhill, Wexford. Tel:
00 353 53-22177
Galway and Kilmacduagh, James McLoughlin, *cons.* 1993.
Clergy, 90. *Diocesan Office*, The Cathedral, Galway. Tel:
00 353 91-63566
Kerry, William Murphy, *cons.* 1995. *Clergy*, 149. *Bishop's
Residence*, Bishop's House, Killarney, Co. Kerry. Tel:
00 353 64-31168
Kildare and Leighlin, Laurence Ryan, *cons.* 1984. *Clergy*, 136.
Bishop's Residence, Bishop's House, Carlow. Tel:
00 353 503-31102
Killala, Thomas Finnegan, *cons.* 1970. *Clergy*, 62. *Bishop's
Residence*, Bishop's House, Ballina, Co. Mayo. Tel:
00 353 96-21518

Killaloe, William Walsh, *cons.* 1994. *Clergy*, 149. *Bishop's Residence*, Westbourne, Ennis, Co. Clare. Tel: 00 353 65-28638

Kilmore, Francis McKiernan, *cons.* 1972. *Coadjutor*, Leo O'Reilly. *Clergy*, 115. *Bishop's Residence*, Bishop's House, Cullies, Co. Cavan. Tel: 00 353 49-31496

Limerick, Donal Murray, *cons.* 1996. *Clergy*, 152. *Diocesan Offices*, 66 O'Connell Street, Limerick. Tel: 00 353 61-315856

Meath, Michael Smith, *cons.* 1984, *apptd* 1990. *Clergy*, 141. *Bishop's Residence*, Bishop's House, Dublin Road, Mullingar, Co. Westmeath. Tel: 00 353 44-48841

Ossory, Laurence Forristal, *cons.* 1980. *Clergy*, 111. *Bishop's Residence*, Sion House, Kilkenny. Tel: 00 353 56-62448

Raphoe, Philip Boyce, *cons.* 1994. *Clergy*, 96. *Bishop's Residence*, Ard Adhamhnáin, Letterkenny, Co. Donegal. Tel: 00 353 74-21208

Waterford and Lismore, William Lee, *cons.* 1993. *Clergy*, 130. *Bishop's Residence*, Woodleigh, Summerville Avenue, Waterford. Tel: 00 353 51-71432

PATRIARCHS IN COMMUNION WITH THE ROMAN CATHOLIC CHURCH

Alexandria, HB Stephanos II Ghattas (Patriarch for Catholic Copts)

Antioch, HB Ignace Antoine II Hayek (Patriarch for Syrian rite Catholics); HB Maximos V. Hakim (Patriarch for Greek Melekite rite Catholics); HE Cardinal Nasrallah Pierre Sfeir (Patriarch for Maronite rite Catholics)

Jerusalem, HB Michel Sabbah (Patriarch for Latin rite Catholics); HB Maximos V. Hakim (Patriarch for Greek Melekite rite Catholics)

Babilonia of the Chaldeans, HB Raphael I Bidawid

Cilicia of the Armenians, HB Jean Pierre XVIII Kasparian (Patriarch for Armenian rite Catholics)

Oriental India, Archbishop Raul Nicolau Gonsalves

Lisbon, vacant

Venice, HE Cardinal Marco Ce

Other Churches in the UK

AFRICAN AND AFRO-CARIBBEAN CHURCHES

There are more than 160 Christian churches or groups of African or Afro-Caribbean origin in the UK. These include the Apostolic Faith Church, the Cherubim and Seraphim Church, the New Testament Church Assembly, the New Testament Church of God, the Wesleyan Holiness Church and the Aladura Churches.

The Afro-West Indian United Council of Churches and the Council of African and Afro-Caribbean Churches UK (which was initiated as the Council of African and Allied Churches in 1979 to give one voice to the various Christian churches of African origin in the UK) are the media through which the member churches can work jointly to provide services they cannot easily provide individually.

There are about 70,000 adherents of African and Afro-Caribbean churches in the UK, and about 1,000 congregations. The Afro-West Indian United Council of Churches has about 30,000 individual members, 135 ministers and 65 places of worship. The Council of African and Afro-

Caribbean Churches UK has about 17,000 members, 250 ministers and 75 congregations.

AFRO-WEST INDIAN UNITED COUNCIL OF CHURCHES, c/o New Testament Church of God, Arcadian Gardens, High Road, London N22 5AA. Tel: 0181-888 9427. *Secretary*, Revd E. Brown

COUNCIL OF AFRICAN AND AFRO-CARIBBEAN CHURCHES UK, 31 Norton House, Sidney Road, London SW9 0UJ. Tel: 0171-274 5589. *Chairman*, His Grace The Most Revd Father Olu A. Abiola

ASSOCIATED PRESBYTERIAN CHURCHES OF SCOTLAND

The Associated Presbyterian Churches came into being in 1989 as a result of a division within the Free Presbyterian Church of Scotland. Following two controversial disciplinary cases, the culmination of deepening differences within the Church, a presbytery was formed calling itself the Associated Presbyterian Churches (APC). The Associated Presbyterian Churches has about 1,000 members, 15 ministers and 20 churches.

Clerk of the Scottish Presbytery, Revd Dr M. MacInnes, Drumalin, 16 Drummond Road, Inverness IV2 4NB. Tel: 01463-223983

THE BAPTIST CHURCH

Baptists trace their origins to John Smyth, who in 1609 in Amsterdam reinstituted the baptism of conscious believers as the basis of the fellowship of a gathered church. Members of Smyth's church established the first Baptist church in England in 1612. They came to be known as 'General' Baptists and their theology was Arminian, whereas a later group of Calvinists who adopted the baptism of believers came to be known as 'Particular' Baptists. The two sections of the Baptists were united into one body, the Baptist Union of Great Britain and Ireland, in 1891. In 1988 the title was changed to the Baptist Union of Great Britain.

Baptists emphasize the complete autonomy of the local church, although individual churches are linked in various kinds of associations. There are international bodies (such as the Baptist World Alliance) and national bodies, but some Baptist churches belong to neither. However, in Great Britain the majority of churches and associations belong to the Baptist Union of Great Britain. There are also Baptist Unions in Wales, Scotland and Ireland which are much smaller than the Baptist Union of Great Britain, and there is some overlap of membership.

There are over 40 million Baptist church members world-wide; in the Baptist Union of Great Britain there are 157,000 members, 1,864 pastors and 2,130 churches. In the Baptist Union of Scotland there are 13,882 members, 160 pastors and 172 churches. In the Baptist Union of Wales there are 22,500 members, 112 pastors and 530 churches. In the Baptist Union of Ireland there are 8,393 members, 90 pastors and 110 churches.

President of the Baptist Union of Great Britain (1998–9), Revd D. G. T. McBain

General Secretary, Revd D. R. Coffey, Baptist House, PO Box 44, 129 Broadway, Didcot, Oxon OX11 8RT. Tel: 01235-512077

THE CONGREGATIONAL FEDERATION

The Congregational Federation was founded by members of Congregational churches in England and Wales who did not join the United Reformed Church (q.v.) in 1972. There are also churches in Scotland and Australia affiliated to the Federation. The Federation exists to encourage congregations of believers to worship in free assembly, but it has no authority over them and emphasizes their right to independence and self-government.

The Federation has 11,923 members, 71 recognized ministers and 313 churches in England, Wales and Scotland.

President of the Federation (1998–9), Revd. I. Gregory
General Secretary, G. M. Adams, The Congregational Centre, 4 Castle Gate, Nottingham NG1 7AS. Tel: 0115-911 1460

THE FREE CHURCH OF ENGLAND

The Free Church of England is a union of two bodies in the Anglican tradition, the Free Church of England, founded in 1844 as a protest against the Oxford Movement in the established Church, and the Reformed Episcopal Church, founded in America in 1873 but which also had congregations in England. As both Churches sought to maintain the historic faith, tradition and practice of the Anglican Church since the Reformation, they decided to unite as one body in England in 1927. The historic episcopate was conferred on the English Church in 1876 through the line of the American bishops, who had pioneered an open table Communion policy towards members of other denominations.

The Free Church of England has 1,500 members, 42 ministers and 25 churches in England. It also has three house churches and three ministers in New Zealand, two churches and two ministers in Queensland, Australia, and one church and one minister in St Petersburg, Russia.

General Secretary, Revd W. J. Lawler, 45 Broughton Road, Wallasey, Merseyside L44 4DT. Tel: 0151-638 2564

THE FREE CHURCH OF SCOTLAND

The Free Church of Scotland was formed in 1843 when over 400 ministers withdrew from the Church of Scotland as a result of interference in the internal affairs of the church by the civil authorities. In 1900, all but 26 ministers joined with others to form the United Free Church (most of which rejoined the Church of Scotland in 1929). In 1904 the remaining 26 ministers were recognized by the House of Lords as continuing the Free Church of Scotland.

The Church maintains strict adherence to the Westminster Confession of Faith (1648) and accepts the Bible as the sole rule of faith and conduct. Its General Assembly meets annually. It also has links with Reformed Churches overseas. The Free Church of Scotland has 6,000 members, 110 ministers and 140 churches.

General Treasurer, I. D. Gill, The Mound, Edinburgh EH1 2LS. Tel: 0131-226 5286

THE FREE PRESBYTERIAN CHURCH OF SCOTLAND

The Free Presbyterian Church of Scotland was formed in 1893 by two ministers of the Free Church of Scotland who refused to accept a Declaratory Act passed by the Free Church General Assembly in 1892. The Free Presbyterian Church of Scotland is Calvinistic in doctrine and emphasizes observance of the Sabbath. It adheres strictly to the Westminster Confession of Faith of 1648.

The Church has about 3,000 members in Scotland and about 7,000 in overseas congregations. It has 26 ministers and 50 churches.

Moderator, Revd D. A. Ross, Free Presbyterian Manse, Laide, Ross-shire IV22 2NB
Clerk of Synod, Revd J. MacLeod, 16 Matheson Road, Stornoway, Isle of Lewis HS1 2LA. Tel: 01851-702755

THE INDEPENDENT METHODIST CHURCHES

The Independent Methodist Churches seceded from the Wesleyan Methodist Church in 1805 and remained independent when the Methodist Church in Great Britain was formed in 1932. They are mainly concentrated in the industrial areas of the north of England.

The churches are Methodist in doctrine but their organization is congregational. All the churches are members of the Independent Methodist Connexion of Churches. The controlling body of the Connexion is the Annual Meeting, to which churches send delegates. The Connexional President is elected annually. Between annual meetings the affairs of the Connexion are handled by departmental committees. Ministers are appointed by the churches and trained through the Connexion. The ministry is open to both men and women and is unpaid.

There are 3,050 members, 106 ministers and 100 churches in Great Britain.

Connexional President (1998–9), M. Bolt
General Secretary, J. M. Day, The Old Police House, Croxton, Stafford ST21 6PE. Tel: 0163-062 0671

THE LUTHERAN CHURCH

Lutheranism is based on the teachings of Martin Luther, the German leader of the Protestant Reformation. The authority of the scriptures is held to be supreme over Church tradition and creeds, and the key doctrine is that of justification by faith alone.

Lutheranism is one of the largest Protestant denominations and it is particularly strong in northern Europe and the USA. Some Lutheran churches are episcopal, while others have a synodal form of organization; unity is based on doctrine rather than structure. Most Lutheran churches are members of the Lutheran World Federation, based in Geneva.

Lutheran services in Great Britain are held in many languages to serve members of different nationalities. English-language congregations are members either of the Lutheran Church in Great Britain-United Synod, or of the Evangelical Lutheran Church of England. The United Synod and most of the various national congregations are members of the Lutheran Council of Great Britain.

There are over 70 million Lutherans world-wide; in Great Britain there are 27,000 members, 45 ministers and 100 churches.
Chairman of the Lutheran Council of Great Britain, Very Revd R. J. Patkai, 30 Thanet Street, London WC1H 9QH. Tel: 0171-383 3081

THE METHODIST CHURCH

The Methodist movement started in England in 1729 when the Revd John Wesley, an Anglican priest, and his brother Charles met with others in Oxford and resolved to conduct their lives and study by 'rule and method'. In 1739 the Wesleys began evangelistic preaching and the first Methodist chapel was founded in Bristol in the same year. In 1744 the first annual conference was held, at which the Articles of Religion were drawn up. Doctrinal emphases included repentance, faith, the assurance of salvation, social concern and the priesthood of all believers. After John Wesley's death in 1791 the Methodists withdrew from the established Church to form the Methodist Church. Methodists gradually drifted into many groups, but in 1932 the Wesleyan Methodist Church, the United Methodist Church and the Primitive Methodist Church united to form the Methodist Church in Great Britain as it now exists.

The governing body and supreme authority of the Methodist Church is the Conference, but there are also 33 district synods, consisting of all the ministers and selected lay people in each district, and circuit meetings of the ministers and lay people of each circuit.

There are over 60 million Methodists world-wide; in Great Britain (1995 figures) there are 380,269 members, 3,660 ministers, 12,611 lay preachers and 6,678 churches.
President of the Conference in Great Britain (1998–9), Revd Prof. W. P. Stephens
Vice-President of the Conference (1998–9), Mrs M. Parker
Secretary of the Conference, Revd Dr N. T. Collinson, Methodist Church, Conference Office, 25 Marylebone Road, London NW1 5JR. Tel: 0171-486 5502

THE METHODIST CHURCH IN IRELAND

The Methodist Church in Ireland is closely linked to British Methodism but is autonomous. It has 17,349 members, 196 ministers, 307 lay preachers and 229 churches.
President of the Methodist Church in Ireland (1998–9), Revd D. J. Kerr, Grosvenor House, 5 Glengall Street, Belfast BT12 5AD. Tel: 01232-241917
Secretary of the Methodist Church in Ireland, Revd E. T. I. Mawhinney, 1 Fountainville Avenue, Belfast BT9 6AN. Tel: 01232-324554

THE (EASTERN) ORTHODOX CHURCH

The Eastern (or Byzantine) Orthodox Church is a communion of self-governing Christian churches recognizing the honorary primacy of the Oecumenical Patriarch of Constantinople.

The position of Orthodox Christians is that the faith was fully defined during the period of the Oecumenical Councils. In doctrine it is strongly trinitarian, and stresses the mystery and importance of the sacraments. It is episcopal in government. The structure of the Orthodox Christian year differs from that of western Churches (*see* page 82).

Orthodox Christians throughout the world are estimated to number about 300 million.

PATRIARCHS OF THE EASTERN ORTHODOX CHURCH
Archbishop of Constantinople, New Rome and Oecumenical Patriarch, Bartholomew, *elected* 1991
Pope and Patriarch of Alexandria and All Africa, Petros VII, *elected* 1997
Patriarch of Antioch and All the East, Ignatios IV, *elected* 1979
Patriarch of Jerusalem and All Palestine, Diodoros, *elected* 1981
Patriarch of Moscow and All Russia, Alexei II, *elected* 1990
Archbishop of Pec, Metropolitan of Belgrade and Karlovci, Patriarch of Serbia, Paul, *elected* 1990
Archbishop of Bucharest and Patriarch of Romania, Teoctist, *elected* 1986
Metropolitan of Sofia and Patriarch of Bulgaria, Maxim, *elected* 1971
Archbishop of Tbilisi and Mtskheta, Catholicos-Patriarch of All Georgia, Ilia II, *elected* 1977

EASTERN ORTHODOX CHURCHES IN THE UK

THE PATRIARCHATE OF ANTIOCH
There are ten parishes served by 12 clergy. In Great Britain the Patriarchate is represented by the Revd Fr Samir Gholam, 1A Redhill Street, London NW1 4BG. Tel: 0171-383 0403.

THE GREEK ORTHODOX CHURCH (PATRIARCHATE OF CONSTANTINOPLE)

The presence of Greek Orthodox Christians in Britain dates back at least to 1677 when Archbishop Joseph Geogirenes of Samos fled from Turkish persecution and came to London. The present Greek cathedral in Moscow Road, Bayswater, was opened for public worship in 1879 and the Diocese of Thyateira and Great Britain was established in 1922. There are now 113 parishes and other communities (including monasteries) in Great Britain, served by six bishops, 97 clergy and 101 churches.

In Great Britain the Patriarchate of Constantinople is represented by Archbishop Gregorios of Thyateira and Great Britain, 5 Craven Hill, London W2 3EN. Tel: 0171-723 4787.

THE RUSSIAN ORTHODOX CHURCH (PATRIARCHATE OF MOSCOW) AND THE RUSSIAN ORTHODOX CHURCH OUTSIDE RUSSIA

The records of Russian Orthodox Church activities in Britain date from the visit to England of Tsar Peter I in the early 18th century. Clergy were sent from Russia to serve the chapel established to minister to the staff of the Imperial Russian Embassy in London.

In Great Britain the Patriarchate of Moscow is represented by Metropolitan Anthony of Sourozh, 67 Ennismore Gardens, London SW7 1NH. Fax only: 0171-584 9864. He is assisted by one archbishop, one vicar bishop and 28 clergy. There are 27 parishes and smaller communities.

The Russian Orthodox Church Outside Russia is represented by Archbishop Mark of Berlin, Germany and Great Britain, c/o 57 Harvard Road, London W4 4ED. Tel: 0181-742 3493. There are eight communities, including two monasteries, served by six priests.

THE SERBIAN ORTHODOX CHURCH (PATRIARCHATE OF SERBIA)

There are 33 parishes and smaller communities in Great Britain served by 12 clergy. The Patriarchate of Serbia is represented by the Episcopal Vicar, the Very Revd Milenko Zebic, 131 Cob Lane, Bournville, Birmingham B30 1QE. Tel: 0121-458 5273.

OTHER NATIONALITIES

Most of the Ukrainian parishes in Britain have joined the Patriarchate of Constantinople, leaving five Ukrainian parishes in Britain under the care of the Patriarch of Kiev (who is not recognized by the other Orthodox churches). The Latvian, Polish and some Belorussian parishes are also under the care of the Patriarchate of Constantinople. The Patriarchate of Romania has one parish served by two clergy. The Patriarchate of Bulgaria has one parish served by one priest. The Belorussian Autocephalous Orthodox Church has five parishes served by two priests.

THE ORIENTAL ORTHODOX CHURCHES

The term 'Oriental Orthodox Churches' is now generally used to describe a group of six ancient eastern churches which reject the Christological definition of the Council of Chalcedon (AD 451) and use Christological terms in different ways from the Eastern Orthodox Church. There are about 34 million members of the Oriental Orthodox Churches.

PATRIARCHS OF THE ORIENTAL ORTHODOX CHURCHES

ARMENIAN ORTHODOX CHURCH – *Supreme Patriarch Catholicos of All Armenians (Etchmiadzin)*, Karekin I, *elected* 1995; *Catholicos of Cilicia*, Aram I, *elected* 1995; *Patriarch of Jerusalem*, Torkom, *elected* 1994; *Patriarch of Constantinople*, vacant
COPTIC ORTHODOX CHURCH – *Pope of Alexandria and Patriarch of the See of St Mark*, Shenouda III, *elected* 1971
ERITREAN ORTHODOX CHURCH – *Patriarch of Eritrea*, Philipos I, *elected* 1998
ETHIOPIAN ORTHODOX CHURCH – *Patriarch of Ethopia*, Paulos, *elected* 1992
MALANKARA ORTHODOX SYRIAN CHURCH – *Catholicos of the East*, Basilios Mar Thoma Mathews II, *elected* 1991
SYRIAN ORTHODOX CHURCH – *Patriarch of Antioch and All the East*, Ignatius Zakka I, *elected* 1980

ORIENTAL ORTHODOX CHURCHES IN THE UK

THE ARMENIAN ORTHODOX CHURCH (PATRIARCHATE OF ETCHMIADZIN)

The Armenian Orthodox Church is the longest-established Oriental Orthodox community in Great Britain. It is represented by Archbishop Yeghishe Gizirian, Armenian Primate of Great Britain, Armenian Vicarage, Iverna Gardens, London W8 6TP. Tel: 0171-937 0152.

THE COPTIC ORTHODOX CHURCH

The Coptic Orthodox Church is the largest Oriental Orthodox community in Great Britain. It has four dioceses (Birmingham; Scotland, Ireland and North-East England; the British Orthodox Church; and churches directly under Pope Shenouda III). The representative in Great Britain of Pope Shenouda III is Fr Antonious Thabit Shenouda, 14 Newton Mansions, Queen's Club Gardens, London W14 9RR. Tel: 0171-385 1991.

THE ERITREAN ORTHODOX CHURCH

In Great Britain the Eritrean Orthodox Church is represented by Bishop Markos, 11 Anfield Close, Weir Road, London SW12 0NT. Tel: 0181-675 5115.

THE ETHIOPIAN ORTHODOX CHURCH

The acting head of the Ethiopian Orthodox Church in Europe is Revd Berhanu Beserat, 33 Jupiter Crescent, London NW1 8HA. Tel: 0956-513700.

THE MALANKARA ORTHODOX SYRIAN CHURCH

The Malankara Orthodox Syrian Church is part of the Diocese of Europe under Metropolitan Thomas Mar Makarios. His representative in Great Britain is Fr M. S. Skariah, Paramula House, 44 Newbury Road, Newbury Park, Ilford, Essex IG2 7HD. Tel: 0181-599 3836.

THE SYRIAN ORTHODOX CHURCH

The Syrian Orthodox Church in Great Britain comes under the Patriarchal Vicar, whose representative is Fr Thomas H. Dawood, Antiochian, 5 Canning Road, Croydon CR0 6QA. Tel: 0181-654 7531. The Indian congregation under the Syrian Patriarch of Antioch is represented by Fr Eldhose Koungampillil, 1 Roslyn Court, Roslyn Avenue, East Barnet, Herts EN4 8DJ. Tel: 0181-368 2794.

THE COUNCIL OF ORIENTAL ORTHODOX CHURCHES, 34 Chertsey Road, Church Square, Shepperton, Middx TW17 9LF. Tel: 0181-368 8447. *Secretary*, Deacon Aziz M. A. Nour

PENTECOSTAL CHURCHES

Pentecostalism is inspired by the descent of the Holy Spirit upon the apostles at Pentecost. The movement began in Los Angeles, USA, in 1906 and is characterized by baptism with the Holy Spirit, divine healing, speaking in tongues (glossolalia), and a literal interpretation of the scriptures. The Pentecostal movement in Britain dates from 1907. Initially, groups of Pentecostalists were led by laymen and did not organize formally. However, in 1915 the Elim Foursquare Gospel Alliance (more usually called the Elim Pentecostal Church) was founded in Ireland by George Jeffreys and in 1924 about 70 independent assemblies formed a fellowship, the Assemblies of God in Great Britain and Ireland. The Apostolic Church grew out of the 1904–5 revivals in South Wales and was established in 1916, and the New Testament Church of God was established in England in 1953. In recent years many aspects of Pentecostalism have been adopted by the growing charismatic movement within the Roman Catholic, Protestant and Eastern Orthodox churches.

There are about 105 million Pentecostalists worldwide, with about 200,000 adult adherents in Great Britain and Ireland.

THE APOSTOLIC CHURCH, International Administration Offices, PO Box 389, 24–27 St Helens Road, Swansea SA1 1ZH. Tel: 01792-473992. *President*, Pastor R. W. Jones; *Administrator*, Pastor A. Saunders. The Apostolic Church has about 130 churches, 5,500 adherents and 83 ministers
THE ASSEMBLIES OF GOD IN GREAT BRITAIN AND IRELAND, General Offices, 16 Bridgford Road, West Bridgford, Nottingham NG2 6AF. Tel: 0115-981 1188. *General Superintendent*, P. Weaver; *General Administrator*, D. H. Gill. The Assemblies of God has 652 churches, about 75,000 adherents (including children) and 1,100 accredited ministers
THE ELIM PENTECOSTAL CHURCH, PO Box 38, Cheltenham, Glos GL50 3HN. Tel: 01242-519904. *General Superintendent*, Pastor I. W. Lewis; *Administrator*, Pastor B. Hunter. The Elim Pentecostal Church has 600 churches, 68,500 adherents and 650 accredited ministers

The New Testament Church of God, Main House, Overstone Park, Overstone, Northampton NN6 OAD. Tel: 01604-643311. *National Overseer*, Revd Dr R. O. Brown. The New Testament Church of God has 110 organized congregations, 7,500 baptized members, about 20,000 adherents and 242 accredited ministers

THE PRESBYTERIAN CHURCH IN IRELAND

The Presbyterian Church in Ireland is Calvinistic in doctrine and presbyterian in constitution. Presbyterianism was established in Ireland as a result of the Ulster plantation in the early 17th century, when English and Scottish Protestants settled in the north of Ireland.

There are 21 presbyteries and five regional synods under the chief court known as the General Assembly. The General Assembly meets annually and is presided over by a Moderator who is elected for one year. The ongoing work of the Church is undertaken by 18 boards under which there are a number of specialist committees.

There are about 295,000 Presbyterians in Ireland, mainly in the north, in 562 congregations and with 400 ministers.

Moderator (1998–9), Rt. Revd S. J. Dixon

Clerk of Assembly and General Secretary (acting), Very Revd Dr S. Hutchinson, Church House, Belfast BT1 6DW. Tel: 01232-322284

THE PRESBYTERIAN CHURCH OF WALES

The Presbyterian Church of Wales or Calvinistic Methodist Church of Wales is Calvinistic in doctrine and presbyterian in constitution. It was formed in 1811 when Welsh Calvinists severed the relationship with the established church by ordaining their own ministers. It secured its own confession of faith in 1823 and a Constitutional Deed in 1826, and since 1864 the General Assembly has met annually, presided over by a Moderator elected for a year. The doctrine and constitutional structure of the Presbyterian Church of Wales was confirmed by Act of Parliament in 1931–2.

The Church has 49,765 members, 130 ministers and 921 churches.

Moderator (1998–9), Revd W. I. Cynwill Williams

General Secretary, Revd D. H. Owen, 53 Richmond Road, Cardiff CF2 3UP. Tel: 01222-494913

THE RELIGIOUS SOCIETY OF FRIENDS (QUAKERS)

Quakerism is a movement, not a church, which was founded in the 17th century by George Fox and others in an attempt to revive what they saw as 'primitive Christianity'. The movement was based originally in the Midlands, Yorkshire and north-west England, but there are now Quakers in 36 countries around the world. The colony of Pennsylvania, founded by William Penn, was originally Quaker.

Emphasis is placed on the experience of God in daily life rather than on sacraments or religious occasions. There is no church calendar. Worship is largely silent and there are no appointed ministers; the responsibility for conducting a meeting is shared equally among those present. Social reform and religious tolerance have always been important

to Quakers, together with a commitment to non-violence in resolving disputes.

There are 213,800 Quakers world-wide, with over 19,000 in Great Britain and Ireland. There are about 490 meeting houses in Great Britain.

CENTRAL OFFICES: (GREAT BRITAIN) Friends House, Euston Road, London NW1 2BJ. Tel: 0171-387 3601; (IRELAND) Swanbrook House, Morehampton Road, Dublin 4. Tel: 00 353 1-683684

THE SALVATION ARMY

The Salvation Army was founded by a Methodist minister, William Booth, in the east end of London in 1865, and has since become established in 103 countries world-wide. It was first known as the Christian Mission, and took its present name in 1878 when it adopted a quasi-military command structure intended to inspire and regulate its endeavours and to reflect its view that the Church was engaged in spiritual warfare. Salvationists emphasize evangelism, social work and the relief of poverty.

The world leader, known as the General, is elected by a High Council composed of the Chief of the Staff and senior ranking officers known as commissioners.

There are about 1.5 million members, 17,389 active officers (full-time ordained ministers) and 16,080 worship centres and outposts world-wide. In Great Britain and Ireland there are 65,168 members, 1,732 active officers and 986 worship centres.

General, P. A. Rader

UK Territorial Commander, Commissioner J. Gowans

TERRITORIAL HEADQUARTERS, 101 Queen Victoria Street, London EC4P 4EP. Tel: 0171-332 0022

THE SEVENTH-DAY ADVENTIST CHURCH

The Seventh-day Adventist Church was founded in 1863 in the USA. Its members look forward to the second coming of Christ and observe the Sabbath (the seventh day) as a day of rest, worship and ministry. The Church bases its faith and practice wholly on the Bible and has developed 27 fundamental beliefs.

The World Church is divided into 14 divisions, each made up of unions of churches. The Seventh-day Adventist Church in the British Isles is known as the British Union of Seventh-day Adventists and is a member of the Trans-European Division. In the British Isles the administrative organization of the church is arranged in three tiers: the local churches; the regional conferences for south England, north England, Wales, Scotland and Ireland; and the national 'union' conference.

There are about 9 million Adventists and 40,905 churches in 208 countries world-wide. In the UK and Ireland there are 19,145 members, 145 ministers and 238 churches.

President of the British Union Conference, Pastor C. R. Perry

BRITISH ISLES HEADQUARTERS, Stanborough Park, Watford WD2 6JP. Tel: 01923-672251

UNDEB YR ANNIBYNWYR CYMRAEG
The Union of Welsh Independents

The Union of Welsh Independents was formed in 1872 and is a voluntary association of Welsh Congregational

Churches and personal members. It is entirely Welsh-speaking. Congregationalism in Wales dates back to 1639 when the first Welsh Congregational Church was opened in Gwent. Member churches are Calvinistic in doctrine and congregationalist in organization. Each church has complete independence in the government and administration of its affairs.

The Union has 39,174 members, 231 ministers and 535 member churches.

President of the Union (1998–9), Revd Dr N. A. Davies
General Secretary, Revd D. Morris Jones, Tŷ John Penry, 11 Heol Sant Helen, Swansea SA1 4AL. Tel: 01792-652542

THE UNITED REFORMED CHURCH

The United Reformed Church was formed by the union of most of the Congregational churches in England and Wales with the Presbyterian Church of England in 1972.

Congregationalism dates from the mid 16th century. It is Calvinistic in doctrine, and its followers form independent self-governing congregations bound under God by covenant, a principle laid down in the writings of Robert Browne (1550–1633). From the late 16th century the movement was driven underground by persecution, but the cause was defended at the Westminster Assembly in 1643 and the Savoy Declaration of 1658 laid down its principles. Congregational churches formed county associations for mutual support and in 1832 these associations merged to form the Congregational Union of England and Wales.

The Presbyterian Church in England also dates from the mid 16th century, and was Calvinistic and evangelical in its doctrine. It was governed by a hierarchy of courts.

In the 1960s there was close co-operation locally and nationally between Congregational and Presbyterian Churches. This led to union negotiations and a Scheme of Union, supported by Act of Parliament in 1972. In 1981 a further unification took place, with the Reformed Association of Churches of Christ becoming part of the URC. In its basis the United Reformed Church reflects local church initiative and responsibility with a conciliar pattern of oversight. The General Assembly is the central body, and is made up of equal numbers of ministers and lay members.

The United Reformed Church is divided into 12 Provinces, each with a Provincial Moderator who chairs the Synod, and 75 Districts. There are 96,917 members, 650 full-time stipendiary ministers, 190 non-stipendiary ministers and 1,739 local churches.

General Secretary, Revd A. G. Burnham, 86 Tavistock Place, London WC1H 9RT. Tel: 0171-916 2020

THE WESLEYAN REFORM UNION

The Wesleyan Reform Union was founded by Methodists who left or were expelled from Wesleyan Methodism in 1849 following a period of internal conflict. Its doctrine is conservative evangelical and its organization is congregational, each church having complete independence in the government and administration of its affairs. The main concentration of churches is in Yorkshire.

The Union has 2,250 members, 20 ministers, 137 lay preachers and 114 churches.

President (1998–9), P. H. Norton
General Secretary, Revd E. W. Downing, Wesleyan Reform Church House, 123 Queen Street, Sheffield S1 2DU. Tel: 0114-272 1938

Non-Trinitarian Churches

THE CHURCH OF CHRIST, SCIENTIST

The Church of Christ, Scientist was founded by Mary Baker Eddy in the USA in 1879 to 'reinstate primitive Christianity and its lost element of healing'. Christian Science teaches the need for spiritual regeneration and salvation from sin, but is best known for its reliance on prayer alone in the healing of sickness. Adherents believe that such healing is a law, or Science, and is in direct line with that practised by Jesus Christ (revered, not as God, but as the Son of God) and by the early Christian Church.

The denomination consists of The First Church of Christ, Scientist, in Boston, Massachusetts, USA (the Mother Church) and its branch churches in over 60 countries world-wide. Branch churches are democratically governed by their members, while a five-member Board of Directors, based in Boston, is authorized to transact the business of the Mother Church. The Bible and Mary Baker Eddy's book, *Science and Health with Key to the Scriptures*, are used at services; there are no clergy. Those engaged in full-time healing are called practitioners, of whom there are 3,500 world-wide.

No membership figures are available, since Mary Baker Eddy felt that numbers are no measure of spiritual vitality and ruled that such statistics should not be published. There are over 2,400 branch churches world-wide, including nearly 200 in the UK.

CHRISTIAN SCIENCE COMMITTEE ON PUBLICATION, 2 Elysium Gate, 126 New Kings Road, London SW6 4LZ. Tel: 0171-371 0600. *District Manager for Great Britain and Ireland*, A. Grayson

THE CHURCH OF JESUS CHRIST OF LATTER-DAY SAINTS

The Church (often referred to as 'the Mormons') was founded in New York State, USA, in 1830, and came to Britain in 1837. The oldest continuous branch in the world is to be found in Preston, Lancs. Mormons are Christians who claim to belong to the 'Restored Church' of Jesus Christ. They believe that true Christianity died when the last original apostle died, but that it was given back to the world by God and Christ through Joseph Smith, the Church's founder and first president. They accept and use the Bible as scripture, but believe in continuing revelation from God and use additional scriptures, including *The Book of Mormon: Another Testament of Jesus Christ*. The importance of the family is central to the Church's beliefs and practices. Church members set aside Monday evenings as Family Home Evenings when Christian family values are taught. Polygamy was formally discontinued in 1890.

The Church has no paid ministry; local congregations are headed by a leader chosen from amongst their number. The world governing body, based in Utah, USA, is the three-man First Presidency, assisted by the Quorum of the Twelve Apostles.

There are more than 10 million members world-wide, with about 180,000 adherents in Britain in over 350 congregations.

President of the Europe North Area (including Britain), Elder S. J. Condie

BRITISH HEADQUARTERS, Church Offices, 751 Warwick
Road, Solihull, W. Midlands B91 3DQ. Tel: 0121-712 1202

JEHOVAH'S WITNESSES

The movement now known as Jehovah's Witnesses grew
from a Bible study group formed by Charles Taze Russell
in 1872 in Pennsylvania, USA. In 1896 it adopted the name
of the Watch Tower Bible and Tract Society, and in 1931
its members became known as Jehovah's Witnesses.
Jehovah's (God's) Witnesses believe in the Bible as the
word of God, and consider it to be inspired and historically
accurate. They take the scriptures literally, except where
there are obvious indications that they are figurative or
symbolic, and reject the doctrine of the Trinity. Witnesses
also believe that the earth will remain for ever and that all
those approved of by Jehovah will have eternal life on a
cleansed and beautified earth; only 144,000 will go to
heaven to rule with Christ. They believe that the second
coming of Christ and his thousand-year reign on earth
have been imminent since 1914, and that Armageddon (a
final battle in which evil will be defeated) will precede
Christ's rule of peace. They refuse to take part in military
service, and do not accept blood transfusions. They publish
two magazines, *The Watchtower* and *Awake!*

The 12-member world governing body is based in New
York, USA. Witnesses world-wide are divided into branches, countries or areas, districts, circuits and congregations. There are overseers at each level, and two assemblies
are held annually for each circuit. There is no paid
ministry, but each congregation has elders assigned to
look after various duties and every Witness is assigned
homes to visit in their congregation.

There are over 5 million Jehovah's Witnesses world-
wide, with 130,000 Witnesses in the UK organized into
over 1,400 congregations.

BRITISH ISLES HEADQUARTERS, Watch Tower House,
The Ridgeway, London NW7 1RN. Tel: 0181-906 2211

UNITARIAN AND FREE CHRISTIAN CHURCHES

Unitarianism has its historical roots in the Judaeo-
Christian tradition but rejects the deity of Christ and the
doctrine of the trinity. It allows the individual to embrace
insights from all the world's faiths and philosophies, as
there is no fixed creed. It is accepted that beliefs may evolve
in the light of personal experience.

Unitarian communities first became established in Poland and Transylvania in the 16th century. The first
avowedly Unitarian place of worship in the British Isles
opened in London in 1774. The General Assembly of
Unitarian and Free Christian Churches came into existence in 1928 as the result of the amalgamation of two
earlier organizations.   There are about 7,000 Unitarians
in Great Britain and Ireland, and 150 Unitarian ministers.
About 200 self-governing congregations and fellowship
groups, including a small number overseas, are members of
the General Assembly.

GENERAL ASSEMBLY OF UNITARIAN AND FREE
CHRISTIAN CHURCHES, Essex Hall, 1–6 Essex Street,
Strand, London WC2R 3HY. Tel: 0171-240 2384. *General
Secretary*, J. J. Teagle

Nobel Prizes

For prize winners for the years 1901–94, *see* earlier editions of *Whitaker's Almanack*.

The Nobel Prizes are awarded each year from the income of a trust fund established by the Swedish scientist Alfred Nobel, the inventor of dynamite, who died on 10 December 1896 leaving a fortune of £1,750,000. The prizes are awarded to those who have contributed most to the common good in the domain of:

Physics – awarded by the Royal Swedish Academy of Sciences
Chemistry – awarded by the Royal Swedish Academy of Sciences
Physiology or Medicine – awarded by the Karolinska Institute
Literature – awarded by the Swedish Academy of Arts
Peace – awarded by a five-person committee elected by the Norwegian Storting
Economic Sciences (instituted 1969) – awarded by the Royal Swedish Academy of Sciences

The prizes are awarded every year on 10 December, the anniversary of Nobel's death. The first awards were made on 10 December 1901.

The Trust is administered by the board of directors of the Nobel Foundation, Stockholm, consisting of five members and three deputy members. The Swedish Government appoints a chairman and a deputy chairman, the remaining members being appointed by the awarding authorities.

The awards have been distributed as follows:

PHYSICS
American 65, British 20, German 19 (1948–90, West German 8), French 12, Soviet 7, Dutch 6, Swedish 4, Austrian 3, Danish 3, Italian 3, Japanese 3, Canadian 2, Chinese 2, Swiss 2, Indian 1, Irish 1, Pakistani 1

CHEMISTRY
American 42, German 27 (1948–90, West German 10), British 25, French 7, Swiss 5, Swedish 4, Canadian 3, Dutch 3, Argentinian 1, Austrian 1, Belgian 1, Czech 1, Finnish 1, Hungarian 1, Italian 1, Japanese 1, Mexican 1, Norwegian 1, Soviet 1

PHYSIOLOGY OR MEDICINE
American 75, British 23, German 15 (1948–90, West German 4), French 7, Swedish 7, Swiss 6, Danish 5, Austrian 4, Belgian 4, Australian 3, Italian 3, Canadian 2, Dutch 2, Hungarian 2, Russian 2, Argentinian 1, Japanese 1, Portuguese 1, South African 1, Spanish 1

LITERATURE
French 12, American 10, British 8, Swedish 7, German 6 (1948–90, West German 1), Italian 6, Spanish 5, Danish 3, Irish 3, Norwegian 3, Polish 3, Soviet 3, Chilean 2, Greek 2, Japanese 2, Swiss 2, Australian 1, Belgian 1, Colombian 1, Czech 1, Egyptian 1, Finnish 1, Guatemalan 1, Icelandic 1, Indian 1, Israeli 1, Mexican 1, Nigerian 1, South African 1, Trinidadian 1, Yugoslav 1, Stateless 1

PEACE
American 18, Institutions 18, British 10, French 9, Swedish 5, German 4 (1948–90, West German 1), South African 4, Belgian 3, Israeli 3, Swiss 3, Argentinian 2, Austrian 2, East Timorese 2, Norwegian 2, Soviet 2, Burmese 1, Canadian 1, Costa Rican 1, Danish 1, Dutch 1, Egyptian 1, Guatemalan 1, Irish 1, Italian 1, Japanese 1, Mexican 1, Palestinian 1, Polish 1, Tibetan 1, Vietnamese 1, Yugoslav 1

ECONOMICS
American 26, British 7, Norwegian 2, Swedish 2, Canadian 1, Dutch 1, French 1, German 1, Soviet 1

The Swedish Embassy (*see* page 1026) can provide a full list of winners.

Prize	1995	1996	1997
Physics	Dr M. Perl (American) Dr F. Reines (American)	Prof. D. Lee (American) Prof. D. Osheroff (American) Prof. R. Richardson (American)	Prof. S. Chu (American) Prof. C. Cohen-Tannoudji (French) Dr W. Phillips (American)
Chemistry	P. Crutzen (Dutch) Dr M. Molina (Mexican) Dr S. Rowland (American)	Prof. R. Curl (American) Sir Harold Kroto, Kt., FRS (British) Prof. R. Smalley (American)	Dr J. Walker (British)
Physiology or Medicine	Dr E. Lewis (American) Dr C. Nuesslein-Volhard (German) Dr E. Wieschaus (American)	Prof. P. Doherty (Australian) Prof. R. Zinkernagel (Swiss)	Prof. S. Prusiner (American)
Literature	S. Heaney (Irish)	W. Szymborska (Polish)	Dario Fo (Italian)
Peace	Prof. J. Rotblat (British) The Pugwash Conference on Science and World Affairs	Bishop Carlos Belo (East Timorese) J. Ramos-Horta (East Timorese)	The International Campaign to Ban Land-mines and the campaign co-ordinator, Jody Williams (American)
Economics	R. Lucas (American)	Prof. J. Mirrlees (British) Prof. W. Vickrey (Canadian)	Prof. M. Scholes (American) Prof. R. Merton (American)

Education

For addresses of national education departments, *see* Government Departments and Public Offices. For other addresses, *see* Education Directory

Responsibility for education in the United Kingdom is largely decentralized. Overall responsibility for all aspects of education lies in England with the Secretary of State for Education and Employment; in Wales with the Secretary of State for Wales; in Scotland with the Secretary of State for Scotland acting through the Scottish Office Education and Industry Department; and in Northern Ireland with the Secretary of State for Northern Ireland.

The main concerns of the education departments (the Department for Education and Employment (DfEE), the Welsh Office, the Scottish Office Education and Industry Department (SOEID), and the Department of Education for Northern Ireland (DENI)) are the formulation of national policies for education and the maintenance of consistency in educational standards. They are responsible for the broad allocation of resources for education, for the rate and distribution of educational building and for the supply, training and superannuation of teachers.

EXPENDITURE

In the UK in 1995–6, expenditure on education was (£ million):

Schools	20,977.9
Further and higher education	9,770.4
Other education and related expenditure	4,680.7

Most of this expenditure is incurred by local authorities, which make their own expenditure decisions according to their local situations and needs. Expenditure on education by central government departments, in real terms, was (£ million):

	1997–8 estimated outturn	1998–9 planned
DfEE	11,692	11,498
Welsh Office	569	527.3
SOEID	1,276	1,182
DENI	1,259	1,284

The bulk of direct expenditure by the DfEE, the Welsh Office and SOEID is directed towards supporting higher education in universities and colleges through the Higher Education Funding Councils (HEFCs) and further education and sixth form colleges through the Further Education Funding Councils (FEFCs) in England and Wales and directly from central government in Scotland. In addition, the DfEE funds student support in England and Wales, the City Technology Colleges (CTCs), the City College for the Technology of the Arts, and pays grants under the specialist schools programme.

The Welsh Office also funds grant-maintained schools, educational services and research, and supports bilingual education and the Welsh language.

In Scotland the main elements of central government expenditure, in addition to those outlined above, are grant-aided special schools, student awards and bursaries (through the Student Award Agency for Scotland), curriculum development, special educational needs and community education.

The Department of Education for Northern Ireland directly funds higher education, teacher education, teacher salaries and superannuation, student awards, further education, grant-maintained integrated schools, and voluntary grammar schools.

Current net expenditure on education by local education authorities in England, Wales, and Scotland, and education and library boards in Northern Ireland is (£ million):

	1997–8 estimated outturn	1998–9 planned
England	18.50	18.40
Wales	1.20	1.30
Scotland	2.40	2.40
Northern Ireland	0.99	0.88

LOCAL EDUCATION ADMINISTRATION

The education service at present is a national service in which the provision of most school education is locally administered.

In England and Wales the education service is administered by local education authorities (LEAs), which carry the day-to-day responsibility for providing most state primary and secondary education in their areas. They share with the FEFCs the duty to provide adult education to meet local needs.

The LEAs own and maintain most schools and some colleges, build new ones and provide equipment. LEAs are financed largely from the council tax and aggregate external finance (AEF) from the Department for the Environment, Transport and the Regions in England and the Welsh Office in Wales.

All LEA-maintained schools manage their own budgets. The LEA allocates funds to the school, largely on the basis of pupil numbers, and the school governing body is responsible for overseeing spending and for most aspects of staffing, including appointments and dismissals. The School Standards and Framework Act has given LEAs greater powers to monitor, maintain and improve standards. An Education Association can be set up to take over the management of failing schools where both the LEA and the governing body have not brought about improvements identified as necessary by inspection.

The duty of providing education locally in Scotland rests with the education authorities. They are responsible for the construction of buildings, the employment of teachers and other staff, and the provision of equipment and materials. Devolved School Management (DSM) is in place for all primary, secondary and special schools.

Education authorities are required to establish school boards consisting of parents and teachers as well as co-opted members, responsible among other things for the appointment of staff.

Education is administered locally in Northern Ireland by five education and library boards, whose costs are met in full by DENI. All grant-aided schools include elected parents and teachers on their boards of governors. Provision has been made for schools wishing to provide integrated education or to have grant-maintained integrated status from the outset. All schools and colleges of further education have full responsibility for their own budgets, including staffing costs. The Council for Catholic Maintained Schools forms an upper tier of management for

Catholic schools and provides advice on matters relating to management and administration.

THE INSPECTORATE

The Office for Standards in Education (OFSTED) is a non-ministerial government department in England headed by HM Chief Inspector of Schools (HMCI). OFSTED's remit is regularly to inspect all maintained schools and report on and thereby improve standards of achievement. All state schools are inspected by teams of OFSTED-trained, self-employed inspectors, including educationalists and lay people and headed by registered inspectors. Registered inspectors are required to follow procedures set out in two key documents, the *Framework for Inspection of Schools* and the *Framework for Nursery Settings* to ensure consistency in the process of inspection and the criteria used. HM Inspectors (HMI) within OFSTED report on good practice in schools and other educational issues based on inspection evidence. From 1997 for secondary and from 1998 for primary, schools will be inspected once every six years or more frequently if there is cause. A summary of the inspection report must be sent to the parents of each pupil by the school, followed by a copy of the governors' action plan thereon. OFSTED's counterpart in Wales is the Office of HM Chief Inspector of Schools in Wales (OHMCI Wales), where inspection of maintained schools is carried out on a five-year cycle. The inspection of further and higher education in England and Wales is the responsibility of inspectors appointed to the respective funding councils. From 2000, each LEA will be inspected on a five-year cycle by OFSTED supported by the Audit Commission.

HM Inspectors of Schools in Scotland inspect schools and publish reports on further education institutions and community education, and are involved in assessing the quality of teacher education. HMIs work in teams alongside lay people and associate assessors, who are practising teachers seconded for the inspection. The inspection of higher education is the responsibility of inspectors appointed to the Higher Education Funding Council for Scotland.

Inspection is carried out in Northern Ireland by the Department of Education's Education and Training Inspectorate, using teams which on occasion include lay people. The Inspectorate also performs an advisory function to the Secretary of State for Northern Ireland. From September 1992 a five-year cycle of inspection was introduced.

There are, in 1998–9, 200 HMIs on OFSTED's permanent staff, 2,000 trained registered inspectors, 9,500 team inspectors in England, 38 HMIs, about 350 registered inspectors and 820 team members in Wales, 78 HMIs and eight Chief Inspectors in Scotland and 58 members of the Inspectorate in Northern Ireland.

SCHOOLS AND PUPILS

Schooling is compulsory in Great Britain for all children between five and 16 years and between four and 16 years in Northern Ireland. Provision is being increased for children under five and many pupils remain at school after the minimum leaving age. No fees are charged in any publicly maintained school in England, Wales and Scotland. In Northern Ireland, fees are paid by pupils in preparatory departments of grammar schools, but pupils admitted to the secondary departments of grammar schools do not pay fees.

In the UK, parents have a right to express a preference for a particular school and have a right to appeal if dissatisfied. The policy, known as more open enrolment, requires schools to admit children up to the limit of their capacity if there is a demand for places, and to publish their criteria for selection if they are over-subscribed, in which case parents have a right of appeal.

The 'Parents' Charter', available free from education departments, is a booklet which tells parents about the education system. Schools are now required to make available information about themselves, their public examination and national test results, truancy rates, and destination of leavers. Corporal punishment is no longer legal in publicly maintained schools in the UK.

FALL AND RISE IN NUMBERS

In primary education, and increasingly in secondary education, pupil numbers in the UK declined through the 1980s. In maintained nursery and primary schools pupil numbers reached their lowest figure of 4.6 million in 1986. They stood at 5.3 million in 1997 and are expected to decline to 5.1 million by 2002. In secondary schools pupil numbers peaked at 4.6 million in 1981. They stood at 3.7 million in 1997 and are projected to rise to about 4 million in 2007.

ENGLAND AND WALES

There are two main types of school in England and Wales: publicly maintained schools, which charge no fees; and independent schools, which charge fees (*see* pages 428–9). Publicly maintained schools are maintained by local education authorities except for grant-maintained schools and City Technology Colleges.

The number of schools by category in 1996 was:

Maintained schools	29,872
County	15,638
Voluntary	7,079
controlled	2,982
aided	4,116
special agreement*	39
Grant-maintained	1,135
Wales	16
CTCs and CCTAs	15
Independent schools	2,318
TOTAL	33,340

* In England only

County schools are owned by LEAs and wholly funded by them. They are non-denominational and provide primary and secondary education. Voluntary schools also provide primary and secondary education. Although the buildings are in many cases provided by the voluntary bodies (mainly religious denominations), they are financially maintained by an LEA. In controlled schools the LEA bears all costs. In aided schools the building is usually provided by the voluntary body. The managers or governors are responsible for repairs to the school building and for improvements and alterations to it, though the DfEE may reimburse up to 85 per cent of approved capital expenditure, while the LEA pays for internal maintenance and other running costs. Special agreement schools are those where the LEA may, by special agreement, pay between one-half and three-quarters of the cost of building a new, or extending an existing, voluntary school, almost always a secondary school.

From September 1999, all existing publicly funded schools will be incorporated into a new school framework. County schools will become community schools. A new voluntary category will be subdivided into two categories, voluntary controlled and voluntary aided schools, which latter will comprise aided and special agreement schools. Most grant-maintained schools will be categorized as foundation schools (*see* below). From 1 September 2000, provision is proposed for schools to opt to transfer between categories.

Under the Local Management of Schools (LMS) initiative, LEAs are required to delegate at least 85 per cent of school budgets, including staffing costs, directly to schools. LEAs continue to retain responsibility for various common services, including transport and school meals.

Governing bodies – All publicly maintained schools have a governing body, usually made up of a number of parent and local community representatives, governors appointed by the LEA if the school is LEA maintained, the headteacher (unless he or she chooses otherwise), and serving teachers. Schools can appoint up to four sponsor governors from business who will be expected to provide financial and managerial assistance. Governors are responsible for the overall policies of schools and their academic aims and objectives; they also control matters of school discipline and the appointment and dismissal of staff. Governing bodies select inspectors for their schools, are responsible for action as a result of inspection reports and are required to make those reports and their action plans thereon available to parents.

The Specialist Schools Programme – The programme is open to all state secondary schools in England which teach the national curriculum and wish to specialize in the teaching of technology, mathematics and science (technology colleges), modern foreign languages (language colleges), sports colleges and arts colleges. In addition to the normal funding arrangements, the schools receive business sponsorship (up to four sponsor governors may sit on governing bodies) and complementary capital grants up to £100,000 from central government, together with extra annual funding of £100 a pupil to assist the delivery of an enhanced curriculum. By September 1998, there were 227 technology colleges, 58 language colleges, 26 sports colleges and 19 arts colleges.

Grant-maintained (GM) schools – Under the Conservative government, all secondary and primary schools, whether maintained or independent, were eligible to apply for grant-maintained status, subject to a ballot of parents. GM schools were maintained directly by the Secretary of State (through the Funding Agency for Schools) and the Welsh Office, not the LEA, and were wholly run by their own governing body. From 1 September 1999, the name and status of GM schools will change. Former county and voluntary controlled schools and those established by the Funding Agency for Schools will become foundation schools, while former voluntary aided and special agreement schools and those founded by promoters will join the voluntary aided subdivision of the voluntary category. They will have the option to express a preference as to category. GM schools will no longer be directly funded and will be included in LEA funding arrangements. About 60 per cent of grant-maintained schools are secondary schools.

City Technology Colleges (CTCs) and *City Colleges for the Technology of the Arts (CCTAs)* are state-aided but independent of LEAs. Their aim is to widen the choice of secondary education in disadvantaged urban areas and to teach a broad curriculum with an emphasis on science, technology, business understanding and arts technologies. Capital costs are shared by government and business sponsors, and running costs are covered by a per capita grant from the DfEE in line with comparable costs in an LEA maintained school. The first city technology college

opened in 1988 in Solihull. The first CCTA, known as Britschool, opened in Croydon in 1991.

SCOTLAND

The number of schools by category in 1997 was:

Publicly maintained schools:

Education authority	3,565
Self-governing	2
Independent schools	114
TOTAL	3,681

Education authority schools (known as public schools) are financed by local government, partly through revenue support grants from central government, and partly from local taxation. A small number of grant-aided schools, mainly in the special sector, are conducted by boards of managers and receive grants direct from the SOEID. Independent schools receive no direct grant and charge fees, but are subject to inspection and registration. An additional category exists of self-governing schools opting to be managed entirely by a board of management. These schools remain in the public sector and are funded by direct government grant set to match the resources the school would receive under education authority management. Two were established, but it is planned to return them to the education authority framework.

Education authorities are required to establish school boards to participate in the administration and management of schools. These boards consist of elected parents and staff members as well as co-opted members.

NORTHERN IRELAND

The number of schools by category in 1997 was:

Grant-aided schools:

Controlled	662
Voluntary maintained	549
Voluntary grammar	53
Integrated schools	32
Independent schools	19
TOTAL	1,296

Controlled schools are maintained by the education and library boards with all costs paid from public funds. Voluntary maintained schools, mainly under Roman Catholic management, receive grants towards capital costs and running costs in whole or in part. Voluntary grammar schools may be under Roman Catholic or non-denominational management and receive grants from DENI. All grant-aided schools include elected parents and teachers on their boards of governors, whose responsibilities also include financial management under the Local Management of Schools (LMS) initiative. All secondary schools now have fully delegated budgets and as of 1996–7 84 per cent of primary schools. Voluntary maintained and voluntary grammar schools can apply for designation as a new category of voluntary school, which is eligible for a 100 per cent as opposed to 85 per cent grant. Such schools are managed by a board of governors on which no single interest group has a majority of nominees.

The majority of children in Northern Ireland are educated in schools which in practice are segregated on religious lines. Integrated schools exist to educate Protestant and Roman Catholic children together. There are two types: grant-maintained integrated schools which are funded by DENI; and controlled integrated schools funded by the education and library boards. Procedures are in place for balloting parents in existing segregated schools to determine whether they want instead to have integrated schools, subject to the satisfaction of certain criteria. By

September 1998, 38 integrated schools had been established, 14 of them secondary.

THE STATE SYSTEM

NURSERY EDUCATION – Nursery education is for children from two to five years and is not compulsory. It takes place in nursery schools (1,538 in the public sector in 1997) or nursery classes in primary schools. The number of children receiving nursery education in the UK in 1996–7 was:

In maintained nursery schools	82,200
In primary schools	989,700
In non-maintained nursery schools	69,300
In special schools	8,000
TOTAL	1,149,200

Many children also attend pre-school playgroups organized by parents and voluntary bodies such as the Pre-School Learning Alliance. The nursery voucher scheme, whereby every parent of a four-year-old received a voucher worth £1,100 exchangeable for up to three terms of pre-school education, was introduced in England and Wales in April 1997. It was discontinued by the present government in summer 1997, before it had been introduced in Northern Ireland. Education authorities are responsible for funding nursery education in their areas using a range of providers on the basis of an Early Years Development Plan after reviewing and consulting on local provision for under-fives. In Scotland vouchers remained in place until June 1998; thereafter local authorities undertook the funding and management of services as elsewhere in the UK. All providers of pre-school education are subject to inspection.

PRIMARY EDUCATION – Primary education begins at five years in Great Britain and four years in Northern Ireland, and is almost always co-educational. In England, Wales and Northern Ireland the transfer to secondary school is generally made at 11 years. In Scotland, the primary school course lasts for seven years and pupils transfer to secondary courses at about the age of 12.

Primary schools consist mainly of infants' schools for children aged five to seven, junior schools for those aged seven to 11, and combined junior and infant schools for both age groups. First schools in some parts of England cater for ages five to ten as the first stage of a three-tier system: first, middle and secondary. Many primary schools provide nursery classes for children under five (*see* above).

Primary schools (UK) 1996–67

No. of primary schools	23,306
No. of pupils	5,380,200
Pupils under five years	989,700

Pupil-teacher ratios in maintained primary schools were:

	1995–6	1996–7
England	23.2	23.4
Wales	22.5	n/a
Scotland	19.6	19.6
Northern Ireland	19.5	19.8
UK	21.2	20.9

The average size of classes 'as taught' was 25.5 in 1996 but rose to 25.6 in 1997.

MIDDLE SCHOOLS – Middle schools (which take children from first schools), mostly in England, cover varying age ranges between eight and 14 and usually lead on to comprehensive upper schools.

SECONDARY EDUCATION – Secondary schools are for children aged 11 to 16 and for those who choose to stay on to 18. At 16, many students prefer to move on to tertiary or sixth form colleges (*see* pages 432–3). Most secondary schools in England, Wales and Scotland are co-educational. The largest secondary schools have over 1,500 pupils but only 30.8 per cent of the schools take over 1,000 pupils.

Secondary schools 1997

	England and Wales	Scotland	N. Ireland
No. of pupils	3,240,100	316,600	152,700
% 16 and 17 years	31.3%	63.1%	41.3%
Average class size	21.2	19.5	n/a
Pupil-teacher ratio	16.3	13.2	14.5

In England and Wales the main types of secondary schools are: comprehensive schools (87.2 per cent of pupils in England, 100 in Wales), whose admission arrangements are without reference to ability or aptitude; middle deemed secondary schools for children aged variously between eight and 14 years who then move on to senior comprehensive schools at 12, 13 or 14 (5.1 per cent of pupils in England); secondary modern schools (2.1 per cent of pupils in England) providing a general education with a practical bias; secondary grammar schools (4.2 per cent of pupils in England) with selective intake providing an academic course from 11 to 16–18 years; and technical schools (0.1 per cent in England), providing an integrated academic and technical education.

In Scotland all pupils in education authority secondary schools attend schools with a comprehensive intake. Most of these schools provide a full range of courses appropriate to all levels of ability from first to sixth year.

In most areas of Northern Ireland there is a selective system of secondary education with pupils transferring either to grammar schools (41 per cent of pupils in 1997) or secondary schools (59 per cent of pupils in 1997) at 11–12 years of age. Parents can choose the school they would like their children to attend and all those who apply must be admitted if they meet the criteria. If a school is over-subscribed beyond its statutory admissions number, selection is on the basis of published criteria, which, for most grammar schools, place emphasis on performance in the transfer procedure tests which are set and administered by the Northern Ireland Council for the Curriculum, Examinations and Assessment. When parents consider that a school has not applied its criteria fairly they have access to independent appeals tribunals. Grammar schools provide an academic type of secondary education with A-levels at the end of the seventh year, while secondary non-grammar schools follow a curriculum suited to a wider range of aptitudes and abilities.

SPECIAL EDUCATION – Special education is provided for children with special educational needs, usually because they have a disability which either prevents or hinders them from making use of educational facilities of a kind generally provided for children of their age in schools within the area of the local authority concerned. Wherever possible, such children are educated in ordinary schools, taking the parents' wishes into account, and schools are required to publish their policy for pupils with special educational needs. LEAs in England and Wales and Education and Library Boards in Northern Ireland are required to identify and secure provision for the needs of children with learning difficulties, to involve the parents in any decision and draw up a formal statement of the child's special educational needs and how they intend to meet them, all within statutory time limits. Parents have a right to appeal to a Special Educational Needs (SEN) Tribunal if they disagree with the statement.

Maintained special schools are run by education authorities which pay all the costs of maintenance, but under the terms of Local Management of Schools (LMS), those able and wishing to manage their own budgets may choose to do so. Non-maintained special schools are run by voluntary bodies; they may receive some grant from central government for capital expenditure and for equipment but their current expenditure is met primarily from the fees charged to education authorities for pupils placed in the schools. Some independent schools provide education wholly or mainly for children with special educational needs and are required to meet similar standards to those for maintained and non-maintained special schools. It is intended that pupils with special education needs should have access to as much of the national curriculum as possible, but there is provision for them to be exempt from it or for it to be modified to suit their capabilities.

The number of full-time pupils with statements of special needs in January 1997 was:

In special schools: total	100,600
England	87,300
Wales*	3,400
Scotland	6,300
N. Ireland	3,600
In public sector primary and secondary	
schools: total	157,100
England	133,700
Wales*	11,600
Scotland	8,000
N. Ireland	3,800

*January 1996 figures

In Scotland, school placing is a matter of agreement between education authorities and parents. Parents have the right to say which school they want their child to attend, and a right of appeal where their wishes are not being met. Whenever possible, children with special needs are integrated into ordinary schools. However, for those who require a different environment or specialized facilities, there are special schools, both grant-aided by central government and independent, and special classes within ordinary schools. Education authorities are required to respond to reasonable requests for independent special schools and to send children with special needs to schools outside Scotland if appropriate provision is not available within the country.

ALTERNATIVE PROVISION

There is no legal obligation on parents in the UK to educate their children at school provided that the local education authority is satisfied that the child is receiving full-time education suited to its age, abilities and aptitudes. The education authority need not be informed that a child is being educated at home unless the child is already registered at a state school. In this case the parents must arrange for the child's name to be removed from the school's register (by writing to the headteacher) before education at home can begin. Failure to do so leaves the parents liable to prosecution for condoning non-attendance.

In most cases an initial visit is made by an education adviser or education welfare officer, and sometimes subsequent inspections are made, but practice varies according to the individual education authority. There is no requirement for parents educating their children at home to be in possession of a teaching qualification.

Information and support on all aspects of home education can be obtained from Education Otherwise (see page 443).

INDEPENDENT SCHOOLS

Independent schools receive no grants from public funds. They charge fees, and are owned and managed under special trusts, with profits being used for the benefit of the schools concerned. There is a wide variety of provision, from kindergartens to large day and boarding schools, and from experimental schools to traditional institutions. A number of independent schools have been instituted by religious and ethnic minorities.

All independent schools in the UK are open to inspection by approved inspectors (see page 425) and must register with the appropriate government education department. The education departments lay down certain minimum standards and can make schools remedy any unacceptable features of their building or instruction and exclude any unsuitable teacher or proprietor. Most independent schools offer a similar range of courses to state schools and enter pupils for the same public examinations. Introduction of the national curriculum and the associated education targets and assessment procedures is not obligatory in the independent sector.

The term public school is often applied to those independent schools in membership of the Headmasters' and Headmistresses' Conference, the Governing Bodies Association or the Governing Bodies of Girls' Schools Association. Most public schools are single-sex but there are some mixed schools and an increasing number of schools have mixed sixth forms.

Preparatory schools are so-called because they prepare pupils for the common entrance examination to senior independent schools. Most cater for pupils from about seven to 13 years. The common entrance examination is set by the Common Entrance Examination Board, but marked by the independent school to which the pupil intends to go. It is taken at 13 by boys, and between 11 and 13 by girls.

The number of schools and pupils in 1996-7 was:

	No. of schools	No. of pupils	Pupil-teacher ratio
England	2,258	567,700	10.3
Wales*	62	10,000	10.1
Scotland	114	32,000	11.5
N. Ireland	19	900	9.7

*1995-6 figures

Most independent schools in Scotland follow the English examination system, i.e. GCSE followed by A-levels, although some take the Scottish Education Certificate at Standard grade followed by Highers or Advanced Highers.

ASSISTED PLACES SCHEME

The Assisted Places Scheme is being phased out after the September 1997 entry. It enables children to attend independent secondary schools which their parents could not otherwise afford. The scheme provides help with tuition fees and other expenses, except boarding costs, on a sliding scale depending on the family's income. The proportion of pupils receiving full fee remission is about 46 per cent. In the 1997-8 academic year, about 38,900 places were offered at the 494 participating schools in England and Wales. In Scotland about 3,800 pupils participated in the scheme in 52 schools in 1997-8. Pupils in secondary education holding their places at the beginning of the 1997-8 school year will keep them until they have completed their education at their current school. Those at the primary stage will hold them until they have completed that phase of their education, although some may exceptionally be allowed to hold their places for a further period to complete their secondary education.

The scheme is administered and funded in England by the DfEE, in Wales by the Welsh Office, and in Scotland by the SOEID. The scheme does not operate in Northern Ireland as the independent sector admits non-fee-paying pupils. There is, however, a similar scheme known as the Talented Children's Scheme to help pupils gifted in music and dance.

Further information can be obtained from the Independent Schools Information Service (*see* page 443).

THE CURRICULUM

ENGLAND AND WALES

The national curriculum was introduced in primary and secondary schools between autumn 1989 and autumn 1996, for the period of compulsory schooling from five to 16. It is mandatory in all maintained schools. As originally proposed, it was widely criticized for being too prescriptive and time-consuming. Following revision in 1994 its requirements were substantially reduced; the revisions were implemented in August 1995 for key stages one to three and from August 1996 for key stage four. Consultation is under way for a revised national curriculum to be introduced in schools from September 2000.

The statutory subjects at key stages one and two (five–11-year olds) are:

Core subjects	*Foundation subjects*
English	Design and technology
Welsh (Welsh-speaking schools in Wales)	Information technology
	History
Mathematics	Geography
Science	Welsh (non-Welsh-speaking schools in Wales)
	Art
	Music
	PE

At key stage three (11- to 14-year-olds) all pupils must study a modern foreign language. At key stage four (14- to 16-year-olds) pupils are required to continue to study the core subjects, PE and, in England only, a modern foreign language, design and technology and information technology. Other foundation subjects are optional. In Wales the national curriculum has separate and distinctive characteristics which are reflected, where appropriate, in the programmes of study. Religious education must be taught across all key stages, following a locally agreed syllabus; parents have the right to remove their children if they wish.

National tests and tasks in English, Welsh (in Welsh-speaking schools in Wales) and mathematics at key stage one, with the addition of science at key stages two and three, are in place. Teachers make their own assessments of their pupils' progress to set alongside the test results. At key stage four the GCSE and vocational equivalents are the main form of assessment.

The DfEE and the Welsh Office publish tables showing pupils' performance in A-level, AS-level, GCSE and GNVQ examinations school by school. In England only, local education authorities are required to publish similar information in November each year showing the results of national curriculum tests and teacher assessments for seven-, 11- and 14-year-olds. Approximately 600,000 pupils in each of the age groups take the tests each year in England and Wales (38,000).

NATIONAL TESTING AND TEACHERS' ASSESSMENT RESULTS IN CORE SUBJECTS 1997

Percentage of pupils reaching the expected level of performance at that age:

	Key stage 1 7-year olds (level 2)	Key stage 2 11-year olds (level 4)	Key stage 3 14-year olds (level 5)
ENGLAND			
English	80.0	63.0	57.5
Mathematics	84.0	63.0	61.5
Science	85.0	69.0	60.5
WALES			
English	80.0	64.5	59.5
Welsh (first language)	85.0	57.0	68.0
Mathematics	83.5	65.0	60.5
Science	84.0	72.0	61.0

National targets have been set for 11-year-olds in England: 80 per cent to reach level four in the English test and 75 per cent to reach level four in the mathematics test by 2002. In Wales the targets are: 70–80 per cent to reach the expected level of performance for that age at key stages two and three by 2002.

In Wales, Welsh is a compulsory subject for all pupils at key stages one, two and three where it is taught either as a first or second language. At key stage four it is compulsory in schools which are Welsh-speaking (as defined by the Education Act 1996). It will also become compulsory at key stage four from September 1999 in schools which are not Welsh-speaking. Schools also use Welsh as the medium of teaching; some 27 per cent of primary schools use Welsh as the sole or main medium of instruction and a further 6 per cent use it for part of the curriculum; nearly 21 per cent of secondary schools use Welsh as the medium of instruction for at least half of their foundation subjects.

In October 1997 in England the Qualifications and Curriculum Authority (QCA) was formed by the amalgamation of the School Curriculum and Assessment Authority (SCAA) and the National Council for Vocational Qualifications. An independent government agency funded by the DfEE, its remit ranges from the under-fives to higher level vocational qualifications. It is responsible for ensuring that the curriculum and qualifications available to young people and adults are of high quality, coherent and flexible. In Wales, the Qualifications, Curriculum and Assessment Authority for Wales/Awdurdod Cymwysterau, Cwricwlwm ac Asesu Cymru (ACCAC) exercises similar functions. ACCAC is funded by the Welsh Office.

SCOTLAND

The content and management of the curriculum in Scotland are not prescribed by statute but are the responsibility of education authorities and individual headteachers. Advice and guidance is provided by the SOEID and the Scottish Consultative Council on the Curriculum, which also has a developmental role. SOEID has produced guidelines on the structure and balance of the curriculum for the five–14 age group as well as for each of the curriculum areas for this age group and a major programme to extend modern language teaching to primary schools is in progress. There are also guidelines on assessment across the whole curriculum, on reporting to parents, and on standardized national tests for English language and mathematics at five levels. The curriculum for 14- to 16-year-olds includes study within each of eight modes: language and communication, mathematical studies, science, technology, social studies, creative activities, physical education, and religious and moral education. There is a recommended percentage of class time to be devoted to each area over the two years. Provision is made for teaching in Gaelic in Gaelic-speaking areas. Testing is carried out on a voluntary basis when the teacher deems it appropriate; most pupils are expected to move from one level to the next at roughly two-year intervals. National testing is largely in place in most primary schools but secondary school participation rates are lower.

For 16- to 18-year-olds, there is available a modular system of vocational courses, certificated by the Scottish Qualifications Authority (SQA), in addition to academic courses. A new unified framework of courses and awards, known as 'Higher Still', which will bring together both academic and vocational courses will be introduced in 1999 (*see* page 431). The SQA will award the new certificates.

NORTHERN IRELAND

A curriculum common to all grant-aided schools exists. Pupils are required to study religious education and, depending on which key stage they have reached, certain subjects from six broad areas of study: English, mathematics, science and technology; the environment and society; creative and expressive studies and, in key stages three and four, language studies. The statutory curriculum requirements at key stages one to three have been revised and new programmes of study were introduced in September 1996. Six cross-curricular educational themes, which include information technology and education for mutual understanding, are woven through the main subjects of the curriculum. Irish is a foundation subject in schools that use it as a medium of instruction.

The assessment of pupils is broadly in line with practice in England and Wales and takes place at the ages of eight, 11 and 14. The GCSE is used to assess 16-year-olds.

NATIONAL TESTING AND TEACHERS' ASSESSMENT RESULTS IN CORE SUBJECTS 1997
Percentage of pupils reaching the expected level of performance at that age:

	Key stage 1 8-year olds (level 2)	Key stage 2 11-year olds (level 4)	Key stage 3 14-year olds (level 5)
English	92.2	63.0	66.5
Mathematics	92.0	69.0	73.0
Science	—	—	63.0

National targets have been set for 11-year-olds: 80 per cent to reach level four in English and mathematics by 2002.

The Northern Ireland Council for the Curriculum, Examinations and Assessment (NICCEA) monitors and advises the department and teachers on all matters relating to the curriculum, assessment arrangements and examinations in grant-aided schools. It conducts GCSE, A- and AS-level examinations, pupil assessment at key stages one, two and three and administers the transfer procedure tests.

RECORDS OF ACHIEVEMENT

The National Record of Achievement (NRA) has been reviewed and will be relaunched in February 1999 as 'Progress File'. It sets down the range of a school-leaver's achievements and activities both inside and outside the classroom, including those not tested by examination, and covers achievement in further and higher education, training and employment. It will be implemented in schools from September 1999. It is not compulsory in Scotland but is available to all education authorities for issue to school leavers. Parents in England and Wales must receive a written yearly progress report on all aspects of their child's achievements. There is a similar commitment

for Northern Ireland. In Scotland the school report card gives parents information on their child's progress.

THE PUBLIC EXAMINATION SYSTEM

ENGLAND, WALES AND NORTHERN IRELAND

Until the end of 1987, secondary school pupils at the end of compulsory schooling around the age of 16, and others, took the General Certificate of Education (GCE) Ordinary-level or the Certificate of Secondary Education (CSE). From 1988 these were replaced by a single system of examinations, the General Certificate of Secondary Education (GCSE), which is usually taken after five years of secondary education. The GCSE is the main method of assessing the performance of pupils at age 16 in all national curriculum subjects required to be assessed at the end of compulsory schooling. The structure of the examination is being adapted in accordance with national curriculum requirements; new subject criteria were published in 1995 to govern GCSE syllabuses introduced in 1996 for first examination in 1998. GCSE short-course qualifications are available in some subjects. As a rule the syllabus takes half the time of a full GCSE course.

The GCSE differs from its predecessors in that there are syllabuses based on national criteria covering course objectives, content and assessment methods; differentiated assessment (i.e. different papers or questions for different ranges of ability); and grade-related criteria (i.e. grades awarded on absolute rather than relative performance). The GCSE certificates are awarded on a seven-point scale, A to G. From 1994 there has been an additional 'starred' A grade (A*), to recognize the achievement of the highest attainers at GCSE. Grades A to C are the equivalent of the corresponding O-level grades A to C or CSE grade 1. Grades D, E, F and G record achievement at least as high as that represented by CSE grades 2 to 5. All GCSE syllabuses, assessments and grading procedures are monitored by the Qualifications and Curriculum Authority (*see* page 429) to ensure that they conform to the national criteria.

In the UK in 1996–7, 94.5 per cent of all 16-year-olds achieved one or more graded GCSE, SCE Standard grade, or equivalent results.

In Wales the Certificate of Education is intended for 16-year-olds for whom no suitable examination exists. In 1996, 24,524 candidates took the examination, of whom 93.4 per cent obtained pass or better.

Many maintained schools offer BTEC Firsts (*see* page 433) and an increasing number offer BTEC Nationals. National Vocational Qualifications in the form of General NVQs are also available to students in schools (*see* page 434). The Part 1 GNVQ is a shortened version of the full GNVQ. Designed for 14- to 16-year-olds, it is a two-year course at foundation and intermediate levels broadly equivalent to two GCSEs at grades A* to C. It has been piloted from 1995 and is planned to be available in schools from September 1998.

Advanced (A-level) examinations are taken by those who choose to continue their education after GCSE. A-level courses last two years and have traditionally provided the foundation for entry to higher education. A-levels are marked on a seven-point scale, from A to E, N (narrow failure) and U (unclassified), which latter grade will not be certificated.

Advanced Supplementary level (AS-level) examinations were introduced in 1987 as an alternative to, and to complement, A-level examinations. AS-levels are for full-time A-level students but are also open to other students. An AS-level syllabus covers not less than half the amount of ground covered by the corresponding A-level syllabus and, where possible, is related to it. An AS-level course lasts two years and requires not less than half the teaching time of the corresponding A-level course, and two AS-levels are equivalent to one A-level. AS-level passes are graded A to E, with grade standards related to the A-level grades.

In the UK in 1996–7, 283,000 students (45.6 per cent boys, 54.4 per cent girls) achieved one or more passes at A-level or SCE H-grade. Of those in Great Britain who entered for at least one A-level, or at least two SCE H-grades, 32 per cent studied sciences (60 per cent boys, 40 per cent girls) and 68 per cent studied arts/social studies (41 per cent of boys, 59 per cent of girls).

Most examining boards allow the option of an additional paper of greater difficulty to be taken by A-level candidates to obtain what is known as a Special-level or Scholarship-level qualification. S-level papers are available in most of the traditional academic subjects and are marked on a three-point scale.

The City & Guilds Diploma of Vocational Education is intended for a wide ability range. The Diploma provides recognition of achievement at two levels: foundation at pre-16 and intermediate at post-16. The intermediate level is being phased in in favour of the corresponding GNVQs. Within guidelines and to meet specified criteria, schools and colleges design their own courses, which stress activity-based learning, core skills which include application of number, communication and information technology, and work experience. The Diploma is of value to those who want to find out what aptitudes they may have and to prepare themselves for work, but who may not yet be committed to a particular occupation. At foundation level, it can be taken alongside GCSEs and can provide a context for the introduction of GNVQ units into the key stage four curriculum.

The various examining boards in England have combined into three unitary awarding bodies, which offer both academic and vocational qualifications: GNVQs, GCSEs and A-levels. The new bodies are Edexcel, the Assessment and Qualifications Alliance (AQA), and Oxford, Cambridge and RSA Examinations (OCR) (see page 444). At present the existing examination boards are still separate bodies, working in alliance to develop single courses.

SCOTLAND

Scotland has its own system of public examinations. At the end of the fourth year of secondary education, at about the age of 16, pupils take the Standard grade (which has replaced the Ordinary grade) of the Scottish Certificate of Education. Standard grade courses and examinations have been designed to suit every level of ability, with assessment against nationally determined standards of performance.

For most courses there are three separate examination papers at the end of the two-year Standard grade course. They are set at Credit (leading to awards at grade 1 or 2), General (leading to awards at grade 3 or 4) and Foundation (leading to awards at grade 5 or 6) levels. Grade 7 is available to those who, although they have completed the course, have not attained any of these levels. Normally pupils will take examinations covering two pairs of grades, either grades 1–4 or grades 3–6. Most candidates take seven or eight Standard grade examinations.

The Higher grade of the Scottish Certificate of Education is normally taken one year after Standard grade, at the age of 17 or thereabouts. It is common for pupils to be presented for four or more Higher grades at a single diet of the examination.

The Certificate of Sixth Year Studies (CSYS) is designed to give direction and purpose to sixth-year work by encouraging pupils who have completed their main subjects at Higher grade to study a maximum of three of

these subjects in depth. Pupils may also use the sixth year to gain improved or additional Higher grades or Standard grades. National Certificates may also be taken in the fifth and six years of secondary school as an alternative to or in addition to Highers.

In 1999–2000 the 'Higher Still' reforms will introduce a new system of courses and qualifications, replacing SCE Highers, CSYS and many national certificate modules, for everyone studying beyond Standard grade in Scottish schools, and for non-advanced students in further education colleges. Qualifications will be available at five levels: Access, Intermediate 1, Intermediate 2, Higher, and Advanced Higher. Courses will be made up of internally assessed units and students possessing a number of units and courses may be able to build them into a Scottish Group Award. Achievement of that award will also indicate that the holder has attained a defined level of competence in the core skills of communication, problem-solving, information technology and working with others.

All of these qualifications are awarded by the Scottish Qualifications Authority (SQA), which on 1 April 1997 assumed the functions of the Scottish Examinations Board and the Scottish Vocational Education Council.

THE INTERNATIONAL BACCALAUREATE

The International Baccalaureate is an internationally recognized two-year pre-university course and examination designed to facilitate the mobility of students and to promote international understanding. Candidates must offer one subject from each of six subject groups, at least three at higher level and the remainder at subsidiary level. Single subjects can be offered, for which a certificate is received. There are 33 schools and colleges in the UK which offer the International Baccalaureate diploma.

TEACHERS

ENGLAND AND WALES

Teachers are appointed by local education authorities, school governing bodies, or school managers. Those in publicly maintained schools must be approved as qualified by the Secretary of State. With certain exceptions the profession at present has an all-graduate entry. To obtain Qualified Teacher Status (QTS) it is necessary to have successfully completed a course of initial teacher training, traditionally either a Bachelor of Education (B.Ed.) degree or the Postgraduate Certificate of Education (PGCE) at an accredited institution. New entrants to the profession are statutorily required to serve a one-year induction period during which they will have a structured programme of support. In recent years various employment-based routes to teaching have been developed. The Graduate Teacher Programme allows graduates with teaching experience to undergo between one term's and one year's school-based training. The Registered Teacher Scheme is designed to attract into the teaching profession entrants over 24 years of age without formal teaching qualifications but with relevant training and experience; entrants are paid a salary and undertake one to two years higher education depending on whether they possess relevant teaching experience. Teachers in further education are not required to have Qualified Teacher Status, though roughly half have a teaching qualification and most have industrial, commercial or professional experience. A mandatory qualification for aspiring head-teachers, the National Professional Qualification for Headship (NPQH), was introduced in September 1997.

From September 1998 the national curriculum for initial teacher training was introduced for primary English and mathematics, and information and communications technology; that for primary science and secondary English, mathematics and science will become mandatory from September 1999.

Teacher training is now largely school-based, with student teachers on secondary PGCE courses spending two-thirds of their training in the classroom. Changes have also been made to primary phase teacher training to make it more school-based and to give schools a role in course design and delivery. Individual schools or consortia of schools and CTCs can bid for funds from the DfEE to carry out their own teacher training, including recruitment of students, subject to approval of their proposed training programme by the Teacher Training Agency (TTA) and monitoring and evaluation by the Office for Standards in Education (OFSTED). Funds are given to schools to meet the costs of designing and delivering the courses.

The TTA accredits institutions in England providing initial teacher training for school teachers which meet certain criteria published by the Secretary of State and quality standards. The TTA funds all types of teacher training in England, whether run by universities, colleges or schools, and some educational research. An independent professional council, the General Teaching Council, is to be established by 2000 to advise the Secretary of State and the TTA, with a separate council for Wales.

The TTA Unit in Wales has a similar remit in respect of Wales. The TTA also acts as a central source of information and advice for both England and Wales about entry to teaching, and has responsibilities relating to the continuing professional development of teachers.

The Specialist Teacher Assistant (STA) scheme was introduced in September 1994 to provide trained support to qualified teachers in the teaching of reading, writing and arithmetic to young pupils.

SCOTLAND

All teachers in maintained schools must be registered with the General Teaching Council for Scotland. They are registered provisionally for a two-year probationary period which can be extended if necessary. Only graduates are accepted as entrants to the profession; primary school teachers undertake either a four-year vocational degree course or a one-year postgraduate course, while teachers of academic subjects in secondary schools undertake the latter. Most initial teacher training is classroom-based. The colleges of education provide both in-service and pre-service training for teachers which is subject to inspection by HM Inspectors. The colleges are funded by the Scottish Higher Education Funding Council.

NORTHERN IRELAND

All new entrants to teaching in grant-aided schools are graduates and hold an approved teaching qualification. Teacher training is provided by the two universities and two colleges of education. The colleges are concerned with teacher education mainly for the primary school sector. They also provide B.Ed. courses for intending secondary school teachers of religious education, commercial studies, and craft, design and technology. With these exceptions, the professional training of teachers for secondary schools is provided in the education departments of the universities. A review of primary and secondary teacher training has taken place as a result of which all student teachers spend more time in the classroom. All newly qualified teachers undertake a two-year induction period.

ACCREDITATION OF TRAINING INSTITUTIONS

Advice to central government on the accreditation, content and quality of initial teacher training courses is given in England by the TTA, in Wales by the HEFCW and in Northern Ireland by validating bodies. These bodies also monitor and disseminate good practice, assisted in Northern Ireland by the Teacher Education Committee. In Scotland the General Teaching Council advises SOEID on the professional suitability of all training courses in colleges of education.

SHORTAGE SUBJECTS

Because of a shortage of teachers in certain secondary subjects, providers of initial teacher training in England and Wales can receive funds from the TTA to help promote courses in certain subjects and to offer students on courses in those subjects financial support. The subjects are: science; mathematics; modern languages (including Welsh in Wales); design and technology; information technology; religious education; music, and geography.

SERVING TEACHERS 1995–6 *(full-time and part-time)* (thousands)

	All	% graduate
Public sector schools	451	62
Nursery and primary	212	50
Secondary	222	72
Special	17	44
FE and HE establishments	127	82
TOTAL	578	72

SALARIES

Qualified teachers in England, Wales and Northern Ireland, other than heads and deputy heads, are paid on an 18-point scale. Entry points and placement depend on qualifications, experience, responsibilities, excellence, and recruitment and retention factors as calculated by the relevant body, i.e. the governing body or the LEA. There is a statutory superannuation scheme in maintained schools.

Teachers in Scotland are paid on a ten-point scale. The entry point depends on type of qualification, and additional allowances are payable under certain circumstances.

Salaries from 1 December 1998*

	England, Wales and N. Ireland	Scotland
Head	£27,204–£59,580	£27,846–£51,582
Deputy head	£26,337–£43,326	£27,846–£38,589
Teacher	£13,362–£35,787	£13,206–£28,893

*From 1 April 1998 for Scotland

FURTHER EDUCATION

Further education is defined as all provision outside schools to people aged over 16 of education up to and including A-level and its equivalent. The Further Education Funding Councils for England and Wales, the Scottish Office Education and Industry Department and the Department of Education for Northern Ireland have a duty to secure provision of adequate facilities for further education in their areas.

ENGLAND AND WALES

Further education and sixth form colleges are funded directly by central government through the Further Education Funding Council for England (FEFCE) and the Further Education Funding Council for Wales (FEFCW). These councils are also responsible for the assessment of quality, in which the Councils' inspectorates play a key role. The colleges are controlled by autonomous further education corporations, which include substantial representation from industry and commerce, and which own their own assets and employ their own staff. Their funding is determined in part by the number of students enrolled.

In England and Wales further education courses are taught at a variety of institutions. These include universities which were formerly polytechnics, colleges of higher education, colleges of further education (some of which also offer higher education courses), and tertiary colleges and sixth form colleges, which concentrate on the provision of normal sixth form school courses as well as a range of vocational courses. A number of institutions specific to a particular form of training, e.g. the Royal College of Music, are also involved.

Teaching staff in further education establishments are not necessarily required to have teaching qualifications although many do so, but they are subject to regular appraisal of teaching performance.

Further education tends to be broadly vocational in purpose and employers are often involved in designing courses. It ranges from lower-level technical and commercial courses through courses for those aiming at higher-level posts in industry, commerce and administration, to professional courses. Facilities exist for GCE A and AS levels, GCSEs, GNVQs and a full range of vocational qualifications (*see* pages 430–1). These courses can form the foundation for progress to higher education qualifications.

The main courses and examinations in the vocational field, all of which link in with the National Vocational Qualification (NVQ) framework (*see* page 434), are offered by the following bodies, but there are also many others.

The Edexcel Foundation was formed by the merger of the Business and Technology Education Council (BTEC) and London Examinations. They provide programmes of study across a wide range of subject areas. The main qualifications offered are GCSEs, A-levels, GNVQs, NVQs, BTEC First, National and Higher National diplomas and certificates, key skills and entry certificates.

City & Guilds specialize in developing qualifications and assessments for work-related and leisure qualifications. They offer nationally and internationally recognized certificates in over 500 qualifications, many of which are NVQs, SVQs and GNVQs. The progressive structure of awards spans seven levels, from foundation to the highest level of professional competence.

RSA Examinations Board schemes cover a wide range of vocational qualifications, including accounting, business administration, customer service, management, language schemes, information technology and teaching qualifications. A wide range of NVQs and GNVQs are offered and a policy operates of credit accumulation, so that candidates can take a single unit or complete qualifications.

There are 480 further education establishments and sixth form colleges in England and Wales. In 1997–8 there were 720,500 full-time and sandwich-course students and 840,900 part-time day students on further education courses.

SCOTLAND

Further education comprises non-advanced courses up to SCE Higher grade, GCE A-level and work-based awards. Courses are taught mainly at colleges of further education, including technical colleges, and in some schools.

There are 46 further education colleges. The responsibility for 43 of these (incorporated colleges) has been transferred to individual boards of management, funded directly by the Secretary of State, which run the colleges and employ staff. The boards include the principal, staff

and student representatives among their ten to 16 members; at least half the members must have experience of commerce, industry or the practice of a profession. Two colleges, on Orkney and Shetland, are under Islands Council control and receive payment from the Secretary of State, as do the trustees of the remaining college, Sabhal Mor Ostaig, the Gaelic college on Skye.

The Scottish Qualifications Authority (SQA) awards qualifications for most occupations. It awards at non-advanced level the National Certificate, which is available in over 4,000 individual modules and covers the whole range of non-advanced further education provision in Scotland. Students may study for the National Certificate on a full-time, part-time, open learning or work-based learning basis. National Certificate modules can be taken in further education colleges, secondary schools and other centres, normally from the age of 16 onwards. In August 1999 the 'Higher Still' reforms will introduce a unified curriculum and assessment system for non-advanced post-16 education. Courses will be available at five levels, replacing SCE Higher grades, CSYS courses and many National Certificate modules. SQA also offers modular advanced-level HNC/HND qualifications, which are available in further education colleges and higher education institutions. SQA accredits and awards Scottish Vocational Qualifications (SVQs) which have mutual recognition with the NVQs available in the rest of the UK. SVQs are work-place assessed, but can also be taken in further education colleges and other centres where work-place conditions can be simulated.

The Record of Education and Training (RET) has been introduced to provide a single certificate recording SQA achievements; an updated version is provided as and when necessary. SQA also administers the National Record of Achievement (now 'Progress File') in Scotland on behalf of the Scottish Office.

In the academic year 1996–7 there were 33,799 full-time and sandwich-course students and 254,065 part-time students on non-advanced vocational courses of further education in the 46 further education colleges.

NORTHERN IRELAND

On 1 April 1998 all further education colleges became free-standing corporate bodies like their counterparts in the rest of the UK. Planning, which was previously undertaken by the Education and Library Boards, is now the responsibility of the Department of Education for Northern Ireland, which also funds the colleges direct. The colleges own their own property, are responsible for their own services and employ their own staff.

The governing bodies of the colleges must include at least 50 per cent membership from the professions, local business or industry, or other fields of employment relevant to the activities of the college.

On reaching school-leaving age, pupils may attend colleges of further education to pursue the same type of vocational courses as are provided in colleges in England and Wales, administered by the same examining bodies.

In 1997–8 Northern Ireland had 17 institutions of further education, and there were 21,642 full-time students and 53,952 part-time students on non-advanced vocational courses of further education.

COURSE INFORMATION

Applications for further education courses are generally made directly to the colleges concerned. Information on further education courses in the UK and addresses of colleges can be found in the *Directory of Further Education* published annually by the Careers Research and Advisory Centre.

Bodies responsible for the regulation of GNVQs and NVQs in the UK are: in England, the Qualifications and Curriculum Authority (QCA); in Wales, the Curriculum and Assessment Authority/Awdurdod Cymwysterau, Cwricwlwm ac Asesu Cymru (ACCAC); in Northern Ireland, the Council for the Curriculum, Examinations and Assessment (NICCEA); and in Scotland, the Scottish Qualifications Authority (SQA). Those bodies do not award qualifications (except for the SQA) but accredit National Vocational Qualifications (NVQs), General National Vocational Qualifications (GNVQs) and core skills. Assessment is carried out through awarding bodies who bestow the qualifications where candidates reach the required standards.

National Vocational Qualifications (NVQs) are workplace based occupational qualifications. In September 1992 General National Vocational Qualifications (GNVQs) were introduced into colleges and schools as a vocational alternative to academic qualifications. They cover broad categories in the NVQ framework and are aimed at those wishing to familiarize themselves with a range of opportunities. Advanced GNVQ or the vocational A-level is equivalent to two A-levels; from September 2000 a revised version equivalent to a single A-level is planned. Intermediate GNVQ is equivalent to four GCSEs at A* to C grade. Foundation GNVQ is equivalent to four GCSEs at D to G grade.

HIGHER EDUCATION

The term higher education is used to describe education above A-level, Higher and Advanced Higher grade and their equivalent, which is provided in universities, colleges of higher education and in some further education colleges.

The Further and Higher Education Act 1992 and parallel legislation in Scotland removed the distinction between higher education provided by the universities, and that provided in England and Wales by the former polytechnics and colleges of higher education and in Scotland by the former central institutions and other institutions, allowing all polytechnics, and other higher education institutions which satisfy the necessary criteria, to award their own taught course and research degrees and to adopt the title of university. All the polytechnics, art colleges and some colleges of higher education have since adopted the title of university. The change of name does not affect the legal constitution of the institutions. All are funded by the Higher Education Funding Councils for England, Wales and Scotland.

The number of students in higher education in the UK in 1996–7 was:

Full-time, sandwich	1,194,600
% female	50.9%
Part-time	696,900
% female	53.3%
TOTAL	1,891,500
of which overseas	201,400

The proportion of 18- to 21-year-olds undertaking full-time and part-time courses in higher education in the UK was 26 per cent in 1995. The number of mature entrants (those aged 21 and over when starting an undergraduate course and 25 and over when starting a postgraduate course) to higher education in Great Britain in 1996–7 (excluding those at the Open University) was 1,560,100.

The number of full-time and part-time students on science courses in 1996–7 was 1,052,900, of whom 22.7 per cent were female.

The universities are self-governing institutions established in most cases by royal charter or Act of Parliament. They have academic freedom and are responsible for their own academic appointments, curricula and student admissions and award their own degrees.

Responsibility for universities in England rests with the Secretary of State for Education and Employment, and in their territories with the Secretaries of State for Scotland, Wales and Northern Ireland. Advice to the Government on matters relating to the universities is provided by the Higher Education Funding Councils for England, Wales and Scotland, and by the Northern Ireland Higher Education Council. The HEFCs receive a block grant from central government which they allocate to the universities and colleges. The grant is allocated directly by central government in Northern Ireland on the advice of the Northern Ireland Higher Education Council.

There are now 88 universities in the UK, where only 47 existed prior to the Further and Higher Education Acts 1992. Of the 88, 71 are in England (including one federal university), two (one a federal institution) in Wales, 13 in Scotland and two in Northern Ireland.

The pre-1992 universities each have their own system of internal government but broad similarities exist. Most are run by two main bodies: the senate, which deals primarily with academic issues and consists of members elected from within the university; and the council, which is the supreme body and is responsible for all appointments and promotions, and bidding for and allocation of financial resources. At least half the members of the council are drawn from outside the university. Joint committees of senate and council are becoming increasingly common.

Those universities which were formerly polytechnics (38) or other higher education institutions (three) and the colleges of higher education (47) are run by higher education corporations (HECs), which are controlled by boards of governors whose members were initially appointed by the Secretaries of State but which will subsequently make their own appointments. At least half the members of each board must be drawn from industry, business, commerce and the professions.

In 1996–7 full-time and part-time student enrolments in England and Wales were:

England

Undergraduates	1,159,600
% overseas	8.5%
Postgraduates	299,100
% overseas	21.2%

Wales

Undergraduates	77,200
% overseas	8.4%
Postgraduates	17,500
% overseas	24.0%

Higher education courses funded by the respective HEFCs are also taught in some further education colleges in England and Wales. In England in 1996–7 there were over 36,000 students (2.5 per cent of total higher education student numbers) on such courses and 549 (0.6 per cent of higher education student numbers) in Wales.

The non-residential Open University provides courses nationally leading to degrees. Teaching is through a combination of television and radio programmes, correspondence, tutorials, short residential courses and local audio-visual centres. No qualifications are needed for entry. The Open University offers a modular programme of undergraduate courses by credit accumulation and post-experience and postgraduate courses, including a programme of higher degrees which comprises B.Phil., M.Phil. and Ph.D. through research, and MA, MBA and M.Sc. through taught courses. The Open University throughout the UK is funded by the Higher Education Funding Council for England. Its recurrent grant for 1996–7 was £110.7 million from the Higher Education Funding Council for England and £6.8 million from the Teacher Training Agency. In 1998, about 116,000 undergraduates were registered at the Open University, of whom about 52 per cent were women. Estimated cost (1998) of a six-credit degree was around £3,800 including course fees of about £2,300.

The independent University of Buckingham provides a two-year course leading to a bachelor's degree and its tuition fees were £9,996 for 1998. It receives no capital or recurrent income from the Government but its students are eligible for mandatory awards from local education authorities. Its academic year consists of four terms of ten weeks each.

ACADEMIC STAFF

Each university and college appoints its own academic staff on its own conditions. However, there is a common salary structure and, except for Oxford and Cambridge, a common career structure in those universities formerly funded by the UFC and a common salary structure for the former PCFC sector. The Universities and Colleges Employers Association (UCEA) acts as a pay agency for universities and colleges.

Teaching staff in higher education require no formal teaching qualification, but teacher trainers are required to spend a certain amount of time in schools to ensure that they have sufficient recent practical experience.

In 1996–7, there were 64,257 full-time and part-time teaching and research staff (UK nationals) in institutions of higher education in the UK.

Salary scales for staff in the pre-1992 universities sector differ from those in the former polytechnics and colleges; it is planned eventually to amalgamate them. The 1998–9 salary scales for non-clinical academic staff in universities formerly funded by the UFC are:

Professor from	£35,120
Senior lecturer	£30,498–£34,464
Lecturer grade B	£22,726–£29,048
Lecturer grade A	£15,735 –£21,815

The salaries of clinical academic staff are kept broadly comparable to those of doctors and dentists in the National Health Service.

Salary scales for lecturers in the former polytechnics, now universities, and colleges of higher education in England, Wales and Northern Ireland are:

	September 1998	March 1999
Head of Department	from £26,304	from £26,304
Principal lecturer	£27,512–£34,543	£27,746–£35,204
Senior lecturer	£22,012–£29,086	£22,400–£29,600
Lecturer	£14,148–£23,585	£14,398–£24,002

The salary scales for staff in Scotland are determined at individual college level.

FINANCE

Although universities and colleges are expected to look to a wider range of funding sources than before, and to generate additional revenue in collaboration with industry, they are still largely financed, directly or indirectly, from government resources.

In 1996–7 the total income of institutions of higher education in the UK was £11,143.5 million (£10,647.4 million in 1995–6). Grants from the funding councils amounted to £4,400 million (£4,428.2 million in 1995–6), forming 39.5 per cent of total income (41.6 per cent in 1995–6). Income from research grants and contracts was £1,642.3 million, 14.7 per cent of total income (14.5 per cent in 1995–6).

In the academic year 1996–7 the HEFCs' recurrent grant to institutions outside their sector and to LEAs for the provision of higher education courses was £84.5 million.

COURSES

In the UK all universities, including the Open University, and some colleges award their own degrees and other qualifications and can act as awarding and validating bodies for neighbouring colleges which are not yet accredited. The Quality Assurance Agency for Higher Education, funded by institutional contributions, advises the Secretaries of State on applications for degree-awarding powers.

Higher education courses last full-time for at least four weeks or, if part-time, involve more than 60 hours of instruction. Facilities exist for full-time and part-time study, day release, sandwich or block release. Credit accumulation and transfer (CATS) is a system of study which is becoming widely available. It allows a student to achieve a final qualification by accumulating credits for courses of study successfully achieved, or even professional experience, over a period. Credit transfer information and values are carried on an electronic database called ECCTIS 2000, which is available in most careers offices and many schools and colleges.

Higher education courses comprise: first degree and postgraduate (including research); Diploma in Higher Education (Dip.HE); Higher National Diploma (HND) and Higher National Certificate (HNC); and preparation for professional examinations. The in-service training of teachers is also included, but from September 1994 has been funded in England by the TTA (see page 432), not the HEFC.

The Diploma of Higher Education (Dip.HE) is a two-year diploma usually intended to serve as a stepping-stone to a degree course or other further study. The Dip.HE is awarded by the institution itself if it is accredited; by an accredited institution of its choice if not. The BTEC Higher National Certificate (HNC) is awarded after two years part-time study. The BTEC Higher National Diploma (HND) is awarded after two years full-time, or three years sandwich-course or part-time study.

With the exception of certain Scottish universities where master is sometimes used for a first degree in arts subjects, undergraduate courses lead to the title of Bachelor, Bachelor of Arts (BA) and Bachelor of Science (B.Sc.) being the most common. For a higher degree the titles are: Master of Arts (MA), Master of Science (M.Sc.) (usually taught courses) and the research degrees of Master of Philosophy (M.Phil.) and Doctor of Philosophy (Ph.D. or, at a few universities, D.Phil.).

Most undergraduate courses at British universities and colleges of higher education run for three years, except modern language courses and those at Scottish universities and at the University of Keele which usually take four years. Professional courses in subjects such as medicine, dentistry and veterinary science take longer. Details of courses on offer and of predicted entry requirements for the following year's intake are provided in *University and*

College Entrance: Official Guide, published annually by the Universities and Colleges Admissions Service (UCAS), which includes degree, Dip.HE and HND courses at all universities (excluding the Open University) and most colleges of HE; it is available from bookshops.

Postgraduate studies vary in length. Taught courses which lead to certificates, diplomas or master's degrees usually take one year full-time and two years part-time. Research degrees take from two to three years full-time and much longer if completed on a part-time basis. Details of taught courses and research degree opportunities can be found in *Graduate Studies,* published annually for the Careers Research and Advisory Centre (CRAC) by Hobsons Publishing plc (for address, *see* page 444).

Post-experience short courses are forming an increasing part of higher education provision, reflecting the need to update professional and technical training. Most of these courses fund themselves.

ADMISSIONS

The target number of students entering full-time higher education has been set at 30 to 31 per cent of the 18- to 19-year-old age group. Institutions suffer financial penalties if the number of students laid down for them by the funding councils is exceeded, but the individual university or college decides which students to accept. The formal entry requirements to most degree courses are two A-levels at grade E or above (or equivalent), and to HND courses one A-level (or equivalent). In practice, most offers of places require qualifications in excess of this, higher requirements usually reflecting the popularity of a course. These requirements do not, however, exclude applications from students with a variety of non-GCSE qualifications or unquantified experience and skills.

For admission to a degree, Dip.HE or HND, potential students apply through a central clearing house. All universities and most colleges providing higher education courses in the UK are members of the Universities and Colleges Admission Service (UCAS). Applicants are supplied with an application form and a *UCAS Handbook,* available from schools, colleges and careers offices or direct from UCAS, and may apply to a maximum of six institutions/courses on the UCAS form. The only exception among universities is the Open University, which conducts its own admissions.

Applications for undergraduate teacher training courses are made through UCAS. Details of initial teacher training courses in Scotland can be obtained from colleges of education and those universities offering such courses, and from the Committee of Scottish Higher Education Principals (COSHEP).

For admission as a postgraduate student, universities and colleges normally require a good first degree in a subject related to the proposed course of study or research, but other experience and qualifications will be considered on merit. Most applications are made to individual institutions but there are two clearing houses of relevance. Postgraduate teacher training courses in England and Wales utilize the Graduate Teacher Training Registry (*see* page 444). Applications to postgraduate teacher training courses in Scotland are made through the Teacher Education Admissions Clearing House (TEACH) (*see* page 444). Applications for PGCE courses at institutions in Northern Ireland are made to the Department of Education for Northern Ireland. For social work the Social Work Admissions System operates (*see* page 444).

SCOTLAND

The Scottish Higher Education Funding Council (SHEFC) funds 21 institutions of higher education, including 13 universities. The universities are broadly managed as described above and each institution of higher education is managed by an independent governing body which includes representatives of industrial, commercial, professional and educational interests. Most of the courses outside the universities have a vocational orientation and a substantial number are sandwich courses.

Student enrolments in 1996–7 in universities and other higher education institutions were:

Undergraduates	125,600
% overseas	8.8%
Postgraduates	37,500
% overseas	29.9%

There were 32,114 students on higher education courses in further education colleges, 19.6 per cent of total higher education students.

NORTHERN IRELAND

In Northern Ireland advanced courses are provided by 17 institutions of further education, the two universities and the two colleges of education. As well as offering first and postgraduate degrees, the University of Ulster offers courses leading to the BTEC Higher National Diploma and professional qualifications. Applications to undertake courses of higher education other than degree courses are made to the institutions direct. Higher education student enrolments in 1996–7 were (thousands):

Undergraduates	30,200
% overseas	16.8%
Postgraduates	9,500
% overseas	18.2%

There were 10,075 students enrolled on advanced courses of higher education in the institutions of further education, 25.4 per cent of higher education student numbers.

FEES

Tuition fees for existing students with mandatory awards (*see* below) are paid by the grant-awarding body. From September 1998, new entrants to undergraduate courses will pay an annual contribution to their fees of up to £1,000, depending on their own level of income and that of their spouse or parents. Students will pay the fee contribution direct to the institution. Among the classes of students exempt from payment are Scottish and EU students in the fourth year of a four-year degree course at a Scottish institution and medical students in the fifth year of their course. Students from EU member countries pay fees at home student rates and will also be liable to make an annual contribution to fees assessed against family income. Since 1980–1 students from outside the EU have paid fees that are meant to cover the cost of their education, but financial help is available under a number of schemes. Information about these schemes is available from British Council offices world-wide.

Universities and colleges are free to set their own charges for students from non-EU countries. Undergraduate fees for the academic year 1998–9 for home and EU students are set at a flat rate of £1,000.

For postgraduate students, the maximum tuition fee that will be reimbursed through the awards system is £2,610 in 1998–9.

GRANTS FOR STUDENTS

Students in the UK who plan to take a full-time or sandwich course of further study after leaving school may currently be eligible for a grant. A parental contribution is deductible on a sliding scale dependent on income. For married students this may be deducted from their spouse's income instead. However, parental contribution is not deducted from the grant to students over 25 years of age who have been self-supporting for at least three years. The main rates of mandatory grant have been frozen since 1991–2 and although existing students will continue to be eligible for grants and loans in similar proportions as now, grants for new entrants to higher education in 1998–9 will be paid at about half the rate for 1997–8, while loans will increase in compensation. From 1999–2000 maintenance grants for the latter category of students and for all new entrants will be replaced entirely by income-related loans.

Grants are paid by local education authorities in England, Wales and Northern Ireland, of which 100 per cent of the cost is reimbursed by central government. Applications are made to the authority in the area in which the student normally lives. In Scotland grants are made by the SOEID through the Student Awards Agency. Applications should not be made earlier than the January preceding the start of the course.

TYPES OF GRANT

Grants are currently of two kinds: mandatory and discretionary. Mandatory grants are those which awarding authorities must pay to students who are attending designated courses and who can satisfy certain other conditions. Such a grant is awarded normally to enable the student to attend only one designated course and there is no general entitlement to an award for any particular number of years. Discretionary grants are those for which each awarding authority has discretion to decide its own policy.

Designated courses are those full-time or sandwich courses leading to: a degree; the Diploma of Higher Education; the Higher National Diploma; initial teacher-training courses, including those for the postgraduate certificate of education and the art teachers' certificate or diploma; a university certificate or diploma course lasting at least three years and other qualifications which are specifically designated as being comparable to first degree courses. The local education authority should be consulted for advice about eligibility for a grant.

A means-tested maintenance grant, usually paid once a term, covers periods of attendance during term as well as the Christmas and Easter vacations, but not the summer vacation. The basic grant rates for 1998–9 (rates for Scottish students in parenthesis) are:

Living in	Existing students	New entrants (1998–9 only)
College/lodgings in London area	£2,225 (£2,145)	£1,225 (£1,145)
College/lodgings outside London area	£1,810 (£1,735)	£810 (£735)
Parental home	1,480 (£1,325)	£480 (£325)

Additional allowances are available if, for example, the course requires a period of study abroad.

LEA and SOEID expenditure on student fees and maintenance in 1996–7 was £2,380.3 million; about 927,900 mandatory awards were made.

STUDENT LOANS

In the academic year 1998–9 students will be eligible to apply for interest-free but indexed loans of up to £2,145 (£3,145 for new entrants).

Students apply direct to the Student Loans Company Ltd (*see* page 444), which will require a certificate of eligibility from their place of study. Loans are available to students on designated courses within the scope of current mandatory awards and certain residency conditions apply. In 1996–7, 589,600 loans were taken up, to the value of £877.2 million. Repayment arrangements differ for exist-ing students and new entrants in 1998–9. Existing students still normally repay over five to seven years, although repayment can be deferred if annual income is at or below 85 per cent of national average earnings (£16,488 at 31 August 1998). New entrants will not be required to make repayments if their annual income is below a designated threshold (£10,000 in 1998–9); otherwise a percentage of the income above that amount is taken to repay the loan.

ACCESS FUNDS

Access funds are allocated by education departments to the appropriate funding councils in England, Wales and Scotland and administered by further and higher education institutions. In Northern Ireland they are allocated by central government to the institutions direct. They are available to students whose access to education might otherwise be inhibited by financial considerations or where real financial difficulties are faced. For the academic year 1998–9, provision in the UK will be £49.4 million.

POSTGRADUATE AWARDS

Grants for postgraduate study are of two types, both discretionary: 30-week bursaries, which are means-tested and are available for certain vocational and diploma courses; and studentship awards, which are dependent on the class of first degree, especially for research degrees, are not means-tested, and cover students undertaking research degrees or taught masters degrees. Postgraduate students, with the exception of students on loan-bearing diploma courses such as teacher training, are not eligible to apply for student loans.

An increasing number of scholarships are available from research charities, endowments, and particular industries or companies. For residents in England and Wales, several schemes of postgraduate bursaries (administered by the British Academy) or studentships are funded by the DfEE, the government research councils, the Ministry of Agriculture, Fisheries and Food, and the British Academy, which awards grants for study in the humanities.

In Scotland postgraduate funding is provided by the SOEID through the Student Awards Agency for Scotland, the Scottish Office Agriculture and Fisheries Department, and the research councils as in England and Wales.

Awards in Northern Ireland are made by DENI, the Department of Agriculture for Northern Ireland, and the Medical Research Council.

The rates for 30-week bursaries for professional and vocational training in 1998–9 (Scottish rates in parenthesis) are:

Living in	
College/lodgings in London area	£4,010 (£3,685)
College/lodgings outside London area	£3,010 (£2,806)
Parental home	£2,520 (£2,180)

Studentship awards are payable at between £5,295 and £6,855 a year (1997–8).

ADULT AND CONTINUING EDUCATION

The term adult education covers a broad spectrum of educational activities ranging from non-vocational courses of general interest, through the acquiring of special vocational skills needed in industry or commerce, to study for a degree at the Open University.

The responsibility for securing adult and continuing education in England and Wales is statutory and shared between the Further Education Funding Councils, which are responsible for and fund those courses which take place in their sector and lead to academic and vocational qualifications, prepare students to undertake further or higher education courses, or confer basic skills; the Higher Education Funding Councils, which fund advanced courses of continuing education; and LEAs, which are responsible for those courses which do not fall within the remit of the funding councils. Funding in Northern Ireland is through the education and library boards and in Scotland by the Scottish Office Education and Industry Department.

PROVIDERS

Courses specifically for adults are provided by many bodies. They include, in the statutory sector: local education authorities in England and Wales; in Scotland the education authorities and the SOEID; education and library boards in Northern Ireland; further education colleges; higher education colleges; universities, especially the Open University and Birkbeck College of the University of London; residential colleges; the BBC, independent television and local radio stations. There are also a number of voluntary bodies.

The LEAs in England and Wales operate through 'area' adult education centres, institutes or colleges, and the adult studies departments of colleges of further education. The SOEID funds adult education, including that provided by the universities and the Workers' Educational Association, at vocational further education colleges (46 in 1997) and evening centres (91 in 1997). In addition, SOEID provides grants to a number of voluntary organizations. Provision in the statutory sector in Northern Ireland is the responsibility of the universities, the education and library boards, the 17 further education colleges and a number of community schools.

The involvement of universities in adult education and continuing education has diversified considerably and is supported by a variety of administrative structures ranging from dedicated departments to a devolved approach. Birkbeck College in the University of London caters solely for part-time students. Those institutions and colleges formerly in the PCFC sector in England and Wales, because of their range of courses and flexible patterns of student attendance, provide opportunities in the field of adult and continuing education. The Forum for the Advancement of Continuing Education (FACE) promotes collaboration between institutions of higher education active in this area. The Open University, in partnership with the BBC, provides distance teaching leading to first degrees, and also offers post-experience and higher degree courses (*see* page 453).

Of the voluntary bodies, the biggest is the Workers' Educational Association (WEA) which operates throughout the UK, reaching about 150,000 adult students annually. The FEFC for England, the SOEID, and LEAs make grants towards provision.

The National Institute of Adult Continuing Education (England and Wales) (NIACE) provides information and advice to organizations and providers on all aspects of adult continuing education. NIACE conducts research, project and development work, and is funded by the DfEE, the LEAs and other funding bodies. The Welsh committee, NIACE Cymru, receives financial support from the Welsh Office, support in kind from Welsh local authorities, and advises government, voluntary bodies and education providers on adult continuing education and training matters in Wales. In Scotland advice on adult and community education, and promotion thereof, is provided by the Scottish Community Education Council. Following the

demise of the Northern Ireland Council for Adult Education, its functions have been taken over by DENI until a successor body can be set up.

Membership of the Universities Association for Continuing Education is open to any university or university college in the UK. It promotes university continuing education, facilitates the interchange of information, and supports research and development work in continuing education.

COURSES

Although lengths vary, most courses are part-time. Long-term residential colleges in England and Wales are grant-aided by the FEFCs and provide full-time courses lasting one or two years. Some colleges and centres offer short-term residential courses, lasting from a few days to a few weeks, in a wide range of subjects. Local education authorities directly sponsor many of the colleges, while others are sponsored by universities or voluntary organizations. A directory of learning holidays, *Time to Learn*, is published by NIACE.

GRANTS

Although full-time courses at first degree level attract mandatory awards or student loans, for courses below that level all students over the age of 19 must pay a fee. However, discretionary grants may be available. Adult education bursaries for students at the long-term residential colleges of adult education are the responsibility of the colleges themselves. The awards are administered for the colleges by the Awards Officer of the Residential Colleges Committee for students resident in England and are funded by the FEFC for England in English colleges; for colleges in Wales they are funded and administered by the FEFC for Wales; and for colleges in Scotland and Northern Ireland they are funded by central government and administered by the education authorities. A booklet, *Adult Education Bursaries*, can be obtained from the Awards Officer, Adult Education Bursaries, c/o Ruskin College (*see* page 454).

Education Directory

LOCAL EDUCATION AUTHORITIES

ENGLAND

County Councils

BEDFORDSHIRE, County Hall, Cauldwell Street, Bedford MK42 9AP. Tel: 01234-362222. *Director*, P. Brett

BUCKINGHAMSHIRE, County Hall, Walton Street, Aylesbury HP20 1UA. Tel: 01296-382641. *Director*, D. McGahey

CAMBRIDGESHIRE, Shire Hall, Castle Hill, Cambridge CB3 0AP. Tel: 01223-717990. *Director*, A. Baxter

CHESHIRE, County Hall, Chester CH1 1SQ. Tel: 01244-602424. *Director*, D. Cracknell

CORNWALL, County Hall, Truro TR1 3AY. Tel: 01872-322400. *Secretary*, J. Harris

CUMBRIA, 5 Portland Square, Carlisle CA1 1PU. Tel: 01228-606868. *Director*, J. Nellist

DERBYSHIRE, County Hall, Matlock DE4 3AG. Tel: 01629-580000. *Chief Education Officer*, Ms V. Hannon

DEVON, County Hall, Topsham Road, Exeter EX2 4QD. Tel: 01392-382059. *Director*, A Smith

DORSET, County Hall, Colliton Park, Dorchester DT1 1XJ. Tel: 01305-224171. *Director*, R. Ely

DURHAM, County Hall, Durham DH1 5UL. Tel: 0191-383 3319. *Director*, K. Mitchell

EAST SUSSEX, County Hall, St Anne's Crescent, Lewes BN7 1SG. Tel: 01273-481000. *County Education Officer*, D. Mallen

ESSEX, PO Box 47, Victoria Road South, Chelmsford CM1 1LD. Tel: 01245-492211. *Director of Learning Services*, P. A. Lincoln

GLOUCESTERSHIRE, Shire Hall, Westgate Street, Gloucester GL1 2TG. Tel: 01452-425300. *Director*, R. Crouch

HAMPSHIRE, The Castle, Winchester SO23 8UG. Tel: 01962-841841. *Director*, P. J. Coles

HERTFORDSHIRE, County Hall, Pegs Lane, Hertford SG13 8DE. Tel: 01992-555704. *Director*, R. Shostak

ISLE OF WIGHT, County Hall, High Street, Newport PO30 1UD. Tel: 01983-823455. *Director*, A. Kaye

KENT, Sessions House, County Hall, Maidstone ME14 1XQ. Tel: 01622-671411. *Director*, N. Henwood

LANCASHIRE, PO Box 61, County Hall, Preston PR1 8RJ. Tel: 01772-254868. *Chief Education Officer*, C. J. Trinick

LEICESTERSHIRE, County Hall, Glenfield, Leicester LE3 8RA. Tel: 0116-265 6631. *Director*, Mrs J. A. M. Strong

LINCOLNSHIRE, County Offices, Newland, Lincoln LN1 1YL. Tel: 01522-553201. *Director*, N. J. Riches

NORFOLK, County Hall, Martineau Lane, Norwich NR1 2DH. Tel: 01603-222300. *Director*, Dr B. Slater

NORTHAMPTONSHIRE, PO Box 233, County Hall, Northampton NN1 1AU. Tel: 01604-236252. *Director*, Mrs B. Bignold

NORTHUMBERLAND, County Hall, Morpeth NE61 2EF. Tel: 01670-533000. *Director*, C. C. Tipple

NORTH YORKSHIRE, County Hall, Northallerton, N. Yorks DL7 8AD. Tel: 01609-780780. *Director*, Miss C. Welbourn

NOTTINGHAMSHIRE, County Hall, West Bridgford, Nottingham NG2 7QP. Tel: 0115-982 3823. *Director*, R. Valentine

OXFORDSHIRE, Macclesfield House, New Road, Oxford OX1 1NA. Tel: 01865-815449. *Director*, G. Badman

SHROPSHIRE, The Shirehall, Abbey Foregate, Shrewsbury SY2 6ND. Tel: 01743-254307. *County Education Officer*, Mrs C. Adams

SOMERSET, County Hall, Taunton TA1 4DY. Tel: 01823-355455. *Chief Education Officer*, M. Jennings

STAFFORDSHIRE, Tipping Street, Stafford ST16 2DH. Tel: 01785-223121. *County Education Officer*, Dr P. J. Hunter

SUFFOLK, St Andrew House, County Hall, Ipswich IP4 1LJ. Tel: 01473-584627. *County Education Officer*, D. J. Peachey

SURREY, County Hall, Penrhyn Road, Kingston upon Thames KT1 2DN. Tel: 0181-541 9500. *County Education Officer*, Dr P. Gray

WARWICKSHIRE, PO Box 24, 22 Northgate Street, Warwick CV34 4SR. Tel: 01926-410410. *Director*, E. Wood

WEST SUSSEX, County Hall, Chichester PO19 1RF. Tel: 01243-777100. *Director*, R. D. C. Bunker

WILTSHIRE, County Hall, Bythesea Road, Trowbridge BA14 8JN. Tel: 01225-713750. *Chief Education Officer*, Dr L. Davies

WORCESTERSHIRE, County Hall, Spetchley Road, Worcester WR5 2NP. Tel: 01905-763763. *Director*, J. Kramer

Unitary Councils

BARNSLEY, Berneslai Close, Barnsley S70 2HS. Tel: 01226-773501. *Programme Director (Education and Leisure)*, D. Dalton

BATH AND NORTH-EAST SOMERSET, PO Box 25, Riverside, Temple Street, Keynsham, Bristol BS31 1EA. Tel: 01225-394200. *Director*, R. Jones

BIRMINGHAM, Margaret Street, Birmingham B3 3BU. Tel: 0121-303 2590. *Chief Education Officer*, Prof. T. Brighouse

BLACKBURN WITH DARWEN, Town Hall, Blackburn BB1 7DY. Tel: 01254-585585. *Director*, Dr M. Pattison

BLACKPOOL, Progress House, Clifton Road, Blackpool FY4 4US. Tel: 01253-476501. *Director*, Dr D. Sanders

BOLTON, Paderborn House, Civic Centre, Bolton BL1 1JW. Tel: 01204-522311. *Director*, Mrs M. Blenkinsop

BOURNEMOUTH, Dorset House, 20–22 Christchurch Road, Bournemouth BH1 3NL. Tel: 01202-451451. *Director*, K. Shaikh

BRACKNELL FOREST, Skimped Hill Lane, Bracknell, Berks RG12 1LY. Tel: 01344-424642. *Director*, A. Ecclestone

BRADFORD, Flockton House, Flockton Road, Bradford BD7 7RY. Tel: 01274-751840. *Director*, Mrs D. Cavanagh

BRIGHTON AND HOVE, PO Box 2503, Kings House, Grand Avenue, Hove BN3 2SR. Tel: 01273-290000. *Director*, Ms D. Stokoe

BRISTOL, Avon House, St James Barton, Bristol BS99 1NB. Tel: 0117-922 4402. *Director*, R. Riddell

BURY, Athenaeum House, Market Street, Bury BL9 0BN. Tel: 0161-253 5603. *Chief Education Officer*, H. Williams

CALDERDALE, Northgate House, Halifax HX1 1UN. Tel: 01422-357257. *Director*, I. Jennings

COVENTRY, New Council Offices, Earl Street, Coventry CV1 5RS. Tel: 01203-831511. *Chief Education Officer*, Ms C. Goodwin

DARLINGTON, Town Hall, Darlington DL1 5QT. Tel: 01325-380651. *Director*, G. Pennington

DERBY, Middleton House, 27 St Mary's Gate, Derby DE1 3NN. Tel: 01332-716922. *Director*, D. D'Hooghe

DONCASTER, PO Box 266, The Council House, College Road, Doncaster DN1 3AD. Tel: 01302-737222. *Director,* M. Simpson

DUDLEY, Westox House, 1 Trinity Road, Dudley DY1 1JB. Tel: 01384-814200. *Chief Education Officer,* R. P. Colligan

EAST RIDING OF YORKSHIRE, County Hall, Beverley HU17 9BA. Tel: 01482-887700. *Director,* J. Ginnever

GATESHEAD, Civic Centre, Regent Street, Gateshead NE8 1HH. Tel: 0191-477 1011. *Director,* B. H. Edwards

HALTON, Grosvenor House, Halton Lea, Runcorn, Cheshire WA7 2WD. Tel: 0151-424 2061. *Director,* G. Talbot

HARTLEPOOL, Civic Centre, Victoria Road, Hartlepool TS24 8AY. Tel: 01429-266522. *Director,* J. J. Fitt

HEREFORDSHIRE, PO Box 185, Herefordshire Council, Blackfriars Street, Hereford HR4 9ZR. Tel: 01432-260908. *Director,* Dr E. Oram

KINGSTON UPON HULL, Essex House, Manor Street, Hull HU1 1YD. Tel: 01482-613161. *Director,* Miss J. E. Taylor

KIRKLEES, Oldgate House, 2 Oldgate, Huddersfield HD1 6QW. Tel: 01484-225242. *Chief Education Officer,* G. Tomkin

KNOWSLEY, Huyton Hey Road, Huyton, Knowsley, Merseyside L36 5YH. Tel: 0151-443 3232. *Director,* P. Wylie

LEEDS, Merrion House, Merrion Way, Leeds LS2 8DT. Tel: 0113-247 5612. *Director (acting),* M. R. Shaw

LEICESTER, Marlborough House, 38 Welford Road, Leicester LE2 7AA. Tel: 0116-252 7700. *Director,* T. Warren

LIVERPOOL, 14 Sir Thomas Street, Liverpool L1 6BJ. Tel: 0151-227 3911. *Director,* M. F. Cogley

LUTON, Unity House, 111 Stuart Street, Luton LU1 5NP. Tel: 01582-548000. *Director,* T. Dessent

MANCHESTER, Cumberland House, Crown Square, Manchester M60 3BB. Tel: 0161-234 7125. *Chief Education Officer,* R. Jobson

MEDWAY, Compass Centre, Chatham Maritime, Chatham, Kent ME7 4OD. Tel: 01634-881638. *Director,* R Bolsin

MIDDLESBROUGH, PO Box 191, 2nd Floor, Civic Centre, Middlesbrough TS1 2XS. Tel: 01642-262001. *Director,* Ms C. Berry

MILTON KEYNES, Saxon Court, 502 Avebury Boulevard, Central Milton Keynes MK9 3HS. Tel: 01908-691691. *Director,* A. Flack

NEWBURY, Avon Bank House, West Street, Newbury, Berks RG14 1BZ. Tel: 01635-519728. *Director,* J. Mercer

NEWCASTLE UPON TYNE, Civic Centre, Newcastle upon Tyne NE1 8PU. Tel: 0191-232 8520. *Director,* D. Bell

NORTH EAST LINCOLNSHIRE, 7 Eleanor Street, Grimsby DN32 9DU. Tel: 01472-323090. *Head of Education,* G. Hill

NORTH LINCOLNSHIRE, PO Box 35, Hewson House, Station Road, Brigg DN20 8XJ. Tel: 01724-297240. *Director,* T. Thomas

NORTH SOMERSET, Town Hall, Weston-super-Mare BS23 1AE. Tel: 01934-888829. *Director,* Ms J. Wreford

NORTH TYNESIDE, Stevenson House, Stevenson Street, North Shields NE30 1QA. Tel: 0191-200 5022. *Director,* L. Watson

NOTTINGHAM CITY, Sandfield Centre, Sandfield Road, Nottingham NG2 6JE. Tel: 0115-915 5555. *Director,* P. Roberts

OLDHAM, PO Box 40, Civic Centre, Oldham OL1 1XJ. Tel: 0161-911 3000. *Director,* M. Willis

PETERBOROUGH, Bayard Place, Broadway, Peterborough PE1 1FB. Tel: 01733-563141. *Director,* W. Goodwin

PLYMOUTH, Civic Centre, Armada Way, Plymouth PL1 2EW. Tel: 01752-304977. *Director,* S. Faruqi

POOLE, Civic Centre, Poole, Dorset BH15 2RU. Tel: 01202-633202. *Policy Director,* Dr S. Goodwin

PORTSMOUTH, Civic Offices, Guildhall Square, Portsmouth PO1 2AL. Tel: 01705-841200. *City Education Officer (acting),* A. Seber

READING, Civic Centre, Reading RG1 7TD. Tel: 0118-939 0120. *Director,* A. Daykin

REDCAR AND CLEVELAND, Council Offices, Kirkleatham Street, Redcar TS10 1RT. Tel: 01642-444342. *Chief Education Officer,* K. Burton

ROCHDALE, PO Box 70, Municipal Offices, Smith Street, Rochdale OL16 1YD. Tel: 01706-647474. *Director,* B. Atkinson

ROTHERHAM, Norfolk House, Walker Place, Rotherham S60 1QT. Tel: 01709-382121. *Education Officer,* H. C. Bower

RUTLAND, Catmose, Oakham, Rutland LE15 6HP. Tel: 01572-772704. *Director,* K. Bartley

ST HELENS, Rivington Centre, Rivington Road, St Helens WA10 4ND. Tel: 01744-456000. *Director,* C. Hilton

SALFORD, Chapel Street, Salford M3 5TL. Tel: 0161-832 9751. *Chief Education Officer,* D. C. Johnston

SANDWELL, PO Box 41, Shaftesbury House, 402 High Street, West Bromwich B70 9LT. Tel: 0121-569 8205. *Director,* S. Gallacher

SEFTON, Town Hall, Oriel Road, Bootle, Merseyside L20 7AE. Tel: 0151-922 4040. *Education Officer,* B. Marsh

SHEFFIELD, Leopold Street, Sheffield S1 1RJ. Tel: 0114-273 5722. *Director,* J. Crossley-Holland

SLOUGH, Town Hall, Bath Road, Slough SL1 3UQ. Tel: 01753-552288. *Director,* J. Christie

SOLIHULL, PO Box 20, Council House, Solihull B91 3QU. Tel: 0121-704 6656. *Director,* D. Nixon

SOUTHAMPTON, 5th Floor, Frobisher House, Commercial Road, Southampton SO15 1GX. Tel: 01703-223855. *Executive Director,* R. Hogg

SOUTH GLOUCESTERSHIRE, Bowling Hill, Chipping Sodbury, S. Glos BS37 6JX. Tel: 01454-863253. *Director,* Ms T. Gillespie

SOUTHEND, Civic Centre, Victoria Avenue, Southend-on-Sea SS2 6ER. Tel: 01702-215921. *Director,* S. Hay

SOUTH TYNESIDE, Town Hall and Civic Offices, Westoe Road, South Shields NE33 2RL. Tel: 0191-427 1717. *Director,* I. Reid

STOCKPORT, Stopford House, Piccadilly, Stockport SK1 3XE. Tel: 0161-474 3813. *Chief Education Officer,* M. Hunt

STOCKTON-ON-TEES, PO Box 228, Municipal Buildings, Church Road, Stockton-on-Tees TS18 1XE. Tel: 01642-393939. *Director,* S. T. Bradford

STOKE-ON-TRENT, PO Box 758, Swann House, Boothen Road, Stoke-on-Trent ST4 1RU. Tel: 01782-232014. *Director of Education,* N. Rigby

SUNDERLAND, Civic Centre, Burdon Road, Sunderland SR2 7DN. Tel: 0191-553 1355. *Director,* Dr J. W. Williams

SWINDON, Civic Offices, Euclid Street, Swindon SN1 2JH. Tel: 01793-463069. *Director,* M. Lusty

TAMESIDE, Council Offices, Wellington Road, Ashton under Lyne, Lancs OL6 6LD. Tel: 0161-342 3200. *Director,* A. M. Webster

TELFORD AND WREKIN, Civic Offices, Telford, Shropshire TF3 4LD. Tel: 01952-202402. *Corporate Director,* Ms C. Davies

THURROCK, PO Box 118, Grays, Essex RM17 6GF. Tel: 01375-652652. *Director,* R. Wilkins

TORBAY, Oldway Mansion, Paignton, Devon TQ3 2TE. Tel: 01803-208201. *Director,* G. Cave

TRAFFORD, PO Box 40, Trafford Town Hall, Talbot Road, Stretford, Trafford, Greater Manchester M32 OEL. Tel: 0161-912 1212. *Director,* Mrs K. August

WAKEFIELD, County Hall, Wakefield WF1 2QL. Tel: 01924-305501. *Education Officer,* J. McLeod

WALSALL, Civic Centre, Darwall Street, Walsall WS1 1TP. Tel: 01922-652301. *Director,* T. Howard

WARRINGTON, New Town House, Buttermarket Street, Warrington, Cheshire WA1 2NH. Tel: 01925-444400. *Director,* M. Roxborgh

WIGAN, Gateway House, Standishgate, Wigan, Lancs WN1 1AE. Tel: 01942-828891. *Education Officer,* R. Clark

WINDSOR AND MAIDENHEAD, Town Hall, St Ives Road, Maidenhead, Berks SL6 1RF. Tel: 01628-796258. *Director,* M. Peckham

WIRRAL, Hamilton Building, Conway Street, Birkenhead L41 4FD. Tel: 0151-666 4288. *Director,* C. Rice

WOKINGHAM, Shute End, Wokingham, Berks RG40 1WQ. Tel: 0118-974 6106. *Director,* Mrs J. Griffin

WOLVERHAMPTON, Civic Centre, St Peter's Square, Wolverhampton WV1 1RR. Tel: 01902-554100. *Director,* R. Lockwood

YORK, 10–12 George Hudson Street, York YO1 1ZG. Tel: 01904-613161. *Director,* M. Peters

LONDON

*Inner London borough

BARKING AND DAGENHAM, Town Hall, Barking, Essex IG11 7LU. Tel: 0181-592 4500. *Education Officer,* A. Larbalestier

BARNET, Former Friern Barnet Town Hall, Friern Barnet Lane, London N11 3DL. Tel: 0181-359 3001. *Director (acting),* M. Kempson

BEXLEY, Hill View, Hill View Drive, Welling, Kent DA16 3RY. Tel: 0181-303 7777. *Director,* P. McGee

BRENT, Chesterfield House, 9 Park Lane, Wembley, Middx HA9 7RW. Tel: 0181-937 3190. *Director,* J. Simpson

BROMLEY, Civic Centre, Stockwell Close, Bromley BR1 3UH. Tel: 0181-464 3333. *Director,* K. Davis

*CAMDEN, Crowndale Centre, 218–220 Eversholt Street, London NW1 1BD. Tel: 0171-911 1525. *Director,* R. Litchfield

*CITY OF LONDON, Education Department, Corporation of London, PO Box 270, Guildhall, London EC2P 2EJ. Tel: 0171-332 1750. *City Education Officer,* D. Smith

*CITY OF WESTMINSTER, City Hall, 64 Victoria Street, London SW1E 6QP. Tel: 0171-641 3338. *Director,* Ms D. McGrath

CROYDON, Taberner House, Park Lane, Croydon CR9 1TP. Tel: 0181-686 4433. *Director,* D. Sands

EALING, Perceval House, 14–16 Uxbridge Road, London W5 2HL. Tel: 0181-758 5410. *Director,* A. Parker

ENFIELD, PO Box 56, Civic Centre, Silver Street, Enfield, Middx EN1 3XQ. Tel: 0181-379 3201. *Director,* Ms E. Graham

*GREENWICH, Riverside House, Beresford Street, London SE18 6DN. Tel: 0181-854 8888. *Director,* G. Gyte

*HACKNEY, Edith Cavell Building, Enfield Road, London N1 5BA. Tel: 0181-356 5000. *Director,* Ms E. Reid

*HAMMERSMITH AND FULHAM, Cambridge House, Cambridge Grove, London W6 0LE. Tel: 0181-748 3020. *Director,* Ms C. Whatford

HARINGEY, 48 Station Road, Wood Green, London N22 4TY. Tel: 0181-975 9700. *Director,* Ms F. Magee

HARROW, PO Box 22, Civic Centre, Station Road, Harrow HA1 2UW. Tel: 0181-424 1304. *Director,* P. Osburn

HAVERING, The Broxhill Centre, Broxhill Road, Harold Hill, Romford RM4 1XN. Tel: 01708-773839. *Director,* C. Hardy

HILLINGDON, Civic Centre, High Street, Uxbridge UB8 1UW. Tel: 01895-250111. *Director (acting),* G. Moss

HOUNSLOW, Civic Centre, Lampton Road, Hounslow TW3 4DN. Tel: 0181-862 5301. *Director,* J. D. Tricket

*ISLINGTON, Laycock Street, London N1 1TH. Tel: 0171-457 5753. *Education Officer,* Dr H. Nicolle

*KENSINGTON AND CHELSEA, Town Hall, Hornton Street, London W8 7NX. Tel: 0171-361 3334. *Director,* R. Wood

KINGSTON UPON THAMES, Guildhall, Kingston upon Thames KT1 1EU. Tel: 0181-547 5220. *Director,* J. Braithwaite

*LAMBETH, Bluestar House, 234–244 Stockwell Road, London SW9 9SP. Tel: 0171-926 1000. *Director,* Ms H. Du Quesnay

*LEWISHAM, Laurence House, Catford, London SE6 4RU. Tel: 0181-314 6200. *Director,* Ms A. Efunshile

MERTON, Civic Centre, London Road, Morden, Surrey SM4 5DX. Tel: 0181-543 2222. *Director,* Ms J. Cairns

NEWHAM, Broadway House, 322 High Street, Stratford, London E15 1AJ. Tel: 0181-555 5552. *Director,* I. Harrison

REDBRIDGE, Lynton House, 255–259 High Road, Ilford IG1 1NN. Tel: 0181-478 3020. *Chief Education Officer,* D. Kapper

RICHMOND UPON THAMES, Regal House, London Road, Twickenham TW1 3QS. Tel: 0181-891 1411. *Director,* R. Hancock

*SOUTHWARK, 1 Bradenham Close, Albany Road, London SE17 2BA. Tel: 0171-525 5000. *Director,* G. Mott

SUTTON, The Grove, Carshalton, Surrey SM5 3AL. Tel: 0181-770 6500. *Director,* Dr I. Birnbaum

*TOWER HAMLETS, Mulberry Place, 5 Clove Crescent, London E14 2BG. Tel: 0171-364 5000. *Director,* Ms C. Gilbert

WALTHAM FOREST, Municipal Offices, High Road, Leyton, London E10 5QJ. Tel: 0181-527 5544. *Chief Education Officer,* A. Lockhart

*WANDSWORTH, Town Hall, Wandsworth High Street, London SW18 2PU. Tel: 0181-871 7890. *Director,* P. Robinson

WALES

ANGLESEY, Swyddfa'r Sir, Llangefni, Anglesey LL77 7EY. Tel: 01248-752900. *Director,* R. L. P. Jones

BLAENAU GWENT, Victoria House, Victoria Business Park, Ebbw Vale NP3 6ER. Tel: 01495-355434. *Director,* B. Mawby

BRIDGEND, Sunnyside, Sunnyside Road, Bridgend CF31 4AR. Tel: 01656-642600. *Director,* D. Matthews

CAERPHILLY, Council Offices, Caerphilly Road, Ystrad Mynach, Hengoed CF82 7EP. Tel: 01443-864956. *Director,* N. Harries

CARDIFF, County Hall, Atlantic Wharf, Cardiff CF1 5UW. Tel: 01222-872700. *Director,* T. Davies

CARMARTHENSHIRE, Pibwrlwyd, Carmarthen SA31 2NH. Tel: 01267-224501. *Director,* K. Davies

CEREDIGION, Swyddfa'r Sir, Marine Terrace, Aberystwyth SY23 2DE. Tel: 01970-633601. *Director,* R Williams

CONWY, Government Buildings, Dinerth Road, Rhos-on-Sea LL28 4UL. Tel: 01492-574000. *Director,* R. E. Williams

DENBIGHSHIRE, County Hall, Mold, Flintshire CH7 6GR. Tel: 01824-706700. *Director,* E. Lewis

FLINTSHIRE, County Hall, Mold, Flintshire CH7 6NW. Tel: 01352-704400. *Director,* K. McDonogh

GWYNEDD, Shire Hall Street, Caernarfon LL55 1SH. Tel: 01286-672255. *Director*, D. Whittall

MERTHYR TYDFIL, Ty Keir Hardie, Riverside Court, Avenue De Clichy, Merthyr Tydfil CF47 8XO. Tel: 01685-724600. *Director*, D. Jones

MONMOUTHSHIRE, County Hall, Cwmbran NP44 2XH. Tel: 01633-644644. *Director*, D. Young

NEATH PORT TALBOT, Civic Centre, Port Talbot SA13 1PJ. Tel: 01639-763333. *Corporate Director*, V. Thomas

NEWPORT, Civic Centre, Newport, South Wales NP9 4UR. Tel: 01633-232204. *Director*, G. Bingham

PEMBROKESHIRE, Cambria House, Haverfordwest SA61 1TP. Tel: 01437-764551. *Director*, G. Davies

POWYS, County Hall, Llandrindod Wells LD1 5LG. Tel: 01597-826006. *Director*, M. Barker

RHONDDA, CYNON, TAFF, Education Centre, Grawen Street, Porth CF39 0BU. Tel: 01443-687666. *Director*, K. Ryley

SWANSEA, County Hall, Oystermouth Road, Swansea SA1 3SN. Tel: 01792-636351. *Director*, R. Parry

TORFAEN, County Hall, Croesyceiliog, Cwmbran, Torfaen NP44 2WN. Tel: 01633-648609. *Director*, M. de Val

VALE OF GLAMORGAN, Civic Offices, Holton Road, Barry CF63 4RU. Tel: 01446-709106. *Director*, A. Davies

WREXHAM, Roxburgh House, Hill Street, Wrexham LL11 1SN. Tel: 01978-297421. *Director*, T. Garner

SCOTLAND

ABERDEEN CITY, Summerhill, Stronsay Drive, Aberdeen AB15 6JA. Tel: 01224-522000. *Director*, J. Stodter

ABERDEENSHIRE, Woodhill House, Westburn Road, Aberdeen AB16 5GB. Tel: 01224-665420. *Director*, M. White

ANGUS, County Buildings, Market Street, Forfar DD8 3WE. Tel: 01307-461460. *Director*, J. Anderson

ARGYLL AND BUTE, Argyll House, Alexandra Parade, Dunoon PA23 8AG. Tel: 01369-704000. *Director*, A. C. Morton

CITY OF EDINBURGH, (*from Dec. 1998*) Wellington Court, 10 Waterloo Place, Edinburgh EH1 3EG. Tel: 0131-200 2000. *Director*, R. Jobson

CLACKMANNANSHIRE, Lime Tree House, Alloa FK10 1EX. Tel: 01259-452431. *Director*, K. Bloomer

DUMFRIES AND GALLOWAY, Education Department, 30 Edinburgh Road, Dumfries DG1 1JG. Tel: 01384-260000. *Director (acting)*, F. Sanderson

DUNDEE CITY, 8th Floor, Tayside House, 28 Crichton Street, Dundee DD1 3RJ. Tel: 01382-433088. *Director*, Ms A. Wilson

EAST AYRSHIRE, Council Headquarters, London Road, Kilmarnock KA3 7BU. Tel: 01563-576017. *Director*, J. Mulgrew

EAST DUNBARTONSHIRE, Boclair House, 100 Milngavie Road, Bearsden, Glasgow G61 2TQ. Tel: 0141-942 9000. *Director*, I. Mills

EAST LOTHIAN, Council Buildings, 25 Court Street, Haddington EH41 3HA. Tel: 01620-827588. *Director*, A. Blackie

EAST RENFREWSHIRE, Council Offices, Eastwood Park, Rouken Glen Road, Giffnock G46 6UG. Tel: 0141-577 3430. *Director*, Ms E. J. Currie

FALKIRK, McLaren House, Marchmont Avenue, Polmont, Falkirk FK2 0NZ. Tel: 01324-506600. *Director*, Dr G. Young

FIFE, Rothesay House, North Street, Glenrothes KY7 5PN. Tel: 01592-413656. *Director*, A. Mackay

GLASGOW CITY, Charing Cross Complex, House 1, 20 India Street, Glasgow G2 4PF. Tel: 0141-287 2000. *Director*, K. Corsar

HIGHLAND, Council Buildings, Glenurquhart Road, Inverness IV3 5NX. Tel: 01463-702802. *Director*, A. Gilchrist

INVERCLYDE, 105 Dalrymple Street, Greenock PA15 1HT. Tel: 01475-712828. *Director*, B. McLeary

MIDLOTHIAN, Fairfield House, 8 Lothian Road, Dalkeith EH22 3ZJ. Tel: 0131-270 7500. *Director*, D. MacKay

MORAY, Council Offices, High Street, Elgin IV30 1BX. Tel: 01343-563134. *Director*, K. Gavin

NORTH AYRSHIRE, Cunninghame House, Irvine KA12 8EE. Tel: 01294-324412. *Director*, J. Travers

NORTH LANARKSHIRE, Municipal Buildings, Kildonan Street, Coatbridge ML5 3BT. Tel: 01236-812222. *Director*, M. O'Neill

ORKNEY ISLANDS, Council Offices, School Place, Kirkwall, Orkney KW15 1NY. Tel: 01856-873535. *Director*, L. Manson

PERTH AND KINROSS, Blackfriars, Perth PH1 5LU. Tel: 01738-476200. *Director*, R. McKay

RENFREWSHIRE, Council Headquarters, South Building, Cotton Street, Paisley PA1 1LE. Tel: 0141-842 5601. *Director*, Ms S. Rae

SCOTTISH BORDERS, Council Headquarters, Newtown St Boswells, Melrose TD6 0SA. Tel: 01835-824000. *Director*, J. Christie

SHETLAND ISLANDS, Hayfield House, Hayfield Lane, Lerwick, Shetland ZE1 0QD. Tel: 01595-744000. *Director*, J. Halcrow

SOUTH AYRSHIRE, County Buildings, Wellington Square, Ayr KA7 1DR. Tel: 01292-612201. *Director*, M. McCabe

SOUTH LANARKSHIRE, Council Headquarters, Almada Street, Hamilton ML3 0AE. Tel: 01698-454379. *Executive Director*, Ms M. Allan

STIRLING, Viewforth, Stirling FK8 2ET. Tel: 01786-442680. *Director*, G. Jeyes

WEST DUNBARTONSHIRE, Garshake Road, Dumbarton G82 3PU. Tel: 01389-737000. *Director*, I. McMurdo

WESTERN ISLES, Council Offices, Sandwick Road, Stornoway, Isle of Lewis HS1 2BW. Tel: 01851-703773. *Director*, N. R. Galbraith

WEST LOTHIAN, Lindsay House, South Bridge Street, Bathgate EH48 1TS. Tel: 01506-776358. *Corporate Manager*, R. Stewart

NORTHERN IRELAND

EDUCATION AND LIBRARY BOARDS

BELFAST, 40 Academy Street, Belfast BT1 2NQ. Tel: 01232-564122. *Chief Executive*, T. G. J. Moag, OBE

NORTH, County Hall, 182 Galgorm Road, Ballymena, Co. Antrim BT42 1HN. Tel: 01266-653333. *Chief Executive*, G. Topping

SOUTH EASTERN, 18 Windsor Avenue, Belfast BT9 6EF. Tel: 01232-381188. *Chief Executive*, J. B. Fitzsimons

SOUTHERN, 3 Charlemont Place, The Mall, Armagh BT61 9AX. Tel: 01861-512200. *Chief Executive*, J. G. Kelly

WESTERN, 1 Hospital Road, Omagh, Co. Tyrone BT79 0AW. Tel: 01662-411411. *Chief Executive*, P. J. Martin

ISLANDS

GUERNSEY, Grange Road, St Peter Port, Guernsey GY1 1RQ. Tel: 01481-710821. *Director*, D. T. Neale

JERSEY, PO Box 142, Jersey JE4 8QJ. Tel: 01534-509500. *Director*, T. W. McKeon

ISLE OF MAN, Murray House, 5–11 Mount Havelock, Douglas, Isle of Man IM1 2SG. Tel: 01624-685820. *Director*, R. B. Cowin

ISLES OF SCILLY, Town Hall, St Mary's, Isles of Scilly TR21 0LW. Tel: 01720-422537 ext. 145. *Secretary for Education*, P. S. Hygate

ADVISORY BODIES

Schools

EDUCATION OTHERWISE, PO Box 7420, London N9 9SG. Tel: Helpline: 0891-518303

BRITISH EDUCATIONAL COMMUNICATIONS AND TECHNOLOGY AGENCY (formerly National Council for Educational Technology), Milburn Hill Road, Science Park, Coventry CV4 7JJ. Tel: 01203-416994. *Chief Executive*, O. Lynch

INTERNATIONAL BACCALAUREATE ORGANIZATION, Peterson House, Fortran Road, St Mellons, Cardiff CF3 0LT. Tel: 01222-774000. *Director of Academic Affairs*, Dr H. Drennan

NATIONAL ADVISORY COUNCIL FOR EDUCATION AND TRAINING TARGETS, 7th Floor, 222 Grays Inn Road, London WC1X 8HL. Tel: 0171-211 5012. *Chairman*, D. Wanless; *Director*, P. Chorley

SPECIAL EDUCATIONAL NEEDS TRIBUNAL, 7th Floor, Windsor House, 50 Victoria Street, London SW1H 0NW. Tel: 0171-925 6925. *President*, T. Aldridge, QC

Independent Schools

GOVERNING BODIES ASSOCIATION, The Ancient Foresters, Bush End, Takeley, Bishop's Stortford, Herts CM22 6NN. Tel: 01279-871865. *Secretary*, F. V. Morgan

GOVERNING BODIES OF GIRLS' SCHOOLS ASSOCIATION, The Ancient Foresters, Bush End, Takeley, Bishop's Stortford, Herts CM22 6NN. Tel: 01279-871865. *Secretary*, F. V. Morgan

INDEPENDENT SCHOOLS COUNCIL, Grosvenor Gardens House, 35–37 Grosvenor Gardens, London SW1W 0BS. Tel: 0171-630 0144. *Administrator*, Ms E. Sutton

INDEPENDENT SCHOOLS EXAMINATIONS BOARD, Jordan House, Christchurch Road, New Milton, Hants BH25 6QJ. Tel: 01425-621111. *Administrator*, Mrs J. Williams

INDEPENDENT SCHOOLS INFORMATION SERVICE, 56 Buckingham Gate, London SW1E 6AG. Tel: 0171-630 8793. *National Director*, D. J. Woodhead

THE ISJC ASSISTED PLACES COMMITTEE, 100 Rochester Row, London SW1P 1JP. Tel: 0171-393 6666. *Secretary*, P. F. V. Waters

Further Education

FURTHER EDUCATION DEVELOPMENT AGENCY, Citadel Place, Tinworth Street, London SE11 5EH. Tel: 0171-962 1280. *Chief Executive*, C. Hughes

Regional Advisory Councils

ASSOCIATION OF COLLEGES IN THE EASTERN REGION, Merlin Place, Milton Road, Cambridge CB4 4DP. Tel: 01223-424022. *Chief Executive*, J. Graystone

CENTRA (EDUCATION AND TRAINING SERVICES) LTD, Duxbury Park, Duxbury Hall Road, Chorley, Lancs PR7 4AT. Tel: 01257-241428. *Chief Executive*, P. Wren

EMFEC (formerly East Midlands Further Education Council), Robins Wood House, Robins Wood Road, Aspley, Nottingham NG8 3NH. Tel: 0115-929 3291. *Chief Executive*, J. Gardiner

NCFE (formerly Northern Council for Further Education), Portland House, 2nd Floor, Block D, New Bridge Street, Newcastle upon Tyne NE1 8AN. Tel: 0191-201 3100. *Chief Executive*, J. F. Pearce

SOUTHERN REGIONAL COUNCIL FOR EDUCATION AND TRAINING, Building 33, The University of Reading, London Road, Reading RG1 5AQ. Tel: 0118-931 6320. *Chief Executive*, B. J. Knowles

SOUTH WEST ASSOCIATION FOR FURTHER EDUCATION AND TRAINING, Bishops Hull House, Bishops Hull, Taunton, Somerset TA1 5RA. Tel: 01823-335491. *Chief Executive*, Ms L. McGrath

WELSH JOINT EDUCATION COMMITTEE, 245 Western Avenue, Cardiff CF5 2YX. Tel: 01222-265000. *Chief Executive*, I. Hume

YORKSHIRE AND HUMBERSIDE ASSOCIATION FOR FURTHER AND HIGHER EDUCATION, 13 Wellington Road East, Dewsbury, W. Yorks WF13 1XG. Tel: 01924-450900. *Director (acting)*, C. Daniel

Higher Education

ASSOCIATION OF COMMONWEALTH UNIVERSITIES, John Foster House, 36 Gordon Square, London WC1H 0PF. Tel: 0171-387 8572. *Secretary-General*, Prof. M. G. Gibbons

COMMITTEE OF SCOTTISH HIGHER EDUCATION PRINCIPALS (COSHEP), St Andrew House, 141 West Nile Street, Glasgow G1 2RN. Tel: 0141-353 1880. *Secretary*, Dr R. L. Crawford

COMMITTEE OF VICE-CHANCELLORS AND PRINCIPALS OF THE UNIVERSITIES OF THE UNITED KINGDOM, Woburn House, 20 Tavistock Square, London WC1H 9HQ. Tel: 0171-419 4111. *Chairman*, Prof. M. Harris; *Chief Executive*, Ms D. Warwick

NORTHERN IRELAND HIGHER EDUCATION COUNCIL, Rathgael House, Balloo Road, Bangor BT19 7PR. Tel: 01247-279333. *Chairman*, Sir Kenneth Bloomfield, KCB; *Secretary*, J. Coote

QUALITY ASSURANCE AGENCY FOR HIGHER EDUCATION, Southgate House, Southgate Street, Gloucester GL1 1UB. Tel: 01452-557000. *Secretary*, S. Bushell

CURRICULUM COUNCILS

AWDURDOD CYMWYSTERAU CWRICWLWM AC ASESU CYMRU/QUALIFICATIONS, CURRICULUM AND ASSESSMENT AUTHORITY FOR WALES, Castle Buildings, Womanby Street, Cardiff CF1 9SX. Tel: 01222-375400. *Chief Executive*, J. V. Williams

NORTHERN IRELAND COUNCIL FOR THE CURRICULUM, EXAMINATIONS AND ASSESSMENT, Clarendon Dock, 29 Clarendon Road, Belfast BT1 3BG. Tel: 01232-261200. *Chief Executive*, Mrs C. Coxhead

QUALIFICATIONS AND CURRICULUM AUTHORITY, 29 Bolton Street, London W1Y 7PD. Tel: 0171-509 5555. *Chairman*, Sir William Stubbs, PH.D; *Chief Executive*, N. Tate, PH.D.

SCOTTISH CONSULTATIVE COUNCIL ON THE CURRICULUM, Gardyne Road, Broughty Ferry, Dundee DD5 1NY. Tel: 01382-455053. *Chief Executive*, M. Baughan

EXAMINING BODIES

UNITARY AWARDING BODIES

ASSESSMENT AND QUALIFICATIONS ALLIANCE (AQA), Stag Hill House, Guildford GU2 5XJ. Tel: 01483-506506. Devas Street, Manchester M15 6EX. Tel: 0161-953 1180. *Director-General*, Ms K. Tattersall

THE EDEXCEL FOUNDATION, Stewart House, 32 Russell Square, London WC1B 5DN. Tel: 0171-393 4444. *Chief Executive*, Ms C. Townsend, PH.D

OXFORD, CAMBRIDGE AND RSA EXAMINATIONS, 1 Regent Street, Cambridge CB2 1GG. Tel: 01223-552552. *Chief Executive*, B. Swift

GCSE

THE EDEXCEL FOUNDATION, *see* above
NORTHERN EXAMINATIONS AND ASSESSMENT BOARD, Devas Street, Manchester M15 6EX. Tel: 0161-953 1180. *Chief Executive*, Ms H. M. James
NORTHERN IRELAND COUNCIL FOR THE CURRICULUM, EXAMINATIONS AND ASSESSMENT, Clarendon Dock, 29 Clarendon Road, Belfast BT1 3BG. Tel: 01232-261200. *Chief Executive*, Mrs C. Coxhead
OXFORD, CAMBRIDGE AND RSA EXAMINATIONS, *see* above
SEG (SOUTHERN EXAMINING GROUP), Stag Hill House, Guildford, Surrey GU2 5XJ. Tel: 01483-506506. *Secretary-General*, Dr C. P. Hughes
WELSH JOINT EDUCATION COMMITTEE, 245 Western Avenue, Cardiff CF5 2YX. Tel: 01222-265000. *Chief Executive*, I. Hume

A-LEVEL

THE ASSOCIATED EXAMINING BOARD, Stag Hill House, Guildford, Surrey GU2 5XJ. Tel: 01483-506506. *Secretary-General*, Dr C. P. Hughes
THE EDEXCEL FOUNDATION, *see* above
NORTHERN EXAMINATIONS AND ASSESSMENT BOARD, Devas Street, Manchester M15 6EX. Tel: 0161-953 1180. *Chief Executive*, Ms H. M. James
NORTHERN IRELAND COUNCIL FOR THE CURRICULUM, EXAMINATIONS AND ASSESSMENT, Clarendon Dock, 29 Clarendon Road, Belfast BT1 3BG. Tel: 01232-261200. *Chief Executive*, Mrs C. Coxhead
OXFORD, CAMBRIDGE AND RSA EXAMINATIONS, *see* above
WELSH JOINT EDUCATION COMMITTEE, 245 Western Avenue, Cardiff CF5 2YX. Tel: 01222-265000. *Chief Executive*, I. Hume

SCOTLAND

SCOTTISH QUALIFICATIONS AUTHORITY, Hanover House, 24 Douglas Street, Glasgow G2 7NQ. Tel: 0141-248 7900. Ironmills Road, Dalkeith EH12 1LE. Tel: 0131-663 6601. *Chief Executive*, R. Tuck

FURTHER EDUCATION

CITY & GUILDS, 1 Giltspur Street, London EC1A 9DD. Tel: 0171-294 2468. *Director-General*, N. Carey, PH.D
THE EDEXCEL FOUNDATION, *see* above
OXFORD, CAMBRIDGE AND RSA EXAMINATIONS, *see* above

FUNDING COUNCILS

SCHOOLS

FUNDING AGENCY FOR SCHOOLS, Albion Wharf, 25 Skeldergate, York YO1 2XL. Tel: 01904-661661. *Chairman*, Vice-Adm. Sir Antony Tippett, KCB; *Chief Executive*, M. Collier

FURTHER EDUCATION

FURTHER EDUCATION FUNDING COUNCIL FOR ENGLAND, Cheylesmore House, Quinton Road, Coventry CV1 2WT. Tel: 01203-863000. *Chief Executive*, Prof. D. Melville
FURTHER EDUCATION FUNDING COUNCIL FOR WALES, Linden Court, The Orchards, Ty Glas Avenue, Cardiff CF4 5DZ. Tel: 01222-761861. *Chief Executive*, Prof. J. Andrews

SCOTTISH FURTHER EDUCATION FUNDING DIVISION, Scottish Office Education and Industry Department, 1st Floor West, Victoria Quay, Edinburgh EH6 6QQ. Tel: 0131-244 0286. *Head of Division*, C. M. Reeves

HIGHER EDUCATION

HIGHER EDUCATION FUNDING COUNCIL FOR ENGLAND, Northavon House, Coldharbour Lane, Bristol BS16 1QD. Tel: 0117-931 7317. *Chief Executive*, Prof. B. Fender
HIGHER EDUCATION FUNDING COUNCIL FOR WALES, Linden Court, The Orchards, Ty Glas Avenue, Cardiff CF4 5DZ. Tel: 01222-761861. *Chief Executive*, Prof. J. A. Andrews
SCOTTISH HIGHER EDUCATION FUNDING COUNCIL, Donaldson House, 97 Haymarket Terrace, Edinburgh EH12 5HD. Tel: 0131-313 6500. *Chief Executive*, Prof. J. Sizer, CBE
STUDENT AWARDS AGENCY FOR SCOTLAND, Gyleview House, 3 Redheughs Rigg, Edinburgh EH12 9HH. Tel: 0131-244 5823. *Chief Executive*, K. MacRae
STUDENT LOANS COMPANY LTD, 100 Bothwell Street, Glasgow G2 7JD. Tel: 0141-306 2000. *Chief Executive*, C. Ward
TEACHER TRAINING AGENCY, Portland House, Stag Place, London SW1E 5TT. Tel: 0171-925 3700. *Chairman*, Prof. C. Booth; *Chief Executive*, Ms A. Millett

ADMISSIONS AND COURSE INFORMATION

CAREERS RESEARCH AND ADVISORY CENTRE, Sheraton House, Castle Park, Cambridge CB3 0AX. Tel: 01223-460277. *Chief Executive*, D. McGregor. *Publishers*, Hobsons Publishing PLC, Bateman Street, Cambridge CB2 1LZ
COMMITTEE OF SCOTTISH HIGHER EDUCATION PRINCIPALS (COSHEP), St Andrew House, 141 West Nile Street, Glasgow Tel: 0141-353 1880. *Secretary*, Dr R. L. Crawford
GRADUATE TEACHER TRAINING REGISTRY, Fulton House, Jessop Avenue, Cheltenham, Glos GL50 3SH. Tel: 01242-544788. *Registrar*, Mrs M. Griffiths
SOCIAL WORK ADMISSIONS SYSTEM, Fulton House, Jessop Avenue, Cheltenham, Glos GL50 3SH. Tel: 01242-544600. *Admissions Officer*, Mrs M. Griffiths
TEACHER EDUCATION ADMISSIONS CLEARING HOUSE (TEACH), PO Box 165, Edinburgh EH12 6YA. Tel: 0131-314 6070.
UNIVERSITIES AND COLLEGES ADMISSIONS SERVICE, Fulton House, Jessop Avenue, Cheltenham, Glos GL50 3SH. Tel: 01242-222444. *Chief Executive*, M. A. Higgins, PH.D

UNIVERSITIES

THE UNIVERSITY OF ABERDEEN (1495)

Regent Walk, Aberdeen AB24 3FX
Tel 01224-272000
Full-time students (1997–8), 11,061
Chancellor, The Lord Wilson of Tillyorn, GCMG (1997)
Vice-Chancellor, Prof. C. D. Rice
Registrar, Dr P. J. Murray
Secretary, S. Cannon
Rector, vacant

THE UNIVERSITY OF ABERTAY DUNDEE
(1994)
Bell Street, Dundee DD1 1HG
Tel 01382-308080
Full-time students (1997–8), 3,577
Chancellor, The Earl of Airlie, KT, GCVO, PC (1994)
Vice-Chancellor, Prof. B. King
Registrar, Dr. D. Button
Secretary, D. Hogarth

ANGLIA POLYTECHNIC UNIVERSITY (1992)
Bishop Hall Lane, Chelmsford CM1 1SQ
Tel 01245-493131
Full-time students (1997–8), 7,672
Chancellor, The Lord Prior, PC (1992)
Vice-Chancellor, M. Malone-Lee, CB
Secretary, S. G. Bennett

ASTON UNIVERSITY (1966)
Aston Triangle, Birmingham B4 7ET
Tel 0121-359 3611
Full-time students (1997–8), 5,346
Chancellor, Sir Adrian Cadbury (1979)
Vice-Chancellor, Prof. M. Wright
Registrar and Secretary, R. D. A. Packham

THE UNIVERSITY OF BATH (1966)
Claverton Down, Bath BA2 7AY
Tel 01225-826826
Full-time students (1997–8), 6,299
Chancellor, The Lord Tugendhat (1998)
Vice-Chancellor, Prof. V. D. Vandelinde
Registrar, J. A. Bursey

THE UNIVERSITY OF BIRMINGHAM (1900)
Edgbaston, Birmingham B15 2TT
Tel 0121-414 3344
Full-time students (1997–8), 17,993
Chancellor, Sir Alexander Jarratt, CB (1983)
Vice-Chancellor, Prof. M. Irvine, PH.D
Registrar and Secretary, D. Allen

BOURNEMOUTH UNIVERSITY (1992)
Talbot Campus, Fern Barrow, Poole BH12 5BB
Tel 01202-524111
Full-time students (1997–8), 4,486
Chancellor, The Baroness Cox (1992)
Vice-Chancellor, Prof. G. Slater
Registrar, N. O. G. Richardson

THE UNIVERSITY OF BRADFORD (1966)
Bradford BD7 1DP
Tel 01274-232323
Full-time students (1997–8), 7,517
Chancellor, The Baroness Lockwood (1997)
Director, Prof. C. Bell
Registrar and Secretary, N. J. Andrew

THE UNIVERSITY OF BRIGHTON (1992)
Mithras House, Lewes Road, Brighton BN2 4AT
Tel 01273-600900
Full-time students (1997–8), 13,000
Chairman of the Board, M. C. M. Hume
Director, Prof. Sir David Watson
Deputy Director, D. E. House

THE UNIVERSITY OF BRISTOL (1909)
Senate House, Tyndall Avenue, Bristol BS8 1TH
Tel 0117-928 9000
Full-time students (1997–8), 11,611
Chancellor, Sir Jeremy Morse, KCMG (1989)
Vice-Chancellor, Sir John Kingman, FRS

Registrar, J. H. M. Parry
Secretary, Ms K. E. McKenzie, D.phil.

BRUNEL UNIVERSITY (1966)
Uxbridge, Middx UB8 3PH
Tel 01895-274000
Full-time students (1997–8), 13,070
Chancellor, The Lord Wakeham, PC (1998)
Vice-Chancellor, Prof. M. J. H. Sterling, PH.D, FEeng.
Registrar, vacant
Academic Secretary, J. B. Alexander

THE UNIVERSITY OF BUCKINGHAM (1983)
(Founded 1976 as University College at Buckingham)
Buckingham MK18 1EG
Tel 01280-814080
Full-time students (1996–7), 798
Chancellor, Sir Martin Jacomb (1998)
Vice-Chancellor, Prof. R. H. Taylor
Registrar and Secretary, J. P. Elder

THE UNIVERSITY OF CAMBRIDGE
University Offices, The Old Schools, Cambridge CB2 1TN
Tel 01223-337733
Undergraduates (1997–8) 11,160

UNIVERSITY OFFICERS, ETC.

Chancellor, HRH The Prince Philip, Duke of Edinburgh,
    KG, KT, OM, GBE, PC (1977)
Vice-Chancellor, Prof. Sir Alec Broers, FRS (1996)
High Steward, The Lord Runcie, PC, DD (1991)
Deputy High Steward, The Lord Richardson of
    Duntisbourne, MBE, TD, PC (1983)
Commissary, The Lord Oliver of Aylmerton, PC (*Trinity
    Hall*) (1989)
Proctors, B. L. Hebbelthwaite (*Queens'*); A. S. Browne, PH.D.
    (*Trinity*) (1998)
Orator, A. J. Bowen (*Jesus*) (1993)
Registrary, T. J. Mead, PH.D. (*Wolfson*) (1997)
Librarian, P. K. Fox (*Selwyn*) (1994)
Treasurer, Mrs J. Womack (*Trinity Hall*) (1993)
Secretary-General of the Faculties, D. A. Livesey, PH.D.
    (*Emmanuel*) (1992)
Director of the Fitzwilliam Museum, D. D. Robinson (*Clare*)
    (1995)

COLLEGES AND HALLS, ETC.
with dates of foundation

CHRIST'S (1505), *Master*, A. J. Munro, PH.D. (1995)
CHURCHILL (1960), *Master*, Sir John Boyd, KCMG (1996)
CLARE (1326), *Master*, Prof. B. A. Hepple, LLD (1993)
CLARE HALL (1966), *President*, Prof. Dame Gillian Beer,
    DBE, Litt. D., FBA (1994)
CORPUS CHRISTI (1352), *Master*, Prof. Sir Tony Wrigley,
    PH.D. (1994)
DARWIN (1964), *Master*, Prof. Sir Geoffrey Lloyd, PH.D.,
    FBA (1989)
DOWNING (1800), *Master*, Prof. D. A. King, FRS (1995)
EMMANUEL (1584), *Master*, Prof. J. E. Ffowcs-Williams,
    SC.D. (1996)
FITZWILLIAM (1966), *Master*, Prof. A. W. Cuthbert, PH.D.,
    FRS (1991)
GIRTON (1869), *Mistress*, Prof. A. M. Strathern, PH.D.
    (1998)
GONVILLE AND CAIUS (1348), *Master*, N. McKendrick
    (1996)
HOMERTON (1824) (for B.Ed. Students), *Principal*, Mrs K.
    B. Pretty, PH.D. (1991)
HUGHES HALL (1885) (for post-graduate students),
    President, Prof. P. Richards (1998)
JESUS (1496), *Master*, Prof. D. G. Crighton, SC.D., FRS (1997)

KING's (1441), *Provost*, Prof. P. P. G. Bateson, SC.D., FRS (1987)
*LUCY CAVENDISH COLLEGE (1965) (for women research students and mature and affiliated undergraduates), *President*, The Baroness Perry of Southwark (1994)
MAGDALENE (1542), *Master*, Prof. Sir John Gurdon, D.phil., FRS (1995)
*NEW HALL (1954), *President*, Mrs A. Lonsdale (1996)
*NEWNHAM (1871), *Principal*, Ms O. S. O'Neill, CBE (1992)
PEMBROKE (1347), *Master*, Sir Roger Tomkys, KCMG (1992)
PETERHOUSE (1284), *Master*, Prof. Sir John Meurig Thomas, FRS (1993)
QUEENS' (1448), *President*, The Lord Eatwell
ROBINSON (1977), *Warden*, Prof. the Lord Lewis of Newnham, SC.D., FRS (1977)
ST CATHARINE'S (1473), *Master*, Prof. Sir Terence English (1993)
ST EDMUND's (1896), *Master*, Prof. R. B. Heap, SC.D. (1996)
ST JOHN's (1511), *Master*, Prof. P. Goddard, PH.D., FRS (1994)
SELWYN (1882), *Master*, Sir David Harrison, CBE, SC.D., F.Eng (1993)
SIDNEY SUSSEX (1596), *Master*, Prof. G. Horn, SC.D., FRS (1992)
TRINITY (1546), *Master*, Prof. A. K. Sen (1998)
TRINITY HALL (1350), *Master*, Sir John Lyons, PH.D. (1984)
WOLFSON (1965), *President*, G. Johnson PH.D. (1994)
*College for women only

UNIVERSITY OF CENTRAL ENGLAND IN BIRMINGHAM (1992)
Perry Barr, Birmingham B42 2SU
Tel 0121-331 5000
Full-time students (1997–8), 18,500
Chancellor, The Lord Mayor of Birmingham
Vice-Chancellor, Dr P. C. Knight, CBE
Registrar and Secretary, Ms M. Penlington

UNIVERSITY OF CENTRAL LANCASHIRE (1992)
Preston PR1 2HE
Tel 01772-201201
Full-time students (1997–8), 14,600
Chancellor, Sir Francis Kennedy, KCMG, CBE (1995)
Vice-Chancellor, Dr M. McVicar
Secretary, Mrs P. M. Ackroyd

CITY UNIVERSITY (1966)
Northampton Square, London EC1V 0HB
Tel 0171-477 8000
Full-time students (1997–8), 6,961
Chancellor, The Rt. Hon. the Lord Mayor of London
Vice-Chancellor, Prof. D. W. Rhind
Academic Registrar, A. H. Seville, PH.D.
Secretary, M. M. O'Hara

COVENTRY UNIVERSITY (1992)
Priory Street, Coventry CV1 5FB
Tel 01203-631313
Full-time students (1997–8), 12,060
Chancellor, The Lord Plumb, MEP (1995)
Vice-Chancellor, M. Goldstein, CBE, PH.D., D.SC.
Academic Registrar, J. Gledhill, PH.D.
Secretary, Ms L. Arlidge

CRANFIELD UNIVERSITY (1969)
(Founded as Cranfield Institute of Technology)
Cranfield, Beds MK43 0AL
Tel 01234-750111

Full-time students (1997–8), 2,321
Chancellor, The Lord Vincent of Coleshill, GBE, KCB, DSO (1998)
Vice-Chancellor, Prof. F. R. Hartley, D.SC.
Secretary and Registrar, J. K. Pettifer

DE MONTFORT UNIVERSITY (1992)
The Gateway, Leicester LE1 9BH
Tel 0116-255 1551
Full-time students (1997–8), 22,700
Chancellor, Dr J. White (1998)
Vice-Chancellor, Prof. K. Barker, CBE
Academic Registrar, V. E. Critchlow

UNIVERSITY OF DERBY (1993)
(formerly Derbyshire College of Higher Education)
Kedleston Road, Derby DE22 1GB
Tel 01332-622222
Full-time students (1997–8), 14,000
Chancellor, Sir Christopher Ball
Vice-Chancellor, Prof. R. Waterhouse
Registrar, Mrs J. Fry
Secretary, R. Gillis

THE UNIVERSITY OF DUNDEE (1967)
Dundee DD1 4HN
Tel 01382-344000
Full-time students (1997–8), 9,835
Chancellor, Sir James Black, FRCP, FRS (1992)
Vice-Chancellor, Dr I. J. Graham-Bryce
Secretary, R. Seaton
Rector, T. Slattery (1998–2001)

THE UNIVERSITY OF DURHAM
(Founded 1832; re-organized 1908, 1937 and 1963)
Old Shire Hall, Durham DH1 3HP
Tel 0191-374 2000
Full-time students (1997–8), 8,157
Chancellor, Sir Peter Ustinov, CBE, FRSL
Vice-Chancellor, Prof. Sir Kenneth Calman, KCB, MD, FRCP, FRCGP, FRCR, FRSE
Registrar and Secretary, J. C. F. Hayward

COLLEGES

COLLINGWOOD, *Principal*, Prof. G. H. Blake, PH.D.
GRADUATE SOCIETY, *Principal*, M. Richardson, PH.D.
GREY, *Master*, V. E. Watts
HATFIELD, *Master*, Prof. T. P. Burt, PH.D.
ST AIDAN's, *Principal*, J. S. Ashworth
ST CHAD's, *Principal*, J. P. M. Cassidy, PH.D.
ST CUTHBERT's SOCIETY, *Principal*, S. G. C. Stoker
ST HILD AND ST BEDE, *Principal*, Prof. D. J. Davies, PH.D.
ST JOHN's, *Principal*, D. V. Day
ST MARY's, *Principal*, Miss J. M. Kenworthy
TREVELYAN, *Principal*, Prof. M. Todd, D.Litt
UNIVERSITY (DURHAM), *Master*, Prof. M. E. Tucker, PH.D.
UNIVERSITY (STOCKTON), *Principal*, J. C. F. Hayward
USHAW, *President*, Revd J. O'Keefe
VAN MILDERT, *Principal*, Prof. I. R. Taylor, PH.D.

THE UNIVERSITY OF EAST ANGLIA (1963)
Norwich NR4 7TJ
Tel 01603-456161
Full-time students (1997–8), 9,750
Chancellor, Sir Geoffrey Allen, FEng, FRS (1994)
Vice-Chancellor, V. Watts
Registrar and Secretary, M. G. E. Paulson-Ellis, OBE

UNIVERSITY OF EAST LONDON (1992)
Longbridge Road, Dagenham, Essex RM8 2AS
Tel 0181-590 7000/7722
Full-time students (1997–8), c.12,000

Chancellor, The Lord Rix, CBE (1997)
Vice-Chancellor, Prof. F. W. Gould
Secretary and Registrar, A. Ingle

THE UNIVERSITY OF EDINBURGH (1583)
Old College, South Bridge, Edinburgh EH8 9YL
Tel 0131-650 1000
Full-time students (1997–8), 17,845
Chancellor, HRH The Prince Philip, Duke of Edinburgh,
 KG, KT, OM, GBE, PC, FRS (1952)
Vice-Chancellor, Prof. Sir Stewart Sutherland, FBA, FRSE
Secretary, M. J. B. Lowe, PH.D.
Rector, J. Colquhoun (1997–2000)

THE UNIVERSITY OF ESSEX (1964)
Wivenhoe Park, Colchester CO4 3SQ
Tel 01206-873333
Full-time students (1997–8), 5,710
Chancellor, The Lord Nolan, PC (1997)
Vice-Chancellor, Prof. I. Crewe
Registrar and Secretary, A. F. Woodburn

THE UNIVERSITY OF EXETER (1955)
Northcote House, The Queen's Drive, Exeter EX4 4QJ
Tel 01392-263263
Full-time students (1997–8), 8,514
Chancellor, The Lord Alexander of Weedon (1998)
Vice-Chancellor, Sir Geoffrey Holland, KCB
Registrar and Secretary, I. H. C. Powell

UNIVERSITY OF GLAMORGAN (1992)
Treforest, Pontypridd CF37 1DL
Tel 01443-480480
Full-time students (1997–8), 10,931
Chancellor, The Lord Merlyn-Rees, PC, QC (1994)
Vice-Chancellor, Prof. A. L. Webb
Academic Registrar, J. O'Shea
Secretary, J. L. Bracegirdle

THE UNIVERSITY OF GLASGOW (1451)
University Avenue, Glasgow G12 8QQ
Tel 0141-330 5911
Full-time students (1997–8), 23,572
Principal, Prof. Sir Graeme Davies, FEng.
Registrar, Mrs C. R. Lowther
Secretary, Mrs J. Ellis
Rector, R. Wilson (1996–9)

GLASGOW CALEDONIAN UNIVERSITY
(1993)
Cowcaddens Road, Glasgow G4 0BA
Tel 0141-331 3000
Full-time students (1997–8), 13,399
Secretary, B. M. Murphy
Chancellor, The Lord Nickson, KBE (1993)
Principal and Vice-Chancellor, W. Laurie
Registrar, B. Ferguson

UNIVERSITY OF GREENWICH (1992)
Bexley Road, Eltham, London SE9 2PQ
Tel 0181-331 8000
Full-time students (1997–8), 14,138
Chancellor, vacant
Vice-Chancellor, Dr D. E. Fussey
Academic Registrar, Ms C. H. Rose
Secretary, J. M. Charles

HERIOT-WATT UNIVERSITY (1966)
Riccarton, Edinburgh EH14 4AS
Tel 0131-449 5111
Full-time students (1997–8), 4,700

Chancellor, The Lord Mackay of Clashfern, PC, QC, FRSE
 (1979)
Vice-Chancellor, Prof. J. S. Archer, FEng.
Secretary, P. L. Wilson

UNIVERSITY OF HERTFORDSHIRE (1992)
College Lane, Hatfield, Herts AL10 9AB
Tel 01707-284000
Full-time students (1997–8), 18,607
Chancellor, The Lord MacLaurin of Knebworth (1996)
Vice-Chancellor, Prof. N. K. Buxton
Registrar and Secretary, P. G. Jeffreys

UNIVERSITY OF HUDDERSFIELD (1992)
Queensgate, Huddersfield HD1 3DH
Tel 01484-422288
Full-time students (1997–8), 10,885
Chancellor, Sir Ernest Hall, OBE (1996)
Vice-Chancellor, Prof. J. R. Tarrant
Registrar and Secretary, Mrs M. H. Andrew

THE UNIVERSITY OF HULL (1954)
Cottingham Road, Hull HU6 7RX
Tel 01482-346311
Full-time students (1997–8), 13,500
Chancellor, The Lord Armstrong of Ilminster, GCB, CVO
 (1994)
Vice-Chancellor, Prof. D. N. Dilks, FRSL
Registrar and Secretary, D. J. Lock

KEELE UNIVERSITY (1962)
Newcastle under Lyme, Staffs ST5 5BG
Tel 01782-621111
Full-time students (1997–8), 6,319
Chancellor, Sir Claus Moser, KCB, CBE, FBA (1986)
Vice-Chancellor, Prof. J. V. Finch
Registrar and Secretary, S. J. Morris

THE UNIVERSITY OF KENT AT
CANTERBURY (1965)
Canterbury CT2 7NZ
Tel 01227-764000
Full-time students (1997–8), 9,904
Chancellor, Sir Crispin Tickell, GCMG, KCVO
Vice-Chancellor, Prof. R. Sibson
Secretary and Registrar, N. A. McHard

KINGSTON UNIVERSITY (1992)
Kingston upon Thames, Surrey KT1 1LQ
Tel 0181-547 2000
Full-time students (1997–8), 12,658
Chancellor, Sir Frank Lampl
Vice-Chancellor, Prof. P. Scott
Secretary, R. Abdulla

THE UNIVERSITY OF LANCASTER (1964)
Bailrigg, Lancaster LA1 4YW
Tel 01524-65201
Full-time students (1997–8), 8,535
Chancellor, HRH Princess Alexandra, the Hon. Lady
 Ogilvy, GCVO (1964)
Vice-Chancellor, Prof. W. Ritchie, OBE
Secretary, S. A. C. Lamley

THE UNIVERSITY OF LEEDS (1904)
Leeds LS2 9JT
Tel 0113-243 1751
Full-time students (1997–8), 19,727
Chancellor, HRH The Duchess of Kent, GCVO (1966)
Vice-Chancellor, Prof. A. G. Wilson
Registrar and Secretary, D. S. Robinson, PH.D.

LEEDS METROPOLITAN UNIVERSITY
(1992)
Calverley Street, Leeds LS1 3HE
Tel 0113-283 2600
Full-time students (1997–8), 15,074
Chairman of the Board of Governors, L. Silver (1989)
Vice-Chancellor, Prof. L. Wagner
Academic Registrar, Ms C. Orange
Secretary, M. Wilkinson

THE UNIVERSITY OF LEICESTER (1957)
University Road, Leicester LE1 7RH
Tel 0116-252 2522
Full-time students (1997–8), 8,657
Chancellor, Sir Michael Atiyah, OM, FRS, PH.D., D.SC. (1995)
Vice-Chancellor, K. J. R. Edwards, PH.D.
Registrar and Secretary, K. J. Julian

**UNIVERSITY OF LINCOLNSHIRE AND
HUMBERSIDE**
(University of Humberside founded 1992; re-organized
1996)
Humberside campus: Hull HU6 7RT
Tel 01482–440550
Lincoln campus: Lincoln LN2 4VF
Tel 01522–882000
Full-time students (1997–8), 10,562
Chancellor, Dr J. H. Hooper, CBE
Vice-Chancellor, Prof. R. P. King
Registrar and Secretary, Dr K. Pardoe

THE UNIVERSITY OF LIVERPOOL (1903)
Senate House, Abercromby Square, Liverpool L69 3BX
Tel 0151-794 2000
Full-time students (1997–8), 13,184
Chancellor, The Lord Owen, CH, PC (1996)
Vice-Chancellor, Prof. P. N. Love, CBE
Registrar and Secretary, M. D. Carr

LIVERPOOL JOHN MOORES UNIVERSITY
(1992)
Rodney House, 70 Mount Pleasant, Liverpool L3 5UX
Tel 0151-231 2121
Full-time students (1997–8), 20,000
Chancellor, J. Moores, CBE
Vice-Chancellor, Prof. P. Toyne
Registrar, Ms A. Wild

THE UNIVERSITY OF LONDON (1836)
Senate House, Malet Street, London WC1E 7HU
Tel 0171-636 8000
Internal students (1997–8), 101,576; External students,
26,000
Visitor, HM The Queen in Council
Chancellor, HRH The Princess Royal, KG, GCVO, FRS (1981)
Vice-Chancellor, Prof. G. Zellick, PH.D.
Chairman of the Council, The Lord Woolf, PC
Chairman of Convocation, D. Leslie

COLLEGES

BIRKBECK COLLEGE, Malet Street, London WC1E 7HX.
Master, Prof. T. O'Shea
CHARING CROSS AND WESTMINSTER MEDICAL SCHOOL,
see Imperial College of Science, Technology and
Medicine
GOLDSMITHS COLLEGE, Lewisham Way, New Cross,
London SE14 6NW. *Warden*, Prof. B. Pimlott, FBA
HEYTHROP COLLEGE, Kensington Square, London
W8 5HQ. *Principal*, B. Callaghan

IMPERIAL COLLEGE OF SCIENCE, TECHNOLOGY AND
MEDICINE (includes Imperial College Schools of
Medicine at Charing Cross, Hammersmith and St
Mary's hospitals and at the National Heart and Lung
Institute), South Kensington, London SW7 2AZ. *Rector*,
Prof. Sir Ronald Oxburgh, KBE, FRS
INSTITUTE OF CANCER RESEARCH, Royal Cancer
Hospital, Chester Beatty Laboratories, 17A Onslow
Gardens, London SW7 3AL. *Chief Executive*, Prof.
P. B. Garland, PH.D., FRSE
INSTITUTE OF EDUCATION, 20 Bedford Way, London
WC1H 0AL. *Director*, Prof. P. Mortimore, OBE
KING'S COLLEGE LONDON (includes King's College
School of Medicine and Dentistry, United Medical and
Dental Schools of Guy's and St Thomas' Hospitals),
Strand, London WC2R 2LS. *Principal*, Prof. A. Lucas, PH.D.
Associated Institute:
Institute of Psychiatry, De Crespigny Park, Denmark Hill,
London SE5 8AF. *Dean*, Prof. S. Checkley.
LONDON BUSINESS SCHOOL, Sussex Place, Regent's Park,
London NW1 4SA. *Principal*, Prof. J. Quelch
THE LONDON HOSPITAL MEDICAL COLLEGE, *see* Queen
Mary and Westfield College.
LONDON SCHOOL OF ECONOMICS AND POLITICAL
SCIENCE, Houghton Street, London WC2A 2AE. *Director*,
Prof. A. Giddens
LONDON SCHOOL OF HYGIENE AND TROPICAL
MEDICINE, Keppel Street, London WC1E 7HT. *Dean*,
Prof. H. Spencer
QUEEN MARY AND WESTFIELD COLLEGE (incorporating
St Bartholomew's and the Royal London School of
Medicine and Dentistry and the London Hospital
Medical College), Mile End Road, London E1 4NS.
Principal, Prof. A. Smith
ROYAL FREE HOSPITAL SCHOOL OF MEDICINE, *see*
University College London
ROYAL HOLLOWAY, Egham Hill, Egham, Surrey TW20
0EX. *Principal*, Prof. N. Gowar
ROYAL POSTGRADUATE MEDICAL SCHOOL, *see* Imperial
College of Science, Technology and Medicine
ROYAL VETERINARY COLLEGE, Royal College Street,
London NW1 0TU. *Principal and Dean*, Prof. L. E. Lanyon,
PH.D.
ST BARTHOLOMEW'S AND THE ROYAL LONDON SCHOOL
OF MEDICINE AND DENTISTRY, *see* Queen Mary and
Westfield College
ST GEORGE'S HOSPITAL MEDICAL SCHOOL, Cranmer
Terrace, London SW17 0RE. *Dean*, Prof. R. Boyd, FRCP
SCHOOL OF ORIENTAL AND AFRICAN STUDIES,
Thornhaugh Street, Russell Square, London WC1H 0XG.
Director, Sir Tim Lankester, KCB
SCHOOL OF PHARMACY, 29–39 Brunswick Square,
London WC1N 1AX. *Dean*, Prof. A. T. Florence, CBE, PH.D.,
FRSE
SCHOOL OF SLAVONIC AND EAST EUROPEAN STUDIES,
Senate House, Malet Street, London WC1E 7HU. *Director*,
Prof. M. A. Branch, PH.D.
UNITED MEDICAL AND DENTAL SCHOOLS OF GUY'S AND
ST THOMAS' HOSPITALS, *see* King's College London
UNIVERSITY COLLEGE LONDON (including UCL
Medical School), Gower Street, London WC1E 6BT.
Provost, Sir Derek Roberts, CBE, FRS, FEng.
WYE COLLEGE, Wye, near Ashford, Kent TN25 5AH.
Principal, Prof. J. H. D. Prescott, PH.D.

INSTITUTES

BRITISH INSTITUTE IN PARIS, 9–11 rue de Constantine,
75340 Paris, Cedex 07, France. *Director*, Prof.
C. L. Campos, CBE, PH.D. *London office:* Senate House,
Malet Street, London WC1E 7HU

CENTRE FOR DEFENCE STUDIES, King's College London, Strand, London WC2R 2LS. *Director,* Prof. L. Freedman, CBE, FBA

COURTAULD INSTITUTE OF ART, North Block, Somerset House, Strand, London WC2R 0RN. *Director,* Prof. E. C. Fernie, CBE, FSA, FRSE

UNIVERSITY MARINE BIOLOGICAL STATION MILLPORT, Isle of Cumbrae, Scotland KA28 0EG. *Director,* Prof. J. Davenport, PH.D., D.SC., FRSE

SCHOOL OF ADVANCED STUDY
Senate House, Malet Street, London WC1E 7HU *Dean,* Prof. T. C. Daintith
Comprises:

CENTRE FOR ENGLISH STUDIES, Senate House, Malet Street, London WC1E 7HU *Director,* Dr W. Gould

INSTITUTE OF ADVANCED LEGAL STUDIES, Charles Clore House, 17 Russell Square, London WC1B 5DR. *Director,* Prof. B. A. K. Rider

INSTITUTE OF CLASSICAL STUDIES, Senate House, Malet Street, London WC1E 7HU. *Director,* Prof. G. B. Waywell, FSA

INSTITUTE OF COMMONWEALTH STUDIES, 27–28 Russell Square, London WC1B 5DS. *Director,* Prof. P. Caplan

INSTITUTE OF GERMANIC STUDIES, 29 Russell Square, London WC1B 5DP. *Hon. Director,* E. M. Batley

INSTITUTE OF HISTORICAL RESEARCH, Senate House, Malet Street, London WC1E 7HU. *Director,* Prof. D. Cannadine

INSTITUTE OF LATIN AMERICAN STUDIES, 31 Tavistock Square, London WC1H 9HA. *Director,* Prof. V. G. Bulmer-Thomas, OBE, D.phil.

INSTITUTE OF ROMANCE STUDIES, Senate House, Malet Street, London WC1E 7HU. *Director,* Prof. J. Labanyi

INSTITUTE OF UNITED STATES STUDIES, Senate House, Malet Street, London WC1E 7HU. *Director,* Prof. G. L. McDowell, PH.D.

WARBURG INSTITUTE, Woburn Square, London WC1H 0AB. *Director,* Prof. C. N. J. Mann, PH.D.

ASSOCIATE INSTITUTIONS
INSTITUTE OF JEWISH STUDIES, 44A Albert Road, London NW4 2SJ. *Principal,* Rabbi Dr D. Sinclair
INSTITUTE OF ZOOLOGY, Royal Zoological Society, Regent's Park, London NW1 4RY. *Director,* Prof. M. Gosling
ROYAL ACADEMY OF MUSIC, Marylebone Road, London NW1 5HT. *Principal,* Prof. C. Price
ROYAL COLLEGE OF MUSIC, Prince Consort Road, London SW7 2BS. *Director,* Dr J. Ritterman
TRINITY COLLEGE OF MUSIC 11–13 Mandeville Place, London W1M 6AQ. *Principal,* G. Henderson

LONDON GUILDHALL UNIVERSITY (1993)
31 Jewry Street, London EC3N 2EY
Tel 0171-320 1000
Full-time students (1997–8), 13,726
Patron, HRH The Prince Philip, Duke of Edinburgh, KG, KT, OM, GBE, PC (1952)
Provost, Prof. R. Floud, D.phil.
Secretary, M. Weaver
Academic Registrar, Ms J. Grinstead

LOUGHBOROUGH UNIVERSITY (1966)
Loughborough, Leics LE11 3TU
Tel 01509-263171
Full-time students (1997–8), 10,500
Chancellor, Sir Denis Rooke, CBE, FRS, FEng (1989)
Vice-Chancellor, Prof. D.Wallace, FRS, FRSE
Registrar, D. E. Fletcher, PH.D.

UNIVERSITY OF LUTON (1993)
Park Square, Luton LU1 3JU
Tel 01582-734111
Full-time students (1997–8), 10,700
Chancellor, Sir David Plastow
Vice-Chancellor, Dr D. John
Registrar, Ms P. Vachon
Secretary, R. Williams

THE UNIVERSITY OF MANCHESTER
(Founded 1851; re-organized 1880 and 1903)
Oxford Road, Manchester M13 9PL
Tel 0161-275 2000
Full-time students (1997–8), 19,508
Chancellor, The Lord Flowers (1994)
Vice-Chancellor, Prof. M. B. Harris, CBE, PH.D.
Registrar and Secretary, E. Newcomb
Academic Registrar, A. McMenemy

UNIVERSITY OF MANCHESTER INSTITUTE OF SCIENCE AND TECHNOLOGY (1824)
PO Box 88, Manchester M60 1QD
Tel 0161-236 3311
Full-time students (1997–8), 6,000
Chancellor, Prof. Sir Roland Smith (1995)
Vice-Chancellor, Prof. R. F. Boucher, FEng.
Registrar, P. C. C. Stephenson

MANCHESTER METROPOLITAN UNIVERSITY (1992)
All Saints, Manchester M15 6BH
Tel 0161-247 2000
Full-time students (1997–8), 22,000
Chancellor, The Duke of Westminster, OBE, TD (1993)
Vice-Chancellor, Mrs A. V. Burslem, OBE
Academic Registrar, J. D. M. Karczewski-Slowikowski
Secretary, T. A. Hendley

MIDDLESEX UNIVERSITY (1992)
White Hart Lane, London N17 8HR N14 4XS
Tel 0181-362 5000
Full-time students (1997–8), 19,790
Chancellor, The Baroness Platt of Writtle (1993)
Vice-Chancellor, Prof. M. Driscoll
Registrar, G. Jones

NAPIER UNIVERSITY (1992)
219 Colinton Road, Edinburgh EH14 1DJ
Tel 0131-444 2266
Full-time students (1997–8), 11,412
Chancellor, The Viscount Younger of Leckie, KCVO, TD, PC, FRSE (1993)
Principal and Vice-Chancellor, Prof. J. Mavor
Secretary and Registrar, I. J. Miller

THE UNIVERSITY OF NEWCASTLE UPON TYNE
(Founded 1852; re-organized 1908, 1937 and 1963)
6 Kensington Terrace, Newcastle upon Tyne NE1 7RU
Tel 0191-222 6000
Full-time students (1997–8), 11,922
Chancellor, The Viscount Ridley, KG, GCVO, TD (*until 31 Dec. 1998*)
Vice-Chancellor, J. R. G. Wright
Registrar, D. E. T. Nicholson

UNIVERSITY OF NORTH LONDON (1992)
166–220 Holloway Road, London N7 8DB
Tel 0171-607 2789

Full-time students (1997–8), *c*.11,500
Secretary, J. McParland
Vice-Chancellor, B. A. Roper
Academic Director, G. Holmes

UNIVERSITY OF NORTHUMBRIA AT NEWCASTLE (1992)
Ellison Place, Newcastle upon Tyne NE1 8ST
Tel 0191-232 6002
Full-time students (1997–8), 18,533
Chancellor, The Lord Glenamara, CH, PC (1984)
Vice-Chancellor, Prof. G. Smith
Registrar, Ms C. Penna
Secretary, R. A. Bott

THE UNIVERSITY OF NOTTINGHAM (1948)
University Park, Nottingham NG7 2RD
Tel 0115-951 5151
Full-time students (1997–8), 16,000
Chancellor, The Lord Dearing, CB (1993)
Vice-Chancellor, Prof. Sir Colin Campbell
Registrar, K. Jones

NOTTINGHAM TRENT UNIVERSITY (1992)
Burton Street, Nottingham NG1 4BU
Tel 0115-948 8418
Full-time students (1997–8), 23,410
Vice-Chancellor, Prof. R. Cowell, PH.D.
Academic Registrar, D. W. Samson
Corporate Secretary and Solicitor, S. Smith

THE UNIVERSITY OF OXFORD
University Offices, Wellington Square, Oxford OX1 2JD
Tel 01865-270001
Students in residence 1997–8, 15,623
Chancellor, The Lord Jenkins of Hillhead, OM, PC (*Balliol*), *elected* 1987
High Steward, The Lord Goff of Chieveley, PC (*Lincoln* and *New College*), *elected* 1990
Vice-Chancellor, Dr C. R. Lucas (*Balliol*), *elected* 1997
Proctors, Dr R. W. Ainsworth (*St Catherine's*); Dr A. M. Hart (*Exeter*), *elected* 1998
Assessor, Dr A. M. Bowie (*Queen's*), *elected* 1998
Public Orator, Prof. J. Griffin (*Balliol*), *elected* 1992
Bodley's Librarian, R. P. Carr (*Balliol*), *elected* 1997
Keeper of Archives, D. G. Vaisey (*Exeter*), *elected* 1995
Director of the Ashmolean Museum, Dr C. Brown (*St Catherine's*), *elected* 1998
Registrar of the University, D. R. Holmes (*Merton*), *elected* 1998
Surveyor to the University, P. M. R. Hill, *elected* 1993
Secretary of Faculties, A. P. Weale (*Worcester*), *elected* 1984
Secretary of the Chest, J. R. Clements, *elected* 1995
Deputy Registrar (Administration), P. W. Jones (*Green*), *elected* 1991

OXFORD COLLEGES AND HALLS
with dates of foundation

ALL SOULS (1438), *Warden*, Prof. J. Davis, FBA (1995)
BALLIOL (1263), *Master*, A. Graham (1998)
BRASENOSE (1509), *Principal*, The Lord Windlesham, CVO, PC (1989)
CHRIST CHURCH (1546), *Dean*, Very Revd J. H. Drury (1991)
CORPUS CHRISTI (1517), *President*, Prof. Sir Keith Thomas, FBA (1986)
EXETER (1314), *Rector*, Dr M. Butler (1993)
GREEN (1979), *Warden*, Sir John Hanson, KCMG, CBE (1997)

HARRIS MANCHESTER (1786), *Principal*, Revd R. Waller, PH.D. (1990)
HERTFORD (1874), *Principal*, Sir Walter Bodmer, FRS (1996)
JESUS (1571), *Principal*, Sir Peter North, CBE, DCL, QC, FBA (1984)
KEBLE (1868), *Warden*, Dr A. Cameron, FBA, FSA (1994)
KELLOGG (1990), *President*, Dr G. P. Thomas (1990)
LADY MARGARET HALL (1878), *Principal*, Sir Brian Fall, GVCO, KCMG (1995)
LINACRE (1962), *Principal*, Dr P. A. Slack, FBA (1996)
LINCOLN (1427), *Rector*, Dr W. E. K. Anderson, FRSE (1994)
MAGDALEN (1458), *President*, A. D. Smith, CBE (1988)
MANSFIELD (1886), *Principal*, Prof. D. I. Marquand (1996)
MERTON (1264), *Warden*, Dr J Rawson, CBE, FBA (1994)
NEW COLLEGE (1379), *Warden*, Dr. A. J. Ryan, FBA (1996)
NUFFIELD (1937), *Warden*, A. Atkinson, FBA (1994)
ORIEL (1326), *Provost*, Dr E. W. Nicholson, DD, FBA (1990)
PEMBROKE (1624), *Master*, Dr R. Stevens, DCL (1993)
QUEEN'S (1340), *Provost*, Dr G. Marshall, FBA (1993)
ST ANNE'S (1952 (Society of Oxford Home-Students (1879)), *Principal*, Mrs R. L. Deech (1991)
ST ANTONY'S (1950), *Warden*, Sir Marrack Goulding, KCMG (1997)
ST CATHERINE'S (1962), *Master*, The Lord Plant of Highfield (1994)
ST CROSS (1965), *Master*, Dr R. C. Repp (1987)
ST EDMUND HALL (*c*.1278), *Principal (acting)*, J. P. D. Dunbabin (1996)
*ST HILDA'S (1893), *Principal*, Miss E. Llewellyn-Smith, CB (1990)
ST HUGH'S (1886), *Principal*, D. Wood, CBE, QC (1991)
ST JOHN'S (1555), *President*, Dr W. Hayes (1987)
ST PETER'S (1929), *Master*, Dr J. P. Barron, FSA (1991)
SOMERVILLE (1879), *Principal*, Dame Fiona Caldicott, DBE, FRCP (1996)
TEMPLETON (1965), *President*, Sir David Rowland (1998)
TRINITY (1554), *President*, The Hon. Michael J. Beloff, QC (1996)
UNIVERSITY (1249), *Master*, Sir Robin Butler, GCB, CVO (1998)
WADHAM (1612), *Warden*, J. S. Flemming, FBA (1993)
WOLFSON (1966), *President*, Sir David Smith, D.Phil., FRS, FRSE (1994)
WORCESTER (1714), *Provost*, R. G. Smethurst (1991)

BLACKFRIARS (1921), *Regent*, Very Revd P. M. Parvis, D.phil (1996)
CAMPION HALL (1896), *Master*, Revd G. J. Hughes, D.phil (1998)
GREYFRIARS (1910), *Warden*, Revd T. G. Weinandy, PH.D (1996)
REGENT'S PARK (1810), *Principal*, Revd P. S. Fiddes, D.phil. (1989)
ST BENET'S HALL (1897), *Master*, Revd H. Wansbrough, OSB (1991)
WYCLIFFE HALL (1877), *Principal*, Revd A. E. McGrath D.phil (1995)

*College for women only

OXFORD BROOKES UNIVERSITY (1993)
Headington, Oxford OX3 0BP
Tel 01865-741111
Full-time students (1997–8), 12,600
Chancellor, Baroness Kennedy of the Shaws, QC
Vice-Chancellor, Prof. G. Upton
Academic Registrar, Ms E. N. Winders
Academic Secretary, B. Summers

UNIVERSITY OF PAISLEY (1992)
Paisley PA1 2BE
Tel 0141-848 3000
Full-time students (1997–8), 10,793
Chancellor, Sir Robert Easton, CBE (1993)
Vice-Chancellor, Prof. R. W. Shaw, CBE
Registrar, D. Rigg
Secretary, J. Fraser

UNIVERSITY OF PLYMOUTH (1992)
Drake Circus, Plymouth PL4 8AA
Tel 01752-600600
Full-time students (1997–8), 15,660
Vice-Chancellor, Prof. J. Bull
Secretary and Academic Registrar, Miss J. Hopkinson

UNIVERSITY OF PORTSMOUTH (1992)
University House, Winston Churchill Avenue, Portsmouth
PO1 2UP
Tel 01705-876543
Full-time students (1997–8), 14,500
Chancellor, The Lord Palumbo (1992)
Vice-Chancellor, Prof. J. Craven
Academic Registrar, A. Rees

THE QUEEN'S UNIVERSITY OF BELFAST
(1908)
Belfast BT7 1NN
Tel 01232-245133
Full-time students (1995–6), 14,500
Chancellor, Sir David Orr, MC (1992)
Vice-Chancellor, Prof. G. Bain
Registrar, J. Town
Administrative Secretary, D. H. Wilson

THE UNIVERSITY OF READING (1926)
Whiteknights, PO Box 217, Reading RG6 6AH
Tel 0118-987 5123
Full-time students (1997–8), 11,096
Chancellor, The Lord Carrington, KG, GCMG, CH, MC, PC
  (1992)
Vice-Chancellor, Prof. R. Williams
Registrar, D. C. R. Frampton

THE ROBERT GORDON UNIVERSITY (1992)
Schoolhill, Aberdeen AB10 1FR
Tel 01224-262000
Full-time students (1997–8), 7,760
Chancellor, Sir Bob Reid (1993)
Vice-Chancellor, Prof. B. Stevely
Secretary, D. Caldwell

THE UNIVERSITY OF ST ANDREWS (1411)
College Gate, St Andrews KY16 9AJ
Tel 01334-476161
Full-time students (1997–8), 5,629
Chancellor, Sir Kenneth Dover, D.Litt., FRSE, FBA (1981)
Vice-Chancellor, Prof. S. Arnott, CBE, FRS, FRSE
Secretary, D. J. Corner
Rector, D. R. Findlay, QC (1997–1999)

THE UNIVERSITY OF SALFORD (1967)
Salford M5 4WT
Tel 0161-295 5000
Full-time students (1997–8), 12,539
Chancellor, Sir Walter Bodmer, PH.D., FRS
Vice-Chancellor, Prof. M. Harloe
Registrar, M. D. Winton, PH.D.

THE UNIVERSITY OF SHEFFIELD (1905)
Western Bank, Sheffield S10 2TN
Tel 0114-222 2000
Full-time students (1997–8), 16,683
Chancellor, vacant
Vice-Chancellor, Prof. Sir Gareth Roberts, FRS
Registrar, vacant
Secretary, J. O'Donovan

SHEFFIELD HALLAM UNIVERSITY (1992)
Howard Street, Sheffield S1 1WB
Tel 0114-225 5555
Full-time students (1997–8), 18,000
Chancellor, Sir Bryan Nicholson (1992)
Vice-Chancellor, Ms D. Green
Registrar, Ms J. Tory
Secretary, Ms S. Neocosmos

THE UNIVERSITY OF SOUTHAMPTON
(1952)
Highfield, Southampton SO17 1BJ
Tel 01703-595000
Full-time students (1997–8), 13,480
Chancellor, The Earl of Selbourne, KBE, FRS (1996)
Vice-Chancellor, Prof. H. Newby, CBE
Secretary and Registrar, J. F. D. Lauwerys

SOUTH BANK UNIVERSITY (1992)
103 Borough Road, London SE1 0AA
Tel 0171-928 8989
Full-time students (1997–8), 15,000
Chancellor, C. McLaren
Vice-Chancellor, Prof. G. Bernbaum
Registrar, R. Phillips
Secretary, Mrs L. Gander

STAFFORDSHIRE UNIVERSITY (1992)
College Road, Stoke-on-Trent ST4 2DE
Tel 01782-294000
Full-time students (1997–8), 14,500
Chancellor, The Lord Ashley of Stoke, CH, PC (1993)
Vice-Chancellor, Prof. C. E. King, PH.D.
Academic Registrar, Ms F. Francis
Secretary, K. Sproston

THE UNIVERSITY OF STIRLING (1967)
Stirling FK9 4LA
Tel 01786-473171
Full-time students (1997–8), 7,500
Chancellor, Dame Diana Rigg, DBE
Vice-Chancellor, Prof. A. Miller, FRSE
Academic Registrar, D. G. Wood
Secretary, K. J. Clarke

THE UNIVERSITY OF STRATHCLYDE (1964)
McCance Building, John Anderson Campus, Glasgow
G1 1XQ
Tel 0141-552 4400
Full-time students (1997–8), 14,300
Chancellor, The Lord Hope of Craighead, PC (1998)
Principal and Vice-Chancellor, Prof. Sir John Arbuthnott,
  FRSE
Secretary, P. W. A. West

UNIVERSITY OF SUNDERLAND (1992)
Langham Tower, Ryhope Road, Sunderland SR2 7EE
Tel 0191-515 2000
Full-time students (1997–8), 11,966
Chancellor, The Lord Puttnam, CBE (1998)
Vice-Chancellor, Ms A. Wright, CBE, PH.D.
Academic Registrar, S. Porteous
Secretary, J. D. Pacey

THE UNIVERSITY OF SURREY (1966)
Guildford, Surrey GU2 5XH
Tel 01483-300800
Full-time students (1997–8), 8,204
Chancellor, HRH The Duke of Kent, KG, GCMG, GCVO (1977)
Vice-Chancellor, Prof. P. J. Dowling, FRS, FEng.
Secretary and Registrar, H. W. B. Davies

THE UNIVERSITY OF SUSSEX (1961)
Falmer, Brighton BN1 9RH
Tel 01273-606755
Full-time students (1997–8), 9,085
Chancellor, The Lord Attenborough (1998)
Vice-Chancellor (acting), Prof. M. A. M. Smith
Registrar and Secretary, B. K. Gooch

UNIVERSITY OF TEESSIDE (1992)
Middlesbrough TS1 3BA
Tel 01642-218121
Full-time students (1997–8), 8,216
Chancellor, The Rt. Hon.Sir Leon Brittan QC (1993)
Vice-Chancellor, Prof. D. Fraser
Secretary, J. M. McClintock

THAMES VALLEY UNIVERSITY (1992)
St Mary's Road, Ealing, London W5 5RF
Tel 0181-579 5000
Full-time students (1997–8), 5,793
Chancellor, The Lord Hamlyn, CBE
Vice-Chancellor, M. Fitzgerald, PH.D.
Director of Registry Services, P. Head

THE UNIVERSITY OF ULSTER (1984)
Cromore Road, Coleraine BT52 1SA
Tel 01265-44141
Full-time students (1997–8), 16,543
Chancellor, Rabbi J. Neuberger (1993)
Vice-Chancellor, Prof. Lord Smith of Clifton (1991)
Academic Registrar, Dr K. Miller

THE UNIVERSITY OF WALES (1893)
King Edward VII Avenue, Cathays Park, Cardiff CF1 3NS
Tel 01222-382656
Students (1997–8), 68,000
Chancellor, HRH The Prince of Wales, KG, KT, GCB, PC (1976)
Senior Vice-Chancellor, Prof. K. G. Robbins, FRSE
Secretary-General, J. D. Pritchard

MEMBER INSTITUTIONS
UNIVERSITY OF WALES, ABERYSTWYTH, Old College, King Street, Aberystwyth SY23 2AX. Tel: 01970-623111. *Vice-Chancellor*, Prof. D. Llwyd Morgan, D.phil. (1995)
UNIVERSITY OF WALES BANGOR, Bangor LL57 2DG. Tel: 01248-351151. *Vice-Chancellor*, Prof. H. R. Evans, PH.D., FEng. (1995)
UNIVERSITY OF WALES, CARDIFF, PO Box 920, Cardiff CF1 3XP. Tel: 01222-874000. *Vice-Chancellor*, Prof. E. B. Smith, PH.D., D.SC. (1993)
UNIVERSITY OF WALES COLLEGE, NEWPORT, Caerleon Campus, PO Box 179, Newport NP6 1YG. Tel: 01633-430088. *Principal*, Prof. K. J. Overshott, PH.D. (1990)
UNIVERSITY OF WALES COLLEGE OF MEDICINE, Heath Park, Cardiff CF4 4XN. Tel: 01222-747747. *Vice-Chancellor*, Prof. I. R. Cameron, DM, FRCP (1994)
UNIVERSITY OF WALES INSTITUTE, CARDIFF, Llandaff Centre, Western Avenue, Cardiff CF5 2SG. Tel: 01222-506070. *Principal*, A. J. Chapman, PH.D. (1998)
UNIVERSITY OF WALES, LAMPETER, Lampeter SA48 7ED. Tel: 01570-422351. *Vice-Chancellor*, Prof. K. G. Robbins, D.Litt., D.phil., FRSE (1992)

UNIVERSITY OF WALES SWANSEA, Singleton Park, Swansea SA2 8PP. Tel: 01792-205678. *Vice-Chancellor*, Prof. R. H. Williams, PH.D., D.SC, FRS (1994)

THE UNIVERSITY OF WARWICK (1965)
Coventry CV4 7AL
Tel 01203-523523
Full-time students (1997–8), 15,291
Chancellor, Sir Shridath Surendranath Ramphal, GCMG, QC (1989)
Vice-Chancellor, Prof. Sir Brian Follett, FRS
Registrar, M. L. Shattock, OBE
Academic Registrar, Dr J. W. Nicholls

UNIVERSITY OF WESTMINSTER (1992)
309 Regent Street, London W1R 8AL
Tel 0171-911 5000
Full-time students (1997–8), 9,825
Vice-Chancellor and Rector, Dr G. M. Copland (1996)
Academic Registrar, E. Green

UNIVERSITY OF THE WEST OF ENGLAND, BRISTOL (BRISTOL UWE) (1992)
Coldharbour Lane, Bristol BS16 1QY
Tel 0117-965 6261
Full-time students (1997–8), 19,769
Academic Secretary, Ms C. Webb
Chancellor, The Rt. Hon. Dame Elizabeth Butler-Sloss, DBE (1993)
Vice-Chancellor, A. C. Morris
Academic Registrar, Ms M. J. Carter

THE UNIVERSITY OF WOLVERHAMPTON (1992)
Wulfruna Street, Wolverhampton WV1 1SB
Tel 01902-321000
Full-time students (1997–8), 14,147
Chancellor, The Earl of Shrewsbury and Talbot (1993)
Vice-Chancellor, Prof. J. S. Brooks, PH.D.
Registrar, J. F. Baldwin
Secretary, A. W. Lee

THE UNIVERSITY OF YORK (1963)
Heslington, York YO10 5DD
Tel 01904-430000
Full-time students (1997–8), 7,000
Chancellor, Dame Janet Baker, CH, DBE (1991)
Vice-Chancellor, Prof. R. U. Cooke, PH.D.
Registrar, D. J. Foster

THE OPEN UNIVERSITY (1969)
Walton Hall, Milton Keynes MK7 6AA
Tel 01908-274066
Students and clients (1998), c.200,000
Tuition by correspondence linked with special radio and television programmes, video and audio cassettes, computing, residential schools and a locally-based tutorial and counselling service. The University awards degrees of BA, B.Sc, B.Phil., MA, MBA, MBA (Technology), M.Eng., M.Maths, M.Sc., M.Phil., PH.D., D.Ed., D.Sc. and D.Litt. There are faculties and schools of arts; education; health and social welfare; law; management; mathematics and computing; modern languages; science; social sciences; technology; and a wide range of qualification courses and study packs.
Chancellor, The Rt. Hon. Betty Boothroyd, MP
Vice-Chancellor, Sir John Daniel
Secretary, D. J. Clinch, OBE

ROYAL COLLEGE OF ART (1837)
Kensington Gore, London SW7 2EU
Tel 0171-590 4444
Students (1998–9), 800 (all postgraduate)
Provost, The Earl of Snowdon, GCVO (1995)
Rector and Vice-Provost, Prof. C. Frayling
Registrar, A. Selby

COLLEGES

It is not possible to name here all the colleges offering courses of higher or further education. The list does not include colleges forming part of a polytechnic or a university. The English colleges that follow are confined to those in the Higher Education Funding Council for England sector; there are many more colleges in England providing higher education courses, some with HEFCFE funding.
The list of colleges in Wales, Scotland and Northern Ireland includes institutions providing at least one full-time course leading to a first degree granted by an accredited validating body.

ENGLAND

BATH SPA UNIVERSITY COLLEGE, Newton Park, Newton St Loe, Bath BA2 9BN. Tel: 01225-875875. *Director*, F. Morgan
BISHOP GROSSETESTE COLLEGE, Lincoln LN1 3DY. Tel: 01522-527347. *Principal*, Ms E. Baker
BOLTON INSTITUTE OF HIGHER EDUCATION, Deane Road, Bolton BL3 5AB. Tel: 01204-528851. *Principal*, Ms M. Temple (*from Jan. 1999*)
BRETTON HALL, West Bretton, Wakefield, W. Yorks WF4 4LG. Tel: 01924-830261. *Principal*, Prof. G. H. Bell
BUCKINGHAMSHIRE CHILTERNS UNIVERSITY COLLEGE, Queen Alexandra Road, High Wycombe, Bucks HP11 2JZ. Tel: 01494-522141. *Director*, Prof. P. B. Mogford
CANTERBURY CHRIST CHURCH UNIVERSITY COLLEGE, North Holmes Road, Canterbury, Kent CT1 1QU. Tel: 01227-767700. *Principal*, Prof. M. Wright
THE CENTRAL SCHOOL OF SPEECH AND DRAMA, Embassy Theatre, 64 Eton Avenue, London NW3 3HY. Tel: 0171-722 8183. *Principal*, Prof. R. S. Fowler
CHELTENHAM AND GLOUCESTER COLLEGE OF HIGHER EDUCATION, PO Box 220, The Park, Cheltenham, Glos GL50 2QF. Tel: 01242-532700. *Director*, Miss J. O. Trotter, OBE
CHICHESTER INSTITUTE OF HIGHER EDUCATION, College Lane, Chichester, W. Sussex PO19 4PE. Tel: 01243-816000. *Director*, P. E. D. Robinson
DARTINGTON COLLEGE OF ARTS, Totnes, Devon TQ9 6EJ. Tel: 01803-862224. *Principal*, Prof. K. Thompson
EDGE HILL UNIVERSITY COLLEGE, St Helens Road, Ormskirk, Lancs L39 4QP. Tel: 01695-575171. *Director*, Dr. J. Cater
FALMOUTH COLLEGE OF ARTS, Woodlane, Falmouth, Cornwall TR11 4RH. Tel: 01326-211077. *Principal*, Prof. A. G. Livingston
HARPER ADAMS AGRICULTURAL COLLEGE, Newport, Shropshire TF10 8NB. Tel: 01952-820280. *Principal*, Prof. E. W. Jones
HOMERTON COLLEGE, Cambridge CB2 2PH. Tel: 01223-507111. *Principal*, Mrs K. Pretty, PH.D.
KENT INSTITUTE OF ART AND DESIGN, Oakwood Park, Maidstone, Kent ME16 8AG (*also* New Dover Road, Canterbury CT1 3AN; and Fort Pitt, Rochester ME1 1DZ). Tel: 01622-757286. *Director*, Prof. V. Grylls

KING ALFRED'S COLLEGE, Sparkford Road, Winchester, Hants SO22 4NR. Tel: 01962-841515. *Principal*, Prof. J. P. Dickinson
LIVERPOOL HOPE UNIVERSITY COLLEGE, Hope Park, Liverpool L16 9JD. Tel: 0151-291 3477. *Rector*, Prof. S. Lee
THE LONDON INSTITUTE, 65 Davies Street, London W1Y 2AA. Tel: 0171-514 6000. *Rector*, Sir William Stubbs
Comprising:
Camberwell College of Arts, Peckham Road, London SE5 8UF
Central St Martins College of Art and Design, Southampton Row, London WC1B 4AP
Chelsea College of Art and Design, Manresa Road, London SW3 6LS
London College of Fashion, 20 John Prince's Street, London W1M 0BJ
London College of Printing, Elephant and Castle, London SE1 6SB
LOUGHBOROUGH COLLEGE OF ART AND DESIGN, Epinal Way, Loughborough, Leics LE11 3GE. Tel: 01509-261515. *Principal*, T. Kavanagh
LSU COLLEGE OF HIGHER EDUCATION, The Avenue, Southampton SO17 1BG. Tel: 01703-216200. *Principal (acting)*, J. Layman
NENE COLLEGE OF HIGHER EDUCATION, Park Campus, Boughton Green Road, Northampton NN2 7AL. Tel: 01604-735500. *Director*, Dr S. M. Gaskell
NEWMAN COLLEGE, Genners Lane, Bartley Green, Birmingham B32 3NT. Tel: 0121-476 1181. *Principal*, Prof. B. Ray
RCN INSTITUTE, The Royal College of Nursing, 20 Cavendish Square, London W1M 0AB. Tel: 0171-409 3333. *Director*, Prof. A. Kitson
ROEHAMPTON INSTITUTE LONDON, Whitelands College, West Hill, London SW15 3SN. Comprises Digby Stuart College, Froebel College, Southlands College and Whitelands College. Tel: 0181-392 3000. *Rector*, Prof. S. C. Holt
ROSE BRUFORD COLLEGE, Lamorbey Park, Sidcup, Kent DA15 9DF. Tel: 0181-300 3024. *Principal*, Prof. R. Ely
ROYAL AGRICULTURAL COLLEGE, Cirencester, Glos GL7 6JS. Tel: 01285-652531. *Principal*, Prof. J. B. Dent
ROYAL NORTHERN COLLEGE OF MUSIC, 124 Oxford Road, Manchester M13 9RD. Tel: 0161-907 5200. *Principal*, Prof. E. Gregson
SOUTHAMPTON INSTITUTE, East Park Terrace, Southampton SO14 0YN. Tel: 01703-319000. *Director*, Dr R. Brown
SURREY INSTITUTE OF ART AND DESIGN, Falkner Road, Farnham, Surrey GU9 7DS. Tel: 01252-722441. *Director*, Prof. N. J. Taylor
TRINITY AND ALL SAINTS' COLLEGE, Brownberrie Lane, Horsforth, Leeds LS18 5HD. Tel: 0113-283 7100. *Principal*, Dr M. J. Coughlan
UNIVERSITY COLLEGE CHESTER, Parkgate Road, Chester CH1 4BJ. Tel: 01244-375444. *Principal*, Prof. T. J. Wheeler
UNIVERSITY COLLEGE OF RIPON AND YORK ST JOHN, Lord Mayor's Walk, York YO3 7EX. Tel: 01904-656771. *Principal*, Prof. R. A. Butlin
UNIVERSITY COLLEGE OF ST MARK AND ST JOHN, Derriford Road, Plymouth PL6 8BH. Tel: 01752-636829. *Principal*, Dr W. J. Rea
UNIVERSITY COLLEGE OF ST MARTIN, Lancaster LA1 3JD. Tel: 01524-384384. *Principal*, Prof. C. J. Carr
UNIVERSITY COLLEGE SCARBOROUGH, Filey Road, Scarborough YO11 3AZ. Tel: 01723-362392. *Principal*, Dr. R. A. Withers

WESTHILL COLLEGE OF HIGHER EDUCATION, Weoley Park Road, Selly Oak, Birmingham B29 6LL. Tel: 0121-472 7245. *Principal*, Prof. J. H. Y. Briggs

WESTMINSTER COLLEGE, Oxford OX2 9AT. Tel: 01865-247644. *Principal*, Revd Dr R. Ralph

WINCHESTER SCHOOL OF ART, Park Avenue, Winchester, Hants SO23 8DL. Tel: 01962-842500. *Head of School*, Prof. K. Crouan

WORCESTER COLLEGE OF HIGHER EDUCATION, Henwick Grove, Worcester WR2 6AJ. Tel: 01905-855000. *Principal*, Ms D. Unwin

WALES

CARMARTHENSHIRE COLLEGE, Graig Campus, Sandy Road, Llanelli SA15 4DN. Tel: 01554-748000. *Principal*, B. Robinson

NORTH EAST WALES INSTITUTE OF HIGHER EDUCATION, Plas Coch, Mold Road, Wrexham LL11 2AW. Tel: 01978-290666. *Principal*, Prof. J. O. Williams

SWANSEA INSTITUTE OF HIGHER EDUCATION, Mount Pleasant, Swansea SA1 6ED. Tel: 01792-481000. *Principal*, Prof. D. Warner

TRINITY COLLEGE, Carmarthen SA31 3EP. Tel: 01267-676767. *Principal*, D. C. Jones-Davies, OBE

WELSH COLLEGE OF MUSIC AND DRAMA, Castle Grounds, Cathays Park, Cardiff CF1 3ER. Tel: 01222-342854. *Principal*, E. Fivet

SCOTLAND

BELL COLLEGE OF TECHNOLOGY, Almada Street, Hamilton, Lanarkshire ML3 0JB. Tel: 01698-283100. *Principal*, Dr K. MacCallum

DUMFRIES AND GALLOWAY COLLEGE, Heathhall, Dumfries DG1 3QZ. Tel: 01387-261261. *Principal*, J. W. M. Neil

FIFE COLLEGE OF FURTHER AND HIGHER EDUCATION, St Brycedale Avenue, Kirkcaldy, Fife KY1 1EX. Tel: 01592-268591. *Principal*, Mrs J. S. R. Johnston

GLASGOW SCHOOL OF ART, 167 Renfrew Street, Glasgow G3 6RQ. Tel: 0141-353 4500. *Director*, Prof. D. Cameron

INVERNESS COLLEGE, Longman Road, Inverness IV1 1SA. Tel: 01463-236681. *Principal*, Ms J. Price

NORTHERN COLLEGE OF EDUCATION, Hilton Place, Aberdeen AB24 4FA. Tel: 01224-283500. Gardyne Road, Dundee DD5 1NY. Tel: 01382-464000. *Principal*, D. A. Adams

QUEEN MARGARET COLLEGE, Duke Street, Edinburgh EH6 8HF. Tel: 0131-317 3000. *Principal*, Dr J. Stringer

ROYAL SCOTTISH ACADEMY OF MUSIC AND DRAMA, 100 Renfrew Street, Glasgow G2 3DB. Tel: 0141-332 4101. *Principal*, Dr P. Ledger, CBE, FRSE

SAC (SCOTTISH AGRICULTURAL COLLEGE), Central Office, West Mains Road, Edinburgh EH9 3JG. Tel: 0131-535 4000. Campuses at Aberdeen, Auchincruive, Ayr and Edinburgh. *Principal*, Prof. P. C. Thomas

ST ANDREW'S COLLEGE OF EDUCATION, Duntocher Road, Bearsden, Glasgow G61 4QA. Tel: 0141-943 3400. *Principal*, Prof. B. J. McGettrick, OBE

NORTHERN IRELAND

EAST DOWN INSTITUTE OF FURTHER AND HIGHER EDUCATION, Market Street, Downpatrick, Co. Down BT30 6ND. Tel: 01396-615815. *Principal*, T. L. Place

ST MARY'S COLLEGE, 191 Falls Road, Belfast BT12 6FE. Tel: 01232-327678. *Principal*, Revd M. O'Callaghan

STRANMILLIS COLLEGE, Stranmillis Road, Belfast BT9 5DY. Tel: 01232-381271. *Principal*, Dr J. R. McMinn

ADULT AND CONTINUING EDUCATION

FORUM FOR THE ADVANCEMENT OF CONTINUING EDUCATION (FACE), Continuing Education, Goldsmiths' College, London SE14 6NW. Tel: 0171-919 7221. *Chair*, M. Barry

NATIONAL INSTITUTE OF ADULT CONTINUING EDUCATION, 21 De Montfort Street, Leicester LE1 7GE. Tel: 0116-204 4200. *Director*, A. Tuckett

NIACE CYMRU, 245 Western Avenue, Cardiff CF5 2YX. Tel: 01222-265002. *Director for Wales*, Ms A. Poole

THE RESIDENTIAL COLLEGES COMMITTEE, c/o Ruskin College, Oxford OX1 2HE. Tel: 01865-556360. *Awards Officer*, Mrs F. A. Bagchi

SCOTTISH COMMUNITY EDUCATION COUNCIL, Rosebery House, 9 Haymarket Terrace, Edinburgh EH12 5EZ. Tel: 0131-313 2488. *Chief Executive*, C. McConnell

THE UNIVERSITIES ASSOCIATION FOR CONTINUING EDUCATION, University of Cambridge Board of Continuing Education, Madingley Hall, Madingley, Cambridge CB3 8AQ. Tel: 01954-210636. *Secretary*, Miss S. E. Rawlings

WORKERS' EDUCATIONAL ASSOCIATION, Temple House, 17 Victoria Park Square, London E2 9PB. Tel: 0181-983 1515. *General Secretary*, R. Lochrie

LONG-TERM RESIDENTIAL COLLEGES FOR ADULT EDUCATION

COLEG HARLECH, Harlech, Gwynedd LL46 2PU. Tel: 01766-780363. *Warden*, J. W. England

CO-OPERATIVE COLLEGE, Stanford Hall, Loughborough, Leics LE12 5QP. Tel: 01509-852333. *Chief Executive*, R. Wildgusp

FIRCROFT COLLEGE, 1018 Bristol Road, Selly Oak, Birmingham B29 6LH. Tel: 0121-471 0116. *Principal*, Ms F. Larden

HILLCROFT COLLEGE, South Bank, Surbiton, Surrey KT6 6DF. Tel: 0181-399 2688. For women only. *Principal*, Ms J. Ireton

NEWBATTLE ABBEY COLLEGE, Dalkeith, Midlothian EH22 3LL. Tel: 0131-663 1921. *Principal*, W. M. Conboy

NORTHERN COLLEGE, Wentworth Castle, Stainborough, Barnsley, S. Yorks S75 3ET. Tel: 01226-776000. *Principal*, Prof. R. H. Fryer

PLATER COLLEGE, Pullens Lane, Oxford OX3 0DT. Tel: 01865-740500. *Principal*, M. Blades

RUSKIN COLLEGE, Walton Street, Oxford OX1 2HE. Tel: 01865-554331. *Principal*, J. Durcan

PROFESSIONAL EDUCATION
Excluding postgraduate study

The organizations listed below are those which, by providing specialist training or conducting examinations, control entry into a profession, or are responsible for maintaining a register of those with professional qualifications in their sector.

Many professions now have a largely graduate entry, and possession of a first degree can exempt entrants from certain of the professional examinations. Enquiries about obtaining professional qualifications should be made to the relevant professional organization(s). Details of higher education providers of first degrees may be found in *University and College Entrance: Official Guide* (available from UCAS, *see* page 444).

EC RECOGNITION

It is now possible for those with professional qualifications obtained in the UK to have these recognized in other European Union countries. A booklet, *Europe Open for Professions*, and further information can be obtained from:
DEPARTMENT OF TRADE AND INDUSTRY, Bay 212 Kingsgate House, 66–74 Victoria Street, London SW1E 6SW. Tel: 0171-215 4648. *Contact*, Ms A. Wilson

ACCOUNTANCY

The main bodies granting membership on examination after a period of practical work are:
ASSOCIATION OF CHARTERED CERTIFIED ACCOUNTANTS, 29 Lincoln's Inn Fields, London WC2A 3EE. Tel: 0171-242 6855. *Chief Executive*, Mrs A. L. Rose
CHARTERED INSTITUTE OF MANAGEMENT ACCOUNTANTS, 63 Portland Place, London W1N 4AB. Tel: 0171-637 2311. *Secretary*, J. S. Chester, OBE
CHARTERED INSTITUTE OF PUBLIC FINANCE AND ACCOUNTANCY, 3 Robert Street, London WC2N 6BH. Tel: 0171-543 5600. *Chief Executive*, D. Adams
INSTITUTE OF CHARTERED ACCOUNTANTS IN ENGLAND AND WALES, Chartered Accountants' Hall, PO Box 433, Moorgate Place, London EC2P 2BJ. Tel: 0171-920 8100. *Chief Executive*, J. Collier
INSTITUTE OF CHARTERED ACCOUNTANTS OF SCOTLAND, 27 Queen Street, Edinburgh EH2 1LA. Tel: 0131-225 5673. *Chief Executive*, P. W. Johnston

ACTUARIAL SCIENCE

Two professional organizations grant qualifications after examination:
FACULTY OF ACTUARIES, 18 Dublin Street, Edinburgh EH1 3PP. Tel: 0131-240 1300. *Secretary*, W. W. Mair
INSTITUTE OF ACTUARIES, Staple Inn Hall, High Holborn, London WC1V 7QJ. Tel: 0171-632 2100. *Secretary-General*, G. B. L. Campbell. Education enquiries to Napier House, 4 Worcester Street, Oxford OX1 2AW. Tel: 01865-268200

ARCHITECTURE

The Education and Professional Development Board of the Royal Institute of British Architects sets standards and guides the whole system of architectural education throughout the UK. The RIBA recognizes courses at 35 schools of architecture in the UK for exemption from their own examinations and at some 50 courses overseas.
ARCHITECTS REGISTRATION BOARD, 73 Hallam Street, London W1N 6EE. Tel: 0171-580 5861. *Chief Officer and Registrar*, A. Finch
THE ROYAL INSTITUTE OF BRITISH ARCHITECTS, 66 Portland Place, London W1N 4AD. Tel: 0171-580 5533. Information Unit: 0891-234400. *President*, D. Rock; *Director-General*, A. Reid, PH.D.

Schools of architecture outside the universities include:
THE ARCHITECTURAL ASSOCIATION, 34–36 Bedford Square, London WC1B 3ES. Tel: 0171-887 4000. *Secretary*, E. A. Le Maistre
PRINCE OF WALES'S INSTITUTE OF ARCHITECTURE, 14–15 Gloucester Gate, London NW1 4HG. Tel: 0171-916 7380. *Director*, Prof. A. Gale

BANKING

Professional organizations granting qualifications after examination are:
CHARTERED INSTITUTE OF BANKERS, 90 Bishopsgate, London EC2N 4AS. Tel: 0171-444 7111. *Chief Executive*, G. Shreeve
CHARTERED INSTITUTE OF BANKERS IN SCOTLAND, Drumsheugh House, 38B Drumsheugh Gardens, Edinburgh EH3 7SW. Tel: 0131-473 7777. *Chief Executive*, Dr C. W. Munn

BUILDING

Examinations are conducted by:
CHARTERED INSTITUTE OF BUILDING, Englemere, King's Ride, Ascot, Berks SL5 7TB. Tel: 01344-630700. *Chief Executive*, K. Banbury
INSTITUTE OF BUILDING CONTROL, 92–104 East Street, Epsom, Surrey KT17 1EB. Tel: 01372-745577. *Chief Executive*, Ms R. Raywood
INSTITUTE OF CLERKS OF WORKS OF GREAT BRITAIN, 41 The Mall, London W5 3TJ. Tel: 0181-579 2917/8. *Secretary*, A. P. Macnamara

BUSINESS, MANAGEMENT AND ADMINISTRATION

Professional bodies conducting training and/or examinations in business, administration, management or commerce include:
AMETS (ASSOCIATION FOR MANAGEMENT EDUCATION AND TRAINING IN SCOTLAND), c/o Cottrell Building, University of Stirling, Stirling FK9 4LA. Tel: 01786-450906. *Chairman*, Prof. F. Pignatelli
THE ASSOCIATION OF MBAS, 15 Duncan Terrace, London N1 8BZ. Tel: 0171-837 3375. Publishes a directory giving details of MBA courses provided at UK institutions. *Director*, M. Jones
CAM FOUNDATION (COMMUNICATIONS, ADVERTISING AND MARKETING EDUCATION FOUNDATION), Abford House, 15 Wilton Road, London SW1V 1NJ. Tel: 0171-828 7506. *General Secretary*, J. Knight
CHARTERED INSTITUTE OF HOUSING, Octavia House, Westwood Business Park, Westwood Way, Coventry CV4 8JP. Tel: 01203-851700. *Chief Executive*, D. Butler
CHARTERED INSTITUTE OF MARKETING, Moor Hall, Cookham, Maidenhead, Berks SL6 9QH. Tel: 01628-427500. *Director-General*, S. Cuthbert
CHARTERED INSTITUTE OF PURCHASING AND SUPPLY, Easton House, Easton on the Hill, Stamford, Lincs PE9 3NZ. Tel: 01780-756777. *Chief Executive*, C. Holden
CHARTERED INSTITUTE OF TRANSPORT, 80 Portland Place, London W1N 4DP. Tel: 0171-467 9400. *Director*, Mrs D. de Carvalho
HENLEY MANAGEMENT COLLEGE, Greenlands, Henley-on-Thames, Oxon RG9 3AU. Tel: 01491-571454. *Principal*, Prof. R. Wild, PH.D., D.SC.
INSTITUTE OF ADMINISTRATIVE MANAGEMENT, 40 Chatsworth Parade, Petts Wood, Orpington, Kent BR5 1RW. Tel: 01689-875555. *Chief Executive*, Prof. G. Robinson
INSTITUTE OF CHARTERED SECRETARIES AND ADMINISTRATORS, 16 Park Crescent, London W1N 4AH. Tel: 0171-580 4741. *Chief Executive*, M. J. Ainsworth
INSTITUTE OF CHARTERED SHIPBROKERS, 3 St Helen's Place, London EC3A 6EJ. Tel: 0171-628 5559. *Director*, Mrs B. Fletcher

INSTITUTE OF EXPORT, Export House, 64 Clifton Street, London EC2A 4HB. Tel: 0171-247 9812. *Director-General*, I. J. Campbell

INSTITUTE OF HEALTH SERVICES MANAGEMENT, 7–10 Chandos Street, London WIM 9DE. Tel: 0171-460 7654. *Director*, Ms K. Caines

INSTITUTE OF MANAGEMENT, Management House, Cottingham Road, Corby, Northants NN17 1TT. Tel: 01536-204222. *Director-General*, Mrs M. Chapman

INSTITUTE OF PERSONNEL AND DEVELOPMENT, IPD House, Camp Road, London SW19 4UX. Tel: 0181-971 9000. *Director-General*, G. Armstrong

INSTITUTE OF PRACTITIONERS IN ADVERTISING, 44 Belgrave Square, London SWIX 8QS. Tel: 0171-235 7020. *Secretary*, J. Raad

INSTITUTE OF QUALITY ASSURANCE, 12 Grosvenor Crescent, London SWIX 7EE. Tel: 0171-245 6722. *Secretary-General*, D. Campbell

CHIROPRACTIC

Chiropractic is accorded statutory regulation by the Chiropractic Act 1994. There are currently four professional associations operating voluntary registration schemes. These schemes will be replaced by a General Chiropractic Council when it opens a new register, probably in late 1998 or early 1999. Once the register is in place it will be illegal for anyone to call themselves a chiropractor unless they have undertaken a recognized course of training and are registered with the General Chiropractic Council.

There are currently five training centres for chiropractic. Two of these provide four-year part-time training programmes leading to internal academic awards; the other three provide full-time training leading to a B.Sc. and M.Sc. in chiropractic. In future, the General Chiropractic Council will determine the training requirements to qualify for registration and accredit courses.

BRITISH CHIROPRACTIC ASSOCIATION, Blagrave House, 17 Blagrave Street, Reading RGI 1QB. Tel: 0118-950 5950. *Executive Director*, Ms S. A. Wakefield

GENERAL CHIROPRACTIC COUNCIL, c/o Department of Science and Technology Studies, University College London, Gower Street, London WCIE 6BT. *Chairman*, Mrs N. Morris

SCOTTISH CHIROPRACTIC ASSOCIATION, St Boswells Chiropractic Clinic, Main Street, St Boswells, Melrose TD6 0AP. Tel: 01835-823645. *Secretary*, Dr C. How

DANCE

IMPERIAL SOCIETY OF TEACHERS OF DANCING, Imperial House, 22–26 Paul Street, London EC2A 4QE. Tel: 0171-377 1577. *Chief Executive*, M. J. Browne

INTERNATIONAL DANCE TEACHERS' ASSOCIATION, International House, 76 Bennett Road, Brighton BN2 5JL. Tel: 01273-685652. *Company Secretary*, J. Dearling

ROYAL ACADEMY OF DANCING, 36 Battersea Square, London SW11 3RA. Tel: 0171-223 0091. *Chief Executive*, D. Watchman; *Artistic Director*, Miss L. Wallis

ROYAL BALLET SCHOOL, 155 Talgarth Road, London W14 9DE. Tel: 0181-748 6335. Also at White Lodge, Richmond Park, Surrey TW10 5HR. Tel: 0181-876 5547. *Director*, Dame Merle Park, DBE

DEFENCE

ROYAL COLLEGE OF DEFENCE STUDIES, Seaford House, 37 Belgrave Square, London SWIX 8NS. Tel: 0171-915 4800. Prepares selected senior officers and officials for responsibilities in the direction and management of defence and security. *Commandant*, Vice-Adm. J. H. S. McNally, LVO

JOINT SERVICES COMMAND AND STAFF COLLEGE, Bracknell, Berks RGI2 9DD. Tel: 01344-54593. *Commandant*, Maj.-Gen. T. Granville-Chapman, CBE; *Dean of Academic Studies*, Prof. G. Till, PH.D.

ROYAL NAVAL COLLEGE

BRITANNIA ROYAL NAVAL COLLEGE, Dartmouth, Devon TQ6 0HJ. Tel: 01803-832141. Provides professional training and education for all new entry RN officers and officers from foreign and Commonwealth navies. *Commodore*, Cdre R. A. G. Clare

MILITARY COLLEGES

DIRECTORATE OF EDUCATIONAL AND TRAINING SERVICES, Trenchard Lines, Upavon, Pewsey, Wilts SN9 6BE. Tel: 01980-618730. *Director*, Brig. C. F. P. Horsfall

ROYAL MILITARY ACADEMY SANDHURST, Camberley, Surrey GU15 4PQ. Tel: 01276-63344. *Commandant*, Maj.-Gen. A. G. Denaro, CBE

ROYAL MILITARY COLLEGE OF SCIENCE, Shrivenham, Swindon, Wilts SN6 8LA. Tel: 01793-785435. Students from UK and overseas study from degree to postgraduate levels in engineering, management, science and technology. The College is a faculty of Cranfield University. *Commandant*, Maj.-Gen. A. S. H. Irwin, CBE; *Principal*, Prof. P. Hutchinson

ROYAL AIR FORCE COLLEGES

ROYAL AIR FORCE COLLEGE, Cranwell, Sleaford, Lincs. NG34 8HB. Selects all officer and aircrew entrants to the RAF and provides initial training for all officer entrants to the RAF. Also provides initial specialist training for junior officers of some ground branches, elementary flying training for all three services, general service training for University Air Squadrons, and supervision of the Air Cadet Organization. *Air Officer Commanding and Commandant*, Air Vice-Marshal T. W. Rimmer, OBE

ROYAL AIR FORCE TRAINING, DEVELOPMENT AND SUPPORT UNIT, RAF Halton, Aylesbury, Bucks HP22 5PG. Tel: 01296-623535. *Commanding Officer*, Gp Capt. A. Harris

DENTISTRY

In order to practise in the UK, a dentist must be entered in the Dentists Register. To be registered, a person must hold the degree or diploma in dental surgery of a university in the UK or the diploma of any of the licensing authorities (the Royal Colleges of Surgeons of England and of Edinburgh, and the Royal College of Physicians and Surgeons of Glasgow). Nationals of EU or European Economic Area member states holding an appropriate European diploma, and holders of certain overseas diplomas, may also be registered. Temporary registration may be available for those dentists who do not hold a diploma described above. The Dentists Register is maintained by:

THE GENERAL DENTAL COUNCIL, 37 Wimpole Street, London WIM 8DQ. Tel: 0171-887 3800. *Chief Executive and Registrar*, Mrs R. M. J. Hepplewhite

DIETETICS
See also FOOD AND NUTRITION SCIENCE

The professional association is the British Dietetic Association. Full membership is open to dietitians holding a recognized qualification, who may also become State Registered Dietitians through the Council for Professions Supplementary to Medicine (*see* Medicine)

THE BRITISH DIETETIC ASSOCIATION, 7th Floor, Elizabeth House, 22 Suffolk Street, Queensway, Birmingham B1 1LS. Tel: 0121-643 5483. *Secretary*, J. Grigg

DRAMA

The national validating body for courses providing training in drama for the professional theatre is the National Council for Drama Training. It currently has accredited courses at the following: Academy of Live and Recorded Arts; Arts Educational Schools; Birmingham School of Speech Training and Dramatic Art; Bristol Old Vic Theatre School; Central School of Speech and Drama; Cygnet Training Theatre, Exeter; Drama Centre, London; Drama Studio, London; Guildford School of Acting; Guildhall School of Music and Drama, London; London Academy of Music and Dramatic Art; Manchester Metropolitan University School of Theatre; Mountview Theatre School; Oxford School of Drama, Woodstock; Queen Margaret College, Edinburgh; Rose Bruford College, Sidcup; Royal Academy of Dramatic Art, London; Royal Scottish Academy of Music and Drama; Webber Douglas Academy of Dramatic Art, London; Welsh College of Music and Drama.

The accreditation of a course in a school does not necessarily imply that other courses of different type or duration in the same school are also accredited.

THE NATIONAL COUNCIL FOR DRAMA TRAINING, 5 Tavistock Place, London WC1H 9SN. *Executive Secretary,* Mrs A. Bailey

ENGINEERING

The Engineering Council supervises the engineering profession through the 39 nominated engineering institutions who are represented on its Board for Engineers' Regulation. Working with and through the institutions, the Council sets the standards for the registration of individuals, and also the accreditation for academic courses in universities and colleges and the practical training in industry.

THE ENGINEERING COUNCIL, 10 Maltravers Street, London WC2R 3ER. Tel: 0171-240 7891. *Director-General,* M. Shirley

The principal qualifying bodies are:

BRITISH COMPUTER SOCIETY, 1 Sanford Street, Swindon SN1 1HJ. Tel: 01793-417417. *Chief Executive,* Mrs J. M. Scott

BRITISH INSTITUTE OF NON-DESTRUCTIVE TESTING, 1 Spencer Parade, Northampton NN1 5AA. Tel: 01604-630124. *Secretary,* M. E. Gallagher

CHARTERED INSTITUTION OF BUILDING SERVICES ENGINEERS, 222 Balham High Road, London SW12 9BS. Tel: 0181-675 5211. *Secretary,* R. John

INSTITUTION OF AGRICULTURAL ENGINEERS, West End Road, Silsoe, Bedford MK45 4DU. Tel: 01525-861096. *Chief Executive,* J. H. Neville

INSTITUTE OF BRITISH FOUNDRYMEN, Bordesley Hall, The Holloway, Alvechurch, Birmingham B48 7QA. Tel: 01527-596100. *Secretary,* G. A. Schofield

INSTITUTION OF CHEMICAL ENGINEERS, Davis Building, 165–189 Railway Terrace, Rugby, Warks CV21 3HQ. Tel: 01788-578214. *Chief Executive,* Dr T. J. Evans

INSTITUTION OF CIVIL ENGINEERS, 1–7 Great George Street, London SW1P 3AA. Tel: 0171-222 7722. *Director-General,* R. S. Dobson, OBE, FEng.

INSTITUTION OF ELECTRICAL ENGINEERS, Savoy Place, London WC2R 0BL. Tel: 0171-240 1871. *Secretary,* Dr J. C. Williams, OBE, FEng.

INSTITUTE OF ENERGY, 18 Devonshire Street, London W1N 2AU. Tel: 0171-580 7124. *Secretary,* Mrs D. Davy

INSTITUTION OF ENGINEERING DESIGNERS, Courtleigh, Westbury Leigh, Westbury, Wilts BA13 3TA. Tel: 01373-822801. Secretary, M. Osborne

INSTITUTION OF FIRE ENGINEERS, 148 New Walk, Leicester LE1 7QB. Tel: 0116-255 3654. *General Secretary,* D. W. Evans

INSTITUTION OF GAS ENGINEERS, 21 Portland Place, London W1N 3AF. Tel: 0171-636 6603. *Secretary,* Mrs S. M. Raine

INSTITUTION OF HEALTHCARE ENGINEERING AND ESTATE MANAGEMENT, 2 Abingdon House, Cumberland Business Centre, Northumberland Road, Portsmouth PO5 1DS. Tel: 01705-823186. *Secretary,* W. R. Pym

INSTITUTION OF INCORPORATED ENGINEERS, Savoy Hill House, Savoy Hill, London WC2R 0BS. Tel: 0171-836 3357. *Chief Executive,* P. F. Wason

INSTITUTION OF INCORPORATED EXECUTIVE ENGINEERS, Wix Hill House, West Horsley, Surrey KT24 6DZ. Tel: 01483-222383. *Secretary,* D. Dacam, OBE

INSTITUTE OF LIGHTING ENGINEERS, Lennox House, 9 Lawford Road, Rugby CV21 2DZ. Tel: 01788-576492. *Chief Executive,* R. G. Frost

INSTITUTE OF MARINE ENGINEERS, The Memorial Building, 76 Mark Lane, London EC3R 7JN. Tel: 0171-481 8493. *Secretary,* J. E. Sloggett, OBE

INSTITUTE OF MATERIALS, 1 Carlton House Terrace, London SW1Y 5DB. Tel: 0171-451 7300. *Secretary,* Dr B. A. Rickinson

INSTITUTE OF MEASUREMENT AND CONTROL, 87 Gower Street, London WC1E 6AA. Tel: 0171-387 4949. *Secretary,* M. J. Yates

INSTITUTION OF MECHANICAL ENGINEERS, 1 Birdcage Walk, London SW1H 9JJ. Tel: 0171-222 7899. *Director-General (acting),* R. Howard-Jones

INSTITUTION OF MINING AND METALLURGY, Danum House, 6A South Parade, Doncaster DN1 2DY. Tel: 01302-320486. *Secretary,* Dr G. J. M. Woodrow

INSTITUTION OF NUCLEAR ENGINEERS, 1 Penerley Road, London SE6 2LQ. Tel: 0181-698 1500. *Secretary,* W. J. Hurst

INSTITUTE OF PHYSICS, 76 Portland Place, London W1N 4AA. Tel: 0171-470 4800. *Chief Executive,* Dr A. D. W. Jones

INSTITUTION OF PLANT ENGINEERS, 77 Great Peter Street, London SW1P 2EZ. Tel: 0171-233 2855. Secretary, P. F. Tye

INSTITUTE OF PLUMBING, 64 Station Lane, Hornchurch, Essex RM12 6NB. Tel: 01708-472791. *Chief Executive,* W. A. Watts, MBE

INSTITUTE OF QUALITY ASSURANCE, 12 Grosvenor Crescent, London SW1X 7EE. Tel: 0171-245 6722. *Secretary-General,* D. Campbell

INSTITUTION OF STRUCTURAL ENGINEERS, 11 Upper Belgrave Street, London SW1X 8BH. Tel: 0171-235 4535. *Chief Executive,* Dr J. W. Dougill, FEng.

INSTITUTION OF WATER OFFICERS, Heriot House, 12 Summerhill Terrace, Newcastle upon Tyne NE4 6EB. Tel: 0191-230 5150. *Company Secretary (acting),* Ms L. Harding

ROYAL AERONAUTICAL SOCIETY, 4 Hamilton Place, London W1V 0BQ. Tel: 0171-499 3515. *Director,* K. Mans

ROYAL INSTITUTION OF NAVAL ARCHITECTS, 10 Upper Belgrave Street, London SW1X 8BQ. Tel: 0171-235 4622. *Chief Executive,* T. Blakeley

THE WELDING INSTITUTE, Abington Hall, Abington, Cambridge CB1 6AL. Tel: 01223-891162. *Chief Executive,* B. Braithwaite, OBE

FILM AND TELEVISION

Postgraduate training for those intending to make a career in film and television production is provided by the National Film and Television School, which provides courses in production, direction, animation, screenwriting, editing, cinematography, screen sound, art direction and screen music. Short post-experience courses to enable professionals to update or expand their skills are also provided.

NATIONAL FILM AND TELEVISION SCHOOL, Station Road, Beaconsfield, Bucks HP9 1LG. Tel: 01494-671234. *Director,* S. Bayly

FOOD AND NUTRITION SCIENCE
See also DIETETICS

Scientific and professional bodies include:
INSTITUTE OF FOOD SCIENCE & TECHNOLOGY, 5 Cambridge Court, 210 Shepherd's Bush Road, London W6 7NJ. Tel: 0171-603 6316. *Chief Executive,* Ms H. G. Wild

FORESTRY AND TIMBER STUDIES

Professional organizations include:
COMMONWEALTH FORESTRY ASSOCIATION, c/o Oxford Forestry Institute, South Parks Road, Oxford OX1 3RB. Tel: 01865-271037. *Chairman,* Dr J. S. Maini
INSTITUTE OF CHARTERED FORESTERS, 7A St Colme Street, Edinburgh EH3 6AA. Tel: 0131-225 2705. *Secretary,* Mrs M. W. Dick
ROYAL FORESTRY SOCIETY OF ENGLAND, WALES AND NORTHERN IRELAND, 102 High Street, Tring, Herts HP23 4AF. Tel: 01442-822028. *Director,* J. E. Jackson, PH.D.
ROYAL SCOTTISH FORESTRY SOCIETY, The Stables, Dalkeith Country Park, Dalkeith, Midlothian EH22 2NA. Tel: 0131-660 9480. *Director,* M. Osborne

FUEL AND ENERGY SCIENCE

The principal professional bodies are:
INSTITUTE OF ENERGY, 18 Devonshire Street, London W1N 2AU. Tel: 0171-580 7124. *Secretary* Mrs D. Davy
INSTITUTION OF GAS ENGINEERS, 21 Portland Place, London W1N 3AF. Tel: 0171-636 6603. *Secretary,* Mrs S. M. Raine
INSTITUTE OF PETROLEUM, 61 New Cavendish Street, London W1M 8AR. Tel: 0171-467 7100. *Director-General,* I. Ward

HOTELKEEPING, CATERING AND INSTITUTIONAL MANAGEMENT
See also DIETETICS, and FOOD AND NUTRITION SCIENCE

The qualifying professional body in these areas is:
HOTEL AND CATERING INTERNATIONAL MANAGEMENT ASSOCIATION, 191 Trinity Road, London SW17 7HN. Tel: 0181-672 4251. *Chief Executive,* D. Wood

INDUSTRIAL AND VOCATIONAL TRAINING

The NTO National Council represents national training organizations (NTOs), a new network of sector training bodies established in 1997. NTOs are independent, employer-owned bodies which represent the education and training interests of their respective sectors to government and ensure the development and adoption of occupational standards, particularly through National and Scottish Vocational Qualifications.
NTO NATIONAL COUNCIL, 10 Meadowcourt, Amos Road, Sheffield S9 1BX. Tel: 0114-261 9926. *Chief Executive,* Dr. A. Powell

INSURANCE

Organizations conducting examinations and awarding diplomas are:

ASSOCIATION OF AVERAGE ADJUSTERS, 200 Aldersgate Street, London EC1A 4JJ. Tel: 0171-956 0099. *Secretary,* D. W. Taylor
CHARTERED INSTITUTE OF LOSS ADJUSTERS, Manfield House, 1 Southampton Street, London WC2R 0LR. Tel: 0171-240 1496. *Director,* A. F. Clack
CHARTERED INSURANCE INSTITUTE, 20 Aldermanbury, London EC2V 7HY. Tel: 0181-989 8464. *Director-General,* Prof. D. E. Bland

JOURNALISM

Courses for trainee newspaper journalists are available at 30 centres. One-year full-time courses are available for selected students and 18-week courses for graduates. Particulars of all these courses are available from the National Council for the Training of Journalists. Short courses for mid-career development can be arranged, as can various distance learning courses. The NCTJ also offers Assessor, Internal Verifier (IV) and Accreditation of Prior Achievement (APA) training, and NVQs.
   For periodical journalists, there are ten centres running courses approved by the Periodicals Training Council.
THE NATIONAL COUNCIL FOR TRAINING OF JOURNALISTS, Latton Bush Centre, Southern Way, Harlow, Essex CM18 7BL. Tel: 01279-430009. *Chief Executive,* R. Selwood
THE PERIODICALS TRAINING COUNCIL, Queen's House, 55–56 Lincoln's Inn Fields, London WC2A 3LJ. Tel: 0171-404 4168. *Director,* Ms J. Butcher

LAW

THE BAR

Admission to the Bar of England and Wales is controlled by the Inns of Court, admission to the Bar of Northern Ireland by the Honorable Society of the Inn of Court of Northern Ireland and admission as an Advocate of the Scottish Bar is controlled by the Faculty of Advocates. The governing body of the barristers' branch of the legal profession in England and Wales is the General Council of the Bar. The governing body in Northern Ireland is the Honorable Society of the Inn of Court of Northern Ireland, and the Faculty of Advocates is the governing body of the Scottish Bar. The education and examination of students training for the Bar of England and Wales is regulated by the General Council of the Bar. Those who intend to practise at the Bar of England and Wales must pass the Bar's vocational course. The Inns of Court School of Law is the largest provider of initial training for those wishing to practise at the Bar, but since September 1997 six other institutions have been validated to provide the course.
FACULTY OF ADVOCATES, Advocates Library, Parliament House, Edinburgh EH1 1RF. Tel: 0131-226 5071. *Dean,* G. N. H. Emslie, QC; *Clerk,* I. G. Armstrong
THE GENERAL COUNCIL OF THE BAR, 3 Bedford Row, London WC1R 4DB. Tel: 0171-242 0082. *Chairman,* H. Hallett, QC; *Chief Executive,* N. Morison
THE HONORABLE SOCIETY OF THE INN OF COURT OF NORTHERN IRELAND, Royal Courts of Justice, Belfast BT1 3JF. Tel: 01232-235111. *Treasurer* (1998), E. A. Comerton, QC; *Under-Treasurer,* J. W. Wilson, QC

The Inns of Court

GRAY'S INN, 8 South Square, London WC1R 5EU. Tel: 0171-405 8164. *Treasurer,* M. Collins, QC; *Under-Treasurer,* D. Machin
THE INNER TEMPLE, London EC4Y 7HL. Tel: 0171-797 8250. *Treasurer,* The Rt. Hon. The Lord Lloyd of Berwick; *Sub-Treasurer,* Brig. P. A. Little, CBE

INNS OF COURT SCHOOL OF LAW 4 Gray's Inn Place, Gray's Inn, London WC1R 5DX. Tel: 0171-404 5787. *Chairman,* The Hon. Mr Justice Hooper; *Principal,* R. Stone

LINCOLN'S INN, London WC2A 3TL. Tel: 0171-405 1393. *Treasurer,* The Rt. Hon. Sir John Balcombe; *Under-Treasurer,* Col. D. H. Hills, MBE

THE MIDDLE TEMPLE, London EC4Y 9AT. Tel: 0171-427 4800. *Treasurer,* Sir David Calcutt, QC; *Under-Treasurer,* Brig. C. T. J. Wright

SOLICITORS

Qualifications for solicitors are obtainable only from one of the Law Societies, which control the education and examination of trainee solicitors and the admission of solicitors.

THE COLLEGE OF LAW provides courses for the Common Professional Examination and Legal Practice Course at Braboeuf Manor, St Catherine's, Guildford, Surrey GU3 1HA; 14 Store Street, London WC1E 7DE; Christleton Hall, Chester CH3 7AB; Bishopthorpe Road, York YO23 2GA. The college also provides the Bar Vocational Course at its London branch

LAW SOCIETY OF ENGLAND AND WALES, 113 Chancery Lane, London WC2A 1PL. Tel: 0171-242 1222. *President* (1998–9), M. Mathews; *Secretary-General,* Mrs J. M. Betts

LAW SOCIETY OF NORTHERN IRELAND, Law Society House, 98 Victoria Street, Belfast BT1 3JZ. Tel: 01232-231614. *Chief Executive,* J. W. Bailie

LAW SOCIETY OF SCOTLAND, Law Society's Hall, 26 Drumsheugh Gardens, Edinburgh EH3 7YR. Tel: 0131-226 7411. *President* (1998–9), P. Dry; *Secretary,* D. R. Mill

OFFICE FOR THE SUPERVISION OF SOLICITORS, Victoria Court, 8 Dormer Place, Leamington Spa, Warks CV32 5AE. Tel: 01926-820082. The Office is an establishment of the Law Society set up to handle complaints about solicitors and regulate solicitors' practices

LIBRARIANSHIP AND INFORMATION SCIENCE/MANAGEMENT

The Library Association accredits degree and post-graduate courses in library and information science which are offered by 17 universities in the UK. A full list of accredited degree and postgraduate courses is available from its Information Services and on its web site (*see* below) The Association also maintains a professional register of Chartered Members open to graduate ordinary members of the Association.

THE LIBRARY ASSOCIATION, 7 Ridgmount Street, London WC1E 7AE. Tel: 0171-636 7543. Web: http:// www.la-hq.org.uk. *Chief Executive,* R. Shimmon

MATERIALS STUDIES

The qualifying body is:
INSTITUTE OF MATERIALS, 1 Carlton House Terrace, London SW1Y 5DB. Tel: 0171-541 7300. *Chief Executive,* Dr B. A. Rickinson

MEDICINE

All doctors must be registered with the General Medical Council. In order to register, medical students must complete a five-year undergraduate degree at one of the 19 universities with medical schools, followed by a year of general clinical training. Once registered, doctors undertake general professional and basic specialist training as senior house officers. Further specialist training is provided by the royal colleges, faculties and societies listed below. The General Medical Council keeps a register of those doctors who have been awarded Certificates of Completion of Specialist Training.

The United Examining Board holds qualifying examinations for candidates who have trained overseas. These candidates must also have spent a period at a UK medical school.

GENERAL MEDICAL COUNCIL, 178 Great Portland Street, London W1N 6JE. Tel: 0171-580 7642. *President,* Sir Donald Irvine, CBE, MD, FRGCP; *Chief Executive,* F. Scott

UNITED EXAMINING BOARD, Apothecaries Hall, Black Friars Lane, London EC4V 6EJ. Tel: 0171-236 1180. *Chairman,* H. B. Devlin; *Registrar,* A. M. Wallington-Smith

COLLEGES/SOCIETIES HOLDING POSTGRADUATE MEMBERSHIP AND DIPLOMA EXAMINATIONS

FACULTY OF ACCIDENT AND EMERGENCY MEDICINE, Royal College of Surgeons of England, 35–43 Lincoln's Inn Fields, London WC2A 3PN. Tel: 0171-405 7071. *President,* Dr K. Little

FACULTY OF OCCUPATIONAL MEDICINE, 6 St Andrew's Place, London NW1 4LB. Tel: 0171-487 3414. *Administrator,* Ms F. M. Quinn

FACULTY OF PHARMACEUTICAL MEDICINE, 1 St Andrew's Place, London NW1 4LB. Tel: 0171-224 0343. *President,* Prof. P. Stonier

FACULTY OF PUBLIC HEALTH MEDICINE, 4 St Andrew's Place, London NW1 4LB. Tel: 0171-935 0243. *Chief Executive,* P. Scourfield

ROYAL COLLEGE OF ANAESTHETISTS, 48–49 Russell Square, London WC1B 4JY. Tel: 0171-813 1900. *President,* Prof. L. Strunin; *Chief Executive,* Ms W. Cogger

ROYAL COLLEGE OF GENERAL PRACTITIONERS, 14 Princes Gate, London SW7 1PU. Tel: 0171-581 3232. *President,* Prof. D. P. Gray, OBE, FRCGP; *Hon. Secretary,* Dr W. Reith, FRCPEd, FRCGP

ROYAL COLLEGE OF OBSTETRICIANS AND GYNAECOLOGISTS, 27 Sussex Place, London NW1 4RG. Tel: 0171-772 6200. *President,* Prof. R. Shaw; *Secretary,* P. A. Barnett

ROYAL COLLEGE OF PAEDIATRICS AND CHILD HEALTH, 50 Hallam Street, London W1N 6DE. Tel: 0171-307 5600. *President,* Prof. J. D. Baum; *Secretary,* Ms L. Tyler

ROYAL COLLEGE OF PATHOLOGISTS, 2 Carlton House Terrace, London SW1Y 5AF. Tel: 0171-930 5861. *President,* Prof. R. N. M. MacSween; *Secretary,* K. Lockyer

ROYAL COLLEGE OF PHYSICIANS, 11 St Andrew's Place, London NW1 4LE. Tel: 0171-935 1174. *President,* Prof. K. G. M. M. Alberti, FRCP; *Secretary,* P. Masterton-Smith

ROYAL COLLEGE OF PHYSICIANS AND SURGEONS OF GLASGOW, 232–242 St Vincent Street, Glasgow G2 5RJ. Tel: 0141-221 6072. *President,* C. Mackay; *Hon. Secretary,* Dr C. Semple

ROYAL COLLEGE OF PHYSICIANS OF EDINBURGH, 9 Queen Street, Edinburgh EH2 1JQ. Tel: 0131-225 7324. *President,* Prof. J. C. Petrie; *Secretary,* Dr J. St J. Thomas

ROYAL COLLEGE OF PSYCHIATRISTS, 17 Belgrave Square, London SW1X 8PG. Tel: 0171-235 2351. *President,* Dr R. E. Kendell, CBE; *Secretary,* Mrs V. Cameron

ROYAL COLLEGE OF RADIOLOGISTS, 38 Portland Place, London W1N 4QJ. Tel: 0171-636 4432. *President,* Prof. P. Armstrong; *Secretary,* A. J. Cowles

ROYAL COLLEGE OF SURGEONS OF EDINBURGH, Nicolson Street, Edinburgh EH8 9DW. Tel: 0131-527 1600. *President,* Prof. A. G. D. Maran; *Secretary,* Ms A. S. Campbell

ROYAL COLLEGE OF SURGEONS OF ENGLAND, 35–43 Lincoln's Inn Fields, London WC2A 3PN. Tel: 0171-405 3474. *President,* B. T. Jackson; *Secretary,* C. Duncan

SOCIETY OF APOTHECARIES OF LONDON, 14 Black Friars Lane, London EC4V 6EJ. Tel: 0171-236 1189. *Clerk,* R. J. Stringer

PROFESSIONS SUPPLEMENTARY TO MEDICINE

The standard of professional education in art, drama and music therapies, biomedical sciences, chiropody, dietetics, occupational therapy, orthoptics, physiotherapy and radiography is the responsibility of nine professional boards, which also publish an annual register of qualified practitioners. The work of the boards is co-ordinated by the Council for Professions Supplementary to Medicine.

In 1997 permission was given for two new boards to be set up, one for prosthetists and orthotists and one for art therapists. These will set up registers of qualified practitioners over the next two years.

THE COUNCIL FOR PROFESSIONS SUPPLEMENTARY TO MEDICINE, Park House, 184 Kennington Park Road, London SE11 4BU. Tel: 0171-582 0866. *Registrar,* M. D. Hall

BIOMEDICAL SCIENCES

Qualifications from higher education establishments and training in medical laboratories are required for membership of the Institute of Biomedical Science.

INSTITUTE OF BIOMEDICAL SCIENCE, 12 Coldbath Square, London EC1R 5HL. Tel: 0171-636 8192. *Chief Executive,* A. Potter

CHIROPODY

Professional recognition is granted by the Society of Chiropodists and Podiatrists to students who are awarded B.Sc. degrees in Podiatry or Podiatric Medicine after attending a course of full-time training for three or four years at one of the 14 recognized schools in the UK (11 in England and Wales, two in Scotland and one in Northern Ireland). Qualifications granted and degrees recognized by the Society are approved by the Chiropodists Board for the purpose of State Registration, which is a condition of employment within the National Health Service.

THE SOCIETY OF CHIROPODISTS AND PODIATRISTS, 53 Welbeck Street, London W1M 7HE. Tel: 0171-486 3381. *General Secretary,* M. Paulson

See also DIETETICS

OCCUPATIONAL THERAPY

The professional qualification may be obtained upon successful completion of a validated course in any of the 28 institutions approved by the College of Occupational Therapists. The courses are normally degree-level courses based in higher education institutions.

COLLEGE OF OCCUPATIONAL THERAPISTS, 106–114 Borough High Street, London SE1 1LB. Tel: 0171-357 6480. *Secretary,* J. Thompson

ORTHOPTICS

Orthoptists undertake the diagnosis and treatment of all types of squint and other anomalies of binocular vision, working in close collaboration with ophthalmologists. The training and maintenance of professional standards are the responsibility of the Orthoptists Board of the Council for the Professions Supplementary to Medicine. The professional body is the British Orthoptic Society. Training is at degree level.

THE BRITISH ORTHOPTIC SOCIETY, Tavistock House North, Tavistock Square, London WC1H 9HX. Hon. Secretary, Ms R. Auld

PHYSIOTHERAPY

Full-time three- or four-year degree courses are available at 28 recognized schools in the UK. Information about courses leading to eligibility for Membership of the Chartered Society of Physiotherapy and to State Registration is available from the Chartered Society of Physiotherapy.

THE CHARTERED SOCIETY OF PHYSIOTHERAPY, 14 Bedford Row, London WC1R 4ED. Tel: 0171-306 6666. *Chief Executive,* P. Gray

RADIOGRAPHY AND RADIOTHERAPY

In order to practise both diagnostic and therapeutic radiography in the UK, it is necessary to have successfully completed a course of education and training recognized by the Privy Council. Such courses are offered by universities throughout the UK and lead to the award of a degree in radiography. Further information is available from the college.

THE COLLEGE OF RADIOGRAPHERS, 2 Carriage Row, 183 Eversholt Street, London NW1 1BU. Tel: 0171-391 4500. *Chief Executive,* S. Evans

COMPLEMENTARY MEDICINE

Professional courses are validated by:

INSTITUTE FOR COMPLEMENTARY MEDICINE, PO Box 194, London SE16 1QZ. Tel: 0171-237 5165. Director A. Baird

MERCHANT NAVY TRAINING SCHOOLS

OFFICERS

WARSASH MARITIME CENTRE, Southampton Institute, Newtown Road, Warsash, Southampton SO31 9ZL. Tel: 01489-576161. *Dean,* Capt. G. B. Angas

SEAFARERS

NATIONAL SEA TRAINING CENTRE, North West Kent College, Dering Way, Gravesend, Kent DA12 2JJ. Tel: 01474-363656. *Director of Faculty,* R. MacDonald

MUSIC

ASSOCIATED BOARD OF THE ROYAL SCHOOLS OF MUSIC, 14 Bedford Square, London WC1B 3JG. Tel: 0171-636 5400. The Board conducts graded music examinations in over 80 countries and provides other services to music education through its professional development department and publishing company. *Chief Executive,* R. Morris

GUILDHALL SCHOOL OF MUSIC AND DRAMA, Silk Street, London EC2Y 8DT. Tel: 0171-628 2571. *Principal,* I. Horsbrugh

LONDON COLLEGE OF MUSIC, Thames Valley University, St Mary's Road, London W5 5RF. Tel: 0181-231 2304. *Dean,* Ms P. Thompson

ROYAL ACADEMY OF MUSIC, Marylebone Road, London NW1 5HT. Tel: 0171-873 7373. *Principal,* Prof. C. Price

ROYAL COLLEGE OF MUSIC, Prince Consort Road, London SW7 2BS. Tel: 0171-589 3643. *Director,* Dr J. Ritterman

ROYAL COLLEGE OF ORGANISTS, 7 St Andrew Street, London EC4A 3LQ. Tel: 0171-936 3606. *Senior Executive,* A. Dear

ROYAL NORTHERN COLLEGE OF MUSIC, 124 Oxford Road, Manchester M13 9RD. Tel: 0161-273 6283. *Principal,* Prof. E. Gregson

ROYAL SCOTTISH ACADEMY OF MUSIC AND DRAMA, 100 Renfrew Street, Glasgow G2 3DB. Tel: 0141-332 4101. *Principal,* Dr P. Ledger, CBE, FRSE

Trinity College of Music, 11–13 Mandeville Place, London wim 6aq. Tel: 0171-935 5773. *Principal,* G. Henderson

NURSING

All nurses must be registered with the UK Central Council for Nursing, Midwifery and Health Visiting. Courses leading to registration as a nurse are at least three years in length. There are also some programmes which are combined with degrees. Students study in colleges of nursing or in institutions of higher education. Courses offer a combination of theoretical and practical experience in a variety of settings. Different courses lead to different types of registration, including: Registered Nurse (RN), Registered Mental Nurse (RMN), Registered Mental Handicap Nurse (RMHN), Registered Sick Children's Nurse (RSCN), Registered Midwife (RM) and Registered Health Visitor (RHV). The various national boards, listed below, are responsible for validating courses in nursing.

The Royal College of Nursing is the main professional union representing nurses and provides higher education through its Institute.

English National Board for Nursing, Midwifery and Health Visiting, Victory House, 170 Tottenham Court Road, London wip oha. Tel: 0171-388 3131. *Chief Executive,* A. P. Smith

National Board for Nursing, Midwifery and Health Visiting for Northern Ireland, Centre House, 79 Chichester Street, Belfast bt1 4je. Tel: 01232-238152. *Chief Executive,* Prof. O. D'A. Slevin, ph.d.

National Board for Nursing, Midwifery and Health Visiting for Scotland, 22 Queen Street, Edinburgh eh2 1nt. Tel: 0131-226 7371. *Chief Executive,* D. C. Benton

The Royal College of Nursing of the United Kingdom, 20 Cavendish Square, London wim oab. Tel: 0171-409 3333. *General Secretary,* Miss C. Hancock; *Director of the RCN Institute,* Prof. A. Kitson

Welsh National Board for Nursing, Midwifery and Health Visiting, 2nd Floor, Golate House, 101 St Mary Street, Cardiff cf1 1dx. Tel: 01222-261400. *Chief Executive,* D. A. Ravey

UK Central Council for Nursing, Midwifery and Health Visiting, 23 Portland Place, London win 4jt. Tel: 0171-637 7181. *Chief Executive and Registrar,* Ms S. Norman

OPHTHALMIC AND DISPENSING OPTICS

Professional bodies are:

The Association of British Dispensing Opticians, 6 Hurlingham Business Park, Sulivan Road, London sw6 3du. Tel: 0171-736 0088. Grants qualifications as a dispensing optician. *Registrar,* D. G. Baker

The College of Optometrists, 42 Craven Street, London wc2n 5ng. Tel: 0171-839 6000. Grants qualifications as an optometrist. *General Secretary,* P. D. Leigh

OSTEOPATHY

Osteopathy is accorded statutory regulation by the Osteopaths Act 1993. The existing voluntary registration schemes were taken over by the General Osteopathic Council, which opened a new statutory register on 9 May 1998. From 2000 it will be an offence for anyone who is not on the statutory register to call themselves an osteopath.

The General Osteopathic Council is now responsible for regulating, developing and promoting the profession. Osteopathic education is currently undergoing considerable change. Courses vary in length from four to six years, granting various qualifications from diploma to honours degree. Shorter courses are available for qualified doctors. Details of accrediting institutions and courses can be obtained from the General Osteopathic Council.

General Osteopathic Council, Premier House, 10 Greycoat Place, London sw1p 1sb. Tel: 0171-799 2442. *Chief Executive and Registrar,* Miss M. Craggs

PHARMACY

Information may be obtained from the Secretary and Registrar of the Royal Pharmaceutical Society of Great Britain.

Royal Pharmaceutical Society of Great Britain, 1 Lambeth High Street, London se1 7jn. Tel: 0171-735 9141. *Secretary and Registrar,* J. Ferguson, obe

PHOTOGRAPHY

The professional body is:

British Institute of Professional Photography, Fox Talbot House, Amwell End, Ware, Herts sg12 9hn. Tel: 01920-464011. *Chief Executive,* A. Mair

PRINTING

Details of training courses in printing can be obtained from the Institute of Printing and the British Printing Industries Federation. In addition to these examining and organizing bodies, examinations are held by various independent regional examining boards in further education.

British Printing Industries Federation, 11 Bedford Row, London wc1r 4dx. Tel: 0171-242 6904. *Chief Executive,* T. P. E. Machin

Institute of Printing, 8a Lonsdale Gardens, Tunbridge Wells, Kent tn1 1nu. Tel: 01892-538118. *Secretary-General,* D. Freeland

SCIENCE

Professional qualifications are awarded by:

Geological Society, Burlington House, Piccadilly, London w1v 0ju. Tel: 0171-434 9944. *Chief Executive,* E. Nickless

Institute of Biology, 20–22 Queensberry Place, London sw7 2dz. Tel: 0171-581 8333. *President,* Dr J. Norris; *Chief Executive,* Prof. A. Malcolm

Institute of Physics, 76 Portland Place, London win 3dh. Tel: 0171-470 4800. *Chief Executive,* Dr A. D. W. Jones

Royal Society of Chemistry, Burlington House, Piccadilly, London w1v 0bn. Tel: 0171-437 8656. *President,* E. Abel, cbe; *Secretary-General,* T. D. Inch, ph.d., d.sc.

SOCIAL WORK

The Central Council for Education and Training in Social Work promotes education and training for social work and social care in the UK. It approves education and training programmes, including those leading to its qualifying award, the Diploma in Social Work.

The Central Council for Education and Training in Social Work, Derbyshire House, St Chad's Street, London wc1h 8ad. Tel: 0171-278 2455. *Chairman,* Ms Z. Alexander; *Chief Executive,* J. Bernard

SPEECH AND LANGUAGE THERAPY

The Royal College of Speech and Language Therapists provides details of courses leading to qualification as a speech and language therapist. Other professionals may become Associates of the College. A directory of registered members is published annually.

THE ROYAL COLLEGE OF SPEECH AND LANGUAGE THERAPISTS, 7 Bath Place, Rivington Street, London EC2A 3DR. Tel: 0171-613 3855. *Director,* Mrs P. Evans

SURVEYING

The qualifying professional bodies include:

ARCHITECTS AND SURVEYORS INSTITUTE, St Mary House, 15 St Mary Street, Chippenham, Wilts SN15 3WD. Tel: 01249-444505. *Chief Executive,* I. N. Norris

ASSOCIATION OF BUILDING ENGINEERS, Jubilee House, Billing Brook Road, Weston Favell, Northampton NN3 8NW. Tel: 01604-404121. *Chief Executive,* D. Gibson

INCORPORATED SOCIETY OF VALUERS AND AUCTIONEERS (1968), 3 Cadogan Gate, London SW1X 0AS. Tel: 0171-235 2282. *Chief Executive,* C. Evans

INSTITUTE OF REVENUES, RATING AND VALUATION, 41 Doughty Street, London WC1N 2LF. Tel: 0171-831 3505. *Director,* C. Farrington

ROYAL INSTITUTION OF CHARTERED SURVEYORS (incorporating The Institute of Quantity Surveyors), 12 Great George Street, London SW1P 3AD. Tel: 0171-222 7000. *Chief Executive,* J. Armstrong

TEACHING

Teachers in maintained schools must have Qualified Teacher Status (QTS). With certain exceptions, teaching is an all-graduate profession, and QTS may be gained by a number of different routes. Those without a first degree may take a Bachelor of Education (B.Ed) or a Bachelor of Arts/Science (BA/B.Sc) with QTS, full-time for three or four years, depending on the programme followed. These degrees combine subject and professional studies with teaching practice. Shortened courses of these degrees are available for those who have successfully completed one or two years of higher education. The Licensed Teacher Scheme, for those with two years higher education who wished to be employed as teachers at the same time as they trained for QTS, was replaced by the Registered Teacher Scheme in 1998; entrants are paid a salary and undertake one to two years higher education.

For those who already have a first degree, the most common route is through a one-year Postgraduate Certificate of Education (PGCE). This may be taken full-time or part-time, or as a distance-learning programme. Postgraduates may also gain QTS through training in a school (School-Centred Initial Teacher Training). Since January 1998, graduates have been able to join the Graduate Teacher Programme which provides teaching and training for one year (*see also* pages 431–2).

Details of courses in England and Wales are contained in the *Handbook of Initial Teacher Training in England and Wales,* published by NATFHE. Further information about teaching in England and Wales is available from the Teaching Information Line, 01245-454454. Details of courses in Scotland can be obtained from colleges of education, universities, COSHEP and TEACH (*see* page 444). Details of courses in Northern Ireland can be obtained from the Department of Education for Northern Ireland. Applications for teacher training courses in Northern Ireland are made to the institutions direct. For applications, *see* page 436.

TEXTILES

THE TEXTILE INSTITUTE, International Headquarters, 10 Blackfriars Street, Manchester M3 5DR. Tel: 0161-834 8457. *Operations Manager,* P. Daniels

THEOLOGICAL COLLEGES

The number of students training for the ministry in the academic year 1997–8 is shown in parenthesis. Those marked * show figures for 1996–7.

ANGLICAN

COLLEGE OF THE RESURRECTION, Mirfield, W. Yorks WF14 0BW. Tel: 01924-481910. (35). *Principal,* Revd C. Irvine

CRANMER HALL, St John's College, Durham DH1 3RJ. Tel: 0191-374 3579. (65). *Principal,* D. V. Day

OAK HILL COLLEGE, Chase Side, London N14 4PS. Tel: 0181-449 0467. (40). *Principal,* Revd Dr D. Peterson

RIDLEY HALL, Cambridge CB3 9HG. Tel: 01223-741080. (50). *Principal,* Revd G. A. Cray

RIPON COLLEGE, Cuddesdon, Oxford OX44 9EX. Tel: 01865-874427. (76). *Principal,* Revd J. Clarke

ST JOHN'S COLLEGE, Chilwell Lane, Bramcote, Nottingham NG9 3DS. Tel: 0115-925 1114. (70). *Principal,* Revd Canon Dr C. Baxter

ST MICHAEL'S THEOLOGICAL COLLEGE, Llandaff, Cardiff CF5 2YJ. Tel: 01222-563379. (32). *Warden,* Revd Dr J. I. Holdsworth

ST STEPHEN'S HOUSE, 16 Marston Street, Oxford OX4 1JX. Tel: 01865-247874. (50). *Principal,* Revd Dr J. P. Sheehy

THEOLOGICAL INSTITUTE OF THE SCOTTISH EPISCOPAL CHURCH, Oldcoates House, 32 Manor Place, Edinburgh EH3 7EB. Tel: 0131-220 2272. (25). *Principal,* Revd Canon R. A. Nixon

TRINITY COLLEGE, Stoke Hill, Bristol BS9 1JP. Tel: 0117-968 2803. (73). *Principal,* Revd Canon D. Gillett

WESTCOTT HOUSE, Jesus Lane, Cambridge CB5 8BP. Tel: 01223-741000. (58). *Principal,* Revd M. G. V. Roberts

WYCLIFFE HALL, 54 Banbury Road, Oxford OX2 6PW. Tel: 01865-274200. (67). *Principal,* Revd Dr A. E. McGrath

BAPTIST

BRISTOL BAPTIST COLLEGE, The Promenade, Clifton, Bristol BS8 3NF. Tel: 0117-946 7050. (23). *Principal,* Revd Dr B. Haymes

NORTHERN BAPTIST COLLEGE, Luther King House, Brighton Grove, Rusholme, Manchester M14 5JP. Tel: 0161-224 2214. (15). *Principal,* Revd Dr R. L. Kidd

NORTH WALES BAPTIST COLLEGE, Ffordd Ffriddoedd, Bangor LL57 2EH. Tel: 01248-362608. (2*). *Warden,* Revd Dr D. D. Morgan

REGENT'S PARK COLLEGE, Oxford OX1 2LB. Tel: 01865-288120. (26). *Principal,* Revd Dr P. S. Fiddes

THE SCOTTISH BAPTIST COLLEGE, 12 Aytoun Road, Glasgow G41 5RN. Tel: 0141-424 0747. (13). *Principal,* Revd Dr K. B. E. Roxburgh

SOUTH WALES BAPTIST COLLEGE, 54 Richmond Road, Cardiff CF2 3UR. Tel: 01222-256066. (23). *Principal,* Revd D. H. Matthews

CHURCH OF SCOTLAND

TRINITY COLLEGE, 4 The Square, University of Glasgow, Glasgow G12 8QQ. Tel: 0141-330 6840. (26). *Principal,* Revd Dr D. M. Murray

CONGREGATIONAL

SCOTTISH CONGREGATIONAL COLLEGE, 18 Inverleith Terrace, Edinburgh EH3 5NS. Tel: 0131-315 3595. (0). *Principal,* Revd Dr J. W. S. Clark

METHODIST

EDGHILL THEOLOGICAL COLLEGE, 9 Lennoxvale, Belfast BT9 5BY. Tel: 01232-665870. (15). *Principal,* Revd Dr W. D. D. Cooke

HARTLEY VICTORIA COLLEGE, Luther King House, Brighton Grove, Manchester M14 5JP. Tel: 0161-224 2215. (25*). *Principal*, Revd Dr J. A. Harrod

WESLEY COLLEGE, College Park Drive, Henbury Road, Bristol BS10 7QD. Tel: 0117-959 1200. (49). *Principal*, Revd Dr N. Richardson

WESLEY HOUSE, Jesus Lane, Cambridge CB5 8BJ. Tel: 01223-741051. (33). *Principal*, Revd Dr I. H. Jones

WESLEY STUDY CENTRE, 55 The Avenue, Durham DH1 4EB. Tel: 0191-386 1833. (24*). *Director*, Revd Dr P. Luscombe

NON-DENOMINATIONAL

CHRIST'S COLLEGE, 25 High Street, Old Aberdeen AB24 3EE. Tel: 01224-272380. (26). *Master*, Revd Prof. D. Fergusson

NEW COLLEGE, Mound Place, Edinburgh EH1 2LX. Tel: 0131-650 8912. (40). *Principal*, Revd Dr R. Page

QUEENS' COLLEGE, Somerset Road, Edgbaston, Birmingham B15 2QH. Tel: 0121-454 1527. (120). *Principal*, Revd P. Fisher

ST MARY'S COLLEGE, The University, St Andrews, Fife KY16 9JU. Tel: 01334-462851. (7*). *Principal*, Dr R. A. Piper

SPURGEON'S COLLEGE, South Norwood Hill, London SE25 6DJ. Tel: 0181-653 0850. (250). *Principal*, Revd M. J. Quicke

PRESBYTERIAN

UNION THEOLOGICAL COLLEGE, 108 Botanic Avenue, Belfast BT7 1JT. Tel: 01232-205080. (40*). *Principal*, Revd Prof. J. C. McCullough

PRESBYTERIAN CHURCH OF WALES

UNITED THEOLOGICAL COLLEGE, Aberystwyth SY23 2LT. Tel: 01970-624574. (9). *Principal*, Revd Dr J. T. Williams

ROMAN CATHOLIC

ALLEN HALL, 28 Beaufort Street, London SW3 5AA. Tel: 0171-351 1296. (30). *Principal*, Revd J. Overton, STL

CAMPION HOUSE COLLEGE, 112 Thornbury Road, Isleworth, Middx TW7 4NN. Tel: 0181-560 1924. (c.15). *Principal*, Revd C. C. Dykehoff, SJ

OSCOTT COLLEGE, Chester Road, Sutton Coldfield, W. Midlands B73 5AA. Tel: 0121-354 7117. (46). *Rector*, Very Revd Mgr K. McDonald

ST JOHN'S SEMINARY, Wonersh, Guildford, Surrey GU5 0QX. Tel: 01483-892217. (56). *Rector*, Revd K. Haggerty, STL

SCOTUS COLLEGE, 2 Chesters Road, Bearsden, Glasgow G61 4AG. Tel: 0141-942 8384. (*35). *Rector*, Rt. Revd M. J. Conway

USHAW COLLEGE, Durham DH7 9RH. Tel: 0191-373 1366. (46). *President*, Revd J. P. O'Keefe

UNITARIAN

UNITARIAN COLLEGE, Luther King House, Brighton Grove, Rusholme, Manchester M14 5JP. Tel: 0161-224 2849. (7). *Principal*, Revd Dr L. Smith

UNITED REFORMED

MANSFIELD COLLEGE, Mansfield Road, Oxford OX1 3TF. Tel: 01865-270999. (20). *Principal*, Prof. D. Marquand

NORTHERN COLLEGE, Luther King House, Brighton Grove, Rusholme, Manchester M14 5JP. Tel: 0161-224 4381. (26). *Principal*, Revd Dr D. R. Peel

WESTMINSTER COLLEGE, Madingley Road, Cambridge CB3 0AA. Tel: 01223-741084. (32). *Principal*, Revd Dr D. G. Cornick

JEWISH

JEWS' COLLEGE, Schaller House, Albert Road, London NW4 2SJ. Tel: 0181-203 6427. (6). *Director*, Prof. D. H. Ruben

LEO BAECK COLLEGE, Sternberg Centre for Judaism, 80 East End Road, London N3 2SY. Tel: 0181-349 4525. (19). *Principal*, Rabbi Prof. J. Magonet

TOWN AND COUNTRY PLANNING

Degree and diploma courses in town planning are accredited by the Royal Town Planning Institute.

THE ROYAL TOWN PLANNING INSTITUTE, 26 Portland Place, London W1N 4BE. Tel: 0171-636 9107. *Secretary-General*, R. Upton

TRANSPORT

Qualifying examinations in transport management and logistics leading to chartered professional status are conducted by the Chartered Institute of Transport.

THE CHARTERED INSTITUTE OF TRANSPORT, 80 Portland Place, London W1N 4DP. Tel: 0171-467 9425. *Director*, Mrs D. de Carvalho

VETERINARY MEDICINE

The regulatory body for veterinary medicine is the Royal College of Veterinary Surgeons, which keeps the register of those entitled to practise veterinary medicine. In order to be registered, a person must complete a five-year undergraduate degree (BvetMed, BVSc., BVMS, BVM and S) at one of the six authorized institutions.

The British Veterinary Association is the professional body representing veterinary surgeons. The British Veterinary Nursing Association is the professional body representing veterinary nurses who are also registered with the Royal College of Veterinary Surgeons.

BRITISH VETERINARY ASSOCIATION, 7 Mansfield Street, London W1M 0AT. Tel: 0171-636 6541. *Chief Executive*, J. Baird

BRITISH VETERINARY NURSING ASSOCIATION, Level 15, Terminus House, Terminus Street, Harlow, Essex CM20 1XA. Tel: 01279-450567. *Chairman*, Ms J. Costello

ROYAL COLLEGE OF VETERINARY SURGEONS, Belgravia House, 62–64 Horseferry Road, London SW1P 2AF. Tel: 0171-222 2001. *President*, Dr A. Brown; *Registrar*, Ms J. Hern

Independent Schools

The following pages list those independent schools whose
Head is a member of the Headmasters' and Headmistress'
Conference, the Society of Headmasters and
Headmistresses of Independent Schools or the Girls'
Schools Association

THE HEADMASTERS' AND HEADMISTRESSES' CONFERENCE

Chairman (1999), J. Sabben-Clare (Winchester College)
Secretary, V. S. Anthony, 130 Regent Road, Leicester
    LEI 7PG. Tel: 0116-285 4810
Membership Secretary, D. E. Prince. Tel: 0116-285 1567
The annual meeting is held early in October

* Woodard Corporation School, 1 The Sanctuary, London
    SWIP 3JT. Tel: 0171-222 5381
† Girls in VI form
‡ Co-educational
° 1997 figures

Name of School	Foun-ded	No. of pupils	Annual fees £		Head (with date of appointment)
			Boarding	Day	
ENGLAND AND WALES					
Abbotsholme School, Rocester	1889	156‡	13,200	8,820	I. M. Allison (1997)
Abingdon School, Oxon	1256	800	11,511	6,246	M. St J. Parker (1975)
Ackworth School, W. Yorks	1779	370‡	10,761	6,120	M. J. Dickinson (1995)
Aldenham School, Elstree, Herts	1597	385‡	13,170	9,075	S. R. Borthwick (1994)
Alleyn's School, London SE22	1619	920‡	—	6,630	Dr C. H. R. Niven (1992)
Ampleforth College (*RC*), N. Yorks	1802	495†	13,305	6,870	Revd G. F. L. Chamberlain, OSB (1993)
*Ardingly College, Haywards Heath	1858	460‡	13,455	10,185	J. Framlin (1998)
Arnold School, Blackpool	1896	800‡	—	4,200	W. T. Gillen (1993)
Ashville College, Harrogate	1877	610‡	10,329	5,550	M. H. Crosby (1987)
Bablake School, Coventry	1560	850‡	—	4,497	Dr S. Nuttall (1991)
Bancroft's School, Woodford Green, Essex	1727	770‡	—	6,681	Dr P. R. Scott (1996)
Barnard Castle School, Co. Durham	1883	500‡	10,047	5,949	M. D. Featherstone (1997)
Batley Grammar School, W. Yorks	1612	510‡	—	4,527	B. Battye (1998)
Bedales School, Petersfield	1893	409‡	15,045	11,502	Mrs A. A. Willcocks (1995)
Bedford Modern School	1566	950	10,575	5,664	S. Smith (1996)
Bedford School	1552	703	12,720	8,010	Dr I. P. Evans (1990)
Berkhamsted Collegiate School, Herts	1541	970†	12,381	7,683	Dr P. Chadwick (*Principal*) (1996)
Birkdale School, Sheffield	1904	530†	—	5,037	R. J. Court (1998)
°Birkenhead School, Merseyside	1860	677	—	4,155	S. J. Haggett (1988)
Bishop's Stortford College, Herts	1868	324‡	11,610	8,370	J. G. Trotman (1997)
*Bloxham School, Banbury	1860	340‡	14,160	11,085	D. K. Exham (1991)
Blundell's School, Tiverton	1604	454‡	13,395	8,175	J. Leigh (1992)
Bolton School	1524	850	—	4,998	A. W. Wright (1983)
Bootham School, York	1823	375‡	11,550	7,515	I. M. Small (1988)
Bradfield College, Reading	1850	580†	14,160	10,620	P. B. Smith (1985)
Bradford Grammar School	1662	850†	—	4,900	S. R. Davidson (1996)
Brentwood School, Essex	1557	1,053‡	11,975	6,875	J. A. B. Kelsall (1993)
Brighton College, E. Sussex	1845	480‡	14,055	9,066	Dr A. F. Seldon (1997)
°Bristol Cathedral School	1140	470†	—	4,362	K. J. Riley (1993)
Bristol Grammar School	1532	1,030‡	—	4,545	C. E. Martin (1986)
Bromsgrove School, Worcs	1553	670‡	11,340	7,110	T. M. Taylor (1986)
Bryanston School, Blandford Forum	1928	640‡	14,982	10,338	T. D. Wheare (1983)
Bury Grammar School, Lancs	1634	700	—	4,194	K. Richards (1990)
Canford School, Wimbourne	1923	554‡	14,415	10,815	J. D. Lever (1992)
Caterham School, Surrey	1811	700‡	12,507	6,747	R. A. E. Davey (1995)
Charterhouse, Godalming	1611	675†	14,706	12,153	Revd J. S. Witheridge (1996)
Cheadle Hulme School, Cheshire	1855	1,015‡	—	4,797	D. J. Wilkinson (1990)
Cheltenham College, Glos	1841	546‡	13,860	10,425	P. A. Chamberlain (1997)
Chetham's School of Music, Manchester	1653	265‡	16,902	13,083	Revd Canon P. F. Hullah (1992)
Chigwell School, Essex	1629	362‡	11,019	7,248	D. F. Gibbs (1996)

Name of School	Foun-ded	No. of pupils	Annual fees £		Head (with date of appointment)
			Boarding	Day	
Christ College, Brecon	1541	340‡	11,364	8,805	D. P. Jones (1996)
Christ's Hospital, Horsham	1553	794‡	varies	—	Dr P. C. D. Southern (1996)
Churcher's College, Petersfield	1722	550‡	—	5,820	G. W. Buttle (1988)
City of London Freemen's School, Ashtead	1854	420‡	11,187	7,002	D. C. Haywood (1987)
City of London, London EC4	1442	875	—	6,741	W. Duggan (1998)
Clifton College, Bristol	1862	666‡	14,085	9,660	A. H. Monro (1990)
Colfe's School, London SE12	1652	710‡	—	5,985	Dr D. J. Richardson (1990)
Colston's Collegiate School, Bristol	1710	501‡	11,460	6,210	D. G. Crawford (1995)
Cranleigh School, Surrey	1863	480‡	14,535	10,755	G. de W. Waller (1997)
Culford School, Bury St Edmunds	1881	360‡	12,330	8,022	J. S. Richardson (1992)
Dame Allan's Boys' School, Newcastle upon Tyne	1705	440†	—	4,305	D. W. Welsh (*Principal*) (1995)
Dauntsey's School, Devizes	1543	670‡	12,318	7,512	S. B. Roberts (1997)
Dean Close School, Cheltenham	1884	453‡	14,055	9,810	Rev. T. M. Hastie-Smith (1998)
*Denstone College, Uttoxeter	1873	335‡	10,248	6,798	D. M. Derbyshire (1997)
Douai School (*RC*), Upper Woolhampton, Reading	1903	200‡	12,114	8,034	Dr P. McLaughlin (1997)
Downside School (*RC*), Somerset	1607	265	12,612	6,402	Revd Dom. A. Sutch (1996)
Dulwich College, London SE21	1619	1,209	13,965	7,080	G. G. Able (*Master*) (1997)
Durham School	1414	275‡	12,360	8,091	N. G. Kern (1997)
Eastbourne College	1867	501‡	13,590	9,360	C. M. P. Bush (1993)
*Ellesmere College, Shropshire	1884	308‡	12,294	8,142	B. J. Wignall (1996)
Eltham College, London SE9	1842	580†	13,227	6,402	D. M. Green (1990)
Emanuel School, London SW11	1594	780‡	—	5,700	Mrs A-M. Sutcliffe (1998)
Epsom College, Surrey	1855	657‡	13,590	10,095	A. H. Beadles (1993)
Eton College, Windsor	1440	1,284	14,796	—	J. E. Lewis (1994)
Exeter School	1633	690‡	9,339	4,929	N. W. Gamble (1992)
Felsted School, Dunmow, Essex	1564	380‡	14,310	11,280	S. C. Roberts (1993)
Forest School, London E17	1834	970†	10,284	6,552	A. G. Boggis (*Warden*) (1992)
Framlingham College, Woodbridge, Suffolk	1864	450‡	11,733	7,299	Mrs. G. M. Randall (1994)
Frensham Heights, Farnham	1925	300‡	13,800	9,150	P. M. de Voil (1993)
Giggleswick School, Settle	1512	326‡	13,515	8,970	A. P. Millard (1993)
The Grange School, Northwich, Cheshire	1978	592‡	—	4,020	Mrs J. E. Stephen (1997)
Gresham's School, Holt, Norfolk	1555	518‡	13,965	9,945	J. H. Arkell (1991)
Haberdashers' Aske's School, Elstree, Herts	1690	1,100	—	6,696	J. W. R. Goulding (1996)
Haileybury, Hertford	1862	630‡	14,640	10,590	S. A. Westley (*Master*) (1996)
Hampton School, Middx	1557	950	—	6,150	B. R. Martin (1987)
Harrow School, Middx	1571	775	15,000	—	N. R. Bomford (1991)
Hereford Cathedral School	1384	620‡	9,555	5,340	Dr H. C. Tomlinson (1987)
Highgate School, London N6	1565	580	—	8,265	R. P. Kennedy (1989)
Hulme Grammar School, Oldham	1611	690	—	4,185	T. J. Turvey (1995)
*Hurstpierpoint College, Hassocks, W. Sussex	1849	360‡	13,170	10,200	S. D. A. Meek (1995)
Hymers College, Hull	1889	750‡	—	4,266	J. C. Morris (1990)
Ipswich School	1390	583‡	10,026	5,823	I. G. Galbraith (1993)
John Lyon School, Harrow	1876	525	—	6,450	Revd T. J. Wright (1986)
Kelly College, Tavistock	1877	350‡	13,095	8,220	M. Turner (1995)
Kent College, Canterbury	1885	480‡	12,100	6,795	E. B. Halse (1995)
Kimbolton School, Huntingdon	1600	560‡	10,560	5,163	R. V. Peel (1987)
King Edward VI School, Southampton	1553	950‡	—	5,625	P. B. Hamilton (1996)
King Edward VII School, Lytham St Annes	1908	490	—	4,260	P. J. Wilde (1993)
King Edward's School, Bath	1552	680‡	—	5,286	P. J. Winter (1994)
King Edward's School, Birmingham	1552	886	—	5,235	R. M. Dancey (*Chief Master*) (1998)
King Edward's School, Witley, Surrey	1553	396‡	10,695	7,320	R. J. Fox (1988)
King Henry VIII School, Coventry	1545	808‡	—	4,497	T. J. Vardon (1994)
*King's College, Taunton	1880	450‡	13,215	8,700	R. S. Funnell (1988)
King's College School, London SW19	1829	720	—	7,800	A. C. V. Evans (1997)
King's School, Bruton, Somerset	1519	352‡	12,360	5,850	R. I. Smyth (1993)
King's School, Canterbury	600	754‡	14,955	10,335	Revd Canon K. H. Wilkinson (1996)
King's School, Chester	1541	520†	—	4,788	A. R. D. Wickson (1981)
King's School, Ely	970	386‡	13,263	9,108	R. H. Youdale (1992)
King's School, Gloucester	1541	320‡	12,500	6,000	P. Lacey (1992)
King's School, Macclesfield	1502	1,200‡	—	4,755	A. G. Silcock (1987)

Name of School	Foun-ded	No. of pupils	Annual fees £ Boarding	Day	Head (with date of appointment)
King's School, Rochester, Kent	604	326‡	14,025	8,085	Dr I. R. Walker (1987)
*King's School, Tynemouth	1860	638‡	—	4,491	Dr D. Younger (1993)
King's School, Worcester	1541	790‡	11,439	5,919	T. H. Keyes (1998)
Kingston Grammar School, Surrey	1561	600‡	—	6,338	C. D. Baxter (1991)
Kingswood School, Bath	1748	495‡	13,266	7,125	G. M. Best (1987)
*Lancing College, W. Sussex	1848	495‡	14,070	10,575	P. M. Tinniswood (1998)
Latymer Upper School, London w6	1624	950†	—	6,966	C. Diggory (1991)
°Leeds Grammar School	1552	1,104	—	5,316	B. W. Collins (1986)
Leicester Grammar School	1981	646‡	—	4,890	J. B. Sugden (1989)
Leighton Park School, Reading	1890	365‡	12,807	9,612	J. Dunston (1996)
The Leys School, Cambridge	1875	450‡	13,290	8,460	Revd Dr J. C. A. Barrett (1990)
Liverpool College	1840	620‡	—	4,515	J. P. Siviter (*Principal*) (1997)
Llandovery College, Carmarthenshire	1848	230‡	11,095	7,368	Dr C. E. Evans (*Warden*) (1988)
Lord Wandsworth College, Long Sutton, Hants	1912	470‡	11,625	9,045	I. G. Power (1997)
Loughborough Grammar School	1495	970	9,999	5,148	P. B. Fisher (1998)
Magdalen College School, Oxford	1480	538	—	5,664	A. D. Halls (*Master*) (1998)
Malvern College, Worcs	1865	555‡	14,175	8,985	H. C. K. Carson (1997)
Manchester Grammar School	1515	1,450	—	4,800	Dr G. M. Stephen (*High Master*) (1994)
Marlborough College, Wilts	1843	820‡	14,790	10,830	E. J. H. Gould (*Master*) (1993)
Merchant Taylors' School, Liverpool	1620	730	—	1,452	S. J. R. Dawkins (1985)
Merchant Taylors' School, Northwood, Middx	1561	774	12,550	7,550	J. R. Gabitass (1991)
Millfield, Street, Somerset	1935	1,248‡	15,105	9,870	P. M. Johnson (1998)
Mill Hill School, London NW7	1807	560‡	13,290	8,700	W. R. Winfield (1995)
Monkton Combe School, Bath	1868	335‡	13,725	9,375	M. J. Cuthbertson (1990)
Monmouth School	1614	568	9,780	5,871	T. H. P. Haynes (1995)
Mount St Mary's College (*RC*), Sheffield	1842	269‡	10,200	6,150	P. Macdonald (1998)
Newcastle-under-Lyme School	1874	1,120‡	—	4,194	Dr R. M. Reynolds (*Principal*) (1990)
Norwich School	1250	633†	—	5,343	C. D. Brown (1984)
°Nottingham High School	1513	834	—	4,923	C. S. Parker (1995)
Oakham School, Rutland	1584	788‡	13,530	8,100	A. R. M. Little (1996)
The Oratory School (*RC*), Woodcote, Berks	1859	356	13,635	9,540	S. W. Barrow (1991)
Oundle School, Northants	1556	845‡	14,616	—	D. B. McMurray (1984)
Pangbourne College, Berks	1917	320‡	13,197	10,485	A. B. E. Hudson (1988)
Perse School, Cambridge	1615	570†	—	5,526	N. P. V. Richardson (1994)
Plymouth College	1877	604‡	10,977	5,721	A. J. Morsley (1992)
Pocklington School, York	1514	600‡	9,900	5,800	J. N. D. Gray (1992)
Portsmouth Grammar School	1732	800‡	—	5,367	Dr T. R. Hands, D.phil. (1997)
Prior Park College (*RC*), Bath	1830	510‡	12,054	6,669	R. G. G. Mercer, D.phil. (1996)
Queen Elizabeth GS, Wakefield	1591	700†	—	5,001	R. P. Mardling (1985)
Queen Elizabeth's GS, Blackburn	1567	840‡	—	4,740	Dr D. S. Hempsall (1995)
Queen Elizabeth's Hospital, Bristol	1590	530	8,385	4,560	Dr R. Gliddon (1985)
Queen's College, Taunton	1843	462‡	10,590	6,945	C. T. Bradnock (1991)
Radley College, Abingdon	1847	620	14,550	—	R. M. Morgan (*Warden*) (1991)
Ratcliffe College (*RC*), Leicester	1844	508‡	10,329	6,888	T. A. Kilbride (1996)
Reading Blue Coat School	1646	614‡	11,082	6,081	S. J. W. McArthur (1997)
Reed's School, Cobham, Surrey	1813	405†	11,970	9,048	D. W. Jarrett (1997)
Reigate Grammar School, Surrey	1675	810‡	—	5,910	P. V. Dixon (1996)
Rendcomb College, Cirencester	1920	242‡	9,270	7,020	J. Tolputt (1987)
Repton School, Derby	1557	554‡	13,400	10,110	G. E. Jones (1987)
RNIB New College, Worcester	1987	42‡	24,667	22,200	Mrs H. Williams (*Principal*) (1995)
Rossall School, Fleetwood, Lancs	1844	253‡	12,600	4,725	R. D. W. Rhodes (1987)
Royal Grammar School, Guildford	1552	850	—	6,660	T. M. S. Young (1992)
Royal Grammar School, Newcastle upon Tyne	1545	915	—	4,527	J. F. X. Miller (1994)
Royal Grammar School, Worcester	1291	745	—	5,130	W. A. Jones (1993)
Royal Hospital School, Ipswich	1712	650‡	12,054	6,450	N. K. D. Ward (1995)
Rugby School	1567	730‡	14,610	8,760	M. B. Mavor, CVO (1990)
Rydal Penrhos School, Colwyn Bay	1880	387‡	11,562	8,152	M. S. James (1998)
Ryde School with Upper Chine, Isle of Wight	1921	450‡	9,690	4,740	Dr N. J. England (1997)
St Albans School	1570	680†	—	6,570	A. R. Grant (1993)
°St Bede's College (*RC*), Manchester	1876	1,002‡	—	4,170	J. Byrne (1983)

Name of School	Founded	No. of pupils	Annual fees £		Head (with date of appointment)
			Boarding	Day	
St Bees School, Cumbria	1583	292‡	12,435	8,556	Mrs J. D. Pickering (1998)
St Benedict's School (*RC*), London w5	1902	582†	—	5,790	Dr A. J. Dachs (1987)
St Dunstan's College, London se6	1888	670‡	—	6,114	D. I. Davies (1998)
St Edmund's College (*RC*), Ware, Herts	1568	400‡	11,535	7,185	D. J. J. McEwen (1984)
St Edmund's School, Canterbury	1749	260‡	13,923	8,988	A. N. Ridley (1994)
St Edward's School, Oxford	1863	555‡	14,250	10,140	D. Christie (*Warden*) (1988)
St George's College (*RC*), Addlestone, Surrey	1869	600‡	—	7,290	J. A. Peake (1995)
St John's School, Leatherhead, Surrey	1851	425‡	12,300	8,550	C. H. Tongue (1993)
St Lawrence College in Thanet, Ramsgate	1879	340‡	13,635	8,745	M. Slater (1996)
St Mary's College (*RC*), Liverpool	1919	617‡	—	4,253	W. Hammond (1991)
St Paul's School, London sw13	1509	770	14,235	9,435	R. S. Baldock (*High Master*) (1992)
St Peter's School, York	627	508‡	11,679	8,061	A. F. Trotman (1995)
Sedbergh School, Cumbria	1525	287	13,920	10,305	C. H. Hirst (1995)
Sevenoaks School, Kent	1418	946‡	14,355	9,108	T. R. Cookson (1996)
Sherborne School, Dorset	1550	555	14,400	10,800	P. H. Lapping (1988)
Shiplake College, Henley-on-Thames	1959	300†	12,945	8,730	N. Bevan (1988)
Shrewsbury School	1552	695	14,325	10,080	F. E. Maidment (1988)
Silcoates School, Wakefield	1820	426‡	—	5,760	A. P. Spillane (1991)
Solihull School	1560	794†	—	4,740	P. S. J. Derham (1996)
°Stamford School, Lincs	1532	550	9,048	4,524	J. Hale (*Principal*) (1997)
Stockport Grammar School	1487	1,000‡	—	4,527	I. Mellor (1996)
Stonyhurst College *(RC)*, Clitheroe	1593	395‡	12,540	7,800	A. J. F. Aylward (1996)
Stowe School, Bucks	1923	580‡	14,940	10,800	J. G. L. Nichols (1989)
Sutton Valence School, Kent	1576	374‡	13,140	8,400	N. A. Sampson (1994)
Taunton School	1847	450‡	12,585	8,070	J. P. Whiteley (1997)
Tettenhall College, Wolverhampton	1863	284‡	9,798	6,039	Dr P. C. Bodkin (1994)
Tonbridge School, Kent	1553	702	15,075	10,650	J. M. Hammond (1990)
Trent College, Nottingham	1868	640‡	11,850	7,300	J. S. Lee (1989)
Trinity School, Croydon	1596	850	—	5,961	B. J. Lenon (1995)
Truro School	1879	780‡	10,065	5,304	G. A. G. Dodd (1993)
University College School, London nw3	1830	700	—	8,010	K. J. Durham (1996)
°Uppingham School, Oakham, Rutland	1584	642†	13,920	9,000	Dr S. C. Winkley, d.phil. (1991)
Warwick School	914	820	11,667	5,466	Dr P. J. Cheshire (1988)
Wellingborough School, Northants	1595	380‡	10,890	6,195	F. R. Ullmann (1993)
Wellington College, Crowthorne, Berks	1856	808‡	14,370	10,560	C. J. Driver (*Master*) (1989)
Wellington School, Somerset	1837	516‡	9,300	5,088	A. J. Rogers (1990)
Wells Cathedral School, Somerset	1180	595‡	11,502	6,831	J. S. Baxter (1986)
West Buckland School, Barnstaple, Devon	1858	493‡	10,380	5,880	J. F. Vick (1997)
Westminster School, London sw1	1560	655‡	15,375	11,550	T. Jones-Parry (1998)
Whitgift School, South Croydon	1596	1,100	—	6,699	C. A. Barnett, d.phil. (1991)
William Hulme's GS, Manchester	1887	725‡	—	4,527	B. J. Purvis (1997)
Winchester College	1382	680	15,345	11,709	J. P. Sabben-Clare (1985)
Wisbech Grammar School, Cambs	1379	630‡	—	5,400	R. S. Repper (1988)
Wolverhampton Grammar School	1512	785‡	—	5,700	Dr B. Trafford (1990)
Woodbridge School, Suffolk	1662	550‡	10,656	6,330	S. H. Cole (1994)
Woodhouse Grove School, Bradford	1812	575‡	10,500	6,120	D. C. Humphreys (1996)
*Worksop College, Notts	1895	370‡	12,375	8,490	R. A. Collard (1994)
Worth School (*RC*), Crawley	1959	320	13,179	9,024	Fr C. Jamison, ocb (1994)
Wrekin College, Telford	1880	320‡	13,080	7,920	S. Drew (1998)
Wycliffe College, Stonehouse, Glos	1882	393‡	14,805	9,660	Dr R. A. Collins (1998)
Yarm School, Stockton-on-Tees	1978	560†	—	5,673	R. N. Tate (1978)

Scotland

Daniel Stewart's and Melville College, Edinburgh	1832	778	9,810	5,091	P. J. F. Tobin (1989)
Dollar Academy, Clackmannanshire	1818	756‡	10,701	4,833	J. S. Robertson (*Rector*) (1994)
The High School of Dundee	1239	715‡	—	4,398	A. M. Duncan (1997)
The Edinburgh Academy	1824	483†	12,159	5,703	J. V. Light (*Rector*) (1995)
Fettes College, Edinburgh	1870	392‡	14,205	9,585	M. C. B. Spens (1998)
George Heriot's School, Edinburgh	1659	931‡	—	4,404	A. G. Hector (1998)
George Watson's College, Edinburgh	1741	1,265‡	9,798	4,800	F. E. Gerstenberg (*Principal*) (1986)
Glasgow Academy	1845	568‡	—	4,875	D. Comins (*Rector*) (1994)
Glenalmond College, Perth	1841	370‡	13,785	9,195	I. G. Templeton (*Warden*) (1992)

Name of School	Foun-ded	No. of pupils	Annual fees £		Head (with date of appointment)
			Boarding	Day	
Gordonstoun School, Elgin	1934	430‡	13,563	8,754	M. C. Pyper (1990)
High School of Glasgow	1124	644‡	—	4,995	R. G. Easton (*Rector*) (1983)
Hutcheson's Grammar School, Glasgow	1641	1,252‡	—	4,473	D. R. Ward (*Rector*) (1987)
Kelvinside Academy, Glasgow	1878	400	—	5,200	J. L. Broadfoot (*Rector*) (1998)
°Loretto School, Musselburgh	1827	319‡	12,195	8,130	K. J. Budge (1995)
Merchiston Castle School, Edinburgh	1833	375	13,470	9,045	A. R. Hunter (1998)
Morrison's Academy, Crieff	1860	393‡	12,450	4,440	G. H. Edwards (*Rector*) (1996)
Robert Gordon's College, Aberdeen	1729	940‡	—	4,800	B. R. W. Lockhart (1996)
°St Aloysius' College, Glasgow	1859	811‡	—	3,500	Revd A. Porter, sj (1995)
St Colomba's School, Kilmacolm	1897	360‡	—	4,473	A. H. Livingstone (1987)
Strathallan School, Perth	1913	420‡	13,500	9,300	A. W. McPhail (1993)
NORTHERN IRELAND					
°Bangor Grammar School	1856	913	—	450	T. W. Patton (1979)
Belfast Royal Academy	1785	1,374‡	—	80	W. M. Sillery (1980)
Campbell College, Belfast	1894	725	6,204	1,317	Dr R. J. I. Pollock (1987)
Coleraine Academical Institution	1856	220	—	75	R. S. Forsythe (1984)
°Methodist College, Belfast	1868	1,864‡	3,449	244	T. W. Mulryne (*Principal*) (1988)
Portora Royal School, Enniskillen	1618	460	—	42	R. L. Bennett (1983)
Royal Belfast Academical Institution	1810	1,050	—	495	R. M. Ridley (*Principal*) (1990)
CHANNEL ISLANDS AND ISLE OF MAN					
Elizabeth College, Guernsey	1563	514†	7,410	2,910	D. E. Toze (1998)
King William's College, Isle of Man	1668	300‡	12,630	9,090	P. K. Fulton-Peebles (*Principal*) (1996)
Victoria College, Jersey	1852	619	—	2,064	J. Hydes (1992)
EUROPE					
Aiglon College, Switzerland	1949	224‡	Fr.58,400	Fr.38,410	R. McDonald (1994)
British School in The Netherlands	1935	560‡	—	Gld.21,720	M. J. Cooper (1990)
British School of Brussels	1970	518‡	—	Fr.697,000	Ms J. M. Bray (*Principal*) (1992)
British School of Paris	1954	340‡	Fr.115,000	Fr.85,000	M. Honour (*Principal*) (1992)
The International School of Geneva	1924	1,074‡	—	Fr.19,420	G. Walker, OBE (*Director-General*) (1991)
King's College, Madrid	1969	580‡	Pesetas 2.18m	Pesetas 1.29m	C. T. G. Leech (1997)
St Columba's College, Dublin	1843	265‡	Ir6,675	Ir3,855	T. E. Macey (*Warden*) (1988)
°St Edward's College, Malta	1929	400†	—	LM.780	G. Briscoe (1989)
°St George's English School, Rome	1958	320‡	—	L.18m	Mrs B. Gardner (1994)
St Julian's School, Portugal	1932	475‡	—	Esc.1.2m	F. D. Styan, OBE (1994)

OTHER OVERSEAS MEMBERS

AFRICA

DIOCESAN COLLEGE, Rondebosch, SA. *Head*, C. N. Watson

FALCON COLLEGE, PO Esigodini, Zimbabwe. *Head*, P. N. Todd

HILTON COLLEGE, Kwazulu-Natal, SA. *Head*, M. J. Nicholson

MICHAELHOUSE, Balgowan, SA. *Head*, R. D. Forde

PETERHOUSE, Marondera, Zimbabwe. *Head*, M. A. Bawden

ST GEORGE'S COLLEGE, Harare, Zimbabwe. *Head*, Fr P. Edwards

ST JOHN'S COLLEGE, Johannesburg, SA. *Head*, R. J. D. Clarence

ST STITHIAN'S COLLEGE, Randburg, SA. *Head*, D. B. Wylde

AUSTRALIA

BRIGHTON GRAMMAR SCHOOL, Brighton, Victoria. *Head*, M. S. Urwin

BRISBANE BOYS' COLLEGE, Toowong, Queensland. *Head*, acting head

CAMBERWELL GRAMMAR SCHOOL, Balwyn, Victoria. *Head*, C. F. Black

CANBERRA GRAMMAR SCHOOL, Red Hill, ACT. *Head*, T. C. Murray

CAULFIELD GRAMMAR SCHOOL, Elsternwick, Victoria. *Head*, S. H. Newton

CHRIST CHURCH GRAMMAR SCHOOL, Claremont, W. Australia. *Head*, J. J. S. Madin

CRANBROOK SCHOOL, Sydney, NSW. *Head*, Dr B. N. Carter

THE GEELONG COLLEGE, Geelong, Victoria. *Head*, Dr P. Turner

GEELONG GRAMMAR SCHOOL, Corio, Victoria. *Head*, L. Hannah

GUILDFORD GRAMMAR SCHOOL, Guildford, W. Australia. *Head*, K. Walton

HAILEYBURY COLLEGE, Keysborough, Victoria. *Head*, A. H. M. Aikman

THE HALE SCHOOL, Wembley Downs, W. Australia. *Head*, R. J. Inverarity

IVANHOE GRAMMAR SCHOOL, Ivanhoe, Victoria. *Head*, R. D. Fraser

Kinross Wolaroi School, Orange, NSW. *Head,*
  A. E. S. Anderson
Knox Grammar School, Wahroonga, NSW. *Head,*
  Dr I. Paterson
Melbourne Grammar School, South Yarra, Victoria.
  Head, A. P. Sheahan
Mentone Grammar School, Mentone, Victoria. *Head,*
  N. Clark
Newington College, Stanmore, NSW. *Head,*
  M. E. Smee
St Peter's College, St Peter's, S. Australia. *Head,*
  R. L. Burchnall
Scotch College, Adelaide, S. Australia. *Head,* K. Webb
Scotch College, Melbourne, Victoria. *Head,*
  Dr F. G. Donaldson
The Scots College, Sydney, NSW. *Head,* Dr R. L. Iles
The Southport School, Southport, Queensland. *Head,*
  B. A. Cook
Sydney Church of England Grammar School,
  Sydney, NSW. *Head,* R. A. I. Grant
Sydney Grammar School, Darlinghurst, NSW. *Head,*
  Dr R. D. Townsend
Trinity Grammar School, Strathfield, NSW. *Head,*
  G. M. Cujes
Wesley College, Melbourne, Victoria. *Head,*
  D. G. McArthur
Westbourne and Williamstown Grammar
  Schools, Hoppers Crossing, Victoria. *Head,* G. G. Ryan

Bermuda

Saltus Grammar School, Hamilton. *Head,*
  R. T. Rowell

Canada

Brentwood College School, Mill Bay, BC. *Head,*
  W. T. Ross
Glenlyon-Norfolk School, Victoria, BC. *Head,*
  D. Brooks
Hillfield Strathallan College, Hamilton, Ontario.
  Head, W. S. Boyer
Ridley College, St Catherine, Ontario. *Head,* R. D. Lane
St Andrew's College, Aurora, Ontario. *Head,*
  R. P. Bedard
Trinity College School, Port Hope, Ontario. *Head,*
  R. C. N. Wright
Upper Canada College, Toronto, Ontario. *Head,*
  J. D. Blakey

Hong Kong

Island School, Borrett Road. *Head,* D. J. James
King George V School, Kowloon. *Head,* M. J. Behennah

India

Bishop Cotton School, Shimla. *Head,* K. K. Mustafi
The Cathedral and John Connon School, Bombay.
  Head, Mrs M. Isaacs
The Lawrence School, Sanawar. *Head,* Dr H. S. Dhillon
The Scindia School, Gwalior. *Head,* A. N. Dar

Korea

Yang Chung High School, Seoul. *Head,* Dr K. B. Uhm

Malaysia

Kolej Tuanku Ja'afar, Negeri Sembilan. *Head,*
  P. D. Briggs

New Zealand

Ballarat and Clarendon College, Victoria. *Head,*
  D. S. Shepherd
Christ's College, Christchurch. *Head,* R. A. Zordan
King's College, Auckland. *Head,* J. S. Taylor

St Andrew's College, Christchurch. *Head,* B. J. Maister
Wanganui Collegiate School, Wanganui. *Head,*
  J. R. Hensman

Pakistan

Aitchison College, Lahore. *Head,* S. Khan
Karachi Grammar School, Karachi. *Head,*
  H. H. A. Pullau

South and Central America

Academia Britanica Cuscatleca, Santa Tecla, El
  Salvador. *Head,* R. Braund
The British Schools, Montevideo, Uruguay. *Head,*
  C. D. T. Smith
Markham College, Lima, Peru. *Head,* W. J. Baker
St Andrew's Scots School, Buenos Aires, Argentina.
  Head, A. G. F. Fisher
St George's College, Buenos Aires, Argentina. *Head,*
  N. P. O. Green
St Pauls' School, São Paulo, Brazil. *Head,*
  M. T. M. C. McCann

USA

St Mark's College, Southborough, Massachusetts.
  Head, A. J. de V. Hill

ADDITIONAL MEMBERS

The headteachers of some maintained schools are by
invitation Additional Members of the HMC. They
include the following:

Bishop Wordsworth's School, Salisbury. *Head,*
  C. D. Barnett
Durham Johnston Comprehensive School, Durham.
  Head, Dr J. Dunford, OBE
Eggbuckland College, Plymouth. *Head,* H. E. Green
Gordano School, Bristol. *Head,* R. Sommers
Haberdashers' Aske's Hatcham College, London
  SE14. *Head,* Dr E. M. Sidwell
Haywards Heath College, W. Sussex. *Head,*
  B. W. Derbyshire
The Judd School, Tonbridge, Kent. *Head,* K. A. Starling
King Edward VI Five Ways School, Birmingham.
  Head, J. Knowles
Lancaster Royal Grammar School, Lancaster. *Head,*
  P. J. Mawby
The London Oratory School, London SW6. *Head,*
  J. C. McIntosh, OBE
Prince Henry's Grammar School, Otley, W Yorks.
  Head, M. Franklin
Prince William School, Oundle, Cambs. *Head,*
  C. J. Lowe
Royal Grammar School, High Wycombe, Bucks. *Head,*
  D. R. Levin
St Ambrose College, Altrincham, Cheshire. *Head,*
  G. E. Hester
St Anselm's College, Birkenhead, Merseyside. *Head,*
  C. J. Cleugh
St Edward's College, Liverpool. *Head,* John Waszek
St Olave's Grammar School, Orpington, Kent. *Head,*
  T. Jarvis

SOCIETY OF HEADMASTERS AND HEADMISTRESSES OF INDEPENDENT SCHOOLS

The Society was founded in 1961 and, in general, represents smaller boarding schools.

General Secretary, I. D. Cleland, Celedston, Rhosesmor Road, Halkyn, Holywell CH8 8DL. Tel: 01352-781102

Headmasters/mistresses of the following schools are members of both HMC and SHMIS; details of these schools appear in the HMC list: Abbotsholme School, Ackworth School, Bedales School, Churcher's College, Colston's Collegiate School, King's School, Gloucester, King's School, Tynemouth, Leighton Park School, Lord Wandsworth College, Pangbourne College, Reading Blue Coat School, Reed's School, Rendcomb College, Royal Hospital School, Rydal Penrhos School, Ryde School, St

George's College, Shiplake College, Silcoates School, Tettenhall College, Wisbech Grammar School, Yarm School

The Headmistress of King Edward VI High School for Girls is a member of both SHMIS and GSA; details of the school are given in the GSA list

CSC Church Schools Company, Church Schools House, Chapel Street, Titchmarsh, Kettering, Northants NN14 3DA. Tel: 01832-735105
* Woodard Corporation School
† Girls in VI form
‡ Co-educational

Name of School	Foun-ded	No. of pupils	Annual fees £		Head (with date of appointment)
			Boarding	Day	
Abbey Gate College, Saighton, Chester	1977	264‡	—	4,755	E. W. Mitchell (1991)
Austin Friars School (*RC*), Carlisle	1951	304‡	9,009	5,215	Revd D. Middleton (1996)
Battle Abbey School, E. Sussex	1912	120‡	10,485	6,510	R. Clark (1998)
Bearwood College, Wokingham	1827	230‡	11,700	6,825	S. G. G. Aiano (1998)
Bedstone College, Bucknell, Shropshire	1948	155‡	11,700	6,450	M. S. Symonds (1990)
Bentham Grammar School, N. Yorks	1726	200‡	10,485	5,640	T. Halliwell (1995)
Bethany School, Cranbrook, Kent	1866	290‡	11,136	7,125	N. Dorey (1998)
Birkdale School, Sheffield	1904	530†	—	5,037	R. Court (1998)
Box Hill School, Dorking	1959	265‡	11,694	6,804	Dr R. A. S. Atwood (1987)
Claremont Fan Court School, Esher	1932	348‡	10,695	6,750	Mrs. P. B. Farrar (*Principal*) (1994)
Clayesmore School, Blandford Forum	1896	307‡	12,726	8,913	D. J. Beeby (1986)
Cokethorpe School, Witney, Oxon	1957	280‡	13,200	7,600	P. J. S. Cantwell (1995)
Duke of York's Royal Military School, Dover	1803	495‡	855	—	G. H. Wilson (1992)
Elmhurst Ballet School, Camberley	1903	200‡	10,965	8,064	J. McNamara (*Principal*) (1995)
Embley Park School, Romsey, Hants	1946	275‡	10,695	6,510	D. F. Chapman (1987)
Ewell Castle School, Epsom	1926	300	—	5205	R. A. Fewtrell (*Principal*) (1983)
Friends' School, Saffron Walden	1702	200‡	11,700	7,020	Ms J. Laing (1996)
Fulneck School (Boys), Pudsey, W. Yorks	1753	260‡	10,095	5,385	Mrs H. Gordon, (*Principal* (1996)
*Grenville College, Bideford	1954	270‡	11,631	5,760	Dr M. C. V. Cane (1992)
Halliford School, Shepperton, Middx	1956	300†	—	5,220	J. R. Crook (1984)
Hipperholme Grammar School, Halifax	1648	335‡	—	4,320	C. C. Robinson (1988)
Keil School, Dumbarton	1915	200‡	11,034	6,186	J. A. Cummings (1993)
Kingham Hill School, Chipping Norton	1886	220‡	10,170	6,090	M. H. Payne (1991)
Kirkham Grammar School, Preston	1549	600‡	8,463	4,335	B. Stacey (1991)
Langley School, Norwich	1910	260‡	11,850	6,120	J. Malcolm (1997)
Lincoln Minster School (*CSC*)	1905	216‡	9,450	5,295	Mrs M. Bradley (1996)
Lomond School, Helensburgh, Argyll and Bute	1977	300‡	11,190	5,220	A. D. Macdonald (1986)
Milton Abbey School, Blandford Forum	1954	210	13,500	9,450	W. J. Hughes-D'Aeth (1995)
Oswestry School, Shropshire	1407	350‡	11,442	6,816	P. K. Smith (1995)
The Purcell School (music), Harrow	1962	151‡	15,348	9,060	K. J. Bain (1983)
Rannoch School, Rannoch, By Pitlochry	1959	230‡	11,655	6,105	Dr J. D. Halliday (1997)
Rishworth School, W. Yorks	1724	360‡	9,720	5,265	R. A. Baker (1998)
Rougemont School, Newport	1974	300‡	—	4,941	I. Brown (1995)
Royal Russell School, Croydon	1853	450‡	11,955	6,165	Dr J. R. Jennings (1996)
Royal School, Dungannon, N. Ireland	1614	690‡	3,970	110	P. D. Hewitt (1986)
Royal Wolverhampton School	1850	298‡	11,625	5,880	Mrs B. A. Evans (1995)
Ruthin School, Denbighshire	1574	169‡	11,235	7,185	J. S. Rowlands (1993)
St Bede's School, Hailsham	1979	500‡	13,050	7,875	R. A. Perrin (1978)
St Christopher School, Letchworth	1915	345‡	11,910	6,750	C. Reid (1981)
St David's College, Llandudno	1965	200	10,740	6,987	W. Seymour (1991)
St Edward's School, Cheltenham	1987	500‡	—	6,075	A. J. Martin (1991)
Scarborough College, N. Yorks	1898	387‡	10,539	5,715	T. L. Kirkup (1996)
Seaford College, Petworth, W. Sussex	1884	275‡	11,400	7,500	T. J. Mullins (1997)
Shebbear College, North Devon	1841	225‡	10,905	5,850	L. D. Clark (1997)
Sibford School, Banbury	1842	252‡	11,700	5,805	Ms S. Freestone (1997)

Name of School	Foun-ded	No. of pupils	Annual fees £		Head (with date of appointment)
			Boarding	Day	
Sidcot School, North Somerset	1808	410‡	11,625	6,450	A. Slesser (1997)
Stafford Grammar School	1982	303‡	—	4,491	M. Darley (1998)
Stanbridge Earls School, Romsey, Hants	1952	186‡	13,500	10,050	H. Moxon (1984)
Sunderland High School (*CSC*)	1887	310‡	—	4,530	Dr A. Slater (1998)
Thetford Grammar School, Norfolk	1119	220‡	—	4,827	J. R. Weeks (1990)
Warminster School, Wilts	1707	272‡	10,605	5,985	D. Dowdles (1998)
Yehudi Menuhin School (music), Surrey	1963	46‡	varies	—	P. N. Chisholm (1988)

GIRLS' SCHOOLS ASSOCIATION

THE GIRLS' SCHOOLS ASSOCIATION, 130 Regent Road, Leicester LEI 7PG. Tel: 0116-254 1619
President, Mrs J. Anderson
Secretary, Ms S. Cooper

Headmasters/mistresses of the following schools are members of both HMC and GSA; details of these schools appear in the HMC list: Berkhamsted Collegiate School, Rydal Penrhos School, Stamford Endowed Schools

CSC Church Schools Company
§ Girls Day School Trust, 100 Rochester Row, London SWIP IJP. Tel: 0171-393 6666
* Woodard Corporation School
† Boys in VI form
‡ Co-educational
° 1997 figures

Name of School	Foun-ded	No. of pupils	Annual fees £		Head (with date of appointment)
ENGLAND AND WALES			Boarding	Day	
Abbey School, Reading	1887	692	—	4,820	Miss B. C. L. Sheldon (1991)
°Abbot's Hill, Hemel Hempstead	1912	153	11,250	6,645	Mrs K. Lewis (1997)
Adcote School for Girls, Shrewsbury	1907	76	10,710	6,150	Mrs A. E. Read (1997)
Alice Ottley School, Worcester	1883	510	—	5,760	Miss C. Sibbit (1986)
Amberfield School, Ipswich	1952	151	—	4,410	Mrs L. A. Lewis (1992)
Ashford School, Kent	1910	400	12,897	7,422	Mrs J. Burnett (1997)
Atherley School, Southampton (*CSC*)	1926	220	—	4,941	Miss A. Burrows (1997)
Badminton School, Bristol	1858	306	13,425	7,425	Mrs J. A. Scarrow (1997)
Bedford High School	1882	700	10,890	5,832	Mrs B. E. Stanley (1995)
Bedgebury School, Goudhurst, Kent	1860	209	12,570	7,806	Mrs L. J. Griffin (1995)
Beechwood Sacred Heart (*RC*), Tunbridge Wells	1915	180	11,940	7,365	Dr S. Price-Cabrera (1997)
§Belvedere School, Liverpool	1880	469	—	4,356	Mrs G. Richards (1997)
Benenden School, Cranbrook, Kent	1923	450	14,997	—	Mrs G. du Charme (1985)
§Birkenhead High School	1901	640	—	4,356	Mrs C. H. Evans (1997)
§Blackheath High School, London SE3	1880	354	—	5,268	Miss R. K. Musgrave (1989)
Bolton School	1877	786	—	4,998	Miss E. J. Panton (1994)
Bradford Girls' Grammar School	1875	659	—	4,728	Mrs L. J. Warrington (1987)
§Brighton and Hove High School	1876	507	—	4,356	Miss R. A. Woodbridge (1989)
Brigidine School, Windsor	1948	192	—	5,280	Mrs M. B. Cairns (1986)
§Bromley High School, Kent	1883	551	—	5,268	Mrs E. J. Hancock (1989)
Bruton School, Somerset	1900	480	9,450	5,200	Mrs A. Napier (*acting*) (1998)
Burgess Hill School, W. Sussex	1906	350	10,635	6,285	Mrs R. F. Lewis (1992)
Bury Grammar School, Lancs	1884	793	—	4,194	Miss C. H. Thompson (1998)
Casterton School, Carnforth, Lancs	1823	351	10,755	6,840	A. F. Thomas (1990)
§Central Newcastle High School	1895	597	—	4,356	Mrs A. M. Chapman (1985)
°Channing School, London N6	1885	335	—	6,210	Mrs I. R. Raphael (1984)
Cheltenham Ladies' College, Glos	1853	856	15,720	10,080	Mrs A. V. Tuck (*Principal*) (1996)
City of London School for Girls, London EC2	1894	566	—	6,237	Mrs Y. A. Burne, PH.D. (1995)
Clifton High School, Bristol	1877	387	8,565	4,965	Mrs M. C. Culligan (1998)
Cobham Hall, Kent	1962	200	12,750	8,700	Mrs R. J. McCarthy (1989)
Colston's Girls' School, Bristol	1891	453	—	4,285	Mrs J. P. Franklin (1989)
Combe Bank School, Sevenoaks	1868	200	—	6,780	Miss N. Spurr (1993)
Commonweal Lodge School, Purley, Surrey	1916	100	—	5,100	Mrs S. C. Law (*Principal*) (1995)
Cranford House School, Moulsford, Oxon	1931	85	—	5,850	Mrs A. B. Gray (1992)
Croham Hurst School, South Croydon	1899	327	—	5,490	Miss S. C. Budgen (1994)
§Croydon High School	1874	685	—	5,268	Miss L. M. Ogilvie (1998)
Dame Alice Harpur School, Bedford	1882	725	—	5,340	Mrs R. Randle (1990)

Name of School	Foun-ded	No. of pupils	Annual fees £ Boarding	Day	Head (with date of appointment)
Dame Allan's Girls' School, Newcastle upon Tyne	1705	390†	—	4,305	D. W. Welsh (*Principal*) (1995)
°Derby High School for Girls	1892	313	—	4,680	G. H. Goddard, ph.d. (1983)
Downe House, Newbury	1907	581	14,175	10,275	Mrs E. McKendrick (1997)
Dunottar School, Reigate	1926	280	—	5,655	Ms M. J. Skinner (1997)
Durham High School for Girls	1884	259	—	5,739	Mrs A. J. Temploman (1998)
Edgbaston Church of England College, Birmingham	1886	149	—	5,100	Mrs A. Varley-Tipton (1992)
Edgbaston High School for Girls, Birmingham	1876	510	—	4,860	Miss E. Mullenger (1998)
Elmslie Girls' School, Blackpool	1918	150	—	4,620	Miss S. J. Woodward (1997)
Farlington School, Horsham	1896	270	11,040	6,795	Mrs P. M. Mawer (1992)
Farnborough Hill, Hants	1889	500	—	5,499	Miss J. Thomas (1998)
°Farringtons and Stratford House, Chislehurst	1911	300	10,914	5,595	Mrs B. J. Stock (1987)
Francis Holland School, London nw1	1878	380	—	6,345	Mrs G. Low (1998)
Francis Holland School, London sw1	1881	250	—	7,110	Miss S. Pattenden (1997)
Gateways School, Harewood, W. Yorks	1941	185	—	4,698	Mrs D. Davidson (1997)
Godolphin and Latymer School, London w6	1905	703	—	6,630	Miss M. Rudland (1986)
Godolphin School, Salisbury	1726	400	12,480	7,476	Miss M. J. Horsburgh (1996)
Greenacre School, Banstead	1933	228	—	5,625	Mrs P. M. Wood (1990)
Guildford High School (*CSC*)	1888	539	—	5,967	Mrs S. H. Singer (1991)
Haberdashers' Aske's School for Girls, Elstree, Herts	1873	850	—	4,980	Mrs P. Penney (1991)
Haberdashers' Monmouth School	1891	585	9,837	5,223	Dr B. Despontin (1997)
Harrogate Ladies' College	1893	356	10,935	6,900	Dr M. J. Hustler (1996)
Headington School, Oxford	1915	530	11,385	5,940	Mrs H. A. Fender (1996)
Heathfield School, Ascot, Berks	1900	220	14,625	—	Mrs J. M. Benammar (1992)
§Heathfield School, Pinner, Middx	1900	326	—	5,268	Miss C. M. Juett (1997)
Hethersett Old Hall School, Norwich	1928	188	10,800	5,430	Mrs V. M. Redington (1983)
Highclare School, Birmingham	1932	196†	—	4,905	Mrs C. A. Hanson (1974)
Hollygirt School, Nottingham	1877	224	—	4,116	Mrs M. I. Connolly (1997)
Holy Child School, Birmingham	1933	147	—	5,109	Mrs J. M. C. Hill (1995)
Holy Trinity College, Bromley	1886	258	—	4,930	Mrs D. A. Bradshaw (1994)
Holy Trinity School, Kidderminster	1903	173	—	4,260	Mrs E. L. Thomas (1998)
Howell's School, Denbigh	1859	200	10,785	7,485	Mrs S. Gordon (1998)
§Howell's School, Llandaff, Cardiff	1860	561	—	4,356	Mrs C. J. Fitz (1991)
Hull High School (*CSC*)	1890	153	—	4,572	Mrs M. A. Benson (1994)
Hulme Grammar School, Oldham	1895	522	—	4,185	Miss M. S. Smolenski (1992)
§Ipswich High School	1878	448	—	4,356	Miss V. C. MacCuish (1993)
James Allen's Girls' School, London se22	1741	740	—	6,501	Mrs M. O. Gibbs (1994)
Kent College, Tunbridge Wells	1885	244	13,080	7,710	Miss B. J. Crompton (1990)
King Edward VI High School for Girls, Birmingham	1883	550	—	5,034	Ms S. H. Evans (1996)
King's High School for Girls, Warwick	1879	550	—	4,980	Mrs J. M. Anderson (1987)
°Kingsley School, Leamington Spa	1884	460	—	4,725	Mrs Mannion Watson (1997)
Lady Eleanor Holles School, Hampton, Middx	1711	726	—	6,600	Miss E. M. Candy (1981)
°La Retraite School, Salisbury	1953	120	—	4,845	Mrs R. A. Simmons (1994)
La Sagesse Convent High School, Newcastle upon Tyne	1906	340	—	4,728	Miss L. Clark (1994)
Lavant House and Rosemead, Chichester	1919	100	11,490	6,450	Mrs S. E. Watkins (1996)
Leeds Girls' High School	1876	617	—	5,199	Mrs S. Fishburn (1997)
Leicester High School	1906	306	—	4,950	Mrs P. A. Watson (1992)
Loughborough High School	1850	549	—	4,689	Miss J. E. L. Harvatt (1978)
Luckley-Oakfield School, Wokingham	1895	264	10,092	5,805	R. C. Blake (1984)
Malvern Girls' College, Worcs	1893	250	13,800	9,210	Mrs P. Leggate (1996)
Manchester High School	1874	726‡	—	4,590	Mrs C. Lee-Jones (1998)
Manor House School, Little Bookham, Surrey	1927	145	8,940	6,210	Mrs L. Mendes (1989)
Marymount International School, Kingston upon Thames	1955	237	15,550	9,050	Sr R. Sheridan (1990)
Maynard School, Exeter	1877	440	—	5,055	Miss F. Murdin (1980)
Merchant Taylors' School, Liverpool	1888	660	—	4,356	Mrs J. I. Mills (1994)
Moira House School, Eastbourne	1875	210	12,930	8,190	Mrs A. Harris (*Principal*) (1997)
More House School, London sw1	1953	220	—	6,300	Miss M. Connell (1991)
Moreton Hall, Oswestry	1913	260	13,230	9,135	J. Forster (1992)
Mount School, York	1831	280	11,655	7,176	Miss B. J. Windle (1986)
Newcastle upon Tyne Church High School	1885	385	—	4,494	Mrs L. G. Smith (1996)

Name of School	Foun-ded	No. of pupils	Annual fees £		Head (with date of appointment)
			Boarding	Day	
New Hall School, Chelmsford	1642	420	12,240	7,950	Sr Anne-Marie (1996)
Northampton High School	1878	599	—	4,650	Mrs L. A. Mayne (1988)
°North Foreland Lodge, Hook	1909	150	11,550	7,050	Miss S. Cameron (1996)
North London Collegiate School, Edgware	1850	760	—	5,850	Mrs B. McCabe (1997)
Northwood College, Middx	1878	451	—	5,790	Mrs J. A. Mayou (1992)
§Norwich High School	1875	662	—	4,356	Mrs V. C. Bidwell (1985)
Notre Dame Senior School, Cobham, Surrey	1937	300	—	5,325	Sr F. Ede (1987)
§Nottingham High School for Girls	1875	849	—	4,356	Mrs A. C. Rees (1996)
§Notting Hill and Ealing High School, London W13	1873	567	—	5,268	Mrs S. M. Whitfield (1991)
Ockbrook School, Derby	1799	480	8,085	4,380	Miss D. P. Bolland (1995)
Old Palace School, Croydon	1887	600	—	4,950	Miss K. L. Hilton (1974)
§Oxford High School	1875	548	—	4,356	Miss F. Lusk (1997)
Palmers Green High School, London N21	1905	150	—	5,235	Mrs S. Grant (1989)
Parsons Mead, Ashtead, Surrey	1897	199	11,010	6,210	Miss E. B. Plant (1990)
Perse School for Girls, Cambridge	1881	540	—	5,499	Miss H. S. Smith (1989)
*Peterborough High School	1939	180	9,930	4,944	Mrs A. J. V. Storey (1977)
Pipers Corner School, High Wycombe	1930	300	11,010	6,588	Mrs V. M. Stattersfield (1996)
Polam Hall School, Darlington	1848	300	10,240	5,034	Mrs H. C. Hamilton (1987)
§Portsmouth High School	1882	458	—	4,356	Mrs J. M. Dawtrey (1984)
°Princess Helena College, Hitchin, Herts	1820	145	10,935	7,605	Mrs A. M. Hodgkiss (*acting*) (1997)
°Prior's Field, Godalming	1902	230	10,905	7,290	Mrs J. M. McCallum (1987)
§Putney High School, London SW15	1893	562	—	5,268	Mrs E. Merchant (1991)
Queen Anne's School, Reading	1698	309	13,215	8,655	Mrs D. Forbes (1993)
Queen Ethelburga's College, York	1912	200	12,675	7,725	Mrs E. I. E. Taylor (1997)
Queen Margaret's School, York	1901	365	11,937	7,653	Dr G. A. H. Chapman (1993)
°Queen Mary School, Lytham St Anne's	1930	470	—	4,062	Miss M. C. Ritchie (1981)
Queen's College, London W1	1848	386	—	6,990	Lady Goodhart (1991)
Queen's Gate School, London SW7	1891	240	—	6,000	Mrs A. M. Holyoak (*Principal*) (1989)
Queen's School, Chester	1878	467	—	4,950	Miss D. M. Skilbeck (1989)
Queenswood, Hatfield, Herts	1894	400	13,425	8,310	Ms C. Farr (*Principal*) (1996)
Redland High School for Girls, Bristol	1882	483	—	4,665	Mrs C. Lear (1989)
Red Maids' School, Bristol	1634	508	8,520	4,260	Miss S. Hampton (1987)
Roedean School, Brighton	1885	422	14,925	9,720	Mrs P. Metham (1997)
§The Royal High School, Bath	1864	670	11,550	4,356	Miss M. A. Winfield (1985)
Royal Masonic School, Herts	1788	500	9,273	5,643	Mrs I. M. Andrews (1992)
Rye St Antony School (*RC*), Oxford	1930	330	9,510	5,565	Miss A. M. Jones (1990)
St Albans High School	1889	560	—	5,640	Mrs C. Y. Daly (1994)
St Andrew's School, Bedford	1897	140	—	4,410	Mrs J. M. Mark (1996)
St Anne's School, Windermere	1863	210	10,590	7,380	R. D. Hunter (1996)
St Antony's-Leweston School (*RC*), Sherborne	1891	250	12,402	8,172	Miss B. A. King (1996)
St Catherine's School, Guildford	1885	481	10,890	6,630	Mrs C. M. Oulton (1994)
St David's School, Ashford, Middx	1716	237†	10,920	6,060	Mrs J. G. Osborne (1985)
St Dunstan's Abbey School, Plymouth	1850	170	9,960	5,580	Mrs B. K. Brown (1998)
St Elphin's School, Matlock	1844	150	11,115	6,474	Mrs V. E. Fisher (1994)
St Felix School, Southwold, Suffolk	1897	170	11,550	7,650	R. Williams (1998)
St Francis' College (*RC*), Letchworth	1933	180	11,535	5,925	Miss M. Hegarty (1993)
St Gabriel's School, Newbury	1929	150	—	5,736	D. J. Cobb (1990)
St George's School, Ascot, Berks	1923	280	13,350	8,550	Mrs A. M. Griggs (1989)
School of St Helen and St Katharine, Abingdon	1903	545	—	5,235	Mrs C. L. Hall (1993)
St Helen's School, Northwood, Middx	1899	630	10,656	5,665	Mrs D. M. Jefkins (1995)
*St Hilary's School, Alderley Edge	1880	100	—	4,635	Ms P. Bristow (1997)
St James' and the Abbey, West Malvern	1896	150	12,366	7,722	Mrs S. Kershaw (1998)
°St Joseph's Convent School (*RC*), Reading	1909	378	—	4,350	Mrs V. Brookes (1990)
St Leonards-Mayfield School, Mayfield	1850	500	12,213	8,142	Sr J. Sinclair (1980)
St Margaret's School, Bushey, Herts	1749	350	10,695	6,405	Miss M. de Villiers (1992)
*St Margaret's School, Exeter	1904	375	—	4,764	Mrs M. D'Albertanson (1993)
St Martin's School, Solihull	1941	245	—	5,025	Mrs S. J. Williams (1988)
*School of S. Mary and S. Anne, Abbots Bromley, Staffs	1874	219	12,180	8,136	Mrs M. Steel (1998)
St Mary's Convent School, Worcester	1934	200	—	4,230	C. Garner (1997)
St Mary's Hall, Brighton	1836	242	10,215	6,675	Mrs S. M. Meek (1997)
St Mary's School (*RC*), Ascot, Berks	1885	353	13,440	8,730	Mrs M. Breen (1998)

Name of School	Founded	No. of pupils	Annual fees £		Head (with date of appointment)
			Boarding	Day	
St Mary's School, Calne, Wilts	1872	300	13,620	8,370	Mrs C. Shaw (1996)
St Mary's School, Cambridge	1898	450	8,745	4,890	Mrs G. Piotrowska (1998)
St Mary's School, Colchester	1908	210	—	4,380	Mrs G. M. G. Mouser (1981)
St Mary's School, Gerrards Cross	1872	140	—	5,900	Mrs F. Balcombe (1995)
St Mary's School (RC), Shaftesbury	1945	262	11,340	7,350	Mrs S. Pennington (1998)
St Mary's School, Wantage, Oxon	1873	210	13,035	8,690	Mrs S. Bodinham (1994)
°St Maur's Senior School, Weybridge	1898	372	—	4,800	Mrs M. E. Dodds (1991)
St Nicholas' School, Fleet, Hants	1935	161	—	4,950	Mrs A. V. Whatmough (1995)
St Paul's Girls' School, London w6	1904	658	—	7,377	Miss E. Diggory (*High Mistress*) (1998)
St Swithun's School, Winchester	1884	465	12,795	7,740	Dr H. Harvey (1995)
St Teresa's School, Dorking	1928	350	11,700	6,450	Mrs M. E. Prescott (1997)
§Sheffield High School	1878	597	—	4,356	Mrs M. A. Houston (1989)
Sherborne School for Girls, Dorset	1899	420	13,950	9,780	Miss J. M. Taylor (1985)
§Shrewsbury High School	1885	353	—	4,356	Miss S. Gardner (1990)
Sir William Perkins's School, Chertsey, Surrey	1725	580	—	4,950	Miss S. Ross (1994)
§South Hampstead High School, London NW3	1876	608	—	5,268	Mrs J. G. Scott (1993)
Stonar School, Melksham, Wilts	1921	340	10,722	5,955	Mrs C. Homan (1997)
Stover School, Newton Abbot	1932	200	9,885	5,085	P. E. Bujak (1994)
§Streatham Hill and Clapham High School, London SW2	1887	419	—	5,268	Miss G. M. Ellis (1979)
°Surbiton High School, Kingston-upon-Thames (CSC)	1884	612	—	5,115	Miss M. G. Perry (1993)
§Sutton High School, Surrey	1884	500	—	5,268	Mrs A. J. Coutts (1995)
§Sydenham High School, London SE26	1887	473	—	5,268	Mrs G. Baker (1988)
Talbot Heath, Bournemouth	1886	431	10,050	5,790	Mrs C. Dipple (1991)
Teesside High School, Stockton-on-Tees	1970	360	—	4,620	Miss J. F. Hamilton (1995)
Tormead School, Guildford	1905	427	—	5,985	Mrs H. E. M. Alleyne (1992)
Truro High School	1880	355	9,285	5,025	J. Graham-Brown (1992)
Tudor Hall School, Banbury	1850	262	11,955	7,455	Miss N. Godfrey (1984)
Wakefield Girls' High School	1878	720†	—	5,001	Mrs P. A. Langham (1987)
Walthamstow Hall, Sevenoaks	1838	260	13,500	7,290	Mrs J. S. Lang (1984)
Wentworth College, Bournemouth	1871	250	10,140	6,360	Miss S. D. Coe (1990)
Westfield School, Newcastle upon Tyne	1962	224	—	4,797	Mrs M. Farndale (1990)
Westholme School, Blackburn	1923	705	—	4,080	Mrs L. Croston (*Principal*) (1988)
Westonbirt School, Tetbury, Glos	1928	200	12,828	8,430	Mrs G. Hylson-Smith (1986)
§Wimbledon High School, London SW19	1880	586	—	5,268	Dr J. L. Clough (1995)
Wispers School, Haslemere, Surrey	1946	107	10,860	6,990	L. H. Beltran (1980)
Withington Girls' School, Manchester	1890	530	—	4,425	Mrs M. Kenyon (1986)
Woldingham School, Surrey	1842	550	13,431	7,124	Mrs M. M. Ribbins (1997)
Wychwood School, Oxford	1897	150	8,040	5,070	Mrs S. Wingfield Digby (1997)
Wycombe Abbey School, High Wycombe	1896	522	14,250	10,689	Mrs P. E. Davies (1998)
Wykeham House School, Fareham, Hants	1913	160	—	4,554	Mrs R. M. Kamaryc (1995)

SCOTLAND

Name of School	Founded	No. of pupils	Boarding	Day	Head
Kilgraston School, Bridge of Earn, Perth	1930	190	10,965	6,750	Mrs J. L. Austin (1993)
Laurel Park School, Glasgow	1996	357	—	4,653	Mrs E. Surber (1995)
Mary Erskine School, Edinburgh	1694	692	9,810	5,091	P. F. J. Tobin (*Principal*) (1989)
St George's School, Edinburgh	1888	550	10,185	5,220	Dr J. McClure (1994)
St Leonards School, St Andrews	1877	255‡	13,110	6,930	Mrs M. James (1988)
St Margaret's School, Aberdeen	1846	206	—	4,536	Miss A. C. Ritchie (1998)
St Margaret's School and St Denis and Cranley, Edinburgh	1890	385	9,675	4,755	Miss A. Mitchell (1994)

CHANNEL ISLANDS

Name of School	Founded	No. of pupils	Boarding	Day	Head
°The Ladies' College, Guernsey	1872	350	—	2,340	Miss M. E. Macdonald (*Principal*) (1992)

Health

SELECTED CAUSES OF DEATH, BY GENDER AND AGE 1996 (United Kingdom)
Percentages and number

	Under 1*	1–14	15–24	25–34	35–54	55–64	65–74	75 and over	All ages
Males									
Circulatory diseases	4	5	4	9	33	43	45	45	42
Cancer	1	16	7	10	28	37	33	22	27
Respiratory diseases	10	7	4	5	5	7	12	20	15
Injury and poisoning	4	30	63	51	15	3	1	1	4
Infectious diseases	7	8	2	5	3	1	—	—	1
Other causes	73	34	19	20	16	9	8	11	11
All males (number)	2,600	1,100	2,800	4,700	22,600	35,100	81,700	155,900	306,500
Females									
Circulatory diseases	6	6	7	12	18	29	39	47	43
Cancer	1	18	17	26	52	48	36	15	23
Respiratory diseases	9	7	5	6	5	9	13	19	16
Injury and poisoning	6	23	43	28	8	2	1	1	2
Infectious diseases	6	8	4	5	1	1	1	—	1
Other causes	73	37	24	24	16	12	11	16	15
All females (number)	1,900	800	1,100	2,200	14,500	21,500	58,200	232,300	332,400

* Excluding deaths at ages under 28 days
Source: The Stationery Office – *Social Trends 28*

NOTIFICATIONS OF INFECTIOUS DISEASES (UK) 1996

Measles	6,865
Mumps	2,182
Rubella	11,720
Whooping cough	2,721
Scarlet fever	6,101
Dysentery	2,641
Food poisoning	89,741
Typhoid and paratyphoid fevers	291
Hepatitis	2,876
Tuberculosis	6,238
Malaria	1,739

Source: The Stationery Office – *Annual Abstract of Statistics 1998*

HIV/AIDS AND SEXUALLY TRANSMITTED DISEASES (ENGLAND)

	1985	1995
HIV cases diagnosed	2,528	2,225
Exposure category		
Homosexual intercourse	67%	57%
Heterosexual intercourse	2%	32%
Injecting drug use	4%	6%
Blood products	24%	1%
Aids cases diagnosed	236	1,524
Sexually transmitted diseases (new cases)		
All, except HIV/Aids	—	404,600
Syphilis	2,400	1,400
Gonorrhoea	46,300	12,400
Chlamydia	—	39,300
Herpes	18,900	27,100
Wart virus	52,200	93,300

Source: The Stationery Office – *Health and Personal Social Services Statistics for England 1997*

PREVALENCE OF SMOKING CIGARETTES (ENGLAND)
Percentages among adults aged 16 and over, by sex

	1986	1996
Males		
Current smoker	34	28
Ex-regular smoker	33	32
Never smoked	33	40
Females		
Current smoker	31	27
Ex-regular smoker	18	20
Never smoked	51	53

Source: The Stationery Office – *Health and Personal Social Services Statistics for England 1997*

ALCOHOL CONSUMPTION - UNITS PER WEEK (ENGLAND) 1996
Percentage

Men	
Non-drinker	7
Under one	7
1–10	31
11–21	24
22–35	17
36–50	7
51 and over	7
Women	
Non-drinker	10
Under one	17
1–10	39
11–21	17
22–35	11
36–50	3
51 and over	3

Source: The Stationery Office – *Health in England 1996*

PEOPLE WHO HAVE EVER TAKEN DRUGS (ENGLAND AND WALES) 1996 *by type of drug and age*

Percentage

Age	16–19	20–24	25–34	35–44	45–59	All aged 16–59
Cannabis	35	42	30	23	8	22
Amphetamines	16	21	11	7	3	9
LSD	10	15	6	4	1	5
Magic mushroom	7	12	8	4	1	5
Ecstasy	9	13	4	1	1	3
Cocaine	2	6	4	3	1	3
Solvents	5	7	3	1	—	2
Crack	1	2	1	1	—	1
Heroin	1	1	1	1	—	1
Any drug	45	49	37	29	13	29

Source: The Stationery Office - *Social Trends 28*

HEALTH IN ENGLAND

A report, *Health in England 1996,* was published by the Health Education Authority and the Office for National Statistics in May 1997. It included the following main findings:

- 31 per cent of men and 29 per cent of women were cigarette smokers
- the mean alcohol consumption was 18.0 units a week for men and 7.7 units a week for women
- 25 per cent of respondents were sedentary
- 38 per cent of men and 26 per cent of women had taken drugs not prescribed by their doctor or bought from the chemist
- 16 per cent of men and 10 per cent of women aged 16–54 had had two or more sexual partners in the previous year

- 80 per cent of men and 78 per cent of women said that their general health was 'very good' or 'good'
- 62 per cent of men and 69 per cent of women had experienced a 'moderate' or 'large' amount of stress in the previous year
- 60 per cent of men and 73 per cent of women had visited their GP in the previous year

HEALTH OF THE NATION TARGETS

The Government in 1992 published a White Paper, *The Health of the Nation,* identifying five key health areas in England (coronary heart disease and stroke, cancers, mental illness, HIV/Aids and sexual health, and accidents) where improvements were deemed to be most necessary. It also identified risk factors associated with the five key areas (including smoking, alcohol, diet and nutrition, obesity and blood pressure). The White Paper set 27 targets, including the following:

- a reduction of 40 per cent in the number of deaths from coronary heart disease and strokes among people under 65 by 2000
- a reduction of 30 per cent in the number of deaths from lung cancer among men and of 15 per cent among women by 2010
- a reduction of 25 per cent in the number of deaths from breast cancer by 2000
- a reduction of 20 per cent in the number of deaths from cervical cancer by 2000
- a reduction of 15 per cent in the number of deaths from suicide by 2000
- a reduction of one third in the number of fatal accidents among children and people over 64 by 2005
- a reduction of 50 per cent in conceptions among girls under 16 by 2000

CONSUMPTION OF FOODS CONTAINING FIBRE AND STARCHY CARBOHYDRATES (ENGLAND) 1996 *by age and sex*

Percentage consuming each food

Age	16–24	25–34	35–44	45–54	55–64	65–74	Total
Men							
Eats wholemeal bread	7	14	16	21	23	22	17
Eats bread daily	83	77	87	84	89	92	84
Eats fruit, vegetables and salad daily	43	51	56	69	72	73	59
Eats potatoes, pasta or rice daily	35	51	55	56	63	66	53
Eats bread; fruit, vegetables and salad; and potatoes, pasta or rice daily	19	31	34	41	45	51	36
Women							
Eats wholemeal bread	16	23	24	30	29	34	25
Eats bread daily	76	75	79	83	83	93	81
Eats fruit, vegetables and salad daily	57	60	74	81	86	83	72
Eats potatoes, pasta or rice daily	44	51	55	62	67	64	56
Eats bread; fruit, vegetables and salad; and potatoes, pasta or rice daily	24	32	38	45	53	53	40

Source: The Stationery Office – *Health in England 1996*

FREQUENCY OF AT LEAST MODERATE-INTENSITY EXERCISE FOR 30 MINUTES OR MORE *by age and sex*

Percentages

Age	16–24	25–34	35–44	45–54	55–64	65–74	Total
Men							
Less than one day a week	9	19	20	26	38	42	24
1–2 days a week	21	20	25	25	23	29	23
3–4 days a week	14	12	12	11	7	14	12
5 or more days a week	56	48	43	39	32	14	41
Women							
Less than one day a week	20	18	19	22	37	46	26
1–2 days a week	29	27	33	28	33	28	30
3–4 days a week	18	15	14	14	9	11	14
5 or more days a week	32	39	34	35	21	14	31

Source: The Stationery Office – *Health in England 1996*

- a reduction of one third in the number of smokers and
of 40 per cent in the number of cigarettes sold by 2000
- a reduction of 25 per cent in obesity levels among men
and of one third among women by 2005
- a reduction of 30 per cent in the number of people
drinking to excess by 2005
- a reduction in the incidence of drug misuse

Annual reports have been published to document
progress towards these targets. Some of the targets have
been met ahead of schedule, others are on course to be
achieved, and others (in particular those relating to obesity
and teenage smoking) are currently showing increases
rather than reductions.

Similar initiatives were undertaken in Scotland, Wales
and Northern Ireland. A policy document, *Scotland's Health:
A Challenge to Us All*, published in 1992, included the
following main targets:
- a reduction of 40 per cent in the number of deaths from
coronary heart disease among people under 65 by 2000
- a reduction of 15 per cent in the number of deaths from
cancer by 2000

NEW HEALTH STRATEGY

In February 1997 the Government published a Green
Paper, *Our Healthier Nation*, which identified four main
areas of illness in England (heart disease and stroke,
accidents, cancer and mental health) to be improved, and
replaced the targets in *The Health of the Nation* with four
main targets:
- a reduction in the number of deaths from coronary
heart disease and strokes by one third by 2010
- a reduction in the number of deaths from cancer by one
fifth by 2010
- a reduction in the number of deaths by suicide by one
sixth by 2010
- a reduction in the number of deaths from accidents by
one fifth by 2010

Similar reviews are being undertaken in Scotland, Wales
and Northern Ireland. A Green Paper, *Working Together for a
Healthier Scotland*, was published in February 1998; it
invited comments on whether current targets should be
revised and/or new targets set. A definitive public health
strategy was to be published by the Government in
summer 1998.

HEALTH EDUCATION

Health education in the UK is the responsibility of the
Health Education Authority, Health Promotion Wales, the
Health Education Board for Scotland and the Health
Promotion Agency for Northern Ireland (*see* page 480).
The role of the four authorities is to provide health
information and advice to the public, health professionals,
and other organizations, and to advise the Government on
health education.

Social Welfare

National Health Service

The National Health Service (NHS) came into being on 5 July 1948 under the National Health Service Act 1946, covering England and Wales, and under separate legislation for Scotland and Northern Ireland. The NHS is administered in England by the Secretary of State for Health, and in Wales, Scotland and Northern Ireland by the respective Secretaries of State. During 1999, responsibility for administering the NHS will transfer from the Secretaries of State for Scotland, Wales and Northern Ireland to the Scottish parliament, Welsh assembly and New Northern Ireland Assembly.

The function of the NHS is to provide a comprehensive health service designed to secure improvement in the physical and mental health of the people and to prevent, diagnose and treat illness. It was founded on the principle that treatment should be provided according to clinical need rather than ability to pay, and should be free at the point of delivery. However, prescription charges were provided for by legislation in 1949 and implemented in 1952, and charges for some dental and ophthalmic treatment have also been introduced.

The NHS covers a comprehensive range of hospital, specialist, family practitioner (medical, dental, ophthalmic and pharmaceutical), artificial limb and appliance, ambulance, and community health services. Everyone normally resident in the UK is entitled to use any of these services.

STRUCTURE

The structure of the NHS remained relatively stable for the first 30 years of its existence. In 1974, a three-tier management structure comprising Regional Health Authorities, Area Health Authorities and District Management Teams was introduced in England, and the NHS became responsible for community health services. In 1979 Area Health Authorities were abolished and District Management Teams were replaced by District Health Authorities.

THE INTERNAL MARKET

The National Health Service and Community Care Act 1990 provided for more streamlined Regional Health Authorities and District Health Authorities, and for the establishment of Family Health Services Authorities (FHSAs) and NHS Trusts. The concept of the 'internal market' was introduced into health care, whereby care was provided through NHS contracts where health authorities or boards and GP fundholders (the purchasers) were responsible for buying health care from hospitals, non-fundholding GPs, community services and ambulance services (the providers).

The Act provided for the establishment of NHS Trusts. Trusts operate as self-governing health care providers independent of health authority control and responsible to the Secretary of State. They derive their income principally from contracts to provide services to health authorities and fund-holding GPs. In Northern Ireland, 20 health and social services trusts are responsible for providing health and social services in an organizational model unique to Northern Ireland.

The Act also paved the way for the Community Care reforms, which were introduced in April 1993 and changed in the way care is administered for elderly people, the mentally ill, the physically handicapped and people with learning disabilities.

The eight Regional Health Authorities in England were abolished in April 1996 and replaced by eight regional offices which, together with the headquarters in Leeds, form the NHS Executive. The regional offices are part of the Department of Health, and their functions include financial and performance monitoring of local purchasers and providers, public health, regional research and development, and education programmes.

In April 1996 the District Health Authorities and Family Health Service Authorities were merged to form 100 unified Health Authorities (HAs) in England. The HAs are responsible for health and health services in their areas. They are also responsible for assessing the health care needs of the local population and developing integrated strategies for meeting these needs in partnership with GPs and in consultation with the public, hospitals and others. HAs' resources are allocated by the NHS Executive headquarters, to which they are also accountable for their performance. HA chairmen are appointed by the Health Secretary and non-executive members by the regional offices of the NHS Executive.

In Wales the chairman and non-executive members of the five HAs which replaced the former 17 HAs and FHSAs in April 1996 are appointed by the Welsh Secretary. The Welsh Health Common Services Authority provides a range of specialist services to the NHS in Wales. In Scotland there are 15 Health Boards with similar responsibilities to those of HAs, and in Northern Ireland there are four Health and Social Services Boards.

There are also Community Health Councils (called Local Health Councils in Scotland and Health and Social Services Councils in Northern Ireland) throughout the UK; their role is to represent the interests of the public to health authorities and boards. The Government announced in March 1998 that public consultation and patient representation in the NHS would be increased.

PROPOSED REFORMS

In December 1997 the Government published a White Paper, *The New NHS*, outlining plans for replacing the NHS internal market in England and establishing teams of GPs and community nurses to work together in primary care groups, with long-term service agreements replacing annual contracts between health authorities, primary care groups and NHS Trusts. The White Paper also proposed to create a National Institute of Clinical Excellence to produce new national guidelines, National Service Frameworks to guarantee consistency in access and quality of care, and a Commission for Health Improvement to promote best practice. Other White Papers, *Putting Patients First* and *Designed to Care*, covered similar plans for reforming the NHS in Wales and Scotland respectively. The reforms should be in place in late 1999 or 2000, subject to the passage of legislation through Parliament. For details, *see* White Papers section.

FINANCE

The NHS is still funded mainly (81.5 per cent) through general taxation, although in recent years more reliance has been placed on the NHS element of National Insurance contributions, patient charges and other sources of income. Total UK expenditure on the NHS in 1997–8 was £44,719 million, of which £42,787 million was from public monies and £1,932 million from patient charges and other receipts. NHS expenditure represented 5.7 per cent of GDP. The total cost per head was £758. The planned expenditure for 1998–9 is £46,844 million. The Government announced in July 1998 that an additional £21,000 million would be spent on the NHS between 1999 and 2002.

ENGLAND

NATIONAL HEALTH CURRENT EXPENDITURE 1996–7

	£ million
National Health Service:	
Hospitals, Community Health Services and Family Health Services	39,425
Departmental administration	265
Other central services	3,124
Less payments by patients	865
TOTAL	41,949

PERSONAL SOCIAL SERVICES CURRENT EXPENDITURE 1996–7

	£ million
Central government	101
Local authorities running expenses	9,996
Capital expenditure	221
TOTAL	10,318

Source: The Stationery Office – Annual Abstract of Statistics 1998

WALES

CENTRAL GOVERNMENT EXPENDITURE 1996–7

	£ thousand
Hospital, community health and family health services	1,769,500
NHS Trusts	46,600
General medical	122,800
Pharmaceutical	206,400
General dental	72,300
General ophthalmic	17,200
Other	100
TOTAL	2,234,900

Source: Welsh Office Departmental Report 1998

SCOTLAND

NET COSTS OF THE NATIONAL HEALTH SERVICE 1995–6

	£ thousand
Central administration	7,651
Total NHS cost	4,384,174
NHS contributions	452,536
Net costs to Exchequer	3,931,638
Health Board administration	95,274
Hospital and community health services	3,160,044
Family practitioner services	914,012
Central health services	145,943
State hospital	21,563
Training	3,243
Research	10,234
Disabled services	2,247
Welfare foods	14,434
Miscellaneous health services	17,180
TOTAL	4,391,825

Source: Scottish Office – Annual Abstract of Statistics 1996

ORGANIZATIONS

HEALTH AUTHORITIES (ENGLAND)

There are 100 health authorities in England. For details, contact the relevant NHS Executive regional office (see below).

NHS EXECUTIVE REGIONAL OFFICES

ANGLIA AND OXFORD, 6–12 Capital Drive, Linford Wood, Milton Keynes MK14 6QP. Tel: 01908-844400. *Chairman*, Mrs R. Varley; *Regional Director*, Ms B. Stocking

NORTHERN AND YORKSHIRE, John Snow House, Durham University Science Park, Durham DH1 3YG. Tel: 0191-301 1300. *Chairman*, Mrs Z. Manzoor; *Regional Director*, Prof. L. Donaldson

NORTH THAMES, 40 Eastbourne Terrace, London W2 3QR. Tel: 0171-725 5300. *Chairman*, I. Mills; *Regional Director*, R. Kerr

NORTH WEST, 930–932 Birchwood Boulevard, Millennium Park, Birchwood, Warrington WA3 7QN. Tel: 01925-704000. *Chairman*, Prof. A. Breckenridge; *Regional Director*, R. Tinston

SOUTH AND WEST, Westward House, Lime Kiln Close, Stoke Gifford, Bristol BS34 8SR. Tel: 0117-984 1750. *Chairman*, Miss J. Trotter, OBE; *Regional Director*, A. Laurance

SOUTH THAMES, 40 Eastbourne Terrace, London W2 3QR. Tel: 0171-725 2500. *Chairman*, Sir William Wells; *Regional Director*, N. Crisp

TRENT, Fulwood House, Old Fulwood Road, Sheffield S10 3TH. Tel: 0114-263 0300. *Chairman*, P. Hammersley; *Regional Director*, N. McKay

WEST MIDLANDS, Bartholomew House, 142 Hagley Road, Birmingham B16 9PA. Tel: 0121-224 4600. *Chairman*, C. Wilkinson; *Regional Director*, S. Day

In April 1999 four of the regional offices will be replaced: North and South Thames will be replaced by London and South-East Regions; Anglia and Oxford by Eastern Region; and South and West by South-West Region. The new regional offices will operate from the addresses of their predecessors.

HEALTH BOARDS (SCOTLAND)

ARGYLL AND CLYDE, Ross House, Hawkhead Road, Paisley PA2 7BN. Tel: 0141-842 7200. *Chairman*, M. D. Jones; *General Manager*, N. McConachie

AYRSHIRE AND ARRAN, PO Box 13, Boswell House, 10 Arthur Street, Ayr KA7 1QJ. Tel: 01292-611040. *Chairman*, Dr J. Morrow; *General Manager*, Mrs W. Hatton

BORDERS, Newstead, Melrose, Roxburghshire TD9 0SE. Tel: 01896-822727. *Chairman*, D. A. C. Kilshaw; *General Manager*, L. Burley

DUMFRIES AND GALLOWAY, Grierson House, Crichton Royal Hospital, Bankend Road, Dumfries DG1 4ZH. Tel: 01387-272700. *Chairman*, J. Ross; *General Manager*, N. Campbell

FIFE, Springfield House, Cupar KY15 9UP. Tel: 01334-656200. *Chairman*, Mrs C. Stenhouse; *General Manager*, Miss P. Frost

FORTH VALLEY, 33 Spittal Street, Stirling FK8 1DX. Tel: 01786-463031. *Chairman*, E. Bell-Scott; *General Manager*, D. Hird

GRAMPIAN, Summerfield House, 2 Eday Road, Aberdeen AB15 6RE. Tel: 01224-663456. *Chairman*, Dr C. MacLeod, CBE; *General Manager*, F. E. L. Hartnett, OBE

GREATER GLASGOW, Dalian House, PO Box 15329, 350 St Vincent Street, Glasgow G3 8YZ. Tel: 0141-201 4444. *Chairman*, Prof. D. Hamblen; *Chief Executive*, C. J. Spry

HIGHLAND, Beechwood Park, Inverness IV2 3HG. Tel: 01463-704800. *Chairman*, Mrs C. Thomson; *General Manager*, Dr G. V. Stone

LANARKSHIRE, 14 Beckford Street, Hamilton, Lanarkshire ML3 0TA. Tel: 01698-281313. *Chairman*, I. Livingstone, CBE; *General Manager*, Prof. T. A. Divers

LOTHIAN, 148 Pleasance, Edinburgh EH8 9RS. Tel: 0131-536 9000. *Chairman*, Mrs M. Ford; *General Manager*, T. Jones

ORKNEY, Garden House, New Scapa Road, Kirkwall, Orkney KW15 1BQ. Tel: 01856-885400. *Chairman*, J. Leslie; *General Manager (acting)*, E. Iseec

SHETLAND, Brevik House, South Road, Lerwick ZE1 0RB. Tel: 01595-696767. *Chairman*, J. Telford; *General Manager*, B. J. Atherton

TAYSIDE, Gateway House, Luna Place, Dundee Technology Park, Dundee DD2 1TP. Tel: 01382-561818. *Chairman*, Mrs F. Havenga; *General Manager*, T. Rett

WESTERN ISLES, 37 South Beach Street, Stornoway, Isle of Lewis HS1 2BN. Tel: 01851-702997. *Chairman*, A. Matheson; *General Manager*, B. Skilbeck

HEALTH AUTHORITIES (WALES)

BRO TAF, Churchill House, Churchill Way, Cardiff CF1 4TW. Tel: 01222-226216. *Chairman*, Mrs K. Thomas; *Chief Executive*, Dr G. Todd

DYFED POWYS, St David's Hospital, Carmarthen SA31 3HB. Tel: 01267-225225. *Chairman*, Ms M. Price; *Chief Executive*, P. Stansbie

GWENT, Mamhilad House, Mamhilad, Pontypool NP4 0YP. Tel: 01495-765065. *Chairman*, Mrs F. Peel; *Chief Executive*, G. Coomber

MORGANNWG, 41 High Street, Swansea SA1 1LT. Tel: 01792-458066. *Chairman*, D. H. Thomas; *Chief Executive*, Mrs J. Williams

NORTH WALES, Preswylfa, Hendy Road, Mold CH7 1PZ. Tel: 01352-700227. *Chairman (acting)*, Mrs A. Roberts; *Chief Executive*, B. Jones

WELSH HEALTH COMMON SERVICES AUTHORITY, Crickhowell House, Pierhead Street, Capital Waterside, Cardiff CF1 5XT. Tel: 01222-500500. Chairman, T. Rees; *Chief Executive*, N. Kirk

NORTHERN IRELAND HEALTH AND SOCIAL SERVICES BOARDS

EASTERN, Champion House, 12-22 Linenhall Street, Belfast BT2 BS. Tel: 01232-321313

NORTHERN, County Hall, 182 Galgorm Road, Ballymena BT42 1QB. Tel: 01266-653333

SOUTHERN, Tower Hill, Armagh BT61 9DR. Tel: 01861-410041

WESTERN, 15 Gransha Park, Clooney Road, Londonderry BT47 6TG. Tel: 01504-860086

HEALTH PROMOTION AUTHORITIES

HEALTH EDUCATION AUTHORITY, Trevelyan House, 30 Great Peter Street, London SW1P 2HW. Tel: 0171-222 5300. *Chairman*, vacant; *Chief Executive*, S. Fortescue

HEALTH PROMOTION WALES, Ffynnon-las, Ty Glas Avenue, Llanishen, Cardiff CF4 5DZ. Tel: 01222-752222. *Chairman*, J. I. Davies; *Chief Executive*, M. Ponton

HEALTH EDUCATION BOARD FOR SCOTLAND, Woodburn House, Canaan Lane, Edinburgh EH10 4SG. Tel 0131-536 5500. *Chairman*, D. Campbell; *Chief Executive*, Prof. A. Tannahill

HEALTH PROMOTION AGENCY FOR NORTHERN IRELAND, 18 Ormeau Avenue, Belfast BT2 8HS. Tel: 01232-311611

EMPLOYEES AND SALARIES

EMPLOYEES

HEALTH AND PERSONAL SOCIAL SERVICES WORKFORCE (*Great Britain*) *as at 30 September 1996*

General medical practitioners	*34,421
General dental practitioners	19,147
Ophthalmic medical practitioners	†766
Ophthalmic opticians	†7,652
Medical staff	62,176
Dental staff	3,127
Nursing and midwifery staff	356,109
Professional and technical staff	105,496
Administrative and clerical staff	178,461
Health care assistants and support staff	93,901
Ambulance staff	16,330
Other Health Service staff	6,834
‡Personal social services staff	233,655

*1994 figure
†Figures for England and Wales relate to 31 December 1996. Figures for Scotland relate to 31 March 1997. Those with contracts with more than one authority/board will be counted more than once.
‡England only
Source: The Stationery Office – *Annual Abstract of Statistics 1998*

SALARIES *as at 1 December 1998*

General Practitioners (GPs), dentists, optometrists and pharmacists are self-employed, and are employed by the NHS under contract. GPs are paid for their NHS work in accordance with a scheme of remuneration which includes a basic practice allowance, capitation fees, reimbursement of certain practice expenses and payments for out-of-hours work. Dentists receive payment for items of treatment for individual adult patients and, in addition, a continuing care payment for those registered with them. Optometrists receive approved fees for each sight test they carry out. Pharmacists receive professional fees from the NHS and are refunded the cost of prescriptions supplied.

Consultant	£45,740–£59,040
Specialist Registrar	£22,510–£32,830
Registrar	£22,510–£27,310
Senior House Officer	£20,135–£26,910
House Officer	£16,145–£18,225
GP	*£49,030
Nursing Grades G–I (Senior Ward Sister)	£19,240–£26,965
Nursing Grade F (Ward Sister)	£16,310–£19,985
Nursing Grade E (Senior Staff Nurse)	£14,705–£17,030
Nursing Grades C–D (Staff/Enrolled Nurse)	£11,210–£14,705
Nursing Grades A–B (Nursing Auxiliary)	£8,315–£11,210

* average intended net remuneration

HEALTH SERVICES

PRIMARY AND COMMUNITY HEALTH CARE SERVICES

Primary and community health care services comprise the family health services (i.e. the general medical, personal medical, pharmaceutical, dental, and ophthalmic services) and community services (including preventive activities such as vaccination, immunization and fluoridation) commissioned by HAs and provided by NHS Trusts, health centres and clinics.

The primary and community nursing services include practice nurses based in general practice, district nurses and health visitors, community psychiatric nursing for mentally ill people living outside hospital, and school nursing for the health surveillance of schoolchildren of all ages. Ante- and post-natal care are also an integral part of the primary health care service.

FAMILY DOCTOR SERVICE

In England and Wales the Family Doctor Service (or General Medical Service) is now the responsibility of the HAs.

Any doctor may take part in the Family Doctor Service (provided the area in which he/she wishes to practise has not already an adequate number of doctors) and about 29,000 GPs in England and Wales do so. The distribution of GPs is controlled by the Medical Practices Committee, a statutory body. The average number of patients on a doctor's list in 1997 was:

England	1,878
Wales	1,706
Scotland	1,478

GPs may also have private fee-paying patients.

The National Health Service and Community Care Act 1990 allowed GP practices to apply for fundholding status, under which the practice is responsible for its own NHS budget for a specified range of goods and services. Since April 1996 there have been three types of GP fundholding: total purchasing (a pilot scheme), under which GPs purchase all hospital and community health services for their patients; standard fundholders, for practices with at least 5,000 patients, who purchase a wide range of in- and out-patient services; and community fundholders, who purchase only community nursing services, drugs and diagnostic tests. There are currently 3,481 fundholding units, comprising 4,243 practices and representing more than 50 per cent of GPs. The Government plans to replace the fundholding system by allowing the new primary care groups to assume one of four levels of responsibility, including managing a single unified budget for health care in their area. Around 480 primary care groups were established in shadow form in August 1998. In April 1999 they will become fully operational and all practices will be represented within a primary care group. A board consisting of GPs, nurses, a social services officer, a health authority representative and a local member of the public will administer each group.

Everyone aged 16 or over can choose their doctor (parents or guardians choose for children under 16); the doctor is free to accept a person or not. Should a patient have difficulty in registering with a doctor, HAs have powers to assign the patient to a GP. A person may change their doctor if they wish, by going to the surgery of a GP of their choice who is willing to accept them, and either handing in their medical card to register or filling in a form. When people are away from home they can still use the Family Doctor Service if they ask to be treated as temporary residents, and in an emergency, any doctor in the service will give treatment and advice.

PHARMACEUTICAL SERVICE

Patients may obtain medicines, appliances and oral contraceptives prescribed under the NHS from any pharmacy whose owner has entered into arrangements with the HA to provide this service; the number of these pharmacies in England and Wales in March 1998 was about 10,500. There are also some appliance suppliers who only provide special appliances. In rural areas, where access to a pharmacy may be difficult, patients may be able to obtain medicines, etc., from their doctor.

Except for contraceptives (for which there is no charge), a charge of £5.80 is payable for each item supplied unless the patient is exempt and the declaration on the back of the prescription form is completed. Prepayment certificates (£30.10 valid for four months, £82.70 valid for a year) may be purchased by those patients not entitled to exemption who require frequent prescriptions.

The following people are exempt from prescription charges:
- children under 16
- full-time students under 19
- men and women aged 60 and over
- pregnant women who hold an exemption certificate
- women who have had a baby in the last 12 months and who hold an exemption certificate
- people suffering from certain medical conditions who hold an exemption certificate
- people who receive income support, family credit, disability working allowance or income-based jobseeker's allowance, and their partners
- people who are named on an HC2 certificate issued by the Health Benefits Division
- war pensioners (for their accepted disablements)

Booklet HC11, available from main post offices and local social security offices, gives further details.

The number of prescriptions dispensed in the community in 1997 was:

England	500,200,000
Wales	38,500,000
Scotland	57,200,000

DENTAL SERVICE

Dentists, like doctors, may take part in the NHS and also have private patients. About 16,000 dentists in England provide NHS general dental services. They are responsible to the HAs in whose areas they provide services.

Patients may go to any dentist who is taking part in the NHS and is willing to accept them. Patients are required to pay 80 per cent of the cost of NHS dental treatment. Since 1 April 1998 the maximum charge for a course of treatment has been £340. There is no charge for arrest of bleeding or repairs to dentures; home visits by the dentist or re-opening a surgery in an emergency are charged for as treatment given in the normal way. The following people are exempt from dental charges or have charges remitted:
- people under 18
- full-time students under 19
- women who were pregnant when accepted for treatment
- women who have had a child in the previous 12 months
- people who receive income support, family credit, disability working allowance or income-based jobseeker's allowance, and their partners
- people who are named on an HC2 certificate issued by the Health Benefits Division

Booklet HC11, available from main post offices and local social security offices, gives further details.

GENERAL DENTAL SERVICE 1996–7 (ENGLAND)

Number of dentists	16,336
Number of patients registered	
Adults	19,524,000
Children	7,270,000
Number of courses of treatment	
Adults	24,580,000
Expenditure (£ million)	
Gross expenditure	1,323.1
Paid by patients	383.0
Paid out of public funds	940.1

Source: The Stationery Office – *Health and Personal Social Services Statistics for England 1997*

General Ophthalmic Services

General Ophthalmic Services are administered by HAs. Testing of sight may be carried out by any ophthalmic medical practitioner or ophthalmic optician (optometrist). The optician must give the prescription to the patient, who can take this to any supplier of glasses to have them dispensed. Only registered opticians can supply glasses to children and to people registered as blind or partially sighted.

The NHS sight test costs £14.10. Those on a low income may qualify for help with the cost. The test is available free to:
– children under 16*
– full-time students under 19*
– people who receive income support, income-based jobseeker's allowance, disability working allowance or family credit, and their partners*
– people who are named on an HC2 certificate issued by the Health Benefits Division*
– people prescribed complex lenses*
– people registered as blind or partially sighted
– diagnosed diabetic and glaucoma patients
– close relatives aged 40 or over of diagnosed glaucoma patients

The categories indicated by * above are automatically entitled to help with the purchase of glasses under an NHS voucher scheme, as are people whose spectacles are lost or damaged as a result of their disability, injury or illness. Booklet HC11, available from main post offices and local social security offices, gives further details.

Diagnosis and specialist treatment of eye conditions, and the provision of special glasses, are available through the Hospital Eye Service.

Community Child Health Services

Pre-school services at GP surgeries or child health clinics provide regular monitoring of children's physical, mental and emotional health and development, and advice to parents on their children's health and welfare.

The School Health Service provides for the medical and dental examination of schoolchildren, and advises the local education authority, the school, the parents and the pupil of any health factors which may require special consideration during the pupil's school life. GPs are increasingly undertaking child health monitoring in order to improve the preventive health care of children.

HOSPITALS AND OTHER SERVICES

Hospital, medical, dental, nursing, ophthalmic and ambulance services are provided by the NHS to meet all reasonable requirements. Facilities for the care of expectant and nursing mothers and young children, and other services required for the diagnosis and treatment of illness, are also provided. Rehabilitation services (occupational therapy, physiotherapy and speech therapy) may also be provided, and surgical and medical appliances are supplied where appropriate.

Specialists and consultants who work in NHS hospitals can also engage in private practice, including the treatment of their private patients in NHS hospitals.

Private Finance Initiative

The Private Finance Initiative (PFI) was launched in 1992, and involves the private sector in designing, building, financing and operating new hospitals, which are then leased to the NHS. In July 1997 a new programme of hospital building under the PFI was announced by the Government.

Charges

Certain hospitals have accommodation in single rooms or small wards which, if not required for patients who need privacy for medical reasons, may be made available to patients who desire it as an amenity for a small charge. These patients are still NHS patients and are treated as such.

In a number of hospitals, accommodation is available for the treatment of private in-patients who undertake to pay the full costs of hospital accommodation and services and (usually) separate medical fees to a specialist as well. The amount of the medical fees is a matter for agreement between doctor and patient. Hospital charges for private in-patients are set locally at a commercial rate.

There is no charge for drugs supplied to NHS hospital in-patients, but out-patients pay £5.80 an item unless they are exempt. With certain exceptions, hospital out-patients have to pay fixed charges for dentures, contact lenses and certain appliances. Glasses may be obtained either from the hospital or an optician, and the charge will be related to the type of lens prescribed and the choice of frame.

Ambulance Service

The NHS provides emergency ambulance services free of charge via the 999 emergency telephone service. There are 44 ambulance services in the UK, all of which are NHS Trusts or form part of larger trusts. Helicopter ambulances are used in some areas where heavy traffic could hinder road progress, and an air ambulance service is available throughout Scotland. Non-emergency ambulance services are provided free of charge to patients who are deemed to require them on medical grounds.

In 1997–8 in England about 3,576,200 emergency calls were made to the ambulance service, an increase of 7 per cent on the previous year. Emergency patient journeys rose from about 2,600,000 to 2,700,000. The Patients' Charter requires emergency ambulances to respond to 95 per cent of calls within 14 minutes in urban areas and 19 minutes in rural areas, and to reach 50 per cent of cases within eight minutes. In 1997 two-thirds of ambulances met the Charter standard.

NHS Direct

NHS Direct is a telephone service staffed by nurses which gives patients advice on how to look after themselves as well as directing them to the appropriate part of the NHS for treatment if necessary. The Government intends that the service will cover 40 per cent of England by April 1999 and all parts of England by the end of 2000.

Blood Services

There are four national bodies which co-ordinate the blood donor programme in each constituent country of the UK. About two million donations of blood are given each year; donors give blood at local centres on a voluntary basis.

National Blood Authority, Oak House, Reeds Crescent, Watford, Herts wd1 1qh. Tel: 01923-486800. *Chairman*, M. Fogden; *Chief Executive*, J. Adey

Scottish National Blood Transfusion Service, 21 Ellens Glen Road, Edinburgh eh17 7qt. Tel: 0131-536 5700. *National Director*, A. McMillan-Douglas

Welsh Blood Service, Ely Valley Road, Talbot Green, Pontyclun cf72 9wb. Tel: 01443-622000. *Director*, Dr F. G. Williams

Northern Ireland Blood Transfusion Service, City Hospital Complex, Lisburn Road, Belfast bt9 7ts. Tel: 01232-321414

HOSPICES

Hospice or palliative care may be available for patients with life-threatening illnesses. It may be provided at the patient's home or in a voluntary or NHS hospice or in hospital, and is intended to ensure the best possible quality of life for the patient during their illness, and to provide help and support to both the patient and the patient's family. The National Council for Hospices and Specialist Palliative Care Services co-ordinates NHS and voluntary services in England, Wales and Northern Ireland; the Scottish Partnership Agency for Palliative and Cancer Care performs the same function in Scotland.

NATIONAL COUNCIL FOR HOSPICE AND SPECIALIST PALLIATIVE CARE SERVICES, 7th Floor, 1 Great Cumberland Place, London WIH 7AL. Tel: 0171-723 1639. *Executive Director,* Mrs J. Gaffin, OBE

SCOTTISH PARTNERSHIP AGENCY FOR PALLIATIVE AND CANCER CARE, 1A Cambridge Street, Edinburgh EH1 2DY. Tel: 0131-229 0538. *Director,* Mrs M. Stevenson

NUMBER OF BEDS AND PATIENT ACTIVITY 1996

	England*	Wales
In-patients:		
Average daily available beds	206,000	15,600
Average daily occupation of beds	n/a	12,200
Persons waiting for admission at 31 March	†1,048,000	65,000
Day-case admissions	2,845,000	286,400
Ordinary admissions	8,379,000	516,400
Out-patient attendances:		
New patients	10,989,000	667,100
Total attendances	40,118,000	2,569,500
Accident and emergency:		
New patients	12,404,000	798,400
Total attendances	14,234,000	975,300

* 1995 figures
† 1996 figure
n/a not available

SCOTLAND
In-patients:	
Average available staffed beds	40,600
Average occupied beds	32,800
Out-patient attendances:	
New patients	2,666,000
Total attendances	6,338,000

Source: The Stationery Office – *Annual Abstract of Statistics 1998*

WAITING LISTS

At the end of March 1998 the total number of patients waiting to be admitted to NHS hospitals in England was 1,297,662, an increase of 12.1 per cent on the previous year. The number of patients who had been waiting more than one year was 68,023, an increase of 118 per cent on the previous year; however, some 70 per cent of elective in-patients are treated within three months of being placed on a waiting list. Under the Patient's Charter, patients are guaranteed admission within 18 months of being placed on a waiting list.

PATIENT'S CHARTERS

The original Patient's Charter was published in 1991 and came into force in 1992; an expanded version was published in 1995. The Charter sets out the rights of patients in relation to the NHS (i.e. the standards of service which all patients will receive at all times); and patients' reasonable expectations (i.e. the standards of service that the NHS aims to provide, even if they cannot in

exceptional circumstances be met). The Charter covers areas such as access to services, personal treatment of patients, the provision of information, registering with a doctor, hospital waiting times, care in hospitals, community services, ambulance waiting times, dental, optical and pharmaceutical services, and maternity services. In England there are separate Patient's Charter leaflets setting out standards in relation to services for children and young people, maternity services, mental health services and blood donation.

The Government is developing a new NHS Charter, expected to be introduced in 1999. Further information is available free of charge from the national Health Information Service (Tel 0800-665544).

Health authorities and boards, NHS Trusts and GP practices may also have their own local charters setting out the standard of service they aim to provide.

COMPLAINTS

The Patient's Charter includes the right to have any complaint about the service provided by the NHS dealt with quickly, with a full written reply being provided by a relevant chief executive. There are two levels to the NHS complaints procedure: the first level involves resolution of a complaint locally, following a direct approach to the relevant service provider; the second level involves an independent review procedure if the complaint is not resolved locally. As a final resort, patients may approach the Health Service Commissioner or Ombudsman (*see* page 311) (in Northern Ireland, the Commissioner for Complaints (*see* page 332)) if they are dissatisfied with the response of the NHS to a complaint.

In 1996–7 there were 92,974 written complaints about hospital and community health services, of which 67 per cent were resolved locally within the target period of four weeks; 1.7 per cent of complainants requested an independent review. There were 36,990 written complaints about family health services and in 1,040 cases the complainant requested an independent review.

NHS TRIBUNALS

The National Health Service Tribunal and the National Health Service Tribunal (Scotland) (*see* page 371) consider representations that the continued inclusion of a doctor, dentist, optician or pharmacist on the list of a health authority or health board would be prejudicial to the efficiency of the service concerned. The Mental Health Review Tribunals (*see* page 371) are responsible for reviewing the cases of patients compulsorily detained under the Mental Health Act 1983.

RECIPROCAL ARRANGEMENTS

Citizens of countries in the European Economic Area (EEA - *see* page 776) are entitled to receive emergency health care either free of charge or for a reduced charge when they are temporarily visiting other member states of the EEA. Form E111, available at post offices, should be obtained before travelling. Non-EEA nationals, or visitors receiving routine, non-emergency care, are normally required to pay for treatment in Britain. There are bilateral agreements with several other countries, including Australia and New Zealand, for the provision of urgent medical treatment either free of charge or for a reduced charge.

Personal Social Services

The Secretary of State for Health is responsible, under the Local Authority Social Services Act 1970, for the provision of social services for elderly people, disabled people, families and children, and those with mental disorders. Personal Social Services are administered by local authorities according to policies and standards set by central government. Each authority has a Director of Social Services and a Social Services Committee responsible for the social services functions placed upon them. Local authorities provide, enable and commission care after assessing the needs of their population. The private and voluntary sectors also play an important role in the delivery of social services, and an estimated six million people in Great Britain provide substantial regular care for a member of their family.

The Community Care reforms introduced in 1993 were intended to enable vulnerable groups to live in the community rather than in residential homes wherever possible, and to offer them as independent a lifestyle as possible.

At 31 March 1997, there were 519,115 places in residential and nursing care homes in England. About 240,000 residents were supported by local authorities (an increase of 12 per cent on the previous year). Of the local authority-supported residents, 24 per cent were in local authority-run homes (down from 29 per cent), 46 per cent were in independent residential care homes (up from 42 per cent) and 27 per cent were in independent nursing homes (the same percentage as in the previous year).

FINANCE

The Personal Social Services programme is financed partly by central government, with decisions on expenditure allocations being made at local authority level.

STAFF

STAFF OF LOCAL AUTHORITY SOCIAL SERVICES DEPARTMENTS 1997 (ENGLAND)
Full-time equivalents

Area office/field work staff	114,900
Residential care staff	65,400
Day care staff	30,800
Central/strategic HQ staff	16,400
Other staff	1,900
Total staff	229,400

Source: Department of Health

ELDERLY PEOPLE

Services for elderly people are designed to enable them to remain living in their own homes for as long as possible. Local authority services include advice, domestic help, meals in the home, alterations to the home to aid mobility, emergency alarm systems, day and/or night attendants, laundry services and the provision of day centres and recreational facilities. Charges may be made for these services. Respite care may also be provided in order to allow carers temporary relief from their responsibilities.

Local authorities and the private sector also provide 'sheltered housing' for elderly people, sometimes with resident wardens.

If an elderly person is admitted to a residential home, charges are made according to a means test; if the person cannot afford to pay, the costs are met by the local authority.

DISABLED PEOPLE

Services for disabled people are designed to enable them to remain living in their own homes wherever possible. Local authority services include advice, adaptations to the home, meals in the home, help with personal care, occupational therapy, educational facilities and recreational facilities. Respite care may also be provided in order to allow carers temporary relief from their responsibilities.

Special housing may be available for disabled people who can live independently, and residential accommodation for those who cannot.

FAMILIES AND CHILDREN

Local authorities are required to provide services aimed at safeguarding the welfare of children in need and, wherever possible, allowing them to be brought up by their families. Services include advice, counselling, help in the home and the provision of family centres. Many authorities also provide short-term refuge accommodation for women and children.

DAY CARE

In allocating day-care places to children, local authorities give priority to children with special needs, whether in terms of their health, learning abilities or social needs. They also provide a registration and inspection service in relation to childminders, play groups and private day nurseries in the local authority area. In England in 1997 there were 6,100 day nurseries providing 194,000 places, 98,500 registered child-minders providing 365,000 places, and 15,800 play groups providing 384,000 places.

A national child care strategy is being developed by the Government, under which day care and out-of-school child care facilities will be extended to match more closely the needs of working parents.

CHILD PROTECTION

Children considered to be at risk of physical injury, neglect or sexual abuse are placed on the local authority's child protection register. Local authority social services staff, school nurses, health visitors and other agencies work together to prevent and detect cases of abuse. In England at 31 March 1997 there were 16,400 boys and 15,700 girls on child protection registers. Of these, 38 per cent were at risk of neglect, 34 per cent of physical abuse, 23 per cent of sexual abuse and 16 per cent of emotional abuse.

LOCAL AUTHORITY CARE

Local authorities are required to provide accommodation for children who have no parent or guardian or whose parents or guardians are unable or unwilling to care for them. A family proceedings court may also issue a care order in cases where a child is being neglected or abused, or is not attending school; the court must be satisfied that this would positively contribute to the well-being of the child.

The welfare of children in local authority care must be properly safeguarded. Children may be placed with foster families, who receive payments to cover the expenses of caring for the child or children, or in residential care. Children's homes may be run by the local authority or by the private or voluntary sectors; all homes are subject to inspection procedures. In England at 31 March 1997, 51,600 children were in the care of local authorities. Of these, 65 per cent were placed with foster parents and 5 per cent were placed for adoption.

ADOPTION

Local authorities are required to provide an adoption service, either directly or via approved voluntary societies.

In England and Wales in 1996, 6,000 children (3,000 boys and 3,000 girls) were adopted.

PEOPLE WITH LEARNING DISABILITIES

Services for people with learning disabilities (i.e. mental handicap) are designed to enable them to remain living in the community wherever possible. Local authority services include short-term care, support in the home, the provision of day care centres, and help with other activities outside the home. Residential care is provided for the severely or profoundly disabled.

MENTALLY ILL PEOPLE

Under the Care Programme Approach, mentally ill people should be assessed by specialist services and receive a care plan, and a key worker should be appointed for each patient. Regular reviews of the patient's progress should be conducted. Local authorities provide help and advice to mentally ill people and their families, and places in day centres and social centres. Social workers can apply for a mentally disturbed person to be compulsorily detained in hospital. Where appropriate, mentally ill people are provided with accommodation in special hospitals, local authority accommodation, or homes run by private or voluntary organizations. Patients who have been discharged from hospitals may be placed on a supervision register. In July 1998 the Government announced that the system of care for mentally ill people would be replaced. A new mental health strategy will be announced in late 1998 and national standards of patient care will be produced by April 1999. The Mental Health Act 1983 will be replaced by new legislation.

TOTAL PLACES IN RESIDENTIAL AND NURSING HOMES (ENGLAND) *as at 31 March 1997*

By client group

Elderly people	374,302
Physically/sensorily disabled adults	11,494
Elderly mentally infirm people	39,373
People with mental illness	22,646
People with learning disabilities	50,872
Other people	20,428
All client groups	519,115

Source: Department of Health

LOCAL AUTHORITY-SUPPORTED RESIDENTS IN STAFFED RESIDENTIAL AND NURSING CARE (ENGLAND) *as at 31 March 1997*

All staffed homes	236,083
Local authority	58,651
Independent residential care	111,444
Independent nursing care	65,988
Elderly people	180,219
Physically/sensorily disabled adults	8,628
People with mental health problems	17,271
People with learning disabilities	26,872
Other people	3,093

Source: The Stationery Office – *Health and Personal Social Services Statistics for England 1997*

LOCAL AUTHORITY PERSONAL SOCIAL SERVICES GROSS EXPENDITURE BY CLIENT GROUP 1995–6 (ENGLAND)
£ million

	Elderly	Children	Learning disability	Adults	Mental health	HQ costs	Total
HQ costs	—	—	—	—	—	122.4	122.4
Area officers/senior managers	99.0	152.1	22.5	29.1	22.7	—	325.5
Care management/care assessment	221.5	289.1	46.9	61.6	69.0	—	688.1
Residential care	2,282.3	631.1	560.7	153.0	147.2	—	3,774.3
Non-residential care	1,405.7	840.9	430.0	333.6	141.2	—	3,151.4
Field social work	61.3	120.1	19.6	18.8	26.1	—	245.8
Other	—	—	—	85.7	—	—	85.7
TOTAL	4,069.8	2,033.2	1,079.7	681.8	406.3	122.4	8,393.0

Source: The Stationery Office – *Health and Personal Social Services Statistics for England 1997*

National Insurance and Related Cash Benefits

NB All leaflets referred to in this section can be obtained from local social security offices unless an alternative source is given

The state insurance and assistance schemes, comprising schemes of national insurance and industrial injuries insurance, national assistance, and non-contributory old age pensions, came into force from 5 July 1948. The Ministry of Social Security Act 1966 replaced national assistance and non-contributory old age pensions with a scheme of non-contributory benefits. These and subsequent measures relating to social security provision in Great Britain were consolidated by the Social Security Act 1975, the Social Security (Consequential Provisions) Act 1975, and the Industrial Injuries and Diseases (Old Cases) Act 1975. Corresponding measures were passed for Northern Ireland. The Social Security Pensions Act 1975 introduced a new state pensions scheme in 1978, and the graduated pension scheme 1961 to 1975 has been wound up, existing rights being preserved. Under the Pensions Act 1995 the age of retirement is to be 65 for both men and women, this being phased in between 2010 and 6 April 2020. The Pensioners' Payments and Social Security Act 1979 provided for a Christmas bonus for pensioners in 1979 and in succeeding years. The Child Benefit Act 1975 replaced family allowances (introduced 1946) with child benefit and one-parent benefit. Some of this legislation has been superseded by the provisions of the Social Security Acts 1969 to 1992. The Government has announced its intention to reform the social security system and a green paper, *New Ambitions for Our Country – A New Contract for Welfare*, was published in March 1998.

NATIONAL INSURANCE SCHEME

The National Insurance (NI) scheme operates under the Social Security Contributions and Benefits Act 1992 and the Social Security Administration Act 1992, and orders and regulations made thereunder. The scheme is financed by contributions payable by earners, employers and others (*see* below) and by a Treasury grant. Money collected under the scheme is used to finance the National Insurance Fund (from which contributory benefits are paid) and to contribute to the cost of the National Health Service.

NATIONAL INSURANCE FUND

Approximate receipts and payments of the National Insurance Fund for the year ended 31 March 1997 were:

Receipts	£'000
Balance, 1 April 1996	7,835,829
Contributions under the Social Security	
Acts (net of SSP and SMP)	41,874,927
Treasury grant	1,901,500
Compensation from	
Consolidated Fund for SSP	
and SMP recoveries	524,000
Income from investments	473,876
Other receipts	107,977
	52,718,109

Payments	£'000	£'000
Unemployment benefit	587,298	
Jobseeker's allowance		
(contributory)	332,708	
Incapacity benefit	7,661,624	
Maternity allowance	32,725	
Widow's benefit	981,241	
Guardian's allowance and		
child's special allowance	1,496	
Retirement pension	31,994,561	
Pensioners' lump sum		
payments	128,614	41,720,267
Personal pensions		1,997,607
Transfers to Northern Ireland		75,000
Administration		1,038,415
Other payments		17,392
Redundancy payments		132,003
Balance, 31 March 1997		7,737,423
		52,718,107

CONTRIBUTIONS

There are five classes of NI contributions:

Class 1   paid by employees and their employers
Class 1A paid by employers who provide employees with cars/fuel for private use
Class 2   paid by self-employed people
Class 3   voluntary contributions paid to protect entitlement to certain benefits
Class 4   paid by the self-employed on their taxable profits over a set limit

The lower and upper earnings limits and the percentage rates referred to below apply from 6 April 1998 to 5 April 1999.

Class 1

Class 1 contributions are paid where a person:
- is an employed earner (employee) or office holder (e.g. company director)
- is 16 or over and under state pension age
- earns at or above the lower earning limit of £64.00 per week (including overtime pay, bonus, commission, etc., without deduction of superannuation contributions)

Class 1 contributions are not paid where a person earns less than the lower earnings limit.

Class 1 contributions are made up of primary and secondary contributions. Primary contributions are those paid by the employee and these are deducted from earnings by the employer. The percentage rates paid by the employee are as follows:
- 2 per cent on all earnings up to and including the lower earnings limit of £64.00
- 10 per cent on earnings between the lower earnings limit and the upper earnings limit of £485.00 per week (8.4 per cent for contracted-out employment, *see* page 488)

Some married women or widows pay a reduced rate of 3.85 per cent on all earnings up to and including the upper earnings limit. It is no longer possible to elect to pay the reduced rate but those who had reduced liability before 12 May 1977 may retain it so long as certain conditions are met. *See* leaflet CA09 (widows) or leaflet CA13 (married women).

Secondary contributions are paid by employers of employed earners on all earnings at or above the lower earnings limit. There is no upper earnings limit for employers' contributions, which are as follows:

Weekly earnings	Percentage of reckonable income		
	Not contracted out	Contracted-out schemes COSR*	COMP*
£64.00–109.99	3.0	0	1.5
110.00–154.99	5.0	2.0	3.5
155.00–209.99	7.0	4.0	5.5
210.00–485.00	10.0	7.0	8.5
over 485.00	10.0	10.0	10.0

* For explanation of COSR and COMP schemes, see page 488

The contracted-out rate applies only to that portion of earnings between the lower and upper earnings limits. Employers' contributions below and above those respective limits are assessed at the appropriate not contracted-out rate.

Class 2

Class 2 contributions are paid where a person is self-employed and is 16 or over and under state pension age. Contributions are paid at a flat rate of £6.35 per week regardless of the amount earned. However, those with earnings of less than £3,590 a year can apply for Small Earnings Exception, i.e. exemption from liability to pay Class 2 contributions. Those granted exemption from Class 2 contributions may pay Class 2 or Class 3 contributions voluntarily. Self-employed earners (whether or not they pay Class 2 contributions) may also be liable to pay Class 4 contributions based on profits. There are special rules for those who are concurrently employed and self-employed.

Married women and widows can no longer choose not to pay Class 2 contributions but those who elected not to pay Class 2 contributions before 12 May 1977 may retain the right so long as certain conditions are met.

Class 2 contributions are collected by the Contributions Agency, an executive agency of the Department of Social Security, by direct debit or quarterly bills. See leaflets CA03 and CA02.

Class 3

Class 3 contributions are voluntary flat-rate contributions of £6.25 per week payable by persons over the age of 16 who would otherwise be unable to qualify for retirement pension and certain other benefits because they have an insufficient record of Class 1 or Class 2 contributions. This may include those who are not working, those not liable for Class 1 or Class 2 contributions or those excepted from Class 2 contributions. Married women and widows who on or before 11 May 1977 elected not to pay Class 1 (full rate) or Class 2 contributions cannot pay Class 3 contributions while they retain this right.

Class 3 contributions are collected by the Contributions Agency by quarterly bills or direct debit. See leaflet CA08.

Class 4

Self-employed people whose profits and gains are over £7,310 a year pay Class 4 contributions in addition to Class 2 contributions. This applies to self-employed earners over 16 and under the state pension age. Class 4 contributions are calculated at 6 per cent of annual profits or gains between £7,310 and £25,220. The maximum Class 4 contribution payable on £25,220 or more is £1,074.60.

Class 4 contributions are assessed and collected by the Inland Revenue together with Schedule D tax. It is possible, in some circumstances, to apply for exceptions from liability to pay Class 4 contributions or to have the amount of contribution reduced (where Class 1 contributions are payable on earnings assessed for Class 4 contributions). See leaflet CA03.

PENSIONS

The Social Security Pensions Act came into force in 1978. It aimed to:
- reduce reliance on means-tested benefit in old age, widowhood and chronic ill-health
- ensure that occupational pension schemes which are contracted out of the state scheme fulfil the conditions of a good scheme
- ensure that pensions are adequately protected against inflation
- ensure that men and women are treated equally in state and occupational schemes

Legislation and regulations introduced since 1978 go further towards fulfilling these aims and more changes came into effect in April 1997 (see below). One of the changes is to equalize the state pension age for men (currently 65 years) and women (currently 60 years) from 6 April 2020. The change will be phased in over the ten years leading up to 6 April 2020. As a result the state pension age is as follows:
- the pension age for men remains at 65
- the pension age for women born on or before 5 April 1950 remains at 60
- the pension age for women born on or after 6 April 1955 is now 65
- for women born after 5 April 1950 and before 6 April 1955, the pension age is 60 plus one month for every month, or part of a month, that their date of birth fell after 5 April 1950

State Pension Scheme

The state pension scheme consists of the basic flat-rate pension and the state earnings-related pension scheme (SERPS), also known as additional pension.

The amount of basic pension paid is dependent on the number of 'qualifying years' a person has in their 'working life'. A 'qualifying year' is a tax year in which a person pays Class 1 (at the standard rate), 2 or 3 NI contributions for the whole year (see above). Those in receipt of invalid care allowance, disability working allowance, jobseeker's allowance, incapacity benefit, severe disablement allowance or approved training have contributions credited to them for each week they receive benefit or fulfil certain other conditions. For those reaching pensionable age on or after 6 April 1999, a Class 3 credit of earnings will be awarded for each week from 6 April 1995 that family credit has been received. 'Working life' is counted from the start of the tax year in which a person reaches 16 to the end of the tax year before the one in which they reach pensionable age: for men this is normally 49 years and for women this varies between 44 and 49 years because the pension ages vary (see above). To get the full rate (100 per cent) basic pension a person must have qualifying years for about 90 per cent of their working life. To get the minimum basic pension (25 per cent) a person will need nine or ten qualifying years. Married women who are not entitled to a pension on their own contributions may get a pension on their husband's contributions. It is possible for people who are unable to work because they care for children or a sick or disabled person at home to reduce the number of qualifying years required. This is called home responsibilities protection (HRP) and can be given for any tax year since April 1978; the number of years for which HRP is given is deducted from the number of qualifying years needed.

The amount of SERPS or additional pension paid depends on the amount of earnings a person has between the lower and upper earnings limits (see page 486) for each complete tax year between 6 April 1978 (when the scheme started) and the tax year before they reach state pension age. The right to additional pension does not depend on the person's right to basic pension. The amount of additional pension paid also depends on when a person reaches retirement; changes being phased in from 6 April 1999 mean that pensions will be calculated differently from that date. Women widowed before 6 April 2000 will inherit all their late husband's additional pension and women widowed on or after this date will inherit half of the husband's additional pension.

There are four categories of state pension provided under the Social Security Contributions and Benefits Act 1992:

- Category A, a contributory pension made up of basic and additional elements, payable to those of pensionable age who satisfy the entitlement conditions described above (see pages 489–90)
- Category B, a contributory pension made up of basic and additional elements, payable to married women and widows and based on their husband's contributions. This category of pension is to be extended to men from 6 April 2010 (see pages 489–90)
- Category C, a non-contributory pension payable to those who reached pensionable age before 5 July 1948 (see page 491)
- Category D, a non-contributory pension for those over 80 (see page 491)

Graduated retirement benefit is also available to those who paid graduated NI contributions into the scheme when it existed between April 1961 and April 1975 (see page 492).

It is possible to find out how much basic and additional pension a person might receive by filling in form BR19, available from local social security offices or by telephoning 0191-225 5240.

CONTRACTED-OUT AND PERSONAL PENSION SCHEMES

Under the Pensions Schemes Act 1993, an employer can contract out of SERPS those employees who are members of an occupational scheme, so long as the occupational scheme satisfies certain conditions. The occupational pension takes the place of the additional pension from April 1997 (previously it took the place of part of the additional pension); the state remains responsible for the basic pension. Until April 1997 members of contracted-out occupational and personal pension schemes accrued additional pension in the same way as someone who is not contracted-out but the rate payable was reduced by contracted-out deductions. Since 5 April 1997, it has not been possible to accrue any SERPS while being a member of a contracted-out occupational or personal pension scheme. Members of a COSR, COMP or personal pension scheme can no longer earn additional pension but they are still entitled to those rights earned before April 1997. From April 1997 there are age-related NI contribution rebates for people who leave SERPS and become members of a COMP or personal pension scheme; these will be lower for younger people and higher for older people.

There are two types of contracted-out occupational schemes.

Contracted-Out Salary Related Scheme (COSR)

- this scheme must provide a pension related to earnings
- the pension provided must not be less than a person's guaranteed minimum pension (GMP), i.e. worth about the same as the additional pension provided by the state scheme
- any additional pension earned from 6 April 1978 to 5 April 1997 will be reduced by the amount of GMP earned during that period

- from 6 April 1997 these schemes no longer have to provide a GMP but do have to satisfy a new scheme-based test in order to be issued with a contracting-out certificate

Contracted-Out Money Purchase Scheme (COMP)

- this scheme must provide a pension based on the value of the fund built up, i.e. the money paid in, along with returns from investment
- part of the pension, known as protected rights, takes the place of the additional pension. A contracted-out deduction, which may be more or less than the pension provided by the scheme, will be made from any additional pension earned from 6 April 1987 to 5 April 1997

In contracted-out occupational pension schemes, both the employee and employer pay lower NI contribution rates in recognition that SERPS will not be paid.

Personal Pension Schemes

The option of a personal pension scheme is open to all employees, even if their employer has an occupational pension scheme. A personal pension scheme must provide a pension based on the value of the fund built up, i.e. the money paid in, along with returns from investment. Part of the pension, known as protected rights, takes the place of the additional pension. A contracted-out deduction, which may be more or less than the pension provided by the scheme, will be made from any additional pension earned from 6 April 1987 to 5 April 1997.

Employees who are members of a personal pension plan and their employers pay NI contributions at the full rate and the DSS pays the difference between the full rate and the contracted-out rate into the personal pension scheme.

A Pensions Ombudsman deals with complaints about maladministration of pensions schemes. The Occupational Pensions Board, which supervised contracting-out and approved personal pension schemes, was abolished in April 1997 and replaced by the Occupational Pensions Regulatory Authority. See leaflet NP46.

BENEFITS

Leaflets relating to the various benefits and contribution conditions for different benefits are available from local social security offices; leaflets NI196 *Social Security Benefit Rates*, FB2 *Which Benefit?* and MG1 *A Guide to Benefits* are general guides to benefits, benefit rates and contributions.

The benefits payable under the Social Security Acts are:

CONTRIBUTORY BENEFITS
Jobseeker's allowance (contribution-based)
Incapacity benefit
Maternity allowance
Widow's benefit (comprising widow's payment, widowed mother's allowance and widow's pension)
Retirement pensions, categories A and B

NON-CONTRIBUTORY BENEFITS
Child benefit
Guardian's allowance
Jobseeker's allowance (income-based)
Invalid care allowance
Severe disablement allowance
Attendance allowance
Disability living allowance
Disability working allowance
Retirement pensions, categories C and D
Income support
Family credit

Housing benefit
Council tax benefit
Social fund

BENEFITS FOR INDUSTRIAL INJURIES AND
DISABLEMENT

OTHER
Statutory sick pay
Statutory maternity pay

CONTRIBUTORY BENEFITS

Entitlement to contributory benefits depends on contribution conditions being satisfied either by the claimant or
by some other person (depending on the kind of benefit).
The class or classes of contribution which for this purpose
are relevant to each benefit are:

Jobseeker's allowance (contribution-based)   Class 1
Incapacity benefit   Class 1 or 2
Maternity allowance   Class 1 or 2
Widow's benefits   Class 1, 2 or 3
Retirement pensions, categories A and B   Class 1, 2 or 3

The system of contribution conditions relates to yearly
levels of earnings on which contributions have been paid.

JOBSEEKER'S ALLOWANCE

Jobseeker's allowance (JSA) replaced unemployment
benefit and income support for unemployed people under
pension age from 7 October 1996. There are two routes of
entitlement. Contribution-based JSA is paid as a personal
rate (i.e. additional benefit for dependants is not paid) to
those who have made sufficient NI contributions. Savings
and partner's earnings are not taken into account and
payment can be made for up to six months. Those who do
not qualify for contribution-based JSA, those who have
exhausted their entitlement to contribution-based JSA or
those for whom contribution-based JSA provides insufficient income may qualify for income-based JSA. The
amount paid depends on age and number of dependants
and income and savings are taken into account. Income-
based JSA may comprise three parts: a personal allowance
for the jobseeker and his/her partner and one for each child
or young person for whom they are responsible; premiums
for groups of people with special needs; and housing costs.
This is payable for the claimant and their dependants for as
long as they satisfy the rules. Rates of jobseeker's allowance
correspond to income support rates.

Claims for this benefit are made through job centres/
employment offices. A person wishing to claim jobseeker's
allowance must be unemployed, capable of work and
available for any work which they can reasonably be
expected to do, usually for at least 40 hours per week. They
must agree and sign a 'jobseeker's agreement', which will
set out each claimant's plans to find work, and must actively
seek work.

A person will be disqualified from jobseeker's allowance
if they have left a job voluntarily or through misconduct, if
they refuse to take up an offer of employment or if they fail
to attend a training scheme or employment programme. In
these circumstances, it may be possible to receive hardship
payments, particularly where the claimant or their family
is vulnerable, e.g. if sick or pregnant, or for those with
children or caring responsibilities. See leaflet JSAL5.

INCAPACITY BENEFIT

Incapacity benefit is available to those who are incapable of
work and cannot get statutory sick pay from their employer.
It is not payable to those over state pension age. However,
people who are already in receipt of short-term incapacity
benefit when they reach state pension age may continue to

receive this benefit for up to 52 weeks. There are three
rates of incapacity benefit:
– short-term lower rate for the first 28 weeks of sickness
– short-term higher rate from weeks 29 to 52
– long-term rate after week 52
The terminally ill and those entitled to the highest rate
care component of disability living allowance are paid the
long-term rate after 28 weeks. Incapacity benefit is taxable
after 28 weeks.

Two rates of age addition are paid with long-term
benefit based on the claimant's age when incapacity started.
The higher rate is payable where incapacity for work
commenced before the age of 35; and the lower rate where
incapacity commenced before the age of 45. Increases for
dependents are also payable with short and long-term
incapacity benefit.

There are two medical tests of incapacity: the 'own
occupation' test and the 'all work' test. Those who worked
before becoming incapable of working will be assessed, for
the first 28 weeks of incapacity, on their ability to do their
own job. After 28 weeks (or from the start of incapacity for
those who were not working) claimants are assessed on
their ability to carry out a range of work-related activities.
The 'all work' test applies to most former sickness and
invalidity benefit claimants. See leaflets IB202 and FB28.

MATERNITY ALLOWANCE

The maternity allowance (MA) scheme covers women
who are self-employed or otherwise do not qualify for
statutory maternity pay (see page 494). In order to qualify
the woman must have been working and paying standard
rate NI contributions for at least 26 weeks in the 66-week
period which ends with the week before the week in which
the baby is due. A woman can choose to start receiving MA
between the beginning of the 11th week before the week in
which the baby is due and the Sunday after the baby is born,
depending on when she stops working. MA is paid for a
period of up to 18 weeks. MA is only paid while the woman
is not working. See leaflet NI17A.

WIDOW'S BENEFITS

Only the late husband's contributions of any class count for
widow's benefit in any of its three forms:
Widow's payment – may be received by a woman who at her
    husband's death is under 60, or whose husband was not
    entitled to a Category A retirement pension when he
    died. It is a single tax-free lump sum payable immedi-
    ately the woman becomes a widow
Widowed mother's allowance – a taxable benefit payable to a
    widow if she is entitled or treated as entitled to child
    benefit, or if she is expecting her husband's baby
Widow's pension – a widow may receive this pension if aged
    45 or over at the time of her husband's death (40 or over
    if widowed before 11 April 1988) or when her widowed
    mother's allowance ends. If aged 55 or over (50 or over if
    widowed before 11 April 1988) she will receive the full
    widow's pension rate
It is not possible to receive widowed mother's allowance
and widow's pension at the same time, and widow's benefit
in any form ceases upon remarriage or during a period in
which a widow lives with a man as his wife. Different rules
and conditions (other than those mentioned) apply to
women widowed before 11 April 1988. See leaflet NP45.

RETIREMENT PENSION: CATEGORIES A AND B

A Category A pension is payable for life to men and women
who reach state pension age and who satisfy the contributions conditions (see page 487). A Category B pension is
payable for life to a woman and is based on her husband's
contributions. It becomes payable only when the husband
has claimed his pension and the woman has reached state

pension age. It is also payable on widowhood after 60 regardless of whether the late husband had qualified for his pension. There are special rules for those who are widowed before reaching pensionable age.

A person may defer claiming their pension for five years after state pension age. In doing so they may earn increments which will increase the weekly amount paid when they claim their pension. If a married man defers his Category A pension, his wife cannot claim a Category B pension on his contributions but she may earn increments on her pension during this time. A woman can defer her Category B pension, and earn increments, even if her husband is claiming his Category A pension.

The basic state pension is £64.70 per week plus any additional (earnings-related) pension the person may be entitled to (*see* page 487). An increase of £38.70 is paid for an adult dependent, providing the dependent's earnings do not exceed the rate of jobseeker's allowance for a single person (*see* below). It is also possible to get an increase of Category A and B pensions for a child or children. An age addition of 25p per week is payable if a retirement pensioner is aged 80 or over.

Since 1989 pensioners have been allowed to have unlimited earnings without affecting their retirement pension. Income support is payable on top of a pension where a pension does not give the person enough to live on and to those who are entitled to retirement pension but who have not claimed it. Pensioners may also be entitled to housing and council tax benefits.

Graduated Retirement Benefit

Graduated NI contributions were first payable from 1961 and were calculated as a percentage of earnings between certain bands. They were discontinued in 1975. Any graduated pension which an employed person over 18 and under 70 (65 for a woman) had earned by paying graduated contributions will be paid when the contributor claims retirement pension or at 70 (65 for a woman), in addition to any retirement pension for which he or she qualifies. A wife can get a graduated pension in return for her own graduated contributions, but not for her husband's.

Graduated retirement benefit is at a weekly rate for each 'unit' of graduated contributions paid by the employee (half a unit or more counts as a whole unit); the rate varies from person to person. A unit of graduated pension can be calculated by adding together all graduated contributions and dividing by 7.5 (men) or 9.0 (women). If a person defers making a claim beyond 65 (60 for a woman), entitlement may be increased by one seventh of a penny per £1 of its weekly rate for each complete week of deferred retirement, as long as the retirement is deferred for a minimum of seven weeks.

Weekly Rates of Benefit
from April 1998

Jobseeker's allowance (contribution-based)
Person under 18	£30.30
Person aged 18–24	39.85
Person over 25	50.35

Short-term incapacity benefit
Person under pension age – lower rate	48.80
*Person under pension age – higher rate	57.70
Increase for adult dependant	30.20
*Person over pension age	62.05
Increase for adult dependant	37.20

Long-term incapacity benefit
Person (under or over pension age)	64.70
Increase for adult dependant	38.70
Age addition – lower rate	6.80
Age addition – higher rate	13.60

Invalidity allowance: maximum amount payable
Higher rate	13.60
Middle rate	8.60
Lower rate	4.30

Maternity allowance
Employed	57.70
Self-employed or unemployed	50.10

Widow's benefits
Widow's payment (lump sum)	1,000.00
*Widowed mother's allowance	64.70
*Widow's pension	64.70

Retirement pension: categories A and B
Single person	64.70
Increase for wife/other adult dependant	38.70

*These benefits attract an increase for each dependent child (in addition to child benefit) of £9.90 for the first or only child and £11.30 for each subsequent child

NON-CONTRIBUTORY BENEFITS

These benefits are paid from general taxation and are not dependent on NI contributions. Unless otherwise stated, a benefit is tax-free and is not means tested.

Child Benefit

Child benefit is payable for virtually all children aged under 16, and for those aged 16 to 18 who are studying full-time up to and including A-level or equivalent standard. It is also payable for a short period if the child has left school recently and is registered for work or work-based training for young people at a careers office.

A higher rate of benefit (child benefit (lone parent)) may be paid to a person who is responsible for bringing up one or more children on his/her own. It is a flat rate benefit payable for the eldest child only. Since 6 July 1998 child benefit (lone parent) has not been available to new lone parents but it may still be payable in certain circumstances. *See* leaflets CH1 and CH11.

Guardian's Allowance

Where the parents of a child are dead, the person who has the child in his/her family may claim a guardian's allowance in addition to child benefit. In exceptional circumstances the allowance is payable on the death of only one parent. *See* leaflet NI14.

Invalid Care Allowance

Invalid care allowance (ICA) is a taxable benefit payable to people of working age who give up the opportunity of full-time paid employment because they are regularly and substantially engaged (spending at least 35 hours per week as a carer) in caring for a severely disabled person. To qualify for ICA a person must be caring for someone in receipt of one of the following benefits:
- the middle or highest rate of disability living allowance care component
- either rate of attendance allowance
- constant attendance allowance, paid at not less than the normal maximum rate, under the industrial injuries or war pension schemes

See leaflets FB31 and FB28.

Severe Disablement Allowance

Persons who have been incapable of work for a continuous period of at least 28 weeks but who do not qualify for contributory incapacity benefit may be entitled to severe disablement allowance (SDA). This benefit is available to people over 16 and under 65. Those who are over 65 can only get SDA if they were entitled to it on the day before their 65th birthday. People who became incapable of work on or before their 20th birthday do not have to have their disability assessed but those who became incapable after their 20th birthday must be assessed as at least 80 per cent disabled. *See* leaflet NI252.

ATTENDANCE ALLOWANCE

This is payable to disabled people over 65 who need a lot of care or supervision because of physical or mental disability for a period of at least six months. People not expected to live for six months because of an illness do not have to wait six months. The allowance has two rates: the lower rate is for day or night care, and the higher rate is for day and night care. *See* leaflets DS702 and FB28.

DISABILITY LIVING ALLOWANCE

This is payable to disabled people under 65 who have personal care and mobility needs because of an illness or disability for a period of at least three months and are likely to have those needs for a further six months or more. People not expected to live for six months because of an illness do not have to wait three months. The allowance has two components: the care component, which has three rates, and the mobility component, which has two rates. The rates depend on the care and mobility needs of the claimant. The mobility component is payable only to those aged five or over. *See* leaflet DS704.

DISABILITY WORKING ALLOWANCE

This is an income-related benefit for people who are working 16 hours per week or more but have an illness or disability which puts them at a disadvantage in getting a job. To qualify a person must be aged 16 or over and must, at the date of the claim, have one of the 'qualifying benefits', such as disability living allowance. The amount payable depends on the size of the family and weekly income. The allowance is not payable if any savings exceed £16,000. *See* leaflet DS703.

RETIREMENT PENSION: CATEGORIES C AND D

A Category C pension is provided, subject to a residence test, for persons who were over pensionable age on 5 July 1948, and for the wives and widows of men who qualified if they are over pension age. A Category D pension is provided for people aged 80 and over if they are not entitled to another category of pension or are entitled to less than the Category D rate.

WEEKLY RATES OF BENEFIT
from April 1998

Child benefit
Eldest child	£11.45
Eldest child of certain lone parents	17.10
Each subsequent child	9.30

Guardian's allowance
Eldest child	9.90
Each subsequent child	11.30

*Invalid care allowance	38.70
Increase for wife/other adult dependant	23.15

*Severe disablement allowance
†Basic rate	39.10
Under 40	13.60
40–49	8.60
50–59	4.30
Increase for wife/other adult dependant	23.20

Attendance allowance
Higher rate	51.30
Lower rate	34.30

Disability living allowance
Care component	
Higher rate	51.30

Middle rate	34.30
Lower rate	13.60
Mobility component	
Higher rate	35.85
Lower rate	13.60

Disability working allowance
Single person	50.75
Couple or single parent	79.40
Child aged under 11	12.35
aged 11–15	20.45
aged 16–18	25.40
Disabled child allowance	21.45
Thirty hours allowance	10.80

‡Applicable amount (income threshold)
Single person	59.25
Couple or single parent	79.00

Retirement pension: categories *C and D
Single person	38.70
Increase for wife/other adult dependant	23.15
(not payable with Category D pension)	

*These benefits attract an increase for each dependent child (in addition to child benefit) of £9.90 for the first or only child and £11.30 for each subsequent child

†The age addition applies to the age when incapacity began

‡70 pence is deducted from the maximum DWA payable (this is obtained by adding up the appropriate allowance for each person in the family) for every £ coming in each week over the appropriate applicable amount. Where weekly income is below the applicable amount, maximum DWA is payable

INCOME SUPPORT

Income support is a benefit for those aged 16 and over whose income is below a certain level. It can be paid to people who are not expected to sign on as unemployed (income support for unemployed people was replaced by jobseeker's allowance in October 1996) and who are:

– incapable of work due to sickness or disability
– bringing up children alone
– 60 or over
– looking after a person who has a disability
– registered blind

Some people who are not in these categories may also be able to claim income support.

Income support is also payable to people who work for less than 16 hours a week on average (or 24 hours for a partner). Some people can claim income support if they work longer hours.

Income support is not payable if the claimant, or claimant and partner, have capital or savings in excess of £8,000. For capital and savings in excess of £3,000, a deduction of £1 is made for every £250 or part of £250 held. The maximum amount of capital is £16,000 for those in residential homes, and £19,000 for those in nursing homes.

Sums payable depend on fixed allowances laid down by law for people in different circumstances. If both partners are entitled to income support, either may claim it for the couple. People receiving income support may be able to receive housing benefit, help with mortgage or home loan interest and help with health care. They may also be eligible for help with exceptional expenses from the Social Fund. Special rates may apply to some people living in residential care or nursing homes. Leaflet IS20 gives a detailed explanation of income support.

In July 1997 the Government initiated a pilot programme for lone parents, and from October 1998 this was extended to the whole of the UK. All lone parents receiving income support are assigned a personal adviser at a jobcentre who will provide guidance and support with a view to enabling the claimant to find work.

INCOME SUPPORT PREMIUMS

Income support premiums are additional weekly payments for those with special needs. People qualifying for more than one premium will normally only receive the highest single premium for which they qualify. However, family premium, disabled child premium, severe disability premium and carer premium are payable in addition to other premiums.

People with children may qualify for:
- the family premium if they have at least one child (a higher rate is paid to lone parents, although from 6 April 1998 it has not generally been available to new claimants)
- the disabled child premium if they have a child who receives disability living allowance or is registered blind

Carers may qualify for:
- the carer premium if they or their partner are in receipt of invalid care allowance

Long-term sick or disabled people may qualify for:
- the disability premium if they or their partner are receiving certain benefits because they are disabled or cannot work; are registered blind; or if the claimant has been incapable of work or receiving statutory sick pay for at least 364 days (196 days if the person is terminally ill), including periods of incapacity separated by eight weeks or less
- the severe disability premium if the person lives alone and receives attendance allowance or the middle or higher rate of disability living allowance care component and no one receives invalid care allowance for caring for that person. This premium is also available to couples where both partners meet the above conditions

People aged 60 and over may qualify for:
- the pensioner premium if they or their partner are aged 60 to 74
- the enhanced pensioner premium if they or their partner are aged 75 to 79
- the higher pensioner premium if they or their partner are aged 80 or over. This is also available to people over 60 who receive attendance allowance, disability living allowance, long-term incapacity benefit or severe disablement allowance, or who are registered blind

WEEKLY RATES OF BENEFIT
from April 1998

Income support

Single person

under 18	£30.30
under 18 (higher)	39.85
aged 18 – 24	39.85
aged 25 and over	50.35
aged 18 and over and a single parent	50.35

Couples*

both under 18	60.10
one or both aged 18 or over	79.00

For each child in a family

until September following 11th birthday	17.30
from September following 11th birthday to September following 16th birthday	25.35
†from September following 16th birthday to day before 19th birthday	30.30

Premiums

Family premium	11.05
Family (lone parent) premium	15.75
Disabled child premium	21.45
Carer premium	13.65
Disability premium	
Single	21.45
Couple	30.60

Severe disability premium

Single	38.50
Couple (one person qualified)	38.50
Couple (both qualified)	77.00
Pensioner premium	
Single	20.10
Couple	30.35
Higher pensioner premium	
Single	27.20
Couple	38.90
Enhanced pensioner premium	
Single	22.85
Couple	33.55

*Where one or both partners are aged under 18, their personal allowance will depend on their situation
†If in full-time education up to A-level or equivalent standard

FAMILY CREDIT

Family credit is a tax-free benefit for working families with children. To qualify, a family must include at least one child under 16 (under 19 if in full-time education up to A-level or equivalent standard) and the claimant, or partner if there is one, must be working for at least 16 hours per week. It does not matter which partner is working and they may be employed or self-employed. Family credit is not payable if the claimant, or claimant and partner, have capital or savings in excess of £8,000. The rate of benefit is affected if capital or savings in excess of £3,000 are held.

Family credit is usually paid at the same rate for 26 weeks, after which a new claim can be made. The rate of family credit depends on:
- the family's net income, excluding child benefit, child benefit (lone-parent) and the first £15.00 of any maintenance in payment
- the number of children and the children's ages
- the number of hours the claimant or their partner work
- in certain circumstances, the amount of childcare charges paid for children under 12

Family credit is claimed by post and in two-parent families the woman should claim. A claim pack, FC1, is available from social security offices or the Family Credit Helpline on 01253-500050. *See* leaflet NI261.

WEEKLY RATES OF BENEFIT
from 7 April 1998

The maximum amount of family credit is payable where income is less than £79.00 per week. For every pound earned over £79.00, 70 pence will be deducted from the maximum amount of family credit that can be paid. The maximum rate consists of:

Adult credit (amount is the same for lone parents and couples)	£48.80
30-hour credit (where one parent works at least 30 hours per week)	10.80

Child credit

each child under 11	12.35
each child aged 11–15	20.45
each child aged 16–18	25.40

HOUSING BENEFIT

Housing benefit is designed to help people with rent (including rent for accommodation in guest houses, lodgings or hostels). It does not cover mortgage payments. The amount of benefit paid depends on:
- the income of the claimant, and partner if there is one, including earned income, unearned income (any other income including some other benefits) and savings
- number of dependents

– certain extra needs of the claimant, partner or any dependants
– number of people sharing the home who are not dependent on the claimant
– how much rent is paid

Housing benefit is not payable if the claimant, or claimant and partner, have savings of over £16,000. The amount of benefit is affected if savings held exceed £3,000. Housing benefit is not paid for meals, fuel or certain service charges that may be included in the rent. Deductions are also made for most non-dependents who live in the same accommodation as the claimant (and their partner).

The maximum amount of benefit (which is not necessarily the same as the amount of rent paid) may be paid where the claimant is in receipt of income support or income-based jobseeker's allowance or where the claimant's income is less than the amount allowed for their needs. Any income over that allowed for their needs will mean that their benefit is reduced.

Claims for housing benefit are made to the local council. Those who are also claiming income support or income-based jobseeker's allowance may claim housing benefit at the local benefits or employment services office. *See* leaflets RR1 and RR2.

COUNCIL TAX BENEFIT

Nearly all the rules which apply to housing benefit apply to council tax benefit, which helps people on low incomes to pay council tax bills. The amount payable depends on how much council tax is paid and who lives with the claimant.

The maximum amount that is payable for those living in properties in council tax bands A to E is 100 per cent of the claimant's council tax liability. This also applies to those living in properties in bands F to H who were in receipt of the benefit at 31 March 1998. From 1 April 1998 council tax benefit for new claimants living in property bands F to H is restricted to the level payable for Band E. This may be available to those receiving income support or income-based jobseeker's allowance or to those whose income is less than that allowed for their needs. Any income over that allowed for their needs will mean that their council tax benefit is reduced. Deductions are made for non-dependents.

If a person shares a home with one or more adults (not their partner) who are on a low income, it may be possible to claim a second adult rebate. Those who are entitled to both council tax benefit and second adult rebate will be awarded whichever is the greater. Second adult rebate may be claimed by those not in receipt of council tax benefit.

THE SOCIAL FUND

The Social Fund helps people with expenses which are difficult to meet from regular income. Regulated maternity and funeral payments are decided by Adjudication Officers and cold weather payments are made automatically. These payments are not limited by the district's Social Fund budget. Discretionary community care grants, and budgeting and crisis loans are decided by Social Fund Officers and come out of a yearly budget which is allocated to each district (1997–8, grants £97 million; loans £370.5 million; £0.5 million set aside as a contingency reserve). *See* leaflet SB16.

REGULATED PAYMENTS
Maternity Payments

A payment of up to £100 for each baby expected, born, adopted, or the subject of a parental order. It is payable to people on income support, income-based jobseeker's allowance, disability working allowance and family credit and does not have to be repaid.

Funeral Payments

Payable for specified funeral director's charges, including the necessary cost of all burial or cremation expenses, plus other funeral expenses reasonably incurred up to £600, by people receiving income support, income-based jobseeker's allowance, disability working allowance, family credit, council tax benefit or housing benefit who have good reason for taking responsibility for the funeral expenses. Savings in excess of £500 (£1,000 for those aged 60 or over) are taken into account. These payments are recoverable from the estate of the deceased.

Cold-Weather Payments

£8.50 for any consecutive seven days when the average temperature is recorded as or forecast to be 0°C or below in their area. Payments are made to people on income support or income-based jobseeker's allowance and who have a child under five or whose benefit includes a pensioner or disability premium. They do not have to be repaid. Winter 1998–9 will be the second of a two-year winter fuel payments scheme helping pensioners with fuel bills. Every eligible pensioner household receives £20 (£50 if they receive income support).

DISCRETIONARY PAYMENTS
Community Care Grants

These are intended to help people on income support or income-based jobseeker's allowance to move into the community or avoid institutional or residential care; ease exceptional pressures on families; care for a prisoner on release on temporary licence; and/or meet certain essential travelling expenses. They do not have to be repaid.

Budgeting Loans

These are interest-free loans to people who have been receiving income support or income-based jobseeker's allowance for at least 26 weeks, for intermittent expenses that may be difficult to budget for.

Crisis Loans

These are interest-free loans to anyone, whether receiving benefit or not, who is without resources in an emergency, where there is no other means of preventing serious damage or serious risk to their health or safety.

SAVINGS

Savings over £500 (£1,000 for people aged 60 or over) are taken into account for maternity and funeral payments, community care grants and budgeting loans. All savings are taken into account for crisis loans. Savings are not taken into account for cold-weather payments.

INDUSTRIAL INJURIES AND DISABLEMENT BENEFITS

The industrial injuries scheme, administered under the Social Security Contributions and Benefits Act 1992, provides a range of benefits designed to compensate for disablement resulting from an industrial accident (i.e. an accident arising out of and in the course of an employed earner's employment) or from a prescribed disease due to the nature of a person's employment. Those who are self-employed are not covered by this scheme.

INDUSTRIAL INJURIES DISABLEMENT BENEFIT

A person must be at least 14 per cent disabled (except for certain respiratory diseases) in order to qualify for this benefit. The amount paid depends on the degree of disablement:

– those assessed as 14–19 per cent disabled are paid at the 20 per cent rate
– those with disablement of over 20 per cent will have the percentage rounded up or down to the nearest 10 per cent, e.g. a disablement of 44 per cent will be paid at the 40 per cent rate while a disablement of 45 per cent will be paid at the 50 per cent rate

Benefit is payable 15 weeks (90 days) after the date of the accident or onset of the disease and may be payable for a limited period or for life. The benefit is payable whether the person works or not and those who are incapable of work are entitled to draw statutory sick pay or incapacity benefit in addition to industrial injuries disablement benefit. It may also be possible to claim the following allowances:

– reduced earnings allowance for those who are unable to return to their regular work or work of the same standard and who had their accident (or whose disease started) before 1 October 1990
– retirement allowance for those who were entitled to reduced earnings allowance who have reached state pension age
– constant attendance allowance for those with a disablement of 95 per cent or more who need constant care. There are four rates of allowance depending on how much care the person needs
– exceptionally severe disablement allowance for those who are entitled to constant care attendance allowance at one of the higher rates and who need constant care permanently

See leaflets NI6 and N12.

OTHER BENEFITS

People who are disabled because of an accident or disease that was the result of work that they did before 5 July 1948 are not entitled to industrial injuries disablement benefit. They may, however, be entitled to payment under the workmen's compensation scheme or the pneumoconiosis, byssinosis and miscellaneous diseases benefit scheme. *See* leaflets WS1 and PN1.

WEEKLY RATES OF BENEFIT
from April 1998

*Disablement benefit/pension
Degree of disablement

100 per cent	£104.70
90	94.23
80	83.76
70	73.29
60	62.82
50	52.35
40	41.85
30	31.41
20	20.94
†Unemployability supplement	64.70
Addition for adult dependant (subject to earnings rule)	38.70
Reduced earnings allowance (maximum)	41.88
Retirement allowance (maximum)	10.47
Constant attendance allowance (normal maximum rate)	42.00
Exceptionally severe disablement allowance	42.00

*There is a weekly benefit for those under 18 with no dependants which is set at a lower rate
†This benefit attracts an increase for each dependent child (in addition to child benefit) of £9.90 for the first child and £11.30 for each subsequent child

CLAIMS AND QUESTIONS

With a few exceptions, claims and questions relating to social security benefits are decided by statutory authorities who act independently of the Department of Social Security and Department for Education and Employment. *See* leaflets NI246 and NI260.

Entitlement to benefit and regulated Social Fund payments is determined by the Adjudication Officer. A claimant who is dissatisfied with that decision has the right of appeal to an independent Social Security Appeal Tribunal. There is a further right of appeal to a Social Security Commissioner against the tribunal's decision but leave to appeal must first be obtained. Appeals to the Commissioner must be on a point of law. Provision is also made for the determination of certain questions by the Secretary of State for Social Security.

Disablement questions are decided by adjudicating medical authorities or medical appeal tribunals. Appeal to the Commissioner against a tribunal's decision is with leave and on a point of law only.

Decisions on applications to the discretionary Social Fund are made by Social Fund Officers. Applicants can ask for a review within 28 days of the date on the decision letter. The Social Fund Review Officer will review the case and there is a further right of review to an independent Social Fund Inspector.

Reviews of housing and council tax benefit decisions are dealt with initially by the council. The claimant must ask for a review within six weeks of being told how much benefit they will receive. Further reviews are dealt with by an independent review board.

OTHER BENEFITS

STATUTORY SICK PAY

Employers usually pay statutory sick pay (SSP) to their employees for up to 28 weeks of sickness in any period of incapacity for work that lasts longer than four days. SSP is paid at £57.70 per week and is subject to PAYE tax and NI deductions. Employees who cannot obtain SSP may be able to claim incapacity benefit. Employers may be able to recover some SSP costs. See leaflets NI244 and NI245.

STATUTORY MATERNITY PAY

In general, employers pay statutory maternity pay (SMP) to pregnant women who have been employed by them full or part-time for at least 26 weeks before the end of the 'qualifying week', which is 15 weeks before the week the baby is due, and whose earnings are on average at least at the lower earnings limit for the payment of NI contributions. All women who meet these conditions receive payment of 90 per cent of their average earnings for six weeks, followed by a maximum of 12 weeks at £57.70. SMP can be paid from the beginning of the 11th week before the week in which the baby is due but women can decide to begin maternity leave later than this. SMP is not payable for any week in which the woman works. Employers are reimbursed for 92 per cent of the SMP they pay (107 per cent for those whose annual NI liability (excluding Class 1A) is £20,000 or less). *See* Leaflet NI17A.

War Pensions

The War Pensions Agency, an executive agency of the Department of Social Security (DSS), awards war pensions under The Naval, Military and Air Forces, Etc. (Disablement and Death) Service Pensions Order 1983 to members of the armed forces in respect of the periods 4 August 1914 to 30 September 1921 and subsequent to 3 September 1939 (including present members of the armed forces). War pensions for the period 1 October 1921 to 2 September 1939 were dealt with by the Ministry of Defence until July 1996 when responsibility passed to the DSS. There is also a scheme for civilians and civil defence workers in respect of the 1939–45 war, and other schemes for groups such as merchant seamen and Polish armed forces who served under British command.

Pensions

War disablement pension is awarded for the disabling effects of any injury, wound or disease which is the result of, or has been aggravated by, conditions of service in the armed forces. It can only be paid once the person has left the armed forces. The amount of pension paid depends on the severity of disablement, which is assessed by comparing the health of the claimant with that of a healthy person of the same age and sex. The person's earning capacity or occupation are not taken into account in this assessment. A pension is awarded if the person has a disablement of 20 per cent or more and a lump sum is usually payable to those with a disablement of less than 20 per cent. No award is made for noise-induced sensorineural hearing loss where the assessment of disablement is less than 20 per cent.

War widow's pension is payable where the husband's death was due to, or hastened by, his service in the armed forces or where the husband was in receipt of a war disablement pension constant attendance allowance (or would have been had he not been in hospital). Since April 1997 a war widow's pension is also payable if the husband was getting unemployability supplement at the time of his death and his pensionable disablement was at least 80 per cent. Most war widows receive a standard rank-related rate but a lower weekly rate is payable to war widows of men below the rank of Lieutenant-Colonel who are under the age of 40, without children and capable of maintaining themselves. This is increased to the standard rate at age 40. Allowances are paid for children (in addition to child benefit) and adult dependants. An age allowance may also be given when the woman reaches 65 and increased at age 70 and age 80.

A war widower's pension may be payable to a man whose wife died because of service in the armed forces, if he was dependent on his wife before her death and cannot support himself.

All war pensions and war widow's pensions are tax-free and pensioners living overseas receive the same amount as those resident in the UK.

Supplementary Allowances

A number of supplementary allowances may be awarded to a war pensioner which are intended to meet various needs which may result from disablement or death and take account of its particular effect on the pensioner or spouse. The principal supplementary allowances are unemployability supplement, allowance for lowered standard of occupation and constant attendance allowance. Others include exceptionally severe disablement allowance, severe disablement occupational allowance, treatment allowance, mobility supplement, comforts allowance, clothing allowance, age allowance and widow's age allowance. There is a rent allowance available on a war widow's pension.

Social Security Benefits

Most social security benefits are paid in addition to the basic war disablement pension or war widow's pension. Any retirement pension for which a war widow qualifies on her own NI contribution record can be paid in addition to her war widow's pension.

A war pensioner or war widow who claims income support, family credit or disability working allowance has the first £10 of pension disregarded. A similar provision operates for housing benefit and council tax benefit; but the local authority may, at its discretion, disregard any or all of the balance.

Claims and Questions

To claim a war pension it is necessary to contact the nearest war pensioners' welfare service office, the address of which is available from local social security offices, or to write to the War Pensions Agency, Norcross, Blackpool FY5 3WP. The war pensioners' welfare service advises and assists war pensioners and war widows on any matters affecting their welfare. General advice can also be obtained from the War Pension Helpline on 01253-858858.

Independent pensions appeal tribunals hear appeals against decisions, made by the DSS, on entitlement and on the assessment of disability with respect to the 1939–45 war and subsequent service cases. War widows from the 1914 war may appeal against decisions about entitlement but there are now no rights of appeal in disablement cases from the 1914 war. Decisions on supplementary allowances are made on a discretionary basis and there is no provision for a statutory right of appeal against them. The DSS send information about how to appeal and the time limits that exist for appeals when they notify claimants of their decision. See leaflet WPA2.

Weekly Rates of Pensions and Allowances
from week commencing 6 April 1998

War disablement pension
Degree of disablement

100 per cent	£111.10
90	99.99
80	88.88
70	77.77
60	66.66
50	55.55
40	44.44
30	33.33
20	22.22

Unemployability supplement

Personal allowance	68.65
Increase for wife/other adult dependant	38.70
Increase for first child	9.90
Increase for other children	11.30

Allowance for lowered standard of occupation (maximum) 41.88
Constant attendance allowance

Half day rate	21.00
Full day rate	42.00
Intermediate rate	63.00
Exceptional rate	84.00

Widow's pension
(widow of Private or equivalent rank)

Standard rate	83.90
Increase for first child	14.25
Increase for other children	15.65
Childless widow under 40	19.41

Widow's age allowance

aged 65–69	9.60
aged 70–79	18.40
aged 80 and over	27.40

The rates for officers and widows of officers differ from those given above. See leaflet WPA9.

Development Corporations

NEW TOWNS

COMMISSION FOR THE NEW TOWNS
Central Business Exchange, 414-428 Midsummer
Boulevard, Central Milton Keynes MK9 2EA
Tel 01908-692692; fax: 01908-691333

The Commission was established under the New Towns
Act 1959. Its remit is to hold, manage and turn to account
the property of development corporations transferred to
the Commission; and to dispose of property so transferred
and any other property held by it, as soon as it considers it
expedient to do so. In carrying out its remit the Commission must have due regard to the convenience and welfare
of persons residing, working or carrying on business there
and, until disposal, the maintenance and enhancement of
the value of the land held and return obtained from it.

The Commission has such responsibilities in Basildon,
Bracknell, Central Lancashire, Corby, Crawley, Harlow,
Hatfield, Hemel Hempstead, Milton Keynes, Northamp-
ton, Peterborough, Redditch, Skelmersdale, Stevenage,
Telford, Warrington and Runcorn, Washington, and
Welwyn Garden City. The Commission has minimal
responsibilities (principally financial and litigation) in
Aycliffe and Peterlee, and Cwmbran following the wind-
ing-up of their development corporations in 1988.

From April 1998 the Commission took over responsi-
bility for any assets and liabilities remaining in the urban
development corporations and housing action trusts of
Tyne and Wear, Teesside, Trafford Park, Merseyside,
Plymouth, Birmingham Heartlands, Black Country and
London Docklands when these were wound up.

Chairman, Sir Alan Cockshaw, CBE
Deputy Chairman, M. H. Mallinson, CBE
Members, J. Trustram Eve; D. Hone; Sir Brian Jenkins,
GBE; J. Walker
Chief Executive, N. J. Walker

REGIONAL OFFICES
NORTH (Central Lancashire, Skelmersdale, Warrington
and Runcorn, Washington, Aycliffe and Peterlee,
Merseyside, Teesside, Trafford Park, and Tyne and
Wear), New Town House, Buttermarket Street,
Warrington WA1 2LF. Tel: 01925-651144. *Director,
Commercial Land Sales,* M. Anderson
CENTRAL (Milton Keynes, Corby, Northampton,
Plymouth), Central Business Exchange, 414–428
Midsummer Boulevard, Central Milton Keynes MK9
2EA. Tel: 01908-692692. *Director, Commercial Land Sales,*
R. Jamieson
WEST MIDLANDS (Redditch, Telford, Birmingham
Heartlands, Black Country), Jordan House West, Hall
Court, Hall Park Way, Telford TF3 4NN. Tel: 01952-
293131. *Director, Land Sales,* E. Jones
SOUTH (Basildon, Bracknell, Crawley, Harlow, Hatfield,
Hemel Hempstead, Peterborough, Stevenage, Welwyn
Garden City, London Docklands), Central Business
Exchange, 414–428 Midsummer Boulevard, Central
Milton Keynes MK9 2EA. Tel: 01908-692692 *Director,
Land Sales,* G. D. Johnston

DEVELOPMENT CORPORATIONS

WALES
DEVELOPMENT BOARD FOR RURAL WALES (1977), merged
with Welsh Development Agency on 1 October 1998 (*see*
page 352)

SCOTLAND
CUMBERNAULD (1956), wound up 31 December 1996
EAST KILBRIDE (1947), wound up 31 December 1995
GLENROTHES (1948), wound up 31 December 1995
IRVINE (1966), wound up 31 March 1997
LIVINGSTON (1962), wound up 31 March 1997

URBAN DEVELOPMENT CORPORATIONS

Urban development corporations were established under
the Local Government, Planning and Land Act 1980, as
short-life public bodies. Their objectives were to bring
land and buildings back into effective use; to develop
existing and new industry and commerce; to improve the
environment; and to ensure that housing and social
facilities are available in the area. All the corporations in
England have now been wound up; the last eight
(Birmingham Heartlands, Black Country, London Docklands, Merseyside, Plymouth, Teesside, Trafford Park and
Tyne and Wear) ceased operations on 31 March 1998.

CARDIFF BAY (1987), Baltic House, Mount Stuart Square,
Cardiff CF1 6DH. Tel: 01222-585858. *Chairman,* Sir
Geoffrey Inkin, OBE; *Chief Executive,* M. Boyce. Area,
1,094 hectares
LAGANSIDE (1989), Clarendon Building, 15 Clarendon
Road, Belfast BT1 3BG. Tel: 01232-328507. *Chairman,* A.
Hopkins; *Chief Executive,* M. Smith. Area, 200 hectares

REGIONAL DEVELOPMENT AGENCIES

The creation of regional development agencies in England
was announced in a White Paper *Building Partnerships for
Prosperity* in December 1997. The agencies' responsibilities
will include economic development and regeneration,
competitiveness, business support and investment, skills,
employment, and sustainable development. There will be
eight in England outside London, to be set up in April 1999,
and one in London, to be set up at a later date. Some of the
functions currently undertaken by English Partnerships,
the Government Offices for the Regions and the Rural
Development Commission (which is to be merged with the
Countryside Commission) will transfer to the agencies.

The Water Industry

ENGLAND AND WALES

In England and Wales the Secretary of State for the
Environment, Transport and the Regions and the Secretary of State for Wales have overall responsibility for water
policy and set the environmental and health and safety
standards for the water industry. The Director-General of
Water Services, as the independent economic regulator, is
responsible for ensuring that the private water companies
are able to fulfil their statutory obligation to provide water
supply and sewerage services, and for protecting the
interests of consumers.

The Minister of Agriculture, Fisheries and Food and the
Secretary of State for Wales are responsible for policy
relating to land drainage, flood protection, sea defences
and the protection and development of fisheries.

The Environment Agency is responsible for water
quality and the control of pollution, the management of
water resources and nature conservation. The Drinking
Water Inspectorate and local authorities are responsible
for the quality of drinking water.

THE WATER COMPANIES

Until 1989 nine regional water authorities in England and
the Welsh Water Authority in Wales were responsible for
water supply and the development of water resources,
sewerage and sewage disposal, pollution control, freshwater fisheries, flood protection, water recreation, and
environmental conservation. The Water Act 1989 provided for the creation of a privatized water industry under
public regulation, and the functions of the regional water
authorities were taken over by ten holding companies and
the regulatory bodies.

Of the 99 per cent of the population of England and
Wales who are connected to a public water supply, 75 per
cent are supplied by the water companies (through their
principal operating subsidiaries, the water service companies). The remaining 25 per cent are supplied by
statutory water companies which were already in the
private sector. Most of these have public limited company
(PLC) status; many are now French-owned and one is
American-owned. They are represented by Water UK,
which also represents the ten water service companies
responsible for sewerage and sewage disposal in England
and Wales, and the state-owned water authorities of
Scotland and Northern Ireland. Water UK is the trade
association for all the water service companies except Mid
Kent Water.

WATER UK, 1 Queen Anne's Gate, London, SW1H 9BT.
Tel: 0171-344 1844. *Chief Executive,* Ms P. Taylor

Water Service Companies

ANGLIAN WATER SERVICES LTD, Anglian House,
Ambury Road, Huntingdon, Cambs PE18 6NZ
DWR CYMRU (WELSH WATER), Cambrian Way, Brecon,
Powys LD3 7HP
NORTHUMBRIAN WATER LTD, Abbey Road, Pity Me,
Durham DH1 5FJ
NORTH WEST WATER LTD, Dawson House, Liverpool
Road, Great Sankey, Warrington WA5 3LW
SEVERN TRENT WATER LTD, 2297 Coventry Road,
Sheldon, Birmingham B26 3PU
SOUTHERN WATER SERVICES LTD, Southern House,
Yeoman Road, Worthing, W. Sussex BN13 3NX
SOUTH WEST WATER SERVICES LTD, Peninsula House,
Rydon Lane, Exeter EX2 7HR
THAMES WATER UTILITIES LTD, Nugent House,
Vastern Road, Reading RG1 8DB
WESSEX WATER SERVICES LTD, Wessex House, Passage
Street, Bristol BS2 0JQ
YORKSHIRE WATER SERVICES LTD, West Riding House,
67 Albion Street, Leeds LS1 5AA

WATER SUPPLY AND CONSUMPTION 1996–7

	Supply		Consumption			
	Supply from treatment works (*Ml/day*)	Total leakage (*Ml/day*)	Household (*l/head/day*) Unmetered	Metered	Non-household (*l/prop/day*) Unmetered	Metered
WATER SERVICE COMPANIES						
Anglian	1,179.3	212.6	177.0	139.8	1,488.6	3,672.6
Dwr Cymru (Welsh)	1,031.2	357.2	173.6	181.1	1,030.6	3,502.0
Northumbrian	798.8	192.4	165.7	133.4	927.2	5,002.2
North West	2,176.5	665.9	157.1	114.7	703.5	3,153.6
Severn Trent	2,022.0	478.6	158.2	138.6	740.0	2.970.6
Southern	622.3	112.7	175.9	140.0	995.1	2,966.6
South West	478.1	129.1	175.3	140.7	1,101.1	1,814.9
Thames	2,857.7	1,082.9	199.3	165.5	1,004.6	3,708.5
Wessex	426.5	128.8	168.0	137.7	1,838.2	2,814.7
Yorkshire	1,350.5	419.8	154.0	130.3	718.3	2,985.9
Total	12,942.9	3,779.8	—	—	—	—
Average	—	—	170.4	138.9	962.5	3,236.3
WATER COMPANIES						
Total	3,422.2	724.9	—	—	—	—
Average	—	—	182.2	156.1	942.5	3,403.4

Source: Office of Water Services

REGULATORY BODIES

The Office of Water Services (Ofwat) (*see* pages 351–2) was set up under the Water Act 1989 and is the independent economic regulator of the water and sewerage companies in England and Wales. Ofwat's main duty is to ensure that the companies can finance and carry out their statutory functions and to protect the interests of water customers. Ofwat is a non-ministerial government department headed by the Director-General of Water Services, who is appointed by the Secretary of State for the Environment, Transport and the Regions and the Secretary of State for Wales.

The Environment Agency (*see* page 301) has statutory duties and powers in relation to water resources, pollution control, flood defence, fisheries, recreation, conservation and navigation in England and Wales.

The Drinking Water Inspectorate is responsible for assessing the quality of the drinking water supplied by the water companies, inspecting the com-panies themselves and investigating any accidents affecting drinking water quality. The Chief Inspector presents an annual report to the Secretary of State for the Environment, Transport and the Regions and the Secretary of State for Wales.

METHODS OF CHARGING

In England and Wales, most domestic customers still pay for domestic water supply and sewerage services through charges based on the old rateable value of their property, although about 10 per cent of householders are now charged according to consumption, which is recorded by meter. Industrial and most commercial customers are charged according to consumption.

Under the Water Industry Act 1991, water companies must discontinue basing their charges on the old rateable value of property after 31 March 2000. In May 1997 the Government announced a review of the system of charging for water. Among other issues, the review considered alternative bases of charging, including continuing the use of rateable values after 2000, the use of council tax bands and metering policy. The Government issued a consulta-tion paper, *Water Charging in England and Wales: A New Approach*, on 1 April 1998.

SCOTLAND

Overall responsibility for national water policy in Scotland rests with the Secretary of State for Scotland. Most aspects of water policy are administered through the Scottish Office Agriculture, Environment and Fisheries Depart-ment.

Water supply and sewerage services were formerly local authority responsibilities and the Central Scotland Water Development Board had the function of developing new sources of water supply for the purpose of providing water in bulk to water authorities whose limits of supply were within the board's area. The Local Government etc. (Scotland) Act 1994 provided for three new public water authorities, covering the north, east and west of Scotland respectively, to be established to take over the provision of water and sewerage services from April 1996. From that date the Central Scotland Water Development Board was abolished. The new authorities are accountable to Parlia-ment through the Secretary of State for Scotland; from July 1999 parliamentary responsibility for the water and sew-erage industry in Scotland and for its regulation will be devolved to the Scottish Parliament. The Act also provi-ded for a Scottish Water and Sewerage Customers Council to be established to represent consumer interests. It monitors the performance of the authorities; approves charges schemes; investigates complaints; and keeps the

Secretary of State advised on standards of service and customer relations.

The Scottish Environment Protection Agency (SEPA) (*see* page 339) is responsible for promoting the cleanliness of Scotland's rivers, lochs and coastal waters. SEPA is also responsible for controlling pollution.

WATER RESOURCES 1996

	No.	Yield (Ml/day)
Reservoirs and lochs	287	2,943
Feeder intakes	27	—
River intakes	223	422
Bore-holes	35	77
Underground springs	103	46
Total	*692	3,487

* Including compensation reservoirs

WATER CONSUMPTION 1996

TOTAL (*Ml/day*)	2,311.6
Potable	2,254.8
Unmetered	1,686.4
Metered	568.4
Non-potable†	56.8*
TOTAL (*l/head/day*)	462.7
Unmetered	337.6
Metered and non-potable†	116.9

† 'Non-potable' supplied for industrial purposes. Metered supplies in general relate to commercial and industrial use and unmetered to domestic use
* Includes 41.6 Ml/d supplied by East of Scotland Water Authority to West of Scotland Water Authority from Loch Lomond
Source: The Scottish Office

EAST OF SCOTLAND WATER AUTHORITY, Pentland Gait, 597 Calder Road, Edinburgh EH11 4HJ. Tel: 0131-453 7500. *Chief Executive*, R. Rennet

NORTH OF SCOTLAND WATER AUTHORITY, Cairngorm House, Beechwood Park North, Inverness IV2 3ED. Tel: 01463-245400. *Chief Executive*, A. Findlay

SCOTTISH WATER AND SEWERAGE CUSTOMERS COUNCIL, Ochil House, Springkerse Business Park, Stirling FK7 7XE. Tel: 01786-430200. *Director*, Dr V. Nash

WEST OF SCOTLAND WATER AUTHORITY, 419 Balmore Road, Glasgow G22 6NU. Tel: 0141-355 5333. *Chief Executive*, E. Chambers

METHODS OF CHARGING

The water authorities set charges for domestic and non-domestic water and sewerage provision through charges schemes which have to be approved by the Scottish Water and Sewerage Customers Council. The authorities must publish a summary of their charges schemes.

NORTHERN IRELAND

In Northern Ireland ministerial responsibility for water services lies with the Secretary of State for Northern Ireland. The Water Service, which is an executive agency of the Department of the Environment for Northern Ireland, is responsible for policy and co-ordination with regard to supply, distribution and cleanliness of water, and the provision and maintenance of sewerage services.

The Water Service (*see* page 330) is divided into four regions, the Eastern, Northern, Western and Southern Divisions. These are based in Belfast, Ballymena, London-derry and Craigavon respectively.

On major issues the Department of the Environment for Northern Ireland seeks the views of the Northern Ireland Water Council, a body appointed to advise the Department on the exercise of its water and sewerage functions. The Council includes representatives from agriculture, angling, industry, commerce, tourism, trade unions and local government.

METHODS OF CHARGING

Usually householders do not pay separately for water and sewerage services; the costs of these services are allowed for in the Northern Ireland regional rate. Water consumed by industry, commerce and agriculture in excess of 100 cubic metres (22,000 gallons) per half year is charged through meters. Traders operating from industrially derated premises are required to pay for the treatment and disposal of the trade effluent which they discharge into the public sewerage system.

HM Coastguard

Founded in 1822, originally to guard the coasts against smuggling, HM Coastguard's role today is the very different one of guarding and saving life at sea. The Service is responsible for co-ordinating all civil maritime search and rescue operations around the 10,500 mile coastline of Great Britain and Northern Ireland and 1,000 miles into the Atlantic. In addition, it co-operates with search and rescue organizations of neighbouring countries in western Europe and around the Atlantic seaboard. The Service maintains a 24-hour radar watch on the Dover Strait, providing a Channel navigation information service for all shipping in one of the busiest sea lanes in the world. It also liaises very closely with the off-shore oil and gas industry and with merchant shipping companies.

Since 1997 HM Coastguard has been organized into five regions, each with a regional controller. Each region is subdivided into districts under district controllers, operating from maritime rescue co-ordination centres or sub-centres. In all there are 21 of these centres. They are on 24-hour watch and are fitted with a comprehensive range of communications equipment. They are supported by smaller stations staffed by part-time auxiliary coastguards under the direction of regulars, each of which keeps its parent centre fully informed of day-to-day casualty risk, particularly on the more remote danger spots around the coast.

Between 1 January and 31 December 1997, HM Coastguard co-ordinated 11,667 incidents requiring search and rescue facilities; 16,884 people were assisted and 251 lives were lost. All distress telephone and radio calls are centralized on the 21 centres, which are on the alert for people or vessels in distress, shipping hazards and pollution incidents. Using telecommunications equipment, including satellite, they can alert and co-ordinate the most appropriate rescue facilities; RNLI lifeboats, Royal Navy, RAF or Coastguard helicopters, fixed-wing aircraft, vessels in the vicinity, or Coastguard shore and cliff rescue teams.

For those who regularly sail in local waters or make longer passages, the Coastguard Yacht and Boat Safety Scheme provides a valuable free service. Its aim is to give the Coastguard a record of the details of craft, their equipment fit and normal operating areas. Yacht and Boat Safety Scheme cards are available from all Coastguard stations, harbourmasters' offices, and most yacht clubs and marinas as well as Coastguard headquarters.

Members of the public who see an accident or a potentially dangerous incident on or around the coast should dial 999 and ask for the Coastguard.

In April 1998 the Coastguard Agency and the Marine Safety Agency merged, forming the Maritime and Coastguard Agency, an executive agency of the Department of the Environment, Transport and the Regions.

Coastguard Headquarters and Office of the Chief Coastguard, Spring Place, 105 Commercial Road, Southampton so15 1EG. Tel: 01703-329100

Energy

The main primary sources of energy in Britain are oil, natural gas, coal, nuclear power and water power. The main secondary sources (i.e. sources derived from the primary sources) are electricity, coke and smokeless fuels, and petroleum products. The Department of the Environment, Transport and the Regions is responsible for promoting energy efficiency.

INDIGENOUS PRODUCTION OF PRIMARY FUELS
Million tonnes of oil equivalent

	1996	1997p
Coal	31.7	30.8
Petroleum	143.1	141.3
Natural gas	84.7	87.0
Primary electricity		
Nuclear	22.12	23.01
Natural flow hydro	0.33	0.38
Total	282.0	282.4

p provisional

INLAND ENERGY CONSUMPTION BY PRIMARY FUEL
Million tonnes of oil equivalent, seasonally adjusted

	1996	1997p
Coal	46.7	41.7
Petroleum	78.6	75.9
Natural gas	82.4	83.4
Primary electricity	23.89	24.85
Nuclear	22.12	23.01
Natural flow hydro	0.33	0.38
Net imports	1.44	1.46
Total	231.6	225.8

p provisional

TRADE IN FUELS AND RELATED MATERIALS 1997p

	Quantity*	Value†
IMPORTS		
Coal and other solid fuel	14.2	714
Crude petroleum	45.3	3,647
Petroleum products	15.3	1,442
Natural gas	1.3	103
Electricity	1.4	406
Total	77.6	6,312
Total (fob)‡	—	5,875
EXPORTS		
Coal and other solid fuel	1.1	82
Crude petroleum	76.7	6,334
Petroleum products	29.2	3,214
Natural gas	1.7	80
Electricity	—	1
Total	108.6	9,712
Total (fob)‡	—	9,712

p provisional
* Million tonnes of oil equivalent
† £ million
‡ Adjusted to exclude estimated costs of insurance, freight, etc.
Source: Department of Trade and Industry

OIL

Until the 1960s Britain imported almost all its oil supplies. In 1969 oil was discovered in the Arbroath field of the UK Continental Shelf (UKCS). The first oilfield to be brought into production was the Argyll field in 1975, and since the mid-1970s Britain has been a major producer of crude oil.

Licences for exploration and production are granted to companies by the Department of Trade and Industry; the leading British oil companies are British Petroleum (BP) and Shell Transport and Trading. At the end of 1997, 938 offshore licences and 129 onshore licences had been awarded, and there were 98 offshore oilfields in production. In 1997 there were 10 oil refineries and four smaller refining units processing crude and process oils. There are estimated to be reserves of 2,015 million tonnes of oil in the UKCS. Royalties are payable on fields approved before April 1982 and petroleum revenue tax is levied on fields approved between 1975 and March 1993.

DRILLING ACTIVITY 1997p

Number of wells started	Offshore	Onshore
Exploration and appraisal	98	13
Exploration	63	—
Appraisal	35	—
Development	256	29

p provisional

VALUE OF UKCS OIL AND GAS PRODUCTION AND INVESTMENT
£ million

	1996	1997p
Total income	21,052	18,955
Operating costs	3,978	4,150
Exploration expenditure	1,097	1,194
Gross trading profits*	14,387	12,638
Percentage contribution to GDP	2.4	2.1
Capital investment	4,440	4,336
Percentage contribution to industrial investment	18	16

* Net of stock appreciation
p provisional

INDIGENOUS PRODUCTION AND REFINERY RECEIPTS

	1996	1997p
Indigenous production (thousand tonnes)	130,007	128,205
Crude oil	121,930	120,116
NGLs*	8,077	8,089
Refinery receipts (thousand tonnes)		
Indigenous	49,449	47,602
Other†	997	794
Net foreign arrivals	48,275	48,636

p provisional
* Natural gas liquids: condensates and petroleum gases derived at onshore treatment plants
† Mainly recycled products

DELIVERIES OF PETROLEUM PRODUCTS FOR INLAND CONSUMPTION BY ENERGY USE
Thousand tonnes

	1996	1997p
Electricity generators	3,316	1,326
Gas works	50	46
Iron and steel industry	737	719
Other industries	6,436	5,813
Transport	46,642	47,322

Domestic	3,167	3,057
Other	3,744	3,264
Total	64,092	61,547

p provisional
Source: Department of Trade and Indusrty

GAS

From the late 18th century gas in Britain was produced from coal. In the 1960s town gas began to be produced from oil-based feedstocks using imported oil. In 1965 gas was discovered in the North Sea in the West Sole field, which became the first gasfield in production in 1967, and from the late 1960s natural gas began to replace town gas. Britain is now the world's fourth largest producer of gas and in 1997 only 1.5 per cent of gas available for consumption in the UK was imported.

By the end of 1997 there were 75 offshore gasfields producing natural gas and associated gas (mainly methane). There are estimated to be between 765,000 million and 1,985,000 million cubic metres of recoverable gas reserves in existing discoveries. There are about 8,704.5 km of major submarine pipelines for transporting hydrocarbons, and onshore pipelines for carrying refined products and chemicals. Natural gas is transported around Britain by about 270,000 km of pipelines supplied by five pipeline terminals. This pipeline system is owned by Transco and transports gas on behalf of suppliers or shippers under a network code.

The Office of Gas Supply (*see* page 304) is the regulatory body for the gas industry. The Government announced in 1998 plans to merge the Office of Gas Supply and the Office of Electricity Regulation to create a single Energy Regulator for Great Britain.

The gas industry in Britain was nationalized in 1949 and operated as the Gas Council. The Gas Council was replaced by the British Gas Corporation in 1972 and the industry became more centralized. The British Gas Corporation was privatized in 1986 as British Gas PLC.

In 1993 the Monopolies and Mergers Commission found that British Gas's integrated business in Great Britain as a gas trader and the owner of the gas transportation system could be expected to operate against the public interest. In February 1997 British Gas demerged its trading arm into two separate companies: BG PLC, which runs the Transco pipeline business in Britain and oil and gas exploration and production in the UK and abroad; and Centrica PLC, which runs the trading, service and retail operations under the British Gas brand name.

Competition was gradually introduced into the industrial gas market from 1986. Supply of gas to the domestic market was opened to companies other than British Gas, starting in April 1996 with a pilot project in the West Country and Wales. From spring 1997 competition was progressively introduced throughout the rest of Britain in stages which were completed in May 1998. Gas companies can now also sell electricity to their customers. Similarly, electricity companies can also offer gas.

BG PLC, 100 Thames Valley Park Drive, Reading RG6 1PT. Tel: 0118-935 3222. *Chairman,* R. V. Giordano; *Chief Executive,* D. Varney

CENTRICA PLC, Charter Court, 50 Windsor Road, Slough, Berks SL1 2HA. Tel: 01753-758000. *Chief Executive,* R. Gardner

NATURAL GAS PRODUCTION AND SUPPLY
GWh

	1996	1997p
Gross gas production	980,064	1,000,676
Exports	15,203	21,666
Imports	19,804	14,062
Gas available	923,260	929,252
Gas transmitted‡	908,647	912,844

p provisional
‡ Figures differ from gas available mainly because of stock changes

NATURAL GAS CONSUMPTION
GWh

	1996	1997p
Electricity generators	190,691	240,346
Iron and steel industry	21,961	20,525
Other industries	169,293	161,763
Domestic	375,841	342,353
Public administration, commerce and agriculture	119,935	108,766
Total	877,721	873,753

p provisional
Source: Deaprtment of Trade and Industry

COAL

Coal has been mined in Britain for centuries and the availability of coal was crucial to the industrial revolution of the 18th and 19th centuries. Mines were in private ownership until 1947 when they were nationalized and came under the management of the National Coal Board, later the British Coal Corporation. In addition to producing coal at its own deep-mine and opencast sites, of which there were 850 in 1955, British Coal was responsible for licensing private mines.

Under the Coal Industry Act 1994, the Coal Authority (*see* page 291) was established to take over ownership of coal reserves and to issue licences to private mining companies as part of the privatization of British Coal. The Coal Authority also deals with the physical legacy of mining, e.g. subsidence damage claims, and is responsible for holding and making available all existing records. The mines were sold as five separate businesses in 1994 and coal production in the UK is now undertaken entirely in the private sector. At the end of 1997 there were 21 large deep mines in operation.

The main UK customer for coal is the electricity supply industry, but the latter's demand for coal declined and National Power (*see* page 502) announced that it expected to close ten of its 18 coal-fired power stations by 2000. However, following a review of energy policy, the Government announced measures in June 1998 which included a freeze on new applications to build gas-fired power stations in order to increase opportunities for coal-fired power stations; there is a possibility that the EU might challenge the Government's plans.

COAL PRODUCTION AND FOREIGN TRADE
Thousand tonnes

	1996	1997p
Total production	50,197	48,540
Deep-mined	32,223	30,351
Opencast	16,315	16,675
Imports	17,799	20,230
Exports	988	1,147

p provisional

INLAND COAL USE
Thousand tonnes

	1996	1997p
Fuel producers		
Collieries	8	8
Electricity generators	54,893	46,990
Coke ovens	8,635	8,750
Other conversion industries	946	864
Total	71,403	63,667
Final users		
Industry	3,639	3,323
Domestic	2,705	3,364
Public administration, commerce		
and agriculture	577	368

p provisional
Source: Department of Trade and Industry

ELECTRICITY

The first power station in Britain generating electricity for public supply began operating in 1882. In the 1930s a national transmission grid was developed, and it was reconstructed and extended in the 1950s and 1960s. Power stations were operated by the Central Electricity Generating Board.

Under the Electricity Act 1989, 12 regional electricity companies (RECs), which are responsible for the distribution of electricity from the national grid to consumers, were formed from the former area electricity boards in England and Wales. Four companies were formed from the Central Electricity Generating Board: three generating companies (National Power PLC, Nuclear Electric PLC and PowerGen PLC) and the National Grid Company PLC, which owns and operates the transmission system. National Power and PowerGen were floated on the stock market in 1991. Nuclear Electric was split into two parts in 1995; the part comprising the more modern nuclear stations was incorporated into a new company, British Energy, which was floated on the stock market in 1996. Magnox Electric, which owns the magnox nuclear reactors, remains in the public sector ans was merged with British Nuclear Fuels (BNFL) in early 1998. Ownership of the National Grid Company was transferred to the RECs and subsequently floated in 1995.

There are now 27 electricity generating companies in Britain. The RECs currently have a monopoly on sales of 100 kW or less to consumers in their franchise areas; over this limit competition has been introduced. Competition was due to be introduced into the domestic electricity market in April 1998, but was postponed due to technical difficulties. Competition is now being introduced from September 1998 and will be completed in June 1999. Generators will sell the electricity they produce into an open commodity market (the Pool) from which buyers will purchase electricity.

Electricity companies can now also sell gas to their customers. Similarly, gas companies can also offer electricity.

In Scotland, three new companies were formed under the Electricity Act 1989: Scottish Power PLC and Scottish Hydro-Electric PLC, which are responsible for generation, transmission, distribution and supply; and Scottish Nuclear Ltd. Scottish Power and Scottish Hydro-Electric were floated on the stock market in 1991; Scottish Nuclear was incorporated into British Energy in 1995.

In Northern Ireland, Northern Ireland Electricity PLC was set up in 1993 under a 1991 Order in Council. It is responsible for transmission, distribution and supply and has been floated on the stock market. There is no Pool in Northern Ireland; three private companies are responsible for electricity generation and the electricity is sold to Northern Ireland Electricity under a series of power purchase agreements.

The Office of Electricity Regulation (*see* page 297) is the regulatory body for the electricity industry. The Government has announced plans to merge the Office of Gas Supply and the Office of Electricity Regulation to create a single Energy Regulator for Great Britain.

The Electricity Association is the electricity industry's main trade association, providing representational and professional services for the electricity companies. EA Technology Ltd provides distribution and utilization research, development and technology transfer.

NUCLEAR POWER

Nuclear reactors began to supply electricity to the national grid in 1956. It is generated at six magnox reactors, seven advanced gas-cooled reactors (AGRs) and one pressurized water reactor (PWR), Sizewell 'B' in Suffolk. Nuclear stations now generate about 28 per cent of the UK's electricity.

In preparation for privatization, the nuclear industry was restructured in December 1995. A holding company, British Energy PLC, was formed with two operational subsidiaries, Nuclear Electric Ltd and Scottish Nuclear Ltd. Nuclear Electric operates the five AGRs and the PWR in England and Wales; Scottish Nuclear operates the two AGRs in Scotland. British Energy was floated on the stock market in 1996. The Magnox reactors were transferred to Magnox Electric PLC, which remained in public ownership. In January 1998 the Government's shareholding in Magnox Electric was transferred to British Nuclear Fuels Ltd (BNFL). BNFL is in public ownership, providing reprocessing, waste management and effluent treatment services. The UK Atomic Energy Authority (*see* page 284) is responsible for the decommissioning of nuclear reactors and other nuclear facilities used in research and development. UK Nirex, which is owned by the nuclear generating companies and the Government, is responsible for the disposal of intermediate and some low-level nuclear waste. The Nuclear Installations Inspectorate of the Health and Safety Executive (*see* page 307) is the nuclear industry's regulator.

SUPPLY COMPANIES

BRITISH ENERGY PLC, 10 Lochside Place, Edinburgh EH12 9DF. Tel: 0131-527 2000. *Chief Executive (acting)*, J. Robb

MAGNOX ELECTRIC PLC, Berkeley Centre, Berkeley, Glos GL13 9PB. Tel: 01453-810451. *Chief Executive*, R. Hall

THE NATIONAL GRID COMPANY PLC, National Grid House, Kirby Corner Road, Coventry CV4 8JY. Tel: 01203-423000. *Chief Executive*, D. Jones

NATIONAL POWER PLC, Windmill Hill Business Park, Whitehill Way, Swindon, Wilts SN5 6PB. Tel: 01793-877777. *Chief Executive*, K. Henry

POWERGEN PLC, Westwood Way, Westwood Business Park, Coventry CV4 8LG. Tel: 01203-424000. *Chairman*, E. Wallis

REGIONAL ELECTRICITY COMPANIES

EASTERN ELECTRICITY PLC, PO Box 40, Wherstead Park, Wherstead, Ipswich IP9 2AQ. Tel: 01473-688688

EAST MIDLANDS ELECTRICITY PLC, PO Box 444, Wollaton, Nottingham NG8 1EZ. Tel: 0115-901 0101

LONDON ELECTRICITY PLC, Templar House, 81–87 High Holborn, London WC1V 6NU. Tel: 0171-242 9050

MANWEB PLC, Manweb House, Kingsfield Court, Chester Business Park, Chester CH4 9RF. Tel: 0845-272 3636

MIDLANDS ELECTRICITY PLC, Mucklow Hill, Halesowen, W. Midlands B62 8BP Tel: 0121-423 2345
NORTHERN ELECTRIC PLC, Carliol House, Market Street, Newcastle upon Tyne NE1 6NE. Tel: 0191-210 2000
NORWEB PLC, Talbot Road, Manchester M16 0HQ. Tel: 0161-873 8000
SEEBOARD PLC, Forest Gate, Brighton Road, Crawley, W. Sussex RH11 9BH. Tel: 01293-565888
SOUTHERN ELECTRIC PLC, Southern Electric House, Westacott Way, Littlewick Green, Maidenhead, Berks SL6 3QB. Tel: 01628-822166
SWALEC PLC, Newport Road, St Mellons, Cardiff CF3 9XW. Tel: 01222-792111
SWEB PLC, 800 Park Avenue, Aztec West, Almondsbury, Bristol BS32 4SE. Tel: 01454-201101
YORKSHIRE ELECTRICITY GROUP PLC, Wetherby Road, Scarcroft, Leeds LS14 3HS. Tel: 0113-289 2123

SCOTLAND

HYDRO-ELECTRIC PLC, Dunkeld Road, Perth PH1 5WA. Tel: 01738-455040. *Chief Executive*, R. Young
SCOTTISH POWER PLC, 1 Atlantic Quay, Glasgow G2 8SP. Tel: 0141-248 8200. *Chief Executive*, I. Robinson

NORTHERN IRELAND

NORTHERN IRELAND ELECTRICITY PLC, 120 Malone Road, Belfast BT 9 5HT. Tel: 01232-661100. *Chief Executive*, Dr P. Haren
ELECTRICITY ASSOCIATION LTD, 30 Millbank, London SW1P 4RD. Tel: 0171-963 5700. *Chief Executive*, P. E. G. Daubeney
EA TECHNOLOGY LTD, Capenhurst, Chester CH1 6ES. Tel: 0151-339 4181. *Managing Director*, Dr S. F. Exell

ELECTRICITY GENERATION, SUPPLY AND CONSUMPTION
GWh

	1995	1996
Electricity generated: total	34,047	347,369
Major power producers: total	310,292	323,155
Conventional steam stations	169,866	160,565
Nuclear stations	85,298	91,040
Gas turbines and oil engines	190	226
Combined cycle gas turbine stations	48,720	65,880
Hydro-electric stations:		
Natural flow	4,096	2,801
Pumped storage	1,552	1,556
Renewables other than hydro	570	1,087
Other generators	23,755	24,214
Electricity used on works: total	17,391	17,728
Major generating companies	15,799	16,064
Other generators	1,592	1,664
Electricity supplied (gross): total	316,655	329,641
Major power producers: total	294,493	307,091
Conventional steam stations	162,084	—
Nuclear stations	77,643	82,871
Gas turbines and oil engines	181	216
Combined cycle gas turbine stations	48,525	65,604
Hydro-electric stations:		
Natural flow	4,051	2,763
Pumped storage	1,502	1,507
Renewables other than hydro	506	960
Other generators	22,163	22,550
Electricity used in pumping		
Major power producers	2,282	2,430

Electricity supplied (net): total	314,374	327,209
Major power producers	292,211	304,659
Other generators	22,163	22,550
Net imports	16,313	16,677
Electricity available	330,687	343,866
Losses in transmission, etc.	28,457	29,601
Electricity consumption: total	302,230	314,285
Fuel industries	8,289	8,629
Final users: total	293,942	305,656
Industrial sector	99,909	103,129
Domestic sector	102,210	107,513
Other sectors	91,823	95,014

Source: The Stationery Office – Annual Abstract of Statistics 1998

RENEWABLE SOURCES

Renewable sources of energy principally include biofuels, hydro, wind, waste and solar. Renewable sources accounted for 2.3 million tonnes of oil equivalent of primary energy use in 1997; of this, about 1.4 million tonnes was used to generate electricity and about 0.9 million tonnes to generate heat.

The Non-Fossil Fuel Obligation (NFFO) Renewables Orders are the Government's principal mechanism for developing renewable energy sources. NFFO Renewables Orders require the regional electricity companies to buy specified amounts of electricity from specified non-fossil fuel sources. The technologies covered by NFFO Orders are landfill gas, municipal and industrial waste, small-scale hydro, onshore wind and energy crops. The fifth NFFO Renewables Order is expected to be made in late 1998.

The Government is reviewing renewable energy policy, including what measures would be necessary and practicable to achieve 10 per cent of the UK's electricity needs from renewables by 2010, and how renewables can contribute to meeting commitments to future reductions in greenhouse gases.

RENEWABLE ENERGY SOURCES 1996

	Percentages
Biofuels	80.3
Landfill gas	14.4
Sewage gas	11.0
Wood combustion	11.8
Straw combustion	4.2
Refuse combustion	25.6
Other biofuels	13.3
Hydro	16.7
Large-scale	16.3
Small-scale	0.4
Wind	2.4
Active solar heating	0.5
Other	0.1
Total	100

Source: Department of Trade and Industry

Transport

CIVIL AVIATION

Since the privatization of British Airways in 1987, UK airlines have been operated entirely by the private sector. In 1997, total capacity on British airlines amounted to 35,539,000 tonne-km, of which 26,504,000 tonne-km was on scheduled services. British airlines carried 84.7 million passengers, 56.2 million on scheduled services and 28.5 million on charter flights.

Leading British airlines include British Airways, Air UK, Britannia Airways, British Midland, Monarch Airlines and Virgin Atlantic.

There are 143 licensed civil aerodromes in Britain, with Heathrow and Gatwick handling the highest volume of passengers. BAA PLC owns and operates the seven major airports: Heathrow, Gatwick, Stansted, Southampton, Glasgow, Edinburgh and Aberdeen, which between them handle about 71 per cent of air passengers and 81 per cent of air cargo traffic in Britain. Many other airports, including Manchester, are controlled by local authorities or private companies.

The Civil Aviation Authority, an independent statutory body, is responsible for the economic regulation of UK airlines and for the safety regulation of the UK civil aviation industry. Through its wholly-owned subsidiary company National Air Traffic Services Ltd the CAA is also responsible for the provision of air traffic control services over Britain and its surrounding seas and at most major British airports. The Government has announced plans to privatize a majority holding in National Air Traffic Services.

The CAA is responsible for ensuring that UK airlines provide services at the lowest charges possible, given the requirement to meet stringent safety standards. It is also responsible for the economic regulation of the larger airports.

All commercial airline companies must be granted an Air Operator's Certificate, which is issued by the CAA to operators meeting the required safety standards. The CAA also issues airport safety licences, which must be obtained by any airport used for public transport and training flights. All British-registered aircraft must be granted an airworthiness certificate, and the CAA also issues professional licences to pilots, flight crew, ground engineers and air traffic controllers.

AIR PASSENGERS 1997*

ALL UK AIRPORTS: TOTAL	148,249,560
LONDON AREA AIRPORTS: TOTAL	94,984,589
Battersea Heliport	5,072
Gatwick (BAA)	26,959,015
Heathrow (BAA)	58,185,398
London City	1,161,121
Luton	3,238,458
Southend	8,666
Stansted (BAA)	5,426,859
OTHER UK AIRPORTS: TOTAL	53,264,971
Aberdeen (BAA)	2,573,376
Barra	8,670
Barrow-in-Furness	206
Belfast City	1,285,712
Belfast International	2,476,834
Benbecula (HIAL)	37,105
Biggin Hill	7,269
Birmingham	6,025,485
Blackpool	84,060
Bournemouth	269,339
Bristol	1,614,837
Cambridge	19,973
Campbeltown (HIAL)	11,361
Cardiff	1,155,186
Carlisle	840
Coventry	1,694
Dundee	18,469
East Midlands	1,885,767
Edinburgh (BAA)	4,214,919
Exeter	228,449
Glasgow (BAA)	6,117,005
Gloucestershire	2,104
Hawarden	4,467
Humberside	334,623
Inverness (HIAL)	401,991
Islay (HIAL)	20,414
Isle of Man	693,012
Kent International	2,936
Kirkwall (HIAL)	97,388
Leeds/Bradford	1,254,853
Lerwick (Tingwall)	4,248
Liverpool	689,468
Londonderry	56,256
Lydd	2,596
Manchester	15,948,373
Newcastle upon Tyne	2,642,615
Norwich	271,848
Penzance Heliport	108,805
Plymouth	130,526
Prestwick (BAA)	581,191
St Mary's, Isles of Scilly	128,265
Scatsta	102,344
Sheffield City	†254
Shoreham	2,685
Southampton	632,472
Stornoway (HIAL)	97,242
Sumburgh (HIAL)	361,505
Teesside	577,532
Tiree (HIAL)	5,201
Tresco, Isles of Scilly (H)	29,694
Unst	2,520
Wick (HIAL)	40,987
CHANNEL IS. AIRPORTS: TOTAL	2,748,432
Alderney	81,048
Guernsey	930,299
Jersey	1,737,085

*Total terminal, transit, scheduled and charter passengers
† Sheffield City began reporting June 1997
Source: Civil Aviation Authority

RAILWAYS

Britain pioneered railways and a railway network was developed across Britain by private companies in the course of the 19th century. In 1948 the main railway companies were nationalized and were run by a public authority, the British Transport Commission. The Commission was replaced by the British Railways Board in 1963, operating as British Rail. On 1 April 1994, responsibility for managing the railway infrastructure passed to a newly-formed company, Railtrack; the British Railways Board continued as operator of all train services until they were sold or franchised to the private sector. All passenger activities have now been franchised and all British Rail's freight, technical support and specialist function businesses have been sold.

PRIVATIZATION

Since 1 April 1994, ownership of operational track and land has been vested in Railtrack, which was floated on the Stock Exchange in 1996. Railtrack manages the track and charges for access to it and is responsible for signalling and timetabling. It does not operate train services. It owns the stations, and leases most of them out to the train operating companies. Infrastructure support functions are now provided by private sector companies. Railtrack invests in infrastructure principally using finance raised by track charges, and takes investment decisions in consultation with rail operators. Railtrack is also responsible for overall safety on the railways.

RAIL REGULATOR

The independent Rail Regulator is responsible for the licensing of new railway operators, approving access agreements, promoting the use and development of the network, preventing anti-competitive practices (in conjunction with the Director General of Fair Trading) and protecting the interests of rail users. The Regulator indicated in July 1998 that he would be looking to tighten the funding regime for Railtrack after 2001 to promote improvements in the infrastructure. The White Paper *New Deal for Transport* contains proposals to strengthen the Regulator's power to impose sanctions and broaden the scope of his duties.

Separate regulations, which took effect on 28 June 1998, established licensing and access arrangements for certain international train services in Great Britain. These will be overseen by the International Rail Regulator, a position at present held by the Rail Regulator.

The White Paper *New Deal for Transport*, published in July 1998, announced plans to establish a Strategic Rail Authority which will manage passenger railway franchising, take responsibility for increasing the use of the railways for freight transport, and lead strategic planning of passenger and freight rail services.

Proposals to privatize part of London Underground were announced in July 1997. The Government intends the infrastructure to be run by between one and three private companies, with the operating company remaining in public ownership.

SERVICES

For privatization, domestic passenger services were divided into 25 train-operating units, which have been franchised to private sector operators via a competitive tendering process overseen by the Director of the Office of Passenger Rail Franchising. The Government continues to subsidize loss-making but socially necessary rail services. The Franchising Director is responsible for monitoring the performance of the franchisees and allocating and administering government subsidy payments.

There are currently 25 train operating companies: Anglia Railways; Cardiff Railway; Central Trains; Chiltern Railways; Connex South Central; Connex South Eastern; Eurostar (which is not subject to a franchise agreement); Gatwick Express; Great Eastern Railway; Great North Eastern Railway; Great Western Trains; Island Line (Isle of Wight); LTS Rail (London to Southend and Shoeburyness); Merseyrail Electrics; Midland Mainline; North Western Trains; Northern Spirit; Scotrail Railways; Silverlink Train Services (North London); South West Trains; Thameslink Rail; Thames Trains; Virgin Trains (which operates two franchises); Wales and West Passenger Trains; and West Anglia Great Northern Railway.

Railtrack publishes a national timetable which contains details of rail services operated over the Railtrack network, coastal shipping information and connections with Ireland, the Isle of Man, the Isle of Wight, the Channel Islands and some European destinations.

The national rail enquiries service offers information about train times and fares for any part of the country:

National Rail Enquiries	0345-484950
London Transport	0171-222 1234
Eurostar	0345-303030

Rail Users' Consultative Committees monitor the policies and performance of train and station operators in their area (there are nine, covering Great Britain). They are statutory bodies and have a legal right to make recommendations for changes. The London Regional Passengers Committee represents users of buses, the Underground and the Docklands Light Railway as well as users of rail services in the London area.

British Rail's passenger rolling stock was divided between three subsidiary companies, which were privatized in 1996. The companies lease rolling stock to passenger service operators. On privatization, British Rail's bulk freight haulage companies and Rail Express Systems, which carries Royal Mail traffic, were sold to English, Welsh and Scottish Railways, which also purchased Railfreight Distribution (international freight) in 1997. In 1997–8 an average 1,159,000 tonnes of freight was transported by an average of 1,900 trains a day.

BRITISH RAILWAYS BOARD, *see* page 287

RAILTRACK, Railtrack House, Euston Square, London NW1 2EE. Tel: 0171-557 8000. *Chairman*, Sir Robert Horton. *Chief Executive*, G. Corbett

ASSOCIATION OF TRAIN OPERATING COMPANIES, 40 Bernard Street, London WC1N 1BY. Tel: 0171-904 3000. *Chairman*, I. W. Warburton

OFFICE OF PASSENGER RAIL FRANCHISING (OPRAF), Golding's House, 2 Hay's Lane, London SE1 2HR. Tel: 0171-940 4200. *Franchising Director*, J. O'Brien

OFFICE OF THE RAIL REGULATOR (ORR) 1 Waterhouse Square, 138–142 Holborn, London EC1N 2ST. Tel: 0171-282 2000. *Rail Regulator*, J. Swift, QC

RAILTRACK

At 31 March 1998, Railtrack had about 20,000 miles of standard gauge lines and sidings in use, representing 10,343 miles of route of which 3,208 miles were electrified. Standard rail on main line has a weight of 110 lb per yard. Railtrack owns 2,495 stations, 90 light maintenance depots, about 40,000 bridges, viaducts and tunnels, and over 9,000 level crossings.

Passenger journeys made in 1997–8 totalled 845.7 million, including 364.8 million made by holders of season tickets. The average distance of each passenger journey on ordinary fare was 27.43 miles; and on season ticket, 15.45 miles. Passenger stations in use numbered 2,500. The number of ticket transactions in the year was 269.5 million, earning a total ticket revenue of £2,957 million.

In 1997–8 Railtrack showed an operating profit of £380 million and a pre-tax profit of £388 million. On 31 March 1997 Railtrack employed 10,937 staff.

	£ million
Income	
Passenger	2,131
Freight	164
Property rental	127
Other	45
Total	2,467
Costs	
Production and management	523
Infrastructure maintenance	702
Asset maintenance plan charge	501
Joint industry costs	213
Depreciation	148
Total	2,087

RAIL SAFETY

The Railways (Safety Case) Regulations 1994 require infrastructure controllers (e.g. Railtrack, London Underground) to have systems in place to manage safety on the railway networks for which they are responsible.

The infrastructure controllers are required to present a safety case to the Railway Inspectorate (part of the Health and Safety Executive). The safety case must be accepted by the Inspectorate, and is subsequently subject to regular compliance audits.

The infrastructure controllers require companies bidding to operate services to present a safety case. The safety case must be accepted by the infrastructure controller before a service operator can receive a licence and begin to provide services. If any variation is required, the safety case must be re-presented. Safety cases must be reviewed at least every three years. The Inspectorate may examine the safety case of service operators as part of its compliance audit of infrastructure operators.

ACCIDENTS ON RAILWAYS

	1995–6	*1996–97
Train accidents: total	989	1,781
Persons killed: total	7	1
Passengers	1	1
Railway staff	1	0
Others	5	0
Persons injured: total	166	257
Passengers	62	182
Railway staff	75	61
Others	29	14
Other accidents through movement of railway vehicles		
Persons killed	17	20
Persons injured	3,078	828
Other accidents on railway premises		
Persons killed	4	4
Passengers	2	3
Railway staff	2	0
Others	0	1
Persons injured	9,046	3,669
Trespassers and suicides		
Persons killed	246	251
Persons injured	82	106

* New accident reporting regulations came into force on 1 April 1996

THE CHANNEL TUNNEL

The earliest recorded scheme for a submarine transport connection between Britain and France was in 1802. Tunnelling has begun simultaneously on both sides of the Channel three times: in 1881, in the early 1970s, and on 1 December 1987, when construction workers began to bore the first of the three tunnels which form the Channel tunnel. They 'holed through' the first tunnel (the service tunnel) on 1 December 1990 and tunnelling was completed in June 1991. The tunnel was officially inaugurated by The Queen and President Mitterrand of France on 6 May 1994.

The submarine link comprises three tunnels. There are two rail tunnels, each carrying trains in one direction, which measure 24.93 ft (7.6 m) in diameter. Between them lies a smaller service tunnel, measuring 15.75 ft (4.8 m) in diameter. The service tunnel is linked to the rail tunnels by 130 cross-passages for maintenance and safety purposes. The tunnels are 31 miles (50 km) long, 24 miles (38 km) of which is under the sea-bed at an average depth of 132 ft (40 m). The rail terminals are situated at Folkestone and Calais, and the tunnels go underground at Shakespeare Cliff, Dover, and Sangatte, west of Calais.

Passenger services (Eurostar) run from Waterloo station in London and Ashford, Kent, to Paris, Brussels and Lille. Connecting services from Edinburgh and Manchester via London began in 1997. The introduction of through services from these cities, not stopping in London, is the subject of a government review, due to report in late 1998. Vehicle shuttle services (Le Shuttle) operate between Folkestone and Calais.

RAIL LINKS

The route for the British Channel Tunnel rail link will run from Folkestone to a new terminal at St Pancras station, London, with new intermediate stations at Ebbsfleet, Kent, and Stratford, east London; at present services run into a terminal at Waterloo station, London.

Construction of the rail link will be financed by the private sector with a substantial government contribution. A private sector consortium, London and Continental Railways Ltd (LCR), is responsible for the design, construction and ownership of the rail link, and has taken over Union Railways and European Passenger Services Ltd, the UK operator of Eurostar (now renamed Eurostar (UK) Ltd). Construction was expected to be completed in 2003, but on 28 January 1998 LCR informed the Government that it was unable to fulfil its obligations. On 3 June 1998 the Government announced a new funding agreement with LCR. The rail link will be constructed in two phases: phase one, from the Channel Tunnel to Fawkham Junction (where an existing connection allows trains to continue to Waterloo), begins in October 1998 and will be completed in 2003; phase two, from Fawkham Junction to St Pancras, will be built between 2001 and 2007. Railtrack will buy phase one when it is completed and has an option to buy phase two by 2003.

Infrastructure developments in France have been completed and high-speed trains run from Calais to Paris, linking the Channel tunnel with the high-speed European network.

ROADS

HIGHWAY AUTHORITIES

The powers and responsibilities of highway authorities in England and Wales are set out in the Highways Acts 1980; for Scotland there is separate legislation.

Responsibility for trunk road motorways and other trunk roads in Great Britain rests in England with the Secretary of State for the Environment, Transport and the Regions, in Scotland with the Secretary of State for Scotland, and in Wales with the Secretary of State for Wales. The costs of construction, improvement and maintenance are paid for by central government. The White Paper *New Deal for Transport*, published in July 1998, proposes that the Highways Agency should take over responsibility for operating, maintaining and improving the trunk road network.

The highway authority for non-trunk roads in England, Wales and Scotland is, in general, the unitary authority, county council or London borough council in whose area the roads lie.

In Northern Ireland the Department of the Environment for Northern Ireland is the statutory road authority responsible for public roads and their maintenance and construction; the Roads Service executive agency (*see* page 330) carries out these functions on behalf of the Department.

FINANCE

The Government contributes towards capital expenditure through Transport Supplementary Grant (TSG) in England and Transport Grant (TG) in Wales. Grant rates are determined by the respective Secretaries of State; at present, grant is paid at 50 per cent of expenditure accepted for grant in England and Wales.

In England TSG is paid towards capital spending on highways and the regulation of traffic; current expenditure is funded by revenue support grant (i.e. central government grants to local authorities for non-specific services). TSG is also paid towards capital spending on bridge assessment and strengthening; towards structural maintenance on the primary route network; and towards all principal 'A' roads. In Wales TG is paid towards capital expenditure only; current expenditure is funded by revenue support grant.

For the financial year 1998–9 local authorities in England will receive £155 million in TSG. Total estimated expenditure on building and maintaining motorways and trunk roads in England in 1996–7 was £1,584 million; estimated outturn for 1997–8 is £1,491 million.

For the financial year 1998–9 local authorities in Wales will receive up to £21.7 million in TG. Total expenditure on motorways and trunk roads in Wales in 1997–8 was £113.5 million and estimated expenditure in 1998–9 is £102.4 million.

The Scottish Office receives a block vote from Parliament and the Secretary of State for Scotland determines how much is allocated towards roads. Total expenditure on building and maintaining trunk roads in Scotland was estimated at £170 million in 1997–8.

In Northern Ireland expenditure on roads in 1997–8 was £154.3 million, and estimated expenditure for 1998–9 is £145.3 million.

The Government is currently considering the possibility of introducing tolls on certain roads. The White Paper *New Deal for Transport* contains proposals to enable local authorities to levy charges for driving cars into town centres and for workplace parking; the income would be used to improve public transport.

PRIVATE FINANCE

Contracts have been let which allow greater involvement by the private sector in the design, finance, construction and operation of roads. Results of research projects carried out into road pricing technology were published in May 1998; further associated research reports were published in July 1998.

ROADS REVIEW

In June 1997 the Government launched a roads review to determine the role which roads should play in an integrated transport policy and to establish a forward investment programme for the road network in England. The review was published in July 1998 and the Government announced a reduction of over two-thirds in the road building programme. Thirty-seven schemes will go ahead and will be built by 2005 at a cost of £1,400 million; 17 schemes were cancelled; 19 will go ahead only if funded by local authorities; 43 schemes are under review, and seven await a decision. In Wales, a review resulted in four schemes going ahead, six being cancelled, eight being referred for further study and three deferred. A separate review of roads policy in Scotland is to be published in November 1998.

ROAD LENGTHS (in miles) *as at April 1997*

	Total roads	Trunk roads (including motorways)	Motorways*
England	175,587	6,522	1,729
Wales	21,270	1,066	83
Scotland	34,348	2,030	214
N. Ireland	15,251	153	70

*There were in addition 43.9 miles of local authority motorway in England

MOTORWAYS

England and Wales:

M1	London to Yorkshire
M2	London to Faversham
M3	London to Southampton
M4	London to South Wales
M5	Birmingham to Exeter
M6	Catthorpe to Carlisle
M10	St Albans spur
M11	London to Cambridge
M18	Rotherham to Goole
M20	London to Folkestone
M23	London to Gatwick
M25	London orbital
M26	M20 to M25 spur
M27	Southampton bypass
M32	M4 to Bristol spur
M40	London to Birmingham
M41	London to West Cross
M42	South-west of Birmingham to Measham
M45	Dunchurch spur
M50	Ross spur
M53	Chester to Birkenhead
M54	M6 to Telford
M55	Preston to Blackpool
M56	Manchester to Chester
M57	Liverpool outer ring
M58	Liverpool to Wigan
M61	Manchester to Preston
M62	Liverpool to Hull
M63	Manchester southern ring road
M65	Calder Valley
M66	Manchester eastern ring road to Rochdale
M67	Manchester Hyde to Denton
M69	Coventry to Leicester
M180	South Humberside

Scotland:

M8	Edinburgh-Newhouse, Baillieston-West Ferry Interchange
M9	Edinburgh to Dunblane
M73	Maryville to Mollinsburn
M74	Glasgow-Paddy's Rickle Bridge, Cleuchbrae-Gretna
M77	Ayr Road Route
M80	Stirling to Haggs/Glasgow (M8) to Stepps
M90	Inverkeithing to Perth
M876	Dennyloanhead (M80) to Kincardine Bridge

Northern Ireland:

M1	Belfast to Dungannon
M2	Belfast to Antrim
M2	Ballymena bypass
M3	Belfast Cross Harbour Bridge
M5	M2 to Greencastle
M12	M1 to Craigavon
M22	Antrim to Randalstown

ROAD USE

ESTIMATED TRAFFIC ON ALL ROADS (GREAT BRITAIN) 1997

Million vehicle kilometres

All motor vehicles	448,900
Cars and taxis	367,800
Two-wheeled motor vehicles	4,000
Buses and coaches	4,900
Light vans	40,500
Other goods vehicles	31,800
Total goods vehicles	72,300
Pedal cycles	4,000

ROAD GOODS TRANSPORT (GREAT BRITAIN) 1997

Analysis by mode of working and by gross weight of vehicle

Estimated tonne kilometres (thousand million)	149.6
Own account	37.4
Public haulage	112.2
By gross weight of vehicle (billion tonne kilometres)	
Not over 25 tonnes	24.3
Over 25 tonnes	125.2
Estimated tonnes carried (millions)	1,643.0
Own account	599.0
Public haulage	1,044.0
By gross weight of vehicle (million tonnes)	
Not over 25 tonnes	419.0
Over 25 tonnes	1,224.0

ROAD PASSENGER SERVICES

Until 1988 most road passenger transport services in Great Britain were provided by the public sector; the National Bus Company was the largest bus and coach operator in England and Wales and the Scottish Bus Group the largest operator in Scotland. The privatization of the National Bus Company was completed in 1988 and that of the Scottish Bus Group in 1991. London Transport's bus operating subsidiaries were privatized by the end of 1994. Almost all bus and coach services in Great Britain are now provided by private sector companies.

Bus services outside London were deregulated in 1986, although local authorities can subsidise the provision of socially necessary services after competitive tendering. In London, London Transport retains overall responsibility for the provision of services.

The largest bus operators in Great Britain are Stagecoach Holdings, FirstGroup (formerly FirstBus) and Arriva (formerly Cowie British Bus), which between them account for over 40 per cent of all passenger journeys. There are also 17 municipal bus companies in England and Wales, and thousands of smaller private sector operators.

National Express runs a national network of coach routes, mainly operating through franchises.

In Northern Ireland, almost all passenger transport services are provided by subsidiaries of Translink (formerly the Northern Ireland Transport Holding Company), which is publicly owned. The two main operators are Citybus Ltd (in Belfast) and Ulsterbus Ltd (outside Belfast). There are also about 75 small private sector operators.

The transport White Paper announced plans to promote bus use, primarily through agreements between local authorities and bus operators to improve the standard and efficiency of services in an area.

There are about 64,000 licensed taxis in Great Britain, of which about 19,000 are in London. There are also about 66,000 licensed private hire vehicles in Great Britain outside London, and an estimated 60,000 in London; an exact figure is not known because there is currently no licensing system in London.

BUSES AND COACHES (GREAT BRITAIN) 1996–7

Number of vehicles (31 March 1997)	75,900
Vehicle kilometres (millions)	4,199
Local bus passenger journeys (millions)	4,355
Passenger receipts (£ million)	3,586

ROAD SAFETY

The Government in 1987 set a target of reducing road traffic casualties by a third by the year 2000 compared to the average for 1981–5. Measures to achieve this were successful in reducing the number of deaths on the road by 36 per cent by 1997, and the number of serious casualties by 42 per cent. Over the same period the number of slight casualties increased by 16 per cent, but as road traffic increased by 52 per cent, the number of casualties per 100 km travelled has increased by only one per cent.

Government consultations with local authorities, the police and road safety organizations in 1996 produced strong support for setting new road safety targets.

Proposals for discussion were produced in autumn 1997, and in late 1998 the Government will set new road safety targets for Britain for the period to 2010; similar targets are being set in Northern Ireland.

ROAD ACCIDENTS 1997

Road accidents	240,046
Vehicles involved:	
Pedal cycles	25,144
Motor vehicles	413,333
Total casualties	327,544
Pedestrians	45,531
Vehicle users	282,013
Killed*	3,599
Pedestrians	973
Pedal cycles	183
All two-wheeled motor vehicles	509
Cars and taxis	1,795
Others	139

*Died within 30 days of accident

	Killed	Injured
1965	7,952	389,985
1970	7,499	355,869
1975	6,366	318,584
1980	6,010	322,590
1985	5,165	312,359
1990	5,217	335,924
1995	3,621	306,885
1996	3,598	316,704
1997	3,599	323,945

Source: Department of the Environment, Transport and the Regions

DRIVING LICENCES

It is necessary to hold a valid full licence in order to drive on public roads in the UK. Learner drivers obtain a provisional driving licence before starting to learn to drive and must then pass a test to obtain a full driving licence. Application forms for a driving licence (form D1) are available from post offices. A phased introduction of driving licences including the driver's photograph began in July 1998; all licences for newly qualified drivers will include a photograph, and qualified drivers will be issued with the new licence when their licence details need updating.

There are separate tests for driving motor cycles, cars, passenger-carrying vehicles (PCVs) and large goods vehicles (LGVs). Drivers must hold full car entitlement before they can apply for PCV or LGV entitlements. At 5 April 1998, 37.6 million people in the UK (20.8 male, 16.8 female) held a valid driving licence (full or provisional). The minimum age for driving motor cars, light goods vehicles up to 3.5 tonnes and motor cycles is 17 (moped, 16). Since June 1997, drivers who collect six or more penalty points within two years of qualifying lose their licence and are required to take another test. A leaflet, *What You Need to Know About Driving Licences* (form D100), is available from post offices.

The Driver and Vehicle Licensing Agency is responsible for issuing driving licences, registering and licensing vehicles, and collecting excise duty in Great Britain. In Northern Ireland the Driver and Vehicle Licensing Agency (Northern Ireland) has similar responsibilities.

DRIVING LICENCE FEES *as at 1 July 1998*

First provisional licence	£21.00
Changing a provisional to a full licence after passing a driving test	free
First full	£6.00
Renewal of licence	£6.00
Renewal of licence including PCV or LGV entitlements	£26.00
Renewal after disqualification	£17.00
Renewal after drinking and driving disqualification	£26.00
Medical renewal	free
Medical renewal (over 70)	£6.00
Duplicate licence	£11.00
Exchange licence	£11.00
Removing endorsements	£11.00
Replacement (change of name or address)	Free

DRIVING TESTS

The Driving Standards Agency is responsible for carrying out driving tests and approving driving instructors in Great Britain. In Northern Ireland the Driver and Vehicle Testing Agency (Northern Ireland) is responsible for testing drivers and vehicles.

More than 1.1 million car driving tests were conducted in Great Britain in 1997–8, of which 46.7 per cent resulted in a pass. In addition over 41,000 lorry tests were undertaken, of which 52.8 per cent were successful. There were more than 5,000 bus tests, with a pass rate of 47.7 per cent. Over 68,000 motorcycle tests were undertaken, of which 68.6 per cent were successful.

Since 1 March 1997 driving test candidates have been required to produce photographic confirmation of their identity.

*DRIVING TEST FEES (weekday rate/evening and Saturday rate) *as at 1 April 1998*

For cars	£32.75/£43
†For motor cycles	£39/£52
For lorries, buses	£73.50/£92
For invalid carriages	free

*Since 1 July 1996 most candidates for car and motor cycle tests have also been required to take a written driving theory test, for which there is a separate fee of £15. Theory tests for lorry and bus drivers were introduced on 1 January 1997
†Before riding on public roads, learner motor cyclists and learner moped riders are required to have completed Compulsory Basic Training, provided by DSA-approved training bodies. Prices vary. All exemptions from CBT were removed on 1 January 1997

An extended driving test was introduced in 1992 for those convicted of dangerous driving. The fee is £65.50/£86 (car) or £78/£104 (motorcycle).

MOTOR VEHICLES

Vehicles must be licensed by the DVLA or the DVLA (Northern Ireland) before they can be driven on public roads. They must also be approved as roadworthy by the Vehicle Certification Agency. The Vehicle Inspectorate carries out annual testing and inspection of goods vehicles, buses and coaches.

There were 39.3 million vehicles registered at the DVLA at March 1998, of which 27.3 million were licensed:

Private and light goods	24,267,758
Motor cycles, scooters, mopeds	655,137
Coaches and buses	79,663
Large goods vehicles	417,646
Electric vehicles	11,651
Others	1,897,227
Total	27,329,082

VEHICLE LICENCES

Registration and first licensing of vehicles is through local offices (known as Vehicle Registration Offices) of the Driver and Vehicle Licensing Agency in Swansea (*see* page 300). Local facilities for relicensing are available at any post office which deals with vehicle licensing. Applicants will need to take their vehicle registration document; if this is not available the applicant must complete form V62 which is held at post offices. Postal applications can be made to the post offices shown on form V100, available at any post office. This form also provides guidance on registering and licensing vehicles.

Details of the present duties chargeable on motor vehicles are available at post offices and Vehicle Registration Offices. The Vehicle Excise and Registration Act 1994 provides *inter alia* that any vehicle kept on a public road but not used on roads is chargeable to excise duty as if it were in use. All non-commercial vehicles constructed before 1 January 1973 are exempt from vehicle excise duty.

VEHICLE EXCISE DUTY RATES *from 15 November 1997*

	Twelve months £	Six months £
Motor Cars		
Light vans, cars, taxis, etc.	150.00	82.50
Motor Cycles		
With or without sidecar, not over 150 cc	15.00	—
With or without sidecar, 150–250 cc	40.00	—
Others	60.00	33.00
Electric motorcycles (including tricycles)	15.00	—
Tricycles (not over 450 kg)		
Not over 150 cc	15.00	—
Others	60.00	33.00
Buses		
Seating 9–16 persons	160.00	88.00
Seating 17–35 persons	210.00	115.50
Seating 36–60 persons	320.00	176.00
Seating over 60 persons	480.00	264.00

MoT TESTING

Cars, motor cycles, motor caravans, light goods and dual-purpose vehicles more than three years old must be covered by a current MoT test certificate. The certificate must be renewed annually. The MoT testing scheme is administered by the Vehicle Inspectorate.

A fee is payable to MoT testing stations, which must be authorized to carry out tests. The maximum fees, which are prescribed by regulations, are:

For cars and light vans	£30.87
For solo motor cycles	£12.74
For motor cycle combinations	£21.28
For three-wheeled vehicles	£25.02
For non-public service vehicle buses	£38.08
For light goods vehicles	£32.77
For goods vehicles up to 3,500 kg	£32.77

SHIPPING AND PORTS

Since earliest times sea trade has played a central role in Britain's economy. By the 17th century Britain had built up a substantial merchant fleet and by the early 20th century it dominated the world shipping industry. In recent years the size and tonnage of the UK-registered trading fleet have declined; the UK-flagged merchant fleet now constitutes about 1 per cent of the world fleet.

Freight is carried by liner and bulk services, almost all scheduled liner services being containerized. About 95 per cent by weight of Britain's overseas trade is carried by sea; this amounts to 77 per cent of its total value. Passengers and vehicles are carried by roll-on, roll-off ferries, hovercraft, hydrofoils and high-speed catamarans. There are about 55 million ferry passengers a year, of whom 35 million travel internationally. The leading British operators of passenger services are Stena Line (which has a Swedish parent company), P. & O. European Ferries and Hoverspeed.

Lloyd's of London provides the most comprehensive shipping intelligence service in the world. *Lloyd's Shipping Index*, published daily, lists some 25,000 ocean-going vessels and gives the latest known report of each.

PORTS

There are about 70 commercially significant ports in Great Britain, including such ports as London, Dover, Forth, Tees and Hartlepool, Grimsby and Immingham, Sullom

Voe, Milford Haven, Southampton, Felixstowe and Liverpool. Belfast is the principal freight port in Northern Ireland.

Broadly speaking, ports are owned and operated by private companies, local authorities or trusts. The largest operator is Associated British Ports (formerly the British Transport Docks Board, privatized in 1981), which owns 23 ports. Total traffic through British ports in 1997 amounted to 557 million tonnes, an increase of 1 per cent on the previous year.

MARINE SAFETY

By 1 October 2002 all roll-on, roll-off ferries operating to and from the UK will be required to meet the new international safety standards on stability established by the Stockholm Agreement.

The Maritime and Coastguard Agency (MCA) was established on 1 April 1998 by the merger of the Coastguard Agency and the Marine Safety Agency. It is an executive agency of the Department of the Environment, Transport and the Regions. The Agency's aims are to develop, promote and enforce high standards of marine safety, to minimize loss of life amongst seafarers and coastal users, and to minimize pollution of the sea and coastline from ships. In 1997 HM Coastguard co-ordinated 11,667 incidents requiring search and rescue facilities; 16,884 people were assisted and 251 lives were lost.

Locations hazardous to shipping in coastal waters are marked by lighthouses and other lights and buoys. The lighthouse authorities are the Corporation of Trinity House (for England, Wales and the Channel Islands), the Northern Lighthouse Board (for Scotland and the Isle of Man), and the Commissioners of Irish Lights (for Northern Ireland and the Republic of Ireland). Trinity House maintains 72 lighthouses, 13 major floating aids to navigation and more than 429 buoys; and the Northern Lighthouse Board 84 lighthouses, 116 minor lights and many buoys.

Harbour authorities are responsible for pilotage within their harbour areas; and the Ports Act 1991 provides for the transfer of lights and buoys to harbour authorities where these are used for mainly local navigation.

PRINCIPAL MERCHANT FLEETS 1997

Flag	No.	Gross tonnage
Panama	6,188	91,127,912
Liberia	1,697	60,058,368
Bahamas	1,221	25,523,201
Greece	1,641	25,288,452
Cyprus	1,650	23,652,626
Malta	1,378	22,984,206
Norway (NIS)	715	19,780,346
Singapore	1,656	18,874,767
Japan	9,310	18,516,363
†China	3,175	16,338,610
Russia	4,814	12,282,373
*United States of America	5,260	11,788,820
Philippines	1,699	8,849,248
St Vincent	1,343	8,374,491
Korea (South)	2,441	7,429,510
Germany	1,125	6,949,555
India	941	6,934,329
Turkey	1,146	6,567,295
Marshall Islands	168	6,314,364
Italy	1,324	6,193,692
Taiwan	692	5,931,264
Hong Kong	375	5,770,563
Denmark (DIS)	468	5,075,438
Malaysia	838	4,842,053
Isle of Man	202	4,759,132
Bermuda	110	4,610,468
Brazil	536	4,372,419
Netherlands	1,178	3,879,532
Iran	417	3,552,950
United Kingdom	1,424	3,485,692
Indonesia	2,383	3,195,007
Norway	1,559	3,058,844
Sweden	588	2,754,113
†Ukraine	1,025	2,689,977
Australia	617	2,606,573
Canada	852	2,526,567
French Antarctic Territory	79	2,462,746
Romania	413	2,344,701
Antigua and Barbuda	516	2,214,334
Thailand	576	2,157,803
Other countries	21,754	46,078,489
WORLD TOTAL	85,494	522,197,193

DIS   Danish International Register of Shipping – offshore registry
NIS   Norwegian International Ship Register – offshore registry
*Excluding ships of United States Reserve Fleet
†Information incomplete

Source: Lloyd's Register of Shipping

MERCHANT SHIPS COMPLETED 1997

Country of Build	No.	Gross tonnage
Japan	624	9,864,236
Korea (South)	202	8,124,454
†China	131	1,394,347
Germany	76	1,088,260
Taiwan	35	722,012
Poland	50	643,223
Denmark	16	465,983
Italy	24	413,107
Finland	6	348,273
Netherlands	98	322,470
Spain	72	225,951
France	15	190,996
Norway	58	163,291
Romania	15	155,263
Croatia	7	121,732
Turkey	26	102,456
Russia	15	87,901
Bulgaria	7	84,339
United Kingdom	17	72,642
†Ukraine	6	71,835
*United States of America	39	70,872
Singapore	42	57,488
Brazil	2	51,861
Malaysia	50	43,742
India	25	41,858
Other countries	162	306,255
For Registration in		
Panama	360	8,119,129
Liberia	65	2,254,515
Germany	146	2,226,880
Singapore	141	1,621,303
Marshall Islands	10	922,058
Norway (NIS)	22	899,978
Bahamas	36	856,269
Hong Kong	27	846,015
Greece	14	791,969
Japan	256	674,487
Philippines	37	630,830
Malaysia	34	474,967
Denmark (DIS)	7	457,188
Barbados	5	389,951
Taiwan	9	322,344
Cyprus	25	286,287
Netherlands	50	249,821
Bermuda	4	243,250
Malta	21	242,888
Israel	8	208,653
Norway	35	181,798
Italy	24	181,440
Korea (South)	26	181,049
Canada	4	157,573
France	13	141,823
Other countries	441	1,672,382
WORLD TOTAL	1,820	25,234,847

DIS   Danish International Register of Shipping – offshore registry
NIS   Norwegian International Ship Register – offshore registry
*Excluding ships of United States Reserve Fleet
†Information incomplete

Source: Lloyd's Register of Shipping

UK-REGISTERED TRADING VESSELS OF 500 GROSS TONS AND OVER *as at end 1996*

Type of vessel	No.	Gross tonnage
Tankers[1]	129	2,958,000
Bulk carriers[2]	42	1,775,000
Specialized carriers[3]	19	87,000
Container (fully cellular)	54	1,491,000
Ro-Ro[4]	87	834,000
Other general cargo	168	681,000
Passenger[5]	15	484,000
TOTAL	514	8,309,000

1 Includes oil, gas, chemical and other specialized tankers
2 Includes combination bulk carriers: ore/oil and ore/bulk/oil carriers
3 Includes livestock, car and chemical carriers
4 Roll-on, roll-off passenger and cargo vessels
5 Cruise liner and other passenger vessels

Source: The Stationery Office – *Annual Abstract of Statistics 1998*

SEABORNE TRADE OF THE UK 1996
EXPORTS (INCLUDING RE-EXPORTS) PLUS IMPORTS BY SEA

	Million tonnes
By weight	
All cargo	354.3
Dry bulk cargo	89.8
Other dry cargo	113.5
Tanker cargo	151.0

	£ million
By value	
All cargo	260,900
Dry bulk cargo	8,500
Other dry cargo	236,200
Tanker cargo	16,200

Source: The Stationery Office – *Annual Abstract of Statistics 1998*

SEAPORT TRAFFIC OF GREAT BRITAIN 1996
BY MODE OF APPEARANCE*

	Million gross tonnes
FOREIGN TRAFFIC: *Imports*	177.6
Bulk fuel traffic	69.4
Other bulk traffic	44.4
Container and roll-on traffic	50.5
Semi-bulk traffic	12.0
Conventional traffic	1.4
FOREIGN TRAFFIC: *Exports*	167.4
Bulk fuel traffic	103.5
Other bulk traffic	15.6
Container and roll-on traffic	42.5
Semi-bulk traffic	4.8
Conventional traffic	1.1
DOMESTIC TRAFFIC†	150.9
Bulk fuel traffic	113.7
Other bulk traffic	29.0
Container and roll-on traffic	5.5
Semi-bulk traffic	0.2
Conventional traffic	0.4
Non-oil traffic with UK offshore installations	2.2
TRAFFIC THROUGH MINOR PORTS‡	35.0
TOTAL FOREIGN AND DOMESTIC TRAFFIC	531.0

* Detailed statistics only available for major ports, i.e. generally those with at least 2 million tonnes of traffic
† Domestic traffic refers to traffic through the ports of Great Britain only, to all parts of the UK, Isle of Man and the Channel Islands. Traffic to and from offshore installations, landing of sea-dredged aggregates and material shipped for dumping at sea included
‡ Ports with less than 2 million tonnes of traffic

Source: The Stationery Office – *Annual Abstract of Statistics 1998*

PASSENGER MOVEMENT BY SEA 1996

Arrivals plus departures at UK seaports by place of embarkation or landing*

All passenger movements	34,828,000
Irish Republic	3,887,000
Belgium	2,053,000
France†	25,470,000
Netherlands	1,956,000
Other EU countries	1,014,000
Other European and Mediterranean countries‡	191,000
USA	20,400
Rest of the world	3,500
Pleasure cruises beginning and/or ending at UK seaports	233,000

* Passengers are included at both departure and arrival if their journeys begin and end at a UK seaport
† Includes hovercraft passengers
‡ Includes North Africa and Middle East Mediterranean countries

Source: The Stationery Office – *Annual Abstract of Statistics 1998*

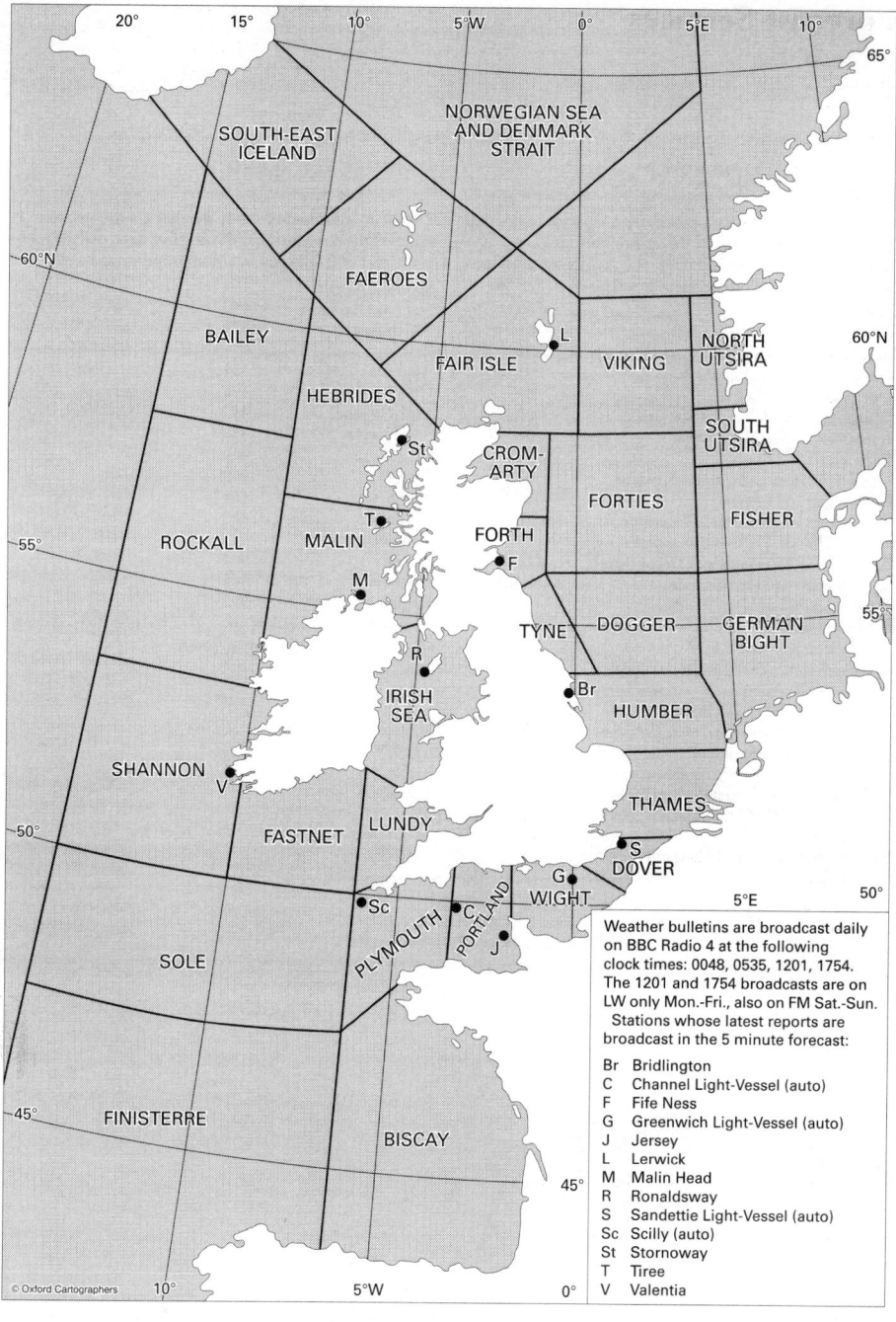

Weather bulletins are broadcast daily
on BBC Radio 4 at the following
clock times: 0048, 0535, 1201, 1754.
The 1201 and 1754 broadcasts are on
LW only Mon.-Fri., also on FM Sat.-Sun.
Stations whose latest reports are
broadcast in the 5 minute forecast:

Br	Bridlington
C	Channel Light-Vessel (auto)
F	Fife Ness
G	Greenwich Light-Vessel (auto)
J	Jersey
L	Lerwick
M	Malin Head
R	Ronaldsway
S	Sandettie Light-Vessel (auto)
Sc	Scilly (auto)
St	Stornoway
T	Tiree
V	Valentia

Forecast Services

WEATHERCALL SERVICE

To obtain local weather forecasts by telephone or fax, dial the prefix code followed by the appropriate area code. The prefix for telephone calls is 0891-500 4; the prefix for faxes is 0897-300 1. A helpdesk can be faxed on 0171-729 8811

National	00
Greater London	01
Kent, Surrey and Sussex	02
Dorset, Hampshire and IOW	03
Devon and Cornwall	04
Wiltshire, Glos, Avon and Somerset	05
Berks, Bucks and Oxfordshire	06
Beds, Herts and Essex	07
Norfolk, Suffolk and Cambridgeshire	08
Glamorgan and Gwent	09
Shropshire, Hereford and Worcester	10
West Midlands, Staffs and Warwickshire	11
Notts, Leics, Northants and Derbyshire	12
Lincolnshire and Humberside	13
Dyfed and Powys	14
Gwynedd and Clwyd	15
North-west England	16
West and South Yorkshire and the Dales	17
North-east England	18
Cumbria and the Lake District	19
Dumfries and Galloway	20
West and Central Scotland	21
Edinburgh, Fife, Lothian and Borders	22
East and Central Scotland	23
Grampian and East Highlands	24
North-west Scotland	25
Highlands, Orkney and Shetland	26
Northern Ireland	27

0891 calls are charged at 50p a minute, 0897 calls at £1.50 per minute (as at September 1998)

MARINECALL SERVICE

To obtain information about weather conditions up to 12 miles off the coast for the following five days, dial the prefix code 0891 500 followed by the appropriate area code

Scotland North	451
Scotland East	452
North-east	453
East	454
Anglia	455
Channel East	456
Mid-Channel	457
South-west	458
Bristol	459
Wales	460
North-west	461
Clyde	462
Caledonia	463
Minch	464
Ulster	465
English Channel	992

0891 calls are charged at 50p a minute, 0897 calls at £1.50 per minute (as at September 1998)

Communications

Postal Services

Responsibility for running postal services rests in the UK with a public authority, the Post Office (*see* pages 333–4). The Secretary of State for Trade and Industry has powers to suspend the letter monopoly of the Post Office in certain areas and to issue licences to other bodies to provide an alternative service. Non-Post Office bodies are permitted to transfer mail between document exchanges and to deliver letters, provided that a minimum fee of £1 per letter is charged. Charitable organizations are allowed to carry and deliver Christmas and New Year cards.

INLAND POSTAL SERVICES AND REGULATIONS

INLAND LETTER POST RATES*

Not over	1st class†	2nd class†
60 g	26p	20p
100 g	39p	31p
150 g	49p	38p
200 g	60p	45p
250 g	70p	55p
300 g	80p	64p
350 g	92p	73p
400 g	£1.04	83p
450 g	£1.17	93p
500 g	£1.30	£1.05
600 g	£1.60	£1.25
700 g	£2.00	£1.45
750 g	£2.15	£1.55 (not
800 g	£2.30	admissible
900 g	£2.55	over 750 g)
1,000 g	£2.50	
Each extra 250 g or part thereof	70p	

UK PARCEL RATES

Not over	
1 kg	£2.70
2 kg	£3.65
4 kg	£5.65
6 kg	£6.15
8 kg	£7.55
10 kg	£7.55
30 kg	£8.85

*Postcards travel at the same rates as letter post
†There is a two-tier postal delivery system in the UK with first class letters normally being delivered the following day and second class post within three days

OVERSEAS POSTAL SERVICES AND REGULATIONS

OVERSEAS SURFACE MAIL RATES

Letters

Not over		Not over	
20 g	31p	450 g	£2.88
60 g	52p	500 g	£3.18
100 g	75p	750 g	£4.70
150 g	£1.06	1,000 g	£6.21
200 g	£1.36	1,250 g	£7.71
250 g	£1.66	1,500 g	£9.21
300 g	£1.97	1,750 g	£10.71
350 g	£2.27	2,000 g	£12.21
400 g	£2.57		

Postcards travel at 20 g letter rate

AIRMAIL LETTER RATES

Europe: Letters

Not over		Not over	
20 g	30p	280 g	£1.95
40 g	44p	300 g	£2.07
60 g	56p	320 g	£2.20
80 g	69p	340 g	£2.32
100 g	82p	360 g	£2.45
120 g	94p	380 g	£2.57
140 g	£1.07	400 g	£2.70
160 g	£1.19	420 g	£2.82
180 g	£1.32	440 g	£2.95
200 g	£1.44	460 g	£3.08
220 g	£1.57	480 g	£3.20
240 g	£1.69	*500 g	£3.33
260 g	£1.82		

* Max. 2 kg
Postcards to Europe travel at 20 g letter rate

Outside Europe: Letters

	Not over 10 g	Not over 20 g	Over 20 g	Post cards
Zone 1	43p	63p	varies	37p
Zone 2	43p	63p	varies	37p

For airmail letter zones outside Europe, *see* pages 520–1

STAMPS

Postage stamps are sold in values of 1p, 2p, 4p, 5p, 6p, 10p, 19p, 20p, 25p, 26p, 29p, 30p, 31p, 35p, 36p, 37p, 38p, 39p, 41p, 43p, 50p, 63p, £1, £1.50, £2.00, £5.00, and £10.00. Books or rolls of first and second class stamps are also available. Stamps are sold at Post Offices and some other outlets, including stationers and newsagents.

PREPAID STATIONERY

Aerogrammes to all destinations are 36p, with a packet of six costing £1.99. Pictorial aerogrammes are 45p; a packet of six, £2.50. Forces aerogrammes are free to certain destinations.

Prepaid envelopes:
Standard services (DL size)

	1st class	2nd class
single	31p	25p
packet of 10	£2.85	£2.25

Guaranteed services	Special Delivery	Registered	Registered Plus
C4, 500g	£3.50	£3.80	£4.85
C5, 250g	3.20	3.60	4.55

Printed postage stamps cut from envelopes, postcards, newspaper wrappers, etc., may be used as stamps in payment of postage, provided that they are not imperfect or defaced.

POSTAL ORDERS

Postal orders (British pattern) are issued and paid at nearly all post offices in the UK and in many other countries.

Postal orders are printed with a counterfoil for denominations of 50p and £1, followed by £1 steps to £10, £15 and £20. Postage stamps may be affixed in the space provided to increase the value of the postal order by up to 49p. Charges (in addition to the value of the postal order): up to £1, 25p; £2–£4, 45p; £5–£7, 65p; £8–£10, 80p; £15, 90p; £20, 95p.

The name of the payee must be inserted on the postal order. If not presented within six months of the last day of the month of issue, orders must be sent to the local customer services manager of Post Office Counters Ltd (listed in the telephone directory) to ascertain whether the order may still be paid. If the counterfoil has been retained postal orders not more than four years out of date may be paid when presented with the counterfoil at a post office.

RESTRICTIONS

Articles which may not be sent in the post include offensive or dangerous articles (such as explosives, articles containing batteries, or aerosol products), packets likely to impede Post Office sorters, and certain kinds of advertisement. Certain other articles (such as biological specimens, liquids, or perishable foodstuffs) may be posted only if packed correctly. Advice is available from Royal Mail (tel: 0345-740740) for letters and small packets; Parcelforce (tel: 0800-224466) for parcels; or local post office counter staff.

The exportation of some goods by post is prohibited except under Department of Trade licence. Enquiries should be addressed to the Export Data Branch, Overseas Trade Divisions, Department of Trade and Industry, 1 Victoria Street, London SWIH OET. Tel: 0171-215 5000.

SPECIAL DELIVERY SERVICES

DATAPOST

A guaranteed service for the delivery of documents and packages: (i) Datapost Sameday offers same working day collection and delivery in many areas; (ii) Datapost 10 (for delivery before 10 a.m.) and Datapost 12 (for delivery before noon) offer next working day delivery nationwide and are available only to certain destinations. Items may be collected or handed in at post offices. There are also Datapost links with a number of overseas countries. Parcelforce 24 (next working day delivery) and 48 (delivery in two working days) offer a similar guaranteed service.

ROYAL MAIL SPECIAL DELIVERY

A guaranteed next-day delivery service by 12.30 p.m. to most UK destinations for first class letters and packets. The fee of £3.20 plus first class postage for a 100 g item is refunded if next working day delivery is not achieved, provided that items are posted before latest recommended posting times.

SWIFTAIR

Express delivery of airmail letters and packets up to 2 kg anywhere in the world. Items are normally placed on the first available flight to the destination country. Charge (in addition to postage), £2.70.

OTHER SERVICES

ADVICE OF DELIVERY

Written confirmation of delivery from the post office at the stated destination. Charge: 33p (inland); 40p (international); plus postage.

CERTIFICATE OF POSTING

Issued free on request at time of posting.

COMPENSATION (INLAND AND INTERNATIONAL)

Inland: compensation up to a maximum of £26 may be paid where it can be shown that a letter was damaged or lost in the post due to the fault of the Post Office, its employees or agents. The Post Office does not accept responsibility for loss or damage arising from faulty packing.

International: if a certificate of posting is produced, compensation up to a maximum of £26 may be given for loss or damage in the UK to uninsured parcels to or from most overseas countries. No compensation will be paid for any loss or damage due to the action of the Queen's Enemies.

INTERNATIONAL REPLY COUPONS

Coupons used to prepay replies to letters, exchangeable abroad for stamps representing the lowest airmail letter rate from the country concerned to the UK. Charge: 60p each.

NEWSPAPER POST

Copies of newspapers registered at the Post Office may be posted only by the publisher or their agents in open-ended wrappers or unsealed envelopes approved by the Post Office, or tied with string removable without cutting. Wrappers and envelopes must be prominently marked 'newspaper post' in the top left-hand corner. The only additional writing or printing permitted is 'with compliments', the name and address of sender, request for return if undeliverable, and a page reference. Items receive first class letter service.

POSTE RESTANTE

Poste Restante is solely for travellers and is for three months in any one town. A packet may be addressed to any post office, except town sub-offices, and should state 'Poste Restante' or 'to be called for' in the address. Redirection from a Poste Restante is undertaken for up to three months. Letters for an expected ship at a port are kept for two months, otherwise letters are kept for two weeks, or one month if from abroad. At the end of this period mail is treated as undeliverable or is returned.

PRIVATE BOX

Provides an alternative address (e.g. PO Box 123) and mail is held at the local delivery office for collection. Charge: £42 (six months); £52 (12 months).

RECORDED MAIL

Provides a record of posting and delivery of letters and ensures a signature on delivery. This service is recommended for items of little or no monetary value. All packets must be handed to the post office and a certificate of posting issued. Charges: 60p plus postage (inland); £2.50 plus postage (international).

REDIRECTION

By agent of addressee: mail other than parcels, business reply and freepost items may be reposted free not later than the day after delivery (not counting Sundays and public holidays) if unopened and if original addressee's name is unobscured. Parcels may be redirected free within the same time limits only if the original and substituted address are in the same local parcel delivery area (or the London postal area). Registered packets must be taken to a post office and are re-registered free up to the day after delivery.

By the Post Office: a printed form obtainable from the Post Office must be signed by the person to whom the letters are to be addressed. A fee is payable for each different surname on the application form. Charges: up to 1 calendar month, £6.00 (abroad, £12.00); up to 3 calendar months, £13.00 (£26.00); up to 12 calendar months, £30.00 (£60.00).

REGISTERED MAIL (INLAND AND INTERNATIONAL)

Inland: all packets must be handed to the post office and a certificate of posting obtained. Charges (plus postage): up to £500 compensation, £3.50; Registered Plus for compensation between £500 and £1,500, £4.10; up to £2,200 compensation, £4.55. Consequential Loss Insurance provides cover up to £10,000:

Compensation up to	Registered fee plus postage
£1,000	£1.20
£2,500	£1.50
£5,000	£2.00
£7,500	£2.50
£10,000	£3.00

Compensation in respect of currency or other forms of monetary worth is given only if money is sent by registered letter post. Compensation cannot be paid in the case of any packet containing prohibited articles (*see* Restrictions). Compensation is only paid for well-packed fragile articles and not for exceptionally fragile or perishable articles.

International: ensures a signature in delivery and compensation for valuables sent by letter or small packet post by air or surface mail. Some countries are not covered. Registered fee plus postage: compensation up to £500, £3.00; up to £2,200, £4.00.

SMALL PACKETS POST AND PRINTED PAPERS (INTERNATIONAL)

Permits the transmission of goods up to 2 kg to all countries, in the same mails as printed papers. Packets can be sealed and can contain personal correspondence relating to the contents. Registration is allowed as insurance as long as the item is packed in a way complying with any insurance regulations. A customs declaration is required and the packet must be marked with 'small packet' and a return address. Instructions for the disposal of undelivered packets must be given at the time of posting. An undeliverable packet will be returned to the sender at his/her expense.

Surface mail: world-wide

Not over		Not over	
100 g	50p	450 g	£1.67
150 g	67p	500 g	£1.84
200 g	84p	750 g	£2.68
250 g	£1.00	1,000 g	£3.51
300 g	£1.17	1,500 g	£5.21
350 g	£1.34	2,000 g	£6.91
400 g	£1.51		

Printed papers only, per extra 50 g, 17p

UNDELIVERED AND UNPAID MAIL

Undelivered mail is returned to the sender provided the return address is indicated either on the outside of the envelope or inside. If the sender's address is not available items not containing property are destroyed. If the packet contains something of value it is retained for up to three months. Undeliverable second class mail containing newspapers, magazines or commercial advertising is destroyed.

All unpaid or underpaid letters are treated as second class mail. The recipient is charged the amount of underpayment plus 15p per item. Parcels over 750 g are charged at first class rates plus 15p.

Public Telecommunications Services

Under the British Telecommunications Act 1981 British Telecom (now BT) was created to provide a national public telecommunications service. The Telecommunications Act 1984 removed BT's monopoly on running the public telecommunications system and BT was privatized in 1984.

The Telecommunications Act 1984 also established the Office of Telecommunications (Oftel) as the independent regulatory body for the telecommunications industry (*see also* Government Departments and Public Offices).

PUBLIC TELECOMMUNICATIONS OPERATORS

Until 1991 the three licensed fixed-link public telecommunications operators (PTOs) in the UK were BT, Mercury Communications Ltd, and Kingston Communications (Hull) PLC. In 1991 the Government announced that it was opening up the existing duopoly of the two major fixed-link operators, BT and Mercury, and would be encouraging applications for telecommunications licences. The Department of Trade and Industry has granted over 280 PTO licences.

BT's obligations under its operating licence continue to include the provision of a universal telecommunications service; a service in rural areas; and essential services, such as public call boxes and emergency services.

Cable and Wireless Communications PLC (which was formed from the merger of Mercury Communications with other communications companies in 1997) is licensed to provide national and international public telecommunications services for residential and business customers. These services utilize the digital network created by Mercury. Cable and Wireless can also provide the following services: public and private telephone services; national and international switched voice and data services; electronic messaging (private circuits and networks (national and international), integrated voice and data); data network services; customer equipment cable television, Internet service provision and mobile communications services.

In December 1996 the Government liberalized international facilities licensing in the UK. The end of the BT/Mercury duopoly means that other operators are now able to apply for licences to own and operate their own international telecommunications networks. By July 1998, 89 operators had been granted international facilities licences. In January 1998 the telecommunications market throughout the European Union was liberalized.

PRIVATE TELEPHONE SERVICES

There are over 260 private telephone companies which offer information on a variety of subjects such as the weather, stock market analysis, horoscopes, etc., on the various networks.

The lines and equipment are provided by BT under condition that services adhere to the codes of practice of the Independent Committee for the Supervision of Standards of Telephone Information Services. Services are charged at different rates from 5p to £1.50 per minute.

MOBILE TELEPHONE SYSTEMS

Cellular telephone network systems allow calls to be made to and from mobile telephones. The four companies licensed by the Department of Trade and Industry to provide competing cellular telephone systems are Cellnet, jointly owned by BT and Securicor; One-2-One, jointly owned by Cable and Wireless and US West; Orange; and Vodafone.

INLAND TELEPHONES

An individual customer can install an extension telephone socket or apparatus in their own home without the need to buy the items from any of the licensed public telecommunications operators. Although an individual need not buy or rent an apparatus from a PTO, a telephone bought from a retail outlet must be of an approved standard compatible with the public network (indicated by a green disc on the label).

BT EXCHANGE LINE RENTALS (*including VAT*)

	Per quarter
Residential, exclusive	£26.62
Light user scheme	from £9.24
Business, exclusive	£43.88

BT TELEPHONE APPARATUS RENTAL *Per quarter*

Residential	from £4.47
Business	from £5.53
Private payphone	from £50.53

EXCHANGE LINE CONNECTION AND TAKE-OVER CHARGES (*including VAT*)
BT

New line	£116.33
Removing customer	£0.00
Take-over of existing lines:	
Simultaneous (same day)	£0.00
Non-simultaneous	£9.99

Cable and Wireless

Monthly line rental	£7.98

RATES

BT and Cable and Wireless local and dialled national calls are charged by the second. Calls made from payphones are charged in 10p units. There is a 5p minimum charge on all BT calls and a 3.5p or 4.2p minimum charge on Cable and Wireless calls depending on the charging package. All charges are subject to VAT, except those from payphones which are VAT inclusive. VAT charges on ordinary lines are calculated as a percentage of the total quarterly (BT)/ monthly (Cable and Wireless) bill.

The charge per second depends on the time of day and the distance of the call:

BT	Cable and Wireless	
Daytime	Daytime	Monday to Friday 8 a.m. to 6 p.m.
Evening and night-time	Evening	Monday to Friday 6 p.m. to 8 a.m.
Weekend	Weekend	Midnight Friday to midnight Sunday

Local rate
Regional rate – up to 35 miles (56 km)
National rate – over 35 miles (56 km) (including Channel Islands and Isle of Man)
Calls to mobile phones

DIALLED CALL TIME pence per minute charges (*including VAT*)*

BT	Local rate
Daytime	4.00
Evening and night-time	1.50
Weekend	1.00
Regional rate	7.91
Daytime	
Evening and night-time	4.00
Weekend	3.00
National rate	
Daytime	7.91
Evening and night-time	4.20
Weekend	3.00
Calls to Cellnet and Vodafone mobile phones	
Daytime	30.00
Evening and night-time	20.00
Weekend	10.00
Calls to Orange and One-2-One mobile phones	
Daytime	30.00
Evening and night-time	20.00
Weekend	10.00

*Cable and Wireless customers choose from a range of packages depending on the time of day they use the telephone most and the distance of their calls. Charges vary with each package.

OPERATOR-CONNECTED CALLS

Operator-connected calls from ordinary lines are generally subject to a one-minute minimum charge (and thereafter by the minute) which varies with distance and time of day. Operator-connected calls from payphones are charged in three-minute periods at the payphone tariff. There is also a £1.80 handling charge for operator-connected calls. For calls that have to be placed through the operator because a dialled call has failed, the charge is equivalent to the dialled rate, subject normally to the one-minute minimum.

Higher charges apply to other operator-connected calls, including special services calls and those to mobile phones, the Irish Republic and the Channel Islands.

PHONECARDS

BT phonecards to the value of £2, £5, £10 and £20 are available from post offices and other outlets for use in specially designated public telephone boxes. Each phonecard unit is equivalent to a 10p coin in a payphone. Special public payphones at major railway stations and airports also accept commercial credit cards.

INTERNATIONAL TELEPHONES

All UK customers have access to International Direct Dialling (IDD) and can dial direct to numbers on most exchanges in over 230 countries world-wide. Details about how to make calls are given in dialling code information and in the International Telephone Guide.

For countries without IDD, calls have to be made through the International Operator. All operator-connected calls are subject to a £1.80 handling charge. Thereafter the call is charged by the minute.

Countries which can be called on IDD fall into one of 18 international charge bands depending on location. Charges in each band also vary according to the time of day; cheap rate dialled calls are available to all countries at certain times, but there is no reduced rate for operator-connected calls. Details of current international telephone charges can be obtained from the International Operator.

For International Dialling Codes, *see* pages 520–1.

OTHER TELECOMMUNICATIONS SERVICES

TELEX SERVICE

There are now more than 240 countries that can be reached by the BT telex network from the UK. Calls can be sent to mobile terminals, including ships via the Inmarsat satellite service. Call charges start at 4.8p per minute for inland calls. International calls are charged by the second.

TELEMESSAGE

Telemessages can be sent by telephone or telex within the UK for 'hard copy' delivery the next working day, including Saturdays. To achieve this, a telemessage must be telephoned/telexed before 10 p.m. Monday to Saturday (7 p.m. Sundays and Bank Holidays). Dial 0800-190190 and ask for the Telemessage Service.

A telemessage costs £8.99 for the first 50 words and £5.00 for each subsequent group of 50 words – the name and address are free. A sender's copy costs £1.20. A selection of cards is available for special occasions at £1.00 per card. (All prices are include VAT.)

BT SERVICES

OPERATOR SERVICES – 100
   For difficulties
   For the following call services: alarm calls (booking charge £2.70); advice of duration and charge (charge £1.80); charge card calls (charge £1.50); freephone calls; international personal calls (charge £2.15–£4.30); transferred charge calls (charge £1.80); subscriber controlled transfer (All charges exclude VAT)
INTERNATIONAL OPERATOR – 155
DIRECTORY ENQUIRIES – 192 (35p charge per call)
INTERNATIONAL DIRECTORY ENQUIRIES – 153 (80p charge per call)
EMERGENCY SERVICES – 999
   Services include fire service; police service; ambulance service; coastguard; lifeboat; cave rescue; mountain rescue
FAULTS   151 (residential), 154 (business)
TELEMESSAGE   0800-190190
INTERNATIONAL TELEGRAMS – 100
MARITIME SERVICES – 100
   Includes Ship's Telegram Service and Ship's Telephone Service
BT INMARSAT SATELLITE SERVICE – 155
ALL OTHER CALL ENQUIRIES – 100

Airmail and IDD Codes

AIRMAIL ZONES (AZ)
The table includes airmail letter zones for countries outside Europe, and destinations to which European and European Union airmail letter rates apply (*see also* page 515).
(*Source*: Post Office)
1   airmail zone 1
2   airmail zone 2
e   Europe

INTERNATIONAL DIRECT DIALLING (IDD)
International dialling codes are composed of four elements which are dialled in sequence:

(i)   the international code
(ii) the country code (*see* below)
(iii) the area code
(iv) the customer's telephone number

Calls to some countries must be made via the international operator. (*Source*: BT)

†   Calls must be made via the international operator
p   A pause in dialling is necessary whilst waiting for a second tone
*   Varies in some areas
**   Varies depending on carrier

Country	AZ	IDD from UK	IDD to UK
Afghanistan	1	00 93	†
Albania	*e*	00 355	00 44
Algeria	1	00 213	00*p*44
Andorra	*e*	00 376	00 44
Angola	1	00 244	00 44
Anguilla	1	00 1 264	00 11 44
Antigua and Barbuda	1	00 1 268	011 44
Argentina	1	00 54	00 44
Armenia	*e*	00 374	810 44
Aruba	1	00 297	00 44
Ascension Island	1	00 247	01 44
Australia	2	00 61	00 11 44
Austria	*e*	00 43	00 44
Azerbaijan	*e*	00 994	810 44
Azores	*e*	00 351	00 44
Bahamas	1	00 1 242	011 44
Bahrain	1	00 973	0 44
Bangladesh	1	00 880	00 44
Barbados	1	00 1 246	011 44
Belarus	*e*	00 375	810 44
Belgium	*e*	00 32	00 44
Belize	1	00 501	011 44
Benin	1	00 229	00*p*44
Bermuda	1	00 1 441	011 44
Bhutan	1	00 975	00 44
Bolivia	1	00 591	00 44
Bosnia-Hercegovina	*e*	00 396	99 44
Botswana	1	00 267	00 44
Brazil	1	00 55	00 44
British Virgin Islands	1	00 1 809	011 44
Brunei	1	00 673	01 44
Bulgaria	*e*	00 359	00 44
Burkina Faso	1	00 226	00 44
Burundi	1	00 257	90 44
Cambodia	1	00 855	00 44
Cameroon	1	00 237	00 44
Canada	1	00 1	011 44
Canary Islands	*e*	00 34	07*p*44
Cape Verde	1	00 238	0 44

Country	AZ	IDD from UK	IDD to UK
Cayman Islands	1	00 1 345	011 44
Central African Republic	1	00 236	00*p*44
Chad	1	00 235	†
Chile	1	00 56	00 44
China	2	00 86	00 44
Hong Kong	1	00 852	001 44
Colombia	1	00 57	90 44
Comoros	1	00 269	10 44
Congo, Dem. Rep. of	1	00 243	00 44
Congo, Republic of	1	00 242	00 44
Cook Islands	2	00 682	00 44
Costa Rica	1	00 506	00 44
Côte d'Ivoire	1	00 225	00 44
Croatia	*e*	00 385	00 44
Cuba	1	00 53	119 44
Cyprus	*e*	00 357	00 44
Czech Republic	*e*	00 420	00 44
Denmark	*e*	00 45	00 44
Djibouti	1	00 253	00 44
Dominica	1	00 1 809	011 44
Dominican Republic	1	00 1 809	011 44
Ecuador	1	00 593	01 44
Egypt	1	00 20	00 44
Equatorial Guinea	1	00 240	19 44
Eritrea	1	00 291	†
Estonia	*e*	00 372	800 44
Ethiopia	1	00 251	00 44
Falkland Islands	1	00 500	01 44
Faroe Islands	*e*	00 298	009 44
Fiji	2	00 679	05 44
Finland	*e*	00 358	00 44**
France	*e*	00 33	00 44
French Guiana	1	00 594	†
French Polynesia	2	00 689	00 44
Gabon	1	00 241	00 44
The Gambia	1	00 220	00 44
Georgia	*e*	00 995	810 44
Germany	*e*	00 49	00 44
Ghana	1	00 233	00 44
Gibraltar	1	00 350	00 44
Greece	*e*	00 30	00 44
Greenland	*e*	00 299	009 44
Grenada	1	00 1 809	011 44
Guadeloupe	1	00 590	19 44
Guam	2	00 671	001 44
Guatemala	1	00 502	00 44
Guinea	1	00 224	00 44
Guinea-Bissau	1	00 245	†
Guyana	1	00 592	001 44
Haiti	1	00 509	†
Honduras	1	00 504	00 44
Hungary	*e*	00 36	00 44
Iceland	*e*	00 354	00 44
India	1	00 91	00 44
Indonesia	1	00 62	001 44** 00844**
Iran	1	00 98	00 44
Iraq	1	00 964	00 44
Ireland, Republic of	*e*	00 353	00 44
Israel	1	00 972	00 44
Italy	*e*	00 39	00 44
Jamaica	1	00 1 809	011 44
Japan	2	00 81	001 44 004144** 006144**
Jordan	1	00 962	00 44*
Kazakhstan	*e*	00 7	810 44
Kenya	1	00 254	00 44

Country	AZ	IDD from UK	IDD to UK	Country	AZ	IDD from UK	IDD to UK
Kiribati	2	00 686	0 44	Russia	e	00 7	810 44
Korea, North	2	00 850	010 44	Rwanda	1	00 250	00 44
Korea, South	2	00 82	001 44**	St Christopher and			
			00244**	Nevis	1	00 1 869	†
Kuwait	1	00 965	00 44	St Helena	1	00 290	01 44
Kyrgystan	e	00 996	810 44	St Lucia	1	00 1 758	01144
Laos	1	00 856	†	St Pierre and			
Latvia	e	00 371	810 44	Miquelon	1	00 508	19p44
Lebanon	1	00 961	00 44	St Vincent and the			
Lesotho	1	00 266	00 44	Grenadines	1	00 1 809	00 44
Liberia	1	00 231	00 44	El Salvador	1	00 503	00 44
Libya	1	00 218	00 44	Samoa	2	00 685	0 44
Liechtenstein	e	00 41	00 44	Samoa, American	2	00 684	144
Lithuania	e	00 370	810 44	San Marino	e	00 378	00 44
Luxembourg	e	00 352	00 44	São Tomé and			
Macao	1	00 853	00 44	Princípe	1	00 239	00 44
Macedonia	e	00 389	99 44	Saudi Arabia	1	00 966	00 44
Madagascar	1	00 261	16p44	Senegal	1	00 221	00p44
Madeira	e	00 351 91	00 44*	Serbia	e	00 381	99 44
Malawi	1	00 265	101 44	Seychelles	1	00 248	0 44
Malaysia	1	00 60	00 44	Sierra Leone	1	00 232	0 44
Maldives	1	00 960	00 44	Singapore	1	00 65	001 44
Mali	1	00 223	00 44	Slovak Republic	e	00 42	00 44
Malta	e	00 356	00 44	Slovenia	e	00 386	00 44
Mariana Islands,				Solomon Islands	2	00 677	00 44
Northern	2	00 1 670	011 44	Somalia	1	00 252	†
Marshall Islands	2	00 692	012 44	South Africa	1	00 27	09 44
Martinique	1	00 596	19p44	Spain	e	00 34	07p44
Mauritania	1	00 222	00 44	Sri Lanka	1	00 94	00 44
Mauritius	1	00 230	00 44	Sudan	1	00 249	00 44
Mayotte	1	00 269	19p44	Suriname	1	00 597	001 44
Mexico	1	00 52	98 44	Swaziland	1	00 268	00 44
Micronesia, Federated				Sweden	e	00 46	007 44**
States of	2	00 691	011 44				00944**
Moldova	e	00 373	810 44				008744**
Monaco	e	00 377 93	00 44	Switzerland	e	00 41	00 44
Mongolia	2	00 976	†	Syria	1	00 963	00 44
Montenegro	e	00 381	99 44	Taiwan	2	00 886	002 44
Montserrat	1	00 1 664	†	Tajikistan	e	00 7	810 44
Morocco	1	00 212	00p44	Tanzania	1	00 255	00 44
Mozambique	1	00 258	00 44	Thailand	1	00 66	001 44
Myanmar	1	00 95	0 44	Tibet	1	00 86	00 44
Namibia	1	00 264	09 44	Togo	1	00 228	00 44
Nauru	2	00 674	00 44	Tonga	2	00 676	00 44
Nepal	1	00 977	00 44	Trinidad and Tobago	1	00 1 868	011 44
Netherlands	e	00 31	00 44	Tristan da Cunha	1	00 2 897	†
Netherlands Antilles	1	00 599	00 44	Tunisia	1	00 216	00 44
New Caledonia	2	00 687	00 44	Turkey	e	00 90	00 44
New Zealand	2	00 64	00 44	Turkmenistan	e	00 993	810 44
Nicaragua	1	00 505	00 44	Turks and Caicos			
Niger	1	00 227	00 44	Islands	1	00 1 649	0 44
Nigeria	1	00 234	009 44	Tuvalu	2	00 688	00 44
Niue	2	00 683	†	Uganda	1	00 256	00 44
Norfolk Island	2	00 672	00 44	Ukraine	e	00 380	810 44
Norway	e	00 47	00 44	United Arab Emirates	1	00 971	00 44
Oman	1	00 968	00 44	Uruguay	1	00 598	00 44
Pakistan	1	00 92	00 44	USA	1	00 1	011 44
Palau	2	00 680	†	Alaska		00 1 907	011 44
Panama	1	00 507	00 44	Hawaii		00 1 808	011 44
Papua New Guinea	2	00 675	05 44	Uzbekistan	e	00 7	810 44
Paraguay	1	00 595	002 44	Vanuatu	2	00 678	00 44
			003 44	Vatican City State	e	00 39 66982	00 44
Peru	1	00 51	00 44	Venezuela	1	00 58	00 44
Philippines	2	00 63	00 44	Vietnam	1	00 84	00 44
Poland	e	00 48	0p044	Virgin Islands (US)	1	00 1 340	011 44
Portugal	e	00 351	00 44	Yemen	1	00 967	00 44
Puerto Rico	1	00 1 787	011 44	Yugoslav Fed. Rep.	e	00 381	99 44
Qatar	1	00 974	044	Zambia	1	00 260	00 44
Réunion	1	00 262	19p44	Zimbabwe	1	00 263	110 44
Romania	e	00 40	00 44				

The Internet

The Internet is a rapidly-growing world-wide network of computer networks which use the same protocols (agreed methods of communication). It has its origins in the Advanced Research Projects Agency Network (ARPA-NET), a government-funded defence network in the USA, and other research and academic networks, such as the UK Joint Academic Network (JANET), a network linking universities and higher education institutions in the UK. JANET has extensive links to international and other national academic networks, and also to commercial and public network services. It is funded by the higher education funding agencies in the UK.

The main protocol used by the networks is Transmission Control Protocol/Internet Protocol (TCP/IP). Other protocols include:
- file transfer protocol (ftp), which allows files to be transferred between computers
- simple mail transfer protocol (smtp), which allows electronic mail (e-mail) to be sent
- hypertext transfer protocol (http), which allows hypertext facilities to be provided
- telnet, a facility which allows users to log on to other computers on the Internet

The most common uses of the Internet include:
- sending and receiving e-mail; text can be sent directly to another computer linked to the Internet
- playing computer games
- commercial transactions
- mailing lists, which enable users to send and receive information on specialist interests
- 'newsgroups' or bulletin boards, where messages on specialist interests can be left for users to read
- the publication of information

The World-Wide Web (WWW or the Web) is a vast collection of computers able to support multi-media formats and accessible via Web 'browsers' (search and navigation tools). Data stored on these computers (servers) is organized into pages with hypertext links; each page has a unique address. It is estimated that the number of pages on the Web trebled between 1995 and 1997 and is now doubling every three months. One estimate put the total number of pages at approximately 320 million in July 1998. For practical purposes the WWW and the Internet are now almost synonymous. The main Web browsers are Netscape Navigator and Internet Explorer. The Internet is increasingly used by commercial organizations for the conduct of electronic business. Policies and standards are being developed to ensure an appropriate level of privacy; tools include access control mechanisms, data labelling and cryptography standards.

The speed of access to Internet sources and of downloading information depends on the number of users on the system (which varies according to the time of day), the location of the information, and the amount of information being downloaded.

CONNECTIONS

Connection to the Internet usually requires access to a computer, a modem and a telephone line, although it is now possible to receive television-based Internet services. Internet service providers (ISPs) supply an Internet address and password, an electronic mailbox and some or all of the necessary software. Most providers provide only a connection to the Internet, but a few also offer more sophisticated on-line services which are usually easier to use but more expensive than direct Internet access. Leading service providers include AOL, CompuServe, Demon, UU net and Microsoft Network. Details of providers are available in computer magazines and specialist Internet publications.

The main methods of connecting to the Internet are by a dial-up connection or a leased-line connection. A dial-up connection may be made over standard telephone lines or over ISDN lines. There are two types of dial-up connection: an online account, which allows the user to log on to an account on a remote computer which is connected to the Internet; and a dial-up IP connection, where a full Internet connection is made from the user's computer. The latter requires more complicated software. A permanent leased-line connection (a data line requiring no modem) is likely to be used where there are a large number of potential users, e.g. where all the users on a local area network (LAN) are to be connected.

In Great Britain, an estimated 6.3 million households own personal computers. Of the 5.5 million people who used the Internet in the first half of 1998, 40 per cent logged on from home compared to 36 per cent from their workplace. The number of Internet users world-wide is estimated to be between 100 million and 130 million.

TERMS

Home page – the introductory section of a site on the Web

Hypertext mark-up language (HTML) – a standard document mark-up language used on the Web

Java – a programming language for writing client/server and networked applications; its uses include creating interactive Web sites

Search engine – a means of finding Web pages or other material on the Internet containing specific words or phrases

Server – a computer storing data and software which can be used by other computers on a network

Uniform/Universal resource locators (URLs) – the address system for the Web

Users' network (USENET) – a large bulletin board system on the Internet

Local Government

Major changes in local government were introduced in England and Wales in 1974 and in Scotland in 1975 by the Local Government Act 1972 and the Local Government (Scotland) Act 1973. Further significant alterations were made in England by the Local Government Acts of 1985 and 1992.

The structure in England was based on two tiers of local authorities (county councils and district councils) in the non-metropolitan areas; and a single tier of metropolitan councils in the six metropolitan areas of England and London borough councils in London.

Following reviews of the structure of local government in England by the Local Government Commission, 46 unitary (all-purpose) authorities were created between April 1995 and April 1998 to cover certain areas in the non-metropolitan counties. The remaining county areas continue to have two tiers of local authorities. The county and district councils in the Isle of Wight were replaced by a single unitary authority on 1 April 1995; the former counties of Avon, Cleveland, Humberside and Berkshire have been replaced by unitary authorities; and Hereford and Worcester was replaced by a new county council for Worcestershire (with district councils) and a unitary authority for Herefordshire.

The Local Government (Wales) Act 1994 and the Local Government etc. (Scotland) Act 1994 abolished the two-tier structure in Wales and Scotland with effect from 1 April 1996, replacing it with a single tier of unitary authorities.

Local authorities are empowered or required by various Acts of Parliament to carry out functions in their areas. The legislation concerned comprises public general Acts and 'local' Acts which local authorities have promoted as private bills.

Elections

Local elections are normally held on the first Thursday in May. Generally, all British subjects and citizens of the Republic of Ireland who are 18 years or over and resident on the qualifying date in the area for which the election is being held, are entitled to vote at local government elections. A register of electors is prepared and published annually by local electoral registration officers.

A returning officer has the overall responsibility for an election. Voting takes place at polling stations, arranged by the local authority and under the supervision of a presiding officer specially appointed for the purpose. Candidates, who are subject to various statutory qualifications and disqualifications designed to ensure that they are suitable persons to hold office, must be nominated by electors for the electoral area concerned.

In England, the Local Government Commission is responsible for carrying out periodic reviews of electoral arrangements and making proposals to the Secretary of State for changes found necessary. In Wales and Scotland these matters are the responsibility of the Local Government Boundary Commission for Wales and the Local Boundary Commission for Scotland respectively.

Local Government Commission for England, Dolphyn Court, 10–11 Great Turnstile, Lincoln's Inn Fields, London wc1v 7ju. Tel: 0171-430 8400
Local Government Boundary Commission for Wales, 1–6 St Andrew's Place, Cardiff cf1 3be. Tel: 01222-395031

Local Government Boundary Commission for Scotland, 3 Drumsheugh Gardens, Edinburgh eh3 7qj. Tel: 0131-538 7510.

Internal Organization

The council as a whole is the final decision-making body within any authority. Councils are free to a great extent to make their own internal organizational arrangements.

Normally, questions of policy are settled by the full council, while the administration of the various services is the responsibility of committees of councillors. Day-to-day decisions are delegated to the council's officers, who act within the policies laid down by the councillors.

Finance

Local government in England, Wales and Scotland is financed from four sources: the council tax, non-domestic rates, government grants, and income from fees and charges for services. (For arrangements in Northern Ireland, *see* page 528.)

Council Tax

Under the Local Government Finance Act 1992, from 1 April 1993 the council tax replaced the community charge (which had been introduced in April 1989 in Scotland and April 1990 in England and Wales in place of domestic rates).

The council tax is a local tax levied by each local council. Liability for the council tax bill usually falls on the owner-occupier or tenant of a dwelling which is their sole or main residence. Council tax bills may be reduced because of the personal circumstances of people resident in a property, and there are discounts in the case of dwellings occupied by fewer than two adults.

In England, each county council, each district council and each police authority sets its own council tax rate. The district councils collect the combined council tax, and the county councils and police authorities claim their share from the district councils' collection funds. In Wales, each unitary authority and each police authority sets its own council tax rate. The unitary authorities collect the combined council tax and the police authorities claim their share from the funds. In Scotland, each island council and unitary authority sets its own rate of council tax.

The tax relates to the value of the dwelling. Each dwelling is placed in one of eight valuation bands, ranging from A to H, based on the property's estimated market value as at 1 April 1991.

The valuation bands and ranges of values in England, Wales and Scotland are:

England

A	Up to £40,000	E	£88,001–£120,000
B	£40,001–£52,000	F	£120,001–£160,000
C	£52,001–£68,000	G	£160,001–£320,000
D	£68,001–£88,000	H	Over £320,000

Wales

A	Up to £30,000	E	£66,001–£90,000
B	£30,001–£39,000	F	£90,001–£120,000
C	£39,001–£51,000	G	£120,001–£240,000
D	£51,001–£66,000	H	Over £240,000

Scotland

A	Up to £27,000	E	£58,001–£80,000
B	£27,001–£35,000	F	£80,001–£106,000
C	£35,001–£45,000	G	£106,001–£212,000
D	£45,001–£58,000	H	Over £212,000

The council tax within a local area varies between the different bands according to proportions laid down by law. The charge attributable to each band as a proportion of the Band D charge set by the council is approximately:

A	67%	E	122%
B	78%	F	144%
C	89%	G	167%
D	100%	H	200%

The band D rate is given in the tables on pages 545–50 (England), 557 (London), 560 (Wales), and 565 (Scotland). There may be variations from the given figure within each district council area because of different parish or community precepts being levied.

NON-DOMESTIC RATES

Non-domestic (business) rates are collected by billing authorities; these are the district councils in those areas of England with two tiers of local government and unitary authorities in other parts of England, in Wales and in Scotland. In respect of England and Wales, the Local Government Finance Act 1988 provides for liability for rates to be assessed on the basis of a poundage (multiplier) tax on the rateable value of property (hereditaments). Separate multipliers are set by the appropriate Secretaries of State in England, Wales and Scotland, and rates are collected by the billing authority for the area where a property is located. Rate income collected by billing authorities is paid into a national non-domestic rating (NNDR) pool and redistributed to individual authorities on the basis of the adult population figure as prescribed by the appropriate Secretary of State. The rates pools are maintained separately in England, Wales and Scotland. For the years 1995–6 to 2000–1 actual payment of rates in certain cases is subject to transitional arrangements, to phase in the larger increases and reductions in rates resulting from the effects of the 1995 revaluation.

Rates are levied in Scotland in accordance with the Local Government (Scotland) Act 1975. For 1995–6, the Secretary of State for Scotland prescribed a single non-domestic rates poundage to apply throughout the country at the same level as the uniform business rate (UBR) in England. Rate income is pooled and redistributed to local authorities on a per capita basis. For the year 1995–6 payment of rates was subject to transitional arrangements to phase in the effect of the 1995 revaluation.

Rateable values for the rating lists came into force on 1 April 1995. They are derived from the rental value of property as at 1 April 1993 and determined on certain statutory assumptions by the Valuation Office Agency in England and Wales, and by Regional Assessors in Scotland. New property which is added to the list, and significant changes to existing property, necessitate amendments to the rateable value on the same basis. Rating lists (valuation rolls in Scotland) remain in force until the next general revaluation. Such revaluations take place every five years, the next being in 2000.

Certain types of property are exempt from rates, e.g. agricultural land and buildings, and places of public religious worship. Charities and other non-profit-making organizations may receive full or partial relief. Empty property is liable to pay rates at 50 per cent, except for certain specified classes which are exempt entirely.

GOVERNMENT GRANTS

In addition to specific grants in support of revenue expenditure on particular services, central government pays revenue support grant to local authorities. This grant is paid to each local authority so that if each authority spends at a level sufficient to provide a standard level of service, all authorities in the same class can set broadly the same council tax.

COMPLAINTS

Commissioners for Local Administration in England, Wales and Scotland (*see* page 320) are responsible for investigating complaints from members of the public who claim to have suffered injustice as a consequence of maladministration in local government or in certain local bodies.

The Northern Ireland Commissioner for Complaints fulfils a similar function in Northern Ireland, investigating complaints about local authorities and certain public bodies.

Complaints are made to the relevant local authority in the first instance and are referred to the Commissioners if the complainant is not satisfied.

THE QUEEN'S REPRESENTATIVES

The Lord-Lieutenant of a county is the permanent local representative of the Crown in that county. The appointment of Lord-Lieutenants is now regulated by the Lieutenancies Act 1997. They are appointed by the Sovereign on the recommendation of the Prime Minister. The retirement age is 75. The office of Lord-Lieutenant dates from 1557, and its holder was originally responsible for the maintenance of order and for local defence in the county. The duties of the post include attending on royalty during official visits to the county, performing certain duties in connection with armed forces of the Crown (and in particular the reserve forces), and making presentations of honours and awards on behalf of the Crown. In England, Wales and Northern Ireland, the Lord-Lieutenant usually also holds the office of *Custos Rotulorum*. As such, he or she acts as head of the county's commission of the peace (which recommends the appointment of magistrates).

The office of Sheriff (from the Old English shire-reeve) of a county was created in the tenth century. The Sheriff was the special nominee of the Sovereign, and the office reached the peak of its influence under the Norman kings. The Provisions of Oxford (1258) laid down a yearly tenure of office. Since the mid-16th century the office has been purely civil, with military duties taken over by the Lord-Lieutenant of the county. The Sheriff (commonly known as 'High Sheriff') attends on royalty during official visits to the county, acts as the returning officer during parliamentary elections in county constituencies, attends the opening ceremony when a High Court judge goes on circuit, executes High Court writs, and appoints under-sheriffs to act as deputies. The appointments and duties of the High Sheriffs in England and Wales are laid down by the Sheriffs Act 1887.

The serving High Sheriff submits a list of names of possible future sheriffs to a tribunal which chooses three names to put to the Sovereign. The tribunal nominates the High Sheriff annually on 12 November and the Sovereign pricks the name of the Sheriff to succeed in the following year. The term of office runs from 25 March to the following 24 March (the civil and legal year before 1752). No person may be chosen twice in three years if there is any other suitable person in the county.

CIVIC DIGNITIES

District councils in England may petition for a royal charter granting borough or 'city' status to the district. Local councils in Wales may petition for a royal charter granting county borough or 'city' status to the council.

In England and Wales the chairman of a borough or county borough council may be called a mayor, and the chairman of a city council a Lord Mayor. Parish councils in England and community councils in Wales may call themselves 'town councils', in which case their chairman is the town mayor.

In Scotland the chairman of a local council may be known as a convenor; a provost is the equivalent of a mayor. The chairmen of the councils for the cities of Aberdeen, Dundee, Edinburgh and Glasgow are Lord Provosts.

ENGLAND
(For London, *see* below)

There are currently 35 non-metropolitan counties; all (apart from the Isle of Wight) are divided into non-metropolitan districts. In addition, there are 45 unitary authorities (13 created in April 1996, 13 in April 1997 and 19 in April 1998). At present there are 237 non-metropolitan districts. The populations of most of the new unitary authorities are in the range of 100,000 to 300,000. The non-metropolitan districts have populations broadly in the range of 60,000 to 100,000; some, however, have larger populations, because of the need to avoid dividing large towns, and some in mainly rural areas have smaller populations.

The main conurbations outside Greater London – Tyne and Wear, West Midlands, Merseyside, Greater Manchester, West Yorkshire and South Yorkshire – are divided into 36 metropolitan districts, most of which have a population of over 200,000.

There are also about 10,000 parishes, in 219 of the non-metropolitan and 18 of the metropolitan districts.

ELECTIONS

For districts, non-metropolitan counties and for about 8,000 parishes, there are elected councils, consisting of directly elected councillors. The councillors elect annually one of their number as chairman.

Generally, councillors serve four years and there are no elections of district and parish councillors in county election years. In metropolitan districts, one-third of the councillors for each ward are elected each year except in the year when county elections take place elsewhere. Non-metropolitan districts can choose whether to have elections by thirds or whole council elections. In the former case, one-third of the council, as nearly as may be, is elected in each year of metropolitan district elections. If whole council elections are chosen, these are held in the year midway between county elections.

FUNCTIONS

In non-metropolitan areas, functions are divided between the districts and counties, those requiring the larger area or population for their efficient performance going to the county. The metropolitan district councils, with the larger population in their areas, already had wider functions than non-metropolitan councils, and following abolition of the metropolitan county councils were given most of their functions also. A few functions continue to be exercised over the larger area by joint bodies, made up of councillors from each district.

The allocation of functions is as follows:

County councils: education; strategic planning; traffic, transport and highways; fire service; consumer protection; refuse disposal; smallholdings; social services; libraries

Non-metropolitan district councils: local planning; housing; highways (maintenance of certain urban roads and off-street car parks); building regulations; environmental health; refuse collection; cemeteries and crematoria

Unitary councils: their functions are all those listed above, except that the fire service is exercised by a joint body

Concurrently by county and district councils: recreation (parks, playing fields, swimming pools); museums; encouragement of the arts, tourism and industry

The Police and Magistrates Court Act 1994 set up police authorities in England and Wales separate from the local authorities.

PARISH COUNCILS

Parishes with 200 or more electors must generally have parish councils, which means that over three-quarters of the parishes have councils. A parish council comprises at least five members, the number being fixed by the district council. Elections are held every four years, at the time of the election of the district councillor for the ward including the parish. All parishes have parish meetings, comprising the electors of the parish. Where there is no council, the meeting must be held at least twice a year.

Parish council functions include: allotments; encouragement of arts and crafts; community halls, recreational facilities (e.g. open spaces, swimming pools), cemeteries and crematoria; and many minor functions. They must also be given an opportunity to comment on planning applications. They may, like county and district councils, spend limited sums for the general benefit of the parish. They levy a precept on the district councils for their funds.

The Local Government and Rating Act 1997 gave additional powers to parish councils to spend money on community transport initiatives and crime prevention equipment.

FINANCE

Aggregate external finance for 1998–9 was originally determined at £37,521 million. Of this, specific and special grants were estimated at £5,372 million; £19,506 million was in respect of revenue support grant and £12,524 million was support from the national non-domestic rate pool. Total standard spending by local authorities considered for grant purposes was £48,192 million.

The average council taxes, expressed in terms of Band C, two-adult properties for 1998–9, were: inner London boroughs and the City of London £585; outer London boroughs £625; metropolitan districts £740; shire areas £655. The average for England was £664.

National non-domestic rate (or uniform business rate) for 1998–9 is 47.4p. The provisional amount estimated to be raised from central, local and Crown lists is £12,500 million. Total rateable value held on draft local authority lists at 31 December 1997 was £29,700 million. The amount to be redistributed to authorities from the pool in 1998–9 is £12,500 million.

Under the Local Government and Housing Act 1989, local authorities have four main ways of paying for capital expenditure: borrowing and other forms of extended credit; capital grants from central government towards some types of capital expenditure; 'usable' capital receipts from the sale of land, houses and other assets; and revenue.

The amount of capital expenditure which a local authority can finance by borrowing (or other forms of credit) is effectively limited by the credit approvals issued to it by central government. Most credit approvals can be used for any local authority service; these are known as basic credit approvals. Others (supplementary credit approvals) are for particular projects or services.

Generally, the 'usable' part of a local authority's capital receipts consists of 25 per cent of receipts from the sale of council houses and 50 per cent of most other receipts. The balance has to be set aside as provision for repaying debt and meeting other credit liabilities.

EXPENDITURE

Local authority budgeted net revenue expenditure for 1998–9 was (1998–9 cash prices):

Service	£m
Education	20,163
Personal social services	8,933
Police	6,809
Highway maintenance	1,702
Fire	1,417
Civil defence and other Home Office services	554
Magistrates courts	312
Public transport and parking	671
Housing benefit administration	5,649
Non-housing revenue account housing	386
Libraries, culture and heritage	864
Sport	517
Local environmental services	5,576
Other services	395
Net current expenditure	53,948
Capital charges	2,168
Capital charged to revenue	759
Other non-current expenditure	4,053
Interest receipts	−810
Gross revenue expenditure	60,118
Specific and special grants outside AEF	−9,218
Revenue expenditure	50,900
Specific and special grants inside AEF	−2,065
Net revenue expenditure	48,835

AEF = aggregate external finance

LONDON

Since the abolition of the Greater London Council in 1986, the Greater London area has not had a single local government body. The area is divided into 32 borough councils, which have a status similar to the metropolitan district councils in the rest of England, and the Corporation of the City of London.

In March 1998 the Government announced proposals for a Greater London Authority (GLA) covering the area of the 32 London boroughs and the City of London, which would comprise a directly elected mayor and a 25-member assembly. A referendum was held in London on 7 May 1998; the turnout was approximately 34 per cent, of whom 72 per cent voted in favour of the GLA. The GLA will be responsible for transport, economic development, strategic planning, culture, health, the environment, the police and fire and emergency planning. The separately elected assembly will scrutinize the mayor's activities and approve plans and budgets. Fourteen of the assembly's members will be directly elected to represent specific areas. The remaining 11 members will be elected on the basis of proportional representation from party political lists. The

Government plans to introduce legislation late in 1998 establishing the new authority, and elections will take place in late 1999 or early 2000.

LONDON BOROUGH COUNCILS

The London boroughs have whole council elections every four years, in the year immediately following the county council election year. The next elections will be in 2002.

The borough councils have responsibility for the following functions: building regulations; cemeteries and crematoria; consumer protection; education; youth employment; environmental health; electoral registration; food; drugs; housing; leisure services; libraries; local planning; local roads; museums; parking; recreation (parks, playing fields, swimming pools); refuse collection and street cleansing; social services; town planning; and traffic management.

THE CORPORATION OF LONDON
(*see also* pages 552–4)
The Corporation of London is the local authority for the City of London. Its legal definition is 'The Mayor and Commonalty and Citizens of the City of London'. It is governed by the Court of Common Council, which consists of the Lord Mayor, 24 other aldermen, and 130 common councilmen. The Lord Mayor and two sheriffs are nominated annually by the City guilds (the livery companies) and elected by the Court of Aldermen. Aldermen and councilmen are elected from the 25 wards into which the City is divided; councilmen must stand for re-election annually. The Council is a legislative assembly, and there are no political parties.

The Corporation has the same functions as the London borough councils. In addition, it runs the City of London Police; is the health authority for the Port of London; has health control of animal imports throughout Greater London, including at Heathrow airport; owns and manages public open spaces throughout Greater London; runs the Central Criminal Court; and runs Billingsgate, Smithfield and Spitalfields markets.

THE CITY GUILDS (LIVERY COMPANIES)
The livery companies of the City of London grew out of early medieval religious fraternities and began to emerge as trade and craft guilds, retaining their religious aspect, in the 12th century. From the early 14th century, only members of the trade and craft guilds could call themselves citizens of the City of London. The guilds began to be called livery companies, because of the distinctive livery worn by the most prosperous guild members on ceremonial occasions, in the late 15th century.

By the early 19th century the power of the companies within their trades had begun to wane, but those wearing the livery of a company continued to play an important role in the government of the City of London. Liverymen still have the right to nominate the Lord Mayor and sheriffs, and most members of the Court of Common Council are liverymen (*see also* page 554).

GREATER LONDON SERVICES
After the abolition of the Greater London Council (GLC) in 1986, the London boroughs took over most of its functions. Successor bodies have also been set up for certain functions. The London Residuary Body (LRB) was set up in 1986 to deal with residual matters of the GLC. It completed its work and was wound up in 1995.

WALES

The Local Government (Wales) Act 1994 abolished the two-tier structure of eight county and 37 district councils which had existed since 1974, and replaced it, from 1 April 1996, with 22 unitary authorities. The new authorities were elected in May 1995. Each unitary authority has inherited all the functions of the previous county and district councils, except fire services (which are provided by three combined fire authorities, composed of representatives of the unitary authorities) and National Parks (which are the responsibility of three independent National Park authorities).

The Police and Magistrates Courts Act 1994 set up four police authorities with effect from 1 April 1995: Dyfed-Powys, Gwent, North Wales, and South Wales.

COMMUNITY COUNCILS

In Wales parishes are known as communities. Unlike England, where many areas are not in any parish, communities have been established for the whole of Wales, approximately 865 communities in all. Community meetings may be convened as and when desired.

Community councils exist in 735 communities and further councils may be established at the request of a community meeting. Community councils have broadly the same range of powers as English parish councils. Community councillors are elected at the same time as a unitary authority election and for a term of four years.

FINANCE

Aggregate external finance for 1998–9 is £2,701.9 million. This comprises revenue support grant of £1,799.9 million, specific grants of £258.9 million, support from the national non-domestic rate pool of £612 million, and £31.2 million in council tax reduction grants. Total standard spending by local authorities considered for grant purposes is £3,090.5 million.

The average Band D council tax levied in Wales for 1998–9 is £555, comprising unitary authorities £513, police authorities £57, community councils £16 and an average grant reduction of £31.

National non-domestic rates (or uniform business rate) in Wales for 1998–9 is 42.9p. The amount estimated to be raised is £612 million. Total rateable value held on local authority lists at 31 December 1997 was £1,342 million.

EXPENDITURE

Local authority budgeted net revenue expenditure for 1998–9 was (1998–9 cash prices):

Service	£m
Education	1,355
Personal social services	578
Police	355
Highway maintenance	147
Fire	88
Civil defence and other Home Office services	33
Magistrates courts	19
Public transport and parking	14
Housing benefit administration	265
Non-housing revenue account housing	17
Libraries, museums and art galleries	47
Swimming pools and recreation	53
Local environmental services	268
Other services	120
Net current expenditure	3,359

Capital charges	256
Capital charged to revenue	20
Other non-current expenditure	136
Interest receipts	−21
Gross revenue expenditure	3,750
Specific grants outside AEF	−488
Revenue expenditure	3,262
Specific grants inside AEF	−73
Net revenue expenditure	3,189

AEF = aggregate external finance

SCOTLAND

The Local Government etc. (Scotland) Act 1994 abolished the two-tier structure of nine regional and 53 district councils which had existed since 1975 and replaced it, from 1 April 1996, with 29 unitary authorities on the mainland; the three islands councils remain. The new authorities were elected in April 1995. Each unitary authority has inherited all the functions of the regional and district councils, except water and sewerage (now provided by three public bodies whose members are appointed by the Secretary of State for Scotland) and reporters panels (now a national agency).

When the Scottish Parliament takes office it will assume responsibility for legislation on local government. The Government has established a Commission on Local Government and the Scottish Parliament to make recommendations on the relationship between local authorities and the new Parliament and on increasing local authorities' accountability. The Commission will report to the First Minister of the Scottish Parliament soon after the Parliament is elected.

ELECTIONS

The unitary authorities consist of directly elected councillors. Elections take place every three years; the next elections are in 1999. In 1998 the register showed 4,005,720 electors in Scotland.

FUNCTIONS

The functions of the councils and islands councils are: education; social work; strategic planning; the provision of infrastructure such as roads; consumer protection; flood prevention; coast protection; valuation and rating; the police and fire services; civil defence; electoral registration; public transport; registration of births, deaths and marriages; housing; leisure and recreation; development control and building control; environmental health; licensing; allotments; public conveniences; and the administration of district courts.

COMMUNITY COUNCILS

Unlike the parish councils and community councils in England and Wales, Scottish community councils are not local authorities. Their purpose as defined in statute is to ascertain and express the views of the communities which they represent, and to take in the interests of their communities such action as appears to be expedient or practicable. Over 1,000 community councils have been established under schemes drawn up by district and islands councils in Scotland.

Since April 1996 community councils have had an enhanced role, becoming statutory consultees on local planning issues and on the decentralization schemes which the new councils have to draw up for delivery of services.

FINANCE

Figures for 1997–8 show total receipts from non-domestic rates of £1,395 million and £991 million from the council tax. The unified business rate for 1997–8 was 44.9p for property with a rateable value of less than £10,000 and 45.8p otherwise. The average Band D council tax payable was £783.

EXPENDITURE

Local authority current expenditure supported by aggregate external finance for 1998–9 was (1998–9 cash prices):

Service	£m
Tourism	8
Roads and transport	340
Housing	3
Other environmental services	701
Law, order and protective services	871
Education	2,703
Arts and libraries	111
Social work services	1,108
Housing benefit administration	32
Sheltered employment	9
Consumer protection	17
Total	5,903
Total excluding housing benefits, sheltered employment and consumer protection	5,845

NORTHERN IRELAND

For the purpose of local government Northern Ireland has a system of 26 single-tier district councils.

ELECTIONS

There are 582 members of the councils, elected for periods of four years at a time on the principle of proportional representation.

FUNCTIONS

The district councils have three main roles. These are:

Executive: responsibility for a wide range of local services including building regulations; community services; consumer protection; cultural facilities; environmental health; miscellaneous licensing and registration provisions, including dog control; litter prevention; recreational and social facilities; refuse collection and disposal; street cleansing; and tourist development

Representative: nominating representatives to sit as members of the various statutory bodies responsible for the administration of regional services such as drainage, education, fire, health and personal social services, housing, and libraries

Consultative: acting as the medium through which the views of local people are expressed on the operation in their area of other regional services, notably conservation (including water supply and sewerage services), planning, and roads, provided by those departments of central government which have an obligation, statutory or otherwise, to consult the district councils about proposals affecting their areas

FINANCE

Local government in Northern Ireland is funded by a system of rates (a local property tax calculated by using the rateable value of a property multiplied by an amount per pound of rateable value). Rates are collected by the Rate Collection Agency, an executive agency within the Department of the Environment for Northern Ireland. A

general revaluation of non-domestic properties became effective on 1 April 1997. As a result of this, separate regional rates are now made at standard uniform amounts by the Department of Finance and Personnel for both domestic and non-domestic sectors. District councils now make their individual district rates on the same basis.

In 1997–8 approximately £495 million was raised in rates. The average domestic poundage levied was 189.59p and the average non-domestic rate poundage was 41.37p.

Political Composition of Local Councils

AS AT END MAY 1998

Abbreviations:

C.	Conservative
Com.	Communist
Dem.	Democrat
Green	Green
Ind.	Independent
Lab.	Labour
Lib.	Liberal
LD	Liberal Democrat
MK	Mebyon Kernow
NP	Non-political/Non-party
PC	Plaid Cymru
RA	Ratepayers'/Residents' Associations
SD	Social Democrat
SNP	Scottish National Party

ENGLAND

COUNTY COUNCILS

*Unitary council

Bedfordshire	*C.* 25, *Lab.* 14, *LD* 10
Buckinghamshire	*C.* 37, *LD* 9, *Lab.* 5, *Ind.* 1, *Ind. C.*1, *Lib.* 1
Cambridgeshire	*C.* 33, *Lab.* 10, *LD* 16
Cheshire	*Lab.* 20, *C.* 19, *LD* 9
Cornwall	*LD, Ind. coalition* 39, *Ind.* 23, *C.* 8, *Lab.* 8, *MK* 1
Cumbria	*Lab.* 44, *C.* 23, *LD* 11, *Ind.* 4, *vacant* 1
Derbyshire	*Lab.* 45, *C.* 12, *LD* 6, *Ind.* 1
Devon	*LD* 31, *C.* 14, *Lab.* 4, *Ind.* 3, *Lib.* 2
Dorset	*LD* 21, *C.* 15, *Lab.* 5, *Ind.* 1
Durham	*Lab.* 53, *Ind.* 4, *C.* 2, *LD* 2
East Sussex	*C.* 21, *LD* 16, *Lab.* 7
Essex	*C.* 39, *Lab.* 24, *LD* 15, *Ind.* 1
Gloucestershire	*LD* 22, *C.* 21, *Lab.* 18, *Ind.* 2
Hampshire	*C.* 42, *LD* 22, *Lab.* 8, *Ind.* 2
Hertfordshire	*C.* 38, *Lab.* 30, *LD* 9
*Isle of Wight	*LD* 16, *C.* 15, *Ind.* 9, *Lab.* 4, *Lib.* 2, *others* 2
Kent	*C.* 46, *Lab.* 22, *LD* 15, *vacant* 1
Lancashire	*Lab.* 47, *C.* 23, *LD* 7, *Ind. Lab.* 1
Leicestershire	*C.* 24, *Lab.* 17, *LD* 11, *Ind. C.* 1, *others* 1
Lincolnshire	*C.* 43, *Lab.* 19, *LD* 11, *Ind.* 3
Norfolk	*C.* 36, *Lab.* 34, *LD* 13, *Ind.* 1
Northamptonshire	*Lab.* 38, *C.* 27, *LD* 3
Northumberland	*Lab.* 43, *C.* 14, *LD* 8, *Ind.* 1
North Yorkshire	*C.* 35, *LD* 21, *Lab.* 12, *Ind.* 6
Nottinghamshire	*Lab.* 42, *C.* 17, *LD* 4
Oxfordshire	*C.* 27, *Lab.* 22, *LD* 19, *Green* 2
Shropshire	*C.* 19, *LD* 13, *Lab.* 7, *Ind. Lab.* 2, *Ind.* 1, *others* 2
Somerset	*LD* 37, *C.* 17, *Lab.* 3
Staffordshire	*Lab.* 40, *C.* 20, *LD* 2
Suffolk	*Lab.* 32, *C.* 31, *LD* 15, *Ind.* 2
Surrey	*C.* 47, *LD* 17, *Lab.* 6, *Ind.* 3, *RA* 3

Warwickshire	*Lab.* 31, *C.* 21, *LD* 7, *Ind.* 3
West Sussex	*C.* 37, *LD* 24, *Lab.* 9, *Ind.* 1
Wiltshire	*C.* 23, *LD* 19, *Lab.* 4, *Ind.* 1
Worcestershire	*C.* 25, *Lab* 22, *LD* 8, *Ind.* 1, *Lib.* 1

UNITARY COUNCILS

Barnsley	*Lab.* 63, *Ind.* 2, *C.* 1
Bath and North-East Somerset	*LD* 28 , *Lab.* 21, *C.* 16
Birmingham	*Lab.* 83, *C.* 17, *LD* 16, *Ind.* 1
Blackburn with Darwen	*Lab.* 46, *C.* 12, *LD* 4
Blackpool	*Lab.* 33, *C.* 8, *LD* 3
Bolton	*Lab.* 47, *C.* 8, *LD* 5
Bournemouth	*LD* 25, *C.* 20, *Ind.* 6, *Lab.* 6
Bracknell Forest	*C.* 23, *Lab.* 17
Bradford	*Lab.* 65, *C.* 18, *LD* 7
Brighton and Hove	*Lab.* 53, *C.* 23, *Green* 1, *Ind.* 1
Bristol	*Lab.* 45, *LD* 16, *C.* 6
Bury	*Lab.* 39, *C.* 6, *LD* 3
Calderdale	*Lab.* 27, *C.* 13, *LD* 13, *Ind.* 1
Coventry	*Lab.* 47, *C.* 6, *SDP* 1
Darlington	*Lab.* 36, *C.* 13, *LD* 2, *Ind.* 1
Derby	*Lab.* 37, *C.* 4, *LD* 3
Doncaster	*Lab.* 49, *LD* 6, *Ind.* 5, *C.* 3
Dudley	*Lab.* 58, *C.* 7, *LD* 7
East Riding of Yorkshire	*Lab.* 22, *C.* 19, *LD* 19, *Ind.* 5, *SDP* 1, *vacant* 1
Gateshead	*Lab.* 50, *LD* 14, *Lib.* 1, *others* 1
Halton	*Lab.* 47, *LD* 8, *C.* 1
Hartlepool	*Lab.* 33, *LD* 8, *C.* 5, *Ind.* 1
Herefordshire	*LD* 32, *Ind.* 18, *C.* 8, *Lab.* 2
Kingston upon Hull	*Lab.* 50, *Ind. Lab.* 5, *LD* 4, *C.* 1
Kirklees	*Lab.* 43, *LD* 20, *C.* 7, *Green* 2
Knowsley	*Lab.* 65, *LD* 1
Leeds	*Lab.* 80, *C.* 9, *LD* 9, *Green* 1
Leicester	*Lab.* 39, *LD* 10, *C.* 7
Liverpool	*LD* 52, *Lab.* 39, *Lib.* 4, *Ind. Lab.* 1, *others* 3
Luton	*Lab.* 36, *LD* 9, *C.* 3
Manchester	*Lab.* 84, *LD* 15
Medway	*Lab.* 39, *LD* 21, *C.* 20
Middlesbrough	*Lab.* 46, *LD* 4, *C.* 2, *Ind.* 1
Milton Keynes	*Lab.* 27, *LD* 19, *C.* 4, *Ind.* 1
Newcastle upon Tyne	*Lab.* 64, *LD* 13, *vacant* 1
North East Lincolnshire	*Lab.* 33, *LD* 6, *C.* 2, *Ind.* 1
North Lincolnshire	*Lab.* 35, *C.* 7
North Somerset	*LD* 29, *C.* 17, *Ind.* 7, *Lab.* 5, *others* 1
North Tyneside	*Lab.* 44, *C.* 8, *LD* 7, *Ind.* 1
Nottingham City	*Lab.* 50, *C.* 3, *LD* 2
Oldham	*Lab.* 36, *LD* 23, *Ind. Lab.* 1
Peterborough	*Lab.* 25, *C.* 24, *Ind. Lab.* 3, *Lib.* 3, *LD* 2
Plymouth	*Lab.* 47, *C.* 13
Poole	*LD* 23, *C.* 13, *Lab.* 3
Portsmouth	*Lab.* 21, *C.* 10, *LD* 8
Reading	*Lab.* 35, *LD* 6, *C.* 3, *Ind.* 1
Redcar and Cleveland	*Lab.* 48, *LD* 8, *Ind. Lab.* 2, *C.* 1
Rochdale	*Lab.* 36, *LD* 18, *C.* 6
Rotherham	*Lab.* 64, *C.* 1, *vacant* 1
Rutland	*Ind.* 8, *LD* 7, *C.* 2, *Lab.* 2, *Green* 1
St Helens	*Lab.* 42, *LD* 10, *C.* 2
Salford	*Lab.* 57, *LD* 3
Sandwell	*Lab.* 60, *LD* 9, *C.* 2, *Ind. Lab.* 1
Sefton	*Lab.* 31, *LD* 23, *C.* 14, *Ind. Lab.* 1
Sheffield	*Lab.* 50, *LD* 36, *C.* 1

Slough	Lab. 34, C. 4, Lib.3
Solihull	C. 20, Lab. 17, LD 11, others 2, vacant 1
Southampton	Lab. 28, LD 14, C. 3
Southend	C. 19, LD 13, Lab. 7
South Gloucestershire	Lab. 31, LD 30, C. 8, others 1
South Tyneside	Lab. 50, LD 6, others 3, vacant 1
Stockport	LD 30, Lab. 26, Ind. 4, C. 3
Stockton-on-Tees	Lab. 43, C. 6, LD 4, Ind. Lab. 1, vacant 1
Stoke-on-Trent	Lab. 54, LD 3, C. 1, Ind. 1, others 1
Sunderland	Lab. 68, C. 4, LD 2, Lib. 1
Swindon	Lab. 40, LD 9, C. 5
Tameside	Lab. 49, C. 2, LD 2, others 4
Telford and Wrekin	Lab. 38, C. 10, LD 5
Thurrock	Lab. 45, C. 4
Torbay	LD 21, C. 9, Lab. 2, others 3, vacant 1
Trafford	Lab. 36, C. 23, LD 4
Wakefield	Lab. 60, C. 2, Ind. Lab. 1
Walsall	Lab. 30, C. 16, LD 5, Ind. 1, others 8
Warrington	Lab. 43, LD 11, C. 4, vacant 2
West Berkshire	LD 37, C. 15, Ind. 1, vacant 1
Wigan	Lab. 70, Ind. Lab. 1, LD 1
Windsor and Maidenhead	LD 29, C. 22, Ind. 7
Wirral	Lab. 41, C. 16, LD 8, Ind. LD 1
Wokingham	C. 31, LD 23
Wolverhampton	Lab. 44, C. 14, LD 2
York	Lab. 30, LD 18, C. 3, Ind. 2

DISTRICT COUNCILS

*Denotes councils where one-third of councillors retire each year except in the year of county council elections

*Adur	LD 21, Lab. 10, C. 6, Ind. 2
Allerdale	Lab. 36, Ind. 7, C. 6, LD 5, vacant 1
Alnwick	LD 12, Rural Alliance 8, Lab. 6, others 3
Amber Valley	Lab. 36, C. 6, vacant 1
Arun	C. 29, LD 14, Lab. 10, Ind. 3
Ashfield	Lab. 33
Ashford	C. 19, LD 14, Lab. 11, Ind. C. 1, Ind. 1, Lib. 1, others 1
Aylesbury Vale	LD 29, C. 14, Ind. 9, Lab. 5, vacant 1
Babergh	Ind. 11, C. 9, Lab. 9, LD 9, Ind. Soc. 2, others 2
*Barrow-in-Furness	Lab. 23, C. 11, others 4
*Basildon	Lab. 22, LD 13, C. 6, vacant 1
*Basingstoke and Deane	C. 25, Lab. 15, LD 13, Ind. 3, NP 1
*Bassetlaw	Lab. 32, C. 9, LD 3, Ind. 2, New Ind. 2, Ind. Lab. 1, vacant 1
*Bedford	Lab. 22, LD 15, C. 9, Ind. 7
Berwick-upon-Tweed	LD 13, Ind. 10, C. 2, Lab. 1, others 2
Blaby	Lab. 17, C. 11, LD 9, Ind. 1, Ind. C. 1
Blyth Valley	Lab. 39, LD 6, Ind. 1, vacant 1
Bolsover	Lab. 35, Ind. 1, RA 1
Boston	Lab. 14, Ind. 7, C. 6, LD 6, vacant 1
Braintree	Lab. 37, C. 10, Ind. 7, LD 6
Breckland	C. 21, Lab. 20, Ind. 8, LD 2, Green 1, vacant 1

*Brentwood	LD 25, C. 10, Lab. 2, Lib. 1, vacant 1
Bridgnorth	Ind. 9, Lab. 6, LD 5, Ind. C. 4, C. 3, Ind. Lab. 1, others 5
Broadland	C. 21, Lab. 16, LD 8, Ind. 4
Bromsgrove	Lab. 24, C. 12, RA 2, Lib. 1
*Broxbourne	C. 30, Lab. 11, vacant 1
Broxtowe	Lab. 36, C. 6, LD 6, Ind. 1
*Burnley	Lab. 31, LD 9, Ind. 5, C. 3
*Cambridge	Lab. 21, LD 18, C. 3
*Cannock Chase	Lab. 39, LD 3
Canterbury	LD 21, Lab. 15, C. 11, Ind. 1, others 1
Caradon	Ind. 18, LD 18, Lab. 2, C. 1, others 2
*Carlisle	Lab. 33, C. 14, LD/Ind. 4
Carrick	LD 17, Ind. 9, C. 8, Lab. 8, MK 1, others 2
Castle Morpeth	Lab. 12, Ind. 9, C. 6, LD 4, Lib. 2, others 1
Castle Point	Lab. 33, C. 5, Ind. Lab. 1
Charnwood	Lab. 30, C. 15, LD 5, Ind. 2
Chelmsford	LD 32, C. 14, Lab. 7, Ind. 3
*Cheltenham	LD 26, C. 9, Lab. 1, others 5
*Cherwell	Lab. 23, C. 18, LD 7, Ind. 3, vacant 1
*Chester	Lab. 26, LD 17, C. 15, Ind. 2
Chesterfield	Lab. 37, LD 10
Chester-le-Street	Lab. 30, C. 1, Ind. 1, LD 1
Chichester	LD 23, C. 22, Ind. 4, Lab. 1
Chiltern	LD 24, C. 21, Ind. 2, RA 2, Lab. 1
*Chorley	Lab. 33, C. 6, LD 6, Ind. 2, Ind. Lab. 1
Christchurch	C. 9, Ind. 8, LD 8
*Colchester	LD 27, Lab. 17, C. 15, RA 1
*Congleton	LD 26, Lab. 11, C. 7, Ind. 1
Copeland	Lab. 32, C. 14, Ind. 2, Ind. Lab. 2, vacant 1
Corby	Lab. 23, C. 1, Ind. Lab. 1, LD 1, vacant 1
Cotswold	Ind. 17, LD 8, Ind. C. 4, Lab. 4, C. 3, others 9
*Craven	C. 13, LD 13, Ind. 4, Lab. 4
*Crawley	Lab. 27, C. 3, LD 2
*Crewe and Nantwich	Lab. 37, C. 15, LD 4, Ind. 1
Dacorum	Lab. 31, C. 20, LD 4, Ind. 3
Dartford	Lab. 34, C. 10, Ind. 3
*Daventry	C. 17, Lab. 13, LD 3, Ind. 2
Derbyshire Dales	LD 16, Ind. C. 15, Lab. 8
Derwentside	Lab. 50, Ind. 5
Dover	Lab. 37, C. 15, LD 3, vacant 1
Durham	Lab. 39, LD 7, Ind. 3
Easington	Lab. 44, Lib. 3, Ind. 2, Ind. Lab. 2
*Eastbourne	LD 18, C. 12
East Cambridgeshire	Ind. 14, LD 13, NP 5, Lab. 4, Ind. C. 1
East Devon	C. 32, LD 19, Ind. 8, Lib. 1
East Dorset	LD 23, C. 12, Ind. C. 1
East Hampshire	LD 25, C. 13, Ind. 3, vacant 1
East Hertfordshire	C. 23, LD 16, Lab. 8, Ind. 2, others 1
*Eastleigh	LD 29, Lab. 8, C. 7
East Lindsey	NP 34, Lab. 14, LD 7, Green 3, others 2
East Northamptonshire	Lab. 24, C. 10, Lib. 2
East Staffordshire	Lab. 34, C. 6, Ind. C. 3, LD 3
Eden	Ind. Group 28, LD 4, Ind. 3, Lab. 2

*Ellesmere Port and
  Neston   *Lab.* 36, *C.* 5
Elmbridge   C. 23, *RA* 21, *LD* 8, *Lab.* 7, *Ind.*
            1
Epping Forest   Lab. 17, *C.* 16, *LD* 15, *RA* 9,
            Ind. 2
Epsom and Ewell   *RA* 32, *LD* 4, *Lab.* 3
Erewash   *Lab.* 39, *C.* 10, *LD* 2, *Ind.* 1
Exeter   Lab. 22, *LD* 8, *C.* 3, *Lib.* 3
Fareham   LD 16, *C.* 14, *Lab.* 8, *Loyal C.* 4
Fenland   *C.* 16, *Lab.* 15, *Ind.* 4, *Socialist*
            Lab. 3, *LD* 2
Forest Heath   *C.* 10, *Ind.* 6, *LD* 5, *Lab.* 4
Forest of Dean   *Lab.* 29, *Ind.* 12, *LD* 5, *C.* 1,
            others 2
Fylde   *C.* 18, *Lab.* 5, *LD* 4, *others* 22
Gedling   *Lab.* 30, *C.* 19, *LD* 7, *Ind.* 1
Gloucester   Lab. 25, *LD* 8, *C.* 6
Gosport   Lab. 10, *C.* 9, *Ind. LD* 8, *LD* 3
Gravesham   *Lab.* 33, *C.* 10, *Ind.* 1
Great Yarmouth   Lab. 36, *C.* 12
Guildford   *LD* 19, *C.* 13, *Ind.* 7, *Lab.* 6
Hambleton   *C./Ind.* 30, *Ind.* 10, *Lab.* 4, *LD* 3
Harborough   *LD* 15, *C.* 12, *Lab.* 8, *Ind.* 2
Harlow   Lab. 38, *LD* 3, *C.* 1
Harrogate   LD 40, *C.* 14, *Lab.* 4, *Ind.* 1
Hart   LD 15, *C.* 14, *Ind.* 4, *Ind. C.* 2
Hastings   Lab. 18, *LD* 13, *C.* 1
Havant   C. 14, *LD* 14, *Lab.* 8, *Ind.* 3, *Ind.*
            Lab. 3
Hertsmere   Lab. 22, *C.* 11, *LD* 6
High Peak   *Lab.* 30, *LD* 6, *C.* 5, *Ind.* 3
Hinckley and Bosworth   *LD* 17, *Lab.* 13, *C.* 4
Horsham   *LD* 22, *C.* 18, *Ind.* 3
Huntingdonshire   C. 34, *LD* 14, *Lab.* 3, *Ind.* 2
Hyndburn   Lab. 35, *C.* 12
Ipswich   Lab. 40, *C.* 8
Kennet   *Ind.* 14, *C.* 9, *Lab.* 9, *LD* 8
Kerrier   *Lab.* 15, *Ind.* 10, *LD* 8, *C.* 2,
            others 9
Kettering   *Lab.* 32, *C.* 7, *Ind.* 3, *LD* 3
King's Lynn and West
  Norfolk   *Lab.* 37, *C./Ind.* 16, *LD* 6, *Ind.* 1
Lancaster   *Lab.* 35, *Ind.* 11, *C.* 8, *LD* 4, *Ind.*
            C. 1, *others* 1
Lewes   *LD* 28, *C.* 16, *Lab.* 2, *Ind.* 1,
            others 1
Lichfield   *Lab.* 31, *C.* 19, *LD* 2, *Ind.* 1, *Ind.*
            Lab. 1, *others* 2
Lincoln   Lab. 28, *Ind. Lab.* 3, *C.* 1, *vacant*
            1
Macclesfield   C. 37, *Lab.* 10, *LD* 10, *others* 3
Maidstone   LD 22, *Lab.* 15, *C.* 13, *Ind.* 5
Maldon   *C.* 15, *Lab.* 8, *Lab.* 7
Malvern Hills   *LD* 19, *C./Ind.* 11, *Ind.* 10, *Lab.*
            1, *vacant* 1
Mansfield   *Lab.* 45, *C.* 1
Melton   *C.* 8, *Lab.* 8, *LD* 6, *Ind.* 4
Mendip   *LD* 19, *Lab.* 9, *C.* 8, *RA* 4, *Ind.* 3
Mid Bedfordshire   *C.* 23, *Lab.* 20, *Ind.* 5, *LD* 5
Mid Devon   *Ind.* 19, *LD* 19, *Lab.* 1, *Lib.* 1
Mid Suffolk   *Lab.* 15, *LD* 11, *C.* 7, *Ind.* 4, *Ind.*
            Lab. 2, *others* 1
Mid Sussex   LD 27, *C.* 19, *Ind.* 4, *Lab.* 4
Mole Valley   LD 16, *C.* 14, *Ind.* 9, *Lab.* 2
Newark and Sherwood   *Lab.* 33, *C.* 12, *LD* 5, *Ind.* 4
Newcastle under Lyme   Lab. 42, *Lib.* 9, *C.* 5
New Forest   *LD* 31, *C.* 23, *Ind.* 4
Northampton   *Lab.* 34, *Lib.* 7, *C.* 1, *vacant* 1
North Cornwall   *Ind.* 27, *LD* 10, *C.* 1

North Devon   *LD* 31, *Ind.* 10, *NP* 2, *C.* 1
North Dorset   *LD* 17, *Ind.* 11, *others* 5
North East Derbyshire   *Lab.* 42, *C.* 5, *LD* 3, *Ind. Lab.* 2,
            Ind. 1
North Hertfordshire   Lab. 26, *C.* 17, *LD* 6, *Ind.* 1
North Kesteven   *Lab.* 16, *LD* 8, *C.* 5, *Ind.* 4,
            others 6
North Norfolk   *Lab.* 19, *LD* 12, *NP* 8, *Ind. C.* 7
North Shropshire   *Ind.* 6, *Lab.* 6, *LD* 4, *C.* 2, *others*
            22
North Warwickshire   *Lab.* 28, *C.* 4, *Ind.* 1, *vacant* 1
North West
  Leicestershire   *Lab.* 35, *C.* 3, *Ind.* 2
North Wiltshire   *LD* 33, *C.* 11, *Lab.* 6, *Ind.* 2
Norwich   Lab. 35, *LD* 13
Nuneaton and Bedworth   Lab. 41, *C.* 4
Oadby and Wigston   LD 25, *C.* 1
Oswestry   *Ind.* 9, *Lab.* 8, *C.* 5, *LD* 5, *others*
            2
Oxford   Lab. 33, *LD* 14, *Green* 4
Pendle   LD 29, *Lab.* 18, *C.* 3, *Ind.* 1
Penwith   LD 12, *C.* 7, *Ind.* 7, *Lab.* 6, *MK*
            2
Preston   Lab. 30, *C.* 13, *LD* 13, *Ind. Lab.*
            1
Purbeck   LD 8, *C.* 6, *Ind.* 5, *Lab.* 3
Redditch   Lab. 23, *C.* 4, *LD* 2
Reigate and Banstead   C. 19, *Lab.* 13, *LD* 11, *RA* 5,
            Ind. 1
Restormel   *LD* 28, *Ind.* 7, *Lab.* 3, *C.* 2, *Ind.*
            LD 1, *others* 2, *vacant* 1
Ribble Valley   *LD* 19, *C.* 18, *Ind.* 1, *Lab.* 1
Richmondshire   *NP* 20, *LD* 8, *C.* 3, *Ind. C.* 1, *SD*
            1, *others* 1
Rochford   LD 18, *Lab.* 12, *C.* 6, *RA* 3, *Ind.*
            1
Rossendale   Lab. 25, *C.* 11
Rother   *C.* 16, *LD* 16, *Ind.* 8, *Lab.* 5
Rugby   Lab. 22, *C.* 12, *LD* 5, *others* 9
Runnymede   C. 23, *Lab.* 12, *Ind.* 6, *LD* 1
Rushcliffe   *C.* 24, *Lab.* 17, *LD* 8, *Ind.* 5
Rushmoor   C. 17, *Lab.* 14, *LD* 14
Ryedale   *Ind.* 10, *LD* 8, *C.* 4, *Lab.* 1
St Albans   LD 30, *Lab.* 16, *C.* 11
St Edmundsbury   *Lab.* 2, *C.* 13, *LD* 6, *Ind.* 3
Salisbury   *LD* 29, *Lab.* 11, *C.* 10, *Ind.* 8
Scarborough   *Lab.* 24, *C.* 13, *Ind.* 8, *LD* 4
Sedgefield   *Lab.* 47, *Ind.* 2
Sedgemoor   *C.* 22, *Lab.* 13, *LD* 12, *Ind.* 2
Selby   *Lab.* 27, *C.* 9, *Ind.* 4, *LD* 1
Sevenoaks   *LD* 19, *C.* 18, *Lab.* 12, *Ind.* 4
Shepway   *C.* 19, *LD* 19, *Lab.* 15, *Ind.* 3
Shrewsbury and Atcham   Lab. 21, *LD* 12, *C.* 11, *Ind.* 4
South Bedfordshire   Lab. 21, *LD* 16, *C.* 13, *RA* 2,
            Ind. 1
South Bucks   *C.* 20, *Ind.* 14, *LD* 5, *NP* 1
South Cambridgeshire   C. 15, *LD* 13, *Lab.* 9
South Derbyshire   *Lab.* 28, *C.* 6
South Hams   *C.* 18, *Ind.* 15, *LD* 9, *Lab.* 2
South Holland   *Ind.* 16, *C.* 9, *Lab.* 8, *others* 5
South Kesteven   *Ind.* 17, *C.* 15, *Lab.* 15, *LD* 7,
            Lib. 2, *vacant* 1
South Lakeland   LD 20, *C.* 13, *Lab.* 10, *Ind.* 9
South Norfolk   *LD* 30, *C.* 12, *Lab.* 3, *Ind.* 2
South Northamptonshire   *C.* 16, *Lab.* 10, *Ind.* 7, *LD* 6,
            vacant 1
South Oxfordshire   *LD* 21, *Lab.* 13, *C.* 9, *Ind.* 5, *RA*
            2
South Ribble   *Lab.* 27, *C.* 16, *LD* 9, *others* 2
South Shropshire   *Ind.* 8, *LD* 7, *Lab.* 1, *NP* 24

South Somerset	LD 44, C. 10, Ind. 5, Lab. 1
South Staffordshire	C. 28, Lab. 15, LD 4, RA 2, Ind. 1
Spelthorne	C. 22, Lab. 14, LD 3, vacant 1
Stafford	Lab. 33, C. 16, LD 10, Ind. C. 1
*Staffordshire Moorlands	Lab. 26, Ind. C. 11, LD 7, Ind. 3, NP 1, RA 8
*Stevenage	Lab. 37, LD 2
*Stratford-on-Avon	LD 23, C. 18, Ind. 7, Lab. 5, others 2
*Stroud	Lab. 26, C. 10, LD 9, Ind. 6, Green 4
Suffolk Coastal	C. 20, Lab. 15, LD 15, Ind. 5
Surrey Heath	C. 24, LD 7, Lab. 4, vacant 1
*Swale	LD 22, Lab. 19, C. 7, Ind. 1
*Tamworth	Lab. 28, C. 1, Ind. 1
*Tandridge	LD 18, C. 17, Lab. 7
Taunton Deane	LD 29, C. 15, Lab. 6, Ind. 3
Teesdale	Ind. 13, Lab. 11, NP 7
Teignbridge	LD 24, Ind. 21, C. 7, Lab. 6
Tendring	Lab. 35, Ind.12, C. 8, LD 5
Test Valley	C. 20, LD 18, Ind. LD 3, Ind. 2, vacant 1
Tewkesbury	Ind. 14, C./Ind. 8, LD 7, Lab. 5, NP 2
Thanet	Lab. 44, C. 4, LD 4, Ind. 2
*Three Rivers	LD 23, C. 17, Lab. 8
*Tonbridge and Malling	C. 23, LD 21, Lab. 11
Torridge	LD 13, Ind. 10, Lab. 5, C. 2, NP 2, others 4
*Tunbridge Wells	C. 27, LD 12, Lab. 7, Ind. 2
Tynedale	Lab. 19, LD 13, C. 11, Ind. 4
Uttlesford	LD 18, C. 14, Ind. 6, Lab. 4
Vale of White Horse	LD 34, C. 11, Lab. 6
Vale Royal	Lab. 41, C. 15, LD 4
Wansbeck	Lab. 46
Warwick	Lab. 17, C. 13, LD 11, Ind. 4
*Watford	Lab. 21, LD 8, C. 7
*Waveney	Lab. 41, C. 3, LD 2, Ind. 1, others 1
Waverley	LD 33, C. 19, Lab. 2, Ind. 1, others 2
Wealden	C. 31, LD 23, NP. 4
Wear Valley	Lab. 35, Ind. 3, LD 2
Wellingborough	Lab. 17, C. 13, Ind. 3, Ind. C. 1
*Welwyn Hatfield	Lab. 27, C. 20
West Devon	LD 15, Ind. 14, Lab. 1
West Dorset	Ind. 20, C. 18, LD 12, Lab. 5
*West Lancashire	Lab. 33, C. 20, Ind. 2
*West Lindsey	LD 18, Ind. 10, Lab. 5, C. 4
*West Oxfordshire	C. 14, Ind. 13, LD 12, Lab. 10
West Somerset	Ind. 13, C. 9, Lab. 8, LD 2
West Wiltshire	C. 27, C. 7, Lab. 5, Ind. 4
*Weymouth and Portland	Lab. 16, LD 13, Ind. 6
*Winchester	LD 37, C. 10, Ind. 4, Lab. 4
*Woking	LD 16, C. 11, Lab. 7, Ind. 1
*Worcester	Lab. 21, C. 10, Ind. 3, LD 2
*Worthing	LD 20, C. 16
Wychavon	C. 18, LD 16, Lab. 10, Ind. 5
Wycombe	C. 24, LD 19, Lab. 15, Ind. 2
Wyre	Lab. 32, C. 18, LD 4, Ind. 1, RA 1
*Wyre Forest	Lab. 28, LD 6, C. 4, Lib. 3, Ind. 1

GREATER LONDON BOROUGHS

Barking and Dagenham	Lab. 47, RA 3, LD 1
Barnet	C. 28, Lab. 26, LD 6
Bexley	C. 32, Lab. 24, LD 6
Brent	Lab. 43, C. 19, LD 4
Bromley	C. 28, LD 25, Lab. 7
Camden	Lab. 43, C. 10, LD 6
City of Westminster	C. 47, Lab. 13
Croydon	Lab. 37, C. 31, LD 1, vacant 1
Ealing	Lab. 53, C. 15, LD 3
Enfield	Lab. 43, C. 23
Greenwich	Lab. 51, C. 8, LD 2
Hackney	Lab. 28, LD 17, C. 12, Green 2, Ind. 1
Hammersmith and Fulham	Lab. 36, C. 14
Haringey	Lab. 54, LD 3, C. 2
Harrow	Lab. 32, C. 20, Lib. 9, Ind. 2
Havering	Lab. 30, RA 16, C. 14, LD 3
Hillingdon	C. 33, Lab. 32, LD 4
Hounslow	Lab. 44, C. 11, LD 4, RA 1
Islington	Lab. 26, LD 26
Kensington and Chelsea	C. 39, Lab. 15
Kingston upon Thames	C. 21, LD 19, Lab. 10
Lambeth	Lab. 47, LD 12, C. 5
Lewisham	Lab. 61, LD 4, C. 2
Merton	Lab. 39, C. 12, Ind. 3, LD 3
Newham	Lab. 59, vacant 1
Redbridge	Lab. 30, C. 23, LD 9
Richmond upon Thames	LD 34, C. 14, Lab. 4
Southwark	Lab. 33, LD 27, C. 4
Sutton	LD 46, C. 5, Lab. 5
Tower Hamlets	Lab. 41, LD 9
Waltham Forest	Lab. 30, C. 14, LD 12, Ind. 1
Wandsworth	C. 50, Lab. 11

WALES

Anglesey	Ind. 22, PC 6, Lab. 4, NP 4, others 3, vacant 1
Blaenau Gwent	Lab. 34, Ind. 5, C. 1, Lib. 1, PC 1
Bridgend	Lab. 39, Ind. 3, C. 2, LD 2, Ind. Lab. 1, PC 1
Caerphilly	Lab. 56, PC 9, Ind. 3
Cardiff	Lab. 56, LD 9, C. 1, PC 1
Carmarthenshire	Lab. 37, Ind. 29, PC 8, Ind. Lab. 2, LD 2, RA 2, others 1
Ceredigion	Ind. 23, LD 10, PC 8, Lab. 1, others 1, vacant 1
Conwy	Lab. 18, C. 10, Ind. 10, LD 6, PC 5, others 11
Denbighshire	Ind. 19, Lab. 16, PC 7, Ind. Lab. 3, LD 3
Flintshire	Lab. 46, Ind. 13, LD 7, C. 3, Ind. 1, others 2
Gwynedd	PC 48, Ind. 18, Lab. 11, LD 4, others 2
Merthyr Tydfil	Lab. 29, Ind. 3, RA 1
Monmouthshire	Lab. 25, C. 11, Ind. 4, LD 1, vacant 1
Neath Port Talbot	Lab. 50, PC 3, RA 3, Ind. 2, LD 2, SD 1, others 2, vacant 1
Newport	Lab. 46, C. 1
Pembrokeshire	Ind. 39, Lab. 11, LD 4, PC 4, others 1, vacant 1
Powys	Ind. 59, Lab. 9, LD 9, C. 3, PC 1, vacant 2
Rhondda, Cynon, Taff	Lab. 57, PC 13, Ind. 4, RA 1
Swansea	Lab. 54, Ind. 9, LD 7, C. 1, vacant 2

Torfaen   *Lab.* 41, *C.* 1, *Ind.* 1, *LD* 1
Vale of Glamorgan   *Lab.* 35, *C.* 7, *PC* 5
Wrexham   *Lab.* 34, *Ind. C.* 6, *Ind. Lab.* 2,
                           others 9

SCOTLAND

Aberdeen City   *Lab.* 29, *LD* 11, *C.* 9, *SNP* 1
Aberdeenshire   *LD* 16, *SNP* 15, *Ind.* 11, *C.* 5
Angus   *SNP* 21, *C.* 2, *LD* 2, *Ind.* 1
Argyll and Bute   *Ind.* 19, *SNP* 5, *LD* 4, *C.* 3, *Lab.*
                           2
City of Edinburgh   *Lab.* 33, *C.* 14, *LD* 10, *SNP* 1
Clackmannanshire   *Lab.* 8, *SNP* 3, *C.* 1
Dumfries and Galloway   *Ind.* 25, *Lab.* 18, *LD* 10, *SNP* 9,
                           C. 2, *Ind. Lab.* 2, *others* 4
Dundee City   *Lab.* 28, *C.* 4, *SNP* 3, *Ind. Lab.* 1
East Ayrshire   *Lab.* 21, *SNP* 9
East Dunbartonshire   *Lab.* 15, *LD* 9, *C.* 2
East Lothian   *Lab.* 15, *C.* 3
East Renfrewshire   *C.* 9, *Lab.* 8, *LD* 2, *RA* 1
Falkirk   *Lab.* 22, *SNP* 8, *C.* 2, *Ind.* 2,
                           others 2
Fife   *Lab.* 54, *LD* 25, *SNP* 9, *Ind.* 4
Glasgow City   *Lab.* 73, *SNP* 4, *C.* 3, *LD* 1,
                           others 1, *vacant* 1
Highland   *Ind.* 50, *LD* 8, *SNP* 7, *Lab.* 6, *C.*
                           1
Inverclyde   *Lab.* 13, *LD* 6, *C.* 1
Midlothian   *Lab.* 14, *SNP* 1
Moray   *SNP* 11, *Lab.* 3, *Ind.* 2, *others* 2
North Ayrshire   *Lab.* 27, *C.* 1, *Ind.* 1, *SNP* 1
North Lanarkshire   *Lab.* 59, *SNP* 7, *Ind.* 2, *vacant* 1
Orkney Islands   *Ind.* 28
Perth and Kinross   *SNP* 18, *Lab.* 6, *LD* 5, *C.* 2, *Ind.*
                           1
Renfrewshire   *Lab.* 20, *SNP* 13, *LD* 3, *C.* 2,
                           Ind. 2
Scottish Borders   *Ind.* 22, *LD* 15, *SNP* 7, *NP* 6,
                           Lab. 4, *C.* 3, *vacant* 1
Shetland Islands   *NP* 11, *Ind.* 5, *LD* 4, *Lab.* 2, *Ind.*
                           Lab. 1, *others* 3
South Ayrshire   *Lab.* 20, *C.* 5
South Lanarkshire   *Lab.* 60, *SNP* 7, *C.* 2, *LD* 2, *Ind.*
                           1, *vacant* 2
Stirling   *Lab.* 12, *C.* 8, *SNP* 2
West Dunbartonshire   *Lab.* 13, *SNP* 9
Western Isles   *NP* 25, *Lab.* 5
West Lothian   *Lab.* 15, *SNP* 11, *C.* 1

England

The Kingdom of England lies between 55° 46' and 49° 57' 30" N. latitude (from a few miles north of the mouth of the Tweed to the Lizard), and between 1° 46' E. and 5° 43' W. (from Lowestoft to Land's End). England is bounded on the north by the Cheviot Hills; on the south by the English Channel; on the east by the Straits of Dover (Pas de Calais) and the North Sea; and on the west by the Atlantic Ocean, Wales and the Irish Sea. It has a total area of 50,351 sq. miles (130,410 sq. km): land 50,058 sq. miles (129,652 sq. km); inland water 293 sq. miles (758 sq. km).

POPULATION

The population at the 1991 census was 46,382,050 (males 22,469,707; females 23,912,343). The average density of the population in 1991 was 3.6 persons per hectare.

FLAG

The flag of England is the cross of St George, a red cross on a white field (cross gules in a field argent). The cross of St George, the patron saint of England, has been used since the 13th century.

RELIEF

There is a marked division between the upland and low-land areas of England. In the extreme north the Cheviot Hills (highest point, The Cheviot, 2,674 ft) form a natural boundary with Scotland. Running south from the Cheviots, though divided from them by the Tyne Gap, is the Pennine range (highest point, Cross Fell, 2,930 ft), the main orological feature of the country. The Pennines culminate in the Peak District of Derbyshire (Kinder Scout, 2,088 ft). West of the Pennines are the Cumbrian mountains, which include Scafell Pike (3,210 ft), the highest peak in England, and to the east are the Yorkshire Moors, their highest point being Urra Moor (1,490 ft).

In the west, the foothills of the Welsh mountains extend into the bordering English counties of Shropshire (the Wrekin, 1,334 ft; Long Mynd, 1,694 ft) and Hereford and Worcester (the Malvern Hills – Worcestershire Beacon, 1,394 ft). Extensive areas of high land and moorland are also to be found in the south-western peninsula formed by Somerset, Devon and Cornwall: principally Exmoor (Dunkery Beacon, 1,704 ft), Dartmoor (High Willhays, 2,038 ft) and Bodmin Moor (Brown Willy, 1,377 ft). Ranges of low, undulating hills run across the south of the country, including the Cotswolds in the Midlands and south-west, the Chilterns to the north of London, and the North (Kent) and South (Sussex) Downs of the south-east coastal areas.

The lowlands of England lie in the Vale of York, East Anglia and the area around the Wash. The lowest-lying are the Cambridgeshire Fens in the valleys of the Great Ouse and the River Nene, which are below sea-level in places. Since the 17th century extensive drainage has brought much of the Fens under cultivation. The North Sea coast between the Thames and the Humber, low-lying and formed of sand and shingle for the most part, is subject to erosion and defences against further incursion have been built along many stretches.

HYDROGRAPHY

The Severn is the longest river in Great Britain, rising in the north-eastern slopes of Plynlimon (Wales) and entering England in Shropshire with a total length of 220 miles (354 km) from its source to its outflow into the Bristol Channel, where it receives on the east the Bristol Avon, and on the west the Wye, its other tributaries being the Vyrnwy, Tern, Stour, Teme and Upper (or Warwickshire) Avon. The Severn is tidal below Gloucester, and a high bore or tidal wave sometimes reverses the flow as high as Tewkesbury (13½ miles above Gloucester). The scenery of the greater part of the river is very picturesque and beautiful, and the Severn is a noted salmon river, some of its tributaries being famous for trout. Navigation is assisted by the Gloucester and Berkeley Ship Canal (16¼ miles), which admits vessels of 350 tons to Gloucester. The Severn Tunnel was begun in 1873 and completed in 1886 at a cost of £2 million and after many difficulties from flooding. It is 4 miles 628 yards in length (of which 2¼ miles are under the river). The Severn road bridge between Haysgate, Gwent, and Almondsbury, Glos, with a centre span of 3,240 ft, was opened in 1966.

The longest river wholly in England is the Thames, with a total length of 215 miles (346 km) from its source in the Cotswold hills to the Nore, and is navigable by ocean-going ships to London Bridge. The Thames is tidal to Teddington (69 miles from its mouth) and forms county boundaries almost throughout its course; on its banks are situated London, Windsor Castle, the oldest royal residence still in regular use, Eton College and Oxford, the oldest university in the kingdom.

Of the remaining English rivers, those flowing into the North Sea are the Tyne, Wear, Tees, Ouse and Trent from the Pennine Range, the Great Ouse (160 miles), which rises in Northamptonshire, and the Orwell and Stour from the hills of East Anglia. Flowing into the English Channel are the Sussex Ouse from the Weald, the Itchen from the Hampshire Hills, and the Axe, Teign, Dart, Tamar and Exe from the Devonian hills. Flowing into the Irish Sea are the Mersey, Ribble and Eden from the western slopes of the Pennines and the Derwent from the Cumbrian mountains.

The English Lakes, noteworthy for their picturesque scenery and poetic associations, lie in Cumbria, the largest being Windermere (10 miles long), Ullswater and Derwent Water.

ISLANDS

The Isle of Wight is separated from Hampshire by the Solent. The capital, Newport, stands at the head of the estuary of the Medina, Cowes (at the mouth) being the chief port. Other centres are Ryde, Sandown, Shanklin, Ventnor, Freshwater, Yarmouth, Totland Bay, Seaview and Bembridge.

Lundy (the name means Puffin Island), 11 miles north-west of Hartland Point, Devon, is about two miles long and about half a mile wide on average, with a total area of about 1,116 acres, and a population of about 20. It became the property of the National Trust in 1969 and is now principally a bird sanctuary.

The Isles of Scilly consist of about 140 islands and skerries (total area, 6 sq. miles/10 sq. km) situated 28 miles south-west of Land's End. Only five are inhabited: St Mary's, St Agnes, Bryher, Tresco and St Martin's. The population is 1,978. The entire group has been designated a Conservation Area, a Heritage Coast, and an Area of Outstanding Natural Beauty, and has been given National Nature Reserve status by the Nature Conservancy Council because of its unique flora and fauna. Tourism and the winter/spring flower trade for the home market form the basis of the economy of the Isles. The island group is a recognized rural development area.

EARLY HISTORY

Archaeological evidence suggests that England has been inhabited since at least the Palaeolithic period, though the extent of the various Palaeolithic cultures was dependent upon the degree of glaciation. The succeeding Neolithic and Bronze Age cultures have left abundant remains throughout the country, the best-known of these being the henges and stone circles of Stonehenge (ten miles north of Salisbury, Wilts) and Avebury (Wilts), both of which are believed to have been of religious significance. In the latter part of the Bronze Age the Goidels, a people of Celtic race, and in the Iron Age other Celtic races of Brythons and Belgae, invaded the country and brought with them Celtic civilization and dialects, place names in England bearing witness to the spread of the invasion over the whole kingdom.

THE ROMAN CONQUEST

The Roman conquest of Gaul (57–50 BC) brought Britain into close contact with Roman civilization, but although Julius Caesar raided the south of Britain in 55 BC and 54 BC, conquest was not undertaken until nearly 100 years later. In AD 43 the Emperor Claudius dispatched Aulus Plautius, with a well-equipped force of 40,000, and himself followed with reinforcements in the same year. Success was delayed by the resistance of Caratacus (Caractacus), the British leader from AD 48–51, who was finally captured and sent to Rome, and by a great revolt in AD 61 led by Boudicca (Boadicea), Queen of the Iceni; but the south of Britain was secured by AD 70, and Wales and the area north to the Tyne by about AD 80.

In AD 122, the Emperor Hadrian visited Britain and built a continuous rampart, since known as Hadrian's Wall, from Wallsend to Bowness (Tyne to Solway). The work was entrusted by the Emperor Hadrian to Aulus Platorius Nepos, legate of Britain from AD 122 to 126, and it was intended to form the northern frontier of the Roman Empire.

The Romans administered Britain as a province under a Governor, with a well-defined system of local government, each Roman municipality ruling itself and its surrounding territory, while London was the centre of the road system and the seat of the financial officials of the Province of Britain. Colchester, Lincoln, York, Gloucester and St Albans stand on the sites of five Roman municipalities, and Wroxeter, Caerleon, Chester, Lincoln and York were at various times the sites of legionary fortresses. Well-preserved Roman towns have been uncovered at or near Silchester (*Calleva Atrebatum*), ten miles south of Reading, Wroxeter (*Viroconium Cornoviorum*), near Shrewsbury, and St Albans (*Verulamium*) in Hertfordshire.

Four main groups of roads radiated from London, and a fifth (the Fosse) ran obliquely from Lincoln through Leicester, Cirencester and Bath to Exeter. Of the four groups radiating from London, one ran south-east to Canterbury and the coast of Kent, a second to Silchester and thence to parts of western Britain and south Wales, a third (later known as Watling Street) ran through Verulamium to Chester, with various branches, and the fourth reached Colchester, Lincoln, York and the eastern counties.

In the fourth century Britain was subject to raids along the east coast by Saxon pirates, which led to the establishment of a system of coast defence from the Wash to Southampton Water, with forts at Brancaster, Burgh Castle (Yarmouth), Walton (Felixstowe), Bradwell, Reculver, Richborough, Dover, Lympne, Pevensey and Porchester (Portsmouth). The Irish (Scoti) and Picts in the north were also becoming more aggressive; from about AD 350 incur-

sions became more frequent and more formidable. As the Roman Empire came under attack increasingly towards the end of the fourth century, many troops were removed from Britain for service in other parts of the empire. The island was eventually cut off from Rome by the Teutonic conquest of Gaul, and with the withdrawal of the last Roman garrison early in the fifth century, the Romano-British were left to themselves.

SAXON SETTLEMENT

According to legend, the British King Vortigern called in the Saxons to defend him against the Picts, the Saxon chieftains being Hengist and Horsa, who landed at Ebbsfleet, Kent, and established themselves in the Isle of Thanet; but the events during the one and a half centuries between the final break with Rome and the re-establishment of Christianity are unclear. However, it would appear that in the course of this period the raids turned into large-scale settlement by invaders traditionally known as Angles (England north of the Wash and East Anglia), Saxons (Essex and southern England) and Jutes (Kent and the Weald), which pushed the Romano-British into the mountainous areas of the north and west, Celtic culture outside Wales and Cornwall surviving only in topographical names. Various kingdoms were established at this time which attempted to claim overlordship of the whole country, hegemony finally being achieved by Wessex (capital, Winchester) in the ninth century. This century also saw the beginning of raids by the Vikings (Danes), which were resisted by Alfred the Great (871–899), who fixed a limit to the advance of Danish settlement by the Treaty of Wedmore (878), giving them the area north and east of Watling Street, on condition that they adopt Christianity.

In the tenth century the kings of Wessex recovered the whole of England from the Danes, but subsequent rulers were unable to resist a second wave of invaders. England paid tribute (*Danegeld*) for many years, and was invaded in 1013 by the Danes and ruled by Danish kings from 1016 until 1042, when Edward the Confessor was recalled from exile in Normandy. On Edward's death in 1066 Harold Godwinson (brother-in-law of Edward and son of Earl Godwin of Wessex) was chosen King of England. After defeating (at Stamford Bridge, Yorkshire, 25 September) an invading army under Harald Hadraada, King of Norway (aided by the outlawed Earl Tostig of Northumbria, Harold's brother), Harold was himself defeated at the Battle of Hastings on 14 October 1066, and the Norman conquest secured the throne of England for Duke William of Normandy, a cousin of Edward the Confessor.

CHRISTIANITY

Christianity reached the Roman province of Britain from Gaul in the third century (or possibly earlier); Alban, traditionally Britain's first martyr, was put to death as a Christian during the persecution of Diocletian (22 June 303), at his native town Verulamium; and the Bishops of Londinium, Eboracum (York), and Lindum (Lincoln) attended the Council of Arles in 314. However, the Anglo-Saxon invasions submerged the Christian religion in England until the sixth century when conversion was undertaken in the north from 563 by Celtic missionaries from Ireland led by St Columba, and in the south by a mission sent from Rome in 597 which was led by St Augustine, who became the first archbishop of Canterbury. England appears to have been converted again by the end of the seventh century and followed, after the Council of Whitby in 663, the practices of the Roman Church, which brought the kingdom into the mainstream of European thought and culture.

PRINCIPAL CITIES

BIRMINGHAM

Birmingham is Britain's second city. It is a focal point in national communications networks with a rapidly expanding international airport. The generally accepted derivation of 'Birmingham' is the *ham* (dwelling-place) of the *ing* (family) of *Beorma*, presumed to have been Saxon. During the Industrial Revolution the town grew into a major manufacturing centre and in 1889 was granted city status.

Despite the decline in manufacturing, Birmingham is still a major hardware trade and motor component industry centre. As well as the National Exhibition Centre and the Aston Science Park, recent developments include the International Convention Centre, the National Indoor Arena and Brindleyplace.

The principal buildings are the Town Hall (1834–50); the Council House (1879); Victoria Law Courts (1891); Birmingham University (1906–9); the 13th-century Church of St Martin-in-the-Bull-Ring (rebuilt 1873); the Cathedral (formerly St Philip's Church) (1711) and the Roman Catholic Cathedral of St Chad (1839–41).

BRADFORD

Bradford lies on the southern edge of the Yorkshire Dales National Park, including within its boundaries the village of Haworth, home of the Brontë sisters, and Ilkley Moor.

Originally a Saxon township, Bradford received a market charter in 1251 but developed only slowly until the industrialization of the textile industry brought rapid growth during the 19th century; it was granted its city charter in 1897. The prosperity of that period is reflected in much of the city's architecture, particularly the public buildings: City Hall (1873), Wool Exchange (1867), St George's Hall (Concert Hall, 1853), Cartwright Hall (Art Gallery, 1904) and the Technical College (1882). Other chief buildings are the Cathedral (15th century) and Bolling Hall (14th century).

Textiles still play an important part in the city's economy but industry is now more broadly based, including engineering, micro-electronics, printing and chemicals. The city has a strong financial services sector, and a growing tourism industry.

BRISTOL

Bristol was a Royal Borough before the Norman Conquest. The earliest form of the name is *Bricgstow*. In 1373 Edward III granted Bristol county status.

The chief buildings include the 12th-century Cathedral (with later additions), with Norman chapter house and gateway, the 14th-century Church of St Mary Redcliffe, Wesley's Chapel, Broadmead, the Merchant Venturers' Almshouses, the Council House (1956), Guildhall, Exchange (erected from the designs of John Wood in 1743), Cabot Tower, the University and Clifton College. The Roman Catholic Cathedral at Clifton was opened in 1973.

The Clifton Suspension Bridge, with a span of 702 feet over the Avon, was projected by Brunel in 1836 but was not completed until 1864. Brunel's SS *Great Britain*, the first ocean-going propeller-driven ship, is now being restored in the City Docks from where she was launched in 1843. The docks themselves have been extensively restored and redeveloped and are becoming a focus for the arts and recreation.

CAMBRIDGE

Cambridge, a settlement far older than its ancient University, lies on the River Cam or Granta. The city is a county town and regional headquarters. Its industries include electronics, high technology research and development, and biotechnology. Among its open spaces are Jesus Green, Sheep's Green, Coe Fen, Parker's Piece, Christ's Pieces, the University Botanic Garden, and the Backs, or lawns and gardens through which the Cam winds behind the principal line of college buildings. East of the Cam, King's Parade, upon which stand Great St Mary's Church, Gibbs' Senate House and King's College Chapel with Wilkins' screen, joins Trumpington Street to form one of the most beautiful throughfares in Europe.

University and college buildings provide the outstanding features of Cambridge architecture but several churches (especially St Benet's, the oldest building in the city, and St Sepulchre's, the Round Church) are also notable. The Guildhall (1939) stands on a site of which at least part has held municipal buildings since 1224.

CANTERBURY

Canterbury, the Metropolitan City of the Anglican Communion, dates back to prehistoric times. It was the Roman *Durovernum Cantiacorum* and the Saxon *Cant-wara-byrig* (stronghold of the men of Kent). Here in 597 St Augustine began the conversion of the English to Christianity, when Ethelbert, King of Kent, was baptized.

Of the Benedictine St Augustine's Abbey, burial place of the Jutish Kings of Kent (whose capital Canterbury was), only ruins remain. St Martin's Church, on the eastern outskirts of the city, is stated by Bede to have been the place of worship of Queen Bertha, the Christian wife of King Ethelbert, before the advent of St Augustine.

In 1170 the rivalry of Church and State culminated in the murder in Canterbury Cathedral, by Henry II's knights, of Archbishop Thomas Becket. His shrine became a great centre of pilgrimage, as described in Chaucer's *Canterbury Tales*. After the Reformation pilgrimages ceased, but the prosperity of the city was strengthened by an influx of Huguenot refugees, who introduced weaving. The poet and playwright Christopher Marlowe was born and reared in Canterbury, and there are also literary associations with Defoe, Dickens, Joseph Conrad and Somerset Maugham.

The Cathedral, with architecture ranging from the 11th to the 15th centuries, is world famous. Modern pilgrims are attracted particularly to the Martyrdom, the Black Prince's Tomb, the Warriors' Chapel and the many examples of medieval stained glass.

The medieval city walls are built on Roman foundations and the 14th-century West Gate is one of the finest buildings of its kind in the country.

The 1,000-seat Marlowe Theatre is a centre for the Canterbury Arts Festival each autumn.

CARLISLE

Carlisle is situated at the confluence of the River Eden and River Caldew, 309 miles north-west of London and about ten miles from the Scottish border. It was granted a charter in 1158.

The city stands at the western end of Hadrian's Wall and dates from the original Roman settlement of *Luguvalium*. Granted to Scotland in the tenth century, Carlisle is not included in the Domesday Book. William Rufus reclaimed the area in 1092 and the castle and city walls were built to guard Carlisle and the western border; the citadel is a Tudor addition to protect the south of the city. Border disputes were common until the problem of the Debate-able Lands was settled in 1552. During the Civil War the city remained Royalist; in 1745 Carlisle was besieged for the last time by the Young Pretender.

The Cathedral, originally a 12th-century Augustinian priory, was enlarged in the 13th and 14th centuries after the diocese was created in 1133. To the south is a restored Tithe Barn and nearby the 18th-century church of St Cuthbert, the third to stand on a site dating from the seventh century.

Carlisle is the major shopping, commercial and agricultural centre for the area, and industries include the manufacture of metal goods, biscuits and textiles. However, the largest employer is the services sector, notably in central and local government, retailing and transport. The city has an important communications position at the centre of a network of major roads, as a stage on the main west coast rail services, and with its own airport at Crosby-on-Eden.

CHESTER

Chester is situated on the River Dee, and was granted borough and city status in 1974. Its recorded history dates from the first century when the Romans founded the fortress of *Deva*. The city's name is derived from the Latin *castra* (a camp or encampment). During the Middle Ages, Chester was the principal port of north-west England but declined with the silting of the Dee estuary and competition from Liverpool. The city was also an important military centre, notably during Edward I's Welsh campaigns and the Elizabethan Irish campaigns. During the Civil War, Chester supported the King and was besieged from 1643 to 1646. Chester's first charter was granted *c.* 1175 and the city was incorporated in 1506. The office of Sheriff is the earliest created in the country (*c.* 1120s), and in 1992 the Mayor was granted the title of Lord Mayor. He/she also enjoys the title 'Admiral of the Dee'.

The city's architectural features include the city walls (an almost complete two-mile circuit), the unique 13th-century Rows (covered galleries above the street-level shops), the Victorian Gothic Town Hall (1869), the Castle (rebuilt 1788 and 1822) and numerous half-timbered buildings. The Cathedral was a Benedictine abbey until the Dissolution. Remaining monastic buildings include the chapter house, refectory and cloisters and there is a modern free-standing bell tower. The Norman church of St John the Baptist was a cathedral church in the early Middle Ages.

Chester is a thriving retail, business and tourist centre.

COVENTRY

Coventry is an important industrial centre, producing vehicles, machine tools, agricultural machinery, man-made fibres, aerospace components and telecommunications equipment. New investment has come from financial services, power transmission, professional services and education.

The city owes its beginning to Leofric, Earl of Mercia, and his wife Godiva who, in 1043, founded a Benedictine monastery. The guildhall of St Mary dates from the 14th century, three of the city's churches date from the 14th and 15th centuries, and 16th-century almshouses may still be seen. Coventry's first cathedral was destroyed at the Reformation, its second in the 1940 blitz (the walls and spire remain) and the new cathedral designed by Sir Basil Spence, consecrated in 1962, now draws innumerable visitors.

Coventry is the home of the University of Warwick and its Science Park, Coventry University, the Westwood Business Park, the Cable and Wireless College, and the Museum of British Road Transport.

DERBY

Derby stands on the banks of the River Derwent, and its name dates back to 880 when the Danes settled in the locality and changed the original Saxon name of *Northworthy* to *Deoraby*.

Derby has a wide range of industries including aero engines, cars, pipework, specialized mechanical engineering equipment, textiles, chemicals, plastics and the Royal Crown Derby porcelain. The city is an established railway centre with rail research, engineering, safety testing, infrastructure and train-operating companies.

Buildings of interest include St Peter's Church and the Old Abbey Building (14th century), the Cathedral (1525), St Mary's Roman Catholic Church (1839) and the Industrial Museum, formerly the Old Silk Mill (1721). The traditional city centre is complemented by the Eagle Centre and 'out-of-centre' retail developments. In addition to the Derby Playhouse, the Assembly Rooms are a multi-purpose venue.

The first charter granting a Mayor and Aldermen was that of Charles I in 1637. Previous charters date back to 1154. It was granted city status in 1977.

DURHAM

The city of Durham is a district in the county of Durham and a major tourist attraction because of its prominent Norman Cathedral and Castle set high on a wooded peninsula overlooking the River Wear. The Cathedral was founded as a shrine for the body of St Cuthbert in 995. The present building dates from 1093 and among its many treasures is the tomb of the Venerable Bede (673–735). Durham's Prince Bishops had unique powers up to 1836, being lay rulers as well as religious leaders. As a palatinate Durham could have its own army, nobility, coinage and courts. The Castle was the main seat of the Prince Bishops for nearly 800 years; it is now used as a college by the University. The University, founded on the initiative of Bishop William Van Mildert, is England's third oldest.

Among other buildings of interest is the Guildhall in the Market Place which dates originally from the 14th century. Work has been carried out to conserve this area as part of the city's contribution to the Council of Europe's Urban Renaissance Campaign. Annual events include Durham's Regatta in June (claimed to be the oldest rowing event in Britain) and the Annual Gala (formerly Durham Miners' Gala) in July.

The economy has undergone a significant change with the replacement of mining as the dominant industry by 'white collar' employment. Although still a predominantly rural area, the industrial and commercial sector is growing and a wide range of manufacturing and service industries are based on industrial estates in and around the city. A research and development centre, linked to the University, also plays an important role in the local economy.

EXETER

Exeter lies on the River Exe ten miles from the sea. It was granted a charter by Henry II. The Romans founded *Isca Dumnoniorum* in the first century AD, and in the third century a stone wall (much of which remains) was built, providing protection against Saxon, and then Danish invasions. After the Conquest, the city led resistance to William in the west until reduced by siege. The Normans built the ringwork castle of Rougemont, the gatehouse and one tower of which remain, although the rest was pulled down in 1784. The first bridge across the Exe was built in the early 13th century. The city's main port was situated downstream at Topsham until the construction in the 1560s of the first true canal in England, the redevelopment of which in 1700 brought seaborne trade direct to the city. Exeter was the Royalist headquarters in the west during the Civil War.

The diocese of Exeter was established by Edward the Confessor in 1050, although a minster existed near the Cathedral site from the late seventh century. A new cathedral was built in the 12th century but the present building was begun c. 1275, although incorporating the Norman towers, and completed about a century later. The Guildhall dates from the 12th century and there are many other medieval buildings in the city, as well as architecture in the Georgian and Regency styles, and the Custom House (1680). Damage suffered by bombing in 1942 led to the redevelopment of the city centre.

Exeter's prosperity from medieval times was based on trade in wool and woollen cloth (commemorated by Tuckers' Hall), which remained at its height until the late 18th century when export trade was hit by the French wars. Subsequently Exeter has developed as an administrative and commercial centre, notably in the distributive trades, light manufacturing industries and tourism.

KINGSTON UPON HULL

Hull (officially Kingston upon Hull) lies at the junction of the River Hull with the Humber, 22 miles from the North Sea. It is one of the major seaports of the United Kingdom, comprising 2,000 acres in four main dock installations. The port provides a wide range of cargo services, including ro-ro and container traffic, and handles a million passengers annually on daily sailings to Rotterdam and Zeebrugge. There is a variety of industry and service industries, as well as increasing tourism and conference business.

The city, restored after heavy air raid damage during the Second World War, has good office and administrative buildings, its municipal centre being the Guildhall, its educational centres the University of Hull and the University of Lincolnshire and Humberside and its religious centre the Parish Church of the Holy Trinity. The old town area has been renovated and includes a marina and shopping complex. Just west of the city is the Humber Bridge, the world's longest single-span suspension bridge. Kingston upon Hull was so named by Edward I. City status was accorded in 1897 and the office of Mayor raised to the dignity of Lord Mayor in 1914.

LEEDS

Leeds, situated in the lower Aire Valley, is a junction for road, rail, canal and air services and an important manufacturing and commercial centre. Seventy-three per cent of employment is in services, notably the distributive trades, public administration, medical services and business services. The main manufacturing industries are mechanical engineering, printing and publishing, metal goods and furniture.

The principal buildings are the Civic Hall (1933), the Town Hall (1858), the Municipal Buildings and Art Gallery (1884) with the Henry Moore Gallery (1982), the Corn Exchange (1863) and the University. The Parish Church (St Peter's) was rebuilt in 1841; the 17th-century St John's Church has a fine interior with a famous English Renaissance screen; the last remaining 18th-century church in the city is Holy Trinity in Boar Lane (1727). Kirkstall Abbey (about three miles from the centre of the city), founded by Henry de Lacy in 1152, is one of the most complete examples of Cistercian houses now remaining. Temple Newsam, birthplace of Lord Darnley, was acquired by the Council in 1922. The present house was largely rebuilt by Sir Arthur Ingram in about 1620. Adel Church, about five miles from the centre of the city, is a fine Norman structure. The new Royal Armouries Museum houses the collection of antique arms and armour formerly held at the Tower of London.

Leeds was first incorporated by Charles I in 1626. The earliest forms of the name are *Loidis* or *Ledes*, the origins of which are obscure.

LEICESTER

Leicester is situated geographically in the centre of England. It dates back to pre-Roman times and was one of the five Danish *Burghs*. In 1589 Queen Elizabeth I granted a charter to the city and the ancient title was confirmed by letters patent in 1919.

The principal industries are hosiery, knitwear, footwear manufacturing and engineering. The growth of Leicester as a hosiery centre increased rapidly from the introduction there of the first stocking frame in 1670 and today it has some of the largest hosiery factories in the world.

The principal buildings are the Town Hall, the New Walk Centre, the University of Leicester, De Montfort University, De Montfort Hall, one of the finest concert halls in the provinces seating over 2,750 people, and the Granby Halls, an indoor sports facility. The ancient churches of St Martin (now Leicester Cathedral), St Nicholas, St Margaret, All Saints, St Mary de Castro, and buildings such as the Guildhall, the 14th-century Newarke Gate, the Castle and the Jewry Wall Roman site still exist. The Haymarket Theatre was opened in 1973 and The Shires shopping centre in 1992.

LINCOLN

Situated 40 miles inland on the River Witham, Lincoln derives its name from a contraction of *Lindum Colonia*, the settlement founded in AD 48 by the Romans to command the crossing of Ermine Street and Fosse Way. Sections of the third-century Roman city wall can be seen, including an extant gateway (Newport Arch), and excavations have discovered traces of a sewerage system unique in Britain. The Romans also drained the surrounding fenland and created a canal system, laying the foundations of Lincoln's agricultural prosperity and also of the city's importance in the medieval wool trade as a port and Staple town.

As one of the Five Boroughs of the Danelaw, Lincoln was an important trading centre in the ninth and tenth centuries and medieval prosperity from the wool trade lasted until the 14th century, enabling local merchants to build parish churches (of which three survive), and attracting in the 12th century a Jewish community (Jew's House and Court, Aaron's House). However, the removal of the Staple to Boston in 1369 heralded a decline from which the city only recovered fully in the 19th century when improved fen drainage made Lincoln agriculturally important and improved canal and rail links led to industrial development, mainly in the manufacture of machinery, components and engineering products.

The castle was built shortly after the Conquest and is unusual in having two mounds; on one motte stands a Keep (Lucy's Tower) added in the 12th century. It currently houses one of the four surviving copies of the Magna Carta. The Cathedral was begun c. 1073 when the first Norman bishop moved the see of Lindsey to Lincoln, but was mostly destroyed by fire and earthquake in the 12th century. Rebuilding was begun by St Hugh and completed over a century later. Other notable architectural features are the 12th-century High Bridge, the oldest in Britain still to carry buildings, and the Guildhall situated above the 15th–16th-century Stonebow gateway.

LIVERPOOL

Liverpool, on the right bank of the River Mersey, three miles from the Irish Sea, is the United Kingdom's foremost port for the Atlantic trade. Tunnels link Liverpool with Birkenhead and Wallasey.

There are 2,100 acres of dockland on both sides of the river and the Gladstone and Royal Seaforth Docks can accommodate Panamax–sized vessels. Approximately 31 million tonnes of cargo is handled annually. The main cargoes are crude oil, grain, fossil fuels, edible oils, timber, scrap metal, containers and break-bulk cargo. Liverpool Free Port, Britain's largest, was opened in 1984.

Liverpool was created a free borough in 1207 and a city in 1880. From the early 18th century it expanded rapidly with the growth of industrialization and the Atlantic trade. Surviving buildings from this period include the Bluecoat Chambers (1717, formerly the Bluecoat School), the Town Hall (1754, rebuilt to the original design 1795), and buildings in Rodney Street, Canning Street and the suburbs. Notable from the 19th and 20th centuries are the Anglican Cathedral, built from the designs of Sir Giles Gilbert Scott (the foundation stone was laid in 1904, and the building was completed only in 1980), the Catholic Metropolitan Cathedral (designed by Sir Frederick Gibberd, consecrated 1967) and St George's Hall (1838–54), regarded as one of the finest modern examples of classical architecture. The refurbished Albert Dock (designed by Jesse Hartley) contains the Merseyside Maritime Museum and Tate Gallery, Liverpool.

In 1852 an Act was obtained for establishing a public library, museum and art gallery; as a result Liverpool had one of the first public libraries in the country. The Brown, Picton and Hornby libraries now form one of the country's major libraries. The Victoria Building of Liverpool University, the Royal Liver, Cunard and Mersey Docks Harbour Company buildings at the Pier Head, the Municipal Buildings and the Philharmonic Hall are other examples of the city's fine buildings.

MANCHESTER

Manchester (the *Mamucium* of the Romans, who occupied it in AD 79) is a commercial and industrial centre with a population engaged in the engineering, chemical, clothing, food processing and textile industries and in education. Banking, insurance and a growing leisure industry are among the prime commercial activities. The city is connected with the sea by the Manchester Ship Canal, opened in 1894, 35½ miles long, and accommodating ships up to 15,000 tons. Manchester Airport handles 15 million passengers yearly.

The principal buildings are the Town Hall, erected in 1877 from the designs of Alfred Waterhouse, with a large extension of 1938; the Royal Exchange (1869, enlarged 1921); the Central Library (1934); Heaton Hall; the 17th-century Chetham Library; the Rylands Library (1900), which includes the Althorp collection; the University precinct; the 15th-century Cathedral (formerly the parish church); G-MEX exhibition centre and the Free Trade Hall. Recent developments include the Manchester Arena, the largest indoor arena in Europe, and the Bridgewater Hall. Manchester is the home of the Hallé Orchestra, the Royal Northern College of Music, the Royal Exchange Theatre and seven public art galleries. Metrolink, the new light rail system, opened in 1992.

The Commonwealth Games are to be held in Manchester in 2002 and new sports facilities include a stadium, a swimming pool complex and the National Cycling Centre.

The town received its first charter of incorporation in 1838 and was created a city in 1853.

NEWCASTLE UPON TYNE

Newcastle upon Tyne, on the north bank of the River Tyne, is eight miles from the North Sea. A cathedral and university city, it is the administrative, commercial and cultural centre for north-east England and the principal port. It is an important manufacturing centre with a wide variety of industries.

The principal buildings include the Castle Keep (12th century), Black Gate (13th century), Blackfriars (13th century), West Walls (13th century), St Nicholas's Cathedral (15th century, fine lantern tower), St Andrew's Church (12th–14th century), St John's (14th–15th century), All Saints (1786 by Stephenson), St Mary's Roman Catholic Cathedral (1844), Trinity House (17th century), Sandhill (16th-century houses), Guildhall (Georgian), Grey Street (1834–9), Central Station (1846–50), Laing Art Gallery (1904), University of Newcastle Physics Building (1962) and Medical Building (1985), Civic Centre (1963), Central Library (1969) and Eldon Square Shopping Development (1976). Open spaces include the Town Moor (927 acres) and Jesmond Dene. Nine bridges span the Tyne at Newcastle.

The city's name is derived from the 'new castle' (1080) erected as a defence against the Scots. In 1400 it was made a county, and in 1882 a city.

NORWICH

Norwich grew from an early Anglo-Saxon settlement near the confluence of the Rivers Yare and Wensum, and now serves as provincial capital for the predominantly agricultural region of East Anglia. The name is thought to relate to the most northerly of a group of Anglo-Saxon villages or *wics*. The city's first known charter was granted in 1158 by Henry II.

Norwich serves its surrounding area as a market town and commercial centre, banking and insurance being prominent among the city's businesses. From the 14th century until the Industrial Revolution, Norwich was the regional centre of the woollen industry, but now the biggest single industry is financial services and principal trades are engineering, printing, shoemaking, double glazing, the production of chemicals and clothing, food processing and technology. Norwich is accessible to seagoing vessels by means of the River Yare, entered at Great Yarmouth, 20 miles to the east.

Among many historic buildings are the Cathedral (completed in the 12th century and surmounted by a 15th-century spire 315 feet in height), the keep of the Norman castle (now a museum and art gallery), the 15th-century flint-walled Guildhall (now a tourist information centre), some thirty medieval parish churches, St Andrew's and Blackfriars' Halls, the Tudor houses preserved in Elm Hill and the Georgian Assembly House. The University of East Anglia is on the city's western boundary.

NOTTINGHAM

Nottingham stands on the River Trent and is connected by canal with the Atlantic Ocean and the North Sea. *Snotingaham* or *Notingeham*, literally the homestead of the people of Snot, is the Anglo-Saxon name for the Celtic settlement of *Tigguocobauc*, or the house of caves. In 878, Nottingham became one of the Five Boroughs of the Danelaw. William the Conqueror ordered the construction of Nottingham Castle, while the town itself developed rapidly under Norman rule. Its laws and rights were later formally recognized by Henry II's charter in 1155. The Castle became a favoured residence of King John. In 1642 King Charles I raised his personal standard at Nottingham Castle at the start of the Civil War.

Nottingham is a major sporting centre, home to Nottingham Forest FC, Notts County FC (the world's oldest football league side), Nottingham Racecourse and the National Watersports Centre. The principal industries include textiles, pharmaceuticals, food manufacturing, engineering and telecommunications. There are two universities within the city boundaries.

Architecturally, Nottingham has a wealth of notable buildings, particularly those designed in the Victorian era by T. C. Hine and Watson Fothergill. The City Council owns the Castle, of Norman origin but restored in 1878, Wollaton Hall (1580–8), Newstead Abbey (home of Lord Byron), the Guildhall (1888) and Council House (1929). St Mary's, St Peter's and St Nicholas's Churches are of interest, as is the Roman Catholic Cathedral (Pugin, 1842–4).

Nottingham was granted city status in 1897.

OXFORD

Oxford is a university city, an important industrial centre, and a market town. Industry played a minor part in Oxford until the motor industry was established in 1912.

It is for its architecture that Oxford is of most interest to the visitor, its oldest specimens being the reputedly Saxon tower of St Michael's church, the remains of the Norman castle and city walls, and the Norman church at Iffley. It is chiefly famous, however, for its Gothic buildings, such as the Divinity Schools, the Old Library at Merton College, William of Wykeham's New College, Magdalen College and Christ Church and many other college buildings. Later centuries are represented by the Laudian quadrangle at St John's College, the Renaissance Sheldonian Theatre by Wren, Trinity College Chapel, and All Saints Church; Hawksmoor's mock-Gothic at All Souls College, and the 18th-century Queen's College. In addition to individual buildings, High Street and Radcliffe Square, just off it, both form architectural compositions of great beauty. Most of the Colleges have gardens, those of Magdalen, New College, St John's and Worcester being the largest.

PLYMOUTH

Plymouth is situated on the borders of Devon and Cornwall at the confluence of the Rivers Tamar and Plym. The city has a long maritime history; it was the home port of Sir Francis Drake and the starting point for his circumnavigation of the world, as well as the last port of call for the *Mayflower* when the Pilgrim Fathers sailed for the New World in 1620. Today Plymouth is host to many international yacht races. The Barbican harbour area has many Elizabethan buildings and on Plymouth Hoe stands Smeaton's lighthouse, the third to be built on the Eddystone Rocks 13 miles offshore.

The city centre was rebuilt following extensive war damage, and comprises a large shopping centre, municipal offices, law courts and public buildings. The main employment is provided at the naval base, though many industrial firms and service industries have become established in the post-war period and the city is a growing tourism centre. In 1982 the Theatre Royal was opened. In conjunction with the Cornwall County Council, the Tamar Bridge was constructed linking the city by road with Cornwall.

PORTSMOUTH

Portsmouth occupies Portsea Island, Hampshire, with boundaries extending to the mainland. It is a centre of industry and commerce, including many high technology and manufacturing industries. It is the British headquarters of several major international companies. The Royal Navy base still has a substantial work-force, although this has decreased in recent years. The commercial port and continental ferry port is owned and run by the City Council, and carries passengers and vehicles to France and northern Spain.

A major port since the 16th century, Portsmouth is also a thriving seaside resort catering for thousands of visitors annually. Among many historic attractions are Lord Nelson's flagship, HMS *Victory*, the Tudor warship *Mary Rose*, Britain's first 'ironclad' warship, HMS *Warrior*, the D-Day Museum, Charles Dickens' birthplace at 393 Old Commercial Road, the Royal Naval and Royal Marine museums, Southsea Castle (built by Henry VIII), Round Tower and Point Battery, which for hundreds of years have guarded the entrance to Portsmouth Harbour, Fort Nelson on Portsdown Hill and the Sealife Centre.

ST ALBANS

The origins of St Albans, situated on the River Ver, stem from the Roman town of *Verulamium*. Named after the first Christian martyr in Britain, who was executed here, St Albans has developed around the Norman Abbey and Cathedral Church (consecrated 1115), built partly of materials from the old Roman city. The museums house Iron Age and Roman artefacts and the Roman Theatre, unique in Britain, has a stage as opposed to an amphitheatre. Archaeological excavations in the city centre have revealed evidence of pre-Roman, Saxon and medieval occupation.

The town's significance grew to the extent that it was a signatory and venue for the drafting of the Magna Carta. It was also the scene of riots during the Peasants' Revolt, the French King John was imprisoned there after the Battle of Poitiers, and heavy fighting took place there during the Wars of the Roses.

Previously controlled by the Abbot, the town achieved a charter in 1553 and city status in 1877. The street market, first established in 1553, is still an important feature of the city, as are many hotels and inns which survive from the days when St Albans was an important coach stop. Tourist attractions include historic churches and houses, and a 15th-century clock tower.

The city now contains a wide range of firms, with special emphasis on information and legal services. In addition, it is the home of the Royal National Rose Society, and of Rothamsted Park, the agricultural research centre.

SHEFFIELD

Sheffield, the centre of the special steel and cutlery trades, is situated at the junction of the Sheaf, Porter, Rivelin and Loxley valleys with the River Don. Though its cutlery, silverware and plate have long been famous, Sheffield has other and now more important industries: special and alloy steels, engineering, tool-making, medical equipment and media-related industries (in its new Cultural Industries Quarter). Sheffield has two universities and is an important research centre.

The parish church of St Peter and St Paul, founded in the 12th century, became the Cathedral Church of the Diocese of Sheffield in 1914. The Roman Catholic Cathedral Church of St Marie (founded 1847) was created Cathedral for the new diocese of Hallam in 1980. Parts of the present building date from *c*.1435. The principal buildings are the Town Hall (1897), the Cutlers' Hall (1832), City Hall (1932), Graves Art Gallery (1934), Mappin Art Gallery, the Crucible Theatre and the restored 19th-century Lyceum theatre, which dates from 1897 and was reopened in 1990. Three major sports venues were opened in 1990 to 1991.

Sheffield was created a city in 1893.

Master Cutler of the Company of Cutlers in Hallamshire 1997–8, P. J. Tear

SOUTHAMPTON

Southampton is the leading British deep-sea port on the Channel and is situated on one of the finest natural harbours in the world. The first charter was granted by Henry II and Southampton was created a county of itself in 1447. In 1964 it was granted city status.

There were Roman and Saxon settlements on the site of the city, which has been an important port since the time of the Conquest due to its natural deep-water harbour. The oldest church is St Michael's (1070) which has an unusually tall spire built in the 18th century as a landmark for navigators of Southampton Water. Other buildings and monuments within the city walls are the Tudor House Museum, God's House Tower, the Bargate museum, the Tudor Merchants Hall, the Weigh-house, West Gate, King John's House, Long House, Wool House, the ruins of Holy Rood Church, St Julien's Church and the Mayflower Memorial. The medieval town walls, built for artillery, are among the most complete in Europe. Public open spaces total over 1,000 acres and comprise 9 per cent of the city's area. The Common covers an area of 328 acres in the central district of the city and is mostly natural parkland. Two recent additions to work in marine technology in Southampton are Europe's leading oceanographic research centre (part of the University) and the marine science and technology business park.

STOKE-ON-TRENT

Stoke-on-Trent, standing on the River Trent and familiarly known as The Potteries, is the main centre of employment for the population of North Staffordshire. The city is the largest clayware producer in the world (china, earthenware, sanitary goods, refractories, bricks and tiles) and also has a wide range of other manufacturing industry, including steel, chemicals, engineering and tyres. Extensive reconstruction has been carried out in recent years.

The city was formed by the federation of the separate municipal authorities of Tunstall, Burslem, Hanley, Stoke, Fenton, and Longton in 1910 and received its city status in 1925.

WINCHESTER

Winchester, the ancient capital of England, is situated on the River Itchen. The city is rich in architecture of all types but the Cathedral takes pride of place. The longest Gothic cathedral in the world, it was built in 1079–93 and exhibits examples of Norman, Early English and Perpendicular styles. Winchester College, founded in 1382, is one of the most famous public schools, the original building (1393) remaining largely unaltered. St Cross Hospital, another great medieval foundation, lies one mile south of the city. The almshouses were founded in 1136 by Bishop Henry de Blois, and Cardinal Henry Beaufort added a new almshouse of 'Noble Poverty' in 1446. The chapel and dwellings are of great architectural interest, and visitors may still receive the 'Wayfarer's Dole' of bread and ale.

Excavations have done much to clarify the origins and development of Winchester. Part of the forum and several of the streets of the Roman town have been discovered; excavations in the Cathedral Close have uncovered the entire site of the Anglo-Saxon cathedral (known as the Old Minster) and parts of the New Minster which was built by Alfred's son Edward the Elder and is the burial place of the Alfredian dynasty. The original burial place of St Swithun, before his remains were translated to a site in the present cathedral, was also uncovered.

Excavations in other parts of the city have thrown much light on Norman Winchester, notably on the site of the Royal Castle (adjacent to which the new Law Courts have been built) and in the grounds of Wolvesey Castle, where the great house built by Bishops Giffard and Henry de Blois in the 12th century has been uncovered. The Great Hall, built by Henry III between 1222 and 1236 survives and houses the Arthurian Round Table.

YORK

The city of York is an archiepiscopal seat. Its recorded history dates from AD 71, when the Roman Ninth Legion established a base under Petilius Cerealis which later became the fortress of *Eburacum*. In Anglo-Saxon times the city was the royal and ecclesiastical centre of Northumbria, and after capture by a Viking army in AD 866 it became the capital of the Viking kingdom of Jorvik. By the 14th century the city had become a great mercantile centre, mainly because of its control of the wool trade, and was used as the chief base against the Scots. Under the Tudors its fortunes declined, though Henry VIII made it the headquarters of the Council of the North. Excavations on many sites, including Coppergate, have greatly expanded knowledge of Roman, Viking and medieval urban life.

With its development as a railway centre in the 19th century the commercial life of York expanded. The principal industries are the manufacture of chocolate, scientific instruments and sugar. It is the location of several government departments.

The city is rich in examples of architecture of all periods. The earliest church was built in AD 627 and, in the 12th to 15th centuries, the present Minster was built in a succession of styles. Other examples within the city are the medieval city walls and gateways, churches and guildhalls. Domestic architecture includes the Georgian mansions of The Mount, Micklegate and Bootham.

English Counties and Shires

LORD-LIEUTENANTS AND HIGH SHERIFFS

County/Shire	Lord-Lieutenant	High Sheriff, 1998–9
Bedfordshire	S. C. Whitbread	G. R. D. Farr
Berkshire	P. L. Wroughton	A. R. Wiseman
Bristol	J. Tidmarsh, MBE	E. H. Webber
Buckinghamshire	Sir Nigel Mobbs	E. R. Verney
Cambridgeshire	J. G. P. Crowden	R. B. Bamford
Cheshire	W. A. Bromley-Davenport	M. A. T. Trevor-Barnston
Cornwall	Lady Holborow	P. R. Thompson
Cumbria	J. A. Cropper	S. P. Pease
Derbyshire	J. K. Bather	G. R. W. Turbutt
Devon	E. Dancer, CBE	The Lady Clinton
Dorset	The Lord Digby	Cdr. P. G. Gregson
Durham	Sir Paul Nicholson	Sir William Gray
East Riding of Yorkshire	R. Marriott, TD	C. A. Maxsted
East Sussex	Admiral Sir Lindsay Bryson, KCB, FRSE, FENG.	Viscountess Brentford, OBE
Essex	The Lord Braybrooke	R. G. Newman
Gloucestershire	H. W. G. Elwes	W. J. Eykyn
Greater London	Field Marshal the Lord Bramall, KG, GCB, OBE, MC	J. P. Gough
Greater Manchester	Col. J. B. Timmins, OBE, TD	J. R. L. Lee
Hampshire	Mrs F. M. Fagan	J. J. L. G. Sheffield
Herefordshire	Sir Thomas Dunne, KCVO	S. W. B. Dereham
Hertfordshire	S. A. Bowes Lyon	The Hon. R. O. Pleydell–Bouverie
Isle of Wight	*C. D. J. Bland	D. C. Biles
Kent	The Lord Kingsdown, KG, PC	J. P. Merricks
Lancashire	The Lord Shuttleworth	C. A. B. Brennan
Leicestershire	T. G. M. Brooks	I. M. McAlpine
Lincolnshire	Mrs B. K. Cracroft-Eley	G. O. Hutchison
Merseyside	A. W. Waterworth	Col. Sir Christopher Hewetson
Norfolk	Sir Timothy Colman, KG	A. E. Buxton
Northamptonshire	Lady Juliet Townsend, LVO	Lady Morton
Northumberland	The Viscount Ridley, KG, GCVO, TD	C. A. F. Baker–Cresswell, OBE, TD
North Yorkshire	Sir Marcus Worsley, Bt.	Lady Clarissa Collin
Nottinghamshire	Sir Andrew Buchanan, Bt.	Mrs J. M. Farr
Oxfordshire	H. L. J. Brunner	R. Ovey
Rutland	Air Chief Marshal Sir Thomas Kennedy, GCB, AFC	Mrs L. L. Taylor
Shropshire	A. E. H. Heber-Percy	L. C. N. Bury
Somerset	Sir John Wills, Bt., KCVO, TD	Mrs M. E. B. Beckett
South Yorkshire	The Earl of Scarbrough	Mrs K. E. Riddle
Staffordshire	J. A. Hawley, TD	A. E. R. Manners
Suffolk	The Lord Belstead, PC	The Hon. P. V. Fisher
Surrey	Mrs S. J. F. Goad	R. H. S. Stilgoe
Tyne and Wear	Sir Ralph Carr-Ellison, TD	J. S. Ward
Warwickshire	M. Dunne	D. J. Barnes
West Midlands	R. R. Taylor, OBE	W. G. K. Carter
West Sussex	Maj.-Gen. Sir Philip Ward, KCVO, CBE	B. S. L. Trafford
West Yorkshire	J. Lyles, CBE	J. J. E. Brennan
Wiltshire	Lt.-Gen. Sir Maurice Johnston, KCB, OBE	Lady Hawley
Worcestershire	Sir Thomas Dunne, KCVO	S. W. B. Dereham

* Lord-Lieutenant and Governor

COUNTY COUNCILS: Area, Population, Finance

Council	Administrative headquarters	Area (hectares)	Population 1996	Total demand upon collection fund 1998–9
Bedfordshire	County Hall, Bedford	123,468	367,300	£83,800,000
Buckinghamshire	County Hall, Aylesbury	188,279	474,600	96,022,000
Cambridgeshire	Shire Hall, Cambridge	306,821	544,600	96,600,000
Cheshire	County Hall, Chester	207,773	668,000	162,108,375
Cornwall	County Hall, Truro	356,442†	483,300†	89,575,000
Cumbria	The Courts, Carlisle	682,451	490,600	102,929,000
Derbyshire	County Hall, Matlock	263,098	728,300	147,817,756
Devon	County Hall, Exeter	656,904	680,100	146,010,000
Dorset	County Hall, Dorchester	265,433	382,090	92,511,952
Durham	County Hall, Durham	243,369	506,900	89,757,000
East Sussex	Pelham House, St Andrew's Lane, Lewes	179,530	485,400	107,110,000
Essex	County Hall, Chelmsford	344,571	1,281,600	277,790,000
Gloucestershire	Shire Hall, Gloucester	264,270	556,300	106,305,850
Hampshire	The Castle, Winchester	378,022	1,222,100	254,437,000
Hertfordshire	County Hall, Hertford	163,601	1,015,800	215,000,000
§Isle of Wight	County Hall, Newport	38,063	125,500	32,345,480
Kent	County Hall, Maidstone	352,556	1,317,800	266,923,000
Lancashire	County Hall, Preston	288,899	1,132,700	237,446,000
Leicestershire	County Hall, Glenfield, Leicester	255,297	597,400	117,462,750
Lincolnshire	County Offices, Newland, Lincoln	591,791	615,900	109,602,000
Norfolk	County Hall, Norwich	537,482	777,000	147,841,234
North Yorkshire	County Hall, Northallerton	803,741	559,600	110,800,000
Northamptonshire	County Hall, Northampton	236,721	604,400	104,406,000
Northumberland	County Hall, Morpeth	503,165	307,400	64,807,000
Nottinghamshire	County Hall, Nottingham	208,620	747,800	158,977,000
Oxfordshire	County Hall, Oxford	260,798	603,200	116,550,537
Shropshire	The Shirehall, Shrewsbury	320,063	277,100	53,720,235
Somerset	County Hall, Taunton	345,233	482,700	95,000,000
Staffordshire	County Buildings, Stafford	271,616	801,300	137,394,388
Suffolk	County Hall, Ipswich	379,664	661,600	120,225,000
Surrey	County Hall, Kingston upon Thames	167,924	1,047,100	248,922,103
Warwickshire	Shire Hall, Warwick	198,052	500,600	105,701,357
West Sussex	County Hall, Chichester	198,935	737,300	161,589,000
Wiltshire	County Hall, Trowbridge	347,883	418,700	87,000,000
Worcestershire	County Hall, Worcester	173,529	505,050	97,586,466

Source for population figures: ONS Monitor PP1 97/1, 28 August 1997
† Including Isles of Scilly
§ Unitary authority since April 1995

COUNTY COUNCILS: Officers and Chairman

Council	Chief Executive	County Treasurer	Chairman of County Council
Bedfordshire	D. Cleggett	°W. Dodds	J. Hawksby
Buckinghamshire	I. Crookall	§§S. Nolan	K. Ross
Cambridgeshire	A. Barnish	D. T. Earle	J. McKay
Cheshire	C. Cheesman (acting)	A. Cope	D. Newton
Cornwall	J. F. Mills	F. P. Twyning	W. R. Hosking
Cumbria	W. A. Swarbrick	R. F. Mather	R. Calvin
Derbyshire	A. R. N. Hodgson	P. Swaby	L. G. Cannon
Devon	P. Jenkinson	§J. Glasby	Mrs M. Rogers
Dorset	P. K. Harvey	A. P. Peel	Mrs P. Hymers
Durham	K. W. Smith	J. Kirkby	M. Nicholls
East Sussex	Mrs C. Miller	J. Davies	M. Skilton
Essex	K. W. S. Ashurst	K. D. Neale	D. F. Rex
Gloucestershire	R. Cockroft	‖R. Cockroft	J. Rawson
Hampshire	P. C. B. Robertson	J. C. Pittam	Capt. M. P. R. Boyle
Hertfordshire	W. D. Ogley	*C. Sweeney	Sir Norman Lindop
Isle of Wight	††F. Hetherington	J. Pulsford	J. Bowker
Kent	M. Pitt	**D. Lewis	Sir John Grugeon
Lancashire	G. A. Johnson	B. G. Aldred	Mrs I. Short
Leicestershire	J. B. Sinnott	A. Youd	Mrs C. Brock
Lincolnshire	M. Spink (acting)	‡‡M. Spink	J. Libell
Norfolk	T. Byles	R. D. Summers	G. B. Hemming
Northamptonshire	J. V. Picking	†R. Paver	M. Young
Northumberland	°°K. Morris	*K. Morris	P. Hillman
North Yorkshire	J. A. Ransford	†J. S. Moore	W. F. Barton
Nottinghamshire	P. J. Housden	R. Latham	Mrs S. M. Smedley
Oxfordshire	J. Harwood	C. Gray	B. Hook
Shropshire	N. T. Pursey	N. T. Pursey	Mrs J. Marsh
Somerset	Dr D. Radford	C. N. Bilsland	R. B. Clark
Staffordshire	B. A. Price, CBE	R. G. Tettenborn, OBE	T. R. Wright
Suffolk	L. Homer	‡‡P. B. Atkinson	D. F. Smith
Surrey	P. Coen	**P. Derrick	Mrs H. Hawker
Warwickshire	I. G. Caulfield	S. R. Freer	R. Sweet
West Sussex	D. P. Rigg	Mrs H. Kilpatrick	I. R. W. Elliott
Wiltshire	Dr K. Robinson	D. Chalker	Mrs B. M. Jay
Worcestershire	R. Sykes	‡M. Weaver	R. Clayton

* Director of Finance
° Corporate Finance Adviser
°° Managing Director
† Chief Financial Services Officer
‡ Director of Finance Services
†† Head of Paid Service
§ Director of Resources
§§ Head of Finance
** Director of Corporate Services
‡‡ Director of Finance and Resources
‖ County Director

Unitary Councils

SMALL CAPITALS denote CITY status
§ Denotes Borough council

Council	Population 1996	Band D charge 1998*	Chief Executive	Mayor (a) Lord Mayor (b) Chairman 1998–9
§Barnsley	227,200	£734.89	J. Edwards, OBE	F. Wright
Bath and North-East Somerset	164,700	762.68	J. Everitt	(b) T. Ball
§BIRMINGHAM	1,020,600	846.00	M. Lyons	(a) Ms S. Anderson
Blackburn with Darwen	139,500	870.41	P. S. Watson	Ms F. Oldfield
Blackpool	152,500	632.93	G. E. Essex-Crosby	H. Mitchell
§Bolton	265,400	845.39	B. Knight	P. Finch
Bournemouth	160,700	702.60	D. Newell	K. Rawlings
Bracknell Forest	110,100	670.30	G. Mitchell	J. Finnie
§BRADFORD	483,400	761.48	R. Penn	(a) T. Miller
Brighton and Hove	249,500	652.00	G. Jones	F. Tonks
BRISTOL	399,600	986.00	Ms L. de Groot	(a) G. Robertson
§Bury	181,900	752.71	D. Taylor	Ms C. M. Fitzgerald
§Calderdale	192,800	839.12	P. Sheehan	A. Worth
§COVENTRY	306,500	897.22	I. Roxburgh	(a) Ms M. Rosher
Darlington	101,300	658.31	B. Keel	Miss P. Buttle
DERBY	233,700	728.67	R. H. Cowlishaw	A. Rehman
§Doncaster	291,800	716.51	A. M. Taylor (acting)	Mrs Y. Woodock
§Dudley	312,200	744.30	A. V. Astling	K. Finch
East Riding of Yorkshire	308,700	808.54	D. Stephenson	(b) D. Ireland
§Gateshead	201,000	927.06	L. N. Elton	B. Richmond
Halton	123,000	643.38	M. Cuff	T. McDermott
Hartlepool	92,100	924.36	B. J. Dinsdale	H. Clouth
Herefordshire	191,550	658.17	N. Pringle	(b) G. Hyde
KINGSTON UPON HULL	266,800	756.79	I. Crookham	(a) B. A. Petch
§Kirklees	388,800	843.00	T. Elson	M. Bower
§Knowsley	154,100	942.83	D. G. Henshaw	S. Byron
§LEEDS	726,900	734.71	†J. P. Smith	(a) G. P. Kirkland
LEICESTER	294,800	764.61	R. Green	(a) J. Mugglestone
§LIVERPOOL	468,000	1,171.54	P. Bounds	(a) H. Herrity
Luton	181,500	653.98	Mrs K. Jones	D. Patten
§MANCHESTER	430,800	949.49	H. Bernstein	(a) G. Conquest
Medway	239,500	634.21	Ms J. Armitt	N. Carter
Middlesbrough	146,800	746.16	¶J. E. Foster	F. Gill
Milton Keynes	197,100	687.00	H. Miller	G. Gillingham
§NEWCASTLE UPON TYNE	282,300	905.89	K. G. Lavery	(a) T. D. Marshall
North East Lincolnshire	158,500	827.35	R. Bentham	Ms C. Dixon
North Lincolnshire	152,800	977.81	Dr M. Garnett	A. Smith
North Somerset	185,300	682.66	P. May	J. Hayes
§North Tyneside	193,600	846.30	Executive Directorate	Ms A. Richardson
NOTTINGHAM CITY	284,000	832.19	E. F. Cantle	(a) J. A. Donn
§Oldham	220,200	865.00	C. Smith	(a) Ms M. Riley
PETERBOROUGH	158,700	695.48	W. E. Samuel	Ms M. Rainey
PLYMOUTH	255,800	645.49	Mrs A. Stone	(a) Mrs E. Evans
Poole	139,200	673.83	J. Brooks	J. G. S. Curtis
PORTSMOUTH	190,400	634.41	N. Gurney	(a) Ms P. Webb
Reading	142,900	799.83	Ms J. Markham	D. Geary
Redcar and Cleveland	139,800	977.00	A. W. Kilburn	G. Houchen
§Rochdale	207,600	820.72	Mrs F. W. Done	H. Hardiker
§Rotherham	255,300	760.14	A. G. Carruthers	R. Windle
Rutland	35,300	864.04	Dr J. R. Morphet	(b) Col. J. M. K. Weir
§St Helens	179,500	948.65	Mrs C. Hudson	D. Craig
§SALFORD	229,200	917.79	J. C. Willis	W. Moores
§Sandwell	292,200	800.47	F. N. Summers	B. James
§Sefton	289,700	872.17	G. J. Haywood	P. J. McVey
§SHEFFIELD	530,400	836.74	B. Kerslake	(a) T. Arber
Slough	110,500	648.73	Ms C. Coppell	G. S. Thind
§Solihull	203,900	693.15	Dr N. H. Perry	P. Hogarth

Council	Population 1996	Band D charge 1998*	Chief Executive	Mayor (a) Lord Mayor (b) Chairman 1998–9
SOUTHAMPTON	214,900	663.66	J. Cairns	vacant
South Gloucestershire	235,100	705.20	M. Robinson	(b) R Springer
Southend	172,300	648.06	J. K. M. Krawiec	Mrs N. T. Goodman
§South Tyneside	156,100	837.97	‡P. J. Haigh	B. Scorer
§Stockport	291,100	871.24	J. Schultz	G. Cooper
Stockton-on-Tees	179,000	801.85	G. Garlick	Mrs A. McCoy
STOKE-ON-TRENT	254,400	707.20	B. Smith	(a) Ms K. M. Banks
§SUNDERLAND	294,300	760.30	Dr C. W. Sinclair	W. Scott
Swindon	174,600	638.77	P. Doherty	B. Ford
§Tameside	220,700	862.20	M. J. Greenwood	J. Middleton
Telford and Wrekin	144,200	522.95	D. Hutchison	(b) M. Smith
Thurrock	132,300	630.27	K. Barnes	A. Bennett
Torbay	123,400	645.26	A. Hodgkiss	V. McCann
§Trafford	218,900	657.00	W. Allan Lewis	Mrs C. S. Merry
§WAKEFIELD	317,300	711.78	R. Mather	A. Barlow
§Walsall	262,600	741.18	D. C. Winchurch	E. W. Newman
Warrington	189,000	688.35	S. Broomhead	A. Clemow
West Berkshire	143,700	799.41	Ms S. Manzie	G. Vernon-Jackson
§Wigan	309,800	747.58	S. M. Jones	S. Little
Windsor and Maidenhead	141,500	708.70	D. C. Lunn	Mrs K. Newbound
§Wirral	329,200	913.99	S. Maddox	Ms M. Green
Wokingham	142,400	765.99	Mrs G. Norton	(b) Mrs P. Helliar-Symons
§Wolverhampton	244,500	913.68	D. Anderson	Mrs G. M. Stafford-Good
YORK	175,100	669.37	D. Clark	(a) D. Smallwood

Source of population figures: ONS Monitor PP1 97/1, 28 August 1997
* For explanation of council tax, *see* pages 523–4
† The Chief Officer
‡ Head of Paid Service
¶ Managing Director

District Councils

SMALL CAPITALS denote CITY status
§ Denotes Borough status
Source of population figures: ONS Monitor PP1 97/2, 28 August 1997
For explanation of council tax, *see* pages 523–4
* Executive Director
† General Manager
‡ Head of Paid Service
†† The Chief Officer
¶ Managing Director

Council	Population 1996	Band D charge 1998	Chief Executive	Chairman 1998–9 (a) Mayor (b) Lord Mayor
Adur	58,900	748.19	I. Lowrie	Ms G. Hammond
§Allerdale	95,700	818.61	C. J. Hart	(a) Mrs J. McKeown
Alnwick	31,100	849.31	L. A. B. St Ruth	J. Hobson
§Amber Valley	115,200	764.76	P. M. Carney	(a) Mrs J. M. Sanders
Arun	138,000	724.75	I. Sumnall	A. M. Williamson
Ashfield	108,600	840.84	E. N. Bernasconi	J. M. A. Wilmott
§Ashford	97,900	689.60	A. Baker	(a) D. S. Madgett
Aylesbury Vale	154,900	683.37	B. Hurley	Mrs F. Roberts, MBE
Babergh	79,000	707.78	D. C. Bishop	R. E. Kemp
§Barrow-in-Furness	71,600	833.92	T. O. Campbell	(a) Mrs M. T. Irwin
Basildon	163,300	760.40	J. Robb	R. Sears
§Basingstoke and Deane	147,900	705.00	Mrs K. Sporle	(a) D. Mirfin
Bassetlaw	106,300	829.05	M. S. Havenhand	Mrs J. Pimperton
§Bedford	137,500	791.16	L. W. Gould	(a) A. Ruffin
§Berwick-upon-Tweed	26,600	818.03	E. O. Cawthorn, TD	(a) J. F. Hills
Blaby	85,600	571.34	E. Hemsley	F. G. H. Jackson
§Blyth Valley	80,000	812.49	D. Crawford	(a) Mrs M. E. Gilchrist

Council	Population 1996	Band D charge 1998	Chief Executive	Chairman 1998–9 (a) Mayor (b) Lord Mayor
Bolsover	70,900	838.58	J. R. Fotherby	S. Patrick
§Boston	54,200	740.96	M. James	(a) A. Day
Braintree	126,200	731.26	Ms A. F. Ralph	Mrs R. Mayes
Breckland	113,700	682.23	R. Garnett	J. Boddy
§Brentwood	71,700	714.69	C. P. Sivell	(a) Ms M. Hogan
Bridgnorth	50,800	715.91	Mrs T. M. Elliott	D. Beechey
Broadland	113,900	699.44	J. Bryant	G. E. Debbage
Bromsgrove	85,200	652.39	D. A. H. Bryant	T. M. Crashley
§Broxbourne	81,800	663.61	M. J. Walker	(a) M. Milovanovic
§Broxtowe	111,400	840.68	M. Brown	(a) R. Todd
§Burnley	90,500	879.79	R. Ellis	(a) E. Selby
CAMBRIDGE	116,700	682.32	R. Hammond	(a) P. Cowell
Cannock Chase	90,800	716.79	M. G. Kemp	Mrs P. Z. Stretton
CANTERBURY	136,500	696.31	C. Carmichael	(b) P. Wales
Caradon	79,700	695.43	Dr. J. Neal	B. G. Wilson, TD
CARLISLE	103,100	843.60	R. S. Brackley	(a) Mrs H. Bradley
Carrick	84,900	711.53	J. P. Winskill	Mrs S. C. Shaw
§Castle Morpeth	49,600	833.73	P. Wilson	(a) N. Weatherly
§Castle Point	84,900	747.36	B. Rollinson	(a) Mrs V. Wells
§Charnwood	155,700	773.54	Mr S. M. Peatfield	(a) Mrs I. Thurlby
§Chelmsford	156,600	723.88	M. Easteal	(a) W. R. C. Lane
§Cheltenham	106,700	705.47	L. Davison	(a) Rev. J. Whales
Cherwell	132,700	643.84	G. J. Handley	Mrs W. Humphries
CHESTER	119,200	820.51	P. F. Durham	(b) D. Neild
§Chesterfield	100,700	795.36	D. R. Shaw	(a) M. Fanshawe
Chester-le-Street	56,100	794.97	J. A. Greensmith	J. Lines
Chichester	104,100	696.00	J. S. Marsland	A. J. French, TD
Chiltern	92,500	711.43	A. Goodrum	S. W. James
§Chorley	96,600	822.17	J. W. Davies	(a) A. Whittaker
§Christchurch	43,200	763.56	M. A. Turvey	(a) J. Lofts
§Colchester	154,200	713.53	J. Cobley	(a) D. Cannon
§Congleton	86,600	811.82	¶P. Cooper	(a) R. Fletcher
§Copeland	70,700	821.89	†Dr J. Stanforth	(a) Mrs H. Richardson
§Corby	52,100	707.12	N. Rudd	(a) G. McCart
Cotswold	81,500	703.46	N. C. Abbott	Mrs P. Pretty
Craven	51,300	625.04	Dr G. Taylor	Mrs J. Gott
§Crawley	93,200	709.56	M. D. Sander	(a) A. Kane
§Crewe and Nantwich	113,700	697.19	A. Wenham	(a) R. Stafford
§Dacorum	134,700	676.60	K. Hunt	(a) Ms M. Flint
§Dartford	83,900	705.87	C. R. Shepherd	(a) I. Jones
Daventry	65,300	677.95	P. Cook	A. Goodridge
Derbyshire Dales	69,600	990.00	D. Wheatcroft	A. S. Thomas
Derwentside	87,700	859.54	‡A. Hodgson	R. McArdle
Dover	107,400	708.21	J. P. Moir, TD	W. V. Newman
DURHAM	90,100	815.91	C. Shearsmith	(a) D. Young
Easington	95,200	885.72	†P. Innes	J. Atkinson
§Eastbourne	89,000	734.18	Mrs S. E. Conway	(a) Mrs B. Healy
East Cambridgeshire	67,500	645.82	R. C. Carr	P. I. Warren
East Devon	123,100	705.30	F. J. Vallender	Miss S. M. Randall Johnson
East Dorset	82,000	778.06	A. Breakwell	D. Mills
East Hampshire	110,800	735.36	Miss J. Hunter	J. Palmer
East Hertfordshire	123,600	656.38	R. J. Bailey	R. Parker
§Eastleigh	111,700	737.00	C. Tapp	(a) Mrs M. Kyrle, OBE
East Lindsey	123,100	722.39	P. Haigh	T. Carpenter
East Northamptonshire	70,800	709.07	R. K. Heath	Mrs E. M. Dicks
§East Staffordshire	100,400	720.08	F. W. Saunders	(a) T. M. Dawn
Eden	48,600	822.17	I. W. Bruce	J. B. Thornborrow
§Ellesmere Port and Neston	80,700	828.83	S. Ewbank	(a) R. J. Santo
§Elmbridge	124,500	721.58	D. W. L. Jenkins	(a) D. Denyer
Epping Forest	119,500	733.50	J. Burgess	M. Heavens
§Epsom and Ewell	69,300	692.44	D. J. Smith	(a) P. Ardern-Jones
§Erewash	106,800	795.03	G. A. Pook	(a) Ms B. White
EXETER	107,700	684.78	P. Bostock	(a) B. McNamara
§Fareham	103,700	702.54	A. A. Davies	(a) G. Neill
Fenland	79,200	660.00	N. R. Topliss	A. R. German

Council	Population 1996	Band D charge 1998	Chief Executive	Chairman 1998–9 (a) Mayor (b) Lord Mayor
Forest Heath	68,600	666.58	††D. W. Burnip, R. D. Bolton, P. Nock	Mrs P. J. Barker
Forest of Dean	76,000	721.62	Ms M. Holborow	Mrs S. M. McDonagh
§Fylde	75,000	821.94	J. R. Wilkinson	(a) Mrs E. A. Smith, OBE
§Gedling	112,200	825.07	D. Kennedy	(a) Mrs J. P. Collins
GLOUCESTER	106,800	698.45	G. Garbutt	(a) Ms J. Lugg
§Gosport	76,400	719.20	M. Crocker	(a) Mrs L. G. Barker
§Gravesham	91,700	672.34	E. C. Anderson	(a) E. A. Brook
§Great Yarmouth	89,300	694.57	R. W. Packham	J. Barnes
§Guildford	124,600	701.65	D. T. Watts	(a) K. Childs
Hambleton	84,700	628.89	P. Simpson	Mrs B. Walkington
Harborough	73,700	762.99	M. C. Wilson	Mrs E. D. Derrick
Harlow	73,400	820.57	†D. F. Byrne	P. Bellairs
§Harrogate	147,600	702.31	P. M. Walsh	(a) Mrs R. Timmis
Hart	85,800	700.00	G. R. Jelbart	Ms S. Wallis
§Hastings	82,000	757.37	R. Mawford	(a) G. Daniel
§Havant	117,300	714.23	R. G. Smith	(a) F. W. G. Pearce
§Hertsmere	94,900	706.98	P. H. Copland	(a) D. Banks
§High Peak	88,200	805.79	R. P. H. Brady	(a) Ms J. Brocklehurst
§Hinckley and Bosworth	97,800	729.87	vacant	(a) G. H. Payne
Horsham	118,600	682.12	M. J. Pearson	Mrs C. A. Sully
Huntingdonshire	152,700	656.63	D. Monks	Mrs P. Newbon
§Hyndburn	79,900	868.45	M. J. Chambers	(a) I. J. Ormerod
§Ipswich	113,600	768.96	J. D. Hehir	(a) G. H. Clarke
Kennet	75,500	715.76	P. L. Owens	Mrs S. Findlay
Kerrier	89,100	710.92	G. G. Fox	N. Stevens
§Kettering	80,800	716.04	P. Walker	(a) D. Whyte
§King's Lynn and West Norfolk	131,200	705.86	A. E. Pask	(a) P. Richards
LANCASTER	136,900	822.31	D. Corker	(a) A. C. Bryning
Lewes	86,900	743.25	J. N. Crawford	P. E. C. McCausland
Lichfield	93,200	707.47	J. T. Thompson	J. A. Brookes
LINCOLN	83,500	750.24	A. Sparke	(a) B. Robinson
§Macclesfield	152,600	807.19	B. W. Longden	(a) T. C. Scanlon
§Maidstone	140,700	730.53	J. D. Makepeace	(a) R. T. Judd
Maldon	54,600	717.10	E. A. P. Plumridge	J. Smith
Malvern Hills	91,000	667.14	C. Brook	Mrs E. Williams
Mansfield	101,400	840.01	R. P. Goad	S. Cornish
§Melton	46,500	758.42	P. M. Murphy	(a) R. F. Moore-Coltman
Mendip	98,400	726.35	G. Jeffs	J. Gilham
Mid Bedfordshire	118,900	771.30	C. A. Tucker	N. Cliff
Mid Devon	66,000	720.27	M. I. R. Bull	D. F. Pugsley
Mid Suffolk	80,400	705.66	G. R. Chilton	R. D. Snell
Mid Sussex	125,300	715.39	W. J. H. Hatton	D. Coombes
Mole Valley	79,400	772.95	Mrs H. Kerswell	J. Butcher
Newark and Sherwood	104,500	896.94	R. G. Dix	A. P. Hannaford
§Newcastle under Lyme	122,300	709.76	F. Harley	(a) Mrs B. Blaise
New Forest	169,500	741.50	¶I. B. Mackintosh	Mrs A. M. Howe
§Northampton	192,400	724.72	R. J. B. Morris	(a) U. E. Gravesande
North Cornwall	78,700	717.53	D. Brown	D. Coad
North Devon	86,200	737.48	D. T. Cunliffe	L. H. Ellway
North Dorset	58,200	734.78	Ms E. Peters	M. F. Lane
North East Derbyshire	99,000	843.31	‡Ms C. A. Gilby	Mrs P. Booker
North Hertfordshire	114,900	706.31	S. Philp	Mrs J. Billing
North Kesteven	86,600	712.21	Mrs R. Barlow	J. C. Rose
North Norfolk	96,900	691.02	B. A. Barrell	T. H. Moore
North Shropshire	54,100	746.43	R. J. Hughes	Ms P. Dee
§North Warwickshire	61,400	804.37	J. Hutchinson	(a) Ms B. Stuart
North West Leicestershire	84,300	784.67	M. J. Diaper	H. Sankey
North Wiltshire	121,700	740.44	R. Marshall	B. E. Atfield
NORWICH	126,200	663.75	J. R. Packer	(b) D. Wood
§Nuneaton and Bedworth	118,300	783.82	Ms C. Kerr	(a) R. Chattaway
§Oadby and Wigston	53,500	755.61	Mrs R. E. Hyde	(a) Mrs L. Thornton
§Oswestry	34,600	727.76	D. A. Towers	(a) S. F. Brown
OXFORD	137,300	759.31	R. S. Block	(b) Ms C. Roberts
§Pendle	84,300	875.06	S. Barnes	(a) C. Waite

Council	Population 1996	Band D charge 1998	Chief Executive	Chairman 1998–9 (a) Mayor (b) Lord Mayor
Penwith	59,600	694.50	‡D. H. Hosken	W. T. Trevorrow
§Preston	134,800	890.61	J. E. Carr	(a) Mrs R. Kinsella
Purbeck	45,300	762.68	P. B. Croft	S. C. S. Hinn
§Redditch	77,200	699.22	Ms K. Kerswell	(a) A. Fry
§Reigate and Banstead	119,300	713.00	M. Bacon	(a) J. H. Prevett, OBE
§Restormel	89,500	697.98	Mrs P. Crowson	(a) M. E. R. Burley
§Ribble Valley	52,700	835.29	D. Morris	(a) D. Smith
Richmondshire	47,300	695.53	H. Tabiner	Mrs S. P. Golding
Rochford	76,500	722.07	R. A. Lovell	G. Fox
§Rossendale	64,900	873.74	J. S. Hartley	(a) Ms M. Disley
Rother	89,500	721.63	D. F. Powell	A. Fleming
§Rugby	87,100	778.50	Mrs D. M. Colley	(a) Mrs H. Bell
§Runnymede	76,000	634.59	T. N. Williams	(a) G. B. Woodger
§Rushcliffe	103,500	823.80	K. Beaumont	(a) P. Smith
§Rushmoor	85,800	717.29	J. A. Lloyd	(a) P. J. Moyle
Ryedale	49,100	717.75	H. W. Mosley	G. W. Hobbs
St Albans	130,300	701.77	E. A. Hackford	(a) B. Peyton
§St Edmundsbury	93,600	692.96	G. R. N. Toft	(a) Mrs M. Martin
Salisbury	112,500	724.86	R. Sheard	M. Humphreys
§Scarborough	108,300	698.00	J. M. Trebble	(a) F. Standing
§Sedgefield	90,000	928.45	N. Vaulks	(a) J. Moran
Sedgemoor	101,900	610.75	A. G. Lovell	P. I. Johnstone
Selby	71,300	719.00	M. Connor	Mrs M. Stone
Sevenoaks	110,500	715.12	N. Howells	Mrs N. Munson
Shepway	98,700	726.91	R. J. Thompson	K. D. Hudson
§Shrewsbury and Atcham	97,100	693.76	D. Bradbury	(a) Ms J. A. Williams
South Bedfordshire	110,900	840.92	J. Ruddick	S. H. M. Owen
South Bucks	63,100	693.40	C. R. Furness	R. J. Worrall
South Cambridgeshire	128,400	596.59	J. S. Ballantyne	A. W. Wyatt
South Derbyshire	77,800	795.86	D. J. Dugdale	J. Ford
South Hams	79,300	722.01	M. S. Carpenter	Miss J. A. Westacott
South Holland	71,400	746.80	C. J. Simpkins	R. B. Hartfil
South Kesteven	120,000	722.01	C. Farmer	Mrs J. Gaffigan
South Lakeland	100,900	816.77	A. F. Winstanley	J. Studholme
South Norfolk	105,800	714.45	A. G. T. Kellett	Mrs S. Beare
South Northamptonshire	75,000	738.22	R. Tinlin	B. Stimpson
South Oxfordshire	124,600	704.99	R. Watson	Ms C. Heath-Whyte
§South Ribble	103,000	821.85	P. Halsall	(a) J. Owen
South Shropshire	40,500	732.44	G. C. Biggs, MBE	R. D. Phillips
South Somerset	150,700	730.08	M. Usher, OBE	N. Speakman
South Staffordshire	103,300	632.25	L. T. Barnfield	K. E. Mackie
§Spelthorne	89,200	707.45	M. B. Taylor	(a) Mrs D. L. Grant
§Stafford	124,500	705.12	D. Rawlings	(a) H. Brunt
Staffordshire Moorlands	94,400	743.87	B. J. Preedy	Mrs D. Lythgoe
§Stevenage	76,800	705.25	I. Paske	(a) W. L. Lawrence
Stratford-on-Avon	111,200	733.51	I. B. Prosser	Ms A. Simpson
Stroud	108,000	757.24	R. M. Ollin	Mrs M. E. A. Nolder
Suffolk Coastal	118,700	697.83	T. K. Griffin	Mrs M. J. Dixon
§Surrey Heath	82,400	703.17	B. R. Catchpole	(a) Mrs J. P. White
§Swale	117,600	687.23	J. C. Edwards	(a) G. Lewin
§Tamworth	72,400	676.50	C. Moore	(a) D. N. Thompson
Tandridge	77,600	712.62	P. J. D. Thomas	R. Harling
§Taunton Deane	98,900	695.61	†Mrs S. Douglas	(a) W. E. Softley
Teesdale	24,500	809.00	C. M. Anderson	Mrs K. M. Mitchell
Teignbridge	116,700	725.00	B. T. Jones	M. J. Haines
Tendring	132,300	722.28	J. Hawkins	L. Randall
§Test Valley	107,200	696.74	A. Jones	(a) A. Jackson
§Tewkesbury	77,300	648.26	H. Davis	(a) Mrs P. E. Stokes
Thanet	125,500	722.65	D. Ralls, CBE, DFC	Mrs M. Davies
Three Rivers	84,600	707.45	A. Robertson	Ms B. Lamb
§Tonbridge and Malling	105,000	718.02	T. Thompson	(a) Ms S. Levett
Torridge	54,400	721.74	R. K. Brasington	F. Howard, MBE
§Tunbridge Wells	102,600	870.39	R. J. Stone	(a) A. J. Baker
Tynedale	58,000	833.45	A. Baty	Mrs D. Elwell
Uttlesford	68,500	734.45	K. Ivory	R. B. Tyler

Council	Population 1996	Band D charge 1998	Chief Executive	Chairman 1998–9 (a) Mayor (b) Lord Mayor
Vale of White Horse	112,500	663.47	T. Stock	Mrs J. Hutchinson
§Vale Royal	115,200	833.71	W. R. T. Woods	(a) K. Musgrave
Wansbeck	62,200	832.00	A. G. White	Ms M. Wallace
Warwick	122,500	754.33	Miss J. Barrett	G. Darmody
§Watford	78,900	768.30	Ms C. Hassan	(a) Ms D. Thornhill
Waveney	107,700	675.08	M. Berridge	F. Devereux
§Waverley	114,100	717.60	Miss C. L. Pointer	(a) J. M. Savage
Wealden	138,000	763.05	D. R. Holness	R. I. F. Parsons
Wear Valley	63,300	832.95	*Mrs C. Hughes	H. Douthwaite
§Wellingborough	67,900	628.43	T. McArdle	(a) M. Prescod
Welwyn Hatfield	95,400	702.10	M. Saminaden	Mrs S. Jones
§West Devon	46,400	743.95	D. J. Incoll	(a) D. Bater
West Dorset	90,300	769.98	R. C. Rennison	Mrs N. M. Penfold
West Lancashire	109,800	840.62	W. J. Taylor	D. Thompson
West Lindsey	77,200	757.98	R. W. Nelsey	C. R. Ireland
West Oxfordshire	96,000	656.45	G. Bonner	A. Walker
West Somerset	32,800	727.47	C. W. Rockall	Mrs A. Cave-Browne-Cave
West Wiltshire	108,900	872.75	J. Ligo	P. J. Bryant
§Weymouth and Portland	62,800	770.54	M. N. Ashby	(a) H. R. Legg
Winchester	106,000	716.96	D. H. Cowan	(a) G. Fothergill
§Woking	90,700	710.46	P. Russell	(a) Mrs R. P. Johnson
Worcester	92,300	661.09	D. Wareing	(a) D. Prodger
§Worthing	99,200	709.29	M. J. Ball	(a) D. Chapman
Wychavon	108,000	677.45	W. S. Nott	J. Payne
Wycombe	164,000	704.28	R. J. Cummins	E. H. Collins
§Wyre	104,300	829.98	M. Brown	(a) R. Sharrock
Wyre Forest	96,700	691.00	W. S. Baldwin	C. D. Nicholls

The Cinque Ports

As their name implies, the Cinque Ports were originally five in number: Hastings, New Romney, Hythe, Dover and Sandwich. They were formed during the 11th century to defend the Channel coast and, after the Norman Conquest, were recognized as a Confederation by a charter of 1278. The 'antient towns' of Winchelsea and Rye were added at some time after the Conquest. The other members of the Confederation, known as Limbs, are Lydd, Faversham, Folkestone, Deal, Tenterden, Margate and Ramsgate.

Until 1855 the duty of the Cinque Ports was to provide ships and men for the defence of the state in return for considerable privileges, such as tax exemptions and the framing of by-laws. Of these privileges only jurisdiction in Admiralty remains.

The Barons of the Cinque Ports have the ancient privilege of attending the Coronation ceremony and are allotted special places in Westminster Abbey.

Lord Warden of the Cinque Ports, HM Queen Elizabeth the Queen Mother

Judge, Court of Admiralty, Hon. Sir Anthony Clarke

Registrar, I. G. Gill, LVO, 7 Rosetower Court, Broadstairs, Kent CT10 3BG. Tel: 01843-861177

LORD WARDENS OF THE CINQUE PORTS *since* 1904

The Marquess Curzon	1904
The Prince of Wales	1905
The Earl Brassey	1908
The Earl Beauchamp	1913
The Marquess of Reading	1934
The Marquess of Willingdon	1936
Winston Churchill	1941
Sir Robert Menzies	1965
HM Queen Elizabeth the Queen Mother	1978

1 Stockton-on-Tees
2 Middlesbrough
3 Blackpool
4 Blackburn
with Darwen
5 Bolton
6 Bury
7 Rochdale
8 Salford
9 Oldham
10 Liverpool
11 Knowsley
12 St Helens
13 Halton
14 Warrington
15 Trafford
16 Manchester
17 Tameside
18 Stockport
19 Nottingham
20 Telford and
Wrekin
21 Wolverhampton

22 Walsall
23 Sandwell
24 Dudley
25 Birmingham
26 Solihull
27 Coventry
28 Peterborough
29 South Glos
30 Bristol
31 Bath and
NE Somerset
32 Windsor and
Maidenhead
33 Slough
34 Reading
35 Wokingham
36 Bracknell Forest
37 Thurrock
38 Southend
39 Medway
40 Plymouth
41 Torbay

LONDON

1 Hillingdon
2 Harrow
3 Barnet
4 Enfield
5 Waltham Forest
6 Redbridge
7 Barking and Dagenham
8 Havering
9 Ealing
10 Brent
11 Camden
12 Haringey
13 Islington
14 Hackney
15 Newham
16 Hounslow
17 Hammersmith and Fulham

18 Kensington and Chelsea
19 City of Westminster
20 City of London
21 Tower Hamlets
22 Richmond upon Thames
23 Wandsworth
24 Lambeth
25 Southwark
26 Lewisham
27 Greenwich
28 Bexley
29 Kingston upon Thames
30 Merton
31 Sutton
32 Croydon
33 Bromley

London

THE CORPORATION OF LONDON
(*see also* page 526)

The City of London is the historic centre at the heart of London known as 'the square mile' around which the vast metropolis has grown over the centuries. The City's residential population is 5,500. The civic government is carried on by the Corporation of London through the Court of Common Council.

The City is an international financial centre, generating over £20 billion a year for the British economy. It includes the head offices of the principal banks, insurance companies and mercantile houses, in addition to buildings ranging from the historic Roman Wall and the 15th-century Guildhall, to the massive splendour of St Paul's Cathedral and the architectural beauty of Wren's spires.

The City of London was described by Tacitus in AD 62 as 'a busy emporium for trade and traders'. Under the Romans it became an important administration centre and hub of the road system. Little is known of London in Saxon times, when it formed part of the kingdom of the East Saxons. In 886 Alfred recovered London from the Danes and reconstituted it a burgh under his son-in-law. In 1066 the citizens submitted to William the Conqueror who in 1067 granted them a charter, which is still preserved, establishing them in the rights and privileges they had hitherto enjoyed.

THE MAYORALTY

The Mayoralty was probably established about 1189, the first Mayor being Henry Fitz Ailwyn who filled the office for 23 years and was succeeded by Fitz Alan (1212–14). A new charter was granted by King John in 1215, directing the Mayor to be chosen annually, which has ever since been done, though in early times the same individual often held the office more than once. A familiar instance is that of 'Whittington, thrice Lord Mayor of London' (in reality four times, 1397, 1398, 1406, 1419); and many modern cases have occurred. The earliest instance of the phrase 'Lord Mayor' in English is in 1414. It was used more generally in the latter part of the 15th century and became invariable from 1535 onwards. At Michaelmas the liverymen in Common Hall choose two Aldermen who have served the office of Sheriff for presentation to the Court of Aldermen, and one is chosen to be Lord Mayor for the following mayoral year.

LORD MAYOR'S DAY

The Lord Mayor of London was previously elected on the feast of St Simon and St Jude (28 October), and from the time of Edward I, at least, was presented to the King or to the Barons of the Exchequer on the following day, unless that day was a Sunday. The day of election was altered to 16 October in 1346, and after some further changes was fixed for Michaelmas Day in 1546, but the ceremonies of admittance and swearing-in of the Lord Mayor continued to take place on 28 and 29 October respectively until 1751. In 1752, at the reform of the calendar, the Lord Mayor was continued in office until 8 November, the 'New Style' equivalent of 28 October. The Lord Mayor is now presented to the Lord Chief Justice at the Royal Courts of Justice on the second Saturday in November to make the final declaration of office, having been sworn in at Guildhall on the preceding day. The procession to the Royal Courts of Justice is popularly known as the Lord Mayor's Show.

REPRESENTATIVES

Aldermen are mentioned in the 11th century and their office is of Saxon origin. They were elected annually between 1377 and 1394, when an Act of Parliament of Richard II directed them to be chosen for life.

The Common Council, elected annually on the first Friday in December, was, at an early date, substituted for a popular assembly called the *Folkmote*. At first only two representatives were sent from each ward, but the number has since been greatly increased.

OFFICERS

Sheriffs were Saxon officers; their predecessors were the *wic-reeves* and *portreeves* of London and Middlesex. At first they were officers of the Crown, and were named by the Barons of the Exchequer; but Henry I (in 1132) gave the citizens permission to choose their own Sheriffs, and the annual election of Sheriffs became fully operative under King John's charter of 1199. The citizens lost this privilege, as far as the election of the Sheriff of Middlesex was concerned, by the Local Government Act 1888; but the liverymen continue to choose two Sheriffs of the City of London, who are appointed on Midsummer Day and take office at Michaelmas.

The office of Chamberlain is an ancient one, the first contemporary record of which is 1237. The Town Clerk (or Common Clerk) is mentioned in 1274.

ACTIVITIES

The work of the Corporation is assigned to a number of committees which present reports to the Court of Common Council. These Committees are: City Lands and Bridge House Grants Estates, Policy and Resources, Finance, Planning and Transportation, Central Markets, Billingsgate and Leadenhall Markets, Spitalfields Market, Police, Port and City of London Health and Social Services, Libraries, Art Galleries and Records, Board of Governors of City of London Freemen's School, Music and Drama (Guildhall School of Music and Drama), Establishment, Housing and Sports Development, Gresham (City side), Hampstead Heath Management, Epping Forest and Open Spaces, West Ham Park, Privileges, Barbican Residential and Barbican Centre (Barbican Arts and Conference Centre).

The City's estate, in the possession of which the Corporation of London differs from other municipalities, is managed by the City Lands and Bridge House Grants Estates Committee, the chairmanship of which carries with it the title of Chief Commoner.

The Honourable the Irish Society, which manages the Corporation's estates in Ulster, consists of a Governor and five other Aldermen, the Recorder, and 19 Common Councilmen, of whom one is elected Deputy Governor.

THE LORD MAYOR 1997–8[*]

The Rt. Hon. the Lord Mayor, Sir Richard Nichols
  Secretary, Air Vice-Marshal M. Dicken, CB

THE SHERIFFS 1998–9

G. F. Arthur (*Alderman, Cripplegate*) and B. N. Harris (*Councilman, Broad Street*); *elected*, 24 June 1998; *assumed office*, 28 September 1998

---

[*] The Lord Mayor for 1998–9 was elected on Michaelmas Day. *See* Stop-press

OFFICERS, ETC

Town Clerk and Chamberlain, B. P. Harty
Chief Commoner (1998), R. G. Scriven
Clerk, The Honourable the Irish Society, S. Waley, The Irish
    Chamber, 1st Floor, 75 Watling Street, London EC4M 9BJ

THE ALDERMEN

Name and Ward	CC	Ald.	Shff.	Lord Mayor
Sir Peter Gadsden, GBE, *Farringdon Wt.*	1969	1971	1970	1979
Sir Christopher Leaver, GBE, *Dowgate*	1973	1974	1979	1981
Sir Alan Traill, GBE, *Langbourn*	1970	1975	1982	1984
Sir David Rowe-Ham, GBE, *Bridge* and *Bridge Wt.*	—	1976	1984	1986
Sir Christopher Collett, GBE, *Broad Street*	1973	1979	1985	1988
Sir Alexander Graham, GBE, *Queenhithe*	1978	1979	1986	1990
Sir Brian Jenkins, GBE, *Cordwainer*	—	1980	1987	1991
Sir Paul Newall, TD, *Walbrook*	1980	1981	1989	1993
Sir Christopher Walford, *Farringdon Wn.*	—	1982	1990	1994
Sir John Chalstrey, *Vintry*	1981	1984	1993	1995
Sir Roger Cork, *Tower*	1978	1983	1992	1996
Richard Nichols, *Candlewick*	1983	1984	1994	1997

All the above have passed the Civic Chair

Lord Levene of Portsoken, KBE, *Portsoken*	1983	1984	1995
Clive Martin, OBE, TD, *Aldgate*	—	1985	1996
David Howard, *Cornhill*	1972	1986	1997
James Oliver, *Bishopsgate*	1980	1987	1997
Peter Bull, *Cheap*	1968	1984	
Gavyn Arthur, *Cripplegate*	1988	1991	1998
Robert Finch, *Coleman Street*	—	1992	
Richard Agutter, *Castle Baynard*	—	1995	
Michael Savory, *Bread Street*	1980	1996	
David Brewer, *Bassishaw*	1992	1996	
Nicholas Anstee, *Aldersgate*	1987	1996	
Michael Everard, CBE, *Lime Street*	—	1996	
John Hughesdon, *Billingsgate*	1991	1997	

THE COMMON COUNCIL

Deputy: Each Common Councilman so described serves as
deputy to the Alderman of her/his ward

Absalom, J. D. (1994)	*Farringdon Wt.*
Altman, L. P. (1996)	*Cripplegate Wn.*
Angell, E. H. (1991)	*Cripplegate Wt.*
Archibald, *Deputy* W. W. (1986)	*Cornhill*
Ayers, K. E. (1996)	*Bassishaw*
Bailey, J. (1993)	*Cripplegate Wt.*
Balls, H. D. (1970)	*Castle Baynard*
Barker, *Deputy* J. A. (1981)	*Cripplegate Wn.*
Barnes-Yallowley, H. M. F. (1986)	*Coleman Street*
Beale, *Deputy* M. J. (1979)	*Lime Street*
Bird, J. L. (1977)	*Bridge*
Biroum-Smith, P. L. (1988)	*Dowgate*
Block, S. A. A. (1983)	*Cheap*
Bowman, J. C. R. (1995)	*Aldgate*
Bradshaw, D. J. (1991)	*Cripplegate Wn.*
Bramwell, F. M. (1983)	*Langbourn*
Branson, N. A. C. (1996)	*Bassishaw*

Brewster, J. W., OBE (1994)	*Bassishaw*
Brighton, R. L. (1984)	*Portsoken*
Brooks, W. I. B. (1988)	*Billingsgate*
Brown, *Deputy* D. T. (1971)	*Walbrook*
Byllam-Barnes, J. (1997)	*Cheap*
Caspi, D. R. (1994)	*Bridge*
Cassidy, *Deputy* M. J. (1989)	*Coleman Street*
Catt, B. F. (1982)	*Farringdon Wn.*
Chadwick, R. A. H. (1994)	*Tower*
Challis, G. H., CBE (1978)	*Langbourn*
Charkham, J. P. (1996)	*Farringdon Wt.*
Cohen, Mrs C. M. (1986)	*Lime Street*
Cole, Lt.-Col. Sir Colin, KCB, KCVO, TD (1964)	*Castle Baynard*
Cotgrove, D. (1991)	*Lime Street*
Coven, *Deputy* Mrs E. O., CBE (1972)	*Dowgate*
Currie, *Deputy* Miss S. E. M. (1985)	*Cripplegate Wt.*
Daily-Hunt, R. B. (1989)	*Cripplegate Wt.*
Darwin, G. E. (1995)	*Farringdon Wt.*
Davis, C. B. (1991)	*Bread Street*
Dove, W. H., MBE (1993)	*Bishopsgate*
Dunitz, A. A. (1984)	*Portsoken*
Eskenzi, A. N. (1970)	*Farringdon Wn.*
Eve, R. A. (1980)	*Cheap*
Everett, K. M. (1984)	*Candlewick*
Falk, F. A., TD (1997)	*Broad Street*
Farrow, M. W. W. (1996)	*Farringdon Wt.*
Farthing, R. B. C. (1981)	*Aldgate*
Fell, J. A. (1982)	*Queenhithe*
FitzGerald, *Deputy* R. C. A. (1981)	*Bread Street*
Forbes, G. B. (1993)	*Bishopsgate*
Fraser, S. J. (1993)	*Coleman Street*
Fraser, W. B. (1981)	*Vintry*
Galloway, A. D. (1981)	*Broad Street*
Gillon, G. M. F. (1995)	*Cordwainer*
Ginsburg, S. (1990)	*Bishopsgate*
Gowman, Miss A. (1991)	*Dowgate*
Graves, A. C. (1985)	*Bishopsgate*
Green, C. (1994)	*Aldersgate*
Griffiths, Mrs R. M. (1996)	*Cripplegate Wt.*
Hall, B. R. H. (1995)	*Farringdon Wn.*
Halliday, Mrs P. (1992)	*Walbrook*
Hardwick, Dr P. B. (1987)	*Aldgate*
Harries, R. E. (1995)	*Cripplegate Wt.*
Harris, B. N. (1996)	*Broad Street*
Hart, *Deputy* M. G. (1970)	*Bridge*
Haynes, J. E. H. (1986)	*Cornhill*
Henderson, *Deputy* J. S., OBE (1975)	*Langbourn*
Henderson-Begg, M. (1977)	*Coleman Street*
Holland, *Deputy* J., CBE (1972)	*Aldgate*
Holliday, Mrs E. H. L. (1987)	*Vintry*
Horlock, *Deputy* H. W. S. (1969)	*Farringdon Wn.*
Jackson, L. St J. T. (1978)	*Bread Street*
Kellett, Mrs M. W. F. (1986)	*Tower*
Kemp, D. L. (1984)	*Coleman Street*
Knowles, S. K. (1984)	*Candlewick*
Lawrence, A. (1994)	*Farringdon Wt.*
Lawson, G. C. H. (1971)	*Portsoken*
Littlestone, N. (1993)	*Aldersgate*
McGuinness, C. (1997)	*Castle Baynard*
MacLellan, A. P. W. (1989)	*Walbrook*
McNeil, I. D. (1977)	*Lime Street*
Malins, *Deputy* J. H., QC (1981)	*Farringdon Wt.*
Martin, R. C. (1986)	*Queenhithe*
Martinelli, *Deputy* P. J. (1994)	*Bassishaw*
Mayhew, Miss J. (1986)	*Queenhithe*
Mayhew, J. P. (1996)	*Aldersgate*
Mitchell, *Deputy* C. R. (1971)	*Castle Baynard*
Mizen, *Deputy* D. H. (1979)	*Broad Street*

Mobsby, *Deputy* D. J. L. (1985)	*Billingsgate*
Morgan, *Deputy* B. L., CBE (1963)	*Bishopsgate*
Moss, A. D. (1989)	*Tower*
Nash, *Deputy* Mrs J. C. (1983)	*Aldersgate*
Newman, Mrs P. B. (1989)	*Aldersgate*
Northall-Laurie, P. D. (1975)	*Walbrook*
O'Ferrall, P. C. K., OBE (1996)	*Aldgate*
Owen, Mrs J. (1975)	*Langbourn*
Owen-Ward, J. R. (1983)	*Bridge*
Parmley, A. C. (1992)	*Vintry*
Pembroke, *Deputy* Mrs A. M. F. (1978)	*Cheap*
Platts-Mills, J. F. F., QC	*Farringdon Wt.*
Ponsonby of Shulbrede, *Deputy* Lady (1981)	*Farringdon Wt.*
Price, E. E. (1996)	*Farringdon Wt.*
Pulman, *Deputy* G. A. G. (1983)	*Tower*
Punter, C. (1993)	*Cripplegate Wn.*
Reed, *Deputy* J. L., MBE (1967)	*Farringdon Wn.*
Revell-Smith, *Deputy* P. A., CBE (1959)	*Vintry*
Rigby, P. P., CBE (1972)	*Farringdon Wn.*
Robinson, Mrs D. C. (1989)	*Bishopsgate*
Roney, *Deputy* E. P. T., CBE (1974)	*Bishopsgate*
Samuel, *Deputy* Mrs I., MBE (1971)	*Portsoken*
Sargant, K. A. (1991)	*Cornhill*
Saunders, *Deputy* R. (1975)	*Candlewick*
Scriven, R. G. (1984)	*Candlewick*
Sellon, S. A., OBE, TD (1990)	*Cordwainer*
Shalit, D. M. (1972)	*Farringdon Wn.*
Sharp, *Deputy* Mrs I. M. (1974)	*Queenhithe*
Sherlock, M. R. C. (1992)	*Dowgate*
Simpson, A. S. J. (1987)	*Aldersgate*
Smith, Miss A. M. (1995)	*Farringdon Wt.*
Snyder, *Deputy* M. J. (1986)	*Cordwainer*
Spanner, J. H., TD (1984)	*Broad Street*
Stevenson, F. P. (1994)	*Cripplegate Wn.*
Taylor, J. A. F., TD (1991)	*Bread Street*
Thorp, C. R. (1996)	*Billingsgate*
Trotter, J. (1993)	*Billingsgate*
Walsh, S. (1989)	*Farringdon Wt.*
Warner, D. W. (1994)	*Cripplegate Wn.*
White, Dr J. W. (1986)	*Cornhill*
Willoughby, P. J. (1985)	*Bishopsgate*
Wilmot, R. T. D. (1973)	*Cordwainer*
Wixley, G. R. A., CBE, TD (1964)	*Coleman Street*
Wooldridge, F. D. (1988)	*Farringdon Wn.*

The City Guilds (Livery Companies)

The constitution of the livery companies has been unchanged for centuries. There are three ranks of membership: freemen, liverymen and assistants. A person can become a freeman by patrimony (through a parent having been a freeman); by servitude (through having served an apprenticeship to a freeman); or by redemption (by purchase).

Election to the livery is the prerogative of the company, who can elect any of its freemen as liverymen. Assistants are usually elected from the livery and form a Court of Assistants which is the governing body of the company. The Master (in some companies called the Prime Warden) is elected annually from the assistants.

As at June 1998, 22,923 liverymen of the guilds were entitled to vote at elections at Common Hall.

The order of precedence, omitting extinct companies, is given in parenthesis after the name of each company in the list below. In certain companies the election of Master or Prime Warden for the year does not take place till the autumn. In such cases the Master or Prime Warden for 1997–8 is given.

THE TWELVE GREAT COMPANIES
In order of civic precedence

MERCERS (*1*). *Hall*, Ironmonger Lane, London EC2V 8HE. *Livery*, 253. *Clerk*, C. H. Parker. *Master*, R. K. Westmacott

GROCERS (*2*). *Hall*, Princes Street, London EC2R 8AD. *Livery*, 316. *Clerk*, C. G. Mattingley, CBE. *Master*, T. V. Carter

DRAPERS (*3*). *Hall*, Throgmorton Avenue, London EC2N 2DQ. *Livery*, 248. *Clerk*, A. L. Lang, MBE. *Master*, N. G. W. Playne

FISHMONGERS (*4*). *Hall*, London Bridge, London EC4R 9EL. *Livery*, 368. *Clerk*, K. S. Waters. *Prime Warden*, The Hon. Sir Mark Lennox-Boyd

GOLDSMITHS (*5*). *Hall*, Foster Lane, London EC2V 6BN. *Livery*, 280. *Clerk*, R. D. Buchanan-Dunlop, CBE. *Prime Warden*, R. F. H. Vanderpump

MERCHANT TAYLORS (*6/7*). *Hall*, 30 Threadneedle Street, London EC2R 8AY. *Livery*, 323. *Clerk*, D. A. Peck. *Master*, P. M. Franklin-Adams

SKINNERS (*6/7*). *Hall*, 8 Dowgate Hill, London EC4R 2SP. *Livery*, 370. *Clerk*, Capt. D. Hart Dyke, CBE, LVO, RN. *Master*, Prof. C. Seymour-Ure

HABERDASHERS (*8*). *Livery*, 320. *Clerk*, Capt. R. J. Fisher, RN, 39–40 Bartholomew Close, London EC1A 7JN. *Master*, D. G. C. Inglefield

SALTERS (*9*). *Hall*, 4 Fore Street, London EC2Y 5DE. *Livery*, 165. *Clerk*, Col. M. P. Barneby. *Master*, The Lord Rockley

IRONMONGERS (*10*). *Hall*, Shaftesbury Place, Barbican, London EC2Y 8AA. *Livery*, 128. *Clerk*, J. A. Oliver. *Master*, H. S. Johnson

VINTNERS (*11*). *Hall*, Upper Thames Street, London EC4V 3BJ. *Livery*, 309. *Clerk*, Brig. M. Smythe, OBE. *Master*, P. E. Cooper

CLOTHWORKERS (*12*). *Hall*, Dunster Court, Mincing Lane, London EC3R 7AH. *Livery*, 200. *Clerk*, M. G. T. Harris. *Master*, A. P. Leslie, TD

OTHER CITY GUILDS
In alphabetical order

ACTUARIES (*91*). *Livery*, 190. *Clerk*, P. D. Esslemont, 16A Cadogan Square, London SW1X 0JU. *Master*, A. S. Fishman

AIR PILOTS AND AIR NAVIGATORS, GUILD OF (*81*). *Livery*, 500. *Grand Master*, HRH The Prince Philip, Duke of Edinburgh, KG, KT, OM, GBE, PC. *Clerk*, Air Vice-Marshal R. G. Peters, CB, Cobham House, 291 Gray's Inn Road, London WC1X 8QF. *Master*, Capt. T. R. Fulton

APOTHECARIES, SOCIETY OF (*58*). *Hall*, 14 Black Friars Lane, London EC4V 6EJ. *Livery*, 1750. *Clerk*, Lt.-Col. R. J. Stringer. *Master*, Dr I. T. Field

ARBITRATORS (*93*). *Livery*, 224. *Clerk*, Lt.-Col. I. R. P. Green, 2 Bolts Hill, Castle Camps, Cambs CB1 6TL. *Master*, I. W. Menzies

ARMOURERS AND BRASIERS (*22*). *Hall*, 81 Coleman Street, London EC2R 5BJ. *Livery*, 120. *Clerk*, Cdr. T. J. K. Sloane, OBE, RN. *Master*, J. H. Hale

BAKERS (*19*). *Hall*, Harp Lane, London EC3R 6DP. *Livery*, 390. *Clerk*, J. W. Tompkins. *Master*, C. Gilford

BARBERS (*17*). *Hall*, Monkwell Square, Wood Street, London EC2Y 5BL. *Livery*, 200. *Clerk*, Brig. A. F. Eastburn. *Master*, Sir John Chalstrey, MD, FRCS

BASKETMAKERS (*52*). *Livery*, 330. *Clerk*, Maj. G. J. Flint-Shipman, TD, 48 Seymour Walk, London SW10 9NF. *Prime Warden*, P. J. Costain

BLACKSMITHS (*40*). *Livery*, 237. *Clerk*, R. C. Jorden, 27 Cheyne Walk, Grange Park, London N21 1DB. *Prime Warden*, J. M. Latham

BOWYERS (*38*). *Livery*, 110. *Clerk*, J. R. Owen-Ward, 11 Aldermans Hill, London N13 4YD. *Master*, W. P. Forrester

BREWERS (*14*). *Hall*, Aldermanbury Square, London EC2V 7HR. *Livery*, 120. *Clerk*, C. W. Dallmeyer. *Master*, C. J. R. Pope

BRODERERS (*48*). *Livery*, 165. *Clerk*, P. J. C. Crouch, 11 Bridge Road, East Molesey, Surrey KT8 9EU. *Master*, C. A. Hart

BUILDERS MERCHANTS (*88*). *Livery*, 180. *Clerk*, Miss S. M. Robinson, TD, 4 College Hill, London EC4R 2RA. *Master*, J. Hauxwell

BUTCHERS (*24*). *Hall*, 87 Bartholomew Close, London EC1A 7EB. *Livery*, 682. *Clerk*, G. J. Sharp. *Master*, R. Moore

CARMEN (*77*). *Livery*, 430. *Clerk*, Cdr. R. M. H. Bawtree, OBE, 35–37 Ludgate Hill, London EC4M 7JN. *Master*, B. J. Hooper, CBE

CARPENTERS (*26*). *Hall*, 1 Throgmorton Avenue, London EC2N 2JJ. *Livery*, 175. *Clerk*, Maj.-Gen. P. T. Stevenson, OBE. *Master*, V. G. Morton-Smith

CHARTERED ACCOUNTANTS (*86*). *Livery*, 345. *Clerk*, C. Bygrave, The Rustlings, Valley Close, Studham, Dunstable LU6 2QN. *Master*, W. K. Gardener

CHARTERED ARCHITECTS (*98*). *Livery*, 104. *Clerk*, J. Griffiths, 28 Palace Road, East Molesey, Surrey KT8 9DL. *Master*, J. H. Penton, MBE

CHARTERED SECRETARIES AND ADMINISTRATORS (*87*). *Livery*, 210. *Clerk*, Maj. I. Stewart, Saddlers' Hall, 3rd Floor, 40 Gutter Lane, London EC2V 6BR. *Master*, Gp Capt. J. Hurn

CHARTERED SURVEYORS (*85*). *Livery*, 350. *Clerk*, Mrs A. L. Jackson, 16 St Mary-at-Hill, London EC3R 8EE. *Master*, S. Hibberdine

CLOCKMAKERS (*61*). *Livery*, 220. *Clerk*, Gp Capt. P. H. Gibson, MBE, Room 66-67 Albert Buildings, 49 Queen Victoria Street, London EC4N 4SE. *Master*, Dr C. R. Lattimore

COACHMAKERS AND COACH-HARNESS MAKERS (*72*). *Livery*, 421. *Clerk*, Gp Capt. G. Bunn, CBE, 8 Chandler's Court, Burwell, Cambridge CB5 0AZ. *Master*, Adm. Sir Derek Reffell, KCB

CONSTRUCTORS (*99*). *Livery*, 118. *Clerk*, L. L. Brace, 181 Fentiman Road, London SW8 1JY. *Master*, P. Heath

COOKS (*35*). *Livery*, 75. *Clerk*, M. C. Thatcher, 55 Great Peter Street, London SW1P 3LR. *Master*, D. Hodgson

COOPERS (*36*). *Hall*, 13 Devonshire Square, London EC2M 4TH. *Livery*, 260. *Clerk*, J. A. Newton. *Master*, J. R. Lawes

CORDWAINERS (*27*). *Livery*, 153. *Clerk*, Lt.-Col. J. R. Blundell, RM, Eldon Chambers, 30 Fleet Street, London EC4Y 1AA. *Master*, J. G. Church, CBE

CURRIERS (*29*). *Livery*, 96. *Clerk*, Gp Capt. F. J. Hamilton, Kestrel Cottage, East Knoyle, Salisbury SP3 6AD. *Master*, D. H. Pertwee

CUTLERS (*18*). *Hall*, Warwick Lane, London EC4M 7BR. *Livery*, 100. *Clerk*, K. S. G. Hinde, OBE, TD. *Master*, P. Watts

DISTILLERS (*69*). *Livery*, 260. *Clerk*, C. V. Hughes, 71 Lincoln's Inn Fields, London WC2A 3JF. *Master*, I. Coombs

DYERS (*13*). *Hall*, 10 Dowgate Hill, London EC4R 2ST. *Livery*, 120. *Clerk*, J. R. Chambers. *Prime Warden*, H. D. M. Morley-Fletcher, FSA

ENGINEERS (*94*). *Livery*, 282. *Clerk*, Cdr. B. D. Gibson, Kiln Bank, Bodle Street Green, Hailsham, E. Sussex BN27 4UA. *Master*, Dr D. S. Mitchell, CBE

ENVIRONMENTAL CLEANERS (*97*). *Livery*, 245. *Clerk*, J. C. M. Chapman, Woodside Cottage, 41 New Road, Bengeo, Hertford SG14 3JL. *Master*, B. Cole

FAN MAKERS (*76*). *Livery*, 202. *Clerk*, Lt.-Col. I. R. P. Green, 2 Bolts Hill, Castle Camps, Cambs CB1 6TL. *Master*, N. G. Crispin

FARMERS (*80*). *Hall*, 3 Cloth Street, London EC1A 7LD. *Livery*, 300. *Clerk*, Miss M. L. Winter. *Master*, C. Pertwee

FARRIERS (*55*). *Livery*, 358. *Clerk*, Mrs C. C. Clifford, 19 Queen Street, Chipperfield, Kings Langley, Herts WD4 9BT. *Master*, T. F. M. Head

FELTMAKERS (*63*). *Livery*, 170. *Clerk*, Lt.-Col. C. J. Holroyd, Providence Cottage, Chute Cadley, Andover, Hants SP11 9EB. *Master*, P. A. Grant

FLETCHERS (*39*). *Hall*, 3 Cloth Street, Long Lane, London EC1A 7LD. *Livery*, 110. *Clerk*, J. R. Owen-Ward. *Master*, R. H. Upton

FOUNDERS (*33*). *Hall*, 1 Cloth Fair, London EC1A 7HT. *Livery*, 170. *Clerk*, A. J. Gillett. *Master*, R. L. Savory

FRAMEWORK KNITTERS (*64*). *Livery*, 211. *Clerk*, H. W. H. Ellis, Whitegarth Chambers, 37 The Uplands, Loughton, Essex IG10 1NQ. *Master*, D. J. Goodenday

FRUITERERS (*45*). *Livery*, 260. *Clerk*, Lt.-Col. L. G. French, Chapelstones, 84 High Street, Codford St Mary, Warminster, Wilts BA12 0ND. *Master*, A. E. Redsell

FUELLERS (*95*). *Livery*, 110. *Clerk*, S. J. Lee, Fords, 134 Ockford Road, Godalming, Surrey GU7 1RG. *Master*, D. R. T. Waring

FURNITURE MAKERS (*83*). *Livery*, 292. *Clerk*, Mrs J. A. Wright, 9 Little Trinity Lane, London EC4V 2AD. *Master*, C. T. A. Hammond

GARDENERS (*66*). *Livery*, 249. *Clerk*, Col. N. G. S. Gray, 25 Luke Street, London EC2A 4AR. *Master*, R. L. Payton

GIRDLERS (*23*). *Hall*, Basinghall Avenue, London EC2V 5DD. *Livery*, 80. *Clerk*, Lt.-Col. R. Sullivan. *Master*, A. R. Westall

GLASS-SELLERS (*71*). *Livery*, 165. *Hon. Clerk*, B. J. Rawles, 43 Aragon Avenue, Thames Ditton, Surrey KT7 0PY. *Master*, C. N. K. Tizard

GLAZIERS AND PAINTERS OF GLASS (*53*). *Hall*, 9 Montague Close, London SE1. *Livery*, 265. *Clerk*, P. R. Batchelor. *Master*, G. D. Cracknell

GLOVERS (*62*). *Livery*, 275. *Clerk*, Mrs M. Hood, 71 Ifield Road, London SW10 9AU. *Master*, M. O. Penney

GOLD AND SILVER WYRE DRAWERS (*74*). *Livery*, 307. *Clerk*, J. R. Williams, 50 Cheyne Avenue, London E18 2DR. *Master*, G. X. Constantinidi

GUNMAKERS (*73*). *Livery*, 265. *Clerk*, J. M. Riches, The Proof House, 48–50 Commercial Road, London E1 1LP. *Master*, Col. D. C. Munn

HORNERS (*54*). *Livery*, 243. *Clerk*, A. R. Layard, c/o EMAP Fashion Ltd, Angel House, 338 Goswell Road, London EC1V 7QP. *Master*, J. J. Cartwright

INFORMATION TECHNOLOGISTS (*100*). *Livery*, 256. *Clerk*, Mrs G. Davies, 30 Aylesbury Street, London EC1R 0ER. *Master*, Mrs P. Drakes

INNHOLDERS (*32*). *Hall*, 30 College Street, London EC4R 2RH. *Livery*, 129. *Clerk*, J. R. Edwardes Jones. *Master*, A. C. Lorkin

INSURERS (*92*). *Hall*, 20 Aldermanbury, London EC2V 7HY. *Livery*, 385. *Clerk*, L. J. Walters. *Master*, P. H. Purchon

JOINERS AND CEILERS (*41*). *Livery*, 125. *Clerk*, Mrs A. L. Jackson, 75 Meadway Drive, Horsell, Woking, Surrey GU21 4TF. *Master*, T. F. K. Boucher

LAUNDERERS (*89*). *Hall*, 9 Montague Close, London SE1 9DD. *Livery*, 230. *Clerk*, Mrs J. Polek. *Master*, M. Bennett

LEATHERSELLERS (*15*). *Hall*, 15 St Helen's Place, London EC3A 6DQ. *Livery*, 150. *Clerk*, Capt. J. G. F. Cooke, OBE, RN. *Master*, G. L. Dove

LIGHTMONGERS (*96*). *Livery*, 155. *Clerk*, D. B. Wheatley, Crown Wharf, 11A Coldharbour, Blackwall Reach, London EI4 9NS. *Master*, J. S. Webb

LORINERS (*57*). *Livery*, 353. *Clerk*, G. B. Forbes, 8 Portland Square, London W1 9QR. *Master*, E. I. Walker-Arnott

MAKERS OF PLAYING CARDS (*75*). *Livery*, 149. *Clerk*, M. J. Smyth, 6 The Priory, Godstone, Surrey RH9 8NL. *Master*, A. H. Wilcox

MARKETORS (*90*). *Livery*, 231. *Clerk*, Mrs G. Duffy, 13 Hall Gardens, Colney Heath, St Albans, Herts AL4 0QF. *Master*, J. Petersen

MASONS (*30*). *Livery*, 125. *Clerk*, T. F. Ackland, 22 Cannon Hill, London N14 6LS. *Master*, N. R. Barnes

MASTER MARINERS, HONOURABLE COMPANY OF (*78*). *Hall*, HQS [Wellington], Temple Stairs, Victoria Embankment, London WC2R 2PN. *Admiral*, HRH The Prince Philip, Duke of Edinburgh, KG, KT, OM, GBE, PC. *Clerk*, J. A. V. Maddock. *Master*, Capt. A. D. Munro

MUSICIANS (*50*). *Livery*, 357. *Clerk*, S. F. N. Waley, 75 Watling Street, London EC4M 9BJ. *Master*, Prof. M. Troup

NEEDLEMAKERS (*65*). *Livery*, 240. *Clerk*, M. G. Cook, 5 Staple Inn, London WC1V 7QH. *Master*, D. A. Culling

PAINTER-STAINERS (*28*). *Hall*, 9 Little Trinity Lane, London EC4V 2AD. *Livery*, 316. *Clerk*, Col. W. J. Chesshyre. *Master*, R. C. Houghton

PATTENMAKERS (*70*). *Livery*, 180. *Clerk*, C. L. K. Ledger, 17 Orchard Close, The Rutts, Bushey Heath, Herts WD2 ILW. *Master*, R. Paice

PAVIORS (*56*). *Livery*, 235. *Clerk*, J. L. White, 3 Ridgemount Gardens, Enfield, Middx EN2 8QL. *Master*, J. H. Lelliott

PEWTERERS (*16*). *Hall*, Oat Lane, London EC2V 7DE. *Livery*, 118. *Clerk*, Cdr. A. St J. Steiner, OBE. *Master*, M. J. W. Piercy

PLAISTERERS (*46*). *Hall*, 1 London Wall, London EC2Y 5JU. *Livery*, 207. *Clerk*, R. Vickers. *Master*, E. Pilgrim

PLUMBERS (*31*). *Livery*, 350. *Clerk*, Lt.-Col. R. J. A. Paterson-Fox, 49 Queen Victoria Street, London EC4N 4SA. *Master*, P. Brunner

POULTERS (*34*). *Livery*, 180. *Clerk*, A. W. Scott, 23 Orchard Drive, Chorleywood, Herts WD3 5QN. *Master*, R. J. C. Gilpin

SADDLERS (*25*). *Hall*, 40 Gutter Lane, London EC2V 6BR. *Livery*, 72. *Clerk*, Gp Capt. W. S. Brereton Martin, CBE. *Master*, D. S. Snowden

SCIENTIFIC INSTRUMENT MAKERS (*84*). *Hall*, 9 Montague Close, London SE1 9DD. *Livery*, 235. *Clerk*, F. G. Everard. *Master*, B. G. Atherton

SCRIVENERS (*44*). *Livery*, 228. *Clerk*, G. A. Hill, HQS [Wellington], Temple Stairs, Victoria Embankment, London WC2R 2PN. *Master*, O. J. R. Kinsey

SHIPWRIGHTS (*59*). *Livery*, 427. *Permanent Master*, HRH The Prince Philip, Duke of Edinburgh, KG, KT, OM, GBE, PC. *Clerk*, Capt. R. F. Channon, RN, Ironmongers' Hall, Barbican, London EC2Y 8AA. *Prime Warden*, The Earl of Inchcape

SOLICITORS (*79*). *Livery*, 267. *Clerk*, Miss S. M. Robinson, TD, 4 College Hill, London EC2R 2RA. *Master*, R. D. Fox

SPECTACLE MAKERS (*60*). *Livery*, 310. *Clerk*, Lt.-Col. J. A. B. Salmon, OBE, Apothecaries' Hall, Black Friars Lane, London EC4V 6EL. *Master*, F. G. Norville

STATIONERS AND NEWSPAPER MAKERS (*47*). *Hall*, Ave Maria Lane, London EC4M 7DD. *Livery*, 446. *Clerk*, Brig. D. G. Sharp, AFC. *Master*, V. F. Sullivan

TALLOW CHANDLERS (*21*). *Hall*, 4 Dowgate Hill, London EC4R 2SH. *Livery*, 180. *Clerk*, Brig. W. K. L. Prosser, CBE, MC. *Master*, R. A. B. Nicolle

TIN PLATE WORKERS (ALIAS WIRE WORKERS) (*67*). *Livery*, 180. *Clerk*, M. Henderson-Begg, Bartholomew House, 66 Westbury Road, New Malden, Surrey KT3 5AS. *Master*, W. A. Warbey

TOBACCO PIPE MAKERS AND TOBACCO BLENDERS (*82*). *Livery*, 161. *Clerk*, N. J. Hallings-Pott, Hackhurst Farm, Lower Dicker, Hailsham, E. Sussex BN27 4BP. *Master*, S. G. Orlik

TURNERS (*51*). *Livery*, 190. *Clerk*, Lt.-Col. J. A. B. Salmon, OBE, c/o Apothecaries' Hall, Black Friars Lane, London EC4V 6EL. *Master*, C. P. J. Field

TYLERS AND BRICKLAYERS (*37*). *Livery*, 123. *Clerk*, J. A. Norris, 28 Palace Road, East Molesey, Surrey KT8 9DL. *Master*, D. R. Munnery

UPHOLDERS (*49*). *Livery*, 225. *Clerk*, J. P. Cody, c/o KES Ltd, 147 Portland Road, London SE25 4UX. *Master*, R. A. Wood

WAX CHANDLERS (*20*). *Hall*, Gresham Street, London EC2V 7AD. *Livery*, 110. *Clerk*, Cdr J. Stevens. *Master*, Lt.-Cdr N. Bailey

WEAVERS (*42*). *Livery*, 127. *Clerk*, Mrs F. Newcombe, Saddlers' House, Gutter Lane, London EC2V 6BR. *Upper Bailiff*, The Hon. G. W. M. Chubb

WHEELWRIGHTS (*68*). *Livery*, 250. *Clerk*, P. J. C. Crouch, 11 Bridge Road, East Molesey, Surrey KT8 9EU. *Master*, E. C. Wakefield

WOOLMEN (*43*). *Livery*, 130. *Clerk*, F. Allen, Hollands, Hedsor Road, Bourne End, Bucks SL8 5EE. *Master*, P. Rippon

FIREFIGHTERS (*No livery*). *Freemen*, 127. *Clerk*, G. P. Ellis, 20 Aldermanbury, London EC2V 7GF. *Master*, K. Knight

PARISH CLERKS (*No livery*). *Members*, 92. *Clerk*, B. J. N. Coombes, 1 Dean Trench Street, London SW1P 3HB. *Master*, J. D. Hebblethwaite

WATER CONSERVATORS (*No livery*). *Hall*, 16 St Mary-at-Hill, London EC2R 8EE. *Freemen*, 183. *Hon. Clerk*, H. B. Berridge, MBE. *Master*, C. Bland

WATERMEN AND LIGHTERMEN (*No livery*). *Hall*, 16 St Mary-at-Hill, London EC3R 8EE. *Craft Owning Freemen*, 360. *Clerk*, C. Middlemiss. *Master*, C. Livett

WORLD TRADERS (*No livery*). *Freemen*, 130. *Clerk*, N. R. Pullman, 36 Ladbroke Grove, London W11 2PA. *Master*, P. Wildblood, OBE

LONDON BOROUGH COUNCILS

Council	Municipal offices	Population 1996	Band D charge 1998	Chief Executive (*Managing Director)	Mayor (a) Lord Mayor 1998–9
Barking and Dagenham	°Dagenham, RM10 7BN	153,700	697.50	W. C. Smith	I. S. Jamu
Barnet	†The Burroughs, Hendon, NW4 4BG	319,400	728.07	M. Caller	Ms U. Chopra
Bexley	‡Bexleyheath, Kent DA6 7LB	219,300	695.20	C. Duffield	C. Ball
Brent	†Forty Lane, Wembley, HA9 9EZ	247,500	588.93	G. Daniel (acting)	Ms B. Joseph
Bromley	°Bromley, BR1 3UH	295,600	609.57	M. Blanch	P. Ayers
§Camden	†Judd Street, WC1H 9JE	189,100	765.38	S. Bundred	R. Hall
§CITY OF WESTMINSTER	City Hall, Victoria Street, SW1E 6QP	204,100	325.00	W. Roots	(a) D. Harvey
Croydon	Taberner House, Park Lane, Croydon, CR9 3JS	333,800	691.93	D. Wechsler	P. Ryan
Ealing	†Uxbridge Road, W5 2HL	297,000	643.00	Ms G. Guy	U. Chander
Enfield	°Enfield, EN1 3XA	262,600	680.00	D. Plank	S. Carter
§Greenwich	†Wellington Street, SE18 6PW	212,100	883.35	D. Brooks (acting)	D. Austen
§Hackney	†Mare Street, E8 1EA	193,800	789.60	A. Elliston	J. Lobenstein, MBE
§Hammersmith and Fulham	†King Street, W6 9JU	156,700	790.00	*N. Newton	A. Slaughter
Haringey	°Wood Green, N22 4LE	216,100	856.00	G. Singh	Ms S. Peacock
Harrow	°Harrow, HA1 2UJ	210,700	723.51	A. Redmond	C. Harrison
Havering	†Romford, RM1 3BD	230,900	724.00	H. W. Tinworth	H. Webb
Hillingdon	°Uxbridge, UB8 1UW	247,700	703.84	D. Leatham	A. Langley
Hounslow	°Lampton Road, Hounslow, TW3 4DN	205,800	730.05	D. Myers	R. Bath
§Islington	†Upper Street, N1 2UD	176,000	912.00	Ms L. Fullick	Ms M. Hillier
§Kensington and Chelsea (RB)	†Hornton Street, W8 7NX	159,000	534.63	A. Taylor	Dr J. Munday
Kingston upon Thames (RB)	Guildhall, Kingston upon Thames, KT1 1EU	141,800	623.65	B. Quoroll	D. Cunningham
§Lambeth	†Brixton Hill, SW2 1RW	264,700	647.00	Ms H. Rabbatts	Ms D. Hayes-Mojon
§Lewisham	†Catford, SE6 4RU	241,500	683.45	Dr B. Quirk	M. Nottingham
Merton	°London Road, Morden, SM4 5DX	182,300	747.41	R. Paine (acting)	Ms L. Kirby
§Newham	†East Ham, E6 2RP	228,900	679.50	Dr W. Thomson	A. K. Sheikh
Redbridge	†Ilford, IG1 1DD	230,600	676.00	M. Frater	J. Lovell
Richmond upon Thames	°Richmond Road, Twickenham, TW1 3AA	179,900	745.00	R. L. Harbord	Ms M. Weber
§Southwark	†Peckham Road, SE5 8UB	229,900	786.58	R. Coomber	Ms J. Heatley
Sutton	‡St Nicholas Way, Sutton, SM1 1EA	175,500	701.73	Mrs P. Hughes	Ms J. Lowne
§Tower Hamlets	107A Commercial Street, E1 6BG	176,600	658.78	Ms S. Pierce	A. Asad
Waltham Forest	†Forest Road, Walthamstow, E17 4JF	220,200	813.66	A. Tobias	T. Bhogal
§Wandsworth	†Wandsworth, SW18 2PU	266,200	318.62	G. K. Jones	Mrs E. Howlett

§   Inner London Borough
RB Royal Borough
°   Civic Centre
†   Town Hall
‡   Civic Offices
Source of population statistics: ONS Monitor PP1 97/1, 28 August 1997
For explanation of council tax, *see* pages 523–4

Wales

The Principality of Wales (Cymru) occupies the extreme west of the central southern portion of the island of Great Britain, with a total area of 8,015 sq. miles (20,758 sq. km): land 7,965 sq. miles (20,628 sq. km); inland water 50 sq. miles (130 sq. km). It is bounded on the north by the Irish Sea, on the south by the Bristol Channel, on the east by the English counties of Cheshire, Shropshire, Worcestershire, and Gloucestershire, and on the west by St George's Channel.

Across the Menai Straits is the island of Anglesey (Ynys Môn) (276 sq. miles), communication with which is facilitated by the Menai Suspension Bridge (1,000 ft long) built by Telford in 1826, and by the tubular railway bridge (1,100 ft long) built by Stephenson in 1850. Holyhead harbour, on Holy Isle (north-west of Anglesey), provides accommodation for ferry services to Dublin (70 miles).

POPULATION

The population at the 1991 census was 2,811,865 (males 1,356,886; females 1,454,979). The average density of population in 1991 was 1.36 persons per hectare.

RELIEF

Wales is a country of extensive tracts of high plateau and shorter stretches of mountain ranges deeply dissected by river valleys. Lower-lying ground is largely confined to the coastal belt and the lower parts of the valleys. The highest mountains are those of Snowdonia in the north-west (Snowdon, 3,559 ft), Berwyn (Aran Fawddwy, 2,971 ft), Cader Idris (Pen y Gadair, 2,928 ft), Dyfed (Plynlimon, 2,467 ft), and the Black Mountain, Brecon Beacons and Black Forest ranges in the south-east (Carmarthen Van, 2,630 ft, Pen y Fan, 2,906 ft, Waun Fâch, 2,660 ft).

HYDROGRAPHY

The principal river rising in Wales is the Severn (*see also* page 534), which flows from the slopes of Plynlimon to the English border. The Wye (130 miles) also rises in the slopes of Plynlimon. The Usk (56 miles) flows into the Bristol Channel, through Gwent. The Dee (70 miles) rises in Bala Lake and flows through the Vale of Llangollen, where an aqueduct (built by Telford in 1805) carries the Pontcysyllte branch of the Shropshire Union Canal across the valley. The estuary of the Dee is the navigable portion, 14 miles in length and about five miles in breadth, and the tide rushes in with dangerous speed over the 'Sands of Dee'. The Towy (68 miles), Teifi (50 miles), Taff (40 miles), Dovey (30 miles), Taf (25 miles) and Conway (24 miles), the last named broad and navigable, are wholly Welsh rivers.

The largest natural lake is Bala (Llyn Tegid) in Gwynedd, nearly four miles long and about one mile wide. Lake Vyrnwy is an artificial reservoir, about the size of Bala, and forms the water supply of Liverpool; Birmingham is supplied from reservoirs in the Elan and Claerwen valleys.

WELSH LANGUAGE

According to the 1991 census results, the percentage of persons of three years and over able to speak Welsh was:

Clwyd	18.2	Powys	20.2
Dyfed	43.7	S. Glamorgan	6.5
Gwent	2.4	W. Glamorgan	15.0
Gwynedd	61.0		
Mid Glamorgan	8.5	Wales	18.7

The 1991 figure represents a slight decline from 18.9 per cent in 1981 (1971, 20.8 per cent; 1961, 26 per cent).

FLAG

The flag of Wales, the Red Dragon (Y Ddraig Goch), is a red dragon on a field divided white over green (per fess argent and vert a dragon passant gules). The flag was augmented in 1953 by a royal badge on a shield encircled with a riband bearing the words *Ddraig Goch Ddyry Cychwyn* and imperially crowned, but this augmented flag is rarely used.

EARLY HISTORY

The earliest inhabitants of whom there is any record appear to have been subdued or exterminated by the Goidels (a people of Celtic race) in the Bronze Age. A further invasion of Celtic Brythons and Belgae followed in the ensuing Iron Age. The Roman conquest of southern Britain and Wales was for some time successfully opposed by Caratacus (Caractacus or Caradog), chieftain of the Catuvellauni and son of Cunobelinus (Cymbeline). South-east Wales was subjugated and the legionary fortress at Caerleon-on-Usk established by about AD 75–77; the conquest of Wales was completed by Agricola about AD 78. Communications were opened up by the construction of military roads from Chester to Caerleon-on-Usk and Caerwent, and from Chester to Conwy (and thence to Carmarthen and Neath). Christianity was introduced during the Roman occupation, in the fourth century.

ANGLO-SAXON ATTACKS

The Anglo-Saxon invaders of southern Britain drove the Celts into the mountain stronghold of Wales, and into Strathclyde (Cumberland and south-west Scotland) and Cornwall, giving them the name of *Waelisc* (Welsh), meaning 'foreign'. The West Saxons' victory of Deorham (AD 577) isolated Wales from Cornwall and the battle of Chester (AD 613) cut off communication with Strathclyde and northern Britain. In the eighth century the boundaries of the Welsh were further restricted by the annexations of Offa, King of Mercia, and counter-attacks were largely prevented by the construction of an artificial boundary from the Dee to the Wye (Offa's Dyke).

In the ninth century Rhodri Mawr (844–878) united the country and successfully resisted further incursions of the Saxons by land and raids of Norse and Danish pirates by sea, but at his death his three provinces of Gwynedd (north), Powys (mid) and Deheubarth (south) were divided among his three sons, Anarawd, Mervyn and Cadell. Cadell's son Hywel Dda ruled a large part of Wales and codified its laws but the provinces were not united again until the rule of Llewelyn ap Seisyllt (husband of the heiress of Gwynedd) from 1018 to 1023.

THE NORMAN CONQUEST

After the Norman conquest of England, William I created palatine counties along the Welsh frontier, and the Norman barons began to make encroachments into Welsh territory. The Welsh princes recovered many of their losses during the civil wars of Stephen's reign and in the early 13th century Owen Gruffydd, prince of Gwynedd, was the dominant figure in Wales. Under Llywelyn ap Iorwerth (1194–1240) the Welsh united in powerful resistance to English incursions and Llywelyn's privileges and *de facto* independence were recognized in Magna Carta. His grandson, Llywelyn ap Gruffydd, was the last native prince; he was killed in 1282 during hostilities between the

Welsh and English, allowing Edward I of England to establish his authority over the country. On 7 February 1301, Edward of Caernarvon, son of Edward I, was created Prince of Wales, a title which has subsequently been borne by the eldest son of the sovereign.

Strong Welsh national feeling continued, expressed in the early 15th century in the rising led by Owain Glyndŵr, but the situation was altered by the accession to the English throne in 1485 of Henry VII of the Welsh House of Tudor. Wales was politically assimilated to England under the Act of Union of 1535, which extended English laws to the Principality and gave it parliamentary representation for the first time.

EISTEDDFOD

The Welsh are a distinct nation, with a language and literature of their own, and the national bardic festival (Eisteddfod), instituted by Prince Rhys ap Griffith in 1176, is still held annually (for date, *see* page 12). These *Eisteddfodau* (sessions) form part of the *Gorsedd* (assembly), which is believed to date from the time of Prydian, a ruling prince in an age many centuries before the Christian era.

PRINCIPAL CITIES

CARDIFF

Cardiff, at the mouth of the Rivers Taff, Rhymney and Ely, is the capital city of Wales and a major administrative, commercial and business centre. It has many industries, including steel, and its flourishing port is within the Cardiff Bay area, subject of a major redevelopment until the year 2000.

The many fine buildings include the City Hall, the National Museum of Wales, University Buildings, Law Courts, Welsh Office, County Hall, Police Headquarters, the Temple of Peace and Health, Llandaff Cathedral, the Welsh National Folk Museum at St Fagans, Cardiff Castle, the New Theatre, the Sherman Theatre and the Welsh College of Music and Drama. More recent buildings include St David's Hall, Cardiff International Arena and World Trade Centre, and the Welsh National Ice Rink. The Millennium Stadium is to be completed for the 1999 rugby World Cup.

SWANSEA

Swansea (*Abertawe*) is a city and a seaport. The Gower peninsula was brought within the city boundary under local government reform in 1974. The trade of the port includes coal, steel products, containerized goods, petroleum products and petrochemicals.

The principal buildings are the Norman Castle (rebuilt *c.*1330), the Royal Institution of South Wales, founded in 1835 (including Library), the University College at Singleton, and the Guildhall, containing the Brangwyn panels. More recent buildings include the Industrial and Maritime Museum, the new Maritime Quarter and Marina and the leisure centre.

Swansea was chartered by the Earl of Warwick, *c.* 1158–84, and further charters were granted by King John, Henry III, Edward II, Edward III and James II, Cromwell (two) and the Marcher Lord William de Breos.

CONSTITUTIONAL DEVELOPMENTS

On 22 July 1997, the Government announced plans to establish a Welsh assembly. The assembly will take over the annual budget of the Welsh Office and pass secondary legislation but will have no tax-raising powers of its own. In a referendum on 18 September 1997 about 50 per cent of the electorate voted, of whom 50.3 per cent voted in favour of the assembly. The assembly will have 60 members, of whom 40 will be representatives of a constituency and the remaining 20 elected by proportional representation on the basis of party political lists. A leader will be elected from the majority party to chair an executive committee of ten members. The assembly will be elected for four years, with the first elections taking place in May 1999.

LOCAL COUNCILS

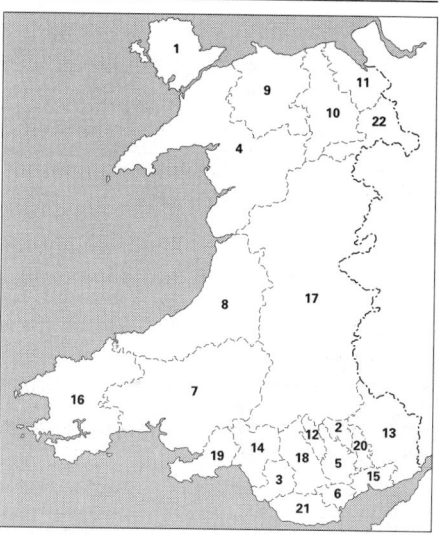

Key	County
1	Anglesey
2	Blaenau Gwent
3	Bridgend
4	Gwynedd
5	Caerphilly
6	Cardiff
7	Carmarthenshire
8	Ceredigion
9	Conwy
10	Denbighshire
11	Flintshire
12	Merthyr Tydfil
13	Monmouthshire
14	Neath and Port Talbot
15	Newport
16	Pembrokeshire
17	Powys
18	Rhondda, Cynon, Taff
19	Swansea
20	Torfaen
21	The Vale of Glamorgan
22	Wrexham

LORD-LIEUTENANTS AND HIGH SHERIFFS

County	Lord-Lieutenant	High Sheriff, 1997–8
Clwyd	Sir William Gladstone, Bt.	Col. H. M. E. Cadogan
Dyfed	Sir David Mansel Lewis, KCVO	J. S. Allen-Mirehouse
Gwent	Sir Richard Hanbury Tenison, KCVO	R. L. Dean
Gwynedd	R. E. Meuric Rees, CBE	Prof. E. Sunderland
Mid Glamorgan	M. A. McLaggan	A. R. Lewis
Powys	The Hon. Mrs S. Legge-Bourke, LVO	J. T. K. Trevor
South Glamorgan	Capt. N. Lloyd-Edwards	D. M. Jones
West Glamorgan	R. C. Hastie, CBE	R. H. Lloyd-Griffiths

LOCAL COUNCILS

SMALL CAPITALS denote CITY status
§ Denotes Borough status

Council	Administrative headquarters	Population 1996	Band D charge 1998	Chief Executive	Chairman 1998–9 (a) Mayor (b) Lord Mayor
Anglesey	Llangefni	67,100	477.32	L. Gibson	H. M. Morgan MBE
§Blaenau Gwent	Ebbw Vale	73,000	567.81	R. Leadbeter, OBE	(a) S. Bartlett
§Bridgend	Bridgend	130,100	601.69	I. K. Lewis	(a) H. C. Davies
§Caerphilly	Hengoed	169,100	601.00	M. Davies	(a) B. Rogers
CARDIFF	Cardiff	315,000	544.58	B. Davies	(b) Ms M. Drake
Carmarthenshire	Carmarthen	169,100	613.33	B. Roynon	J. A. Harries
Ceredigion	Aberaeron	69,500	622.66	O. Watkin	H. Lewis
§Conwy	Conwy	110,600	459.50	C. D. Barker	D. Parry-Jones
Denbighshire	Ruthin	92,200	582.03	H. V. Thomas	P. Williams
Flintshire	Mold	144,900	562.75	P. McGreevy	A. Jones
Gwynedd	Caernarfon	117,800	568.14	G. R. Jones	J. E. James
§Merthyr Tydfil	Merthyr Tydfil	58,100	638.31	G. Meredith	(a) E. C. Galsworthy
Monmouthshire	Cwmbran	86,800	451.88	Ms J. Redfearn	A. R. Carrington
§Neath Port Talbot	Port Talbot	139,500	687.00	K. R. Sawyers	(a) M. Jones
§Newport	Newport	136,800	461.78	R. D. Blair	(a) K. Powell
Pembrokeshire	Haverfordwest	113,600	490.09	B. Parry-Jones	A. Luke
Powys	Llandrindod Wells	124,400	500.89	Ms J. Tonge	M. W. Shaw
§Rhondda, Cynon, Taff	Tonypandy	240,100	600.00	G. R. Thomas	(a) J. David
SWANSEA	Swansea	230,200	542.22	Ms V. Sugar	(b) D. J. E. Jones
§Torfaen	Pontypool	90,500	532.34	Dr C. Grace	(a) B. Smith
§Vale of Glamorgan	Barry	119,400	485.07	D. Foster	J. Batey
§Wrexham	Wrexham	123,300	574.70	D. Griffin	(a) B. Williams

For explanation of council tax, see pages 523–4
Source of population figures: ONS Monitor PP1 97/1, 28 August 1997

Scotland

The Kingdom of Scotland occupies the northern portion of the main island of Great Britain and includes the Inner and Outer Hebrides, and the Orkney, Shetland, and many other islands. It lies between 60° 51′ 30″ and 54° 38′ N. latitude and between 1° 45′ 32″ and 6° 14′ W. longitude, with England to the south, the Atlantic Ocean on the north and west, and the North Sea on the east.

The greatest length of the mainland (Cape Wrath to the Mull of Galloway) is 274 miles, and the greatest breadth (Buchan Ness to Applecross) is 154 miles. The customary measurement of the island of Great Britain is from the site of John o' Groats house, near Duncansby Head, Caithness, to Land's End, Cornwall, a total distance of 603 miles in a straight line and approximately 900 miles by road.

The total area of Scotland is 30,420 sq. miles (78,789 sq. km); land 29,767 sq. miles (77,097 sq. km), inland water 653 sq. miles (1,692 sq. km).

POPULATION

The population at the 1991 census was 4,998,567 (males 2,391,961; females 2,606,606). The average density of the population in 1991 was 0.65 persons per hectare.

RELIEF

There are three natural orographic divisions of Scotland. The southern uplands have their highest points in Merrick (2,766 ft), Rhinns of Kells (2,669 ft), and Cairnsmuir of Carsphairn (2,614 ft), in the west; and the Tweedsmuir Hills in the east (Hartfell 2,651 ft, Dollar Law 2,682 ft, Broad Law 2,756 ft).

The central lowlands, formed by the valleys of the Clyde, Forth and Tay, divide the southern uplands from the northern Highlands, which extend almost from the extreme north of the mainland to the central lowlands, and are divided into a northern and a southern system by the Great Glen.

The Grampian Mountains, which entirely cover the southern Highland area, include in the west Ben Nevis (4,406 ft), the highest point in the British Isles, and in the east the Cairngorm Mountains (Cairn Gorm 4,084 ft, Braeriach 4,248 ft, Ben Macdui 4,296 ft). The north-western Highland area contains the mountains of Wester and Easter Ross (Carn Eige 3,880 ft, Sgurr na Lapaich 3,775 ft).

Created, like the central lowlands, by a major geological fault, the Great Glen (60 miles long) runs between Inverness and Fort William, and contains Loch Ness, Loch Oich and Loch Lochy. These are linked to each other and to the north-east and south-west coasts of Scotland by the Caledonian Canal, providing a navigable passage between the Moray Firth and the Inner Hebrides.

HYDROGRAPHY

The western coast is fragmented by peninsulas and islands, and indented by fjords (sea-lochs), the longest of which is Loch Fyne (42 miles long) in Argyll. Although the east coast tends to be less fractured and lower, there are several great drowned inlets (firths), e.g. Firth of Forth, Firth of Tay, Moray Firth, as well as the Firth of Clyde in the west.

The lochs are the principal hydrographic feature. The largest in Scotland and in Britain is Loch Lomond (27 sq. miles), in the Grampian valleys; the longest and deepest is Loch Ness (24 miles long and 800 feet deep), in the Great Glen; and Loch Shin (20 miles long) and Loch Maree in the Highlands.

The longest river is the Tay (117 miles), noted for its salmon. It flows into the North Sea, with Dundee on the estuary, which is spanned by the Tay Bridge (10,289 ft) opened in 1887 and the Tay Road Bridge (7,365 ft) opened

in 1966. Other noted salmon rivers are the Dee (90 miles) which flows into the North Sea at Aberdeen, and the Spey (110 miles), the swiftest flowing river in the British Isles, which flows into Moray Firth. The Tweed, which gave its name to the woollen cloth produced along its banks, marks in the lower stretches of its 96-mile course the border between Scotland and England.

The most important river commercially is the Clyde (106 miles), formed by the junction of the Daer and Portrail water, which flows through the city of Glasgow to the Firth of Clyde. During its course it passes over the picturesque Falls of Clyde, Bonnington Linn (30 ft), Corra Linn (84 ft), Dundaff Linn (10 ft) and Stonebyres Linn (80 ft), above and below Lanark. The Forth (66 miles), upon which stands Edinburgh, the capital, is spanned by the Forth (Railway) Bridge (1890), which is 5,330 feet long, and the Forth (Road) Bridge (1964), which has a total length of 6,156 feet (over water) and a single span of 3,000 feet.

The highest waterfall in Scotland, and the British Isles, is Eas a'Chùal Aluinn with a total height of 658 feet (200 m), which falls from Glas Bheinn in Sutherland. The Falls of Glomach, on a head-stream of the Elchaig in Wester Ross, have a drop of 370 feet.

GAELIC LANGUAGE

According to the 1991 census, 1.4 per cent of the population of Scotland, mainly in the Highlands and western coastal regions, were able to speak the Scottish form of Gaelic.

FLAG

The flag of Scotland is known as the Saltire. It is a white diagonal cross on a blue field (saltire argent in a field azure) and represents St Andrew, the patron saint of Scotland.

THE SCOTTISH ISLANDS

ORKNEY

The Orkney Islands (total area 375½ sq. miles) lie about six miles north of the mainland, separated from it by the Pentland Firth. Of the 90 islands and islets (holms and skerries) in the group, about one-third are inhabited.

The total population at the 1991 census was 19,612; the 1991 populations of the islands shown here include those of smaller islands forming part of the same civil parish.

Mainland, 15,128	Rousay, 291
Burray, 363	Sanday, 533
Eday, 166	Shapinsay, 322
Flotta and Fara, 126	South Ronaldsay, 943
Graemsay and Hoy, 477	Stronsay, 382
North Ronaldsay, 92	Westray, 704
Papa Westray, 85	

The islands are rich in prehistoric and Scandinavian remains, the most notable being the Stone Age village of Skara Brae, the burial chamber of Maeshowe, the many brochs (towers) and the 12th-century St Magnus Cathedral. Scapa Flow, between the Mainland and Hoy, was the war station of the British Grand Fleet from 1914 to 1919 and the scene of the scuttling of the surrendered German High Seas Fleet (21 June 1919).

Most of the islands are low-lying and fertile, and farming (principally beef cattle) is the main industry. Flotta, to the south of Scapa Flow, is the site of the oil terminal for the Piper, Claymore and Tartan fields in the North Sea.

The capital is Kirkwall (population 6,881) on Mainland.

SHETLAND

The Shetland Islands have a total area of 551 sq. miles and a population at the 1991 census of 22,522. They lie about 50 miles north of the Orkneys, with Fair Isle about half-way between the two groups. Out Stack, off Muckle Flugga, one mile north of Unst, is the most northerly part of the British Isles (60° 51′ 30″ N. lat.).

There are over 100 islands, of which 16 are inhabited. Populations at the 1991 census were:

Mainland, 17,596	Muckle Roe, 115
Bressay, 352	Trondra, 117
East Burra, 72	Unst, 1,055
Fair Isle, 67	West Burra, 857
Fetlar, 90	Whalsay, 1,041
Housay, 85	Yell, 1,075

Shetland's many archaeological sites include Jarlshof, Mousa and Clickhimin, and its long connection with Scandinavia has resulted in a strong Norse influence on its place-names and dialect.

Industries include fishing, knitwear and farming. In addition to the fishing fleet there are fish processing factories, while the traditional handknitting of Fair Isle and Unst is supplemented now with machine-knitted garments. Farming is mainly crofting, with sheep being raised on the moorland and hills of the islands. Latterly the islands have become a centre of the North Sea oil industry, with pipelines from the Brent and Ninian fields running to the terminal at Sullom Voe, the largest of its kind in Europe. Lerwick is the main centre for supply services for offshore oil exploration and development.

The capital is Lerwick (population 7,901) on Mainland.

THE HEBRIDES

Until the late 13th century the Hebrides included other Scottish islands in the Firth of Clyde, the peninsula of Kintyre (Argyll), the Isle of Man, and the (Irish) Isle of Rathlin. The origin of the name is stated to be the Greek *Eboudai*, latinized as *Hebudes* by Pliny, and corrupted to its present form. The Norwegian name *Sudreyjar* (Southern Islands) was latinized as *Sodorenses*, a name that survives in the Anglican bishopric of Sodor and Man.

There are over 500 islands and islets, of which about 100 are inhabited, though mountainous terrain and extensive peat bogs mean that only a fraction of the total area is under cultivation. Stone, Bronze and Iron Age settlement has left many remains, including those at Callanish on Lewis, and Norse colonization influenced language, customs and place-names. Occupations include farming (mostly crofting and stock-raising), fishing and the manufacture of tweeds and other woollens. Tourism is also an important factor in the economy.

The Inner Hebrides lie off the west coast of Scotland and relatively close to the mainland. The largest and best-known is Skye (area 643 sq. miles; pop. 8,868; chief town, Portree), which contains the Cuillin Hills (Sgurr Alasdair 3,257 ft), the Red Hills (Beinn na Caillich 2,403 ft), Bla Bheinn (3,046 ft) and The Storr (2,358 ft). Skye is also famous as the refuge of the Young Pretender in 1746. Other islands in the Highland council area include Raasay (pop. 163), Rum, Eigg and Muck.

Further south the Inner Hebridean islands include Arran (pop. 4,474) containing Goat Fell (2,868 ft); Coll and Tiree (pop. 940); Colonsay and Oronsay (pop. 106); Islay (area 235 sq. miles; pop. 3,538); Jura (area 160 sq. miles; pop. 196) with a range of hills culminating in the Paps of Jura (Beinn-an-Oir, 2,576 ft, and Beinn Chaolais, 2,477 ft); and Mull (area 367 sq. miles; pop. 2,708; chief town Tobermory) containing Ben More (3,171 ft).

The Outer Hebrides, separated from the mainland by the Minch, now form the Western Isles Islands Council

area (area 1,119 sq. miles; population at the 1991 census 29,600). The main islands are Lewis with Harris (area 770 sq. miles, pop. 21,737), whose chief town, Stornoway, is the administrative headquarters; North Uist (pop. 1,404); South Uist (pop. 2,106); Baleshare (55); Benbecula (pop. 1,803) and Barra (pop. 1,244). Other inhabited islands include Bernera (262), Berneray (141), Eriskay (179), Grimsay (215), Scalpay (382) and Vatersay (72).

EARLY HISTORY

There is evidence of human settlement in Scotland dating from the third millennium BC, the earliest settlers being Middle Stone Age hunters and fishermen. Early in the second millennium BC, New Stone Age farmers began to cultivate crops and rear livestock; their settlements were on the west coast and in the north, and included Skara Brae and Maeshowe (Orkney). Settlement by the Early Bronze Age 'Beaker folk', so-called from the shape of their drinking vessels, in eastern Scotland dates from about 1800 BC. Further settlement is believed to have occurred from 700 BC onwards, as tribes were displaced from further south by new incursions from the Continent and the Roman invasions from AD 43.

Julius Agricola, the Roman governor of Britain AD 77–84, extended the Roman conquests in Britain by advancing into Caledonia, culminating in a victory at Mons Graupius, probably in AD 84; he was recalled to Rome shortly afterwards and his forward policy was not pursued. Hadrian's Wall, mostly completed by AD 30, marked the northern frontier of the Roman empire except for the period between about AD 144 and 190 when the frontier moved north to the Forth–Clyde isthmus and a turf wall, the Antonine Wall, was manned.

After the Roman withdrawal from Britain, there were centuries of warfare between the Picts, Scots, Britons, Angles and Vikings. The Picts, believed to be a non-Indo-European race, occupied the area north of the Forth. The Scots, a Gaelic-speaking people of northern Ireland, colonized the area of Argyll and Bute (the kingdom of Dalriada) in the fifth century AD and then expanded eastwards and northwards. The Britons, speaking a Brythonic Celtic language, colonized Scotland from the south from the first century BC; they lost control of south-eastern Scotland (incorporated into the kingdom of Northumbria) to the Angles in the early seventh century but retained Strathclyde (south-western Scotland and Cumbria). Viking raids from the late eighth century were followed by Norse settlement in the western and northern isles, Argyll, Caithness and Sutherland from the mid-ninth century onwards.

UNIFICATION

The union of the areas which now comprise Scotland began in AD 843 when Kenneth mac Alpin, king of the Scots from c.834, became also king of the Picts, joining the two lands to form the kingdom of Alba (comprising Scotland north of a line between the Forth and Clyde rivers). Lothian, the eastern part of the area between the Forth and the Tweed, seems to have been leased to Kenneth II of Alba (reigned 971–995) by Edgar of England c.973/4, and Scottish possession was confirmed by Malcolm II's victory over a Northumbrian army at Carham c.1016. At about this time Malcolm II (reigned 1005–34) placed his grandson Duncan on the throne of the British kingdom of Strathclyde, bringing under Scots rule virtually all of what is now Scotland.

The Norse possessions were incorporated into the kingdom of Scotland from the 12th century onwards. An uprising in the mid-12th century drove the Norse from most of mainland Argyll. The Hebrides were ceded to Scotland by the Treaty of Perth in 1266 after a Norwegian expedition in 1263 failed to maintain Norse authority over the islands. Orkney and Shetland fell to Scotland in 1468–9 as a pledge for the unpaid dowry of Margaret of Denmark, wife of James III, though Danish claims of suzerainty were relinquished only with the marriage of Anne of Denmark to James VI in 1590.

From the 11th century, there were frequent wars between Scotland and England over territory and the extent of England's political influence. The failure of the Scottish royal line with the death of Margaret of Norway in 1290 led to disputes over the throne which were resolved by the adjudication of Edward I of England. He awarded the throne to John Balliol in 1292 but Balliol's refusal to be a puppet king led to war. Balliol surrendered to Edward I in 1296 and Edward attempted to rule Scotland himself. Resistance to Scotland's loss of independence was led by William Wallace, who defeated the English at Stirling Bridge (1297), and Robert Bruce, crowned in 1306, who held most of Scotland by 1311 and routed Edward II's army at Bannockburn (1314). England recognized the independence of Scotland in the Treaty of Northampton in 1328. Subsequent clashes include the disastrous battle of Flodden (1513) in which James IV and many of his nobles fell.

THE UNION

In 1603 James VI of Scotland succeeded Elizabeth I on the throne of England (his mother, Mary Queen of Scots, was the great-granddaughter of Henry VII), his successors reigning as sovereigns of Great Britain. Political union of the two countries did not occur until 1707.

THE JACOBITE REVOLTS

After the abdication (by flight) in 1688 of James VII and II, the crown devolved upon William III (grandson of Charles I) and Mary II (elder daughter of James VII and II). In 1689 Graham of Claverhouse roused the Highlands on behalf of James VII and II, but died after a military success at Killiecrankie.

After the death of Anne (younger daughter of James VII and II), the throne devolved upon George I (great-grandson of James VI and I). In 1715, armed risings on behalf of James Stuart (the Old Pretender, son of James VII and II) led to the indecisive battle of Sheriffmuir, and the Jacobite movement died down until 1745, when Charles Stuart (the Young Pretender) defeated the Royalist troops at Prestonpans and advanced to Derby (1746). From Derby, the adherents of 'James VIII and III' (the title claimed for his father by Charles Stuart) fell back on the defensive and were finally crushed at Culloden (16 April 1746).

PRINCIPAL CITIES

ABERDEEN

Aberdeen, 130 miles north-east of Edinburgh, received its charter as a Royal Burgh in 1179. Scotland's third largest city, Aberdeen is the second largest Scottish fishing port and the main centre for offshore oil exploration and production. It is also an ancient university town and distinguished research centre. Other industries include engineering, food processing, textiles, paper manufacturing and chemicals.

Places of interest include King's College, St Machar's Cathedral, Brig o' Balgownie, Duthie Park and Winter Gardens, Hazlehead Park, the Kirk of St Nicholas, Mercat Cross, Marischal College and Marischal Museum, Provost Skene's House, Art Gallery, Gordon Highlanders

Museum, Satrosphere Hands-On Discovery Centre, and Aberdeen Maritime Museum in Provost Ross's House.

DUNDEE

Dundee, a Royal Burgh, is situated on the north bank of the Tay estuary. The city's port and dock installations are important to the offshore oil industry and the airport also provides servicing facilities. Principal industries include textiles, computers and other electronic industries, lasers, printing, tyre manufacture, food processing, carpets, engineering, clothing manufacture and tourism.

The unique City Churches – three churches under one roof, together with the 15th-century St Mary's Tower – are the most prominent architectural feature. Dundee has two historic ships: the Dundee-built RRS *Discovery* which took Capt. Scott to the Antarctic lies alongside Discovery Quay, and the frigate *Unicorn*, the only British-built wooden warship still afloat, is moored in Victoria Dock. Places of interest include Mills Public Observatory, the Tay road and rail bridges, McManus Galleries, Barrack Street Museum, Claypotts Castle, Broughty Castle and Verdant Works (Textile Heritage Centre).

EDINBURGH

Edinburgh is the capital of and seat of government in Scotland. The city is built on a group of hills and contains in Princes Street one of the most beautiful thoroughfares in the world.

The principal buildings are the Castle, which now houses the Stone of Scone and also includes St Margaret's Chapel, the oldest building in Edinburgh, and near it, the Scottish National War Memorial; the Palace of Holyroodhouse; Parliament House, the present seat of the judicature; three universities (Edinburgh, Heriot-Watt, Napier); St Giles' Cathedral; St Mary's (Scottish Episcopal) Cathedral (Sir George Gilbert Scott); the General Register House (Robert Adam); the National and the Signet Libraries; the National Gallery; the Royal Scottish Academy; the National Portrait Gallery; and the Edinburgh International Conference Centre, opened in 1995.

GLASGOW

Glasgow, a Royal Burgh, is the principal commercial and industrial centre in Scotland. The city occupies the north and south banks of the Clyde, formerly one of the chief commercial estuaries in the world. The principal industries include engineering, electronics, finance, chemicals and printing. The city has also developed recently as a tourism and conference centre.

The chief buildings are the 13th-century Gothic Cathedral, the University (Sir George Gilbert Scott), the City Chambers, the Royal Concert Hall, St Mungo Museum of Religious Life and Art, Pollok House, the School of Art (Mackintosh), Kelvingrove Art Galleries, the Gallery of Modern Art, the Burrell Collection museum and the Mitchell Library. The city is home to the Scottish National Orchestra, Scottish Opera and Scottish Ballet.

CONSTITUTIONAL DEVELOPMENTS

On 24 July 1997, the Government announced plans to establish a Scottish parliament. The parliament will have responsibility for areas such as education, health, law, the environment, economic development and local government, with such areas as foreign and economic policy, defence and security being retained by Westminster. The parliament will also be able to raise or reduce the basic rate of income tax by up to three pence. In a referendum in

Scotland on 11 September 1997 about 62 per cent of the electorate turned out, of whom 74.3 per cent voted in favour of the parliament and 63.5 per cent in favour of its having tax-raising powers.

There will be 129 members in the new parliament, of whom 73 will be elected by majority vote in a constituency and the remaining 56 by proportional representation on the basis of party political lists. Elections will be held every four years, with the first elections taking place in May 1999. A First Minister will be appointed by The Queen to head a Scottish executive comprising ministers and law officers. The parliament is due to begin sitting in 2000, although there is a possibility of the timetable being brought forward. The number of Scottish MPs at Westminster is to be cut by about 12 by 2007.

The Secretary of State for Scotland will remain a Cabinet minister, responsible for communication between the Scottish and Westminster parliaments and for representing Scottish interests in those policy areas not devolved. In the event of a dispute between the two parliaments, the judicial committee of the Privy Council will act as arbiter.

LORD-LIEUTENANTS

Title	Name
Aberdeenshire	A. Farquharson
Angus	The Earl of Airlie, KT, GCVO, PC
Argyll and Bute	The Duke of Argyll
Ayrshire and Arran	Maj. R. Y. Henderson, TD
Banffshire	J. A. S. McPherson, CBE
Berwickshire	Maj.-Gen. Sir John Swinton, KCVO, OBE
Caithness	Maj. G. T. Dunnett, TD
Clackmannan	Lt.-Col. R. C. Stewart, CBE, TD
Dumfries	Capt. R. C. Cunningham-Jardine
Dumbartonshire	Brig. D. D. G. Hardie, TD
East Lothian	Sir Hew Hamilton-Dalrymple, Bt., KCVO
Fife	The Earl of Elgin and Kincardine, KT
Inverness	The Lord Gray of Contin, PC
	The Viscount of Arbuthnott, KT, CBE, DSC, FRSE
Kincardineshire	H. B. Sneddon, CBE
Lanarkshire	Capt. G. W. Burnet, LVO
Midlothian	Air Vice-Marshal G. A. Chesworth, CB, OBE, DFC
Moray	
Nairn	The Earl of Leven and Melville
Orkney	G. R. Marwick
Perth and Kinross	Sir David Montgomery, Bt.
Renfrewshire	C. H. Parker, OBE
Ross and Cromarty	Capt. R. W. K. Stirling of Fairburn, TD
Roxburgh, Ettrick and Lauderdale	Dr June Paterson-Brown
Shetland	J. H. Scott
Stirling and Falkirk	Lt.-Col. J. Stirling of Garden, CBE, TD, FRICS
Sutherland	Maj.-Gen. D. Houston, CBE
The Stewartry of Kirkcudbright	Lt.-Gen. Sir Norman Arthur, KCB
Tweeddale	Capt. J. D. B. Younger
West Lothian	The Earl of Morton
Western Isles	The Viscount Dunrossil, CMG
Wigtown	Maj. E. S. Orr-Ewing

The Lord Provosts of the four city districts of Aberdeen, Dundee, Edinburgh and Glasgow are Lord-Lieutenants for those districts *ex officio*

LOCAL COUNCILS

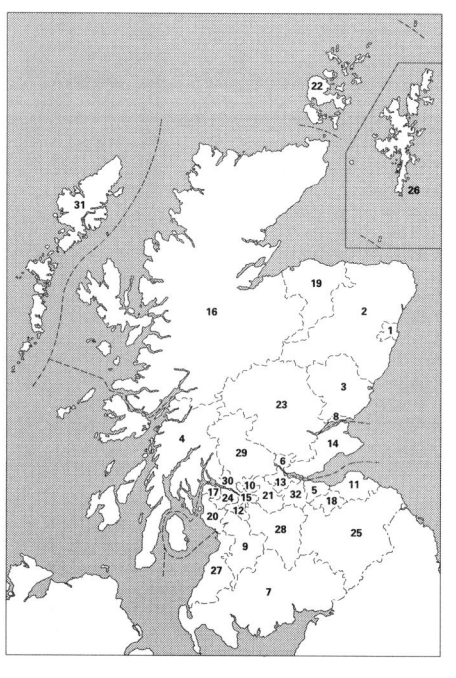

Key	Council
1	Aberdeen City
2	Aberdeenshire
3	Angus
4	Argyll and Bute
5	City of Edinburgh
6	Clackmannanshire
7	Dumfries and Galloway
8	Dundee City
9	East Ayrshire
10	East Dumbartonshire
11	East Lothian
12	East Renfrewshire
13	Falkirk
14	Fife
15	Glasgow City
16	Highland
17	Inverclyde
18	Midlothian
19	Moray
20	North Ayrshire
21	North Lanarkshire
22	Orkney
23	Perth and Kinross
24	Renfrewshire
25	Scottish Borders
26	Shetland
27	South Ayrshire
28	South Lanarkshire
29	Stirling
30	West Dumbartonshire
31	Western Isles
32	West Lothian

LOCAL COUNCILS

Council	Administrative headquarters	Population (latest estimate)	Band D charge 1998	Chief Executive	Chairman (a) Convener (b) Provost (c) Lord Provost
Aberdeen City	Aberdeen	217,260	£794.00	D. Paterson	(c) Ms M. Farquhar
Aberdeenshire	Aberdeen	227,430	695.00	A. G. Campbell	(a) Dr C. S. Millar
Angus	Forfar	111,750	709.00	A. B. Watson	(b) Mrs F. E. Duncan
Argyll and Bute	Lochgilphead	90,550	881.00	J. A. McLellan	(a) J. Wilson
City of Edinburgh	Edinburgh	448,850	867.00	T. N. Aitchison	(c) Rt. Hon. E. Milligan
Clackmannanshire	Alloa	48,810	959.73	R. Allan	(b) R. Elder
Dumfries and Galloway	Dumfries	147,300	886.33	I. F. Smith	(a) A. T. Baldwick
Dundee City	Dundee	149,160	1,148.52	A. Stephen	(c) M. J. Rolfe
East Ayrshire	Kilmarnock	124,000	974.33	D. Montgomery	(b) R. Stirling
East Dunbartonshire	Glasgow	110,679	790.00	C. Mallon	(b) J. Dempsey
East Lothian	Haddington	88,140	760.00	J. Lindsay	(a) P. O'Brien
East Renfrewshire	Glasgow	89,383	682.00	P. Daniels	(b) A. Steele
Falkirk	Falkirk	143,040	699.00	Ms M. Pitcaithly	(b) A. H. Fowler
Fife	Glenrothes	349,300	917.73	J. Markland	(a) J. MacDougall
Glasgow City	Glasgow	611,660	1,229.33	J. Andrews (acting)	(c) P. J. Lally
Highland	Inverness	208,700	776.47	A. D. McCourt	(a) P. J. Peacock, CBE
Inverclyde	Greenock	86,500	1,018.33	R. Cleary	(b) Mrs C. Allan
Midlothian	Dalkeith	80,000	892.00	T. Muir	(b) D. Molloy
Moray	Elgin	86,030	699.00	A. A. Connell	(a) G. McDonald
North Ayrshire	Irvine	139,000	906.33	B. Devine	(a) G. Steven
North Lanarkshire	Motherwell	325,940	967.33	A. Cowe	(b) V. Mathieson
Orkney Islands	Kirkwall	20,000	765.52	A. Buchan	(a) H. Halcro-Johnston
Perth and Kinross	Perth	132,750	884.63	H. Robertson	(b) J. Culliven
Renfrewshire	Paisley	178,260	938.33	T. Scholes	(b) Ms N. Allison
Scottish Borders	Melrose	106,100	639.00	A. M. Croall	(a) A. L Tulley
Shetland Islands	Lerwick	22,522	558.00	N. Reiter	(a) L. S. Smith
South Ayrshire	Ayr	114,247	792.00	G. W. F. Thorley	(b) R. Campbell
South Lanarkshire	Hamilton	307,350	859.00	A. MacNish	(b) S. Casserly
Stirling	Stirling	83,580	910.73	K. Yates	(b) J. Paterson
West Dunbartonshire	Dumbarton	95,760	1,166.00	M. Waters	(b) G. Cairney
Western Isles	Stornoway	28,240	656.00	B. W. Stewart	(a) D. M. Mackay
West Lothian	Livingston	149,540	792.00	A. M. Linkston	(b) J. Thomas

For explanation of council tax, see pages 523–4

Northern Ireland

Northern Ireland has a total area of 5,467 sq. miles (14,144 sq. km): land, 5,225 sq. miles (13,532 sq. km); inland water and tideways, 249 sq. miles (628 sq. km).

The population of Northern Ireland at the 1991 census was 1,577,836 (males, 769,071; females, 808,765). The average density of population in 1991 was 1.11 persons per hectare.

In 1991 the number of persons in the various religious denominations (expressed as percentages of the total population) were: Roman Catholic, 38.4; Presbyterian, 21.4; Church of Ireland, 17.7; Methodist, 3.8; others 7.7; none, 3.7; not stated, 7.3.

FLAG

The official national flag of Northern Ireland is now the Union Flag. The flag formerly in use (a white, six-pointed star in the centre of a red cross on a white field, enclosing a red hand and surmounted by a crown) has not been used since the imposition of direct rule.

PRINCIPAL CITIES

BELFAST

Belfast, the administrative centre of Northern Ireland, is situated at the mouth of the River Lagan at its entrance to Belfast Lough. The city grew, owing to its easy access by sea to Scottish coal and iron, to be a great industrial centre.

The principal buildings are of a relatively recent date and include the Parliament Buildings at Stormont, the City Hall, the Law Courts, the Public Library and the Museum and Art Gallery.

Belfast received its first charter of incorporation in 1613 and was created a city in 1888; the title of Lord Mayor was conferred in 1892.

LONDONDERRY

Londonderry (originally Derry) is situated on the River Foyle, and has important associations with the City of London. The Irish Society was created by the City of London in 1610, and under its royal charter of 1613 it fortified the city and was for long closely associated with its administration. Because of this connection the city was incorporated in 1613 under the new name of Londonderry.

The city is famous for the great siege of 1688–9, when for 105 days the town held out against the forces of James II until relieved by sea. The city walls are still intact and form a circuit of almost a mile around the old city.

Interesting buildings are the Protestant Cathedral of St Columb's (1633) and the Guildhall, reconstructed in 1912 and containing a number of beautiful stained glass windows, many of which were presented by the livery companies of London.

CONSTITUTION AND GOVERNMENT

Northern Ireland is subject to the same fundamental constitutional provisions which apply to the rest of the United Kingdom. It had its own parliament and government from 1921 to 1972, but after increasing civil unrest the Northern Ireland (Temporary Provisions) Act 1972 transferred the legislative and executive powers of the Northern Ireland parliament and government to the UK Parliament and a Secretary of State. The Northern Ireland Constitution Act 1973 provided for devolution in North-

ern Ireland through an assembly and executive, but a power-sharing executive formed by the Northern Ireland political parties in January 1974 collapsed in May 1974; since then Northern Ireland has been governed by direct rule under the provisions of the Northern Ireland Act 1974. This allows Parliament to approve all laws for Northern Ireland and places the Northern Ireland department under the direction and control of the Secretary of State for Northern Ireland.

Attempts were made by successive governments to find a means of restoring a widely acceptable form of devolved government to Northern Ireland. In 1985 the governments of the United Kingdom and the Republic of Ireland signed the Anglo-Irish Agreement, establishing an intergovernmental conference in which the Irish government may put forward views and proposals on certain aspects of Northern Ireland affairs.

Discussions between the British and Irish governments and the main Northern Ireland parties began in 1991. It was agreed that any political settlement would need to address three key relationships: those within Northern Ireland; those within the island of Ireland (north/south); and those between the British and Irish governments (east/west). Although round table talks ended in 1992 the process continued from September 1993 as separate bilateral discussions with three of the Northern Ireland parties (the DUP declined to participate).

In December 1993 the British and Irish governments published the Joint Declaration complementing the political talks, and making clear that any settlement would need to be founded on principles of democracy and consent. The declaration also stated that all democratically mandated parties could be involved in political talks as long as they permanently renounced paramilitary violence.

The provisional IRA and loyalist paramilitary groups announced cease-fires on 31 August and 13 October 1994 respectively. The Government initiated exploratory meetings with Sinn Fein and loyalist representatives in December 1994.

In February 1995 the Prime Minister (John Major) launched *A Framework for Accountable Government in Northern Ireland* and, with the Irish Prime Minister, *A New Framework for Agreement*. These outlined what a comprehensive political settlement might look like. The ideas were intended to facilitate multilateral dialogue involving the Northern Ireland parties and the British government. To this end the Secretary of State for Northern Ireland (Sir Patrick Mayhew) initiated separate bilateral meetings with the leaders of the main parties.

In autumn 1995 the Prime Minister said that Sinn Fein would not be invited to all-party talks until the IRA had decommissioned its arms; the IRA ruled out any decommissioning of weapons in advance of a political settlement. In November 1995 the Prime Minister and the Irish Prime Minister agreed to set up a three-member international body chaired by a former US senator, George Mitchell, to advise both governments on suitable methods of decommissioning arms. The international body reported in January 1996 that no weapons would be decommissioned before the start of all-party talks and that a compromise agreement was necessary under which weapons would be decommissioned during negotiations. The Prime Minister accepted the report and proposed that elections should be held to provide a pool of representatives to conduct all-party talks. On 9 February 1996 the IRA called off its cease-fire.

PEACE TALKS

Following elections on 30 May 1996, all-party talks opened at Stormont Castle on 10 June 1996 which included nine of the ten parties returned at the election; Sinn Fein representatives were turned away because the IRA had failed to reinstate its cease-fire.

The participants of the all-party talks agreed the rules of procedure and set up a business committee. On 29 July 1996 the all-party talks were suspended after disagreements over the issue of decommissioning arms. From September 1996 discussion focused on the issue of decommissioning arms, and an opening agenda for the talks was agreed in October 1996. The talks were suspended from 5 March 1997 until 3 June because of the UK general election and local government elections in Northern Ireland.

On 25 June 1997 the newly-elected Labour Government said that substantive negotiations should begin in September 1997 with a view to reaching conclusions by May 1998. The British and Irish governments issued a joint paper outlining their proposals for resolving the decommissioning issue. The Government also indicated that if the IRA were to call a cease-fire, it would assess whether it was genuine over a period of six weeks, and if satisfied that it was so, would then invite Sinn Fein to the talks. An IRA cease-fire was declared on 20 July 1997.

The Northern Ireland Secretary (Mo Mowlam) met a Sinn Fein delegation on 6 August 1997 and later announced that Sinn Fein would be present when the substantive talks opened on 15 September. The Unionist and loyalist parties, unhappy at the terms on which Sinn Fein had been admitted, boycotted the opening of the talks. The Ulster Unionist Party, the Progressive Unionist Party and the Ulster Democratic Party re-entered the negotiations on 17 September. Full-scale peace talks began on 7 October. The parties had agreed to concentrate on constitutional issues, with the issue of decommissioning terrorist weapons to be handled by a new independent commission.

On 12 January 1998 the British and Irish governments issued a joint document, *Propositions on Heads of Agreement*, proposing the establishment of various new cross-border bodies; further proposals were presented on 27 January. A draft peace settlement was issued by the talks' chairman, Sen. George Mitchell, on 6 April 1998 but was rejected by the Unionists the following day. On 10 April agreement was reached between the British and Irish governments and the eight Northern Ireland political parties still involved in the talks. The agreement provided for an elected New Northern Ireland Assembly; a North/South Ministerial Council, and a British-Irish Council comprising representatives of the British, Irish, Channel Islands and Isle of Man governments and members of the new assemblies for Scotland, Wales and Northern Ireland. Further points included the abandonment of the Republic of Ireland's constitutional claim to Northern Ireland; the decommissioning of weapons; the release of paramilitary prisoners; and changes in policing (*see also* Events of the Year).

Referendums on the agreement were held in Northern Ireland and the Republic of Ireland on 22 May 1998. In Northern Ireland the turnout was 81 per cent, of which 71.12 per cent voted in favour of the agreement. In the Republic of Ireland, the turnout was about 55 per cent, of which 94.4 per cent voted in favour of both the agreement and the necessary constitutional change.

NORTHERN IRELAND ASSEMBLY

Elections to the New Northern Ireland Assembly took place on 25 June 1998 and members met for the first time on 1 July 1998. The Assembly will meet in shadow form until early 1999, when it will become fully operational. It will have executive and legislative authority over those areas formerly the responsibility of the Northern Ireland government departments: agriculture, economic development, education, the environment, finance, health and social security. Its powers might be extended further in future.

The Assembly has 108 members elected by single transferable vote (six from each of the 18 Westminster constituencies). Safeguards ensure that key decisions have cross-community support. The executive powers of the Assembly will be discharged by an executive committee comprising a First Minister and Deputy First Minister (jointly elected by the Assembly on a cross-community basis) and up to ten ministers with departmental responsibilities. Ministerial posts are allocated on the basis of the number of seats each party holds.

Composition

Party	Seats
UUP	28
SDLP	24
DUP	20
Sinn Fein	18
Alliance Party	6
UK Unionist Party	5
Progressive Unionist Party	2
Northern Ireland Women's Coalition	2
Others	3

Presiding Officer, Lord Alderdice
First Minister, David Trimble, MP (UUP)
Deputy First Minister, Seamus Mallon, MP (SDLP)

OTHER BODIES

By 31 October 1998 the Northern Ireland Assembly will identify at least 12 areas in which decisions are to be reached by a North/South Ministerial Council comprising ministers from the Assembly and the Irish government. In at least six of these categories, cross-border agencies will be established.

The intergovernmental conference established by the 1985 Anglo-Irish Agreement (*see* above) was replaced by a new British-Irish Intergovernmental Conference which will discuss all areas of mutual bilateral interest.

The British-Irish Council will operate on the basis of consensus and may reach agreements and pursue common policies in areas of mutual interest.

ECONOMY

FINANCE

Taxation in Northern Ireland is largely imposed and collected by the UK government. After deducting the cost of collection and of Northern Ireland's contributions to the European Union, the balance, known as the Attributed Share of Taxation, is paid over to the Northern Ireland Consolidated Fund. Northern Ireland's revenue is insufficient to meet its expenditure and is supplemented by a grant-in-aid.

	1997–8*	1998–9**
Public income	£6,830,248,928	£7,422,000,000
Public expenditure	6,862,559,199	7,422,000,000

* Outturn
** Estimate

PRODUCTION

The products of the engineering and allied industries, which employed 26,100 persons in 1995, were valued at £2,090 million. The textiles industry (manufacture of textiles and textile products), employing about 24,300 persons, produced goods valued at approximately £999 million. The food products, beverages and tobacco industry, employing about 19,400 persons, produced goods valued at £3,910 million.

In 1997, 1,478 persons were employed in mining and quarrying operations in Northern Ireland and the minerals raised (21,591,000 tonnes) were valued at £55,553,000.

COMMUNICATIONS

The total tonnage handled by Northern Ireland ports in 1997 was 19.5 million. Regular ferry, freight and container services operate to ports in Great Britain and Europe from a number of ports, with most trade passing through Belfast (60 per cent of the total), Larne and Warrenpoint.

The Northern Ireland Transport Holding Company is largely responsible for the supervision of the subsidiary companies, Ulsterbus and Citybus (which operate the public road passenger services) and Northern Ireland Railways (collectively known as Translink). Road freight services are also provided by a large number of hauliers operating competitively under licence.

Belfast International Airport was privatized in July 1994. It provides scheduled and chartered services on domestic and international routes. In 1997–8 the airport handled approximately 2.5 million passengers and 41,000 tonnes of freight. Scheduled services also operate from Belfast City Airport (BCA) to 20 UK destinations. In 1997–8 the airport handled approximately 1.3 million passengers. City of Derry Airport (Londonderry) provides services to 14 UK and four European destinations and to Belfast, providing links to many of the locations serviced by BCA. In 1997–8 City of Derry Airport handled approximately 68,000 passengers.

NORTHERN IRELAND COUNTIES

County	Area* (sq. miles)	Lord-Lieutenant	High Sheriff, 1998
Antrim	1,093	The Lord O'Neill, TD	R. Conway
Armagh	484	The Earl of Caledon	Dr D. E. Dorman
‡Belfast City	25	Col. J. E. Wilson, OBE	J. Clarke
Down	945	Maj. W. J. Hall	B. L. Henderson
Fermanagh	647	The Earl of Erne	R. A. D. Kells
†Londonderry	798	Sir Michael McCorkell, KCVO, OBE, TD	Maj.-Gen. P. M. Welsh
‡Londonderry City	3.4	J. T. Eaton, CBE, TD	A. D. McClure
Tyrone	1,211	The Duke of Abercorn	Capt. G. H. Caldecott

* Excluding inland waters and tideways
‡ Denotes County Borough
† Excluding the City of Londonderry

DISTRICT COUNCILS

SMALL CAPITALS denotes CITY status
§ Denotes Borough Council

Council	Population (30 June 1996)	Net Annual Value	Council Clerk	Chairman †Mayor 1998
§Antrim, Co. Antrim	47,100	£30,178,161	S. J. Magee	†P. Marks
§Ards, Co. Down	67,500	29,070,618	D. J. Fallows	†G. Ennis
§ARMAGH, Co. Armagh	52,900	19,660,325	D. R. D. Mitchell	†P. Brannigan
§Ballymena, Co. Antrim	58,000	33,959,906	M. G. Rankin	†J. Currie
§Ballymoney, Co. Antrim	24,800	8,699,661	J. Dempsey	†F. Campbell
Banbridge, Co. Down	37,400	14,154,306	R. Gilmore	Mrs J. Baird
BELFAST, Co. Antrim and Co. Down	296,200	287,078,814	B. Hanna	A. Maginnis
§Carrickfergus, Co. Antrim	35,400	15,715,675	R. Boyd	†D. W. Hilditch
§Castlereagh, Co. Down	64,200	30,267,118	A. Donaldson	†J. Norris
§Coleraine, Co. Londonderry	54,500	28,265,513	W. Moore	†J. McClure
Cookstown, Co. Tyrone	31,700	13,755,959	M. J. McGuckin	S. Begley
§Craigavon, Co. Armagh	78,400	43,269,959	T. Reaney	†K. Twyble
DERRY, Co. Londonderry	103,500	60,139,480	T. J. Keaney	†M. Bradley
Down, Co. Down	60,900	22,586,030	O. O'Connor	P. Toman
Dungannon, Co. Tyrone	46,800	22,971,711	W. J. Beattie	P. Daly
Fermanagh, Co. Fermanagh	55,200	27,285,345	Mrs A. McGinley	F. McQuillan
§Larne, Co. Antrim	30,200	17,868,183	C. McGarry	†Mrs J. Drummond
§Limavady, Co. Londonderry	30,500	11,679,636	J. K. Stevenson	†G. Lynch
§Lisburn, Co. Antrim and Co. Down	105,700	56,847,179	N. Davidson	†G. Morrison
Magherafelt, Co. Londonderry	37,500	14,780,022	J. A. McLaughlin	P. Groogan
Moyle, Co. Antrim	14,900	4,703,049	R. G. Lewis	R. Kerr
Newry and Mourne, Co. Down and Co. Armagh	83,900	33,920,343	K. O'Neill	C. Smyth
§Newtownabbey, Co. Antrim	79,200	43,063,458	N. Dunn	†N. Crilly
§North Down, Co. Down	73,400	38,068,752	A. McDowell	†Mrs R. Cooling
Omagh, Co. Tyrone	46,600	21,958,441	J. P. McKinney	J. Byrne
Strabane, Co. Tyrone	36,500	13,004,829	Dr V. R. Eakin	E. Mullen

The Isle of Man

Ellan Vannin

The Isle of Man is an island situated in the Irish Sea, in latitude 54° 3′–54° 25′ N. and longitude 4° 18′–4° 47′ W., nearly equidistant from England, Scotland and Ireland. Although the early inhabitants were of Celtic origin, the Isle of Man was part of the Norwegian Kingdom of the Hebrides until 1266, when this was ceded to Scotland. Subsequently granted to the Stanleys (Earls of Derby) in the 15th century and later to the Dukes of Atholl, it was brought under the administration of the Crown in 1765. The island forms the bishopric of Sodor and Man.

The total land area is 221 sq. miles (572 sq. km). The report on the 1991 census showed a resident population of 69,788 (males, 33,693; females, 36,095). The main language in use is English. There are no remaining native speakers of Manx Gaelic but 643 people are able to speak the language.

CAPITAL – ΨDouglas; population (1991), 22,214.ΨCastletown (3,152) is the ancient capital; the other towns are ΨPeel (3,829) and ΨRamsey (6,496)

FLAG – A red flag charged with three conjoined armoured legs in white and gold

TYNWALD DAY – 5 July

GOVERNMENT

The Isle of Man is a self-governing Crown dependency, having its own parliamentary, legal and administrative system. The British Government is responsible for international relations and defence. Under the UK Act of Accession, Protocol 3, the island's relationship with the European Union is limited to trade alone and does not extend to financial aid. The Lieutenant-Governor is The Queen's personal representative in the island.

The legislature, Tynwald, is the oldest parliament in the world in continuous existence. It has two branches: the Legislative Council and the House of Keys. The Council consists of the President of Tynwald, the Bishop of Sodor and Man, the Attorney-General (who does not have a vote) and eight members elected by the House of Keys. The House of Keys has 24 members, elected by universal adult suffrage. The branches sit separately to consider legislation and sit together, as Tynwald Court, for most other parliamentary purposes.

The presiding officer in Tynwald Court is the President of Tynwald, elected by the members, who also presides over sittings of the Legislative Council. The presiding officer of the House of Keys is Mr Speaker, who is elected by members of the House.

The principal members of the Manx Government are the Chief Minister and nine departmental ministers, who comprise the Council of Ministers.

Lieutenant-Governor, HE Sir Timothy Daunt, KCMG
   ADC to the Lieutenant-Governor, vacant
President of Tynwald, The Hon. Sir Charles Kerruish, OBE
Speaker, House of Keys, The Hon. N. Q. Cringle
The First Deemster and Clerk of the Rolls, His Honour T. W. Cain
Clerk of Tynwald, Secretary to the House of Keys and Counsel to the Speaker, Prof. T. St J. N. Bates
Clerk of Legislative Council and Clerk Assistant of Tynwald, T. A. Bawden
Attorney-General, W. J. H. Corlett
Chief Minister, The Hon. D. J. Gelling
Chief Secretary, J. F. Kissack
Chief Financial Officer, J. A. Cashen

ECONOMY

Most of the income generated in the island is earned in the services sector with financial and professional services accounting for just over half of the national income. Tourism and manufacturing are also major generators of income whilst the island's other traditional industries of agriculture and fishing now play a smaller role in the economy.

Under the terms of Protocol 3, the island has tariff-free access to EU markets for its goods.

The island's unemployment rate is approximately 1.5 per cent and price inflation is around 3 per cent per annum.

FINANCE

The budget for 1998–9 provided for net revenue expenditure of £264 million. The principal sources of government revenue are taxes on income and expenditure. Income tax is payable at a rate of 15 per cent on the first £9,500 of taxable income for single resident individuals and 20 per cent on the balance, after personal allowances of £7,070. These bands are doubled for married couples. The rate of income tax is 20 per cent on the whole taxable income of non-residents and companies. By agreement with the British Government, the island keeps most of its rates of indirect taxation (VAT and duties) the same as those in the United Kingdom, but this agreement may be terminated by either party. However, VAT on tourist accommodation is charged at 5 per cent. A reciprocal agreement on national insurance benefits and pensions exists between the governments of the Isle of Man and the United Kingdom. Taxes are also charged on property (rates), but these are comparatively low.

The major government expenditure items are health, social security and education, which account for 60 per cent of the government budget. The island makes a voluntary annual contribution to the United Kingdom for defence and other external services.

The island has a special relationship with the European Union and neither contributes money to nor receives funds from the EU budget.

The Channel Islands

The Channel Islands, situated off the north-west coast of France (at distances of from ten to 30 miles), are the only portions of the Dukedom of Normandy still belonging to the Crown, to which they have been attached since the Conquest. They were the only British territory to come under German occupation during the Second World War, following invasion on 30 June to 1 July 1940. The islands were relieved by British forces on 9 May 1945, and 9 May (Liberation Day) is now observed as a bank and public holiday.

The islands consist of Jersey (28,717 acres/11,630 ha), Guernsey (15,654 acres/6,340 ha), and the dependencies of Guernsey: Alderney (1,962 acres/795 ha), Brechou (74/30), Great Sark (1,035/419), Little Sark (239/97), Herm (320/130), Jethou (44/18) and Lihou (38/15) – a total of 48,083 acres/19,474 ha, or 75 sq. miles/194 sq. km. In 1991 the population of Jersey was 84,082; and of Guernsey, 58,867; Alderney, 2,297 and Sark, 575. The official languages are English and French but French is being supplanted by English, which is the language in daily use. In country districts of Jersey and Guernsey and throughout Sark a Norman-French *patois* is also in use, though to a declining extent.

GOVERNMENT

The islands are Crown dependencies with their own legislative assemblies (the States in Jersey, Guernsey and Alderney, and the Court of Chief Pleas in Sark), and systems of local administration and of law, and their own courts. Acts passed by the States require the sanction of The Queen-in-Council. The British Government is responsible for defence and international relations. The Channel Islands have trading rights alone within the European Union; these rights do not include financial aid.

In both Bailiwicks the Lieutenant-Governor and Commander-in-Chief, who is appointed by the Crown, is the personal representative of The Queen and the channel of communication between the Crown (via the Privy Council) and the island's government.

The government of each Bailiwick is conducted by committees appointed by the States. Justice is administered by the Royal Courts of Jersey and Guernsey, each consisting of the Bailiff and 12 elected Jurats. The Bailiffs of Jersey and Guernsey, appointed by the Crown, are President of the States and of the Royal Courts of their respective islands.

Each Bailiwick constitutes a deanery under the jurisdiction of the Bishop of Winchester (*see* Index).

ECONOMY

A mild climate and good soil have led to the development of intensive systems of agriculture and horticulture, which form a significant part of the economy. Equally important are invisible earnings, principally from tourism and banking and finance, the low rate of income tax (20p in the £ in Jersey and Guernsey; no tax of any kind in Sark) and the absence of super-tax and death duties making the islands a popular tax-haven.

Principal exports are agricultural produce and flowers; imports are chiefly machinery, manufactured goods, food, fuel and chemicals. Trade with the UK is regarded as internal.

British currency is legal tender in the Channel Islands but each Bailiwick issues its own coins and notes (*see* page 612). They also issue their own postage stamps; UK stamps are not valid.

JERSEY

Lieutenant-Governor and Commander-in-Chief of Jersey, HE Gen. Sir Michael Wilkes, KCB, CBE, *apptd* 1995
   Secretary and ADC, Lt.-Col. A. J. C. Woodrow, OBE, MC
Bailiff of Jersey, Sir Philip Bailhache, Kt.
Deputy Bailiff, F. C. Hamon
Attorney-General, M. C. St J. Burt, QC
Receiver-General, Gp Capt. R. Green, OBE
Solicitor-General, Miss S. C. Nicolle, QC
Greffier of the States, G. H. C. Coppock
States Treasurer, G. M. Baird

FINANCE

Year to 31 Dec.	1996	1997
Revenue income	£427,619,424	£423,764,968
Revenue expenditure	395,666,525	395,662,095
Capital expenditure	86,728,614*	93,476,388
Public debt	0	0

* restated

CHIEF TOWN – ΨSt Helier, on the south coast of Jersey
FLAG – A white field charged with a red saltire cross, and the arms of Jersey in the upper centre

---

GUERNSEY AND DEPENDENCIES

Lieutenant-Governor and Commander-in-Chief of the Bailiwick of Guernsey and its Dependencies, HE Vice-Adm. Sir John Coward, KCB, DSO, *apptd* 1994
   Secretary and ADC, Capt. D. P. L. Hodgetts
Bailiff of Guernsey, Sir Graham Dorey
Deputy Bailiff, de V. G. Carey
HM Procureur and Receiver-General, A. C. K. Day, QC
HM Comptroller, G. R. Rowland, QC
States Supervisor, M. J. Brown

FINANCE

Year to 31 Dec.	1996	1997
Revenue	£182,016,695	£183,273,000
Expenditure	166,817,571	168,712,000

CHIEF TOWNS – ΨSt Peter Port, on the east coast of Guernsey; St Anne on Alderney
FLAG – White, bearing a red cross of St George, with a gold cross overall in the centre

ALDERNEY

President of the States, J. Kay-Mouat, OBE
Clerk of the States, D. V. Jenkins
Clerk of the Court, A. Johnson

SARK

Seigneur of Sark, J. M. Beaumont
The Seneschal, L. P. de Carteret
The Greffier, J. P. Hamon

OTHER DEPENDENCIES

Brechou, Lihou and Jethou are leased by the Crown. Herm is leased by the States of Guernsey.

The Environment

THE RIO EARTH SUMMIT

The UN Conference on Environment and Development (UNCED) took place in Rio, Brazil, in 1992. At the conference 103 heads of state or government adopted the Rio Declaration, 27 principles intended to guide governments in pursuing economic development in ways that would benefit all and protect the environment. In particular the declaration stressed that the environment should be protected as part of development and that poorer developing countries should be helped so that they could develop in ways that would minimize damage to the environment. The measures needed to ensure such sustainable development were outlined in the document *Agenda 21*. Neither the Rio Declaration nor Agenda 21 were binding agreements. The UN Commission on Sustainable Development was set up to monitor the progress of Agenda 21.

The second UNCED took place in New York in June 1997. It was found that progress towards the goals set at Rio had been slow. The UK agreed to reverse the decline in the amount of aid it was giving to developing countries and to reduce greenhouse gas emissions to 20 per cent below their 1990 levels by 2010.

CONVENTION ON BIOLOGICAL DIVERSITY

This binding agreement was adopted by 153 states at Rio, came into force in December 1993 and was ratified by the UK in June 1994. Its aim is to lessen the destruction of biological species and habitats, and parties to the convention are required to take inventories of their plants and animals, to protect endangered species and to ensure the diversity of species and habitats in the world. The convention is being implemented through a series of scientific advisory meetings (the third of which took place in September 1997) and meetings of parties (the fourth of which took place in May 1998).

FRAMEWORK CONVENTION ON CLIMATE CHANGE

This convention, also a binding agreement, was adopted by 153 states at Rio, ratified by the UK in December 1993 and came into force in March 1994. It is intended to reduce the risks of global warming by limiting 'greenhouse' gas emissions. It recommended that industrialized countries reduce 'greenhouse' gas emissions to 1990 levels by 2000. Parties are required to reduce emissions but are not bound to the recommended targets.

Progress towards the convention's targets is reviewed at regular conferences. The most recent of these was held in Kyoto, Japan, in December 1997 and the 159 countries represented agreed the Kyoto Protocol, which covers the six main 'greenhouse' gases (carbon dioxide, methane, nitrous oxide, hydrofluorocarbons (HFCs), perfluorocarbons (PFCs), sulphur hexafluoride (SF_6)). Under the protocol:
- 38 industrial countries agreed to legally binding targets for cutting their emissions of greenhouse gases to at least 5.2 per cent below 1990 levels between 2008 and 2012. EU members agreed to an 8 per cent reduction in emissions
- nations are permitted to trade carbon permits, i.e. those close to their ceiling of allowed emissions could buy the right to pollute from those who had not used up their capacity
- nations can also offset emissions by using features such as forests that absorb carbon gases

Sanctions for those not meeting their targets are to be agreed at a later date. A framework convention detailing how these commitments will be met is to be agreed before the protocol comes into force. Follow-up talks are to take place in Buenos Aires, Argentina, in November 1998.

STATEMENT OF PRINCIPLES ON FORESTS

This non-binding agreement was intended to preserve tropical rain forests. It was recognized that forests must meet human needs (as a national resource providing timber and fuel) and that forests are important for absorbing carbon dioxide. The statement recommends the development of sustainable forest management policies and financial aid to developing countries so that they can preserve their forests.

EUROPEAN UNION PROGRAMMES

The EC environmental action programmes are underpinned by the following principles: preventative action; the rectification of environmental damage at source where possible; and the 'polluter pays' principle (i.e. the polluter meets the full cost of the control of pollution). Since the first environmental action plan was adopted in 1972 over 300 EC directives concerning the protection of the environment have been agreed. These must be transposed into national law and policy to be effective.

The EC Fifth Environmental Action Programme, called 'Towards Sustainability', was endorsed in December 1992 and is the EC programme for sustainable development to 2000. It is based on the concept of joint action by national governments, local authorities, private companies and individuals. A review of the programme, setting out priorities for further action, including further integration of environmental considerations into other policy areas, was completed in 1998.

The European Environment Agency was established in 1993 to monitor the state of the environment in Europe and to provide comparable environmental information at pan-European level.

UK MEASURES

The UK's international commitments on the environment have been incorporated into annual white papers called *This Common Inheritance*. These reports summarize the Government's commitments, state what has been achieved in the previous year and outline future action and targets. Among the issues covered by the reports are climate change, wildlife and habitats, rural and urban development, air and water quality, pollution and waste, forestry and soil, and transport.

UK governments have increasingly seen environmental policy as part of a broader concept of sustainable development. This involves achieving environmental, economic and social objectives simultaneously, with environmental impact taken into account in all areas of policy (including transport and agriculture) rather than being considered in isolation. Government policy and operations are subject to scrutiny by the parliamentary environmental audit committee.

The UK produced its first national sustainable development strategy in 1994 and its first set of sustainable development indicators in 1996. Consultation on a new strategy took place in early 1998 and a White Paper is to be published (probably in 1999) which will include revised indicators and targets. (For targets set in 1995 and achievements, *see* below.)

BIOLOGICAL DIVERSITY

The UK Biodiversity Group was set up after the Rio Earth Summit to identify and draw up costed action plans to protect the most threatened and declining species in the UK. The group's report, published in December 1995, identified 1,250 species and 38 key habitats which require action to protect them. Action plans for 116 species and 14 habitats have been produced so far, and a further 286 species and 24 habitat plans are expected to be completed by the end of 1998.

CLIMATE CHANGE AND POLLUTION

The Climate Change Impact Review Group was set up after Rio to review all previously published work on the effects of climate change. In July 1996 the group published the *Review of the Potential Effects of Climate Change in the UK*, a sector by sector analysis of the impacts of climate change on sea level, the natural environment, energy and transport for the 2020s and 2050s in the UK.

The National Air Quality Strategy was adopted in March 1997. It is a framework for improving air quality. It sets quality standards for the main air pollutants and specific air quality objectives to be met by 2005, and outlines how industry, central and local government, transport and other sectors can contribute to improving air quality.

Progress towards sustainable development is measured by indicators first published in 1996. There are 118 indicators in 21 categories, e.g. economy, leisure and tourism, wildlife and habitats. A revised set of indicators is to be published in 1998 and the Ministry of Agriculture, Fisheries and Food has also begun work on a set of indicators of some of the pressures that agriculture exerts on the environment.

LOCAL AGENDA 21

Local authorities (and local communities) are being encouraged to play their part in meeting the UK's commitments under Agenda 21 and to a lesser degree the Biological Diversity and Climate Change Conventions. Under Local Agenda 21, local authorities draw up a sustainable development strategy for their areas. The main aims of the strategy are to protect and enhance the local environment while meeting social needs and promoting economic success.

Each strategy should identify the local sustainability issues, set explicit objectives and priorities, state which organizations or sectors will take which actions, show how the objectives will be achieved and progress assessed, and outline the procedures for updating the strategy over time. Issues that might be covered by a local sustainability strategy include health, housing, home energy conservation, development plans, transport, air quality, biodiversity and recycling.

Local Agenda 21 is managed by the Local Agenda 21 Steering Group, made up of representatives from the Local Government Association, the Convention of Scottish Local Authorities, the Association of Local Authorities of Northern Ireland, the TUC, the Advisory Committee on Business and the Environment, the World-Wide Fund for Nature, and other organizations. The International Council for Local Environmental Initiatives (ICLEI) is co-ordinating the international Local Agenda 21 initiative and the results of these efforts are reported via local government associations to the United Nations Commission on Sustainable Development.

Local authorities are under no statutory obligation to take part in Local Agenda 21 but a survey in 1996 found that 70 per cent of local authorities are engaged in or committed to Local Agenda 21. The Government would like all local authorities to adopt a Local Agenda 21 strategy by 2000.

BUSINESSES

The Environmental Technology Best Practice Programme was set up in 1994 to help businesses to improve their environmental performance. Businesses are advised on how to minimize waste and to reduce waste at source and in the production process in ways that are low-cost or offer potential savings. The programme publishes free guides to good practice and case studies on low-cost waste minimization measures, cleaner technologies and on specific sectors and pollutants. The specific sectors covered so far are foundries, metal finishing, volatile organic compounds (solvents), textiles, paper and board, glass, printing, food and drink, and chemicals. Work is currently being carried out on guides for engineering and ceramics.

The Environmental Helpline offers advice to business on any environmental issue.

UK TARGETS AND RECENT ACHIEVEMENTS *as at February 1997*

Global Atmosphere
– return carbon dioxide and other greenhouse gas emissions to 1990 levels by 2000
– phase out production and supply of CFCs by end of 1994 (*achieved*)
– return atmospheric chlorine and bromide to 1994 levels by 2012
– phase out HCFCs by 2015 and cut consumption of methyl bromide by 25 per cent by 1998

Air Quality and Noise
– reduce sulphur dioxide emissions by 80 per cent on 1980 levels by 2010
– maintain emissions of oxides of nitrogen at 1987 levels from 1994 (*being achieved*)
– cut emissions from large combustion plants by 60 per cent between 1980 and 2003 (sulphur dioxide) and by 30 per cent between 1980 and 1988 (oxides of nitrogen)

Fresh Water and the Sea
– bring drinking water standards up to EC Directive standards by the mid-1990s (*largely achieved: in 1995, 99.5 per cent of tests in England and Wales met standards*)
– bring bathing waters fully up to EC Directive standards by the mid-1990s (*90 per cent of UK bathing waters met the standards in 1996*)
– phase out dumping of waste from collieries at sea by 1997 (*achieved in 1995*) and dumping of sewage sludge at sea by end of 1998
– halve atmospheric inputs of 17 harmful substances by 1999

Forestry
– double England's forest in the next 50 years (currently 7.5 per cent of total land area), subject to the necessary Common Agricultural Policy reform
– increase woodland cover in Wales by 50 per cent in next 50 years (currently 12 per cent of total land area)

Energy
– achieve energy savings of 250 petajoules per year by 2000

– achieve 15 per cent improvement in energy efficiency of government estate over five years to March 1996 (*achieved 14.5 per cent improvement*). New target set of 20 per cent improvement by 2000
– create 1500 MW of new electricity generating capacity from renewable resources by 2000

Waste
Reduce proportion of controlled waste going to landfill from 70 per cent to 60 per cent by 2005:
– recycle or compost 25 per cent of household waste by 2000
– 1 million tonnes of organic household waste a year to be composted by 2000, and 40 per cent of domestic properties with a garden to carry out composting by 2000
– 40 per cent of soil improvers and growing media in UK to be supplied by non-peat materials by 2005
– maintain at least 90 per cent recycling rate for waste lead-acid batteries
– increase use of waste/recycled materials as aggregates in England from about 30 to 55 million tonnes a year by 2006
– recover 50–65 per cent of packaging waste by 2001 and recycle 25–45 per cent by 2001 (minimum of 15 per cent for each material)
– ensure 40 per cent of UK newspaper feedstock to be waste paper by 2000
– recover 65 per cent of scrap tyres
– achieve easily accessible recycling facilities for 80 per cent of households by 2000

Housing
– reduce the proportion of homes lying empty to 3 per cent by 2005
– ensure that half of all new housing is built on re-used sites by 2005
– reduce number of government-owned empty homes. By April 1997 Home and Scottish Offices to have vacant (for no more than six months) only 1 per cent of their homes which are or could be made habitable, Welsh Office 5 per cent and Department of Transport 7 per cent

ADDRESSES
ADVISORY COMMITTEE ON BUSINESS AND THE ENVIRONMENT, Floor 6/D9, Ashdown House, 123 Victoria Street, London SWIE 6DE. Tel: 0171-890 6624
ENVIRONMENT AGENCY, *see* page 301
ENVIRONMENTAL TECHNOLOGY BEST PRACTICE PROGRAMME, The Environmental Helpline: 0800-585794
EUROPEAN ENVIRONMENT AGENCY, Kongens Nytorv 6, DK-1050 Copenhagen K, Denmark. Tel: Copenhagen 3336 7100. Web: http://www.eea.eu.int
GOVERNMENT PANEL ON SUSTAINABLE DEVELOPMENT, Zone 4/F5 Ashdown House, 123 Victoria Street, London SWIE 6DE. Tel: 0171-890 4962
· INTERNATIONAL COUNCIL FOR LOCAL ENVIRONMENTAL INITIATIVES (ICLEI), City Hall, East Tower, 8th Floor, Toronto, Ontario M5H 2N2, Canada. Tel: Toronto 392 1462. Web: http://wwww.iclei.org
LOCAL AGENDA 21, The Local Government Management Board, Layden House, 76-78 Turnmill Street, London ECIM 5QU. Tel: 0171-296 6599. Web: http://www.lgmb.gov.uk
ROYAL COMMISSION ON ENVIRONMENTAL POLLUTION, *see* page 301
SCOTTISH ENVIRONMENT PROTECTION AGENCY, *see* page 339

UK BIODIVERSITY GROUP, c/o Biodiversity Action Plan Secretariat, European Wildlife Division, Department of the Environment, Transport and the Regions, Room 902D Tollgate House, Houlton Street, Bristol BS2 9DJ. Tel: 0117-987 8974
UK ROUND TABLE ON SUSTAINABLE DEVELOPMENT, Zone 4/F4 Ashdown House, 123 Victoria Street, London SWIE 6DE. Tel: 0171-890 4962
UN COMMISSION ON SUSTAINABLE DEVELOPMENT, Division for Sustainable Development, Room DC2, 2220 United Nations, New York, NY 10017, USA. Tel: New York 963 3170

Conservation and Heritage

Conservation of the Countryside

NATIONAL PARKS

ENGLAND AND WALES

The ten National Parks of England and Wales were set up under the provisions of the National Parks and Access to the Countryside Act 1949 to conserve and protect scenic landscapes from inappropriate development and to provide access to the land for public enjoyment.

The Countryside Commission is the statutory body which has the power to designate National Parks in England, and the Countryside Council for Wales is responsible for National Parks in Wales. Designations in England are confirmed by the Secretary of State for the Environment, and those in Wales by the Secretary of State for Wales. The designation of a National Park does not affect the ownership of the land or remove the rights of the local community. The majority of the land in the National Parks is owned by private landowners (74 per cent) or by bodies such as the National Trust (7 per cent) and the Forestry Commission (7 per cent). The National Park Authorities own only 2.3 per cent of the land.

The Environment Act 1995 replaced the existing National Park boards and committees with free-standing National Park Authorities (NPAs). NPAs are the sole local planning authorities for their areas and as such influence land use and development, and deal with planning applications. Their duties include conserving and enhancing the natural beauty, wildlife and cultural heritage of the National Parks; promoting opportunities for public understanding and enjoyment of the National Parks; and fostering the economic and social well-being of the communities within National Parks. The NPAs publish management plans as statements of their policies and appoint their own officers and staff.

Membership of the NPAs differs slightly between England and Wales. In England membership is split between representatives of the constituent local authorities and members appointed by the Secretary of State (of whom one half minus one are nominated by the parish councils in the park), with the local authority representatives in a majority of one. The Countryside Commission advises the Secretary of State on appointments not nominated by the parish councils. In Wales two-thirds of NPA members are appointed by the constituent local authorities and one-third are appointed by the Secretary of State for Wales, advised by the Countryside Council for Wales.

Central government provides 75 per cent of the funding for the parks through the National Park Grant. The remaining 25 per cent is supplied by the local authorities concerned. Approved net expenditure for all National Parks in 1998–9 was £23,285,900 for England and £8,045,333 for Wales.

Two areas considered as having equivalent status are the Broads and the New Forest (*see* page 575).

The National Parks (with date designation confirmed) are:

BRECON BEACONS (1957), Powys (66 per cent)/Carmarthenshire/Rhondda, Cynon and Taff/Merthyr Tydfil/Blaenau Gwent/Monmouthshire, 1,351 sq. km/522 sq. miles – The park is centred on the Beacons, Pen y Fan, Corn Du and Cribyn, but also includes the valley of the Usk, the Black Mountains to the east and the Black Mountain to the west. There are information centres at Brecon, Craig-y-nos Country Park, Abergavenny and Llandovery, a study centre at Danywenallt and a day visitor centre near Libanus. *Information Office*, 7 Glamorgan Street, Brecon, Powys LD3 7DP. Tel: 01874-624437. *National Park Officer*, M. Fitton

DARTMOOR (1951 and 1994), Devon, 954 sq. km/368 sq. miles – The park consists of moorland and rocky granite tors, and is rich in prehistoric remains. There are information centres at Newbridge, Tavistock, Bovey Tracey, Steps Bridge, Princetown and Postbridge. *Information Office*, Parke, Haytor Road, Bovey Tracey, Devon TQ13 9JQ. Tel: 01626-832093. *National Park Officer*, N. Atkinson

EXMOOR (1954), Somerset (71 per cent)/Devon, 693 sq. km/268 sq. miles – Exmoor is a moorland plateau inhabited by wild ponies and red deer. There are many ancient remains and burial mounds. There are information centres at Lynmouth, County Gate, Dulverton and Combe Martin. *Information Office*, Exmoor House, Dulverton, Somerset TA22 9HL. Tel: 01398-23665. *National Park Officer*, K. Bungay

LAKE DISTRICT (1951), Cumbria, 2,292 sq. km/885 sq. miles – The Lake District includes England's highest mountains (Scafell Pike, Helvellyn and Skiddaw) but it is most famous for its glaciated lakes. There are information centres at Keswick, Waterhead, Hawkshead, Seatoller, Bowness, Grasmere, Coniston, Glenridding and Pooley Bridge, an information van at Gosforth and a park centre at Brockhole, Windermere. *Information Office*, Brockhole, Windermere, Cumbria LA23 1LJ. Tel: 01539-446601. *National Park Officer*, P. Tiplady

NORTHUMBERLAND (1956), Northumberland, 1,049 sq. km/405 sq. miles – The park is an area of hill country stretching from Hadrian's Wall to the Scottish Border. There are information centres at Ingram, Once Brewed, Rothbury, Housesteads, Harbottle and Kielder, and an information caravan at Cawfields. *Information Office*, Eastburn, South Park, Hexham, Northumberland NE46 1BS. Tel: 01434-605555. *National Park Officer*, G. Taylor

NORTH YORK MOORS (1952), North Yorkshire (96 per cent)/Redcar and Cleveland, 1,436 sq. km/554 sq. miles – The park consists of woodland and moorland, and includes the Hambleton Hills and the Cleveland Way. There are information centres at Danby, Pickering, Sutton Bank, Ravenscar, Helmsley and Hutton-le-Hole, and a day study centre at Danby. *Information Office*, The Old Vicarage, Bondgate, Helmsley, York YO6 5BP. Tel: 01439-70657. *National Park Officer*, D. Arnold-Forster

PEAK DISTRICT (1951), Derbyshire (64 per cent)/Staffordshire/South Yorkshire/Cheshire/West Yorkshire/Greater Manchester, 1,438 sq. km/555 sq. miles – The Peak District includes the gritstone moors

of the 'Dark Peak' and the limestone dales of the 'White Peak'. There are information centres at Bakewell, Edale, Fairholmes and Castleton, and information points at Torside (in the Longdendale Valley) and at Hartington (former station).
Information Office, Aldern House, Baslow Road, Bakewell, Derbyshire DE45 1AE. Tel: 01629-814321. *National Park Officer*, C. Harrison

PEMBROKESHIRE COAST (1952 and 1995), Pembrokeshire, 584 sq. km/225 sq. miles – The park includes cliffs, moorland and a number of islands, including Skomer. There are information centres at Tenby, St David's, Pembroke, Newport, Kilgetty, Haverfordwest and Broad Haven.
Information Office, Winch Lane, Haverfordwest, Pembrokeshire SA61 1PY. Tel: 01437-764636. *National Park Officer*, N. Wheeler

SNOWDONIA (1951), Gwynedd/Conwy, 2,142 sq. km/ 827 sq. miles – Snowdonia is an area of deep valleys and rugged mountains. There are information centres at Aberdyfi, Bala, Betws y Coed, Blaenau Ffestiniog, Conwy, Harlech, Dolgellau and Llanberis.
Information Office, Penrhyndeudraeth, Gwynedd LL48 6LF. Tel: 01766-770274. *National Park Officer*, I. Huws

YORKSHIRE DALES (1954), North Yorkshire (88 per cent)/ Cumbria, 1,769 sq. km/683 sq. miles – The Yorkshire Dales are composed primarily of limestone overlaid in places by millstone grit. The three peaks of Ingleborough, Whernside and Pen-y-Ghent are within the park. There are information centres at Clapham, Grassington, Hawes, Aysgarth Falls, Malham and Sedbergh.
Information Office, Yorebridge House, Bainbridge, Leyburn, N. Yorks DL8 3BP. Tel: 01969-50456. *National Park Officer*, H. Hancock

Two other areas considered to have equivalent status to national parks are the Broads and the New Forest. The Broads Authority, a special statutory authority, was established in 1989 to develop, conserve and manage the Norfolk and Suffolk Broads (*see also* page 287). The Government declared in 1992 its intention of giving the New Forest a status equivalent to that of a National Park by declaring it an 'area of national significance'.

THE BROADS (1989), Norfolk, 303 sq. km/117 sq. miles – The Broads are located between Norwich and Great Yarmouth on the flood plains of the five rivers flowing through the area to the sea. The area is one of fens, winding waterways, woodland and marsh. The 40 or so broads are man-made, and are connected to the rivers by dykes, providing over 200 km of navigable waterways. There are information centres at Beccles, Hoveton, North-west Tower (Yarmouth), Ranworth and Toad Hole.
Broads Authority, Thomas Harvey House, 18 Colegate, Norwich NR3 1BQ. Tel: 01603-610734. *Chief Executive*, A. Clark

THE NEW FOREST, Hampshire, 376 sq. km/145 sq. miles – The forest has been protected since 1079 when it was declared a royal hunting forest. The area consists of forest, ancient woodland and heathland. Much of the Forest is managed by the Forestry Commission, which provides several camp-sites. The main villages are Brockenhurst, Burley and Lyndhurst, which has a visitor centre.
The Forestry Commission, Office of the Deputy Surveyor of the New Forest and the New Forest Committee, The Queen's House, Lyndhurst, Hants SO43 7NH. Tel: 01703-284149

SCOTLAND AND NORTHERN IRELAND
The National Parks and Access to the Countryside Act 1949 dealt only with England and Wales and made no provision for Scotland or Northern Ireland. Although there are no national parks in these two countries, there is power to designate them in Northern Ireland under the Amenity Lands Act 1965 and the Nature Conservation and Amenity Lands Order (Northern Ireland) 1985. In 1989 the Scottish Office asked Scottish Natural Heritage to report on whether national parks should be designated in Scotland.

AREAS OF OUTSTANDING NATURAL BEAUTY

ENGLAND AND WALES
Under the National Parks and Access to the Countryside Act 1949, provision was made for the designation of Areas of Outstanding Natural Beauty (AONBs) by the Countryside Commission. The Countryside Commission continues to be responsible for AONBs in England but since April 1991 the Countryside Council for Wales has been responsible for the Welsh AONBs. Designations in England are confirmed by the Secretary of State for the Environment and those in Wales by the Secretary of State for Wales.

Although less emphasis is placed upon the provision of open-air enjoyment for the public than in the national parks, AONBs are areas which are no less beautiful and require the same degree of protection to conserve and enhance the natural beauty of the countryside. This includes protecting flora and fauna, geological and other landscape features. In AONBs planning and management responsibilities are split between county and district councils; where unitary authorities exist they have sole responsibility for planning and management. Several AONBs cross local authority boundaries. Finance for the AONBs is provided by grant-aid.

The 41 Areas of Outstanding Natural Beauty (with date designation confirmed) are:

ANGLESEY (1967), Anglesey, 221 sq. km/85 sq. miles
ARNSIDE AND SILVERDALE (1972), Cumbria/Lancashire, 75 sq. km/29 sq. miles
BLACKDOWN HILLS (1991), Devon/Somerset, 370 sq. km/143 sq. miles
CANNOCK CHASE (1958), Staffordshire, 68 sq. km/26 sq. miles
CHICHESTER HARBOUR (1964), Hampshire/West Sussex, 74 sq. km/29 sq. miles
CHILTERNS (1965; extended 1990), Bedfordshire/ Hertfordshire/Buckinghamshire/Oxfordshire, 833 sq. km/322 sq. miles
CLWYDIAN RANGE (1985), Denbighshire/Flintshire, 157 sq. km/60 sq. miles
CORNWALL (1959; Camel estuary 1983), 958 sq. km/370 sq. miles
COTSWOLDS (1966; extended 1990), Gloucestershire/ Wiltshire/Warwickshire/Worcestershire/Somerset, 2,038 sq. km/787 sq. miles
CRANBORNE CHASE AND WEST WILTSHIRE DOWNS (1983), Dorset/Hampshire/Somerset/Wiltshire, 983 sq. km/379 sq. miles
DEDHAM VALE (1970; extended 1978, 1991), Essex/ Suffolk, 90 sq. km/35 sq. miles
DORSET (1959), 1,129 sq. km/436 sq. miles
EAST DEVON (1963), 268 sq. km/103 sq. miles
EAST HAMPSHIRE (1962), 383 sq. km/148 sq. miles
FOREST OF BOWLAND (1964), Lancashire/North Yorkshire, 802 sq. km/310 sq. miles

GOWER (1956), Swansea/Carmarthenshire, 189 sq. km/73 sq. miles

HIGH WEALD (1983), Kent/Surrey/East Sussex/West Sussex, 1,460 sq. km/564 sq. miles

HOWARDIAN HILLS (1987), North Yorkshire, 204 sq. km/ 79 sq. miles

ISLE OF WIGHT (1963), 189 sq. km/73 sq. miles

ISLES OF SCILLY (1976), 16 sq. km/6 sq. miles

KENT DOWNS (1968), 878 sq. km/339 sq. miles

LINCOLNSHIRE WOLDS (1973), 558 sq. km/215 sq. miles

LLŶN (1957), Gwynedd, 161 sq. km/62 sq. miles

MALVERN HILLS (1959), Herefordshire/Worcestershire/ Gloucestershire, 105 sq. km/40 sq. miles

MENDIP HILLS (1972; extended 1989), Somerset, 198 sq. km/76 sq. miles

NIDDERDALE (1994), North Yorkshire, 603 sq. km/233 sq. miles

NORFOLK COAST (1968), 451 sq. km/174 sq. miles

NORTH DEVON (1960), 171 sq. km/66 sq. miles

NORTH PENNINES (1988), Cumbria/Durham/ Northumberland, 1,983 sq. km/766 sq. miles

NORTHUMBERLAND COAST (1958), 135 sq. km/52 sq. miles

QUANTOCK HILLS (1957), Somerset, 99 sq. km/38 sq. miles

SHROPSHIRE HILLS (1959), 804 sq. km/310 sq. miles

SOLWAY COAST (1964), Cumbria, 115 sq. km/44 sq. miles

SOUTH DEVON (1960), 337 sq. km/130 sq. miles

SOUTH HAMPSHIRE COAST (1967), 77 sq. km/30 sq.miles

SUFFOLK COAST AND HEATHS (1970), 403 sq. km/156 sq. miles

SURREY HILLS (1958), 419 sq. km/162 sq. miles

SUSSEX DOWNS (1966), 983 sq. km/379 sq. miles

TAMAR VALLEY (1995), Cornwall/Devon, 195 sq. km/115 sq. miles

NORTH WESSEX DOWNS (1972), Berkshire/Hampshire/ Oxfordshire/Wiltshire, 1,730 sq. km/668 sq. miles

WYE VALLEY (1971), Monmouthshire/Gloucestershire/ Herefordshire, 326 sq. km/126 sq. miles

NORTHERN IRELAND

The Department of the Environment for Northern Ireland, with advice from the Council for Nature Conservation and the Countryside, designates Areas of Outstanding Natural Beauty in Northern Ireland. At present there are nine and these cover a total area of approximately 284,948 hectares (704,121 acres).

ANTRIM COAST AND GLENS , Co. Antrim, 70,600 ha/ 174,452 acres

CAUSEWAY COAST , Co. Antrim, 4,200 ha/10,378 acres

LAGAN VALLEY , Co. Down, 2,072 ha/5,119 acres

LECALE COAST , Co. Down, 3,108 ha/7,679 acres

MOURNE , Co. Down, 57,012 ha/140,876 acres

NORTH DERRY , Co. Londonderry, 12,950 ha/31,999 acres

RING OF GULLION , Co. Armagh, 15,353 ha/37,938 acres

SPERRIN , Co. Tyrone/Co. Londonderry, 101,006 ha/ 249,585 acres

STRANGFORD LOUGH , Co. Down, 18,647 ha/46,077 acres

NATIONAL SCENIC AREAS

No Areas of Outstanding Natural Beauty are designated in Scotland. However, National Scenic Areas have a broadly equivalent status. Scottish Natural Heritage recognizes areas of national scenic significance. At mid 1998 there were 40, covering a total area of 1,001,800 hectares (2,475,448 acres).

Development within National Scenic Areas is dealt with by the local planning authority, who are required to consult Scottish Natural Heritage concerning certain categories of development. Land management uses can also be modified in the interest of scenic conservation. The Secretary of State for Scotland has limited powers of intervention should a planning authority and Scottish Natural Heritage disagree.

ASSYNT-COIGACH, Highland, 90,200 ha/222,884 acres

BEN NEVIS AND GLEN COE, Highland/Argyll and Bute/ Perthshire and Kinross, 101,600 ha/251,053 acres

CAIRNGORM MOUNTAINS, Highland/Aberdeenshire/ Moray, 67,200 ha/166,051 acres

CUILLIN HILLS, Highland, 21,900 ha/54,115 acres

DEESIDE AND LOCHNAGAR, Aberdeenshire/Angus, 40,000 ha/98,840 acres

DORNOCH FIRTH, Highland, 7,500 ha/18,532 acres

EAST STEWARTRY COAST, Dumfries and Galloway, 4,500 ha/11,119 acres

EILDON AND LEADERFOOT, Borders, 3,600 ha/8,896 acres

FLEET VALLEY, Dumfries and Galloway, 5,300 ha/13,096 acres

GLEN AFFRIC, Highland, 19,300 ha/47,690 acres

GLEN STRATHFARRAR, Highland, 3,800 ha/9,390 acres

HOY AND WEST MAINLAND, Orkney Islands, 14,800 ha/ 36,571 acres

JURA, Argyll and Bute, 21,800 ha/53,868 acres

KINTAIL, Highland, 15,500 ha/38,300 acres

KNAPDALE, Argyll and Bute, 19,800 ha/48,926 acres

KNOYDART, Highland, 39,500 ha/97,604 acres

KYLE OF TONGUE, Highland, 18,500 ha/45,713 acres

KYLES OF BUTE, Argyll and Bute, 4,400 ha/10,872 acres

LOCH NA KEAL, MULL, Argyll and Bute, 12,700 ha/ 31,382 acres

LOCH LOMOND, Argyll and Bute/Stirling/West Dumbartonshire, 27,400 ha/67,705 acres

LOCH RANNOCH AND GLEN LYON, Perthshire and Kinross/Stirling, 48,400 ha/119,596 acres

LOCH SHIEL, Highland, 13,400 ha/33,111 acres

LOCH TUMMEL, Perthshire and Kinross, 9,200 ha/22,733 acres

LYNN OF LORN, Argyll and Bute, 4,800 ha/11,861 acres

MORAR, MOIDART AND ARDNAMURCHAN, Highland, 13,500 ha/33,358 acres

NORTH-WEST SUTHERLAND, Highland, 20,500 ha/50,655 acres

NITH ESTUARY, Dumfries and Galloway, 9,300 ha/ 22,980 acres

NORTH ARRAN, North Ayrshire, 23,800 ha/58,810 acres

RIVER EARN, Perthshire and Kinross, 3,000 ha/7,413 acres

RIVER TAY, Perthshire and Kinross, 5,600 ha/13,838 acres

ST KILDA, Western Isles, 900 ha/2,224 acres

SCARBA, LUNGA AND THE GARVELLACHS, Argyll and Bute, 1,900 ha/4,695 acres

SHETLAND, Shetland Islands, 11,600 ha/28,664 acres

SMALL ISLES, Highland, 15,500 ha/38,300 acres

SOUTH LEWIS, HARRIS AND NORTH UIST, Western Isles, 109,600 ha/270,822 acres

SOUTH UIST MACHAIR, Western Isles, 6,100 ha/15,073 acres

THE TROSSACHS, Stirling, 4,600 ha/11,367 acres

TROTTERNISH, Highland, 5,000 ha/12,355 acres

UPPER TWEEDDALE, Borders, 10,500 ha/25,945 acres

WESTER ROSS, Highland, 145,300 ha/359,036 acres

THE NATIONAL FOREST

The National Forest is being planted in about 200 square miles of Derbyshire, Leicestershire and Staffordshire. About 30 million trees, of mixed species but mainly broadleaved, will be planted over the next 20 years and beyond, and will eventually cover about one-third of the designated area. The project is funded by the Department of the Environment, Transport and the Regions. It was developed in 1992–5 by the Countryside Commission and is now run by the National Forest Company. Competitive bids for woodland creation projects are submitted to the National Forest Company by anybody who wishes to undertake a project, and are considered under the National Forest tender scheme. Sixteen tenders were approved in the first round of the scheme in 1995. Approval of tenders in the second round of the scheme was given in autumn 1996 and the results of the third round were announced in autumn 1997.

NATIONAL FOREST COMPANY, Enterprise Glade, Bath Lane, Moira, Swadlincote, Derbys DE12 6BD. Tel: 01283-551211. *Chief Executive*, Miss S. Bell

Nature Conservation Areas

SITES OF SPECIAL SCIENTIFIC INTEREST

Site of Special Scientific Interest (SSSI) is a legal notification applied to land in England, Scotland or Wales which English Nature (EN), Scottish Natural Heritage (SNH), or the Countryside Council for Wales (CCW) identifies as being of special interest because of its flora, fauna, geological or physiographical features. In some cases, SSSIs are managed as nature reserves.

EN, SNH and CCW must notify the designation of a SSSI to the local planning authority, every owner/occupier of the land, and the relevant Secretary of State. Forestry and agricultural departments and a number of other bodies are also informed of this notification.

Objections to the notification of a SSSI can be made and ultimately considered at a full meeting of the Council of EN or CCW. In Scotland an objection will be dealt with by the appropriate regional board or the main board of SNH, depending on the nature of the objection. Unresolved objections on scientific grounds must be referred to the Advisory Committee for SSSI.

The protection of these sites depends on the co-operation of individual landowners and occupiers. Owner/occupiers must consult EN, SNH or CCW and gain written consent before they can undertake certain listed activities on the site. Funds are available through management agreements and grants to assist owners and occupiers in conserving sites' interests. As a last resort a site can be purchased.

The number and area of SSSIs in Britain as at 31 March 1998 was:

	no.	hectares	acres
England	4,000	955,000	2,359,805
Scotland	1,442	916,080	2,263,634
Wales	942	217,807	538,202

NORTHERN IRELAND

In Northern Ireland 142 Areas of Special Scientific Interest (ASSIs) have been established by the Department of the Environment for Northern Ireland. These cover a total area of 79,822.206 hectares (197,160.8 acres).

NATIONAL NATURE RESERVES

National Nature Reserves are defined in the National Parks and Access to the Countryside Act 1949 as land designated for the study and preservation of flora and fauna, or of geological or physiographical features.

English Nature (EN), Scottish Natural Heritage (SNH) or the Countryside Council for Wales (CCW) can designate as a National Nature Reserve land which is being managed as a nature reserve under an agreement with one of the statutory nature conservation agencies; land held and managed by EN, SNH or CCW; or land held and managed as a nature reserve by another approved body. EN, SNH or CCW can make by-laws to protect reserves from undesirable activities; these are subject to confirmation by the relevant Secretary of State.

The number and area of National Nature Reserves in Britain as at 31 March 1998 was:

	no.	hectares	acres
England	189	70,623	174,509
Scotland	70	113,238	279,811
Wales	62	18,592	45,922

NORTHERN IRELAND

National Nature Reserves are established and managed by the Department of the Environment for Northern Ireland, with advice from the Council for Nature Conservation and the Countryside. There are 45 National Nature Reserves covering 4,322.1 hectares (10,676 acres).

LOCAL NATURE RESERVES

Local Nature Reserves are defined in the National Parks and Access to the Countryside Act 1949 as land designated for the study and preservation of flora and fauna, or of geological or physiographical features. The Act gives local authorities in England, Scotland and Wales the power to acquire, declare and manage local nature reserves in consultation with English Nature, Scottish Natural Heritage and the Countryside Council for Wales. Conservation trusts can also own and manage non-statutory local nature reserves.

The number and area of designated Local Nature Reserves in Britain as at 31 March 1998 was:

	no.	hectares	acres
England	566	20,428	50,479
Scotland	26	8,031	19,845
Wales	40	4,256	10,517

An additional 38 km of linear trails are designated as Local Nature Reserves.

FOREST NATURE RESERVES

Forest Enterprise (an executive agency of the Forestry Commission) is responsible for the management of the Commission's forests. It has created 46 Forest Nature Reserves with the aim of protecting and conserving special forms of natural habitat, flora and fauna. There are about 300 SSSIs on the estates, some of which are also Nature Reserves.

Forest Nature Reserves extend in size from under 50 hectares (124 acres) to over 500 hectares (1,236 acres). The largest include the Black Wood of Rannoch, by Loch Rannoch; Cannop Valley Oakwoods, Forest of Dean; Culbin Forest, near Forres; Glen Affric, near Fort Augustus; Kylerhea, Skye; Pembrey, Carmarthen Bay; Starr Forest, in Galloway Forest Park; and Wyre Forest, near Kidderminster.

Forest Enterprise also manages 18 Caledonian Forest Reserves in Scotland. These reserves are intended to protect and expand 16,000 hectares of native oak and pine woods in the Scottish highlands.

NORTHERN IRELAND

There are 36 Forest Nature Reserves in Northern Ireland, covering 1,759 hectares (4,346 acres). They are designated and administered by the Forest Service, an agency of the Department of Agriculture for Northern Ireland. There are also 15 National Nature Reserves on Forest Service-owned property.

MARINE NATURE RESERVES

The Wildlife and Countryside Act 1981 gives the Secretary of State for the Environment (and the Secretaries of State for Wales and for Scotland where appropriate) power to designate Marine Nature Reserves, and English Nature, Scottish Natural Heritage and the Countryside Council for Wales powers to select and manage these reserves. Marine Nature Reserves may be established in Northern Ireland under a 1985 Order.

Marine Nature Reserves provide protection for marine flora and fauna, and geological and physiographical features on land covered by tidal waters or parts of the sea in or adjacent to the UK. Reserves also provide opportunities for study and research.

The three statutory Marine Nature Reserves are:

LUNDY (1986), Bristol Channel
SKOMER (1990), Dyfed
STRANGFORD LOUGH (1995), Northern Ireland

Two other areas proposed for designation as reserves are: the Menai Strait, and Bardsey Island and part of the Llŷn peninsula, both in Wales.

A number of non-statutory marine reserves have been set up by conservation groups.

Conservation of Wildlife and Habitats

The United Kingdom is party to a number of international conservation conventions.

RAMSAR CONVENTION

The Convention on Wetlands of International Importance especially as Waterfowl Habitat was adopted at Ramsar, Iran, in 1971 and ratified by the UK in 1976. By June 1998, 110 countries were party to the convention. The aim of the convention is to promote the protection and conservation of wetlands (e.g. areas of marsh, fen) and their flora and fauna, especially waterfowl. Governments who are party to the convention are obliged to designate wetlands in their territory for inclusion in the List of Wetlands of International Importance and to include wetland conservation considerations in their national land-use planning. As at 30 March 1998, there were 124 sites in the UK.

RAMSAR CONVENTION BUREAU, Rue Mauverney 28, CH-1196 Gland, Switzerland. Tel: Gland 999 0170. Web: http://ramsar.org

BONN CONVENTION

The Bonn Convention on the Conservation of Migratory Species of Wild Animals was adopted in 1979 and came into force in the UK on 1 October 1979. The convention requires the protection of listed endangered migratory species and encourages international agreements covering these and other threatened species.

The United Kingdom has signed and ratified two regional agreements under the convention: the Agreement on the Conservation of Small Cetaceans of the Baltic and North Seas (ASCOBANS), protecting dolphins and porpoises, etc; and the Agreement on the Conservation of Bats in Europe. The UK is also a signatory to the African-Eurasian Migratory Waterbird Agreement (AEWA), which is aimed at protecting migrant waterbirds, and is working towards becoming a signatory (on behalf of Gibraltar) to the Agreement on the Conservation of Cetaceans in the Mediterranean and Black Seas (ACCOBAMS).

UNEP/CMS SECRETARIAT, United Nations Premises in Bonn, Martin-Luther-King Strasse 8, D-53175 Bonn, Germany. Tel: Bonn 815 2401. Web: http://www.wcmc.org.uk/cms

BERN CONVENTION

The Convention on the Conservation of European Wildlife and Natural Habitats was adopted in 1979 and ratified by the UK in 1982. The aim of the convention is to conserve flora and fauna and their natural habitats in Europe. Particular emphasis is placed on the protection of endangered and vulnerable species (both endemic and migratory) and on those species and habitats whose conservation requires the co-operation of several states.

Parties to the convention undertake to maintain populations (or take steps to increase populations where necessary) of species covered by the convention while taking account of local cultural, economic and recreational requirements and the requirements of sub-species. They must also ensure that national and local planning and development policies take account of wildlife and fauna.

SECRETARIAT OF THE BERN CONVENTION STANDING COMMITTEE, Council of Europe, F-67075 Strasbourg Cedex, France. Tel: Strasbourg 8841 2253. Web: http://www.coe.com

HABITATS DIRECTIVE

The Council (EC) Directive on the Conservation of Natural Habitats of Wild Fauna and Flora was adopted by the Council in 1992 and became law in the UK in 1994 as the Conservation (Natural Habitats) Regulations. Under this directive EU members are required to maintain or restore natural habitats and wild species (other than birds) and to designate Special Areas of Conservation (SACs). SACs are those areas that are considered to be of European-wide importance because they are rare, threatened or important for the maintenance of biological diversity in Europe. The directive specifies the habitat types and species which require site designation: 75 habitat types and 47 species are proposed for site designation in the UK.

Member states compile a national list from which a final list of European importance will be drawn by 2004. By June 1998 the UK had submitted a total of 315 candidate sites to the Commission.

BIRDS DIRECTIVE

The Council (EC) Directive on the Conservation of Wild Birds was adopted by the Council in 1979 and came into force in April 1981. Under this directive EU members are required to maintain populations of wild birds and to preserve the diversity and area of their habitats. The species that are to be protected are listed in Annex 1 to the directive and are those species that are in danger of extinction, rare, or vulnerable to changes in their habitat.

Members are also obliged, under the directive, to notify the Commission of sites which are of particular importance to the conservation of wild birds. These sites are designated as Special Protection Areas (SPAs). Any site that is to be designated as a SPA in the UK must first have been notified as a Site of Special Scientific Interest or Area of Special Scientific Interest (*see* page 577). Sites may be designated as SPAs if they are of national or international importance.

By February 1998, a total of 1,740 SPAs had been designated, of which 169 are in the UK. The UK designations cover over 700,000 hectares.

CITES

The Convention on Trade in Endangered Species of Wild Fauna and Flora (CITES) was agreed in 1973 and came into force in 1975. It aims to prevent international trade in wildlife and their products, e.g. skins, from threatening species with extinction. Plant and animal species subject to regulation are listed according to the degree of protection they need:

– appendix I is a list of species threatened with extinction that are, or may be, affected by trade. International trade in these species is prohibited
– appendix II is a list of species which might become threatened if trade in them is not controlled. A permit is required to trade in these species
– appendix III is a list of species, protected within individual countries, where the country has asked other parties to the convention to assist in controlling international trade. A permit is required to trade in these species

Approximately 30,000 species are covered by the regulations.

The Wildlife Licensing and Registration Service (Wildlife and Countryside Directorate) of the Department of Environment, Transport and the Regions (*see* page 299) is responsible for issuing permits and compiling annual trade reports. The Joint Nature Conservation Committee (*see* page 329) and the Royal Botanic Gardens (*see* page 338) are the officially designated scientific authorities (on animals and plants respectively) who provide the expertise on which import and export approvals are based. CITES is financed by contributions from the member countries. CITES SECRETARIAT, 15 Chemin des Anémones, CH-1219 Châtelaine, Geneva, Switzerland. Tel: Geneva 2979 9139

EUROPEAN WILDLIFE TRADE REGULATION

The Council (EC) Regulation on the Protection of Species of Wild Fauna and Flora by Regulating Trade Therein came into force in the UK on 1 June 1997. It is intended to standardize wildlife trade regulations across Europe and to improve the application of CITES. Approximately 30,000 plant and animal species are protected under the regulation.

UK LEGISLATION

The Wildlife and Countryside Act 1981 gives legal protection to a wide range of wild animals and plants. Subject to parliamentary approval, the Secretary of State for the Environment may vary the animals and plants given legal protection. The most recent variation of Schedules 5 and 8 came into effect in March and April 1998.

Under Section 9 and Schedule 5 of the Act it is illegal without a licence to kill, injure, take, possess or sell any of the listed animals (whether alive or dead) and to disturb its place of shelter and protection or to destroy that place.

Under Section 13 and Schedule 8 of the Act it is illegal without a licence to pick, uproot, sell or destroy any of the listed plants and, unless authorized, to uproot any wild plant.

The Act lays down a close season for wild birds (other than game birds) from 1 February to 31 August inclusive, each year. Exceptions to these dates are made for:

Capercaillie and (except Scotland) *Woodcock* – 1 February to 30 September
Snipe – 1 February to 11 August
Wild Duck and *Wild Goose* (below high water mark) – 21 February to 31 August

Birds which may be killed or taken outside the close season (except on Sundays and on Christmas Day in Scotland, and on Sundays in prescribed areas of England and Wales) are the above-named, plus coot, certain wild duck (gadwall, goldeneye, mallard, pintail, pochard, shoveler, teal, tufted duck, wigeon), certain wild geese (Canada, greylag, pink-footed, white-fronted (in England and Wales only)), moorhen, golden plover and woodcock.

Certain wild birds may be killed or taken subject to the conditions of a general licence at any time by authorized persons: crow, collared dove, gull (great and lesser black-backed or herring), jackdaw, jay, magpie, pigeon (feral or wood), rook, sparrow (house), and starling. Conditions usually apply where the birds pose a threat to agriculture, public health, air safety, other bird species, and to prevent the spread of disease.

All other British birds are fully protected by law throughout the year.

Animals

‡Adder (*Vipera berus*)
Anemone, Ivell's Sea (*Edwardsia ivelli*)
Anemone, Starlet Sea (*Nematosella vectensis*)
Apus, Tadpole shrimp (*Triops cancriformis*)
Bat, Horseshoe (*Rhinolophidae*, all species)
Bat, Typical (*Vespertilionidae*, all species)
Beetle (*Graphoderus zonatus*)
Beetle (*Hypebaeus flavipes*)

Beetle, Lesser Silver Water (*Hydrochara caraboides*)
§§Beetle, Mire Pill (*Curimopsis nigrita*)
Beetle, Rainbow Leaf (*Chrysolina cerealis*)
*Beetle, Stag (*Lucanus cervus*)
Beetle, Violet Click (*Limoniscus violaceus*)
Beetle, Water (*Graphoderus zonatus*)
Beetle, Water (*Paracymus aeneus*)
Burbot (*Lota lota*)
*Butterfly, Adonis Blue (*Lysandra bellargus*)
*Butterfly, Black Hairstreak (*Strymonidia pruni*)
*Butterfly, Brown Hairstreak (*Thecla betulae*)
*Butterfly, Chalkhill Blue (*Lysandra coridon*)
*Butterfly, Chequered Skipper (*Carterocephalus palaemon*)
*Butterfly, Duke of Burgundy Fritillary (*Hamearis lucina*)
*Butterfly, Glanville Fritillary (*Melitaea cinxia*)
Butterfly, Heath Fritillary (*Mellicta athalia* (or *Melitaea athalia*))
Butterfly, High Brown Fritillary (*Argynnis adippe*)
Butterfly, Large Blue (*Maculinea arion*)
Butterfly, Large Copper (*Lycaena dispar*)
*Butterfly, Large Heath (*Coenonympha tullia*)
*Butterfly, Large Tortoiseshell (*Nymphalis polychloros*)
*Butterfly, Lulworth Skipper (*Thymelicus acteon*)
Butterfly, Marsh Fritillary (*Eurodryas aurinia*)
*Butterfly, Mountain Ringlet (*Erebia epiphron*)
*Butterfly, Northern Brown Argus (*Aricia artaxerxes*)
*Butterfly, Pearl-bordered Fritillary (*Boloria euphrosyne*)
*Butterfly, Purple Emperor (*Apatura iris*)
*Butterfly, Silver Spotted Skipper (*Hesperia comma*)
*Butterfly, Silver-studded Blue (*Plebejus argus*)
*Butterfly, Small Blue (*Cupido minimus*)
Butterfly, Swallowtail (*Papilio machaon*)
*Butterfly, White Letter Hairstreak (*Stymonida w-album*)
*Butterfly, Wood White (*Leptidea sinapis*)
Cat, Wild (*Felis silvestris*)
Cicada, New Forest (*Cicadetta montana*)
**Crayfish, Atlantic stream (*Austropotamobius pallipes*)
Cricket, Field (*Gryllus campestris*)
Cricket, Mole (*Gryllotalpa gryllotalpa*)
Damselfly, Southern (*Coenagrion mercuriale*)
Dolphin (*Cetacea*)
Dormouse (*Muscardinus avellanarius*)
Dragonfly, Norfolk Aeshna (*Aeshna isosceles*)
*Frog, Common (*Rana temporaria*)
Goby, Couch's (*Gobius couchii*)
Goby, Giant (*Gobius cobitis*)
Grasshopper, Wart-biter (*Decticus verrucivorus*)
Hatchet Shell, Northern (*Thyasira gouldi*)
Hydroid, Marine (*Clavopsella navis*)
Lagoon Snail (*Paludinella littorina*)
Lagoon Snail, De Folin's (*Caecum armoricum*)
Lagoon Worm, Tentacled (*Alkmaria romijni*)
Leech, Medicinal (*Hirudo medicinalis*)
Lizard, Sand (*Lacerta agilis*)
‡Lizard, Viviparous (*Lacerta vivipara*)
Marten, Pine (*Martes martes*)
Moth, Barberry Carpet (*Pareulype berberata*)
Moth, Black-veined (*Siona lineata* (or *Idaea lineata*))
Moth, Essex Emerald (*Thetidia smaragdaria*)
Moth, Fiery clearwing (*Bembecia chrysidiformis*)

---

*   The offence relates to sale only
**   The offence relates to 'taking' and 'sale' only
†   The offence relates to 'killing and injuring' only
‡   The offence relates to 'killing, injuring and sale'
§   The offence relates to 'killing, injuring and taking'
§§ The offence relates only to damaging, destroying or obstructing access to a shelter or protection
†† The offence relates to killing, injuring, taking, possession and sale
‡‡ The offence relates to killing, injuring, taking and damaging, etc., a shelter

Moth, Fisher's estuarine (*Gortyna borelii*)
Moth, New Forest Burnet (*Zygaena viciae*)
Moth, Reddish Buff (*Acosmetia caliginosa*)
Moth, Sussex Emerald (*Thalera fimbrialis*)
††Mussel, Fan (*Atrina fragilis*)
†Mussel, Freshwater Pearl (*Margaritifera margaritifera*)
Newt, Great Crested (or Warty) (*Triturus cristatus*)
*Newt, Palmate (*Triturus helveticus*)
*Newt, Smooth (*Triturus vulgaris*)
Otter, Common (*Lutra lutra*)
Porpoise (*Cetacea*)
Sandworm, Lagoon (*Armandia cirrhosa*)
††Sea Fan, Pink (*Eunicella verrucosa*)
Sea-Mat, Trembling (*Victorella pavida*)
Sea Slug, Lagoon (*Tenellia adspersa*)
‡‡Shad, Allis (*alosa alosa*)
§§Shad, Twaite (*alosa fallax*)
Shark, Basking (*Cetorhinus maximus*)
Shrimp, Fairy (*Chirocephalus diaphanus*)
Shrimp, Lagoon Sand (*Gammarus insensibilis*)
‡Slow-worm (*Anguis fragilis*)
Snail, Glutinous (*Myxas glutinosa*)
Snail, Sandbowl (*Catinella arenaria*)
‡Snake, Grass (*Natrix natrix* (*Natrix helvetica*))
Snake, Smooth (*Coronella austriaca*)
Spider, Fen Raft (*Dolomedes plantarius*)
Spider, Ladybird (*Eresus niger*)
Squirrel, Red (*Sciurus vulgaris*)
Sturgeon (*Acipenser sturio*)
*Toad, Common (*Bufo bufo*)
Toad, Natterjack (*Bufo calamita*)
Turtle, Marine (*Dermochelyidae* and *Cheloniidae*, all species)
Vendace (*Coregonus albula*)
§§Vole, Water (*Arvicola terrestris*)
Walrus (*Odobenus rosmarus*)
Whale (*Cetacea*)
Whitefish (*Coregonus lavaretus*)

Plants

Adder's tongue, Least (*Ophioglossum lusitanicum*)
Alison, Small (*Alyssum alyssoides*)
Blackwort (*Southbya nigrella*)
°Bluebell (*Hyacinthoides non-scripta*)
Broomrape, Bedstraw (*Orobanche caryophyllacea*)
Broomrape, Oxtongue (*Orobanche loricata*)
Broomrape, Thistle (*Orobanche reticulata*)
Cabbage, Lundy (*Rhynchosinapis wrightii*)
Calamint, Wood (*Calamintha sylvatica*)
Caloplaca, Snow (*Caloplaca nivalis*)
Catapyrenium, Tree (*Catapyrenium psoromoides*)
Catchfly, Alpine (*Lychnis alpina*)
Catillaria, Laurer's (*Catellaria laureri*)
Centaury, Slender (*Centaurium tenuiflorum*)
Cinquefoil, Rock (*Potentilla rupestris*)
Clary, Meadow (*Salvia pratensis*)
Club-rush, Triangular (*Scirpus triquetrus*)
Colt's-foot, Purple (*Homogyne alpina*)
Cotoneaster, Wild (*Cotoneaster integerrimus*)
Cottongrass, Slender (*Eriophorum gracile*)
Cow-wheat, Field (*Melampyrum arvense*)
Crocus, Sand (*Romulea columnae*)
Crystalwort, Lizard (*Riccia bifurca*)
Cudweed, Broad-leaved (*Filago pyramidata*)
Cudweed, Jersey (*Gnaphalium luteoalbum*)
Cudweed, Red-tipped (*Filago lutescens*)
Cut-grass (*Leersia oryzoides*)

Diapensia (*Diapensia lapponica*)
Dock, Shore (*Rumex rupestris*)
Earwort, Marsh (*Jamesoniella undulifolia*)
Eryngo, Field (*Eryngium campestre*)
Fern, Dickie's bladder (*Cystopteris dickieana*)
Fern, Killarney (*Trichomanes speciosum*)
Flapwort, Norfolk (*Leiocolea rutheana*)
Fleabane, Alpine (*Erigeron borealis*)
Fleabane, Small (*Pulicaria vulgaris*)
Fleawort, South stack (*Tephroseris integrifolia* (*ssp maritima*))
Frostwort, Pointed (*Gymnomitrion apiculatum*)
Fungus, Hedgehog (*Hericium erinaceum*)
Fungus, Oak polypore (*Buglossoporus pulvinus*)
Fungus, Royal bolete (*Boletus regius*)
Fungus, Sandy stilt puffball (*Battarraea phalloides*)
Galingale, Brown (*Cyperus fuscus*)
Gentian, Alpine (*Gentiana nivalis*)
Gentian, Dune (*Gentianella uliginosa*)
Gentian, Early (*Gentianella anglica*)
Gentian, Fringed (*Gentianella ciliata*)
Gentian, Spring (*Gentiana verna*)
Germander, Cut-leaved (*Teucrium botrys*)
Germander, Water (*Teucrium scordium*)
Gladiolus, Wild (*Gladiolus illyricus*)
Goosefoot, Stinking (*Chenopodium vulvaria*)
Grass-poly (*Lythrum hyssopifolia*)
Grimmia, Blunt-leaved (*Grimmia unicolor*)
Gyalecta, Elm (*Gyalecta ulmi*)
Hare's-ear, Sickle-leaved (*Bupleurum falcatum*)
Hare's-ear, Small (*Bupleurum baldense*)
Hawk's-beard, Stinking (*Crepis foetida*)
Hawkweed, Northroe (*Hieracium northroense*)
Hawkweed, Shetland (*Hieracium zetlandicum*)
Hawkweed, Weak-leaved (*Hieracium attenuatifolium*)
Heath, Blue (*Phyllodoce caerulea*)
Helleborine, Red (*Cephalanthera rubra*)
Helleborine, Young's (*Epipactis youngiana*)
Horsetail, Branched (*Equisetum ramosissimum*)
Hound's-tongue, Green (*Cynoglossum germanicum*)
Knawel, Perennial (*Scleranthus perennis*)
Knotgrass, Sea (*Polygonum maritimum*)
Lady's-slipper (*Cypripedium calceolus*)
Lecanactis, Churchyard (*Lecanactis hemisphaerica*)
Lecanora, Tarn (*Lecanora archariana*)
Lecidea, Copper (*Lecidea inops*)
Leek, Round-headed (*Allium sphaerocephalon*)
Lettuce, Least (*Lactuca saligna*)
Lichen, Alpine sulphur-tresses (*Alectoria ochroleuca*)
Lichen, Arctic kidney (*Nephroma arcticum*)
Lichen, Ciliate strap (*Heterodermia leucomelos*)
Lichen, Convoluted cladonia (*Cladonia convoluta*)
Lichen, Coralloid rosette (*Heterodermia propagulifera*)
Lichen, Ear-lobed dog (*Peltigera lepidophora*)
Lichen, Forked hair (*Bryoria furcellata*)
Lichen, Goblin lights (*Catolechia wahlenbergii*)
Lichen, Golden hair (*Teloschistes flavicans*)
Lichen, New Forest beech-lichen (*Enterographa elaborata*)
Lichen, Orange fruited Elm (*Caloplaca luteoalba*)
Lichen, River jelly (*Collema dichotomum*)
Lichen, Scaly breck (*Squamarina lentigera*)
Lichen, Stary breck (*Buellia asterella*)
Lichen, Upright mountain cladonia (*Cladonia stricta*)
Lily, Snowdon (*Lloydia serotina*)
Liverwort, Leafy (*Petallophyllum ralfsi*)
Liverwort, Lindenberg's (*Adelanthus lindenbergianus*)
Marsh-mallow, Rough (*Althaea hirsuta*)
Marshwort, Creeping (*Apium repens*)
Milk-parsley, Cambridge (*Selinum carvifolia*)
Moss (*Drepanocladius vernicosus*)
Moss, Alpine copper (*Mielichoferia mielichoferi*)
Moss, Anomodon, long-leaved (*Anomodon longifolius*)

° The sale of plants taken from the wild is prohibited; the sale of cultivated plants is still permitted

Moss, Baltic bog (*Sphagnum balticum*)
Moss, Blue dew (*Saelania glaucescens*)
Moss, Blunt-leaved bristle (*Orthotrichum obtusifolium*)
Moss, Bright green cave (*Cyclodictyon laetevirens*)
Moss, Cordate beard (*Barbula cordata*)
Moss, Cornish path (*Ditrichum cornubicum*)
Moss, Derbyshire feather (*Thamnobryum angustifolium*)
Moss, Dune thread (*Bryum mamillatum*)
Moss, Flamingo (*Desmatodon cernuus*)
Moss, Glaucous beard (*Barbula glauca*)
Moss, Green shield (*Buxbaumia viridis*)
Moss, Hair silk (*Plagiothecium piliferum*)
Moss, Knothole (*Zygodon forsteri*)
Moss, Large yellow feather (*Scorpidium turgescens*)
Moss, Millimetre (*Micromitrium tenerum*)
Moss, Multifruited river (*Cryphaea lamyana*)
Moss, Nowell's limestone (*Zygodon gracilis*)
Moss, Polar feather-moss (*Hygrohypnum polare*)
Moss, Rigid apple (*Bartramia stricta*)
Moss, Round-leaved feather (*Rhyncostegium rotundifolium*)
Moss, Schleicher's thread (*Bryum schleicheri*)
Moss, Threadmoss, long-leaved (*Bryum neodamense*)
Moss, Triangular pygmy (*Acaulon triquetrum*)
Moss, Vaucher's feather (*Hypnum vaucheri*)
Mudwort, Welsh (*Limosella austeralis*)
Naiad, Holly-leaved (*Najas marina*)
Naiad, Slender (*Najas flexilis*)
Orache, Stalked (*Halimione pedunculata*)
Orchid, Early spider (*Ophrys sphegodes*)
Orchid, Fen (*Liparis loeselii*)
Orchid, Ghost (*Epipogium aphyllum*)
Orchid, Lapland marsh (*Dactylorhiza lapponica*)
Orchid, Late spider (*Ophrys fuciflora*)
Orchid, Lizard (*Himantoglossum hircinum*)
Orchid, Military (*Orchis militaris*)
Orchid, Monkey (*Orchis simia*)
Panneria, Caledonia (*Panneria ignobilis*)
Parmelia, New Forest (*Parmelia minarum*)
Parmentaria, Oil stain (*Parmentaria chilensis*)
Pear, Plymouth (*Pyrus cordata*)
Penny-cress, Perfoliate (*Thlaspi perfoliatum*)
Pennyroyal (*Mentha pulegium*)
Pertusaria, Alpine moss (*Pertusaria bryontha*)
Physcia, Southern grey (*Physcia tribacioides*)
Pigmyweed (*Crassula aquatica*)
Pine, Ground (*Ajuga chamaepitys*)
Pink, Cheddar (*Dianthus gratianopolitanus*)
Pink, Childing (*Petroraghia nanteuilii*)
Pink, Deptford (*Dianthus armeria*) (England and Wales only)
Plantain, Floating water (*Luronium natans*)
Pseudocyphellaria, Ragged (*Pseudocyphellaria lacerata*)
Psora, Rusty Alpine (*Psora rubiformis*)
Ragwort, Fen (*Senecio paludosus*)
Ramping-fumitory, Martin's (*Fumaria martinii*)
Rampion, Spiked (*Phyteuma spicatum*)
Restharrow, Small (*Ononis reclinata*)
Rock-cress, Alpine (*Arabis alpina*)
Rock-cress, Bristol (*Arabis stricta*)
Rustwort, Western (*Marsupella profunda*)
Sandwort, Norwegian (*Arenaria norvegica*)
Sandwort, Teesdale (*Minuartia stricta*)
Saxifrage, Drooping (*Saxifraga cernua*)
Saxifrage, Marsh (*Saxifrage hirulus*)
Saxifrage, Tufted (*Saxifraga cespitosa*)
Solenopsora, Serpentine (*Solenopsora liparina*)
Solomon's-seal, Whorled (*Polygonatum verticillatum*)
Sow-thistle, Alpine (*Cicerbita alpina*)
Spearwort, Adder's-tongue (*Ranunculus ophioglossifolius*)
Speedwell, Fingered (*Veronica triphyllos*)

Speedwell, Spiked (*Veronica spicata*)
Spike rush, Dwarf (*Eleocharis parvula*)
Star-of-Bethlehem, Early (*Gagea bohemica*)
Starfruit (*Damasonium alisma*)
Stonewort, Bearded (*Chara canescens*)
Stonewort, Foxtail (*Lamprothamnium papulosum*)
Strapwort (*Corrigiola litoralis*)
Turpswort (*Geocalyx graveolens*)
Violet, Fen (*Viola persicifolia*)
Viper's-grass (*Scorzonera humilis*)
Water-plantain, Ribbon-leaved (*Alisma gramineum*)
Wood-sedge, Starved (*Carex depauperata*)
Woodsia, Alpine (*Woodsia alpina*)
Woodsia, Oblong (*Woodsia ilvenis*)
Wormwood, Field (*Artemisia campestris*)
Woundwort, Downy (*Stachys germanica*)
Woundwort, Limestone (*Stachys alpina*)
Yellow-rattle, Greater (*Rhinanthus serotinus*)

MOST UNDER THREAT

The animals and birds considered to be most under threat in Great Britain by the Joint Nature Conservation Committee are the high brown fritillary butterfly; violet click beetle; new forest burnet moth; corncrake; aquatic warbler; tree sparrow; wryneck; water vole; red squirrel; allis shad; and twaite shad.

Close Seasons and Times

GAME BIRDS

In each case the dates are inclusive:

Black game – 11 December to 19 August (31 August in Somerset, Devon and New Forest)

*Grouse – 11 December to 11 August

*Partridge – 2 February to 31 August

*Pheasant – 2 February to 30 September

*Ptarmigan – (Scotland only) 11 December to 11 August

*It is also unlawful in England and Wales to kill this game on a Sunday or Christmas Day

HUNTING AND GROUND GAME

There is no statutory close time for fox-hunting or rabbit-shooting, nor for hares. However, by an Act passed in 1892 the sale of hares or leverets in Great Britain is prohibited from 1 March to 31 July inclusive. The recognized date for the opening of the fox-hunting season is 1 November, and it continues till the following April.

DEER

The statutory close seasons for deer (all dates inclusive) are:

	England and Wales	*Scotland*
Fallow deer		
Male	1 May–31 July	1 May–31 July
Female	1 Mar.–31 Oct.	16 Feb.–20 Oct.
Red deer		
Male	1 May–31 July	21 Oct.–30 June
Female	1 Mar.–31 Oct.	16 Feb.–20 Oct.
Roe deer		
Male	1 Nov.–31 Mar.	21 Oct.–31 Mar.
Female	1 Mar.–31 Oct.	1 April–20 Oct.
Sika deer		
Male	1 May–31 July	21 Oct.–30 June
Female	1 Mar.–31 Oct.	16 Feb.–20 Oct.
Red/Sika hybrids		
Male	—	21 Oct.–30 June
Female	—	16 Feb.–20 Oct

ANGLING

GAME FISHING

Where local by-laws neither specify nor dispense with an annual close season, the statutory close times for game fishing are: Trout, 1 October to end February; Salmon, 1 November to 31 January.

COARSE FISHING

Responsibility for the fisheries function of the National Rivers Authority, including licensing and regulation, passed to the Environment Agency on 1 April 1996. The statutory close season for coarse fish in England and Wales runs from 15 March to 15 June on all rivers, streams and drains. Close season arrangements for canals vary from region to region. The close season on all lakes, ponds and reservoirs is at the discretion of the fishery owner, except on the Norfolk Broads and certain Sites of Special Scientific Interest where the statutory close season still applies. It is necessary in all cases to check with the Environment Agency regional office concerning the area (details can be found in the local telephone directory).

LICENCES

Purchase of a national rod fishing licence is legally required of anglers wishing to fish with rod and line in all waters within the area of the Environment Agency.

	Salmon and sea trout	*Non-migratory trout and coarse fish*
Full	£55.00	£16.00
Concessionary	27.50	8.00
Eight-day	15.00	6.00
One-day	5.00	2.00

Concessionary licences are available for juniors (12–16 years), for senior citizens (65 years and over), and disabled who are in receipt of long-term incapacity benefit, short-term incapacity benefit (at the higher rate) or severe disablement allowance. Those in receipt of a war pension which includes unemployability supplements are also eligible.

Historic Buildings and Monuments

Under the Planning (Listed Buildings and Conservation Areas) Act 1990, the Secretary of State for National Heritage has a statutory duty to compile lists of buildings or groups of buildings in England which are of special architectural or historic interest. Under the Ancient Monuments and Archaeological Areas Act 1979 as amended by the National Heritage Act 1983, the Secretary of State is also responsible for compiling a schedule of ancient monuments. Decisions are taken on the advice of English Heritage (*see* page 308).

Listed buildings are classified into Grade I, Grade II* and Grade II. There are currently about 500,000 individual listed buildings in England, of which about 95 per cent are Grade II listed. Almost all pre-1700 buildings are listed, and most buildings of 1700 to 1840. English Heritage is carrying out thematic surveys of particular types of buildings with a view to making recommendations for listing, and members of the public may propose a building for consideration. The main purpose of listing is to ensure that care is taken in deciding the future of a building. No changes which affect the architectural or historic character of a listed building can be made without listed building consent (in addition to planning permission where relevant). Applications for listed building consent are normally dealt with by the local planning authority, although English Heritage is always consulted about proposals affecting Grade I and Grade II* properties. It is a criminal offence to demolish a listed building, or alter it in such a way as to affect its character, without consent.

There are currently about 22,500 scheduled monuments in England. English Heritage is carrying out a Monuments Protection Programme assessing archaeological sites with a view to making recommendations for scheduling, and members of the public may propose a monument for consideration. All monuments proposed for scheduling are considered to be of national importance. Where buildings are both scheduled and listed, ancient monuments legislation takes precedence. The main purpose of scheduling a monument is to preserve it for the future and to protect it from damage, destruction or any unnecessary interference. Once a monument has been scheduled, scheduled monument consent is required before any works are carried out which would damage or alter the monument in any way. The scope of the control is more extensive and more detailed than that applied to listed buildings, but certain minor works, as detailed in the Ancient Monuments Class Consents Order 1994, may be carried out without consent. It is a criminal offence to carry out unauthorized work to scheduled monuments.

Under the Planning (Listed Buildings and Conservation Areas) Act 1990 and the Ancient Monuments and Archaeological Areas Act 1979, the Secretary of State for Wales is responsible for listing buildings and scheduling monuments in Wales on the advice of Cadw (*see* page 353), the Historic Buildings Council for Wales (*see* page 308) and the Ancient Monuments Board for Wales (*see* page 309). The criteria for evaluating buildings are similar to those in England and the same listing system is used. In April 1997 there were 19,161 listed buildings and 2,999 scheduled monuments in Wales.

Under the Town and Country Planning (Scotland) Act 1972 and the Ancient Monuments and Archaeological Areas Act 1979, the Secretary of State for Scotland is responsible for listing buildings and scheduling monu-

ments in Scotland on the advice of Historic Scotland (*see* page 341), the Historic Buildings Council for Scotland (*see* page 308) and the Ancient Monuments Board for Scotland (*see* page 309). The criteria for evaluating buildings are similar to those in England but an A, B, C grading system is used. There are about 43,783 listed buildings and about 6,800 scheduled monuments in Scotland.

Under the Planning (Northern Ireland) Order 1991 and the Historic Monuments and Archaeological Objects (Northern Ireland) Order 1995, the Department of the Environment for Northern Ireland (*see* page 330) is responsible for listing buildings and scheduling monuments in Northern Ireland on the advice of the Historic Buildings Council for Northern Ireland and the Historic Monuments Council for Northern Ireland. The criteria for evaluating buildings are similar to those in England but no statutory grading system is used. In June 1997 there were 8,589 listed buildings and 1,295 scheduled monuments in Northern Ireland.

The following is a selection of the many historic buildings and monuments open to the public. The admission charges given are the standard charges for 1998–9; many properties have concessionary rates for children, etc. Opening hours vary. Many properties are closed in winter and some are also closed in the mornings. Most properties are closed on Christmas Eve, Christmas Day, Boxing Day and New Year's Day, and many are closed on Good Friday. During the winter season, most English Heritage monuments are closed on Mondays and Tuesdays and monuments in the care of Cadw are closed on Sunday mornings. In Northern Ireland most monuments are closed on Mondays except on bank holidays. Information about a specific property should be checked by telephone.

*Closed in winter (usually November-March)
†Closed in winter, and in mornings in summer

ENGLAND

EH English Heritage property
NT National Trust property

*A LA RONDE (NT), Exmouth, Devon. Tel: 01395-265514. Closed Fri. and Sat. Adm. £3.20. Unique 16-sided house completed *c.*1796

†ALNWICK CASTLE, Northumberland. Tel: 01665-510777. Closed Fri. (except Good Friday). Adm. charge. Seat of the Dukes of Northumberland since 1309; Italian Renaissance-style interior

ALTHORP, Northants. Tel: 01604-770107, ticket reservations 01604-592020. Open 1 July to 30 August. Adm £9.50. Spencer family seat. Diana, Princess of Wales memorabilia

†ANGLESEY ABBEY (NT), Cambs. Tel: 01223-811200. Closed Mon. (except Bank Holidays) and Tues. Gardens open daily July to Sept. Adm. £5.80 (£6.80 Sun. and Bank Holidays); gardens only, £3.40. House built *c.*1600. Outstanding grounds with unique statuary

APSLEY HOUSE, London W1. Tel: 0171-499 5676. Closed Mon. Adm. £4.50. Built by Robert Adam 1771-8, home of the Dukes of Wellington since 1817 and known as 'No. 1 London'. Collection of fine and decorative arts

†Arundel Castle, W. Sussex. Tel: 01903-883136. Closed Sat. Adm. charge. Castle dating from the Norman Conquest. Seat of the Dukes of Norfolk

Avebury (nt), Wilts. Adm. free. Remains of stone circles constructed 4,000 years ago surrounding the later village of Avebury. Also *Alexander Keiller Museum.* Tel: 01672-539250. Adm. £1.60

Banqueting House, Whitehall, London sw1. Tel: 0171-930 4179. Closed Sun. and Bank Holidays. Adm. £3.55. Designed by Inigo Jones; ceiling paintings by Rubens. Site of the execution of Charles I

†Basildon Park, Berks. Tel: 0118-984 3040. Closed Mon. (except Bank Holidays), Tues. and Good Friday. Adm. £4.00; grounds only, £1.60. Palladian house built in 1776

Battle Abbey (eh), E. Sussex. Tel: 01424-773792. Adm. £4.00. Remains of the abbey founded by William the Conqueror on the site of the Battle of Hastings

Beaulieu, Hants. Tel: 01590-612345. Adm. charge. House and gardens, Beaulieu Abbey and exhibition of monastic life, National Motor Museum (*see also* page 591)

Beeston Castle (eh), Cheshire. Tel: 01829-260464. Adm. £2.70. Thirteenth-century inner ward with gatehouse and towers, and remains of outer ward

†Belton House (nt), Grantham, Lincs. Tel: 01476-566116. Closed Mon. (except Bank Holidays), Tues. and Good Friday. Adm. £5.00. Fine 17th-century house in landscaped park

*Belvoir Castle, nr Grantham, Lincs. Tel: 01476-870262. Closed Mon. (except Bank Holidays) and Fri.; also closed Mon.-Sat. in Oct. Adm. £5.00. Seat of the Dukes of Rutland; 19th-century Gothic-style castle

*Berkeley Castle, Glos. Tel: 01453-810332. Opening times vary. Adm. £4.95. Completed 1153; site of the murder of Edward II (1327)

*Blenheim Palace, Woodstock, Oxon. Tel: 01993-811325. Adm. charge. Seat of the Dukes of Marlborough and Winston Churchill's birthplace; designed by Vanbrugh

†Blickling Hall (nt), Norfolk. Tel: 01263-733084. Opening times vary. Adm. £6.00; garden only, £3.30. Jacobean house with state rooms, temple and 18th-century orangery

Bodiam Castle (nt), E. Sussex. Tel: 01580-830436. Closed Mon. in winter. Adm. £3.30. Well-preserved medieval moated castle

Bolsover Castle (eh), Derbys. Tel: 01246-823349. Closed Mon. and Tues. in winter. Adm. £2.95. Notable 17th-century buildings

Boscobel House (eh), Shropshire. Tel: 01902-850244. Closed Mon. and Tues. in winter; also closed in Jan. Adm. £3.95. Timber-framed 17th-century hunting lodge, refuge of fugitive Charles II

†Boughton House, Northants. Tel: 01536-515731. House open Aug. only; grounds May to Sept. except Fri.; state rooms by prior booking. Adm. £4.00; grounds, £1.50. A 17th-century house with French-style additions

*Bowood House, Wilts. Tel: 01249-812102. Adm. charge. An 18th-century house in Capability Brown park, with lake, temple and arboretum

†Broadlands, Hants. Tel: 01794-517888. Open June-Sept. Adm. £5.00. Palladian mansion in Capability Brown parkland. Mountbatten exhibition

Brontë Parsonage, Haworth, W. Yorks. Tel: 01535-642323. Closed Jan.-Feb. Adm. charge. Home of the Brontë sisters; museum and memorabilia

Buckfast Abbey, Devon. Tel: 01364-642519. Adm. free. Benedictine monastery on medieval foundations

*Buckingham Palace, London sw1. Tel: 0171-839 1377. Open daily for eight weeks from early Aug. each year. Adm. £9.50. Purchased by George III in 1762, and the Sovereign's official London residence since 1837. Eighteen state rooms, including the Throne Room, and Picture Gallery

Buckland Abbey (nt), Devon. Tel: 01822-853607. Closed Thurs.; in winter open only weekend afternoons, closed 4-22 January 1999. Adm. £4.30; grounds only, £2.20. A 13th-century Cistercian monastery. Home of Sir Francis Drake

Burghley House, Stamford, Lincs. Tel: 01780-752451. Adm. £5.85. Late Elizabethan house; vast state apartments

†Calke Abbey (nt), Derbys. Tel: 01332-863822. Closed Thurs. and Fri. Adm. £4.90, by timed ticket; garden only, £2.20. Baroque 18th-century mansion

Carisbrooke Castle (eh), Isle of Wight. Tel: 01983-522107. Adm. £4.00. Norman castle; prison of Charles I 1647-8

Carlisle Castle (eh), Cumbria. Tel: 01228-591922. Adm. £2.90. Medieval castle, prison of Mary Queen of Scots

*Carlyle's House (nt), Cheyne Row, London sw3. Tel: 0171-352 7087. Closed Mon. (except Bank Holidays), Tues. and Good Friday. Adm. £3.20. Home of Thomas Carlyle

Castle Acre Priory (eh), Norfolk. Tel: 01760-755394. Closed Mon. and Tues. in winter. Adm. £2.95. Remains include 12th-century church and prior's lodgings

*Castle Drogo (nt), Devon. Tel: 01647-433306. Castle closed Fri. (except Good Friday). Adm. £5.20; grounds only, £2.40. Granite castle designed by Lutyens

*Castle Howard, N. Yorks. Tel: 01653-648444. Adm. £6.50; grounds only, £4.00. Designed by Vanbrugh 1699-1726; mausoleum designed by Hawksmoor

Castle Rising Castle (eh), Norfolk. Tel: 01553-631330. Closed Mon. and Tues. in winter. Adm. £2.30. A 12th-century keep in a massive earthwork with gatehouse and bridge

†Chartwell (nt), Kent. Tel: 01732-866368. Closed Mon. (except Bank Holidays) and Tues. (except July and Aug.). Adm. £5.20 by timed ticket; grounds only, £2.60. Home of Sir Winston Churchill

*Chatsworth, Derbys. Tel: 01246-582204. Adm. charge. Tudor mansion in magnificent parkland

Chesters Roman Fort (eh), Northumberland. Tel: 01434-681379. Adm. £2.70. Roman cavalry fort

*Chysauster Ancient Village (eh), Cornwall. Adm. £1.60. Romano-Cornish village, 2nd and 3rd century AD, on a probably late Iron Age site

Clifford's Tower (eh), York. Tel: 01904-646940. Adm. £1.70. A 13th-century tower built on a mound

†Cliveden (nt), Berks. Tel: 01628-605069. House open Thurs. and Sun. only, gardens daily. Adm. £4.80; £1.00 extra for house. Former home of the Astors, now an hotel set in garden and woodland

Corbridge Roman Site (eh), Northumberland. Tel: 01434-632349. Closed Mon. and Tues. in winter. Adm. £2.70. Excavated central area of a Roman town and successive military bases ·

Corfe Castle (nt), Dorset. Tel: 01929-481294. Adm. £3.80. Ruined former royal castle dating from 11th century

†Croft Castle (nt), Herefordshire. Tel: 01568-780246. Closed Mon. (except Bank Holidays), Tues. and Good Friday; April and Oct. open weekends only; grounds open all year. Adm. £3.30; grounds only, £1.50 per car. Pre-Conquest border castle with Georgian-Gothic interior

DEAL CASTLE (EH), Kent. Tel: 01304-372762. Closed Mon. and Tues. in winter. Adm. £3.00. Largest of the coastal defence forts built by Henry VIII

DICKENS HOUSE, Doughty Street, London WC1. Tel: 0171-405 2127. Closed Sun. Adm. £3.50. House occupied by Dickens 1837-9; manuscripts, furniture and portraits

DR JOHNSON'S HOUSE, 17 Gough Square, London EC4. Tel: 0171-353 3745. Closed Sun. and Bank Holidays. Adm. charge. Home of Samuel Johnson

DOVE COTTAGE, Grasmere, Cumbria. Tel: 01539-435544. Closed Jan. and early Feb. Adm. £4.40; museum only, £2.20. Wordsworth's home 1799-1808; museum

DOVER CASTLE (EH), Kent. Tel: 01304-201628. Adm. £6.50. Castle with Roman, Saxon and Norman features; wartime operations rooms

DUNSTANBURGH CASTLE (EH), Northumberland. Tel: 01665-576231. Closed Mon. and Tues. in winter. Adm. £1.70. A 14th-century castle on a cliff, with a substantial gatehouse-keep

FARLEIGH HUNGERFORD CASTLE (EH), Somerset. Tel: 01225-754026. Closed Mon. and Tues. in winter. Adm. £2.10. Late 14th-century castle with two courts; chapel with tomb of Sir Thomas Hungerford

*FARNHAM CASTLE KEEP (EH), Surrey. Tel: 01252-713393. Adm. £2.00. Large 12th-century shell-keep

FOUNTAINS ABBEY (NT), nr Ripon, N. Yorks. Tel: 01765-608888. Closed Fri. Nov.-Jan.; deer park open daily all year. Adm. £4.20; visitor centre, deer park and St Mary's Church free. Ruined Cistercian monastery; 18th-century landscaped gardens of Studley Royal estate

FRAMLINGHAM CASTLE (EH), Suffolk. Tel: 01728-724189. Adm. £2.95. Castle (c.1200) with high curtain walls enclosing an almshouse (1639)

FURNESS ABBEY (EH), Cumbria. Tel: 01229-823420. Closed Mon. and Tues. in winter. Adm. £2.50. Remains of church and conventual buildings founded in 1123

GLASTONBURY ABBEY, Somerset. Tel: 01458-832267. Adm. £2.50. Ruins of 12th-century abbey rebuilt after fire. Site of an early Christian settlement

GOODRICH CASTLE (EH), Herefordshire. Tel: 01600-890538. Adm. £2.95. Remains of 13th- and 14th-century castle with 12th-century keep

GREENWICH, London SE10. Royal Observatory. Tel: 0181-858 4422. Adm. £5.00 (joint ticket for Royal Observatory, The Queen's House and National Maritime Museum). Former Royal Observatory (founded 1675) housing the time ball and zero meridian of longitude. The Queen's House. Tel: 0181-858 4422. Closed Sun. mornings. Adm. charge. Designed for Queen Anne, wife of James I, by Inigo Jones. Painted Hall and Chapel (Royal Naval College). Closed mornings. Visitors admitted to Sunday service (11 a.m.) in the chapel during college term

GRIME'S GRAVES (EH), Norfolk. Tel: 01842-810656. Closed Mon. and Tues. in winter. Adm. £1.75. Neolithic flint mines. One shaft can be descended

GUILDHALL, London EC2. Tel: 0171-332 1460. Closed Sun. in winter. Adm. free. Centre of civic government of the City. Built c.1440; facade built 1788-9

*HADDON HALL, Derbys. Tel: 01629-812855. Adm. £5.50. Well-preserved 12th-century manor house

HAILES ABBEY (EH), Glos. Tel: 01242-602398. Closed Mon. to Fri. in winter. Adm. £2.50. Ruins of a 13th-century Cistercian monastery

†HAM HOUSE (NT), Richmond, Surrey. Tel: 0181-940 1950. Closed Thurs. and Fri. Adm. £5.00. Garden open all year except Thurs. and Fri. Adm. £1.50. Stuart house with fine interiors

HAMPTON COURT PALACE, East Molesey, Surrey. Tel: 0181-781 9500. Adm. £9.25. A 16th-century palace with additions by Wren. Gardens with maze; Tudor tennis court (summer only)

†HARDWICK HALL (NT), Derbys. Tel: 01246-850430. Closed Mon. (except Bank Holidays), Tues. and Fri.; grounds open daily, all year. Adm. £6.00; grounds only, £2.70. Built 1591-7 for Bess of Hardwick; notable furnishings

*HARDY'S COTTAGE (NT), Higher Bockhampton, Dorset. Tel: 01305-262366. Closed Fri. (except Good Friday) and Sat. Adm. £2.60. Birthplace of Thomas Hardy

*HAREWOOD HOUSE, W. Yorks. Tel: 0113-288 6331. Closed 5 June. Adm. £6.75. An 18th-century house designed by John Carr and Robert Adam; park by Capability Brown

†HATFIELD HOUSE, Herts. Tel: 01707-262823. Closed Mon. (except Bank Holidays). Adm. £5.70; grounds, £3.10. Jacobean house built by Robert Cecil; surviving wing of Royal Palace of Hatfield (1497)

HELMSLEY CASTLE (EH), N. Yorks. Tel: 01439-770442. Closed Mon. and Tues. in winter. Adm. £2.20. A 12th-century keep and curtain wall with 16th-century buildings. Spectacular earthwork defences

†HEVER CASTLE, Kent. Tel: 01732-865224. Adm. charge. A 13th-century double-moated castle, childhood home of Anne Boleyn

*HOLKER HALL, Cumbria. Tel: 015395-58328. Closed Sat. Adm. charge. Former home of the Dukes of Devonshire; award-winning gardens

†HOLKHAM HALL, Norfolk. Tel: 01328-710227. Closed Fri. and Sat. Adm. £4.00. Fine Palladian mansion

HOUSESTEADS ROMAN FORT (EH), Northumberland. Tel: 01434-344363. Adm. £2.70. Excavated infantry fort on Hadrian's Wall with extra-mural civilian settlement

†HUGHENDEN MANOR (NT), High Wycombe. Tel: 01494-532580. Closed Mon. (except Bank Holidays) and Tues.; open weekends only in March. Adm. £4.00. Home of Disraeli; small formal garden

JANE AUSTEN'S HOUSE, Chawton, Hants. Tel: 01420-83262. Closed Mon.-Fri. in Jan. and Feb. Adm. charge. Jane Austen's home 1809-17

*KELMSCOTT MANOR, nr Lechlade, Oxon. Tel: 01367-252486. Open Wed. and afternoon of third Sat. in every month, Thurs. and Fri. by appointment. Adm. £6.00. Summer home of William Morris, with products of Morris and Co.

KENILWORTH CASTLE (EH), Warks. Tel: 01926-852078. Adm. £3.10. Castle with building styles from 1155 to 1649

*KENSINGTON PALACE, London W8. Closed Mon. and Tues. in winter. Adm. £7.50. Built in 1605 and enlarged by Wren; bought by William and Mary in 1689. Birthplace of Queen Victoria. Royal Ceremonial Dress Collection

KENWOOD (EH), Hampstead Lane, London NW3. Tel: 0181-348 1286. Adm. free. Adam villa housing the Iveagh bequest of paintings and furniture. Open-air concerts in summer

*KEW PALACE, Surrey. Tel: 0181-332 5189. Closed for refurbishment until spring 1999. Also Queen Charlotte's Cottage, weekends and Bank Holidays in May-Sept. Adm. free (but £4.50 adm. to Kew Gardens)

†KINGSTON LACY HOUSE (NT), Dorset. Tel: 01202-883402. Closed Thurs. and Fri. Adm. £6.00; grounds only, £2.50. A 17th-century house with 19th-century alterations; important art collection

†KNEBWORTH HOUSE, Herts. Tel: 01438-812661. Closed Mon. (except Bank Holidays); grounds open daily except mid-Sept. Mon.-Fri. Adm. charge. Tudor manor house concealed by 19th-century Gothic decoration; Lutyens gardens

*Knole (NT), Kent. Tel: 01732-450608. Closed Mon. (except Bank Holidays) and Tues.; park open daily; garden open first Wed. of each month. Adm. £5.00; garden,£1.00; park free to pedestrians. House dating from 1456 set in parkland; fine art treasures

Lambeth Palace, London SE1. Tel: 0171-928 8282. Visits by written application. Official residence of the Archbishop of Canterbury. A 19th-century house with parts dating from the 12th century

*Lanercost Priory (EH), Cumbria. Tel: 01697-73030. Adm. £1.90. The nave of the Augustinian priory church, c.1166, is still used; remains of other claustral buildings

*Lanhydrock (NT), Cornwall. Tel: 01208-73320. Closed Mon. (except Bank Holidays). Garden open all year. Adm. £6.20; garden and grounds only, £3.10. House dating from the 17th century; 45 rooms, including kitchen and nursery

Leeds Castle, Kent. Tel: 01622-765400. Adm. charge. Castle dating from 9th century, on two islands in lake

*Levens Hall, Cumbria. Tel: 015395-60321. Closed Fri. and Sat. Adm. £5.20; grounds only, £3.80. Elizabethan house with unique topiary garden (1694). Steam engine collection

Lincoln Castle. Tel: 01522-511068. Adm. charge. Closed Mon.-Fri. in summer. Built by William the Conqueror in 1068

Lindisfarne Priory (EH), Northumberland. Tel: 01289-389200. Open all year, subject to tide times. Adm. £2.70. Bishopric of the Northumbrian kingdom destroyed by the Danes; re-established in the 11th century as a Benedictine priory, now ruined

†Little Moreton Hall (NT), Cheshire. Tel: 01260-272018. Closed Mon. (except Bank Holidays) and Tues.; 7 Nov.-20 Dec. open Sat. and Sun. only. Adm. £4.00; free 7 Nov.-20 Dec. Timber-framed moated manor house with knot garden

Longleat House, Warminster, Wilts. Tel: 01985-844400. Open daily; safari park closed winter. Adm. charge. Elizabethan house in Italian Renaissance style

Lullingstone Roman Villa (EH), Kent. Tel: 01322-863467. Adm. £2.50. Large villa occupied for much of the Roman period; fine mosaics

†Luton Hoo, Beds. Tel: 01582-722955. Open Fri.-Sun. and Bank Holiday Mon. Adm. charge. Houses the Wernher collection of china, glass, pictures and other *objets d'art*

Mansion-House, London EC4. Tel: 0171-626 2500. Group visits only, by prior arrangement. Adm. free. The official residence of the Lord Mayor of London

Marble Hill House (EH), Twickenham, Middx. Tel: 0181-892 5115. Closed Mon. and Tues. in winter. Adm. £3.00. English Palladian villa with Georgian paintings and furniture

*Michelham Priory, E. Sussex. Closed Mon. and Tues. except in Aug. Tel: 01323-844224. Adm. £4.00. Tudor house built onto an Augustinian priory

Middleham Castle (EH), N. Yorks. Tel: 01969-623899. Closed Mon. and Tues. in winter. Adm. £2.20. A 12th-century keep within later fortifications. Childhood home of Richard III

†Montacute House (NT), Somerset. Tel: 01935-823289. Closed Tues; grounds open all year. Adm. £5.20; grounds only, £2.90. Elizabethan house with National Portrait Gallery portraits from period

Mount Grace Priory (EH), N. Yorks. Tel: 01609-883494. Closed Mon. and Tues. in winter. Adm. £2.70. Carthusian monastery, with remains of monastic buildings

Netley Abbey (EH), Hants. Tel: 01703-453076. Adm. free. Remains of Cistercian abbey, used as house in Tudor period

Old Sarum (EH), Wilts. Tel: 01722-335398. Adm. £2.00. Earthworks enclosing remains of the castle and the 11th-century cathedral

Orford Castle (EH), Suffolk. Tel: 01394-450472. Closed Mon. and Tues. in winter. Adm. £2.30. Circular keep of c.1170 and remains of coastal defence castle built by Henry II

*Osborne House (EH), Isle of Wight. Tel: 01983-200022. Adm. £6.50; grounds only, £3.50. Queen Victoria's seaside residence

†Osterley Park House (NT), Isleworth, Middx. Tel: 0181-560 3918. Closed Mon. (except Bank Holidays), Tues. and Good Friday; grounds open all year. Adm. £4.00; grounds free. Elizabethan mansion set in parkland

*Pendennis Castle (EH), Cornwall. Tel: 01326-316594. Adm. £3.00. Well-preserved coastal defence castle built by Henry VIII

†Penshurst Place, Kent. Tel: 01892-870307. Closed Mon.-Fri. in Mar. Adm. £5.70; grounds only, £4.20. House with medieval Baron's Hall and 14th-century gardens

†Petworth (NT), W. Sussex. Tel: 01798-342207. Closed Thur. and Fri. (except Good Friday); grounds open all year. Adm. £5.00; grounds free. Late 17th-century house set in deer park

Pevensey Castle (EH), E. Sussex. Tel: 01323-762604. Closed Mon. and Tues. in winter. Adm. £2.50. Walls of a 4th-century Roman fort; remains of an 11th-century castle

Peveril Castle (EH), Derbys. Tel: 01433-620613. Closed Mon. and Tues. in winter. Adm. £1.75. A 12th-century castle defended on two sides by precipitous rocks

†Polesden Lacy (NT), Surrey. Tel: 01372-458203. Closed Mon. (except Bank Holidays) and Tues.; grounds open daily all year. Adm. £6.00; grounds only, £3.00. Regency villa remodelled in the Edwardian era. Fine paintings and furnishings

Portchester Castle (EH), Hants. Tel: 01705-378291. Adm. £2.50. Walls of a late Roman fort enclosing a Norman keep and an Augustinian priory church

*Powderham Castle, Devon. Tel: 01626-890243. Closed Sat. Adm. charge. Medieval castle with 18th- and 19th-century alterations

†Raby Castle, Co. Durham. Tel: 01833-660202. Closed Sat. (except Bank Holiday weekends); open Wed. and Sun. only in May and June. Adm. charge. A 14th-century castle with walled gardens

*Ragley Hall, Warks. Tel: 01789-762090. Closed Mon.-Wed.; grounds open daily in July and Aug. Adm. charge. A 17th-century house with gardens, park and lake

*Richborough Roman Fort (EH), Kent. Tel: 01304-612013. Closed Mon. and Tues. in Nov. and March, Mon.-Fri. Dec.-Feb. Adm. £2.50. Landing-site of the Claudian invasion in AD 43, with 3rd-century stone walls

Richmond Castle (EH), N. Yorks. Tel: 01748-822493. Adm. £2.20. A 12th-century keep with 11th-century curtain wall and domestic buildings

Rievaulx Abbey (EH), N. Yorks. Tel: 01439-798228. Adm. £2.90. Remains of a Cistercian abbey founded c.1131

Rochester Castle (EH), Kent. Tel: 01634-402276. Adm. £2.60. An 11th-century castle partly on the Roman city wall, with a square keep of c.1130

†ROCKINGHAM CASTLE, Northants. Tel: 01536-770240. Open Sun. and Thurs. only (and Bank Holiday Mon. and Tues., and Tues. in Aug.). Adm. £3.90; gardens only, £2.50. Built by William the Conqueror

ROYAL PAVILION, Brighton. Tel: 01273-290900. Adm. charge. Palace of George IV, in Chinese style with Indian exterior and Regency gardens

†RUFFORD OLD HALL (NT), Lancs. Tel: 01704-821254. Closed Thurs. and Fri. Adm. £3.50; garden only, £1.80. A 16th-century hall with unique screen

ST AUGUSTINE'S ABBEY (EH), Canterbury, Kent. Tel: 01227-767345. Adm. £2.50. Remains of Benedictine monastery, with Norman church, on site of abbey founded AD 598 by St Augustine

ST MAWES CASTLE (EH), Cornwall. Tel: 01326-270526. Closed Wed. and Thurs. in winter. Adm. £2.50. Coastal defence castle built by Henry VIII

ST MICHAEL'S MOUNT (NT), Cornwall. Tel: 01736-710507. Opening times vary. Adm. £3.90. A 14th-century castle with later additions, off the coast at Marazion

*SANDRINGHAM, Norfolk. Tel: 01553-772675. Closed for two weeks in summer and when the Royal Family is in residence. Adm. £4.50; grounds only, £3.50. The Queen's private residence; a neo-Jacobean house built in 1870

SCARBOROUGH CASTLE (EH), N. Yorks. Tel: 01723-372451. Closed Mon. and Tues. in winter. Adm. £2.20. Remains of 12th-century keep and curtain walls

†SHERBORNE CASTLE, Dorset. Tel: 01935-813182. Open Tues., Thurs., Sat., Sun. and Bank Holiday Mon. Adm. charge. Sixteenth-century castle built by Sir Walter Raleigh

*SHUGBOROUGH (NT), Staffs. Tel: 01889-881388. Open Sun. only in October; open for booked parties in winter. Adm. house, county museum and farm, £8.00; each site alone, £3.50. House set in 18th-century park with monuments, temples and pavilions in the Greek Revival style

SKIPTON CASTLE, N. Yorks. Tel: 01756-792442. Closed Sun. mornings. Adm. £3.80. D-shaped castle with six round towers and beautiful inner courtyard

†SMALLHYTHE PLACE (NT), Kent. Tel: 01580-762334. Closed Thurs. and Fri. (except Good Friday). Adm. £3.00. Half-timbered 16th-century house; home of Ellen Terry 1899-1928

†STANFORD HALL, Leics. Tel: 01788-860250. Open Sat.-Sun.; also Bank Holiday Mon. and Tues. Adm. £3.80; grounds only, £2.10. William and Mary house with Stuart portraits. Motorcycle museum

STONEHENGE (EH), Wilts. Tel: 01980-624715. Adm. £3.90. Prehistoric monument consisting of concentric stone circles surrounded by a ditch and bank

†STONOR PARK, Oxon. Tel: 01491-638587. Opening days vary. Adm. £4.50. Medieval house with Georgian facade. Centre of Roman Catholicism after the Reformation

†STOURHEAD (NT), Wilts. Tel: 01747-841152. Closed Thurs.-Fri. Gardens open daily all year. Adm. £4.40; gardens, £3.40; combined ticket £7.90. English Palladian mansion with famous gardens

*STRATFIELD SAYE HOUSE, Hants. Tel: 01256-882882. Closed Fri.; May and Sept. open weekends and Bank Holidays only. Adm. charge. House built 1630-40; home of the Dukes of Wellington since 1817

STRATFORD-UPON-AVON, Warks. Shakespeare's Birthplace with Shakespeare Centre; Anne Hathaway's Cottage, home of Shakespeare's wife; Mary Arden's House, home of Shakespeare's mother; New Place, where Shakespeare died; and Hall's Croft, home of Shakespeare's daughter.

Tel: 01789-204016. Adm. charges. Also Grammar School attended by Shakespeare, Holy Trinity Church, where Shakespeare is buried, Royal Shakespeare Theatre (burnt down 1926, rebuilt 1932) and Swan Theatre (opened 1986)

*SUDELEY CASTLE, Glos. Tel: 01242-602308. Adm. £5.50; grounds only, £4.00. Castle built in 1442; restored in the 19th century

SYON HOUSE, Brentford, Middx. Tel: 0181-560 0881. Opening times vary. Adm. charges vary. Built on the site of a former monastery; Adam interior

TILBURY FORT (EH), Essex. Tel: 01375-858489. Closed Mon. and Tues. in winter. Adm. £2.30. A 17th-century coastal fort

TINTAGEL CASTLE (EH), Cornwall. Tel: 01840-770328. Adm. £2.80. A 12th-century cliff-top castle and Dark Age settlement site

TOWER OF LONDON, London EC3. Tel: 0171-709 0765. Adm. £9.00. Royal palace and fortress begun by William the Conqueror in 1078. Houses the Crown Jewels

*TRERICE (NT), Cornwall. Tel: 01637-875404. Closed Tues. and Sat. (except in Aug.). Adm. £4.00. Elizabethan manor house

TYNEMOUTH PRIORY AND CASTLE (EH), Tyne and Wear. Tel: 0191-257 1090. Closed Mon.-Tues. in winter. Adm. £1.70. Remains of a Benedictine priory, founded c.1090, on Saxon monastic site

†UPPARK (NT), W. Sussex. Tel: 01730-825415. Closed Fri. and Sat. Adm. £5.50 by timed ticket. Late 17th-century house, completely restored after fire. Fetherstonhaugh art collection

WALMER CASTLE (EH), Kent. Tel: 01304-364288. Closed Mon. and Tues. in winter; closed Jan.-Feb. and when the Lord Warden is in residence. Adm. £4.00. One of Henry VIII's coastal defence castles, now the residence of the Lord Warden of the Cinque Ports

WALTHAM ABBEY (EH), Essex. Tel: 01992-702200. Adm. free. Ruined abbey including the nave of the abbey church, 'Harold's Bridge' and late 14th-century gatehouse. Traditionally the burial place of Harold II (1066)

WARKWORTH CASTLE (EH), Northumberland. Tel: 01665-711423. Adm. £2.70. A 15th-century keep amidst earlier ruins, with 14th-century hermitage (open Wed., Sun. and Bank Holidays in summer) upstream

WARWICK CASTLE. Tel: 01926-406600. Adm. charge. Medieval castle with Madame Tussaud's waxworks, in Capability Brown parkland

WHITBY ABBEY (EH), N. Yorks. Tel: 01947-603568. Adm. £1.70. Remains of Norman church on the site of a monastery founded in AD 657

*WILTON HOUSE, Wilts. Tel: 01722-746729. Adm. £6.50. A 17th-century house on the site of a Tudor house and Saxon abbey

WINDSOR CASTLE, Berks. Tel: 01753-831118 for recorded information on opening times. Adm. £9.50, including the Castle precincts. Official residence of The Queen; oldest royal residence still in regular use. Also St George's Chapel

WOBURN ABBEY, Beds. Tel: 01525-290666. Closed Nov. and Dec.; also Mon.-Fri. in Jan. and Feb. Adm. charge. Built on the site of a Cistercian abbey; seat of the Dukes of Bedford. Important art collection; antiques centre

WROXETER ROMAN CITY (EH), Shropshire. Tel: 01743-761330. Closed Mon. and Tues. in winter. Adm. £2.95. Second-century public baths and part of the forum of the Roman town of Viroconium

WALES

c Property of Cadw: Welsh Historic Monuments
nt National Trust property

Beaumaris Castle (c), Anglesey. Tel: 01222-500200. Adm. £2.20. Concentrically-planned castle, still almost intact

Caerleon Roman Baths and Amphitheatre (c), nr Newport. Tel: 01633-422518. Closed Sun. morning in winter. Adm. £2.00, joint ticket with Roman Legionary Museum £3.30. Rare example of a legionary bath-house and late 1st-century arena surrounded by bank for spectators

Caernarfon Castle (c). Tel: 01222-500200. Adm. £4.00. Important Edwardian castle built, with the town wall, between 1283 and 1330

Caerphilly Castle (c). Tel: 01222-500200. Adm. £2.40. Concentrically-planned castle (c.1270) notable for its scale and use of water defences

Cardiff Castle. Tel: 01222-878100. Adm. charge. Castle built on the site of a Roman fort; spectacular towers and rich interior

Castell Coch (c), nr Cardiff. Tel: 01222-500200. Adm. £2.50. Rebuilt 1875-90 on medieval foundations

Chepstow Castle (c). Tel: 01222-500200. Adm. £3.00. Rectangular keep amid extensive fortifications

Conwy Castle (c). Tel: 01222-500200. Adm. £3.50. Built by Edward I, 1283-7

***Criccieth Castle** (c). Tel: 01222-500200. Adm. £2.20. Native Welsh 13th-century castle, altered by Edward I

Denbigh Castle (c). Tel: 01222-500200. Adm. £1.70. Remains of the castle (begun 1282), including triple-towered gatehouse

Harlech Castle (c). Tel: 01222-500200. Adm. £3.00. Well-preserved Edwardian castle, constructed 1283-90, on an outcrop above the former shore-line

Pembroke Castle. Tel: 01646-681510. Adm. £3.00. Castle founded in 1093; Great Tower built 1200; birthplace of King Henry VII

†**Penrhyn Castle** (nt), Bangor. Tel: 01248-353084. Closed Tues. Adm. £4.80; grounds only, £3.00. Neo-Norman castle built in the 19th century. Industrial railway museum

Portmeirion, Penrhyndeudraeth. Tel: 01766-770228. Adm. £3.75. Village in Italianate style

†**Powis Castle** (nt), nr Welshpool. Tel: 01938-554338. Closed Mon. (except Bank Holidays) and Tues. (except July and Aug.). Adm. £7.50; garden only, £5.00. Medieval castle with interior in variety of styles; 17th-century gardens and Clive of India museum

Raglan Castle (c). Tel: 01222-500200. Adm. £2.40. Remains of 15th-century castle with moated hexagonal keep

St Davids Bishop's Palace (c), St Davids. Tel: 01222-500200. Closed Sun. mornings in winter. Adm. £1.70. Remains of residence of Bishops of St Davids built 1328-47

Tintern Abbey (c), nr Chepstow. Tel: 01222-500200. Adm. £2.20. Remains of 13th-century church and conventual buildings of a Cistercian monastery

***Tretower Court and Castle** (c), nr Crickhowell. Tel: 01222-500200. Adm. £2.20. Medieval house with remains of 12th-century castle nearby

SCOTLAND

hs Historic Scotland property
nts National Trust for Scotland property

Antonine Wall (hs), between the Clyde and the Forth. Adm. free. Built about AD 142, consists of ditch, turf rampart and road, with forts every two miles

Balmoral Castle, nr Braemar. Tel: 013397-42334. Open mid-April to end July; closed Sun. in April and May. Adm. £4.00. Baronial-style castle built for Victoria and Albert. The Queen's private residence

Black House, Arnol (hs), Lewis, Western Isles. Tel: 01851-710395. Closed Sun.; also Fri. in winter. Adm. £1.80. Traditional Lewis thatched house

***Blair Castle**, Blair Atholl. Tel: 01796-481207. Adm. £5.50. Mid 18th-century mansion with 13th-century tower; seat of the Dukes of Atholl

***Bonawe Iron Furnace** (hs), Argyll and Bute. Tel: 01866-822432. Closed Sun. mornings. Adm. £2.30. Charcoal-fuelled ironworks founded in 1753

†**Bowhill**, Selkirk. Tel: 01750-22204. House open July only; grounds open April-Aug. except Fri. Adm. £4.00; grounds only, £1.00. Seat of the Dukes of Buccleuch and Queensberry; fine collection of paintings, including portrait miniatures

Brough of Birsay (hs), Orkney. Adm. £1.00. Remains of Norse church and village on the tidal island of Birsay

Caerlaverock Castle (hs), nr Dumfries. Tel: 01387-770244. Closed Sun. mornings. Adm. £2.30. Fine early classical Renaissance building

Calanais Standing Stones (hs), Lewis, Western Isles. Tel: 01851-621422. Adm. £1.50. Standing stones in a cross-shaped setting, dating from 3000 BC

Cathertuns (Brown and White) (hs), nr Brechin. Adm. free. Two large Iron Age hill forts

***Cawdor Castle**, Inverness. Tel: 01667-404615. Adm. £5.20; grounds only, £2.80. A 14th-century keep with 15th- and 17th-century additions

Clava Cairns (hs), Highland. Adm. free. Late Neolithic or early Bronze Age cairns

***Crathes Castle** (nts), nr Banchory. Tel: 01330-844525. Garden and grounds open all year. Adm. castle, garden and grounds, £4.80; each site, £2.00. A 16th-century baronial castle in woodland, fields and gardens

***Culzean Castle** (nts), S. Ayrshire. Tel: 01655-760274. Country park open all year. Adm. £6.50; country park only, £3.50. An 18th-century Adam castle with oval staircase and circular saloon

Dryburgh Abbey (hs), Scottish Borders. Tel: 01835-822381. Closed Sun. mornings. Adm. £2.30. A 12th-century abbey containing tomb of Sir Walter Scott

***Dunvegan Castle**, Skye. Tel: 01470-521206. Adm. £5.00; gardens only, £3.50. A 13th-century castle with later additions; home of the chiefs of the Clan MacLeod; trips to seal colony

Edinburgh Castle (hs). Tel: 0131-225 9846. Adm. £6.00; war memorial free. Includes the Scottish National War Memorial, Scottish United Services Museum and historic apartments

Edzell Castle (hs), nr Brechin. Tel: 01356-648631. Closed Sun. mornings, Thurs. afternoons and Fri. in winter. Adm. £2.30. Medieval tower house; unique walled garden

***Eilean Donan Castle**, Wester Ross. Tel: 01599-555202. Adm. £3.00. A 13th-century castle with Jacobite relics

Elgin Cathedral (hs), Moray. Tel: 01343-547171. Closed Sun. mornings, Thurs. afternoons and Fri. in winter. Adm. £1.80. A 13th-century cathedral with fine chapterhouse

***Floors Castle**, Kelso. Tel: 01573-223333. Adm. charge. Largest inhabited castle in Scotland; seat of the Dukes of Roxburghe

FORT GEORGE (HS), Highland. Tel: 01667-462777. Closed Sunday mornings in winter. Adm. £3.00. An 18th-century fort

*GLAMIS CASTLE, Angus. Tel: 01307-840393. Adm. £5.20; grounds only, £2.40. Seat of the Lyon family (later Earls of Strathmore and Kinghorne) since 1372

GLASGOW CATHEDRAL (HS). Tel: 0141-552 6891. Closed Sun. mornings. Adm. free. Medieval cathedral with elaborately vaulted crypt

GLENELG BROCH (HS), Highland. Adm. free. Two broch towers with well-preserved structural features

*HOPETOUN HOUSE, nr Edinburgh. Tel: 0131-331 2451. Adm. £4.70. House designed by Sir William Bruce, enlarged by William Adam

HUNTLY CASTLE (HS). Tel: 01466-793191. Closed Sun. mornings; also Thurs. afternoons and Fri. in winter. Adm. £2.30. Ruin of a 16th- and 17th-century house

*INVERARAY CASTLE, Argyll. Tel: 01499-302203. Adm. charge. Gothic-style 18th-century castle; seat of the Dukes of Argyll

IONA ABBEY, Inner Hebrides. Tel: 01828-640411. Adm. £2.00. Monastery founded by St Columba in AD 563

*JARLSHOF (HS), Shetland. Tel: 01950-460112. Closed Sun. mornings. Adm. £2.30. Remains from Stone Age

JEDBURGH ABBEY (HS), Scottish Borders. Tel: 01835-863925. Closed Sun. mornings in winter. Adm. £2.80. Romanesque and early Gothic church founded c.1138

KELSO ABBEY (HS), Scottish Borders. Adm. free. Remains of great abbey church founded 1128

LINLITHGOW PALACE (HS). Tel: 01506-842896. Closed Sun. mornings in winter. Adm. £2.30. Ruin of royal palace in park setting. Birthplace of Mary, Queen of Scots

MAES HOWE (HS), Orkney. Tel: 01856-761606. Closed Sun. mornings, Thurs. afternoons and Fri. in winter. Adm. £2.30. Neolithic tomb

*MEIGLE SCULPTURED STONE (HS), Angus. Tel: 01828-640612. Adm. £1.50. Celtic Christian stones

MELROSE ABBEY (HS), Scottish Borders. Tel: 01896-822562. Closed Sun. mornings in winter. Adm. £2.80. Ruin of Cistercian abbey founded c.1136

MOUSA BROCH (HS), Shetland. Adm. free. Finest surviving Iron Age broch tower

NETHER LARGIE CAIRNS (HS), Argyll and Bute. Adm. free. Bronze Age and Neolithic cairns

NEW ABBEY CORN MILL (HS), nr Dumfries. Tel: 01387-850260. Closed Sun. mornings, Thurs. afternoons and Fri. in winter. Adm. £2.30. Water-powered mill

PALACE OF HOLYROODHOUSE, Edinburgh. Tel: 0131-556 7371. Closed when The Queen is in residence. Adm. £5.30. The Queen's official Scottish residence. Main part of the palace built 1671-9

RING OF BROGAR (HS), Orkney. Adm. free. Neolithic circle of upright stones with an enclosing ditch

RUTHWELL CROSS (HS), Dumfries and Galloway. Adm. free. Seventh-century Anglian cross

ST ANDREWS CASTLE AND CATHEDRAL (HS), Fife. Tel: 01334-477196 (castle); 01334-472563 (cathedral). Adm. £2.30 (castle); £1.80 (cathedral); £3.50 (combined ticket). Closed Sun. mornings in winter. Ruins of 13th-century castle and remains of the largest cathedral in Scotland

*SCONE PALACE, Perth. Tel: 01738-552300. Adm. £5.20. House built 1802-13 on the site of a medieval palace

SKARA BRAE (HS), Orkney. Tel: 01856-841815. Closed Sun. mornings in winter. Adm. £3.20 (winter); £4.00 (summer, joint ticket with Skaill House). Stone-Age village with adjacent 17th-century house

*SMAILHOLM TOWER (HS), Scottish Borders. Tel: 01573-460365. Closed Sun. mornings. Adm. £1.80. Well-preserved tower-house

STIRLING CASTLE (HS). Tel: 01786-450000. Adm. £4.50. Great Hall and gatehouse of James IV, palace of James V, Chapel Royal remodelled by James VI

TANTALLON CASTLE (HS), E. Lothian. Tel: 01620-892727. Closed Sun. mornings, Thurs. afternoons and Fri. in winter. Adm. £2.30. Fortification with earthwork defences and a 14th-century curtain wall with towers

*THREAVE CASTLE (HS), Dumfries and Galloway. Tel: 0831-168512. Adm. £1.80, including ferry trip. Late 14th-century tower on an island; reached by boat, long walk to castle

URQUHART CASTLE (HS), Loch Ness. Tel: 01456-450551. Adm. £3.50. Castle remains with well-preserved tower

NORTHERN IRELAND

DE Property in the care of the Northern Ireland Department of the Environment

NT National Trust property

CARRICKFERGUS CASTLE (DE), Co. Antrim. Tel: 01960-351273. Closed Sun. mornings. Adm. £2.70. Castle begun in 1180 and garrisoned until 1928

†CASTLE COOLE (NT), Enniskillen. Tel: 01365-322690. Closed Thurs, also Mon.-Fri. in April and Sept. (except Bank Holidays). Adm. house, £2.80; estate, £2.00 per car. An 18th-century mansion by James Wyatt in parkland

†CASTLE WARD (NT), Co. Down. Tel: 01396-881204. Closed Thurs; also closed Mon.-Fri. in April, Sept. and Oct.; grounds open all year. Adm. £2.60. An 18th-century house with Classical and Gothic facades

*DEVENISH ISLAND (DE), Co. Fermanagh. Closed Sun. mornings and Mon. Adm. £2.25. Island monastery founded in the 6th century by St Molaise

DOWNHILL CASTLE (NT), Co. Londonderry. Tel: 01265-848728. Adm. free. Ruins of palatial house in landscaped estate including Mussenden Temple. Opening times of temple vary

DUNLUCE CASTLE (DE), Co. Antrim. Tel: 012657-31938. Closed Sun. morning (except July and Aug.). Adm. £1.50. Ruins of 16th-century stronghold of the MacDonnells

†FLORENCE COURT (NT), Co. Fermanagh. Tel: 01365-348249. Closed Tues.; also closed Mon.-Fri. (except Bank Holidays) in April and Sept.; grounds open all year. Adm. £2.80; estate £2.00 per car. Mid 18th-century house with rococo plasterwork

*GREY ABBEY (DE), Co. Down. Tel: 01247-788585. Closed Sun. morning and Mon. Adm £1.00. Substantial remains of a Cistercian abbey founded in 1193

HILLSBOROUGH FORT (DE), Co. Down. Closed Sun. mornings and Mon. Adm. free. Built in 1650

†MOUNT STEWART (NT), Co. Down. Tel: 012477-88387. Closed Tues.; also closed Mon.-Fri. in April and Oct. Adm. £3.50; garden only, £3.00. An 18th-century house, childhood home of Lord Castlereagh

NENDRUM MONASTERY (DE), Mahee Island, Co. Down. Closed Sun. mornings and Mon.; also Mon.-Fri. in winter. Adm. 75p. Founded in the 5th century by St Machaoi

*TULLY CASTLE (DE), Co. Fermanagh. Closed Sun. mornings and Mon. Adm. £1.00. Fortified house and bawn built in 1613

*WHITE ISLAND (DE), Co. Fermanagh. Closed Sun. mornings and Mon. Adm. £2.25. Tenth-century monastery and 12th-century church. Access by ferry

Museums and Galleries

There are more than 2,500 museums and galleries in the United Kingdom. Over 1,700 are registered with the Museums and Galleries Commission (*see* page 323), which indicates that they have an appropriate constitution, are soundly financed, have adequate collection management standards and public services, and have access to professional curatorial advice. Museums must achieve full or provisional registration status in order to be eligible for grants from the Museums and Galleries Commission and from Area Museums Councils. Over 700 of the registered museums are run by a local authority.

The national museums and galleries receive direct government grant-in-aid. These are:
- British Museum
- Imperial War Museum
- National Army Museum
- National Galleries of Scotland
- National Gallery
- National Maritime Museum
- National Museums and Galleries on Merseyside
- National Museum of Wales
- National Museums of Scotland
- National Portrait Gallery
- Natural History Museum
- RAF Museum
- Royal Armouries
- Science Museum
- Tate Gallery
- Ulster Folk and Transport Museum
- Ulster Museum
- Victoria and Albert Museum
- Wallace Collection

Local authority museums are funded by the local authority and may also receive grants from the Museums and Galleries Commission. Independent museums and galleries mainly rely on their own resources but are also eligible for grants from the Museums and Galleries Commission.

The Museums and Galleries Commission has identified 26 non-national museum bodies which have pre-eminent collections of more than local or regional importance. Some of those designated are museum services with a wide variety of collections; others are small and more focused in a particular field. Ten Area Museum Councils in the UK, which are independent charities that receive an annual grant from the Museums and Galleries Commission, give advice and support to the museums in their area and may offer improvement grants. They also circulate exhibitions and assist with training and marketing.

OPENING TO THE PUBLIC

The following is a selection of the museums and art galleries in the United Kingdom. The admission charges given are the standard charges for 1998–9, where a charge is made; many museums have concessionary rates for children, etc. Opening hours vary. Most museums are closed on Christmas Eve, Christmas Day, Boxing Day and New Year's Day; many are closed on Good Friday, and some are closed on May Day Bank Holiday. Some smaller museums close at lunchtimes. Information about a specific museum or gallery should be checked by telephone.

* Local authority museum/gallery
† Museum/gallery contains a collection designated pre-eminent

ENGLAND

BARNARD CASTLE, Co. Durham – *† *The Bowes Museum,* Westwick Road. Tel: 01833-690606. Closed Sun. mornings. Adm. £3.50. European art from the late medieval period to the 19th century; music and costume galleries; English period rooms from Elizabeth I to Victoria; local archaeology

BATH – *American Museum in Britain,* Claverton Manor. Tel: 01225-460503. Closed mornings and Mon. (except Bank Holidays); also closed in winter (except on application). Adm. £5.00 (including house); grounds and galleries only, £2.50. American decorative arts from the 17th to 19th century

**Museum of Costume,* Bennett Street. Tel: 01225-477752. Adm. £3.80. Fashion from the 16th century to the present day

**Roman Baths Museum,* Abbey Church Yard. Tel: 01225-477774. Adm. (excluding 18th-century Pump Room, which is free) £6.30. Museum adjoins the remains of a Roman baths and temple complex

**Victoria Art Gallery,* Bridge Street. Tel: 01225-477772. Closed Bank Holidays. Adm. free. European Old Masters and British art since the 18th century

BEAMISH, Co. Durham – *† *Beamish, The North of England Open Air Museum.* Tel: 01207-231811. Closed Mon. and Fri. in winter. Adm. charge. Recreated northern town *c.*1900, with rebuilt and furnished local buildings, colliery village, farm, railway station, tramway, Pockerley Manor and horse-yard (set *c.*1800)

BEAULIEU, Hants – † *National Motor Museum.* Tel: 01590-612345. Adm. charge. Displays of over 250 vehicles dating from 1895 to the present day

BIRMINGHAM – *† *Aston Hall,* Albert Road. Tel: 0121-327 0062. Closed mornings and in winter. Adm. free. Jacobean house containing paintings, furniture and tapestries from 17th to 19th century

**Birmingham Nature Centre,* Edgbaston. Tel: 0121-472 7775. Closed Mon.-Sat. in winter. Adm. £1.50. Indoor and outdoor enclosures displaying British wildlife

*† *City Museum and Art Gallery,* Chamberlain Square. Tel: 0121-303 2834. Closed Sun. mornings. Adm. free (except Gas Hall). Includes notable collection of Pre-Raphaelites

*† *Museum of the Jewellery Quarter,* Vyse Street, Hockley. Tel: 0121-554 3598. Closed Sun. Adm. £2.00. Built around a real jewellery workshop

*† *Soho House,* Soho Avenue. Tel: 0121-554 9122. Closed Sun. mornings and Mon. (except Bank Holidays). Adm. £2.00. Eighteenth-century home of industrialist Matthew Boulton

BOVINGTON CAMP, Dorset – *Tank Museum.* Tel: 01929-405096. Adm. £6.00. Collection of 300 tanks from the earliest days of tank warfare to the present

BRADFORD – * *Cartwright Hall Art Gallery,* Lister Park. Tel: 01274-493313. Closed Sun. mornings and Mon. (except Bank Holidays). Adm. free. British 19th- and 20th-century fine art

**Industrial Museum and Horses at Work,* Moorside Road. Tel: 01274-631756. Closed Sun. mornings and Mon. (except Bank Holidays). Adm. charge. Engineering, textiles, transport and social history exhibits, including recreated back-to-back cottages, shire horses and horse tram-rides

BRIGHTON – *†Booth Museum of Natural History, Dyke Road. Tel: 01273-292777. Closed Thurs. and Sun. mornings. Adm. free. Zoology, botany and geology collections; British birds in recreated habitats

*† *Brighton Museum and Art Gallery*, Church Street. Tel: 01273-290900. Closed Sun. mornings and Wed. Adm. free. Includes fine art, design, fashion, archaeology, Brighton history

BRISTOL – *Arnolfini Gallery*, Narrow Quay. Tel: 0117-929 9191. Adm. free; charge for cinema and events. Contemporary visual arts, dance, theatre, film and music

*† *Blaise Castle House Museum*, Henbury. Tel: 0117-950 6789. Closed Thurs. and Fri.; also closed 1 Nov. to 31 Mar. Adm. free. Agricultural and social history collections in an 18th-century mansion

*† *Bristol Industrial Museum*, Prince Street. Tel: 0117-925 1470. Closed Thurs. and Fri.; closed Mon.-Fri. in winter. Adm. charge (except on Sun.). Industrial, maritime and transport collections

*† *City Museum and Art Gallery*, Queen's Road. Tel: 0117-922 3571. Adm. charge (except on Sun.). Includes fine and decorative art, oriental art, Egyptology and Bristol ceramics and paintings

CAMBRIDGE – *Duxford Airfield*, Duxford. Tel: 01223-835000. Adm. £5.95. Displays of military and civil aircraft, tanks, guns and naval exhibits

† *Fitzwilliam Museum*, Trumpington Street. Tel: 01223-332900. Closed Mon. (except some Bank Holidays) and Sun. mornings. Adm. free. Antiquities, fine and applied arts, clocks, ceramics, manuscripts, furniture, sculpture, coins and medals, temporary exhibitions

† *University Museum of Archaeology and Anthropology*, Downing Street. Tel: 01223-333516. Closed Sun., Mon. and mornings. Adm. free. Archaeology and anthropology from all parts of the world

† *Whipple Museum of the History of Science*, Free School Lane. Tel: 01223-330906. Closed mornings and weekends. Adm. free. Scientific instruments from the 14th century to the present day

CARLISLE – *Tullie House Museum and Art Gallery*, Castle Street. Tel: 01228-34781. Closed Sun. mornings. Adm. charge to Border galleries only; ground floor, Old Tullie House and Jacobean galleries, adm. free. Prehistoric archaeology, Hadrian's Wall, Viking and medieval Cumbria, and the social history of Carlisle; also British 19th- and 20th-century art and English porcelain

CHATHAM – *The Historic Dockyard*. Tel: 01634-823800. Closed Mon., Tues., Thurs. and Fri. in Feb., Mar. and Nov., also closed Dec.-Jan. Adm. charge. Maritime attractions including lifeboat collection

† *Royal Engineers Museum*, Brompton Barracks. Tel: 01634-406397. Closed Fri. Adm. £3.00. Regimental history, ethnography, decorative art and photography

CHESTER – *Grosvenor Museum*, Grosvenor Street. Tel: 01244-321616. Closed Sun. mornings. Adm. free. Roman collections, natural history, art, Chester silver, local history and costume

CHICHESTER – † *Weald and Downland Open Air Museum*, Singleton. Tel: 01243-811348. Closed Mon.,Tues., Thurs., Fri. in winter. Adm. £5.20. Rebuilt vernacular buildings from south-east England; includes medieval houses, agricultural and rural craft buildings and a working watermill

COLCHESTER – *† *Colchester Castle Museum*, Castle Park. Tel: 01206-282939. Closed Sun. mornings. Adm. £3.60. Local archaeological antiquities and displays on Roman Colchester; tours of the Roman vaults, castle walls and chapel with medieval and prison displays

COVENTRY – *Herbert Art Gallery and Museum*, Jordan Well. Tel: 01203-832381. Closed Sun. mornings. Local

history, archaeology and industry, oriental ceramics, and fine and decorative art

*† *Museum of British Road Transport*, Hales Street. Tel: 01203-832425. Adm. free. Hundreds of motor vehicles and bicycles

CRICH, nr Matlock, Derbys – † *National Tramway Museum*. Tel: 01773-852565. Closed in winter and most Fri. in April, Sept. and Oct. Adm. £5.90. Open-air working museum with tram rides

DERBY – *Derby Museum and Art Gallery*, The Strand. Tel: 01332-716659. Closed Bank Holiday mornings and Sun. Adm. free. Includes paintings by Joseph Wright of Derby and Derby porcelain

* *Industrial Museum*, off Full Street. Tel: 01332-255308. Closed Bank Holiday mornings and Sun. Adm. free. Rolls-Royce aero engine collection and a railway engineering gallery

DEVIZES – † *Devizes Museum*, Long Street. Tel: 01380-727369. Closed Sun. Adm. £2.00. Natural and local history, art gallery, archaeological finds from Bronze Age, Iron Age, Roman and Saxon sites

DORCHESTER – *Dorset County Museum*, High West Street. Tel: 01305-262735. Closed Sun. (except July and Aug.). Adm. charge. Includes a collection of Thomas Hardy's manuscripts, books, notebooks and drawings

EXETER – *† *Royal Albert Memorial Museum*, Queen Street. Tel: 01392-265858. Closed Sun. Adm. free. Natural history, archaeology, and fine and decorative art including Exeter silver

GAYDON, Warwick – *British Motor Industry Heritage Trust*, Heritage Motor Centre, Banbury Road. Tel: 019626-641188. Adm. charge. History of British motor industry from 1895 to present; classic vehicles; engineering gallery; Corgi and Lucas collections

GLOUCESTER, – *National Waterways Museum*, Llanthony Warehouse, The Docks. Tel: 01452-318054. Adm. £4.50. Two-hundred-year history of Britain's canals and inland waterways

GOSPORT, Hants – *Royal Navy Submarine Museum*, Haslar Jetty Road. Tel: 01705-529217. Adm. £3.75. Underwater warfare, including the submarine *Alliance*, historical and nuclear galleries; and first Royal Navy submarine

GRASMERE, Cumbria – † *Dove Cottage* and the *Wordsworth Museum* (*see* page 586)

HALIFAX – *Eureka! The Museum for Children*, Discovery Road. Tel: 01426-983191. Adm. £4.75 (over age 12), £3.75 (ages 3-12), free (under age 3). Saver ticket £14.75. Hands-on museum designed for children up to age 12

HULL – *Ferens Art Gallery*, Queen Victoria Square. Tel: 01482-613902. Closed Sun. mornings. Adm. non-residents £1.00; residents free. European art, especially Dutch 17th-century paintings, British portraits from 17th to 20th century, and marine paintings

Town Docks Museum, Queen Victoria Square. Tel: 01482-613902. Closed Sun. mornings. Adm.: non-residents £1.00; residents free. Whaling, fishing and navigation exhibits

HUNTINGDON – *Cromwell Museum*, Grammar School Walk. Tel: 01480-375830. Closed Mon., and mornings (except Sat.) in winter. Adm. free. Portraits and memorabilia relating to Oliver Cromwell

IPSWICH – *Christchurch Mansion and Wolsey Art Gallery*, Christchurch Park. Tel: 01473-253246. Closed Sun. mornings and Mon. (except Bank Holidays). Adm. free. Tudor house with paintings by Gainsborough, Constable and other Suffolk artists; furniture and 18th-century ceramics. Art gallery for temporary exhibitions

LEEDS – *† *City Art Gallery*, The Headrow. Tel: 0113-247 8248. Closed Sun. mornings. Adm. free. British and

European paintings including English watercolours, modern sculpture, Henry Moore gallery, print room
*†*City Museum*, Calverley Street. Tel: 0113-247 8275. Closed Sun. and Mon. Adm. free. Natural history, archaeology, ethnography and coin collections
*†*Lotherton Hall*, Aberford. Tel: 0113-281 3259. Closed Sun. mornings and Mon.; also closed Jan.-Feb. Adm. charge. Costume and oriental collections in furnished Edwardian house; deer park and bird garden
Royal Armouries Museum, Armouries Drive. Tel: 0990-106666. Adm. £4.95 low season, £7.95 high season. National collection of arms and armour from BC to present; demonstrations of foot combat in museum's five galleries; falconry and mounted combat in the tiltyard
*† *Temple Newsam House*. Tel: 0113-264 7321. Closed Sun. mornings and Mon.; also closed Jan.-Feb. Adm. charge. Old Masters and 17th- and 18th-century decorative art in furnished Jacobean/Tudor house
LEICESTER – **Jewry Wall Museum*, St Nicholas Circle. Tel: 0116-247 3021. Closed Sun. mornings. Adm. free. Archaeology, Roman Jewry Wall and baths, and mosaics
**New Walk Museum and Art Gallery*, New Walk. Tel: 0116-255 4100. Closed Sun. mornings. Adm. free. Natural history, geology, ancient Egypt gallery, European art and decorative arts
**Snibston Discovery Park*, Coalville. Tel: 01530-510851. Adm. £4.75. Open-air science and industry museum on site of a coal mine; country park with nature trail
LINCOLN – **Museum of Lincolnshire Life*, Burton Road. Tel: 01522-528448. Closed Sun. mornings in winter. Adm. charge. Social history and agricultural collection
*Usher Gallery, Lindum Road. Tel: 01522-527980. Closed Sun. mornings. Adm. £2.00. Watches, miniatures, porcelain, silver; collection of Peter de Wint works; Lincolnshire topography; Royal Lincs Regiment and Tennyson memorabilia
LIVERPOOL – *Lady Lever Art Gallery*, Wirral. Tel: 0151-478 4136. Closed Sun. mornings. Adm. £3.00 for an 'Eight Pass' which is valid for 12 months and for all National Museums and Galleries on Merseyside. Paintings, furniture and porcelain
Liverpool Museum, William Brown Street. Tel: 0151-478 4399. Closed Sun. mornings. Adm. 'Eight Pass' as above. Includes Egyptian mummies, weapons and classical sculpture; planetarium, aquarium, vivarium and natural history centre
Merseyside Maritime Museum, Albert Dock. Tel: 0151-478 4499. Adm. 'Eight Pass' as above. Floating exhibits, working displays and craft demonstrations; incorporates HM Customs and Excise National Museum
Museum of Liverpool Life, Mann Island. Tel: 0151-478 4080. Adm. 'Eight Pass' as above. The history of Liverpool
Sudley House, Mossley Hill Road. Tel: 0151-724 3245. Closed Sun. mornings. Adm. 'Eight Pass' as above. Late 18th- and 19th-century British paintings in former shipowner's home
Tate Gallery Liverpool, Albert Dock. Tel: 0151-709 3223. Twentieth-century painting and sculpture
Walker Art Gallery, William Brown Street. Tel: 0151-478 4199. Closed Sun. mornings. Adm. 'Eight Pass' as above. Paintings from the 14th to 20th century
LONDON: GALLERIES – **Barbican Art Gallery*, Barbican Centre, EC2. Tel: 0171-382 7105. Temporary exhibitions
†*Courtauld Gallery*, Somerset House, Strand, WC2. Tel: 0171-873 2526. Closed Sun. mornings. Adm. £4.00. The University of London galleries
†*Dulwich Picture Gallery*, College Road, SE21. Tel: 0181-693 5254. Closed Sun. mornings and Mon. (except Bank

Holidays). Adm. £3.00 (free on Fri.). Built by Sir John Soane to house 17th- and 18th-century paintings
Hayward Gallery, South Bank, SE1. Tel: 0171-928 3144. Adm. £5.00. Temporary exhibitions
National Gallery, Trafalgar Square, WC2. Tel: 0171-839 3321. Closed Sun. mornings. Adm. free. Western painting from the 13th to 20th century; early Renaissance collection in the Sainsbury wing
National Portrait Gallery, St Martin's Place, WC2. Tel: 0171-306 0055. Closed Sun. mornings and some Bank Holidays. Adm. free (except for some special exhibitions). Portraits of eminent people in British history
Percival David Foundation of Chinese Art, Gordon Square, WC1. Tel: 0171-387 3909. Closed weekends and Bank Holidays. Adm. free (charge for use of reference library). Chinese ceramics from tenth to 18th century
Photographers Gallery, Great Newport Street, WC2. Tel: 0171-831 1772. Closed Sun. mornings. Adm. free. Temporary exhibitions
The Queen's Gallery, Buckingham Palace, SW1. Tel: 0171-839 1377. Adm. £3.50. Art from the Royal Collection
Royal Academy of Arts, Piccadilly, W1. Tel: 0171-300 8000. Adm. charge. British art since 1750 and temporary exhibitions; annual Summer Exhibition
Saatchi Gallery, Boundary Road, NW8. Tel: 0171-624 8299. Closed mornings and Mon.-Wed. Adm. £4.00. Contemporary art including paintings, photographs, sculpture and installations
Serpentine Gallery, Kensington Gardens, W2. Tel: 0171-402 6075. Adm. free. Temporary exhibitions of British and international contemporary art
Tate Gallery, Millbank, SW1. Tel: 0171-887 8000. Adm. free (charge for special exhibitions). British painting and 20th-century painting and sculpture
Wallace Collection, Manchester Square, W1. Tel: 0171-935 0687. Closed Sun. mornings. Adm. free. Paintings and drawings, French 18th-century furniture, armour, porcelain and clocks
Whitechapel Art Gallery, Whitechapel High Street, E1. Tel: 0171-522 7878. Closed Mon. Adm. free to most exhibitions. Temporary exhibitions of modern art
LONDON: MUSEUMS – *Bank of England Museum*, Threadneedle Street, EC2 (entrance from Bartholomew Lane). Tel: 0171-601 5545. Closed weekends and Bank Holidays. Adm. free. History of the Bank since 1694
Bethnal Green Museum of Childhood, Cambridge Heath Road, E2. Tel: 0181-983 5200. Closed Sun. mornings and Fri. Adm. free but donations invited. Toys, games and exhibits relating to the social history of childhood
British Museum, Great Russell Street, WC1. Tel: 0171-636 1555. Closed Sun. mornings. Adm. free. Antiquities, coins, medals, prints and drawings
Cabinet War Rooms, King Charles Street, SW1. Tel: 0171-930 6961. Adm. £4.40. Underground rooms used by Churchill and the Government during the Second World War
Commonwealth Experience, Kensington High Street, W8. Tel: 0171-603 4535. Exhibitions on Commonwealth nations, visual arts and crafts; Interactive World
Cutty Sark, Greenwich, SE10. Tel: 0181-858 3445. Adm. £3.50. Restored and rerigged tea clipper with exhibits on board. Sir Francis Chichester's round-the-world yacht, *Gipsy Moth IV*, can also be seen
Design Museum, Shad Thames, SE1. Tel: 0171-378 6055. Adm. £5.25. The development of design and the mass-production of consumer objects
Geffrye Museum, Kingsland Road, E2. Tel: 0171-739 9893. Closed Mon.; also Sun. and Bank Holiday mornings. Adm. free. English urban domestic interiors from 1600

to present day; also paintings, furniture, decorative arts, walled herb garden

HMS Belfast, Morgans Lane, Tooley Street, SE1. Tel: 0171-407 6434. Adm £4.40. Life on a warship, illustrated on World War II warship

†*Horniman Museum and Gardens*, London Road, SE23. Tel: 0181-699 1872. Adm. free. Museum of ethnography, musical instruments, natural history and aquarium; reference library; sunken, water and flower gardens

Imperial War Museum, Lambeth Road, SE1. Tel: 0171-416 5000. Reference departments closed Sat. (except by appointment) and Sun. Adm. £4.70 (free after 4.30 p.m. daily). All aspects of the two world wars and other military operations involving Britain and the Commonwealth since 1914

†*Jewish Museum*, Albert Street, NW1. Tel: 0171-284 1997. Closed Fri., Sat., public and Jewish holidays. Adm. £3.00. Jewish life, history and religion

Jewish Museum, East End Road, N3. Tel: 0181-349 1143. Closed Fri., Sat., public and Jewish holidays. Adm. £2.00. Jewish life in London and Holocaust education

†*London Transport Museum*, Covent Garden, WC2. Tel: 0171-379 6344. Adm. charge. Vehicles, photographs and graphic art relating to the history of transport in London

MCC Museum, Lord's, NW8. Tel: 0171-289 1611. Open match days (closed most Sun. mornings); also conducted tours by appointment with Tours Manager. Adm. charge. Cricket museum

Museum of Garden History, Lambeth Palace Road SE1. Tel: 0171-401 8865. Closed Sat. and Dec.-Feb. Adm. free. Exhibition of aspects of garden history and re-created 17th-century garden

†*Museum of London*, London Wall, EC2. Tel: 0171-600 3699. Adm. £5.00 (ticket valid for one year); free after 4.30 p.m. History of London from prehistoric times to present day

Museum of the Moving Image, South Bank, SE1. Tel: 0171-401 2636. Adm. £6.25. History of the moving image in cinema and television

National Army Museum, Royal Hospital Road, SW3. Tel: 0171-730 0717. Adm. free. Five-hundred-year history of the British soldier; exhibits include model of the Battle of Waterloo and *Army for Today* gallery

National Maritime Museum, Greenwich, SE10. Tel: 0181-858 4422. Reference library closed Sat. (except by appointment) and Sun. Adm. £5.50. Comprises the main building, the Old Royal Observatory and the Queen's House (*see page* 586). Maritime history of Britain; collections include globes, clocks, telescopes and paintings

Natural History Museum, Cromwell Road, SW7. Tel: 0171-938 9123. Adm. £6.00. Natural history collections

Royal Air Force Museum, Colindale, NW9. Tel: 0181-205 2266. Adm. £5.85. National museum of aviation with over 70 full-size aircraft; aviation from before the Wright brothers to the present-day RAF; flight simulator

Royal Mews, Buckingham Palace, SW1. Tel: 0171-839 1377. Open Tues.-Thurs. afternoons. Adm. £4.00. Carriages, coaches, stables and horses

Science Museum, Exhibition Road, SW7. Tel: 0171-938 8000. Adm. charge. Science, technology, industry and medicine collections

Shakespeare Globe Exhibition, Bankside, SE1. Tel: 0171-902 1500. Adm. £5.00. Recreation of Elizabethan theatre using 16th-century techniques

Sherlock Holmes Museum, Baker Street, NW1. Tel: 0171-935 8866. Adm. £5.00. Recreated rooms of the fictional detective

Sir John Soane's Museum, Lincoln's Inn Fields, WC2. Tel: 0171-430 0175. Closed Sun. and Mon. Adm. free (groups by appointment only). Art and antiques

Theatre Museum, Russell Street, WC2. Tel: 0171-836 2330. Closed Mon. Adm. £3.50. History of the performing arts

*Tower Bridge Experience, SE1. Tel: 0171-378 1928. Adm. £5.95. History of the bridge and display of Victorian steam machinery; panoramic views from walkways

Victoria and Albert Museum, Cromwell Road, SW7. Tel: 0171-938 8500. Closed Mon. mornings. Adm. £5.00. Includes National Art Library and Print Room (closed Sun. and Mon.). Fine and applied art and design, including furniture, glass, textiles, dress collections (British Galleries closed 1998-9)

Wellington Museum, Apsley House, W1 (*see* page 584)

Wimbledon Lawn Tennis Museum, Church Road, SW19. Tel: 0181-946 6131. Closed Sun. mornings and Mon. (except summer Bank Holidays). Adm. £3.00. Tennis trophies, fashion and memorabilia; view of Centre Court

MANCHESTER – **Gallery of Costume*, Rusholme. Tel: 0161-224 5217. Closed Sun., Mon. Adm. free. Exhibits from the 16th to 20th century

†*Manchester Museum*, Oxford Road. Tel: 0161-275 2634. Closed Sun. Adm. free. Archaeology, archery, botany, Egyptology, entomology, ethnography, geology, natural history, numismatics, oriental and zoology collections

†*Museum of Science and Industry*, Castlefield. Tel: 0161-832 1830. Adm. £6.50. On site of world's oldest passenger railway station; galleries relating to space, energy, power, transport, aviation and social history; interactive science centre

†*Whitworth Art Gallery*, Oxford Road. Tel: 0161-275 7450. Closed Sun. mornings. Adm. free. Watercolours, drawings, prints, textiles, wallpapers and 20th-century British art

NEWCASTLE UPON TYNE – **Laing Art Gallery*, New Bridge Street. Tel: 0191-232 7734. Closed Sun. mornings. Adm. free. British and European art, ceramics, glass, silver, textiles and costume; *Art on Tyneside* display

*†Newcastle Discovery Museum, West Blandford Square. Tel: 0191-232 6789. Closed Sun. mornings. Adm. free. Science and industry, local history, fashion and Tyneside's maritime history; Turbinia (first steam-driven engine) gallery

NEWMARKET – *National Horseracing Museum*, High Street. Tel: 01638-667333. Closed Mon. (except July and Aug.) and Nov.-March. Adm. £3.50. Paintings, trophies and exhibits relating to horseracing and tours of local trainers' yards and studs

NORWICH – **†Castle Museum*. Tel: 01603-493624. Closed Sun. mornings. Adm. £3.20 (£2.40 in winter). Art (including Norwich school), archaeology, natural history, teapot collection; guided tours of battlements and dungeons

NOTTINGHAM – **Brewhouse Yard Museum*, Castle Boulevard. Tel: 0115-915 3600. Adm. free (except weekends and Bank Holidays). Daily life from the 17th to 20th century

*Castle Museum. Tel: 0115-915 3700. Adm. free (except weekends and Bank Holidays). Paintings, ceramics, silver and glass; history of Nottingham

*Industrial Museum, Wollaton Park. Tel: 0115-915 3910. Adm. free (except weekends and Bank Holidays). Lacemaking machinery, steam engines and transport exhibits

*Museum of Costume and Textiles, Castle Gate. Tel: 0115-915 3500. Closed Mon. and Tues. Adm. free. Costume

displays from 1790 to the mid-20th century in period rooms

Natural History Museum, Wollaton Park. Tel: 0115-915 3900. Adm. free (except weekends and Bank Holidays). Local natural history and wildlife dioramas

OXFORD – †*Ashmolean Museum*, Beaumont Street. Tel: 01865-278000. Closed Mon. (except Bank Holidays) and Sun. mornings. Adm. free. European and Oriental fine and applied arts, archaeology, Egyptology and numismatics

Museum of Modern Art, Pembroke Street. Tel: 01865-722733. Closed Mon. Adm. £2.50. Temporary exhibitions

†*Museum of the History of Science*, Broad Street. Tel: 01865-277280. Closed mornings and Sun.-Mon. Adm. free. Displays include early scientific instruments, chemical apparatus, clocks and watches

†*Oxford University Museum of Natural History*, Parks Road. Tel: 01865-272950. Closed mornings (except for school parties by appointment) and Sun. Adm. free. Entomology, geology, mineralogy and zoology

†*Pitt Rivers Museum*, South Parks Road. Tel: 01865-270927. Closed mornings (except by appointment) and Sun. Adm. free. Ethnological and archaeological artefacts. Check for periods of closure in 1999

PLYMOUTH – *†*City Museum and Art Gallery*, Drake Circus. Tel: 01752-264878. Closed Mon. (except Bank Holidays) and Sun. Adm. free. Local and natural history, ceramics, silver, Old Masters, temporary exhibitions

The Dome, The Hoe. Tel: 01752-603300. Adm. charge. Maritime history museum

PORTSMOUTH – *Charles Dickens Birthplace Museum*, Old Commercial Road. Tel: 01705-827261. Closed in winter. Adm. charge. Dickens memorabilia

D-Day Museum, Clarence Esplanade. Tel: 01705-827261. Adm. charge. Includes the Overlord Embroidery

Flagship Portsmouth, HM Naval Base. Incorporates the *Royal Naval Museum* (tel: 01705-727562), HMS *Victory* (tel: 01705-822034), HMS *Warrior* (tel: 01705-291379), the †*Mary Rose* (tel: 01705-750521) and the *Dockyard Museum*. Adm. charge to each (combined ticket available). History of the Royal Navy and the dockyard and the trades in it

PRESTON – *Harris Museum and Art Gallery*, Market Square. Tel: 01772-258248. Closed Sun. and Bank Holidays. Adm. free. British art since the 18th century, ceramics, glass, costume and local history; also contemporary exhibitions

READING – †*Rural History Centre*, University of Reading. Tel: 0118-931 8660. Closed Sun. and Mon. Adm. £1.00. History of farming and the countryside over the last 200 years

ST ALBANS – *Verulamium Museum*, St Michael's. Tel: 01727-819339. Closed Sun. mornings. Adm. £2.80. Iron Age and Roman Verulamium, including wall plasters, jewellery, mosaics and room reconstructions

ST IVES, Cornwall – *Tate Gallery St Ives*, Porthmeor Beach. Tel: 01736-796226. Opening times vary seasonally; closed Mon. Oct.-March. Adm. £3.50. Painting and sculpture by artists associated with St Ives

SHEFFIELD – *City Museum and Mappin Art Gallery*, Weston Park. Tel: 0114-276 8588. Closed Mon. and Tues. Adm. free. Includes applied arts, natural history, Bronze Age archaeology and ethnography, 19th- and 20th-century art

Graves Art Gallery, Surrey Street. Tel: 0114-273 5158. Closed Sun. and Mon. Adm. free. 20th-century British art, Grice Collection of Chinese ivories

Kelham Island Industrial Museum, off Alma Street. Tel: 0114-272 2106. Closed Fri. and Sat. Adm. charge. Local industrial and social history

STOKE-ON-TRENT – *Etruria Industrial Museum*, Etruria. Tel: 01782-287557. Closed Mon. and Tues. Adm. charge. Britain's sole surviving steam-powered potter's mill

Gladstone Pottery Museum, Longton. Tel: 01782-319232. Adm. charge. A working Victorian pottery. Pottery factory tours are available by arrangement Mon.-Fri., except during factory holidays, at the following: *Royal Doulton*, Burslem; *Spode*, Stoke; *Wedgwood*, Barlaston; *W. Moorcroft*, Cobridge; *H R Johnson Tiles*, Tunstall; *Moorland Pottery*, Burslem; *Peggy Davies Ceramics*, Stoke; *Staffordshire Enamels*, Longton; *St George's Fine Bone China*, Hanley

*†*Potteries Museum and Art Gallery*, Hanley. Tel: 01782-232323. Closed Sun. mornings. Adm. free. Pottery, china and porcelain collections

STYAL, Cheshire – *Quarry Bank Mill*. Tel: 01625-527468. Closed Mon. in winter. Adm. charge. Working mill illustrating history of cotton industry; costumed guides at restored Apprentice House

TELFORD – *†*Ironbridge Gorge Museums*. Tel: 01952-433522. Smaller sites closed in winter. Adm. charge for each site; £9.50 for all sites (ticket valid until all sites have been visited). Includes first iron bridge; Blists Hill (late Victorian working town); Museum of Iron; Jackfield Tile Museum; Coalport China Museum; Tar Tunnel; Broseley Pipeworks

TRING, Herts – *Tring Zoological Museum*, Akeman Street. Tel: 01442-824181. Closed Sun. mornings. Adm. £2.50. Display of more than 4,000 animal species

WAKEFIELD – *Yorkshire Sculpture Park*, West Bretton. Tel: 01924-830302. Adm. free. Open-air sculpture gallery including works by Moore, Hepworth, Frink and others

WORCESTER – *City Museum and Art Gallery*, Foregate Street. Tel: 01905-25371. Closed Thurs. and Sun. Adm. free. Includes a military museum, 19th-century chemist's shop and changing art exhibitions

Museum of Worcester Porcelain and Royal Worcester Factory, Severn Street. Tel: 01905-23221. Factory tours on weekdays

WROUGHTON, nr Swindon, Wilts – *Science Museum*, Wroughton Airfield. Tel: 01793-814466. Open selected summer weekends only. Adm. charge. Aircraft displays and some of the Science Museum's transport and agricultural collection

YEOVIL, Somerset – *Fleet Air Arm Museum*, Royal Naval Air Station, Yeovilton. Tel: 01935-840565. Adm. charge. History of naval aviation; historic aircraft, including Concorde 002

Montacute House, Montacute (*see* page 587). Elizabethan and Jacobean portraits from the National Portrait Gallery

YORK – *Beningbrough Hall*, Shipton-by-Beningbrough. Tel: 01904-470666. Closed Thurs. and Fri. (except Good Friday and July-Aug.); also closed in winter. Adm. £4.75. Portraits from the National Portrait Gallery

*†*Castle Museum*. Tel: 01904-653611. Adm. £4.75. Reconstructed streets; costume and military collections

*†*City Art Gallery*, Exhibition Square. Tel: 01904-551861. Closed Sun. mornings. Adm. free. European and British painting spanning seven centuries; modern pottery

Jorvik Viking Centre, Coppergate. Tel: 01904-643211. Adm. £4.99. Reconstruction of Viking York

National Railway Museum, Leeman Road. Tel: 01904-621261. Adm. £4.80. Includes locomotives, rolling stock and carriages

*†*Yorkshire Museum*, Museum Gardens. Tel: 01904-629745. Adm. £3.75. Yorkshire life from Roman to medieval times; geology gallery

WALES

BODELWYDDAN, Denbighshire – *Bodelwyddan Castle*. Tel: 01745-584060. Opening times vary. Adm. charge. Portraits from the National Portrait Gallery, furniture from the Victoria and Albert Museum and sculptures from the Royal Academy

CAERLEON – *Roman Legionary Museum*. Tel: 01633-423134. Adm. charge. Material from the site of the Roman fortress of Isca and its suburbs

CARDIFF – *National Museum and Gallery Cardiff*, Cathays Park. Tel: 01222-397951. Closed Mon. (except Bank Holidays). Adm. charge. Includes natural sciences, archaeology and Impressionist paintings
Museum of Welsh Life, St Fagans. Tel: 01222-573500. Adm. charge. Open-air museum with re-erected buildings, agricultural equipment and costume

DRE-FACH FELINDRE, nr Llandysul – *Museum of the Welsh Woollen Industry*. Tel: 01559-370929. Closed Sun., and Sat. in winter. Adm. charge. Exhibitions, a working woollen mill and craft workshops

LLANBERIS, nr Caernarfon – *Welsh Slate Museum*. Tel: 01286-870630. Closed in winter (except by appointment). Adm. charge. Former slate quarry with original machinery and plant; slate crafts demonstrations

LLANDRINDOD WELLS – *National Cycle Exhibition*, Exhibition Palace, Temple Street. Tel: 01597-825531. Adm £2.50. Over 200 bicycles on display, from 1818 to the present day

SWANSEA – *Glyn Vivian Art Gallery and Museum*, Alexandra Road. Tel: 01792-655006. Closed Mon. (except Bank Holidays). Adm. free. Paintings, ceramics, Swansea pottery and porcelain, clocks, glass and Welsh art
Swansea Maritime and Industrial Museum, Museum Square. Tel: 01792-650351. Closed Mon. (except Bank Holidays). Adm. free. Includes a working woollen mill and historic boats afloat

SCOTLAND

ABERDEEN – *Aberdeen Art Gallery*, Schoolhill. Tel: 01224-646333. Closed Sun. mornings. Adm. free. Art from the 18th to 20th century
Aberdeen Maritime Museum, Shiprow. Tel: 01224-337700. Adm. £3.50. Maritime history, including shipbuilding and North Sea oil

EDINBURGH – *Britannia*, Leith docks. Tel: 0131-555 8800. Former royal yacht; opening Oct. 1998
City Art Centre, Market Street. Tel: 0131-529 3993. Closed Sun. Adm. free. Late 19th- and 20th-century art and temporary exhibitions
Huntly House Museum, Canongate. Tel: 0131-529 4143. Closed Sun. Adm. free. Local history, silver, glass and Scottish pottery
Museum of Childhood, High Street. Tel: 0131-529 4142. Closed Sun. Adm. free. Toys, games, clothes and exhibits relating to the social history of childhood
Museum of Flight, East Fortune Airfield, nr North Berwick. Tel: 01620-880308. Closed in winter. Adm. £3.00. Display of aircraft
National Gallery of Scotland, The Mound. Tel: 0131-624 6200. Closed Sun. mornings. Adm. free. Paintings, drawings and prints from the 16th to 20th century, and the national collection of Scottish art
The People's Story, Canongate. Tel: 0131-529 4057. Closed Sun. Adm. free. Edinburgh life since the 18th century

Royal Museum of Scotland, Chambers Street. Tel: 0131-225 7534. Closed Sun. mornings. Adm. £3.00. Scottish and international collections from prehistoric times to the present
Scottish Agricultural Museum, Ingliston. Tel: 0131-225 7534. Closed Sat. and Sun. Adm. free. History of agriculture in Scotland
Scottish National Portrait Gallery, Queen Street. Tel: 0131-624 6200. Closed Sun. mornings. Adm. free. Portraits of eminent people in Scottish history, and the national collection of photography
Scottish National Gallery of Modern Art, Belford Road. Tel: 0131-624 6200. Closed Sun. mornings. Adm. free. Twentieth-century painting, sculpture and graphic art
The Writer's Museum, Lawnmarket. Tel: 0131-529 4901. Closed Sun. Adm. free. Robert Louis Stevenson, Walter Scott and Robert Burns exhibits

FORT WILLIAM – *West Highland Museum*, Cameron Square. Tel: 01397-702169. Closed Sun. Adm. £2.00. Includes tartan collections and exhibits relating to 1745 uprising

GLASGOW – *Burrell Collection*, Pollokshaws Road. Tel: 0141-649 7151. Adm. free. Paintings, textiles, furniture, ceramics, stained glass and silver from classical times to the 19th century
Gallery of Modern Art, Queen Street. Tel: 0141-229 1996. Adm. free. Collection of contemporary Scottish and world art
Glasgow Art Gallery and Museum, Kelvingrove. Tel: 0141-287 2699. Adm. free. Includes Old Masters, 19th-century French paintings and armour collection
Hunterian Art Gallery, Hillhead Street. Tel: 0141-330 5431. Closed Sun. Adm. free. Rennie Mackintosh and Whistler collections; Old Masters, Scottish paintings and modern paintings, sculpture and prints
McLellan Galleries, Sauchiehall Street. Tel: 0141-331 1854. Adm. charge. Temporary exhibitions
Museum of Transport, Bunhouse Road. Tel: 0141-287 2720. Adm. free. Includes a reproduction of a 1938 Glasgow street, cars since the 1930s, trams and a Glasgow subway station
People's Palace Museum, Glasgow Green. Tel: 0141-554 0223. Adm. free. History of Glasgow since 1175
St Mungo Museum of Religious Life and Art, Castle Street. Tel: 0141-553 2557. Adm. free. Explores universal themes through objects of all the main world religions

NORTHERN IRELAND

BELFAST – *Ulster Museum*, Botanic Gardens. Tel: 01232-383000. Closed weekend mornings. Adm. free. Irish antiquities, natural and local history, fine and applied arts

HOLYWOOD, Co. Down – *Ulster Folk and Transport Museum*, Cultra. Tel: 01232-428428. Closed Sun. mornings. Adm. £4.00. Open-air museum with original buildings from Ulster town and rural life *c*. 1900; indoor galleries including Irish rail and road transport and Titanic exhibitions

LONDONDERRY – *The Tower Museum*, Union Hall Place. Tel: 01504-372411. Closed Sun. and Mon. Adm. £3.25. Tells the story of Ireland through the history of Londonderry

OMAGH, Co. Tyrone – *Ulster American Folk Park*, Castletown. Tel: 01662-243292. Closed in winter. Adm. £3.50. Open-air museum telling the story of Ulster's emigrants to America; restored or recreated dwellings and workshops; ship and dockside gallery

Sights of London

For historic buildings and museums and galleries in London, *see* pages 584–90 and 593–4

ALEXANDRA PALACE, Alexandra Palace Way, Wood Green, London N22 4AY. Tel: 0181-365 2121. The Victorian Palace was severely damaged by fire in 1980 but was restored, and reopened in 1988. Alexandra Palace now provides modern facilities for exhibitions, conferences, banquets and leisure activities. There is an ice rink, open daily, and a boating lake.

BARBICAN CENTRE, Silk Street, London EC2Y 8DS. Tel: 0171-638 4141. Owned, funded and managed by the Corporation of London, the Barbican Centre opened in 1982 and houses the 1,156-seat Barbican Theatre, a 200-seat studio theatre (The Pit), and the 1,989-seat Barbican Hall. There are also three cinemas, two art galleries, a sculpture court, a lending library, conference, trade and banqueting facilities, conservatory, shops, restaurants, cafés and bars.

BRIDGES. The bridges over the Thames (from east to west) are:

The Queen Elizabeth II Bridge, opened 1991, from Dartford to Thurrock

Tower Bridge, opened 1894 (*see also* page 594)

London Bridge, opened after rebuilding by Rennie, 1831; the new London Bridge opened 1973

Alexandra Bridge (railway bridge), built 1863–6

Southwark Bridge (Rennie), built 1814–19; rebuilt 1912–21

Blackfriars Railway Bridge, completed 1864

Blackfriars Bridge, built 1760–9; rebuilt 1860–9; widened 1907–10

Waterloo Bridge (Rennie), opened 1817; rebuilt 1937–42

Hungerford Railway Bridge (Brunel), suspension bridge built 1841–5; replaced by present railway and footbridge 1863

Westminster Bridge (width 84 ft), opened 1750; rebuilt 1854–62

Lambeth Bridge, built 1862; rebuilt 1929–32

Vauxhall Bridge, built 1811–16; rebuilt 1895–1906

Grosvenor Bridge (railway bridge), built 1859–60; rebuilt 1963–7

Chelsea Bridge, built 1851–8; replaced by suspension bridge 1934; widened 1937

Albert Bridge, opened 1873; restructured (Bazalgette) 1884; strengthened 1971–3

Battersea Bridge (Holland), opened 1772; rebuilt (Bazalgette) 1890

Battersea Railway Bridge, opened 1863

Wandsworth Bridge, opened 1873; rebuilt 1940

Putney Railway Bridge, opened 1889

Putney Bridge, built 1727–9; rebuilt (Bazalgette) 1882–6; starting point of Oxford and Cambridge Boat Race

Hammersmith Bridge, built 1824–7; rebuilt (Bazalgette) 1883–7; closed in 1997 for safety work

Barnes Railway Bridge (also pedestrian), built 1846–9; restructured 1893

Chiswick Bridge, opened 1933

Kew Railway Bridge, opened 1869

Kew Bridge, built 1758–9; rebuilt and renamed King Edward VII Bridge 1903

Richmond Lock, lock, weir and footbridge opened 1894

Twickenham Bridge, opened 1933

Richmond Railway Bridge, opened 1848; restructured 1906–8

Richmond Bridge, built 1774–7; widened 1937

Teddington Lock, footbridge opened 1889; marks the end of the tidal reach of the Thames

Kingston Bridge, built 1825–8; widened 1914

Hampton Court Bridge, built 1753; replaced by iron bridge 1865; present bridge built 1933

CEMETERIES. *Abney Park*, Stamford Hill, N16 (35 acres), tomb of General Booth, founder of the Salvation Army, and memorials to many Nonconformist divines. *Brompton*, Old Brompton Road, SW10 (40 acres), graves of Sir Henry Cole, Emmeline Pankhurst, John Wisden. *City of London Cemetery and Crematorium*, Aldersbrook Road, E12 (200 acres). *Golders Green Crematorium*, Hoop Lane, NW11 (12 acres), with Garden of Rest and memorials to many famous men and women. *Hampstead*, Fortune Green Road, NW6 (36 acres), graves of Kate Greenaway, Lord Lister, Marie Lloyd. *Highgate*, Swains Lane, N6 (38 acres), tombs of George Eliot, Faraday and Marx; guided tours only, west side, £3.00. *Kensal Green*, Harrow Road, W10 (70 acres), tombs of Thackeray, Trollope, Sydney Smith, Wilkie Collins, Tom Hood, George Cruikshank, Leigh Hunt, I. K. Brunel and Charles Kemble. Churchyard of the former *Marylebone Chapel*, Marylebone High Street, W1, Charles Wesley and his son Samuel Wesley buried; chapel demolished in 1949, now Garden of Rest. *Nunhead*, Linden Grove, SE15 (26 acres), closed in 1969, recently restored and opened for burials. *St Marylebone Cemetery and Crematorium*, East End Road, N2 (47 acres). *West Norwood Cemetery and Crematorium*, Norwood High Street, SE27 (42 acres), tombs of Sir Henry Bessemer, Mrs Beeton, Sir Henry Tate and Joseph Whitaker (*Whitaker's Almanack*).

CENOTAPH, Whitehall, London SW1. The word 'cenotaph' means 'empty tomb'. The monument, erected 'To the Glorious Dead', is a memorial to all ranks of the sea, land and air forces who gave their lives in the service of the Empire during the First World War. Designed by Sir Edwin Lutyens and erected as a temporary memorial in 1919, it was replaced by a permanent structure unveiled by George V on Armistice Day 1920. An additional inscription was made after the Second World War to commemorate those who gave their lives in that conflict.

CHARTERHOUSE, Sutton's Hospital, Charterhouse Square, London EC1M 6AN. Tel: 0171-253 9503. A Carthusian monastery from 1371 to 1537, purchased in 1611 by Thomas Sutton, who endowed it as a hospital for aged men 'of gentle birth' and a school for poor scholars (removed to Godalming in 1872). Open to visitors on Wednesdays at 2.15 (April–July). Admission £3.00. *Registrar and Clerk to the Governors*, Lt.-Col. I. Macdonald.

CHELSEA PHYSIC GARDEN, 66 Royal Hospital Road, London SW3 4HS. Tel: 0171-352 5646. A garden of general botanical research, maintaining a wide range of rare and unusual plants. The garden was established in 1673 by the Society of Apothecaries. Open Wednesday and Sunday p.m. during summer months. All enquiries to the Curator.

DOWNING STREET, London SW1. Number 10 Downing Street is the official town residence of the Prime Minister, No. 11 of the Chancellor of the Exchequer and No. 12 is the office of the Government Whips. The street was named after Sir George Downing, Bt., soldier and diplomatist, who was MP for Morpeth from 1660 to 1684.

Chequers, a Tudor mansion in the Chilterns near Princes Risborough, was presented by Lord and Lady Lee of

Fareham in 1917 to serve, from 1921, as a country residence for the Prime Minister of the day.

GEORGE INN, Borough High Street, London SE1. The last galleried inn in London, built in 1677. Now run as an ordinary public house.

GREENWICH, London SE10. *The Royal Naval College* was until 1873 the Greenwich Hospital. It was built by Charles II, largely from designs by John Webb, and by Queen Anne and William III, from designs by Wren. It stands on the site of an ancient royal palace and of the more recent Palace of Placentia constructed by Humphrey, Duke of Gloucester (1391–1447), son of Henry IV. Henry VIII, Mary I and Elizabeth I were born in the royal palace (which reverted to the Crown in 1447) and Edward VI died there. *Greenwich Park* (196½ acres) was enclosed by Humphrey, Duke of Gloucester, and laid out by Charles II from the designs of Le Nôtre. On a hill in Greenwich Park is the former Royal Observatory (founded 1675). Its buildings are now managed by the National Maritime Museum (*see* page 594) and the first observatory is named Flamsteed House, after John Flamsteed (1646–1719), the first Astronomer Royal (*see* page 586). *The Cutty Sark*, the last of the famous tea clippers, has been preserved as a memorial to ships and men of a past era. The yacht *Gipsy Moth IV* is preserved alongside the *Cutty Sark*.

HORSE GUARDS, Whitehall, London SW1. Archway and offices built about 1753. The mounting of the guard takes place at 11 a.m. (10 a.m. on Sundays) and the dismounted inspection at 4 p.m. Only those on the Lord Chamberlain's list may drive through the gates and archway into *Horse Guards' Parade* (230,000 sq. ft), where the Colour is 'trooped' on The Queen's official birthday.

THE HOUSES OF PARLIAMENT, Westminster, London SW1. The royal palace of Westminster, originally built by Edward the Confessor, was the normal meeting place of Parliament from about 1340. St Stephen's Chapel was used from about 1550 for the meetings of the House of Commons, which had previously been held in the Chapter House or Refectory of Westminster Abbey. The House of Lords met in an apartment of the royal palace.

The fire of 1834 destroyed much of the palace and the present Houses of Parliament were erected on the site from the designs of Sir Charles Barry and Augustus Welby Pugin between 1840 and 1867. The chamber of the House of Commons was destroyed by bombing in 1941 and a new Chamber designed by Sir Giles Gilbert Scott was used for the first time in 1950.

Lord Chancellor's Residence, Lord Chancellor's Office, House of Lords, London, SW1A 0PW. Tel: 0171-219 2394. Open 10.30 a.m.–12 noon, days vary. Postal requests in advance to 'Residence visit', Lord Chancellor's Office.

Westminster Hall was the only part of the old palace of Westminster to survive the fire of 1834. It was built by William Rufus (1097–9) and altered by Richard II (1394–9). The hammerbeam roof of carved oak dates from 1396–8. The Hall was the scene of the trial of Charles I.

The Victoria Tower of the House of Lords is about 330 ft high, and when Parliament is sitting the Union flag flies by day from its flagstaff. *The Clock Tower* of the House of Commons is about 320 ft high and contains 'Big Ben', the hour bell said to be named after Sir Benjamin Hall, First Commissioner of Works when the original bell was cast in 1856. This bell, which weighed 16 tons 11 cwt, was found to be cracked in 1857. The present bell (13½ tons) is a recasting of the original and was first brought into use in 1859. The dials of the clock are 23 ft in diameter, the hands being 9 ft and 14 ft long (including balance piece).

A light is displayed from the Clock Tower at night when Parliament is sitting.

For security reasons tours of the Houses of Parliament are available only to those who have made advance arrangements through an MP or peer.

Admission to the Strangers' Gallery of the House of Lords is arranged by a peer or by queue via St Stephen's Entrance. Admission to the Strangers' Gallery of the House of Commons is by Members' order (Members' orders should be sought several weeks in advance), or by queue via St Stephen's Entrance. Queues are usually shorter after 6 p.m. Monday–Thursday and on Wednesday morning. Overseas visitors may write to the Parliamentary Education Unit to obtain a permit to tour the Houses of Parliament, or obtain cards of introduction from their Embassy or High Commission to attend the public gallery.

INNS OF COURT. The *Inner* and *Middle Temple,* Fleet Street/Victoria Embankment, London EC4, have occupied since the early 14th century the site of the buildings of the Order of Knights Templars. *Inner Temple Hall* is open by appointment on application to the Treasurer's Office. *Middle Temple Hall* (1562–70) is open when not in use, Monday–Friday 10–11.30 and 3–4; closed on public holidays. In Middle Temple Gardens (open to the public May–July, Monday–Friday 12–3) Shakespeare (Henry VI, Part I) places the incident which led to the 'Wars of the Roses' (1455–85).

Temple Church, London EC4, has a nave which forms one of five remaining round churches in England. Open Wednesday–Friday 10–4. Services: 8.30 and 11.15 a.m. except in August and September. *Master of the Temple,* Revd Canon J. Robinson.

Lincoln's Inn, Chancery Lane/Lincoln's Inn Fields, London WC2, occupies the site of the palace of a former Bishop of Chichester and of a Black Friars monastery. The hall and library buildings are of 1845, although the library is first mentioned in 1474; the old hall (late 15th century) and the chapel were rebuilt *c.* 1619–23. Halls open by appointment, chapel and gardens, Monday–Friday 12–2.30. Chapel services Sunday 11.30 a.m. during law terms. *Lincoln's Inn Fields* (7 acres). The square was laid out by Inigo Jones.

Gray's Inn, Holborn/Gray's Inn Road, London WC1. Early 14th century; Hall 1556–8. Matins 11.15 a.m. (during dining term only). Holy Communion first Sunday in every month except January, August and September. Gardens open Monday–Friday 12–2.30 (except Public Holidays). Tel: 0171-405 8164.

No other 'Inns' are active, but there are remains of *Staple Inn,* a gabled front on Holborn (opposite Gray's Inn Road). *Clement's Inn* (near St Clement Danes Church), *Clifford's Inn,* Fleet Street, and *Thavies Inn,* Holborn Circus, are all rebuilt. *Serjeants' Inn,* Fleet Street, and another (demolished 1910) of the same name in Chancery Lane, were composed of Serjeants-at-Law, the last of whom died in 1922.

LLOYD'S, Lime Street, London EC3M 7HA. International insurance market which evolved during the 17th century from Lloyds Coffee House. The present building was opened for business in May 1986, and houses the Lutine Bell. Underwriting is on three floors with a total area of 114,000 sq. feet.

LONDON PARKS, ETC.

Royal Parks

Bushy Park (1,099 acres), Surrey. Adjoining Hampton Court, contains avenue of horse-chestnuts enclosed in a fourfold avenue of limes planted by William III. 'Chestnut Sunday' (when the trees are in full bloom with their 'candles') is usually about 1 to 15 May

Green Park (49 acres), London w1. Between Piccadilly and St James's Park, with Constitution Hill leading to Hyde Park Corner

Greenwich Park (196½ acres), London se10

Hampton Court Gardens (54 acres), Surrey

Hampton Court Green (17 acres), Surrey

Hampton Court Park (622 acres), Surrey

Hyde Park (341 acres), London w1/w2. From Park Lane to Kensington Gardens, containing the Serpentine. Fine gateway at Hyde Park Corner, with Apsley House, the Achilles Statue, Rotten Row and the Ladies' Mile. To the north-east is the Marble Arch, originally erected by George IV at the entrance to Buckingham Palace and re-erected in the present position in 1851

Kensington Gardens (275 acres), London w2/w8. From the western boundary of Hyde Park to Kensington Palace, containing the Albert Memorial and Peter Pan statue

Kew, Royal Botanic Gardens, see page 338

Regent's Park and *Primrose Hill* (464 acres), London nw1. From Marylebone Road to Primrose Hill surrounded by the Outer Circle and divided by the Broad Walk leading to the Zoological Gardens

Richmond Park (2,469 acres), Surrey

St James's Park (93 acres), London sw1. From Whitehall to Buckingham Palace. Ornamental lake of 12 acres. The original suspension bridge built in 1857 was replaced in 1957. The Mall leads from the Admiralty Arch to Buckingham Palace, Birdcage Walk from Storey's Gate to Buckingham Palace

Maintained by the Corporation of London

Ashtead Common (500 acres), Surrey

Burnham Beeches and *Fleet Wood* (540 acres), Bucks. Purchased by the Corporation for the benefit of the public in 1880, Fleet Wood (65 acres) being presented in 1921

Coulsdon Common (133 acres), Surrey

Epping Forest (6,000 acres), Essex. Purchased by the Corporation and opened to the public in 1882. The present forest is 12 miles long by 1 to 2 miles wide, about one-tenth of its original area

Farthing Downs (121 acres), Surrey

Hampstead Heath (789 acres), London nw3. Including Golders Hill (36 acres) and Parliament Hill (271 acres)

Highgate Wood (70 acres), London n6/n10

Kenley Common (138 acres), Surrey

Queen's Park (30 acres), London nw6

Riddlesdown (90 acres), Surrey

Spring Park (51 acres), Kent

West Ham Park (77 acres), London e15

West Wickham Common (25 acres), Kent

Woodredon and *Warlies Park Estate* (740 acres), Waltham Abbey

Also smaller open spaces within the City of London, including *Finsbury Circus Gardens*

London Planetarium, Marylebone Road, London nw1 5lr. Tel: 0171-935 6861. Open daily (except Christmas Day), star show and interactive exhibits 12.20–5.00. Admission charge.

London Zoo, Regent's Park, London nw1. Tel: 0171-722 3333. Opened in 1828. Open daily (except Christmas Day) 10–5.30 March–September, 10–4 in winter. Admission £8.50.

Madame Tussaud's, Marylebone Road, London nw1 5lr. Tel: 0171-935 6861. Waxwork exhibition. Open daily (except Christmas Day) 9.30–5.30 (earlier at weekends and during school holidays). Admission charge.

Markets. The London markets are mostly administered by the Corporation of London. *Billingsgate* (fish), Thames Street site dating from 1875, a market site for over 1,000 years, moved to the Isle of Dogs in 1982. *Borough* se1 (vegetables, fruit, flowers, etc.), established

on present site 1756, privately owned and run. *Covent Garden* (vegetables, fruit, flowers, etc.), established in 1661 under a charter of Charles II, moved in 1973 to Nine Elms. *Leadenhall,* ec3 (meat, poultry, fish, etc.), built 1881, part recently demolished. *London Fruit Exchange,* Brushfield Street, built by Corporation of London 1928–9 as buildings for Spitalfields market; not connected with the market since it moved in 1991. *Petticoat Lane,* Middlesex Street, e1, a market has existed on the site for over 500 years, now a Sunday morning market selling almost anything. *Portobello Road,* w11, originally for herbs and horse-trading from 1870; became famous for antiques after the closure of the Caledonian Market in 1948; Saturdays. *Smithfield, Central Meat, Fish, Fruit, Vegetable and Poultry Markets,* built 1851–66, the site of St Bartholomew's Fair from 12th to 19th century, new hall built 1963, market refurbished 1993–4. *Spitalfields,* e1 (vegetables, fruit, etc.), established 1682, modernized 1928, moved to Leyton in 1991.

Marlborough House, Pall Mall, London sw1a 5hx. Built by Wren for the first Duke of Marlborough and completed in 1711, the house reverted to the Crown in 1835. In 1863 it became the London house of the Prince of Wales and was the London home of Queen Mary until her death in 1953. In 1959 Marlborough House was given by The Queen as a centre for Commonwealth government conferences and it was opened as such in 1962. The Queen's Chapel, Marlborough Gate, begun in 1623 from the designs of Inigo Jones for the Infanta Maria of Spain, and completed for Queen Henrietta Maria, is open to the public for services on Sundays at 8.30 a.m. and 11.15 a.m. between Easter Day and end July (*see* St James's Palace for winter services in The Chapel Royal).

London Monument (commonly called The Monument), Monument Street, London ec3. Built from designs of Wren, 1671–7, to commemorate the Great Fire of London, which broke out in Pudding Lane on 2 September 1666. The fluted Doric column is 120 ft high; the moulded cylinder above the balcony supporting a flaming vase of gilt bronze is an additional 42 ft; and the column is based on a square plinth 40 ft high (with fine carvings on the west face) making a total height of 202 ft. Splendid views of London from gallery at top of column (311 steps).

Monuments (sculptor's name in parenthesis). *Albert Memorial* (Durham), Kensington Gore; *Royal Air Force* (Blomfield), Victoria Embankment; *Viscount Alanbrooke,* Whitehall; *Beaconsfield,* Parliament Square; *Beatty* (Macmillan), Trafalgar Square; *Belgian Gratitude* (setting by Blomfield, statue by Rousseau), Victoria Embankment; *Boadicea* (or Boudicca), Queen of the Iceni (Thornycroft), Westminster Bridge; *Brunel* (Marochetti), Victoria Embankment; *Burghers of Calais* (Rodin), Victoria Tower Gardens, Westminster; *Burns* (Steell), Embankment Gardens; *Canada Memorial* (Granche), Green Park; *Carlyle* (Boehm), Chelsea Embankment; *Cavalry* (Jones), Hyde Park; *Edith Cavell* (Frampton), St Martin's Place; *Cenotaph* (Lutyens), Whitehall; *Charles I* (Le Sueur), Trafalgar Square; *Charles II* (Gibbons), South Court, Chelsea Hospital; *Churchill* (Roberts-Jones), Parliament Square; *Cleopatra's Needle* (68½ ft high, c.1500 bc, erected on the Thames Embankment in 1877–8; the sphinxes are Victorian); *Clive* (Tweed), King Charles Street; *Captain Cook* (Brock), The Mall; *Crimean,* Broad Sanctuary; *Oliver Cromwell* (Thornycroft), outside Westminster Hall; *Cunningham* (Belsky), Trafalgar Square; *Gen. Charles de Gaulle,* Carlton Gardens; *Lord Dowding* (Faith Winter), Strand; *Duke of Cambridge* (Jones), Whitehall; *Duke of York* (124 ft), Carlton House Terrace;

Edward VII (Mackennal), Waterloo Place; *Elizabeth I* (1586, oldest outdoor statue in London; from Ludgate), Fleet Street; *Eros* (Shaftesbury Memorial) (Gilbert), Piccadilly Circus; *Marechal Foch* (Mallisard, copy of one in Cassel, France), Grosvenor Gardens; *Charles James Fox* (Westmacott), Bloomsbury Square; *George III* (Cotes Wyatt), Cockspur Street; *George IV* (Chantrey), riding without stirrups, Trafalgar Square; *George V* (Reid Dick), Old Palace Yard; *George VI* (Macmillan), Carlton Gardens; *Gladstone* (Thornycroft), Strand; *Guards'* (Crimea) (Bell), Waterloo Place; (Great War) (Ledward, figures, Bradshaw, cenotaph), Horse Guards' Parade; *Haig* (Hardiman), Whitehall; *Sir Arthur (Bomber) Harris* (Faith Winter), Strand; *Irving* (Brock), north side of National Portrait Gallery; *James II* (Gibbons and/or pupils), Trafalgar Square; *Jellicoe* (Wheeler), Trafalgar Square; *Samuel Johnson* (Fitzgerald), opposite St Clement Danes; *Kitchener* (Tweed), Horse Guards' Parade; *Abraham Lincoln* (Saint-Gaudens, copy of one in Chicago), Parliament Square; *Milton* (Montford), St Giles, Cripplegate; *The Monument* (*see* above); *Mountbatten*, Foreign Office Green; *Nelson* (170 ft 2 in), Trafalgar Square, with Landseer's lions (cast from guns recovered from the wreck of the *Royal George*); *Florence Nightingale* (Walker), Waterloo Place; *Palmerston* (Woolner), Parliament Square; *Peel* (Noble), Parliament Square; *Pitt* (Chantrey), Hanover Square; *Portal* (Nemon), Embankment Gardens; *Prince Consort* (Bacon), Holborn Circus; *Queen Elizabeth Gate*, Hyde Park Corner; *Raleigh* (Macmillan), Whitehall; *Richard I (Coeur de Lion)* (Marochetti), Old Palace Yard; *Roberts* (Bates), Horse Guards' Parade; *Franklin D. Roosevelt* (Reid Dick), Grosvenor Square; *Royal Artillery* (South Africa) (Colton), The Mall; (Great War), Hyde Park Corner; *Captain Scott* (Lady Scott), Waterloo Place; *Shackleton* (Sarjeant Jagger), Kensington Gore; *Shakespeare* (Fontana, copy of one by Scheemakers in Westminster Abbey), Leicester Square; *Smuts* (Epstein), Parliament Square; *Sullivan* (Goscombe John), Victoria Embankment; *Trenchard* (Macmillan), Victoria Embankment; *Victoria Memorial*, in front of Buckingham Palace; *Raoul Wallenberg* (Phillip Jackson), Great Cumberland Place; *George Washington* (Houdon copy), Trafalgar Square; *Wellington* (Boehm), Hyde Park Corner; (Chantrey) riding without stirrups, outside Royal Exchange; *John Wesley* (Adams Acton), City Road; *William III* (Bacon), St James's Square; *Wolseley* (Goscombe John), Horse Guards' Parade.

PORT OF LONDON. The Port of London covers the tidal section of the River Thames from Teddington to the seaward limit (the outer Tongue buoy and the Sunk light vessel), a distance of 150 km. The governing body is the Port of London Authority (PLA). Each year 56 million tonnes of cargo is handled at privately operated riverside terminals between Fulham and Canvey Island, including the enclosed dock at Tilbury, 40 km below London Bridge. Passenger vessels and cruise liners can be handled at moorings at Greenwich, Tower Bridge and Tilbury.

ROMAN REMAINS. The city wall of Roman *Londinium* was largely rebuilt during the medieval period but sections may be seen near the White Tower in the Tower of London; at Tower Hill; at Coopers' Row; at All Hallows, London Wall, its vestry being built on the remains of a semi-circular Roman bastion; at St Alphage, London Wall, showing a succession of building repairs from the Roman until the late medieval period; and at St Giles, Cripplegate. Sections of the great forum and basilica, more than 165 metres square, have been encountered during excavations in the area of Leadenhall, Gracechurch Street and Lombard Street. Traces of Roman activity along the river include a massive riverside wall built in the late Roman period, and a succession of Roman timber quays along Lower and Upper Thames Street. Finds from these sites can be seen at the Museum of London (*see* page 594).

Other major buildings are the amphitheatre at Guildhall; remains of bath-buildings in Upper and Lower Thames Street; and the temple of Mithras in Walbrook.

ROYAL ALBERT HALL, Kensington Gore, London SW7 2AP. Tel: 0171-589 3203. The elliptical hall, one of the largest in the world, was completed in 1871, and since 1941 has been the venue each summer for the Promenade Concerts founded in 1895 by Sir Henry Wood. Other events include pop and classical music concerts, dance, opera, sporting events, conferences and banquets.

ROYAL HOSPITAL, CHELSEA, Royal Hospital Road, London SW3 4SR. Tel: 0171-730 0161. Founded by Charles II in 1682, and built by Wren; opened in 1692 for old and disabled soldiers. Open Monday–Saturday 10–12, daily 2–4. The extensive grounds include the former Ranelagh Gardens and are the venue for the Chelsea Flower Show each May. *Governor*, Gen. Sir Brian Kenny, GCB, CBE.

ROYAL OPERA HOUSE, Covent Garden, London WC2E 9DD. Home of The Royal Ballet (1931) and The Royal Opera (1946). The Royal Opera House is the third theatre to be built on the site, opening 1858; the first was opened in 1732. The theatre is closed for redevelopment until winter 1999.

ST JAMES'S PALACE, Pall Mall, London SW1. Built by Henry VIII; the Gatehouse and Presence Chamber remain; later alterations were made by Wren and Kent. The Chapel Royal is open for services on Sundays at 8.30 a.m. and 11.15 a.m. between the beginning of October and Good Friday (*see* Marlborough House for summer services in The Queen's Chapel). Representatives of foreign powers are still accredited 'to the Court of St James's'. *Clarence House* (1825) in the palace precinct is the home of The Queen Mother.

ST PAUL'S CATHEDRAL, London EC4M 8AD. Built 1675–1710, cost £747,660. The cross on the dome is 365 ft above the ground level, the inner cupola 218 ft above the floor. 'Great Paul' in the south-west tower weighs nearly 17 tons. The organ by Father Smith (enlarged by Willis and rebuilt by Mander) is in a case carved by Grinling Gibbons, who also carved the choir stalls. Open for sightseeing Monday–Saturday 8.30–4.00. Admission to cathedral and crypt: £4.00, children £2.00; Galleries £3.50/£1.50. Services: Sundays, 8, 10, 11, 3.15 and 6. Weekdays, 7.30, 8, 12.30 and 5 (Saturday Matins 8.30 a.m.).

SOMERSET HOUSE, Strand and Victoria Embankment, London WC2. The river façade (600 ft. long) was built in 1776–86 from the designs of Sir William Chambers; the eastern extension, which houses part of King's College, was built by Smirke in 1829. Somerset House was the property of Lord Protector Somerset, at whose attainder in 1552 the palace passed to the Crown, and it was a royal residence until 1692.

SOUTH BANK, London SE1. The arts complex on the south bank of the River Thames which consists of the 2,903-seat *Royal Festival Hall* (opened in 1951 for the Festival of Britain), the adjacent 1,056-seat *Queen Elizabeth Hall*, the 368-seat *Purcell Room*, and the 77-seat *Voice Box*. Tel: 0171-960 4242.

THE *National Film Theatre* (opened 1952), administered by the British Film Institute, has three auditoria showing over 2,000 films a year. The London Film Festival is held here every November. Tel: 0171-928 3232.

The *Royal National Theatre* opened in 1976 and stages classical, modern, new and neglected plays in its three auditoria: the 1,160-seat Olivier theatre, the 890-seat Lyttelton theatre and the Cottesloe theatre which seats up to 400. Tel: 0171-928 3000.

SOUTHWARK CATHEDRAL, London SE1 9DA. Mainly 13th century, but the nave is largely rebuilt. The tomb of John Gower (1330–1408) is between the Bunyan and Chaucer memorial windows in the north aisle; Shakespeare's effigy backed by a view of Southwark and the Globe Theatre in the south aisle; the tomb of Bishop Andrewes (died 1626) is near the screen. The lady chapel was the scene of the consistory courts of the reign of Mary (Gardiner and Bonner) and is still used as a consistory court. John Harvard, after whom Harvard University is named, was baptized here in 1607, and the chapel by the north choir aisle is his memorial chapel. Open 9–6, admission free (suggested donation £2). Services: Sundays, 9, 11, 3. Weekdays, 8, 12.45, 5.30 (sung on Tuesdays and Fridays), Saturdays, 9, 4.

THAMES EMBANKMENTS. The *Victoria Embankment*, on the north side from Westminster to Blackfriars, was constructed by Sir Joseph Bazalgette (1819–91) for the Metropolitan Board of Works, 1864–70; the seats, of which the supports of some are a kneeling camel, laden with spicery, and of others a winged sphinx, were presented by the Grocers' Company and by W. H. Smith, MP, in 1874; the *Albert Embankment*, on the south side from Westminster Bridge to Vauxhall, 1866–9; the *Chelsea Embankment*, 1871–4. The total cost exceeded £2,000,000. Bazalgette also inaugurated the London main drainage system, 1858–65. A medallion (*Flumini vincula posuit*) has been placed on a pier of the Victoria Embankment to commemorate the engineer.

THAMES FLOOD BARRIER. Officially opened in May 1984, though first used in February 1983, the barrier consists of ten rising sector gates which span 570 yards from bank to bank of the Thames at Woolwich Reach. When not in use the gates lie horizontally, allowing shipping to navigate the river normally; when the barrier is closed, the gates turn through 90 degrees to stand vertically more than 50 feet above the river bed. The barrier took eight years to complete and can be raised within about 30 minutes.

THAMES TUNNELS. The *Rotherhithe Tunnel*, opened 1908, connects Commercial Road, London E14, with Lower Road, Rotherhithe; it is 1 mile 332 yards long, of which 525 yards are under the river. The first *Blackwall Tunnel* (northbound vehicles only), opened 1897, connects East India Dock Road, Poplar, with Blackwall Lane, East Greenwich. The height restriction on the northbound tunnel is 13ft 4in. A second tunnel (for southbound vehicles only) opened 1967. The lengths of the tunnels measured from East India Dock Road to the Gate House on the south side are 6,215 ft (old tunnel) and 6,152 ft. *Greenwich Tunnel* (pedestrians only), opened 1902, connects the Isle of Dogs, Poplar, with Greenwich; it is 406 yards long. The *Woolwich Tunnel* (pedestrians only), opened 1912, connects North and South Woolwich below the passenger and vehicular ferry from North Woolwich Station, London E16, to High Street, Woolwich, London SE18; it is 552 yards long.

WALTHAM CROSS, Herts. At Waltham Cross is one of the crosses (partly restored) erected by Edward I to mark a resting place of the corpse of Queen Eleanor on its way to Westminster Abbey. Ten crosses were erected, but only those at Geddington, Northampton and Waltham survive; 'Charing' Cross originally stood near the spot now occupied by the statue of Charles I at Whitehall.

WESTMINSTER ABBEY, London SW1. Built between 1050 and 1745; contains the chapel of Henry VII, chapter house and cloisters, Edward the Confessor's shrine, tombs of kings and queens and many other monuments, including the grave of 'The Unknown Warrior' and Poets' Corner. The Coronation Chair formerly enclosed the Stone of Scone, removed from Scotland by Edward I in 1296 and returned to Scotland in 1996. Open on weekdays 9.20–4.45. Admission £5.00. Last admission Monday–Friday 3.45 p.m., Saturday 1.45 p.m. No sightseeing on Sundays. Services: Sundays, 8, 10, 11.15, 3, 6.30 (generally preceded by an organ recital). Monday–Friday, 7.30, 8, 12.30, 5. Saturdays, 8, 9.20, 3.

WESTMINSTER CATHEDRAL, Ashley Place, London SW1P 1QW. Roman Catholic cathedral built 1895–1903 from the designs of J. F. Bentley. The campanile is 283 feet high. Cathedral open 6.50 a.m.–7 p.m. Masses: Sundays, 7, 8, 9, 10.30 (sung), 12, 5.30 and 7; Solemn Vespers and Benediction 3.30. Monday–Friday, 7, 8, 8.30, 9, 10.30, 12.30, 1.05 and 5.30 (sung), Morning Prayer 7.40, Vespers 5. Saturdays 8, 8.30, 9, 10.30 (sung), 12.30 and 6, Morning Prayer 10.00, Rosary, Benediction 7.00. Holy days of obligation, Low Masses 7, 8, 8.30, 9, 10.30, 12.30, 1.05, 5.30 (sung) and 7.

LONDON TOURIST BOARD AND CONVENTION BUREAU, Glen House, Stag Place, London, SW1E 5LT. Tourist information: 0839-123456

Hallmarks

Hallmarks are the symbols stamped on gold, silver or platinum articles to indicate that they have been tested at an official Assay Office and that they conform to one of the legal standards. With certain exceptions, all gold, silver or platinum articles are required by law to be hallmarked before they are offered for sale. Hallmarking was instituted in England in 1300 under a statute of Edward I.

MODERN HALLMARKS

At present, a complete modern hallmark consists of four symbols – the sponsor's mark, the assay office mark, the fineness (standard) mark and the date letter. Under proposed amendments to the Hallmarking Act 1973, expected to come into effect from 1 January 1999, the sponsor's mark, the assay office mark and the fineness mark will remain compulsory; the date letter, and the Britannia for 958 silver, the lion passant for 925 silver and the orb for 950 platinum may become additional voluntary marks; and the assay office import marks will no longer be used. Additional finenesses (indicated by * below) will become legal, reflecting the more common finenesses used in Europe.

SPONSOR'S MARK

Instituted in England in 1363, the sponsor's mark was originally a device such as a bird or fleur-de-lis. Now it consists of the initial letters of the name or names of the manufacturer or firm. Where two or more sponsors have the same initials, there is a variation in the surrounding shield or style of letters.

FINENESS (STANDARD) MARK

The fineness (standard) mark indicates that the content of the precious metal in the alloy from which the article is made, is not less than the legal standard. The legal standard is the minimum content of precious metal by weight in parts per thousand, and the standards are:

Gold	916.6	(22 carat)
	750	(18 carat)
	585	(14 carat)
	375	(9 carat)
Silver	958.4	(Britannia)
	925	(sterling)
Platinum	950	

The metals are marked, if they are manufactured in the United Kingdom prior to the amendments becoming effective, as follows:

GOLD – a crown followed by the millesimal figure for the standard, e.g. 916 for 22 carat (*see* table above)

SILVER – Britannia silver: a full-length figure of Britannia. Sterling silver: a lion passant (England) or a lion rampant (Scotland)

 Britannia Silver

 Sterling Silver (England)

 Sterling Silver (Scotland)

PLATINUM – an orb

ASSAY OFFICE MARK

This mark identifies the particular assay office at which the article was tested and marked. The British assay offices are:

LONDON, Goldsmiths' Hall, London EC2V 8AQ.
Tel: 0171-606 8975

BIRMINGHAM, Newhall Street, Birmingham B3 1SB.
Tel: 0121-236 6951

 Gold and platinum

 Silver

SHEFFIELD, 137 Portobello Street, Sheffield S1 4DS.
Tel: 0114-275 5111

EDINBURGH, 39 Manor Place, Edinburgh EH3 7EB.
Tel: 0131-226 1122

Assay offices formerly existed in other towns, e.g. Chester, Exeter, Glasgow, Newcastle, Norwich and York, each having its own distinguishing mark.

DATE LETTER

The date letter shows the year in which an article was assayed and hallmarked. Each alphabetical cycle has a distinctive style of lettering or shape of shield. The date letters were different at the various assay offices and the particular office must be established from the assay office mark before reference is made to tables of date letters. Date letter marks may become voluntary from 1 January 1999.

The table on page 603 shows specimen shields and letters used by the London Assay Office on silver articles in each period from 1498. The same letters are found on gold articles but the surrounding shield may differ. Since 1 January 1975, each office has used the same style of date letter and shield for all articles.

OTHER MARKS

FOREIGN GOODS

Since 1842 foreign goods imported into Britain have been required to be hallmarked before sale. The marks consist of the importer's mark, a special assay office mark, the figure denoting fineness (fineness mark) and the annual date letter.

The following are the assay office marks for gold imported articles. For silver and platinum the symbols remain the same but the shields differ in shape.

 London

 Birmingham

 Sheffield

 Edinburgh

CONVENTION HALLMARKS

Special marks at authorized assay offices of the signatory countries of the International Convention (Austria, Denmark, Finland, Ireland, Norway, Portugal, Sweden, Switzerland and the UK) are legally recognized in the United Kingdom as approved hallmarks. These consist of a sponsor's mark, a common control mark, a fineness mark (arabic numerals showing the standard in parts per thousand), and an assay office mark. There is no date letter.

The fineness marks are:

Gold	750	(18 carat)
	585	(14 carat)
	375	(9 carat)
Silver	925	(sterling)
Platinum	950	

The common control marks are:

 Gold (18 carat)

 Silver

 Platinum

DUTY MARKS

In 1784 an additional mark of the reigning sovereign's head was introduced to signify that the excise duty had been paid. The mark became obsolete on the abolition of the duty in 1890.

COMMEMORATIVE MARKS

There are three other marks to commemorate special events: the silver jubilee of King George V and Queen Mary in 1935, the coronation of Queen Elizabeth II in 1953, and her silver jubilee in 1977.

LONDON (GOLDSMITHS' HALL) DATE LETTERS FROM 1498

---

		from	to
	Black letter, small	1498–9	1517–8
	Lombardic	1518–9	1537–8
	Roman and other capitals	1538–9	1557–8
	Black letter, small	1558–9	1577–8
	Roman letter, capitals	1578–9	1597–8

		from	to
	Lombardic, external cusps	1598–9	1617–8
	Italic letter, small	1618–9	1637–8
	Court hand	1638–9	1657–8
	Black letter, capitals	1658–9	1677–8
	Black letter, small	1678–9	1696–7
	Court hand	1697	1715–6
	Roman letter, capitals	1716–7	1735–6
	Roman letter, small	1736–7	1738–9
	Roman letter, small	1739–40	1755–6
	Old English, capitals	1756–7	1775–6
	Roman letter, small	1776–7	1795–6
	Roman letter, capitals	1796–7	1815–6
	Roman letter, small	1816–7	1835–6
	Old English, capitals	1836–7	1855–6
	Old English, small	1856–7	1875–6
	Roman letter, capitals [A to M square shield N to Z as shown]	1876–7	1895–6
	Roman letter, small	1896–7	1915–6
	Black letter, small	1916–7	1935–6
	Roman letter, capitals	1936–7	1955–6
	Italic letter, small	1956–7	1974
	Italic letter, capitals	1975	

Economic Statistics

The Budget 1998

GOVERNMENT RECEIPTS £ billion

	Outturn 1996–7	Estimate 1997–8	Forecast 1998–9
Inland Revenue	103.7	117.4	126.1
Income tax (gross)	71.5	79.4	86.1
Income tax credits	−2.4	−2.7	−1.8
Corporation tax[1]	27.8	30.5	30.0
Windfall tax	—	2.6	2.6
Petroleum revenue tax	1.7	1.1	0.5
Capital gains tax	1.1	1.4	2.2
Inheritance tax	1.6	1.7	1.9
Stamp duties	2.5	3.4	4.6
Customs and Excise	82.4	89.9	95.6
Value added tax	46.7	51.0	53.3
Fuel duties	17.2	19.1	21.5
Tobacco duties	8.0	8.3	8.9
Spirits duties	1.6	1.5	1.6
Wine duties	1.3	1.4	1.5
Beer and cider duties	2.8	2.8	2.9
Betting and gaming duties	1.4	1.5	1.6
Air passenger duty	0.4	0.5	0.7
Insurance premium tax	0.7	1.0	1.3
Landfill tax	0.1	0.4	0.4
Customs duties and levies	2.3	2.3	2.0
Vehicle excise duties	4.2	4.6	4.6
Oil royalties	0.7	0.5	0.3
Business rates[2]	14.7	14.7	15.0
Social security contributions	47.1	50.5	53.7
Council tax	10.1	11.1	11.6
Other taxes and royalties	7.9	7.6	7.2
Net taxes and social security contributions	270.7	296.1	314.1
Interest and dividends	5.2	5.1	4.5
Gross trading surpluses and rent	4.9	4.8	4.9
Other receipts and accounting adjustments	5.6	7.1	6.6
Total general government receipts	286.4	313.1	330.1
North Sea revenues[3]	3.6	3.4	2.6

1. Includes advance corporation tax. Also includes North Sea corporation tax after ACT set-off and corporation tax on gains
2. Includes district council rates in Northern Ireland
3. North Sea corporation tax (before ACT set-off), petroleum revenue tax and royalties
Source: HM Treasury – *Financial Statement and Budget Report March 1998*

GOVERNMENT EXPENDITURE

THE CONTROL TOTAL AND GENERAL GOVERNMENT EXPENDITURE
(*excluding privatization proceeds*) £ billion

	Outturn 1996–7	Estimate 1997–8	Forecast 1998–9
Control Total	259.8	264.1	274.9
Welfare to Work spending	—	0.2	1.1
Local authority spending under the capital receipts initiative	—	0.2	0.7
Cyclical social security	14.0	12.8	13.0
Central government debt interest	22.0	24.3	24.6
Accounting adjustments	12.2	11.0	12.2
Net general government expenditure[1]	307.9	312.6	326.5
Privatization proceeds	−4.4	−1.8	0.0
Other adjustments	5.6	6.2	6.1
General government expenditure	309.1	317.1	332.5
GGE as a percentage of GDP	41.1%	39.8%	39.9%

1. Excluding privatization proceeds and lottery-financed spending and net of interest and dividend receipts
Source: HM Treasury – *Financial Statement and Budget Report March 1998*

CONTROL TOTAL EXPENDITURE BY DEPARTMENT £ million

	Outturn 1996–7	Estimate 1997–8	Plans 1998–9
Defence	22,345	21,840	22,240
sale of married quarters	−962	−700	0
Foreign Office	1,053	1,090	1,040
International Development	2,344	2,260	2,310
Agriculture, Fisheries and Food	4,229	3,620	3,370
Trade and Industry – programmes	3,064	3,140	2,960
Trade and Industry – nationalized industries	−394	−140	−140
ECGD	15	40	60
DETR[1]	12,975	12,600	12,150
DETR – Local government	31,321	31,380	32,760
of which education SSA	17,764	18.370	19,380
Home Office	6,486	6,890	6,890
Legal departments	2,674	2,740	2,690
Education and Employment[2]	14,495	14,620	13,070
Culture, Media and Sport	959	910	910

CONTROL TOTAL EXPENDITURE BY DEPARTMENT *contd.*
£ million

	Outturn 1996–7	Estimate 1997–8	Plans 1998–9
Health	33,816	35,340	37,170
of which NHS	33,043	34,690	36,510
Social security	76,905	79,620	83,620
Scotland	14,421	14,520	14,580
Wales	6,817	6,950	6,970
Northern Ireland	8,026	8,280	8,400
Chancellor of the Exchequer's departments	3,190	3,250	3,100
Cabinet Office	1,157	970	1,310
European Communities	1,717	1,780	2,440
Local Authority self-financed expenditure	13,182	13,600	14,000
Allowance for shortfall	0	−400	0
Reserve	0	0	3,000
Control total	259,834	264,100	274,900

1. Includes payments of revenue support grant and national non-domestic rates to English local authorities. These finance, at local authorities' discretion, a range of local services, including education, social services and other environmental services
2. Does not include local authority total standard spending on education, shown under DETR – Local government. Figures for 1997–8 and 1998–9 are distorted by the effect of sales of student loans and abolition of nursery vouchers
Source: HM Treasury – *Financial Statement and Budget Report March 1998*

LOCAL AUTHORITY TRANSACTIONS   *£ million*

	Outturn 1996–7	Estimate 1997–8	Forecast 1998–9
Receipts			
Council tax[1]	10.2	11.3	11.8
Current grants from central government	59.3	58.7	61.1
Other receipts[2]	7.8	8.1	8.3
Capital grants from central government	2.9	3.5	3.6
Total receipts	80.2	81.6	84.8
Expenditure			
Current expenditure on goods and services	55.0	56.0	58.8
Current grants and subsidies	14.3	14.1	14.4
Interest	4.2	4.4	4.2
Capital expenditure before depreciation	6.4	6.4	7.0
Total expenditure	79.9	80.9	84.3[3]
Financial deficit	−0.3	−0.7	−0.5
Net financial transactions	−0.6	0.0	0.0
Net borrowing	−0.8	−0.7	−0.5

1. Net of rebates and council tax benefit. Includes district council rates in Northern Ireland
2. Includes interest receipts, rent and gross trading surplus
3. Assumes no allocation from the reserve
Source: HM Treasury – *Financial Statement and Budget Report March 1998*

PUBLIC SECTOR BORROWING REQUIREMENT *£ billion*

	Outturn 1996–7	Estimate 1997–8	Forecast 1998–9
General government expenditure	309.1	317.1	332.5
General government receipts[1]	286.4	313.1	330.1
General government borrowing requirement	22.7	3.9	2.4
Public corporations' market and overseas borrowing	0.0	−1.4	−0.1
PSBR (£ billion)	22.7	2.6	2.3
PSBR excluding windfall tax	22.7	5.0	3.9
PSBR as % of GDP	3.0%	0.6%	0.5%

1. On a cash basis
Source: HM Treasury – *Financial Statement and Budget Report March 1998*

GDP BY INDUSTRY 1996 BEFORE DEPRECIATION BUT AFTER STOCK APPRECIATION
£ million

Agriculture, hunting, forestry and fishing	11,790
Mining and quarrying, including oil and gas extraction	18,068
Manufacturing (revised definition)	137,006
Electricity, gas and water supply	13,606
Construction	33,746
Wholesale and retail trade; repairs; hotels and restaurants	93,091
Transport, storage and communication	54,056
Financial intermediation; real estate; renting and business activities	164,282
Public administration, national defence and compulsory social security	38,244
Education; health; social work	81,876
Other services, including sewage and refuse disposal	24,713
TOTAL	670,479
less adjustment for financial services	26,968
Statistical discrepancy (income adjustment)	−595
GROSS DOMESTIC PRODUCT	642,916

Source: The Stationery Office – *Annual Abstract of Statistics 1998* (Crown copyright)

BALANCE OF PAYMENTS 1996   *£ million*

CURRENT ACCOUNT

Trade in goods	
Exports (fob)	166,340
Imports (fob)	178,938
Trade in goods balance	−12,598
Services balance	7,142
Investment income	9,652
Transfers balance	−4,631
CURRENT BALANCE	−435

*TRANSACTIONS IN EXTERNAL ASSETS AND LIABILITIES

Investment overseas by UK residents	
Direct	−28,560
Portfolio	−60,691
Total UK investment overseas	−89,251
Investment in the UK by overseas residents	
Direct	20,758
Portfolio	27,701
Total overseas investment in UK	48,459
Foreign currency lending abroad by UK banks	−55,589
Foreign currency borrowing abroad by UK banks	78,136
Net foreign currency transactions of UK banks	22,547
Sterling lending abroad by UK banks	−7,737
Sterling borrowing and deposit liabilities abroad of UK banks	−3,411
Net sterling transactions of UK banks	−11,148
Deposits with and lending to banks abroad by UK non-bank private sector	−10,821
Borrowing from banks abroad by:	
UK non-bank private sector	33,629
Public corporations	−14
General government	−79
Official reserves (additions to −, drawings on +)	1,966
Other external assets of:	
UK non-bank private sector and public corporations	−55,751
General government	−653
Other external liabilities of:	
UK non-bank private sector and public corporations	61,088
General government	−713
NET TRANSACTIONS IN ASSETS AND LIABILITIES	−2,198
BALANCING ITEM	2,633

* Assets: increase −/decrease +
Liabilities: increase +/decrease−
Source: The Stationery Office – *Annual Abstract of Statistics 1998*
(Crown copyright)

UK TRADE ON A BALANCE OF PAYMENTS BASIS
£ million

	Exports	Imports	Balance
1986	72,627	82,186	−9,559
1987	79,153	90,735	−11,582
1988	80,346	101,826	−21,480
1989	92,154	116,837	−24,683
1990	101,718	120,527	−18,809
1991	103,413	113,697	−10,284
1992	107,343	120,447	−13,104
1993	121,398	134,858	−13,460
1994	134,664	145,793	−11,129
1995	153,077	164,659	−11,582
1996	166,340	178,938	−12,598

Source: The Stationery Office – *Annual Abstract of Statistics 1998*
(Crown copyright)

VALUE OF UK EXPORTS 1997
BY DESTINATION   *£ million*

European Community	95,033.3
Other western Europe	7,992.7
Eastern Europe	5,179.5
North America	23,946.9
Other America	3,193.2
Middle East and North Africa	10,686.0
Sub-Saharan Africa	3,577.0
Asia and Oceania	21,812.3
Low-value exports	563.3
Total non-EC exports	76,950.9
Total exports	171,984.2

Source: HM Customs and Excise

VALUE OF UK IMPORTS 1997
BY SOURCE   *£ million*

European Community	100,204.2
Other western Europe	11,342.1
Eastern Europe	4,347.0
North America	28,066.8
Other America	3,066.9
Middle East and North Africa	3,991.9
Sub-Saharan Africa	2,839.8
Asia and Oceania	33,911.3
Low-value imports	472.0
Total non-EC imports	88,037.8
Total imports	188,242.0

Source: HM Customs and Excise

EMPLOYMENT

LABOUR FORCE BY AGE 1997 (UK)

Age	Male	Female
16–24	2,400,000	2,000,000
25–44	8,100,000	6,400,000
45–59	4,500,000	3,700,000
60–64	700,000	400,000
65 and over	300,000	200,000
Total	16,000,000	12,700,000

ECONOMIC STATUS OF PEOPLE OF WORKING AGE (UK)
as at spring 1997

	Male	Female
All in employment	14,500,000	11,400,000
Working full-time	11,000,000	6,000,000
Working part-time	900,000	4,500,000
Self-employed	2,400,000	800,000
Others in employment	200,000	200,000
Unemployed	1,300,000	700,000
All economically active	15,700,000	12,100,000
Economically inactive	2,900,000	4,900,000
TOTAL	18,700,000	17,000,000

Source: The Stationery Office – *Social Trends 28* (Crown copyright)

THE WORKFORCE IN EMPLOYMENT (UK)
SEASONALLY ADJUSTED, AT DECEMBER 1997

Employees in employment	23,082,000
Self-employed	3,543,000
*HM Forces	211,000
*Work-related government-supported training	169,000
Total workforce in employment	27,005,000

* not seasonally adjusted

EMPLOYEES IN EMPLOYMENT, BY MAIN SECTOR (UK)
SEASONALLY ADJUSTED, AT DECEMBER 1997

Service industries	17,505,000
Manufacturing industries	4,091,000
Energy and water supply	221,000
Other industries	1,265,000
Total employees in employment	23,082,000

AVERAGE GROSS WEEKLY EARNINGS OF EMPLOYEES (GREAT BRITAIN) *as at April 1997*

	Full–time	Part–time
All adults	£368	£114
All men	409	133
Men, manual	314	—
Men, non-manual	484	—
All women	297	110
Women, manual	201	—
Women, non-manual	318	—

Source: Office for National Statistics

UNEMPLOYMENT BY REGIONS
January to March 1998

	Total	% of total economically active
United Kingdom	1,844,000	6.4
England:	1,495,000	6.2
Eastern	147,000	5.4
East Midlands	111,000	5.3
London	279,000	8.0
Merseyside	66,000	11.0
North East	101,000	8.7
North West	150,000	5.7
South East	182,000	4.5
South West	116,000	4.8
West Midlands	165,000	6.3
Yorkshire and the Humber	178,000	7.4
Wales	97,000	7.5
Scotland	194,000	7.8
Northern Ireland	59,000	8.0

Source: Office for National Statistics

UNEMPLOYMENT RATES BY AGE 1997 (UK)
Percentages

Age	Male	Female
16–19	18.2	14.0
20–24	14.0	8.9
25–44	7.0	5.4
45–54	6.1	3.8
55–59	8.0	4.8
60–64	7.6	—
60 and over	—	2.0
65 and over	4.0	—
All ages	8.1	5.8

Source: The Stationery Office – *Social Trends 28* (Crown copyright)

INDUSTRIAL STOPPAGES 1996 (UK)
Duration

Not more than 5 days	196,000
6–10 days	20,000
11–20 days	7,000
21–30 days	6,000
31–50 days	10,000
More than 50 days	5,000
Total number of stoppages	244,000

Source: The Stationery Office – *Annual Abstract of Statistics 1998* (Crown copyright)

TRADE UNIONS (UK)

Year	No. of unions at end of year	Total membership at end of year
1970	543	11,187,000
1975	470	12,026,000
1980	438	12,947,000
1985	370	10,821,000
1990	287	9,947,000
1995	238	8,089,000
1996*	245	7,934,000

* Figures for Great Britain only
Source: Office for National Statistics; Department of Trade and Industry

HOUSEHOLDS AND THEIR EXPENDITURE 1996–7[1]

NUMBER OF HOUSEHOLDS

SUPPLYING DATA	6,415
Total number of persons	15,732
Total number of adults[2]	11,495

DISTRIBUTION BY TENURE

Rented unfurnished	27.9%
Rented furnished	4.5%
Rent-free	1.7%
Owner-occupied	65.9%

AVERAGE NUMBER OF PERSONS
PER HOUSEHOLD

All persons	2.452
Males	1.178
Females	1.275
Adults[2]	1.792
Persons under 65	1.436
Persons 65 and over	0.356
Children[2]	0.660
Children under 2	0.079
Children 2 and under 5	0.116
Children 5 and under 18	0.465
Persons economically active	1.161
Persons not economically active	1.292
Men 65 and over, women 60 and over	0.378
Others	0.913

HOUSEHOLD EXPENDITURE ON COMMODITIES AND
SERVICES – WEEKLY AVERAGE

	£	As % of total
Housing[3]	49.10	15.9
Fuel and power	13.35	4.3
Food	55.15	17.8
Alcoholic drink	12.41	4.0
Tobacco	6.07	2.0
Clothing and footwear	18.27	5.9
Household goods	26.74	8.7
Household services	16.36	5.3
Personal goods and services	11.64	3.8
Motoring expenditure	41.20	13.3
Fares and other travel costs	7.45	2.4
Leisure goods	15.17	4.9
Leisure services	33.95	11.0
Miscellaneous	2.21	0.7
Total	309.07	100.0

1. Information derived from the Family Expenditure Survey; relates to the UK
2. Adults = all persons 18 and over and married persons under 18
Children = all unmarried persons under 18
3. Excludes mortgage payments but includes imputed expenditure (i.e. the weekly equivalent of rateable value)
Source: The Stationery Office – *Annual Abstract of Statistics 1998* (Crown copyright)

SOURCES OF HOUSEHOLD INCOME 1996–7*

AVERAGE WEEKLY INCOME BY SOURCE (£)

Wages and salaries	256.28
Self-employment	37.48
Investments	17.75
Annuities and pensions (other than social security benefits)	25.95
Social security benefits	54.09
Other sources	5.31
Total	396.86

SOURCES AS A PERCENTAGE OF TOTAL HOUSEHOLD
INCOME (%)

Wages and salaries	64.6
Self-employment	9.4
Investments	4.5
Annuities and pensions (other than social security benefits)	6.5
Social security benefits	13.6
Other sources	1.3
Total	100.0

* Information derived from the Family Expenditure Survey; relates to the UK. Number of households supplying data, 6,415
Source: The Stationery Office – *Annual Abstract of Statistics 1998* (Crown copyright)

AVAILABILITY OF CERTAIN DURABLE GOODS 1996–7*

	% of households
Car	69.0
One	43.0
Two	21.5
Three or more	4.5
Central heating, full or partial	87.3
Washing machine	91.0
Fridge/freezer or deep freezer	90.7
Refrigerator	49.4
Television	98.3†
Telephone	93.1
Home computer	26.7
Video recorder	81.8

* Information derived from the Family Expenditure Survey; relates to the UK. Number of households supplying data, 6,415
† 1992 figure
Source: The Stationery Office – *Annual Abstract of Statistics 1998* (Crown copyright)

Cost of Living and Inflation Rates

The first cost of living index to be calculated took July 1914 as 100 and was based on the pattern of expenditure of working-class families in 1914. The cost of living index was superseded in 1947 by the general index of retail prices (RPI), although the older term is still popularly applied to it.

GENERAL INDEX OF RETAIL PRICES

The general index of retail prices measures the changes month by month in the average level of prices of goods and services purchased by most households in the United Kingdom. The spending pattern on which the index is based is revised each year, mainly using information from the Family Expenditure Survey. The expenditure of certain higher income households and of households mainly dependent on state pensions is excluded.

The index is compiled using a selection of over 600 goods and services, and the prices charged for these items are collected at regular intervals in about 146 locations throughout the country. For the index, the price changes are weighted in accordance with the pattern of consumption of the average family.

INFLATION RATE

The twelve-monthly percentage change in the 'all items' index of the RPI is usually referred to as the rate of inflation. The percentage change in prices between any two months/years can be obtained using the following formula:

$$\frac{\text{Later date RPI} - \text{Earlier date RPI}}{\text{Earlier date RPI}} \times 100$$

e.g. to find the rate of inflation for 1988, using the annual averages for 1987 and 1988:

$$\frac{106.9 - 101.9}{101.9} \times 100 = 4.9\%$$

PURCHASING POWER OF THE POUND

Changes in the internal purchasing power of the pound may be defined as the 'inverse' of changes in the level of prices; when prices go up, the amount which can be purchased with a given sum of money goes down. To find the purchasing power of the pound in one month or year, given that it was 100p in a previous month or year, the calculation would be:

$$100p \times \frac{\text{Earlier month/year RPI}}{\text{Later month/year RPI}}$$

Thus, if the purchasing power of the pound is taken to be 100p in 1975, the comparable purchasing power in 1997 would be:

$$100p \times \frac{34.2}{157.5} = 21.71p$$

For longer term comparisons, it has been the practice to use an index which has been constructed by linking together the RPI for the period 1962 to date; an index derived from the consumers expenditure deflator for the period from 1938 to 1962; and the prewar 'cost of living' index for the

period 1914 to 1938. This long-term index enables the internal purchasing power of the pound to be calculated for any year from 1914 onwards. It should be noted that these figures can only be approximate.

	Long-term index of consumer goods and services (Jan. 1987 = 100)	Comparable purchasing power of £1 in 1997	Rate of inflation (annual average)
1914	2.8	56.25	
1915	3.5	45.00	
1920	7.0	22.50	
1925	5.0	31.50	
1930	4.5	35.00	
1935	4.0	39.38	
1938	4.4	35.80	
There are no official figures for 1939–45			
1946	7.4	21.28	
1950	9.0	17.50	
1955	11.2	14.06	
1960	12.6	12.50	
1965	14.8	10.64	
1970	18.5	8.51	
1975	34.2	4.61	
1980	66.8	2.36	18.0
1981	74.8	2.11	11.9
1982	81.2	1.94	8.6
1983	84.9	1.86	4.6
1984	89.2	1.77	5.0
1985	94.6	1.66	6.1
1986	97.8	1.61	3.4
1987	101.9	1.55	4.2
1988	106.9	1.47	4.9
1989	115.2	1.37	7.8
1990	126.1	1.25	9.5
1991	133.5	1.18	5.9
1992	138.5	1.14	3.7
1993	140.7	1.12	1.6
1994	144.1	1.09	2.4
1995	149.1	1.06	3.5
1996	152.7	1.03	2.4
1997	157.5	1.00	3.1

Gaming and Lotteries

Gaming and lotteries in the UK are officially regulated and may only be run by licensed operators or in licensed premises. Responsibility for policy and the laws on gaming and lotteries rests with the Home Secretary. Supervision of gaming and lottery operations is mostly the responsibility of the Gaming Board of Great Britain, although the National Lottery (*see* below) is regulated by the Director-General of the National Lottery through the Office of the National Lottery.

Most betting is on horseracing and greyhound racing, and may take place at racecourses and greyhound tracks, or at off-course betting offices. The amount spent on on-course betting cannot be calculated precisely since no duty is payable on it and therefore no returns are made; however, it is estimated to be about 10 per cent of the figures for off-course betting.

OFF-COURSE BETTING (UK)

	£ million
1995–6	6,313
1996–7	6,718
1997–8	6,838p

p provisional
Source: Horserace Totalisator Board

Other forms of gaming and lotteries include the following (for National Lottery, *see* below):

Number of casinos operating	118
Total drop (1996–7)	£2,599m
Bingo clubs holding gaming licences	908
Amount staked (1996–7)	£967m
Gaming machines licensed	*c.*262,000
Society lottery schemes registered	614
Local authority lottery schemes registered	11
Number of lotteries held under registered schemes	2,443
Total ticket sales (£ million)	£115m

In 1996–7 sales of society lottery tickets increased by 46 per cent to £115 million. Of this, £40 million (35 per cent) was spent on prizes, £30 million (26 per cent) on expenses and £45 million (39 per cent) went to good causes.
Source: Report of the Gaming Board for Great Britain 1996–7

THE NATIONAL LOTTERY

The National Lottery is currently run by a private company, Camelot Group PLC. The seven-year licence granted to Camelot expires in 2001 and the Government has announced its intention to reform the system for operating the National Lottery.

The Office of the National Lottery (Oflot) regulates the National Lottery operations and licenses games promoted as part of the lottery. In early 1999 Oflot will be replaced by a five-member National Lottery Commission.

The first National Lottery tickets draw was made on 19 November 1994 and Instants (scratchcards) were introduced on 25 March 1995. A second weekly draw was introduced on Wednesday 5 February 1997. Tickets for the main lottery game cost £1. If the jackpot prize is not won, it is 'rolled over' to the following week. The highest win on a single ticket to date was £22,590,829 on 10 June 1995. By mid-1998, 597 millionaires had been created.

SALES 1997–8

Average number of tickets sold per week	*c.*90m
Average number of people playing weekly	*c.*30m
% of adult population buying tickets regularly	*c.*65%

Amount raised by ticket sales, 1994 to mid-1998 — £17,860m
Sources: Camelot, Oflot

DISTRIBUTION OF PROCEEDS
over the seven-year licence period

Allocated to:	%
Prize money	50
Tax	13
Retailer commission	5
Camelot (operating costs and profit)	4
Good causes	28

The 'good causes' originally benefitting from lottery funds were the arts, sport, heritage, charities and the Millennium Commission. In July 1998 the National Lottery Act created a sixth good cause, the New Opportunities Fund, to fund health, education and environmental initiatives. The Act also created a National Endowment for Science, Technology and the Arts (NESTA), a non-departmental public body whose objectives are: to help talented individuals; to enable inventions and ideas to be commercially exploited; and to promote public knowledge of science, technology and the arts. NESTA received an initial £200 million from the New Opportunities Fund but thereafter is to generate its own income.

From October 1997 the percentage of all the funds allocated to the good causes received by each cause is as follows: the arts, sport, heritage and charities 16.66 per cent each; the Millennium Commission 20 per cent; and the New Opportunities Fund 13.33 per cent. From October 1999 the share going to the Millennium Commission will be reduced to 13.33 per cent and that going to the New Opportunities Fund will rise to 20 per cent.

Awards were initially given only to capital projects, but since April 1996 it has been possible to obtain lottery funding for projects to develop individuals' talents and potential and to increase access to the arts. In late 1997 lottery funding was made available for access, education and youth initiatives in the heritage field.

The cumulative amount allocated to the good causes from November 1994 to March 1998 was £5,310 million.

AWARDS 1997–8

Most awards are conditional on partnership funding being obtained from other sources.

	Number	Total value £
Total	13,377	2,206,907,271
Arts, total	4,891	378,706,294
Arts Council of England	4,124	305,764,112
Arts Council of Wales	409	26,575,384
Scottish Arts Council	248	40,844,269
Arts Council of Northern Ireland	110	5,522,529
Millennium Commission		
awards to projects	83	400,071,996
awards to schemes funding individuals	21	20,120,000
Heritage Lottery Fund	964	813,211,545
National Lottery Charities Board	6,340	306,822,535
Sport, total	1,078	287,974,901
Sports Council	791	249,145,000
Sports Council for Wales	73	16,159,980
Scottish Sports Council	118	15,485,558
Sports Council for Northern Ireland	96	7,184,363

Finance

British Currency

The unit of currency is the pound sterling (£) of 100 pence. The decimal system was introduced on 15 February 1971.

COIN

Gold Coins	‡*Bi-colour Coins*
*One hundred pounds £100	Two pounds £2
*Fifty pounds £50	*Nickel-Brass Coins*
*Twenty-five pounds £25	§Two pounds £2
*Ten pounds £10	One pound £1
Five pounds £5	
Two pounds £2	*Cupro-Nickel Coins*
Sovereign £1	Crown £5 (since 1990)
Half-Sovereign 50p	50 pence 50p
	Crown 25p (pre-1990)
Silver Coins	20 pence 20p
(*Britannia coins*)	10 pence 10p
Two pounds £2	5 pence 5p
One pound £1	
50 pence 50p	*Bronze Coins*
Twenty pence 20p	2 pence 2p
(†*Maundy Money*)	1 penny 1p
Fourpence 4p	
Threepence 3p	*Copper-plated Steel Coins*
Twopence 2p	2 penny 2p
Penny 1p	1 penny 1p

*Britannia coins: gold bullion coins introduced 1987; silver coins introduced 1997
†Gifts of special money distributed by the Sovereign annually on Maundy Thursday to the number of aged poor men and women corresponding to the Sovereign's own age
‡Cupro-nickel centre and nickel-brass outer ring
§Commemorative coins; not intended for general circulation

GOLD COIN

Gold ceased to circulate during the First World War. Since then controls on buying, selling and holding gold coin have been imposed at various times but subsequently have been revoked. Under the Exchange Control (Gold Coins Exemption) Order 1979, gold coins may now be imported and exported without restriction, except gold coins which are more than 50 years old and valued at a sum in excess of £8,000; these cannot be exported without specific authorization from the Department of Trade and Industry.

In 1982 the Government introduced VAT on sales of all gold coin.

SILVER COIN

Prior to 1920 silver coins were struck from sterling silver, an alloy of which 925 parts in 1,000 were silver. In 1920 the proportion of silver was reduced to 500 parts. From 1 January 1947 all 'silver' coins, except Maundy money, have been struck from cupro-nickel, an alloy of copper 75 parts and nickel 25 parts, except for the 20p, composed of copper 84 parts, nickel 16 parts. Maundy coins continue to be struck from sterling silver.

BRONZE COIN

Bronze, introduced in 1860 to replace copper, is an alloy of copper 97 parts, zinc 2.5 parts and tin 0.5 part. These proportions have been subject to slight variations in the past. Bronze was replaced by copper-plated steel in September 1992 and reintroduced in April 1997.

LEGAL TENDER

Gold (dated 1838 onwards, if not below least current weight)	to any amount
£5 (Crown since 1990)	to any amount
£2	to any amount
£1	to any amount
50p	up to £10
25p (Crown pre-1990)	up to £10
20p	up to £10
10p	up to £5
5p	up to £5
2p	up to 20p
1p	up to 20p

The £1 coin was introduced in 1983 to replace the £1 note.

These coins ceased to be legal tender on the following dates:

Farthing	31 December 1960
Halfpenny ($\frac{1}{2}$d)	1 August 1969
Half-crown	1 January 1970
Threepence	31 August 1971
Penny (1d)	31 August 1971
Sixpence	30 June 1980
Halfpenny ($\frac{1}{2}$p)	31 December 1984
old 5 pence	31 December 1990
old 10 pence	30 June 1993
old 50 pence	28 February 1998

Since 1982 the word 'new' in 'new pence' displayed on decimal coins has been dropped.

The Channel Islands and the Isle of Man issue their own coinage, which are legal tender only in the island of issue. For denominations, *see* page 612.

	Metal	Standard weight (g)	Standard diameter (cm)
Penny	bronze	3.564	2.032
Penny	copper-plated steel	3.564	2.032
2 pence	bronze	7.128	2.591
2 pence	copper-plated steel	7.128	2.591
5p	cupro-nickel	3.25	1.80
10p	cupro-nickel	6.5	2.45
20p	cupro-nickel	5.0	2.14
25p Crown	cupro-nickel	28.28	3.861
50p	cupro-nickel	13.5	3.0
¶50p	cupro-nickel	8.00	2.73
£1	nickel-brass	9.5	2.25
£2	nickel-brass	15.98	2.84
‡£2	cupro-nickel, nickel-brass	12.00	2.84
£5 Crown	cupro-nickel	28.28	3.861

¶New 50p coin introduced on 1 September 1997

The 'remedy' is the amount of variation from standard permitted in weight and fineness of coins when first issued from the Mint.

The Trial of the Pyx is the examination by a jury to ascertain that coins made by the Royal Mint, which have been set aside in the pyx (or box), are of the proper weight, diameter and composition required by law. The trial is held annually, presided over by the Queen's

Remembrancer (the Senior Master of the Supreme Court), with a jury of freemen of the Company of Goldsmiths.

BANKNOTES

Bank of England notes are currently issued in denominations of £5, £10, £20 and £50 for the amount of the fiduciary note issue, and are legal tender in England and Wales.

The current E series of notes was introduced from June 1990, replacing the D series (*see* below). The historical figures portrayed in this series are:

£5	June 1990–	George Stephenson
£10	April 1992–	Charles Dickens
£20	June 1991–	Michael Faraday
£50	April 1994–	Sir John Houblon

Note Circulation

Note circulation is highest at the two peak spending periods of the year, around Christmas and during the summer holiday period. The total value of notes in circulation at 24 December 1997 was £26,105 million, compared to £22,407 million at 18 December 1996.

The value of notes in circulation at end February 1997 and 1998 was:

	1997	1998
£1*	£56m	£55m
£5	£1,047m	£1,034m
£10	£5,915m	£5,960m
£20	£9,559m	£10,621m
£50	£3,273m	£3,636m
Other notes†	£2,161m	£2,242m
Total	£22,011m	£23,548m

* No £1 notes have been issued since 1984
† Includes higher value notes used internally in the Bank of England, e.g. as cover for the note issues of banks in Scotland and Northern Ireland in excess of their permitted issue

Legal Tender

Banknotes which are no longer legal tender are payable when presented at the head office of the Bank of England in London.

The white notes for £10, £20, £50, £100, £500 and £1,000, which were issued until April 1943, ceased to be legal tender in May 1945, and the white £5 note in March 1946.

The white £5 note issued between October 1945 and September 1956, the £5 notes issued between 1957 and 1963 (bearing a portrait of Britannia) and the first series to bear a portrait of The Queen, issued between 1963 and 1971, ceased to be legal tender in March 1961, June 1967 and September 1973 respectively.

The series of £1 notes issued during the years 1928 to 1960 and the 10 shilling notes issued from 1928 to 1961 (those without the royal portrait) ceased to be legal tender in May and October 1962 respectively. The £1 note first issued in March 1960 (bearing on the back a representation of Britannia) and the £10 note first issued in February 1964 (bearing a lion on the back), both bearing a portrait of The Queen on the front, ceased to be legal tender in June 1979. The £1 note first issued in 1978 ceased to be legal tender on 11 March 1988. The 10 shilling note was replaced by the 50p coin in October 1969, and ceased to be legal tender on 21 November 1970.

The D series of banknotes was introduced from 1970 and ceased to be legal tender from the dates shown below.

The predominant identifying feature of each note was the portrayal on the back of a prominent figure from British history:

£1	Feb. 1978–March 1988	Sir Isaac Newton
£5	Nov. 1971–Nov. 1991	The Duke of Wellington
£10	Feb. 1975–May 1994	Florence Nightingale
£20	July 1970–March 1993	William Shakespeare
£50	March 1981–Sept. 1996	Sir Christopher Wren

The £1 coin was introduced on 21 April 1983 to replace the £1 note.

Other Banknotes

Scotland – Banknotes are issued by three Scottish banks. The Royal Bank of Scotland issues notes for £1, £5, £10, £20 and £100. The Bank of Scotland and the Clydesdale Bank issue notes for £5, £10, £20, £50 and £100. Scottish notes are not legal tender in Scotland but they are an authorized currency and enjoy a status comparable to that of Bank of England notes.

Northern Ireland – Banknotes are issued by four banks in Northern Ireland. The Bank of Ireland, the Northern Bank and the Ulster Bank issue notes for £5, £10, £20, £50 and £100. The First Trust Bank issues notes for £10, £20, £50 and £100. Northern Ireland notes are not legal tender in Northern Ireland but they circulate widely and enjoy a status comparable to that of Bank of England notes.

Channel Islands – The States of Guernsey issues its own currency notes and coinage. The notes are for £1, £5, £10, £20 and £50, and the coins are for 1p, 2p, 5p, 10p, 20p, 50p, £1, £2 and £5. The States of Jersey issues its own currency notes and coinage. The notes are for £1, £5, £10, £20 and £50, and the coins are for 1p, 2p, 5p, 10p, 20p, 50p, £1 and £2.

The Isle of Man – The Isle of Man Government issues notes for £1, £5, £10, £20 and £50. Although these notes are only legal tender in the Isle of Man, they are accepted at face value in branches of the clearing banks in the UK. The Isle of Man issues coins for 1p, 2p, 5p, 10p, 20p, 50p, £1, £2 and £5.

Although none of the series of notes specified above is legal tender in the UK, they are generally accepted by the banks irrespective of their place of issue. At one time the banks made a commission charge for handling Scottish and Irish notes but this was abolished some years ago.

Banking

Deposit-taking institutions may be broadly divided into two sectors: the monetary sector, which is predominantly banks, and those institutions outside the monetary sector, of which the most important are the building societies (*see* pages 619–22) and National Savings (*see* pages 623–5). Both sectors are supervised by the Financial Services Authority. As a result of the conversion of several building societies into banks in recent years, the size of the banking sector, which was already substantially greater than the non-bank deposit-taking sector, has increased further.

The main institutions within the British banking system are the Bank of England (the central bank), the retail banks, the merchant banks and the overseas banks. In its role as the central bank, the Bank of England acts as banker to the Government and as a note-issuing authority; it also oversees the efficient functioning of payment and settlement systems.

Since May 1997, the Bank of England has had operational responsibility for monetary policy. At monthly meetings of its monetary policy committee the Bank sets the interest rate at which it will lend to the money markets.

OFFICIAL INTEREST RATES 1997–8

7 August 1997	7.00%
6 November 1997	7.25%
4 June 1998	7.50%

RETAIL BANKS

The major retail banks are Abbey National, Bank of Scotland, Barclays, Halifax, Lloyds/TSB, Midland, National Westminster and the Royal Bank of Scotland.

Retail banks offer a wide variety of financial services to companies and individuals, including current and deposit accounts, loan and overdraft facilities, automated teller (cashpoint) machines, cheque guarantee cards, credit cards and debit cards.

The Banking Ombudsman scheme provides independent and impartial arbitration in disputes between a bank and its customer (*see also* page 635).

Banking hours differ throughout the UK. Many banks now open longer hours and some at weekends, and hours vary from branch to branch. Current core opening hours are:

ENGLAND AND WALES: Monday–Friday 9.30–4.30
SCOTLAND: Monday–Friday, 9.00–5.00
NORTHERN IRELAND: Monday–Friday 9.30–4.30
(Wednesdays 10.00–4.30, except Ulster Bank Ltd);
Northern Bank, 10.00–3.30, Saturdays 9.30–12.30

PAYMENT CLEARINGS

The Association for Payment Clearing Services (APACS) is an umbrella organization for payment clearings in the UK. It operates three clearing companies:
– BACS Ltd is the UK's automated clearing house for bulk clearing of electronic debits and credits (e.g. direct debits and salary credits)
– the Cheque and Credit Clearing Company Ltd operates bulk clearing systems for inter-bank cheques and paper credit items in Great Britain
– CHAPS Clearing Company Ltd provides same-day clearing for high-value electronic funds transfers throughout the UK in sterling and euros

Membership of APACS and the clearing companies is open to any appropriately regulated financial institution providing payment services and meeting the relevant membership criteria. As at June 1998, APACS had 23 members, comprising the major banks and building societies.

ASSOCIATION FOR PAYMENT CLEARING SERVICES (APACS), Mercury House, Triton Court, 14 Finsbury Square, London EC2A 1BR. Tel: 0171-711 6200. *Head of Public Affairs*, R. Tyson-Davies

BACS LTD, De Havilland Road, Edgware, Middx HA8 5QA. *Chief Executive*, G. Younger

CHEQUE AND CREDIT CLEARING COMPANY LTD, Mercury House, Triton Court, 14 Finsbury Square, London EC2A 1BR

CHAPS CLEARING COMPANY LTD, Mercury House, Triton Court, 14 Finsbury Square, London EC2A 1BR

AUTHORIZED INSTITUTIONS

Banking in the UK is regulated by the Banking Act 1987 as amended by the European Community's Second Banking Co-ordination Directive, which came into effect on 1 January 1993. The Banking Act 1987 established a single category of banks eligible to carry out banking business; these are known as authorized institutions. Authorization under the Act is granted by the Bank of England; it is an offence for anyone not on the Bank's list of authorized institutions to conduct deposit-taking business, unless they are exempted from the requirements of the Act (e.g. building societies).

The implementation of the Second Banking Co-ordination Directive permits banks incorporated in one EU member state to carry on certain banking activities in

MAJOR RETAIL BANKS: FINANCIAL RESULTS 1997

Bank Group	Profit before taxation £m	Profit after taxation £m	Total assets £m	Number of UK branches
Abbey National	1,279	953	150,808	800
Bank of Scotland	742	531.5	54,697	325
Barclays	1,716	1,174	226,500	1,975
Halifax	1,631	1,091	131,100	c.900
Lloyds/TSB Group	3,162	2,349	158,106	2,900
Midland	1,625	1,066	102,076	1,720
NatWest Group	1,011	702	185,400	1,750
Royal Bank of Scotland Group	760	541	72,601	700

another member state without the need for authorization by that state. Consequently, the Bank of England no longer authorizes banks incorporated in other EU states with branches in the UK; the authorization of their home state supervisor is sufficient provided that certain notification requirements are met.

In May 1997, the Chancellor of the Exchequer announced that he planned to amend the Banking Act 1987 to transfer responsibility for banking supervision from the Bank of England to a new supervisory body, the Financial Services Authority, which will be responsible for supervision of the financial services industry. Once the necessary legislation has been passed (probably in 1998–9), the FSA will be responsible for the authorization and supervision of banks and the supervision of clearing and settlement systems.

As at end February 1998, a total of 579 institutions were authorized to carry out banking business in the UK, 362 authorized under the Banking Act 1987 and 217 recognized under the Second Banking Co-ordination Directive as European authorized institutions (EAIs):

UK-incorporated	213
Incorporated outside the EEA	149
EAIs with UK branches entitled to accept deposits in UK	71
EAIs entitled to accept deposits in UK on cross-border basis	71
Other EAIs	41

The following institutions were authorized or entitled to accept deposits through presences in the UK as at 15 July 1998.

AUTHORIZED BY THE BANK OF ENGLAND

UK-Incorporated
(Including partnerships formed under the law of any part of the UK)

ABC International Bank PLC
AMC Bank Ltd
AY Bank Ltd
Abbey National PLC
Abbey National Treasury Services PLC
Adam & Company PLC
Afghan National Credit and Finance Ltd
Airdrie Savings Bank
Alliance and Leicester PLC
Alliance and Leicester Group Treasury PLC
Alliance Trust (Finance) Ltd
Allied Bank Philippines (UK) PLC
Allied Irish Bank (GB)/First Trust Bank – (AIB Group (UK) PLC)
Alpha Bank London Ltd
Anglo-Romanian Bank Ltd
Henry Ansbacher & Co. Ltd
Arbuthnot Latham & Co. Ltd
Assemblies of God Property Trust
Associates Capital Corporation Ltd
Avco Trust PLC

Bank Leumi (UK) PLC
Bank of America International Ltd
Bank of China International (UK) Ltd
Bank of Cyprus (London) Ltd
Bank of Montreal Europe Ltd
Bank of Scotland
Bank of Scotland Treasury Services PLC
Bank of Wales PLC
Bankers Trust International PLC
Bankgesellschaft Berlin (UK) PLC
Banque Nationale de Paris PLC

Baptist Union Corporation Ltd
Barclays Bank PLC
Barclays Bank Trust Company Ltd
Barclays Capital Finance Ltd
Barclays Private Bank Ltd
Baring Brothers Ltd
Beneficial Bank PLC
Bristol and West PLC
British Arab Commercial Bank Ltd
British Bank of the Middle East
British Linen Bank Ltd
Brown, Shipley & Co. Ltd

CIBC Wood Gundy Bank PLC
Cafcash Ltd
Capital Bank PLC
Cater Allen Ltd
Chartered Trust PLC
Charterhouse Bank Ltd
Chase Manhattan International Ltd
Cheltenham and Gloucester PLC
Citibank International PLC
Clive Discount Company Ltd
Close Brothers Ltd
Clydesdale Bank PLC
Consolidated Credits Bank Ltd
Co-operative Bank PLC
Coutts & Co.
Crédit Agricole Lazard Financial Products Bank
Crédit Suisse Financial Products
Crown Agents Financial Services Ltd

Daiwa Europe Bank PLC
Dalbeattie Finance Co. Ltd
Dao Heng Bank (London) PLC
Dexia Municipal Bank PLC
Direct Line Financial Services Ltd
Dorset, Somerset and Wilts Investment Society Ltd
Dryfield Trust PLC
Dunbar Bank PLC
Duncan Lawrie Ltd

EFG Private Bank Ltd
Eccles Savings and Loans Ltd

FCE Bank PLC
FIBI Bank (UK) PLC
Fairmount Capital Management Ltd
Financial and General Bank PLC
First National Bank PLC
First National Commercial Bank PLC
Robert Fleming & Co. Ltd
Forward Trust Group Ltd
Frizzell Bank Ltd

Gartmore Money Management Ltd
GE Capital Bank Ltd
Gerrard and King Ltd
Ghana International Bank PLC
Girobank PLC
Goldman Sachs International Bank
Granville Bank Ltd
Gresham Trust PLC
Guinness Mahon & Co. Ltd

HFC Bank PLC
HSBC Equator Bank PLC
HSBC Investment Bank PLC
Habibsons Bank Ltd
Halifax PLC
Hambros Bank Ltd
Hampshire Trust PLC
Hardware Federation Finance Co. Ltd
Harrods Bank Ltd

Harton Bank Ltd
Havana International Bank Ltd
Heritable and General Investment Bank Ltd
Hill Samuel Bank Ltd
C. Hoare & Co.
Julian Hodge Bank Ltd
Humberclyde Finance Group Ltd

3i PLC
3i Group PLC
IBJ International PLC
Investec Bank (UK) Ltd
Iran Overseas Investment Bank Ltd
Italian International Bank PLC

Jordan International Bank PLC
Leopold Joseph and Sons Ltd

KDB Bank (UK) Ltd
KEXIM Bank (UK) Ltd
Kleinwort Benson Ltd
Kleinwort Benson Investment Management Ltd
Korea Long Term Credit Bank International Ltd

Lazard Brothers & Co. Ltd
Legal and General Bank Ltd
Lloyds Bank PLC
Lloyds Bank (BLSA) Ltd
Lloyds Bowmaker Ltd
Lloyds Private Banking Ltd
Lombard and Ulster Ltd
Lombard Bank Ltd
Lombard North Central PLC
London Scottish Bank PLC
London Trust Bank PLC

MBNA International Bank Ltd
W. M. Mann & Co. (Investments) Ltd
Marks and Spencer Financial Services Ltd
Matheson Bank Ltd
Matlock Bank Ltd
Meghraj Bank Ltd
Merrill Lynch International Bank Ltd
Methodist Chapel Aid Association Ltd
Midland Bank PLC
Midland Bank Trust Company Ltd
Minster Trust Ltd
Samuel Montagu & Co. Ltd
Morgan Grenfell & Co. Ltd
Moscow Narodny Bank Ltd
Mutual Trust and Savings Ltd

National Bank of Egypt International Ltd
National Bank of Kuwait (International) PLC
National Westminster Bank PLC
NationsBank Europe Ltd
Nikko Bank (UK) PLC
Noble Grossart Ltd
Nomura Bank International PLC
Northern Bank Ltd
Northern Bank Executor and Trustee Company Ltd
Northern Rock PLC

PaineWebber International Bank Ltd
Philippine National Bank (Europe) PLC
Pointon York Ltd
Prudential-Bache International Bank Ltd
Prudential Banking PLC

RBS Trust Bank Ltd
R. Raphael and Sons PLC
Rathbone Bros & Co. Ltd
Rea Brothers Ltd
Reliance Bank Ltd
Riggs Bank Europe Ltd
Riyad Bank Europe Ltd
N. M. Rothschild and Sons Ltd

Royal Bank of Canada Europe Ltd
Royal Bank of Scotland PLC
RoyScot Trust PLC
Ruffler Bank PLC

SBI European Bank PLC
Sabanci Bank PLC
Sainsbury's Bank PLC
Sanwa International PLC
Saudi American Bank (UK) Ltd
Saudi International Bank (Al-Bank Al-Saudi Al-Alami Ltd)
Schroder Leasing Ltd
J. Henry Schroder & Co. Ltd
Scotiabank Europe PLC
Scottish Widows Bank PLC
Secure Trust Bank PLC
Singer and Friedlander Ltd
Smith and Williamson Investment Management Ltd
Southsea Mortgage and Investment Co. Ltd
Standard Bank London Ltd
Standard Chartered Bank
Standard Life Bank Ltd
State Street Bank Europe Ltd
Sun Bank PLC

TSB Bank PLC
TSB Bank Scotland PLC
Tesco Personal Finance Ltd
Tokai Bank Europe PLC
Toronto Dominion Bank Europe Ltd
Turkish Bank (UK) Ltd

UCB Bank PLC
Ulster Bank Ltd
Union Discount Company Ltd
United Bank of Kuwait PLC
United Dominions Trust Ltd
United Trust Bank Ltd
Unity Trust Bank PLC

Weatherbys & Co. Ltd
Wesleyan Savings Bank Ltd
West Merchant Bank Ltd
Whiteaway Laidlaw Bank Ltd
Wintrust Securities Ltd
Woolwich PLC

Yorkshire Bank PLC

INCORPORATED OUTSIDE THE EUROPEAN ECONOMIC AREA
(Including partnerships or other unincorporated associations formed under the law of any member state of the European Union other than the UK)
†Provisional liquidator appointed

ABSA Bank Ltd
Allied Bank of Pakistan Ltd
American Express Bank Ltd
Arab African International Bank
Arab Bank PLC
Arab National Bank
Asahi Bank Ltd
Australia and New Zealand Banking Group Ltd

BSI – Banca della Svizzera Italiana
Banca Serfin SA
Banco de la Nación Argentina
Banco do Brasil SA
Banco do Estado de São Paulo SA
Banco Mercantil de São Paulo SA-Finasa
Banco Nacional de Mexico SA
Banco Real SA
Bancomer SA

Bangkok Bank Public Company Ltd
Bank Julius Baer & Co. Ltd
BankBoston NA
Bank Bumiputra Malaysia Berhad
PT Bank Ekspor Impor Indonesia (Persero)
Bank Handlowy w Warszawie SA
Bank Hapoalim BM
Bank Mellat
Bank Melli Iran
PT Bank Negara Indonesia (Persero) Tbk
Bank of America NT & SA
Bank of Baroda
Bank of Ceylon
Bank of China
Bank of Cyprus Ltd
Bank of East Asia Ltd
Bank of Fukuoka Ltd
Bank of India
Bank of Montreal
Bank of New York
Bank of Nova Scotia
Bank of Tokyo-Mitsubishi Ltd
Bank of Yokohama Ltd
Bank Saderat Iran
Bank Sepah-Iran
Bank Tejarat
Bankers Trust Company
Beirut Riyad Bank SAL

Canadian Imperial Bank of Commerce
Canara Bank
Capital One Bank
Chang Hwa Commercial Bank Ltd
Chase Manhattan Bank
Chiba Bank Ltd
Cho Hung Bank
Chuo Trust and Banking Co. Ltd
Citibank NA
Commercial Bank of Korea Ltd
Commonwealth Bank of Australia
Crédit Suisse First Boston
Cyprus Popular Bank Ltd

Dai-Ichi Kangyo Bank Ltd
Daiwa Bank Ltd
Development Bank of Singapore Ltd
Discount Bank and Trust Company

Emirates Bank International PJSC

First Bank of Nigeria PLC
First Commercial Bank
First National Bank of Chicago
First Union National Bank
Fuji Bank Ltd

Gulf International Bank BSC

Habib Bank AG Zurich
Habib Bank Ltd
Hanil Bank
Hongkong and Shanghai Banking Corporation Ltd
Housing and Commercial Bank, Korea

Industrial Bank of Japan Ltd

Joyo Bank Ltd

KorAm Bank
Korea Development Bank
Korea Exchange Bank
Korea First Bank

Long-Term Credit Bank of Japan Ltd

Macquarie Bank Ltd

Malayan Banking Berhad
MashreqBank PSC
Mellon Bank NA
Mitsubishi Trust and Banking Corporation
Mitsui Trust and Banking Co. Ltd
Morgan Guaranty Trust Company of New York

Nacional Financiera SNC
National Australia Bank Ltd
National Bank of Abu Dhabi
National Bank of Canada
National Bank of Dubai Public Joint Stock Company
National Bank of Pakistan
NationsBank NA
Nedcor Bank Ltd
Norinchukin Bank
Northern Trust Company

Oversea-Chinese Banking Corporation Ltd
Overseas Trust Bank Ltd
Overseas Union Bank Ltd

People's Bank
Philippine National Bank

Qatar National Bank SAQ

†Rafidain Bank
Republic National Bank of New York
Riggs Bank NA
Riyad Bank
Royal Bank of Canada

Sakura Bank Ltd
Sanwa Bank Ltd
Saudi American Bank
Saudi British Bank
SEOULBANK
Shanghai Commercial Bank Ltd
Shinhan Bank
Siam Commercial Bank Public Company Ltd
Sonali Bank
State Bank of India
State Street Bank and Trust Company
Sumitomo Bank Ltd
Sumitomo Trust and Banking Co. Ltd
Syndicate Bank

TC Ziraat Bankasi
Thai Farmers Bank Public Company Ltd
Tokai Bank Ltd
Toronto-Dominion Bank
Toyo Trust and Banking Company Ltd
Türkiye Iş Bankasi AŞ

UBS AG
Uco Bank
Union Bancaire Privée CBI-TDB
Union Bank of Nigeria PLC
United Bank Ltd
United Mizrahi Bank Ltd
United Overseas Bank Ltd

Wachovia Bank NA
Westpac Banking Corporation

Yasuda Trust and Banking Co. Ltd

Zambia National Commercial Bank Ltd
Zivnostenská Banka AS

EUROPEAN AUTHORIZED INSTITUTIONS
ENTITLED TO ESTABLISH UK BRANCHES

The following are entitled to establish branches in the UK
for the purpose of accepting deposits in the UK. The

country of the home state supervisory authority is in parenthesis.

ABN AMRO Bank NV (Netherlands)
Allied Irish Banks PLC (Republic of Ireland)
Alpha Credit Bank AE (Greece)
Anglo Irish Bank Corporation PLC (Republic of Ireland)

BfG Bank AG (Germany)
BHF Bank AG (Germany)
Banca Cassa di Risparmio di Torino SpA (Italy)
Banca Commerciale Italiana (Italy)
Banca di Roma SpA (Italy)
Banca March SA (Spain)
Banca Monte dei Paschi di Siena SpA (Italy)
Banca Nazionale dell'Agricoltura SpA (Italy)
Banca Nazionale del Lavoro SpA (Italy)
Banca Popolare di Milano (Italy)
Banca Popolare di Novara (Italy)
Banco Ambrosiano Veneto SpA (Italy)
Banco Bilbao-Vizcaya (Spain)
Banco Central Hispanoamericano SA (Spain)
Banco de Sabadell (Spain)
Banco di Napoli SpA (Italy)
Banco di Sicilia SpA (Italy)
Banco Español de Crédito SA (Spain)
Banco Espirito Santo e Comercial de Lisboa (Portugal)
Banco Exterior de España SA (Spain)
Banco Nacional Ultramarino SA (Portugal)
Banco Português do Atlântico (Portugal)
Banco Santander (Spain)
Banco Santander de Negocios SA (Spain)
Banco Totta & Açores SA (Portugal)
Bank Austria AG (Austria)
Bank Brussels Lambert (Belgium)
Bankgesellschaft Berlin AG (Germany)
Bank of Ireland (Republic of Ireland)
Banque AIG (France)
Banque Arabe et Internationale d'Investissement (France)
Banque Banorabe (France)
Banque CPR (France)
Banque Française de l'Orient (France)
Banque Internationale à Luxembourg SA (Luxembourg)
Banque Nationale de Paris (France)
Bayerische Hypotheken-und Wechsel-Bank AG (Germany)
Bayerische Landesbank Girozentrale (Germany)
Bayerische Vereinsbank AG (Germany)
Belgolaise SA (Belgium)
Berliner Bank AG (Germany)
Byblos Bank Europe SA (Belgium)

CARIPLO (Cassa di Risparmio delle Provincie Lombarde SpA) (Italy)
CETELEM (France)
Caisse Nationale de Crédit Agricole (France)
Cariverona Banca SpA (Italy)
Christiania Bank og Kreditkasse (Norway)
Commerzbank AG (Germany)
Compagnie Financière de CIC et de l'Union Européenne (France)
Confederación Española de Cajas de Ahorros (Spain)
Crédit Agricole IndoSuez (France)
Creditanstalt Aktiengesellschaft (Austria)
Crédit Commercial de France (France)
Crédit du Nord (France)
Crédit Lyonnais (France)
Credito Italiano (Italy)

De Nationale Investeringsbank NV (Netherlands)
Den Danske Bank Aktieselskab (Denmark)
Den norske Bank ASA (Norway)

Deutsche Bank AG (Germany)
Deutsche Bau- und Bodenbank AG (Germany)
Deutsche Genossenschaftsbank (Germany)
Dresdner Bank AG (Germany)

Equity Bank Ltd (Republic of Ireland)
Ergobank SA (Greece)
Erste Bank der oesterreichischen Sparkassen AG (Austria)

FIMAT International Banque (France)
First National Building Society (Republic of Ireland)
Frankfurter Hypothekenbank Centalboden AG (Germany)

Generale Bank (Belgium)

Hamburgische Landesbank Girozentrale (Germany)

ICC Bank PLC (Republic of Ireland)
ING Bank NV (Netherlands)
Industrial Bank of Korea Europe SA (Luxembourg)
Ionian and Popular Bank of Greece SA (Greece)
Irish Nationwide Building Society (Republic of Ireland)
Irish Permanent PLC (Republic of Ireland)
Istituto Bancario San Paolo di Torino SpA (Italy)

Jyske Bank (Denmark)

KBC Bank NV (Belgium)
Kas-Associatie NV (Netherlands)

Landesbank Berlin Girozentrale (Germany)
Landesbank Hessen-Thüringen Girozentrale (Germany)
Lehman Brothers Bankhaus AG (Germany)

MeesPierson NV (Netherlands)
Merita Bank Ltd (Finland)

Natexis Banque (France)
National Bank of Greece SA (Greece)
Norddeutsche Landesbank Girozentrale (Germany)

Paribas (France)
Postipankki Ltd (Finland)

Rabobank International (Coöperatieve Centrale Raiffeisen-Boerenleenbank BA) (Netherlands)
Raiffeisen Zentralbank Osterreich AG (Austria)

Skandinaviska Enskilda Banken AB (publ) (Sweden)
Société Générale (France)
Südwestdeutsche Landesbank Girozentrale (Germany)
Svenska Handelsbanken AB (publ) (Sweden)
SwedBank (FöreningsSparbanken AB (publ)) (Sweden)

Triodosbank NV (Netherlands)

Ulster Bank Markets Ltd (Republic of Ireland)
Unibank A/S (Denmark)

Westdeutsche Landesbank Girozentrale (Germany)

Mutual Societies

In July 1997 the Government announced that responsibility for regulation of mutual societies would be transferred to a single new regulatory organization.

On 30 July 1998 the Chief Secretary to the Treasury announced that from January 1999 the new organization, the Financial Services Authority, would take responsibility for supporting the Building Societies Commission, the Friendly Societies Commission and, in relation to credit unions, the Chief Registrar of Friendly Societies. This announcement coincided with the publication of the draft Financial Services and Markets Bill which will underpin the work of the FSA. A decision on the early integration of the registration and records work of the Chief Registrar (other than for credit unions) was deferred to enable Ministers to take account of representations during the consultation period for the draft Bill.

FRIENDLY SOCIETIES IN BRITAIN

Friendly societies are voluntary mutual organizations, the main purposes of which are the provision of relief or maintenance during sickness, unemployment or retirement, and the provision of life assurance. Many of the older traditional societies complement their business activities by social activity and a general care for individual members in ways normally outside the scope of a purely commercial organization. There are three main categories of friendly societies: societies with separately registered branches, commonly called orders; centralized societies, which conduct business directly with members (having no separately registered branches); and collecting societies. Collecting societies conduct industrial assurance business and are subject to the requirements of the Industrial Assurance Acts in addition to the Friendly Societies Acts. Industrial assurance is life assurance for which the premiums are payable at intervals of less than two months and are received by means of collectors who make house-to-house visits for the purpose.

The Friendly Societies Act 1974 allowed three other main classes of society to be registered: benevolent societies, working men's clubs and specially authorized societies. Benevolent societies are established for any charitable or benevolent purpose, to provide the same type of benefits as would be permissible for a friendly society, but in contrast the benefits must be for persons who are not members instead of, or in addition to, members. Working men's clubs provide social and recreational facilities for members. Specially authorized societies are registered for any purpose authorized by the Treasury as a purpose to which some or all of the provisions of the 1974 Act ought to be extended. Examples are societies for the promotion of science, literature and the fine arts, or to enable members to pursue an interest in sports and games. No new societies of any type may now be registered under this Act.

The most recent legislation, the Friendly Societies Act 1992, created a new legislative framework for friendly societies, enabling them to provide a wider range of services to their members and allowing them to compete on more equal terms with other financial institutions. At the same time it provided for more flexible prudential supervision to safeguard members of societies.

The Act enables friendly societies to incorporate and establish subsidiaries to provide various financial and other

services to their members and the public. The activities which subsidiaries are able to conduct include those to establish and manage unit trust schemes and personal equity plans; to arrange for the provision of credit, whether as agents or providers; to carry on long-term or general insurance business; to provide insurance intermediary services; to provide fund management services for trustees of pension funds; to administer estates and execute trusts of wills; and to establish and manage sheltered housing, residential homes for the elderly, hospitals and nursing homes.

The Act established a new framework to oversee friendly societies, including a Friendly Societies Commission, whose principal functions are to regulate the activities of friendly societies, promote their financial stability and protect members' funds. All friendly societies carrying on insurance or non-insurance business require authorization by the Commission, which has a broad range of prudential powers. Friendly societies were also to be brought within the scope of the Policyholders Protection Act 1975, the statutory investor protection scheme covering insurance policyholders.

By the end of May 1998, there were 118 societies authorized to write new business. Thirty-five societies had taken advantage of the 1992 Act to incorporate and 19 of them had established subsidiary companies providing a wide range of services.

The Friendly Societies (Activities of a Subsidiary) Order 1996 came into force on 6 January 1997. The Order extended the range of activities which a subsidiary of an incorporated society may undertake, by allowing them to:

- establish and manage open ended investment companies (OEICs)
- convert unit trusts into OEICs
- establish and manage investment trusts
- provide fund management services to other bodies in addition to the trustees of pension funds

OEICs are collective investment schemes, similar to unit trusts, but in a corporate form.

The principal statistics at the end of 1996 are given below.

FRIENDLY SOCIETIES – Membership, Income and Funds

	No. of societies	No. of members 000s	Income £000s	Funds £000s
Orders	15*	254	34,611	239,109
Collecting societies	17	5,803†	781,980	5,392,252
Other centralized societies	277	2,650	948,383	4,721,782
ALL SOCIETIES	309	8,708	1,764,973	10,353,143

* 893 branches
† Includes 4.3 million policies rather than members in the case of six collecting societies

OTHER SOCIETIES ON REGISTER *at end 1996*

Benevolent societies	67
Working men's clubs	2,206
Specially authorized societies	126

INDUSTRIAL AND PROVIDENT SOCIETIES IN BRITAIN

The familiar 'Co-op' societies are amongst the wide variety which are registered under the Industrial and Provident Societies Act 1965. This consolidating Act, which is administered by the Chief Registrar of Friendly Societies, provides for the registration of societies and lays down the broad framework within which they must operate. Internal relations of societies are governed by their registered rules.

Registration under the Act confers upon a society corporate status by its registered name with perpetual succession and a common seal, and limited liability. A society qualifies for registration if it is carrying on an industry, business or trade, and it satisfies the Registrar either (a) that it is a bona fide co-operative society, or (b) that in view of the fact that its business is being, or is intended to be, conducted for the benefit of the community, there are special reasons why it should be registered under the Act rather than as a company under the Companies Act.

The Credit Unions Act 1979 added a new class of society registerable under the 1965 Act. It also made provision for the supervision of these savings and loan bodies. Unlike other classes, where the role of the Registry is solely that of a registration authority, it is for credit unions the prudential supervisor, seeking to encourage the prudent safe-keeping of investors' money.

During 1996 the number of registered societies of all classes decreased by 55 to 10,601 but the number of credit unions increased by 19 to 550. Assets of industrial and provident societies totalled £41,528 million, almost half of which is held in the 3,985 housing societies. The principal statistics at the end of 1996 are given in the table below.

	No. of socie-ties	No. of mem-bers 000s	Funds of members £000s	Total assets £000s
Retail	127	5,965	1,414,127	2,595,902
Wholesale and productive	127	45	682,975	1,434,757
Agricultural	958	251	260,228	744,790
Fishing	83	4	8,699	19,819
Clubs	3,662	2,089	337,119	552,350
General service	1,109	407	1,827,113	16,923,606
Housing	3,985	176	7,406,086	19,156,844
Credit unions	550	191	95,752	100,348
Total	10,601	9,128	12,032,099	41,528,416

BUILDING SOCIETIES IN THE UK

The Building Societies Act 1997, which received royal assent on 21 March 1997, makes substantive amendments to, but does not replace, the Building Societies Act 1986. It liberalizes the statutory regime for building societies to enable them to compete on more level terms with other financial institutions without having to forego their mutual status.

The Building Societies Act 1986 gave building societies a completely new legal framework for the first time since the initial comprehensive building society legislation in 1874. The 1986 Act sets out detailed provisions in relation to:

– the constitution of building societies

– building societies' powers in relation to raising funds, advances, loans, other assets and the provision of services
– the powers of control of the Building Societies Commission
– protection of investors, and complaints and disputes
– management of building societies, accounts and audit
– mergers and transfers of business

The 1986 Act was prescriptive in respect of building societies' powers and the way in which they were exercised. However, it gave numerous powers to the Building Societies Commission and/or the Treasury to make statutory instruments which, subject to parliamentary approval, can amend, extend and supplement the provisions of the Act. Since it came into force on 1 January 1987 the Act had been amended and extended considerably, especially in respect of building societies' powers.

The main purposes of the Building Societies Act 1997 are:

– to remove the prescriptive powers' regime relating to building societies and to replace it with a permissive regime with appropriately revised balance-sheet 'nature limits', thus increasing the commercial freedom of societies and allowing increased competiton and wider choice for customers
– to enhance the powers of control of the Building Societies Commission
– to introduce a package of measures to enhance the accountability of building societies' boards to their members
– to make changes to the provisions relating to the transfer of a building society's business to a company

The Act came fully into force on 21 October 1997. Under it a building society may pursue any activities set out in its memorandum, subject only to:

– principal purpose: its purpose or principal purpose must be that of making loans which are secured on residential properties and are funded substantially by its members
– lending limit: at least 75 per cent of its business assets must be loans fully secured on residential property
– funding limit: at least 50 per cent of its funds must be raised in the form of shares held by individual members
– restrictions: subject to certain exceptions, it must not act as a market maker in securities, commodities or currencies; trade in commodities or currencies; enter into transactions involving derivatives, except in relation to hedging; nor create a floating charge over its assets
– prudential: it must comply with the criteria of prudential management

By the end of 1998 almost all societies will have gained the approval of their members to amend their memorandum and rules in line with the Act and will be operating under the new statutory regime.

CONVERSIONS AND TAKE-OVERS

The Alliance and Leicester, Halifax, Northern Rock and Woolwich building societies completed their conversions to PLC status during 1997, whilst Bristol and West transferred to the Bank of Ireland and Greenwich transferred to the Portman.

On 12 August 1997 the directors of Birmingham Midshires Building Society announced their intention to seek their members' approval of a proposed takeover of the business by the Royal Bank of Scotland PLC. Following a takeover approach to the society by Halifax PLC on 9 March 1998, the Building Societies Commission indicated to the society on 23 March that, under the Building Societies

(Transfer of Business) Regulations 1998, it could not approve a transfer statement covering the Royal Bank offer which did not include a recommendation to society members that they accept the offer. Subsequently the agreement between the Royal Bank and the Birmingham Midshires was cancelled by agreement between the two parties.

OMBUDSMAN SCHEME

Societies must belong to an ombudsman scheme for the investigation of complaints. Matters to be covered by the scheme include operation of share and deposit accounts, loans (but not the making of new loans), money transmission services, foreign exchange services, agency payments and receipts, and the provision of credit. Grounds for complaint include breach of the Act or contract, unfair treatment or maladministration, and where the complainant has suffered pecuniary loss or expense or inconvenience. A society must agree to be bound by decisions of the adjudicator unless it agrees to give notice to its members

and the public of its reasons for not doing so. For address of the Building Societies Ombudsman scheme, *see* page 635.

BUILDING SOCIETIES 1996–7

	1996	1997
No. of societies – total	88	82
– authorized	77	71
No. of shareholders (000s)	37,768	19,234
No. of depositors (000s)	6,889	964
No. of borrowers (000s)	6,859	2,872
Share balances (£m)	196,546	90,092
Deposit balances (£m)	76,231	31,207
Mortgage balances (£m)	236,930	105,803
Total assets (£m)	318,392	137,864
Advances during year		
No. (000s)	1,115	522
Amount (£m)	43,881	22,730

MORTGAGE ARREARS AND REPOSSESSIONS

The recession resulted in a sharp rise in mortgage arrears and repossessions, with more than 75,000 properties repossessed in 1991. That total fell by 7,000 in 1992 as a result of a greater willingness by lenders to enter into arrangements with borrowers. The number continued to decline in the following four years. Under 33,000 proper-

ties were taken into possession in 1997, the lowest figure since 1989. Details of loans outstanding and properties repossessed for recent years, based on statistics of the largest building society and non-building society lenders, are shown below.

	1990	1991	1992	1993	1994	1995	1996	1997
No. of loans at end year (000s)	9,415	9,815	9,922	10,137	10,410	10,521	10,637	10,738
Properties repossessed in year								
Number	43,890	75,540	68,540	58,540	49,190	49,410	42,560	32,770
%	0.47	0.77	0.70	0.58	0.47	0.47	0.40	0.31

INTEREST RATES: MORTGAGE AND SHARE 1993–8

The interest rates prevailing on mortgage lending and share investment vary from society to society and in relation to the type or amount of loan or investment.

The interval between the payments or compounding of interest is crucial in determining the competitiveness of

particular societies' accounts. In order to make a true comparison of interest rates, the annual percentage rate or APR, which should appear in all advertisements and leaflets, must be used.

	1993	1994	1995	1996	1997	1998 1st quarter
Average bank base rate	6.01	5.46	6.70	5.96	6.56	7.25
Building societies average mortgage rate	8.09	7.68	7.84	6.72	7.03	7.71
Building societies average share rate	5.78	5.36	5.62	4.54	5.49	6.19

SOCIETIES WITH TOTAL ASSETS EXCEEDING £1 MILLION AT END OF FINANCIAL YEAR 1996

Name of Society* and head office address	Share investors	Total assets £'000
Barnsley, Regent Street, Barnsley, S. Yorks S70 2EH	41,939	217,544
Bath Investment, 20 Charles Street, Bath BA1 1HY	19,750	76,152
Beverley, 57 Market Place, Beverley, E. Yorks HU17 8AA	10,645	47,310
Birmingham Midshires, PO Box 81, Pendeford Business Park, Wobaston Road, Wolverhampton WV9 5HZ	848,563	7,682,900
Bradford and Bingley, Crossflatts, Bingley, W. Yorks BD16 2UA	1,701,988	18,754,792
Britannia, Britannia House, Cheadle Road, Leek, Staffs ST13 5RG	1,470,151	17,751,000
Buckinghamshire, High Street, Chalfont St Giles, Bucks HP8 4QB	9,000	82,030
Cambridge, 51 Newmarket Road, Cambridge CB5 8FF	59,700	418,812
Catholic, 7 Strutton Ground, London SW1P 2HY	3,555	30,485
Century, 21 Albany Street, Edinburgh EH1 3QW	2,806	13,167
Chelsea, Thirlestaine Hall, Thirlestaine Road, Cheltenham, Glos GL53 7AL	279,818	3,500,580
Chesham, 12 Market Square, Chesham, Bucks HP5 1ER	18,430	119,408
Cheshire, Castle Street, Macclesfield, Cheshire SK11 6AF	328,751	1,887,664
Chorley and District, Key House, Foxhole Road, Chorley, Lancs PR7 1NZ	15,450	79,369
Clay Cross, Eyre Street, Clay Cross, Chesterfield S45 9NS	3,500	16,706
Coventry, PO Box 9, High Street, Coventry CV1 5QN	686,331	4,359,782
Cumberland, Cumberland House, Castle Street, Carlisle CA3 8RX	160,000	699,752
Darlington, Sentinel House, Lingfield Way, Darlington, Co. Durham DL1 4PR	66,001	338,009
Derbyshire, Duffield Hall, Duffield, Derby DE56 1AG	323,962	2,247,665
Dudley, Dudley House, Stone Street, Dudley DY1 1NP	26,552	95,915
Dunfermline, Caledonia House, Carnegie Avenue, Dunfermline, Fife KY11 5PJ	177,400	1,220,361
Earl Shilton, 22 The Hollow, Earl Shilton, Leicester LE9 7NB	11,265	61,333
Ecology, 18 Station Road, Cross Hills, Keighley, W. Yorks BD20 7EH	5,172	22,433
Furness, 51–55 Duke Street, Barrow-in-Furness LA14 1RT	82,446	392,141
Gainsborough, 9 Lord Street, Gainsborough, Lincs DN21 2DD	7,677	30,957
Hanley Economic, Granville House, Festival Park, Hanley, Stoke-on-Trent, Staffs ST1 5TB	31,070	202,190
Harpenden, 14 Station Road, Harpenden, Herts AL5 4SE	12,713	54,470
Hinckley and Rugby, Upper Bond Street, Hinckley, Leics LE10 1DG	84,000	380,097
Holmesdale, 43 Church Street, Reigate, Surrey RH2 0AE	7,506	82,730
Ilkeston Permanent, 24–26 South Street, Ilkeston, Derby DE7 5HQ	4,500	16,658
Ipswich, 44 Upper Brook Street, Ipswich IP4 1DP	47,000	213,520
Kent Reliance, Reliance House, Manor Road, Chatham, Kent ME4 6AF	56,900	292,372
Lambeth, 118–120 Westminster Bridge Road, London SE1 7XE	49,427	651,746
Leeds and Holbeck, 105 Albion Street, Leeds LS1 5AS	325,000	2,857,251
Leek United, 50 St Edward Street, Leek, Staffs ST13 5DH	60,589	420,505
Londonderry Provident, 31A Carlisle Road, Londonderry BT48 6JJ	1,386	10,804
Loughborough, 6 High Street, Loughborough, Leics LE11 2QB	21,647	137,287
Manchester, 24 Queen Street, Manchester M2 5AH	16,261	151,909
Mansfield, Regent House, Regent Street, Mansfield, Notts NG18 1SS	20,125	126,44
Market Harborough, Welland House, The Square, Market Harborough, Leics LE16 7PD	48,521	256,738
Marsden, 6–20 Russell Street, Nelson, Lancs BB9 7NJ	66,991	270,731
Melton Mowbray, 39 Nottingham Street, Melton Mowbray, Leics LE13 1NR	49,230	219,234
Mercantile, Mercantile House, Silverbank Business Park, Wallsend, Tyne and Wear NE28 9NY	33,959	152,130
Monmouthshire, John Frost Square, Newport, Gwent NP9 1PX	32,617	210,634
National Counties, National Counties House, Church Street, Epsom, Surrey KT17 4NL	22,822	517,936
Nationwide, Nationwide House, Pipers Way, Swindon SN38 1NW	7,980,146	47,078,200
Newbury, 17–20 Bartholomew Street, Newbury, Berks RG14 5LY	36,000	81,246
Newcastle, Portland House, New Bridge Street, Newcastle upon Tyne NE1 8AL	200,000	1,755,152
Norwich and Peterborough, Peterborough Business Park, Lynchwood, Peterborough PE2 6WZ	211,887	1,856,099
Nottingham, 5–13 Upper Parliament Street, Nottingham NG1 2BX	163,614	1,158,839
Nottingham Imperial, Imperial House, 72 Bridgford Road, West Bridgford, Nottingham NG2 6AP	10,688	56,648
Penrith, 7 King Street, Penrith, Cumbria CA11 7AR	6,156	53,076
Portman, Portman House, Richmond Hill, Bournemouth, Dorset BH2 6EP	1,144,731	4,726,237
Principality, PO Box 89, Principality Buildings, Queen Street, Cardiff CF1 1UA	250,566	1,720,543
Progressive, 33–37 Wellington Place, Belfast BT1 6HH	66,381	506,325
Saffron Walden, Herts and Essex, 1A Market Street, Saffron Walden, Essex CB10 1HX	58,806	281,678
Scarborough, Prospect House, PO Box 6, Scarborough, N. Yorks YO12 6EQ	114,207	703,831
Scottish, 23 Manor Place, Edinburgh EH3 7XE	25,685	133,022
Shepshed, Bull Ring, Shepshed, Loughborough, Leics LE12 9QD	7,933	37,581
Skipton, The Bailey, Skipton, N. Yorks BD23 1DN	352,159	3,773,473

Name of Building Society* and head office address	Share investors	Total assets £'000
Stafford Railway, 4 Market Square, Stafford ST16 2JH	11,132	60,540
Staffordshire, Jubilee House, PO Box 66, 84 Salop Street, Wolverhampton WV3 0SA	222,566	1,191,295
Standard, 64 Church Way, North Shields, Tyne and Wear NE29 0AF	2,500	15,496
Stroud and Swindon, Rowcroft, Stroud, Glos GL5 3BG	136,163	1,012,846
Swansea, 11 Cradock Street, Swansea SA1 3EW	3,747	32,327
Teachers, Allenview House, Hanham Road, Wimborne, Dorset BH21 1AG	15,070	144,392
Tipton and Coseley, 70 Owen Street, Tipton, W. Midlands DY4 8HG	25,709	132,950
Universal, Universal House, Kings Manor, Newcastle upon Tyne NE1 6PA	48,000	304,878
Vernon, 19 St Petersgate, Stockport, Cheshire SK1 1HF	29,975	141,085
West Bromwich, 374 High Street, West Bromwich, W. Midlands B70 8LR	462,000	2,158,800
Yorkshire, Yorkshire House, Yorkshire Drive, Bradford BD5 8LJ	1,000,000	8,230,720

* 'Building Society' are the last words in every society's name

National Savings

Investment and Ordinary Accounts

On 31 May 1998, there were about 16,110,318 accounts with the sum of approximately £1,324.1 million due to depositors in ordinary accounts and about 4,260,275 accounts with the sum of approximately £8,255.2 million due to depositors in investment accounts.

Interest is earned at 3 per cent per year on each ordinary account for every complete calendar month in which the balance is £500 or more; and at 2 per cent per year for other months. The minimum deposit is £10; maximum balance £10,000 plus interest credited. On 31 May 1998 the average amount held in ordinary accounts was approximately £82.

The investment account pays a higher rate of interest depending on the account balance (the current rate can be found at any post office). The minimum deposit is £20; maximum balance £100,000 plus interest credited. On 31 May 1998 the average amount held in investment accounts was approximately £1,937.

Premium Bonds

Premium Bonds are a government security which were first introduced in 1956. Premium Bonds enable savers to enter a regular draw for tax-free prizes, while retaining the right to get their money back. A sum equivalent to interest on each bond is put into a prize fund and distributed by monthly prize draws. (The rate of interest is 5 per cent a year from 1 November 1997.) The prizes are drawn by ERNIE (electronic random number indicator equipment) and are free of all UK income tax and capital gains tax.

Bonds are in units of £1, with a minimum purchase of £100; above this, purchases must be in multiples of £10, up to a maximum holding limit of £20,000 per person. The scheme offers a facility to reinvest prize wins automatically. Upon completion of an automatic prize reinvestment mandate, holders receive new bonds which are immediately eligible for future prize draws. Bonds can only be held in the name of an individual and not by organizations.

Bonds become eligible for prizes once they have been held for one clear calendar month following the month of purchase. Each £1 unit can win only one prize per draw, but it will be awarded the highest for which it is drawn. Bonds remain eligible for prizes until they are repaid. When a holder dies, bonds remain eligible for prizes up to and including the twelfth monthly draw after the month in which the holder dies.

By April 1998 bonds to the value of £16,255 million had been sold. Of these £6,087 million had been cashed, leaving £10,168 million still invested. By the July 1998 prize draw, 63.7 million prizes totalling £4,020 million had been distributed since the first prize draw in June 1957.

Income Bonds

National Savings Income Bonds were introduced in 1982. They are suitable for those who want to receive regular monthly payments of interest while preserving the full cash value of their capital. The bonds are sold in multiples of £1,000. The minimum holding is £2,000 and the maximum £250,000 (sole or joint holding).

Interest is calculated on a day-to-day basis and paid monthly. Interest is taxable but is paid without deduction of tax at source. The bonds have a guaranteed life of ten years, but may be repaid at par before maturity on giving three months' notice. Repayment is also possible without giving notice but incurs a penalty. If the sole or sole surviving holder dies, however, no fixed period of notice is required and there is no loss of interest for repayment made within the first year.

Net investment in National Savings Income Bonds was £10,256 million at the end of April 1998.

Pensioners Guaranteed Income Bonds

Pensioners Guaranteed Income Bonds were introduced in January 1994 and are designed for people aged 60 and over who wish to receive regular monthly payments with a rate of interest that is fixed for a five-year period whilst preserving the full cash value of their investment.

The minimum limit for each purchase is £500. The maximum holding is £50,000 (£100,000 for a joint holding); within those limits bonds can be bought for any amount in pounds and pence. The rate of interest is fixed and guaranteed for the first five years. Interest is taxable but is paid without deduction of tax at source.

Holders can apply for repayment (or part repayment of a bond subject to the minimum holding limits) by giving 60 days notice (if repayment is before the fifth anniversary date). No interest is earned during the notice period. If repayment is requested within two weeks of any fifth anniversary of purchase, there is no formal period of notice. Repayment is possible without giving notice but a penalty is incurred. On the death of a holder or sole surviving investor in a joint holding, repayment will be made without notice. Interest will be paid in full up to the date of repayment.

Net investment in Pensioners Guaranteed Income Bonds was £7,393 million at the end of April 1998.

Children's Bonus Bonds

Children's Bonus Bonds were introduced in 1991. The latest issue, Issue J, was introduced in March 1998. They can be bought for any child under 16 and will go on growing in value until he or she is 21. The bonds are sold in multiples of £25. The minimum holding is £25. The maximum holding in Issue J is £1,000 per child. This is in addition to holdings of earlier issues of the bond (excluding interest and bonuses). Bonds for children under 16 must be held by a parent or guardian.

Children's Bonus Bonds (Issue J) earn 5 per cent a year over five years. A bonus (6.2 per cent) of the purchase price is added at the fifth anniversary. This is equal to 6 per cent a year compound. All returns are totally exempt from UK income tax. No interest is earned on bonds cashed in before the first anniversary of purchase. Bonuses are only payable if the bond is held until the next bonus date. Bonds over five years old continue to earn interest and bonuses until the holder is 21, when they should be cashed in. If bonds are not cashed in on the holder's 21st birthday, they earn no interest after that birthday.

FIRST Option Bonds

FIRST (Fixed Interest Rate Savings Tax-paid) Option Bonds were introduced in 1992. They offer guaranteed rates without the need for long-term commitment for personal savers over 16. They may be held indefinitely and will continue to grow in value at rates of interest fixed for 12 months at a time. Tax is deducted from the interest at source. The minimum purchase is £1,000 and the maximum holding is £250,000. Withdrawals can be made without penalty at any anniversary date and there is no formal notice period for repayment. No interest is earned on repayments before the first anniversary.

CAPITAL BONDS

National Savings Capital Bonds were introduced in 1989. The latest series, Series L, was introduced in March 1998. Capital Bonds offer capital growth over five years with guaranteed returns at fixed rates. The interest is taxable each year (for those who pay income tax) but is not deducted at source. The minimum purchase is £100. There is a maximum holding limit of £250,000 from Series B onwards.

Capital Bonds will be repaid in full with all interest gained at the end of five years. No interest is earned on bonds repaid in the first year. Reinvestment or extension terms may also be available.

NATIONAL SAVINGS TREASURER'S ACCOUNT

The Treasurer's Account, introduced in September 1996, offers attractive rates and security to non-profit making organizations such as charities, friendly societies, clubs, etc. The minimum holding is £10,000 and the maximum is £2 million. Interest is paid at the rate of 6.2 per cent a year on holdings of £10,000 to £24,999, 6.45 per cent a year on holdings of £25,000 to £99,999, and 7 per cent a year on holdings of £100,000 and above.

NATIONAL SAVINGS CERTIFICATES

RECENT ISSUES

The amount, including accrued interest, index-linked increase or bonus remaining to the credit of investors in National Savings Certificates on 30 April 1998 was approximately £20,077 million. In 1997–8, approximately £4,393.8 million was subscribed and £4,059.7 million (excluding interest, index-linked increase or bonus) was repaid. Interest, index-linked increase, bonus or other sum payable is free of UK income tax (including investment income surcharge) and capital gains tax.

From June 1982, savings certificates of the 7th to 40th Issues will be extended on general extension rates as they reach the end of their existing extension periods. The percentage interest rate is determined by the Treasury and any change in this general extension rate will be applicable from the first of the month following its announcement. Under the system, a certificate earns interest for each complete period of three months beyond the expiry of the previous extension terms. Within each three-month period, interest is calculated separately for each month at the rate applicable from the beginning of that month. The interest for each month is one-twelfth of the annual rate (i.e. it does not vary with the number of days in the month) and is capitalized annually on the anniversary of the date of purchase. The current rate of interest under the general extension rate is given in leaflets available at post offices.

FIFTH INDEX-LINKED ISSUE

2 July 1990–12 November 1992
Maximum holding: 400 units, plus special facilities to hold up to a further 400 units
Unit cost: £25
Interest per unit: the repayment value, subject to their being held for one year, is related to the movement of the UK General Index of Retail Prices. In addition, there is guaranteed extra interest which is paid from the date of purchase for each full year the certificates are held. After the first year the return is the Retail Price Index (RPI) only. Certificates repaid before the first anniversary date earn RPI for each complete month held from the purchase date. For the second year, the RPI plus 0.5 per cent; for the third, the RPI plus 1 per cent; for the fourth, the RPI plus 2 per cent; and at the fifth anniversary, RPI plus 4.5 per cent. Certificates held beyond the fifth anniversary earn the index-linked return only

FORTIETH ISSUE

7 December 1992–16 December 1993

Maximum holding: 400 units, plus special facilities to hold up to a further 800
Unit cost: £100; reinvestment certificates £25
Value after five years: £132.25
Interest per unit: after one year the repayment value increases by 4 per cent for ordinarily held 40th Issue. However, reinvestment certificates earn interest during the first year at a rate of 4 per cent a year. On a £100 unit after one year, £4 is added; during the second year, £1.15 per completed three months; during the third year, £1.56 per completed three months; during the fourth year, £1.54 per completed three months; and during the fifth year, £2.42 per completed three months

SIXTH INDEX-LINKED ISSUE

7 December 1992–16 December 1993
Maximum holding: 400 units, plus special facilities to hold up to a further 800
Unit cost: £100; reinvestment certificates £25
Interest per unit: the repayment value, subject to their being held for one year, is related to the movement of the UK General Index of Retail Prices. In addition, there is a guaranteed extra interest of 1.5 per cent for the first year; 2 per cent for the second year; 2.75 per cent for the third year; 3.75 per cent for the fourth year; and 6.32 per cent for the fifth year. This is worth 3.25 per cent compound over the full five years. Reinvestment certificates repaid before the first anniversary date earn RPI plus extra interest of 1.5 per cent a year for each complete month

SEVENTH INDEX-LINKED ISSUE

17 December 1993–19 September 1994
Maximum holding: 400 units, plus special facilities to hold up to a further 800
Unit cost: £100; reinvestment certificates £25
Interest per unit: the repayment value, subject to their being held for one year, is related to the movement of the UK General Index of Retail Prices. In addition, there is a guaranteed extra interest of 1.25 per cent for the first year; 1.75 per cent for the second year; 2.5 per cent for the third year; 3.5 per cent for the fourth year and 6.07 per cent for the fifth year. This is worth 3 per cent compound over the full five years. Reinvestment certificates repaid before the first anniversary date will earn RPI plus extra interest of 1.25 per cent a year for each complete month

FORTY-FIRST ISSUE

17 December 1993–19 December 1994
Maximum holding: 400 units, plus special facilities to hold up to a further 800
Unit cost: £100; reinvestment certificates £25
Value after five years: £130.08
Interest per unit: after one year the repayment value increases by 3.65 per cent for ordinarily held 41st Issue. However, reinvestment certificates if encashed before the first anniversary earn interest at 3.65 per cent for each complete period of three months. On a £100 unit after one year, £3.65 is added; during the second year, £1.05 per completed three months; during the third year, £1.45 per completed three months; during the fourth year, £1.82 per completed three months; and during the fifth year, £2.28 per completed three months

FORTY-SECOND ISSUE

20 September 1994–25 January 1996
Maximum holding: £10,000, plus special facilities to hold up to a further £20,000
Unit cost: certificates may be purchased for any amount, subject to a minimum purchase at any time of £100; reinvestment certificates are available for any amount and are not subject to a minimum purchase requirement
Value after five years: £132.88
Interest: after one year the repayment value increases by 4 per cent for ordinarily held 42nd Issue. However, reinvestment certificates if encashed before the first anniversary earn interest at 4 per cent for each complete period of three months. On a £100 certificate after one year £4.00 is added; during the second year £1.19 per completed three months; during the third year, £1.49 per completed three months; during the fourth year, £1.93 per completed three months; and during the fifth year, £2.59 per completed three months

EIGHTH INDEX-LINKED ISSUE

20 September 1994–25 January 1996
Maximum holding: £10,000, plus special facilities to hold up to a further £20,000

Unit cost: certificates may be purchased for any amount, subject to a minimum purchase at any time of £100; reinvestment certificates are available for any amount and are not subject to a minimum purchase requirement

Interest: the repayment value, subject to their being held for one year, is related to the movement of the UK General Index of Retail Prices. In addition, there is a guaranteed extra interest of 1.25 per cent for the first year, 1.75 per cent for the second year, 2.5 per cent for the third year, 3.5 per cent for the fourth year and 6.07 per cent for the fifth year. This is worth 3 per cent compound over the full five years. Reinvestment certificates repaid before the first anniversary date will earn RPI plus extra interest of 1.25 per cent a year for each complete month

FORTY-THIRD ISSUE
26 January 1996–31 March 1997
Maximum holding: £10,000, plus special facilities to hold up to a further £20,000
Unit cost: certificates may be purchased for any amount, subject to a minimum purchase at any time of £100; reinvestment certificates are available for any amount and are not subject to a minimum purchase requirement
Value after five years: £129.77
Interest: after one year the repayment value increases by 3.75 per cent for ordinarily held 43rd Issue. However, reinvestment certificates if encashed before the first anniversary earn interest at 3.75 per cent a year for each complete period of three months. On a £100 unit after one year, £3.75 is added; during the second year, £1.07 per completed three months; during the third year, £1.35 per completed three months; during the fourth year, £1.74 per completed three months; and during the fifth year, £2.33 per completed three months

NINTH INDEX-LINKED ISSUE
26 January 1996–31 March 1997
Maximum holding: £10,000, plus special facilities to hold up to a further £20,000
Unit cost: certificates may be purchased for any amount, subject to a minimum purchase at any time of £100; reinvestment certificates are available for any amount and are not subject to a minimum purchase requirement
Interest: the repayment value, subject to their being held for one year, is related to the movement of the UK General Index of Retail Prices. In addition, there is a guaranteed extra interest of 1 per cent for the first year, 1.25 per cent for the second year, 2 per cent for the third year, 3 per cent for the fourth year and 5.31 per cent for the fifth year. This is worth 2.5 per cent a year compound over the full five years. Reinvestment certificates repaid before the first anniversary date will earn RPI plus extra interest of 1 per cent a year for each complete month

FORTY-FOURTH ISSUE
1 April 1997–
Maximum holding: £10,000, plus special facility to reinvest an unlimited amount
Unit cost: certificates may be purchased for any amount, subject to a minimum purchase at any time of £100; reinvestment certificates are available for any amount and are not subject to a minimum or maximum requirement
Interest: after one year the repayment value increases by 3.75 per cent for ordinarily held 44th Issue. However, reinvestment certificates if encashed before the first anniversary earn interest at 3.75 per cent a year for each complete period of three months. On a £100 certificate after one year £3.75 is added; during the second year, £1.07 per completed three months; during the third year, £1.35 per completed three months; during the fourth year, £1.74 per completed three months; and during the fifth year, £2.33 per completed three months

TENTH INDEX-LINKED ISSUE
1 April 1997–
Maximum holding: £10,000, plus special facility to reinvest an unlimited amount
Unit cost: certificates may be purchased for any amount, subject to a minimum purchase at any time of £100; reinvestment certificates are available for any amount and are not subject to a minimum or maximum requirement
Interest: the repayment value, subject to their being held for one year, is related to the movement of the UK General Index of Retail Prices. In addition, there is a guaranteed extra interest of 1 per cent for the first year, 1.25 per cent for the second year, 2 per cent

for the third year, 3 per cent for the fourth year and 5.31 per cent for the fifth year. This is worth 2.5 per cent a year compound over the full five years. Reinvestment certificates repaid before the first anniversary date will earn RPI plus extra interest of 1 per cent a year for each complete month.

Insurance

AUTHORIZATION

The Insurance Companies Act 1982 empowers the Insurance Directorate of HM Treasury to authorize corporate bodies to transact insurance in the United Kingdom provided they comply with the financial and other regulations detailed in the Act. At the end of 1997 there were 814 insurance companies with authorization from the Treasury to transact one or more classes of insurance business. However, with the establishment of the single European insurance market on 1 July 1994 an insurer authorized in any of the European Union (EU) countries can now transact insurance in the UK without further formality; this creates a potential market of over 5,000 insurance companies.

REGULATION

Under the Financial Services Act 1986, the Securities and Investments Board (SIB) is empowered to make, monitor and enforce rules about the conduct of investment business. Insurance companies offering investment contracts like life insurance, pensions, unit trusts and annuities can either obtain authorization direct from SIB or from one of the self-regulating organizations (SROs). For life insurance the SRO is currently the Personal Investment Authority (PIA) (*see* page 634). In May 1997, the Chancellor of the Exchequer announced the reform of financial services regulation. The three SROs, including the PIA, will be wound up and their functions passed to the Financial Services Authority (FSA), an enlarged and enhanced regulator which will oversee all forms of retail investment. The legislation to establish the FSA is scheduled for autumn 1998 but pressure on parliamentary time may delay this.

Disputes between policy holders and insurers may be referred to the Insurance Ombudsman or, if appropriate, the PIA Ombudsman or the Pensions Ombudsman (*see* page 635). These functions will also pass to the FSA Ombudsman.

ASSOCIATION OF BRITISH INSURERS

Over 96 per cent of the world-wide business of UK insurance companies is transacted by the 453 members of the Association of British Insurers (ABI) (51 Gresham Street, London EC2V 7HQ), a trade association which represents both life and general insurers. On general insurance (motor, household, holiday, etc.), ABI acts as a regulatory organization for insurance intermediaries.

INSURANCE BROKERS

Under the Insurance Brokers Registration Act 1977, the Insurance Brokers Registration Council (IBRC) (63 St Mary Axe, London EC3A 8NB) is the statutory body responsible for the registration of insurance brokers. The Council is responsible for the registration and training of insurance brokers, conduct of business, and discipline, and it lays down rules relating to such matters as accounting practice, staff qualifications, advertising, etc.

It is possible to act as an insurance intermediary without being registered with the IBRC but unregistered intermediaries are forbidden to use the words 'Insurance Broker' as a title.

It is expected that the legislation to set up the Financial Services Authority will include measures to repeal the Insurance Brokers Registration Act, abolishing the IBRC.

IBRC Registered Brokers 1997

Registered individuals	16,973
Limited companies registered	2,128
Sole traders and partnerships	1,005
(containing 1,807 partners and directors)	

BALANCE OF PAYMENTS

The overseas earnings of UK insurance institutions fell 11 per cent in 1996, to £6,141 million, but the insurance industry was still the second largest contributor to the UK's balance of payments.

GENERAL INSURANCE

The predictions of a downturn in profits for the general insurance market for 1997 proved incorrect as the world-wide general insurance trading profit for UK insurers increased by 6.5 per cent to £3,140 million. The main reason for the increase was a reduction in underwriting loss from £1,880 million in 1996 to £1,630 million in 1997.

In the UK, motor underwriting losses increased by 62.6 per cent to £1,140 million; although fierce competition has meant no increases in premiums during 1997, this level of loss is not sustainable. The only improvement on the UK motor account was the reduction in theft claims.

On the non-motor side, underwriting profit rose by 8.1 per cent from £74 million to £80 million. Problem areas in 1997 included fire claims, which rose by 4.5 per cent, business interruption claims, up by 33 per cent, and domestic subsidence claims, up by 18 per cent. However, weather damage claims fell by 24.5 per cent and theft claims by 7.3 per cent.

Overseas, there were mixed results, with premiums for motor and non-motor business falling in all countries. In other EU countries motor premiums fell from £1,828 million to £1,696 million, in the USA from £1,585 million to £1,533 million, and in other territories from £1,768 million to £1,753 million. The motor underwriting loss worsened by 22.5 per cent to £354 million. Premiums for non-motor business fell from £6,600 million to £6,320 million (4.3 per cent) but the underwriting loss was reduced by just over 50 per cent from £633 million to £314 million.

Commentators expect results to worsen in 1998 unless premium rates can be increased, an unlikely prospect given the competitive climate and over-capacity in most markets.

LONDON INSURANCE MARKET

The London Insurance Market is a distinct, separate sector of the UK insurance and reinsurance industry. It is the world's leading market for internationally traded insurances and reinsurance, its business comprising mainly overseas non-life large and high-exposure risks. It is based in the City of London with participating insurers having an underwriting room either within the Lloyd's building or situated nearby. Currently there are 139 Lloyd's syndicates, about 140 insurance companies and 39 Marine Protection and Indemnity Clubs active in the market. In 1995 the market had a written gross premium income of £14,558 million.

The trade association for the international insurance and reinsurance companies writing primarily non-marine insurance and all classes of reinsurance business in the London Market is the London International Insurance and Reinsurance Market Association (LIRMA) (Lower Ground Floor, London Underwriting Centre, 3 Minster Court, Mincing Lane, London EC3R 7DD). However, LIRMA is to merge with the Institute of London Underwriters (ILU) (49 Leadenhall Street, London EC3A 2BE). The new organization, to be known as the International Underwriting Association of London, is expected to begin work at the start of 1999.

BRITISH INSURANCE COMPANIES

The following insurance company figures refer to members and certain non-members of the ABI.

CLAIMS STATISTICS (£ million)

	1996	1997
Domestic claims		
Theft	551	513
Fire	223	247
Weather	525	377
Subsidence	333	393
Business interruption	n/a	n/a
Total	1,632	1,530
Commercial claims		
Theft	180	167
Fire	484	492
Weather	201	171
Subsidence	n/a	n/a
Business interruption	203	270
Total	1,068	1,100

WORLD-WIDE GENERAL BUSINESS TRADING RESULT

	1996 £m	1997 £m
Net written premiums	35,177	35,330
Underwriting profit (loss) for one year account business	(1,766)	(1,707)
Transfer to profit and loss account for other business		
Marine, Aviation, Transport	(61)	(42)
Other	(60)	115
Total underwriting result	(1,888)	(1,633)
Net investment income	4,840	4,777
Overall trading profit	2,952	3,144
Profit as % of premium income	8.4	8.9

LLOYD'S OF LONDON

Lloyd's of London is an international market for almost all types of insurance. Lloyd's currently earns a gross premium income of around £8,000 million for underwriters each year. Much of this business comes from outside Great Britain and makes a valuable contribution to the balance of payments.

A policy is underwritten at Lloyd's by a mixture of private and corporate members, corporate members having been admitted for the first time in 1992. Specialist underwriters accept insurance risks at Lloyd's on behalf of members (referred to as 'names') grouped in syndicates. There are currently around 170 syndicates of varying sizes, some with over 2,000 names, each managed by an underwriting agent approved by the Council of Lloyd's.

Individual members are still in the majority at Lloyd's with a total of 6,825 individuals as opposed to 435 corporate members. However, in 1995 the market capacity of the corporate sector exceeded for the first time that of the individuals, individuals representing £4,105 million of capacity and corporate members £6,064 million. This trend is likely to continue in future, bringing about a fundamental change in the structure of the market.

WORLD-WIDE GENERAL BUSINESS UNDERWRITING RESULT

	1996					1997				
	UK	Other EU	USA	Other	Total	UK	Other EU	USA	Other	Total
Motor										
Premiums: £m	5,913	1,828	1,585	1,768	11,094	6,182	1,696	1,533	1,753	11,164
Profit (loss): £m	(698)	(173)	(67)	(49)	(987)	(1,135)	(244)	(66)	(44)	(1,489)
% of premiums	(11.8)	(9.4)	(4.2)	(2.8)	(8.89)	(18.4)	(14.4)	(4.3)	(2.5)	(13.33)
Non-motor										
Premiums: £m	12,519	2,389	1,995	2,218	19,121	13,018	2,389	1,890	2,075	19,372
Profit (loss): £m	74	(98)	(426)	(109)	(559)	80	(98)	(184)	(6)	(208)
% of premiums	0.6	(4.1)	(21.3)	(4.9)	(2.92)	0.6	(4.1)	(9.7)	(0.3)	(1.07)

NET PREMIUM INCOME BY TERRITORY 1997

	UK £m	Other EU £m	USA £m	Other £m	Total £m
Motor	6,182	1,696	1,533	1,753	11,165
Non-motor	13,018	2,351	1,890	2,075	19,333
Marine, Aviation and Transport	1,239	210	237	180	1,866
Non-MAT reinsurance	1,805	484	0	180	2,470
Other funded business	489	4	0	3	496
Total general business	22,734	4,745	3,660	4,191	35,330
Ordinary long-term	59,333	5,709	4,270	4,442	73,755
Industrial long-term	1,052	—	—	—	1,052
Total long-term business	60,385	5,709	4,270	4,442	74,807

Lloyd's is incorporated by an Act of Parliament (Lloyd's Acts 1971 onwards) and is governed by a council of 19 members. Market management is handled by a Market Board of 18 members (comprising three working members and three external members of the Council, three Corporation executives (including the chief executive officer), eight additional market practitioners and one external member. Regulation is supervised by a Board of 14 members, comprising four nominated members of the Council, two external members of the Council, four appointed working members, two other appointed external members and the Director, Regulatory Division.

The Corporation is a non-profit making body chiefly financed by its members' subscriptions. It provides the premises, administrative staff and services enabling Lloyd's underwriting syndicates to conduct their business. It does not, however, assume corporate liability for the risks accepted by its members, who remain responsible to the full extent of their personal means for their underwriting affairs.

Lloyd's syndicates have no direct contact with the public. All business is transacted through insurance brokers accredited by the Corporation of Lloyd's. In addition, non-Lloyd's brokers in the UK, when guaranteed by Lloyd's brokers, are able to deal directly with Lloyd's motor syndicates, a facility which has made the Lloyd's market more accessible to the insuring public.

Lloyd's also provides the most comprehensive shipping intelligence service in the world. The shipping and other information received from Lloyd's agents, shipowners, news agencies and other sources throughout the world is collated and distributed to the media as well as to the maritime and commercial sectors in general. *Lloyd's List* is London's oldest daily newspaper and contains news of general commercial interest as well as shipping information. *Lloyd's Shipping Index*, also published daily, lists some 25,000 ocean-going vessels in alphabetical order and gives the latest known report of each.

DEVELOPMENTS IN 1997

The 1995 year of account produced a profit after expenses of more than £1,000 million for the third successive year. This was gratifying for the market as it exceeded the profitability of the majority of Lloyd's competitors. Of the 170 syndicates trading in the 1995 year of account, 137 traded profitably.

One major factor in this result was the fall in the number of major catastrophes during 1995. There were six non-marine catastrophes, with hurricane *Marilyn* in the USA and subsidence in the UK producing the most significant claims. No serious marine catastrophes were recorded during the year.

It is expected, however, that the results for 1996 onwards will begin to show a downturn in profitability. Evidence of this is already becoming apparent with the falls in premium rates in most sectors.

In November 1997 a review of Lloyd's regulatory arrangements, chaired by Sir Alan Hardcastle, concluded that it was advisable for Lloyd's to be accountable to an external regulator. This was endorsed by the Council of Lloyd's. Subsequently, the government announced its intention to introduce legislation to achieve this and it is now expected that Lloyd's will join other financial and insurance institutions under the auspices of the new Financial Services Authority.

Chairman, M. Taylor
Chief Executive, R. Sandler

LLOYD'S MEMBERSHIP

	1995	1996	1997
Total no. of underwriting members participating			
Individuals	14,744	12,798	9,958
Corporate	140	162	202

TOTAL MARKET CAPACITY

	1995 £m	1996 £m	1997 £m
Individual	7,835	6,985	5,824
Corporate	2,360	3,009	4,500
Total	10,195	9.994	10,324

LLOYD'S GLOBAL ACCOUNTS
as at 31 December 1997

	1994 and prior years of account £m	1995 pure year result £m
Gross premiums written (net of brokerage)	7,657	8,005
Outward reinsurance premiums	1,969	2,089
Net premiums	5,688	5,916
Reinsurance to close premiums received from earlier years of account	1,385	—
Amounts retained to meet all known and unknown outstanding liabilities brought forward	223	—
	7,296	5,916
Gross claims paid	3,667	3,468
Reinsurers' share	847	795
Net claims	2,820	2,673
Other reinsurance premiums paid to close the year of account	2,558	1,698
Amounts retained to meet all known and unknown outstanding liabilities carried forward	256	30
	5,634	4,401
Underwriting result	1,662	1,515
Other profit (loss) on exchange	14	8
Syndicate operating expenses	(426)	(390)
Balance on technical account	1,250	1,133
Investment income	515	520
Investment expenses and charges	(10)	(9)
Investment gains less losses	(6)	13
Result before personal expenses	1,749	1,657
Personal expenses	(654)	(652)
Result after personal expenses	1,095	1,005

LLOYD'S RESULTS 1995

	Marine 1994 £m	Marine 1995 £m	Non-marine 1994 £m	Non-marine 1995 £m	Aviation 1994 £m	Aviation 1995 £m	Motor 1994 £m	Motor 1995 £m
Net premiums	1,254	1,274	2,921	3,194	510	620	976	828
Pure year result	565	514	837	856	148	283	117	4

LIFE INSURANCE AND PENSIONS

The total world-wide long-term premium income of UK insurers increased by 12.4 per cent to £74,800 million in 1997, reflecting sustained consumer interest in life, incapacity and pension policies as a means of saving and protection. UK premium income was £60,400 million, an increase of 14.3 per cent, while overseas premiums rose by 5.2 per cent to £14,400 million. The highest performing sector was UK single premium pensions, where premiums increased by 32.7 per cent to £20,400 million. Most other sectors also showed increases.

REVIEW OF PENSIONS SELLING

The review of the selling of personal pensions continued throughout 1997. The pensions concerned were contracts sold between April 1988 and July 1994 to up to 1,500,000 people who were advised to take out a personal pension plan; in many cases this was in preference to remaining in a company pension scheme. In 1993 the Securities and Investments Board (SIB) first brought the problem of mis-selling of these pensions to public notice. SIB, and later the Personal Investment Authority (PIA), issued guidance to insurance companies and others on conducting a proactive review of the sales of these products.

By spring 1997, the number of cases actually settled was very low, and the regulators and subsequently the Government increased the pressure on the companies concerned. The result was the setting of targets, the 'naming and shaming' of the companies most heavily involved by Treasury ministers and, more recently, disciplinary action. The number of cases settled accelerated and by the end of September 1997 64 per cent of cases identified as 'priority one' had been dealt with. Progress is now being made but the Government and regulators continue to monitor the situation.

PREMIUM INCOME FOR WORLD-WIDE LONG-TERM INSURANCE BUSINESS

	1996 £m	1997 £m
Ordinary Branch		
Business written in UK		
Annual premiums		
Life	11,976	12,571
Annuities	52	65
Pensions	10,283	11,241
Single premiums		
Life	12,545	13,811
Annuities	789	342
Pensions	15,389	20,423
Income protection	54	68
Business written overseas		
Annual premiums	5,495	8,214
Single premiums	8,214	9,293
Industrial Business	1,145	1,052
Total	66,544	74,807

PAYMENTS TO POLICYHOLDERS

	1996 £m	1997 £m
Payments to UK policyholders	38,298	46,126
Payments to overseas policyholders	8,957	10,035
Total	47,255	56,161

INVESTMENTS OF INSURANCE COMPANIES 1997

Investment of funds	Long-term business £m	General business £m
Index-linked British Government securities	16,570	1,770
Non-index-linked British Government securities	86,670	12,921
Other UK public sector debt securities	4,493	527
Overseas government, provincial and municipal securities	25,837	15,539
Debentures, loan shares, preference and guaranteed stocks and shares		
UK	48,035	6,234
Overseas	36,353	4,427
Ordinary stocks and shares		
UK	272,536	14,358
Overseas	68,850	8,216
Unit trusts		
Equities	47,080	1,269
Fixed interest	3,108	322
Loans secured on property	11,189	2,016
Real property and ground rents	41,851	3,854
Other invested assets	49,193	12,703
Total invested assets	711,766	84,156
Net current assets	4,028	12,888
Total	707,738	97,044
Net investment income	35,840	4,777

INDIVIDUAL PENSIONS: NEW BUSINESS 1996–7

	Annual premium policies		Single premium policies	
	No. new policies	New premiums £m	No. new policies	New premiums £m
1996				
1st quarter	210,000	245	71,000	1,035
2nd quarter	238,000	300	96,000	1,380
3rd quarter	203,000	257	67,000	922
4th quarter	213,000	279	63,000	993
1997				
1st quarter	248,000	281	75,000	1,180
2nd quarter	310,000	375	120,000	1,818
3rd quarter	266,000	327	85,000	1,248
4th quarter	236,000	308	65,000	1,112

DIRECTORY OF INSURANCE COMPANIES

Classes of insurance undertaken
G   General
L   Life
M   Marine
Re   Reinsurance

Group membership
(CGU)   Commercial Union/General Accident
(ES)   Eagle Star
(G)   Guardian
(NU)   Norwich Union
(RSA)   Royal and SunAlliance

Nature of business	*Name of company*	*Head Office address*
GLM Re	AGF	500 Avebury Boulevard, Milton Keynes MK9 2LA
L	Abbey Life	100 Holdenhurst Road, Bournemouth BH8 8AL
L	AIG Life (UK)	Alico House, 22 Addiscombe Road, Croydon CR9 5AZ
GM Re	Albion	Hill Place House, 55 High Street, Wimbledon SW19 5BA
L	Alico	Alico House, 22 Addiscombe Road, Croydon CR9 5AZ
GLM	Alliance Assurance (RSA)	1 Bartholomew Lane, London EC2N 2AB
L	Allied Dunbar	Allied Dunbar Centre, Swindon SN1 1EL
G	Ansvar	31 St Leonards Road, Eastbourne BN21 3UR
GM	Atlas (G)	Royal Exchange, London EC3V 3LS
L	Australian Mutual Provident	AMP House, Dingwall Road, Croydon CR9 2AP
L	Axa Equity and Law Life	Amersham Road, High Wycombe HP13 5AL
G	Axa Provincial	107 Cheapside, London EC2V 6DU
G	Baptist	1 Merchant Street, London E3 4LY
L	Barclays Life	9 Fleetway House, 25 Farringdon Street, London EC4A 4JA
G Re	Black Sea and Baltic	65 Fenchurch Street, London EC3M 4EV
M	Bradford (RSA)	Bowling Mill, Dean Clough, Halifax HX3 5WA
L	Britannia Life	Britannia Court, 50 Bothwell Street, Glasgow G2 6HR
GL	Britannic Assurance	1 Wythall Green Way, Wythall, Birmingham B47 6WG
M	British and Foreign Marine (RSA)	New Hall Place, Liverpool
GLM	British Equitable (G)	Royal Exchange, London EC3V 3LS
L	British Life Office	Reliance House, Mount Ephraim, Tunbridge Wells, Kent TN4 8BL
G	British Oak (G)	Royal Exchange, London EC3V 3LS
L	Caledonian (G)	Royal Exchange, London EC3V 3LS
GM	Cambrian (G)	Royal Exchange, London EC3V 3LS
L	Canada Life	Canada Life House, Potters Bar, Herts EN6 5BA
GM	Car and General (G)	Royal Exchange, London EC3V 3LS
L	Century Life	Century House, 5 Old Bailey, London EC4M 7BA
GL	CIGNA	PO Box 42, Greenock PA15 1AB
L	Clerical, Medical Group	Narrow Plain, Bristol BS2 0JH
L	Colonial Mutual	Colonial Mutual House, Chatham Maritime, Kent ME14 4YY
GLM Re	Commercial Union (CGU)	St Helen's, 1 Undershaft, London EC3P 3DQ
L	Commercial Union Life (CGU)	St Helen's, 1 Undershaft, London EC3P 3DQ
L	Confederation Life	Lytton Way, Stevenage, Herts SG1 1AN
G	Congregational and General	Currer House, Currer Street, Bradford BD1 5BA
GLM Re	Co-operative	Miller Street, Manchester M60 0AL
GLM Re	Cornhill	57 Ladymead, Guildford GU1 1DB
GL	Direct Line Insurance	3 Edridge Road, Croydon CR9 1AG
GLM Re	Eagle Star (ES)	60 St Mary Axe, London EC3A 8JQ
GL Re	Ecclesiastical	Beaufort House, Brunswick Road, Gloucester GL1 1JZ
G	Equine and Livestock	PO Box 100, Ouseburn, York YO5 9SZ
L	Equitable Life	Walton Street, Aylesbury HP21 7QW
L	Friends' Provident	Pixham End, Pixham Lane, Dorking, Surrey RH4 1QA
GM Re	Gan	Gan House, 12 Arthur Street, London EC4R 9BT
GM Re	General Accident (CGU)	Pitheavlis, Perth PH2 0NH
L	General Accident Life (CGU)	2 Rougier Street, York YO1 1HR
G	Gresham Fire and Accident	11 Queen Victoria Street, London EC4N 4XP
GM	Guarantee Society (CGU)	42–47 Minories, London EC3N 1BX
L	Guardian Insurance (G)	Civic Drive, Ipswich IP1 2AN
GLM Re	Guardian Royal Exchange (G)	Civic Drive, Ipswich IP1 2AN
GLM Re	Hibernian	Haddington Road, Dublin 4
G	Hiscox Insurance Co.	52 Leadenhall Street, London EC3A 2BJ
GL	Ideal	Pitmaston, Moseley, Birmingham B13 8NG
L	Irish Life	Irish Life Centre, Victoria Street, St Albans AL1 5TS
GF	Iron Trades	Iron Trades House, 21–24 Grosvenor Place, London SW1X 7JA
GM	ITT London and Edinburgh	The Warren, Worthing, W. Sussex BN14 9QD
GLM Re	Legal and General	Temple Court, 11 Queen Victoria Street, London EC4N 4TP

Nature of business	Name of company	Head Office address
GF	Licenses and General (G)	Royal Exchange, London EC3V 3LS
L	Lincoln	The Quays, 101–105 Oxford Road, Uxbridge UB8 1LZ
GM	Liverpool Marine and General (RSA)	1 Bartholomew Lane, London EC2N 2AB
GL	Liverpool Victoria Friendly	135 Poole Road, Bournemouth BH4 9BG
GM	Local Government Guarantee (G)	Royal Exchange, London EC3V 3LS
GM Re	Lombard General	Lombard House, 182 High Street, Tonbridge, Kent TN9 1BY
L	London and Manchester	Winslade Park, Exeter EX5 1DS
L	M and G Assurance	Three Quays, Tower Hill, London EC3R 6BQ
L	Manulife	St George's Way, Stevenage SG1 1HP
M	Marine (RSA)	1 Cornhill, London EC3V 3QR
M Re	Maritime (NU)	PO Box 6, Surrey Street, Norwich NR1 3NS
L	Medical, Sickness, Annuity and Life	Pynes Hill House, Rydon Lane, Exeter EX2 5SP
Re	Mercantile and General	Moorfields House, Moorfields, London EC4R 9BJ
L	Merchant Investors	St Bartholomew's House, Lewins Mead, Bristol BS1 2NH
G Re	Methodist	Brazennose House, Brazennose Street, Manchester M2 5AS
L	MGM Insurance	MGM House, Heene Road, Worthing BN11 2DY
G	Motor Union (G)	Royal Exchange, London EC3V 3LS
L	National Mutual Life	The Priory, Hitchin, Herts SG5 2DW
GM	Navigators and General (ES)	Lanchester House, Trafalgar Place, Trafalgar Street, Brighton BN1 4DA
GL Re	NFU Avon	Tiddington Road, Stratford-upon-Avon CV37 7BJ
G	NIG Skandia	Crown House, 145 City Road, London EC1V 1LP
L	NM Financial Management	Enterprise House, Isambard Brunel Road, Portsmouth PO1 2AW
GM	Norwich Union Fire	PO Box 6, Surrey Street, Norwich NR1 3NS
L	Norwich Union Life	8 Surrey Street, Norwich NR1 3NG
L	NPI	NPI House, Tunbridge Wells, Kent TN1 2UE
GLM Re	Pearl	The Pearl Centre, Lynchwood, Peterborough PE2 6FY
L Sickness	Permanent	Pynes Hill House, Rydon Lane, Exeter EX2 5SP
GLM	Phoenix (RSA)	1 Bartholomew Lane, London EC2N 2AB
L	Property Growth (RSA)	Phoenix House, Redcliff Hill, Bristol BS1 6SX
GLM Re	Prudential	142 Holborn Bars, London EC1N 2NH
GL	Refuge	Refuge House, Alderley Road, Wilmslow, Cheshire SK9 1PF
GM	Reliance Marine (G)	Royal Exchange, London EC3V 3LS
L	Reliance Mutual	Reliance House, Mount Ephraim, Tunbridge Wells, Kent TN4 8BL
G	Road Transport and General (CGU)	Pitheavlis, Perth PH2 0NH
G	Royal Exchange (G)	Royal Exchange, London EC3V 3LS
L	Royal Heritage Life (RSA)	Royal Insurance House, Business Park, Peterborough PE2 6GG
GLM Re	Royal and SunAlliance (RSA)	1 Bartholomew Lane, London EC2N 2AB
Engineering	Royal and SunAlliance Engineering (RSA)	17 York Street, Manchester M2 3RS
L	Royal Liver	Royal Liver Building, Pier Head, Liverpool L3 1HT
GL	Royal London	Royal London House, Middleborough, Colchester CO1 1RA
L	Royal National Pension Fund for Nurses	Burdett House, 15 Buckingham Street, Strand, London WC2N 6ED
F	Salvation Army	117–121 Judd Street, London WC1H 9NN
L	Save and Prosper	Hexagon House, 28 Western Road, Romford RM1 3LB
L	Scottish Amicable	Craigforth, PO Box 25, Stirling FK9 4UE
Engineering	Scottish Boiler (CGU)	PO Box 131, 825 Wilmslow Road, Didsbury, Manchester M20 8GS
L	Scottish Equitable	28 St Andrew Square, Edinburgh EH2 2QZ
L	Scottish Friendly	16 Blythswood Square, Glasgow G2 6HJ
M	Scottish General (CGU)	PO Box 896, 103 Westerhill Road, Bishopbriggs, Glasgow G64 2QX
L	Scottish Legal Life	95 Bothwell Street, Glasgow G2 7HY
L	Scottish Life	19 St Andrew Square, Edinburgh EH2 1YE
L	Scottish Mutual	301 St Vincent Street, Glasgow G2 5HN
L	Scottish Provident Institution	6 St Andrew Square, Edinburgh EH2 2YA
GLM	Scottish Union and National (NU)	Surrey Street, Norwich NR1 3NS
L	Scottish Widows'	15 Dalkeith Road, Edinburgh EH16 5BU
GM	Sea (RSA)	1 Bartholomew Lane, London EC2N 2AB
L	Stalwart Assurance	Stalwart House, Station Road, Dorking, Surrey RH4 1HL
L	Standard Life	30 Lothian Road, Edinburgh EH1 2DH
GM	State Assurance (G)	Royal Exchange, London EC3V 3LS
GLM	Sun Alliance (RSA)	1 Bartholomew Lane, London EC2N 2AB
GM	Sun Insurance Office (RSA)	1 Bartholomew Lane, London EC2N 2AB
L	Sun Life Assurance	Sun Life Centre, PO Box 1810, Bristol BS99 5SN

Nature of business	*Name of company*	*Head Office address*
L Re	Sun Life of Canada	Basing View, Basingstoke RG21 2DZ
L	Swiss Life	Swiss Life House, South Park, Sevenoaks TN13 1BG
GL	Teacher's Assurance	Tringham House, Wessex Fields, Deansleigh Road, Bournemouth BH7 7DT
L	Tunstall Assurance	Station Chambers, The Boulevard, Tunstall, Stoke-on-Trent ST6 6DU
M	Ulster Marine (G)	Pitheavlis, Perth PH2 0NH
GL	UIA Insurance	Kings Court, London Road, Stevenage SG1 2TP
GM	Union Insurance Society of Canton (G)	Royal Exchange, London EC3V 3LS
GL	United Friendly	42 Southwark Bridge Road, London SE1 9HE
GL Re	Wesleyan Assurance	Colmore Circus, Birmingham B4 6AR
L	Windsor Life	Windsor House, Telford TF3 4NB
L	Winterthur Life	Winterthur Way, Basingstoke RG21 6SZ
GM Re	Zurich	Zurich House, Stanhope Road, Portsmouth PO1 1DU
L	Zurich Life	3000 Parkway, Whiteley, Fareham PO15 7JY

The London Stock Exchange

The London Stock Exchange Ltd serves the needs of government, industry and investors by providing facilities for raising capital and a central market-place for securities trading. This market-place covers government stocks (called gilts), UK and overseas company shares (called equities and fixed interest stocks), and traditional options.

PRIMARY MARKETS

The Exchange enables companies to raise capital for development and growth through the issue of securities. For a company entering the market for the first time there is a choice of Exchange markets, depending upon the size, history and requirements of the company. The first is the Official List, the main market, which exists for well-established companies; these must comply with stringent criteria relating to all aspects of their operations. At present, companies coming to this market require a minimum market capitalization of £700,000 and a three-year trading record with a minimum of 25 per cent of the shares held in public hands. The Alternative Investment Market (AIM) began trading in June 1995. It enables small, young and growing companies to raise capital, widen their investor base and have their shares traded on a regulated market without the expense of a full Exchange listing.

Once admitted to the Exchange, all companies are obliged to keep their shareholders informed of their progress, making announcements of a price-sensitive nature through the Exchange's company announcements department.

At the end of 1997 there were 2,157 UK companies listed on the London Stock Exchange; their equity capital had a total market value of £1,251,400 million. Also, 526 foreign companies were listed, with a total equity market value of £2,429,100 million. By the end of 1997 the Alternative Investment Market had attracted 310 companies, with a total capitalization of £5,704 million.

UK equity turnover in 1997 was £1,012,534.8 million, with an average 52,752 bargains and £4,002.11 million value a day. Foreign equity turnover in 1997 totalled £1,443,200 million.

BIG BANG

During 1986 the London Stock Exchange went through the greatest period of change in its 200-year history. In March 1986 it opened its doors for the first time to overseas and corporate membership of the Exchange, allowing banks, insurance companies and overseas securities houses to become members of the Exchange and to buy existing member firms. On 27 October 1986, three major reforms took place, changes which became known as 'Big Bang':

- the abolition of scales of minimum commissions, allowing clients to negotiate freely with their brokers about the charge for their services
- the abolition of the separation of member firms into brokers and jobbers: firms are now broker/dealers, able to act as agents on behalf of clients; to act as principals buying and selling shares for their own account; and to become registered market makers, making continuous buying and selling prices in specific securities
- the introduction of the Stock Exchange automated quotations (SEAQ) system

Since the introduction of SEAQ, dealing in stocks and shares takes place via the telephone in the firms' own dealing rooms, rather than face to face on the floor of the Exchange, or can be done through the Stock Exchange Electronic Trading Service (SETS), launched in 1997. The new systems also provide increased investor protection. All deals taking place via the Exchange's SEAQ system are recorded on a database which can be used to resolve disputes or to carry out investigations.

Members of the London Stock Exchange buy and sell shares on behalf of the public, as well as institutions such as pension funds or insurance companies. In return for transacting the deal, the broker will charge a commission, which is usually based upon the value of the transaction. The market makers, or wholesalers, in each security do not charge a commission for their services, but will quote the broker two prices, a price at which they will buy and a price at which they will sell. It is the middle of these two prices which is published in lists of Stock Exchange prices in newspapers.

REGULATORY BODIES

The London Stock Exchange Ltd and the Securities and Futures Authority are the two regulatory bodies (*see* pages 634–5). They were formed under the provisions of the Financial Services Act 1986, which requires investment businesses to be authorized and regulated by a self-regulating organization (SRO), of which the Securities and Futures Authority is one. The Act also requires business to be conducted through a recognized investment exchange (RIE). The London Stock Exchange is an RIE, regulating three main markets: UK equities, international equities and gilts. The changes to the financial regulatory system which are to be introduced in the next few years will affect the Stock Exchange's role as a regulatory body.

THE GOVERNING BOARD

The London Stock Exchange has its headquarters in London, and representative offices around the UK. At present there are about 273 member firms.

The governing board is responsible for overall policy and the strategic direction of the Exchange. The board consists of representatives drawn from listed companies, investors and other major users, elected at the annual general meeting, and the Government Broker, the Chief Executive and up to five senior executives of the Stock Exchange.

LONDON STOCK EXCHANGE LTD, Old Broad Street, London EC2N 1HP. Tel: 0171-797 1000
Chairman, J. Kemp-Welch
Chief Executive, G. Casey
Government Broker, I. Plenderleith (*Deputy Chairman*)
Other Board members, G. Allen, CBE; G. Allen; J. Bond; Ms C. Dann; M. Marks; P. Meinertzhagen; S. Robertson; I. Salter; H. Sants; N. Sherlock; M. Wheatley

Financial Services Regulation

In May 1997 the Government announced plans to establish a new statutory single financial regulator responsible for the supervision of banks, building societies, insurance companies, investment firms and markets. It will replace the current supervisory framework, established under a number of different statutes. The new regulator is the Financial Services Authority (FSA), which in corporate and legal terms is the Securities and Investments Board (SIB) renamed.

The FSA will acquire its full range of responsibilties in two stages. The first stage was completed on 1 June 1998 when the FSA acquired responsibility, under the Bank of England Act 1998, for supervising banks, listed money market institutions and related clearing houses; the Bank of England had previously exercised this responsibility. The second stage will follow the enactment of the Financial Services and Markets Bill, published in draft form for consultation in July 1998. When this bill is passed by Parliament, a date commonly referred to as N2, the FSA will acquire its full range of powers and will take on responsibility for the regulation and registration functions of the following regulators and supervisors:

SELF-REGULATING ORGANIZATIONS

INVESTMENT MANAGEMENT REGULATORY
ORGANIZATION (IMRO), 5th Floor, Lloyd's
Chambers, Portsoken Street, London EI 8BT. Tel: 0171-390 5000
PERSONAL INVESTMENT AUTHORITY (PIA), 1 Canada
Square, Canary Wharf, London E14 5AZ. Tel: 0171-538 8860
SECURITIES AND FUTURES AUTHORITY LTD (SFA),
Cottons Centre, Cottons Lane, London SE1 2QB. Tel: 0171-378 9000

OTHERS

BUILDING SOCIETIES COMMISSION, Victory House,
30–34 Kingsway, London WC2B 6ES. Tel: 0171-663 5000
FRIENDLY SOCIETIES COMMISSION, Victory House,
30–34 Kingsway, London WC2B 6ES. Tel: 0171-663 5000
INSURANCE DIRECTORATE OF HM TREASURY (including
Lloyd's of London), 1 Victoria Street, London SWIH
0ET. Tel: 0171-215 5000
REGISTRY OF FRIENDLY SOCIETIES, Victory House,
30–34 Kingsway, London WC2B 6ES. Tel: 0171-663 5000

It is intended that all the above organizations will be based at the FSA's offices in Canary Wharf from early 1999.

The FSA also supervises the recognized professional bodies and recognized clearing houses, ensuring that they continue to fulfil their regulatory responsibilities.

Until N2, the above organizations will continue to have legal responsibility for regulating their firms under the existing statutory or contractual arrangements. However, in order to facilitate speedy operational integration, the staff of the SROs transferred contracts of employment to the FSA on 1 June 1998 and now operate under a single management structure It is planned that staff currently employed by the Insurance Directorate of HM Treasury and by the Registry of Friendly Societies will similarly transfer in early 1999. Detailed contracts have been put in place providing the services of the FSA staff to these bodies to enable them to carry out their work.

The Government has said that the FSA will have statutory objectives in four main areas:
– maintaining confidence in the UK financial system
– promoting public understanding of the financial system, including awareness of the benefits and risks associated with different kinds of investment or other financial dealing
– securing the appropriate degree of protection for consumers, having regard to the differing degrees of risk involved in different kinds of investment or other transaction, the differing degrees of experience and expertise which different consumers may have, and the general principle that consumers should take responsibility for their decisions
– reducing the extent to which it is possible for a business carried out by a regulated person to be used for a purpose connected with financial crime

It is the Government's intention that the FSA should pursue its objectives in a way which is efficient and economic; facilitates innovation in financial services; and takes account of the international nature of financial regulation and financial services business.

CENTRAL REGISTER/PUBLIC ENQUIRIES

The FSA maintains the Central Register of all firms who are authorized to carry on investment business. The entry for each firm gives its name, address and telephone number; a reference number; its authorization status; states which organization regulates it; and whether it can handle client money.
PUBLIC ENQUIRIES OFFICE: 0845-606 1234

INVESTORS COMPENSATION SCHEME

The Investors Compensation Scheme is part of the overall investor protection system. This comes into play when a regulated investment firm becomes insolvent owing money to private investors. It is funded by a levy on all regulated firms. The maximum compensation that the scheme can pay to an investor is £48,000.

DEPOSIT PROTECTION SCHEME

This scheme provides investors with protection when a bank becomes insolvent. It provides protection for depositors of up to a maximum compensation payment of £18,000 (or ECU 20,000 if greater).

FINANCIAL SERVICES AUTHORITY, 25 The North
Colonnade, Canary Wharf, London E14 5HS. Tel: 0171-676 1000. Web: http://www.fsa.gov.uk. *Chairman*, H. Davies

AUTHORIZED DEPOSIT-TAKING INSTUTITIONS

For deposit-taking institutions, *see* Banking

RECOGNIZED PROFESSIONAL BODIES

The FSA is empowered to recognize professional bodies (RPBs) who, as a result, can authorize their members to conduct investment business. Such business must not form the whole or main part of the total business undertaken by the firm.

INSTITUTE OF CHARTERED ACCOUNTANTS IN ENGLAND
AND WALES, Chartered Accountants' Hall, PO Box 433,
Moorgate Place, London EC2P 2BJ. Tel: 0171-920 8100
INSTITUTE OF CHARTERED ACCOUNTANTS OF
SCOTLAND, 27 Queen Street, Edinburgh EH2 1LA. Tel: 0131-225 5673
THE ULSTER SOCIETY OF THE INSTITUTE OF
CHARTERED ACCOUNTANTS IN IRELAND, 11 Donegall
Square South, Belfast BT1 5JE. Tel: 01232-321600

ASSOCIATION OF CHARTERED CERTIFIED
ACCOUNTANTS, 29 Lincoln's Inn Fields, London WC2A
3EE. Tel: 0171-242 6855
INSTITUTE OF ACTUARIES, Staple Inn Hall, High
Holborn, London WC1V 7QJ. Tel: 0171-242 0106
THE LAW SOCIETY, 113 Chancery Lane, London WC2A
1PL. Tel: 0171-242 1222
LAW SOCIETY OF NORTHERN IRELAND, Law Society
House, 98 Victoria Street, Belfast BT1 3JZ. Tel: 01232-
231614
LAW SOCIETY OF SCOTLAND, Law Society's Hall, 26
Drumsheugh Gardens, Edinburgh EH3 7YR. Tel: 0131-
226 7411

RECOGNIZED INVESTMENT EXCHANGES

Investment exchanges are exempt from needing authorization under the Financial Services Act. To be a recognized
investment exchange (RIE), it must fulfil the following
requirements: adequate financial resources; proper conduct of business rules; a proper market in its products;
procedures for recording transactions; effective monitoring and enforcement of rules; proper arrangements for the
clearing and performance of contracts.

FINANCIAL NETWORKS PLC (TRADEPOINT), 35 King
Street, London WC2E 8JD. Tel: 0171-240 8000
INTERNATIONAL PETROLEUM EXCHANGE (IPE),
International House, 1 St Katharine's Way, London E1
9UN. Tel: 0171-481 0643
LONDON STOCK EXCHANGE (LSE), Old Broad Street,
London EC2N 1HP. Tel: 0171-797 1000
LONDON INTERNATIONAL FINANCIAL FUTURES AND
OPTIONS EXCHANGE (LIFFE), Cannon Bridge,
London EC4R 3XX. Tel: 0171-623 0444
LONDON METAL EXCHANGE LTD (LME), 56 Leadenhall
Street, London EC3A 2BJ. Tel: 0171-264 5555
THE LONDON SECURITIES AND DERIVATIVES
EXCHANGE LTD (OMLX), Milestone House, 107
Cannon Street, London EC4N 5AD. Tel: 0171-283 0678

Following the implementation of the EC Investment
Services Directive, recognition by the UK authorities is
no longer required by exchanges within the European
Economic Area (with certain exceptions).

RECOGNIZED CLEARING HOUSES

A recognized clearing house (RCH) must satisfy similar
criteria to those which apply to be an RIE. There are two
RCHs which act as clearing houses for some of the above
RIEs. In addition, Crest also operates a system for
dematerialized settlement of share transactions.

CRESTCO LTD, 10th Floor, Trinity Tower, 9 Thomas
More Street, London E1 9YN. Tel: 0171-459 3000
LONDON CLEARING HOUSE LTD (LCH), Roman Wall
House, 1–2 Crutched Friars, London EC3N 2AN. Tel:
0171-265 2000

DESIGNATED INVESTMENT EXCHANGES

The FSA has drawn up a list of 52 designated overseas
investment exchanges. These are deemed to provide
protection for investors of an equivalent standard to that
provided by RIEs.

OMBUDSMAN SCHEMES

Independent ombudsman schemes have been set up for
banks, building societies, insurance companies, financial
institutions and independent financial advisers. They
provide an independent and impartial method of resolving

disputes that arise between a company and a customer. In
most ombudsman schemes there is a council which
appoints and supervises the Ombudsman. The Ombudsman Council is composed of people representing public
and consumer interests and member companies. The
schemes are funded in various ways: annual subscription
from member companies, a levy on member companies
according to the size of their assets, a charge for each
complaint handled against a particular company, or a
combination of these.

The Investment Ombudsman is responsible for resolving disputes that arise between a customer and a
company regulated by IMRO. The Personal Investment
Authority (PIA) Ombudsman is primarily responsible for
resolving complaints against PIA members about personal
investments.

The Pensions Ombudsman is appointed and operates
under the Pension Schemes Act 1993 as amended by the
Pensions Act 1995; he is responsible to Parliament. He
investigates and decides complaints and disputes concerning occupational pension schemes, primarily alleged
maladministration by the persons responsible for managing an occupational pension scheme. Personal pension
complaints are normally dealt with only if outside the
jurisdiction of the Personal Investment Authority.

THE OFFICE OF THE BANKING OMBUDSMAN, 70 Gray's
Inn Road, London WC1X 8NB. Tel: 0171-404 9944.
Banking Ombudsman, D. Thomas
THE OFFICE OF THE BUILDING SOCIETIES OMBUDSMAN,
Millbank Tower, Millbank, London SW1P 4XS. Tel:
0171-931 0044. *Building Societies Ombudsman*, B. Murphy
THE INSURANCE OMBUDSMAN BUREAU, City Gate One,
135 Park Street, London SE1 9EA. Tel: 0171-928 4488.
Insurance Ombudsman, W. Merricks
THE OFFICE OF THE INVESTMENT OMBUDSMAN, 6
Frederick's Place, London EC2R 8BT. Tel: 0171-796
3065. *Investment Ombudsman*, P. Dean, CBE
THE PENSIONS OMBUDSMAN, 6th Floor, 11 Belgrave
Road, London SW1V 1RB. Tel: 0171-834 9144. *Pensions
Ombudsman*, Dr J. T. Farrand
THE PIA OMBUDSMAN BUREAU, Hertsmere House,
Hertsmere Road, London E14 4AB. Tel: 0171-216 0016.
Principal Ombudsman, A. J. Holland

THE TAKEOVER PANEL

The Takeover Panel is a non-statutory body that operates
the City code on take-overs and mergers. Its principal
objective is to ensure equality of treatment, and fair
opportunity for all shareholders to consider on its merits an
offer that would result in the change of control of a
company.

The chairman, deputy chairmen and three lay members
of the panel are appointed by the Bank of England. The
remainder are representatives of the banking, insurance,
investment, pension fund and accountancy professional
bodies, the CBI, IMRO and the Stock Exchange.

THE TAKEOVER PANEL, PO Box 226, The Stock
Exchange Building, London, EC2P 2JX. Tel: 0171-382
9026. *Chairman*, Sir David Calcutt, QC

Stamp Duties

Stamp duty is a tax on documents. There are a number of separate duties, under different heads of charge.

A stampable instrument may, subject to exceptions, be stamped without penalty if presented for stamping within 30 days after its date of first execution. Where wholly executed abroad, the period begins to run from the date of arrival in the UK.

Instruments presented after the proper time (subject to special provisions in some cases and subject to the Commissioner's power to mitigate) are subject to a penalty equal to the unpaid duty (and interest thereon if duty exceeds £10) plus £10.

AGREEMENT FOR SALE OF PROPERTY

Charged with *ad valorem* duty as if an actual conveyance on sale, with certain exceptions, e.g. agreements for the sale of land, stocks and shares, goods, wares or merchandise, or a ship (*see* S. 59 (1), Stamp Act 1891). If *ad valorem* duty is paid on an agreement in accordance with this provision, the subsequent conveyance or transfer is not chargeable with any *ad valorem* duty and the Commissioners will upon application either place a denoting stamp on such conveyance or transfer or will transfer the *ad valorem* duty thereto. Further, if such an agreement is rescinded, not performed, etc., the Commissioners will return the *ad valorem* duty paid.

BEARER INSTRUMENT

Inland bearer instrument, 1.5 per cent
Overseas bearer instrument, 1.5 per cent

CONVEYANCE OR TRANSFER ON SALE

(In the case of a Voluntary Disposition, *see* below)

Conveyance or transfer on sale of any property (except stock or marketable securities), where the conveyance or transfer contains a certificate of value certifying that the transaction does not form part of a larger transaction or a series of transactions in respect of which the aggregate amount or value of the consideration exceeds £60,000, *nil*
Value of £60,001–£250,000 (for every £100 or fraction of £100), £1
Value of £250,001–£500,000 (for every £100 or fraction of £100), £2
Value exceeds £500,000 (for every £100 or fraction of £100), £3

Conveyances to charities are exempt from duty under this head provided the instrument is stamped with a denoting stamp.

CONVEYANCE OR TRANSFER OF ANY OTHER KIND

Fixed duty, 50p

However, under the Stamp Duty (Exempt Instruments) Regulations 1987, instruments which would otherwise fall under this head are exempt from stamp duty provided that the document is duly certified. The certificate must contain a sufficient description of the category into which the instrument falls, and must be signed by the transferor, his solicitor or agent: 'I/We hereby certify that this instrument falls within category ... in the Schedule to the Stamp Duty (Exempt Instruments) Regulations 1987.'

COVENANT, for original creation and sale of any annuity, *see* CONVEYANCE

DECLARATION OF TRUST

Not being a will or settlement, 50p

DUPLICATE OR COUNTERPART

Same duty as original, but not to exceed 50p

LEASES (INCLUDING AGREEMENTS FOR LEASES)

Lease or tack for any definite term less than a year of any furnished dwelling-house or apartments where the rent for such term exceeds £500, £1

Of any lands, tenements, etc., in consideration of any rent, according to the following:

| Annual rent not exceeding | † Term not exceeding | | | Exceeding |
	7 yrs	35 yrs	100 yrs	100 yrs
£	£ p	£ p	£ p	£ p
5	nil	0.10	0.60	1.20
10	nil	0.20	1.20	2.40
15	nil	0.30	1.80	3.60
20	nil	0.40	2.40	4.80
25	nil	0.50	3.00	6.00
50	nil	1.00	6.00	12.00
75	nil	1.50	9.00	18.00
100	nil	2.00	12.00	24.00
150	nil	3.00	18.00	36.00
200	nil	4.00	24.00	48.00
250	nil	5.00	30.00	60.00
300	nil	6.00	36.00	72.00
350	nil	7.00	42.00	84.00
400	nil	8.00	48.00	96.00
450	nil	9.00	54.00	108.00
500	nil	10.00	60.00	120.00
Exceeding £500, for every £50 or fraction thereof	0.50	1.00	6.00	12.00

†If the term is indefinite the same duty is payable as if the term did not exceed seven years.

Where a consideration other than rent is payable, the same rule applies where the consideration does not exceed £60,000 as under conveyance or transfer on sale (except stock or marketable securities), provided that any rent payable does not exceed £600 a year and a certificate of value is included in the conveyance or transfer.

Where a lease is granted pursuant to a prior agreement for lease, the agreement itself is liable to duty. Credit for any duty paid on the agreement will be given against the duty payable on the lease and the Commissioners will place a denoting stamp on the lease. Where there is no prior agreement for lease, the lease must contain a certificate that it has not been made in pursuance of an agreement.

Leases to charities are exempt from duty under this head provided the instrument is stamped with a denoting stamp.

MORTGAGES, exempt

TRANSFER OF STOCK AND SHARES BY SALE, 0.5 per cent

UNIT TRUST INSTRUMENT

Unit Trust Instrument duty was abolished in the Finance Act 1988. Transfer of property to a unit trust or agreement to transfer units is generally subject to Conveyance on Sale duty.

By the Finance Act 1989, the transfer of units in certain authorized unit trusts is no longer subject to duty.

VOLUNTARY DISPOSITION, *inter vivos*

Fixed duty, 50p

However, under the Stamp Duty (Exempt Intruments) Regulations 1987, instruments which would otherwise fall under this head are exempt from stamp duty provided that the document is certified as falling within category L in the schedule to the Regulations. *See* Conveyance or Transfer of Any Other Kind, above.

Taxation

INCOME TAX

Income tax is charged on the income of individuals for a year of assessment commencing on 6 April and ending on the following 5 April. The rates of tax and the calculation of liability frequently differ from one year of assessment to another. The following information is confined to the year of assessment 1998–9, ending on 5 April 1999 and has only limited application to earlier years. However, a number of changes which will come into effect subsequently are also noted.

Liability to income tax is determined by establishing the taxable income for a year of assessment. The taxable income will be reduced by an individual's personal allowance and perhaps by other allowances or reliefs. The first £4,300 of taxable income remaining is assessable to income tax at the lower rate of 20 per cent. Disregarding income from 'savings', the next £22,800 is taxed at the basic rate of 23 per cent. Should any excess over £27,100 (£4,300 plus £22,800) remain, this will be taxable at the higher rate of 40 per cent.

Company dividends, interest and other forms of 'savings income' do not incur liability at the basic rate of 23 per cent. Income of this nature is taxable at 20 per cent unless the individual's taxable income exceeds £27,100, when liability may arise at 40 per cent on the excess.

Certain allowances and reliefs are given at the rate of 15 or 20 per cent as a deduction from income tax payable. These adjustments can only be made once the full amount of tax otherwise due has been calculated.

The tables below show the income tax payable for 1998–9 by an individual on the amount of income speci-fied, after deducting the personal allowance and providing relief for the married couple's allowance, where appropriate. Persons over the age of 74 years may pay less tax, unless their income is substantial. Some taxpayers may be entitled to further allowances and reliefs which reduce the tax payable below the amount shown by the tables. These tables have been structured on the assumption that none of the income arises from savings. Should income of this nature be received, less tax may be due.

Trustees administering settled property and personal representatives dealing with the estate of a deceased person are chargeable to income tax at the basic rate of 23 per cent. Where trustees retain discretionary powers or income is accumulated, liability may be increased to 34 per cent. Companies residing in the UK are not liable to income tax but suffer corporation tax on income, profits and gains (see pages 648–9).

The charge to income tax arises on all taxable income accruing from sources in the UK. Individuals who are resident in this territory may also become liable on income arising overseas. An individual is resident in the UK if he/she normally resides here. Persons not normally residing in the UK may be treated as resident if they visit this territory for periods which average three months or more through-out a period of years, or are present for at least 183 days in a particular year.

Income arising overseas will often incur liability to foreign taxation. If that income is also chargeable to UK income tax, excessive liability could arise. The UK has concluded double taxation agreements with many over-seas territories and these ensure that the same slice of income is not doubly taxed. In the absence of such an agreement, foreign tax suffered can usually be relieved when calculating liability to UK income tax.

SINGLE PERSONS AND MARRIED WOMEN					MARRIED MEN				
Income	Persons under 65		Persons 65 or over*		Income	Couples under 65		Couples 65 or over†	
£	Income tax £	Average rate %	Income tax £	Average rate %	£	Income tax £	Average rate %	Income tax £	Average rate %
4,500	61	1.4	—	—	4,500	—	—	—	—
5,000	161	3.2	—	—	5,000	—	—	—	—
6,000	361	6.0	118	2.0	6,000	76	1.3	—	—
7,000	561	8.0	318	4.5	7,000	276	3.9	—	—
8,000	761	9.5	518	6.5	8,000	476	6.0	22	0.3
9,000	976	10.8	718	8.0	9,000	691	7.7	222	2.5
10,000	1,206	12.1	927	9.3	10,000	921	9.2	431	4.3
12,000	1,666	13.9	1,387	11.6	12,000	1,381	11.5	891	7.4
14,000	2,126	15.2	1,847	13.2	14,000	1,841	13.2	1,351	9.7
16,000	2,586	16.2	2,307	14.4	16,000	2,301	14.4	1,811	11.3
18,000	3,046	16.9	2,974	16.5	18,000	2,761	15.3	2,478	13.8
20,000	3,506	17.5	3,506	17.5	20,000	3,221	16.1	3,113	15.6
25,000	4,656	18.6	4,656	18.6	25,000	4,371	17.5	4,371	17.5
30,000	5,806	19.4	5,806	19.4	30,000	5,521	18.4	5,521	18.4
40,000	9,586	24.0	9,586	24.0	40,000	9,301	23.3	9,301	23.3
50,000	13,586	27.2	13,586	27.2	50,000	13,301	26.6	13,301	26.6
60,000	17,586	29.3	17,586	29.3	60,000	17,301	28.8	17,301	28.8
100,000	33,586	33.6	33,586	33.6	100,000	33,301	33.3	33,301	33.3

* Persons aged 75 or over suffer less tax on income falling below £18,000 on this table

† Persons aged 75 or over suffer less tax on income falling below £25,000 on this table

Husband and Wife

A husband and wife are separately taxed, with each entitled to his or her personal allowance. A married man 'living with' his wife can obtain a married couple's allowance. In the absence of any claim, this allowance must be used by the husband but where any balance remains the surplus may be transferred to the wife. It is possible for a married woman to claim half the basic married couple's allowance as of right. In addition, the entire basic allowance may be claimed by the wife, if her husband so agrees.

Each spouse may obtain other allowances and reliefs where the required conditions are satisfied. Income must be accurately allocated between the couple by reference to the individual beneficially entitled to that income. Where income arises from jointly-held assets, this must be apportioned equally between husband and wife. However, in those cases where the beneficial interests in jointly-held assets are not equal, a special declaration can be made to apportion income by reference to the actual interests in that income.

Self-Assessment

Self-assessment, introduced on 6 April 1996, affects individuals, trustees and personal representatives. Central to self-assessment is the requirement to deliver a completed tax return. This must normally be submitted by 31 January following the end of the year of assessment to which the return relates. In addition to completing the return, the taxpayer must calculate the amount of income tax due. If a taxpayer wishes the Inland Revenue to calculate the tax due, the return must be forwarded to the Inland Revenue not later than the previous 30 September.

It is the responsibility of the taxpayer to submit payments of income tax on time. There are three different dates on which payments may fall due:

(a) an interim payment due on 31 January in the year of assessment itself
(b) a second interim payment due on the following 31 July
(c) a balancing payment, or possibly a repayment, on the following 31 January

The two interim payments will be based on tax payable for the previous year of assessment but liability may be reduced where income has fallen or even avoided entirely where the amounts are not substantial.

The impact of self-assessment is largely restricted to fewer than nine million persons receiving tax returns. These comprise self-employed individuals, those receiving income from the exploitation of land in the UK, company directors, others with investment income liable to higher rate income tax, trustees and personal representatives. Individuals whose only source of income is earnings from an employment where the PAYE system applies are largely unaffected. Separate tax return forms are issued to a husband and wife, where such forms are needed.

Failure to submit completed tax returns by 31 January or to discharge payments of income tax on time will incur a liability to interest, surcharges and penalties.

Income Taxable

Income tax is assessed under several Schedules. Each Schedule determines the extent of liability and establishes the amount to be included in taxable income. In some instances the actual income arising in a year of assessment will be charged to income tax for that year.

A different basis of assessment may be used for income taxable under Cases I to V of Schedule D. For many years income was assessed under these Cases on a 'preceding year' basis. This involved measuring income for the year by reference to that arising in a previous year or period but there were special rules where a new source was acquired or an existing source discontinued. The 'preceding year' basis has been replaced by a 'current year' basis of assessment. This requires that business profits assessable under Case I or Case II of Schedule D will be those for the accounting period ending in the year of assessment, with special adjustments for the opening and closing years of a business. Other income assessable under Schedule D will be that which arises in the actual year of assessment.

Following the withdrawal of income tax liability for most commercial woodlands in the UK, Schedule B no longer applies. Schedule C has also been withdrawn as the result of further changes. The contents of the remaining schedules are shown below.

Schedule A

Tax is charged under Schedule A on the annual profits or gains arising from any business carried on for the exploitation of land in the UK. As the result of recent amendments, the determination of profits from a Schedule A business adopts principles identical to those used when establishing the profits or gains of a trade, profession or vocation. Rents and other income from the exploitation of land are included in the calculation, and outgoings incurred wholly and exclusively for the purposes of the Schedule A business may be deducted from income.

Schedule A does not extend to profits from farming, market gardening or woodlands, nor does it apply to mineral rents and royalties. Premiums arising on the grant of a lease for a period not exceeding 50 years in duration are treated as rents. However, the amount of the taxable premium may be reduced by 2 per cent for each complete year, after the first 12 months, of the leasing period. Income arising from the provision of certain furnished holiday accommodation attracts a number of tax advantages not otherwise available for most income chargeable under Schedule A.

Receipts not exceeding £4,250 annually and accruing to an individual from letting property furnished in his or her own home are usually excluded from liability to income tax.

Schedule D

This Schedule is divided into six Cases:

Cases I and II – profits arising from trades, professions and vocations, including farming and market gardening. Capital expenditure incurred on assets used for business purposes will often produce an entitlement to capital allowances which reduce the profits chargeable. These profits may also be reduced by claims for loss relief and other matters.

Case III – interest on government stocks not taxed at source, interest on National Savings Bank deposits and discounts. Interest up to £70 on ordinary National Savings Bank deposits is exempt from income tax. The exemption applies to both husband and wife separately. Interest on National Savings Bank special investment accounts is not exempt. Interest and other items of savings income incur no liability at the basic rate.

Cases IV and V – interest from overseas securities, rents, dividends and all other income accruing outside the UK. Assessment is based on the full amount of income arising, whether remitted to the UK or retained overseas, but individuals who are either not domiciled in the UK or who are ordinarily resident overseas may be taxed on a remittance basis. Overseas pensions are taxable but the amount arising may be reduced by 10 per cent for assessment purposes. Dividends and interest on most overseas investments are chargeable only at the lower rate of 20 per cent and the higher rate of 40 per cent.

Case VI – sundry profits and annual receipts not assessed under any other Case or Schedule. These may include insurance commissions, post-cessation receipts and numerous other receipts specifically charged under Case VI.

Schedule E

All earnings from an office or employment are assessable under this Schedule. There are three Cases:

Case I – applies to all earnings of an individual resident and ordinarily resident in the UK.

Case II – of application where the individual is not resident or not ordinarily resident and extends to earnings for duties undertaken in the UK.

Case III – applies in rare situations to other earnings remitted to the UK.

When calculating liability under Case 1 or foreign earnings, deduction of 100 per cent was previously available where earnings arose from duties performed overseas. After 16 March 1998, this deduction is confined to certain seafarers.

A 'receipts basis' applies for determining the year of assessment in which earnings must be taxed. Where earnings are assessable under Case I or Case II, the date of receipt will comprise the earlier of the date of payment, or the date entitlement arises. In the case of company directors it is the earlier of these two dates, with the addition of the following three which establish the time of receipt: the date earnings are credited in the company's books; where earnings for a period are determined after the end of that period, the date of determination; where earnings for a period are determined in that period, the last day of that period.

The earnings assessable under Schedule E include all salaries, wages, director's fees and other money sums. In addition, the value of a wide range of benefits must be added to taxable earnings. These include the provision of living accommodation on advantageous terms and advantages arising from the use of vouchers.

Further taxable benefits accrue to directors and also to employees receiving earnings of £8,500 or more in the year of assessment. Such benefits include the reimbursement of expenses, the availability of motor cars for private motoring, the provision of petrol or other fuel for private motoring, the use of vans, the provision of interest-free loans, and other benefits provided at the employer's expense. The cost of providing a limited range of child care facilities may be excluded.

In arriving at the amount to be assessed under Schedule E, all expenses incurred wholly, exclusively and necessarily in the performance of the duties, together with the cost of business travel, may be deducted. Fees and subscriptions paid to certain professional bodies and learned societies may also be deducted. Fees paid to managers by entertainers, actors and others assessable under Schedule E may be deducted, up to a maximum of 17.5 per cent of earnings.

Compensation for loss of office and other sums received on the termination of an office or employment are assessable to tax. However, the first £30,000 may be excluded with only the balance remaining chargeable, unless the compensatory payment is linked with the retirement of the recipient.

For several years earnings received from an approved profit-related pay scheme have been exempt from income tax. However, this exemption is being phased out and will cease to apply entirely after 31 December 1999.

Schedule F

This Schedule is concerned with dividends and distributions received from a UK resident company. A shareholder residing in the UK and obtaining a receipt of this nature may expect to have a tax credit attached equal to one-quarter of the sum received for 1998–9. The gross dividend or distrubition (sum received plus tax credit) is regarded as having suffered income tax, equal to the tax credit, at the lower rate of 20 per cent. Where the shareholder is not liable, or not fully liable, at that rate a repayment can usually be obtained. Dividends and distributions comprise income from savings and incur no liability to income tax at the basic rate of 23 per cent (*see* below). Taxpayers with substantial income suffer tax on the gross sum at 40 per cent, less the tax credit of 20 per cent.

The tax credit will be reduced from one-quarter to one-ninth after 5 April 1999 with no part of that credit qualifying for repayment. To compensate for the reduction in the amount of the tax credit it is expected that dividends and distributions will be subject to an ordinary rate of 10 per cent for 1999–2000. This will match the tax credit of 10 per cent on the gross sum. Shareholders liable to the higher rate will suffer tax at the upper rate of 32.5 per cent less the tax credit of one-ninth.

Pension funds have been unable to recover the tax credit for dividends paid after 1 July 1997.

Building society and bank interest

Many payments of interest by building societies and banks are received after the deduction of income tax at the lower rate of 20 per cent. However, investors not liable to income tax may arrange to receive interest gross, with no tax being deducted on payment. Others who suffer income tax by deduction can obtain a repayment in whole or in part if they are not fully liable at the lower rate. This income also comprises income from savings, which is taxable as outlined below.

Income From Savings

Some forms of investment income attract a reduced rate of income tax for 1998–9. This is limited to 'income from savings', which includes interest on bank and building society accounts, government securities, the income element of purchased life annuities, and dividends from UK companies. In addition, 'income from savings' may extend to dividends and other income of a similar nature arising outside the UK. Not all forms of investment income are included in the list; a notable exception is income from letting property.

A great deal of interest will be received after deduction of income tax at the lower rate of 20 per cent. Dividends have a tax credit attached which effectively represents tax at the rate of 20 per cent on the grossed-up equivalent. The significance of these rates is that income from savings will be taxed at 20 per cent where the income of the recipient is sufficiently substantial. There is no liability at the basic rate of 23 per cent but where taxable income exceeds £27,100, the excess is liable at the higher rate of 40 per cent. As tax will usually have been deducted at source at 20 per cent, higher rate liability arises at a further 20 per cent (40 per cent less 20 per cent). When calculating liability, income from savings is treated as the 'top slice' of the taxpayer's income.

Income Not Taxable

Income which is not taxable in 1998–9 includes interest on National Savings certificates, most scholarship income, bounty payments to members of the armed services and annuities payable to the holders of certain awards. Dividend income arising from investments in personal equity plans (PEPs) and venture capital trusts may be exempt from tax. Income received under most maintenance agreements and court orders made after 30 June 1988 will not be liable to tax. Nor will payments made under many deeds of covenant be recognized for tax purposes, unless the recipient is a charity. Interest arising on a tax exempt special savings account (TESSA) opened with a building society or bank will be exempt from tax if the account is maintained throughout a five-year period.

Most items of income mentioned above and which are not taxable in 1998–9 continue to avoid liability in future years, but changes will affect certain other items. Interest on TESSAs opened before 6 April 1999 will retain exemption throughout the remaining part of the five-year period but no new accounts will be available. PEPs held on the same date also continue to retain income tax exemption for the future, and for 1999–2000 and the four following years, tax credits on PEPs will be repayable. However, no investments in PEPs can take place after 5 April 1999.

A new vehicle, the individual savings account (ISA), is to become available on 6 April 1999 for investment by UK resident individuals aged 18 or over. The ISA may have three components: cash; stocks and shares; and life assurance. Interest on the cash component, usually comprising bank or building society deposits, will be exempt from income tax. Dividends on most quoted holdings in the stocks and shares component will also be immune from liability to income tax, with tax credits being repaid in the first five years. It is likely that income and gains accruing to the provider of the life assurance component will be free of all liability to taxation.

A maximum subscription of £7,000 can be made by an individual to an ISA during 1999–2000. Of this sum, no more than £3,000 can be allocated to the cash component and £1,000 to the life assurance component. For later years the maximum subscription is reduced to £5,000, with no more than £1,000 being allocated to each of the cash and life assurance components.

Social Security Benefits

Many social security benefits are not liable to income tax. These include income support, family credit, maternity allowance, child benefit, war widow's pension and disability living allowance. The benefits which are taxable include the retirement pension, widow's pension, widowed mother's allowance and jobseeker's allowance. Short-term sick pay and maternity pay payable by an employer are also chargeable to tax. Incapacity benefit is chargeable to tax but no liability arises for the first 28 weeks of receiving benefit.

It is expected that a new working families' tax credit system will replace family credit in autumn 1999.

Pay As You Earn

The Pay As You Earn (PAYE) system is not an independent form of taxation but is designed to collect income tax by deduction from most earnings. When paying earnings to employees, an employer is usually required to deduct income tax and account for that tax to the Inland Revenue. In many cases this deduction procedure will fully exhaust the individual's liability to income tax, unless there is other income. The date of 'receipt' used for assessment purposes (see page 639) also identifies the date of 'payment' when establishing liability for PAYE.

The PAYE system is used to collect tax on certain payments made 'in kind'. This includes payment in the form of gold bullion, diamonds and marketable securities, among others.

Allowances

The allowances available to individuals for 1998–9 are:

Personal allowance

Basic personal allowance	£4,195
Those over 64 on 5 April 1999	£5,410
Those over 74 on 5 April 1999	£5,600

The increased allowance is available for those who died during the year of assessment but who would otherwise have achieved the appropriate age not later than 5 April 1999.

The amount of the increased personal allowance for older taxpayers will be reduced by one-half of total income in excess of £16,200. This reduction in the allowance will continue until it has been reduced to the basic personal allowance of £4,195.

The personal allowance is given as a deduction in calculating taxable income and may therefore produce relief at the rate of 20, 23 or 40 per cent, as appropriate.

Married couple's allowance

A married man who was 'living with' his wife at any time in the year ending on 5 April 1999 is entitled to a married couple's allowance. The basic allowance is £1,900. This may be increased to £3,305 if either the husband or the wife is 65 years or over at any time in the year ending on 5 April 1999. A further increase to £3,345 can be obtained where either party to the marriage was 75 or over on 5 April 1999. Where an individual would otherwise have reached either age by 5 April 1999, but who died earlier in the year, the increased allowance is given.

The amount of the increased married couple's allowance may be reduced where the income of the husband (excluding the income of the wife) exceeds £16,200. The reduction will comprise:

(a) one-half of the husband's total income in excess of £16,200, less
(b) the amount of any reduction made when calculating the husband's increased personal allowance

This reduction in the married couple's allowance cannot reduce that allowance below the basic amount of £1,900.

If husband and wife were married during 1998–9 the married couple's allowance of £1,900, or any increased sum, must be reduced by one-twelfth for each complete month commencing on 6 April 1998 and preceding the date of marriage.

Unlike the personal allowance, the married couple's allowance does not reduce taxable income. Relief is granted by reducing the tax payable by 15 per cent of the allowance. Should the allowance exceed taxable income, no tax will be due, nor will any repayment arise.

In the absence of any further action the married couple's allowance will be given to the husband. If he is unable to utilize all or any part of that allowance due to an absence of income, the husband may transfer the unused portion to his wife. The decision whether or not to transfer remains at the discretion of the husband.

However, a wife may file an election to obtain one-half of the basic married couple's allowance as of right, leaving the husband with the balance of that allowance. Alternatively, the couple may jointly elect that the entire basic allowance should be allocated to the wife only. Should either spouse be unable to utilize his or her share of the married couple's allowance the unused part may be transferred to the other spouse.

Relief for the married couple's allowance will be reduced from 15 per cent to 10 per cent for 1999–2000.

Additional personal allowance

An allowance of £1,900 is available to a single person who has a qualifying child resident with him/her in 1998–9. The allowance can also be obtained by a married man or a married woman whose spouse is totally incapacitated by physical or mental infirmity throughout the year.

A 'qualifying child' for 1998–9 must be born during the year, be under the age of 16 years at the commencement of the year, or be over the age of 16 at the commencement of the year and either receiving full-time instruction at a university, college, school or other educational establishment or undergoing training for a trade, profession or vocation throughout a minimum period of two years. It is also necessary that the child is the claimant's own, a stepchild of the claimant, an illegitimate child if the parents married after the child's birth, or an adopted child under the age of 18 at the time of adoption. Alternatively it must be shown that the child was either born during 1998–9 or under the age of 18 at the commencement of the year and maintained by the claimant at his or her own expense during the whole of the succeeding 12-month period.

Only one additional personal allowance of £1,900 can be obtained by an individual notwithstanding the number of children involved. Where an unmarried couple are living together as husband and wife, it is not possible for both to obtain the additional personal allowance. The allowance is given by reducing tax payable at the rate of 15 per cent of £1,900. This rate falls to 10 per cent for 1999–2000.

Widow's bereavement allowance

For the year of assessment in which a husband dies his surviving widow may obtain a widow's bereavement allowance, which is £1,900 for 1998–9. It is a requirement that the parties were 'living together' immediately before the husband's death. A similar allowance will be available in the year following death, unless the widow remarried in the year of death. No widow's bereavement allowance can be obtained for future years. Relief is granted by reducing tax payable at the rate of 15 per cent of £1,900, or 10 per cent for 1999–2000.

Blind person's allowance

An allowance of £1,330 is available to an individual if at any time during the year ending on 5 April 1999, he or she was registered as blind on a register maintained by a local authority. If the individual is 'living with' a wife or husband, any unused part of the blind person's allowance can be transferred to the other spouse. The allowance reduces taxable income and may therefore give rise to relief at the taxpayer's highest rate of tax suffered.

Transitional allowances

There are two remaining transitional allowances which are intended to ensure that the independent taxation of husband and wife, introduced on 6 April 1990, did not increase liability to income tax for subsequent years. These allowances comprise:
(a) an increased personal allowance available to a wife where the husband cannot fully use that allowance in 1998–9
(b) a married couple's allowance available to a separated husband not 'living with' his wife if the separation occurred before 6 April 1990
These allowances are of limited application.

INTEREST

In addition to personal and blind person's allowances, which reduce taxable income, and other allowances which reduce tax payable, further reliefs may be available to an individual. These include payments of interest.

In some instances, interest paid by a business proprietor may be included when calculating profits chargeable to income tax under Case I or Case II of Schedule D. In addition, relief for interest paid on a loan applied to acquire or develop land and buildings for letting may be obtained by including the outlay in the calculation of income chargeable under Schedule A. However, many private individuals cannot obtain relief in this manner and must satisfy stringent requirements before relief will be forthcoming. In general terms it is a requirement that before interest can qualify for relief it must be paid for a qualifying purpose. Relief will not be available to the extent that interest exceeds a reasonable commercial rate and no relief is forthcoming for interest on an overdraft.

For 1998–9 relief will be available on the following payments:
(a) Interest on a loan to purchase, develop or improve an interest in land owned by the individual and used as the only or main residence of that individual. 'Land' includes large houseboats and also caravans used for residential purposes. No relief is available for interest on loans applied after 5 April 1988 for the development or improvement of land, unless the work involves the construction of a new building. Relief is available for interest paid on a loan applied to acquire a property which is the only or main residence of a dependent relative, a separated spouse or a divorced former spouse, but only where that person occupied the property before 6 April 1988. Relief may also be forthcoming for interest on a loan used to acquire some other property, perhaps to be used as the only or main residence on retirement, by an individual who is compelled to occupy property by reason of his or her work. If the loan, or aggregate of several loans, exceeds £30,000, relief is restricted to interest on that amount. Where two or more persons apply loans after 31 July 1988 to acquire interests in a single building, those persons cannot, collectively, obtain relief for interest on more than £30,000 in relation to that building. Relief is given by reducing the income tax payable by 10 per cent of the qualifying interest paid in 1998–9
(b) Interest on a loan made to acquire an interest in a close company or in a partnership, or to advance money to such a person
(c) Interest on a loan to a member of a partnership to acquire machinery or plant for use in the partnership business
(d) Interest on a loan to an employed person to acquire machinery or plant for the purposes of his/her employment
(e) Interest on a loan made for the purpose of contributing capital to an industrial co-operative
(f) Interest on a loan applied for investment in an employee-controlled company
(g) Interest on a loan made to elderly persons for the purchase of an annuity where the loan is secured on land. If the loan exceeds £30,000, relief is limited to interest on this amount. This relief is restricted to income tax at the basic rate of 23 per cent
(h) Interest on a loan to personal representatives to provide funds for the payment of inheritance tax

Relief for many payments of mortgage interest is obtained through MIRAS (mortgage interest relief at source). This applies to interest paid to a building society, bank, insurance company and certain other approved persons. When making payments of this nature in 1998–9 the payer will deduct and retain income tax at the rate of 10 per cent. This will provide the payer with full relief at that rate and no other relief will be necessary. Qualifying payments of interest outside the MIRAS scheme continue to produce relief by reducing tax payable at the rate of 10 per cent.

Other relief under headings (b) to (h) (but not (g)) are given by deducting interest from taxable income. This enables the taxpayer to obtain relief at his or her top rate suffered.

OTHER OUTGOINGS

Many employees pay contributions to an approved occupational pension scheme. The amount of their contributions may be deducted when calculating earnings assessable under Schedule E. Relief should also be available for any additional voluntary contributions paid.

Self-employed individuals and those receiving earnings not covered by an occupational pension scheme may contribute under personal pension scheme arrangements. These individuals may also pay premiums under retirement annuity schemes if the arrangements were concluded before 1 July 1988. Contributions paid under both headings and which do not exceed upper limits may obtain income tax relief by deduction from taxable income.

Subject to a maximum of £150,000 in 1998–9, the cost of subscribing for shares in an unquoted trading company or companies may qualify for relief under the Enterprise Investment Scheme. Many requirements must be satisfied before this relief can be obtained, but a husband and wife may each take advantage of the £150,000 maximum. Relief is given by reducing tax payable at the rate of 20 per cent of the share subscription cost. Further relief, up to a maximum of £100,000 and given at the rate of 20 per cent, is available for a subscription of shares in a venture capital trust company.

CAPITAL GAINS TAX

An individual is potentially chargeable to capital gains tax on chargeable gains which accrue to him/her during a year of assessment ending on 5 April. The application of the tax has been amended several times in recent years and further alterations were made in spring 1998. The following information is largely confined to the year of assessment 1998–9, ending on 5 April 1999.

Liability extends to individuals who are either resident or ordinarily resident for the year but special rules apply where a person permanently leaves the UK or comes to this territory for the purpose of acquiring residence. Non-residents are not liable to capital gains tax unless they carry on a business in the UK through a branch or agency. However, individuals who leave the UK after 16 March 1998 and who have been resident or ordinarily resident in at least four of the seven previous years may remain liable to capital gains tax unless they reside overseas throughout a period of five complete tax years. Exceptions from this may apply where there is a disposal of assets acquired in the period of absence.

Trustees residing in the UK are chargeable to capital gains tax but chargeable gains accruing to companies are assessable to corporation tax.

For 1997–8 and earlier years, capital gains tax was chargeable on the net chargeable gains accruing to a person in a year of assessment after subtracting the annual exemption for that year. Net chargeable gains represented capital gains less capital losses arising from disposals carried out during the year. Unused losses brought forward from an earlier year could be offset against current net chargeable gains, but in the case of individuals must not reduce the net gains for 1997–8 below £6,500. It was possible to utilize trading losses against chargeable gains where those losses had not been offset against income.

TAPER RELIEF

The calculation of net gains chargeable to capital gains tax for 1998–9 and future years is affected by the introduction of taper relief. The purpose of this relief, which replaces the indexation allowance (see page 643), is to require that only a percentage of gains become chargeable to capital gains tax. The percentage is governed by the number of complete years of ownership falling after 5 April 1998, although one additional 'bonus year' can be obtained for most assets acquired before 17 March 1998.

Taper relief, which is limited to disposals made after 5 April 1998, draws a distinction between business assets and non-business assets. The expression 'business asset' broadly identifies an asset used for business purposes, in addition to some holdings of shares in trading companies. Where the nature of an asset has changed during the period of ownership from a business asset to a non-business asset, or vice versa, the asset must be effectively broken down into two parts. The percentages attributable to each type of asset are:

No. of whole years	Percentage of gain chargeable	
	Business assets	Non-business assets
	%	%
1	92.5	100
2	85.0	100
3	77.5	95
4	70.0	90
5	62.5	85
6	55.0	80
7	47.5	75
8	40.0	70
9	32.5	65
10	25.0	60

If only chargeable gains arise from disposals carried out in 1998–9, the taper relief, if any, must be calculated by reference to each disposal. The aggregate sum will then be subtracted from the total chargeable gains and the net sum reduced, or perhaps eliminated, by the annual exemption of £6,800.

Where disposals in 1998–9 produce both gains and losses, the losses must be subtracted from the gains and taper relief calculated on the new sum remaining. It is necessary to allocate the losses between the gains where there are two or more disposals. Losses brought forward from an earlier year must also be subtracted when calculating the net gains qualifying for taper relief. However, losses brought forward are not to reduce the net gains below the annual exemption of £6,800.

RATE OF TAX

The net gains remaining, if any, after subtracting taper relief and the annual exemption incur liability to capital gains tax for 1998–9 by using the taxpayer's marginal rate of income tax. This is achieved by adding the remaining net chargeable gains to the amount of income chargeable to income tax. The rate attributable to this top slice will disclose the rate of capital gains tax payable, which may be at 20 per cent, 23 per cent, 40 per cent, or a combination of the three. Although income tax rates are used, capital gains tax remains a separate tax.

Capital gains tax for 1998–9 falls due for payment in full on 31 January 2000. If payment is delayed beyond that date, interest or surcharges may be imposed.

HUSBAND AND WIFE

Independent taxation requires that a husband and wife 'living together' are separately assessed to capital gains tax. Each spouse must independently calculate his or her gains and losses, with each entitled to the benefit of taper relief, if any, and the annual exemption of £6,800 for 1998–9. No liability to capital gains tax arises from the transfer of assets between husband and wife 'living together'.

DISPOSAL OF ASSETS

Before chargeable gains potentially liable to capital gains tax can arise, a disposal or deemed disposal of an asset must take place. This occurs not only where assets are sold or exchanged but applies on the making of a gift. There is also a disposal of assets where any capital sum is derived from assets, e.g. where compensation is received for loss or damage to an asset.

The date on which a disposal must be treated as having taken place will determine the year of assessment into which the chargeable gain or allowable loss falls. In those cases where a disposal is made under an unconditional contract, the time of disposal will be that when the contract was entered into and not the subsequent date of conveyance or transfer. A disposal under a conditional contract or option is treated as taking place when the contract becomes unconditional or the option is exercised. Disposals by way of gift are undertaken when the gift becomes effective.

VALUATION OF ASSETS

The amount actually received as consideration for the disposal of an asset will be the sum from which very limited outgoings must be deducted for the purpose of establishing the gain or loss. In cases where the consideration does not accurately reflect the value of the asset, a different basis must be used. This applies, in particular, where an asset is transferred by way of gift or otherwise than by a bargain made at arm's length. Such transactions are deemed to take place for a consideration representing market value, which will determine both the disposal proceeds accruing to the transferor and the cost of acquisition to the transferee.

Market value represents the price which an asset might reasonably be expected to fetch on a sale in the open market. In the case of unquoted shares or securities, it is to be assumed that the hypothetical purchaser in the open market would have available all the information which a prudent prospective purchaser of shares or securities might reasonably require if he were proposing to purchase them from a willing vendor by private treaty and at arm's length. This is important as the amount of information deemed to be available to a hypothetical purchaser may materially affect the price 'reasonably' offered in an open market situation. The market value of unquoted shares or securities will often be established following negotiations with the Shares Valuation Division of the Capital Taxes Office. The valuation of land and interests in land in the UK will be dealt with by the District Valuer. Special rules apply to determine the market value of shares quoted on the Stock Exchange.

DEDUCTION FOR OUTGOINGS

Once the actual or notional disposal proceeds have been determined, it only remains to subtract eligible outgoings for the purpose of computing the gain or loss. There is the general rule that any outgoings deducted, or which are available to be deducted, when calculating income tax liability must be ignored. Subject to this, deductions will usually be limited to:

(a) the cost of acquiring the asset, together with incidental costs wholly and exclusively incurred in connection with the acquisition

(b) expenditure incurred wholly and exclusively on the asset in enhancing its value, being expenditure reflected in the state or nature of the asset at the time of the disposal, and any other expenditure wholly and exclusively incurred in establishing, preserving or defending title to, or a right over, the asset

(c) the incidental costs of making the disposal

Where the disposal concerns a leasehold interest having less than 50 years to run, any expenditure falling under (a) and (b) must be written off throughout the duration of the lease.

ASSETS HELD ON 31 MARCH 1982

Where the disposal relates to assets held on 31 March 1982, the actual cost of acquisition will not usually enter into the calculation of gain. It is to be assumed that such assets were acquired on 31 March 1982 for a consideration representing market value on that date. The increase in value, if any, occurring before 31 March 1982 will not be assessable to capital gains tax.

INDEXATION ALLOWANCE

In recent years an indexation allowance has been available when calculating a gain on the disposal of an asset. The allowance was based on percentage increases in the retail prices index between the month of March 1982, or the month in which expenditure was incurred if later, and the month of disposal. The indexation allowance calculated on this basis entered into the calculation of chargeable gain arising on the disposal of an asset. For several years it had not been possible to use the allowance to increase or to create an allowable loss.

With the introduction of taper relief for disposals taking place after 6 April 1998, the amount and use of the indexation allowance has been restricted; and for periods after April 1998 the indexation allowance can no longer run. However, where an asset was acquired before April 1998, the indexation allowance will be calculated to that month and then frozen. The frozen allowance will then enter into the calculation of chargeable gain, if any, when the asset is disposed of at some later date. The adjustment for the indexation allowance will be made before calculating taper relief on the net sum remaining.

EXEMPTIONS

There is a general exemption from liability to capital gains tax where the net gains of an individual for 1998–9 do not exceed £6,800. This general exemption applies separately to a husband and wife whether or not the parties are 'living together'.

The disposal of many assets will not give rise to chargeable gains or allowable losses and these assets include:

(a) private motor cars
(b) government securities
(c) loan stock and other securities (but not shares)
(d) options and contracts relating to securities within (b) and (c)
(e) National Savings Certificates, Premium Bonds, Defence Bonds and National Development Bonds
(f) currency of any description acquired for personal expenditure outside the UK
(g) decorations awarded for valour
(h) betting wins and pools, lottery or games prizes
(i) compensation or damages for any wrong or injury

suffered by an individual in his/her person, profession or vocation

(j) life assurance and deferred annuity contracts where the person making the disposal is the original beneficial owner

(k) dwelling-houses and land enjoyed with the residence which is an individual's only or main residence

(l) tangible movable property, the consideration for the disposal of which does not exceed £6,000

(m) certain tangible movable property which is a wasting asset having a life not exceeding 50 years

(n) assets transferred to charities and other bodies

(o) works of art, historic buildings and similar assets

(p) assets used to provide maintenance funds for historic buildings

(q) assets transferred to trustees for the benefit of employees

(r) assets held in an Individual Savings Account

DWELLING-HOUSES

Exemption from capital gains tax will usually be available for any gain which accrues to an individual from the disposal of, or of an interest in, a dwelling-house or part of a dwelling-house which has been his/her only or main residence. The exemption extends to land which has been occupied and enjoyed with the residence as its garden or grounds. Some restriction may be necessary where the land exceeds half a hectare.

The gain will not be chargeable to capital gains tax if the dwelling-house, or part, has been the individual's only or main residence throughout the period of ownership, or throughout the entire period except for all or any part of the last three years. A proportionate part of the gain will be exempt in other cases if the dwelling-house has been the individual's only or main residence for part only of the period of ownership. In the case of property acquired before 31 March 1982, the period of ownership is treated as commencing on this date.

Where part of the dwelling-house has been used exclusively for business purposes, that part of the gain attributable to business use will not be exempt.

In those cases where part of a qualifying dwelling-house has been used to provide rented residential accommodation, this non-personal use may frequently be ignored when calculating exemption from capital gains tax, unless relatively substantial sums are involved.

Dwellings occupied by dependent relatives, separated spouses or divorced former spouses, may also qualify for the exemption, but only where occupation commenced before 6 April 1988.

ROLL-OVER RELIEF – BUSINESS ASSETS

Persons carrying on business will often undertake the disposal of an asset and use the proceeds to finance the acquisition of a replacement asset. Where this situation arises, a claim for roll-over relief may be available. The broad effect of such a claim is that all or part of the gain arising on the disposal of the old asset may be disregarded. The gain or part is then subtracted from the cost of acquiring the replacement asset. As this cost is reduced, any gain arising from the future disposal of the replacement asset will be correspondingly increased, unless a further roll-over situation then develops.

It remains a requirement that both the old and the replacement asset must be used for the purpose of the taxpayer's business. Relief will only be available if the acquisition of the replacement asset takes place within a period commencing twelve months before, and ending three years after, the disposal of the old asset, although the Inland Revenue retain a discretion to extend this period

where the circumstances were such that it was impossible for the taxpayer to acquire the replacement asset before the expiration of the normal time limit.

Whilst many business assets qualify for roll-over relief there are exceptions.

DEFERRAL RELIEF

A form of roll-over relief enables gains arising on the disposal of an asset to be matched, in whole or in part, with a subscription for shares in a restricted range of unquoted companies, including certain companies whose shares are dealt in on the Alternative Investment Market. Where matching can be achieved any part of the gain arising on disposal, not exceeding the cost of the qualifying share subscription, may become the subject of a claim. Unlike the usual form of roll-over relief, this claim does not eliminate or reduce the chargeable gain. It has the effect of deferring that gain until the time of some future event, which will usually be identified by the disposal of the newly acquired shares or the lost of UK residential status. The relief, referred to as deferral relief, applied also to transactions taking place before 6 April 1998 but was limited to a subscription for shares qualifying for enterprise investment scheme income tax relief.

A similar form of deferral relief is available for gains arising on other disposals which are matched with a qualifying investment in a venture capital trust company. To the extent of the gain arising, which must not exceed the amount of the investment qualifying for income tax relief, that gain is deferred until the time of a future event, which will normally comprise the disposal of shares in the venture capital trust or the loss of UK residential status.

HOLD-OVER RELIEF – GIFTS

The gift of an asset is treated as a disposal made for a consideration equal to market value, with a corresponding acquisition by the transferee at an identical value. In the case of gifts made by individuals and a limited range of trustees to a transferee resident in the UK, a form of hold-over relief may be available. Relief is limited to the transfer of certain assets, including the following:

(a) assets used for the purposes of a trade or similar activity carried on by the transferor or his/her personal company

(b) shares or securities of a trading company which is not listed on a stock exchange

(c) shares or securities of a trading company which is listed but which is the transferor's personal company

(d) many interests in agricultural property qualifying for agricultural property relief for inheritance tax purposes

(e) assets involved in transactions which are lifetime transfers for inheritance tax purposes, other than potentially exempt transfers

The effect of the claim is similar to that following a claim for roll-over relief on the disposal of business assets, but adjustments are necessary where some consideration is given for the transfer, the asset has not been used for business purposes throughout the period of ownership, or not all assets of a company are used for business purposes.

RETIREMENT RELIEF

Retirement relief is available to an individual who disposes by way of sale or gift of the whole or part of a business. The isolated disposal of assets used for the purpose of a business will not necessarily represent the disposal of the whole or part of a business. The main condition for granting this relief is that throughout a period of at least one year the business has been owned either by the individual or by a trading company in which the individual retained a sufficient shareholding interest. The relief extends also to cases where an individual disposes by way of sale or gift of shares or securities of a company. It must be demonstrated that the company was a trading company, that the individual retained a sufficient shareholding interest, and that he/she was engaged as a full-time working officer or employee.

An individual who has attained the age of 50 years at the time of a disposal may now obtain substantial retirement relief which shelters gains from liability to capital gains tax. Full relief is available for disposals taking place not later than 5 April 1999. The amount of relief then reduces on an annual basis before being abolished entirely for disposals taking place on and after 6 April 2003.

No retirement relief will be forthcoming if the disposal occurs before the individual's 50th birthday, except where an individual is compelled to retire early on the grounds of ill-health.

Retirement relief must be subtracted from the net gains arising on disposal, leaving the balance, if any, chargeable to capital gains tax in the normal manner. Taper relief applies only to this balance of net gains and not to the gains eliminated by retirement relief.

DEATH

No capital gains tax is chargeable on the value of assets retained at the time of death. However, the personal representatives administering the deceased's estate are deemed to acquire those assets for a consideration representing market value on death. This ensures that any increase in value occurring before the date of death will not be chargeable to capital gains tax. If a legatee or other person acquires an asset under a will or intestacy no chargeable gain will accrue to the personal representatives, and the person taking the asset will also be treated as having acquired it at the time of death for its then market value.

INHERITANCE TAX

Liability to inheritance tax may arise on a limited range of lifetime gifts and other dispositions and also on the value of assets retained, or deemed to be retained, at the time of death. An individual's domicile at the time of any gift or on death is an important matter. Domicile will generally be determined by applying normal rules, although special considerations may be necessary where an individual was previously domiciled in the UK but subsequently acquired a domicile of choice overseas. In addition, individuals who have been resident in the UK for at least 17 of the previous 20 years at the time of an event are treated as domiciled in the UK.

Where a person was domiciled, or treated as domiciled, in the UK at the time of a disposition or on death the location of assets is immaterial and full liability to inheritance tax arises. Individuals domiciled outside the UK are, however, chargeable to inheritance tax only on transactions affecting assets located in the UK.

The assets of husband and wife are not merged for inheritance tax purposes. Each spouse is treated as a separate individual entitled to receive the benefit of his or her exemptions, reliefs and rates of tax. Where husband and wife retain similar assets, e.g. shares in the same family company, special 'related property' provisions may require the merger of those assets for valuation purposes only.

LIFETIME GIFTS AND DISPOSITIONS

Gifts and dispositions made during lifetime fall under four broad headings, namely:
(a) dispositions which are not transfers of value
(b) exempt transfers
(c) potentially exempt transfers
(d) chargeable transfers

Dispositions which are not transfers of value

Several lifetime transactions are not treated as transfers of value and may be entirely disregarded for inheritance tax purposes. These include transactions not intended to confer gratuitous benefit, the provision of family maintenance, the waiver of the right to receive remuneration or dividends, and the grant of agricultural tenancies for full consideration.

Exempt transfers

Certain transfers are treated as exempt transfers and incur no liability to inheritance tax. The main exempt transfers are listed below:

Transfers between spouses – Transfers between husband and wife are usually exempt. However, if the transferor is, but the transferee spouse is not, domiciled in the UK, transfers will be exempt only to the extent that the total does not exceed £55,000. Unlike the requirement used for income tax and capital gains tax purposes, it is immaterial whether husband and wife are living together.

Annual exemption – The first £3,000 of gifts and other dispositions made in a year ending on 5 April is exempt. If the exemption is not used, or not wholly used, in any year the balance may be carried forward to the following year only. The annual exemption will only be available for a potentially exempt transfer if that transfer becomes chargeable by reason of the donor's subsequent death.

Small gifts – Outright gifts of £250 or less to any person in one year ending 5 April are exempt.

Normal expenditure – A transfer made during lifetime and comprising normal expenditure is exempt. To obtain this exemption it must be shown that:
(a) the transfer was made as part of the normal expenditure of the transferor
(b) taking one year with another, the transfer was made out of income
(c) after allowing for all transfers of value forming part of normal expenditure the transferor was left with sufficient income to maintain his or her usual standard of living

Gifts in consideration of marriage – These are exempt if they satisfy certain requirements. The amount allowed will be governed by the relationship between the donor and a party to the marriage. The allowable amounts comprise:
(a) gifts by a parent, £5,000
(b) gifts by a grandparent, £2,500
(c) gifts by a party to the marriage, £2,500
(d) gifts by other persons, £1,000

Gifts to charities – These are exempt from liability.

Gifts to political parties – Gifts which satisfy certain requirements are generally exempt.

Gifts for national purposes – Gifts made to certain bodies are exempt from liability. These bodies include, among others, the National Gallery, the British Museum, the National Trust, the National Art Collections Fund, the National Heritage Memorial Fund, the Historic Buildings and Monuments Commission for England (English Heritage), any local authority, and any university or university college in the UK.

A number of other gifts made for the public benefit are also exempt.

Potentially exempt transfers

Lifetime gifts and dispositions which are neither to be ignored nor comprise exempt transfers incur possible liability to inheritance tax. However, relief is available for a range of potentially exempt transfers. These comprise gifts made by an individual to:

(a) a second individual
(b) trustees administering an accumulation and maintenance trust
(c) trustees administering a disabled person's trust

The accumulation and maintenance trust mentioned in (b) must provide that on reaching a specified age, not exceeding 25 years, a beneficiary will become absolutely entitled to trust assets or obtain an interest in possession in the income from those assets.

Additions to the above list affect settled property administered by trustees where an individual, or individuals, retain an interest in possession. The transfer of assets to, the removal of assets from, or the rearrangement of interests in such property comprise potentially exempt transfers if the person transferring an interest and the person benefiting from the transfer are both individuals.

No immediate liability to inheritance tax will arise on the making of a potentially exempt transfer. Should the donor survive for a period of seven years, immunity from liability will be confirmed. However, the donor's death within the seven-year *inter vivos* period produces liability if the amounts involved are sufficiently substantial (*see* below).

Chargeable transfers

Any remaining lifetime gifts or dispositions which are neither to be ignored nor represent exempt transfers or potentially exempt transfers, incur liability to inheritance tax. The range of such chargeable transfers is severely limited and is broadly confined to transfers made to or affecting discretionary trusts, transfers to non-individuals and transfers involving companies.

GIFTS WITH RESERVATION

A lifetime gift of assets made at any time after 17 March 1986 may incur additional liability to inheritance tax if the donor retains some interest in the subject matter of the gift. This may arise, for example, where a parent transfers a dwelling-house to a son or daughter and continues to occupy the property or to enjoy some benefit from that property. The retention of a benefit may be ignored where it is enjoyed in return for full consideration, perhaps a commercial rent, or where the benefit arises from changed circumstances which could not have been foreseen at the time of the original gift. The gift with reservation provisions will not usually apply to most exempt transfers.

There are three possibilities which may arise where the donor reserves or enjoys some benefit from the subject matter of a previous gift and subsequently dies, namely:

(a) if no benefit is enjoyed within a period of seven years before death there can be no further liability
(b) if the benefit ceased to be enjoyed within a period of seven years before the date of death, the original donor is deemed to have made a potentially exempt transfer representing the value of the asset at the time of cessation
(c) if the benefit is enjoyed at the time of death, the value of the asset must be included in the value of the deceased's estate on death

It must be emphasized that the existence of a benefit enjoyed at any time within a period of seven years before death will establish liability to tax on gifts with reservation, notwithstanding that the gift may have been made many years earlier, providing it was undertaken after 17 March 1986.

DEATH

Immediately before the time of death an individual is deemed to make a transfer of value. This transfer will comprise the value of assets forming part of the deceased's estate after subtracting most liabilities. Any exempt transfers may, however, be excluded. These include transfers for the benefit of a surviving spouse, a charity and a qualifying political party, together with bequests to approved bodies and for national purposes.

Death may also trigger three additional liabilities:

(a) A potentially exempt transfer made within the period of seven years ending on death loses its potential status and becomes chargeable to inheritance tax
(b) The value of gifts made with reservation may incur liability if any benefit was enjoyed within a period of seven years preceding death
(c) Additional tax may become payable for chargeable lifetime transfers made within seven years before death

VALUATIONS

The valuation of assets establishes the value transferred for lifetime dispositions and also the value of a person's estate at the time of death. The value of property will represent the price which might reasonably be expected from a sale in the open market.

In some cases it may be necessary to incorporate the value of 'related property'. This will include property comprised in the estate of the transferor's spouse and certain property previously transferred to charities. The purpose of the related property valuation rules is not to add the value of the property to the estate of the transferor. Related property must be merged to establish the aggregate value of the respective interests and this value is then apportioned, usually on a *pro rata* basis, to the separate interests.

The value of shares and securities listed on the Stock Exchange will be determined by extracting figures from the daily list of official prices.

Where quoted shares and securities are sold or the quotation is suspended within a period of 12 months following the date of death, a claim may be made to substitute the proceeds or subsequent value for the value on death. This claim will only be beneficial if the gross proceeds realized are lower or the value has fallen below market value at the time of death. A similar claim may be available for interests in land sold within a period of four years following death.

RELIEF FOR SELECTED ASSETS

Special relief is made available for certain assets, notably:

Woodlands

Where woodlands pass on death the value will usually be included in the deceased's estate. However, an election may be made in respect of land in the UK on which trees or underwood is growing to delete the value of those assets. Relief is confined to the value of trees or underwood and does not extend to the land on which they are growing. Liability to inheritance tax will arise if and when the trees or underwood are sold.

Agricultural property

Relief is available for the agricultural value of agricultural property. Such property must be occupied and used for agricultural purposes and relief is confined to the agricultural value only.

The value transferred, either on a lifetime gift or on death, must be determined. This value may then be reduced by a percentage. For events taking place after 9 March 1992, a 100 per cent deduction will be available if the transferor retained vacant possession or could have obtained that possession within a period of 12 months following the transfer. In other cases, notably including land let to tenants, a lower deduction of 50 per cent is usually available. However, this lower deduction may be increased to 100 per cent if the letting was made after 31 August 1995.

It remains a requirement that the agricultural property was either occupied by the transferor for the purposes of agriculture throughout a two-year period ending on the date of the transfer, or was owned by him/her throughout a period of seven years ending on that date and also occupied for agricultural purposes.

Business property

Where the value transferred is attributable to relevant business property, that value may be reduced by a percentage. The reduction in value applies to:

(a) property consisting of a business or an interest in a business (i.e. a partnership)
(b) shares or securities of an unquoted company which provided the transferor with more than 25 per cent of voting rights
(c) other unquoted shares or securities
(d) shares or securities of a quoted company which provided the transferor with control
(e) any land, building, machinery or plant which, immediately before the transfer, was used wholly or mainly for the purposes of a business carried on by a company of which the transferor had control
(f) any land, building, machinery or plant which, immediately before the transfer, was used wholly or mainly for the purposes of a business carried on by a partnership of which the transferor was a partner
(g) any land, building, machinery or plant which, immediately before the transfer, was used wholly or mainly for the purposes of a business carried on by the transferor and was then settled property in which he/ she retained an interest in possession

For events occurring after 9 March 1992, a deduction of 100 per cent is available for assets falling within (a) and (b). The deductions for unquoted shares in (c) is 100 per cent for events taking place after 5 April 1996. A deduction of 50 per cent remains for assets within (d) to (g).

It is a general requirement that the property must have been retained for a period of two years before the transfer or death and restrictions may be necessary if the property has not been used wholly for business purposes. The same property cannot obtain both business property relief and the relief available for agricultural property.

CALCULATION OF TAX PAYABLE

The calculation of inheritance tax payable adopts the use of a cumulative total. Each chargeable lifetime transfer is added to the total with a final addition made on death. The top slice added to the total for the current event determines the rate at which inheritance tax must be paid. However, the cumulative total will only include transfers made within a period of seven years before the current event and those undertaken outside this period must be excluded.

Lifetime chargeable transfers

The value transferred by the limited range of lifetime chargeable transfers must be added to the seven-year cumulative total to calculate whether any inheritance tax is due. Should the nil rate band be exceeded, tax will be imposed on the excess at one-half of the rate shown below, i.e. at the rate of 20 per cent. However, if the donor dies within a period of seven years from the date of the chargeable lifetime transfer, additional tax may be due. This is calculated by applying tax at the full rate (in substitution for the one-half rate previously used). The amount of tax is then reduced to a percentage by applying tapering relief. This percentage is governed by the number of years from the date of the lifetime gift to the date of death, as follows:

Period of years before death	
Not more than 3	100%
More than 3 but not more than 4	80%
More than 4 but not more than 5	60%
More than 5 but not more than 6	40%
More than 6 but not more than 7	20%

Should this exercise produce liability greater than that previously paid at the one-half rate on the lifetime transfer, additional tax, representing the difference, must be discharged. Where the calculation shows an amount falling below tax paid on the lifetime transfer, no additional liability can arise nor will the shortfall become repayable.

Tapering relief will, of course, only be available if the calculation discloses a liability to inheritance tax. There can be no liability to the extent that the lifetime transfer falls within the nil rate band.

Potentially exempt transfers

Where a potentially exempt transfer loses immunity from liability due to the donor's death within the seven-year *inter vivos* period, the value transferred by that transfer enters into the cumulative total. Any liability to inheritance tax will be calculated by applying the full rate shown below, reduced to the percentage governed by tapering relief if the original transfer occurred more than three years before death. Liability can only arise to the extent, if any, that the nil rate band is exceeded.

Death

The final addition to the seven-year cumulative total will comprise the value of an estate on death. Inheritance tax will be calculated by applying the full rate shown below to the extent the nil rate band is exceeded. No tapering relief can be obtained.

RATES OF TAX

In earlier times there were several rates of inheritance tax which progressively increased as the value transferred grew in size. However, for events taking place after 5 April 1998, a nil rate applies to the first £223,000. Any excess is charged at the single positive rate of 40 per cent.

Only one-half of the 40 per cent rate (namely 20 per cent) will be applicable for chargeable lifetime transfers.

PAYMENT OF TAX

Inheritance tax usually falls due for payment six months after the end of the month in which the chargeable transaction takes place. Where a transfer other than that made on death occurs after 5 April and before the following 1 October, tax falls due on the following 30 April, although there are some exceptions to this.

Inheritance tax attributable to the transfer of certain land, controlling shareholding interests, unquoted shares, businesses and interests in businesses, together with agricultural property, may usually be satisfied by instalments spread over ten years. Except in the case of non-agricultural land, where interest is charged on outstanding instalments, no liability to interest arises where tax is paid on the due date. In all cases, delay in the payment of tax may incur liability to interest.

SETTLED PROPERTY

Complex rules apply to establish inheritance tax liability on settled property. Where a person is beneficially entitled to an interest in possession, that person is effectively deemed to own the property in which the interest subsists. It follows that where the interest comes to an end during the beneficiary's lifetime and some other person becomes entitled to the property or interest, the beneficiary is treated as having made a transfer of value. However, this will usually comprise a potentially exempt transfer. In addition, no liability will arise where the property vests in the absolute ownership of the previous beneficiary. The death of a person entitled to an interest in possession will require the value of the underlying property to be added to the value of the deceased's estate.

In the case of other settled property where there is no interest in possession (e.g. discretionary trusts), liability to tax will arise on each ten-year anniversary of the trust. There will also be liability if property ceases to be held on discretionary trusts before the first ten-year anniversary date is reached or between anniversaries. The rate of tax suffered will be governed by several considerations, including previous dispositions made by the settlor of the trust, transactions concluded by the trustees, and the period throughout which property has been held in trust.

Accumulation and maintenance settlements which require assets to be distributed, or interests in income to be created, not later than a beneficiary's 25th birthday may be exempt from any liability to inheritance tax.

CORPORATION TAX

Profits, gains and income accruing to companies resident in the UK incur liability to corporation tax. Non-resident companies are immune from this tax unless they carry on a trade in the UK through a permanent establishment, branch or office. Companies residing outside the UK may be liable to income tax at the basic rate on other income arising in the UK, perhaps from letting property. The following comments are confined to companies resident in the UK.

Liability to corporation tax is governed by the profits, gains or income for an accounting period. This is usually the period for which financial accounts are made up, and in the case of companies preparing accounts to the same accounting date annually will comprise successive periods of 12 months.

RATE OF TAX

The amount of profits or income for an accounting period must be determined on normal taxation principles. The special rules which apply to individuals where a source of income is acquired or discontinued are ignored and consideration is confined to the actual profits or income for an accounting period.

The rate of corporation tax is fixed for a financial year ending on 31 March. Where the accounting period of a company overlaps this date and there is a change in the rate of corporation tax, profits and income must be apportioned.

The full rate of corporation tax for recent years and that which applies for the immediate future is:

Financial year

Ending 31 March 1995, 1996 and 1997	33%
31 March 1998 and 1999	31%
31 March 2000	30%

SMALL COMPANIES' RATE

Where the profits of a company do not exceed stated limits, corporation tax becomes payable at the small companies' rate. It is the amount of profits and not the size of the company which governs the application of this rate.

In recent years and for the immediate future, the small companies' rate is:

Financial year

Ending 31 March 1995 and 1996	25%
31 March 1997	24%
31 March 1998 and 1999	21%
31 March 2000	20%

The level of profits which a company may derive without losing the benefit of the small companies' rate is frequently changed. For each year ending on 31 March 1995 to 31 March 2000, the limit is £300,000. However, if profits exceed £300,000 but fall below £1,500,000, marginal small companies' rate relief applies. The effect of marginal relief is that the average rate of corporation tax imposed on all profits steadily increases from the lower small companies' rate to the full rate of 33, 31 or 30 per cent, with tax being imposed on profits in the margin at an increased rate. Where the accounting period of a company overlaps 31 March, profits must be apportioned to establish the appropriate rate for each part of those profits.

The lower limit of £300,000 and the upper limit of £1,500,000 apply to a period of 12 months and must be proportionately reduced for shorter periods. Some restriction in the small companies' rate and the marginal rate may be necessary if there are two or more associated companies, namely companies under common control.

The small companies' rate is not available for close investment-holding companies.

PAYMENT OF TAX

Corporation tax charged on profits for an accounting period falls due for payment in a single lump sum nine months after the end of that period. Most companies will continue to discharge corporation tax on this basis in the future but a change affects large companies for accounting periods ending on or after 1 July 1999. It is proposed that these companies should discharge their liability by four instalments, with the amount of earlier instalments being increased over a number of years. Annual profits of at least £1,500,000 broadly identifies a large company. Where a company is a member of a group, the profits of the entire group must be merged to establish whether it is large.

CAPITAL GAINS

Chargeable gains arising to a company are calculated in a manner similar to that used for individuals. The withdrawal of the indexation allowance after April 1998 and the introduction of taper relief have no application to companies, although this may change at some later date. Nor are companies entitled to the annual exemption of £6,800. Companies do not suffer capital gains tax on chargeable gains but incur liability to corporation tax. Tax is suffered on the full chargeable gain of an accounting period after subtracting relief for losses, if any.

DISTRIBUTIONS

Dividends and other qualifying distributions made by a UK resident company on or before 5 April 1999 are not satisfied after deduction of income tax. However, when making such a distribution, a company is required to account to the Inland Revenue for advance corporation tax. The amount of this tax has changed from time to time but for distributions between 6 April 1994 and 5 April 1999 it is calculated at the rate of one-quarter of the distribution.

Advance corporation tax accounted for in this manner in relation to distributions made in an accounting period may usually be set against a company's corporation tax liability for the same period. Some restrictions are imposed on the amount which can be offset but any surplus may be carried backwards, and perhaps carried forward, to be set against corporation tax paid or due for other accounting periods.

Liability to account for advance corporation tax will no longer apply where distributions are made on or after 6 April 1999. As previously, there will be no deduction of income tax and apart from removal of the obligation to account for advance corporation tax there will be little effect on most companies. Special rules apply when using surplus advance corporation tax brought forward on 6 April 1999.

Interest

On making many payments of interest after 5 April 1996 a company is required to deduct income tax at the lower rate of 20 per cent and account for the tax deducted to the Inland Revenue. The gross amount of interest paid will usually be included in the calculation of profits on which corporation tax becomes payable.

Groups of Companies

Each company within a group is separately charged to corporation tax on profits, gains and income. However, where one group member realizes a loss, other than a capital loss, a claim may be made to offset the deficiency against profits of some other member of the same group.

Claims are also available to avoid the payment of advance corporation tax on distributions made before 6 April 1999, or the deduction of income tax on the payment of interest, for transactions between members of a group of companies. The transfer of capital assets from one member of a group to a fellow member will incur no liability to tax on chargeable gains.

Compliance

A 'pay and file' system currently affects all companies. Under this system tax is payable nine months following the end of the accounting period involved, with accounts and returns being submitted three months later. Failure to satisfy corporation tax or to submit documents within these time limits will result in a liability to interest and penalties.

Although 'pay and file' remains, some change will apply once self-assessment affects all companies for accounting periods ending after 30 June 1999.

VALUE ADDED TAX

Value added tax (VAT) is charged on the value of the supplies made by a registered trader and extends to both the supply of goods and the supply of services. It is administered by Customs and Excise.

Liability to account for VAT arises on the value of goods imported into the UK from sources outside the European Community. In contrast goods imported by a trader from a second trader in a member state of the European Community attract no VAT on importation. Instead there is an acquisition tax whereby a trader who acquires goods must include the acquisition in his normal VAT return and account for the tax due. A UK trader who exports goods to a member state will not be required to account for VAT on

the supply, if that trader observes the requirements laid down by regulations.

Registration

All traders, including professional men and women and companies, making taxable supplies of a value exceeding stated limits are required to register for VAT purposes. Taxable supplies represent the supply of goods and services potentially chargeable with VAT. The limits which govern mandatory registration are amended periodically, and from 1 April 1998 an unregistered trader must register:

(a) at any time, if there are reasonable grounds for believing that the value of taxable supplies in the next 30 days will exceed £50,000

(b) at the end of any month if the value of taxable supplies in the 12 months then ending has exceeded £50,000.

Liability to register under (b) may be avoided if it can be shown that the value of supplies in the period of 12 months then beginning will not exceed £48,000. There may, however, be liability to register immediately where a business is taken over from another trader as a 'going concern'. Other limits apply where goods are acquired from within the European Community.

Where the limits governing mandatory registration have been exceeded, the trader must notify Customs and Excise. In the event of failure to provide prompt notification, the person concerned will be required to account for VAT from the proper registration date.

A trader whose taxable supplies do not reach the mandatory registration limits may apply for voluntary registration. This step may be thought advisable to recover input tax or to compete with other registered traders.

A registered trader may submit an application for deregistration if the value of taxable supplies subsequently falls. From 1 April 1998, an application for deregistration can be made if the value of taxable supplies for the year beginning on the application date is not expected to exceed £48,000.

Input Tax

A registered trader will both suffer tax (input tax) when obtaining goods or services for the purposes of his business and also become liable to account for tax (output tax) on the value of goods and services which he supplies. Relief can usually be obtained for input tax suffered, either by setting that tax against output tax due or by repayment. Most items of input tax can be relieved in this manner but there are exceptions, including the prohibition of relief for the cost of business entertaining. Where a registered trader makes both exempt supplies and taxable supplies to his customers or clients, there may be some restriction in the amount of input tax which can be recovered.

Output Tax

When making a taxable supply of goods or services, a registered trader must account for output tax, if any, on the value of the supply. Usually the price charged by the registered trader will be increased by adding VAT but failure to make the required addition will not remove liability to account for output tax.

The liability to account for output tax, and also relief for input tax, may be affected where a trader is using the special second-hand goods scheme.

Exempt Supplies

No VAT is chargeable on the supply of goods or services which are treated as exempt supplies. These include the provision of burial and cremation facilities, insurance, finance and education. The granting of a lease to occupy land or the sale of land will usually comprise an exempt supply, but there are numerous exceptions. In particular, the sale of new non-domestic buildings or certain buildings used by charities cannot be treated as exempt supplies.

A taxable person may elect to tax rents and other supplies relating to buildings and agricultural land not used for residential or charitable purposes.

Exempt supplies do not enter into the calculation of taxable supplies which governs liability to mandatory registration. Such supplies made by a registered trader may, however, limit the amount of input tax which can be relieved. It is for this reason that the election may be useful.

RATES OF TAX

Two rates of VAT have applied since 1 April 1991, namely:
(a) a zero, or nil, rate
(b) a standard rate of 17.5 per cent
In addition, a special reduced rate of 8 per cent applied to supplies of domestic fuel after March 1994. This rate was reduced to 5 per cent for supplies made after 1 September 1997.

ZERO-RATING

A large number of supplies are zero-rated. The following list is not exhaustive but indicates the wide range of supplies which may be included under this heading:
(a) the supply of many items of food and drink for human consumption. This does not include ice creams, chocolates, sweets, potato crisps and alcoholic drinks. Nor does it extend to supplies made in the course of catering or to items supplied for consumption in a restaurant or café. Whilst the supply of cold items, e.g. sandwiches, for consumption away from the supplier's premises, is zero-rated, the supply of hot food, e.g. fish and chips, is not
(b) animal feeding stuffs
(c) sewerage and water, unless for industrial purposes
(d) books, brochures, pamphlets, leaflets, newspapers, maps and charts
(e) talking books for the blind and handicapped, and wireless sets for the blind
(f) supplies of services, other than professional services, when constructing a new domestic building or a building to be used by a charity. The supply of materials for such a building is zero-rated, together with the sale or the grant of a long lease. Alterations to some protected buildings are zero-rated
(g) the transportation of persons in a vehicle, ship or aircraft designed to carry not less than 12 persons
(h) supplies of drugs, medicines and other aids for the handicapped
(i) supplies of clothing and footwear for young persons
(j) exports
Although no tax is due on a zero-rated supply, this does comprise a taxable supply which must be included in the calculation governing liability to register.

COLLECTION OF TAX

Registered traders submit VAT returns for accounting periods usually of three months duration but arrangements can be made to submit returns on a monthly basis. Very large traders must account for tax on a monthly basis but this does not affect the three-monthly return. The return will show both the output tax due for supplies made by the trader in the accounting period and also the input tax for which relief is claimed. If the output tax exceeds input tax the balance must be remitted with the VAT return. Where input tax suffered exceeds the output tax due the registered trader may claim recovery of the excess from Customs and Excise.

This basis for collecting tax explains the structure of VAT. Where supplies are made between registered traders the supplier will account for an amount of tax which will usually be identical to the tax recovered by the person to whom the supply is made. However, where the supply is made to a person who is not a registered trader there can be no recovery of input tax and it is on this person that the final burden of VAT eventually falls.

Where goods are acquired by a UK trader from a supplier within a member state of the European Community, the trader must also account for the tax due on acquisition.

An optional scheme is available for registered traders having an annual turnover of taxable supplies not exceeding £300,000. Such traders may render returns annually. Nine interim payments of VAT will be made on account, with a final balancing payment accompanying submission of the return. The number of interim payments may be reduced if turnover does not exceed £100,000.

BAD DEBTS

Many retailers operate special retail schemes for calculating the amount of VAT due. These schemes are based on the volume of consideration received in an accounting period. Should a customer fail to pay for goods or services supplied, there will be no consideration on which to calculate VAT.

To avoid the problem of bad debts incurred by traders not operating a special retail scheme, an optional system of cash accounting is available. This scheme, confined to traders with annual taxable supplies not exceeding £350,000, enables returns to be made on a cash basis, in substitution for the normal supply basis. Traders using such a scheme will not include bad debts in the calculation of cash receipts.

Where neither the cash accounting arrangements nor the special retail scheme applies, output tax falls due on the value of the supply and liability is not affected by failure to receive consideration. However, where a debt is more than six months old, relief for bad debts will be forthcoming. The calculation of the six-month period commences from the date on which payment for the supply falls due.

In those cases where a supplier obtains relief for a bad debt, the person to whom the supply has been made must refund to Customs and Excise any input tax relief which may have been granted.

OTHER SPECIAL SCHEMES

In addition to the schemes for retailers, there are several special schemes applied to calculate the amount of VAT due and which also limit the ability to recover input tax. The supply of virtually all second-hand goods has now been brought within special margin schemes.

FARMERS

Farmers may elect to apply a special flat rate scheme. This scheme is available to farmers who are not registered traders. Under the scheme a flat-rate addition of 4 per cent may be made on sales, with the amount of the addition being retained by the farmer. Registered traders to whom such a supply is made may treat the 4 per cent addition as recoverable input tax.

Legal Notes

IMPORTANT

These notes outline certain aspects of the law as they might affect the average person. They are intended only as a broad guideline and are by no means definitive. The information is believed to be correct at the time of going to press but the law is constantly changing so expert advice should always be taken. In some cases, sources of further information are given in these notes.

It is always advisable to consult a solicitor without delay; timely advice will set your mind at rest but sitting on your rights can mean that you lose them. Anyone who does not have a solicitor already can contact the Citizens' Advice Bureau (addresses in the telephone directory or at any post office or town hall), the Law Society of England and Wales (113 Chancery Lane, London WC2A 1PL) or the Law Society of Scotland (26 Drumsheugh Gardens, Edinburgh EH3 7YR) for assistance in finding one.

The legal aid and legal aid and assistance schemes exist to make the help of a lawyer available to those who would not otherwise be able to afford one. Entitlement depends upon an individual's means (see pages 662–4) but a solicitor or Citizens' Advice Bureau will be able to advise about entitlement.

ADOPTION OF CHILDREN

In England and Wales the adoption of children is mainly governed by the Adoption Act 1976 and the Children Act 1989.

Anyone over 21, whether married, single, widowed or divorced, can legally adopt a child. Married couples must adopt 'jointly', unless one partner cannot be found, is incapable of making an application, or if a separation is likely to be permanent. Unmarried couples may not adopt 'jointly' although one partner in that couple may adopt. The only organizations allowed to arrange adoptions are the social services departments of local authorities or voluntary agencies such as Barnardo's which are registered as adoption agencies with the local authorities.

Once an adoption has been arranged, a court order is necessary to make it legal. These are obtained from the High Court (Family Division) or from a county or family proceedings court. The child's natural parents (or guardians) must consent to the adoption, unless the court dispenses with the consent, e.g. where the natural parent has neglected the child or is incapable of giving consent. Once adopted, the child has the same status as a child born to the adoptive parents and the natural parents cease to have any rights or responsibilities where the child is concerned. The adopted child will be treated as the natural child of the adoptive parents for the purposes of intestate succession, national insurance, family allowances, etc. The adopted child ceases to have any rights to the estates of his/her natural parents.

REGISTRATION AND CERTIFICATES

All adoptions in England and Wales are registered in the Adopted Children Register kept by the Office of National Statistics, and by the General Register Office for adoptions in Scotland. Certificates from the registers can be obtained in a similar way to birth certificates (see page 652).

TRACING NATURAL PARENTS OR CHILDREN WHO HAVE BEEN ADOPTED

An adult adopted person may apply to the Registrar-General for information to enable him/her to obtain a full birth certificate. For those adopted before 12 November 1975 it is obligatory to receive counselling services before this information is given; for those adopted after that date counselling services are optional. There is also an Adoption Contact Register (created after the 1989 Act) in which details of adult adopted people and of their relatives may be recorded. The BAAF (see below) can provide addresses of organizations which offer advice, information and counselling to adopted people, adoptive parents and people who have had their children adopted.

SCOTLAND

The relevant legislation is the Adoption (Scotland) Act 1978 (as amended by the Children Act 1995) and the provisions are similar to those described above. In Scotland, petitions for adoption are made to the Sheriff Court or the Court of Session.

Further information can be obtained from:
BRITISH AGENCIES FOR ADOPTION AND FOSTERING (BAAF), Skyline House, 200 Union Street, London SE1 0LX. Tel: 0171-593 2000

BIRTHS (REGISTRATION)

The birth of a child must be registered within 42 days of birth at the register office of the district in which the baby was born. In England and Wales it is possible to give the particulars to be registered at any other register office. Responsibility for registering the birth rests with the parents, except in the case of an illegitimate child, when the mother is responsible for registration. Responsibility rests firstly with the parents but if they fail, particulars may be given to the registrar by:
– a relative of either parent (in Scotland only)
– the occupier of the house in which the baby was born
– a person present at the birth
– the person having charge of the child
Failure to register the birth within 42 days without reasonable cause may leave the parents liable to a penalty.

If the parents were married at the time of the birth, either parent may register the birth and details about both parents will be entered on the register. If the parents were unmarried at the time of the birth, the father's details are entered only if both parents attend or if the parents have made a statutory declaration confirming the identity of the father. Copies of the forms necessary to make such a declaration are available at the register offices. A short birth certificate is issued free when the birth is registered.

STILL BIRTHS

If a baby is stillborn, i.e. born dead after the 24th week of pregnancy, the birth must be registered. The doctor or midwife who attends the birth or afterwards examines the body of the child will issue a Medical Certificate of Stillbirth and this must be presented at the register office.

RE-REGISTRATION

In certain circumstances it may be necessary to re-register a birth, e.g. where the birth of an illegitimate child is legitimated by the subsequent marriage of the parents. It is also possible to re-register the birth of an illegitimate child so that the father's name is entered on the register.

BIRTH AT SEA

The master of a British ship must record any birth on board and send particulars to the Registrar-General of Shipping.

BIRTH ABROAD

Births of British subjects occurring abroad are registered with consular officers and certificates of birth are subsequently available from the Registrar-General. The registration of births among members of the armed forces that occur abroad or on military ships or aircraft is governed by the Registration of Births, Deaths and Marriages (Special Provisions) Act 1957.

SCOTLAND

In Scotland the birth of a child must be registered within 21 days at the register office of either the district in which the baby was born or the district in which the mother was resident at the time of the birth.

If the child is born, either in or out of Scotland, on a ship, aircraft or land vehicle that ends its journey at any place in Scotland, the child, in most cases, will be registered as if born in that place.

CERTIFICATES OF BIRTHS, DEATHS OR MARRIAGES

Certificates of births, deaths or marriages that have taken place in England and Wales since 1837 can be obtained from the Office of National Statistics (General Register Office). Applications can be made:
– by a personal visit to the Family Records Centre, London (for opening hours, *see* below)
– by postal application to the General Register Office, Southport
Certificates are also available from the Superintendent Registrar for the district in which the event took place or, in the case of marriage certificates, from the minister of the church in which the marriage took place. Any register office can advise about the best way to obtain certificates.

There is no charge for the short birth certificate issued when a birth is registered. The fees for other certificates (from 1 April 1998) are:

Obtained from Registrar who registered the birth, death or marriage
Standard certificate, £3.50
Special certificate for certain statutory purposes, £3.50
Short certificate of birth, £3.50

Obtained from Superintendent Registrar
Standard certificate, £6.50
Special certificate for certain statutory purposes, £3.50
Short certificate of birth, £5.00

From the Family Records Centre, London / by post from the General Register Office, Southport
Standard certificate of birth, death or marriage
Personal application, £6.50
Postal application, £12.00
Postal application and information from ONS Index supplied, £9.00
Standard certificate of adoption
Personal application, £6.50
Postal application, £10.50

Short certificate of birth
Personal application, £6.50
Postal application, £12.00
Postal application and information from ONS Index supplied, £9.00
Short certificate of adoption
Personal application, £3.50
Postal application, £9.00

Indexes prepared from the registers are available for searching by the public at the Family Records Centre in London or at a Superintendent Registrar's Office; indexes at the latter relate only to births, deaths and marriages which occurred in that registration district. There is no charge for searching the indexes in the Public Search Room at the Family Records Centre but a general search fee is charged for searches at a Superintendent Registrar's Office. A fee is charged for verifying index references against the records.

The Society of Genealogists has many records of baptisms, marriages and deaths prior to 1837.

SCOTLAND

Certificates of births, deaths or marriages that have taken place in Scotland since 1855 can be obtained from the General Register Office or from the appropriate local registrar. The General Register Office also keeps the Register of Divorces (including decrees of declaration of nullity of marriage), and holds parish registers dating from before 1855.

Fees for certificates (from 1 April 1998) are:

Certificates (full or abbreviated) of birth, death, marriage or adoption, £8.00
Electronic mail application, £10.00

Particular search for each period of five years or part thereof, whether specified entry is traced or not:
Personal application, £3.00
Postal application, £5.00
Electronic mail application, £7.00

General search in the indexes to the statutory registers and parochial registers, per day or part thereof:
Payment not less than 14 days in advance, £13.00
In any other case, £17.00

Further information can be obtained from:
THE GENERAL REGISTER OFFICE, Office for National Statistics, Smedley Hydro, Trafalgar Road, Birkdale, Southport, Merseyside PR8 2HH. Tel: 01704-569824
FAMILY RECORDS CENTRE, 1 Myddelton Street, London ECIR 1UW. Opens 9 a.m. on Monday, Wednesday, Thursday, Friday, 10 a.m. Tuesday, 9.30 a.m. Saturday. Closes 5 p.m. Monday, Wednesday, Friday, Saturday, 7 p.m. Tuesday, Thursday
THE GENERAL REGISTER OFFICE, New Register House, Edinburgh EH1 3YT. Tel: 0131-334 0380
THE SOCIETY OF GENEALOGISTS, 14 Charterhouse Buildings, Goswell Road, London ECIM 7BA. Tel: 0171-251 8799

BRITISH CITIZENSHIP

The British Nationality Act 1981 which came into force on 1 January 1983 established three types of citizenship to replace the single form of Citizenship of the UK and Colonies created by the British Nationality Act 1948. The three forms of citizenship are: British Citizenship; British Dependent Territories Citizenship; and British Overseas Citizenship. Three residual categories were created:

British Subjects; British Protected Persons; and British Nationals (Overseas).

BRITISH CITIZENSHIP

Almost everyone who was a citizen of the UK and colonies and had a right of abode in the UK prior to the 1981 Act became British citizens when the Act came into force. British citizens have the right to live permanently in the UK and are free to leave and re-enter the UK at any time.

A person born on or after 1 January 1983 in the UK (including, for this purpose, the Channel Islands and the Isle of Man) is entitled to British citizenship if he/she falls into one of the following categories:
– he/she has a parent who is a British citizen
– he/she has a parent who is settled in the UK
– he/she is a newborn infant found abandoned in the UK
– his/her parents subsequently settle in the UK
– he/she lives in the UK for the first ten years of his/her life and is not absent for more than 90 days in each of those years
– he/she is adopted in the UK and one of the adopters is a British Citizen

A person born outside the UK may acquire British citizenship if he/she falls into one of the following categories:
– he/she has a parent who is a British citizen otherwise than by descent, e.g. a parent who was born in the UK
– he/she has a parent who is a British citizen serving the Crown overseas
– the Home Secretary consents to his/her registration while he/she is a minor
– he/she is a British Dependent Territories citizen, a British Overseas citizen, a British subject or a British protected person and has been lawfully resident in the UK for five years
– he/she is a British Dependent Territories citizen who acquired that citizenship from a connection with Gibraltar
– he/she is adopted (*see* above) or naturalized (*see* below)

Where parents are married, the status of either may confer citizenship on their child. If a child is illegitimate, the status of the mother determines the child's citizenship.

Under the 1981 Act, Commonwealth citizens and citizens of the Republic of Ireland were entitled to registration as British citizens before 1 January 1988. In 1985 citizens of the Falkland Islands were granted British citizenship.

Renunciation of British citizenship must be registered with the Home Secretary and will be revoked if no new citizenship or nationality is acquired within six months. If the renunciation was required in order to retain or acquire another citizenship or nationality, the citizenship may be reacquired once.

BRITISH DEPENDENT TERRITORIES CITIZENSHIP

Under the 1981 Act, this type of citizenship was conferred on citizens of the UK and colonies by birth, naturalization or registration in British Dependent Territories. British Dependent Territories citizens may be entitled to registration as British citizens on completion of five years' legal residence in the UK.

On 1 July 1997 citizens of Hong Kong who did not qualify to register as British citizens under the British Nationality (Hong Kong) Act 1990 lost their British Dependent Territories citizenship on the handover of sovereignty to China; they may, however, have applied to register as British Nationals (Overseas).

Eligibility for British Dependent Territories citizenship is determined by similar rules to those for acquiring British citizenship, except that the connection is with the dependent territory rather than with the UK.

BRITISH OVERSEAS CITIZENSHIP

Under the 1981 Act, this type of citizenship was conferred on any UK and colonies citizens who did not qualify for British citizenship or citizenship of the British Dependent Territories. British Overseas citizenship may be acquired by the wife and minor children of a British Overseas citizen in certain circumstances. British Overseas citizens may be entitled to registration as British citizens on completion of five years' legal residence in the UK.

RESIDUAL CATEGORIES

British subjects, British protected persons and British Nationals (Overseas) may be entitled to registration as British citizens on completion of five years' legal residence in the UK.

Citizens of the Republic of Ireland who were also British subjects before 1 January 1949 can retain that status if they fulfill certain conditions.

EUROPEAN UNION CITIZENSHIP

British citizens (including Gibraltarians who are registered as such) are also EU citizens and are entitled to travel freely to other EU countries to work, study, reside and set up a business. EU citizens have the same rights with respect to the United Kingdom.

NATURALIZATION

Naturalization is granted at the discretion of the Home Secretary. The basic requirements are five years' residence (three years if the applicant is married to a British citizen), good character, adequate knowledge of the English, Welsh or Scottish Gaelic language, and an intention to reside permanently in the UK.

STATUS OF ALIENS

Aliens may not hold public office or vote in Britain and they may not own a British ship or aircraft. Citizens of the Republic of Ireland are not deemed to be aliens.

Further information can be obtained from the Home Office, Nationality Directorate, 3rd Floor, India Buildings, Water Street, Liverpool L2 0QN. Tel: 0151-237 5200

CONSUMER LAW

SALE OF GOODS

A sale of goods contract is the most common type of contract. It is governed by the Sale of Goods Act 1979 (as amended by the Sale and Supply of Goods Act 1994). The Act provides protection for buyers by implying terms into every sale of goods contract. These terms are:
– a condition that the seller will pass good title to the buyer (unless the seller agrees to transfer only such title as he has)
– where the seller sells goods by reference to a description, a condition that the goods will match that description and, where the sale is by sample and description, a condition that the bulk of the goods will correspond with such sample and description
– where goods are sold by a business seller, a condition that the goods will be of satisfactory quality if they meet the standard that a reasonable person would regard as satisfactory taking into account any description of the goods, the price, and all other relevant circumstances.

The quality of the goods includes their state and condition, relevant aspects being whether they are suitable for their common purpose, their appearance and finish, freedom from minor defects and their safety and durability. This term will not be implied, however, if a buyer has examined the goods and should have noticed the defect or if the seller specifically drew the buyer's attention to the defect

– where goods are sold by a business seller, a condition that the goods are reasonably fit for any purpose made known to the seller by the buyer, unless the buyer does not rely on the seller's judgement, or it is not reasonable for him/her to do so

– where goods are sold by sample, conditions that the bulk of the sample will correspond with the sample in quality, that the buyer will have a reasonable opportunity of comparing the two and that the goods are free from any defect rendering them unsatisfactory which would not be obvious from the sample

Some of the above terms can be excluded from contracts by the seller. The seller's right to do this is, however, restricted by the Unfair Contract Terms Act 1977. The Act offers more protection to a buyer who 'deals as a consumer', that is where the sale is a business sale, the goods are ordinarily bought for private use and the goods are bought by a buyer who is not a business buyer. In a sale by auction or competitive tender, a buyer never deals as consumer. Also, a seller can never exclude the implied term as to title mentioned above.

HIRE-PURCHASE AGREEMENTS

Terms similar to those implied in contracts of sales of goods are implied into contracts of hire-purchase, under the Supply of Goods (Implied Terms) Act 1973. The 1977 Act limits the exclusion of these implied terms as before.

SUPPLY OF GOODS AND SERVICES

Under the Supply of Goods and Services Act 1982, similar terms are also implied in other types of contract under which ownership of goods passes, e.g. a contract for 'work and materials' such as supplying new parts while servicing a car, and contracts for the hire of goods. These types of contracts have additional implied terms:

– that the supplier will use reasonable care and skill
– that the supplier will carry out the service in a reasonable time (unless the time has been agreed)
– that the supplier will make a reasonable charge (unless the charge has already been agreed)

The 1977 Act limits the exclusion of these implied terms in a similar manner as before.

UNFAIR TERMS

The Unfair Terms in Consumer Contracts Regulations 1994 apply to contracts between business sellers (or suppliers of goods and services) and consumers, where the terms have not been individually negotiated, i.e. where the terms were drafted in advance so that the consumer was unable to influence those terms. An unfair term is one which operates to the detriment of the consumer. An unfair term does not bind the consumer but the contract will continue to bind the parties if it is capable of existing without the unfair term. The regulations contain a non-exhaustive list of terms which are regarded as unfair. Whether a term is regarded as fair or not will depend on many factors, including the nature of the goods or services, the surrounding circumstances (such as the bargaining strength of both parties) and the other terms in the contract.

TRADE DESCRIPTIONS

It is a criminal offence under the Trade Descriptions Act 1968 for a business seller to apply a false trade description of goods or to supply or offer to supply any goods to which a false description has been applied. A 'trade description' includes descriptions of quality, size, composition, fitness for purpose and method, and place and date of manufacture of the goods. It is also an offence to give a false indication of the price of goods. Prosecutions are brought by trading standards inspectors.

FAIR TRADING

The Fair Trading Act 1973 is designed to protect the consumer. It provides for the appointment of a Director-General of Fair Trading, one of whose duties is to review commercial activities in the UK relating to the supply of goods and services to consumers. An example of a practice which has been prohibited by a reference made under this Act is that of business sellers posing in advertisements as private sellers.

CONSUMER PROTECTION

Under the Consumer Protection Act 1987, producers of goods are liable for any injury or for any damage exceeding £275 caused by a defect in their product (subject to certain defences).

The Consumer Protection (Cancellation of Contracts Concluded Away from Business Premises) Regulations 1987 allow consumers a seven-day period in which to cancel contracts for the supply of goods and services, where the contracts were made during an unsolicited visit to the consumer's home or workplace. This only applies to contracts where the cost exceeds £35.

CONSUMER CREDIT

In matters relating to the provision of credit (or the supply of goods on hire or hire-purchase), consumers are also protected by the Consumer Credit Act 1974. Under this Act a licence, issued by the Director-General of Fair Trading, is required to conduct a consumer credit or consumer hire business or to deal in credit brokerage, debt adjusting, counselling or collecting. Any 'fit' person may apply to the Director-General of Fair Trading for a licence, which is normally renewable after ten years. A licence is not necessary if such types of business are only transacted occasionally, or if only exempt agreements are involved. The provisions of the Act only apply to 'regulated' agreements, i.e. those that are with individuals or partnerships, those that are not exempt (such as certain local authority and building society loans), and those where the total credit does not exceed £25,000. Provisions include:

– the terms of the regulated agreement can be altered by the creditor provided the agreement gives him/her the right to do so; in such cases the debtor must be given proper notice of this

– in order for a creditor to enforce a regulated agreement, the agreement must comply with certain formalities and must be properly executed. The debtor must also be given specified information by the creditor or his/her broker or agent during the negotiations which take place before the signing of the agreement. The agreement must state certain information such as the amount of credit, the annual percentage rate of interest and the amount and timing of repayments

– if an agreement is signed other than at the creditor's (or credit broker's or negotiator's) place of business and oral representations were made in the debtor's presence during discussions pre-agreement, the debtor has a right to cancel the agreement. Time for cancellation expires

five clear days after the debtor receives a second copy of the agreement. The agreement must inform the debtor of his right to cancel and how to cancel
- if the debtor is in arrears (or otherwise in breach of the agreement), the creditor must serve a default notice before taking any action such as repossessing the goods
- if the agreement is a hire-purchase or conditional sale agreement, the creditor cannot repossess the goods without a court order if the debtor has paid one-third of the total price of the goods
- in agreements where the debtor is required to make grossly exorbitant payments or where the agreement grossly contravenes the ordinary principles of fair trading, the debtor may request that the court alter or set aside some of the terms of the agreement. The agreement can also be reopened during enforcement proceedings by the court itself

Where a credit reference agency has been used to check the debtor's financial standing, the creditor must give the agency's name to the debtor, who is entitled to see the agency's file on him. A fee of £1 is payable to the agency.

SCOTLAND

The legislation governing the sale and supply of goods applies to Scotland as follows:
- the Sale of Goods Act 1979 applies with some modifications and it has been amended by the Sale and Supply of Goods Act 1994
- the Supply of Goods (Implied Terms) Act 1973 applies
- the Supply of Goods and Services Act 1982 does not extend to Scotland but some of its provisions were introduced by the Sale and Supply of Goods Act 1994
- only Parts II and III of the Unfair Contract Terms Act 1977 apply
- the Trade Descriptions Act 1968 applies with minor modifications
- the Consumer Credit Act 1974 applies

PROCEEDINGS AGAINST THE CROWN

Until 1947, proceedings against the Crown were generally possible only by a procedure known as a petition of right, which put the litigant at a considerable disadvantage. The Crown Proceedings Act 1947 placed the Crown (not the Sovereign in his/her private capacity, but as the embodiment of the State) largely in the same position as a private individual. The Act did not, however, extinguish or limit the Crown's prerogative or statutory powers, and it granted immunity to HM ships and aircraft. It also left certain Crown privileges unaffected. The Act largely abolished the special procedures which previously applied to civil proceedings by and against the Crown. Civil proceedings may be instituted against the appropriate government department or against the Attorney-General.

In Scotland proceedings against the Crown founded on breach of contract could be taken before the 1947 Act and no special procedures applied. The Crown could, however, claim certain special pleas. The 1947 Act applies in part to Scotland and brings the practice of the two countries as closely together as the different legal systems permit. Civil proceedings may be instituted against the Lord Advocate representing the appropriate government department.

DEATHS

WHEN A DEATH OCCURS

If the death was expected, the doctor who attended the deceased during their final illness should be contacted. If the death was sudden or unexpected, the family doctor (if known) and police should be contacted. For stillbirths, see page 651.

If the cause of death is quite clear the doctor will provide:
- a medical certificate that shows the cause of death (this will be in a sealed envelope, addressed to the registrar)
- a formal notice that states that the doctor has signed the medical certificate and that explains how to get the death registered

If the death was known to be caused by a natural illness but the doctor wishes to know more about the cause of death, he/she may ask the relatives for permission to carry out a post-mortem examination. This should not delay the funeral.

In England and Wales a coroner is responsible for investigating deaths occurring in the following circumstances:
- when no doctor has treated the deceased during his or her last illness or when the doctor attending the patient did not see him or her within 14 days before death, or after death; or
- when the death occured during an operation or before recovery from the effect of an anaesthetic; or
- when the death was sudden and unexplained or attended by suspicious circumstances; or
- when the death might be due to an industrial injury or disease, or to accident, violence, neglect or abortion, or to any kind of poisoning; or
- the death occurred in prison or in police custody

The doctor will write on the formal notice that the death has been referred to the coroner; if the post mortem shows that death was due to natural causes, the coroner may issue a notification which gives the cause of death so that the death can be registered. If the cause of death was violent or unnatural, the coroner is obliged to hold an inquest.

In Scotland the office of coroner does not exist. The local procurator fiscal inquires into sudden or suspicious deaths. A fatal accident inquiry will be held before the sheriff where the death has resulted from an accident during the course of the employment of the person who has died, or where the person who has died was in legal custody, or where the Lord Advocate deems it in the public interest that an inquiry be held.

REGISTERING A DEATH

In England and Wales the death must be registered by the registrar of births and deaths for the district in which it occurred; details can be obtained from the telephone directory (under registration of births and deaths and marriages), from the doctor or local council, or at a post office or police station. From April 1997, information concerning a death can be given before any registrar of births and deaths in England and Wales. The registrar will pass the relevant details to the registrar for the district where the death occurred, who will then register the death. In Scotland a death may be registered in any registration district in which the deceased was ordinarily resident immediately before his/her death.

In England and Wales the death must normally be registered within five days; in Scotland it must be registered within eight days. If the death has been referred to the coroner it cannot be registered until the registrar has received authority from the coroner to do so. Failure to register a death involves a penalty.

If the death occurred at a house, the death may be registered by:

– any relative of the deceased present at the death or in attendance during the last illness
– any relative of the deceased residing or being in the sub-district where the death occurred
– any person present at the death
– the occupier or any inmate of the house if he/she knew of the occurrence of the death
– any person causing the disposal of the body

The person registering the death should take the medical certificate of the cause of death with them; it is also useful, though not essential, to take the deceased's birth and marriage certificates, medical card (if possible), pension documents and life assurance details. The registrar will issue a certificate for burial or cremation and a certificate of registration of death; both are free of charge. A death certificate is a certified copy of the entry in the death register; these can be provided on payment of a fee and may be required for the following purposes:

– the will
– bank and building society accounts
– savings bank certificates and premium bonds
– insurance policies
– pension claims

If the death occurred abroad or on a foreign ship or aircraft, the death should be registered according to the local regulations of the relevant country and a death certificate should be obtained. The death can also be registered with the British Consul in that country and a record will be kept at the General Register Office. This avoids the expense of bringing the body back.

After 12 months of death or the finding of a dead body, no death can be registered without the consent of the Registrar-General.

BURIAL AND CREMATION

In most circumstances in England and Wales a certificate for burial or cremation must be obtained from the registrar before the burial or cremation can take place. If the death has been referred to the coroner, an order for burial or a certificate for cremation must be obtained. In Scotland a body may be buried (but not cremated) before the death is registered.

Most funerals are arranged by a funeral director. The funeral costs can normally be repaid out of the deceased's estate and will be given priority over any other claims. If the deceased has left a will it may contain directions concerning the funeral; however, these directions need not be followed by the executor.

The deceased's papers should also indicate whether a grave space had already been arranged. Most town churchyards and many suburban churchyards are no longer open for burial because they are full. Most cemeteries are non-denominational and may be owned by local authorities or private companies; fees vary.

If the body is to be cremated, an application form, two cremation certificates (for which there is a charge) or a certificate for cremation if the death was referred to the coroner, and a certificate signed by the medical referee must be completed in addition to the certificate for burial or cremation (the form is not required if the coroner has issued a certificate for cremation). All the forms are available from the funeral director or crematorium. Most crematoria are run by local authorities; the fees usually include the medical referee's fee and the use of the chapel. Ashes may be scattered, buried in a churchyard or cemetery, or kept.

The registrar must be notified of the date, place and means of disposal of the body within 96 hours (England and Wales) or three days (Scotland).

If the death occurred abroad or on a foreign ship or aircraft, a local burial or cremation may be arranged. If the body is to be brought back to England or Wales, a death certificate from the relevant country or an authorization for the removal of the body from the country of death from the coroner or relevant authority will be required. To arrange a funeral in England or Wales an authenticated translation of a foreign death certificate or a death certificate issued in Scotland or Northern Ireland which must show the cause of death, is needed, together with a certificate of no liability to register from the registrar in England and Wales in whose sub-district it is intended to bury or cremate the body. If it is intended to cremate the body a cremation order will be required from the Home Office or a certificate for cremation.

Further information can be obtained from:

THE GENERAL REGISTER OFFICE, Office for National Statistics, Smedley Hydro, Trafalgar Road, Birkdale, Southport, Merseyside PR8 2HH. Tel: 01704-569824

THE GENERAL REGISTER OFFICE, New Register House, Edinburgh EH1 3YT. Tel: 0131-334 0380

DIVORCE AND RELATED MATTERS

ENGLAND AND WALES

There are two types of matrimonial suit: those seeking the annulment of a marriage, and those seeking a judicial separation or divorce. To obtain an annulment, judicial separation or divorce in England and Wales, one or both of the parties must have their permanent home in England and Wales when the petition is started, or have been living in England and Wales for at least a year on the day the petition is started. All cases are commenced in divorce county courts or in the Divorce Registry in London. If a suit is defended it may be transferred to the High Court.

NULLITY OF MARRIAGE

A marriage is invalid from the beginning if:

– the parties were within the prohibited degrees of consanguinity, affinity or adoption (*see* page 664)
– the parties were not male and female
– either of the parties was already married (if the polygamous marriage was entered into outside England and Wales, it is invalid if either of the parties lived in England or Wales at the time of the marriage)
– either of the parties was under the age of 16
– the formalities of the marriage were defective, e.g. the marriage did not take place in an authorized building, and both parties knew of the defect

In the case of those aged 16 to 17, absence of parental consent does not invalidate the marriage.

A marriage may be voidable (i.e. a decree of nullity may be obtained but in the meantime the marriage remains valid) on the following grounds:

– either party was unable to consummate the marriage
– the respondent wilfully refused to consummate the marriage (insistence on the use of contraceptives does not constitute wilful refusal to consummate, but may constitute unreasonable behaviour for the purpose of divorce and may be allowed as a defence to a charge of desertion)

- either party did not validly consent to the marriage, in consequence of duress, mistake, unsoundness of mind, or otherwise
- either party was suffering from a mental disorder at the time of the marriage
- the respondent was suffering from a communicable venereal disease at the time of the marriage, and the petitioner did not know this
- the respondent was pregnant by another man at the time of the marriage, and the petitioner did not know this

In the last four circumstances, proceedings must generally be instituted within three years of the date of the marriage.

A decree of nullity only annuls the marriage from the date of the decree, and any children of the marriage are legitimate. Children of a void marriage are illegitimate unless the father lived in England and Wales at the time of the birth (or father's death, if earlier) and at the time of conception (or marriage, if later) both or either of the parents reasonably believed the marriage was valid.

When a marriage has been annulled, both parties are free to marry again.

Separation

A couple may enter into an agreement to separate by consent but for the agreement to be valid it must be followed by an immediate separation; a solicitor should be contacted.

Judicial separation does not dissolve a marriage and it is not necessary to prove that the marriage has irretrievably broken down. Either party can petition for a judicial separation at any time; the grounds listed below as grounds for divorce are also grounds for judicial separation.

Divorce

Divorce dissolves the marriage and leaves both parties at liberty to marry again. Neither party can petition for divorce until at least one year after the date of the marriage. The fee for starting a divorce petition is £150. The sole ground for divorce is the irretrievable breakdown of the marriage; this must be proved on one or more of the following grounds:

- the respondent has committed adultery and the petitioner finds it intolerable to live with him/her; however the petitioner cannot rely on an act of adultery by the other party if they have lived together for more than six months after the discovery that adultery had been committed
- the respondent has behaved in such a way that the petitioner cannot reasonably be expected to continue living with him/her
- the respondent deserted the petitioner for two years immediately before the petition. Desertion may be defined as a voluntary withdrawal from cohabitation by the respondent without just cause and against the wishes of the petitioner; where one party is guilty of serious misconduct which forces the other party to leave, the party at fault is said to be guilty of constructive desertion
- the respondent and the petitioner have lived separately for two years immediately before the petition and the respondent consents to the decree
- the respondent and the petitioner have lived separately for five years immediately before the petition

A total period of less than six months during which the parties have resumed living together is disregarded in determining whether the prescribed period of separation or desertion has been continuous (but cannot be included as part of the period of separation).

The Matrimonial Causes Act 1973 requires the solicitor for the petitioner in certain cases to certify whether the possibility of a reconciliation has been discussed with the petitioner.

The Decree Nisi

A decree nisi does not dissolve or annul the marriage but must be obtained before a divorce or annulment can take place.

Where the suit is undefended, the evidence normally takes the form of a sworn written statement made by the petitioner which is considered by a district judge. If the judge is satisfied that the petitioner has proved the contents of the petition, he/she will set a date for the pronouncement of the decree nisi in open court; neither party need attend.

If the judge is not satisfied that the petitioner has proved the contents of the petition, or if the suit is defended, the petition will be heard in open court with the parties giving oral evidence.

The Decree Absolute

The decree nisi is usually made absolute after six weeks and on the application of the petitioner. The fee for applying for a decree absolute is £20. If the judge thinks it may be necessary to exercise any of his/her powers under the Children Act 1989, he/she can in exceptional circumstances delay the granting of the decree absolute. The decree absolute dissolves or annuls the marriage.

Children

Neither parent is now awarded 'custody' of any children of the marriage in England and Wales. Both parents, if married, have 'parental responsibility'. Either parent can exercise this, independently of the other. Any dispute between the parents can be resolved by the courts. In all court cases concerning children, whether connected to a matrimonial suit or not, the welfare of the child is the paramount consideration.

Maintenance, etc.

Either party may be liable to pay maintenance to their former spouse. If there were any children of the marriage, both parents have a legal responsibility to support them financially if they can afford to do so. These so-called ancillary matters, including any property settlements, may be settled before the divorce goes through but currently can go on long after the marriage is dissolved.

The courts are responsible for assessing maintenance for the former spouse, taking into account each party's income and essential outgoings and other aspects of the case. The court also deals with any maintenance for a child which has been treated by the spouses as a 'child of the family', e.g. a stepchild, and any property settlements.

The Child Support Agency (CSA) was set up under the Child Support Act 1991 and is now responsible for assessing the maintenance that absent parents should pay for their natural or adopted children (whether or not a marriage has taken place). The CSA accepts applications only when all the people involved are habitually resident in the UK; the courts will continue to deal with cases where one of the people involved lives abroad. The CSA deals with all new cases, and is gradually taking on cases where the parent with care (or his/her new partner) was already receiving income support, family credit or disability working allowance before 5 April 1993. People with existing court orders or written maintenance agreements made before 5 April 1993 should continue to use the courts. Where it is already collecting child maintenance, the CSA has the power to offer a collection and enforcement service for certain other payments of maintenance.

A formula is used to work out how much child maintenance is payable. The formula ensures that after the payment of child maintenance the absent parent's income, and that of any second family he/she may now have, remains significantly above basic income support rates. Also, no absent parent will normally be assessed to pay more than 30 per cent of his/her net income in current child maintenance, or more than 33 per cent if he/she is also liable for any arrears. Absent parents are normally expected to pay at least a minimum amount of child maintenance (currently about £2.50 a week).

A scheme has begun to be introduced since the end of 1996 which allows departures from the formula in certain tightly defined circumstances, e.g. the high costs of travel to maintain contact with a child, or to have a property and capital transfer ('clean break' settlement) entered into before April 1993 taken into account; there will also be some additional grounds which may result in liability being increased.

Some cases involving unusual circumstances are treated as special cases and the assessment is modified. Where there is financial need (e.g. because of disability or continuing education), maintenance may be ordered by the court for children even beyond the age of 18.

The level of maintenance is reviewed automatically every two years. Either parent can report a change of circumstances and request a review at any time. An independent complaints examiner for the CSA was appointed in early 1997.

If the absent parent does not pay the child maintenance, the CSA may make an order for payments to be deducted directly from his/her salary or wages; if all other methods fail, the CSA may take court action to enforce the payment.

Court Orders

Magistrates' courts used for domestic proceedings are now called family proceedings courts. A spouse can apply to the family proceedings court for a court order on the ground that the other spouse:
– has failed to pay reasonable maintenance for the applicant
– has failed to make a proper contribution towards the reasonable maintenance of a 'child of the family'
– has deserted the applicant
– has behaved in such a way that the applicant cannot reasonably be expected to live with the respondent
   If the case is proved, the court can order:
– periodical payments for the applicant and/or a 'child of the family'
– a lump sum payment (not exceeding £1,000) to the applicant and/or a 'child of the family'
   In deciding what orders (if any) to make, the court must consider guidelines which are similar to those governing financial orders in divorce cases. There are also special provisions relating to consent orders and separation by agreement. An order may be enforceable even if the parties are living together, but in some cases it will cease to have effect if they continue to do so for six months.

Domestic Violence

If one spouse has been subjected to violence at the hands of the other, it is now possible to obtain a court order very quickly to restrain further violence and if necessary to have the other spouse excluded from the home. Such orders may also relate to unmarried couples. A person disobeying such a court order is liable to be imprisoned for contempt of court.

Impending Legislation

A recent Act of Parliament provides that irretrievable breakdown would be the sole ground for divorce; the partner initiating the divorce would be required to attend an information session about the nature of divorce and the options available; and divorce would be granted after one year, or 18 months if the couple have children, during which time the couple would have the chance to take part in mediation sessions to make arrangements concerning children, property and money. These changes are unlikely to be effective until 2000 at the earliest.

SCOTLAND

Although there is separate legislation for Scotland covering nullity of marriage, judicial separation, divorce and ancillary matters, the provisions are in most respects the same as those for England and Wales. The following is confined to those points on which the law in Scotland differs.

A suit for judicial separation or divorce may be raised in the Court of Session; it may also be raised in the Sheriff Court if either party was resident in the sheriffdom for 40 days immediately before the date of the action or for 40 days ending not more than 40 days before the date of the action. The fee for starting a divorce petition is £72 in the Sheriff Court.

When adultery is cited as proof that the marriage has broken down irretrievably, it is not necessary in Scotland to prove also that it is intolerable for the petitioner to live with the respondent. In the case of desertion, irretrievable breakdown is not established if cohabitation is resumed for a period of more than three months after the two-year desertion period has expired.

The court is responsible for seeking to promote a reconciliation between the spouses. Where a divorce action has been raised, it may be postponed by the court to enable the parties to seek to effect a reconciliation if the court feels that there may be a reasonable prospect of such reconciliation. If the parties do cohabit during such postponement, no account is taken of the cohabitation if the action later proceeds.

In actions for divorce and separation, the court has the power to award a residence order in respect of any children of the marriage. The welfare of the children is of paramount importance, and the fact that a spouse has caused the breakdown of the marriage does not in itself preclude him/her from being awarded residence.

A simplified procedure for 'do-it-yourself' divorce was introduced in 1983 for certain divorces. If the action is based on two or five years' separation and will not be opposed, and if there are no children under 16 and no financial claims, the applicant can write directly to the local sheriff court or to the Court of Session for the appropriate forms to enable him or her to proceed. The fee is £56, unless the applicant receives income support, family credit or legal advice and assistance, in which case there is no fee. The decree absolute is known in Scotland as the extract decree. The fee for applying for an extract decree is £16.

Further information can be obtained from any divorce county court, solicitor or Citizens' Advice Bureau, the Lord Chancellor's Department or the Lord Advocate's Department (for entries, *see* Index), or the following:

The Principal Registry, First Avenue House, 42–49 High Holborn, London wciv 6np. Tel: 0171-936 6000

The Court of Session, Divorce Section (SP), Parliament House, Parliament Square, Edinburgh ehi irq. Tel: 0131-225 2595

THE CHILD SUPPORT AGENCY, Longbenton, Newcastle upon Tyne NE98 IYX. Tel: 0191-213 5000

EMPLOYMENT LAW

PAY AND CONDITIONS

The Employment Rights Act 1996 consolidates the statutory provisions relating to employees' rights. Employers must give each employee based in Great Britain and employed for more than one month a written statement containing the following information:
– names of employer and employee
– date when employment began
– remuneration and intervals at which it will be paid
– job title or description of job
– hours and place(s) of work
– holiday entitlement and holiday pay
– entitlement to sick leave and sick pay
– details of pension scheme(s)
– length of notice period that employer and employee need to give to terminate employment, or the end date for a fixed-term contract
– details of any collective agreement which affects the terms of employment
– details of disciplinary and grievance procedures
– if the employee is to work outside the UK for more than one month, the period of such work and the currency in which payment is made
This must be given to the employee within two months of the start of their employment.

SICK PAY

Employees absent from work through illness or injury are entitled to receive Statutory Sick Pay (SSP) from the employer for a maximum period of 28 weeks in any three-year period. This applies to all employees, both men and women, up to the age of 65.

DEDUCTIONS FROM PAY

Employers may not make deductions from an employee's wages without the employee's prior written consent or unless authorized by statute (e.g. deductions for national insurance or tax).

PART-TIME EMPLOYEES

The rights of part-time workers are in most circumstances in line with the treatment of full-time workers.

SUNDAY TRADING

The Sunday Trading Act 1994 gave new rights to shop workers. They have the right not to be dismissed, selected for redundancy or to suffer any detriment (such as the denial of overtime, promotion or training) if they refuse to work on Sundays. This does not apply to those who, under their contracts, are employed to work on Sundays.

TRADE UNION MEMBERSHIP

Under employment legislation, employees or potential employees may not be penalized because they are or are not a member of a trade union.

DISPUTES

Where it has not been possible to settle a dispute in the workplace, it may be possible for employees to make a complaint to an industrial tribunal. ACAS (the Advisory, Conciliation and Arbitration Service; for entry, see Index) offers advice and conciliation in employment disputes.

TERMINATION OF EMPLOYMENT

An employee may be dismissed without notice if guilty of gross misconduct but in other cases a period of notice must be given by the employer. The minimum periods of notice specified in the Employment Rights Act 1996 are:
– at least one week if the employee has been continuously employed for one month or more but for less than two years
– at least two weeks if the employee has been continuously employed for two years or more. A week is added for every complete year of continuous employment up to 12 years
– at least 12 weeks for those who have been continuously employed for 12 years or more
– longer periods apply if these are specified in the contract of employment
If an employee is dismissed with less notice than he/she is entitled to, the employer is generally liable to pay wages for the period of proper notice (or for the period of the contract for those on fixed-term contracts). Generally, no notice needs to be given of the expiry of a fixed-term contract.

REDUNDANCY

An employee dismissed because of redundancy may be entitled to a lump sum. This applies if:
– the employee has at least two years' continuous service (qualified as for unfair dismissal, below)
– the employee is actually dismissed by the employer (even in cases of voluntary redundancy)
– dismissal is due to a reduction in the work force
An employee may not be entitled to a redundancy payment if offered a new job by the same employer. The amount of payment depends on the length of service, the salary and the age of the employee.

UNFAIR DISMISSAL

Complaints about unfair dismissal are dealt with by an industrial tribunal. Any employee, with two years' continuous service (although this requirement has been referred by the House of Lords to the European Court of Justice) subject to exceptions, regardless of their hours of work, can make a complaint to the tribunal. At the tribunal the employer must prove that he/she acted reasonably in dismissing the employee and that the dismissal was due to one or more of the following reasons:
– the employee's capability for the job
– the employee's conduct
– redundancy
– a legal restriction preventing the continuation of the employee's contract
– some other substantial reason
If the employee is found to have been unfairly dismissed, the tribunal can order that he/she be reinstated or compensated.

DISCRIMINATION

Discrimination in employment on the grounds of sex, race or (subject to wide exceptions) disability is unlawful. The following legislation applies to those employed in Great Britain but not to employees in Northern Ireland or (subject to EC exceptions) to those who work mainly abroad:
– The Equal Pay Act 1970 (as amended) entitles men and women to equality in matters related to their contracts of employment. Those doing like work for the same employer are entitled to the same pay and conditions regardless of their sex
– The Sex Discrimination Act 1975 (as amended by the Sex Discrimination Act 1986) makes it unlawful to

discriminate on grounds of sex or marital status. This covers all aspects of employment, including advertising for recruits, terms offered, opportunities for promotion and training, and dismissal procedures
- The Race Relations Act 1976 gives individuals the right not to be discriminated against in employment matters on the grounds of race, colour, nationality, or ethnic or national origins. It applies to all aspects of employment
- The Disability Discrimination Act 1995 makes discrimination against a disabled person in all aspects of employment unlawful. Unlike sex and race discrimination, an employer may show that the treatment is justified and that the employer acted reasonably. Employers with 20 or fewer employees are exempt

The Equal Opportunities Commission and the Commission for Racial Equality (for entries, *see* Index) have the function of eliminating such discriminations in the workplace and can provide further information and assistance.

In Northern Ireland like provisions exist but are constituted in separate legislation. The Fair Employment (Northern Ireland) Act 1989 adds specific provisions aimed at preventing religious discrimination.

ILLEGITIMACY AND LEGITIMATION

The Children Act 1989 gives the mother parental responsibility for the child when she is not married to the father. The father can acquire parental responsibility either by agreement with her (in prescribed form) or by applying to the court. If an illegitimate child is to be adopted, the father's consent is required only where he has been awarded parental rights by the court.

Every child born to a married woman during marriage is presumed to be legitimate, unless the couple are separated under court order when the child is conceived, in which case the child is presumed not to be the husband's child. It is possible to challenge the presumption of legitimacy or illegitimacy through court proceedings.

In Scotland, the father of an illegitimate child has a responsibility to provide for that child until he/she is 16. The mother of the child can take action in court if this is not done. The court will also decide on residence and contact issues.

LEGITIMATION
Under the Legitimacy Act 1976, an illegitimate person automatically becomes legitimate when his/her parents marry. This applies even where one of the parents was married to a third person at the time of the birth. In such cases it is necessary to re-register the birth of the child. In Scotland, the relevant legislation is the Legitimation (Scotland) Act 1968 which came into operation on 8 June 1968, on which date thousands of existing illegitimate children were regarded as legitimate.

RIGHTS OF ILLEGITIMATE PEOPLE
For the purposes of most legislation, illegitimate and legitimate people have the same rights and responsibilities. In particular, under the Family Law Reform Acts 1969 and 1987, legitimate and illegitimate children have broadly the same rights on an intestacy. Furthermore, in any will made after 31 December 1969, it is assumed that any reference to children or relatives will include those who are illegitimate and those related through another person who is illegitimate. In Scotland, illegitimate and legitimate people are given equal status under the Law Reform (Parent and Child) Scotland Act 1986.

JURY SERVICE

A person charged with any but the most minor offences is entitled to be tried by jury, although jury trials are now unusual in civil cases. In England and Wales there are 12 members of a jury in a criminal case and eight members in a civil case. In Scotland there are 12 members of a jury in a civil case in the Court of Session, seven in the Sheriff Court, and 15 in a criminal trial. Jurors are normally asked to serve for ten working days, although jurors selected for longer cases are expected to sit for the duration of the trial.

Every parliamentary or local elector between the ages of 18 and 70 who has lived in the UK (including, for this purpose, the Channel Islands and the Isle of Man) for any period of at least five years since reaching the age of 13 is qualified to serve on a jury unless he/she is ineligible or disqualified.

ENGLAND AND WALES
Those ineligible for jury service include:
- those who have at any time been judges, magistrates or senior court officials
- those who have within the previous ten years been concerned with the adminstration of justice (e.g. barristers, solicitors and their clerks, court officials, coroners, police officers, prison officers and probation officers)
- priests of any religion and vowed members of religious communities
- certain sufferers from mental illness

Those disqualified from jury service include:
- those who have at any time been sentenced by a court in the UK (including, for this purpose, the Channel Islands and the Isle of Man) to a term of imprisonment or custody of five years or more
- those who have within the previous ten years served any part of a sentence of imprisonment, youth custody or detention, been detained in a young offenders' institution, received a suspended sentence of imprisonment or order for detention, or received a community service order
- those who have within the previous five years been placed on probation

Those who may be excused as of right from jury service include:
- persons over the age of 65
- members and officers of the Houses of Parliament
- full-time serving members of the armed forces
- registered and practising members of the medical, dental, nursing, veterinary and pharmaceutical professions
- those who have served on a jury in the previous two years

The court has the discretion to excuse a juror from service, or defer the date of service, if the service would be a hardship to the juror. If a person serves on a jury knowing himself/herself to be ineligible or disqualified, he/she is liable to be fined up to £5,000 if disqualified and up to £1,000 for all other offences. The defendant can object to any juror if he/she can show cause.

A juror may claim travelling expenses, a subsistence allowance and an allowance for other financial loss (e.g. loss of earnings or benefits, fees paid to carers or child-minders) up to a stated limit.

It is an offence for a juror to disclose what happened in the jury room even after the trial is over. A jury's verdict must normally be unanimous, but if no verdict has been reached after two hours' consideration (or such longer period as the court deems to be reasonable) a majority verdict is acceptable if ten jurors agree to it.

It is an offence to intimidate, threaten or harm a juror.

SCOTLAND

Qualification criteria for jury service in Scotland are similar to those in England and Wales, except that the maximum age for a juror is 65, and those who have within the previous five years been concerned with the administration of justice are ineligible for service. Ministers of religion, persons in holy orders and those who have served on a jury in the previous five years are excusable as of right.

The maximum fine for a person serving on a jury knowing himself/herself to be ineligible is £1,000. The maximum fine for failing to attend without good cause is also £1,000.

Further information can obtained from:

THE COURT SERVICE, Southside, 105 Victoria Street, London SW1E 6QT. Tel: 0171-210 1775

THE CLERK OF JUSTICIARY, High Court of Justiciary, Parliament House, Parliament Square, Edinburgh EH1 1RQ. Tel: 0131-225 2595

LANDLORD AND TENANT

When a property is rented to a tenant, the rights and responsibilities of the landlord and the tenant are determined largely by the tenancy agreement but also by statutory provisions. Some of the main provisions are outlined below but it is advisable to contact the Citizens' Advice Bureau or the local authority housing department for further information.

RESIDENTIAL LETTINGS

The provisions outlined here apply only where the tenant lives in a separate dwelling from the landlord and where the dwelling is the tenant's only or main home. It does not apply to licensees such as lodgers, guests or service occupiers.

The 1996 Housing Act radically changes certain aspects of the legislation referred to below, in particular the grant of assured and assured shorthold tenancies under the Housing Act 1988. It is advisable to check whether the new legislation has come into force before relying on the provisions set out below.

ASSURED SHORTHOLD TENANCIES

If a tenancy was granted on or after 15 January 1989 and before 28 February 1997, the tenant may have an assured tenancy giving that tenant greater rights. The tenant could, for example, stay in possession of the dwelling for as long as the tenant observed the terms of the tenancy. The landlord cannot obtain possession from such a tenant unless the landlord can establish a specific ground for possession (set out in the Housing Act 1988) and obtains a court order. The rent payable is that agreed with the landlord unless the rent has been fixed by the rent assessment committee of the local authority. The tenant or the landlord may request that the committee set the rent in line with open market rents for that type of property. Any rent increases that are to take place should be written into the agreement but failing that, the landlord must give advance notice of the increase.

Under the Housing Act 1996, most new lettings entered into on or after 28 February 1997 will be assured shorthold tenancies. This means that tenants are given limited rights. The landlord must obtain a court order, however, to obtain possession if the tenant refuses to vacate at the end of the tenancy.

REGULATED TENANCIES

Before the Housing Act 1988 came into force (15 January 1989) there were regulated tenancies; some are still in existence and are protected by the Rent Act 1977. Under this Act it is possible for the landlord or the tenant to apply to the local rent officer to have a 'fair' rent registered. The fair rent is then the maximum rent payable.

SECURE TENANCIES

Secure tenancies are generally given to tenants of local authorities, housing associations and certain other bodies. This gives the tenant lifelong tenure unless the terms of the agreement are broken by the tenant. In certain circumstances those with secure tenancies may have the right to buy their property. In practice this right is generally only available to council tenants.

AGRICULTURAL PROPERTY

Tenancies in agricultural properties are governed by the Agricultural Holdings Act 1986 and the Rent (Agricultural) Act 1976, which give similar protections to those described above, e.g. security of tenure, right to compensation for disturbance, etc. The Agricultural Holdings (Scotland) Act 1991 applies similar provisions to Scotland.

EVICTION

Under the Protection from Eviction Act 1977 (as amended by the Housing Act 1988), a landlord must give reasonable notice that he/she is to evict the tenant, and in most cases a possession order, granted in court, is necessary. Notice is generally to be at least four weeks and in prescribed statutory form (notices are available from law stationers). It is illegal for a landlord to evict a person by putting their belongings onto the street, by changing the locks and so on. It is also illegal for a landlord to harass a tenant in any way in order to persuade him/her to give up the tenancy.

LANDLORD RESPONSIBILITIES

Under the Landlord and Tenant Act 1985, where the term of the lease is less than seven years the landlord is responsible for maintaining the structure and exterior of the property and all installations for the supply of water, gas and electricity, for sanitation, and for heating and hot water.

LEASEHOLDERS

Legally leaseholders have bought a long lease rather than a property and in certain limited circumstances the landlord can end the tenancy. Under the Leasehold Reform Act 1967 (as amended by the Housing Acts 1969, 1974 and 1980), leaseholders of houses may have the right to buy the freehold or to take an extended lease for a term of 50 years. This applies to leases where the term of the lease is over 21 years and where the leaseholder has occupied the house as his/her main residence for the last three years, or for a total of three years over the last ten.

The Leasehold Reform, Housing and Urban Development Act came into force in 1993 and allows the leaseholders of flats in certain circumstances to buy the freehold of the building in which they live.

Responsibility for maintenance of the structure, exterior and interior of the building should be set out in the lease. Usually the upkeep of the interior of his/her part of the property is the responsibility of the leaseholder, and responsibility for the structure, exterior and common interior areas is shared between the freeholder and the leaseholder(s).

BUSINESS LETTINGS

The Landlord and Tenant Acts 1927 and 1954 (as amended) give security of tenure to the tenants of most business premises. The landlord can only evict the tenant on one of the grounds laid down in the 1954 Act, and in some cases where the landlord repossesses the property the tenant may be entitled to compensation.

SCOTLAND

In Scotland assured and short assured tenancies exist for lettings after 2 January 1989 and are similar to assured tenancies in England and Wales. The relevant legislation is the Housing (Scotland) Act 1988.

Most tenancies created before 2 January 1989 were regulated tenancies and the Rent (Scotland) Act 1984 still applies where these exist. The Act defines, among other things, the circumstances in which a landlord can increase the rent when improvements are made to the property. The provisions of the Rent Act do not apply to tenancies where the landlord is the Crown, a local authority, the development corporation of a new town or a housing corporation.

The Housing (Scotland) Act 1987 and its provisions relate to local authority responsibilities for housing, the right to buy, and local authority secured tenancies. The provisions are broadly similar to England and Wales.

In Scotland, business premises are not controlled by statute to the same extent as in England and Wales, although the Shops (Scotland) Act 1949 gives some security to tenants of shops. Tenants of shops can apply to the sheriff for a renewal of tenancy if threatened with eviction. This application may be dismissed if the landlord has offered to sell the property to the tenant at an agreed price. The Act extends to properties where the Crown or government departments are the landlords or the tenants.

Under the Leases Act 1449 the landlord's successors (either purchasers or creditors) are bound by the agreement made with any tenants so long as the following conditions are met:
– the lease, if for more than one year, must be in writing
– there must be a rent
– there must be a term of expiry
– the tenant must have entered into possession

Many leases contain references to term and quarter days. The statutory dates of these are listed on page 9.

LEGAL AID

Under the Legal Aid Act 1988 (as amended) and the Legal Aid (Scotland) Act 1986, people on low or moderate incomes may qualify for help with the costs of legal advice or representation. The scheme is administered in England and Wales by the Legal Aid Board and in Scotland by the Scottish Legal Aid Board (for entries, *see* Index). There are three types of legal aid: civil legal aid, legal advice and assistance, and criminal legal aid.

CIVIL LEGAL AID

Applications for legal aid are made through a solicitor; the Citizens' Advice Bureau will have addresses for local solicitors. Franchised solicitors are those approved by the Legal Aid Boards, which can provide details.

Civil legal aid is available for proceedings in the following:
– the House of Lords
– the High Court
– the Court of Appeal
– county courts
– lands tribunals
– the Employment Appeal Tribunal
– the Restrictive Practices Court
– the Commons Commissioners
– civil proceedings in magistrates' courts
– family proceedings courts

It is not available for the following:
– tribunals other than those mentioned above
– defamation proceedings
– obtaining the decree in undefended divorce and judicial separation
– court cases outside England and Wales

ELIGIBILITY

The Legal Aid Board will only grant a civil legal aid certificate where:
– the applicant qualifies financially, and
– the applicant has reasonable grounds for taking or defending the action, and
– it is reasonable to grant legal aid in the circumstances of the case. For example, civil legal aid will not be granted where it appears that the applicant will gain only trivial advantage from the proceedings

In order to qualify for civil legal aid, a person's disposable income must be £7,777 a year or less and their disposable capital must be £6,750 or less. (The financial limits are different for pensioners and in personal injury claims). Disposable income is the total income, less outgoings such as tax and national insurance contributions, rent, council tax, mortgage payments, etc., with allowances made for dependants. The income of a spouse or cohabitee is taken into account unless they are living apart or have a contrary interest in the proceedings. Disposable capital includes savings, insurances, any personal possessions of substantial value and property owned. For applications from 1 June 1996, the applicant's dwelling house is treated as follows:
– the capital value of the property (i.e. market value, less amount outstanding on any mortgage) will be taken into account in so far as it exceeds £100,000
– the capital amount allowed in respect of mortgage debt or charge over the property cannot exceed £100,000
– if the mortgage debt exceeds £100,000, the amount allowed against income for mortgage payments will be reduced in proportion
– the total amount of mortgage debt allowed for all properties (including second and subsequent dwellings) cannot exceed £100,000

CONTRIBUTIONS

Some of those who qualify for legal aid will have to contribute towards their legal costs:
– if in receipt of income support, no contributions are due
– if annual disposable income is between £2,625 and £7,777, a contribution must be made from disposable income
– if disposable capital is over £3,000, all disposable capital in excess of £3,000 must be paid as a contribution

Contributions from disposable income are paid monthly for as long as the person has legal aid. The amount of the contribution depends on the amount of disposable income in excess of £2,625; the greater the excess income, the greater the contribution. Contributions from capital are payable immediately.

STATUTORY CHARGES

A statutory charge is made if a person receives money or property in a case for which they have received legal aid. This means that the amount paid by the Legal Aid Fund on their behalf is deducted from the amount that the person receives. This does not apply if the court has ordered that the costs be paid by the other party or if the payments are for maintenance. In family proceedings cases, the first £2,500 is exempt and the statutory charge is taken from anything in excess of that.

In urgent cases, e.g. domestic violence, legal aid may be granted without the means test. This will be carried out later and the person will have to reimburse the Legal Aid Fund for any aid that they received which exceeded their entitlement.

SCOTLAND

Civil legal aid is available for cases in the following:
- the House of Lords
- the Court of Session
- the Lands Valuation Appeal Court
- the Scottish Land Court
- sheriff courts
- the Lands Tribunal for Scotland
- the Employment Appeal Tribunals
- the Restrictive Practices Court

Eligibility for civil legal aid is assessed in a similar way to that in England and Wales, though the financial limits differ in some respects and are as follows:
- a person is eligible if disposable income is £8,571 or less and disposable capital is £8,560 or less
- if disposable income is between £2,625 and £8,571, contributions are payable
- if disposable capital exceeds £3,000, contributions are payable

LEGAL ADVICE AND ASSISTANCE

The legal aid and assistance scheme (commonly referred to as the green form scheme) covers the costs of getting advice and help from a solicitor, and, in some cases, representation in court under the 'assistance by way of representation' scheme (*see* below).

A person is eligible for legal advice and assistance if:
- they have a disposable income of £80 a week or less and disposable capital of £1,000 or less (£1,335 if the person has one dependant, £1,535 if two dependants)
- they are eligible for income support, family credit, income-based jobseeker's allowance or disability working allowance (unless they have disposable capital of more than £1,000)

There are no contributions under this scheme.

If a person is eligible, the Legal Aid Board will pay for up to two hours' work by a solicitor on behalf of the person (three hours where drafting a petition for divorce). The solicitor must seek the approval of the Legal Aid Board to claim for longer periods of time. The work the solicitor does may include giving advice, writing letters, making an application for civil/criminal legal aid, seeking the advice of a barrister, etc. The scheme does not cover any form of proceedings before a court or tribunal.

Any money or property recovered with the help of legal advice and assistance will be subject to a 'solicitor's charge', which is similar to a statutory charge in civil legal aid but with some differences.

ASSISTANCE BY WAY OF REPRESENTATION

This type of assistance is available for most cases in a family proceedings court and to patients before a mental health review tribunal. It covers the cost of preparing a case and of legal representation in the court.

Under this scheme the two-hour limit does not apply and the approval of the Legal Aid Board is needed in all cases. The income and capital limits are different to legal advice and assistance. In order to qualify, a person's disposable income must be £172 a week or less and their savings must not exceed £3,000. There is no means test for patients due before a mental health review tribunal. Contributions may have to be made and a solicitor's charge will apply to money or property recovered (as with legal advice and assistance).

DUTY SOLICITORS

The Legal Aid Act 1988 also provides free advice and assistance to anyone questioned by the police (whether under arrest or helping the police with their enquiries). No means test or contributions are required for this. The advice or assistance can be from the duty solicitor at the police station, from a person's own solicitor or from any local solicitor (a list is available at police stations).

Duty solicitors are usually available at the magistrates' court, in criminal cases, for advice and/or representation on first appearances. This assistance is not means-tested.

The Legal Aid Fund also covers the costs of a solicitor present in the buildings of family proceedings or county courts who may be requested by the court to advise or represent someone in need of help.

SCOTLAND

Legal advice and assistance operates in a similar way in Scotland. A person is eligible:
- if disposable income does not exceed £172 a week. If disposable income is between £72 and £172 a week, contributions are payable
- if disposable capital does not exceed £1,000 (£1,335 if the person has one dependant, £1,535 if two dependants). There are no contributions from capital

CRIMINAL LEGAL AID

It is up to the criminal court in which proceedings are to take place to grant criminal legal aid. The court will do this if it is desirable in the interests of justice (e.g. if there are important questions of law to be argued or the case is so serious that if found guilty the person may go to prison) and the person needs help to pay their legal costs.

Criminal legal aid covers the cost of preparing a case and legal representation (including the cost of a barrister) in criminal proceedings. It is also available for appeals against verdicts or sentences in magistrates' courts, the Crown Court or the Court of Appeal. It is not available for bringing a private prosecution in a criminal court.

If granted criminal legal aid, either the person may choose their own solicitor or the court will assign one. Contributions to the legal costs must be paid by anyone who has a disposable income of over £50 a week or disposable capital of over £3,000. These contributions are payable each month and will probably be returned to the person if they are acquitted. If the payments are not made, the legal aid order may be revoked.

SCOTLAND

The procedure for application for criminal legal aid depends on the circumstances of each case. In solemn cases (more serious cases, e.g. homicide) heard before a jury, it is for the court to decide whether to grant legal aid. In summary cases (less serious) the procedure depends on whether the person is in custody:

– anyone taken into custody has the right to free legal aid from the duty solicitor up to and including the first court appearance
– if the person is not in custody and wishes to plead guilty, they are not entitled to criminal legal aid but may be entitled to legal advice and assistance, including assistance by way of representation
– if the person is not in custody and wishes to plead not guilty, they can apply for criminal legal aid. This must be done within 14 days of the first court appearance at which they made the plea
The criteria used to assess whether or not criminal legal aid should be granted is similar to the criteria for England and Wales.

MARRIAGE

Any two persons may marry provided that:
– they are at least 16 years old on the day of the marriage (in England and Wales persons under the age of 18 must generally obtain the consent of their parents; if consent is refused an appeal may be made to the High Court, the county court or a court of summary jurisdiction)
– they are not related to one another in a way which would prevent their marrying (see below)
– they are unmarried (a person who has already been married must produce documentary evidence that the previous marriage has been ended by death, divorce or annulment)
– they are not of the same sex
– they are capable of understanding the nature of a marriage ceremony and of consenting to marriage
– the marriage would be regarded as valid in any foreign country of which either party is a citizen

Degrees of Relationship

A marriage between persons within the prohibited degrees of consanguinity, affinity or adoption is void.

A man may not marry his mother, daughter, grandmother, granddaughter, sister, aunt, niece, great-grandmother, great-granddaughter, adoptive mother, former adoptive mother, adopted daughter or former adopted daughter. In some circumstances he may now be allowed to marry his former wife's daughter, former wife's granddaughter, father's former wife or grandfather's former wife.

A woman may not marry her father, son, grandfather, grandson, brother, uncle, nephew, great-grandfather, great-grandson, adoptive father, former adoptive father, adopted son or former adopted son. In some circumstances she may now be allowed to marry her former husband's son, former husband's grandson, mother's former husband or grandmother's former husband.

ENGLAND AND WALES

Types of Marriage Ceremony

It is possible to marry by either religious or civil ceremony. A religious ceremony can take place at a church or chapel of the Church of England or the Church in Wales, or at any other place of worship which has been formally registered by the Registrar-General.

A civil ceremony can take place at a register office, a registered building or any other premises approved by the local authority. A list of approved premises for the area can be obtained from the local authority.

An application for an approved premises licence must be made by the owners or trustees of the building concerned; it cannot be made by the prospective marriage couple.

Approved premises must be regularly open to the public so that the marriage can be witnessed; the venue must be deemed to be a permanent and immovable structure. Open-air ceremonies are prohibited.

Non-Anglican marriages may also be solemnized following the issue of a Registrar-General's licence in unregistered premises where one of the parties is seriously ill, is not expected to recover, and cannot be moved to registered premises. Detained and housebound persons may be married at their place of residence.

Marriage in the Church of England or the Church in Wales

Marriage by banns

The marriage must take place in a parish in which one of the parties lives, or in a church in another parish if it is the usual place of worship of either or both of the parties. The banns must be called in the parish in which the marriage is to take place on three Sundays before the day of the ceremony; if either or both of the parties lives in a different parish the banns must also be called there. After three months the banns are no longer valid.

Marriage by common licence

The vicar who is to conduct the marriage will arrange for a common licence to be issued by the diocesan bishop; this dispenses with the necessity for banns. One of the parties must have lived in the parish for 15 days immediately before the issuing of the licence or must usually worship at the church. Affidavits are prepared from the personal instructions of one of the parties and the licence will be given to the applicant in person.

Marriage by special licence

A special licence is granted by the Archbishop of Canterbury in special circumstances for the marriage to take place at any place, with or without previous residence in the parish, or at any time. Application must be made to the Faculty Office of the Archbishop of Canterbury, 1 The Sanctuary, London SW1P 3JT. Tel: 0171-222 5381.

Marriage by certificate

The marriage can be conducted on the authority of the superintendent registrar's certificate, provided that the vicar's consent is obtained. One of the parties must live in the parish or must usually worship at the church.

Marriage by Other Religious Ceremony

One of the parties must normally live in the registration district where the marriage is to take place. In addition to giving notice to the superintendent registrar (see page 665), it may also be necessary to book a registrar to be present at the ceremony.

Civil Marriage

A marriage may be solemnized at any register office, registered building or approved premises in England and Wales. The superintendent registrar of the district should be contacted, and, if the marriage is to take place at approved premises, the necessary arrangements at the venue must also be made.

Notice of Marriage

Unless it is to take place by banns or under common or special licence in the Church of England or the Church in Wales, a notice of the marriage must be given in person to the superintendent registrar. Notice of marriage may be given in the following ways:

– by certificate. Both parties must have lived in a registration district in England or Wales for at least seven days immediately before giving notice at the local register office. If they live in different registration districts, notice must be given in both districts. The marriage can take place in any register office in England and Wales 21 days after notice has been given

– by licence (often known as 'special licence'). One of the parties must have lived in a registration district in England or Wales for at least 15 days before giving notice at the register office; the other party need only be a resident of, or be physically in, England and Wales on the day notice is given. The marriage can take place one clear day (other than a Sunday, Christmas Day or Good Friday) after notice has been given

A notice of marriage is valid for 12 months. It is not therefore possible to give formal notice of a marriage more than three months before it is to take place, but it should be possible to make an advance (provisional) booking 12 months before the ceremony. In this case it is still necessary to give formal notice three months before the marriage. When giving notice of the marriage it is necessary to produce official proof, if relevant, that any previous marriage has ended in divorce or death by producing a decree absolute or death certificate; it is also useful, but not necessary, to take birth certificates or passports as proof of age and identity.

SOLEMNIZATION OF THE MARRIAGE

On the day of the wedding there must be at least two other people present who are prepared to act as witnesses and sign the marriage register. A registrar of marriages must be present at a marriage in a register office or at approved premises, but an authorized person may act in the capacity of registrar in a registered building.

If the marriage takes place at approved premises, the room must be separate from any other activity on the premises at the time of the ceremony, and no food or drink can be sold or consumed in the room during the ceremony or for one hour beforehand.

The marriage must be solemnized between 8 a.m. and 6 p.m., with open doors. At some time during the ceremony the parties must make a declaration that they know of no legal impediment to the marriage and they must also say the contracting words; the declaratory and contracting words may vary according to the form of service in use but the most basic forms are:

– (*declaratory words*) 'I declare that I know of no legal reason why I, A. B., may not be joined in marriage to C. D.' Alternatively, the couple may answer 'I am' to the question 'Are you, A. B., free lawfully to marry C. D.?'
– (*contracting words*) 'I, A. B., take you, C. D., to be my wedded wife [or husband]'

A civil marriage cannot contain any religious aspects, but it may be possible for non-religious music and/or poetry readings to be included. It may also be possible to embellish the marriage vows taken by the couple.

If both parties are Jewish, they may be married in a synagogue, in a private house or elsewhere. The wedding may take place at any time of day and must be registered by the secretary of the synagogue of which the man is a member. The presence of a registrar of marriages is not necessary.

If both parties are members of the Society of Friends (Quakers), they may be married in a Friends' meeting-house. The marriage must be registered by the registering officer of the Society appointed to act for the district in which the meeting-house is situated. The presence of a registrar of marriages is not necessary.

CIVIL FEES *from 1 April 1998*

Registrar
Attending a marriage at a register office, £30.00
Attending a marriage at a registered building/residence of a housebound person, £36.00
Attending a marriage by Registrar-General's licence, £2.00

Superintendent Registrar
Entering a notice of marriage in marriage notice book, £21.00
Entering notice of marriage by Registrar-General's licence in marriage notice book, £3.00
Attending outside office to be given notice of marriage of housebound/detained person, £40.00
Issuing licence for marriage, £46.50
Attending marriage at residence of housebound/detained person, £40.00
Attending a marriage by Registrar-General's licence, £2.00
Attending with a registrar a marriage on approved premises, fee set by local authority
Marriage certificate on day of marriage, £3.50

ECCLESIASTICAL FEES *since 1 January 1997*
(Church of England and Church in Wales*)
Marriage by banns
For publication of banns, £13.00
For certificate of banns issued at time of publication, £7.00
For marriage service, £117.00
Marriage by common licence
Fee for licence, £53.00
Marriage by special licence
Fee for licence, £120.00
Further fees may be payable for additional facilities at the marriage, e.g. the organist's fee.

*Some of these fees may not apply to the Church in Wales

SCOTLAND

REGULAR MARRIAGES

A regular marriage is one which is celebrated by a minister of religion or authorized registrar or other celebrant. Proclamation of banns is not required in Scotland. Each of the parties must complete a marriage notice form and return it to the district registrar for the area in which they are to be married, irrespective of where they live, at least 15 days before the ceremony is due to take place.

A marriage schedule, which is prepared by the registrar, will be issued to one or both of the parties in person up to seven days before a religious marriage; for a civil marriage the schedule will be available at the ceremony. The schedule must be handed to the celebrant before the ceremony starts; it must be signed immediately after the wedding and the marriage must be registered within three days.

The authority to conduct a marriage is deemed to be vested in the person conducting the ceremony rather than in the building in which it takes place; open-air ceremonies are therefore permissible in Scotland.

MARRIAGE BY HABIT AND REPUTE

If two people live together constantly as husband and wife and are generally held to be such by the neighbourhood and among their friends and relations, there may arise a presumption from which marriage can be inferred. Before such a marriage can be registered, however, a decree of declarator of marriage must be obtained from the Deputy Principal Clerk of the Court of Session.

CIVIL FEES *from 1 April 1998*
The basic statutory fee is £72.00, comprising a £12.00 per person fee for a statutory notice of intention to marry, a £40.00 fee for solemnization of the marriage in a register office, and an £8.00 fee for a copy of the marriage certificate.

Further information can be obtained from:

THE GENERAL REGISTER OFFICE, Office for National Statistics, Smedley Hydro, Trafalgar Road, Birkdale, Southport, Merseyside PR8 2HH. Tel: 01704-569824

THE GENERAL REGISTER OFFICE FOR SCOTLAND, New Register House, Edinburgh EH1 3YT. Tel: 0131-334 0380

TOWN AND COUNTRY PLANNING

The principal legislation governing the development of land and buildings in England and Wales is the Town and Country Planning Act 1990 (as amended by the Planning and Compensation Act 1991). The equivalent legislation in Scotland is the Town and Country Planning (Scotland) Act 1997. The uses of buildings are classified by the Town and Country Planning (Use Classes) Order 1987 (as amended) in England and Wales, and in Scotland by the Town and Country Planning (Use Classes) (Scotland) Order 1997. It is advisable in all cases to contact the planning department of the local authority to check whether planning or other permission is needed.

PLANNING PERMISSION

Planning permission is needed if the work involves:
– making a material change in use, such as dividing off part of the house so that it can be used as a separate home or dividing off part of the house for commercial use, e.g. for a workshop
– going against the terms of the original planning permission, e.g. there may be a restriction on fences in front gardens on an open-plan estate
– building, engineering for mining, except for the permissions below
– new or wider access to a main road
– additions or extensions to flats or maisonettes

Planning permission is not needed to carry out internal alterations or work which does not affect the external appearance of the building.

There are certain types of development for which the Secretary of State for the Environment has granted general permissions. These include:
– house extensions and additions (including conservatories, loft conversions, garages and dormer windows). Up to 10 per cent or up to 50 cubic metres (whichever is the greater) can be added to the original house for terraced houses. Up to 15 per cent or 70 cubic metres (whichever is the greater) to other kinds of houses. The maximum that can be added to any house is 115 cubic metres
– buildings such as garden sheds and greenhouses so long as they are no more than 3 metres high (or 4 metres if the roof is ridged), are no nearer to a highway than the house, and at least half the ground around the house remains uncovered by buildings
– adding a porch with a ground area of less than 3 square metres and that is less than 3 metres in height
– putting up fences, walls and gates of under 1 metre in height if next to a road and under 2 metres elsewhere
– laying patios, paths or driveways for domestic use

OTHER RESTRICTIONS

It may be necessary to obtain other types of permissions before carrying out any development. These permissions are separate from planning permission and apply regardless of whether or not planning permission is needed, e.g.:
– building regulations will probably apply if a new building is to be erected, if an existing one is to be altered or extended, or if the work involves building over a drain or sewer. The building control department of the local authority will advise on this
– any alterations to a listed building or the grounds of a listed building must be approved by the local authority
– local authority approval is necessary if a building (or, in some circumstances, gates, walls, fences or railings) in a conservation area is to be demolished; each local authority keeps a register of all local buildings that are in conservation areas
– many trees are protected by tree preservation orders and must not be pruned or taken down without local authority consent
– bats and other species are protected and English Nature, the Countryside Council for Wales or Scottish Natural Heritage (for entries, *see* Index) must be notified before any work is carried out that will affect the habitat of protected species, e.g. timber treatment, renovation or extensions of lofts
– any development in areas designated as a National Park, an Area of Outstanding National Beauty, a National Scenic Area or in the Norfolk or Suffolk Broads is subject to greater restrictions. The local planning authority will advise or refer enquirers to the relevant authority

VOTERS' QUALIFICATIONS

Those entitled to vote at parliamentary, European Union (EU) and local government elections are those who are:
– resident in the constituency or ward on the qualifying date i.e. 10 October in the year before the electoral register (*see* below) comes into effect; in Northern Ireland the qualifying date is 15 September and voters must have been resident in Northern Ireland for the three months leading up to that date
– over 18 years old
– Commonwealth (which includes British) citizens or citizens of the Republic of Ireland

British citizens resident abroad are entitled to vote, for 20 years after leaving Britain, as overseas electors in parliamentary and EU elections in the constituency in which they were last resident. Members of the armed forces, Crown servants and employees of the British Council who are overseas and their spouses are entitled to vote regardless of how long they have been abroad.

European Union citizens resident in the UK may vote in EU and local government elections.

The following people are not entitled to vote:
– peers, and peeresses in their own right, who are members of the House of Lords (except that they may vote in EU and local government elections)
– patients detained under mental health legislation
– voluntary mental patients (unless they make a prescribed declaration)
– those serving prison sentences
– those convicted within the previous five years of corrupt or illegal election practices

REGISTERING TO VOTE

Voters must be entered on an electoral register, which runs from 16 February in one year to 15 February in the following year. The registration officer for each constituency is responsible for preparing and publishing the register. A registration form is sent to all households in the autumn of each year and the householder is required to provide details of all occupants who are eligible to vote, including ones who will reach their 18th birthday in the year covered by the register. Those who fail to give the required information or who give false information are liable to be fined. A draft register is usually published at the end of November. Any person whose name has been omitted may ask to be registered and should contact the registration officer. Anyone on the register may object to the inclusion of another person's name, in which case he/she should notify the registration officer, who will investigate that person's eligibility. Supplementary electors lists are published throughout the duration of the register.

VOTING

Voting is not compulsory in the UK. Those who wish to vote must generally vote in person at the allotted polling station. Those who will be away at the time of the election, those who will not be able to attend in person due to physical incapacity or the nature of their occupation, and those who have changed address during the period for which the register is valid, may apply for a postal vote or nominate a proxy to vote for them. Overseas electors who wish to vote must do so by proxy.

Further information can be obtained from the local authority's electoral registration officer in England and Wales or the regional valuation assessor in Scotland (details in local telephone directories), or the Chief Electoral Officer in Northern Ireland (3rd Floor, St Anne's House, 15 Church Street, Belfast BT1 1ER. Tel: 01232-245353).

WILLS AND INTESTACY

In a will a person leaves instructions as to the disposal of their property after they die. A will is also used to appoint executors (who will administer the estate), give directions as to the disposal of the body, appoint guardians for children and, for larger estates, can operate to reduce the level of inheritance tax. It is best to have a will drawn up by a solicitor but if a solicitor is not employed, the following points must be taken into account:
- if possible the will must not be prepared on behalf of another person by someone who is to benefit from it or who is a close relative of a major beneficiary
- the language used must be clear and unambiguous and it is better to avoid the use of legal terms where the same thing can be expressed in plain language
- it is better to rewrite the whole document if a mistake is made. If necessary, alterations can be made by striking through the words with a pen, and the signature or initials of the testator and the witnesses must be put in the margin opposite the alteration. No alteration of any kind should be made after the will has been executed
- if the person later wishes to change the will or part of it, it is better to write a new will revoking the old. The use of codicils (documents written as supplements or containing modifications to the will) should be left to a solicitor
- the will should be typed or printed, or if handwritten be legible and preferably in ink. Commercial will forms can be obtained from some stationers

The form of a will varies to suit different cases; the following is an example of how a will might be written. The notes after this example explain the terms used and procedures that need to be followed in drawing up a will.

This is the last will and testament of me [*Thomas Smith*] of [*Heather Cottage, Prospero Road, Manchester* M1 4DK] which I make this [*seventeenth*] day of [*May* 1998] and I revoke all previous wills and testamentary dispositions.
1. I appoint as my executors and trustees [*Ann Green of _____ and Richard Brown of _____*]. In my will the expression 'my Trustees' means any executors and trustees for the time being of my will and of any trust arising under it.
2. I give all my property to [*such of my children as shall survive me by 28 days and if more than one in equal shares* or as the case may be].
or
2. I give to [*Pamela Henderson of _____*] the sum of [£____] and to [*Michael Broadbent of _____*] the sum of [£____] and to [*Ruth Walker of _____*] all of my [*jewellery, books* or as the case may be]
and
3. I give everything not otherwise disposed of to [*Richard Black of _____*]
Signed by the testator in our joint presence and then by us in his.

Thomas Smith
[*Signature of the person making the will*]
Elizabeth Wall
[*Signature of witness*] of 67 Beatrice Lane, Manchester M1 4DK, journalist
William Jones
[*Signature of witness*] of 17 Paris Road, Manchester M1 4EN, tailor

TERMS TO AVOID USING

Keep the will as simple as possible. Try to avoid using the following terms, as they have specific legal meaning:
- real property
- personal property
- goods and chattels
- my money

SPECIFIC GIFTS AND LEGACIES

Gifts of specific items usually fail if the property is not owned by the person making the will on their death. This problem can be avoided by making a gift of any property fulfilling a particular description, e.g. a car, which is owned at the date of death. It is better in all cases where such gifts are made, to insert a clause which reads 'I give everything not otherwise disposed of to [Richard Black of _____], even if it seems that all property has already been disposed of in the will.

LAPSED LEGATEES

If a person who has been left property in a will dies before the person who made the will, the gift fails and will pass to the person entitled to everything not otherwise disposed of (the residuary estate).

If the person left the residuary estate dies before the person who made the will, their share will generally pass to the closest relative(s) of the person who made the will (as in intestacy) unless the will names a beneficiary such as a charity who will take as a 'long stop' if this gift is unable to take effect for any reason.

It is always better to draw up a new will if a beneficiary predeceases the person who made the will.

EXECUTORS

It is usual to appoint two executors, although one is sufficient. No more than four persons can deal with the estate of the person who has died. The name and address of each executor should be given in full (the addresses are not essential but including them adds clarity to the document).

Executors should be 18 years of age or over. An executor may be a beneficiary of the will.

WITNESSES

A person who is a beneficiary of a will, or the spouse of a beneficiary at the time the will is signed, must not act as a witness or else he/she will be unable to take his/her gift. Husband and wife can both act as witnesses provided neither benefits from the will. A blind person cannot witness a will.

It is better that a person does not act as an executor and as a witness, as he/she can take no benefit under a will to which he/she is witness. The identity of the witnesses should be made as explicit as possible.

EXECUTION OF A WILL

The person making the will should sign his/her name at the foot of the document, in the presence of the two witnesses. The witnesses must then sign their names while the person making the will looks on. If this procedure is not adhered to, the will will be considered invalid. There are certain exceptional circumstances where these rules are relaxed, e.g. where the person may be too ill to sign, and in these cases the attestation clause which normally reads 'signed by the testator in our joint presence and then by us in his/hers' should be reworded as follows:

The will was read over to Thomas Smith in our presence when he stated that he understood it. It was then signed on his behalf by Thomas Brown in the presence of the testator and by his direction in our joint presence and then by us in his.

CAPACITY TO MAKE A WILL

Anyone aged 18 or over can make a will. However, if there is any suspicion that the person making the will is not, through reasons of infirmity or age, fully in command of his/her faculties, it is advisable to arrange for a medical practitioner to examine the person making the will at the time it is to be executed to verify his/her mental capacity and to record that medical opinion in writing, and to ask the examining practitioner to act as a witness. If a person is not mentally able to make a will, the Court may do this for him/her under provisions contained in the Mental Health Act 1983.

REVOCATION

A will may be revoked or cancelled in a number of ways:
- a later will revokes an earlier one if it says so; otherwise the earlier will will be impliedly revoked by the later one to the extent that it contradicts or repeats the earlier one
- a will is also revoked if the physical document on which it is written is destroyed by the person whose will it is. There must be an intention to revoke the will. It may not be sufficient to obliterate the will with a pen
- a will is revoked when the person marries, unless it is clear from the will that the person intended the will to stand after the marriage
- where a marriage ends in divorce or is annulled or declared void, gifts to the spouse and the appointment of the spouse as executor fail unless the will says that this is not to happen. A former spouse is treated as having predeceased the testator. A separation does not change the effect of a married person's will.

PROBATE AND LETTERS OF ADMINISTRATION

Probate is granted to the executors named in a will and once granted, the executors are obliged to carry out the instructions of the will. Letters of administration are granted where no executor is named in a will or is willing or able to act or where there is no will or no valid will; this gives a person, often the next of kin, similar powers and duties to those of an executor.

Applications for probate or for letters of administration can be made to the Principal Registry of the Family Division, to a district probate registry or to a probate sub-registry. Applicants will need the following documents: the original will (if any); a certificate of death; oath for executors or administrators; particulars of all property and assets left by the deceased; a list of debts and funeral expenses. Certain property, up to the value of £5,000, may be disposed of without a grant of probate or letters of administration.

WHERE TO FIND A PROVED WILL

Since 1858 wills which have been proved, that is wills on which probate or letters of administration have been granted, must have been proved at the Principal Registry of the Family Division or at a district probate registry. The Lord Chancellor has power to direct where the original documents are kept but most are filed where they were proved and may be inspected there and a copy obtained. The Principal Registry also holds copies of all wills proved at district probate registries and these may be inspected at Somerset House. An index of all grants, both of probate and of letters of administration, is compiled by the Principal Registry and may be seen either at the Principal Registry or at a district probate registry.

It is also possible to discover when a grant of probate or letters of administration is issued by requesting a standing search. In response to a request and for a small fee, a district probate registry will supply the names and addresses of executors or administrators and the registry in which the grant was made, of any grant in the estate of a specified person made in the previous 12 months or following six months. This is useful for applicants under the Inheritance (Provision for Family and Dependants) Act 1975 (*see* Intestacy, page 669) and for creditors of the deceased.

SCOTLAND

In Scotland any person over 12 and of sound mind can make a will. The person making the will can only freely dispose of what is known as the 'dead's part' of the estate because:
- the spouse has the right to inherit one-third of the moveable estate if there are children or other descendants, and one-half of it if there are not
- children are entitled to one-third of the moveable estate if there is a surviving spouse, and one-half of it if there is not

The remaining portion is the dead's part, and legacies and bequests are payable from this. Debts are payable out of the whole estate before any division.

From August 1995, wills no longer needed to be 'holographed' and it is now only necessary to have one witness. The person making the will still needs to sign each page. It is better that the will is not witnessed by a beneficiary although the attestation would still be sound and the beneficiary would not have to relinquish the gift (as is the case in England and Wales).

Subsequent marriage does not revoke a will but the birth of a child who is not provided for may do so. A will may be revoked by a subsequent will, either expressly or by implication, but in so far as the two can be read together both have effect. If a subsequent will is revoked, the earlier will is revived.

Wills may be registered in the Books of the Sheriffdom in which the deceased lived or in the Books of Council and Session at the Registers of Scotland. The original will can be inspected and a copy obtained for a small fee.

CONFIRMATION

Confirmation (probate) is obtained in the sheriff court of the sheriffdom in which the deceased was resident at the time of death. Executives are either 'nominate' (named by the deceased in the will) or 'dative' (appointed by the court in cases where no executor is named in a will or in cases of intestacy). Applicants for confirmation must first provide an inventory of the deceased's estate and a schedule of debts, with an affidavit. In estates under £17,000 gross, confirmation can be obtained under a simplified procedure at reduced fees. The local sheriff clerk's office can provide assistance.

Further information can be obtained from:

PRINCIPAL REGISTRY (FAMILY DIVISION), First Avenue House, 42–49 High Holborn, London, WCIV 6NP. Tel: 0171-936 6000

REGISTERS OF SCOTLAND, Meadowbank House, 153 London Road, Edinburgh, EH8 7AU. Tel: 0131-659 6111

INTESTACY

Intestacy occurs when someone dies without leaving a will or leaves a will which is invalid or which does not take effect for some reason. In such cases the person's estate (property, possessions, other assets following the payment of debts) passes to certain members of the family. The relevant legislation is the Administration of Estates Act 1925, as amended by various legislation including the Intestates Estates Act 1952, the Law Reform (Succession) Act 1995, and the Trusts of Land and Appointment of Trustees Act 1996 and Orders made there under. Some of the provisions of this legislation are described below. If a will has been written that disposes of only part of a person's property, these rules apply to the part which is undisposed of.

If the person (intestate) leaves a spouse who survives for 28 days and children (legitimate, illegitimate and adopted children and other descendants), the estate is divided as follows:

- the spouse takes the 'personal chattels' (household articles, including cars, but nothing used for business purposes), £125,000 free of tax (with interest payable at 6 per cent from the time of the death until payment) and a life interest in half of the rest of the estate (which can be capitalized by the spouse if he/she wishes)
- the rest of the estate goes to the children*

If the person leaves a spouse who survives for 28 days but no children:

- the spouse takes the personal chattels, £200,000 free of tax (interest payable as before) and full ownership of half of the rest of the estate
- the other half of the rest of the estate goes to the parents (equally, if both alive) or, if none, to the brothers and sisters of the whole blood*
- if there are no parents or brothers or sisters of the whole blood or their children, the spouse takes the whole estate

If there is no surviving spouse, the estate is distributed among those who survive the intestate as follows:

- to surviving children*, but if none to
- parents (equally, if both alive), but if none to
- brothers and sisters of the whole blood*, but if none to
- brothers and sisters of the half blood*, but if none to
- grandparents (equally, if more than one), but if none to
- aunts and uncles of the whole blood*, but if none to
- aunts and uncles of the half blood*, but if none to
- the Crown, Duchy of Lancaster or the Duke of Cornwall (bona vacantia)

* To inherit, a member of these groups must survive the intestate and attain 18, or marry under that age. If they die under 18 (unless married

under that age), their share goes to others, if any, in the same group. If any member of these groups predeceases the intestate leaving children, their share is divided equally among their children.

In England and Wales the provisions of the Inheritance (Provision for Family and Dependants) Act 1975 may allow other people to claim provision from the deceased's assets. This Act also applies to cases where a will has been made and allows a person to apply to the Court if they feel that the will or rules of intestacy or both do not make adequate provision for them. The Court can order payment from the deceased's assets or the transfer of property from them if the applicant's claim is accepted. The application must be made within six months of the grant of probate or letters of administration and the following people can make an application:

- the spouse
- a former spouse who has not remarried
- a child of the deceased
- someone treated as a child of the deceased's family
- someone maintained by the deceased
- someone who has cohabited for two years before the death in the same household as the deceased and as the husband or wife of the deceased

SCOTLAND

Under the Succession (Scotland) Act 1964, no distinction is made between 'moveable' and 'heritable' property in intestacy cases.

A surviving spouse is entitled to 'prior rights'. This means that the spouse has the right to inherit:

- the matrimonial home up to a value of £110,000, or one matrimonial home if there is more than one, or, in certain circumstances, the value of the matrimonial home
- the furnishings and contents of that home, up to the value of £20,000
- £30,000 if the deceased left children or other descendants, or £50,000 if not

These figures are increased from time to time by order of the Secretary of State.

Once prior rights have been satisfied, what remains of the estate is generally divided between the surviving spouse and children (legitimate and illegitimate) according to 'legal' rights. Legal rights are:

Jus relicti(ae) – the right of a surviving spouse to one-half of the net moveable estate, after satisfaction of prior rights, if there are no surviving children; if there are surviving children, the spouse is entitled to one-third of the net moveable estate

Legitim – the right of surviving children to one-half of the net moveable estate if there is no surviving spouse; if there is a surviving spouse, the children are entitled to one-third of the net moveable estate after the satisfaction of prior rights

Where there is no surviving spouse or children, half of the estate is taken by the parents and half by the brothers and sisters. Failing that, the lines of succession, in general, are:

- to descendants
- if no descendants, then to collaterals (i.e. brothers and sisters) and parents
- surviving spouse
- if no collaterals or parents or spouse, then to ascendants collaterals (i.e. aunts and uncles), and so on in an ascending scale
- if all lines of succession fail, then to the Crown

Relatives of the whole blood are preferred to relatives of the half blood. The right of representation, i.e. the right of the issue of a person who would have succeeded if he/she had survived the intestate, also applies.

The Queen's Awards

The Queen's Award for Export Achievement and The Queen's Award for Technological Achievement were instituted by royal warrant in 1975. The two separate awards took the place of The Queen's Award to Industry, which had been instituted in 1965. In 1992 the scheme was extended with the launch of a third award, The Queen's Award for Environmental Achievement.

The export and technological awards are designed to recognize and encourage outstanding achievements in exporting goods or services from the United Kingdom and in advancing process or product technology. The purpose of the environmental award is to recognize and encourage product and process development which has major benefits for the environment and which is commercially successful.

The awards differ from a personal royal honour in that they are given to a unit as a whole, management and employees working as a team. They may be applied for by any organization within the United Kingdom, the Channel Islands or the Isle of Man producing goods or services which meet the criteria for the awards. Eligibility is not influenced in any way by the particular activities, location or size of the unit applying. Units or agencies of central and local government with industrial functions, as well as research associations, educational institutions and bodies of a similar character, are also eligible provided that they can show they have contributed to industrial efficiency.

Each award is formally conferred by a grant of appointment and is symbolized by a representation of its emblem cast in stainless steel and encapsulated in a transparent acrylic block.

Awards are held for five years and holders are entitled to fly the appropriate award flag and to display the emblem on the packaging of goods produced in this country, on the goods themselves, on the unit's stationery, in advertising and on certain articles used by employees. Units may also display the emblem of any previous current awards during the five years.

Awards are announced on 21 April (the birthday of The Queen) and published formally in a special supplement to the London Gazette.

AWARDS OFFICE

All enquiries about the scheme and requests for application forms (completed forms must be returned by 31 October) should be made to: The Secretary, The Queen's Awards Office, 151 Buckingham Palace Road, London SW1W 9SS. Tel: 0171-222 2277.

EXPORT ACHIEVEMENT

The criterion upon which recommendations for an award for export achievement are based is a substantial and sustained increase in export earnings to a level which is outstanding for the products or services concerned and for the size of the applicant unit's operations. Account will be taken of any special market factors described in the application. Applicants for the award will be expected to explain the basis of the achievement (e.g. improved marketing organization or new initiative to cater for export markets) and this will be taken into consideration. Export earnings considered will include receipts by the applicant unit in this country from the export of goods produced in this country, the provision of services to non-residents, merchant profit on re-export of foreign goods and/or trade arranged between overseas countries and royalties and fees from abroad. Account will be taken of the overseas expenses incurred other than marketing expenses. Income from profits (after overseas tax) remitted to this country from the applicant unit's direct investments in its overseas branches, subsidiaries or associates in the same general line of business will be taken into account, but not receipts from profits on other overseas investments or by interest on overseas loans or credits. Commissions or fees received by applicants for selling UK goods or services overseas as agents for other UK firms are also regarded as eligible export earnings.

In 1998, The Queen's Award for Export Achievement was conferred on the following concerns:

ADC Metrica, Richmond, Surrey – *computer software and services*

Abbeyvet Export Ltd, Sherburn-in-Elmet, N. Yorks – *veterinary products*

Aber Instruments Ltd, Aberystwyth – *yeast and biomass monitors*

Accuracy International Ltd, Portsmouth – *precision rifles and accessories*

Applied Communications Inc. Ltd, Watford – *computer software and services*

Aquaman (UK) Ltd, London SE24 – *waterproof plastic cases for cameras and communications equipment*

Ariella Fashions 80's Ltd, London N22 – *ladies' fashion outerwear*

Aston Martin Lagonda Ltd, Newport Pagnell, Bucks – *luxury sports and grand touring cars, parts and restoration services*

Aston Packaging Ltd, Birmingham – *recycled packaging and packaging production machinery*

Atlas Ward Structures Ltd, Malton, N. Yorks – *steel-framed structures and pre-engineered package buildings*

W. W. Bellamy (Bakers) Ltd, Trafford Park, Manchester – *breakfast muffins, crumpets and pancakes*

Bio-Rad Micromeasurements Ltd, York – *advanced measuring systems*

Enid Blyton Ltd, London W1 – *rights to the works of Enid Blyton*

Braime Elevator Components Ltd, Leeds – *components for material handling equipment*

Brintons Ltd, Kidderminster, Worcs – *Axminster and Wilton carpets*

H. P. Bulmer Ltd, Hereford – *cider*

Cable and Wireless Marine Ltd, Chelmsford – *installation and maintenance of submarine telecommunications cables*

Calcarb Ltd, Bellshill, Lanarkshire – *carbon-bonded carbon fibre thermal insulation*

Cambridge Animation Systems Ltd, Cambridge – *cartoon software*

Cambridge University Press, Cambridge – *publishing of academic books, journals and Bibles*

Cape Boards Ltd, Uxbridge, Middx – *high-performance asbestos-free building products*

Cleveland Cascades, Middlesbrough – *dry bulk loading chutes*

COBE Laboratories Ltd, Quedgeley, Glos – *medical products for open-heart surgery and blood transfusions*

Corney and Barrow (Broker Services) Ltd, London EC1 – *fine and rare wines*

Cussons Technology, Broughton, Manchester – *educational technology in internal combustion engines*

De La Rue Holographics (a division of De La Rue International Ltd), Basingstoke, Hants – *security holograms*

The Dudson Group of Companies, Stoke-on-Trent – *durable tableware for the catering industry*

Electro Furnace Products Ltd, Hull – *magnesia powder*

Energy for Sustainable Development Ltd, Corsham, Wilts – *energy consultancy*

Euro/DPC Ltd, Caernarfon – *diagnostic reagents and systems*

Europa Scientific Ltd, Crewe – *scientific instruments – mass spectrometers*

The Folio Society Ltd, London WC1 – *publishing*

France Angleterre Ltd, Sundridge, Kent – *tour operator*

GEC ALSTHOM Ruston Diesels Ltd, Newton-le-Willows, Merseyside – *medium-speed diesel engines*

Gordon and Innes Ltd, Huntly, Aberdeenshire – *seed potatoes*

William Grant and Sons Ltd, Bellshill, Lanarkshire – *Scotch whisky*

Griffin-Woodhouse Ltd, Cradley Heath, W. Midlands – *mooring systems*

Hammersmith Medicines Research Ltd, London NW10 – *medicines research*

Hawker Energy Products Ltd, Newport, Gwent – *lead acid batteries*

Heatric Ltd, Poole, Dorset – *heat exchangers*

K. Home Engineering Ltd, Thornaby-on-Tees, Cleveland – *project management and engineering design services*

John Horsfall and Sons (Greetland) Ltd, Halifax, W. Yorks – *blankets for air travel*

Huf UK Ltd, Willenhall, W. Midlands – *locks and handles for the automotive industry*

Domnick Hunter Ltd, Birtley, Co. Durham – *compressed air purification, liquid and air sterilization filters and gas generating equipment*

IMI Watson Smith Ltd, Leeds – *pneumatic control instrumentation*

ITE Group PLC, London W9 – *organization of international trade exhibitions and conferences*

Innovative Tooling Solutions (a division of Forth Tool and Valve Ltd), Glenrothes, Fife – *specialized machine tooling for controlled boring operations*

Inspec Fine Chemicals Ltd, Wolverhampton – *intermediate fine chemicals*

International Sorbent Technology Ltd, Hengoed, Mid Glam. – *scientific sample preparation products*

JCB Parts and Attachments, Rocester, Staffs – *spare parts and equipment*

Johnson and Johnson Medical Ltd, Ascot, Berks – *surgical and medical devices*

Joy Mining Machinery Ltd, Wigan – *underground mining equipment*

Kingspan Building Products Ltd, Holywell, Flintshire – *insulated roof and wall cladding*

Lloyd Loom of Spalding Ltd, Spalding, Lincs – *woven fibre furniture*

Load-Lok Manufacturing Ltd, Merthyr Tydfil, Mid Glam. – *cargo restraint systems*

Mabey and Johnson Ltd, Reading – *steel bridges*

The Macallan Distillers Ltd, Craigellachie, Banffshire – *malt Scotch whisky*

Merechoice Ltd, Worthing, W. Sussex – *radio pagers, mobile telephones and related components and equipment*

Micro Medical Ltd, Gillingham, Kent – *medical electronic devices and instruments*

Mondiale Corporation Ltd, Hitchin, Herts – *publishing and conference management for the office products industry*

Morrison Bowmore Distillers Ltd, Glasgow – *malt Scotch whisky*

Mott MacDonald Group Ltd, Croydon – *engineering consultancy services*

Nauticalia Ltd, Shepperton-on-Thames, Middx – *reproduction nautical artefacts*

Newall Measurement Systems Ltd, Leicester – *digital read-out systems*

News Digital Systems PLC, West Drayton, Middx – *digital television compression and transmission encryption systems*

Norbar Torque Tools Ltd, Banbury, Oxon – *torque tools and wrenches*

The Northampton Machinery Company Ltd, Northampton – *machinery for high-speed stranding and winding of cable*

Novartis Grimsby, Grimsby, Lincs – *fine organic chemicals*

Ocular Sciences Ltd, Eastleigh, Hants – *soft contact lenses*

Pace Micro Technology PLC, Shipley, W. Yorks – *analogue and digital set-top boxes for the reception of satellite, cable and terrestrial television transmissions*

Prestwick Circuits Ltd, Ayr – *printed circuit boards*

Prigee International Ltd, Perivale, Middx – *automotive components*

Quest International, Fragrance Division, Ashford, Kent – *fragrance ingredients and compounds*

Rhône-Poulenc Rorer Ltd, West Malling, Kent – *pharmaceutical products*

Rolls-Royce Commercial Aero Engines Ltd, Derby – *aero engines*

Rotary (International) Ltd, Mallusk, Co. Antrim – *mechanical and electrical installations*

Rover Group Ltd, Warwick – *motor vehicles*

SMC Transit International, Milton Keynes – *train door systems*

Samsung Electronics Manufacturing (UK) Ltd, Wynyard, Cleveland – *colour television sets, microwave ovens and monitors for personal computers*

Sanyo Electric Manufacturing (UK) Ltd, Newton Aycliffe, Co. Durham – *microwave ovens and magnetrons*

Scheibler Filters Ltd, Retford, Notts – *liquid chemical filters*

J. Henry Schroder and Co Ltd, International Energy and Projects Division, London EC2 – *financial advisory services*

Scomark Engineering Ltd, Swadlincote, Derbys – *pipeline fittings*

Scottish and Newcastle PLC, International Division, Edinburgh – *beer*

Seafood Marketing International PLC, Droylsden, Manchester – *frozen shrimps*

Seal Sands Chemicals Ltd, Seal Sands, Middlesbrough – *synthetic organic fine chemicals*

Sema Group Telecoms (a division of Sema Group UK Ltd), London WC1 – *software for the telecommunications industry*

SEOS Displays Ltd, Burgess Hill, W. Sussex – *visual display systems for training simulators*

Sibert Instruments Ltd, Guildford, Surrey – *instruments and equipment for use within the CD industry*

Software 2000 Ltd, Oxford – *computer software*

Solid State Logic Ltd, Begbroke, Oxon – *professional audio recording and mixing equipment*

Statestrong Ltd, Lytham, Lancs – *aerosol toiletries*

Steffen, Robertson and Kirsten (UK) Ltd, Cardiff – *engineering and scientific consulting services*

Sterling International Movers Ltd, Perivale, Middx – *international corporate relocating services*

Strix Ltd, Ronaldsway, Isle of Man – *controls for the domestic appliance industry*

Sulzer Vascutek Ltd, Inchinnan, Renfrewshire – *sterile implantable polyester fibre vascular grafts*

Sutcliffe Speakman Carbons Ltd, Ashton-in-Makerfield, Lancs – *speciality activated carbon*

Svitzer Ltd, Great Yarmouth, Norfolk – *specialized offshore surveying*

TSL Group PLC, Wallsend, Tyne and Wear – *fused quartz and silica products*

Thames Distributors Ltd, Hounslow, Middx – *sound recordings, wholesale merchants*

Thermoteknix Systems Ltd, Cambridge – *specialized electronics and products for infra-red imaging and line scanning*

W. H. Tracey Textile Recyclers, Bury – *second-hand clothing and footwear*

UCB Films PLC, Wigton, Cumbria – *cellulose and polypropylene films*

UWG Ltd, Norwich – *engineering and management services and products to the offshore oil and gas industry*

UNECIA Ltd (Universities of England Consortium for International Activities), Sheffield – *academic and technical assistance, consultancy and training*

VZS Technical Ceramics Ltd, Glenrothes, Fife – *technical ceramics*

Visual Communications Group Ltd, London E14 – *stock photographs*

Vosper Thornycroft Holdings PLC, Southampton – *Naval ships, support packages and spares*

Ward Shoes, Sheffield – *end-of-range and imperfect footwear*

Wavespec Ltd, Maldon, Essex – *marine consultancy*

Weardale Steel (Wolsingham) Ltd, Bishop Auckland, Co. Durham – *ships' stern castings and fabrications*

Wesley Jessen PBH Ltd, Southampton – *contact lenses*

Vivienne Westwood Ltd, London SW11 – *fashion clothing and accessories*

York International Ltd, Manufacturing Division, Basildon, Essex – *chillers for air conditioning and refrigeration*

Zeneca LifeScience Molecules, Blackley, Manchester – *fine chemicals and biotechnology-based products*

TECHNOLOGICAL ACHIEVEMENT

The criterion upon which recommendations for an award for technological achievement are based is a significant advance, leading to increased efficiency, in the application of technology to a production or development process in British industry or the production for sale of goods which incorporate new and advanced technological qualities. An award is only granted for production or development processes which have achieved commercial success.

In 1998 The Queen's Award for Technological Achievement was conferred on the following concerns:

Advent Communications Ltd, Chesham, Bucks – *motorized mobile satellite communications system 'NewSwift'*

BBC Research and Development, Tadworth, Surrey – *motion compensated television standards converter*

DRS Hadland Ltd, Tring, Herts – *Imacon 468 ultra high-speed imaging system*

Electronic Techniques (Anglia) Ltd, Ipswich – *high-speed vacuum encapsulation of minute safety-critical electronic components*

Institute of Laryngology and Otology, London WC1 – *screening technology for detecting hearing deficiencies in newborn babies*

Nycomed Amersham PLC, Imaging Division, Little Chalfont, Bucks – *Myoview™ imaging agent for the study of heart disease*

Otodynamics Ltd, Hatfield, Herts – *screening technology for detecting hearing deficiencies in newborn babies*

Rolls-Royce PLC, Engineering and Technology, Derby – *gas turbine high-temperature technology*

SEOS Displays Ltd, Burgess Hill, W. Sussex – *multi-projector wide field-of-view display systems*

Smiths Industries Aerospace; Civil Systems UK, Cheltenham – *Electrical Load Management System (ELMS) for civil passenger aircraft*

Snell and Wilcox Ltd, Petersfield, Hants – *motion compensated television standards converter*

Stewart Hughes Ltd, Eastleigh, Hants – *monitoring systems for detecting defects in helicopter engines and systems*

Surface Technology Systems Ltd, Newport, Gwent – *anisotropic plasma etching of silicon*

Surrey Satellite Technology Ltd, Guildford, Surrey – *modular microsatellite*

ENVIRONMENTAL ACHIEVEMENT

The criterion upon which recommendations for an award for environmental achievement are based is a significant advance in the application by British industry of the development of products, technology or processes which offer major benefits in environmental terms compared to existing products, technology or processes. An award is only granted for products, technology or processes which have achieved commercial success. Applicants are expected to show the significance and difficulty of the environmental problem addressed, the extent to which the product, technology or process addresses the problem's cause as opposed to its effect, and the potential for wider application or transfer.

In 1998 The Queen's Award for Environmental Achievement was conferred on the following concerns:

Energy Technology and Control Ltd, Lewes, E. Sussex – *energy conservation and reduction of harmful emissions to air from combustion processes in industrial boilers*

Euro Chemical Control PLC, Leeds – *Devex developer recycling management system for the film processing industries*

Pilkington PLC, St Helens, Merseyside – *Pilkington 3R™ technology to reduce NO_x emissions in glass melting furnaces*

Rolls-Royce PLC, Aerospace, Derby – *low NO_x aeroengine combustor*

The Media

CROSS-MEDIA OWNERSHIP

There are rules on cross-media ownership to prevent undue concentration of ownership. These were amended by the Broadcasting Act 1996. Radio companies are now permitted to own one AM, one FM and one other (AM or FM) service; ownership of the third licence is subject to a public interest test. Local newspapers with a circulation under 20 per cent in an area are also allowed to own one AM, one FM and one other service, and may control a regional Channel 3 television service subject to a public interest test. Local newspapers with a circulation between 20 and 50 per cent in an area may own one AM and one FM service, subject to a public interest test, but may not control a regional Channel 3 service. Those with a circulation over 50 per cent may own one radio service in the area (provided that more than one independent local radio service serves the area) subject to a public interest test.

Ownership controls on the number of television or radio licences have been removed; holdings are now restricted to 15 per cent of the total television audience or 15 per cent of the total points available in the radio points scheme. Ownership controls on cable operators have also been removed. National newspapers with less than 20 per cent of national circulation may apply to control any broadcasting licences, subject to a public interest test. National newspapers with more than 20 per cent of national circulation may not have more than a 20 per cent interest in a licence to provide a Channel 3 service, Channel 5 or national and local analogue radio services.

Broadcasting

The British Broadcasting Corporation (*see* pages 285–6) is responsible for public service broadcasting in the UK. Its role is to provide high-quality programmes with wide-ranging appeal that educate, inform and entertain. Its constitution and finances are governed by royal charter and agreement. On 1 May 1996 a new royal charter came into force, establishing the framework for the BBC's activities until 2006.

The Independent Television Commission (*see* page 313) and the Radio Authority (*see* pages 335–6) were set up under the terms of the Broadcasting Act 1990. The ITC is the regulator and licensing authority for all commercially-funded television services, including cable and satellite services. The Radio Authority is the regulator and licensing authority for all independent radio services.

COMPLAINTS

The Broadcasting Standards Commisson was set up in April 1997 under the Broadcasting Act 1996 and was formed from the merger of the Broadcasting Complaints Commission and the Broadcasting Standards Council. The Commission considers and adjudicates upon complaints of unfair treatment or unwarranted infringement of privacy in all broadcast programmes and advertisements on television, radio, cable, satellite and digital services. It also monitors the portrayal of violence and sex, and matters of taste and decency. Its new code of practice came into force on 1 January 1998.

BROADCASTING STANDARDS COMMISSION, 7 The Sanctuary, London SW1P 3JS. Tel: 0171-233 0544. *Chairman*, The Lady Howe of Aberavon; *Deputy Chairmen*, Ms J. Leighton, Mrs S. Warner; *Director*, S. Whittle

---

TELEVISION

All channels are broadcast in colour on 625 lines UHF from a network of transmitting stations. The BBC's transmission network was sold to the Castle Tower Consortium in February 1997; ITV transmission services are owned and operated by National Transcommunications Ltd. Transmissions are available to more than 99 per cent of the population.

The total number of receiving television licences in the UK at July 1998 was 21,634,000. Annual television licence fees are: monochrome £32.50; colour £97.50.

No overall statistics are available for subscriptions in the UK to satellite television services; British Sky Broadcasting had 6.2 million subscribers at March 1997, though an increasing number of these view through cable. At April 1998 there were 2,469,754 subscribers to cable television.

DIGITAL TELEVISION

Digital television broadcasting is a new technique which may improve the quality of the current reception of television programmes. It uses digital modulation to improve reception and digital compression to make more effective use of the frequency channels available than PAL, the analogue system currently used.

The Broadcasting Act 1996 provided for the licensing of 20 or more digital terrestrial television channels (on six frequency channels or 'multiplexes'). Two multiplexes were allocated to existing national television broadcasters (one to the BBC and one to ITV and Channel 4). A third multiplex, with guaranteed space for Channel 5, S4C in Wales and Gaelic programmes in Scotland, was awarded to SDN Ltd, the only bidder. All programmes broadcast on existing analogue channels will have to be broadcast on the equivalent digital service. Analogue broadcasting will eventually be discontinued.

In June 1997 the licences to run the remaining digital multiplexes were awarded by the ITC to British Digital Broadcasting (now called ONdigital), a consortium led by Carlton Communications and Granada. The first digital services are due to be on air by autumn 1998. Until digital television sets are on the market it will be necessary to purchase a set-top box to convert the digital signals into analogue sound and picture waves in order to watch the digital channels. Digital television services are also offered by cable and satellite companies.

AUDIENCE SHARE

ESTIMATED AUDIENCE SHARE *for 12 months to 31 March 1998*

	Percentage
ITV companies	32.4
BBC 1	30.4
BBC 2	11.3
Cable and satellite channels	11.2
Channel 4	10.0
Channel 5	3.2
S4C Wales	0.4

Source: Independent Television Commission

BBC TELEVISION

Television Centre, Wood Lane, London W12 7RJ
Tel 0181-743 8000

The BBC's experiments in television broadcasting started in 1929 and in 1936 the BBC began the world's first public service of high-definition television from Alexandra Palace. The BBC broadcasts two UK-wide television services, BBC 1 and BBC 2; outside England these services are designated BBC Scotland on 1, BBC Scotland on 2, BBC 1 Northern Ireland, BBC 2 Northern Ireland, BBC Wales on 1 and BBC Wales on 2. On 9 November 1997 the BBC launched News 24, a 24-hour television news service broadcast by cable during the day and on BBC 1 at night.

BBC WORLDWIDE LTD

Woodlands, 80 Wood Lane, London W12 0TT
Tel 0181-576 2000

BBC Worldwide was formed in May 1994 to develop a co-ordinated approach to the BBC's international and commercial activities. The World Service broadcasts in 46 languages to a weekly audience of 143 million. Worldwide Ltd provides commercial products and services in a range of media including television channels.

INDEPENDENT TELEVISION

The ITV franchises for the 15 regional companies and for breakfast television were allocated new ten-year licences from January 1993. A new independent national television channel was due to be established by autumn 1993, but the ITC decided not to award the licence to Channel Five Holdings Ltd, the only applicant. The ITC received a further four bids for the licence in May 1995. The winner was Channel 5 Broadcasting Ltd and the new channel was launched on 30 March 1997.

ITV NETWORK CENTRE/ITV ASSOCIATION

200 Gray's Inn Road, London WC1X 8HF
Tel 0171-843 8000

The ITV Network Centre is wholly owned by the ITV companies and undertakes the commissioning and scheduling of those television programmes which are shown across the ITV network. Through its sister organization, the ITV Association, it also provides a range of services to the ITV companies where a common approach is required.
Chief Executive, R. Eyre

INDEPENDENT TELEVISION NETWORK COMPANIES

ANGLIA TELEVISION LTD (owned by MAI) (*eastern England*), Anglia House, Norwich NR1 3JG. Tel: 01603-615151

BORDER TELEVISION PLC (*the Borders*), The Television Centre, Carlisle CA1 3NT. Tel: 01228-25101

CARLTON UK TELEVISION (*London (weekdays*)), 101 St Martin's Lane, London WC2N 4AZ. Tel: 0171-240 4000

CENTRAL INDEPENDENT TELEVISION LTD (owned by Carlton Communications) (*the Midlands*), Central Court, Gas Street, Birmingham B1 2JT. Tel: 0121-643 9898

CHANNEL TELEVISION LTD (*Channel Islands*), The Television Centre, St Helier, Jersey JE2 3ZD. Tel: 01534-816816

GRAMPIAN TELEVISION PLC (owned by Scottish Media) (*northern Scotland*), Queen's Cross, Aberdeen AB15 2XJ. Tel: 01224-846846

GRANADA TELEVISION LTD (owned by Granada Media) (*north-west England*), Quay Street, Manchester M60 9EA. Tel: 0161-832 7211

HTV GROUP PLC (*Wales and western England*), HTV Wales, The Television Centre, Culverhouse Cross, Cardiff CF5 6XJ. Tel: 01222-590590; HTV West, The Television Centre, Bath Road, Bristol BS4 3HG. Tel: 0117-977 8366

LONDON WEEKEND TELEVISION LTD (owned by Granada Media) (*London (weekends*)), The London Television Centre, Upper Ground, London SE1 9LT. Tel: 0171-620 1620

MERIDIAN BROADCASTING LTD (owned by MAI) (*south and south-east England*), The Television Centre, Southampton SO14 0PZ. Tel: 01703-222555

SCOTTISH TELEVISION PLC (owned by Scottish Media) (*central Scotland*), Cowcaddens, Glasgow G2 3PR. Tel: 0141-300 3000

TYNE TEES TELEVISION LTD (owned by Granada Media) (*north-east England*), The Television Centre, City Road, Newcastle upon Tyne NE1 2AL. Tel: 0191-261 0181

ULSTER TELEVISION PLC (*Northern Ireland*), Havelock House, Ormeau Road, Belfast BT7 1EB. Tel: 01232-328122

WESTCOUNTRY TELEVISION LTD (owned by Carlton Communications) (*south-west England*), Langage Science Park, Plymouth PL7 5BG. Tel: 01752-333333

YORKSHIRE TELEVISION LTD (owned by Granada Media) (*Yorkshire*), The Television Centre, Leeds LS3 1JS. Tel: 0113-243 8283

OTHER INDEPENDENT TELEVISION COMPANIES

CHANNEL 5 BROADCASTING LTD, 22 Long Acre, London WC2E 9LY. Tel: 0171-550 5555

CHANNEL FOUR TELEVISION CORPORATION , 124 Horseferry Road, London SW1P 2TX. Tel: 0171-396 4444. Provides a service to the UK except Wales, and is charged to cater for interests under-represented by the ITV network companies. Channel 4 sells its own advertising

GMTV LTD (*breakfast television*), The London Television Centre, Upper Ground, London SE1 9TT. Tel: 0171-827 7000

INDEPENDENT TELEVISION NEWS LTD , 200 Gray's Inn Road, London WC1X 8XZ. Tel: 0171-833 3000

TELETEXT LTD, 101 Farm Lane, London SW6 1QJ. Tel: 0171-386 5000. Provides teletext services for the ITV companies and Channel 4

WELSH FOURTH CHANNEL AUTHORITY (Sianel Pedwar Cymru), Parc Ty Glas, Llanishen, Cardiff CF4 5DU. Tel: 01222-747444. S4C schedules Welsh language programmes and relays most Channel 4 programmes

DIRECT BROADCASTING BY SATELLITE TELEVISION

BRITISH SKY BROADCASTING LTD, Grant Way, Isleworth, Middx TW7 5QD. Tel: 0171-705 3000. Broadcasts 11 channels which are wholly owned by Sky (Sky One, Sky News, Sky Sports 1, Sky Sports 2, Sky Sports 3, Sky Movies, The Movie Channel, Sky Movies Gold, Sky Soap, Sky Travel and The Computer Channel). Sky also co-operates with 14 joint venture channels and distributes 16 multi-channels for third parties.

RADIO

UK domestic radio services are broadcast across three wavebands: FM (or VHF), medium wave (also referred to as AM) and long wave (used by BBC Radio 4). In the UK the FM waveband extends in frequency from 87.5 MHz to 108 MHz and the medium wave band extends from 531 kHz to 1602 kHz. Some radios are still calibrated in wavelengths rather than frequency. To convert frequency to wavelength, divide 300,000 by the frequency in kHz.

DIGITAL RADIO

Digital radio is a new technique for improving the robustness of high fidelity radio services, especially compared with current FM and AM radio transmissions. It was developed in a collaborative research project under the pan-European EUREKA initiative and has been adopted as a world standard for new digital radio systems. Digital radio allows more services to be broadcast to a higher technical quality in a given amount of radio spectrum, and provides the data facility for text or pictures associated with sound programmes. The frequencies allocated for terrestrial digital radio in the UK are 217.5 to 230 MHz.

The Broadcasting Act 1996 provided for the licensing of up to 42 digital radio services (on seven frequency channels or 'multiplexes'). The BBC has been allocated a multiplex capable of broadcasting six to eight national stereo services; BBC digital broadcasts began in the London area in September 1995. A national digital multiplex has also been made available, on which the three independent national radio stations have a guaranteed place, and local and regional services will use the remaining five multiplexes. The Radio Authority will be responsible for awarding licences for capacity on the non-BBC multiplexes; the national licence was advertised in spring 1998 and will be awarded in autumn 1998, with the first independent digital services due to be broadcast in 1999. The first local multiplex licences are to be advertised by autumn 1998. Analogue services will eventually be discontinued.

AUDIENCE SHARE

ESTIMATED AUDIENCE SHARE *January to March 1998*

	Percentage
BBC Radio 1	9.4
BBC Radio 2	13.2
BBC Radio 3	1.3
BBC Radio 4	10.4
BBC Radio 5 Live	3.9
BBC Local/Regional	9.6
Atlantic 252	2.0
Classic FM	3.6
Talk Radio	1.7
Virgin Radio (AM only)	2.9
Local commercial	39.9
Other	2.2

Source: RAJAR/RSL

BBC RADIO

Broadcasting House, Portland Place, London WIA IAA
Tel 0171-580 4468

BBC Radio broadcasts five national services to the UK, Isle of Man and the Channel Islands. There is also a tier of national regional services in Wales, Scotland and Northern Ireland and 39 local radio stations in England and the Channel Islands. In Wales there are two national regional services based on the Welsh and English languages respectively.

BBC NATIONAL SERVICES

RADIO 1 (Contemporary pop music, social action campaigns and entertainment news) – 24 hours a day. *Frequencies:* 97.6–99.8 FM, coverage 99%

RADIO 2 (Popular music, entertainment, comedy and the arts) – 24 hours a day. *Frequencies:* 88–90.2 FM, coverage 99%

RADIO 3 (Classical music, classic drama, documentaries and features) – 24 hours a day. *Frequencies:* 90.2–92.4 FM, coverage 99%

RADIO 4 (News, documentaries, drama, entertainment, and cricket on long wave in season) – 5.55 a.m.–1.00 a.m. daily, with BBC World Service overnight. *Frequencies:* 94.6–96.1 FM and 103.5–105 FM, coverage 99%;1449 AM, plus eight local fillers on AM

RADIO 5 LIVE (News and sport) – 24 hours a day. *Frequencies:* 693 AM and 909 AM, plus one local filler

BBC NATIONAL REGIONAL SERVICES

RADIO SCOTLAND *Frequencies:* 810 AM plus two local fillers; 92.4–94.7 FM, coverage 99%. Local programmes on FM as above: HIGHLANDS; NORTH-EAST; BORDERS; SOUTH-WEST (also 585 AM); ORKNEY; SHETLAND; RADIO NAN GAIDHEAL (Gaelic service) (103.5–105 FM) available in Western Highlands and Islands, Moray Firth and central Scotland; also available on 990 AM in Aberdeen

RADIO ULSTER *Frequencies:* 1341 AM (873 AM Enniskillen), plus two local fillers; 92.4–95.4 FM, coverage 96%. Local programmes on RADIO FOYLE *Frequencies:* 792 AM; 93.1 FM

RADIO WALES *Frequencies:* 882 AM plus two local fillers; 95.1 FM, 95.9 FM (*Gwent*), coverage 97%

RADIO CYMRU (Welsh-language) *Frequencies:* 92.4–94.6 FM, 95.7 FM (*Llanfyllin*), 96.1 FM (*Llandinam*), 96.8 FM and 103.5–105 FM, coverage 97%

BBC LOCAL RADIO STATIONS

There are 39 local stations serving England and the Channel Islands:

ASIAN NETWORK, Epic House, Charles Street, Leicester LEI 3SH. Tel: 0116-251 6688. *Frequencies:* 828/837/1458 AM

BRISTOL, PO Box 194, Bristol BS99 7QT. Tel: 0117-974 1111; 14–15 Paul Street, Taunton TAI 3PF. Tel: 01823-252437. *Frequencies:* 1548 AM, 1323 AM (*Somerset Sound*), 94.9/95.5/104.6 FM

CAMBRIDGESHIRE, Broadcasting House, 104 Hills Road, Cambridge CB2 ILD. Tel: 01223-259696. *Frequencies:* 96.0/95.7 FM

CLEVELAND, PO Box 95 FM, Newport Road, Middlesbrough TSI 5DG. Tel: 01642-225211. *Frequencies:* 95.0/95.8 FM

CORNWALL, Phoenix Wharf, Truro, Cornwall TRI IUA. Tel: 01872-275421. *Frequencies:* 95.2/96.0/103.9 FM

COVENTRY AND WARWICKSHIRE, Holt Court, 1 Greyfriars Road, Coventry CVI 2WR. Tel: 01203-860086. *Frequencies:* 94.8/103.7/104.0 FM

CUMBRIA, Annetwell Street, Carlisle CA3 8BB. Tel: 01228-592444. *Frequencies:* 95.6/96.1/104.1 FM

DERBY, PO Box 269, Derby DEI 3HL. Tel: 01332-361111. *Frequencies:* 1116 AM, 95.3/104.5 FM

DEVON, PO Box 5, Broadcasting House, Seymour Road, Plymouth PL3 5BD. Tel: 01752-260323. *Frequencies:* 103.4/96.0/95.8/94.8 FM

ESSEX, 198 New London Road, Chelmsford CM2 9XB. Tel: 01245-262393. *Frequencies:* 103.5/95.3 FM

GLOUCESTERSHIRE, London Road, Gloucester GLI ISW. Tel: 01452-308585. *Frequencies:* 1413 AM, 104.7 FM

GLR (GREATER LONDON RADIO), 35c Marylebone High Street, London WIA 4LG. Tel: 0171-224 2424. *Frequency:* 94.9 FM

GMR (GREATER MANCHESTER RADIO), PO Box 951, Oxford Road, Manchester M60 ISD. Tel: 0161-200 2000. *Frequencies:* 95.1/104.6 FM

GUERNSEY, Commerce House, Les Banques, St Peter Port, Guernsey GY1 2HS. Tel: 01481-728977. *Frequencies:* 1116 AM, 93.2 FM

HEREFORD AND WORCESTER, Hylton Road, Worcester WR2 5WW. Tel: 01905-748485. *Frequencies:* 104.6/104.0/ 94.7 FM

HUMBERSIDE, 9 Chapel Street, Hull HU1 3NU. Tel: 01482-323232. *Frequency:* 95.9 FM

JERSEY, 18 Parade Road, St Helier, Jersey JE2 3PL. Tel: 01534-870000. *Frequencies:* 1026 AM, 88.8 FM

KENT, Sun Pier, Chatham, Kent ME4 4EZ. Tel: 01634-830505. *Frequencies:* 96.7/97.6/104.2 FM

LANCASHIRE, 26 Darwen Street, Blackburn BB2 2EA. Tel: 01254-262411. *Frequencies:* 95.5/104.5/103.9 FM

LEEDS, Broadcasting House, Woodhouse Lane, Leeds LS2 9PN. Tel: 0113-244 2131. *Frequencies:* 774 AM, 92.4/95.3 FM

LEICESTER, Epic House, Charles Street, Leicester LE1 3SH. Tel: 0116-251 6688. *Frequency:* 104.9 FM

LINCOLNSHIRE, PO Box 219, Newport, Lincoln LN1 3XY. Tel: 01522-511411. *Frequencies:* 1368 AM, 94.9/104.7 FM

MERSEYSIDE, 55 Paradise Street, Liverpool L1 3BP. Tel: 0151-708 5500. *Frequency:* 95.8 FM

NEWCASTLE, Broadcasting Centre, Barrack Road, Newcastle upon Tyne NE99 IRN. Tel: 0191-232 4141. *Frequencies:* 95.4/104.4/96.0/103.7 FM

NORFOLK, Norfolk Tower, Surrey Street, Norwich NR1 3PA. Tel: 01603-617411. *Frequencies:* 95.1/104.4 FM

NORTHAMPTON, Broadcasting House, Abington Street, Northampton NN1 2BH. Tel: 01604-239100. *Frequencies:* 104.2/103.6 FM

NOTTINGHAM, York House, Mansfield Road, Nottingham NG1 3JB. Tel: 0115-955 0500. *Frequencies:* 103.8/95.5 FM

SHEFFIELD, Ashdell Grove, 60 Westbourne Road, Sheffield S10 2QU. Tel: 0114-268 6185. *Frequencies:* 94.7/ 104.1/88.6 FM

SHROPSHIRE, 2–4 Boscobel Drive, Shrewsbury SY1 3TT. Tel: 01743-248484. *Frequencies:* 95.0/96.0 FM

SOLENT, Broadcasting House, Havelock Road, Southampton SO14 7PW. Tel: 01703-631311. *Frequencies:* 96.1/103.8 FM

SOUTHERN COUNTIES, Broadcasting Centre, Guildford GU2 5AP. Tel: 01483-306306. *Frequencies:* 95–95.3/ 104–104.8 FM

STOKE, Cheapside, Hanley, Stoke-on-Trent ST1 1JJ. Tel: 01782-208080. *Frequencies:* 94.6/104.1 FM

SUFFOLK, Broadcasting House, St Matthew's Street, Ipswich IP1 3EP. Tel: 01473-250000. *Frequencies:* 103.9/ 104.6/95.5 FM

THAMES VALLEY, 269 Banbury Road, Oxford OX2 7DW. Tel: 01865-311444. *Frequencies:* 95.2/95.4/104.0/104.1 FM

THREE COUNTIES RADIO , PO Box 3CR, Luton, Beds LU1 5XL. Tel: 01582-441000. *Frequencies:* 630 AM, 104.5/ 95.5/103.8 FM

WILTSHIRE SOUND, Broadcasting House, Prospect Place, Swindon SN1 3RW. Tel: 01793-513626. *Frequencies:* 103.6/ 104.3/103.5 FM

WM (WEST MIDLANDS), Pebble Mill Road, Birmingham B5 7SD. Tel: 0121-432 8484. *Frequency:* 95.6 FM

YORK, 20 Bootham Row, York YO3 7BR. Tel: 01904-641351. *Frequencies:* 103.7/104.3/95.5 FM

BBC WORLD SERVICE

Bush House, Strand, London WC2B 4PH
Tel 0171-240 3456

The BBC World Service broadcasts over 1,000 hours of programmes a week in 44 languages including English. Of the 111 transmitters in use, 40 are in the UK and 71 overseas.

The World Service is organized into five world regions, each responsible for programmes in English as well as regional languages.

AFRICA AND THE MIDDLE EAST, Arabic, French, Hausa, Kinyarwanda/Kirundi, Portuguese, Somali and Swahili; English programmes including *Network Africa* and *Focus on Africa.*

ASIA AND THE PACIFIC, Bengali, Burmese, Cantonese, Hindi, Indonesian, Mandarin, Nepali, Sinhala, Tamil, Thai, Urdu and Vietnamese; English programmes including *East Asia Today* and *South Asia Report.*

EUROPE, Albanian, Bulgarian, Croatian, Czech, German, Greek, Hungarian, Macedonian, Polish, Romanian, Serbian, Slovak and Slovene; English programmes including *The World Today for Europe.*

FORMER SOVIET UNION AND SOUTH-WEST ASIA, Azeri, Kazakh, Kyrgyz, Pashto, Persian, Russian, Turkish, Ukrainian and Uzbek.

THE AMERICAS, Portuguese for Brazil, Spanish; English programmes including *The World* (a global news magazine for American listeners), *Caribbean Report* and *Calling the Falklands.*

BBC ENGLISH teaches English world-wide through radio, television and a wide range of published courses

BBC INTERNATIONAL BROADCASTING AND AUDIENCE RESEARCH carries out audience research and sells printed publications and data

BBC MONITORING supplies news and information from the output of overseas radio and television stations and news agency sources

BBC MPM (Marshall Plan of the Mind) makes programmes about business, democracy and management for countries of the former Soviet Union

BBC WORLD SERVICE TRAINING runs journalism, management and skills training courses for overseas broadcasters

INDEPENDENT RADIO

The Radio Authority began advertising new licences for the development of commercial radio in January 1991. Since then it has awarded three national licences, 101 new local radio licences (including ten regional licences) and one additional service licence (to use the spare capacity in an existing channel which is not used by the programme service). The Authority has also issued about 2,000 restricted service licences (for temporary low-powered radio services). The Authority will continue to advertise about two local licences a month in 1998–9.

COMMERCIAL RADIO COMPANIES ASSOCIATION, 77 Shaftesbury Avenue, London W1V 7AD. Tel: 0171-306 2603. *Chief Executive,* P. Brown

INDEPENDENT NATIONAL RADIO STATIONS

CLASSIC FM , Academic House, 24–28 Oval Road, London NW1 7DQ. Tel: 0171-284 3000. 24 hours a day. *Frequencies:* 99.9–101.9 FM

TALK RADIO , 76 Oxford Street, London W1N 0TR Tel: 0171-636 1089. 24 hours a day. *Frequencies:* 1053/1089 AM

VIRGIN RADIO , 1 Golden Square, London WIR 4DJ. Tel: 0171-434 1215. 24 hours a day. *Frequencies:* 1215/1197/ 1233/1242/1260 AM

INDEPENDENT REGIONAL LOCAL RADIO STATIONS

100.7 HEART FM (*West Midlands*), 1 The Square, 111 Broad Street, Birmingham B15 1AS. Tel: 0121-626 1007. *Frequency:* 100.7 FM

CENTURY 105 (*north-west*), Century House, Waterfront Quay, Salford Quays, Manchester M5 2XW. Tel: 0161-400 0105. *Frequency:* 105.4 FM

CENTURY 106 (*east Midlands*), City Link, Nottingham NG2 4NG. Tel: 0115-910 6100. *Frequency:* 106.0 FM

CENTURY RADIO (*north-east*), Century House, PO Box 100, Gateshead NE8 2YX. Tel: 0191-477 6666. *Frequencies:* 100.7/101.8/96.2/96.4 FM

GALAXY 101 (*Severn estuary*), Millennium House, 26 Baldwin Street, Bristol BS1 1SE. Tel: 0117-901 0101. *Frequencies:* 101.0/97.2 FM (Bristol)

GALAXY 105 (*Yorkshire*), Joseph's Well, Westgate, Leeds LS3 1AB. Tel: 0113-213 0105. *Frequencies:* 105.1 FM (Leeds);105.6 FM (Bradford and Sheffield); 105.8 FM (Hull)

JAZZ FM 100.4 (*north-west*), The World Trade Centre, Exchange Quay, Manchester M5 3EJ. Tel: 0161-877 1004. *Frequency:* 100.4 FM

SCOT FM (*central Scotland*), 1 Albert Quay, Leith EH6 7DN. Tel: 0131-554 6677. *Frequencies:* 100.3/101.1 FM

VIBE FM (*east*), Reflection House, The Anderson Centre, Olding Road, Bury St Edmunds, Suffolk IP33 3TA. Tel: 01284-718800. *Frequencies:* 107.7 FM (Peterborough); 105.6 FM (Cambridge); 106.1 FM (Norwich); 106.4 FM (Ipswich)

WAVE 105 FM (*Solent*), 5 Manor Court, Barnes Wallis Road, Segensworth East, Fareham, Hants PO15 5TH. Tel: 01489-481050. *Frequencies:* 105.2 FM (Solent); 105.8 FM (Poole)

INDEPENDENT LOCAL RADIO STATIONS

England

2-TEN FM, PO Box 2020, Reading RG31 7FG. Tel: 0118-945 4400. *Frequencies:* 97.0/102.9/103.4 FM

2CR FM, 5 Southcote Road, Bournemouth BH1 3LR. Tel: 01202-259259. *Frequency:* 102.3 FM

96 TRENT FM, 29–31 Castle Gate, Nottingham NG1 7AP. Tel: 0115-952 7000. *Frequencies:* 96.2/96.5 FM

96.3 AIRE FM, PO Box 2000, 51 Burley Road, Leeds LS3 1LR. Tel: 0113-283 5500. *Frequency:* 96.3 FM

96.4 FM BRMB, Radio House, Aston Road North, Birmingham B6 4BX. Tel: 0121-359 4481. *Frequency:* 96.4 FM

96.4 THE EAGLE, Dolphin House, North Street, Guildford, Surrey GU1 4AA. Tel: 01483-300964. *Frequency:* 96.4 FM

96.6 OASIS FM, 9 Christopher Place Shopping Centre, St Albans, Herts AL3 5DQ. Tel: 01727-831966. *Frequency:* 96.6 FM

96.9 VIKING FM, Commercial Road, Hull HU1 2SG. Tel: 01482-325141. *Frequency:* 96.9 FM

97.2 STRAY FM, PO Box 972, Station Parade, Harrogate HG1 5YF. Tel: 01423-522972. *Frequency:* 97.2 FM

97.4 GOLD RADIO, Longmead, Shaftesbury, Dorset SP7 8QQ. Tel: 01747-855711. *Frequency:* 97.4 FM

102.4 WISH FM, Orrell Lodge, Orrell Road, Orrell, Wigan WN5 8HJ. Tel: 01942-761024. *Frequency:* 102.4 FM

102.7 HEREWARD FM, PO Box 225, Queensgate Centre, Peterborough PE1 1XJ. Tel: 01733-460460. *Frequency:* 102.7 FM

103.4 THE BEACH, PO Box 103.4, Lowestoft, Suffolk NR32 2TL. Tel: 07000-001035. *Frequency:* 103.4 FM

106 CTFM RADIO, 16 Lower Bridge Street, Canterbury, Kent CT1 2HQ. Tel: 01227-789106. *Frequency:* 106.0 FM

107.2 WIRE FM, c/o The Lodge, Orrell Road, Orrell, Wigan WN5 8HJ. Tel: 01942-777666. Expected on air September 1998. *Frequency:* 107.2 FM

107.6 KESTREL FM, 2nd Floor, Paddington House, The Walks Shopping Centre, Basingstoke, Hants RG21 7LJ. Tel: 01256-694000. *Frequency:* 107.6 FM

107.7 THE WOLF, 10th Floor, Mander House, Wolverhampton WV1 3NB. Tel: 01902-571070. *Frequency:* 107.7 FM

107.8 ARROW FM, Priory Meadow Centre, Hastings, E. Sussex TN34 1PJ. Tel: 01424-461177. *Frequency:* 107.8 FM

107.8 FM THAMES RADIO, Brentham Court, 45C High Street, Hampton Wick, Kingston upon Thames KT1 4DG. Tel: 0181-288 1300. *Frequency:* 107.8 FM

963/972 LIBERTY RADIO, 7th Floor, Trevor House, 100 Brompton Road, London SW3 1ER. Tel: 0171-893 8966. *Frequency:* 963/972 AM

1458 LITE AM, PO Box 1458, Quay West, Trafford Park, Manchester M17 1FL. Tel: 0161-872 1458. *Frequency:* 1458 AM

ACTIVE 107.5 FM, Lambourne House, 7 Western Road, Romford, Essex RM1 3LD. Tel: 01708-731643. *Frequency:* 107.5 FM

ALPHA 103.2, Radio House, 11 Woodland Road, Darlington DL3 7BJ. Tel: 01325-255552. *Frequency:* 103.2 FM

ASIAN SOUND RADIO, Globe House, Southall Street, Manchester M3 1LG. Tel: 0161-288 1000. *Frequencies:* 1377/963 AM

B 97 CHILTERN FM, 55 Goldington Road, Bedford MK40 3LT. Tel: 01234-272400. *Frequency:* 96.9 FM

THE BAY, PO Box 969, St George's Quay, Lancaster LA1 3LD. Tel: 01524-848747. *Frequencies:* 96.9/102.3/103.2 FM

BEACON FM, 267 Tettenhall Road, Wolverhampton WV6 0DQ. Tel: 01902-838383. *Frequencies:* 97.2 FM (Wolverhampton and Black Country); 103.1 FM (Shrewsbury and Telford)

THE BREEZE, Radio House, Clifftown Road, Southend-on-Sea, Essex SS1 1SX. Tel: 01702-333711. *Frequencies:* 1359 AM (Chelmsford); 1431 AM (Southend)

BROADLAND 102, St George's Plain, 47–49 Colegate, Norwich NR3 1DB. Tel: 01603-630621. *Frequency:* 102.4 FM

CAMBRIDGE CAFÉ RADIO, PO Box 1079, Cambridge CB5 8FX. Tel: 01223-722300. *Frequency:* 107.9 FM

CAPITAL FM AND GOLD, 30 Leicester Square, London WC2H 7LA. Tel: 0171-766 6000. *Frequencies:* 1548 AM (*Gold*), 95.8 FM

CAPITAL GOLD (1152), Radio House, Aston Road North, Birmingham B6 4BX. Tel: 0121-359 4481. *Frequency:* 1152 AM

CAPITAL GOLD (1170 and 1557), Radio House, Whittle Avenue, Segensworth West, Fareham, Hants PO15 5SH. Tel: 01489-589911. *Frequencies:* 1170/1557 AM

CAPITAL GOLD (1242 and 603), Radio House, John Wilson Business Park, Whitstable, Kent CT5 3QX. Tel: 01227-772004. *Frequencies:* 603 AM (East Kent); 1242 AM (Maidstone and Medway)

CAPITAL GOLD (1323 and 945), Radio House, PO Box 2000, Brighton BN4I 2SS. Tel: 01273-430111. *Frequencies:* 945/1323 AM

CENTRE FM, 5–6 Aldergate, Tamworth, Staffs B79 7DJ. Tel: 01827-318000. *Frequencies:* 101.6/102.4 FM

CFM, PO Box 964, Carlisle, Cumbria CA1 3NG. Tel: 01228-818964. *Frequencies:* 96.4 FM (Penrith); 102.5 FM (Carlisle); 102.2 FM (Workington); 103.4 FM (Whitehaven)

CHANNEL TRAVEL RADIO, Main Control Building, PO Box 2000, Eurotunnel UK Terminal, Folkestone, Kent CT18 8XY. Tel: 01303-283873. *Frequency:* 107.6 FM

CHELMER FM, Duke House, Victoria Road South, Chelmsford, Essex CM1 1LN. Tel: 01245-259400. Expected on air winter 1998. *Frequency:* to be announced

CHELTENHAM RADIO (will become THE CAT, broadcasting on an FM frequency from September 1998), Regent Arcade, Cheltenham, Glos GL50 1JZ. Tel: 01242-699555. *Frequency:* 603 AM

CHILTERN FM, Chiltern Road, Dunstable, Beds LU6 1HQ. Tel: 01582-676200. *Frequency:* 97.6 FM

CHOICE FM (BIRMINGHAM) 95 Broad Street, Birmingham B15 1AU. Tel: 0121-616 1000. *Frequency:* 102.2 FM

CHOICE FM LONDON, 16–18 Trinity Gardens, London SW9 8DP. Tel: 0171-738 7969. *Frequency:* 96.9 FM

RADIO CITY 96.7, 8–10 Stanley Street, Liverpool L1 6AF. Tel: 0151-227 5100. *Frequency:* 96.7 FM

CLASSIC GOLD 774, Old Talbot House, Southgate Street, Gloucester GL1 2DQ. Tel: 01452-423791. *Frequency:* 774 AM

CLASSIC GOLD 792/828, Chiltern Road, Dunstable, Beds LU6 1HQ. Tel: 01582-676200. *Frequencies:* 792 AM (Bedford); 828 AM (Luton)

CLASSIC GOLD 828, 5 Southcote Road, Bournemouth, Dorset BH1 3LR. Tel: 01202-259259. *Frequency:* 828 AM

CLASSIC GOLD 936/1161 AM, PO Box 2000, Swindon SN4 7EX. Tel: 01793-842600. *Frequencies:* 936 AM (West Wilts); 1161 AM (Swindon)

CLASSIC GOLD 954/1530, 5 Barbourne Terrace, Worcester WR1 3JZ. Tel: 01905-612212. *Frequencies:* 954 AM (Hereford); 1530 AM (Worcester)

CLASSIC GOLD 1260, PO Box 2020, Watershed, Canons Road, Bristol BS99 7SN. Tel: 0117-984 3200. *Frequency:* 1260 AM

CLASSIC GOLD 1278/1530, Forster Square, Bradford BD1 5NE. Tel: 01274-203040. *Frequencies:* 1278/1530 AM

CLASSIC GOLD 1332 AM, PO Box 2020, Queensgate Centre, Peterborough PE1 1LL. Tel: 01733-460460. *Frequency:* 1332 AM

CLASSIC GOLD 1359, Hertford Place, Coventry CV1 3TT. Tel: 01203-868200. *Frequency:* 1359 AM

CLASSIC GOLD 1431/1485, PO Box 2020, Reading RG31 7FG. Tel: 0118-945 4400. *Frequencies:* 1431/1485 AM

CLASSIC GOLD 1557, 19–21 St Edmunds Road, Northampton NN1 5DY. Tel: 01604-795600. *Frequency:* 1557 AM

CLASSIC GOLD AMBER, St George's Plain, 47–49 Colegate, Norwich NR3 1DB. Tel: 01603-630321. *Frequency:* 1152 AM

CLASSIC GOLD AMBER (SUFFOLK), Radio House, Alpha Business Park, White House Road, Ipswich IP1 5LT. Tel: 01473-461000. *Frequency:* 1170 AM (Ipswich); 1251 AM (Bury St Edmunds)

CLASSIC GOLD GEM, 29–31 Castle Gate, Nottingham NG1 7AP. Tel: 0115-952 7000. *Frequencies:* 945/999 AM

CLASSIC GOLD WABC, 267 Tettenhall Road, Wolverhampton WV6 0DQ. Tel: 01902-838383. *Frequencies:* 990 AM (Wolverhampton); 1017 AM (Shrewsbury and Telford)

CONNECT FM, Church Street, Wellingborough, Northants NN8 4XX. Tel: 01933-224972. *Frequency:* 97.2 FM

COUNTY SOUND RADIO 1476 AM, Dolphin House, North Street, Guildford GU1 4AA. Tel: 01483-300964. *Frequency:* 1476 AM

CRASH FM, 27 Fleet Street, Liverpool L1 4AR. Tel: 0151-707 3107. *Frequency:* 107.6 FM

DELTA RADIO 97.1 FM, 65 Weyhill, Haslemere, Surrey GU27 1HN. Tel: 01428-651971. *Frequency:* 97.1 FM

DUNE FM, The Power Station, Victoria Way, Southport PR8 1RR. Tel: 01704-502500

ELEVEN SEVENTY , PO Box 1170, High Wycombe, Bucks HP13 6YT. Tel: 01494-446611. *Frequency:* 1170 FM

ESSEX FM, Radio House, Clifftown Road, Southend-on-Sea, Essex SS1 1SX. Tel: 01702-333711. *Frequencies:* 96.3 FM (Southend); 102.6 FM (Chelmsford)

FAME 1521, The Stanley Centre, Kelvin Way, Crawley, W. Sussex RH10 2SE. Tel: 01293-519161. *Frequency:* 1521 AM

FLR 107.3, PO Box 1073, London SE8 4WU. Tel: 0181-469 3981. *Frequency:* 107.3 FM (on air November 1998)

FM 102 – THE BEAR, The Guard House Studios, Banbury Road, Stratford-upon-Avon, Warks CV37 7HX. Tel: 01789-262636. *Frequency:* 102.0 FM

FM 103 HORIZON, The Broadcast Centre, Vincent Avenue, Crownhill Industry, Milton Keynes MK8 0AB. Tel: 01908-269111. *Frequency:* 103.3 FM

FOX FM, Brush House, Pony Road, Oxford OX4 2XR. Tel: 01865-871000. *Frequencies:* 102.6/97.4 FM

GALAXY 102, 127–129 Portland Street, Manchester M1 6ED. Tel: 0161-228 0102. *Frequency:* 102.0 FM

GEMINI AM AND FM, Hawthorn House, Exeter Business Park, Exeter EX1 3QS. Tel: 01392-444444. *Frequencies:* 666/954 AM, 96.4/97.0/103.0 FM

GWR FM (BRISTOL AND BATH), PO Box 2000, Watershed, Canon's Road, Bristol BS99 7SN. Tel: 0117-984 3200. *Frequencies:* 96.3 FM (Bristol); 103.0 FM (Bath)

GWR FM (SWINDON AND WEST WILTSHIRE), PO Box 2000, Swindon SN4 7EX. Tel: 01793-842600. *Frequencies:* 97.2 FM (Swindon); 102.2 FM (West Wilts); 96.5 FM (Marlborough)

HALLAM FM, Radio House, 900 Herries Road, Sheffield S6 1RH. Tel: 0114-285 3333. *Frequencies:* 97.4 FM (Sheffield); 102.9/103.4 FM (Rotherham); 102.9 FM (Barnsley); 103.4 FM (Doncaster)

HEART 106.2, The Chrysalis Building, Bramley Road, London W10 6SP. Tel: 0171-468 1062. *Frequency:* 106.2 FM

HUDDERSFIELD FM, The Old Stableblock, Brewery Drive, Lockwood Park, Huddersfield HD1 3UR. Tel: 01484-321107. *Frequency:* 107.9 FM

INVICTA FM, Radio House, John Wilson Business Park, Whitstable, Kent CT5 3QX. Tel: 01227-772004. *Frequencies:* 103.1 FM (Maidstone and Medway); 102.8 FM (Canterbury); 95.9 FM (Thanet); 97.0 FM (Dover); 96.1 FM (Ashford)

ISLE OF WIGHT RADIO, Dodnor Park, Newport, Isle of Wight PO30 5XE. Tel: 01983-822557. *Frequencies:* 102.0/107.0 FM

JAZZ FM 102.2, 26–27 Castlereagh Street, London W1H 6DJ. Tel: 0171-706 4100. *Frequency:* 102.2 FM

KCBC, PO Box 1074, Centre 2000, Kettering, Northants NN16 8PU. Tel: 07000-1074 1074. *Frequency:* 107.4 FM

KEY 103, Castle Quay, Castlefield, Manchester M1 4AW. Tel: 0161-288 5000. *Frequency:* 103.0 FM

KFM, 1 East Street, Tonbridge, Kent TN9 1AR. Tel: 01732-369200. *Frequencies:* 96.2 FM (South); 101.6 FM (North)

KISS 100 FM, Kiss House, 80 Holloway Road, London N7 8JG. Tel: 0171-700 6100. *Frequency:* 100.0 FM

KIX 96, St Mark's Church Annexe, Bird Street, Stoney Stanton Road, Coventry CV1 4FH. Tel: 01203-525656. *Frequency:* 96.2 FM

KL.FM 96.7 , PO Box 77, 18 Blackfriars Street, King's Lynn, Norfolk PE30 1NN. Tel: 01553-772777. *Frequency:* 96.7 FM

LANTERN FM, The Light House, 17 Market Place, Bideford, N. Devon EX39 2DR. Tel: 01237-424444. *Frequency:* 96.2 FM

LBC 1152 AM, 200 Gray's Inn Road, London WC1X 8XZ. Tel: 0171-973 1152. *Frequency:* 1152 AM

LEICESTER SOUND, Granville House, Granville Road, Leicester LE1 7RW. Tel: 0116-256 1300. *Frequency:* 105.4 FM

LINCS FM, Witham Park, Waterside South, Lincoln LN5 7JN. Tel: 01522-549900. *Frequencies:* 102.2 FM/96.7 FM (Grantham Relay)

LONDON GREEK RADIO, Florentia Village, Vale Road, London N4 1TD. Tel: 0181-800 8001. *Frequency:* 103.3 FM

LONDON TURKISH RADIO LTR, 185B High Road, Wood Green, London N22 6BA. Tel: 0181-881 0606. *Frequency:* 1584 AM

MAGIC 828, PO Box 2000, 51 Burley Road, Leeds LS3 1LR. Tel: 0113-283 5500. *Frequency:* 828 AM

MAGIC 1152, Newcastle upon Tyne NE99 1BB. Tel: 0191-420 3040. *Frequency:* 1152 AM

MAGIC 1161 AM, Commercial Road, Hull HU1 2SG. Tel: 01482-325141. *Frequency:* 1161 AM

MAGIC (1170), Radio House, Yale Crescent, Thornaby, Stockton-on-Tees , Cleveland TS17 6AA. Tel: 01642-888222. *Frequency:* 1170 AM

MAGIC 1548, 8–10 Stanley Street, Liverpool L1 6AF. Tel: 0151-227 5100. *Frequency:* 1548 AM

MAGIC AM, Radio House, 900 Herries Road, Sheffield S6 1RH. Tel: 0114-285 2121. *Frequencies:* 990/1305/1548 AM

MARCHER GOLD, The Studios, Mold Road, Wrexham LL11 4AF. Tel: 01978-752202. *Frequency:* 1260 AM

MEDWAY FM, Berkeley House, 186 High Street, Rochester MEI 1EY. Tel: 01634-841111. *Frequencies:* 107.9/100.4 FM

MELLOW 1557, Media Centre, 2 St Johns Wynd, Culver Square, Colchester CO1 1WG. Tel: 01206-764466. *Frequency:* 1557 AM

MELODY FM, 97 Tottenham Court Road, London W1P 9HF. Tel: 0171-504 6000. *Frequency:* 105.4 FM

MERCIA FM, Hertford Place, Coventry CV1 3TT. Tel: 01203-868200. *Frequencies:* 97.0/102.9 FM

MERCURY FM, The Stanley Centre, Kelvin Way, Crawley, W. Sussex RH10 2SE. Tel: 01293-519161. *Frequencies:* 97.5/102.7 FM

METRO FM, Newcastle upon Tyne NE99 1BB. Tel: 0191-420 0971. *Frequencies:* 97.1 FM (Northumberland, Tyne and Wear, Durham); 103.0 FM (Tyne Valley); 102.6 FM (Alnwick); 103.2 FM (Hexham)

MFM 97.1, Media House, Claughton Road, Birkenhead, Merseyside L45 6EY. Tel: 0151-650 1700. *Frequency:* 97.1 FM

MFM 103.4, The Studios, Mold Road, Gwersyllt, Nr Wrexham LL11 4AF. Tel: 01978-752202. *Frequency:* 103.4 FM

MILLENNIUM RADIO, Harrow Manor Way, Thamesmead, London SE2 9XH. Tel: 0181-311 3112. *Frequency:* 106.8 FM

MINSTER FM, PO Box 123, Dunnington, York YO1 5ZX. Tel: 01904-488888. *Frequencies:* 104.7 FM (York); 102.3 FM (Thirsk)

MIX 96, Friars Square Studios, 11 Bourbon Street, Aylesbury, Bucks HP20 2PZ. Tel: 01296-399396. *Frequency:* 96.2 FM

NEPTUNE RADIO, PO Box 1068, Dover CT16 1GB; PO Box 964, Folkestone CT18 8GG. Tel: 01304-202505. *Frequencies:* 96.4 FM (Folkestone); 106.8 FM (Dover)

NEWS DIRECT 97.3 FM, 200 Gray's Inn Road, London WC1X 8XZ. Tel: 0171-973 1152. *Frequency:* 97.3 FM

NORTHANTS 96, 19–21 St Edmunds Road, Northampton NN1 5DY. Tel: 01604-795600. *Frequency:* 96.6 FM

OAK FM, 18 Jubilee Drive, Loughborough, Leics LE11 5TQ. Tel: 01509-217080. Expected on air November 1998. *Frequency:* to be announced

OCEAN FM, Radio House, Whittle Avenue, Segensworth West, Fareham, Hants PO15 5SH. Tel: 01489-589911. *Frequencies:* 96.7/97.5 FM

ORCHARD FM, Haygrove House, Taunton, Somerset TA3 7BT. Tel: 01823-338448. *Frequencies:* 96.5 FM (Taunton); 97.1 FM (Yeovil); 102.6 FM (Somerset)

OXYGEN 107.9 FM, Suite 41, Westgate Centre, Oxford OX1 1PD. Tel: 01865-724442. *Frequency:* 107.9 FM

PEAK 107 FM, Radio House, Foxwood Road, Chesterfield, Derbys S41 9RF. Tel: 01246-269107. Expected on air 1 October 1998. *Frequency:* to be announced

PICCADILLY RADIO 1152 AM, Castle Quay, Castlefield, Manchester M5 4PR. Tel: 0161-288 5000. *Frequency:* 1152 AM

PIRATE FM 102, Carn Brea Studios, Wilson Way, Redruth, Cornwall TR15 3XX. Tel: 01209-314400. *Frequencies:* 102.2 FM (East Cornwall and West Devon); 102.8 FM (West Cornwall and Isles of Scilly)

PLYMOUTH SOUND AM AND FM, Earl's Acre, Plymouth PL3 4HX. Tel: 01752-227272. *Frequencies:* 1152 AM, 97.0/96.6 FM

POWER FM, Radio House, Whittle Avenue, Segensworth West, Fareham, Hants PO15 5SH. Tel: 01489-589911. *Frequency:* 103.2 FM

PREMIER RADIO, Glen House, Stag Place, London SW1E 5AG. Tel: 0171-316 1300. *Frequencies:* 1305/1332/1413 AM

THE PULSE, Pennine House, Forster Square, Bradford BD1 5NE. Tel: 01274-203040. *Frequencies:* 97.5 FM (Bradford); 102.5 FM (Huddersfield and Halifax)

Q 103 FM, Enterprise House, The Vision Park, Chivers Way, Histon, Cambridge CB4 4WW. Tel: 01223-235255. *Frequencies:* 103.0 FM (Cambridge); 97.4 FM (Newmarket)

QUAY WEST RADIO, Harbour Studios, The Esplanade, Watchet, Somerset TA23 0AJ. Tel: 01984-634900. *Frequency:* 102.4 FM

RADIO MANSFIELD, The Media Suite, Brunts Business Centre, Samuel Brunts Way, Mansfield, Notts NG18 2AH. Tel: 01623-646666. Expected on air 1 October 1998. *Frequency:* to be announced

RADIO XL 1296 AM, KMS House, Bradford Street, Birmingham B12 0JD. Tel: 0121-753 5353. *Frequency:* 1296 AM

RAM FM , The Market Place, Derby DE1 3AA. Tel: 01332-292945. *Frequency:* 102.8 FM

RED ROSE 999, PO Box 999, Preston PR1 1XR. Tel: 01772-556301. *Frequency:* 999 AM

ROCK FM, PO Box 974, Preston PR1 1XS. Tel: 01772-556301. *Frequency:* 97.4 FM

RTL COUNTRY 1035 AM, PO Box 1035, London W1A 2ZT. Tel: 0171-546 1010. *Frequency:* 1035 AM

RUTLAND RADIO, Rutland Business Centre, Gaol Street, Oakham, Rutland LE15 6AQ. Tel: 01572-757868. Expected on air autumn 1998. *Frequency:* to be announced

SABRAS, Radio House, 63 Melton Road, Leicester LE4
6PN. Tel: 0116-261 0666. *Frequency:* 1260 AM
SEVERN SOUND FM, Old Talbot House, Southgate
Street, Gloucester GL1 2DQ. Tel: 01452-423791.
Frequencies: 103.0/102.4 FM
SGR COLCHESTER , Abbeygate Two, 9 Whitewell Road,
Colchester CO2 7DE. Tel: 01206-575859. *Frequency:* 96.1
FM
SGR-FM , Radio House, Alpha Business Park, White
House Road, Ipswich IP1 5LT. Tel: 01473-461000.
Frequencies: 97.1 FM (Ipswich); 96.4 FM (Bury St
Edmunds)
SIGNAL FM, Regent House, Heaton Lane, Stockport SK4
1BX. Tel: 0161-285 4545. *Frequencies:* 104.9 FM
(Stockport); 96.4 FM (Cheshire)
SIGNAL ONE (FM) AND TWO (AM), Stoke Road, Stoke-
on-Trent ST4 2SR. Tel: 01782-747047. *Frequencies:* 1170
AM, 102.6 FM/96.9 FM (Stafford)
SILK FM, Radio House, Bridge Street, Macclesfield,
Cheshire SK11 6DJ. Tel: 01625-268000. *Frequency:* 106.9
FM
SOUTHERN FM, Radio House, PO Box 2000, Brighton
BN41 2SS. Tel: 01273-430111. *Frequencies:* 102.0 FM
(Hastings); 102.4 FM (Eastbourne); 96.9 FM
(Newhaven); 103.5 FM (Brighton)
SOVEREIGN RADIO, 14 St Mary's Walk, Hailsham, E.
Sussex BN27 1AF. Tel: 01323-442700. *Frequency:* 107.5
FM
SPECTRUM INTERNATIONAL RADIO, International Radio
Centre, 204–206 Queenstown Road, London SW8 3NR.
Tel: 0171-627 4433. *Frequency:* 558 AM
SPIRE FM, City Hall Studios, Malthouse Lane, Salisbury,
Wilts SP2 7QQ. Tel: 01722-416644. *Frequency:* 102.0 FM
SPIRIT FM, Dukes Court, Bognor Road, Chichester,
W. Sussex PO19 2FX. Tel: 01243-773600. *Frequencies:*
96.6/102.3 FM
STAR FM, The Observatory Shopping Centre, Slough,
Berks SL1 1LH. Tel: 01753-551066. *Frequency:* 106.6 FM
SUN FM, PO Box 1034, Sunderland SR1 3YZ. Tel: 0191-567
3333. *Frequency:* 103.4 FM
SUNRISE FM, Sunrise House, 30 Chapel Street, Little
Germany, Bradford BD1 5DN. Tel: 01274-735043.
Frequency: 103.2 FM
SUNRISE RADIO, Sunrise House, Sunrise Road, Southall,
Middx UB2 4AU. Tel: 0181-574 6666. *Frequency:* 1458
AM
SUNSHINE 855, Sunshine House, Waterside, Ludlow,
Shropshire SY8 1GS. Tel: 01584-873795. *Frequency:* 855
AM
SURF 107, PO Box 107, Brighton BN1 1QG. Tel: 01273-
386107. Frequency: 107.2 FM
TEN 17, Latton Bush Centre, Southern Way, Harlow,
Essex CM18 7BU. Tel: 01279-432415. *Frequency:* 101.7 FM
TFM, Radio House, Yale Crescent, Thornaby, Stockton-
on-Tees TS17 6AA. Tel: 01642-888222. *Frequency:* 96.6
FM
THANET LOCAL RADIO, Imperial House, 2–14 High
Street, Margate, Kent CT9 1DH. Tel: 01843-220222.
Frequency: 107.2 FM
TRAX FM, PO Box 444, Worksop, Notts S81 9YW. Tel:
01909-500611. Expected on air autumn 1998. *Frequency:*
to be announced
VIRGIN 105.8, 1 Golden Square, London W1R 4DJ. Tel:
0171-434 1215. *Frequency:* 105.8 FM
THE WAVE 96.5, 965 Mowbray Drive, Blackpool FY3 7JR.
Tel: 01253-304965. *Frequency:* 96.5 FM
WESSEX FM, Radio House, Trinity Street, Dorchester
DT1 1DJ. Tel: 01305-250333. *Frequencies:* 97.2/96.0 FM

WEY VALLEY RADIO, Prospect Place, Mill Lane, Alton,
Hants GU34 2SY. Tel: 01420-544444. *Frequencies:* 102.0/
101.6 FM
WYVERN FM, 5 Barbourne Terrace, Worcester WR1 3JZ.
Tel: 01905-612212. *Frequencies:* 97.6 FM (Hereford);
102.8 FM (Worcester); 96.7 FM (Kidderminster)
XFM, 97 Charlotte Street, London W1P 1LB. Tel: 0171-299
4000. *Frequency:* 104.9 FM
YORKSHIRE COAST RADIO, PO Box 962, Scarborough,
N. Yorks YO12 5YX. Tel: 01723-500962. *Frequencies:* 96.2/
103.1 FM
YORKSHIRE DALES RADIO LTD, YDR House, Gargrave
Road, Skipton, N. Yorks BD23 1YD. Tel: 01756-799991.
Frequencies: 936 AM (Hawes); 1413 AM (Skipton)

Wales

CHAMPION FM, PO Box 103, Caernarfon LL55 1ZD. Tel:
01978-752202. *Frequency:* 103.0 FM
COAST FM, Media House, Conway Road, Colwyn Bay
LL28 5AB. Tel: 01492-534555. *Frequency:* 96.3 FM
RADIO CEREDIGION, Yr Hen Ysgol Gymraeg, Ffordd
Alexandra, Aberystwyth SY23 1LF. Tel: 01970-627999.
Frequencies: 103.3/97.4/96.6 FM
RADIO MALDWYN, The Studios, The Park, Newtown,
Powys SY16 2NZ. Tel: 01686-623555. *Frequency:* 756 AM
RED DRAGON FM, Radio House, West Canal Wharf,
Cardiff CF1 5XJ. Tel: 01222-384041. *Frequencies:* 103.2
FM (Cardiff); 97.4 FM (Newport)
SWANSEA SOUND, PO Box 1170, Victoria Road,
Gowerton, Swansea SA4 3AB. Tel: 01792-511170.
Frequency: 1170 AM
TOUCH RADIO, West Canal Wharf, Cardiff CF1 5XL. Tel:
01222-237878. *Frequencies:* 1359 AM (Cardiff); 1305
AM (Newport)
VALLEYS RADIO, Festival Park, Victoria, Ebbw Vale
NP3 6XW. Tel: 01495-301116. *Frequencies:* 999/1116 AM
THE WAVE 96.4 FM , PO Box 964, Victoria Road,
Gowerton, Swansea SA4 3AB. Tel: 01792-511964.
Frequency: 96.4 FM

Scotland

96.3 QFM, 26 Lady Lane, Paisley PA1 2LG. Tel: 0141-887
9630. *Frequency:* 96.3 FM
CENTRAL FM, 201 High Street, Falkirk FK1 1DU. Tel:
01324-611164. *Frequency:* 103.1 FM
CLYDE 1 (FM) AND 2 (AM), Clydebank Business Park,
Clydebank, Glasgow G81 2RX. Tel: 0141-565 2200.
Frequencies: 102.5 FM; 103.3 FM (Firth of Clyde); 97.0
FM (Vale of Leven); 1152 AM
FORTH AM AND FM, Forth House, Forth Street,
Edinburgh EH1 3LF. Tel: 0131-556 9255. *Frequencies:* 1548
AM, 97.3/97.6 FM
HEARTLAND FM, Atholl Curling Rink, Lower Oakfield,
Pitlochry, Perthshire PH16 5HQ. Tel: 01796-474040.
Frequency: 97.5 FM
ISLES FM, PO Box 333, Stornoway, Isle of Lewis HS1 2PU.
Tel: 01851-703333. *Frequency:* 103.0 FM
KINGDOM FM, Gilmerton House, By St Andrews, Fife
KY16 8NB. Tel: 01382-776403. *Frequencies:* 95.2/96.2 FM
LOCHBROOM FM, Mill Street Industrial Estate, Ullapool,
Wester Ross IV26 2UN. Tel: 01854-613131. *Frequency:*
102.2 FM
MORAY FIRTH RADIO, Scorguie Place, Inverness IV3 6SF.
Tel: 01463-224433. *Frequencies:* 97.4 FM, 1107 AM
NECR (NORTH-EAST COMMUNITY RADIO), Town
House, Kintore, Inverurie, Aberdeenshire AB51 0US. Tel:
01467-632909. *Frequencies:* 102.1 FM (Inverurie); 102.6
FM (Kildrummy); 103.2 FM (Colpy)

NEVIS RADIO, Inverlochy, Fort William, Inverness-shire PH33 6LU. Tel: 01397-700007. *Frequencies:* 96.6 FM (Fort William); 97.0 FM (Glencoe); 102.3 FM (Skye); 102.4 FM (Loch Leven)

NORTHSOUND ONE (FM) AND TWO (AM), 45 Kings Gate, Aberdeen AB15 4EL. Tel: 01224-337000. *Frequencies:* 1035 AM, 96.9/97.6/103.0 FM

OBAN FM, McLeod Units, Lochavullin Estate, Oban, Argyll. Tel: 01631-570057. *Frequency:* 103.3 FM

RADIO BORDERS, Tweedside Park, Galashiels TD1 3TD. Tel: 01896-759444. *Frequencies:* 96.8/97.5/103.1/103.4 FM

RADIO TAY AM AND TAY FM, 6 North Isla Street, Dundee DD3 7JQ. Tel: 01382-200800. *Frequencies:* 1161 AM, 102.8 FM (Dundee); 1584 AM, 96.4 FM (Perth)

SIBC, Market Street, Lerwick, Shetland ZE1 0JN. Tel: 01595-695299. *Frequencies:* 96.2/102.2 FM

SOUTH WEST SOUND, Campbell House, Bankend Road, Dumfries DG1 4TH. Tel: 01387-250999. *Frequencies:* 97.0/96.5/103.0 FM

WAVES RADIO PETERHEAD, Unit 2, Blackhouse Industrial Estate, Peterhead AB42 1BW. Tel: 01779-491012. *Frequency:* 101.2 FM

WEST SOUND AM AND FM, Radio House, 54A Holmston Road, Ayr KA7 3BE. Tel: 01292-283662. *Frequencies:* 1035 AM, 96.7 FM (Ayr); 97.5 FM (Girvan)

Northern Ireland

CITY BEAT 96.7, Lamont Buildings, Stranmillis Embankment, Belfast BT9 5FN. Tel: 01232-205967. *Frequency:* 96.7 FM

COOL FM, PO Box 974, Belfast BT1 1RT. Tel: 01247-817181. *Frequency:* 97.4 FM

DOWNTOWN RADIO, Newtownards, Co. Down BT23 4ES. Tel: 01247-815555. *Frequencies:* 1026 AM (Belfast); 102.4 FM (Londonderry); 96.4 FM (Limavady); 96.6 FM (Enniskillen); 103.1 FM (Newry); 102.3 FM Ballymena

GOLD BEAT 828, 2C Park Avenue, Cookstown, Co. Tyrone BT80 8AH. Tel: 016487-64828. *Frequency:* 828 AM

HEART BEAT 1521, Carn Business Park, Craigavon, Co. Armagh BT63 5RH. Tel: 01762-330033. *Frequency:* 1521 AM

Q 102.9 FM, The Riverside Suite, Old Waterside Railway Station, Duke Street, Londonderry BT47 6DH. Tel: 01504-344449. *Frequency:* 102.9 FM

Channel Islands

CHANNEL 103 FM, 6 Tunnell Street, St Helier, Jersey JE2 4LU. Tel: 01534-888103. *Frequency:* 103.7 FM

ISLAND FM, 12 Westerbrook, St Sampson, Guernsey GY2 4QQ. Tel: 01481-42000. *Frequencies:* 104.7 FM (Guernsey); 93.7 FM (Alderney)

SERVICES BROADCASTING

The British Forces Broadcasting Service (BFBS) and Teleport London International (TLI), both part of the Services Sound and Vision Corporation (SSVC) group of companies, provide HM Forces and their families with radio and television broadcasting. The broadcasting service covers Britain and Northern Ireland, Cyprus, Germany, Gibraltar, the Falkland Islands, Belize, Bosnia, Brunei, Kuwait and Saudi Arabia.

SSVC, Chalfont Grove, Gerrards Cross, Bucks SL9 8TN. Tel: 01494-874461. *Managing Director,* D. O. Crwys-Williams, CB

The Press

The newspaper and periodical press in the UK is large and diverse, catering for a wide variety of views and interests. There is no state control or censorship of the press, though it is subject to the laws on publication and the Press Complaints Commission (*see* below) was set up by the industry as a means of self-regulation.

The press is not state-subsidized and receives few tax concessions. The income of most newspapers and periodicals is derived largely from sales and from advertising; the press is the largest advertising medium in Britain.

SELF-REGULATION

The report of the Committee on Privacy and Related Matters, chaired by David Calcutt, QC, was published in June 1990 and led to the setting up of a non-statutory Press Complaints Commission. The performance of the Press Complaints Commission was reviewed after 18 months of operation (the *Calcutt Review of Press Self-Regulation*, presented to Parliament in January 1993) to determine whether statutory measures were required. No proposals for replacing the self-regulation system have been made to date.

COMPLAINTS

The Press Complaints Commission was founded by the newspaper and magazine industry in January 1991 to replace the Press Council (established in 1953). It is a voluntary, non-statutory body set up to operate the press's self-regulation system, and funded by the industry through the Press Standards Board of Finance.

The Commission's objects are to consider, adjudicate, conciliate, and resolve complaints of unfair treatment by the press; and to ensure that the press maintains the highest professional standards with respect for generally recognized freedoms, including freedom of expression, the public's right to know, and the right of the press to operate free from improper pressure. The Commission judges newspaper and magazine conduct by a code of practice drafted by editors, agreed by the industry and ratified by the Commission.

Seven of the Commission's members are editors of national, regional and local newspapers and magazines, and nine, including the chairman, are drawn from other fields. One member has been appointed Privacy Commissioner with special powers to investigate complaints about invasion of privacy.

PRESS COMPLAINTS COMMISSION, 1 Salisbury Square, London EC4Y 8AE. Tel: 0171-353 1248. *Chairman,* Lord Wakeham, PC; *Director,* G. Black

---

NEWSPAPERS

Newspapers are usually financially independent of any political party, though most adopt a political stance in their editorial comments, usually reflecting proprietorial influence. Ownership of the national and regional daily newspapers is concentrated in the hands of large corporations whose interests cover publishing and communications. The rules on cross-media ownership, as amended by the Broadcasting Act 1996, limit the extent to which newspaper organizations with over 20 per cent of national circulation may become involved in broadcasting (*see* page 674).

There are 16 daily and about 14 Sunday national papers, about 80 regional daily papers, and several hundred local papers that are published weekly or twice-weekly. Scotland, Wales and Northern Ireland all have at least one daily and one Sunday national paper.

Newspapers are usually published in either broadsheet or tabloid format. The 'quality' daily papers, i.e. those providing detailed coverage of a wide range of public matters, have a broadsheet format. The tabloid papers take a more popular approach and are more illustrated.

CIRCULATION

NATIONAL DAILY NEWSPAPERS

Daily Mail	2,267,000
Daily Sport	230,000
Daily Star	574,000
Daily Telegraph	1,070,000
The Express	1,142,000
Financial Times	358,000
The Guardian	396,000
The Independent	220,000
The Mirror	2,292,000
Racing Post	73,000
The Scotsman	81,000
The Sun	3,651,000
The Times	753,000

NATIONAL SUNDAY NEWSPAPERS

The Express on Sunday	1,069,000
Independent on Sunday	255,000
The Mail on Sunday	2,191,000
News of the World	4,206,000
The Observer	402,000
The People	1,733,000
Scotland on Sunday	123,000
Sunday Mirror	2,033,000
Sunday Sport	234,000
The Sunday Telegraph	826,000
The Sunday Times	1,340,000

NATIONAL DAILY NEWSPAPERS

DAILY MAIL, Northcliffe House, 2 Derry Street, London W8 5TT. Tel: 0171-938 6000. Fax: 0171-937 3745

DAILY STAR, Ludgate House, 245 Blackfriars Road, London SE1 9UX. Tel: 0171-928 8000. Fax: 0171-633 0244

DAILY TELEGRAPH, 1 Canada Square, Canary Wharf, London E14 5DT. Tel: 0171-538 5000. Fax: 0171-538 6242

THE EUROPEAN, 200 Gray's Inn Road, London WC1X 8NE. Tel: 0171-418 7777. Fax: 0171-713 1840

THE EXPRESS, Ludgate House, 245 Blackfriars Road, London SE1 9UX. Tel: 0171-928 8000. Fax: 0171-633 0244

FINANCIAL TIMES, 1 Southwark Bridge, London SE1 9HL. Tel: 0171-873 3000. Fax: 0171-407 5700

THE GUARDIAN, 119 Farringdon Road, London EC1R 3ER. Tel: 0171-278 2332. Fax: 0171-837 2114

THE HERALD, 195 Albion Street, Glasgow G1 1QP. Tel: 0141-552 6255. Fax: 0141-552 1344

THE INDEPENDENT, 1 Canada Square, Canary Wharf, London E14 5DL. Tel: 0171-293 2000. Fax: 0171-293 2435

THE MIRROR, 1 Canada Square, Canary Wharf, London E14 5AP. Tel: 0171-293 3000. Fax: 0171-293 3405

MORNING STAR, 1–3 Ardleigh Road, London N1 4HS. Tel: 0171-254 0033. Fax: 0171-254 5950

RACING POST, 1 Canada Square, Canary Wharf, London EI4 5AP. Tel: 0171-293 3000

THE SCOTSMAN, 20 North Bridge, Edinburgh EHI IYT. Tel: 0131-225 2468. Fax: 0131-220 3714

THE SUN, 1 Virginia Street, London EI 9XR. Tel: 0171-782 4000. Fax: 0171-583 9504

THE TIMES, 1 Pennington Street, London EI 9XN. Tel: 0171-782 5000. Fax: 0171-782 5988

REGIONAL DAILY NEWSPAPERS

BERKSHIRE

READING EVENING POST, 8 Tessa Road, Reading RGI 8NS

CAMBRIDGESHIRE

CAMBRIDGE EVENING NEWS, Winship Road, Milton, Cambridge CB4 6PP

PETERBOROUGH EVENING TELEGRAPH, New Priestgate House, 57 Priestgate, Peterborough PEI IJW

CUMBRIA

NEWS AND STAR, Newspaper House, Dalston Road, Carlisle CA2 5UA

NORTH-WEST EVENING MAIL, Newspaper House, Abbey Road, Barrow-in-Furness LA14 5QS

DERBYSHIRE

DERBY EVENING TELEGRAPH, Northcliffe House, Meadow Road, Derby DEI 2DW

DEVON

EVENING HERALD, 17 Brest Road, Derriford Business Park, Plymouth PL6 5AA

EXPRESS AND ECHO, Heron Road, Sowton, Exeter EX2 7NF

HERALD EXPRESS, Harmsworth House, Barton Hill Road, Torquay TQ2 8JN

WESTERN MORNING NEWS, 17 Brest Road, Derriford Business Park, Plymouth PL6 5AA

DORSET

THE DAILY ECHO, Richmond Hill, Bournemouth BH2 6HH

DORSET EVENING ECHO, 57 St Thomas Street, Weymouth DT4 8EU

DURHAM

NORTHERN ECHO, Priestgate, Darlington DLI INF

EAST SUSSEX

THE ARGUS/EVENING ARGUS, Argus House, Crowhurst Road, Hollingbury, Brighton BNI 8AR

ESSEX

EVENING ECHO, Newspaper House, Chester Hall Lane, Basildon SS14 3BL

EVENING GAZETTE, Oriel House, 43–44 North Hill, Colchester COI ITZ

GLOUCESTERSHIRE

THE CITIZEN, St John's Lane, Gloucester GLI 2AY

GLOUCESTERSHIRE ECHO, 1–3 Clarence Parade, Cheltenham GL50 3NZ

HAMPSHIRE

THE NEWS, The News Centre, Hilsea, Portsmouth PO2 9SX

SOUTHERN DAILY ECHO, Newspaper House, Test Lane, Retbridge, Southampton SOI6 9JX

HEREFORD AND WORCESTER

WORCESTER EVENING NEWS, Hylton Road, Worcester WR2 5JX

KENT

KENT TODAY, Messenger House, New Hythe Lane, Larkfield, Aylesford ME20 6SG

LANCASHIRE

BOLTON EVENING NEWS, Churchgate, Bolton BLI IDE

EVENING CHRONICLE, 172 Union Street, Oldham OLI IEQ

THE GAZETTE, PO Box 20, Preston New Road, Blackpool FY4 4AU

LANCASHIRE EVENING POST, Oliver's Place, Fulwood, Preston PR2 9ZA

LANCASHIRE EVENING TELEGRAPH, Newspaper House, High Street, Blackburn BBI IHT

MANCHESTER EVENING NEWS, 164 Deansgate, Manchester M60 2RD

WIGAN EVENING POST, Oliver's Place, Fulwood, Preston PR2 9ZA

LEICESTERSHIRE

LEICESTER MERCURY, St George Street, Leicester LEI 9FQ

LINCOLNSHIRE

GRIMSBY EVENING TELEGRAPH, 80 Cleethorpe Road, Grimsby DN31 3EH

LINCOLNSHIRE ECHO, Brayford Wharf East, Lincoln LN5 7AT

SCUNTHORPE EVENING TELEGRAPH, Telegraph House, Doncaster Road, Scunthorpe DN15 7RE

LONDON

THE EVENING STANDARD, Northcliffe House, 2 Derry Street, London W8 5TT

MERSEYSIDE

DAILY POST, and LIVERPOOL ECHO, PO Box 48, Old Hall Street, Liverpool L69 3EB

NORFOLK

EASTERN DAILY PRESS, and EVENING NEWS, Prospect House, Rouen Road, Norwich NRI IRE

NORTHAMPTONSHIRE

CHRONICLE AND ECHO, Upper Mounts, Northampton NNI 3HR

NORTHAMPTONSHIRE EVENING TELEGRAPH, Northfield Avenue, Kettering NN16 9TT

NOTTINGHAMSHIRE

NOTTINGHAM EVENING POST, Forman Street, Nottingham NGI 4AB

OXFORDSHIRE

THE OXFORD MAIL, Newspaper House, Osney Mead, Oxford OX2 0EJ

SHROPSHIRE

SHROPSHIRE STAR, Ketley, Telford TFI 4HU

SOMERSET

THE BATH CHRONICLE, Windsor House, Windsor Bridge, Bath BA2 3AJ

BRISTOL EVENING POST, and WESTERN DAILY PRESS, Temple Way, Bristol BS99 7HD

STAFFORDSHIRE

BURTON MAIL, 65–68 High Street, Burton-on-Trent DEI4 ILE

THE SENTINEL, Sentinel House, Etruria, Stoke-on-Trent STI 5SS

SUFFOLK

EAST ANGLIAN DAILY TIMES, and EVENING STAR, 30 Lower Brook Street, Ipswich IP4 IAN

TYNE AND WEAR

EVENING CHRONICLE, and THE JOURNAL, Thomson House, Groat Market, Newcastle upon Tyne NEI IED
SHIELDS GAZETTE, Chapter Row, South Shields NE33 IBL
SUNDERLAND ECHO, Echo House, Pennywell, Sunderland SR4 9ER

WARWICKSHIRE

HEARTLAND EVENING NEWS, Newspaper House, 11–15 Newtown Road, Nuneaton CVII 4HR

WEST MIDLANDS

THE BIRMINGHAM POST, AND BIRMINGHAM EVENING MAIL, 28 Colmore Circus, Queensway, Birmingham B4 6AX
COVENTRY EVENING TELEGRAPH, Corporation Street, Coventry CVI IFP
EXPRESS AND STAR, 51–53 Queen Street, Wolverhampton WVI IES

WILTSHIRE

EVENING ADVERTISER, Newspaper House, 100 Victoria Road, Swindon SNI 3BE

YORKSHIRE

BARNSLEY STAR, York Street, Sheffield SI IPU
THE DONCASTER STAR, York Street, Sheffield SI IPU
EVENING GAZETTE, Gazette Buildings, Borough Road, Middlesbrough TSI 3AZ
HALIFAX EVENING COURIER, PO Box 19, Courier Buildings, King Cross Street, Halifax HXI 2SF
HUDDERSFIELD DAILY EXAMINER, PO Box A26, Queen Street South, Huddersfield HDI 2TD
HULL DAILY MAIL, Blundell's Corner, Beverley Road, Hull HU3 IXS
ROTHERHAM STAR, York Street, Sheffield SI IPU
SCARBOROUGH EVENING NEWS, 17–23 Aberdeen Walk, Scarborough YOII IBB
THE STAR, York Street, Sheffield SI IPU
TELEGRAPH AND ARGUS, Hall Ings, Bradford BDI IJR
YORKSHIRE EVENING POST, PO Box 168, Wellington Street, Leeds LSI IRF
YORKSHIRE EVENING PRESS, PO Box 29, 76–86 Walmgate, York YOI IYN
YORKSHIRE POST, PO Box 168, Wellington Street, Leeds LSI IRF

WALES

EVENING LEADER, Mold Business Park, Wrexham Road, Mold CH7 IXY
SOUTH WALES ARGUS, Cardiff Road, Maesglas, Newport NP9 IQW
SOUTH WALES ECHO, Thomson House, Havelock Street, Cardiff CFI IXR
SOUTH WALES EVENING POST, Adelaide Street, Swansea SAI IQT
WESTERN MAIL, Thomson House, Havelock Street, Cardiff CFI IXR

SCOTLAND

COURIER AND ADVERTISER, 2 Albert Square, Dundee DDI 9QJ
DAILY RECORD, 40 Anderston Quay, Glasgow G3 8DA
EDINBURGH EVENING NEWS, 20 North Bridge, Edinburgh EHI IYT

EVENING EXPRESS, PO Box 43, Lang Stracht, Mastrick, Aberdeen ABI5 6DF
EVENING TELEGRAPH AND POST, 2 Albert Square, Dundee DDI 9QJ
EVENING TIMES, 195 Albion Street, Glasgow GI IQP
GREENOCK TELEGRAPH, Pitreavie Business Park, Dunfermline KYII 5QS
PAISLEY DAILY EXPRESS, 1 Woodside Terrace, Glasgow G3 7UY
PRESS AND JOURNAL, PO Box 43, Lang Stracht, Mastrick, Aberdeen ABI5 6DF

NORTHERN IRELAND

BELFAST TELEGRAPH, 124–144 Royal Avenue, Belfast BTI IEB

CHANNEL ISLANDS

GUERNSEY EVENING PRESS AND STAR, PO Box 57, Guernsey GYI 3BW
JERSEY EVENING POST, PO Box 582, Five Oaks, St Saviour, Jersey JE4 8XQ

WEEKLY NEWSPAPERS

THE EXPRESS ON SUNDAY, Ludgate House, 245 Blackfriars Road, London SEI 9UX. Tel: 0171-928 8000. Fax: 0171-633 0244
INDEPENDENT ON SUNDAY, 1 Canada Square, Canary Wharf, London EI4 5DL. Tel: 0171-293 2000. Fax: 0171-293 2435
INDIA TIMES, Global House, 90 Ascot Gardens, Southall, Middx UBI 2SB. Tel: 0181-575 0151. Fax: 0181-575 5661
THE MAIL ON SUNDAY, Northcliffe House, 2 Derry Street, London W8 5TS. Tel: 0171-938 6000. Fax: 0171-937 7896
NEWS OF THE WORLD, 1 Virginia Street, London EI 9XR. Tel: 0171-782 4000. Fax: 0171-583 9504
THE OBSERVER, 119 Farringdon Road, London ECIR 3ER. Tel: 0171-278 2332. Fax: 0171-837 2114
THE PEOPLE, 1 Canada Square, Canary Wharf, London EI4 5AP. Tel: 0171-293 3000. Fax: 0171-293 3405
SCOTLAND ON SUNDAY, 20 North Bridge, Edinburgh EHI IYT. Tel: 0131-225 2468. Fax: 0131-220 2443
SUNDAY MAIL, 40 Anderston Quay, Glasgow G3 8DA. Tel: 0141-248 7000. Fax: 0141-242 3340
SUNDAY MIRROR, 1 Canada Square, Canary Wharf, London EI4 5AP. Tel: 0171-293 3000. Fax: 0171-293 3405
SUNDAY POST, Courier Place, Dundee DDI 9QJ. Tel: 01382-223131. Fax: 01382-201064
SUNDAY SPORT, 19 Great Ancoats Street, Manchester M60 4BT. Tel: 0161-236 4466. Fax: 0161-236 4535
THE SUNDAY TELEGRAPH, 1 Canada Square, Canary Wharf, London EI4 5DT. Tel: 0171-538 5000. Fax: 0171-512 2504
THE SUNDAY TIMES, 1 Pennington Street, London EI 9XN. Tel: 0171-782 5000. Fax: 0171-782 5988
WALES ON SUNDAY, Thomson House, Havelock Street, Cardiff CFI IXR. Tel: 01222-583583. Fax: 01222-583451
WEEKLY NEWS, Courier Place, Dundee DDI 9QJ. Tel: 01382-223131. Fax: 01382-201390

RELIGIOUS PAPERS

Alt = Alternate; *M* = Monthly; *Q* = Quarterly; *W* = Weekly

BAPTIST TIMES, PO Box 54, 129 The Broadway, Didcot, Oxon OXII 8XB. *W*
CATHOLIC HERALD, Herald House, Lambs Passage, Bunhill Row, London ECIY 8TQ. *W*
CHALLENGE - THE GOOD NEWS PAPER, PO Box 300, Kingstown Broadway, Carlisle, Cumbria CA3 OQS. *M*

THE CHURCH OF ENGLAND NEWSPAPER, 10 Little College Street, London SW1P 3SH. *W*

CHURCH OF IRELAND GAZETTE, 36 Bachelor's Walk, Lisburn, Co. Antrim BT28 1XN. *W*

CHURCH TIMES, 33 Upper Street, London N1 0PN. *W*

ENGLISH CHURCHMAN, 22 Lesley Avenue, Canterbury, Kent CT1 3LF. *Alt. W*

THE FRIEND, Drayton House, 30 Gordon Street, London WC1H 0BQ. *W*

JEWISH CHRONICLE, 25 Furnival Street, London EC4A 1JT. *W*

JEWISH TELEGRAPH, Telegraph House, 11 Park Hill, Bury Old Road, Prestwich, Manchester M25 0HH. *W*

LIFE AND WORK, Church of Scotland, 121 George Street, Edinburgh EH2 4YN. *M*

METHODIST RECORDER, 122 Golden Lane, London EC1Y 0TL. *W*

MIDDLE WAY, Buddhist Society, 58 Eccleston Square, London SW1V 1PH. *Q*

ORTHODOX OUTLOOK, 42 Withens Lane, Wallasey, Merseyside L45 7NN. *Alt. M*

PRESBYTERIAN HERALD, Church House, Fisherwick Place, Belfast BT1 6DW. *Ten times a year*

QUAKER MONTHLY, Friends House, Euston Road, London NW1 2BJ. *M*

REFORM, United Reformed Church, 86 Tavistock Place, London WC1H 9RT. *Eleven times a year*

THE SIKH COURIER INTERNATIONAL, The Sikh Cultural Society of Great Britain, 33 Wargrave Road, Harrow, Middx HA2 8LL. *Q*

THE SIKH MESSENGER, 43 Dorset Road, London SW19 3EZ. *Q*

THE TABLET, 1 King Street Cloisters, Clifton Walk, London W6 0QZ. *W*

THE UNIVERSE, 1st Floor, St James Building, Oxford Street, Manchester M1 6FP. *W*

THE WAR CRY, 101 Queen Victoria Street, London EC4P 4EP. *W*

PERIODICALS

There are about 6,500 periodicals published in Britain. These are classified as consumer, i.e. general interest, or as trade, professional or academic.

CONSUMER PERIODICALS

Alt = Alternate; *M* = Monthly; *Q* = Quarterly; *W* = Weekly

AL MAJALLA, Arab Press House, 184 High Holborn, London WC1V 7AP. *W*

AMATEUR GARDENING, Westover House, West Quay Road, Poole, Dorset BH15 1JG. *W*

AMATEUR PHOTOGRAPHER, King's Reach Tower, Stamford Street, London SE1 9LS. *W*

ANGLING TIMES, Bretton Court, Bretton, Peterborough PE3 8DZ. *W*

ANTIQUE, 10–11 Lower John Street, London W1R 3PE. *Q*

APOLLO, 1 Castle Lane, London SW1E 6DR. *M*

ARENA, 3rd Floor, Block A, Exmouth House, Pine Street, London EC1R 0JL. *M*

ART MONTHLY, Suite 17, 26 Charing Cross Road, London WC2H 0DG. *Ten times a year*

ASIAN TIMES, 148 Cambridge Heath Road, London E1 5QJ. *W*

ASTRONOMY NOW, PO Box 175, Tonbridge, Kent TN10 4ZY. *M*

ATHLETICS WEEKLY, Bretton Court, Bretton, Peterborough PE3 8DZ. *W*

AUTOCAR, 38–42 Hampton Road, Teddington, Middx TW11 0JE. *W*

BBC GARDENER'S WORLD, Woodlands, 80 Wood Lane, London W12 0TT. *M*

BBC GOOD FOOD, Woodlands, 80 Wood Lane, London W12 0TT. *M*

BBC VEGETARIAN GOOD FOOD, Woodlands, 80 Wood Lane, London W12 0TT. *M*

BBC WILDLIFE MAGAZINE, Woodlands, 80 Wood Lane, London W12 0TT. *M*

BELFAST GAZETTE (*Official*), The Stationery Office, PO Box 276, London SW8 5DT. *W*

BELLA, 2nd Floor, Shirley House, 25–27 Camden Road, London NW1 9LL. *W*

BEST, 10th Floor, Portland House, Stag Place, London SW1E 5AU. *W*

THE BIG ISSUE, Fleet House, 57–61 Clerkenwell Road, London EC1M 5NP. *W*

BIKE, Bushfield House, Orton Centre, Peterborough PE2 5UW. *M*

BIRD WATCHING, Bretton Court, Bretton, Peterborough PE3 8DZ. *M*

BIRDS, RSPB, The Lodge, Sandy, Beds SG19 2DL. *Q*

BOXING MONTHLY, 24 Notting Hill Gate, London W11 3JE. *M*

BRIDES AND SETTING UP HOME, Vogue House, Hanover Square, London W1R 0AD. *Alt. M*

BRITISH PHILATELIC BULLETIN, 20 Brandon Street, Edinburgh EH3 5TT. *M*

CAMPING AND CARAVANNING, Greenfields House, Westwood Way, Coventry CV4 8JH. *M*

CAR, Abbots Court, 34 Farringdon Lane, London EC1R 3AU. *M*

CARIBBEAN TIMES, 3rd Floor, Tower House, 141–149 Fonthill Road, London N4 3HF. *W*

CAT WORLD, 10 Western Road, Shoreham-by-Sea, W. Sussex BN43 5WD. *M*

CHAT, King's Reach Tower, Stamford Street, London SE1 9LS. *W*

CLASSIC AND SPORTSCAR, 38–42 Hampton Road, Teddington, Middx TW11 0JE. *M*

CLASSIC CARS, Abbots Court, 34 Farringdon Lane, London EC1R 3AU. *M*

CLASSIC CD, Beauford Court, 30 Monmouth Street, Bath BA1 2BW. *Thirteen times a year*

CLOTHES SHOW MAGAZINE, Woodlands, 80 Wood Lane, London W12 0TT. *M*

COARSE FISHERMAN, 67 Tyrrell Street, Leicester LE3 5SB. *M*

COIN NEWS, PO Box 14, Honiton, Devon EX14 9YP. *M*

COMPANY, National Magazine House, 72 Broadwick Street, London W1V 2BP. *M*

COMPUTER AND VIDEO GAMES, Priory Court, 30–32 Farringdon Lane, London EC1R 3AU. *M*

COMPUTER SHOPPER, 19 Bolsover Street, London W1P 7HJ. *M*

COSMOPOLITAN, National Magazine House, 72 Broadwick Street, London W1V 2BP. *M*

COUNTRY HOMES AND INTERIORS, King's Reach Tower, Stamford Street, London SE1 9LS. *M*

COUNTRY LIFE, King's Reach Tower, Stamford Street, London SE1 9LS. *W*

COUNTRY LIVING MAGAZINE, National Magazine House, 72 Broadwick Street, London W1V 2BP. *M*

COUNTRY WALKING, Bretton Court, Bretton, Peterborough PE3 8DZ. *M*

THE COUNTRYMAN, Link House Magazines Ltd, Sheep Street, Burford, Oxon OX18 4LH. *Alt. M*

THE CRICKETER INTERNATIONAL, Beech Hanger, Ashurst, Tunbridge Wells, Kent TN3 9ST. *M*

CYCLING WEEKLY, King's Reach Tower, Stamford Street, London SE1 9LS. *W*

THE DALESMAN, Stable Courtyard, Broughton Hall, Skipton, N. Yorks BD23 3AE. *M*

DALTONS WEEKLY, CI Tower, St George's Square, New Malden, Surrey KT3 4JA. *W*

DANCE THEATRE JOURNAL, Laban Centre London, Laurie Grove, London SE14 6NH. *Three times a year*

DANCING TIMES, Clerkenwell House, 45–47 Clerkenwell Green, London ECIR 0EB. *M*

DOG WORLD, 9 Tufton Street, Ashford, Kent TN23 IQN. *W*

DOGS TODAY, Pankhurst Farm, Bagshot Road, West End, Woking, Surrey GU24 9QR. *M*

THE ECOLOGIST, Agriculture House, Bath Road, Sturminster Newton, Dorset DT10 IDU. *Alt. M*

THE ECONOMIST, 25 St James's Street, London SW1A IHG. *W*

EDINBURGH GAZETTE (*Official*), The Stationery Office, PO Box 276, London SW8 5DT. *Two times a week*

ELLE, Victory House, 14 Leicester Place, London WC2H 7BP. *M*

EMPIRE, Mappin House, 4 Winsley Street, London W1N 7AR. *M*

ESQUIRE, National Magazine House, 72 Broadwick Street, London W1V 2BP. *M*

ESSENTIALS, King's Reach Tower, Stamford Street, London SE1 9LS. *M*

EXCHANGE AND MART, Link House, 25 West Street, Poole, Dorset BH15 ILL. *W*

THE FACE, 3rd Floor, Block A, Exmouth House, Pine Street, London ECIR 0JL. *M*

FAMILY CIRCLE, King's Reach Tower, Stamford Street, London SE1 9LS. *M*

FHM, Mappin House, 4 Winsley Street, London W1N 7AR. *M*

THE FIELD, King's Reach Tower, Stamford Street, London SE1 9LS. *M*

FILM REVIEW, 9 Blades Court, Deodar Road, London SW15 2NU. *M*

FORE!, Bretton Court, Bretton, Peterborough PE3 8DZ. *M*

GARDEN NEWS, Apex House, Oundle Road, Peterborough PE2 9NP. *W*

GAY TIMES, Ground Floor, Worldwide House, 116–134 Bayham Street, London NW1 0BA. *M*

GEOGRAPHICAL JOURNAL, Royal Geographical Society, 1 Kensington Gore, London SW7 2AR. *Three times a year*

GOLF WORLD, Mappin House, 4 Winsley Street, London W1N 7AR. *M*

GOOD HOLIDAY MAGAZINE, 91 High Street, Esher, Surrey KT10 9QA. *Q*

GOOD HOUSEKEEPING, National Magazine House, 72 Broadwick Street, London W1V 2BP. *M*

THE GOOD SKI GUIDE, 91 High Street, Esher, Surrey KT10 9QA. *Five times a year*

GQ, Vogue House, Hanover Square, London W1R 0AD. *M*

GRAMOPHONE, 135 Greenford Road, Harrow, Middx HA1 3YD. *M*

GRANTA, 2–3 Hanover Yard, Noel Road, London N1 8BE. *Q*

THE GUARDIAN WEEKLY, 119 Farringdon Road, London ECIR 3ER. *W*

GUIDING, 17–19 Buckingham Palace Road, London SW1W 0PT. *M*

HANSARD *see* Parliamentary Debates

HARPERS AND QUEEN, National Magazine House, 72 Broadwick Street, London W1V 2BP. *M*

HAVING A BABY, National Magazine House, 72 Broadwick Street, London W1V 2BP. *Q*

HEALTH AND FITNESS MAGAZINE, Nexus House, Azalea Drive, Swanley, Kent BR8 8HY. *M*

HELLO!, 69–71 Upper Ground, London SE1 9PQ. *W*

HOMES AND GARDENS, King's Reach Tower, Stamford Street, London SE1 9LS. *M*

HORSE AND HOUND, King's Reach Tower, Stamford Street, London SE1 9LS. *W*

HOUSE AND GARDEN, Vogue House, Hanover Square, London W1R 0AD. *M*

HOUSE BEAUTIFUL, National Magazine House, 72 Broadwick Street, London W1V 2BP. *M*

i-D Magazine, Universal House, 251 Tottenham Court Road, London W1P 0AB. *M*

IDEAL HOME, King's Reach Tower, Stamford Street, London SE1 9LS. *M*

ILLUSTRATED LONDON NEWS, 20 Upper Ground, London SE1 9PF. *Twice a year*

IN BRITAIN, Haymarket House, 1 Oxendon Street, London SW1Y 4EE. *M*

INVESTORS CHRONICLE, Greystoke Place, Fetter Lane, London EC4A 1ND. *W*

IRISH POST, Uxbridge House, 464 Uxbridge Road, Hayes, Middx UB4 0SP. *W*

JAZZ JOURNAL INTERNATIONAL, 1–5 Clerkenwell Road, London ECIM 5PA. *M*

JUST SEVENTEEN, Victory House, 14 Leicester Place, London WC2H 7BP. *W*

LABOUR RESEARCH, 78 Blackfriars Road, London SE1 8HF. *M*

THE LADY, 39–40 Bedford Street, London WC2E 9ER. *W*

LAND AND LIBERTY, 177 Vauxhall Bridge Road, London SW1V IEU. *Q*

LITERARY REVIEW, 44 Lexington Street, London W1R 3LH. *M*

LONDON GAZETTE (*Official*), The Stationery Office, PO Box 276, London SW8 5DT. *Five times a week*

LONDON REVIEW OF BOOKS, 28–30 Little Russell Street, London WC1A 2HN. *Alt. W*

M, National Magazine House, 72 Broadwick Street, London W1V 2BP. *Q*

MAJESTY, 26–28 Hallam Street, London W1N 6NP. *M*

MARIE CLAIRE, 2 Hatfields, London SE1 9PG. *M*

MAX POWER, Bushfield House, Orton Centre, Peterborough PE2 5UW. *M*

MELODY MAKER (MM), King's Reach Tower, Stamford Street, London SE1 9LS. *W*

METEOROLOGICAL MAGAZINE, The Stationery Office, PO Box 276, London SW8 5DT. *M*

MIZZ, King's Reach Tower, Stamford Street, London SE1 9LS. *Alt. W*

MODEL BOATS, Nexus House, Boundary Way, Hemel Hempstead, Herts HP2 7ST. *M*

MONEYWISE, 11 Westferry Circus, Canary Wharf, London E14 4HE. *M*

MORE!, Victory House, 14 Leicester Place, London WC2H 7BP. *Alt. W*

MOTHER AND BABY, Victory House, 14 Leicester Place, London WC2H 7BP. *M*

MY WEEKLY, 80 Kingsway East, Dundee DD4 8SL. *W*

NATURE, Porters South, Crinan Street, London N1 9SQ. *W*

NEEDLECRAFT, Beauford Court, 30 Monmouth Street, Bath BA1 2BW. *Thirteen times a year*

NEW INTERNATIONALIST, 55 Rectory Road, Oxford OX4 1BW. *M*

NEW MUSICAL EXPRESS (NME), King's Reach Tower, Stamford Street, London SE1 9LS. *W*

NEW SCIENTIST, 1st Floor, 151 Wardour Street, London W1V 4BN. *W*

NEW STATESMAN, 7th Floor, Victoria Station House, 191 Victoria Street, London SW1E 5NE. *W*

NEW WOMAN, Victory House, 14 Leicester Place, London WC2H 7BP. *M*

NEWSWEEK, 18 Park Street, London W1Y 4HH. *W*

19, King's Reach Tower, Stamford Street, London SE1 9LS. *M*

OK!, Northern and Shell Tower, City Harbour, London E14 9GL. *M*

THE OLDIE, 45–46 Poland Street, London W1V 4AU. *M*

OPERA, 1A Mountgrove Road, London N5 2LU. *M*

OPERA NOW, 241 Shaftesbury Avenue, London WC2H 8EH. *Alt. M*

OPTIONS, King's Reach Tower, Stamford Street, London SE1 9LS. *M*

OUR DOGS, 5 Oxford Road, Station Approach, Manchester M60 1SX. *W*

PARENTS, Victory House, 14 Leicester Place, London WC2H 7BP. *M*

PARLIAMENTARY DEBATES (COMMONS) (HANSARD), The Stationery Office, PO Box 276, London SW8 5DT. *W*

PARLIAMENTARY DEBATES (LORDS) (HANSARD), The Stationery Office, PO Box 276, London SW8 5DT. *W*

PEOPLE'S FRIEND, 80 Kingsway East, Dundee DD4 8SL. *W*

PHILOSOPHY NOW, 226 Bramford Road, Ipswich IP1 4AS. *Q*

POETRY REVIEW, 22 Betterton Street, London WC2H 9BU. *Q*

PONY, Haslemere House, Lower Street, Haslemere, Surrey GU27 2PE. *M*

PRACTICAL BOAT OWNER, Westover House, West Quay Road, Poole, Dorset BH15 1JG. *M*

PRACTICAL CARAVAN, 60 Waldegrave Road, Teddington, Middx TW11 8LG. *M*

PRACTICAL HOUSEHOLDER, Boundary Way, Hemel Hempstead, Herts HP2 7ST. *M*

PRACTICAL PARENTING, King's Reach Tower, Stamford Street, London SE1 9LS. *M*

PRACTICAL PHOTOGRAPHY, Apex House, Oundle Road, Peterborough PE2 9NP. *M*

PRIMA, 10th Floor, Portland House, Stag Place, London SW1E 5AU. *M*

PRIVATE EYE, 6 Carlisle Street, London W1V 5RG. *Alt. W*

PROGRESS (*Braille type*), RNIB, Technical Consumer Services Division, Orton Southgate, Peterborough PE2 6XU. *M*

PROSPECT, 4 Bedford Square, London WC1B 3RA. *M*

THE PUZZLER, Glenthorne House, Hammersmith Grove, London W6 0LG. *M*

Q, Mappin House, 4 Winsley Street, London W1M 7AR. *M*

THE RACING CALENDAR, British Horseracing Board Publications, c/o Weatherbys Group Ltd, Sanders Road, Wellingborough, Northants NN8 4BX. *W*

RADIO TIMES, Woodlands, 80 Wood Lane, London W12 0TT. *W*

RAILWAY MAGAZINE, King's Reach Tower, Stamford Street, London SE1 9LS. *M*

RAILWAY MODELLER, Peco Publications and Publicity Ltd, Beer, Seaton, Devon EX12 3NA. *M*

READER'S DIGEST, 11 Westferry Circus, Canary Wharf, London E14 4HE. *M*

RiDE, Abbots Court, 34 Farringdon Lane, London EC1R 3AU. *M*

RIDING, 2 West Street, Bourne, Lincs PE10 9NE. *M*

RUGBY LEAGUER, Martland Mill, Martland Mill Lane, Wigan, Lancs WN5 0LX. *W*

SCOTS MAGAZINE, 2 Albert Square, Dundee DD1 9QJ. *M*

SCOTTISH FIELD, Royston House, Caroline Park, Edinburgh EH5 1QJ. *M*

SCOUTING, Baden-Powell House, Queen's Gate, London SW7 5JS. *M*

SEA ANGLER, Bretton Court, Bretton, Peterborough PE3 8DZ. *M*

SHE, National Magazine House, 72 Broadwick Street, London W1V 2BP. *M*

SHOOT, King's Reach Tower, Stamford Street, London SE1 9LS. *W*

SHOOTING TIMES AND COUNTRY MAGAZINE, King's Reach Tower, Stamford Street, London SE1 9LS. *W*

SKY MAGAZINE, 5th Floor, Mappin House, 4 Winsley Street, London W1N 7AR. *M*

SLIMMING MAGAZINE, Victory House, 14 Leicester Place, London WC2H 7BP. *Ten times a year*

SMASH HITS, 5th Floor, Mappin House, 4 Winsley Street, London W1M 7AR. *Alt. W*

THE SPECTATOR, 56 Doughty Street, London WC1N 2LL. *W*

THE STRAD, 7 St John's Road, Harrow, Middx HA1 2EE. *M*

TATLER, Vogue House, Hanover Square, London W1R 0AD. *Ten times a year*

TENNIS WORLD, The Spendlove Centre, Enstone Road, Charlbury, Chipping Norton, Oxon OX7 3PQ. *M*

THIS ENGLAND, Alma House, 73 Rodney Road, Cheltenham, Glos GL50 1HT. *Q*

TIME MAGAZINE, Brettenham House, Lancaster Place, London WC2E 7TL. *W*

TIME OUT, Universal House, 251 Tottenham Court Road, London W1P 0AB. *W*

THE TIMES EDUCATIONAL SUPPLEMENT, Admiral House, 66–68 East Smithfield, London E1 9XY. *W*

THE TIMES HIGHER EDUCATION SUPPLEMENT, Admiral House, 66–68 East Smithfield, London E1 9XY. *W*

THE TIMES LITERARY SUPPLEMENT, Admiral House, 66–68 East Smithfield, London E1 9XY. *W*

TOP GEAR, Woodlands, 80 Wood Lane, London W12 0TT. *M*

TRIBUNE, 308 Gray's Inn Road, London WC1X 8DY. *W*

TROUT AND SALMON, Bretton Court, Bretton, Peterborough PE3 8DZ. *M*

TV TIMES, King's Reach Tower, Stamford Street, London SE1 9LS. *W*

VACHER'S PARLIAMENTARY COMPANION, 113 High Street, Berkhamsted, Herts HP4 2DJ. *Q*

VANITY FAIR, Vogue House, Hanover Square, London W1R 0AD. *M*

VIZ MAGAZINE, The Boat House, 136-142 Bramley Road, London W10 6SR. *Alt. M*

VOGUE, Vogue House, Hanover Square, London W1R 0AD. *M*

THE VOICE, 370 Coldharbour Lane, London SW9 8PL. *W*

VOX, King's Reach Tower, Stamford Street, London SE1 9LS. *M*

WEATHER, 104 Oxford Road, Reading RG1 7LJ. *M*

THE WEEKLY TELEGRAPH, 1 Canada Square, Canary Wharf, London E14 5DT. *W*

WELSH NATION (Plaid Cymru), 18 Park Grove, Cardiff CF1 3NB. *Q*

WHAT CAR?, 38–42 Hampton Road, Teddington, Middx TW11 0JE. *M*

WHICH?, 2 Marylebone Road, London NW1 4DF. *M*

WOMAN, King's Reach Tower, Stamford Street, London SE1 9LS. *W*

WOMAN AND HOME, King's Reach Tower, Stamford Street, London SE1 9LS. *M*

WOMAN'S JOURNAL, King's Reach Tower, Stamford Street, London SE1 9LS. *M*

WOMAN'S OWN, King's Reach Tower, Stamford Street, London SE1 9LS. *W*

WOMAN'S REALM, King's Reach Tower, Stamford Street, London SE1 9LS. *W*

WOMAN'S WEEKLY, King's Reach Tower, Stamford Street, London SE1 9LS. *W*

THE WORLD OF INTERIORS, Vogue House, Hanover Square, London W1R 0AD. *Eleven times a year*

YACHTING MONTHLY, King's Reach Tower, Stamford Street, London SE1 9LS. *M*

YOUR GARDEN, Westover House, West Quay Road, Poole, Dorset BH15 1JG. *M*

ZEST, National Magazine House, 72 Broadwick Street, London W1V 2BP. *M*

TRADE PERIODICALS

ACCOUNTANCY, Institute of Chartered Accountants, 40 Bernard Street, London WC1N 1LD. *M*

ACCOUNTANCY AGE, VNU House, 32–34 Broadwick Street, London W1A 2HG. *W*

THE ACTUARY, 7th Floor, The Plaza Tower, East Kilbride, Glasgow G74 1LW. *M*

AGRICULTURE AND EQUIPMENT INTERNATIONAL, Nottingham Trent University, Library and Information Services, Dryden Street, Nottingham NG1 4FZ. *Alt. M*

ANTIQUARIAN BOOK MONTHLY (ABM), PO Box 97, High Wycombe, Bucks HP10 8QT. *M*

ANTIQUE DEALER AND COLLECTORS GUIDE, PO Box 805, London SE10 8TD. *M*

ANTIQUES TRADE GAZETTE, 17 Whitcomb Street, London WC2H 7PL. *W*

THE ARCHITECTS' JOURNAL, 151 Rosebery Avenue, London EC1R 4QX. *W*

THE ARCHITECTURAL REVIEW, 151 Rosebery Avenue, London EC1R 4QX. *M*

THE AUTHOR, Society of Authors, 84 Drayton Gardens, London SW10 9SB. *Q*

THE BIOCHEMIST, The Biochemical Society, 59 Portland Place, London W1N 3AJ. *Alt. M*

BIOLOGIST, Institute of Biology, 20–22 Queensberry Place, London SW7 2DZ. *Five times a year*

THE BOOKSELLER, 12 Dyott Street, London WC1A 1DF. *W*

BRAIN: A JOURNAL OF NEUROLOGY, Oxford University Press, Science, Medical and Journal Division, Great Clarendon Street, Oxford OX2 6DP. *M*

BREWING AND DISTILLING INTERNATIONAL, Southbound House, 163 Burton Road, Branston, Burton-on-Trent, Staffs DE14 3DP. *M*

BRITISH BAKER, Maclaren House, 19 Scarbrook Road, Croydon CR9 1QH. *W*

BRITISH DENTAL JOURNAL, BMA House, Tavistock Square, London WC1H 9JR. *Alt. W*

BRITISH FOOD JOURNAL, 60–62 Toller Lane, Bradford, W. Yorks BD8 9BY. *Eleven times a year*

BRITISH JOURNAL OF PHOTOGRAPHY, 39 Earlham Street, London WC2H 9LD. *W*

BRITISH JOURNAL OF PSYCHIATRY, Royal College of Psychiatrists, 17 Belgrave Square, London SW1X 8PG. *M*

BRITISH JOURNAL OF PSYCHOLOGY, British Psychological Society, 13A Church Lane, London N2 8DX. *Q*

BRITISH MEDICAL JOURNAL, British Medical Association, BMA House, Tavistock Square, London WC1H 9JR. *W*

BRITISH PRINTER, Miller Freeman House, Sovereign Way, Tonbridge, Kent TN9 1RW. *M*

BRITISH TAX REVIEW, 100 Avenue Road, London NW3 3PF. *Alt. M*

BUILDING, 40 Marsh Wall, London E14 9TP. *W*

BUILDING TRADE AND INDUSTRY, 131–133 Duckmoor Road, Ashton Gate, Bristol BS3 2BH. *M*

BUSINESS CONNECTIONS, Node Court, Drivers End, Codicot, Hitchin, Herts SG4 8TR. *Q*

BUSINESS EDUCATION TODAY, Pitman Publishing, 128 Long Acre, London WC2E 9AN. *Alt. M*

CA MAGAZINE, Institute of Chartered Accountants of Scotland, 27 Queen Street, Edinburgh EH2 1LA. *M*

CABINET MAKER, Miller Freeman House, Sovereign Way, Tonbridge, Kent TN9 1RW. *W*

CAMPAIGN, 174 Hammersmith Road, London W6 7JP. *W*

CARPET AND FLOORCOVERINGS REVIEW, Miller Freeman House, Sovereign Way, Tonbridge, Kent TN9 1RW. *Alt. W*

CATERER AND HOTELKEEPER, Quadrant House, The Quadrant, Sutton, Surrey SM2 5AS. *W*

CHARTERED BANKER, 4–9 Burgate Lane, Canterbury, Kent CT1 2XJ. *M*

CHEMIST AND DRUGGIST, Miller Freeman House, Sovereign Way, Tonbridge, Kent TN9 1RW. *W*

CHEMISTRY AND INDUSTRY, 15 Belgrave Square, London SW1X 8PS. *Alt. W*

CHEMISTRY IN BRITAIN, Royal Society of Chemistry, Burlington House, Piccadilly, London W1V 0BN. *M*

CHILD EDUCATION, Villiers House, Clarendon Avenue, Leamington Spa, Warks CV32 5PR. *M*

CLASSICAL MUSIC, 241 Shaftesbury Avenue, London WC2H 8EH. *Alt. W*

COMMUNITY CARE, Quadrant House, The Quadrant, Sutton, Surrey SM2 5AS. *W*

COMPUTER WEEKLY, Quadrant House, The Quadrant, Sutton, Surrey SM2 5AS. *W*

COMPUTING, VNU House, 32–34 Broadwick Street, London W1A 2HG. *W*

CONSTRUCTION NEWS, 151 Rosebery Avenue, London EC1R 4QX. *W*

CONTAINER MANAGEMENT, 4th Floor, Regal House, 70 London Road, Twickenham, Middx TW1 3QS. *M*

CONTRACT JOURNAL, Quadrant House, The Quadrant, Sutton, Surrey SM2 5AS. *W*

CONTROL AND INSTRUMENTATION, Miller Freeman House, 30 Calderwood Street, London SE18 6QH. *M*

COUNTRYSIDE, The Countryside Commission, John Dower House, Crescent Place, Cheltenham, Glos GL50 3RA. *Q*

CRAFTS MAGAZINE, Crafts Council, 44A Pentonville Road, London N1 9BY. *Alt. M*

THE CRIMINOLOGIST, Tolley House, 2 Addiscombe Road, Croydon CR9 5AF. *Q*

DAIRY FARMER AND DAIRY BEEF PRODUCER, 2 Wharfedale Road, Ipswich IP1 4LG. *Thirteen times a year*

DAIRY INDUSTRIES INTERNATIONAL, Wilmington House, Church Hill, Wilmington, Dartford, Kent DA2 7EF. *M*

THE DENTIST, Unit 2, Riverview Business Park, Walnut Tree Close, Guildford, Surrey GU1 4QT. *M*

DESIGN WEEK, St Giles House, 49–50 Poland Street, London W1A 4AX. *W*

THE DIRECTOR, Institute of Directors, Mountbarrow House, 6–20 Elizabeth Street, London SW1W 9RB. *M*

DRAPERS RECORD, 67 Clerkenwell Road, London EC1R 5BH. *W*

THE ECONOMIC JOURNAL, 108 Cowley Road, Oxford OX4 1JF. *Alt. M*

EDUCATION TODAY, Datateam Publishing Ltd, Fairmeadow, Maidstone, Kent ME14 1NG. *Nine times a year*

ELECTRICAL AND RADIO TRADING, Queensway House, 2 Queensway, Redhill, Surrey RH1 1QS. *W*

ELECTRICAL REVIEW, Quadrant House, The Quadrant, Sutton, Surrey SM2 5AS. *Alt. W*

ELECTRICAL TIMES, Quadrant House, The Quadrant, Sutton, Surrey SM2 5AS. *M*

ELECTRONIC ENGINEERING, Miller Freeman House, 30 Calderwood Street, London SE18 6QH. *M*

ENERGY MANAGEMENT, 19 Scarbrook Road, Croydon, Surrey CR9 1QH. *Alt. M*

THE ENGINEER, Miller Freeman House, 30 Calderwood Street, London SE18 6QH. *W*

ENGINEERING, Chester Court, High Street, Knowle, Solihull, W. Midlands B93 0LL. *Eleven times a year*

THE ENGLISH HISTORICAL REVIEW, Addison Wesley Longman, Edinburgh Gate, Harlow, Essex CM20 2JE. *Five times a year*

ENGLISH TODAY, Cambridge University Press, The Edinburgh Building, Shaftesbury Road, Cambridge CB2 2RU. *Q*

EQUITY JOURNAL, Guild House, Upper St Martin's Lane, London WC2H 9EG. *Q*

ESTATES GAZETTE, 151 Wardour Street, London WIV 4BN. W

FAIRPLAY INTERNATIONAL SHIPPING WEEKLY, 20 Ullswater Crescent, Ullswater Business Park, Coulsdon, Surrey CR5 2HR. W

FARMERS WEEKLY, Quadrant House, The Quadrant, Sutton, Surrey SM2 5AS. W

FIRE, Queensway House, 2 Queensway, Redhill, Surrey RH1 IQS. M

FIRE PREVENTION, Fire Protection Association, Melrose Avenue, Borehamwood, Herts WD6 2BJ. Ten times a year

FISH TRADER, Queensway House, 2 Queensway, Redhill, Surrey RH1 IQS. M

FISHING NEWS INTERNATIONAL, Meed House, 21 John Street, London WC1N 2BP. M

FLIGHT INTERNATIONAL, Quadrant House, The Quadrant, Sutton, Surrey SM2 5AS. W

FOOD TRADE REVIEW, Station House, Hortons Way, Westerham, Kent TN16 1BZ. M

FORESTRY AND BRITISH TIMBER, Miller Freeman House, Sovereign Way, Tonbridge, Kent TN9 IRW. M

FOUNDRY TRADE JOURNAL, Queensway House, 2 Queensway, Redhill, Surrey RH1 IQS. Alt. W

FROZEN AND CHILLED FOODS, Queensway House, 2 Queensway, Redhill, Surrey RH1 IQS. M

FUEL, The Boulevard, Langford Lane, Kidlington, Oxon OX5 1GB. Fifteen times a year

GAS ENGINEERING AND MANAGEMENT, Institution of Gas Engineers, 21 Portland Place, London W1N 3AF. Ten times a year

GEOGRAPHY, Geographical Association, 343 Fulwood Road, Sheffield S10 3BP. Q

GEOLOGICAL MAGAZINE, Cambridge University Press, The Edinburgh Building, Shaftesbury Road, Cambridge CB2 2RU. Alt. M

THE GROCER, Broadfield Park, Crawley, W. Sussex RH11 9RT. W

GROWER, Nexus House, Azalea Drive, Swanley, Kent BR8 8HY. W

HAIRDRESSERS' JOURNAL INTERNATIONAL, Quadrant House, The Quadrant, Sutton, Surrey SM2 5AS. W

THE HEALTH SERVICE JOURNAL, Porters South, 4–6 Crinan Street, London N1 9SQ. W

HEATING, VENTILATING AND PLUMBING, Hereford House, Bridle Path, Croydon, Surrey CR9 4NL. M

HISTORY, 108 Cowley Road, Oxford OX4 1JF. Q

HISTORY TODAY, 20 Old Compton Street, London W1V 5PE. M

INDEX ON CENSORSHIP, Writers and Scholars International Ltd, 33 Islington High Street, London N1 9LH. Ten times a year

INDUSTRIAL EXCHANGE AND MART, Link House, 25 West Street, Poole, Dorset BH15 1LL. W

INDUSTRIAL RELATIONS JOURNAL, 108 Cowley Road, Oxford OX4 1JF. Alt. M

INTERNATIONAL AFFAIRS, Cambridge University Press, The Edinburgh Building, Shaftesbury Road, Cambridge CB2 2RU. Q

JANE'S DEFENCE WEEKLY, Sentinel House, 163 Brighton Road, Coulsdon, Surrey CR5 2NH. W

JOURNAL OF ALTERNATIVE AND COMPLEMENTARY MEDICINE, 9 Rickett Street, London SW6 1RU. M

JOURNAL OF THE BRITISH ASTRONOMICAL ASSOCIATION, Burlington House, Piccadilly, London W1V 9AG. Alt. M

JOURNAL OF THE CHEMICAL SOCIETY, Thomas Graham House, Science Park, Milton Road, Cambridge CB4 4WF. Irregular

THE JOURNALIST, National Union of Journalists, Acorn House, 314 Gray's Inn Road, London WC1X 8DP. Alt. M

JUSTICE OF THE PEACE REPORTS, Tolley House, 2 Addiscombe Road, Croydon CR9 5AF. Alt. W

THE LANCET, 42 Bedford Square, London WC1B 3SL. W

LAW QUARTERLY REVIEW, 100 Avenue Road, London NW3 3PF. Q

THE LAW REPORTS, 3 Stone Buildings, Lincoln's Inn, London WC2A 3XN. M

LAW SOCIETY'S GAZETTE, 50 Chancery Lane, London WC2A 1SX. W

LEATHER: THE INTERNATIONAL JOURNAL, Miller Freeman House, Sovereign Way, Tonbridge, Kent TN9 1RW. M

LEISURE WEEK, St Giles House, 49–50 Poland Street, London W1V 4AX. Alt. W

LIBRARY ASSOCIATION RECORD, 7 Ridgmount Street, London WC1E 7AE. M

LLOYD'S LOADING LIST, Sheepen Place, Colchester, Essex CO3 3LP. W

LLOYD'S SHIPPING INDEX, Sheepen Place, Colchester, Essex CO3 3LP. W

LOCAL GOVERNMENT CHRONICLE, 33–39 Bowling Green Lane, London EC1R 0DA. W

MACHINERY AND PRODUCTION ENGINEERING, Franks Hall, Franks Lane, Horton Kirby, Dartford DA4 9LL. Alt. W

MACHINERY MARKET, 6 Blyth Road, Bromley, Kent BR1 3RX. W

MANAGEMENT ACCOUNTING, Chartered Institute of Management Accountants, 63 Portland Place, London W1N 4AB. M

MANAGEMENT TODAY, 174 Hammersmith Road, London W6 7JP. M

MANAGING INFORMATION, Aslib, Staple Hall, Stone House Court, London EC3A 7PB. M

MANUFACTURING CHEMIST, Miller Freeman House, 30 Calderwood Street, London SE18 6QH. M

MARKETING, 174 Hammersmith Road, London W6 7JP. W

MARKETING WEEK, St Giles House, 49–50 Poland Street, London W1V 4AX. W

MATERIALS RECYCLING WEEKLY, Maclaren House, 19 Scarbrook Road, Croydon, Surrey CR9 1QH. W

MATERIALS WORLD, Institute of Materials, 1 Carlton House Terrace, London SW1Y 5DB. M

MEAT TRADES JOURNAL, Maclaren House, 19 Scarbrook Road, Croydon, Surrey CR9 1QH. W

MEDIA WEEK, 33–39 Bowling Green Lane, London EC1R 0DA. W

METALS INDUSTRY NEWS, Queensway House, 2 Queensway, Redhill, Surrey RH1 IQS. Q

MINING JOURNAL, 60 Worship Street, London EC2A 2HD. W

MOTOR TRANSPORT, Quadrant House, The Quadrant, Sutton, Surrey SM2 5AS. W

MUNICIPAL JOURNAL, 32 Vauxhall Bridge Road, London SW1V 2SS. W

MUSIC JOURNAL, Incorporated Society of Musicians, 10 Stratford Place, London W1N 9AE. M

MUSIC WEEK, 8 Montague Close, London Bridge, London SE1 9UR. W

MUSICIAN, 241 Shaftesbury Avenue, London WC2H 8EH. Q

NUCLEAR ENGINEERING INTERNATIONAL, Wilmington House, Church Hill, Wilmington, Dartford, Kent DA2 7EF. M

NURSING TIMES, Porters South, Crinan Street, London N1 9SQ. W

OFF-LICENCE NEWS, Broadfield Park, Crawley, W. Sussex RH11 9RT. W

OPERA NOW, 241 Shaftesbury Avenue, London WC2H 8EH. Alt. M

OPTICIAN, Quadrant House, The Quadrant, Sutton, Surrey SM2 5AS. W

PACKAGING WEEK, Miller Freeman House, Sovereign Way, Tonbridge, Kent TN9 1RW. W

PATENT WORLD, 3rd Floor, Brigade House, Parsons Green, London SW6 4TH. *Ten times a year*

PC PLUS, Kingsgate House, 536 Kings Road, London SW10 OTE. *M*

PEOPLE MANAGEMENT, Institute of Personnel and Development, 17 Britton Street, London EC1M 9NQ. *Alt. W*

PERSONAL COMPUTER WORLD, VNU House, 32–34 Broadwick Street, London W1A 2HG. *M*

PHARMACEUTICAL JOURNAL, Royal Pharmaceutical Society of Great Britain, 1 Lambeth High Street, London SE1 7JN. *W*

PHILOSOPHY (ROYAL INSTITUTE OF PHILOSOPHY), Cambridge University Press, The Edinburgh Building, Shaftesbury Road, Cambridge CB2 2RU. *Q*

THE PHOTOGRAPHER, British Institute of Professional Photography, Fox Talbot House, Amwell End, Ware, Herts SG12 9HN. *Ten times a year*

PHYSICS WORLD, Dirac House, Temple Back, Bristol BS1 6BE. *M*

POLICE REVIEW, 5th Floor, Celcon House, 289–293 High Holborn, London WC1V 7HU. *W*

THE PRACTITIONER, Miller Freeman House, 30 Calderwood Street, London SE18 6QH. *M*

PRESS GAZETTE, 33–39 Bowling Green Lane, London EC1R 0DA. *W*

PRINTING WORLD, Miller Freeman House, Sovereign Way, Tonbridge, Kent TN9 1RW. *W*

PROBATION JOURNAL, National Association of Probation Officers, 3–4 Chivalry Road, London SW11 1HT. *Q*

PROFESSIONAL CARE OF MOTHER AND CHILD, PO Box 100, Chichester, W. Sussex PO18 8HD. *Alt. M*

THE PSYCHOLOGIST, British Psychological Society, St Andrews House, 48 Princess Road East, Leicester LE1 7DR. *M*

QUARRY MANAGEMENT, 7 Regent Street, Nottingham NG1 5BS. *M*

RAILWAY GAZETTE INTERNATIONAL, Quadrant House, The Quadrant, Sutton, Surrey SM2 5AS. *M*

RATING AND VALUATION REPORTER, 4 Breams Buildings, London EC4A 1AQ. *M*

RETAIL NEWSAGENT, Robert Taylor House, 11 Angel Gate, City Road, London EC1V 2PT. *W*

RETAIL WEEK, Maclaren House, PO Box 109, Croydon CR9 1QH. *W*

RUSI JOURNAL, Royal United Services Institute for Defence Studies, Whitehall, London SW1A 2ET. *Alt. M*

SCREEN INTERNATIONAL, 33–39 Bowling Green Lane, London EC1R 0DA. *W*

SHIPPING WORLD AND SHIPBUILDER, 4 Hubbard Road, Houndsmill, Basingstoke, Hants RG21 6UH. *M*

SHOE AND LEATHER NEWS, 67 Clerkenwell Road, London EC1R 5BH. *M*

SMALLHOLDER, Reliance House, Long Street, Dursley, Glos GL11 4LF. *M*

SOCIOLOGICAL REVIEW, 108 Cowley Road, Oxford OX4 1JF. *Q*

SOLICITORS' JOURNAL, 21–27 Lamb's Conduit Street, London WC1N 3NJ. *W*

THE STAGE, 47 Bermondsey Street, London SE1 3XT. *W*

THE STRUCTURAL ENGINEER (Institution of Structural Engineers), 11 Upper Belgrave Street, London SW1X 8BH. *Alt. W*

THE SURVEYOR, 32 Vauxhall Bridge Road, London SW1V 2SS. *W*

TAXATION PRACTITIONER (Chartered Institute of Taxation), 12 Upper Belgrave Street, London SW1X 8BB. *M*

TAXI, Taxi House, 7–11 Woodfield Road, London W9 2BA. *Alt. W*

THE TEACHER, National Union of Teachers, Hamilton House, Mabledon Place, London WC1H 9BD. *Eight times a year*

TEACHING HISTORY, The Historical Association, 59A Kennington Park Road, London SE11 4JH. *Q*

TELEVISION, Royal Television Society, Holborn Hall, 100 Gray's Inn Road, London WC1X 8AL. *Eight times a year*

TEXTILE HORIZONS INTERNATIONAL, 8 De Montfort Street, Leicester LE1 7GA. *Ten times a year*

TEXTILE MONTH, Perkin House, 1 Longlands Street, Bradford, W. Yorks BD1 2TB. *M*

TIMBER AND WOOD PRODUCTS, Miller Freeman House, Sovereign Way, Tonbridge, Kent TN9 1RW. *W*

TOBACCO EUROPE, Queensway House, 2 Queensway, Redhill, Surrey RH1 1QS. *Alt. M*

TOWN AND COUNTRY PLANNING, Town and Country Planning Association, 17 Carlton House Terrace, London SW1Y 5AS. *M*

TOWN PLANNING REVIEW, Liverpool University Press, Senate House, Abercromby Square, Liverpool L69 3BX. *Q*

TRADE MARKS JOURNAL, Patent Office, Cardiff Road, Newport, Gwent NP9 1RH. *W*

THE TRADER, Link House, 25 West Street, Poole, Dorset BH15 1LL. *M*

TRAVEL TRADE GAZETTE (UK AND IRELAND), 1st Floor, City Reach, 5 Greenwich View Place, Mill Harbour, London E14 9NN. *W*

VETERINARY RECORD, British Veterinary Association, 24–28 Oval Road, London NW1 7DX. *W*

WEEKLY LAW REPORTS, 3 Stone Buildings, Lincoln's Inn, London WC2A 3XN. *W*

WOODCARVING, 86 High Street, Lewes, E. Sussex BN7 1XN. *Alt. M*

WORLD'S FAIR, 2 Daltry Street, Oldham, Lancs OL1 4BB. *W*

NEWS AGENCIES IN LONDON

THE ASSOCIATED PRESS LTD (AP), 12 Norwich Street, London EC4A 4BP. Tel: 0171-353 1515. Fax: 0171-353 8118

CENTRAL PRESS FEATURES LTD, 5th Floor, Evening Post Building, Temple Way, Bristol BS99 7HD. Tel: 0117-934 3600. Fax: 0117-934 3639

EXTEL FINANCIAL LTD, Fitzroy House, 13–17 Epworth Street, London EC2A 4DL. Tel: 0171-825 8000

HAYTERS, 146–148 Clerkenwell Road, London EC1R 5DP. Tel: 0171-837 7171. Fax: 0171-837 2420

PARLIAMENTARY AND EEC NEWS SERVICE, 19 Douglas Street, London SW1P 4PA. Tel: 0171-233 8283

PRESS ASSOCIATION LTD, 292 Vauxhall Bridge Road, London SW1V 1AE. Tel: 0171-963 7000. Fax: 0171-963 7192

REUTERS LTD, 85 Fleet Street, London EC4P 4AJ. Tel: 0171-250 1122. Fax: 0171-542 7921

TWO-TEN COMMUNICATIONS LTD, Communications House, 210 Old Street, London EC1V 9UN. Tel: 0171-490 8111. Fax: 0171-490 1255

UNITED PRESS INTERNATIONAL (UK) LTD (UPI), 2 Greenwich View, Millharbour, London E14 9NN. Tel: 0171-333 1690. Fax: 0171-538 1051

Book Publishers

More than 18,000 firms, individuals and societies have published one or more books in recent years. The list which follows is a selective one comprising those firms whose names are most familiar to the general public. A fuller list, *Whitaker Directory of Publishers*, containing some 3,450 names and addresses is published annually in March by J. Whitaker and Sons Ltd.

ACADEMIC PRESS INC.(LONDON), *see* Harcourt Brace
ADDISON WESLEY LONGMAN, Edinburgh Gate, Harlow CM20 2JE. Tel: 01279-623623
ALLAN (IAN), Riverdene Business Park, Molesey Road, Hersham KT12 4RG. Tel: 01923-266600
ALLEN (J. A.), 1 Lower Grosvenor Place, London SW1W 0EL. Tel: 0171-834 0090
ALLISON & BUSBY, 114 New Cavendish Street, London W1M 7FD. Tel: 0171-636 2942
APPLE PRESS, Fitzpatrick Building, 188–194 York Way, London N7 9QR. Tel: 0171-700 8521/7
ARNOLD, 338 Euston Road, London NW1 3BH. Tel: 0171-873 6000
ARROW BOOKS, 20 Vauxhall Bridge Road, London SW1V 2SA. Tel: 0171-840 8400
ASHGATE, Croft Road, Aldershot GU11 3HR. Tel: 01252-331551
ATHLONE PRESS, 1 Park Drive, London NW11 7SG. Tel: 0181-458 0888
AURUM PRESS, 25 Bedford Avenue, London WC1B 3AT. Tel: 0171-637 3225
AUTOMOBILE ASSOCIATION, Norfolk House, Priestly Road, Basingstoke, Hants RG24 9NY. Tel: 01256-491524
BANTAM BOOKS, 61 Uxbridge Road, London W5 5SA. Tel: 0181-579 2652
BARRIE & JENKINS, 20 Vauxhall Bridge Road, London SW1V 2SA. Tel: 0171-840 8400
BARTHOLOMEW, 77 Fulham Palace Road, London W6 8JB. Tel: 0181-741 7070
BATSFORD (B. T.), 583 Fulham Road, London SW6 5BY. Tel: 0171-471 1100
BBC BOOKS, 80 Wood Lane, London W12 0TT. Tel: 0181-576 2570
BLACK (A. & C.), 35 Bedford Row, London WC1R 4JH. Tel: 0171-242 0946
BLACKWELL PUBLISHERS, 108 Cowley Road, Oxford OX4 1JF. Tel: 01865-791100
BLOOMSBURY PUBLISHING, 38 Soho Square, London W1V 5DF. Tel: 0171-494 2111
BODLEY HEAD, 20 Vauxhall Bridge Road, London SW1V 2SA. Tel: 0171-840 8400
BOWKER-SAUR, Windsor Court, East Grinstead House, East Grinstead RH19 1XA. Tel: 01342-326972
BOXTREE, 25 Eccleston Place, London SW1W 9NF. Tel: 0171-881 8000
BOYARS (MARION), 24 Lacy Road, London SW15 1NL. Tel: 0181-788 9522
BRIMAX BOOKS, Studlands Park Industrial Estate, Exning Road, Newmarket, Suffolk CB8 7AU. Tel: 01638-664611
BRITISH COUNCIL, 10 Spring Gardens, London SW1A 2BN. Tel: 0171-930 8466
BRITISH MUSEUM PRESS, 46 Bloomsbury Street, London WC1B 3QQ. Tel: 0171-323 1234
BUTTERWORTH & CO., 35 Chancery Lane, London WC2A 1ER. Tel: 0171-400 2500
CADOGAN BOOKS, Morris Communications, 29 Berwick Street, London W1V 3RF. Tel: 0171-287 6555

CALDER PUBLICATIONS, 126 Cornwall Road, London SE1 8TQ. Tel: 0171-633 0599
CAMBRIDGE UNIVERSITY PRESS, The Edinburgh Building, Shaftesbury Road, Cambridge CB2 2RU. Tel: 01223-312393
CANONGATE BOOKS, 14 High Street, Edinburgh EH1 1TE. Tel: 0131-557 5111
CAPE (JONATHAN), 20 Vauxhall Bridge Road, London SW1V 2SA. Tel: 0171-840 8400
CASSELL, 125 Strand, London WC2R 0BB. Tel: 0171-420 5555
CAVENDISH PUBLISHING, The Glass House, Wharton Street, London WC1X 9PX. Tel: 0171-278 8000
CENTURY PUBLISHING CO., *see* Random House UK
CHAMBERS, 43–45 Annandale Street, Edinburgh EH7 4AZ. Tel: 0131-557 4571
CHAPMAN & HALL, 2 Boundary Row, London SE1 8HN. Tel: 0171-865 0066
CHAPMAN (GEOFFREY), *see* Cassell
CHAPMANS PUBLISHERS, 5 Upper St Martin's Lane, London WC2H 9EA. Tel: 0171-240 3444
CHATTO & WINDUS, 20 Vauxhall Bridge Road, London SW1V 2SA. Tel: 0171-840 8400
CHIVERS PRESS, Windsor Bridge Road, Bath BA2 3AX. Tel: 01225-335336
CHURCH HOUSE PUBLISHING, Church House, Great Smith Street, London SW1P 3NZ. Tel: 0171-222 9011
CHURCHILL LIVINGSTONE, 24–28 Oval Road, London NW1 7DX . Tel: 0171-267 4466
CLARK (T. & T.), 50 George Street, Edinburgh EH2 2LQ. Tel: 0131-225 4703
COLLINS (WILLIAM), *see* HarperCollins Publishers
CONSTABLE & Co., 3 The Lanchesters, 162 Fulham Palace Road, London W6 9ER. Tel: 0181-741 3663
CONSUMERS' ASSOCIATION, see Which? Books
CORGI BOOKS, 61 Uxbridge Road, London W5 5SA. Tel: 0181-579 2652
CROWOOD PRESS, The Stable Block, Crowood Lane, Ramsbury, Marlborough, Wilts SN8 2HR. Tel: 01672-520320
DARTON, LONGMAN & TODD, 1 Spencer Court, 140–142 Wandsworth High Street, London SW18 4JJ. Tel: 0181-875 0134
DAVID & CHARLES, Brunel House, Newton Abbot, Devon TQ12 4PU. Tel: 01626-361121
DEAN & SON, 81 Fulham Road, London SW3 6RB. Tel: 0171-581 9393
DENT (J. M.) & SONS, 5 Upper St Martin's Lane, London WC2H 9EA. Tel: 0171-240 3444
DEUTSCH (ANDRE), 76 Dean Street, London W1V 5HA. Tel: 0171-580 2746
DORLING KINDERSLEY, 9 Henrietta Street, London WC2E 8PS. Tel: 0171-836 5411
DOUBLEDAY, 61 Uxbridge Road, London W5 5SA. Tel: 0181-579 2652
DUCKWORTH & Co., 48 Hoxton Square, London N1 6PB. Tel: 0171-729 5986
EBURY PRESS, 20 Vauxhall Bridge Road, London SW1V 2SA. Tel: 0171-840 8400
ELEMENT BOOKS, The Old School House, The Courtyard, Bell Street, Shaftesbury, Dorset SP7 8BP. Tel: 01747-851448
ELLIOT RIGHT WAY BOOKS, Kingswood Building, Lower Kingswood, Tadworth, Surrey KT20 6TD. Tel: 01737-832202

ELSEVIER SCIENCE, Oxford Spires, The Boulevard, Langford Lane, Kidlington, Oxon OX5 1GB. Tel: 01865-843000

ENCYCLOPAEDIA BRITANNICA INTERNATIONAL, Chancery House, St Nicholas Way, Sutton SM1 1JB. Tel: 0181-770 7766

EPWORTH PRESS, c/o SCM Press, 9–17 St Albans Place, London N1 0NX. Tel: 0171-359 8033

EVANS BROS, 2A Portman Mansions, Chiltern Street, London W1M 1LE. Tel: 0171-935 7160

EVERYMAN, see Orion Publishing Group

EVERYMAN'S LIBRARY, 79 Berwick Street, London W1V 3PF. Tel: 0171-287 0035

FABER & FABER, 3 Queen Square, London WC1N 3AU. Tel: 0171-465 0045

FLAMINGO, see HarperCollins Publishers

FONTANA, see HarperCollins Publishers

FOULIS (G. T.), Sparkford, Yeovil, Somerset BA22 7JJ. Tel: 01963-440635

FOULSHAM (W.) & Co., Bennetts Close, Cippenham, Slough SL1 5AP. Tel: 01753-526769

FOURTH ESTATE, 6 Salem Road, London W2 4BU. Tel: 0171-727 8993

FRENCH (SAMUEL), 52 Fitzroy Street, London W1P 6JR. Tel: 0171-387 9373

GAIA BOOKS, 20 High Street, Stroud GL5 1AS. Tel: 01453-752985

GIBBONS (STANLEY), 5 Parkside, Christchurch Road, Ringwood, Hants BH24 3SH. Tel: 01425-472363

GINN & Co., Prebendal House, Parson's Fee, Aylesbury, Bucks HP20 2QZ. Tel: 01296-488411

GOLLANCZ (VICTOR), see Cassell

GOWER PUBLISHING Co., Croft Road, Aldershot, Hants GU11 3HR. Tel: 01252-331551

GRANTA BOOKS, 2 Hanover Yard, London N1 8BE. Tel: 0171-704 9776

GUINNESS PUBLISHING, 338 Euston Road, London NW1 3BD. Tel: 0171-891 4567

HALE (ROBERT), 45 Clerkenwell Green, London EC1R 0HT. Tel: 0171-251 2661

HAMILTON (HAMISH), 27 Wrights Lane, London W8 5TZ. Tel: 0171-416 3000

HAMLYN (PAUL), 81 Fulham Road, London SW3 6RB. Tel: 0171-581 9393

HARCOURT BRACE, 24 Oval Road, London NW1 7DX. Tel: 0171-424 4200

HARPERCOLLINS PUBLISHERS, 77 Fulham Palace Road, London W6 8JB. Tel: 0181-741 7070

HARRAP, New Penderel House, 283–288 High Holborn, London, WC1V 7HZ. Tel: 0171-903 9999

HAYNES (J. H.), Sparkford, Yeovil, Somerset BA22 7JJ. Tel: 01963-440635

HEADLINE BOOK PUBLISHING, see Hodder Headline

HEINEMANN (WILLIAM), (Adults' books), see Random House

HEINEMANN (WILLIAM), (Children's books), 81 Fulham Road, London SW3 6RB. Tel: 0171-581 9393

HERBERT PRESS, 35 Bedford Row, London WC1R 4JH. Tel: 0171-242 0946

HIPPO BOOKS, 1–19 New Oxford Street, London WC1A 1NU. Tel: 0171-421 9000

HMSO, see Stationery Office Books

HODDER & STOUGHTON, see Hodder Headline

HODDER HEADLINE, 338 Euston Road, London NW1 3BH. Tel: 0171-873 6000

HOGARTH PRESS, 20 Vauxhall Bridge Road, London SW1V 2SA. Tel: 0171-973 9740

HUTCHINSON, see Random House UK

ISIS LARGE PRINT BOOKS, 7 Centremead Road, Osney Mead, Oxford OX2 0ES. Tel: 01865-250333

JARROLD PUBLISHING, Whitefriars, Norwich NR3 1TR. Tel: 01603-763300

JORDAN PUBLISHING, 21 St Thomas Street, Bristol BS1 6JS. Tel: 0117-923 0600

JOSEPH (MICHAEL), 27 Wrights Lane, London W8 5TZ. Tel: 0171-416 3000

KEGAN PAUL INTERNATIONAL, PO Box 256, London WC1B 3SW. Tel: 0171-580 5511

KINGFISHER BOOKS, New Penderel House, 283–288 High Holborn, London, WC1V 7HZ. Tel: 0171-903 9999

KINGSWAY PUBLICATIONS, Lottbridge Drove, Eastbourne BN23 6NT. Tel: 01323-410930

KOGAN PAGE, 120 Pentonville Road, London N1 9JN. Tel: 0171-278 0433

LADYBIRD BOOKS, Beeches Road, Loughborough LE11 2NQ. Tel: 01509-268021

LAROUSSE, New Penderel House, 283–288 High Holborn, London, WC1V 7HZ. Tel: 0171-903 9999

LASCELLES (ROGER), 47 York Road, Brentford, Middx TW8 0QP. Tel: 0181-847 0935

LAWRENCE & WISHART, 99A Wallis Road, London E9 5LN. Tel: 0181-533 2506

LENNARD PUBLISHING, Windmill Cottage, Mackerye End, Harpenden, Herts AL5 5DR. Tel: 01582-715866

LETTS OF LONDON, 24 Nutford Place, London W1H 6DQ. Tel: 0171-724 7773

LINCOLN (FRANCES), 4 Torriano Mews, Torriano Avenue, London NW5 2RZ. Tel: 0171-284 4009

LION PUBLISHING, Sandy Lane West, Oxford OX4 5HG. Tel: 01865-747550

LITTLE, BROWN & Co., Brettenham House, Lancaster Place, London WC2E 7EN. Tel: 0171-911 8000

LONGMAN, see Addison Wesley Longman

LUND HUMPHRIES, 1 Russell Gardens, London NW11 9NN. Tel: 0181-458 6314

LUTTERWORTH PRESS, PO Box 60, Cambridge CB1 2NT. Tel: 01223-350865

MACDONALD & EVANS, 128 Long Acre, London WC2E 9AN. Tel: 0171-447 2000

MACDONALD YOUNG BOOKS, 61 Western Road, Hove, E. Sussex BN3 1JD. Tel: 01273-722561

McGRAW-HILL, Shoppenhangers Road, Maidenhead, Berks SL6 2QL. Tel: 01628-23432

MACMILLAN PUBLISHERS, 25 Eccleston Place, London SW1W 9NF. Tel: 0171-881 8000

MACRAE (JULIA), 20 Vauxhall Bridge Road, London SW1V 2SA. Tel: 0171-840 8400

MAINSTREAM PUBLISHING CO. (EDINBURGH), 7 Albany Street, Edinburgh EH1 3UG. Tel: 0131-557 2959

MAMMOTH, 81 Fulham Road, London SW3 6RB. Tel: 0171-581 9393

MANDARIN, 20 Vauxhall Bridge Road, London SW1V 2SA. Tel: 0171-840 8400

METHUEN LONDON, 20 Vauxhall Bridge Road, London SW1V 2SA. Tel: 0171-840 8400

MILLS & BOON, 18–24 Paradise Road, Richmond, Surrey TW9 1SR. Tel: 0181-948 0444

MINERVA PRESS, 195 Knightsbridge, London SW7 1RE. Tel: 0171-581 5612

MITCHELL BEAZLEY, 81 Fulham Road, London SW3 6RB. Tel: 0171-581 9393

MOWBRAY, see Cassell

MURRAY (JOHN), 50 Albemarle Street, London W1X 4BD. Tel: 0171-493 4361

NATIONAL CHRISTIAN EDUCATION COUNCIL, 1020 Bristol Road, Selly Oak, Birmingham B29 6LB. Tel: 0121-472 4242

NELSON (THOMAS), Mayfield Road, Walton-on-Thames KT12 5PL. Tel: 01932-252211

NEW HOLLAND PUBLISHERS, 24 Nutford Place, London WIH 6DQ. Tel: 0171-724 7773

NEXUS SPECIAL INTEREST, Nexus House, Boundary Way, Hemel Hempstead, Herts HP2 7ST. Tel: 01442-66551

NISBET & CO., 78 Tilehouse Street, Hitchin, Herts SG5 2DY. Tel: 01462-438331

NOVELLO & CO., 8 Frith Street, London W1V 5TZ. Tel: 0171-434 0066

OCTOPUS BOOKS, 81 Fulham Road, London SW3 6RB. Tel: 0171-581 9393

OLIVER & BOYD, Edinburgh Gate, Harlow, Essex CM20 2JE. Tel: 01279-623623

O'MARA (MICHAEL) BOOKS, 9 Lion Yard, Tremadoc Road, London SW4 7NQ. Tel: 0171-720 8643

ORCHARD BOOKS, 96 Leonard Street, London EC2A 4RH. Tel: 0171-739 2929

ORION PUBLISHING GROUP, 5 Upper St Martin's Lane, London WC2H 9EA. Tel: 0171-240 3444

OSPREY PUBLISHING, 1st Floor, Elms Court, Chapel Way, Botley, Oxford OX2 9LP. Tel: 01865-727022

OWEN (PETER), 73 Kenway Road, London SW5 0RE. Tel: 0171-373 5628

OXFORD UNIVERSITY PRESS, Great Clarendon Street, Oxford OX2 6DP. Tel: 01865-556767

PAN BOOKS, 25 Eccleston Place, London SW1W 9NF. Tel: 0171-881 8000

PAVILION BOOKS, London House, Great Eastern Wharf, Parkgate Road, London SW11 4NQ. Tel: 0171-350 1230

PENGUIN BOOKS, 27 Wrights Lane, London W8 5TZ. Tel: 0171-416 3000

PERGAMON PRESS, Oxford Spires, The Boulevard, Langford Lane, Kidlington, Oxon OX5 1GB. Tel: 01865-843000

PHAIDON PRESS, Regent's Wharf, All Saints Street, London N1 9PA. Tel: 0171-843 1234

PHILIP (GEORGE), 81 Fulham Road, London SW3 6RB. Tel: 0171-581 9393

PIATKUS BOOKS, 5 Windmill Street, London W1P 1HF. Tel: 0171-631 0710

PICADOR, see Pan Books

PINTER PUBLISHERS, see Cassell

PITKIN UNICHROME, Healey House, Dene Road, Andover, Hants SP10 2AA. Tel: 01264-334303

PITMAN PUBLISHING, 128 Long Acre, London WC2E 9AN. Tel: 0171-447 2000

PRENTICE HALL, Campus 400, Maylands Avenue, Hemel Hempstead HP2 7EZ. Tel: 01442-881900

QUARTET BOOKS, 27 Goodge Street, London W1P 2LD. Tel: 0171-636 3992

QUILLER PRESS, 46 Lillie Road, London SW6 1TN. Tel: 0171-499 6529

RANDOM HOUSE UK, 20 Vauxhall Bridge Road, London SW1V 2SA. Tel: 0171-840 8400

READER'S DIGEST, 11 West Ferry Circus, London E14 4HE. Tel: 0171-715 8000

RELIGIOUS & MORAL EDUCATION PRESS, St Mary's Works, St Mary's Plain, Norwich NR3 3BH. Tel: 01603-615995

ROUGH GUIDES, 1 Mercer Street, London WC2H 9QJ. Tel: 0171-379 3329

ROUTLEDGE, 11 New Fetter Lane, London EC4P 4EE. Tel: 0171-583 9855

ST ANDREW PRESS, 121 George Street, Edinburgh EH2 4YN. Tel: 0131-225 5722

SCM PRESS, 9–17 St Albans Place, London N1 0NX. Tel: 0171-359 8033

SCRIPTURE UNION, 207–209 Queensway, Bletchley, Milton Keynes, MK2 2EB. Tel: 01908-856000

SECKER & WARBURG, 20 Vauxhall Bridge Road, London SW1V 2SA. Tel: 0171-840 8400

SERPENT'S TAIL PUBLISHING, 4 Blackstock Mews, London N4 2BT. Tel: 0171-354 1949

SEVERN HOUSE, 9 Sutton High Street, Sutton SM1 1DF. Tel: 0181-770 3930

SIDGWICK & JACKSON, 25 Eccleston Place, London SW1W 9NF. Tel: 0171-881 8000

SIMON & SCHUSTER, Campus 400, Maylands Avenue, Hemel Hempstead HP2 7EZ. Tel: 01442-881900

SOUVENIR PRESS, 43 Great Russell Street, London WC1B 3PA. Tel: 0171-580 9307

SPCK, Holy Trinity Church, Marylebone Road, London NW1 4DU. Tel: 0171-387 5282

STATIONERY OFFICE BOOKS, PO Box 276, London SW8 5DT. Tel: 0171-873 0011

STEPHENS (PATRICK), Sparkford, Yeovil BA22 7JJ. Tel: 01963-440635

SUTTON PUBLISHING, Phoenix Mill, Far Thrupp, Stroud, Glos GL5 2BU. Tel: 01453-731114

SWEET & MAXWELL, 100 Avenue Road, London NW3 3PS. Tel: 0171-449 1104

TAYLOR & FRANCIS, 1 Gunpowder Square, London EC4A 3DE. Tel: 0171-583 0490

THAMES & HUDSON, 30 Bloomsbury Street, London WC1B 3QP. Tel: 0171-636 5488

THORNES (STANLEY) (PUBLISHERS), Ellenborough House, Wellington Street, Cheltenham, Glos GL50 1YW. Tel: 01242-228888

THORSONS, 77 Fulham Palace Road, London W6 8JB. Tel: 0181-741 7070

TIMES BOOKS, 77 Fulham Palace Road, London W6 8JB. Tel: 0181-741 7070

TRANSWORLD PUBLISHERS, 61-63 Uxbridge Road, London W5 5SA. Tel: 0181-579 2652

UNIVERSITY OF WALES PRESS, 6 Gwennyth Street, Cardiff CF2 4YD. Tel: 01222-231919

USBORNE PUBLISHING, Usborne House, 83–85 Saffron Hill, London EC1N 8RT. Tel: 0171-430 2800

VIKING, 27 Wrights Lane, London W8 5TZ. Tel: 0171-416 3000

VIRAGO PRESS, Brettenham House, Lancaster Place, London WC2E 7EN. Tel: 0171-911 8000

VIRGIN PUBLISHING, Units 5 and 6, Thames Wharf, Rainville Road, London W6 9HT. Tel: 0171-386 3300

WALKER BOOKS, 87 Vauxhall Walk, London SE11 5HJ. Tel: 0171-793 0909

WARD LOCK EDUCATIONAL CO., 1 Christopher Road, East Grinstead, W. Sussex RH19 3BT. Tel: 01342-318980

WARNE (FREDERICK), see Penguin Books

WATTS (FRANKLIN), 96 Leonard Street, London EC2A 4RH. Tel: 0171-739 2929

WAYLAND (PUBLISHERS), 61 Western Road, Hove, E. Sussex BN3 1JD. Tel: 01273-722561

WEIDENFELD & NICOLSON, 5 Upper St Martin's Lane, London WC2H 9EA. Tel: 0171-240 3444

WHICH? BOOKS, Consumer's Association, 2 Marylebone Road, London NW1 4DF. Tel: 0171-830 6000

WHITAKER (J.), Woolmead House West, Bear Lane, Farnham GU9 7LG. Tel: 01252-742500

WILEY (JOHN) & SONS, 1 Oldlands Way, Bognor Regis PO22 9SA. Tel: 01243-779777

YALE UNIVERSITY PRESS, 23 Pond Street, London NW3 2PN. Tel: 0171-431 4422

Annual Reference Books

If the address of the editorial office of a publication differs from the address to which orders should be sent, the address given is usually the one for orders

AA HOTEL GUIDE, Distribution Centre, Colchester Road, Frating Green, Colchester CO7 7DW. (Oct.) £14.99

ADVERTISER'S ANNUAL, Windsor Court, East Grinstead House, London Road, East Grinstead, W. Sussex RH19 1XA. £195.00

AEROSPACE EUROPE, Riverbank House, Angel Lane, Tonbridge, Kent TN9 1SE. £87.00

ALLIED DUNBAR INVESTMENT AND SAVINGS HANDBOOK, 12–14 Slaidburn Crescent, Southport, Merseyside PR9 9YF. £25.99

ALLIED DUNBAR TAX HANDBOOK, 12–14 Slaidburn Crescent, Southport, Merseyside PR9 9YF. £25.99

ALMANACH DE GOTHA, 27 Manchester Street, London WIM 5PG. £45.00

ANNUAL ABSTRACT OF STATISTICS, PO Box 276, London SW8 5DT. (Jan.) £39.50

ANNUAL REGISTER: A RECORD OF WORLD EVENTS, 5 Five Mile Drive, Oxford OX2 8HT. £109.00

ANTIQUE SHOPS OF BRITAIN, GUIDE TO THE, 5 Church Street, Woodbridge, Suffolk IP12 1DS. £14.95

ART SALES INDEX, 1 Thames Street, Weybridge, Surrey KT13 8JG. 2 vol. £110.00

ART YEAR REVIEW, 1 Stewarts Court, 220 Stewarts Road, London SW8 4UO. (Jan.) £9.95

ASLIB DIRECTORY OF INFORMATION SOURCES IN THE UNITED KINGDOM, Commerce Way, Colchester CO2 8HP. £250.00

ASSOCIATION OF CONSULTING ENGINEERS DIRECTORY OF MEMBERS FIRMS, Alliance House, 12 Caxton Street, London SWIH 0QL. £10.00

ASTRONOMICAL ALMANAC, PO Box 276, London SW8 5DT. (Dec.) £27.50

ATHLETICS: ASSOCIATION OF TRACK AND FIELD STATISTICIANS YEAR BOOK, Waldenbury, North Common, North Chailey, Lewes, E. Sussex BN8 4DR. (May) £14.95

AUTOMOBILE YEAR, Waldenbury, North Common, North Chailey, Lewes, E. Sussex BN8 4DR. £30.95

BAILY'S HUNTING DIRECTORY, Chesterton Mill, French's Road, Cambridge CB4 3NP. (Nov.) £34.95

BANKER'S ALMANAC, East Grinstead House, East Grinstead, W. Sussex RH19 1XA. (Feb.) 5 vol. £399.00

BENEDICTINE AND CISTERCIAN MONASTIC YEAR BOOK, Ampleforth Abbey, York YO6 4EN. (Dec.) £2.25

BENN'S MEDIA: UNITED KINGDOM, Riverbank House, Angel Lane, Tonbridge, Kent TN9 1SE. £133.00

BIRMINGHAM POST AND MAIL YEAR BOOK AND WHO'S WHO, 137 Newhall Street, Birmingham B3 1SF. (Sept.) £30.00

BPIF PRINT BUYER'S DIRECTORY, 11 Bedford Row, London WCIR 4DX. £95.00

BRASSEY'S DEFENCE YEAR BOOK, PO Box 269, Abingdon, Oxon OX14 4YN. £40.00

BRITAIN: AN OFFICIAL HANDBOOK, PO Box 276, London SW8 5DT. (Jan.) £32.00

BRITANNICA BOOK OF THE YEAR, St Nicholas Way, Sutton SMI 1JB. (May) £60.00

BRITISH CLOTHING INDUSTRY YEAR BOOK, 11 The Swan Courtyard, Charles Edward Road, Yardley, Birmingham B26 1BU. £50.00

BRITISH EXPORTS, East Grinstead House, East Grinstead, W. Sussex RH19 1XA. £170.00

BRITISH MUSIC YEAR BOOK, 241 Shaftesbury Avenue, London WC2H 8EH. £23.95

BRITISH PERFORMING ARTS YEAR BOOK, Albert House, Apex Business Centre, Boscombe Road, Dunstable, Beds LU5 4RL. (Jan.) £23.95

BRITISH PLASTICS AND RUBBER DIRECTORY, Catalyst House, 159 Clapham High Street, London SW4 7SS. £10.00

BRITISH THEATRE DIRECTORY, Douglas House, 3 Richmond Buildings, London WIV 5AE. (April) £34.95

BROWN'S NAUTICAL ALMANAC DAILY TIDE TABLES, 4–10 Darnley Street, Glasgow G41 2SD. (Sept.) £38.00

BUILDING AND CONSTRUCTION INDEX, Riverbank House, Angel Lane, Tonbridge, Kent TN9 1SE. (Jan.) £74.00

BUILDING SOCIETIES YEAR BOOK, 4 Tabernacle Street, London EC2A 4LU. £50.00

BUSES YEAR BOOK, Riverdene Business Park, Molesey Road, Hersham KT12 4RG. £12.99

BUTTERWORTHS LAW DIRECTORY AND LEGAL SERVICES DIRECTORY, Maypole House, Maypole Road, East Grinstead, W. Sussex RH19 1HH. (Feb.) 2 vol. £58.00

CATHOLIC DIRECTORY OF ENGLAND AND WALES, St James's Buildings, Oxford Street, Manchester MI 6FP. £23.50

CBI SKILLS AND TRAINING HANDBOOK, 120 Pentonville Road, London NI 9JN. £30.00

CHARITIES CHOICE, Paulton House, 8 Shepherdess Walk, London NI 7LB. £69.95

CHEMICAL INDUSTRY EUROPE, Riverbank House, Angel Lane, Tonbridge, Kent TN9 1SE. £96.00

CHEMIST AND DRUGGIST DIRECTORY, Riverbank House, Angel Lane, Tonbridge, Kent TN9 1SE. £112.00

CHRISTIES' REVIEW OF THE YEAR, 1 Stewart's Court, 220 Stewart's Road, London SW8 4UD. (Nov.) £35.00

CHURCH OF ENGLAND YEARBOOK, St Mary's Works, St Mary's Plain, Norwich NR3 3BH. (Jan.) £22.50

CHURCH OF SCOTLAND YEAR BOOK, 121 George Street, Edinburgh EH2 4YN. (Oct.) £11.00

CITY OF LONDON DIRECTORY AND LIVERY COMPANIES GUIDE, Seatrade House, 42–48 North Station Road, Colchester CO1 1RB. £21.50

CIVIL SERVICE YEAR BOOK, PO Box 276, London SW8 5DT. (Feb.) £27.50

COMMONWEALTH UNIVERSITIES YEAR BOOK, 36 Gordon Square, London WCIH 0PF. (July) 2 vol. £140.00

COMMONWEALTH YEAR BOOK, Jordan House, 47 Brunswick Place, London NI 6EB (May) £55.00

COMPUTER USERS' YEAR BOOK, Woodside, Hinksey Hill, Oxford OXI 5BE. 3 vol. £295.00

CONCRETE YEAR BOOK, Thomas Telford House, 1 Heron Quay, London E14 4JD. £66.00

CURRENT LAW YEAR BOOK, Cheriton House, North Way, Andover, Hants SPIO 5BE. £130.00

DEBRETT'S PEOPLE OF TODAY, 73–77 Britannia Road, London SW6 2JY (April) £97.50

DIPLOMATIC SERVICE LIST, PO Box 276, London SW8 5DT. (April) £25.00

DIRECTORY OF DIRECTORS, Windsor Court, East Grinstead House, East Grinstead, W. Sussex RH19 1XA. (Jan.) 2 vol. £225.00

DIRECTORY OF FURTHER EDUCATION, Star Road, Partridge Green, Horsham, W. Sussex RH13 8LD. (June) £69.50

DIRECTORY OF GRADUATE STUDIES, Star Road, Partridge Green, Horsham, W. Sussex RH13 8LD. (July) £99.99

DIRECTORY OF LOCAL AUTHORITIES, 12–14 Slaidburn Crescent, Southport, Merseyside PR9 9YF. (May) £24.95

DIY TRADE BUYERS GUIDE, Riverbank House, Angel Lane, Tonbridge, Kent TN9 1SE. £75.00

DOD'S PARLIAMENTARY COMPANION, PO Box 3700, London SW1E 5NP. £100.00

EDUCATION AUTHORITIES' DIRECTORY AND ANNUAL, Derby House, Bletchingley Road, Merstham, Surrey RH1 3DN. (Jan.) £72.00, £60.00

EDUCATION YEAR BOOK, 12–14 Slaidburn Crescent, Southport, Merseyside PR9 9YF. £89.00

ELECTRICAL AND ELECTRONIC TRADES DIRECTORY, Michael Faraday House, Six Hills Way, Stevenage, Herts SG1 2AY. (Feb.) £82.00

ELECTRICITY SUPPLY HANDBOOK, PO Box 935, Finchingfield, Braintree, Essex CM7 4LN. (Feb.) £98.00

EUROPA WORLD YEAR BOOK, 18 Bedford Square, London WC1B 3JN. 2 vol. £395.00

EUROPEAN GLASS DIRECTORY AND BUYER'S GUIDE, 2 Queensway, Redhill, Surrey RH1 1QS. £146.85

FLIGHT INTERNATIONAL DIRECTORY, PO Box 1315, Potters Bar, Herts EN6 1PU. £68.00

FOOD TRADES DIRECTORY OF THE UK AND EUROPE, 32 Vauxhall Bridge Road, London SW1V 2SS. 2 vol. £150.00

FROZEN AND CHILLED FOODS YEAR BOOK, Queensway House, 2 Queensway, Redhill, Surrey RH1 1QS. £114.75

FURNITURE AND FURNISHINGS INDUSTRY, DIRECTORY OF THE, Riverbank House, Angel Lane, Tonbridge, Kent TN9 1SE. £107.00

GAS INDUSTRY DIRECTORY, Riverbank House, Angel Lane, Tonbridge, Kent TN9 1SE. (Oct.) £102.00

GIBBONS' SIMPLIFIED CATALOGUE OF STAMPS OF THE WORLD, 5 Parkside, Christchurch Road, Ringwood, Hants BH24 3SH. (Oct.) 3 vol. £24.95, £24.95, £22.95

GOOD FOOD GUIDE, Bath Road, Harmondsworth, West Drayton, Middx UB7 0DA. £14.99

GOOD GUIDE TO BRITAIN, Church Road, Tiptree, Colchester CO5 0SR. (Nov.) £14.99

GOOD HOTEL GUIDE, Church Road, Tiptree, Colchester CO5 0SR. £14.99

GUINNESS BOOK OF KNOWLEDGE, Brunel Road, Houndmills, Basingstoke, Hants RG21 2XS. (Oct.) £20.00

GUINNESS BOOK OF RECORDS, Brunel Road, Houndmills, Basingstoke, Hants RG21 2XS. (Oct.) £18.00

HEALTH AND SOCIAL SERVICES YEARBOOK, 12–14 Slaidburn Crescent, Southport, Merseyside PR9 9YF. £125.00

HEALTH CARE BUYERS GUIDE, Riverbank House, Angel Lane, Tonbridge, Kent TN9 1SE. £86.00

HISTORIC HOUSES, CASTLES AND GARDENS, Star Road, Partridge Green, Horsham, W. Sussex RH13 8LD. (March) £6.95

HOLLIS UK PRESS AND PR ANNUAL, Harlequin House, 7 High Street, Teddington TW11 8EY. (Oct.) £92.50

HOUSING AND PLANNING YEAR BOOK, 12–14 Slaidburn Crescent, Southport, Merseyside PR9 9YF. £92.00

HUTCHINS' PRICED SCHEDULES, Halley Court, Jordan Hill, Oxford OX2 8EJ. £69.99

INDEPENDENT SCHOOLS YEAR BOOK, PO Box 19, Huntingdon, Cambs PE19 3SF. £26.00

INSURANCE DIRECTORY, 39 Earlham Street, London WC2H 9LD (Feb.) £250.00

INTERNATIONAL PAPER DIRECTORY, PHILLIPS', Riverbank House, Angel Lane, Tonbridge, Kent TN9 1SE. £132.00

INTERNATIONAL WHO'S WHO, 18 Bedford Square, London WC1R 4JH. (July) £180.00

INTERNATIONAL YEARBOOK AND STATESMEN'S WHO'S WHO, Maypole House, Maypole Road, East Grinstead, W. Sussex RH19 1HU. (April) £175.00

JANE'S ALL THE WORLD'S AIRCRAFT, Sentinel House, 163 Brighton Road, Coulsdon, Surrey CR5 2NH. (Oct.) £270.00

JANE'S ARMOUR AND ARTILLERY, Sentinel House, 163 Brighton Road, Coulsdon, Surrey CR5 2NH. (Nov.) £270.00

JANE'S FIGHTING SHIPS, Sentinel House, 163 Brighton Road, Coulsdon, Surrey CR5 2NH. £270.00

JANE'S HIGH SPEED MARINE TRANSPORTATION, Sentinel House, 163 Brighton Road, Coulsdon, Surrey CR5 2NH. £235.00

JANE'S INFANTRY WEAPONS, Sentinel House, 163 Brighton Road, Coulsdon, Surrey CR5 2NH. (Aug.) £235.00

JANE'S NAVAL WEAPON SYSTEMS, Sentinel House, 163 Brighton Road, Coulsdon, Surrey CR5 2NH. £390.00

JANE'S WORLD RAILWAYS, Sentinel House, 163 Brighton Road, Coulsdon, Surrey CR5 2NH. £280.00

JEWISH YEAR BOOK, Star Road, Partridge Green, Horsham, W. Sussex RH13 8LD. (Feb.) £24.00

KELLY'S BUSINESS DIRECTORY, East Grinstead House, East Grinstead, W. Sussex RH19 1XA. £235.00

KEMPE'S ENGINEERS YEAR BOOK, Riverbank House, Angel Lane, Tonbridge, Kent TN9 1SE. £115.00

KIME'S INTERNATIONAL LAW DIRECTORY, 12–14 Slaidburn Crescent, Southport, Merseyside PR9 9YF. (Dec.) £77.00

LAXTON'S BUILDING PRICE BOOK, Halley Court, Jordan Hill, Oxford OX2 8EJ. 2 vol. £94.00

LIBRARY ASSOCIATION YEAR BOOK, 39 Milton Park, Abingdon, Oxon OX14 4TD. (June) £37.50

LLOYD'S LIST OF SHIPOWNERS, 100 Leadenhall Street, London EC3A 3BP (Sept.) £145.00

LLOYD'S MARITIME DIRECTORY, Sheepen Place, Colchester CO3 3LP. (Jan.) £247.50

LLOYD'S NAUTICAL YEAR BOOK, Sheepen Place, Colchester CO3 3LP. (Sept.) £68.00

LLOYD'S REGISTER OF SHIPS, 100 Leadenhall Street, London EC3A 3BP. (July) 3 vol. £525.00

LYLE OFFICIAL ANTIQUES PRICE GUIDE, Glenmayne, Galashiels TD1 3NR. £19.99

MACMILLAN NAUTICAL ALMANAC, Brunel Road, Houndmills, Basingstoke, Hants RG21 2XS. £29.95

MAGISTRATES' COURT GUIDE, Halsbury House, 35 Chancery Lane, London WC2A 1EL. £27.50

MEDICAL DIRECTORY, 12–14 Slaidburn Crescent, Southport, Merseyside PR9 9YF. (June) 2 vol. £175.00

MEDICAL REGISTER, 178 Great Portland Street, London W1N 6JE. (March) 4 vol. £110.00

MIDDLE EAST AND NORTH AFRICA, 18 Bedford Square, London WC1B 3JN. (Oct.) £215.00

MILLER'S ANTIQUES PRICE GUIDE, Christchurch House, Units 1–16 Beaufort Court, Sir Thomas Langley Road, Rochester, Kent ME2 4FX. £22.50

MINING ANNUAL REVIEW AND METALS AND MINERALS ANNUAL REVIEW, PO Box 10, Edenbridge, Kent TN8 5NE. £85.00

MINING INTERNATIONAL YEAR BOOK, 12–14 Slaidburn Crescent, Southport, Merseyside PR9 9YF. (June) £175.00

MOTOR INDUSTRY OF GREAT BRITAIN WORLD AUTOMOTIVE STATISTICS, Forbes House, Halkin Street, London SW1X 7DS. (Oct.) £75.00

MOTOR SHIP DIRECTORY, PO Box 935, Finchingfield, Braintree, Essex CM7 4LN. £110.00

MUNICIPAL YEARBOOK, 32 Vauxhall Bridge Road, London SW1V 2SS. (Dec.) £160.00

MUSEUMS AND GALLERIES IN GREAT BRITAIN AND IRELAND, Star Road, Partridge Green, Horsham, W. Sussex RH13 8LD. (Oct.) £8.95

NAUTICAL ALMANAC, PO Box 276, London SW8 5DT. (Oct.) £24.00

PACKAGING INDUSTRY DIRECTORY, Riverbank House, Angel Lane, Tonbridge, Kent TN9 1SE. £92.00

PEARS CYCLOPEDIA, PO Box 11, West Drayton, Middx UB7 0DA. £16.99

PHOTOGRAPHY YEAR BOOK, Fountain House, 2 Gladstone Road, Kingston-upon-Thames, Surrey KT1 3HD. £24.95

POLYMERS, PAINT AND COLOUR YEAR BOOK, Queensway House, 2 Queensway, Redhill, Surrey RH1 1QS. £119.50

PORTS OF THE WORLD, Sheepen Place, Colchester CO3 3LP. £210.00

PRINTING TRADES DIRECTORY, Riverbank House, Angel Lane, Tonbridge, Kent TN9 1SE. £107.00

PUBLIC AUTHORITIES DIRECTORY, Audit House, 260 Field End Road, Ruislip, Middx HA4 9LT. (Jan.) £105.00

PUBLIC SERVICES YEARBOOK, 12–14 Slaidburn Crescent, Southport, Merseyside PR9 9YF. (April) £28.00

PUBLISHING, DIRECTORY OF, Stanley House, 3 Fleets Lane, Poole, Dorset BH15 3AJ. (Oct.) £60.00

RAC EUROPE FOR THE INDEPENDENT TRAVELLER, 39 Milton Park, Abingdon, Oxon OX14 4TD. £8.99

RAC INSPECTED HOTELS, BRITAIN AND IRELAND, 39 Milton Park, Abingdon, Oxon OX14 4TD. £12.99

RAILWAY DIRECTORY, PO Box 935, Finchingfield, Braintree, Essex CM7 4LN. (Dec.) £95.00

REGIONAL TRENDS, PO Box 276, London SW8 5DT. (July) £37.50

RETAIL DIRECTORY OF THE UNITED KINGDOM, 32 Vauxhall Bridge Road, London SW1V 2SS. £139.00

RIBA DIRECTORY OF PRACTICES, 39 Moreland Street, London EC1V 8BB. (Oct.) £60.00

ROTHMAN'S FOOTBALL YEAR BOOK, 39 Milton Park, Abingdon, Oxon OX14 4TD. (Aug.) £30.00, £17.99

ROTHMAN'S RUGBY LEAGUE YEAR BOOK, 39 Milton Park, Abingdon, Oxon OX14 4TD. (Sept.) £16.99

ROTHMAN'S RUGBY UNION YEAR BOOK, 39 Milton Park, Abingdon, Oxon OX14 4TD. (Sept.) £17.99

ROYAL AND ANCIENT GOLFER'S HANDBOOK, Brunel Road, Houndmills, Basingstoke, Hants RG21 2XS. (April) £49.99, £19.99

ROYAL SOCIETY YEAR BOOK, 6 Carlton House Terrace, London SW1Y 5AG. (Feb.) £22.00

SALVATION ARMY YEAR BOOK, 117–121 Judd Street, London WC1H 9NN. (April) £5.50

SCOTTISH LAW DIRECTORY, 59 George Street, Edinburgh EH2 2LQ. £34.00

SEABY STANDARD CATALOGUE OF BRITISH COINAGE, 5–7 King Street, London SW1Y 6QS. (Sept.) £15.00

SELL'S PRODUCTS AND SERVICES DIRECTORY, Riverbank House, Angel Lane, Tonbridge, Kent TN9 1SE. (June) £95.00

SHEET METAL INDUSTRIES YEAR BOOK, Queensway House, 2 Queensway, Redhill, Surrey RH1 1QS. £82.70

SHOWCASE INTERNATIONAL MUSIC BOOK, 38C The Broadway, London N8 9SU. £35.00

SOCIAL SERVICES YEAR BOOK, 12–14 Slaidburn Crescent, Southport, Merseyside PR9 9YF. (April) £120.00

SOCIAL TRENDS, PO Box 276, London SW8 5DT. (Jan.) £39.50

SOLICITORS AND BARRISTERS, DIRECTORY OF, PO Box 269, Abingdon, Oxon OX14 4YN. £54.95, £39.95

SPON'S ARCHITECTS' AND BUILDERS' PRICE BOOK, Cheriton House, North Way, Andover, Hants SP10 5BE. £72.50

SPON'S MECHANICAL AND ELECTRICAL SERVICES PRICE BOOK, Cheriton House, North Way, Andover, Hants SP10 5BE. £75.00

STATESMAN'S YEARBOOK, Brunel Road, Houndmills, Basingstoke, Hants RG21 2XS. (Aug.) £50.00

STOCK EXCHANGE YEARBOOK, Brunel Road, Houndmills, Basingstoke, Hants RG21 2XS. £245.00

STONE'S JUSTICES' MANUAL, PO Box 3000, Halsbury House, 35 Chancery Lane, London WC2A 1EL. 3 vol. (May) £265.00

STUDENT BOOK, 12 Hill Rise, Richmond, Surrey TW10 6UA. (June) £9.99

TANKER REGISTER, 12 Camomile Street, London EC3A 7BP. (April) £155.00

TIMBER TRADES ADDRESS BOOK, Riverbank House, Angel Lane, Tonbridge, Kent TN9 1SE. £72.00

TRAVEL TRADE GAZETTE DIRECTORY, Riverbank House, Angel Lane, Tonbridge, Kent TN9 1SE. (April) £53.00

UK KOMPASS REGISTER, East Grinstead House, East Grinstead, W. Sussex RH19 1XA. 2 vol. £320.00

UNITED KINGDOM MINERALS YEARBOOK, British Geological Survey, Keyworth, Nottingham NG12 5GG. £35.00

UNITED REFORMED CHURCH YEAR BOOK, 86 Tavistock Place, London WC1H 9RT. (Sept.) £17.50

UNIT TRUST YEAR BOOK, Maple House, 149 Tottenham Court Road, London W1P 9LL. £325.00

UNIVERSITY AND COLLEGE ENTRANCE, 14 Cooper's Row, London EC3N 2BH. (June) £19.95

VETERINARY ANNUAL, PO Box 269, Abingdon, Oxon. OX14 4YN. £70.00

WATER SERVICES YEAR BOOK, Queensway House, 2 Queensway, Redhill, Surrey RH1 1QS. (Oct.) £84.80

WHITAKER DIRECTORY OF PUBLISHERS, 12 Dyott Street, London WC1A 1DF. (March) £22.50

WHITAKER'S ALMANACK, PO Box 276, London SW8 5DT. (Oct.) £65.00, £35.00

WHITAKER'S BOOKS IN PRINT, 12 Dyott Street, London WC1A 1DF. (Jan.) 5 vol. £410.00

WHITAKER'S CONCISE ALMANACK, PO Box 276, London SW8 5DT. (Oct.) £14.99

WHO OWNS WHOM?, Holmers Farm Way, High Wycombe, Bucks HP12 4UL. 6 vol. £1,174.00

WHO'S WHO, PO Box 19, Huntingdon, Cambs PE19 3SF. £105.00

WILLING'S PRESS GUIDE, Harlequin House, 7 High Street, Teddington, Middx TW11 8EY. (Feb.) 2 vol. £189.00

WISDEN CRICKETERS' ALMANACK, Bath Road, Harmondsworth, West Drayton, Middx UB7 0DA. (April) £27.50

WORLD HOTEL DIRECTORY, 12–14 Slaidburn Crescent, Southport, Merseyside PR9 9YF. £140.00

WORLD INSURANCE, 12–14 Slaidburn Crescent, Southport, Merseyside PR9 9YF. £195.00

WORLD MINERAL STATISTICS, British Geological Survey, Keyworth, Notts NG12 5GG. (Sept.) 2 vol. £83.60

WORLD OF LEARNING, 18 Bedford Square, London WC1B 3JN. (Jan.) 2 vol. £240.00

WORLD SHIPPING DIRECTORY, PO Box 96, Coulsdon, Surrey CR5 2TE. £99.00

WRITERS' AND ARTISTS' YEAR BOOK, PO Box 19, Huntingdon, Cambs PE19 3SF. (Sept.) £11.99

Employers' and Trade Associations

At 31 December 1997 there were 107 employers' associations listed by the Certification Officer (*see* page 290) and 107 which had not sought to be listed. Most national employers' associations are members of the Confederation of British Industry (CBI). For ACAS, the Certification Office, the Commission for Racial Equality, the Equal Opportunities Commission, the Health and Safety Commission, the Industrial Tribunals and Review Bodies, *see* Index.

CONFEDERATION OF BRITISH INDUSTRY

Centre Point, 103 New Oxford Street, London wc1a 1du
Tel 0171-379 7400

The Confederation of British Industry was founded in 1965 and is an independent non-party political body financed by industry and commerce. It exists primarily to ensure that the Government understands the intentions, needs and problems of British business. It is the recognized spokesman for the business viewpoint and is consulted as such by the Government.

The CBI represents, directly and indirectly, some 250,000 companies, large and small, from all sectors.

The governing body of the CBI is the 200-strong Council, which meets four times a year in London under the chairmanship of the President. It is assisted by 17 expert standing committees which advise on the main aspects of policy. There are 13 regional councils and offices covering the administrative regions of England, Wales, Scotland and Northern Ireland. There is also an office in Brussels.

President, Sir Clive Thompson
Director-General, J. Adair Turner
Secretary, P. Forder

ASSOCIATIONS

ADVERTISING ASSOCIATION, Abford House, 15 Wilton Road, London sw1v 1nj. Tel: 0171-828 2771. *Director-General*, A. Brown
AEROSPACE COMPANIES LTD, SOCIETY OF BRITISH, 60 Petty France, London sw1h 9eu. Tel: 0171-227 1000. *Director-General*, D. Marshall
APPAREL AND TEXTILE CONFEDERATION LTD, BRITISH, 5 Portland Place, London w1n 3aa. Tel: 0171-636 7788. *Director-General*, J. R. Wilson
BAKERS, FEDERATION OF, 6 Catherine Street, London wc2b 5jw. Tel: 0171-420 7190. *Executive Director*, Mrs A. Linehan
BANKERS' ASSOCIATION, BRITISH, 105–108 Old Broad Street, London ec2n 1ex. Tel: 0171-216 8800. *Director-General*, T. P. Sweeney
BLC LEATHER TECHNOLOGY CENTRE, Leather Trade House, Kings Park Road, Moulton Park, Northampton nn3 6jd. Tel: 01604-679999. *Chief Executive*, K. T. W. Alexander, ph.d
BREWERS AND LICENSED RETAILERS ASSOCIATION, 42 Portman Square, London w1h 0bb. Tel: 0171-486 4831. *Director*, R. W. Simpson

BRF (BRITISH ROAD FEDERATION), Pillar House, 194–202 Old Kent Road, London se1 5tg. Tel: 0171-703 9769. *Director*, R. Diment
BUILDING MATERIAL PRODUCERS, NATIONAL COUNCIL OF, 26 Store Street, London wc1e 7bt. Tel: 0171-323 3770. *Director-General*, N. M. Chaldecott, obe
CHAMBER OF SHIPPING LTD, Carthusian Court, 12 Carthusian Street, London ec1m 6eb. Tel: 0171-417 8400. *Director-General*, Vice-Adm. Sir Christopher Morgan, kbe
CHEMICAL INDUSTRIES ASSOCIATION LTD, Kings Buildings, Smith Square, London sw1p 3jj. Tel: 0171-834 3399. *Director-General*, Dr E. G. Finer
CLOTHING INDUSTRY ASSOCIATION LTD, BRITISH, 5 Portland Place, London w1n 3aa. Tel: 0171-636 7788. *Director*, J. R. Wilson
CONSTRUCTION CONFEDERATION, Construction House, 56–64 Leonard Street, London ec2a 4jx. Tel: 0171-608 5000. *Chief Executive*, I. A. Deslandes
DAIRY INDUSTRY FEDERATION, 19 Cornwall Terrace, London nw1 4qp. Tel: 0171-486 7244. *Director-General*, J. Begg
ELECTROTECHNICAL AND ALLIED MANUFACTURERS' ASSOCIATIONS, FEDERATION OF BRITISH (BEAMA), Westminster Tower, 3 Albert Embankment, London se1 7sl. Tel: 0171-793 3000. *Director-General*, D. P. Dossett
ENGINEERING EMPLOYERS' FEDERATION, Broadway House, Tothill Street, London sw1h 9nq. Tel: 0171-222 7777. *Director-General*, G. R. Mackenzie, obe, f.eng.
FARMERS' UNION, NATIONAL (NFU), 164 Shaftesbury Avenue, London wc2h 8hl. Tel: 0171-331 7290. *Director-General*, R. Macdonald
FARMERS' UNION OF SCOTLAND, NATIONAL, Rural Centre–West Mains, Ingliston, Newbridge, Midlothian eh28 8lt. Tel: 0131-472 4000. *Chief Executive*, E. R. Brown
FARMERS' UNION, ULSTER, 475 Antrim Road, Belfast bt15 3da. Tel: 01232-370222. *Director-General*, A. MacLaughlin
FINANCE AND LEASING ASSOCIATION, 15–19 Imperial House, Kingsway, London wc2b 6un. Tel: 0171-836 6511. *Director-General*, M. A. Hall, mvo
FOOD AND DRINK FEDERATION, 6 Catherine Street, London wc2b 5jj. Tel: 0171-836 2460. *Director-General*, M. P. Mackenzie
FOREST PRODUCTS ASSOCIATION, UNITED KINGDOM, Office 14, John Player Building, Stirling Enterprise Park, Springbank Road, Stirling fk7 7rs. Tel: 01786-449029. *Executive Director*, D. J. Sulman
FREIGHT TRANSPORT ASSOCIATION LTD, Hermes House, 157 St John's Road, Tunbridge Wells, Kent tn4 9uz. Tel: 01892-526171. *Director-General*, D. C. Green
INSURERS, ASSOCIATION OF BRITISH, 51 Gresham Street, London ec2v 7hq. Tel: 0171-600 3333. *Director-General*, M. Boléat
KNITTING INDUSTRIES' FEDERATION LTD, 53 Oxford Street, Leicester le1 5xy. Tel: 0116-254 1608. *Director*, J. P. Harrison
LEATHER PRODUCERS' ASSOCIATION, Leather Trade House, Kings Park Road, Moulton Park, Northampton nn3 6jd. Tel: 01604-679999. *Chief Executive*, Dr K. Alexander

MANAGEMENT CONSULTANCIES ASSOCIATION, 11 West Halkin Street, London SW1X 8JL. Tel: 0171-235 3897. *Executive Director*, B. Petter

MARINE INDUSTRIES FEDERATION, BRITISH, Meadlake Place, Thorpe Lea Road, Egham, Surrey TW20 8HE. Tel: 01784-473377. *Executive Chairman*, A. V. Beechey

MARKET TRADERS' FEDERATION, NATIONAL, Hampton House, Hawshaw Lane, Hoyland, Barnsley S74 0HA. Tel: 01226-749021. *General Secretary*, D. E. Feeny

MASTER BUILDERS, FEDERATION OF, Gordon Fisher House, 14–15 Great James Street, London WC1N 3DP. Tel: 0171-242 7583. *Director-General*, I. Davis

MOTOR MANUFACTURERS AND TRADERS LTD, SOCIETY OF, Forbes House, Halkin Street, London SW1X 7DS. Tel: 0171-235 7000. *Chief Executive*, R. E. Thompson

NEWSPAPER PUBLISHERS ASSOCIATION LTD, 34 Southwark Bridge Road, London SE1 9EU. Tel: 0171-207 2200. *Director*, S. Oram

NEWSPAPER SOCIETY, Bloomsbury House, 74–77 Great Russell Street, London WC1B 3DA. Tel: 0171-636 7014. *Director*, D. Newell

OFFICE SYSTEMS AND STATIONERY FEDERATION, BRITISH, 6 Wimpole Street, London W1M 8AS. Tel: 0171-637 7692. *Chief Executive*, K. Davies

PAPER FEDERATION OF GREAT BRITAIN LTD, Papermakers House, Rivenhall Road, Swindon SN5 7BD. Tel: 01793-886086. *Director-General*, W. J. Bartlett

PASSENGER TRANSPORT UK, CONFEDERATION OF, Imperial House, 15–19 Kingsway, London WC2B 6UN. Tel: 0171-240 3131. *Director-General*, Mrs V. Palmer, OBE

PLASTICS FEDERATION, BRITISH, 6 Bath Place, Rivington Street, London EC2A 3JE. Tel: 0171-457 5000. *Director-General*, P. Davis, OBE

PORTS ASSOCIATION, BRITISH, Africa House, 64–78 Kingsway, London WC2B 6AH. Tel: 0171-242 1200. *Director*, D. Whitehead

PRINTING INDUSTRIES FEDERATION, BRITISH, 11 Bedford Row, London WC1R 4DX. Tel: 0171-242 6904. *Chief Executive*, T. P. E. Machin

PRIVATE MARKET OPERATORS, ASSOCIATION OF, 4 Worrygoose Lane, Whiston, Rotherham S60 4AD. Tel: 01709-700072. *Secretary*, D. J. Glasby

PROPERTY FEDERATION, BRITISH, 35 Catherine Place, London SW1E 6DY. Tel: 0171-828 0111. *Director-General*, W. A. McKee

PUBLISHERS ASSOCIATION, THE, 1 Kingsway, London WC2B 6XF. Tel: 0171-565 7474. *Chief Executive*, R. Williams, OBE

RADIO COMPANIES ASSOCIATION, COMMERCIAL, 77 Shaftesbury Avenue, London W1V 7AD. Tel: 0171-306 2603. *Chief Executive*, P. Brown

RETAIL CONSORTIUM, BRITISH, 5 Grafton Street, London W1X 3LB. Tel: 0171-647 1500. *Director-General*, Ms A. Robinson

RETAIL NEWSAGENTS, NATIONAL FEDERATION OF, Yeoman House, Sekforde Street, London EC1R 0HD. Tel: 0171-253 4225. *Chief Executive*, R. Clarke

ROAD HAULAGE ASSOCIATION LTD, Roadway House, 35 Monument Hill, Weybridge, Surrey KT13 8RN. Tel: 01932-841555. *Director-General*, S. J. Norris

RUBBER MANUFACTURERS' ASSOCIATION LTD, BRITISH, 90 Tottenham Court Road, London W1P 0BR. Tel: 0171-580 2794. *Director*, A. J. Dorken

SPORT INDUSTRIES FEDERATION, Federation House, National Agricultural Centre, Stoneleigh Park, Kenilworth, Warks CV8 2RF. Tel: 01203-414999. *Chief Executive*, M. Johnson

TIMBER GROWERS ASSOCIATION LTD, 5 Dublin Street Lane South, Edinburgh EH1 3PX. Tel: 0131-538 7111. *Chief Executive*, P. H. Wilson

TIMBER TRADE FEDERATION, Clareville House, 26–27 Oxendon Street, London SW1Y 4EL. Tel: 0171-839 1891. *Director-General*, P. G. Harris

UK OFFSHORE OPERATORS ASSOCIATION LTD, First Floor, 30 Buckingham Gate, London SW1E 6NN. Tel: 0171-802 2400. *Director-General*, J. May

UK PETROLEUM INDUSTRY ASSOCIATION LTD, 9 Kingsway, London WC2B 6XF. Tel: 0171-240 0289. *Director-General*, Dr M. A. Frend

Trade Unions

At 31 December 1997 there were 233 trade unions listed by the Certification Officer (*see* page 290). In 1996 7,938,213 people were members of listed trade unions, compared with 8,031,326 in 1995. Nearly 80 per cent of trade union members belong to unions affiliated to the TUC (*see* below).

The Central Arbitration Committee arbitrates in industrial disputes between trade unions and employers, and determines disclosure of information complaints. The Commissioner for the Rights of Trade Union Members provides assistance to individuals taking action against their trade union when they have not been afforded their statutory rights or when specific union rules have been breached. The Commissioner for Protection Against Unlawful Industrial Action assists individuals who have been, or are likely to be, deprived of goods or services because of industrial action unlawfully organized by a trade union.

For ACAS, the Certification Office, the Commission for Racial Equality, the Equal Opportunities Commission, the Health and Safety Commission, the Industrial Tribunals and Review Bodies, *see* Index.

THE CENTRAL ARBITRATION COMMITTEE, Brandon House, 180 Borough High Street, London SE1 1LW. Tel: 0171-210 3737/8. *Chairman*, Prof. Sir John Wood, CBE; *Secretary*, S. Gouldstone

THE COMMISSIONER FOR THE RIGHTS OF TRADE UNION MEMBERS, 1st Floor, Bank Chambers, 2A Rylands Street, Warrington, Cheshire WA1 1EN. Tel: 01925-415771. *Commissioner*, G. Corless

THE COMMISSIONER FOR PROTECTION AGAINST UNLAWFUL INDUSTRIAL ACTION, 2nd Floor, Bank Chambers, 2A Rylands Street, Warrington, Cheshire WA1 1EN. Tel: 01925-414128. *Commissioner*, G. Corless

TUC-AFFILIATED TRADE UNIONS

TRADES UNION CONGRESS (TUC)
Congress House, 23–28 Great Russell Street, London WC1B 3LS
Tel 0171-636 4030

The Trades Union Congress, founded in 1868, is an independent association of trade unions. The TUC promotes the rights and welfare of those in work and helps the unemployed. It helps its member unions promote membership in new areas and industries, and campaigns for rights at work for all employees, including part-time and temporary workers, whether union members or not. TUC representatives sit on many public bodies at national and international level. It makes representations to government, political parties, employers and international bodies such as the European Union.

The governing body of the TUC is the annual Congress. Between Congresses, business is conducted by a General Council, which meets five times a year, and an Executive Committee, which meets monthly. The full-time staff is headed by the General Secretary who is elected by Congress and is a permanent member of the General Council.

Affiliated unions (in 1997–8) totalled 73 with a total membership of nearly 6,700,000.

President (1997–8), J. Edmonds (GMB). (The President for 1998–9 was elected in September 1998. *See* Stop-press)
General Secretary, J. Monks, *elected* 1993

SCOTTISH TRADES UNION CONGRESS
333 Woodlands Road, Glasgow G3 6NS
Tel 0141-337 8100

The Congress was formed in 1897 and acts as a national centre for the trade union movement in Scotland. In 1998 it consisted of 48 unions with a membership of 647,744 and 31 directly affiliated Trades Councils.

The Annual Congress in April elects a 37-member General Council on the basis of eight industrial sections.
Chairperson, Ms A. Middleton
General Secretary, B. Speirs

MERGERS

In 1997–8 the Government Communications Staff Federation merged with the Public Services, Tax and Commerce Union. The Public Services, Tax and Commerce Union merged with the Civil and Public Services Association to form the Public and Commercial Services Union.

The Communication Managers' Association merged with the Manufacturing, Science and Finance Union, The National Association of Licensed House Managers merged with the Transport and General Workers' Union.

AFFILIATED UNIONS AS AT 1 SEPTEMBER 1998 (Number of members in parenthesis)

AMALGAMATED ENGINEERING AND ELECTRICAL UNION (AEEU) (720,000), Hayes Court, West Common Road, Bromley, Kent BR2 7AU. Tel: 0181-462 7755. *General Secretary*, K. Jackson

ANSA (INDEPENDENT UNION FOR ABBEY NATIONAL STAFF) (8,000), ANSA House, 15B Mile End Road, Colchester, Essex CO4 5BT. Tel: 01206-577545. *General Secretary*, Ms L. Rolph

ASSOCIATED METALWORKERS UNION (AMU) (1,000), 92 Worsley Road North, Worsley, Manchester M28 5QW. Tel: 01204-793245. *General Secretary*, R. Marron

ASSOCIATED SOCIETY OF LOCOMOTIVE ENGINEERS AND FIREMEN (ASLEF) (14,260), 9 Arkwright Road, London NW3 6AB. Tel: 0171-317 8600. *General Secretary*, D. Rix (from Jan. 1999)

ASSOCIATION OF FIRST DIVISION CIVIL SERVANTS (10,387), 2 Caxton Street, London SW1H 0QH. Tel: 0171-343 1111. *General Secretary*, J. Baume

ASSOCIATION OF FLIGHT ATTENDANTS – COUNCIL 7 (900), United Airlines Cargo Centre, Shoreham Road East, Heathrow Airport, Hounslow TW6 3RD. Tel: 0181-750 9723. *President*, K. Creighan

ASSOCIATION OF MAGISTERIAL OFFICERS (5,900), 231 Vauxhall Bridge Road, London SW1V 1EG. Tel: 0171-630 5455. *General Secretary*, Ms R. Eagleson

ASSOCIATION OF UNIVERSITY TEACHERS (40,000), Egmont House, 25–31 Tavistock Place, London WC1H 9UT. Tel: 0171-670 9700. *General Secretary*, D. Triesman

BAKERS, FOOD AND ALLIED WORKERS' UNION (31,200), Stanborough House, Great North Road, Stanborough, Welwyn Garden City, Herts AL8 7TA. Tel: 01707-260150. *General Secretary*, J. R. Marino

BANKING, INSURANCE AND FINANCE UNION (116,000), Sheffield House, 1B Amity Grove, London SW20 0LG. Tel: 0181-946 9151. *General Secretary*, E. Sweeney

BRITISH ACTORS' EQUITY ASSOCIATION (38,000), Guild House, Upper St Martin's Lane, London WC2H 9EG. Tel: 0171-379 6000. *General Secretary*, I. McGarry

BRITISH AIR LINE PILOTS ASSOCIATION (BALPA) (6,020), 81 New Road, Harlington, Hayes, Middx UB3 5BG. Tel: 0181-476 4000. *General Secretary*, C. Darke

BRITISH ASSOCIATION OF COLLIERY MANAGEMENT (4,204), 17 South Parade, Doncaster, S. Yorks DN1 2DR. Tel: 01302-815551. *General Secretary*, P. M. Carragher

BRITISH DIETETIC ASSOCIATION (3,300), 7th Floor, Elizabeth House, 22 Suffolk Street, Queensway, Birmingham B1 1LS. Tel: 0121-643 5483. *Secretary*, J. Grigg

BRITISH ORTHOPTIC SOCIETY (888), Tavistock House North, Tavistock Square, London WC1H 9HX. Tel: 0171-387 7992. *Executive Secretary*, Mrs S. Armour

BROADCASTING, ENTERTAINMENT, CINEMATOGRAPH AND THEATRE UNION (BECTU) (30,000), 111 Wardour Street, London W1V 4AY. Tel: 0171-437 8506. *General Secretary*, R. Bolton

CARD SETTING MACHINE TENTERS' SOCIETY (88), 48 Scar End Lane, Staincliffe, Dewsbury, W. Yorks WF12 4NY. Tel: 01924-400206. *Secretary*, A. Moorhouse

CERAMIC AND ALLIED TRADES UNION (20,000), Hillcrest House, Garth Street, Hanley, Stoke-on-Trent ST1 2AB. Tel: 01782-272755. *General Secretary*, G. Bagnall

THE CHARTERED SOCIETY OF PHYSIOTHERAPY (30,296), 14 Bedford Row, London WC1R 4ED. Tel: 0171-306 6682. *Secretary*, P. Gray

COMMUNICATION WORKERS UNION (271,000), 150 The Broadway, Wimbledon, London SW19 1RX. Tel: 0181-971 7200. *General Secretary*, D. Hodgson

COMMUNITY AND DISTRICT NURSING ASSOCIATION (5,750), Thames Valley University, 8 University House, Ealing Green, London W5 5ED. Tel: 0181-231 2776. *Hon. General Secretary*, Ms A. Keen

COMMUNITY AND YOUTH WORKERS UNION (2,890), Unit 302, The Argent Centre, 60 Frederick Street, Birmingham B1 3HS. Tel: 0121-244 3344. *General Secretary*, D. Nicholls

THE EDUCATIONAL INSTITUTE OF SCOTLAND (50,800), 46 Moray Place, Edinburgh EH3 6BH. Tel: 0131-225 6244. *General Secretary*, R. A. Smith

ENGINEERING AND FASTENER TRADE UNION (150), 42 Galton Road, Warley, West Midlands B67 5JU. Tel: 0121-429 2594. *General Secretary*, J. Burdis

ENGINEERS' AND MANAGERS' ASSOCIATION (30,000), Flaxman House, Gogmore Lane, Chertsey, Surrey KT16 9JS. Tel: 01932-577011. *General Secretary*, D. A. Cooper

THE FIRE BRIGADES UNION (53,000), Bradley House, 68 Coombe Road, Kingston upon Thames, Surrey KT2 7AE. Tel: 0181-541 1765. *General Secretary*, K. Cameron

GENERAL UNION OF LOOM OVERLOOKERS (340), 9 Wellington Street, St Johns, Blackburn, Lancs BB1 8AF. Tel: 01254-51760. *General Secretary*, D. J. Rishton

GMB (formerly GENERAL, MUNICIPAL, BOILERMAKERS AND ALLIED TRADES UNION) (700,000), 22–24 Worple Road, London SW19 4DD. Tel: 0181-947 3131. *General Secretary*, J. Edmonds

GRAPHICAL, PAPER AND MEDIA UNION (216,991), 63–67 Bromham Road, Bedford MK40 2AG. Tel: 01234-351521. *General Secretary*, A. D. Dubbins

GUINNESS STAFF ASSOCIATION (575), Sun Works Cottage, Park Royal Brewery, London NW10 7RR. Tel: 0181-965 7700. *General Secretary*, J. Collins

HOSPITAL CONSULTANTS AND SPECIALISTS ASSOCIATION (2,500), 1 Kingsclere Road, Overton, Basingstoke, Hants RG25 3JA. Tel: 01256-771777. *Chief Executive*, S. J. Charkham

INDEPENDENT UNION OF HALIFAX STAFF (25,000), Simmons House, 46 Old Bath Road, Charvil, Reading RG10 9QR. Tel: 0118-934 1808. *General Secretary*, G. Nichols

INSTITUTION OF PROFESSIONALS, MANAGERS AND SPECIALISTS (75,000), 75–79 York Road, London SE1 7AQ. Tel: 0171-902 6704. *General Secretary*, W. Brett

IRON AND STEEL TRADES CONFEDERATION (50,000), Swinton House, 324 Gray's Inn Road, London WC1X 8DD. Tel: 0171-837 6691. *General Secretary*, D. K. Brookman

MANAGERIAL AND PROFESSIONAL OFFICERS UNION (10,000), Terminus House, The High, Harlow, Essex CM20 1TZ. Tel: 01279-434444. *General Secretary*, R. Newland

MANUFACTURING, SCIENCE AND FINANCE UNION (MSF) (400,000), MSF Centre, 33–37 Moreland Street, London EC1V 8BB. Tel: 0171-505 3000. *General Secretary*, R. Lyons

MILITARY AND ORCHESTRAL MUSICAL INSTRUMENT MAKERS TRADE SOCIETY (62), 2 Whitehouse Avenue, Borehamwood, Herts WD6 1HD. *General Secretary*, F. McKenzie

MUSICIANS' UNION (35,000), 60–62 Clapham Road, London SW9 0JJ. Tel: 0171-582 5566. *General Secretary*, D. Scard

NASUWT (NATIONAL ASSOCIATION OF SCHOOLMASTERS/UNION OF WOMEN TEACHERS) (172,852), 5 King Street, London WC2E 8HN. Tel: 0171-379 9499. *General Secretary*, N. de Gruchy

NATFHE (UNIVERSITY AND COLLEGE LECTURERS UNION) (66,000), 27 Britannia Street, London WC1X 9JP. Tel: 0171-837 3636. *General Secretary*, P. Mackney

NATIONAL ASSOCIATION OF COLLIERY OVERMEN, DEPUTIES AND SHOTFIRERS (645), Simpson House, 48 Nether Hall Road, Doncaster DN1 2PZ. Tel: 01302-368015. *Secretary*, P. McNestry

NATIONAL ASSOCIATION OF CO-OPERATIVE OFFICIALS (3,150), Coronation House, Arndale Centre, Manchester M4 2HW. Tel: 0161-834 6029. *General Secretary*, L. W. Ewing

NATIONAL ASSOCIATION OF PROBATION OFFICERS (6,955), 4 Chivalry Road, London SW11 1HT. Tel: 0171-223 4887. *General Secretary*, Ms J. McKnight

NATIONAL LEAGUE OF THE BLIND AND DISABLED (2,200), 2 Tenterden Road, London N17 8BE. Tel: 0181-808 6030. *General Secretary*, J. Mann

NATIONAL UNION OF DOMESTIC APPLIANCES AND GENERAL OPERATIVES (2,500), 7–8 Imperial Buildings, Corporation Street, Rotherham, S. Yorks S60 1PB. Tel: 01709-382820. *General Secretary*, A. McCarthy

NATIONAL UNION OF INSURANCE WORKERS (10,347), 27 Old Gloucester Street, London WC1N 3AF. Tel: 0171-405 6798. *General Secretary*, K. Perry

NATIONAL UNION OF JOURNALISTS (NUJ) (20,000), Acorn House, 314–320 Gray's Inn Road, London WC1X 8DP. Tel: 0171-278 7916. *General Secretary*, J. Foster

NATIONAL UNION OF KNITWEAR, FOOTWEAR AND APPAREL TRADES (38,075), 55 New Walk, Leicester LE1 7EB. Tel: 0116-255 6703. *General Secretary*, P. Gates

NATIONAL UNION OF LOCK AND METAL WORKERS (4,000), Bellamy House, Wilkes Street, Willenhall, W. Midlands WV13 2BS. Tel: 01902-366651. *General Secretary*, R. Ward

NATIONAL UNION OF MARINE, AVIATION AND SHIPPING TRANSPORT OFFICERS (18,600), Oceanair House, 750–760 High Road, London E11 3BB. Tel: 0181-989 6677. *General Secretary*, B. Orrell

NATIONAL UNION OF MINEWORKERS (NUM) (5,000), Miners' Offices, 2 Huddersfield Road, Barnsley, S. Yorks S70 2LS. Tel: 01226-215555. *President*, A. Scargill

NATIONAL UNION OF RAIL, MARITIME AND TRANSPORT WORKERS (RMT) (56,000), Unity House, 205 Euston Road, London NW1 2BL. Tel: 0171-387 4771. *General Secretary*, J. Knapp

NATIONAL UNION OF TEACHERS (NUT) (191,800), Hamilton House, Mabledon Place, London WC1H 9BD. Tel: 0171-388 6191. *General Secretary*, D. McAvoy

NORTHERN CARPET TRADES' UNION (655), 22 Clare Road, Halifax HX1 2HX. Tel: 01422-360492. *General Secretary*, K. Edmondson

POWER LOOM CARPET WEAVERS' AND TEXTILE WORKERS' UNION (2,000), 148 Hurcott Road, Kidderminster, Worcs DY10 2RL. Tel: 01562-823192. *General Secretary*, G. Rudd

PRISON OFFICERS' ASSOCIATION (28,699), Cronin House, 245 Church Street, London N9 9HW. Tel: 0181-803 0255. *General Secretary*, D. Evans

PROFESSIONAL FOOTBALLERS' ASSOCIATION (1,200), 2 Oxford Court, Bishopsgate, Manchester M2 3WQ. Tel: 0161-236 0575. *Chief Executive*, G. Taylor

PUBLIC AND COMMERCIAL SERVICES UNION (250,000), 160 Falcon Road, London SW11 2LN. Tel: 0171-924 2727. *Joint General Secretaries*, B. Reamsbottom; J. Sheldon

SCOTTISH PRISON OFFICERS' ASSOCIATION (3,302), 21 Calder Road, Edinburgh EH11 3PF. Tel: 0131-443 8105. *General Secretary*, D. Turner

SCOTTISH UNION OF POWER-LOOM OVERLOOKERS (42), 3 Napier Terrace, Dundee DD2 2SL. Tel: 01382-612196. *Secretary*, J. D. Reilly

SHEFFIELD WOOL SHEAR WORKERS' UNION (11), 5 Collin Avenue, Sheffield S6 4ES. Tel: 0114-220 6748. *Secretary*, B. Bell

SOCIETY OF CHIROPODISTS AND PODIATRISTS (7,000), 53 Welbeck Street, London W1M 7HE. Tel: 0171-486 3381. *General Secretary*, M. Paulson

THE SOCIETY OF RADIOGRAPHERS (14,000), 2 Carriage Row, 183 Eversholt Street, London NW1 1BU. Tel: 0171-391 4500. *General Secretary*, S. Evans

SOCIETY OF TELECOM EXECUTIVES (17,000), 1 Park Road, Teddington, Middx TW11 0AR. Tel: 0181-943 5181. *General Secretary*, S. Petch

TRANSPORT AND GENERAL WORKERS' UNION (TGWU) (882,272), Transport House, 16 Palace Street, London SW1E 5JD. Tel: 0171-828 7788. *General Secretary*, W. Morris

TRANSPORT SALARIED STAFFS' ASSOCIATION (31,000), Walkden House, 10 Melton Street, London NW1 2EJ. Tel: 0171-387 2101. *General Secretary*, R. A. Rosser

UNDEB CENEDLAETHOL ATHRAWON CYMRU (NATIONAL ASSOCIATION OF TEACHERS OF WALES) (3,641), Pen Roc, Rhodfa'r Môr, Aberystwyth, Ceredigion SY23 2AZ. Tel: 01970-615577. *General Secretary*, G. W. James

UN1FI (43,000), Oathall House, Oathall Road, Haywards Heath, W. Sussex RH16 3DG. Tel: 01444-419701. *General Secretary*, J. S. P. Snowball

UNION OF CONSTRUCTION, ALLIED TRADES AND TECHNICIANS (UCATT) (114,000), UCATT House, 177 Abbeville Road, London SW4 9RL. Tel: 0171-622 2442. *Secretary*, G. Brumwell

UNION OF SHOP, DISTRIBUTIVE AND ALLIED WORKERS (USDAW) (290,170), Oakley, 188 Wilmslow Road, Fallowfield, Manchester M14 6LJ. Tel: 0161-224 2804. *Secretary*, W. Connor

UNION OF TEXTILE WORKERS (1,553), Foxlowe, Market Place, Leek, Staffs ST13 6AD. Tel: 01538-382068. *General Secretary*, A. Hitchmough

UNISON (1,300,000), 1 Mabledon Place, London WC1H 9AJ. Tel: 0171-388 2366. *General Secretary*, R. Bickerstaffe

WRITERS' GUILD OF GREAT BRITAIN (2,000), 430 Edgware Road, London W2 1EH. Tel: 0171-723 8074. *General Secretary*, Ms A. Gray

NON-AFFILIATED TRADE UNIONS

ASSOCIATION OF TEACHERS AND LECTURERS (150,000), 7 Northumberland Street, London WC2N 5DA. Tel: 0171-930 6441. *General Secretary*, P. Smith

BRITISH DENTAL ASSOCIATION (15,525), 64 Wimpole Street, London W1M 8AL. Tel: 0171-935 0875. *Chief Executive*, J. M. G. Hunt

CHARTERED INSTITUTE OF JOURNALISTS (1,100), 2 Dock Offices, Surrey Quays Road, London SE16 2XU. Tel: 0171-252 1187. *General Secretary*, C. Underwood

NATIONAL ASSOCIATION OF HEAD TEACHERS (NAHT) (32,000), 1 Heath Square, Boltro Road, Haywards Heath, W. Sussex RH16 1BL. Tel: 01444-472472. *General Secretary*, D. Hart, OBE

NATIONAL SOCIETY FOR EDUCATION IN ART AND DESIGN (2,500), The Gatehouse, Corsham Court, Corsham, Wilts SN13 0BZ. Tel: 01249-714825. *General Secretary*, Dr J. H. M. Steers

PATTERN WEAVERS SOCIETY (40), 24 Fortis Way, Salendine Park, Huddersfield HD3 3WW. Tel: 01484-656886. *Secretary*, D. Mellor

PRISON GOVERNORS ASSOCIATION (935), Room 718, Horseferry House, Dean Ryle Street, London SW1P 2AW. Tel: 0171-217 8591. *General Secretary*, D. Roddan

RETAIL BOOK, STATIONERY AND ALLIED TRADES EMPLOYEES' ASSOCIATION (5,500), 8–9 Commercial Road, Swindon SN1 5RB. Tel: 01793-615811. *President*, D. Pickles

ROYAL COLLEGE OF MIDWIVES (37,000), 15 Mansfield Street, London W1M 0BE. Tel: 0171-312 3535. *General Secretary*, Mrs K. Davis

SCOTTISH SECONDARY TEACHERS' ASSOCIATION (6,900), 15 Dundas Street, Edinburgh EH3 6QG. Tel: 0131-556 5919. *General Secretary*, D. H. Eaglesham

SECONDARY HEADS ASSOCIATION (8,500), 130 Regent Road, Leicester LE1 7PG. Tel: 0116-299 1122. *General Secretary*, J. Dunford, OBE

SOCIETY OF AUTHORS (6,000), 84 Drayton Gardens, London SW10 9SB. Tel: 0171-373 6642. *General Secretary*, M. Le Fanu, OBE

UNITED ROAD TRANSPORT UNION (18,000), 76 High Lane, Chorlton-cum-Hardy, Manchester M21 9EF. Tel: 0161-881 6245. *General Secretary*, D. Higginbottom

National Academies of Scholarship

THE BRITISH ACADEMY (1901)
10 Carlton House Terrace, London SW1Y 5AH
Tel 0171-969 5200

The British Academy is an independent, self-governing learned society for the promotion of historical, philosophical and philological studies. It supports advanced academic research in the humanities and social sciences, and is a channel for the Government's support of research in those disciplines. The Humanities Research Board is responsible for the administration of the majority of the Academy's grant programmes.

The Fellows are scholars who have attained distinction in one of the branches of study that the Academy exists to promote. Candidates must be nominated by existing Fellows. At 1 June 1998 there were 666 Fellows, 15 Honorary Fellows, and 320 Corresponding Fellows overseas.

President, Sir Tony Wrigley, PBA
Vice-President, Prof. R. J. P. Kain, FBA (second Vice-President to be appointed)
Treasurer, J. S. Flemming, FBA
Foreign Secretary, Prof. B. E. Supple, FBA
Publications Secretary, Prof. F. G. B. Millar, FBA
Chair, Committee on Academy Research Projects, Prof. R. R. Davies, FBA
Secretary, P. W. H. Brown, CBE

THE ROYAL ACADEMY (1768)
Burlington House, London W1V 0DS
Tel 0171-439 7438

The Royal Academy of Arts is an independent, self-governing society devoted to the encouragement and promotion of the fine arts.

Membership of the Academy is limited to 80 Royal Academicians, all being painters, engravers, sculptors or architects. Candidates are nominated and elected by the existing Academicians. There is also a limited class of honorary membership and there were 14 honorary members as at mid-1998.
President, Sir Philip Dowson, CBE, PRA
Treasurer, M. Kenny, RA
Keeper, B. Neiland, RA
Secretary, D. Gordon

THE ROYAL ACADEMY OF ENGINEERING (1976)
29 Great Peter Street, London SW1P 3LW
Tel 0171-222 2688

The Royal Academy of Engineering was established as the Fellowship of Engineering in 1976. It was granted a royal charter in 1983 and its present title in 1992. It is an independent, self-governing body whose object is the pursuit, encouragement and maintenance of excellence in the whole field of engineering, in order to promote the advancement of the science, art and practice of engineering for the benefit of the public.

Election to the Fellowship is by invitation only from nominations supported by the body of Fellows. Fellows are chosen from among chartered engineers of all disciplines. At July 1998 there were 1,096 Fellows, 18 Honorary Fellows and 74 Foreign Members. The Duke of Edinburgh is the Senior Fellow and the Duke of Kent is a Royal Fellow.

President, Sir David Davies, CBE, FRS, F.Eng
Senior Vice-President, B. R. R. Butler, CBE, F.Eng
Vice-Presidents, Dr J. R. Forrest, F.Eng; Sir Gordon Higginson, F.Eng; S. N. Mustow, CBE, F.Eng
Hon. Treasurer, J. W. Herbert, F.Eng
Hon. Secretaries, Prof. J. M. Brady FRS, F.Eng (*Electrical Engineering*); Prof. P. Braiden, F.Eng (*Mechanical Engineering*); J. R. Darley, F.Eng (*Process Engineering*); B. R. R. Butler, CBE, F.Eng (*International Activities*); Dr J. R. Forrest, F.Eng (*Education and Training*)
Executive Secretary, J. R. Appleton

THE ROYAL SCOTTISH ACADEMY (1838)
The Mound, Edinburgh EH2 2EL
Tel 0131-225 6671

The Scottish Academy was founded in 1826 to arrange exhibitions of contemporary paintings and to establish a society of fine art in Scotland. The Academy was granted a royal charter in 1838.

Members are elected from the disciplines of painting, sculpture, architecture and printmaking. Elections are from nominations put forward by the existing membership. At mid-1998 there were seven Senior Academicians, four Senior Associates, 34 Academicians, 45 Associates, four non-resident Associates and 22 Honorary Members.
President, W. J. L. Baillie, CBE, PRSA
Secretary, I. McKenzie Smith, RSA
Treasurer, J. Morris, RSA
Librarian, P. Collins, RSA
Administrative Secretary, B. Laidlaw

ROYAL SOCIETY (1660)
6 Carlton House Terrace, London SW1Y 5AG
Tel 0171-839 5561

The Royal Society is the United Kingdom academy of science. It is an independent, self-governing body under a royal charter, promoting and advancing all fields of physical and biological sciences, of mathematics and engineering, medical and agricultural sciences, their applications and place in society.

Election to Fellowship of the Royal Society is limited to those distinguished for original scientific work. Each year up to 40 new Fellows and six Foreign Members are elected from the most distinguished scientists. In addition, the Council can recommend for election members of the royal family and, on average, one person each year for conspicuous service to the cause of science. At June 1998, there were 1,193 Fellows, 110 Foreign Members and six Royal Fellows or Patrons.
President, Sir Aaron Klug, OM, PRS
Treasurer, Sir John Horlock, FRS, F.Eng

Biological Secretary, Prof. P. J. Lachmann, FRS
Physical Secretary, Prof. J. S. Rowlinson, FRS, F.Eng
Foreign Secretary, Prof. R. B. Heap, CBE, FRS
Executive Secretary, S. Cox

THE ROYAL SOCIETY OF EDINBURGH
(1783)
22–24 George Street, Edinburgh EH2 2PQ
Tel 0131-240 5000

The Royal Society of Edinburgh is Scotland's premier learned society. The Society was founded by royal charter in 1783 for 'the advancement of learning and useful knowledge', and its principal role is the promotion of scholarship in all its branches. It provides a forum for broadly-based interdisciplinary activity in Scotland, including organizing public lectures, conferences and specialist research seminars; providing advice to Parliament and government; administering a range of research fellowships held in Scotland; and publishing learned journals.

Fellows are elected by ballot after being nominated by at least four existing Fellows. At 30 April 1998 there were 1,151 Ordinary Fellows and 64 Honorary Fellows.
President, Prof. M. A. Jeeves, CBE
Treasurer, Sir Lewis Robertson, CBE, FRSE
General Secretary, Prof. P. N. Wilson, CBE
Executive Secretary, Dr W. Duncan

Royal Academicians

*Senior Academician

1989	Abrahams, Ivor	1979	Dowson, Sir Philip, CBE	1982	Lawson, Sonia
1988	Ackroyd, Prof. Norman	1990	Draper, Kenneth	1996	Le Brun, Christopher
1967	Adams, Norman	1959	*Dunstan, Bernard	1975	Levene, Ben
1978	Aitchison, Craigie	1994	Durrant, Jennifer	1987	McComb, Leonard
1989	*Armfield, Diana	1976	Eyton, Anthony	1993	MacCormac, Richard, CBE
1994	*Armitage, Kenneth	1998	Farthing, Stephen	1998	Mach, David
1986	Bellany, John, CBE	1992	*Fedden, Mary	1947	*Machin, Sir Arnold, OBE
1992	Berg, Adrian	1987	Flanagan, Barry, OBE	1995	Maine, John
1971	Blackadder, Elizabeth, OBE	1983	Foster, Sir Norman	1976	*Manasseh, Leonard, OBE
1974	Blake, Peter, CBE	1975	Fraser, Donald Hamilton	1994	Manser, Michael
1970	*Blamey, Norman	1990	Freeth, Peter	1985	*Martin, Sir Leslie
1971	Blow, Sandra	1992	*Frost, Sir Terry	1991	Mistry, Dhruva
1970	Bowey, Olwyn	1964	*Gore, Frederick, CBE	1994	Moon, Mick
1974	Bowyer, William	1971	Green, Anthony	1992	Neiland, Prof. Brendan
1968	Brown, Ralph	1994	Grimshaw, Nicholas	1995	Orr, Christopher
1964	Butler, James	1963	*Hayes, Colin	1979	Paolozzi, Sir Eduardo, CBE
1971	*Cadbury-Brown, Prof. H. T., OBE	1990	*Herman, Josef, OBE	1980	Partridge, John, CBE
		1985	Hockney, David	1984	Phillips, Tom
1974	Camp, Jeffery	1974	*Hogarth, Paul, OBE	1972	*Powell, Sir Philip, CH, OBE
1962	*Casson, Sir Hugh, CH, KCVO	1992	Hopkins, Sir Michael, CBE	1996	Procktor, Patrick
1993	Caulfield, Patrick, CBE	1983	Howard, Ken	1978	Rogers of Riverside, Lord
1980	Christopher, Ann	1983	Hoyland, John	1990	Rooney, Michael
1970	Clarke, Geoffrey	1987	Huxley, Prof. Paul	1960	*Rosoman, Leonard, OBE
1968	Clatworthy, Robert	1996	*Irwin, Flavia	1975	Stephenson, Ian
1965	Coker, Peter	1989	Jacklin, Bill	1977	Sutton, Philip
1965	Cooke, Jean	1997	Jiricna, Eva	1985	Tilson, Joe
1994	Cragg, Prof. Tony	1981	Jones, Allen	1973	Tindle, David
1993	Craxton, John	1976	Kenny, Michael	1992	Tucker, William
1989	Cullinan, Edward, CBE	1989	Kiff, Ken	1980	Whishaw, Anthony
1969	Cuming, Frederick	1977	King, Prof. Phillip, CBE	1970	*Williams, Kyffin, OBE
1992	Cummins, Gus	1984	Kitaj, R. B.	1990	*Wilson, Colin St J.
1977	*Dannatt, Prof. Trevor	1970	Kneale, Bryan	1983	Wragg, John
1998	Deacon, Richard	1986	Koralek, Paul, CBE		
1970	Dickson, Jennifer	1991	*Lasdun, Sir Dennis, CBE		

The Research Councils

The Government funds basic and applied civil science research, mostly through the seven research councils, which are supported by the Department of Trade and Industry. The councils support research and training in universities and other higher education establishments. They also receive income for research commissioned by government departments and the private sector. In July 1998, the Government announced additional funding for research of £1,100 million over the three years 1999–2002.

The Government science budget for 1998–9 was £1,338.326 million in total and included the following allocations:

	1997–8 £m	1998–9 £m
BBSRC	183.30	185.74
ESRC	64.90	65.99
EPSRC	386.37	382.98
MRC	289.07	290.21
NERC	165.12	171.771
PPARC	191.85	191.27
International subscription reserve	8.80	3.03
CCLRC	1.45	1.46
Pensions	11.53	12.30
Royal Society	22.27	22.62
Royal Academy of Engineering	3.37	3.44
OST initiatives	2.30	2.38
Joint Research Equipment Initiative	—	4.15
LINK/Foresight	—	1.00

BIOTECHNOLOGY AND BIOLOGICAL SCIENCES RESEARCH COUNCIL (BBSRC)
Polaris House, North Star Avenue, Swindon SN2 1UH
Tel 01793-413200

The BBSRC promotes and supports research and post-graduate training relating to the understanding and exploitation of biological systems; advances knowledge and technology, and provides trained scientists to meet the needs of biotechnological-related industries; and provides advice, disseminates knowledge, and promotes public understanding of biotechnology and the biological sciences.
Chairman, Dr P. Doyle, CBE, FRSE
Chief Executive, Prof. R. Baker, FRS

INSTITUTES

BABRAHAM INSTITUTE
Director, Dr R. G. Dyer, Babraham Hall, Babraham, Cambridge CB2 4AT. Tel: 01223-832312

INSTITUTE FOR ANIMAL HEALTH
Director, Dr C. J. Bostock, Compton, Newbury, Berks RG20 7NN. Tel: 01635-578411

BBSRC AND MRC NEUROPATHOGENESIS UNIT, Ogston Building, West Mains Road, Edinburgh EH9 3JF. Tel: 0131-667 5204/5.
COMPTON LABORATORY, Compton, Newbury, Berks RG20 7NN. Tel: 01635-578411.
PIRBRIGHT LABORATORY, Ash Road, Pirbright, Woking, Surrey GU24 0NF. Tel: 01483-232441. *Head*, Dr A. I. Donaldson

INSTITUTE OF ARABLE CROPS RESEARCH
Director, Prof. B. J. Miflin, Rothamsted, Harpenden, Herts AL5 2JQ. Tel: 01582-763133
IACR – BROOM'S BARN, Higham, Bury St Edmunds, Suffolk IP28 6NP. Tel: 01284-812200. *Head*, Dr J. D. Pidgeon
IACR – LONG ASHTON RESEARCH STATION, Department of Agricultural Sciences, University of Bristol, Long Ashton, Bristol BS18 9AF. Tel: 01275-392181. *Head*, Prof. P. R. Shewry
IACR – ROTHAMSTED, Harpenden, Herts AL5 2JQ. Tel: 01582-763133. *Head*, Prof. B. J. Miflin.

INSTITUTE OF FOOD RESEARCH
Director (acting), Prof. H. J. H. MacFie, Earley Gate, Whiteknights Road, Reading RG6 6BZ. Tel: 0118-935 7055
NORWICH LABORATORY, Norwich Research Park, Colney Lane, Norwich NR4 7UA. Tel: 01603-255000. *Head of Laboratory*, Prof. P. S. Belton
READING LABORATORY, Earley Gate, Whiteknights Road, Reading RG6 6BZ. Tel: 01189-357000. *Head of Laboratory*, Prof. H. J. H. MacFie

INSTITUTE OF GRASSLAND AND ENVIRONMENTAL RESEARCH
Director, Prof. C. J. Pollock, Plas Gogerddan, Aberystwyth, Ceredigion SY23 3EB. Tel: 01970-828255
ABERYSTWYTH RESEARCH CENTRE, Plas Gogerddan, Aberystwyth, Ceredigion SY23 3EB. Tel: 01970-828255
BRONYDD MAWR RESEARCH STATION, Trecastle, Brecon, Powys LD3 8RD. Tel: 01874-636480
NORTH WYKE RESEARCH STATION, Okehampton, Devon EX20 2SB. Tel: 01837-82558. *Head*, Prof. R. J. Wilkins
TRAWSGOED RESEARCH FARM, T rawsgoed, Aberystwyth, Ceredigion SY23 4LL. T el: 01974-261615

JOHN INNES CENTRE
Director, Prof. R. B. Flavell, Norwich Research Park, Colney, Norwich NR4 7UH. Tel: 01603-452571

ROSLIN INSTITUTE
Director, Prof. G. Bulfield, Roslin, Midlothian EH25 9PS. Tel: 0131-527 4200

SILSOE RESEARCH INSTITUTE
Director, Prof. B. J. Legg, Wrest Park, Silsoe, Bedford MK45 4HS. Tel: 01525-860000

INTERDISCIPLINARY RESEARCH CENTRES

ADVANCED CENTRE FOR BIOCHEMICAL ENGINEERING
Director, Prof. P. Dunnill, FEng., University College London, Torrington Place, London WC1E 7JE. Tel: 0171-380 7031
CENTRE FOR GENOME RESEARCH
Director, Dr A. Smith, University of Edinburgh, King's Buildings, West Mains Road, Edinburgh EH9 3JQ. Tel: 0131-650 5890
EDWARD JENNER INSTITUTE FOR VACCINE RESEARCH
Scientific Head, Prof. P. C. L. Beverley, Compton, Newbury, Berks RG20 7NN. Tel: 01635-577900
OXFORD CENTRE FOR MOLECULAR SCIENCES
Director, Prof. J. E. Baldwin, FRS, New Chemistry Laboratory, University of Oxford, South Parks Road, Oxford OX1 3QT. Tel: 01865-275654

Sussex Centre for Neuroscience
Director, Prof. M. O'Shea, School of Biological Sciences, University of Sussex, Brighton BNI 9QG. Tel: 01273-678055

SCOTTISH AGRICULTURAL AND BIOLOGICAL RESEARCH INSTITUTES

Hannah Research Institute, Ayr KA6 5HL. Tel: 01292-674000. *Director,* Prof. M. Peaker, FRS
Macaulay Land Use Research Institute, Craigiebuckler, Aberdeen AB15 8QH. Tel: 01224-318611. *Director,* Prof. T. J. Maxwell, FRSE
Moredun Research Institute, Pentlands Science Park, Bush Loan, Penicuik, Midlothian EH26 OPZ.Tel: 0131-445 5111. *Director,* Prof. Q. A. McKellar
Rowett Research Institute, Greenburn Road, Bucksburn, Aberdeen AB21 9SB. Tel: 01224-712751. *Director,* Prof. W. P. T. James, CBE, FRSE
Scottish Crop Research Institute (SCRI), Invergowrie, Dundee DD2 5DA. Tel: 01382-562731. *Director,* Prof. J. Hillman, FRSE
Biomathematics and Statistics Scotland (BioSS) (Administered by SCRI), University of Edinburgh, James Clerk Maxwell Building, The King's Buildings, Mayfield Road, Edinburgh EH9 3JZ. Tel: 0131-650 4900. *Director,* R. A. Kempton

COUNCIL FOR THE CENTRAL LABORATORY OF THE RESEARCH COUNCILS (CCLRC)
Chilton, Didcot, Oxon OXII OQX
Tel 01235-821900

The CCLRC was set up in April 1995 and is responsible for the Daresbury and Rutherford Appleton Laboratories, which provide advanced facilities and specialist expertise to support academic and industrial research in the physical and life sciences. Eighty per cent of the CCLRC's programme supports academic research, funded mainly by the other research councils, and the remaining 20 per cent is research for industry, government and other institutions world-wide.
Chairman and Chief Executive, Dr A. R. C. Westwood, FENg

Daresbury Laboratory, Daresbury, Warrington, Cheshire WA4 4AD. Tel: 01925-603000
Rutherford Appleton Laboratory, Chilton, Didcot, Oxon OXII OQX. Tel: 01235-821900

ECONOMIC AND SOCIAL RESEARCH COUNCIL (ESRC)
Polaris House, North Star Avenue, Swindon SN2 IUJ
Tel 01793-413000

The purpose of the ESRC is to promote and support research and postgraduate training in the social sciences; to advance knowledge and provide trained social scientists; to provide advice on, and disseminate knowledge and promote public understanding of, the social sciences.
Chairman, Dr B. Smith, OBE
Chief Executive, Prof. R. Amann

RESEARCH CENTRES

Cambridge Group for the History of Population and Social Structure, 27 Trumpington Street, Cambridge CB2 IQA. Tel: 01223-333181. *Director,* Prof. R. Smith
Centre for the Analysis of Social Exclusion, London School of Economics, Houghton Street, London WC2A 2AE. Tel: 0171-955 6679. *Director,* Prof. J. Hills
Centre for Business Research, Department of Applied Economics, University of Cambridge, Sidgwick Avenue, Cambridge CB3 9DE. Tel: 01223-335248. *Director,* A. Hughes
Centre for Economic Learning and Social Evolution, Department of Economics, University College London, 8 Alfred Place, London WCIE 6BT. Tel: 0171-387 7050. *Research Director,* Prof. K. Binmore
Centre for Economic Performance, London School of Economics, Houghton Street, London WC2A 2AE. Tel: 0171-955 7048. *Director,* Prof. R. Layard
Centre for Fiscal Policy, Institute for Fiscal Studies, 7 Ridgmount Street, London WCIE 7AE. Tel: 0171-636 3784. *Director,* Prof. R. Blundell
Centre for Housing Research and Urban Studies, Department of Urban Studies, University of Glasgow, 25 Bute Gardens, Glasgow G12 8RS. Tel: 0141-330 4615. *Director,* Prof. P. A. Kemp
Centre for International Employment Relations Research, School of Industrial and Business Studies, University of Warwick, Coventry CV4 7AL. Tel: 01203-524265. *Director,* Prof. K. Sisson
Centre for Organization and Innovation, Institute of Work Psychology, University of Sheffield, Sheffield SIO 2TN. Tel: 0114-276 8555. *Director,* Prof. T. Wall
Centre for Research in Development, Instruction and Training, Department of Psychology, University of Nottingham, Nottingham NG7 2RD. Tel: 0115-951 5312. *Director,* Prof. D. J. Wood
Centre for Research in Ethnic Relations, University of Warwick, Coventry CV4 7AL. Tel: 01203-523607. *Director,* Prof. Z. Layton-Henry
Centre for Research into Elections and Social Trends, Social and Community Planning Research, 35 Northampton Square, London ECIV OAX. Tel: 0171-250 1866. *Director,* Prof. R. Jowell
Centre for Research on Innovation and Competition, Faculty of Economic and Social Studies, University of Manchester MI3 9PL. Tel: 0161-275 2000. *Director,* Prof. S. Metcalfe; Manchester School of Management, UMIST, Manchester M60 IQD. Tel: 0161-236 3311. *Director,* Prof. R. Coombs
Centre for Social and Economic Research on the Global Environment, School of Environmental Sciences, University of East Anglia, Norwich NR4 7TJ. Tel: 01603-593176. *Director,* Prof. K. Turner
Centre for the Study of African Economies, Institute of Economics and Statistics, University of Oxford, St Cross Building, Manor Road, Oxford OXI 3UL. Tel: 01865-271084. *Director,* Prof. P. Collier
Centre for the Study of Globalization and Regionalization, Department of Political Science, University of Warwick, Coventry CV4 7AL. Tel: 01203-523916. *Director,* Prof. R. Higgott
Complex Product System Innovation Centre, SPRU, Mantell Building, University of Sussex, Brighton BNI 9RF. Tel: 01273-686758. *Director,* Dr M. Hobday; CENTRIM, University of Brighton, Brighton BNI 9PH. Tel: 01273-642188. *Director,* H. Rush

FINANCIAL MARKETS CENTRE, London School of Economics, Houghton Street, London WC2A 2AE. Tel: 0171-955 7275. *Director,* Prof. D. Webb

HUMAN COMMUNICATION RESEARCH CENTRE, University of Edinburgh, 2 Buccleuch Place, Edinburgh EH8 9LW. Tel: 0131-650 4444. *Director,* Prof. K. Stenning

RESEARCH CENTRE ON MICRO-SOCIAL CHANGE, University of Essex, Wivenhoe Park, Colchester, Essex CO4 3SQ. Tel: 01206-872957. *Director,* Prof. J. Gershuny

TRANSPORT STUDIES UNIT, Centre for Transport Studies, University College London, Gower Street, London WCIE 6BT. Tel: 0171-391 1580. *Director,* Dr P. Goodwin

RESOURCE CENTRES

BUSINESS PROCESS RESOURCE CENTRE, Warwick Manufacturing Group, University of Warwick, Coventry CV4 7AL. Tel: 01203-524173. *Director,* Dr S. Manton

CENTRE FOR APPLIED SOCIAL SURVEYS, Social and Community Planning Research, 35 Northampton Square, London ECIV OAX. Tel: 0171-250 1866. *Director,* R. Thomas

CENTRE FOR ECONOMIC POLICY RESEARCH, 25–28 Old Burlington Street, London WIX ILB. Tel: 0171-734 9110. *Director,* Prof. R. Portes

ESRC DATA ARCHIVE, University of Essex, Wivenhoe Park, Colchester, Essex CO4 3SQ. Tel: 01206-872006. *Director,* Prof. D. Lievesley

INTERNATIONAL BIBLIOGRAPHY OF THE SOCIAL SCIENCES, British Library of Political and Economic Science, London School of Economics, Houghton Street, London WC2A 2AE. Tel: 0171-955 7000. *Director,* Ms L. Brindley

QUALITATIVE DATA ARCHIVAL RESOURCE CENTRE, Department of Sociology, University of Essex, Wivenhoe Park, Colchester, Essex CO4 3SQ. Tel: 01206-873333. *Director,* Prof. P. Thompson

RESOURCE CENTRE FOR ACCESS TO DATA IN EUROPE, Department of Geography, University of Durham, Durham DHI 3HP. Tel: 0191-374 7350. *Director,* Prof. R. Hudson

ENGINEERING AND PHYSICAL SCIENCES RESEARCH COUNCIL (EPSRC)
Polaris House, North Star Avenue, Swindon SN2 IET
Tel 01793-444000

The purpose of the EPSRC is to encourage and support all basic and strategic research and training in UK higher education institutions in the natural and physical sciences and engineering. It no longer has any research institutions.
Chairman, Dr A. Rudge, CBE, FRS, FEng.
Chief Executive, Prof. R. Brook, OBE

INTERDISCIPLINARY RESEARCH CENTRES

The EPSRC supports eight interdisciplinary research centres (IRCs) based at universities throughout the UK and specializing in strategic research areas. These were originally funded for a ten-year period (which expires in 1998 for the first IRC and 2000 for the last). It is envisaged that after the ten-year period the IRCs will seek funding from the EPSRC as well as obtaining money from other sources, e.g. industry, to make up their budgets.

CENTRE FOR PROCESS SYSTEMS ENGINEERING – University College London and Imperial College London

IRC FOR SEMICONDUCTOR MATERIALS – Imperial College London, Universities of Oxford and Sheffield, University College London

IRC IN BIOMEDICAL MATERIALS – Queen Mary and Westfield College, London Hospital Medical College, Royal Free Hospital School of Medicine, Royal National Orthopaedic Hospital

IRC IN MATERIALS FOR HIGH PERFORMANCE APPLICATIONS – Universities of Birmingham and Swansea

IRC IN SUPERCONDUCTIVITY – University of Cambridge

OPTOELECTRONICS RESEARCH CENTRE – University of Southampton

POLYMER SCIENCE AND TECHNOLOGY IRC – Universities of Bradford, Leeds and Durham

SURFACE SCIENCE IRC – Universities of Liverpool and Manchester

MEDICAL RESEARCH COUNCIL (MRC)
20 Park Crescent, London WIN 4AL
Tel 0171-636 5422

The purpose of the MRC is to promote medical and related biological research. The council employs its own research staff and funds research by other institutions and individuals, complementing the research resources of the universities and hospitals.
Chairman, Sir Anthony Cleaver
Chief Executive, Prof. G. K. Radda, CBE, D.phil., FRS
Chairman, Neurosciences and Mental Health Board, Dr T. W. Robbins
Chairman, Molecular and Cellular Medicine Board, Prof. L. K. Borysiewicz
Chairman, Physiological Medicine and Infections Board, Prof. A. M. McGregor, MD, FRCP
Chairman, Health Services and Public Health Research Board, Prof. R. Fitzpatrick, ph.D.

NATIONAL INSTITUTE FOR MEDICAL RESEARCH, The Ridgeway, Mill Hill, London NW7 IAA. Tel: 0181-959 3666. *Director,* Sir John Skehel, ph.D., FRS

CLINICAL SCIENCES CENTRE, Royal Postgraduate Medical School, Du Cane Road, London WI2 ONN. Tel: 0181-743 2030. *Director,* Prof. C. Higgins, ph.D., FRSE

LABORATORY OF MOLECULAR BIOLOGY, Hills Road, Cambridge CB2 2QH. Tel: 01223-248011. *Director,* R. Henderson, ph.D., FRS

RESEARCH UNITS

ANATOMICAL NEUROPHARMACOLOGY UNIT, Mansfield Road, Oxford OXI 3TH. Tel: 01865-271865. *Director,* Prof. P. Somogyi, ph.D.

BBSRC/MRC NEUROPATHOGENESIS UNIT, Ogston Building, West Mains Road, Edinburgh EH9 3JF. Tel: 0131-667 5204. *Director,* C. Bostock, ph.D.

BIOCHEMICAL AND CLINICAL MAGNETIC RESONANCE UNIT, Magnetic Resonance Spectroscopy, John Radcliffe Hospital, Headington, Oxford OXI 9DU. Tel: 01865-275274. *Director (acting),* P. Styles, D.phil.

BIOSTATISTICS UNIT, Institute of Public Health, University Forvie Site, Robinson Way, Cambridge CB2 2SR. Tel: 01223-330366. *Hon. Director,* Prof. N. E. Day, ph.D.

BRAIN METABOLISM UNIT, University Department of Pharmacology, University of Edinburgh, 1 George Square, Edinburgh EH8 9JZ. Tel: 0131-650 3543. *Director,* Prof. G. Fink, MD, D.phil., FRSE

CANCER TRIALS OFFICE, 5 Shaftesbury Road, Cambridge CB2 2BW. Tel: 01223-311110

CELL MUTATION UNIT, University of Sussex, Falmer, Brighton BN1 9RR. Tel: 01273-678123. *Director,* Prof. B. A. Bridges, PH.D., FIBiol.

CELLULAR IMMUNOLOGY UNIT, Sir William Dunn School of Pathology, Oxford OX1 3RE. Tel: 01865-275594. *Director (acting),* D. W. Mason

CENTRE FOR BRAIN REPAIR, E. D. Adrian Building, University Forrie Site, Robinson Way, Cambridge CB2 2PY. Tel: 01223-331160. *Chairman,* Prof. D. A. S. Compston, MD, FRCP

CENTRE FOR MECHANISMS OF HUMAN TOXICITY, Hodgkin Building, University of Leicester, PO Box 138, Lancaster Road, Leicester LE1 9HN. Tel: 0116-252 5525. *Director,* Prof. G. C. K. Roberts, PH.D.

CENTRE FOR MOLECULAR SCIENCES, New Chemistry Laboratory, South Parks Road, Oxford OX1 3QT. Tel: 01865-275627. *Director,* Prof. J. E. Baldwin, FRS

CENTRE FOR PROTEIN ENGINEERING, MRC Centre, Hills Road, Cambridge CB2 2QH. Tel: 01223-248011. *Director,* Prof. A. Fersht, PH.D., FRS

CHILD PSYCHIATRY UNIT, Institute of Psychiatry, De Crespigny Park, Denmark Hill, London SE5 8AF. Tel: 0171-703 5411. *Hon. Director,* Prof. Sir Michael Rutter, CBE, FRS, MD, FRCP, FRCPsych.

COGNITION AND BRAIN SCIENCES UNIT, 15 Chaucer Road, Cambridge CB2 2EF. Tel: 01223-355294. *Director,* Prof. W. Marslen-Wilson, FBA

CYCLOTRON UNIT, MRC Clinical Sciences Centre, RPMS Hammersmith Hospital, Du Cane Road, London W12 0NN. Tel: 0181-740 3162. *Director,* Prof. C. Higgins, PH.D., FRSE

DUNN NUTRITION UNIT, Downhams Lane, Milton Road, Cambridge CB4 1XJ. Tel: 01223-426356. *Director,* Prof. J. Walker, FRS

ENVIRONMENTAL EPIDEMIOLOGY UNIT, Southampton General Hospital, Southampton SO16 6YD. Tel: 01703-777624. *Director,* Prof. D. J. P. Barker, MD, PH.D., FRCP, FRCOG

EPIDEMIOLOGY AND MEDICAL CARE UNIT, Wolfson Institute of Preventive Medicine, St Bartholomew's and the Royal London Hospital School of Medicine and Dentistry, Charterhouse Square, London EC1M 6BQ. Tel: 0171-982 6000. *Director,* Prof. T. W. Meade, CBE, DM, FRCP

HEALTH SERVICES RESEARCH COLLABORATION, University of Bristol, Canynge Hall, Whiteladies Road, Bristol BS8 2PR. TEL: 0117-928 7343. Director, Prof. P. Dieppe, MD, FRCP

HUMAN BIOCHEMICAL GENETICS UNIT, The Galton Laboratory, University College London, Wolfson House, 4 Stephenson Way, London NW1 2HE. Tel: 0171-387 7050. *Director,* Prof. D. A. Hopkinson, MD

HUMAN GENETICS UNIT, Western General Hospital, Crewe Road, Edinburgh EH4 2XU. Tel: 0131-332 2471. *Director,* Prof. N. D. Hastie, PH.D., FRSE

HUMAN GENOME MAPPING PROJECT RESOURCE CENTRE, Hinxton Hall, Hinxton, Cambridge CB10 1SB. Tel: 01223-494500. *Director,* D. Campbell, PH.D.

HUMAN MOVEMENT AND BALANCE UNIT, Institute of Neurology, National Hospital for Neurology and Neuro-surgery, Queen Square, London WC1 3BG. Tel: 0171-837 3611. *Hon. Director,* Prof. C. D. Marsden, D.S C., FRCP, FRS

IMMUNOCHEMISTRY UNIT, University Department of Biochemistry, South Parks Road, Oxford OX1 3QU. Tel: 01865-275354. *Director,* Prof. K. B. M. Reid, PH.D.

INSTITUTE FOR ENVIRONMENT AND HEALTH, University of Leicester, PO Box 138, Lancaster Road, Leicester LE1 9HN. Tel: 0116-223 1600. *Director,* vacant

INSTITUTE OF HEARING RESEARCH, University of Nottingham, Nottingham NG7 2RD. Tel: 0115-922 3431. *Director,* Prof. M. P. Haggard, PH.D.

INSTITUTE OF MOLECULAR MEDICINE, John Radcliffe Hospital, Headington, Oxford OX3 9DU. Tel: 01865-222443. *Hon. Director,* Prof. Sir David Weatherall, MD, FRCP, FRCPath., FRS

INTERDISCIPLINARY RESEARCH CENTRE FOR COGNITIVE NEURO-SCIENCE, University Laboratory of Physiology, Parks Road, Oxford OX1 3PT. Tel: 01865-272470. *Director,* Prof. C. Blakemore, FRS

INTERDISCIPLINARY RESEARCH CENTRE IN CELL BIOLOGY, MRC Laboratory for Molecular Cell Biology, University College London, Gower Street, London WC1E 6BT. Tel: 0171-380 7806. *Director,* Prof. C. R. Hopkins, PH.D.

MAMMALIAN GENETICS UNIT, Harwell Site, Chilton, Didcot, Oxon OX11 0RD. Tel: 01235-834393. *Director,* Prof. S. Brown, PH.D.

MEDICAL SOCIOLOGY UNIT, 6 Lilybank Gardens, Glasgow G12 8QQ. Tel: 0141-357 3949. *Director,* Prof. S. Macintyre, OBE, PH.D.

MOLECULAR HAEMATOLOGY UNIT, Institute of Molecular Medicine, John Radcliffe Hospital, Headington, Oxford OX1 9DU. Tel: 01865-222359. *Hon. Director,* Prof. Sir David Weatherall, MD, FRCP, FRCPath., FRS

MOUSE GENOME CENTRE, Harwell Site, Chilton, Didcot, Oxon OX11 0RD. Tel: 01235-834393. *Director,* Prof. S. Brown, PH.D.

MRC CENTRE, CAMBRIDGE, Hills Road, Cambridge CB2 2QH. Tel: 01223-248011. *Head of Centre,* M. B. Davies, PH.D.

MRC CENTRE, OXFORD, Manor House, John Radcliffe Hospital, Headington, Oxford OX3 9DU. Tel: 01865-222124. *Head of Centre,* D. McLaren, PH.D.

MRC LABORATORIES, THE GAMBIA, PO Box 273, Banjul, The Gambia, W. Africa. *Director,* Prof. K. McAdam, FRCP

MRC LABORATORIES, JAMAICA, University of the West Indies, Mona, Kingston 7, Jamaica. *Director,* Prof. G. R. Serjeant, CMG, MD, FRCP

MUSCLE AND CELL MOTILITY UNIT, Division of Biophysics, King's College London, 26–29 Drury Lane, London WC2B 5RL. Tel: 0171-836 8851. *Hon. Director,* Prof. R. M. Simmons, PH.D.

NEUROCHEMICAL PATHOLOGY UNIT, Newcastle General Hospital, Westgate Road, Newcastle upon Tyne NE4 6BE. Tel: 0191-273 5251. *Director,* Prof. J. A. Edwardson, PH.D.

PROTEIN PHOSPHORYLATION UNIT, Department of Biochemistry, Medical Sciences Institute, University of Dundee, Dundee DD1 4HN. Tel: 01382-344241. *Hon. Director,* Prof. P. Cohen, PH.D., FRS, FRSE

RADIATION AND GENOME STABILITY UNIT, Harwell Site, Chilton, Didcot, Oxon OX11 0RD. Tel: 01235-834393. *Director,* Prof. D. Goodhead, D.phil.

REPRODUCTIVE BIOLOGY UNIT, Centre for Reproductive Biology, 37 Chalmers Street, Edinburgh EH3 9EW. Tel: 0131-229 2575. *Director,* Prof. A. S. McNeilly, PH.D., D.SC., FRSE

SOCIAL, GENETIC AND DEVELOPMENTAL PSYCHIATRY RESEARCH CENTRE, Institute of Psychiatry, De Crespigny Park, Denmark Hill, London SE5 8AF. Tel: 0171-740 5121. *Director,* Sir Michael Rutter, CBE, FRS, FRCP, FRCPsych.

Toxicology Unit, Hodgkin Building, University of Leicester, PO Box 138, Lancaster Road, Leicester LEI 9HN. Tel: 0116-252 5600. *Director*, vacant

Virology Unit, Institute of Virology, Church Street, Glasgow GII 5JR. Tel: 0141-330 4017. *Director*, Prof. D. J. McGeoch

NATURAL ENVIRONMENT RESEARCH COUNCIL (NERC)
Polaris House, North Star Avenue, Swindon SN2 IEU
Tel 01793-411500

The purpose of the NERC is to promote and support research, survey, long-term environmental monitoring and related postgraduate training in terrestrial, marine and freshwater biology, and Earth, atmospheric, hydrological, oceanographic and polar sciences and Earth observation; to advance knowledge and technology, and to provide services and trained scientists and engineers; to provide advice, disseminate knowledge and promote public understanding in these fields.
Chairman, J. C. Smith, CBE, FEng., FRSE
Chief Executive, Prof. J. R. Krebs, FRS

CENTRES/SURVEYS

British Antarctic Survey, High Cross, Madingley Road, Cambridge CB3 OET. Tel: 01223-221400. *Director*, Dr C. Rapley

British Geological Survey, Kingsley Dunham Centre, Nicker Hill, Keyworth, Nottingham NGI2 5GG. Tel: 0115-936 3100. *Director*, Dr D. Falvey

Centre for Coastal and Marine Science
Director, Prof. J. McGlade (based at Plymouth Marine Laboratory)
Plymouth Marine Laboratory, Prospect Place, West Hoe, Plymouth PLI 3DH. Tel: 01752-633100. *Director*, Prof. R. F. Mantoura
Proudman Oceanographic Laboratory, Bidston Observatory, Birkenhead L43 7RA. Tel: 0151-653 8633. *Director (acting)*, Dr J. Huthnance
Dunstaffnage Marine Laboratory, PO Box 3, Oban, Argyll PA34 4AD. Tel: 01631-562244. *Director*, Dr G. B. Shimmield

Centre for Ecology and Hydrology
Director, Prof. W. B. Wilkinson (based at Institute of Hydrology)
Institute of Freshwater Ecology, The Ferry House, Far Sawrey, Ambleside, Cumbria LA22 OLP. Tel: 015394-42468. *Director*, Prof. A. D. Pickering
Institute of Hydrology, Maclean Building, Crowmarsh Gifford, Wallingford, Oxon OXI0 8BB. Tel: 01491-838800. *Director*, Dr J. Wallace
Institute of Terrestrial Ecology, Monks Wood, Abbots Ripton, Huntingdon PEI7 2LS. Tel: 01487-773381. *Director*, Prof T. M. Roberts
Institute of Virology and Environmental Microbiology, Mansfield Road, Oxford OXI 3SR. Tel: 01865-281630. *Director*, Dr P. Nuttall

Southampton Oceanography Centre, University of Southampton, Empress Dock, Southampton SOI4 3ZH. Tel: 01703-596888. *Director*, Dr J. Shepherd

UNITS

Atmospheric Chemistry Modelling Support Unit, University Chemical Laboratory, University of Cambridge, Lensfield Road, Cambridge CB2 IEP. Tel: 01223-336473. *Director*, Dr J. A. Pyle

Centre for Global Atmospheric Modelling, Department of Meteorology, University of Reading, 2 Earley Gate, Whiteknights, Reading RG6 2AU. Tel: 0118-931 8315. *Director*, Prof. A. O'Neill

Centre for Population Biology, Imperial College, Silwood Park, Ascot, Berks SL5 7PY. Tel: 01344-294346. *Director*, Prof. J. Lawton, CBE, FRS

Environmental Systems Science Centre, Department of Geography, Reading University, Whiteknights, Reading RG6 2AB. Tel: 0118-931 8741. *Director*, Prof. R. Gurney

Sea Mammal Research Unit, Gatty Marine Laboratory, University of St Andrews, St Andrews, Fife KYI6 8LB. Tel: 01334-462630. *Head*, Dr. P. Hammond

PARTICLE PHYSICS AND ASTRONOMY RESEARCH COUNCIL (PPARC)
Polaris House, North Star Avenue, Swindon SN2 ISZ
Tel 01793-442000

The purpose of the PPARC is to support research into elementary particles and the fundamental forces of nature, planetary and solar research, including space physics, and astronomy, astrophysics and cosmology. It funds research in the universities and is responsible for funding both national and international facilities, including the European Laboratory for Particle Physics (CERN) and the European Space Agency. In July 1997 the Government announced that the work of the two Royal Observatories was to be concentrated in a new UK Astronomy Technology Centre (UKATC) at Edinburgh.
Chairman, Dr P. Williams, CBE
Chief Executive, Prof. I. Halliday

Royal Observatory, Edinburgh, Blackford Hill, Edinburgh EH9 3HJ. Tel: 0131-668 8100. *Director*, S. G. Pitt

Isaac Newton Group of Telescopes, Apartado de Coreos 321, Santa Cruz de la Palma, Tenerife 38780, Canary Islands. Tel: 00 3422-411048. *Director*, R. Rutten

Joint Astronomy Centre, 660 N A'ohoku Place, University Park, Hilo, Hawaii 96720. Tel: 00 808-961 3756. *Head*, Prof. I. Robson

UK Astronomy Technology Centre, Blackford Hill, Edinburgh EH9 3HJ. Tel: 0131-668100. *Director*, Dr. A. Russell

Research and Technology Organizations

The following industrial and technological research bodies are members of the Association of Independent Research and Technology Organizations (AIRTO). Members' activities span a wide range of disciplines from life sciences to engineering. Their work includes basic research, development and design of innovative products or processes, instrumentation testing and certification, and technology and management consultancy. AIRTO publishes a directory to help clients identify the organizations which might be able to assist them.
AIRTO, PO Box 85, Leatherhead, Surrey KT22 7YG. Tel: 01372-802260. *President*, B. Blunden, OBE

ADVANCED MANUFACTURING TECHNOLOGY RESEARCH INSTITUTE, Hulley Road, Macclesfield, Cheshire SK10 2NE. Tel: 01625-425421. *Managing Director,* D. Palethorpe

AIRCRAFT RESEARCH ASSOCIATION LTD, Manton Lane, Bedford MK41 7PF. Tel: 01234-350681. *Chief Executive,* B. Timmins

BHR GROUP LTD (*Fluid mechanics and process technology*), The Fluid Engineering Centre, Cranfield, Bedford MK43 0AJ. Tel: 01234-750422. *Chief Executive,* I. Cooper

BIBRA INTERNATIONAL (*Assessment of toxicity of food and chemicals to humans*), Woodmansterne Road, Carshalton, Surrey SM5 4DS. Tel: 0181-652 1000. *Director,* Dr S. E. Jaggers

BLC (THE LEATHER TECHNOLOGY CENTRE), Leather Trade House, Kings Park Road, Moulton Park, Northants NN3 6JD. Tel: 01604-679999. *Chief Executive,* Dr K. Alexander

BRITISH GLASS, Northumberland Road, Sheffield S10 2UA. Tel: 0114-268 6201. *Director-General,* Dr W. Cook

BRITISH MARITIME TECHNOLOGY LTD, Orlando House, 1 Waldegrave Road, Teddington, Middx TW11 8LZ. Tel: 0181-943 5544. *Chief Executive,* D. Goodrich

BREWING RESEARCH INTERNATIONAL (*Alcoholic beverages*), Lyttel Hall, Coopers Hill Road, Nutfield, Surrey RH1 4HY. Tel: 01737-822272. *Director-General,* Prof. R. Righelato

BRITISH TEXTILE TECHNOLOGY GROUP, Wira House, West Park Ring Road, Leeds LS16 6QL. Tel: 0113-259 1999; Shirley House, Wilmslow Road, Didsbury, Manchester M20 2RB. Tel: 0161-445 8141. *Chief Executive,* A. King

BUILDING RESEARCH ESTABLISHMENT, Garston, Watford WD2 7JR. Tel: 01923-664000. *Managing Director,* Dr. M. Wyatt

BUILDING SERVICES RESEARCH AND INFORMATION ASSOCIATION, Old Bracknell Lane West, Bracknell, Berks RG12 7AH. Tel: 01344-426511. *Chief Executive,* G. J. Baker

CAMBRIDGE CONSULTANTS LTD (*Products, systems and manufacturing processes design and development*), Science Park, Milton Road, Cambridge CB4 4DW. Tel: 01223-420024. *Chief Executive,* Dr J. P. Auton

CAMBRIDGE REFRIGERATION TECHNOLOGY (CRT), 140 Newmarket Road, Cambridge CB5 8HE. Tel: 01223-365101. *Managing Director,* A. Robertson

CAMPDEN AND CHORLEYWOOD FOOD RESEARCH ASSOCIATION, Chipping Campden, Glos GL55 6LD. Tel: 01386-842000. *Director-General,* Prof. C. Dennis

CENTRE FOR MARINE AND PETROLEUM TECHNOLOGY, Exploration House, Offshore Technology Park, Aberdeen AB23 8GX. Tel: 01224-853400; 19 Buckingham Street, London WC2N 6EF. Tel: 0171-321 0674; Research Park North, Riccarton, Edinburgh EH14 4AP. Tel: 0131-451 5231. *Chief Executive,* R. Lane-Nott, CB

CERAM RESEARCH (BRITISH CERAMIC RESEARCH LTD), Queen's Road, Penkhull, Stoke-on-Trent ST4 7LQ. Tel: 01782-764444. *Chief Executive,* Dr N. E. Sanderson

CIRIA (CONSTRUCTION INDUSTRY RESEARCH AND INFORMATION ASSOCIATION), 6 Storey's Gate, London SW1P 3AU. Tel: 0171-222 8891. *Director-General,* Dr P. L. Bransby

CRL (*Specialist products, technology licences, research and development*), Dawley Road, Hayes, Middx UB3 1HH. Tel: 0181-848 9779. *Managing Director,* Dr J. White

CUTLERY AND ALLIED TRADES RESEARCH ASSOCIATION, Henry Street, Sheffield S3 7EQ. Tel: 0114-276 9736. *Director of Research,* R. C. Hamby

EA TECHNOLOGY (*Use and distribution of electricity*), Capenhurst, Chester CH1 6ES. Tel: 0151-339 4181. *Chief Executive,* Dr S. F. Exell

ERA TECHNOLOGY LTD (*Electronic, electrical, materials and structural engineering*), Cleeve Road, Leatherhead, Surrey KT22 7SA. Tel: 01372-367000. *Managing Director and Chief Executive,* Prof. M. J. Withers

FABRIC CARE RESEARCH ASSOCIATION, Forest House Laboratories, Knaresborough Road, Harrogate, N. Yorks HG2 7LZ. Tel: 01423-885977. *Managing Director,* C. Tebbs

FIRA INTERNATIONAL LTD (FURNITURE INDUSTRY RESEARCH ASSOCIATION), Maxwell Road, Stevenage, Herts SG1 2EW. Tel: 01438-313433. *Managing Director,* H. Davies

HR WALLINGFORD GROUP LTD (*Hydroinformatics and engineering*), Howbery Park, Wallingford, Oxon OX10 8BA. Tel: 01491-835381. *Chief Executive,* Dr J. Weare, OBE

LABORATORY OF THE GOVERNMENT CHEMIST, Queens Road, Teddington, Middx TW11 OLY. Tel: 0181-943 7300. *Chief Executive and Government Chemist,* Dr R. Worswick

LEATHERHEAD FOOD RESEARCH ASSOCIATION, Randalls Road, Leatherhead, Surrey KT22 7RY. Tel: 01372-376761. *Director,* Dr M. P. J. Kierstan

MATERIALS ENGINEERING RESEARCH LABORATORY LTD, Tamworth Road, Hertford SG13 7DG. Tel: 01992-500120. *Managing Director,* Dr A. Stevenson

MINERAL INDUSTRY RESEARCH ORGANIZATION, Expert House, Sandford Street, Lichfield, Staffs WS13 6QA. Tel: 01543-262957. *Director,* N. Roberts

MOTOR INDUSTRY RESEARCH ASSOCIATION, Watling Street, Nuneaton, Warks CV10 OTU. Tel: 01203-355000. *Managing Director,* J. R. Wood

MOTOR INSURANCE REPAIR RESEARCH CENTRE, Colthorp Lane, Thatcham, Berks RG19 4NP. Tel: 01635-868855. *Chief Executive,* M. Smith

THE NATIONAL COMPUTING CENTRE LTD, Oxford House, Oxford Road, Manchester M1 7ED. Tel: 0161-228 6333. *Managing Director,* C. Pearse

NATIONAL PHYSICAL LABORATORY, Queens Road, Teddington, Middx TW11 OLW. Tel: 0181-977 3222. *Deputy Director,* Dr A. Wallard

PAINT RESEARCH ASSOCIATION, 8 Waldegrave Road, Teddington, Middx TW11 8LD. Tel: 0181-977 4427. *Managing Director,* J. A. Bernie

PERA GROUP (*Multi-disciplinary research, design, development and consultancy*), Middle Aston House, Middle Aston, Oxon OX6 3PT. Tel: 01869-347755. *Chief Executive,* R. A. Armstrong

PIRA INTERNATIONAL (*Paper and board, printing, publishing and packaging*), Randalls Road, Leatherhead, Surrey KT22 7RU. Tel: 01372-802000. *Managing Director,* M. Hancock

RAPRA TECHNOLOGY LTD (*Rubber and plastics*), Shawbury, Shrewsbury SY4 4NR. Tel: 01939-250383; North East Centre, 18 Belasis Court, Belasis Technology Park, Billingham TS23 4AZ. Tel: 01642-370406. *Chief Executive,* Dr P. Extance

SATRA TECHNOLOGY CENTRE (Footwear, apparel, safety products and furniture), Satra House, Rockingham Road, Kettering, Northants NN16 9JH. Tel: 01536-410000. *Chief Executive,* Dr R. E. Whittaker

SIRA LTD (*Measurement, instrumentation, control and optical systems technology*), South Hill, Chislehurst, Kent BR7 5EH. Tel: 0181-467 2636. *Managing Director,* Prof. R. A. Brook

SMITH INSTITUTE (*Mathematics and computing*), PO Box 183, Guildford, Surrey GU2 5GG. Tel: 01483-579108. *Director,* Dr L. Wallen

SMITH SYSTEM ENGINEERING LTD, Surrey Research Park, Guildford, Surrey GU2 5YP. Tel: 01483-442000. *Managing Director,* Dr T. Black

SPORTS TURF RESEARCH INSTITUTE, St Ives Estate, Bingley, W. Yorks BD16 1AU. Tel: 01274-565131. *Chief Executive*, Dr M. Canaway
STEEL CONSTRUCTION INSTITUTE, Silwood Park, Ascot, Berks SL5 7QN. Tel: 01344-623345. *Director*, Dr G. Owens
TRADA TECHNOLOGY LTD (*Timber and wood-based products*), Chiltern House, Stocking Lane, Hughenden Valley, High Wycombe, Bucks HP14 4ND. Tel: 01494-563091. *Managing Director*, A. Abbott

TRANSPORT RESEARCH LABORATORY, Old Wokingham Road, Crowthorne, Berks RG45 6AU. Tel: 01344-773131. *Chief Executive*, G. Clarke
TWI (*Welding*), Abington Hall, Abington, Cambridge CB1 6AL. Tel: 01223-891162. *Chief Executive*, A. B. M. Braithwaite, OBE

Royal Scottish Academicians

SENIOR ACADEMICIANS
1958   Armour, Dr Mary
1979   Baillie, William, CBE
1974   Crosbie, William
1976   Malcolm, Ellen
1977   Robertson, R. Ross
1975   Wheeler, Sir Anthony, OBE
1977   Whiston, Peter

ROYAL SCOTTISH ACADEMICIANS
1972   Blackadder, Elizabeth, OBE
1993   Bryce, Gordon
1991   Buchan, Dennis
1986   Bushe, Fred, OBE
1977   Butler, Vincent
1981   Campbell, Alex
1974   Collins, Peter
1992   Donald, George
1989   Evans, David
1989   Fraser, Alexander
1989   Harvey, Jake
1972   Houston, John
1979   Knox, John
1973   Littlejohn, William
1991   Maclean, William
1990   MacMillan, Andrew, OBE
1991   Merrylees, Andrew
1990   Metzstein, Isi
1972   Michie, David, OBE
1989   Morris, James
1992   Morrison, James
1990   Pelly, Frances

1991   Pottinger, Frank
1992   Rae, Barbara
1997   Renton, Stuart, MBE
1976   Reeves, Philip
1989   Richards, John, CBE
1989   Robertson, James
1984   Scott, Bill
1990   Shanks, Duncan
1987   Smith, Ian McKenzie, OBE
1985   Snowden, Michael
1979   Steedman, Robert, OBE
1982   Walker, Frances

ASSOCIATES
Arnott, Ian
Black, Robert
Boys, John
Brotherston, William
Busby, John
Bytautus, Alfons
Cairns, Joyce
Campbell, A. Buchanan
Clarke, Derek
Clifford, J. G.
Cocker, Douglas
Convery, Frank
Crowe, Victoria
Dean, Fiona
Docherty, Michael
Dunbar, Lennox
Fairgrieve, James
Fisher, Beth

The Earl Haig
Howard, Ian
Johnstone, John
Lamb, Elspeth
Lawrence, Eileen
Low, Bet
McCulloch, Ian
McIntosh, Iain
MacPherson, George
Main, Kirkland
Mitchell, Gordon
Mooney, John
Murphy, Richard
Onwin, Glen
Page, David
Rayner, Martin
Rodger, Willie
Ross, Alastair
Smith, Marion
Squire, Geoffrey
Stenhouse, Andrew
Watson, Arthur
Webster, Robin
Wedgwood, Roland
Wishart, Sylvia
Wiszhewski, Adrian
Wyllie, George

NON-RESIDENT ASSOCIATES
Balmer, Barbara
Gasson, Barry
Morrocco, Leon

Sports Bodies

* Governing body for the sport

Sports Councils

CENTRAL COUNCIL OF PHYSICAL RECREATION, Francis House, Francis Street, London SW1P 1DE. Tel: 0171-828 3163. *General Secretary*, M. Denton

THE ENGLISH SPORTS COUNCIL, 16 Upper Woburn Place, London WC1H 0QP. Tel: 0171-273 1500. *Chief Executive Officer*, D. Casey

SCOTTISH SPORTS COUNCIL, Caledonia House, South Gyle, Edinburgh EH12 9DQ. Tel: 0131-317 7200. *Chief Executive*, F. A. L. Alstead, CBE

SPORTS COUNCIL FOR NORTHERN IRELAND, House of Sport, Upper Malone Road, Belfast BT9 5LA. Tel: 01232-381222. *Chief Executive*, E. McCartan

SPORTS COUNCIL FOR WALES, Sophia Gardens, Cardiff CF1 9SW. Tel: 01222-300500. *Chief Executive*, Dr H. Jones

UK SPORTS COUNCIL, Walkden House, 10 Melton Street, London NW1 2EB. Tel: 0171-380 8000. *Chief Executive*, D. Chesterton

Angling

*NATIONAL FEDERATION OF ANGLERS, Halliday House, Egginton Junction, Derbys DE65 6GU. Tel: 01283-734735. *Chief Administration Officer*, W. Hall

Archery

*GRAND NATIONAL ARCHERY SOCIETY, National Agricultural Centre, 7th Street, Stoneleigh, Kenilworth, Warks CV8 2LG. Tel: 01203-696631. *Chief Executive*, J. S. Middleton

Association Football

*THE FOOTBALL ASSOCIATION, 16 Lancaster Gate, London W2 3LW. Tel: 0171-402 7151. *Chief Executive*, R. H. G. Kelly

*FOOTBALL ASSOCIATION OF WALES, Plymouth Chambers, 3 Westgate Street, Cardiff CF1 1DD. Tel: 01222-372325. *Secretary-General*, D. G. Collins

THE FOOTBALL LEAGUE LTD, 319 Clifton Drive South, Lytham St Annes, Lancs FY8 1JG. Tel: 01253-729421. *Chief Executive*, R. C. Scudamore

*IRISH FOOTBALL ASSOCIATION, 20 Windsor Avenue, Belfast BT9 6EE. Tel: 01232-669458. *General Secretary*, D. I. Bowen

IRISH FOOTBALL LEAGUE, 96 University Street, Belfast BT7 1HE. Tel: 01232-242888. *Secretary*, H. Wallace

*SCOTTISH FOOTBALL ASSOCIATION, 6 Park Gardens, Glasgow G3 7YF. Tel: 0141-332 6372. *Chief Executive*, J. Farry

SCOTTISH FOOTBALL LEAGUE, 188 West Regent Street, Glasgow G2 4RY. Tel: 0141-248 3844. *Secretary*, P. Donald

Athletics

ATHLETICS ASSOCIATION OF WALES, Morfa Stadium, Landore, Swansea SA1 7DF. Tel: 01792-456237. *Chief Executive*, D. Turner

NORTHERN IRELAND ATHLETIC FEDERATION, Athletics House, Old Coach Road, Belfast BT9 5PR. Tel: 01232-602707. *Secretary*, J. Allen

SCOTTISH ATHLETICS FEDERATION, Caledonia House, South Gyle, Edinburgh EH12 9DQ. Tel: 0131-317 7320. *Administrator*, N. F. Park

UK ATHLETICS '98, 30A Harborne Road, Birmingham B15 3AA. Tel: 0121-456 5098. *Information Officer*, W. Adcocks

Badminton

*BADMINTON ASSOCIATION OF ENGLAND LTD, National Badminton Centre, Bradwell Road, Loughton Lodge, Milton Keynes MK8 9LA. Tel: 01908-268400. *Chief Executive*, S. Baddeley

*SCOTTISH BADMINTON UNION, Cockburn Centre, 40 Bogmoor Place, Glasgow G51 4TQ. Tel: 0141-445 1218. *Chief Executive*, Miss A. Smillie

*WELSH BADMINTON UNION, Fourth Floor, 3 Westgate Street, Cardiff CF1 1ND. Tel: 01222-222082. *Coaching Development Manager*, L. Williams

Baseball

*BRITISH BASEBALL FEDERATION, PO Box 45, Hessle, E. Yorks HU13 0YQ. Tel: 01482-643551. *Secretary*, Ms W. Macadam

Basketball

*BASKETBALL ASSOCIATION OF WALES, Connies House, Rhymney River Bridge Road, Cardiff CF3 7YZ. Tel: 01222-454395. *Administrator*, F. M. Daw

*ENGLISH BASKETBALL ASSOCIATION, 48 Bradford Road, Stanningley, Leeds LS28 6DF. Tel: 0113-236 1166. *Chief Executive (acting)*, S. Kirkland

*SCOTTISH BASKETBALL ASSOCIATION, Caledonia House, South Gyle, Edinburgh EH12 9DQ. Tel: 0131-317 7260. *Chief Executive Officer*, Mrs S. F. E. Mason

Billiards

*WORLD LADIES BILLIARDS AND SNOOKER ASSOCIATION, 27 Oakfield Road, Clifton, Bristol BS8 2AT. Tel: 0117-974 4491. *Company Secretary*, M. D. Blake

*WORLD PROFESSIONAL BILLIARDS AND SNOOKER ASSOCIATION, 27 Oakfield Road, Clifton, Bristol BS8 2AT. Tel: 0117-974 4491. *Chief Executive*, M. D. Blake

Bobsleigh

*BRITISH BOBSLEIGH ASSOCIATION, The Chestnuts, 85 High Street, Codford, Warminster, Wilts BA12 0ND. Tel: 01985-850064. *General Secretary*, Ms H. Alderman

Bowls

*BRITISH ISLES BOWLS COUNCIL, 2 Pentland Avenue, Gowkshill, Gorebridge, Midlothian EH23 4PG. Tel: 01875-821105. *Hon. Secretary*, J. P. Darling

*BRITISH ISLES INDOOR BOWLS COUNCIL, 9 Highlight Lane, Barry CF62 8AA. Tel: 01446-733978. *Hon. Secretary*, J. R. Thomas, MBE

*BRITISH ISLES WOMEN'S BOWLING COUNCIL, 2 Case Gardens, Seaton, Devon EX12 2AP. Tel: 01297-21317. *Hon. Secretary*, Mrs N. Colling, MBE

*BRITISH ISLES WOMEN'S INDOOR BOWLS COUNCIL, 101 Skyline Drive, Lambeg, Lisburn, Co. Antrim BT27 4HU. Tel: 01846-663516. *Hon. Secretary*, Mrs D. Miskelly

*ENGLISH BOWLING ASSOCIATION, Lyndhurst Road, Worthing, W. Sussex BN11 2AZ. Tel: 01903-820222. *Secretary*, G. D. Shaw

*ENGLISH INDOOR BOWLING ASSOCIATION, David Cornwell House, Bowling Green, Leicester Road, Melton Mowbray, Leics LE13 0DA. Tel: 01664-481900. *Secretary*, D. N. Brown

*English Women's Bowling Association, 2 Case Gardens, Seaton, Devon EX12 2AP. Tel: 01297-21317. *Hon. Secretary*, Mrs N. Colling, MBE

*English Women's Indoor Bowling Association, 3 Scirocco Close, Moulton Park, Northampton NN3 6AP. Tel: 01604-494163. *Secretary*, Mrs M. E. Ruff

Boxing

*Amateur Boxing Association of England Ltd, Crystal Palace National Sports Centre, London SE19 2BB. Tel: 0181-778 0251. *Secretary*, C. Brown

*British Amateur Boxing Association, 96 High Street, Lochee, Dundee DD2 3AY. Tel: 01382-611412. *Chief Executive*, F. Hendry

*British Boxing Board of Control Ltd, Jack Petersen House, 52A Borough High Street, London SE1 1XW. Tel: 0171-403 5879. *General Secretary*, J. Morris

Canoeing

*British Canoe Union, Adbolton Lane, West Bridgford, Nottingham NG2 5AS. Tel: 0115-982 1100. *Chief Executive*, P. Owen

Chess

*British Chess Federation, 9A Grand Parade, St Leonard's-on-Sea, E. Sussex TN38 0DD. Tel: 01424-442500. *Manager*, Mrs G. White

Clay Pigeon Shooting

*Clay Pigeon Shooting Association Ltd, Earlstrees Court, Earlstrees Road, Corby, Northants NN17 4AX. Tel: 01536-443566. *Director*, E. G. Orduna

Cricket

*England and Wales Cricket Board, Lord's Cricket Ground, London NW8 8QZ. Tel: 0171-432 1200. *Chief Executive*, T. Lamb

MCC, Lord's Cricket Ground, London NW8 8QN. Tel: 0171-289 1611. *Secretary*, R. D. V. Knight

Croquet

*Croquet Association, c/o The Hurlingham Club, Ranelagh Gardens, London SW6 3PR. Tel: 0171-736 3148. *Secretary*, P. W. P. Campion

Cycling

*British Cycling Federation, National Cycling Centre, Stuart Street, Manchester M11 4DQ. Tel: 0161-230 2301. *Chief Executive*, P. King

*Road Time Trials Council, 77 Arlington Drive, Pennington, Leigh, Lancs WN7 3QP. Tel: 01942-603976. *National Secretary*, P. Heaton

Darts

British Darts Organization, 2 Pages Lane, Muswell Hill, London N10 1PS. Tel: 0181-883 5544. *General Secretary*, O. A. Croft

Diving

*Great Britain Diving Federation, PO Box 222, Batley, W. Yorks WF17 8XD. Tel: 01924-422322. *Director of Administration*, J. Cryer

Equestrianism

*British Equestrian Federation, Stoneleigh Park, Kenilworth, Warks CV8 2RH. Tel: 01203-698871. *Director-General*, vacant

*British Horse Trials Association, National Agricultural Centre, Stoneleigh Park, Kenilworth, Warks CV8 2RN. Tel: 01203-698856. *Director*, Maj. T. Taylor

Eton Fives

*Eton Fives Association, 74 Clarence Road, St Albans, Herts AL1 4NG. Tel: 01727-837099. *Secretary*, R. Beament

Fencing

*British Fencing Association, 1 Baron's Gate, 33–35 Rothschild Road, London W4 5HT. Tel: 0181-742 3032. *General Secretary*, Miss G. Kenneally

Gliding

*British Gliding Association, Kimberley House, Vaughan Way, Leicester LE1 4SE. Tel: 0116-253 1051. *Secretary*, B. Rolfe

Golf

*Ladies' Golf Union, The Scores, St Andrews, Fife KY16 9AT. Tel: 01334-475811. *Secretary*, Mrs J. Hall

*Royal and Ancient Golf Club of St Andrews, Golf Place, St Andrews, Fife KY16 9JD. Tel: 01334-472112. *Secretary*, M. F. Bonallack, OBE

Greyhound Racing

*National Greyhound Racing Club Ltd, Twyman House, 16 Bonny Street, London NW1 9QD. Tel: 0171-267 9256. *Chief Executive*, F. Melville

Gymnastics

*British Gymnastics, Ford Hall, Lilleshall National Sports Centre, Newport, Shropshire TF10 9NB. Tel: 01952-820330. *General Secretary*, D. Minnery

Hockey

*English Hockey Association, The Stadium, Silbury Boulevard, Milton Keynes MK9 1NR. Tel: 01908-689290. *Chief Executive*, S. P. Baines

*Scottish Hockey Union, 48 Pleasance, Edinburgh EH8 9TJ. Tel: 0131-650 8170. *Chairman*, P. Monaghan

*Welsh Hockey Union, 80 Woodville Road, Cathays, Cardiff CF2 4ED. Tel: 01222-233257. *Executive Secretary*, J. G. Williams

Horse-racing

*British Horseracing Board, 42 Portman Square, London W1H 0EN. Tel: 0171-396 0011. *Chief Executive*, R. T. Ricketts

The Jockey Club, 42 Portman Square, London W1H 0EN. Tel: 0171-486 4921. *Senior Steward*, C. Spence

Ice Hockey

*British Ice Hockey Association, 2nd Floor Suite, 517 Christchurch Road, Boscombe, Bournemouth BH1 4AG. Tel: 01202-303946. *General Secretary*, D. Pickles

Ice Skating

*National Ice Skating Association of the UK Ltd, First Floor, 114–116 Curtain Road, London EC2A 3AH. Tel: 0171-613 1188. *Chief Executive*, Ms C. Godsall

Judo

*British Judo Association, 7A Rutland Street, Leicester LE1 1RB. Tel: 0116-255 9669. *Office Manager*, Mrs S. Startin

Lacrosse

*English Lacrosse Association, 4 Western Court, Bromley Street, Digbeth, Birmingham B9 4AN. Tel: 0121-773 4422. *Chief Executive Officer*, D. Shuttleworth

Lawn Tennis

*Lawn Tennis Association, The Queen's Club, London W14 9EG. Tel: 0171-381 7000. *Secretary*, J. C. U. James

Lugeing

*Great Britain Luge Association, 1 Highfield House, Hampton Bishop, Hereford HR1 4JN. Tel: 01432-271982. *General Secretary*, J. G. Evans

Martial Arts
MARTIAL ARTS DEVELOPMENT COMMISSION, PO Box 381, Erith, Kent DA8 1TF. Tel: 01322-431440. *Office Administrator,* Mrs E. Jewell

Motor Sports
*AUTO-CYCLE UNION, ACU House, Wood Street, Rugby, Warks CV21 2YX. Tel: 01788 566400. *Chief Executive,* G. Wilson
MOTORCYCLE CIRCUIT RACING CONTROL BOARD, PO Box 72, Castle Donington, Derbys DE74 2ZQ. Tel: 01332-853822. *Manager,* D. R. Barnfield
*RAC MOTOR SPORTS ASSOCIATION LTD, Motor Sports House, Riverside Park, Colnbrook, Slough SL3 0HG. Tel: 01753-681736. *Chief Executive,* J. R. Quenby
*SCOTTISH AUTO CYCLE UNION LTD, Block 2, Unit 6, Whiteside Industrial Estate, Bathgate, W. Lothian EH48 2RX. Tel: 01506-630262. *Secretary,* A. M. Brownlie

Mountaineering
*BRITISH MOUNTAINEERING COUNCIL, 177–179 Burton Road, West Didsbury, Manchester M20 2BB. Tel: 0161-445 4747. *General Secretary,* R. Payne

Multi-Sport Bodies
BRITISH OLYMPIC ASSOCIATION, 1 Wandsworth Plain, London SW18 1EH. Tel: 0181-871 2677. *Chief Executive,* S. Clegg
BRITISH UNIVERSITIES SPORTS ASSOCIATION, 8 Union Street, London SE1 1SZ. Tel: 0171-357 8555. *Chief Executive,* G. Gregory-Jones
COMMONWEALTH GAMES COUNCIL FOR ENGLAND, Tavistock House South, Tavistock Square, London WC1H 9JZ. Tel: 0171-388 6643. *General Secretary,* Miss A. Hogbin
COMMONWEALTH GAMES FEDERATION, Walkden House, 3–10 Melton Street, London NW1 2EB. Tel: 0171-383 5596. *Hon. Secretary,* D. Dixon, CVO

Netball
*ALL ENGLAND NETBALL ASSOCIATION LTD, Netball House, 9 Paynes Park, Hitchin, Herts SG5 1EH. Tel: 01462-442344. *Chief Executive,* Mrs E. M. Nicholl
*NORTHERN IRELAND NETBALL ASSOCIATION, House of Sport, Upper Malone Road, Belfast BT9 5LA. Tel: 01232-381222. *Secretary,* Mrs R. McWhinney
*SCOTTISH NETBALL ASSOCIATION, 24 Ainslie Road, Hillington Business Park, Hillington, Glasgow G52 4RU. Tel: 0141-570 4016. *Administrator,* Ms M. Martin
*WELSH NETBALL ASSOCIATION, 50 Cathedral Road, Cardiff CF1 9LL. Tel: 01222-237048. *Chief Executive Officer,* Mrs S. J. Holvey

Orienteering
*BRITISH ORIENTEERING FEDERATION, Riversdale, Dale Road North, Darley Dale, Matlock, Derbys DE4 2HX. Tel: 01629-734042. *Secretary-General,* D. Locke

Polo
*THE HURLINGHAM POLO ASSOCIATION, Winterlake, Kirtlington, Kidlington, Oxon OX5 3HG. Tel: 01869-350044. *Secretary,* J. W. M. Crisp

Rackets and Real Tennis
*TENNIS AND RACKETS ASSOCIATION, c/o The Queen's Club, Palliser Road, London W14 9EQ. Tel: 0171-386 3447. *Chief Executive,* Brig. A. D. Myrtle, CB, CBE

Rifle Shooting
*NATIONAL RIFLE ASSOCIATION, Bisley Camp, Brookwood, Woking, Surrey GU24 0PB. Tel: 01483-797777. *Chief Executive,* Col. C. C. C. Cheshire, OBE

*NATIONAL SMALL-BORE RIFLE ASSOCIATION, Lord Roberts House, Bisley Camp, Brookwood, Woking, Surrey GU24 0NP. Tel: 01483-476969. *Secretary,* Lt.-Col. J. D. Hoare

Rowing
*AMATEUR ROWING ASSOCIATION LTD, The Priory, 6 Lower Mall, London W6 9DJ. Tel: 0181-748 3632. *National Manager,* Mrs R. Napp
HENLEY ROYAL REGATTA, Regatta Headquarters, Henley-on-Thames, Oxon RG9 2LY. Tel: 01491-572153. *Secretary,* R. S. Goddard
SCOTTISH AMATEUR ROWING ASSOCIATION, 18 Daniel McLauchlin Place, Kirkintilloch, Glasgow G66 2LH. Tel: 0141-775 0522. *Secretary,* Miss R. Clarke
*WELSH AMATEUR ROWING ASSOCIATION, Lyndhurst, 77 Hereford Road, Monmouth NP5 4JZ. Tel: 01600-714244. *Secretary,* M. C. Hargaden

Rugby Fives
*RUGBY FIVES ASSOCIATION, The Old Forge, Sutton Valence, Maidstone, Kent ME17 3AW. Tel: 01622-842278. *General Secretary,* M. F. Beaman

Rugby League
*BRITISH AMATEUR RUGBY LEAGUE ASSOCIATION, West Yorkshire House, 4 New North Parade, Huddersfield HD1 5JP. Tel: 01484-544131. *Chief Executive,* M. F. Oldroyd
*THE RUGBY FOOTBALL LEAGUE, Red Hall, Red Hall Lane, Leeds LS17 8NB. Tel: 0113-232 9111. *Chief Executive,* J. N. Tunnicliffe

Rugby Union
*IRISH RUGBY FOOTBALL UNION, 62 Lansdowne Road, Ballsbridge, Dublin 4, Republic of Ireland. Tel: 00 353-1-668 4601. *Secretary,* P. R. Browne
IRISH WOMEN'S RUGBY UNION, 140 Georgian Village, Castleknock, Dublin 15, Republic of Ireland. Tel: 00 353-1-821 4237. *Secretary,* Ms R. Hanley
*RUGBY FOOTBALL UNION, Rugby House, Rugby Road, Twickenham TW1 1DS. Tel: 0181-892 2000. *Chief Executive,* vacant
RUGBY FOOTBALL UNION FOR WOMEN (ENGLAND), 33 Rice Mews, St Thomas, Exeter EX2 9AY. Tel: 01635-278177. *Secretary,* Ms. S. Eakers
*SCOTTISH RUGBY UNION, Murrayfield, Edinburgh EH12 5PJ. Tel: 0131-346 5000. *Chief Executive,* W. Watson
SCOTTISH WOMEN'S RUGBY UNION, 11 Bavelaw Crescent, Penicuik, Midlothian EH26 9AX. Tel: 01968-673355.
*WELSH RUGBY UNION, PO Box 22, Hodge House, St Mary Street, Cardiff CF1 1DY. Tel: 01222-781700. *Secretary,* D. Gethin
WELSH WOMEN'S RUGBY UNION, 40 Wolseley Street, Pilwenlly, Newport NP9 2HP. Tel: 01633-220249. *Secretary,* Ms. F. Margerison

Skiing
*BRITISH SKI AND SNOWBOARD FEDERATION, 258 Main Street, East Calder, Livingston, W. Lothian EH53 0EE. Tel: 01506-884343. *Chief Executive,* M. Jardine

Snooker
*WORLD LADIES BILLIARDS AND SNOOKER ASSOCIATION, 27 Oakfield Road, Clifton, Bristol BS8 2AT. Tel: 0117-974 4491. *Company Secretary,* M. D. Blake
*WORLD PROFESSIONAL BILLIARDS AND SNOOKER ASSOCIATION, 27 Oakfield Road, Clifton, Bristol BS8 2AT. Tel: 0117-974 4491. *Chief Executive,* M. D. Blake

Speedway
*SPEEDWAY CONTROL BOARD LTD, ACU Headquarters,
Wood Street, Rugby, Warks CV21 2YX. Tel: 01788-
540096. *Manager,* D. Hughes

Squash Rackets
*SCOTTISH SQUASH, Caledonia House, South Gyle,
Edinburgh EH12 9DQ. Tel: 0131-317 7343. *Secretary,*
N. Brydon
*SQUASH RACKETS ASSOCIATION, PO Box 1106, London
W3 0ZD. Tel: 0181-746 1616. *Chief Executive,*
S. H. Courtney
*WELSH SQUASH, PO Box 56, Penarth CF64 1XP. Tel: 01222-
704096. *Administrator,* Ms D. Selley

Sub-Aqua
*BRITISH SUB-AQUA CLUB, Telfords Quay, Ellesmere
Port, Cheshire L65 4FY. Tel: 0151-350 6255. *Chief
Executive Officer,* D. Roberts

Swimming
*AMATEUR SWIMMING ASSOCIATION, Harold Fern House,
Derby Square, Loughborough, Leics LE11 5AL. Tel:
01509-618700. *Chief Executive,* D. Sparkes
*SCOTTISH AMATEUR SWIMMING ASSOCIATION,
Holmhills Farm, Greenlees Road, Cambuslang,
Glasgow G72 8DT. Tel: 0141-641 8818. *Administration
Manager,* Mrs E. Mackenzie
*WELSH AMATEUR SWIMMING ASSOCIATION, Roath Park
House, Ninian Road, Cardiff CF2 5ER. Tel: 01222-
488820. *Hon. General Secretary,* vacant

Table Tennis
*ENGLISH TABLE TENNIS ASSOCIATION, Queensbury
House, Havelock Road, Hastings, E. Sussex TN34 1HF.
Tel: 01424-722525. *Chief Executive,* R. Yule

Volleyball
*ENGLISH VOLLEYBALL ASSOCIATION, 27 South Road,
West Bridgford, Nottingham NG2 7AG. Tel: 0115-
981 6324. *Chief Executive Officer,* vacant
*SCOTTISH VOLLEYBALL ASSOCIATION, 48 Pleasance,
Edinburgh EH8 9TJ. Tel: 0131-315 4997. *Director,*
N. S. Moody
*WELSH VOLLEYBALL ASSOCIATION, 9 St Dennis Road,
Heath, Cardiff CF4 4NA. Tel: 01222-758427. *Secretary,*
Ms T. Shaw

Walking
*RACE WALKING ASSOCIATION, Hufflers, Heard's Lane,
Shenfield, Brentwood, Essex CM15 0SF. Tel: 01277-
220687. *Hon. General Secretary,* P. J. Cassidy

Water Skiing
*BRITISH WATER SKI FEDERATION, 390 City Road,
London EC1V 2QA. Tel: 0171-833 2855. *Executive Officer,*
Ms G. Hill

Weightlifting
*BRITISH AMATEUR WEIGHTLIFTERS ASSOCIATION, 3
Iffley Turn, Oxford OX4 4DU. Tel: 01865-778319. *Hon.
Secretary,* W. Holland, OBE

Wrestling
*BRITISH AMATEUR WRESTLING ASSOCIATION, 41 Great
Clowes Street, Salford, Manchester M7 1RQ. Tel: 0161-
832 9209. *National Development Officer,* R. Tomlinson

Yachting
*ROYAL YACHTING ASSOCIATION, RYA House, Romsey
Road, Eastleigh, Hants SO50 9YA. Tel: 01703-627400.
Secretary-General, R. Duchesne, OBE

Clubs

ALPINE CLUB (1857), 55 Charlotte Road, London
EC2A 3QT. Tel: 0171-613 0755. *Hon. Secretary*,
G. D. Hughes

AMERICAN WOMEN'S CLUB (1899), 68 Old Brompton
Road, London SW7 3LQ. Tel: 0171-589 8292. *Secretary*,
Mrs S. Byrnes

ANGLO-BELGIAN CLUB (1955), 60 Knightsbridge,
London SW1X 7LF. Tel: 0171-235 2121. *Secretary*,
Baronne van Havre

ARMY AND NAVY CLUB (1837), 36 Pall Mall, London
SW1Y 5JN. Tel: 0171-930 9721. *Secretary*, Cdr. J. A. Holt,
MBE

ARTS CLUB (1863), 40 Dover Street, London W1X 3RB. Tel:
0171-499 8581. *Secretary*, Ms J. Downing

ARTS THEATRE CLUB (1927), 50 Frith Street, London
W1V 5TE. Tel: 0171-287 9236. *Hon. Secretary*, S. Labisko

THE ATHENAEUM (1824), 107 Pall Mall, London SW1Y 5ER.
Tel: 0171-930 4843. *Secretary*, J. G. F. Stoy

AUTHORS' CLUB (1892), 40 Dover Street, London W1X 3RB.
Tel: 0171-499 8581. *Secretary*, Mrs A. de la Grange

BEEFSTEAK CLUB (1876), 9 Irving Street, London
WC2H 7AT. Tel: 0171-930 5722. *Secretary*,
Sir John Lucas-Tooth, Bt.

BOODLE'S (1762), 28 St James's Street, London SW1A 1HJ.
Tel: 0171-930 7166. *Secretary*, R. R. T. Smith

BROOKS'S (1764), St James's Street, London SW1A 1LN. Tel:
0171-493 4411. *Secretary*, G. Snell

BUCK'S CLUB (1919), 18 Clifford Street, London W1X 1RG.
Tel: 0171-734 6896. *Secretary*, Capt. P. G. J. Murison, RN

CALEDONIAN CLUB (1891), 9 Halkin Street, London
SW1X 7DR. Tel: 0171-235 5162. *Secretary*, P. J. Varney

CANNING CLUB (1910), (from Jan. 1999) 4 St James's
Square, London SW1Y 4JU. Tel: 0171-499 5163. *Secretary*,
T. M. Harrington

CARLTON CLUB (1832), 69 St James's Street, London
SW1A 1PJ. Tel: 0171-493 1164. *Secretary*, A. E. Telfer

CAVALRY AND GUARDS CLUB (1893), 127 Piccadilly,
London W1V 0PX. Tel: 0171-499 1261. *Secretary*,
N. J. Walford

CHELSEA ARTS CLUB (1891), 143 Old Church Street,
London SW3 6EB. Tel: 0171-376 3311. *Secretary*,
D. Winterbottom

CITY LIVERY CLUB (1914), 20 Aldermanbury, London
EC2V 7HP. Tel: 0171-814 0200. *Hon. Secretary*,
J. C. F. B. Byllam-Barnes

CITY OF LONDON CLUB (1832), 19 Old Broad Street,
London EC2N 1DS. Tel: 0171-588 7991. *Secretary*,
G. S. Jones

CITY UNIVERSITY CLUB (1895), 50 Cornhill, London
EC3V 3PD. Tel: 0171-626 8571. *Secretary*,
Miss R. C. Graham

EAST INDIA CLUB (1849), 16 St James's Square, London
SW1Y 4LH. Tel: 0171-930 1000. *Secretary*, D. Taylor

FARMERS CLUB (1842), 3 Whitehall Court, London
SW1A 2EL. Tel: 0171-930 3751. *Secretary*,
Gp Capt G. P. Carson

FLYFISHERS' CLUB (1884), 69 Brook Street, London
W1Y 2ER. Tel: 0171-629 5958. *Secretary*,
Cdr. T. H. Boycott, OBE

GARRICK CLUB (1831), 15 Garrick Street, London
WC2E 9AY. Tel: 0171-379 6478. *Secretary*, M. J. Harvey

GREEN ROOM CLUB (1877), 9 Adam Street, London
WC2N 6AA. Tel: 0171-836 7453. *Secretary*, Ms J. Mander

GROUCHO CLUB (1985), 45 Dean Street, London W1V 5AP.
Tel: 0171-439 4685. *Company Secretary*, Miss Z. Noordin

HURLINGHAM CLUB (1869), Ranelagh Gardens, London
SW6 3PR. Tel: 0171-736 8411. *Secretary*, P. H. Covell

THE KENNEL CLUB (1873), 1–5 Clarges Street, London
W1Y 8AB. Tel: 0171-493 6651. *Chief Executive*, R. French

LANSDOWNE CLUB (1934), 9 Fitzmaurice Place, London
W1X 6JD. Tel: 0171-629 7200. *Secretary*, Lt.-
Cdr. T. P. Havers

LONDON ROWING CLUB (1856), Embankment, Putney,
London SW15 1LB. Tel: 0181-788 1400. *Hon. Secretary*,
N. A. Smith

MCC (MARYLEBONE CRICKET CLUB) (1787), Lord's
Cricket Ground, London NW8 8QN. Tel: 0171-289 1611.
Secretary, R. D. V. Knight

NATIONAL CLUB (1845), c/o The Carlton Club, 69 St
James's Street, London SW1A 1PJ. Tel: 0171-493 1164.
Hon. Secretary, I. A. Sowton

NATIONAL LIBERAL CLUB (1882), Whitehall Place,
London SW1A 2HE. Tel: 0171-930 9871. *Secretary*,
S. J. Roberts

NAVAL AND MILITARY CLUB (1862), (from Jan. 1999) 4 St
James's Square, London SW1Y 4JU. Tel: 0171-499 5163.
Secretary, M. G. G. Ebbitt

NAVAL CLUB (1946), 38 Hill Street, London W1X 8DP. Tel:
0171-493 7672. *Chief Executive*, Cdr. J. L. L. Pritchard

NEW CAVENDISH CLUB (1984), 44 Great Cumberland
Place, London W1H 8BS. Tel: 0171-723 0391. *Secretary*,
J. P. Dauvergne

DEN NORSKE KLUB LTD (1924), 5 Wimbledon Close,
London SW20 8HW. Tel: 0181-879 3463. *Secretary*,
Ms J. P. Okkenhaug

ORIENTAL CLUB (1824), Stratford House, Stratford Place,
London W1N 0ES. Tel: 0171-629 5126. *Secretary*,
S. C. Doble

PORTLAND CLUB (1816), 42 Half Moon Street, London
W1Y 7RD. Tel: 0171-499 1523. *Secretary*, J. Burns, CBE

PRATT'S CLUB (1841), 14 Park Place, London SW1A 1LP.
Tel: 0171-493 0397. *Secretary*, G. Snell

QUEEN'S CLUB (1886), Palliser Road, London W14 9EQ.
Tel: 0171-385 3421. *Secretary*, J. A. S. Edwardes

RAILWAY CLUB (1899), Room 208, 25 Marylebone Road,
London NW1 5JS. Tel: 0173-781 2175. *Hon. Secretary*,
A. G. Wells

REFORM CLUB (1836), 104–105 Pall Mall, London
SW1Y 5EW. Tel: 0171-930 9374. *Secretary*, R. A. M. Forrest

ROEHAMPTON CLUB (1901), Roehampton Lane, London
SW15 5LR. Tel: 0181-876 5505. *Chief Executive*, M. Yates

ROYAL AIR FORCE CLUB (1918), 128 Piccadilly, London
W1V 0PY. Tel: 0171-399 1000. *Secretary*, P. N. Owen

ROYAL AUTOMOBILE CLUB (1897), 89–91 Pall Mall,
London SW1Y 5HS. Tel: 0171-930 2345. *General Secretary*,
N. A. Johnson, OBE

ROYAL OCEAN RACING CLUB (1925), 20 St James's Place,
London SW1A 1NN. Tel: 0171-493 2248. *General Manager*,
D. J. Minords, OBE

ROYAL OVER-SEAS LEAGUE (1910), Over-Seas House,
Park Place, St James's Street, London SW1A 1LR. Tel:
0171-408 0214. *Director-General*, R. F. Newell

ROYAL THAMES YACHT CLUB (1775), 60 Knightsbridge, London SW1X 7LF. Tel: 0171-235 2121. *Secretary*, Capt. D. Goldson, RN

ST STEPHEN'S CONSTITUTIONAL CLUB (1870), 34 Queen Anne's Gate, London SW1H 9AB. Tel: 0171-222 1382. *Secretary*, L. D. Mawby

SAVAGE CLUB (1857), 1 Whitehall Place, London SW1A 2HD. Tel: 0171-930 8118. *Hon. Secretary*, D. Stirling

SAVILE CLUB (1868), 69 Brook Street, London W1Y 2ER. Tel: 0171-629 5462. *Secretary*, N. Storey

SKI CLUB OF GREAT BRITAIN (1903), The White House, 57–63 Church Road, Wimbledon SW19 5DQ. Tel: 0181-410 2000. *Managing Director*, Ms C. Stuart-Taylor

THAMES ROWING CLUB (1860), Embankment, Putney, London SW15 1LB. Tel: 0181-788 0798. *Hon. Secretary*, J. McConnell

TRAVELLERS CLUB (1819), 106 Pall Mall, London SW1Y 5EP. Tel: 0171-930 8688. *Secretary*, M. S. Allcock

TURF CLUB (1868), 5 Carlton House Terrace, London SW1Y 5AQ. Tel: 0171-930 8555. *Secretary*, Col. J. G. B. Rigby, OBE

UNITED OXFORD AND CAMBRIDGE UNIVERSITY CLUB (1972), 71 Pall Mall, London SW1Y 5HD. Tel: 0171-930 5151. *Secretary*, G. R. Buchanan

UNIVERSITY WOMEN'S CLUB (1886), 2 Audley Square, South Audley Street, London W1Y 6DB. Tel: 0171-499 2268. *Secretary*, J. Robson

VICTORIA CLUB (1863), 1 North Court, Great Peter Street, London SW1P 3LL. *Secretary*, Ms S. David

VICTORY SERVICES CLUB (1907), 63–79 Seymour Street, London W2 2HF. Tel: 0171-723 4474. *General Manager*, G. F. Taylor

WHITE'S (1693), 37–38 St James's Street, London SW1A 1JG. Tel: 0171-493 6671. *Secretary*, D. A. Anderson

WIG AND PEN CLUB (1908), 229–230 Strand, London WC2R 1BA. Tel: 0171-583 7255. *Chairman*, B. Coral

---

CLUBS OUTSIDE LONDON

Bath: BATH AND COUNTY CLUB (1865), Queen's Parade, Bath BA1 2NJ. Tel: 01225-423732. *Secretary*, R. M. Lockert

Birmingham: THE BIRMINGHAM CLUB (1872), Winston Churchill House, 8 Ethel Street, Birmingham B2 4BG. Tel: 0121-643 3357. *Hon. Secretary*, T. R. Pepper

ST PAUL'S CLUB (1859), 34 St Paul's Square, Birmingham B3 1QZ. Tel: 0121-236 1950. *Hon. Secretary*, E. A. Fellowes

Bishop Auckland: THE CLUB (1868), Lightfoot Institute, Kingsway, Bishop Auckland, Co. Durham DL14 7JN. Tel: 01388-603219. *Hon. Secretary*, R. Kellett

Blackburn: DISTRICT AND UNION CLUB (1849), Northwood, 1 West Park Road, Blackburn BB2 6DE. Tel: 01254-51474. *Hon. Secretary*, R. W. Edge

Bristol: CLIFTON CLUB (1882), 22 The Mall, Clifton, Bristol BS8 4DS. Tel: 0117-973 5527. *Secretary*, R. G. M. Henry

Cambridge: CAMBRIDGE UNIVERSITY AMATEUR DRAMATIC CLUB (1855), ADC Theatre, Park Street, Cambridge CB5 8AS. Tel: 01223-359547. *Secretary*, Ms F. Beauman

THE UNION (1815), 9A Bridge Street, Cambridge CB2 1UB. Tel: 01223-566421. *Chief Clerk*, Mrs S. Finding

Canterbury: KENT AND CANTERBURY CLUB (1868), The Elms, 17 Old Dover Road, Canterbury CT1 3JB. Tel: 01227-462181. *Secretary*, K. D. Bassey

Cheltenham: NEW CLUB (1874), 2 Montpellier Parade, Cheltenham GL50 1UD. Tel: 01242-523285. *Hon. Secretary*, N. S. Parrack

Chichester: REGNUM CLUB (1862), 45A South Street, Chichester, W. Sussex PO19 1DS. Tel: 01243-780219. *Hon. Secretary*, A. H. Murray

Durham: COUNTY CLUB (1890), 52 Old Elvet, Durham DH1 3HJ. Tel: 0191-384 8156. *Secretary*, Mrs C. Arnot

NORTH BAILEY CLUB (1842), 24 North Bailey, Durham DH1 3EW. Tel: 0191-384 3724. *Permanent Secretary*, Mrs E. M. Hardcastle

Guildford: THE COUNTY CLUB, 158 High Street, Guildford GU1 3HJ. Tel: 01483-560677. *Hon. Secretary*, R. W. D. Hemingway

Henley-on-Thames: LEANDER CLUB (1818), Henley-on-Thames, Oxon RG9 2LP. Tel: 01491-575782. *Hon. Secretary*, J. Beveridge

PHYLLIS COURT CLUB (1906), Marlow Road, Henley-on-Thames, Oxon RG9 2HT. Tel: 01491-570500. *Secretary*, R. Edwards

Hove: HOVE CLUB (1882), 28 Fourth Avenue, Hove, E. Sussex BN3 2PJ. Tel: 01273-730872. *Secretary*, J. L. C. Young

Leamington Spa: TENNIS COURT CLUB (1846), 50 Bedford Street, Leamington Spa, Warks CV32 5DT. Tel: 01926-424977. *Hon. Secretary*, P. J. Lloyd

Leeds: THE LEEDS CLUB (1849), 3 Albion Place, Leeds LS1 6JL. Tel: 0113-242 1591. *Administrator*, Mrs I. Sigsworth

Leicester: LEICESTERSHIRE CLUB (1873), 9 Welford Place, Leicester LE1 6ZH. Tel: 0116-254 0399. *Secretary*, T. M. Bedingfield

Liverpool: THE ATHENAEUM (1797), Church Alley, Liverpool L1 3DD. Tel: 0151-709 7770. *Secretary*, B. H. Denton

Macclesfield: OLD BOYS' AND PARK GREEN CLUB, 7 Churchside, Macclesfield, Cheshire SK10 1HG. Tel: 01625-423292. *Hon. Secretary*, J. G. P. van der Feltz

Newcastle upon Tyne: NORTHERN CONSTITUTIONAL CLUB (1882), 37 Pilgrim Street, Newcastle upon Tyne NE1 6QE. Tel: 0191-232 0884. *Hon. Secretary*, J. L. Browne

Northampton: NORTHAMPTON AND COUNTY CLUB (1873), George Row, Northampton NN1 1DF. Tel: 01604-632962. *Secretary*, J. Green

Norwich: NORFOLK CLUB (1770), 17 Upper King Street, Norwich NR3 1RB. Tel: 01603-610652. *Secretary*, G. G. Hardaker

Nottingham: NOTTINGHAM AND NOTTS UNITED SERVICES CLUB (1920), Newdigate House, Castle Gate, Nottingham NG1 6AF. Tel: 0115-912 6220. *Secretary*, K. Goodman

Oxford: FREWEN CLUB (1869), 98 St Aldate's, Oxford OX1 1BT. Tel: 01865-243816. *Hon. Secretary*, B. R. Boyt

VINCENT'S CLUB (1863), 1A King Edward Street, Oxford OX1 4HS. Tel: 01865-722984. *Steward*, H. Dean

Paignton: PAIGNTON CLUB (1882), The Esplanade, Paignton, Devon TQ4 6ED. Tel: 01803-559682. *Hon. Secretary*, P. Grafton

Shrewsbury: SALOP CLUB (1974), The Old House, Dogpole, Shrewsbury SY1 1EP. *Secretary*, J. W. Rouse

Stourbridge: STOURBRIDGE OLD EDWARDIAN CLUB (1898), Drury Lane, Stourbridge, West Midlands DY8 1BL. Tel: 01384-395635. *Hon. Secretary*, D. J. Lucas

Teddington: ROYAL CANOE CLUB (1866), Trowlock Island, Teddington, Middx TW11 9QZ. Tel: 0181-977 5269. *Hon. Secretary*, Mrs J. S. Evans

WALES

Cardiff: CARDIFF AND COUNTY CLUB (1866), Westgate Street, Cardiff CF1 1DA. Tel: 01222-220846. *Hon. Secretary*, Cdr. J. E. Payn, RD, RNR

SCOTLAND

Aberdeen: ROYAL NORTHERN AND UNIVERSITY CLUB (1854/1889, amal. 1979), 9 Albyn Place, Aberdeen AB10 1YE. Tel: 01224-583292. *Secretary,* Miss R. A. Black
Ayr: AYR COUNTY CLUB (1872), Savoy Park Hotel, Racecourse Road, Ayr KA7 2UT. Tel: 01292-266112. *Hon. Secretary,* G. A. Hay
Edinburgh: CALEDONIAN CLUB, 32 Abercromby Place, Edinburgh EH3 6QE. Tel: 0131-557 2675. *Secretary,* P. Walker
NEW CLUB (1787), 86 Princes Street, Edinburgh EH2 2BB. Tel: 0131-226 4881. *Secretary,* A. D. Orr Ewing
Glasgow: GLASGOW ART CLUB (1867), 185 Bath Street, Glasgow G2 4HU. Tel: 0141-248 5210. *Secretary,* L. J. McIntyre
ROYAL SCOTTISH AUTOMOBILE CLUB (1899), 11 Blythswood Square, Glasgow G2 4AG. Tel: 0141-221 3850. *Secretary,* J. C. Lord
WESTERN CLUB (1825), 32 Royal Exchange Square, Glasgow G1 3AB. Tel: 0141-221 2016. *Secretary,* D. H. Gifford

NORTHERN IRELAND

Belfast: ULSTER REFORM CLUB (1885), 4 Royal Avenue, Belfast BT1 1DA. Tel: 01232-323411. *Secretary,* Miss M. P. Mackintosh
Londonderry: NORTHERN COUNTIES CLUB (1880), 24 Bishop Street, Londonderry BT48 6PP. Tel: 01504-262012. *Hon. Secretary,* N. Dykes

CHANNEL ISLANDS

Guernsey: UNITED CLUB (1870), Pier Steps, St Peter Port, Guernsey GY1 2LF. Tel: 01481-725722. *Hon. Secretary,* J. J. L. Morgan
Jersey: VICTORIA CLUB (1853), Beresford Street, St Helier, Jersey JE2 4WN. Tel: 01534-23381. *Secretary,* W. A. F. Hurst

YACHT CLUBS

Bembridge: BEMBRIDGE SAILING CLUB (1886), Embankment Road, Bembridge, IOW PO35 5NR. Tel: 01983-872237. *Secretary,* Lt.-Col. M. J. Samuelson, RM
Birkenhead: ROYAL MERSEY YACHT CLUB (1844), Bedford Road East, Rock Ferry, Birkenhead, Merseyside L42 1LS. Tel: 0151-645 3204. *Hon. Secretary,* P. A. Bastow
Bridlington: ROYAL YORKSHIRE YACHT CLUB (1847), 1 Windsor Crescent, Bridlington, E. Yorks YO15 3HX. Tel: 01262-672041. *Secretary,* J. H. Evans
Burnham-on-Crouch: ROYAL CORINTHIAN YACHT CLUB (1872), The Quay, Burnham-on-Crouch, Essex CM0 8AX. Tel: 01621-782105. *Hon. Secretary,* B. Stanford
Chichester: CHICHESTER YACHT CLUB (1965), Chichester Yacht Basin, Birdham, Chichester, W. Sussex PO20 7EJ. Tel: 01243-512918. *Secretary,* I. M. Clark
Cowes: ROYAL YACHT SQUADRON (1815), The Castle, Cowes, IOW PO31 7QT. Tel: 01983-292191. *Secretary,* Maj. R. P. Rising, RM
Dartmouth: ROYAL DART YACHT CLUB (1866), Priory Street, Kingswear, Dartmouth, Devon TQ6 0AB. Tel: 01803-752496. *Hon. Secretary,* Mrs. R. Hine-Haycock
Dover: ROYAL CINQUE PORTS YACHT CLUB (1872), 5 Waterloo Crescent, Dover, Kent CT16 1LA. Tel: 01304-206262. *Secretary,* Mrs C. A. Partridge

Fowey: ROYAL FOWEY YACHT CLUB (1881), Whitford Yard, Fowey, Cornwall PL23 1BH. Tel: 01726-833573. *Hon. Secretary,* P. J. Selbie
Ipswich: ROYAL HARWICH YACHT CLUB (1843), Woolverstone, Ipswich IP9 1AT. Tel: 01473-780319. *Secretary,* Cdr. J. A. Adams, RD
Leigh-on-Sea: ESSEX YACHT CLUB (1890), HQS Bembridge, Foreshore, Leigh-on-Sea, Essex SS9 1BD. Tel: 01702-478404. *Hon. Secretary,* Ms L. Kelly
London: THE CRUISING ASSOCIATION (1908), CA House, 1 Northey Street, Limehouse Basin, London E14 8BT. Tel: 0171-537 2828. *General Secretary,* Mrs. L. Hammett
ROYAL THAMES YACHT CLUB (1775), 60 Knightsbridge, London SW1X 7LF. Tel: 0171-235 2121. *Secretary,* Capt. D Goldson, RN
Lowestoft: ROYAL NORFOLK AND SUFFOLK YACHT CLUB (1859), Royal Plain, Lowestoft, Suffolk NR33 0AQ. Tel: 01502-566726. *General Manager,* A. Donovan
Lymington: ROYAL LYMINGTON YACHT CLUB (1922), Bath Road, Lymington, Hants SO41 3SE. Tel: 01590-672677. *Secretary,* I. Gawn
Plymouth: ROYAL PLYMOUTH CORINTHIAN YACHT CLUB (1877), Madeira Road, Plymouth PL1 2NY. Tel: 01752-664327. *Hon. Secretary,* W. E. Roberts
ROYAL WESTERN YACHT CLUB OF ENGLAND (1827), Queen Anne's Battery, Plymouth PL4 0TW. Tel: 01752-660077. *Chief Executive,* J. Lewis
Poole: EAST DORSET SAILING CLUB (1875), 352 Sandbanks Road, Poole, Dorset BH14 8HY. Tel: 01202-706111. *Hon. Secretary,* Mrs T. Neely
PARKSTONE YACHT CLUB (1895), Pearce Avenue, Poole, Dorset BH14 8EH. Tel: 01202-743610. *General Manager,* M. Simms
POOLE HARBOUR YACHT CLUB (1949), 38 Salterns Way, Lilliput, Poole, Dorset BH14 8JR. Tel: 01202-707321. *Secretary,* J. N. J. Smith
POOLE YACHT CLUB (1865), New Harbour Road West, Hamworthy, Poole, Dorset BH15 4AQ. Tel: 01202-672687. *Secretary/Manager,* Miss L. Clark
Portsmouth: ROYAL NAVAL AND ROYAL ALBERT YACHT CLUB (1867), 17 Pembroke Road, Portsmouth PO1 2NT. Tel: 01705-824491. *Secretary,* J. McDermott, MBE
Ramsgate: ROYAL TEMPLE YACHT CLUB (1857), 6 Westcliff Mansions, Ramsgate, Kent CT11 9HY. Tel: 01843-591766. *Hon. Secretary,* Maj. B. A. Cook
Southampton: ROYAL AIR FORCE YACHT CLUB (1932), Riverside House, Rope Walk, Hamble, Southampton SO31 4HD. Tel: 01703-452208. *Secretary,* W. J. Oakley
ROYAL SOUTHAMPTON YACHT CLUB, 1 Channel Way, Ocean Village, Southampton SO14 3QF. Tel: 01703-223352. *Secretary,* A. M. Paterson
ROYAL SOUTHERN YACHT CLUB (1837), Rope Walk, Hamble, Southampton SO31 4HB. Tel: 01703-453271. *Secretary,* P. J. F. Allen, MBE
Torquay: ROYAL TORBAY YACHT CLUB (1863), 12 Beacon Terrace, Torquay, Devon TQ1 2BH. Tel: 01803-292006. *Secretary,* R. M. Porteous
Westcliff-on-Sea: THAMES ESTUARY YACHT CLUB (1895), 3 The Leas, Westcliff-on-Sea, Essex SS0 7ST. Tel: 01702-345967. *Hon. Secretary,* D. G. Brown
Weymouth: ROYAL DORSET YACHT CLUB (1875), 11 Custom House Quay, Weymouth, Dorset DT4 8BG. Tel: 01305-786258. *Secretary,* Mrs M. Tye
Windermere: ROYAL WINDERMERE YACHT CLUB (1860), Fallbarrow Road, Bowness-on-Windermere, Windermere, Cumbria LA23 3DJ. Tel: 015394-43106. *Hon. Secretary,* Mrs. F. Bentley

Yarmouth: ROYAL SOLENT YACHT CLUB (1878), Yarmouth,
IOW PO41 ONS. Tel: 01983-760256. *Secretary,*
Mrs S. Tribe

WALES

Beaumaris: ROYAL ANGLESEY YACHT CLUB (1802), 5–6
Green Edge, Beaumaris, Anglesey LL58 8BY. Tel: 01248-
810295. *Hon. Secretary,* J. E. de Leyland-Berry
Caernarfon: ROYAL WELSH YACHT CLUB (1847),
Porth–Yr–Aur, Caernarfon LL55 1SN. Tel: 01286-672599.
Hon. Secretary, J. H. Long
Penarth: PENARTH YACHT CLUB (1880), The Esplanade,
Penarth, Vale of Glamorgan CF64 3AU. Tel: 01222-
708196. *Hon. Secretary,* R. S. McGregor
Swansea: BRISTOL CHANNEL YACHT CLUB (1875), 744
Mumbles Road, Mumbles, Swansea SA3 4EL. Tel: 01792-
366000. *Hon. Secretary,* R. L. Morgan

SCOTLAND

Dundee: ROYAL TAY YACHT CLUB (1885), 34 Dundee
Road, West Ferry, Dundee DD5 1LX. Tel: 01382-477516.
Hon. Secretary, S. Buchanan
Edinburgh: ROYAL FORTH YACHT CLUB (1868), Middle
Pier, Granton Harbour, Edinburgh EH5 1HF. Tel: 0131-
552 8560. *Hon. Secretary,* C. D. Hurn
Helensburgh: ROYAL NORTHERN AND CLYDE YACHT CLUB
(1824, amal. 1978), Rhu, Helensburgh, Argyll and Bute
G84 8NG. Tel: 01436-820322. *General Manager,*
Capt. A. T. Lightoller
ROYAL WESTERN YACHT CLUB (1875), Braidhurst
Cottage, Shandon, Helensburgh, Argyll and Bute
G84 8NP. Tel: 01436-820256. *Hon. Secretary,*
T. J. Henderson
Slockavullin: ROYAL HIGHLAND YACHT CLUB (1881),
Raslie House, Slockavullin, Argyll PA31 8QG. Tel: 01546-
510261. *Secretary,* Mrs A. Wood

NORTHERN IRELAND

Bangor: ROYAL ULSTER YACHT CLUB (1866), 101 Clifton
Road, Bangor, Co. Down BT20 5HY. Tel: 01247-270568.
Secretary, Mrs V. F. M. Boyd

CHANNEL ISLANDS

Jersey: ROYAL CHANNEL ISLANDS YACHT CLUB (1862), Le
Boulevard, Bulwarks, St Aubin, Jersey JE3 8GW. Tel:
01534-45783. *Hon. Secretary,* D. C. Dale

Societies and Institutions

Although this section is arranged in alphabetical order, organizations are usually listed by the keyword in their title. The date in parenthesis after the organization's title is the year of its foundation.

ABBEYFIELD SOCIETY (1956), Abbeyfield House, 53 Victoria Street, St Albans, Herts ALI 3UW. Tel: 01727-857536. *Chief Executive*, F. Murphy

ACCOUNTANTS, ASSOCIATION OF CHARTERED CERTIFIED (1904), 29 Lincoln's Inn Fields, London WC2A 3EE. Tel: 0171-242 6855. *Chief Executive*, Mrs A. L. Rose

ACCOUNTANTS IN ENGLAND AND WALES, INSTITUTE OF CHARTERED (1880), Chartered Accountants' Hall, PO Box 433, Moorgate Place, London EC2P 2BJ. Tel: 0171-920 8100. *Chief Executive*, J. Collier

ACCOUNTANTS, INSTITUTE OF COMPANY (1974), 40 Tyndalls Park Road, Bristol BS8 IPL. Tel: 0117-973 8261. *Director-General*, B. T. Banks

ACCOUNTANTS, INSTITUTE OF FINANCIAL (1916), Burford House, 44 London Road, Sevenoaks, Kent TNI3 IAS. Tel: 01732-458080. *Chief Executive*, J. M. Dean

ACCOUNTANTS OF SCOTLAND, INSTITUTE OF CHARTERED (1854), 27 Queen Street, Edinburgh EH2 ILA. Tel: 0131-225 5673. *Chief Executive*, P. W. Johnston

ACCOUNTING TECHNICIANS, ASSOCIATION OF (1980), 154 Clerkenwell Road, London ECIR 5AD. Tel: 0171-837 8600. *Chief Executive*, Ms J. Scott Paul

ACE STUDY TOURS (formerly Association for Cultural Exchange), Babraham, Cambridge CB2 4AP. Tel: 01223-835055. *General Secretary*, P. B. Barnes

ACTION RESEARCH (1952), Vincent House, Horsham, W. Sussex RHI2 2DP. Tel: 01403-210406. *Director-General*, Mrs A. Luther

ACTORS' BENEVOLENT FUND (1882), 6 Adam Street, London WC2N 6AA. Tel: 0171-836 6378. *General Secretary*, Mrs J. Skerrett

ACTORS' CHARITABLE TRUST (1896), 255–256 Africa House, 64–78 Kingsway, London WC2B 6BD. Tel: 0171-242 0111. *General Secretary*, B. Batchelor

ACTORS' CHURCH UNION (1899), St Paul's Church, Bedford Street, London WC2E 9ED. Tel: 0171-602 8748. *Senior Chaplain*, Canon W. Hall

ACTUARIES IN SCOTLAND, FACULTY OF (1856), 17 Thistle Street, Edinburgh EH2 IDF. Tel: 0131-220 4555. *Secretary*, W. W. Mair

ACTUARIES, INSTITUTE OF (1848), Staple Inn Hall, High Holborn, London WCIV 7QJ. Tel: 0171-632 2100. *Secretary-General*, G. B. L. Campbell

ADAM SMITH INSTITUTE (1977), 23 Great Smith Street, London SWIP 3BL. Tel: 0171-222 4995. *President*, Dr M. Pirie

ADMINISTRATIVE MANAGEMENT, INSTITUTE OF (1915), 40 Chatsworth Parade, Petts Wood, Orpington, Kent BR5 IRW. Tel: 01689-875555. *Chief Executive*, Prof. G. Robinson

ADULT SCHOOL ORGANIZATION, NATIONAL (1899), MASU Centre, Gaywood Croft, Cregoe Street, Birmingham BI5 2ED. Tel: 0121-622 3400. *General Secretary*, Mrs P. C. Dean

ADVERTISING, INSTITUTE OF PRACTITIONERS IN (1927), 44 Belgrave Square, London SWIX 8QS. Tel: 0171-235 7020. *Director-General*, N. Phillips

ADVERTISING STANDARDS AUTHORITY (1962), 2 Torrington Place, London WCIE 7HW. Tel: 0171-580 5555. *Director-General*, Mrs M. Alderson

AERONAUTICAL SOCIETY, ROYAL (1866), 4 Hamilton Place, London WIV 0BQ. Tel: 0171-499 6230. *Director*, K. Mans

AFRICAN INSTITUTE, INTERNATIONAL (1926), SOAS, Thornhaugh Street, Russell Square, London WCIH 0XG. Tel: 0171-323 6035. *Hon. Director*, Prof. P. Spencer

AFRICAN MEDICAL AND RESEARCH FOUNDATION, 11 Old Queen Street, London SWIH 9JA. Tel: 0171-233 0066. *Executive Director*, A. Heroys

AGE CONCERN CYMRU, 4th Floor, 1 Cathedral Road, Cardiff CFI 9SD. Tel: 01222-371566. *Director*, R. W. Taylor

AGE CONCERN ENGLAND (1940), Astral House, 1268 London Road, London SWI6 4ER. Tel: 0181-679 8000. *Director-General*, Ms S. Greengross, OBE

AGE CONCERN NORTHERN IRELAND (1976), 3 Lower Crescent, Belfast BT7 INR. Tel: 01232-245729. *Director*, C. J. Common

AGE CONCERN SCOTLAND (1943), 113 Rose Street, Edinburgh EH2 3DT. Tel: 0131-220 3345. *Director*, Ms M. O'Neill

AGEING, CENTRE FOR POLICY ON (1947), 25–31 Ironmonger Row, London ECIV 3QP. Tel: 0171-253 1787. *Director*, Dr G. Dalley

AGEING, RESEARCH INTO (1978), Baird House, 15–17 St Cross Street, London ECIN 8UN. Tel: 0171-404 6878. *Director*, Mrs E. Mills

AGRICULTURAL BENEVOLENT INSTITUTION, ROYAL (1860), Shaw House, 27 West Way, Oxford OX2 0QH. Tel: 01865-724931. *Chief Executive*, Air Cdre R. B. Duckett, CVO, AFC

AGRICULTURAL BENEVOLENT INSTITUTION, ROYAL SCOTTISH (1897), Ingliston, Edinburgh EH28 8NB. Tel: 0131-333 1023. *Director*, I. C. Purves-Hume

AGRICULTURAL ENGINEERS ASSOCIATION (1875), Samuelson House, Paxton Road, Orton Centre, Peterborough PE2 5LT. Tel: 01733-371381. *Director-General*, J. Vowles

AGRICULTURAL SOCIETY, EAST OF ENGLAND, East of England Showground, Peterborough PE2 6XE. Tel: 01733-234451. *Chief Executive*, T. Gibson, OBE

AGRICULTURAL SOCIETY OF ENGLAND, ROYAL (1838), National Agricultural Centre, Stoneleigh Park, Kenilworth, Warks CV8 2LZ. Tel: 01203-696969. *Chief Executive*, C. Runge

AGRICULTURAL SOCIETY OF THE COMMONWEALTH, ROYAL (1957), 2 Grosvenor Gardens, London SWIW 3DF. Tel: 0171-259 9678. *Hon. Secretary*, J. Anderson, FRICS

AGRICULTURAL SOCIETY, ROYAL ULSTER (1826), The King's Hall, Balmoral, Belfast BT9 6GW. Tel: 01232-665225. *Chief Executive*, W. H. Yarr, OBE

AIR LEAGUE (1909), Broadway House, Tothill Street, London SWIH 9NS. Tel: 0171-222 8463. *Director*, Gp Capt E. R. Cox

ALCOHOLICS ANONYMOUS (1947), PO Box 1, Stonebow House, Stonebow, York YO1 2NJ. Tel: 01904-644026. *General Secretary*, J. Keeney

ALEXANDRA ROSE DAY (1912), 2A Ferry Road, Barnes, London SW13 9RX. Tel: 0181-748 4824. *National Director*, Mrs G. Greenwood

ALLIANCE PARTY OF NORTHERN IRELAND (1970), 88 University Street, Belfast BT7 1HE. Tel: 01232-324274. *Party Leader*, Lord Alderdice

ALLOTMENT AND LEISURE GARDENERS, NATIONAL SOCIETY OF (1930), Hunters Road, Corby, Northants NN17 5JE. Tel: 01536-266576. *National Secretary*, G. W. Stokes

ALMSHOUSES, NATIONAL ASSOCIATION OF (1946), Billingbear Lodge, Carter's Hill, Wokingham, Berks RG40 5RU. Tel: 01344-52922. *Director*, Maj.-Gen. A. deC. L. Leask

ALZHEIMER'S DISEASE SOCIETY (1979), Gordon House, 10 Greencoat Place, London SW1P 1PH. Tel: 0171-306 0606. *Executive Director*, H. Cayton

AMNESTY INTERNATIONAL UNITED KINGDOM (1961), 99–119 Rosebery Avenue, London EC1R 4RE. Tel: 0171-814 6200. *Director*, D. Bull

ANAESTHETISTS OF GREAT BRITAIN AND IRELAND, ASSOCIATION OF (1932), 9 Bedford Square, London WC1B 3RA. Tel: 0171-631 1650. *Hon. Secretary*, Dr. P. G. M. Wallace

ANCIENT BUILDINGS, SOCIETY FOR THE PROTECTION OF (1877), 37 Spital Square, London E1 6DY. Tel: 0171-377 1644. *Secretary*, P. Venning, FSA

ANCIENT MONUMENTS SOCIETY (1924), St Ann's Vestry Hall, 2 Church Entry, London EC4V 5HB. Tel: 0171-236 3934. *Secretary*, M. J. Saunders, MBE

ANGLO-ARAB ASSOCIATION (1961), The Arab British Centre, 21 Collingham Road, London SW5 0NU. Tel: 0171-373 8414. *Executive Director*, A. C. W. Lee

ANGLO-BELGIAN SOCIETY (1982), 5 Hartley Close, Bickley, Kent BR1 2TP. Tel: 0181-467 8442. *Hon. Secretary*, P. R. Bresnan

ANGLO-BRAZILIAN SOCIETY (1943), 32 Green Street, London W1Y 3FD. Tel: 0171-493 8493. *Secretary*, Mrs M. Lee

ANGLO-DANISH SOCIETY (1924), 25 New Street Square, London EC4A 3LN. Tel: 01753-884846. *Chairman*, H. Castenskiold, OBE

ANGLO-NORSE SOCIETY (1918), 25 Belgrave Square, London SW1X 8QD. Tel: 0171-591 5500. *Chairman*, Sir John Robson, KCMG

ANIMAL CONCERN (1988), PO Box 3982, Glasgow G51 4WD. Tel: 0141-445 3570. *Organizing Secretary*, Dr M. Daly

ANIMAL HEALTH TRUST (1942), Lanwades Park, Kentford, Newmarket, Suffolk CB8 7UU. Tel: 01638-751000. *Director*, A. J. Higgins, PH.D.

ANTHROPOLOGICAL INSTITUTE, ROYAL (1843), 50 Fitzroy Street, London W1P 5HS. Tel: 0171-387 0455. *Director*, J. C. M. Benthall

ANTHROPOSOPHICAL SOCIETY IN GREAT BRITAIN (1923), Rudolf Steiner House, 35 Park Road, London NW1 6XT. Tel: 0171-723 4400. *General Secretary*, N. C. Thomas

ANTIQUARIES OF LONDON, SOCIETY OF (1717), Burlington House, Piccadilly, London W1V 0HS. Tel: 0171-734 0193. *General Secretary*, D. Morgan Evans, FSA

ANTIQUARIES OF SCOTLAND, SOCIETY OF (1780), Royal Museum of Scotland, Chambers Street, Edinburgh EH1 1JF. Tel: 0131-247 4115. *Director*, Mrs F. Ashmore, FSA

ANTIQUE DEALERS' ASSOCIATION, BRITISH (1918), 20 Rutland Gate, London SW7 1BD. Tel: 0171-589 4128. *Secretary-General*, Mrs E. J. Dean

ANTI-SLAVERY INTERNATIONAL (1839), Unit 4, Stableyard, Broomgrove Road, London SW9 9TL. Tel: 0171-924 9555. *Director*, M. Dottridge

ANTI-VIVISECTION: BRITISH UNION FOR THE ABOLITION OF VIVISECTION (1898), 16A Crane Grove, London N7 8NN. Tel: 0171-700 4888. *Chief Executive*, M. Baker

ANTI-VIVISECTION SOCIETY, NATIONAL (1875), 261 Goldhawk Road, London W12 9PE. Tel: 0181-846 9777. *Director*, Ms J. Creamer

APOSTLESHIP OF THE SEA (1920), Stella Maris, 66 Dock Road, Tilbury, Essex RM18 7BX. Tel: 01375-850801. *National Director*, T. J. MacGuire

APOTHECARIES OF LONDON, SOCIETY OF (1617), 14 Black Friars Lane, London EC4V 6EJ. Tel: 0171-236 1189. *Clerk*, R. J. Stringer

ARBITRATORS, CHARTERED INSTITUTE OF (1915), 24 Angel Gate, City Road, London EC1R 2RS. Tel: 0171-837 4483. *Secretary-General*, K. Harding

ARCHAEOLOGICAL ASSOCIATION, CAMBRIAN (1846), Cochwillan, Tal-y-bont, Bangor, Gwynedd LL57 3AZ. Tel: 01633-262449. *General Secretary*, P. Llewellyn

ARCHAEOLOGICAL INSTITUTE, ROYAL (1843), c/o Society of Antiquaries of London, Burlington House, Piccadilly, London W1V 0HS. *Secretary*, J. G. Coad, FSA

ARCHAEOLOGY, COUNCIL FOR BRITISH (1944), Bowes Morrell House, 111 Walmgate, York YO1 9WA. Tel: 01904-671417. *Director*, R. K. Morris

ARCHITECTS AND SURVEYORS INSTITUTE (1926), St Mary House, 15 St Mary Street, Chippenham, Wilts SN15 3WD. Tel: 01249-444505. *Chief Executive*, I. N. Norris

ARCHITECTS BENEVOLENT SOCIETY (1850), 43 Portland Place, London W1N 3AG. Tel: 0171-580 2823. *Secretary*, R. Roth

ARCHITECTS IN SCOTLAND, ROYAL INCORPORATION OF (1922), 15 Rutland Square, Edinburgh EH1 2BE. Tel: 0131-229 7545. *Secretary*, S. Tombs

ARCHITECTS REGISTRATION BOARD (1931), 73 Hallam Street, London W1N 6EE. Tel: 0171-580 5861. *Registrar*, A. Finch

ARCHITECTS, ROYAL INSTITUTE OF BRITISH (1834), 66 Portland Place, London W1N 4AD. Tel: 0891-234400. *Director-General*, A. Reid, PH.D.

ARCHITECTURAL ASSOCIATION (1847), 34–36 Bedford Square, London WC1B 3ES. Tel: 0171-887 4000. *Secretary*, E. Le Maistre

ARCHITECTURAL HERITAGE FUND (1976), Clareville House, 26–27 Oxendon Street, London SW1Y 4EL. Tel: 0171-925 0199. *Secretary*, Lady Weir

ARCHIVISTS, SOCIETY OF (1947), 40 Northampton Road, London EC1R 0HB. Tel: 0171-278 8630. *Executive Secretary*, P. S. Cleary

ARK ENVIRONMENTAL FOUNDATION (1988), Suite 640–643, Linen Hall, 162–168 Regent Street, London W1R 5TB. Tel: 0171-439 4567. *Co-ordinator*, R. Boorer

ARLIS/UK and Ireland (The Art Libraries Society) (1969), 18 College Road, Bromsgrove, Worcs B60 2NE. Tel: 01527-579298. *Administrator*, Ms S. French

Army Benevolent Fund (1944), 41 Queen's Gate, London SW7 5HR. Tel: 0171-584 5232. *Controller*, Maj.-Gen. M. D. Regan, CB, OBE

Army Cadet Force Association (1930), E Block, Duke of York's HQ, London SW3 4RR. Tel: 0171-730 9733/4. *General Secretary*, Brig. R. B. MacGregor-Oakford, CBE, MC

Art Collections Fund, National (1903), Millais House, 7 Cromwell Place, London SW7 2JN. Tel: 0171-225 4800. *Director*, D. Barrie

Arthritis Care (1949), 18 Stephenson Way, London NW1 2HD. Tel: 0171-916 1500. *Chief Executive*, R. Gutch

Arthritis Research Campaign (1936), Copeman House, St Mary's Court, St Mary's Gate, Chesterfield, Derbys S41 7TD. Tel: 01246-558033. *Chief Executive*, F. Logan

Artists, Federation of British, 17 Carlton House Terrace, London SW1Y 5BD. Tel: 0171-930 6844. *Chairman*, T. Muir

Artists' General Benevolent Institution (1814) and Artists' Orphan Fund (1871), Burlington House, Piccadilly, London W1V 0DJ. Tel: 0171-734 1193. *Secretary*, Ms A. Connett-Dance

Art, Royal Cambrian Academy of (1882), Crown Lane, Conwy LL32 8BH. Tel: 01492-593413. *Curator and Secretary*, Ms V. Macdonald

Arts, National Campaign for the (1984), Francis House, Francis Street, London SW1P 1DE. Tel: 0171-828 4448. *Director*, Ms J. Edwards

Asian Family Counselling Service (1985), 74 The Avenue, London W13 8LB. Tel: 0181-997 5749. *Director*, R. Atma

Aslib (The Association for Information Management) (1924), Staple Hall, Stone House Court, London EC3A 7PB. Tel: 0171-903 0000. *Chief Executive*, R. Bowes

Asthma Campaign, National (1927), Providence House, Providence Place, London N1 0NT. Tel: 0171-226 2260. Helpline: 0345-010203. *Chief Executive*, Ms A. Bradley

Astronomical Association, British (1890), Burlington House, Piccadilly, London W1V 9AG. *Assistant Secretary*, Miss P. M. Barber

ATS/WRAC Association Benevolent Funds (1964), AGC Centre, Worthy Down, Winchester, Hants SO21 2RG. Tel: 01962-887612/478. *Secretaries*, Mrs A. H. S. Matthews; Mrs F. M. White

Audit Bureau of Circulations Ltd (1931), Black Prince Yard, 207– 209 High Street, Berkhamsted, Herts HP4 1AD. Tel: 01442-870800. *Director (acting)*, A. Peacham

Authors, Society of (1884), 84 Drayton Gardens, London SW10 9SB. Tel: 0171-373 6642. *General Secretary*, M. Le Fanu, OBE

Automobile Association (1905), Norfolk House, Priestley Road, Basingstoke, Hants RG24 9NY. Tel: 0990-500600. *Director-General*, J. Maxwell

Ayrshire Cattle Society of Great Britain and Ireland (1877), 1 Racecourse Road, Ayr KA7 2DE. Tel: 01292-267123. *Chief Executive*, S. J. Thomson

Back Pain Association, National (1968), 16 Elmtree Road, Teddington, Middx TW11 8ST. Tel: 0181-977 5474. *Executive Director*, G. Thomas

Baltic Air Charter Association (1949), The Baltic Exchange, St Mary Axe, London EC3A 8BH. Tel: 0171-623 5501. *Chairman*, Mrs G. Malempré

Baltic Exchange (1903), St Mary Axe, London EC3A 8BH. Tel: 0171-369 1621. *Chief Executive*, J. Buckley

Baltic Exchange Charitable Society (1978), 38 St Mary Axe, London EC3A 8BH. Tel: 0171-369 1643. *Secretary*, D. A. Painter

Balzan Foundation, International (1956), Piazzetta U Giordano 4, Milan, Italy 20122. Tel: 00 392-7600 2212. *Secretary-General*, Mrs P. Rognoni

Bankers, Chartered Institute of (1879), 90 Bishopsgate, London EC2N 4AS. Tel: 0171-444 7111. *Chief Executive*, G. Shreeve

Bankers in Scotland, Chartered Institute of (1875), Drumsheugh House, 38B Drumsheugh Gardens, Edinburgh EH3 7SW. Tel: 0131-473 7777. *Chief Executive*, Dr C. W. Munn

Baptist Missionary Society (1792), Baptist House, PO Box 49, 129 Broadway, Didcot, Oxon OX11 8XA. Tel: 01235-512077. *General Director*, Revd Dr A. Brown

Bar Association for Local Government and the Public Service (1945), c/o Head of Legal Services, Bolton MBC, Town Hall, Bolton BL1 1RU. Tel: 01204-522311 ext. 1111. *Chairman*, M. F. N. Ahmad

Barnardo's (1866), Tanners Lane, Barkingside, Ilford, Essex IG6 1QG. Tel: 0181-550 8822. *Senior Director*, R. Singleton

Baronetage, Standing Council of the (1898), The Church House, Bibury, Cirencester, Glos GL7 5NR. *Chairman*, Sir Brian Barttelot, Bt.

Barristers' Benevolent Association (1873), 14 Gray's Inn Square, London WC1R 5JP. Tel: 0171-242 4761. *Secretary*, Mrs A. Ashley

Bee-Keepers' Association, British (1874), National Agricultural Centre, Stoneleigh Park, Kenilworth, Warks CV8 2LZ. Tel: 01203-696679. *General Secretary*, A. C. Waring

Bell Ringers, Central Council of Church (1891), 50 Cramhurst Lane, Witley, Godalming, Surrey GU8 5QZ. Tel: 01428-682790. *Hon. Secretary*, C. H. Rogers

Bevin Boys Association (1989), 147 Cannock Road, Stafford ST17 0QN. Tel: 01785-661042. *Hon. Secretary*, G. K. Thomas

Bible Society, British and Foreign (1804), Stonehill Green, Westlea, Swindon SN5 7DG. Tel: 01793-418100. *Chief Executive*, N. Crosbie

Bibliographical Society (1892), c/o The Wellcome Institute, 183 Euston Road, London NW1 2BE. Tel: 0171-611 7244. *Hon. Secretary*, D. Pearson

Bibliographical Society, Edinburgh (1890), c/o Rare Books Division, National Library of Scotland, George IV Bridge, Edinburgh EH1 1EW. Tel: 0131-226 4531. *Hon. Secretary*, R. Ovenden

Biochemical Society (1911), 59 Portland Place, London W1N 3AJ. Tel: 0171-580 5530. *Executive Secretary*, G. D. Jones

Biology, Institute of (1950), 20– 22 Queensberry Place, London SW7 2DZ. Tel: 0171-581 8333. *Chief Executive*, Prof. A. Malcolm

Birds, *see* Royal Society for the Protection of and Scottish Society for the Protection of Wild

BIRMINGHAM AND MIDLAND INSTITUTE (1854) and PRIESTLEY LIBRARY (1779), Margaret Street, Birmingham B3 3BS. Tel: 0121-236 3591. *Administrator and General Secretary*, P. A. Fisher

BLIND, GUIDE DOGS FOR THE, *see* GUIDE DOGS FOR THE BLIND ASSOCIATION

BLIND, NATIONAL LIBRARY FOR THE (1882), Far Cromwell Road, Bredbury, Stockport, Cheshire SK6 2SG. Tel: 0161-355 2000. *Chief Executive*, Ms M. Bennett

BLIND PEOPLE, ACTION FOR (1857), 14–16 Verney Road, London SE16 3DZ. Tel: 0171-732 8771. *Chief Executive*, S. Remington

BLIND, ROYAL LONDON SOCIETY FOR THE (1838), Dorton House, Seal, Sevenoaks, Kent TN15 0ED. Tel: 01732-761477. *Chief Executive*, P. Talbot

BLIND, ROYAL NATIONAL COLLEGE FOR THE (1872), College Road, Hereford HR1 1EB. Tel: 01432-265725. *Principal*, C. Housby-Smith, PH.D.

BLIND, ROYAL NATIONAL INSTITUTE FOR THE, *see* ROYAL NATIONAL INSTITUTE FOR THE BLIND

BLIND, ROYAL SCHOOL FOR THE, *see* ABILITY

BLOOD AUTHORITY, NATIONAL (1948), Oak House, Reeds Crescent, Watford, Herts WD1 1QH. Tel: 01923-486800. *Chairman*, M. Fogden

BLOOD TRANSFUSION ASSOCIATION, SCOTTISH NATIONAL (1940), c/o Scottish National Blood Transfusion Service, Ellen's Glen Road, Edinburgh EH17 7QT. Tel: 0131-664 2317. *Secretary*, W. Mack

BLUE CROSS (1897), Shilton Road, Burford, Oxon OX18 4PF. Tel: 01993-822651. *Secretary and Chief Executive*, A. Kennard, MBE

BODLEIAN, FRIENDS OF THE (1925), Bodleian Library, Oxford OX1 3BG. Tel: 01865-277022/277234. *Secretary*, G. Groom

BOOK AID INTERNATIONAL (1954), 39–41 Coldharbour Lane, London SE5 9NR. Tel: 0171-733 3577. *Director*, Mrs S. Harrity, MBE

BOOKSELLERS ASSOCIATION OF GREAT BRITAIN AND IRELAND (1895), Minster House, 272 Vauxhall Bridge Road, London SW1V 1BA. Tel: 0171-834 5477. *Chief Executive*, T. E. Godfray

BOOK TRADE BENEVOLENT SOCIETY (1967), Dillon Lodge, The Retreat, Kings Langley, Herts WD4 8LT. Tel: 01923-263128. *Chief Executive*, D. Hicks

BOOK TRUST (1986), Book House, 45 East Hill, London SW18 2QZ. Tel: 0181-516 2977. *Executive Director*, B. Perman

BORN FREE FOUNDATION (1984), 3 Grove House, Foundry Lane, Horsham, W. Sussex RH13 5PL. Tel: 01403-240170. *Director*, W. Travers

BOTANICAL SOCIETY OF SCOTLAND, c/o Royal Botanic Garden, Inverleith Row, Edinburgh EH3 5LR. Tel: 0131-552 7171. *Hon. General Secretary*, R. Galt

BOTANICAL SOCIETY OF THE BRITISH ISLES (1836), c/o Department of Botany, The Natural History Museum, Cromwell Road, London SW7 5BD. *Hon. General Secretary*, R. Gwynn Ellis

BOY SCOUTS ASSOCIATION, *see* SCOUT ASSOCIATION

BOYS' AND GIRLS' CLUBS OF NORTHERN IRELAND (1940), 2nd Floor, 38 Dublin Road, Belfast BT2 7HN. Tel: 01232-241924. *General Secretary*, K. Culbert

BOYS' BRIGADE (1883), Felden Lodge, Hemel Hempstead, Herts HP3 0BL. Tel: 01442-231681. *Brigade Secretary*, S. Jones, OBE

BREWING, INSTITUTE OF (1886), 33 Clarges Street, London W1Y 8EE. Tel: 0171-499 8144. *Chief Executive*, P. W. E. Istead

BRIDEWELL ROYAL HOSPITAL (1553), Witley, Godalming, Surrey GU8 5SG. Tel: 01428-682371. *Clerk*, D. W. Hanson

BRITAIN-NEPAL SOCIETY (1960), 3C Gunnersbury Avenue, London W5 3NH. Tel: 0181-992 0173. *Hon. Secretary*, Mrs P. Mellor

BRITAIN-RUSSIA CENTRE and BRITISH EAST WEST CENTRE (1959), 14 Grosvenor Place, London SW1X 7HW. Tel: 0171-235 2116. *Director*, Dr I. Elliot

BRITISH AND FOREIGN SCHOOL SOCIETY (1808), Croudace House, Godstone Road, Caterham, Surrey CR3 6RE. Tel: 01883-331177. *Director*, J. Kidd

BRITISH EXECUTIVE SERVICE OVERSEAS (1976), 164 Vauxhall Bridge Road, London SW1V 4RB. Tel: 0171-630 0644. *Chief Executive*, G. Ramsey, CBE

BRITISH INSTITUTE IN EASTERN AFRICA (1959), 20–22 Queensberry Place, London SW7 2DZ. Tel: 0171-584 4653. *London Secretary*, Mrs J. Moyo

BRITISH INSTITUTE OF ARCHAEOLOGY AT ANKARA (1948), Senate House, Malet Street, London WC1E 7HU. Tel: 0171-862 8734. *Director*, Dr R. J. Matthews

BRITISH INSTITUTE OF PERSIAN STUDIES (1961), c/o The British Academy, 10 Carlton House Terrace, London SW1Y 5AH. Tel: 0171-969 5203. *Hon. Secretary*, Dr R. Gleave

BRITISH INTERPLANETARY SOCIETY (1933), 27–29 South Lambeth Road, London SW8 1SZ. Tel: 0171-735 3160. *Executive Secretary*, Ms S. A. Jones

BRITISH ISRAEL WORLD FEDERATION (1919), 8 Blades Court, Deodar Road, London SW15 2NU. Tel: 0181-877 9010. *Secretary*, A. E. Gibb

BRITISH LEGION, ROYAL (1921), 48 Pall Mall, London SW1Y 5JY. Tel: 0345-725725. *Secretary-General*, Brig. I. G. Townsend

BRITISH LEGION SCOTLAND, ROYAL (1921), New Haig House, Logie Green Road, Edinburgh EH7 4HR. Tel: 0131-557 2782. *General Secretary*, Maj.-Gen. J. D. MacDonald, CB, CBE

BRITISH MEDICAL ASSOCIATION (1832), BMA House, Tavistock Square, London WC1H 9JP. Tel: 0171-387 4499. *Secretary*, Dr E. M. Armstrong

BRITISH NATIONAL PARTY (1982), PO Box 117, Welling, Kent DA16 3DW. Tel: 0374-454893. *Chairman*, J. Tyndall

BRITISH RED CROSS (1870), 9 Grosvenor Crescent, London SW1X 7EJ. Tel: 0171-235 5454. *Director-General*, M. R. Whitlam

BRITISH RESEARCH IN THE LEVANT, COUNCIL FOR (1998), 29 The Walk, Southport, Merseyside PR8 4GB. Tel: 01704-569664. *Secretary*, Miss C. Middleton

BUDDHIST SOCIETY (1924), 58 Eccleston Square, London SW1V 1PH. Tel: 0171-834 5858. *General Secretary*, R. C. Maddox

BUDGERIGAR SOCIETY (1925), 49–53 Hazelwood Road, Northampton NN1 1LG. Tel: 01604-624549. *General Secretary*, D. Whittaker

BUILDING, CHARTERED INSTITUTE OF (1834), Englemere, King's Ride, Ascot, Berks SL5 7TB. Tel: 01344-630700. *Chief Executive*, K. Banbury

BUILDING ENGINEERS, ASSOCIATION OF (1925), Jubilee House, Billing Brook Road, Weston Favell, Northampton NN3 8NW. Tel: 01604-404121. *Chief Executive*, D. Gibson

BUILDING SERVICES ENGINEERS, CHARTERED
INSTITUTION OF (1897), Delta House, 222 Balham
High Road, London SW12 9BS. Tel: 0181-675 5211. *Chief
Executive*, R. John

BUILDING SOCIETIES ASSOCIATION (1936), 3 Savile Row,
London W1X 1AF. Tel: 0171-437 0655. *Director-General*, A.
Coles

BUSINESS AND PROFESSIONAL WOMEN UK LTD (1938),
23 Ansdell Street, London W8 5BN. Tel: 0171-938 1729.
General Secretary, vacant

BUSINESS ARCHIVES COUNCIL (1934), The Clove
Building, 4 Maguire Street, London SE1 2NQ. Tel: 0171-
407 6110. *Secretary-General*, Ms W. S. Quinn

BUSINESS IN THE COMMUNITY (1982), 44 Baker Street,
London W1M 1DH. Tel: 0171-224 1600. *Chief Executive*,
Ms J. Cleverdon, CBE

BUSINESS SOFTWARE ALLIANCE (1989), 79
Knightsbridge, London SW1X 7RB. Tel: 0171-245 0304.
Managing Director, Mrs E. Knight

CADET FORCE ASSOCIATION, COMBINED (1952), E
Block, The Duke of York's HQ, London SW3 4RR. Tel:
0171-730 9733/4. *Secretary*, Brig. R. B. MacGregor-
Oakford, CBE, MC

CAFOD (CATHOLIC FUND FOR OVERSEAS
DEVELOPMENT) (1962), Romero Close, Stockwell
Road, London SW9 9TY. Tel: 0171-733 7900. *Director*, J.
Filochowski

CALOUSTE GULBENKIAN FOUNDATION (1956), 98
Portland Place, London W1N 4ET. Tel: 0171-636 5313.
Director, B. Whitaker

CAMBRIDGE PRESERVATION SOCIETY (1929),
Wandlebury Ring, Gog Magog Hills, Babraham,
Cambridge CB2 4AE. Tel: 01223-243830. *Director*, R.
Whittaker; *Secretary*, D. J. Carrott

CAMERON FUND (1971), Tavistock House North,
Tavistock Square, London WC1H 9HR. Tel: 0171-
388 0796. *Secretary*, Mrs J. Martin

CAMPAIGN FOR COURTESY, *see* POLITE SOCIETY

CAMPAIGN FOR NUCLEAR DISARMAMENT (CND)
(1958), 162 Holloway Road, London N7 8DQ. Tel: 0171-
700 2393. *Chair*, D. Knight

CancerBACUP (FORMERLY BRITISH ASSOCIATION OF
CANCER UNITED PATIENTS (BACUP)) (1985), 3 Bath
Place, Rivington Street, London EC2A 3JR. Tel: 0800-
181199. *Chief Executive*, Mrs J. Mossman

CANCER CARE, MARIE CURIE, *see* MARIE CURIE CANCER
CARE

CANCER CARE FOR CHILDREN, SARGENT (1968), 14
Abingdon Road, London W8 6AF. Tel: 0171-565 5100.
Chief Executive, Mrs D. Yeo

CANCER RELIEF, MACMILLAN (1911), Anchor House,
15–19 Britten Street, London SW3 3TZ. Tel: 0171-
351 7811. *Chief Executive*, N. Young

CANCER RESEARCH CAMPAIGN, 10 Cambridge Terrace,
London NW1 4JL. Tel: 0171-224 1333. *Director-General*,
Prof. J. G. McVie

CANCER RESEARCH FUND, IMPERIAL (1902), PO Box 123,
Lincoln's Inn Fields, London WC2A 3PX. Tel: 0171-
242 0200. *Director-General*, Dr P. Nurse, FRS

CANCER RESEARCH: ROYAL CANCER HOSPITAL,
INSTITUTE OF, 17A Onslow Gardens, London SW7 3AL.
Tel: 0171-352 8133. *Chief Executive*, Prof. P. B. Garland

CARERS NATIONAL ASSOCIATION (1988), Ruth Pitter
House, 20–25 Glasshouse Yard, London EC1A 4JS. Tel:
0171-490 8818. *Chief Executive*, Baroness Pitkeathley,
OBE

CARNEGIE DUNFERMLINE TRUST (1903), Abbey Park
House, Dunfermline, Fife KY12 7PB. Tel: 01383-723638.
Secretary, W. C. Runciman

CARNEGIE HERO FUND TRUST (1908), Abbey Park
House, Dunfermline, Fife KY12 7PB. Tel: 01383-723638.
Secretary, W. C. Runciman

CARNEGIE UNITED KINGDOM TRUST (1913), Comely
Park House, Dunfermline, Fife KY12 7EJ. Tel: 01383-
721445. *Secretary*, C. J. Naylor, OBE

CATHEDRALS FABRIC COMMISSION FOR ENGLAND
(1949), Fielden House, 13 Little College Street,
London SW1P 3SH. Tel: 0171-222 3793. *Secretary*, Dr R.
Gem

CATHOLIC ENQUIRY OFFICE (1954), The Chase Centre,
114 West Heath Road, London NW3 7TX. Tel: 0181-
458 3316. *Secretary*, Fr J. O'Toole

CATHOLIC RECORD SOCIETY (1904), c/o 12 Melbourne
Place, Wolsingham, Co. Durham DL13 3EH. Tel: 01388-
527747. *Hon. Secretary*, Dr L. Gooch

CATHOLIC TRUTH SOCIETY (1868), 40–46 Harleyford
Road, London SE11 5AY. Tel: 0171-640 0042. *General
Secretary*, F. Martin

CATHOLIC UNION OF GREAT BRITAIN (1872), St
Maximilian Kolbe House, 63 Jeddo Road, London
W12 9EE. Tel: 0181-749 1321. *Secretary*, P. H. Higgs

CATTLE ASSOCIATION, NATIONAL, 60 Kenilworth Road,
Leamington Spa, Warks CV32 6JX. Tel: 01926-337378.
Secretary, Miss K. S. Brake

CATTLE BREEDERS' CLUB LTD, BRITISH (1945), Hayleys
Manor, Upland Road, Thornwood, Epping, Essex
CM16 6PQ. Tel: 01992-572511. *Secretary*, Mrs J. Padfield

CENTRAL AND CECIL HOUSING TRUST (1926), 2 Priory
Road, Kew, Richmond, Surrey TW9 3DG. Tel: 0181-
940 9828. *Director and Secretary*, G. Brighton

CENTRAL BUREAU FOR EDUCATIONAL VISITS AND
EXCHANGES (1948), 10 Spring Gardens, London
SW1A 2BN. Tel: 0171-389 4004. *Director*, A. H. Male

CENTREPOINT (1969), Bewlay House, 2 Swallow Place,
London W1R 7AA. Tel: 0171-544 5000. *Chief Executive*, V.
O. Adebowale

CHADWICK TRUST (1895), Department of Civil and
Environmental Engineering, University College,
Gower Street, London WC1E 6BT. Tel: 0171-380 7327/
7766. *Secretary to the Trustees*, I. K. Orchardson, PH.D.

CHANTREY BEQUEST (1875), Royal Academy of Arts,
Burlington House, Piccadilly, London W1V 0DS. Tel:
0171-439 7438. *Secretary*, P. Rodgers

CHARITIES AID FOUNDATION (1974), Kings Hill, West
Malling, Kent ME19 4TA. Tel: 01732-520000. *Chief
Executive*, M. Brophy

CHEMICAL ENGINEERS, INSTITUTION OF (1922), Davis
Building, 165–189 Railway Terrace, Rugby, Warks
CV21 3HQ. Tel: 01788-578214. *Chief Executive*, Dr T. J.
Evans

CHEMISTRY, ROYAL SOCIETY OF, Burlington House,
Piccadilly, London W1V 0BN. Tel: 0171-437 8656.
Secretary-General, Dr T. D. Inch

CHESHIRE (LEONARD) FOUNDATION, *see* LEONARD
CHESHIRE

CHESS FEDERATION, BRITISH (1904), 9A Grand Parade,
St Leonards-on-Sea, E. Sussex TN38 0DD. Tel: 01424-
442500. *Manager*, Mrs G. White

CHEST, HEART AND STROKE ASSOCIATION, *see* STROKE
ASSOCIATION

CHILDBIRTH TRUST, NATIONAL (1956), Alexandra House, Oldham Terrace, London W3 6NH. Tel: 0181-992 8637. *Director*, Ms C. Swarbrick

CHILDREN 1ST (ROYAL SCOTTISH SOCIETY FOR PREVENTION OF CRUELTY TO CHILDREN) (1884), Melville House, 41 Polwarth Terrace, Edinburgh EH11 1NU. Tel: 0131-337 8539. *Chief Executive*, A. M. M. Wood, OBE

CHILDREN'S SOCIETY, THE (1881), Edward Rudolf House, Margery Street, London WC1X 0JL. Tel: 0171-837 4299. *Chief Executive*, I. Sparks

CHINA ASSOCIATION (1889), Swire House, 59 Buckingham Gate, London SW1E 6AJ. Tel: 0171-821 3220. *Executive Director*, D. F. L. Turner

CHIROPODISTS AND PODIATRISTS, SOCIETY OF (1945), 53 Welbeck Street, London W1M 7HE. Tel: 0171-486 3381. *General Secretary*, J. G. C. Trouncer

CHIROPRACTIC ASSOCIATION, BRITISH (1925), Blagrave House, 17 Blagrave Street, Reading, Berks RG1 1QB. Tel: 0118-950 5950. *Executive Director*, Miss S. A. Wakefield

CHOIRS SCHOOLS ASSOCIATION (1921), The Minster School, Deangate, York YO1 2JA. Tel: 01904-624900. *Administrator*, Mrs W. Jackson

CHRISTIAN AID (1945), PO Box 100, London SE1 7RT. Tel: 0171-620 4444. *Director*, Revd M. H. Taylor

CHRISTIAN EDUCATION COUNCIL, NATIONAL (1809), 1020 Bristol Road, Selly Oak, Birmingham B29 6LB. Tel: 0121-472 4242. *General Manager*, Mrs. S. Sharman

CHRISTIAN EDUCATION MOVEMENT (1965), Royal Buildings, Victoria Street, Derby DE1 1GW. Tel: 01332-296655. *Director*, Revd Dr S. Orchard

CHRISTIAN KNOWLEDGE, SOCIETY FOR PROMOTING (SPCK) (1698), Holy Trinity Church, Marylebone Road, London NW1 4DU. Tel: 0171-387 5282. *General Secretary*, P. Chandler

CHRISTIANS AND JEWS, COUNCIL OF (1942), Drayton House, 30 Gordon Street, London WC1H 0AN. Tel: 0171-388 3322. *Director*, P. Mendel

CHURCH ARMY (1882), Independents Road, London SE3 9LG. Tel: 0181-318 1226. *Chief Secretary*, Capt. P. Johanson

CHURCH BUILDING SOCIETY, INCORPORATED (1818), Fulham Palace, London SW6 6EA. Tel: 0171-736 3054. *Secretary*, M. W. Tippen

CHURCH EDUCATION CORPORATION, Bedgebury School, Goudhurst, Cranbrook, Kent TN17 2SH. Tel: 01580-211211. *Secretary*, Mr N. Willoughby, FCIS

CHURCH HOUSE, THE CORPORATION OF (1888), Church House, Dean's Yard, London SW1P 3NZ. Tel: 0171-222 5261. *Secretary*, C. D. L. Menzies

CHURCH LADS' AND CHURCH GIRLS' BRIGADE (1891), 2 Barnsley Road, Wath upon Dearne, Rotherham, S. Yorks S63 6PY. Tel: 01709-876535. *General Secretary*, J. S. Cresswell

CHURCH MISSION SOCIETY (1799), Partnership House, 157 Waterloo Road, London SE1 8UU. Tel: 0171-928 8681. *General Secretary*, Canon D. K. Witts

CHURCH MONUMENTS SOCIETY (1979), c/o Society of Antiquaries, Burlington House, Piccadilly, London W1V 0HS. Tel: 0171-734 0193. *Hon. Secretary*, C. J. Easter

CHURCH MUSIC, ROYAL SCHOOL OF (1927), Cleveland Lodge, Westhumble, Dorking, Surrey RH5 6BW. Tel: 01306-877676. *Director-General*, Prof. J. Harper

CHURCH OF ENGLAND PENSIONS BOARD (1926), 7 Little College Street, London SW1P 3SF. Tel: 0171-222 2091. *Secretary*, R. G. Radford

CHURCH SOCIETY, INTERCONTINENTAL (1823), 1 Athena Drive, Tachbrook Park, Warwick CV34 6NL. Tel: 01926-430347. *International Director*, Revd Canon J. R. Moore

CHURCH UNION (1859), Faith House, 7 Tufton Street, London SW1P 3QN. Tel: 0171-222 6952. *House Manager*, Mrs J. Miller

CHURCHES, COUNCIL FOR THE CARE OF (1921), Fielden House, 13 Little College Street, London SW1P 3SH. Tel: 0171-222 3793. *Secretary*, Dr T. Cocke

CHURCHES, FRIENDS OF FRIENDLESS (1957), St Ann's Vestry Hall, 2 Church Entry, London EC4V 5HB. Tel: 0171-236 3934. *Hon. Director*, M. Saunders, MBE

CHURCHES MAIN COMMITTEE (1941), Fielden House, 13 Little College Street, London SW1P 3SH. Tel: 0171-222 4984. *Secretary*, D. Taylor Thompson, CB

CHURCHILL SOCIETY (1990), 18 Grove Lane, Ipswich, Suffolk IP4 1NR. Tel: 01473-413533. *General Secretary*, N. H. Rogers

CITIZEN'S ADVICE BUREAUX, NATIONAL ASSOCIATION OF (1931), Myddelton House, 115–123 Pentonville Road, London N1 9LZ. Tel: 0171-833 2181. *Chief Executive*, D. Harker

CITY BUSINESS LIBRARY, Brewers Hall Garden, London EC2V 5BX. Tel: 0171-638 8215.

CITY PAROCHIAL FOUNDATION (1891), 6 Middle Street, London EC1A 7PH. Tel: 0171-606 6145. *Clerk*, B. Mehta

CIVIC TRUST (1957), 17 Carlton House Terrace, London SW1Y 5AW. Tel: 0171-930 0914. *Director*, M. Gwilliam

CIVIL ENGINEERS, INSTITUTION OF (1818), 1–7 Great George Street, London SW1A 3AA. Tel: 0171-222 7722. *Director-General*, R. S. Dobson, OBE, FEng.

CIVIL LIBERTIES, NATIONAL COUNCIL FOR, *see* LIBERTY

CLASSICAL ASSOCIATION (1903), Department of Classics, University of Keele, Keele, Newcastle under Lyme, Staffs ST5 5BG. Tel: 01782-583048. *Hon. Treasurer*, R. Wallace

CLEAR AIR AND ENVIRONMENTAL PROTECTION, NATIONAL SOCIETY FOR (1899), 136 North Street, Brighton BN1 1RG. Tel: 01273-326313. *Secretary-General*, R. Mills

CLERGY ORPHAN CORPORATION (1749), 1 Dean Trench Street, London SW1P 3HB. Tel: 0171-799 3696. *Registrar*, R. C. F. Leach

CLERKS OF WORKS OF GREAT BRITAIN, INSTITUTE OF (1882), 41 The Mall, London W5 3TJ. Tel: 0181-579 2917. *General Secretary*, A. P. Macnamara

COACHING CLUB (1871), Craigmore, 24 Barton View, Penrith, Cumbria CA11 8AX. *Secretary*, A. S. Cowdery

COLITIS AND CROHN'S DISEASE, NATIONAL ASSOCIATION FOR (1979), PO Box 205, St Albans, Herts AL1 1AB. Tel: 01727-844296/830038. *Director*, R. Driscoll

COMMERCE, BRITISH CHAMBERS OF (1860), Manning House, 22 Carlisle Place, London SW1P 1JA. Tel: 0171-565 2000. *Director-General*, C. Humphries

COMMERCE AND INDUSTRY, LONDON CHAMBER OF, 33 Queen Street, London EC4R 1AP. Tel: 0171-248 4444. *Chief Executive*, S. G. Sperryn

COMMERCE AND MANUFACTURERS, EDINBURGH CHAMBER OF (1786), 3 Randolph Crescent, Edinburgh EH3 7UD. Tel: 0131-225 5851. *Chief Executive*, D. I. Brown

COMMERCE AND MANUFACTURES, GLASGOW CHAMBER OF (1783), 30 George Square, Glasgow G2 1EQ. Tel: 0141-204 2121. *Chief Executive*, P. V. Burdon

COMMERCE, CANADA-UNITED KINGDOM CHAMBER OF (1921), 38 Grosvenor Street, London W1X 0DP. Tel: 0171-258 6572. *Executive Director*, M. Hall

COMMERCE, SCOTTISH CHAMBERS OF, Conference House, The Exchange, 152 Morrison Street, Edinburgh EH3 8EB. Tel: 0131-477 8025. *Director*, L. Gold

COMMERCIAL TRAVELLERS' BENEVOLENT INSTITUTION (1849), 54 Rothbury Avenue, Regent Farm Estate, Gosforth, Newcastle upon Tyne NE3 3HL. Tel: 0191-284 9100. *Secretary*, Mrs G. Tate

COMMISSIONAIRES, THE CORPS OF (1859), Market House, 85 Cowcross Street, London EC1M 6BP. Tel: 0171-490 1125. *Managing Director*, C. J. Salt

COMMUNICATORS IN BUSINESS, BRITISH ASSOCIATION OF (1949), 42 Borough High Street, London SE1 1XW. Tel: 0171-378 7139. *Director*, Mrs. K. Jones

COMPLEMENTARY AND ALTERNATIVE MEDICINE, COUNCIL FOR (1985), 179 Gloucester Place, London NW1 6DX. Tel: 0171-724 9103. *Secretary*, Ms C. Daglish

COMPLEMENTARY MEDICINE, INSTITUTE FOR (1856), PO Box 194, London SE16 1QZ. Tel: 0171-237 5165. *Director*, A. Baird

COMPOSERS' GUILD OF GREAT BRITAIN (1945), The Penthouse, 4 Brook Street, London W1Y 1AA. Tel: 0171-629 0886. *General Secretary*, Ms N. Moskovic

COMPUTER SOCIETY, BRITISH (1957), 1 Sanford Street, Swindon SN1 1HJ. Tel: 01793-417417. *Chief Executive*, Ms J. M. Scott

CONSERVATION OF HISTORIC AND ARTISTIC WORKS, INTERNATIONAL INSTITUTE FOR (1950), 6 Buckingham Street, London WC2N 6BA. Tel: 0171-839 5975. *Secretary-General*, D. Bomford

CONSERVATION VOLUNTEERS, BRITISH TRUST FOR (BTCV) (1970), 36 St Mary's Street, Wallingford, Oxon OX10 0EU. Tel: 01491-839766. *Chief Executive*, T. O. Flood

CONSULTANTS BUREAU, BRITISH (1965), 1 Westminster Palace Gardens, 1–7 Artillery Row, London SW1P 1RJ. Tel: 0171-222 3651. *Director*, C. Adams, CBE

CONSULTING ECONOMISTS' ASSOCIATION, INTERNATIONAL (1986), 3 St George's Court, Putney Bridge Road, London SW15 2PA. Tel: 0181-875 9960. *Secretary*, J. Butler

CONSULTING ENGINEERS, ASSOCIATION OF (1913), Alliance House, 12 Caxton Street, London SW1H 0QL. Tel: 0171-222 6557. *Chief Executive*, N. Bennett

CONSULTING SCIENTISTS, ASSOCIATION OF (1958), PO Box 4040, Thorpe-le-Soken, Clacton-on-Sea CO16 0EL. Tel: 01225-862526. *Hon. Secretary*, W. G. Simpson

CONSUMERS' ASSOCIATION (1957), c/o The Association for Consumer Research, 2 Marylebone Road, London NW1 4DF. Tel: 0171-830 6000. *Director*, Ms S. McKechnie, OBE

CONTEMPORARY APPLIED ARTS (1948), 2 Percy Street, London W1P 9FA. Tel: 0171-436 2344. *Director*, Ms M. La Trobe-Bateman

CONVENIENCE STORES, ASSOCIATION OF (1890), Federation House, 17 Farnborough Street, Farnborough, Hants GU14 8AG. Tel: 01252-515001. *Chief Executive*, T. Dixon

CONVEYANCERS, COUNCIL FOR LICENSED (1986), 16 Glebe Road, Chelmsford, Essex CM1 1QG. Tel: 01245-349599. *Director*, Mrs V. Eden

CO-OPERATIVE PARTY, Victory House, 10–14 Leicester Square, London WC2H 7QH. Tel: 0171-439 0123. *Secretary*, P. Hunt

CO-OPERATIVE UNION LTD (1869), Holyoake House, Hanover Street, Manchester M60 0AS. Tel: 0161-832 4300. *Chief Executive*, D. L. Wilkinson

CO-OPERATIVE WHOLESALE SOCIETY LTD (1863), PO Box 53, New Century House, Manchester M60 4ES. Tel: 0161-834 1212. *Chief Executive*, G. J. Melmoth

COPYRIGHT COUNCIL, BRITISH (1953), 29–33 Berners Street, London W1P 4AA. Tel: 01986-788122. *Secretary*, Ms J. Ibbotson

CORONERS' SOCIETY OF ENGLAND AND WALES (1846), 44 Ormond Avenue, Hampton, Middx TW12 2RX. *Hon. Secretary*, M. J. G. Burgess

CORPORATE TREASURERS, ASSOCIATION OF (1979), Ocean House, 10–12 Little Trinity Lane, London EC4V 2AA. Tel: 0171-213 9728. *Director-General*, Dr D. Creed

CORPORATE TRUSTEES, ASSOCIATION OF (1974), The Glen House, 43 Surrey Road, Westbourne, Bournemouth, Dorset BH4 9HR. Tel: 01202-765559. *Secretary*, R. J. Payne

CORRESPONDENCE COLLEGES, ASSOCIATION OF BRITISH (1955), PO Box 17926, London SW19 3WB. Tel: 0181-544 9559. *Secretary*, Mrs H. Owen

CORRYMEELA COMMUNITY (1965), Corrymeela House, 8 Upper Crescent, Belfast BT7 1NT. Tel: 01232-325008. *Leader*, Revd T. Williams

COTTON GROWING ASSOCIATION, BRITISH (1904), Knowle Hill Park, Fairmile Lane, Cobham, Surrey KT11 2PD. Tel: 01932-861000. *Managing Director*, P. R. Walters

COUNCIL FOR THE PROTECTION OF RURAL ENGLAND, *see* CPRE

COUNCIL SECRETARIES AND SOLICITORS, ASSOCIATION OF (1974, merged 1996), Foxcroft, Gill Lane, Longton, Preston PR4 4SR. Tel: 01772-611167. *Executive Officer*, N. Yates

COUNSEL AND CARE (1954), Twyman House, 16 Bonny Street, London NW1 9PG. Tel: 0845-300 7585. *General Manager*, J. Smith

COUNTRY HOUSES ASSOCIATION (1955), Suite 10, Aynhoe Park, Aynho, Banbury, Oxon OX17 3BQ. Tel: 01869-812800. *Chief Executive*, A. R. A. Bennett

COUNTRY LANDOWNERS ASSOCIATION (1907), 16 Belgrave Square, London SW1X 8PQ. Tel: 0171-235 0511. *Director-General*, J. A. Anderson

COUNTRYSIDE ALLIANCE (1930), Old Town Hall, 367 Kennington Road, London SE11 4PT. Tel: 0171-582 5432. *Chief Executive*, vacant

COUNTY CHIEF EXECUTIVES, ASSOCIATION OF (1974), Office of the Chief Executive, County Hall, West Bridgeford, Nottingham NG2 7QP. Tel: 0115-977 3582. *Hon. Secretary*, P. Housden

COUNTY EMERGENCY PLANNING OFFICERS' SOCIETY, *see* EMERGENCY PLANNING SOCIETY

COUNTY SECRETARIES, SOCIETY OF, *see* COUNCIL SECRETARIES AND SOLICITORS, ASSOCIATION OF

COUNTY SURVEYORS' SOCIETY, *see* CSS

COUNTY TREASURERS, SOCIETY OF (1903), County Hall, West Bridgford, Nottingham NG2 7QP. *Hon. Secretary*, R. Latham

CPRE (COUNCIL FOR THE PROTECTION OF RURAL ENGLAND) (1926), Warwick House, 25 Buckingham Palace Road, London SW1W 0PP. Tel: 0171-976 6433. *Director*, Ms K. Parminter

CRAFTS COUNCIL (1971), 44A Pentonville Road, London N1 9BY. Tel: 0171-278 7700. *Director*, T. Ford

CRISIS (1967), 1st Floor, Challenger House, 42 Adler Street, London E1 1EE. Tel: 0171-377 0489. *Director*, S. Ghosh

CROSSLINKS (1922), 251 Lewisham Way, London SE4 1XF. Tel: 0181-691 6111. *General Secretary*, Revd R. Bowen

CRUEL SPORTS, LEAGUE AGAINST (1924), 83–87 Union Street, London SE1 1SG. Tel: 0171-403 6155. *Chief Officer*, G. Sirl

CRUELTY TO ANIMALS, SOCIETY FOR THE PREVENTION OF, *see* ROYAL and SCOTTISH

CRUELTY TO CHILDREN, SOCIETY FOR THE PREVENTION OF, *see* CHILDREN 1ST and NATIONAL

CRUSE BEREAVEMENT CARE (1959), 126 Sheen Road, Richmond, Surrey TW9 1UR. Tel: 0181-940 4818. Bereavement line: 0181-332 7227. *Executive Director*, Dr C. Easton

CSS (formerly County Surveyors' Society) (1884), c/o Director of Environmental Services, County Offices, Matlock DE4 3AG. Tel: 01629-585730. *Hon. Secretary*, D. Harvey

CTC (CYCLISTS' TOURING CLUB) (1878), Cotterell House, 69 Meadrow, Godalming, Surrey GU7 3HS. Tel: 01483-417217. *Director*, K. Mayne

CURWEN INSTITUTE (1875), 5 Bigbury Close, Styvechale, Coventry CV3 5AJ. Tel: 01203-413010. *Director*, J. Dowding

CWMNI URDD GOBAITH CYMRU (1922), Swyddfa'r Urdd, Aberystwyth, Dyfed SY23 1EN. Tel: 01970-623744. *Chief Executive*, J. O'Rourke

CYCLISTS' TOURING CLUB, *see* CTC

CYMMRODORION, THE HONOURABLE SOCIETY OF (1751), 30 Eastcastle Street, London W1N 7PD. Tel: 0171-631 0502. *Hon. Secretary*, J. Samuel

CYSTIC FIBROSIS TRUST (1964), 11 London Road, Bromley, Kent BR1 1BY. Tel: 0181-464 7211. *Chief Executive*, Ms R. Barnes

DAIRY FARMERS, ROYAL ASSOCIATION OF BRITISH (1876), Dairy House, 60 Kenilworth Road, Leamington Spa, Warks CV32 6JX. Tel: 01926 887477. *Chief Executive*, P. M. Gilbert

DAIRY TECHNOLOGY, SOCIETY OF (1943), 72 Ermine Street, Huntingdon, Cambs PE18 6EZ. Tel: 01480-450741. *National Secretary*, Mrs R. Gale

DATA (DESIGN AND TECHNOLOGY ASSOCIATION), 16 Wellesbourne House, Walton Road, Wellesbourne, Warks CV35 9JB. Tel: 01789-470007. *Chairman*, Dr R. V. Peacock, OBE

D-DAY AND NORMANDY FELLOWSHIP (1968), 9 South Parade, Southsea, Hants PO5 2JB. Tel: 01705-812180. *Hon. Secretary*, Mrs L. R. Reed

DEAF, COMMONWEALTH SOCIETY FOR THE (SOUND SEEKERS) (1959), 138 Buckingham Palace Road, London SW1W 9SA. Tel: 0171-259 0200. *Chief Executive*, Brig. J. A. Davies

DEAF ASSOCIATION, BRITISH (formerly British Deaf and Dumb Association) (1890), 1 Worship Street, London EC2A 2AB. Tel: 0171-588 3520. *Chief Executive*, J. McWhinney

DEAF CHILDREN, ROYAL SCHOOL FOR (1792), Victoria Road, Margate, Kent CT9 1NB. Tel: 01843-227561. *Secretary*, J. C. Gunnell, OBE

DEAF PEOPLE, FOLEY HOUSE RESIDENTIAL HOME FOR (1851), Foley House, 115 High Garrett, Braintree, Essex CM7 5NU. Tel: 01376-326552. *Director*, J. Bethell

DEAF PEOPLE, ROYAL ASSOCIATION IN AID OF (1841), 27 Old Oak Road, London W3 7HN. Tel: 0181-743 6187. *General Secretary*, B. Edmond

DEAF PEOPLE, ROYAL NATIONAL INSTITUTE FOR (1911), 19–23 Featherstone Street, London EC1Y 8SL. Tel: 0870-605 0123 (voice); 0870-603 3007 (text). *Chief Executive*, J. Strachan

DEFENCE STUDIES, ROYAL UNITED SERVICES INSTITUTE FOR (1831), Whitehall, London SW1A 2ET. Tel: 0171-930 5854. *Director*, Rear-Adm. R. Cobbold, CB

DEMOCRATIC LEFT (1991), 6 Cynthia Street, London N1 9JF. Tel: 0171-278 4443. *Secretary*, Ms N. Temple

DENTAL ASSOCIATION, BRITISH (1880), 64 Wimpole Street, London W1M 8AL. Tel: 0171-935 0875. *Chief Executive*, J. M. G. Hunt

DENTAL COUNCIL, GENERAL (1956), 37 Wimpole Street, London W1M 8DQ. Tel: 0171-887 3800. *Chief Executive*, Mrs R. M. Hepplewhite

DENTAL HOSPITALS OF THE UNITED KINGDOM, ASSOCIATION OF (1942), Birmingham Dental Hospital, St Chad's Queensway, Birmingham B4 6NN. Tel: 0121-236 8611. *Hon. Secretary*, Mrs P. Harrington

DESIGN AND INDUSTRIES ASSOCIATION (1915), Business Design Centre, 52 Upper Street, London N1 0QH. Tel: 0171-288 6212. *Chairman*, G. Adams

DESIGNERS, CHARTERED SOCIETY OF (1930), 32–38 Saffron Hill, London EC1N 8FH. Tel: 0171-831 9777. *President*, Ms A. Leman

DESIGNERS FOR INDUSTRY, FACULTY OF ROYAL (1936), RSA, 8 John Adam Street, London WC2N 6EZ. Tel: 0171-930 5115. *Administrator*, Ms J. Thackray

DIABETIC ASSOCIATION, BRITISH (1934), 10 Queen Anne Street, London W1M 0BD. Tel: 0171-323 1531. *Director-General*, M. Cooper

DIANA, PRINCESS OF WALES MEMORIAL FUND (1997), County Hall, Westminster Bridge Road, London SE1 7PB. Tel: 0171-902 5500. *Chief Executive*, Dr A. Purkis

DICKENS FELLOWSHIP (1902), Dickens House, 48 Doughty Street, London W1 2LF. Tel: 0171-405 2127. *Hon. General Secretary*, E. G. Preston

DIRECTORS, INSTITUTE OF (1903), 116 Pall Mall, London SW1Y 5ED. Tel: 0171-839 1233. *Director-General*, T. Melville-Ross

DIRECTORS OF PUBLIC HEALTH, ASSOCIATION OF (1982), Walsall Health Authority, Lichfield House, 27–31 Lichfield Street, Walsall, West Midlands WS1 1TE. Tel: 01922-720255. *Hon. Secretary*, Dr S. Ramaiah

DIRECTORY AND DATABASE PUBLISHERS ASSOCIATION (1970), 93A Blenheim Crescent, London W11 2EQ. Tel: 0171-221 9089. *Secretary*, Ms R. Pettit

DISPENSING OPTICIANS, ASSOCIATION OF BRITISH (1925), 6 Hurlingham Business Park, Sulivan Road, London SW6 3DU. Tel: 0171-736 0088. *Registrar*, D. S. Baker

DISTRICT SECRETARIES, ASSOCIATION OF, *see* COUNCIL SECRETARIES AND SOLICITORS, ASSOCIATION OF

DITCHLEY FOUNDATION, Ditchley Park, Enstone, Chipping Norton, Oxon OX7 4ER. Tel: 01608-677346. *Director,* Sir Michael Quinlan, GCB

DOWNS SYNDROME ASSOCIATION (1970), 155 Mitcham Road, London SW17 9PG. Tel: 0181-682 4001. *Director,* Ms C. Boys

DOWSERS, BRITISH SOCIETY OF (1933), Sycamore Barn, Hastingleigh, Ashford, Kent TN25 5HW. Tel: 01233-750253. *Secretary,* M. D. Rust

DRAINAGE AUTHORITIES, ASSOCIATION OF (1937), The Mews, 3 Royal Oak Passage, High Street, Huntingdon, Cambs PE18 6EA. Tel: 01480-411123. *Secretary,* D. Noble

DRINKING FOUNTAIN AND CATTLE TROUGH ASSOCIATION, METROPOLITAN (1859), Oaklands, 5 Queensborough Gardens, Chislehurst, Kent BR7 6NP. Tel: 0181-467 1261. *Secretary,* R. P. Baber

DRIVING SOCIETY, BRITISH (1957), 27 Dugard Place, Barford, Warwick CV35 8DX. Tel: 01926-624420. *Secretary,* Mrs J. M. Dillon

DRUG DEPENDENCE, INSTITUTE FOR THE STUDY OF (1968), 32 Loman Street, London SE1 0EE. Tel: 0171-928 1211. *Director,* Ms A. Bradley

DUKE OF EDINBURGH'S AWARD, THE (1956), Gulliver House, Madeira Walk, Windsor, Berks SL4 1EU. Tel: 01753-810753. *Director,* Vice-Adm. M. P. Gretton, CB

DYERS AND COLOURISTS, SOCIETY OF (1884), PO Box 244, Perkin House, 82 Grattan Road, Bradford BD1 2JB. Tel: 01274-725138. *General Secretary,* K. M. McGhee

DYSLEXIA INSTITUTE (1972), 133 Gresham Road, Staines, Middlesex TW18 2AJ. Tel: 01784-463851. *Executive Director,* Mrs E. J. Brooks

EARLY CHILDHOOD EDUCATION, BRITISH ASSOCIATION FOR (1923), 111 City View House, 463 Bethnal Green Road, London E2 9QY. Tel: 0171-739 7594. *Secretary,* Mrs B. Boon

EATING DISORDERS ASSOCIATION (1989), First Floor, Wensum House, 103 Prince of Wales Road, Norwich NR1 1DW. Tel: 01603-619090. Helpline: 01603-621414. *Chief Executive,* Mrs. N. Bryant

ECCLESIASTICAL HISTORY SOCIETY (1961), Department of History (Medieval), University of Glasgow, Glasgow G12 8QQ. Tel: 0141-330 4087. *Secretary,* M. J. Kennedy

ECCLESIOLOGICAL SOCIETY (1839), Underedge, Back Lane, Hathersage, Sheffield S32 1AR. Tel: 01433-650833. *Hon. Secretary,* Prof. K. H. Murta, FRIBA

ECONOMIC AFFAIRS, INSTITUTE OF (1955), 2 Lord North Street, London SW1P 3LB. Tel: 0171-799 3745. *General Director,* J. Blundell

EDITH CAVELL AND NATION'S FUND FOR NURSES (1917), Flints, Petersfield Road, Winchester, Hants SO23 0JD. Tel: 01962-860900. *Administrator,* Mrs A. Rich

EDITORS, GUILD OF (1946), Bloomsbury House, 74–77 Great Russell Street, London WC1B 3DA. Tel: 0171-436 2445. *Secretary,* Mrs V. L. Hird

EDUCATION OFFICERS' SOCIETY, COUNTY (1889), Education Department, Northamptonshire County Council, PO Box 149, County Hall, Northampton NN1 1AU. Tel: 01604-236250. *Secretary,* J. R. Atkinson

EDUCATION OFFICERS, SOCIETY OF (1971), Boulton House, 17–21 Chorlton Street, Manchester M1 3HY. Tel: 0161-236 5766. *General Secretary,* A. Collier

EDUCATIONAL RESEARCH IN ENGLAND AND WALES, NATIONAL FOUNDATION FOR (1946), The Mere, Upton Park, Slough SL1 2DQ. Tel: 01753-574123. *Director,* Dr S. Hegarty

EGYPT EXPLORATION SOCIETY (1882), 3 Doughty Mews, London WC1N 2PG. Tel: 0171-242 1880. *Secretary,* Dr P. A. Spencer

ELECTORAL REFORM SOCIETY, 6 Chancel Street, London SE1 0UU. Tel: 0171-928 1622. *President,* Baroness Seear

ELECTRICAL ENGINEERS, INSTITUTION OF (1871), Savoy Place, London WC2R 0BL. Tel: 0171-240 1871. *Secretary,* J. C. Williams, OBE, PH.D., FEng.

ELGAR FOUNDATION (1973), Pippins, Kinnersley, Severn Stoke, Worcs WR8 9JR. *Secretary to the Trustees,* Air Cdre B. W. Opie

ELGAR SOCIETY (1951), c/o 29 Van Diemens Close, Chinnor, Oxon OX9 4QE. Tel: 01844-354096. *Hon. Secretary,* Ms W. Hillary

EMERGENCY PLANNING SOCIETY (1966), Emergency Planning Officer, London Borough of Brent, Pyramid House, Forthway, Wembley, Middx HA9 0LJ. Tel: 0181-908 7035. *Hon. Secretary,* K. D. Gosling

ENABLE (SCOTTISH SOCIETY FOR THE MENTALLY HANDICAPPED) (1954), 7 Buchanan Street, Glasgow G1 3HL. Tel: 0141-226 4541. *Director,* N. Dunning

ENERGY ASSOCIATION, BRITISH (1924), 34 St James's Street, London SW1A 1HD. Tel: 0171-930 1211. *Director,* M. Jefferson

ENERGY, INSTITUTE OF (1927), 18 Devonshire Street, London W1N 2AU. Tel: 0171-580 7124. *Secretary,* J. E. H. Leach

ENERGY SAVING TRUST (1992), 21 Dartmouth Street, London SW1H 9BP. Tel: 0171-222 0101. *Chief Executive,* Dr E. Lees

ENGINEERING COUNCIL, THE (1981), 10 Maltravers Street, London WC2R 3ER. Tel: 0171-240 7891. *Director-General,* M. Shirley

ENGINEERING DESIGNERS, INSTITUTION OF (1945), Courtleigh, Westbury Leigh, Westbury, Wilts BA13 3TA. Tel: 01373-822801. *Secretary,* M. J. Osborne

ENGINEERING INDUSTRIES ASSOCIATION (1941), Broadway House, Tothill Street, London SW1H 9NS. Tel: 0171-222 2367. *Chief Executive,* Mrs J. Moore

ENGINEERS, INSTITUTION OF BRITISH (1928), Royal Liver Building, 6 Hampton Place, Brighton BN1 3DD. Tel: 01273-734274. *Secretary,* Ms J. Busby

ENGINEERS, SOCIETY OF (1854), Guinea Wiggs, Nayland, Colchester, Essex CO6 4NF. Tel: 01206-263332. *Secretary,* Mrs L. C. A. Wright

ENGLISH ASSOCIATION (1906), University of Leicester, University Road, Leicester LE1 7RH. Tel: 0116-252 3982. *Chief Executive,* Ms H. Lucas

ENGLISH FOLK DANCE AND SONG SOCIETY (1932), Cecil Sharp House, 2 Regent's Park Road, London NW1 7AY. Tel: 0171-485 2206. *Chief Executive,* M. Frost

ENGLISH PLACE-NAME SURVEY (1923), Grey College, Durham DH1 3LG. Tel: 0115-951 5919. *Hon. Director,* V. E. Watts, FSA

ENGLISH-SPEAKING UNION OF THE COMMONWEALTH (1918), Dartmouth House, 37 Charles Street, London W1X 8AB. Tel: 0171-493 3328. *Director-General,* Mrs V. Mitchell

ENTOMOLOGICAL SOCIETY OF LONDON, ROYAL (1833), 41 Queen's Gate, London SW7 5HR. Tel: 0171-584 8361. *Registrar,* G. G. Bentley

ENVIRONMENTAL HEALTH, CHARTERED INSTITUTE OF (1883), Chadwick Court, 15 Hatfields, London SE1 8DJ. Tel: 0171-928 6006. *Chief Executive,* M. Cooke

ENVIRONMENT COUNCIL (1969), 212 High Holborn, London WC1V 7VW. Tel: 0171-836 2626. *Chief Executive*, S. Robinson

EPILEPSY ASSOCIATION, BRITISH (1949), Anstey House, 40 Hanover Square, Leeds LS3 1BE. Tel: 0800-309030. *Chief Executive*, P. Lee

EPILEPSY, NATIONAL SOCIETY FOR (1892), Chalfont St Peter, Gerrards Cross, Bucks SL9 0RJ. Tel: 01494-601300. Helpline: 01494-601400. *Chief Executive*, D. Bennett

EQUESTRIAN FEDERATION, BRITISH (1972), British Equestrian Centre, Stoneleigh Park, Kenilworth, Warks CV8 2RH. Tel: 01203-698871. *Director-General*, vacant

ERSKINE HOSPITAL (formerly Princess Louise Scottish Hospital) (1916), Bishopton, Renfrewshire PA7 5PU. Tel: 0141-812 1100. *Chief Executive*, Col. M. F. Gibson, OBE

ESPERANTO ASSOCIATION OF BRITAIN (1977), 140 Holland Park Avenue, London W11 4UF. Tel: 0171-727 7821. *Office Manager*, M. McClelland

ESTATE AGENTS, NATIONAL ASSOCIATION OF (1962), Arbon House, 21 Jury Street, Warwick CV34 4EH. Tel: 01926-496800. *Chief Executive*, H. Dunsmore-Hardy

ESTATE AGENTS, OMBUDSMAN FOR (1990), Beckett House, 4 Bridge Street, Salisbury, Wilts SP1 2LX. Tel: 01722-333306. *Ombudsman*, T. D. G. Quayle, CB

EUGENICS SOCIETY, *see* GALTON INSTITUTE

EVANGELICAL LIBRARY (1928), 78A Chiltern Street, London W1M 2HB. Tel: 0171-935 6997. *Librarian*, S. J. Taylor

EXPORT, INSTITUTE OF (1935), Export House, 64 Clifton Street, London EC2A 4HB. Tel: 0171-247 9812. *Director-General*, I. J. Campbell

EX-SERVICES LEAGUE, BRITISH COMMONWEALTH (1921), 48 Pall Mall, London SW1Y 5JG. Tel: 0171-973 7263. *Secretary-General*, Lt.-Col. S. Pope, OBE, RM

EX-SERVICES MENTAL WELFARE SOCIETY (1919), Broadway House, The Broadway, London SW19 1RL. Tel: 0181-543 6333. *Director*, Brig. A. K. Dixon, OBE

FABIAN SOCIETY (1884), 11 Dartmouth Street, London SW1H 9BN. Tel: 0171-222 8877. *General Secretary*, M. Jacobs

FAIR ISLE BIRD OBSERVATORY TRUST (1948), Fair Isle Bird Observatory, Fair Isle, Shetland ZE2 9JU. Tel: 01595-760258. *Administrator*, M. Newell

FALSE MEMORY SOCIETY, BRITISH (1993), Bradford on Avon, Wilts BA15 1NF. Tel: 01225-868682. *Director*, R. Scotford

FAMILY HISTORY SOCIETIES, FEDERATION OF (1974), The Benson Room, Birmingham and Midland Institute, Margaret Street, Birmingham B3 3BS. *Administrator*, Mrs P. A. Saul

FAMILY MEDIATION, NATIONAL (1982), 9 Tavistock Place, London WC1H 9SN. Tel: 0171-383 5993. *Director*, Ms T. Fisher

FAMILY PLANNING ASSOCIATION (1939), 2–12 Pentonville Road, London N1 9FP. Tel: 0171-837 5432. *Chief Executive*, Ms A. Weyman

FAMILY WELFARE ASSOCIATION (1869), 501–505 Kingsland Road, London E8 4AU. Tel: 0171-254 6251. *Chief Executive*, Ms H. Dent

FAUNA AND FLORA INTERNATIONAL (1903), Great Eastern House, Tenison Road, Cambridge CB1 2DT. Tel: 01223-571000. *Director*, M. Rose

FELLOWSHIP HOUSES TRUST (1937), Clock House, 192 High Road, Byfleet, Surrey KT14 7RN. Tel: 01932-343172. *Secretary*, Mrs A. J. Elliot

FIELD ARCHAEOLOGISTS, INSTITUTE OF (1982), University of Reading, PO Box 239, Reading RG6 6AU. Tel: 0118-931 6446. *Director*, P. Hinton

FIELD STUDIES COUNCIL (1943), Preston Montford, Montford Bridge, Shrewsbury SY4 1HW. Tel: 01743-850674. *Chief Executive*, A. D. Thomas

FILM CLASSIFICATION, BRITISH BOARD OF (1912), 3 Soho Square, London W1V 6HD. Tel: 0171-439 7961. *Director*, J. Ferman

FIRE ENGINEERS, INSTITUTION OF (1918), 148 New Walk, Leicester LE1 7QB. Tel: 0116-255 3654. *General Secretary*, D. W. Evans

FIRE PROTECTION ASSOCIATION (1946), Melrose Avenue, Borehamwood, Herts WD6 2BJ. Tel: 0181-207 2345. *Director*, Dr J. Denney

FIRE SERVICES NATIONAL BENEVOLENT FUND (1943), Marine Court, Fitzalan Road, Littlehampton, W. Sussex BN17 5NF. Tel: 01903-736063. *General Manager*, C. W. Pile

FLAG INSTITUTE (1971), 9 Laurel Grove, Chester CH2 3HU. Tel: 01244-351335. *General Secretary*, G. Bartram

FLEET AIR ARM OFFICERS' ASSOCIATION (1957), 94 Piccadilly, London W1V 0BP. Tel: 0171-499 0360. *Secretary*, Cdr. J. D. O. Macdonald

FOLKLORE SOCIETY, c/o University College, Gower Street, London WC1E 6BT. Tel: 0171-387 5894. *Hon. Secretary*, Dr J. Simpson

FOOD FROM BRITAIN (1983), 123 Buckingham Palace Road, London SW1W 9SA. Tel: 0171-233 5111. *Chairman*, G. John, CBE

FOOD SCIENCE AND TECHNOLOGY, INSTITUTE OF (1964), 5 Cambridge Court, 210 Shepherd's Bush Road, London W6 7NJ. Tel: 0171-603 6316. *Chief Executive*, Ms H. G. Wild

FORCES HELP SOCIETY AND LORD ROBERTS WORKSHOPS, *see* SSAFA FORCES HELP

FOREIGN PRESS ASSOCIATION IN LONDON (1888), 11 Carlton House Terrace, London SW1Y 5AJ. Tel: 0171-930 0445. *Secretary*, Ms D. Crole

FORENSIC SCIENCE SOCIETY (1959), Clarke House, 18A Mount Parade, Harrogate, N. Yorks HG1 1BX. Tel: 01423-506068. *Hon. Secretary*, Dr A. R. W. Forrest

FORENSIC SCIENCES, BRITISH ACADEMY OF (1959), Anaesthetic Unit, The Royal London Hospital, Whitechapel, London E1 1BB. Tel: 0171-377 9201. *Secretary-General*, Dr P. J. Flynn

FORESTERS, INSTITUTE OF CHARTERED (1982), 7A St Colme Street, Edinburgh EH3 6AA. Tel: 0131-225 2705. *Executive Director*, Mrs M. W. Dick

FORESTRY ASSOCIATION, COMMONWEALTH (1921), c/o Oxford Forestry Institute, South Parks Road, Oxford OX1 3RB. Tel: 01865-271037. *Chairman*, Dr J. S. Maini

FORESTRY SOCIETY OF ENGLAND, WALES AND NORTHERN IRELAND, ROYAL (1882), 102 High Street, Tring, Herts HP23 4AF. Tel: 01442-822028. *Director*, J. E. Jackson, PH.D.

FORESTRY SOCIETY, ROYAL SCOTTISH (1854), The Stables, Dalkeith Country Park, Dalkeith, Midlothian EH22 2NA. Tel: 0131-660 9480. *Director*, M. Osborne

FOUNDRYMEN, INSTITUTE OF BRITISH (1904), Bordesley Hall, The Holloway, Alvechurch, Birmingham B48 7QA. Tel: 01527-596100. *Secretary*, G. A. Schofield

FRANCO-BRITISH SOCIETY (1924), Room 623, Linen Hall, 162–168 Regent Street, London WIR 5TB. Tel: 0171-734 0815. *Executive Secretary*, Mrs M. Clarke

FREEDOM ASSOCIATION (1975), 35 Westminster Bridge Road, London SEI 7JB. Tel: 0171-928 9925. *Administrator*, Mrs P. North

FREEMASONS: GRAND LODGE OF ANTIENT FREE AND ACCEPTED MASONS OF SCOTLAND (1736), Freemasons' Hall, 96 George Street, Edinburgh EH2 3DH. Tel: 0131-225 5304. *Grand Master Mason of Scotland*, The Lord Burton; *Grand Secretary*, C. M. McGibbon

FREEMASONS: UNITED GRAND LODGE OF ENGLAND (1717), Freemasons' Hall, Great Queen Street, London WC2B 5AZ. Tel: 0171-831 9811. *Grand Master*, HRH The Duke of Kent, KG, GCMG, GCVO; *Grand Secretary*, Cdr. M. B. S. Higham

FREEMEN OF ENGLAND AND WALES (1966), Glenrise, Churchfields, Stonesfield, Witney, Oxon OX8 8PP. Tel: 01993-891414. *President*, R. J. M. Bishop

FREEMEN OF THE CITY OF LONDON, GUILD OF (1908), PO Box 153, 40A Ludgate Hill, London EC4M 7DE. Tel: 0171-223 7638. *Clerk*, Col. D. Ivy

FREEMEN OF THE CITY OF YORK, GILD OF (1953), 29 Albemarle Road, York YO23 IEW. Tel: 01904-653698. *Hon. Clerk*, R. Lee

FREEMEN'S GUILD, CITY OF COVENTRY (1946), 47 Brownshill Green Road, Coventry CV6 2AP. Tel: 01203-333980. *Hon. Clerk*, K. Talbot

FRIENDLY SOCIETIES, ASSOCIATION OF (1887), Royex House, Aldermanbury Square, London EC2V 7HR. Tel: 0171-606 1881. *General Secretary*, Miss M. Poole

FRIENDS OF CATHEDRAL MUSIC (1956), Aeron House, Llangeitho, Tregaron, Dyfed SY24 6SU. *Secretary*, M. J. Cooke

FRIENDS OF THE EARTH (1971), 26–28 Underwood Street, London NI 7JQ. Tel: 0171-490 1555. *Director*, C. Secrett

FRIENDS OF THE ELDERLY (1905), 40–42 Ebury Street, London SWIW OLZ. Tel: 0171-730 8263. *Chief Executive*, Mrs S. Levett

FRIENDS OF THE NATIONAL LIBRARIES (1931), c/o Department of Manuscripts, The British Library, 96 Euston Road, London NWI 2DB. Tel: 0171-412 7559. *Hon. Secretary*, M. Borrie, OBE, FSA

FURNITURE HISTORY SOCIETY (1964), 1 Mercedes Cottages, St John's Road, Haywards Heath, W. Sussex RHI6 4EH. Tel: 01444-413845. *Membership Secretary*, Dr B. Austen

GALLIPOLI ASSOCIATION (1915), Earleydene Orchard, Earleydene, Ascot, Berks SL5 9JY. Tel: 01344-626523. *Hon. Secretary*, J. C. Watson Smith

GALTON INSTITUTE (1907), 19 Northfields Prospect, London SWI8 IPE. *General Secretary*, Mrs B. Nixon

GAMBLERS ANONYMOUS (1954), PO Box 88, London SWIO OEU. Tel: 01709-553089.

GAME CONSERVANCY TRUST (1969), Fordingbridge, Hants SP6 IEF. Tel: 01425-652381. *Director-General*, Dr G. R. Potts

GARDEN HISTORY SOCIETY (1965), 77 Cowcross Street, London ECIM 6BP. Tel: 0171-608 2409. *Director*, Ms L. Wigley

GARDENERS' ASSOCIATION, THE GOOD (1968), Pinetum, Churcham, Glos GL2 8AD. Tel: 01452-750402. *Hon. Director*, D. Wilkin

GARDENERS' ROYAL BENEVOLENT SOCIETY (1839), Bridge House, 139 Kingston Road, Leatherhead, Surrey KT22 7NT. Tel: 01372-373962. *Chief Executive*, K. Moller

GARDENS SCHEME CHARITABLE TRUST, NATIONAL (1927), Hatchlands Park, East Clandon, Guildford, Surrey GU4 7RT. Tel: 01483-211535. *Director*, C. Barham Carter

GAS CONSUMERS COUNCIL (1986), 6th Floor, Abford House, 15 Wilton Road, London SWIV ILT. Tel: 0171-931 0977. *Director*, Ms S. Slipman, OBE

GAS ENGINEERS, INSTITUTION OF (1863), 21 Portland Place, London WIN 3AF. Tel: 0171-636 6603. *Chief Executive*, Mrs S. M. Razne

GEMMOLOGICAL ASSOCIATION AND GEM TESTING LABORATORY OF GREAT BRITAIN (1931), 27 Greville Street, (Saffron Hill entrance), London ECIN 8SU. Tel: 0171-404 3334. *Director*, Dr R. R. Harding

GENEALOGICAL RESEARCH SOCIETY, IRISH (1936), c/o The Irish Club, 82 Eaton Square, London SWIW 9AJ. *Hon. Librarian*, J. G. Chartres

GENEALOGISTS AND RECORD AGENTS, ASSOCIATION OF (1968), 29 Badgers Close, Horsham, W. Sussex RHI2 5RU.

GENEALOGISTS, SOCIETY OF (1911), 14 Charterhouse Buildings, Goswell Road, London ECIM 7BA. Tel: 0171-251 8799. *Director*, R. I. N. Gordon

GENERAL PRACTITIONERS, ROYAL COLLEGE OF (1952), 14 Princes Gate, London SW7 IPU. Tel: 0171-581 3232. *Hon. Secretary*, Dr W. Reith

GENTLEPEOPLE, GUILD OF AID FOR (1904), 10 St Christopher's Place, London WIM 6HY. Tel: 0171-935 0641.

GEOGRAPHICAL ASSOCIATION, 160 Solly Street, Sheffield SI 4BF. Tel: 0114-269 0088. *Senior Administrator*, Miss F. M. Soar

GEOGRAPHICAL SOCIETY, ROYAL and THE INSTITUTE OF BRITISH GEOGRAPHERS (1830), 1 Kensington Gore, London SW7 2AR. Tel: 0171-591 3000. *President*, The Earl of Selborne, KBE, FRS; *Director*, Dr R. Gardner

GEOGRAPHICAL SOCIETY, ROYAL SCOTTISH (1884), Graham Hills Building, 40 George Street, Glasgow GI IQE. Tel: 0141-552 3330. *Director*, Dr D. M. Munro

GEOLOGICAL SOCIETY (1807), Burlington House, Piccadilly, London WIV OJU. Tel: 0171-434 9944. *Chief Executive Officer*, E. Nickless

GEOLOGISTS' ASSOCIATION (1858), Burlington House, Piccadilly, London WIV 9AG. Tel: 0171-434 9298. *Executive Secretary*, Mrs S. Stafford

GEORGIAN GROUP (1937), 6 Fitzroy Square, London WIP 6DX. Tel: 0171-387 1720. *Secretary*, N. Burton

GIFTED CHILDREN, NATIONAL ASSOCIATION FOR (1966), Elder House, Milton Keynes MK9 ILR. Tel: 01908-673677. *Executive Director*, P. Carey

GILBERT AND SULLIVAN SOCIETY (1924), 1 Nethercourt Avenue, London N3 IPS. *Hon. Secretary*, Ms M. Bowden

GINGERBREAD (1970), 16–17 Clerkenwell Close, London ECIR OAA. Tel: 0171-336 8183. An association for one-parent families and their children. *Chief Executive*, Ms L. Sewell

GIRL GUIDES, *see* GUIDE ASSOCIATION

GIRLS' BRIGADE, Girls' Brigade House, 62 Foxhall Road, Didcot, Oxon OXII 7BQ. Tel: 01235-510425. *Brigade Secretary*, Mrs S. P. Bunting

GIRLS' FRIENDLY SOCIETY IN ENGLAND AND WALES (1875), 126 Queens Gate, London SW7 5LQ. Tel: 0171-589 9628. *General Secretary,* Mrs H. Crompton

GIRLS' VENTURE CORPS AIR CADETS (1964), Redhill Aerodrome, Kings Mill Lane, South Nutfield, Redhill RH1 5JY. Tel: 01737-823345. *Corps Director,* Mrs M. A. Rowland

GLASS ENGRAVERS, GUILD OF (1975), 35 Ossulton Way, London N2 0JY. Tel: 0181-731 9352. *Secretary,* Mrs C. Weatherhead

GLASS TECHNOLOGY, SOCIETY OF (1916), Thornton, 20 Hallam Gate Road, Sheffield S10 5BT. Tel: 0114-266 3168. *Administration Manager,* Ms J. Costello

GLIDING ASSOCIATION, BRITISH (1930), Kimberley House, Vaughan Way, Leicester LE1 4SE. Tel: 0116-253 1051. *Secretary,* B. Rolfe

GOAT SOCIETY, BRITISH (1879), 34–36 Fore Street, Bovey Tracey, Newton Abbot, Devon TQ13 9AD. Tel: 01626-833168. *Secretary,* Ms S. Knowles

GRAPHOLOGISTS, BRITISH INSTITUTE OF (1983), 24–26 High Street, Hampton Hill, Hampton, Middx TW12 1PD. Tel: 01753-891241. *Chairman,* E. Rees

GREEK INSTITUTE (1969), 34 Bush Hill Road, London N21 2DS. Tel: 0181-360 7968. *Director,* Dr K. Tofallis

GREEN PARTY (1973), 1A Waterlow Road, London N19 5NJ. Tel: 0171-272 4474. *Executive Chair,* Ms J. Jones

GREENPEACE UK (1971), Canonbury Villas, London N1 2PN. Tel: 0171-865 8100. *Executive Director,* P. Melchett

GUIDE ASSOCIATION (1910), 17–19 Buckingham Palace Road, London SW1W 0PT. Tel: 0171-834 6242. *Chief Executive,* Mrs T. Ryall; *Chief Guide,* Miss B. Towle

GUIDE DOGS FOR THE BLIND ASSOCIATION (1931), Hillfields, Burghfield Common, Reading, Berks RG7 3YG. Tel: 0118-983 5555. *Chief Executive,* Mrs G. Peacock

GULBENKIAN FOUNDATION, *see* CALOUSTE GULBENKIAN FOUNDATION

GURKHA WELFARE TRUST (1969), 3rd Floor, 88 Baker Street, London W1M 2AX. Tel: 0171-707 1925. *Director,* E. D. Powell-Jones

HAEMOPHILIA SOCIETY (1950), Chesterfield House, 385 Euston Road, London NW1 3AU. Tel: 0171-380 0600. *Chief Executive,* Ms K. Pappenheim

HAIG HOMES (1928), Alban Dobson House, Green Lane, Morden, Surrey SM4 5NS. Tel: 0181-648 0335. Housing for ex-service people. *Director,* A. N. Carlier

HAKLUYT SOCIETY (1846), c/o Map Library, The British Library, 96 Euston Road, London NW1 2BD. Tel: 01986-788359. *Hon. Secretary,* A. P. Payne

HANSARD SOCIETY FOR PARLIAMENTARY GOVERNMENT (1944), St Philips Building North, Sheffield Street, London WC2A 2EX. Tel: 0171-955 7478. *Director,* Mrs S. Diplock

HARD OF HEARING, BRITISH ASSOCIATION OF THE, *see* HEARING CONCERN

HARVEIAN SOCIETY OF EDINBURGH (1782), Respiratory Medicine Unit, Department of Medicine, The Royal Infirmary, Edinburgh EH3 9YW. Tel: 0131-536 2351. *Joint Secretaries,* A. B. MacGregor; Prof. N. J. Douglas

HARVEIAN SOCIETY OF LONDON (1831), Lettsom House, 11 Chandos Street, London W1M 0EB. Tel: 0171-580 1043. *Executive Secretary,* M. C. Griffiths, TD

HEALTH CARE ASSOCIATION, BRITISH (1931), 24A Main Street, Garforth, Leeds LS25 1AA. Tel: 0113-232 0903. *Chief Executive,* Mrs C. Bell

HEALTH EDUCATION, INSTITUTE OF (1962), Department of Oral Health and Development, University Dental Hospital, Higher Cambridge Street, Manchester M15 6FH. Tel: 0161-275 6610. *Hon. Secretary,* Prof. A. S. Blinkhorn

HEALTH, GUILD OF (1904), Edward Wilson House, 26 Queen Anne Street, London W1M 9LB. Tel: 0171-580 2492. *General Secretary,* Revd A. Lynn

HEALTH SERVICES MANAGEMENT, INSTITUTE OF (1902), 7–10 Chandos Street, London W9DE. Tel: 0171-460 7654. *Director,* Ms K. Caines

HEARING CONCERN (BRITISH ASSOCIATION OF THE HARD OF HEARING) (1948), 7–11 Armstrong Road, London W3 7JL. Tel: 0181-743 1110. Helpline: 01245-344600. *Director,* C. J. Meyer, OBE

HEART FOUNDATION, BRITISH (1963), 14 Fitzhardinge Street, London W1H 4DH. Tel: 0171-935 0185. *Director-General,* Maj.-Gen. L. F. H. Busk, CB

HEDGEHOG PRESERVATION SOCIETY, BRITISH (1982), Knowbury House, Knowbury, Ludlow, Shropshire SY8 3LQ. Tel: 01584-890287. *Founder,* Maj. A. H. Coles, TD

HELLENIC STUDIES, SOCIETY FOR THE PROMOTION OF (1879), Senate House, Malet Street, London WC1E 7HU. Tel: 0171-862 8730. *Secretary,* R. W. Shone

HELP THE AGED (1960), St James's Walk, Clerkenwell Green, London EC1R 0BE. Tel: 0171-253 0253. *Director-General,* C. M. Lake, CBE

HERALDIC AND GENEALOGICAL STUDIES, INSTITUTE OF (1961), 79–82 Northgate, Canterbury, Kent CT1 1BA. Tel: 01227-768664. *Registrar,* J. Palmer

HERALDRY SOCIETY (1947), PO Box 32, Maidenhead, Berks SL6 3FD. Tel: 0118-932 0210. *Secretary,* Mrs M. Miles, MBE, RD

HERPETOLOGICAL SOCIETY, BRITISH (1947), c/o Zoological Society of London, Regent's Park, London NW1 4RY. Tel: 0181-452 9578. *Secretary,* Mrs M. Green

HISPANIC AND LUSO BRAZILIAN COUNCIL (1943), Canning House, 2 Belgrave Square, London SW1X 8PJ. Tel: 0171-235 2303. *Director-General,* J. Amey

HISTORICAL ASSOCIATION (1906), 59A Kennington Park Road, London SE11 4JH. Tel: 0171-735 3901. *Chief Executive,* Mrs M. Stiles

HISTORICAL SOCIETY, ROYAL (1868), University College London, Gower Street, London WC1E 6BT. Tel: 0171-387 7532. *Executive Secretary,* Mrs J. N. McCarthy

HISTORIC HOUSES ASSOCIATION (1973), 2 Chester Street, London SW1X 7BB. Tel: 0171-259 5688. *Director-General,* R. Wilkin

HOME FARM TRUST (1962), Merchants House, Wapping Road, Bristol BS1 4RW. Tel: 0117-927 3746. *Director-General,* C. Carey

HOMEOPATHIC ASSOCIATION, BRITISH (1902), 27A Devonshire Street, London W1N 1RJ. Tel: 0171-935 2163. *General Secretary,* Mrs E. Segall

HONG KONG ASSOCIATION (1961), Swire House, 59 Buckingham Gate, London SW1E 6AJ. Tel: 0171-821 3220. *Executive Director,* D. F. L. Turner

HOROLOGICAL INSTITUTE, BRITISH (1858), Upton Hall, Upton, Newark, Notts NG23 5TE. Tel: 01636-813795. *Secretary,* Ms H. Bartlett

HOROLOGICAL SOCIETY, ANTIQUARIAN (1953), New House, High Street, Ticehurst, Wadhurst, E. Sussex TN5 7AL. Tel: 01580-200155. *Secretary,* Mrs P. Hossbach

Horse Society, British (1947), British Equestrian Centre, Stoneleigh Park, Kenilworth, Warks CV8 2LR. Tel: 01203-696697. *Chief Executive*, Col. T. Eastwood

Hospital Federation, International (1947), 4 Abbot's Place, London NW6 4NP. Tel: 0171-372 7181. *Director-General*, Dr E. N. Pickering

Hospitality Association, British (1907), Queens House, 55–56 Lincoln's Inn Fields, London WC2A 3BH. Tel: 0171-404 7744. *Chief Executive*, J. Logie

Hospital Saturday Fund (1873), 24 Upper Ground, London SE1 9PD. Tel: 0171-928 6662. *Chief Executive*, K. R. Bradley

Hospital Saving Association, Hambleden House, Andover, Hants SP10 1LQ. Tel: 01264-353211. *Chief Executive*, J. A. Young

Hostelling International Northern Ireland (formerly Youth Hostels Association of Northern Ireland) (1931), 22–32 Donegall Road, Belfast BT12 5JN. Tel: 01232-324733. *Hon. Secretary*, D. Forsythe

Hotel and Catering International Management Association (1971), 191 Trinity Road, London SW17 7HN. Tel: 0181-672 4251. *Chief Executive*, D. Wood

House of St Barnabas-in-Soho (1846), 1 Greek Street, London W1V 6NQ. Tel: 0171-434 1846. *Director*, Ms S. Dixon

Housing Aid Society, Catholic (1956), 209 Old Marylebone Road, London NW1 5QT. Tel: 0171-723 7273. Advice line: 0171-723 5928. *Director*, Ms R. Rafferty

Housing and Town Planning Council, National (1900), 14–18 Old Street, London EC1V 9AB. Tel: 0171-251 2363. *Director*, K. MacDonald

Housing, Chartered Institute of, Octavia House, Westwood Business Park, Westwood Way, Coventry CV4 8JP. Tel: 01203-851700. *Chief Executive*, D. Butler

Hovercraft Society (1971), 15 St Mark's Road, Alverstoke, Gosport, Hants PO12 2DA. Tel: 01705-601310. *Chairman*, J. Gifford

Howard League for Penal Reform (1866), 708 Holloway Road, London N19 3NL. Tel: 0171-281 7722. *Director*, Ms F. Crook

Huguenot Society of Great Britain and Ireland (1885), The Huguenot Library, University College, Gower Street, London WC1E 6BT. Tel: 0171-380 7094. *Hon. Secretary*, Mrs M. Bayliss

Humane Research Trust (1974), Brook House, 29 Bramhall Lane South, Bramhall, Stockport, Cheshire SK7 2DN. Tel: 0161-439 8041. *Chairman*, K. Cholerton

Humanist Association, British (1963), 47 Theobald's Road, London WC1X 8SP. Tel: 0171-430 0908. *Executive Director*, R. Ashby

Human Rights, British Institute of (1970), King's College London, Strand, London WC2R 2LS. Tel: 0171-873 2352. *Director*, Ms S. Cooke

Hydrographic Society (1972), c/o University of East London, Longbridge Road, Dagenham, Essex RM8 2AS. Tel: 0181-597 1946. *Hon. Secretary*, P. J. H. Warden

Hymn Society of Great Britain and Ireland (1936), 7 Paganel Road, Minehead, Somerset TA24 5ET. Tel: 01643-703530. *Secretary*, Revd G. Wrayford

ICAN (Invalid Children's Aid Nationwide) (1888), Barbican Citygate, 1–3 Dufferin Street, London EC1Y 8NA. Tel: 0171-374 4422. *Chief Executive*, Ms G. Edelman

Immigration Advisory Service (1970), County House, 190 Great Dover Street, London SE1 4YB. Tel: 0171-357 7511. Appeals and refusals helpline: 0171-378 9191. *Chief Executive*, K. Best

Independent Britain, Campaign for an (1976), 81 Ashmole Street, London SW8 1NF. Tel: 0181-340 0314. *Hon. Secretary*, Sir Robin Williams, Bt.

Independent Schools' Bursars Association (1933), 5 Chapel Close, Old Basing, Basingstoke, Hants RG24 7BY. Tel: 01256-330369. *General Secretary*, M. J. Sant

Independent Schools Careers Organization (1942), 12A Princess Way, Camberley, Surrey GU15 3SP. Tel: 01276-21188. *National Director*, J. D. Stuart

Independent Schools Council (1974), Grosvenor Gardens House, 35–37 Grosvenor Gardens, London SW1W 0BS. Tel: 0171-630 0144. *General Secretary*, Dr A. B. Cooke, OBE, PH.D

Independent Schools Information Service (1972), 56 Buckingham Gate, London SW1E 6AG. Tel: 0171-630 8793. *Director*, D. J. Woodhead

Indexers, Society of (1957), 1 Mermaid House, Mermaid Court, London SE1 1HR. Tel: 0171-403 4947. *Secretary*, Ms L. Weinhove

Industrial Society (1918), Robert Hyde House, 48 Bryanston Square, London W1H 7LN. Tel: 0171-479 2000. *Chief Executive*, T. Morgan

Industry and Parliament Trust, 1 Buckingham Place, London SW1E 6HR. Tel: 0171-976 5311. *Director*, F. R. Hyde-Chambers

Industry Churches Forum (formerly Industrial Churches Fellowship) (1877), 86 Leadenhall Street, London EC3A 3DH. Tel: 0181-656 1644. *Chairman*, Revd Canon G. Brown

Industry Training Organizations, National Council of (1988), 10 Meadowcourt, Amos Road, Sheffield S9 1BX. Tel: 0114-261 9926. *Chief Executive*, Dr A. Powell

Infant Deaths, Foundation for the Study of (1971), 14 Halkin Street, London SW1X 7DP. Tel: 0171-235 0965. Helpline: 0171-235 1721. *Secretary-General*, Mrs J. Epstein

Information Scientists, Institute of (1958), 44–45 Museum Street, London WC1A 1LY. Tel: 0171-831 8003. *Director*, E. Hyams

Inner Wheel Clubs in Great Britain and Ireland, Association of (1934), 51 Warwick Square, London SW1V 2AT. Tel: 0171-834 4600. *Secretary*, Miss J. Dobson

Insolvency, Society of Practitioners of (1990), Halton House, 20–23 Holborn, London EC1N 2JE. Tel: 0171-831 6563. *General Secretary*, R. M. Stancombe

Insurance and Investment Brokers' Association, British, BIIBA House, 14 Bevis Marks, London EC3A 7NT. Tel: 0171-623 9043. *Chief Executive*, R. M. Williams

Insurance Brokers Registration Council, 63 St Mary Axe, London EC3A 8NB. Tel: 0171-621 1061. *Registrar*, Miss E. J. Rees

Insurance Institute, Chartered (1897), 20 Aldermanbury, London EC2V 7HY. Tel: 0181-989 8464. *Director-General*, D. E. Bland, OBE, PH.D.

Insurers, Association of British (1985), 51 Gresham Street, London EC2V 7HQ. Tel: 0171-600 3333. *Director-General*, M. Boléat

INTERNATIONAL AFFAIRS, ROYAL INSTITUTE OF (1920), Chatham House, 10 St James's Square, London SW1Y 4LE. Tel: 0171-957 5700. *Director*, C. Gamble, PH.D. (from Dec. 1998)

INTERNATIONAL FRIENDSHIP LEAGUE (1931), 3 Creswick Road, London W3 9HE. *Secretary*, Miss J. Nelson

INTERNATIONAL POLICE ASSOCIATION (British Section) (1950), 1 Fox Road, West Bridgford, Nottingham NG2 6AJ. Tel: 0115-981 3638. *Chief Executive Officer*, A. F. Carter

INTERNATIONAL STUDENTS HOUSE (1962), 229 Great Portland Street, London W1N 5HD. Tel: 0171-631 8300. *Executive Director*, P. Anwyl

INTERSERVE (1852), 325 Kennington Road, London SE11 4QH. Tel: 0171-735 8227. *National Director*, R. Clark

INTER VARSITY CLUBS, ASSOCIATION OF (1946), 2nd Floor, Grosvenor House, 94–96 Grosvenor Square, Manchester M1 7HL. Tel: 0161-273 2316. *Secretary*, S. Craven

INVALIDS-AT-HOME (1966), 17 Lapstone Gardens, Kenton, Harrow, Middx HA3 0EB. Tel: 0181-907 1706. *Executive Officer*, Mrs S. Lomas

INVISIBLES, BRITISH (1983), 6th Floor, Windsor House, 39 King Street, London EC2V 8DQ. Tel: 0171-600 1198. *Director-General*, E. J. Seddon

INVOLVEMENT AND PARTICIPATION ASSOCIATION (1884), 42 Colebrooke Row, London N1 8AF. Tel: 0171-354 8040. *Director*, B. C. Stevens

IRAN SOCIETY (1936), 2 Belgrave Square, London SW1X 8PJ. Tel: 0171-235 5122. *Hon. Secretary*, A. D. Ashmole

ITRI (formerly International Tin Research Institute) (1932), Kingston Lane, Uxbridge, Middx UB8 3PJ. Tel: 01895-272406. *Director*, R. Bedder

JACQUELINE DU PRÉ MUSIC BUILDING APPEAL (1988), St Hilda's College, Oxford OX4 1DY. Tel: 01865-276803. *Chairman*, Dr J. H. Mellanby

JAPAN ASSOCIATION (1950), Swire House, 59 Buckingham Gate, London SW1E 6AJ. Tel: 0171-821 3220. *Executive Director*, D. F. L. Turner

JERUSALEM AND THE MIDDLE EAST CHURCH ASSOCIATION (1887), 1 Hart House, The Hart, Farnham, Surrey GU9 7HA. Tel: 01252-726994. *Secretary*, Mrs V. Wells

JEWISH HISTORICAL SOCIETY OF ENGLAND (1893), 33 Seymour Place, London W1H 5AP. Tel: 0171-723 5852. *Hon. Secretary*, C. M. Drukker

JEWISH PEOPLE, CHURCH'S MINISTRY AMONG (1809), 30c Clarence Road, St Albans, Herts AL1 4JJ. Tel: 01727-833114. *General Director*, Revd Dr W. Riggans

JEWISH YOUTH, ASSOCIATION FOR (part of Norwood Ravenswood) (1899), Norwood House, Harmony Way, Victoria Road, London NW4 2BZ. Tel: 0181-203 3030. *Head*, E. Finestone

JOURNALISTS, CHARTERED INSTITUTE OF (1883), 2 Dock Offices, Surrey Quays Road, London SE16 2XU. Tel: 0171-252 1187. *General Secretary*, C. J. Underwood

JUSTICE (British Section of the International Commission of Jurists) (1957), 59 Carter Lane, London EC4V 5AQ. Tel: 0171-329 5100. *Director*, Ms A. Owers

JUSTICES' CLERKS' SOCIETY (1839), The Magistrates' Court, 107 Dale Street, Liverpool L2 2JQ. Tel: 0151-255 0790. *Hon. Secretary*, M. Marsh

KING GEORGE'S FUND FOR SAILORS (1917), 8 Hatherley Street, London SW1P 2YY. Tel: 0171-932 0000. *Director-General*, Capt. M. J. Appleton, RN

KING'S FUND, THE (formerly King Edward's Hospital Fund for London) (1897), 11–13 Cavendish Square, London W1M 0AN. Tel: 0171-307 2400. *Chief Executive*, Rabbi J. Neuberger

KIPLING SOCIETY (1927), Tree Cottage, 2 Brownleaf Road, Brighton, E. Sussex BN2 6LB. Tel: 01273-303719. *Hon. Secretary*, J. W. M. Smith

LADIES IN REDUCED CIRCUMSTANCES, SOCIETY FOR THE ASSISTANCE OF (1886), Lancaster House, 25 Hornyold Road, Malvern, Worcs WR14 1QQ. Tel: 01684-574645.

LANDSCAPE INSTITUTE (1929), 6–8 Barnard Mews, London SW11 1QU. Tel: 0171-738 9166. *Director-General*, S. Royston

LAND-VALUE TAXATION AND FREE TRADE, INTERNATIONAL UNION FOR, 177 Vauxhall Bridge Road, London SW1V 1EU. Tel: 0171-834 4266. *Hon. Secretary*, Mrs B. P. Sobrielo

LANGUAGE LEARNING, ASSOCIATION FOR (1990), 150 Railway Terrace, Rugby CV21 3HN. Tel: 01788-546443. *Director*, Dr. B. Boyce

LAW REPORTING FOR ENGLAND AND WALES, INCORPORATED COUNCIL OF (1865), 3 Stone Buildings, Lincoln's Inn, London WC2A 3XN. Tel: 0171-242 6471. *Secretary*, J. Cobbett

LEAGUE OF THE HELPING HAND (1908), Petersham Hollow, 226 Petersham Road, Petersham, Richmond, Surrey TW10 7AL. Tel: 0181-940 7303. *Secretary*, Mrs I. Goodlad

LEAGUE OF WELLDOERS (1893), 119–133 Limekiln Lane, Liverpool L5 8SN. Tel: 0151-207 1984. *Chief Executive*, P. Rooney

LEATHER AND HIDE TRADES' BENEVOLENT INSTITUTION (1860), 60 Wickham Hill, Hurstpierpoint, Hassocks, W. Sussex BN6 9NP. Tel: 01273-843488. *Secretary*, Mrs G. M. Stapleton, MBE

LEGAL EXECUTIVES, INSTITUTE OF (1892), Kempston Manor, Kempston, Bedford MK42 7AB. Tel: 01234-841000. *Chief Executive*, vacant

LEONARD CHESHIRE (1955), 30 Millbank, London SW1P 4QD. Tel: 0171-802 8200. *Director-General*, B. Dutton

LEPROSY MISSION (ENGLAND AND WALES) (1874), Goldhay Way, Orton Goldhay, Peterborough PE2 5GZ. Tel: 01733-370505. *Executive Director*, Revd J. A. Lloyd, PH.D.

LEUKAEMIA RESEARCH FUND (1962), 43 Great Ormond Street, London WC1N 3JJ. Tel: 0171-405 0101. *Executive Director*, D. L. Osborne

LIBERAL PARTY (1877; relaunched 1989), The Pine Grove Centre, 1A Pine Grove, Southport PR9 9AQ. Tel: 01704-500115. *Communications Director*, D. Green

LIBERTY (NATIONAL COUNCIL FOR CIVIL LIBERTIES) (1934), 21 Tabard Street, London SE1 4LA. Tel: 0171-403 3888. *Director*, J. Wadham

LIBRARY ASSOCIATION (1877), 7 Ridgmount Street, London WC1E 7AE. Tel: 0171-636 7543. *Chief Executive*, R. Shimmon

LIFEBOATS, *see* ROYAL NATIONAL LIFEBOAT INSTITUTION

LIGHT HORSE BREEDING SOCIETY, NATIONAL (1885), 96 High Street, Edenbridge, Kent TN8 5AR. Tel: 01732-866277. *General Secretary*, Mrs K. P. Hall

LINGUISTS, INSTITUTE OF (1910), Saxon House, 48 Southwark Street, London SE1 1UN. Tel: 0171-940 3100. *Director*, H. Pavlovich

LINNEAN SOCIETY OF LONDON (1788), Burlington House, Piccadilly, London W1V 0LQ. Tel: 0171-434 4479. *President*, Prof. Sir Ghillean Prance, FRS

LIONS CLUBS INTERNATIONAL (BRITISH ISLES AND IRELAND) (1949), 257 Alcester Road South, Kings Heath, Birmingham B14 6BT. Tel: 0121-441 4544. *Office Manager*, Mrs J. Davis

LISTENING BOOKS (formerly The Listening Library), 12 Lant Street, London SE1 1QH. Tel: 0171-407 9417. *Chief Executive*, T. Taylor

LLOYD'S OF LONDON, 1 Lime Street, London EC3M 7HA. Tel: 0171-327 1000. *Chief Executive*, R. Sandler

LLOYD'S REGISTER OF SHIPPING, 100 Leadenhall Street, London EC3A 3BP. Tel: 0171-709 9166. *Chief Executive Officer*, T. Jones

LOCAL AUTHORITY CHIEF EXECUTIVES AND SENIOR MANAGERS, SOCIETY OF (1974), PO Box 21, Archway Road, Huyton, Knowsley, Merseyside L36 9YU. Tel: 0151-443 3931. *Hon. Secretary*, D. Henshaw

LOCAL COUNCILS, NATIONAL ASSOCIATION OF (1947), 109 Great Russell Street, London WC1B 3LD. Tel: 0171-637 1865. *Director*, P. Clayden, OBE

LOCAL GOVERNMENT ASSOCIATION (1974), 26 Chapter Street, London SW1P 4ND. Tel: 0171-664 3000. *Chief Executive*, B. Briscoe

LOCAL GOVERNMENT INTERNATIONAL BUREAU (1913); *also* Council of European Municipalities and Regions (British Section) and International Union of Local Authorities (British Section) (1951), 35 Great Smith Street, London SW1P 3BJ. Tel: 0171-664 3100. *Director*, J. Smith

LOCAL HISTORY, BRITISH ASSOCIATION FOR (1843), 24 Lower Street, Harnham, Salisbury, Wilts SP2 8EY. Tel: 01722-332158. *Secretary*, M. Cowan

LONDON APPRECIATION SOCIETY (1932), 7–20 Hampden Gurney Street, London W1H 5AL. Tel: 0171-724 0221. *Chairman*, Miss V. C. Colin-Russ

LONDON CITY MISSION (1835), 175 Tower Bridge Road, London SE1 2AH. Tel: 0171-407 7585. *General Secretary*, Revd J. McAllen

LONDON COURT OF INTERNATIONAL ARBITRATION (1892), Hulton House, 6th Floor, 161–166 Fleet Street, London EC4A 2DY. Tel: 0171-936 3530. *Executive Director*, Ms M. May, CBE

LONDON FLOTILLA (1937), 40 Endlesham Road, London SW12 8JL. *Hon. Secretary*, Lt.-Cdr. H. C. R. Upton, RD, RNR

LONDON GOVERNMENT, ASSOCIATION OF (1964), 36 Old Queen Street, London SW1H 9JF. Tel: 0171-222 7799. *Chief Executive*, M. Pilgrim

LONDON LIBRARY, THE (1841), 14 St James's Square, London SW1Y 4LG. Tel: 0171-930 7705. *Librarian*, A. S. Bell

LONDON MAGISTRATES' CLERKS' ASSOCIATION (1889), c/o Thames Magistrates' Court, 58 Bow Road, London E3 4DJ. Tel: 0181-980 1000 ext. 3708. *Hon. Chairman*, J. Mulhern; *Hon. Secretary*, J. Mulreany

LONDON PLAYING FIELDS SOCIETY (1890), Boston Manor Playing Field, Boston Gardens, Brentford, Middx TW8 9LR. Tel: 0181-560 3667. *Chief Executive*, Dr C. Goodson-Wickes

LONDON SOCIETY (1912), 4th Floor, Senate House, Malet Street, London WC1E 7HU. Tel: 0171-580 5537. *Hon. Secretary*, Mrs B. Jones

LORD'S DAY OBSERVANCE SOCIETY (1831), 3 Epsom Business Park, Kiln Lane, Epsom, Surrey KT17 1JF. Tel: 01372-728300. *General Secretary*, J. G. Roberts

LOTTERIES COUNCIL (1979), Windermere House, Kendal Avenue, London W3 0XA. Tel: 0181-896 8101. *Hon. Secretary*, G. Wilson, CBE

LUNG FOUNDATION, BRITISH (1985), 78 Hatton Garden, London EC1N 8JR. Tel: 0171-831 5831. *Chief Executive*, B. Walden

MACA – PARTNERS IN MENTAL HEALTH (formerly Mental After Care Association) (1879), 25 Bedford Square, London WC1B 3HW. Tel: 0171-436 6194. *Chief Executive*, G. Hitchon

MAGISTRATES' ASSOCIATION (1920), 28 Fitzroy Square, London W1P 6DD. Tel: 0171-387 2353. *Secretary*, Ms S. Dickinson

MAILING PREFERENCE SERVICE (1983), 5 Reef House, Plantation Wharf, London SW11 3UF. Tel: 0345-034599. *Chief Executive*, Ms K. Beckett

MAIL USERS' ASSOCIATION (1976), 70 Main Road, Hermitage, Near Emsworth, W. Sussex PO10 8AX. Tel: 0976-710315. *Chairman*, D. Thomas

MANAGEMENT, INSTITUTE OF (1992), Management House, Cottingham Road, Corby, Northants NN17 1TT. Tel: 01536-204222. *Director-General*, Mrs M. Chapman

MANAGEMENT AND PROFESSIONAL STAFFS, ASSOCIATION OF (1972), Parkgates, Bury New Road, Prestwich, Manchester M25 0JW. Tel: 0161-773 8621. *Executive Secretary*, A. J. Casey

MANAGEMENT SERVICES, INSTITUTE OF, 1 Cecil Court, London Road, Enfield, Middx EN2 6DD. Tel: 0181-363 7452. *Director-General*, P. Symes

MANIC DEPRESSION FELLOWSHIP (1983), 8–10 High Street, Kingston upon Thames, Surrey KT1 1EY. Tel: 0181-974 6550. *Director*, Ms M. Fulford

MANORIAL SOCIETY OF GREAT BRITAIN (1906), 104 Kennington Road, London SE11 6RE. Tel: 0171-735 6633. *Hon. Chairman*, R. A. Smith

MANPOWER SOCIETY (1969), 39 Apple Tree Walk, Climping, Littlehampton, W. Sussex BN17 5QN. Tel: 01903-731728. *Administration Manager*, Mrs H. Gale

MARIE CURIE CANCER CARE (1948), 28 Belgrave Square, London SW1X 8QG. Tel: 0171-235 3325. Scottish Office: 21 Rutland Street, Edinburgh EH1 2AH. *Chief Executive*, Sir Nicholas Fenn, GCMG

MARINE ARTISTS, ROYAL SOCIETY OF (1939), 17 Carlton House Terrace, London SW1Y 5BD. Tel: 0171-930 6844. *Secretary*, Ms S. Robinson

MARINE BIOLOGICAL ASSOCIATION OF THE UK (1884), Citadel Hill, Plymouth PL1 2PB. Tel: 01752-633100. *Director*, Prof. M. Whitfield

MARINE ENGINEERS, INSTITUTE OF (1889), The Memorial Building, 76 Mark Lane, London EC3R 7JN. Tel: 0171-481 8493. *Secretary*, J. E. Sloggett, OBE

MARINE SCIENCE, SCOTTISH ASSOCIATION FOR (1914), PO Box 3, Oban, Argyll PA34 4AD. Tel: 01631-562244. *Director*, Dr G. B. Shimmield

MARINE SOCIETY, THE (1756), 202 Lambeth Road, London SE1 7JW. Tel: 0171-261 9535. *Director*, Capt. J. J. Howard

MARIO LANZA EDUCATIONAL FOUNDATION (1976), 646 Portway, Avonmouth, Bristol BS11 9NZ. *Hon. Secretary*, Mrs C. Jacobs

MARKET AUTHORITIES, NATIONAL ASSOCIATION OF BRITISH (1948), NABMA House, 21 Tarnside Road, Orrell, Wigan, Lancs WN5 8RN. Tel: 01695-623860. *Secretary*, J. Edwards

MARKETING, CHARTERED INSTITUTE OF (1911), Moor Hall, Cookham, Maidenhead, Berks SL6 9QH. Tel: 01628-427500. *Director-General*, S. Cuthbert

MARK MASTER MASONS, GRAND LODGE OF (1856), Mark Masons' Hall, 86 St James's Street, London SW1A 1PL. Tel: 0171-839 5274. *Grand Secretary*, T. J. Lewis; *Grand Master*, HRH Prince Michael of Kent

MARRIAGE CARE (formerly the Catholic Marriage Advisory Council) (1946), Clitherow House, 1 Blythe Mews, Blythe Road, London W14 0NW. Tel: 0171-371 1341. *Chief Executive*, Mrs M. Corbett

MASONIC BENEVOLENT INSTITUTION, ROYAL (1842), 20 Great Queen Street, London WC2B 5BG. Tel: 0171-405 8341. *Chief Executive*, Miss J. Reynolds

MASONIC TRUST FOR GIRLS AND BOYS (1985), 31 Great Queen Street, London WC2B 5AG. Tel: 0171-405 2644. *Secretary*, Lt.-Col. J. C. Chambers

MASTERS OF WINE, INSTITUTE OF (1955), Five Kings House, 1 Queen Street Place, London EC4R 1QS. Tel: 0171-236 4427. *Executive Director*, J. F. Casson

MATERIALS, INSTITUTE OF (1985), 1 Carlton House Terrace, London SW1Y 5DB. Tel: 0171-451 7300. *Chief Executive*, Dr B. A. Rickinson

MATERNAL AND CHILD WELFARE, NATIONAL ASSOCIATION FOR (1911), 1st Floor, 40–42 Osnaburgh Street, London NW4 3ND. Tel: 0171-383 4117. *Administrator*, Mrs V. A. Farebrother

MATERNITY ALLIANCE (1980), 45 Beech Street, London EC2P 2LX. Tel: 0171-588 8583. *Director*, Ms C. Gowdridge

MATHEMATICAL ASSOCIATION (1871), 259 London Road, Leicester LE2 3BE. Tel: 0116-270 3877. *Executive Secretary*, Ms H. Whitby

MATHEMATICS AND ITS APPLICATIONS, INSTITUTE OF (1964), Catherine Richards House, 16 Nelson Street, Southend-on-Sea, Essex SS1 1EF. Tel: 01702-354020. *Executive Secretary*, Dr A. M. Lepper

ME ASSOCIATION (1976), 4 Corringham Road, Stanford-le-Hope, Essex SS17 0AH. Tel: 01375-642466. *Chief Executive*, Ms M. Moore

MEASUREMENT AND CONTROL, INSTITUTE OF (1944), 87 Gower Street, London WC1E 6AA. Tel: 0171-387 4949. *Secretary*, M. J. Yates

MECHANICAL ENGINEERS, INSTITUTION OF (1847), 1 Birdcage Walk, London SW1H 9JJ. Tel: 0171-222 7899. *Director-General (acting)*, R. Howard-Jones

MEDICAL COUNCIL, GENERAL (1858), 178 Great Portland Street, London W1N 6JE. Tel: 0171-580 7642. *Chief Executive*, F. M. Scott, TD

MEDIC-ALERT FOUNDATION, 1 Bridge Wharf, 156 Caledonian Road, London N1 9UU. Tel: 0171-833 3034. *Chief Executive*, Miss J. Friend

MEDICAL FOUNDATION FOR THE CARE OF VICTIMS OF TORTURE (1986), 96–98 Grafton Road, London NW5 3EJ. Tel: 0171-813 7777. *Director*, Ms H. Bamber

MEDICAL SOCIETY OF LONDON (1773), Lettsom House, 11 Chandos Street, London W1M 0EB. Tel: 0171-580 1043. *Registrar*, M. C. Griffiths, TD

MEDICAL WOMEN'S FEDERATION (1917), Tavistock House North, Tavistock Square, London WC1H 9HX. Tel: 0171-387 7765. *Hon. Secretary*, Dr S. Glendinning

MENCAP (THE ROYAL SOCIETY FOR MENTALLY HANDICAPPED CHILDREN AND ADULTS) (1946), 123 Golden Lane, London EC1Y 0RT. Tel: 0171-454 0454. *Chief Executive*, F. Heddell

MENSA, BRITISH (1946), Mensa House, St Johns Square, Wolverhampton WV2 4AH. Tel: 01902-772771. *General Manager*, D. Chatten

MENTAL HEALTH FOUNDATION (1949), 37 Mortimer Street, London W1N 8JU. Tel: 0171-580 0145. *Director*, Ms J. McKerrow

MENTAL HEALTH, NATIONAL ASSOCIATION FOR, *see* MIND

MENTAL HEALTH, SCOTTISH ASSOCIATION FOR (1923), Cumbrae House, 15 Carlton Court, Glasgow G5 9JP. Tel: 0141-568 7000. *Chief Executive*, Ms S. M. Barcus

MENTALLY HANDICAPPED, SCOTTISH SOCIETY FOR THE, *see* ENABLE

MERCHANT NAVY WELFARE BOARD (1948), 19–21 Lancaster Gate, London W2 3LN. Tel: 0171-723 3642. *General Secretary*, Capt. D. A. Parsons

METAL TRADES BENEVOLENT SOCIETY, ROYAL (1843), Brooke House, 4 The Lakes, Bedford Road, Northampton NN4 7YD. Tel: 01604-622023. *General Secretary*, A. G. Johnson

METEOROLOGICAL SOCIETY, ROYAL (1850), 104 Oxford Road, Reading, Berks RG1 7LJ. Tel: 01734-568500. *Executive Secretary*, R. P. C. Swash

METROPOLITAN HOSPITAL-SUNDAY FUND (1872), 45 Westminster Bridge Road, London SE1 7JB. Tel: 0171-922 0200. *Secretary*, H. F. Doe

MIDDLE EAST ASSOCIATION (1961), Bury House, 33 Bury Street, London SW1Y 6AX. Tel: 0171-839 2137. *Director-General*, B. P. Constant

MIDWIVES, ROYAL COLLEGE OF (1881), 15 Mansfield Street, London W1M 0BE. Tel: 0171-312 3535. *General Secretary*, Mrs K. Davis

MIGRAINE ACTION ASSOCIATION, (formerly British Migraine Association) (1858), 178A High Road, Byfleet, West Byfleet, Surrey KT14 7ED. Tel: 01932-352468. *Director*, Mrs A. Turner

MIGRAINE TRUST (1965), 45 Great Ormond Street, London WC1N 3HZ. Tel: 0171-278 2676. *Director*, Ms A. Rush

MILITARY HISTORICAL SOCIETY, National Army Museum, Royal Hospital Road, London SW3 4HT. Tel: 01380-723371. *The Secretary*, Lt.-Col. R. E. L. Hodges

MIND (NATIONAL ASSOCIATION FOR MENTAL HEALTH), Granta House, 15–19 Broadway, London E15 4BQ. Tel: 0181-519 2122. Information lines: 0181-522 1728/0345-660063. *Chief Executive*, Ms J. Clements

MINERALOGICAL SOCIETY (1876), 41 Queen's Gate, London SW7 5HR. Tel: 0171-584 7516. *Hon. General Secretary*, Dr B. A. Cressey

MINIATURE PAINTERS, SCULPTORS AND GRAVERS, ROYAL SOCIETY OF (1895), 1 Knapp Cottages, Wyke, Gillingham, Dorset SP8 4NQ. Tel: 01747-825718. *Executive Secretary*, Mrs P. Henderson

MINING AND METALLURGY, INSTITUTION OF (1889), Danum House, 6A South Parade, Doncaster, S. Yorks DN1 2DY. Tel: 01302-320486. *Secretary,* Dr G. J. M. Woodrow

MISSING PERSONS HELPLINE, NATIONAL (1992), Roebuck House, 284–286 Upper Richmond Road West, London SW14 7JE. Tel: 0181-392 4545. Helpline: 0500-700700. *Co-Founders,* Mrs M. Asprey, OBE; Mrs J. Newman, OBE

MISSION TO DEEP SEA FISHERMEN, ROYAL NATIONAL (1881), 43 Nottingham Place, London W1M 4BX. Tel: 0171-487 5101. *Chief Executive,* A. D. Marsden

MISSIONS TO SEAMEN (1856), St Michael Paternoster Royal, College Hill, London EC4R 2RL. Tel: 0171-248 5202. *Secretary-General,* Revd Canon G. Jones

MODERN CHURCHPEOPLE'S UNION (1898), MCU Office, 25 Birch Grove, London W3 9SP. Tel: 0181-932 4379. *General Secretary,* Revd N. P. Henderson

MONUMENTAL BRASS SOCIETY (1887), Lowe Hill House, Stratford St Mary, Colchester, Essex CO7 6JX. Tel: 01206-337239. *Hon. Secretary,* H. M. Stuchfield

MORAVIAN MISSIONS, LONDON ASSOCIATION IN AID OF (1817), Moravian Church House, 5–7 Muswell Hill, London N10 3TJ. Tel: 0181-883 3409. *Secretary,* Ms J. Morten

MOTHERS' UNION (1876), Mary Sumner House, 24 Tufton Street, London SW1P 3RB. Tel: 0171-222 5533. *Chief Executive,* Mrs A. Ridler

MOTOR INDUSTRY, INSTITUTE OF THE, Fanshaws, Brickendon, Hertford SG13 8PQ. Tel: 01992-511521. *Director-General,* R. Ward

MOUNTBATTEN MEMORIAL TRUST (1979), 1 Grosvenor Crescent, London SW1X 7EF. Tel: 0171-235 5231 ext 255. *Director,* J. Boyd-Brent

MOUNTBATTEN TRUST, THE EDWINA (1960), 1 Grosvenor Crescent, London SW1X 7EF. Tel: 0171-235 5231 ext 255. *Secretary,* J. Boyd-Brent

MULTIPLE SCLEROSIS SOCIETY (1953), 25 Effie Road, London SW6 1EE. Tel: 0171-610 7171. *Chief Executive,* P. Cardy

MUNICIPAL ENGINEERS, ASSOCIATION OF, Institution of Civil Engineers, Great George Street, London SW1P 3AA. Tel: 0171-222 7722. *Director,* A. Bhogal

MUSEUMS ASSOCIATION (1889), 42 Clerkenwell Close, London EC1R 0PA. Tel: 0171-608 2933. *Director,* M. Taylor

MUSIC ALLIANCE, THE, Copyright House, 29–33 Berners Street, London W1P 4AA. Tel: 0171-580 5544. *Chief Executive,* J. Hutchinson

MUSIC HALL SOCIETY, BRITISH (1963), c/o Brodie and Middleton Ltd, 68 Drury Lane, London WC2B 5SP. Tel: 0171-836 3289. *Hon. Secretary,* Mrs D. Masterton

MUSICIANS BENEVOLENT FUND (1921), 16 Ogle Street, London W1P 8JB. Tel: 0171-636 4481. *Secretary,* Ms H. Faulkner

MUSICIANS, INCORPORATED SOCIETY OF (1882), 10 Stratford Place, London W1N 9AE. Tel: 0171-629 4413. *Chief Executive,* N. Hoyle

MUSICIANS OF GREAT BRITAIN, ROYAL SOCIETY OF (1738), 10 Stratford Place, London W1N 9AE. Tel: 0171-629 6137. *Secretary,* Mrs M. Gibb

MUSIC INFORMATION CENTRE, BRITISH (1967), 10 Stratford Place, London W1N 9AE. Tel: 0171-499 8567. *Directors,* M. Greenall; T. Morgan

MUSIC SOCIETIES, NATIONAL FEDERATION OF (1935), Francis House, Francis Street, London SW1P 1DE. Tel: 0171-828 7320. *Chief Executive,* R. Jones

NABC - CLUBS FOR YOUNG PEOPLE (1925), 371 Kennington Lane, London SE11 5QY. Tel: 0171-793 0787. *National Director,* C. Groves, FIPD, F.I.MGT

NABS (formerly National Advertising Benevolent Society) (1913), 32 Wigmore Street, London W1H 9DF. Tel: 0171-299 2888. *Director,* Ms H. Tridgell

NACRO (NATIONAL ASSOCIATION FOR THE CARE AND RESETTLEMENT OF OFFENDERS) (1966), 169 Clapham Road, London SW9 0PU. Tel: 0171-582 6500. *Chief Executive,* Ms H. Edwards

NATIONAL BENEVOLENT INSTITUTION (1812), 61 Bayswater Road, London W2 3PG. Tel: 0171-723 0021. *Secretary,* Gp Capt D. St J. Homer, MVO

NATIONAL COUNCIL FOR VOLUNTARY ORGANIZATIONS, *see* VOLUNTARY ORGANIZATIONS, NATIONAL COUNCIL FOR

NATIONAL COUNCIL OF WOMEN OF GREAT BRITAIN (1895), 36 Danbury Street, London N1 8JU. Tel: 0171-354 2395. *President,* Mrs G. Wedekind

NATIONAL DEMOCRATS (formerly National Front) (1967), PO Box 2269, London E6 3RF. Tel: 0181-471 6872. *Chairman,* I. Anderson

NATIONAL EXTENSION COLLEGE (1963), 18 Brooklands Avenue, Cambridge CB2 2HN. Tel: 01223-450200. *Director,* Dr R. Morpeth

NATIONAL SOCIETY, THE (1811), Church House, Great Smith Street, London SW1P 3NZ. Tel: 0171-222 1672. *General Secretary,* Canon J. Hall

NATIONAL SOCIETY FOR THE PREVENTION OF CRUELTY TO CHILDREN (NSPCC) (1884), 42 Curtain Road, London EC2A 3NH. Tel: 0171-825 2500. *Director,* J. Harding

NATIONAL TRUST, THE (1895), 36 Queen Anne's Gate, London SW1H 9AS. Tel: 0171-222 9251. *Director-General,* M. Drury

NATIONAL TRUST FOR SCOTLAND (1931), 5 Charlotte Square, Edinburgh EH2 4DU. Tel: 0131-226 5922. *Director,* T. Croft

NATIONAL UNION OF STUDENTS (1922), Nelson Mandela House, 461 Holloway Road, London N7 6LJ. Tel: 0171-272 8900. *National President,* A. Pakes

NATIONAL VIEWERS' AND LISTENERS' ASSOCIATION (1964), All Saints House, High Street, Colchester CO1 1UG. Tel: 01206-561155. *Director,* J. C. Beyer

NATIONAL WOMEN'S REGISTER (1960), 3A Vulcan House, Vulcan Road North, Norwich NR6 6AQ. Tel: 01603-406767. *National Organizer,* Mrs M. Dodkins

NATURALISTS' ASSOCIATION, BRITISH (1905), 1 Bracken Mews, London E4 7UT. *Hon. Membership Secretary,* Mrs Y. H. Griffiths

NAUTICAL RESEARCH, SOCIETY FOR (1911), c/o National Maritime Museum, Greenwich, London SE10 9NF. *Hon. Secretary,* Lt.-Cdr. W. J. R. Gardner

NAVAL ARCHITECTS, ROYAL INSTITUTION OF (1860), 10 Upper Belgrave Street, London SW1X 8BQ. Tel: 0171-235 4622. *Chief Executive,* T. Blakeley

NAVAL, MILITARY AND AIR FORCE BIBLE SOCIETY (1780), Radstock House, 3 Eccleston Street, London SW1W 9LZ. Tel: 0171-730 2155. *General Secretary,* J. M. Hines

NAVIGATION, ROYAL INSTITUTE OF (1947), 1 Kensington Gore, London SW7 2AT. Tel: 0171-589 5021. *Director,* Gp Capt D. W. Broughton, MBE

NAVY RECORDS SOCIETY (1893), c/o Department of War Studies, King's College, The Strand, London WC2R 2LS. *Hon. Secretary*, Dr A. D. Lambert

NCH ACTION FOR CHILDREN (1869), 85 Highbury Park, London N5 IUD. Tel: 0171-226 2033. *Chief Executive*, D. Mead

NEEDLEWORK, ROYAL SCHOOL OF (1872), Apartment 12A, Hampton Court Palace, East Molesey, Surrey KT8 9AU. Tel: 0181-943 1432. *Principal*, Mrs E. Elvin

NEWCOMEN SOCIETY (1920), The Science Museum, London SW7 2DD. Tel: 0171-589 1793. *Executive Secretary*, C. Armstrong

NEWSPAPER PRESS FUND (1864), Dickens House, 35 Wathen Road, Dorking, Surrey RH4 IJY. Tel: 01306-887511. *Director*, P. W. Evans

NEWSTRAID BENEVOLENT SOCIETY (1839), PO Box 306, Dunmow, Essex CM6 IHY. Tel: 01371-874198. *President*, A. Cameron

NHS CONFEDERATION (1974), 26 Chapter Street, London SW1P 4ND. Tel: 0171-233 7388. *Chief Executive*, S. Thornton

NOISE ABATEMENT SOCIETY (1959), PO Box 518, Eynsford, Dartford, Kent DA4 0LL. Tel: 01322-862789. *Chairman*, J. Connell, OBE

NON-SMOKERS, NATIONAL SOCIETY OF, *see* QUIT

NORWOOD RAVENSWOOD (formerly Norwood Childcare) (1795), Broadway House, 80–82 The Broadway, Stanmore, Middx HA7 4HB. Tel: 0181-954 4555. *Executive Directors*, Ms N. Brier; S. Brier

NOTARIES' SOCIETY (1907), 7 Lower Brook Street, Ipswich IP4 IAF. Tel: 01473-214762. *Secretary*, A. G. Dunford

NUCLEAR ENERGY SOCIETY, BRITISH (1962), 1–7 Great George Street, London SW1P 3AA. Tel: 0171-665 2241. *Executive Officer*, A. Tillbrook

NUFFIELD FOUNDATION (1943), 28 Bedford Square, London WC1B 3EG. Tel: 0171-631 0566. *Director*, A. Tomei

NUFFIELD TRUST (formerly the Nuffield Provincial Hospitals Trust) (1939), 59 New Cavendish Street, London W1M 7RD. Tel: 0171-631 8450. *Secretary*, J. Wyn Owen, CB

NURSES' NATIONAL HOME, RETIRED (1934), Riverside Avenue, Bournemouth BH7 7EE. Tel: 01202-396418. *Chairman*, R. Forder

NURSES, ROYAL NATIONAL PENSION FUND FOR, Burdett House, 15 Buckingham Street, London WC2N 6ED. Tel: 0171-839 6785. *General Manager*, V. G. West

NURSING, MIDWIFERY AND HEALTH VISITING, ENGLISH NATIONAL BOARD FOR, Victory House, 170 Tottenham Court Road, London W1P 0HA. Tel: 0171-388 3131. *Chief Executive Officer*, A. P. Smith, CBE

NURSING, MIDWIFERY AND HEALTH VISITING FOR NORTHERN IRELAND, NATIONAL BOARD FOR, Centre House, 79 Chichester Street, Belfast BT1 4JE. Tel: 01232-238152. *Chief Executive*, Prof. O. D'A. Slevin

NURSING, MIDWIFERY AND HEALTH VISITING FOR SCOTLAND, NATIONAL BOARD FOR, 22 Queen Street, Edinburgh EH2 INT. Tel: 0131-226 7371. *Chief Executive*, D. C. Benton

NURSING, MIDWIFERY AND HEALTH VISITING, UK CENTRAL COUNCIL FOR, 23 Portland Place, London W1N 4JT. Tel: 0171-637 7181. *Chief Executive*, Ms S. Norman

NURSING, MIDWIFERY AND HEALTH VISITING, WELSH NATIONAL BOARD FOR, 2nd Floor, Golate House, 101 St Mary Street, Cardiff CF1 IDX. Tel: 01222-261400. *Chief Executive*, D. A. Ravey

NURSING, ROYAL COLLEGE OF (1916), 20 Cavendish Square, London W1M 0AB. Tel: 0171-409 3333. *General Secretary*, Miss C. Hancock

NUTRITION FOUNDATION, BRITISH (1967), High Holborn House, 52–54 High Holborn, London WC1V 6RQ. Tel: 0171-404 6504. *Director-General*, Prof. R. Pickard, PH.D

NUTRITION SOCIETY (1941), 10 Cambridge Court, 210 Shepherds Bush Road, London W6 7NJ. Tel: 0171-602 0228. *Hon. Secretary*, Dr J. D. Oldham

OBSTETRICIANS AND GYNAECOLOGISTS, ROYAL COLLEGE OF (1929), 27 Sussex Place, London NW1 4RG. Tel: 0171-772 6200. *Secretary*, P. A. Barnett

OCCUPATIONAL HEALTH AND SAFETY AGENCY, *see* OHSA

OCCUPATIONAL SAFETY AND HEALTH, INSTITUTION OF (1946), The Grange, Highfield Drive, Wigston, Leics LE18 INN. Tel: 0116-257 3100. *Chief Executive*, J. R. Barrell, OBE

OFFICERS' ASSOCIATION, THE (1920), 48 Pall Mall, London SW1Y 5JY. Tel: 0171-930 0125. *General Secretary*, Brig. J. M. A. Norton, OBE, MC

OFFICERS' PENSIONS SOCIETY (1946), 68 South Lambeth Road, London SW8 IRL. Tel: 0171-820 9988. *General Secretary*, Maj.-Gen. P. R. F. Bonnet, CB, MBE

OHSA (formerly Occupational Health and Safety Agency), Communications HQ, Dacre House, 17–19 Dacre Street, London SW1H 0DH. Tel: 0171-222 1202. *Managing Director*, Ms W. Gill

OIL PAINTERS, ROYAL INSTITUTE OF (1883), 17 Carlton House Terrace, London SW1Y 5BD. Tel: 0171-930 6844. *Secretary*, B. Bennett

ONE-PARENT FAMILIES, NATIONAL COUNCIL FOR, 255 Kentish Town Road, London NW5 2LX. Tel: 0171-267 1361. *Director*, Ms K. Pappenheim

OPAS (PENSIONS ADVISORY SERVICE) (1982), 11 Belgrave Road, London SW1V IRB. Tel: 0171-233 8080. *Chief Executive*, M. McLean, OBE

OPEN-AIR MISSION (1853), 19 John Street, London WC1N 2DL. Tel: 0171-405 6135. *Secretary*, A. J. Greenbank

OPEN SPACES SOCIETY (1865), 25A Bell Street, Henley-on-Thames, Oxon RG9 2BA. Tel: 01491-573535. *General Secretary*, Miss K. Ashbrook

OPERATIC AND DRAMATIC ASSOCIATION, NATIONAL (1899), NODA House, 1 Crestfield Street, London WC1H 8AU. Tel: 0171-837 5655. *Chief Executive*, M. Thorburn

OPSIS (NATIONAL ASSOCIATION FOR THE EDUCATION, TRAINING AND SUPPORT OF BLIND AND PARTIALLY SIGHTED PEOPLE) (1992), 67–71 Goswell Road, London EC1V 7EN. Tel: 0171-608 3161. *Secretary-General*, C. Binks

OPTICAL COUNCIL, GENERAL (1958), 41 Harley Street, London W1N 2DJ. Tel: 0171-580 3898. *Registrar*, R. Wilshin

OPTOMETRISTS, COLLEGE OF, 42 Craven Street, London WC2N 5NG. Tel: 0171-839 6000. *Secretary*, P. D. Leigh

ORDERS AND MEDALS RESEARCH SOCIETY (1942), 123 Turnpike Link, Croydon CR0 5NU. Tel: 0181-680 2701. *General Secretary*, N. G. Gooding

ORIENTAL CERAMIC SOCIETY (1921), 30B Torrington Square, London WC1E 7LJ. Tel: 0171-636 7985. *Hon. Secretary*, Dr. F. Wood

ORNITHOLOGISTS' CLUB, SCOTTISH (1936), 21 Regent Terrace, Edinburgh EH7 5BT. Tel: 0131-556 6042. *Secretary*, Ms S. Laing

ORNITHOLOGISTS' UNION, BRITISH (1858), c/o The Natural History Museum, Akeman Street, Tring, Herts HP23 6AP. Tel: 01442-890080. *Administrator*, S. P. Dudley

ORNITHOLOGY, BRITISH TRUST FOR (1932), National Centre for Ornithology, The Nunnery, Thetford, Norfolk IP24 2PU. Tel: 01842-750050. *Director*, Dr J. J. D. Greenwood

ORTHOPAEDIC ASSOCIATION, BRITISH (1918), c/o The Royal College of Surgeons, 35–43 Lincoln's Inn Fields, London WC2A 3PN. Tel: 0171-405 6507. *Chief Executive*, D. C. Adams

OSTEOPATHIC COUNCIL, GENERAL (formerly General Council and Register of Osteopaths) (1936), Room 432, Premier House, 10 Greycoat Place, London SW1P 1SB. Tel: 0171-799 2442. *Registrar*, Miss M. J. Craggs

OSTEOPATHIC MEDICINE, LONDON COLLEGE OF, 8–10 Boston Place, London NW1 6QH. Tel: 0171-262 5250. *Clinic Manager*, Mrs A. Dalby

OSTEOPOROSIS SOCIETY, NATIONAL (1986), PO Box 10, Radstock, Bath BA3 3YB. Tel: 01761-471771. *Communications Manager*, Miss C. Chisholm

OUTWARD BOUND TRUST (1941), Award House, 7–11 St Matthew Street, London SW1P 2JT. Tel: 0171-222 3059. *Director*, Sir Michael Hobbs, KCVO, CBE

OVERSEAS DEVELOPMENT INSTITUTE (1960), Portland House, Stag Place, London SW1E 5DP. Tel: 0171-393 1600. *Director*, S. Maxwell

OVERSEAS SERVICE PENSIONERS' ASSOCIATION (1960), 138 High Street, Tonbridge, Kent TN9 1AX. Tel: 01732-363836. *Secretary*, D. F. B. Le Breton, CBE

OVERSEAS SETTLEMENT (1925), Church of England Board for Social Responsibility, Great Smith Street, London SW1P 3NZ. Tel: 0171-222 9011. *Administration Secretary*, Miss P. J. Hallett

OXFAM UK/IRELAND (1942), 274 Banbury Road, Oxford OX2 7DZ. Tel: 01865-311311. *Director*, D. Bryer, CMG

OXFORD PRESERVATION TRUST (1927), 10 Turn Again Lane, St Ebbes, Oxford OX1 1QL. Tel: 01865-242918. *Secretary*, vacant

OXFORD SOCIETY (1932), 41 Wellington Square, Oxford OX1 2JF. Tel: 01865-270088. *Secretary*, T. J. Lewis

PAEDIATRICS AND CHILD HEALTH, ROYAL COLLEGE OF (1928), 5 St Andrews Place, Regents Park, London NW1 4LB. Tel: 0171-486 6151. *Hon. Secretary*, Dr K. Dodd

PAINTER-PRINTMAKERS, ROYAL SOCIETY OF (1880), Bankside Gallery, 48 Hopton Street, London SE1 9JH. Tel: 0171-928 7521. *President*, Prof. D. Carpanini

PAINTERS IN WATER COLOURS, ROYAL INSTITUTE OF (1831), 17 Carlton House Terrace, London SW1Y 5BD. Tel: 0171-930 6844. *Secretary*, T. Hunt

PALAEONTOLOGICAL ASSOCIATION (1957), c/o Lapworth Museum, School of Earth Sciences, University of Birmingham, Birmingham B15 2TT. Tel: 0121-414 4173. *Secretary*, Dr P. Smith

PARENTS AT WORK (1985), 45 Beech Street, Barbican, London EC2Y 8AD. Tel: 0171-628 3578. *Joint Chief Executives*, Ms S. Jackson; Ms S. Monk

PARKINSON'S DISEASE SOCIETY OF THE UNITED KINGDOM (1969), 215 Vauxhall Bridge Road, London SW1V 1EJ. Tel: 0171-931 8080. Helpline: 0171-233 5373. *Chief Executive*, B. A. Brooking, MBE

PARLIAMENTARY AND SCIENTIFIC COMMITTEE (1939), 48 Westminster Palace Gardens, 1–7 Artillery Row, London SW1P 1RR. Tel: 0171-222 7085. *Administrative Secretary*, Dr A. Whitehouse

PASTORAL PSYCHOLOGY, GUILD OF (1936), PO Box 1107, London W3 6ZP. Tel: 0181-993 8366. *Administrator*, Mrs N. Stanley

PATENT AGENTS, CHARTERED INSTITUTE OF (1882), Staple Inn Buildings, High Holborn, London WC1V 7PZ. Tel: 0171-405 9450. *Secretary*, M. C. Ralph

PATENTEES AND INVENTORS, INSTITUTE OF (1919), Suite 505A, Triumph House, 189 Regent Street, London W1R 7WF. Tel: 0171-434 1818. *Secretary*, R. Magnus

PATHOLOGISTS, ROYAL COLLEGE OF, 2 Carlton House Terrace, London SW1Y 5AF. Tel: 0171-930 5863. *Secretary*, K. Lockyer

PATIENTS ASSOCIATION (1963), PO Box 935, Harrow, Middx HA1 3YJ. Tel: 0181-423 9111. Helpline: 0181-423 8999. *General Manager*, Ms E. Richardson

PDSA (PEOPLE'S DISPENSARY FOR SICK ANIMALS) (1917), Whitechapel Way, Priorslee, Telford, Shropshire TF2 9PQ. Tel: 01952-290999. *Director-General*, M. R. Curtis, MBE

PEACE COUNCIL, NATIONAL (1908), 88 Islington High Street, London N1 8EG. Tel: 0171-354 5200.

PEAK AND NORTHERN FOOTPATHS SOCIETY (1894), 15 Parkfield Drive, Tyldesley, Manchester M29 8NR. Tel: 0161-790 4383. *Hon. General Secretary*, D. Taylor

PEARSON'S HOLIDAY FUND, PO Box 123, Bishops Waltham, Southampton SO32 1ZE. Tel: 01489-893260. *General Secretary*, R. Heasman

PEDESTRIANS ASSOCIATION (1929), 126 Aldersgate Street, London EC1A 4JQ. Tel: 0171-490 0750. *Director*, B. Plowden

PEN, INTERNATIONAL (1921), 9–10 Charterhouse Buildings, Goswell Road, London EC1M 7AT. Tel: 0171-253 4308. English Centre: 7 Dilke Street, London SW3 4JE. Tel: 0171-352 6303. World association of writers. *International Secretary*, A. Blokh

PENSION FUNDS LTD, NATIONAL ASSOCIATION OF (1923), 12–18 Grosvenor Gardens, London SW1W 0DH. Tel: 0171-730 0585. *Director-General*, Dr A. Robinson

PENSIONS ADVISORY SERVICE, *see* OPAS

PERFORMING RIGHT SOCIETY LTD (1914), Copyright House, 29–33 Berners Street, London W1P 4AA. Tel: 0171-580 5544. *Chief Executive*, J. Hutchinson

PERIODICAL PUBLISHERS ASSOCIATION LTD (1913), Queens House, 28 Kingsway, London WC2B 6JR. Tel: 0171-404 4166. *Chief Executive*, I. Locks

PESTALOZZI CHILDREN'S VILLAGE TRUST (1959), Sedlescombe, Battle, E. Sussex TN33 0RR. Tel: 01424-870444. *Director*, M. Phillips

PETROLEUM, INSTITUTE OF (1913), 61 New Cavendish Street, London W1M 8AR. Tel: 0171-467 7100. *Director-General*, I. Ward

PHARMACEUTICAL SOCIETY OF GREAT BRITAIN, ROYAL (1841), 1 Lambeth High Street, London SE1 7JN. Tel: 0171-735 9141. *Secretary*, J. Ferguson, OBE

PHARMACOLOGICAL SOCIETY, BRITISH (1931), 16 Angel Gate, City Road, London EC1V 2PT. *Hon. General Secretary*, Dr T. P. Blackburn

PHILOLOGICAL SOCIETY (1842), School of Oriental and African Studies, University of London, Thornhaugh Street, London WC1H OXG. *Hon. Secretary*, Prof. N. Sims-Williams

PHILOSOPHY, ROYAL INSTITUTE OF (1925), 14 Gordon Square, London WC1H OAG. Tel: 0171-387 4130. *Director*, Prof. A. O'Hear

PHOTOGRAPHY, BRITISH INSTITUTE OF PROFESSIONAL (1901), Fox Talbot House, Amwell End, Ware, Herts SG12 9HN. Tel: 01920-464011. *Chief Executive*, A. Mair

PHYSICAL RECREATION, CENTRAL COUNCIL OF (1935), Francis House, Francis Street, London SW1P 1DE. Tel: 0171-828 3163. *General Secretary*, M. Denton

PHYSICIANS, ROYAL COLLEGE OF (1518), 11 St Andrews Place, London NW1 4LE. Tel: 0171-935 1174. *Secretary*, P. Masterton-Smith

PHYSICIANS AND SURGEONS OF GLASGOW, ROYAL COLLEGE OF (1599), 232–242 St Vincent Street, Glasgow G2 5RJ. Tel: 0141-221 6072. *Hon. Secretary*, Dr C. Semple

PHYSICIANS OF EDINBURGH, ROYAL COLLEGE OF (1681), 9 Queen Street, Edinburgh EH2 1JQ. Tel: 0131-225 7324. *Secretary*, Dr J. St. J. Thomas

PHYSICS AND ENGINEERING IN MEDICINE, INSTITUTE OF, 53 Piccadilly, York YO1 1PL. Tel: 01904-610821. *General Secretary*, R. W. Neilson

PHYSICS, INSTITUTE OF (1874), 76 Portland Place, London W1N 3DH. Tel: 0171-470 4800. *Chief Executive*, Dr A. D. W. Jones

PHYSIOLOGICAL SOCIETY, THE (1876), PO Box 11319, London WC1E 7JF. Tel: 0171-631 1456. *Hon. Secretary*, Prof. P. Stanfield

PHYSIOTHERAPY, CHARTERED SOCIETY OF (1894), 14 Bedford Row, London WC1R 4ED. Tel: 0171-306 6682. *Secretary*, P. Grey

PIG ASSOCIATION, BRITISH (1884), 7 Rickmansworth Road, Watford WD1 7HE. Tel: 01923-234377/230421. *Chief Executive*, G. E. Welsh

PILGRIM TRUST (1930), Fielden House, Little College Street, London SW1P 3SH. Tel: 0171-222 4723. *Director*, Miss G. Nayler

PILGRIMS OF GREAT BRITAIN (1902), c/o 32 Old Queen Street, London SW1H 9HP. Tel: 0171-222 0232. *Hon. Secretary*, M. P. S. Barton

PLAIN ENGLISH CAMPAIGN (1979), PO Box 3, New Mills, Stockport SK22 4QP. Tel: 01663-744409. *Director*, Ms C. Maher, OBE

PLANT ENGINEERS, INSTITUTION OF, 77 Great Peter Street, London SW1P 2EZ. Tel: 0171-233 2855. *Secretary*, P. F. Tye

PLAYING FIELDS ASSOCIATION, NATIONAL (1925), 25 Ovington Square, London SW3 1LQ. Tel: 0171-584 6445. *Director*, Ms E. Davies

PLUNKETT FOUNDATION (1919), 23 Hanborough Business Park, Long Hanborough, Oxford OX8 8LH. Tel: 01993-883636. *Director*, S. Rawlinson

POETRY SOCIETY (1909), 22 Betterton Street, London WC2H 9BU. Tel: 0171-420 9880. *Director*, C. Meade

POLICY STUDIES INSTITUTE (1978), 100 Park Village East, London NW1 3SR. Tel: 0171-468 0468. *Director*, Ms P. Meadows

POLIO FELLOWSHIP, BRITISH (1939), Ground Floor, Unit A, Eagle Office Centre, The Runway, South Ruislip, Middx HA4 6SE. Tel: 0181-842 1898. *Chief Executive*, A. Kemp, CQSW

POLITE SOCIETY and CAMPAIGN FOR COURTESY (1986), 6 Norman Avenue, Henley-on-Thames, Oxon RG9 1SG. Tel: 01491-572794. *Hon. Secretary*, Miss G. Mackenzie

PONY CLUB (1929), National Agricultural Centre, Stoneleigh Park, Kenilworth, Warks CV8 2RW. Tel: 01203-698300. *Chief Executive*, R. J. R. Symonds

PORTRAIT PAINTERS, ROYAL SOCIETY OF (1891), 17 Carlton House Terrace, London SW1Y 5BD. Tel: 0171-930 6844. *Secretary*, P. Brason

POST OFFICE USERS' NATIONAL COUNCIL (1970), 6 Hercules Road, London SE1 7DN. Tel: 0171-928 9458. *Secretary*, J. Dobbs

PRAYER BOOK SOCIETY (1975), St James Garlickhythe, Garlick Hill, London EC4V 2AL. Tel: 01923-824278. *Chairman*, C. A. A. Kilmister

PRE-SCHOOL LEARNING ALLIANCE, 69 Kings Cross Road, London WC1X 9LL. Tel: 0171-833 0991. *Chief Executive Officer*, Ms M. Lochrie

PRESS UNION, COMMONWEALTH (1909), 17 Fleet Street, London EC4Y 1AA. Tel: 0171-583 7733. *Director*, M. Robinson

PREVENTION OF ACCIDENTS, ROYAL SOCIETY FOR THE (1916), Edgbaston Park, 353 Bristol Road, Birmingham B5 7ST. Tel: 0121-248 2000. *Chief Executive*, Dr J. Hooper

PRINCESS LOUISE SCOTTISH HOSPITAL, *see* ERSKINE HOSPITAL

PRINCE'S SCOTTISH YOUTH BUSINESS TRUST (1989), 6th Floor, Mercantile Chambers, 53 Bothwell Street, Glasgow G2 6TS. Tel: 0141-248 4999. *Director*, D. W. Cooper

PRINCESS ROYAL TRUST FOR CARERS (1990), 142 Minories, London EC3N 1LS. Tel: 0171-480 7788. *Chief Executive*, D. Butler

PRINCE'S TRUST (1976) and ROYAL JUBILEE TRUSTS (1935, 1977), 18 Park Square East, London NW1 4LH. Tel: 0800-842842. *Director*, T. Shebbeare, CVO

PRINCE'S YOUTH BUSINESS TRUST, *see* PRINCE'S TRUST

PRINTERS' CHARITABLE CORPORATION (1827), 7 Cantelupe Mews, Cantelupe Road, East Grinstead, W. Sussex RH19 3BG. Tel: 01342-318882. *Director*, Ms T. Searle

PRINTING HISTORICAL SOCIETY (1964), St Bride Institute, Bride Lane, London EC4Y 8EE. *Hon. Secretary*, P. Wickens

PRINTING, INSTITUTE OF (1961), 8A Lonsdale Gardens, Tunbridge Wells, Kent TN1 1NU. Tel: 01892-538118. *Secretary-General*, D. Freeland

PRISONERS ABROAD (1978), 72–82 Rosebery Avenue, London EC1R 4RR. Tel: 0171-833 3467. *Director*, C. Laurenzi

PRISON VISITORS, NATIONAL ASSOCIATION OF (1922), 29 Kimbolton Road, Bedford MK40 2PB. Tel: 01234-359763. *General Secretary*, Mrs A. G. McKenna

PRIVATE LIBRARIES ASSOCIATION (1957), Ravelston, South View Road, Pinner, Middx HA5 3YD. *Hon. Secretary*, F. Broomhead

PROCURATORS IN GLASGOW, ROYAL FACULTY OF (1600), 12 Nelson Mandela Place, Glasgow G2 1BT. Tel: 0141-552 3422. *Clerk*, A. J. Campbell

PROFESSIONAL CLASSES AID COUNCIL (1921), 10 St Christopher's Place, London W1M 6HY. Tel: 0171-935 0641.

PROFESSIONAL FOOTBALLERS' ASSOCIATION, 2 Oxford Court, Bishopsgate, Manchester M2 3WQ. Tel: 0161-236 0575. *Chief Executive*, G. Taylor

PROFESSIONS SUPPLEMENTARY TO MEDICINE, COUNCIL FOR, Park House, 184 Kennington Park Road, London SE11 4BU. Tel: 0171-582 0866. *Registrar*, M. D. Hall

PROTECTION OF UNBORN CHILDREN, SOCIETY FOR THE (1967), Phyllis Bowman House, 5–6 St Matthew Street, London SW1P 2JT. Tel: 0171-222 5845. *National Director*, J. Smeaton

PROTESTANT ALLIANCE (1845), 77 Ampthill Road, Flitwick, Bedford MK45 1BD. Tel: 01525-712348. *General Secretary*, Dr S. J. Scott-Pearson

PSORIASIS ASSOCIATION (1968), 7 Milton Street, Northampton NN2 7JG. Tel: 01604-711129. *National Secretary*, Mrs L. Henley

PSYCHIATRISTS, ROYAL COLLEGE OF (1971), 17 Belgrave Square, London SW1X 8PG. Tel: 0171-235 2351. *Secretary*, Mrs V. Cameron

PSYCHICAL RESEARCH, SOCIETY FOR (1882), 49 Marloes Road, London W8 6LA. Tel: 0171-937 8984. *Secretary*, Ms E. J. O'Keeffe

PSYCHOLOGICAL SOCIETY, BRITISH (1901), St Andrews House, 48 Princess Road East, Leicester LE1 7DR. Tel: 0116-254 9568. *Executive Secretary*, C. V. Newman, PH.D.

PUBLIC FINANCE AND ACCOUNTANCY, CHARTERED INSTITUTE OF (1885), 3 Robert Street, London WC2N 6BH. Tel: 0171-543 5600. *Chief Executive*, D. Adams

PUBLIC HEALTH AND HYGIENE, ROYAL INSTITUTE OF, and SOCIETY OF PUBLIC HEALTH (1937), 28 Portland Place, London W1N 4DE. Tel: 0171-580 2731. *Secretary*, Gp Capt R. A. Smith

PUBLIC RELATIONS, INSTITUTE OF (1948), The Old Trading House, 15 Northburgh Street, London EC1V 0PR. Tel: 0171-253 5151. *Executive Director*, J. B. Lavelle

PUBLIC TEACHERS OF LAW, SOCIETY OF (1908), School of Law, Kings College London, Strand, London WC2R 2LS. Tel: 0171-873 2849. *Hon. Secretary*, Prof. D. Hayton

PURCHASING AND SUPPLY, CHARTERED INSTITUTE OF (1967), Easton House, Easton on the Hill, Stamford, Lincs PE9 3NZ. Tel: 01780-756777. *Chief Executive*, C. Holden

QUAKER SOCIAL RESPONSIBILITY AND EDUCATION, Friends House, 173–177 Euston Road, London NW1 2BJ. Tel: 0171-663 1000. *General Secretary*, Ms B. Smith

QUALITY ASSURANCE, INSTITUTE OF, 12 Grosvenor Crescent, London SW1X 7EE. Tel: 0171-245 6722. *Secretary-General*, D. G. Campbell

QUARRIERS (formerly Quarriers Homes) (1871), Bridge of Weir, Renfrewshire PA11 3SA. Tel: 01505-612224. *Director*, G. E. Lee

QUARRYING, INSTITUTE OF (1917), 7 Regent Street, Nottingham NG1 5BS. Tel: 0115-941 1315. *Secretary*, M. J. Arthur

QUEEN ELIZABETH'S FOUNDATION FOR DISABLED PEOPLE (1967), Leatherhead Court, Leatherhead, Surrey KT22 0BN. Tel: 01372-842204. *Director*, M. B. Clark, PH.D.

QUEEN'S ENGLISH SOCIETY, THE (1972), 20 Jessica Road, London SW18 2QN. Tel: 0181-874 2200. *Hon. Secretary*, Miss P. Raper

QUEEN'S NURSING INSTITUTE (1887), 3 Albemarle Way, London EC1V 4JB. Tel: 0171-490 4227. *Director*, Mrs J. Hesketh

QUEEN VICTORIA CLERGY FUND (1897), Church House, Dean's Yard, London SW1P 3NZ. Tel: 0171-222 5261. *Secretary*, C. D. L. Menzies

QUEEN VICTORIA SCHOOL (1908), Dunblane, Perthshire FK15 0JY. Tel: 01786-822288. *Headmaster*, B. Raine

QUEKETT MICROSCOPICAL CLUB (1865), Flat 3, Romagna, 101 Truro Road, London N22 4DL. *Hon. Business Secretary*, Miss P. Hamer

QUIT (NATIONAL SOCIETY OF NON-SMOKERS) (1926), Victory House, 170 Tottenham Court Road, London W1P 0HA. Tel: 0171-388 5775. Helpline: 0800-002200. *Chief Executive*, P. McCabe

RADAR (ROYAL ASSOCIATION FOR DISABILITY AND REHABILITATION) (1977), 12 City Forum, 250 City Road, London EC1V 8AF. Tel: 0171-250 3222. *Director*, B. Massie, OBE

RADIOLOGISTS, ROYAL COLLEGE OF (1934), 38 Portland Place, London W1N 4JQ. Tel: 0171-636 4432. *General Secretary*, A. J. Cowles

RADIOLOGY, BRITISH INSTITUTE OF (1897), 36 Portland Place, London W1N 4AT. Tel: 0171-580 4085. *Chief Executive*, Ms M.A. Piggott

RAIL USERS' CONSULTATIVE COMMITTEE, CENTRAL (1948), Clements House, 14–18 Gresham Street, London EC2V 7NL. Tel: 0171-505 9090. *National Director*, P. Hadley

RAILWAY AND CANAL HISTORICAL SOCIETY, 17 Clumber Crescent North, The Park, Nottingham NG7 1EY. Tel: 0115-941 4844. *Hon. Secretary*, G. H. R. Gwatkin

RAILWAY BENEVOLENT INSTITUTION (1858), Foundation House, 7–11 Macon Court, Herald Drive, Crewe, Cheshire CW1 6WA. Tel: 01270-251316. *Director*, B. R. Whitnall

RAMBLERS' ASSOCIATION (1935), 1–5 Wandsworth Road, London SW8 2XX. Tel: 0171-339 8500. *Director*, A. Mattingly

RARE BREEDS SURVIVAL TRUST (1973), National Agricultural Centre, Stoneleigh Park, Kenilworth, Warks CV8 2LG. Tel: 01203-696551. *Executive Director*, G. L. H. Alderson

RATHBONE COMMUNITY INDUSTRY (1919), 1st Floor, The Excalibur Building, 77 Whitworth Street, Manchester M1 6EZ. Tel: 0161-236 5358. Helpline: 0161-236 1877. *Chief Executive*, Ms A. Weinstock, CBE

RECORDS ASSOCIATION, BRITISH (1932), 40 Northampton Road, London EC1R 0HB. Tel: 0171-833 0428. *Hon. Secretary*, Mrs E. Hughes

RECORD SOCIETY, SCOTTISH (1897), Department of Scottish History, University of Glasgow, Glasgow G12 8QH. Tel: 0141-339 8855 ext 5682. *Hon. Secretary*, J. Kirk, PH.D.

RED CROSS SOCIETY, BRITISH, *see* BRITISH RED CROSS

RED POLL CATTLE SOCIETY (1888), The Market Hill, Woodbridge, Suffolk IP12 4LU. Tel: 01394-380643. *Secretary*, P. Ryder-Davies

REFRIGERATION, INSTITUTE OF (1899), Kelvin House, 76 Mill Lane, Carshalton, Surrey SM5 2JR. Tel: 0181-647 7033. *Secretary*, M. J. Horlick

REFUGEE COUNCIL, BRITISH (1981), Bondway House, 3–9 Bondway, London SW8 1SJ. Tel: 0171-820 3000. *Chief Executive*, N. Hardwick

REGIONAL STUDIES ASSOCIATION (1965), Wharfdale Projects, 15 Micawber Street, London N1 7TB. Tel: 0171-490 1128. *Director*, Mrs S. Hardy

REGULAR FORCES EMPLOYMENT ASSOCIATION (1885), 49 Pall Mall, London SW1Y 5JG. Tel: 0171-321 2011. *Chief Executive*, Maj.-Gen. M. F. L. Shellard, CBE

RELATE: NATIONAL MARRIAGE GUIDANCE (1938), Herbert Gray College, Little Church Street, Rugby, Warks CV21 3AP. Tel: 01788-573241. *Chief Executive*, Ms S. Bowler

RENT OFFICERS AND RENTAL VALUERS, INSTITUTE OF (1966), Beaufort House, Hamble Lane, Bursledon, Southampton SO31 8BR. Tel: 01703-403716. *General Secretary*, A. E. Corcoran, FRV

RESEARCH DEFENCE SOCIETY (1908), 58 Great Marlborough Street, London W1V 1DD. Tel: 0171-287 2818. *Executive Director*, Dr M. Matfield

RESERVE FORCES ASSOCIATION (formerly Council of Territorial, Auxiliary and Volunteer Reserve Associations) (1908), Duke of York's HQ, London SW3 4SG. Tel: 0171-414 5588. *Secretary-General*, Maj.-Gen. W. A. Evans, CB

RETIREMENT PENSIONS ASSOCIATIONS, NATIONAL FEDERATION OF (1938), Thwaites House, Railway Road, Blackburn BB1 5AX. Tel: 01254-52606. *General Secretary*, R. Stansfield

REVENUES, RATING AND VALUATION, INSTITUTE OF (1882), 41 Doughty Street, London WC1N 2LF. Tel: 0171-831 3505. *Director*, C. Farrington

RICHARD III SOCIETY (1924), 4 Oakley Street, London SW3 5NN. *Secretary*, Miss E. M. Nokes

ROAD SAFETY OFFICERS, INSTITUTE OF (1971), c/o 11 Parkside, Groby, Leicester LE6 0EB. Tel: 0116-265 7229. *Chairman*, Mrs R. Duffield

ROAD TRANSPORT ENGINEERS, INSTITUTE OF (1945), 22 Greencoat Place, London SW1P 1PR. Tel: 0171-630 1111. *Chief Executive*, A. F. Stroud

ROMAN STUDIES, SOCIETY FOR THE PROMOTION OF (1910), Senate House, Malet Street, London WC1E 7HU. Tel: 0171-862 8727. *Secretary*, Dr H. M. Cockle

ROTARY INTERNATIONAL IN GREAT BRITAIN AND IRELAND (1914), Kinwarton Road, Alcester, Warks B49 6BP. Tel: 01789-765411. *Secretary*, R. Freeman

ROUND TABLES OF GREAT BRITAIN AND IRELAND, NATIONAL ASSOCIATION OF (1927), Marchesi House, 4 Embassy Drive, Edgbaston, Birmingham B15 1TP. Tel: 0121-456 4402. *General Secretary*, J. R. Ollerton

ROYAL AIR FORCE BENEVOLENT FUND (1919), 67 Portland Place, London W1N 4AR. Tel: 0171-580 8343. *Controller*, Air Chief Marshal Sir David Cousins, KCB, AFC

ROYAL AIR FORCES ASSOCIATION (1943), 43 Grove Park Road, London W4 3RX. Tel: 0181-994 8504. *Secretary-General*, J. G. Hargreaves, CBE

ROYAL ALEXANDRA AND ALBERT SCHOOL (1758), Gatton Park, Reigate, Surrey RH2 0TW. Tel: 01737-642576. *Secretary*, Wg Cdr. N. J. Wright

ROYAL ALFRED SEAFARERS' SOCIETY (1865), Weston Acres, Woodmansterne Lane, Banstead, Surrey SM7 3HB. Tel: 01737-352231. *General Secretary*, A. R. Quinton

ROYAL ARMOURED CORPS WAR MEMORIAL BENEVOLENT FUND (1946), c/o RHQ RTR, Bovington Camp, Wareham, Dorset BH20 6JA. Tel: 01929-403331. *Secretary*, Maj. A. Henzie, MBE

ROYAL ARTILLERY ASSOCIATION, Artillery House, Front Parade, Royal Artillery Barracks, Woolwich, London SE18 4BH. Tel: 0181-781 3005. *General Secretary*, Lt.-Col. M. G. Felton

ROYAL ASIATIC SOCIETY (1823), 60 Queen's Gardens, London W2 3AF. Tel: 0171-724 4742. *Secretary*, T. N. Guina, MVO

ROYAL BRITISH LEGION, *see* BRITISH LEGION, ROYAL

ROYAL CALEDONIAN EDUCATIONAL TRUST (1815), 80A High Street, Bushey, Watford, Herts WD2 3DE. Tel: 0181-421 8845. *Chief Executive*, J. Horsfield

ROYAL CELTIC SOCIETY (1820), 23 Rutland Street, Edinburgh EH1 2RN. Tel: 0131-228 6449. *Secretary*, J. G. Cameron, WS

ROYAL CHORAL SOCIETY (1871), Unit 9, 92 Lots Road, London SW10 0QD. Tel: 0171-376 3718. *Administrator*, G. Tonge

ROYAL ENGINEERS ASSOCIATION, RHQ Royal Engineers, Brompton Barracks, Chatham, Kent ME4 4UG. Tel: 01634-822394. *Controller*, Lt.-Col. J. W. Ray (retd)

ROYAL ENGINEERS, INSTITUTION OF (1875), Brompton Barracks, Chatham, Kent ME4 4UG. Tel: 01634-842669. *Secretary*, Col. M. R. Cooper

ROYAL HIGHLAND AND AGRICULTURAL SOCIETY OF SCOTLAND (1784), Royal Highland Centre, Ingliston, Edinburgh EH28 8NF. Tel: 0131-335 6200. *Chief Executive*, R. Jones

ROYAL HORTICULTURAL SOCIETY (1804), 80 Vincent Square, London SW1P 2PE. Tel: 0171-834 4333. *Director-General*, G. H. Rae

ROYAL HOSPITAL FOR NEURO-DISABILITY (1854), West Hill, Putney, London SW15 3SW. Tel: 0181-780 4500. *Chief Executive*, V. J. Beauchamp

ROYAL HUMANE SOCIETY (1774), Brettenham House, Lancaster Place, London WC2E 7EP. Tel: 0171-836 8155. *Secretary*, Maj.-Gen. C. Tyler, CB

ROYAL INSTITUTION OF GREAT BRITAIN (1799), 21 Albemarle Street, London W1X 4BS. Tel: 0171-409 2992. *Director*, Prof. S. Greenfield

ROYAL LIFE SAVING SOCIETY UK (1891), River House, High Street, Broom, Warks B50 4HN. Tel: 01789-773994. *Director-General*, S. Lear

ROYAL LITERARY FUND (1790), 144 Temple Chambers, Temple Avenue, London EC4Y 0DA. Tel: 0171-353 7150. *Secretary*, Mrs F. M. Clark

ROYAL MEDICAL BENEVOLENT FUND (1836), 24 King's Road, London SW19 8QN. Tel: 0181-540 9194. *Secretary*, Mrs G. A. R. Wells

ROYAL MEDICAL SOCIETY (1737), Students Centre, 5/5 Bristo Square, Edinburgh EH8 9AL. Tel: 0131-650 2672. *Senior President*, C. Parsons

ROYAL MICROSCOPICAL SOCIETY (1839), 37–38 St Clements, Oxford OX4 1AJ. Tel: 01865-248768. *Administrator*, P. B. Hirst

ROYAL MUSICAL ASSOCIATION (1874), Department of Music, The University of Leeds, Leeds LS2 9JT. *President*, J. Rushton

ROYAL NATIONAL INSTITUTE FOR THE BLIND (1868), 224 Great Portland Street, London W1N 6AA. Tel: 0171-388 1266. *Director-General*, I. Bruce

ROYAL NATIONAL LIFEBOAT INSTITUTION (1824), West Quay Road, Poole, Dorset BH15 1HZ. Tel: 01202-663000. *Director (until Dec. 1998)*, B. Miles, CBE, RD

ROYAL NAVAL AND ROYAL MARINES CHILDREN'S TRUST (1834), HMS Nelson, Portsmouth PO1 3HH. Tel: 01705-817435. *Secretary*, Mrs M. Bateman

ROYAL NAVAL ASSOCIATION (1950), 82 Chelsea Manor Street, London SW3 5QJ. Tel: 0171-352 6764. *General Secretary*, Capt. R. McQueen, CBE, RN

ROYAL NAVAL BENEVOLENT SOCIETY FOR OFFICERS (1739), 1 Fleet Street, London EC4Y 1BD. Tel: 0171-353 4080 ext 471. *Secretary*, Capt. I. B. Sutherland

ROYAL NAVAL BENEVOLENT TRUST (1922), Castaway House, 311 Twyford Avenue, Portsmouth PO2 8PE. Tel: 01705-690112. *Chief Executive*, Cdr. J. Owens

ROYAL NAVY OFFICERS, ASSOCIATION OF (1920), 70 Porchester Terrace, London W2 3TP. Tel: 0171-402 5231. *Secretary*, Lt.-Cdr. I. M. P. Coombes

ROYAL OVER-SEAS LEAGUE (1910), Over–Seas House, Park Place, St James's Street, London SW1A 1LR. Tel: 0171-408 0214. *Director-General*, R. F. Newell

ROYAL PATRIOTIC FUND CORPORATION (1854), 40 Queen Anne's Gate, London SW1H 9AP. Tel: 0171-233 1894. *Secretary*, Brig. T. G. Williams, CBE

ROYAL PHILATELIC SOCIETY LONDON (1869), 41 Devonshire Place, London W1N 1PE. Tel: 0171-486 1044. *Hon. Secretary*, Prof. B. S. Jay

ROYAL PHOTOGRAPHIC SOCIETY (1853), The Octagon, Milsom Street, Bath BA1 1DN. Tel: 01225-462841. *Secretary-General*, B. Lane

ROYAL PINNER SCHOOL FOUNDATION, 110 Old Brompton Road, London SW7 3RA. Tel: 0171-373 6168. *Secretary*, D. Crawford

ROYAL SAILORS' RESTS (1876), 5 St Georges Business Centre, St Georges Square, Portsmouth PO1 1EY. Tel: 01705-296096. *Executive Director*, Revd J. Martin

ROYAL SOCIETY FOR ASIAN AFFAIRS (1901), 2 Belgrave Square, London SW1X 8PJ. Tel: 0171-235 5122. *Secretary*, D. J. Easton

ROYAL SOCIETY FOR THE ENCOURAGEMENT OF ARTS, MANUFACTURES AND COMMERCE (RSA) (1754), 8 John Adam Street, London WC2N 6EZ. Tel: 0171-930 5115. *Chairman*, R. Onians

ROYAL SOCIETY FOR THE PREVENTION OF CRUELTY TO ANIMALS (RSPCA) (1824), Causeway, Horsham, W. Sussex RH12 1HG. Tel: 01403-264181. *Director-General*, P. R. Davies, CB

ROYAL SOCIETY FOR THE PROMOTION OF HEALTH (formerly Royal Society of Health) (1876), RSH House, 38 St George's Drive, London SW1V 4BH. Tel: 0171-630 0121. *Secretary*, Mrs H. Brandon

ROYAL SOCIETY FOR THE PROTECTION OF BIRDS (RSPB) (1889), The Lodge, Sandy, Beds SG19 2DL. Tel: 01767-680551. *Chief Executive*, G. R. Wynne

ROYAL SOCIETY OF LITERATURE (1823), 1 Hyde Park Gardens, London W2 2LT. Tel: 0171-723 5104. *Secretary*, Mrs M. Fergusson

ROYAL SOCIETY OF MEDICINE (1805), 1 Wimpole Street, London W1M 8AE. Tel: 0171-290 2900. *Executive Director*, Dr A. Grocock

ROYAL SOCIETY OF ST GEORGE (1894), 127 Sandgate Road, Folkestone, Kent CT20 2BL. Tel: 01303-241795. *Chairman*, W. M. Firth

ROYAL STAR AND GARTER HOME FOR DISABLED SAILORS, SOLDIERS AND AIRMEN (1916), Richmond Hill, Richmond upon Thames, Surrey TW10 6RR. Tel: 0181-940 3314. *Chief Executive*, I. Lashbrooke

ROYAL STATISTICAL SOCIETY (1834), 12 Errol Street, London EC1Y 8LX. Tel: 0171-638 8998. *Executive Secretary*, I. J. Goddard

ROYAL TANK REGIMENT BENEVOLENT FUND (1919), RHQ RTR, Bovington Camp, Wareham, Dorset BH20 6JA. Tel: 01929-403331. *Regimental Secretary*, Maj. A. Henzie, MBE

ROYAL TELEVISION SOCIETY (1927), Holborn Hall, 100 Gray's Inn Road, London WC1X 8AL. Tel: 0171-430 1000. *Executive Director*, M. Bunce

ROYAL UNITED KINGDOM BENEFICENT ASSOCIATION (1863), 6 Avonmore Road, London W14 8RL. Tel: 0171-602 6274. *Director*, W. Rathbone

RURAL ENGLAND, COUNCIL FOR THE PROTECTION OF, *see* CPRE

RURAL SCOTLAND, ASSOCIATION FOR THE PROTECTION OF (1926), 3rd Floor, Gladstone's Land, 483 Lawnmarket, Edinburgh EH1 2NT. Tel: 0131-225 7012. *Manager*, Mrs E. J. Garland

RURAL WALES, CAMPAIGN FOR THE PROTECTION OF (1928), Ty Gwyn, 31 High Street, Welshpool, Powys SY21 7YD. Tel: 01938-552525. *Director*, M. Williams

SAFETY COUNCIL, BRITISH (1957), National Safety Centre, 70 Chancellor's Road, London W6 9RS. Tel: 0181-741 1231. *Director-General*, Sir Neville Purvis, KCB

SAILORS' FAMILIES' SOCIETY (1821), Newland, Hull HU6 7RJ. Tel: 01482-342331. *Chief Executive*, G. J. Powell

SAILORS' SOCIETY, BRITISH AND INTERNATIONAL (1818), 3 Orchard Place, Southampton SO14 3AT. Tel: 01703-337333. *General Secretary*, G. Chambers

ST DEINIOL'S RESIDENTIAL LIBRARY (1902), Hawarden, Deeside, Flintshire CH5 3DF. Tel: 01244-532350. *Warden and Chief Librarian*, Revd P. B. Francis

ST DUNSTAN'S, 12–14 Harcourt Street, London W1A 4XB. Tel: 0171-723 5021. For men and women blinded in the service of their country. *Chief Executive*, G. B. J. Frost

ST JOHN AMBULANCE (1887), 1 Grosvenor Crescent, London SW1X 7EF. Tel: 0171-235 5231. *Executive Director*, L. Martin

SALES AND MARKETING MANAGEMENT, INSTITUTE OF (1966), Romeland House, Romeland Hill, St Albans AL3 4ET. Tel: 01727-812500. *Chief Executive*, P. Joiner

SALMON AND TROUT ASSOCIATION (1903), Fishmongers' Hall, London Bridge, London EC4R 9EL. Tel: 0171-283 5838. *Director*, C. W. Poupard

SALTIRE SOCIETY (1936), 9 Fountain Close, 22 High Street, Edinburgh EH1 1TF. Tel: 0131-556 1836. *Administrator*, Mrs K. Munro

SAMARITANS, THE (1953), 10 The Grove, Slough SL1 1QP. Tel: 01753-532713. Helpline: 0345-909090. PO Box 9090, Stirling FK8 2SA. Tel: 08457-909192. *Chief Executive*, S. Armson

SANE (1986), 1st Floor, Cityside House, 40 Alder Street, London E1 1EE. Tel: 0171-375 1002. *Chief Executive*, Ms M. Wallace, MBE

SAVE BRITAIN'S HERITAGE (1975), 77 Cowcross Street, London EC1M 6BP. Tel: 0171-253 3500. *Secretary*, R. Pollard

SAVE THE CHILDREN FUND (1919), 17 Grove Lane, London SE5 8RD. Tel: 0171-703 5400. *Director-General*, M. Aaronson

SCHIZOPHRENIA FELLOWSHIP, NATIONAL (1970), 28 Castle Street, Kingston upon Thames, Surrey KT1 1SS. Tel: 0181-547 3937. *Chief Executive*, C. Prior

SCHOOL LIBRARY ASSOCIATION (1937), Liden Library, Barrington Close, Liden, Swindon SN3 6HF. Tel: 01793-617838. *Executive Secretary*, Ms K. Lemaire

SCHOOLMASTERS, SOCIETY OF (1798), Dolton's Farm, Woburn, Milton Keynes MK17 9HX. Tel: 01525-290093. *Secretary*, Mrs B. A. Skipper

SCHOOLMISTRESSES AND GOVERNESSES BENEVOLENT INSTITUTION (1843), Queen Mary House, Manor Park Road, Chislehurst, Kent BR7 5PY. Tel: 0181-468 7997. *Director*, L. I. Baggott

SCIENCE, BRITISH ASSOCIATION FOR THE ADVANCEMENT OF (1831), 23 Savile Row, London W1X 2NB. Tel: 0171-973 3500. *Chief Executive*, Dr P. Briggs

SCIENCE EDUCATION, ASSOCIATION FOR (1963), College Lane, Hatfield, Herts AL10 9AA. Tel: 01707-283000. *Chief Executive*, Dr D. S. Moore

SCOPE (formerly The Spastics Society) (1952), 12 Park Crescent, London W1N 4EQ. Tel: 0171-636 5020. *Chief Executive*, R. P. Brewster

SCOTCH WHISKY ASSOCIATION (1919), 20 Atholl Crescent, Edinburgh EH3 8HF. Tel: 0131-222 9200. *Director-General*, H. Morison

SCOTTISH CHIEFS, STANDING COUNCIL OF (1952), Hope Chambers, 52 Leith Walk, Edinburgh EH6 5HW. Tel: 0131-554 6321. *General Secretary*, G. A. Way of Plean

SCOTTISH CHURCH HISTORY SOCIETY (1922), St Serf's Manse, 1 Denham Green Terrace, Edinburgh EH5 3PG. Tel: 0131-552 4059. *Hon. Secretary*, Revd Dr P. H. Donald

SCOTTISH COUNTRY DANCE SOCIETY, ROYAL (1923), 12 Coates Crescent, Edinburgh EH3 7AF. Tel: 0131-225 3854. *Secretary*, Miss G. S. Parker

SCOTTISH GENEALOGY SOCIETY (1953), Library and Family History Centre, 15 Victoria Terrace, Edinburgh EH1 2JL. Tel: 0131-220 3677. *Hon. Secretary*, Miss J. P. S. Ferguson

SCOTTISH HISTORY SOCIETY (1886), Department of Scottish History, 17 Buccleuch Place, University of Edinburgh, Edinburgh EH8 9LN. Tel: 0131-650 4030. *Hon. Secretary*, Dr S. Boardman

SCOTTISH LANDOWNERS' FEDERATION (1906), 25 Maritime Street, Edinburgh EH6 5PW. Tel: 0131-555 1031. *Director*, Dr M. S. Hankey

SCOTTISH LAW AGENTS SOCIETY, Signet Library, Parliament Square, Edinburgh EH1 1RD. Tel: 0131-225 5051. *Secretary*, Mrs J. H. Webster, WS

SCOTTISH NATIONAL INSTITUTION FOR THE WAR BLINDED (1915), PO Box 500, Gillespie Crescent, Edinburgh EH10 4HZ. Tel: 0131-229 1456. *Secretary*, J. B. M. Munro

SCOTTISH NATIONAL WAR MEMORIAL (1927), The Castle, Edinburgh EH1 2YT. Tel: 0131-226 7393. *Secretary*, Lt.-Col. H. D. R. Mackay

SCOTTISH SOCIETY FOR THE PREVENTION OF CRUELTY TO ANIMALS (1839), Braehead Mains, 603 Queensferry Road, Edinburgh EH4 6EA. Tel: 0131-339 0222. *Chief Executive*, J. Morris, CBE

SCOTTISH SOCIETY FOR THE PROTECTION OF WILD BIRDS (1927), Foremount House, Kilbarchan, Renfrewshire PA10 2EZ. Tel: 01505-702419. *Secretary*, Dr J. A. Gibson

SCOTTISH WILDLIFE TRUST (1964), Cramond House, Kirk Cramond, Cramond Glebe Road, Edinburgh EH4 6NS. Tel: 0131-312 7765. *Director*, D. J. Hughes-Hallett

SCOUT ASSOCIATION (1907), Baden–Powell House, Queen's Gate, London SW7 5JS. Tel: 0171-584 7030. *Chief Executive*, D. M. Twine; *Chief Scout*, W. G. Purdy

SCRIBES AND ILLUMINATORS, SOCIETY OF (1921), 6 Queen Square, London 3AR. Tel: 01483-894155. *Hon. Secretary*, Ms C. Turvey

SCRIPTURE GIFT MISSION INCORPORATED (1888), Radstock House, 3 Eccleston Street, London SW1W 9LZ. Tel: 0171-730 2155. *International Director*, H. Q. Davies

SCRIPTURE UNION (1867), 207–209 Queensway, Bletchley, Milton Keynes MK2 2EB. Tel: 01908-856000. *Chief Executive*, P. Kimber

SEA CADET ASSOCIATION (1895), 202 Lambeth Road, London SE1 7JF. Tel: 0171-928 8978. *General Secretary*, Cdre. R. M. Parker

SEAMEN'S BOY'S HOME, BRITISH (1863), Outdoor Educational Activity Centre, Grenville House, Berry Head Road, Brixham, Devon TQ5 9AF. Tel: 01803-852797. *Secretary*, R. M. Williams

SEAMEN'S CHRISTIAN FRIEND SOCIETY (1846), 48 South Street, Alderley Edge, Cheshire SK9 7ES. Tel: 01625-590010. *Director*, M. J. Wilson

SEAMEN'S PENSION FUND, ROYAL (1919), 65 High Street, Ewell, Epsom, Surrey KT17 1RX. Tel: 0181-393 5873. *Secretary*, D. Barker

SECRETARIES AND ADMINISTRATORS, INSTITUTE OF CHARTERED (1891), 16 Park Crescent, London W1N 4AH. Tel: 0171-580 4741. *Chief Executive*, M. J. Ainsworth

SECULAR SOCIETY, NATIONAL (1866), 25 Red Lion Square, London WC1R 4RL. Tel: 0171-404 3126. *General Secretary*, K. P. Wood

SeeABILITY (formerly Royal School for the Blind) (1799), 56–66 Highlands Road, Leatherhead, Surrey KT22 8NR. Tel: 01372-373086. *Chief Executive*, R. M. Perkins

SELDEN SOCIETY (1887), Faculty of Laws, Queen Mary College, Mile End Road, London E1 4NS. Tel: 0171-975 5136. *Secretary*, V. Tunkel

SENSE (NATIONAL DEAFBLIND AND RUBELLA ASSOCIATION) (1955), 11–13 Clifton Terrace, London N4 3SR. Tel: 0171-272 7774. *Chief Executive*, R. Clark

SHAFTESBURY HOMES AND *Arethusa* (1843), 3 Rectory Grove, London SW4 0DX. Tel: 0171-720 8709. *Director*, Capt. N. C. Baird-Murray, CBE, RN

SHAFTESBURY SOCIETY (1844), 16 Kingston Road, London SW19 1JZ. Tel: 0181-239 5555. *Chief Executive*, Ms F. Beckett

SHELLFISH ASSOCIATION OF GREAT BRITAIN (1904), Fishmongers' Hall, London Bridge, London EC4R 9EL. Tel: 0171-283 8305. *Director*, E. Edwards, OBE, Ph.D.

SHELTER (THE NATIONAL CAMPAIGN FOR HOMELESS PEOPLE) (1966), 88 Old Street, London EC1V 9HU. Tel: 0171-505 2000. *Director*, C. Holmes, CBE

SHERLOCK HOLMES SOCIETY OF LONDON (1951), 13 Crofton Avenue, Orpinton, Kent BR6 8DW. Tel: 01689-811314. *General Secretary*, R. J. Ellis

SHIPBROKERS, INSTITUTE OF CHARTERED (1911), 3 St Helen's Place, London EC3A 6EJ. Tel: 0171-628 5559. *Director*, Mrs B. Fletcher

SHIRE HORSE SOCIETY (1878), East of England Showground, Peterborough PE2 6XE. Tel: 01733-234451. *Secretary*, T. Gibson, OBE

SHRIEVALTY ASSOCIATION (1971), Office of the High Sheriffs, Duncombe Place, York YO1 7DY. Tel: 01904-634771. *Secretary*, J. H. N. Towers

SIGHT SAVERS INTERNATIONAL (ROYAL COMMONWEALTH SOCIETY FOR THE BLIND) (1950), Grosvenor Hall, Bolnore Road, Haywards Heath, W. Sussex RH16 4BX. Tel: 01444-446600. *Executive Director*, R. Porter

SIMPLIFIED SPELLING SOCIETY (1908), Tailours, High Road, Chigwell, Essex IG7 6DL. Tel: 0181-501 0405. *Chairman*, C. J. H. Jolly

SIR OSWALD STOLL FOUNDATION (1916), 446 Fulham Road, London SW6 1DT. Tel: 0171-385 2110. *Director*, R. C. Brunwin

SMALL BUSINESSES, FEDERATION OF (1974), 2 Catherine Place, London SW1E 6HF. Tel: 0171-233 7900. *Hon. National Chairman*, I. Handford

SOCIAL CONCERN, NATIONAL COUNCIL FOR, Montague Chambers, Montague Place, London SE1 9DA. Tel: 0171-403 0977. *Director*, P. Carlin

SOCIALIST PARTY, THE (formerly Socialist Party of Great Britain) (1904), 52 Clapham High Street, London SW4 7UN. Tel: 0171-622 3811. *General Secretary*, Ms J. Carter

SOCIAL WORKERS, BRITISH ASSOCIATION OF (1970), 16 Kent Street, Birmingham B5 6RD. Tel: 0121-622 3911. *Director*, vacant

SOIL ASSOCIATION (1946), Bristol House, 40–56 Victoria Street, Bristol BS1 6BY. Tel: 0117-929 0661. *Director*, P. Holden

SOLDIERS' AND AIRMEN'S SCRIPTURE READERS ASSOCIATION (1838), Havelock House, Barrack Road, Aldershot, Hants GU11 3NP. Tel: 01252-310033. *General Secretary*, Lt.-Col. M. Hitchcott

SOLDIERS' WIDOWS, ROYAL CAMBRIDGE HOME FOR (1851), 82–84 Hurst Road, East Molesey, Surrey KT8 9AH. Tel: 0181-979 3788. *Superintendent*, Mrs I. O. Yarnell

SOLICITORS IN THE SUPREME COURT OF SCOTLAND, SOCIETY OF (1784), SSC Library, Parliament House, 11 Parliament Square, Edinburgh EH1 1RF. Tel: 0131-225 6268. *Secretary*, I. L. S. Balfour

SOROPTIMIST INTERNATIONAL OF GREAT BRITAIN AND IRELAND (1923), 127 Wellington Road South, Stockport SK1 3TS. Tel: 0161-480 7686. *Executive Officer*, Ms K. Heward

SOS SOCIETY, *see* 2CARE

SOUTH AMERICAN MISSION SOCIETY (1844), Allen Gardiner House, Pembury Road, Tunbridge Wells, Kent TN2 3QU. Tel: 01892-538647. *General Secretary*, Rt. Revd D. R. J. Evans

SOUTH WALES INSTITUTE OF ENGINEERS (1857), 2nd Floor, Empire House, Mount Stuart Square, Cardiff CF1 6DN. Tel: 01222-481726. *Hon. Secretary*, R. E. Lindsay

SPEAKERS CLUBS, ASSOCIATION OF (1971), 28 High Street, Auchterarder, Perthshire PH3 1DF. Tel: 01764-662457. *National Secretary*, D. Williams

SPINA BIFIDA AND HYDROCEPHALUS, ASSOCIATION FOR (ASBAH), 42 Park Road, Peterborough PE1 2UQ. Tel: 01733-555988. *Executive Director*, A. Russell

SPORT AND THE ARTS, FOUNDATION FOR (1991), PO Box 20, Liverpool L13 1HB. Tel: 0151-259 5505. *Secretary to the Trustees*, G. Endicott, OBE

SPORTS MEDICINE, INSTITUTE OF (1963), Room 212, Charles Bell House, University College London Medical School, 67–73 Riding House Street, London W1P 7LD. Tel: 0171-813 2832. *Hon. Secretary*, Dr W. T. Orton

SPURGEON'S CHILD CARE (1867), 74 Wellingborough Road, Rushden, Northants NN10 9TY. Tel: 01933-412412. *Chief Executive*, D. C. Culwick

SSAFA FORCES HELP (1885, merged 1997), 19 Queen Elizabeth Street, London SE1 2LP. Tel: 0171-403 8783. *Controller*, Maj.-Gen. P. Sheppard, CB, CBE

STANDING CONFERENCE OF NATIONAL AND UNIVERSITY LIBRARIES (SCONUL) (1950), 102 Euston Street, London NW1 2HA. Tel: 0171-387 0317. *Secretary*, A. J. C. Bainton

STATISTICIANS, INSTITUTE OF, *see* ROYAL STATISTICAL SOCIETY

STEWART SOCIETY (1899), 17 Dublin Street, Edinburgh EH1 3PG. Tel: 0131-557 6824. *Hon. Secretary*, Mrs M. Walker

STRATEGIC PLANNING SOCIETY (1967), 17 Portland Place, London W1N 3AF. Tel: 0171-636 7737. *General Manager*, D. Lambert

STRATEGIC STUDIES, INTERNATIONAL INSTITUTE FOR (1958), 23 Tavistock Street, London WC2E 7NQ. Tel: 0171-379 7676. *Director*, Dr J. Chipman

STROKE ASSOCIATION (1899), Stroke House, Whitecross Street, London EC1V 8JJ. Tel: 0171-566 0300. *Chief Executive Officer*, Miss M. Goose

STRUCTURAL ENGINEERS, INSTITUTION OF (1908), 11 Upper Belgrave Street, London SW1X 8BH. Tel: 0171-235 4535. *Chief Executive*, Dr J. W. Dougill, FEng.

STUDENT CHRISTIAN MOVEMENT (1889), Westhill College, 14–16 Weoley Park Road, Selly Oak, Birmingham B29 6LL. Tel: 0121-471 2404. *Co-ordinator*, Ms. C. Clayton

SUFFOLK HORSE SOCIETY (1878), The Market Hill, Woodbridge, Suffolk IP12 4LU. Tel: 01394-380643. *Secretary*, P. Ryder-Davies

SURGEONS OF EDINBURGH, ROYAL COLLEGE OF (1505), Nicolson Street, Edinburgh EH8 9DW. Tel: 0131-527 1600. *Executive Secretary*, Miss A. Campbell; *President*, Prof. Sir Robert Shields

SURGEONS OF ENGLAND, ROYAL COLLEGE OF (1800), 35–43 Lincoln's Inn Fields, London WC2A 3PN. Tel: 0171-405 3474. *Secretary*, C. Duncan

SURVEYORS, ROYAL INSTITUTION OF CHARTERED (1868), 12 Great George Street, London SW1P 3AD. Tel: 0171-222 7000. *Chief Executive*, Ms C. Makin

SURVIVAL INTERNATIONAL (1969), 11–15 Emerald Street, London WC1N 3QT. Tel: 0171-242 1441. *Director*, S. Corry

SUZY LAMPLUGH TRUST (1986), 14 East Sheen Avenue, London SW14 8AS . Tel: 0181-392 1839. Promotes personal safety. *Executive Secretary*, P. Lamplugh

SWEDENBORG SOCIETY (1810), 20–21 Bloomsbury Way, London WC1A 2TH. Tel: 0171-405 7986. *Secretary*, Miss M. G. Waters

TAVISTOCK INSTITUTE, THE (1947), 30 Tabernacle Street, London EC2A 4DD. Tel: 0171-417 0407. *Secretary*, J. Margarson

TAXATION, CHARTERED INSTITUTE OF (1930), 12 Upper Belgrave Street, London SW1X 8BB. Tel: 0171-235 9381. *Secretary-General*, R. A. Dommett

TEACHERS, COLLEGE OF (formerly College of Preceptors) (1846), Coppice Row, Theydon Bois, Epping, Essex CM16 7DN. Tel: 01992-812727. *Chief Executive Officer*, R. Page

TEACHERS OF HOME ECONOMICS AND TECHNOLOGY, NATIONAL ASSOCIATION OF (1896), Hamilton House, Mabledon Place, London WC1H 9BJ. Tel: 0171-387 1441. *General Secretary*, G. Thompson

TEACHERS OF MATHEMATICS, ASSOCIATION OF (1952), 7 Shaftesbury Street, Derby DE23 8YB. Tel: 01332-346599. *Hon. Secretary*, Ms A. Gammon

TEACHERS OF THE DEAF, BRITISH ASSOCIATION OF (1977), 41 The Orchard, Leven, Beverley, E. Yorks HU17 5QA. Tel: 01964-544243. *Hon. Secretary*, P. A. Simpson

TEACHERS' UNION, ULSTER (1919), 94 Malone Road, Belfast BT9 5HP. Tel: 01232-662216. *General Secretary*, R. Calvin

TELECOMMUNICATION USERS' ASSOCIATION (1965), Woodgate Studios, 2–8 Games Road, Cockfosters, Herts EN4 9HN. Tel: 0181-449 8844. *Executive Chairman*, W. E. Mieran

TEMPERANCE COUNCIL, NATIONAL UNITED (1880), Alliance House, 12 Caxton Street, London SW1H 0QS. Tel: 0181-444 5004. *General Secretary*, Mrs G. O. Stretton

TEMPERANCE FRIENDLY SOCIETY, ORDER OF THE SONS OF (1855), 176 Blackfriars Road, London SE1 8ET. Tel: 0171-928 7384. *Secretary*, Mrs M. C. Scroby

TEMPERANCE LEAGUE, BRITISH NATIONAL (1834), Westbrook Court, 2 Sharrow Vale Road, Sheffield S11 8YZ. Tel: 0114-267 9976. *Executive Director*, A. Willis

TEMPERANCE SOCIETY, ROYAL NAVAL (1876), 5 St George's Business Centre, St George's Square, Portsmouth PO1 3EY. Tel: 01705-296096. *General Secretary*, Revd J. P. M. Martin

TEMPLETON FOUNDATION (1973), 18 Eastgate Gardens, Taunton, Somerset TA1 1RD. Tel: 01823-324522. *UK Representative*, Mrs N. Pearse

TERRENCE HIGGINS TRUST (1982), 52–54 Grays Inn Road, London WC1X 8JU. Tel: 0171-831 0330. *Chairman*, N. Partridge

TEXTILE INSTITUTE, THE (1910), 10 Blackfriars Street, Manchester M3 5DR. Tel: 0161-834 8457. *Chief Executive*, R. G. Denyer

THEATRE RESEARCH, SOCIETY FOR (1948), c/o The Theatre Museum, 1E Tavistock Street, London WC2E 7PA. *Joint Hon. Secretaries*, Ms E. Cottis; Ms F. Dann

THEATRES TRUST, THE (1976), 22 Charing Cross Road, London WC2H 0HR. Tel: 0171-836 8591. *Director*, P. Longman

THEATRICAL FUND, ROYAL (1839), 11 Garrick Street, London WC2E 9AR. Tel: 0171-836 3322. *Secretary*, Mrs R. M. Foster

THEOSOPHICAL SOCIETY IN ENGLAND (1875), 50 Gloucester Place, London W1H 4EA. Tel: 0171-935 9261. *General Secretary*, P. Barton

THISTLE FOUNDATION (1945), Niddrie Mains Road, Edinburgh EH16 4EA. Tel: 0131-661 3366. *Director*, Ms J. Fisher

THOMAS CORAM FOUNDATION FOR CHILDREN (formerly The Foundling Hospital) (1739), 40 Brunswick Square, London WC1N 1AZ. Tel: 0171-520 0300. *Director*, Dr G. Pugh, OBE

TIDY BRITAIN GROUP (1953), The Pier, Wigan WN3 4EX. Tel: 01942-824620. *Director-General*, Prof. G. Ashworth, CBE

TOC H (1915), 1 Forest Close, Wendover, Aylesbury, Bucks HP22 6BT. Tel: 01296-623911. *Director*, M. Lyddiard

TOURIST BOARD, ENGLISH, Thames Tower, Black's Road, London W6 9EL. Tel: 0181-846 9000. *Chief Executive*, T. Bartlett

TOURIST BOARD, NORTHERN IRELAND, St Anne's Court, 59 North Street, Belfast BT1 1NB. Tel: 01232-231221. *Chief Executive*, I. G. Henderson

TOURIST BOARD, SCOTTISH (1969), 23 Ravelston Terrace, Edinburgh EH4 3EU. Tel: 0131-332 2433. *Chief Executive*, T. Buncle

TOURIST BOARD, WALES, Brunel House, 2 Fitzalan Road, Cardiff CF2 1UY. Tel: 01222-499909. *Chief Executive*, J. French

TOWN AND COUNTRY PLANNING ASSOCIATION (1899), 17 Carlton House Terrace, London SW1Y 5AS. Tel: 0171-930 8903/4/5. *Director*, vacant

TOWN PLANNING INSTITUTE, ROYAL (1914), 26 Portland Place, London W1N 4BE. Tel: 0171-636 9107. *Secretary-General*, R. Upton

TOWNSWOMEN'S GUILDS (1929), Chamber of Commerce House, 75 Harborne Road, Birmingham B15 3DA. Tel: 0121-456 3435. *National Secretary*, Mrs P. Wilkes

TOYNBEE HALL (1884), 28 Commercial Street, London E1 6LS. Tel: 0171-247 6943. *Chief Executive*, A. Prescott

TRADE MARK AGENTS, INSTITUTE OF (1934), Canterbury House, 2–6 Sydenham Road, Croydon CR0 9XE. Tel: 0181-686 2052. *Secretary*, Mrs M. J. Tyler

TRADING STANDARDS ADMINISTRATION, INSTITUTE OF (1881), 3–5 Hadleigh Business Centre, 351 London Road, Hadleigh, Essex SS7 2BT. Tel: 01702-559922. *Chief Executive*, A. J. Street

TRANSLATION AND INTERPRETING, INSTITUTE OF (1986), 377 City Road, London EC1V 1NA. Tel: 0171-713 7600. *Chairman*, G. Cross

TRANSPORT ADMINISTRATION, INSTITUTE OF (1944), 32 Palmerston Road, Southampton SO14 1LL. Tel: 01703-631380. *Director*, J. K. Millar

TRANSPORT, CHARTERED INSTITUTE OF (1919), 80 Portland Place, London W1N 4DP. Tel: 0171-467 9400. *Director*, Mrs D. de Carvalho

TRAVEL AGENTS, ASSOCIATION OF BRITISH (ABTA) (1950), 68–71 Newman Street, London W1P 4AH. Tel: 0171-637 2444. *Chief Executive*, I. Reynolds

TREE COUNCIL (1974), 51 Catherine Place, London SW1E 6DY. Tel: 0171-828 9928. *Director*, R. Osborne

TREE FOUNDATION, INTERNATIONAL (formerly Men of the Trees) (1922), Sandy Lane, Crawley Down, W. Sussex RH10 4HS. Tel: 01342-712536. *Chairman*, S. G. Keys

TROPICAL MEDICINE AND HYGIENE, ROYAL SOCIETY OF (1907), Manson House, 26 Portland Place, London W1N 4EY. Tel: 0171-580 2127. *Hon. Secretaries*, Dr D. C. Barker; Dr S. B. Squire

TURNER SOCIETY (1975), BCM Box Turner, London WC1N 3XX. *Chairman*, E. Joll

2CARE (formerly The SOS Society) (1929), 11–13 Harwood Road, London SW6 4QP. Tel: 0171-371 0118. *Chief Executive*, Miss E. C. R. O'Sullivan

UFAW (UNIVERSITIES FEDERATION FOR ANIMAL WELFARE) (1926), The Old School, Brewhouse Hill, Wheathampstead, Herts AL4 8AN. Tel: 01582-831818. *Director*, Dr J. K. Kirkwood

UK INDEPENDENCE PARTY, 80 Regent Street, London WIR 5PE. Tel: 0171-434 4559. *Secretary*, A. Scholefield

UNBORN CHILDREN, SOCIETY FOR THE PROTECTION OF, *see* PROTECTION OF UNBORN CHILDREN

UNITED KINGDOM ALLIANCE (1863), 176 Blackfriars Road, London SE1 8ET. *General Secretary*, Revd B. Kinman

UNITED NATIONS ASSOCIATION OF GREAT BRITAIN AND NORTHERN IRELAND (1945), 3 Whitehall Court, London SW1A 2EL. Tel: 0171-930 2931. *Director*, M. C. Harper

UNITED REFORMED CHURCH HISTORY SOCIETY (1972), Westminster College, Madingley Road, Cambridge CB3 0AA. Tel: 01223-741084. *Hon. Secretary*, Revd E. J. Brown

UNITED SOCIETY FOR CHRISTIAN LITERATURE (1799), Albany House, 67 Sydenham Road, Guildford, Surrey GUI 3RY. Tel: 01483-888580. *General Secretary*, Dr A. Marriage

UNITED SOCIETY FOR THE PROPAGATION OF THE GOSPEL (USPG) (1701), Partnership House, 157 Waterloo Road, London SE1 8XA. Tel: 0171-928 8681. *Secretary*, Rt Revd M. Rumalshah

UNIVERSITIES OF THE UNITED KINGDOM, COMMITTEE OF VICE-CHANCELLORS AND PRINCIPALS OF THE (1918), Woburn House, 20 Tavistock Square, London WC1H 9HQ. Tel: 0171-419 4111. *Chief Executive*, Ms D. Warwick

VALUERS AND AUCTIONEERS, INCORPORATED SOCIETY OF (1968), 3 Cadogan Gate, London SW1X 0AS. Tel: 0171-235 2282. *Chief Executive*, C. Evans

VEGAN SOCIETY (1944), Donald Watson House, 7 Battle Road, St Leonards-on-Sea, E. Sussex TN37 7AA. Tel: 01424-427393. *Information Officer*, Ms A. Rofe

VEGETARIAN SOCIETY OF THE UNITED KINGDOM, Parkdale, Dunham Road, Altrincham, Cheshire WA14 4QG. Tel: 0161-928 0793. *Chief Executive*, Ms T. Fox

VENEREAL DISEASES, MEDICAL SOCIETY FOR THE STUDY OF (1922), 1 Wimpole Street, London W1M 8AE. Tel: 0171-290 2968. *Hon. Secretary*, Dr A. J. Robinson

VERNACULAR ARCHITECTURE GROUP (1953), 16 Falna Crescent, Coton Green, Tamworth, Staffs B79 8JS. Tel: 01827-69434. *Hon. Secretary*, R. A. Meeson

VETERINARY ASSOCIATION, BRITISH (1881), 7 Mansfield Street, London W1M 0AT. Tel: 0171-636 6541. *Chief Executive*, J. H. Baird

VETERINARY SURGEONS, ROYAL COLLEGE OF (1844), Belgravia House, 62–64 Horseferry Road, London SW1P 2AF. Tel: 0171-222 2001. *Registrar*, J. C. Hern

VICTIM SUPPORT (NATIONAL ASSOCIATION OF VICTIMS SUPPORT SCHEMES) (1979), National Office, Cranmer House, 39 Brixton Road, London SW9 6DZ. Tel: 0171-735 9166. *Director*, Ms H. Reeves, OBE

VICTORIA CROSS AND GEORGE CROSS ASSOCIATION, Room 028, The Old War Office, London SW1A 2EU. Tel: 0171-930 3506. *Secretary*, Mrs D. Grahame, MVO

VICTORIA INSTITUTE (PHILOSOPHICAL SOCIETY OF GREAT BRITAIN), 41 Marne Avenue, Welling, Kent DA16 2EY. Tel: 0181-303 0465. *Chairman of Council*, T. C. Mitchell

VICTORIAN SOCIETY (1958), 1 Priory Gardens, Bedford Park, London W4 1TT. Tel: 0181-994 1019. *Director*, Dr W. Filmer-Sankey

VICTORY (SERVICES) ASSOCIATION LTD AND CLUB (1907), 63–79 Seymour Street, London W2 2HF. Tel: 0171-723 4474. *General Manager*, G. F. Taylor

VIKING SOCIETY FOR NORTHERN RESEARCH (1892), Department of Scandinavian Studies, University College, Gower Street, London WC1E 6BT. *Hon. Secretaries*, Prof. M. P. Barnes; Dr J. Jesh

VOLUNTARY ORGANIZATIONS, NATIONAL COUNCIL FOR (1919), Regents Wharf, 8 All Saints Street, London N1 9RL. Tel: 0171-713 6161. *Chief Executive*, S. Etherington

VOLUNTARY ORGANIZATIONS, SCOTTISH COUNCIL FOR (1943), 18–19 Claremont Crescent, Edinburgh EH7 4QD. Tel: 0131-556 3882. *Director*, M. Sime

VSO (VOLUNTARY SERVICE OVERSEAS) (1958), 317 Putney Bridge Road, London SW15 2PN. Tel: 0181-780 7500. *Director*, D. Green

WAR ON WANT (1952), Fenner Brockway House, 37–39 Great Guildford Street, London SE1 0ES. Tel: 0171-620 1111. *Director*, Ms M. Lynch

WAR WIDOWS ASSOCIATION (1971), 3 Claudians Close, Abbeymead, Gloucester GL4 5FB. Tel: 01452-611593. *Chairman*, Mrs I. M. Thorogood

WASTES MANAGEMENT, INSTITUTE OF (1898), 9 Saxon Court, St Peter's Gardens, Northampton NN1 1SX. Tel: 01604-620426. *Chief Executive*, M. J. Philpott

WATER AND ENVIRONMENTAL MANAGEMENT, CHARTERED INSTITUTION OF (1987), 15 John Street, London WC1N 2EB. Tel: 0171-831 3110. *Executive Director*, N. Reeves

WATERCOLOUR SOCIETY, ROYAL (1804), Bankside Gallery, 48 Hopton Street, London SE1 9JH. Tel: 0171-928 7521. *Secretary*, Ms J. Dixey

WELLBEING (1964), 27 Sussex Place, London NW1 4SP. Tel: 0171-262 5337. Health research society for women and babies. *Director*, Mrs C. Lebus

WELLCOME TRUST (1936), The Wellcome Building, 183 Euston Road, London NW1 2BE. Tel: 0171-611 8888. *Director*, Dr M. Dexter, FRS

WESLEY HISTORICAL SOCIETY (1893), 34 Spiceland Road, Northfield, Birmingham B31 1NJ. Tel: 0121-475 4914. *General Secretary*, Dr E. D. Graham

WEST LONDON MISSION (1887), 19 Thayer Street, London W1M 5LJ. Tel: 0171-935 6179. *Superintendent*, Revd D. S. Cruise

WESTMINSTER FOUNDATION FOR DEMOCRACY (1992), Clutha House, 10 Storey's Gate, London SW1P 3AY. Tel: 0171-976 7565. *Chief Executive*, Ms A. Jones

WES WORLD-WIDE EDUCATION SERVICE (1888), Canada House, 272 Field End Road, Eastcote, Ruislip, Middx HA4 9NA. Tel: 0181-582 0317. *Head of Consultancy*, Mrs T. Mulder-Reynolds

WILDFOWL AND WETLANDS TRUST (1946), The New Grounds, Slimbridge, Glos GL2 7BT. Tel: 01453-890333. *Managing Director*, A. E. Richardson

WILDLIFE TRUSTS, THE (1912), The Green, Witham Park, Waterside South, Lincoln LN5 7JR. Tel: 01522-544400. *Director-General*, Dr S. Lyster

WILLIAM MORRIS SOCIETY AND KELMSCOTT FELLOWSHIP (1918), Kelmscott House, 26 Upper Mall, London W6 9TA. Tel: 0181-741 3735. *Hon. Secretary*, P. Faulkner

WINE AND SPIRIT ASSOCIATION OF GREAT BRITAIN AND NORTHERN IRELAND (c.1825), Five Kings House, 1 Queen Street Place, London EC4R 1XX. Tel: 0171-248 5377. *Director*, P. Lewis

WOMEN, SOCIETY FOR PROMOTING THE TRAINING OF (1859), Meadowbrook, Carlby Road, Greatford, Stamford, Lincs PE9 4PR. Tel: 01778-560978. *Hon. Secretary*, Revd B. Harris

WOMEN ARTISTS, SOCIETY OF (1855), 1 Knapp Cottages, Wyke, Gillingham, Dorset SP8 4NQ. Tel: 01747-825718. *Executive Secretary*, Mrs P. Henderson

WOMEN GRADUATES, BRITISH FEDERATION OF (1907), 4 Mandeville Courtyard, 142 Battersea Park Road, London SW11 4NB. Tel: 0171-498 8037. *Secretary*, Mrs A. B. Stein

WOMEN'S ENGINEERING SOCIETY (1920), 2 Queen Anne's Gate Buildings, Dartmouth Street, London SW1H 9BP. Tel: 0171-233 1974. *Secretary*, Mrs C. MacGillivray

WOMEN'S INSTITUTES, NATIONAL FEDERATION OF (1915), 104 New Kings Road, London SW6 4LY. Tel: 0171-371 9300. *General Secretary*, Mrs J. Osborne

WOMEN'S INSTITUTES OF NORTHERN IRELAND, FEDERATION OF (1932), 209–211 Upper Lisburn Road, Belfast BT10 0LL. Tel: 01232-301506/601781. *General Secretary*, Mrs I. A. Sproule

WOMEN'S NATIONWIDE CANCER CONTROL CAMPAIGN (1964), Suna House, 128–130 Curtain Road, London EC2A 3AR. Tel: 0171-729 4688/1735. *Administrator*, Miss J. Harding

WOMEN'S ROYAL NAVAL SERVICE BENEVOLENT TRUST (1942), 311 Twyford Avenue, Portsmouth PO2 8PE. Tel: 01705-655301. *General Secretary*, Mrs S. Torabella

WOMEN'S ROYAL VOLUNTARY SERVICE (WRVS), Milton Hill House, Milton Hill, Abingdon, Oxfordshire OX13 6AF. Tel: 01235-442900. *National Chairman*, Lady Toulson

WOMEN'S RURAL INSTITUTES, SCOTTISH (1917), 42 Heriot Row, Edinburgh EH3 6ES. Tel: 0131-225 1724. *General Secretary*, Mrs A. Peacock

WOMEN'S TRANSPORT SERVICE (FANY) (1907), Mercury House, Duke of York's Headquarters, London SW3 4RX. Tel: 0171-730 2058. *Corps Commander*, Mrs L. Rose

WOODLAND TRUST (1972), Autumn Park, Dysart Road, Grantham, Lincs NG31 6LL. Tel: 01476-581111. *Chief Executive*, M. J. Townsend

WOOD PRESERVING AND DAMP-PROOFING ASSOCIATION, BRITISH (1930), 6 The Office Village, 4 Romford Road, London E15 4EA. Tel: 0181-519 2588. *Director*, Dr C. R. Coggins

WORKERS' EDUCATIONAL ASSOCIATION, Temple House, 17 Victoria Park Square, London E2 9PB. Tel: 0181-983 1515. *General Secretary*, R. Lochrie

WORLD EDUCATION FELLOWSHIP (1921), International Headquarters, 58 Dickens Rise, Chigwell, Essex IG7 6NY. Tel: 0181-281 7122. *General Secretary*, G. John

WORLD ENERGY COUNCIL (1924), 34 St James's Street, London SW1A 1HD. Tel: 0171-930 3966. *Secretary-General*, G. W. Doucet

WORLD MISSION, COUNCIL FOR (1977), 32–34 Great Peter Street, London SW1P 2DB. Tel: 0171-222 4214. *General Secretary*, D. P. Niles, PH.D.

WORLD SHIP SOCIETY (1946), 101 The Everglades, Hempstead, Gillingham, Kent ME7 3PZ. Tel: 01634-372015. *Secretary*, J. Poole

WORLD SOCIETY FOR THE PROTECTION OF ANIMALS (1981), 2 Langley Lane, London SW8 1TJ. Tel: 0171-793 0540. *Chief Executive*, A. Dickson

WRITERS TO HM SIGNET, SOCIETY OF (1532), Signet Library, Parliament Square, Edinburgh EH1 1RF. Tel: 0131-225 4923. *General Manager*, J. R. C. Foster

WWF-UK (WORLD WIDE FUND FOR NATURE) (1961), Panda House, Weyside Park, Godalming, Surrey GU7 1XR. Tel: 01483-426444. *Director*, Dr R. Pellew

YEOMANRY BENEVOLENT FUND (1902), 10 Stone Buildings, Lincoln's Inn, London WC2A 3TG. Tel: 0171-831 6727. *Secretary*, Mrs C. W. Chrystie

YORKSHIRE AGRICULTURAL SOCIETY (1837), Great Yorkshire Showground, Harrogate, N. Yorks HG2 8PW. Tel: 01423-541000. *Chief Executive*, R. T. Keigwin

YORKSHIRE SOCIETY (1812), 35 Waldorf Heights, Camberley, Surrey GU17 9JH. Tel: 01276-36342. *Secretary*, G. G. Prince, TD

YOUNG FARMERS' CLUBS, NATIONAL FEDERATION OF, YFC Centre, National Agricultural Centre, Stoneleigh Park, Kenilworth, Warks CV8 2LG. Tel: 01203-696544. *Chief Executive*, B. Loughran

YOUNG MEN'S CHRISTIAN ASSOCIATION (YMCA) (1844), National Council of YMCAs, 640 Forest Road, London E17 3DZ. Tel: 0181-520 5599. *National Secretary*, E. Thomas

YOUNG WOMEN'S CHRISTIAN ASSOCIATION OF GREAT BRITAIN (YWCA) (1855), Clarendon House, 52 Cornmarket Street, Oxford OX1 3EJ. Tel: 01865-304200. *Chief Executive*, Ms G. Tishler

YOUTH ACTION, NORTHERN IRELAND (1944), Hampton, Glenmachan Park, Belfast BT4 2PJ. Tel: 01232-760067. *Director*, P. Graham

YOUTH CLUBS UK (1911), 2nd Floor, Kirby House, 20–24 Kirby Street, London EC1N 8TS. Tel: 0171-242 4045. *Chief Executive*, J. Bateman

YOUTH HOSTELS ASSOCIATION (ENGLAND AND WALES) (1930), Trevelyan House, 8 St Stephen's Hill, St Albans, Herts AL1 2DY. Tel: 01727-855215. *Chief Executive*, C. Logan

YOUTH HOSTELS ASSOCIATION, SCOTTISH (1931), 7 Glebe Crescent, Stirling FK8 2JA. Tel: 01786-891400. *General Secretary*, W. Forsyth

ZOOLOGICAL SOCIETY, NORTH OF ENGLAND (1934), Chester Zoo, Upton by Chester, Chester CH2 1LH. Tel: 01244-380280. *Director*, Dr G. McGregor Reid

ZOOLOGICAL SOCIETY OF LONDON (1826), Regent's Park, London NW1 4RY. Tel: 0171-722 3333. *Director-General*, R. D. A. Burge

ZOOLOGICAL SOCIETY OF SCOTLAND, ROYAL (1913), Scottish National Zoological Park, Edinburgh Zoo, 134 Corstorphine Road, Edinburgh EH12 6TS. Tel: 0131-334 9171. *Director*, Dr D. Waugh, PH.D.

LOCAL HISTORY AND ARCHAEOLOGICAL SOCIETIES

ENGLAND

Berkshire: BERKSHIRE ARCHAEOLOGICAL SOCIETY. *Hon. Secretary,* L. J. Over, 43 Laburnham Road, Maidenhead, Berks SL6 4DE. Tel: 01628-31225.

Buckinghamshire: BUCKINGHAMSHIRE ARCHAEOLOGICAL SOCIETY. *Hon. Secretary,* G. J. Aylett, County Museum, Church Street, Aylesbury, Bucks HP20 2QP.

Cambridgeshire: CAMBRIDGE ANTIQUARIAN SOCIETY. *Hon. Secretary,* Mrs S. Oosthuizen, Board of Continuing Education, Madingley Hall, Madingley, Cambs CB3 8AQ.

Cheshire: CHESTER ARCHAEOLOGICAL SOCIETY. *Secretary,* Dr D. J. P. Mason, FSA, Ochr Cottage, Porch Lane, Hope Mountain, Caergwrle, Flintshire LL12 9LS. Tel: 01978-760834.

Cornwall: CORNWALL ARCHAEOLOGICAL SOCIETY. *Hon. Secretary,* Mrs P. M. Fryer, Little Pengelly Cottage, Lower Sticker, St Austell, Cornwall PL26 7JJ.

Cumberland and Westmorland: CUMBERLAND AND WESTMORLAND ANTIQUARIAN AND ARCHAEOLOGICAL SOCIETY. *Hon. Secretary,* R. Hall, 2 High Tenterfell, Kendal, Cumbria LA9 4PG. Tel: 01539-728288.

Derbyshire: DERBYSHIRE ARCHAEOLOGICAL SOCIETY. *Hon. Secretary,* C. McGee, 25 Bridgeness Road, Heatherton, Littleover, Derby DE23 7UJ.

Devonshire: DEVON ARCHAEOLOGICAL SOCIETY. *Hon. Secretary,* H. Bishop, RAM Museum, Queen Street, Exeter, Devon EX4 3RX. Tel: 01392-265858.

Dorset: DORSET NATURAL HISTORY AND ARCHAEOLOGICAL SOCIETY. *Secretary,* R. M. de Peyer, Dorset County Museum, Dorchester, Dorset DT1 1XA. Tel: 01305-262735.

Durham: DURHAM AND NORTHUMBERLAND ARCHITECTURAL AND ARCHAEOLOGICAL SOCIETY. *Hon. Secretary,* S Cousins, 24 Toll House Road, Durham DH1 4HU. Tel: 0191-384 2724.

Essex: ESSEX SOCIETY FOR ARCHAEOLOGY AND HISTORY. *Secretary,* Dr C. Thornton, Hollytrees Museum, High Street, Colchester CO1 1UG. Tel: 01206-271458.

Gloucestershire: BRISTOL AND GLOUCESTERSHIRE ARCHAEOLOGICAL SOCIETY. *Hon. Secretary,* D. J. H. Smith, 22 Beaumont Road, Gloucester GL2 0EJ. Tel: 01452-302610.

Hampshire: HAMPSHIRE FIELD CLUB AND ARCHAEOLOGICAL SOCIETY. *Secretary,* R. Iles, Hyde Historic Resources Centre, 75 Hyde Street, Winchester, Hants SO23 7DW. Tel: 01962-848269.

Herefordshire: WOOLHOPE NATURALISTS' FIELD CLUB. *Hon. Secretary,* J. W. Tonkin, Chy an Whyloryon, Wigmore, Leominster, Herefordshire HR6 9UD. Tel: 01568-770356.

Hertfordshire: EAST HERTFORDSHIRE ARCHAEOLOGICAL SOCIETY. *Hon. Secretary,* Mrs M. C. Readman, 1 Marsh Lane, Stanstead Abbots, Ware, Herts SG12 8HH. Tel: 01920-870664.

ST ALBANS AND HERTFORDSHIRE ARCHITECTURAL AND ARCHAEOLOGICAL SOCIETY. *Hon. Secretary,* B. E. Moody, 24 Rose Walk, St Albans, Herts AL4 9AF. Tel: 01727-853204.

Isle of Wight: ISLE OF WIGHT NATURAL HISTORY AND ARCHAEOLOGICAL SOCIETY. *Hon. Secretary,* Dr. M. Jackson, Island Countryside Centre, Rylstone Gardens, Shanklin, Isle of Wight PO37 6RG. Tel: 01983-867016.

Kent: KENT ARCHAEOLOGICAL SOCIETY. *Hon. General Secretary,* A. I. Moffat, Three Elms, Woodlands Lane, Shorne, Gravesend, Kent DA12 3HH.

Leicestershire: LEICESTERSHIRE ARCHAEOLOGICAL AND HISTORICAL SOCIETY. *Hon. Secretary,* Dr A. D. McWhirr, The Guildhall, Leicester LE1 5FQ. Tel: 0116-270 3031.

Lincolnshire: SOCIETY FOR LINCOLNSHIRE HISTORY AND ARCHAEOLOGY. *Hon. Secretary,* Mrs M. A. Birch, Jew's Court, Steep Hill, Lincoln LN2 1LS. Tel: 01522-521337.

London and Middlesex: CITY OF LONDON ARCHAEOLOGICAL SOCIETY. *Hon. Secretary,* Ms M. Bowen, 34 College Cross, London N1 1PR. Tel: 0171-609 2930.

LONDON AND MIDDLESEX ARCHAEOLOGICAL SOCIETY. *Hon. Secretary,* M. Curtis, 34 Alexandra Road, Wimbledon, London SW19 7JZ. Tel: 0181-879 7109.

Norfolk: NORFOLK AND NORWICH ARCHAEOLOGICAL SOCIETY. *Hon. General Secretary,* R. Bellinger, 30 Brettingham Avenue, Norwich NR4 6XG. Tel: 01603-455913.

Northumberland and Tyne and Wear: SOCIETY OF ANTIQUARIES OF NEWCASTLE UPON TYNE. *Secretary,* N. Hodgson, Black Gate, Castle Garth, Newcastle upon Tyne NE1 1RQ. Tel: 0191-261 5390.

Northumberland: SUNDERLAND ANTIQUARIAN SOCIETY. *Hon. Secretary,* Mrs V. M. Stevens, 16 Grizedale Court, Seaburn Dene, Sunderland SR6 8JP. Tel: 0191-548 7541.

Oxfordshire: OXFORDSHIRE ARCHITECTURAL AND HISTORICAL SOCIETY. *Hon. Secretary,* Dr A. J. Dodd, 53 Radley Road, Abingdon, Oxon OX14 3PN. Tel: 01235-525960.

Shropshire: SHROPSHIRE ARCHAEOLOGICAL AND HISTORICAL SOCIETY. *Chairman,* J. B. Lawson, Westcott Farm, Pontesbury, Shrewsbury SY5 0SQ. Tel: 01743-790531.

Somerset: SOMERSET ARCHAEOLOGICAL AND NATURAL HISTORY SOCIETY. *Hon. Secretary,* Dr I. J. Sinclair, Taunton Castle, Taunton, Somerset TA1 4AD. Tel: 01823-272429.

Staffordshire: CITY OF STOKE-ON-TRENT MUSEUM ARCHAEOLOGICAL SOCIETY. *Chairman,* E. E. Royle, The Potteries Museum and Art Gallery, Hanley, Stoke-on-Trent ST1 3DW. Tel: 01782-232323.

Suffolk: SUFFOLK INSTITUTE OF ARCHAEOLOGY AND HISTORY. *Hon. Secretary,* E. A. Martin, Oak Tree Farm, Finborough Road, Hitcham, Ipswich IP7 7LS. Tel: 01449-741266.

Surrey: SURREY ARCHAEOLOGICAL SOCIETY. *Hon. Secretary,* Miss A. J. Monk, Castle Arch, Guildford, Surrey GU1 3SX. Tel: 01483-532454.

Sussex: SUSSEX ARCHAEOLOGICAL SOCIETY. *Chief Executive,* J. Manley, Bull House, 92 High Street, Lewes, E. Sussex BN7 1XH. Tel: 01273-486260.

Warwickshire: COVENTRY AND DISTRICT ARCHAEOLOGICAL SOCIETY. *Hon. Secretary,* Mrs J. Smith, 1 Holloway Field, Coventry CV6 2DA. Tel: 01203-591078.

BIRMINGHAM AND WARWICKSHIRE ARCHAEOLOGICAL SOCIETY. *Hon. Secretary,* Miss S. Middleton, c/o Birmingham and Midland Institute, Margaret Street, Birmingham B3 3BS.

Wiltshire: WILTSHIRE ARCHAEOLOGICAL AND NATURAL
HISTORY SOCIETY. *Secretary,* Cdr. P. M. M. Coston,
Devizes Museum, 41 Long Street, Devizes, Wilts
SN10 1NS. Tel: 01380-727369.

Worcestershire: WORCESTERSHIRE ARCHAEOLOGICAL
SOCIETY. *Hon. Secretary,* Ms S. L. Lamb, c/o
Worcestershire County Museum, Hartlebury Castle,
Hartlebury, Nr Kidderminster, Worcs DY11 7XZ. Tel:
01299 250416.

Yorkshire: HALIFAX ANTIQUARIAN SOCIETY. *Hon. Secretary,*
Dr J. A. Hargreaves, 7 Hyde Park Gardens, Haugh Shaw
Road, Halifax, W. Yorks HX1 3AH. Tel: 01422-250780.
THORESBY SOCIETY. *Hon. Secretary,* B. Harrison,
Claremont, 23 Clarendon Road, Leeds LS2 9NZ.
YORKSHIRE ARCHAEOLOGICAL SOCIETY. *Hon. Secretary,*
Ms J. Heron, Claremont, 23 Clarendon Road, Leeds
LS2 9NZ. Tel: 0113-245 7910.

SCOTLAND

AYRSHIRE ARCHAEOLOGICAL AND NATURAL HISTORY
SOCIETY. *Hon. Secretary,* Dr T. Mathews, 10 Longlands
Park, Ayr KA7 4RJ. Tel: 01292-441915.

DUMFRIESSHIRE AND GALLOWAY NATURAL HISTORY
AND ANTIQUARIAN SOCIETY. *Hon. Secretary,* M. White,
Smithy Cottage, Crocketford Road, Milton, Dumfries
DG2 8QT.

HAWICK ARCHAEOLOGICAL SOCIETY. *Hon. Secretary,* I. W.
Landles, Orrock House, Stirches Road, Hawick,
Roxburghshire TD9 7HF. Tel: 01450-375546.

INVERNESS FIELD CLUB. *Hon. Secretary,* Miss I. McLean, 6
Drumblair Crescent, Inverness IV2 4RG.

WALES

Dyfed: CEREDIGION ANTIQUARIAN SOCIETY. *Hon.
Secretary,* T. G. Davies, Henllys, Lôn Tyllwyd,
Llanfarian, Aberystwyth SY23 4UH. Tel: 01970-625818.

Powys: POWYSLAND CLUB. *Hon. Secretary,* Miss P. M.
Davies, Llygad y Dyffryn, Llanidloes, Powys SY18 6JD.
Tel: 01686-412277.

CHANNEL ISLANDS

SOCIÉTÉ JERSIAISE, ARCHAEOLOGICAL SECTION. *Hon.
Secretary,* Mrs D. Shute, La Hougue Bie Museum,
Grouville, Jersey. Tel: 01534-758314.

International Organizations

ASSOCIATION OF SOUTH EAST ASIAN NATIONS
70 A. Jl. Sisingamangaraja Kebayoran Baru, Jakarta Selatan, PO Box 2072, Jakarta, Indonesia

The Association of South East Asian Nations (ASEAN) was formed in 1967 with the aims of fostering economic growth, social progress and cultural development, and ensuring regional stability.

The heads of government meeting, which convenes every three years, is ASEAN's highest authority. Its main policy-making body is the annual meeting of foreign ministers of the member countries, which appoints the secretary-general. The founding members are Indonesia, Malaysia, the Philippines, Singapore and Thailand. Brunei and Vietnam joined in 1984 and 1995 respectively. Laos and Myanmar were admitted in July 1997, although Cambodia, which was expected to join at the same time, had its entry deferred following internal conflict; it retains observer status.

The heads of government summit in 1992 agreed to set up the ASEAN Free Trade Area (AFTA), which is to be implemented by 2003, with Vietnam likely to join by 2006. A common preferential tariff was introduced in 1993. At the annual summit in 1995, a South East Asia nuclear weapon-free zone was declared by ASEAN, Cambodia, Laos and Myanmar.

Secretary-General, Rodolfo C. Severino (Philippines)

BANK FOR INTERNATIONAL SETTLEMENTS
Centralbahnplatz 2, 4002 Basle, Switzerland
Tel: Basle 280 8080; fax: Basle 280 9100
Web: http://www.bis.org

The objectives of the Bank for International Settlements (founded in 1930) are to promote co-operation between central banks; to provide facilities for international financial operations; and to act as trustee or agent in international financial settlements entrusted to it. There are 41 members. The London agent is the Bank of England, and the Governor of the Bank of England is a member of the Board of Directors, in which administrative control is vested.

Chairman of the Board of Directors and President of the Bank for International Settlements, Alfons Verplaetse (Belgium)

CAB INTERNATIONAL
Wallingford, Oxon OXIO 8DE
Tel: 01491-832111; fax: 01491-833508
E-mail: cabi@cabi.org
Web: http://www.cabi.org

CAB International (formerly the Commonwealth Agricultural Bureaux) was founded in 1929. It generates, disseminates and applies scientific knowledge in support of sustainable development, with an emphasis on the needs of developing countries. The organization is owned and governed by its 40 member governments, each represented on an Executive Council. A Governing Board provides guidance to management on policy issues.

CABI has three divisions: bioscience, information and publishing. These undertake research and consultancy aimed at raising agricultural productivity, conserving biological resources, protecting the environment and controlling disease. The organization publishes books, journals and newsletters and produces bibliographic databases on agriculture, health and allied disciplines. It also undertakes contracted scientific research and provides consultancy services and information support to developing countries.

Director-General, James H. Gilmore

CARIBBEAN COMMUNITY AND COMMON MARKET
PO Box 10827, Georgetown, Guyana
Tel: Georgetown 69281; fax: Georgetown 67816
E-mail: carisec2@caricom.org
Web: http://www.caricom.org

The Caribbean Community and Common Market (CARICOM) was established in 1973 with three objectives: economic co-operation through the Caribbean Common Market, the co-ordination of member states' foreign policy, and the provision of common services and co-operation in health, education, culture, communications and industrial relations.

The supreme organ is the Conference of Heads of Government, which determines policy, takes strategic decisions and is responsible for resolving conflicts and all matters relating to the founding treaty. The Community Council of Ministers consists of ministers of government responsible for CARICOM affairs and any other ministers designated by member states and is responsible for strategic planning in the areas of economic integration, functional co-operation and external relations. The principal administrative arm is the Secretariat, based in Guyana. The Bureau of the Conference of Heads of Government is the executive body. It comprises the Chairman of the Conference, the outgoing Chairman and the Secretary-General, who are authorized to initiate proposals and to secure the implementation of CARICOM decisions.

The 14 member states are Antigua and Barbuda, The Bahamas (which is not a member of the Common Market), Barbados, Belize, Dominica, Grenada, Guyana, Jamaica, Montserrat, St Christopher and Nevis, St Lucia, St Vincent and the Grenadines, Suriname, and Trinidad and Tobago. The British Virgin Islands and the Turks and Caicos Islands are associate members. The Dominican Republic, Haiti, Mexico, Puerto Rico and Venezuela have observer status. At the 1997 annual summit, the member countries agreed to admit Haiti as a full member, subject to an economic evaluation.

Secretary-General, Edwin W. Carrington

THE COMMONWEALTH

The Commonwealth is a voluntary association of 54 sovereign independent states together with their associated states and dependencies. All of the states were formerly parts of the British Empire or League of Nations (later UN) mandated territories, except for Mozambique which was admitted as a unique case because it was surrounded by Commonwealth nations.

The status and relationship of member nations were first defined by the Inter-Imperial Relations Committee of the 1926 Imperial Conference, when the six existing dominions (Australia, Canada, the Irish Free State, Newfoundland, New Zealand and South Africa) were described as 'autonomous Communities within the British Empire, equal in status, in no way subordinate one to another in any aspect of their domestic or external affairs, though united by a common allegiance to the Crown and freely associated as Members of the British Commonwealth of Nations'. This formula was given legal substance by the Statute of Westminster 1931.

This concept of a group of countries owing allegiance to a single Crown changed in 1949 when India decided to become a republic. Her continued membership of the Commonwealth was agreed by the other members on the basis of her 'acceptance of The King as the symbol of the free association of its independent member nations and as such the head of the Commonwealth'. This paved the way for other republics to join the association in due course. Member nations agreed at the time of the accession of Queen Elizabeth II to recognize Her Majesty as the new Head of the Commonwealth. However, the position is not vested in the British Crown.

THE MODERN COMMONWEALTH

As the UK's former colonies joined, initially with India and Pakistan in 1947, the Commonwealth was transformed from a grouping of all-white dominions into a multi-racial association of equal, sovereign nations. It increasingly focused on promoting development and racial equality, most notably imposing sanctions against South Africa in the 1970s over its policy of apartheid.

The new goals of advocating democracy, the rule of law, good government and social justice were enshrined in the Harare Commonwealth Declaration (1991), which formed the basis of new membership guidelines agreed in Cyprus in 1993. It was under these guidelines that Nigeria and Sierra Leone were suspended for anti-democratic behaviour, though Sierra Leone's suspension was revoked when the legitimate government was returned to power. The heads of government meeting in Edinburgh in 1997 established a set of economic principles for the Commonwealth, promoting economic growth whilst protecting smaller member states from the effects of globalization.

MEMBERSHIP

Membership of the Commonwealth involves acceptance of the association's basic principles and is subject to the approval of existing members. There are 54 members at present. (The date of joining the Commonwealth is shown in parenthesis.)

*Antigua and Barbuda (1981)	Brunei (1984)
*Australia (1931)	Cameroon (1995)
*The Bahamas (1973)	*Canada (1931)
Bangladesh (1972)	Cyprus (1961)
*Barbados (1966)	Dominica (1978)
*Belize (1981)	Fiji (1970, 1997)
Botswana (1966)	The Gambia (1965)

Ghana (1957)	*St Lucia (1979)
*Grenada (1974)	*St Vincent and the
Guyana (1966)	Grenadines (1979)
India (1947)	Seychelles (1976)
*Jamaica (1962)	Sierra Leone (1961)
Kenya (1963)	Singapore (1965)
Kiribati (1979)	*Solomon Islands (1978)
Lesotho (1966)	South Africa (1931)
Malawi (1964)	Sri Lanka (1948)
Malaysia (1957)	Swaziland (1968)
The Maldives (1982)	Tanzania (1961)
Malta (1964)	Tonga (1970)
Mauritius (1968)	Trinidad and Tobago
Mozambique (1995)	(1962)
Namibia (1990)	*Tuvalu (1978)
Nauru (1968)	Uganda (1962)
*New Zealand (1931)	*United Kingdom
†Nigeria (1960)	Vanuatu (1980)
Pakistan (1947)	Western Samoa (1970)
*Papua New Guinea (1975)	Zambia (1964)
*St Christopher and Nevis	Zimbabwe (1980)
(1983)	

*Realms of Queen Elizabeth II
†Suspended in 1995

Nauru and Tuvalu are special members, with the right to participate in all functional Commonwealth meetings and activities, but not to attend meetings of Commonwealth heads of government.

Countries which have left the Commonwealth
Fiji (1987, rejoined 1997)
Republic of Ireland (1949)
Pakistan (1972, rejoined 1989)
South Africa (1961, rejoined 1994)

Of the 54 member states, 16 have Queen Elizabeth II as head of state, 33 are republics, and five have national monarchies.

In each of the realms where Queen Elizabeth II is head of state (except for the UK), she is personally represented by a Governor-General, who holds in all essential respects the same position in relation to the administration of public affairs in the realm as is held by Her Majesty in Britain. The Governor-General is appointed by The Queen on the advice of the government of the state concerned.

INTERGOVERNMENTAL AND OTHER LINKS

The main forum for consultation is the Commonwealth heads of government meetings held biennially to discuss international developments and to consider co-operation among members. Decisions are reached by consensus, and the views of the meeting are set out in a communiqué. There are also annual meetings of finance ministers and frequent meetings of ministers and officials in other fields, such as education, health, women's affairs, agriculture, and science. Intergovernmental links are complemented by the activities of some 300 Commonwealth non-governmental organizations linking professionals, sportsmen and sportswomen, and interest groups, forming a 'people's Commonwealth'. The Commonwealth Games take place every four years.

Assistance to other Commonwealth countries normally has priority in the bilateral aid programmes of the association's developed members (Australia, Britain, Canada and New Zealand), who direct about 30 per cent of their aid to other member countries. Developing Commonwealth nations also assist their poorer partners, and many Commonwealth voluntary organizations promote development.

COMMONWEALTH SECRETARIAT

The Commonwealth has a secretariat, established in 1965 in London, which is funded by all member governments. This is the main agency for multilateral communication between member governments on issues relating to the Commonwealth as a whole. It promotes consultation and co-operation, disseminates information on matters of common concern, organizes meetings including the biennial summits, co-ordinates Commonwealth activities, and provides technical assistance for economic and social development through the Commonwealth Fund for Technical Co-operation.

The Commonwealth Foundation was established by Commonwealth governments in 1966 as an autonomous body with a board of governors representing Commonwealth governments that fund the Foundation. It promotes and funds exchanges and other activities aimed at strengthening the skills and effectiveness of professionals and non-governmental organizations. It also promotes culture, rural development, social welfare and the role of women.

COMMONWEALTH SECRETARIAT, Marlborough House, Pall Mall, London SW1Y 5HX. Tel: 0171-839 3411; fax: 0171-839 9081. Web: http://www.tcol.co.uk and http://www.thecommonwealth.org. *Secretary-General*, Chief Emeka Anyaoku (Nigeria)

COMMONWEALTH FOUNDATION, Marlborough House, Pall Mall, London SW1Y 5HY. Tel: 0171-930 3783. *Director*, Dr Humayun Khan (Pakistan)

COMMONWEALTH INSTITUTE, Kensington High Street, London W8 6NQ. Tel: 0171-603 4535. *Director-General*, David French

---

COMMONWEALTH OF INDEPENDENT STATES

Minsk, Belarus
Web: http://www.cis.minsk.by

The Commonwealth of Independent States (CIS) is a multilateral grouping of 12 sovereign states which were formerly constituent republics of the USSR. It was formed by Russia, Ukraine and Belarus on 8 December 1991, the remaining republics, apart from the Baltic states and Georgia, joining on 21 December. Georgia joined in December 1993. Azerbaijani and Moldovan membership effectively lapsed because of non-ratification until September 1993 and April 1994 respectively. The CIS charter, signed in 1993 by seven states (Armenia, Belarus, Kazakhstan, Kyrgyzstan, Russia, Tajikistan, Uzbekistan) and open for signing by the other states, formally established the functions of the organization and the obligations of its member states.

The CIS acts as a co-ordinating mechanism for foreign, defence and economic policies, and is a forum for addressing problems which have specifically arisen from the break-up of the USSR. These matters are addressed in more than 50 inter-state, intergovernmental co-ordinating and consultative statutory bodies. However, member states have criticized the CIS for operating ineffectively, and for failing to carry through decisions made by CIS organs.

STRUCTURE

The two supreme CIS bodies are the Council of Heads of State and the Council of Heads of Government. The Council of Heads of State is the highest organ of the CIS and meets not less than twice yearly. It is chaired by the heads of state of the members in (Russian) alphabetical order. The Council of Heads of Government meets not less than once every three months to co-ordinate military and economic activity. Other important bodies are the Council of Heads of Collective Security (defence ministers), the Joint Staff for Co-ordinating Military Co-operation, the CIS Inter-Parliamentary Assembly, the Economic Arbitration Court and the Co-ordinating Consultative Committee. Administrative support is provided by the Executive Secretariat based in Minsk.

DEFENCE CO-OPERATION

On becoming member states of the CIS, the 11 original states agreed to recognize their existing borders, respect one another's territorial integrity and reject the use of military force or other forms of coercion to settle disputes between them. Agreement was also reached on fulfilling all the international treaty obligations of the former USSR, together with the establishment of CIS joint armed forces.

The members agreed on a central CIS command for all nuclear weapons, the control over which was passed to CIS commander-in-chief Marshal Shaposhnikov in December 1991. All tactical nuclear weapons had been transferred to Russia by May 1992. An agreement was reached with the USA in May 1992 by the four republics with strategic nuclear weapons (Russia, Ukraine, Belarus, Kazakhstan) on implementing the strategic arms reduction talks (START) treaty previously signed by the USA and USSR, and the START I treaty was ratified by the five parties between October 1992 and February 1994. Under this agreement Ukraine, Belarus and Kazakhstan agreed to eliminate all their strategic nuclear weapons over a seven-year period and Russia has agreed to reduce its strategic nuclear weapons.

A CIS high command and a joint conventional force were created in 1992 to operate in parallel with member states' own armed forces. In the same year, a Treaty on Collective Security was signed by six states and a joint peacemaking force, to intervene in CIS conflicts, was agreed upon by nine states. Deployment of these forces was made conditional on consensus in the Council of Heads of State. Fear of Russian domination by some states led to the downgrading of the high command into a Joint Staff for Co-ordinating Military Co-operation in 1993. Russia responded by concluding bilateral and multilateral agreements with other CIS states under the supervision of the Council of Heads of Collective Security (established 1993). These have been gradually upgraded into CIS agreements under the umbrella of the Treaty on Collective Security, enabling Russia to station troops in ten of the other 11 CIS states (not Ukraine), and giving Russian forces *de facto* control of virtually all of the former USSR's external borders. Only Ukraine and Moldova remain outside the defence co-operation framework and have not signed the Treaty on Collective Security. In November 1995, the ten agreed to recreate a joint air defence system.

ECONOMIC CO-OPERATION

In 1991, 11 republics signed a treaty forming an economic community. The principles of the treaty were embodied within the CIS and formed the basis of its economic co-operation. Members agreed to refrain from economic actions that would damage each other and to co-ordinate economic and monetary policies. A Co-ordinating Consultative Committee, an economic arbitration court and an inter-state bank were established. A single monetary unit, the rouble, was originally agreed upon by all member states, and the members recognized that the basis of recovery for their economies was private ownership, free enterprise and competition.

Russia effectively forced the collapse of the rouble zone in July 1993 by withdrawing all pre-1993 roubles and forcing the remaining states using roubles to accept Russian monetary control or introduce their own currencies, which all did apart from Tajikistan. The resulting economic collapse of the non-Russian economies led to renewed interest in economic co-operation and the signing of a Treaty on Economic Union in September 1993. The 11 CIS members who have signed the Treaty (Ukraine is an associate member of the economic union) are committed to a common market without internal barriers to trade, common fiscal policies and an eventual currency union with currencies semi-fixed against the rouble. In order to facilitate faster economic integration 11 states (not Turkmenistan) agreed in October 1994 to establish an Inter-state Economic Committee, and in May 1995 a monetary committee to facilitate payments in different currencies was agreed. Belarus has withdrawn its currency and rejoined Russia and Tajikistan in the rouble zone. A treaty creating a common market was signed by Kazakhstan, Kyrgyzstan, Russia and Belarus in March 1996, with other CIS states originally excluded from membership, although Tajikistan has since joined.
Executive Secretary, Boris Berezovsky

THE COUNCIL OF EUROPE
67075 Strasbourg, France
Tel: Strasbourg 8841 2000; fax: Strasbourg 8841 2781/2/3
E-mail: information.point@seddoc.coe.fr
Web: http://www.coe.fr

The Council of Europe was founded in 1949. Its aim is to achieve greater unity between its members, to safeguard their European heritage and to facilitate their progress in economic, social, cultural, educational, scientific, legal and administrative matters, and in the furtherance of pluralist democracy, human rights and fundamental freedoms.

The 40 members are Albania, Andorra, Austria, Belgium, Bulgaria, Croatia, Cyprus, Czech Republic, Denmark, Estonia, Finland, France, Germany, Greece, Hungary, Iceland, the Republic of Ireland, Italy, Latvia, Liechtenstein, Lithuania, Luxembourg, Macedonia (Former Yugoslav Republic of), Malta, Moldova, the Netherlands, Norway, Poland, Portugal, Romania, Russia, San Marino, Slovakia, Slovenia, Spain, Sweden, Switzerland, Turkey, the UK and Ukraine. 'Special guest status' has been granted to Armenia, Azerbaijan, Bosnia-Hercegovina and Georgia. Turkey's membership was suspended from April 1995 to September 1996 over its military offensive against Kurdish guerrillas in northern Iraq.

The organs are the Committee of Ministers, consisting of the foreign ministers of member countries, who meet twice yearly, and the Parliamentary Assembly of 286 members, elected or chosen by the national parliaments of member countries in proportion to the relative strength of political parties. There is also a Joint Committee of Ministers and Representatives of the Parliamentary Assembly.

The Committee of Ministers is the executive organ. The majority of its conclusions take the form of international agreements (known as European Conventions) or recommendations to governments. Decisions of the Ministers may also be embodied in partial agreements to which a limited number of member governments are party. Member governments accredit Permanent Representatives to the Council in Strasbourg, who are also the Ministers' Deputies. The Committee of Deputies meets

every month to transact business and to take decisions on behalf of Ministers.

The Parliamentary Assembly holds three week-long sessions a year. Its 13 permanent committees meet once or twice between each public plenary session of the Assembly. The Congress of Local and Regional Authorities of Europe each year brings together mayors and municipal councillors in the same numbers as the members of the Parliamentary Assembly.

One of the principal achievements of the Council of Europe is the European Convention on Human Rights (1950) under which was established the European Commission and the European Court of Human Rights, which were merged in 1993. The reorganized European Court of Human Rights sits in chambers of seven judges or exceptionally as a grand chamber of 17 judges. Litigants must exhaust legal processes in their own country before bringing cases before the court.

Among other conventions and agreements are the European Social Charter, the European Cultural Convention, the European Code of Social Security, the European Convention on the Protection of National Minorities, and conventions on extradition, the legal status of migrant workers, torture prevention, conservation, and the transfer of sentenced prisoners. Most recently, the specialized bodies of the Venice Commission and Demosthenes have been set up to assist in developing legislative, administrative and constitutional reforms in central and eastern Europe.

Non-member states take part in certain Council of Europe activities on a regular or *ad hoc* basis; thus the Holy See participates in all the educational, cultural and sports activities. The European Youth Centre is an educational residential centre for young people. The European Youth Foundation provides youth organizations with funds for their international activities.
Secretary-General, Daniel Tarschys (Sweden)
Permanent UK Representative, HE Andrew Carter, CMG, *apptd* 1997

THE ECONOMIC COMMUNITY OF WEST AFRICAN STATES
Secretariat Building, Asokoro, Abuja, Nigeria
Tel: Abuja 523 1858

The Economic Community of West African States (ECOWAS) was founded in 1975 and came into operation in 1977. It aims to promote the cultural, economic and social development of West Africa through mutual co-operation. A revised ECOWAS Treaty was signed in 1993 and came into effect in July 1995. It makes the prevention and control of regional conflicts an aim of ECOWAS and provides for the imposition of a community tax and for the establishment of a regional parliament, an economic and social council, and a court of justice.

The supreme authority of ECOWAS is vested in the annual summit of heads of government of all 16 member states. A Council of Ministers, two from each member state, meets biannually to monitor the organization and make recommendations to the summit. ECOWAS operates through a Secretariat, headed by the Executive Secretary. In addition there is a financial controller, an external auditor, the Disputes Tribunal and the Defence Council.

A Fund for Co-operation, Compensation and Development, situated at Lomé, Togo, finances development projects and provides compensation to member states who have suffered losses as a result of ECOWAS's policies, particularly trade liberalization.

An ECOWAS Monitoring Group (ECOMOG) peace-keeping force has been involved in attempts to restore peace in Liberia (1990–6) and Sierra Leone (1997–8).
Executive Secretary, Lansana Kouyate (Guinea)

THE EUROPEAN BANK FOR RECONSTRUCTION AND DEVELOPMENT
One Exchange Square, London EC2A 2EH
Tel: 0171-338 6000; fax: 0171-338 6100
Web: http://www.ebrd.com

The charter of the European Bank for Reconstruction and Development (EBRD) was signed by 40 countries, the European Commission and the European Investment Bank in May 1990 and was inaugurated in April 1991.

The aim of the EBRD is to facilitate the transformation of the states of central and eastern Europe (Albania, Bulgaria, Czech Republic, Hungary, Poland, Romania, Slovakia, the republics of the former USSR and former Yugoslavia) from centrally-planned to free-market economies, and to promote multi-party democracy, entrepreneurial initiative, and respect for human rights and the environment.

The EBRD provides technical assistance, training and investment in the upgrading of infrastructure; the mobilization of domestic capital; privatization; the strengthening of legal systems; gaining foreign direct investment; the creation of modern financial systems; tourism; the exploitation of natural resources; and the restructuring of state industries. No more than 40 per cent of the EBRD's investment can be made in state-owned concerns. It works in co-operation with its members, private companies, and international organizations such as the OECD, the IMF, the World Bank and the UN specialized agencies.

The EBRD has a subscribed capital of 20 billion ECU, of which 30 per cent is paid in. The EBRD is also able to borrow on world capital markets. Its major subscribers are the USA, 10 per cent; Britain, France, Germany and Japan, 8.5 per cent each. The EBRD offers a range of financing instruments including loans, equity investments and guarantees. As of 31 December 1997, the total number of projects approved since its establishment was 575, involving ECU 13,900 million of EBRD funds.

The EBRD has 60 members. The highest authority is the Board of Governors; each member appoints one Governor and one Alternate. The Governors delegate most powers to a 23-member Board of Directors; the Directors are responsible for the EBRD's operations and budget, and are elected by the Governors for three-year terms. The Governors also elect the President of the Board of Directors, who acts as the Bank's president, for a four-year term. A Secretary-General liaises between the Directors and EBRD staff.
President of the Board of Directors, Horst Koehler (Germany)
UK Executive Director, Michael McCulloch
Secretary-General, Antonio Maria Costa (Italy)

EUROPEAN FREE TRADE ASSOCIATION
Headquarters: 9–11 rue de Varembé, 1211 Geneva 20, Switzerland
Tel: Geneva 749 1111; fax: Geneva 733 9291
E-mail: efta-mailbox@secrbru.efta.int
Web: http://www.efta.int
EEA matters: 74 rue de Trèves, B-1040 Brussels, Belgium
Tel: Brussels 286 1726; fax: Brussels 286 1750

The European Free Trade Association (EFTA) was established in 1960 by Austria, Denmark, Norway, Portugal, Sweden, Switzerland and the UK, and was subsequently joined by Finland (associate member 1961, full member 1986), Iceland (1970) and Liechtenstein (1991). Six members have left to join the European Union: Denmark and the UK (1973), Portugal (1986), Austria, Finland and Sweden (1995). The existing members are Iceland, Liechtenstein, Norway and Switzerland.

The first objective of EFTA was to establish free trade in industrial goods between members; this was achieved in 1966. Its second objective was the creation of a single market in western Europe and in 1972 EFTA signed free trade agreements with the EC covering trade in industrial goods; the remaining tariffs on industrial products were abolished in 1984.

An agreement on the creation of the European Economic Area (EEA), an extension of the EC single market to the EFTA states, was signed in 1992 and entered into force on 1 January 1994. Switzerland rejected EEA membership in a referendum in 1992 and Liechtenstein joined on 1 May 1995 after adapting its customs union with Switzerland.

EFTA has expanded its relations with other non-EU states in recent years, signing free trade agreements with Turkey (1991), Israel, Poland and Romania (1992), Bulgaria, Hungary, the Czech Republic and Slovakia (1993), Estonia, Latvia, Lithuania and Slovenia (1995) and Morocco (1997). In addition, EFTA has signed declarations of economic co-operation with Albania (1992), Egypt and Tunisia (1995), the Former Yugoslav Republic of Macedonia and the PLO (1996), and Jordan and Lebanon (1997).

The EFTA Council is the principle organ of the Association. It generally meets twice a month at the level of heads of the permanent national delegations to the EFTA Secretariat in Geneva and twice a year at ministerial level.
Secretary-General, Kjartan Jóhannsson (Iceland)
Deputy Secretary-General (Geneva), Aldo Matteucci (Switzerland)
Deputy Secretary-General (Brussels), Guttorm Vik (Norway)

EUROPEAN ORGANIZATION FOR NUCLEAR RESEARCH (CERN)
CH-1211 Geneva 23, Switzerland
Tel: Geneva 767 4101; fax: Geneva 785 0247 Web: http://www.cern.ch

The Convention establishing the European Organization for Nuclear Research (CERN) came into force in 1954. CERN promotes European collaboration in high energy physics of a scientific, rather than a military nature.

The member countries are Austria, Belgium, the Czech Republic, Denmark, Finland, France, Germany, Greece,

Hungary, Italy, the Netherlands, Norway, Poland, Portugal, Slovakia, Spain, Sweden, Switzerland and the UK. Israel, Russia, Turkey, the EU Commission and UNESCO have observer status.

The Council is the highest policy-making body and comprises two delegates from each member state. There is also a Committee of the Council comprising a single delegate from each member state (who is also a Council member) and the chairmen of the scientific policy and finance advisory committees. The Council is chaired by the President who is elected by the Council in Session. The Council also elects the Director-General, who is responsible for the internal organization of CERN. The Director-General heads a workforce of approximately 3,000, including physicists, craftsmen, technicians and administrative staff. At present over 6,500 physicists use CERN's facilities.

The member countries contribute to the budget in proportion to their net national revenue. The 1997 budget was SFr 873 million.

President of the Council, Eschel Bacher (Germany)
Director-General (1994–9), Prof. Christopher Llewellyn-Smith (UK)

EUROPEAN SPACE AGENCY
8–10 rue Mario Nikis, 75738 Paris, France
Tel: Paris 5369 7654; fax: Paris 5369 7560
Web: http://www.esa.int

The European Space Agency (ESA) was created in 1975 by the merger of the European Space Research Organization (ESRO) and the European Launcher Development Organization (ELDO). Its aims include the advancement of space research and technology and the implementation of a long-term European space policy.

The member countries are Austria, Belgium, Denmark, Finland, France, Germany, Republic of Ireland, Italy, Netherlands, Norway, Spain, Sweden, Switzerland and the UK. Canada is a co-operating state.

The agency is directed by a Council composed of the representatives of the member states; its chief officer is the Director-General.

Director-General, Antonio Rodotà, *apptd* 1997

FOOD AND AGRICULTURE
ORGANIZATION OF THE UNITED
NATIONS
Viale delle Terme di Caracalla, I-00100 Rome, Italy
Tel: Rome 57051; fax: Rome 5705 3152
E-mail: fao-hq@fao.org
Web: http://www.fao.org

The Food and Agriculture Organization (FAO) is a specialized UN agency, established in 1945. It assists rural populations by raising levels of nutrition and living standards, and by encouraging greater efficiency in food production and distribution. It analyses and disseminates information on agriculture and natural resources. The FAO also advises governments on national agricultural policy and planning; its Investment Centre, together with the World Bank and other financial institutions, helps to prepare development projects. The FAO's field programme covers a range of activities, including strengthening crop production, rural and livestock development, and conservation.

The FAO's top priorities are sustainable agriculture, rural development and food security. The Organization attempts to ensure the availability of adequate food supplies, stability in the flow of supplies and the securing of access to food by the poor. The FAO monitors potential famine areas. The Special Relief Operations Service channels emergency aid from governments and other agencies, and assists in rehabilitation. The Technical Co-operation Programme provides schemes for countries facing agricultural crises.

The FAO had 176 members (175 states and the EU) as at May 1998. It is governed by a biennial conference of its members which sets a programme and budget. The budget for 1998–9 is US$650million, funded by member countries in proportion to their gross national products. The FAO is also funded by the UN Development Programme, donor governments and other institutions.

The Conference elects a Director-General and a 49-member Council which governs between conferences. The Regular and Field Programmes are administered by a Secretariat, headed by the Director-General. Five regional, five sub-regional and 80 national offices help administer the Field Programme.

Director-General, Jacques Diouf (Senegal)
UK Representative, Anthony Beattie, British Embassy, Rome

INMARSAT
99 City Road, London ECIY IAX
Tel: 0171-728 1000; fax: 0171-728 1044
Web: http://www.inmarsat.org/inmarsat/index.html

Inmarsat (formerly the International Mobile Satellite Organization) was founded in 1979 as the International Maritime Satellite Organization and began operations in 1982. Inmarsat is an internationally-owned co-operative which operates a system of satellites to provide global mobile communications. Inmarsat satellite terminals are used world-wide on ships, aircraft and on land for telecommunications, as well as maritime safety, position reporting and distress communications.

Inmarsat comprises three bodies: the Assembly, the Council and the Directorate. The Assembly is composed of representatives of the 80 member countries, each having one vote. It meets every two years to review activities and objectives, and to make recommendations to the Council. The Council is the main decision-making body and consists of representatives of the 18 members with the largest investment shares, and four members representing the interests of developing countries who are elected to the Council on the basis of geographical representation. Members have voting powers equal to their investment shares. The Council meets at least three times a year and oversees the activities of the Directorate, the permanent staff of Inmarsat.

Director-General, Warren Grace (Australia)

INTERNATIONAL ATOMIC ENERGY
AGENCY
Vienna International Centre, Wagramerstrasse 5,
PO Box 100, 1400 Vienna, Austria
Tel: Vienna 20600; fax: Vienna 20607
E-mail: Official.Mail@iaea.org
Web: http://www.iaea.or.at/worldatom

The International Atomic Energy Agency (IAEA) was established in 1957. It is an intergovernmental organization which reports to, but is not a specialized agency of, the UN.

The IAEA aims to enhance the contribution of atomic energy to peace, health and prosperity, and to ensure that any assistance that it provides is not used for military purposes. It establishes atomic energy safety standards and offers services to its member states for the safe operation of their nuclear facilities and for radiation protection. It is the focal point for international conventions on the early notification of a nuclear accident, assistance in the case of a nuclear accident, civil liability for nuclear damage, physical protection of nuclear material, nuclear safety and the safety of spent fuel and radioactive waste management. The IAEA also encourages research and training in nuclear power. It is additionally charged with drawing up safeguards and verifying their use in accordance with the Nuclear Non-Proliferation Treaty (NPT) 1968, the Treaty for the Prohibition of Nuclear Weapons in Latin America (Tlatelolco Treaty) 1968, the Treaty on a South Pacific Nuclear Free Zone (Rarotonga Treaty), and the African Nuclear Weapon-Free Zone Treaty (Pelindaba Treaty) 1996. Together with the Food and Agriculture Organization and the World Health Organization, the IAEA established an International Consultative Group on Food Irradiation in 1983.

The IAEA concluded a safeguards agreement with North Korea in April 1992 and began inspections to verify that its nuclear programme was for peaceful purposes only. In 1994 the IAEA informed the UN Security Council that North Korea had violated its NPT obligations and all technical aid to North Korea was suspended. North Korea resigned from the IAEA in 1994, but permitted IAEA inspections under the terms of an agreement with the USA which enabled the IAEA to resume safeguards inspections.

The IAEA had 127 members as at May 1998. A General Conference of all its members meets annually to decide policy, a programme and a budget (1998, US$222 million), as well as electing a Director-General and a 35-member Board of Governors. The Board meets four times a year to formulate policy which is implemented by the Secretariat under a Director-General.

Director-General, Mohamed El Baradei (Egypt)
Permanent UK Representative, Dr John Freeman, Jaurèsgasse 12, 1030 Vienna, Austria

INTERNATIONAL CIVIL AVIATION ORGANIZATION

1000 Sherbrooke Street West, Montreal, Quebec, Canada H3A 2R2
Tel: Montreal 954 8221; fax: Montreal 954 6376
Web: http://www.icao.org

The International Civil Aviation Organization (ICAO) was founded with the signing of the Chicago Convention on International Civil Aviation in 1944, and became a specialized agency of the United Nations in 1947. It sets international technical standards and recommended practices for all areas of civil aviation, including airworthiness, air navigation, traffic control and pilot licensing. It encourages uniformity and simplicity in ground regulations and operations at international airports, including immigration and customs control. The ICAO also promotes regional air navigation, plans for ground facilities, and collects and distributes air transport statistics worldwide. It is dedicated to improving safety and to the orderly development of civil aviation throughout the world.

The ICAO had 185 members as at 10 June 1998. It is governed by an assembly of its members which meets at least once every three years. A Council of 33 members is elected, which represents leading air transport nations as well as less developed countries. The Council elects the President, appoints the Secretary-General and supervises the organization through subsidiary committees, serviced by a Secretariat.

President of the Council, Dr Assad Kotaite (Lebanon)
Secretary-General, R. C. Costa Pereira (Brazil)
UK Representative, D. S. Evans, CMG, Suite 14.15, 999 University Street, Montreal, Quebec, Canada H3C 5J9

INTERNATIONAL CONFEDERATION OF FREE TRADE UNIONS

Boulevard Emile Jacqmain 155 B1, B-1210 Brussels, Belgium
Tel: Brussels 224 0211; fax: Brussels 203 0756
E-mail: internetpo@icftu.org
Web: http://www.icftu.org

The International Confederation of Free Trade Unions (ICFTU) was created in 1949. It aims to establish, maintain and promote free trade unions, and to promote peace with economic security and social justice.

Affiliated to the ICFTU are 206 individual unions and representative bodies in 141 countries and territories. There were 125 million members on 19 December 1997.

The Congress, the supreme authority of the ICFTU, convenes at least every four years. It is composed of delegates from the affiliated trade union organizations. The Congress elects an Executive Board of 49 members which meets not less than once a year. The Board establishes the budget and receives suggestions and proposals from affiliates as well as acting on behalf of the Confederation. The Congress also elects the General Secretary.

General Secretary, Bill Jordan (UK)
UK Affiliate, TUC, Congress House, 23–28 Great Russell Street, London WC1B 3LS. Tel: 0171-636 4030

INTERNATIONAL CRIMINAL POLICE ORGANIZATION

200 Quai Charles de Gaulle, 69006 Lyon, France
Tel: Lyon 7244 7000; fax: Lyon 7244 7163
Web: http://www.interpol.com

The International Criminal Police Commission (Interpol) was set up in 1923 to establish an international criminal records office and to harmonize extradition procedures. As of 1 January 1998, the organization comprised 177 member states.

Interpol's aims are to promote co-operation between criminal police authorities, and to support government agencies concerned with combating crime, whilst respecting national sovereignty. It is financed by annual contributions from the governments of member states.

Interpol's policy is decided by the General Assembly which meets annually; it is composed of delegates appointed by the member states. The 13-member Executive Committee is elected by the General Assembly from among the member states' delegates, and is chaired by the President, who has a four-year term of office. The permanent administrative organ is the General Secretariat, headed by the Secretary-General, who is appointed by the General Assembly.

Secretary-General, Raymond Kendall, QPM (UK)

UK Office, NCIS-Interpol, PO Box 8000, London
seii 5en. Tel: 0171-238 8000. *UK Representative,* J. M.
Abbott, qpm

INTERNATIONAL ENERGY AGENCY
9 rue de la Fédération, 75739 Paris Cedex 15, France
Tel: Paris 4057 6554; fax: Paris 4057 6559
Web: http://www.iea.org

The International Energy Agency (IEA), founded in 1974,
is an autonomous agency within the framework of the
Organization for Economic Co-operation and Development (OECD). The IEA had 24 member countries as at
June 1998.

The IEA's objectives include improvement of energy
co-operation world-wide, increased efficiency, development of alternative energy sources and the promotion of
relations between oil producing and oil consuming
countries. The IEA also maintains an emergency system
to alleviate the effects of severe oil supply disruptions.

The main decision-making body is the Governing
Board composed of senior energy officials from member
countries. Various standing groups and special committees
exist to facilitate the work of the Board. The IEA
Secretariat, with a staff of energy experts, carries out the
work of the Governing Board and its subordinate bodies.
The Executive Director is appointed by the Board.
Executive Director, Robert Priddle (UK)

INTERNATIONAL FUND FOR
AGRICULTURAL DEVELOPMENT
107 Via del Serafico, 00142 Rome, Italy
Tel: Rome 54591; fax: Rome 504 3463
E-mail: ifad@ifad.org
Web: http://www.ifad.org

The establishment of the International Fund for Agricultural Development (IFAD) was proposed by the 1974
World Food Conference and IFAD began operations as a
UN specialized agency in 1977. Its purpose is to mobilize
additional funds for agricultural and rural development
projects in developing countries that benefit the poorest
rural populations; provide employment and additional
income for poor farmers; reduce malnutrition; and
improve food distribution systems.

IFAD had 161 members as at April 1998. Membership is
divided into three lists: List A (OECD countries), List B
(OPEC countries), and List C (developing countries)
which is subdivided into C1 (Africa), C2 (Africa, Asia and
the Pacific) and C3 (Latin America and the Caribbean). All
powers are vested in a Governing Council of all member
countries. It elects an 18-member Executive Board (with
17 alternate members) responsible for IFAD's operations.
The Council meets annually and elects a President who is
also chairman of the Board. He is assisted by a Vice-
President and three Assistant Presidents.

At the end of December 1997 IFAD's loan portfolio
comprised commitments of US$5,645.8 million for 489
approved projects in 111 developing countries. In 1997 the
Executive Board approved 30 projects, including loans
worth US$397.7 million.
President, Fawzi H. Al-Sultan (Kuwait)

INTERNATIONAL LABOUR
ORGANIZATION
4 route des Morillons, CH 1211 Geneva 22, Switzerland
Tel: Geneva 799 6111; fax: Geneva 798 8685
Web: http://www.ilo.org

The International Labour Organization (ILO) was established in 1919 as an autonomous body of the League of
Nations and became the UN's first specialized agency in
1946. The ILO aims to increase employment, improve
working conditions, raise living standards and encourage
democratic development. It sets minimum international
labour standards through the drafting of international
conventions. Member countries are obliged to submit
these to their domestic authorities for ratification, and thus
undertake to bring their domestic legislation in line with
the conventions. Members must report to the ILO
periodically on how these regulations are being implemented. The ILO plays a major role in helping developing
countries achieve economic stability and job expansion
through its wide-ranging programme of technical co-
operation. The ILO is also the world's principal resource
centre for information, analysis and guidance on labour
and employment. The organization aims to improve
working and living conditions throughout the world and
to support the transition to democracy and market
economics under way in many states.

The ILO had 174 members as at June 1998. It is
composed of the International Labour Conference, the
Governing Body and the International Labour Office. The
Conference of members meets annually, and is attended by
national delegations comprising two government delegates, one worker delegate and one employer delegate. It
formulates international labour conventions and recommendations, provides a forum for discussion of world
employment and social issues, and approves the ILO's
programme and budget (1998–9, US$481 million).

The 56-member Governing Body, composed of 28
government, 14 worker and 14 employer members, acts as
the ILO's executive council. Ten governments, including
Britain, hold seats on the Governing Body because of their
industrial importance. There are also various regional
conferences and advisory committees. The International
Labour Office acts as a secretariat and as a centre for
operations, publishing and research.
Director-General, Michel Hansenne (Belgium); *(from 4
March 1999)* Juan Somavia (Chile)
UK Office, Millbank Tower, 21-24 Millbank, London
swip 4qp. Tel: 0171-828 6401; fax: 0171-233-5925

INTERNATIONAL MARITIME
ORGANIZATION
4 Albert Embankment, London sei 7sr
Tel: 0171-735 7611; fax: 0171-587 3210
E-mail: info@imo.org
Web: http://www.imo.org

The International Maritime Organization (IMO) was
established as a UN specialized agency in 1948. Owing to
delays in treaty ratification it did not commence operations until 1958. Originally it was called the Inter-
Governmental Maritime Consultative Organization
(IMCO) but changed its name in 1982.

The IMO fosters intergovernmental co-operation in
technical matters relating to international shipping,
especially with regard to safety at sea. It is also charged

with preventing and controlling marine pollution caused by shipping and facilitating marine traffic. The IMO is responsible for convening maritime conferences and drafting marine conventions. It also provides technical aid to countries wishing to develop their activities at sea.

The IMO had 155 members as at April 1998. It is governed by an Assembly comprising delegates of all its members. It meets biennially to formulate policy, set a budget (1998–9, £36.6 million), vote on specific recommendations on pollution and maritime safety and elect the Council. The Council fulfils the functions of the Assembly between sessions and appoints the Secretary-General. It consists of 32 members: eight from the world's largest shipping nations, eight from the nations most dependent on seaborne trade, and 16 other members to ensure a fair geographical representation. The Maritime Safety Committee, through its sub-committees, makes reports and recommendations to the Council and the Assembly. There are a number of other specialist subsidiary committees, including one for marine environmental protection.

The IMO acts as the secretariat for the London Convention (1972) which regulates the disposal of land-generated waste at sea.

Secretary-General, William A. O'Neil (Canada)

INTERNATIONAL MONETARY FUND
700 19th Street NW, Washington DC 20431, USA
Tel: Washington DC 623 7000; fax: Washington DC 623 4661
E-mail: publicaffairs@imf.org
Web: http://ww.imf.org

The International Monetary Fund (IMF) was established in 1944, at the UN Monetary and Financial Conference held at Bretton Woods, New Hampshire. Its Articles of Agreement entered into force in 1945 and it began operations in 1946.

The IMF exists to promote international monetary co-operation, the expansion of world trade, and exchange stability, and to eliminate foreign exchange restrictions. The IMF advises members on their economic and financial policies; promotes policy co-ordination among the major industrial countries; and gives technical assistance in central banking, balance of payments accounting, taxation, and other financial matters. The IMF serves as a forum for members to discuss important financial and monetary issues and seeks the balanced growth of international trade and, through this, high levels of employment, income and productive capacity. As at April 1998 the IMF had 182 members. The voting rights of Sudan and the Democratic Republic of Congo have been suspended.

Upon joining the IMF, a member is assigned a 'quota', based on the member's relative standing in the world economy and its balance of payments position, that determines its capital subscription to the Fund, its access to IMF resources, its voting power, and its share in the allocation of Special Drawing Rights (SDRs). Quotas are reviewed every five years and adjusted accordingly. Since the Ninth General Review of quotas in 1994, total Fund quotas stand at SDR 145.3 billion, although the Board of Governors has proposed a quota increase of 45 per cent to SDR 212 billion. The SDR, an international reserve asset issued by the IMF, is calculated daily on a basket of usable currencies and is the IMF's unit of account; on 30 April 1998, SDR 1 equalled US$1.34666. SDRs are allocated at intervals to supplement members' reserves and thereby improve international financial liquidity.

IMF financial resources derive primarily from members' capital subscriptions, which are equivalent to their quotas. In addition, the IMF is authorized to borrow from official lenders. It may also draw on a line of credit of SDR 18.5 billion from various countries under the so-called General Arrangements to Borrow (GAB). Periodic charges are also levied on financial assistance. At the end of April 1998, total outstanding IMF credits amounted to SDR 49.7 billion.

The IMF is not a bank and does not lend money; it provides temporary financial assistance by selling a member's SDRs or other members' currencies in exchange for the member's own currency. The member can then use the purchased currency to alleviate its balance of payments difficulties. The IMF's credit under its regular facilities is made available to members in tranches or segments of 25 per cent of quota. For first credit tranche purchases, members are required to demonstrate reasonable efforts to overcome their balance of payments difficulties. There are no performance criteria and the total amount is repaid in three and a quarter to five years. Upper credit tranche purchases are normally associated with stand-by arrangements. These typically cover periods of one to two years. They focus on macroeconomic policies aimed at overcoming balance of payment difficulties and are required to meet certain performance criteria. Repurchases are made in three and a quarter to five years.

The IMF supports long-term efforts at economic reform and transformation, such as the re-establishment of market economies in the countries of eastern Europe and the former Soviet Union. In addition, the IMF supports medium-term programmes under the extended Fund facility, which runs for three to four years and is aimed at overcoming balance of payments difficulties stemming from macroeconomic and structural problems. Members experiencing a temporary balance of payments shortfall have access to the compensatory and contingency financing facility. The IMF also offers credits to low-income countries engaged in economic reform through its structural adjustment facility (SAF) and enhanced structural adjustment facility (ESAF). As at 30 April 1998, SDR 6.2 billion in SAF and ESAF loans is outstanding.

The IMF is headed by a Board of Governors, comprising representatives of all members, which meets annually. The Governors delegate powers to 24 Executive Directors, who are appointed or elected by member countries. The Executive Directors operate the Fund on a daily basis under a Managing Director, whom they elect.

Managing Director, Michel Camdessus (France)
UK Executive Director, Gus O'Donnell, Room 11-120, IMF, 700 19th Street NW, Washington DC 20431

INTERNATIONAL RED CROSS AND RED CRESCENT MOVEMENT
17 avenue de la Paix, 1211 Geneva, Switzerland
Web: http://www.icrc.org

The International Red Cross and Red Crescent Movement is composed of three elements. The International Committee of the Red Cross (ICRC), the organization's founding body, was formed in 1863. It aims to negotiate between warring factions and to protect and assist victims of armed conflict. It also seeks to ensure the application of the Geneva Conventions with regard to prisoners of war and detainees.

The International Federation of Red Cross and Red Crescent Societies was founded in 1919 to contribute to the development of the humanitarian activities of national societies, to co-ordinate their relief operations for victims of natural disasters, and to care for refugees outside areas of conflict. There are Red Cross and Red Crescent Societies in 175 countries, with a total membership of 250 million.

The International Conference of the Red Cross and Red Crescent meets every four years, bringing together delegates of the ICRC, the International Federation and the national societies, as well as representatives of nations bound by the Geneva Conventions.

President of the ICRC, Cornelio Sommaruga
BRITISH RED CROSS, 9 Grosvenor Crescent, London SW1X 7EJ. Tel: 0171-235 5454; fax: 0171-245 6315. E-mail: information@redcross.org.uk. Web: http://www.redcross.org.uk/vauxhall.htm. *Director-General*, Michael R. Whitlam.

INTERNATIONAL TELECOMMUNICATIONS SATELLITE ORGANIZATION

3400 International Drive NW, Washington DC 20008–3098, USA
Tel: Washington DC 944 6800; fax: Washington DC 944 7898
E-mail: customer.service@intelsat.int
Web: http://www.intelsat.int

The International Telecommunications Satellite Organization (Intelsat) was formed in 1964. It owns and operates the world-wide commercial communications satellite system which is composed of 20 satellites and more than 4,000 antennas which connect over 200 countries, territories and dependencies. Intelsat provides international and domestic voice/data and video services.

Each of the 142 member states contributes to the capital costs of the organization in proportion to its investment share, which is based on its relative usage of the system.

There is a four-tier hierarchy. The Assembly of Parties to the agreement meets every two years to consider long-term objectives and is composed of representatives of the member governments. The Meeting of Signatories annually considers the financial, technical and operational aspects of the system. The Board of Governors has 28 members; INTELSAT Management is the permanent staff of the organization and is headed by a Director-General who reports to the Board of Governors.

Director-General, Irving Goldstein (USA)

INTERNATIONAL TELECOMMUNICATION UNION

Place des Nations, 1211 Geneva 20, Switzerland
Tel: Geneva 730 5111; fax: Geneva 733 7256
E-mail: intumail@itu.int
Web: http://www.itu.org

The International Telecommunication Union (ITU) was founded in Paris in 1865 as the International Telegraph Union and became a UN specialized agency in 1947. It promotes international co-operation and sets standards and regulations for the interconnection of telecommunications systems of all kinds. It assists the development of telecommunications in developing countries by providing technical assistance, management, investment financing and network installation. The ITU adopts international regulations and treaties to allocate the radio frequency spectrum and registers radio frequency assignments in order to avoid harmful interference between radio stations

of different countries. It also governs and allocates the use of the geostationary-satellite orbit and collects and disseminates telecommunications information.

The ITU had 187 member states and 433 members (scientific and industrial companies, broadcasters, public and private operators, and international organizations) as at June 1997. The supreme authority is the Plenipotentiary Conference, composed of representatives of all the members, which meets once every four years. It elects the Administrative Council of 46 members which meets annually to supervise the Union and set the budget (1996–7, SFr 295 million). The Conference also elects the Secretary-General, who heads the General Secretariat. The ITU is structured into three sectors: the radiocommunication sector, including world and regional radiocommunication conferences, radiocommunication assemblies and the Radio Regulations Board; the telecommunication standardization sector; and the telecommunication development sector.

Secretary-General, Dr P. Tarjanne (Finland)

LEAGUE OF ARAB STATES

Maidane Al-Tahrir, Cairo, Egypt
Tel: Cairo 750 511; fax: Cairo 574 0331

The purpose of the League of Arab States, founded in 1945, is to ensure co-operation among member states and protect their independence and sovereignty, to supervise the affairs and interests of Arab countries, to control the execution of agreements concluded among the member states, and to promote the process of integration among them. The League considers itself a regional organization and has observer status at the United Nations.

Member states are Algeria, Bahrain, Comoros, Djibouti, Egypt, Iraq, Jordan, Kuwait, Lebanon, Libya, Mauritania, Morocco, Oman, Palestine, Qatar, Saudi Arabia, Somalia, Sudan, Syria, Tunisia, UAE and Yemen.

Member states participate in various specialized agencies of the League whose role is to develop specific areas of co-operation between Arab states. These include: the Arab Organization for Mineral Resources; the Arab Monetary Fund; the Arab Satellite Communications Organization; the Arab Academy of Maritime Transport; the Arab Bank for Economic Development in Africa; the Arab League Educational, Cultural and Scientific Organization and the Council of Arab Economic Unity.

Secretary-General, Dr Ahmed Esmat Abdul-Maguid (Egypt)
UK OFFICE, 52 Green Street, London W1Y 3RH. Tel: 0171-629 0044; fax: 0171-493 7943

THE NORDIC COUNCIL

The Nordic Council was established in March 1952 as an advisory body on economic and social co-operation, comprising parliamentary delegates from Denmark, Iceland, Norway and Sweden. It was subsequently joined by Finland (1956), and representatives from the Faröes (1970), the Åland Islands (1970), and Greenland (1984).

Co-operation is regulated by the Treaty of Helsinki signed in 1962. This was amended in 1971 to create the Nordic Council of Ministers, which discusses all matters except defence and foreign affairs. Matters are given preparatory consideration by a Committee of Co-operation Ministers' Deputies and joint committees of officials. Decisions of the Council of Ministers, which are taken by consensus, are binding, although if ratification by member parliaments is required, decisions only become effective following parliamentary approval. The Council of Ministers is advised by the Nordic Council, to which it reports annually. There are Ministers for Nordic Co-operation in every member government.

The Nordic Council, comprising 87 voting delegates nominated from member parliaments and about 80 non-voting government representatives, meets at least once a year in plenary sessions. The full Council chooses an 11-member Praesidium, comprising two delegates from each sovereign member and one party group-nominated delegate, which conducts business between sessions. A Secretariat, located in Stockholm and headed by a Secretary-General, liaises with the Council of Ministers and provides administrative support, as well as acting as a publishing house and information centre. The Council of Ministers has a separate Secretariat, based in Copenhagen.

SECRETARIAT OF THE PRAESIDIUM OF THE NORDIC
  COUNCIL, Tyrgatan 7, PO Box 19506, S -10432
  Stockholm, Sweden. Tel: Stockholm 414 3420/453
  4700; fax: Stockholm 411 7536. Web: http://www.
  norden.org. *Secretary-General*, Anders Wenström
  (Sweden)
SECRETARIAT OF THE NORDIC COUNCIL OF MINISTERS,
  Store Strandgade 18, 1255 Copenhagen K, Denmark.
  Secretary-General, Per Stenback (Finland)

NORTH ATLANTIC TREATY ORGANIZATION
Brussels 1110, Belgium
Tel: Brussels 707 4111; fax: Brussels 707 4579
E-mail: natodoc@hq.nato.int
Web: http://www.nato.int

The North Atlantic Treaty (Treaty of Washington) was signed in 1949 by Belgium, Canada, Denmark, France, Iceland, Italy, Luxembourg, the Netherlands, Norway, Portugal, the UK and the USA. Greece and Turkey acceded to the Treaty in 1952, the Federal Republic of Germany in 1955 (the reunited Germany acceded in October 1990), and Spain in 1982.

The North Atlantic Treaty Organization (NATO) is the structural framework for a defensive political and military alliance designed to provide common security for its members through co-operation and consultation in political, military and economic as well as scientific and other non-military fields.

STRUCTURE

The North Atlantic Council (NAC), chaired by the Secretary-General, is the highest authority of the Alliance and is composed of permanent representatives of the 16 member countries. It meets at ministerial level (foreign ministers) at least twice a year. The permanent representatives (ambassadors) head national delegations of advisers and experts. Defence matters are dealt with by the Defence Planning Committee (DPC), composed of representatives of all member countries. The DPC also meets at ministerial level (defence ministers) at least twice a year. Nuclear matters are dealt with in the Nuclear Planning Group (NPG), composed of representatives of all countries except for France (Iceland being an observer). The NPG meets regularly at Permanent Representative level and twice a year at ministerial level (defence ministers). The NATO Secretary-General chairs the Council, the DPC and the NPG.

The Council and DPC are forums for constant inter-governmental consultation and are the main decision-making bodies within the Alliance. They are assisted by an International Staff, divided into five divisions: political affairs; defence planning and policy; defence support; infrastructure, logistics and civil emergency planning; scientific and environmental affairs.

The senior military authority in NATO, under the Council and DPC, is the Military Committee composed of the Chief of Defence Staffs of each member country except Iceland, which has no military and may be represented by a civilian. The Military Committee, which is assisted by an integrated international military staff, also meets in permanent session with permanent military representatives and is responsible for making recommendations to the Council and DPC on measures considered necessary for the common defence of the NATO area and for supplying guidance on military matters to the major NATO commanders. The Chairman of the Military Committee, elected for a period of two to three years, represents the committee on the Council.

The strategic area covered by the North Atlantic Treaty is divided between two major NATO commands (MNCs), European and Atlantic; and three major subordinate commands (MSCs) within Allied Command Europe, South, Central and North-West. There is also a Regional Planning Group (Canada and the United States).

The major NATO commanders are responsible for the development of defence plans for their respective areas, for the determination of force requirements and for the deployment and exercise of the forces under their command. The major NATO commanders report to the Military Committee. From 1995 the reorganized NATO force structure consists of three components: the Allied Rapid Reaction Corps of four divisions, with air and sea components (the majority of which are British forces); the main defence force of four corps (one Danish-German, one Dutch-German, two US-German); and the augmentation forces of reserves and territorials.

POST-COLD WAR DEVELOPMENTS

In response to the new security environment arising from the demise of the Warsaw Pact and the end of the Cold War in 1990, NATO issued a Declaration of Peace and Co-operation in 1991, and published a new strategic concept which introduced organizational changes and force reductions of around 30 per cent.

The Euro-Atlantic Partnership Council (EAPC), which was established in 1997 as a replacement for the North Atlantic Co-operation Council (NACC), was formed to develop closer security links with eastern European and former Soviet states. It focuses on defence planning, defence industry conversion, defence management and force structuring, and the democratic concepts of civilian-military relations. The EAPC provides the framework for consultations and co-operation under the Partnership for Peace (PFP) programme, a form of associate membership launched in 1994. NATO will consult with any PFP partner which perceives a direct threat to its territorial integrity, political independence or security. Most of the 27 PFP partners send liaison officers to NATO headquarters in Brussels and to the Partnership Co-ordination Cell in Mons, Belgium, and participate in joint military exercises co-ordinated by NATO. EAPC membership is open to all former NACC members and PFP participants. It meets monthly at ambassadorial level in Brussels and twice a year at foreign minister and defence minister level.

In 1994, NATO announced that it would consider admitting new members, and in 1997 announced that Poland, the Czech Republic and Hungary would be admitted to the Alliance by April 1999. At the same time, the NATO-Ukraine Charter recognized the importance to European security of a democratic and independent Ukraine, and set up a programme for further co-operation in the future. Russian opposition to expansion was tempered by the signing of a Founding Act on Mutual Relations, Co-operation and Security in May 1997 which provided for the creation of a Permanent Joint Council. In exchange for dropping its objections to NATO's eastern expansion, Russia will have ambassadorial representation at NATO, attend NATO meetings and have equal status in preparing for peacekeeping operations. It will have no right to veto NATO actions.

In 1996 the NAC proposed the creation of combined joint task forces which would provide European NATO members with a framework for operations without US involvement, under the auspices of the Western Europe Union.

From 1992 until the end of 1995, NATO provided support for UN peacekeeping efforts in the former Yugoslavia. With the signing of the Bosnian peace agreement in 1995, a NATO-led multinational Implementation Force (IFOR) embarked on Operation Joint Endeavour to implement the peace accord. IFOR was replaced by the Sustaining Force (SFOR) in December 1996.

Secretary-General and Chairman of the North Atlantic Council, of the DPC and of the NPG, Javier Solana (Spain)

UK Permanent Representative on the North Atlantic Council, Sir John Goulden, KCMG

Chairman of the Military Committee, Gen. Klaus Naumann (Germany)

Supreme Allied Commander, Europe, Gen. Wesley Clark (USA)

Supreme Allied Commander, Atlantic, Gen. John Sheehan (USA)

ORGANIZATION FOR ECONOMIC CO-OPERATION AND DEVELOPMENT

2 rue André-Pascal, 75116 Paris
Tel: Paris 4524 8200; fax: Paris 4524 8500
Web: http://www.oecd.org

The Organization for Economic Co-operation and Development (OECD) was formed in 1961 to replace the Organization for European Economic Co-operation. It is the instrument for international co-operation among industrialized member countries on economic and social policies. Its objectives are to assist its member governments in the formulation and co-ordination of policies designed to achieve high, sustained economic growth while maintaining financial stability, to contribute to world trade on a multilateral basis and to stimulate members' aid to developing countries.

The members are Australia, Austria, Belgium, Canada, the Czech Republic, Denmark, Finland, France, Germany, Greece, Hungary, Iceland, Republic of Ireland, Italy, Japan, Republic of Korea, Luxembourg, Mexico, the Netherlands, New Zealand, Norway, Poland, Portugal, Spain, Sweden, Switzerland, Turkey, the UK and the USA.

The Council is the supreme body of the organization. It is composed of one representative for each member country and meets at permanent representative level under the chairmanship of the Secretary-General, or at ministerial level (usually once a year) under the chairmanship of a minister elected annually. Decisions and recommendations are adopted by the unanimous agreement of all members. An executive committee comprising 14 members of the Council is chosen annually, although most of the OECD's work is undertaken in over 200 specialized committees and working parties. Five autonomous or semi-autonomous bodies are associated in varying degrees to the Organization: the Nuclear Energy Agency, the International Energy Agency, the Development Centre, the Centre for Educational Research and Innova-

tion, and the European Conference of Ministers of Transport. These bodies, the committees and the Council are serviced by an international Secretariat headed by the Secretary-General.

Secretary-General, Donald J. Johnston (Canada)

UK Permanent Representative, HE Peter Vereker, 19 rue de Franqueville, Paris 75116

ORGANIZATION FOR SECURITY AND CO-OPERATION IN EUROPE

Kärntner Ring 5–7, A-1010 Vienna, Austria
Tel: Vienna 514 360; fax: Vienna 514 3696
Web: http://www.osce.org

The Organization for Security and Co-operation in Europe (OSCE) was launched in 1975 (as the Conference on Security and Co-operation in Europe (CSCE)) under the Helsinki Final Act. This established agreements between NATO members, Warsaw Pact members, and neutral and non-aligned European countries covering security in Europe; economic, scientific, technological and environmental co-operation; and humanitarian principles. Further conferences were held at Belgrade (1977–8), Madrid (1980–3) and Vienna (1986–9).

With the end of the Cold War, it was decided that the CSCE should be institutionalized to provide a new security framework for Europe. The Charter of Paris for a New Europe, signed on 21 November 1990, committed members to support multi-party democracy, free-market economics, the rule of law, and human rights. The signatories also agreed to regular meetings of heads of government, ministers and officials. The first institutionalized heads of state and government summit was held in Helsinki in December 1992, at which the Helsinki Document was adopted. This declared the CSCE to be a regional organization and defined the structures of the organization. The summit also appointed a High Commissioner on National Minorities. At its December 1994 summit the CSCE was renamed the Organization for Security and Co-operation in Europe.

Three structures have been established: the Ministerial Council of foreign ministers, the central decision-making and governing body, which meets at least once a year; the Senior Council, which prepares work for the Ministerial Council, carries out its decisions and is responsible for the overview, management and co-ordination of OSCE activities and meets at least three times a year; and the Permanent Council, which is responsible for the day-to-day operational tasks of the OSCE and is the regular body for political consultation, meeting weekly. The chairmanship of the Ministerial Council, Senior Council and Permanent Council rotates among participating states with the Senior Council meeting in Prague and the Permanent Council in Vienna.

The OSCE is also underpinned by four permanent institutions: a Secretariat (Vienna); a Forum for Security Co-operation (Vienna), which meets weekly to discuss arms control, disarmament and security-building measures; an Office for Democratic Institutions and Human Rights (Warsaw), which is charged with furthering human rights, democracy and the rule of law; and an office of the High Commissioner on National Minorities (The Hague), which identifies ethnic tensions that might endanger peace and promotes their resolution. There is also a documentation and conference centre in Prague, an OSCE Parliamentary Assembly with a secretariat based in Copenhagen, and a Court of Conciliation and Arbitration in Geneva.

In June 1991 the CSCE agreed upon new crisis prevention mechanisms to prevent or manage violent conflict between and within member countries. The OSCE has monitoring missions in ten OSCE countries, has sent an assistance group to Chechenia, co-ordinates the international presence in Albania, and has an advisory and monitoring group in Belarus. It is also organizing a peacekeeping force in Nagorno-Karabakh. The OSCE supervised all elections in Bosnia-Hercegovina between 1996 and 1998. A Joint Consultative Group of the OSCE promotes the objectives and implementation of the Conventional Armed Forces in Europe (CFE) Treaty (1990) which limits conventional ground and air forces.

The OSCE has 55 participating states: Albania, Andorra, Armenia, Austria, Azerbaijan, Belarus, Belgium, Bosnia-Hercegovina, Bulgaria, Canada, Croatia, Cyprus, Czech Republic, Denmark, Estonia, Finland, France, Georgia, Germany, Greece, Hungary, Iceland, Ireland, Italy, Kazakhstan, Kyrgyzstan, Latvia, Liechtenstein, Lithuania, Luxembourg, Macedonia (Former Yugoslav Republic of), Malta, Moldova, Monaco, the Netherlands, Norway, Poland, Portugal, Romania, Russia, San Marino, Slovakia, Slovenia, Spain, Sweden, Switzerland, Tajikistan, Turkey, Turkmenistan, UK, Ukraine, USA, Uzbekistan, the Vatican and Yugoslavia (suspended from activities July 1992).
Chair of the OSCE: Poland (1998); Norway (1999)
Secretary-General of the OSCE, Giancarlo Aragona (Italy)
Director of the Office for Democratic Institutions and Human Rights, Gérard Stoudmann (Switzerland)
OSCE High Commissioner on National Minorities, Max van der Stoel (Netherlands)

ORGANIZATION OF AFRICAN UNITY
PO Box 3243, Addis Ababa, Ethiopia
Tel: Addis Ababa 517700; fax: Addis Ababa 513036

The Organization of African Unity (OAU) was established in 1963 and has 53 members; Morocco suspended its participation in 1985 in protest at the Polisario-proclaimed Saharan Arab Democratic Republic (SADR), representing Western Sahara, being admitted as a member. The OAU aims to further African unity and solidarity, to co-ordinate political, economic, social and defence policies, and to eliminate colonialism in Africa.

The chief organs are the Assembly of heads of state or government, which is the supreme organ of the OAU and meets once a year to consider matters of common African concern and to co-ordinate the Organization's policies; the Council of foreign ministers, which is the Organization's executive body responsible for the implementation of the Assembly's policies, and which meets twice a year; and the Commission of Mediation, Conciliation and Arbitration which promotes the peaceful settlement of disputes between member countries. The main administrative body is the General Secretariat, based in Addis Ababa, headed by a Secretary-General who is elected by the Assembly for a four-year term.

Substantial budgetary arrears due to delays in the payment of national contributions has meant that the OAU continually faces difficulties in furthering its aims. Its budget for 1997–8 was set at US$30.85 million; several OAU programmes have been suspended since November 1994 after unpaid contributions reached US$77 million, although by June 1995 arrears had dropped to US$38.3 million. In June 1991 the Assembly adopted an African Economic Community Treaty which envisages establishment of the Economic Community after ratification by two-thirds of the OAU's membership. In June 1993 a mechanism was created for conflict prevention, management and resolution, and a peace fund was established.
Secretary-General, Salim Ahmed Salim (Tanzania)

ORGANIZATION OF AMERICAN STATES
17th Street and Constitution Avenue NW, Washington DC 20006, USA
Tel: Washington DC 458 3000; fax: Washington DC 458 6421
E-mail: info@oas.org
Web: http://www.oas.org

Originally founded in 1890 for largely commercial purposes, the Organization of American States (OAS) adopted its present name and charter in 1948. The charter entered into force in 1951 and was amended in 1967, 1985 and 1996; the 1992 Protocol of Washington will enter into force upon ratification by two-thirds of member states.

The OAS aims to strengthen the peace and security of the continent; to promote and consolidate representative democracy with due respect for the principle of non-intervention; to prevent possible causes of difficulties and to ensure the peaceful resolution of disputes arising among its member states; to provide for common action on the part of those states in the event of aggression; to seek the resolution of political, judicial and economic problems that may arise among them; to promote, by co-operative action, their economic, social and cultural development; and to achieve an effective limitation of conventional weapons so that resources can be devoted to economic and social development.

Policy is determined by the annual General Assembly, which is the supreme authority and elects the Secretary-General for a five-year term. The Meeting of Consultation of ministers of foreign affairs considers urgent problems on an *ad hoc* basis. The Permanent Council, comprising one representative from each member state, promotes friendly inter-state relations, acts as an intermediary in case of disputes arising between states and oversees the General Secretariat, the main administrative body. The Inter-American Council for Integral Development was created in 1996 by the ratification of the Protocol of Managua to promote sustainable development.

The 35 member states are Antigua and Barbuda, Argentina, Bahamas, Barbados, Belize, Bolivia, Brazil, Canada, Chile, Colombia, Costa Rica, Cuba, Dominica, Dominican Republic, Ecuador, Grenada, Guatemala, Guyana, Haiti, Honduras, Jamaica, Mexico, Nicaragua, Panama, Paraguay, Peru, St Christopher and Nevis, St Lucia, St Vincent and the Grenadines, El Salvador, Suriname, Trinidad and Tobago, Uruguay, USA and Venezuela. The European Union and 39 non-American states have permanent observer status.
Secretary-General, Dr César Gaviria Trujillo (Colombia)

ORGANIZATION OF ARAB PETROLEUM EXPORTING COUNTRIES
PO Box 20501, Safat 13066, Kuwait
Tel: Kuwait 484 4500; fax: Kuwait 481 5747
E-mail: oapec@kuwait.net
Web: http://www.kuwait.net/oapec

The Organization of Arab Petroleum and Exporting Countries (OAPEC) was founded in 1968. Its objectives are to promote co-operation in economic activities, to safeguard members' interests, to unite efforts to ensure the flow of oil to consumer markets, and to create a favourable climate for the investment of capital and expertise.

The Ministerial Council is composed of oil ministers from the member countries and meets twice a year to determine policy and to approve the budgets and accounts of the General Secretariat and the Judicial Tribunal. The Judicial Tribunal is composed of seven part-time judges who rule on disputes between member countries and disputes between countries and oil companies. The executive organ of OAPEC is the General Secretariat.

The members are Algeria, Bahrain, Egypt, Iraq, Kuwait, Libya, Qatar, Saudi Arabia, Syria and the United Arab Emirates. Tunisia's membership has been inactive since 1987.

Secretary-General, Abdel-Aziz A. Al-Turki

ORGANIZATION OF THE ISLAMIC CONFERENCE
PO Box 178, Jeddah 21411, Saudi Arabia
Tel: Jeddah 680 0800; fax: Jeddah 687 3568

The Organization of the Islamic Conference (OIC) was established in 1971 with the purpose of promoting solidarity and co-operation between Islamic countries. It also has the specific aims of co-ordinating efforts to safeguard the Muslim holy places, supporting the formation of a Palestinian state, assisting member states to maintain their independence, co-ordinating the views of member states in international forums such as the UN, and improving co-operation in the economic, cultural and scientific fields.

The OIC has three central organs, supreme among them the Conference of the Heads of State which meets once every three years to discuss issues of importance to Islamic states. The Conference of Foreign Ministers meets annually to prepare reports for the Conference of Heads of State. The General Secretariat carries out administrative tasks. It is headed by a Secretary-General who is elected by the Conference of Foreign Ministers for a non-renewable four-year term.

In addition to this structure, the OIC has several subsidiary bodies and specialized bodies. These include the Islamic Solidarity Fund, to aid Islamic institutions in member countries, and the Islamic Development Bank, to finance development projects in poorer member states. An Islamic Court of Justice is planned. The OIC runs various offices to organize the economic boycott of Israel.

The achievement of the OIC's aims has often been prevented by political rivalry and conflicts between member states, such as the Iran-Iraq war and the Iraqi invasion of Kuwait. Egypt's membership was suspended from 1979 to 1984 because of its peace treaty with Israel. Saudi Arabia, the main source of funding, exercises great influence within the OIC. Since 1991 the OIC has become more united and has spoken out against violence against Muslims in India, the Occupied Territories and Bosnia-Hercegovina. From 1993 to 1995 the OIC co-ordinated the offering of troops to the UN by Muslim states to protect Muslim areas of Bosnia-Hercegovina.

The Organization has 55 members (54 sovereign Muslim states in Africa, the Middle East, central and south-east Asia and Europe, plus the Palestine Liberation Organization) and three observers, the Central African Republic, Turkish Northern Cyprus and Côte d'Ivoire. It has an annual budget of £5 million.

Secretary-General, Azzedine Laraki (Morocco)

ORGANIZATION OF THE PETROLEUM EXPORTING COUNTRIES
Obere Donaustrasse 93, 1020 Vienna, Austria
Tel: Vienna 211 120; fax: Vienna 214 9827
E-mail: info@opec.org
Web: http://www.opec.org

The Organization of the Petroleum Exporting Countries (OPEC) was created in 1960 as a permanent intergovernmental organization with the principal aims of unifying and co-ordinating the petroleum policies of its members, determining ways of protecting their interests individually and collectively, and ensuring the stabilization of prices in international oil markets with a view to eliminating unnecessary fluctuations. Since 1982 OPEC has attempted (only partially successfully) to impose overall production limits and production quotas in an attempt to maintain stable oil prices. In March 1998, OPEC members and a number of the main non-OPEC producers agreed to reduce oil production by 1.5 million barrels per day to boost oil prices, which had fallen to their lowest level in real terms since 1973.

The supreme authority is the Conference of Ministers of oil, mines and energy of member countries, which meets at least twice a year to formulate policy. The Board of Governors, nominated by member countries, directs the management of OPEC and implements conference resolutions. The Secretariat carries out executive functions under the direction of the Board of Governors.

The member states are Algeria, Indonesia, Iran, Iraq, Kuwait, Libya, Nigeria, Qatar, Saudi Arabia, UAE and Venezuela. Ecuador withdrew in 1992 and Gabon in 1995.

Secretary-General, HE Dr Rilwanu Lukman (Nigeria)

THE PACIFIC COMMUNITY
BP D5, 98848Nouméa Cedex, New Caledonia
Tel: Nouméa 262000; fax: Nouméa 263818
E-mail: spc@spc.org.nc
Web: http://www.spc.org.nc

The Pacific Community (formerly the South Pacific Commission) was established in 1947 by Australia, France, the Netherlands, New Zealand, the UK and the USA with the aim of promoting the economic and social stability of the islands in the region. The Community now numbers 27 member states and territories: the five remaining founder states (the Netherlands has withdrawn), in which no programmes are run, and the other 22 states and territories of Melanesia, Micronesia and Polynesia.

The Secretariat of the Pacific Community (SPC) is a technical assistance agency with programmes in agriculture and plant protection, fisheries and marine resources, community health, socio-economic and statistical services, and community education services.

The governing body is the Conference of the Pacific Community, which meets every two years. The Director-General is the chief executive.

Director-General, Bob Dun (Australia)
Deputy Directors-General, Jimmie Rodgers (Solomon Islands); Lourdes Pangelinan (Guam)

THE UNITED NATIONS
UN Plaza, New York, NY 10017, USA
Tel: New York 963 1234
Web: http://www.un.org

The United Nations (UN) is an intergovernmental organization of member states, dedicated through signature of the UN Charter to the maintenance of international peace and security and the solution of economic, social and political problems through international co-operation.

The UN was founded as a successor to the League of Nations and inherited many of its procedures and institutions. The name 'United Nations' was first used in the Washington Declaration 1942 to describe the 26 states which had allied to fight the Axis powers. The UN Charter developed from discussions at the Moscow Conference of the foreign ministers of China, the UK, the USA and the Soviet Union in 1943. Further progress was made at Dumbarton Oaks, Washington, in 1944 during talks involving the same states. The role of the Security Council was formulated at the Yalta Conference in 1945. The Charter was formally drawn up by 50 allied nations at the San Francisco Conference between April and 26 June 1945, when it was signed. Following ratification the UN came into effect on 24 October 1945, which is celebrated annually as United Nations Day. The UN flag is light blue with the UN emblem centred in white.

The principal organs of the UN are the General Assembly, the Security Council, the Economic and Social Council, the Trusteeship Council, the Secretariat and the International Court of Justice. The Economic and Social Council and the Trusteeship Council are auxiliaries, charged with assisting and advising the General Assembly and Security Council. The official languages used are Arabic, Chinese, English, French, Russian and Spanish. Deliberations at the International Court of Justice are in English and French only.

MEMBERSHIP

Membership is open to all countries which accept the Charter and its principle of peaceful co-existence. New members are admitted by the General Assembly on the recommendation of the Security Council. The original membership of 51 states has grown to 185:

Afghanistan
Albania
Algeria
Andorra
Angola
Antigua and Barbuda
*Argentina
Armenia
*Australia
Austria
Azerbaijan
The Bahamas
Bahrain
Bangladesh
Barbados
*Belarus
*Belgium
Belize
Benin
Bhutan
*Bolivia
Bosnia-Hercegovina
Botswana
*Brazil
Brunei

Bulgaria
Burkina
Burundi
Cambodia (suspended)
Cameroon
*Canada
Cape Verde
Central African Rep.
Chad
*Chile
*China
*Colombia
Comoros
Congo, Democratic Rep.
Congo, Rep. of
*Costa Rica
Côte d'Ivoire
Croatia
*Cuba
Cyprus
*Czech Republic
*Denmark
Djibouti
Dominica
*Dominican Republic

*Ecuador
*Egypt
Equatorial Guinea
Eritrea
Estonia
*Ethiopia
Federated States of
  Micronesia
Fiji
Finland
*France
Gabon
Gambia
Georgia
Germany
Ghana
*Greece
Grenada
*Guatemala
Guinea
Guinea-Bissau
Guyana
*Haiti
*Honduras
Hungary
Iceland
*India
Indonesia
*Iran
*Iraq
Ireland, Republic of
Israel
Italy
Jamaica
Japan
Jordan
Kazakhstan
Kenya
Korea, D. P. Rep. (North)
Korea, Rep. of (South)
Kuwait
Kyrgyzstan
Laos
Latvia
*Lebanon
Lesotho
*Liberia
Libya
Liechtenstein
Lithuania
*Luxembourg
Macedonia (Former Yugo-
  slav Republic of)
Madagascar
Malawi
Malaysia
Maldives
Mali
Malta
Marshall Islands
Mauritania
Mauritius
*Mexico
Moldova
Monaco
Mongolia
Morocco
Mozambique
Myanmar (Burma)

Namibia
Nepal
*Netherlands
*New Zealand
*Nicaragua
Niger
Nigeria
*Norway
Oman
Pakistan
Palau
*Panama
Papua New Guinea
*Paraguay
*Peru
*Philippines
*Poland
Portugal
Qatar
Romania
*Russian Federation
Rwanda
St Christopher and Nevis
St Lucia
St Vincent and the Grena-
  dines
*El Salvador
Samoa
San Marino
São Tomé and Princípe
*Saudi Arabia
Senegal
Seychelles
Sierra Leone
Singapore
*Slovakia
Slovenia
Solomon Islands
Somalia
*South Africa
Spain
Sri Lanka
Sudan
Suriname
Swaziland
Sweden
*Syria
Tajikistan
Tanzania
Thailand
Togo
Trinidad and Tobago
Tunisia
*Turkey
Turkmenistan
Uganda
*Ukraine
United Arab Emirates
*United Kingdom
*United States of America
*Uruguay
Uzbekistan
Vanuatu
*Venezuela
Vietnam
Yemen
*Yugoslavia (suspended)
Zambia
Zimbabwe

*Original member (i.e. from 1945)

From 25 October 1971 'China' was taken to mean the People's Republic of China. Czechoslovakia was an original member in 1945 and a member until 31 December 1992; the successor states of the Czech Republic and Slovakia were admitted as members in January 1993.

The Russian Federation took over the membership of the Soviet Union in the Security Council and all other UN organs on 24 December 1991. Belarus (formerly Belorussia) and the Ukraine on becoming independent sovereign states continued their existing memberships of the UN, both having been granted separate UN membership in 1945 as a concession to the Soviet Union.

OBSERVERS

Permanent observer status is held by the Holy See and Switzerland. The Palestine Liberation Organization has special observer status.

NON-MEMBERS

A number of countries are not members, usually due to their small size and limited financial resources. Notable exceptions include Switzerland, which follows a policy of absolute neutrality, and Taiwan, which was replaced by the People's Republic of China in 1971. The others are Kiribati, Nauru, Tonga, Tuvalu and the Holy See.

THE GENERAL ASSEMBLY
UN Plaza, New York, NY 10017, USA

The General Assembly is the main deliberative organ of the UN. It consists of all members, each entitled to five representatives but having only one vote. The annual session begins on the third Tuesday of September, when the President is elected, and usually continues until mid-December. Special sessions are held on specific issues and emergency special sessions can be called within 24 hours.

The Assembly is empowered to discuss any matter within the scope of the Charter, except when it is under consideration by the Security Council, and to make recommendations. Under the 'uniting for peace' resolution, adopted in 1950, the Assembly may also take action to maintain international peace and security when the Security Council fails to do so because of a lack of unanimity of its permanent members. Important decisions, such as those on peace and security, the election of officers, the budget, etc., need a two-thirds majority. Others need a simple majority. The Assembly has effective power only over the internal operations of the UN itself; external recommendations are not legally binding.

The work of the General Assembly is divided among six main committees, on each of which every member has the right to be represented: disarmament and international security; economic and financial; social, humanitarian and cultural; special political issues and decolonization (including non-self governing territories); administrative and budgetary; and legal. In addition, the General Assembly appoints *ad hoc* committees to consider special issues, such as human rights, peacekeeping, disarmament and international law. All committees consider items referred to them by the Assembly and recommend draft resolutions to its plenary meeting.

The Assembly is assisted by a number of functional committees. The General Committee co-ordinates its proceedings and operations, while the Credentials Committee verifies the credentials of representatives. There are also two standing committees, the Advisory Committee on Administration and Budgetary Questions and the Committee on Contributions, which suggests the scale of members' payments to the UN.

President of the General Assembly (1997), Hennadiy Udovenko (Ukraine)

The Assembly has created a large number of specialized bodies over the years, which are supervised jointly with the Economic and Social Council. They are supported by UN and voluntary contributions from governments, non-governmental organizations and individuals. These organizations include:

THE CONFERENCE ON DISARMAMENT (CD)
Palais des Nations, 1211 Geneva 10, Switzerland
Established by the UN as the Committee on Disarmament in 1962, the CD is the single multilateral disarmament negotiating forum. The present title of the organization was adopted in 1984. There were 40 members as at June 1994.

A Chemical Weapons Convention was agreed in Paris in 1993 and came into force in April 1997 after being ratified by 87 countries. It bans the use, production, stockpiling and transfer of all chemical weapons. All US and Russian weapons must be destroyed within 15 years of the Convention entering into force and all other states' weapons must be destroyed within ten years.
Secretary-General, Vladimir Petrovsky (Russia)
UK Representative, I. Soutar, 37–39 rue de Vermont, 1211 Geneva 20, Switzerland

THE UNITED NATIONS CHILDREN'S FUND (UNICEF)
3 UN Plaza, New York, NY 10017, USA
Established in 1947 to assist children and mothers in the immediate post-war period, UNICEF now concentrates on developing countries. It provides primary health-care and health education. In particular, it conducts programmes in oral hydration, immunization against leading diseases, child growth monitoring, and the encouragement of breast-feeding. Its operations are often conducted in co-operation with the World Health Organization (WHO).
Executive Director, Carol Bellamy (USA)

THE UNITED NATIONS DEVELOPMENT PROGRAMME (UNDP)
1 UN Plaza, New York, NY 10017, USA
Established in 1966 from the merger of the UN Expanded Programme of Technical Assistance and the UN Special Fund, UNDP is the central funding agency for economic and social development projects around the world. Much of its annual expenditure is channelled through UN specialized agencies, governments and non-governmental organizations.
Administrator, James G. Speth (USA)

THE UNITED NATIONS HIGH COMMISSIONER FOR REFUGEES (UNHCR)
Centre William Rappard, 154 rue de Lausanne, PO Box 2500, 1211 Geneva 2, Switzerland
Established in 1951 to protect the rights and interests of refugees, UNHCR organizes emergency relief and longer-term solutions, such as voluntary repatriation, local integration or resettlement.
High Commissioner, Sadako Ogata (Japan)
UK OFFICE, 76 Westminster Palace Gardens, London SWIP IRL. Tel: 0171-828 9191

THE UN RELIEF AND WORKS AGENCY FOR PALESTINE REFUGEES IN THE NEAR EAST (UNRWA)
Vienna International Centre, Wagramerstrasse 5, PO Box 100, 1400 Vienna, Austria
Established in 1949 to bring relief to the Palestinians displaced by the Arab-Israeli conflict.
Commissioner-General, Ilter Turkman (Turkey)

THE UNITED NATIONS HIGH COMMISSIONER FOR HUMAN RIGHTS

Established in 1993 to secure respect for, and prevent violations of human rights by engaging in dialogue with governments and international organizations. Responsible for the co-ordination of all UN human rights activities.

High Commissioner, Mary Robinson (Ireland)

Other bodies include:

THE UN CENTRE FOR HUMAN SETTLEMENTS (Habitat), PO Box 30030, Nairobi, Kenya
THE UN CONFERENCE ON TRADE AND DEVELOPMENT (UNCTAD), Palais des Nations, 1211 Geneva 10, Switzerland
THE DEPARTMENT OF HUMANITARIAN AFFAIRS (DHA), Palais des Nations, 1211 Geneva 10, Switzerland
THE INTERNATIONAL SEABED AUTHORITY, Kingston, Jamaica
THE UN ENVIRONMENT PROGRAMME (UNEP), PO Box 30552, Nairobi, Kenya
THE UN POPULATION FUND (UNFPA), 220 East 42nd Street, New York, NY 10017, USA
THE UN INSTITUTE FOR THE ADVANCEMENT OF WOMEN (INSTRAW), PO Box 21747, Santo Domingo, Dominican Republic
THE UN UNIVERSITY (UNU), Toho Seimei Building, 15-1, Shibuya, 2-Chome, Shibuya-ku, Tokyo 150, Japan
THE WORLD FOOD COUNCIL (WFC), Via delle Terme di Caracalla, 00100 Rome, Italy
THE WORLD FOOD PROGRAMME (WFP), Via delle Terme di Caracalla, 00100 Rome, Italy

BUDGET OF THE UNITED NATIONS

The budget adopted for the biennium 1998–9 was US$2,387 million. The scale of assessment contributions of 88 UN members is set at the minimum 0.01 per cent. The ten largest assessments are: USA, 25 per cent; Japan, 12.45; Germany, 8.93; Russia, 6.91; France, 6.00; UK, 5.02; Italy, 4.29; Canada, 3.11; Spain, 1.98; Australia, 1.51.

THE SECURITY COUNCIL
UN Plaza, New York, NY 10017, USA

The Security Council is the senior arm of the UN and has the primary responsibility for maintaining world peace and security. It consists of 15 members, each with one representative and one vote. There are five permanent members, China, France, Russia, the UK and the USA, and ten non-permanent members. Each of the non-permanent members is elected for a two-year term by a two-thirds majority of the General Assembly and is ineligible for immediate re-election. Five of the elective seats are allocated to Africa and Asia, one to eastern Europe, two to Latin America and two to western Europe and remaining countries. Procedural questions are determined by a majority vote. Other matters require a majority inclusive of the votes of the permanent members; they thus have a right of veto. The abstention of a permanent member does not constitute a veto. The presidency rotates each month by state in (English) alphabetical order. Parties to a dispute, other non-members and individuals can be invited to participate in Security Council debates but are not permitted to vote. In 1998 the ten non-permanent members were: Costa Rica, Japan, Kenya, Portugal, Sweden (*term expires 31 December 1998*), Bahrain, Brazil, Gabon, Gambia, Slovenia (*term expires 31 December 1999*).

The Security Council is empowered to settle or adjudicate in disputes or situations which threaten international peace and security. It can adopt political, economic and military measures to achieve this end. Any matter considered to be a threat to or breach of the peace or an act of aggression can be brought to the Security Council's attention by any member state or by the Secretary-General. The Charter envisaged members placing at the disposal of the Security Council armed forces and other facilities which would be co-ordinated by the Military Staff Committee, composed of military representatives of the five permanent members. The Security Council is also supported by a Committee of Experts, to advise on procedural and technical matters, and a Committee on Admission of New Members.

Owing to superpower disunity, the Security Council rarely played the decisive role set out in the Charter; the Military Staff Committee was effectively suspended from 1948 until 1990, when a meeting was convened during the Gulf Crisis on the formation and control of UN-supervised armed forces. However, at an extraordinary meeting of the Security Council in January 1992, heads of government laid plans to transform the UN in light of the changed post-Cold War world. The Secretary-General was asked to draw up a report on enhancing the UN's preventive diplomacy, peacemaking and peacekeeping ability. The report, *An Agenda for Peace,* was produced in June 1992 and centred on the establishment of a UN army composed of national contingents on permanent standby, as envisaged at the time of the UN's formation.

PEACEKEEPING FORCES

The Security Council has established a number of peace-keeping forces since its foundation, comprising contingents provided mainly by neutral and non-aligned UN members. Current forces include: the UN Truce Supervision Organization (UNTSO), Israel, 1948; the UN Military Observer Group in India and Pakistan (UNMOGIP), 1949; the UN Peacekeeping Force in Cyprus (UNFICYP), 1964; the UN Disengagement Observer Force (UNDOF), Golan Heights, Syria, 1974; the UN Interim Force in Lebanon (UNIFIL), 1978; the UN Iraq-Kuwait Observation Mission (UNIKOM), 1991; the UN Mission for the Referendum in Western Sahara (MINURSO), 1991; the UN Observer Mission in Georgia (UNOMIG), 1993; the UN Observer Mission in Liberia (UNOMIL), 1993; the UN Observer Mission in Guatemala (MINUGA), 1994; the UN Observer Mission in Tajikistan (UNMOT), 1994; the UN Preventive Deployment Force (UNPREDEP), Former Yugoslav Republic of Macedonia, 1995; the UN Mission in Bosnia-Hercegovina (UNMIBH), 1995; the UN Mission of Observers in Prevlaka (UNMOP), 1996; the UN Observer Mission in Angola (UNOMA), 1997.

THE ECONOMIC AND SOCIAL COUNCIL
UN Plaza, New York, NY 10017, USA

The Economic and Social Council is responsible under the General Assembly for the economic and social work of the UN and for the co-ordination of the activities of the 15 specialized agencies and other UN bodies. It makes reports and recommendations on economic, social, cultural, educational, health and related matters, often in consultation with non-governmental organizations, passing the reports to the General Assembly and other UN bodies. It also drafts conventions for submission to the Assembly and calls conferences on matters within its remit.

The Council consists of 54 members, 18 of whom are elected annually by the General Assembly for a three-year term. Each has one vote and can be immediately re-elected on retirement. A President is elected annually and is also eligible for re-election. One substantive session is held annually and decisions are reached by simple majority vote of those present.

The Council has established a number of standing committees on particular issues and several commissions. Commissions include: Statistical, Human Rights, Social Development, Sustainable Development, Status of Women, Crime Prevention and Criminal Justice, Narcotic Drugs, Science and Technology for Development, and Population; and Regional Economic Commissions for Europe, Asia and the Pacific, Western Asia, Latin America and Africa.

THE TRUSTEESHIP COUNCIL
UN Plaza, New York, NY10017, USA

The Trusteeship Council supervised the administration of territories within the UN Trusteeship system inherited from the League of Nations. It consists of the five permanent members of the Security Council. With the independence of the Republic of Palau in October 1994, all eleven trusteeships have now progressed to independence or merged with neighbouring states and the Trusteeship Council suspended its operations on 1 November 1994.

THE SECRETARIAT
UN Plaza, New York, NY 10017, USA

The Secretariat services the other UN organs and is headed by a Secretary-General elected by a majority vote of the General Assembly on the recommendation of the Security Council. He is assisted by an international staff, chosen to represent the international character of the organization. The Secretary-General is charged with bringing to the attention of the Security Council any matter which he considers poses a threat to international peace and security. He may also bring other matters to the attention of the General Assembly and other UN bodies and may be entrusted by them with additional duties. As chief administrator to the UN, the Secretary-General is present in person or via representatives at all meetings of the other five main organs of the UN. He may also act as an impartial mediator in disputes between member states.

The power and influence of the Secretary-General has been determined largely by the character of the office-holder and by the state of relations between the super-powers. The thaw in these relations since the mid-1980s has increased the effectiveness of the UN, particularly in its attempts to intervene in international disputes. It helped to end the Iran-Iraq war and sponsored peace in Central America. Following Iraq's invasion of Kuwait in 1990 the UN took its first collective security action since the Korean War. UN action to protect the Kurds in northern Iraq has widened its legal authority by breaching the prohibition on its intervention in the essentially domestic affairs of states. Currently the UN is involved in peace-keeping, aid distribution and negotiations in the former Yugoslavia; and is addressing the global problems of Aids and environmental destruction.

Secretary-General, Kofi Annan, apptd 1996 (Ghana)
Deputy Secretary-General, Louise Frechette, apptd 1998 (Canada)

UNDER-SECRETARIES-GENERAL

Administration and Management, Joseph Connor (USA)
Chef de Cabinet, Iqbal Riza (Pakistan)
Development Support and Management Services, Jin Yongjian (China)
Humanitarian Affairs, Sergio Vieira de Mello (Brazil)
Legal Affairs and UN Legal Counsel, Hans Corell (Sweden)
Peacekeeping Operations, Bernard Miyet (France)

Policy Co-ordination and Sustainable Development, Nitin Desai (India)
Political Affairs, Sir Kieran Prendergast (UK)

FORMER SECRETARIES-GENERAL

1946–53	Trygve Lie (Norway)
1953–61	Dag Hammarskjöld (Sweden)
1961–71	U Thant (Burma)
1971–81	Kurt Waldheim (Austria)
1981–91	Javier Pérez de Cuéllar (Peru)
1991–6	Boutros Boutros-Ghali (Egypt)

INTERNATIONAL COURT OF JUSTICE
The Peace Palace, 2517 KJ The Hague, The Netherlands

The International Court of Justice is the principal judicial organ of the UN. The Statute of the Court is an integral part of the Charter and all members of the UN are *ipso facto* parties to it. The Court is composed of 15 judges, elected by both the General Assembly and the Security Council for nine-year terms which are renewable. Judges may deliberate over cases in which their country is involved. If no judge on the bench is from a country which is a party to a dispute under consideration, that party may designate a judge to participate *ad hoc* in that particular deliberation. If any party to a case fails to adhere to the judgment of the Court, the other party may have recourse to the Security Council.

President, Mohammed Bedjaoui (Algeria) (2006)
Vice-President, Stephen M. Schwebel (USA) (2006)
Judges, Carl-August Fleischhauer (Germany) (2003); Gilbert Guillaume (France) (2000); Geza Herczegh (Hungary) (2003); Rosalyn Higgins (UK) (2000); Shi Jiuyong (China) (2003); Pieter H. Kooijmans (Netherlands) (2006); Abdul G. Koroma (Sierra Leone) (2003); Shigeru Oda (Japan) (2003); Gonzalo Parra-Aranguren (Venezuela) (2000); Raymond Ranjeva (Madagascar) (2000); José Francisco Rezek (Brazil) (2006); Christopher G. Weeramantry (Sri Lanka) (2000); Vladlen S. Vereshchetin (Russia) (2006)

INTERNATIONAL WAR CRIMES TRIBUNAL FOR THE FORMER YUGOSLAVIA
Churchill Plein 1, PO Box 13888, 2501 EW The Hague, The Netherlands

In February 1993, the Security Council voted to establish a war crimes tribunal for the former Yugoslavia to hear cases covering grave breaches of the Geneva Conventions and crimes against humanity. The Court was inaugurated in November 1993 in The Hague with 11 judges elected by the UN General Assembly from 11 states, divided into two trial chambers of three judges each and an appeal chamber of five judges. The court is unable to force suspects to stand trial but is empowered to pass verdicts in the absence of suspects and can put suspects under an 'act of accusation' which prevents them from leaving their own country.

In October 1995, the tribunal formally charged the Bosnian Serb leaders Radovan Karadzic and Gen. Ratko Mladic, and the Croatian Serb President Milan Martic and 21 others with genocide and crimes against humanity. As at January 1997 only one of the 75 suspected war criminals to be indicted has been imprisoned.

President, Antonio Cassese (Italy)
Chief Prosecutor, Louise Arbour (Canada)

INTERNATIONAL CRIMINAL TRIBUNAL FOR RWANDA
In November 1994, the UN Security Council voted to establish a tribunal to try those responsible for genocide and other violations of international humanitarian law in Rwanda between 1 January and 31 December 1994. The

tribunal, based in Arusha, Tanzania, is empowered to try the most senior people responsible for the massacre. It formally opened in November 1995 to consider 463 indictments.

Chief Prosecutor, Louise Arbour (Canada)

SPECIALIZED AGENCIES

Fifteen independent international organizations, each with its own membership, budget and headquarters, carry out their responsibilities in co-ordination with the UN under agreements made with the Economic and Social Council. An entry for each appears elsewhere in the International Organizations section. They are: the Food and Agriculture Organization of the UN; International Civil Aviation Organization; International Fund for Agricultural Development; International Labour Organization; International Maritime Organization; the International Monetary Fund; International Telecommunications Union; UN Educational, Scientific and Cultural Organization; UN Industrial Development Organization; Universal Postal Union; World Bank (International Bank for Reconstruction and Development, International Development Agency, International Finance Corporation); World Health Organization; World Intellectual Property Organization; and World Meteorological Organization. The International Atomic Energy Agency and the World Trade Organization are linked to the UN but are not specialized agencies.

UK MISSION TO THE UNITED NATIONS
One Dag Hammarskjöld Plaza, 885 Second Avenue, New York, NY 10017, USA
Permanent Representative to the United Nations and Representative on the Security Council, Sir John Weston, KCMG, *apptd* 1995
Deputy Permanent Representative, S. J. Gomersall, CMG

UK MISSION TO THE OFFICE OF THE UN AND OTHER INTERNATIONAL ORGANIZATIONS IN GENEVA
37–39 rue de Vermont, 1211 Geneva 20, Switzerland
Permanent UK Representative, R. M. J. Lyne, CMG, *apptd* 1997
Deputy Permanent Representative, P. R. Jenkins

UK MISSION TO THE INTERNATIONAL ATOMIC ENERGY AGENCY, THE UN INDUSTRIAL DEVELOPMENT ORGANIZATION AND THE UN OFFICE AT VIENNA
Jaurèsgasse 12, 1030 Vienna, Austria
Permanent UK Representative, Dr J. P. Freeman, *apptd* 1997
Deputy Permanent Representative, G. D. Cole

UN OFFICE AND INFORMATION CENTRE
Millbank Tower, 21–24 Millbank, London, SWIP 4QH
Tel: 0171-630 1981; fax: 0171-976 6478

UNITED NATIONS EDUCATIONAL, SCIENTIFIC AND CULTURAL ORGANIZATION

7 place de Fontenoy, 75352 Paris 07SP, France
Tel: Paris 4568 1000; fax: Paris 4567 1690
Web: http://www.unesco.org

The United Nations Educational, Scientific and Cultural Organization (UNESCO) was established in 1946. It promotes collaboration among its member states in education, science, culture and communication. It aims to further a universal respect for human rights, justice and the rule of law, without distinction of race, sex, language or religion, in accordance with the UN Charter.

UNESCO runs a number of programmes to improve education and extend access to it. It provides assistance to ensure the free flow of information and its wider and better balanced dissemination without any obstacle to freedom of expression, and to maintain cultural heritage in the face of development. It fosters research and study in all areas of the social and environmental sciences.

UNESCO had 186 member states as at July 1997. There are three associate members. The General Conference, consisting of representatives of all the members, meets biennially to decide the programme and the budget (1998–9, US$544,367,250). It elects the 51-member Executive Board, which supervises operations, and appoints a Director-General who heads a Secretariat responsible for carrying out the organization's programmes. In most member states national commissions liaise with UNESCO to execute its programme.

The UK withdrew from UNESCO in 1985; it rejoined on 1 July 1997.

Director-General, Federico Mayor Zaragoza (Spain)

UNITED NATIONS INDUSTRIAL DEVELOPMENT ORGANIZATION

Vienna International Centre, Wagramerstrasse 5, PO Box 300, A-1400 Vienna, Austria
Tel: Vienna 21131; fax: Vienna 232156
E-mail: unido-pinfo@unido.org
Web: http://www.unido.org

The United Nations Industrial Development Organization (UNIDO) was established in 1966 by the UN General Assembly to act as the central co-ordinating body for industrial activities within the UN. It became a UN specialized agency in 1985 with the aim of promoting the industrialization of developing countries, with special emphasis upon the manufacturing sector. To this end it provides technical assistance and advice, provides investment promotion and helps with planning. UNIDO assists both public and private sectors and has made its services available to former centrally planned economies in transition to a market economy.

UNIDO had 168 members as at June 1998. It is funded by the UN, member states and non-governmental organizations. A General Conference of all the members meets biennially to discuss strategy and policy, approve the budget (1998–9, US$129.5 million) and elect the Director-General. The Industrial Development Board is composed of members from 53 member states and reviews implementation of the regular work programme and the budget, which is prepared by the Programme and Budget Committee.

Director-General, Carlos Magariños (Argentina)
Permanent UK Representative, Dr John Freeman, British Embassy, Vienna

UNIVERSAL POSTAL UNION

Weltpoststrasse 4, 3000 Berne 15, Switzerland
Tel: Berne 350 3111; fax: Berne 350 3110
E-Mail: ib.info@ib.upu.org
Web: http://www.ibis.ib.upu.org

The Universal Postal Union (UPU) was established by the Treaty of Berne 1874, taking effect from 1875, and became a UN specialized agency in 1948. The UPU is an intergovernmental organization which exists to form and regulate a single postal territory of all member countries for the reciprocal exchange of correspondence without discrimination. It also assists and advises on the improvement of postal services.

The UPU had 189 members as at June 1998. A Universal Postal Congress of all its members is the UPU's supreme authority and meets every five years to review the Treaty. A Council of Administration composed of 41 members was established by the 1994 Congress. It meets annually to ensure continuity between congresses, study regulatory developments and broad policies, approve the budget and examine proposed Treaty changes. A Postal Operations Council also meets annually to deal with specific technical and operational issues. The three UPU bodies are served by the International Bureau, a secretariat headed by a Director-General.

Funding is provided by members according to a scale of contributions drawn up by the Congress. The Council sets the annual budget (1998, SFr35,747,000) within a five-year figure decided by the Congress.

Director-General, Thomas E. Leavey (USA)

WESTERN EUROPEAN UNION
4 rue de la Régence, 1000 Brussels, Belgium
Tel: Brussels 500 4455; fax: Brussels 511 3519
E-mail: ueo.presse@skynet.be
Web: http://www.weu.int

The Western European Union (WEU) originated as the Brussels Treaty Organization (BTO) established under the Treaty of Brussels, signed in 1948 by Belgium, France, Luxembourg, the Netherlands and the UK, to provide collective self-defence and economic and social collaboration amongst its signatories. With the collapse of the European Defence Community and the decision of NATO to incorporate the Federal Republic of Germany into the Western security system, the BTO was modified to become the WEU in 1954 with the admission of West Germany and Italy. However, owing to the overlap with NATO and the Council of Europe, the Union became largely defunct.

From the late 1970s onwards efforts were made to add a security dimension to the EC's European Political Co-operation. Opposition to these efforts from Denmark, Greece and Ireland led the remaining EC countries, all WEU members, to decide to reactivate the Union in 1984. Members committed themselves to harmonizing their views on defence and security and developing a European security identity, while bearing in mind the importance of transatlantic relations. Portugal and Spain joined the WEU in 1988, and Greece became a full member in 1995.

After much debate about its future, the EU Maastricht Treaty designated the WEU as the future defence component of the European Union. WEU foreign ministers agreed in the Petersberg Declaration 1992 to assign forces to WEU command for 'peacemaking' operations in Europe. In November 1992 the WEU's role as the common security dimension of the EU was enhanced when WEU ministers signed a declaration with remaining European NATO members to give them various forms of WEU membership. Iceland, Norway and Turkey became associate members; Ireland, Denmark, Austria, Finland and Sweden became observer members. In 1994 the WEU reached agreements with Estonia, Latvia, Lithuania, Poland, Czech Republic, Slovak Republic, Hungary, Romania and Bulgaria, under which they all became associate partners; Slovenia became an associate partner in 1996.

The WEU works in close co-operation with the Atlantic Alliance, and relations between the WEU and NATO are developing on the basis of transparency and complementarity. The 1993 Luxembourg Declaration states that the WEU is ready to participate in the future work of the NATO Alliance as its European pillar, and at the Atlantic Alliance summit in January 1994, NATO expressed its readiness to make Alliance assets and capabilities available for WEU operations. In June 1996, NATO foreign and defence ministers approved the Combined Joint Task Force (CJTF) concept and the elaboration of multinational European command arrangements for WEU-led operations.

The formation of a 'Eurocorps' based on the Franco-German brigade as a force answerable to the WEU was announced in 1992. The 'Eurocorps' was inaugurated in 1993 and became fully operational in 1995 with 51,000 troops comprising French, German, Belgian, Luxembourg and Spanish forces.

A Council of Ministers (foreign and defence) meets biannually in the capital of the presiding country; the presidency rotates biannually, and from 1999 the sequence of WEU presidencies will be harmonized with those of the EU Council of Ministers. A Permanent Council of the member states' permanent representatives meets weekly in Brussels. The Permanent Council is chaired by the Secretary-General and serviced by the Secretariat. A planning cell has been established to draw up contingency plans in the areas of humanitarian relief, peacekeeping and crisis management. The Assembly of the WEU is composed of 115 parliamentarians of member states and meets twice annually in Paris to debate matters within the scope of the revised Brussels Treaty.

Presidency (1998), Greece, Italy; (1999) Germany, Luxembourg

Secretary-General, José Cutileiro (Portugal)

UK Representative on the Permanent Council, Sir John Goulden, KCMG

ASSEMBLY, 43 avenue du Président Wilson, 75775 Paris Cedex 16, France

---

THE WORLD BANK
1818 H Street NW, Washington DC 20433, USA
Tel: Washington DC 477 1234; fax: Washington DC 477 6391
Web: http://www.worldbank.org

The World Bank, more formally known as the International Bank for Reconstruction and Development (IBRD), is a specialized agency of the UN. It developed from the international monetary and financial conference held at Bretton Woods, New Hampshire, in 1944 and was established by 44 nations in 1945 to encourage economic growth in developing countries through the provision of loans and technical assistance to their respective governments. The IBRD now has 181 members.

The Bank is owned by the governments of member countries and its capital is subscribed by its members. It finances its lending primarily from borrowing in world capital markets, and derives a substantial contribution to its resources from its retained earnings and the repayment of loans. The interest rate on its loans is calculated in relation to its cost of borrowing. Loans generally have a grace period of five years and are repayable within 20 years. The loans made by the Bank since its inception to 30 June 1997 totalled US$295,263.9 million to 131 countries. Total capital is US$182,426 million.

Originally directed towards post-war reconstruction in Europe, the Bank has subsequently turned towards assisting less-developed countries with the establishment of two affiliates, the International Finance Corporation (IFC) in 1956 and the International Development Association (IDA) in 1960. The IFC promotes the growth of the private sector in developing member countries by mobilizing domestic and foreign capital. The IFC's subscribed share capital was US$2.36 million at 30 June 1997. It is also empowered to borrow up to two and a half times the amount of its unimpaired subscribed capital and accumulated earnings for use in its lending programme. At 30 June 1997, the IFC had committed financing totalling more than US$6.7 billion in 129 countries.

The IDA performs the same function as the World Bank but primarily to less-developed countries and on terms that bear less heavily on their balance of payments than IBRD loans. Eligible countries typically have a per capita gross national product of less than US$925 (1996). Funds (called credits to distinguish them from IBRD loans) come mostly in the form of subscriptions and contributions from the IDA's richer members and transfers from the net income of the IBRD. The terms for IDA credits, which bear no interest and are made to governments only, are ten-year grace periods and 35- or 40-year maturities. By 30 June 1997, the IDA had extended development credits totalling US$101,563.4 million to 100 countries.

The IBRD and its affiliates are financially and legally distinct but share headquarters. The IBRD is headed by a Board of Governors, consisting of one Governor and one alternate Governor appointed by each member country. Twenty-four Executive Directors exercise all powers of the Bank except those reserved to the Board of Governors. The President, elected by the Executive Directors, conducts the business of the Bank, assisted by an international staff. Membership in both the IFC (162 members) and the IDA (160 members) is open to all IBRD countries. The IDA is administered by the same staff as the Bank; the IFC has its own personnel but draws on the IBRD for administrative and other support. All share the same President.

In 1988 a third affiliate, the Multilateral Investment Guarantee Agency (MIGA) was formed. MIGA encourages foreign investment in developing states by providing investment guarantees to potential investors and advisory services to developing member countries. At 30 December 1994 128 countries were members of MIGA.
President (IBRD, IFC, IDA, MIGA), James D. Wolfensohn (USA)
UK Executive Director, A. O'Donnell, Room 11-120, IMF, 700 19th Street NW, Washington DC 20431
EUROPEAN OFFICE, 66 avenue d'Iena, 75116 Paris, France
JAPAN OFFICE, 10F, Fukoku Seimei Building, 2-2-2 Uchisaiwai-cho, Chiyoda-ku, Tokyo 100-0011, Japan
UK OFFICE, New Zealand House, Haymarket, London SW1Y 4TQ. Tel: 0171-930 8511; fax: 0171-930 8515

THE WORLD COUNCIL OF CHURCHES
PO Box 2100, 1211 Geneva 2, Switzerland
Tel: Geneva 791 6111; fax: Geneva 798 1346
E-mail: info@wcc-coe.org
Web: http://www.wcc-coe.org

The World Council of Churches (WCC) was constituted in 1948 to promote unity among Christian churches. The 332 member churches have adherents in more than 100 countries. With the exception of Roman Catholicism, virtually all Christian traditions are represented.

The policies of the Council are determined by delegates of the member churches meeting in Assembly, roughly every seven years; the seventh Assembly was held in Canberra, Australia, in February 1991 and the eighth Assembly is scheduled to be held in Harare, Zimbabwe, in December 1998. More detailed decisions are taken by a 156-member Central Committee which is elected by the Assembly and meets, with the eight WCC Presidents, annually. The Central Committee in turn appoints a smaller Executive Committee and also nominates commissions to guide the various programmes.
General Secretary, Dr Konrad Raiser (Germany)

WORLD HEALTH ORGANIZATION
20 avenue Appia, 1211 Geneva 27, Switzerland
Tel: Geneva 791 2111; fax: Geneva 791 0746
E-mail: info@who.ch
Web: http://www.who.ch

The UN International Health Conference, held in 1946, established the World Health Organization (WHO) as a UN specialized agency, with effect from 1948. It is dedicated to attaining the highest possible level of health for all. It collaborates with member governments, UN agencies and other bodies to improve health standards, control communicable diseases and promote all aspects of family and environmental health. It seeks to raise the standards of health teaching and training, and promotes research through collaborating research centres worldwide. Its other services include the *International Pharmacopoeia*, epidemiological surveillance, and the collation and publication of statistics. WHO activities are orientated to achieving 'Health for All'.

WHO had 191 members as at April 1998. It is governed by the annual World Health Assembly of members which meets to set policy, approve the budget (1997–8, US$1,800 million), appoint a Director-General, and adopt health conventions and regulations. It also elects 32 members who designate one expert to serve on the Executive Board. The Board effects the programme, suggests initiatives and is empowered to deal with emergencies. A Secretariat, headed by the Director-General, supervises the activities of six regional offices.
Director-General, Gro Harlem Bruntland (Norway)

WORLD INTELLECTUAL PROPERTY ORGANIZATION
34 chemin des Colombettes, 1211 Geneva 20, Switzerland
Tel: Geneva 338 9111; fax: Geneva 733 5428
E-mail: publicinf.mail@wipo.int
Web: http://www.wipo.int

The World Intellectual Property Organization (WIPO) was established in 1967 by the Stockholm Convention, which entered into force in 1970. In addition to that Convention, WIPO administers 19 treaties, the principal ones being the Paris Convention for the Protection of Industrial Property and the Berne Convention for the Protection of Literary and Artistic Works. WIPO became a UN specialized agency in 1974.

WIPO promotes the protection of intellectual property throughout the world through co-operation among states, and the administration of various 'Unions', each founded on a multilateral treaty and dealing with the legal and administrative aspects of intellectual property.

Intellectual property comprises two main branches: industrial property (inventions, trademarks, industrial designs and appellations of origin); and copyright (literary, musical, photographic, audiovisual and artistic works, etc.). WIPO also assists creative intellectual activity and facilitates technology transfer, particularly to developing countries.

WIPO had 169 members as at June 1998. The biennial session of all its governing bodies sets policy, a programme and a budget (1998–9, SFr400 million). WIPO has three governing bodies: the General Assembly, composed of WIPO members who are also members of the Paris or Berne conventions; the Conference, composed of all WIPO members; and the Co-ordination Committee, composed of member states elected by members of WIPO and the Paris and Berne conventions. The General Assembly elects a Director-General, who heads the International Bureau (secretariat).

A separate International Union for the Protection of New Varieties of Plants (UPOV), established by convention in 1961, is linked to WIPO. It has 37 members.

Director-General, Dr Kamil Idris (Sudan)

WORLD METEOROLOGICAL ORGANIZATION
41 avenue Giuseppe Motta, PO Box 2300, 1211 Geneva 20, Switzerland
Tel: Geneva 730 8111; fax: Geneva 734 2326

The World Meteorological Organization (WMO) was established as a UN specialized agency in 1950, succeeding the International Meteorological Organization founded in 1873. It facilitates co-operation in the establishment of networks for making meteorological, climatological, hydrological and geophysical observations, as well as their exchange, processing and standardization, and assists technology transfer, training and research. It also fosters collaboration between meteorological and hydrological services, and furthers the application of meteorology to aviation, shipping, environment, water problems, agriculture, etc.

The WMO had 179 member states and six member territories as at 30 December 1997. The supreme authority is the World Meteorological Congress of member states and member territories, which meets every four years to determine general policy, make recommendations and set a budget (1996–9, SFr255 million). It also elects 26 members of the 36-member Executive Council, the other members being the President and three Vice-Presidents of the WMO, and the Presidents of the six regional associations, who are ex-officio members. The Council supervises the implementation of Congress decisions, initiates studies and makes recommendations on matters needing international action. The WMO functions through six regional associations and eight technical commissions. Each of the regional associations has responsibility for co-ordinating meteorological activities within its region. The technical commissions study meteorological and hydrological problems, lay down the necessary methodologies and procedures, and make recommendations to the Executive Council and Congress. The Secretariat is headed by a Secretary-General, appointed by the Congress.

Secretary-General, G. O. P. Obasi (Nigeria)

WORLD TRADE ORGANIZATION
Centre William Rappard, 154 rue de Lausanne, 1211 Geneva 21, Switzerland
Tel: Geneva 739 5111; fax: Geneva 739 5458
E-mail: enquiries@wto.org
Web: http://www.wto.org

The World Trade Organization was established on 1 January 1995 as the successor to the General Agreement on Tariffs and Trade (GATT). GATT was established in 1948 as an interim agreement until the charter of a new international trade organization could be drafted by a committee of the UN Economic and Social Council and ratified by member states. The charter was never ratified and GATT became the only regime for the regulation of world trade, evolving its own rules and procedures.

GATT was dedicated to the expansion of non-discriminatory international trade and progressively extended free trade via 'rounds' of multilateral negotiations. Eight rounds were concluded: Geneva (1947), Annecy (1948), Torquay (1950), Geneva (1956), Dillon (1960–1), Kennedy (1964–7), Tokyo (1973–9) and Uruguay (1986–94). By the time the measures of the Uruguay Round are fully implemented in 2002, the average duties on manufactured goods will have been reduced from 40 per cent in the 1940s to 3 per cent. The Final Act of the Uruguay Round was signed by trade ministers from the 128 GATT negotiating states and the EU in Marrakesh, Morocco, on 15 April 1994. It established the World Trade Organization (WTO) to supersede GATT and implement the Uruguay Round agreements.

The WTO is the legal and institutional foundation of the multilateral trading system. It provides the contractual obligations determining how governments frame and implement trade policy and provides the forum for the debate, negotiation and adjudication of trade problems. The WTO's principal aims are to liberalize world trade and place it on a secure basis, and it seeks to achieve this partly by an agreed set of trade rules and market access agreements and partly through further trade liberalization negotiations. The WTO also administers and implements a further 29 multilateral agreements in fields such as agriculture, textiles and clothing, services, government procurement, rules of origin and intellectual property.

The highest authority of the WTO is the Ministerial Conference composed of all members, which meets at least once every two years. The General Council meets as required and acts on behalf of the Ministerial Conference in regard to the regular working of the WTO. Composed of all members, the General Council also convenes in two particular forms: as the Dispute Settlement Body, dealing with disputes between members arising from the Uruguay Round Final Act; and as the Trade Policy Review Body, conducting regular reviews of the trade policies of members. A secretariat of 450 staff headed by a Director-General services WTO bodies and provides trade performance and trade policy analysis.

As at April 1998 there were 132 WTO members, and a further 31 governments had applied to join. The WTO budget for 1998 was SFr115 million, with members' contributions calculated on the basis of their share of the total trade conducted by WTO members. The official languages of the WTO are English, French and Spanish.

Director-General, Renato Ruggiero (Italy)
Permanent UK Representative, R. M. J. Lyne, 37–39 rue de Vermont, 1211 Geneva 20

The European Union

MEMBERS

State	Accession Date	Population (million)	GNP (US$ million)	GDP per head‡	Council Votes	EP Seats
Austria	1 January 1995	8.05	226,510	22,516	4	21
Belgium	1 January 1958*	10.11	268,633	20,998	5	25
Denmark	1 January 1973	5.23	168,917	26,537	3	16
Finland	1 January 1995	5.11	119,086	20,368	3	16
France	1 January 1958*	58.14	1,533,619	20,869	10	87
Germany	1 January 1958*†	81.64	2,364,632	22,585	10	99
Greece	1 January 1981	10.56	120,021	10,051	5	25
Ireland	1 January 1973	3.58	62,040	18,169	3	15
Italy	1 January 1958*	57.19	1,140,484	17,276	10	87
Luxembourg	1 January 1958*	0.41	18,850	33,035	2	6
Netherlands	1 January 1958*	15.45	402,565	20,392	5	31
Portugal	1 January 1986	10.80	100,934	8,919	5	25
Spain	1 January 1986	39.21	563,249	11,887	8	64
Sweden	1 January 1995	8.83	227,315	22,803	4	22
UK	1 January 1973	58.26	1,152,136	19,234	10	87
TOTAL		372.57	8,468,991		87	626

* Acceded to the European Coal and Steel Community (ECSC) on its formation in 1952
† Federal Republic of Germany (West) 1952/1958; German Democratic Republic (East) acceded on German reunification (3 October 1990)
EP European Parliament

DEVELOPMENT

1950　Robert Schuman (French foreign minister) proposes that France and West Germany pool their coal and steel industries under a supranational authority (Schuman Plan)

1951　Paris Treaty signed by France, West Germany, Belgium, Italy, Luxembourg and the Netherlands establishes the European Coal and Steel Community (ECSC)

1952　ECSC treaty enters into force

1957　25 March: Treaty of Rome signed by the six, establishes the European Economic Community (EEC) and the European Atomic Energy Authority (EURATOM). Treaty aims to create a customs union; remove obstacles to free movement of capital, goods, people and services; establish common external trade policy and common agricultural and fisheries policies; co-ordinate economic policies; harmonize social policies; promote co-operation in nuclear research

1958　1 January: EEC and EURATOM begin operation. Joint Parliament and Court of Justice established for all three communities, and the Commission, Council of Ministers, Economic and Social Committee and Investment Bank for the EEC

1962　Common Agricultural Policy (CAP) agreed (*see* page 771)

1967　EEC, ECSC and EURATOM merge to form the European Communities (EC), with a single Council of Ministers and Commission

1968　EEC customs union completed
Implementation of CAP completed

1970　Foreign policy co-ordination begins

1971　The Common Fisheries Policy comes into operation

1972　European Social Fund established

1974　Regular heads of governments summits begin

1975　'Own resources' funding of EC budget introduced (*see* pages 770–1)
UK renegotiates its terms of accession
European Regional Development Fund created

1979　European Monetary System (EMS) comes into operation (*see* page 772)
First direct elections to European Parliament (June)

1984　Fontainebleau summit settles UK annual budget rebate and agrees first major CAP reform
European Parliament elections (June)

1986　Single European Act (SEA) signed (*see* page 771)
European Political Co-operation (EPC) established (*see* page 772)

1988　Second major CAP reform

1989　European Parliament elections (June)

1991　Maastricht Treaty agreed (*see* page 772)

1992　31 December: Single internal market programme completed

1993　September: the exchange rate mechanism (ERM) of the EMS effectively suspended
1 November: The Maastricht Treaty enters into force, establishing the European Union (EU)

1994　1 January: European Economic Area (EEA) agreement comes into operation (*see* pages 771–2)
Norway rejects EU membership in referendum

1997　Amsterdam Treaty agreed

1998　11 states chosen to enter first round of EMU
European Central Bank replaces European Monetary Institute.

ENLARGEMENT AND EXTERNAL RELATIONS

The procedure for accession to the EU is laid down in the Treaty of Rome; states must be stable European democracies governed by the rule of law with free market economies. A membership application is studied by the Commission, which produces an Opinion. If the Opinion is positive, negotiations may be opened leading to an Accession Treaty which must be approved by all member state governments and parliaments, the European Parliament, and the applicant state's government and parliament. *Applicants:* Morocco (applied 1987/rejected 1987), Turkey (applied 1987/negative Opinion 1989), Cyprus (applied 1990/rejected 1993/negotiations begun 1998), Malta (applied 1990/negative Opinion 1993), Switzerland (applied 1992/no Opinion yet), Hungary (applied 1994/negotiations begun 1998), Poland (applied 1994/negotiations begun 1998), Bulgaria (applied 1995/offered partnership 1998), Estonia (applied 1995/negotiations begun 1998), Latvia (applied 1995/offered partnership 1998), Lithuania (applied 1995/offered partnership 1998), Romania (applied 1995/offered partnership 1998), Slovakia (applied 1995/offered partnership 1998), the Czech Republic (applied 1996/negotiations begun 1998), Slovenia (applied 1995/negotiations begun 1998).

Apart from the EEA Agreement (*see* page 771), the EU has three types of agreements with other European and CIS states. 'Europe' Agreements commit the EU and signatory states to long-term political and economic integration, a free trade zone (apart from agriculture and labour movement) and eventual EU membership. Government representatives from the signatory states are entitled to attend one summit and two finance and foreign council meetings a year. Association agreements include a commitment to EU financial aid and to eventual membership; agreements have been signed with Malta (1971), Cyprus (1972), Turkey (1974) and Slovenia (1996). Partnership and co-operation agreements are based on regulating and improving political and economic relations and mutual trade concessions but exclude any possibility of membership. Agreements have been signed with Ukraine, Russia, Moldova (1994), Kyrgyzstan and Belarus (1995).

In March 1998, formal accession negotiations were begun with Hungary, Poland, Estonia, the Czech Republic, Slovenia and Cyprus; full membership of the EU is not expected until 2001 at the earliest, and more likely 2003. Bulgaria, Romania, Latvia, Lithuania and Slovakia have been invited into partnerships with the EU to help speed up preparations for their eventual membership.

THE COUNCIL OF THE EUROPEAN UNION
175 rue de la Loi, 1048 Brussels, Belgium

The Council of the European Union (Council of Ministers) consists of ministers from the government of each of the member states. It formally comprises the foreign ministers of the member states but in practice the minister depends on the subject under discussion, e.g. when EC environment matters are under discussion, the meeting is informally known as the Environment Council. Council decisions are taken by qualified majority vote (in which members' votes are weighted), by a simple majority, or by unanimity. Council meetings are prepared by the Committee of Permanent Representatives (COREPER) of the member states, which acts as the 'gatekeeper' between national governments and the supranational EC, often negotiating on proposals with the Commission during the legislative process.

Unanimity votes are taken on sensitive issues such as taxation and constitutional matters; in preparation for an expanded Union, the Amsterdam Treaty extended areas where qualified majority votes may be taken, to areas such as Single Market laws and harmonization, environment policy, health and safety, transport policy, overseas aid, research and development, culture, consumer protection, education and training, the development of a single currency and social policy. Member states have weighted votes in the Council loosely proportional to their relative population sizes (*see* introductory table), with a total of 87 votes. For a proposal from the Commission to pass, it must receive 62 votes; 26 votes are necessary to block a proposal, and 23 votes constitute a temporary blocking minority. For other proposals to be passed they must receive 62 votes cast by at least ten member states.

The European Council, comprising the heads of government of the member states, meets twice a year to provide overall policy direction. The presidency of the EC is held in rotation for six-month periods, setting the agenda for and chairing all Council meetings. The presidency provides the incumbent nation with an opportunity to pursue its own policy priorities. The European Council holds a summit in the country holding the presidency at the end of its period in office. The holders of the presidency for the years 1998–2000 are:

1998 UK, Austria
1999 Germany, Finland
2000 Portugal, France

OFFICE OF THE UNITED KINGDOM PERMANENT REPRESENTATIVE TO THE EUROPEAN COMMUNITIES
avenue d'Auderghem, 1040 Brussels, Belgium
Ambassador and UK Permanent Representative, HE Sir Stephen Wall, KCMG, LVO, *apptd* 1995
Minister and Deputy Permanent Representative, D. Bostock

THE EUROPEAN COMMISSION
200 rue de la Loi, 1049 Brussels, Belgium

The Commission consists of 20 Commissioners, two each from France, Germany, Italy, Spain and the UK, and one each from the remaining member states. The members of the Commission are appointed for five-year renewable terms by the agreement of the member states; the present Commission came into office on 23 January 1995 and in future the five-year term will run concurrently with the term of the European Parliament. The President and Vice-Presidents are elected by the Commissioners from among their number, and under the terms of the Amsterdam Treaty, the appointment of President must henceforth also be endorsed by the European Parliament. The Commissioners pledge sole allegiance to the EC. The Commission initiates and implements EC legislation and is the guardian of the EC treaties. It is the exponent of Community-wide interests rather than the national preoccupations of the Council. Each Commissioner is supported by advisers and oversees whichever of the 24 departments, known as Directorates-General (DGs), is assigned to him. Each Directorate-General is headed by a Director-General. The Commission has a total staff of around 15,000 civil servants.

COMMISSIONERS *as at June 1998*
President
Secretariat-General; Forward Studies Unit; Inspectorate-General; Legal Service; Spokesman's Service; Joint Interpreting and Conference Service; Security Office; Overall responsibility for monetary matters, common foreign and security policy, institutional questions and intergovernmental conference, Jacques Santer (Luxembourg)

Vice-Presidents
External Relations with North America, Australia, Japan, New Zealand, China, South Korea, Taiwan, Hong Kong, Macao, Common Commercial Policy, Relations with the OECD and WTO, Sir Leon Brittan (UK)
External Relations with the Mediterranean, the Middle East, Latin America and parts of Asia, Manuel Marin (Spain)

Members
Industrial Affairs, Information Technology and Telecommunications, Martin Bangemann (Germany)
Immigration, Interior and Judicial Affairs, Financial Control, Anti-Fraud Measures, Relations with the Ombudsman, Anita Gradin (Sweden)
Agriculture and Rural Development, Franz Fischler (Austria)
Budget, Personnel and Administration, Translation, Erkki Liikanen (Finland)
Economic and Financial Affairs, Monetary matters, Credit and Investments, Statistical Office, Yves-Thibault de Silguy (France)
Energy and Euratom Supply Agency, Small and Medium Enterprises, Tourism, Christos Papoutis (Greece)
Institutional Questions, Intergovernmental Conference, Relations with the European Parliament, Culture and Audiovisual, Publications Office, Openness, Communications and Information, Marcelino Oreja (Spain)
Transport, Neil Kinnock (UK)
Regional Policy, Relations with the Committee of the Regions, Cohesion Fund, Monika Wulf-Mathies (Germany)
Science, Research and Development, Joint Research Centre, Human Resources, Education, Training and Youth, Edith Cresson (France)
Competition, Karel Van Miert (Belgium)
External Relations with Central and Eastern Europe, the former Soviet Union and other European states, Common Foreign and Security Policy, External Service, Hans van den Broek (Netherlands)
External Relations with African, Caribbean and Pacific states, Lomé Convention, João de Deus Pinheiro (Portugal)
Social Affairs and Employment, Relations with the Economic and Social Committee, Padraig Flynn (Ireland)
Fisheries, Consumer Policy, EC Humanitarian Office, Emma Bonino (Italy)
Environment, Nuclear Safety, Ritt Bjerregaard (Denmark)
Internal Market, Financial Services, Customs, Taxation, Mario Monti (Italy)
Secretary-General, Carlo Trojan (Netherlands)

THE EUROPEAN PARLIAMENT

The European Parliament (EP) originated as the Common Assembly of the ECSC; it acquired its present name in 1962. Members (MEPs) were initially appointed from the membership of national parliaments; direct elections to the Parliament were first held in 1979. Elections to the Parliament are held on differing bases throughout the EC; from June 1999, British MEPs will be elected for the first time by a 'regional list' system of proportional representa-

EUROPEAN PARLIAMENT POLITICAL GROUPINGS

	PES	EPP	UFE	ELDR	EUL/NGL	Green	ERA	IEN	Ind.	Total
Austria	6	7	–	1	–	1	–	–	6	21
Belgium	6	7	–	6	–	2	1	–	3	25
Denmark	4	3	–	5	–	–	–	4	–	16
Finland	4	4	–	5	2	1	–	–	–	16
France	15	12	17	1	7	1	12	11	11	87
Germany	40	47	–	–	–	12	–	–	–	99
Greece	10	9	2	–	4	–	–	–	–	25
Ireland	1	4	7	1	–	2	–	–	–	15
Italy	18	15	24	4	5	4	2	–	15	87
Luxembourg	2	2	–	1	–	–	1	–	–	6
Netherlands	7	9	2	10	–	1	–	2	–	31
Portugal	10	9	3	–	3	–	–	–	–	25
Spain	21	30	–	2	9	–	2	–	–	64
Sweden	7	5	–	3	3	4	–	–	–	22
UK	63	18	–	2	–	–	2	1	1	87
TOTAL	214	181	55	41	33	28	20	18	36	626

PES   Party of European Socialists (including British Labour Party, Northern Ireland Social Democratic and Labour Party, Italian Democratic Left Party) Socialist, Social Democratic and Labour parties

EPP   European People's Party (including British Conservative Party, Northern Ireland Official Unionist Party, Spanish Popular Party, French UDF, Irish Fine Gael, Swedish Moderate Party) Christian Democrats and Conservatives

UFE   Union for Europe (including Forza Italia Party, French Gaullists, Irish Fianna Fáil Party, Greek Political Spring Party, Portuguese Centre Party)

ELDR   European Liberal Democratic and Reformist Group (including British Liberal Democratic Party, Portuguese Social Democrats) centre and liberal parties

EUL/NGL   Confederal Group of the European United Left/Nordic Green Left (French, Greek and Portuguese Communist Parties, Italian Refounded Communist Party, some Spanish regionalists, Danish, Swedish, Finnish, Greek, Italian and Spanish Green/Left parties)

Green   Green and Ecologist parties

ERA   European Radical Alliance (Scottish National Party, French Radicals of the Left, Italian Radical Party, Belgian Flemish and Spanish regionalists)

IEN   Independent Europe of the Nations Group (French Other Europe Group, Dutch and Danish Euro-sceptics)

Ind   Independents (Italian National Alliance, French National Front, Belgian Vlaams Blok, Northern Ireland Democratic Unionist Party)

tion. The latest elections were held in June 1994, when the Parliament expanded from 518 to 567 seats to include representatives from the former East Germany and concurrent increases in other member states' representatives. It expanded to 626 seats on 1 January 1995 with the accession of Austria, Finland and Sweden to the EU. The next elections will be in June 1999. For total number of seats per member and political groupings, *see* table below. MEPs serve on 20 committees, which scrutinise draft EC legislation and the activities of the Commission. A minimum of 12 plenary sessions a year are held in Strasbourg and Brussels, committees meet in Brussels, and the Secretariat's headquarters is in Luxembourg.

The EP has gradually expanded its influence within the EU through the Single European Act, which introduced the co-operation procedure, the Maastricht Treaty, which extended the co-operation procedure and introduced the co-decision procedure (*see* Legislative Process), and the Amsterdam Treaty, which effectively extended co-decision to all areas except economic and monetary union. It has general powers of supervision over the Commission, and consultation and co-decision with the Council; it votes to approve a newly appointed Commission and can dismiss it at any time by a two-thirds majority. Under the Maastricht Treaty it has the right to be consulted on the appointment of the new Commission and can veto its appointment. It can reject the EU budget as a whole, alter non-compulsory expenditure not specified in the EU primary legislation, and can question the Commission's management of the budget and call in the Court of Auditors. Although the EP cannot directly initiate legislation, its reports can spur the Commission into action. In accordance with the Maastricht Treaty the EP appointed an ombudsman in October 1995, to provide citizens with redress against maladministration by EU institutions.

The Parliament's organization is deliberately biased in favour of multi-national political groupings, recognition of a political grouping in the parliament entitling it to offices, funding, representation on committees and influence in debates and legislation. A political grouping with members from only one country needs a minimum of 29 members for recognition, whereas one with members from two countries needs 23 members, a grouping with members from three countries needs 18 members, and a grouping with members from four or more countries needs only 14 members.

PARLIAMENT , Palais de l'Europe, 67006 Strasbourg Cedex, France; 97–113 rue Belliard, 1047 Brussels, Belgium

SECRETARIAT, Centre Européen, Kirchberg, L-2929 Luxembourg

President, José Maria Gil-Robles Gil-Delgado (Spain)

Ombudsman, Jacob Söderman (Finland), 1 avenue du Président Robert Schuman, BP403, F-67001, Strasbourg, France

(For a full list of British MEPs, *see* pages 268–9)

THE LEGISLATIVE PROCESS

The core of the EU policymaking process is a dialogue between the Commission, which initiates and implements policy, and the Council of Ministers, which takes policy decisions. A degree of democratic control is exercised by the European Parliament.

The original legislative process is known as the consultative procedure. The Commission drafts a proposal which it submits to the Council and to the Parliament. The Council then consults the Economic and Social Committee (ESC), the Parliament and the Committee of the Regions; the Parliament may request that amendments are made. With or without these amendments, the proposal is then adopted by the Council and becomes law.

Under the Single European Act (SEA), the role of the Parliament was strengthened by the introduction of the co-operation procedure. The Parliament now has a second reading of proposals in some fields, and after the second reading its rejection of a proposal can only be overturned by a unanimous decision of the Council. The Maastricht Treaty extends the scope of the co-operation procedure, which now applies to Single Market laws and harmonization, trans-European networks, development policy, the social fund, and some aspects of transport, environment, research, social policy and competition policy.

The SEA introduced the assent procedure, whereby an absolute majority of the Parliament must vote to approve laws in certain fields before they are passed. Issues covered by the assent procedure include foreign treaties, accession treaties, international agreements with budgetary implications, citizenship, residence rights, the CAP, and regional and structural funds.

The Maastricht Treaty introduced the co-decision procedure; if, after the Parliament's second reading of a proposal, the Council and Parliament fail to agree, a conciliation committee of the two will reach a compromise. If a compromise is not reached, the Parliament can reject the legislation by the vote of an absolute majority of its members. The Amsterdam Treaty extended co-decision to all areas covered by qualified majority voting.

The Council issues the following legislation:
– Regulations, which are binding in their entirety and directly applicable to all member states; they do not need to be incorporated into national law to come into effect
– Directives, which are less specific, binding as to the result to be achieved but leaving the method of implementation open to member states; a directive thus has no force until it is incorporated into national law
– Decisions, which are also binding but are addressed solely to one or more member states or individuals in a member state
– Recommendations
– Opinions, which are merely persuasive

The Council also has certain budgetary powers, including the power to reject the budget as a whole and to increase expenditure or redistribute money within sectors.

THE COMMUNITY BUDGET

The principles of funding the European Community budget were established by the Treaty of Rome and remain with modifications to this day. There is a legally binding limit on the overall level of resources (known as 'own resources') that the Community can raise from its member states; this limit is defined as a percentage of gross national product (GNP). Budget revenue and expenditure must balance and there is therefore no deficit financing. The own resources decision, which came into effect in 1975, states that there are four sources of Community funding under which each member state makes contributions: levies charged on agricultural imports into the Community from non-member states; customs duties on imports from non-member states; contributions based on member states' shares of a notional Community harmonized VAT base; and contributions based on member states' shares of Community GNP. The latter is the budget-balancing item and covers the difference between total expenditure and the revenue from the other three sources. Since 1984 the UK has had an annual rebate equivalent to 66 per cent of the difference between what the UK contributes to the budget and what it receives. This was introduced to compensate the UK for disproportionate

contributions caused by its high proportion of agricultural and non-agricultural imports from non-member states and its relatively small receipts from the Common Agricultural Policy, the most important portion of Community expenditure.

BUDGET 1997

	Billion ECU*	As % of total
Agriculture	41.3	50.9
Regional and Social	26.3	32.4
External Action	4.8	5.9
Administration	4.3	5.3
Research and Technology	3.2	3.9
Consumer Protection, Industry, Internal Market	0.7	0.9
Energy and Environment	0.2	0.2
Foreign and Security Policy	0.3	0.4
TOTAL	81.1	99.9

EC BUDGET BY MEMBER STATE 1996 (billion ECU*)

	Contributions		Receipts	Net gain‡
Germany	19.94	(29.0%)	10.16	−9.83
France	11.95	(17.5%)	12.09	+0.14
UK	7.92	(11.6%)	6.01	−1.91
Italy	8.67	(12.7%)	7.79	−0.88
Netherlands	4.23	(6.2%)	2.05	−2.18
Spain	4.37	(6.4%)	10.65	+6.28
Belgium	2.66	(3.9%)	2.11	−0.55
Austria	1.78	(2.6%)	1.64	−0.14
Sweden	1.91	(2.8%)	1.30	−0.61
Denmark	1.30	(1.9%)	1.57	+0.27
Greece	1.09	(1.6%)	5.19	+4.10
Finland	0.96	(1.4%)	1.02	+0.06
Portugal	0.82	(1.2%)	3.69	+2.87
Ireland	0.68	(1.0%)	3.01	+2.33
Luxembourg	0.14	(0.2%)	0.14	—
TOTAL	68.42	(100%)	68.42	—

* 1 ECU = £0.691 as at 17 September 1998
‡ Net contributor (−)/net recipient (+)

Under the Edinburgh summit agreement (December 1992) the EC budget will rise in stages from 1.2 per cent of Community (Union) GNP in 1992 to 1.27 per cent in 1999.

THE COMMON AGRICULTURAL POLICY

The Common Agricultural Policy (CAP) was established to increase agricultural production, provide a fair standard of living for farmers and ensure the availability of food at reasonable prices. This aim is achieved by a number of mechanisms:
– import levies (the EC sets a target price for a particular product in the Community, the world price is monitored and if it falls below the guide price, an import levy can be imposed equivalent to the difference between the two)
– intervention purchase (if the price of a product falls below the level indicated by the Council, member states must purchase supplies of the product, provided that they are of suitable quality)
– export subsidies (the EC pays a food exporter a subsidy equivalent to the difference between the price at which the product is bought in the EC and the lower sale price on the world market)

These measures stimulated production but also placed increasing demands on the EC budget which were exacerbated by the increase in EC members and yields enlarged by technological innovation; CAP now accounts for almost 50 per cent of EC expenditure. To surmount these problems reforms were agreed in 1984, 1988, 1992 and 1997.

REFORMS

The 1984 reforms created the system of co-responsibility levies: farm payments to the EC by volume of product sold. This system was supplemented by national quotas for particular products, such as milk. The 1988 reforms emphasized 'set-aside', whereby farmers are given direct grants to take land out of production as a means of reducing surpluses. The set-aside reforms were extended in 1993 for another five years and to every farm in the EC, which must set aside at least 18 per cent of its land. The 1992 reforms were based on the reduction of target prices for cereals, beef and dairy produce, which were reduced by 29 per cent, 15 per cent and 5 per cent respectively. The 1997 reforms seek to further reduce surpluses of cereals, beef and milk by cutting the intervention prices by up to 30 per cent and compensating producers by making area payments. Under the new reforms, CAP rules will also be greatly simplified, eliminating inconsistencies between policies.

Under the Uruguay round agreement of GATT concluded in 1993, the EU must, over a six-year period from 1 January 1995, reduce its import levies by 36 per cent, reduce its domestic subsidies by 20 per cent, reduce its export subsidies by 36 per cent in value, and reduce its subsidized exports by 21 per cent in volume.

THE SINGLE MARKET

Throughout the 1970s and early 1980s, EC members became concerned at the slow growth of the European economy. Although tariffs and quotas had been removed between member states, the EC was still separated into a number of national markets by a series of non-tariff barriers. It was to overcome these internal barriers to trade that the concept of the Single Market was developed. The measures to be undertaken were outlined in the Cockfield report (1985) and codified in the Single European Act (SEA) 1986, which came into force in 1987 with a target date of 31 December 1992 for completion.

The SEA includes articles removing obstacles that distort the internal market: the elimination of frontier controls; the mutual recognition of professional qualifications; the harmonization of product specifications, largely by the mutual recognition of national standards; open tendering for public procurement contracts; the free movement of capital; the harmonization of VAT and excise duties; and the reduction of state aid to particular industries. The SEA changed the legislative process within the EC, particularly with the introduction of qualified majority voting in the Council of Ministers for some policy areas, and the introduction of the assent procedure in the European Parliament. The SEA also extends EC competence into the fields of technology, the environment, regional policy, monetary policy and external policy. The Single Market came into effect on 1 January 1993 and is expected to result in at least a 5 per cent increase in the collective GNP of EC member states. The full implementation of the elimination of frontier controls and harmonization of taxes have, however, been repeatedly delayed.

THE EUROPEAN ECONOMIC AREA (see also EFTA, page 749)

The EC Single Market programme spurred European non-member states to open negotiations with the EC on preferential access for their goods, services, labour and capital to the Single Market. Principal among these states were European Free Trade Association (EFTA) members who opened negotiations on extending the Single Market to EFTA by the formation of the European Economic Area (EEA) encompassing all 19 EC and EFTA states. Agreement was reached in May 1992 but the operation of the EEA was delayed by its rejection in a Swiss referendum, necessitating an additional protocol agreed by the remaining 18 states. The EEA came into effect on 1 January 1994 after ratification by 17 member states (Liechtenstein joined on 1 May 1995 after adapting its customs union with Switzerland).

Austria, Finland and Sweden joined the EU itself on 1 January 1995, leaving only Norway, Iceland and Liechtenstein as the non-EU EEA members. Under the EEA agreement, the three states are to adopt the EU's *acquis communautaire*, apart from in the fields of agriculture, fisheries, and coal and steel.

The EEA is controlled by regular ministerial meetings and by a joint EU-EFTA committee which extends relevant EU legislation to EEA states. Apart from single market measures, there is co-operation in education, research and development, consumer policy and tourism. An EFTA Court of Justice has been established in Luxembourg and an EFTA Surveillance Authority in Brussels to supervise the implementation of the EEA Agreement.

THE EUROPEAN MONETARY SYSTEM

The European monetary system (EMS) began operation in March 1979 with three main purposes. The first was to establish monetary stability in Europe, initially in exchange rates between EC member state currencies, and in the longer term to be part of a wider stabilization process, overcoming inflation and budget and trade deficits. The second purpose was to overcome the constraints resulting from the interdependence of EC economies, and the third was to aid the long-term process of European monetary integration. All EC member state currencies are members of the EMS.

The EMS has three components: the ECU; the exchange rate mechanism (ERM); and the credit mechanisms. The ECU is a monetary unit, the value of which is calculated as a basket of set amounts of each member state currency. The relative weighting given to each currency in the ECU basket is proportional to the size of an EU member's economy and the state's share of EU trade. The German Deutsche Mark (DM) has the largest weighting of 32 per cent. The ECU is used for officially fixing the central rates in the ERM and as a means of settlement among central banks in the EMS.

The ERM is the central component of the EMS. Officially all member currencies of the ERM have a central rate against the ECU, the anchor of the mechanism. In practice, the Deutsche Mark has become the anchor currency, with all other currencies' central rates expressed against the DM. Central banks are obliged to maintain their currencies within set margins of their central rate (either 2.25 per cent or 6 per cent above or below) by intervening in the foreign currency markets. Currencies may be revalued or devalued by up to 10 per cent by agreement with all other ERM members. To do this, central banks co-ordinate their actions and can use the credit mechanisms to borrow money from each other and from the Central European Monetary Co-operation Fund where they each deposit 20 per cent of their reserves. Financial assistance is available to central banks over very short-term, short-term and medium-term periods.

Five currencies (Deutsche Mark, French franc, Belgian franc, Dutch guilder, Danish krone) joined the ERM with 2.25 per cent fluctuation margins, and two currencies

(Irish punt and Italian lira) with 6 per cent margins in 1979. Subsequently the punt and lira reduced to 2.25 per cent margins. The Spanish peseta (1989), UK pound sterling (1990) and Portuguese escudo (1992) joined the ERM with 6 per cent margins. The pound and the lira were forced out of the mechanism by speculation in September 1992; the lira rejoined in November 1996. Speculation forced the widening of the fluctuation margins to 15 per cent from August 1993 for six of the remaining ERM member currencies (the Deutsche Mark and Dutch guilder remain within 2.25 per cent margins). By April 1994 the French franc, Belgian franc, Irish punt and Danish krone were informally operating within 2.25 per cent fluctuation margins again. The Austrian schilling joined the ERM in January 1995, operating within 15 per cent margins.

THE MAASTRICHT TREATY

The Treaty on European Union was agreed at a meeting of the European Council in Maastricht, the Netherlands, in December 1991. It came into effect in November 1993 following ratification by the member states.

Three 'pillars' formed the basis of the new treaty:
– the European Community with its established institutions and decision-making processes
– a Common Foreign and Security Policy (see below) with the Western European Union as the potential defence component of the EU
– co-operation in justice and home affairs, with the Council of Ministers to co-ordinate policies on asylum, immigration, conditions of entry, cross-border crime, drug trafficking and terrorism

The Treaty established a common European citizenship for nationals of all member states and introduced the principle of subsidiarity whereby decisions are taken at the most appropriate level: national, regional or local. It extended EC competency into the areas of environmental and industrial policies, consumer affairs, health, and education and training, and extended qualified majority voting in the Council of Ministers to cover areas which had previously required a unanimous vote. The powers of the European Parliament over the budget and over the Commission were also enhanced and a co-decision procedure enabled the Parliament to override decisions made by the Council of Ministers (see page 770). A separate

protocol to the Maastricht Treaty on social policy was adopted by 11 states and was incorporated into the Amsterdam Treaty in 1997 following adoption by the UK.

COMMON FOREIGN AND SECURITY POLICY

The Common Foreign and Security Policy (CFSP) was created as a pillar of the EU by the Maastricht Treaty (see above). It adopted the machinery of the European Political Co-operation (EPC) framework which it replaced and was charged with providing a forum for member states and EU institutions to consult on foreign affairs.

The CFSP system is headed by the European Council, which provides general lines of policy. Specific policy decisions are taken by the Council of Foreign Ministers, which meets at least four times a year to determine areas for joint action. The foreign minister of the state holding the EU presidency initiates action, manages the CFSP and represents it abroad. He is supported by a secretariat based in Brussels and is advised by the past and future holders of the presidency, forming a so-called troika. The Council of Ministers is supported by the Political Committee which meets monthly, or within 48 hours if there is a crisis, to prepare for ministerial discussions. A group of correspondents, designated diplomats in each member's foreign ministry, provides day-to-day contact.

The Amsterdam Treaty introduced qualified majority voting for foreign affairs and created a high representative on CFSP to act as a spokesperson. It also established a new policy planning and early warning unit to monitor international developments. The unit is to consist of specialists from the member states, the Council and the Commission, as well as from the WEU.

ECONOMIC AND MONETARY UNION

The Maastricht Treaty set in motion timetables for achieving economic and monetary union (EMU) and a single currency (the euro). At the Brussels summit in May 1998, 11 member states were chosen to participate in the first stage of EMU: Austria, Belgium, Finland, France, Germany, Ireland, Italy, Luxembourg, the Netherlands, Portugal and Spain. On 1 January 1999 member states will fix their exchange rates against each other and against the euro, the European Central Bank will take charge of the

PROGRESS TOWARDS MEETING EMU CRITERIA

State	Budget deficit*	National debt*	Inflation rate (%)†	Interest rate (%)†	Year of joining ERM
Austria	−2.5	66.1	1.1	5.5	1995
Belgium	−2.1	122.2	1.2	5.6	1979
Denmark	+0.7	65.1	1.8	6.0	1979
Finland	−0.9	55.8	1.5	5.7	1996
France	−3.0	58.0	1.1	5.4	1979
Germany	−2.7	61.3	1.3	5.5	1979
Greece	−4.0	108.7	4.9	9.8	1998
Ireland	+0.9	66.3	1.2	6.0	1979
Italy	−2.7	121.6	1.8	6.3	1979–92, 1996
Luxembourg	+1.7	6.7	1.4	5.5	1979
Netherlands	+1.4	72.1	2.0	5.4	1979
Portugal	−2.5	62.0	1.6	6.0	1992
Spain	−2.6	68.8	1.7	6.0	1989
Sweden	−0.8	76.6	2.0	6.3	—
UK	−1.9	53.4	1.7	6.8	1990–2

* percentage of GDP
† as at March 1997
Source: IMF

single monetary policy and the euro will replace the ecu. Euros will circulate alongside national currencies for six months from 1 January 2002, after which national currencies will be abolished.

To participate in EMU, member states have to conform to, or be close to conforming to and moving towards, the following criteria:
– the budget deficit should be 3 per cent or less of gross domestic product (GDP)
– total national debt must not exceed 60 per cent of GDP
– inflation should be no more than 1.5 per cent above the average rate of the three best performing economies in the EU
– long-term interest rates should be no more than 2 per cent above the average of the three best performing economies in the EU in the previous 12 months
– applicants must have been a member of the ERM for two years without having realigned or devalued their currency

The table below indicates progress towards achieving the qualifying criteria for economic and monetary union. Budget deficit/surplus, national debt and interest rate figures are based on estimates for 1997.

A growth and stability pact was agreed in Dublin in December 1996 which establishes penalties to be imposed on EMU members with high budget deficits. Governments with deficits exceeding 3 per cent of GDP will receive a warning and will be obliged to pay up to 0.5 per cent of their GDP into a fund after ten months. This will become a fine if the budget deficit is not rectified within two years. A member state with negative growth will be allowed to apply for an exemption from the fine in 'exceptional circumstances', e.g. a recession whereby GDP had fallen by 0.75 per cent or more during one year.

A special protocol was agreed allowing the UK to 'opt out' of a single currency if it so wishes in January 1999. Denmark also secured an 'opt-out' from the single currency.

THE SCHENGEN AGREEMENT

The Schengen Agreement was signed by France, Germany, Belgium, Luxembourg and the Netherlands in 1990 to replace an accord on border controls agreed in Schengen, Luxembourg, in 1985. The Agreement committed the five states to abolishing internal border controls and erecting external frontiers against illegal immigrants, drug traffickers, terrorists and organized crime.

Subsequently signed by Spain and Portugal, the Agreement was ratified by the seven signatory states and entered into force in March 1995 with the removal of frontier, passport, customs and immigration controls. Provisional agreement was reached in June 1995 between the signatory states and the Nordic Union on a merger of the two frontier-free zones, enabling Denmark, Finland and Sweden to become full members in December 1996. Italy and Austria became full members in April 1998; Greece has applied for membership.

The Schengen Agreement originated as an intergovernmental agreement but became part of the EU following the signing of the Amsterdam Treaty.

THE ECONOMIC AND SOCIAL COMMITTEE
2 rue Ravenstein, 1000 Brussels, Belgium

The Economic and Social Committee (ESC) is an advisory and consultative body. It has 222 members, nominated by member states, and is divided into three groups: employers, workers, and other interest groups such as consumers, farmers and the self-employed. It issues opinions on draft EC legislation and can bring matters to the attention of the Commission, Council and Parliament. Consultation of the ESC by the Parliament is enshrined in the Amsterdam Treaty, formally recognizing the importance of the opinions of the EU's economic and social partners.
President, Tom Jenkins (UK)

THE EUROPEAN COURT OF AUDITORS
12 rue A. De Gasperi, L-1615 Luxembourg

The European Court of Auditors, established in 1977, is responsible for the audit of the legality and regularity as well as of the sound financial management of the resources managed by the European Communities and Community bodies. The Court of Auditors may also submit observations on specific questions and deliver opinions. The Court of Auditors draws up an annual report and a statement of assurance on the accounts and underlying operations of the Communities. The Maastricht Treaty designated the Court of Auditors as a full institution of the European Union, enabling it to take other institutions to the Court of Justice. It has 15 members appointed for six-year terms by the Council of Ministers following consultation with the European Parliament.
President, Bernhard Friedmann (Germany)

COURT OF JUSTICE OF THE EUROPEAN COMMUNITIES
L–2925 Luxembourg

The European Court superseded the Court of Justice of the ECSC and is common to the three European Communities. It exists to safeguard the law in the interpretation and application of the Community treaties, to decide on the legality of decisions of the Council of Ministers or the Commission, and to determine infringements of the treaties. Cases may be brought to it by the member states, the Community institutions, firms or individuals. Its decisions are directly binding in the member countries, and the Maastricht Treaty enhanced the Court's powers by permitting it to impose fines on member states. The 15 judges and nine advocates-general of the Court are appointed for renewable six-year terms by the member governments in concert. During 1997, 445 new cases were lodged at the court, 456 cases were concluded and 242 judgments were delivered.

Composition of the Court, in order of precedence, with effect from 5 March 1998:
G. C. Rodríguez Iglesias (*President*); C. Gulmann (*President of the 3rd and 5th Chambers*); G. Cosmas (*First Advocate General*); H. Ragnemalm (*President of the 4th and 6th Chambers*); M. Wathelet (*President of the 1st Chamber*); R. Schintgen (*President of the 2nd Chamber*); G. F. Mancini (*Judge*); J. C. Moitinho de Almeida (*Judge*); F. G. Jacobs (*Advocate-General*); P. J. G. Kapteyn (*Judge*); J. L. Murray (*Judge*); D. A. O. Edward (*Judge*); A. M. La Pergola (*Advocate-General*); J.-P. Puissochet (*Judge*); P. Léger (*Advocate-General*); G. Hirsch (*Judge*); P. Jann (*Judge*); L. Sevón (*Judge*); N. Fennelly (*Advocate-General*); D. Ruiz-Jarabo Colomer (*Advocate-General*); K. M. Ioannou (*Judge*); S. Alber (*Advocate-General*); J. Mischo (*Advocate-General*); A. Saggio (*Advocate-General*); R. Grass (*Registrar*)

COURT OF FIRST INSTANCE
L-2925 Luxembourg

Established under powers conferred by the Single European Act, the Court of First Instance started to exercise its functions at the end of October 1989. It had jurisdiction to hear and determine certain categories of cases brought by natural or legal persons, in particular cases brought by European Community officials, or cases on competition law. By a Council decision of 1993 the court had its jurisdiction enlarged to hear and determine all actions brought by natural or legal persons. During 1997, 624 new cases were lodged at the court, 186 cases were concluded and 94 judgments were delivered.

Composition of the Court, in order of precedence, for the judicial year 1997–8:

B. Vesterdorf (*President of the Court of First Instance*); A. Kalogeropoulos (*President of Chamber*); V. Tiili (*President of Chamber*); P. Lindh (*President of Chamber*); J. Azizi (*President of Chamber*); C. P. Briët (*Judge*); R. García-Valdecasas y Fernández (*Judge*); K. Lenaerts (*Judge*); C. W. Bellamy (*Judge*); A. Potocki (*Judge*); R. Moura Ramos (*Judge*); J. D. Cooke (*Judge*); M. Jaeger (*Judge*); J. Pirrung (*Judge*); P. Mengozzi (*Judge*); H. Jung (*Registrar*)

THE EUROPEAN INVESTMENT BANK
100 Boulevard Konrad Adenauer, L-2950 Luxembourg

The European Investment Bank (EIB) was set up in 1958 under the terms of the Treaty of Rome to finance capital investment projects promoting the balanced development of the European Community.

It grants long-term loans to private and public enterprises, public authorities and financial institutions, to finance projects which further the economic development of less advanced regions (Assisted Areas); improvement of European communications; environmental protection; attainment of the EU's energy policy objectives; modernization of enterprises, co-operation between undertakings in the different member states, and the activities of small and medium-sized enterprises.

EIB activities have also been extended outside member countries as part of the EU's development co-operation policy, under the terms of different association or co-operation agreements with 12 countries in the Mediterranean region, 11 in central and eastern Europe, 30 in Latin America and Asia, and, under the Lomé Conventions, 70 in Africa, the Caribbean and the Pacific.

The Bank's total financing operations in 1997 amounted to 26,202 million ECU, of which 22,958 million was for investment in the EU and 3,244 million for investment outside the EU. Between 1993 and 1997 the EIB made available a total of more than 104,611 million ECU for investment.

The members of the EIB are the 15 member states of the EU, who have all subscribed to the Bank's capital of 62,013 million ECU. The bulk of the funds required by the Bank to carry out its tasks are borrowed on the capital markets of the EU and non-member countries, and on the international market.

As it operates on a non-profit-making basis, the interest rates charged by the EIB reflect the cost of the Bank's borrowings and closely follow conditions on world capital markets.

The Board of Governors of the EIB consists of one government minister nominated by each of the member countries, usually the finance minister, who lay down general directives on the policy of the Bank and appoint members to the Board of Directors (24 nominated by the member states, one by the European Commission), which takes decisions on the granting and raising of loans and the fixing of interest rates. A Management Committee, composed of the Bank's President and seven Vice-Presidents, also appointed by the Board of Governors, is responsible for the day-to-day operations of the Bank. The President and Vice-Presidents also preside as Chairman and Vice-Chairmen at meetings of the Board of Directors.
President, Sir Brian Unwin, KCB
Vice-Presidents, Wolfgang Roth; Panagiotis-Loukas Gennimatas; Massimo Ponzellini; Louis Martí; Ariane Obolensky; Rudolf de Korte; Claes de Neergaard
UK OFFICE: 68 Pall Mall, London SW1Y 5ES. Tel: 0171-343 1200

NEW INSTITUTIONS AND AGENCIES

The Maastricht Treaty, together with the 1993 Brussels Council summit, established a number of new institutions and agencies:

THE COMMITTEE OF THE REGIONS
79 rue Belliard, 1040 Brussels, Belgium

The Committee of the Regions (COR) is an advisory and consultative body established to redress the lack of a role for regional and local authorities in the EU democratic system. The COR is composed of 222 appointed and indirectly elected members, of whom half are from large regions and half are from small local authorities, who meet five times each year for two days. The COR delivers opinions on policies affecting regions, such as trans-border transport links, economic and social cohesion, education and training, social policy, culture and regional policy.
President, Manfred Dammeyer (Germany)

THE EUROPEAN CENTRAL BANK
29 Kaiserstrasse, 60311 Frankfurt-am-Main, Germany

The European Central Bank (ECB), which superseded the European Monetary Institute, was established on 1 July 1998. It consists of the President, the Vice-President and four members of the executive board, who are appointed by the governments of the participating states, from people with recognized standing and professional experience. The ECB is independent of national governments. It will become fully operational on 1 January 1999, and will define and implement the single monetary policy necessary for EMU. It will work with the European System of Central Banks (ESCB), which is made up of the governors of the central banks of member states.
President, Willem Duisenberg (Netherlands)
Vice-President, Christian Noyer (France)

THE EUROPEAN POLICE OFFICE
Raamweg 47, 2596HN The Hague, The Netherlands

The European Police Office (Europol), which comes into being on 1 October 1998 when it will supersede the European Drugs Agency, has been created to improve police co-operation between member states and to combat terrorism, illicit traffic in drugs and other serious forms of international crime. Each member state will set up a national unit to liaise with Europol, and the units will send at least one liaison officer to represent its interests at Europol headquarters. Europol will maintain a computerized information system, designed to facilitate the exchange of information between member states; the system is maintained by the national units and may be consulted by Europol agents. The computerized database may contain both personal and non-personal data; individuals are entitled to request access to data concerning themselves. All Europol activities will be monitored by an independent joint supervisory body, to ensure the rights of the individual are upheld.

Co-ordinator, Juergen Storbeck (Germany)

Other bodies include:

THE EUROPEAN MEDICINE EVALUATION AGENCY, London

THE EUROPEAN TRADEMARK OFFICE, Alicante

THE EUROPEAN AGENCY FOR HEALTH AND SAFETY AT WORK, Bilbao

THE EUROPEAN OFFICE FOR VETERINARY AND PLANT HEALTH INSPECTION, Dublin

THE EUROPEAN DRUGS OBSERVATORY, Lisbon

THE EUROPEAN FOUNDATION FOR TRAINING, Turin

THE EUROPEAN CENTRE FOR THE DEVELOPMENT OF VOCATIONAL TRAINING, Salonika

THE EUROPEAN ENVIRONMENT AGENCY, Copenhagen

THE EUROPEAN TRANSLATION AGENCY, Luxembourg

EUROPEAN COMMUNITY INFORMATION

EUROPEAN COMMISSION REPRESENTATIVE OFFICES

ENGLAND, 8 Storey's Gate, London SW1P 3AT. Tel: 0171-973 1992

WALES, 4 Cathedral Road, Cardiff CF1 9SG. Tel: 01222-371631

SCOTLAND, 9 Alva Street, Edinburgh EH2 4HP. Tel: 0131-225 2058

NORTHERN IRELAND, Windsor House, 9–15 Bedford Street, Belfast BT2 7EG. Tel: 01232-240708

REPUBLIC OF IRELAND, 39 Molesworth Street, Dublin 2

USA, 2100 M Street NW (Suite 707), Washington DC 20037; 1 Dag Hammarskjöld Plaza, 254 East 47th Street, New York, NY 10017

CANADA, Inn of the Provinces, Office Tower (Suite 1110), 350 Sparks Street, Ottawa, Ontario, KIR 7SA

AUSTRALIA, 18 Alakana Street, Yarralumia, ACT 2600, and a number of other cities

UK EUROPEAN PARLIAMENT INFORMATION OFFICE
2 Queen Anne's Gate, London SW1H 9AA. Tel: 0171-227 4300

There are European Information Centres, set up to give information and advice to small businesses, in 21 British towns and cities. A number of universities maintain European Documentation Centres.

Countries of the World

WORLD AREA AND POPULATION

The total population of the world in mid-1990 was estimated at 5,292 million, compared with 3,019 million in 1960 and 2,070 million in 1930.

Continent, etc.	Area sq. miles '000	sq. km '000	Estimated population mid-1990
Africa	11,704	30,313	642,000,000
North America[1]	8,311	21,525	276,000,000
Latin America[2]	7,933	20,547	448,000,000
Asia[3]	10,637	27,549	3,113,000,000
Europe[4]	1,915	4,961	498,000,000
Former USSR	8,649	22,402	289,000,000
Oceania[5]	3,286	8,510	26,500,000
TOTAL	52,435	135,807	5,292,000,000

[1] Includes Greenland and Hawaii
[2] Mexico and the remainder of the Americas south of the USA
[3] Includes European Turkey, excludes former USSR
[4] Excludes European Turkey and former USSR
[5] Includes Australia, New Zealand and the islands inhabited by Micronesian, Melanesian and Polynesian peoples
Source: UN Demographic Yearbook 1990 (pub. 1992)

A United Nations report *The Sex and Age Distribution of the World Populations* (revised 1994) puts the world's population in the late 20th and the 21st centuries at the following levels (medium variant data):

1995	5,716.4m	2030	8,670.6m
2000	6,158.0m	2040	9,318.2m
2010	7,032.3m	2050	9,833.2m
2020	7,887.8m		

The population forecast for the years 2000 and 2050 is:

Continent, etc.	Estimated population (million) 2000	2050
Africa	831.596	2,140.844
North America[1]	306.280	388.997
Latin America[2]	523.875	838.527
Asia	3,753.846	5,741.005
Europe	729.803	677.764
Oceania	30.651	46.070
TOTAL	6,158.051	9,833.207

[1] Includes Bermuda, Greenland, and St Pierre and Miquelon
[2] Mexico and the remainder of the Americas south of the USA

AREA AND POPULATION BY CONTINENT

No complete survey of many countries has yet been achieved and consequently accurate area figures are not always available. Similarly, many countries have not recently, or have never, taken a census. The areas of countries given below are derived from estimated figures published by the United Nations. The conversion factors used are:
(i) to convert square miles to square km, multiply by 2.589988
(ii) to convert square km to square miles, multiply by 0.3861022
Population figures for countries are derived from the most recent estimates available. Accurate and up-to-date data for the populations of capital cities are scarce, and definitions of cities' extent differ. The figures given below are the latest estimates available.

Ψ   seaport

AFRICA

COUNTRY/TERRITORY	AREA sq. miles	sq. km	POPULATION	CAPITAL	POPULATION OF CAPITAL
Algeria	919,595	2,381,741	28,548,000	Ψ Algiers	1,740,461
Angola	481,354	1,246,700	11,072,000	Ψ Luanda	475,328
Benin	43,484	112,622	5,561,000	Ψ Porto Novo	179,138
Botswana	224,607	581,730	1,456,000	Gaborone	133,468
Burkina Faso	105,792	274,000	10,200,000	Ouagadougou	634,479
Burundi	10,747	27,834	5,982,000	Bujumbura	235,440
Cameroon	183,569	475,442	13,277,000	Yaoundé	653,670
Cape Verde	1,557	4,033	392,000	Ψ Praia	80,000
Central African Republic	240,535	622,984	3,315,000	Bangui	473,817
Chad	495,755	1,284,000	6,361,000	N'Djaména	179,000
The Comoros	863	2,235	653,000	Moroni	17,267
Congo, Dem. Rep. of	905,355	2,344,858	43,901,000	Kinshasa	2,664,309
Congo, Rep. of	132,047	342,000	2,590,000	Brazzaville	596,200
Côte d'Ivoire	124,504	322,463	14,230,000	Yamoussoukro	126,191
Djibouti	8,958	23,200	577,000	Ψ Djibouti	340,700
Egypt	386,662	1,001,449	59,226,000	Cairo	13,000,000
Equatorial Guinea	10,831	28,051	400,000	Ψ Malabo	30,418
Eritrea	45,406	117,600	3,531,000	Asmara	358,100
Ethiopia	426,373	1,104,300	56,677,000	Addis Ababa	2,316,400
Gabon	103,347	267,668	1,320,000	Ψ Libreville	251,000

Country/Territory	Area sq. miles	sq. km	Population	Capital	Population of Capital
Gambia	4,361	11,295	1,118,000	Ψ Banjul	109,986
Ghana	92,098	238,533	17,453,000	Ψ Accra	738,498
Guinea	94,926	245,857	6,700,000	Ψ Conakry	763,000
Guinea-Bissau	13,948	36,125	1,073,000	Ψ Bissau	109,214
Kenya	224,081	580,367	30,522,000	Nairobi	1,400,000
Lesotho	11,720	30,355	2,050,000	Maseru	288,951
Liberia	43,000	111,369	2,760,000	Ψ Monrovia	421,053
Libya	679,362	1,759,540	5,407,000	Ψ Tripoli	1,000,000
Madagascar	226,658	587,041	14,763,000	Antananarivo	377,600
Malawi	45,747	118,484	9,788,000	Lilongwe	233,973
Mali	478,841	1,240,192	10,795,000	Bamako	658,275
Mauritania	395,956	1,025,520	2,284,000	Nouakchott	850,000
Mauritius	788	2,040	1,122,000	Ψ Port Louis	144,776
Mayotte (Fr.)	144	372	94,410	Mamoudzou	12,000
Morocco	172,414	446,550	27,111,000	Ψ Rabat	1,300,000
Western Sahara	102,703	266,000	283,000	Laayoune	96,784
Mozambique	309,496	801,590	17,423,000	Ψ Maputo	882,601
Namibia	318,261	824,292	1,540,000	Windhoek	169,000
Niger	489,191	1,267,000	9,151,000	Niamey	392,169
Nigeria	356,669	923,768	111,721,000	Abuja	378,671
Réunion (Fr.)	969	2,510	653,000	St Denis	121,999
Rwanda	10,169	26,338	7,952,000	Kigali	156,000
St Helena (UK)	47	122	7,000	Ψ Jamestown	1,332
Ascension Island (UK)	34	88	1,051	Ψ Georgetown	—
Tristan da Cunha (UK)	38	98	288	Ψ Edinburgh of the Seven Seas	—
São Tomé and Príncipe	372	964	127,000	Ψ São Tomé	43,420
Senegal	75,955	196,722	8,312,000	Ψ Dakar	1,641,358
Seychelles	176	455	75,000	Ψ Victoria	24,324
Sierra Leone	27,699	71,740	4,509,000	Ψ Freetown	469,776
Somalia	246,201	637,657	9,250,000	Ψ Mogadishu	1,000,000
South Africa	471,445	1,221,031	41,244,000	Pretoria / Ψ Cape Town	525,583 / 1,911,521
Sudan	967,500	2,505,813	28,098,000	Khartoum	924,505
Swaziland	6,704	17,364	908,000	Mbabane	38,290
Tanzania	362,162	938,000	30,337,000	Dodoma	88,474
Togo	21,925	56,785	4,138,000	Ψ Lomé	366,476
Tunisia	62,592	162,155	8,896,000	Ψ Tunis	1,830,634
Uganda	93,065	241,038	21,297,000	Kampala	750,000
Zambia	290,587	752,618	9,373,000	Lusaka	982,362
Zimbabwe	150,872	390,757	11,526,000	Harare	1,189,103

AMERICA

North America

Canada	3,849,674	9,970,610	29,606,000	Ottawa	1,010,288
Greenland (Den.)	840,004	2,175,600	58,000	Ψ Godthåb	12,483
Mexico	756,066	1,958,201	90,487,000	Mexico City	15,047,685
St Pierre and Miquelon (Fr.)	93	242	6,000	Ψ St Pierre	5,416
United States	3,540,321	9,169,389	263,034,000	Washington DC	7,051,495

Central America and the West Indies

Anguilla (UK)	37	96	8,000	The Valley	1,400
Antigua and Barbuda	171	442	66,000	Ψ St John's	22,342
Aruba (Neth.)	75	193	70,000	Ψ Oranjestad	25,000
Bahamas	5,358	13,878	278,000	Ψ Nassau	172,196
Barbados	166	430	264,000	Ψ Bridgetown	108,000
Belize	8,763	22,696	217,000	Belmopan	44,087
Bermuda (UK)	20	53	63,000	Ψ Hamilton	2,277
Cayman Islands (UK)	102	264	35,000	Ψ George Town	20,000
Costa Rica	19,730	51,100	3,333,000	San José	1,186,417
Cuba	42,804	110,861	11,041,000	Ψ Havana	2,175,888
Dominica	290	751	71,000	Ψ Roseau	16,243
Dominican Republic	18,816	48,734	7,915,000	Ψ Santo Domingo	2,134,779

Country/Territory	Area sq. miles	sq. km	Population	Capital	Population of Capital
Grenada	133	344	92,000	Ψ St George's	4,788
Guadeloupe (*Fr.*)	658	1,705	428,000	Ψ Basse Terre	29,522
Guatemala	42,042	108,889	10,621,000	Guatemala City	1,675,589
Haiti	10,714	27,750	7,180,000	Ψ Port-au-Prince	690,168
Honduras	43,277	112,088	5,953,000	Tegucigalpa	670,100
Jamaica	4,243	10,990	2,530,000	Ψ Kingston	103,962
Martinique (*Fr.*)	425	1,102	379,000	Ψ Fort de France	97,814
Montserrat (*UK*)	39	102	3,500	Ψ Plymouth	—
Netherlands Antilles (*Neth.*)	309	800	199,000	Ψ Willemstad	50,000
Nicaragua	50,193	130,000	4,539,000	Managua	608,020
Panama	29,157	75,517	2,631,000	Ψ Panama City	658,000
Puerto Rico (*USA*)	3,427	8,875	3,674,000	Ψ San Juan	1,222,316
Saint Christopher and Nevis	101	261	41,000	Ψ Basseterre	14,161
St Lucia	240	622	145,000	Ψ Castries	56,000
St Vincent and the Grenadines	150	388	111,000	Ψ Kingstown	33,694
El Salvador	8,124	21,041	5,768,000	San Salvador	422,570
Trinidad and Tobago	1,981	5,130	1,306,000	Ψ Port of Spain	46,222
Turks and Caicos Is. (*UK*)	166	430	19,000	Ψ Grand Turk	3,691
Virgin Islands:					
British (*UK*)	58	151	19,107	Ψ Road Town	3,983
US (*USA*)	134	347	105,000	Ψ Charlotte Amalie	11,842
South America					
Argentina	1,073,518	2,780,400	34,587,000	Ψ Buenos Aires	10,686,163
Bolivia	424,165	1,098,581	7,414,000	La Paz	784,976
Brazil	3,300,171	8,547,403	155,822,000	Brasilia	1,601,094
Chile	292,135	756,626	14,210,000	Santiago	5,257,937
Colombia	439,737	1,138,914	35,099,000	Bogotá	8,000,000
Ecuador	109,484	283,561	11,460,000	Quito	1,387,887
Falkland Islands (*UK*)	4,700	12,173	2,000	Ψ Stanley	1,636
French Guiana (*Fr.*)	34,749	90,000	147,000	Ψ Cayenne	41,164
Guyana	83,000	214,969	835,000	Ψ Georgetown	250,000
Paraguay	157,048	406,752	5,085,325	Asunción	718,690
Peru	496,225	1,285,216	23,532,000	Lima	6,483,901
South Georgia (*UK*)	1,580	4,092	—	—	—
Suriname	63,037	163,265	423,000	Ψ Paramaribo	200,970
Uruguay	68,500	177,414	3,186,000	Ψ Montevideo	1,383,660
Venezuela	352,145	912,050	21,644,000	Caracas	2,784,042

ASIA

Afghanistan	251,773	652,090	20,141,000	Kabul	1,424,400
Bahrain	268	694	586,000	Ψ Manama	140,401
Bangladesh	55,598	143,998	120,433,000	Dhaka	3,397,187
Bhutan	18,147	47,000	1,638,000	Thimphu	15,000
Brunei	2,226	5,765	285,000	Bandar Seri Begawan	49,902
Cambodia	69,898	181,035	9,836,000	Ψ Phnom Penh	832,000
China[1]	3,705,408	9,596,961	1,221,462,000	Beijing (Peking)	7,362,426
Hong Kong (*China*)	415	1,075	6,311,000	—	—
India	1,269,346	3,287,590	935,744,000	New Delhi	301,297
Indonesia	735,358	1,904,569	193,750,000	Ψ Jakarta	9,160,500
Iran	630,577	1,633,188	67,283,000	Tehran	6,750,043
Iraq	169,235	438,317	20,449,000	Baghdad	3,841,268
Israel[2]	8,130	21,056	5,695,000	Tel Aviv	1,880,200
West Bank and Gaza Strip	2,406	6,231	1,635,000	Gaza City	120,000
Japan	145,870	377,801	125,197,000	Tokyo	11,927,457
Jordan	37,738	97,740	5,439,000	Amman	1,270,000
Kazakhstan	1,049,156	2,717,300	15,671,000	Astana	292,000
Korea, (D.P.R.) (North)	46,540	120,538	23,917,000	Pyongyang	2,000,000
Korea, Rep. of (South)	38,330	99,274	46,430,000	Seoul	10,412,000
Kuwait	6,880	17,818	1,691,000	Ψ Kuwait City	400,000
Kyrgyzstan	76,641	198,500	4,500,000	Bishkek	627,800
Laos	91,429	236,800	4,882,000	Vientiane	132,253
Lebanon	4,015	10,400	3,009,000	Ψ Beirut	1,500,000
Macao (*Port.*)	7	18	418,000	Ψ Macao	—
Malaysia	127,320	329,758	20,140,000	Kuala Lumpur	1,145,075

Country/Territory	Area sq. miles	sq. km	Population	Capital	Population of Capital
Maldives	115	298	254,000	Ψ Malé	62,973
Mongolia	604,829	1,566,500	2,410,000	Ulan Bator	515,100
Myanmar (Burma)	261,228	676,578	46,527,000	Ψ Yangon (Rangoon)	2,513,023
Nepal	56,827	147,181	21,918,000	Kathmandu	419,073
Oman	119,498	309,500	2,020,000	Ψ Muscat	400,000
Pakistan	307,374	796,095	129,808,000	Islamabad	350,000
Philippines	115,831	300,000	70,267,000	Ψ Manila	8,594,150
Qatar	4,247	11,000	551,000	Ψ Doha	217,294
Saudi Arabia	830,000	2,149,690	17,880,000	Riyadh	1,800,000
Singapore	239	618	2,987,000	—	—
Sri Lanka	25,332	65,610	18,354,000	Ψ Colombo	615,000
Syria	71,498	185,180	14,315,000	Damascus	1,549,000
Taiwan	13,800	35,742	21,450,183	Taipei	2,607,010
Tajikistan	55,251	143,100	5,513,400	Dushanbe	602,000
Thailand	198,115	513,115	60,206,000	Ψ Bangkok	5,876,000
Turkey[3]	299,158	774,815	61,644,000	Ankara	3,103,000
Turkmenistan	188,456	488,100	3,808,900	Ashkhabad	407,000
United Arab Emirates	32,278	83,600	2,377,453	Abu Dhabi	450,000
Uzbekistan	172,742	447,400	21,206,800	Tashkent	2,094,000
Vietnam	128,066	331,689	74,545,000	Hanoi	3,056,146
Yemen	203,850	527,968	14,501,000	Sana'a	926,595

[1] Including Tibet
[2] Including East Jerusalem, the Golan Heights and Israeli citizens on the West Bank
[3] Including Turkey in Europe

EUROPE

Albania	11,099	28,748	3,645,000	Tirana	244,153
Andorra	175	453	68,000	Andorra la Vella	16,151
Armenia	11,506	29,800	3,762,000	Yerevan	1,254,400
Austria	32,378	83,859	8,053,000	Vienna	1,806,737
Azerbaijan	33,436	86,600	7,499,000	Ψ Baku	1,149,000
Belarus	80,155	207,600	10,141,000	Minsk	1,687,400
Belgium	11,783	30,519	10,113,000	Brussels	960,324
Bosnia-Hercegovina	19,735	51,129	4,484,000	Sarajevo	415,631
Bulgaria	42,823	110,912	8,402,000	Sofia	1,188,563
Croatia	34,022	88,117	4,495,000	Zagreb	867,717
Cyprus	3,572	9,251	742,000	Nicosia	188,800
Czech Republic	30,450	78,864	10,331,000	Prague	1,216,568
Denmark	16,639	43,094	5,228,000	Ψ Copenhagen	1,353,333
Faroe Islands	540	1,399	47,000	Ψ Tórshavn	16,218
Estonia	17,413	45,100	1,530,000	Tallinn	447,672
Finland	130,559	338,145	5,108,000	Ψ Helsinki	1,016,291
France	212,935	551,500	58,143,000	Paris	9,319,367
Georgia	26,911	69,700	5,401,000	Tbilisi	1,268,000
Germany	137,735	356,733	81,642,000	Berlin	3,472,009
Gibraltar (UK)	2.3	6	28,000	Ψ Gibraltar	
Greece	50,949	131,957	10,458,000	Athens	3,027,922
Hungary	35,920	93,032	10,225,000	Budapest	2,002,121
Iceland	39,769	103,000	272,064	Ψ Reykjavik	106,617
Ireland, Republic of	27,137	70,284	3,626,087	Ψ Dublin	952,700
Italy	116,320	301,268	57,187,000	Rome	2,693,383
Latvia	24,942	64,600	2,479,870	Riga	847,976
Liechtenstein	62	160	31,000	Vaduz	5,072
Lithuania	25,174	65,200	3,715,000	Vilnius	581,500
Luxembourg	998	2,586	418,300	Luxembourg	76,446
Macedonia, Former Yugoslav Republic of	9,928	25,713	2,163,000	Skopje	448,229
Malta	122	316	371,000	Ψ Valletta	9,144
Moldova	13,012	33,700	4,335,000	Kishinev	667,100
Monaco	0.4	1	32,000	Monaco-Ville	27,063
Netherlands	15,770	40,844	15,451,000	Ψ Amsterdam	1,100,764
Norway[1]	125,050	323,877	4,360,000	Ψ Oslo	758,949
Poland	124,808	323,250	38,588,000	Warsaw	1,643,203
Portugal[2]	35,514	91,982	9,920,760	Ψ Lisbon	2,561,225

Country/Territory	Area sq. miles	sq. km	Population	Capital	Population of Capital
Romania	92,043	238,391	22,680,000	Bucharest	2,060,551
Russia[3]	6,592,850	17,075,400	147,500,000	Moscow	8,600,000
San Marino	24	61	25,000	San Marino	4,251
Slovakia	18,924	49,012	5,364,000	Bratislava	451,272
Slovenia	7,821	20,256	1,984,000	Ljubljana	330,000
Spain[4]	195,365	505,992	39,210,000	Madrid	3,084,673
Sweden	173,732	449,964	8,831,000	Ψ Stockholm	1,532,803
Switzerland	15,940	41,284	7,040,000	Berne	321,932
Ukraine	233,090	603,700	50,500,000	Kiev	2,646,100
United Kingdom[5]	94,248	244,101	58,258,000	Ψ London	6,962,319
England	50,351	130,410	48,903,000	—	—
Wales	8,015	20,758	2,917,000	Ψ Cardiff	303,000
Scotland	30,420	78,789	5,137,000	Ψ Edinburgh	448,000
Northern Ireland	5,467	14,160	1,649,000	Ψ Belfast	297,000
Vatican City State	0.2	0.44	1,000	Vatican City	766
Yugoslavia, Fed. Rep. of	39,449	102,173	10,544,000	Belgrade	1,136,786

[1] Excludes Svalbard and Jan Mayen Islands (approx. 24,101 sq. miles (62,422 sq. km) and 3,000 population)
[2] Includes Madeira (314 sq. miles) and the Azores (922 sq. miles)
[3] Includes Russia in Asia
[4] Includes Balearic Islands, Canary Islands, Ceuta and Melilla
[5] Excludes Isle of Man (221 sq. miles (572 sq. km), 69,788 population), and Channel Islands (75 sq. miles (194 sq. km), 142,949 population)

OCEANIA

Country/Territory	Area sq. miles	sq. km	Population	Capital	Population of Capital
American Samoa (*USA*)	77	199	56,000	Ψ Pago Pago	3,519
Australia	2,988,902	7,741,220	18,054,000	Ψ Canberra	307,100
Norfolk Island (*Aust.*)	14	36	1,772	Ψ Kingston	—
Fiji	7,056	18,274	796,000	Ψ Suva	141,273
French Polynesia (*Fr.*)	1,544	4,000	220,000	Ψ Papeete	36,784
Guam (*USA*)	212	549	149,000	Hagatna	1,139
Kiribati	280	726	79,000	Tarawa	17,921
Marshall Islands	70	181	56,000	Dalap-Uliga-Darrit	20,000
Micronesia, Fed. States of	271	702	105,000	Palikir	—
Nauru	8	21	11,000	Ψ Nauru	—
New Caledonia (*Fr.*)	7,172	18,575	186,000	Ψ Noumea	97,581
New Zealand	104,454	270,534	3,681,546	Ψ Wellington	326,900
Cook Islands	91	236	19,000	Rarotonga	—
Niue	100	260	2,000	Alofi	—
Ross Dependency[1]	175,000	453,248	—	—	—
Tokelau	5	12	2,000	—	—
Northern Mariana Islands (*USA*)	179	464	47,000	Saipan	52,706
Palau (*USA*)	177	459	17,000	Koror	10,493
Papua New Guinea	178,704	462,840	4,074,000	Ψ Port Moresby	173,500
Pitcairn Islands (*UK*)	2	5	42	—	—
Samoa	1,093	2,831	171,000	Ψ Apia	36,000
Solomon Islands	11,157	28,896	378,000	Ψ Honiara	40,000
Tonga	288	747	98,000	Ψ Nuku'alofa	29,018
Tuvalu	10	26	10,000	Ψ Funafuti	2,856
Vanuatu	4,706	12,189	165,000	Ψ Port Vila	26,100
Wallis and Futuna Islands (*Fr.*)	77	200	14,000	Ψ Mata-Utu	—

[1] Includes permanent shelf ice

THE ANTARCTIC

The Antarctic is generally defined as the area lying within the Antarctic Convergence, the zone where cold northward-flowing Antarctic sea water sinks below warmer southward-flowing water. This zone is at about latitude 50° S. in the Atlantic Ocean and latitude 55°–62° S. in the Pacific Ocean. The continent itself lies almost entirely within the Antarctic Circle, an area of about 13.66 million sq. km (5.3 million sq. miles), 99.67 per cent of which is permanently ice-covered. The average thickness of the ice is 2,450 m (7,100 ft) but in places exceeds 4,500 m (14,500 ft). Some mountains protrude, the highest being Vinson Massif, 4,897 m (16,067 ft). The ice amounts to some 30 million cubic km (7.2 million cubic miles) and represents more than 90 per cent of the world's fresh water.

Along 43 per cent of the Antarctic coastline, land-ice flowing outwards forms extensive ice shelves, fragments of which break off to form tabular icebergs, leaving ice-cliffs up to 50 m (150 ft) high. Much of the sea freezes in winter, forming fast ice which breaks up in summer and drifts north as pack ice.

The most conspicuous physical features of the continent are its high inland plateau (much of it over 3,000 m (10,000 ft)), the Transantarctic Mountains (which together with the large embayments of the Weddell Sea and Ross Sea mark the approximate boundary between East and West Antarctica), and the mountainous Antarctic Peninsula and off-lying islands which extend northwards towards South America.

CLIMATE

On land, summer temperatures range from just above freezing around the coast to −34° C (about −30° F) on the plateau, and in winter from −20° C (about −4° F) on the coast to −65° C (about −85° F) inland. Over a large area the maxima do not exceed −15° C (+5° F).

Precipitation is scant over the plateau but amounts to 25–76 cm (10–30 in) (water equivalent) along the coast and some scientific stations are permanently buried by snow. Some rain falls over the more northerly areas in summer. Gravity winds on the plateau slopes and cyclonic storms further north can both exceed 160 km/h (100 m.p.h.) and gusts have been known to reach 240 km/h (150 m.p.h.). Visibility can be reduced to zero in blizzards.

FLORA AND FAUNA

Although a small number of flowering plants, ferns and clubmosses occur on the sub-Antarctic islands, only two (a grass and a pearlwort) extend south of 60° S. Antarctic vegetation is dominated by lichens and mosses, with a few liverworts, algae and fungi. Most of these occur around the coast or on islands, but lichens and some mosses also occur inland.

The only land animals are tiny insects and mites with nematodes, rotifers, and tardigrades in the mosses, but large numbers of seals, penguins and other sea-birds go ashore to breed in the summer. The emperor penguin is the only species which breeds ashore throughout the winter. By contrast, the Antarctic seas abound with life, a wide variety of invertebrates (including krill) and fish providing food for the seals, penguins and other birds, and a residual population of whales.

In 1994 the International Whaling Commission agreed to establish a whale sanctuary around Antarctica in which commercial whaling will be banned for ten years. The sanctuary covers all sea areas south of 60°S. latitude, apart from the south-west Atlantic and south-east Pacific where it will be south of 40°S. latitude.

POTENTIAL RESOURCES

In the 180 years from Captain James Cook's circumnavigation of the Antarctic in 1772–5 to the mid-1950s, expeditions to the Antarctic made major contributions to geographical and scientific knowledge of the area.

Increasing pressure on the world's food and mineral supplies has stimulated interest in the potential resources even in the extremely hostile polar environment. Minerals may be present in great variety but not in commercially exploitable concentrations in accessible localities. There are indications that off-shore hydrocarbons may be present but mostly below great depths of stormy, ice-infested seas. A 50-year ban on Antarctic mineral exploitation came into effect in January 1998 (see below).

Currently, the chief interest is in marine protein, including the shrimp-like krill already fished commercially by Japan and Poland. Research to ensure management of stocks of this organism is being continued by international groups, but it is estimated that they could sustain a yield equal to the present total annual world fish catch.

THE ANTARCTIC TREATY

The International Geophysical Year 1957–8 gave great impetus to Antarctic research, increasing the number of stations from 17 to 44 and the number of nations involved in research from four to 12 by 1957. The co-operative scientific effort proved so fruitful that the 12 nations involved (Argentina, Australia, Belgium, Chile, France, Japan, New Zealand, Norway, South Africa, the Soviet Union, the UK and the USA) pledged themselves to promote scientific and technical co-operation unhampered by politics, and the Antarctic Treaty was signed by the 12 states in 1959.

The 12 signatories to the treaty agreed to establish free use of the Antarctic continent for peaceful scientific purposes; to freeze all territorial claims and disputes in the Antarctic; to ban all military activities in the area; and to prohibit nuclear explosions and the disposal of radioactive waste. Since then additional agreements have been reached to promote conservation and regulate tourism, waste disposal and pollution.

The Antarctic Treaty was defined as covering areas south of latitude 60° S., excluding the high seas but including the ice shelves, and came into force in 1961. It has since been signed by a further 31 states, 14 of which are active in the Antarctic and have therefore been accorded consultative status, bringing the number of consultative parties to 26. In 1998 an extension to the treaty came into effect, placing a 50-year ban on mining, oil exploration and mineral extraction in Antarctica. Furthermore, all tourists, explorers and expeditions will now need permission to enter the Antarctic.

TERRITORIAL CLAIMS

Under the provisions of the Antarctic Treaty all territorial claims and disputes were frozen without the acceptance or denial of the claims of the various claimants. The US and Soviet governments also made it clear that although they had not made any specific territorial claims, they did not relinquish the right to make such claims.

Seven states have made claims in the Antarctic: Argentina claims the part of Antarctica between 74° W. and

25° W.; Chile that part between 90° W. and 53° W.; Britain claims the British Antarctic Territory, an area of 1,709,340 sq. km (660,000 sq. miles) between 20° and 80° W. longitude; France claims Terre Adélie, 432,000 sq. km (166,800 sq. miles) between 136° and 142° E.; Australia claims the Australian Antarctic Territory, 6,120,000 sq. km (2,320,000 sq. miles) between 160° and 45° E. longitude excluding Terre Adélie; Norway claims Queen Maud Land between 20° W. and 45° E.; and New Zealand claims the Ross Dependency, 450,000 sq. km (175,000 sq. miles) between 160° E. and 150° W. longitude. The Argentinian, British and Chilean claims overlap; the part of the continent between 90° W. and 150° W. is unclaimed by any state.

SCIENTIFIC RESEARCH

There were 35 permanently occupied stations in 1997–8 operated by the following nations: Argentina (6), Australia (3), Brazil (1), Chile (3), China (2), France (1), Germany (1), India (1), Japan (2), New Zealand (1), Poland (1), Russia (4), South Africa (1), South Korea (1), UK (2), Ukraine (1), Uruguay (1), USA (3, including one at the South Pole).

The staff of these stations and summer field-workers are the only people present on the continent and off-lying islands. There are no indigenous inhabitants.

DISTANCES FROM LONDON BY AIR

Distances in statute miles from London, Heathrow, to various cities (airport) abroad, supplied by the publishers of *IATA/Serco Aviation Services Air Distances Manual*, Southall, Middx.

To	Miles
Abidjan	3,197
Abu Dhabi (International)	3,425
Addis Ababa	3,675
Adelaide (International)	10,111
Aden	3,670
Algiers	1,035
Amman (Queen Alia)	2,287
Amsterdam	230
Ankara (Esenboga)	1,770
Athens	1,500
Auckland	11,404
Baghdad (Saddam)	2,551
Bahrain	3,163
Baku	2,485
Bangkok	5,928
Barbados	4,193
Barcelona (Muntadas)	712
Basle	447
Beijing (Capital)	5,063
Beirut	2,161
Belfast (Aldergrove)	325
Belgrade	1,056
Berlin (Tegel)	588
Bermuda	3,428
Berne	476
Bogotá	5,262
Bombay (Mumbai)	4,478
Boston	3,255
Brasilia	5,452
Bratislava	817
Brisbane (Eagle Farm)	10,273
Brussels	217
Bucharest (Otopeni)	1,307
Budapest	923
Buenos Aires	6,915
Cairo (International)	2,194
Calcutta	4,958
Canberra	10,563
Cape Town	6,011
Caracas	4,639
Chicago (O'Hare)	3,941
Cologne	331
Colombo (Katunayake)	5,411
Copenhagen	608
Dakar	2,706
Dallas (Fort Worth)	4,736
Damascus (International)	2,223

Dar-es-Salaam	4,662
Darwin	8,613
Delhi	4,180
Detroit (Metropolitan)	3,754
Dhaka	4,976
Dubai	3,414
Dublin	279
Durban	5,937
Düsseldorf	310
Entebbe	4,033
Frankfurt (Main)	406
Freetown	3,046
Geneva	468
Gibraltar	1,084
Gothenburg (Landvetter)	664
Harare	5,156
Havana	4,647
Helsinki (Vantaa)	1,148
Hobart	10,826
Ho Chi Minh City	6,345
Hong Kong	5,990
Honolulu	7,220
Houston (Intercontinental)	4,821
Islamabad	3,767
Istanbul	1,560
Jakarta	7,295
Jeddah	2,947
Johannesburg	5,634
Kabul	3,558
Karachi	3,935
Kathmandu	4,570
Khartoum	3,071
Kiev (Borispol)	1,357
Kiev (Julyany)	1,337
Kingston, Jamaica	4,668
Kuala Lumpur (Subang)	6,557
Kuwait	2,903
Lagos	3,107
Larnaca	2,036
Lima	6,303
Lisbon	972
Lomé	3,129
Los Angeles (International)	5,439
Madrid	773
Malta	1,305
Manila	6,685
Marseille	614
Mauritius	6,075
Melbourne (Essendon)	10,504
Melbourne (Tullamarine)	10,499
Mexico City	5,529
Miami	4,414
Milan (Linate)	609
Montevideo	6,841

Montreal (Mirabel)	3,241
Moscow (Sheremetievo)	1,557
Munich (Franz Josef Strauss)	584
Muscat	3,621
Nairobi (Jomo Kenyatta)	4,248
Nassau	4,333
New York (J. F. Kennedy)	3,440
Nice	645
Oslo (Fornebu)	722
Ottawa	3,321
Palma, Majorca	836
Paris (Charles de Gaulle)	215
Paris (Orly)	227
Perth, Australia	9,008
Port of Spain	4,404
Prague	649
Pretoria	5,602
Reykjavik (Keflavik)	1,177
Rhodes	1,743
Rio de Janeiro	5,745
Riyadh International	3,067
Rome (Fiumicino)	895
St John's, Newfoundland	2,308
St Petersburg	1,314
San Francisco	5,351
São Paulo	5,892
Sarajevo	1,017
Seoul (Kimpo)	5,507
Shanghai	5,725
Shannon	369
Singapore (Changi)	6,756
Sofia	1,266
Stockholm (Arlanda)	908
Suva	10,119
Sydney (Kingsford Smith)	10,568
Tangier	1,120
Tehran	2,741
Tel Aviv	2,227
Tokyo (Narita)	5,956
Toronto	3,544
Tripoli (International)	1,468
Tunis	1,137
Turin (Caselle)	570
Ulan Bator	4,340
Vancouver	4,707
Venice (Tessera)	715
Vienna (Schwechat)	790
Vladivostok	5,298
Warsaw	912
Washington (Dulles)	3,665
Wellington	11,692
Yangon/Rangoon	5,582
Zagreb	848
Zürich	490

Currencies of the World
AND EXCHANGE RATES AGAINST £ STERLING

Franc CFA = Franc de la Communauté financière africaine
Franc CFP = Franc des Comptoirs français du Pacifique
*Rouble rebased 1 January 1998: 1 new rouble=1,000 old roubles

COUNTRY/TERRITORY	MONETARY UNIT	AVERAGE RATE TO £ 5 September 1997	AVERAGE RATE TO £ 4 September 1998
Afghanistan	Afghani (Af) of 100 puls	Af 7531.12	Af 7947.70
Albania	Lek (Lk) of 100 qindarka	Lk 242.978	Lk 251.231
Algeria	Algerian dinar (DA) of 100 centimes	DA 95.1300	DA 98.4813
American Samoa	Currency is that of the USA	US$ 1.5855	US$ 1.6732
Andorra	French and Spanish currencies in use	—	—
Angola	Readjusted kwanza (Kzrl) of 100 lwei	Kzrl 407676.4	Kzrl 430226.7
Anguilla	East Caribbean dollar (EC$) of 100 cents	EC$ 4.2809	EC$ 4.5177
Antigua and Barbuda	East Caribbean dollar (EC$) of 100 cents	EC$ 4.2809	EC$ 4.5177
Argentina	Peso of 10,000 australes	Pesos 1.5847	Pesos 1.6720
Armenia	Dram of 100 louma	Dram 794.494*	Dram 840.583*
Aruba	Aruban florin	Florins 2.8381	Florins 2.9950
Ascension Island	Currency is that of St Helena	at parity with £ sterling	
Australia	Australian dollar ($A) of 100 cents	$A 2.1703	$A 2.8507
Norfolk Island	Currency is that of Australia	$A 2.1703	$A 2.8507
Austria	Schilling of 100 Groschen	Schilling 20.1585	Schilling 20.4216
Azerbaijan	Manat of 100 gopik	Manat 6262.72*	Manat 6609.14*
The Bahamas	Bahamian dollar (B$) of 100 cents	B$ 1.5855	B$ 1.6732
Bahrain	Bahraini dinar (BD) of 1,000 fils	BD 0.5977	BD 0.6308
Bangladesh	Taka (Tk) of 100 poisha	Tk 70.6341	Tk 78.8078
Barbados	Barbados dollar (BD$) of 100 cents	BD$ 3.1889	BD$ 3.3653
Belarus	Rouble of 100 kopeks	Roubles 68710.7*	Roubles 402404.7*
Belgium	Belgian franc (or frank) of 100 centimes (centiemen)	Francs 59.1551	Francs 59.8839
Belize	Belize dollar (BZ$) of 100 cents	BZ$ 3.1710	BZ$ 3.3464
Benin	Franc CFA	Francs 964.080	Francs 973.140
Bermuda	Bermuda dollar of 100 cents	$ 1.5855	$ 1.6732
Bhutan	Ngultrum of 100 chetrum (Indian currency is also legal tender)	Ngultrum 58.0294	Ngultrum 71.2156
Bolivia	Boliviano ($b) of 100 centavos	$b 8.3715	$b 9.3365
Bosnia-Hercegovina	Convertible marka	—	—
Botswana	Pula (P) of 100 thebe	P 5.8511	P 7.8389
Brazil	Real of 100 centavos	Real 1.7330	Real 1.9711
Brunei	Brunei dollar (B$) of 100 sen (fully interchangeable with Singapore currency)	$ 2.4021	$ 2.9256
Bulgaria	Lev of 100 stotinki	Leva 2857.07	Leva 2894.22
Burkina Faso	Franc CFA	Francs 964.080	Francs 973.140
Burundi	Burundi franc of 100 centimes	Francs 562.187	Francs 747.541
Cambodia	Riel of 100 sen	Riel 4785.04	Riel 6241.04
Cameroon	Franc CFA	Francs 964.080	Francs 973.140
Canada	Canadian dollar (C$) of 100 cents	C$ 2.1930	C$ 2.5605
Cape Verde	Escudo Caboverdiano of 100 centavos	Esc 154.142	Esc 166.795
Cayman Islands	Cayman Islands dollar (CI$) of 100 cents	CI$ 1.3131	CI$ 1.3858
Central African Republic	Franc CFA	Francs 964.080	Francs 973.140
Chad	Franc CFA	Francs 964.080	Francs 973.140
Chile	Chilean peso of 100 centavos	Pesos 657.824	Pesos 793.515
China	Renminbi Yuan of 10 jiao or 100 fen	Yuan 13.1413	Yuan 13.8534
Hong Kong	Hong Kong dollar (HK$) of 100 cents	HK$ 12.2837	HK$ 12.9481
Colombia	Colombian peso of 100 centavos	Pesos 1880.09	Pesos 2585.26
Comoros	Comorian franc (KMF) of 100 centimes	Francs 726.996	Francs 729.663
Congo, Dem. Rep. of	Congolese franc	Zaïre 218006.2	CFr 230065.1
Congo, Rep. of	Franc CFA	Francs 964.080	Francs 973.140
Costa Rica	Costa Rican colón (₡) of 100 céntimos	₡ 375.779	₡ 437.793
Côte d'Ivoire	Franc CFA	Francs 964.080	Francs 973.140
Croatia	Kuna of 100 lipas	Kuna 10.1121	Kuna 10.5468
Cuba	Cuban peso of 100 centavos	Pesos 33.2955	Pesos 38.4836
Cyprus	Cyprus pound (C£) of 100 cents	C£ 0.8458	C£ 0.8558
Czech Republic	Koruna (Kčs) of 100 haléřu	Kčs 54.3629	Kčs 51.6208

Country/Territory	Monetary Unit	Average Rate to £ 5 September 1997	Average Rate to £ 4 September 1998
Denmark	Danish krone of 100 øre	Kroner 10.9075	Kroner 11.0523
Faroe Islands	Currency is that of Denmark	Kroner 10.9075	Kroner 11.0523
Djibouti	Djibouti franc of 100 centimes	Francs 281.775	Francs 297.361
Dominica	East Caribbean dollar (EC$) of 100 cents	EC$ 4.2809	EC$ 4.5177
Dominican Republic	Dominican Republic peso (RD$) of 100 centavos	RD$ 22.3476	RD$ 25.7673
Ecuador	Sucre of 100 centavos	Sucres 6536.22*	Sucres 9283.75*
Egypt	Egyptian pound (£E) of 100 piastres or 1,000 millièmes	£E 5.3879	£E 5.7203
Equatorial Guinea	Franc CFA	Francs 964.080	Francs 973.140
Eritrea	Nakfa	—	Nakfa 7.45
Estonia	Kroon of 100 sents	Kroons 22.9141	Kroons 23.4228
Ethiopia	Ethiopian birr (EB) of 100 cents	EB 10.6609	EB 11.6923
Falkland Islands	Falkland pound of 100 pence	*at parity with £ sterling*	
Fiji	Fiji dollar (F$) of 100 cents	F$ 2.3163	F$ 3.4536
Finland	Markka (Mk) of 100 penniä	Mk 8.5887	Mk 8.8297
France	Franc of 100 centimes	Francs 9.6408	Francs 9.7314
French Guiana	Currency is that of France	Francs 9.6408	Francs 9.7314
French Polynesia	Franc CFP	Francs 176.241	Francs 176.887
Gabon	Franc CFA	Francs 964.080	Francs 973.140
The Gambia	Dalasi (D) of 100 butut	D 15.9057	D 17.0918
Georgia	Lari of 100 tetri	—	—
Germany	Deutsche Mark (DM) of 100 Pfennig	DM 2.8647	DM 2.9023
Ghana	Cedi of 100 pesewas	Cedi 3472.25	Cedi 3890.20
Gibraltar	Gibraltar pound of 100 pence	*at parity with £ sterling*	
Greece	Drachma of 100 leptae	Drachmae 451.519	Drachmae 501.358
Greenland	Currency is that of Denmark	Kroner 10.9075	Kroner 11.0523
Grenada	East Caribbean dollar (EC$) of 100 cents	EC$ 4.2809	EC$ 4.5177
Guadeloupe	Currency is that of France	Francs 9.6408	Francs 9.7314
Guam	Currency is that of USA	US$ 1.5855	US$ 1.6732
Guatemala	Quetzal (Q) of 100 centavos	Q 9.6459	Q 10.9173
Guinea	Guinea franc of 100 centimes	Francs 1759.90	Francs 2079.79
Guinea-Bissau	Franc CFA	Francs 964.080	Francs 973.140
Guyana	Guyana dollar (G$) of 100 cents	G$ 225.934	G$ 271.561
Haiti	Gourde of 100 centimes	Gourdes 26.1766	Gourdes 27.5488
Honduras	Lempira of 100 centavos	Lempiras 20.6115	Lempiras 22.7555
Hungary	Forint of 100 fillér	Forints 311.939	Forints 372.505
Iceland	Icelandic króna (Kr) of 100 aurar	Kr 114.568	Kr 118.496
India	Indian rupee (Rs) of 100 paisa	Rs 58.0294	Rs 71.2156
Indonesia	Rupiah (Rp) of 100 sen	Rp 4653.45	Rp 18321.6
Iran	Rial	Rials 4756.50	Rials 5019.60
Iraq	Iraqi dinar (ID) of 1,000 fils	ID 0.4929*	ID 0.5202*
Ireland, Rep. of	Punt (IR£) of 100 pence	IR£ 1.0672	IR£ 1.1582
Israel	Shekel of 100 agora	Shekels 5.5770	Shekels 6.4222
Italy	Lira of 100 centesimi	Lire 2792.53	Lire 2866.48
Jamaica	Jamaican dollar (J$) of 100 cents	J$ 54.6205	J$ 59.9006
Japan	Yen of 100 sen	Yen 192.171	Yen 224.769
Jordan	Jordanian dinar (JD) of 1,000 fils	JD 1.1249	JD 1.1913
Kazakhstan	Tenge	Tenge 120.260	Tenge 132.518
Kenya	Kenya shilling (Ksh) of 100 cents	Ksh 100.481	Ksh 99.8064
Kiribati	Australian dollar ($A) of 100 cents	$A 2.1703	$A 2.8507
Korea, North	Won of 100 chon	Won 3.4881	Won 3.6811
Korea, South	Won of 100 jeon	Won 1437.26	Won 2247.11
Kuwait	Kuwaiti dinar (KD) of 1,000 fils	KD 0.4838	KD 0.5094
Kyrgyzstan	Som	—	—
Laos	Kip (K) of 100 at	K 1523.67	K 4353.67
Latvia	Lats of 100 santimes	Lats 0.9287	Lats 0.9952
Lebanon	Lebanese pound (L£) of 100 piastres	L£ 2439.29	L£ 2539.08
Lesotho	Loti (M) of 100 lisente	M 7.4384	M 10.4153
Liberia	Liberian dollar (L$) of 100 cents	L$ 1.5855	L$ 1.6732
Libya	Libyan dinar (LD) of 1,000 dirhams	LD 0.6081	LD 0.6454
Liechtenstein	Swiss franc of 100 rappen (or centimes)	Francs 2.3467	Francs 2.3816
Lithuania	Litas	Litas 6.3429	Litas 6.6946
Luxembourg	Luxembourg franc (LF) of 100 centimes (Belgian currency is also legal tender)	LF 59.1551	LF 59.8839
Macao	Pataca of 100 avos	Pataca 12.6877	Pataca 13.3943

COUNTRY/TERRITORY	MONETARY UNIT	AVERAGE RATE TO £ 5 September 1997	AVERAGE RATE TO £ 4 September 1998
Macedonia (Former Yugoslav Republic of)	Dinar of 100 paras	Dinars 89.2816	Dinars 90.8466
Madagascar	Franc malgache (FMG) of 100 centimes	FMG 7848.22	FMG 9035.28
Malawi	Kwacha (K) of 100 tambala	K 27.3118	K 69.6029
Malaysia	Malaysian dollar (ringgit) (M$) of 100 sen	M$ 4.6713	M$ 6.3582
Maldives	Rufiyaa of 100 laaris	Rufiyaa 18.6613	Rufiyaa 19.6936
Mali	Franc CFA	Francs 964.080	Francs 973.140
Malta	Maltese lira (LM) of 100 cents or 1,000 mils	LM 0.6337	LM 0.6432
Marshall Islands	Currency is that of USA	US$ 1.5855	US$ 1.6732
Martinique	Currency is that of France	Francs 9.6408	Francs 9.7314
Mauritania	Ouguiya (UM) of 5 khoums	UM 246.142	UM 338.932
Mauritius	Mauritius rupee of 100 cents	Rs 34.6749	Rs 40.7843
Mayotte	Currency is that of France	Francs 9.6408	Francs 9.7314
Mexico	Peso of 100 centavos	Pesos 12.3733	Pesos 16.9704
Federated States of Micronesia	Currency is that of USA	US$ 1.5855	US$ 1.6732
Moldova	Leu	Leu 7.2457	Leu 8.0565
Monaco	French franc of 100 centimes	Francs 9.6408	Francs 9.7314
Mongolia	Tugrik of 100 möngö	Tugriks 1244.24	Tugriks 1368.03
Montserrat	East Caribbean dollar (EC$) of 100 cents	EC$ 4.2809	EC$ 4.5177
Morocco	Dirham (DH) of 100 centimes	DH 15.5997	DH 15.8718
Mozambique	Metical (MT) of 100 centavos	MT 18226.1	MT 19233.4
Myanmar	Kyat (K) of 100 pyas	K 9.8541	K 10.4604
Namibia	Namibian dollar of 100 cents	*at parity with SA Rand*	
Nauru	Australian dollar ($A) of 100 cents	$A 2.1703	$A 2.8507
Nepal	Nepalese rupee of 100 paisa	Rs 90.2942	Rs 114.330
The Netherlands	Gulden (guilder) or florin of 100 cents	Guilders 3.2267	Guilders 3.2753
Netherlands Antilles	Netherlands Antilles guilder of 100 cents	Guilders 2.8381	Guilders 2.9950
New Caledonia	Franc CFP	Francs 176.241	Francs 176.887
New Zealand	New Zealand dollar (NZ$) of 100 cents	NZ$ 2.4912	NZ$ 3.3058
Cook Islands	Currency is that of New Zealand	NZ$ 2.4912	NZ$ 3.3058
Niue	Currency is that of New Zealand	NZ$ 2.4912	NZ$ 3.3058
Tokelau	Currency is that of New Zealand	NZ$ 2.4912	NZ$ 3.3058
Nicaragua	Córdoba (C$) of 100 centavos	C$ 15.2761	C$ 17.9869
Niger	Franc CFA	Francs 964.080	Francs 973.140
Nigeria	Naira (N) of 100 kobo	N 34.7003*	N 36.6197*
Northern Mariana Islands	Currency is that of USA	US$ 1.5855	US$ 1.6732
Norway	Krone of 100 øre	Kroner 11.7812	Kroner 12.8929
Oman	Rial Omani (OR) of 1,000 baiza	OR 0.6105	OR 0.6442
Pakistan	Pakistan rupee of 100 paisa	Rs 64.1803	Rs 83.5680
Palau	Currency is that of the USA	US$ 1.5855	US$ 1.6732
Panama	Balboa of 100 centésimos (US notes are also in circulation)	Balboa 1.5855	Balboa 1.6732
Papua New Guinea	Kina (K) of 100 toea	K 2.2554	K 3.9376
Paraguay	Guaraní (Gs) of 100 céntimos	Gs 3448.46	Gs 4718.43
Peru	New Sol of 100 cénts	New Sol 4.1960	New Sol 5.0966
The Philippines	Philippine peso (P) of 100 centavos	P 50.8946	P 76.1189
Pitcairn Islands	Currency is that of New Zealand	NZ$ 2.4912	NZ$ 3.3058
Poland	Złoty of 100 groszy	Złotys 5.5532	Złotys 6.1658
Portugal	Escudo (Esc) of 100 centavos	Esc 290.543	Esc 297.403
Puerto Rico	Currency is that of USA	US$ 1.5855	US$ 1.6732
Qatar	Qatar riyal of 100 dirhams	Riyals 5.7723	Riyals 6.0913
Réunion	Currency is that of France	Francs 9.6408	Francs 9.7314
Romania	Leu (Lei) of 100 bani	Lei 11851.6	Lei 15038.7
Russia	*New Rouble of 100 kopeks	Roubles 9260.91	Roubles 33.0877
Rwanda	Rwanda franc of 100 centimes	Francs 478.907	Francs 522.708
St Christopher and Nevis	East Caribbean dollar (EC$) of 100 cents	EC$ 4.2809	EC$ 4.5177
St Helena	St Helena pound (£) of 100 pence	*at parity with £ sterling*	
St Lucia	East Caribbean dollar (EC$) of 100 cents	EC$ 4.2809	EC$ 4.5177
St Pierre and Miquelon	Currency is that of France	Francs 9.6408	Francs 9.7314
St Vincent and the Grenadines	East Caribbean dollar (EC$) of 100 cents	EC$ 4.2809	EC$ 4.5177
El Salvador	El Salvador colón (₡) of 100 centavos	₡ 13.8811	₡ 14.6489
Samoa	Tala (S$) of 100 sene	S$ 4.1515	S$ 5.1546

Country/Territory	Monetary Unit	Average Rate to £ 5 September 1997	Average Rate to £ 4 September 1998
San Marino	San Marino and Italian currencies are in circulation	Lire 2792.53	Lire 2866.48
São Tomé and Príncipe	Dobra of 100 centavos	Dobra 3781.62	Dobra 3998.95
Saudi Arabia	Saudi riyal (SR) of 20 qursh or 100 halala	SR 5.9465	SR 6.2754
Senegal	Franc CFA	Francs 964.080	Francs 973.140
Seychelles	Seychelles rupee of 100 cents	Rs 8.0861	Rs 8.7007
Sierra Leone	Leone (Le) of 100 cents	Le 1236.69	Le 2526.53
Singapore	Singapore dollar (S$) of 100 cents	S$ 2.4021	S$ 2.9253
Slovakia	Koruna (Sk) of 100 haliers	Kčs 55.3197	Kčs 58.8113
Slovenia	Tolar (SIT) of 100 stotin	Tolars 268.058	Tolars 273.541
Solomon Islands	Solomon Islands dollar (SI$) of 100 cents	SI$ 5.8184	SI$ 8.0261
Somalia	Somali shilling of 100 cents	Shillings 4154.01	Shillings 4383.79
South Africa	Rand (R) of 100 cents	R 7.4384	R 10.4153
Spain	Peseta of 100 céntimos	Pesetas 241.694	Pesetas 246.396
Sri Lanka	Sri Lankan rupee of 100 cents	Rs 94.3373	Rs 110.808
Sudan	Sudanese dinar (SD) of 10 pounds	SD 244.167	SD 305.526
Suriname	Suriname guilder of 100 cents	Guilders 635.785	Guilders 670.953
Swaziland	Lilangeni (E) of 100 cents (South African currency is also in circulation)	E 7.4384	E 10.4153
Sweden	Swedish krona of 100 öre	Kronor 12.3493	Kronor 13.2891
Switzerland	Swiss franc of 100 rappen (or centimes)	Francs 2.3467	Francs 2.3816
Syria	Syrian pound (S$) of 100 piastres	S£ 63.4200	S£ 66.9280
Taiwan	New Taiwan dollar (NT$) of 100 cents	NT$ 45.3730	NT$ 58.0508
Tajikistan	Tajik rouble (TJR) of 100 tanga	—	—
Tanzania	Tanzanian shilling of 100 cents	Shillings 976.589	Shillings 1102.97
Thailand	Baht of 100 satang	Baht 58.7825	Baht 68.2415
Togo	Franc CFA	Francs 964.080	Francs 973.140
Tonga	Pa'anga (T$) of 100 seniti	T$ 2.1703	T$ 2.8507
Trinidad and Tobago	Trinidad and Tobago dollar (TT$) of 100 cents	TT$ 9.6795	TT$ 10.4441
Tristan da Cunha	Currency is that of the UK	—	—
Tunisia	Tunisian dinar of 1,000 millimes	Dinars 1.8103	Dinars 1.8806
Turkey	Turkish lira (TL) of 100 kurus	TL 269281.4	TL 464062.1
Turkmenistan	Manat of 100 tenesi	—	—
Turks and Caicos Islands	US dollar (US$)	US$ 1.5855	US$ 1.6732
Tuvalu	Australian dollar ($A) of 100 cents	$A 2.1703	$A 2.8507
Uganda	Uganda shilling of 100 cents	Shillings 1744.05	Shillings 2098.19
Ukraine	Hryvna of 100 kopiykas	Hryvnas 2.9494	Hryvnas 5.1033
United Arab Emirates	UAE dirham of 100 fils	Dirham 5.8234	Dirham 6.1457
United Kingdom	Pound sterling (£) of 100 pence	£ 1.00	£ 1.00
United States of America	US dollar (US$) of 100 cents	US$ 1.5855	US$ 1.6732
Uruguay	Uruguayan peso of 100 centésimos	Pesos 15.4586	Pesos 17.9702
Uzbekistan	Sum	—	Sum 481.045
Vanuatu	Vatu of 100 centimes	Vatu 186.479	Vatu 221.700
Vatican City State	Italian currency is legal tender	Lire 2792.53	Lire 2866.48
Venezuela	Bolívar (Bs) of 100 céntimos	Bs 786.606	Bs 976.530
Vietnam	Dông of 10 hào or 100 xu	Dông 18545.6	Dông 23270.0
Virgin Islands, British	US dollar (US$) (£ sterling and EC$ also circulate)	US$ 1.5855	US$ 1.6732
Virgin Islands, US	Currency is that of the USA	US$ 1.5855	US$ 1.6732
Wallis and Futuna Islands	Franc CFP	Francs 176.241	Francs 176.887
Yemen	Riyal of 100 fils	Riyals 206.115	Riyals 219.173
Yugoslavia	New dinar of 100 paras	New Dinars 9.0507	New Dinars 17.5608
Zambia	Kwacha (K) of 100 ngwee	K 2100.00	K 3363.15
Zimbabwe	Zimbabwe dollar (Z$) of 100 cents	Z$ 18.9626	Z$ 41.4120

Time Zones

Standard time differences from the
Greenwich meridian

+   hours ahead of GMT
−   hours behind GMT
*   may vary from standard time at
    some part of the year (Summer
    Time or Daylight Saving Time)
h   hours
m   minutes

	h m
Afghanistan	+ 4 30
*Albania	+ 1
Algeria	+ 1
*Andorra	+ 1
Angola	+ 1
Anguilla	− 4
Antigua and Barbuda	− 4
Argentina	− 3
*Armenia	+ 3
Aruba	− 4
Ascension Island	0
*Australia	+10
*Broken Hill area	
(NSW)	+ 9 30
*Lord Howe Island	+10 30
Northern Territory	+ 9 30
*South Australia	+ 9 30
Western Australia	+ 8
*Austria	+ 1
*Azerbaijan ·	+ 4
*Azores	− 1
*Bahamas	− 5
Bahrain	+ 3
Bangladesh	+ 6
Barbados	− 4
*Belarus	+ 2
*Belgium	+ 1
Belize	− 6
Benin	+ 1
*Bermuda	− 4
Bhutan	+ 6
Bolivia	− 4
*Bosnia-Hercegovina	+ 1
Botswana	+ 2
Brazil	
Acre	− 5
*eastern, including all	
coast and Brasilia	− 3
Fernando de Noronha	
Island	− 2
*southern	− 4
western	− 4
British Antarctic Territory	− 3
British Indian Ocean	
Territory	+ 5
Diego Garcia	+ 6
British Virgin Islands	− 4
Brunei	+ 8
*Bulgaria	+ 2
Burkina Faso	0
Burundi	+ 2
Cambodia	+ 7
Cameroon	+ 1
Canada	
*Alberta	− 7
*British Columbia	− 8
*Labrador	− 4

	h m
*Manitoba	− 6
*New Brunswick	− 4
*Newfoundland	− 3 30
*Northwest Territories	
east of 85° W.	− 5
85° W.–102° W.	− 6
west of 102° W.	− 7
*Nova Scotia	− 4
*Ontario	
east of 90° W.	− 5
west of 90° W.	− 6
*Prince Edward Island	− 4
Quebec	
east of 63° W.	− 4
*west of 63° W.	− 5
Saskatchewan	− 6
*Yukon	− 8
*Canary Islands	0
Cape Verde	− 1
Cayman Islands	− 5
Central African Republic	+ 1
Chad	+ 1
*Chatham Islands	+12 45
*Chile	− 4
China	+ 8
Christmas Island (Indian	
Ocean)	+ 7
Cocos Keeling Islands	+ 6 30
Colombia	− 5
Comoros	+ 3
Congo (Dem. Rep.)	
east	+ 2
west	+ 1
Congo (Rep. of)	+ 1
Cook Islands	− 10
Costa Rica	− 6
Côte d'Ivoire	0
*Croatia	+ 1
*Cuba	− 5
*Cyprus	+ 2
*Czech Republic	+ 1
*Denmark	+ 1
Djibouti	+ 3
Dominica	− 4
Dominican Republic	− 4
Ecuador	− 5
Galápagos Islands	− 6
*Egypt	+ 2
Equatorial Guinea	+ 1
Eritrea	+ 3
*Estonia	+ 2
Ethiopia	+ 3
*Falkland Islands	− 4
*Faröe Islands	0
Fiji	+12
*Finland	+ 2
*France	+ 1
French Guiana	− 3
French Polynesia	−10
Marquesas Islands	− 9 30
Gabon	+ 1
The Gambia	0
Georgia	+ 5
*Germany	+ 1
Ghana	0
*Gibraltar	+ 1
*Greece	+ 2

	h m
*Greenland	− 3
Danmarkshavn	0
Mesters Vig	0
*Scoresby Sound	− 1
*Thule area	− 4
Grenada	− 4
Guadeloupe	− 4
Guam	+10
Guatemala	− 6
Guinea	0
Guinea-Bissau	0
Guyana	− 4
*Haiti	− 5
Honduras	− 6
*Hungary	+ 1
Iceland	0
India	+ 5 30
Indonesia	
Bali	+ 8
Flores	+ 8
Irian Jaya	+ 9
Java	+ 7
Kalimantan (south and	
east)	+ 8
Kalimantan (west and	
central)	+ 7
Molucca Islands	+ 9
Sulawesi	+ 8
Sumatra	+ 7
Sumbawa	+ 8
Tanimbar	+ 9
Timor	+ 8
*Iran	+ 3 30
*Iraq	+ 3
*Ireland, Republic of	0
*Israel	+ 2
*Italy	+ 1
Jamaica	− 5
Japan	+ 9
*Jordan	+ 2
*Kazakhstan	
western (Aktau)	+ 4
central (Atyrau)	+ 5
eastern	+ 6
Kenya	+ 3
Kiribati	+12
Line Islands	+14
Phoenix Islands	+13
Korea, North	+ 9
Korea, South	+ 9
Kuwait	+ 3
*Kyrgyzstan	+ 5
Laos	+ 7
*Latvia	+ 2
*Lebanon	+ 2
Lesotho	+ 2
Liberia	0
*Libya	+ 1
*Liechtenstein	+ 1
Line Islands not part of	
Kiribati	−10
*Lithuania	+ 2
*Luxembourg	+ 1
Macao	+ 8
*Macedonia (Former Yug.	
Rep. of)	+ 1
Madagascar	+ 3

	h m		h m
*Madeira	0	St Lucia	− 4
Malawi	+ 2	*St Pierre and Miquelon	− 3
Malaysia	+ 8	St Vincent and the	
Maldives	+ 5	Grenadines	− 4
Mali	0	El Salvador	− 6
*Malta	+ 1	Samoa	−11
Marshall Islands	+12	Samoa, American	−11
Ebon Atoll	−12	*San Marino	+ 1
Martinique	− 4	São Tomé and Princípe	0
Mauritania	0	Saudi Arabia	+ 3
Mauritius	+ 4	Senegal	0
*Mexico	− 6	Seychelles	+ 4
central	− 7	Sierra Leone	0
*Quintana Roo	− 5	Singapore	+ 8
western	− 8	*Slovakia	+ 1
Micronesia		*Slovenia	+ 1
Caroline Islands	+10	Solomon Islands	+11
Kosrae	+11	Somalia	+ 3
Pingelap	+11	South Africa	+ 2
Pohnpei	+11	South Georgia	− 2
*Moldova	+ 2	*Spain	+ 1
*Monaco	+ 1	Sri Lanka	+ 6
*Mongolia	+ 8	Sudan	+ 2
Montserrat	− 4	Suriname	− 3
Morocco	0	Swaziland	+ 2
Mozambique	+ 2	*Sweden	+ 1
Myanmar	+ 6 30	*Switzerland	+ 1
*Namibia	+ 1	*Syria	+ 2
Nauru	+12	Taiwan	+ 8
Nepal	+ 5 45	Tajikistan	+ 5
*Netherlands	+ 1	Tanzania	+ 3
Netherlands Antilles	− 4	Thailand	+ 7
New Caledonia	+11	Togo	0
*New Zealand	+12	Tonga	+13
Nicaragua	− 6	Trinidad and Tobago	− 4
Niger	+ 1	Tristan da Cunha	0
Nigeria	+ 1	Tunisia	+ 1
Niue	−11	*Turkey	+ 2
Norfolk Island	+11 30	Turkmenistan	+ 5
Northern Mariana Islands	+10	*Turks and Caicos Islands	− 5
*Norway	+ 1	Tuvalu	+12
Oman	+ 4	Uganda	+ 3
Pakistan	+ 5	*Ukraine	+ 2
Palau	+ 9	United Arab Emirates	+ 4
Panama	− 5	*United Kingdom	0
Papua New Guinea	+10	*United States of America	
*Paraguay	− 4	Alaska	− 9
Peru	− 5	Aleutian Islands, east of	
Philippines	+ 8	169° 30′ W.	− 9
*Poland	+ 1	Aleutian Islands, west	
*Portugal	+ 0	of 169° 30′ W.	−10
Puerto Rico	− 4	eastern time	− 5
Qatar	+ 3	central time	− 6
Réunion	+ 4	Hawaii	−10
*Romania	+ 2	mountain time	− 7
*Russia		Pacific time	− 8
Zone 1	+ 2	Uruguay	− 3
Zone 2	+ 3	Uzbekistan	+ 5
Zone 3	+ 4	Vanuatu	+11
Zone 4	+ 5	*Vatican City State	+ 1
Zone 5	+ 6	Venezuela	− 4
Zone 6	+ 7	Vietnam	+ 7
Zone 7	+ 8	Virgin Islands (US)	− 4
Zone 8	+ 9	Yemen	+ 3
Zone 9	+10	*Yugoslavia (Fed. Rep. of)	+ 1
Zone 10	+11	Zambia	+ 2
Zone 11	+12	Zimbabwe	+ 2
Rwanda	+ 2		
St Helena	0		
St Christopher and Nevis	− 4		

Source: reproduced with permission from data produced by HM Nautical Almanac Office

Countries of the World: A–Z

AFGHANISTAN
Da Afghanistan Jamhuriat

AREA – 251,773 sq. miles (652,090 sq. km). Neighbours: Iran (west), Pakistan (south), Tajikistan, Uzbekistan and Turkmenistan (north), Pakistan and China (east)
POPULATION – 20,141,000 (1994 UN estimate): Pushtuns (38 per cent) predominate in the south and west; Tajiks (25 per cent); Hazaras (19 per cent) in the centre; Uzbeks (6 per cent) in the north; Aimaqs (4 per cent); Baluchis (0.5 per cent). The principal languages are Dari (a form of Persian) and Pushtu
CAPITAL – Kabul (population, 1,424,400, 1988)
MAJOR CITIES – Herat (177,300); Jalalabad (55,000); Kandahar (225,500); Mazar-i-Sharif (130,600) (1988 UN estimates)
CURRENCY – Afghani (Af) of 100 puls
NATIONAL ANTHEM – Soroud-e-Melli
NATIONAL DAY – 19 August
NATIONAL FLAG – Three horizontal stripes of green, white, black with the national arms in gold
LIFE EXPECTANCY (years) – male 43.00; female 44.00
POPULATION DENSITY – 31 per sq. km (1995)
Mountains, chief among which are the Hindu Kush, cover three-quarters of the country. There are three great river basins, the Oxus, Helmand, and Kabul. The climate is dry, with extreme temperatures.

HISTORY AND POLITICS

The constitutional monarchy, introduced by the 1964 constitution, was overthrown by a coup in 1973. The country was ruled by presidential decree until 1977 when Mohammad Daoud was elected president. He was over-thrown in 1978 by the armed forces and power was handed to the People's Democratic Party of Afghanistan (PDPA). In December 1979 Soviet troops invaded Afghanistan and installed Babrak Karmal as head of state. Armed Islamic resistance groups, the mujahidin, fought against Soviet and Afghan forces until the withdrawal of Soviet troops in 1988. Mujahidin opposition to the Homeland Party (formerly PDPA) government continued until the government collapsed in April 1992. Mujahidin forces overran Kabul bringing an end to the war, and declared an Islamic state.
The new government appointed Burhanuddin Rabbani as interim president, but infighting between factions of the mujahidin resumed in December 1992. A cease-fire and power sharing agreement between them collapsed in October 1993. In the winter of 1994–5, divided mujahidin forces suffered heavy defeats at the hands of the Taliban (armed Islamic students), which extended its power across half of the country. In March 1996, the mujahidin agreed to combine their forces against the Taliban but failed to prevent the Taliban from seizing Kabul in September 1996. The forces of the former government were forced northwards. The United Islamic Front for the Salvation of Afghanistan (UIFSA) or Northern Alliance was formed by the four main mujahidin factions which together con-trolled one-third of Afghanistan. The Taliban, thought to be backed by Pakistan and Saudi Arabia, imposed strict Sharia law in Kabul. In May 1997 the Taliban temporarily gained control of Mazar-i-Sharif after forming an alliance with Gen. Malik Pahlawan who had defected from the opposition.
In April 1998, Bill Richardson, the US Permanent Representative to the UN, visited Afghanistan to meet representatives of the Taliban militia and the anti-Taliban coalition. On 27 April the two sides met for peace talks in Islamabad, Pakistan, and agreed on the formation of a peace commission to be made up of Islamic scholars; fighting continues throughout the country.

POLITICAL SYSTEM

There are 29 provinces, 20 of which are under Taliban control and governed through an interim council (*shura*).

EMBASSY OF THE ISLAMIC STATE OF AFGHANISTAN
31 Prince's Gate, London SW7 1QQ
Tel 0171-589 8891
Ambassador Extraordinary and Plenipotentiary, new appointment awaited
Minister-Counsellor and Chargé d'Affaires, Ahmad Wali Masud

BRITISH EMBASSY
Karte Parwan, Kabul
Staff were withdrawn from post in February 1989. Ambassador is now resident in Islamabad.

ECONOMY

The economy has been devastated by the political upheavals of the last 17 years. Traditional industries have diminished as the narcotics trade has grown. In 1995 heroin worth £50,000 million was produced. Afghanistan is also the world's second largest producer of opium; the Taliban impose a 10 per cent tax on opium sales. In November 1997, the UN Drug Control Programme brokered an agreement with the Taliban to limit poppy production, and to give UN inspectors access to opium-producing areas.
Agriculture and sheep raising were traditionally the principal industries. Silk, woollen and hair cloths and carpets were manufactured. Salt, silver, copper, coal, iron, lead, rubies, lapis lazuli, gold, chrome, barite, uranium, and talc are found.
There are thought be considerable fuel reserves. US and Saudi Arabian companies have attempted to negotiate with the Taliban and mujahidin for permission to construct an oil pipeline from Pakistan to Turkmenistan crossing Afghanistan.
GDP – US$17,418 million (1994); US$3,937 per capita (1994)
INFLATION RATE – 56.7 per cent (1991); estimated to be 400 per cent in 1996

TRADE

Trade is now largely limited to narcotics, but in the past exports have been Persian lambskins (Karakul), dried fruits, nuts, cotton, raw wool, carpets, spice and natural gas, while the imports are chiefly oil, cotton yarn and piece goods, tea, sugar, machinery and transport equipment.
In 1991 imports totalled US$616 million and exports US$188 million. There was a current account deficit of US$143 million in 1989.

Trade with UK	1996	1997
Imports from UK	£7,581,000	£9,579,000
Exports to UK	2,693,000	2,948,000

COMMUNICATIONS

Main roads run from Kabul to Kandahar, Herat, Maimana via Mazar-i-Sharif and Faizabad via Khanabad. Roads cross the border with Pakistan at Chaman and via the Khyber Pass, and there are roads from Herat to the borders of Central Asia and Iran. Much of the country's road system has been damaged during the fighting.

In 1982 the Afghan and Uzbek shores of the River Oxus were linked by a road and rail bridge which joins the Afghan port of Hairatan and the Uzbek port of Termez.

EDUCATION

Education is free and nominally compulsory, elementary schools having been established in most centres; there are secondary schools in large urban areas and four universities, in Kabul (established 1932), Jalalabad (established 1962), Balkh and Herat (both established 1988). Kabul's 26 newspapers were closed by the Taliban and women were prohibited from teaching or studying at schools and universities.

ILLITERACY RATE – 68.5 per cent

ENROLMENT (percentage of age group) – primary 29 per cent (1993); tertiary 1.8 per cent (1990)

ALBANIA
Republika e Shqipërisë

AREA – 11,099 sq. miles (28,748 sq. km). Neighbours: Montenegro (north), Serbia and Macedonia (east), Greece (south)

POPULATION – 3,645,000 (1994 UN estimate). Muslim (70 per cent), Greek Orthodox (20 per cent), Roman Catholic (10 per cent). The language is Albanian

CAPITAL – Tirana (population, 244,153, 1990)

CURRENCY – Lek (Lk) of 100 qindarka

NATIONAL DAY – 28 November

NATIONAL FLAG – Black two-headed eagle on a red field

LIFE EXPECTANCY (years) – male 69.60; female 75.50

POPULATION GROWTH RATE – 2.3 per cent (1995)

POPULATION DENSITY – 127 per sq. km (1995)

URBAN POPULATION – 36.7 per cent (1991)

ENROLMENT (percentage of age group) – primary 96 per cent (1995); tertiary 9.6 per cent (1993)

HISTORY AND POLITICS

Albania was under Turkish suzerainty from 1468 until 1912, when independence was declared. After a period of unrest, a republic was declared in 1925, and in 1928 a monarchy. The King went into exile in 1939 when the country was occupied by the Italians; Albania was liberated in November 1944. Elections in 1945 resulted in a Communist-controlled Assembly; the King was deposed in absentia and a republic declared in January 1946.

From 1946 to 1991 Albania was a one-party, Communist state. In March 1991 multiparty elections were won by the Socialist Party (the renamed Communist Party of Labour) and a coalition government was formed in June 1991. In December 1991 the Democratic Party withdrew from the government and won new elections which were held in March 1992. A coalition government was formed with the Social Democrat and Republican parties. In April 1992 the Democratic Party leader Dr Sali Berisha was elected by parliament as Albania's first non-Communist president. The general election of June 1996 was boycotted by opposition parties amid allegations of electoral malpractice, enabling the Democratic Party to win 122 of the 140

seats in parliament. Rioting broke out in January 1997 following the collapse of several pyramid investment schemes. Anti-government protests, taking the form of armed rebellion, spread throughout the country. A state of emergency was declared in March, and an interim government held power until elections could take place. Legislative elections were held in June 1997 and were won by a Socialist-led coalition. President Berisha resigned following the announcement of the result and was replaced by Rexhep Mejdani.

HEAD OF STATE

President, Prof. Rexhep Mejdani, *elected by parliament* 24 July 1997

COUNCIL OF MINISTERS *as at July 1998*

Prime Minister, Fatos Nano (SP)

Deputy PM, Government Co-ordination, Kastriot Islami (SP)

Deputy PM, Local Administration, Bashkim Fino (SP)

Agriculture and Food, Lufter Xhuveli (AP)

Culture, Youth and Sport, Edi Rama (Ind.)

Defence, Luan Hajdaraga (SP)

Economic Co-operation and Trade, Ermelinda Meksi (SP)

Education and Science, Et'hem Ruka (SP)

Finance, Arben Malaj (SP)

Foreign Affairs, Paskal Milo (SDP)

Health and Environment, Leonard Solis (HRUP)

Justice, Thimio Kondi (Ind.)

Labour and Social Affairs, Anastas Angjeli (SP)

Legislative Reform and Parliamentary Relations, Arben Imami (DAP)

Public Economy and Privatization, Ylli Bufi (SP)

Public Order, Perikli Teta (DAP)

Public Works and Transport, Gaqo Apostoli (SDP)

AP Agrarian Party; DAP Democratic Alliance Party; HRUP Human Rights Union Party; SP Socialist Party; SDP Social Democratic Party

EMBASSY OF THE REPUBLIC OF ALBANIA

4th Floor, 38 Grosvenor Gardens, London SW1W 0EB

Tel 0171-730 5709

Ambassador Extraordinary and Plenipotentiary, HE Agim Besim Fagu, apptd 1998

BRITISH EMBASSY

Rruga Vaso Pasha, 7–1, Tirana

Tel: Tirana 34973/4/5

Ambassador Extraordinary and Plenipotentiary, HE Andrew Tesoriere, apptd 1996

DEFENCE

The Army has 859 main battle tanks, 103 armoured personnel carriers and 823 artillery pieces. The Navy has one submarine and 31 patrol and coastal combatant vessels at six bases. The Air Force has 98 combat aircraft.

MILITARY EXPENDITURE – 3.9 per cent of GDP (1996)

MILITARY PERSONNEL – Armed Forces yet to be reconstituted following civil unrest

ECONOMY

Much of the country is mountainous and nearly a half is covered by forest. The main crops are wheat, maize, sugar beet, potatoes and fruit. There are large chromium deposits. The principal industries are agricultural product processing, textiles, oil products and cement.

Since April 1992, the government has imposed austerity measures in an attempt to reduce the budget deficit and to cut inflation. Up to US$1,200 million worth of personal savings were lost in the collapse of several fraudulent pyramid savings schemes in January 1997, and the value of the lek fell heavily.

Remittances from 500,000 overseas workers remain an important source of revenue. Albania has received $1 billion in aid from Western donors and was promised £2,800 million in food and medical aid by the EU in March 1997. An international donors' conference in October 1997 approved a US$600 million aid package dependent on the closure of all remaining pyramid schemes, and in November 1997, the IMF approved credit of approximately US$12 million.

GNP – US$2,705 million (1996); US$820 per capita (1996)
GDP – US$1,689 million (1994); estimated to be US$2,300 million (1996); US$700 per capita (1994)
INFLATION RATE – 7.8 per cent (1995)
UNEMPLOYMENT – 9.1 per cent (1991)
TOTAL EXTERNAL DEBT – US$781 million (1996)

TRADE

Exports include crude oil, minerals (bitumen, chrome, nickel, copper), tobacco, fruit and vegetables. In 1996 Albania had a trade deficit of US$678 million and a current account deficit of US$107 million.

TRADE WITH UK	1996	1997
Imports from UK	£14,664,000	£9,076,000
Exports to UK	318,000	2,124,000

ALGERIA
Al-Jumhuriya al-Jazairiya ad-Dimuqratiya ash-Shabiya

AREA – 919,595 sq. miles (2,381,741 sq. km). Neighbours: Morocco and Western Sahara (west), Mauritania and Mali (south-west), Niger (south-east) and Libya and Tunisia (east)
POPULATION – 28,548,000 (1994 UN estimate); 22,971,558 (1987 census). Arabic is the official language although French and Berber are also spoken
CAPITAL – ΨAlgiers (population, 1,740,461, 1977; now roughly 3,250,000). It is one of the principal ports of the Mediterranean
MAJOR CITIES – ΨAnnaba; ΨBejaia; Blida; Constantine; ΨMostaganem; ΨOran; Setif; Sidi-Bel-Abbès; ΨSkida; Tizi Ouzou and Tlemcen
CURRENCY – Algerian dinar (DA) of 100 centimes
NATIONAL ANTHEM – Qassaman
NATIONAL DAY – 1 November
NATIONAL FLAG – Divided vertically green and white with a red crescent and star over all in the centre
LIFE EXPECTANCY (years) – male 65.75; female 66.34
POPULATION GROWTH RATE – 2.4 per cent (1995)
POPULATION DENSITY – 12 per sq. km (1995)
ILLITERACY RATE – 38.4 per cent
ENROLMENT (percentage of age group) – primary 95 per cent (1995); secondary 56 per cent (1995); tertiary 10.9 per cent (1995)

HISTORY AND POLITICS

Algeria was annexed to France in 1842, with the departments of Algiers, Oran and Constantine forming an integral part of France. President de Gaulle declared Algeria independent in July 1962 following an eight-year armed rebellion by the (Arab) Front de Libération Nationale (FLN), whose leader, Ben Bella, was elected president in 1963. Ben Bella was deposed in 1965 by a military junta presided over by Col. Boumediène, who was

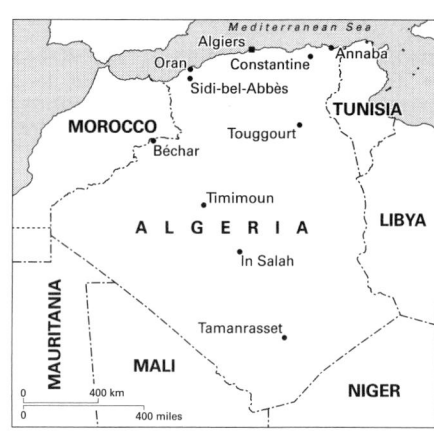

formally elected president in 1976. Boumediène died in 1978 and was succeeded by Chadli Bendjedid.

A new constitution agreed by referendum in 1989 moved Algeria towards pluralism. However, the 1991 legislative elections were abandoned in anticipation of the success of the opposition Islamic Salvation Front (FIS), which had campaigned on a radical 'Islamist' platform. The Army forced President Bendjedid to resign and a military-backed Higher Committee of State (HCS), headed by former FLN veteran Mohammed Boudiaf, took power. The HCS declared a state of emergency in 1992 which was extended indefinitely in 1993. The FIS was banned in 1992 but continued to operate covertly and was suspected of assassinating Boudiaf in June 1992.

A national reconciliation conference in January 1994 was boycotted by the FIS but nevertheless it appointed Brig.-Gen. Liamine Zeroual as president to replace the HCS, which disbanded itself. Zeroual was elected president for a five-year term in November 1995. Multiparty elections on 5 June 1997 were won by a newly-formed pro-Zeroual party, National Democratic Rally (RND), which captured 155 seats. Hamas (Movement for a Society of Peace) (MSP) won 69 seats; the FLN 64 seats; Annahda (Renaissance Movement) 34; Rally for Culture and Democracy 19; Socialist Forces Front 19. Elections to the National Council (the upper house) took place in December 1997 and were dominated by RND, which won 80 of the 96 elected seats.

INSURGENCY

Since the abortive elections in 1992, the FIS-backed Islamic Salvation Army (AIS) and the more extreme Armed Islamic Group (GIA) have waged an armed campaign against the military regime in favour of an Islamic state. The two groups have targeted the military and security forces, their secular supporters in the population, and foreign expatriates. The army has had little success in stopping the killings, and there have been suggestions from diplomatic observers of complicity between the army and the death squads. More than 75,000 people have died in the fighting since 1992.

POLITICAL SYSTEM

The legislature is bicameral. The National Assembly (the lower chamber) has 380 members, directly elected for a five-year term. The *Majlis el-Umma* (Council of the Nation) is the upper chamber, with a third of its 144 members appointed by the president; two-thirds are indirectly elected for six-year terms.

HEAD OF STATE
President, Brig.-Gen. Liamine Zeroual, *elected* November
1995

GOVERNMENT *as at June 1998*
Prime Minister, Ahmed Ouyahia (RND)
Agriculture and Fisheries, Belhouadjeb Benalia (FLN)
Communications and Culture, Habib Chawki Hamraoui
(RND)
Energy and Mines, Youcef Yousfi (RND)
Equipment, National and Regional Development, Abderrahmane
Belayat (FLN)
Finance, Abdelkrim Harchaoui (RND)
Foreign Affairs, Ahmed Attaf (RND)
Health and Population, Yahia Guidoum (RND)
Higher Education and Scientific Research, Amar Tou (FLN)
Housing, Abdelkader Bounekraf (FLN)
Industry and Restructuring, Abdelmajid Menasra (MSP)
Interior, Local Authorities, Environment, Mostefa Benmansour
(RND)
Justice, Mohamed Adami (RND)
Labour, Social Services and Vocational Training, Hacene Laskri
(RND)
National Education, Boubakeur Benbouzid (RND)
National Solidarity and Family Matters, Rabea Mercherchene
(RND)
Posts and Telecommunications, Mohamed-Salah Youyou
(RND)
Relations with Parliament, Mohamed Kechoud (RND)
Religious Affairs, Bouabdellah Ghlamallah (RND)
Small and Medium-sized Enterprises, Bouguerra Soltani
(MSP)
Tourism and Handicrafts, Abdelkader Bengrina (MSP)
Trade, Bakhti Belaib (RND)
Transport, Sid Ahmed Boulil (MSP)
War Veterans, Mohamed Said Abadou (RND)
Youth and Sports, Mohammed Aziz Derouaz (RND)

ALGERIAN EMBASSY
54 Holland Park, London WII 3RS
Tel 0171-221 7800
Ambassador Extraordinary and Plenipotentiary, HE Ahmed
Benyamina, apptd 1996

BRITISH EMBASSY
7 Chemin des Glycines,
BP 08, Alger-Gare 16000, Algiers
Tel: Algiers 230068
Ambassador Extraordinary and Plenipotentiary, HE François
Gordon, apptd 1996

DEFENCE

The Army has 890 main battle tanks, 530 armoured
personnel carriers and 303 artillery pieces. The Navy has
two submarines, three frigates and 22 patrol and coastal
vessels. The Air Force has 181 combat aircraft and 65
armed helicopters.
MILITARY EXPENDITURE – 4.0 per cent of GDP (1996)
MILITARY PERSONNEL – 270,200: Army 107,000, Navy
7,000, Air Force 10,000, Paramilitaries 146,200
CONSCRIPTION DURATION – 18 months

ECONOMY

The main industry is the hydrocarbons industry. Oil and
natural gas are pumped from the Sahara to terminals on the
coast before being exported; the gas is first liquefied at
liquefaction plants at Skikda and Arzew, although pipelines serve Libya and Italy direct. In November 1996 a 750-
mile gas pipeline to Spain was opened, enabling Algeria to
double its gas exports to Morocco, Spain, Germany and

France. Its initial annual capacity of 8,000 million cubic
metres is projected to rise to 20,000 million cubic metres a
year by 2000.
  Other major industries include a steel industry, motor
vehicles, building materials, paper making, chemical
products and metal manufactures. Most major industrial
enterprises are still under state control.
  Prior to 1989 the economy was centrally planned and
state-controlled in most sectors. Economic reform, begun
in 1987, was speeded up in 1988 and now includes
industrial and financial sectors. In 1994 the government
finally accepted full economic reform and liberalization
under a reform programme agreed with the IMF. The
government has cut the budget deficit, devalued the
currency and freed price controls. The first stock exchange
in Algiers opened on 15 December 1997.
GNP – US$43,726 million (1996); US$1,520 per capita
(1996)
GDP – US$50,464 million (1994); US$563 per capita
(1994)
ANNUAL AVERAGE GROWTH OF GDP – –5.3 per cent
(1982)
INFLATION RATE – 32.2 per cent (1995)
UNEMPLOYMENT – 23.8 per cent (1992)
TOTAL EXTERNAL DEBT – US$33,260 million (1996)

TRADE

Export earnings come mainly from crude oil and liquefied
natural gas sales. Algeria's main trading partners are
France, Italy, USA, Spain and Germany.
  In 1991 Algeria had a trade surplus of US$5,468 million
and a current account surplus of US$2,367 million. In
1995 imports totalled US$10,250 million and exports
US$10,240 million.

TRADE WITH UK	1996	1997
Imports from UK	£70,939,000	£91,094,000
Exports to UK	202,428,000	85,239,000

ANDORRA
Principat d'Andorra

AREA – 175 sq. miles (453 sq. km). Neighbours: Spain and
France
POPULATION – 68,000 (1996); less than one-quarter of the
population are native Andorrans. The official language
is Catalan, but French and Spanish (Castilian) are also
spoken. The established religion is Roman Catholicism
CAPITAL – Andorra la Vella (population, 16,151, 1986)
CURRENCY – French and Spanish currencies in use
NATIONAL DAY – 8 September
NATIONAL FLAG – Three vertical bands, blue, yellow, red;
Andorran coat of arms frequently imposed on central
(yellow) band but not essential
POPULATION GROWTH RATE – 5.1 per cent (1995)
POPULATION DENSITY – 150 per sq. km (1995)
URBAN POPULATION – 95.6 per cent (1991)

HISTORY AND POLITICS

Andorra is a small, neutral principality formed by a treaty
in 1278. The first elections under the new constitution
were held in December 1993, and on 20 January 1994 the
first sovereign government of Andorra took office.

POLITICAL SYSTEM

Under a new constitution promulgated in May 1993,
Andorra became an independent, democratic parliament-

ary co-principality, with sovereignty vested in the people rather than in the two co-princes, as had previously been the case. The constitution enables Andorra to establish an independent judiciary and to carry out its own foreign policy, whilst its people may now join trade unions and political parties. The two co-princes, the President of the French Republic and the Spanish Bishop of Urgel, remain heads of state but now only have the power to veto treaties with France and Spain which affect the state's borders and security. The co-princes are represented by Permanent Delegates of whom one is the French Prefect of the Pyrénées Orientales department at Perpignan and the other is the Spanish Vicar-General of the diocese of Urgel.

Andorra has a unicameral legislature of 28 members known as the *Consell General de las Valls d'Andorra* (Valleys of Andorra General Council). Fourteen members are elected on a national list basis and 14 in seven dual-member constituencies based on Andorra's seven parishes. The Council appoints the head of the executive government, who designates the members of his government.

Permanent French Delegate, Jean Caullet
Permanent Episcopal Delegate, Nemesi Marqués Oste

EXECUTIVE GOVERNMENT *as at June 1998*
President, Marc Forné Molné
Culture, Pere Canturri Montanya
Economy, Enric Casadevall Medrano
Education, Youth and Sports, Carme Sala Sansa
Environment and Tourism, Enric Pujal Areny
Finance, Susagna Arasanz Serra
Foreign Affairs, Albert Pintat Santolària
Health and Welfare, Josep Maria Goicoechea Utrillo
Interior, Lluís Montanya Tarrés
Planning, Josep Garralla Rossell
Presidency, Estanislau Sangrà Cardona

ANDORRAN DELEGATION, 63 Westover Road, London sw18 2rf. Tel: 0181-874 4806
BRITISH AMBASSADOR – HE David Brighty, cmg, cvo, resident at Madrid

ECONOMY

Potatoes are produced in the highlands and tobacco in the valleys. The economy is largely based on tourism, banking, commerce, tobacco, construction and forestry; a third of the country is classified as forest. Andorra has negotiated a customs union with the European Union which came into force in 1991. The economy is now diversifying rapidly into offshore financial services.

GDP – US$781 million (1994); US$11,462 per capita (1994)

TRADE WITH UK	1996	1997
Imports from UK	£19,096,000	£30,967,000
Exports to UK	3,394,000	118,000

COMMUNICATIONS

A road into the valleys from Spain is open all year round, and that from France is closed only occasionally in winter. There are two radio stations in Andorra, one privately owned and Radio Andorra, operated by the government, as well as a state-owned television station.

ANGOLA
República de Angola

AREA – 481,354 sq. miles (1,246,700 sq. km). Neighbours: Democratic Republic of Congo (north and east), Zambia (east) and Namibia (south). The enclave of Cabinda is separated from the rest of Angola by the Democratic Republic of Congo and also borders on the Republic of the Congo
POPULATION – 11,072,000 (1994 UN estimate). The official language is Portuguese; Ovimbundu, Kimbundu, Bakongo and Chokwe are widely spoken
CAPITAL – ΨLuanda (population, 475,328, 1970; now estimated at 3,000,000)
CURRENCY – Readjusted kwanza (Kzrl) of 100 lwei
NATIONAL ANTHEM – Angola Avante
NATIONAL DAY – 11 November (Independence Day)
NATIONAL FLAG – Red and black with a yellow star, machete and cog-wheel
LIFE EXPECTANCY (years) – male 44.90; female 48.10
POPULATION GROWTH RATE – 2.0 per cent (1995)
POPULATION DENSITY – 9 per sq. km (1995)
ENROLMENT (percentage of age group) – tertiary 0.7 per cent (1991)

HISTORY AND POLITICS

After a Portuguese presence of five centuries, and an anti-colonial war since 1961, Angola became independent on 1 November 1975 in the midst of civil war. Soviet-Cuban military assistance to the Popular Movement for the Liberation of Angola (MPLA) enabled it to defeat its rival early in 1976. The MPLA government remained under pressure from the National Union for the Total Independence of Angola (UNITA) guerrilla movement, led by Dr Jonas Savimbi. In 1988 a cease-fire between South African, Cuban and Angolan forces took place and an agreement providing for the withdrawal of South African and Cuban troops by July 1991 was signed. A peace agreement was signed between the government and UNITA in 1991; multiparty legislative and presidential elections took place in 1992, and were won by the MPLA and its leader José Eduardo dos Santos. UNITA refused to accept the results and the civil war resumed in 1993, with UNITA at one point controlling an estimated 75% of the country.

UNITA and the MPLA government signed a peace agreement (the Lusaka Protocol) under UN mediation in November 1994. By September 1996 more than 70,000 UNITA troops had been confined by the UN peacekeeping force, UNAVEM III, although many subsequently fled. A government of national reconciliation was formed in April 1997 and 70 UNITA legislators took up their seats in parliament, although Savimbi rejected an offer of the vice presidency and refused to enter Luanda. UNITA also refused to allow central state administration to be restored in key areas, and following the fall from power of Zaïre's President Mobutu (one of UNITA's key supporters) fighting resumed in May 1997.

On 31 October 1997 the UN Security Council ordered sanctions against UNITA for failing to meet its obligations under the Lusaka Protocol. UNITA returned much of its territory to government control in December, and in January 1998 a new schedule for implementation of the Lusaka Protocol was agreed; UNITA returned the Cuango valley diamond mines to the government, and in March UNITA became a legitimate political party. Three of its representatives were appointed governors of provinces of Angola.

SECESSION

In the northern enclave of Cabinda, the Front for the Liberation of the Cabinda Enclave (FLEC) fought a 20-year war of independence until the signing of a cease-fire with the government in September 1995, which was followed by the initialling of a peace agreement in April 1996.

POLITICAL SYSTEM

The MPLA, formerly a Marxist-Leninist party, was the sole legal party until early 1991 when a multiparty system was adopted. The constitution declares Angola to be a democratic state and provides for a president, who appoints a Council of Ministers to assist him, and a 220-member National Assembly. In November 1996 the National Assembly adopted a constitutional amendment extending its mandate for between two and four years.

HEAD OF STATE

President, José Eduardo dos Santos, *re-elected* 30 September 1992

COUNCIL OF MINISTERS *as at June 1998*

Prime Minister, Fernando Franca van Dunem
Agriculture, Carlos Antonio Fernandes
Education, Antonio Buletim da Silva Neto
Finance, Mario de Alcantra Monteiro
Foreign Affairs, Venancio da Silva Moura
Geology and Mines, Marcos Samondo
Health, Anastacio Ruben Sikatu
Industry, Manuel Diamantino Borges Duque
Interior, Andre Pitra Petroff
Justice, Paulo Tjipilica
National Defence, Gen. Pedro Sebastião
Petroleum, Albina Faria de Assis
Public Administration, Antonio Pitra Costa Neto
Science and Technology, Francisco Mubengai
Telecommunications, Licinio Tavares Ribeiro
Territorial Administration, Fernando Faustino Muteka
Trade, Victorino Domingos Hossi
Women's Affairs, Joana Lina Ramos Baptista Cristiano
Youth and Sports, José da Rocha Sardinha de Castro

EMBASSY OF ANGOLA

98 Park Lane, London W1Y 3TA
Tel 0171-495 1752
Ambassador Extraordinary and Plenipotentiary, HE Antonio da Costa Fernandes, apptd 1993

BRITISH EMBASSY

Rua Diogo Cão 4 (Caixa Postal 1244), Luanda
Tel: Luanda 334582
Ambassador Extraordinary and Plenipotentiary, HE Roger Hart, apptd 1995

DEFENCE

The army has 250 main battle tanks, 100 armoured personnel carriers and 300 artillery pieces. The Navy has seven patrol vessels at three bases. The Air Force has 27 combat aircraft and 26 armed helicopters.
MILITARY EXPENDITURE – 6.4 per cent of GDP (1996)
MILITARY PERSONNEL – 126,000: Army 98,000, Navy 2,000, Air Force 11,000, Paramilitaries 15,000

ECONOMY

Angola has valuable oil and diamond deposits and exports of these two commodities account for over 90 per cent of total exports. Principal agricultural crops are cassava, maize, bananas, coffee, palm oil and kernels, cotton and sisal. Coffee, sisal, maize and palm oil are exported; exports also include mahogany and other hardwoods from the tropical rain forests in the north of the country.

The government is attempting to reform the socialist economy by free market reforms but is making little progress, with high inflation and a collapsing economy. Following implementation of the peace accord, UNITA transferred diamond mines in the Cuango valley back to the government in January; the estimated annual revenue from the mines is US$400 million.

In 1994 Angola had a trade surplus of US$1,563 million and a current account deficit of US$340 million.
GNP – US$2,972 million (1996); US$270 per capita (1996)
GDP – US$8,524 million (1994); US$384 per capita (1994)
TOTAL EXTERNAL DEBT – US$10,612 million (1996)

TRADE WITH UK	1996	1997
Imports from UK	£45,631,000	£81,371,000
Exports to UK	8,852,000	18,012,000

ANTIGUA AND BARBUDA
State of Antigua and Barbuda

AREA – 171 sq. miles (442 sq. km); Antigua 108 sq. miles (279 sq. km); Barbuda 62 sq.miles (160 sq. km); Redonda $\frac{1}{2}$sq. mile (1.2 sq. km)
POPULATION – 66,000 (1994 UN estimate); 65,962, Antigua 64,562, Barbuda 1,400 (official census 1991); the official language is English.
CAPITAL – ΨSt John's (population, 22,342, 1991)
MAJOR TOWNS – The town of Barbuda is Codrington
CURRENCY – East Caribbean dollar (EC$) of 100 cents
NATIONAL ANTHEM – Fair Antigua and Barbuda
NATIONAL DAY – 1 November (Independence Day)
NATIONAL FLAG – Red with an inverted triangle divided black over blue over white, with a rising gold sun on the white band
POPULATION GROWTH RATE – 0.6 per cent (1995)
POPULATION DENSITY – 149 per sq. km (1995)
MILITARY EXPENDITURE – 0.8 per cent of GDP (1996)

Antigua is part of the Leeward Islands in the eastern Caribbean. It is distinguished from the rest of the Leeward group by its absence of high hills and forest, and a drier climate than most of the West Indies. Barbuda, formerly a possession of the Codrington family, is very flat, mainly scrub-covered, with a large lagoon.

HISTORY AND POLITICS

Antigua was first settled by the English in 1632, and was granted to Lord Willoughby by Charles II. It became internally self-governing in 1967 and fully independent on 1 November 1981.

The Antigua Labour party won the general election of March 1994 and a fifth successive term of office with 11 seats in the House of Representatives compared to five seats for the United Progressive Party.

POLITICAL SYSTEM

Antigua and Barbuda is a constitutional monarchy with Queen Elizabeth II as Head of State, represented by the Governor-General. There is a Senate of 17 appointed members and a House of Representatives of 17 members elected every five years. The Attorney-General may be appointed.

Governor-General, HE Sir James Carlisle, GCMG

CABINET *as at June 1998*
Prime Minister, Foreign Affairs, Social Affairs, Lester Bird
*Agriculture, Lands, Fisheries, Co-operatives; Finance and Social
  Security,* John St Luce
Cabinet Secretary, Lounel Stevens
Education, Youth, Sports, Community Development, Bernard
  Percival
Health and Civil Service Affairs, Samuel Aymer
Justice, Legal Affairs and Attorney-General, Radford Hill
Labour and Home Affairs, Adolphus Freeland
Planning, Implementation and Environment, Molwyn Joseph
Prime Minister's Office, Housing, Henderson Simon
Public Utilities, Public Works, Robin Yearwood
Tourism and Culture, Dr Rodney Williams
Trade, Industry, Commerce, Consumer Affairs, Hilroy
  Humphreys

HIGH COMMISSION FOR ANTIGUA AND BARBUDA
15 Thayer Street, London WIM 5LD
Tel 0171-486 7073/5
High Commissioner, HE Ronald Sanders, CMG, apptd 1995

BRITISH HIGH COMMISSION
11 Old Parham Road (PO 483), St John's
Tel: St John's 462 0008/9
High Commissioner, HE Gordon Baker, resident at
  Bridgetown, Barbados
Resident High Commissioner, M. Maxwell, MVO

ECONOMY

The economy is largely based on tourism and related
services. For many years sugar was the dominant crop but
is no longer produced. Agricultural production includes
livestock, sea island cotton, mixed market gardening and
fishing. An offshore banking centre has been developed.

  In 1994 Antigua and Barbuda had a trade deficit of
US$254 million and a current account deficit of US$18
million.

GNP – US$482 million (1996); US$7,330 per capita (1996)
GDP – US$377 million (1994); US$5,666 per capita (1994)
ANNUAL AVERAGE GROWTH OF GDP – 3.4 per cent (1993)
INFLATION RATE – 1.0 per cent (1985)

TRADE WITH UK	1996	1997
Imports from UK	£36,792,000	£42,825,000
Exports to UK	3,207,000	3,449,000

ARGENTINA
República Argentina

AREA – 1,073,518 sq. miles (2,780,400 sq. km). Neighbours:
Bolivia (north), Paraguay, Brazil and Uruguay (north-
east), Chile (west) from which it is separated by the
Cordillera de los Andes
POPULATION – 34,587,000 (1994 UN estimate); 32,370,298
(1991 census). The language is Spanish
CAPITAL – ΨBuenos Aires (population, 10,686,163, 1991);
metropolitan area 2,960,976
MAJOR CITIES – Córdoba (1,148,305); ΨLa Plata
(640,344); ΨMar del Plata (519,707); Mendoza
(773,559); ΨRosario (894,645); San Miguel de
Tucumán (622,348)
CURRENCY – Peso of 10,000 australes
NATIONAL ANTHEM – ¡Oíd Mortales! (Hear, oh mortals!)
NATIONAL DAY – 25 May
NATIONAL FLAG – Horizontal bands of blue, white, blue;
gold sun in centre of white band
LIFE EXPECTANCY (years) – male 68.17; female 73.09

POPULATION GROWTH RATE – 1.2 per cent (1995)
POPULATION DENSITY – 12 per sq. km (1995)

Argentina occupies the greater portion of the southern
part of the South American continent, and extends from
Bolivia to Cape Horn.

HISTORY AND POLITICS

The estuary of La Plata was discovered in 1515 by Juan
Díaz de Solís and the region was subsequently colonized by
the Spanish. Spain ruled the territory from the 16th
century until 1810. In 1816, after a long campaign of
liberation conducted by General José de San Martín,
independence was declared by the Congress of Tucumán.

  President Juan Domingo Perón was overthrown in
1955, and there followed 18 years of instability until 1973
when he was recalled from exile. Perón died within a year
and was succeeded by his widow, Vice-President María
Estela Martínez de Perón. A coup led to the establishment
of a military junta in 1976. Following the Falkland Islands
defeat in 1982 the President, Gen. Galtieri, resigned and
the Army appointed Gen. Bignone. A civilian president
was elected in 1983. Presidential elections in 1989 were
won by the Justicialist Party (Perónist) candidate Carlos
Menem. In the October 1997 elections, which followed
widespread protests against the government's free market
policies and a general strike in August 1997, the Justicialist
Party lost its overall majority, holding 118 out of the 257
seats. It is still the largest single party in the Chamber of
Deputies.

POLITICAL SYSTEM
The 1853 constitution was amended in 1994. Power is
vested in the president who appoints the Cabinet and is
directly elected for a once-renewable four-year term. A
presidential candidate must win at least 45 per cent of the
vote, or 40 per cent with a 10 per cent lead over the nearest
challenger, to gain victory. The legislature consists of a 72-
member (three for each province) Senate and a 259-
member Chamber of Deputies. A third of the Senate is
elected every three years and half of the Chamber of
Deputies is elected every two years. Senators serve for a
nine-year term and Deputies for a four-year term.

FEDERAL STRUCTURE
The republic is divided into 23 provinces, each with an
elected Governor and legislature, and one federal district
(Buenos Aires), with an elected mayor and autonomous
government.

Provinces	Area (sq. km)	Population (1991 census)	Capital
Buenos Aires	307,571	12,594,974	La Plata
Catamarca	102,602	264,234	Catamarca
Chaco	99,633	839,677	Resistencia
Chubut	224,686	357,189	Rawson
Córdoba	165,321	2,766,683	Córdoba
Corrientes	88,199	795,594	Corrientes
Entre Ríos	78,781	1,020,257	Paraná
Federal Capital	200	2,965,403	Buenos Aires
Formosa	72,066	398,413	Formosa
Jujuy	53,219	512,329	San Salvador de Jujuy
La Pampa	143,440	259,996	Santa Rosa
La Rioja	89,680	229,729	La Rioja
Mendoza	148,827	1,412,481	Mendoza
Misiones	29,801	788,915	Posadas
Neuquén	94,078	388,833	Neuquén
Rio Negro	203,013	506,772	Viedma
Salta	155,488	866,153	Salta
San Juan	89,651	528,715	San Juan

Provinces	Area (sq. km)	Population (1991 census)	Capital
San Luis	76,748	286,458	San Luis
Santa Cruz	243,943	159,839	Rio Gallegos
Santa Fé	133,007	2,798,422	Santa Fé
Santiago del Estero	136,351	671,988	Santiago del Estero
Tierra del Fuego	21,571	69,369	Ushuaia
Tucumán	22,524	1,142,105	San Miguel de Tucumán

HEAD OF STATE
President, Dr Carlos Saúl Menem, *elected* May 1989, *re-elected* 14 May 1995
Vice-President, Dr Carlos Federico Ruckauf

CABINET *as at June 1998*
Cabinet Chief, Jorge Alberto Rodríguez
Defence, Jorge Domínguez
Economy and Public Works, Roque Fernández
Education and Culture, Susana Decibe
Environment, María Julia Alsogaray
Foreign Affairs, Guido di Tella
Health and Social Welfare, Alberto José Mazza
Interior, Carlos Corach
Justice, Raúl Granillo Ocampo
Labour and Social Security, Antonio Erman González
Secretary-General of the Presidency, Alberto Kohan
Social Development, Ramón Ortega

EMBASSY OF THE ARGENTINE REPUBLIC
65 Brook Street, London WIY IYE
Tel 0171-318 1300
Ambassador Extraordinary and Plenipotentiary, HE Rogelio Pfirter, apptd 1995
Defence Attaché, Capt. Eduardo Rodriguez
Counsellor (Economic and Commercial Affairs), Gustavo Martino

BRITISH EMBASSY
Dr Luis Agote 2141/52, 1425 Buenos Aires
Tel: Buenos Aires 8037 070/1
Ambassador Extraordinary and Plenipotentiary, HE William Marsden, CMG, apptd 1997
Deputy Head of Mission and Minister, Dominic Asquith
Defence and Air Attaché, Gp Capt. D. McDonnell, OBE
Naval and Military Attaché, Col. H. Massey
First Secretary (Commercial), H. Wiles
Cultural Attaché and British Council Representative, M. Potter, OBE, Marcelo T. de Alvear 590, 1058 Buenos Aires
BRITISH CHAMBER OF COMMERCE, Av. Corrientes 457, 10 piso, 1043 Buenos Aires

DEFENCE

The Army has 326 main battle tanks, 646 armoured infantry fighting vehicles and armoured personnel carriers, 40 helicopters and 217 artillery pieces. The Navy has three submarines, six destroyers, seven frigates, 18 patrol and coastal vessels, 30 combat aircraft and 11 armed helicopters. The Air Force has 202 combat aircraft, and 14 armed helicopters.
MILITARY EXPENDITURE – 1.5 per cent of GDP (1996)
MILITARY PERSONNEL – 104,240: Army 41,000, Navy 20,000, Air Force 12,000, Paramilitaries 31,240
CONSCRIPTION DURATION – none

ECONOMY

A large proportion of the land is still held in large estates devoted to cattle raising but the number of small farms is increasing. The principal crops are wheat, maize, oats, barley, rye, linseed, sunflower seed, alfalfa, sugar, fruit and cotton. Argentina is pre-eminent in the production of beef, mutton and wool. There is an oil refinery in San Lorenzo (Santa Fé province). Natural gas is also produced. Coal, lead, zinc, tungsten, iron ore, sulphur, mica and salt are the other chief minerals being exploited. There are small worked deposits of beryllium, manganese, bismuth, uranium, antimony, copper, kaolin, arsenate, gold, silver and tin. Coal is produced at the Rio Turbio mine in the province of Santa Cruz.

Meat-packing is one of the principal industries; flour-milling, sugar-refining, and the wine industry are also important. In recent years progress has been made by the textile, plastic and machine tool industries and engineering, especially in the production of motor vehicles and steel manufactures.

The Menem government introduced an economic reform programme in 1991 involving the privatization of most state-owned industries, widespread deregulation, exchange-rate stabilization and lower trade barriers. This led to economic growth, increased foreign investment and much lower inflation. Economic growth was 8 per cent in 1996–7. The IMF approved a three-year credit of $2.8 billion in March 1998. The peso has been pegged to the US dollar since 1991.

Severe flooding along the Paraná basin in April 1998 is estimated to have cost the country $2.5 billion.
GNP – US$295,131 million (1996); US$8,380 per capita (1996)
GDP – US$190,523 million (1994); US$8,248 per capita (1994)
ANNUAL AVERAGE GROWTH OF GDP – 4.3 per cent (1996)
INFLATION RATE – 0.2 per cent (1996)
UNEMPLOYMENT – 18.8 per cent (1995)
TOTAL EXTERNAL DEBT – US$93,841 million (1996)

TRADE

The chief imports are machinery, industrial and transport equipment, chemicals, metals and plastics. The chief exports are vegetable products, processed foods, minerals, live animals and oils. Argentina's main trading partners are Brazil and the USA.

In 1996 Argentina had a trade surplus of US$1,612 million and a current account deficit of US$4,013 million. In 1996 imports totalled US$23,762 million and exports US$23,811 million.

TRADE WITH UK	1996	1997
Imports from UK	£331,631,000	£487,127,000
Exports to UK	285,487,000	269,864,000

COMMUNICATIONS

The 25,386 miles of railway are state-owned. The combined national and provincial road network totals approximately 137,000 miles of which 23,180 miles are surfaced.

CULTURE AND EDUCATION

The literature of Spain is part of the culture. There is little indigenous literature before the break from Spain, but all branches have flourished since the latter half of the 19th century. About 450 daily newspapers are published in Argentina, including seven major ones in the city of Buenos Aires. The English language newspaper is the *Buenos Aires Herald* (daily).

Education is compulsory for the seven grades of primary school (six to 13). Secondary schools (14 to 17+) are available in and around Buenos Aires and in most of the important towns in the interior of the country. Most secondary schools are administered by the Central Ministry of Education in Buenos Aires, while primary schools are administered by the Central Ministry or by Provincial Ministries of Education. Private schools, of which there are many, are also loosely controlled by the Central Ministry. The total number of universities is over 50 with 24 national, 25 private and a small number of provincial universities.

ILLITERACY RATE – 3.8 per cent

ENROLMENT (percentage of age group) – primary 95 per cent (1991); secondary 59 per cent (1991); tertiary 35.8 per cent (1994)

ARMENIA
Hayastany Hanrapetoutioun

AREA – 11,506 sq. miles (29,800 sq. km). Neighbours: Azerbaijan (east and south-west), Georgia (north), Iran (south) and Turkey (west)

POPULATION – 3,762,000 (1994 UN estimate). Armenians 93.8 per cent, Kurds 1.7 per cent and Russians 1.6 per cent. Azerbaijanis formed 2.6 per cent of the population, but most fled or were expelled after the outbreak of war with Azerbaijan. There are also Ukrainians, Greeks and Assyrians. The Armenian diaspora numbers some 5,300,000. Armenian is the official language, though Russian is widely spoken and understood. The main religion is Armenian Orthodox Christian (Armenian Church centred in Etchmiadzin). Armenia adopted Christianity as its official religion in AD 301, the first state in the world to do so

CAPITAL – Yerevan (population, 1,254,400, 1990)

CURRENCY – Dram of 100 louma

NATIONAL DAY – 21 September (Independence Day)

NATIONAL FLAG – Three horizontal stripes of red, blue and orange

LIFE EXPECTANCY (years) – male 68.66; female 75.51

POPULATION GROWTH RATE – 1.2 per cent (1995)

POPULATION DENSITY – 126 per sq. km (1995)

URBAN POPULATION – 68.5 per cent (1992)

Armenia lies between the Black and Caspian Seas, occupying the south-western part of the Caucasus region of the former Soviet Union. It is very mountainous, consisting of several vast tablelands surrounded by ridges. The climate is continental, dry and cold, but the Ararat valley has a long, hot and dry summer.

HISTORY AND POLITICS

Armenia was first unified in 95 BC but was divided between the Persian and Byzantine Empires in AD 387 and then conquered in the 11th century by the Seljuk Turks and the Mongols. In the 16th century most of Armenia was incorporated into the Ottoman Empire. In 1639 the country was divided again, the easternmost portions, now the republic of Armenia, becoming part of the Persian Empire. In 1828 eastern Armenia became part of the Russian Empire while western Armenia remained under Ottoman rule. The Ottomans launched pogroms against the Armenians from 1894 onwards, and in 1915 to 1918 massacred 1,500,000 Armenians.

Armenia declared its independence on 28 May 1918, but was crushed and divided between Turkish and Soviet forces in 1920, with the area under Soviet control proclaimed a Soviet Socialist Republic on 29 November 1920. The Soviet government was overthrown by a nationalist revolt in 1921 but reinstated by the Red Army a few months later. In early 1922 Armenia acceded to the USSR.

An Armenian nationalist movement swept to power in national elections in mid-1990. In a referendum in 1991, 99 per cent of the electorate voted for independence, which was declared on 21 September 1991.

FOREIGN RELATIONS

The dispute between the (ethnic Armenian) Nagorno-Karabakh forces supported by Armenia and the Azeri government over Nagorny-Karabakh erupted into all-out war in May 1992, when Nagorno-Karabakh forces breached Azerbaijan's defences to form a land bridge to Armenia. By the end of summer 1992 all of Nagorno-Karabakh was under Armenian control, and by the end of 1993 all Azeri territory that separated Nagorno-Karabakh from Armenia and all mountainous Azeri territory around Nagorny-Karabakh was under the control of Nagorny-Karabakh Armenians. Armenia claims this territory as historically Armenian land arbitrarily given to Azerbaijan by Stalin in 1921–2. A cease-fire agreement between Armenia, Azerbaijan and Nagorny-Karabakh was reached in May 1994, and talks mediated by the OSCE continue to seek a peaceful resolution to the dispute.

In August 1997 Armenia and Russia renewed a Treaty of Friendship, Co-operation and Mutual Assistance in effect since 1991.

POLITICAL SYSTEM

In April 1995, a law was passed creating a 190-member National Assembly, to be elected every four years by a combined constituency and party-list system. In the first elections to the new body in July 1995, the ruling Republican coalition led by the Pan-Armenian National Movement won a majority of seats. A new constitution was approved by a referendum in July 1995.

On 3 February 1998, President Levon Ter-Petrossian resigned after 40 deputies withdrew their support for his coalition government, in protest at his policy on Nagorny-Karabakh. Robert Kocharian, the Prime Minister and a former President of Nagorny-Karabakh, was elected to succeed him on 30 March.

Armenia is divided into 11 Administrative Regions.

HEAD OF STATE
President, Robert Kocharian, *sworn in* 9 April 1998

CABINET *as at May 1998*
Prime Minister, Armen Darbinian
Agriculture, Vladimir Movsisian
Communications, Artak Vardanian
Defence, Vazgen Sarkissian
Director of State Taxation Agency, Artashes Toumanian
Director of Statistics, State Register and Analysis Department, Stepan Mnatsakanian
Ecology and Natural Resources, Sargis Shahazizian
Economic Structural Reform, Vahram Avanessian
Education and Science, Levon Mkrtchian
Emergency Situations, Vyacheslav Haroutiounian
Energy, Gagik Martirossian
Finance and Economy, Edward Sandoyan
Foreign Affairs, Vardan Oskanian
Government Chief of Staff, Shahen Karamanoukian
Health, Dr Gagik Stamboltsian
Internal Affairs and National Security, Serge Sarkissian
Justice, David Haroutiounian
Privatization, Pavel Khaltakchian
Social Security, Gagik Yekanian
Trade, Services, Tourism and Industry, Garnik Nanagoulian
Transport, Yervand Zakarian
Urban Planning and Construction, Felix Pirumian

Chairman of the National Assembly, Khosrov Haroutiounian

EMBASSY OF THE REPUBLIC OF ARMENIA
25A Cheniston Gardens, London w8 6TG
Tel 0171-938 5415
Chargé d'Affaires, Nounoufar Sarkassian

BRITISH EMBASSY
28 Charents Street, Yerevan
Tel: Yerevan 151 841/2
Ambassador Extraordinary and Plenipotentiary, HE Dr John
Mitchiner, apptd 1996

DEFENCE

The Army has 102 main battle tanks, 228 armoured
infantry fighting vehicles and armoured personnel carriers, 225 artillery pieces, six combat aircraft and seven
armed helicopters.

Russia maintains 4,300 army personnel in Armenia. An
agreement on military co-operation with Russia was
signed in 1996 which paved the way for joint military
exercises. A protocol was also signed on the establishment
of coalition troops in Transcaucasia and the planned use of
Russian and Armenian armed forces as part of coalition
troops in cases of mutual interest.
MILITARY EXPENDITURE – 5.6 per cent of GDP (1996)
MILITARY PERSONNEL – 59,600: Army 58,600,
Paramilitaries 1,000
CONSCRIPTION DURATION – 18 months

ECONOMY

The Armenian economy has been badly affected by the
Azeri and Turkish economic embargoes which have been
in place since 1988. The main trade and transportation
routes now lie via Georgia and Iran.

Armenia has a strong agricultural sector in low-lying
areas, where industrial and fruit crops are grown. Grain is
grown in the hills and the country is also noted for its wine
and brandy. There are large copper ore and molybdenum
deposits and other minerals. The country also has developed chemicals, industrial vehicles and textiles
industries.

The government introduced a programme of economic
reforms in November 1994 with IMF support, including
the liberalization of prices, stabilization of the currency
and privatization.

In 1996 Armenia had a trade deficit of US$468 million
and a current account deficit of US$319 million.
GNP – US$2,387 million (1996); US$630 per capita (1996)
GDP – US$5,487 million (1994); US$117 per capita (1994)
TOTAL EXTERNAL DEBT – US$552 million (1996)

TRADE WITH UK	1996	1997
Imports from UK	£3,856,000	£7,172,000
Exports to UK	283,000	111,000

CULTURE AND EDUCATION

The Armenian alphabet was established in AD 405. Major
writers include the poets Narekatsi (10th century), Frick
(13th century), Nahapet Kuchak (16th century) and Sayat-
Nova (18th century). The composer Aram Khachaturian
(1903–78) was Armenian.
ILLITERACY RATE – 0.4 per cent
ENROLMENT (percentage of age group) – tertiary 41.8 per
cent (1990)

AUSTRALIA
The Commonwealth of Australia

AREA – 2,988,902 sq. miles (7,741,220 sq. km)
POPULATION – 18,054,000 (1996 estimate): 265,459 (1.6
per cent) of Aboriginal and Torres Strait Islander origin
(1991 census). The language is English
CAPITAL – Canberra, in the Australian Capital Territory
(population, 307,100, 1996 estimate). It has been the seat
of government since 1927
MAJOR CITIES – Adelaide (1,482,900); Brisbane
(1,548,346); Hobart (195,000); Melbourne (3,248,800);
Perth, including Fremantle (1,319,000); Sydney
(3,934,700)
CURRENCY – Australian dollar ($A) of 100 cents
NATIONAL ANTHEM – Advance Australia Fair
NATIONAL DAY – 26 January (Australia Day)
NATIONAL FLAG – The British Blue Ensign with five stars
of the Southern Cross in the fly and the white
Commonwealth Star of seven points beneath the Union
Flag
LIFE EXPECTANCY (years) – male 75.04; female 80.94
POPULATION GROWTH RATE – 1.1 per cent (1995)
POPULATION DENSITY – 2 per sq. km (1995)
URBAN POPULATION – 85.4 per cent (1986)

Australia is a continent in the southern hemisphere. The
highest point is Mt. Kosciusko (2,228 m) and the lowest,
Lake Eyre (–15 m). Climatic conditions range from the
alpine to the tropical. Two-thirds of the continent is arid or
semi-arid although good rainfalls (over 800 mm annually)
occur in the northern monsoonal belt and along the eastern
and southern highland regions.

HISTORY AND POLITICS

Australia was discovered in the 18th century and was
colonized by the British, initially as a penal colony. The
Commonwealth of Australia was inaugurated on 1 January
1901, at which time Australia gained dominion status
within the British Empire. Australia became independent
within the British Commonwealth by the 1931 Statute of
Westminster.

POLITICAL SYSTEM

The government is that of a federal commonwealth within
the Commonwealth, the executive power being vested in
the Sovereign (through the Governor-General), assisted
by a federal government. Under the constitution the
federal government has acquired and may acquire certain
defined powers as surrendered by the states, residuary
legislative power remaining with the states. The right of a
state to legislate on any matter is not abrogated except in
connection with matters exclusively under federal control,
but where a state law is inconsistent with a law of the
Commonwealth the latter prevails to the extent of the
inconsistency.

Parliament consists of Queen Elizabeth II, the Senate
and the House of Representatives. The constitution
provides that the number of members of the House of
Representatives shall be, as nearly as practicable, twice the
number of senators. Members of the Senate are elected for
six years by universal suffrage, half the members retiring
every third year. Each of the six states returns 12 senators,
and the Australian Capital Territory and the Northern
Territory two each. The House of Representatives,
similarly elected for a maximum of three years, contains
members proportionate to the population, with a minimum of five members for each state. There are now 148

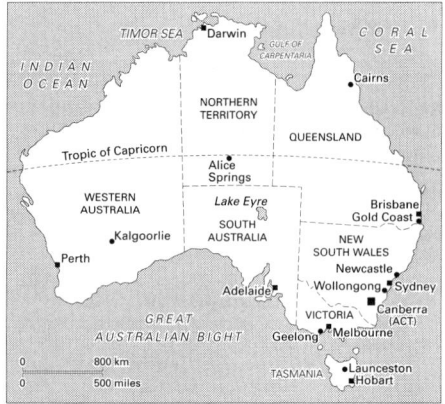

members in the House of Representatives, including one member for the Northern Territory and two for the Australian Capital Territory.

The High Court exercises jurisdiction over all matters arising under the constitution, all matters arising between the states and between residents of different states, matters to which the Commonwealth of Australia is a party, matters arising under any treaty, and matters affecting foreign representatives in Australia. The High Court also hears appeals from the Federal Court and from the Supreme Courts of states and territories.

The Federal Court of Australia has jurisdiction over important industrial, trade practices, intellectual property, administrative law, admiralty law and bankruptcy matters. It also acts as a court of appeal for decisions from the Australian Capital Territory Supreme Court and certain decisions of state Supreme Courts exercising federal jurisdiction. Each state has its own judicature of supreme, superior and minor courts for criminal and civil cases.

On 13 February 1998, the Constitutional Convention voted by 89 votes to 52 to sever constitutional links with the United Kingdom monarchy. A national referendum will be held on the issue in late 1999.

FEDERAL STRUCTURE

In the states, executive authority is vested in a Governor (appointed by the Crown), assisted by a Council of Ministers or Executive Council. Each state has a legislature comprising a Legislative Council and a Legislative Assembly or House of Assembly which are elected for four-year terms, except Queensland, which has a Legislative Assembly only.

Administration of the Northern Territory became a federal responsibility in 1911. Since 1978 Northern Territory ministers have had responsibility for Territory finances and administration.

GOVERNOR-GENERAL

Governor-General, HE Sir William Deane, AC, KBE, *assumed office* 16 February 1996

CABINET *as at June 1998*
Prime Minister, John Howard
Deputy Prime Minister, Trade, Tim Fischer
Attorney-General, Daryl Williams
Communications, Arts, Information Economy, Sen. Richard Alston
Defence, Ian McLachlan
Employment, Education, Training and Youth Affairs, Dr David Kemp
Finance and Administration, John Fahey
Foreign Affairs, Alexander Downer
Health and Family Services, Dr Michael Wooldridge
Industry, Science and Tourism, John Moore
Leader of the Government in the Senate, Environment, Sen. Robert Hill
Leader of the House, Industrial Relations, Peter Reith
Primary Industries and Energy, John Anderson
Social Security, Sen. Jocelyn Newman
Transport and Regional Development, Mark Vaile
Treasurer, Peter Costello

President of the Senate, Sen. Kerry Sibraa
Speaker, House of Representatives, Stephen Martin

AUSTRALIAN HIGH COMMISSION
Australia House, Strand, London WC2B 4LA
Tel 0171-379 4334
High Commissioner, HE Philip Flood, apptd May 1998
Deputy High Commissioner, R. McGovern
Minister-Counsellor, C. J. Walsh *(Industry, Science and Technology)*
Head of Defence Staff, Brig. P. L. McGuiness

NEW SOUTH WALES GOVERNMENT OFFICE, The Australia Centre, Strand, London WC2B 4LG. Tel: 0171-887 5871

STATES AND TERRITORIES

	Area (sq. km)	Resident population 31 December 1997p	Capital	Governor	Premier
Australian Capital Territory (ACT)	2,400	309,000	Canberra	—	—
New South Wales (NSW)	801,600	6,306,300	Sydney	HE Gordon Samuels, AC	Bob Carr
Northern Territory (NT)	1,346,200	189,200	Darwin*	Dr Neil Conn†	Shane Stone‡
Queensland (Qld)	1,727,200	3,430,400	Brisbane	HE Maj.-Gen. Peter Arnison, AO	Peter Beattie
South Australia (SA)	984,000	1,482,900	Adelaide	HE Sir Eric Neal, AC, CVO	John Olsen
Tasmania (Tas.)	67,800	471,800	Hobart	HE Sir Guy Greene, AC, KBE	Tony Rundle
Victoria (Vic.)	227,600	4,627,300	Melbourne	HE James Gobbo	Jeff Kennett
Western Australia (WA)	2,525,500	1,811,100	Perth	HE Maj.-Gen. Philip Jeffery, AO, MC	Richard Court

p preliminary
* Seat of administration
† Administrator
‡ Chief Minister

AGENT-GENERAL FOR QUEENSLAND, 392 Strand, London WC2R OLZ. Tel: 0171-836 1333. *Agent-General*, D. A. McManus
AGENT-GENERAL FOR SOUTH AUSTRALIA, 115 Strand, London WC2R OAJ. *Agent-General*, G. Walls
AGENT-GENERAL FOR VICTORIA, Victoria House, Melbourne Place, Strand, London WC2B 4LG. *Agent-General*, Alan J. Brown
AGENT-GENERAL FOR WESTERN AUSTRALIA, Australia Centre, Strand, London WC2B 4LG. *Agent-General*, C. E. Griffiths

BRITISH HIGH COMMISSION
Commonwealth Avenue, Yarralumla, Canberra, ACT 2600
Tel: Canberra 270 6666
High Commissioner, HE Alexander Allan, apptd 1997
Deputy High Commissioner, A. J. Pocock
First Secretary, B. J. Davidson *(Economic and Agricultural)*
Defence and Naval Adviser and Head of British Defence Liaison Staff, Cdre A. J. Lyall, MBE
Consuls-General, S. J. Hiscock (*Brisbane*); G. Finlayson (*Melbourne*); M. J. Horne (*Perth*); P. Morrice (*Sydney*)
Cultural Adviser and British Council Representative, J. Potts, OBE, Edgecliff Centre, 401/203 New South Head Road (PO Box 88), Edgecliff, Sydney, NSW 2027

DEFENCE

The Army has 71 main battle tanks, 620 armoured personnel carriers and armoured infantry fighting vehicles, 385 artillery pieces, four aircraft and 128 armed helicopters. The Navy has three submarines, three destroyers, seven frigates, 15 patrol and coastal vessels and 16 armed helicopters. There are bases at Sydney, Garden Island, Cairns and Darwin. The Air Force has 126 combat aircraft.

MILITARY EXPENDITURE – 2.2 per cent of GDP (1996)
MILITARY PERSONNEL – 57,400: Army 25,400, Navy 14,300, Air Force 17,700

ECONOMY

The wide range of climatic and soil conditions has resulted in a diversity of crops. Generally, cereal crops (excluding rice and sorghum) are widely grown, while other crops are confined to specific locations in a few states. However, scant or erratic rainfall, limited potential for irrigation and unsuitable soils or topography have restricted intensive agriculture.

Significant mineral resources include bauxite, coal, copper, crude petroleum, gems, gold, ilmenite, iron ore, lead, limestone, manganese, nickel, rutile, salt, silver, tin, tungsten, uranium, zinc and zircon. In 1995–6 248,773,000 tonnes of coal, 30,763 million litres of crude oil, 19,169 billion litres of natural gas, 137,267,000 tonnes of iron ore, 774,000 tonnes of lead, and 291,965 kilograms of gold were produced.

GNP – US$367,802 million (1996); US$20,090 per capita (1996)
GDP – US$335,527 million (1994); US$18,561 per capita (1994)
ANNUAL AVERAGE GROWTH OF GDP – 4.0 per cent (1996)
INFLATION RATE – 2.6 per cent (1996)
UNEMPLOYMENT – 8.5 per cent (1995)

TRADE

In 1996–7 the main exports were coal and gas (12.5 per cent); aluminium and aluminium oxide (6.3 per cent); iron, iron ore and steel (6.1 per cent); gold (6 per cent); wheat (5.5 per cent); petroleum oils and products (4.8 per cent). The major imports are motor vehicles and parts (10.1 per cent); computer technology (7.2 per cent); petroleum oils (6.1 per cent); telecommunications equipment (3.1 per cent); aircraft and spacecraft (2.3 per cent).

Australia's main trading partners are Japan, the USA, New Zealand, China, Korea, Germany and the UK.

In 1996 Australia had a trade deficit of US$726 million and a current account deficit of US$15,371 million. In 1996 imports totalled US$65,427 million and exports US$60,535 million.

Trade with UK	1996	1997
Imports from UK	£2,465,635,000	£2,454,988,000
Exports to UK	1,296,021,000	1,371,268,000

COMMUNICATIONS

There are six government-owned railway systems, operated by the State Rail Authority of NSW, Victorian Railways, Queensland Government Railways, Western Australian Government Railways, the State Transport Authority of Southern Australia, and the Australian National Railways Commission (ANRC). The ANRC incorporates the former Commonwealth Railways system, and the Tasmanian and non-metropolitan South Australian railways (urban rail services in Southern Australia remain the responsibility of the State Transport Authority).

The Northern Territory has three main ports: Darwin, and the private mining ports of Gove and Groote Eylandt. Most freight in the Territory is moved by road trains. These are massive trucks hauling two or three trailers, having a net capacity of about 100 tonnes and measuring up to 45 metres in length.

EDUCATION

Education is administered by the state governments and is compulsory between the ages of five or six and 15 years. It is available at government schools controlled by the state education department and at private or independent schools, some of which are denominational. Tertiary education is available through universities, and technical and further education colleges. New South Wales has ten universities, South Australia three, the University of Tasmania in Tasmania, Victoria nine and Western Australia four.

ENROLMENT (percentage of age group) – primary 98 per cent (1995); secondary 89 per cent (1995); tertiary 71.7 per cent (1995)

EXTERNAL TERRITORIES

ASHMORE AND CARTIER ISLANDS

Ashmore Islands (known as Middle, East and West Islands) and Cartier Island are situated in the Indian Ocean 850 km and 790 km west of Darwin respectively. The islands are uninhabited. The territory has been administered by the Australian Government since 1933.

THE AUSTRALIAN ANTARCTIC TERRITORY

The Australian Antarctic Territory was established in 1933 and comprises all the islands and territories, other than Adélie Land, which are situated south of the latitude 60° S. and lying between 160° E. longitude and 45° E. longitude. The territory is administered by the Antarctic Division of the Department of the Environment. There are nine scientific research stations.

CHRISTMAS ISLAND

AREA – 52 sq. miles (135 sq. km)

POPULATION – 1,906 (1996 census)

Christmas Island is situated in the Indian Ocean about 1,408 km NW of North West Cape in Western Australia. The island became an Australian territory in 1958. The Administrator is responsible to the Australian Minister for Regional Development, Territories and Local Government in Canberra. The Shire of Christmas Island (SOCI) has nine elected members. SOCI is responsible for municipal functions and services on the island.

Administrator, R. G. Harvey, CVO

COCOS (KEELING) ISLANDS

AREA – 5.4 sq. miles (14 sq. km)
POPULATION – 655 (1996 census)

The Cocos (Keeling) Islands are two separate atolls (North Keeling Island and, 24 km to the south, the main atoll) comprising some 27 small coral islands, situated in the Indian Ocean. The main islands of the southern atoll are West Island (about 9 km in length); Home Island, where the Cocos Malay community lives; Direction Island, Horsburgh and South Island.

The islands were declared a British possession in 1857. All land in the islands was granted to George Clunies-Ross and his heirs by Queen Victoria in 1886. In 1978 the Australian Government purchased all Clunies-Ross land and property interests except for the family home and grounds; the last of the remaining grounds were purchased in 1993. Between 1979 and 1984 most of the land was transferred to the Cocos (Keeling) Islands Council, the local government body established in 1979 which was replaced by the Shire of the Cocos (Keeling) Islands in July 1992.

On 6 April 1984 the Cocos community, in a UN-supervised Act of Self-Determination, chose to integrate with Australia. The islands are administered by the Australian Government through the Department of Transport and Regional Development in Canberra.

Administrator, R. G. Harvey, CVO (*acting*)

CORAL SEA ISLANDS TERRITORY

The Coral Sea Islands Territory lies east of Queensland between the Great Barrier Reef and longitude 156° 06′ E., and between latitudes 12° and 24° S. It comprises scattered islands, spread over a sea area of 780,000 sq. km. The islands are formed mainly of coral and sand, and most are extremely small. There is a manned meteorological station in the Willis Group but the remaining islands are uninhabited.

The territory is administered through the Department of Transport and Regional Development in Canberra.

HEARD ISLAND AND McDONALD ISLANDS

The Heard and McDonald islands, about 4,100 km south-west of Perth, comprise all the islands and rocks lying between 52° 30′ and 53° 30′ S. latitude and 72° and 74° 30′ E. longitude. The islands are administered by the Antarctic Division of the Department of the Environment.

NORFOLK ISLAND

AREA – 13.3 sq. miles (34.5 sq. km)
POPULATION – 1,772 (1996 census)
SEAT OF GOVERNMENT – Kingston

Norfolk Island is situated in the South Pacific Ocean. It is about 8 km long by 5 km wide. The climate is mild and subtropical.

The island, discovered by Captain Cook in 1774, served as a penal colony from 1788 to 1814 and 1825 to 1855. In 1856, 194 descendants of the *Bounty* mutineers accepted an invitation to leave Pitcairn and settle on Norfolk Island. Since 1914 Norfolk Island has been regarded as an integral part of Australia.

In 1979 Norfolk Island gained a substantial degree of self-government. Wide powers are exercised by a nine-member Legislative Assembly. The Administrator is responsible to the Australian Minister for Regional Development, Territories and Local Government.

Administrator, A. J. Messner

AUSTRIA
Republik Österreich

AREA – 32,378 sq. miles (83,859 sq. km). Neighbours: the Czech Republic and Slovakia (north), Italy and Slovenia (south) Hungary (east), Germany (north-west), Switzerland and Liechtenstein (west)
POPULATION – 8,053,000 (1995 estimate); 7,813,000 (1991 census). The language is German, but the rights of the Slovene- and Croat-speaking minorities in Carinthia, Styria and Burgenland are protected. The predominant religion is Roman Catholicism
CAPITAL – Vienna, on the Danube (population, 1,806,737, 1995 estimate)
MAJOR CITIES – Graz (237,810); Innsbruck (118,112); Klagenfurt (89,415); Linz (203,044); Salzburg (143,978)
CURRENCY – Schilling of 100 Groschen
NATIONAL ANTHEM – Land der Berge, Land am Strome (Land of mountains, land on the river)
NATIONAL DAY – 26 October
NATIONAL FLAG – Three equal horizontal stripes of red, white, red
LIFE EXPECTANCY (years) – male 73.34; female 79.73
POPULATION GROWTH RATE – 0.8 per cent (1995)
POPULATION DENSITY – 96 per sq. km (1995)
URBAN POPULATION – 64.6 per cent (1991)

HISTORY AND POLITICS

The Republic of Austria was established in 1918 on the break-up of the Austro-Hungarian Empire. In March 1938 Austria was incorporated into Nazi Germany under the name *Ostmark*. After the liberation of Vienna in 1945, the Republic of Austria was reconstituted within the 1937 frontiers and a freely-elected government took office in December 1945. The country was divided into four zones occupied respectively by the UK, USA, USSR and France, while Vienna was jointly occupied by the four Powers. In 1955 the Austrian State Treaty was signed by the foreign ministers of the four Powers and of Austria. This treaty recognized the re-establishment of Austria as a sovereign, independent and democratic state, having the same frontiers as on 1 January 1938. Austria acceded to the European Union on 1 January 1995.

After the general election of 17 December 1995 the Social Democrats and the People's Party formed a coalition government.

POLITICAL SYSTEM

There is a bicameral national assembly; the lower house (*Nationalrat*) has 183 members and the upper house (*Bundesrat*) has 64 members. There is a 4 per cent qualification for parliamentary representation.

FEDERAL STRUCTURE

There are nine provinces:

Provinces	Area (sq. km)	Population	Capital
Burgenland	3,965	274,334	Eisenstadt
Carinthia	9,533	560,994	Klagenfurt
Lower Austria	19,174	1,518,254	St Pölten
Salzburg	7,154	506,850	Salzburg
Styria	16,388	1,206,317	Graz
Tirol	12,648	658,312	Innsbruck
Upper Austria	11,980	1,385,769	Linz
Vienna	415	1,592,596	Vienna
Vorarlberg	2,601	343,109	Bregenz

HEAD OF STATE

President of the Republic of Austria, Dr Thomas Klestil, *took office* 8 July 1992, *re-elected* 19 April 1998

CABINET *as at June 1998*

Chancellor, Viktor Klima (SPÖ)
Vice Chancellor, Foreign Affairs, Wolfgang Schüssel (ÖVP)
Agriculture and Forestry, Wilhelm Molterer (ÖVP)
Defence, Werner Fasslabend (ÖVP)
Economic Affairs, Johann Farnleitner (ÖVP)
Education and Cultural Affairs, Elisabeth Gehrer (ÖVP)
Environment, Youth and Family, Martin Bartenstein (ÖVP)
Finance, Rudolf Edlinger (SPÖ)
Interior, Karl Schlögl (SPÖ)
Justice, Nikolaus Michalek (Ind.)
Labour, Health and Social Affairs, Eleonore Hostasch (SPÖ)
Science and Transport, Caspar Einem (SPÖ)
Women's Affairs and Consumer Protection, Barbara Prammer (SPÖ)

SPÖ Social Democratic Party; ÖVP People's Party; Ind. Independent

AUSTRIAN EMBASSY

18 Belgrave Mews West, London SW1X 8HU
Tel 0171–235 3731
Ambassador Extraordinary and Plenipotentiary, Eva Nowotny, apptd 1997
Minister, Dr Herbert Krauss
Defence Attaché, Brig. H. Rüdiger Sulzgruber
Consul-General, Hella Naumann
Commercial Counsellor and Trade Commissioner, Dr Rudolf Engel

BRITISH EMBASSY

Jaurèsgasse 12, 1030 Vienna
Tel: Vienna 716130
Ambassador Extraordinary and Plenipotentiary, HE Sir Anthony Figgis, KCVO, CMG, apptd 1996
Deputy Head of Mission, Counsellor and Consul-General, I. Cliffe, OBE
Defence Attaché, Lt.-Col. A. Manton
First Secretary (Economic), W. Brandon

BRITISH CONSULAR OFFICES – There is a consular office at Vienna, and Honorary Consulates at Bregenz, Graz, Innsbruck and Salzburg.

BRITISH COUNCIL REPRESENTATIVE, M. Evans, Schenkenstrasse 4, A–1010 Vienna

DEFENCE

The Army has 169 main battle tanks, 533 armoured personnel carriers and 176 artillery pieces. The Air Force has 53 combat aircraft.

Women were permitted to join the army for the first time in February 1998.

MILITARY EXPENDITURE – 0.9 per cent of GDP (1996)
MILITARY PERSONNEL – 49,750: Army 45,500, Air Force 4,250
CONSCRIPTION DURATION – Seven to eight months plus refresher training

ECONOMY

Austria produces wheat, rye, barley, oats, maize, potatoes, sugar beet and turnips. Timber forms a valuable source of Austria's indigenous wealth, about 47 per cent of the total land area consisting of forest areas. Foreign exchange receipts from tourism were a major contribution to the balance of payments.

In 1996 Austria had a current account deficit of US$4,202 million and a trade deficit of US$4,722 million.
GNP – US$226,510 million (1996); US$28,110 per capita (1996)
GDP – US$170,558 million (1994); US$24,823 per capita (1994)
ANNUAL AVERAGE GROWTH OF GDP – 1.8 per cent (1995)
INFLATION RATE – 1.8 per cent (1996)
UNEMPLOYMENT – 4.5 per cent (1995)

TRADE

Main exports are processed goods (iron and steel, other metal goods, textiles, paper and cardboard products), machinery and transport equipment, other finished goods (including clothing), raw materials, chemical products and foodstuffs. Main imports are machinery and transport equipment, processed goods, chemical products, foodstuffs, fuel and energy. Austria's main trading partners are Germany, Italy, France and Switzerland.

In 1995, imports totalled US$66,263 million, and exports US$57,532 million.

Trade with UK	1996	1997
Imports from UK	£1,209,400,000	£1,329,000,000
Exports to UK	1,082,100,000	1,082,600,000

COMMUNICATIONS

Internal communications are partly restricted because of the mountainous nature of the country, although there is now a network of 1,567 km of *Autobahn* between major cities which also links up with the German and Italian networks. The railways are state-owned and in 1993 had 5,605 km of track, 58.8 per cent of which is electrified. Of the 425 km of waterways, 350 km are navigable and there is considerable trade through the Danube ports by both local and foreign shipping. There are six commercial airports catering for 5,527,600 passengers in 1995.

There are four national radio and two national television channels, together with three national and twelve regional newspapers.

EDUCATION

Education is free and compulsory between the ages of six and 15 and there are good facilities for secondary, technical and professional education. There are 12 state-maintained universities and six colleges of art.
ENROLMENT (percentage of age group) – primary 100 per cent (1994); secondary 90 per cent (1994); tertiary 44.8 per cent (1994)

AZERBAIJAN
Azarbaijchan Respublikasy

AREA – 33,436 sq. miles (86,600 sq. km). Neighbours: Iran (south), Armenia (west) and Georgia and Russia (north)
POPULATION – 7,499,000 (1996 estimate): 83 per cent Azeri, 6 per cent Russian and 6 per cent Armenian. There are also Kurds, Jews, Georgians and Turks. There are more Azeris in Iran than in Azerbaijan. The population is predominantly Shia Muslim although it was heavily secularized during the Soviet era. The language is Azeri
CAPITAL – ΨBaku (population, 1,149,000, 1990)
CURRENCY – Manat of 100 gopik
NATIONAL DAY – 28 May (Independence Day)
NATIONAL FLAG – Three horizontal stripes of blue, red and green with a white crescent and eight-pointed star in the centre
LIFE EXPECTANCY (years) – male 66.60; female 74.20
POPULATION GROWTH RATE – 0.9 per cent (1995)
POPULATION DENSITY – 87 per sq. km (1995)
URBAN POPULATION – 54.2 per cent (1989)

Azerbaijan occupies the eastern part of the Caucasus region of the former Soviet Union, on the shore of the Caspian Sea. The north-eastern part of the republic is taken up by the south-eastern end of the main Caucasus ridge, its south-western part by the smaller Caucasus hills, and its south-eastern corner by the spurs of the Talysh Ridge. Its central part is a depression irrigated by the River Kura and the lower reaches of its tributary the Araks. Azerbaijan has a continental climate.

Azerbaijan has 64 administrative districts and also includes the Nakhichevan Autonomous Republic, which is geographically separated from the rest of Azerbaijan by Armenia and borders on Iran and Turkey, and the Nagorno-Karabakh Autonomous Province.

HISTORY AND POLITICS

The territory that is now Azerbaijan was successively part of the Assyrian, Persian, Median and Greek empires. With the influx of Huns and Khazars in the first century BC, the Turkic Azerbaijani people evolved and formed an independent state. This was invaded by the Arab Caliphates in the seventh century AD and under their 300-year rule Islam was introduced and became the dominant religion. In the 16th century Azerbaijan was again invaded by Persia and became a Persian province. The country was divided during the Russo-Persian wars of the early 19th century, the northern portion (the present-day Azerbaijan) becoming part of the Russian Empire and the southern portion remaining Persian and subsequently Iranian.

In 1918 the Azerbaijan Democratic Republic was established. It was overthrown by Communists in 1918 and Azerbaijan acceded to the USSR in 1922.

In January 1990, the Azerbaijani Popular Front took power from the local Communist Party and declared independence from the Soviet Union. Soviet troops overthrew the Popular Front and restored the Communist regime under President Ayaz Mutalibov. This government declared Azerbaijan's independence in August 1991. Mutalibov won the presidential election held in September 1991, but widespread civil unrest forced him to resign. At the presidential election in June 1992 the Popular Front leader Abulfaz Elchibey was elected.

Popular discontent at military defeats caused Elchibey to flee Baku in June 1993 and the former Azerbaijani Communist Party First Secretary Heydar Aliyev took over

the presidency. The new regime was confirmed in office in a referendum in August and Aliyev won the presidential election in October 1993.

In November 1995, elections were held to the *Milli Majlis* (parliament), which had been increased to 125 seats: 100 directly elected and 25 allocated by proportional representation. The New Azerbaijan party, founded by Aliyev, won 70 per cent of the vote and a majority of seats.

SECESSION

In 1988 fighting broke out in the predominantly Armenian-populated region of Nagorny-Karabakh between Soviet Azerbaijani forces and ethnic Armenians demanding unification with Armenia. In late 1993 Nagorno-Karabakh forces captured all of the region, together with all Azeri territory separating the region from Armenia (20 per cent of Azeri territory). Azeri forces pushed back the Nagorno-Karabakh forces in early 1994 before a cease-fire agreement was signed in May 1994. Between 500,000 and one million Azeris have been displaced by the fighting, which briefly flared up again along the Azeri-Armenian border in April and May 1997. Peace talks, held under the auspices of the OSCE, have yet to yield any significant results, although both sides reaffirmed their commitment to finding a peaceful solution at a meeting in October 1997, in which both sides rejected the idea of full independence for Nagorny-Karabakh as 'unrealistic'.

POLITICAL SYSTEM

A new constitution was approved by a referendum in November 1995, which created a presidential republic with executive power to be exercised by the president and with legislative power vested in the *Milli Majlis*.

HEAD OF STATE
President, Heydar Aliyev, *assumed office* 18 June 1993, *elected* 3 October 1993

GOVERNMENT *as at June 1998*
Prime Minister, Artur Rasizade
First Deputy Prime Minister, Abbas Abbasov
Deputy Prime Ministers, Tofig Azizov; Elchin Efendiyev; Rafik Khalafov; Izzet Rustamov; Abid Sharifov
Agriculture, Irshad Aliyev
Communications, Nadyr Akhmadov
Culture, Polad Byulbyulogly
Defence, Lt.-Gen. Safar Abiyev
Economy, Namik Nasrullayev
Education (acting), Ahmed Abdinov
Finance, Fikret Yusifov
Foreign Affairs, Tofik Zulfugarov
Health, Ali Insanov
Interior, Ramil Usubov
Justice, Sudaba Hasanova
Labour and Social Protection of the Population, Ali Nagiyev
Media and Information, Siruz Tebrizli
National Security, Namig Abbasov
Trade, Farkhad Aliyev
Youth and Sports, Abulfaz Garaev

AZERBAIJANI EMBASSY
4 Kensington Court, London W8 5DL
Tel 0171-938 3412
Ambassador Extraordinary and Plenipotentiary, HE Mahmud Mamed-Kuliyev, apptd 1994

BRITISH EMBASSY
2 Izmir Street, Baku 370065
Tel: Baku 985558
Ambassador Extraordinary and Plenipotentiary, HE David R. Thomas, apptd 1997

DEFENCE

The Army has 270 main battle tanks, 287 armoured infantry fighting vehicles, 270 armoured personnel carriers and 301 artillery pieces. The Navy is based at Baku, with a share of the former Soviet Caspian Fleet Flotilla, comprising two frigates and 18 patrol and coastal vessels. The Air Force has 36 combat aircraft and 15 attack helicopters.

MILITARY EXPENDITURE – 5.3 per cent of GDP (1996)
MILITARY PERSONNEL – 106,700: Army 53,300, Navy 2,200, Air Force 11,200, Paramilitaries 40,000
CONSCRIPTION DURATION – 17 months

ECONOMY

Azerbaijan was heavily industrialized as part of the Russian Empire. Industry is dominated by oil and natural gas extraction and related industries centred on Baku and Sumgait and the large oil deposits in the Caspian Sea, estimated at more than 6,000 million barrels. Five contracts to explore and exploit oilfields in the Caspian Sea have been signed since 1994.

The republic is also rich in mineral resources, with iron, copper, lead and salt, and is important as a cotton-growing area and a silkworm-breeding area.

The Azeri economy was devastated by the war although it is now showing signs of recovery. There was a 67 per cent growth in investment activity in 1997.

GNP – US$3,642 million (1996); US$480 per capita (1996)
GDP – US$10,148 million (1994); US$176 per capita (1994)
TOTAL EXTERNAL DEBT – US$435 million (1996)

TRADE WITH UK	1996	1997
Imports from UK	£30,145,000	£55,728,000
Exports to UK	2,238,000	10,088,000

CULTURE AND EDUCATION

Azerbaijan was the birthplace of the prophet Zoroaster, who founded one of the first monotheistic religions in the world. The country has witnessed a succession of three religions: Zoroastrianism, Christianity and Islam.

Azeri is one of the Turkic languages. Previously written in the Russian script, Azeri in the Latin script was adopted as the official language in December 1992. In the 18th and 19th centuries Azerbaijani literature produced the poets and dramatists Vagif, Vazekhi, Zakir, Akhundov and Vezirov.

ILLITERACY RATE – 0.4 per cent
ENROLMENT (percentage of age group) – tertiary 19.8 per cent (1993)

THE BAHAMAS
The Commonwealth of The Bahamas

AREA – 5,358 sq. miles (13,878 sq. km)
POPULATION – 278,000 (1996 estimate). The language is English
CAPITAL – ΨNassau (population, 172,196, 1996 estimate)
CURRENCY – Bahamian dollar (B$) of 100 cents
NATIONAL ANTHEM – March on, Bahamaland
NATIONAL DAY – 10 July (Independence Day)
NATIONAL FLAG – Horizontal stripes of aquamarine, gold and aquamarine, with a black equilateral triangle on the hoist
LIFE EXPECTANCY (years) – male 68.32; female 75.28
POPULATION GROWTH RATE – 1.7 per cent (1995)

POPULATION DENSITY – 20 per sq. km (1995)
URBAN POPULATION – 83.5 per cent (1990)

The Bahamas extend from the coast of Florida on the north-west almost to Haiti on the south-east. The group consists of 700 islands, of which 30 are inhabited, and 2,400 cays. The principal islands include: Abaco, Acklins, Andros, Berry Islands, Bimini, Cat Island, Crooked Island, Eleuthera, Exuma, Grand Bahama, Harbour Island, Inagua, Long Island, Mayaguana, New Providence (on which is located the capital, Nassau), Ragged Island, Rum Cay, San Salvador and Spanish Wells. San Salvador was the first landfall in the New World of Christopher Columbus on 12 October 1492.

HISTORY AND POLITICS

The Bahamas were settled by the British and became a Crown colony in 1717. Taken over in 1782 by the Spanish, the Treaty of Versailles in 1783 restored them to the British. The Bahamas gained independence on 10 July 1973.

A general election held in March 1997 was won by the Free National Movement which defeated the Progressive Liberal Party. The Free National Movement hold 35 seats in the House of Assembly and the Progressive Liberal Party six seats.

POLITICAL SYSTEM

The head of state is Queen Elizabeth II who is represented in the islands by a Governor-General. There is an appointed Senate of 16 members and an elected House of Assembly of 40 members.

Governor-General, HE Sir Orville Turnquest, GCMG, QC, apptd 1994

CABINET *as at May 1998*

Prime Minister, Hubert Ingraham
Deputy Prime Minister, National Security, Frank Watson
Agriculture and Fisheries, Earl Deveaux
Attorney-General, Justice, Tennyson Wells
Consumer Welfare and Aviation, Pierre Dupuch
Education, Dame Ivy Dumont, DCMG
Finance and Planning, William Allen
Foreign Affairs, Janet Bostwick
Health and Environment, Ronald Knowles
Labour, Immigration and Training, Theresa Moxey-Ingraham
Public Works, Orville Turnquest
Social Development and Housing, Algernon Allen
Tourism, Cornelius Smith
Transport, James Knowles

President of the Court of Appeal, Sir Joaquim Gonsalves-Sabola, KCMG
Chief Justice, Dame Joan Sawyer

BAHAMAS HIGH COMMISSION
Bahamas House, 10 Chesterfield Street, London W1X 8AH
Tel 0171-408 4488
High Commissioner, HE Arthur A. Foulkes, apptd 1992

BRITISH HIGH COMMISSION
PO Box N-7516, Nassau
Tel: Nassau 325 7471
High Commissioner, HE Peter Young, MBE, apptd 1996

DEFENCE

The Navy has seven patrol and coastal vessels, six harbour patrol units and two light aircraft.

Military Expenditure – 0.5 per cent of GDP (1996)
Military Personnel – 860: Navy

ECONOMY

Tourism employs about half of the labour force and provides about half of government revenue and about half the country's foreign exchange earnings. International banking and trust business is also important. The absence of direct taxation coupled with internal stability have enabled the country to become one of the world's leading offshore financial centres. In February 1998, Finance Minister William Allen announced that regulations were in place for the establishment of a stock exchange, which is scheduled to start operating by the end of 1998.

Agricultural production is mainly of fresh vegetables, fruit, meat and eggs for the domestic market, and crawfish, mostly for export. Reserves of aragonite, limestone and salt are being commercially exploited. Freeport is the country's leading industrial centre, with a pharmaceutical and chemicals plant, an oil trans-shipment and storage terminal, and port and bunkering facilities. There are also a brewery and a rum distillery on New Providence.

GNP – US$3,297 million (1995); US$11,940 per capita (1995)
GDP – US$3,229 million (1994); US$12,342 per capita (1994)
Annual Average Growth of GDP – 4.9 per cent (1987)
Inflation Rate – 1.4 per cent (1996)
Unemployment – 13.3 per cent (1994)

Trade

The imports are chiefly foodstuffs, manufactured articles, building materials, vehicles and machinery, chemicals and petroleum. The chief exports are rum, petroleum, hormones, salt, crawfish and aragonite.

In 1996 the Bahamas had a trade deficit of US$990 million and a current account deficit of US$187 million.

Trade with UK	1996	1997
Imports from UK	£18,825,000	£19,110,000
Exports to UK	62,769,000	56,850,000

COMMUNICATIONS

The main ports are Nassau (New Providence), Freeport (Grand Bahama) and Matthew Town (Inagua). International air services are operated from Abaco, Bimini, Eleuthera, Exuma, Grand Bahama and New Providence. About 50 smaller airports and landing strips facilitate services between the islands, the services being mainly provided by Bahamasair, the national carrier. There are roads on the larger islands, and roads are under construction on the smaller islands. There are no railways.

EDUCATION

Education is compulsory between the ages of five and 16. More than 60,000 students are enrolled in Ministry of Education and independent schools in New Providence and the Family Islands.
Illiteracy Rate – 1.8 per cent
Enrolment (percentage of age group) – primary 95 per cent (1993); secondary 87 per cent (1993); tertiary 17.7 per cent (1985)

BAHRAIN
Dawlet al-Bahrein

Area – 268 sq. miles (694 sq. km)
Population – 586,000 (1994 UN estimate); about 70 per cent are Bahraini; about 40 per cent of the Bahrainis are Sunni Muslims, the remaining 60 per cent being Shias; the ruling family and many of the most prominent merchants are Sunnis. The official language is Arabic; English is often used for business, and Farsi, Hindi and Urdu are also spoken
Capital – ΨManama (population, 140,401, 1991 census)
Currency – Bahraini dinar (BD) of 1,000 fils
National Day – 16 December
National Flag – Red, with vertical serrated white bar next to staff
Life Expectancy (years) – male 66.83; female 69.43
Population Growth Rate – 3.1 per cent (1995)
Population Density – 844 per sq. km (1995)
Urban Population – 88.4 per cent (1991)
Illiteracy Rate – 14.8 per cent
Enrolment (percentage of age group) – primary 100 per cent (1995); secondary 85 per cent (1994); tertiary 20.2 per cent (1993)

Bahrain consists of a group of low-lying islands situated about half-way down the Gulf, some 20 miles off the east coast of Saudi Arabia. The largest of these, Bahrain Island, is about 30 miles long and 10 miles wide at its broadest, with the capital, Manama, situated on the north shore. The second largest, Muharraq, with the town and Bahrain International Airport, is connected to Manama by a causeway 1½ miles long.

Insurgencies

Since 1994 Shi'ite protestors demanding the re-establishment of the National Assembly have regularly clashed with security forces and Shi'ite leaders have been detained. Opponents of the government have engaged in a sustained bombing campaign.

Political System

Bahrain is a constitutional monarchy and has been fully independent since 1971, when British protectorate status was ended. The 1973 constitution provides for a National Assembly but this was dissolved in 1975. A 40-member Consultative Council was appointed in September 1996; it is an advisory body with no legislative powers.

Head of State

HH The Amir of Bahrain, Shaikh Isa bin Sulman al-Khalifa, GCMG, *born* 1932; *acceded* 16 December 1961
Crown Prince (and C.-in-C., Bahrain Defence Force), HE Shaikh Hamad bin Isa al-Khalifa, KCMG

Cabinet *as at May 1998*

Prime Minister, HH Shaikh Khalifa bin Sulman al-Khalifa
Agriculture and Public Works, HE Majid Jawad Al-Jishi
Amiri Court Affairs, HH Shaikh Ali bin Isa bin Sulman Al-Khalifa
Cabinet Affairs and Information, HE Mohammed Ibrahim al-Mutawwa
Commerce, HE Ali Saleh Abdullah al-Saleh
Consultative Council President, Ibrahim Mohammed Humaidan
Defence, HE Maj.-Gen. Shaikh Khalifa bin Ahmed Al-Khalifa
Education, HE Brig.-Gen. Abdul-Aziz Mohammed al-Fadhil

Finance and National Economy, HE Ibrahim Abdul-Karim Mohammed
Foreign Affairs, HE Shaikh Mohammed bin Mubarak Al-Khalifa
Health, HE Faisal Radhi al-Mousawi
Housing, Municipalities, Shaikh Khalid bin Abdullah Al-Khalifa
Interior, HE Shaikh Mohammed bin Khalifa Al-Khalifa
Justice and Islamic Affairs, HE Shaikh Abdullah bin Khalid Al-Khalifa
Labour and Social Affairs, HE Abdul-Nabi al-Shula
Minister of State, HE Jawad Salim al-Arrayed
Oil and Industry, HE Shaikh Isa bin Ali bin Hamad Al-Khalifa
Power and Water, Abdulla Mohammed Juma
Transport, Civil Aviation, HH Shaikh Ali bin Khalifa bin Sulman Al-Khalifa

EMBASSY OF THE STATE OF BAHRAIN
98 Gloucester Road, London SW7 4AU
Tel 0171-370 5132
Ambassador Extraordinary and Plenipotentiary, HE Shaikh Abdul-Aziz bin Mubarak Al-Khalifa, apptd 1996

BRITISH EMBASSY
21 Government Avenue, Manama 306, PO Box 114
Tel: Manama 534404
Ambassador Extraordinary and Plenipotentiary, HE Ian Lewty, apptd 1996

BRITISH COUNCIL REPRESENTATIVE, J. Shorter, AMA Centre, PO Box 452, Manama 356

DEFENCE

The Army has 106 main battle tanks, 340 armoured personnel carriers and 49 artillery pieces. The Navy, based at Mina Sulman, has one frigate and 12 patrol and coastal vessels. The Air Force has 24 combat aircraft and 24 armed helicopters.
MILITARY EXPENDITURE – 5.6 per cent of GDP (1996)
MILITARY PERSONNEL – 20,850: Army 8,500, Navy 1,000, Air Force 1,500, Paramilitaries 9,850

ECONOMY

The largest sources of revenue are oil production and refining. The Bahrain field, discovered in 1932, is wholly owned by the Bahrain National Oil Co. The Sitra refinery derives about 70 per cent of its crude oil by submarine pipeline from Saudi Arabia. Bahrain also has a half share with Saudi Arabia in the profits of the offshore Abu Sa'afa field. A reservoir of unassociated gas has recently been developed on Bahrain Island.
There is some heavy industry on the islands and a number of small to medium-sized industrial units.
The state has developed as a financial centre. Apart from several commercial banks, many international banks have been licensed as offshore banking units; there are also money brokers and merchant banks.
GNP – US$4,525 million (1995); US$7,840 per capita (1995)
GDP – US$4,455 million (1994); US$8,223 per capita (1994)
ANNUAL AVERAGE GROWTH OF GDP – 2.2 per cent (1995)
INFLATION RATE – – 0.3 per cent (1996)

TRADE

In 1996 imports totalled US$4,093 million and exports US$4,602 million. In 1995 the government had a trade surplus of US$769 million and a current account surplus of US$557 million.

TRADE WITH UK	1996	1997
Imports from UK	£161,180,000	£157,936,000
Exports to UK	20,677,000	33,397,000

COMMUNICATIONS

Bahrain International airport is one of the main air traffic centres of the Gulf; it is the headquarters of Gulf Air, and a stopping point on routes between Europe and Australia and the Far East for other airlines. A causeway links Bahrain to Saudi Arabia.
A world-wide telephone and telex service, by satellite and cable, is operated by Bahrain Telecommunications Company.

BANGLADESH
Ghana Praja Tantri Bangladesh

AREA – 55,598 sq. miles (143,998 sq. km). Neighbours: India (west, north and east) and Myanmar (east)
POPULATION – 120,433,000 (1994 UN estimate). The state language is Bengali. Use of Bengali is compulsory in all government departments. English is understood and is used widely as an unofficial second language. The faith of 88 per cent of the population is Islam and 10.5 per cent Hinduism. Islam has been declared the state religion
CAPITAL – Dhaka (population, 3,397,187, 1991 census)
CURRENCY – Taka (Tk) of 100 poisha
NATIONAL ANTHEM – Amar Sonar Bangla
NATIONAL DAY – 26 March (Independence Day)
NATIONAL FLAG – Red circle on a bottle-green ground
LIFE EXPECTANCY (years) – male 56.91; female 55.97
POPULATION GROWTH RATE – 2.2 per cent (1995)
POPULATION DENSITY – 836 per sq. km (1995)
URBAN POPULATION – 13.8 per cent (1986)

The country is crossed by a network of rivers, including the eastern arms of the Ganges, the Jamuna (Brahmaputra) and the Meghna, flowing into the Bay of Bengal. The climate is tropical and monsoon; hot and extremely humid during the summer, and mild and dry during the short winter.

HISTORY AND POLITICS

Prior to becoming East Pakistan, Bangladesh had been the province of East Bengal and the Sylhet district of Assam of British India. The territory acceded to Pakistan in August 1947, which became a republic on 23 March 1956. Bangladesh achieved its independence from Pakistan on 16 December 1971, following the conclusion of the Indo-Pakistan war. Pakistan and Bangladesh accorded one another mutual recognition in 1974.
In 1975 a one-party presidential system was introduced, with Prime Minister Sheikh Mujibur Rahman assuming the presidency under martial law until his assassination in 1975. A presidential election in 1978 was won by Maj.-Gen. Zia Rahman, who introduced a multiparty presidential system of government. Zia was assassinated in 1981. His replacement, Justice Abdus Sattar, was overthrown in 1982 in a coup led by the then Chief of Army Staff, Gen. Ershad. Following parliamentary elections in 1986, a civilian Cabinet was appointed and Gen. Ershad was elected president. Popular unrest forced Gen. Ershad's resignation in December 1990; the Bangladesh Nationalist Party (BNP) won the subsequent parliamentary elections and its leader, Begum Khaleda Zia, was sworn in as prime

minister. In August 1991 a constitutional amendment returned Bangladesh to parliamentary rule.

In December 1994, the opposition parties resigned from parliament and organized a series of mass rallies and strikes demanding fresh elections. Public disorder persisted despite a general election in February 1996 which was won by the BNP, although turnout was a mere five per cent. In March 1996, Prime Minister Zia agreed to new elections; these elections in June 1996 produced a majority for the Awami League under Prime Minister Sheikh Hasina Wajed. In November 1997, the BNP walked out of parliament, accusing the government of repression. They returned in March 1998 after signing a memorandum of understanding with the government.

INSURGENCIES

Since 1975, the Shanti Bahini rebels have been fighting for the autonomy of the Chittagong Hill Tracts in the south-east of the country; 10,000 people have died since fighting began. Following peace talks in December 1997, an agreement was signed granting an amnesty for all members of Shanti Bahini and its political wing, the Parbatya Chattagram Janasanghati Samiti, on condition that they surrender their arms; additionally, a regional council is to be set up to give more representative power to the area.

POLITICAL SYSTEM

There is a unicameral parliament (*Jatiya Sangshad*) of 330 members which can amend the constitution by a two-thirds majority. The country is divided into six administrative divisions, sub-divided into 64 districts.

HEAD OF STATE

President, Shahabuddin Ahmed, *sworn in* 9 October 1996

CABINET *as at May 1998*

Prime Minister, Armed Forces Division, Cabinet Division, Special Affairs, Defence, Establishment, Energy, Shaikh Hasina Wajed
Agriculture and Food, Matia Choudhry
Civil Aviation and Tourism, Mosharraf Hossain
Commerce and Industry, Tofail Ahmed
Communications, Anwar Hussain Manju
Education, Science and Technology, A. S. H. K. Sadek
Environment and Forests, Syeda Sajeda Chowdhury
Finance, S. A. M. S. Kibria
Foreign Affairs, Abdus Samad Azad
Health and Family Welfare, Salahuddin Yousuf
Home Affairs, Maj. (retd) Rafiqul Islam Bir Uttam
Labour and Manpower, Abdul Mannan
Law, Justice and Parliamentary Affairs, Abdul Matin Khasru
Local Government, Rural Development and Co-operatives, Mohammad Zillur Rahman
Post and Telecommunications, Housing and Public Works, Mohammad Nasim
Shipping, A. S. M. Abdur Rab
Water Resources, Irrigation and Flood Control, Abdur Razzak
Without Portfolio, Kalpa Ranjan Chakma; Lt.-Gen. (retd) Nooruddin Khan

There are 15 Ministers of State.

BANGLADESH HIGH COMMISSION
28 Queen's Gate, London SW7 5JA
Tel 0171–584 0081
High Commissioner, HE Mahmood Ali, apptd 1997
Deputy High Commissioner, Munshi Faiz Ahmad
Defence Adviser, Brig. A. M. Mahmuduzzaman

BRITISH HIGH COMMISSION
United Nations Road, Baridhara, Dhaka
PO Box 6079, Dhaka-12
Tel: Dhaka 882705
High Commissioner, HE David Walker, CMG, CVO, apptd 1996
Deputy High Commissioner, M. McIntosh
Defence Adviser, Col. J. M. Philips

BRITISH COUNCIL REPRESENTATIVE, T. Cowin, 5 Fuller Road (PO Box 161), Dhaka 1000

DEFENCE

The army has 80 main battle tanks, 20 armoured personnel carriers and 140 artillery pieces. The Navy, based at Chittagong, has four frigates and 41 patrol and coastal vessels. The Air Force has 49 combat aircraft.
MILITARY EXPENDITURE – 1.7 per cent of GDP (1996)
MILITARY PERSONNEL – 170,700: Army 101,000, Navy 10,500, Air Force 9,500, Paramilitaries 49,700

ECONOMY

Between 1991–5, the government implemented an IMF economic reform plan which delivered stable prices and inflation, and reduced the budget deficit. In November 1997, the Paris Club promised US$1.9 billion of aid.

Bangladesh is self-sufficient in food production. Agricultural products include rice, wheat, tobacco, tea, oil seeds, pulses and sugar cane. The chief industries are jute, cotton, tea, leather, pharmaceuticals, fertilizer, sugar, prawn fishing and natural gas. Garment manufacturing is the main export. Remittances sent home by Bangladeshis abroad are of considerable significance to the economy.
GNP – US$31,217 million (1996); US$260 per capita (1996)
GDP – US$28,734 million (1994); US$234 per capita (1994)
ANNUAL AVERAGE GROWTH OF GDP – 5.3 per cent (1996)
INFLATION RATE – 2.7 per cent (1996)
TOTAL EXTERNAL DEBT – US$16,083 million (1996)

TRADE

In 1995 Bangladesh had a current account deficit of US$824 million and a trade deficit of US$2,324 million. In 1996 imports totalled US$6,615 million and exports US$3,297 million.

TRADE WITH UK	1996	1997
Imports from UK	£71,557,000	£81,517,000
Exports to UK	279,573,000	246,401,000

COMMUNICATIONS

Principal seaports are Chittagong and Mongla. The Bangladesh Shipping Corporation was set up by the Government to operate the Bangladesh merchant fleet. The principal airports are Dhaka (Zia International) and Chittagong. The international airline, Bangladesh Biman, serves Europe, the Middle East, South and South-East Asia, and an internal network.

EDUCATION

Primary education is free and planned to be universal by 2000. There are 11 universities.
ILLITERACY RATE – 61.9 per cent
ENROLMENT (percentage of age group) – primary 62 per cent (1990); secondary 20 per cent (1990); tertiary 4.4 per cent (1990)

BARBADOS

AREA – 166 sq. miles (430 sq. km); nearly 21 miles long by 14 miles broad
POPULATION – 264,000 (1994 UN estimate). The official language is English; Bajan is also spoken
CAPITAL – ΨBridgetown in the parish of St Michael (population, 108,000, 1990)
MAJOR TOWNS – Holetown in St James, Oistins in Christ Church and Speightstown in St Peter
CURRENCY – Barbados dollar (BD$) of 100 cents
NATIONAL ANTHEM – In Plenty and in Time of Need
NATIONAL DAY – 30 November (Independence Day)
NATIONAL FLAG – Three vertical stripes, dark blue, gold and dark blue, with a trident head on gold stripe
LIFE EXPECTANCY (years) – male 67.15; female 72.46
POPULATION GROWTH RATE – 0.5 per cent (1995)
POPULATION DENSITY – 614 per sq. km (1995)
MILITARY EXPENDITURE – 0.7 per cent of GDP (1996)
MILITARY PERSONNEL – 610: Army 500, Navy 110

Barbados is the most easterly of the Caribbean islands. The land rises in a series of terraced tablelands to the highest point, Mt Hillaby (1,116 ft). The annual average temperature is 26.6°C (79.8°F) with rainfall varying from a yearly average of 75 inches in the high central district to 50 inches in the low-lying coastal areas.

HISTORY AND POLITICS

The first inhabitants of Barbados were Arawak Indians but the island was uninhabited when first settled by the British in 1627. It was a Crown Colony from 1652 until it became an independent state within the Commonwealth on 30 November 1966.
   The last general election took place on 6 September 1994 and seats in the House of Assembly were distributed as follows: Barbados Labour Party 19, Democratic Labour Party 8, National Democratic Party 1.

POLITICAL SYSTEM

The head of state is the British sovereign. The legislature consists of the Governor-General, a Senate and a House of Assembly. The Senate comprises 21 Senators appointed by the Governor-General, of whom 12 are appointed on the advice of the prime minister, two on the advice of the Leader of the Opposition and seven by the Governor-General at his/her discretion to represent religious, economic or social interests. The House of Assembly comprises 28 members elected every five years by adult suffrage.
   There are 11 administrative areas (parishes): St Michael, Christ Church, St Andrew, St George, St James, St John, St Joseph, St Lucy, St Peter, St Philip and St Thomas.

Governor-General, HE Sir Clifford Husbands, GCMG, KA, apptd 1996

CABINET *as at May 1998*

Prime Minister, Defence and Security, Finance and Information, Economic Affairs, Owen Arthur
Deputy Prime Minister, Foreign Affairs, Tourism and International Transport, Billie Miller
Agriculture and Rural Development, Rawle Eastmond
Attorney-General and Home Affairs, David Simmons, QC
Chief Justice, Sir Denys Williams, KCMG
Education, Youth and Culture, Mia Mottley
Health and Environment, Elizabeth Thompson
Industry and Commerce, Reginald Farley

International Trade, Philip Goddard
Labour, Community Development and Sport, Rudolph Greenidge
Minister of State, Foreign Affairs, International Transport and Tourism, Ronald Toppin
Minister of State, Prime Minister's Office, Glyne Murray
Public Works, Transport and Housing, George Payne

BARBADOS HIGH COMMISSION
1 Great Russell Street, London WC1B 3JY
Tel 0171–631 4975
High Commissioner, HE Peter Simmons, apptd 1995
Deputy High Commissioner, H. Yearwood
First Secretary (Commercial), K. Campbell

BRITISH HIGH COMMISSION
Lower Collymore Rock, PO Box 676, Bridgetown C
Tel: Bridgetown 436 6694
High Commissioner, HE Gordon Baker, apptd 1998
Deputy High Commissioner, P. J. Mathers, LVO
Defence Adviser, Capt. I. M. Hime
First Secretary, P. Curwen

ECONOMY

The economy is based on tourism, sugar and light manufacturing. In 1995, 442,107 tourists visited Barbados and 484,670 cruise ship passengers. Chief exports are sugar, chemicals, electronic components and clothing.
GNP – US$1,745 million (1995); US$6,560 per capita (1995)
GDP – US$1,641 million (1994); US$6,505 per capita (1994)
ANNUAL AVERAGE GROWTH OF GDP – 2.7 per cent (1995)
INFLATION RATE – 2.4 per cent (1996)
UNEMPLOYMENT – 19.7 per cent (1995)
TOTAL EXTERNAL DEBT – US$581 million (1996)

TRADE

In 1995 Barbados had a current account surplus of US$88 million and a trade deficit of US$440 million. In 1996 exports totalled US$281 million and imports US$830 million.

TRADE WITH UK	1996	1997
Imports from UK	£35,538,000	£37,182,000
Exports to UK	65,524,000	30,897,000

COMMUNICATIONS

Barbados has some 965 miles of roads, of which about 917 miles are asphalted. The Grantley Adams International airport is situated at Seawell, 12 miles from Bridgetown. Bridgetown, the only port of entry, has a deep-water harbour with berths for eight ships; oil is pumped ashore at Spring Garden and at an Esso installation on the West Coast.

EDUCATION

Education is free in government schools. There are 105 primary schools, 22 government secondary schools and 15 approved government secondary schools.
ILLITERACY RATE – 2.6 per cent
ENROLMENT (percentage of age group) – primary 78 per cent (1991); secondary 75 per cent (1989); tertiary 28.1 per cent (1994)

BELARUS
Respublika Belarus

AREA – 80,155 sq. miles (207,600 sq. km). Neighbours: Latvia and Lithuania (north), Russia (east), Ukraine (south) and Poland (west)

POPULATION – 10,141,000 (1998 estimate): 78 per cent Belarusian, 13 per cent Russian, 4 per cent Polish and 3 per cent Ukrainian, with smaller numbers of Jews and Lithuanians. Belarusian, a Slavonic language written in the Cyrillic script, and Russian have equal official language status. Most of the population are Belarusian Orthodox with a minority of Roman Catholics

CAPITAL – Minsk (population, 1,687,400, 1993 estimate); the administrative centre of the CIS

MAJOR CITIES – Brest (290,600); Gomel (514,900); Grodno 298,400); Mogilev (364,600); Vitebsk (370,800), 1993 estimates

CURRENCY – Rouble of 100 kopeks

NATIONAL ANTHEM – The former Soviet national anthem but with the words omitted

NATIONAL DAY – 3 July (Independence Day)

NATIONAL FLAG – Red with a green strip along the lower edge, and in the hoist a vertical red and white ornamental pattern

LIFE EXPECTANCY (years) – male 63.75; female 74.43

POPULATION GROWTH RATE – −0.2 per cent (1995)

POPULATION DENSITY – 49 per sq. km (1995)

URBAN POPULATION – 68.1 per cent (1993)

Belarus is situated in the western part of the European area of the former USSR. The main rivers are the upper reaches of the Dnieper, of the Niemen and of the Western Dvina. Much of the land is a plain, with many lakes, swamps and marshy areas. The climate is continental with mild, humid winters and relatively cool and rainy summers.

HISTORY AND POLITICS

In the ninth century AD the Kievan Rus state was a unified state encompassing all the Russian, Ukrainian and Belarusian populations. After being absorbed into Lithuania in the 13th and 14th centuries, the Belarusian nationality, language and culture flourished until it came under Polish rule in the mid-16th century. Two hundred years of Polish rule followed until Belarus was re-absorbed into the Russian Empire.

Much of Belarus was under German control at the time of the Russian revolution and it was not until German forces withdrew that a Byelorussian Soviet Socialist Republic was declared on 1 January 1919. Western Belarus was ceded to Poland after the Soviet defeat in the Polish-Soviet war of 1919–20, and was not recovered until Soviet forces occupied the area under the 1939 Nazi-Soviet Pact. Belarus was devastated by the German invasion in the Second World War; 25 per cent of the population was killed and thousands deported.

Belarus issued a Declaration of State Sovereignty on 27 July 1990 and declared its independence from the Soviet Union after the failed coup in Moscow in August 1991. Stanislav Shuskevich became Belarusian leader at the head of a coalition of Communists and democrats. Until 1994, however, parliament and the government remained under the control of former Communists, who thwarted all attempts at economic and political reform. Shuskevich was forced to resign in January 1994 and was replaced by Gen. Mecheslav Grib who pursued closer political, economic and trade relations with Russia. The presidential election in July 1994 was won by Alexandr Lukashenka.

FOREIGN RELATIONS

An agreement was signed with Russia in April 1996 to form a Commonwealth of Sovereign Republics. In April 1997 a treaty of union was signed with Russia. It provided for the creation of a supreme council, chaired by the state presidents on a two-year rotating basis, which will co-ordinate foreign affairs and economic and defence co-operation.

POLITICAL SYSTEM

The president's term of office is five years, although a referendum in 1996 extended Lukashenka's term until 2002; the president has authority to appoint half the members of the constitutional court and the electoral commission. The legislature is the bicameral National Assembly, comprising a 110-member House of Representatives (lower chamber) and a 64-member Council of the Republic (upper chamber). Eight members of the upper chamber are appointed by the president, the rest are indirectly elected by members of the local soviets in each region.

The republic is divided into six regions (*oblasts*): Brest, Gomel, Grodno, Minsk, Mogilev and Vitebsk.

HEAD OF STATE
President, Aleksandr Lukashenka, *elected* 10 July 1994

COUNCIL OF MINISTERS *as at May 1998*
Prime Minister, Sergei Ling
First Deputy Prime Minister, Leonid Kozik
Deputy Prime Ministers, Uladzimir Garkun; Valeriy Kokarau; Uladzimir Zamyatalin; Vasil Dalgalyow; Genadz Navitsky
Agriculture and Food, Ivan Shakola
Architecture and Construction, Viktar Vetraw
CIS Affairs, Valentsin Vyalichka
Communications and Information Technology, Uladzimir Gancharenka
Culture, Aleksandr Sasnouski
Defence, Lt.-Gen. Alexsandr Chumakow
Economy, Uladzimir Shymow
Education, Vasil Strazhau
Emergency Situations, Ivan Kenik
Enterprise and Investments, Aleksandr Sazonau
Finance, Mikhaly Korbut
Foreign Affairs, Ivan Antanovich
Foreign Economic Relations, Mikhail Marynich
Forestry, Valentsin Zorin
Health, Igor Zelenkevich
Housing and Municipal Services, Boris Batura
Industry, Anatol Kharlap
Internal Affairs, Maj.-Gen. Valentsin Agalets
Justice, Genadz Varantsou
Labour, Ivan Lyakh
Natural Resources and Environmental Protection, Mikhail Rusy
Social Security, Volga Dargel
Sport and Tourism, Nikolai Ananiev
State-owned Property and Privatization, Vasil Novak
Statistics and Analysis, Uladzimir Nichyparovich
Trade, Pyotr Kazlou
Transport, Aleksandr Lukashou

EMBASSY OF THE REPUBLIC OF BELARUS
6 Kensington Court, London w8 5DL
Tel 0171-937 3288
Ambassador Extraordinary and Plenipotentiary, HE Uladzimir Shchasny, apptd 1995

BRITISH EMBASSY
37 Karl Marx Street, Minsk 220030
Tel: Minsk 292303/4/5

Ambassador Extraordinary and Plenipotentiary, HE Jessica
   Pearce, apptd 1996

DEFENCE

The Army has 1,778 main battle tanks, 1,020 armoured
personnel carriers and 1,519 artillery pieces. The Air Force
has 230 combat aircraft and 74 armed helicopters.
MILITARY EXPENDITURE – 4.2 per cent of GDP (1996)
MILITARY PERSONNEL – 80,500: Army 50,500, Air Force
   22,000, Paramilitaries 8,000
CONSCRIPTION DURATION – 18 months

ECONOMY

Agricultural productivity was severely affected by nuclear
fallout from the Chernobyl disaster in 1986 although
Belarus is now self-sufficient in the production of foodstuffs. As a result of the collapse of the Soviet centrally
planned economic system, the country lost cheap supplies
of energy and raw materials. Energy from Russia is still the
largest import.
   Economic reform and privatization have been introduced and in May 1995 a customs union agreement with
Russia took effect. A treaty was signed with Kazakhstan,
Kyrgyzstan and Russia in March 1996 aimed at the
establishment of a single customs territory. In 1997
investment activity rose by 20 per cent; trade with Russia
rose by 40 per cent during 1997, and in December 1997 the
first Russia-Belarus joint budget was endorsed, with
projects estimated to cost US$100 billion.
   In 1996 the government had a budget deficit equivalent
to 1.9 per cent of GDP. In 1996 imports totalled US$6,939
million and exports US$5,463 million.
GNP – US$22,452 million (1996); US$2,070 per capita
   (1996)
GDP – US$40,342 million (1994); US$517 per capita
   (1994)
INFLATION RATE – 52.7 per cent (1996)
UNEMPLOYMENT – 2.7 per cent (1995)
TOTAL EXTERNAL DEBT – US$1,071 million (1996)

TRADE WITH UK	1996	1997
Imports from UK	£27,661,000	£35,242,000
Exports to UK	13,596,000	15,615,000

EDUCATION

The national system comprises pre-school, general sec-
ondary, out-of-school, vocational training and trade
schools, secondary specialized and higher education.
General secondary education begins at the age of six.
There are also 22 private educational institutions.
ILLITERACY RATE – 0.5 per cent
ENROLMENT (percentage of age group) – primary 95 per
cent (1994); tertiary 42.6 per cent (1995)

BELGIUM
Royaume de Belgique

AREA – 11,783 sq. miles (30,519 sq. km). Neighbours: the
Netherlands (north), France (south), and Germany and
Luxembourg (east)
POPULATION – 10,113,000 (1994 UN estimate). Greater
Brussels 949,070; Flanders 5,847,022; Wallonia
3,304,539, of whom 68,741 are German-speaking.
Roman Catholicism is the religion of 86 per cent of the
population. The official languages are Flemish, French
and German
CAPITAL – Brussels (population, 960,324, 1991 estimate)

MAJOR CITIES – ΨAntwerp, the chief port (455,852);
Bruges (115,815); Charleroi (205,591); ΨGhent
(226,464); Liège (190,525); Leuven (87,132); Mons
(92,260); Namur (105,059)
CURRENCY – Belgian franc (or frank) of 100 centimes
(centiemen)
NATIONAL ANTHEM – La Brabançonne
NATIONAL DAY – 21 July (Accession of King Leopold I,
1831)
NATIONAL FLAG – Three vertical bands, black, yellow, red
LIFE EXPECTANCY (years) – male 72.43; female 79.13
POPULATION GROWTH RATE – 0.3 per cent (1995)
POPULATION DENSITY – 331 per sq. km (1995)

The Meuse and its tributary, the Sambre, divide Belgium
into two distinct regions, that in the west being generally
level and fertile, while the tableland of the Ardennes, in the
east, has mostly poor soil. The polders near the coast,
which are protected by dykes against floods, cover an area
of 193 sq. miles. The principal rivers are the Scheldt and the
Meuse.
   Belgium is divided between those who speak Dutch (the
Flemings) and those who speak French (the Walloons).
Dutch is recognized as the official language in the northern
areas and French in the southern (Walloon) area and there
are guarantees for the respective linguistic minorities.
Brussels is officially bilingual. There is a small German-
speaking area (Eupen and Malmédy) along the German
border, east of Liège.

HISTORY AND POLITICS

The kingdom formed part of the Low Countries (Netherlands) from 1815 until 14 October 1830, when a National
Congress proclaimed its independence. On 4 June 1831,
Prince Leopold of Coburg was chosen as the hereditary
king. The neutrality and inviolability of Belgium were
guaranteed by a Conference of the European powers, and
by the Treaty of London 1839. On 4 August 1914 the
Germans invaded Belgium, in violation of the terms of the
treaty, and this led the Allies to declare war. Eupen and
Malmédy were ceded by Germany under the Versailles
Treaty 1919. The kingdom was again invaded by Germany
in 1940 and was occupied by Nazi troops until liberated by
the Allies in September 1944.
   The last general election was held on 21 May 1995. The
results were as follows (seats):
   Chamber of Deputies: Christian Social Party (CVP)
(Flemish) 29; Socialist Party (PS) (Francophone) 21;

Flemish Liberals and Democrats (VLD) 21; SP 20; Liberal Reform Party-Democratic Front (PRL-FDF) (Francophone) 18; Christian Social Party (PSC) (Francophone) 12; Vlaams Blok (Flemish Nationalist Party) 11; Ecolo (Francophone Ecology Party) 6; Agalev (Flemish Environmental Party) 5; Flemish People's Union (VU) 5; Front National (FN) 2.

Senate: of the 40 seats directly elected, CVP 7; SP 6; VLD 6; PRL-FDF 5; PS 5; PSC 3; Vlaams Blok 3; VU 2; Ecolo 2; Agalev 1. A further 31 Senators are indirectly elected or co-opted (*see* below).

POLITICAL SYSTEM

Belgium is a constitutional representative and hereditary monarchy with a bicameral legislature, consisting of the King, the Senate and the Chamber of Representatives. The parliamentary term is four years. Amendments to the constitution enacted since 1968 have devolved power to the regions. The national government retains competence only in foreign and defence policies, the national budget and monetary policy, social security, and the judicial, legal and penal systems. The Senate has 71 seats, of which 40 are directly elected, 21 indirectly elected and ten co-opted by the Flemish and Francophone Communities. The Chamber of Representatives has 150 seats. There are four levels of sub-national government: community, regional, provincial, and communal.

FEDERAL STRUCTURE

There are three communities: Flemish; Francophone; Germanophone. Each community has its own assembly, which elects the community government. At this level, Flanders is covered by the Flemish Community Assembly; most of Wallonia is covered by the Francophone Community Assembly, and the areas of Wallonia in the German-speaking communities of Eupen and Malmédy are covered by the Germanophone Community Assembly; Brussels is covered by a Joint Community Commission of the Flemish and Francophone Community Assemblies.

At regional level, Belgium is divided into the three regions of Wallonia, Brussels and Flanders. Each region has its own assembly and government.

There are ten provinces; five French-speaking in Wallonia (Hainaut, Liège, Luxembourg, Namur and French Brabant); and five Dutch-speaking in Flanders (Antwerp, East Flanders, West Flanders, Limbourg and Flemish Brabant). In addition, Belgium has 589 communes as the lowest level of local government.

Minister-President of the Flemish Government, Luc van den Brande (CVP)
Minister-President of the Walloon Regional Government, Robert Collignon (PS)

Head of City Government in Brussels, Charles Picqué

HEAD OF STATE

HM The King of the Belgians, King Albert II, *born* 6 June 1934; *succeeded* 9 August 1993; *married* 2 July 1959, Donna Paola Ruffo di Calabria, and has *issue* Prince Philippe (*see* below); Princess Astrid, *b.* 5 June 1962; Prince Laurent, *b.* 20 October 1963
Heir, HRH Prince Philippe Léopold Louis Marie, *born* 15 April 1960

CABINET *as at June 1998*

Prime Minister, Jean-Luc Dehaene (CVP)
Deputy PM, Budget, Herman Van Rompuy (CVP)
Deputy PM, Economic Affairs, Telecommunications, Elio di Rupo (PS)
Deputy PM, Finance, Foreign Trade, Philippe Maystadt (PSC)
Deputy PM, Interior, Louis Tobback (SP)
Agriculture and Small and Medium-sized Enterprises, Karel Pinxten (CVP)
Civil Service, André Flahaut (PS)
Defence, Jean-Pol Poncelet (PSC)
Employment, Equal Opportunities, Miet Smet (CVP)
Foreign Affairs, Eric Derycke (SP)
Justice, Tony van Parys (CVP)
Pensions and Public Health, Marcel Colla (SP)
Scientific Policy, Yvan Ylieff (PS)
Social Affairs, Magda De Galan (PS)
Transport, Michel Daerden (PS)

CVP Christian Social Party (Flemish); PS Socialist Party (Francophone); SP Socialist Party (Flemish); PSC Christian Social Party (Francophone)

BELGIAN EMBASSY

103-105 Eaton Square, London SW1W 9AB
Tel 0171-470 3700
Ambassador Extraordinary and Plenipotentiary, HE Lode Willems, apptd 1997
Minister-Counsellors, M. Vanmerk (*Political*); F. De Sutter (*Economic*)
Military, Naval and Air Attaché, Col. J. Bouzette

BRITISH EMBASSY

rue d'Arlon 85, 1040 Brussels
Tel: Brussels 287 6211
Ambassador Extraordinary and Plenipotentiary, HE David Colvin, CMG, apptd 1993
Deputy Ambassador, Counsellor and Consul-General, E. C. Glover, MVO
Counsellors (Commercial), M. T. Jones; I. McRory
Defence and Military Attaché, Col. T. E. Hall
There are British Consular Offices at Brussels, Antwerp and Liège.

Province	Area (sq. km)	Population (1996)	Main Town	Population (1996)
FLANDERS				
Antwerp	2,867	1,631,243	Antwerp	455,852
East Flanders	2,982	1,351,777	Ghent	226,464
Flemish Brabant	2,106	999,186	Leuven	87,132
Limbourg	2,422	775,302	Hasselt	67,456
West Flanders	3,144	1,122,849	Bruges	115,815
WALLONIA				
Hainaut	3,786	1,284,761	Mons	92,260
Liège	3,862	1,013,729	Liège	190,525
Luxembourg	4,440	241,339	Arlon	15,000
Namur	3,666	435,677	Namur	105,059
Walloon Brabant	1,091	339,062	Wavre	27,000

British Council Representative to Belgium and Luxembourg – Dr Ken Churchill, OBE, rue de la Charité 15, Liefdadigheidstraat 15, 1210 Brussels
British Chamber of Commerce for Belgium and Luxembourg (Inc.), rue Joseph II 30, 1040 Brussels

DEFENCE

The Army has 326 main battle tanks, 434 armoured personnel carriers, 236 armoured infantry fighting vehicles, 255 artillery pieces and 78 helicopters. The Navy is based at Ostend and Zeebrugge and has three frigates and three helicopters. The Air Force has 132 combat aircraft.

The headquarters of NATO, SHAPE and the Western European Union Military Planning Cell are in Belgium; 1,365 US personnel are stationed in the country.
Military Expenditure – 1.6 per cent of GDP (1996)
Military Personnel – 43,200: Army 28,500, Navy 2,700, Air Force 12,000

ECONOMY

With no natural resources except coal, production of which has now ceased, industry is based largely on the processing for re-export of imported raw materials. Principal industries are steel and metal products, chemicals and petrochemicals, textiles, glass, and foodstuffs.

On 1 May 1998, it was announced that Belgium had satisfied the convergence criteria and would be one of 11 countries to participate in the European Single Currency from 1 January 1999.

In 1996 there was a budget deficit of 3.2 per cent of GDP and public debt was 130.1 per cent of GDP.
GNP – US$268,633 million (1996); US$26,440 per capita (1996)
GDP – US$201,125 million (1994); US$21,765 per capita (1994)
Annual Average Growth of GDP – 2.2 per cent (1994)
Inflation Rate – 2.1 per cent (1996)
Unemployment – 9.3 per cent (1995)

TRADE

External trade figures relate to Luxembourg as well as Belgium since the two countries formed an economic union in 1921. The main trading partners are Germany, France and the Netherlands.

In 1996 Belgium and Luxembourg had a trade surplus of US$9,146 million and a current account surplus of US$14,387 million. In 1996 exports totalled US$168,095 million and imports US$154,935 million.

Trade with UK (Belgium and Luxembourg)

	1996	1997
Imports from UK	£8,114,000,000	£8,005,500,000
Exports to UK	8,096,000,000	8,716,000,000

COMMUNICATIONS

The railways are operated by the Belgian National Railways. Ship canals include Ghent-Terneuzen (18 miles, half in the Netherlands) by which ships up to 60,000 tons reach Ghent; Willebroek Rupel-Brussels (20 miles, by which ships drawing 18 ft reach Brussels from the sea); Bruges (from Zeebrugge on the North Sea to Bruges, 6¼ miles); and Albert (79 miles), Liège to Antwerp for barges up to 1,350 tons. The River Meuse from the Dutch to the French frontiers, the River Sambre between Namur and Monceau, the River Scheldt from Antwerp to Ghent and the Brussels-Charleroi Canal are being widened or deepened to take barges up to 1,350 tons. Most maritime trade is carried in foreign shipping.

In 1986 there were 14,260 km of trunk road, of which about 1,550 km were motorways. The Belgian national airline Sabena operates regular services between Brussels and European centres, as well as intercontinental services worldwide.

CULTURE AND EDUCATION

The literature of France and the Netherlands is supplemented by an indigenous Belgian literary activity in both French and Dutch. Maurice Maeterlinck (1862–1949) was awarded the Nobel Prize for Literature in 1911. Emile Verhaeren (1855–1916) was a poet of international standing. Of contemporary Belgian writers, the most celebrated was Georges Simenon (1903–89).

Nursery schools provide free education for children from two and a half to six years. There are over 4,000 primary schools (6 to 12 years), more than 1,000 secondary schools offering a general academic education slightly over half of which are free institutions (predominantly Roman Catholic but subsidized by the state) and the remainder official institutions. The official school-leaving age is 18.
Enrolment (percentage of age group) – primary 98 per cent (1993); secondary 98 per cent (1993); tertiary 49.1 per cent (1993)

BELIZE

Area – 8,763 sq. miles (22,696 sq. km). Neighbours: Mexico (north and north-west) and Guatemala (west and south)
Population – 217,000 (1994 UN estimate): 44 per cent Mestizo (Maya-Spanish); 30 per cent Creole; 11 per cent Maya; plus a number of East Indian and Spanish descent. The races are now inter-mixed. The majority of the population is Christian, about 58 per cent Catholic and 34 per cent Protestant. The official language and language of instruction is English. Spanish is also widely spoken and English Creole is the vernacular. There are also Garifuna and Maya speakers
Capital – Belmopan (population, 44,087, 1991)
Major Cities – ΨBelize City (1993 census 46,342), the former capital; Corozal (7,420); Dangriga (6,761); Orange Walk (11,573); San Ignacio (9,417)
Currency – Belize dollar (BZ$) of 100 cents. The Belize dollar is tied to the US dollar, BZ$2 = US$1
National Anthem – Land of the Free
National Day – 21 September (Independence Day)
National Flag – Blue ground with red band along top and bottom edges, and in centre a white disc containing the coat of arms surrounded by a green garland
Life Expectancy (years) – male 69.95; female 74.07
Population Growth Rate – 2.7 per cent (1995)
Population Density – 10 per sq. km (1995)
Urban Population – 47.5 per cent (1994)
Military Expenditure – 2.4 per cent of GDP (1996)
Military Personnel – 1,000: Army

The coastal areas are mostly flat and swampy with many islets but the country rises gradually towards the interior, which is mainly forest. The northern and western districts are hilly, and in the south the Maya Mountains and the Cockscombs form the backbone of the country, reaching a height of 3,700 feet at Victoria Peak. The climate is subtropical.

HISTORY AND POLITICS

Numerous ruins in the area indicate that Belize was heavily populated by the Maya Indians. The first British settlement was established in 1638 but was subject to repeated attacks by the Spanish, who claimed sovereignty until defeated by the Royal Navy and settlers in 1798. In 1871 the area was recognized by Britain as a colony and called British Honduras. In 1973 the colony was renamed Belize, and was granted independence on 21 September 1981.

The 1993 elections were won by the United Democratic Party. The next elections are due to be held in August 1998.

FOREIGN RELATIONS

A long-standing territorial dispute with Guatemala was provisionally resolved in 1992 when the Guatemalan Congress and Supreme Court voted to recognize Belize and establish diplomatic relations. Guatemala still retains its claim, subject to arbitration by the International Court of Justice.

POLITICAL SYSTEM

Queen Elizabeth II is head of state, represented in Belize by a Governor-General. There is a National Assembly, comprising a House of Representatives (29 members elected for five years) and a Senate (eight members appointed by the Governor-General). Executive power is vested in the Cabinet, which is responsible to the National Assembly.

Governor-General, HE Sir Colville Norbert Young, GCMG, apptd 17 November 1993

CABINET *as at May 1998*

Prime Minister, Finance and Economic Development, Manuel Esquivel
Deputy PM, National Security, Attorney-General, Foreign Affairs, Dean Barrow
Agriculture and Fisheries, Russell García
Education, Public Service, Elodio Aragón
Energy, Science, Technology and Transport, Joseph Cayetano
Health and Sports, Salvador Fernández
Housing, Urban Development and Co-operatives, Home Affairs, Labour, Hubert Elrington
Human Resources, Women's Affairs and Youth Development, Philip Goldson
National Co-ordination and Mobilization, Ruben Campos
Natural Resources, Eduardo Dito Juan
Public Works, Melvin Hulse
Tourism and Environment, Henry Young
Trade and Industry, Alfredo Martínez

BELIZE HIGH COMMISSION
22 Harcourt House, 19a Cavendish Square, London WIM 9AD
Tel 0171-499 9728
High Commissioner, HE Dr Ursula Barrow, apptd 1993

BRITISH HIGH COMMISSION
PO Box 91, Belmopan
Tel: Belmopan 22146/7
High Commissioner, HE Timothy David, apptd 1998

ECONOMY

About 30 per cent of the population is engaged in agriculture. The country is more or less self-sufficient in fresh beef, pork and poultry, but processed meat and dairy products are imported. About 25 per cent of timber production (mostly mahogany) is exported, and there is a large US market for lobster, conch and scale fish. Tourism is also a valuable source of income.

In 1995 Belize had a trade deficit of US$66 million and a current account deficit of US$17 million. In 1996 imports totalled US$256 million and exports US$154 million.

GNP – US$600 million (1996); US$2,700 per capita (1996)
GDP – US$422 million (1994); US$2,630 per capita (1994)
ANNUAL AVERAGE GROWTH OF GDP – 1.4 per cent (1996)
INFLATION RATE – 6.4 per cent (1996)
UNEMPLOYMENT – 11.1 per cent (1994)
TOTAL EXTERNAL DEBT – US$288 million (1996)

Trade with UK	1996	1997
Imports from UK	£10,192,000	£13,561,000
Exports to UK	47,863,000	36,291,000

COMMUNICATIONS

There is a government-operated radio service and three privately-owned radio stations but no official television service in the country. An automatic telephone service operated by Belize Telecommunications Ltd covers the whole country.

The principal airport is at Belize City and various airlines operate international flights to the USA and other Central American states. The main port is also Belize City, which has deep water quays. Several inland waterways are also navigable. There are 1,865 miles of road, including four main highways, but there is no railway system.

EDUCATION

Education is compulsory from six to 14 years of age. In 1992 primary education was provided by 241 schools, most of which are government-aided. Secondary education is provided by 40 secondary and post-secondary institutions. A University College of Belize has been established. There is an extra-mural faculty of the University of the West Indies, with a resident tutor.
ENROLMENT (percentage of age group) – primary 99 per cent (1994); secondary 36 per cent (1992)

BENIN
République du Benin

AREA – 43,484 sq. miles (112,622 sq. km). Neighbours: Togo (west), Burkina Faso and Niger (north), Nigeria (east)
POPULATION – 5,561,000 (1994 UN estimate). The official language is French
CAPITAL – ΨPorto Novo (population, 179,138, 1992)
MAJOR TOWNS – ΨCotonou (487,020, 1992) is the principal commercial town and port
CURRENCY – Franc CFA of 100 centimes
NATIONAL DAY – 30 November
NATIONAL FLAG – Two horizontal stripes of yellow over red with a vertical green band in the hoist
LIFE EXPECTANCY (years) – male 45.92; female 49.29
POPULATION GROWTH RATE – 3.2 per cent (1995)
POPULATION DENSITY – 49 per sq. km (1995)
URBAN POPULATION – 35.7 per cent (1992)
MILITARY EXPENDITURE – 1.2 per cent of GDP (1996)
MILITARY PERSONNEL – 7,300: Army 4,500, Navy 150, Air Force 150, Paramilitaries 2,500
CONSCRIPTION DURATION – 18 months
ILLITERACY RATE – 63.0 per cent
ENROLMENT (percentage of age group) – primary 59 per cent (1995); tertiary 2.6 per cent (1995)

Benin (formerly known as Dahomey) has a short coastline of 78 miles on the Gulf of Guinea but extends northwards inland for 437 miles. The four main regions, running horizontally, are a narrow sandy coastal strip, a succession of inter-communicating lagoons, a clay belt and a sandy plateau in the north.

HISTORY AND POLITICS

Benin was placed under French administration in 1892 and became an independent republic within the French Community in December 1958; full independence outside the Community was proclaimed on 1 August 1960. Between 1963 and 1972 successive governments were overthrown by the military until a coup d'état in 1972 brought to power a Marxist-Leninist military government headed by Lt.-Col. Kérékou.

The government dropped Marxism-Leninism as the official ideology in 1989, revoked the constitution in March 1990 and changed the country's official name from the People's Republic of Benin to the Republic of Benin. The Revolutionary National Assembly (legislature) was replaced by a High Council of the Republic (HCR).

A pluralistic constitution was adopted in December 1990 and legislative and presidential elections were held in 1991. Nicéphore Soglo was sworn in as president and appointed a Benin Resistance Party (PRB)-dominated provisional government. Legislative elections to the 83-seat National Assembly in March 1995 gave the PRB and allies 32 seats and opposition parties 49 seats. Soglo was defeated by Gen. Kérékou in a presidential election in March 1996.

POLITICAL SYSTEM

The president is head of government as well as head of state, and is directly elected for a five-year term, renewable once only. The president appoints and presides over the Council of Ministers. The National Assembly has 83 members, directly elected for a maximum of four years.

HEAD OF STATE

President and Head of the Armed Forces, HE Gen. Mathieu Kérékou, *sworn in* 4 April 1996

CABINET *as at May 1998*

Prime Minister, Adrien Houngbedji
Civil Service, Labour and Administrative Reform, Yacoubou Assouma
Culture and Communication, Timothée Zannou
Defence, Sévérin Adjovi
Environment, Housing and Urban Affairs, Sahidou Dango-Nadey
Finance, Moïse Mensah
Foreign Affairs and Co-operation, Pierre Osho
Health, Social Welfare and Women's Affairs, Marina d'Almeida-Massougbodji
Industry, Small and Medium-sized Enterprises, Félix Adimi
Interior, Security and Territorial Administration, Théophile N'da
Justice, Legislation and Human Rights, Ismaël Tidjani Serpos
Mines, Energy and Water Resources, Emmanuel Golon
National Education and Scientific Research, Djidjoho Léonard Padonou
Planning, Economic Reconstruction and Employment Promotion, Albert Tevoedjre
Public Works and Transport, Kamarou Fassassi
Rural Development, Jérôme-Desiré Sacca Kina
Trade, Tourism and Handicrafts, Gatien Houngbedji
Youth, Sports and Leisure, Damien Alahassa

EMBASSY OF THE REPUBLIC OF BENIN

87 Avenue Victor Hugo, 75116 Paris, France
Tel: Paris 4500 9882
Ambassador Extraordinary and Plenipotentiary, HE Andres Ologoudou, apptd 1998

HONORARY CONSULATE, 16 The Broadway, Stanmore, Middx HA7 4DW. Tel: 081–954 8800. *Honorary Consul*, Lawrence Landau

BRITISH AMBASSADOR, HE Graham Burton, CMG, resident at Lagos, Nigeria

ECONOMY

The principal exports are cotton, palm products, ground-nuts, shea-nuts, and coffee. Small deposits of gold, iron and chrome have been found. Oil production started in 1983.

In 1994 Benin had a trade deficit of US$65 million and a current account surplus of US$36 million. In 1995 imports totalled US$692 million and exports US$180 million.
GNP – US$1,998 million (1996); US$350 per capita (1996)
GDP – US$2,032 million (1994); US$278 per capita (1994)
ANNUAL AVERAGE GROWTH OF GDP – 6.0 per cent (1995)
INFLATION RATE – 4.8 per cent (1996)
TOTAL EXTERNAL DEBT – US$1,594 million (1996)

TRADE WITH UK	1996	1997
Imports from UK	£43,636,000	£47,211,000
Exports to UK	3,097,000,	1,249,000

BHUTAN
Druk-yul

AREA – 18,147 sq. miles (47,000 sq. km). Neighbours: Tibet (north), India (west, south and east)
POPULATION – 1,638,000 (1994 UN estimate): about 80 per cent are Buddhists, the remainder (mostly the Nepali Bhutanese) are Hindu. The official language, for administrative and religious purposes, is Dzongkha, a variant of Tibetan, which functions as a lingua franca amongst a variety of languages and dialects. Nepali remains a recognized language and English remains the medium of instruction and the working language of the administration
CAPITAL – Thimphu (population, 15,000, 1987 estimate)
CURRENCY – Ngultrum of 100 chetrum (Indian currency is also legal tender)
NATIONAL DAY – 17 December
NATIONAL FLAG – Saffron yellow and orange-red divided diagonally, with dragon device in centre
LIFE EXPECTANCY (years) – male 49.10; female 52.40
POPULATION GROWTH RATE – 1.2 per cent (1995)
POPULATION DENSITY – 35 per sq. km (1995)
ILLITERACY RATE – 57.8 per cent

There is a mountainous northern region which is infertile and sparsely populated, a central zone of upland valleys where most of the population and cultivated land is found, and in the south the densely forested foothills of the Himalayas, which are mainly inhabited by Nepalese settlers and indigenous tribespeople.

INSURGENCIES

In January 1989 the King introduced a code of national etiquette designed to protect the national culture and language from Nepali encroachment. These measures, together with the granting of citizenship only to Nepalis settled in Bhutan before 1958, led to an exodus of ethnic Nepalis to Nepal, where about 80,000 live in camps. A low-level insurgency has been waged in the south of the country against the King's policies by ethnic Nepalis since 1990. Talks between the Nepali and Bhutan governments continue in an attempt to resolve the fate of the refugees.

FOREIGN RELATIONS

Under a 1949 treaty Bhutan is guided by the advice of India in regard to its external relations. It retains its own diplomatic representatives and is a member of the UN. It also receives from India an annual payment of Rs500,000 as compensation for portions of its territory annexed by the British Government in India in 1864.

POLITICAL SYSTEM

Bhutan has a 150-member National Assembly which meets twice a year. The ten-member Royal Advisory Council, nominated by the King and the National Assembly, acts as a consultative body when the National Assembly is not in session. The King is also assisted by the *Lhengyal Sgungtsog* (Cabinet). There are no political parties.

HEAD OF STATE

HM The King of Bhutan, Jigme Singye Wangchuk, *born* 11 November 1955; *succeeded his father* July 1972; *crowned* 2 June 1974
Heir, Crown Prince Jigme Gesar Namgyal Wangchuk, *designated* 31 October 1988

COUNCIL OF MINISTERS *as at May 1998*

Representative of the King in the Ministry of Agriculture, HRH Ashi Sonam Chhoden Wangchuk
Representative of the King in the Ministry of Communications, HRH Ashi Dechan Wangmo Wangchuk
Representative of the King in the Ministry of Social Services, HRH Namgyal Wangchuck
Cabinet Secretary, Foreign Affairs, Lyonpo Dawa Tshering
Chief Operations Officer, Royal Bhutan Army, Goongloan Gongma Lam Dorji
Finance, Lyonpo Dorji Tshering
Home Affairs, Lyonpo Dago Tshering
Planning, Lyonpo Chenkyab Dorji
Trade and Industry, Lyonpo Om Pradhan

ECONOMY

The economy is based on agriculture and animal husbandry, which engage over 90 per cent of the workforce in what is largely a self-sufficient rural society. The principal food crops are rice, wheat, maize and barley. Vegetables and fruit are also produced. Bhutan is the world's largest producer of cardamom, which forms its principal export to countries other than India. Agriculture is, however, limited by the country's mountainous topography and 60 per cent forest cover.

The mountains contain rich deposits of limestone, gypsum, dolomite and graphite and small amounts of coal, which are exported to India. A modest industrial base is being developed. A distillery and cement, chemicals and food-processing plants are in production; a forestry industries complex is being expanded. Tourism and postage stamps are increasingly important sources of foreign exchange.

The government budget deficit was equivalent to 0.26 per cent of GDP in 1993. In 1994 imports totalled US$114 million and exports US$71 million.

GNP – US$282 million (1996); US$390 per capita (1996)
GDP – US$345 million (1994); US$163 per capita (1994)
ANNUAL AVERAGE GROWTH OF GDP – 6.4 per cent (1996)
INFLATION RATE – 8.4 per cent (1995)
TOTAL EXTERNAL DEBT – US$87 million (1996)

TRADE

Over 90 per cent of foreign trade is with India. Principal exports are agricultural products, timber, cement and coal; main imports are textiles, cereals and consumer goods.

Bhutan's airline, Druk Air, flies between Paro, New Delhi and Calcutta.

Trade with UK	1996	1997
Imports from UK	£1,313,000	£1,491,000
Exports to UK	394,000	964,000

BOLIVIA
República de Bolivia

AREA – 424,165 sq. miles (1,098,581 sq. km). Neighbours: Brazil (north and east), Paraguay and Argentina (south) and Chile and Peru (west)
POPULATION – 7,414,000 (1994 UN estimate): 12 per cent is of white European descent, 30 per cent Mestizo (mixed European-Indian), 25 per cent Quechua Indian and 17 per cent Aymará Indian. The official language is Spanish; Quechua and Aymará are also spoken. Roman Catholicism was the state religion until disestablishment in 1961
CAPITAL – La Paz (population, 784,976, 1993 estimate)
MAJOR CITIES – Cochabamba (448,756); El Alto (446,189); Oruro (201,831); Potosí (123,327); Santa Cruz (767,260); Sucre, the legal capital and seat of the judiciary (144,994)
CURRENCY – Boliviano ($b) of 100 centavos
NATIONAL ANTHEM – Bolivianos, El Hado Propicio (Oh Bolivia, our long-felt desires)
NATIONAL DAY – 6 August (Independence Day)
NATIONAL FLAG – Three horizontal bands, red, yellow, green
LIFE EXPECTANCY (years) – male 57.74; female 61.00
POPULATION GROWTH RATE – 2.4 per cent (1995)
POPULATION DENSITY – 7 per sq. km (1995)
URBAN POPULATION – 57.5 per cent (1992)

The chief topographical feature is the great central plateau over 500 miles in length, at an average altitude of 12,500 feet above sea level, between the two great chains of the Andes, which traverse the country from south to north. The total length of the navigable rivers is about 12,000 miles, the principal rivers being the Itenez, Beni, Mamore and Madre de Dios.

HISTORY AND POLITICS

Bolivia won its independence from Spain in 1825 after a war of liberation led by Simon Bolivar (1783–1830), from whom the country derives its name. From 1964 to 1982 Bolivia was ruled by military juntas until civilian rule was restored.

Congressional and presidential elections were held in June 1997. No party won an outright majority in Congress and a multiparty government was formed.

POLITICAL SYSTEM

The constitution provides for a directly elected executive president who appoints the Cabinet. The legislature (Congress) consists of a 27-member Senate and a 130-member Chamber of Deputies; both chambers are elected for four-year terms, and the president for five years.

HEAD OF STATE

President of the Republic, Gen. (retd) Hugo Bánzer Suárez, *inaugurated* 6 August 1997
Vice President, Jorge Quiroga Ramírez

CABINET *as at May 1998*

Agriculture, Luís Freddy Conde López (C)
Economic Development, Ivo Kuljis (UCS)
Education, Tito Hoz de Vila (ADN)

Finance, Edgar Millares Ardaya (Ind.)
Foreign Affairs, Javier Murillo de la Rocha (ADN)
Home Affairs, Guido Nayar Parad (ADN)
Housing, Javier Escobar (C)
Human Development and Health, Tonchi Marinkovic (MIR)
International Trade and Investment, Jorge Crespo (MIR)
Justice, Ana María Cortéz de Soriano (ADN)
Labour, Leopoldo López Cossio (MIR)
National Defence, Fernando Kieffer Guzmán (ADN)
Presidency, Carlos Iturralde Ballivian (ADN)
Sustainable Development and Environment, Erick Reyes Villa (NFR)

ADN Democratic Nationalist Action; C Conscience of the Fatherland; MIR Movement of the Revolutionary Left; NFR New Republican Force; UCS Civic Solidarity Union

BOLIVIAN EMBASSY
106 Eaton Square, London SW1W 9AD
Tel 0171-235 2257/4248
Ambassador Extraordinary and Plenipotentiary, Jaime Quiroga Matos, apptd 1998

BRITISH EMBASSY
Avenida Arce 2732, (Casilla 694) La Paz
Tel: La Paz 433424
Ambassador Extraordinary and Plenipotentiary, HE Graham Minter, apptd 1998
Deputy Head of Mission, J. Gardner

There is an Honorary Consulate at Santa Cruz.

DEFENCE

The Army has 108 armoured personnel carriers and 146 artillery pieces. The Navy has 17 patrol vessels. The Air Force has 33 combat aircraft and 10 armed helicopters.
MILITARY EXPENDITURE – 2.0 per cent of GDP (1996)
MILITARY PERSONNEL – 70,600: Army 25,000, Navy 4,500, Air Force 4,000, Paramilitaries 37,100
CONSCRIPTION DURATION – 12 months

ECONOMY

Mining, natural gas, petroleum and agriculture are the principal industries. The ancient silver mines of Potosí are now worked chiefly for tin, but gold is obtained on the Eastern Cordillera of the Andes. Tin output, together with other minerals (copper, tungsten, antimony, lead, zinc, asbestos, wolfram, bismuth salt and sulphur), provides over one-third of exports. Following a decline in the price of tin, many workers have taken to growing coca, which has become a significant export. A government plan to reduce coca production by offering growers alternative means of support has only been of limited success. Small quantities of oil are produced for internal consumption, and gas (currently providing about a quarter of export income) is piped to Argentina; in December 1997 the World Bank approved financing for the 3,150 km Bolivia-Brazil gas pipeline, estimated to cost around US$2 billion.

The economy deteriorated badly in the late 1970s and early 1980s; in the mid-1980s economic reforms were introduced with privatization of some state-owned firms and the encouragement of foreign investment. The peso was replaced in 1987 with the Boliviano of 1,000,000 old pesos in a successful effort to stem hyperinflation. The economy and currency have stabilized.

In 1996 the government signed an agreement with the South American Common Market (Mercosur) to create a free trade zone within 18 years.
GNP – US$6,302 million (1996); US$830 per capita (1996)
GDP – US$6,229 million (1994); US$867 per capita (1994)
ANNUAL AVERAGE GROWTH OF GDP – 4.4 per cent (1995)

INFLATION RATE – 12.4 per cent (1996)
UNEMPLOYMENT – 3.6 per cent (1995)
TOTAL EXTERNAL DEBT – US$5,174 million (1996)

TRADE

Mineral exports represent about 35 per cent of total trade. Bolivia has now developed its own smelters and is exporting metals. The chief imports are wheat and flour, iron and steel products, machinery, vehicles and textiles.

In 1995 Bolivia had a trade deficit of US$182 million and a current account deficit of US$328 million. In 1996 imports totalled US$1,635 million and exports US$1,137 million.

Trade with UK	1996	1997
Imports from UK	£11,270,000	£15,241,000
Exports to UK	39,142,000	16,436,000

COMMUNICATIONS

There are 2,200 miles of railways in operation. Communication with Peru is by road from La Paz via Copacabana and thence to the railhead at Puno. In 1993 Bolivia and Peru signed an agreement granting Bolivia a concession of 162 hectares at the southern Peruvian port of Ilo for 98 years to construct a free trade zone.

Commercial aviation is conducted by the national airline, Lloyd Aereo Boliviano and Transporte Aereo Militar between the major towns; Lloyd Aereo Boliviano and a number of foreign airlines provide international flights to the USA, South and Central America and Europe.

Most towns have radio, telephone or telegraph communication with the main cities. There are 16 principal daily newspapers.

EDUCATION

Elementary education is compulsory and free and there are secondary schools in urban centres. Provision is also made for higher education; in addition to St Francisco Xavier's University at Sucre, founded in 1624, there are seven other universities, the largest being the University of San Andrés at La Paz, and ten private universities.
ILLITERACY RATE – 16.9 per cent
ENROLMENT (percentage of age group) – primary 91 per cent (1990); secondary 29 per cent (1990); tertiary 22.2 per cent (1990)

BOSNIA-HERCEGOVINA

AREA – 19,735 sq. miles (51,129 sq. km). Neighbours: Serbia (east), Montenegro (south-east), Croatia (north and west)
POPULATION – 4,484,000 (1994 UN estimate); 4.4 million (1991 census): 44 per cent Bosniac, 33 per cent Serbs and 17 per cent Croats. The languages are Serbo-Croat (spoken by Serbs and written in the Cyrillic alphabet) and Croato-Serb (spoken by Croats and written in the Latin script)
CAPITAL – Sarajevo (population, 415,631, 1991 estimate)
MAJOR CITIES – Banja Luka (195,994); Mostar (127,034); Tuzla (131,866); Zenica (145,837)
CURRENCY – Convertible marka
NATIONAL DAY – 1 March (anniversary of 1992 declaration of independence)
NATIONAL FLAG – Blue, bearing a yellow triangle above a line of white stars
LIFE EXPECTANCY (years) – male 69.55; female 75.11
POPULATION GROWTH RATE – 0.0 per cent (1995)

POPULATION DENSITY – 88 per sq. km (1995)
URBAN POPULATION – 39.6 per cent (1991)
MILITARY EXPENDITURE – 6.25 per cent of GDP (1996)
MILITARY PERSONNEL – Bosnian Muslim Army (BiH):
   40,000; Croat Defence Council (HVO): 16,000; Bosnian
   Serb Army: 30,000
GDP – US$7,768 million (1994); US$1,307 per capita
   (1994)

HISTORY AND POLITICS

The country was settled by Slavs in the seventh century and conquered by the Ottoman Turks in 1463. Ruled by the Turks for over 400 years, the country came under Austro-Hungarian control in 1878. Austria-Hungary's annexation of Bosnia-Hercegovina in 1908 was never accepted by Serbia because of the large ethnic Serb population in the country; the assassination of the heir to the Austro-Hungarian throne in Sarajevo by an ethnic Serb precipitated the First World War. Bosnia-Hercegovina became part of the 'Kingdom of Serbs, Croats and Slovenes' (renamed Yugoslavia in 1929) under the Versailles Treaty (1919). It was occupied by German and Axis forces between 1941 and 1945. At the end of the war Bosnia-Hercegovina came under Communist rule as part of the Socialist Federal Republic of Yugoslavia, which eventually collapsed with the secession of Slovenia and Croatia in 1991.

The Bosnia-Hercegovina government issued a declaration of sovereignty in October 1991 against the wishes of the ethnic Serb Democratic Party. Independence was declared on 1 March 1992 following a referendum which was boycotted by the Bosnian Serbs. Bosnia-Hercegovina was recognized as an independent state by the EC and USA in April 1992 and admitted to UN membership in May 1992.

THE WAR

Fighting broke out in March 1992 between the pro-independence Muslims and Bosnian Serbs who wanted to merge with the Serbian republic to form a Greater Serbia. The Bosnian Serbs, assisted by the Serb-dominated Federal Yugoslav Army (JNA) rapidly gained control of 70 per cent of Bosnia and in August 1992 declared their own 'Republika Srpska' with its capital at Pale. International pressure eventually forced the JNA to withdraw but it handed over its weapons to the Bosnian Serb forces.

The Bosnian government (Muslim) forces formed an alliance with Bosnian Croat and Croat forces in early 1992 which collapsed in 1993. The Muslims then came under fire from both Bosnian Serb and Bosnian Croat forces. In January 1993 the UN and EU attempted to negotiate an end to the war by proposing a peace plan at a conference in Geneva. The Vance-Owen plan was accepted by all parties including the Bosnian president Radovan Karadzic but was rejected by the Bosnian Serb parliament and the fighting continued.

The Bosnian Serbs began to shell Sarajevo and government-held enclaves following the collapse of a three-month détente between the Serbs and the Muslims which lasted until December 1993. The attack on the enclaves and the siege of Sarajevo prompted the UN to declare Srebrenica, Zepa, Gorazde, Sarajevo, Tuzla and Bihac 'safe areas'.

In August 1993 the Bosnian Croats declared a 'Republic of Herceg-Bosna', with its capital in Mostar, and following a cease-fire in February 1994 joined the government forces in a Muslim-Croat Federation.

A Bosnian Serb artillery attack on a Sarajevo market in February 1994 killed 68 people and resulted in the imposition of a heavy weapons exclusion zone around the city by the UN and NATO. Bosnian Serb forces captured most of the enclave of Gorazde in April despite NATO air strikes. NATO widened its threat of air strikes to all UN 'safe areas' and galvanized the USA, Britain, France, Germany and Russia to form the Contact Group (CG) to co-ordinate peace efforts. The CG brought about a cease-fire in June 1994 and presented a peace plan, proposing a 51:49 division of territory between the Muslim-Croat Federation and the Bosnian Serbs. The Bosnian Serbs rejected the plan and the CG attempted to isolate them, with the support of Serbia, which had agreed to blockade Bosnian Serb forces in exchange for a relaxation of sanctions.

NATO air strikes against Bosnian Serbs in December 1994 resulted in the seizure of 350 UN peacekeepers, who were released as part of a cease-fire agreement in January. Bosnian Serbs retaliating against a Federation offensive in March resumed artillery attacks on Sarajevo, prompting a NATO bombing campaign and a second hostage crisis.

Fighting intensified in 1995, climaxing in a land-grab during the final months of the war. Bosnian Serb forces overran the UN safe areas of Zepa and Srebrenica in July, allegedly massacring thousands of fleeing Muslims, and then laid siege to the Bihac 'safe area' together with Croatian Serbs and rebel Muslims. Bosnian government and Croatian forces lifted the siege of Bihac in August, enabling a joint attack on Serb-held central Bosnia.

A Serb artillery attack on Sarajevo on 28 August which killed 37 people prompted NATO to bomb military and infrastructure targets and to issue an ultimatum to the Bosnian Serbs to remove their heavy weapons from around Sarajevo. The ultimatum was met by 20 September, following coercion from President Milosevic of Serbia.

The foreign ministers of Bosnia, Croatia and Serbia (rump Yugoslavia) met in Geneva in September 1995 and agreed to a US-sponsored peace accord. A cease-fire agreement was signed on 5 October and observed from 22 October, delayed by a Federation advance in the west and north-west, and Bosnian Serbs overrunning Tuzla.

THE PEACE AGREEMENT

The Presidents of Bosnia, Serbia and Croatia met in Dayton, Ohio, USA, for negotiations which culminated in an agreement on 21 November 1995. The Dayton Peace

Treaty was signed in Paris on 14 December. It was agreed to preserve Bosnia as a single state with a 51:49 division of territory between the Bosnian and Croat Federation and the Republika Srpska (Bosnian Serbs). A Republican (national) government, presidency and democratically elected institutions, based in Federation-controlled Sarajevo, were provided for. The Bosnian Serbs agreed to return five Sarajevo suburbs to the Federation and were given access to the sea in a land-swap with Croatia. The Federation gained a land corridor between Sarajevo and Gorazde but was obliged to return Mrkonjic Grad to the Bosnian Serbs.

The Dayton agreement provided for the deployment of a 60,000-strong NATO-led Peace Implementation Force (IFOR) which took over from UNPROFOR on 20 December 1995 and was mandated until December 1996. IFOR was replaced by a 31,000-strong, NATO-led Stabilization Force (SFOR), mandated until June 1998. SFOR in turn was replaced by a Dissuasion Force (DFOR) with no formal end date.

Mostar, which had been divided during the war between the Muslims and Croats of the Federation and administered by the EU, held elections in June 1996. The EU withdrew in December 1996. Control of the northern town of Brcko is still contested but remains under Bosnian Serb control. The Bosnian Croat state of Herceg-Bosna ceased to exist on 17 December 1996.

The Dayton peace agreement uses the term 'Bosniac' to refer to Bosnian Muslims.

POLITICAL SYSTEM

Under the Dayton peace agreement, the Bosnian republican (national) government was made responsible for foreign affairs, currency, citizenship and immigration. Executive authority was vested in a democratically elected rotating presidential triumvirate comprising a representative from each community.

Legislative authority is vested in a bicameral parliament, the Assembly of Bosnia-Hercegovina, comprising a House of Peoples and a House of Representatives. Both houses have two-year terms. The House of Peoples has 15 members, five from each community, who are selected by the House of Representatives. The House of Representatives has 42 directly elected members; two-thirds of the members come from the Federation and one-third from Republika Srpska. Within the Bosniac-Croat Federation there is a 140-member House of Representatives and ten cantonal assemblies; in the Republika Srpska there is an 83-member People's Assembly.

HEADS OF STATE (FOR ALL BOSNIA)
Current President, Alija Izetbegovic (Bosniac); Presidency Members, Momcilo Krajisnik (Serb); Kresimir Zubak (Croat), elected 14 September 1996

HEAD OF THE FEDERATION
President, Ejup Ganic (Bosniac)
Vice-President, Vladimir Soljic (Croat)

HEAD OF REPUBLIKA SRPSKA
President, Biljana Plavsic, elected 14 September 1996
Vice-President, Dragljub Mirjanic

COUNCIL OF MINISTERS (FOR ALL BOSNIA) as at June 1998
Co-Prime Ministers, Haris Silajdzic (Bosniac); Boro Bosic (Serb)
Deputy Prime Minister, Neven Tomic (Croat)
Communications and Civilian Affairs, Spasoje Albijanic (Serb)
Foreign Affairs, Jadranko Prlic (Croat)
Foreign Trade and Economic Relations, Mirsad Kurtovic (Bosniac)

FEDERATION CABINET as at June 1998
Prime Minister, Edhem Bicakcic (Bosniac)
Deputy PM, Finance, Drago Bilandzija (Croat)
Agriculture, Water-power and Forestry, Ahmed Smajic (Bosniac)
Defence, Ante Jelavic (Croat)
Education, Science, Culture and Sport, Fahrudin Rizvanbegovic (Bosniac)
Energy, Mining and Industry, Mirsad Salkic (Bosniac)
Environment, Ibrahim Morankic (Bosniac)
Health, Bozo Ljubic (Croat)
Interior, Mehmed Zilic (Bosniac)
Justice, Mate Tadic (Croat)
Social Welfare, Displaced Persons and Refugees, Rasim Kadic (Bosniac)
Trade, Ile Krezo (Croat)
Transport and Communications, Kemal Bubalo (Bosniac)
Without Portfolio, Nikola Antunovic (Croat); Nedeljko Despotovic (Serb)

REPUBLIKA SRPSKA GOVERNMENT as at June 1998
Prime Minister, Milorad Dodik
Deputy PMs, Durad Banjac (Industry and Technology); Ostoja Kremenovic (Internal Administration)
Agriculture, Waterways and Forestry, Milenko Savic
Defence, Manojlo Milovanovic
Education, Nenad Suzic
Finance, Novak Kondic
Foreign Economic Relations, Savo Loncar
Health and Social Welfare, Zeljko Rodic
Energy and Mining, Vladimir Dokic
Information, Rajko Vasic
Internal Affairs, Milovan Stankovic
Justice, Petko Cancar
Labour, Veterans and War Casualties, Tihomir Gligoric
Refugees and Displaced Persons, Miladin Dragicevic
Religion, Jovo Turanjanin
Science and Culture, Zivojin Eric
Sport and Youth, Milorad Karalic
Trade and Tourism, Nikola Kragulj
Transport and Communications, Marko Pavic
Urban Planning, Construction, Housing, Public Services and Environment, Jovo Basic

EMBASSY OF THE REPUBLIC OF BOSNIA-HERCEGOVINA
4th Floor, Morley House, 314–22 Regent Street, London WIR 5AB
Tel 0171-255 3758
Ambassador Extraordinary and Plenipotentiary, HE Osman Topcagic, apptd 1998

BRITISH EMBASSY
8 Tina Ujevica, Sarajevo
Tel: Sarajevo 663922
Ambassador Extraordinary and Plenipotentiary, HE Graham Hand, apptd 1998

BRITISH COUNCIL REPRESENTATIVE, Sue Barnes, 2nd Floor, Obala Kulina Bana 4, Sarajevo 71000

TRADE WITH UK	1996	1997
Imports from UK	£16,644,000	£10,015,000
Exports to UK	635,000	1,368,000

BOTSWANA
The Republic of Botswana

AREA – 224,607 sq. miles (581,730 sq. km). Neighbours: South Africa (south and east), Zimbabwe (north and north-east), Namibia (west)

POPULATION – 1,456,000 (1994 UN estimate). The national language is Setswana and the official language is English
CAPITAL – Gaborone (population, 133,468, 1991 census)
MAJOR CITIES – Francistown (55,244); Lobatse (26,052); Selebi-Phikwe (39,772)
CURRENCY – Pula (P) of 100 thebe
NATIONAL ANTHEM – Fatshe La Rona
NATIONAL DAY – 30 September
NATIONAL FLAG – Light blue with a horizontal black stripe fimbriated in white across the centre
LIFE EXPECTANCY (years) – male 52.32; female 59.70
POPULATION GROWTH RATE – 2.3 per cent (1995)
POPULATION DENSITY – 3 per sq. km (1995)
URBAN POPULATION – 48.1 per cent (1995)

A plateau at a height of about 4,000 feet divides Botswana into two main topographical regions. To the east of the plateau streams flow into the Marico, Notwani and Limpopo rivers; to the west lies a flat region comprising the Kgalagadi Desert, the Okavango Swamps and the Northern State Lands area. The climate is generally sub-tropical.

HISTORY AND POLITICS

On 30 September 1966 the British Protectorate of Bechuanaland became a republic within the Commonwealth under the name Botswana.

The last general election on 15 October 1994 was won by the Botswana Democratic Party with 26 seats to the Botswana National Front's 13 seats.

POLITICAL SYSTEM

The president is head of state and is elected by an absolute majority in the National Assembly. He appoints as vice-president a member of the National Assembly who is leader of government business in the National Assembly. The Assembly consists of the president, 40 members elected on a basis of universal adult suffrage, four specially elected members, the Attorney-General (non-voting) and the Speaker. Presidential and legislative elections are held every five years. There is also a 15-member House of Chiefs which considers legislation affecting the constitution and chieftaincy matters. In August 1997 the minimum voting age was lowered from 21 to 18.

HEAD OF STATE
President, HE Festus Mogae, *sworn in* 2 April 1998

CABINET *as at May 1998*
The President
Vice-President, Minister for Presidential Affairs and Public Administration, Lt.-Gen. Ian Khama
Agriculture, Ronald Sebego
Assistant Ministers, Lesedi Mothibamele *(Agriculture)*; Jacob Nkate *(Finance and Development Planning)*; Joy Phumaphi, Boometswe Mokgothu *(Local Government, Lands and Housing)*
Commerce and Industry, George Kgoroba
Education, Gaositwe Chiepe
Finance and Development Planning, Ponatshego Kedikilwe
Foreign Affairs, Lt.-Gen. Mompati Merafhe
Health, Chapson Butale
Labour and Home Affairs, Bahiti Temane
Local Government, Lands and Housing, Daniel Kwelagobe
Mineral Resources, Energy and Water Affairs, Margaret Nasha
Works, Transport and Communications, David Magang

BOTSWANA HIGH COMMISSION
6 Stratford Place, London WIN 9AE
Tel 0171–499 0031

High Commissioner, HE Tuelonyana Ditlhabi-Oliphant, apptd 1996

BRITISH HIGH COMMISSION
Private Bag 0023, Gaborone
Tel: Gaborone 352841/2/3
High Commissioner, HE David Beaumont, apptd 1994

BRITISH COUNCIL REPRESENTATIVE, P. Mitchell, British High Commission Building, Queen's Road, The Mall, PO Box 439, Gaborone

DEFENCE

The Army has 30 armoured personnel carriers and 16 artillery pieces. The Air Wing has 38 combat aircraft.
MILITARY EXPENDITURE – 5.2 per cent of GDP (1996)
MILITARY PERSONNEL – 8,500: Army 7,000, Air Wing 500, Paramilitaries 1,000

ECONOMY

Agriculture is predominantly pastoral. The national herd is around 2.2 million cattle and one million sheep and goats. Cattle rearing accounts for about 85 per cent of agricultural output, and livestock products, particularly beef, are a major source of foreign exchange earnings.

Mineral extraction and processing is now the major source of income following the opening of large mines for diamonds and copper-nickel. Botswana is one of the largest producers of diamonds in the world, with diamonds accounting for 80 per cent of export revenue. Large deposits of coal have been discovered and are now being mined. Manufacturing industry is growing but it is still a small sector of the economy. Tourism is the third largest industry, generating about 7 per cent of GDP.

In 1995 the government had a trade surplus of US$586 million and a current account surplus of US$342 million. Imports totalled US$1,914 million and exports US$2,143 million.
GNP – US$4,381 million (1995); US$3,020 per capita (1995)
GDP – US$3,959 million (1994); US$2,666 per capita (1994)
ANNUAL AVERAGE GROWTH OF GDP – 7.0 per cent (1996)
INFLATION RATE – 10.1 per cent (1996)
TOTAL EXTERNAL DEBT – US$613 million (1996)

Trade with UK	1996	1997
Imports from UK	£23,444,000	£20,460,000
Exports to UK	48,269,000	108,978,000

COMMUNICATIONS

The railway from Cape Town to Zimbabwe passes through eastern Botswana. The main roads are the north-south road, which closely follows the railway, and the road running east-west that links Francistown and Maun. Air services are provided on a scheduled basis between the main towns.

EDUCATION

There are 657 primary schools, 163 community junior secondary schools and 23 government and government-aided senior secondary schools. Total enrolment in the tertiary sector (teacher training establishments, colleges of education and the University of Botswana) numbers 6,923.
ILLITERACY RATE – 30.2 per cent
ENROLMENT (percentage of age group) – primary 96 per cent (1994); secondary 45 per cent (1994); tertiary 4.1 per cent (1994)

BRAZIL
República Federativa do Brasil

AREA – 3,300,171 sq. miles (8,547,403 sq. km). Neighbours: Guyana, Suriname, French Guiana, Colombia and Venezuela (north), Peru, Bolivia, Paraguay and Argentina (west), Uruguay (south)
POPULATION – 155,822,000 (1994 UN estimate). Portuguese is the national language but Italian, Spanish, German, Japanese and Arabic are also spoken
CAPITAL – Brasilia (population, 1,601,094, 1994 estimate)
MAJOR CITIES – Belo Horizonte (2,029,160); ΨFortaleza (1,768,637); ΨRecife (1,298,227); ΨRio de Janeiro (5,480,786), the former capital; ΨSalvador (2,075,275); São Paulo (9,646,187), 1996 census
CURRENCY – Real of 100 centavos
NATIONAL ANTHEM – Ouviram do Ipirangas às Margens Placidas (From peaceful Ypiranga's banks)
NATIONAL DAY – 7 September (Independence Day)
NATIONAL FLAG – Green with a yellow lozenge containing a blue sphere studded with white stars, and crossed by a white band with the motto *Ordem e Progresso*
LIFE EXPECTANCY (years) – male 63.81; female 70.38
POPULATION GROWTH RATE – 1.5 per cent (1995)
POPULATION DENSITY – 18 per sq. km (1995)
URBAN POPULATION – 75.6 per cent (1991)

The north is mainly wide, low-lying, forest-clad plains. The central areas are principally plateau land and the east and south are traversed by successive mountain ranges interspersed with fertile valleys. The principal ranges are the Serra do Mar, the Serra da Mantiqueira and the Serra do Espinhaco along the east coast. The River Amazon flows from the Peruvian Andes to the Atlantic.

HISTORY AND POLITICS

Brazil was discovered by the Portuguese navigator Pedro Alvares Cabral in 1500 and colonized by Portugal in the early 16th century. In 1822 it became independent under Dom Pedro, son of King Joao VI of Portugal, who had been forced to flee to Brazil during the Napoleonic Wars. In 1889, Dom Pedro II was dethroned and a republic was proclaimed. In 1985 Brazil returned to democratic rule after two decades of military government.

Fernando Cardoso of the Social Democratic Party, part of the Liberal Front coalition, won the presidential election of October 1994. In the November 1994 legislative elections the Liberal Front won 33 Senate seats, 175 seats in the Chamber of Deputies and nine state governorships.

POLITICAL SYSTEM

The Federative Republic of Brazil is composed of the federal district and 26 states. Under the 1988 constitution the president, who heads the executive, is directly elected for a four-year term; in June 1997 the constitution was amended to allow the president to stand for a second term. The Congress consists of an 81-member Senate (three senators per state elected for an eight-year term) and a 517-member Chamber of Deputies which is elected every four years; the number of deputies per state depends upon the state's population. Each state has a Governor, and a Legislative Assembly with a four-year term.

FEDERAL STRUCTURE

Federal Unit	Area (sq. km)	Population (1991)	Capital
Central west			
Distrito Federal	5,822	1,601,094	Brasília
Goiás	341,290	4,018,903	Goiânia
Matto Grosso	906,807	2,027,231	Cuiabá
Matto Grosso do Sul	358,159	1,780,373	Campo Grande
North			
Acre	153,150	417,718	Rio Branco
Amapá	143,454	289,397	Macapá
Amazonas	1,577,820	2,103,243	Manaus
Pará	1,253,165	4,950,060	Belém
Rondônia	238,513	1,132,692	Pôrto Velho
Roraima	225,116	217,583	Boa Vista
Tocantins	278,421	919,863	Palmas
North-east			
Alagoas	27,933	2,514,100	Maceió
Bahia	567,295	11,867,991	Salvador
Ceará	146,348	6,366,647	Fortaleza
Maranhão	333,366	4,930,253	São Luís
Paraíba	56,585	3,201,114	João Pessoa
Pernambuco	98,938	7,127,855	Recife
Piaui	252,378	2,582,137	Teresina
Rio Grande do Norte	53,307	2,415,567	Natal
Sergipe	22,050	1,491,876	Aracajú
South			
Paraná	199,709	8,448,713	Curitiba
Rio Grande do Sul	282,062	9,138,670	Pôrto Alegre
Santa Catarina	95,443	4,541,994	Florianópolis
South-east			
Espírito Santo	46,184	2,600,618	Vitória
Minas Gerais	588,384	15,743,152	Belo Horizonte
Rio de Janeiro	43,910	12,807,706	Rio de Janeiro
São Paulo	248,809	31,588,925	São Paulo

HEAD OF STATE

President, Fernando Henrique Cardoso, *sworn in* 1 January 1995
Vice-President, Marco Maciel

CABINET *as at May 1998*

Agriculture and Supplies, Francisco Turra
Air Force, Air Chief Marshal Lélio Lobo
Armed Forces Chief of Staff, Gen. Benedito Bezerra Leonel
Army, Gen. Zenildo Gonzaga Zoroastro de Lucena
Civilian Household of the Presidency, Clovis de Barros Carvalho
Communications, Luiz Carlos Membriça de Barros
Culture, Francisco Correa Weffort
Education, Paulo Renato de Souza
Energy and Mines, Raimundo Brito
Environment, Gustavo Krause
Finance, Pedro Malan
Foreign Affairs, Luiz Felipe Lampreia
Health, José Serra
Industry, Commerce and Tourism, José Botafogo Goncalves
Institutional Reform, Antonio Freitas Neto
Justice, José Renan Calheiros
Labour, Edward Joaquim Amadeo
Land Reform, Raúl Jungmann
Military Household of the Presidency, Gen. Alberto Cardoso
National Social Communications Secretary, Sergio Silva do Amaral
Navy, Adm. Mauro Cesar Rodrigues Pereira
Planning, Budget and Co-ordination, Paolo Paiva
Science and Technology, José Israel Vargas

Secretary-General of the Presidency, Eduardo Jorge Caldas
Pereira
Social Security, Waldeck Vieira Ornelas
State Reform, Luis Carlos Bresser Pereira
Strategic Affairs Secretariat, Ronaldo Sardenberg
Transport, Eliseu Padilha

BRAZILIAN EMBASSY
32 Green Street, London WIY 4AT
Tel 0171-499 0877
Ambassador Extraordinary and Plenipotentiary, HE Rubens
Antonio Barbosa, LVO, apptd 1994
Military Attaché, Fernando Drubski de Campos
Counsellor (Financial and Economic Affairs), Bezerra Abbott
Galvão

There is also a Brazilian Consulate-General in London and
honorary consular offices at Cardiff and Glasgow.

BRITISH EMBASSY
Sector de Embaixadus Sul, Quadra 801, Conjunto K, CEP
70.408 Brasilia DF
Tel: Brasilia 225 2710
Ambassador Extraordinary and Plenipotentiary, HE Keith
Haskell, CMG, CVO, apptd 1995
Deputy Head of Mission, Consul-General, J. A. Penney
Defence Attaché, Col. D. M. Black
First Secretary (Commercial), M. A. Patterson

There are British Consulates-General at Rio de Janeiro
and São Paulo.

BRITISH COUNCIL REPRESENTATIVE, Howard
Thompson, OBE, Edificio Morro Vermilho, Quadra 1.
Bloco H, SCS, 70399–900, Brasilia. Regional directors
in Recife, Rio de Janeiro and São Paulo

BRITISH AND COMMONWEALTH CHAMBER OF
COMMERCE IN SÃO PAULO, Rua Barão de Itapetininga
275, 7th Floor, 01042, São Paulo (*Postal Address,* PO Box
1621, 01000 São Paulo) and Rua Real Grandeza 99,
22281 Rio de Janeiro

DEFENCE

The Army has 61 main battle tanks, 823 armoured
personnel carriers, 765 artillery pieces, three aircraft and
97 helicopters. The Navy has bases at Rio de Janeiro,
Salvador, Recife, Belém, Florianpolis, Ladario and Manaus. It is equipped with six submarines, one aircraft carrier,
three destroyers, 18 frigates, and 35 patrol and coastal
vessels. Naval aviation has 54 armed helicopters, the
Marines have 33 armoured personnel carriers and 39
artillery pieces. The Air Force has 269 combat aircraft and
29 armed helicopters.
MILITARY EXPENDITURE – 2.8 per cent of GDP (1996)
MILITARY PERSONNEL – 314,700: Army 200,000, Navy
64,700, Air Force 50,000
CONSCRIPTION DURATION – 12 months (can be extended
to 18 months)

ECONOMY

There are large mineral deposits including iron ore
(hematite), manganese, bauxite, beryllium, chrome, nickel,
tungsten, cassiterite, lead, gold, monazite (containing rare
earths and thorium) and zirconium. Diamonds and precious and semi-precious stones are also found. Brazil is the
world's largest producer of coffee; the other main agricultural products are cassava, maize, soya, rice, wheat, black
beans, potatoes, cotton, cocoa, tobacco and peanuts.
    Since the return to civilian rule in 1985 successive
governments have attempted to curb high inflation and
large budget deficits. In February 1994 the government

and Congress agreed the first balanced budget in 20 years
and created a US$16 billion social emergency fund. An
interim currency pegged to the US dollar, known as the
Real Unit Value, was introduced in March 1994 and
replaced by a new non-inflationary currency, the real, in
July 1994.
    By mid-1995 inflation was down and the economy had
stabilized. Privatization was reactivated and the oil, telecommunications, electricity, gas and shipping industries
were opened to private investment. In November 1997, the
government announced a R$20 billion austerity package to
counter the economic threats resulting from the Asian
financial crisis. The plan doubled interest rates, increased
taxes and cut budgets. In March 1998, unemployment
reached its highest level since 1985.
GNP – US$709,591 million (1996); US$4,400 per capita
(1996)
GDP – US$523,392 million (1994); US$3,786 per capita
(1994)
ANNUAL AVERAGE GROWTH OF GDP – 4.1 per cent (1995)
INFLATION RATE – 18.2 per cent (1996)
UNEMPLOYMENT – 6.2 per cent (1993)
TOTAL EXTERNAL DEBT – US$179,047 million (1996)

TRADE

Principal imports are machinery, fuel and lubricants,
mineral products, transport equipment and chemicals.
Principal exports are industrial goods, coffee, iron ore and
soya. In 1994 the Brazilian automobile industry produced
1,400,000 vehicles. Of these, 374,000 vehicles were exported. The main trading partners are the USA, Argentina
and the EU.
    In 1995 Brazil had a trade deficit of US$3,157 million
and a current account deficit of US$18,136 million. In 1996
imports totalled US$56,947 million and exports
US$47,762.

Trade with UK	1996	1997
Imports from UK	£846,505,000	£1,027,974,000
Exports to UK	983,041,000	954,936,000

COMMUNICATIONS

There are 1,670,148 km of highways and the route-length
of railways is 30,129 km. There are ten international
airports and internal air services are highly developed.
There are 21,944 miles of navigable inland waterways. Rio
de Janeiro and Santos are the two leading ports.

EDUCATION

The education system includes both public and private
institutions. Public education is free at all levels.
ILLITERACY RATE – 16.7 per cent
ENROLMENT (percentage of age group) – primary 90 per
cent (1994); secondary 19 per cent (1994); tertiary 11.3
per cent (1994)

BRUNEI
Negara Brunei Darussalam

AREA – 2,226 sq. miles (5,765 sq. km). Neighbour: Malaysia
POPULATION – 285,000 (1996 official estimate): 66.9 per
cent Malay, 15.2 per cent Chinese, 5.9 per cent
indigenous races and 12 per cent European, Indian and
other races. The majority are Sunni Muslims. The
official language is Malay; English and dialects of
Chinese are also spoken

CAPITAL – Bandar Seri Begawan (population, 49,902, 1994 estimate)
CURRENCY – Brunei dollar (B$) of 100 sen (fully interchangeable with Singapore currency)
NATIONAL ANTHEM – Allah Peliharakan Sultan (God Bless His Majesty)
NATIONAL DAY – 23 February
NATIONAL FLAG – Yellow with diagonal stripes of white over black and the arms in red all over the centre
LIFE EXPECTANCY (years) – male 70.13; female 72.69
POPULATION GROWTH RATE – 2.4 per cent (1995)
POPULATION DENSITY – 49 per sq. km (1995)
URBAN POPULATION – 66.6 per cent (1991)
ILLITERACY RATE – 11.8 per cent
ENROLMENT (percentage of age group) – primary 91 per cent (1994); secondary 68 per cent (1994); tertiary 6.6 per cent (1994)

Brunei is situated on the north-west coast of the island of Borneo. It has a humid tropical climate.

HISTORY AND POLITICS

Formerly a powerful Muslim sultanate, Brunei was reduced to its present size by the mid-19th century and became a British Protectorate in 1888. In 1959 the Sultan promulgated the first written constitution, and on 1 January 1984 Brunei resumed full independence from Britain.

POLITICAL SYSTEM

Supreme executive authority rests with the Sultan, who presides over and is advised by the Privy Council, the Religious Council and the Council of Ministers. The Sultan effectively rules by decree as a state of emergency has been in effect since a revolt in 1962; there are no political parties and no elections.

HEAD OF STATE

HM The Sultan of Brunei, HM Sultan Haji Hassanal Bolkiah Mu'izzaddin Waddaullah, Sultan and Yang Di-Pertuan, GCB, acceded 1967, crowned 1 August 1968

COUNCIL OF MINISTERS as at May 1998
Prime Minister, Defence, Finance, HM The Sultan
Communications, Pehin Dato Zakaria
Development, Pengiran Dato Haji Ismail
Education; Health (acting), Pehin Dato Haji Abdul Aziz
Foreign Affairs, Prince Mohamed Bolkiah
Home Affairs, Special Adviser to the Sultan, Pehin Dato Haji Isa
Industry and Primary Resources, Pehin Dato Haji Abdul Rahman
Law, Pengiran Haji Bahrin
Religious Affairs, Pehin Dato Haji Mohammad Zain
Youth, Sports and Culture, Pehin Dato Haji Hussein

BRUNEI DARUSSALAM HIGH COMMISSION
19 – 20 Belgrave Square, London SW1X 8PG
Tel 0171-581 0521
High Commissioner, HE Pehin Dato Jaya Abdul Latif, apptd 1997

BRITISH HIGH COMMISSION
2/01 2nd Floor Block D, Komplexs Bangunan Yayasan, Sultan Haji Hassanal Bolkiah, Jalan Pretty, PO Box 2197
Bandar Seri Begawan
Tel: Bandar Seri Begawan 222231
High Commissioner, HE Ivan Callan, CMG, apptd 1994

BRITISH COUNCIL REPRESENTATIVE, T. Walsh, 45 Simpang 100, Jalan Tungku Link, Gadong, Bandar Seri Begawan 3192

DEFENCE

The Army has 26 armoured personnel carriers. The Navy, based in Muara, has nine patrol and coastal vessels. The Air Force has six armed helicopters.
MILITARY EXPENDITURE – 6.5 per cent of GDP (1996)
MILITARY PERSONNEL – 9,050: Army 3,900, Navy 700, Air Force 400, Paramilitaries 4,050

ECONOMY

The economy is based on the production of oil and natural gas. Royalties and taxes from these operations form the bulk of government revenue and have enabled the construction of free health, education and welfare services. However, the Asian economic slump coupled with a 40 per cent drop in the price of oil have damaged the economy.

The country has eight hospitals, 350 schools and one university. Royal Brunei Airlines operates scheduled flights to the UK, Australia and throughout the Far East. Radio Television Brunei broadcasts one television and three radio channels from the capital.

In 1995 Brunei produced 7,738,000 tonnes of crude petroleum and 9,350 cubic metres of natural gas. In 1994 imports totalled US$1,634 million and exports US$2,215 million.
GNP – US$3,975 million (1994); US$14,240 per capita (1994)
GDP – US$3,731 million (1994); US$16,270 per capita (1994)

TRADE WITH UK	1996	1997
Imports from UK	£562,396,000	£560,184,000
Exports to UK	291,711,000	336,627,000

BULGARIA
Republika Bulgaria

AREA – 42,823 sq. miles (110,912 sq. km). Neighbours: Romania (north), Serbia and the Former Yugoslav Republic of Macedonia (west), Greece and Turkey (south)
POPULATION – 8,402,000 (1994 UN estimate). The language is Bulgarian, a Southern Slavonic tongue closely allied to Serbo-Croat and Russian with local admixtures of modern Greek, Albanian and Turkish words. The alphabet is Cyrillic. The predominant religion is the Bulgarian Orthodox Church
CAPITAL – Sofia (population, 1,188,563, 1992 estimate)
MAJOR CITIES – ΨBourgas (210,788); Dobritch (104,485); Plévène (160,383); Plovdiv (341,374); Roussé (186,869); Slivène (144,045); Stara Zagora (175,385); ΨVarna (314,357), 1992 estimates
CURRENCY – Lev of 100 stotinki
NATIONAL DAY – 3 March
NATIONAL FLAG – Three horizontal bands, white, green, red
LIFE EXPECTANCY (years) – male 67.71; female 74.72
POPULATION GROWTH RATE – –1.4 per cent (1995)
POPULATION DENSITY – 76 per sq. km (1995)
URBAN POPULATION – 67.4 per cent (1993)

HISTORY AND POLITICS

A principality of Bulgaria was created by the Treaty of Berlin 1878, and in 1908 the country was declared an independent kingdom. A coup d'état in September 1944 gave power to the Fatherland Front, a coalition of Communists, Agrarians and Social Democrats. In August

1945, the main body of Agrarians and Social Democrats left the government. A referendum in September 1946 led to the abolition of the monarchy and the establishment of a republic.

The post-war period was dominated by the Communist Party (BCP), led by Todor Zhivkov. He was forced to resign in November 1989, and in January 1990 the National Assembly voted to abolish the BCP's constitutional guarantee of power. Multiparty elections to a Grand National Assembly (parliament) were held in June 1990 and won by the BCP, renamed the Bulgarian Socialist Party (BSP). This government lasted only two months, and in December 1990 a multiparty government was formed which began to implement a programme of economic and political reform.

After legislative elections in October 1991 a coalition government of the Union of Democratic Forces (UDF) and the Turkish Movement for Rights and Freedom Party (MRF) was formed. This government was replaced in December 1992 by a weak government of non-party technocrats which also collapsed. The BSP won the ensuing general election in December 1994 and formed a government with the Agrarian National Union (ANU). In November 1996 the UDF candidate, Petar Stoyanov, became president. The following month the BSP Prime Minister Jan Videnov resigned following protests about falling standards of living. The UDF won the resulting elections in April 1997.

POLITICAL SYSTEM

A new constitution enshrining democracy and the free market was adopted in 1991. It provides for a directly-elected president who serves for no more than two five-year terms. The chief executive is the prime minister who is appointed by the president, and is usually the leader of the largest party in the legislature. There is a unicameral National Assembly of 240 members who are directly elected by proportional representation for five-year terms.

HEAD OF STATE
President, Petar Stoyanov, *elected* 3 November 1996

COUNCIL OF MINISTERS *as at June 1998*

Prime Minister, Ivan Kostov
Deputy PM, Education and Science, Vesselin Metodiev
Deputy PM, Industry, Aleksander Bozhkov
Deputy PM, Regional and Urban Development, Evgenii Bakurdjiev
Agriculture, Forestry and Land Reform, Ventsislav Vurbanov
Culture, Emma Moskova
Defence, Georgi Ananiev
Environment and Water, Evdokia Maneva
Finance, Mouravei Radev
Foreign Affairs, Nadezhda Mihailova
Health, Peter Boyadjiev
Interior, Bogomil Bonev
Justice and European Legal Integration, Vassil Gotsev
Labour and Social Affairs, Ivan Neikov
Secretary-General to the Cabinet, State Administration, Mario Tagarinski
Trade and Tourism, Valentin Vassilev
Transport, Wilhelm Kraus

EMBASSY OF THE REPUBLIC OF BULGARIA
186–188 Queen's Gate, London SW7 5HL
Tel 0171–584 9400
Ambassador Extraordinary and Plenipotentiary, HE Valentin Dobrev, apptd 1998
Counsellor (Commercial/Economic), D. Georgiev
Military, Air and Naval Attaché, Capt. Ivan Mladenov Yordanov

BRITISH EMBASSY
38 Boulevard Vassil Levski, Sofia
Tel: Sofia 2980 1220
Ambassador Extraordinary and Plenipotentiary, HE Richard Stagg, apptd 1998
Deputy Head of Mission, Consul and First Secretary, M. Tatham
Defence Attaché, Col. R. E. Fielding
First Secretary (Commercial), M. J. Carbine

BRITISH COUNCIL REPRESENTATIVE, K. Lewis, 7 Tulovo Street, 1504, Sofia

DEFENCE

The Army has 1,475 main battle tanks, 100 armoured infantry fighting vehicles, 1,894 armoured personnel carriers and 1,750 artillery pieces. The Navy has two submarines, one frigate, 23 patrol and coastal vessels, and nine armed helicopters. The Air Force has 217 combat aircraft and 44 armed helicopters.

MILITARY EXPENDITURE – 3.3 per cent of GDP (1996)
MILITARY PERSONNEL – 109,800: Army 50,400, Navy 6,100, Air Force 19,300, Paramilitaries 34,000
CONSCRIPTION DURATION – 18 months

ECONOMY

The principal crops are wheat, maize, beet, tomatoes, tobacco, oleaginous seeds, fruit, vegetables and cotton. The livestock includes cattle, sheep, goats, pigs, horses, asses, mules and water buffaloes. Cadmium, coal, copper, pig iron, kaolin, lead, silver and zinc are produced.

The lack of radical economic reform has hampered economic development; in 1996, the value of the lev plummeted by 70 per cent and food shortages were commonplace. The government responded by adopting a radical reform package including the closure of 70 state companies, but interest rates and inflation reached 300 per cent a year.

The lev was pegged to the Deutsche Mark from 1 July 1997, at a rate of DM1=1,000 leva. Privatizations in 1997 were expected to raise 600 billion leva. Following the implementation of fiscal reforms, Bulgaria received some US$385 million in loans from the EU and the World Bank to help economic recovery.

GNP – US$9,924 million (1996); US$1,190 per capita (1996)
GDP – US$16,985 million (1994); US$1,106 per capita (1994)
UNEMPLOYMENT – 11.1 per cent (1995)
TOTAL EXTERNAL DEBT – US$9,819 million (1996)

TRADE

The principal imports are fuels, minerals and metals, engineering goods and industrial equipment. The principal exports are agricultural produce, engineering goods and industrial equipment, industrial consumer goods, chemicals and fuels, minerals and metals.

In 1993 Bulgaria signed an Association Agreement with the EU, and EU duties on Bulgarian industrial goods were abolished by 1995 and levies on agricultural goods significantly lowered.

In 1996 Bulgaria had a trade surplus of US$144 million and a current account deficit of US$23 million. The principal trading partners are Russia and Germany.

Trade with UK	1996	1997
Imports from UK	£87,260,000	£77,181,000
Exports to UK	116,018,000	91,029,000

EDUCATION

Education is free and compulsory for children from seven to 15 years inclusive. There are three universities (at Sofia, Plovdiv and Veliko Turnovo), an American University and 21 higher education establishments.

ILLITERACY RATE – 1.7 per cent

ENROLMENT (percentage of age group) – primary 97 per cent (1995); secondary 75 per cent (1995); tertiary 39.4 per cent (1995)

BURKINA FASO

AREA – 105,792 sq. miles (274,000 sq. km). Neighbours: Mali (west), Niger and Benin (east), Togo, Ghana and Côte d'Ivoire (south)

POPULATION – 10,200,000 (1994 UN estimate). The official language is French. Mossi, More, Dioula and Goumantche are indigenous languages

CAPITAL – Ouagadougou (population, 634,479, 1991 estimate)

MAJOR CITIES – Bobo-Dioulasso (228,668); Koudougou (30,000)

CURRENCY – Franc CFA

NATIONAL ANTHEM – Ditanyé

NATIONAL DAY – 11 December

NATIONAL FLAG – Equal bands of red over green, with a yellow star in centre

LIFE EXPECTANCY (years) – male 45.84; female 49.01

POPULATION GROWTH RATE – 2.5 per cent (1995)

POPULATION DENSITY – 37 per sq. km (1995)

URBAN POPULATION – 15.0 per cent (1995)

MILITARY EXPENDITURE – 2.0 per cent of GDP (1996)

MILITARY PERSONNEL – 10,000: Army 5,600, Air Force 200, Paramilitaries 4,200

ILLITERACY RATE – 80.8 per cent

ENROLMENT (percentage of age group) – primary 31 per cent (1994); secondary 7 per cent (1993); tertiary 1.1 per cent (1994)

Burkina Faso (formerly Upper Volta) is an inland savannah state in West Africa. The largest tribe is the Mossi whose king, the Moro Naba, still wields a certain moral influence.

HISTORY AND POLITICS

Burkina Faso was annexed by France in 1896 and between 1932 and 1947 was administered as part of the Colony of the Ivory Coast. It decided on 11 December 1958 to remain an autonomous republic within the French Community; full independence outside the Community was proclaimed on 5 August 1960.

In 1966 the Army assumed power; a constitution allowing for a partial return to civilian rule was adopted in 1970, but was suspended in 1974. Full legislative and presidential elections were held again in 1978.

Following a number of military coups, Capt. Blaise Compaoré seized power in 1987. A new constitution was adopted in 1991. Presidential elections were held in December 1991 and won by Compaoré in the face of a boycott by the opposition parties, who were unhappy with the new constitution. Opposition parties also boycotted the 1992 legislative elections, which were won by Compaoré's Organization for Popular Democracy-Labour Movement (ODP-MT) party; it formed the government in coalition with several smaller parties.

HEAD OF STATE

President, Capt. Blaise Compaoré, *assumed office* October 1987, *elected* December 1991

COUNCIL OF MINISTERS *as at May 1998*

Prime Minister, Economy and Finance, Kadré Désiré Ouedraogo

Agriculture, Michel Koutaba

Animal Resources, Alassane Seré

Basic and Mass Education, Baworo Seydou Sanou

Civil Service and Institutional Development, Paramanga Ernest Yonli

Communications and Culture, Mahamoudou Ouedraogo

Defence, Albert D. Milogo

Economy and Finance (government spokesman), Tertius Zongo

Employment, Labour, Social Security, Elie Saré

Energy and Mines, Elie Ouedraogo

Foreign Affairs, Ablassé Ouedraogo

Health, Alain Ludovic Tou

Infrastructure, Housing, Urban Planning, Joseph Kaboré

Justice, Keeper of the Seals, Larba Yarga

Presidency of the Republic, Bognessan Arsene Yé

Regional Integration, Viviane Yolande Compaoré

Relations with Parliament, Cyril Goungounga

Secondary and Higher Education, Scientific Research, Christophe Dabiré

Social Affairs and Family, Bana Ouandaogo

Territorial Administration and Security, Yéro Boli

Trade, Industry and Crafts, Idrissa Zampaligré

Transport and Tourism, Bedouma Alain Yoda

Water and Environment, Salif Diallo

Women's Promotion, Alice Tiendrebeogo

Youth and Sports, Joseph André Tiendrebeogo

EMBASSY OF BURKINA FASO

16 Place Guy d'Arezzo, 1060 Brussels, Belgium

Tel: Brussels 345 9912

Ambassador Extraordinary and Plenipotentiary, HE Youssouf Ouedraogo, apptd 1995, resident in Brussels

HONORARY CONSULATE, 5 Cinnamon Row, Plantation Wharf, London SW11 3TW. Tel: 0171-738 1800. *Honorary Consul-General,* S. G. Singer

BRITISH AMBASSADOR, HE Haydon Warren-Gash, CMG, resident at Abidjan, Côte d'Ivoire

ECONOMY

The principal industry is cattle and sheep rearing. Agriculture employs one fifth of the workforce and contributes 10 per cent of GDP. The chief exports are livestock, groundnuts, millet and sorghum. Small deposits of gold, manganese, copper, bauxite and graphite have been found.

In 1994 Burkina Faso had a trade deficit of US$129 million and a current account surplus of US$15 million. In 1996 imports totalled US$545 million and exports US$305 million.

GNP – US$2,410million (1996); US$230 per capita (1996)

GDP – US$2,798 million (1994); US$186 per capita (1994)

ANNUAL AVERAGE GROWTH OF GDP – 2.7 per cent (1992)

INFLATION RATE – 6.2 per cent (1996)

TOTAL EXTERNAL DEBT – US$1,294 million (1996)

TRADE WITH UK	1996	1997
Imports from UK	£11,283,000	£5,798,000
Exports to UK	1,015,000	1,193,000

BURUNDI
République du Burundi

AREA – 10,747 sq. miles (27,834 sq. km). Neighbours: Rwanda (north), Tanzania (east and south), Democratic Republic of Congo (west)

POPULATION – 5,982,000 (1994 UN estimate): 83 per cent Hutu, 15 per cent Tutsi. The official languages are Kirundi, a Bantu language, and French. Kiswahili is also used

CAPITAL – Bujumbura (formerly Usumbura) (population, 235,440, 1994)

MAJOR CITIES – Kitega (18,000)

CURRENCY – Burundi franc of 100 centimes

NATIONAL DAY – 1 July

NATIONAL FLAG – Divided diagonally by a white saltire into red and green triangles; on a white disc in the centre three red six-pointed stars edged in green

NATIONAL ANTHEM – Uburundi Bwacu

LIFE EXPECTANCY (years) – male 48.42; female 51.92

POPULATION GROWTH RATE – 1.8 per cent (1995)

POPULATION DENSITY – 215 per sq. km (1995)

URBAN POPULATION – 5.0 per cent (1990)

MILITARY EXPENDITURE – 4.8 per cent of GDP (1996)

MILITARY PERSONNEL – 22,000: Army 18,500, Paramilitaries 3,500

ILLITERACY RATE – 64.7 per cent

ENROLMENT (percentage of age group) – primary 52 per cent (1992); secondary 5 per cent (1992); tertiary 0.9 per cent (1992)

HISTORY AND POLITICS

Formerly a Belgian trusteeship under the United Nations, Burundi became independent as a constitutional monarchy on 1 July 1962. However, the monarchy was overthrown in 1966 and the country became a republic. After a coup in 1987 the Military Committee of National Redemption came to power, led by Maj. Pierre Buyoya, a Tutsi.

Although most of the population is Hutu, political and military power has traditionally rested with the Tutsi minority. Since the 1960s, Hutu attempts to overthrow Tutsi rule have resulted in ethnic massacres. The National Unity and Progress Party (UPRONA) government's attempts to introduce multiparty non-tribal politics were approved by national referendum in 1992. The legislative elections in 1993 were won by the Front for Democracy in Burundi (FRODEBU). However, the identification of the government with Hutu interests led the Tutsi-dominated army to attempt a coup in October 1993 in which President Melchior Ndadaye was killed. The government regained control in December but two months of inter-racial fighting left more than 50,000 dead and 500,000 refugees.

FRODEBU and UPRONA agreed to form a coalition government in February 1994 with a Tutsi prime minister and Hutu president. The constitution was amended to specify that the 25-member Cabinet must include ten Tutsi, ten Hutu and five neutral ministers. However, the government was unable to halt attacks by the Tutsi-dominated army and Hutu militias on each other's communities. The fighting claimed 200,000 lives in 1993–5.

In July 1996 the army again seized power and installed Maj. Buyoya as president. Political parties were banned and the National Assembly was suspended until October 1996 when fewer than half its deputies attended. A multi-ethnic government of national unity was formed in August 1996. Clashes between the army and Hutu militias, and massacres of civilians have continued, despite talks aimed at finding a peaceful solution. More than 300,000 refugees remain in camps in Tanzania and the Democratic Republic of Congo.

HEAD OF STATE
President, Maj. Pierre Buyoya, *appointed* 25 July 1996

COUNCIL OF MINISTERS *as at May 1998*
Prime Minister, Pascal-Firmin Ndimira
Agriculture and Livestock, Damas Nyiraniwangira
Communal Development, Pierre Bambasi
Communications, Pierre Claver Ndayicarye
Defence, Lt.-Col. Alfred Ngurunziza
Development Planning and Reconstruction, Evariste Minani
Energy and Mines, Bernard Barandereka
Finance, Astère Girukwigomba
Foreign Affairs, Luc Rukingama
Human Rights, Social Action and Women's Promotion, Christine Ruhuza
Institutional Reforms, Eugène Niindorera
Interior and Public Security, Col. Epitace Bayaganakandi
Justice, Terence Sinunguruza
Labour, Handicrafts and Professional Training, Barnabé Muteragiranwa
Peace Process, Ambroise Niyonsaba
Primary Education and Literacy, Joseph Ndayisaba
Public Service, Monique Ndakozi
Public Works and Equipment, Vital Nzobonimpa
Reintegration and Resettlement of Displaced Persons and Repatriates, Pascal Ngurunziza
Secondary Schools, Higher Education and Scientific Research, Rogatien Ndoricimpa
Territorial Management and Environment, Samuel Bigawa
Trade, Industry and Tourism, Grégoire Banyiyezako
Transport, Posts and Telecommunications, Vénérand Nzohabonayo
Youth, Sports and Culture, Bonaventure Gasutwa

EMBASSY OF THE REPUBLIC OF BURUNDI
Square Marie Louise 46, 1040 Brussels, Belgium
Tel: Brussels 2304535
Ambassador Extraordinary and Plenipotentiary, Leonidas Ndoricampa, resident in Brussels
BRITISH AMBASSADOR, HE Kaye Oliver, OBE, resident at Kigali, Rwanda

ECONOMY

The chief crops are coffee, tea and cotton, accounting for over 80 per cent of export earnings. Mineral, hide and skin exports are also important.

A total economic blockade was imposed by Cameroon, Ethiopia, Kenya, Rwanda, Tanzania, Uganda and Zaïre (now the Democratic Republic of Congo) following the 1996 coup. This was relaxed slightly in April 1997 to allow food and medicine into the country.

In 1995 there was a trade deficit of US$63 million and a current account deficit of US$6 million. In 1996 imports totalled US$127 million and exports US$40 million.

GNP – US$1,066 million (1996); US$170 per capita (1996)
GDP – US$1,264 million (1994); US$172 per capita (1994)
ANNUAL AVERAGE GROWTH OF GDP – 2.3 per cent (1992)
INFLATION RATE – 26.4 per cent (1996)
TOTAL EXTERNAL DEBT – US$1,127 million (1996)

TRADE WITH UK	1996	1997
Imports from UK	£2,439,000	£2,224,000
Exports to UK	2,712,000	8,867,000

CAMBODIA

AREA – 69,898 sq. miles (181,035 sq. km). Neighbours: Laos (north), Thailand (north and west), and Vietnam (east)
POPULATION – 9,836,000 (1997 estimate). The language is Khmer. Chinese and Vietnamese are also spoken
CAPITAL – ΨPhnom Penh (population, 832,000, 1997)
CURRENCY – Riel of 100 sen
NATIONAL ANTHEM – Nokoreach
NATIONAL DAY – 9 November (Independence Day)
NATIONAL FLAG – Three horizontal stripes of blue, red, blue, with the blue of double width and containing a representation of the temple of Angkor in white
LIFE EXPECTANCY (years) – male 50.10; female 52.90
POPULATION GROWTH RATE – 2.8 per cent (1995)
POPULATION DENSITY – 54 per sq. km (1995)
URBAN POPULATION – 12.6 per cent (1990)
ILLITERACY RATE – 34.7 per cent
ENROLMENT (percentage of age group) – tertiary 1.6 per cent (1994)

HISTORY AND POLITICS

Cambodia became a French protectorate in 1863 and was granted independence within the French Union as an Associate State in 1949. Full independence was proclaimed on 9 November 1953, and Prince Norodom Sihanouk became head of state. In March 1970 Prince Sihanouk was deposed and a Khmer Republic was declared in October 1970.

In April 1975, after a five-year civil war, Phnom Penh fell to the North Vietnamese-backed Khmer Rouge. Pol Pot, the leader of the Khmer Rouge (Communist) party, formed a new government and the state was renamed Democratic Kampuchea. During Khmer Rouge rule hundreds of thousands of Cambodians fled into exile and an estimated two million were killed.

In December 1978, Vietnamese troops invaded Cambodia and the state was renamed The People's Republic of Kampuchea (PRK); in April 1989 it became the State of Cambodia (SOC). With support from the Vietnamese army, PRK forces won control of most of the country from the forces of the Coalition Government of Democratic Kampuchea (CGDK), formed in June 1982 by the Khmer Rouge and two non-Communist groups. Following the Vietnamese withdrawal in 1989, the resistance forces regained ground.

In September 1990, the SOC and the CGDK established a Supreme National Council. A permanent cease-fire began on 23 June and peace agreements were signed on 23 October 1991. In March 1992 the United Nations Transitional Authority for Cambodia (UNTAC) assumed authority from the SOC government in the run-up to the May 1993 elections.

Multiparty elections were held in May 1993. Prince Sihanouk brokered a coalition government agreement under which he became head of state and the leaders of the United Front for an Independent, Neutral, Peaceful and Co-operative Cambodia (FUNCINPEC) and the Cambodian People's Party (CPP) (the former SOC party), Prince Ranariddh and Hun Sen, became co-prime ministers. In September 1993 a new constitution was adopted under which Cambodia became a pluralist liberal democracy with a constitutional monarchy. Prince Sihanouk was elected king and he appointed a new government.

Prince Ranariddh was ousted from power following a coup by soldiers loyal to Hun Sen in July 1997, and armed conflicts between the rival factions broke out throughout the country. At the opening of the United Nations General Assembly in September, a resolution was adopted that prevented Cambodia from taking its seat until the merits of the rival delegations, those of Prince Ranariddh and Hun Sen, could be assessed. On 27 February 1998, both sides declared a cease-fire in a Japanese-brokered peace plan. Under the terms of the deal Prince Ranariddh would be tried by the Hun Sen government and unconditionally pardoned if found guilty; he would then return to the country for democratic elections in July 1998.

INSURGENCIES

In July 1994 the Royal Government outlawed the Khmer Rouge, which responded by declaring a provisional government. Large numbers of Khmer Rouge have defected to the Royal Government including more than 2,500 led by Ieng Sary, who formally joined the Royal Cambodian Armed Forces in November 1996. Khmer Rouge leader Pol Pot was captured by a group of defectors in June 1997 and died in captivity on 15 April 1998.

About 3,000 Khmer Rouge members are still active in northern Cambodia and control 5 per cent of the territory.

POLITICAL SYSTEM

Legislative power is vested in the National Assembly, which has 120 members elected for five-year terms. Executive power rests in the Royal Government, with the King having the power only to make appointments and declare a state of emergency, in consultation with the government.

HEAD OF STATE

HM The King of Cambodia, Norodom Sihanouk, *elected by the Council of the Throne* 24 September 1993

ROYAL GOVERNMENT OF CAMBODIA *as at July 1998*

First Prime Minister, Ung Huot (F)
Second Prime Minister, Hun Sen (CPP)
Deputy Prime Minister, Interior and National Security, Sar Kheng (CPP)

Deputy Prime Minister, Public Works and Transport, Ing Kieth (F)
Agriculture, Forestry and Fishing, Tao Senghuo (F)
Commerce, Cham Prasit (CPP)
Culture and Fine Arts, Nut Narang (CPP)
Education, Youth and Sport, Tol Loas (F)
Environment Management, Mok Maret (CPP)
Health, Chhea Thang (CPP)
Industry, Mines and Energy, Pu Sothirak (F)
Information Adviser, Sieng Lapresse (F)
Information and Press, Ieng Muli (BLDP)
Interior and National Security, Yu Hokkri (F)
Military Adviser to the Prime Minister, Gen. Ea Chuo-Kimmeng (F)
National Defence, Gen. Tea Banh (CPP); Gen. Tie Chamrat (F)
Office of the Council of Ministers, Sok An (CPP); Nadi Tan (F)
Planning, Chea Chanto (CPP)
Rural Development, Hong Sun-huot (F)
State Minister for Cultural Affairs, Van Molivan (CPP)
State Minister for Inspection, Ung Phan (F)
State Minister for Justice, Chem Snguon (CPP)
State Minister for Rehabilitation and Development, Economy and Finance, Keat Chhon (CPP)
Tourism, Veng Sereivut (F)

BLDP Buddhist Liberal Democrat Party; CPP Cambodian People's Party; F FUNCINPEC

BRITISH EMBASSY
29, Street 75, Phnom Penh
Tel: Phnom Penh 427124
Ambassador Extraordinary and Plenipotentiary, HE George Edgar, apptd 1997

DEFENCE

The Army has 100 main battle tanks, 250 armoured personnel carriers and 400 artillery pieces. The Navy has 13 patrol and coastal vessels. The Air Force has 23 combat aircraft.
MILITARY EXPENDITURE – 3.9 per cent of GDP (1996)
MILITARY PERSONNEL – 140,500: Army 84,000, Navy 5,000, Air Force 1,500, Provincial Forces 50,000
CONSCRIPTION DURATION – Not implemented since 1993

ECONOMY

The economy is based on agriculture, fishing and forestry. In addition to rice, which is the staple crop, the major products are rubber, livestock, maize, timber, pepper, palm sugar, fresh and dried fish, kapok, beans, soya and tobacco. Rice, rubber and wood used to be the main exports, though production was brought to a standstill by the hostilities.

Under the Khmer Rouge, the urban population was forced to work on the land, and re-establish plantations producing such crops as cotton, rubber and bananas. Following the Vietnamese invasion of 1978 the towns were repopulated and factories, in particular textile mills, iron smelting works and cement works, were put back in production.

In 1996 there was a trade deficit of US$428 million and a current account deficit of US$298 million.
GNP – US$3,088 million (1996); US$300 per capita (1996)
GDP – US$1,036 million (1994); US$422 per capita (1994)
INFLATION RATE – 10.1 per cent (1996)
TOTAL EXTERNAL DEBT – US$2,111 million (1996)

TRADE WITH UK	1996	1997
Imports from UK	£3,343,000	£2,454,000
Exports to UK	21,932,000	24,582,000

COMMUNICATIONS

The country has over 5,000 kilometres of roads, although most are now in a state of disrepair. There are two railways, one from Phnom Penh to the Thai border, the other from Phnom Penh to Kampot and Sihanoukville (Kompong Som). Phnom Penh is on a river capable of receiving ships of up to 2,500 tons all the year round. The deep water port at Sihanoukville (Kompong Som) on the Gulf of Thailand can receive ships of up to 10,000 tons. The port is linked to Phnom Penh by a modern highway.

CAMEROON
République du Cameroun

AREA – 183,569 sq. miles (475,442 sq. km). Neighbours: Nigeria (north and west), Chad and Central African Republic (east), Republic of Congo, Gabon and Equatorial Guinea (south)
POPULATION – 13,277,000 (1994 UN estimate). French and English are both official languages and enjoy equal status
CAPITAL – Yaoundé (population, 653,670, 1986 estimate)
MAJOR CITIES – ΨDouala (1,029,736) is the commercial centre
CURRENCY – Franc CFA of 100 centimes
NATIONAL ANTHEM – O Cameroun, Berceau de Nos Ancêtres (O Cameroon, thou cradle of our forefathers)
NATIONAL DAY – 20 May
NATIONAL FLAG – Vertical stripes of green, red and yellow with single five-pointed yellow star in centre of red stripe
LIFE EXPECTANCY (years) – male 54.50; female 57.50
POPULATION GROWTH RATE – 2.8 per cent (1995)
POPULATION DENSITY – 28 per sq. km (1995)
MILITARY EXPENDITURE – 2.4 per cent of GDP (1996)
MILITARY PERSONNEL – 22,100: Army 11,500, Navy 1,300, Air Force 300, Paramilitaries 9,000
ILLITERACY RATE – 36.6 per cent
ENROLMENT (percentage of age group) – secondary 15 per cent (1980); tertiary 3.3 per cent (1990)

HISTORY AND POLITICS

The German colony of the Cameroons, established in 1884, was captured by British and French forces in 1916 and divided into the League of Nations-mandated territories (later UN trusteeships) of East (French) and West (British) Cameroon. On 1 January 1960 East Cameroon became independent as the Republic of Cameroon. This was joined on 1 October 1961 by the southern part of West Cameroon after a plebiscite held under United Nations auspices; the northern part joined Nigeria. Cameroon became a federal republic with separate East and West Cameroon state governments. After a plebiscite held in 1972, Cameroon became a unitary republic and a one-party state.

After extensive unrest, multiparty elections were held in March 1992, although they were boycotted by two of the main opposition parties. The ruling People's Democratic Movement emerged short of a parliamentary majority but formed a coalition government with a small opposition party, the Movement for the Defence of the Republic.

Presidential elections were held in October 1992 and won by the incumbent Paul Biya. The results were disputed by opponents and foreign observers, who accused the authorities of malpractice. In November a new coalition government was formed with the addition of the

Union for Democracy and Progress and the Union of Peoples of Cameroon. A legislative election held in May 1997 was dominated by the ruling Cameroon People's Democratic Movement (CPDM) which won 109 of the 180 seats, though Commonwealth observers reported widespread fraud and voter intimidation.

INTERNATIONAL RELATIONS

There have been armed clashes with Nigeria over the disputed Bakassi peninsula. The dispute is under consideration at the International Court of Justice.

POLITICAL SYSTEM

The president is directly elected for a seven-year term, and appoints the prime minister and Cabinet. The National Assembly comprises 180 members, directly elected for a five-year term. Under the 1995 constitutional amendments a Senate is to be created.

HEAD OF STATE

President and Commander in Chief of the Armed Forces, Paul Biya, *acceded* 6 November 1982, *elected* 14 January 1984, *re-elected* 24 April 1988, 10 October 1992, 12 October 1997

CABINET *as at July 1998*

Prime Minister, Peter Mafany Musonge
Agriculture, Zacharie Perevet; Aboubakari Abdoulaye
Animal Breeding, Fisheries and Animal Industries, Ajoudji Hamadjoda
City Affairs, Antoine Zanga
Civil Service and Administrative Reform, Sali Dairou
Communication, René Ze Nguele
Culture, Ferdinand Leopold Oyono
Defence and National Police Force, Emmanuel Edou
Delegate at the Foreign Ministry in charge of Commonwealth Relations, Joseph Dion Ngute
Delegate at the Foreign Ministry in charge of Islamic Relations, Gargoum Adoum
Delegate at the Ministry of Finance in charge of Budget, Roger Melingui
Delegate at the Ministry of Finance in charge of the Plan for Stability, Jean-Marie Gankou
Delegate at the Presidency in charge of Defence, Ali Amadou
Delegate at the Presidency in charge of Relations with the Assemblies, Grégoire Owona
Delegate at the Presidency in charge of State Control, Lucy Gwanmesia
Economy and Finance, Edouard Akame Mfoumdou
Education, Charles Etoundi
Employment, Labour and Social Causes, Pius Ondoua
Environment and Forests, Sylvester Naah Ondoua
Foreign Affairs, Augustin Kontchou Kouemegni
Health, Alim Hayatou
Higher Education, Jean-Marie Atangana Mebara
Industrial and Commercial Development, Maigari Bello Bouba (UNDP); Edmond Mouampea Mbio
Investment and National Development, Tsala Messi
Justice, Keeper of the Seals, Laurent Esso
Mines, Water Resources and Energy, Yves Mbelle
National Education, Joseph Yunga Teghen
Post and Telecommunications, Saidou Mountchipou; Denis Oumarou
Public Health, Gotlieb Monekosso
Public Investment and Regional Planning, Justin Ndioro a Yombo
Public Works, Jérome Etah; Emmanuel Bonde
Scientific and Technical Research, Henri Hogbe Nlend
Social Affairs, Madaleine Fouda

Special Duties at the Presidency, Peter Abety; Martin Okouda; Amadou Baba; Elvis Ngole Ngole
Territorial Administration, Samson Ename Ename; Antar Gassagaye
Tourism, Claude Joseph Mbafou
Town Planning and Housing, Pierre Hele; Shey Johnes Yembe
Transport, Joseph Tsanga Abanda; Nana Aboubakar Diallo
Women's Affairs, Aissatou Yaou
Youth and Sports, Joseph Owona

EMBASSY OF THE REPUBLIC OF CAMEROON

84 Holland Park, London WII 3SB
Tel 0171–727 0771/3
Ambassador Extraordinary and Plenipotentiary, HE Samuel Libock Mbei, apptd 1995

BRITISH HIGH COMMISSION

Avenue Winston Churchill, BP 547 Yaoundé
Tel: Yaoundé 220545
High Commissioner, HE Peter Boon, MBE, apptd 1998
There is also a British Consulate at Douala.

BRITISH COUNCIL DIRECTOR, Terence Humphreys, Avenue Charles de Gaulle (BP 818), Yaoundé

ECONOMY

Principal products are cocoa, coffee, bananas, cotton, timber, groundnuts, aluminium, rubber and palm products. Crude petroleum is also one of Cameroon's principal products.

France, Italy and other European Union states are Cameroon's main trading partners. In 1993 there was a trade surplus of US$502 million and a current account deficit of US$565 million. In 1995 exports totalled US$2,040 million and imports US$1,241 million.
GNP – US$8,356 million (1996); US$610 per capita (1996)
GDP – US$10,481 million (1994); US$526 per capita (1994)
ANNUAL AVERAGE GROWTH OF GDP – 2.1 per cent (1990)
INFLATION RATE – 4.5 per cent (1996)
TOTAL EXTERNAL DEBT – US$9,515 million (1996)

TRADE WITH UK	1996	1997
Imports from UK	£33,745,000	£30,264,000
Exports to UK	42,682,000	42,025,000

CANADA

AREA – 3,849,674 sq. miles (9,970,610 sq. km). Neighbours: USA (south), Alaska (USA) (west)
POPULATION – 29,606,000 (1994 UN estimate). The languages are English and French
CAPITAL – Ottawa (population, 1,010,288, 1994 estimate). The population of the metropolitan area of Ottawa–Hull was estimated at 1,024,657 in 1995
CURRENCY – Canadian dollar (C$) of 100 cents
NATIONAL ANTHEM – O Canada
NATIONAL DAY – 1 July (Dominion Day)
NATIONAL FLAG – Red maple leaf with 11 points on white square, flanked by vertical red bars one-half the width of the square
LIFE EXPECTANCY (years) – male 73.02; female 79.79
POPULATION GROWTH RATE – 2.2 per cent (1995)
POPULATION DENSITY – 3 per sq. km (1995)
URBAN POPULATION – 76.6 per cent (1991)

Canada occupies the whole of the northern part of the North American continent, with the exception of Alaska.

FEDERAL STRUCTURE

Provinces or Territories (with official contractions)	Area (sq. miles)	Population, census 1996	Capital	Lieutenant-Governor	Premier
Alberta (AB)	255,290	2,696,826	Edmonton	H. A. Olson	Ralph Klein
British Columbia (BC)	365,950	3,724,500	ΨVictoria	Garde Gardom	Glen Clarke
Manitoba (MB)	250,950	1,113,898	Winnipeg	Yvon Dumont	Gary Filmon
New Brunswick (NB)	28,360	738,133	Fredericton	Marilyn Counsell	Raymond Frenette
Newfoundland and Labrador (NF)	156,650	551,792	ΨSt John's	A. M. House	Brian Tobin
Nova Scotia (NS)	21,420	909,282	ΨHalifax	James Kinley	Russel MacLellan
Ontario (ON)	412,580	10,753,573	ΨToronto	Hilary Weston	Michael Harris
Prince Edward Island (PE)	2,180	134,557	ΨCharlottetown	Gilbert Clements	Patrick Binns
Quebec (QC)	594,860	7,138,795	ΨQuébec	Lise Thibeault	Lucien Bouchard
Saskatchewan (SK)	251,870	990,237	Regina	John Wiebe	John Roy Romanow
Yukon Territory (YT)	186,660	30,766	*Whitehorse	†Judy Gingell	‡John Otashek
Northwest Territories (NT)	1,322,900	64,402	*Yellowknife	†Helen Maksagak	‡Don Morin

Area figures include land and water area   † Commissioner
* seat of government   ‡ Government Leader

In eastern Canada, the southernmost point is Middle Island in Lake Erie. Canada has six main physiographic divisions: the Appalachian-Acadian region, the Canadian shield, which comprises more than half the country, the St Lawrence-Great Lakes lowland, the interior plains, the Cordilleran region and the Arctic archipelago.

The climate of the eastern and central portions presents greater extremes than in corresponding latitudes in Europe, but in the south-western portion of the prairie region and the southern portions of the Pacific slope the climate is milder.

HISTORY AND POLITICS

Canada was originally discovered by Cabot in 1497 but its history dates from 1534, when the French took possession of the country. The first permanent settlement at Port Royal (now Annapolis), Nova Scotia, was founded in 1605, and Quebec was founded in 1608. In 1759 Quebec was captured by British forces under General Wolfe and in 1763 the whole territory of Canada became a possession of Great Britain by the Treaty of Paris 1763. Nova Scotia was ceded in 1713 by the Treaty of Utrecht, the provinces of New Brunswick and Prince Edward Island being subsequently formed out of it. British Columbia was formed into a Crown colony in 1858, having previously been a part of the Hudson Bay Territory, and was united to Vancouver Island in 1866.

The constitution of Canada has its source in the British North America Act of 1867 which formed a Dominion, under the name of Canada, of the four provinces of Ontario, Quebec, New Brunswick and Nova Scotia. To this federation the other provinces have subsequently been admitted: Manitoba (1870), British Columbia (1871), Prince Edward Island (1873), Alberta and Saskatchewan (1905) and Newfoundland (1949). In 1982, the constitution was patriated (severed from the British parliament) with the approval of all provinces except Quebec. In 1985, the federal prime minister and the provincial premiers concluded the Meech Lake Accord which provided for Quebec to be recognized as a distinct society within Canada. However, two provincial legislatures withheld approval and the accord did not come into force. In Quebec, a referendum calling for sovereignty and a new political and economic partnership was defeated in October 1995. In September 1997 Quebec was recognized as having a 'unique character' by leaders of the other provinces and territories.

In the federal election on 2 June 1997 the Liberal Party was returned to power. The state of parties in the House of Commons following the election was Liberals 155, Reform Party 60, Bloc Québécois 44, New Democrats 21, Progressive Conservatives 20, Independent 1.

POLITICAL SYSTEM

Executive power is vested in a Governor-General appointed by the Sovereign on the advice of the Canadian government.

Parliament consists of a Senate and a House of Commons. The Senate consists of 104 members, nominated by the Governor-General on the advice of the prime minister, the seats being distributed between the various provinces. The House of Commons has 301 members directly elected for a five-year term. Representation is proportional to the population of each province.

The judicature is administered by judges following the civil law in Quebec province and common law in other provinces. Each province has a Court of Appeal. All superior, county and district court judges are appointed by the Governor-General, the others by the Lieutenant-Governors of the provinces.

The highest federal court is the Supreme Court of Canada, which exercises general appellate jurisdiction throughout Canada in civil and criminal cases. There is one other federally constituted court, the Federal Court of Canada, which has jurisdiction on appeals from its trial division, from federal tribunals and reviews of decisions and references by federal boards and commissions.

GOVERNOR-GENERAL
Governor-General and Commander-in-Chief, HE Roméo LeBlanc, PC, CC, CMM, CD

CABINET *as at July 1998*
Prime Minister, Jean Chrétien
Deputy Prime Minister, Herbert Gray
Agriculture and Agri-Food, Lyle Vanclief
Citizenship and Immigration, Lucienne Robillard
Environment, Christine Stewart
Finance, Paul Martin
Fisheries and Oceans, David Anderson
Foreign Affairs, Lloyd Axworthy
Health, Allan Rock
Heritage, Sheila Copps
Human Resources Development, Pierre Pettigrew
Indian Affairs and Northern Development, Jane Stewart
Industry, John Manley
Infrastructure, President of the Treasury Board, Marcel Massé
Intergovernmental Affairs, President of the Privy Council, Stéphane Dion
International Co-operation and Francophonie, Diane Marleau
International Trade, Sergio Marchi
Justice and Attorney-General, Anne McLellan
Labour, Lawrence MacAulay
Leader of the Government in the House of Commons, Don Boudria
Leader of the Government in the Senate, Bernard Graham
National Defence, Arthur C. Eggleton
Natural Resources, Canadian Wheat Board, Ralph Goodale

Public Works and Government Services, Alfonso Gagliano
Secretary of State for Asia-Pacific, Raymond Chan
Secretary of State for Atlantic Canada Opportunities Agency; Veterans Affairs, Fred Mifflin
Secretary of State for Children and Youth, Ethel Blondin-Andrews
Secretary of State for International Financial Institutions, James Scott Peterson
Secretary of State for Latin America and Africa, David Kilgour
Secretary of State for Multiculturalism and the Status of Women, Hedy Fry
Secretary of State for Parks, Andrew Mitchell
Secretary of State for Regional Development in Quebec, Martin Cauchon
Secretary of State for Science, Research and Development; Western Economic Diversification, Ronald Duhamel
Solicitor-General, Andy Scott
Transport, David Collenette

CANADIAN HIGH COMMISSION
1 Grosvenor Square, London WIX OAB
Tel 0171-258 6600
Canada House, 5 Trafalgar Square, London SWIY 5BJ
High Commissioner, HE Roy MacLaren, apptd 1996
Deputy High Commissioner, J. Bilodeau
Minister, T. MacDonald (*Commercial/Economic*)
Defence Adviser, Brig.-Gen. R. Bastien

BRITISH HIGH COMMISSION
80 Elgin Street, Ottawa KIP 5K7
Tel: Ottawa 237 1530
High Commissioner, HE Sir Anthony Goodenough, KCMG, apptd 1996
Deputy High Commissioner, L. J. Duffield
Counsellor, M. Uden (*Economic*)
Defence and Military Adviser, Brig. E. Springfield, CBE
CONSULATES-GENERAL – Montreal, Toronto, Vancouver
CONSULATES – Halifax/Dartmouth, St John's, Winnipeg
BRITISH COUNCIL DIRECTOR, Dr S. Lewis (*Cultural Counsellor*)
BRITISH COUNCIL REPRESENTATIVE IN QUEBEC, S. Dawbarn, 1000 ouest rue de La Gauchetière, Montreal, Quebec H3B 4W5

DEFENCE

The Canadian armed forces are unified and organized into three functional commands: Land Force Command; Maritime Command; Air Command.

The Army (Land Forces) has 114 main battle tanks, 1,858 armoured personnel carriers and 272 artillery pieces. The Navy (Maritime Forces) has three submarines, four destroyers, 16 frigates and 16 patrol and coastal vessels. The Air Force has 140 combat aircraft and 30 armed helicopters.

MILITARY EXPENDITURE – 1.5 per cent of GDP (1996)
MILITARY PERSONNEL – 57,000: Army 21,900, Navy 9,400, Air Force 14,600, Other 11,100

ECONOMY

About 7.3 per cent of the total land area is farmed. Over 60 per cent of this is under cultivation, the remainder being predominantly classified as unimproved pasture. More than 80 per cent of the cultivated land is in the prairie region of western Canada.

Farm cash receipts from the sale of farm products in 1996 were C$28,379 million. Livestock and animal products contributed C$13,648 million; field crops C$13,846 million; grain and oilseed C$9,538 million.

In 1995–6 Canada produced pelts valued at C$83 million. Wildlife pelts made up 30.2 per cent of the total, with a value of C$25 million.

The marketed value of fish catches in 1994 was C$3,149 million (preliminary).

In 1991 about 42 per cent of the total land area was considered as inventoried forest area. The value of shipments and other revenue from forestry-related industries in 1994 was: logging $10,144.8 million; sawmill and planing mill products $15,075.9 million; shingle and shake $254.4 million; veneer and plywood $1,482.9 million; and paper and allied products $25,647.8 million.

In 1995, Canada was the world's largest producer of zinc, potash and uranium, the second largest of nickel, asbestos, cadmium and elemental sulphur. The country is also rich in gold, copper, lead, molybdenum, platinum group metals, gypsum, cobalt, titanium concentrates, and aluminium. The total value of mineral production in 1996 was C$49,171.8 million.

Production of gold was 151,257 kg in 1995 and of silver 1,245,939 kg. Uranium production in 1995 was 10,518 tonnes.

GNP – US$569,899 million (1996); US$19,020 per capita (1996)

GDP – US$599,578 million (1994); US$18,635 per capita (1994)

ANNUAL AVERAGE GROWTH OF GDP – 1.5 per cent (1996)

INFLATION RATE – 1.6 per cent (1996)

UNEMPLOYMENT – 9.5 per cent (1995)

TRADE

The main exports in 1996 were passenger automobiles and chassis, motor vehicle parts except engines, lumber and softwood, crude petroleum, trucks, truck tractors and chassis, newsprint paper, other telecommunication and related equipment, wood pulp and similar pulp, natural gas, petroleum and coal products.. Trade with the USA accounts for about 80 per cent of Canada's exports and 75 per cent of its imports.

In 1996 imports totalled US$175,158 million and exports US$201,633 million. In 1996 Canada had a trade surplus of US$27,164 million and a current account deficit of US$2,076 million.

Trade with UK	1996	1997
Imports from UK	£1,974,524,000	£2,155,968,000
Exports to UK	2,484,044,000	2,553,935,000

COMMUNICATIONS

In 1991 there were 290,194 km of federal and provincial territorial roads and highways and 85,563 km of railway track in operation.

The registered shipping on 1 January 1991 including inland vessels, was 43,787 vessels with gross tonnage 4,956,845. The bulk of canal shipping in Canada is handled through the two sections of the St Lawrence Seaway, which provide access to the Great Lakes for ocean-going ships.

EDUCATION

Education is under the control of the provincial governments, the cost of the publicly controlled schools being met by local taxation, aided by provincial grants. Education is compulsory between the ages of five or six and fifteen or sixteen.

In 1995–6 there were 16,096 elementary and secondary schools with 5,899,943 pupils. There were 70 degree-granting universities.

ENROLMENT (percentage of age group) – primary 95 per cent (1994); secondary 92 per cent (1994); tertiary 102.9 per cent (1993)

Source: for some financial and economic statistics, Statistics Canada

CAPE VERDE
República de Cabo Verde

AREA – 1,557 sq. miles (4,033 sq. km). Comprising the Windward Islands (Santo Antão, São Vicente, Santa Luzia, São Nicolau, Boa Vista and Sal) and Leeward Islands (Maio, São Tiago, Fogo and Brava)

POPULATION – 392,000, (1995 estimate), the majority of whom are Roman Catholic. The official language is Portuguese; a creole is spoken by most of the population

CAPITAL – ΨPraia (population, 80,000, 1995 estimate)

CURRENCY – Escudo Caboverdiano of 100 centavos

NATIONAL DAY – 5 July (Independence Day)

NATIONAL FLAG – Blue with three horizontal stripes of white, red, white near the bottom; over all on these near the hoist a ring of ten yellow stars

LIFE EXPECTANCY (years) – male 63.53; female 71.33

POPULATION GROWTH RATE – 2.8 per cent (1995)

POPULATION DENSITY – 97 per sq. km (1995)

URBAN POPULATION – 44.1 per cent (1990)

MILITARY EXPENDITURE – 1.7 per cent of GDP (1996)

MILITARY PERSONNEL – 1,100: Army 1,000, Air Force 100

CONSCRIPTION DURATION – Selective conscription

ILLITERACY RATE – 28.4 per cent

ENROLMENT (percentage of age group) – primary 100 per cent (1993); secondary 22 per cent (1993)

HISTORY AND POLITICS

The islands, colonized *c.*1460, achieved independence from Portugal on 5 July 1975 under the Partido Africano da Independência da Guiné e Cabo Verde (PAIGC). A federation of the islands with Guinea Bissau was planned but this was dropped following the 1980 coup in Guinea Bissau.

The republic was a one-party state under the African Party for the Independence of Cape Verde (PAICV) until the constitution was amended in 1990. Multiparty elections, held in January 1991, were won by the opposition Movement for Democracy (MPD). The MPD government was re-elected in December 1995 with 50 of the 72 seats in the National Assembly. President António Mascarenhas Monteiro was re-elected unopposed in February 1996.

HEAD OF STATE

President, António Mascarenhas Monteiro, *assumed office* 22 March 1991, *re-elected* 18 February 1996

COUNCIL OF MINISTERS *as at July 1998*

Prime Minister, Carlos Veiga

Deputy Prime Minister, Economic Co-ordination, António Gualberto do Rosario

Assistant to the Prime Minister (Social Communication), José António dos Reis

Agriculture, Food, Supply and the Environment, José António Pinto Monteiro

Culture, António Jorge Delgado

Defence, Ulpio Napoleão Fernandes

Deputy Secretary of State for Finance, Olavo Correia

Education, Science, Youth and Sport, José Luis Livramento

Employment, Training and Social Integration, Orlanda Santos Ferreira

Foreign Affairs and Communities, José Luis de Jesus
Health and Social Promotion, João Baptista Medina
Infrastructure and Housing, António Fernandes
Justice and Internal Administration, Simão Gomes Monteiro
Minister of the Presidency of the Council of Ministers, Rui
Figueiredo Silva
Secretary of State for Communities, Marly Meneses
Secretary of State for Decentralization, Cesar Almeida
Secretary of State for the Fight Against Poverty, Manuela Teresa
Silva
Secretary of State for Public Administration, Anna Paula
Almeida
Secretary of State for Youth and Sports, Victor Osório
Speaker of the National Assembly, Antonio Espirito Santo
Fonseca
Tourism, Transport and Marine Affairs, Maria Helena
Semedo

EMBASSY OF THE REPUBLIC OF CAPE VERDE
44 Koninginnegracht, 2514 AD, The Hague, The
Netherlands
Tel: The Hague 346 9623
Chargé d'Affaires, M. Rodrigues de Almeida Pereira

BRITISH AMBASSADOR, HE David Snoxell, resident at
Dakar, Senegal
There is a British Consulate on São Vicente.

ECONOMY

The islands have little rain and agriculture is mostly
confined to irrigated inland valleys. The chief products are
bananas and coffee (for export), maize, sugar cane and nuts.
Fish and shellfish are important exports. Salt is obtained on
Sal, Boa Vista and Maio; volcanic rock is also mined for
export.

In 1993 the government announced a programme of
reform to institute a change to a market economy and to
privatize most industry within four years. In 1995 there
was a trade deficit of US$224 million and a current account
deficit of US$39 million. In 1994 imports totalled US$209
million and exports US$5 million.

The main ports are Praia and Mindelo, and there is an
international airport on Sal.
GNP – US$393 million (1996); US$1,010 per capita (1996)
GDP – US$382 million (1994); US$900 per capita (1994)
TOTAL EXTERNAL DEBT – US$211 million (1996)

TRADE WITH UK	1996	1997
Imports from UK	£6,942,000	£5,483,000
Exports to UK	803,000	881,000

CENTRAL AFRICAN REPUBLIC
République Centrafricaine

AREA – 240,535 sq. miles (622,984 sq. km). Neighbours:
Chad (north), Sudan (east), Congo and Democratic
Republic of Congo (south), Cameroon (west)
POPULATION – 3,315,000 (1994 UN estimate). French is
the official language; the native language is Sango
CAPITAL – Bangui (population, 473,817, 1984 estimate)
CURRENCY – Franc CFA of 100 centimes
NATIONAL DAY – 1 December
NATIONAL FLAG – Four horizontal stripes, blue, white,
green, yellow, crossed by central vertical red stripe with
a yellow five-pointed star in top left-hand corner
LIFE EXPECTANCY (years) – male 46.87; female 51.88
POPULATION GROWTH RATE – 2.5 per cent (1995)
POPULATION DENSITY – 5 per sq. km (1995)
MILITARY EXPENDITURE – 2.7 per cent of GDP (1996)
MILITARY PERSONNEL – 4,950: Army 2,500, Air Force 150,
Paramilitaries 2,300
CONSCRIPTION DURATION – Two years
ILLITERACY RATE – 40.0 per cent
ENROLMENT (percentage of age group) – primary 54 per
cent (1990); tertiary 1.4 per cent (1991)

HISTORY AND POLITICS

In December 1958 the French colony of Ubanghi Shari
elected to remain within the French Community and
adopted the title of the Central African Republic. It
became fully independent on 17 August 1960. The first
president, David Dacko, was overthrown in 1966 by the
then Col. Bokassa, who in 1976 proclaimed himself
Emperor and renamed the country the Central African
Empire. In 1979 Bokassa was deposed by Dacko in a
bloodless coup and the country reverted to a republic.
President Dacko surrendered power in 1981 to Gen. André
Kolingba, who instituted military rule until 1985, when a
civilian-dominated Cabinet was appointed. In November
1986 a referendum was held which approved a new
constitution and the establishment of a one-party state.

Multiparty presidential and legislative elections were
held in October 1992 but were annulled due to irregularities. President Kolingba formed a coalition government in February 1993. Presidential and legislative elections held in 1993 were won by Ange-Felix Patasse
(MLPC), and the Central African People's Liberation
Party (MLPC). The MLPC formed a coalition government in October 1993.

POLITICAL SYSTEM

Constitutional reforms were passed in a national referendum in December 1994 which created a constitutional
court, introduced elected local assemblies, extended the
presidential mandate to a maximum of two six-year terms
and subordinated the government to the president.

INSURGENCY

The army is divided between southerners loyal to former
President Gen. Kolingba and northerners loyal to President Patasse. The 1,100 French troops stationed near
Bangui have been called upon to quell frequent mutinies
by Gen. Kolingba's supporters; in March 1998 the French
troops were replaced by the UN MINURCA peacekeeping force.

HEAD OF STATE
President, Ange-Felix Patasse, *elected* 19 September 1993

COUNCIL OF MINISTERS *as at July 1998*
Prime Minister, Michel Gbezera-Bria (Ind.)
Civil Service, Jean-Claude Gouanga (FPP)
Communications, Thierry Ignifolo Vanden-Boss (PLD)
Economy, Planning and International Co-operation, Christophe
Bremaidou (CN)
Environment, Joseph Yomba (MDREC)
Family and Social Affairs, Eliane Mokodopo (MESAN)
Finance and Budget, Anicet Georges Doleguele (MLPC)
Foreign Affairs, Jean Mete Yapende (MLPC)
Higher Education, Théophile Touba (RDC)
Housing, Clement Belibanga (ADP)
Human Rights, Democratic Culture and National Reconciliation,
Laurent Gomina-Pampali (RDC)
Industry and Commerce, Simon Bongolapke (MDD)
Justice, Marcel Metefara (MLPC)
National Defence, War Veterans and War Victims, Pascal Kado
(MLPC)
National Education, Albert Mberio (MLPC)

Parliamentary Relations, Charles Armel Doubane (ADP)
Posts and Telecommunications, Michel Bindo (RDC)
Public Health, Fernand Djengo (RDC)
Public Works, Jackson Madeck (MLPC)
Secretary of State for Administration, Gilbert Moussa Labbe (Ind.)
Secretary of State for National Solidarity, Albertine Mbissa (PSD)
Territorial Administration and Public Security, Gen. François Ndjadder Bedaya (MLPC)
Tourism, Arts and Culture, Gaston Beina Gbandi (MLPC)
Transport, André Gombako (FPP)
Youth and Sports, Bertin Bea (MDD)

ADP Alliance for Democracy and Progress; CN National Convention; FPP Patriotic Front for Progress; Ind. Independent; MDD Movement for Democracy and Development; MDREC Democratic Movement for the Renaissance and Evolution of the Central African Republic; MESAN Movement for the Social Evolution of Black Africa; MLPC Movement for the Liberation of the Central African People; PLD Liberal Democratic Party; PSD Social Democraatic Party; RDC Central African Democratic Rally

EMBASSY OF THE CENTRAL AFRICAN REPUBLIC
30 rue des Perchamps, 75016, Paris
Tel: Paris 4224 4256
Ambassador Extraordinary and Plenipotentiary, new appointment awaited

BRITISH AMBASSADOR, HE Peter Boon, resident at Yaoundé, Cameroon
Honorary Consul, J. Y. Lauge, BP 977, Bangui

ECONOMY

The IMF approved a US$23 million credit to support economic reform in 1994. Cotton, diamonds, coffee and timber are the major exports.

In 1994 there was a trade surplus of US$15 million and a current account deficit of US$25 million. In 1995 exports totalled US$171 million and imports US$174 million.
GNP – US$1,024 million (1996); US$310 per capita (1996)
GDP – US$1,642 million (1994); US$313 per capita (1994)
INFLATION RATE – 19.2 per cent (1995)
TOTAL EXTERNAL DEBT – US$928 million (1996)

TRADE WITH UK	1996	1997
Imports from UK	£749,000	£1,183,000
Exports to UK	87,000	63,000

CHAD
République du Tchad

AREA – 495,755 sq. miles (1,284,000 sq. km). Neighbours: Niger, Nigeria and Cameroon (west), Libya (north), Sudan (east), Central African Republic (south)
POPULATION – 6,361,000 (1994 UN estimate); French and Arabic are the official languages; there are more than 50 indigenous languages, of which the most widely spoken is Sara
CAPITAL – N'Djaména (population, 179,000, 1972 estimate)
CURRENCY – Franc CFA of 100 centimes
NATIONAL DAY – 13 April
NATIONAL FLAG – Vertical stripes, blue, yellow and red
LIFE EXPECTANCY (years) – male 45.93; female 49.12
POPULATION GROWTH RATE – 2.2 per cent (1995)
POPULATION DENSITY – 5 per sq. km (1995)

URBAN POPULATION – 21.7 per cent (1993)
MILITARY EXPENDITURE – 3.8 per cent of GDP (1996)
MILITARY PERSONNEL – 29,850: Army 25,000, Air Force 350, Paramilitaries 4,500
ILLITERACY RATE – 51.9 per cent
ENROLMENT (percentage of age group) – tertiary 0.8 per cent (1994)

HISTORY AND POLITICS

Chad became a member state of the French Community in 1958, and was proclaimed fully independent on 11 August 1960. The constitution was suspended in 1975 when President Tombalbaye was killed in a coup by Gen. Felix Malloum; following a succession of further coups, Idriss Déby came to power in 1990 and announced the adoption of a multiparty system, allowing the legalization of political parties in 1991 and 1992. A Higher Transitional Council (CST) was elected in 1993 to serve as the transitional legislature and appointed a transitional government in conjunction with President Déby. The CST has twice extended the transitional period by one year to allow sufficient time to organize elections. In March 1996, the government concluded the Franceville agreement with opposition parties which provided for a national cease-fire and an independent commission to oversee the election. A new constitution, establishing a unified, democratic state, was confirmed by a referendum. Déby won the first multiparty presidential elections in 1996. Elections to the 125-member National Assembly in January and February 1997 were won by the pro-Déby Patriotic Salvation Movement (MPS).

FOREIGN RELATIONS

The Aouzou strip was claimed by Libya, which occupied the area from 1973 to 1994. A war over the territory ended in 1987. In 1990 Chad and Libya presented their claims to the International Court of Justice, which in 1994 awarded jurisdiction over the whole of the strip to Chad.

HEAD OF STATE
President, Idriss Déby, *took power* December 1990, *elected* 3 July 1996

GOVERNMENT *as at July 1998*
Prime Minister, Nassour Owaido Guelendouksia
Agriculture, Moctar Moussa
Civil Service and Labour, Salibou Ngarba
Communication, Haroun Kabadi
Culture, Youth and Sport, Mansoungaral Nassingar
Defence, Oumar Kadjalami
Education, Abderahim Breme Hamid
Environment and Water, Mariam Mahamat Nour
Finance and Economy, Bichara Cherif Daoussa
Foreign Affairs, Mohamat Saleh Annadif
Government Secretary, Houdeingar David
Higher Education, Adoum Goudja
Industrial Development, Djitangar Djibangar
Interior, Abderrahmane Salah
Justice, Limane Mahamat
Livestock, Mahamat Nouri
Planning, Ahmat Hamid
Posts and Telecommunications, Mahamat Ahmat Karambal
Public Health, Kedallah Younouss Hamit
Public Works, Transport, Housing, Ahmat Lamine
Social Affairs, Agnes Alafi
Tourism, Pascal Yoadimnadji

EMBASSY OF THE REPUBLIC OF CHAD
Boulevard Lambermont 52, 1030 Brussels, Belgium
Tel: Brussels 215 1975
Ambassador Extraordinary and Plenipotentiary, new
appointment awaited

BRITISH AMBASSADOR, HE Peter Boon, resident at Abuja,
Nigeria

Honorary Consul, E. Abtour, BP877, Avenue Charles de
Gaulle, N'Djaména

ECONOMY

About 90 per cent of the workforce is occupied in
agriculture, fishing and forestry. There is an oilfield in
Kanem and salt is mined around Lake Chad, but the most
important activities are cotton growing and animal husbandry. Raw cotton and meat are the main exports. Chad's
main trading partners are France and Nigeria.

In 1994 Chad had a trade deficit of US$77 million and a
current account deficit of US$38 million. In 1995 imports
totalled US$220 million and exports US$252 million.
GNP – US$1,035 million (1996); US$160 per capita (1996)
GDP – US$1,535 million (1994); US$162 per capita (1994)
ANNUAL AVERAGE GROWTH OF GDP – ;5.6 per cent
(1987)
INFLATION RATE – 9.1 per cent (1995)
TOTAL EXTERNAL DEBT – US$997 million (1996)

TRADE WITH UK	1996	1997
Imports from UK	£3,708,000	£1,182,000
Exports to UK	1,180,000	479,000

CHILE
República de Chile

AREA – 292,135 sq. miles (756,626 sq. km). Neighbours:
Peru (north), Bolivia and Argentina (east)
POPULATION – 14,210,000 (1994 UN estimate). The main
groups are: indigenous Araucanian Indians, Fuegians,
Rapanui and Changos; Spanish settlers and their
descendants; mixed Spanish Indians; and European
immigrants. Because of extensive intermarriage only a
few indigenous Indians are racially separate. The
language is Spanish, with admixtures of local words of
Indian origin. The main religion is Roman Catholicism
CAPITAL – Santiago (population, 5,257,937, 1992)
MAJOR CITIES – ΨAntofagasta (236,730); Concepción
(350,268); Puente Alto (318,898); Temuco (239,340);
ΨValparaíso (282,168); ΨPunta Arenas (117,206), on
the Straits of Magellan, is the southernmost city in the
world
CURRENCY – Chilean peso of 100 centavos
NATIONAL ANTHEM – Canción Nacional de Chile
NATIONAL DAY – 18 September (National Anniversary)
NATIONAL FLAG – Two horizontal bands, white, red; in
top sixth a white star on blue square, next staff
LIFE EXPECTANCY (years) – male 71.83; female 77.77
POPULATION GROWTH RATE – 1.6 per cent (1995)
POPULATION DENSITY – 19 per sq. km (1995)
URBAN POPULATION – 84.5 per cent (1995)

Chile lies between the Andes (5,000 to 15,000 feet above
sea level) and the shores of the South Pacific, extending
coastwise from the arid north around Arica to Cape Horn.
The extreme length of the country is about 2,800 miles,
with an average breadth, north of 41°, of 100 miles.

Island possessions include the Juan Fernández group
(three islands) about 360 miles from Valparaíso; one of
these islands is the reputed scene of Alexander Selkirk's
(Robinson Crusoe) shipwreck. Easter Island, about 2,000
miles away in the South Pacific Ocean, contains stone
platforms and hundreds of stone figures.

HISTORY AND POLITICS

Chile was discovered by Spanish adventurers in the 16th
century and remained under Spanish rule until 1810, when
the first autonomous government was established. Full
independence was consolidated in 1818 after a revolutionary war.

A Marxist, Salvador Allende, was elected president in
1970, but was overthrown in a military coup in 1973. In
1981, Gen. Pinochet was sworn in to serve as president
until 1989; a plebiscite to permit a second eight-year term
of office was rejected in 1988. Presidential and congressional elections were held in 1989, beginning the transition
to full democracy. Gen. Pinochet retired as commander-
in-chief of the Army but took up an unelected seat for life
in the Senate, despite public protests and government
attempts to prevent it.

Presidential and legislative elections were held in 1993.
Eduardo Frei won the presidential election and his ruling
Coalition for Democracy (CPD) (centre and centre-left
parties) won 70 seats in the Chamber of Deputies and 22 in
the Senate. In the 1997 legislative elections the CPD
maintained its 70-seat majority in the Chamber of Deputies.

POLITICAL SYSTEM

Executive power is held by the president. Legislative
power is exercised by a Congress which comprises a Senate
of 48 Senators (40 elected and eight appointed) and a
Chamber of Deputies of 120 elected members. A joint
session of Congress in 1994 reduced the presidential term
from eight to six years with no possibility of re-election.

Chile is divided into 12 regions and the Metropolitan
Area.

HEAD OF STATE

President of the Republic, Eduardo Frei Ruíz-Tagle, *elected* 11
December 1993, *sworn in* 11 March 1994

CABINET *as at July 1998*

Agriculture, Carlos Mladinic (Ind.)
Corporation for the Development of Production, Felipe Sandoval
(PDC)
Defence, Raúl Troncoso Castillo
Economy, Development and Reconstruction, Alvaro García
Hurtado (PPD)
Education, José Pablo Arellano (PDC)
Energy, Alejandro Jadresic (Ind.)
Finance, Eduardo Aninat Ureta (PDC)
Foreign Affairs, José Miguel Insulza (PS)
Health, Alex Figueroa (PDC)
Housing and Urban Development, Sergio Henríquez
Interior, Carlos Figueroa Serrano (PDC)
Justice, Soledad Alvear (PDC)
Labour and Social Security, Jorge Arrate MacNiven (PS)
Mining, Sergio Jiménez Moraga
National Resources, Adriana Delpiano Puelma (PPD)
Planning and Co-operation, Germán Quintana (PS)
Public Works, Ricardo Lagos Escobar (PS/PPD)
Secretary-General of the Government, José Joaquín Brunner
(PPD)
Secretary-General of the Presidency, Juan Villarzú (PDC)
Transport and Telecommunications, Claudio Hohmann
(PDC)
Women's Affairs, Josefina Bilbao (Ind.)

840　Countries of the World

PDC Christian Democratic Party; PPD Party for Democracy; PS Socialist Party; Ind. Independent

EMBASSY OF CHILE
12 Devonshire Street, London WIN 2DS
Tel 0171–580 6392
Ambassador Extraordinary and Plenipotentiary, HE Mario
Artaza, apptd 1996

BRITISH EMBASSY
Avenida El Bosque Norte 0125
Casilla 72-D, Santiago 9
Tel: Santiago 231 3737
Ambassador Extraordinary and Plenipotentiary, HE Glynne
Evans, CMG, apptd 1997
Deputy Head of Mission, Counsellor and Consul-General, D.
Roberts
Defence Attaché, Capt. P. Ellis
First Secretary (Commercial), T. Torlot
CONSULAR OFFICES – Antofagasta, Arica, Concepción,
Santiago, Punta Arenas, Valparaíso.

BRITISH COUNCIL DIRECTOR, D. Stokes (*Cultural Attaché*),
Eliodoro Yañez 832, Casilla 115 Correa 55, Santiago
British-Chilean Chamber of Commerce, Av. Suecia
155-C, Casilla 536, Santiago

DEFENCE

The Army has 130 main battle tanks, 20 armoured infantry fighting vehicles, 438 armoured personnel carriers and 126 artillery pieces. The Navy has four submarines, four destroyers, four frigates, 30 patrol and coastal vessels, 12 combat aircraft and 12 armed helicopters. The Air Force has 92 combat aircraft.
MILITARY EXPENDITURE – 3.4 per cent of GDP (1996)
MILITARY PERSONNEL – 125,500: Army 51,000, Navy 29,800, Air Force 13,500, Paramilitaries 31,200
CONSCRIPTION DURATION – 12–22 months

ECONOMY

Economic reforms during the late 1970s and the 1980s, with large-scale privatization and deregulation, have made Chile one of the most successful economies in Latin America. Cereals, vegetables, fruit, tobacco, hemp and vines are grown extensively and livestock accounts for nearly 40 per cent of agricultural production. Sheep farming predominates in the extreme south. There are large timber tracts in the central and southern zones which produce timber, cellulose and wood for export. Fishing is also a major industry.

Chile is rich in copper-ore, iron-ore and nitrates, and has the only commercial production of nitrate of soda (Chile saltpetre) from natural resources in the world. There are large deposits of high grade sulphur. Oil and natural gas are produced in the Magallanes area, but domestic production is now declining.

In 1996 there was a trade deficit of US$1,146 million and a current account deficit of US$2,921 million.
GNP – US$70,060 million (1996); US$4,860 per capita (1996)
GDP – US$39,365 million (1994); US$3,685 per capita (1994)
ANNUAL AVERAGE GROWTH OF GDP – 7.2 per cent (1996)
INFLATION RATE – 7.4 per cent (1996)
UNEMPLOYMENT – 4.7 per cent (1995)
TOTAL EXTERNAL DEBT – US$27,411 million (1996)

TRADE

The principal exports are minerals, timber and metal products, fish products and vegetables. The principal imports are food products, industrial raw materials,

machinery, and equipment and spares. The main trade partners are Japan and the USA; in 1996 Chile joined the Mercosur Free Trade Zone, and in March 1998 signed an extension to a free trade agreement with Mexico. In 1996 imports totalled US$17,828 million and exports US$15,353 million.

Trade with UK	1996	1997
Imports from UK	£166,129,000	£210,516,000
Exports to UK	377,549,000	393,731,000

COMMUNICATIONS

With the improvement of the roads an increasing share of internal transportation is moving by road and rail, although shipping is still important. The road system is about 80,000 km in length.

A railway line runs from Valparaíso through La Calera and Santiago to Puerto Montt. With the completion of a section of 435 miles from Corumba, Brazil, to Santa Cruz, Bolivia, the Trans-Continental Line will link the Chilean Pacific port of Arica with Rio de Janeiro on the Atlantic. A line runs from Antofagasta to Salta (Argentina).

Domestic air traffic is carried by Linea Aerea Nacional (LAN) and LADECO, which also operate internationally, and smaller regional carriers.

CULTURE AND EDUCATION

Chilean Nobel Prize winners include the writers Gabriela Mistral (1945) and Pablo Neruda (1971).

Elementary education is free and compulsory. There are eight state universities (three in Santiago, two in Valparaíso, one each in Antofagasta, Concepción and Valdivia), and many private universities.
ILLITERACY RATE – 4.8 per cent
ENROLMENT (percentage of age group) – primary 86 per cent (1995); secondary 55 per cent (1995); tertiary 30.3 per cent (1996)

CHINA
Zhonghua Renmin Gongheguo – The People's Republic of China

AREA – 3,705,408 sq. miles (9,596,961 sq. km). Neighbours: Russia and Mongolia (north), North Korea (east), Vietnam, Laos, Myanmar, India, Bhutan and Nepal (south), India, Pakistan, Afghanistan, Tajikistan, Kyrgyzstan and Kazakhstan (west)
POPULATION – 1,221,462,000 (1994 UN estimate). A census (the fourth) was held in 1990 and recorded a total population of 1,130 million. About 6 per cent of the population belong to around 55 ethnic minorities. Among the largest are the Zhuang of Guangxi, the Uygurs of Xinjiang, the Tibetans and the Mongols. The indigenous religions are Confucianism, Taoism and Buddhism. There are also Muslims (officially estimated at about 12 million) and Christians (unofficially estimated at about 50 million). The official language is Mandarin Chinese; of the many local dialects the largest are Cantonese, Fukienese, Xiamenhua and Hakka. The autonomous regions of Mongolia, Tibet and Xinjiang have their own languages
CAPITAL – Beijing (Peking) (population, 7,362,426, 1990)
MAJOR CITIES – Chengdu (3,483,834); Chongqing (3,122,704); Dalian (3,473,832); Guangzhou (Canton) (3,918,010); Harbin (3,597,404); Qingdo (5,124,868); ΨShanghai (8,205,598); Shenyang (4,655,280); Tianjin (5,804,023); Wuhan (3,832,536); Wuxi (3,181,985); Yantai (3,204,669); Zaozhuang (3,191,974)
CURRENCY – Renminbi Yuan of 10 jiao or 100 fen

NATIONAL ANTHEM – March of the Volunteers
NATIONAL DAY – 1 October (Founding of People's
Republic)
NATIONAL FLAG – Red, with large gold five-point star and
four small gold stars in crescent, all in upper quarter next
staff
LIFE EXPECTANCY (years) – male 66.70; female 70.45
POPULATION GROWTH RATE – 1.1 per cent (1995)
POPULATION DENSITY – 127 per sq. km (1995)
URBAN POPULATION – 26.2 per cent (1990)

HISTORY AND POLITICS

China was ruled by imperial dynasties for over 20
centuries until revolutionaries led by Sun Yat-sen forced
the Emperor to abdicate on 10 October 1911. Neither the
new Nationalist Party (Kuomintang (KMT)) government
nor the emergent Chinese Communist Party (CCP) were
able to unify China, or to agree on the basis for further
reform. Warlord infighting rendered China weak, enabling
Japan to occupy Manchuria and all the important northern
and coastal areas of China by 1939. Japan's occupation was
ended by its defeat by the allies in 1945.

The Communists' initial five-year co-operation with
the KMT ended in 1927, although the KMT was unable to
suppress the CCP. The CCP had successfully politicized
the rural population, setting up a 'Soviet Republic' in
Jiangxi in the early 1930s, but were forced to flee by the
KMT and began the 'Long March' to Shanxi in 1934. The
Communists established control over large areas of China
in the early 1940s, seizing the territory abandoned by Japan
in 1945. Civil war lasted until 1949 when the CCP, led by

Mao Zedong (Mao Tse-tung), inaugurated the People's
Republic of China (PRC), and the KMT under Chiang
Kai-shek went into exile in Taiwan. The USA continued to
recognize the Chiang Kai-shek regime as the rightful
government of China until 1971, when the PRC took over
China's membership of the United Nations from Taiwan.

Under Mao Zedong China was ruled on the basis of four
'cardinal principles': Marxist–Leninist–Maoist thought,
the Socialist Road, the dictatorship of the proletariat, and
the leadership of the CCP. Mao's 'Great Leap Forward'
(1958–61) was an attempt to industrialize rural areas
which resulted in a famine in which 30–40 million people
died. China was plunged into chaos during the Cultural
Revolution (1966–70) when the Red Guards were used to
rid the country of 'rightist elements'.

Following the death of Mao Zedong in 1976, the
disgraced Deng Xiaoping was recalled. In 1977 he was
elected Vice-Chairman of the CCP, becoming the dominant force within the party by eliminating leftist influence,
rehabilitating fallen leaders and promoting an 'open door'
policy of economic liberalization. The Congresses of 1982
and 1987 reaffirmed Deng's policies, and in 1987 most of
the revolutionary generation were replaced in the top
posts by younger, more liberal supporters of reform.

Student-led pro-democracy demonstrations in April
and May 1989, centred on Tiananmen Square in Beijing,
ended on 3–4 June when the army took control of Beijing,
killing thousands of protesters. This strengthened the
position of hardliners within the leadership, who re-
adopted policies of centralization based on Marxist ideology. Deng retired from his last official post in November
1989 but retained effective control until late 1994.

At Deng's instigation during 1992 the emphasis switched back to economic reform and the power of the hardliners waned. The 14th Party Congress in 1992 endorsed Deng's calls for faster, bolder economic reforms and his 'socialist market economy'. Deng died on 19 February 1997 and Jiang Zemin assumed the mantle of leader.

In addition to continuing economic reforms, Jiang has sought to improve China's standing in the international community. In June 1998, President Clinton became the first US president to visit China since the 1989 Tiananmen Square massacre. The visit brought no significant new agreements between the two countries, although a debate between the two leaders and a speech by President Clinton were broadcast live on state television, the first time a foreign statesman has been allowed such open coverage.

INSURGENCIES

Separatists from the Uygur Muslim minority group in Xinjiang Autonomous Region have demonstrated against Han rule. They have claimed responsibility for bomb attacks in the provincial capital, Urumqi, and in Beijing.

POLITICAL SYSTEM

Under the 1982 constitution, the National People's Congress is the highest organ of state power. It is elected for a term of five years and is supposed to hold one session a year. It is empowered to amend the constitution, make laws, select the president and vice-president and other leading officials of the state, approve the national economic plan, the state budget and the final state accounts, and to decide on questions of war and peace. The State Council is the highest organ of the state administration. It is composed of the Premier, the Vice-Premiers, the State Councillors, heads of Ministries and Commissions, the Auditor-General and the Secretary-General. Command over the armed forces is vested in the Central Military Commission.

Deputies to Congresses at the primary level are 'directly elected' by the voters 'through a secret ballot after democratic consultation'. This is now extended to county level. These Congresses elect the deputies to the Congress at the next higher level. Deputies to the National People's Congress are elected by the People's Congresses of the provinces, autonomous regions and municipalities directly under the central government, and by the armed forces.

Local government is conducted through People's Governments at provincial, municipal and county levels. Autonomous regions, prefectures and counties exist for national minorities and are described as self-governing.

HEAD OF STATE

President of the People's Republic of China, Jiang Zemin, *elected* April 1993

Vice-President, Hu Jintao

Chairman of the Standing Committee of the National People's Congress, Li Peng

Chairman of the Central Military Committee, Jiang Zemin

STATE COUNCIL *as at July 1998*

Premier, Zhu Rongji

Vice-Premiers, Qian Qichen; Li Lanqing; Wen Jiabao; Wu Bangguo

State Councillors, Gen. Chi Haotian; Ismail Amat; Luo Gan; Wu Yi; Wang Zhongyu

MINISTERS

Agriculture, Chen Yaobang
Civil Affairs, Doje Cering

Communications, Huang Zhendong
Construction, Yu Zhengsheng
Culture, Sun Jiazheng
Defence, Gen. Chi Haotian
Education, Chen Zhili
Finance, Xiang Huaicheng
Foreign Affairs, Tang Jiaxuan
Foreign Trade and Economic Co-operation, Shi Guansheng
Health, Zhang Wenkang
Information Industry, Wu Jichuan
Justice, Gao Changli
Labour and Social Security, Zhang Zuoji
Land and Natural Resources, Zhou Yongkang
Personnel, Song Defu
Public Security, Jia Chunwang
Railways, Fu Zhihuan
Science and Technology, Zhu Lilan
State Security, Xu Yongyue
Supervision, He Yong
Water Resources, Niu Maosheng

MINISTERS IN CHARGE OF STATE COMMISSIONS

Development Planning, Zeng Peiyan
Economics and Trade, Sheng Huaren
Ethnic Affairs, Li Dezhu
Family Planning, Zhang Weiqing
Legislative Affairs, Yang Jingyu
Science, Technology and Industry for National Defence, Liu Jibin
Auditor-General, Li Jinhua
Governor of the People's Bank of China, Dai Xianglong

THE CHINESE COMMUNIST PARTY

General Secretary, Jiang Zemin
Politburo Standing Committee, Jiang Zemin; Li Peng; Zhu Rongji; Li Ruihuan; Hu Jintao; Wei Jianxing; Li Lanqing
Politburo of the Central Committee, Tian Jiyun; Jiang Zemin; Li Tieying; Li Ruihuan; Zhu Rongji; Hu Jintao; Ding Guangen; Qian Qichen; Li Lanqing; Wei Jianxing; Wu Bangguo; Xie Fei; Li Peng; Huang Ju; Wen Jiabao; Li Changchun; Wu Guanzheng; Chi Haotian; Zhang Wannian; Luo Gan; Jia Qinglin; Jiang Chunyun (*full members*); Zeng Qinghong; Wu Yi (*alternate members*)
Secretariat of the Central Committee, Ding Guangen; Hu Jintao; Wei Jianxing; Wen Jiabao; Zhang Wannian; Luo Gan; Zeng Qinghong (*full members*)
Membership, 52,000,000 (1993)

EMBASSY OF THE PEOPLE'S REPUBLIC OF CHINA

49–51 Portland Place, London WIN 4JL
Tel 0171–636 0288/5726
Ambassador Extraordinary and Plenipotentiary, HE Ma Zhengang, apptd 1997
Minister-Counsellor, Lu Kexing (*Commercial*)
Defence Attaché, Maj.-Gen. Yan Kunsheng

BRITISH EMBASSY

11 Guang Hua Lu, Jian Guo Men Wai, Beijing 100 600
Tel: Beijing 6532 1961/2/3/4
Ambassador, HE Anthony Galsworthy, CMG, apptd 1997
Minister, Consul-General and Deputy Head of Mission, A. D. Sprake
Counsellors, J. V. Everard (*Political and Economic*); C. Segar (*Commercial*); M. Davidson (*Cultural, and British Council Representative*)
Defence, Military and Air Attaché, Brig. J. G. Kerr

BRITISH CONSULATES-GENERAL – Shanghai and Guangzhou

DEFENCE

All three military arms are parts of the People's Liberation Army (PLA). China has at least 17 intercontinental and 46 intermediate range land-based, and 12 submarine-launched nuclear ballistic missiles. The Army has up to 8,500 main battle tanks, 5,500 armoured personnel carriers and armoured infantry fighting vehicles, and more than 14,500 artillery pieces.

The Navy has 61 submarines, 18 destroyers, 36 frigates, 830 patrol and coastal vessels, 535 combat aircraft and 20 armed helicopters. The Air Force has 3,740 combat aircraft.

MILITARY EXPENDITURE – 6.2 per cent of GDP (1996)
MILITARY PERSONNEL – 3,640,000: Army 2,090,000, Navy 280,000, Air Force 470,000, Paramilitaries 800,000
CONSCRIPTION DURATION – Three to four years

ECONOMY

Economic liberalization in the early 1980s reduced central planning and broadened the role of the market, which has led to an explosion in manufacturing, concentrated in China's coastal regions. Foreign direct investment, especially from Hong Kong and Taiwan, has enabled the construction of a significant industrial base and transport infrastructure. In the coastal regions the economy has become a free market in all but name, with several stock markets and Shanghai's emergence as a financial centre. The economy is prone to bouts of 'overheating', fuelled by excessive investment in capital construction, which required austerity measures in 1993–5 in an attempt to control inflation. The measures have also caused widespread unemployment, with an estimated 50–100 million migrant workers unemployed in 1995–6. By 1994, 50–60 per cent of industrial output was produced by private or collective firms which employed a total of 120 million people.

Agriculture remains of great importance, with 70 per cent of the population still living in rural areas. Agricultural policies have devolved responsibility for agricultural production to individual households. Cereals, with peas and beans, are grown in the northern provinces, and rice, tea and sugar in the south. Rice is the staple food of the inhabitants. Cotton (mostly in valleys of the Yangtze and Yellow Rivers), tea (in the west and south), with hemp, jute and flax, are the most important crops. Livestock is raised in large numbers. Sericulture is one of the oldest industries. Cottons, woollens and silks are manufactured in large quantities.

Coal, iron ore, tin, antimony, wolfram, bismuth and molybdenum are abundant. Oil is produced in several northern provinces, particularly in Heilongjiang and Shandong, and off-shore deposits are being sought in co-operation with western and Japanese companies. In November 1997, a deal was reached with Russia over the construction of a US$12 billion liquefied natural gas (LNG) pipeline to take LNG from Siberia to China's Pacific coast. In March 1998, China announced the construction of a US$2.3 billion 1,875-mile oil pipeline along the Silk Road to Kazakhstan.

In January 1998, reforms of the banking sector were announced in response to the south-east Asian financial crisis. The reforms introduce stricter controls on loan management, increased competition in the banking sector, and the dropping of import duties to encourage foreign investment. China's refusal to devalue the yuan has helped restore a degree of stability to the region.

In 1995 the government had a current account surplus of US$1,618 million.

GNP – US$906,079 million (1996); US$750 per capita (1996)
GDP – US$613,617 million (1994); US$440 per capita (1994)
ANNUAL AVERAGE GROWTH OF GDP – 10.5 per cent (1995)
INFLATION RATE – 8.3 per cent (1996)
UNEMPLOYMENT – 2.8 per cent (1994)
TOTAL EXTERNAL DEBT – US$128,817 million (1996)

TRADE

Foreign trade and external economic relations have grown enormously since 1978. In 1995, import tariffs were cut to an average 23 per cent in line with China's attempts to join the World Trade Organization. The principal exports are animals and animal products, oil, textiles, ores, metals, tea, electronics and manufactured goods. The principal imports are motor vehicles, machinery, chemical fertilizer, plants, aircraft, books, paper and paper-making materials, chemicals, metals and ores, and dyes.

In 1995 China had a trade surplus of US$18,050 million. In 1996 imports totalled US$138,944 million and exports US$151,197 million.

Trade with UK	1996	1997
Imports from UK	£738,514,000	£920,261,000
Exports to UK	2,202,081,000	2,494,987,000

COMMUNICATIONS

There are more than 53,400 km of railway lines and 1,041,100 km of highway (1991). In addition, internal civil aviation has been developed, with routes totalling more than 471,900 km.

In the past the principal means of communication east to west was by the rivers, the most important of which are the Yangtze (Changjiang) (3,400 miles), the Yellow River (Huanghe) (2,600 miles) and the West River (Xihe) (1,650 miles). These, together with the network of canals connecting them, are still much used but their overall importance has declined. Coastal port facilities are being improved and the merchant fleet expanded.

Postal services and telecommunications have developed in recent years and it is claimed that 95 per cent of all rural townships are on the telephone and that postal routes reach practically every production brigade headquarters.

EDUCATION

Primary education lasts five years and secondary education lasts five years (three years in junior middle school and two years in senior middle school). There are over 1,000 universities, colleges and institutes.

ILLITERACY RATE – 18.5 per cent
ENROLMENT (percentage of age group) – primary 99 per cent (1995); tertiary 5.7 per cent (1996)

CULTURE

The Chinese language has many dialects, notably Cantonese, Hakka, Amoy, Foochow, Changsha, Nanchang, Wu (Shanghai) and the northern dialect. The Common Speech or *putonghua* (often referred to as Mandarin) is based on the northern dialect. The Communists have promoted it as the national language and it is taught throughout the country. As *putonghua* encourages the use of the spoken language in writing, the old literary style and ideographic form of writing has fallen into disuse. Since 1956 simplified characters have been introduced to make reading and writing easier. In 1958 the National People's Congress adopted a system of romanization known as pinyin.

Chinese literature is one of the richest in the world. Paper has been employed for writing and printing for nearly 2,000 years. The Confucian classics which formed the basis of traditional Chinese culture date from the Warring States period (fourth to third centuries BC), as do the earliest texts of Taoism. Histories, philosophical and scientific works, poetry, literary and art criticism, novels and romances survive from most periods.

The most important among the newspapers and magazines are the *People's Daily* and the twice-monthly *Qiushi*, which replaced *Red Flag* as the CCP's mouthpiece in 1989.

TIBET

AREA – 463,000 sq. miles (1,199,164 sq. km)
POPULATION – 2,260,000 (1993)
CAPITAL – Lhasa

Tibet is a plateau seldom lower than 10,000 feet, which forms the northern frontier of India (boundary imperfectly demarcated), from Kashmir to Myanmar, but is separated therefrom by the Himalayas.

From 1911 to 1950, Tibet was virtually an independent country though its status was never officially so recognized. In 1950 Chinese Communist forces invaded eastern Tibet. In 1951 an agreement was reached whereby the Chinese army was allowed entry into Tibet, and a Communist military and administrative headquarters was set up. A series of revolts against Chinese rule culminated in 1959 in a rising in Lhasa, the capital. Fighting continued for several days before the rebellion was crushed and military rule was imposed. The Dalai Lama fled to India where he and his followers were granted political asylum and established a government in exile.

In 1964 the Dalai Lama and the Panchen Lama were dismissed, marking the end of co-operation between the Chinese government and the traditional religious authorities. Tibet became an Autonomous Region of China in 1965. Martial law was declared in Tibet in 1989 after serious unrest, and sporadic outbursts of unrest continue.

The Panchen Lama died in 1989. China rejected the Dalai Lama's choice of successor, which is believed to have been executed, and enthroned its own candidate.

In December 1997, the International Commission of Jurists issued a report declaring that Tibet was 'under alien subjugation' and called for a UN-managed referendum to decide its future status. China contested that the report failed to acknowledge its historical claims to the region.

HONG KONG

AREA – 415 sq. miles (1,075 sq. km)
POPULATION – 6,311,000 (1996)
CURRENCY – Hong Kong dollar (HK$) of 100 cents
FLAG – Red, with a white bauhinia flower of five petals each containing a red star
LIFE EXPECTANCY (years) – male 75.84; female 81.16
POPULATION GROWTH RATE – 1.6 per cent (1995)
POPULATION DENSITY – 5,758 per sq. km (1995)
URBAN POPULATION – 93.1 per cent (1986)

Hong Kong, consisting of more than 230 islands and of a portion of the mainland (Kowloon and the New Territories) on the south-east coast of China, is situated at the eastern side of the mouth of the Pearl River. Hong Kong Island is about 11 miles (18 km) long and from two to five miles (three to eight km) broad. It is separated from the mainland by a narrow strait.

The climate is sub-tropical, tending towards the temperate for nearly half the year. The mean monthly temperature ranges from 16° C to 29° C. The average annual rainfall is 2,214 mm, of which nearly 80 per cent falls between May and September. Tropical cyclones occur between May and November, causing high winds and heavy rain.

HISTORY AND POLITICS

Hong Kong Island was first occupied by Great Britain in 1841 and formally ceded by the Treaty of Nanking in 1842. Kowloon was acquired by the Peking Convention of 1860 and the New Territories, consisting of a peninsula in the southern part of the Guangdong province together with adjacent islands, by a 99-year lease signed on 9 June 1898.

On 19 December 1984 the UK and China signed a Joint Declaration in which it was agreed that China would resume sovereignty over Hong Kong on 1 July 1997. In the run-up to the 1997 handover, the Chinese government's insistence on a greater say in the running of the colony and Governor Patten's plan for an extension of democracy prompted acrimonious disputes. The Chinese government refused to accept the reforms and replaced the Legislative Council with a Provisional Legislative Council (*see* below).

Hong Kong became, with effect from 1 July 1997, a Special Administrative Region (SAR) of the People's Republic of China.

The Joint Declaration which took effect in May 1985 guarantees: the free movement of goods and capital; the retention of Hong Kong's free port status, separate customs territory and freely convertible currency; the protection of property rights and foreign investment; the right of free movement to and from Hong Kong; Hong Kong's autonomy in the conduct of its external commercial relations and its own monetary and financial policies; and judicial independence. Hong Kong's constitution is the Basic Law which was passed by China's National People's Congress in 1990 and guarantees that the SAR's social and economic systems will remain unchanged for 50 years.

POLITICAL SYSTEM

Hong Kong is administered by the Hong Kong government, headed by the Chief Executive, who is aided by an Executive Council and a Provisional Legislative Council. The Executive Council consists of three ex-officio members (the Chief Secretary, the Financial Secretary and the Attorney-General) together with ten other members.

The Provisional Legislative Council consists of 60 members and replaced the Legislative Council (Legco). Both the Chief Executive and the Provisional Legislative Council were elected by a 400-strong committee which in turn was chosen by a 150-member Preparatory Committee, headed by the Chinese foreign minister, from a shortlist drawn up by China. The President of the Legislative Council is elected by the members. Legislative elections in May 1998 used a proportional representation system in five geographical constituencies, each with three to five seats. Thirty members were elected in functional constituencies and ten more from a committee.

The Urban Council provides services relating to public health and sanitation, culture and recreation in the urban area. A Regional Council was set up in 1986 to provide similar services in the New Territories. There are also 18 district boards (nine in the urban areas and nine in the New Territories) which are statutory bodies that provide a forum for public consultation and participation in the administration of the districts.

Chief Executive, Tung Chee-hwa, *sworn in* 1 July 1997

EXECUTIVE COUNCIL *as at July 1997*
Non-official Members, Dr Chung Sze-yuen *(convenor);* Dr
Raymond Ch'ien; Chung Shui-ming; Nellie Fong;
Charles Lee; Anthony Leung; Leung Chun-ying; Tam
Yiu-chung; Henry Tang; Rosanna Wong; Yang Ti-liang
Ex-officio Members, Anson Chan; Donald Tsang; Elsie
Leung

GOVERNMENT SECRETARIAT *as at July 1997*
Administrative Secretary, Anson Chan
Financial Secretary, Donald Tsang
Justice, Elsie Leung
Broadcasting, Culture and Sport, Chau Tak-hay
Civil Service, Lam Woon-kwong
Constitutional Affairs, Michael Suen
Economic Services, Stephen Ip
Education and Manpower, Joseph Wong
Financial Services, Rafael Hui
Health and Welfare, Katherine Fok, OBE
Home Affairs, D. H. T. Lan
Housing, Dominic Wong
Planning, Environment and Lands, Bowen Leung
Security, Peter Lai
Trade and Industry, Denise Yue
Transport, Nicholas Ng
Treasury, Kwong Ki-chi
Works, Benedict Kwong
Speaker of the Provisional Legislative Council, Rita Fan

CONSUL-GENERAL, Sir Andrew Burns, KCMG, 1 Supreme
Court Road, Central, (PO Box 528), Hong Kong. Tel:
Hong Kong 2901 3000
BRITISH COUNCIL REPRESENTATIVE, D. Lauder
HONG KONG ECONOMIC AND TRADE OFFICE, 6 Grafton
Street, London WIX 3LB. Tel: 0171-499 9821.
Commissioner, John Tsang, apptd 1998

ECONOMY
The main economic sector is the services industry,
especially financial services. It employs roughly two thirds
of the workforce and contributed 84 per cent to GDP in
1996. The manufacturing sector contributed 8.8 per cent to
GDP. Principal exports are clothing, electrical machinery
and apparatus, and textiles.
  Diversification in terms of products and markets continues to be the main feature of recent industrial development, as are industrial partnerships with overseas companies. The economy is based on export rather than the
domestic market. Tourism is very important to the
economy; over 12 million people visited Hong Kong in
1996.
  In October 1997, the financial crisis in south-east Asia
reached Hong Kong, causing the Hang Seng index to fall by
33.4 per cent in two weeks. The Hong Kong Monetary
Authority used its foreign exchange reserves to fend off
speculators and preserve the Hong Kong currency's peg to
the US dollar, which stabilized the currency. In January
1998, the region's largest investment bank, Peregrine
Investment Holdings, filed for liquidation, plunging the
financial market back into turmoil; between September
1997 and January 1998 the Hang Seng index lost half its
value. By April 1998, unemployment was at a near-record
level of 3.5 per cent.
GNP – US$153,288 million (1996); US$24,290 per capita
  (1996)
GDP – US$93,223 million (1994); US$22,590 per capita
  (1994)
INFLATION RATE – 6.0 per cent (1996)
UNEMPLOYMENT – 3.2 per cent (1995)

TRADE
In 1996 imports totalled US$198,560 million and exports
US$180,745 million. Hong Kong's principal customers for
its domestic products, in order of value of trade, were
China, USA, Japan and Germany. China was its principal
supplier.

Trade with UK	1996	1997
Imports from UK	£2,923,391,000	£3,210,841,000
Exports to UK	4,072,935,000	4,348,846,000

COMMUNICATIONS
Hong Kong has one of the world's finest natural harbours,
and it is the busiest container port in the world, with eight
terminals, as well as large modern cargo and liner terminals. Dockyard facilities include eight floating drydocks,
the largest being capable of docking vessels up to 150,000
tonnes deadweight. A new 17-berth container port will
open in stages between 1997 and 2003.
  An international airport built on reclaimed land at Chek
Lap Kok opened in July 1998. When fully operational, it
will be capable of handling 35 million passengers and 1.5
million tonnes of cargo annually.

EDUCATION
Free education for children up to the age of 15 is
compulsory. Post-secondary education is provided by six
universities and one college. The Open Learning Institute
of Hong Kong provides university education. There are
also seven technical institutes and the Hong Kong Institute
of Education.
ILLITERACY RATE – 7.8 per cent
ENROLMENT (percentage of age group) – primary 91 per
  cent (1995); secondary 71 per cent (1995); tertiary 21.9
  per cent (1993)

COLOMBIA
República de Colombia

AREA – 439,737 sq. miles (1,138,914 sq. km). Neighbours:
  Venezuela (north and east), Brazil (south-east), Peru
  (south), Ecuador (south-west), Panama (north-west)
POPULATION – 35,099,000 (1994 UN estimate). The
  language is Spanish. Roman Catholicism is the
  established religion
CAPITAL – Bogotá (population, 8,000,000, 1992)
MAJOR CITIES – ΨBarranquilla (1,400,000), the major
  port on the Caribbean; Bucaramanga (350,000);
  ΨBuenaventura (130,000), the major port on the Pacific;
  Cali (1,800,000); ΨCartagena (700,000); Medellín
  (2,400,000)
CURRENCY – Colombian peso of 100 centavos
NATIONAL ANTHEM – Oh gloria inmarcesible
NATIONAL DAY – 20 July (National Independence Day)
NATIONAL FLAG – Broad yellow band in upper half,
  surmounting equal bands of blue and red
LIFE EXPECTANCY (years) – male 66.36; female 72.26
POPULATION GROWTH RATE – 1.7 per cent (1995)
POPULATION DENSITY – 31 per sq. km (1995)
URBAN POPULATION – 67.2 per cent (1985)

Colombia lies in the extreme north-west of South America, having a coastline on both the Caribbean Sea and
Pacific Ocean.
  The country is divided by the Cordillera de los Andes
into a coastal region in the north and west and extensive
plains in the east. The eastern range of the Colombian
Andes is a series of vast tablelands. This temperate region is

the most densely peopled portion of the country. The principal rivers are the Magdalena, Guaviare, Cauca, Atrato, Caquetá, Putumayo and Patia.

HISTORY AND POLITICS

The Colombian coast was visited in 1502 by Columbus, and in 1536 a Spanish expedition penetrated the interior and established a government. The country remained under Spanish rule until 1819 when Simón Bolivar established the Republic of Colombia, consisting of the territories now known as Colombia, Panama, Venezuela and Ecuador. In 1829–30 Venezuela and Ecuador withdrew, and in 1831 the remaining territories formed the Republic of New Granada. The name was changed to the Granadine Confederation in 1858, to the United States of Colombia in 1861 and to the Republic of Colombia in 1866. Panama seceded in 1903.

During the early 1950s Colombia suffered a period of virtual civil war between the supporters of the Conservative and the Liberal parties. From 1957 to 1974 the country was governed under the 'National Front' agreement with an alternating presidency and equal numbers of ministerial posts. The alternation of the presidency ended in 1974 and parity in appointments in 1978.

A new constitution was promulgated in 1991. In the 1994 presidential election the Liberal candidate Ernesto Samper narrowly defeated the Social Conservative Party (PSC) candidate. President Samper appointed a Liberal–PSC coalition government in August 1994. The March 1998 legislative elections were won by the Liberal Party, who remained the largest party in both houses with 56 per cent of the vote in the House of Representatives and 54 per cent in the Senate. The presidential election in June 1998 was won by the PSC candidate Andrés Pastrana Arango.

INSURGENCIES

Colombia is dogged by insurgency from left-wing guerrillas and from the drugs cartels centred on Cali. The main active guerrilla factions are the Revolutionary Armed Forces of Colombia (FARC) and the National Liberation Army (ELN). Preliminary discussions regarding peace talks were held in June 1997 but have yet to yield significant results. The security threat from the Medellín drugs cartel effectively ended with the death of Pablo Escobar, the cartel leader, in December 1993. In 1995, the government came under suspicion of having links with the cartel and President Samper was accused of authorizing the use of cartel money to fund his 1994 election campaign.

POLITICAL SYSTEM

The Congress is a bicameral legislature. The lower house (the House of Representatives) has 163 members elected for a four-year term. The upper house (the Senate) has 102 members, 99 of whom are directly elected for four years; three seats are reserved for representatives of indigenous people. The president, who appoints the Cabinet, is directly elected for a four-year term.

HEAD OF STATE

President, Andrés Pastrana Arango, *elected* 21 June 1998

CABINET *as at May 1998*

Agriculture and Rural Development, Antonio Gómez Merlano
Communications, José Fernando Bautista
Culture, Ramiro Osorio
Defence, Gilberto Echeverri Mejía
Economic Development, Carlos Julio Gaitan
Education, Jaime Niño Diez
Environment, Eduardo Verano de la Rosa
Finance, Antonio José Urdinola

Foreign Affairs, Camilo Reyes Rodríguez
Foreign Trade, Carlos Ronderos
Health, María Teresa Forero de Saade
Interior, Alfonso López Caballero
Justice, Almabeatriz Rengifo López
Labour and Social Welfare, Carlos Bula
Mines and Energy, Orlando Cabrales Martínez
Planning, Cecilia López Montaño
Transport, Rodrigo Marín

COLOMBIAN EMBASSY
Flat 3A, 3 Hans Crescent, London SWIX OLR
Tel 0171–589 9177/5037
Ambassador Extraordinary and Plenipotentiary, new appointment awaited

BRITISH EMBASSY
Edificio Ing Barings, Carrera 9 No 76-49 Piso 9, Bogotá
Tel: Bogotá 317 6690
Ambassador Extraordinary and Plenipotentiary, HE Jeremy Thorpe, apptd 1998
BRITISH CONSULAR OFFICES – Barranquilla, Bogotá, Cali and Medellín

BRITISH COUNCIL DIRECTOR, K. Board, Calle 87 No. 12–79, Bogotá DE

COLOMBO-BRITISH CHAMBER OF COMMERCE, Apartado Aereo 054 728, Av. 39 No. 13–62, Bogotá DE

DEFENCE

The Army has 12 light tanks, 160 armoured personnel carriers, and 130 artillery pieces. The Navy has two submarines, four frigates, 39 patrol and coastal vessels, four aircraft and two helicopters at eight bases. The Air Force has 72 combat aircraft and 63 armed helicopters.

MILITARY EXPENDITURE – 2.2 per cent of GDP (1996)
MILITARY PERSONNEL – 146,300: Army 121,000, Navy 18,000, Air Force 7,300
CONSCRIPTION DURATION – 12–18 months

ECONOMY

Coal, natural gas and hydroelectricity resources are largely unexploited, although development of coal is being given priority. The hydrocarbon sector accounts for over half of the mining output, precious metals (gold, platinum and silver) and iron ore accounting for the remainder. Other mineral deposits include nickel, bauxite, copper, gypsum, limestone, phosphates, sulphur and uranium. Colombia is also the world's largest producer of emeralds.

Major cash crops are coffee, sugar, bananas, cut flowers and cotton. Cattle are raised in large numbers, and meat and cured skins and hides are also exported.

The government has encouraged diversification to reduce dependence on coffee as the major export and this has led to the growth of new export-orientated industries, particularly textiles, paper products and leather goods. Stimulus to the economy has been provided by loans from the World Bank and IADB for project development.

Since the late 1980s the government has introduced trade liberalization and privatization measures which have effectively freed foreign exchange transactions, increased foreign competition, ended protectionism and reduced inflation.

In 1995 there was a trade deficit of US$2,548 million and a current account deficit of US$4,116 million. In 1996 and 1997 Colombia was blacklisted by the USA for failing to curb levels of drug production sufficiently. These sanctions were ended in March 1998 in recognition of new efforts made by the Colombian government in the fight against drugs; however, Colombia was not included on the

USA's list of countries whose co-operation over narcotics was deemed to be 'satisfactory'.

GNP – US$80,174 million (1996); US$2,140 per capita (1996)

GDP – US$46,145 million (1994); US$1,847 per capita (1994)

ANNUAL AVERAGE GROWTH OF GDP – 2.1 per cent (1996)

INFLATION RATE – 20.2 per cent (1996)

TOTAL EXTERNAL DEBT – US$28,859 million (1996)

TRADE

Principal exports are petroleum and derivatives, coffee, bananas, cut flowers, clothing and textiles, ferro-nickel and coal. Principal trading partners are USA, the EU and Latin America.

In 1996 imports totalled US$13,684 million and exports US$10,587 million.

Trade with UK	1996	1997
Imports from UK	£177,767,000	£170,503,000
Exports to UK	211,476,000	185,657,000

COMMUNICATIONS

The Andes make surface transport difficult so air transport is used extensively. There are daily air services between Bogotá and all the principal towns, as well as frequent services to other countries. The 'Atlantic Railway' links the departmental lines running down to the River Magdalena, and completes the connection between Bogotá and Santa Marta. Although the railways are in a poor state, there are about 2,600 miles of rail in use at present. The road network consists of 105,201 km of roads of all types, of which 21,800 km are classified as main trunk and transversal roads. A canal to link the Pacific Ocean and the Caribbean Sea has been planned.

There are three national television channels.

CULTURE AND EDUCATION

There is a flourishing press in urban areas and a national literature supplements the rich inheritance from the time of Spanish colonial rule. State education is free.

ILLITERACY RATE – 8.7 per cent

ENROLMENT (percentage of age group) – primary 85 per cent (1995); secondary 50 per cent (1995); tertiary 17.2 per cent (1995)

THE COMOROS

République Fédérale Islamique des Comores

AREA – 863 sq. miles (2,235 sq. km). The Comoro archipelago includes the islands of Great Comoro, Anjouan, Mayotte and Moheli and certain islets in the Indian Ocean

POPULATION – 653,000 (1994 UN estimate), mostly Muslim. French and Arabic are the official languages; the majority of the population speak Comoran, a blend of Arabic and Swahili

CAPITAL – Moroni (population, 17,267, 1980 estimate), on Great Comoro

CURRENCY – Comorian franc (KMF) of 100 centimes. The Franc CFA of 100 centimes is also used

NATIONAL DAY – 6 July (Independence Day)

NATIONAL FLAG – Green ground, with a white crescent and four white stars, horns towards the fly. The name of *Allah,* in Arabic script in the upper fly and the name of *Mohammed* in the lower hoist

LIFE EXPECTANCY (years) – male 55.50; female 56.50

POPULATION GROWTH RATE – 3.7 per cent (1995)

POPULATION DENSITY – 292 per sq. km (1995)

URBAN POPULATION – 28.5 per cent (1991)

ILLITERACY RATE – 42.7 per cent

ENROLMENT (percentage of age group) – primary 53 per cent (1993); tertiary 0.6 per cent (1995)

HISTORY AND POLITICS

The islanders voted for independence from France in December 1974 and three islands became independent on 6 July 1975. The island of Mayotte opposed independence and has remained under French administration.

An election in 1993 brought President Djohar's PDR party to power. Djohar was temporarily ousted in a coup in 1995 which was thwarted by French troops. While Djohar was abroad for medical attention, the Prime Minister of the newly installed unity government, Caabiel Yachroutou, declared himself interim president and refused to acknowledge Djohar's authority, resulting in the formation of a rival government. Djohar returned to the Comoros in January 1996 but was prohibited from contesting the March 1996 presidential election, which was won by Mohammad Taki Abdoulkarim of the National Union for Democracy in the Comoros. Taki dissolved the National Assembly and legislative elections were held in December 1996 although boycotted by the opposition FAR.

In August 1997, separatists on the islands of Anjouan and Moheli demanded independence from the Comoros and a return to French rule. Following a failed attempt to resolve the situation by force, President Taki assumed absolute power and established a State Transition Commission to function as a Cabinet. In a referendum in October, the inhabitants of Anjouan voted overwhelmingly for independence. Talks mediated by the OAU began in December 1997 and are continuing.

In March 1998, Anjouan's self-proclaimed President Abdallah Ibrahim appointed a prime minister and Cabinet, though their legitimacy has not been recognized internationally. In May President Taki dismissed his whole Cabinet on grounds of 'incompetence'; to date, one new minister has been appointed, with a wide range of portfolios, but no prime minister.

POLITICAL SYSTEM

In October 1996 a new constitution was approved by referendum. The president may be elected for an unlimited number of six-year terms and has the authority to appoint a prime minister and Governors, and reports to the Federal Assembly.

Each island is administered by a Governor, assisted by up to four Commissioners whom he appoints, and has an elected Legislative Council.

HEAD OF STATE

President, Mohammad Taki Abdoulkarim, *sworn in 25 March 1996*

COUNCIL OF MINISTERS *as at July 1998*

Justice, Public Works, Employment, Training, Administrative Decentralization and Institutional Reforms, Mohamed Abdou Mahdi

EMBASSY OF THE FEDERAL ISLAMIC REPUBLIC OF THE COMOROS
20 rue Marbeau, 75016 Paris, France
Tel Paris 4067 9054

BRITISH AMBASSADOR, HE Robert Dewar, resident at Antananarivo, Madagascar

ECONOMY

The most important products are vanilla, copra, cloves and essential oils, which are the principal exports; cacao, sisal and coffee are also cultivated. Great Comoro is well forested and produces some timber.

GNP – US$228million (1996); US$450 per capita (1996)
GDP – US$259 million (1994); US$301 per capita (1994)
TOTAL EXTERNAL DEBT – US$206 million (1996)

TRADE WITH UK	1996	1997
Imports from UK	£907,000	£457,000
Exports to UK	68,000	35,000

DEMOCRATIC REPUBLIC OF CONGO

AREA – 905,355 sq. miles (2,344,858 sq. km). Neighbours: Central African Republic (north), Sudan (north-east), Uganda, Rwanda, Burundi and Tanzania (east), Zambia (south), Angola (south-west), Republic of Congo (north-west)

POPULATION – 43,901,000 (1994 UN estimate). The population was 34,671,607 at the 1985 census, composed almost entirely of Bantu groups, divided into roughly 300 semi-autonomous tribes. Minorities include Sudanese, Nilotes, Pygmies and Hamites, as well as refugees from Angola. Swahili, a Bantu dialect with an admixture of Arabic, is the nearest approach to a common language in the east and south, while Lingala is the language of a large area along the river and in the north, and Kikongo of the region between Kinshasa and the sea. French is the language of administration

CAPITAL – Kinshasa (population, 2,664,309, 1985)
MAJOR CITIES – Kananga (601,239); Kisangani (310,705); Likasi (146,394); Lubumbashi (403,623); ΨMatadi (143,598); Mbandaka (134,495)
CURRENCY – Congolese franc
NATIONAL DAY – 24 November
NATIONAL FLAG – Blue with a large yellow five-pointed star in the centre and five small yellow five-pointed stars in a vertical line down the hoist
LIFE EXPECTANCY (years) – male 50.40; female 53.66
POPULATION GROWTH RATE – 4.2 per cent (1995)
POPULATION DENSITY – 19 per sq. km (1995)
URBAN POPULATION – 39.5 per cent (1985)
MILITARY EXPENDITURE – 2.8 per cent of GDP (1996)
MILITARY PERSONNEL – 20,000–40,000: Army being reorganized following change of government
ILLITERACY RATE – 22.7 per cent
ENROLMENT (percentage of age group) – primary 61 per cent (1994); secondary 23 per cent (1994); tertiary 2.3 per cent (1994)

The Democratic Republic of Congo (formerly Zaïre) is Africa's second largest state. Apart from the coastal district in the west which is fairly dry, the rainfall averages between 60 and 80 inches. The average temperature is about 27°C, but in the south the winter temperature can fall nearly to freezing point. Extensive forest covers the central districts.

HISTORY AND POLITICS

The state of the Congo, founded in 1885, became a Belgian colony in 1908 and was administered by Belgium until independence in 1960. Mobutu Sésé Seko, formerly commander-in-chief of the Congolese National Army, came to power in a coup in 1965 and was elected president in 1970. Legislative power was vested in a unicameral National Legislative Council, with candidates proposed by the sole legal political party, Mouvement Populaire de la Révolution (MPR).

Political reforms were announced in April 1990 and President Mobutu called a National Conference to draft a new constitution although the government refused to grant it sovereign status. Mobutu accepted an opposition-dominated government under Prime Minister Etienne Tshisekedi in October 1991. His attempts to replace this with MPR-dominated governments failed and the National Conference confirmed the Tshisekedi government as legitimate in August 1992.

From 1992 to 1995 the president and the opposition were locked in a power struggle. In January 1994 President Mobutu dissolved the government and on 9 April 1994 promulgated a Transitional Constitutional Act which regulated a 15-month period of transition to democracy. In July 1995 the transition period was extended by a further two years.

In October 1996 fighting broke out between Zaïrean Tutsis (*Banyamulenge)* and the Zaïrean army in North and South Kivu provinces which had received an influx of Hutu refugees from Rwanda. The pro-Hutu army attempted to expel the Tutsis from the region but found themselves outgunned by the rebels, under the leadership of Laurent Kabila, who were backed by the Rwandan and Ugandan governments. Kabila's Alliance of Democratic Forces for the Liberation of Congo-Zaïre (AFDL) captured Kinshasa in May 1997 and President Mobutu fled. Zaïre was renamed the Democratic Republic of Congo. Unrest in the Kivu provinces has continued since the change of government.

SECESSION

Since 1992 ethnic Katangans have been forcing ethnic Kasai mineworkers and their families out of the southern region of Shaba (Katanga) in a wave of ethnic violence which is a repeat of the Katanga secessionist war in 1960. In December 1993 the Governor of Shaba declared total autonomy and announced the reversion of the region's name to Katanga.

POLITICAL SYSTEM

President Kabila announced a two-year transitional period before elections in April 1999. A Constituent Council was set up to draft a new constitution that will be approved or rejected in a referendum in December 1998. Political parties have been banned.

There are 11 regions, each under a Governor and provincial administration: Bas-Zaïre (provincial capital, Matadi); Bandundu (Bandundu); Equateur (Mbandaka); Haut-Zaïre (Kisangani); Kinshasa (Kinshasa); Maniema (Kindu); North Kivu (Goma); South Kivu (Bukavu); Shaba (Katanga) (Lubumbashi); East Kasai (Mbuji-Mayi); West Kasai (Kananga).

HEAD OF STATE
President and Minister of Defence, Laurent Désiré Kabila, *sworn in* 29 May 1997

CABINET *as at* July 1998

Agriculture and Animal Husbandry, Mawampanga Mwana Nanga
Civil Service, Paul-Gabriel Kapita Shabanga
Commerce, Paul Bandoma
Culture, Juliana Lumumba
Deputy Minister for Commerce and Petroleum Products, Banyaku Luarte
Deputy Minister for Foreign Affairs, David Mbwankiem
Deputy Ministers for the Interior, Mulumba Katchy; Cdt Faustin Munene
Deputy Minister for Oil Development, Pierre Talema Losona
Deputy Minister for Primary, Secondary and Professional Education, Ebaba Kubutio
Deputy Minister for Social Affairs, Milulu Mamboleo
Development Areas, Umba Kyamitala
Economy, Nyembo Kabemba
Energy, Eleko Botula
Environment, Fisheries and Forest Resources, Edi Angulu
Finance, Fernand Tala Ngai
Foreign Affairs, Bizima Karaha
Health, Jean Baptiste Sondji
Human Rights, Cheick Okitundu
Industry, Small and Medium-sized Enterprises, Babi Mbayi
Information, Didier Mumengi
International Co-operation, Celestin Luangi
Justice, Mwenze Kongolo
Labour and Social Security, Thomas Kanza
Land, Anatole Bisikwabo Tshiumbaka
Mines, Frederic Kibassa-Maliba
Minister attached to the Presidency, Pierre-Victor Mpoyo; Deogratias Buguera
Minister of State for the Interior, Gaetan Kakudji
Minister of State for Planning, Badimani Bilembo Mulumba
National Education, Kamara Rwakaikara
Post and Telecommunications, Kinkela Vinkasi
Public Works, Bruno Luwawula
State Firms, Prosper Kibue Molambo
Transport, Henri Mova Sakanyi
Youth and Sports, Dumba Kimaya

EMBASSY OF THE DEMOCRATIC REPUBLIC OF CONGO
26 Chesham Place, London SW1X 8HH
Tel 0171-235 6137
Chargé d'Affaires, Nsangolo Iwula

BRITISH EMBASSY
Avenue des Trois 'Z', Gombe, Kinshasa
Tel: Kinshasa 34775
Ambassador Extraordinary and Plenipotentiary, HE Douglas Scrafton, apptd 1996
CONSULATE – Kisangani

ECONOMY

Palm oil is the most important agricultural cash product though it is no longer exported. Coffee, rubber, cocoa and timber are the most important agricultural exports. The production of cotton, pyrethrum and copal is increasing. Copper is widely exploited, and industrial diamonds and cobalt are also produced. Oil deposits are exploited off the Zaïre estuary and reef-gold is mined in the north-east of the country.

The main industrial products are foodstuffs, beverages, tobacco, textiles, leather, wood products, cement and building materials, metallurgy, small river craft and bicycles. There are reserves of hydroelectric power and the Inga dam on the river Zaïre supplies electricity to Matadi, Kinshasa and Shaba.

Rampant hyperinflation and corruption have left the economy and the state's finances in a parlous state. Multilateral and bilateral aid were greatly reduced because of President Mobutu's refusal to leave office.

In 1993 the government had a budget deficit equivalent to 13.72 per cent of GDP.
GNP – US$5,727 million (1996); US$130 per capita (1996)
GDP – US$9,642 million (at current prices) (1994); US$227 per capita (1994)
ANNUAL AVERAGE GROWTH OF GDP – – 10.5 per cent (1992)
INFLATION RATE – 658.8 per cent (1996)
TOTAL EXTERNAL DEBT – US$12,826 million (1996)

TRADE

The chief exports are copper, crude oil, coffee, diamonds, rubber, cobalt, gold, zinc and other metals.

In 1995 imports totalled US$397 million and exports US$438 million.

Trade with UK	1996	1997
Imports from UK	£17,090,000	£14,827,000
Exports to UK	14,754,000	5,073,000

COMMUNICATIONS

There are approximately 20,500 km of roads (earth-surfaced) of national importance, and 6,000 km of railways. The country has four international and 40 principal airports.

REPUBLIC OF CONGO
République du Congo

AREA – 132,047 sq. miles (342,000 sq. km). Neighbours: Gabon (west), Cameroon and Central African Republic (north), Angola (Cabinda) (south-west), the Democratic Republic of Congo (east and south)
POPULATION – 2,590,000 (1994 UN estimate). The official language is French; Lingala and Kikongo are widely spoken
CAPITAL – Brazzaville (population, 596,200, 1984)
MAJOR CITIES – ΨPointe Noire (350,000), the main commercial centre
CURRENCY – Franc CFA of 100 centimes
NATIONAL DAY – 15 August
NATIONAL FLAG – Divided diagonally into green, yellow and red bands
LIFE EXPECTANCY (years) – male 48.91; female 53.77
POPULATION GROWTH RATE – 3.0 per cent (1995)
POPULATION DENSITY – 8 per sq. km (1995)
MILITARY EXPENDITURE – 2.3 per cent of GDP (1996)

MILITARY PERSONNEL – 12,000: Army 8,000, Navy 800, Air Force 1,200, Paramilitaries 2,000
ILLITERACY RATE – 25.1 per cent
ENROLMENT (percentage of age group) –primary 96 per cent (1980); tertiary 5.3 per cent (1990)

HISTORY AND POLITICS

Formerly the French colony of Middle Congo, the Congo became a member state of the French Community on 28 November 1958 and fully independent on 17 August 1960.

In 1968, a National Council of army officers took power and created the Parti Congolais du Travail (PCT) and the People's Republic of Congo. After popular pressure, the PCT abandoned its monopoly of power and renounced Marxism in 1990. A transitional government was formed in January 1991 and a national conference suspended the constitution, stripped President Sassou-Nguesso of all powers and formed itself into the Higher Council of the Republic (CSR). In December 1991 the CSR adopted a new multiparty constitution with a directly-elected president and a bicameral parliament. The new constitution was approved by a referendum in 1992 and in the ensuing elections the Pan-African Union for Social Democracy (UPADS) emerged as the largest party.

The lack of a parliamentary majority forced President Lissouba to call fresh elections in 1993. These too were won by the UPADS but the results were disputed by opposition groups and violence broke out between rival parties. An international panel, called to investigate the 1993 election, annulled the results in nine seats, for which by-elections were held in 1995. A new UPADS-dominated government was appointed in January 1995. In June 1997, fighting broke out between forces of President Lissouba and followers of former president Sassou-Nguesso. Lissouba was ousted from power in October 1997 and Sassou-Nguesso was reinstalled as president. Elections scheduled for July 1997 were called off and a National Forum for Unity and Democracy was set up to schedule legislative elections. It declared a three-year transition period after which democratic elections will be held.

HEAD OF STATE
President, Minister of Defence, Denis Sassou-Nguesso, *sworn in* 25 October 1997

CABINET *as at July 1998*
Agriculture and Livestock, Nkoua Celestin Gongara
Civil Service and Administrative Reforms, Charles Dambenzet
Communication and Government Spokesman, François Ibovi
Culture, Arts and Francophonie, Mambou Elie Niamy
Energy and Water Resources, Jean-Marie Tassoua
Family Affairs, Women in Development Efforts, Cécile Matingou
Finance and Budget, Mathias Dzon
Fishing and Fish Resources, Pierre Gassay
Foreign Affairs and Co-operation, Rodolphe Adada
Forestry, Henri Djombo
Health and Population, Mamadou Dekamo
Higher Education and Scientific Research, François Loumouamou
Industry and Mines, Michel Mampoya
Interior, Security and Territorial Administration, Col. Pierre Oba
Keeper of the Seals, Justice, Pierre Nze
Labour and Social Security, Jean-Martin M'bemba
National Solidarity, Disasters, War Victims and Relief Actions, Léon Alfred Opimba
Organization of National Forum, Relations with National Council, Fulmin Ayessa
Permanent Undersecretary at the Presidency, Isidore Mvouba

Petroleum Affairs, Jean-Baptiste Taty-Loutard
Posts and Telecommunications, Jean-Félix Demba Delo
Primary and Secondary Education, Pierre Tsiba
Programming and Privatization, Paul Kaya
Reconstruction and Urban Development, Itihi Lekounzou Ossetoumba
Small and Medium-sized Enterprises, Handicrafts, Pierre Damien Boussoukou Boumba
Social Amenities and Public Works, Col. Florent Tsiba
State Control, Gérard Bitsindou
Technical Education and Vocational Training, André Okombi Salissan
Territorial and Regional Development, Pierre Moussa
Tourism and Environment, Nobert Ngoua
Town Planning and Housing, Mannze Nguele
Trade, Consumer Affairs and Supplies, Félix Ngoulou
Transport, Civil Aviation and Merchant Navy, Martin M'beri
Youth Redeployment, Sports and Civic Education, Claude-Ernest Ndalla-Graille

EMBASSY OF THE REPUBLIC OF CONGO
37 bis rue Paul Valéry, 75016 Paris, France
Tel: Paris 4500 6057
Ambassador Extraordinary and Plenipotentiary, HE Pierre-Michel Nguimbi, apptd 1996

HONORARY CONSULATE, 4 Wendle Court, 131–137 Wandsworth Road, London sw8 2LH. Tel: 0171-622 0419. *Honorary Consul,* L. Muzzu

BRITISH AMBASSADOR, HE Marcus Hope, resident at Kinshasa, Democratic Republic of Congo
HONORARY CONSULATES – Brazzaville and Pointe Noire

ECONOMY

Congo has its own oil deposits, producing about 9 million tonnes annually. It also produces lead, zinc and gold. The principal agricultural products are timber, cassava and yams. Imports are mainly of machinery.

In 1996 Congo had a trade surplus of US$63 million and a current account deficit of US$1,034 million. Imports in 1995 totalled US$670 million and exports US$842 million. In 1996 the UN approved a three-year loan of US$100 million and the Paris Club cancelled 67 per cent of the debt owed to it by Congo.

GNP – US$1,813 million (1996); US$670 per capita (1996)
GDP – US$2,832 million (1994); US$860 per capita (1994)
ANNUAL AVERAGE GROWTH OF GDP – 1.8 per cent (1989)
INFLATION RATE – 21.4 per cent (1995)
TOTAL EXTERNAL DEBT – US$5,240 million (1996)

TRADE WITH UK	1996	1997
Imports from UK	£29,000,000	£28,472,000
Exports to UK	22,698,000	4,918,000

COSTA RICA
República de Costa Rica

AREA – 19,730 sq. miles (51,100 sq. km). Neighbours: Nicaragua, Panama
POPULATION – 3,333,000 (1994 UN estimate), mainly of European origin. The language is Spanish
CAPITAL – San José (population, 1,186,417, 1994 estimate)
MAJOR CITIES – Alajuela (170,080); Cartago (117,004)
CURRENCY – Costa Rican colón (₡) of 100 céntimos
NATIONAL ANTHEM – Himno Nacional de Costa Rica
NATIONAL DAY – 15 September

NATIONAL FLAG – Five horizontal bands, blue, white, red, white, blue (the red band twice the width of the others with emblem near staff)
LIFE EXPECTANCY (years) – male 72.89; female 77.60
POPULATION GROWTH RATE – 3.5 per cent (1995)
POPULATION DENSITY – 65 per sq. km (1995)
URBAN POPULATION – 44.0 per cent (1994)
MILITARY EXPENDITURE – 0.5 per cent of GDP (1996)
MILITARY PERSONNEL – 7,000: Paramilitaries
ILLITERACY RATE – 5.2 per cent
ENROLMENT (percentage of age group) – primary 92 per cent (1995); secondary 43 per cent (1995); tertiary 31.9 per cent (1994)

The coastal lowlands have a tropical climate but the interior plateau, with a mean elevation of 4,000 feet, enjoys a temperate climate.

HISTORY AND POLITICS

For nearly three centuries (1530–1821) Costa Rica was under Spanish rule. In 1821 the country obtained its independence, although from 1824 to 1839 it was one of the United States of Central America.

In 1948 the Army was abolished, the President declaring it unnecessary. The main political parties are the Social Christian Unity Party (PUSC) and the National Liberation Party (PLN). The last presidential and legislative elections were held on 1 February 1998, when PUSC candidate Miguel Angel Rodríguez won the presidential election, and the PUSC won 27 seats in the Legislative Assembly.

POLITICAL SYSTEM

Executive power is vested in the president, who is head of state and government, with legislative power vested in the 57-member Legislative Assembly. Under the constitution both the president and the members of the Legislative Assembly are elected for a single four-year term and may not be re-elected.

HEAD OF STATE
President, Miguel Angel Rodríguez , *elected 1 February 1998*

CABINET *as at July 1998*

Vice-President, Minister of Culture, Astrid Fischel
Vice-President, Minister of Environment, Elizabeth Odio
Agriculture and Livestock, Esteban Brenes
Economy and Foreign Trade, Samuel Guzowski
Finance, Leonel Baruch
Foreign Affairs, Roberto Rojas
Health, Rogelio Pardo
Housing, José Antonio Lobo
Justice, Mónica Nágel
Labour and Social Security, Victor Morales
Presidency and Planning, Roberto Tovar
President of the Central Bank, Eduardo Lizano
Public Education, Claudio Gutiérrez
Public Security, Juan Rafael Lizano
Public Works and Transport, Rodolfo Mendez
Women's Affairs, Yolanda Ingianna

COSTA RICAN EMBASSY
Flat 1, 14 Lancaster Gate, London W2 3LH
Tel 0171-706 8844
Ambassador Extraordinary and Plenipotentiary, Jorge Borbón

BRITISH EMBASSY
Apartado 815, Edificio Centro Colón (11th Floor), San José 1007
Tel: San José 221 5566

Ambassador Extraordinary and Plenipotentiary and Consul-General, HE Alan Green

ECONOMY

Tourism is the largest single industry, with ecotourism a growing area; one third of the country is national parkland or nature reserve. Industrial activity is principally in the manufacturing sector and manufactured goods include computer components, foodstuffs, textiles and clothing, plastic goods and pharmaceuticals. The principal agricultural products are coffee, bananas, sugar and cattle (for meat).
GNP – US$9,081 million (1996); US$2,640 per capita (1996)
GDP – US$6,996 million (1994); US$2,463 per capita (1994)
ANNUAL AVERAGE GROWTH OF GDP – –0.7 per cent (1996)
INFLATION RATE – 17.5 per cent (1996)
UNEMPLOYMENT – 5.2 per cent (1995)
TOTAL EXTERNAL DEBT – US$3,454 million (1996)

TRADE
The chief exports are manufactured goods, coffee, bananas, cocoa and sugar. The chief imports are machinery, including transport equipment, manufactures, chemicals, fuel and mineral oils and foodstuffs. In 1995 there was a trade deficit of US$474 million and a current account deficit of US$143 million. In 1996 imports totalled US$3,433 million and exports US$2,946 million.

Trade with UK	1996	1997
Imports from UK	£36,030,000	£38,845,000
Exports to UK	93,051,000	71,585,000

COMMUNICATIONS

The chief ports are Limón on the Atlantic coast, through which passes most of the coffee exported, and Caldera on the Pacific coast. LACSA is the national airline, operating flights throughout Central and South America, the Caribbean and USA, besides internal flights to local airports by SANSA.

CÔTE D'IVOIRE
République de la Côte d'Ivoire

AREA – 124,504 sq. miles (322,463 sq. km). Neighbours: Guinea and Liberia (west), Mali and Burkina Faso (north), Ghana (east)
POPULATION – 14,230,000 (1994 UN estimate): 39 per cent Muslim, 28 per cent Christian (mainly Roman Catholic) and 17 per cent maintain traditional beliefs. The official language is French, but Agni, Baoulé, Dioula, Senoufo and Yacouba are spoken
CAPITAL – Yamoussoukro (population, 126,191, 1988), the political and administrative capital since 1983
MAJOR CITIES – ΨAbidjan (2,700,000), the economic and financial centre
CURRENCY – Franc CFA of 100 centimes
NATIONAL ANTHEM – L'Abidjanaise
NATIONAL DAY – 7 August
NATIONAL FLAG – Three vertical stripes, orange, white and green
LIFE EXPECTANCY (years) – male 49.69; female 52.38
POPULATION GROWTH RATE – 3.9 per cent (1995)
POPULATION DENSITY – 44 per sq. km (1995)
URBAN POPULATION – 45.6 per cent (1993)

MILITARY EXPENDITURE – 0.9 per cent of GDP (1996)
MILITARY PERSONNEL – 15,400: Army 6,800, Navy 900, Air Force 700, Paramilitaries 7,000
CONSCRIPTION DURATION – Six months
ILLITERACY RATE – 59.9 per cent
ENROLMENT (percentage of age group) – primary 47 per cent (1990); tertiary 4.4 per cent (1993)

The climate is equatorial in the south and west, which are mainly forested; tropical in the centre and east, which are savanna regions with trees; dry and tropical in the north, which is a grassy savannah region.

HISTORY AND POLITICS

Although French contact was made in the first half of the 19th century, Côte d'Ivoire became a colony only in 1893 and was finally pacified in 1912. It decided on 5 December 1958 to remain an autonomous republic within the French Community; full independence outside the Community was proclaimed on 7 August 1960.

The PDCI won multiparty elections held in November 1990 amid allegations of electoral fraud. After having been president since independence in 1960, President Houphouët-Boigny died in December 1993 and was replaced by the parliamentary speaker Henri Konan-Bédié. Konan-Bédié was elected by an overwhelming majority following an opposition party boycott in the October 1995 presidential election. The PDCI won 148 of the 175 seats in the November 1995 elections to the National Assembly.

POLITICAL SYSTEM

Côte d'Ivoire has a presidential system of government and a single-chamber National Assembly of 175 members, directly elected for a five-year term. It has been a multiparty system since 1990. In May 1998, the president's term of office was increased from five to seven years.

HEAD OF STATE

President, Henri Konan-Bédié, *took office* 7 December 1993, *elected* 22 October 1995

CABINET *as at July 1998*

Prime Minister, Planning and Industrial Development, Daniel Kablan Duncan
Agriculture and Animal Resources, Lambert Kouassi Konan
Commerce, Nicolas Kouassi Akon
Communications, Government Spokesperson, Danielle Boni-Claverie
Culture, Bernard Zadi Zaourou
Defence, Bandama N'Gatta
Economic Infrastructure, Ezan Akele
Economy and Finance, Niamien N'Goran
Employment and Civil Service, Social Welfare, Achi Atsain
Energy, Safiatou Françoise Ba N'daw
Family and Women's Promotion, Albertine Gnanazan Epie
Foreign Affairs, Amara Essy
High Commissioners, Tchere Seka *(Development in Mountainous Areas);* Ahmadou Ahmed Timite *(Development of Central and Northern Areas);* Sekou Toure *(Hydraulics);* Eugène Kindo Bouadi *(Tourism)*
Higher Education, Scientific Research and Technological Innovation, Saliou Toure
Housing, Living Conditions and Environment, Albert Kacou Tiapani
Industrial Development, Ahoua N'doli
Interior, National Integration, Emile Constant Bombet
Justice and Public Liberty, Kouakou Brou
Mines and Petroleum Resources, Lamine Fadika
National Education and Basic Training, Pierre Kipre
National Solidarity, Laurent Dona-Fologo

Presidential Affairs, Faustin Kouamé
President of the National Assembly, Emile Brou
Public Health, Maurice Kacou Guikahue
Raw Material, Guy-Alain Emmanuel Gauze
Relations with Institutions, Timothée Ahoua N'Guetta
Security, Marcel Dibona Koné
Sports, Sidibé Soumahoro
Technical Education, Professional Training and Handicrafts, Komenan Zapka
Transport, Adama Coulibaly
Yamoussoukro, Jean Konan Banny
Youth Promotion and Civil Education, Vlami Bi Dou

EMBASSY OF THE REPUBLIC OF CÔTE D'IVOIRE
2 Upper Belgrave Street, London SW1X 8BJ
Tel 0171–235 6991
Chargé d'Affaires, Florent Kouassi Ekra

BRITISH EMBASSY
Immeuble Les Harmonies, 01 BP 2581, Abidjan 01
Tel: Abidjan 226850
Ambassador Extraordinary and Plenipotentiary, HE Haydon Warren-Gash

ECONOMY

Côte d'Ivoire became wealthy in the 1970s because of the high prices of its two principal export earners, coffee and cocoa. In the late 1980s the economy contracted considerably as its exports deteriorated in competitiveness and its rivals devalued their currencies while the franc CFA remained pegged to the French franc. An economic reform and stabilization programme began in 1989 under IMF auspices and has brought down inflation, increased investment and led to GDP growth. The devaluation of the CFA franc in January 1994 has increased exports considerably and restored a trade surplus. In February 1998 a further economic reform programme began, aided by a US$385 million loan from the IMF. Under the terms of the loan, the government will liberalize the economy and introduce tighter fiscal controls.

The principal exports are coffee, cocoa, timber, palm oil, sugar, rubber, pineapples, bananas, and cotton. There are a few deposits of diamonds and minerals including manganese and iron. Oil and gas deposits began to be exploited in 1995.

There was a trade surplus of US$1,860 million in 1996 and a current account deficit of US$203 million. Imports totalled US$3,207 million and exports US$4,314 million.
GNP – US$9,434 million (1996); US$660 per capita (1996)
GDP – US$11,645 million (1994); US$544 per capita (1994)
ANNUAL AVERAGE GROWTH OF GDP – 3.5 per cent (1981)
INFLATION RATE – 2.5 per cent (1996)
TOTAL EXTERNAL DEBT – US$19,713 million (1996)

TRADE WITH UK	1996	1997
Imports from UK	£54,165,000	£58,844,000
Exports to UK	91,470,000	68,451,000

CROATIA

AREA – 34,022 sq. miles (88,117 sq. km). Neighbours: Slovenia, Hungary (north), the rump Federal Yugoslav state (east), Bosnia-Hercegovina (south, and east of Adriatic coastal strip)
POPULATION – 4,495,000 (1994 UN estimate); 4,784,265 (1991 census): 78 per cent Croat, 12 per cent Serb, 2 per cent Yugoslav; also Hungarians, Italians, Albanians, Czechs, Ukrainians and Jews. Roman Catholic 76.5 per

cent, Eastern Orthodox 11.1 per cent, Protestant 1.4 per cent, Muslim 1.2 per cent. The language is Croatian in the Latin script

CAPITAL – Zagreb (population, 867,717, 1991)

MAJOR CITIES – Osijek (129,792); Rijeka (167,964); Split (200,459), 1991

CURRENCY – Kuna of 100 lipas

NATIONAL ANTHEM – Lijepa naša domovina (Our Beautiful Homeland)

NATIONAL DAY – 30 May (Statehood Day)

NATIONAL FLAG – Three horizontal stripes of red, white, blue, with the national arms over all in the centre

LIFE EXPECTANCY (years) – male 68.29; female 75.63

POPULATION GROWTH RATE – – 1.2 per cent (1995)

POPULATION DENSITY – 51 per sq. km (1995)

URBAN POPULATION – 54.3 per cent (1991)

ILLITERACY RATE – 2.4 per cent

ENROLMENT (percentage of age group) – primary 82 per cent (1994); secondary 66 per cent (1994); tertiary 28.3 per cent (1995)

Croatia is divided into three major geographic regions: the Pannonian region in the north, the central mountain belt, and the Adriatic coast region of Istria and Dalmatia which has 1,185 islands and islets and 1,104 miles (1,778 km) of coastline.

HISTORY AND POLITICS

Croatia was part of the Austro-Hungarian Empire from 1526 to 1918. On 29 October 1918 the Croatian parliament declared Croatia independent and soon after Croatia joined with Slovenia, Bosnia-Hercegovina, Serbia and Montenegro to form the 'Kingdom of Serbs, Croats and Slovenes' (renamed Yugoslavia in 1929). From 1941 to 1945 Yugoslavia was occupied by the Axis powers, with Italy and Hungary annexing parts of Croatia and a pro-Nazi Croat puppet state being established in the remainder of Croatia and Bosnia-Hercegovina. The armed extremists of this state (Ustashe) engaged in fierce fighting with Serbian royalists, Communist partisans and pro-Allied Croat partisans.

At the end of the war Yugoslavia was re-established as a federal republic under Communist rule but gradually disintegrated following the death of the wartime partisan leader Josep Tito in 1980. When Croatia informed Belgrade of its independence in June 1991, the Federal Yugoslav Army (JNA) intervened against local defence forces to prevent the disintegration of the federation. Croatia's ethnic Serb minority, which rejected Croatia's independence, began fighting with the Croat defence forces. By September 1991 this had escalated into war between Croatia and Serbia, which had assumed control of the JNA.

The war in Croatia continued until January 1992 when a cease-fire was declared. The JNA and Serb forces had secured control of virtually all ethnic Serb areas in Croatia. Four UN protected areas, Northern and Southern Krajina and Eastern and Western Slavonia, were created from the Serb-controlled areas in Croatia and UN troops arrived to police the areas. The JNA withdrew from Croatia but the ethnic Serb forces refused to disarm.

In April and May 1990 Croatia's first free, democratic elections were won by the Croatian Democratic Union (HDZ) of Dr Franjo Tudjman. A new constitution was adopted by parliament in December 1990 and a referendum in May 1991 backed independence from Yugoslavia. Croatia declared its independence on 30 May 1991.

The HDZ won a majority of seats in the 1995 elections to the Chamber of Representatives and in the April 1997 elections to the Chamber of Districts. Tudjman was re-elected in June 1997 with 61 per cent of the vote, although OSCE observers declared that the elections had not met the minimum standards for democracies.

SECESSION

Croatia's ethnic Serbs voted to establish a Republic of Serbian Krajina (RSK) in 1993 and elected Milan Martic as president in January 1994. Fighting between Croatian Serbs and government troops continued until a cease-fire agreement was concluded in the UN-protected areas of Slavonia and Krajina in April 1994. A new mandate agreed for the UN Confidence Rebuilding Operation (UNCRO) was annulled in Western Slavonia following the capture of the area by Croatian forces in May 1995. The government seized the whole of Krajina in August 1995 prompting the withdrawal of 10,000 UNCRO peacekeepers and the flight of 150,000 Serbs. The last Croatian Serb-held area of Eastern Slavonia agreed in November 1995 to its eventual reintegration into Croatia in 1997–8. A 5,000-strong UN force was dispatched to the area in 1996 to oversee the formation of a two-year transitional government. In April 1996, the regional council of Eastern Slavonia, the sole remaining component of the RSK, appointed Goran Hadzic as president. The council was dissolved and replaced by a regional assembly based in Vukovar. On 15 January 1998, the UN pulled out of Eastern Slavonia and Croatia resumed full control of the territory.

FOREIGN RELATIONS

An agreement to normalize relations with Yugoslavia was signed in August 1996. Croatia was sworn in as a member of the Council of Europe in November 1996.

POLITICAL SYSTEM

Executive power is vested in a president and government. The president is directly elected for five-year terms. Legislative power is vested in the bicameral parliament (*Sabor*), comprising the 68-member Chamber of Districts and the 127-member Chamber of Representatives.

Croatia is divided into 20 counties; each county elects three members to the Chamber of Districts. Counties are composed of groups of districts and function both as units of local government and as regional offices for the central administration. There are 102 districts.

HEAD OF STATE

President, Franjo Tudjman, *elected* May 1990, *re-elected* 2 August 1992, 15 June 1997, *sworn in* 5 August 1997

CABINET *as at July 1998*

Prime Minister, Zlatko Matesa

Deputy PMs, Jure Radic *(Development and Reconstruction)*; Borislav Skegro *(Economy and Finance)*; Mate Granic *(Foreign Affairs and Refugees)*; Ivica Kostovic *(Humanitarian Issues, Science and Technology)*; Ljerka Mintas-Hodak *(Internal and Social Affairs, European Integration)*; Milan Ramljak *(Justice)*

Administration, Marijan Ramuscak

Agriculture and Forestry, Zlatko Dominikovic

Culture, Bozo Biskupic

Defence, Andrija Hebrang

Economy, Nenad Porges

Education and Sport, Bozidar Pugelnik

Government Secretary, Jagoda Premuzic

Health, Zeljko Rajner

Internal Affairs, Ivan Penic

Labour and Social Welfare, Joso Skara

Maritime Affairs, Transport and Communications, Zeljko Luzavec

Privatization and Property Management, Milan Kovic

Return and Immigration, Marijan Petrovic
Tourism, Sergej Morsan
Urban Planning, Construction and Housing, Marko Sirac
Without Portfolio, Branko Mocibob; Juraj Njauro

EMBASSY OF THE REPUBLIC OF CROATIA
21 Conway Street, London WIP 5HL
Tel 0171-387 2022
Ambassador Extraordinary and Plenipotentiary, HE Andrija
Kojakovic, apptd 1997

BRITISH EMBASSY
Vlaska 121/III Floor, PO Box 454, 4100 Zagreb
Tel: Zagreb 455 5310
Ambassador Extraordinary and Plenipotentiary, HE Colin
Munro, apptd 1997
BRITISH CONSULATES – Split and Dubrovnik
BRITISH COUNCIL DIRECTOR, R. Evans, PO Box 55,
10000 Zagreb

DEFENCE

The Army has 285 main battle tanks, 150 armoured
personnel carriers, 100 armoured infantry fighting vehicles and 2,500 artillery pieces. The Air Force has 30 combat
aircraft and 15 armed helicopters. The Navy has one
submarine and eight patrol and coastal combatants at five
bases.
MILITARY EXPENDITURE – 6.9 per cent of GDP (1996)
MILITARY PERSONNEL – 98,000: Army 50,000, Navy
3,000, Air Force 5,000, Paramilitaries 40,000
CONSCRIPTION DURATION – Ten months

ECONOMY

Production was severely hampered during the conflict in
1991–5; the material damage was estimated by the
government to be US$27 billion, with the loss of 13,583
lives. Large areas of farmland were destroyed and the
tourist industry, which provided one third of total foreign
exchange earnings in 1990, was decimated.
Shipbuilding and fishing are major industries on the
Adriatic coast. Inland there is a light manufacturing sector,
food-processing industries, bauxite deposits, thermal mineral springs, hydroelectric potential, and agriculture
based on grain, horticulture, livestock and tobacco. Textiles is one of the most important industries employing
more than 17 per cent of the population. In April 1996,
Croatia agreed to pay 29.5 per cent of Yugoslavia's debt,
totalling US$1.45 billion.
In 1996 Croatia had a trade deficit of US$2,497 million
and a current account deficit of US$1,452 million. In 1996
imports totalled US$7,788 million and exports US$4,513
million.
GNP – US$18,130 million (1996); US$3,800 per capita
(1996)
GDP – US$16,915 million (1994); US$3,867 per capita
(1994)
INFLATION RATE – 4.3 per cent (1996)
UNEMPLOYMENT – 16.8 per cent (1993)
TOTAL EXTERNAL DEBT – US$4,634 million (1996)

TRADE

Trade with UK	1996	1997
Imports from UK	£135,333,000	£107,136,000
Exports to UK	37,066,000	35,830,000

CUBA
República de Cuba

AREA – 42,804 sq. miles (110,861 sq. km)
POPULATION – 11,041,000 (1994 UN estimate). The
language is Spanish
CAPITAL – ΨHavana (population, 2,175,888, 1992
estimate)
MAJOR CITIES – Camagüey (294,332); Guantánamo
(207,796); Holguín (242,085); Santa Clara (205,400);
ΨSantiago (430,494)
CURRENCY – Cuban peso of 100 centavos
NATIONAL ANTHEM – Al Combate, Corred Bayameses
(To battle, men of Bayamo)
NATIONAL DAY – 1 January (Day of Liberation)
NATIONAL FLAG – Five horizontal bands, blue and white
(blue at top and bottom) with red triangle, close to staff,
charged with five-point star
LIFE EXPECTANCY (years) – male 72.89; female 76.80
POPULATION GROWTH RATE – 0.8 per cent (1995)
POPULATION DENSITY – 100 per sq. km (1995)
URBAN POPULATION – 74.4 per cent (1993)

HISTORY AND POLITICS

The island was visited by Columbus in 1492. Early in the
16th century the island was conquered by the Spanish, and
for almost four centuries remained under Spanish rule.
Separatist agitation culminated in the closing years of the
19th century in open warfare. In 1898 the USA intervened
and demanded the evacuation of Cuba by Spanish forces.
The Spanish–American war led to the abandonment of the
island, which came under American military rule from
1899 until 1902, when an autonomous government was
inaugurated with an elected president, and bicameral
legislature.
A revolution led by Dr Fidel Castro overthrew the
government of Gen. Batista in 1959. In 1965 the Communist Party of Cuba (PCC) was formed to succeed the
United Party of the Socialist Revolution; it is the only
authorized political party. A new Socialist constitution
came into force in 1976 and indirect elections to the
National Assembly of People's Power were subsequently
held. The first direct elections to the 589-member
National Assembly were held in February 1993; all
candidates were officially approved by the Communist
Party and ran for election unopposed. The 14 provincial
assemblies were elected in the same manner. The fifth
congress of the PCC was held in October 1997. At the
election of deputies to the National Assembly in January
1998, all 601 PCC candidates received the required 50 per
cent of the vote, and in February the National Assembly
confirmed Dr Castro as president for a further five-year
term.

HEAD OF STATE
President of Council of State and Council of Ministers, Dr Fidel
Castro Ruz, *appointed* 2 November 1976, *re-elected* 15
March 1993, 24 February 1998

COUNCIL OF STATE *as at July 1998*
President, Dr Fidel Castro Ruz
First Vice-President, Gen. Raúl Castro Ruz
Vice-Presidents, Carlos Lage Dávila; Juan Almeida Bosque;
Abelardo Colomé Ibarra; Esteban Lazo Hernández; José
Ramón Machado Ventura
Secretary, José Miyar Barrueco

COUNCIL OF MINISTERS *as at July 1998*
President, Dr Fidel Castro Ruz

First Vice-President, Revolutionary Armed Forces, Gen. Raúl
Castro Ruz
Vice-Presidents, Dr Carlos Rafael Rodríguez Rodríguez;
Osmani Cienfuegos Gorriarán; Pedro Miret Prieto; José
Ramón Fernández Alvárez; Jaime Crombet Hernández
Baquero; Adolfo Diaz Suárez
Secretary, Carlos Lage Dávila

Ministers, Alfredo Jordán Morales (Agriculture); Gen.
Silvano Colás Sánchez (Communications); Juan Mario
Junco del Pino (Construction); José M. Cañete Alvárez
(Construction Materials Industry); Abel Prieto Jiménez
(Culture); Barbara Castillo Cuesta (Domestic Trade); José
Luis Rodríguez García (Economy and Planning); Luís
Ignacio Gómez Gutiérrez (Education); Manuel Millares
Rodríguez (Finance and Prices); Orlando Felipe
Rodríguez Romay (Fishing Industry); Alejandro Rocas
Iglesias (Food Industry); Ibrahim Farradaz (Foreign
Investment and Economic Co-operation); Roberto Robaina
González (Foreign Relations); Ricardo Cabrisas Ruíz
(Foreign Trade); Marcos J. Portal León (Heavy Industries);
Fernando Vecino Alegret (Higher Education); Gen.
Abelardo Colomé Ibarra (Interior); Roberto Díaz
Sotolongo (Justice); Salvador Valdez Mesa (Labour and
Social Security); Jesús Pérez Othon (Light Industry);
Roberto Ignacio González Planas (Metalworking and
Electronics Industries); Carlos Dotres Martínez (Public
Health); Rosa Eleana Simeón Negrín (Science, Technology
and Environment); Div.-Gen. Ulises Rosales del Toro
(Sugar Industry); Osmani Cienfuegos Gorriarán
(Tourism); Alvaro Pérez Morales (Transport); Wilfredo
López Rodríguez (Without Portfolio)

EMBASSY OF THE REPUBLIC OF CUBA
167 High Holborn, London WCIV 6PA
Tel 0171– 240 2488

Ambassador Extraordinary and Plenipotentiary, HE Rodney
Alejandro López Clemente, apptd 1995

BRITISH EMBASSY
e7 ma Y 17, Miramar, Havana.
Tel: Havana 241 771
Ambassador Extraordinary and Plenipotentiary, HE David
Ridgeway, OBE, apptd 1998

DEFENCE

The Army has 1,500 main battle tanks, 400 armoured
infantry fighting vehicles, 700 armoured personnel carriers and 740 artillery pieces. The Navy has two submarines,
one frigate and five patrol and coastal vessels at six bases.
The Air Force has 130 combat aircraft and 45 armed
helicopters.

The last former Soviet combat personnel left Cuba in
1993, but 810 Russian military advisers remain to operate
military intelligence facilities. The United States has 1,640
naval personnel at Guantánamo Bay Naval Base, which has
been leased since before the 1959 revolution.
MILITARY EXPENDITURE – 5.4 per cent of GDP (1996)
MILITARY PERSONNEL – 72,000: Army 38,000, Navy
5,000, Air Force 10,000, Paramilitaries 19,000
CONSCRIPTION DURATION – Two years

ECONOMY

After the revolution virtually all land and industrial and
commercial enterprises were nationalized. Following the
curtailing of Cuba's privileged trading relationships with
the Soviet bloc in 1989, the economy deteriorated sharply.
GDP fell by 75 per cent between 1989 and 1994, and the
government was forced to introduce reforms. Since 1993,
the government has legalized the holding of US dollars by
private individuals, permitted private enterprise, cut sub-

sidies to loss-making state industries, allowed prices for some goods and services to rise, and introduced income tax. State farms have been transformed into co-operatives run by private individuals and permitted to sell 20 per cent of produce on the open market, but remain relatively unproductive. In 1995, foreign investors were permitted to buy property and own Cuban-based companies, with British and Canadian firms becoming involved in the oil and mining industries.

Following austerity measures imposed in 1993, the economy has slowly started to grow. Sugar is still the mainstay of the economy and the principal source of foreign exchange; production dropped from 8.04 million tons in 1989–90 to 4.4 million tons in 1996–7. Domestic oil production is rising and reached 1.285 million tonnes in 1995. In March 1998, Japan agreed to renegotiate Cuba's US$782 million debt, payments on which had been suspended since 1987. Lack of external finance has been a major obstacle to economic recovery.

The tourism industry has expanded since 1986 to become the country's largest foreign exchange earner. In 1995 738,200 tourists visited Cuba, generating some US$1,100 million.

GDP – US$14,131 million (1994); US$1,627 per capita (1994)

TRADE

Cuba's exports dropped from US$8.1 billion in 1989 to US$1.7 billion in 1993 while imports declined by 73 per cent. Trade between Cuba and the former socialist economies of Europe is now less than 10 per cent of pre-1989 levels. A trade deal was signed with Russia in 1995 providing for the exchange of sugar for oil. The US trade and economic embargo remains in force, though it was relaxed in March 1998 to allow food and medicine into the country. Principal exports are sugar, nickel, seafood, citrus fruits, tobacco and rum.

Trade with UK	1996	1997
Imports from UK	£24,504,000	£19,484,000
Exports to UK	19,378,000	15,093,000

COMMUNICATIONS

There are 12,700 km of railway track, of which 5,000 km are in public service. In 1986 there were 13,247 km of road. Scheduled international air services run to Central and South American countries and Europe. In March 1998 the ban on direct flights between Cuba and USA was lifted.

CULTURE AND EDUCATION

The press and broadcasting are under the control of the government. Education is compulsory and free. In 1964 illiteracy was officially declared to be eliminated.

ILLITERACY RATE – 4.3 per cent

ENROLMENT (percentage of age group) – primary 99 per cent (1995); secondary 59 per cent (1993); tertiary 12.7 per cent (1995)

CYPRUS
Kypriaki Dimokratia/Kibris Cumhuriyeti

AREA – 3,572 sq. miles (9,251 sq. km)

POPULATION – 742,000 (1994 UN estimate): 85 per cent Greek, 12 per cent Turkish. Greek and Turkish are official languages

CAPITAL – Nicosia (Lefkosia) (population in the government-controlled area, 188,800)

MAJOR CITIES – ΨFamagusta; ΨLarnaca; ΨLimassol; Paphos

CURRENCY – Cyprus pound (C£) of 100 cents

NATIONAL ANTHEM – Ode to Freedom

NATIONAL DAY – 1 October (Independence Day)

NATIONAL FLAG – White with a gold map of Cyprus above a wreath of olive

LIFE EXPECTANCY (years) – male 74.64; female 79.05

POPULATION GROWTH RATE – 1.7 per cent (1995)

POPULATION DENSITY – 80 per sq. km (1995)

URBAN POPULATION – 67.7 per cent (1992)

ENROLMENT (percentage of age group) – primary 96 per cent (1995); secondary 93 per cent (1995); tertiary 20.0 per cent (1995)

The climate is Mediterranean, with a hot dry summer and a variable warm winter.

HISTORY AND POLITICS

Cyprus came under British administration from 1878, and was formally annexed to Britain in 1914 on the outbreak of war with Turkey. From 1925 to 1960 it was a Crown Colony. Following the launching in 1955 of an armed campaign by EOKA in support of union with Greece, a state of emergency was declared which lasted for four years. An agreement was signed on 19 February 1959 between the United Kingdom, Greece, Turkey, and the Greek and Turkish Cypriots which provided that Cyprus would be an independent republic.

The island became independent on 16 August 1960. The constitution provided for a Greek Cypriot president and a Turkish Cypriot vice-president. The constitution proved unworkable and led to intercommunal trouble. The UN Peacekeeping Force in Cyprus (UNFICYP) was set up in 1964.

A general election was held for the House of Representatives (56 Greek Cypriot and 24 vacant Turkish Cypriot seats) on 26 May 1996, resulting in the parties gaining the following seats: Democratic Rally-Liberal Party 20; AKEL (Communist) 19; Democratic Party (DIKO) 10; EDEK (Socialist) 5; Free Democrats 2. In February 1998, Glafcos Clerides of the Democratic Rally-Liberal Party was re-elected president with 51 per cent of the vote. On 30 March 1998, formal accession talks with the EU began.

HEAD OF STATE

President, Glafcos Clerides, *elected* 14 February 1993, *re-elected* 15 February 1998

CABINET *as at July 1998*

Agriculture, Environment and Natural Resources, Konstantinos Themistokleous

Commerce, Industry and Tourism, Nikolaos Rolandhis

Communications and Works, Leondios Ierodhiakonou

Defence, Ioannis Omirou

Deputy Minister to the President, Pandelis Kouros

Education and Culture, Likourghos Kappas

Finance, Christodhoulos Christodhoulou

Foreign Affairs, Ioannis Kasoulidhis

Government Spokesman, Khristos Stilianidhis

Health, Khristos Solomis

Interior, Konstantinos Mikhailidhis

Justice and Public Order, Nicolaos Kosis

Labour and Social Insurance, Andhreas Mousiouttas

CYPRUS HIGH COMMISSION

93 Park Street, London W1Y 4ET

Tel 0171-499 8272

High Commissioner, HE Michalis Attalides, apptd 1998

Counsellors, P. Kyriakou (*Consular Affairs*); K. Avgoustinos (*Cultural Affairs*); A. Georgiades (*Commerce*)

BRITISH HIGH COMMISSION
Alexander Pallis Street (PO Box 1978), Nicosia
Tel: Nicosia 2-473131
High Commissioner, HE David Madden, CMG, apptd 1994
Counsellor and Deputy High Commissioner, J. S. Buck
Defence Adviser, Col. C. S. Wakelin, OBE
First Secretary (Commercial), W. Preston

BRITISH COUNCIL DIRECTOR, Robert Ness, PO Box 5654,
3 Museum Street, 1097 Nicosia

BRITISH SOVEREIGN AREAS
The UK retained full sovereignty and jurisdiction over
two areas of 99 square miles in all: Akrotiri–Episkopi–Par-
amali and Dhekelia–Pergamos–Ayios Nicolaos–Xylopha-
gou. The British Administrator of these areas is appointed
by The Queen and is responsible to the Secretary of State
for Defence. The combined total of army and RAF
personnel stationed in the areas is 5,000.
Administrator of the British Sovereign Areas, Air Vice-Marshal
P. Millar

DEFENCE

The National Guard has 102 main battle tanks, 70
armoured infantry fighting vehicles, 302 armoured personnel carriers and 134 artillery pieces. Turkey has 30,000
troops in northern Cyprus.
   In January 1998, a military airfield in Paphos was
completed. It is intended to provide a base for Greek
military aircraft, as Cyprus does not possess its own air
force.
MILITARY EXPENDITURE – 5.0 per cent of GDP (1996)
MILITARY PERSONNEL – 10,000 National Guard
CONSCRIPTION DURATION – 26 months

ECONOMY

Agriculture employs 12 per cent of the workforce. Main
products are citrus fruits, grapes and vine products, meat,
milk, potatoes and other vegetables. Manufacturing, construction, distribution and other service industries are
other major employers. Tourism is the main growth
industry with over two million tourists producing
C£1,200 million in foreign exchange earnings in 1995; it
contributed 25 per cent of GDP and employed 25 per cent
of the workforce. Over 5,000 foreign firms and individuals
have registered as offshore companies in Cyprus, and 20
per cent of the world's ships are Cypriot registered.
GDP – US$6,620 million (1994); US$9,754 per capita
   (1994)
ANNUAL AVERAGE GROWTH OF GDP – 5.0 per cent (1995)
INFLATION RATE – 3.0 per cent (1996)
UNEMPLOYMENT – 2.6 per cent (1995)

TRADE
The UK is the main trading partner, taking 29 per cent of
exports in 1994 and supplying 12 per cent of imports. In
1995 there was a trade deficit of US$2,085 million and a
current account deficit of US$213 million. In 1996 imports
totalled US$3,983 million and exports US$1,395 million.

Trade with UK	1996	1997
Imports from UK	£290,735,000	£265,959,000
Exports to UK	158,728,000	122,413,000

TURKISH REPUBLIC OF NORTHERN
CYPRUS

In 1974, mainland Greek officers under instructions from
the military junta in Athens launched a coup and installed a
former EOKA member, Nikos Sampson, as president.
Turkey invaded northern Cyprus and occupied over a

third of the island. In 1975 a 'Turkish Federated State of
Cyprus' under Rauf Denktash was declared in this area, its
constitution being approved by referendum. In 1983 a
'Declaration of Statehood' was issued which purported to
establish the 'Turkish Republic of Northern Cyprus'. The
declaration was condemned by the UN Security Council
and only Turkey has recognized the new 'state'. In 1985 a
referendum in the north of Cyprus approved a constitution
for the 'Turkish Republic of Northern Cyprus', Denktash
was elected president and a general election was held.
Denktash was re-elected in 1990 and April 1995, and
general elections were held in 1990 and 1993.

CZECH REPUBLIC
Česká Republika

AREA – 30,450 sq. miles (78,864 sq. km). Neighbours:
   Poland (north-east), Germany (west and north-west),
   Austria (south), Slovakia (south-east)
POPULATION – 10,331,000 (1994 UN estimate),
   10,302,000 (1991 census): 95 per cent Czech, 3 per cent
   Slovak. Czech is the official language. The majority of
   the population is Roman Catholic, with a small
   Protestant minority
CAPITAL – Prague (Praha) on the Vltava (Moldau)
   (population, 1,216,568, 1994 estimate)
MAJOR CITIES – Brno (Brün) (390,073); Ostrava (326,049);
   Plzeň (172,055)
CURRENCY – Koruna (Kčs) of 100 haléřu
NATIONAL ANTHEM – Kde Domov Müj (Where is my
   Motherland)
NATIONAL DAY – 28 October
NATIONAL FLAG – White over red horizontally with a
   blue triangle extending from the hoist to the centre of
   the flag
LIFE EXPECTANCY (years) – male 69.53; female 76.55
POPULATION GROWTH RATE – −0.1 per cent (1995)
POPULATION DENSITY – 131 per sq. km (1995)
URBAN POPULATION – 74.7 per cent (1993)

The Czech Republic is composed of Bohemia and
Moravia. Bohemia is surrounded by mountain ranges
while Moravian land stretches to the Danubian basin.

HISTORY AND POLITICS

The area which is now the Czech Republic came under the
rule of the Habsburg dynasty in 1526 and remained part of
the Austro-Hungarian Empire until 1918. Austrian attempts to Germanize the Czech lands in the 18th and 19th
centuries led to the rise of Czech nationalism in the late
19th century. The independence of Czechoslovakia was
proclaimed on 28 October 1918 following an amalgamation of Bohemia, Moravia, Slovakia and Ruthenia and was
confirmed by the Versailles Peace Conference in 1919.
   Czechoslovakia was forced to cede the ethnic German
Sudetenland to Nazi Germany in 1938 after the Munich
Agreement. German forces invaded the Czech Republic in
March 1939 and incorporated it into Germany while
Slovakia became a puppet state. The Czech Republic was
liberated by Soviet and American forces in May 1945. The
pre-war democratic Czechoslovak state was re-established
in 1945, having ceded Ruthenia to the Soviet Union. The
Communists took power in a coup in 1948 and remained in
power until 1989.
   In 1968 the Communist Party under Alexander Dubček
embarked on a political and economic reform programme
(the Prague Spring). The reforms were suppressed following an invasion by Warsaw Pact troops on the night of 20

August 1968, and were abandoned when Gustáv Husák became leader of the Communist Party in 1969.

Mass protests in November 1989 led to the resignation of the Communist Party Central Committee. The Party was forced to concede its monopoly of power and on 10 December a new government was appointed in which only half the ministers were Communists. Husák resigned as president and was replaced by the dissident writer Václav Havel. Free elections were held in June 1990 in which the Communist Party was defeated.

In late 1992 the leaders of the Czech and Slovak republics agreed to dissolve the federation and form two sovereign states; this took effect on 1 January 1993.

The elections of June 1992 had returned the Civil Democratic Party (ODS) as the largest party in the Czech parliament, and it formed a coalition government with three other centre-right parties in July 1992 which was sworn in as the government of the Czech Republic on 1 January 1993. The former federal President Havel was elected president. Following the general election of 31 May 1996, the ODS and its coalition partners, two seats short of a majority, agreed to slow the rate of privatization in return for support from the opposition Social Democrats. The general election in June 1998 produced no outright winner. Miloš Zeman, leader of the Czech Social Democratic Party (CSSD), formed a coalition government; all ministers are members of the CSSD except the Justice Minister, who is non-partisan.

POLITICAL SYSTEM

The constitution vests legislative power in the bicameral parliament, comprising a 200-member Chamber of Deputies elected for a four-year term and an 81-member Senate elected for a six-year term, one-third being renewed every two years. The president is elected by parliament for a five-year term. Executive power is held by the prime minister and Council of Ministers. A two-thirds majority in parliament is necessary to amend the constitution, and federal laws remain in place unless superseded by Czech ones. A Constitutional Court has been established comprising 15 judges nominated by the president for ten-year terms with Senate approval.

HEAD OF STATE

President, Václav Havel (ODS), *elected* 26 January 1993, *re-elected* 20 January 1998

COUNCIL OF MINISTERS *as at July 1998*

Prime Minister, Miloš Zeman
Deputy Prime Minister, Employment and Social Affairs, Vladimír Spidla
Deputy Prime Ministers, Pavel Mertlík; Pavel Rychetsky; Egon Lánsky
Agriculture, Jan Fencl
Culture, Pavel Dostál
Defence, Vladimír Vetchy
Education, Youth and Sports, Eduard Zeman
Environment, Miloš Kužvart
Finance, Ivo Svoboda
Foreign Affairs, Jan Kavan
Health, Ivan David
Interior, Václav Grulich
Justice, Otakar Motejl
Regional Development, Jaromir Cisař
Trade and Industry, Miroslav Grégr
Transport and Communications, Antonín Peltrám
Without Portfolio, Jaroslav Bašta

EMBASSY OF THE CZECH REPUBLIC
26–30 Kensington Palace Gardens, London w8 4qy
Tel 0171–243 1115

Ambassador Extraordinary and Plenipotentiary, HE Pavel Seifter, apptd 1998
Minister-Counsellor, Milan Jakobec
Military Attaché, Col. Milan Skalický
Counsellor (Commercial), Karel Antropius

BRITISH EMBASSY
Thunovská 14, 11800 Prague 1
Tel: Prague 5732 0355
Ambassador Extraordinary and Plenipotentiary, HE David Broucher, apptd 1997
Deputy Head of Mission, D. E. P. P. Keefe
Defence Attaché, Col. A. F. Davidson, MBE
First Secretary (Commercial), M. L. Connor
Cultural Attaché, M. O'Neill (*British Council Director*)

DEFENCE

The army has 952 main battle tanks, 945 armoured infantry fighting vehicles, 422 armoured personnel carriers and 767 artillery pieces. The Air Force has 129 combat aircraft and 36 attack helicopters. The Czech Republic has been accepted for membership of NATO.

MILITARY EXPENDITURE – 1.9 per cent of GDP (1996)
MILITARY PERSONNEL – 49,600: Army 27,000, Air Force 17,000, Paramilitaries 5,600
CONSCRIPTION DURATION – 12 months

ECONOMY

Under Communist rule industry and most agricultural land was state-owned. An economic reform programme began in 1990 to produce a free-market economy, and the government of the Czech Republic has continued to follow the policies of the former federal government. This has necessitated a restrictive monetary policy to stem inflation and a restructuring of industry to be competitive, and these were major reasons for the break with Slovakia. As a result, foreign investment (US$4,000 million in 1989–94) and private enterprises have grown and reliance on trade with the former Soviet bloc countries has ended. By late 1995 over 90 per cent of the economy had been privatized, with two-thirds of the population owning shares.

A trade-liberalizing association agreement with the EU is in operation, and formal EU accession talks began in March 1998.

A customs union between the Czech and Slovak Republics is in place but separate currencies were introduced in February 1993 following speculation. The Koruna was made fully convertible in October 1995.

Principal agricultural products are sugar beet, potatoes and cereal crops; the timber industry is also very important. Having been the major industrial area of the Austro-Hungarian Empire, the country has long been industrialized, and machinery, industrial consumer goods and raw materials are major exports.

In 1994 the government had a budget surplus equivalent to 0.88 per cent of GDP. In 1996 there was a trade deficit of US$5,971 million and a current account deficit of US$4,479 million. In 1996 imports totalled US$29,162 million and exports US$21,918 million.

GNP – US$48,861 million (1996); US$4,740 per capita (1996)
GDP – US$25,777 million (1994); US$3,498 per capita (1994)
ANNUAL AVERAGE GROWTH OF GDP – 4.4 per cent (1996)
INFLATION RATE – 8.8 per cent (1996)
UNEMPLOYMENT – 3.4 per cent (1995)
TOTAL EXTERNAL DEBT – US$20,094 million (1996)

Trade with UK	1996	1997
Imports from UK	£714,613,000	£709,754,000
Exports to UK	372,796,000	465,478,000

EDUCATION

Education is compulsory and free for all children from the ages of six to 16. There are seven universities of which the oldest and most famous is Charles University in Prague (founded 1348).
ENROLMENT (percentage of age group) – primary 98 per cent (1994); secondary 88 per cent (1994); tertiary 20.8 per cent (1994)

CULTURE

The Reformation gave a widespread impetus to Czech literature, the writings of Jan Hus (martyred in 1415 as a religious and social reformer) familiarizing the people with Wyclif's teaching. This lasted until the close of the 17th century when Jan Amos Komensky or Comenius (1592–1670) was expelled from the country. Under Austrian rule and with the pursuit of Germanization, there was a period of stagnation until the national revival in the 19th century. Authors of international reputation include Jaroslav Hašek (1883–1923), Jaroslav Seifert (1901–86, Nobel Prize for Literature, 1985), Václav Havel (b. 1936) and Milan Kundera (b. 1929).

DENMARK
Kongeriget Danmark

AREA – 16,639 sq. miles (43,094 sq. km). Neighbour: Germany (south)
POPULATION – 5,228,000 (1996 estimate). The majority of the population is Lutheran. The language is Danish
CAPITAL – ΨCopenhagen (population, 1,353,333, 1996 estimate)
MAJOR CITIES – ΨÅlborg (116,567); ΨÅrhus (209,404); Esbjerg (73,149); ΨOdense (143,029); Randers (55,515)
CURRENCY – Danish krone of 100 øre
NATIONAL ANTHEMS – Kong Kristian; Det er et yndigt land
NATIONAL DAY – 5 June (Constitution Day)
NATIONAL FLAG – Red, with white cross
LIFE EXPECTANCY (years) – male 72.49; female 77.76
POPULATION GROWTH RATE – 0.3 per cent (1995)
POPULATION DENSITY – 121 per sq. km (1995)

Denmark is a kingdom, consisting of the islands of Zealand, Funen, Lolland, etc., the peninsula of Jutland, the outlying island of Bornholm in the Baltic, and the Faröes and Greenland.

HISTORY AND POLITICS

Denmark derives its name from the Dan people of southern Sweden who invaded the area of present-day Denmark and established a unified state under Gorm the Old in the tenth century. The Danes were at the forefront of Viking expansionism and briefly united England and Scandinavia under Canute (995–1035).
From the 12th to 19th centuries the Danes contended for domination in Scandinavia and the Baltic region. The Union of Kalmar (1397) brought Norway and Sweden (including Finland) under Danish rule. Danish power waned during the 16th century, however, enabling Sweden to re-establish its independence in 1523. Sweden achieved ascendancy in the following two centuries, subjecting

Denmark to defeat in the Thirty Years' War (1618–48) and the Great Northern War (1700–21). In the 19th century Norway was ceded to Sweden under the Treaty of Kiel (1814) and both Schleswig and Holstein, which had been subsumed in 1460, were surrendered to Germany.
Denmark remained neutral during the First World War, and in a plebiscite held in accordance with the Versailles Treaty (1919), northern Schleswig voted to return to Danish sovereignty. In 1939 Denmark signed a non-aggression pact with Germany but was invaded on 9 April 1940 and coerced into contributing to the German war effort. Iceland declared its independence from Denmark in 1944. Social Democrat-led coalitions dominated the post-war era until 1982 when a right-wing government was elected. Denmark joined the European Community in 1973.
On 21 September 1994, a new coalition government of the Social Democrat, Social Liberal and Centre Democrat parties was formed. On 12 March 1998, Poul Nyrop Rasmussen's centre-left coalition was re-elected, winning 90 of the 179 seats in the parliament, giving a majority of a single seat. The EU Amsterdam Treaty was ratified in a national referendum in May 1998.

POLITICAL SYSTEM

The legislature consists of one chamber, the *Folketing*, of not more than 179 members, including two for the Faröes and two for Greenland, which is elected for a four-year term. The voting age is 18 with voting based on a proportional representation system with a 2 per cent threshold for parliamentary representation.

HEAD OF STATE

HM *The Queen of Denmark*, Queen Margrethe II, KG, *born* 16 April 1940, *succeeded* 14 January 1972, *married* 10 June 1967, Count Henri de Monpezat (Prince Henrik of Denmark), and *has issue* Crown Prince Frederik (*see* below); Prince Joachim, *born* 7 June 1969; *married* 18 November 1995, Miss Alexandra Manley (Princess Alexandra of Denmark)
Heir, HRH Crown Prince Frederik, *born* 26 May 1968

860   Countries of the World

CABINET *as at July 1998*
Prime Minister, Poul Nyrup Rasmussen (S)
Culture, Elsebeth Gerner Nielsen (RV)
Defence, Hans Haekkerup (S)
Development Co-operation, Poul Nielson (S)
Economic Affairs and Nordic Co-operation, Marianne Jelved (RV)
Education and Ecclesiastical Affairs, Margrethe Vestager (RV)
Environment and Energy, Svend Auken (S)
Finance, Mogens Lykketoft (S)
Food, Agriculture and Fisheries, Henrik Dam Christensen (S)
Foreign Affairs, Niels Helveg Petersen (RV)
Health, Carsten Koch (S)
Interior, Thorkild Simonsen (S)
Justice, Frank Jensen (S)
Labour, Ove Hygum (S)
Research, Jan Troejborg (S)
Social Affairs, Karen Jespersen (S)
Taxation, Ole Stavad (S)
Trade and Industry, Pia Gjellerup (S)
Transport, Sonja Mikkelsen (S)
Urban Affairs and Housing, Jytte Andersen (S)
S Social Democrat Party; RV Social Liberal Party

ROYAL DANISH EMBASSY
55 Sloane Street, London SW1X 9SR
Tel 0171–333 0200
Ambassador Extraordinary and Plenipotentiary, HE Ole Lønsmann Poulsen, apptd 1996
Counsellor (Commercial), Gunner Tetler
Defence Attaché, Capt. P. Grooss

BRITISH EMBASSY
36–40 Kastelsvej, DK-2100 Copenhagen Ø
Tel: Copenhagen 3544 5200
Ambassador Extraordinary and Plenipotentiary, HE Andrew Bache, CMG, apptd 1996
Counsellor and Deputy Head of Mission, P. B. Yaghmourian
Defence Attaché, Cmdr. A. Gordon-Lennox, RN
First Secretary (Commercial), D. T. Cox

BRITISH CONSULATES – Åbenraa, Ålborg, Århus, Esbjerg, Fredericia, Herning, Odense, Rønne (Bornholm); Tórshavn (Faröe Islands)

BRITISH COUNCIL REPRESENTATIVE, Dr M. Sørensen-Jones, Gammel Mont 12.3, 1117 Copenhagen K

DEFENCE

The Army has 353 main battle tanks, 50 armoured infantry fighting vechicles, 594 armoured personnel carriers, 503 artillery pieces and 12 attack helicopters. The Navy has five submarines, three frigates and 65 patrol and coastal vessels at two bases. The Air Force has 64 combat aircraft.
MILITARY EXPENDITURE – 1.7 per cent of GDP (1996)
MILITARY PERSONNEL – 32,900: Army 19,000, Navy 6,000, Air Force 7,900
CONSCRIPTION DURATION – Four to 12 months

ECONOMY

Of the labour force, in 1996 45 per cent was employed in the professional services and administration; 18 per cent in commerce; 19 per cent in manufacturing and 5 per cent in agriculture. The chief agricultural products are pigs, dairy products, poultry and eggs, seeds and cereals; manufactures are mostly based on imported raw materials but there are also considerable imports of finished goods. Denmark is self-sufficient in oil and natural gas.
GNP – US$168,917 million (1996); US$32,100 per capita (1996)

GDP – US$139,826 million (1994); US$ 28,245 per capita (1994)
ANNUAL AVERAGE GROWTH OF GDP – 2.4 per cent (1996); forecast to be 2.9 per cent in 1997
INFLATION RATE – 2.1 per cent (1996)
UNEMPLOYMENT – 7.0 per cent (1995)

TRADE

The principal imports are industrial raw materials, consumer goods, construction inputs, machinery, raw materials, vehicles and textile products. The chief exports are manufactured articles, and agricultural and dairy products. Germany and Sweden are Denmark's main trading partners.
In 1996 Denmark had a trade surplus of US$7,313 million and a current account surplus of US$1,920 million. Imports totalled US$43,504 million and exports US$48,883 million.

Trade with UK	1996	1997
Imports from UK	£2,111,700,000	£1,986,300,000
Exports to UK	2,239,400,000	2,223,000,000

COMMUNICATIONS

In 1996, the Danish mercantile fleet numbered 584 ships of more than 100 gross tonnage. There were 3,000 km of railway, 85 per cent of which belonged to the state and 15 per cent to privately-owned companies. A rail tunnel and bridge linking the islands of Zealand and Funen was opened in 1997.

CULTURE AND EDUCATION

The Danish language is akin to Swedish and Norwegian. Danish literature, ancient and modern, embraces all forms of expression, familiar names being Hans Christian Andersen (1805–75), Søren Kierkegaard (1813–55) and Karen Blixen (1885–1962). Some 38 newspapers are published in Denmark; eight daily papers are published in Copenhagen.
Education is free and compulsory. Special schools are numerous, commercial, technical and agricultural predominating. There are universities at Copenhagen (founded in 1479), Århus (1928), Odense (1966), Roskilde (1972) and Ålborg (1974).
ENROLMENT (percentage of age group) – primary 99 per cent (1994); secondary 86 per cent (1994); tertiary 45.0 per cent (1994)

THE FARÖE ISLANDS

AREA – 540 sq. miles (1,399 sq. km)
POPULATION – 43,700 (1995)
CAPITAL – Tórshavn (population, 16,218, 1992)

Since 1948 the Faröes or Sheep Islands have had a degree of home rule. The islands are governed by a *Lagting* of 32 members and a *Landsstyret* of four members which deals with special Faröes affairs, and send two representatives to the *Folketing* at Copenhagen. The Faröes are not part of the EU.

Prime Minister, Edmund Joensen

TRADE WITH UK	1996	1997
Imports from UK	£15,499,000	£8,551,000
Exports to UK	116,630,000	109,790,000

GREENLAND

AREA – 840,004 sq. miles (2,175,600 sq. km) of which about 16 per cent is ice-free
POPULATION – 55,700 (1995)
CAPITAL – Godthåb (Nuuk) (population, 13,148, 1995)

Greenland attained a status of internal autonomy in May 1979 and a government (*Landsstyret*) was established. It has a *Landsting* (parliament) of 31 members and sends two representatives to the *Folketing* at Copenhagen. Greenland negotiated its withdrawal from the EU, without discontinuing relations with Denmark, and left on 1 February 1985.

The USA has acquired certain rights to maintain air bases in Greenland.

Prime Minister, Jonathan Motzfeldt

TRADE WITH UK	1996	1997
Imports from UK	£2,772,000	£672,000
Exports to UK	9,666,000	8,525,000

DJIBOUTI
Jumhouriyya Djibouti

AREA – 8,958 sq. miles (23,200 sq. km). Neighbours: Eritrea (north), Ethiopia (west and south), Somalia (south-east)
POPULATION – 577,000 (1994 UN estimate), 520,000 (1991 census), mostly Afar or Issas. The official languages are Arabic and French; Afar and Somali are also spoken
CAPITAL – ΨDjibouti (population, 340,700, 1991)
CURRENCY – Djibouti franc of 100 centimes
NATIONAL DAY – 27 June (Independence Day)
NATIONAL FLAG – Blue over green with white triangle in the hoist containing a red star
LIFE EXPECTANCY (years) – male 46.72; female 50.00
POPULATION GROWTH RATE – 2.2 per cent (1995)
POPULATION DENSITY – 25 per sq. km (1995)
MILITARY EXPENDITURE – 5.1 per cent of GDP (1996)
MILITARY PERSONNEL – 11,400: Army 8,000, Navy 200, Air Force 200, Paramilitaries 3,000
GDP – US$493 million (1994); US$926 per capita (1994)
TOTAL EXTERNAL DEBT – US$241 million (1996)
ILLITERACY RATE – 53.8 per cent
ENROLMENT (percentage of age group) – primary 32 per cent (1995); secondary 11 per cent (1985); tertiary 0.2 per cent (1995)

The climate is harsh and much of the country is semi-arid desert.

HISTORY AND POLITICS

Formerly French Somaliland and then the French Territory of the Afars and the Issas, the Republic of Djibouti became independent on 27 June 1977. A multiparty constitution was adopted by referendum in 1992 and subsequent multiparty elections held in December 1992 were won by the *Rassemblement Populaire pour le Progrès* (RPP, the Popular Rally for Progress). President Aptidon was re-elected for a fourth six-year term in 1993. However, less than half the electorate voted in either election and the Front for the Restoration of Unity and Democracy (FRUD) boycotted both. In December 1997, in the first elections since the 1994 peace accord, the RPP and the FRUD formed an alliance and won all 65 seats in the Chamber of Deputies.

INSURGENCY

Armed FRUD rebels, their support based among ethnic Afars, have been fighting the government since 1991 in protest at the concentration of political power in the hands of the Somali-speaking Issas. A formal peace agreement with the government was signed by the majority faction of FRUD in December 1994 and FRUD was recognized as a political party in March 1996. A minority faction has condemned the agreement and continues to fight.

HEAD OF STATE
President, Hassan Gouled Aptidon, *elected* 1977, *re-elected* 1981, 1987 and 8 May 1993

COUNCIL OF MINISTERS *as at July 1998*
Prime Minister, National and Regional Development, Barkat Gourad Hamadou
Agriculture, Farming, Fisheries and Hydraulic Resources, Ibrahim Idriss Djibril
Civil Service and Administrative Reform, Ougoure Kifle Ahmed
Defence, Abdallah Chirwa Djibril
Economy, Finance, Planning and Privatization, Yacin Elmi Bouh
Energy and Natural Resources, Ali Abdi Farah
Environment, Tourism and Handicrafts, Osman Robleh Daach
Foreign Affairs and International Co-operation, Mohamed Moussa Chehem
Interior, Decentralization, Elmi Obsieh Farah
Justice, Islamic Affairs and Prisons, Mohamed Dini Farah
Labour and Vocational Training, Muhummad Ali Muhammad
National Education, Ahmed Guirreh Waberi
Public Health and Social Affairs, Ali Muhammad Daoud
Public Works, Town Planning and Housing, Hassan Farah Miguil
Trade and Industry, Mohamed Barkat Abdillahi
Transport and Telecommunications, Abdallah Abdillahi Miguil
Youth, Sport and Cultural Affairs, Rifki Abdoulkader Bamakhrama

EMBASSY OF THE REPUBLIC OF DJIBOUTI
26 rue Emile Ménier, 75016 Paris, France
Tel: Paris 4727 4922
Ambassador Extraordinary and Plenipotentiary, HE Djama Omar Idleh, apptd 1998

BRITISH AMBASSADOR, HE Gordon Wetherell, resides at Addis Ababa, Ethiopia

BRITISH CONSULATE
PO Box 81, 9–11 Rue de Geneve, Djibouti
Honorary Consul, P. Lambrecht

The French continue to maintain army, navy and air force bases in Djibouti, with a total strength of 2,600 personnel. Djibouti has an excellent port, an international airport, and a railway line runs to Addis Ababa. In 1995 Djibouti had a trade deficit of US$171 million and a current account deficit of US$23 million.

TRADE WITH UK	1996	1997
Imports from UK	£12,911,000	£15,380,000
Exports to UK	74,000	411,000

DOMINICA
The Commonwealth of Dominica

AREA – 290 sq. miles (751 sq. km)
POPULATION – 71,000 (1994 UN estimate). English is the official language although Creole French is more commonly used
CAPITAL – ΨRoseau (population, 16,243, 1991)
MAJOR TOWNS – Portsmouth (3,620)
CURRENCY – East Caribbean dollar (EC$) of 100 cents
NATIONAL ANTHEM – Isle of Beauty
NATIONAL DAY – 3 November (Independence Day)

NATIONAL FLAG – Green ground with a cross overall of yellow, black and white stripes, and in the centre a red disc charged with a Sisserou parrot in natural colours within a ring of ten green stars
POPULATION GROWTH RATE – –0.1 per cent (1995)
POPULATION DENSITY – 95 per sq. km (1995)

Dominica, in the Lesser Antilles, lies in the Windward Islands group 95 miles south of Antigua. It is about 29 miles long and 16 miles wide. The island is of volcanic origin and very mountainous, and the soil is very fertile. The temperature varies, according to the altitude, from 13° to 29°C.

HISTORY AND POLITICS

The island was discovered by Columbus in 1493, when it was a stronghold of the Caribs, who remained virtually the sole inhabitants until the French established settlements in the 18th century. It was captured by the British in 1759 but passed back and forth between France and Britain until 1805, after which British possession was not challenged. From 1871 to 1939 Dominica was part of the Leeward Islands Colony, then from 1940 the island was a unit of the Windward Islands group. Internal self-government from 1967 was followed on 3 November 1978 by independence as a republic.

The most recent general election was held in June 1995 and won by the Dominica United Workers' Party, which captured 11 seats, with five seats each going to the Dominica Freedom Party and the Dominica Labour Party.

POLITICAL SYSTEM

Executive authority is vested in the president, who is elected by the House of Assembly for not more than two terms of five years. Parliament consists of the president and the House of Assembly (21 representatives elected by universal adult suffrage for a five-year term) and nine senators, five of whom are appointed on the advice of the prime minister and the other four on the advice of the Leader of the Opposition.

HEAD OF STATE

President, HE Crispin Sorhaindo, OBE, *elected* 4 October 1993, *took office* 25 October 1993

CABINET *as at July 1998*

Prime Minister, External Affairs, Legal Affairs and Labour, Edison James
Agriculture and Environment, Peter Carbon
Communications, Works and Housing, Earl Williams
Community Development and Women's Affairs, Gertrude Roberts
Education, Sports and Youth Affairs, Ronald Green
Finance, Industry and Planning, Julius Timothy
Health and Social Security, Doreen Paul
Tourism, Ports and Employment, Norris Prevost
Trade and Marketing, Norris Charles

HIGH COMMISSION FOR THE COMMONWEALTH OF DOMINICA
1 Collingham Gardens, London SW5 OHW
Tel 0171–370 5194/5
High Commissioner, HE George Williams, apptd 1996

BRITISH HIGH COMMISSIONER, HE Gordon Baker, resides at Bridgetown, Barbados

BRITISH CONSULATE
PO Box 2269, Roseau
Honorary Consul, P. Fletcher

ECONOMY

Agriculture is the principal occupation, with tropical and citrus fruits the main crops. Products for export are bananas, fruit juices, lime oil, bay oil, copra and rum. Forestry, fisheries and agro-processing are being encouraged. The only commercially exploitable mineral is pumice, used chiefly for building purposes. Manufacturing consists largely of the processing of agricultural products although there have been attempts to diversify into light industry.
GNP – US$228 million (1996); US$3,090 per capita (1996)
GDP – US$204 million (1994); US$2,902 per capita (1994)
ANNUAL AVERAGE GROWTH OF GDP – 1.8 per cent (1993)
INFLATION RATE – 1.7 per cent (1996)
TOTAL EXTERNAL DEBT – US$111 million (1996)

TRADE WITH UK	1996	1997
Imports from UK	£11,166,000	£11,575,000
Exports to UK	19,110,000	19,933,000

DOMINICAN REPUBLIC
República Dominicana

AREA – 18,816 sq. miles (48,734 sq. km). Neighbour: Haiti (west)
POPULATION – 7,915,000 (1994 UN estimate). The language is Spanish
CAPITAL – Ψ Santo Domingo (population, 2,134,779, 1993)
MAJOR CITIES – Duarte (272,227); La Vega (335,140); Puerto Plata (255,061); San Cristóbal (409,381); San Juan (247,029); Santiago de los Caballeros (690,458), 1993 UN estimates
CURRENCY – Dominican Republic peso (RD$) of 100 centavos
NATIONAL FLAG – Divided into blue and red quarters by a white cross
NATIONAL ANTHEM – Quisqueyanos Valientes, Alcemos (Brave men of Quisqueya, let's raise our song)
NATIONAL DAY – 27 February (Independence Day 1844)
LIFE EXPECTANCY (years) – male 67.63; female 71.69
POPULATION GROWTH RATE – 2.0 per cent (1995)
POPULATION DENSITY – 162 per sq. km (1995)
URBAN POPULATION – 61.7 per cent (1995)
MILITARY EXPENDITURE – 1.1 per cent of GDP (1996)
MILITARY PERSONNEL – 39,500: Army 15,000, Navy 4,000, Air Force 5,500, Paramilitaries 15,000
ILLITERACY RATE – 17.9 per cent
ENROLMENT (percentage of age group) – primary 81 per cent (1994); secondary 22 per cent (1994); tertiary 18 per cent (1985)

The Dominican Republic, the eastern part of the island of Hispaniola (Haiti is the western part), is the oldest European settlement in America. The climate is tropical in the lowlands and semi-tropical to temperate in the higher altitudes.

HISTORY AND POLITICS

Santo Domingo was discovered by Columbus in 1492, and was a Spanish colony until 1821. In 1822 it was subjugated by the neighbouring Haitians who remained in control until 1844, when the Dominican Republic was proclaimed. The country was occupied by American marines from 1916 until 1924. Gen. Rafael Trujillo ruled from 1930 until 1961.

President Juan Bosch held office from December 1962 to September 1963, when he was deposed by a military junta. A left-wing revolt in favour of ex-President Bosch in April 1965 developed into civil war lasting until September the same year, when Bosch's supporters were defeated by the arrival of US troops, and a provisional president was elected. A presidential election in May 1994 was won by the incumbent President Balaguer. Balaguer was replaced by opposition Dominican Liberation Party (PLD) candidate, Leonel Fernández, who defeated the ruling Christian Social Reform Party (PRSC) candidate, Jacinto Peynado, in a run-off election on 30 June 1996.

POLITICAL SYSTEM

Executive power is vested in the president, who is directly elected for four-year terms and appoints the Cabinet. Legislative power is exercised by the Congress, which has a term of four years concurrent with the presidency. The Congress comprises the Senate of 30 senators, one for each province and one for Santo Domingo, and the 120-member Chamber of Deputies.

HEAD OF STATE

President, Leonel Fernández, *elected* 30 June 1996

CABINET *as at July 1998*

Agriculture, Frank Rodríguez
Defence, Rear-Adm. Rubén Paulino Alvárez
Education and Culture, Ligia Amada Melo de Córdova
Finance, Daniel Toribio
Foreign Affairs, Eduardo Latorre
Health, Alejandra Guzmán
Industry and Commerce, Luis Manuel Bonetti
Information, Virgilio Alcantara
Interior, Norge Botello
Labour, Rafael Albuquerque de Castro
Procurator-General, Abel Rodríguez del Orbe
Public Works, Jaime Durán
Sports, Juan Marichal
Tourism, Felix Jimenéz
Without Portfolio, Lidio Cadet; Ramón Ventura Carnejo

EMBASSY OF THE DOMINICAN REPUBLIC
15 Brechin Place, London, SW7 4QB
Tel 0171–727 6232
Ambassador Extraordinary and Plenipotentiary, HE Dr Pedro
  Padilla Tonos, apptd 1997

BRITISH EMBASSY
Edificio Corominas Pepin, Ave 27 de Fabrero No 233, Santo
  Domingo
Tel: Santo Domingo 472 7111
Ambassador Extraordinary and Plenipotentiary, HE Dick
  Thomson, apptd 1995
BRITISH CONSULAR OFFICES – Santo Domingo, Puerto
  Plata

ECONOMY

Since 1990 the government has successfully reduced inflation and increased output. Large amounts of foreign debt have been paid off but unemployment remains high. State subsidies were ended in 1995 in an attempt to reduce the budget deficit.

Sugar, cocoa, coffee, bananas, rice and tobacco are the most important crops. Other products are maize, molasses, beans, tomatoes, cement, ferro-nickel, gold, silver and cattle. Light industry produces beer, tinned foodstuffs, glass products, textiles, soap, cigarettes, construction materials, plastic articles, paint, rum, matches and peanut oil.

GNP – US$12,765 million (1996); US$1,600 per capita (1996)

GDP – US$8,892 million (1994); US$1,347 per capita (1994)
ANNUAL AVERAGE GROWTH OF GDP – 7.3 per cent (1996)
INFLATION RATE – 12.5 per cent (1995)
TOTAL EXTERNAL DEBT – US$4,310 million (1996)

TRADE

The chief imports are machinery, foodstuffs, iron and steel, cotton textiles and yarns, mineral oils (including petrol), motor vehicles, chemical and pharmaceutical products, electrical equipment and accessories, construction materials, paper and paper products, and rubber and rubber products. The chief exports are sugar, coffee, cocoa, tobacco, chocolate, molasses, ferro-nickel and gold.

In 1995 there was a trade deficit of US$1,792 million and a current account deficit of US$125 million. In 1996 imports totalled US$3,686 million and exports US$815 million.

Trade with UK	1996	1997
Imports from UK	£27,322,000	£38,857,000
Exports to UK	25,725,000	34,665,000

COMMUNICATIONS

There are over 4,000 miles of roads and a direct road from Santo Domingo to Port-au-Prince, the capital of Haiti, but that part of it in the border area has fallen into disuse. The frontier has been closed since 1967, except for the section crossed by the main road linking the two capitals. A telephone system connects all the principal towns. There are more than 90 commercial broadcasting stations and six television stations.

ECUADOR
República del Ecuador

AREA – 109,484 sq. miles (283,561 sq. km). Neighbours:
  Colombia (north), Peru (east and south)
POPULATION – 11,460,000 (1994 UN estimate),
  descendants of the Spanish, aboriginal Indians, and
  Mestizos. Spanish is the principal language but Quechua
  is also a recognized language and is spoken by most
  Indians
CAPITAL – Quito (population, 1,387,887, 1991 estimate)
MAJOR CITIES – Cuenca (332,117); ΨGuayaquil
  (1,531,229), the chief port
CURRENCY – Sucre of 100 centavos
NATIONAL DAY – 10 August (Independence Day)
NATIONAL FLAG – Three horizontal bands, yellow, blue
  and red (the yellow band twice the width of the others);
  emblem in centre
LIFE EXPECTANCY (years) – male 67.32; female 72.49
POPULATION GROWTH RATE – 2.2 per cent (1995)
POPULATION DENSITY – 40 per sq. km (1995)
URBAN POPULATION – 59.2 per cent (1995)
MILITARY EXPENDITURE – 2.8 per cent of GDP (1996)
MILITARY PERSONNEL – 57,370: Army 50,000, Navy
  4,100, Air Force 3,000, Paramilitaries 270
CONSCRIPTION DURATION – 12 months

Ecuador is an equatorial state of South America. It extends across the Western Andes, the highest peaks being Chimborazo (20,408 ft) and Ilinza (17,405 ft) in the Western Cordillera; and Cotopaxi (19,612 ft) and Cayambe (19,160 ft) in the Eastern Cordillera. Ecuador is watered by the Upper Amazon, and by the rivers Guayas, Mira, Santiago, Chone, and Esmeraldas on the Pacific coast. There are extensive forests.

HISTORY AND POLITICS

The former kingdom of Quito was conquered by the Incas of Peru in the 15th century. Early in the 16th century Pizarro's conquests led to the inclusion of the present territory of Ecuador in the Spanish Vice-royalty of Quito. Independence was achieved in a revolutionary war which culminated in the battle of Mount Pichincha (1822).

After seven years of military rule, Ecuador returned to democracy in 1979. In the 1992 legislative election a loose coalition of parties enabled President Ballén to introduce a programme of economic reform, financial liberalization and privatization. This, together with reductions in state spending, caused social unrest in 1992–4 and led to the government's defeat in the May 1994 legislative elections. In the July 1996 elections the ruling Social Christian Party (PSC) won a majority of seats. Abdala Bucaram was elected president in July 1996, and appointed a coalition government. Bucaram was ousted by the legislature on the grounds of insanity and replaced firstly by Vice-President Arteaga and then by the Speaker of the National Congress Fabián Alarcón. The presidential elections in July 1998 were won by Jamil Mahaud, the former Mayor of Quito, who gained 51 per cent of the vote.

FOREIGN RELATIONS

The border with Peru was demarcated by a 1942 treaty which was partly revoked by Ecuador in 1960 in relation to a disputed 50-mile stretch. An inconclusive four-week border war was fought with Peru in February 1995 until a cease-fire was signed on 1 March 1995. A 54-mile demilitarized zone was agreed in July 1995. Talks over the disputed border are continuing.

POLITICAL SYSTEM

The 1978 constitution provides for an elected president and vice-president who serve for a single four-year term. There is a unicameral National Congress which meets for two months a year and has 82 members, 12 of whom are elected on a national basis every four years and 70 on a provincial basis every two years. Voting is compulsory for all literate and voluntary for all illiterate citizens over the age of 18. The republic is divided into 21 provinces.

A Constituent Assembly, formed in November 1997 to oversee constitutional reform, proposed an increase in the number of seats in Congress to 121, and declared that in the event of the President being unable to perform his duties, the Vice President, and not the Speaker of Congress, would take over presidential duties.

HEAD OF STATE

President, Jamil Mahaud, *elected* 20 July 1998
Vice-President, Gustavo Noboa Bejarno

CABINET *as at August 1998*

Agriculture, Emilio Gallardo
Defence, José Gallardo
Education, Wladimiro Alvarez
Energy and Mines, Patricio Rivadeneira
Environment, Yolanda Kakabadse
Finance, Fidel Jaramillo
Foreign Affairs, José Ayala Lasso
Foreign Trade, Héctor Plaza
Health, Edgar Rodas
Home Affairs, Ana Lucía Armijos
Housing, Teodoro Peña
Labour, Angel Polibio Chávez
Public Works, Raúl Samaniego
Social Welfare, Guillermo Celi
Tourism, Rocío Vásquez

General Secretaries, Jaime Durán (*Administration*); Ramón Yulee (*Presidency*)

EMBASSY OF ECUADOR
Flat 3B, 3 Hans Crescent, London SW1X 0LS
Tel 0171–584 1367
Ambassador Extraordinary and Plenipotentiary, HE Osvaldo Ramírez-Landázuri

BRITISH EMBASSY
Calle González Suárez 111, Casilla 314, Quito
Tel: Quito 560670
Ambassador Extraordinary and Plenipotentiary, HE John Forbes-Meyler, OBE, apptd 1997
BRITISH CONSULAR OFFICES – Cuenca, Galápagos and Guayaquil

BRITISH COUNCIL REPRESENTATIVE, Anthony Deyes, Av. Amazonas 1646, Casilla 17-07-8829, Quito

ECONOMY

Agriculture is the most important sector of the economy. The main products for export are fish, bananas, which provide a third of agricultural exports, cocoa and coffee. Other important crops are sugar, soya, rice, cotton, African palm, vegetables, fruit and timber. The main imports are manufactured goods and machinery.

The economy was transformed by the discovery in 1972 of major oil fields in the Oriente area which are evacuated by a trans-Andean pipeline to the port of Balao. Ecuador withdrew from OPEC in 1992 in order to raise its production to 19,303,000 tonnes in 1994.

In 1996 there was a trade surplus of US$1,402 million and a current account surplus of US$296 million. Imports totalled US$3,724 million and exports US$4,890 million.
GNP – US$17,531 million (1996); US$1,500 per capita (1996)
GDP – US$12,322 million (1994); US$1,597 per capita (1994)
ANNUAL AVERAGE GROWTH OF GDP – 2.9 per cent (1996)
INFLATION RATE – 24.4 per cent (1996)
UNEMPLOYMENT – 7.1 per cent (1994)
TOTAL EXTERNAL DEBT – US$14,491 million (1996)

TRADE WITH UK	1996	1997
Imports from UK	£41,430,000	£45,501,000
Exports to UK	29,150,000	36,184,000

COMMUNICATIONS

There are 23,256 km of permanent roads and 5,044 km of roads which are only open during the dry season. Ten commercial airlines operate international flights and there are internal services between all important towns. Two daily newspapers are published at Quito and four at Guayaquil.

EDUCATION

Elementary education is free and compulsory. There are ten universities (three at Quito, three at Guayaquil, and one each at Cuenca, Machala, Loja and Portoviejo), polytechnic schools at Quito and Guayaquil and eight technical colleges in other provincial capitals.
ILLITERACY RATE – 9.9 per cent
ENROLMENT (percentage of age group) – primary 92 per cent (1994); tertiary 20.0 per cent (1990)

GALÁPAGOS ISLANDS

The Galápagos (Giant Tortoise) Islands, forming the province of the Archipelago de Colón, were annexed by Ecuador in 1832. The archipelago lies in the Pacific, about

500 miles from the mainland. There are 12 large and several hundred smaller islands with a total area of about 3,000 sq. miles and an estimated population (1982) of 6,119. The capital is San Cristóbal, on Chatham Island. Although the archipelago lies on the equator, the temperature of the surrounding water is well below equatorial average owing to the Humboldt current. The province consists for the most part of National Park Territory, where unique marine birds, iguanas, and the giant tortoises are conserved. There is some local subsistence farming; the main industry, apart from tourism, is tuna and lobster fishing.

EGYPT
Al-Jumhuriyat Misr al-Arabiya

AREA – 386,662 sq. miles (1,001,449 sq. km). Neighbours: Sudan (south), Libya (west), Gaza Strip and Israel (east)

POPULATION – 59,226,000 (official estimate 1995). The largest, or 'Egyptian' element, is a Hamito-Semite race. A second element is the *Bedouin*, or nomadic Arabs of the Western and Eastern deserts, who are now mainly semi-sedentary tent-dwellers. The third element is the *Nubian* of the Nile Valley of mixed Arab and Negro blood. Over 90 per cent of the population are Muslims of the Sunni denomination, and most of the rest are Coptic Christians. Arabic is the official language

CAPITAL – Cairo (population, 13,000,000, 1994 estimate) stands on the Nile about 14 miles from the head of the delta

MAJOR CITIES – ΨAlexandria (3,328,196, 1997 estimate), founded 332 BC by Alexander the Great, was the capital for over 1,000 years; Asyût (2,802,185); Faiyûm (1,989,881); Ismailia (715,009); ΨPort Said (469,533); ΨSuez (417,610)

CURRENCY – Egyptian pound (£E) of 100 piastres or 1,000 millièmes

NATIONAL DAY – 23 July (Anniversary of Revolution in 1952)

NATIONAL FLAG – Horizontal bands of red, white and black, with an eagle in the centre of the white band

LIFE EXPECTANCY (years) – male 62.86; female 66.39

POPULATION GROWTH RATE – 2.1 per cent (1995)

POPULATION DENSITY – 59 per sq. km (1995)

URBAN POPULATION – 44.0 per cent (1994)

ILLITERACY RATE – 48.6 per cent

ENROLMENT (percentage of age group) – primary 89 per cent (1993); secondary 65 per cent (1993); tertiary 18.1 per cent (1994)

Egypt comprises Egypt proper, the peninsula of Sinai and a number of islands in the Gulf of Suez and Red Sea, of which the principal are Jubal, Shadwan, Gafatin and Zeberged (or St John's Island).

The country is mainly flat but there are mountainous areas in the south-west, along the Red Sea coast and in the south of the Sinai peninsula; the highest peak is Mt Catherina (8,668 ft). Most of the land is desert and the Nile valley and delta were the only fertile areas until the opening of the Aswan Dam allowed areas of desert to be reclaimed. West of the Nile Valley is the Western Desert, containing some depressions whose springs irrigate oases. The Eastern Desert between the Nile and the mountains along the Red Sea coast is mostly plateaux dissected by wadis (dry water-courses).

HISTORY AND POLITICS

The unification of the kingdoms of Lower and Upper Egypt under the Pharaohs *c.*3100 BC marked the establishment of the Egyptian state, with Memphis as its capital. Egypt was ruled for nearly 2,800 years by a succession of 31 Pharaonic dynasties which built the pyramids at Gizeh. A period of Hellenic rule began in 332 BC, followed by a period of rule by Rome (30 BC to AD 324) and then by the Byzantine Empire. In AD 640 Egypt was subjugated by Arab Muslim invaders. In 1517 the country was incorporated in the Ottoman Empire, under which it remained until the early 19th century. A British Protectorate over Egypt lasted from 1914 to 1922, when Sultan Ahmed Fuad was proclaimed King of Egypt. In 1953 the monarchy was deposed and Egypt became a republic.

In 1956, as a result of Egypt's trade agreements with Communist countries, Britain and the USA withdrew offers of financial aid and in retaliation President Nasser seized the assets of the Suez Canal Company. Egyptian occupation of the Canal Zone while repulsing an Israeli attack was used as a pretext for military action by Britain and France in support of their Suez Canal Company interests. A cease-fire and Anglo-French withdrawal were negotiated by the UN.

The Israeli invasion of 1956 overran the Sinai peninsula but six months later Israel withdrew. However, mounting tension culminated in a second invasion of Sinai (the Six Day War in June 1967) and occupation of the peninsula by Israel. Egypt's attempt to recapture the territory (the Yom Kippur War in October 1973) was unsuccessful but Sinai was returned to Egypt in 1982 under the treaty of 1979 which resulted from the Camp David talks and formally terminated a 31-year-old state of war between the two countries.

The ruling National Democratic Party won the general election held in November and December 1995. President Mubarak was nominated by the legislature to run unopposed for a third six-year term in July 1993, and was elected in October.

INSURGENCY

Militant Muslim fundamentalists re-emerged in 1992, carrying out attacks on tourists, Coptic Christians, government ministers, civil servants and the security forces. Attacks continued in 1993–7 and are concentrated in Upper Egypt and the Cairo area. The government has reacted vigorously to the armed campaign with the arrest of 20,000 militants.

POLITICAL SYSTEM

The constitution of 1971 provides for an executive president who appoints the Council of Ministers and determines government policy. The president is elected by the legislature every six years. The legislature is the People's Assembly which has 454 members, 444 of whom are elected, the remaining ten nominated by the president. The Shura Council or Consultative Assembly (210 members) has an advisory role.

HEAD OF STATE
President, Muhammad Hosni Mubarak, *elected* 1981, *re-elected* 1987, 13 October 1993

COUNCIL OF MINISTERS *as at July 1998*

Prime Minister, Planning, International Co-operation, Kamal Ahmed al-Ganzuri

Deputy PM, Agriculture and Land Reclamation, Yousef Amin Wali

Administrative Development, Mahmoud Zaki Abu Amer

Cabinet Affairs and Follow-up of Economic Affairs, Tala'at
 Sayyed Ahmed Hammad
Culture, Farouk Hosni Abdel Aziz
Defence and Military Production, Field Marshal Mohammad
 Hussein Tantawi
Economy, Yussef Boutros Ghali
Education, Hussein Kamel Bahaeddin
Electricity and Energy, Mohamed Maher Othman Abaza
Environment, Nadia Makram Obeid
Finance, Mohieddin Abu Bakr al Ghareeb
Foreign Affairs, Amr Mahmoud Moussa
Health and Population, Ismail Awadallah Sallam
Higher Education and Scientific Research, Mufid Shehab
Housing, Utilities and New Urban Communities, Mohammed
 Ibrahim Soliman
Industry and Mineral Resources, Soliman Reda Ali Soliman
Information, Safwat El-Sherif
Interior, Brig. Habib al-Adli
Justice, Farouk Seif El-Nasr
Labour and Emigration, Ahmed al-Amawi
Military Production, Mohammad al-Ghamrawi Daoud
 Hasan
People's National Assembly and Consultative Council Affairs,
 Kamal Mohammed Al Shazli
Petroleum, Hamdi Abdel Wahab al-Banbi
Planning and International Co-operation, Zafir Selim Al-
 Beshri
Public Business Sector, Atef Mohammad Obeid
Public Works and Water Resources, Mahmoud Abdul Halim
 Abu Zaid
Religious Endowments (Wakfs), Mahmoud Hamdi Zakzouk
Rural Development, Mahmoud El-Sherif Sayeed Ahmed
Scientific Research, Venise Kamel Gouda
Social Insurance and Social Affairs, Marwat al-Tilawi
Tourism, Mamdouh Ahmed Al-Beltagui
Trade and Supply, Ahmed Ahmed Gowaili
Transport and Communications, Soliman Mutwalli

EMBASSY OF THE ARAB REPUBLIC OF EGYPT
26 South Street, London WIY 6DD
Tel 0171-499 2401
Ambassador Extraordinary and Plenipotentiary, HE Abdel El-
 Gazar, apptd 1997
Ministers Plenipotentiary, Samiha Abou Steit (*Consul-
 General*); Ismail Roushdy (*Commercial*)
Defence Attaché, Cdre. Mohamed F. E. Genina
Cultural Counsellor, Mohamed A. El-Sharkawy

BRITISH EMBASSY
Ahmed Ragheb Street, Garden City, Cairo
Tel: Cairo 354 0850
Ambassador Extraordinary and Plenipotentiary, HE Sir David
 Blatherwick, KCMG, OBE, apptd 1995
Counsellor and Deputy Head of Mission, G. D. Adams
Defence and Military Attaché, Col. A. Snook, OBE
First Secretaries, P. Byrde (*Consul*); D. G. Reader (*Commercial*)
BRITISH CONSULAR OFFICES – *Consulate-General,*
 Alexandria; *Consulates,* Luxor, Suez, Port Said, Aswan

BRITISH COUNCIL DIRECTOR, D. Marler OBE (*Cultural
 First Secretary*), 192 Sharia el Nil, Agouza, Cairo

DEFENCE

The Army has 3,700 main battle tanks, 790 armoured
infantry fighting vehicles, 3,904 armoured personnel
carriers and 1,247 artillery pieces. The Navy has one
destroyer, eight frigates, eight submarines, 43 patrol and
coastal vessels and 24 armed helicopters at six bases. The
Air Force has 572 combat aircraft and 125 armed helicopters.

MILITARY EXPENDITURE – 3.5 per cent of GDP (1996)
MILITARY PERSONNEL – 680,000: Army 320,000, Navy
 20,000, Air Force 30,000, Air Defence Command
 80,000, Paramilitaries 230,000
CONSCRIPTION DURATION – Three years

ECONOMY

Despite increasing industrialization, agriculture remains
the most important economic activity, employing 35 per
cent of the labour force and producing 22 per cent of GDP
in 1995. Egypt is still a net importer of foodstuffs,
especially grain, and a food security programme has been
set up with the aim of achieving self-sufficiency. The main
cash crop is cotton, of which Egypt is one of the world's
main producers. Other important crops are maize, rice,
sugar cane, wheat and potatoes. Other fruits and vegetables
are also grown.

With its considerable reserves of petroleum and natural
gas, and the hydroelectric power produced by the Aswan
and High Dams, Egypt is self-sufficient in energy. The
major manufacturing industries are food processing,
motor cars, electrical goods, steel, chemical products,
yarns and textiles. In 1996 more than two million tourists
visited Egypt, though in 1997 the tourism industry was
badly affected following attacks on foreign tourists by
Islamic militants.

In 1995 the government had a trade deficit of US$7,597
million and a current account deficit of US$254 million.

GNP – US$64,275 million (1996); US$1,080 per capita
 (1996)
GDP – US$48,691 million (1994); US$760 per capita
 (1994)
ANNUAL AVERAGE GROWTH OF GDP – 5.1 per cent (1996)
INFLATION RATE – 7.2 per cent (1996)
UNEMPLOYMENT – 11.0 per cent (1994)
TOTAL EXTERNAL DEBT – US$31,407 million (1996)

TRADE

The main imports are wheat, maize, chemicals and motor
vehicles and parts. The main exports are crude petroleum,
cotton, cotton yarn, oranges, rice and cotton textiles.

In 1995 Egypt's imports totalled US$11,739 million and
exports US$3,435 million.

Trade with UK	1996	1997
Imports from UK	£431,424,000	£498,582,000
Exports to UK	281,502,000	270,027,000

COMMUNICATIONS

There are international airports at Cairo and Luxor. The
road and rail networks link the Nile valley and delta with
the main development areas east and west of the river. The
Suez Canal was reopened in 1975 and a two-stage
development project begun to widen and deepen the canal
to allow the passage of larger shipping and to permit two-
way traffic. Port Said and Suez have been reconstructed
and the port of Alexandria is being improved.

EQUATORIAL GUINEA
República de Guinea Ecuatorial

AREA – 10,831 sq. miles (28,051 sq. km). Neighbours:
 Cameroon (north), Gabon (east and south)
POPULATION – 400,000 (1994 UN estimate). The official
 languages are Spanish and French
CAPITAL – ΨMalabo on the island of Bioko (population,
 30,418, 1983 estimate)

MAJOR TOWN – ΨBata is the principal town and port of Rio Muni
CURRENCY – Franc CFA of 100 centimes
NATIONAL DAY – 12 October
NATIONAL FLAG – Three horizontal bands, green over white over red; blue triangle next staff; coat of arms in centre of white band
LIFE EXPECTANCY (years) – male 44.86; female 47.78
POPULATION GROWTH RATE – 2.8 per cent (1995)
POPULATION DENSITY – 14 per sq. km (1995)
URBAN POPULATION – 37.0 per cent (1991)
MILITARY EXPENDITURE – 1.1 per cent of GDP (1996)
MILITARY PERSONNEL – 1,320: Army 1,100, Navy 120, Air Force 100
ILLITERACY RATE – 21.5 per cent

Equatorial Guinea consists of the island of Bioko, in the Bight of Biafra about 20 miles from the west coast of Africa, Annonbón Island in the Gulf of Guinea, the Corisco Islands (Corisco, Elobey Grande and Elobey Chico), and Rio Muni, a mainland area between Cameroon and Gabon.

HISTORY AND POLITICS

Formerly colonies of Spain, the territories now forming Equatorial Guinea were constituted as two provinces of Metropolitan Spain in 1959, became autonomous in 1963 and fully independent in 1968.

In 1979 President Macias was deposed by a revolutionary military council headed by Col. Obiang Nguema. Constitutional amendments in 1982 provided for legislative elections, which were held in 1983 and 1988, but all candidates were chosen by the president.

A multiparty political system under a new constitution was approved by a referendum in 1991 and ten opposition parties have been legalized, operating alongside the ruling Equatorial Guinea Democratic Party (PDGE). A National Pact was agreed and signed in March 1993 but legislative elections in November were boycotted by most of the electorate and opposition parties. The PDGE won 68 out of 80 National Assembly seats and formed a government. In the February 1996 election, the president claimed to have won more than 99 per cent of the vote. Most opposition parties boycotted the ballot. In June 1997 the Progress Party, the largest opposition party, was banned by the government, and in February 1998 opposition party coalitions were deemed illegal. There have been widespread allegations of government repression from several opposition parties.

HEAD OF STATE
President of the Supreme Military Council and Minister of Defence, Brig.-Gen. Teodoro Obiang Nguema Mbasogo, *took office* August 1979, *re-elected* June 1989, 25 February 1996

MINISTERS *as at July 1998*
Prime Minister, Angel Serafiín Dougan
Deputy PM, Foreign Affairs, Miguel Oyono Ndong Mifumu
Deputy PM, Interior, Demetrio Elo Ndong
Minister of State, Health and Social Welfare, Salomón Nguema Owono
Minister of State, Labour and Social Security, Carmelo Modu Akune
Minister of State, Missions, Alejandro Evuna Owono Asangono
Minister of State, Planning, Economic Development, Government Spokesman, Antonio Fernando Nve Ngu
Minister of State, Public Works and Urban Affairs, Francisco Pascual Eyegue Obama Asue

Minister of State, Secretary-General at the Presidency, Ricardo Mangue Obama Nfue
Minister of State, Transport and Communication, Marcelino Oyono Ntutumu
Agriculture, Fisheries and Animal Husbandry, Constantine Eko Nsue
Civil Service and Administrative Reform, Fernando Mabale Mba
Economy and Finance, Baltazar Engonga Edjo
Education, Science and Francophonie, Santiago Ngua Nfumu
Forestry and Environment, Nguema Teodoro Obiang
Industry, Commerce, Small and Medium-sized Enterprises, Vidal Djoni Becoba
Information, Tourism and Culture, Lucas Nguema Esono
Interior and Local Corporations, Angel Esono Abaga
Justice and Religious Affairs, Rubén Mye Nsue
Mines and Energy, Juan Olo Mba Nseng
Social Affairs, Women's Affairs, Margarita Alene Mba
Youth and Sports, Ignacio Minlane Ntang

EMBASSY OF THE REPUBLIC OF EQUATORIAL GUINEA
6 rue Alfred de Vigny, 75008, Paris
Tel: Paris 4766 4433
Ambassador Extraordinary and Plenipotentiary, HE Lino-Sima Ekua Avomo

BRITISH AMBASSADOR, HE Peter Boon, resident at Yaoundé, Cameroon

ECONOMY

The chief products are cocoa, coffee and wood. Production has declined and except for cocoa there is little commercial agriculture. The economy is heavily dependent on outside aid, principally from Spain. Oil and gas production is increasing. Equatorial Guinea entered the 'franc zone' in 1985.

In 1995 imports totalled US$50 million and exports US$86 million.
GNP – US$217 million (1996); US$530 per capita (1996)
GDP – US$174 million (1994); US$342 per capita (1994)
INFLATION RATE – 4.0 per cent (1993)
TOTAL EXTERNAL DEBT – US$282 million (1996)

TRADE WITH UK	1996	1997
Imports from UK	£1,504,000	£10,594,000
Exports to UK	108,000	626,000

ERITREA

AREA – 45,406 sq. miles (117,600 sq. km). Neighbours: Sudan (north and north-west), Ethiopia (south and south-west), Djibouti (south-east)
POPULATION – 3,531,000 (1994 UN estimate), roughly half Coptic Christian (mainly highlanders) and half Muslim (mainly lowlanders). Arabic and Tigrinya are official languages, but English and Italian are widely spoken. There are nine indigenous language groups: Afar; Bilen; Hadareb; Kunama; Nara; Rashida; Saho; Tigre; Tigrinya
CAPITAL – Asmara (population, 358,100, 1990 estimate)
MAJOR TOWNS – ΨAssab; ΨMassawa
CURRENCY – Nakfa
NATIONAL DAY – 24 May (Independence Day)
NATIONAL FLAG – Divided into three triangles; the one based on the hoist is red and bears a gold olive wreath; the upper triangle is green and the lower one light blue
LIFE EXPECTANCY (years) – male 48.85; female 52.06
POPULATION GROWTH RATE – 2.7 per cent (1995)
POPULATION DENSITY – 30 per sq. km (1995)

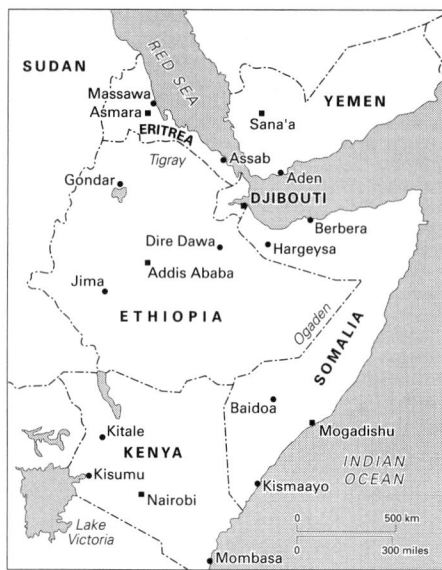

MILITARY EXPENDITURE – 8.4 per cent of GDP (1996)
CONSCRIPTION DURATION – Two years
ENROLMENT (percentage of age group) – primary 31 per cent (1995); secondary 15 per cent (1995); tertiary 1.1 per cent (1994)

HISTORY AND POLITICS

Eritrea was colonized by Italy in the late 19th century and was the base for the 1936 Italian invasion of Abyssinia (Ethiopia). After the Italian defeat in East Africa in 1941 by British and Commonwealth forces, Eritrea became a British protectorate. This lasted until 15 September 1952 when Eritrea was federated with Ethiopia. The Ethiopian Emperor Haile Selassie incorporated Eritrea as a province of Ethiopia in 1962. An armed campaign for independence began in the 1970s, first against Emperor Haile Selassie's forces and from 1974 against the Mengistu regime.

In 1991 the Mengistu government was overthrown by the Eritrean People's Liberation Front (EPLF) and the Ethiopian People's Revolutionary Democratic Front (EPRDF). The new EPRDF-led government in Ethiopia agreed to an Eritrean referendum on independence which was held in April 1993 and recorded a 99 per cent vote in favour. Independence was declared on 24 May 1993.

FOREIGN RELATIONS

Eritrea claims the three Hanish Islands in the Red Sea, the largest of which, Hanish al Kabir, was seized from Yemen in December 1995. The land border with Djibouti is also disputed.

In June 1998 fighting flared up on the border with Ethiopia, with both countries accusing the other of sending troops across the border. Talks to resolve the crisis are continuing.

POLITICAL SYSTEM

Under the 1997 constitution, the head of state is the president, elected for a five-year term by the National Assembly, of which he is chair. The 150-member unicameral legislature (the *Hagerawi Baito*) is directly elected for four years. The president is head of government and presides over a State Council.

HEAD OF STATE
President, Chairman of the National Assembly, Issaias Afewerki, *elected by National Assembly* 22 May 1993

STATE COUNCIL *as at July 1998*
Chairman, The President
Agriculture, Arefaine Berhe
Defence, Sebhat Efraim
Education, Osman Salih Muhammad
Energy and Mining, Tesfay Gebreselassie
Environment and Water, Tesfaye Ghirmatsion
Eritrean Relief, Refugee Commission, Werku Tesfamichael
Finance and Development, Ghebresellsie Yossief
Fisheries, Petros Solomon
Foreign Affairs, Haile Weldetensae
Health, Saleh Mekki
Industry and Trade, Ali Said Abdella
Information, Beraki Gebreselassie
Justice, Fozia Hashim
Labour and Social Security, Okbe Abraha
Local Government, Mahammud Ahmed Sharifo
Public Works, Abraha Asfeha
Tourism, Ahmed Haji Ali
Transport and Communications, Saleh Kekia

EMBASSY OF THE STATE OF ERITREA
15–17 avenue Wolvendael, 1180 Brussels, Belgium
Tel: Brussels 374 4434
Ambassador Extraordinary and Plenipotentiary, HE Andebrhan Weldegiorgis, apptd 1996
HONORARY CONSULATE, 96 White Lion Street, London N1 9PF. Tel: 0171–713 0096. *Honorary Consul,* Afewerki Abraha

BRITISH AMBASSADOR, HE Gordon Wetherell, resident at Addis Ababa, Ethiopia

BRITISH CONSULATE
PO Box 997, Asmara
Tel: Asmara 411 4242
Honorary Consul, S. J. Burgess

BRITISH COUNCIL DIRECTOR – Dr Negusse Araya, PO Box 997, Asmara

ECONOMY

Since 1991 the government has attempted to rebuild industry, agriculture and infrastructure which were devastated by the war of independence. The rebuilding programme has focused on the ports of Massawa and Assab, the roads from the ports to Ethiopia, and the railway from Massawa to Sudan via Asmara. Before 1962 Eritrea was one of the most industrialized areas of Africa and some industry remains, producing textiles and footwear. The government hopes to base the rebuilding of the economy on the return of well-educated exiles, international aid and investment, the development of tourism along the coast, and the diversification of the economy away from agriculture.

GDP – US$581 million (1994); US$96 per capita (1994)
TOTAL EXTERNAL DEBT – US$46 million (1996)

TRADE WITH UK	1996	1997
Imports from UK	£2,348,000	£7,042,000
Exports to UK	39,000	84,000

ESTONIA
The Republic of Estonia

AREA – 17,413 sq. miles (45,100 sq. km). Neighbours:
    Russia (east), Latvia (south)
POPULATION – 1,530,000 (1997 UN estimate): 64.6 per
    cent Estonian, 28.5 per cent Russian, 2.6 per cent
    Ukrainian, 1.5 per cent Belarusian, 0.7 per cent Finnish,
    others 1.9 per cent. The majority religion is Lutheran,
    with Russian Orthodox and Baptist minorities. Estonian
    is the first language of 64.2 per cent and Russian of 28.7
    per cent
CAPITAL – Tallinn (population, 447,672, 1993 estimate)
MAJOR TOWNS AND CITIES – Kohtla-Järve (53,485);
    Narva (75,211); Tartu (101,901)
CURRENCY – Kroon of 100 sents
NATIONAL ANTHEM – Mu Isamaa, mu õnn ja rõõm (My
    Native Land, My Joy, Delight)
NATIONAL DAY – 24 February (Independence Day)
NATIONAL FLAG – Three horizontal stripes of blue, black,
    white
LIFE EXPECTANCY (years) – male 64.05; female 75.03
POPULATION GROWTH RATE – −0.5 per cent (1995)
POPULATION DENSITY – 34 per sq. km (1995)
URBAN POPULATION – 70.4 per cent (1993)
MILITARY EXPENDITURE – 2.4 per cent of GDP (1996)
MILITARY PERSONNEL – 3,510: Army 3,350, Navy 160
CONSCRIPTION DURATION – 12 months

Estonia includes 1,500 islands in the Baltic Sea and the
Gulf of Riga. Forests cover roughly 20 per cent of the
country, which also has many lakes. The climate is mild
and maritime.

HISTORY AND POLITICS

Estonia, a former province of the Russian Empire, declared
its independence on 24 February 1918. A war of independence was fought against the German army until November 1918, and then against Soviet forces until the peace
treaty of Tartu was signed in 1920. By this treaty the Soviet
Union recognized Estonia's independence.

The Soviet Union annexed Estonia in 1940 under the
terms of the Molotov-Ribbentrop pact with Germany.
Estonia was occupied when Germany invaded the Soviet
Union during the Second World War. In 1944 the Soviet
Union recaptured the country from Germany and con-
firmed its annexation.

The Estonian Supreme Soviet in November 1989
declared the republic to be sovereign and its 1940 annexation by the Soviet Union to be illegal. In February 1990 the
leading role of the Communist Party was abolished, and
following multiparty elections in March 1990 a period of
transition to independence was inaugurated. Independence was declared on 20 August 1991.

Presidential and legislative elections were held in
September 1992 on the basis of special provisions different
from the 1992 constitution. The president was directly
elected for a four-year term and the Riigikogu for a three-
year term. A radical right-wing coalition government was
elected which held power until September 1994. At the
legislative election of March 1995 a centre-left government of the Coalition Party and Rural People's Union
(KMÜ) and the Centre Party was formed; the government
collapsed in October 1995. A new coalition government
formed by the KMÜ and the Reform Party (AP) lasted
until the withdrawal of the Reform Party in November
1996, after which the KMÜ formed a minority government.

POLITICAL SYSTEM

Legislative power is exercised by the unicameral *Riigikogu*
of 101 members elected by proportional representation
every four years. The president is elected for a five-year
term by the Riigikogu by a two-thirds majority or, if no
candidate receives this majority after three rounds of
voting, by an electoral body composed of Riigikogu
members and local government officials. Executive authority is vested in a prime minister who is nominated by
the president and who forms a government. Members of
the government need not be members of the Riigikogu.

Estonia is divided into 46 towns and 15 districts for local
administration purposes.

HEAD OF STATE
President, Lennart Meri, *elected* 5 October 1992, *re-elected* 20
    September 1996

GOVERNMENT *as at July 1998*
Prime Minister, Mart Siimann (KMÜ)
Agriculture, Andres Varik (KMÜ)
Culture, Jaak Allik (KMÜ)
Defence, Andrus Öövel (Ind.)
Economics, Jaak Leimann (Ind.)
Education, Mait Klaassen (Ind.)
Environment, Villu Reiljan (KMÜ)
Finance, Mart Opmann (KMÜ)
Foreign Affairs, Toomas Hendrik Ilves (Ind.)
Interior, Olari Taal (Ind.)
Justice, Paul Varul (KMÜ)
Social Affairs, Tiiu Aro (KMÜ)
Transport and Communications, Raivo Vare (Ind.)
Without Portfolio, Peep Aru (KMÜ); Andra Veidemann (AP)

EMBASSY OF THE REPUBLIC OF ESTONIA
16 Hyde Park Gate, London SW7 5DG
Tel 0171-589 3428
Ambassador Extraordinary and Plenipotentiary, HE Raul Mälk,
    apptd 1996

BRITISH EMBASSY
Kentmanni 20, Tallinn EE0100
Tel: Tallinn 631 3353
Ambassador Extraordinary and Plenipotentiary, HE Timothy
   Craddock, apptd 1997

ECONOMY

Since 1992 the government has introduced free-market reforms, privatization and restructuring. Privatization has gained momentum with foreign direct investment quadrupling in 1994. Estonia is still dependent on Russian natural gas supplies.

Agriculture and dairy-farming are a major sector of the economy, the main products being rye, oats, barley, flax, potatoes, meat, milk, butter and eggs.

Light industry is the other major sector, concentrating on textiles, clothing and footwear, forestry, wood and paper products, and food and fish processing. Some heavy industry exists, mostly chemicals and the manufacture of power equipment.

The kroon is pegged to the Deutsche Mark.

GNP – US$4,509 million (1996); US$3,080 per capita (1996)

GDP – US$85,956 million (1994); US$1,510 per capita (1994)

ANNUAL AVERAGE GROWTH OF GDP – 2.9 per cent (1995)

INFLATION RATE – 23.1 per cent (1996)

UNEMPLOYMENT – 8.9 per cent (1994)

TOTAL EXTERNAL DEBT – US$405 million (1996). The IMF approved a stand-by credit of US$22 million in December 1997

TRADE

Although Estonia signed a free trade deal with Russia in 1992, it has greatly reduced its trade with the former Soviet states. In 1994 over 70 per cent of trade was with EU and EFTA states and Estonia's trade rose by 50 per cent. Free trade and association agreements with the EU came into effect in 1995; Estonia has a partnership agreement with the EU with a view to becoming a full member at a future date.

In 1996 there was a trade deficit of US$1,058 million and a current account deficit of US$447 million. Imports totalled US$3,188 million and exports US$2,043 million.

Trade with UK	1996	1997
Imports from UK	£55,421,000	£63,728,000
Exports to UK	144,150,000	154,680,000

COMMUNICATIONS

Freedom of the press is guaranteed in the constitution, and the state monopoly on television and radio ended soon after independence. All newspapers have been privatized and broadcasting channels are in the process of being privatized. Russian-language news and programmes are provided on Estonian Television. There are five Estonian- and three Russian-language daily newspapers.

EDUCATION

Estonia has a three-tier education system, consisting of primary level (four years), secondary level (six years) and university level (four to six years). Primary- and secondary-level education is compulsory.

ILLITERACY RATE – 0.2 per cent

ENROLMENT (percentage of age group) – primary 94 per cent (1995); secondary 77 per cent (1995); tertiary 38.1 per cent (1995)

ETHIOPIA
Federal Democratic Republic of Ethiopia

AREA – 426,373 sq. miles (1,104,300 sq. km). Neighbours: Sudan (west), Kenya (south), Djibouti and Somalia (east), Eritrea (north)

POPULATION – 56,677,000 (1994 UN estimate). About one-third are of Semitic origin (Amharas and Tigreans) and the remainder mainly Oromos (40 per cent), Somalis (6 per cent) and Afar (4 per cent). Amharas, Tigreans and many Oromos are Ethiopian Orthodox Christians. The Afar people in the north and the Somalis in the southeast, as well as some Oromos, are Muslim. Amharic is the most widely used of the 70 languages

CAPITAL – Addis Ababa (population, 2,316,400, 1994 estimate)

MAJOR CITIES – Dire Dawa (population, 194,587, 1994 estimate)

CURRENCY – Ethiopian birr (EB) of 100 cents

NATIONAL ANTHEM – Ityopya, Ityopya Kidemi

NATIONAL DAY – 28 May

NATIONAL FLAG – Three horizontal bands: green, yellow, red; in the centre a blue disc, containing a yellow pentagram

LIFE EXPECTANCY (years) – male 45.93; female 49.06

POPULATION GROWTH RATE – 3.2 per cent (1995)

POPULATION DENSITY – 51 per sq. km (1995)

URBAN POPULATION – 15.3 per cent (1995)

MILITARY EXPENDITURE – 2.0 per cent of GDP (1996)

HISTORY AND POLITICS

The Hamitic culture was heavily influenced by Semitic immigration from Arabia at about the time of Christ. Christianity was introduced in the fourth century. The empire attained its zenith in the sixth century under the Axum rulers but was checked by Islamic expansion from the east. Modern Ethiopia dates from 1855 when Theodore established supremacy over the various tribes. The last emperor was Haile Selassie who reigned from 1930 until 1974, when he was deposed by the armed forces. After ten years of military rule, a Workers' Party on the Soviet model was formed with Lt.-Col. Mengistu Haile Mariam as General Secretary. The People's Democratic Republic of Ethiopia was established under a new constitution in 1987 with Lt.-Col. Mengistu as president. Armed insurgencies by the Eritrean People's Liberation Front (EPLF) and the Ethiopian People's Revolutionary Democratic Front (EPRDF), originating in Tigre, brought down Mengistu's government in May 1991.

A transitional administration comprising the EPRDF and other opposition groups formed a Council of Representatives which governed until 1995 under President Meles Zenawi. In 1994, the Council agreed on a draft federal constitution which was adopted by an elected Constituent Assembly on 8 December 1994. Multiparty elections in May and June 1995 were won by the EPRDF, which gained 80 per cent of the seats in the newly-created 526-seat Council of People's Representatives; a 117-member Federal Council to represent the 22 ethnic groups was also created. The Council of People's Representatives elected Dr Negaso Gidada to the non-executive office of president and Meles Zenawi as prime minister. The Federal Democratic Republic of Ethiopia was proclaimed on 22 August 1995.

FOREIGN RELATIONS

Eritrea, which since 1962 had been a province of Ethiopia, seceded and became independent on 24 May 1993. Relations between the two countries had been good until fighting broke out along the border in June 1998, with each side accusing the other of sending troops across the border. American and Italian mediators are attempting to resolve the dispute peacefully.

POLITICAL SYSTEM

The constitution provides for a federal government responsible for foreign affairs, defence and economic policy, and for nine regional administrations (Tigre, Afar, Amara, Oromia, Somai, Benshangui, Gambela, Harer and Southern), with a degree of autonomy and the right to secede.

HEAD OF STATE

President, Dr Negaso Gidada, *elected by the Council of People's Representatives* 22 August 1995

COUNCIL OF MINISTERS *as at July 1998*

Prime Minister, Meles Zenawi
Deputy PMs, Tefera Walwa *(Defence)*; Kassu Ylala *(Economic Affairs)*
Agriculture, Seifu Ketema
Commerce and Industry, Kasahun Ayele
Economic Development and Co-operation, Giram Biru
Education, Genet Zewdie
Finance, Sufyan Ahmad
Foreign Affairs, Seyoum Mesfin
Health, Adem Ibrahim
Information and Culture, Wolde Mikael Chamo
Justice, Werede Woldemichael
Mines and Energy, Ezedin Ali
Revenue Collectors' Board, Desta Amare
Speaker, Council of People's Representatives, Davit Yohanes
Transport and Communications, Abdulmejid Hussein
Water Resources, Shiferaw Jarso
Works and Urban Development, Haile Asegde

EMBASSY OF ETHIOPIA

17 Prince's Gate, London SW7 1PZ
Tel 0171-589 7212/3/4/5
Ambassador Extraordinary and Plenipotentiary, HE Dr Solomon Gidada, apptd 1992
Counsellor, Osman Yemam (*Commercial*)

BRITISH EMBASSY

Fikre Mariam Abatechan Street (PO Box 858), Addis Ababa
Tel: Addis Ababa 161 2354
Ambassador Extraordinary and Plenipotentiary, HE Gordon Wetherell, apptd 1997
Deputy Head of Mission and First Secretary, C. O. Pigott

BRITISH COUNCIL REPRESENTATIVE, M. Sargent, OBE, Artistic Building, Adwa Avenue (PO Box 1043), Addis Ababa

ECONOMY

The post-Mengistu government implemented a programme of free-market economic reform which reduced government spending and inflation. The currency was devalued, the civil service reduced and the army cut by two-thirds. Western states have responded with debt relief and loans. An agreement waiving customs levies was concluded with Eritrea in April 1995.

Agriculture accounts for approximately 50 per cent of GDP and employs around 80 per cent of the workforce. The major food crops are teff, maize, barley, sorghum, wheat, pulses and oil seeds. Famine conditions in 1984–5 recurred to a lesser extent in 1992 and 1997. However, agricultural liberalization has led to dramatic progress in food production.

Manufacturing industry accounts for less than 9 per cent of GDP and is heavily dependent on agriculture. Ethiopia's known, but as yet largely unexploited, natural resources include gold, platinum, copper and potash. Traces of oil and natural gas have been found.

In 1996 there was a trade deficit of US$817 million and a current account deficit of US$102 million.
GNP – US$6,042 million (1996); US$100 per capita (1996)
GDP – US$8,941 million (1994); US$96 per capita (1994)
ANNUAL AVERAGE GROWTH OF GDP – –6.0 per cent (1991)
INFLATION RATE – –5.1 per cent (1996)
TOTAL EXTERNAL DEBT – US$10,077 million (1996)

TRADE

The chief imports by value are machinery and transport equipment, manufactured goods and chemicals; the principal exports by value are coffee, oil seeds, hides and skins, and pulses.

Trade with UK	1996	1997
Imports from UK	£49,377,000	£58,070,000
Exports to UK	26,260,000	16,686,000

COMMUNICATIONS

A network of roads in rural areas links the major cities with each other, with the Sudanese and Kenyan borders and through Eritrea to the Red Sea coast.

There is a railway link from Addis Ababa to Djibouti. Ethiopian Airlines maintains regular services from Addis Ababa to many provincial towns, throughout Africa and to Europe.

EDUCATION

Elementary and secondary education are provided by government schools in the main centres of population; there are also mission schools. The National University (founded 1961) co-ordinates the institutions of higher education. There is a separate university at Alemaya (agricultural).
ILLITERACY RATE – 64.5 per cent
ENROLMENT (percentage of age group) – primary 24 per cent (1994); tertiary 0.7 per cent (1994)

FIJI

Matanitu Ko Viti – Republic of Fiji

AREA – 7,056 sq. miles (18,274 sq. km)
POPULATION – 796,000 (1994 UN estimate), 715,373 (1986 census): 48.6 per cent Indians, 46.2 per cent Fijians, and 5.2 per cent other races. Since the 1987 coup many ethnic Indians have left and by 1994 Melanesian Fijians formed the largest population group. The main languages are Fijian and Hindi
CAPITAL – Ψ Suva (population, 141,273, 1986), on the island of Viti Levu
CURRENCY – Fiji dollar (F$) of 100 cents
NATIONAL ANTHEM – God Bless Fiji
NATIONAL DAY – 10 October (Fiji Day)
NATIONAL FLAG – Light blue ground with Union flag in top left quarter and the shield of Fiji in the fly
LIFE EXPECTANCY (years) – male 60.72; female 63.87
POPULATION GROWTH RATE – 1.7 per cent (1995)

Population Density – 44 per sq. km (1995)
Urban Population – 38.7 per cent (1987)
Military Expenditure – 2.3 per cent of GDP (1996)
Military Personnel – 3,600: Army 3,300, Navy 300
Illiteracy Rate – 8.4 per cent
Enrolment (percentage of age group) – primary 99 per
cent (1992); tertiary 11.9 per cent (1991)

Fiji is composed of roughly 332 islands (about 100 permanently inhabited) and over 500 islets in the South Pacific, about 1,100 miles north of New Zealand. The group extends 300 miles from east to west and 300 miles north to south. The International Date Line has been diverted to the east of the island group. The largest islands are Viti Levu and Vanua Levu. The main groups of islands are Lomaiviti, Lau and Yasawas. The climate is tropical without extremes of heat.

HISTORY AND POLITICS

Fiji was a British colony from 1874 until 10 October 1970 when it became an independent state and a member of the Commonwealth.

A coalition under Dr Timoci Bavadra won a general election in April 1987, but was overthrown by the military on 14 May by Lt.-Col. Sitiveni Rabuka. An Advisory Council was set up as an interim government, but it too was overthrown on 25 September 1987. On 7 October Rabuka declared Fiji a republic; the Governor-General resigned on 15 October; Fiji's Commonwealth membership lapsed and another interim government was formed.

The constitution was changed in 1990 to give greater power to indigenous Melanesian Fijians at the expense of the Indian community. The Fijian Political Party led by Rabuka won the general elections in May 1992 and February 1994 and has formed a coalition government. Following constitutional reform in July 1997, Fiji was readmitted to the Commonwealth on 1 October 1997.

POLITICAL SYSTEM

The 1990 constitution was reformed in July 1997 to reduce the political dominance of Melanesians within the government. The parliament is bicameral; the upper house or Senate has 32 members appointed by the president, of which 14 seats are reserved for Melanesian Fijians, one for the Polynesian island of Rotuma and nine for other races. The House of Representatives has 71 seats, of which 23 are reserved for Melanesians, 19 for Indians, one for Rotuma, and three for other races. The president is elected by the (Melanesian) Great Council of Chiefs, and appoints a prime minister who must establish a multiparty government.

HEAD OF STATE

President, Ratu Sir Kamisese Mara, *inaugurated* 18 January 1994

CABINET *as at July 1998*

Prime Minister, Constitution Review, Multi-ethnic Affairs, Regional Development, Maj.-Gen. Sitiveni Rabuka
Deputy Prime Minister, Education and Technology, Taufa Vakatale
Agriculture, Fisheries and Forestry, Militoni Leweniqila
Attorney-General, Ratu Eruate Tavai
Commerce, Industry, Co-operatives and Public Enterprises, Isimeli Bose
Communications, Public Works and Energy, Ratu Inoke Kubuabola
Fijian Affairs and the Agricultural Landlords and Tenants Act, Ratu Finau Mara
Finance and Economic Planning, James Ah Koy

Foreign Affairs and External Trade, Berenado Vunibobo
Health and Social Welfare, Leo Smith
Home Affairs, Justice and Immigration, Col. Paul Manueli
Information, Women and Culture, Seruwaia Hong Tiy
Labour and Industrial Relations, Vincent Lobendahn
Lands and Mining, Ratu Timoci Vesikula
National Planning, Filipe Bole
Transport and Tourism, David Pickering
Urban Development, Housing and Environment, Vilisoni Cagimaivei
Youth, Employment Opportunities and Sport, Jonetani Kaukimoce

Embassy of the Republic of Fiji
34 Hyde Park Gate, London sw7 5DN
Tel 0171-584 3661
Ambassador Extraordinary and Plenipotentiary, HE Filimone Jitoko, apptd 1996

British Embassy
Victoria House, 47 Gladstone Road, PO Box 1355, Suva
Tel: Suva 311033
Ambassador Extraordinary and Plenipotentiary, HE Michael Dibben, apptd 1997

ECONOMY

The economy is primarily agrarian. The principal cash crop is sugar cane, which is the main export, followed by coconuts, ginger and copra. A variety of other fruit, vegetables and root crops are also grown, and self-sufficiency in rice is a major aim. Forestry, fishing and beef production are being encouraged in order to diversify the economy. The processing of agricultural, marine and timber products are the main industries, along with gold mining and textiles. Tourism is second only to sugar as a money-earner.

In January 1998 the Reserve Bank of Fiji devalued the Fijian dollar by 20 per cent in response to poor growth in 1997 and anxieties about the Asian financial crisis.

GNP – US$1,983 million (1996); US$2,470 per capita (1996)
GDP – US$1,466 million (1994); US$2,369 per capita (1994)
Annual Average Growth of GDP – 6.7 per cent (1990)
Inflation Rate – 3.1 per cent (1996)
Unemployment – 5.4 per cent (1995)
Total External Debt – US$217 million (1996)

TRADE

The chief imports are foodstuffs, machinery, mineral fuels, chemicals, beverages, tobacco and manufactured articles. Chief exports are sugar, coconut oil, fish, lumber, molasses and ginger.

In 1996 there was a trade deficit of US$182 million and a current account surplus of US$10 million. Imports totalled US$980 million and exports US$745 million.

Trade with UK	1996	1997
Imports from UK	£7,362,000	£10,560,000
Exports to UK	89,508,000	60,281,000

COMMUNICATIONS

Fiji is one of the main aerial crossroads in the Pacific, providing services to New Zealand, Australia, Tonga, Western Samoa, Vanuatu, the Solomon Islands, Kiribati, Tuvalu, New Caledonia and American Samoa. Fiji has three ports of entry, at Suva, Lautoka and Levuka. There are 5,100 km of roads.

FINLAND
Suomen Tasavalta

AREA – 130,559 sq. miles (338,145 sq. km). Neighbours: Norway (north-west and north), Russia (east), Sweden (west)
POPULATION – 5,108,000 (1994 UN estimate). Finnish and Swedish are both official languages, 93.6 per cent speaking Finnish as their first language and 6.2 per cent Swedish. Lapp is spoken by the 2,500 Lapps who live in the far north. The population is predominantly Lutheran
CAPITAL – ΨHelsinki (Helsingfors) (population, 1,016,291, 1993 estimate)
MAJOR CITIES – Espoo (Esbo) (200,834); ΨOulu (Oleåborg) (113,567); Tampere (Tammerfors) (188,726); ΨTurku (Åbo) (168,772); Vantaa (Vanda) (171,297), 1997 estimates
CURRENCY – Markka (Mk) of 100 penniä
NATIONAL DAY – 6 December (Independence Day)
NATIONAL FLAG – White with blue cross
LIFE EXPECTANCY (years) – male 72.82; female 80.15
POPULATION GROWTH RATE – 0.5 per cent (1995)
POPULATION DENSITY – 15 per sq. km (1995)
URBAN POPULATION – 64.2 per cent (1994)

The Åland archipelago (Ahvenanmaa), a group of small islands at the entrance to the Gulf of Bothnia, covers about 572 square miles, with a population (1994) of 25,158 (95.2 per cent Swedish-speaking). The islands have semi-autonomous status.

HISTORY AND POLITICS

Finland was part of the Swedish Empire from the Middle Ages until it was ceded to Russia in 1809 and became an autonomous grand duchy of the Russian Empire. Finland became independent after the Russian revolution of 1917, but was forced to cede around one-tenth of its land to the Soviet Union and to resettle 10 per cent of its population under the Treaty of Paris (1947). A Soviet-Finnish Co-operation Treaty forced Finland to demilitarize its Soviet border, to enter into a barter trade agreement and to adopt a stance of neutrality. These terms lasted until the demise of the Soviet Union in 1991.

The present government took office in April 1995. The five parties in the ruling coalition are the Social Democratic Party, the National Coalition Party (conservative), the Left-wing Alliance, the Swedish People's Party, and the Greens, with a total of 145 out of 200 seats.

Finland joined the European Union on 1 January 1995 following a referendum in October 1994 in which accession was approved by 57 per cent in Finland and by 74 per cent in a separate Åland Islands referendum.

POLITICAL SYSTEM

Under the constitution there is a unicameral legislature, the *Eduskunta*, composed of 200 members elected by universal suffrage for a four-year term. The highest executive power is held by the president who is directly elected for a period of six years. The first direct elections for the presidency were held in 1994, the president having previously been elected by an electoral college.

HEAD OF STATE
President, Martti Ahtisaari, *inaugurated* 1 March 1994

CABINET *as at July 1998*
Prime Minister, Paavo Lipponen (SDP)
Deputy PM, Finance, Sauli Niinistö (NCP)
Administrative Affairs, Jouni Backman (SDP)
Agriculture and Forestry, Kalevi Hemilä (Ind.)
Culture, Youth, Universities, Science, Outi Siimes (LA)
Defence, Anneli Taina (NCP)
Education, Olli-Pekka Heinonen (NCP)
Environment, Development Co-operation, Pekka Haavisto (Greens)
European Affairs and Foreign Trade, Ole Norrback (SPP)
Finance, PM's Office (Planning), Jouko Skinnari (SDP)
Foreign Affairs, Tarja Halonen (SDP)
Interior, Jan-Erik Enestam (SPP)
Justice, Jussi Järventaus (NCP)
Labour, Liisa Jaakonsaari (SDP)
Social Affairs and Health, Housing and Building, Sinikka Mönkäre (SDP)
Social and Health Services, Equality Affairs, Labour Protection, Terttu Huttu-Juntunen (LA)
Trade and Industry, Antti Kalliomäki (SDP)
Transport, Matti Aura (NCP)

SDP Social Democratic Party; NCP National Coalition Party; LA Left-wing Alliance; SPP Swedish People's Party

EMBASSY OF FINLAND
38 Chesham Place, London SW1X 8HW
Tel 0171-838 6200
Ambassador Extraordinary and Plenipotentiary, HE Pertti Salolainen, apptd 1996
Minister, Kirsti Eskelinen
Counsellor (Commercial), Marcus Moberg
Defence Attaché, Col. Ilpo Eerik Bergholm

BRITISH EMBASSY
Itäinen Puistotie 17, 00140 Helsinki
Tel: Helsinki 2286 5100
Ambassador Extraordinary and Plenipotentiary, HE Gavin Hewitt, CMG, apptd 1997
Deputy Head of Mission and Counsellor, D. J. Gowan
First Secretary (Commercial), H. B. Formstone, OBE
Defence Attaché, Lt.-Col. G. A. Grant

BRITISH CONSULAR OFFICES – Helsinki, Jyväskylä, Kotka, Kuopio, Oulu, Pori, Tampere, Turku, Vaasa, Mariehamn

BRITISH COUNCIL REPRESENTATIVE, Tuija Talvitie, Hakaniemenkatu 2, 00530 Helsinki

DEFENCE

The Army has 196 main battle tanks, 1,063 armoured infantry fighting vehicles and armoured personnel carriers, and 1,008 artillery pieces. The Navy has 14 patrol and coastal vessels. The Air Force has 98 combat aircraft.
MILITARY EXPENDITURE – 1.8 per cent of GDP (1996)
MILITARY PERSONNEL – 31,000: Army 27,000, Navy 2,100, Air Force 1,900
CONSCRIPTION DURATION – Eight to 11 months

ECONOMY

Finland produces a wide range of capital and consumer goods. Metal-working, electronics and engineering now account for around half of exports, and timber and timber-based products account for a third. The glass, ceramics and furniture industries enjoy international reputations. Other important industries are mobile phones, rubber, plastics, chemicals and pharmaceuticals, footwear, foodstuffs and shipbuilding.

The markka joined the ERM in August 1996, and on 1 May 1998 it was announced that Finland had satisfied the convergence criteria and would be one of the 11 countries to participate in the European Single Currency from January 1999.

In 1997 the budget deficit was equivalent to 4.5 per cent of GDP, and public debt was 67.7 per cent of GDP.

GNP – US$119,086 million (1996); US$23,240 per capita (1996)

GDP – US$123,720 million (1994); US$19,048 per capita (1994)

ANNUAL AVERAGE GROWTH OF GDP – 3.7 per cent (1996); estimated to be 4.1 per cent in 1997

INFLATION RATE – 0.6 per cent (1996); estimated to be 2.0 per cent in 1997

UNEMPLOYMENT – 17.4 per cent (1995); estimated to be 15.3 per cent in 1997

TRADE

The principal imports are raw materials, machinery and manufactured goods. The barter-trade relationship with the former Soviet Union collapsed in 1991 and exports to the countries of the former Soviet Union fell from 20 per cent of the total in the early 1980s to 5 per cent in 1994. Trade with EU countries accounts for more than half of Finland's total trade.

In 1996 there was a trade surplus of US$10,946 million and a current account surplus of US$4,178 million. Imports totalled US$29,264 million and exports US$38,435 million.

Trade with UK	1996	1997
Imports from UK	£1,729,300,000	£1,485,300,000
Exports to UK	2,467,600,000	2,449,000,000

COMMUNICATIONS

There are 9,000 km of railroad, railway connections with Sweden and Russia, and passenger boat connections with Sweden, Germany, Poland, Russia and the Baltic states. There are also passenger/cargo services between Britain and Helsinki, Kotka and other Finnish ports. External air services are maintained by most European airlines.

CULTURE AND EDUCATION

Newspapers, books, plays and films appear in both Finnish and Swedish. There is a vigorous modern literature. F. E. Sillanpää, who died in 1964, was awarded the Nobel Prize for Literature in 1939. In 1995 there were 56 daily newspapers.

Primary education (co-educational comprehensive school) is free and compulsory for children from seven to 16 years.

ENROLMENT (percentage of age group) – primary 99 per cent (1994); secondary 93 per cent (1994); tertiary 66.9 per cent (1994)

FRANCE
La République Française

AREA – 212,935 sq. miles (551,500 sq. km). Neighbours: Belgium and Luxembourg (north-east), Germany, Switzerland and Italy (east), Spain and Andorra (south-west)

POPULATION – 58,143,000 (1994 UN estimate); 57,218,000 (Metropolitan France), and 58,745,000 including overseas departments (1992 official estimate): 72 per cent Catholic, 8 per cent Muslim, 2 per cent

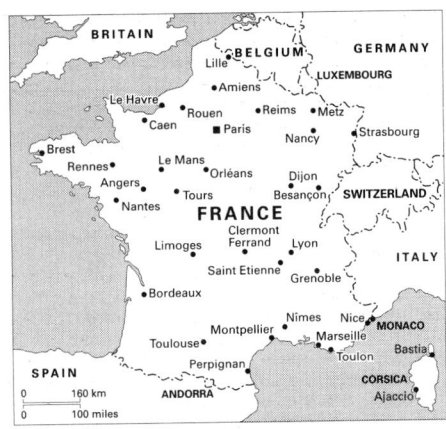

Jewish. The language is French; there are several regional dialects including Basque and Breton

CAPITAL – Paris (population, 9,319,367, 1990), on the Seine

MAJOR CITIES – ΨBordeaux (696,819); Grenoble (404,837); Lille (959,433); Lyon (1,262,342); ΨMarseille (1,230,871); Nantes (495,229); Nice (517,291); Strasbourg (388,466); Toulon (437,825); Toulouse (650,311). The chief towns of Corsica are ΨAjaccio (58,315) and ΨBastia (52,446)

CURRENCY – Franc of 100 centimes

NATIONAL ANTHEM – La Marseillaise

NATIONAL DAY – 14 July (Bastille Day 1789)

NATIONAL FLAG – The tricolour, three vertical bands, blue, white, red (blue next to flagstaff)

LIFE EXPECTANCY (years) – male 72.94; female 81.15

POPULATION GROWTH RATE – 0.5 per cent (1995)

POPULATION DENSITY – 105 per sq. km (1995)

URBAN POPULATION – 73.9 per cent (1992)

HISTORY AND POLITICS

There are dolmens and menhirs in Brittany, prehistoric remains and cave drawings in Dordogne and Ariège, and throughout France various megalithic monuments erected by primitive tribes, predecessors of Iberian invaders from Spain (now represented by the Basques), Ligurians from northern Italy and Celts or Gauls from the valley of the Danube. Julius Caesar found Gaul 'divided into three parts' and described three political groups: Aquitanians south of the Garonne, Celts between the Garonne and the Seine and Marne, and Belgae from the Seine to the Rhine. Roman remains are plentiful throughout France in the form of aqueducts, arenas, triumphal arches, etc. The celebrated Norman and Gothic cathedrals, including Notre Dame in Paris and those of Chartres, Reims, Amiens, Bourges, Beauvais, Rouen, etc., have survived invasions and bombardments with only partial damage, and many of the Renaissance and the 17th- and 18th-century chateaux survived the French Revolution.

The state of the parties in the Senate at August 1996 was: Rassemblement pour la République (RPR) 102; Socialist Party (PS) 78; Centrist Union (UDC) 64; Republican and Independent Union (RI) 47; Democratic and European Rally (RDE) 26; Communists (PCF) 15; Independents 9.

In the last elections to the National Assembly in May and June 1997 the PS won 241 seats, the Gaullist RPR 134, Union pour la Démocratie Française (UDF) 108, PCF 38, Independent Left 21, Independent Right 14, Radical

Socialist Party 12, Green Party 7, National Front 1, Independent 1.

POLITICAL SYSTEM

The legislature consists of the National Assembly of 577 deputies (555 for Metropolitan France and 22 for the overseas departments and territories) and the Senate of 321 Senators (296 for Metropolitan France, 13 for the overseas departments and territories and 12 for French citizens abroad). Deputies in the National Assembly are directly elected for a five-year term. One-third of the Senate is indirectly elected every three years.

The prime minister is appointed by the president, as is the Council of Ministers on the prime minister's recommendation. They are responsible to the legislature, but as the executive is constitutionally separate from the legislature, ministers may not sit in the legislature and must hand over their seats to a substitute.

France is divided into 95 departments, including the island of Corsica, in the Mediterranean off the west coast of Italy.

HEAD OF STATE
President of the French Republic, Jacques Chirac, *elected* 7 May 1995, *took office* 17 May 1995

COUNCIL OF MINISTERS *as at July 1998*
Prime Minister, Lionel Jospin
Agriculture and Fisheries, Louis Le Pensec
Capital Works, Transport and Housing, Jean-Claude Gayssot
Civil Service, Administrative Reform and Decentralization, Emile Zuccarelli
Culture and Communications, Catherine Trautmann
Defence, Alain Richard
Economy, Finance and Industry, Dominique Strauss-Kahn
Employment and Solidarity, Martine Aubry
Foreign Affairs, Hubert Vedrine
Interior, Jean-Pierre Chevènement
Justice, Keeper of the Seals, Elisabeth Guigou
National Education, Research and Technology, Claude Allegre
Relations with Parliament, Daniel Vaillant
Town and Country Planning and the Environment, Dominique Voynet
Youth and Sport, Marie-George Buffet

President of the Senate, René Monory
President of the National Assembly, Laurent Fabius

FRENCH EMBASSY
58 Knightsbridge, London SW1X 7JT
Tel 0171-201 1000
Ambassador Extraordinary and Plenipotentiary, new appointment awaited
Minister-Counsellor, G. Keller
Defence Attaché, Contre-Amiral J. Gheerbrant
Cultural Counsellor, O. Poivre D'Arvor
Minister-Counsellor (Economic and Commercial Affairs), O. Louis

BRITISH EMBASSY
35 rue du Faubourg St Honoré, 75383 Paris Cedex 08
Tel: Paris 4451 3100
Ambassador Extraordinary and Plenipotentiary, HE Sir Michael Jay, KCMG, apptd 1996
Minister, S. F. Howarth
Defence and Air Attaché, Air Cdre D. N. Adams
Counsellor, V. Caton (*Finance and Economic*)
First Secretary and Consul-General, K. C. Moss

BRITISH CONSULAR OFFICES – Amiens, Biarritz, Bordeaux, Boulogne, Calais, Cherbourg, Dunkirk, Le Havre, Lille, Lyon, Marseille, Montpellier, Nantes, Nice, Paris, Perpignan, St Malo, Toulouse; overseas in

Cayenne (French Guiana), Papeete (French Polynesia), Fort de France (Martinique), Pointe à Pitre (Guadeloupe) and St Denis (Réunion)
BRITISH COUNCIL DIRECTOR, C. Gamble, 9/11 rue de Constantine, 75007 Paris
FRANCO-BRITISH CHAMBER OF COMMERCE, 8 rue Cimarosa, 75116 Paris. *President,* R. Lyon. *Vice-President,* B. Cordery, OBE

DEFENCE

The Army has 768 main battle tanks, 4,533 armoured personnel carriers and armoured infantry fighting vehicles, 1,081 artillery pieces, seven aircraft and 508 helicopters.

The Navy has 14 submarines, two aircraft carriers, one cruiser, four destroyers, 35 frigates and 36 patrol and coastal vessels, 69 combat aircraft and 25 armed helicopters. The Navy has four domestic and five overseas bases.

The Air Force has 505 combat aircraft including 45 short-range nuclear attack aircraft and 15 strategic bombers, and 18 intermediate-range ballistic missiles.

France deploys 44,083 armed forces personnel abroad; 11,700 in Germany; 20,300 in French Overseas Departments and Territories; 7,900 in former French colonies in Africa; and 4,183 on UN and peacekeeping duties.
MILITARY EXPENDITURE – 3.1 per cent of GDP (1996)
MILITARY PERSONNEL – 469,320: Army 219,900, Strategic Nuclear Forces 10,400, Navy 63,300, Air Force 83,420, Paramilitaries 92,300
CONSCRIPTION DURATION – Ten to 24 months. Conscription is to be phased out over six years, beginning in 1997

ECONOMY

Viniculture is extensive, regions famous for their wines including Bordeaux, Burgundy and Champagne. Production of wine in 1995 was 5,300,000 tonnes. Cognac, liqueurs and cider are also important products.

Oil is produced from fields in the Landes area, but France is a net importer of crude oil, for processing by its important oil-refining industry. Natural gas is produced in the foothills of the Pyrenees.

Heavy industries include oil-refining and the production of iron and steel, and aluminium. In 1995 production of pig iron was 13,154,000 tonnes and steel 18,104,000 tonnes. Other important industries produce chemicals, tyres, aluminium, textiles, paper products and processed food. Engineering products include motor vehicles, and television and radio sets.

In 1993 the government announced the privatization of most public sector companies, which was expected to generate F300,000 million over five years.

The Banque de France was made independent in 1994 with the formation of a nine-member monetary policy council to define and implement monetary policy independent of the government.

In 1995–6, the government introduced austerity measures to enable France to meet the Maastricht criteria for European monetary union. Cost-cutting reforms targeted the welfare budget, provoking a series of strikes by public-sector workers in December 1995 and early 1996. On 1 May 1998 it was announced that, having satisfied the convergence criteria, France would be one of the 11 states to participate in the European Single Currency from January 1999.
GNP – US$1,533,619 million (1996); US$26,270 per capita (1996)
GDP – US$1,241,147 million (1994); US$24,608 per capita (1994)

ANNUAL AVERAGE GROWTH OF GDP – 1.5 per cent (1996); forecast to be 2.4 per cent in 1997

INFLATION RATE – 2.0 per cent (1996); forecast to be 1.6 per cent in 1997

UNEMPLOYMENT – 11.6 per cent (1995); forecast to be 12.1 per cent in 1997

TRADE

The principal imports are raw materials for the heavy and manufacturing industries (e.g. oil, minerals, chemicals), machinery and precision instruments, agricultural products, chemicals and vehicles. Raw materials, semi-manufactured and manufactured goods, chemicals and vehicles are also the principal exports. Most of France's trade is done with other EU countries.

In 1996 there was a trade surplus of US$15,099 million and a current account surplus of US$20,511 million. Imports totalled US$276,053 million and exports US$289,614 million.

Trade with UK	1996	1997
Imports from UK	£16,190,100,000	£15,721,300,000
Exports to UK	16,624,500,000	16,971,200,000

COMMUNICATIONS

The length of roads in 1996 was 964,356 km, of which 7,396 km were motorways.

The railroad system is extensive. The length of lines open for traffic in 1996 was 31,940 km.

The French mercantile marine consisted in 1995 of 208 ships of a total of 4,300,000 tonnes which transported 91,500,000 tonnes of freight.

CULTURE AND EDUCATION

French is the official language. The work of the French Academy, founded in 1635, has established *le bon usage*, equivalent to 'The Queen's English' in Britain. French authors have been awarded the Nobel Prize for Literature on 12 occasions and include R. F. A. Sully-Prudhomme (1901), Anatole France (1921), André Gide (1947), François Mauriac (1952), Albert Camus (1957), Jean-Paul Sartre (1964) and Claude Simon (1985).

Education is compulsory, free and secular from six to 16. Schools may be single-sex or co-educational. Primary education is given in nursery schools, primary schools and *collèges d'enseignement général* (four-year secondary modern course); secondary education in *collèges d'enseignement technique, collèges d'enseignement secondaire* and *lycées* (seven-year course leading to one of the five *baccalauréats*). Special schools are numerous.

There are many *grandes écoles* in France which award diplomas in many subjects not taught at university, especially applied science and engineering. Most of these are state institutions but have a competitive system of entry, unlike universities. There are universities in 24 towns including 13 in Paris and the immediate area.

In 1993 the government gave German official parity with French in Alsace schools.

ENROLMENT (percentage of age group) – primary 99 per cent (1993); secondary 92 per cent (1993); tertiary 49.6 per cent (1993)

OVERSEAS DEPARTMENTS

Greater powers of self-government were granted to French Guiana, Guadeloupe, Martinique and Réunion in 1982. These former colonies had enjoyed departmental status since 1946 and the status of regions since 1974. Their directly elected Assemblies operate in parallel with the existing, indirectly constituted Regional Councils. The French government is represented by a Prefect in each.

FRENCH GUIANA

AREA – 34,749 sq. miles (90,000 sq. km)

POPULATION – 147,000 (1994)

CAPITAL – ΨCayenne (41,164)

Situated on the north-eastern coast of South America, French Guiana is flanked by Suriname on the west and by Brazil on the south and east. Under the administration of French Guiana is a group of islands (St Joseph, Ile Royal and Ile du Diable), known as Iles du Salut.

Prefect, P. Dartout

Trade with UK	1995	1996
Imports from UK	£3,734,000	£11,713,000
Exports to UK	591,000	1,149,000

GUADELOUPE

AREA – 658 sq. miles (1,705 sq. km)

POPULATION – 428,000 (1994)

CAPITAL – ΨBasse Terre (29,522) on Guadeloupe

A number of islands in the Leeward Islands group of the West Indies, consisting of the two main islands of Guadeloupe (or Basse-Terre) and Grande-Terre, with the adjacent islands of Marie-Galante, La Désirade and Îles des Saintes, and the islands of St Martin and St Barthélemy over 150 miles to the north-west. The main towns are ΨPointe à Pitre (26,000) in Grande-Terre and ΨGrand Bourg (6,611) in Marie-Galante.

Prefect, M. Diefenbacher

Trade with UK	1995	1996
Imports from UK	£6,896,000	£10,029,000
Exports to UK	211,000	68,000

MARTINIQUE

AREA – 425 sq. miles (1,102 sq. km)

POPULATION – 379,000 (1994)

CAPITAL – ΨFort de France (97,814)

An island situated in the Windward Islands group of the West Indies, between Dominica in the north and St Lucia in the south. The main towns are ΨTrinité (11,214) and ΨMarin (6,104).

Prefect, J.-F. Cordet

Trade with UK	1995	1996
Imports from UK	£13,839,000	£16,422,000
Exports to UK	14,000	196,000

RÉUNION

AREA – 969 sq. miles (2,510 sq. km)

POPULATION – 653,000 (1994)

CAPITAL – St Denis (121,999)

Réunion, which became a French possession in 1638, lies in the Indian Ocean, about 569 miles east of Madagascar and 110 miles south-west of Mauritius. Other towns are Saint-Paul (71,669) and Saint-Pierre (58,846). The smaller, uninhabited islands of Bassas da India, Europa, Îles Glorieuses, Juan de Nova and Tromelin are administered from Réunion.

Prefect, H. Fournier

Trade with UK	1995	1996
Imports from UK	£15,345,000	£15,374,000
Exports to UK	2,278,000	2,910,000

TERRITORIAL COLLECTIVITÉS

MAYOTTE

AREA – 144 sq. miles (372 sq. km)
POPULATION – 94,410 (1991 census)
CAPITAL – Mamoudzou (12,000)

Part of the Comoros Islands group, Mayotte remained a French dependency when the other three islands became independent as the Comoros Republic in 1975. Since 1976 the island has been a *collectivité territoriale*, an intermediate status between Overseas Department and Overseas Territory.

Prefect, P. Boisadam

Trade with UK	1996	1997
Imports from UK	£5,823,000	£6,294,000
Exports to UK	447,000	427,000

ST PIERRE AND MIQUELON

AREA – 93 sq. miles (242 sq. km)
POPULATION – 6,000 (1990)
CAPITAL – ΨSt Pierre (5,416)

These two small groups of islands off the coast of Newfoundland became a *collectivité territoriale* in 1985.

Prefect, R. Thuau

Trade with UK	1996	1997
Imports from UK	£1,542,000	£708,000
Exports to UK	—	—

OVERSEAS TERRITORIES

FRENCH POLYNESIA

AREA – 1,544 sq. miles (4,000 sq. km)
POPULATION – 220,000 (1994)
CAPITAL – ΨPapeete (36,784), in Tahiti

Five archipelagos in the south Pacific, comprising the Society Islands (Windward Islands group includes Tahiti, Moorea, Makatea, Mehetia, Tetiaroa, Tubuai Manu; Leeward Islands group includes Huahine, Raiatea, Tahaa, Bora-Bora, Maupiti), the Tuamotu Islands (Rangiroa, Hao, Turéia, etc.), the Gambier Islands (Mangareva, etc.), the Tubuai Islands (Rimatara, Rurutu, Tubuai, Raivavae, Rapa, etc.) and the Marquesas Islands (Nuku-Hiva, Hiva-Oa, Fatu-Hiva, Tahuata, Ua Huka, etc.).

High Commissioner, P. Roncière

Trade with UK	1996	1997
Imports from UK	£6,327,000	£5,622,000
Exports to UK	207,000	124,000

NEW CALEDONIA

AREA – 7,172 sq. miles (18,575 sq. km)
POPULATION – 186,000 (1994)
CAPITAL – ΨNoumea (97,581)

New Caledonia is a large island in the western Pacific, 700 miles east of Queensland. Dependencies are the Isles of Pines, the Loyalty Islands (Mahé, Lifou, Urea, etc.), the Bélep Archipelago, the Chesterfield Islands, the Huon Islands and Walpole.

New Caledonia was discovered in 1774 and annexed by France in 1854; from 1871 to 1896 it was a convict settlement. In 1995, the territory was divided into three provinces, each with a provincial assembly which combined to form the Territorial Assembly. In elections in July 1995, Kanaks won majorities in North province and the Loyalty Islands, whereas pro-French settlers won a majority in the South province.

A referendum in 1987 on the question of independence was boycotted by the indigenous Kanaks, and New Caledonia therefore voted to remain French. In April 1998 an agreement was reached between the pro-independence Kanak Socialist National Liberation Front, the anti-independence Rally for Caledonia in the Republic and the French government to hold a referendum on independence in 15–20 years' time, and for greater autonomy for the indigenous people in the intervening period.

High Commissioner, D. Bur

Trade with UK	1996	1997
Imports from UK	£10,529,000	£16,558,000
Exports to UK	10,891,000	5,209,000

SOUTHERN AND ANTARCTIC TERRITORIES

Created in 1955 from former Réunion dependencies, the territory comprises the islands of Amsterdam (25 sq. miles) and St Paul (2.7 sq. miles), the Kerguelen Islands (2,700 sq. miles) and Crozet Islands (116 sq. miles) archipelagos and Adélie Land (116,800 sq. miles) in the Antarctic continent. The only population are members of staff of the scientific stations.

WALLIS AND FUTUNA ISLANDS

AREA – 77 sq. miles (200 sq. km)
POPULATION – 14,000 (1990 census)
CAPITAL – Mata-Utu on Uvea, the main island of the Wallis group

Two groups of islands (the Wallis Archipelago and the Îles de Hoorn) in the central Pacific, north-east of Fiji.

Prefect, L. Legrand

Trade with UK	1996	1997
Imports from UK	£20,000	£45,000
Exports to UK	—	—

THE FRENCH COMMUNITY

The constitution of the Fifth French Republic, promulgated in 1958, envisaged the establishment of a French Community of States. A number of the former French states in Africa have seceded from the Community but for all practical purposes continue to enjoy the same close links with France as those that remain formally members. Most former French African colonies are closely linked to France by financial, technical and economic agreements.

GABON
République Gabonaise

AREA – 103,347 sq. miles (267,668 sq. km). Neighbours: Equatorial Guinea and Cameroon (north), Republic of Congo (east and south)
POPULATION – 1,320,000 (1994 UN estimate). The official language is French; Fang is widely spoken
CAPITAL – ΨLibreville (population, 251,000)
CURRENCY – Franc CFA of 100 centimes
NATIONAL ANTHEM – La Concorde
NATIONAL DAY – 17 August
NATIONAL FLAG – Horizontal bands, green, yellow and blue
LIFE EXPECTANCY (years) – male 51.86; female 55.18
POPULATION GROWTH RATE – 2.8 per cent (1995)
POPULATION DENSITY – 5 per sq. km (1995)
URBAN POPULATION – 73.2 per cent (1993)

MILITARY EXPENDITURE – 2.2 per cent of GDP (1996)
MILITARY PERSONNEL – 9,500: Army 3,200, Navy 500, Air
  Force 1,000, Paramilitary 4,800
ILLITERACY RATE – 36.8 per cent

HISTORY AND POLITICS

The first Europeans to visit the region were the Portuguese in the 15th century, and Dutch, French and English traders arrived over the following decades. In 1849 a slave ship was captured by the French, and the freed slaves formed a settlement which they called Libreville, the current capital. The territory was annexed to French Congo in 1888.

Gabon elected on 28 November 1958 to remain an autonomous republic within the French Community and gained full independence on 17 August 1960.

Multiparty elections held in autumn 1990 were won by the ruling Parti Démocratique Gabonais (PDG), amid allegations of fraud. The PDG formed a coalition government, although the other parties left the government in 1991 in protest at PDG domination. A presidential election in 1993 was won by the incumbent, President Bongo of the PDG, amid accusations of corruption, which led to riots in Libreville. In September 1994, the government and opposition parties signed the Paris Agreement, which provided for a new coalition government and parliamentary elections. The elections, held in December 1996, returned the PDG to power.

POLITICAL SYSTEM

The constitution provides for an executive president, directly elected for a seven-year term, who appoints the Council of Ministers. There is a 120-member National Assembly and a 91-member Senate.

HEAD OF STATE

President, El Hadj Omar Bongo, *assumed office* December 1967, *re-elected* 1973, 1979, 1986 and 5 December 1993
Vice-President, Divungui-Di-Ndinge Didjob

COUNCIL OF MINISTERS *as at July 1998*

Prime Minister, Dr Paulin Obame-Nguema
Minister of State, Agriculture, Livestock and Rural Economy, Emmanuel Ondo Methogo
Minister of State, Equipment and Construction, Zacharie Myboto
Minister of State, Foreign Affairs and Co-operation, Casimir Oyé Mba
Minister of State, Habitat, Lands, Urban Planning, Welfare, Jean-François Ntoutoume-Emane
Minister of State, Interior, Antoine Mboumbou Miyakou
Minister of State, Justice, Keeper of the Seals, Human Rights, Marcel Eloi Rahandi Chambrier
Minister of State, Labour, Employment, Human Resources and Training, Jean-Rémy Pendy Bouyiki
Minister of State, National Education, Women's Affairs, Government Spokesperson, Paulette Moussavou Missambo
Civil Service, Administrative Reform, Patrice Nziengui
Commerce, Industry, Small and Medium-sized Enterprises, Handicrafts, Martin Fidèle Magnaga
Communication, Culture, Art, Mass Education, Jacques Adiahenot
Finance, Economy, Budget and Participation, Privatization, Marcel Doupambi Matoka
Higher Education, Scientific Research, Lazare Digombé
Merchant Marine and Fishing, Jean Félix Sibi
Mines, Energy and Oil, Paul Toungui
National Defence, Security and Immigration, Posts and Telecommunications, Gen. Idriss Ngari
Planning, Environment and Tourism, Jean Ping
Public Health and Population, Faustin Boukoubi

Relations with Parliament and the Assemblies, Government Spokesperson, André Mba Obame
Social Affairs, National Solidarity and the Family, Zeng Ebome
Transport, Civil Aviation, Gen. Albert Ndjavé-Ndjoy
Water, Forests and Re-afforestation, André Dieudonné Berre
Youth and Sports, Alexandre Sambat

EMBASSY OF THE REPUBLIC OF GABON
27 Elvaston Place, London SW7 5NL
Tel 0171–823 9986
Ambassador Extraordinary and Plenipotentiary, HE Honorine Dossou-Naki, apptd 1996

BRITISH AMBASSADOR, HE Peter Boon, OBE, resident at Yaoundé, Cameroon

ECONOMY

The economy is heavily dependent on oil and, to a lesser extent, other mineral resources, including manganese and uranium. Gabon has considerable timber reserves with 80 per cent of the country still forested, although production has stagnated in recent years.

France and the USA are the main trading partners. In 1994 there was a trade surplus of US$1,593 million and a current account surplus of US$320 million. In 1995 imports totalled US$882 million and exports US$2,713 million.

GNP – US$4,444 million (1996); US$3,950 per capita (1996)
GDP – US$5,851 million (1994); US$3,086 per capita (1994)
INFLATION RATE – 4.2 per cent (1996)
TOTAL EXTERNAL DEBT – US$4,213 million (1996)

TRADE WITH UK	1996	1997
Imports from UK	£20,900,000	£27,191,000
Exports to UK	8,433,000	6,965,000

THE GAMBIA
The Republic of the Gambia

AREA – 4,361 sq. miles (11,295 sq. km). Neighbour: Senegal, which surrounds the Gambia except at the coast
POPULATION – 1,118,000 (1994 UN estimate), mainly Wollof, Mandinka and Fula peoples who originally migrated from the north and east. The official language is English; Fula, Jola, Mandinka, Serahule and Wollof are indigenous languages
CAPITAL – ΨBanjul (population, 109,986, 1980 estimate)
CURRENCY – Dalasi (D) of 100 butut
NATIONAL ANTHEM – For The Gambia, Our Homeland
NATIONAL DAY – 18 February (Independence Day)
NATIONAL FLAG – Horizontal stripes of red, blue and green, separated by narrow white stripes
LIFE EXPECTANCY (years) – male 43.41; female 46.63
POPULATION GROWTH RATE – 3.8 per cent (1995)
POPULATION DENSITY – 99 per sq. km (1995)
MILITARY EXPENDITURE – 3.9 per cent of GDP (1996)
MILITARY PERSONNEL – 800: Army 800

The Gambia is named after the Gambia River, which it straddles for over 200 miles inland from the west coast of Africa. The climate is Sahelian, with a dry season between October and May and heavy rainfall in July and August.

HISTORY AND POLITICS

The Gambia River basin was part of the region dominated in the tenth to 16th centuries by the Songhai and Mali kingdoms centred on the upper Niger. The Portuguese reached the Gambia River in 1447; English merchants began to trade along the river from 1588. Merchants from France, Courland (now Latvia) and the Netherlands also established trading posts. In 1816 the British stationed a garrison on an island at the river mouth which became the capital of a small British-administered colony. In 1889 France agreed that the British rights along the upper river should extend to 10 km from the river on either bank. British administration was extended from the Colony to this Protectorate. The Gambia became independent within the Commonwealth on 18 February 1965, and a republic on 24 April 1970.

In July 1994 junior army officers launched a coup which ousted the president and the government, and a military council was formed. The coup leader, Lt. (later Capt.) Jammeh, assumed the presidency, the constitution was suspended and a civilian-military government was formed to rule in conjunction with the Ruling Military Council. A referendum approved a new constitution in August 1996, Jammeh was elected president the following month and the Ruling Military Council was dissolved. A pro-presidential party won 33 of the 49 seats in the new parliament in a legislative election in January 1997.

FOREIGN RELATIONS

The relationship with Senegal remains an important factor in political and economic policy. Moves towards a closer association were accelerated after an abortive coup in 1981 was put down with the help of Senegalese troops. In 1982 the Senegambia Confederation was instituted but following disagreements it was dissolved in 1989. A treaty of friendship and co-operation was signed with Senegal in 1991.

POLITICAL SYSTEM

The constitution gives enhanced powers to the president who is elected for an indefinite term.

HEAD OF STATE

President, Defence, Capt. Yahya Jammeh, *took power* 23 July 1994, *elected* 26 September 1996
Vice-President, Health and Social Affairs, Isatou Njie-Saidy

CABINET *as at July 1998*
Agriculture, Musa Mbenga
Education, Satang Jow
External Affairs, Lamine Sedat Jobe
Finance and Economic Affairs, Famara Jatta
Interior, Momodou Bojang
Justice, Awa Ceesay-Sabally
Presidency, National Assembly, Fisheries and Natural Resources, Capt. Edward Singhateh
Public Works, Communications, Information, Ebrima Ceesay
Territorial Administration, Capt. Lamin Bayo
Tourism and Culture, Susan Ogoo
Trade, Industry and Employment, Dominic Mendy
Youth and Sports, Capt. Yankouba Touray

GAMBIA HIGH COMMISSION
57 Kensington Court, London W8 5DG
Tel 0171-937 6316/7/8
High Commissioner, HE John P. Bojang, apptd 1997

BRITISH HIGH COMMISSION
48 Atlantic Road, Fajara (PO Box 507), Banjul
Tel: Banjul 495133
High Commissioner, HE Tony Millson, apptd 1998

ECONOMY

Agriculture accounts for 75 per cent of employment and contributes roughly 20 per cent of GDP. The chief product, groundnuts, also forms over 80 per cent of domestic exports. Other crops are cotton, rice, millet, sorghum and maize. Fishing and livestock industries are being developed.

Manufactures are limited to groundnut processing, minor metal fabrications, paints, furniture, soap and bottling. Tourism is developing quickly with more than 80,000 visitors in 1996–7. Trade through the Gambia, re-exporting imported goods to neighbouring countries, is an important element in the economy. In 1995 there was a trade deficit of US$40 million and a current account deficit of US$8 million. Imports totalled US$140 million and exports US$16 million.

GNP – US$354 million (1995); US$320 per capita (1995)
GDP – US$330 million (1994); US$332 per capita (1994)
ANNUAL AVERAGE GROWTH OF GDP – –4.1 per cent (1995)
INFLATION RATE – 1.1 per cent (1996)
TOTAL EXTERNAL DEBT – US$452 million (1996)

TRADE WITH UK	1996	1997
Imports from UK	£16,443,000	£19,182,000
Exports to UK	3,207,000	3,104,000

COMMUNICATIONS

There is an international airport at Yundum, 17 miles from Banjul, with scheduled services flying to other West African states and to the UK and Belgium. Banjul is the main port. Internal communication is by road and river. There are five broadcasting stations and a UHF telephone service linking Banjul with the principal towns in the provinces. There is one television station.

EDUCATION

There are 24 secondary schools (eight high and 16 technical). Two high schools provide A-level education. Gambia College provides post-secondary courses in education, agriculture, public health and nursing. There are seven vocational training institutions. Higher education and advanced training courses are taken outside The Gambia, currently by over 200 students.
ILLITERACY RATE – 61.4 per cent
ENROLMENT (percentage of age group) – primary 55 per cent (1992); secondary 18 per cent (1992); tertiary 1.7 per cent (1994)

GEORGIA
Sakartvelos Respublika

AREA – 26,911 sq. miles (69,700 sq. km). Neighbours: Russia (north), Azerbaijan (south-east), Armenia (south), Turkey (south-west)
POPULATION – 5,401,000 (1998 estimate): 70 per cent Georgian, 8 per cent Armenian, 6 per cent Russian, 6 per cent Azerbaijani, 3 per cent Ossetian and 2 per cent Abkhazian, with smaller groups of Greeks, Ukrainians, Jews and Kurds. The majority religion is the Georgian Orthodox Church. There is also a small Muslim minority. Georgian, Russian and Armenian are the most commonly used languages. Georgian is one of the oldest languages in the world to have been continually in use, the alphabet having emerged in the third century BC
CAPITAL – Tbilisi (population, 1,268,000, 1990 estimate)
MAJOR CITIES – Batumi (137,000); Kutaisi (236,000); Rustavi (160,000); Sukhumi (capital of Abkhazia) (122,000)
CURRENCY – Lari of 100 tetri
NATIONAL DAY – 26 May (Independence Day)
NATIONAL FLAG – Cherry red with a canton in the upper hoist divided black over white

LIFE EXPECTANCY (years) – male 68.10; female 75.70
POPULATION GROWTH RATE – – 0.0 per cent (1995)
POPULATION DENSITY – 78 per sq. km (1995)
URBAN POPULATION – 55.4 per cent (1989)
MILITARY EXPENDITURE – 3.4 per cent of GDP (1996)
MILITARY PERSONNEL – 17,600: Army 12,600, Navy 2,000, Air Force 3,000
CONSCRIPTION DURATION – Two years
ILLITERACY RATE – 0.5 per cent
ENROLMENT (percentage of age group) – primary 82 per cent (1995); secondary 71 per cent (1995); tertiary 38.1 per cent (1995)

Georgia occupies the north-western part of the Caucasus region of the former Soviet Union. It contains the two autonomous republics of Abkhazia and Adjaria and the disputed region of South Ossetia (Tskhinvali).

Georgia is mountainous, with the Greater Caucasus in the north and the Lesser Caucasus in the south. Western Georgia has a mild and damp climate, eastern Georgia is more continental and dry. The Black Sea shore and the Rioni lowland are subtropical.

HISTORY AND POLITICS

The Georgians formed two states, Colchis and Iberia, on the edge of the Black Sea around 1000 BC. After centuries of invasions by Arabs, Turks and Khazars, Georgia entered its 'Golden Age' in the 12th century AD when trade, irrigation and communications were developed. Invasions by the Khazars and Mongols led to the division of Georgia into several states. These struggled against the Turkish and the Persian empires from the 16th to the 18th centuries, gradually turning to the Russian Empire for protection and support. Eastern Georgia signed a treaty of alliance with Russia which recognized Russian supremacy in 1783 and joined the Russian Empire in 1801, followed soon after by Western Georgia.

In the late 19th century, nationalist and Marxist movements competed for limited political influence under autocratic Russian rule. One of the most prominent Marxist activists was Iosif Dzhugashvili (Josef Stalin). After the Russian revolution of 1917, a nationalist government came to power in Georgia supported by allied intervention forces. In 1921 Soviet forces occupied Tbilisi, and in 1922 Georgia joined the Soviet Union as part of the Transcaucasian Soviet Socialist Republic.

In March 1990 the Georgian Supreme Soviet declared illegal the treaties of 1921–2 by which Georgia had joined the Soviet Union. The Communist Party's monopoly on power was abolished and in multiparty elections held in October and November 1990 the nationalist leader Zviad Gamsakhurdia was elected president. Georgia declared its independence from the Soviet Union in May 1991 and was admitted to UN membership on 31 July 1992.

Gamsakhurdia's government faced armed opposition from 1991 onwards. Defeat in the ensuing civil war in Tbilisi led to Gamsakhurdia's overthrow in January 1992, and in March 1992 a state council was appointed with the former Soviet foreign minister Eduard Shevardnadze as chairman. Fighting continued throughout 1992 and 1993. In October 1992 Shevardnadze was elected head of state and Chairman of the Parliament, and a loose alliance of pro-Shevardnadze parties formed a government.

Gamsakhurdia returned to western Georgia in September 1993, a month after economic chaos had forced the government to resign. President Shevardnadze assumed full executive powers at the head of an emergency council, but failed to prevent the advance of Gamsakhurdia's rebels as most government forces were engaged in Abkhazia. Shevardnadze was forced to accept Russian armaments and troops to defeat the rebellion and in return agreed to join the CIS. Presidential and legislative elections, held on 5 November 1995, were won by President Shevardnadze and his Citizens' Union of Georgia party.

SECESSION

In late 1990 the South Ossetians took up arms against Georgian rule in an attempt to join North Ossetia, itself part of Russia. The South Ossetian provincial parliament voted in November 1992 to secede from Georgia and join Russia. Fighting ceased in June 1992 and a joint Russian-Georgian-Ossetian peacekeeping force was dispatched. Representatives of the South Ossetian and Georgian governments met in April 1996 to agree security and confidence-building measures. South Ossetia was renamed Tskhinvali under Georgia's 1995 constitution. Presidential elections in South Ossetia were won by Ludvig Chibirov, the chair of the Supreme Council, in November 1996.

In July 1992 the Abkhazian republican parliament declared Abkhazia independent. Fighting broke out between Georgian forces and Abkhazian separatists supported by Russian arms and irregulars; Georgian forces were defeated and were forced to withdraw in September 1993. Negotiations under Russian auspices led to an Abkhaz-Georgian cease-fire and separation of forces agreement being signed in May 1994 and the deployment of 2,500 Russian UN peacekeepers on the Abkhaz-Georgian border. In November 1994 the Abkhaz Supreme Soviet declared Abkhazia's independence again and elected Vladislav Ardzinba as president. Abkhazia was given autonomous republic status under the 1995 constitution; this was rejected by the republican parliament. Elections to the self-declared Abkhaz People's Assembly were held in November 1996. Although the CIS peacekeeping mandate expired on 31 January 1998, troops have remained in the area as talks between the two sides continue.

FOREIGN RELATIONS

In September 1997, President Shevardnadze signed an accord with President Maskhadov of Chechenya, calling for closer co-operation between the two states. In October 1997, a Georgian-Ukrainian declaration was signed, promising a development of co-operation with NATO within the framework of the Partnership for Peace programme. Georgia has signed a Partnership and Co-operation Agreement with the European Union.

POLITICAL SYSTEM

The 1995 constitution provides for a federal republic with a unicameral legislature, to become bicameral 'following the creation of appropriate conditions'; and a popularly elected president who serves a maximum of two five-year terms.

HEAD OF STATE
President, Eduard Shevardnadze, *elected* 11 October 1992, re-elected 5 November 1995

CABINET *as at June 1998*
Minister of State, Head of Chancellery, Nikoloz Lekishvili
Agriculture and Food, Bakur Gulua
Communications and Posts, Fridon Injia
Culture, Valeri Asatiani
Defence, David Tevzadze
Economics, Vladimir Papava
Education, Tamaz Kvachantiradze
Energy, Teimuraz Giorgadze
Environmental Protection, Natural Resources, Nino Chkhobadze
Finances, Micheil Chkuaseli
Foreign Affairs, Irakli Menagarishvili
Health Care, Avtandil Jorbenadze
Industry, Tamaz Agladze
Internal Affairs, Kakha Targamadze
Justice, Tedo Ninidze
Refugees and Accommodation, Valeri Vashakidze
Social Protection, Labour, Employment, Tengiz Gazdeliani
State Property Management, Avtandil Silagadze
State Security, Jemal Gakhokidze
Trade, Foreign Economic Relations, Konstantin Zaldastanishvili
Transport, Merab Adeishvili
Urbanization and Construction, Merab Chkhenkeli

EMBASSY OF THE REPUBLIC OF GEORGIA
3 Hornton Place, London, W8 4LZ
Tel 0171–937 8233
Ambassador Extraordinary and Plenipotentiary, HE Teimuraz Mamatsashvili, apptd 1995

BRITISH EMBASSY
Metechi Palace Hotel, 380003 Tbilisi
Tel: Tbilisi 955497
Ambassador Extraordinary and Plenipotentiary, HE Richard Jenkins, OBE, apptd 1997

ECONOMY

The economy was brought to the brink of collapse by civil and secessionist wars and the ending of former Soviet trading relationships. Industrial production fell by 70 per cent between 1991 and 1995. Although Georgia has deposits of coal, they have not been exploited and it is desperately short of energy supplies. A large proportion of production is stolen by black marketeers, whilst the tourist industry on the Black Sea coast has been destroyed by the fighting. The only productive sector of the economy is agriculture, with a concentration on viniculture, tea and tobacco-growing and citrus fruits.

Economic performance improved in 1995 with inflation dropping from 7,500 per cent in 1994 to 2 per cent per month in 1995. Reforms included the introduction of a new currency in October 1995, and new legislation permitting the private ownership of arable land and stricter bank regulation. GDP has grown gradually in the past two years, and in 1997 investment activity grew by 87 per cent. In May 1998, a co-operation agreement was signed with US company Enron to build a trans-Caspian pipeline for transporting oil and gas.
GNP – US$4,590 million (1996); US$850 per capita (1996)
GDP – US$4,547 million (1994); US$256 per capita (1994)
TOTAL EXTERNAL DEBT – US$1,356 million (1996)

TRADE WITH UK	1996	1997
Imports from UK	£3,784,000	£12,100,000
Exports to UK	579,000	1,257,000

GERMANY
Bundesrepublik Deutschland – Federal Republic of Germany

AREA – 137,735 sq. miles (356,733 sq. km). Neighbours: Denmark (north), Poland (east), Czech Republic (east and south-east), Austria (south-east and south), Switzerland (south), France, Luxembourg, Belgium and the Netherlands (west)
POPULATION – 81,642,000 (1995 UN estimate). Approximately 80 per cent of the population live in the former West Germany. In 1994 there were 28,197,000 Protestants, 27,909,797 Roman Catholics, 2,700,000 Muslims and 53,797 Jews. The language is German; there is a Danish-speaking minority in Schleswig-Holstein
CAPITAL – Berlin (population, 3,472,009, 1996). The seat of government and parliament is to be transferred from Bonn to Berlin by 2000
MAJOR CITIES – Bremen (549,182); Cologne (963,817); Dortmund (600,918); Dresden (474,443); Duisburg (536,106); Düsseldorf (572,638); Essen (617,955); Frankfurt am Main (652,412); Hamburg (1,705,872); Hannover (524,823); Leipzig (481,121); Munich (1,244,676); Nuremberg (495,845); Stuttgart (588,482)
CURRENCY – Deutsche Mark (DM) of 100 Pfennig
NATIONAL ANTHEM – Einigkeit und Recht und Freiheit (Unity and right and freedom)
NATIONAL DAY – 3 October (Anniversary of 1990 Unification)
NATIONAL FLAG – Horizontal bars of black, red and gold
LIFE EXPECTANCY (years) – male 72.77; female 79.30
POPULATION GROWTH RATE – 0.6 per cent (1995)
POPULATION DENSITY – 229 per sq. km (1995)
URBAN POPULATION – 76.3 per cent (1990)

HISTORY AND POLITICS

The term 'deutsch' (German) was probably first used in the eighth century and described the language spoken in the eastern part of the Frankish realm. The first German realm was the Holy Roman Empire, established in AD 962 when Otto I of Saxony was crowned Emperor. The Empire endured until 1806, but the achievement of a national state was prevented by fragmentation into small principalities and dukedoms.

The Empire was replaced by a loose association of sovereign states known as the German Confederation, which was dissolved in 1866 and replaced by the Prussian-dominated North German Federation. Prussia had translated its earlier economic predominance into political hegemony by the annexation of the duchies of Schleswig and Holstein from Denmark in 1864 and a decisive defeat of Austria in 1866 (the Seven Weeks' War). After the Franco-Prussian War of 1870–1, which resulted in the defeat of France and the cession of Alsace and part of Lorraine, the south German principalities united with the northern federation to form a second German Empire, the King of Prussia being proclaimed Emperor in 1871.

Defeat in the First World War led to the abdication of the Emperor, and the country became a republic. The Treaty of Versailles (1919) returned Alsace-Lorraine to France, and large areas in the east were lost to Poland. The world economic crisis of 1929 contributed to the collapse of the Weimar Republic and the subsequent rise to power

government was established in the Soviet zone (henceforth the German Democratic Republic (GDR)). In 1961 the Soviet zone of Berlin was sealed off, and the Berlin Wall was built along the zonal boundary, partitioning the western sectors of the city from the eastern.

Soviet-initiated reform in eastern Europe during the late 1980s led to unrest in the GDR. The mass exodus of its citizens to the west via Hungary and Czechoslovakia culminated in the opening of the Berlin Wall in November 1989 and the collapse of Communist government. The 'Treaty on the Final Settlement with Respect to Germany', concluded between the FRG, GDR and the four former occupying powers in September 1990, unified Germany with effect from 3 October 1990 as a fully sovereign state. Economic and monetary union preceded formal union on 1 July 1990. Unification is constitutionally the accession of Berlin and the five reformed *Länder* of the GDR to the FRG, which remains in being. The first government of the new Germany took office in January 1991 following all-German elections on 2 December 1990.

The distribution of seats following the last election for the Bundestag on 16 October 1994 was: Christian Democratic Union, 244; Social Democrats, 252; Free Democrats, 47; Christian Social Union, 50; Democratic Socialists, 30; The Greens, 49. The next elections are due to be held in September 1998.

of the National Socialist movement of Adolf Hitler, who became Chancellor in 1933.

After concluding a Treaty of Non-Aggression with the Soviet Union in August 1939, Germany invaded Poland (1 September 1939), precipitating the Second World War, which lasted until 1945. Hitler committed suicide on 30 April 1945. On 8 May 1945, Germany unconditionally surrendered.

THE POST-WAR PERIOD

Germany was divided into American, French, British and Soviet zones of occupation. Supreme authority was exercised by the respective Commanders-in-Chief, and jointly through the Control Council of the four Commanders, with Berlin under joint administration. The USSR withdrew from the Control Council in 1948 and the rift divided Germany *de facto* into east and west.

The Federal Republic of Germany (FRG) was created out of the three western zones in 1949. A Communist

POLITICAL SYSTEM

The Basic Law provides for a president, elected by a Federal Convention (electoral college) for a five-year term, a lower house (*Bundestag*) of 672 members elected by direct universal suffrage for a four-year term of office, and an upper house (*Bundesrat*) composed of 69 members appointed by the governments of the *Länder* in proportion to *Länder* populations, without a fixed term of office.

Judicial authority is exercised by the Federal Constitutional Court, the federal courts provided for in the Basic Law and the courts of the Länder.

FEDERAL STRUCTURE

Germany is a federal republic composed of 16 states (*Länder*) (ten from the former West, five from the former East and Berlin). Each *Land* has its own directly elected legislature and government led by Minister-Presidents (prime ministers) or equivalents. The 1949 Basic Law vests

Land	Area (sq. km)	Population (1995)	Capital	Minister-President (June 1998)
Baden-Württemberg	35,751	10.3m	Stuttgart	Erwin Teufel (CDU)
Bavaria	70,552	12.0m	Munich	Dr Edmund Stoiber (CSU)
Berlin	891	3.5m	—	Eberhard Diepgen (CDU)*
Brandenburg	29,476	2.5m	Potsdam	Dr Manfred Stolpe (SPD)
Bremen	404	0.7m	—	Dr Henning Scherf (SPD)*
Hamburg	755	1.7m	—	Ortwin Runde (SPD)*
Hesse	21,114	6.0m	Wiesbaden	Hans Eichel (SPD)
Lower Saxony	47,612	7.7m	Hannover	Gerhard Schröder (SPD)
Mecklenburg-Western Pomerania	23,170	1.8m	Schwerin	Dr Berndt Seite (CDU)
North Rhine-Westphalia	34,079	17.8m	Düsseldorf	Dr Johannes Rau (SPD)
Rhineland-Palatinate	19,853	4.0m	Mainz	Kurt Beck (SPD)
Saarland	2,570	1.1m	Saarbrücken	Oskar Lafontaine (SPD)
Saxony	18,413	4.6m	Dresden	Prof. Kurt Biedenkopf (CDU)
Saxony-Anhalt	20,446	2.8m	Magdeburg	Dr Reinhard Höppner (SPD)
Schleswig-Holstein	15,771	2.7m	Kiel	Heide Simonis (SPD)
Thuringia	16,171	2.5m	Erfurt	Dr Bernhard Vogel (CDU)

*Berlin, *Governing Mayor*; Bremen, *Mayor*; Hamburg, *First Mayor*

CDU Christian Democratic Union; CSU Christian Social Union; SPD Social Democratic Party

executive power in the *Länder* governments except in those areas reserved for the federal government.

HEAD OF STATE
Federal President, Professor Roman Herzog, *born* 1934, *elected* 23 May 1994, *sworn in* 1 July 1994

CABINET *as at July 1998*
Federal Chancellor, Dr Helmut Kohl (CDU)
Federal Vice-Chancellor, Foreign Affairs, Dr Klaus Kinkel (FDP)
Defence, Volker Rühe (CDU)
Economic Co-operation and Development, Carl-Dieter Spranger (CSU)
Economics, Dr Günter Rexrodt (FDP)
Education, Science, Research and Technology, Dr Jürgen Rüttgers (CDU)
Environment, Nature Conservation and Reactor Safety, Dr Angela Merkel (CDU)
Family, Youth, Women and the Elderly, Claudia Nolte (CDU)
Finance, Dr Theo Waigel (CSU)
Head of Chancery, Friedrich Bohl (CDU)
Health, Horst Seehofer (CSU)
Interior, Manfred Kanther (CDU)
Justice, Prof. Edzard Schmidt-Jortzig (FDP)
Labour and Social Affairs, Dr Norbert Blüm (CDU)
Nutrition, Agriculture, Forestry, Jochen Borchert (CDU)
Regional Planning and Urban Development, Eduard Oswald (CSU)
Transport, Matthias Wissmann (CDU)
CDU Christian Democratic Union; CSU Christian Social Union; FDP Free Democratic Party

EMBASSY OF THE FEDERAL REPUBLIC OF GERMANY
23 Belgrave Square, London SWIX 8PZ
Tel 0171-824 1300
Ambassador Extraordinary and Plenipotentiary, HE Gebhardt von Moltke, apptd 1997
Minister, Peter von Butler
Minister-Counsellor, Paul von Maltzahn
Counsellors, F. Burbach (*Cultural Affairs*); F. J. Kremp (*Economic Affairs*)
Defence Attaché, Brig.-Gen. Eckart Fischer

BRITISH EMBASSY
Friedrich-Ebert-Allée 77, 53113 Bonn
Tel: Bonn 91670
Ambassador Extraordinary and Plenipotentiary, HE Sir Paul Lever, CMG, apptd 1997
Deputy Head of Mission, Minister, R. F. Cooper, MVO
Defence Attaché, Brig. B. R. Isbell, MBE
Counsellor (Economic), R. L. Turner
Counsellor (Management and Consular), S. C. Johns

BRITISH EMBASSY OFFICE, BERLIN
Unter den Linden 32/34, 0-10117 Berlin
Tel: Berlin 201 840
Counsellor, Deputy Head of Mission, D. L. Corner
Minister, A. Ford, CMG
First Secretary (Commercial), D. S. Schroeder
BRITISH CONSULATES-GENERAL – Düsseldorf, Frankfurt, Hamburg, Munich, Stuttgart
BRITISH CONSULATES – Bremen, Hannover, Kiel and Nuremberg

BRITISH COUNCIL REPRESENTATIVE, K. Dobson, OBE, Hahnenstrasse 6, 50667 Köln. Offices at Berlin, Hamburg, Leipzig and Munich

BRITISH CHAMBER OF COMMERCE, Neumarkt 14, D-5000 Köln 1. *Director*, Herr Heumann

DEFENCE
The Army has 3,248 main battle tanks, 5,733 armoured personnel carriers and armoured infantry fighting vehicles, 2,058 artillery pieces, and 204 attack helicopters. The Navy has 16 submarines, three destroyers, 12 frigates, 34 patrol and coastal vessels, 53 combat aircraft and 17 armed helicopters. The Air Force has 455 combat aircraft.

There remain 120,285 NATO personnel in Germany (USA 75,665; UK 27,920; Belgium 2,000; France 11,700; Netherlands 3,000).

During 1993 both the Constitutional Court and the Bundestag agreed that German armed forces may operate outside Germany and the NATO area in UN and other peacekeeping operations for the first time since 1945. In 1994 the Constitutional Court ruled that German forces could serve in armed peacekeeping missions.
MILITARY EXPENDITURE – 1.7 per cent of GDP (1996)
MILITARY PERSONNEL – 344,610: Army 239,950, Navy 27,760, Air Force 76,900. Under the terms of the Treaty of Unification, the German armed forces have been limited to 370,000 active personnel since the end of 1994
CONSCRIPTION DURATION – Ten to 23 months

ECONOMY
Germany has a predominantly industrial economy. Principal industries are coal mining, iron and steel production, machine construction, the electrical industry, the manufacture of steel and metal products, chemicals, automobile production, electronics, textiles and the processing of foodstuffs.

In 1996, Germany produced 235,377,000 tonnes of coal and 2,850,000 tonnes of crude petroleum.

After a mini-boom generated by new East German demand in 1990 and 1991, Germany entered its most severe recession since the war induced by the costs of reunification. In 1993 a 'Solidarity Pact' was agreed by federal and länder governments, opposition parties, and employers and trade unions, to take effect from 1995. The pact lays down the basis of future funding transfers to the East based on a 5.5 per cent rise in income taxes, wage restraint in the West, more private investment in the East, and the distribution of the funding burden between the federal and länder governments. The government, under pressure to meet the criteria for European monetary union in 1999, announced proposed spending cuts of 2.5 per cent for 1996. In December 1997 unemployment reached a post-war high of 4.5 million, with the former East Germany worst affected. On 1 May 1998 it was announced that, having satisfied the convergence criteria, Germany would participate in the European Single Currency from 1 January 1999.

In 1996 there was a trade surplus of US$73,356 million and a current account deficit of US$13,919 million. Imports totalled US$455,683 million and exports US$521,111 million.
GNP – US$2,364,632 million (1996); US$28,870 per capita (1996)
GDP – US$1,767,217 million (1994); US$25,179 per capita (1994)
ANNUAL AVERAGE GROWTH OF GDP – 1.3 per cent (1996); expected to be 2.4 per cent in 1997
INFLATION RATE – 1.5 per cent (1996)
UNEMPLOYMENT – 12.9 per cent (1995); expected to be 10 per cent in 1997

Trade with UK	1996	1997
Imports from UK	£19,753,800,000	£19,501,400,000
Exports to UK	25,560,400,000	24,546,900,000

COMMUNICATIONS

In 1995 the state-owned railways measured 40,209 km of which 17,054 km were electrified, and the privately owned railways totalled approximately 2,807 km. Classified roads measured 228,860 km in 1996, of which motorways were 11,190 km. Merchant shipping under the German flag in 1994 amounted to 5,696,088 tonnes gross. Inland waterways are 6,929 km long.

EDUCATION

School attendance is compulsory between the ages of six and 18 and comprises nine years of full-time education at primary and main schools and three years of vocational education on a part-time basis. The secondary school leaving examination (*Abitur*) entitles the holder to a place of study at a university or another institution of higher education.

Children below the age of 18 who are not attending a general secondary or a full-time vocational school have compulsory day-release at a vocational school.

The largest universities are in Munich, Berlin, Hamburg, Bonn, Frankfurt and Cologne.

ENROLMENT (percentage of age group) – primary 100 per cent (1994); secondary 88 per cent (1994); tertiary 42.7 per cent (1994)

CULTURE

Modern (or New High) German has developed from the time of the Reformation to the present day, with differences of dialect in Austria, Alsace, Luxembourg, Liechtenstein and the German-speaking cantons of Switzerland.

The literary language is usually regarded as having become fixed by Luther and Zwingli at the Reformation, since which time many great names occur in all branches, notably philosophy, from Leibnitz (1646–1716) to Kant (1724–1804), Schelling (1775–1854) and Hegel (1770–1831); drama, from Goethe (1749–1832) and Schiller (1759–1805) to Gerhart Hauptmann (1862–1946); and poetry, Heine (1797–1856). Seven German authors have received the Nobel Prize for Literature: Theodor Mommsen (1902), R. Eucken (1908), P. Heyse (1909), Gerhart Hauptmann (1912), Thomas Mann (1929), N. Sachs (1966) and Heinrich Böll (1972).

GHANA
The Republic of Ghana

AREA – 92,098 sq. miles (238,533 sq. km). Neighbours: Burkina Faso (north), Côte d'Ivoire (west), Togo (east)
POPULATION – 17,453,000 (1997 estimate); most are Sudanese Negroes, although Hamitic strains are common in the north. The official language is English. The principal indigenous language group is Akan, of which Twi and Fanti are the most commonly used. Ga, Ewe and languages of the Mole-Dagbani group are common in certain regions. Most Ghanaians are Christians, although there is a substantial Muslim minority in the north
CAPITAL – ΨAccra (population, 738,498, 1970), Greater Accra Region (including Tema) 1,781,100 (1990 estimate)
MAJOR CITIES – Kumasi (385,192); ΨSekondi-Takoradi (103,653); Tamale (151,069); Tema (109,975)
CURRENCY – Cedi of 100 pesewas
NATIONAL FLAG – Equal horizontal bands of red over gold over green; five-point black star on gold stripe

NATIONAL ANTHEM – God Bless our Homeland Ghana
NATIONAL DAY – 6 March (Independence Day)
LIFE EXPECTANCY (years) – male 54.22; female 57.84
POPULATION GROWTH RATE – 3.0 per cent (1995)
POPULATION DENSITY – 73 per sq. km (1995)
MILITARY EXPENDITURE – 1.9 per cent of GDP (1996)
MILITARY PERSONNEL – 7,800: Army 5,000, Navy 1,000, Air Force 1,000, Paramilitaries 800
ILLITERACY RATE – 35.5 per cent
ENROLMENT (percentage of age group) – tertiary 1.4 per cent (1990)

HISTORY AND POLITICS

First reached by Europeans in the 15th century, the constituent parts of Ghana came under British administration at various times, the original Gold Coast Colony being constituted in 1874, and Ashanti and the Northern Territories Protectorate in 1901. Trans-Volta-Togoland, part of the former German colony of Togo, was mandated to Britain by the League of Nations after the First World War, and became a United Nations Trusteeship under British administration after the Second World War. After a plebiscite in 1956, the territory was integrated with the Gold Coast Colony. The former Gold Coast Colony and associated territories became the independent state of Ghana on 6 March 1957 and became a republic in 1960.

Since 1966, Ghana has experienced long periods of military rule interspersed with short-lived civilian governments. A coup in 1979 led to the formation of an Armed Forces Revolutionary Council chaired by Flt. Lt. Jerry Rawlings. Civilian rule was restored in 1979 but another coup in December 1981 brought Rawlings back to power.

A referendum in 1992 approved a new multiparty constitution and the legalization of political parties. The National Democratic Congress (NDC) was established as a political party from the ruling Provisional National Defence Council. The presidential and parliamentary elections in late 1992 were won by Rawlings and the NDC, following a boycott by most opposition parties and most of the electorate. The Fourth Republic was declared on 7 January 1993 and a new government nominated by the president took office in March 1993. In legislative elections in December 1996, the NDC retained its absolute majority; President Rawlings was also re-elected.

POLITICAL SYSTEM

The head of state is an executive president elected for a four-year term, renewable only once. The president appoints the Council of Ministers. The unicameral legislature, the Parliament, has 200 members directly elected for a four-year term.

For political and administrative purposes Ghana is divided into ten regions, each headed by a Regional Minister who is the representative of the central government.

HEAD OF STATE

President, Flt. Lt. (retd) Jerry John Rawlings, *took power* 31 December 1981, *elected* 3 November 1992, *re-elected* 7 December 1996
Vice-President, John Evans Mills

COUNCIL OF MINISTERS *as at July 1998*

Communications, Ekwow Spio Garbrah
Defence, Mahama Iddrissu
Education, Christine Amoako-Nuamah
Employment and Social Welfare, Alhaji Mohammed Mumuni
Environment, Science and Technology, J. E. Afful
Finance, Richard Kwame Peprah
Food and Agriculture, Kwabana Adjei

Foreign Affairs, James Victor Gbeho
Health, Eunice Brookman-Amissah
Interior, Nii Okaija Adamafio
Justice and Attorney-General, Obed Asamoah
Lands and Forestry, Cletus Avoka
Local Government and Rural Development, Kwamena Ahwoi
Parliamentary Affairs, J. H. Owusu-Acheampong
Roads and Transport, Edward Salia
Tourism, Mike Gizo
Trade and Industry, John Abu
Without Portfolio, Margaret Clarke-Kwesie
Works and Housing, Isaac Adjei-Mensah
Youth and Sports, E. T. Mensah

GHANA HIGH COMMISSION
13 Belgrave Square, London SW1 8PN
Tel 0171-235 4142
High Commissioner, HE James E. K. Aggrey-Orleans
Defence Adviser, Capt. Nii Coleman
Counsellor, Ato Kwamina Budu-Amoako (*Trade*)

BRITISH HIGH COMMISSION
PO Box 296, Osu Link, Accra
Tel: Accra 221665
High Commissioner, HE Ian Mackley, CMG, apptd 1996
Deputy High Commissioner, I. C. Orr
Defence Adviser, Lt.-Col. E. Glover
First Secretary (Commercial), M. A. Ives

BRITISH COUNCIL DIRECTOR, C. Stevenson, 11 Liberia
Road (PO Box 771), Accra. There is also an office in
Kumasi.

ECONOMY

Agriculture is the basis of the economy, employing 70 per
cent of the workforce. Crops include cocoa, the largest
single source of revenue, rice, cassava, plantains, oranges
and pineapples, groundnuts, corn, millet, oil palms, yams,
maize and vegetables. Livestock is raised in uncultivated
areas. Attempts are being made to diversify agricultural
production, with cash crops such as coffee and tobacco
being cultivated for export. Fishing is important in coastal
areas and in the Volta lake and river system.

Manganese production ranks among the world's largest,
with 186,902 tonnes of ore being produced in 1995;
diamonds and bauxite are also produced. The Ashanti
Goldfields Corporation is one of the world's largest
producers and was privatized in 1994 with estimated gold
reserves of 20.3 million ounces. Some 30,000 persons are
employed by the mining companies.

Small-scale traditional industries include tailoring,
goldsmithing and carpentry. Priority has been given in
recent years to establishing manufacturing industries and a
modern industrial complex has developed in the Accra-
Tema area. In 1995, 335,000 tourists visited Ghana.

Since 1966 the Volta Dams at Akosombo and Kpong
have generated hydroelectric power for the processing of
bauxite and fed a power transmission network for most of
Ghana, Togo and Benin.

In 1994 there was a trade deficit of US$353 million and a
current account deficit of US$264 million. Imports totalled
US$2,109 million.

GNP – US$6,223 million (1996); US$360 per capita (1996)
GDP – US$7,710 million (1994); US$333 per capita (1994)
ANNUAL AVERAGE GROWTH OF GDP – 4.5 per cent (1995)
INFLATION RATE – 34.0 per cent (1996)
TOTAL EXTERNAL DEBT – US$6,202 million (1996)

TRADE
Principal exports are cocoa, timber, minerals and gold.
Principal imports are road vehicles, manufacturing equip-
ment, petroleum, raw materials and food.

Trade with UK	1996	1997
Imports from UK	£299,791,000	£270,189,000
Exports to UK	190,386,000	134,978,000

COMMUNICATIONS

The Kotoka Airport at Accra is an international airport and
Ghana Airways is the national airline. There are also
internal airports at Takoradi, Kumasi, Sunyani, and
Tamale.

There are more than 20,000 miles of motorable roads.
There are 600 miles of railway, linking Accra and the
principal ports of Takoradi and Tema with their hinter-
lands, the mining centres and with each other.

Takoradi Harbour consists of seven quay berths: one is
leased specially for manganese exports. Tema Harbour has
ten berths for larger ocean-going vessels and the largest dry
dock on the West African coast. An oil berth has also been
built to serve the refinery at Tema.

GREECE
Elliniki Dimokratia

AREA – 50,949 sq. miles (131,957 sq. km). Neighbours:
Albania, Bulgaria and the Former Yugoslav Republic of
Macedonia (north), Turkey (east)
POPULATION – 10,458,000 (1994 UN estimate), 10,256,464
(1991 census): 98 per cent Greek Orthodox, 1 per cent
Catholic, 1 per cent Muslim. The language is Greek
CAPITAL – Athens (population 3,027,922, 1991); including
ΨPiraeus and suburbs, 3,096,775 (1991 census)
MAJOR CITIES – ΨCanea (Crete) (65,519); ΨHeraklion
(Crete) (127,600); ΨKavalla (58,576); Larissa (113,426);
ΨPatras (172,763); ΨRhodes (43,619); ΨThessaloniki
(Salonika) (739,998); ΨVolos (115,732)
CURRENCY – Drachma of 100 leptae
NATIONAL ANTHEM – Imnos Eis Tin Eleftherian (Hymn
to Freedom)
NATIONAL DAY – March 25 (Independence Day)
NATIONAL FLAG – Blue and white stripes with a white
cross on a blue field in the canton
LIFE EXPECTANCY (years) – male 74.61; female 79.96
POPULATION GROWTH RATE – 0.6 per cent (1995)
POPULATION DENSITY – 79 per sq. km (1995)
URBAN POPULATION – 58.9 per cent (1991)

The main areas are: Macedonia (which includes Mt Athos
and the island of Thasos), Thrace (including the island of
Samothrace), Epirus, Thessaly, Continental Greece
(which includes the island of Euboea and the Sporades),
Crete and the Peloponnese. The main island groups are the
Sporades (of which the largest is Skyros), the Dodecanese
or Southern Sporades (Rhodes, Astypalaia, Karpathos,
Kassos, Nisyros, Kalymnos, Leros, Patmos, Kos, Symi,
Khalki, Tilos), the Cyclades (about 200, including Syros,
Andros, Tinos, Mykonos, Naxos, Paros, Santorini, Milos
and Serifos), the Ionian Islands (Corfu, Paxos, Levkas,
Ithaca, Cephalonia, Zante and Cerigo), and the Aegean
Islands (Chios, Lesbos, Limnos and Samos). In Crete from
about 3000 to 1400 BC a civilization flourished which
spread its influence throughout the Aegean, and the ruins
of the palace of Minos at Knossos afford evidence of
astonishing comfort and luxury.

HISTORY AND POLITICS

Greece was under Turkish rule from the mid-15th century until a war of independence (1821–7) led to the establishment of a Greek kingdom in the Peloponnese in 1829. The remainder of Greece gradually became independent until the Dodecanese were returned by Italy in 1947. After the Nazi German occupation of 1941–4, a civil war between monarchist and Communist groups lasted from 1946 to 1949, and tension between right-wing and radical groups continued after 1949. In 1967 right-wing elements in the army seized power and established a military regime (the 'Greek Colonels'). The King went into voluntary exile in 1967; in 1974 the monarchy was abolished and a republic established. Unrest in Athens in 1973–4 intensified after the government was involved in the overthrow of President Makarios of Cyprus in July 1974, and led the Colonels to surrender power. Konstantinos Karamanlis (prime minister 1955–63) returned from exile to form a provisional government, and the first elections for ten years were held in 1974. The restoration of the monarchy was rejected by referendum on 8 December 1974 and Greece became a republic.

The most recent general election was held on 22 September 1996 with the Panhellenic Socialist Party (PASOK) winning 162 seats, the New Democracy Party (Christian Democrats) 108 seats, the Communist Party 11 seats, the Coalition of the Left and Progress ten seats, and the Democratic Social Movement nine seats.

POLITICAL SYSTEM

In 1986 most executive power was transferred from the president to the government. The unicameral 300-member Chamber of Deputies (*Vouli*) is elected for a four-year term by universal adult suffrage under a system of proportional representation, with a three per cent threshold for parliamentary representation.

HEAD OF STATE

President of the Hellenic Republic, Constantine Stephanopoulos, *elected by parliament* 8 March 1995

CABINET *as at July 1998*

Prime Minister, Costas Simitis
Aegean, Elisabeth Papazoi
Agriculture, Stephanos Tzoumakas
Culture, Evangelos Venizelos
Development, Vasso Papandreou
Education and Religion, Gerasimos Arsenis
Environment, Town Planning and Public Works, Costas Laliotis
Foreign Affairs, Theodoros Pangalos
Foreign Affairs (Alternate), George Papandreou
Health and Welfare, Costas Geitonas
Interior, Public Administration and Decentralization, Alekos Papadopoulos
Justice, Evangelos Yiannopoulos
Labour and Social Security, Militiades Papaioannou
Macedonia and Thrace, Phillipos Petsalnikos
Merchant Marine, Stavros Soumakis
National Defence, Akis Tsohatzopoulos
National Economy and Finance, Yiannos Papantoniou
Press and Media, Government Spokesman, Dimitris Reppas
Public Order, George Romeos
Transport and Communications, Tassos Mantelis

EMBASSY OF GREECE
1A Holland Park, London WII 3TP
Tel 0171-229 3850
Ambassador Extraordinary and Plenipotentiary, HE Vassilis Zafiropoulos, apptd 1996
Defence Attaché, Capt. N. Kostakis
Minister-Counsellor, M. Spinellis

HONORARY CONSULATES – Belfast, Birmingham, Edinburgh, Falmouth, Glasgow, Leeds and Southampton

BRITISH EMBASSY
1 Ploutarchou Street, 10675 Athens
Tel: Athens 723 6211
Ambassador Extraordinary and Plenipotentiary, HE Sir Michael Llewellyn Smith, KCVO, CMG, apptd 1996
Deputy Head of Mission, Counsellor and Consul-General, P. J. Millet
Defence and Military Attaché, Brig. W. A. McMahon
First Secretary (Commercial), G. G. Thomas

BRITISH CONSULAR OFFICES – Athens, Corfu, Heraklion (Crete), Kos, Patras, Rhodes, Salonika, Syros and Zakynthos

BRITISH COUNCIL DIRECTOR, P. Chenery, 17 Kolonaki Square, Athens 10673. There is also an office at Salonika.

BRITISH-HELLENIC CHAMBER OF COMMERCE, 25 Vas. Sofias Avenue, GR-106 74 Athens. Tel: 721 0361

DEFENCE

The Army has 1,735 main battle tanks, 809 armoured personnel carriers and armoured infantry fighting vehicles, and 1,878 artillery pieces. The Navy has eight submarines, four destroyers, 11 frigates, 41 patrol and coastal vessels, six combat aircraft and 15 armed helicopters. The Air Force has a total of 342 combat aircraft.

Greece maintains 1,250 army personnel in Cyprus. There are 435 US military personnel stationed in Greece.
MILITARY EXPENDITURE – 4.7 per cent of GDP (1996)
MILITARY PERSONNEL – 166,300: Army 116,000, Navy 19,500, Air Force 26,800, Paramilitary 4,000
CONSCRIPTION DURATION – Up to 21 months

ECONOMY

The principal minerals are nickel, bauxite, iron ore, iron pyrites, manganese magnesite, chrome, lead, zinc and emery. The chief industries are textiles (cotton, woollen and synthetics), chemicals, cement, glass, metallurgy, shipbuilding, domestic electrical equipment and footwear, the production of aluminium, nickel, iron and steel products, tyres, chemicals, fertilizers and sugar (from locally-grown beet). Food processing and ancillary industries are also growing.

The development of the country's electric power resources, irrigation and land reclamation schemes, and the exploitation of lignite resources for fuel and industrial purposes are continuing. Tourism is also a major industry, with over 10 million visitors in 1995.

Though there has been substantial industrialization, agriculture still employs about a fifth of the working population and contributes 12 per cent of GDP. The most important agricultural products are tobacco, wheat, cotton, sugar, rice, fruit (olives, peaches, vines, oranges, lemons, figs, almonds and currant-vines). Exports of fresh fruit, currants and vegetables are an important contributor to the economy.

The IMF austerity programme of privatization and reduction of the public sector has been partially reversed by the current government, which has slowed privatization. Further austerity measures imposed in an attempt to meet the EU's economic and monetary union criteria have prompted strikes. In March 1998 the drachma was devalued by 14 per cent and admitted to the ERM; Greece intends to participate in EMU in 2001, subject to meeting the economic criteria.

In 1996 there was a trade deficit of US$15,505 million and a current account deficit of US$4,554 million. In 1994 imports totalled US$21,466 million and exports US$9,384 million.

GNP – US$120,021 million (1996); US$11,460 per capita (1996)
GDP – US$70,897 million (1994); US$7,465 per capita (1994)
ANNUAL AVERAGE GROWTH OF GDP – 1.5 per cent (1994)
INFLATION RATE – 8.2 per cent (1996)
UNEMPLOYMENT – 10.0 per cent (1995)

Trade with UK	1996	1997
Imports from UK	£1,090,400,000	£996,600,000
Exports to UK	368,800,000	375,200,000

COMMUNICATIONS

The 2,650 km of railways are state-owned, with the exception of the Athens–Piraeus Electric Railway. Roads total over 38,500 km, of which about 25 per cent are national highways and just under 30,000 km are provincial roads. The Greek mercantile fleet numbers 1,864 ships over 100 tons gross with a total tonnage of 53,778,128 tons gross. Athens has direct airline links with Australasia, North America, most countries in Europe, Africa and the Middle East.

EDUCATION

Education is free and compulsory from the age of six to 15 and is maintained by state grants. There are eighteen universities and several other institutes of higher learning.
ILLITERACY RATE – 3.3 per cent
ENROLMENT (percentage of age group) – primary 98 per cent (1990); secondary 85 per cent (1994); tertiary 38.1 per cent (1994)

CULTURE

Greek civilization emerged c.1300 BC and the poems of Homer, which were probably current c.800 BC, record the struggle between the Achaeans of Greece and the Phrygians of Troy (1194 to 1184 BC).

The spoken language of modern Greece is descended from the Common Greek of Alexander the Great's empire. *Katharevousa*, a conservative literary dialect evolved by Adamantios Corais (Diamant Coray) (1748–1833) and used for official and technical matters, has been phased out. Novels and poetry are mostly in *dimotiki*, a progressive literary dialect which owes much to John Psycharis (1854–1929). The poets Solomos, Palamas, Cavafy and Sikelianos have won a European reputation. George Seferis (1963) and Odysseus Elytis (1979) have won the Nobel Prize for Literature.

GRENADA
The State of Grenada

AREA – 133 sq. miles (344 sq. km)
POPULATION – 92,000 (1994 UN estimate), 95,000 (1992 census). The language is English
CAPITAL – Ψ St George's (population, 4,788, 1981)
CURRENCY – East Caribbean dollar (EC$) of 100 cents
NATIONAL DAY – 7 February (Independence Day)
NATIONAL FLAG – Divided diagonally into yellow and green triangles within a red border containing six yellow stars, a yellow star on a red disc in the centre and a nutmeg on the green triangle in the hoist
POPULATION GROWTH RATE – 0.2 per cent (1995)
POPULATION DENSITY – 267 per sq. km (1995)

The island is about 21 miles long and 12 miles wide. Also a part of Grenada are some of the Grenadines islets, the largest of which is Carriacou, 13 square miles in area.

HISTORY AND POLITICS

Discovered by Columbus in 1498, and named Concepción, Grenada was originally colonized by France and was ceded to Great Britain by the Treaty of Versailles in 1783. It became an Associated State in 1967 and an independent nation within the Commonwealth on 7 February 1974.

The government was overthrown in 1979 by the New Jewel Movement and a People's Revolutionary Government was set up. In October 1983 disagreements within the PRG led to the death of Prime Minister Maurice Bishop, whose government was replaced by a Revolutionary Military Council. These events prompted the intervention of Caribbean and US forces. The Governor-General installed an advisory council to act as an interim government until a general election was held in December 1984. A phased withdrawal of US forces was completed by June 1985.

The general election held on 20 June 1995 was won by the New National Party led by Dr Keith Mitchell, with eight seats in the House of Representatives to the National Democratic Congress's five seats.

POLITICAL SYSTEM

Queen Elizabeth II is head of state and is represented by a Governor-General. Legislative power is vested in a bicameral parliament consisting of an elected 15-member House of Representatives and a 13-member Senate appointed by the Governor-General.

Governor-General, HE Sir Daniel Williams, GCMG, QC, apptd 1996

CABINET *as at July 1998*
Prime Minister, Finance, National Security, Information, Foreign Affairs, Keith Mitchell
Minister of State, Agriculture, Forestry, Lands and Fisheries, Michael Baptiste
Minister of State, Carriacou and Petit Martinique Affairs, Elvin Nimrod

Minister of State, Communications, Works and Public Utilities,
Oliver Archibald
Minister of State, Finance, Patrick Bubb
Minister of State, Youth, Sports, Culture and Community
Development, William Dewsbury
Agiculture, Lands, Forestry and Fisheries, Mark Isaacs
Communications, Works and Public Utilities, Gregory Bowen
Education and Labour, Lawrence Joseph
Health, Roger Radix
Housing, Social Security, Women's Affairs, National Insurance,
Laurina Waldron
Legal Affairs, Local Government, Caricom Affairs, Raphael
Fletcher
Tourism, Civil Aviation, Co-operatives, Joslyn Whiteman
Youth, Sports, Culture and Community Development, Adrian
Mitchell

GRENADA HIGH COMMISSION
1 Collingham Gardens, London SW5 0HW
Tel 0171-373 7809
High Commissioner, HE Marcelle Gairy, apptd 1997

BRITISH HIGH COMMISSIONER, HE Richard Thomas,
CMG, resident at Bridgetown, Barbados

ECONOMY

The economy is principally agrarian, with cocoa, nutmegs
and bananas the major crops. Fruit and vegetables are
grown and livestock raised for domestic consumption. The
fishing industry is being developed. Manufacturing consists of processing agricultural products and the production of textiles, concrete, aluminium and handicrafts.
Tourism is the main foreign exchange earner. In 1996
there were 386,013 tourists.
GNP – US$285 million (1996); US$2,880 per capita (1996)
GDP – US$208 million (1994); US$2,437 per capita (1994)
ANNUAL AVERAGE GROWTH OF GDP – 0.6 per cent (1992)
INFLATION RATE – 3.0 per cent (1995)
TOTAL EXTERNAL DEBT – US$120 million (1996)

TRADE

In 1994 there was a trade deficit of US$99 million and a
current account deficit of US$33 million.

Trade with UK	1996	1997
Imports from UK	£7,503,000	£7,010,000
Exports to UK	1,767,000	1,050,000

GUATEMALA
República de Guatemala

AREA – 42,042 sq. miles (108,889 sq. km). Neighbours:
Mexico (north and west), El Salvador, Honduras and
Belize (east)
POPULATION – 10,621,000 (1994 UN estimate). The
language is Spanish, but 40 per cent of the population
speak an Indian language
CAPITAL – Guatemala City (population, 1,675,589, 1990
estimate)
MAJOR CITIES – Antigua (30,000); Mazatenango (21,000);
ΨPuerto Barrios (23,000); Quezaltenango (100,000)
CURRENCY – Quetzal (Q) of 100 centavos
NATIONAL ANTHEM – Guatemala Feliz (Guatemala be
praised)
NATIONAL DAY – 15 September
NATIONAL FLAG – Three vertical bands, blue, white, blue;
coat of arms on white stripe
LIFE EXPECTANCY (years) – male 55.11; female 59.43
POPULATION GROWTH RATE – 2.9 per cent (1995)

POPULATION DENSITY – 98 per sq. km (1995)
URBAN POPULATION – 38.7 per cent (1995)
MILITARY EXPENDITURE – 1.3 per cent of GDP (1996)
MILITARY PERSONNEL – 50,500: Army 38,500, Navy
1,500, Air Force 700, Paramilitaries 9,800
CONSCRIPTION DURATION – 30 months
ILLITERACY RATE – 44.4 per cent
ENROLMENT (percentage of age group) – primary 58 per
cent (1980); secondary 13 per cent (1980); tertiary 8.1 per
cent (1995)

Guatemala is traversed from west to east by mountains
containing volcanic summits rising to 13,000 feet above sea
level; earthquakes are frequent. There are numerous
rivers. The climate is hot and malarial near the coast,
temperate in the higher regions.

HISTORY AND POLITICS

Guatemala was under Spanish rule from 1524 until gaining
independence in 1821. It formed part of the Confederation
of Central America from 1823 to 1839.
    After a series of military coups, civilian rule was restored
with the election of a Constituent Assembly in 1984 and
the promulgation of a new constitution in 1985. In May
1993 President Serrano partially suspended the constitution and attempted to rule by decree but was effectively
ousted by the army on 1 June. Ramiro de León Carpio was
elected president by Congress to serve out Serrano's term
to January 1996.
    President de León continued attempts to curb political
corruption and in November 1993 forced Congress and the
Supreme Court to dissolve themselves and to agree to
constitutional changes, including reducing the presidential term to four years, which were ratified by a referendum
in January 1994. Legislative elections to a smaller 80-seat
National Congress were held in August 1994. Elections to
the National Congress in November 1995 were won by the
National Advancement Party (PAN) which won 43 seats to
the Guatemalan Republican Front's 21. The presidential
election in January 1996 was won by Alvaro Arzú of the
PAN.

INSURGENCY

Since 1960 the armed forces have been fighting insurgency
by the left-wing, mainly Mayan Indian, guerrillas of the
Guatemalan Revolutionary National Unity Movement
(URNG). Some 150,000 have been killed in the fighting.
Government–URNG negotiations began in 1991 and have
continued since, leading to a reduction in fighting and
agreements in 1993. In March 1994 a human rights accord
was reached under which a 300-strong UN Observer
Mission (MINUGUA) was established in November 1994
to supervise the implementation of government–URNG
accords. An accord recognizing the rights of the indigenous
population was signed in March 1995. Representatives of
the four rebel groups comprising the URNG signed a
peace treaty with the government in December 1996
under which they would become a political party. In
August 1997, Ricardo Ramírez was elected secretary-
general of the URNG's political executive committee.

POLITICAL SYSTEM

Executive power is vested in the president, who is directly
elected for a single four-year term. He appoints the
Cabinet. Legislative authority is vested in the National
Congress, whose 80 members are directly elected for a
four-year term.
    The republic is divided into 22 departments.

HEAD OF STATE
President, Alvaro Arzú Irigoyen, *sworn in* 14 January 1996
Vice-President, Luís Alberto Flores Asturias

GOVERNMENT *as at July 1998*
The President
The Vice-President
Agriculture, Livestock and Food, Mariano Ventura
Communications, Fritz García Gallont
Culture, Augusto Vela
Defence, Gen. Héctor Mario Barrios Zelada
Economy, Juan Mauricio Wurmser
Education, Roberto Moreno Godoy
Energy, Leonel López Rodas
Foreign Affairs, Eduardo Stein
Interior, Rodolfo Mendoza
Labour and Social Security, Héctor Cifuentes
Public Finance, José Alejandro Arevalo
Public Health, Marco Tulio Sosa
Secretary-General of the Presidency, Carlos García Regas

EMBASSY OF GUATEMALA
13 Fawcett Street, London SW10 9HN
Tel 0171-351 3042
Ambassador Extraordinary and Plenipotentiary, HE Fernando
Andrade Díaz-Duran, apptd 1996

BRITISH EMBASSY
Edificio Centro Financiero (7th Floor), Tower Two,
Seventh Avenue 5–10, Zone 4, Guatemala City
Tel: Guatemala City 332 1601
Ambassador Extraordinary and Plenipotentiary, HE Andrew
Caie, apptd 1998

ECONOMY

Agriculture provides 25 per cent of GDP and employs nearly two thirds of the workforce. The principal export is coffee, other articles being manufactured goods, sugar, bananas and cardamom. The chief imports are petroleum, vehicles, machinery and foodstuffs.

The chief seaports are San José de Guatemala and Champerico on the Pacific and Santo Tomás de Castilla and Puerto Barrios on the Atlantic side.

In 1995 there was a trade deficit of US$877 million and a current account deficit of US$572 million. In 1996 imports totalled US$3,146 million and exports US$2,031 million.
GNP – US$16,018 million (1996) (1996); US$1,470 per capita (1996)
GDP – US$8,969 million (1994); US$1,252 per capita (1994)
ANNUAL AVERAGE GROWTH OF GDP – 3.0 per cent (1996)
INFLATION RATE – 11.1 per cent (1996)
TOTAL EXTERNAL DEBT – US$3,785 million (1996)

TRADE WITH UK	1996	1997
Imports from UK	£27,878,000	£33,052,000
Exports to UK	19,635,000	15,893,000

GUINEA
République de Guinée

AREA – 94,926 sq. miles (245,857 sq. km). Neighbours: Guinea-Bissau (east), Senegal, Mali (north), Côte d'Ivoire (west), Sierra Leone and Liberia (south)
POPULATION – 6,700,000 (1994 UN estimate); the official language is French; Fullah, Malinké and Soussou are indigenous languages
CAPITAL – ΨConakry (population, 763,000)

MAJOR CITIES – Kankan; Kindia; Labé; Mamou; N'Zérékoré; Siguiri
CURRENCY – Guinea franc of 100 centimes
NATIONAL DAY – 2 October (Anniversary of Proclamation of Independence)
NATIONAL FLAG – Three vertical stripes of red, yellow and green
LIFE EXPECTANCY (years) – male 44.00; female 45.00
POPULATION GROWTH RATE – 3.0 per cent (1995)
POPULATION DENSITY – 27 per sq. km (1995)
MILITARY EXPENDITURE – 1.4 per cent of GDP (1996)
MILITARY PERSONNEL – 12,300: Army 8,500, Navy 400, Air Force 800, Paramilitaries 2,600
CONSCRIPTION DURATION – Two years
ILLITERACY RATE – 64.1 per cent
ENROLMENT (percentage of age group) – primary 37 per cent (1993); secondary 9 per cent (1985); tertiary 1.1 per cent (1990)

HISTORY AND POLITICS

Guinea was separated from Senegal in 1891 and administered by France as a separate colony. On 2 October 1958 Guinea became an independent republic.

M. Sékou Touré assumed office as head of the new government, and was elected president in 1961. His death in 1984 was followed by a military coup. Guinea was ruled by a military government directed by a Military Committee for National Recovery (CMRN). A new constitution, providing for the end of military rule, was approved by referendum in 1990.

In January 1991 the CMRN was dissolved and a mixed civilian-military Transitional Committee for National Recovery (CTRN) was established which appointed a new government. Civil disturbances in 1991 caused the government to introduce a full multiparty system in April 1992, since when 40 opposition parties have been legalized. A presidential election held in 1993 was won by the incumbent President Conté with 51 per cent of the vote amid opposition claims of electoral fraud. Legislative elections in June 1995 were won by President Conté's Party of Unity and Progress (PUP), which gained 71 of the 114 National Assembly seats.

HEAD OF STATE
President, Maj.-Gen. Lansana Conté, *took power* 3 April 1984, *elected* 19 December 1993

COUNCIL OF MINISTERS *as at July 1998*
Prime Minister, Co-ordinator of Government Actions, Sidia Touré
Agriculture, Water and Forests, Jean-Paul Sarr
Communication and Culture, Ibrahima Mongo Diallo
Defence, Dorank Assifat Diasseny
Economic Affairs, Finance, Ibrahima Kassory Fofana
Employment and Civil Service, Almane Fode Sylla
Fishing and Animal Husbandry, Boubacar Barry
Foreign Affairs, Lamine Camara
Interior, Decentralization, Abidine Zainoul Sanoussy
Justice, Moussa Sampil
National Education and Scientific Research, Eugene Camara
Natural Resources and Energy, Facinet Fofana
Planning and International Co-operation, Mamadou Cellou Diallo
Pre-University Teaching, Germain Doualamou
Private Sector, Industry and Commerce, Madikaba Camara
Public Health, Kandjoura Drame
Public Works, Environment, Transport and Telecommunications, Cellou Dalen Diallo
Secretary-General to the President, Fode Bangoura
Security, Govreissi Conde
Social Affairs, Promotion of Women and Children, Saran Daraba

Technical Education and Vocational Training, Almany Diaby
Tourism and Hotels, Kozo Zoumanigui
Urbanization and Housing, Alpha Ousmane Diallo
Youth, Sports and Civil Education, Koumba Diakite

EMBASSY OF THE REPUBLIC OF GUINEA
51 rue de la Faisanderie, 75016 Paris, France
Tel: Paris 4704 8148/4553 8545
Ambassador Extraordinary and Plenipotentiary, HE Ibrahima
    Sylla, apptd 1997

BRITISH CONSULATE
BP 834 Conakry, Guinea
British Ambassador, HE David Snoxell, resident at Dakar,
    Senegal

ECONOMY

The principal products are bauxite, alumina, palm kernels,
millet, cassava, bananas, plantains and rubber. Deposits of
iron ore, gold, diamonds and uranium have been discovered. Principal imports are cotton goods, petroleum
products, sugar, flour and salt; exports, bauxite, alumina,
iron ore, diamonds, coffee, bananas, palm kernels and
pineapples.

In 1995 there was a trade deficit of US$39 million and a
current account deficit of US$197 million.
GNP – US$3,804 million (1996); US$560 per capita (1996)
GDP – US$3,223 million (1994); US$461 per capita (1994)
TOTAL EXTERNAL DEBT – US$3,240 million (1996)

TRADE WITH UK	1996	1997
Imports from UK	£19,911,000	£17,091,000
Exports to UK	1,064,000	1,017,000

GUINEA–BISSAU
República da Guiné-Bissau

AREA – 13,948 sq. miles (36,125 sq. km). Neighbours:
    Senegal (north), Guinea (east and south)
POPULATION – 1,073,000 (1994 UN estimate). The main
    ethnic groups are the Balante, Malinké, Fulani,
    Mandjako and Pepel. The official language is
    Portuguese; most of the population speak Guinean
    Creole
CAPITAL – ΨBissau (population, 109,214, 1979)
CURRENCY – Franc CFA
NATIONAL DAY – 24 September (Independence Day)
NATIONAL FLAG – Horizontal bands of yellow over green
    with vertical red band in the hoist charged with a black
    star
LIFE EXPECTANCY (years) – male 41.92; female 45.12
POPULATION GROWTH RATE – 2.1 per cent (1995)
POPULATION DENSITY – 30 per sq. km (1995)
MILITARY EXPENDITURE – 2.8 per cent of GDP (1996)
MILITARY PERSONNEL – 9,250: Army 6,800, Navy 350, Air
    Force 100, Paramilitaries 2,000
CONSCRIPTION DURATION – Selective conscription
ILLITERACY RATE – 45.1 per cent
ENROLMENT (percentage of age group) – primary 46 per
    cent (1986); secondary 3 per cent (1980); tertiary 0.5 per
    cent (1988)

HISTORY AND POLITICS

Guinea-Bissau, formerly Portuguese Guinea, achieved
independence on 24 September 1974. Following a coup led
by Maj. (now Brig.-Gen.) Vieira in 1980, a Revolutionary
Council was established. Under a new constitution
adopted in 1984, the Revolutionary Council became a 15-
member Council of State and an Assembly of 150 members

was set up. The ruling African Party for the Independence
of Guinea and Cape Verde (PAIGC) introduced a multiparty system in January 1991. Ten opposition parties have
been legalized since November 1991. Elections to a new
100-seat legislature were held in July 1994; the PAIGC
won 64 seats. Brig.-Gen. Vieira won the second round of
the presidential election in August 1994 with 52 per cent of
the vote.

In June 1998, several hundred people were killed when
fighting broke out in Bissau between troops loyal to
President Vieira and supporters of the sacked army chief
Ansumane Mane. Senegal sent in troops to support Vieira,
and talks to resolve the crisis continue.

HEAD OF STATE
*President, Chairman of the Council of State, C.-in-C. of the Armed
    Forces,* Brig.-Gen. João Bernardo Vieira, *took power*
    November 1980, *elected* June 1989, *re-elected for a five-year
    term* 6 August 1994

COUNCIL OF MINISTERS *as at July 1998*
Prime Minister, Carlos Correia
Defence, Samba Lamine Mane
Economy and Finance, Issuf Sanha
Equipment, João Gomes Cardoso
Foreign Affairs and Co-operation, Fernando Delfim da Silva
Interior, Francisca Pereira
Justice and Labour, Daniel Ferreira
National Education, Odette Semedo
Parliamentary Affairs and Information, Malal Sane
Public Health, Brandao Gomes Co
Rural Development, Natural Resources and Environment, José
    Avito da Silva
Social Affairs and Women's Promotion, Nharebat N'Inçaia
    N'Tchasso
Territorial Administration, Nicandro Barreto Pereira
Veterans' Affairs, Arafan Mane

EMBASSY OF THE REPUBLIC OF GUINEA-BISSAU
94 rue St Lazare, Paris 75009, France
Tel: Paris 4526 1851
Chargé d'Affaires, Maria Filomena Araujo Vieira

HONORARY CONSULATE
Flat 5, 8 Palace Gate, London W8 5NF
Tel: 0171-589 5253
Honorary Consul, Raja Makarem

BRITISH CONSULATE
Mavegro Int., CP100, Bissau
British Ambassador, HE David Snoxell, resident at Dakar,
    Senegal

ECONOMY

Guinea-Bissau produces rice, coconuts, groundnuts and
plantains. Cattle are raised, and there are bauxite and
phosphate deposits. In May 1997 Guinea-Bissau joined the
French Franc Zone, and the CFA Franc replaced the peso
as currency.

In 1995 there was a trade deficit of US$35 million and a
current account deficit of US$41 million. In 1996 imports
totalled US$63 million and exports US$21 million.
GNP – US$270 million (1996); US$250 per capita (1996)
GDP – US$262 million (1994); US$182 per capita (1994)
ANNUAL AVERAGE GROWTH OF GDP – 3.0 per cent (1993)
INFLATION RATE – 50.7 per cent (1996)
TOTAL EXTERNAL DEBT – US$937 million (1996)

TRADE WITH UK	1996	1997
Imports from UK	£1,695,000	£1,348,000
Exports to UK	94,000	168,000

GUYANA
The Co-operative Republic of Guyana

AREA – 83,000 sq. miles (214,969 sq. km). Neighbours: Venezuela (west), Brazil (west and south), Suriname (east)

POPULATION – 835,000 (1994 UN estimate): 51 per cent East Indian (mainly rural), 30 per cent African (mainly urban), Amerindians, Europeans, Chinese and people of mixed descent; 50 per cent Christian, 35 per cent Hindu, less than 10 per cent Muslim. Guyana is the only English-speaking country in South America

CAPITAL – ΨGeorgetown (population, 250,000)

MAJOR TOWNS – Corriverton (24,000); Linden (35,000); ΨNew Amsterdam (25,000)

CURRENCY – Guyana dollar (G$) of 100 cents

NATIONAL ANTHEM – Dear Land of Guyana

NATIONAL DAYS – 26 May (Independence Day); 23 February (Republic Day)

NATIONAL FLAG – Green with a yellow, white-bordered triangle based on the hoist and surmounted by a red, black-bordered triangle

LIFE EXPECTANCY (years) – male 62.44; female 68.02

POPULATION GROWTH RATE – 1.0 per cent (1995)

POPULATION DENSITY – 4 per sq. km (1995)

MILITARY EXPENDITURE – 1.0 per cent of GDP (1996)

MILITARY PERSONNEL – 1,500: Army 1,400, Air Force 100

HISTORY AND POLITICS

Guyana (formerly British Guiana) became independent on 26 May 1966, with a Governor-General appointed by Queen Elizabeth II. It became a republic on 23 February 1970.

Elections were held in October 1992 after voter registration lists and electoral machinery had finally been established after many years. In the presidential election Dr Cheddi Jagan defeated the incumbent Desmond Hoyte and in the legislative election Jagan's People's Progressive Party (PPP) defeated the People's National Congress (PNC) which had governed since independence. Jagan died in March 1997 and was replaced by former Prime Minister Samuel Hinds. In the December 1997 election, Janet Jagan (who had previously served as prime minister and was the widow of the late president) was elected president and the PPP returned to power. The PNC claimed the result was fixed and their demonstrations against the government became violent; in January 1998 an agreement was reached between the PNC and the PPP whereby the constitution would be reviewed within 18 months and new elections would be held within three years rather than five.

POLITICAL SYSTEM

The 1980 constitution provides for an executive president who serves a five-year term, and a National Assembly of 65 members, of which 53 are elected nationally by proportional representation and 12 are regional representatives.

HEAD OF STATE

President, Janet Jagan, *elected* 15 December 1997

CABINET *as at July 1998*

The President
Prime Minister, Home Affairs and Public Works, Sam Hinds
Agriculture, Reepu Daman Persaud
Amerindian Affairs, Vilbert de Souza
Attorney-General, Legal Affairs, Charles Ramson
Education and Cultural Development, Dale Bisnauth

Finance, Bharrat Jagdeo
Foreign Affairs, Clement Rohee
Housing and Water, Shaik Baksh
Human Services, Social Security, Indranie Chandarpal
Information, Moses Nagamootoo
Labour, Health, Henry Jeffrey
Marine Resources, Satyadcow Sawh
Presidential Secretariat, Roger Luncheon
Public Service, George Fung-on
Regional and Local Government, Clinton Collymore; Harripersaud Nokta
Trade, Tourism and Industry, Michael Shree Chan
Transport and Hydraulics, Anthony Xavier
Youth, Sport and Culture, Gail Teixera

GUYANA HIGH COMMISSION
3 Palace Court, Bayswater Road, London W2 4LP
Tel 0171-229 7684
High Commissioner, HE Laleshwar Singh, apptd 1993

BRITISH HIGH COMMISSION
44 Main Street (PO Box 10849), Georgetown
Tel: Georgetown 65881/4
High Commissioner, HE Ian Whitehead, apptd 1998

ECONOMY

Agriculture is the principal economic activity. The economy is based almost entirely on the main export items of Demerara sugar, rice, shrimps, gold and rum. Diamonds are also mined. There is some cattle ranching in the savanna country, and oil deposits have been found there. Industry is fairly small-scale. Much emphasis is now being placed on eco-tourism. Foreign aid covers much of the government deficit.

In 1995 there was a trade deficit of US$41 million and a current account deficit of US$135 million. in 1996 exports totalled US$546 million.

GNP – US$582 million (1996); US$690 per capita (1996)

GDP – US$531 million (1994); US$655 per capita (1994)

ANNUAL AVERAGE GROWTH OF GDP – 8.2 per cent (1993)

INFLATION RATE – 2.6 per cent (1992)

TOTAL EXTERNAL DEBT – US$1,631 million (1996)

TRADE WITH UK	1996	1997
Imports from UK	£33,984,000	£25,774,000
Exports to UK	91,558,000	81,852,000

COMMUNICATIONS

Georgetown and New Amsterdam are the principal ports, though bauxite ships also sail to Linden, on the Demerara, and Everton, on the Berbice. There are no public railways and the few roads are confined mainly to the coastal areas. Paved roads total about 430 miles out of a total network of 1,459 miles. Air transport is the easiest form of communication between the coast and the interior. The state-owned national airline is called Guyana Airways.

There is a state-owned radio broadcasting station which operates two channels and a fledgling television service.

EDUCATION

Education is compulsory between the ages of five and 14; nursery, primary and secondary schooling are free. The government assumed total control of the education system in 1976 and made education free. The government instituted fees for study at the University of Guyana in 1994.

There are several technical and vocational institutions, as well as some 30 adult education schools. There are also a number of technical and vocational institutions not under the aegis of the Ministry of Education.

ILLITERACY RATE – 1.9 per cent
ENROLMENT (percentage of age group) – primary 90 per cent (1994); secondary 66 per cent (1992); tertiary 8.6 per cent (1994)

HAITI
République d'Haiti

AREA – 10,714 sq. miles (27,750 sq. km). Neighbour: Dominican Republic (east)
POPULATION – 7,180,000 (1994 UN estimate) of which 90 per cent are black and 10 per cent mulatto (mixed race). Both French and Creole are regarded as official languages. French is the language of government and the press but it is only spoken by the educated mulatto minority. The usual language is Creole
CAPITAL – ΨPort-au-Prince (population, 690,168, 1990 estimate)
MAJOR CITIES – ΨCap Haitien (54,691); Gonaives (36,736); Jérémie (25,117); Les Cayes (27,222)
CURRENCY – Gourde of 100 centimes
NATIONAL ANTHEM – La Dessalinienne
NATIONAL DAY – 1 January
NATIONAL FLAG – Horizontally blue over red
LIFE EXPECTANCY (years) – male 54.95; female 58.34
POPULATION GROWTH RATE – 2.0 per cent (1995)
POPULATION DENSITY – 259 per sq. km (1995)
URBAN POPULATION – 32.6 per cent (1995)
MILITARY EXPENDITURE – 3.5 per cent of GDP (1996)
ILLITERACY RATE – 55.0 per cent
ENROLMENT (percentage of age group) – primary 26 per cent (1990); tertiary 1.1 per cent (1985)

The Republic of Haiti occupies the western third of the Caribbean island of Hispaniola. The climate is tropical with high humidity and an almost constant temperature.

HISTORY AND POLITICS

Haiti was a French slave colony under the name of Saint-Domingue from 1697 until 1791, when French rule was overthrown in a revolt led by Toussaint L'Ouverture. French rule was restored by Napoleon in 1802 but in 1803 French forces surrendered to a British naval blockade and on 1 January 1804 the colony was declared independent as Haiti by Jean Jacques Dessalines. Dessalines became Emperor of Haiti but was assassinated in 1806.

Haiti was under US military occupation from 1915 to 1934. Dr François 'Papa Doc' Duvalier was elected in 1957 and became life president in 1964. He was succeeded in 1971 by his son Jean-Claude 'Baby Doc' Duvalier who fled to France in 1986 in the face of sustained popular unrest. Five years of military government followed until Father Jean-Bertrand Aristide, leader of the National Front for Change and Democracy, won a free presidential election in 1990.

Aristide fled to the USA following a military coup in September 1991. The UN and OAS imposed an oil and arms embargo and froze the military élite's foreign assets, forcing the regime to negotiate the Governor's Island Agreement in July 1993, which provided for Aristide's return. In September 1993, the military reneged on the agreement and the UN imposed a naval blockade and a total economic, trade and travel ban. In September 1994, an agreement was reached on President Aristide's return and the flight of the military junta members abroad. Sanctions were lifted and Aristide returned on 15 October to appoint a new government. Forces of the UN Mission in Haiti

(UNMIH) took over responsibility for internal security and retraining Army personnel on 31 March 1995. At the expiration of the UNMIH peacekeeping mandate in November 1997, the UN Security Council agreed to establish a civilian police mission to continue training the Haitian police force for a further 12 months.

Elections to the 27-member Senate and 83-member Chamber of Deputies in June to August 1995 were won by the pro-Aristide Lavalas party. The presidential election in December 1995 was won by Lavalas candidate René Préval. The nomination of Hervé Denis as prime minister twice failed to gain ratification from the Senate. He was the second nominee to be rejected, leaving the government without a leader and threatening the successful implementation of economic reforms necessary for development loans.

POLITICAL SYSTEM

The head of state is a president, directly elected for a five-year term that may not be renewed immediately. The National Assembly is the bicameral legislature; the lower house, the Chamber of Deputies, has 83 members directly elected for four years. The upper house or Senate has 27 members elected for six years; one third of the senators are elected every two years. The president appoints the prime minister, who must be approved by the National Assembly. The prime minister chooses the Cabinet.

HEAD OF STATE
President, René Préval, *sworn in* 7 February 1996

CABINET *as at July 1998*
Prime Minister, vacant
Commerce and Industry, Frenel Germain
Economy, Finance, Agriculture, Fred Joseph
Education, Jacques Edouard Alexis
Foreign Affairs, Fritz Longchamp
Haitians Abroad, Paul Gijem
Interior and Defence, Jean-Joseph Molière
Justice, Pierre Max Antoine
Planning, External Co-operation, Jean-Eric Dérice
Public Works, Transport, Communications, Environment, Jacques Dorcéan
Social Affairs, Culture, Women's Affairs, Pierre-Denis Amédée

BRITISH AMBASSADOR, HE A. R. Thomas, CMG, resident at Kingston, Jamaica

ECONOMY

Coffee accounts for about one third of total exports. Cocoa is the second largest export earner. Corn, sorghum and rice are also grown. Increased production of tropical fruits and vegetables is being encouraged.

Leather goods, textiles, electronic components and sports equipment are manufactured, using imported raw materials, for re-export. Principal imports are raw materials for the export assembly sector, foodstuffs, machinery, vehicles, mineral oils and textiles.

Privatization of several large state enterprises and a programme of land redistribution have begun.

In 1995 Haiti had a trade deficit of US$415 million and a current account deficit of US$67 million. In 1996 imports totalled US$665 million and exports US$90 million.
GNP – US$2,282 million (1996); US$310 per capita (1996)
GDP – US$1,959 million (1994); US$266 per capita (1994)
ANNUAL AVERAGE GROWTH OF GDP – 2.8 per cent (1996)
INFLATION RATE – 17.1 per cent (1996)
TOTAL EXTERNAL DEBT – US$897 million (1996)

TRADE WITH UK	1996	1997
Imports from UK	£9,732,000	£8,746,000
Exports to UK	1,789,000	1,359,000

COMMUNICATIONS

There are more than 4,000 km of roads. Air services are maintained between the capital and the principal provincial towns and to the USA and Caribbean and South American countries. The principal towns and villages are connected by telephone and/or telegraph. There are several commercial radio stations and two television stations at Port-au-Prince.

HOLY SEE, *see* VATICAN CITY STATE

HONDURAS
República de Honduras

AREA – 43,277 sq. miles (112,088 sq. km). Neighbours: Guatemala (north-west), El Salvador (south-west), Nicaragua (south)

POPULATION – 5,953,000 (1994 UN estimate) of mixed Spanish and Indian blood. The Garifunas in the north are of West Indian origin. The language is Spanish, although English is the first language of many in the islands and on the north coast

CAPITAL – Tegucigalpa (population, 670,100, 1991 estimate)

MAJOR CITIES – Choluteca (63,200); ΨLa Ceiba (77,100); ΨPuerto Cortes (32,500); San Pedro Sula (325,900); ΨTela (24,000)

CURRENCY – Lempira of 100 centavos

NATIONAL ANTHEM – Tu Bandera Es Un Lampo De Cielo (Your flag is a heavenly light)

NATIONAL DAY – 15 September

NATIONAL FLAG – Three horizontal bands, blue, white, blue (with five blue stars on white band)

LIFE EXPECTANCY (years) – male 65.43; female 70.06

POPULATION GROWTH RATE – 3.1 per cent (1995)

POPULATION DENSITY – 53 per sq. km (1995)

URBAN POPULATION – 47.5 per cent (1995)

MILITARY EXPENDITURE – 1.1 per cent of GDP (1996)

MILITARY PERSONNEL – 24,300: Army 16,000, Navy 1,000, Air Force 1,800, Paramilitaries 5,500

CONSCRIPTION DURATION – Two years (ended 1995)

The country is mountainous, being traversed by the Cordilleras, with peaks rising to 1,500 and 2,400 metres above sea level. Rainfall is seasonal, May to October being wet and November to April dry.

HISTORY AND POLITICS

Discovered and settled by the Spanish in the 16th century, Honduras formed part of the Spanish American dominions until 1821 when independence was proclaimed. Under military government from 1972, Honduras returned to civilian rule in 1981 with an executive presidency, a 128-seat unicameral Congress, and a multiparty system. The most recent legislative elections were held on 30 November 1997 and won by the Liberal Party. In October 1997, Congress approved a constitutional amendment reducing the legislature to 80 members. The amendment must also be ratified by the current session of Congress before it becomes law.

The country is divided into 18 departments.

HEAD OF STATE

President of the Republic, Carlos Roberto Flores (Liberal), *elected* 30 November 1997

CABINET *as at July 1998*

Agriculture and Livestock, Pedro Arturo Sevilla
Culture, Arts and Sports, Herman Allan Padget
Defence, Col. Cristóbal Corrales Calix
Education, Aristides Mejia Casco
Foreign Affairs, José Fernando Martínez
Health, Marco Antonio Rosa
Home Office, Delmer Urbizo Panting
Industry, Trade, Tourism, Reginaldo Panting
Labour and Social Security, Andrés Victor Artiles
Natural Resources, Environment, Elvin Santos
Presidential Office, Gustavo Alfaro
Public Works, Transport and Housing, Tomás Lozano Reyes
Secretary of the Treasury, Gabriela Nuñez López

EMBASSY OF HONDURAS
115 Gloucester Place, London WIH 3PJ
Tel 0171-486 4880
Ambassador Extraordinary and Plenipotentiary, HE Roberto Flores-Bermúdez, apptd 1998

BRITISH EMBASSY
Apartado Postal 290, Tegucigalpa
Tel: Honduras 232 0612/18
Ambassador Extraordinary and Plenipotentiary, HE David Osbourne, apptd 1998
BRITISH CONSULATE – San Pedro Sula

ECONOMY

Three-quarters of the country is covered by pine forests. Agriculture and cattle raising is mainly confined to the fertile coastal plain on the Caribbean and the extensive valleys in the Comayagua and Olancho regions of the interior. The Mosquitia tropical forest covers the area from the coast to the border with Nicaragua and provides valuable reserves of timber. Lead, zinc and silver are mined on a small scale.

The chief exports are coffee, bananas, frozen meat, shrimps, lobsters and timber, the most important woods being pine, mahogany and cedar. The main imports are machinery and electrical equipment, industrial chemicals and lubricants.

In 1995 Honduras had a trade deficit of US$141 million and a current account deficit of US$201 million. In 1996 imports totalled US$1,694 million and exports US$1,106 million.

GNP – US$4,012 million (1996); US$660 per capita (1996)
GDP – US$7,136 million (1994); US$532 per capita (1994)
ANNUAL AVERAGE GROWTH OF GDP – 3.0 per cent (1996)
INFLATION RATE – 23.8 per cent (1996)
UNEMPLOYMENT – 3.2 per cent (1995)
TOTAL EXTERNAL DEBT – US$4,453 million (1996)

TRADE WITH UK	1996	1997
Imports from UK	£12,203,000	£13,677,000
Exports to UK	13,772,000	35,596,000

COMMUNICATIONS

There are about 1,004 km of railway in operation, chiefly to serve the banana plantations and the Caribbean ports. There are 17,947 km of roads, of which 2,613 km are paved. There are 33 smaller airstrips and four international airports, Tegucigalpa, San Pedro Sula, La Ceiba and Roatan (Bay Island).

The chief ports are Puerto Cortes, Tela and La Ceiba on the north coast, through which passes the bulk of the trade with the USA and Europe. Puerto Castilla is being developed as a deep-water container port, and San Lorenzo is also experiencing rapid growth.

EDUCATION

Primary and secondary education is free, primary education being compulsory, and the government has launched a campaign to eradicate illiteracy.

ILLITERACY RATE – 27.3 per cent

ENROLMENT (percentage of age group) – primary 90 per cent (1993); secondary 21 per cent (1991); tertiary 10.0 per cent (1994)

HUNGARY
Magyar Köztársaság

AREA – 35,920 sq. miles (93,032 sq. km). Neighbours: Slovakia (north), Ukraine and Romania (east), the rump Yugoslav Federal state and Croatia (south), Slovenia and Austria (west)

POPULATION – 10,225,000 (1994 UN estimate). There are minorities of gypsies (4.8 per cent), ethnic Germans (1.9 per cent) and Slovaks (0.9 per cent). About two-thirds of the population are Roman Catholic and the remainder mostly Calvinist. The language is Hungarian (Magyar)

CAPITAL – Budapest, on the Danube (population, 2,002,121, 1993 estimate)

MAJOR CITIES – Debrecen (214,245); Miskolc (185,877); Pécs (167,772); Szeged (173,860)

CURRENCY – Forint of 100 fillér

NATIONAL ANTHEM – Isten Aldd Meg A Magyart (God Bless the Hungarians)

NATIONAL DAYS – 15 March, 20 August, 23 October

NATIONAL FLAG – Red, white, green (horizontally)

LIFE EXPECTANCY (years) – male 64.84; female 74.23

POPULATION GROWTH RATE – –0.3 per cent (1995)

POPULATION DENSITY – 110 per sq. km (1995)

URBAN POPULATION – 63.3 per cent (1994)

HISTORY AND POLITICS

Hungary, reconstituted as a kingdom in 1920 after having been declared a republic on 17 November 1918, joined the Anti-Comintern Pact in February 1939 and entered the Second World War on the side of Germany in 1941. On 20 January 1945 a Hungarian provisional government of liberation signed an armistice under the terms of which the frontiers of Hungary were withdrawn to the 1937 limits.

After the liberation, a coalition of parties carried out land reform and nationalization. By 1949 the Communists had succeeded in gaining a monopoly of power and by 1952 practically the entire economy had been 'socialized'.

Divisions within the Communist Party and popular demand for free elections and Soviet troop withdrawals grew from July 1956 onwards. An uprising on 23 October was quelled by Soviet forces the following morning. By 30 October the Soviets had withdrawn from Budapest and on 3 November an all-party coalition government under Imre Nagy was formed. This government was overthrown and the attempted revolution suppressed by a renewed attack by Soviet forces on Budapest on 4 November. The formation of a new Hungarian Revolutionary Worker Peasant (Communist) government under János Kádár was announced the same day.

From 1968 the government gradually introduced economic reforms and some political liberalization. Kádár was forced to resign in May 1989. In October 1989 the National

Assembly (*Országgyülés*) approved an amended constitution which described Hungary as an independent, democratic state. The 386-seat National Assembly is elected on a mixed first past the post and proportional representation basis with a 5 per cent threshold for representation. The first free multiparty elections took place in March and April 1990 and were won by the (conservative) Hungarian Democratic Forum.

In the legislative elections in May 1998, no party won an overall majority. The Federation of Young Democrats-Hungarian Party (Fidesz-MPP) won the largest number of seats and its leader, Viktor Orbàn, was asked by President Göncz to form a coalition government. The composition of the National Assembly in June 1998 was: Fidesz-MPP 147, Hungarian Socialist Party (HSP) 134, Independent Smallholders Party (FKGP) 48, Alliance of Free Democrats (AFD) 24, Hungarian Democratic Forum (MDF) 18, Hungarian Justice and Life Party 14, others 1.

HEAD OF STATE

President, Árpád Göncz, *sworn in* 3 August 1990, *re-elected by parliament* 19 June 1995

CABINET *as at July 1998*

Prime Minister, Viktor Orbán (F)

Agriculture and Rural Development, József Torgyán (FKGP)

Defence, János Szabó (FKGP)

Economic Affairs, Attila Chikán (F)

Education, Zoltán Pokorni (F)

Environmental Protection, Pál Pepó (FKGP)

Finance, Zsigmond Járai (F)

Foreign Affairs, János Martonyi (F)

Health, Árpád Gógl (F)

Home Affairs, Sándor Pintér (Ind.)

Justice, Ibolya Dávid (MDF)

National Cultural Heritage, József Hámori (Ind.)

Social and Family Affairs, Péter Harrach (MKSZ)

Transport, Telecommunications and Water Management, Kálmán Katona (F)

Without Portfolio, László Kövér (F) *(Civil Security Services)*; Imre Boros (FKGP) *(PHARE Programme)*; István Stumpf (F) *(Prime Minister's Office)*

F Fidesz-MPP; FKGP Independent Smallholders Party; Ind. Independent; MDF Hungarian Democratic Forum; MKSZ Hungarian Christian Democratic Alliance

EMBASSY OF THE REPUBLIC OF HUNGARY

35 Eaton Place, London SW1X 8BY

Tel 0171–235 5218

Ambassador Extraordinary and Plenipotentiary, HE Gábor Szentiványi, apptd 1997

Minister Plenipotentiary, Sándor Juhász

Counsellor and Consul-General, Dr Péter Kallós

Commercial Counsellor, Dr Jenó Hámori

Defence and Military Attaché, Col. László Hajdú

BRITISH EMBASSY

Harmincad Utca 6, Budapest V

Tel: Budapest 266–2888

Ambassador Extraordinary and Plenipotentiary, HE Nigel Thorpe, CVO, RCDS, apptd 1998

Counsellor and Deputy Head of Mission, G. B. Reid

Defence Attaché, Col. A. T. B. Kimber

First Secretary (Commercial), S. C. Martin

First Secretary (Management) and Consul, I. H. Davies

BRITISH COUNCIL DIRECTOR, P. Dick, OBE, Benczur Utca 26, H–1068 Budapest VI

DEFENCE

The Army has 797 main battle tanks, 1,300 armoured infantry fighting vehicles and armoured personnel carriers and 840 pieces of artillery. The Air Force has 80 combat aircraft and 59 attack helicopters. Hungary will join Nato by April 1999.

MILITARY EXPENDITURE – 1.2 per cent of GDP (1996)
MILITARY PERSONNEL – 63,200: Army 31,600, Air Force 17,500, Paramilitaries 14,100
CONSCRIPTION DURATION – Nine months

ECONOMY

Agriculture accounts for around 8 per cent of GDP and employs 8 per cent of the workforce. Production is concentrated on maize, wheat, sugar beet, barley, rye and oats.

Industry is mainly based on imported raw materials but Hungary has its own coal, bauxite, considerable deposits of natural gas, some iron ore and oil. Output figures in 1995 were: coal 14,461,000 tonnes; aluminium 34,900 tonnes; rolled steel 1,865,000 tonnes; crude petroleum 1,669,000 tonnes. Natural gas production totalled 5,365 million cubic metres.

The economy has suffered from the loss of export markets in the Soviet Union and the former Yugoslavia, and the transition to a market economy. With the exception of the engineering sector, industrial output declined in 1996.

Privatization and the establishment of small businesses proved successful in 1990–4, aided by large-scale foreign investment. Some 40 per cent of state enterprises have been privatized. Hungary joined the OECD in March 1996. In February 1998, the IMF announced its decision not to renew Hungary's stand-by credit arrangement, on the basis that the Hungarian economy was now strong enough to operate without outside assistance.

In 1996 Hungary had a trade deficit of US$2,652 million and a current account deficit of US$1,689 million. Imports totalled US$15,896 million and exports US$12,686 million.

GNP – US$44,274 million (1996); US$4,340 per capita (1996)
GDP – US$31,155 million (1994); US$4,072 per capita (1994)
ANNUAL AVERAGE GROWTH OF GDP – 2.9 per cent (1994); estimated to be 3.2 per cent in 1997
INFLATION RATE – 23.5 per cent (1996); estimated to be 17.6 per cent in 1997
UNEMPLOYMENT – 10.3 per cent (1995)
TOTAL EXTERNAL DEBT – US$26,958 million (1996)

Trade with UK	1996	1997
Imports from UK	£347,111,000	£435,817,000
Exports to UK	423,294,000	485,383,000

EDUCATION

There are five types of schools under the Ministry of Education: kindergartens for age three to six, general schools for age six to 14 (compulsory), vocational schools (15–18), secondary schools (15–18), universities and adult training schools (over 18).

ILLITERACY RATE – 0.8 per cent
ENROLMENT (percentage of age group) – primary 93 per cent (1994); secondary 73 per cent (1994); tertiary 19.1 per cent (1994)

CULTURE

Magyar, or Hungarian, is one of the Finno-Ugrian languages. Hungarian literature began to flourish in the second half of the 16th century. Among the greatest writers of the 19th and 20th centuries are Mihály Vörösmarty (1800–55), Sándor Petöfi (1823–49), János Arany (1817–82), Imre Madách (1823–64), Kálmán Mikszáth (1847–1910), Endre Ady (1877–1918), Attila József (1905–37), Mihály Babits (1883–1941), Dezsö Kosztolányi (1885–1936), Gyula Illyes (1902–83), János Pilinszky (1921–81) and Sándor Weöres (1913–89).

ICELAND
Island

AREA – 39,769 sq. miles (103,000 sq. km)
POPULATION – 272,064 (1997). Some 92.2 per cent of the population are members of the (Lutheran) Church of Iceland. The language is Icelandic
CAPITAL – ΨReykjavik (population, 106,617, 1997)
MAJOR CITIES – Akranes; ΨAkureyri; ΨHafnarfjördur; Isafjördur; Keflavík; Kópavogur; ΨSiglufjördur; Westman Islands
CURRENCY – Icelandic króna (Kr) of 100 aurar
NATIONAL ANTHEM – O Gud Vors Lands (Our Country's God)
NATIONAL DAY – 17 June
NATIONAL FLAG – Blue, with white-bordered red cross
LIFE EXPECTANCY (years) – male 76.85; female 80.75
POPULATION GROWTH RATE – 1.1 per cent (1995)
POPULATION DENSITY – 3 per sq. km (1995)
URBAN POPULATION – 91.3 per cent (1993)
MILITARY EXPENDITURE – 0.1 per cent of GDP (1996)
MILITARY PERSONNEL – 120 Paramilitaries

HISTORY AND POLITICS

Iceland was uninhabited before the ninth century, when settlers came from Norway. For several centuries a form of republican government prevailed, with an annual assembly of leading men called the *Althing*, but in 1262 Iceland became subject to Norway, and later to Denmark. During the colonial period, Iceland maintained its cultural integrity but a deterioration in the climate, together with frequent volcanic eruptions and outbreaks of disease, led to a serious drop in living standards and to a decline in the population to little more than 40,000. In the 19th century a struggle for independence led to home rule in 1918 and to independence as a republic in 1944.

The parliamentary (*Althing*) elections on 8 April 1995 gave the Independence Party 25 seats, Progressives 15, Social Democratic Party 7, People's Alliance 9, Awakening of the Nation 4, and Women's Alliance 3. A coalition government of the Independence Party and the Progressive Party was formed after the election.

HEAD OF STATE
President, Olafur Ragnar Grimsson, *elected* 29 June 1996

CABINET *as at May 1998*
Prime Minister, Statistical Bureau of Iceland, David Oddsson (IP)

Agriculture and Environment, Gudmundur Bjarnason (PP)
Communications, Halldór Blöndal (IP)
Education and Culture, Björn Bjarnason (IP)
Finance, Geir Haarde (IP)
Fisheries, Justice and Ecclesiastical Affairs, Thorsteinn
  Pálsson (IP)
Foreign Affairs and External Trade, Halldór Ásgrímsson (PP)
Health and Social Security, Ingibjörg Pálmadóttir (PP)
Social Affairs, Páll Pétursson (PP)
Trade and Industry, Finnur Ingólfsson (PP)
IP Independence Party; PP Progressive Party

EMBASSY OF ICELAND
1 Eaton Terrace, London SW1W 8EY
Tel 0171–590 1100
Ambassador Extraordinary and Plenipotentiary, HE Benedikt
  Ásgeirsson, apptd 1995

BRITISH EMBASSY
Laufásvegur 31, 101 Reykjavík
Tel: Reykjavík 5100
*Ambassador Extraordinary and Plenipotentiary and Consul-
General*, HE James McCulloch, apptd 1996
CONSULATE – Akureyri

ECONOMY

Iceland has considerable resources of hydroelectric and geothermal energy. Heavy industry includes an aluminium smelter, a nitrogen fertilizer factory, a cement factory, a diatomite plant and a ferro-silicon plant.

The major sectors of the economy are fishing and fish processing, manufacturing, agriculture, energy production and tourism, which is of growing importance with 201,655 visitors in 1997.

As a member of the European Free Trade Association (EFTA), Iceland has become a member of the European Economic Area (EEA) which extends most of the provisions of the EU's single market to EFTA states.

In 1995 Iceland had a trade surplus of US$206 million and a current account surplus of US$51 million. In 1996 imports totalled US$2,005 million and exports US$1,898 million.
GNP – US$7,175 million (1996); US$26,580 per capita
  (1996)
GDP – US$6,345 million (1994); US$23,280 per capita
  (1994)
ANNUAL AVERAGE GROWTH OF GDP – 5.7 per cent (1996)
INFLATION RATE – 1.8 per cent (1997)
UNEMPLOYMENT – 3.9 per cent (1997)

TRADE

The principal exports are fish and fish products, ferro-silicon and aluminium; the chief imports are consumer durables, petroleum products, transport equipment, textiles, foodstuffs, animal feeds and timber.

Trade with UK	1996	1997
Imports from UK	£153,975,000	£158,329,000
Exports to UK	267,876,000	242,664,000

COMMUNICATIONS

At 1 January 1997, the mercantile marine consisted of 989 registered vessels (254,532 gross tons). There are regular shipping services between Reykjavík and Felixstowe, Humber ports, Europe and the USA.

A regular air service is maintained by Icelandair between Glasgow and London and Reykjavík. There are also air services to Scandinavia, USA, Germany, France and Luxembourg.

Road communications are adequate in summer but greatly restricted by snow in winter. Only roads in town centres and key highways are metalled, the rest being of gravel, sand and lava dust. The climate and terrain make first-class surfaces for highways out of the question. There are no railways.

There are three television channels (one public, two private) and several private and public radio stations.

CULTURE

The ancient Norraena (or Northern tongue) has close affinities to Anglo-Saxon and as spoken and written in Iceland today differs little from that introduced into the island in the ninth century. There is a rich literature with two distinct periods of development, from the mid-11th to the late 13th century and from the early 19th century to the present.
ENROLMENT (percentage of age group) – tertiary 35.2 per
  cent (1994)

INDIA
The Republic of India

AREA – 1,269,346 sq. miles (3,287,590 sq. km). Neighbours: Pakistan (north-west), China, Tibet, Nepal and Bhutan (north), Myanmar (east), Bangladesh
POPULATION – 935,744,000 (1994 UN estimate), 846,302,688 (1991 census): Hindu (82.6 per cent), the rest being Muslim (11.4 per cent), Christian (2.4 per cent), Sikh (2.0 per cent), Buddhist (0.7 per cent) and Jain (0.5 per cent). The official languages are Hindi in the Devanagari script and English, though 17 regional languages also are recognized for adoption as official state languages
CAPITAL – New Delhi (population, 301,297; 8,419,084 including Delhi/Dilli), 1991
MAJOR CITIES – Ahmedabad (3,312,216); Bangalore (4,130,288); ΨBombay/Mumbai (12,596,243); ΨCalcutta (11,021,918); Hyderabad (4,344,437); Kanpur (2,029,889); Lucknow (1,669,204); ΨMadras/ Chinnai (5,421,985); Pune (2,493,987) (1991 figures)
CURRENCY – Indian rupee (Rs) of 100 paisa
NATIONAL ANTHEM – Jana-gana-mana
NATIONAL DAY – 26 January (Republic Day)
NATIONAL FLAG – A horizontal tricolour with bands of deep saffron, white and dark green in equal proportions. In the centre of the white band appears an Asoka wheel in navy blue
LIFE EXPECTANCY (years) – male 57.70; female 58.10
POPULATION GROWTH RATE – 2.3 per cent (1995)
POPULATION DENSITY – 285 per sq. km (1995)
URBAN POPULATION – 26.3 per cent (1993)
ILLITERACY RATE – 48.0 per cent
ENROLMENT (percentage of age group) – tertiary 6.4 per
  cent (1995)
India has three well-defined regions: the mountain range of the Himalayas, the Indo–Gangetic plain, and the southern peninsula. The main mountain ranges are the Himalayas (over 29,000 feet) and the Western and Eastern Ghats (over 8,000 feet). Major rivers include the Ganges, Indus, Krishna, Godavari and Mahanadi.

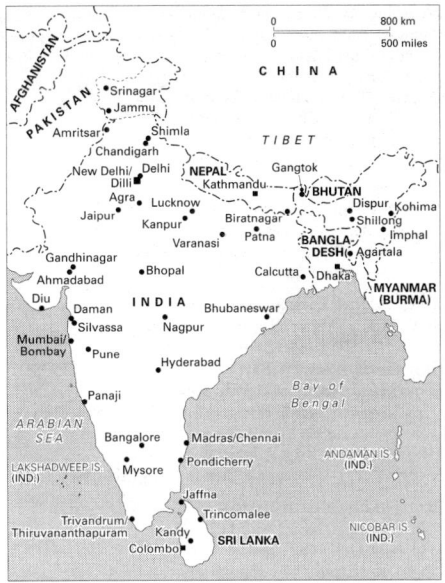

0   800 km
0   500 miles

AFGHANISTAN
PAKISTAN

CHINA

Srinagar
Jammu
Amritsar   Shimla
Chandigarh   TIBET
New Delhi/ Delhi   NEPAL   Gangtok
Dilli   Kathmandu   BHUTAN
Agra   Lucknow   Dispur Kohima
Jaipur   Biratnagar   Shillong
Kanpur   Patna   Imphal
Varanasi   BANGLA-
DESH   Agartala
Gandhinagar   Calcutta   Dhaka   MYANMAR
Ahmadabad   Bhopal   (BURMA)
Diu
Daman   INDIA   Bhubaneswar
Silvassa   Nagpur
Mumbai/
Bombay   Pune
Hyderabad
Panaji
Bay of
Bengal
ARABIAN
SEA   Bangalore   Madras/Chennai
Pondicherry   ANDAMAN IS
LAKSHADWEEP IS   Mysore   (IND.)
(IND.)
Jaffna
Trivandrum   Trincomalee
Thiruvananthapuram Kandy   NICOBAR IS
Colombo   SRI LANKA   (IND.)

Temperatures vary over the country between averages of about 10°C and 33°C, reaching over 38°C in some parts during the hot season. There are similar variations in rainfall, from only a few inches a year falling in the western Thar Desert to over 400 inches in Meghalaya.

HISTORY AND POLITICS

The Indus civilization was fully developed by *c.*2500 BC but collapsed *c.*1750 BC, and was replaced by an Aryan civilization from the west. Arab invasions of the north-west began in the seventh century and Muslim, Hindu and Buddhist states developed until the establishment of the Mogul dynasty in 1526. The British East India Company established settlements throughout the 17th century; clashes with the French and native princes led to the British government taking control of the company in 1784 and gradually extending sovereignty over the whole subcontinent. The separate dominions of India and Pakistan became independent within the Commonwealth on 15 August 1947 and India became a republic in 1950.

Between 1947 and 1996, India was ruled by the Congress (I) Party for all but four years (March 1977–January 1980, November 1989–June 1991). Congress (I) has been led by members of the Nehru-Gandhi dynasty for most of the post-independence period: Prime Ministers Jawaharlal Nehru (1947–64), Indira Gandhi (1966–1977, 1980–84) and Rajiv Gandhi (1984–89). Indira Gandhi was assassinated by Sikh extremists seeking an independent Sikh state in Punjab; her son Rajiv was assassinated by Sri Lankan Tamils.

In November 1997, the United Front government (a coalition of Communist and low-caste parties) collapsed after Congress (I) withdrew its support. The last parliamentary elections in February 1998 produced no outright winner; in March 1998, the BJP formed a coalition government under Atal Bihari Vajpayee.

SECESSION

The Hindu Maharaja of Kashmir signed his state's instrument of accession to India in October 1947, two months after India and Pakistan became independent. This was disputed by Pakistan, on the basis that the majority of the state's population was Muslim. After three Indian-Pakistani wars, a line of control was agreed under the 1972 Simla agreement (China has also occupied some of Kashmir since the 1962 Sino-Indian war). The line was rejected by armed groups which have waged a campaign of violence against the Hindu population and against Indian security forces. Kashmir was placed under direct rule in 1990 but state assembly elections, held in September 1996, were won by Jammu and Kashmir National Conference.

INSURGENCIES

Groups of Bodo separatists in Assam have been fighting for a separate Bodoland since the 1980s.

FOREIGN RELATIONS

India and Pakistan have fought three major wars since independence, in 1947–8, 1965 and 1971. Since 1985 they have continued a low-level war at altitude for control of the Siachen glacier in Kashmir.

In May 1998, India conducted five underground nuclear tests, confirming its status as a nuclear power. The tests were condemned by the international community. Within three weeks, Pakistan had conducted its own nuclear tests, leading to fears that border confrontations between the two countries could escalate into nuclear conflict.

POLITICAL SYSTEM

Executive power is vested in the president, elected for a five-year term by an electoral college consisting of the elected members of the Union and State legislatures. The president appoints the prime minister and, on the latter's advice, the ministers, and can dismiss them. The Council of Ministers is collectively responsible to the *Lok Sabha* (lower house). The vice-president is ex-officio chairman of the *Rajya Sabha* (upper house).

Legislative power rests with the president, the Rajya Sabha (245 members serving six-year terms) and the Lok Sabha (545 members). Twelve members of the Rajya Sabha are presidential nominees, the rest are indirectly elected representatives of the State and Union Territories. The 530 members of the Lok Sabha representing the States are directly elected by universal adult franchise, and 15 representatives of the Union Territories are chosen, for a maximum term of five years.

The Supreme Court consists of the Chief Justice and not more than 25 other judges, appointed by the president. It is the highest court in respect of all constitutional matters and the final Court of Appeal and is situated in New Delhi. Each state or group of states also has a High Court with a hierarchy of subordinate courts. The judges of the High Court of a state are appointed by the president.

FEDERAL STRUCTURE

There are 25 States and seven Union Territories. Each state is headed by a Governor, who is appointed by the president and holds office for five years, and by a Council of Ministers. All states have a Legislative Assembly, and some have also a Legislative Council, elected directly by adult suffrage for a maximum period of five years.

The Union Territories are administered, except where otherwise provided by Parliament, by the president acting through an Administrator or Lieutenant-Governor, or other authority appointed by him.

	Area (sq. km)	Population (1991 census)	Capital
STATES			
Andhra Pradesh	275,100	66,304,854	Hyderabad
Arunachal Pradesh	83,700	858,392	Itanagar
Assam	78,400	22,414,322	Dispur
Bihar	173,900	86,374,465	Patna
Goa	3,700	1,168,622	Panaji
Gujarat	196,000	41,309,582	Gandhinagar
Haryana	44,200	16,463,648	Chandigarh
Himachal Pradesh	55,700	5,170,877	Shimla
Jammu and Kashmir*	222,200	5,987,389	Srinagar/ Jammu
Karnataka	191,800	44,977,201	Bangalore
Kerala	38,900	29,011,237	Trivandrum
Madhya Pradesh	443,500	66,135,862	Bhopal
Maharashtra	307,700	78,937,187	Bombay (Mumbai)
Manipur	22,300	1,826,714	Imphal
Meghalaya	22,400	1,774,778	Shillong
Mizoram	21,100	686,217	Aizawl
Nagaland	16,600	1,209,549	Kohima
Orissa	155,700	31,659,736	Bhubaneswar
Punjab	50,400	20,190,795	Chandigarh
Rajasthan	342,200	44,005,990	Jaipur
Sikkim	7,100	405,550	Gangtok
Tamil Nadu	130,100	55,638,318	Madras (Chinnai)
Tripura	10,500	2,744,827	Agartala
Uttar Pradesh	294,400	139,112,287	Lucknow
West Bengal	88,800	67,982,732	Calcutta
UNION TERRITORIES			
Andaman and Nicobar Is.	8,200	280,661	Port Blair
Chandigarh	114	642,015	
Dadra and Nagar Haveli	500	138,477	Silvassa
Daman and Diu	112	101,586	
Delhi	1,500	9,420,644	
Lakshadweep	30	51,681	Kavaratti
Pondicherry	500	807,785	

* The area figure includes those parts occupied by Pakistan and China, which are claimed by India, but the population figure excludes the population of these areas, where the census was not taken. The state's capital is at Srinagar in summer and Jammu in winter.

HEAD OF STATE
President of the Republic of India, Kocheril Raman Narayanan, *elected* 17 July 1997
Vice-President, Krishan Kant, *elected* 16 August 1997

COUNCIL OF MINISTERS *as at July 1998*
Prime Minister, Atal Bihari Vajpayee (BJP)
Chemicals, Fertilizers and Food, Surjit Singh Barnala (SAD)
Civil Aviation, Anant Kumar (BJP)
Commerce, Ram Krishna Hegde (LS)
Defence, George Fernandes (SP)
Environment, Suresh Prabhu (SS)
Finance, Yashwant Sinha (BJP)
Home Affairs, Jammu and Kashmir, Lal Krishna Advani (BJP)
Human Resource Development, Science and Technology, Murli Manohar Joshi (BJP)
Industry, Sikander Bakht (BJP)
Information, Broadcasting, Communications, Sushma Swaraj (BJP)
Labour, Satynarayan Jatiya (BJP)
Law, Justice, Company Affairs, M. Thambi Durai (AIADMK)
Parliamentary Affairs, Tourism, Madan Lal Khurana (BJP)

Petroleum and Natural Gas, K. Ramamurthy (TRC)
Power, R. Kumaramangalam (BJP)
Railways, Nitish Kumar (SP)
Rural Development, Babagouda Patil (BJP)
Steel, Mines, Naveen Patnaik (BJD)
Surface Transport, Debendra Pradhan (BJP)
Textiles, Kashiram Rana (BJP)
Urban Development, Ram Jethmalani (Ind.)

BJP Bharatiya Janata Party; SAD Sikh Akali Dal; LS Lok Shakti (People's Power); SP Samta (Equality) Party; SS Shivaji's Army; AIADMK All India Dravidian Progressive Party; TRC Tamil Rajiv Congress; BJD Biju Danata Dal; Ind. Independent

INDIAN HIGH COMMISSION
India House, Aldwych, London WC2B 4NA
Tel 0171–836 8484
High Commissioner, HE Shri Salman Haider, apptd 1998
Deputy High Commissioner, P. K. Singh
First Secretaries, Shashi Bhushan Singh (*Commerce*); Rajiv Kumar (*Consular*); Anup Ranjan Basu (*Culture*)
Military Adviser, Brig. R. Dhir
CONSULATES-GENERAL – Birmingham, Glasgow

BRITISH HIGH COMMISSION
Chanakyapuri, New Delhi 1100021
Tel: New Delhi 687 2161
High Commissioner, new appointment awaited
Deputy High Commissioner and Minister, Dr D. Carter
Deputy High Commissioners, M. C. Bates (*Bombay*); S. M. Scaddan (*Calcutta*); S. H. Palmer (*Madras*)
Defence and Military Adviser, Brig. S. M. A. Lee, OBE
Counsellor (Economic and Commercial), W. Morris
Minister for Cultural Affairs and British Council Representative, C.W. Perchard, OBE
BRITISH COUNCIL – offices at New Delhi, Bombay, Calcutta and Madras. British Council libraries at these four centres and British libraries at Ahmedabad, Bangalore, Bhopal, Hyderabad, Lucknow, Patna, Pune and Trivandrum

DEFENCE

The Army has 3,314 main battle tanks, 1,507 armoured infantry fighting vehicles and armoured personnel carriers and 4,175 artillery pieces. The Navy has 17 submarines, one aircraft carrier, six destroyers, 18 frigates, 45 patrol and coastal vessels, 68 combat aircraft and 83 armed helicopters. It has nine bases including one under construction. The Air Force has 777 combat aircraft and 34 armed helicopters.

India exploded its first nuclear weapon in 1974 and is since believed to have acquired a stockpile of nuclear arms. It conducted further nuclear tests in May 1998. In 1993–4 India successfully test-fired its intermediate-range 'Agni' and 'Prithvi' ballistic missiles, and the latter went into production in September 1997.
MILITARY EXPENDITURE – 2.8 per cent of GDP (1996)
MILITARY PERSONNEL – 1,145,000: Army 980,000, Navy 55,000, Air Force 110,000

ECONOMY

Agriculture supports about 70 per cent of the population, and contributes nearly 29 per cent of GDP. Production has grown by 2.6 per cent each year since 1951, remaining slightly ahead of the 2 per cent increase necessary to keep pace with the rising population. Food crops occupy three-quarters of the total cultivated area. The main food crops are rice, cereals (principally wheat) and pulses. The major cash crops include sugar cane, jute, cotton and tea. Other products include oil seeds, spices, groundnuts, soya bean, tobacco, rubber and coffee. Livestock is raised, principally for dairy purposes or for the hides.

Industry is based on the exploitation and processing of mineral resources, principally coal, oil and iron, and on the production of textiles. The coal industry reached an output in 1996 of 319,000,000 tonnes; production of crude petroleum was 33,000,000 tonnes. Steel production is mainly in the hands of the public sector, with five public and one private sector integrated steel plants producing 12,972,000 tonnes of ingot steel in 1996. The engineering industry, heavy and light, is increasingly being privatized.

The manufacture of paper, cement, pharmaceuticals, chemicals, fertilizers, petrochemicals, motor vehicles and commercial vehicles has been expanded. Other principal manufactures are those derived from agricultural products, textiles, jute goods, sugar and leather, which along with tea, tobacco, rubber, fish and iron ore are major exports.

India introduced free market reforms in 1991. Subsidies were cut, state corporations privatized and the economy opened up to foreign competition and investment. To integrate India into the international trading system proper, the 1993–5 budgets floated the rupee, cut interest rates and duties on imports, reduced subsidies to farmers, restructured the taxation system, removed industrial controls and dismantled protectionist structures.

The reforms have been successful, encouraging high levels of foreign investment, a fall in inflation, a 24 per cent increase in exports, a rise in foreign currency reserves from US$1,000 million to US$16,000 million in 1996, improved agricultural efficiency and an increase in the average annual industrial growth rate from 1 per cent to 12 per cent.

In 1995 there was a trade deficit of US$4,788 million and a current account deficit of US$5,563 million. In 1996 imports totalled US$37,375 million and exports US$33,054 million.

GNP – US$357,759 million (1996); US$380 per capita (1996)
GDP – US$349,071 million (1994); US$309 per capita (1994)
ANNUAL AVERAGE GROWTH OF GDP – 7.3 per cent (1995)
INFLATION RATE – 9.0 per cent (1996)
TOTAL EXTERNAL DEBT – US$89,827 million (1996)

TRADE WITH UK	1996	1997
Imports from UK	£1,706,606,000	£1,575,431,000
Exports to UK	1,610,996,000	1,622,330,000

COMMUNICATIONS

The International Airports Authority manages five international airports: Palam (Delhi), Sahar (Bombay), Dum Dum (Calcutta), Meenambakkam (Madras) and Trivandrum. The other 88 aerodromes are controlled and operated by the Civil Aviation Department of the government. The national airlines are Indian Airlines (internal) and Air India (international).

The railways are grouped into nine administrative zones, Southern, Central, Western, Northern, North-Eastern, North-East Frontier, Eastern, South-Eastern and South-Central, with a total track length of 62,660 km, about 19 per cent of which is electrified. The total length of the road network is 2,065,209 km of which 964,072 km is surfaced.

The chief seaports are Bombay/Mumbai, Calcutta, Haldia, Madras/Chinnai, Mormugao, Cochin, Visakhapatnam, Kandla, Paradip, Mangalore and Tuticorin; these handled a cargo of 179.3 million tonnes in 1993–4. There are 139 minor working ports with varying capacity.

INDONESIA
Republik Indonesia

AREA – 735,358 sq. miles (1,904,569 sq. km). Indonesia shares borders with Malaysia (on Borneo) and Papua New Guinea (on New Guinea)
POPULATION – 193,750,000 (1994 UN estimate): 87 per cent Muslim, with Christian, Buddhist, Hindu and Animist minorities. Bahasa Indonesian, a variant of Malay, is the national language, although more than 250 dialects are spoken
CAPITAL – ΨJakarta (population, 9,160,500)
MAJOR CITIES – (Irian Jaya) Jayapura (180,400); (Java) Bandung (2,368,200), ΨSemarang (1,366,500), ΨSurabaya (2,701,300); (Kalimantan) Banjarmasin (534,600), ΨPontianak (449,100); (Moluccas) Ambon (313,100); (Sulawesi) ΨUjung Pandang (1,091,800); (Sumatra) Medan (1,909,700), Palembang (1,352,300)
CURRENCY – Rupiah (Rp) of 100 sen
NATIONAL ANTHEM – Indonesia Raya (Great Indonesia)
NATIONAL DAY – 17 August (Anniversary of Proclamation of Independence)
NATIONAL FLAG – Equal bands of red over white
LIFE EXPECTANCY (years) – male 61.00; female 64.50
POPULATION GROWTH RATE – 1.5 per cent (1995)
POPULATION DENSITY – 102 per sq. km (1995)
URBAN POPULATION – 30.9 per cent (1990)
ILLITERACY RATE – 16.2 per cent
ENROLMENT (percentage of age group) – primary 97 per cent (1994); secondary 42 per cent (1994); tertiary 11.1 per cent (1994)

Indonesia comprises the islands of Java, Madura, Sumatra, the Riouw-Lingga archipelago, Bangka and Billiton, part of the island of Borneo (Kalimantan), Sulawesi (formerly Celebes), the Molucca Islands, the islands of Bali, Lombok, Sumbawa, Sumba, Flores, Timor and others comprising the provinces of East and West Nusa Tenggara and the western half of the island of New Guinea (Irian Jaya).

HISTORY AND POLITICS

From the early part of the 17th century much of the Indonesian archipelago was under Dutch rule. Following the Second World War, during which the archipelago was occupied by the Japanese, a strong nationalistic movement formed and after sporadic fighting all the former Dutch East Indies except western New Guinea became independent as Indonesia on 27 December 1949. Western New Guinea became part of Indonesia in 1963 under the name West Irian (now Irian Jaya), this interpretation being confirmed in an 'Act of Free Choice' in July 1969.

The Army Minister Gen. Suharto assumed effective political power in March 1966. Gen. Suharto was appointed president in 1968 and was reappointed by the People's Consultative Assembly at every subsequent presidential election. The House of People's Representatives is composed of 425 elected members and 75 military appointees. The military has effectively ruled since 1966 through its political organization Golkar, which won 74 per cent of the votes cast in the general election on 29 May 1997. The presidential election held in March 1998 was won by Gen. Suharto.

Following attacks on the rupiah by currency speculators in August 1997, the government abandoned fixed exchange rates and allowed the rupiah to float freely. This temporarily stabilized the currency, but despite an IMF stand-by credit of US$10 billion, approved in November, the value of the rupiah dropped dramatically at the end of

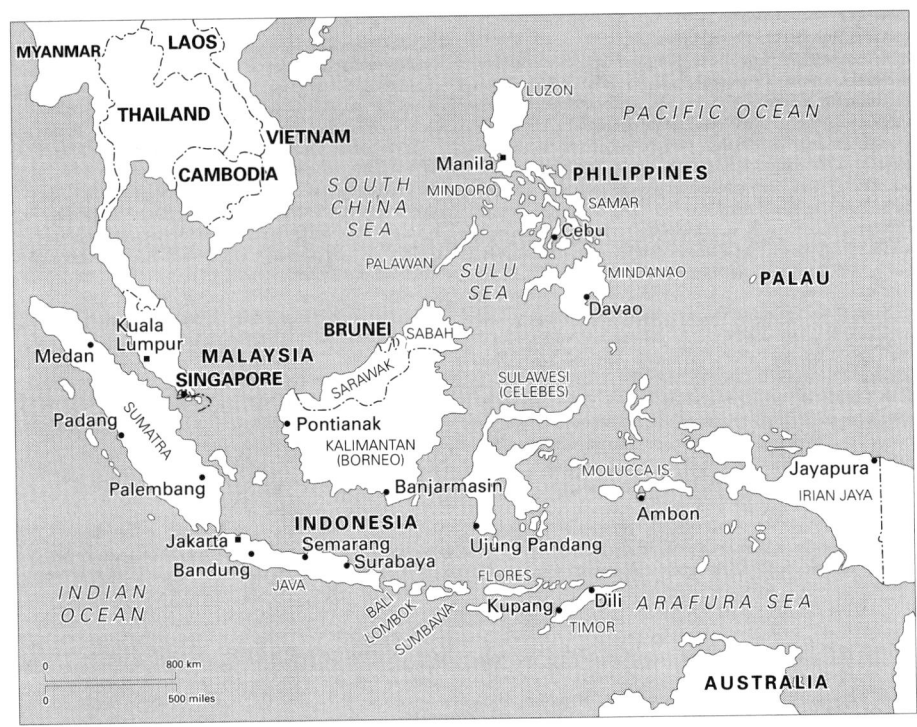

the year, falling from 2,700 to the dollar in August to 10,000 to the dollar in January 1998. A US$45-billion IMF rescue package was announced, conditional on economic reforms ending state monopolies and curtailing corruption. Government measures to combat the crisis were widely regarded as inadequate, and following the imposition of austerity measures, there was widespread ill-feeling towards Suharto and his family, many of whom had amassed large personal fortunes presiding over state businesses. Rampant inflation and high food and fuel prices provoked civil unrest, and by April 1998 riots and protests calling for Suharto's resignation were frequent. On 21 May 1998, following weeks of rioting, Suharto announced he would step down. He was replaced by his deputy B. J. Habibie.

INSURGENCIES

There are two armed secessionist movements based on ethnic and nationalist groups, which are fighting perceived Javanese domination. In Irian Jaya government forces are fighting the Papua Independent Organization (OPM) guerrillas who claim the 1969 referendum was rigged and oppose Indonesian settlement. In northern Sumatra the Free Aceh Movement is active.
See also East Timor, page 901.

HEAD OF STATE
President, Bacharuddin Jusuf Habibie, *sworn in* 21 May 1998

CABINET *as at July 1998*

Co-ordinating Ministers, Hartarto Sastrosoenarto (*Development Supervision, State Administrative Reform*); Air Vice-Marshal (retd) Ginajar Kartasasmita (*Economy, Finance, Industry, National Development Planning Agency*); Haryono Suyono (*People's Welfare, Poverty Eradication,*

National Family Planning Board); Feisal Tanjung (*Political and Security Affairs*)
Ministers, Akbar Tanjung (*State Secretary*); Budiono (*National Development Planning*); Zuhal (*Research, Science and Technology*); A. M. Saefuddin (*Food Affairs*); Ida Bagus Oka (*Population, National Family Planning Board*); Hamzah Haz (*Investment Affairs, National Investment Co-ordinating Board*); Hasan Basri Durin (*Land Affairs*); Tanri Abeng (*State Enterprises*); Panagian Siregar (*Environment*); Theo Sambuaga (*Public Housing*); Agung Laksono (*Youth and Sports Affairs*); Tutty Alawiyah (*Women's Affairs*); Lt.-Gen. Syarwan Hamid (*Home Affairs*); Ali Alatas (*Foreign Affairs*); Lt.-Gen. Wiranto (*Defence and Security, Commander-in-Chief of the Armed Forces, Head of Co-ordinating Agency for Reinforcement of National Stability*); Muladi (*Justice*); Lt.-Gen. Yunus Yosfiah (*Information*); Bambang Subianto (*Finance*); Rahardi Ramelan (*Trade and Industry*); Adi Sasono (*Co-operatives, Guidance of Small Business*); Soleh Solahuddin (*Agriculture*); Muslimin Nasution (*Forestry and Plantation*); Kuntoro Mangkusubroto (*Mines and Energy*); Yustika Baharsyah (*Social Affairs*); Rahmadi Bambang Sumadhyo (*Public Works*); Malik Fajar (*Religious Affairs*); Marzuki Usman (*Tourism, Arts and Culture*); Fahmi Idris (*Manpower*); Abdullah Makhmud Hendropriyono (*Transmigration*); Juwono Sudarsono (*Education and Culture*); Farid Anfasa Muluk (*Health*); Lt.-Gen. Muhammad Andi Ghalib (*Attorney-General*); Giri Suseno Hadihardjono (*Transport*)
Leading Members of the Armed Forces, Lt.-Gen. Wiranto (*Commander-in-Chief of Armed Forces*); Lt.-Gen. Subagio Hadsiswoyo (*Army Chief of Staff*); Rear-Adm. Widodo (*Navy Chief of Staff*); Air Vice-Marshal Hanafie Asnan (*Air Force Chief of Staff*); Maj.-Gen. Jamari Chaniago (*Commander of Army Strategic Command*)

INDONESIAN EMBASSY
38 Grosvenor Square, London WIX 9AD
Tel 0171–499 7661
Ambassador Extraordinary and Plenipotentiary, HE Rahardjo
Jamtomo
Minister, H. Sudirman (*Deputy Chief of Mission*)
Commercial Attaché, Andreas Anugerah

BRITISH EMBASSY
Jalan M. H. Thamrin 75, Jakarta 10310
Tel: Jakarta 315 6264
Ambassador Extraordinary and Plenipotentiary, HE Robin
Christopher, CMG, apptd 1997
Deputy Ambassador, Counsellor and Consul-General,
Q. M. Quayle
Counsellor (Commercial / Development), P. J. Johnstone
Defence Attaché, Col. D. S. MacFarlane
BRITISH CONSULAR OFFICES – Jakarta, Medan, Surabaya

BRITISH COUNCIL DIRECTOR, Dr N. Kemp, S Widjojo
Centre, Jalan Jenderal Sudirman 71, Jakarta 12190

DEFENCE

The Army has 591 armoured personnel carriers, 181
artillery pieces and 32 aircraft. The Navy has two
submarines, 17 frigates, 59 patrol and coastal vessels, 40
combat aircraft and ten armed helicopters. There are five
principal naval bases. The Air Force has 92 combat aircraft.
MILITARY EXPENDITURE – 2.1 per cent of GDP (1996)
MILITARY PERSONNEL – 284,000: Army 220,000, Navy
43,000, Air Force 21,000
CONSCRIPTION DURATION – Two years

ECONOMY

Nearly 70 per cent of the population is engaged in
agriculture and related production. Copra, nutmeg, pepper, palm oil, sugar, fibres, rubber, tea, coffee and tobacco
are produced. Rice is a staple food and Java, Sulawesi and
Sumatra are important producers. In September and
October 1997, more than 600,000 hectares of land was
destroyed in forest fires, execerbated by unusually dry
weather conditions.

Oil and liquefied natural gas are the most important
assets. Timber is the second largest foreign exchange
earner after oil. Indonesia is rich in minerals, particularly
tin, of which the country is the world's third biggest
producer; coal, nickel and bauxite are the other principal
mineral products. There are also considerable deposits of
gold, silver, manganese phosphates and sulphur.

Principal exports are petroleum, textiles and clothing,
timber, natural gas and rubber. Principal imports are
machinery and transport equipment, electrical equipment
and chemicals.

Indonesia was one of the countries worst affected by the
Asian economic crisis, which began in the latter half of
1997. An IMF programme to stabilize and rebuild the
economy is under way.

In 1995 there was a trade surplus of US$5,710 million
and a current account deficit of US$7,023 million. In 1996
imports totalled US$42,929 million and exports
US$49,814 million.
GNP – US$213,384 million (1996); US$1,080 per capita
(1996)
GDP – US$136,934 million (1994); US$792 per capita
(1994)
ANNUAL AVERAGE GROWTH OF GDP – 7.8 per cent (1996)
INFLATION RATE – 7.9 per cent (1996)
TOTAL EXTERNAL DEBT – US$129,033 million (1996)

TRADE WITH UK	1996	1997
Imports from UK	£828,268,000	£701,496,000
Exports to UK	980,680,000	1,028,914,000

COMMUNICATIONS

There are railway systems in Java and Sumatra linking the
main towns. There are about 50,000 miles of roads.

Sea communications are maintained by the state-run
shipping companies Djakarta-Lloyd (ocean-going) and
Pelni (coastal and inter-island) and other small concerns.
Transport by small craft on the rivers of the larger islands
plays an important part in trade.

Air services are operated by Garuda Indonesian Airways
and other local airlines, and Jakarta is served by various
international services.

EAST TIMOR

East Timor was a Portuguese colony from 1702 until
Portuguese control collapsed following the 1974 coup in
Portugal. An independence war waged by the Marxist
Fretilin (Revolutionary Front for an Independent East
Timor) developed into a civil war between Fretilin and
local conservative forces in 1975. After gaining control,
Fretilin declared East Timor independent on 27 Novem-
ber 1975 and this was recognized by Portugal. Indonesian
forces invaded East Timor on 7 December 1975 and
declared East Timor Indonesia's 27th province.

Since 1975 Fretilin has waged an armed campaign for
independence; resistance has left 200,000 East Timorese
dead. About 150,000 Muslims have been settled in East
Timor alongside the predominantly Roman Catholic
population (80 per cent in 1975). The UN does not
recognize the annexation and considers Portugal to exercise sovereignty still. A massacre of pro-independence
demonstrators in the capital, Dili, in 1991 provoked
international outrage. Following the collapse of the
Suharto regime, talks over the future of East Timor have
been conducted.

IRAN
Jomhuri-e-Islami-e-Iran

AREA – 630,577 sq. miles (1,633,188 sq. km). Neighbours:
Armenia, Azerbaijan, Turkmenistan (north),
Afghanistan (north-east), Pakistan (south-east), Iraq
(south-west), Turkey (north-west)
POPULATION – 67,283,000 (1996 census): 99 per cent
Muslims (Shia 91 per cent and Sunni 8 per cent) with
small minorities of Zoroastrians, Bahais, Jews, and
Armenian and Assyrian Christians. The official
language is Persian (Farsi). Turkish, Kurdish, Arabic,
Lori, Guilani, Mazandarani and Baluchi are also spoken
CAPITAL – Tehran, (population 6,750,043, 1994 estimate)
MAJOR CITIES – Ahwaz (828,380); Esfahan (1,220,595);
Mashhad (1,964,489); Qom (780,453); Shiraz
(1,042,801); Tabriz (1,166,203), 1994
CURRENCY – Rial
NATIONAL ANTHEM – Sorood-e Jomhoori-e Eslami
NATIONAL DAY – 11 February
NATIONAL FLAG – Three horizontal stripes of green,
white, red, with the slogan *Allahu Akbar* repeated 22 times
along the edges of the green and red stripes, and the
national emblem in the centre
LIFE EXPECTANCY (years) – male 58.38; female 59.70

POPULATION GROWTH RATE – 4.2 per cent (1995)
POPULATION DENSITY – 41 per sq. km (1995)
URBAN POPULATION – 57.5 per cent (1993)

Iran is mostly an arid tableland, encircled, except in the east, by mountains, the highest in the north rising to 18,934 ft. The central and eastern portion is a vast salt desert.

HISTORY AND POLITICS

Iran was ruled from the end of the 18th century by Shahs of the Qajar dynasty. In 1925 the last of the dynasty, Sultan Ahmed Shah, was deposed in his absence by the National Assembly, which handed executive power to Prime Minister Reza Khan. Reza Khan was elected Shah as Reza Shah Pahlavi by the Constituent Assembly in December 1925. In 1941 Reza Shah abdicated in favour of the Crown Prince, who ascended the throne as Mohammed Reza Shah Pahlavi.

In January 1979, the Shah left Iran, handing over power to the Prime Minister, who was ousted by Ayatollah Khomeini, the spiritual leader of the Shia Muslims, on his return from exile. Following a national referendum, an Islamic Republic was declared on 1 April 1979. A new constitution, providing for a president, prime minister, Consultative Assembly, and leadership by Ayatollah Khomeini, was approved by referendum in December 1979. In June 1989 Khomeini died and President Khamenei was appointed Leader of the Islamic Republic. Rafsanjani was elected president in July 1989, and the post of prime minister was abolished. The 1997 presidential election was won by Mohammad Khatami, leader of a centre-left coalition. He was seen as a moderate, and following his election has pursued reformist policies, including calling for 'a thoughtful dialogue with the American people'. Iran and the USA broke all diplomatic links in 1980.

FOREIGN RELATIONS

Iran was at war with Iraq following the Iraqi invasion of Iran in September 1980. International efforts to end the fighting resulted in a cease-fire in August 1988. In August 1990 Iraq accepted Iran's conditions for settling the conflict, including a return to the 1975 border, but a formal peace treaty has not been signed.

POLITICAL SYSTEM

The leader of the republic is elected by the Council of Experts whose 83 members are popularly elected every eight years. The president, who is the chief executive, is directly elected for a four-year term, renewable once. Ministers are nominated by the president and must obtain a vote of confidence in the Majlis. The Majlis comprises 270 representatives who are directly elected for a four-year term. Laws passed by the Majlis must be approved by the 12-member Guardian Council. In November 1997, President Khatami announced the establishment of the Committee for the Implementation and Supervision of the Constitution, a five-member body to ensure the constitution was abided by and that people's rights were respected.

Leader of the Islamic Republic, Ayatollah Seyed Ali Khamenei, *appointed* June 1989
President, Seyed Mohammad Khatami, *elected* 23 May 1997
First Vice-President, Hassan Ebrahim Habibi

COUNCIL OF MINISTERS *as at July 1998*

Vice-Presidents, Gholamreza Aqazadeh (*Atomic Energy*); Abdollah Nouri (*Development and Social Affairs*);

Masoumeh Ebtekar (*Environmental Protection*); Mohammad Hashemi (*Executive Affairs*); Abdulvahed Moussavi-Lari (*Legal and Parliamentary Affairs*); Mostafa Hashemi-Taba (*Physical Education*); Mohammad Ali Najafi (*Planning and Budget*); Mohammad Baqerian (*State Employment and Administrative Affairs*)
Agriculture and Rural Affairs, Isa Kalantari
Commerce, Mohammad Shariatmadari
Co-operatives, Morteza Hajji
Culture and Islamic Guidance, Ataollah Mohajerani
Defence and Logistics, Ali Shamkhani
Economic Affairs and Finance, Hossain Namazi
Education, Hossain Mozafar
Energy, Habibollah Bitaraf
Foreign Affairs, Kamal Kharrazi
Health, Mohamad Farhadi
Higher Education, Mostafa Moin
Housing and Urban Development, Ali Abol-Alizadeh
Industries, Gholamreza Shafei
Information, Qorbanali Dorri Najafabadi
Interior (acting), Mostafa Tajzadeh
Jihad for Reconstruction, Mohamad Saidi Kya
Justice, Hojjatolislam Ismail Shostari
Labour and Social Affairs, Hossein Kamali
Mines and Metals, Eshaq Jahangiri
Oil, Bijan Namdar Zanganeh
Posts, Telephones and Telegraphs, Mohammad Reza Aref
Roads and Transport, Mahmoud Hojjati

EMBASSY OF THE ISLAMIC REPUBLIC OF IRAN
16 Prince's Gate, London SW7 1PT
Tel 0171-225 3000
Chargé d'Affaires, G. Ansari

BRITISH EMBASSY
143 Ferdowsi Avenue, PO Box 11365–4474, Tehran 11344
Tel: Tehran 675011
Counsellor and Chargé d'Affaires, Nicholas W. Browne
First Secretary (Commercial), A. F. Bedford

DEFENCE

The Army has 1,390 main battle tanks, 950 armoured personnel carriers and armoured infantry fighting vehicles, 1,995 artillery pieces, 77 aircraft and 100 attack helicopters. The Navy has three submarines, one destroyer, three frigates, 48 patrol and coastal vessels and nine armed helicopters. There are six naval bases. The Air Force has some 295 combat aircraft, of which only about 50 per cent are serviceable due to the US armaments embargo, in operation since 1979.

MILITARY EXPENDITURE – 2.1 per cent of GDP (1996)
MILITARY PERSONNEL – 668,000: Army 350,000,
   Revolutionary Guard Corps 120,000, Navy 18,000, Air
   Force 30,000, Paramilitaries 150,000
CONSCRIPTION DURATION – Two years

ECONOMY

Iran's alleged support for international terrorism and its suspected nuclear weapons programme prompted the USA to impose a full trade and investment embargo in June 1995, and to impose sanctions on foreign companies investing more than £26 million a year in Iran's energy sector, in July 1996. However, in August 1996, Turkey signed a £13-billion deal to buy Iranian gas and for the construction of a gas pipeline.

Agricultural output rose following the end of the Iran–Iraq war and an attempt is being made to reduce dependence on food imports. Wheat is the principal crop; other important crops are barley, rice, cotton, sugar beet, fruit, nuts and vegetables. Wool is also a major product.

The oilfields, which lie in south-western Iran, were nationalized in 1951. In 1979, the National Iranian Oil Company assumed control of the production, refining and sale of oil. Oil production was 180,911,000 tonnes in 1995. Apart from oil, the principal industrial products are carpets, textiles, sugar, cement and other construction materials, ginned cotton, vegetable oil and other food products, leather and shoes, metal manufactures, pharmaceuticals, motor vehicles, fertilizers and plastics. Privatization began in 1991.

In 1995 there was a trade surplus of US$5,697 million and a current account surplus of US$3,478 million.

GDP – US$656,589 million (1994); US$1,151 per capita (1994)

ANNUAL AVERAGE GROWTH OF GDP – 4.2 per cent (1995)

INFLATION RATE – 28.9 per cent (1996)

TOTAL EXTERNAL DEBT – US$21,183 million (1996)

TRADE

Imports are mainly industrial and agricultural machinery, motor vehicles and components for assembly, iron and steel, electrical machinery and goods, foodstuffs and certain textile fabrics and yarns. The principal exports, apart from oil and gas, are carpets and fruit. Japan, Germany, France, the UAE and Italy are Iran's main trading partners.

Trade with UK	1996	1997
Imports from UK	£396,561,000	£395,845,000
Exports to UK	118,771,000	36,158,000

COMMUNICATIONS

Tehran is the centre of a network of highways linking the major towns, ports, the Caspian Sea and the national frontiers.

The Trans-Iranian Railway runs from Bandar Turcoman, on the Caspian Sea, via Tehran to Bandar Khomeini, on the Persian Gulf. Other lines link Tehran with Tabriz and Mashhad; Tabriz to Julfa; Zahedan to Quetta; Ahvaz to Khorramshahr; Qom to Kerman; and Bandar Turcoman to Gorgan. The rail system is linked to the Turkish system via Van. A track between Mashhad and Tedzhen in Turkmenistan, opened in May 1996, has re-established the ancient Silk Road between China and the Mediterranean.

There is an international airport at Tehran (Mehrabad), and airports at all the major provincial centres. The national airline, Iranair, is government-owned and operates international and domestic routes.

EDUCATION AND CULTURE

Since 1943 primary education has been compulsory and free. There are 57 universities in Iran. The educational system has been reformed following the revolution.

Persian or Farsi is an Indo-European language with many Arabic elements added; the alphabet is mainly Arabic, with writing from right to left. Among the great names in Persian literature are those of Abu'l Kásim Mansúr, or Firdausi (AD 939–1020), Omar Khayyám, the astronomer-poet (died AD 1122), Muslihu'd-Din, known as Sa'di (born AD 1184), and Shems-ed-Din Muhammad, or Hafiz (died AD 1389).

ILLITERACY RATE – 27.9 per cent

ENROLMENT (percentage of age group) – primary 79 per cent (1985); tertiary 14.8 per cent (1994)

IRAQ
Al-Jumhouriya al-'Iraqia

AREA – 169,235 sq. miles (438,317 sq. km). Neighbours: Iran (east), Saudi Arabia, Kuwait (south), Jordan (west), Syria (north-west), Turkey (north)

POPULATION – 20,449,000 (1994 UN estimate), 16,278,316 (1987 census). The official language is Arabic. Minority languages include Kurdish (about 15 per cent), Turkic and Aramaic

CAPITAL – Baghdad (population, 3,841,268, 1987)

MAJOR CITIES – ΨBasra (406,296); Kirkuk (418,624); Mosul (664,221)

CURRENCY – Iraqi dinar (ID) of 1,000 fils

NATIONAL DAY – 17 July (Revolution Day)

NATIONAL FLAG – Three horizontal stripes of red, white, black; on the white stripe three stars and the slogan *Allahu Akbar* all in green

LIFE EXPECTANCY (years) – male 77.43; female 78.22

POPULATION GROWTH RATE – 3.3 per cent (1995)

POPULATION DENSITY – 47 per sq. km (1995)

URBAN POPULATION – 69.9 per cent (1990)

ILLITERACY RATE – 42.0 per cent

ENROLMENT (percentage of age group) – primary 79 per cent (1992); secondary 37 per cent (1992); tertiary 12.6 per cent (1990)

In 1993 the border between Iraq and Kuwait was formally demarcated, moving a few hundred metres northwards and giving part of the port of Umm Qasr to Kuwait. The rivers Euphrates (1,700 miles) and Tigris (1,150 miles) rise in Turkey and traverse Iraq to their junction at Qurna, from where the Euphrates flows the 70 miles to the Gulf.

HISTORY AND POLITICS

Iraq is the site of the remains of several ancient civilizations: one site at Tel Hassuna, near Shura, dates back to 5000 BC; Tel Abu Shahrain near 'Ur of the Chaldees' is the site of the Sumerian city of Eridu; the ancient city of Hillah, 70 miles south of Baghdad, is near the site of Babylon and the Tower of Babel. Mosul governorate covers a great part of the ancient kingdom of Assyria, the ruins of Nineveh, the Assyrian capital, being visible on the banks of the Tigris, opposite Mosul. Qurna, at the junction of the Tigris and Euphrates, is traditionally supposed to be the site of the Garden of Eden.

Under the Treaty of Lausanne (1923), Turkey renounced sovereignty over Mesopotamia. A provisional government was set up in 1920, and in 1921 the Emir Faisal was elected King of Iraq. The country was a monarchy until July 1958, when King Faisal II was assassinated. From 1958 Iraq has been under the rule of the Ba'ath Party.

The Arab Ba'ath Socialist Party held a majority of Assembly seats following the 1989 elections; no party affiliations were ascribed in the results of the most recent election, held on 24 March 1996.

FOREIGN RELATIONS

Iraq invaded Iran in September 1980 and was at war until the August 1988 cease-fire. In 1990 Iraq accepted Iran's conditions for peace, including a return to the 1975 border, but a formal peace treaty has not been signed.

Iraq invaded Kuwait on 2 August 1990 and declared Kuwait a province of Iraq. The UN Security Council declared the annexation void. After months of diplomatic attempts to secure an Iraqi withdrawal from Kuwait, an alliance of NATO and Middle East countries launched an

offensive in January 1991 and liberated Kuwait in February 1991.

A United Nations Special Committee (UNSCOM), charged with securing Iraq's full nuclear, biological and chemical disarmament, has frequently been hindered in its task by Iraqi officials. In November 1997, an UNSCOM team was denied access to the Presidential Palaces, following UNSCOM's discovery of undeclared Iraqi chemical weapons. A military conflict was averted in February 1998 when UN Secretary-General Kofi Annan signed an agreement with the Iraqi government allowing unlimited access for UN weapons inspectors. The USA recognized the deal but maintained its forces on alert in the Gulf for a further six months. In August 1998, the Iraqi government announced that it was suspending all co-operation with UNSCOM officials in protest at the continuing sanctions.

INSURGENCIES

Following the allied victory in Kuwait in February 1991, rebellion broke out in the Kurdish north and the Shi'ite south. Although the revolt was quickly suppressed, Iraqi attacks on Kurdish civilians led Western governments to set up a security zone and a UN safe haven in northern Iraq to protect them. An air exclusion zone north of the 36th parallel was also established. Saddam Hussein withdrew his administration from Kurdish northern Iraq in October 1991, enabling the Kurds to establish a *de facto* administration with its capital at Arbil. In 1992 the Kurds voted for a 100-seat parliament and a 'political leader'. The Kurdish Democratic Party (KDP) and the Patriotic Union of Kurdistan (PUK) both gained 50 seats and a coalition government was formed. Trading difficulties, fuel and food shortages, and land disputes led to fighting between the two parties. A cease-fire lasted from September 1995 to August 1996 when the KDP invited Iraqi troops to invade the safe haven. Another cease-fire was signed in October 1996. There are 25,000 KDP members and 12,000 PUK members.

Although the Shi'ite revolt in southern Iraq was defeated in April 1991, a low-level insurgency continued in the southern marshlands. Continued Iraqi bombing of Shi'ite refugees in these areas led to an air exclusion zone being established south of the 32nd parallel in August 1992, patrolled by US, British and French aircraft. Since then the Iraqi regime has systematically drained the southern marshes by canal construction and river diversion; with continued ground offensives, this had effectively ended the Shi'ite rebellion by late 1994.

POLITICAL SYSTEM

According to the provisional constitution, the highest state authority is the Revolutionary Command Council (RCC), which elects the president from among its members. A constitutional amendment approved in September 1995 provided for the confirmation of the RCC's choice of president by the National Assembly and by a popular referendum. The president appoints the Council of Ministers. Legislative authority is shared by the RCC and the 250-member National Assembly, which is elected every four years by universal adult suffrage. Following the amendment to the constitution, a referendum on a further seven-year term for President Saddam was approved by a claimed 99.96 per cent of voters on 15 October 1995.

HEAD OF STATE

President, Saddam Hussein, *assumed office* 16 July 1979, *reappointed* 17 October 1995
Vice President, Taha Mohieddin Maarouf

REVOLUTIONARY COMMAND COUNCIL

Chairman, The President
Vice-Chairman, Izzat Ibrahim
Secretary-General, Khaled Abdel-Moneim Rasheed
Members, Taha Yassin Ramadan; Sa'adoun Shaker; Tariq Aziz; Taha Mohieddin Maarouf; Mohammad Hamzah al-Zubaydi; Mizban Khader Hadi

CABINET *as at July 1998*

The President
Deputy Prime Ministers, Tariq Aziz; Taha Yassin Ramadan; Mohammad Hamzah al-Zubaydi
Agriculture, Abd al-Ilah Hamid Muhammad Salih
Defence, Gen. Abd al-Jabbar Shanshal
Education, Fahd Salem al-Shaqra
Finance, Hikmat Mizban Ibrahim al-Azzawi
Foreign Affairs, Muhammad Said Kazim al-Sahhaf
Health, Umid Midhat Mubarak
Higher Education and Scientific Research, Abd al-Jabbar Tawfiq Muhammad
Housing and Reconstruction, Ma'n Abdullah al-Sarsam
Industry, Minerals, Adnan Abd al Majid Jasim al-Ani
Information and Culture, Humam Abd al-Khaliq abd al-Ghafur
Interior, Muhammad Ziman Abd al-Razzaq
Irrigation, Mahmud Dhiyab al-Ahmad
Justice, Shabib Lazim al-Maliki
Labour and Social Affairs, Staff Gen. Sa'di Tu'mah Abbas
Ministers of State, Gen. Abdel-Jabbar Khalil Shanshal (*Military Affairs*); Abdel Wahhab Omar Mirza al-Atrushi (*Without Portfolio*); Arshad Muhammad Ahmad al-Zibari (*Without Portfolio*)
Oil, Lt.-Gen. Amir Muhammad Rashid al-Ubaydi
Religious Endowments and Religious Affairs, Abd al-Munim Ahmad Salih
Trade, Mohammad Mehdi Salih
Transport and Communications, Ahmad Murtada Khalil

IRAQI DIPLOMATIC MISSION IN LONDON

Since Iraq's breach of diplomatic relations with Britain in February 1991, the Jordanian Embassy has handled Iraqi interests in the UK.
Minister/Head of Interests Section, Zuhair Ibrahim

BRITISH DIPLOMATIC REPRESENTATION

The British Embassy was closed in January 1991. The Russian Embassy has since handled British interests in Iraq.

DEFENCE

The Army has roughly 2,700 main battle tanks, 2,900 armoured personnel carriers and armoured infantry fighting vehicles, 1,800 artillery pieces and 120 armed helicopters. The Navy has two frigates and six patrol and coastal vessels at two bases.

In 1991, the UN demanded the destruction of all weapons of mass destruction and their means of production as a prerequisite for the lifting of sanctions. By mid-1995 it was believed that most of these weapons had been destroyed and a long-term monitoring operation was under way to ensure production did not restart. In late 1995, evidence of a ballistic missile programme and large biological weapons stockpiles was discovered; in 1997 evidence of further Iraqi chemical weapons, including missiles loaded with VX gas, was discovered.

MILITARY EXPENDITURE – 8.7 per cent of GDP (1996)
MILITARY PERSONNEL – 437,500: Army 350,000, Navy 2,500, Air Force 35,000, Paramilitaries 50,000
CONSCRIPTION DURATION – 18–24 months

ECONOMY

Increasing industrialization is taking place but production has been hampered by war damage and sanctions. Iraq's major industry is oil production which was nationalized in 1972 and usually accounts for approximately 98 per cent of the total government revenue and 45 per cent of GNP. Production was 3.5 million barrels per day in 1979 but has been reduced by war damage from the Iran–Iraq and Gulf wars, the closure of Syrian, Turkish and Saudi pipelines and UN economic sanctions. A £2.2 million deal with Russia was signed in March 1997 to develop the Qurnah oilfield in southern Iraq.

Agricultural production is important, with two harvests usually gathered in a year, depending on rainfall. Salinity and soil erosion limit productivity.

The UN imposed economic sanctions and a world-wide ban on Iraqi oil exports in August 1990. In May 1996, Iraq agreed to a UN-proposed 'oil-for-food' deal, permitting the sale of £2.6 billion of oil a year to buy food and medicine. Limited oil exports resumed in December 1996. Thirty per cent of the revenue will pay for reparations to Gulf War victims, and up to 15 per cent will provide aid to Iraqi Kurds.

GDP – US$25,219 million (1994); US$2,855 per capita (1994)
ANNUAL AVERAGE GROWTH OF GDP – –7.2 per cent (1989)

TRADE

The principal imports are normally iron and steel, military equipment, building materials, mechanical and electrical machinery, motor vehicles, textiles and clothing, essential foodstuffs and raw industrial materials. The chief exports are normally crude petroleum, dates, raw wool, raw hides and skins and raw cotton.

Trade with UK	1996	1997
Imports from UK	£10,927,000	£6,431,000
Exports to UK	105,000	29,000

COMMUNICATIONS

The port of Basra has not been used since the outbreak of hostilities with Iran in 1980. Continuous dredging of the Shatt-al-Arab has also been suspended by hostilities and the channel has seriously silted. The port of Umm Qasr on the Kuwaiti border, which was developed for freight and sulphur handling and includes a container terminal, was opened in late 1993. All external borders, except that of Jordan, are closed to Iraqi traffic.

There is an international airport at Baghdad. Iraqi Airways provided flights between Baghdad and London, and other international airlines operated to Europe. Iraqi Republican Railways provided regular passenger and goods services between Basra, Baghdad and Mosul. There is also a metre gauge rail line connecting Baghdad with Khanaqin, Kirkuk and Arbil.

Iraqi communications were greatly affected by the Gulf War; large numbers of bridges were destroyed and the railway system extensively disrupted.

REPUBLIC OF IRELAND
Poblacht Na hEireann

AREA – 27,137 sq. miles (70,284 sq. km). Neighbour: Northern Ireland (north)
POPULATION – 3,626,087 (1996 census). At the 1991 census religious adherence was: Roman Catholic, 3,228,327; Church of Ireland, 89,187; Presbyterians, 13,199; Methodists, 5,037; others, 189,969. Irish is the first official language; English is recognized as a second official language, but is more commonly used
CAPITAL – ΨDublin (*Baile Atha Cliath*), (population, 952,700, 1996 census)
MAJOR CITIES – ΨCork (180,000); ΨGalway (57,400); ΨLimerick (79,100); Waterford (44,200), 1996 census
CURRENCY – Punt (IR£) of 100 pence
NATIONAL ANTHEM – Amhrán na BhFiann (The Soldier's Song)
NATIONAL DAY – 17 March (St Patrick's Day)
NATIONAL FLAG – Equal vertical stripes of green, white and orange
LIFE EXPECTANCY (years) – male 72.30; female 77.87
POPULATION GROWTH RATE – 0.4 per cent (1995)
POPULATION DENSITY – 51 per sq. km (1995)
URBAN POPULATION – 57.0 per cent (1991)
MILITARY EXPENDITURE – 1.1 per cent of GDP (1996)
MILITARY PERSONNEL – 12,700: Army 10,500, Navy 1,100, Air Force 1,100
CONSCRIPTION DURATION – Three–year terms

Ireland is separated from Scotland by the North Channel and from England and Wales by the Irish Sea and St George's Channel. The greatest length of the island, from north-east to south-west (Torr Head to Mizen Head), is 302 miles, and the greatest breadth, from east to west (Dundrum Bay to Annagh Head), is 174 miles. On the north coast of Achill Island (Co. Mayo) are the highest cliffs in the British Isles, 2,000 feet sheer above the sea.

The highest point is Carrantuohill (3,414 ft). The principal river is the Shannon (240 miles), which drains the central plain. The Slaney flows into Wexford Harbour, the Liffey to Dublin Bay, the Boyne to Drogheda, the Lee to Cork Harbour, the Blackwater to Youghal Harbour, and the Suir, Barrow and Nore to Waterford Harbour.

The principal hydrographic feature is the loughs; the Shannon chain of Allen, Boderg, Forbes, Ree and Derg, and the Erne chain of Gowna, Oughter, Lower Erne, and Erne; Melvin, Gill, Gara and Conn in the north-west; and Corrib and Mask (joined by a hidden channel) in the west.

The Republic of Ireland is divided into four provinces of 26 counties: Leinster (Carlow, Dublin, Kildare, Kilkenny, Laoighis, Longford, Louth, Meath, Offaly, Westmeath, Wexford and Wicklow); Munster (Clare, Cork, Kerry, Limerick, Tipperary and Waterford); Connacht

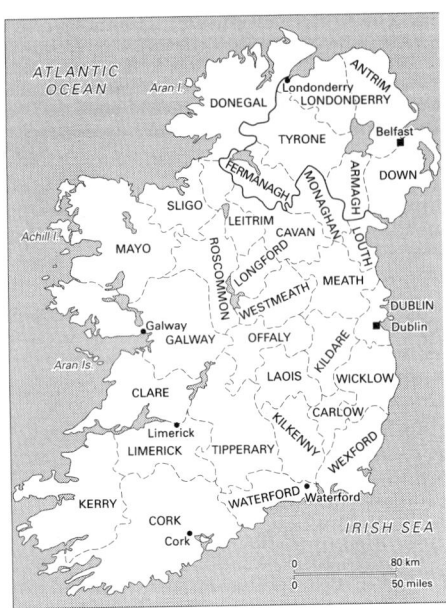

(Galway, Leitrim, Mayo, Roscommon and Sligo); and part of Ulster (Cavan, Donegal and Monaghan).

HISTORY AND POLITICS

The first inhabitants of Ireland, hunters from mainland Britain, arrived in 7,000 BC, and were joined by Celts from central Europe from the sixth century BC until about the time of Christ. The introduction of Christianity in the fifth century is traditionally associated with St Patrick and inspired 300 years of rich cultural achievements. The Vikings, who established most of the major towns, including Dublin and Cork, invaded around AD 800 and controlled Ireland until their defeat at the Battle of Clontarf (1014) by Brian Boru, who had become king of all Ireland in 1002.

In the 12th century the Norman English invaded at the invitation of Dermod MacMurrough, the deposed king of Leinster, and established feudal control over most of the island; this lasted for 300 years. King Henry VIII of England reconquered Ireland and in 1541 declared himself king of Ireland, the first English monarch to do so. Protestantism was introduced but failed to take root, except in Ulster where English and Scottish Presbyterians settled during the reign of James I (1603–25). A rebellion initiated by Ulster Catholics in 1641 was ruthlessly crushed by Oliver Cromwell's army. Catholicism was repressed and further Protestant colonization encouraged. Following the abdication of the Catholic King James II in 1688, Irish Protestants supported William of Orange's accession to the throne. James II was defeated in Ireland, most famously at the Battle of the Boyne (1690), and Protestant ascendancy was restored, enduring throughout the 18th century.

The Irish parliament was granted independence in 1782, although the Dublin administration was still appointed by the king. The parliament was abolished by the Act of Union in 1801 following a rebellion by the Society of the United Irishmen in 1798, and subsequently Irish MPs sat at Westminster. Demands for the restoration of the Irish parliament and home rule for Ireland were successful in

1914, but were delayed when World War I broke out. A rebellion, the Easter Rising of 1916, was suppressed by the British, fuelling support for the *Sinn Féin* party, which won the 1918 election in Ireland and withdrew from the British parliament to form a legislature in Dublin under the leadership of Éamon de Valera. The resulting two-year war of independence between the Irish Republican Army and British forces ended in a truce, followed by negotiations leading to the signing of the Anglo-Irish Treaty in December 1921. The island was partitioned, the 26 counties of the Irish Free State accepting dominion status within the British Empire, while six of the nine counties of Ulster, where the majority Protestant population opposed home rule, remained part of the United Kingdom, governed by a Northern Ireland parliament.

Civil war broke out between the new Irish government and opponents of the treaty until a truce was reached in May 1923. Constitutional links between the Irish Free State and the UK were gradually removed by the Irish parliament and a new constitution enacted in 1937 declared the Irish Free State a sovereign, independent state with a republican government. However, it continued in association with the states of the British Commonwealth until 1949, when constitutional links with Britain were severed and the state was renamed the Republic of Ireland.

Under the terms of the 1998 Belfast Agreement, the Irish Republic gave up its territorial claim to the six counties of Northern Ireland. Additionally, a North-South Ministerial Council, comprising officials from both countries, would meet to regulate areas of common interest.

The presidential election in October 1997 was won by Mary McAleese with almost 59 per cent of second-round votes. The composition of the Dáil Eireann as of July 1998 was: Fianna Fáil 76; Fine Gael 54; Labour 16; Democratic Left 4; Progressive Democrats 4; Green Party 2; Sinn Fein 1; Socialist 1; others 6. Fianna Fail and the Progressive Democrats formed a coalition government.

POLITICAL SYSTEM

The president (*Uachtarán na hEireann*) is directly elected for a term of seven years, and is eligible for a second term. The president is aided and advised by a Council of State.

The National Parliament (*Oireachtas*) consists of the president, House of Representatives (*Dáil Éireann*) and Senate (*Seanad Éireann*). Dáil Éireann is composed of 166 members elected for a five-year term on a basis of proportional representation by means of the single transferable vote. Seanad Éireann is composed of 60 members, of whom 11 are nominated by the prime minister (*Taoiseach*) and 49 are elected, six by institutions of higher education and 43 from panels of candidates established on a vocational basis.

Executive power is vested in the government subject to the constitution. The government is responsible to the Dáil. The taoiseach is appointed by the president on the nomination of the Dáil. The other members of the government are appointed by the president on the nomination of the taoiseach with the previous approval of the Dáil. The taoiseach appoints a member of the government to be his deputy (the *tánaiste*).

The judicial system comprises courts of first instance and a court of final appeal called the Supreme Court (*Cúirt Uachtarach*). The courts of first instance include a High Court (*Ard-Chúirt*) and courts of local and limited jurisdiction, with a right of appeal as determined by law. The High Court alone has original jurisdiction to consider the question of the validity of any law having regard to the provisions of the constitution. The Supreme Court has appellate jurisdiction from decisions of the High Court.

HEAD OF STATE

President, Mary McAleese, *elected* 30 October 1997, *sworn in* 11 November 1997

CABINET *as at July 1998*

Taoiseach (PM), Bertie Ahern
Tánaiste (Deputy PM), *Enterprise, Trade and Employment*, Mary Harney
Agriculture and Food, Joe Walsh
Arts, Heritage, Gaeltachta and Islands, Síle de Valera
Attorney-General, David Byrne
Defence, Michael Smith
Education, Michael Martin
Environment and Local Government, Noel Dempsey
Finance, Charlie McCreevy
Foreign Affairs, David Andrews
Government Chief Whip, Seamus Brennan
Health and Children, Brian Cowen
Justice and Equality, Law Reform, John O'Donoghue
Marine and Natural Resources, Michael Woods
Minister of State to the Government, Robert Molloy
Public Enterprise, Mary O'Rourke
Social, Community and Family Affairs, Dermot Ahern
Tourism, Sport and Recreation, Jim McDaid

IRISH EMBASSY

17 Grosvenor Place, London SW1X 7HR
Tel 0171-235 2171
Ambassador Extraordinary and Plenipotentiary, HE Edward Barrington, apptd 1995
Counsellor, E. Carey (*Economic*)

BRITISH EMBASSY

29 Merrion Road, Dublin 4
Tel: Dublin 205 3700
Ambassador Extraordinary and Plenipotentiary, HE Veronica Sutherland, CMG, apptd 1995
Counsellor and Deputy Head of Mission, R. I. Clarke
Defence Attaché, Col. J. A. Wilson
First Secretary (Commercial), R. N. J. Baker

BRITISH COUNCIL REPRESENTATIVE, Harold Fish, OBE, Newmount House, 22/24 Lower Mount Street, Dublin 2

ECONOMY

Although industry has expanded greatly since Ireland's entry into the European Community in 1973, agriculture remains important; in 1997, 10 per cent of the workforce was employed in agriculture. The main crops are wheat, barley, oats, potatoes and sugar beet. Agriculture has benefited considerably from the EU Common Agricultural Policy and support funds but has suffered from the drift of the rural population to urban areas and abroad.

Industry accounted for about 38 per cent of GNP and about 27 per cent of employment in 1996. The traditional brewing, spirits and food-processing sectors have expanded and have been joined by the manufacture of textiles, chemicals, pharmaceuticals, electronics, office machinery and transportation equipment. The services sector is currently the fastest-growing sector of the economy and accounted for 58 per cent of GNP and 62 per cent of employment in 1996. Tourism is the most important part of the service sector and in recent years has provided substantial revenue, with over five million visitors in 1997.

The Kinsale gas field off the south coast provides 69 per cent of Ireland's gas needs, with the rest coming via an undersea pipeline from Moffat, Scotland. There are seven government-funded milled peat power-generating stations. Hydroelectric power from the Shannon barrage and other schemes is also important but Ireland still imports 53 per cent of oil and coal for power generation. Metal content of ores raised (1997) was lead, 45,100 tonnes; zinc, 194,800 tonnes; silver 13,300,000 grammes. An estimated 15,500 persons were employed in the fisheries in 1997.

Animal products, dairy products and livestock, especially cattle, are the main exports. The UK, USA, Germany, France and Japan are Ireland's main trading partners.

On 1 May 1998, it was announced that Ireland had satisfied the Maastricht convergence criteria and would participate in the European Single Currency from 1 January 1999.

In 1996 Ireland had a trade surplus of US$15,194 million and a current account surplus of US$1,406 million. Imports totalled US$35,771 million and exports US$48,180 million.

GNP – US$62,040 million (1996); US$17,110 per capita (1996)
GDP – US$53,727 million (1994); US$14,735 per capita (1994)
ANNUAL AVERAGE GROWTH OF GDP – 7.7 per cent (1996)
INFLATION RATE – 1.7 per cent (1996)
UNEMPLOYMENT – 12.15 per cent (1995)

Trade with UK	1996	1997
Imports from UK	£8,272,700,000	£8,829,500,000
Exports to UK	6,825,000,000	7,047,800,000

COMMUNICATIONS

In 1997 there were 1,945 km of railway operated by *Iarnród Eireann*. In 1996 the number of ships with cargo which arrived at Irish ports was 16,787 (54,602,000 net registered tons), with a total weight of goods handled of 33.9 million tonnes.

Shannon Airport, Co. Clare, is on the main transatlantic air route. In 1997 the airport handled 1,822,427 passengers. Dublin Airport serves the cross-channel and European services operated by the Irish national airline Aer Lingus and other airlines. In 1997 the airport handled 10,333,202 passengers. In 1997 Cork Airport handled 1,196,261 passengers.

EDUCATION

Primary education is directed by the state, with the exception of 62 private primary schools. There were 3,192 state-aided primary schools in 1996–7.

In 1996–7 there were 440 recognized secondary schools under private management (mainly religious orders), and 243 vocational schools. There were 16 state comprehensive schools and 64 community schools.

Third-level education is catered for by seven university colleges, and also by third-level courses offered by the technical colleges and regional technical colleges and other third-level institutions.

ENROLMENT (percentage of age group) – primary 100 per cent (1994); secondary 85 per cent (1994); tertiary 37.0 per cent (1994)

ISRAEL

Medinat Israel

AREA – 8,130 sq. miles (21,056 sq. km). Neighbours: Lebanon (north), Syria (north-east), Jordan and the West Bank (east), the Gaza Strip and the Egyptian province of Sinai (south-west)

south-east which divides the hill region; the Negev, a semi-desert triangular-shaped region, extending from a base south of Beersheba, to an apex at the head of the Gulf of Aqaba; and parts of the Jordan valley, including the Hula region, Tiberias and the south-western extremity of the Dead Sea.

The principal river is the Jordan, which rises from three main sources in Israel, the Lebanon and Syria, and flows through the Hula valley, Lake Tiberias/Kinneret (Sea of Galilee) and the Jordan Valley into the Dead Sea, falling 1,517 ft from Hulata to the Dead Sea. The other principal rivers are the Yarkon and Kishon. The Dead Sea is a lake (shared between Israel, the West Bank and Jordan), 1,286 ft below sea-level; it has no outlet, the surplus being carried off by evaporation.

The climate is variable, modified by altitude and distance from the sea, with hot summers and rainy winters.

HISTORY AND POLITICS

The Ottoman Empire province of Palestine was captured by British forces in 1917, the same year that the British Government issued the Balfour Declaration which 'viewed with favour the establishment of a national home for the Jewish people in Palestine'. The Balfour Declaration's terms were enshrined in Britain's League of Nations mandate over Palestine, leading to steady Jewish immigration in the inter-war years and a post-1945 flood by Nazi concentration camp survivors. The Arab Palestinian population revolted against Jewish immigration from 1936 onwards, while Jewish groups conducted a terrorist campaign against the British administration from 1945 onwards.

In 1947 Britain announced its withdrawal from Palestine with effect from May 1948, handing over to the UN responsibility for resolving the conflict between Arabs and Jews. Both sides ignored the UN partition plan; on the withdrawal of British forces on 14 May 1948 the State of Israel was proclaimed and the first Arab-Israeli war began. By the time of the January 1949 cease-fire Israeli forces controlled all of the former mandate territory apart from the West Bank (and East Jerusalem) and the Gaza Strip, which had come under Jordanian and Egyptian control respectively.

During the 1967 Six-Day War Israel captured the West Bank and the Gaza Strip, together with Sinai from Egypt and the Golan Heights from Syria, and annexed East Jerusalem. Israel held on to its gains in the 1973 Yom Kippur War. The Golan Heights were annexed in 1981; Sinai was returned to Egypt in 1982 in accordance with the 1979 Israeli–Egyptian peace treaty, and the South Lebanon Security Zone was established after the 1982–5 invasion of Lebanon. The annexations of East Jerusalem and the Golan Heights remain unrecognized internationally.

The Labour leader of the coalition government formed after the 1992 general election, Yitzhak Rabin, was assassinated by a Jewish extremist on 4 November 1995, and was replaced by Foreign Minister Shimon Peres. A general election on 29 May 1996, the first to have separate ballots for the prime minister and legislature, was won by Likud leader Binyamin Netanyahu, although no party gained outright control of the Knesset. Netanyahu formed an eight-party coalition government which commanded 66 seats in the Knesset.

FOREIGN RELATIONS

A peace process, started in October 1991 in Madrid, led to agreements with the Palestine Liberation Organization (*see* page 910), and with Jordan on 14 September 1993. A

POPULATION – 5,695,000 (1997 estimate): roughly 82 per cent Jewish, 14 per cent Arab Muslims, 2.5 per cent Christians of which 90 per cent are Arab, and 2 per cent Druze. Since independence Israel has had a policy of granting an immigration visa to every Jew who expresses a desire to settle in Israel. Between 1948 and 1992, 2.3 million immigrants had entered Israel from over 100 different countries. Hebrew and Arabic are the official languages. Arabs are entitled to transact all official business with government departments in Arabic

CAPITAL – Most of the government departments are in Jerusalem, population 662,700 (1995 estimate). A resolution proclaiming Jerusalem as the capital of Israel was adopted by the *Knesset* in 1950. It is not, however, recognized as the capital by the UN because East Jerusalem is part of the Occupied Territories captured in 1967. The UN and international law continues to reject the Israeli annexation of East Jerusalem and considers the pre-1950 capital Tel Aviv (population, 1,880,200) to be the capital

MAJOR CITIES – Beersheba (and district 122,000); ΨHaifa (and district 491,000)

CURRENCY – Shekel of 100 agora

NATIONAL ANTHEM – Hatikvah (The Hope)

NATIONAL FLAG – White, with two horizontal blue stripes, the Shield of David in the centre

LIFE EXPECTANCY (years) – male 75.33; female 79.10

POPULATION GROWTH RATE – 3.5 per cent (1995)

POPULATION DENSITY – 263 per sq. km (1995)

URBAN POPULATION – 89.7 per cent (1994)

Israel comprises the hill country of Galilee and parts of Judea and Samaria, rising to heights of nearly 4,000 ft; the coastal plain from the Gaza strip to north of Acre, including the plain of Esdraelon running from Haifa Bay to the

full peace agreement with Jordan was signed on 26 October 1994 and provides for the return to Jordan of land occupied by Israel since 1967 in the southern Araba valley (completed 9 February 1995).

Intermittent peace talks with Syria have stumbled over control of the Golan Heights and Israel's role in southern Lebanon.

POLITICAL SYSTEM

Israel is a sovereign democratic republic with executive power vested in a prime minister and Cabinet, and legislative power in a unicameral legislature (*Knesset*) of 120 members elected by proportional representation for a maximum term of four years. The prime minister is elected separately from the legislature. The president is head of state and is elected by the Knesset for a maximum of two five-year terms.

HEAD OF STATE

President of Israel, Ezer Weizman, *elected* 24 March 1993, *re-elected* 4 March 1998

CABINET *as at July 1998*

Prime Minister, Construction and Housing, Foreign Affairs,
   Binyamin Netanyahu (L)
Deputy PM, Agriculture and Rural Development, Environment,
   Rafael Eitan (T)
Deputy PM, Tourism, Moshe Katzav (L)
Communications, Limor Livnat (L)
Defence, Yitzhak Mordechai (L)
Education, Culture and Sport, Yitzhak Levy (NRP)
Finance, Prof. Yaacov Ne'eman (Ind.)
Health, Yehoshua Matza (L)
Immigrant Absorption, Yuli Edelstein (YB)
Industry, Trade, CIS Relations, Natan Sharansky (YB)
Interior and Religious Affairs, Eli Suissa (S)
Justice, Tzachi Hanegbi (L)
Labour and Social Affairs, Eliyahu Yishai (S)
National Infrastructure, Ariel Sharon (L)
Public Security, Avigdor Kahalani (TW)
Science, Michael Eitan (L)
Transport, Shaoul Yahalom (NRP)

L Likud; T Tsomet; NRP National Religious Party; S Shas; YB Yisrael Ba'aliya; TW Third Way; Ind. Independent

EMBASSY OF ISRAEL

2 Palace Green, Kensington, London w8 4QB
Tel 0171-957 9500
Ambassador Extraordinary and Plenipotentiary, HE Dror
   Zeigerman, apptd 1998
Minister Plenipotentiary, A. Magid
Defence Attaché, Brig.-Gen. I. Chen
Minister, M. Bar-On (*Consular*)
Counsellor, A. Wohl (*Commercial*)

BRITISH EMBASSY

192 Hayarkon Street, Tel Aviv 63405
Tel: Tel Aviv 524 9171
Ambassador Extraordinary and Plenipotentiary,
   HE David G. Manning, CMG, apptd 1995
Counsellor, Consul-General and Deputy Head of Mission, S.
   Pease
Defence and Military Attaché, Col. E. Houstoun, OBE
First Secretary (Commercial), W. W. Magor
CONSULATES – Tel Aviv, Eilat

BRITISH COUNCIL DIRECTOR, D. Elliot, 140 Hayarkon
   Street, PO Box 3302, Tel Aviv 61032
ISRAEL -BRITISH CHAMBER OF COMMERCE, 76 IBN Guirol
   Street, Tel Aviv 64162

DEFENCE

Israel is believed to have a nuclear capacity of around 100 warheads which could be delivered by aircraft or Jericho I and II missiles.

The Army has 4,300 main battle tanks, more than 9,400 armoured personnel carriers and 1,550 artillery pieces. The Navy has three submarines and 53 patrol and coastal vessels at three bases. The Air Force has 448 combat aircraft and 130 armed helicopters.

MILITARY EXPENDITURE – 10.2 per cent of GDP (1996)
MILITARY PERSONNEL – 181,050: Army 134,000, Navy
   9,000, Air Force 32,000, Paramilitaries 6,050
CONSCRIPTION DURATION – 21–48 months (Jews and
   Druze only)

ECONOMY

The country is generally fertile although water supply for irrigation restricts production. Agriculture accounts for 5 per cent of GNP and 4 per cent of exports.

The 'Jaffa' orange is produced in large quantities for export, along with other summer fruits, seasonal vegetables and glasshouse crops. Olives are cultivated, mainly for the production of oil. The main winter crops are wheat, barley and various kinds of pulses, while in summer sorghum, millet, maize, sesame and summer pulses are grown. Beef, cattle and poultry farming have been developed. Tobacco and cotton are now grown.

Polished diamonds account for about 23 per cent of total exports. Amongst the most important industries are textiles, foodstuffs and chemicals (mainly fertilizers and pharmaceuticals). Metal-working and science-based industries are sophisticated and technologically advanced and include the aircraft and military industries. Other important manufacturing industries include plastics, rubber, cement, glass, paper and oil refining. Industry accounts for 30 per cent of GNP.

GNP – US$90,310 million (1996); US$15,870 per capita
   (1996)
GDP – US$69,831 million (1994); US$14,333 per capita
   (1994)
ANNUAL AVERAGE GROWTH OF GDP – 4.4 per cent (1996)
INFLATION RATE – 11.3 per cent (1996)
UNEMPLOYMENT – 6.9 per cent (1995)

TRADE

The principal imports are foodstuffs, crude oil, machinery and vehicles, iron, steel and chemicals. The principal exports are metal machinery, electronic goods, chemicals, rubber, plastics, textiles, food and beverages, minerals, citrus produce and polished diamonds.

In 1996 Israel had a trade deficit of US$8,069 million and a current account deficit of US$6,298 million. Exports totalled US$20,489 million.

Trade with UK	1996	1997
Imports from UK	£1,265,773,000	£1,178,664,000
Exports to UK	831,845,000	879,922,000

COMMUNICATIONS

Israel State Railways serves Haifa, Tel Aviv, Jerusalem, Lod, Nahariya, Beersheba, Dimona, Ashdod and intermediate stations with a network of 528 km. There were 12,823 km of paved road in 1986. A major road building programme has been underway in the West Bank since 1992.

The chief ports are Haifa and Ashdod on the Mediterranean, and Eilat on the Red Sea; Acre has an anchorage for small vessels. The chief international airport is Ben Gurion between Tel Aviv and Jerusalem.

EDUCATION

Education from six to 16 years is free and compulsory. The law also provides for working youth aged 16–18, who for some reason have not completed their education, to be exempted from work in order to do so. There are seven universities including two engineering and technological institutes.

ILLITERACY RATE – 4.4 per cent

ENROLMENT (percentage of age group) – tertiary 41.1 per cent (1995)

CULTURE

Important historic sites in Israel include: *Jerusalem* – the Church of the Holy Sepulchre, the Al Aqsa Mosque and Dome of the Rock standing on the remains of the Temple Mount of Herod the Great of which the Western (wailing) Wall is a fragment, the Church of the Dormition and the Coenaculum on Mount Zion, Ein Karem, Church of the Visitation, Church of St John the Baptist; *Galilee* – the Sea, Church and Mount of the Beatitudes, ruins of Capernaum and other sites connected with the life of Christ; *Mount Tabor* – Church of the Transfiguration; *Nazareth* – Church of the Annunciation, and other Christian shrines associated with the childhood of Christ; there are also numerous sites dating from biblical and medieval days, such as Ascalon, Caesarea, Atlit, Massada, Megiddo and Hazor.

PALESTINIAN AUTONOMOUS AREAS

AREA – The total area is 2,406 sq. miles (6,231 sq. km). The area which is fully autonomous is 159 sq. miles (412 sq. km), of which the Gaza Strip is 136 sq. miles (352 sq. km) and the Jericho enclave 23 sq. miles (60 sq. km). The partially autonomous area is the remainder of the West Bank, some 2,247 sq. miles (5,819 sq. km). The UN and the international community also recognize East Jerusalem as part of the Occupied Territories

POPULATION – 2,920,454 (1998 census), of whom 210,209 live in East Jerusalem. In addition there are 141,000 Jewish settlers in the West Bank and 4,000 in the Gaza Strip who remain under Israeli administration and jurisdiction. Some 90 per cent of Palestinians are Muslim (the vast majority Sunni) and 10 per cent are Christians

CAPITAL – Although Palestinians claim East Jerusalem as their capital, the administrative capital has been established in Gaza City (population 120,000)

MAJOR TOWNS – Khan Yunis, Rafah in the Gaza Strip; Nablus, Hebron, Jericho, Ramallah and Bethlehem on the West Bank

FLAG – Three horizontal stripes of black, white, green with a red triangle based on the hoist (the PLO flag)

NATIONAL ANTHEM – Fidai, Fidai (Freedom Fighter, Freedom Fighter)

HISTORY AND POLITICS

Israel captured the Gaza Strip, East Jerusalem and the West Bank during the 1967 Six-Day War and annexed East Jerusalem. After the war the Israeli government began to establish settlements in the Occupied Territories. Palestinian resistance to Israeli rule was led by the Palestine Liberation Organization (PLO) which was established in 1964. Frustration at continued Israeli occupation led to the start of the *intifada*, a campaign of sustained unrest, in 1987. When the 1991 Madrid peace process stalled, Israeli and PLO officials engaged in secret negotiations in Norway which led to the signing of the 'Declaration of Principles on Interim Self-Government Arrangements' on 13 September 1993. Under this agreement the PLO renounced

terrorism and recognized Israel's right to exist in secure borders, while Israel recognized the PLO as the legitimate representative of the Palestinian people.

The Declaration of Principles established a timetable for progress towards a final settlement: negotiations leading to an Israeli military withdrawal from the Gaza Strip and Jericho by 13 April 1994, when power was to be transferred to a nominated Palestinian National Authority (PNA); elections to a new Palestinian Council, which would also exercise control over six policy areas in the rest of the West Bank (culture, tourism, health, education, social welfare, direct taxation), and the Israeli military administration dissolved by 13 July 1994; negotiations on a permanent settlement, including Jewish settlers and East Jerusalem, to begin by 13 April 1996; and a permanent settlement to be in place by 13 April 1999.

The timetable has slipped, with the Israeli military not finally redeploying in the Gaza Strip and withdrawing from Jericho until 18 May 1994, when the five-year period of interim self-government under the PNA began.

Israel and the Palestinians struggled to reach agreement on the extension of self-rule until 28 September 1995, when the 'Oslo B' or Taba Accord was signed which provided for Israeli withdrawal from six towns and 85 per cent of Hebron; the extension of self-rule to most of the West Bank by 1998; the release of 5,300 Palestinian prisoners; and the striking out of the demand for Israel's destruction from the PLO's charter. On 29 December 1995 an agreement was reached on the transfer of 17 areas of civilian power to the PNA in Hebron.

Implementation of the agreement began with the release of 1,100 Palestinian prisoners in October 1995; Israeli troops left Ramallah, the last of the six West Bank towns, on 27 December 1995 and the inaugural Palestinian National Council meeting on 23 April 1996 voted to amend the PLO charter. The final element of the Declaration of Principles, the 'final status talks' opened in Taba, Egypt, on 5 May 1996 to decide the final status of the West Bank, Gaza and Jerusalem. The election of a Likud-led government opposed to the establishment of a Palestinian state resulted in a deadlock in negotiations in 1997 and delays in the withdrawal of Israeli troops from Hebron.

Legislative elections on 20 January 1996 were won by the mainstream al-Fatah faction of the PLO, with its leader Yasser Arafat winning 88.1 per cent of the vote to become the president of the Palestinian National Authority.

Talks between the Palestinians and Israelis continued intermittently throughout 1997, but little of substance was achieved. Yasser Arafat and Binyamin Netanyahu met separately with American diplomats in London in May 1998, but talks broke down over the precise extent of Israeli troop withdrawals, the Israelis rejecting an American proposal of a 13 per cent withdrawal as unsatisfactory.

POLITICAL SYSTEM

The Oslo B accord laid down the political structure of the nascent Palestinian state. Executive authority is vested in the Palestinian National Authority which is headed by a popularly elected leader (*rais*). Legislative authority is vested in the 88-member Palestinian Council which is directly elected by means of a first-past-the-post system, and itself elects the four-fifths of the PNA not appointed by the leader.

PALESTINIAN NATIONAL AUTHORITY *as at August 1998*

Leader, Yasser Arafat
Agriculture, Hekmat Zaid
Bethlehem 2000 Affairs, Dr Nabeel Qais
Civil Affairs, Jamil Tarifi
Economy and Trade, Maher Al-Massri

Environment, Dr Yousef Abu Safia
Finance, Mohammed Zuhdi Al-Nashashibi
Higher Education, Dr Munzer Salah
Housing, Dr Abdel Rahman Hamad
Industry, Dr Saadi Al-Karnaz
Justice, Freih Abu Midein
Labour, Rafeek Al-Natsha
Local Government, Dr Saeb Erikat
Media and Culture, Yasser Abd Rabbo
Parliament, Nabeel Amr
Planning, International Co-operation, Dr Nabeel Shaath
Post and Telecommunications, Imad Al-Falouji
Prisoners' Affairs, Hisham Abdel Razek
Public Works, Azzam Al-Ahmad
Social Affairs, Intisar Al-Wazir
Supply, Abdul Aziz Shahin
Tourism and Antiquities, Metri Abu Attia
Transport, Dr Ali Al-Kawasmi
Without Portfolio, Assad Abdel Kader; Ziad Abu Ziad;
    Hassan Asfour; Talal Sadr

British Consulate-General
19 Nashashibi Street, PO Box 19690, East Jerusalem 97200
Consul-General, R. A. Kealy
British Council Director, P. Skelton, OBE (*Cultural Attaché*), Al-Nuzha Building, 2 Abu Obeida Street, PO Box 19136, Jerusalem

---

ITALY
Repubblica Italiana

AREA – 116,320 sq. miles (301,268 sq. km). Neighbours: Switzerland and Austria (north), Slovenia (east), France (west)
POPULATION – 57,187,000 (1994 UN estimate): 83 per cent Catholic. The language is Italian, a Romance language derived from Latin. It is spoken in its purest form in Tuscany, but there are numerous dialects, showing variously French, German, Spanish and Arabic influences. Sard, the dialect of Sardinia, is accorded by some authorities the status of a distinct Romance language
CAPITAL – Rome (population, 2,693,383, 1991). The Eternal City was founded, according to legend, by Romulus in 753 BC. It was the centre of Latin civilization and capital of the Roman Republic and Roman Empire
MAJOR CITIES – Bologna (404,322); Florence (402,316); ΨGenoa (675,639); Milan (1,371,008); ΨNaples (1,054,601); Turin (961,916); Sicily, ΨPalermo (697,162); *Sardinia*, ΨCagliari (203,254), 1991 census
CURRENCY – Lira of 100 centesimi
NATIONAL ANTHEM – Inno di Mameli
NATIONAL DAY – 2 June
NATIONAL FLAG – Vertical stripes of green, white and red
LIFE EXPECTANCY (years) – male 73.79; female 80.36
POPULATION GROWTH RATE – –0.2 per cent (1995)
POPULATION DENSITY – 190 per sq. km (1995)
URBAN POPULATION – 96.6 per cent (1991)

Italy consists of a peninsula, the islands of Sicily, Sardinia, Elba and about 70 other small islands. The peninsula is for the most part mountainous, but between the Apennines, which form its spine, and the eastern coastline are two large fertile plains: Emilia/Romagna in the north and Apulia in the south. The Alps divide Italy from France, Switzerland, Austria and Slovenia. Partly within the Italian borders are Monte Rosa (15,217 ft), the Matterhorn (14,780 ft) and several peaks from 12,000 to 14,000 ft. The chief rivers are

the Po (405 miles), flowing through Piedmont, Lombardy and the Veneto; the Adige (Trentino and Veneto); the Arno (Florentine plain); and the Tiber (flowing through Rome to Ostia).

HISTORY AND POLITICS

Italian unity was accomplished under the House of Savoy after a struggle from 1848 to 1870 in which Mazzini (1805–72), Garibaldi (1807–82) and Cavour (1810–61) were the principal figures. It was completed when Lombardy was ceded by Austria in 1859 and Venice in 1866, and through the evacuation of Rome by the French in 1870. In 1871 the King of Italy entered Rome, and that city was declared to be the capital.

A fascist regime came to power in 1922 under Benito Mussolini, known as *Il Duce* (The Leader), who was prime minister from 1922 until 25 July 1943, when the regime was abolished. Mussolini was captured by Italian partisans while attempting to escape across the Swiss frontier and killed on 28 April 1945.

In fulfilment of a promise given in April 1944 that he would retire when the Allies entered Rome, a decree was signed in June 1944 by King Victor Emmanuel III under which Prince Umberto, his son, became Lieutenant-General of the Realm. The King remained head of the House of Savoy and retained the title King of Italy until his abdication in May 1946, when he was succeeded by the Crown Prince. A referendum on the future of the monarchy was held in June 1946, in which a majority favoured a republic, and the royal family left the country.

Political instability and widespread corruption, often with Mafia links, led to public disenchantment with the major political parties. Their support collapsed in the April 1992 general election, which produced an increase in support for Northern League and anti-Mafia parties. The so-called 'clean hands' investigation into corruption and Mafia links that began in Milan in February 1992 has led to the arrest by magistrates of thousands of politicians and businessmen.

The first general election under the new electoral system, on 27–28 March 1994, resulted in victory for the right-wing Freedom Alliance, who formed a government led by millionaire businessman Silvio Berlusconi in May 1994. The coalition government collapsed in December

1994 following Berlusconi's indictment on charges of bribery and corruption. The independent Treasury minister Lamberto Dini formed a government of technocrats in January 1995. Dini resigned in January 1996 and a general election on 21 April 1996 was won by the left-wing Olive Tree alliance led by the Democratic Party of the Left, whose leader, Romano Prodi, became prime minister. The government won 157 seats in the Senate and 284 seats in the Chamber of Deputies where it required the support of the Communist Refoundation (RC) to win a vote of confidence. In October 1997, the RC refused to support the government budget and Prodi offered his resignation. Seeking to avoid a crisis which could affect Italy's participation in the European Single Currency, President Scalfaro refused to accept the resignation and after negotiations Prodi and the RC signed a one-year agreement.

POLITICAL SYSTEM

The constitution provides for the election of the president for a seven-year term by an electoral college which consists of the two houses of the parliament (the Chamber of Deputies and the Senate) sitting in joint session, together with three delegates from each region (one in the case of the Valle d'Aosta). The president, who must be over 50 years of age, has the right to dissolve one or both houses after consultation with the Speakers. Members of both houses were elected wholly by proportional representation until 1993. Now 75 per cent (232) of the 315 elected seats in the Senate are elected on a first-past-the-post basis and the remaining elected seats are filled by proportional representation. There are 11 life senators, who are past presidents and prime ministers. In the Chamber of Deputies 75 per cent (472) of seats are elected on a first-past-the-post basis, and 25 per cent (158) by proportional representation, with a 4 per cent threshold for parliamentary representation.

HEAD OF STATE
President, Oscar Luigi Scalfaro, *elected by electoral college* 25 May 1992

COUNCIL OF MINISTERS *as at July 1998*
Prime Minister, Romano Prodi (IPP)
Deputy PM, Culture, Valter Veltroni (DPL)
Defence, Benjamino Andreatta (IPP)
Education and Research, Luigi Berlinguer (DPL)
Environment, Edo Ronchi (Green)
Equal Opportunity, Anna Finocchiaro (DPL)
Finance, Vincenzo Visco (DPL)
Food, Farm and Forest Resources, Michele Pinto (IPP)
Foreign Affairs, Lamberto Dini (IR)
Foreign Trade, Augusto Fantozzi (IR)
Health, Rosaria Bindi (DPL)
Industry and Tourism, Pierluigi Bersani (DPL)
Interior, Giorgio Napolitano (DPL)
Justice, Giovanni Maria Flick (Ind.)
Labour and Social Security, Tiziano Treu (IR)
Post and Telecommunications, Antonio Maccanico (Ind.)
Public Works, Paolo Costa (Ind.)
Regional Affairs, Civil Service, Franco Bassanini (DPL)
Social Solidarity, Livia Turco (DPL)
Transport and Navigation, Claudio Burlando (DPL)
Treasury, Carlo Azeglio Ciampi (Ind.)

IPP Italian Popular Party; DPL Democratic Party of the Left; Green Green Party; IR Italian Renewal; Ind. Independent

ITALIAN EMBASSY
14 Three Kings Yard, Davies Street, London WIY 2EH
Tel 0171-312 2200
Ambassador Extraordinary and Plenipotentiary,
  HE Dr Paolo Galli, apptd 1995
Minister-Counsellor, A. Armellini
Defence Attaché, Capt. P. Rizzo
Cultural Attaché, Prof. B. Abruzzese
Consul-General, L. Savoia
First Counsellor, A. Cevese (*Commercial*)
CONSULAR OFFICES – Bedford, Edinburgh, Manchester

BRITISH EMBASSY
Via XX Settembre 80A, 00187 Rome
Tel: Rome 482-5441
Ambassador Extraordinary and Plenipotentiary,
  HE Thomas L. Richardson, CMG, apptd 1996
Deputy Head of Mission, K. G. Bloomfield
Defence and Military Attaché, Brig. J. A. Anderson
Director-General for British Trade Development in Italy and Consul-General, C. De Chassiron (*Milan*)
Counsellor (Economic and Commercial), M. A. Hatful
CONSULATES-GENERAL – Milan, Naples
CONSULATES – Rome, Bari, Florence, Genoa, Trieste, Turin, Venice, Messina, Brindisi, Palermo, Cagliari

BRITISH COUNCIL REPRESENTATIVE, R. Alford, OBE, Palazzo del Drago, Via Quattro Fontane 20, 00184 Rome. There are British Council Offices at Milan, Bologna, Naples and Turin

BRITISH CHAMBER OF COMMERCE, Via San Paolo 7, 20121 Milan

DEFENCE

The Army has 1,325 main battle tanks, 2,867 armoured personnel carriers and 1,939 artillery pieces. The Navy has eight submarines, one aircraft carrier, one cruiser, four destroyers, 26 frigates, 14 patrol and coastal vessels, 18 combat aircraft and 74 armed helicopters. There are ten naval bases. The Air Force has 286 combat aircraft.
MILITARY EXPENDITURE – 1.9 per cent of GDP (1996)
MILITARY PERSONNEL – 551,600: Army 188,300, Navy 44,000, Air Force 63,600, Paramilitaries 255,700
CONSCRIPTION DURATION – Ten months

ECONOMY

Deposits of natural methane gas and oil have been discovered, mainly south of Sicily, and have been rapidly exploited. Production of lignite has also increased. Other minerals include iron ores and pyrites, mercury (over one-quarter of the world production), lead, zinc and aluminium. Rich gold veins were discovered in Sardinia in 1996. Marble is a traditional product of the Massa Carrara district.

Agricultural production is concentrated in Tuscany, Emilia-Romagna, Sicily and the whole of the southern third of the country. The principal products are wine, tobacco, citrus fruits, tomatoes, almonds, sugar beet, wheat and maize.

Tourism is a major contributor to the economy; in 1996, more than 56 million people visited Italy. The commercial and banking services are concentrated in Rome and in Milan, where the stock market is located.

The state-owned sector of Italian industry is still important, dominated by the holding companies IRI (mechanical, steel, airlines), ENI (petrochemicals), and ENEL (electricity). Industry is centred around Milan (steel, machine tools, motor cars), Turin (motor cars, steel, roller bearings, textiles), Rome (light industries), Venice (shipbuilding, paper, mechanical equipment, electrical goods, woollens), Bologna/Florence (food industry, footwear and textiles, reproduction furniture, glassware, pottery, ceramics), Naples, Bari (valves, vehicle bodies, tyres), Taranto (steel, oil refining), Trieste (shipbuilding) and Cagliari (aluminium production, petrochemicals).

Following a programme of severe austerity measures, it was announced on 1 May 1998 that Italy had satisfied the convergence criteria and would be one of the 11 states to participate in the European Single Currency from 1 January 1999.

In 1996 there was a trade surplus of US$60,821 million and a current account surplus of US$41,040 million. Imports totalled US$206,901 million and exports US$250,843 million.

Italy's chief exports are industrial and agricultural machinery, textiles and clothing, electrical equipment and chemicals. Chief imports are chemicals, motor vehicles and metals. Italy's main trading partners are Germany, France, the UK and the USA.

GNP – US$1,140,484 million (1996); US$19,880 per capita (1996)
GDP – US$1,134,661 million (1994); US$17,921 per capita (1994)
ANNUAL AVERAGE GROWTH OF GDP – 0.7 per cent (1996)
INFLATION RATE – 4.0 per cent (1996)
UNEMPLOYMENT – 12 per cent (1995); forecast to be 11.5 per cent in 1997

TRADE WITH UK	1996	1997
Imports from UK	£7,659,900,000	£7,786,400,000
Exports to UK	8,949,200,000	9,106,900,000

COMMUNICATIONS

The main railway system is state-run by the *Ferrovia dello Stato*. A network of motorways (*autostrade*) covers the country, built and operated mainly by the IRI state holding company and ANAS, the state highway authority. Alitalia, the principal international and domestic airline, is also state-controlled by the IRI group. Other smaller companies, including ATI (an Alitalia subsidiary) and Air Mediterranea, operate on domestic routes. Genoa is the major port, handling about one-third of Italy's foreign trade.

EDUCATION

Education is free and compulsory between the ages of six and 14; this comprises five years at primary school and three in 'middle school', of which there are about 8,000. Pupils who obtain the middle school certificate may seek admission to any 'senior secondary school', which may be a lyceum with a classical or scientific or artistic bias, or an institute directed at technology (of which there are eight different types), trade or industry (including vocational schools), or teacher-training. Courses at the lyceums and technical institutes usually last for five years and success in the final examination qualifies for admission to university.

There are 35 state and 14 private universities, some of ancient foundation; those at Bologna, Modena, Parma and Padua were started in the 12th century. University education is not free, but entrants with higher qualifications are charged reduced fees according to a sliding scale.

In general, schools, lyceums and universities are financed by local taxation and central government grants.
ILLITERACY RATE – 1.9 per cent
ENROLMENT (percentage of age group) – primary 97 per cent (1994); tertiary 40.6 per cent (1994)

CULTURE

Florence, the capital of Tuscany, was one of the greatest cities in Europe from the 11th to the 16th centuries, and the cradle of the Renaissance. Under the Medici family in the 15th century flourished many of the greatest names in Italian art, including Filippo Lippi, Botticelli, Donatello and Brunelleschi, and in the 16th century Michelangelo and Leonardo da Vinci.

Italian literature (in addition to Latin literature, which is the common inheritance of western Europe) is one of the richest in Europe, particularly in its golden age (Dante, 1265–1321; Petrarch, 1304–74; Boccaccio, 1313–75) and in the Renaissance (Ariosto, 1474–1533; Machiavelli, 1469–1527; Tasso, 1544–95). Notable in modern Italian literature are Manzoni (1785–1873), Carducci (1835–1907) and Gabriele d'Annunzio (1864–1938). The Nobel Prize for Literature has been awarded to Italian authors on six occasions: G. Cariducci (1906), Signora G. Deledda (1926), Luigi Pirandello (1934), Salvatore Quasimodo (1959), Eugenio Montale (1975) and Dario Fo (1997).

ISLANDS

CAPRI
EOLIAN ISLANDS, including Lipari; area 45 sq. miles (116 sq. km); population 18,636
FLEGREAN ISLANDS, including Ischia; area 23 sq. miles (60 sq. km); population 51,883
PANTELLERIA ISLAND (part of Trapani Province) in the Sicilian Narrows; area 31 sq. miles (80 sq. km); population 9,601
THE PELAGIAN ISLANDS (Lampedusa, Linosa and Lampione) are part of the province of Agrigento; area 8 sq. miles (21 sq. km); population 4,811
PONTINE ARCHIPELAGO, including Ponza; area 4 sq. miles (10 sq. km); population 2,515
TREMITI ISLANDS; area 1 sq. mile (3 sq. km); population 426
THE TUSCAN ARCHIPELAGO (including Elba); area 113 sq. miles (293 sq. km); population 31,861

JAMAICA

AREA – 4,243 sq. miles (10,990 sq. km)
POPULATION – 2,530,000 (1994 UN estimate). The official language is English; a local patois is also spoken
CAPITAL – ΨKingston (population, 103,962, 1991)
MAJOR CITIES – Mandeville; May Pen; ΨMontego Bay; Ocho Rios; Spanish Town
CURRENCY – Jamaican dollar (J$) of 100 cents
NATIONAL ANTHEM – Jamaica, Land We Love
NATIONAL DAY – First Monday in August (Independence Day)
NATIONAL FLAG – Gold diagonal cross forming triangles of green at top and bottom, triangles of black at hoist and in fly
LIFE EXPECTANCY (years) – male 71.41; female 75.82
POPULATION GROWTH RATE – 0.9 per cent (1995)
POPULATION DENSITY – 230 per sq. km (1995)
MILITARY EXPENDITURE – 0.5 per cent of GDP (1996)
MILITARY PERSONNEL – 3,320: Army 3,000, Coast Guard 150, Air Wing 170
ILLITERACY RATE – 15.0 per cent
ENROLMENT (percentage of age group) – primary 100 per cent (1992); secondary 64 per cent (1992); tertiary 6.0 per cent (1992)

Jamaica is divided into three counties (Surrey, Middlesex and Cornwall) and 14 parishes. The island consists mainly of coastal plains, divided by the Blue Mountain range in the east and the hills and limestone plateaux in the central and western areas of the interior. The central chain of the Blue Mountains is over 6,000 feet above sea level, and the Blue Mountain Peak is 7,402 feet.

HISTORY AND POLITICS

The island was discovered by Columbus in 1494, and occupied by Spain from 1509 until 1655 when an English expedition under Admiral Penn and General Venables captured the island. In 1670 it was formally ceded to England by the Treaty of Madrid. Jamaica became an independent state within the Commonwealth on 6 August 1962.

At the general election of 18 December 1997, the People's National Party won 50 out of a total of 60 seats, securing a third term as prime minister for Percival Patterson.

POLITICAL SYSTEM

Queen Elizabeth II is the head of state, represented by the Governor-General. The legislature consists of a Senate of 21 nominated members and a House of Representatives consisting of 60 members elected by universal adult suffrage for a five-year term. The prime minister is the leader of the majority party in the House.

Governor-General, HE Sir Howard Felix Hanlon Cooke, GCMG, GCVO, apptd 1991

CABINET *as at July 1998*

Prime Minister, Percival J. Patterson, QC
Deputy PM, Foreign Affairs and Foreign Trade, Seymour Mullings
Agriculture, Roger Clarke
Commerce and Technology, Phillip Paulwell
Education, Youth and Culture, Burchel Whiteman
Environment and Housing, Easton Douglas
Finance and Planning, Omar Davies
Health, John Archbald Junor
Industry, Investments and Commerce, Paul Robertson
Labour, Social Security and Sports, Portia Simpson
Local Government and Community Development, Arnold Bertram
Mining and Energy, Robert Pickersgill
National Security and Justice, Keith Desmond Knight
Tourism, Francis Tulloch
Transportation and Works, Peter Phillips
Water, Karl Blythe
Without Portfolio, Maxine Henry-Wilson

JAMAICAN HIGH COMMISSION
1–2 Prince Consort Road, London SW7 2BZ
Tel 0171-823 9911
High Commissioner, HE Derick Heaven, apptd 1994
Deputy High Commissioners, O. Singh; J. K. Pringle, CBE, OJ (*Trade*)
Minister-Counsellor, L. Wilks (*Consular Affairs*)
Defence Adviser, Col. B. Blake

BRITISH HIGH COMMISSION
PO Box 575, Trafalgar Road, Kingston 10
Tel: Kingston 926 9050
High Commissioner, HE Richard Thomas, CMG, apptd 1995
Deputy High Commissioner, J. Malcolm
Defence Adviser, Col. A. Moorby
First Secretary (Management/Consular), P. Duffy

BRITISH COUNCIL REPRESENTATIVE IN THE CARIBBEAN, J. Day, 4th Floor, PCMB Building, 64 Knutsford Boulevard, PO Box 235, Kingston 5

ECONOMY

Alumina, bananas, bauxite and sugar are the main exports. Other exports include garments, processed food products, limestone and horticultural products.

Since 1989 the PNP government has abolished price subsidies, removed foreign exchange controls and introduced a 10 per cent consumption tax. Jamaica is a popular tourist resort, attracting more than 1,700,000 visitors in 1995.

In 1995 Jamaica had a trade deficit of US$813 million and a current account deficit of US$245 million. In 1996 imports totalled US$2,922 million and exports US$1,360 million.
GNP – US$4,066 million (1996); US$1,600 per capita (1996)
GDP – US$4,484 million (1994); US$1,650 per capita (1994)
ANNUAL AVERAGE GROWTH OF GDP – 0.8 per cent (1994)
INFLATION RATE – 26.4 per cent (1996)
UNEMPLOYMENT – 15.9 per cent (1992)
TOTAL EXTERNAL DEBT – US$4,041 million (1996)

Trade with UK	1996	1997
Imports from UK	£67,749,000	£59,888,000
Exports to UK	151,410,000	138,379,000

COMMUNICATIONS

There are several excellent harbours, Kingston being the principal port. The island has 2,944 miles of main roads and 7,264 miles of subsidiary roads.

There are two international airports, the Norman Manley International Airport on the south coast serving Kingston, and Sangster Airport on the north coast serving the major tourist areas. In addition there are licensed aerodromes at Port Antonio, Ocho Rios, Mandeville and Negril. There are 16 privately owned, seven public and two military airstrips. Air Jamaica, the national airline, operates international services.

JAPAN
Nihon Koku – Land of the Rising Sun

AREA – 145,870 sq. miles (377,801 sq. km)
POPULATION – 125,197,000 (1994 UN estimate). The principal religions are Mahayana Buddhism and Shinto. About 1 per cent of Japanese are Christians. The language is Japanese
CAPITAL – Tokyo (population, 11,927,457, 1993 estimate)
MAJOR CITIES – ΨFukuoka (1,275,165); ΨKobé (1,518,982); Kyoto, the ancient capital (1,448,377); ΨNagoya (2,153,293); ΨOsaka (2,575,042); Sapporo (1,744,806); ΨYokohama (3,300,513), 1994
CURRENCY – Yen of 100 sen
NATIONAL ANTHEM – Kimigayo
NATIONAL DAY – 23 December (the Emperor's Birthday)
NATIONAL FLAG – White, charged with sun (red)
LIFE EXPECTANCY (years) – male 76.57; female 82.98
POPULATION GROWTH RATE – 0.3 per cent (1995)
POPULATION DENSITY – 331 per sq. km (1995)
URBAN POPULATION – 77.4 per cent (1990)

Japan consists of four large islands: *Honshu* (or Mainland) 88,839 sq. miles (230,448 sq. km), *Shikoku,* 7,231 sq. miles (18,757 sq. km), *Kyushu,* 16,170 sq. miles (42,079 sq. km), *Hokkaido,* 30,265 sq. miles (78,508 sq. km), and many small islands (including Okinawa).

The interior is very mountainous, and crossing the mainland from the Sea of Japan to the Pacific is a group of volcanoes, mainly extinct or dormant. Mount Fuji, the

Party 40; Japan Communist Party 26; SDP 14; Sakigake 2; Independent 10.

POLITICAL SYSTEM

Legislative authority rests with the bicameral *Diet*, which comprises a 500-member House of Representatives, and a 252-member House of Councillors. The House of Representatives chooses the prime minister from among its ranks, ratifies treaties and passes budget bills. Since 1996, 200 of its members are elected by proportional representation in 11 regional blocks and 300 in single-member, first-past-the-post constituencies. All members serve four-year terms. The House of Councillors elects half its members every three years for six-year terms. Unlike the lower House it cannot be dissolved by the prime minister. Executive authority is vested in the Cabinet which is responsible to the legislature.

HEAD OF STATE

His Imperial Majesty The Emperor of Japan, Emperor Akihito, *born* 23 December 1933; *succeeded* 8 January 1989; *enthroned* 12 November 1990; *married* 10 April 1959, Miss Michiko Shoda, and has *issue*: the Crown Prince (*see* below); Prince Fumihito, *born* 30 November 1965; and Princess Sayako, *born* 18 April 1969

Heir, HRH Crown Prince Naruhito Hironomiya, *born* 23 February 1960, *married* 9 June 1993 Miss Masako Owada

CABINET *as at August 1998*

Prime Minister, Keizo Obuchi
Agriculture, Forestry and Fisheries, Shoichi Nakagawa
Chief Cabinet Secretary, Hiromu Nonaka
Construction, Katsutsugu Sekiya
Defence Agency, Fukushiro Nukaga
Economic Planning Agency, Taichi Sakaiya
Education, Akito Arima
Environment Agency, Kenji Manabe
Finance, Kiichi Miyazawa
Foreign Affairs, Masahiko Koumura
Health and Welfare, Sohei Miyashita
Hokkaido and Okinawa Development Agency, Kichio Inoue
Home Affairs, Mamoru Nishida
International Trade and Industry, Kaoru Yosano
Justice, Shozaburo Nakamura
Labour, Akira Amari
Management and Co-ordination Agency, Seiichi Ota
National Land Agency, Hakuo Yanagisawa
Post and Telecommunications, Seiko Noda
Science and Technology Agency, Yutaka Takeyama
Transport, Jiro Kawasaki
Without Portfolio, Masasuke Omori

EMBASSY OF JAPAN

101–104 Piccadilly, London WIV 9FN
Tel 0171-465 6500
Ambassador Extraordinary and Plenipotentiary, HE Sadayuki Hayashi, apptd 1998
Ministers, I. Umezu (*Plenipotentiary*); M. Muto (*Cultural*); M. Amano (*Commercial*); M. Kohno; K. Hayashi; T. Taga; T. Uranishi; C. Harada

BRITISH EMBASSY

No. 1 Ichiban-cho, Chiyoda-ku, Tokyo 102
Tel: Tokyo 5211-1100
Ambassador Extraordinary and Plenipotentiary, HE David J. Wright, KCMG, LVO, apptd 1996
Minister, C. T. W. Humfrey
Counsellors, P. Bateman (*Commercial*); P. V. Rollitt (*Management and Consul-General*)
Defence and Naval Attaché, Capt. N. D. V. Robertson

most sacred mountain of Japan, is 12,370 ft high and has been dormant since 1707, but volcanoes which are active include Mount Aso in Kyushu. There are frequent earthquakes, mainly along the Pacific coast near the Bay of Tokyo. The climate varies from sub-tropical in the south to cool temperate in the north.

HISTORY AND POLITICS

According to tradition, Jimmu, the first Emperor of Japan, ascended the throne on 11 February 660 BC. Under the *Meiji* constitution (1889), the monarchy is hereditary in the male heirs of the Imperial house.

After the unconditional surrender to the Allied nations (14 August 1945), Japan was occupied by Allied forces under General MacArthur. A Japanese peace treaty became effective on 28 April 1952. Japan then resumed her status as an independent power.

The (conservative) Liberal Democratic Party (LDP) governed Japan almost without interruption from the Second World War until 1993. During the 1990s public disenchantment at political corruption led to a loss of support for the LDP and the formation of several splinter parties. Support for the new parties caused the LDP to lose its majority at the 1993 election, following which a seven-party coalition formed a government.

The government led by Morihiro Hosokawa (JNP) reached a compromise with the LDP-controlled House of Councillors to phase out corporate donations to individual MPs by 2000. State funding for political parties was introduced and the electoral system altered. The LDP returned to power in June 1994 in coalition with the SDPJ and Sakigake parties, with SDPJ leader Tomiichi Murayama becoming Japan's first socialist prime minister. Five reformist opposition parties (JNP, JRP, Komeito, DSP, USDP) merged in November 1994 to form the New Frontier Party (NFP) (Shinshinto) as a rival centre-right conservative party to the LDP. Murayama resigned in January 1996 and was replaced by LDP leader Ryutaro Hashimoto. The NFP disbanded in December 1997. In March 1998 four opposition parties merged to form the Democratic Party of Japan.

Hashimoto was elected to a second term as prime minister, but resigned in July 1998 following a heavy defeat for the LDP in the upper house elections, seen as largely due to his handling of the economic crisis. He was replaced as prime minister and leader of the LDP by Foreign Minister Keizo Obuchi. The LDP have 263 seats in the House of Representatives. The standing of the other parties is: Democratic Party 91; Heiwa Kaikaku 47; Liberal

CONSULATES-GENERAL – Tokyo, Osaka, Sapporo
HONORARY CONSULATES – Fukuoka, Hiroshima

BRITISH COUNCIL REPRESENTATIVE, M. Barrett, OBE
(*Cultural Attaché*), 2 Kagurazaka 1-Chome, Shinjuku-ku,
Tokyo 162

BRITISH CHAMBER OF COMMERCE, No. 16 Kowa Building,
1–9–20 Akasaka, Minato-ku, Tokyo 107

DEFENCE

The constitution prohibits the maintenance of armed
forces, although internal security forces were created in the
1950s and their mission was extended in 1954 to include
the defence of Japan against aggression. In the 1990s
legislation was passed permitting the armed forces limited
participation in UN peacekeeping missions and allowing
them to enter foreign conflicts in order to rescue Japanese
nationals. A revision to the USA–Japan defence co-
operation guidelines agreed in 1997 permits Japan to play
a supporting role in US military operations in areas
surrounding Japan.

The Ground Self-Defence Force (GSDF) has 1,110
main battle tanks, around 950 armoured personnel carriers
and infantry fighting vehicles, 800 artillery pieces, 20
aircraft and 90 attack helicopters. The Maritime Self-
Defence Force (MSDF) has 17 submarines, nine destroyers, 50 frigates, 110 combat aircraft and 99 armed helicopters at five bases. The Air Self-Defence Force (ASDF) has
368 combat aircraft.

The USA has 36,530 personnel stationed in Japan.
Following an agreement in December 1996 the USA is due
to vacate 21 per cent of the land it occupies in Japan and
close part or all of 11 military facilities.

MILITARY EXPENDITURE – 1.0 per cent of GDP (1996)
MILITARY PERSONNEL – 246,300: Army 147,700, Navy
42,500, Air Force 44,100, Paramilitaries 12,000

ECONOMY

Owing to the mountainous nature of the country less than
20 per cent of its area can be cultivated and only 14 per cent
is used for agriculture; 67 per cent is wooded. The soil is
only moderately fertile but intensive cultivation secures
good crops. Tobacco, tea, potatoes, rice, maize, wheat and
other cereals are all cultivated. Rice is the staple food of the
people. Fruit is abundant and pigs and chickens are widely
reared.

Mineral resources include gold, silver, copper, lead,
zinc, iron chromite, white arsenic, coal, sulphur, petroleum, salt and uranium. However, iron ore, coal and crude
oil are among the principal imports.

Japan is one of the most highly industrialized nations in
the world, with the whole range of modern light and heavy
industries, including steel, aerospace, computers, office
machinery, motor vehicles, electronics, metals, machinery,
chemicals, textiles (cotton, silk, wool and synthetics),
cement, pottery, glass, rubber, lumber, paper, oil refining
and shipbuilding.

Japan's economy has been severely affected by the
financial crisis in Asia. Its banks have made loans totalling
some US$200 billion to tiger economies, and following
widespread economic collapse in the region, Japan's
financial institutions have suffered; Yamaichi Securities
became Japan's largest ever commercial failure when it
folded in November 1997. The Nikkei Dow lost a quarter
of its value in 1997, and in May 1998 unemployment was at
4.1 per cent, its highest level since 1945. Emergency
measures announced by the government were perceived
by the markets as inadequate; the US government agreed a

US$2 billion rescue package for the yen, in exchange for
fiscal reforms.

GNP – US$5,149,185 million (1996); US$40,940 per
capita (1996)
GDP – US$3,152,205 million (1994); US$36,782 per capita
(1994)
ANNUAL AVERAGE GROWTH OF GDP – 3.6 per cent (1996)
INFLATION RATE – 0.1 per cent (1996)
UNEMPLOYMENT – 3.2 per cent (1995)

TRADE

Being deficient in natural resources, Japan has had to
develop a complex foreign trade. Principal imports include
mineral fuels, food, raw materials and metal ores. Principal
exports include machinery, transport equipment, chemicals, metal products and textiles.

In 1996 Japan had a trade surplus of US$83,561 million
and a current account surplus of US$65,884 million.
Imports totalled US$349,152 million and exports
US$410,901 million. The USA, China, Australia, Hong
Kong, South Korea, Taiwan and Singapore are Japan's
main trading partners.

Trade with UK	1996	1997
Imports from UK	£4,263,666,000	£4,177,609,000
Exports to UK	8,994,299,000	9,409,949,000

COMMUNICATIONS

Japan National Railways was privatized in 1987 and is
known as Japan Railways (JR). There are six regional
companies and one goods company. Shinkansen (bullet
train) tracks are currently being expanded. The opening in
1988 of the Seikan rail tunnel and the Seto Ohashi rail
bridge means that the four major islands are now linked for
the first time.

EDUCATION

Education at elementary (six-year course) and lower
secondary (three-year course) schools is free, compulsory
and co-educational. The (three-year) upper secondary
schools are attended by 96.7 per cent of the age group.

There are two- or three-year junior colleges and four-
year universities. Some of the universities have graduate
schools. In 1993 there were 1,129 universities and junior
colleges, most of which are privately maintained. The most
prominent universities are the seven state universities of
Tokyo, Kyoto, Tohoku (Sendai), Hokkaido (Sapporo),
Kyushu (Fukuoka), Osaka and Nagoya, and the two private
universities of Keio and Waseda.

ENROLMENT (percentage of age group) – primary 100 per
cent (1993); secondary 96 per cent (1993); tertiary 40.3
per cent (1994)

CULTURE

Japanese is said to be one of the Uro-Altaic group of
languages and remained a spoken tongue until the fifth to
seventh centuries AD, when Chinese characters came into
use. Japanese who have received school education can read
and write the Chinese characters in current use (about
1,800) and also the syllabary characters called Kana.

JORDAN
Al-Mamlaka al Urduniya al-Hashemiyah

AREA – 37,738 sq. miles (97,740 sq. km). Neighbours: Syria (north), Israel and the West Bank (west), Saudi Arabia (south and east), Iraq (east)

POPULATION – 5,439,000 (1994 UN estimate); 4,095,579 (1994 census). The majority are Sunni Muslims and Islam is the religion of the state; however, freedom of belief is guaranteed by the constitution

CAPITAL – Amman (population, 1,270,000, 1994)

MAJOR CITIES – Irbid (216,000); Zarqa (359,000), 1991

CURRENCY – Jordanian dinar (JD) of 1,000 fils

NATIONAL ANTHEM – Long Live the King

NATIONAL DAY – 25 May (Independence Day)

NATIONAL FLAG – Three horizontal stripes of black, white, green and a red triangle based on the hoist, containing a seven-pointed white star

LIFE EXPECTANCY (years) – male 66.16; female 69.84

POPULATION GROWTH RATE – 4.9 per cent (1995)

POPULATION DENSITY – 56 per sq. km (1995)

ILLITERACY RATE – 13.4 per cent

ENROLMENT (percentage of age group) – primary 89 per cent (1992); secondary 42 per cent (1989); tertiary 24.5 per cent (1989)

HISTORY AND POLITICS

After the defeat of Turkey in the First World War, the Amirate of Transjordan was established in the area east of the River Jordan as a state under British mandate. The mandate was terminated after the Second World War and the Amirate, still ruled by its founder the Amir Abdullah, became the Hashemite Kingdom of Jordan. Following the 1948–9 war between Israel and the Arab states, that part of Palestine remaining in Arab hands (the West Bank and East Jerusalem, but excluding Gaza) was, with Palestinian agreement, incorporated into the Hashemite Kingdom. King Abdullah was assassinated in 1951; his son Talal ruled briefly but abdicated in favour of King Hussein in 1952.

The West Bank has been under Israeli occupation since its capture from Jordan in the 1967 war, and East Jerusalem was annexed by Israel in 1967. In 1988 Jordan severed its legal and administrative ties with the occupied West Bank, but did not formally renounce sovereignty over the area. As a result of the wars of 1948–9 and 1967 there are about one million Palestinian refugees and displaced persons living in East Jordan, about 200,000 of whom live in refugee and displaced persons camps established by the UN Relief and Works Agency (UNRWA). In addition there are 300,000 self-supporting Palestinians in East Jordan.

In 1993, multiparty parliamentary elections were held for the first time since 1956. In the most recent elections, held on 4 November 1997, pro-government candidates won 62 out of 80 seats; the main opposition parties boycotted the elections.

FOREIGN RELATIONS

The Middle East peace process begun in 1991 led to Jordan signing an agreement on a 'common agenda' for peace with Israel in 1993. Intensive bilateral negotiations continued throughout 1993–4 with Israel agreeing to return two narrow strips of territory in the Arava desert seized in 1967. On 25 July 1994 King Hussein and the Israeli Prime Minister signed a framework agreement for peace which ended the state of war existing since 1948. The first Israeli–Jordanian border crossing was opened between Eilat and Aqaba in August 1994. A full peace treaty was signed on 26 October 1994 which established full diplomatic and economic relations between the two states. It included agreements on sharing water from the Jordan and Yarmouk rivers; co-operating in the fields of commerce, transport, tourism, communications, energy and agriculture; and granted King Hussein custodianship of Islamic holy sites in Jerusalem. Israeli forces completed their withdrawal from Jordanian land in the Arava valley on 9 February 1995.

POLITICAL SYSTEM

The constitution provides for a Senate of 40 members (all appointed by the King) and an elected House of Representatives which until 1988 had 60 members representing both the East and West Banks. Legislation passed in 1989 stipulated that in future elections seats would be contested on the East Bank only. The first parliamentary elections since 1967 took place in 1989 to a new 80-member House of Representatives.

The King appoints the members of the Council of Ministers. Crown Prince Hassan normally acts as regent when King Hussein is abroad. In 1991 a new national charter was formulated which lifted the ban on political parties, imposed in 1957.

HEAD OF STATE

His Majesty The King of the Jordan, King Hussein, GCVO, born 14 November 1935, *succeeded* on the abdication of his father, King Talal, 11 August 1952, *assumed constitutional powers* 2 May 1953, on coming of age

Crown Prince, Prince Hassan, third son of King Talal of Jordan, *born* 1947, *appointed Crown Prince* 1 April 1965

COUNCIL OF MINISTERS *as at July 1998*

Prime Minister, Defence, Abd al-Salam al-Majali

Deputy PM, Foreign Affairs, Development, Jawad al-Anani

Deputy PM, Information, Abdullah al-Nusur

Administrative Development, Bassam Amoush

Agriculture, Mijhim al-Khurayshah

Culture and Youth, Talal al-Hassan

Education, Higher Education, Mohammed Hamdane

Energy and Mineral Resources, Muhammad Salah al-Hurani

Finance, Sulayman Hafiz

Health, Ashraf al-Kurdi

Industry, Trade and Supply, Hani al-Mulqi

Interior, Nazir Rashid

Justice, Riyadh al-Shak'ah

Labour, Mehdi Ferhane

Municipal, Rural and Environmental Affairs, Tawfiq Kurayshan

Planning, Rima Khalaf al-Hunaydi

Public Works and Housing, Nasir al-Lawzi

Religious Endowments (Waqfs), Islamic Affairs, Abdul Salam al-Abbadi

Social Development, Muhammad Khayr Mamsar

Tourism and Antiquities, Aql Biltaji

Transport and Communication, Sami Qammou

Water and Irrigation, Mundhir Haddadin

EMBASSY OF THE HASHEMITE KINGDOM OF JORDAN

6 Upper Phillimore Gardens, London W8 7HB

Tel 0171-937 3685

Ambassador Extraordinary and Plenipotentiary, HE Fouad Ayoub, apptd 1991

Defence Attaché, Brig. Ahmad Bataineh

British Embassy
Abdoun (PO Box 87), Amman
Tel: Amman 592 3100
Ambassador Extraordinary and Plenipotentiary, HE
    Christopher Battiscombe, CMG, apptd 1997
Counsellor, S. P. Collis (*Deputy Head of Mission and Consul-
    General*)
Defence Attaché, Col. R. J. Sandy
First Secretary, R. Leadbetter (*Consul and Management*)
British Council Director, Dr D. Burton, Rainbow
    Street (PO Box 634), Amman 11118

DEFENCE

The Army has 1,141 main battle tanks, 1,135 armoured personnel carriers and armoured infantry fighting vehicles, and 485 artillery pieces. The Navy has five patrol and coastal vessels at its base at Aqaba. The Air Force has 97 combat aircraft and 24 armed helicopters.
Military Expenditure – 5.5 per cent of GDP (1996)
Military Personnel – 114,050: Army 90,000, Navy 650, Air Force 13,400, Paramilitaries 10,000

ECONOMY

The main agricultural areas are the Jordan valley, the hills overlooking the valley, and the flatter country to the south of Amman and around Madaba and Irbid. However, several large farms, which depend for irrigation on water pumped from deep aquifers, have been established in the southern desert area. The rest of the country is desert and semi-desert. The principal crops are wheat, barley, vegetables, olives and fruit. Agricultural production has increased considerably in recent years due to improvements in production and irrigation techniques.

Important industrial products are raw phosphates (1995, 4.9 million tonnes) and potash (1995, 1.06 million tonnes), most of which is exported, together with fertilizers and pharmaceuticals. The Trans-Arabian oil pipeline (Tapline) runs through north Jordan from Saudi Arabia to the Lebanese port of Sidon. A branch pipeline, together with oil trucked by road from Iraq, feeds a refinery at Zerqa (production 1994, 2.9 million tons) which meets most of Jordan's requirements for refined petroleum products. Sufficient reserves of natural gas have been discovered in the north-east to produce electricity for the national grid since 1989.

The peace with Israel, including a preferential trade agreement signed in October 1995, has created a mini-boom, with a 40 per cent rise in tourism and 25 per cent rise in exports. Tourism has developed, principally in Amman, Aqaba, Zerka Ma'in and on the shores of the Dead Sea. In 1995, Jordan had more than 800,000 visitors.

In 1994 there was a trade deficit of US$1,579 million and a current account deficit of US$398 million. In 1996 imports totalled US$4,428 million and exports US$1,817 million.
GNP – US$7,088 million (1996); US$1,650 per capita (1996)
GDP – US$4,938 million (1994); US$1,095 per capita (1994)
Annual Average Growth of GDP – 5.2 per cent (1996)
Inflation Rate – 6.5 per cent (1996)
Total External Debt – US$8,118 million (1996)

Trade with UK	1996	1997
Imports from UK	£140,044,000	£147,603,000
Exports to UK	25,081,000	23,369,000

COMMUNICATIONS

Amman is linked to Aqaba, Damascus, Baghdad and Jeddah by roads which are of considerable importance in the overland trade of the Middle East.

The former Hejaz Railway runs from Syria through Jordan, and is used mainly for freight between Amman and Damascus. The Aqaba railway carries phosphate rock from the mines of al Hasa and al Abiad to Aqaba.

The Royal Jordanian Airline operates from Amman to Aqaba and has an extensive network of routes to the Middle East, Europe, North America and the Far East.

KAZAKHSTAN
Kazak Respublikasy

Area – 1,049,156 sq. miles (2,717,300 sq. km). Neighbours: Russia (north and west), Turkmenistan, Uzbekistan and Kyrgyzstan (south), China (east)
Population – 15,671,000 (1998 estimate): Kazakhs (43 per cent), Russians (36 per cent), Ukrainians (5 per cent) and ethnic Germans (4 per cent), with smaller numbers of Tatars, Uzbeks, Koreans and Belarusians. The Russian population is concentrated in the north of the country, where it forms a significant majority, and in Almaty. The majority of ethnic Kazakhs are Sunni Muslims, and this is the main religion of the republic. Kazakh (one of the Turkic languages) became the official language in 1993; a law passed in July 1997 decreed Kazakh as the language of state administration; Russian has a special status as the 'social language between peoples'. Otherwise each ethnic group uses its own language
Capital – Astana (population, 292,000, 1993 estimate. Known as Akmola until May 1998). The capital was moved from Alma-Ata (Almaty) in December 1997
Major Cities – Almaty (1,198,000); Karaganda (596,000); Pavlograd (367,000); Shimkent (447,000), 1993 estimates
Currency – Tenge
National Day – 25 October (Republic Day)
National Flag – Dark blue with a sun and a soaring eagle in the centre all in gold, and a red vertical ornamentation stripe near the hoist
Life Expectancy (years) – male 63.83; female 73.06
Population Growth Rate – −0.1 per cent (1995)
Population Density – 6 per sq. km (1995)
Urban Population – 56.7 per cent (1993)
Illiteracy Rate – 0.4 per cent
Enrolment (percentage of age group) – tertiary 32.7 per cent (1995)

Kazakhstan occupies the northern part of what was Soviet Central Asia. It stretches from the Volga and the Caspian Sea in the west to the Altai and Tienshan mountains in the east. The country consists of arid steppes and semi-deserts, flat in the west, hilly in the east and mountainous in the south-east (Southern Altai and Tienshan mountains). The main rivers are the Irtysh, the Ural, the Syr-Darya and the Ili. The climate is continental and very dry.

HISTORY AND POLITICS

Kazakhstan was inhabited by nomadic tribes before being invaded by Ghenghiz Khan and incorporated into his empire in 1218. After his empire disintegrated, feudal towns emerged based on large oases. These towns affiliated and established a Kazakh state in the late 15th century which engaged in almost continuous warfare with the

marauding Khanates on its southern border. After appeal-
ing to Russia for aid and protection, in 1731 Kazakhstan
acceded to the Russian Empire under a voluntary act of
accession.

The First World War brought privation to Kazakhstan,
leading to an uprising in 1916 against the conscription of
male Kazakhs. After the 1917 Russian revolution, Kazakhstan came under the control of White Russian forces until
1919. On 26 August 1920 a constitution was signed under
which Kazakhstan became a Soviet Socialist Republic.
Under Soviet rule in the 1920s and 1930s there was rapid
industrial development and the traditional nomadic way of
life disappeared. The Kazakhs suffered greatly in the
Stalinist purges, the merchant and religious classes being
murdered and thousands dying in the desert on collective
farms. Other nationalities, such as Tatars and Germans,
were forcibly transported to Kazakhstan by Stalin. Kazakhstan was the last of the former USSR republics to declare its
independence (16 December 1991).

The Communist-derived Congress of People's Unity of
Kazakhstan (SNEK) won the March 1994 legislative
elections which were ruled invalid by the Constitutional
Court. The President responded by dissolving the Supreme Kenges in March 1995. Elections to the new
legislature were held in December 1995; the requirement
for candidates to achieve an absolute majority made run-
offs necessary. A referendum on 29 April 1995 extended
President Nazarbayev's term until 2000.

POLITICAL SYSTEM

Executive power is vested in the president and government. The president must be a Kazakh speaker and has the
power to appoint the prime minister, other senior
ministers and all ambassadors. The parliament does not
have the power to impeach the president but the president
can dissolve parliament.

A new constitution approved by referendum on 30
August 1995 granted the president the power to dissolve
the legislature and to rule by decree. It also nominated
Kazakh as the sole official language; prohibited dual
citizenship; and created a new bicameral legislature
composed of a 47-member Senate and a 67-member
Majlis. The Constitutional Court, which opposed the
new constitution, was replaced by a Constitutional Council which was made subject to presidential veto.

HEAD OF STATE

President, Nursultan Nazarbayev, *elected* 1 December 1991,
  confirmed in office until 2000 by referendum 29 April 1995

GOVERNMENT *as at June 1998*

Prime Minister, Nurlan Balgymbayev
First Deputy PM, Uraz Jandosor
Deputy PMs, Zhanybek Karibzhanov; Alexander Pavlov
Agriculture, Sergei Kulagin
Chief of Presidential Staff, Akhmetzhan Yesimov
Defence, Gen. Mukhtar Altynbaev
Ecology and Natural Resources, Serikbek Daukeyev
Education, Culture and Health, Krymbek Kusherbayev
Finance, Sauat Mynbayev
Foreign Affairs, Kasymzhomart Tokayev
Information and Public Accord, Altynbek Sarsenbayev
Internal Affairs, Kairbek Suleimenov
Justice, Bauyrzhan Mukhamedzhanov
Labour and Social Protection, Natalia Korzhova
Power, Industry and Trade, Mukhtar Ablyazov
Science, Vladimir Shkolnik
State Secretary, Abish Kekilbayev
Transport and Communications, Yerkin Kaliyev

EMBASSY OF THE REPUBLIC OF KAZAKHSTAN
33 Thurloe Square, London SW7 2SD
Tel 0171-581 4646
Ambassador Extraordinary and Plenipotentiary,
  HE Kanat Saudabaev, apptd 1997

BRITISH EMBASSY
U1 Furmanova 173, Almaty
Tel: Almaty 506191
Ambassador Extraordinary and Plenipotentiary,
  HE Douglas B. McAdam, apptd 1996

BRITISH COUNCIL DIRECTOR, E. White, Panfilova 158,
  Almaty 480091

DEFENCE

In 1993–4 Kazakhstan established its own armed forces
from forces that were formerly under joint CIS control
with Russia. An agreement signed with Russia in January
1995 provides for eventual reunification of the two states'
armed forces. The CIS mutual defence treaty of 1993, to
which Kazakhstan is a signatory, retains a common air
defence force, while Kazakh forces also take part in the CIS
peacekeeping force along the Tajikistan–Afghanistan
border. A military union with a joint staff is being formed
in co-operation with Kyrgyzstan and Uzbekistan. Kazakhstan ratified the Start 1 Treaty in 1992 and signed the
Nuclear Non-Proliferation Treaty in December 1994. By
1996, all nuclear warheads had been returned to Russia
although Kazakhstan retained 48 SS-18 intercontinental
ballistic missiles. Kazakhstan participates in the NATO
Partnership for Peace programme.

The Army has 630 main battle tanks and 1,000 artillery
pieces. The Caspian Sea Flotilla, which Kazakhstan shares
with Russia and Turkmenistan, operates under Russian
command. The Air Force has 113 combat aircraft.

MILITARY EXPENDITURE – 2.7 per cent of GDP (1996)
MILITARY PERSONNEL – 69,600: Army 20,000, Navy 100,
  Air Force 15,000, Paramilitaries 34,500
CONSCRIPTION DURATION – 31 months

ECONOMY

Kazakhstan is rich in minerals, with copper, lead, gold,
uranium, chromium, silver, zinc, iron ore, coal, oil and
natural gas. In 1995 production of coal was 82.2 million
tonnes and of iron ore was 2.3 million tonnes. The oil and
gas industry, concentrated in the west of the country, has
been expanded by foreign investment, which is also being
used to explore the Karachaganak (gas) and Tengiz (oil)
fields in the Caspian Sea. In November 1997, a deal was
signed with the USA that provided for a US$26 billion
investment in the energy sector.

An agreement was signed in 1996 to begin the construction of a pipeline between Russia and Kazakhstan. Oil
production in 1997 was 25.8 million tonnes and gas output
was 8.1 billion cubic metres. Industry is dominated by food
processing and mining and metals production; textiles,
steel and tractors are also produced. The main centres of
the metal industry are in the Altai mountains, in Shimkent,
north of Lake Balkhash and in central Kazakhstan.

Agriculture, including stock-raising, is highly developed, particularly in the central and south-west of the
republic. Grain is grown in the north and north-east, and
cotton and wool produced in the south and south-east. 12.3
million tonnes of grain crop was grown in 1997 and 1.5
million tonnes of meat produced in 1993.

In 1993 the government announced a privatization
programme under which most state-owned enterprises
were to be sold. Small businesses and retail outlets have
been sold at auction since 1992. The economy was

weakened by the ending of preferential trading links to other CIS states at the break-up of the Soviet Union although a single market was formed with Kyrgyzstan and Uzbekistan in 1994. A treaty on further economic and humanitarian co-operation, as well as a customs union, was signed with Belarus, Kyrgyzstan and Russia in March 1996.

In 1997 investment activity rose by 19 per cent. In 1996 imports totalled US$4,261 million and exports US$6,230 million.

GNP – US$22,213 million (1996); US$1,350 per capita (1996)

GDP – US$37,288 million (1994); US$120 per capita (1994)

UNEMPLOYMENT – 1.0 per cent (1993)

INFLATION RATE – 39.2 per cent (1996)

TOTAL EXTERNAL DEBT – US$2,920 million (1996)

TRADE WITH UK	1996	1997
Imports from UK	£33,653,000	£53,847,000
Exports to UK	47,375,000	10,391,000

KENYA
Jamhuri ya Kenya

AREA – 224,081 sq. miles (580,367 sq. km). Neighbours: Somalia (east), Ethiopia (north), Sudan (north-west), Uganda (west), Tanzania (south)

POPULATION – 30,522,000 (1994 UN estimate). The main tribal groups are the Kikuyu, Luhya, Luo, Kalenjin, Kamba and Masai. The official languages are Swahili, which is generally understood throughout Kenya, and English; numerous indigenous languages are also spoken

CAPITAL – Nairobi (population, 1,400,000, 1989 estimate)

MAJOR CITIES –ΨKisumu (192,733); ΨMombasa (461,753); Nakuru (163,927), 1989 estimate

CURRENCY – Kenya shilling (Ksh) of 100 cents

NATIONAL DAY – 12 December (Independence Day)

NATIONAL FLAG – Horizontally black, red and green with the red fimbriated in white, and with a shield and crossed spears all over in the centre

LIFE EXPECTANCY (years) – male 54.18; female 57.29

POPULATION DENSITY – 53 per sq. km (1995)

MILITARY EXPENDITURE – 2.2 per cent of GDP (1996)

MILITARY PERSONNEL – 29,200: Army 20,500, Navy 1,200, Air Force 2,500, Paramilitaries 5,000

ILLITERACY RATE – 21.9 per cent

ENROLMENT (percentage of age group) – primary 91 per cent (1980); tertiary 1.6 per cent (1990)

HISTORY AND POLITICS

Kenya became an independent state and a member of the British Commonwealth on 12 December 1963 and a republic in 1964. In 1982 the government introduced amendments to the constitution making the country a one-party state, with the Kenya African National Union (KANU) as the ruling party. In December 1991, the government yielded to internal and international pressure and introduced a multiparty democracy.

Multiparty presidential and legislative elections were held in December 1992 and were won by President Moi and KANU respectively, though Commonwealth observers declared that the elections were not free and fair. KANU formed a new government in January 1993. In July and August 1997, pro-democracy rallies were violently broken up by police and 14 demonstrators were killed, provoking outrage at home and abroad. In November 1997,

Moi responded to pressure and granted limited reforms, repealing laws suppressing political debate, and granting equal media access to all parties. On 29 December 1997, in elections hampered by heavy flooding and marred by allegations of electoral malpractice, KANU won 109 out of 210 seats in the National Assembly, and Moi won just over 40 per cent of the vote to win a fifth term in office.

Following the elections, fighting broke out in the Rift Valley; by April 1998, more than 100 people had died and 300,000 had been driven from their homes. The victims were mainly from the Kikuyu tribe, and the perpetrators appeared to be members of Moi's Kalenjin tribe. The army was sent into the area to confiscate weapons and end the conflict in May 1998.

The country is divided into eight provinces (Central, Coast, Eastern, Nairobi, Nyanza, North Eastern, Rift Valley, Western).

HEAD OF STATE
President and C.-in-C. Armed Forces, Daniel T. arap Moi (KANU), *took office* 14 October 1978, *re-elected* 1979, 1983, 1988, 1992 and 29 December 1997

CABINET *as at May 1998*
The President
Agriculture, Musalia Mudavadi
Attorney-General, Amos Wako
Co-operative Development, Dr Frederick Amukowa Anangwe
East African and Regional Co-operation, Nicholas Biwott
Education, Human Resources Development, Stephen Kalonzo Musyoka
Energy, Chrisanthus Okemo
Environmental Conservation, Francis Nyenze
Finance, Simeon Nyachae
Foreign Affairs, Bonaya Godana
Health, Jackson Kalweo
Home Affairs, National Heritage, Culture and Social Services, Shariff Nasir
Industrial Development, Yekoyada Masakalia
Information and Broadcasting, Joseph Nyagah
Labour, Joseph Kimen Ngutu
Lands and Settlement, Noah Katana Ngala
Local Authorities, Samson Ongeri
Ministers of State in the President's Office, Gideon Ndambuki; Marsden Madoka
Natural Resources, Francis Lotodo
Planning and National Development, George Saitoti
Public Works and Housing, Kipkalya Kones
Regional Development, Hussein Maalim
Research and Technology, Andrew Kiptoon
Tourism, Henry Kosgei
Trade, Joseph Kamotho
Transport and Communications, William Ole Ntimama
Water Resources, Kigng'eno Arap Ngeny
Women and Youth Affairs, Mohamud Mohamed

KENYA HIGH COMMISSION
45 Portland Place, London WIN 4AS
Tel 0171-636 2371
High Commissioner, HE Mwanyengela Ngali, apptd 1996
Defence Adviser, Col. G. L. Okanga
Commercial Attaché, D. Mbugua

BRITISH HIGH COMMISSION
Bruce House, Upper Hill Road, PO Box 30465 Nairobi
Tel: Nairobi 714699
High Commissioner, HE Jeffrey James, CMG, apptd 1997
Deputy High Commissioner, A. Tucker
Defence Adviser, Col. T. Merritt, OBE
First Secretary (Commercial), S. Martin
First Secretary (Consular), J. Dunlop

CONSULAR OFFICES – Nairobi, Mombasa, Malindi

BRITISH COUNCIL REPRESENTATIVE, B. Harvey, (PO Box 40751) ICEA Building, Kenyatta Avenue, Nairobi. There are offices at Kisumu and Mombasa

ECONOMY

Agriculture provides about 30 per cent of GDP. The great variation in altitude and ecology provides conditions under which a wide range of crops can be grown. These include wheat, barley, pyrethrum, coffee, tea, sisal, coconuts, cashew nuts, cotton, maize and a wide variety of tropical and temperate fruits and vegetables. The total area of well-farmed land on which concentrated mixed farming can be practised is small and the remainder is arid or semi-arid country but population pressure and the need to increase agricultural production for export has led to attempts to develop such areas.

Mineral production consists of soda ash, salt and limestone. Hydroelectric power has been developed, particularly on the Upper Tana River, and Kenya is now almost self-sufficient in electric power generation.

There has been considerable industrial development over the last 15 years and Kenya has a variety of industries processing agricultural produce and manufacturing products from local and imported raw materials. New industries are steel, textile mills, dehydrated vegetable processing and motor tyre manufacture. Smaller schemes have added to the country's consumer goods manufacturing base. There is an oil refinery in Mombasa supplying both Kenya and Uganda, and a fuel pipeline now connects Mombasa and Nairobi. Tourism generates some US$400 million per year.

GNP – US$8,661 million (1996); US$320 per capita (1996)
GDP – US$9,016 million (1994); US$254 per capita (1994)
ANNUAL AVERAGE GROWTH OF GDP – 4.2 per cent (1996)
INFLATION RATE – 8.8 per cent (1996)
TOTAL EXTERNAL DEBT – US$6,893 million (1996)

TRADE

Principal exports are coffee and tea, which account for roughly a third of total export earnings. Also exported are fruit, vegetables, and crude animal and vegetable material. Industrial machinery is the largest single import; other imports are transport equipment, petroleum and petroleum products, metals, pharmaceuticals and chemicals. In 1995 Kenya had a trade deficit of US$738 million and a current account deficit of US$400 million. In 1996 imports totalled US$2,912 million and exports US$2,067 million.

Trade with UK	1996	1997
Imports from UK	£241,132,000	£238,190,000
Exports to UK	191,262,000	195,731,000

COMMUNICATIONS

The Kenya Railways Corporation has 1,700 miles of railway open to traffic. There are also 67,000 km of road, of which 8,900 are bitumen surfaced.

The principal port is Mombasa, operated by the Kenya Ports Authority. International air services operate from airports at Nairobi and Mombasa. The national airline is Kenya Airways.

KIRIBATI
Ribaberikin Kiribati – Republic of Kiribati

AREA – 280 sq. miles (726 sq. km)
POPULATION – 79,000 (1994 UN estimate): predominantly Christian. The languages are I-Kiribati and English
CAPITAL – Tarawa (population, 17,921, 1978)
CURRENCY – Australian dollar ($A) of 100 cents
NATIONAL ANTHEM – Teirake Kain Kiribati (Stand Kiribati)
NATIONAL DAY – 12 July (Independence Day)
NATIONAL FLAG – Red, with blue and white wavy lines in base, and in the centre a gold rising sun and a flying frigate bird
POPULATION GROWTH RATE – 1.9 per cent (1995)
POPULATION DENSITY – 109 per sq. km (1995)

Kiribati (pronounced Kiribas) comprises 36 islands: the Gilberts Group (17) including Banaba (formerly Ocean Island), the Phoenix Islands (8), and the Line Islands (11), which are situated in the south-west central Pacific around the point at which the International Date Line cuts the Equator. The total land area is spread over some 2 million square miles of ocean. Few of the atolls are more than half a mile in width or more than 12 feet high. The vegetation consists mainly of coconut palms, breadfruit trees and pandanus.

HISTORY AND POLITICS

The Gilbert and Ellice Islands were proclaimed a British protectorate in 1892 and annexed as the Gilbert and Ellice Islands Colony on 10 November 1915 (taking effect 12 January 1916). The Gilbert Islands were occupied by the Japanese army during World War II. Nuclear tests were carried out by the British off Kiritimati (Christmas Island) in 1957. In October 1975 the Ellice Islands seceded to become the independent state of Tuvalu. The Gilbert Islands achieved independence on 12 July 1979 as the Republic of Kiribati.

The next legislative election will be held in autumn 1998; the last presidential election, on 30 September 1994, was won by Teburoro Tito.

POLITICAL SYSTEM

The president is head of state as well as head of government and is elected nationally. There is a House of Assembly of 41 members (39 elected members, the Attorney-General and a representative of Banaba Island). Executive authority is vested in the Cabinet.

HEAD OF STATE

President, Foreign Affairs, Teburoro Tito, *sworn in* 1 October 1994
Vice-President, Home Affairs, Rural Development, Tewareka Tentoa

CABINET *as at July 1998*

The President
The Vice-President
Commerce, Industry and Tourism, Tim Taekiti
Education, Training and Technology, Teiraoi Tetabea
Environment, Social Development, Tewareka Boorau
Finance and Economic Planning, Beniamina Tiinga
Health and Family Planning, Kataotika Tekee
Labour, Employment and Co-operatives, Tanieru Awerika

Line and Phoenix Islands, Timbo Keariki
Natural Resources Development, Willie Tokataake
Transport, Communications and Information, Manraoi Kaiea
Works and Energy, Emile Schutz

HONORARY CONSULATE
The Great House, Llanddewi Rhydderch, Monmouthshire
NP7 9UY
Tel 01873-840 375
Honorary Consul, M. Walsh

BRITISH HIGH COMMISSIONER, HE Michael Dibben,
apptd 1998, resident at Suva, Fiji

ECONOMY

Many people still practise a semi-subsistence economy,
the main staples of their diet being coconuts and fish.
    The principal imports are foodstuffs, consumer goods,
machinery and transport equipment. The principal exports are copra and fish.
    In 1994 there was a trade deficit of US$21 million and a
current account surplus of US$1 million.
GNP – US$75 million (1996); US$920 per capita (1996)
GDP – US$41 million (1994); US$602 per capita (1994)

TRADE WITH UK	1996	1997
Imports from UK	£231,000	£174,000
Exports to UK	10,000	13,000

COMMUNICATIONS

Air communication exists between most of the islands and
is operated by Air Tungaru, a statutory corporation. Air
Marshall Islands operates a weekly service between
Majuro, Tarawa, Funafuti and Nadi, and Air Nauru
between Tarawa, Nauru and Nadi. Inter-island shipping
is operated by a statutory corporation, the Shipping
Corporation of Kiribati.

EDUCATION AND SOCIAL WELFARE

The government maintains a teacher training college and a
secondary school. Five junior secondary schools are
maintained by missions. Throughout the republic there
are about a hundred primary schools. The total enrolment
of children of school age is about 16,000.
    There is a general hospital at Tarawa. The other
inhabited islands have dispensaries.

KOREA

Korea's southern and western coasts are fringed with
innumerable islands, of which the largest, forming a
province of its own, is Cheju. The Korean language is of
the Ural-Altaic Group. Its script, Hangul, was invented in
the 15th century; prior to this Chinese characters alone
were used. Despite the great cultural influence of the
Chinese, Koreans have developed and preserved their own
cultural heritage.

HISTORY

The Korean peninsula was first unified in AD 676 when
Silla, having emerged as the dominant tribal state, drove
out the Chinese. The Kim dynasty was succeeded by the
Wang dynasty in 918. The last native dynasty (Yi) ruled
from 1392 until 1910 when Japan formally annexed Korea.
The country remained part of the Japanese Empire until
the defeat of Japan in 1945, when it was occupied by troops
of the USA and the USSR, the 38th parallel being fixed as
the boundary between the two zones of occupation.

Attempts to reunite Korea failed and the issue was
referred to the UN General Assembly. The UN in
November 1947 resolved that elections should be held for
a National Assembly which, when elected, should set up a
government. The Soviet government refused to comply
and a UN commission was only allowed to operate south of
the 38th parallel.
    A general election was held on 10 May 1948, and the first
National Assembly met in Seoul on 31 May. The
Assembly passed a constitution on 12 July and on 15
August 1948 the republic was formally inaugurated and
American military government came to an end. Meanwhile, in the Soviet-occupied zone north of the 38th
parallel the Democratic People's Republic had been
established with its capital at Pyongyang. A Supreme
People's Soviet was elected in September 1948, and a
Soviet-style constitution adopted.

THE KOREAN WAR

Korea remained divided along the 38th parallel until June
1950, when North Korean forces invaded South Korea. In
response to Security Council recommendations, 16 nations, including the USA and the UK, came to the aid of the
Republic of Korea. China entered the war on the side of
North Korea in November 1950. The fighting was ended
by an armistice agreement signed on 27 July 1953. By this
agreement (which was not signed by the Republic of
Korea), the line of division between North and South
Korea remained close to the 38th parallel, and a Military
Armistice Commission (MAC) was established to monitor
the cease-fire. North Korea and China withdrew from the
MAC in 1994.
    Talks between North and South Korea on the reunifica-
tion of the country have taken place intermittently. A non-
aggression accord was signed between the North and
South in 1991 and an agreement on the denuclearization of
the Korean peninsula was reached in 1992. A summit of
North and South Korean presidents was scheduled for July
1994 but Kim Il-sung died before it could take place. Four-
party talks between China, the USA and the two Koreas
took place in December 1997 and again in March 1998, but
no new agreements were reached.

DEMOCRATIC PEOPLE'S REPUBLIC OF KOREA
Chosun Minchu-chui Inmin Kongwa-guk

AREA – 46,540 sq. miles (120,538 sq. km). Neighbours:
    China, Russia (north), Republic of Korea (south)
POPULATION – 23,917,000 (1994 UN estimate). The
    language is Korean
CAPITAL – Pyongyang (approximate population,
    2,000,000)
CURRENCY – Won of 100 chon
NATIONAL ANTHEM – A Chi Mun Bin No Ra I Gang San
    (Shine bright, oh dawn, on this land so fair)
NATIONAL DAY – 16 February (Kim Jong-il's birthday)
NATIONAL FLAG – Red with white fimbriations and blue
    borders at top and bottom; a large red star on a white disc
    near the hoist
LIFE EXPECTANCY (years) – male 67.70; female 73.95
POPULATION GROWTH RATE – 1.9 per cent (1995)
POPULATION DENSITY – 198 per sq. km (1995)

POLITICAL SYSTEM

The constitution of the Democratic People's Republic of
Korea provides for a Supreme People's Assembly, presently consisting of 687 deputies, which is elected every five

years by universal suffrage. The Assembly elects a president for a five-year term, and the Central People's Committee. In turn, the Central People's Committee directs the Administrative Council which implements the policy formulated by the Committee.

The Administrative Council (51 members), the government of North Korea, includes the prime minister and various ministers. In practice, however, the country is ruled by the Korean Workers' Party which elects a Central Committee; this in turn appoints a Politburo. The senior ministers of the Administrative Council are all members of the Communist Party Central Committee and the majority are also members of the Politburo. Kim Il-sung, who had been head of the state, party and military since the country's inception in 1948, died on 8 July 1994. His son Kim Jong-il has not yet assumed his father's positions.

HEAD OF STATE
President, vacant
Vice-Presidents, Kim Yong-ju; Kim Pyong-sik; Pak Song-chol; Yi Jong-ok
General Secretary, Korean Workers' Party; Member of Presidium, Kim Jong-il
Politburo of the Central Committee, Kim Jong-il; Pak Son-chol; Yi Chong-ok; Yon Hyong-muk; Kang Song-san; So Yun-sok; Ho Dam; Kim Yong-nam; Kye Ung-tae; Kang Song-san; Han Song-yong; Kim Yong-ju (*full members*); the politburo also contains 17 alternate members

ADMINISTRATION COUNCIL *as at July 1998*
Prime Minister (acting), Foreign Affairs, Kim Yong-nam
Deputy Prime Ministers, Kim Pok-sin (*Light Industry Commission*); Kim Chang-chu; Kim Hwan (*Chemical Industry*); Cho Yong-nim (*Metal Industry*); Chang Chol (*Culture and Art*); Hong Song-nam; Kang Hui-won; Kong Chin-tae; Kim Yun-hyok

MINISTERS
Academy of Sciences, Kim Kil-yon
Atomic Energy Industry, Cho Hak-kun
Building Materials, Yi Tong-chun
Central Bank President, Chong Song-taek
Central Statistics Bureau, Sin Kyong-sik
Chair, Agriculture Commission, Kim Won-chin
Chair, Educational Commission, Choe Ki-chong
Chair, Electronics and Automation Industry, Kim Chang-ho
Chair, External Economic Committee, Yi Song-tae
Chair, Materials Supplying Commission, No Tu-chol
Chair, Mining Industry Commission, Cho Chang-tok
Chair, People's Service Commission, Kong Chin-tae
Chair, Power Industry Commission, Yi Chi-chan
Chair, State Construction Commission, Kim Ung-sang
Chair, State Inspection Commission, Chon Mun-sop
Chair, State Planning Committee, Hong Sok-hyong
Chair, State Scientific and Technological Commission, Yi Cha-pang
Chair, State Sports Commission, Pak Myong-chol
Chair, Transport Commission, Yi Yong-mu
Coal Industry, Kim Ni-kyong
Commerce, Han Chan-kun
Construction, Cho Yun-hui
External Economic Affairs, Chong Song-nam
Finance, Yun Ki-chong
Forestry, Yi Chun-sok
General Central Materials Supply Association, Chae Gyu-bin
Korean Central Physical Education Guidance Commission, Kim Yu-sun
Labour Administration, Yi Chae-yun
Local Industry, Cho Chong-ung
Machine Industry, Kwak Pom-ki

Marine Transport, O Song-yol
Mining Industry, Kim Pyong-kil
Posts and Telecommunications, Kim Hak-sop
Public Health, Kim Su-hak
Public Security, Lt.-Gen. Paek Hak-nom
Railways, Kim In-kap
Reception of Overseas Compatriots, Kim Chu-ho
Secretariat and State Administration Council, Chong Mun-sang
Urban Management, Yi Chol-pong

DEFENCE
The Army has 3,000 main battle tanks, 2,500 armoured personnel carriers and 10,600 artillery pieces. The Navy has 26 submarines, three frigates and about 422 patrol and coastal vessels at 15 bases. The Air Force has 607 combat aircraft.

Between 1992 and 1994 North Korea embarked on a clandestine nuclear weapons programme despite being a signatory of the Nuclear Non-Proliferation Treaty (NPT). The NPT's enforcing arm, the International Atomic Energy Authority (IAEA), was repeatedly refused access to inspect military installations. North Korea withdrew from the NPT following an IAEA report that the country was attempting to reprocess plutonium for use in nuclear weapons. An agreement was signed with the USA on 21 October 1994 under which North Korea vowed to remain a party to the NPT; to permit IAEA inspections; and to switch to light-water reactors unsuitable for plutonium production. In return the USA agreed to establish diplomatic and economic relations and to pay for interim energy requirements. The IAEA verified the halting of North Korea's nuclear programme in November 1994 although a final settlement was only achieved in June 1995.

MILITARY EXPENDITURE – 27.0 per cent of GDP (1996)
MILITARY PERSONNEL – 1,244,000: Army 923,000, Navy 47,000, Air Force 85,000, Paramilitaries 189,000
CONSCRIPTION DURATION – Three to ten years

ECONOMY
North Korea is rich in minerals and industry was developed, but the economy has stagnated owing to poor planning and a shortage of foreign exchange. The current economic crisis was precipitated by the curtailment of barter trade with the Soviet Union after 1991, and the end of subsidized oil and grain from China. Industrial output has collapsed, with industry operating at one-third of capacity. The economy has been sustained by foreign exchange sent by ethnic Koreans in Japan. In April 1998, South Korea lifted its ban on investment in North Korea, allowing South Koreans to send money to their relatives in the north.

In 1995–8, a slump in agricultural production was exacerbated by widespread flooding which devastated the rice harvest and threatened potential famine. In January 1998, the UN World Food Programme launched a food aid operation to provide 658,000 tonnes of food to North Korea, where daily rations of grain had fallen from 300 grams in January 1998 to 100 grams in March.

Under the nuclear agreement, North Korea is to receive 500,000 tonnes of oil a year and is hoping to export manganese to the USA; it has lifted the embargo on the import of US commodities.

GDP – US$19,566 million (1994); US$1,155 per capita (1994)

TRADE WITH UK	1996	1997
Imports from UK	£23,625,000	£24,800,000
Exports to UK	231,000	442,000

REPUBLIC OF KOREA
Daehanminkuk

AREA – 38,330 sq. miles (99,274 sq. km). Neighbour: Democratic People's Republic of Korea (north)
POPULATION – 46,430,000 (1998 estimate). The largest religions are Buddhism (10.3 million) and Christianity (8.8 million Protestants, 2.9 million Roman Catholics). The language is Korean
CAPITAL – Seoul (population, 10,412,000, 1996)
MAJOR CITIES – ΨInchon (2,390,000); ΨPusan (3,865,000); Taegu (2,478,000)
CURRENCY – Won of 100 jeon
NATIONAL ANTHEM – Aegukka (Song of the Mother Country)
NATIONAL DAY – 15 August (Independence Day)
NATIONAL FLAG – White with a red and blue yin-yang in the centre, surrounded by four black trigrams
LIFE EXPECTANCY (years) – male 67.66; female 75.67
POPULATION GROWTH RATE – 0.9 per cent (1995)
POPULATION DENSITY – 452 per sq. km (1995)
URBAN POPULATION – 74.4 per cent (1990)

HISTORY AND POLITICS

The Republic of Korea was not officially recognized by any former Communist bloc country until 1989, and not by the People's Republic of China until 1992.

The most recent elections to the National Assembly in April 1996 produced no outright majority although the ruling New Korea Party (formerly Democratic Liberal Party) was able to form a government following defections from opposition parties. In the most recent presidential election of 18 December 1997, Kim Dae-jung of the National Congress for New Politics was elected president with just over 40 per cent of the vote. He nominated Kim Jong-pil as prime minister, but this was rejected by the National Assembly. Kim Jong-pil was nevertheless appointed acting prime minister and formed a government.

POLITICAL SYSTEM
A new constitution was adopted in 1988 following a year of political unrest. The president, who is head of state, chief of the executive and commander-in-chief of the armed forces, is directly elected for a single term of five years. He appoints the prime minister with the consent of the National Assembly, and members of the State Council (Cabinet) on the recommendation of the prime minister. The president is also empowered to take wide-ranging measures in an emergency, including the declaration of martial law, but must obtain the agreement of the National Assembly. The National Assembly of 299 members is directly elected for a four-year term.

HEAD OF STATE
President, Kim Dae-jung, *elected* 18 December 1997, *sworn in* 25 February 1998

CABINET *as at June 1998*
Prime Minister (acting), Kim Jong-pil
Agriculture and Forestry, Kim Sung-hoon
Construction and Transportation, Lee Jung-moo
Culture and Tourism, Shin Nak-yun
Defence, Chun Yong-taek

Education, Lee Hai-chan
Environment, Choi Jae-wook
Finance and Economy, Lee Kyu-sung
Foreign Affairs, Trade, Park Chung-soo
Government Administration, Home Affairs, Kim Jung-kil
Health and Welfare, Kim Mo-im
Information and Communications, Bae Soon-hoon
Justice, Park Sang-cheon
Labour, Lee Ki-ho
Legislation, Kim Hong-tae
Maritime Affairs and Fisheries, Kim Sun-kil
National Unification, Kang In-duk
Patriots' and Veterans' Affairs, Kim Ui-chae
Science and Technology, Kang Chang-hee
Trade, Industry and Energy, Park Tae-yung

EMBASSY OF THE REPUBLIC OF KOREA
60 Buckingham Gate, London SW1E 6AJ
Tel 0171-227 5500
Ambassador Extraordinary and Plenipotentiary, HE Choi Dong-jin, apptd 1996
Defence Attaché, Capt. Lee Byun-moon
Consul, Lee Jong-kug
Counsellor, Kim Chil-doo *(Commercial Affairs)*

BRITISH EMBASSY
No. 4, Chung-Dong, Chung-Ku, Seoul 100
Tel: Seoul 735–7341/3
Ambassador Extraordinary and Plenipotentiary, HE Stephen Brown, apptd 1997
Counsellor (Economic) and Deputy Head of Mission, D. R. Marsh
Defence and Military Attaché, Brig. C. D. Parr, OBE
First Secretary (Commercial), D. F. Graham
There is a Trade Office and an Honorary British Consul at Pusan.

BRITISH COUNCIL REPRESENTATIVE, T. Toney, 1st Floor, Anglican Church Building, 3–7 Chung Dong, Choong-ku, Seoul 100–120

BRITISH CHAMBER OF COMMERCE, c/o Chartered Bank, 1st and 2nd Floors, Samsung Building, 50, 1-Ka Ulchi Ro, Chung-Ku, Seoul

DEFENCE

The Army has 2,130 main battle tanks, 2,490 armoured personnel carriers, 3,500 artillery pieces and 143 armed helicopters. The Navy has six submarines, seven destroyers, 33 frigates, 105 patrol and coastal vessels, 23 combat aircraft, 47 armed helicopters, 60 main battle tanks and 60 armoured personnel carriers. There are eight naval bases. The Air Force has 461 combat aircraft.

The USA maintains 35,920 personnel in the country.
MILITARY EXPENDITURE – 3.2 per cent of GDP (1996)
MILITARY PERSONNEL – 676,500: Army 560,000, Navy 60,000, Air Force 52,000, Paramilitaries 4,500
CONSCRIPTION DURATION – 26–30 months

ECONOMY

In January 1997, the steel and construction firm Hanbo, one of Korea's largest companies, collapsed amid allegations of corruption and incompetence. Several other major Korean companies collapsed in 1997, putting enormous strain on the Korean financial sector that had loaned money to the failed enterprises. Following economic problems elsewhere in Asia, the South Korean stock market fell heavily in October 1997. The value of the won also fell, raising the cost of borrowing for the already troubled banking sector exposed to bad loans in other Asian economies. On 3 December 1997, a record IMF rescue package totalling US$57 billion was announced. Having already fallen to 912 won to the US dollar in October, the won reached an all-time low of 1,962 to the dollar on 23 December 1997; the next day, the government announced further austerity measures to stabilize the economy; the markets responded well, and the won regained ground. In January 1998, the government began implementing economic reforms required by the IMF, and in March 1998 negotiated an agreement to restructure US$21 billion of its short-term debt.

Land redistribution and US aid (US$6,000 million from 1945 to 1978) enabled the rapid industrialization of South Korea in the 1950s and 1960s. Former land owners formed *chaebols* (industrial conglomerates) which benefited from a highly-educated workforce and import substitution policies. From 1961 to 1979 exports increased by an average of 10 per cent a year. From 1985 to 1994, economic growth averaged 7.8 per cent. Major industries include shipbuilding, construction, iron and steel, textiles, electrical and electronic goods, footwear, passenger vehicles and railway rolling stock.

The soil is fertile but arable land is limited by the mountainous nature of the country. Staple agricultural products are rice, cereals, beans and potatoes. Fruit-growing, sericulture and the growing of the medicinal root ginseng are also practised. The fishing industry is a major contributor to both food supply and exports.

Korea is deficient in mineral resources, except for deposits of coal on the east coast and tungsten. There are some prospects of discovering oil in the sea between Korea and Japan.

In 1995 there was a trade deficit of US$4,746 million and a current account deficit of US$8,251 million. In 1996 imports totalled US$150,339 million and exports US$129,715 million.

GNP – US$483,130 million (1996); US$10,610 per capita (1996)

GDP – US$317,891 million (1994); US$8,519 per capita (1994)

UNEMPLOYMENT – 2.0 per cent (1995)

TRADE WITH UK	1996	1997
Imports from UK	£1,303,560,000	£1,223,293,000
Exports to UK	2,038,376,000	2,238,623,000

COMMUNICATIONS

Korean Air and Asiana operate regular flights to Europe, the USA, the Middle East and south-east Asia. Pusan and Inchon are the major ports with Pusan serving the industrial areas of the south-east. Inchon, 28 miles from Seoul, serves the capital, but development and operation at Inchon are hampered by a tidal variation of 9–10 metres.

EDUCATION

Primary education is compulsory for six years from the age of six. Secondary and higher education is extensive with the option of middle school to age 15 and high school to age 18.

ILLITERACY RATE – 2.0 per cent

ENROLMENT (percentage of age group) – primary 99 per cent (1993); secondary 96 per cent (1995); tertiary 52.0 per cent (1995)

KUWAIT
Dowlat al- Kuwait

AREA – 6,880 sq. miles (17,818 sq. km). Neighbours: Iraq (north and west); Saudi Arabia (south and south-west)

POPULATION – 1,691,000 (1995 census): 41.6 per cent were Kuwaiti citizens, the remainder being other Arabs, Iranians, Indians and Pakistanis. The total Western population was 14,240. Islam is the official religion, though religious freedom is constitutionally guaranteed. The official language is Arabic, and English is widely spoken as a second language

CAPITAL – ΨKuwait City (population, 400,000, 1975)

CURRENCY – Kuwaiti dinar (KD) of 1,000 fils

NATIONAL DAY – 25 February

NATIONAL FLAG – Three horizontal stripes of green, white and red, with black trapezoid next to staff

LIFE EXPECTANCY (years) – male 71.77; female 73.32

POPULATION GROWTH RATE – –4.7 per cent (1995)

POPULATION DENSITY – 95 per sq. km (1995)

MILITARY EXPENDITURE – 14.5 per cent of GDP (1996)

MILITARY PERSONNEL – 20,300: Army 11,000, Navy 1,800, Air Force 2,500, Paramilitaries 5,000

CONSCRIPTION DURATION – Two years

In 1993 the UN settled the dispute between Kuwait and Iraq, moving the border some few hundred metres northwards. Kuwait has since completed a 130-mile ditch, sand wall and barbed wire system along its border.

Kuwait has a dry, desert climate with summer extending from April to September. The mean temperature varies between 29–45°C in summer, and 8–18°C in winter. Humidity rarely exceeds 60 per cent except in July and August.

HISTORY AND POLITICS

Although Kuwait had been independent for some years, the 'exclusive agreement' of 1899 between the Sheikh of Kuwait and the British government was formally abrogated by an exchange of letters dated 19 June 1961. Iraq invaded Kuwait on 2 August 1990 and it was liberated on 26 February 1991 by an alliance of Western and Arab forces. Iraq built up its armed forces on Kuwait's border in October 1994, until it was deterred by the arrival of US and British forces. Iraq formally recognized the sovereignty and territorial integrity of Kuwait as well as the UN-demarcated border in November 1994. Roughly 600 Kuwaitis are still held in Iraq.

Voting took place for a new National Assembly in October 1996. Pro-government candidates won 19 of the 25 seats, although all were independent.

POLITICAL SYSTEM

Under the constitution legislative power is vested in the Amir and the 50-member National Assembly, and executive power in the Amir and the Cabinet. Following popular pressure after the liberation, elections for the National Assembly were held in October 1992. The electorate consists of all Kuwaiti male nationals over 21 whose families have lived in the Emirate since before 1921.

There are five governorates: Capital, Hawally, Ahmadi, Jara and Al Farwaniya.

HEAD OF STATE

HH The Amir of Kuwait, Shaikh Jabir al-Ahmad al Jabir al-Sabah, *born* 1928, acceded 31 December 1977

Crown Prince, HH Shaikh Saad al-Abdullah al-Salim al-Sabah

CABINET *as at July 1998*
Prime Minister, HH The Crown Prince
First Deputy PM, Foreign Affairs, Shaikh Sabah al-Ahmed al-Jabir al-Sabah
Second Deputy PM, Cabinet Affairs, Nasser Abdullah al-Roudhan
Deputy PM, Defence, Shaikh Salem Sabah al-Salem al-Sabah
Commerce and Industry, Abdulaziz Abdullah al-Dakheel
Communications, Finance, Shaikh Ali Salim al-Sabah
Education and Higher Education, Abdul Aziz al-Ghanim
Information, Yusuf Muhammad al-Samit
Interior, Shaikh Mohammed Khaled al-Hamad al-Sabah
Justice, Waqfs and Islamic Affairs, Ahmed Khalid al-Kulaib
Labour, Social Affairs and Housing, Jassem Mohammed al-Oun
Minister of State for National Assembly, Mohammed Dhaifallah Sharar
Oil, Shaikh Sa'ud Nasir al-Sabah
Planning and Administrative Development Affairs, Ali Musa al-Musa
Public Health, Adil Khaled al-Sabih
Public Works, Electricity and Water, Hamud Abdullah al-Raqubah

EMBASSY OF THE STATE OF KUWAIT
2 Albert Gate, London SW1X 7JU
Tel 0171-590 3400
Ambassador Extraordinary and Plenipotentiary, HE Khaled al-Duwaisan, GCVO, apptd 1993
Cultural Attaché, Dr Ajeel al-Zaher

BRITISH EMBASSY
PO Box 2 Safat, 13001 Safat, Kuwait
Tel: Kuwait 240 3334/5/6
Ambassador Extraordinary and Plenipotentiary, HE Graham H. Boyce, CMG, apptd 1996
Counsellor and Deputy Head of Mission, B. E. Stewart
First Secretaries, L. Hartley (*Management and Consul*); M. Hurley (*Commercial*)
Defence Attaché, Col. G. Sayle, OBE

BRITISH COUNCIL REPRESENTATIVE, C. Reuter, 2 Al Arabi Street (PO Box 345), 13004 Safat, Mansouriyah, Kuwait City

ECONOMY

Despite the desert terrain, 8.4 per cent of land is under cultivation, tomatoes, onions and melons being the main crops. Shrimp fishing has declined through oil pollution of coastal waters.

The oil industry was brought into government ownership in 1975. Since reorganization in 1980, the national industry has been run by the Kuwait Petroleum Corporation. Oil installations were extensively damaged when Iraqi forces set light to oil wells prior to their retreat. Oil exports were resumed in July 1991 and production (including output from the neutral zone) reached 2,000,000 barrels per day in 1993. Capacity is 2,500,000 barrels per day.

There are four power stations capable of generating almost 7,000 MW of electricity. The country depends on desalination plants for its water supply. Both water and power facilities were heavily damaged during the war, although electricity and water distillation capacity were restored to pre-invasion levels in 1995.

GNP – US$28,941 million (1995); US$17,390 per capita (1995)
GDP – US$22,946 million (1994); US$16,285 per capita (1994)
ANNUAL AVERAGE GROWTH OF GDP – 1.0 per cent (1995)
INFLATION RATE – 3.2 per cent (1996)

TRADE

Oil is the major export. Non-oil exports, mainly to Asian countries and the Indian sub-continent, have included chemical fertilizers, ammonia and other chemicals, metal pipes, shrimps and building materials. Re-exports to neighbouring states traditionally accounted for a major proportion of non-oil exports but were brought to a halt by the Iraqi invasion. Major trading partners are Japan, the USA, the UAE, Saudi Arabia and Western Europe.

In 1996 Kuwait had a trade surplus of US$7,034 million and a current account surplus of US$6,773 million. Imports totalled US$7,542 million and exports US$14,803 million.

Trade with UK	1996	1997
Imports from UK	£579,097,000	£503,529,000
Exports to UK	179,865,000	201,064,000

COMMUNICATIONS

Ports and airport were damaged during the Iraqi occupation, but have been reopened since liberation. There is a network of dual-carriageway roads and more are under construction. Telecommunications and postal services are conducted by the government. Its earth satellite station and telecommunications network were severely damaged during the Iraqi occupation but domestic and international telephone services have been fully restored.

SOCIAL WELFARE

The government invested its considerable oil revenues in comprehensive social services. Education and medical treatment are free. Kuwait University opened in 1966, and in 1987–8 had 15,602 students. In 1987–8 there were over 489,000 pupils at government and private schools. These numbers have declined along with the total population since the Iraqi invasion and a number of schools did not reopen after Kuwait's liberation.
ILLITERACY RATE – 21.4 per cent
ENROLMENT (percentage of age group) – primary 65 per cent (1995); secondary 54 per cent (1993); tertiary 25.4 per cent (1995)

KYRGYZSTAN
Kyrgyz Respublikasy

AREA – 76,641 sq. miles (198,500 sq. km). Neighbours: Kazakhstan (north), China (east), Tajikistan (south and south-west), Uzbekistan (west)
POPULATION – 4,500,000 (1998 estimate): 52.4 per cent Kirghiz (Turkic origin), 21.5 per cent Russian and 12.9 per cent Uzbek, with smaller numbers of Ukrainians, Germans, Tatars and Kazakhs. Islam is the main religion. Kirghiz is a Turkic language which was given an alphabet in the 1930s and became the official language after independence. Russian is an equal official language in the fields of science, industry and the health service, and in all regions where there is a large Russian population. Otherwise the ethnic groups use their own languages
CAPITAL – Bishkek (population, 627,800, 1991 estimate; 616,000, 1989 census)
CURRENCY – Som of 100 tyin (introduced on 10 May 1993 at rate of 1:200 against the rouble)
NATIONAL DAY – 31 August (Independence Day)
NATIONAL FLAG – Red with a rayed sun containing a representation of a yurt, all in gold
LIFE EXPECTANCY (years) – male 64.23; female 72.23

POPULATION GROWTH RATE – 1.2 per cent (1995)
POPULATION DENSITY – 24 per sq. km (1995)
URBAN POPULATION – 39.3 per cent (1995)
MILITARY EXPENDITURE – 2.6 per cent of GDP (1996)
MILITARY PERSONNEL – 17,200: Army 9,800, Air Force 2,400, Paramilitaries 5,000
CONSCRIPTION DURATION – 18 months

Kyrgyzstan (formerly Kirghizia) is mountainous, the major part being covered by the ridge of the Central Tienshan, while the Pamir-Altai system occupies its southern part. There are a number of spacious mountain valleys, the Alai, Susamyr and others. Kyrgyzstan is divided into six administrative regions.

HISTORY AND POLITICS

The Kirghiz people were first mentioned in Chinese chronicles in the second millennium BC. They are a merger of two ethnic groups, a Turkic-speaking people driven into the area by the Mongols from the River Yenisei area of Central Asia, and indigenous peoples who spoke a similar language. After a long period under Mongol, Chinese and Persian rule, the Kirghiz became part of the Russian Empire in the 1860s and 1870s. Kyrgyzstan became part of the Soviet Union in 1920 and underwent some industrialization.

Kyrgyzstan declared independence just after the failed Moscow coup on 31 August 1991.

Ethnic tensions between the rural nomadic Kirghiz, the urban Russians and the wealthy Uzbeks who own many businesses and form the majority in the second largest town of Osh, are never far from the surface. By presidential decree the sphere of official usage of the Russian language has been expanded to encourage Russians to remain, and a treaty on dual citizenship has been signed with Russia. The government is also committed to the fair representation of ethnic Russians in the civil service.

President Akaev had difficulty in introducing economic reforms because of obstruction by the bureaucracy and the *Uluk Kenesh* (parliament) over the reforms enshrined in the constitution. The president won a referendum on his plans for greater economic reform in January 1994. Elections to the new parliament, the *Zhogorku Kenesh*, were held in February 1995. A new government was appointed by the president in February 1996 in the wake of the referendum increasing his powers.

POLITICAL SYSTEM

The head of state is a president directly elected for a five-year term. There is a bicameral legislature composed of a 35-member Legislative Assembly and a 70-member People's Assembly, both of which are elected for five-year terms. The president appoints the prime minister and the other members of the government. The Assembly of the People of Kyrgyzstan, which comprises the leaders of the republic's ethnic communities, was designated a consultative body in January 1997.

HEAD OF STATE
President, Askar Akayev, *elected* 12 October 1991, *re-elected* 24 December 1995

GOVERNMENT *as at June 1998*
Prime Minister, Kubanychbek Zhumaliyev
Deputy PM, Boris Silayev
Agriculture and Water Resources, Karimsher Abdimomunov
Chair, Assembly of People's Representatives, Abdygany Erkrbayev
Chair, Legislative Assembly, Usup Mukambayer
Defence, Col.-Gen. Myrzakan Subanov

Education, Science and Culture, Sovetbek Toktomyshev
Emergency Situations and Civil Defence, Sultan Urmanayev
Environmental Protection, Kulubek Bokonbayev
Finance, Taalaibek Koiychumanov
Foreign Affairs, Muratbek Imanaliyev
Foreign Trade and Industry, Orozmat Abdykalykov
Health, Naken Kasiyev
Interior, Maj.-Gen. Omurbek Kutuyev
Justice, Nelya Beishenaliyeva
Labour and Social Security, Imankadyr Rysaliyev
National Security, Misir Ashirkulov
Transport and Communications, Zhantoro Satybaldiev

EMBASSY OF THE KYRGYZ REPUBLIC
Ascot House, 119 Crawford Street, London WIH IAF
Tel 0171–935 1462
Ambassador Extraordinary and Plenipotentiary, HE Roza Otunbayeva, apptd 1997

BRITISH AMBASSADOR, HE Douglas B. McAdam, resident at Almaty, Kazakhstan

ECONOMY

Agriculture is the main sector of the economy, with sugar beet, grain and sheep the main products. Private ownership of land was legalized in 1997. Industry is concentrated in the food-processing, textiles, timber and mining fields. Since 1992, some 60 per cent of state-owned enterprises have been privatized. Hydroelectric power is abundant and Kyrgyzstan has reserves of gold, coal, mercury and uranium, although only gold has so far been exploited and is the country's largest export. In 1997, industry grew by 47 per cent and agriculture by 10 per cent.

The government introduced the som in May 1993 to break the link with the depreciating rouble, the cause of high inflation in 1992 and early 1993. The president and government have also made the Central Bank independent of government and parliamentary control. However, the country needs direct foreign investment desperately and has had most of its trading links with other Central Asian republics reduced because of their refusal to accept payments in soms, although this has been ameliorated by the signing of an economic union agreement with Kazakhstan and Uzbekistan in February 1994. Subsidized goods supplies from Russia have also been reduced. In March 1996, a treaty was signed with Belarus, Kazakhstan and Russia enhancing economic co-operation and working towards a single customs territory.

GNP – US$2,486 million (1996); US$550 per capita (1996)
GDP – US$3,117 million (1994); US$222 per capita (1994)
TOTAL EXTERNAL DEBT – US$789 million (1996)

TRADE WITH UK	1996	1997
Imports from UK	£5,565,000	£3,056,000
Exports to UK	344,000	2,722,000

CULTURE AND EDUCATION

Until the 1930s the Kirghiz language had an oral tradition of literature which included the epic poem *Manas*, which tells the history of the Kirghiz people. Internationally, one of the best-known writers of the former Soviet Union is the Kirghiz writer Chingiz Aitmatov (1928–).

ILLITERACY RATE – 0.4 per cent
ENROLMENT (percentage of age group) – primary 97 per cent (1995); tertiary 12.2 per cent (1995)

LAOS
Satharanarath Pasathipatai Pasason Lao

AREA – 91,429 sq. miles (236,800 sq. km). Neighbours:
China (north), Vietnam (north-east and east), Cambodia
(south), Thailand (west), Myanmar (north-west)
POPULATION – 4,882,000 (1995 census). Lao is the official
language; French and English are spoken
CAPITAL – Vientiane (population, 132,253, 1966; 120,000,
1984 estimate)
CURRENCY – Kip (K) of 100 at
NATIONAL DAY – 2 December
NATIONAL FLAG – Blue background with a central white
circle, framed by two horizontal red stripes
LIFE EXPECTANCY (years) – male 49.50; female 52.50
POPULATION GROWTH RATE – 3.0 per cent (1995)
POPULATION DENSITY – 21 per sq. km (1995)
MILITARY EXPENDITURE – 3.9 per cent of GDP (1996)
MILITARY PERSONNEL – 29,000: Army 25,000, Navy 500,
Air Force 3,500
CONSCRIPTION DURATION – 18 months minimum
ILLITERACY RATE – 43.4 per cent
ENROLMENT (percentage of age group) – primary 68 per
cent (1993); secondary 18 per cent (1993); tertiary 1.5 per
cent (1993)

HISTORY AND POLITICS

The kingdom of Lane Xang, the Land of a Million
Elephants, was founded in the 14th century but broke up
at the beginning of the 16th century into the separate
kingdoms of Luang Prabang and Vientiane and the
principality of Champassac, which together came under
French protection in 1893. In 1945 the Japanese staged a
coup and suppressed the French administration. In 1947
Laos became a constitutional monarchy under King
Sisvang Vong, and an independent sovereign state in
1953. The next 22 years in Laos were marked by power
struggles and civil war, eventually won by the North
Vietnamese-backed Pathet Lao, a Communist-dominated
organization.

The Lao People's Democratic Republic was proclaimed
in December 1975 following victory by the Pathet Lao and
the abdication of the King. A president and Council of
Ministers were installed, and a 45-member Supreme
People's Council was appointed to draft a constitution,
which was approved in 1991. The Lao People's Revolutionary Party (LPRP) is the sole legal political organization. A general election to the enlarged 99-member
National Assembly was held on 21 December 1997; all the
candidates were approved by the LPRP. The president,
prime minister and Council of Ministers were confirmed
in their posts by the National Assembly on 24 February
1998.

HEAD OF STATE
President, Gen. Khamtay Siphandone, *elected by Supreme
People's Assembly* 24 February 1998
Vice-President, Oudom Khatti-Gna

COUNCIL OF MINISTERS *as at July 1998*

Prime Minister, Gen. Sisavat Keobounphanh
Deputy PMs, Khamphoui Keoboualapha (*Finance*);
Somsavat Lengsavad (*Foreign Affairs*); Gen. Choumaly
Sayasone (*National Defence*); Boungnang Vorachith
Agriculture and Forestry, Siene Saphangthong
Commerce and Tourism, Phoumy Thipphavone
Communications, Transport, Posts and Construction, Phao
Bounnaphol

Education, Phimmasone Leuangkhamma
Governor of the State Bank, Cheuang Sombounekhanh
Industry and Handicrafts, Soulivong Daravong
Information and Culture, Sileua Bounkham
Interior, Gen. Asang Laoly
Justice, Khamouane Boupha
Labour and Social Welfare, Somphan Phengkhammy
National Economic Institute, Minister attached to Prime Minister,
Khamxay Souphanouvong
Public Health, Ponemek Daraloy
State Planning Committee, Bouathong Vonglokham

EMBASSY OF THE LAO PEOPLE'S DEMOCRATIC REPUBLIC
74 Avenue Raymond-Poincaré 75116 Paris
Tel: Paris 4553 0298
Ambassador Extraordinary and Plenipotentiary, HE Kamphan
Simmalavong, apptd 1995

BRITISH AMBASSADOR, HE Sir James Hodge, KCVO, CMG,
resident at Bangkok, Thailand

ECONOMY

A 'new economic mechanism' programme was introduced
in 1986 which began the liberalization of the economy,
with greater autonomy for state enterprises, the relaxation
of price controls and the encouragement of private
business and investors. These reforms have produced a
market-orientated economic system which has increased
growth and reduced inflation. The economy is dominated
by the agricultural sector, which contributed 55 per cent of
real GDP in 1996. Laos is a major producer of opium.

Although Laos is one of the poorest states in the world,
there is potential for increased hydroelectric power
exports to Thailand and there are deposits of coal, tin,
iron ore, gold, bauxite and lignite. Foreign capital investment in infrastructure began with the 1994 opening of the
Friendship Bridge over the Mekong river border with
Thailand which links road routes from Singapore to China.
Hydroelectric power is the main export, followed by
wood.

In 1995 Laos had a trade deficit of US$199 million and a
current account deficit of US$230 million. Imports totalled
US$587 million and exports US$348 million.
GNP – US$1,895 million (1996); US$400 per capita (1996)
GDP – US$990 million (1994); US$290 per capita (1994)
ANNUAL AVERAGE GROWTH OF GDP – 6.7 per cent (1996)
INFLATION RATE – 19.6 per cent (1995)
TOTAL EXTERNAL DEBT – US$2,263 million (1996)

TRADE WITH UK	1996	1997
Imports from UK	£5,264,000	£3,069,000
Exports to UK	6,988,000	6,030,000

LATVIA
The Republic of Latvia

AREA – 24,942 sq. miles (64,600 sq. km). Neighbours:
Estonia (north), Lithuania and Belarus (south), the
Russian Federation (east)
POPULATION – 2,479,870 (1997): 55.3 per cent Latvian, 32.5
per cent Russian, 4.0 per cent Belarusian, with small
Ukrainian and Polish minorities. The main religions are
Lutheran, Roman Catholic and Russian Orthodox. The
official language is Latvian; Russian is also spoken.
Education is in Latvian and Russian. Public sector
employees must pass language tests in Latvian to a level
commensurate with the nature of their employment.
The right of minorities to use their mother tongue has
been acknowledged

CAPITAL – Riga (population, 847,976, 1995)
MAJOR CITIES – Daugavpils (117,502); Jelgava (70,962);
   Jurmala (58,977); Liepaja (97,278); Ventspils (46,564)
CURRENCY – Lats of 100 santims
NATIONAL ANTHEM – Dievs, svētī Latviju (God bless
   Latvia)
NATIONAL DAY – 18 November (Independence Day
   1918)
NATIONAL FLAG – Crimson, with a white horizontal
   stripe across the centre
LIFE EXPECTANCY (years) – male 60.72; female 72.87
POPULATION GROWTH RATE – – 1.2 per cent (1995)
POPULATION DENSITY – 39 per sq. km (1995)
URBAN POPULATION – 69.1 per cent (1994)

HISTORY AND POLITICS

Latvia came under the control of the German Teutonic
Knights at the end of the 13th century. During the next few
centuries the country endured sporadic invasions by the
Swedes, Poles and Russians. By 1795 Latvia was entirely
under Russian control. On 18 November 1918, Latvia
declared its independence and this was confirmed by the
Versailles Treaty in 1919. Several years of fighting with the
new Soviet Russia ensued until a peace treaty was signed
under which Soviet Russia renounced all claims to Latvian
territory.

The Soviet Union annexed Latvia in 1940 under the
terms of the Molotov–Ribbentrop pact with Germany.
Latvia was invaded and occupied when Germany invaded
the Soviet Union during the Second World War. In 1944
the Soviet Union recaptured Latvia from Germany and
confirmed its annexation, though this was never accepted
as legal by most states.

In 1988 the Popular Front of Latvia was formed to
campaign for greater sovereignty and democracy for
Latvia. It won the elections to the Supreme Council in
1989, and on 4 May 1990 the Supreme Council declared
the independent republic of Latvia to be, *de jure*, still in
existence. Agitation in Latvia against Soviet rule led in
1990 and early 1991 to clashes between independence
supporters and Latvian Communists and the Soviet
military. Violence reached a peak in January 1991 with
deaths caused by Soviet Interior Ministry troops and
attacks on Baltic border posts. A national referendum was
held in March 1991 in which 73 per cent voted in favour of
independence, and this was declared on 21 August 1991.
The State Council of the Soviet Union recognized the
independence of Latvia on 10 September 1991.

On 25 July 1997, Prime Minister Andris Skele announced the resignation of his coalition government
following allegations of corruption. A new coalition under
Guntars Krasts was approved by 73 of the 100 members of
the *Saéima* on 7 August 1997.

POLITICAL SYSTEM

Executive authority is vested in a prime minister and
Cabinet of Ministers. Legislative power is exercised by the
unicameral parliament (*Saéima*), which comprises 100
deputies elected for four-year terms by proportional
representation, with a 5 per cent threshold for parliamentary representation. The deputies elect a president of state,
serving for three years, who in turn appoints the prime
minister. The prime minister appoints, and the Saéima
approves, the Cabinet of Ministers.

The electorate and citizenship had been restricted to
descendants of Latvian citizens before the 1940 Soviet
occupation and to those who could pass the required
Latvian language tests, until 1994 when a law was passed
enabling naturalization of long-term residents.

HEAD OF STATE
President, Guntis Ulmanis, *elected* 7 July 1993, *re-elected* 18
   June 1996

COUNCIL OF MINISTERS *as at June 1998*
Prime Minister, Guntars Krasts (TB)
*Deputy PM, Environmental Protection and Regional
   Development*, Anatolijs Gorbunovs (LC)
Agriculture, Andris Rāvinš (LZS)
Culture, Ramona Umblija (TB)
Defence, Tālavs Jundzis (KDS)
Economy, Laimonis Strujevičs (LZS)
Education and Science, Jānis Gaigals (LC)
Finance, Roberts Zīle (TB)
Foreign Affairs, Valdis Birkavs (LC)
Interior, Andrejs Krastinš (NRP)
Justice, Dzintars Rasnačs (TB)
Transport, Vilis Krištopāns (LC)
Welfare, Vladimirs Makarovs (TB)

TB For Fatherland and Freedom; LZS Latvia's Farmers'
Union; KDS Christian Democratic Union; LC Latvia's
Way; NRP National Reform Party

EMBASSY OF THE REPUBLIC OF LATVIA
45 Nottingham Place, London WIM 3FE
Tel 0171-312 0040
Ambassador Extraordinary and Plenipotentiary, HE Normans
   Penke, apptd 1997

BRITISH EMBASSY
5, Alunana Iela Street, Riga LV1010
Tel: Riga 733 8126
Ambassador Extraordinary and Plenipotentiary, HE Nicholas
   R. Jarrold, apptd 1996

BRITISH COUNCIL DIRECTOR, I. Stewart, 5a Blaumana
   iela 3, Riga LV-1010

DEFENCE

The Army has 13 armoured personnel carriers and 24
artillery pieces, the Navy has 13 patrol craft at two bases
and the Air Force has two aircraft and five helicopters.

All remaining Russian forces withdrew from Latvia on
31 August 1994 except for those stationed at the anti-
ballistic missile early-warning radar at Skrunda, which will
continue to operate until 1999.
MILITARY EXPENDITURE – 2.6 per cent of GDP (1996)
MILITARY PERSONNEL – 8,100: Army 3,400, Navy 980, Air
   Force 120, Paramilitaries 3,600
CONSCRIPTION DURATION – 12 months

ECONOMY

Attempts to move from a command economy to a market
economy resulted in low growth and high unemployment
in the early 1990s, though economic reforms have begun to
show results. The government has initiated a privatization
process which has made many industrial facilities available
for purchase both by Latvian and foreign private investors.
The privatization of state industries will be complete by
the end of 1998.

Latvia is an agricultural exporter, specializing in cattle
and pig breeding, dairy farming and crops, including sugar
beet, flax, cereals and potatoes. Natural resources include
limestone, gypsum, peat and timber.

Industry is specialized in certain areas including the
production of food and beverages, motor vehicles, textiles
and timber and paper products.

Tourism is being developed, capitalizing on Latvia's
beach resorts, nature reserves and parks. Latvia is also

geographically well-placed for the development of transport services.

GNP – US$5,730 million (1996); US$2,300 per capita (1996)

GDP – US$9,370 million (1994); US$1,173 per capita (1994)

ANNUAL AVERAGE GROWTH OF GDP – 2.8 per cent (1996)

INFLATION RATE – 17.6 per cent (1996)

UNEMPLOYMENT – 6.6 per cent (1995)

TOTAL EXTERNAL DEBT – US$472 million (1996)

TRADE

In 1997, 48.9 per cent of Latvia's exports were to EU states, compared to 19.7 per cent to the CIS. In 1996, a free trade regime was agreed with the EU and EFTA. The main imports are oil and energy, and the main exports are wood and wood products, artificial fibres, meat and dairy products.

In 1996 there was a trade deficit of US$927 million and a current account deficit of US$454 million. Imports totalled US$2,311 million and exports US$1,424 million.

Trade with UK	1996	1997
Imports from UK	£78,986,000	£86,828,000
Exports to UK	307,121,000	346,686,000

COMMUNICATIONS

Latvia has 2,413 km of railways and some 20,300 km of roads, of which 18,800 km is hard-surfaced. Many of the exports from former CIS states are transported to Western Europe via Latvia. Latvia is also being developed as a transportation route from Scandinavia to central and southern Europe. Several warm-water ports exist, of which three, Riga, Ventspils and Liepaja, are developed for commercial transport. The national airline, Latvijas Aviolinijas, operates regular flights to Russia, Scandinavia and Europe. 531,000 people came through the international airport in Riga in 1997.

CULTURE AND EDUCATION

The Latvian language belongs to the Baltic branch of the Indo-European languages, and as such is distinct from Russian. The Latin alphabet is used. Independent Latvian literature appeared in the late 18th and early 19th centuries and played a role in the fight for independence in 1918.

There are 17 higher education institutions, of which four are universities.

ILLITERACY RATE – 0.3 per cent

ENROLMENT (percentage of age group) – primary 84 per cent (1995); secondary 78 per cent (1995); tertiary 25.7 per cent (1995)

LEBANON
Al-Jumhouriya al-Lubnaniya

AREA – 4,015 sq. miles (10,400 sq. km). Neighbours: Syria (north and east), Israel (south)

POPULATION – 3,009,000 (1994 UN estimate): 30 per cent Christian, 6 per cent Druze, 4 per cent Armenian. Arabic is the official language, and French and English are also widely used

CAPITAL – ΨBeirut (population, 1,500,000, 1991)

MAJOR CITIES – ΨSidon (100,000); ΨTripoli (200,000); ΨTyre (70,000)

CURRENCY – Lebanese pound (L£) of 100 piastres

NATIONAL ANTHEM – Kulluna Lil Watan Lil'ula Lil'alam (We all belong to the homeland)

NATIONAL DAY – 22 November

NATIONAL FLAG – Horizontal bands of red, white and red with a green cedar of Lebanon in the centre of the white band

LIFE EXPECTANCY (years) – male 66.60; female 70.50

POPULATION GROWTH RATE – 3.3 per cent (1995)

POPULATION DENSITY – 289 per sq. km (1995)

HISTORY AND POLITICS

Lebanon has some important historical remains, notably Baalbek (Heliopolis) which contains the ruins of first- to third-century Roman temples and Jbeil (Byblos), one of the oldest continuously inhabited towns in the world, and ancient Tyre.

Lebanon became an independent state in 1920, administered under French mandate until 22 November 1943. Powers were transferred to the Lebanese government from January 1944 and French troops were withdrawn in 1946.

In 1975, fighting broke out in Beirut between Maronite, Sunni and Shia factions. In 1976 the Arab Deterrent Forces, composed mainly of Syrian troops, imposed a cease-fire but fighting resumed and continued until the end of the civil war in 1990. In 1978 Israeli forces invaded but withdrew some months later, handing over their positions, except for a belt in the south, to the UN Interim Force in Lebanon (UNIFIL). In 1982 Israeli forces again invaded, penetrating as far as Beirut. Although the bulk of Israeli troops withdrew from southern Lebanon in 1985, a buffer zone controlled by the Israeli-backed South Lebanon Army (SLA), a Christian militia, was established along the Israeli–Lebanon border. Syrian forces are deployed in west Beirut and in the north and the east of the country.

The Taif Accord 'for national conciliation', drawn up by an Arab League-appointed committee, gained the approval of most Lebanese MPs in 1989, but was resisted by Gen. Aoun, who insisted on an immediate withdrawal of the 35,000 Syrian troops in Lebanon. The Lebanese government with the backing of Syrian troops ousted Gen. Aoun in October 1990 and a new government incorporating the main militia leaders was formed in December 1990. Since then the government has attempted to clear the militias from the Greater Beirut area and restore its authority throughout most of the country. The Beqa'a valley remains under Syrian control and the South Lebanon Security Zone under Israeli control. All militias have been disarmed apart from Hezbollah and the SLA. Since 1993 the Lebanese Army has deployed in southern villages alongside UNIFIL forces but has not disarmed Hezbollah forces, who are financed, armed and trained by Syria and Iran to continue fighting against Israel and the SLA.

Low-level fighting continued throughout 1993–8. In April 1996, Israel began a two-week missile bombardment of Hezbollah targets in Beirut and southern Lebanon. The mission, code-named 'Grapes of Wrath', was in retaliation for suicide attacks and Hezbollah strikes against Israel's northern cities. An agreement was reached on 15 April to confine hostilities to southern Lebanon.

The first parliamentary elections since 1972 were held between August and October 1992. The 128-seat National Assembly was directly elected by universal suffrage and divided equally between Christians and Muslims. The polls were widely boycotted in Christian areas because of the continuing presence of Syrian troops, in breach of the Taif Accord. A government was formed under Prime Minister Rafiq Al-Hariri in October 1992 which has focused on the economy and reconstruction. National

Assembly elections were held in August and September 1996, and the first local elections for 35 years were held in May and June 1998.

POLITICAL SYSTEM

The National Covenant (1943) is characterized by the division of power between the religious communities. The executive comprises the president, prime minister and Cabinet. The president is elected by the National Assembly for a non-renewable term of six years and must be a Maronite Christian. The prime minister is appointed following consultation between the president and National Assembly and must be a Sunni Muslim. The 128-member unicameral National Assembly comprises equal numbers of Christians and Muslims although the speaker must be a Shia Muslim. Political parties are banned. There are six governorates divided into 26 districts.

HEAD OF STATE

President of the Republic of Lebanon, Elias Hrawi, *took office* 25 November 1989 (term extended by three years by National Assembly on 19 October 1995)

CABINET *as at July 1998*

Prime Minister, Posts and Telecommunications, Finance, Rafiq al-Hariri
Deputy PM, Interior, Michel al-Murr
Administrative Reform, Besharah Merhej
Agriculture, Chawki Fakhouri
Culture and Higher Education, Fawzi Hobeish
Economy and Trade, Yassine Jaber
Environment, Akram Chehayeb
Expatriates, Talal Arslan
Foreign Affairs, Fares Boueiz
Housing and Co-operatives, Mahmoud Abou Hamdan
Industry, Nadim Salem
Information, Basem al-Sabaa
Justice, Bahij Tabbarah
Labour, Asaad Hardan
Ministers of State, Fouad Siniora *(Financial Affairs);* Nadim Salem *(Industrial Affairs);* Michel Eddé; Elias Hanne; Ghazi Seifeddine
Municipalities and Rural Affairs, Hagop Yarwan Damarjian
National Defence, Mohsein Dalloul
National Education, Jean Obeid
Oil, Shahi Barsoumian
Public Health, Sleiman Franjieh
Public Works, Ali Harajli
Refugee Affairs, Walid Jumblatt
Social Affairs, Ayoub Hmayed
Tourism, Nicholas Fattouch
Transport, Omar Meskaoui
Vocational and Technical Education, Farouk al-Barbir
Water and Electricity Resources, Elias Hobeika

LEBANESE EMBASSY

21 Kensington Palace Gardens, London W8 4QM
Tel 0171–229 7265/6
Ambassador Extraordinary and Plenipotentiary, HE Mahmoud Hammoud, apptd 1990

BRITISH EMBASSY

Autostrade Jal El Dib, Coolrite Building (PO Box 60180), Beirut
Tel: Beirut 406330
Ambassador Extraordinary and Plenipotentiary, HE David MacLennan, apptd 1996

BRITISH COUNCIL DIRECTOR, A. Malamah-Thomas, MBE, Sidani Street, Fawzi Azar Building, Beirut

DEFENCE

The Army has 315 main battle tanks, 895 armoured personnel carriers and 153 artillery pieces. The Navy has 14 patrol and coastal vessels at three bases. The Air Force has three combat aircraft and four armed helicopters.

There are a 4,468-strong UN peacekeeping force, 30,000 Syrian troops and 150 Iranian Revolutionary Guards operating in Lebanon.

MILITARY EXPENDITURE – 3.7 per cent of GDP (1996)
MILITARY PERSONNEL – 68,100: Army 53,300, Navy 1,000, Air Force 800, Paramilitaries 13,000
CONSCRIPTION DURATION – 12 months

ECONOMY

Fruits are the most important products and include citrus fruit, apples, grapes, bananas and olives. There is some light industry, mostly for the production of consumer goods, but most factories are still in need of reconstruction because of the civil war.

A ten-year plan has been initiated to repair war damage and to restore Lebanon's position as a regional financial services and light industrial centre. The 1993–2002 reconstruction plan is estimated to cost US$12,900 million, of which US$7,600 million is to come from foreign loans and grants and US$5,300 million from budget surpluses. It is to concentrate on rebuilding housing, transport, services, education and health services, and aiding industry and agriculture.

A plan to reconstruct the commercial centre of Beirut has been started, with the issue in January 1994 of US$650 million of shares in the US$1,800 million Solidère company which will reconstruct the 400-acre site. The government has also obtained US$1,600 million in loans and grants for its national reconstruction programme, mainly from Arab states and international agencies.

GNP – US$12,118 million (1996); US$2,970 per capita (1996)
GDP – US$4,977 million (1994); US$1,692 per capita (1994)
INFLATION RATE – 6.8 per cent (1994)
TOTAL EXTERNAL DEBT – US$3,996 million (1996)

TRADE

Principal imports are gold and precious metals, machinery and electrical equipment, textiles and yarns, vegetable products, iron and steel goods, and motor vehicles. There had been a gradual decline in the overall amount of imports as a result of continued instability. A free trade agreement with Syria will be phased in from 1999.

Principal exports include gold and precious metals, fruits and vegetables, textiles, building materials, furniture, plastic goods, foodstuffs, tobacco and wine.

At one time there was a considerable transit trade through Beirut into the Arab hinterland. Lebanon is the terminal for two oil pipelines, one formerly belonging to the Iraq Petroleum Company, debouching at Tripoli, the other belonging to the Trans Arabian Pipeline Company, at Sidon. These lines have not functioned for some years.

In 1996 imports totalled US$7,582 million and exports US$1,017 million.

Trade with UK	1996	1997
Imports from UK	£173,766,000	£191,206,000
Exports to UK	12,200,000	16,876,000

COMMUNICATIONS

The railways are not functioning as a result of the civil war. There is an international airport at Beirut, served by the national carrier Middle East Airlines and other airlines. An internal service operates from Beirut to Tripoli.

EDUCATION

There are six universities in Beirut, the American and the French universities, and the Lebanese National University, the Beirut University College, the Kaslik Saint Esprit University and the Arab University, with the University of Balamand situated near Tripoli. There are several institutions for vocational training, and there is a good provision throughout the country of primary and secondary schools, among which are a great number of private schools.
ILLITERACY RATE – 7.6 per cent
ENROLMENT (percentage of age group) – tertiary 27.0 per cent (1995)

LESOTHO
'Muso oa Lesotho

AREA – 11,720 sq. miles (30,355 sq. km). Neighbour: South Africa, which completely surrounds Lesotho
POPULATION – 2,050,000 (1994 UN estimate). The languages are Sesotho and English
CAPITAL – Maseru (population, 288,951, 1986)
CURRENCY – Loti (M) of 100 lisente. The South African rand is also legal tender
NATIONAL ANTHEM – Pina ea Sechaba
NATIONAL DAY – 4 October (Independence Day)
NATIONAL FLAG – Diagonally white over blue over green with the white of double width, and an assegai and knobkerrie on a Basotho shield in brown in the upper hoist
LIFE EXPECTANCY (years) – male 58.00; female 63.00
POPULATION GROWTH RATE – 2.7 per cent (1995)
POPULATION DENSITY – 68 per sq. km (1995)
MILITARY EXPENDITURE – 3.3 per cent of GDP (1996)
MILITARY PERSONNEL – 2,000 Army

HISTORY AND POLITICS

Lesotho (formerly Basutoland) became a constitutional monarchy within the Commonwealth on 4 October 1966. The independence constitution was suspended in 1970 and the country was governed by a Council of Ministers headed by Leabua Jonathan until the establishment of a National Assembly in 1974.

Jonathan's government was overthrown in 1986, and executive and legislative powers were conferred on the King, to be advised by the Military Council and Council of Ministers led by Maj.-Gen. Justin Lekhanya. In March 1990, King Moshoeshoe II's powers were formally revoked and in November the King was deposed and replaced by his son, who assumed the title of Letsie III. Maj.-Gen. Lekhanya was overthrown in 1991 in a coup led by Col. Elias Ramaema. Elections were held in March 1993 and the Basotho Congress Party (BCP) won all 65 seats in the new National Assembly. A BCP government led by Ntsu Mokhele was formed, King Letsie III swore allegiance to a new multiparty democratic constitution and the Military Council was dissolved.

On 17 August 1994 King Letsie III and sections of the military mounted a coup attempt and announced the dismissal of the government and the dissolution of parliament. After mediation, the government, which had refused to leave office, was restored by the King. King Letsie also announced his intention to abdicate in favour of his father, Moshoeshoe II, who was restored on 25 January 1995.

When King Moshoeshoe II died in a car crash on 15 January 1996, King Letsie III again ascended to the throne.

The country is divided into ten administrative districts. In each district there is a district secretary who co-ordinates all government activity in the area, working in co-operation with hereditary chiefs. At the last legislative elections in May 1998, the Lesotho Congress for Democracy won 78 of the 80 seats in the National Assembly.

HEAD OF STATE
HM *The King of Lesotho*, King Letsie III, *acceded* February 1996, *crowned* 31 October 1997

COUNCIL OF MINISTERS *as at July 1998*
Prime Minister, Defence, Public Service, Bethuel Pakalitha Mosisili
Agriculture, Co-operatives, Kelebone Albert Maope
Education, Manpower Development, Lesao Lehohla
Environment, Women, Youth Affairs, Mamoshebi Kabi
Finance and Development Planning, Leketekete Ketso
Foreign Affairs, Tom Thabane
Health and Social Welfare, Vova Bulane
Home Affairs, Local Government, Mopshatla Mabitle
Industry, Trade and Marketing, Mpho Malie
Information, Broadcasting, Post and Telecommunications, Nyane Mphafi
Justice, Human Rights, Law and Constitutional Affairs, Sephiri Motanyane
Labour and Employment, Not'si Molopo
Natural Resources, Monyane Moleleki
Prime Minister's Office, Mofelehetsi Moerane
Tourism, Sport and Culture, Hlalele Motaung
Works and Transport, Shakhane Robong Mokhehle

HIGH COMMISSION FOR THE KINGDOM OF LESOTHO
7 Chesham Place, London SW1 8HN
Tel 0171-235 5686
High Commissioner, HE Benjamin Masilo, apptd 1996

BRITISH HIGH COMMISSION
PO Box 521, Maseru 100
Tel: Maseru 313961
High Commissioner, HE Peter J. Smith, OBE, apptd 1996

BRITISH COUNCIL REPRESENTATIVE, S. Cweba, Hobson's Square, PO Box 429, Maseru 100

ECONOMY

The economy is based on agriculture and animal husbandry, and the adverse balance of trade (mainly consumer and capital goods) is offset by the earnings of the large numbers of the population who work in South Africa. Apart from some diamonds, Lesotho has few natural resources. Agriculture contributes 15 per cent of GDP and the main crops are maize, sorghum and vegetables. The Lesotho National Development Corporation was set up to promote the development of industry, mining, trade and tourism; a number of light manufacturing and processing industries have recently been established. The main sources of revenue are customs and excise duty.

In 1994 Lesotho had a trade deficit of US$667 million and a current account surplus of US$108 million.
GNP – US$1,331 million (1996); US$660 per capita (1996)
GDP – US$684 million (1994); US$424 per capita (1994)
TOTAL EXTERNAL DEBT – US$654 million (1996)

TRADE WITH UK	1996	1997
Imports from UK	£1,864,000	£4,847,000
Exports to UK	60,000	105,000

COMMUNICATIONS

A tarred road links Maseru to several of the main lowland towns, and this is being extended in the south of the country. The mountainous areas are linked by tarred, gravelled and earth roads and tracks. Roads link border towns in South Africa with the main towns in Lesotho. Maseru is also connected by rail with the main Bloemfontein–Natal line of the South African Railways. Scheduled international air services are operated daily between Maseru and Johannesburg, and other scheduled international flights are to Gaborone, Harare, Manzini and Maputo. There are around 30 airstrips. Internal scheduled services are operated by the Lesotho Airways Corporation.

The telephone network is fully automated in all urban centres. Radio telephone communication is used extensively in the remote rural areas.

EDUCATION

Most schools are mission-controlled, the government providing grants for salaries and buildings. There are over 1,000 primary and over 100 secondary schools, with emphasis being laid on agricultural and vocational education. The National University of Lesotho at Roma was established as a university in 1975.

ILLITERACY RATE – 28.7 per cent
ENROLMENT (percentage of age group) – primary 65 per cent (1994); secondary 16 per cent (1994); tertiary 2.4 per cent (1994)

LIBERIA
Republic of Liberia

AREA – 43,000 sq. miles (111,369 sq. km). Neighbours: Guinea (north), Côte d'Ivoire (east), Sierra Leone (north-west)
POPULATION – 2,760,000 (1994 UN estimate). The official language is English. The main African languages are Bassa, Kpelle and Kru, though some 16 ethnic languages are spoken
CAPITAL – ΨMonrovia (population, 421,053, 1984)
MAJOR CITIES – ΨBuchanan (Grand Bassa); ΨGreenville (Sinoe); ΨHarper (Cape Palmas)
CURRENCY – Liberian dollar (L$) of 100 cents
NATIONAL ANTHEM – All Hail, Liberia, Hail
NATIONAL DAY – 26 July
NATIONAL FLAG – Alternate horizontal stripes (five white, six red), with five-pointed white star on blue field in upper corner next to flagstaff
LIFE EXPECTANCY (years) – male 45.80; female 44.00
POPULATION GROWTH RATE – 2.7 per cent (1995)
POPULATION DENSITY – 25 per sq. km (1995)
URBAN POPULATION – 44.6 per cent (1995)
MILITARY EXPENDITURE – 3.5 per cent of GDP (1996)
ILLITERACY RATE – 61.7 per cent

HISTORY AND POLITICS

Liberia was founded by the American Colonization Society in 1822 as a colony for freed American slaves, and has been recognized since 1847 as an independent state.

William V. S. Tubman, President since 1944, died in 1971 and was succeeded by Dr Tolbert. The constitution was suspended following a military coup in 1980 during which Tolbert was killed. M/Sgt. Samuel Doe assumed power as chairman of a military council. A new constitution was endorsed by a referendum in 1984. Doe and his party, the National Democratic Party of Liberia (NDPL)

won the elections held in 1985, amid allegations of electoral fraud, and a civilian government was formally installed in 1986.

CIVIL WAR

A rebel incursion in 1989 by the National Patriotic Front of Liberia (NPFL) led by Charles Taylor developed into a full-scale civil war in 1990. A five-nation ECOWAS peacekeeping force (known as ECOMOG) landed in Monrovia in an effort to end the conflict but in September 1990 President Doe was killed, having refused to step down.

The Interim Government of National Unity (IGNU) was formed in August 1990 in The Gambia and arrived in Monrovia in November. An agreement to establish a cease-fire and confine troops to barracks under ECOMOG supervision broke down in October 1992 when the NPFL attempted to seize Monrovia. In response ECOMOG assumed a more offensive role, driving NPFL forces out of Monrovia's suburbs. By March 1993 the NPFL had been driven into eastern parts of Liberia and peace negotiations between the warring factions had begun. A peace agreement was signed by the IGNU, NPFL and another rebel group, ULIMO, on 25 July 1993 which brought about a cease-fire on 1 August. Interim President Amos Sawyer was due to be replaced within one month by a five-member Council of State to govern the country during a transitional period, together with a 35-member transitional legislature including members from all three factions. The Council of State and legislature did not take power until March 1994 and the transitional government of IGNU, NPFL and ULIMO members not until May 1994.

Continued fighting and the fracturing of the three factions led to further negotiations and an agreement in December 1994 on a new Council of State. A Council of State comprising the faction leaders was inaugurated on 1 September 1995 and a transitional government formed. Fighting resumed briefly in April 1996, although a cease-fire in July 1996 enabled elections to be held in July 1997. Legislative elections were won by the NPFL, and Charles Taylor was elected president with 75 per cent of the vote in elections deemed free and fair by international observers. The ECOMOG mandate expired in February 1998.

HEAD OF STATE

President, Charles Taylor, *elected* 19 July 1997, *inaugurated* 3 August 1997
Vice-President, Enoch Dogolea Junior

CABINET *as at July 1998*

Agriculture, Roland Massaquoi
Commerce, Ibrahim Kaba
Defence, Daniel Chea
Education, Evelyne Kandakai
Finance, Elias Saleeby
Foreign Affairs, Monie Captan
Forestry Development Authority, Bob Taylor
Health and Social Welfare, Peter Coleman
Information, Culture and Tourism, Joe Mulbah
Interior, Edward Sackor
Junior Legal Adviser to the President, James Teah
Justice, Eddington Varmah
Labour, Thomas Woewiyu
Land, Mines, Energy, Jenkins Dunbar
Liberia Electricity Corporation, Samuel Burnette
Liberia Telecommunications Corporation, Charles Roberts
Maritime Affairs Commissioner, Benoni Uray
Minister of State for Presidential Affairs, T. Ernest Eastman
Minister of State Without Portfolio, Augustine Zayzay
National Bank Governor, Charles Bright

Planning and Economic Affairs, Amelia Ward
Post and Telecommunications, Maxwell Kaba
Press Secretary, Reginald Goodrich
Public Works, John Richardson
Rural Development, Roosevelt Johnson
Transport, Larmin Kawah
Youth and Sports, François Massaquoi

EMBASSY OF THE REPUBLIC OF LIBERIA
2 Pembridge Place, London W2 4XB
Tel 0171-221 1036
Minister-Counsellor, Chargé d'Affaires, Ishmael Grant

BRITISH AMBASSADOR, HE Haydon Warren-Gash, resident
at Abidjan, Côte d'Ivoire

ECONOMY

Before the civil war began principal exports were iron ore,
crude rubber, timber, uncut diamonds, palm kernels, cocoa
and coffee, but the civil war has resulted in the suspension
of most economic activity.
GDP – US$1,442 million (1994); US$718 per capita (1994)
ANNUAL AVERAGE GROWTH OF GDP – 2.7 per cent (1987)
INFLATION RATE – 9.1 per cent (1989)
TOTAL EXTERNAL DEBT – US$2,107 million (1996)

	1996	1997
TRADE WITH UK		
Imports from UK	£6,095,000	£12,677,000
Exports to UK	11,707,000	318,000

COMMUNICATIONS

The artificial harbour and free port of Monrovia was
opened in 1948. There are nine ports of entry, including
three river ports. Robertsfield International Airport is
under NPFL control and not yet in use. Spriggs Payne
airfield, on the outskirts of Monrovia, normally used for
internal flights, is currently being used for flights to other
West African countries.

LIBYA
Al-Jamahiriya Al-Arabiya
Al-Libiya Al-Shabiya Al-Ishtirakiya Al-Uthma

AREA – 679,362 sq. miles (1,759,540 sq. km). Neighbours:
  Egypt and Sudan (east), Chad and Niger (south), Algeria
  and Tunisia (west)
POPULATION – 5,407,000 (1994 UN estimate). The people
  of Libya are principally Arab with some Berbers in the
  west and some Tuareg tribesmen in the Fezzan. Islam is
  the official religion but other religions are tolerated. The
  official language is Arabic
CAPITAL – ΨTripoli (population, 1,000,000, 1991
  estimate)
MAJOR CITIES – ΨBenghazi (500,000); ΨMisurata
  (200,000); Sirte (100,000)
CURRENCY – Libyan dinar (LD) of 1,000 dirhams
NATIONAL DAY – 1 September
NATIONAL FLAG – Libya uses a plain emerald green flag
LIFE EXPECTANCY (years) – male 61.58; female 65.00
POPULATION DENSITY – 3 per sq. km (1995)
ILLITERACY RATE – 23.8 per cent
ENROLMENT (percentage of age group) – primary 97 per
  cent (1992); secondary 62 per cent (1980); tertiary 16.4
  per cent (1991)

Vast sand and rock deserts, almost completely barren,
occupy the greater part of Libya. The southern part of the
country lies within the Sahara Desert. There are few rivers

and as rainfall is irregular outside parts of Cyrenaica and
Tripolitania, good harvests are rare.
   The ancient ruins in Cyrenaica, at Cyrene, Ptolemais
(Tolmeta) and Apollonia, are outstanding, as are those at
Leptis Magna, 70 miles east, and at Sabratha, 40 miles west
of Tripoli. An Italian expedition found in the south-west of
the Fezzan a series of rock-paintings more than 5,000 years
old.

HISTORY AND POLITICS

From the 16th century Libya was dominated by the
Ottoman Empire, until occupied by Italy in 1911–12 in the
course of the Italo-Turkish War. Under the 1912 Treaty of
Ouchy, sovereignty over the province was transferred by
Turkey to Italy, and in 1939 the four provinces of Libya
(Tripoli, Misurata, Benghazi and Derna) were incorporated in the national territory of Italy as *Libia Italiana.* After
the Second World War Tripolitania and Cyrenaica were
placed provisionally under British and the Fezzan under
French administration, and in conformity with a resolution
of the UN General Assembly in 1949, Libya became on 24
December 1951 the first independent state to be created by
the UN. The monarchy was overthrown by a revolution in
1969 and the country was declared a republic. It was ruled
by the Revolutionary Command Council (RCC) under
the leadership of Col. Muammar al-Gadhafi.
   In 1977, a new form of direct democracy, the 'Jamahiriya' (state of the masses) was promulgated and the official
name of the country was changed to Socialist People's
Libyan Arab Jamahiriya. Since a reorganization in 1979,
neither Col. Gadhafi nor his former RCC colleagues have
held formal posts in the administration. Gadhafi continues
to hold the ceremonial title 'Leader of the Revolution'.

POLITICAL SYSTEM

At local level authority is vested in about 1,500 Basic and 14
Municipal People's Congresses which appoint Popular
Committees to execute policy. Officials of these congresses and committees, together with representatives from
unions and other organizations, form the General People's
Congress, which normally meets for about a week each
year. In addition, a number of extraordinary sessions are
held throughout the year. This is the highest policy-
making body in the country.
   The General People's Congress appoints its own General Secretariat and the General People's Committee,
whose members head the government departments which
execute policy at national level. The Secretary of the
General People's Committee has functions similar to those
of a prime minister.

*Leader of the Revolution and Supreme Commander of the Armed
  Forces,* Col. Muammar al-Gadhafi

SECRETARIAT OF THE GENERAL PEOPLE'S CONGRESS *as at
  July 1998*
Secretary, Affairs of People's Committees, Al Baghdadi Ali Al
  Mahmoudi
Secretary, Foreign Affairs, Abdel Rahman Shalgam
Secretary, Trade Unions, Abdallah Idris Ibrahim
Speaker, Al Zenati Mohammad Al Zenati
Assistant Secretaries, Ahmed Mohamed Ibrahim (*Affairs of
  People's Congresses);* Noura Han Abu-Sefrian (*Women's
  Affairs);* Abd Al-Hameed Al Saed Al Zentani

GENERAL PEOPLE'S COMMITTEE (CABINET)
Secretary (Premier), Mohammad Ahmed al-Manqoush
Agriculture, Mohamed Ali ben Ramadhan
Animal Resources, Masoud Said Abu Souwah
Arab Unity, Gumaa al-Mahdi al-Fazzani

Communications and Transport, Izzidin Mohamed al-Hinshiri
Economy and Trade, Abdel Hafez Mahmoud al-Zelinti
Education and Scientific Research, Al-Mahdi Muftah Embresh
Energy, Abdallah Salem al-Badri
Finance, Mohammad Abdallah Beit al-Mal
Foreign Liaison and International Co-operation, Omar Mustafa al-Muntasser
Formation and Training, Maatoug Mohamed Maatoug
General Provisional Committee for Defence, Abu Bakr Jaber Yunes
Great Man-made River Project, Abd al-Majad al-Qa'ud
Housing and Utilities, Mubarak Abdallah al-Shamikh
Industry and Mines, Muftah Ali Azouza
Information, Culture and Jamahiri Mobilization, Fawziya Basheer Shalabi
Justice, Mohamed Abu al-Gasem al-Zowi
Maritime Resources, Bashir Ramadhan
Planning, Jadallah Azouz al-Talahi
Public Accounting and Control, Abdul Rahman al-Abbar
Public Security, Maj.-Gen. Mohamed Mahmoud al-Hijazi
Social Security, Suleimon al-Ghamari Abdallah
Tourism, al-Bokhari Salem Houda
Youth and Jamahiri Sports, Ali Mursi al-Shaeri

LIBYAN DIPLOMATIC MISSION IN LONDON
Since the break of diplomatic relations with Libya in April 1984, the Royal Embassy of Saudi Arabia has handled Libyan interests in Britain.
Head of Interests Section, Isa Baruni Edaeki

BRITISH EMBASSY
British interests are currently handled by the British Interests Section of the Italian Embassy, Sharia Uahran 1 (PO Box 4206), Tripoli.
Head of Interests Section, D. G. Ward

DEFENCE
The Army has 2,210 main battle tanks, 1,990 armoured infantry fighting vehicles and armoured personnel carriers, and 1,170 artillery pieces. The Navy has four submarines, three frigates, 36 patrol and coastal vessels, and 32 armed helicopters at six bases. The Air Force has 420 combat aircraft and 52 armed helicopters.

Libya is alleged to have built at least one chemical weapons plant. The USA claims that a plant at Rabta, closed in 1990, was reopened in 1995, and that a plant has been constructed near Tahunah, south of Tripoli.

As part of the UN economic sanctions imposed in April 1992, there is a total embargo on arms sales to Libya.
MILITARY EXPENDITURE – 1.8 per cent of GDP (1996)
MILITARY PERSONNEL – 65,000: Army 35,000, Navy 8,000, Air Force 22,000
CONSCRIPTION DURATION – Selective conscription, one to two years

ECONOMY
Economic sanctions were imposed on Libya in April 1992 by the UN Security Council following Libya's failure to hand over two suspects in the bombing of Pan-Am flight 103 over Lockerbie, Scotland, in 1988. The UN imposed additional sanctions in December 1993, including freezing assets abroad and restricting imports of spare parts and equipment for the oil and aviation sectors. All the sanctions remain in place and are renewed every 120 days. The USA also enacted legislation in July 1996 penalizing foreign companies that invest more than £26 million a year in Libya's energy sector.

Agriculture is confined mainly to the coastal areas of Tripolitania and Cyrenaica, where barley, wheat, olives, almonds, citrus fruits and dates are produced, and to the areas of the oases, many of which are well supplied with springs supporting small fertile areas. Among the important oases are Jaghbub, Ghadames, Jofra, Sebha, Murzuq, Brak, Ghat, Jalo and the Kufra group in the south-east.

The main industry is oil and gas production. There are pipelines from Zelten to the terminal at Mersa Brega, from Dahra to Ras-es-Sider, from Amal to Ras Lanuf, and from the Intisar field to Zuetina. In 1995, 66.6 million tonnes of crude oil was produced. A major petrochemical complex has been built at Ras Lanuf. The construction of an iron and steel plant at Misurata has been completed. Economic constraints have delayed some projects, particularly since Libya decided in 1983 to go ahead with a major irrigation scheme, the 'Great Man-Made River'.

Libya has technical assistance agreements with a number of countries, and also employs large numbers of foreign labourers and experts.
GDP – US$29,274 million (1994); US$4,220 per capita (1994)

TRADE
Exports are dominated by crude oil, but some wool, cattle, sheep and horses, olive oil, and hides and skins are also exported. Principal imports are foodstuffs, including sugar, tea and coffee, and most construction materials and consumer goods. After the revolution the private sector was virtually eliminated and Libya became a state trading country with imports controlled by state monopolies. Since reforms in 1988, however, a small private sector has been re-established.

Trade with UK	1996	1997
Imports from UK	£248,818,000	£268,959,000
Exports to UK	150,380,000	231,403,000

COMMUNICATIONS
The coastal road running from the Tunisian frontier through Tripoli to Benghazi, Tobruk and the Egyptian border serves the main population centres. Main roads also link the provincial centres, and the oil-producing areas of the south with the coastal towns.

There are airports at Tripoli and Benghazi (Benina), Tobruk, Mersa Brega, Sebha, Ghadames and Kufra regularly used by commercial airlines. Since April 1992 a UN embargo on air links with Libya has been in force.

LIECHTENSTEIN
Fürstentum Liechtenstein

AREA – 62 sq. miles (160 sq. km). Neighbours: Austria, Switzerland
POPULATION – 31,000 (1994 UN estimate). The language of the principality is German
CAPITAL – Vaduz (population, 5,072, 1993)
CURRENCY – Swiss franc of 100 rappen (or centimes)
NATIONAL ANTHEM – Oben am Jungen Rhein (High on the Rhine)
NATIONAL DAY – 15 August
NATIONAL FLAG – Equal horizontal bands of blue over red; gold crown on blue band near staff
LIFE EXPECTANCY (years) – male 66.07; female 72.94
POPULATION GROWTH RATE – 1.3 per cent (1995)
POPULATION DENSITY – 194 per sq. km (1995)

HISTORY AND POLITICS

The Principality of Liechtenstein was established by Emperor Charles VI in 1719. Following the First World War, Liechtenstein severed its ties with Austria and began its association with Switzerland, taking up the Swiss currency in 1921.

The Patriotic Union and Progressive Citizens' parties have governed the country in coalition since 1938. There is a threshold of 8 per cent for parties to gain representation in the Landtag. At the general election on 31 January and 2 February 1997 the Patriotic Union won 13 seats, Progressive Citizens' Party 11, and Free List 2. The Patriotic Union is the first government to face an opposition since 1938.

HEAD OF STATE

HSH The Prince of Liechtenstein, Hans Adam II, *born* 14 February 1945; *succeeded* 13 November 1989; *married* 30 July 1967, Countess Marie Kinsky; and has *issue*: Prince Alois (*see* below); Prince Maximilian, *b.* 16 May 1969; Prince Constantin, *b.* 15 March 1972; Princess Tatjana, *b.* 10 April 1973

Heir, HSH Prince Alois, *b.* 11 June 1968, *married* 1993 Duchess Sophie of Bavaria; and has *issue*: Prince Wenzel, *b.* 24 May 1995

MINISTRY *as at July 1998*

Prime Minister, Finance, Construction, Mario Frick
Education, Environment, Transport, Norbert Marxer
Foreign Affairs, Family and Equal Opportunities, Culture and Sport, Andrea Willi
Internal Affairs, Economy, Health and Welfare, Michael Ritter
Justice, Heinz Frommelt

DIPLOMATIC REPRESENTATION

Liechtenstein is represented in diplomatic and consular matters in the United Kingdom by the Swiss Embassy.

BRITISH AMBASSADOR, Christopher Hulse, CMG, resident at Berne, Switzerland

ECONOMY

The main industries are high and ultra-high vacuum engineering, the semiconductor industry, roller bearings, artificial teeth, heating equipment, synthetic fibres, woollen and homespun fabrics.

In 1991 Liechtenstein became a member of the European Free Trade Association, and as such is a party to the European Economic Area (EEA) Agreement with the EU which came into force on 1 January 1994. In December 1992 in separate referenda, Switzerland voted against EEA membership while Liechtenstein voted in favour. After adapting its customs union with Switzerland, and again voting in favour of joining the EEA in a referendum in April 1995, Liechtenstein joined the EEA on 1 May 1995.

In 1997, imports from the UK totalled £11,043,000 and exports to the UK £25,693,000.
GDP – US$1,296 million (1994); US$49,368 per capita (1994)

LITHUANIA
Lietuva

AREA – 25,174 sq. miles (65,200 sq. km). Neighbours: Latvia (north), Belarus (east and south), Poland and the Kaliningrad region of the Russian Federation (south-west)

POPULATION – 3,715,000 (1997): 81.6 per cent Lithuanian, 8.2 per cent Russian, 6.9 per cent Polish, 1.5 per cent Belarusian, 1 per cent Ukrainian. The majority are Roman Catholic, with Russian Orthodox and Lutheran minorities. Lithuanian is the state language
CAPITAL – Vilnius (population, 581,500, 1997)
MAJOR CITIES – Kaunas (421,600); Klaipéda (204,300), 1993 estimates
CURRENCY – Litas, pegged to the dollar, US$1 = 4 litas
NATIONAL ANTHEM – Tautiška Giesmé (The National Song)
NATIONAL DAY – 16 February (Independence Day)
NATIONAL FLAG – Three horizontal stripes of yellow, green, red
LIFE EXPECTANCY (years) – male 63.27; female 75.04
POPULATION GROWTH RATE – -0.0 per cent (1995)
POPULATION DENSITY – 57 per sq. km (1995)
URBAN POPULATION – 67.9 per cent (1995)

Lithuania lies in the middle and lower basin of the river Nemunas. Along the coast is a lowland plain which rises inland to form uplands in east and central Lithuania. These uplands, the Middle Lowlands, give way to the Baltic Highlands in east and south-east Lithuania; the highest point is 294 m (965 ft). There is a network of rivers and over 2,800 lakes, which mainly lie in the east of the country. The climate varies between maritime and continental.

HISTORY AND POLITICS

The first independent Lithuanian state emerged as the Kingdom of Lithuania in 1251, and over the next few centuries acted as a buffer state between Germans to the west and Mongols and Tartars to the east. After forming a joint Commonwealth and Kingdom with Poland in 1561, Lithuania was taken over by the Russian Empire in the partitions of Poland that occurred in 1772, 1792 and 1795.

Lithuania declared its independence from the Russian Empire on 16 February 1918 and then fought against German and Soviet forces until its independence was recognized by the Versailles Treaty (1919) and the peace treaty signed with the Soviet Union on 12 July 1920. The Soviet Union annexed Lithuania in 1940 under the terms of the Molotov–Ribbentrop pact with Germany. Lithuania was invaded and occupied when Germany invaded Soviet Union during the Second World War. In 1944, the Soviet Union recaptured the country and confirmed its annexation, though this was never accepted as legal by most states.

In December 1989, public pressure forced the Lithuanian Communist Party to agree to multiparty elections, which were held in February 1990. These were won by the nationalist Sajudis movement, and the Supreme Council (parliament) declared the restoration of independence on 11 March 1990. Clashes occurred throughout 1990 between Lithuanians and Soviet military forces. Over 90 per cent of the population voted for independence in a referendum in February 1991. The Soviet Union recognized the independence of Lithuania on 10 September 1991.

The ruling Lithuanian Democratic Labour Party (former Communist Party) was defeated in a legislative election in October and November 1996. The Homeland Union (Conservative Party) and the Christian Democratic Party formed a coalition government. On 4 January 1998, the independent candidate Valdas Adamkus won the presidential election with 50.3 per cent of the vote.

FOREIGN RELATIONS

Lithuania applied for membership of the EU in December 1995; a treaty of association with the EU was ratified by parliament on 20 June 1996.

POLITICAL SYSTEM

Under the 1992 constitution, executive authority is vested in the government, consisting of the prime minister, who is appointed by the president with the approval of the *Seimas*, and ministers appointed upon the recommendation of the prime minister. The government is accountable to the Seimas, and presidential powers are subject to strict parliamentary control.

Legislative power is exercised by the Seimas, a uni-cameral parliament of 141 members elected for four-year terms. Seventy-one members are elected in first-past-the-post constituencies and 70 by proportional representation, with a 5 per cent threshold for representation. The constitution bans an alignment of Lithuania with any post-Soviet eastern alliance.

Lithuania is divided into 11 cities and 44 rural districts. Each has a municipal council elected by the local population for a period of three years.

HEAD OF STATE

President, Valdas Adamkus, *inaugurated* 26 February 1998

GOVERNMENT *as at July 1998*

Prime Minister, Gediminas Vagnorius (HU)
Agriculture and Forestry, Edvardas Makelis (Ind.)
Culture, Saulius Šaltenis (HU)
Economy, Vincas Babilius (Ind.)
Education and Science, Kornelijus Platelis (Ind.)
Environmental Protection, Algis Čaplikas (CU)
Finance, Algirdas Šemeta (Ind.)
Foreign Affairs, Algirdas Saudargas (CD)
Health, Laurynas Mindaugas Stankevičius (LDLP)
Interior, Stasys Šedbaras (Ind.)
Justice, Vytautas Pakalniškis (HU)
National Defence, Česlovas Vytautas Stankevičius (CD)
*Public Administration Reforms and Local Government
    Authorities*, Kstutis Skrebys (HU)
Social Welfare and Labour, Irena Degutiene (HU)
Transport, Algis Žvaliauskas (HU)

HU Homeland Union; CU Centre Union; CD Christian Democrat; LDLP Lithuanian Democratic Labour Party; Ind. Independent

EMBASSY OF LITHUANIA
84 Gloucester Place, London WIH 3HN
Tel 0171-486 6401
Ambassador Extraordinary and Plenipotentiary, HE Justas
    Paleckis, apptd 1996

BRITISH EMBASSY
2 Antakalnio, 2055 Vilnius
Tel: Vilnius 222 2070
Ambassador Extraordinary and Plenipotentiary, HE
    Christopher Robbins, apptd 1998

BRITISH COUNCIL REPRESENTATIVE, L. Balenaite,
    Vilniaus 39/6,2600 Vilnius

DEFENCE

The Army has 24 armoured personnel carriers; the Navy has two frigates and three patrol and coastal vessels based at Klaipéda; the Air Force has three helicopters but no combat aircraft. The last Russian troops withdrew in 1993.
MILITARY EXPENDITURE – 1.6 per cent of GDP (1996)

MILITARY PERSONNEL – 5,250: Army 4,200, Navy 500, Air
    Force 550
CONSCRIPTION DURATION – 12 months

ECONOMY

The economy was largely agricultural prior to rapid industrialization during the Soviet era. A privatization programme began in 1991 and progress in the sale of small enterprises has been quick and successful. In 1997, the privatization of communication, energy and transport companies was begun.

In 1996, agriculture and forestry accounted for 10 per cent of GDP, the chief products being beef, pork, rye, oats, wheat, flax, barley, sugar beet and potatoes. The main industries are chemicals and petrochemicals, food processing, wood products, textiles, leather goods, machinery, machine tools and household appliances.
GNP – US$8,455 million (1996); US$2,280 per capita
    (1996)
GDP – US$7,596 million (1994); US$1,132 per capita
    (1994)
ANNUAL AVERAGE GROWTH OF GDP – 3.6 per cent (1996)
INFLATION RATE – 24.6 per cent (1996)
UNEMPLOYMENT – 7.3 per cent (1995)
TOTAL EXTERNAL DEBT – US$1,286 million (1996)

TRADE

Lithuania's main trading partners are Russia, Germany and Belarus. The Lithuanian economy is still heavily dependent on Russian supplies of oil, gas and metals. In 1997, total foreign investment in Lithuania reached US$1 billion.

In 1996 there was a trade deficit of US$887 million and a current account deficit of US$700 million. Imports totalled US$4,405 million and exports US$3,280 million.

Trade with UK	1996	1997
Imports from UK	£83,539,000	£106,240,000
Exports to UK	184,542,000	147,649,000

COMMUNICATIONS

There is a relatively well-developed railway system of 1,240 miles (2,000 km) running east-west and north-south and linking the major towns with Vilnius and Klaipéda, the main international port. Vilnius has an international airport and there are smaller ones at Kaunas, Palanga and Siauliai.

CULTURE AND EDUCATION

Lithuanian culture and literature are closely linked to the national liberation movements of the 19th and early 20th centuries, and the literature of Lithuanians who went into exile during the Soviet era.

Lithuania re-established a national education system in 1990. Education begins at age 6–7 years, with the system comprising elementary schools (four years), nine-year schools (five years), and secondary schools (three years). The language of instruction is predominantly Lithuanian, but there are also Russian and Polish schools. There are 105 vocational schools and 65 colleges. Lithuania has eight universities and seven other institutes of higher education. Vilnius University, founded in 1579, is one of the oldest universities in eastern Europe.
ILLITERACY RATE – 0.5 per cent
ENROLMENT (percentage of age group) – secondary 80 per
    cent (1994); tertiary 28.2 per cent (1995)

LUXEMBOURG
Grand-Duché de Luxembourg

AREA – 998 sq. miles (2,586 sq. km). Neighbours: Germany (east), Belgium (west and north), France (south)

POPULATION – 418,300 (1997), nearly all Roman Catholic. The officially designated 'national language' is Letzebuergesch (Luxembourgish), a mainly spoken language. French and German are the official languages for written purposes, and French is the language of administration

CAPITAL – Luxembourg (population, 76,446, 1996), a dismantled fortress

CURRENCY – Luxembourg franc (LF) of 100 centimes (Belgian currency is also legal tender). The Luxembourg franc is linked in a currency union with the Belgian franc

NATIONAL ANTHEM – Ons Hémécht (Our homeland)

NATIONAL DAY – 23 June

NATIONAL FLAG – Three horizontal bands, red, white and blue

LIFE EXPECTANCY (years) – male 70.61; female 77.87

POPULATION GROWTH RATE – 1.2 per cent (1995)

POPULATION DENSITY – 157 per sq. km (1995)

ENROLMENT (percentage of age group) – primary 81 per cent (1985); secondary 66 per cent (1985); tertiary 2.6 per cent (1985)

HISTORY AND POLITICS

Established as an independent state under the sovereignty of the King of the Netherlands as Grand Duke by the Congress of Vienna in 1815, Luxembourg formed part of the Germanic Confederation from 1815 to 1866, and was included in the German 'Zollverein'. In 1867 the Treaty of London declared it a neutral territory. On the death of the King of the Netherlands in 1890 it passed to the Duke of Nassau.

The territory was invaded and overrun by the Germans at the beginning of the war in 1914 but was liberated in 1918. By the Treaty of Versailles (1919), Germany renounced its former agreements with Luxembourg and in 1921 an economic union was formed with Belgium. The Grand Duchy was again invaded and occupied by Germany in 1940, and liberated in 1944.

FOREIGN RELATIONS

The constitution was modified in 1948 and the stipulation of permanent neutrality was abandoned. Luxembourg is now a signatory of the Brussels and North Atlantic treaties, and also a member of the EU. Luxembourg is a member of the Belgium-Netherlands-Luxembourg Customs Union (Benelux 1960).

POLITICAL SYSTEM

There is a Chamber of 60 deputies, elected by universal suffrage for five years. Legislation is submitted to the Council of State. The last general election was held on 12 June 1994 and a coalition government was installed. In March 1998, Grand Duke Jean passed certain constitutional powers on to his son and heir, Prince Henri.

HEAD OF STATE

HRH The Grand Duke of Luxembourg, Grand Duke Jean, KG, *born* 5 January 1921; *succeeded* (on the abdication of his mother) 12 November 1964; *married* 9 April 1953, Princess Joséphine-Charlotte of Belgium, and has *issue*, three sons and two daughters

Heir, HRH Prince Henri, *born* 16 April 1955, *married* 14 February 1981, Maria Teresa Mestre, and has *issue*, Prince Guillaume, *b.* 11 November 1981; Prince Felix, *b.* 3 June 1984; Prince Louis, *b.* 3 August 1986; Princess Alexandra, *b.* 2 February 1991; Prince Sébastien, *b.* 16 April 1992, Princess Gabriella, *b.* 26 March 1994

CABINET *as at June 1998*

Prime Minister, Minister of State, Employment, Finance and Treasury, Jean-Claude Juncker (CD)
Deputy PM, Foreign Affairs, Trade, Overseas Aid and Development, Jacques Poos (SOC)
Agriculture, Viticulture, Rural Development, Small Businesses, Housing and Tourism, Fernand Boden (CD)
Economy, Trade, Public Works, Energy, Robert Goebbels (SOC)
Education, Cultural and Religious Affairs, Erna Hennicot-Schoepges (CD)
Family, Women and the Disabled, Marie-Josée Jacobs (CD)
Health, Youth and Sports, Georges Wohlfart (SOC)
Home Affairs, Civil Service and Administrative Reforms, Michel Wolter (CD)
Justice, Budget, Relations with Parliament, Luc Frieden (CD)
Land Planning, Defence, Environment, Alex Bodry (SOC)
Secretary of State, Lydie Err (SOC)
Social Security, Transport, Post and Communication, Mady Delvaux-Stehres (SOC)

CD Christian Social People's Party; SOC Luxembourg Socialist Workers' Party

EMBASSY OF LUXEMBOURG
27 Wilton Crescent, London SW1X 8SD
Tel 0171-235 6961
Ambassador Extraordinary and Plenipotentiary, HE Joseph Weyland, apptd 1993

BRITISH EMBASSY
14 Boulevard F. D. Roosevelt, L-2450 Luxembourg Ville
Tel: Luxembourg 229864/5/6
Ambassador Extraordinary and Plenipotentiary, HE John Elam, CMG, apptd 1994

DEFENCE

For legal reasons, NATO's squadron of 18 E-3A Sentry airborne early warning aircraft is registered in Luxembourg.

MILITARY EXPENDITURE – 0.7 per cent of GDP (1996)
MILITARY PERSONNEL – 1,360: Army 800, Paramilitaries 560

ECONOMY

The country has an important iron and steel industry and is an important financial centre. In 1996, 667,000 tourists visited Luxembourg.

GNP – US$18,850 million (1996); US$45,360 per capita (1996)
GDP – US$9,973 million (1994); US$27,611 per capita (1994)
ANNUAL AVERAGE GROWTH OF GDP – 1.8 per cent (1992)
INFLATION RATE – 1.4 per cent (1996)
UNEMPLOYMENT – 2.8 per cent (1995)

TRADE WITH UK
(Belgium and Luxembourg)

	1996	1997
Imports from UK	£8,114,000,000	£8,005,500,000
Exports to UK	8,096,000,000	8,716,000,000

MACEDONIA (FORMER YUGOSLAV REPUBLIC OF)

AREA – 9,928 sq. miles (25,713 sq. km). Neighbours: Federal Republic of Yugoslavia (north), Bulgaria (east), Greece (south), Albania (west)

POPULATION – 2,163,000 (1994 UN estimate); 1,936,877 (1994 census): 66.5 per cent Macedonian, 22.9 per cent Albanian, 4.0 per cent ethnic Turks, 2.3 per cent gypsies, 2.3 per cent Serbs and 0.4 per cent Vlachs. The census results are disputed by the ethnic Albanians and Serbs. Macedonian Orthodox Christianity is the majority religion, with a Muslim minority. The main language is Macedonian (a south Slavic language), which is written in the Cyrillic script

CAPITAL – Skopje (population, 448,229, 1991)

MAJOR CITIES – Bitola (84,002); Kumanov (69,231); Prilep (70,152)

CURRENCY – Dinar of 100 paras

NATIONAL ANTHEM – Today over Macedonia

NATIONAL FLAG – Red with an eight-rayed sun displayed over the whole field

LIFE EXPECTANCY (years) – male 68.80; female 74.95

POPULATION GROWTH RATE – 1.3 per cent (1995)

POPULATION DENSITY – 84 per sq. km (1995)

URBAN POPULATION – 58.1 per cent (1991)

MILITARY EXPENDITURE – 7.5 per cent of GDP (1996)

MILITARY PERSONNEL – 22,900: Army 15,400, Paramilitaries 7,500

CONSCRIPTION DURATION – Nine months

ENROLMENT (percentage of age group) – primary 85 per cent (1995); secondary 51 per cent (1995); tertiary 17.5 per cent (1995)

HISTORY AND POLITICS

From the ninth to the 14th centuries AD Macedonia was ruled alternately by the Bulgars and the Byzantine Empire. In the middle of the 14th century the area was conquered by the Turks and remained under the Ottoman Empire for over 500 years. After the defeat of Turkey in the two Balkan wars of 1912–13 the geographical area of Macedonia was divided, the major part becoming Serbian (the areas of the present-day Macedonia) and the remainder given to Greece and Bulgaria. In 1918 on the formation of the Kingdom of the Serbs, Croats and Slovenes (later Yugoslavia), Serbian Macedonia was incorporated into Serbia as South Serbia. When Yugoslavia was reconstituted in 1944 as a Communist federal republic under President Tito, Macedonia became a constituent republic.

Multiparty elections for the 120-seat assembly held in November and December 1990 produced the first non-Communist government since the Second World War. The electorate overwhelmingly approved Macedonian sovereignty and independence in a referendum and independence was declared on 18 September 1991.

Presidential and legislative elections were held in October 1994, and the presidential election was won by the incumbent, Kiro Gligorov. The parliamentary elections to the 120-seat *Sobranje* (National Assembly) were marred by allegations of ballot-rigging and partially boycotted by the Democratic Party and the nationalist UMRO party. The elections were won by the ruling Alliance for Macedonia (a coalition of the Social Democrat, Liberal and Socialist parties) with 95 seats; the ethnic Albanian parties won 19 seats, and independents six. A coalition government was formed in December 1994 by the Social Democratic Alliance of Macedonia, the Party of Demo-

cratic Prosperity (an ethnic Albanian party) and the Socialist Party of Macedonia.

FOREIGN RELATIONS

A new constitution was adopted in November 1991 and then amended at the EC's request to make it clear that Macedonia had no territorial claim on its neighbours. Macedonia applied for EC recognition in December 1991 but was refused because of Greece's objections to the state's name, flag and currency which, according to the Greek government, amounted to a territorial claim on the Greek province of Macedonia. The peaceful withdrawal of the Yugoslav Army (JNA) from Macedonia was completed in April 1992.

Tensions between Macedonia and its neighbours grew in late 1992, with Greece imposing a virtual economic blockade and Albania alleging discrimination against ethnic Albanians. Fearing conflict, the UN sent 1,000 peacekeepers in 1992–3 to man border posts with Serbia and Albania. A full UN peacekeeping force, the UN Preventive Deployment Force (UNPREDEP) was established in March 1995. Its mandate is due to expire at the end of August 1998.

Macedonia gained UN membership on 8 April 1993 following a compromise with Greece by which it is temporarily known as the 'Former Yugoslav Republic of Macedonia' (FYROM). Greece subsequently reopened its border to Macedonian trade in September 1993, but reimposed its economic blockade in February 1994 after the majority of EU states established diplomatic relations with Macedonia. An agreement was signed in September 1995 under which Greece agreed to lift the embargo on 15 October 1995 in exchange for Macedonia removing the contentious Star of Vergina from its flag.

HEAD OF STATE

President, Kiro Gligorov, *elected* 27 January 1991, *re-elected* 16 October 1994

Vice-Presidents, Dimitar Buzlevski (SDSM);Zlatka Popovski (SPM); Naser Ziberi (PDP) (*Labour and Social Policy*)

CABINET *as at July 1998*

Prime Minister, Branko Crvenkovski (SDSM)

Agriculture, Forestry and Water Management, Kiro Dokuzovski (SDSM)

Culture, Slobodan Unkovski (SDSM)

Defence, Lazar Kitanoski

Development, Abdimenaf Neziri (PDP)

Economy, Boris Rikalovski (SDSM)

Education and Physical Culture, Sofija Todorova (SDSM)

Finance, Taki Fiti (SDSM)

Foreign Affairs, Blagoj Handziski (SDSM)

Health, Petar Iliovski (SPM)

Interior, Tomislav Cokrevski (SDSM)

Justice, Gjorgji Spasov (SDSM)

Science, Aslan Selmani (PDP)

Transport and Communications, Abdulmenaf Bedzeti (PDP)

Urbanism, Civil Engineering and Environment, Tome Trombev (SDSM)

Without Portfolio, Vladimir Naumovski (SPM)

SDSM Social Democratic Alliance of Macedonia; PDP Party of Democratic Prosperity; SPM Socialist Party of Macedonia

EMBASSY OF THE FORMER YUGOSLAV REPUBLIC OF MACEDONIA

10 Harcourt House, 19A Cavendish Square, London WIM 9AD

Tel 0171-499 5152

Ambassador Extraordinary and Plenipotentiary, HE Stevo
Crvenkovski, apptd 1997

BRITISH EMBASSY
Veljko Vlahovíc 26, 9100 Skopje
Tel: Skopje 116772
Ambassador Extraordinary and Plenipotentiary, HE Mark
Dickinson, apptd 1997

ECONOMY

The economy was decimated by the UN trade sanctions
against the rump Yugoslavia (from May 1992 until
November 1995), with which Macedonia had conducted
60 per cent of its trade. The Greek economic blockade
(from February 1994 until October 1995) deprived Macedonia of most of its oil supplies and industry survived on
imports from Turkey and Bulgaria. In February 1998 the
World Bank approved a US$35 million loan to modernize
six power plants. Macedonia is attempting to transform its
economy to a market-orientated one and to introduce
privatization. Foreign investment has been minimal because of the lack of international recognition.

In 1991 41.2 per cent of GDP was produced by industry
and mining and 14 per cent by agriculture. Mineral
resources include lead, zinc, copper, manganese and iron
ore. The main industrial sectors are basic metal industries,
chemicals, textiles and food processing. Important agricultural products are grain, tobacco, lamb, tomatoes and sugar
beet.

In 1994 there was a trade deficit of US$208 million and a
current account deficit of US$207 million.

GNP – US$1,956 million (1996); US$990 per capita (1996)
GDP – US$3,470 million (1994); US$1,552 per capita
(1994)
UNEMPLOYMENT – 35.6 per cent (1995)
TOTAL EXTERNAL DEBT – US$1,659 million (1996)

TRADE WITH UK	1996	1997
Imports from UK	£17,955,000	£15,618,000
Exports to UK	9,282,000	10,043,000

MADAGASCAR
Repoblika n'i Madagaskar

AREA – 226,658 sq. miles (587,041 sq. km)
POPULATION – 14,763,000 (1994 UN estimate). The
people are of mixed Malayo-Polynesian, Arab and
African origin. There are sizeable French, Chinese and
Indian communities. The official languages are
Malagasy and French
CAPITAL – Antananarivo (population, 377,600, 1971
estimate)
MAJOR CITIES – ΨAntsiranana (220,000); Fianarantsoa
(300,000); ΨMahajanga (200,000); ΨToamasina
(230,000), the chief port
CURRENCY – Franc malgache (FMG) of 100 centimes
NATIONAL DAY – 26 June (Independence Day)
NATIONAL FLAG – Equal horizontal bands of red (above)
and green, with vertical white band by staff
LIFE EXPECTANCY (years) – male 55.00; female 58.00
POPULATION DENSITY – 25 per sq. km (1995)
MILITARY EXPENDITURE – 0.8 per cent of GDP (1996)
MILITARY PERSONNEL – 28,500: Army 20,000, Navy 500,
Air Force 500, Paramilitaries 7,500
CONSCRIPTION DURATION – 18 months
ILLITERACY RATE – 54.3 per cent
ENROLMENT (percentage of age group) – tertiary 3.4 per
cent (1992)

Madagascar lies 240 miles off the east coast of Africa and is
the fourth largest island in the world.

HISTORY AND POLITICS

Madagascar (known from 1958 to 1975 as the Malagasy
Republic) became a French protectorate in 1895, and a
French colony in 1896 when the former queen was exiled.
Republican status was adopted on 14 October 1958, and
independence was proclaimed on 26 June 1960.

The post-independence civilian government was replaced by a military government in 1975 and martial law
was declared. A Supreme Council of the Revolution under
Capitaine de Frégate (subsequently Admiral) Didier
Ratsiraka was established.

In November 1991, after six months of agitation against
his one-party socialist rule, President Ratsiraka relinquished executive power to a new prime minister, Guy
Razanamasy. However, the president retained his official
position and the main opposition grouping, the *Forces
Vives,* established a rival government led by Albert Zafy. In
December 1991 a transitional government including
Forces Vives and Razanamasy supporters was formed to
draft a new constitution, approved by referendum in
August 1992. Presidential elections were held in two
rounds in November 1992 and February 1993, Albert Zafy
emerging victorious with 67 per cent of the vote. He
became the first president of the Third Republic, which
came into being at the same time.

President Zafy was impeached in September 1996 and
defeated in a presidential election in November and
December 1996 by former president Ratsiraka. Following
legislative elections held in May 1998, Ratsiraka's *Avant-
garde de la révolution malgache* (AREMA) party became the
largest party in the National Assembly.

HEAD OF STATE
President, Adm. Didier Ratsiraka, *elected* 29 December 1996,
inaugurated 9 February 1997

COUNCIL OF MINISTERS *as at July 1998*

Prime Minister, Pascal Rakotomavo
Deputy PMs, Pierrot Rajaonarivelo *(Decentralization and the
Budget);* Tantely Andrianarivo *(Finance and Economy);*
Herizo Razafimahaleo *(Foreign Affairs)*
Agriculture, M. Ranjakason
Armed Forces, Gen. Marcel Ranjeva
Basic and Secondary Education, Simon Jacquit
Civil Service, Labour and Social Legislation, Abel Jean Désiré
Ratovonelinjafy
Energy and Mines, Charles Rasoja
Environment, Colette Vaohita
Fishing and Marine Resources, Abdallah Hussein
Health, Henriette Rahantalalao
Higher Education, Ange Andrianarisoa
Industrialization and Cottage Industry, Manassé
Esoavelomandroso
Information, Culture and Communication, Fredo Betsimifira
Interior, Col. Jean-Jacques Rasolondraibe
Justice, Keeper of the Seals, Anaclet Imbiky
Livestock, Lt.-Cmdr. Ndrianasolo
Population and Solidarity, Ernest Njara
Posts and Telecommunications, Ny Hasina Andriamanjato
Private Sector and Privatization, Horace Constant
Public Works, Col. Jean Emile Tsaranazy
Regional and Town Planning, Herivelona Ramanantsoa
Scientific Research, Lila Ratsifandriamanana
Secretaries of State, Brig. Jean-Paul Bory *(Gendarmerie);*
Azaly Ben Marouf *(Public Security)*
Technical Education and Vocational Training, Boniface Levelo

Tourism, Juliette Raharisoa
Trade and Consumption, Auguste Paraina
Transport and Meteorology, Naivo Ramamonjisoa
Water and Forests, Rija Rajohnson
Youth and Sports, Lina Andriamifidimanana

EMBASSY OF THE REPUBLIC OF MADAGASCAR
4 avenue Raphael, 75016 Paris, France
Tel: Paris 4504 6211
Ambassador Extraordinary and Plenipotentiary, new
appointment awaited

HONORARY CONSULATE OF THE REPUBLIC OF
MADAGASCAR
16 Lanark Mansions, Pennard Road, London W12 8DT
Tel 0181-746 0133
Honorary Consul, Stephen Hobbs

BRITISH EMBASSY
1st Floor, Immeuble 'Ny Havana', Cite de 67 Ha,
BP 167, Antananarivo
Tel: Antananarivo 27749
Ambassador Extraordinary and Plenipotentiary, HE Robert S.
Dewar, apptd 1996

ECONOMY

The economy is still largely based on agriculture, which
employs more than 80 per cent of the workforce. The main
products are rice, cassava, sugar cane and sweet potatoes.
Development plans have placed emphasis on improving
communications, the exploitation of mineral deposits and
the creation of small industries.

In 1995 there was a trade deficit of US$122 million and a
current account deficit of US$276 million. Imports totalled
US$499 million and exports US$364 million.

GNP – US$3,428 million (1996); US$250 per capita (1996)
GDP – US$2,979 million (1994); US$208 per capita (1994)
ANNUAL AVERAGE GROWTH OF GDP – 1.8 per cent (1995)
INFLATION RATE – 19.8 per cent (1996)
TOTAL EXTERNAL DEBT – US$4,175 million (1996)

TRADE WITH UK	1996	1997
Imports from UK	£6,430,000	£8,191,000
Exports to UK	22,372,000	24,432,000

MALAWI
Dziko La Malawi

AREA – 45,747 sq. miles (118,484 sq. km). Neighbours:
Tanzania (north-east), Zambia (west), Mozambique
(south)
POPULATION – 9,788,000 (1994 UN estimate). The official
languages are Chichewa and English
CAPITAL – Lilongwe (population, 233,973, 1987)
MAJOR CITIES – Blantyre (331,588), incorporating
Blantyre and Limbe, the major commercial and
industrial centre; Mzuzu (44,238); Zomba (42,878), the
former capital
CURRENCY – Kwacha (K) of 100 tambala
NATIONAL ANTHEM – O God Bless Our Land of Malawi
NATIONAL DAY – 6 July (Independence Day)
NATIONAL FLAG – Horizontal stripes of black, red and
green, with rising sun in the centre of the black stripe
LIFE EXPECTANCY (years) – male 43.51; female 46.75
POPULATION GROWTH RATE – 3.3 per cent (1995)
POPULATION DENSITY – 83 per sq. km (1995)
URBAN POPULATION – 18.9 per cent (1995)
MILITARY EXPENDITURE – 1.2 per cent of GDP (1996)
MILITARY PERSONNEL – 6,000: Army 5,000,
Paramilitaries 1,000

ILLITERACY RATE – 43.6 per cent
ENROLMENT (percentage of age group) – primary 100 per
cent (1994); secondary 2 per cent (1994); tertiary 0.8 per
cent (1993)

Malawi lies in south-eastern Africa. Much of the eastern
border of Malawi is formed by Lake Malawi (formerly
Lake Nyasa), which covers nearly half of the north of the
country. The valley of the River Shire runs south from the
lake, its watershed with the Zambezi lying on the western
border with Mozambique and its tributary, the Ruo, with
lakes Chinta and Chirwa, lying on the eastern border with
Mozambique. The north and centre are plateaux, and the
south highlands.

HISTORY AND POLITICS

Malawi (formerly Nyasaland) assumed internal self-government on 1 February 1963, and became independent on
6 July 1964. It became a republic on 6 July 1966.

In 1991–2 Life President Hastings Banda, who had
ruled since independence, came under increasing pressure
to introduce a multiparty democratic system of government. In May 1992 aid donors tied new loans to improvements in the human rights record and moves to multiparty
democracy. A referendum was held on the adoption of a
multiparty democracy in June 1993 and approved by 63
per cent of voters. President Banda and the Malawi
Congress Party refused to resign but parliament passed a
law to amend the constitution to allow multiparty politics
and Banda announced a political amnesty to allow exiles to
return. Multiparty presidential and legislative elections
held in May 1994 were won by Bakili Muluzi and the
United Democratic Front (UDF) respectively. Foreign
and multilateral aid has since been restored. A coalition
UDF-Alliance for Democracy (AFORD) government was
formed although AFORD withdrew from the coalition in
June 1996. Former President Banda died on 25 November
1997.

POLITICAL SYSTEM
There is a Cabinet consisting of the president and
ministers. The National Assembly, which usually meets
three times a year, consists of 177 members elected by
universal suffrage. A new multiparty constitution took
effect on 17 May 1994. It reduces presidential powers,
limits the presidential term to five years, establishes the
posts of first and second vice-president and provides for a
Senate, to come into being by May 1999.

HEAD OF STATE
President, Bakili Muluzi, *elected* 17 May 1994, *sworn in* 21
May 1994
Vice-President, Privatization, Justin Malewezi

CABINET *as at July 1998*
The President
The Vice-President
Agriculture and Irrigation, Aleke Banda
Attorney-General, Justice, Peter Fachi
Commerce and Industry, Matembo Nzunda
Defence, Joseph Kubwalo
Education, Sports and Culture, Brown Mpinganjira
Finance, Cassim Chilumpha
Foreign Affairs, Mapopa Chipeta
Forestry, Fisheries and Environmental Affairs, Mayinga
Mkandawire
Health and Population, Harry Thomson
Home Affairs, Melvyn Moyo
Information, Sam Mpasu
Labour and Vocational Training, Samuel Kaliyoma Phumisa

Lands, Housing, Physical Planning and Services, Richard Sembereka
Ministers of State in the President's Office, George Bundaunda Phiri (*District and Local Government Administration*); Edda Chitalo (*Human Resource Mangement and Development*); Dumbo Lemani (*Statutory Corporations*)
Tourism, Parks and Wildlife, Patrick Mbewe
Transport, Kamangadazi Chambalo
Water Development, Edward Bwanali
Women, Youth and Community Services, Lilian Patel
Works and Supplies, Abdul Pillane

MALAWI HIGH COMMISSION
33 Grosvenor Street, London WIX ODE
Tel 0171-491 4172/7
High Commissioner, new appointment awaited

BRITISH HIGH COMMISSION
PO Box 30042, Lilongwe 3
Tel: Lilongwe 782400
High Commissioner, G. Finlayson, apptd 1998

BRITISH COUNCIL REPRESENTATIVE, J. Kennedy, Plot No. 13/20, City Centre, PO Box 30222, Lilongwe 3

ECONOMY

The economy is largely agricultural, providing 90 per cent of export earnings; maize is the main subsistence crop, and tobacco, sugar, tea, groundnuts and cotton are the main cash crops and principal exports. There are two sugar mills. A number of light manufacturing industries have been established, mainly in agricultural processing, clothing/textiles and building materials.

In 1994 there was a trade deficit of US$276 million and a current account deficit of US$450 million. In 1995 imports totalled US$475 million and exports US$405 million.
GNP – US$1,832 million (1996); US$180 per capita (1996)
GDP – US$2,079 million (1994); US$130 per capita (1994)
ANNUAL AVERAGE GROWTH OF GDP – –9.3 per cent (1994)
INFLATION RATE – 83.3 per cent (1995)
TOTAL EXTERNAL DEBT – US$2,312 million (1996)

TRADE WITH UK	1996	1997
Imports from UK	£20,558,000	£18,188,000
Exports to UK	16,062,000	13,241,000

COMMUNICATIONS

A single-track railway runs from Mchinji on the Zambian border, through Lilongwe and Salima on Lake Malawi (itself served by two passenger and a number of cargo boats) through to Blantyre. The route south to the Mozambique port of Beira was severed by the Mozambican civil war, but the route to Nacala in Mozambique is open again. There are 14,077 km of roads in Malawi of which about 18 per cent are bituminized. There is an international airport 26 km from Lilongwe, which handles regional and intercontinental flights, and another airport at Chileka.

MALAYSIA
Persekutuan Tanah Malaysia

AREA – 127,320 sq. miles (329,758 sq. km). Thailand borders the Malay peninsula to the north. On Borneo, Malaysia (Sarawak and Sabah) borders Indonesia to the south, and surrounds Brunei to the north

POPULATION – 20,140,000 (1995); 16,921,300 (1988 census): Malays (53 per cent), Chinese (35 per cent), and those of Indian and Sri Lankan origin, as well as the indigenous races of Sarawak and Sabah. Bahasa Malaysia (Malay) is the official language, but English, various dialects of Chinese, and Tamil are also widely spoken. There are a few indigenous languages widely spoken in Sabah and Sarawak. Islam is the official religion of Malaysia, each ruler being the head of religion in his state (except in Sabah and Sarawak). The Yang di-Pertuan Agong is the head of religion in Melaka and Penang. The constitution guarantees religious freedom
CAPITAL – Kuala Lumpur (population, 1,145,075, 1991)
MAJOR CITIES – Ipoh (382,633); Johore Bharu (328,646); Petaling Jaya (254,849)
CURRENCY – Malaysian dollar (ringgit) (M$) of 100 sen
NATIONAL ANTHEM – Negara-Ku
NATIONAL DAY – 31 August (*Hari Kebangsaan*)
NATIONAL FLAG – Equal horizontal stripes of red (seven) and white (seven); 14-point yellow star and crescent in blue canton
LIFE EXPECTANCY (years) – male 68.68; female 73.04
POPULATION GROWTH RATE – 2.5 per cent (1995)
POPULATION DENSITY – 61 per sq. km (1995)
URBAN POPULATION – 50.6 per cent (1991)
ILLITERACY RATE – 16.5 per cent
ENROLMENT (percentage of age group) – primary 91 per cent (1994); tertiary 10.6 per cent (1994)

Malaysia comprises the 11 states of peninsular Malaya plus Sabah and Sarawak. It occupies two distinct regions, the Malay peninsula which extends from the isthmus of Kra to the Singapore Strait, and the north-western coastal area of the island of Borneo. Each is separated from the other by the South China Sea.

The year is commonly divided into the south-west and north-west monsoon seasons. Rainfall averages about 100 inches throughout the year. The average daily temperature varies from 21° C to 32° C, though in higher areas temperatures are lower and vary widely.

HISTORY AND POLITICS

The Federation of Malaya became an independent country within the Commonwealth on 31 August 1957. On 16 September 1963 the federation was enlarged by the accession of the states of Singapore, Sabah (formerly British North Borneo) and Sarawak, and the name of Malaysia was adopted from that date. On 9 August 1965 Singapore seceded from the federation.

The National Front (Barisan Nasional) Coalition led by Dr Mahathir Mohamed won a fourth term in office in a general election held on 25 April 1995, winning 162 of the 192 seats.

POLITICAL SYSTEM

The constitution provides for a strong federal government and a degree of autonomy for the state governments. It created a constitutional Supreme Head of the Federation (HM the *Yang di-Pertuan Agong*) and a Deputy Supreme Head (HRH *Timbalan Yang di-Pertuan Agong*) to be elected for a term of five years by the rulers from among their number. The Malay rulers are either chosen or succeed to their position in accordance with the custom of the particular state. In other states of Malaysia, choice of the head of state is at the discretion of the Yang di-Pertuan Agong after consultation with the Chief Minister of the state.

The Federal Parliament consists of two houses, the Senate and the House of Representatives. The Senate (*Dewan Negara*) consists of 69 members who serve a six-year term, 26 being elected by the Legislative Assemblies of the states (two from each) and 43 appointed by the Yang di-Pertuan Agong. The House of Representatives (*Dewan Rakyat*) consists of 192 members elected for a five-year term by universal adult suffrage with a common electoral roll.

The judicial system consists of a Federal Court and two High Courts, one in peninsular Malaysia and one for Sabah and Sarawak. The Federal Court comprises a president, the two Chief Justices of the High Courts and other judges. It possesses appellate, original and advisory jurisdiction. Each of the High Courts consists of a Chief Justice and not less than four other judges.

FEDERAL STRUCTURE

According to the constitution, each state shall have its own constitution not inconsistent with the federal constitution, with the ruler or governor acting on the advice of an Executive Council appointed on the advice of the Chief Minister and a single-chamber Legislative Assembly. The Legislative Assemblies are fully elected on the same basis as the federal parliament.

State	Area (sq. km)	Population (1997 estimate)	Main Town
Johore	18,986	2,554,100	ΨJohore Bahru
Kedah	9,426	1,530,100	Alor Setar
Kelantan	14,943	1,447,000	Kota Bahru
Melaka	1,650	582,000	ΨMelaka
Negri Sembilan	6,643	810,500	Seremban
Pahang	35,965	1,239,000	ΨKuantan
Penang	1,031	1,222,100	ΨGeorgetown
Perak	21,005	2,094,800	Ipoh
Perlis	795	217,400	Kangar
Sabah	73,711	2,593,400	ΨKota Kinabalu
Sarawak	124,449	1,954,300	ΨKuching
Selangor	7,956	2,999,800	ΨShah Alam
Terengganu	12,955	975,800	ΨKuala Terengganu

Federal Territories

Kuala Lumpur Labuan	} 1,231,500

HEAD OF STATE

Supreme Head of State, HM Tuanku Ja'afar ibni Al-Marhum Tuanku Abdul Rahman (Yang Dipertuan Besar of Negeri Sembilan), *sworn in* 26 April 1994, *crowned* 22 September 1994

Deputy Supreme Head of State, HRH Sultan Salahuddin Abdul Aziz Shah Al-Haj ibni Almarhum Sultan Hishamuddin Alam Shah Al-Haj (Sultan of Selangor)

CABINET *as at July 1998*

Prime Minister, Home Affairs, Datuk Seri Dr Mahathir Mohamed
Deputy PM, Finance, Datuk Seri Anwar Ibrahim
Agriculture, Datuk Dr Sulaiman bin Daud
Culture, Datuk Sabbaruddin Chik
Defence, Datuk Syed Hamid Albar
Domestic Trade and Consumer Affairs, Dato Megat Junid Ayob
Economic Development Issues, Tun Daim Zainuddin
Education, Datuk Seri Najib Tun Razak
Energy, Telecommunications and Posts, Datuk Leo Moggie Anak Irok
Entrepreneurial Development, Datuk Mustapha Mohamad
Foreign Affairs, Dato Abdullah Ahmad Badawi
Health, Chua Jui Meng
Housing and Local Government, Datuk Ting Chew Peh
Human Resources, Datuk Lim Ah Lek

Information, Dato Mohamad Rahmat
International Trade and Industry, Datuk Seri Rafidah Aziz
Lands and Co-operative Development, Dato Osu Sukam
National Unity and Social Development, Datin Paduka Zaleha Ismail
Primary Industries, Datuk Seri Dr Lim Keng Yaik
Prime Minister's Department, Datuk Abang Abu Bakar Mustafa (*Legal and Justice Affairs*); Dato Dr Haji Abdul Hamid Osman; Dato Ibrahim Saad; Datuk Nazri Abdul Aziz
Public Works, Datuk Seri S. Samy Vellu
Rural Development, Dato Haji Anuar bin Musa
Sabah Affairs, Datuk Chong Kah Kiet
Science, Datuk Law Hieng Ding
Transport, Datuk Seri Dr Ling Liong Sik
Youth and Sports, Tan Sri Dato Muhyiddin Yasin

NOTE: Tunku/Tengku, Tun, Tan Sri, and Datuk/Dato are titles. Tunku/Tengku is equivalent to Prince. Tun denotes membership of the highest order of Malaysian chivalry. Tan Sri and Datuk/Dato (Datuk Seri in Perak and Datu in Sabah) are the equivalent of a knighthood. The wife of a Tun is styled Toh Puan, that of a Tan Sri is styled Puan Sri and of a Datuk, Datin. Tuan or Encik is equivalent to Mr and Puan is equivalent to Mrs.

MALAYSIAN HIGH COMMISSION
45 Belgrave Square, London SW1X 8QT
Tel 0171-235 8033
High Commissioner, HE Dato Mohamad Amir bin Ja'afar, apptd 1998
Deputy High Commissioner (acting), Husni Zai Yaacob
Defence Adviser, Col. Kamaruddin Mattan

BRITISH HIGH COMMISSION
185 Jalan Ampang (PO Box 11030), 50450 Kuala Lumpur
Tel: Kuala Lumpur 248 2122
High Commissioner, HE David Moss, CMG, apptd 1994
Deputy High Commissioner, T. N. Byrne
Counsellor (Commercial/Economic), H. Parkinson
Defence Adviser, Col. M. B. Cooper

BRITISH COUNCIL DIRECTOR, T. Edmundson, PO Box 10539, Jalan Bukit Aman, Kuala Lumpur 50916. There are also offices at Penang, Kota Kinabalu (Sabah) and Kuching (Sarawak).

DEFENCE

The Army has 816 armoured personnel carriers and 127 artillery pieces. The Royal Malaysian Navy has six frigates, 37 patrol and coastal vessels and 12 armed helicopters at five bases. The Royal Malaysian Air Force has 94 combat aircraft.

Australia maintains an infantry company and an air force detachment in Malaysia.

MILITARY EXPENDITURE – 3.6 per cent of GDP (1996)
MILITARY PERSONNEL – 131,600: Army 85,000, Navy 14,000, Air Force 12,500, Paramilitaries 20,100

ECONOMY

From being an agriculturally-based economy reliant on raw materials exports at independence, Malaysia has undergone an industrialization programme and now produces clothing, textiles, rubber goods, electronics, office equipment, cars, household appliances, semi-conductors, food processing and chemicals. Under the New Economic Policy of 1970–90, the economy grew at an average rate of 6.7 per cent a year. The National Development Policy 1990–2000 is seen as the second stage in making Malaysia a fully-developed industrial state by 2020, though recent economic difficulties may delay this.

In 1995 44 per cent of GDP was produced by services, 35 per cent by manufacturing and 14 per cent by agriculture.

Malaysia has been severely affected by the economic crisis in Asia. During 1997, the Malaysian stock market lost 60 per cent of its value, and between July 1997 and January 1998 the ringgit fell by 33 per cent against the US dollar. The crisis was to some extent exacerbated by sudden policy changes by the government, though austerity measures and economic reforms averted the need to apply for IMF assistance. In January 1998 the government announced that it would deport all foreign workers except Indonesians; during the economic boom some two million workers arrived in Malaysia, but more than half will now leave.

GNP – US$89,800 million (1996); US$4,370 per capita (1996)
GDP – US$58,941 million (1994); US$3,582 per capita (1994)
ANNUAL AVERAGE GROWTH OF GDP – 9.6 per cent (1995)
INFLATION RATE – 3.5 per cent (1996)
UNEMPLOYMENT – 2.8 per cent (1995)
TOTAL EXTERNAL DEBT – US$39,777 million (1996)

TRADE
Malaysia is the largest exporter of natural rubber, tin, palm oil and tropical hardwoods. Other major export commodities are manufactured and processed products, petroleum, oil and other minerals, palm kernel oil, tea and pepper. Imports consist mainly of machinery and transport equipment, manufactured goods, foods, consumer durables and metal products. Japan, the USA and Singapore are the main trading partners.

In 1995 Malaysia had a trade deficit of US$100 million and a current account deficit of US$7,362 million. In 1996 imports totalled US$78,422 million and exports US$78,246 million.

Trade with UK	1996	1997
Imports from UK	£1,160,025,000	£1,205,390,000
Exports to UK	2,380,115,000	2,025,491,000

MALDIVES
Dhivehi Jumhooriyya

AREA – 115 sq. miles (298 sq. km)
POPULATION – 254,000 (1996). The people are Sunni Muslims and the Maldivian (Dhivehi) language is akin to Elu or old Sinhalese
CAPITAL – ΨMalé (population, 62,973, 1995)
CURRENCY – Rufiyaa of 100 laaris
NATIONAL DAY – 26 July
NATIONAL FLAG – Green field bearing a white crescent, with wide red border
LIFE EXPECTANCY (years) – male 67.15; female 66.60
POPULATION GROWTH RATE – 3.3 per cent (1995)
POPULATION DENSITY – 852 per sq. km (1995)
URBAN POPULATION – 25.9 per cent (1990)
ILLITERACY RATE – 6.8 per cent

The Maldives are a chain of coral atolls 400 miles to the south-west of Sri Lanka, stretching north for about 600 miles from just south of the Equator. There are about 19 coral atolls comprising over 1,200 islands, 198 of which are inhabited. No point in the entire chain of islands is more than eight feet above sea-level.

HISTORY AND POLITICS
Until 1952 the islands were a sultanate under the protection of the British Crown. Internal self-government was achieved in 1948 and full independence in 1965. The Maldives became a special member of the Commonwealth in 1982 and a full member in 1985.

The Maldives form a republic which is elective. The legislature, the Citizens' Assembly (*Majlis*), has 40 representatives elected from all the atolls, and eight appointed by the president, for a five-year term. The government consists of a Cabinet, which is responsible to the Majlis. Under the 1998 constitution, the president is elected by the Majlis and confirmed by a referendum.

HEAD OF STATE
President, HE Maumoon Abdul Gayoom, *elected* 1978, *re-elected* 1983, 1989, 1 October 1993

CABINET *as at July 1998*
Attorney-General, Mohamed Munnavaru
Construction and Public Works, Umar Zahir
Defence, National Security, Finance and Treasury, The President
Education, Dr Mohamed Latheef
Fisheries and Agriculture, Hassan Sobir
Foreign Affairs, Fathullah Jameel
Health, Ahmed Abdulla
Home Affairs and Housing, Abdulla Jameel
Information, Arts and Culture, Ibrahim Manik
Justice and Islamic Affairs, Ahmed Zahir
Ministers of State, Mohamed Rashid Ibrahim *(Chief Justice)*; Maj.-Gen. Ambaree Abdul Sattar *(Defence and National Security)*; Arif Hilmy *(Finance and Treasury)*; Mohamed Hussain *(Presidential Affairs)*; Moosa Fathuhy *(Supreme Council on Islamic Affairs)*; Abdulla Hameed *(Atolls Administration, Majlis Speaker)*; Ismail Fathy
Planning, Human Resources and Environment, Abdul Rasheed Hussain
Tourism, Ibrahim Hussain Zaki
Trade and Industries, Abdulla Yameen
Transport and Communication, Ismail Shafeeu
Women's Affairs and Social Welfare, Rashida Yoosuf
Youth and Sports, Mohamed Zahir Hussain

HIGH COMMISSION OF THE REPUBLIC OF MALDIVES
22 Nottingham Place, London W1M 3FB
Tel 0171–224 2135
Acting High Commissioner, Adam Hassan

BRITISH HIGH COMMISSIONER, HE David E. Tatham, CMG, resident at Colombo, Sri Lanka

ECONOMY
The vegetation of the islands is coconut palms with some scrub. Hardly any cultivation of crops is possible and nearly all food to supplement the basic fish diet has to be imported. Tourism is expanding rapidly (338,733 visitors in 1996). The principal industry is fishing, which together with tourism accounts for about 30 per cent of GDP. The Maldives National Ship Management Ltd (MNSML) has a fleet of nine merchant ships. There is an international airport at Malé.

In 1993 the Maldives had a trade deficit of US$139 million and a current account deficit of US$48 million. In 1996 imports totalled US$302 million and exports US$59 million.
GNP – US$277 million (1996); US$1,080 per capita (1996)
GDP – US$180 million (1994); US$1,032 per capita (1994)
ANNUAL AVERAGE GROWTH OF GDP – 7.2 per cent (1995)
INFLATION RATE – 6.3 per cent (1996)

TOTAL EXTERNAL DEBT – US$167 million (1996)

TRADE WITH UK	1996	1997
Imports from UK	£5,895,000	£7,394,000
Exports to UK	7,549,000	9,658,000

MALI
République du Mali

AREA – 478,841 sq. miles (1,240,192 sq. km). Neighbours: Senegal (west), Mauritania (north-west), Algeria (north-east), Niger (east), Burkina Faso and Côte d'Ivoire (south), Guinea (south-west)
POPULATION – 10,795,000 (1994 UN estimate). The official language is French; Bambara is the largest local language
CAPITAL – Bamako (population, 658,275, 1987)
MAJOR CITIES – Gao; Kayes; Mopti; Segou; Sikasso; Timbuktu (all regional capitals)
CURRENCY – Franc CFA of 100 centimes
NATIONAL DAY – 22 September
NATIONAL FLAG – Vertical stripes of green (by staff), yellow and red
LIFE EXPECTANCY (years) – male 55.24; female 58.66
POPULATION DENSITY – 9 per sq. km (1995)
URBAN POPULATION – 22.0 per cent (1987)
MILITARY EXPENDITURE – 1.8 per cent of GDP (1996)
MILITARY PERSONNEL – 12,150: Army 7,350, Paramilitaries 4,800
CONSCRIPTION DURATION – Two years
ILLITERACY RATE – 69.0 per cent
ENROLMENT (percentage of age group) – primary 25 per cent (1994); secondary 5 per cent (1990); tertiary 0.8 per cent (1990)

HISTORY AND POLITICS

Formerly the French colony of Soudan, the territory elected on 24 November 1958 to remain an autonomous republic within the French Community. It associated with Senegal in the Federation of Mali, which was granted full independence on 20 June 1960. The Federation was effectively dissolved in August 1960 by the secession of Senegal. The title of the Republic of Mali was adopted in September 1960.

The regime of Modibo Keita was overthrown in 1968 by a group of army officers who formed a National Liberation Committee and appointed a prime minister. Moussa Traoré assumed the functions of head of state. A civil constitution came into being in 1979.

President Traoré was overthrown in March 1991 by troops led by Lt.-Col. Touré. A military National Reconciliation Committee joined with democratic parties to form a Transitional Committee for the Salvation of the People which suspended the constitution and dissolved the Mali People's Democratic Union (UPDM), formerly the sole party. A transitional government was formed in April 1991 and a new constitution was approved by referendum in January 1992. The new constitution provided for a multiparty political system, and legislative elections were held in February and March 1992 with the Alliance for Democracy in Mali (ADEMA) emerging victorious. Alpha Konaré, the ADEMA leader, won the presidential elections in April 1992 and was re-elected in May 1997. In legislative elections in July and August 1997, ADEMA won 129 out of 147 seats in the National Assembly.

HEAD OF STATE
President, Alpha Oumar Konaré, *elected* 1992, *re-elected* 11 May 1997

CABINET *as at July 1998*
Prime Minister, Ibrahim Boubacar Keita
Armed Forces and Veterans, Mohamed Salia Sokona
Basic Education, Government Spokesperson, Adama Samassekou
Communications, Ascofaré Ouleymatou
Culture and Tourism, Aminata Dramane Traoré
Economy, Planning and Integration, Ahmed El Madani Diallo
Employment, Civil Service and Labour, Ousmane Oumarou Sidibé
Environment, Mohamed Ag Erlaf
Finance, Soumaila Cissé
Foreign Affairs, Malians Abroad, Maj. Modibo Sidibé
Health, Solidarity and the Elderly, Diakité Fatoumata N'Diayé
Industry, Commerce, Cottage Industries, Fatou Haidara
Justice and Keeper of the Seals, Hamidou Diabaté
Mines and Energy, Yoro Diakité
Public Works and Transport, Ibréhima Siby
Relations with Political Institutions and Parties, Hassane Barry
Rural Development and Water, Modibo Traoré
Secondary and Higher Education and Scientific Research, Younous Hamaye Dicko
Sports, Adama Koné
Territorial Administration and Security, Lt.-Col. Sada Samaké
Urban Development and Housing, Sy Kadiatou Sow
Women, Children and the Family, Diarra Afsata Thiero
Youth Promotion, Boubacar Karamoko Coulibaly

EMBASSY OF THE REPUBLIC OF MALI
Avenue Molière 487, 1060 Brussels, Belgium
Tel: Brussels 345 7432
Ambassador Extraordinary and Plenipotentiary, HE N'Tji Laico Traoré, apptd 1993
BRITISH AMBASSADOR, HE David Snoxell, resident at Dakar, Senegal
BRITISH CONSULATE – Bamako

ECONOMY

Mali's principal exports are gold, groundnuts, cotton fibres, meat and dried fish. Principal imports include petroleum, textiles and machinery. Mali rejoined the CFA Franc Zone in 1984.

In 1994 Mali had a trade deficit of US$102 million and a current account deficit of US$164 million. In 1995 imports totalled US$755 million and exports US$452 million.
GNP – US$2,422 million (1996); US$240 per capita (1996)
GDP – US$2,895 million (1994); US$183 per capita (1994)
ANNUAL AVERAGE GROWTH OF GDP – –0.2 per cent (1991)
INFLATION RATE – 6.8 per cent (1996)
TOTAL EXTERNAL DEBT – US$3,020 million (1996)

TRADE WITH UK	1996	1997
Imports from UK	£24,335,000	£24,051,000
Exports to UK	681,000	613,000

MALTA
Repubblika ta' Malta

AREA – 122 sq. miles (316 sq. km)
POPULATION – 371,000 (1995). The Maltese are mainly Roman Catholic. The Maltese language is of Semitic origin and held by some to be derived from the Carthaginian and Phoenician tongues. Maltese and English are the official languages of administration. Maltese is the official language in all the courts of law and the language of general use in the islands
CAPITAL – ΨValletta (population, 9,144, 1995 census)
CURRENCY – Maltese lira (LM) of 100 cents or 1,000 mils
NATIONAL ANTHEM – L-Innu Malti
NATIONAL DAYS – 31 March (Freedom Day); 8 September (Lady of Victories); 7 June; 21 September (Independence Day); 13 December (Republic Day)
NATIONAL FLAG – Two equal vertical stripes, white at the hoist and red at the fly. A representation of the George Cross is carried edged with red in the canton of the white stripe
LIFE EXPECTANCY (years) – male 74.86; female 79.11
POPULATION GROWTH RATE – 0.9 per cent (1995)
POPULATION DENSITY – 1,173 per sq. km (1995)
MILITARY EXPENDITURE – 1.1 per cent of GDP (1996)
MILITARY PERSONNEL – 1,950

Malta lies in the Mediterranean Sea, 58 miles (93 km) from Sicily and about 180 miles (288 km) from the African coast. It is about 17 miles (27 km) in length and 9 miles (14.5 km) in breadth. Malta also includes the islands of Gozo (area 25.9 sq. miles (67 sq. km)), Comino and minor islets.

HISTORY AND POLITICS

Malta was in turn held by the Phoenicians, Carthaginians, Romans and Arabs. In 1090 it was conquered by Count Roger of Normandy and in 1530 handed over to the Knights of St John. In 1565 it sustained the famous siege, when the Turks were successfully withstood by Grand-master La Valette. The Knights fortified the islands and built Valletta before being expelled by Napoleon in 1798. The Maltese rose against the French garrison soon after-wards and the island was subsequently blockaded by the British fleet. The Maltese people requested the protection of the British Crown in 1802 on condition that their rights would be respected. The islands were finally annexed to the British Crown by the Treaty of Paris in 1814.
Malta was again besieged during the Second World War. From June 1940 to the end of the war, 432 members of the garrison and 1,540 civilians were killed by enemy aircraft. The island was awarded the George Cross for gallantry on 15 April 1942.
On 21 September 1964 Malta became an independent state within the Commonwealth, and on 13 December 1974 a republic within the Commonwealth.
Elections to the unicameral parliament of 65 members are held every five years by a system of proportional representation. The Malta Labour Party was elected in the general election in October 1996, winning 35 seats to the Nationalist Party's 34.

FOREIGN RELATIONS

Malta applied for EC membership in 1990 and in June 1993 the Commission issued its Opinion that Malta should be accepted as a member subsequent to the implementation of a series of economic reforms. In October 1996 the Labour government announced its intention to withdraw Malta's EU application and its participation in NATO's partner-ship for peace programme.

HEAD OF STATE
President, Dr Ugo Mifsud Bonnici, *took office* 4 April 1994

CABINET *as at July 1998*
Prime Minister, Home Affairs, Information, Shipping, Dr Alfred Sant
Deputy PM, Foreign Affairs, Environment, Dr George Vella
Agriculture and Fisheries, Noel Farrugia
Economic Affairs and Industry, Dr John Attard Montalto
Education and National Culture, Evarist Bartolo
Finance and Commerce, Leo Brincat
Health, Care of the Elderly and Family Affairs, Michael Farrugia
Housing and Local Councils, Freddie Portelli
Justice, Gavin Gulia
Office of the Prime Minister, Joe Mizzi
Public Works and Construction, Charles Buhagiar
Social Welfare, Edwin Grech
Tourism, the Self-Employed, Karmenu Vella
Transport and Ports, Joe Debono Grech

MALTA HIGH COMMISSION
Malta House, 36–38 Piccadilly, London WIV OPQ
Tel 0171-292 4800
High Commissioner, HE Richard Matrenza, apptd 1997

BRITISH HIGH COMMISSION
7 St Anne Street, Floriana (PO Box 506), Malta
Tel: Floriana 233134/7
High Commissioner, HE Graham Archer, CMG, apptd 1995
BRITISH COUNCIL REPRESENTATIVE, A. Bradley, c/o British High Commission

ECONOMY

Tourism has assumed primary importance, with more than 1,100,000 tourists visiting the island in 1997. In 1996 2,443,502 passengers passed through Malta airport.
Agriculture and fisheries are also important. Principal products are potatoes, tomatoes, animal products, fruit, flowers and cuttings.
The island's leading industry is the state-owned Malta Drydocks, employing about 3,350 people. Malta Freeport was opened in 1990 in the southern port of Marsaxlokk and comprises a container distribution centre, an oil products terminal and warehouse facilities. A second container terminal is being built.
In 1994 manufacturing employed 22.1 per cent of the workforce and accounted for 24 per cent of GDP. Industries include food processing, textiles, footwear and clothing, plastics and chemical products, electronic equip-ment, machinery and components. Value Added Tax was abolished in July 1997.
In 1995 there was a trade deficit of US$748 million and a current account deficit of US$402 million. In 1996 imports totalled US$2,802 million and exports US$1,743 million.
GDP – US$2,804 million (1994); US$7,394 per capita (1994)
ANNUAL AVERAGE GROWTH OF GDP – 9.0 per cent (1995)
INFLATION RATE – 2.5 per cent (1996)
UNEMPLOYMENT – 4.5 per cent (1993)
TOTAL EXTERNAL DEBT – US$953 million (1996)

TRADE

The principal imports are foodstuffs (mainly wheat, meats, milk and fruit), fodder, beverages and tobacco, fuels, chemicals, textiles and machinery (industrial, agricultural and transport). The chief exports are processed food, electronics, textiles, and other manufactures.

Trade with UK	1996	1997
Imports from UK	£242,572,000	£253,777,000
Exports to UK	94,910,000	85,753,000

EDUCATION

Education is compulsory between the ages of five and 16 and is free at all levels. Secondary education in state schools is provided in secondary schools, junior lyceums and trade schools. There are ten junior lyceums, 18 secondary schools and five centres catering for low achievers.

A Junior College, administered by the University of Malta, prepares students specifically for a university course. Tertiary education is available at the University of Malta. There are also schools administered by the Catholic Church and other private schools.

ILLITERACY RATE – 8.7 per cent

ENROLMENT (percentage of age group) – primary 100 per cent (1994); secondary 84 per cent (1994); tertiary 21.8 per cent (1994)

MARSHALL ISLANDS
Republic of the Marshall Islands

AREA – 70 sq. miles (181 sq. km)

POPULATION – 56,000 (1994 UN estimate): 99 per cent are Micronesian. Over half the population is under 15. About 60 per cent of the population is concentrated on the two atolls of Majuro and Kwajalein. The population is Christian, primarily Protestant but with a substantial Catholic minority. Marshallese and English are the official languages

CAPITAL – Dalap-Uliga-Darrit, on Majuro Atoll (population, 20,000)

MAJOR TOWN – Ebeye (9,200)

CURRENCY – Currency is that of the USA

NATIONAL DAY – 21 October (Compact Day)

NATIONAL FLAG – Blue with a diagonal ray divided white over orange running from the lower hoist to the upper fly; in the canton a white sun

LIFE EXPECTANCY (years) – male 59.06; female 62.96

POPULATION GROWTH RATE – 3.7 per cent (1995)

POPULATION DENSITY – 307 per sq. km (1995)

The Republic of the Marshall Islands consists of 29 atolls and five islands in the central Pacific. The islands and atolls form two parallel chains running north-west to south-east: the Ratak (Sunrise) chain and the Ralik (Sunset) chain. The largest atoll is Kwajalein in the Ralik chain. The atolls are coral and the islands are volcanic. None of the islands rises more than a few metres above sea level. The climate is hot and humid with little seasonal variation in temperature.

HISTORY AND POLITICS

The Marshall Islands were claimed by Spain in 1592 but were left undisturbed by the Spanish Empire for 300 years. In 1886 the Marshall Islands formally became a German protectorate. On the outbreak of the First World War in 1914, Japan took control of the islands on behalf of the Allied powers, and after the war administered the territory as a League of Nations mandate. During the Second World War US armed forces seized the islands from the Japanese after intense fighting. In 1947 the USA entered into agreement with the UN Security Council to administer the Micronesia area, of which the Marshall Islands are a part, as the UN Trust Territory of the Pacific Islands.

The islands became internally self-governing in 1979, and the US Trusteeship administration came to an end on 21 October 1986, when a Compact of Free Association between the USA and the Republic of the Marshall Islands came into effect. By this agreement the USA recognized the Republic of the Marshall Islands as a fully sovereign and independent state. The UN Security Council terminated the UN Trust Territory of the Pacific in relation to the Marshall Islands and recognized its independence in December 1990.

FOREIGN RELATIONS

The Republic of the Marshall Islands has no defence forces. The Compact of Free Association places full responsibility for defence of the Marshall Islands on the USA. The US Department of Defense retains control of islands within Kwajalein Atoll where it has a missile test range.

POLITICAL SYSTEM

The republic is a democracy based on a parliamentary system of government. The executive is headed by the president, who is elected by the *Nitijela* from among its members. The president serves for a four-year term. The legislature has two chambers, the Council of Chiefs (*Iroij*) of 12 members and the Nitijela of 33 members. The Nitijela is the law-making chamber, to which the president and government are accountable. The Iroij has an advisory role.

There are 24 local government districts, each of which usually consists of an elected council, a mayor and appointed local officials.

HEAD OF STATE

President, Imata Kabua, *elected* 14 January 1997

GOVERNMENT *as at July 1998*

The President

Education, Justin DeBrum

Finance, Ruben Zackhras

Foreign Affairs, Trade, Phillip Muller

Health and Environment, Tom Kijiner

Interior and Social Welfare, Brenson Wase

Justice, Lomes McKay

Resources and Development, Jiba Kabua

Transportation and Communication, Kunio Lemari

Without Portfolio, Christopher Loeak; Litokwa Tomeing

BRITISH AMBASSADOR, HE Vernon Scarborough, resident at Suva, Fiji

ECONOMY

The economy is a mixture of subsistence and a service-based sector. About half the working population is engaged in agriculture and fishing, with coconut oil and copra production comprising 90 per cent of total exports. Imports include oil, food and machinery. The service sector is based in Majuro and Ebeye and concentrated in banking and insurance, construction, transportation and tourism. Direct US aid under the Compact accounts for two-thirds of the islands' budget. The islands charge foreign fishing fleets licences for fishing tuna in the waters around the islands. Japanese fleets pay some US$3 million a year. The USA, Japan and Australia are the main trading partners.

GNP – US$108 million (1996); US$1,890 per capita (1996)

GDP – US$72 million (1994); US$1,719 per capita (1994)

TRADE WITH UK	1996	1997
Imports from UK	£2,562,000	£15,635,000
Exports to UK	383,000	441,000

COMMUNICATIONS

Air Marshall Islands provides air services within the islands and to Hawaii. Continental Air Micronesia serves Majuro and Kwajalein with flights to Hawaii and Guam. Majuro also has shipping links to Hawaii, Australia, Japan and throughout the Pacific.

SOCIAL WELFARE

Majuro and Ebeye have hospitals run by the government with aid from the US Public Health Service. Each outer island community has a health assistant.

The state school system provides education up to age 18, but only 25 per cent of students proceed beyond elementary level because of inadequate resources.

MAURITANIA
République Islamique de Mauritanie

AREA – 395,956 sq. miles (1,025,520 sq. km). Neighbours: Senegal (south-west), Mali (east and south), Algeria and Western Sahara (north)
POPULATION – 2,284,000 (1994 UN estimate). The official language is Arabic. Pulaar, Soninke, Wolof and French are also spoken
CAPITAL – Nouakchott (population, 850,000)
CURRENCY – Ouguiya (UM) of 5 khoums
NATIONAL DAY – 28 November
NATIONAL FLAG – Yellow star and crescent on green ground
LIFE EXPECTANCY (years) – male 49.90; female 53.10
POPULATION GROWTH RATE – 2.6 per cent (1995)
POPULATION DENSITY – 2 per sq. km (1995)
MILITARY EXPENDITURE – 2.9 per cent of GDP (1996)
MILITARY PERSONNEL – 20,650: Army 15,000, Navy 500, Air Force 150, Paramilitaries 5,000
CONSCRIPTION DURATION – Two years
ILLITERACY RATE – 62.3 per cent
ENROLMENT (percentage of age group) – primary 60 per cent (1995); tertiary 4.1 per cent (1993)

HISTORY AND POLITICS

Mauritania elected on 28 November 1958 to remain within the French Community as an autonomous republic. It became fully independent on 28 November 1960. In 1972 Mauritania left the Franc Zone.

Mauritania and Morocco occupied the Western Sahara territory in February 1976 when Spain formally relinquished it and in April 1976 agreed on a new frontier dividing the territory between them. In August 1979, Mauritania relinquished all claim to the southern sector of the Western Sahara after a three-year war against Polisario Front guerrillas.

After a military coup in 1978, Mauritania was ruled by a Military Committee for National Salvation. In April 1991 President Ould Taya announced a political amnesty, followed by multiparty elections for a reconvened Senate and National Assembly. The constitution was approved by referendum in July 1991. Multiparty legislative elections were held in March 1992 and won by the Republican Democratic and Social Party (PRDS) led by President Ould Taya. The president appointed a Cabinet of PRDS members in April 1992 but the legitimacy of the new government was undermined by the boycott of the elections by the main opposition grouping, the Union of Democratic Forces (UDF).

Legislative elections in October 1996 were won by the PRDS after the UDF pulled out after the first round accusing the government of fraud. In presidential elections in December 1997, President Ould Taya was re-elected following a boycott by opposition parties.

HEAD OF STATE
President, Col. Moaouia ould Sidi Ahmed Taya (PRDS), *took power* 12 December 1984, *elected* 17 January 1992, *re-elected* 12 December 1997

COUNCIL OF MINISTERS *as at July 1998*
Prime Minister, Mohamed Lemine ould Guig
Civil Service, Labour, Youth, Sports, Baba ould Sidi
Communications and Relations with Parliament, Rachid ould Saleh
Culture, Islamic Orientation, Khattry ould Jiddou
Defence, Kaba ould Elewa
Education, Ahmedou ould Moustapha ould Senhouri
Equipment and Transport, Sgheyer ould M'Barek
Finance, Kamara Ali Gueladio
Fisheries and Marine Economy, Mohamed El-Moctar ould Zamel
Foreign Affairs, Mohamed El-Hacen ould Lebbatt
Health and Social Affairs, Dia Ba
Interior, Post and Telecommunications, Col. Ahmed ould Minnih
Justice, Mohamed Lemine ould Ahmed
Mines and Industry, N'Gaidé Lamine Kayou
Planning, Sid'el Moctar Naji
Rural Development and Environment, Abderrahmane ould Hamma Vezaz
Trade, Handicrafts and Tourism, Sidi Mohamed ould Mohamed Boual
Water Power, Energy, Mohamed Salem ould Merzoug

EMBASSY OF THE ISLAMIC REPUBLIC OF MAURITANIA
5 rue de Montevideo, Paris XVIe, France
Tel: Paris 45048854
Ambassador Extraordinary and Plenipotentiary, Dah ould Abdi, apptd 1996

BRITISH AMBASSADOR, HE William H. Fullerton, CMG, resident at Rabat, Morocco

ECONOMY

The main source of potential wealth lies in rich deposits of iron ore around Zouérate, in the north of the country, and rich fishing grounds off the coast.

In 1995 Mauritania had a trade surplus of US$184 million and a current account surplus of US$22 million. In 1994 imports totalled US$403 million and exports US$487 million.
GNP – US$1,089 million (1996); US$470 per capita (1996)
GDP – US$1,193 million (1994); US$411 per capita (1994)
INFLATION RATE – 4.7 per cent (1996)
TOTAL EXTERNAL DEBT – US$2,363 million (1996)

TRADE WITH UK	1996	1997
Imports from UK	£14,150,000	£8,555,000
Exports to UK	13,982,000	16,357,000

MAURITIUS

AREA – 788 sq. miles (2,040 sq. km)
POPULATION – 1,122,000 (1996 estimate): Asiatic races (Hindus 51.8 per cent, Muslims 16.5 per cent, Chinese 2.8 per cent), and persons of European (mainly French) extraction, mixed and African descent (28.6 per cent). English is the official language but French may be used in the National Assembly and lower law courts. Creole is the most commonly used language and several Indian languages are also used
CAPITAL – ΨPort Louis (population, 144,776, 1994 estimate)

MAJOR TOWNS – Beau Bassin-Rose Hill (97,050); Curepipe (76,971); Quatre Bornes (73,870); Vacoas-Phoenix (94,558), 1994 estimates
CURRENCY – Mauritius rupee of 100 cents
NATIONAL ANTHEM – Glory to thee, Motherland
NATIONAL DAY – 12 March
NATIONAL FLAG – Red, blue, yellow and green horizontal stripes
LIFE EXPECTANCY (years) – male 66.44; female 73.95
POPULATION GROWTH RATE – 1.2 per cent (1995)
POPULATION DENSITY – 550 per sq. km (1995)
URBAN POPULATION – 43.6 per cent (1994)
MILITARY EXPENDITURE – 1.4 per cent of GDP (1996)
MILITARY PERSONNEL – 1,800 Paramilitaries

Mauritius is an island group lying in the Indian Ocean, 550 miles east of Madagascar. The climate is sub-tropical and maritime, with a wide range of rainfall and temperature resulting from the mountainous nature of the island. Humidity is high throughout the year.

HISTORY AND POLITICS

Mauritius was discovered in 1511 by the Portuguese; the Dutch visited it in 1598 and named it Mauritius after Prince Maurice of Nassau. From 1638 to 1710 it was held as a Dutch colony; the French took possession in 1715 but did not settle it until 1721. Mauritius was taken by a British force in 1810 and became a Crown Colony. It became an independent state within the Commonwealth on 12 March 1968 and a republic on 12 March 1992.

The last general election was held on 20 December 1995. The present government was formed by the Parti des Travailleurs Mauricien (PTM).

POLITICAL SYSTEM

The president is head of state and is elected by the National Assembly. The prime minister, appointed by the president, is the member of the National Assembly who appears to the president best able to command the support of the majority of members of the Assembly. Other ministers are appointed by the president acting on the advice of the prime minister.

The National Assembly has a five-year term and consists of 62 elected members (the island of Mauritius is divided into 20 three-member constituencies and Rodrigues returns two members), and eight specially-elected members. Of the latter, four seats go to the 'best loser' of whichever communities in the island are under-represented in the Assembly after the general election and the four remaining seats are allocated on the basis of both party and community.

HEAD OF STATE

President, Cassam Uteem, *elected* June 1992, *re-elected* 28 June 1997
Vice-President, Angidi Verriah Chettjar

COUNCIL OF MINISTERS *as at July 1998*

Prime Minister, Defence and Home Affairs, External Communications and Outer Islands, Civil Service Affairs, Urban and Rural Development, Dr Navinchandra Ramgoolam
Deputy PM, Foreign Affairs and International Trade, Rajkeswur Purryag
Agriculture, Fisheries, Co-operatives, Arvin Boolell
Arts and Culture, Tsang Fan Hin Tsang Man Kin
Attorney-General, Justice, Human Rights and Corporate Affairs, Labour and Industrial Relations, Abdul Razack Mohamed Amin Peeroo
Economic Development and Regional Co-operation, Rundheersing Bheenick

Education and Human Resource Development, Ramsamy Chedumbarum Pillay
Finance, Vasant Kumar Bunwaree
Health and Quality of Life, Nankeswarsingh Deerpalsingh
Housing, Land Development, Clarel Désiré Malherbe
Industry and Commerce, Sathiamoorthy Sunassee
Land Transport, Shipping and Public Safety, Ahmed Rashid Beebeejaun
Local Government, Environment, James Burty David
Public Infrastructure, Mohamed Siddick Chady
Public Utilities, Devanand Virahsawmy
Rodrigues Island, Bénoît Jolicoeur
Social Security and National Solidarity, Dhurma Gian Nath
Telecommunications and Information Technology, Sarat Dutt Lallah
Tourism and Leisure, Marie Joseph Jacques Chasteau de Balyon
Women, Family Welfare and Child Development, Indira Savitree Thacoor-Sidaya
Youth and Sports, Sachindev Mahess Kumar Soonarane

MAURITIUS HIGH COMMISSION
32–33 Elvaston Place, London SW7 5NW
Tel 0171-581 0294/5
High Commissioner, HE Sir Satcam Boolell, QC, apptd 1996

BRITISH HIGH COMMISSION
Les Cascades Building, Edith Cavell Street, Port Louis (PO Box 1063)
Tel: Port Louis 211 1361
High Commissioner, HE James Daly, CVO, apptd 1997

BRITISH COUNCIL DIRECTOR, S. Ponnappa, PO Box 111, Rose Hill

ECONOMY

The major cash crop is sugar cane. Tea and tobacco are grown commercially on a smaller scale. Production in 1996 was: sugar, 560,138 tonnes; tea (manufactured), 2,497 tonnes; tobacco (leaves), 878 tonnes. In 1994 production of molasses, mainly for export, was 138,421 tonnes. Other products include alcohol, rum, denatured spirits, perfumed spirits and vinegar.

The bulk of the island's requirements in manufactured products still has to be imported. However, the number of export-orientated enterprises had risen from ten in 1971 to 481 in 1996. The biggest firms are in clothing manufacture, particularly woollen knitwear, but the range of goods produced includes toys, plastic products, leather goods, diamond cutting and polishing, watches, television sets and telephones.

Tourism is a major source of income, with an estimated 486,867 tourists in 1996. France is the most important source of tourists, followed closely by the neighbouring French island of Réunion.
GNP – US$4,205 million (1996); US$3,710 per capita (1996)
GDP – US$4,810 million (1994); US$3,134 per capita (1994)
ANNUAL AVERAGE GROWTH OF GDP – 5.5 per cent (1996)
INFLATION RATE – 6.6 per cent (1996)
TOTAL EXTERNAL DEBT – US$1,818 million (1996)

TRADE

Most foodstuffs and raw materials have to be imported from abroad. Apart from local consumption (about 36,500 tonnes a year), the sugar produced is exported, mainly to Britain.

In 1996 Mauritius had a trade deficit of US$295 million and a current account surplus of US$17 million. In 1995 imports totalled US$1,958 million and exports US$1,538 million.

Trade with UK	1996	1997
Imports from UK	£73,417,000	£65,751,000
Exports to UK	344,161,000	339,214,000

COMMUNICATIONS

Port Louis, on the north-west coast, handles the bulk of the island's external trade. A bulk sugar terminal capable of handling the total sugar crop began operating in 1980. The international airport is located at Plaisance, about five miles from Mahébourg. There are seven daily newspapers and 15 weeklies, mostly in French. The Mauritius Broadcasting Corporation operates television and radio broadcasting in the country.

EDUCATION

Primary and secondary education are free and primary education is compulsory. There are a number of training facilities offering vocational training. The Institute of Education is responsible for training primary and secondary school teachers and for curriculum development. The University of Mauritius had 2,496 students in 1996–7.

ILLITERACY RATE – 17.1 per cent

ENROLMENT (percentage of age group) – primary 96 per cent (1995); tertiary 6.3 per cent (1995)

RODRIGUES AND DEPENDENCIES

Rodrigues, formerly a dependency but now part of Mauritius, is about 350 miles east of Mauritius, with an area of 40 square miles. Population (1996) 35,019. Cattle, salt fish, sheep, goats, pigs, maize and onions are the principal exports. The island is administered by an Island Secretary.

Island Secretary, B. Juggoo

The islands of Agalega and St Brandon are dependencies of Mauritius. Total population (1996) 170.

MEXICO
Estados Unidos Mexicanos

AREA – 756,066 sq. miles (1,958,201 sq. km). Neighbours: USA (north), Guatemala and Belize (south-east)

POPULATION – 90,487,000 (1994 UN estimate). Spanish is the official language and is spoken by about 95 per cent of the population. There are five main groups of Indian languages (Náhuatl, Maya, Zapotec, Otomí, Mixtec) and 59 dialects derived from them

CAPITAL – Mexico City (population, 15,047,685, 1990)

MAJOR CITIES – Ciudad Juárez (797,679); Guadalajara (2,846,000); León (956,070); Monterrey (2,521,697); Puebla (1,454,526); Tijuana (742,686); Toluca (827,339); Torreón (876,456), 1990 census

CURRENCY – Peso of 100 centavos

NATIONAL ANTHEM – Mexicanos, Al Grito De Guerra (Mexicans, to the war cry)

NATIONAL DAY – 16 September (Proclamation of Independence)

NATIONAL FLAG – Three vertical bands in green, white, red, with the Mexican emblem (an eagle on a cactus devouring a snake) in the centre

LIFE EXPECTANCY (years) – male 62.10; female 66.00

POPULATION GROWTH RATE – 1.8 per cent (1995)

POPULATION DENSITY – 46 per sq. km (1995)

ILLITERACY RATE – 10.4 per cent

ENROLMENT (percentage of age group) – primary 100 per cent (1993); secondary 45 per cent (1990); tertiary 14.3 per cent (1994)

The Sierra Nevada, known in Mexico as the Sierra Madre, and Rocky Mountains continue south from the northern border with the USA, running parallel to the west and east coasts. The interior consists of an elevated plateau between the two ranges. In the west is the peninsula of Lower California, separated from the mainland by the Gulf of California. The main rivers are the Rio Grande (Rio Bravo) del Norte, which forms part of the northern boundary and is navigable for about 70 miles from its mouth in the Gulf of Mexico, and the Rio Grande de Santiago, the Rio Balsas and Rio Papaloapan.

HISTORY AND POLITICS

Present-day Mexico and Guatemala were once the centre of a civilization which flowered in the periods from AD 500 to 1100 and 1300 to 1500 and collapsed before the army of Spanish adventurers under Hernán Cortés in the years following 1519. Pre-Columbian Mexico was divided between different Indian cultures, each of which has left distinctive archaeological remains, most notably the Mayan, Teotihuacáno, Zapotec, Totonac and Toltec cultures. The last and most famous Indian culture, the Aztec, based on Tenochtitlán, suffered more than the others at the hands of the Spanish and very few Aztec monuments remain.

After the conquest, the Spanish appointed a Viceroy to rule their new dominions, which they called New Spain. The country was largely converted to Christianity and a distinctive colonial civilization, representing a marriage of Indian and Spanish traditions, developed. In 1810 a revolt began against Spanish rule. This was finally successful in 1821, when a precarious independence was proclaimed.

Friction with the USA led to the war of 1845–8, at the end of which Mexico was forced to cede the northern provinces of Texas, California and New Mexico. In 1862 Mexican insolvency led to invasion by French forces which installed Archduke Maximilian of Austria as Emperor. The empire collapsed with the execution of the Emperor in 1867 and the austere reformer Juárez restored the republic. Juárez's death was followed by the dictatorship of Porfirio Díaz, which saw an enormous increase in foreign, particularly British and American, investment in the country. In 1910 began the Mexican Revolution which reformed the social structure and the land system, curbed the power of foreign companies and ushered in the independent industrial Mexico of today.

There are nine registered political parties, of which the largest is the Partido Revolucionario Institucional (PRI) which has constituted the governing party for more than 60 years. The main opposition parties are the Partido de Acción Nacional (PAN) and the Partido de la Revolución Democrática (PRD). On 6 July 1997 voting took place in the first fully democratic elections for the Chamber of Deputies, a quarter of the Senate, six state governorships and the Mayor of Mexico. Though still the largest party, the PRI no longer has an overall majority in the Chamber of Deputies.

INSURGENCIES

An armed revolt of Zapatista peasant Indians in the southern state of Chiapas in January 1994 highlighted continuing charges against the PRI of corruption, and these continued up to the August 1994 elections.

A further armed revolt by the Zapatista National Liberation Army (ZNLA) in Chiapas from December 1994 to February 1995 caused a political and economic crisis. President Zedillo introduced political reforms agreed with the PAN and PRD, making the electoral commission fully independent and providing for the re-examination of contentious elections by impartial observers. Negotiations with the Zapatistas produced a preliminary agreement on indigenous rights in February 1996, but talks broke down and were suspended in September 1996.

New guerrilla groups, the People's Revolutionary Army (EPR) and the Popular Insurgency Revolutionary Army (ERIP), emerged in 1996. There were nationwide protests after the police and senior officials were implicated in the massacre of 45 Indians in Chiapas on 22 December 1997. There were renewed calls for the Army to withdraw from the province, and discussions over new peace talks resumed in February 1998.

POLITICAL SYSTEM

Congress consists of a Senate of 128 members, elected for six years, and of a Chamber of Deputies, at present numbering 500, elected for three years. The chief executive of the government is the president, who is elected for a six-year term and may not be re-elected.

FEDERAL STRUCTURE

State	Area (sq. km)	Population (1995)	Capital
Federal District	1,499	8,489,007	Mexico City
Aguascalientes	5,589	862,720	Aguascalientes
Baja California	70,113	2,112,140	Mexicali
Baja California Sur	73,677	375,494	La Paz
Campeche	51,833	642,516	Campeche
Coahuila	151,571	2,173,775	Saltillo
Colima	5,455	488,028	Colima
Chiapas	73,887	3,584,786	Tuxtla Gutiérrez
Chihuahua	247,087	2,793,537	Chihuahua
Durango	119,648	1,431,748	Victoria de Durango
Guanajuato	30,589	4,406,568	Guanajuato
Guerrero	63,794	2,916,567	Chilpancingo
Hidalgo	20,987	2,112,473	Pachuca de Soto
Jalisco	80,137	5,991,176	Guadalajara
México	21,461	11,707,964	Toluca de Lerdo
Michoacán	59,864	3,870,604	Morelia
Morelos	4,941	1,442,662	Cuernavaca
Nayarit	27,621	896,702	Tepic
Nuevo Léon	64,555	3,550,114	Monterrey
Oaxaca	95,364	3,228,895	Oaxaca de Juárez
Puebla	33,919	4,624,365	Puebla de Zaragoza
Querétaro	11,769	1,250,476	Querétaro
Quintana Roo	50,350	703,536	Chetumal
San Luis Potosí	62,848	2,200,763	San Luis Potosí
Sinaloa	58,092	2,425,675	Culiacán Rosales
Sonora	184,934	2,085,536	Hermosillo
Tabasco	24,661	1,748,769	Villahermosa
Tamaulipas	79,829	2,527,328	Ciudad Victoria
Tlaxcala	3,914	883,924	Tlaxcala
Veracruz	72,815	6,737,324	Jalapa Enríquez
Yucatán	39,340	1,556,622	Mérida
Zacatecas	75,040	1,336,496	Zacatecas

HEAD OF STATE

President, Dr Ernesto Zedillo Ponce de León, *elected* August 1994, *took office* 1 December 1994

CABINET *as at July 1998*

Agrarian Reform, Arturo Warman Gryj
Agriculture, Livestock and Rural Development, Romárico Arroyo Marroquin
Attorney-General, Jorge Madrazo Cuéllar
Communications and Transport, Carlos Ruiz Sacristan
Comptroller-General, Arsenio Farell Cubillas

Defence, Gen. Enrique Cervantes Aguirre
Education, Miguel Limón Rojas
Energy, Luis Téllez Kuenzler
Environment, Natural Resources and Fisheries, Julia Carabias Lillo
Finance and Public Credit, José Ángel Gurría Treviño
Foreign Affairs, Rosario Green Macias
Health, Juan Ramón de la Fuente Ramírez
Interior, Francisco Labastida Ochoa
Labour and Social Welfare, José Antonio González Fernández
Mayor of Mexico City, Cuauhtémoc Cárdenas Solórzano
Naval Affairs, Adm. José Ramón Lorenzo Franco
Social Development, Esteban Moctezuma
Tourism, Oscar Espinosa Villareal
Trade and Industry, Herminio Blanco Mendoza

MEXICAN EMBASSY

42 Hertford Street, London WIY 7TF
Tel 0171-499 8586
Ambassador Extraordinary and Plenipotentiary, HE Santiago Oñate, apptd 1997
Minister, Deputy Ambassador, J. Brito-Moncada
Military Attaché, Col. F. A. Espitia-Hernández
Minister, Consul-General, J. Ibarra-Morales
Counsellor, F. Estandía-González (*Commercial*)

BRITISH EMBASSY

Calle Río Lerma 71, Colonia Cuauhtémoc, 06500 Mexico City
Tel: Mexico City 207 2089
Ambassador Extraordinary and Plenipotentiary, HE Adrian Beamish, CMG, apptd 1994
Deputy Head of Mission, Minister-Counsellor and Consul-General, Dr P. Tibber
Defence Attaché, Col. J. Watson
First Secretary (*Commercial*), A. Stephens

CONSULAR OFFICES – Mexico City, Acapulco, Cancun, Ciudad Juárez, Guadalajara, Mérida, Monterrey, Oaxaca, Tampico, Tijuana, Veracruz

BRITISH COUNCIL DIRECTOR, A. Curry, Maestro Antonio Caso 127, Col. San Rafael, Delegación Cuauhtémoc, (PO Box 30-588), Mexico 06470

BRITISH CHAMBER OF COMMERCE, British Trade Centre, Rio de la Plata 30, Col. Cuauhtémoc, CP 06500, Mexico City DF. *Manager,* Stephen Grant

DEFENCE

The Army has 720 armoured personnel carriers and 123 artillery pieces. The Navy has three destroyers, four frigates, 106 patrol and coastal vessels, and nine combat aircraft. There are 20 naval bases. The Air Force has 125 combat aircraft and 95 armed helicopters.
MILITARY EXPENDITURE – 0.8 per cent of GDP (1996)
MILITARY PERSONNEL – 175,000: Army 130,000, Navy 37,000, Air Force 8,000
CONSCRIPTION DURATION – 12 months (four hours per week) by lottery

ECONOMY

The principal crops are maize, beans, sorghum, rice, wheat, barley, sugar cane, coffee, cotton, tomatoes, chillies, tobacco, chick-peas, groundnuts, cocoa and many kinds of fruit. The maguey, or Mexican cactus, yields several fermented drinks, mezcal and tequila (distilled) and pulque (undistilled). Another species of the plant supplies sisal-hemp (henequen). The forests contain mahogany, rosewood, ebony and chicle trees. Agriculture employs an estimated 20 per cent of the working population.

The principal industries are mining and petroleum, although there has been considerable expansion of both light and heavy industries; exports of manufactured goods now average about 56 per cent of total exports. The steel industry expanded steadily until recently and current production is around 5.8 million tons. In 1996, 1,212,586 motor vehicles were produced.

The mineral wealth is great, and principal minerals are gold, silver, copper, lead, zinc, quicksilver, iron and sulphur. Substantial reserves of uranium have been found. Mexico produces 25 per cent of the world's supply of fluorspar.

Oil exports were 1.5 million barrels per day in 1996. Oil reserves have increased substantially due to discoveries in the Gulf of Campeche. A refinery at Tula is the nation's largest; and new refineries in Monterrey, State of Nuevo León, and Salina Cruz, State of Oaxaca, are under construction.

Following economic difficulties in late 1994, the government introduced austerity measures in January 1995, increasing interest rates and petrol taxes, curbing pay levels and reducing public expenditure in an attempt to keep inflation and debt levels under control and to rein back a runaway trade deficit. In June 1997 the government announced a three-year National Programme for the Financing of Development intended to stimulate the economy. Mexico repaid the last of its debt to the USA in 1997.

In November 1997 the stock market and the peso fell as a result of the economic crisis in south-east Asia. In response, the government secured a contingency loan of US$2.5 billion, which successfully halted the slide. The currency and the stock market quickly recovered to their pre-November levels.

Mexico joined GATT in 1986 and the OECD in 1994.

GNP – US$341,718 million (1996); US$3,670 per capita (1996)
GDP – US$270,699 million (1994); US$4,041 per capita (1994)
ANNUAL AVERAGE GROWTH OF GDP – 5.1 per cent (1996)
INFLATION RATE – 34.4 per cent (1996)
UNEMPLOYMENT – 4.7 per cent (1995)
TOTAL EXTERNAL DEBT – US$157,125 million (1996)

TRADE

Major imports include computers, auto assembly material, electrical parts, auto and truck parts, powdered milk, corn and sorghum, transport, sound-recording and power-generating equipment, chemicals, industrial machinery, pharmaceuticals and specialized appliances. Principal exports include oil, automobiles, auto engines, fruits and vegetables, shrimps, coffee, computers, cattle, glass, iron and steel pipes, and copper. The main trading partners are the USA (65.6 per cent), EU (15 per cent), Latin America (5.2 per cent) and Japan (5 per cent). The North American Free Trade Agreement, to which Mexico is a signatory, came into effect on 1 January 1994; trade with the USA rose by 21 per cent. Mexico has free trade deals with Bolivia, Chile, Colombia, Costa Rica, Nicaragua and Venezuela, and negotiations are under way to create free trade agreements with other South American countries as well as the EU and Israel.

In 1995 Mexico had a trade surplus of US$7,089 million and a current account deficit of US$654 million. In 1996 imports totalled US$98,411 million and exports US$95,991 million.

Trade with UK	1996	1997
Imports from UK	£317,428,000	£429,254,000
Exports to UK	334,765,000	382,321,000

COMMUNICATIONS

Veracruz, Tampico and Coatzacoalcos are the chief ports on the Atlantic, and Guaymas, Mazatlán, Puerto Lázaro Cárdenas and Salina Cruz on the Pacific. Work is proceeding on the reorganization and re-equipment of the whole rail system. Total track length of the railways was 240,186 km in 1990. Mexico City may be reached by at least three highways from the USA, and from the south from Yucatán as well as on two principal highways from the Guatemalan border.

There are 1,113 airports and landing fields in Mexico, of which 18 are equipped to handle long-distance flights. There are 166 airline companies, including two major, now private, national airlines, Mexicana de Aviación and Aeroméxico.

Teléfonos de México, now privatized, controls about 98 per cent of all telephone services.

FEDERATED STATES OF MICRONESIA

AREA – 271 sq. miles (702 sq. km)
POPULATION – 105,000 (1994 UN estimate). Pohnpei: population, 31,000; capital, Kolonia; Chuuk (Truk): population, 52,000; capital, Moen; Yap: population, 12,000; capital, Colonia; Kosrae: population, 6,500; capital, Lelu. The population is Micronesian and predominantly Christian. English (official) and eight other languages are used in different parts of the Federated States: Yapese, Ulithian, Woleaian, Ponapean, Nukuoran, Kapingamarangi, Trukese and Kosraen
FEDERAL CAPITAL – Palikir, on Pohnpei
CURRENCY – Currency is that of the USA
NATIONAL FLAG – United Nations blue with four white stars in the centre
POPULATION GROWTH RATE – 1.0 per cent (1995)
POPULATION DENSITY – 150 per sq. km (1995)

The Federated States of Micronesia comprise more than 600 islands extending 2,900 km (1,800 miles) across the archipelago of the Caroline Islands in the western Pacific Ocean. The islands vary geologically from mountainous islands to low coral atolls. The climate is tropical. Storms are common between August and December, and typhoons between July and November.

HISTORY AND POLITICS

The Spanish Empire claimed sovereignty over the Caroline Islands until 1899, when Spain withdrew from her Pacific territories and sold her possessions in the Caroline Islands to Germany. The Caroline Islands became a German protectorate until the outbreak of the First World War in 1914, when Japan took control of the islands on behalf of the Allied powers. After the war Japan continued to administer the territory under a League of Nations mandate. During the Second World War, US armed forces took control of the islands from the Japanese. In 1947 the USA entered into agreement with the UN Security Council to administer the Micronesia area, of which the Federated States of Micronesia were a part, as the UN Trust Territory of the Pacific Islands.

The US Trusteeship administration came to an end on 3 November 1986, when a Compact of Free Association between the USA and the Federated States of Micronesia came into effect. By this agreement the USA recognized the Federated States of Micronesia as a fully sovereign and independent state. The independence of the Federated States of Micronesia was recognized by the UN in December 1990.

POLITICAL SYSTEM

The constitution separates the executive, legislative and judicial branches. There is a bill of rights and provision for traditional rights. The executive comprises a federal president and vice-president, both of whom must be chosen from amongst the four nationally-elected senators. There is a single-chamber Congress of 14 members, four members elected on a nation-wide basis and ten members elected from congressional districts apportioned by population.

The Compact of Free Association places full responsibility for the defence of the Federated States of Micronesia on the USA.

The judiciary is headed by the Supreme Court, which is divided into trial and appellate divisions. Below this, each state has its own judicial system.

FEDERAL STRUCTURE

The Federated States of Micronesia is a federal republic of four constituent states: Chuuk, Kosrae, Pohnpei and Yap. Each of the constituent states has its own government and legislative system.

State	Area (sq. km)	Population (1994)	Headquarters
Chuuk	127	52,870	Weno
Kosrae	109	7,354	Tofol
Pohnpei	344	33,372	Kolonia
Yap	119	11,128	Colonia

HEAD OF STATE

President, Jacob Nena (Kosrae)
Vice-President, Leo Falcam (Pohnpei)

CABINET *as at July 1998*

Administrative Services, Kapilly Capelle
Budget, Aloysius Tuuth
External Affairs, Asterio Takesy
Finance, Patrick MacKenzie
Health, Eliuel Pretrick
National Planning, Bermin Weilbacher
Resources and Development, Sabastian Anefel
Transportation and Communications, Lukner Weilbacher

BRITISH AMBASSADOR, HE Vernon Scarborough, resident at Suva, Fiji

ECONOMY

The economy is dependent mainly on subsistence agriculture and government spending. Copra and fish are the two main exports. The majority of the working population is engaged in government administration, subsistence farming, fishing, copra production and the tourist industry. In 1990, there were 20,475 visitors.
GNP – US$225 million (1996); US$2,070 per capita (1996)
GDP – US$259 million (1994); US$2,560 per capita (1994)

TRADE WITH UK	1996	1997
Imports from UK	£19,000	£95,000
Exports to UK	—	1,000

MOLDOVA
Republica Moldova

AREA – 13,012 sq. miles (33,700 sq. km). Neighbours: Ukraine (north, east and south-east), Romania (west)
POPULATION – 4,335,000 (1996 official estimate): 65 per cent are Moldovan, 14.2 per cent Ukrainian and 13 per cent Russian, together with smaller numbers of Gagauz (ethnic Turks), Jews and Bulgarians. Most of the population are adherents of the Moldovan Orthodox Church. Moldovan was made the official language (written in the Latin script) in 1989 but the use of Russian in official business is permitted
CAPITAL – Kishinev (population, 667,100)
CURRENCY – Leu (plural lei)
NATIONAL DAY – 27 August (Independence Day)
NATIONAL FLAG – Vertical stripes of blue, yellow, red, with the national arms in the centre
LIFE EXPECTANCY (years) – male 64.28; female 70.99
POPULATION GROWTH RATE – 0.3 per cent (1995)
POPULATION DENSITY – 132 per sq. km (1995)
URBAN POPULATION – 46.9 per cent (1992)
MILITARY EXPENDITURE – 2.1 per cent of GDP (1996)
MILITARY PERSONNEL – 14,430: Army 9,300, Air Force 1,730, Paramilitaries 3,400
CONSCRIPTION DURATION – Up to 18 months
ILLITERACY RATE – 1.1 per cent
ENROLMENT (percentage of age group) – tertiary 25.0 per cent (1995)

HISTORY AND POLITICS

A Moldovan feudal state was established in the 14th century when Slavic tribes who had previously lived under Roman and Byzantine rule integrated with Slavic tribes from further east. In the 15th century a Moldovan principality was formed which entered into military and political alliances with Muscovy before being absorbed into the Turkish Empire in the 16th century. Moldova became the site of many Russo-Turkish battles and skirmishes in the 18th century before the area between the Dniester and Prut rivers (later known as Bessarabia) was annexed to the Russian Empire by the Bucharest Peace Treaty of 1812.

After the Russian Revolution in 1917, Bessarabia came under the control of White Russian forces and was annexed to Romania under the Versailles Peace Treaty (1919). In 1924 the Moldavian Autonomous Soviet Socialist Republic (ASSR) was established on the east bank of the Dniester river as part of Soviet Ukraine. In August 1940 the Soviet Union forced Romania to cede Bessarabia and the Moldavian Soviet Socialist Republic was formed from the majority of Bessarabia (the southernmost parts were incorporated into the Ukraine) and the Moldavian ASSR.

Moldova (formerly Moldavia) declared its independence from the USSR in August 1991. Reunification with Romania was rejected in a referendum on 6 March 1994, following which the Moldovan parliament voted to join the CIS. In July 1994 the Moldovan parliament adopted a new constitution which defines Moldova as a 'presidential parliamentary republic' based on political pluralism. It also provides for autonomous status for the Gagauz and Transdniester regions, with the Gagauz region having its own elected National Assembly.

Parliament now has 101 seats and is elected by proportional representation for a four-year term. President Petru Lucinschi replaced former Communist president Mircea Snegur in presidential elections in November–December 1996. In legislative elections in March 1998, no party won an overall majority, and a right-wing coalition government under Ion Ciubuc was formed.

INSURGENCIES

After independence was declared, the majority ethnic Romanian (Moldovan) population expressed a wish to rejoin Romania. This alienated the ethnic Ukrainian and Russian populations, who formed a majority east of the Dniester, and they declared their independence from Moldova as the Transdniester republic in December 1991. The Moldovan government refused to recognize this and in 1992 a war was waged between government forces and Transdniester forces, who were supported by the former Soviet 14th Army stationed in Transdniester and by Cossack volunteers from Russia.

A mainly Russian CIS peacekeeping force (later changed to a joint Russian-Moldovan-Transdniester force) was deployed in July 1992 and a cease-fire has held since August 1992. Although no political solution has been finalized and a state of armed truce remains, the Moldovan government in February 1994 agreed to an OSCE plan for the Transdniester area to have a high degree of autonomy within Moldova but no independent or federal status. In October 1994 the Russian and Moldovan presidents signed an agreement on the withdrawal of the 14th Army over a three-year period, the first troops leaving in February 1996. A memorandum of understanding on the normalization of relations between the two sides was signed in May 1997, which committed both parties to hold further talks within 'the framework of a single state'.

A referendum in Transdniester on 24 December 1995 approved independence. President Igor Smirnov was re-elected in presidential elections in Transdniester in December 1996.

HEAD OF STATE
President, Petru Lucinschi, *elected* 1 December 1996

GOVERNMENT *as at July 1998*

Prime Minister, Ion Ciubuc
Deputy PMs, Ion Sturza *(Economy and Reform);* Valentin Dolganiuc *(Industrial and Agrarian Policies);* Nicolae Andronic *(Legal Issues);* Oleg Stratulat *(Social Policy and Science)*
Agriculture, Food Industry and Forestry, Valeriu Bulgari
Chairman of the Parliament, Dumitru Dyakov
Culture, Ghenadie Ciobanu
Defence, Valeriu Pasat
Education and Science, Anatol Grimalschi
Environmental Protection, Arcadie Capcelea
Finance, Anatol Arapu
Foreign Affairs, Nicolae Tabacaru
Health, Eugen Gladun
Industry and Trade, Georgy Kuku
Interior, Victor Catan
Justice, Ion Paduraru
Labour, Social Security and Family Affairs, Vladimir Guritenco
Minister of State, Nicolae Cernomaz
National Security, Tudor Botnaru
Territorial Development, Public Utilities and Construction, Mihai Severovan
Trade and Industry, Ion Tanase
Transport and Communications, Tudor Leanca

EMBASSY OF THE REPUBLIC OF MOLDOVA
175 Avenue Emile Max, 1040 Brussels, Belgium
Tel: Brussels 732 9659
Ambassador Extraordinary and Plenipotentiary, HE Tudor Botnaru

BRITISH AMBASSADOR, HE Sir Andrew Wood, KCMG, resident at Moscow

ECONOMY

The main sector is agriculture, especially viniculture, fruit-growing and market gardening. Industry is small and concentrated east of the Dniester. Severe drought in 1992, the severance of most trading ties with former Soviet republics, war damage and reductions in Russian fuel deliveries paralysed the economy from 1992 to 1994. An economic reform programme aiming to attract foreign investment began in summer 1993; a privatization pro-

gramme, completed in November 1995, sold off 1,132 large enterprises. Moldova is dependent on Russia for energy supplies and owes roughly US$6,000 million. In September 1997 the World Bank approved a US$100 million loan to aid structural reform of the economy.

In 1996 there was a trade deficit of US$254 million and a current account deficit of US$300 million. Imports totalled US$1,079 million and exports US$802 million.
GNP – US$2,542 million (1996); US$590 per capita (1996)
GDP – US$7,396 million (1994); US$322 per capita (1994)
UNEMPLOYMENT – 1.0 per cent (1995)
TOTAL EXTERNAL DEBT – US$834 million (1996)

TRADE WITH UK	1996	1997
Imports from UK	£3,181,000	£4,458,000
Exports to UK	866,000	1,031,000

MONACO
Principauté de Monaco

AREA – 0.4 sq. miles (1 sq. km). Neighbour: France
POPULATION – 32,000 (1994 UN estimate). Only 5,000 residents have full Monégasque citizenship and thus the right to vote. The official language is French. Monégasque, a mixture of Provençal and Ligurian, is also spoken
CAPITAL – Monaco (population, 27,063, 1982)
CURRENCY – French franc of 100 centimes
NATIONAL ANTHEM – Hymne Monégasque
NATIONAL DAY – 19 November
NATIONAL FLAG – Two equal horizontal stripes, red over white
POPULATION GROWTH RATE – 1.3 per cent (1995)
POPULATION DENSITY – 21,477 per sq. km (1995)

A small principality on the Mediterranean, with land frontiers joining France at every point, Monaco is divided into the districts of Monaco-Ville, La Condamine, Fontvielle and Monte Carlo.

HISTORY AND POLITICS

The principality, ruled by the Grimaldi family since 1297, was abolished during the French Revolution and re-established in 1815 under the protection of the kingdom of Sardinia. In 1861 Monaco came under French protection.

The 1962 constitution, which can be modified only with the approval of the National Council, maintains the traditional hereditary monarchy and guarantees freedom of association, trade union freedom and the right to strike. Legislative power is held jointly by the Prince and a unicameral, 18-member National Council elected by universal suffrage. Executive power is exercised by the Prince and a four-member Council of Government, headed by a Minister of State. The judicial code is based on that of France.

HEAD OF STATE

HSH The Prince of Monaco, Prince Rainier III Louis-Henri-Maxence Bertrand, *born* 31 May 1923, *succeeded* 9 May 1949; *married* 19 April 1956, Miss Grace Patricia Kelly (died 14 September 1982) and *has issue* Prince Albert *(see below)*; Princess Caroline Louise Marguerite, *born* 23 January 1957; and Princess Stephanie Marie Elisabeth, *born* 1 February 1965
Heir, HRH Prince Albert Alexandre Louis Pierre, *born* 14 March 1958

President of the Crown Council, Charles Ballerio
President of the National Council, Dr Jean-Louis Campora

Minister of State, Michel Lévêque
Finance and Economy, Henri Fissore
Interior, Jean Aribaud
Public Works and Social Affairs, Michel Sosso

CONSULATE-GENERAL OF MONACO
4 Cromwell Place, London SW7 2JE
Tel 0171-225 2679
Consul-General, I. B. Ivanovic

BRITISH CONSUL -GENERAL, I. Davies, apptd 1997,
resident at Marseilles, France

ECONOMY

The whole available ground is built over so that there is no
cultivation, though there are some notable public and
private gardens. The economy is based on real estate
revenues, the financial sector and tourism (226,421 visitors
in 1996). Monaco has a small harbour (30 ft alongside quay)
and the import duties are the same as in France.
GDP – US\$668 million (1994); US\$24,693 per capita
(1994)

MONGOLIA
State of Mongolia

AREA – 604,829 sq. miles (1,566,500 sq. km). Neighbours:
Russia (north), China (south)
POPULATION – 2,410,000 (1994 UN estimate). Mongolians
also live in China and in the neighbouring regions of
Russia, especially the Mongolian Buryat Autonomous
Region. The official language is Khalkha Mongolian
CAPITAL – Ulan Bator (population, 515,100, 1987
estimate)
CURRENCY – Tugrik of 100 möngö
NATIONAL DAY – 11 July
NATIONAL FLAG – Vertical tricolour red, blue, red and in
the hoist the traditional Soyombo symbol in gold
LIFE EXPECTANCY (years) – male 62.32; female 65.00
POPULATION GROWTH RATE – 2.0 per cent (1995)
POPULATION DENSITY – 2 per sq. km (1995)
URBAN POPULATION – 57.1 per cent (1989)
MILITARY EXPENDITURE – 1.5 per cent of GDP (1996)
MILITARY PERSONNEL – 14,900: Army 8,500, Air Defence
500, Paramilitaries 5,900
CONSCRIPTION DURATION – 12 months
ILLITERACY RATE – 17.1 per cent
ENROLMENT (percentage of age group) – primary 80 per
cent (1995); secondary 57 per cent (1995); tertiary 15.2
per cent (1995)

Mongolia, which is almost entirely at least 1,000 metres
above sea level, forms part of the central Asiatic plateau
and rises towards the west in the mountains of the
Mongolian Altai and Hangai ranges. The Hentai range,
situated to the north-east of the capital Ulan Bator, is lower.
The Gobi region covers much of the southern half of the
country and contains sand deserts interspersed with semi-
desert. There are several long rivers and many lakes but
good water is scarce as much of the lake water is salty. The
climate is harsh, with a short mild summer giving way to a
long winter when temperatures can drop as low as −50°C.

HISTORY AND POLITICS

Mongolia, under Genghis Khan the conqueror of China
and much of Asia, was for many years a buffer state between
Tsarist Russia and China, although it was under general
Chinese suzerainty. The Chinese Revolution in 1911 led
to a declaration of autonomy under Chinese suzerainty

which was confirmed by the Sino-Russian Treaty of
Kiakhta (1915) but cancelled by a unilateral Chinese
declaration in 1919. Later the country became a battleground of the Russian civil war, and Soviet and Mongolian
troops occupied Ulan Bator in 1921; this was followed by
another declaration of independence. In 1924 the Soviet
Union in a treaty with China again recognized the latter's
sovereignty over Mongolia, but this was never properly
exercised because of China's preoccupation with internal
affairs and later by the war with Japan. The Mongolian
People's Republic was formally established in 1924. Under
the Yalta Agreement, President Chiang Kai-shek of China
agreed to a plebiscite, held in 1945, in which the Mongolians declared their desire for independence and this was
formally recognized by China.

The Mongolian People's Revolutionary Party (MPRP)
was the sole political party from 1924 to 1990. Demonstrations in favour of political and economic reform began in
December 1989 and led to changes in the MPRP leadership in March 1990. The MPRP's constitutionally guaranteed monopoly of power was subsequently relinquished,
and the introduction of a multiparty system was approved
by the Great People's Hural (parliament). The MPRP won
the first multiparty elections, held in July 1990. Since then,
and following Moscow's lead, Mongolia has embarked on a
programme of political and economic reforms.

The most recent legislative election, held on 30 June
1996, was won by the Democratic Union Coalition (Mongolian National Democratic Party and Mongolian Social
Democratic Party) which won 50 seats. The country's first
direct presidential election was held in 1993 and won by
the incumbent Punsalmaagiyn Ochirbat, who stood as an
opposition candidate after the MPRP refused to endorse
him as its candidate. Ochirbat was ousted in May 1997 by
the leader of the MPRP, Natsagyn Bagabandi. Prime
Minister Mendsayhany Enhsayhan resigned in April 1998
and was replaced by Tsahiagiyn Elbegdorj.

The country and three city districts (Ulan Bator,
Darkhan and Erdenet) are divided into 21 *aimaks* (provinces) and beneath these into 258 *somons* (districts), and
these form the basis of the state organization of the country.
The last remaining former Soviet armed forces personnel
were withdrawn in late 1992.

POLITICAL SYSTEM

A new constitution was approved in January 1992 which
enshrines the concepts of democracy, a mixed economy,
free speech and neutrality in foreign affairs. The Great and
Little Hurals were abolished, and a new unicameral Great
Hural became the legislative body of the country. There
are 76 members of the Great Hural, elected for four-year
terms by a simple majority amounting to at least 25 per
cent of the votes cast.

HEAD OF STATE
President, Natsagyn Bagabandi, *elected* 18 May 1997

CABINET *as at July 1998*
Prime Minister, Tsahiagiyn Elbegdorj
Agriculture and Industry, Noroviin Altanhuyag
Defence, D. Enhbaatar
Education, Culture and Science, Ch. Sayhanbileg
Finance, Bat-Erdeniin Batbayar
Foreign Affairs, Renchinnyamyn Amarjargal
Health and Social Protection, Sharavjamtsyn Batbayar
Infrastructure Development, Sanjahsurengiin Zorig
Justice, Sarigiin Batchuluun
Nature and Environment Protection, Sangajaviin Bayartsogt
Chairman of the Great Hural, Radnaasumbereliin
  Gonchigdorj

EMBASSY OF MONGOLIA
7 Kensington Court, London W8 5DL
Tel 0171-937 0150
Ambassador Extraordinary and Plenipotentiary, HE
    Tsedenjavyn Suhbaatar, apptd 1997

BRITISH EMBASSY
30 Enkh Taivny Gudamzh (PO Box 703), Ulan Bator 13
Tel: Ulan Bator 358133
Ambassador Extraordinary and Plenipotentiary, HE John
    Durham, apptd 1997

ECONOMY

Traditionally the Mongolians led a nomadic life tending
flocks of sheep, goats, horses, cows and camels. With the
coming of the Communist regime, and especially after
1952, great efforts were made to settle the population but a
proportion still live nomadically or semi-nomadically in
the traditional *ger* (circular tent). Collectivization at the
end of the 1950s into huge *negdels* (co-operatives) and state
farms hastened the process of settlement, but within these
the herdsmen and their families still move with their *gers*
from pasture to pasture as the seasons change. Total
livestock was 25 million in 1993.

The semi-desert areas of the Gobi region provide
pasture for sheep, goats, camels, horses and some cattle. In
the steppe areas to the north of the Gobi pasturage is better
and livestock more abundant. Even further north, in the
better-watered provinces, grain, fodder and vegetable
crops are grown.

Although the economy remains predominantly pastoral,
factories have started up, coal, copper and molybdenum
are mined and the electricity industry has been developed.
Ulan Bator and Darkhan are the main seats of industry,
which includes lime, cement and building materials, a
flour mill and a power station. Choibalsan is also being
developed industrially.

Mongolia's economic difficulties stem from its small
labour force, and its undeveloped infrastructure. To
address this problem, in September 1997 the government
launched a plan to sell off almost all state-owned enterprises before 2000, in order to provide the necessary capital
to develop infrastructure. Communication is still difficult
as there are very few tarmac roads and horses are still the
characteristic means of transport for the rural population.
The trans-Mongolian railway links Mongolia with both
China and Russia. All trade barriers were abolished in May
1997. In October 1997, the Mongolian Assistance Group
pledged US$250 million in aid for 1998.
GNP – US$902 million (1996); US$360 per capita (1996)
GDP – US$609 million (1994); US$290 per capita (1994)
ANNUAL AVERAGE GROWTH OF GDP – –11.6 per cent
    (1992)
INFLATION RATE – 45.8 per cent (1996)
TOTAL EXTERNAL DEBT – US$524 million (1996)

TRADE

Foreign trade was formerly dominated by the Soviet
Union and other Eastern bloc countries. Following the
collapse of the COMECON trading system, trade with
Western countries, Japan and South Korea is increasing.
Since January 1991, trade has been in hard currency,
causing particular strain. The principal exports are animal
by-products (especially wool, hides and furs) and cattle.
In 1995 there was a trade surplus of US$25 million and a
current account surplus of US$39 million. In 1996 imports
totalled US$439 million and exports US$423 million.

Trade with UK	1996	1997
Imports from UK	£2,518,000	£3,872,000
Exports to UK	11,696,000	9,847,000

MOROCCO
Al-Mamlaka Al-Maghrebia

AREA – 172,414 sq. miles (446,550 sq. km). Neighbours:
    Algeria (east and south-east), Western Sahara (south-
    west)
POPULATION – 27,111,000 (1994 UN estimate). Arabic is
    the official language. Berber is the vernacular, mainly in
    the mountain regions. French and Spanish are also
    spoken, mainly in the towns. Islam is the state religion
CAPITAL – ΨRabat (population, 1,300,000, 1993 estimate)
MAJOR CITIES – ΨAgadir (923,000); ΨCasablanca
    (3,100,000); Fez (554,000); Marrakesh (878,000);
    Meknès (614,000); Oujda (430,000), 1997 estimates
CURRENCY – Dirham (DH) of 100 centimes
NATIONAL DAY – 3 March (Anniversary of the Throne)
NATIONAL FLAG – Red, with green pentagram (the Seal of
    Solomon)
LIFE EXPECTANCY (years) – male 61.58; female 65.00
POPULATION GROWTH RATE – 2.0 per cent (1995)
POPULATION DENSITY – 61 per sq. km (1995)
URBAN POPULATION – 51.6 per cent (1995)

Morocco is traversed in the north by the Rif mountains
and, in a south-west to north-east direction, by the Middle
Atlas, the High Atlas, the Anti-Atlas and the Sarrho ranges.
Much of the country is desert. The north-westerly point of
Morocco is the peninsula of Tangier dominated by the
Jebel Mousa which, with the rocky eminence of Gibraltar,
was known to the ancients as the Pillars of Hercules, the
western gateway of the Mediterranean.

HISTORY AND POLITICS

Morocco became an independent sovereign state in 1956,
following joint declarations made with France on 2 March
1956 and with Spain on 7 April 1956. The Sultan of
Morocco, Sidi Mohammad ben Youssef, adopted the title
of King Mohammad V.

Elections were held on 14 November 1997 to the new
House of Representatives; no party won an overall
majority, but Abderrahmane El Youssoufi was appointed
prime minister as the leader of the Socialist Union of
Popular Forces, the largest party in the House of Representatives. On 5 December 1997, elections to the Chamber
of Councillors were held. The pro-government *Wifaq* bloc
and centre parties won 166 seats; the opposition *Koutla* bloc
won 44 seats.

POLITICAL SYSTEM

The King nominates the prime minister and, on the latter's
recommendation, appoints the members of the Council of
Ministers. The government is responsible both to parliament and to the King. There is a bicameral legislature. The
Chamber of Representatives has 325 members elected by
universal suffrage using a first-past-the-post system. The
Chamber of Councillors has 270 members, 60 per cent of
whom are elected by local councils, 20 per cent by
employers' associations and 20 per cent by trade unions.
One third of its members are elected every three years.

HEAD OF STATE

HM The King of Morocco, King Hassan II (Moulay Hassan
    Ben Mohammed), *born* 9 July 1929; *acceded* 3 March 1961
Heir, HRH Crown Prince Sidi Mohamed, *born* 21 August
    1963

COUNCIL OF MINISTERS *as at July 1998*

Prime Minister, Abderrahmane El Youssoufi
Agriculture, Development, Maritime Fishing, Habib Malki

Communications, Larbi Messari
Country Planning, Environment, Town Planning, Housing,
  Mohamed El Yazghi
Cultural Affairs, Mohamed Achaari
Economy and Finance, Fathallah Oualalou
Energy and Mining, Youssef Tahiri
Equipment, Bouamar Tighouane
General Secretary of the Government, Abdessadek Rabii
Health, Abdelouahed El Fassi
Higher Education, Executive Training, Scientific Research, Najib
  Zerouali
Human Rights, Mohamed Aoujar
Industry, Commerce and Handicrafts, Alami Tazi
Justice, Omar Azziman
Minister of State for Foreign Affairs and Co-operation, Abdellatif
  Filali
Minister of State for the Interior, Driss Basri
National Education, Ismail Alaoui
Public Sector and Privatization, Rachid Filali
Public Service and Administrative Development, Aziz Hocine
Relations with Parliament, Mohamed Bouzoubaa
Social Development, Solidarity, Employment, Vocational Training,
  Government Spokesman, Khalid Alioua
Tourism, Hassan Sebbar
Transport and Merchant Navy, Mustapha Mansouri
Waqf and Islamic Affairs, Abdelkabir M'Daghri Alaoui
Youth and Sports, Ahmed Moussaoui

EMBASSY OF THE KINGDOM OF MOROCCO
49 Queen's Gate Gardens, London SW7 5NE
Tel 0171–581 5001/4
Ambassador Extraordinary and Plenipotentiary, HE Khalil
  Haddaoui, apptd 1991

BRITISH EMBASSY
17 Boulevard de la Tour Hassan (BP 45), Rabat
Tel: Rabat 720905/6
Ambassador Extraordinary and Plenipotentiary, HE William H.
  Fullerton, CMG, apptd 1996
CONSULATE-GENERAL – Casablanca
CONSULATES - Agadir, Marrakesh, Tangier

BRITISH COUNCIL DIRECTOR, P. Wingate-Saul, BP 427,
  36 rue de Tanger, Rabat
BRITISH CHAMBER OF COMMERCE, 1st Floor, 185
  Boulevard Zerktouni, Casablanca. Tel: 256920

DEFENCE

The Army has 524 main battle tanks, 100 light tanks, 890
armoured infantry fighting vehicles and armoured personnel carriers, and 190 artillery pieces.

The Navy has one frigate and 26 patrol and coastal
combatant vessels at five bases. The Air Force has 89
combat aircraft and 24 armed helicopters.

The UN has some 238 personnel in Western Sahara
pending the referendum (see below). Polisario deploys
3,000 – 6,000 troops in Western Sahara with Algerian-
supplied and captured Moroccan tanks, armoured personnel carriers, anti-tank and anti-aircraft weapons.
MILITARY EXPENDITURE – 4.3 per cent of GDP (1996)
MILITARY PERSONNEL – 238,300: Army 175,000, Navy
  7,800, Air Force 13,500, Paramilitaries 42,000
CONSCRIPTION DURATION – 18 months

ECONOMY

Morocco's main sources of wealth are agricultural and
mineral. The latest development plan (1987 onwards)
emphasizes social improvement, industrial development,
agriculture, fisheries and tourism. Economic reform has
also been implemented to reduce debt and inflation. A

large-scale privatization programme has attracted substantial foreign investment.

Agriculture contributes roughly four-fifths of GDP.
The main agricultural exports are fruit and vegetables,
with cereals and sugar beet produced and sheep reared for
domestic consumption. Cork and wood pulp are the most
important commercial forest products. Esparto grass is also
produced. There is a fishing industry and substantial
quantities of canned fish are exported.

For a developing country Morocco has a large industrial
sector. The main sectors are chemicals, textiles and leather
goods, food processing and cement production. Manufacturing industries are centred in Casablanca, Fez, Tangier
and Safi.

Morocco's mineral exports are phosphates, fluorite,
barite, manganese, iron ore, lead, zinc, cobalt, copper and
antimony. Morocco possesses nearly three-quarters of the
world's estimated reserves of phosphates. There are oil
refineries at Mohammedia and Sidi Kacem handling about
four million tonnes of crude oil a year.

Tourism is of increasing importance to the economy,
with development concentrated in Agadir and Marrakesh.
In 1994, 2,293,744 foreign tourists visited Morocco. Work-
ers' remittances, US$1,959 million in 1993, are also
important to the economy.
GNP – US$34,936 million (1996); US$1,290 per capita
  (1996)
GDP – US$26,925 million (1994); US$1,098 per capita
  (1994)
ANNUAL AVERAGE GROWTH OF GDP – 12.0 per cent
  (1996)
INFLATION RATE – 3.0 per cent (1996)
UNEMPLOYMENT – 16.0 per cent (1992)
TOTAL EXTERNAL DEBT – US$21,767 million (1996)

TRADE

The main imports are petroleum products, motor vehicles,
building materials, agricultural and other machinery,
chemical products, sugar, green tea and other foodstuffs.
The EU, with which an association agreement was signed
in November 1995, is Morocco's largest trading partner
and in May 1998 awarded Morocco grants totalling US$98
million. The main exports are textiles, phosphates and
phosphoric acid, fertilizers, citrus fruits, and fish and
seafoods.

In 1995 Morocco had a trade deficit of US$2,397 million
and a current account deficit of US$1,521 million. In 1996
imports totalled US$9,713 million and exports US$6,904
million.

Trade with UK	1996	1997
Imports from UK	£281,575,000	£356,677,000
Exports to UK	303,998,000	346,992,000

COMMUNICATIONS

Railroads cover 1,175 miles (1,893 km), linking the major
towns. An extensive network of 9,880 miles (15,900 km) of
well-surfaced roads covers all the main towns. There are
air services between Casablanca, Tangier, Agadir (seasonal), Marrakesh and London, and also between Tangier and
Gibraltar connecting with London. Royal-Air-Maroc is
the national airline.

EDUCATION

Education is compulsory between the ages of seven and 13.
There are government primary, secondary and technical
schools. In 1991 there were 4,890 government schools. At
Fez there is a theological university of great repute in the
Muslim world. There is a secular university at Rabat.

Schools for special denominations, Jewish and Catholic, are permitted and may receive government grants. American schools operate in Rabat and Casablanca.
ILLITERACY RATE – 56.3 per cent
ENROLMENT (percentage of age group) – primary 72 per cent (1995); secondary 20 per cent (1980); tertiary 11.3 per cent (1994)

WESTERN SAHARA

Formerly the Spanish Sahara, the territory was split between Morocco and Mauritania in 1976 after Spain withdrew in December 1975. In 1976 the Polisario Front (Frente Popular para la Liberación de Saguia y Río de Oro) declared Western Sahara to be an independent state, the Saharan Arab Democratic Republic, and formed a government led by Bouchraya Bayoune which remains in exile. The Polisario Front has been recognized as the legitimate government of Western Sahara by over 70 states and the Organization of African Unity. In 1979 Mauritania renounced its claim to its share of the territory, which was added by Morocco to its area.

In 1988, Morocco and the Polisario Front accepted a UN peace plan under which a cease-fire came into effect in September 1991. A referendum to determine the future of the area was to have been held in January 1992 but has not yet taken place because the Moroccan government and Polisario have not agreed on the referendum terms or voter eligibility. The UN Security Council intervened to break the impasse, passing a resolution which stipulates that the referendum should be a straight choice between independence or integration with Morocco. A further resolution provided for the drawing up of a new voter registration list. Voter identification began in August 1994 but the failure to agree on eligibility prompted the UN to threaten the suspension of the UN Mission for the Referendum in Western Sahara (MINURSO), which had been deployed since 1991. The date for the referendum on the future of Western Sahara has now been set for 6 December 1998, with MINURSO responsible for identifying voters.

MOZAMBIQUE
República de Moçambique

AREA – 309,496 sq. miles (801,590 sq. km). Neighbours: Swaziland (south), South Africa (south and west), Zimbabwe (west), Zambia and Malawi (north-west), Tanzania (north)
POPULATION – 17,423,000 (1995 official estimate). The official language is Portuguese
CAPITAL – ΨMaputo (population, 882,601, 1986 estimate)
MAJOR CITIES – ΨBeira (264,202); ΨNacala (182,505), 1986 estimates
CURRENCY – Metical (MT) of 100 centavos
NATIONAL DAY – 25 June (Independence Day)
NATIONAL FLAG – Horizontally green, black, yellow with white fimbriations; a red triangle based on the hoist containing the national emblem
LIFE EXPECTANCY (years) – male 44.88; female 48.01
POPULATION GROWTH RATE – 4.2 per cent (1995)
POPULATION DENSITY – 22 per sq. km (1995)
MILITARY EXPENDITURE – 3.6 per cent of GDP (1996)
MILITARY PERSONNEL – 6,100: Army 5,000, Navy 100, Air Force 1,000
ILLITERACY RATE – 59.9 per cent
ENROLMENT (percentage of age group) – primary 40 per cent (1995); secondary 6 per cent (1995); tertiary 0.5 per cent (1995)

HISTORY AND POLITICS

Mozambique, discovered by Vasco da Gama in 1498 and colonized by Portugal, achieved independence on 25 June 1975. It was a Marxist one-party (Frelimo) state until a multiparty system was adopted in 1990. The legislative assembly has 250 members.

Following two years of negotiations, the Frelimo government and the rebel Mozambican National Resistance (Renamo) signed a peace agreement in October 1992 which ended 16 years of civil war. Under the peace agreement, demobilization of government and Renamo troops was due to begin within one month of parliamentary ratification of the peace accord (which occurred on 9 October 1992) although the belated arrival of the UN Operation for Mozambique (ONUMOZ) delayed demobilization until 1994.

Presidential and legislative elections were held on 27–29 October 1994. The incumbent, Joaquim Chissano of Frelimo, won the presidential election in the first round with 53 per cent of the vote. Frelimo also won the legislative election, gaining 129 seats to Renamo's 112 seats and the Democratic Union's 9 seats. The last ONUMOZ troops left in January 1995.

Mozambique was admitted to the Commonwealth on 13 November 1995 as a special case, because of its close links with Commonwealth countries.

HEAD OF STATE
President, Joaquim Alberto Chissano, *sworn in* November 1986, *elected* 29 October 1994

COUNCIL OF MINISTERS *as at July 1998*
Prime Minister, Pascoal Mocumbi
Agriculture and Fisheries, Carlos Rosario
Culture, Youth and Sports, Mateus Kathupa
Education, Arnaldo Nhavoto
Environmental Action Co-ordination, Bernardo Ferraz
Foreign Affairs and Co-operation, Leonardo Simão
Health, Aurelio Zihao
Industry, Trade and Tourism, Oldemiro Baloi
Justice, José Abudo
Labour, Guilherme Mavila
Mineral Resources and Energy, John Katchamila
Ministers in the President's Office, Armirinho da Cruz Marcos Manhanze (*Defence, Security Affairs and Interior*); Eneias da Conceiçao Comiche (*Economic and Social Affairs*); Francisco Madeira (*Parliamentary Affairs*); Isaac Murargy (*Secretary-General*)
National Defence, Aguiar Real Mazula
Planning and Finance, Tomas Salomao
Public Construction and Housing, Roberto White
Secretary-General of the Council of Ministers, Carlos Taju
Social Action, Filipe Mandlate *(acting)*
State Administration, Alfredo Gamito
Transport and Communications, Paulo Muxanga

HIGH COMMISSION FOR THE REPUBLIC OF MOZAMBIQUE
21 Fitzroy Square, London WIP 5HJ
Tel 0171–383 3800
High Commissioner, HE Dr Eduardo José Baciao Koloma, apptd 1996

BRITISH HIGH COMMISSION
Av. Vladimir I Lenine 310, CP 55, Maputo
Tel: Maputo 420111/2/5/6/7
High Commissioner, HE Bernard J. Everett, apptd 1996

BRITISH COUNCIL DIRECTOR, P. Woods, PO Box 4178, Maputo

ECONOMY

The basis of the economy is subsistence agriculture, but there is an industrial sector based mainly in Beira and Maputo. There are substantial coal deposits in Tete province and an offshore gas field at Pande. The government launched an economic rehabilitation programme in 1987 to attract foreign investment and boost production. Economic subsidies have been removed and an IMF reform programme is being implemented. The economy is still heavily dependent on aid. A five-year plan has been launched with the priorities of rural development, education, health and land reform.

GNP – US$1,472 million (1996); US$80 per capita (1996)
GDP – US$1,676 million (1994); US$92 per capita (1994)
ANNUAL AVERAGE GROWTH OF GDP – 5.7 per cent (1994)
INFLATION RATE – 45.0 per cent (1996)
TOTAL EXTERNAL DEBT – US$5,842 million (1996)

TRADE

The main exports are shellfish, cotton, sugar, cashew nuts, copra, tea and sisal. In 1995 exports totalled US$169 million and imports US$784 million. Mozambique's main trading partners are South Africa, Portugal, Spain and Japan.

Trade with UK	1996	1997
Imports from UK	£14,421,000	£14,183,000
Exports to UK	2,195,000	3,350,000

MYANMAR
Pyidaungsu Myanma Naingngandaw – Union of Myanmar

AREA – 261,228 sq. miles (676,578 sq. km). Neighbours: Bangladesh (west), India (north-west), China (north-east), Laos and Thailand (east)
POPULATION – 46,527,000 (1994 UN estimate).The indigenous inhabitants are of similar racial types and speak languages of the Tibeto-Burman, Mon-Khmer and Thai groups. The three significant non-indigenous elements are Indians, Chinese and those from Bangladesh. Burmese is the official language, but minority languages include Shan, Karen, Chin, Kayah and the various Kachin dialects. English is spoken in educated circles. Buddhism is the religion of 85 per cent of the people, with 5 per cent Animists, 4 per cent Muslims, 4 per cent Hindus and less than 3 per cent Christians
CAPITAL – ΨYangon (Rangoon) (population, 2,513,023, 1983)
MAJOR CITIES – Mandalay (532,949); Mawlamyine/Moulmein (219,961); Pathein/Bassein (144,096)
CURRENCY – Kyat (K) of 100 pyas
NATIONAL DAY – 4 January
NATIONAL FLAG – Red, with a canton of dark blue, inside which are a cogwheel and two rice ears surrounded by 14 white stars
LIFE EXPECTANCY (years) – male 57.89; female 63.14
POPULATION GROWTH RATE – 2.1 per cent (1995)
POPULATION DENSITY – 69 per sq. km (1995)

HISTORY AND POLITICS

The Union of Burma (the name was officially changed to the Union of Myanmar in 1989) became an independent republic outside the British Commonwealth on 4 January 1948 and remained a parliamentary democracy for 14 years. In 1962 the army took power and suspended the parliamentary constitution. A Revolutionary Council of senior officers under Gen. Ne Win instituted a socialist state.

After months of popular demonstrations and a series of presidents during 1988, Gen. Saw Maung, leader of the armed forces, assumed power in September 1988. The People's Assembly, the Council of State and the Council of Ministers were abolished and replaced by the State Law and Order Restoration Council (SLORC). The constitution was effectively abrogated.

A People's Assembly Election Law was published in 1989 committing the SLORC to hold multiparty elections. These were held on 27 May 1990, resulting in a majority for the National League for Democracy (NLD) even though its leader Aung San Suu Kyi had been under house arrest since July 1989. The SLORC refused to transfer power to a civilian government and large numbers of NLD MPs and supporters were detained. Others fled to the border areas with Thailand where an exile government led by Sein Win, the National Coalition Government of the Union of Burma (NCGUB), was set up. However, following the replacement of Saw Maung by Than Shwe as SLORC chairman and prime minister in April 1992, the government began a dialogue with some elements of the opposition. A Constitutional Convention of delegates appointed by the SLORC to discuss a future constitution convened in January 1993 and has continued fitfully since, but with minimal progress. The SLORC released Aung San Suu Kyi (who won the Nobel Peace Prize in 1991) on 10 July 1995, although on several occasions subsequently she has been forcibly prevented from attending political meetings by government troops. Many other opposition figures remain in detention or under house arrest. In November 1997, the SLORC was renamed the State Peace and Development Council (SPDC).

Myanmar is comprised of seven states (Chin, Kachin, Kayin (Karen), Kayah, Mon, Rakhine, Shan) and seven divisions (Irrawaddy, Magwe, Mandalay, Pegu, Yangon (Rangoon), Sagaing, Tenasserim).

INSURGENCIES

Since independence in 1948 the government has fought various armed insurgent groups, the largest of which were derived from the Kachin, Karen, Karenni, and Wa ethnic groups but the Shan, Mon, Arakan and Chin ethnic minorities have also formed armed groups.

Since 1992, as a result of government offensives, 15 ethnic groups have signed cease-fire agreements with the government, including the Kachin Independence Army, the Karenni National People's Liberation Front and the Shan State Liberation Organization in 1994, and Mon rebels in July 1995. In 1995–6, government forces launched successful offensives against the Karen National Union, the Karenni National Progressive Party and the Mong Tai army, whose leader, the drugs warlord Khun Sa, surrendered in January 1996.

STATE PEACE AND DEVELOPMENT COUNCIL *as at July 1998*

Chairman, Senior Gen. Than Shwe
Vice-Chairman, Gen. Maung Aye
Members, Rear-Adml Nyunt Thein; Maj.-Gen. Kyaw Than; Maj.-Gen. Aung Htwe; Maj.-Gen. Ye Myint; Maj.-Gen. Khin Maung Than; Maj.-Gen. Kyaw Win; Maj.-Gen. Thein Sein; Maj.-Gen. Thura Thiha Thura Sit Maung; Brig.-Gen. Thura Shwe Mahn; Brig.-Gen. Myint Aung; Brig.-Gen. Maung Bo; Brig.-Gen. Thiha Thura Tin Aung Myint Oo; Brig.-Gen. Soe Win; Brig.-Gen. Tin Aye
Secretaries, Lt.-Gen. Khin Nyunt; Lt.-Gen. Tin Oo; Lt.-Gen. Win Myint

CABINET *as at July 1998*
Prime Minister, Defence, Gen. Than Shwe
Deputy PMs, Vice-Adm. Maung Maung Khin (*Burma Investment Commission*); Lt.-Gen. Tin Tun
Agriculture and Irrigation, Maj.-Gen. Nyunt Tin
Border Areas and National Races, Col. Thein Nyunt
Commerce, Maj.-Gen. Kyaw Than
Construction, Maj.-Gen. Saw Tun
Co-operatives, U Aung San
Culture, U Win Sein
Education, U Than Aung
Electric Power, Maj.-Gen. Tin Htut
Energy, Brig.-Gen. Lun Thi
Finance and Revenue, U Khin Maung Thein
Foreign Affairs, U Ohn Gyaw
Forestry, U Aung Phone
Health, Maj.-Gen. Ket Sein
Home Affairs, Col. Tin Hlaing
Hotels and Tourism, Maj.-Gen. Saw Lwin
Immigration and Population, U Saw Tun
Industry, U Aung Thaung; Maj.-Gen. Hla Myint Swe
Information, Maj.-Gen. Kyi Aung
Labour, Vice-Adm. Tin Aye
Livestock Breeding and Fisheries, Brig.-Gen. Maung Maung Thein
Military Affairs, Lt.-Gen. Tin Hla
Mines, Brig.-Gen. Ohn Myint
Ministers in the Office of the SPDC Chairman, Lt.-Gen. Min Thein; Brig.-Gen. Maung Maung; Brig.-Gen. David Abel
National Planning and Economic Development, U Soe Tha
Prime Minister's Office, Brig.-Gen. Lun Maung; U Than Shwe; Maj.-Gen. Tin Ngwe
Rail Transport, U Pan Aung
Religious Affairs, Maj.-Gen. Sein Htwa
Science and Technology, U Thaung
Social Welfare, Relief and Resettlement, Brig.-Gen. Pyi Sone
Sports, Col. Sein Win
Telecommunications, Posts and Telegraphs, Brig.-Gen. Win Tin
Transport, Lt.-Gen. Tin Ngwe

EMBASSY OF THE UNION OF MYANMAR
19A Charles Street, Berkeley Square, London WIX 8ER
Tel 0171-499 8841
Ambassador Extraordinary and Plenipotentiary, U Win Aung, apptd 1996

BRITISH EMBASSY
80 Strand Road (Box No. 638), Yangon
Tel: Yangon 295300
Ambassador Extraordinary and Plenipotentiary, HE Robert A. E. Gordon, OBE, apptd 1995
Cultural Attaché and British Council Director, C. Henning, OBE

DEFENCE

The Army has some 130 main battle tanks, 270 armoured personnel carriers and 246 artillery pieces. The Navy has 65 patrol and coastal vessels at six bases.
MILITARY EXPENDITURE – 3.2 per cent of GDP (1996)
MILITARY PERSONNEL – 429,000: Army 400,000, Navy 20,000, Air Force 9,000

ECONOMY

The chief sources of revenue are profits on state trading, taxes and duties; the chief heads of expenditure are defence, education and police.

Three-quarters of the population depend on agriculture; the chief products are rice, oilseeds (sesamum and groundnut), maize, millet, cotton, beans, wheat, grain, tea, sugar cane, tobacco, jute and rubber. Following legislation in 1990, farmers are permitted to grow crops of their choice.

Myanmar is rich in minerals, including petroleum, zinc, nickel, lead, silver, tungsten, wolfram and gemstones. Production of crude petroleum in 1995 totalled 823,000 tonnes. There are refineries at Chauk, the main oilfield, Syriam and Mann. Major reserves of natural gas have been discovered in the Martaban Gulf. Timber production is an important industry and timber is a major export. Fisheries produce pearls and oyster shells in addition to significant quantities of fish.

A new ministry was established in 1992 with the task of attracting 500,000 tourists; less than 10,000 visited in 1991 but visitors and revenues are increasing. Foreign hotels have opened in Yangon and Mandalay, and in 1995 there were over 105,000 visitors.

In 1993 the government began to open the economy to foreign investment, signing 50 joint ventures in the fields of oil and gas exploration, hotel construction and forestry.

Myanmar is thought to be the world's leading producer of opium with an estimated annual output of 2,600 tons.

In July 1997, Myanmar became a member of ASEAN. In 1997 the EU stripped Myanmar of trading privileges and the USA imposed economic sanctions.

In 1996 imports totalled US$1,364 million and exports US$693 million.
GDP – US$29,769 million (1994); US$1,485 per capita (1994)
ANNUAL AVERAGE GROWTH OF GDP – 5.7 per cent (1996)
INFLATION RATE – 16.3 per cent (1996)
TOTAL EXTERNAL DEBT – US$5,184 million (1996)

TRADE WITH UK	1996	1997
Imports from UK	£21,421,000	£15,363,000
Exports to UK	13,732,000	19,450,000

COMMUNICATIONS

The Irrawaddy and its chief tributary, the Chindwin, are important waterways, the main stream being navigable 900 miles from its mouth and carrying much traffic. The chief seaports are Yangon (Rangoon), Mawlamyine (Moulmein), Akyab (Sittwe) and Pathein (Bassein).

The railway network covers 3,955 route miles, extending to Myitkyina on the Upper Irrawaddy. There are 2,452 miles of highways and 14,318 miles of other main roads. The airport at Mingaladon, about 13 miles north of Yangon (Rangoon), handles limited international air traffic.

EDUCATION

Most children attend primary school, and about six million are currently enrolled; in middle and high schools, enrolment is about two million. There are universities at Yangon (Rangoon), Mandalay, Taunggyi, Sagaing and Mawlamyine (Moulmein). Under the universities are three affiliated degree colleges and the Workers' College, Yangon.

Vocational training is provided at 17 teachers' training institutes, seven government technical institutes, 14 technical high schools, 17 agricultural institutes and schools, and 34 vocational schools for handicrafts, etc.
ILLITERACY RATE – 16.9 per cent
ENROLMENT (percentage of age group) – tertiary 5.4 per cent (1994)

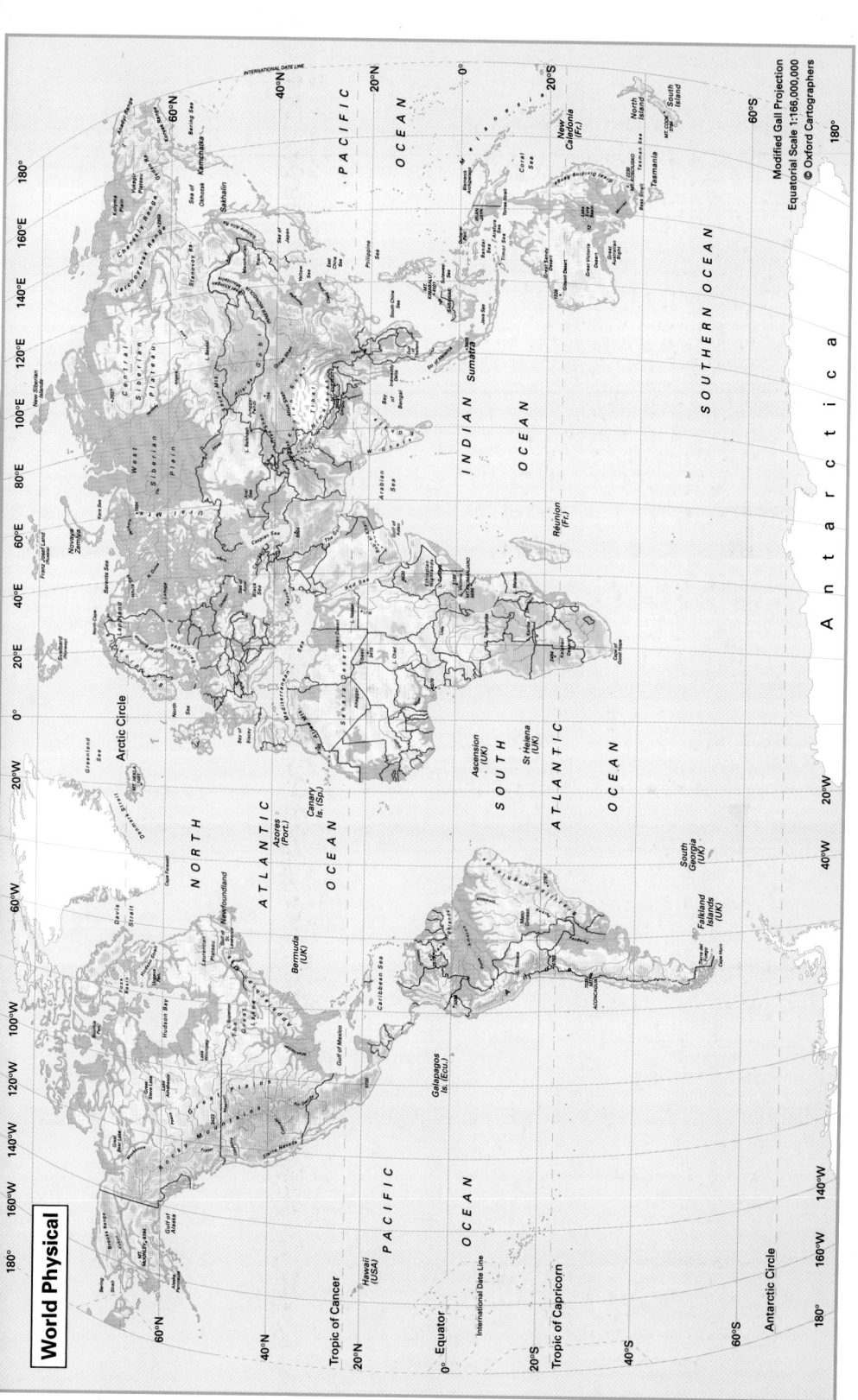

World Physical

Scale 1:20 000 000

| 0 | 200 | 400 | 600 km |

| 0 | 100 | 200 | 300 miles |

30°W 20°W 10°W 0° 10°

60°N

55°N

50°N

45°N

40°N

30°N

ICELAND
Vatnajökull
Reykjavik

Faröe Is.
(Den.)

Shetland Is.

Orkney Is

Hebrides

Trondheim
Ålesund

Bergen
Stavanger
Oslo
Dram
Kristiansand

Skagerrak

Bo
G
Ålborg
Århus
DENMARK
Odense
Kiel R
Hamburg
Elbe
Bremen Hannover
Ma

A T L A N T I C

O C E A N

Bay of

B i s c a y

Londonderry
Belfast
Glasgow
Aberdeen
Dundee
Edinburgh
UNITED
KINGDOM Newcastle
Middlesbrough

REPUBLIC
OF
IRELAND Dublin
Cork
St. George's Channel
Swansea
Cardiff
Bristol
Southampton
Plymouth

Liverpool
Leeds Hull
Manchester
Sheffield
Stoke Nottingham
Birmingham Norwich
London Thames
Dover
Calais Lille

North

Sea

NETHERLANDS
The Amsterdam
Hague Rotterdam
Antwerp
Gent **BELGIUM**
Brussels
Dortmund
Essen Kassel
Düsseldorf
Cologne Leipzig
Bonn Erfurt

Wiesbaden Frankfurt-
GERMANY Pra
Mannheim am-Main
Nürnbe

Stuttgart

English Channel
Cherbourg
Le Havre Luxembourg **LUX**
Reims
Brest
Rennes
Seine **Paris**
Le Mans Nancy
Loire Strasbourg
Saarbrücken
Nantes

F R A N C E

Corunna
Gijón
Vigo
Oporto
Coimbra

P O R T U G A L

Lisbon
Tagus
Guadiana
Badajoz

San
Sebastián
Bilbao
Valladolid
Zaragoza
Madrid
S P A I N
Ebro

Sabadell
Barcelona

Limoges
Clermont
Ferrand
Bordeaux
Garonne
Toulouse
ANDORRA

Dijon

Lyon
Massif
Central
Nîmes
Marseilles
Nice **MONACO**

Freiburg
Basle Zürich Innsbruck
Bern **LIECH.**
SWITZERLAND
Geneva

Milan Brescia
Turin Verona
Parma Bologna
Genoa **SAN**
MARINO
Florence

Munich

A

Tries
Venic
Padua

A P E n
Rome

Pyrenees

Valencia

Balearic Is.

Palma

Corsica

Ajaccio

Sardinia

Sassari

Cagliari

Nap
Tyrrhenian

Sea

Sicily

M e d i t e r r a n e a n

Seville
Málaga
Cádiz
Murcia Alicante
Córdoba
Cartagena

Tangier
Gibraltar
Ceuta(Sp.)
Tetuán
Melilla(Sp.)
MOROCCO Oujda
Rabat Fès
El Jadida **Casablanca**
Moulouya
Tlemcen

Cheliff
Oran
Medéa
Sidi-bel-Abbès
Djelfa

Algiers
Bejaia
A L G E R I A Annaba
Constantine
Batna

Skikda
Binzert

Tunis
TUNISIA Sousse

Sfax

Corsica

Sardinia

Conical Orthomorphic Projection

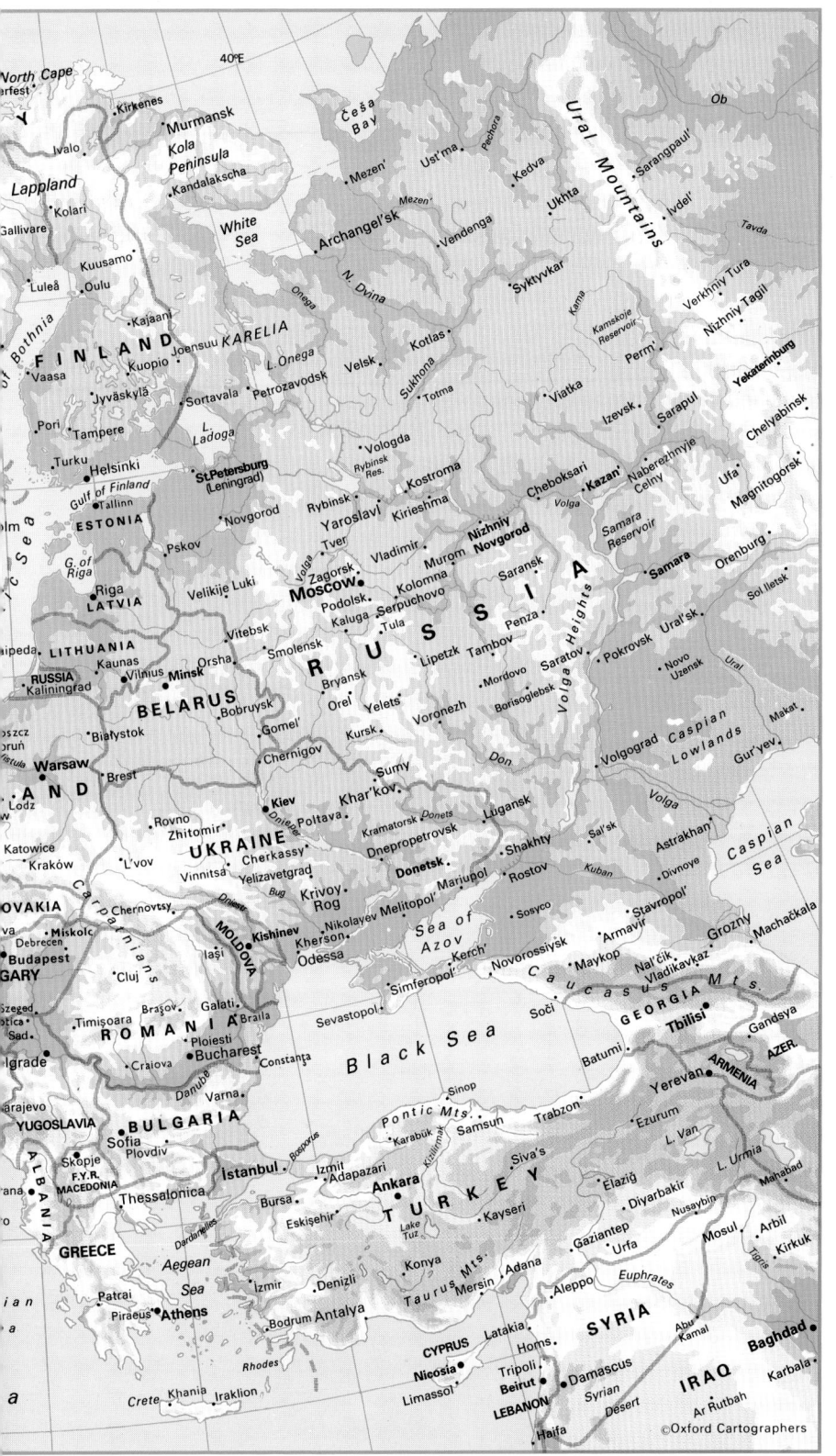

North Cape
arfest
Y
Ivalo
Kirkenes
Murmansk
Kola
Peninsula
Kandalakscha
Češa
Bay
Mezen'
Ust'ma
Pechora
Ob
Sarangpaul'
Ural Mountains
Lappland
Kolari
Kadva
Ukhta
Ivdel'
Gallivare
Kuusamo
White
Sea
Mezen'
Vendenga
Tavda
Luleå
Oulu
Kajaani
Archangel'sk
N. Dvina
Syktyvkar
Kama
Verkhniy Tura
Nizhniy Tagil
FINLAND
Joensuu KARELIA
Onega
Kamskoje
Reservoir
Perm'
Yekaterinburg
Vaasa
Kuopio
L.Onega
Velsk
Kotlas
Sukhona
Totma
Viatka
Izevsk
Sarapul
Chelyabinsk
Jyväskylä
Sortavala
Petrozavodsk
L.
Ladoga
Vologda
Rybinsk
Res.
Cheboksari
Kazan'
Naberezhnyje
Celny
Uta
Magnitogorsk
Pori
Tampere
Turku
Helsinki
St.Petersburg
(Leningrad)
Novgorod
Rybinsk
Yaroslavl
Kostroma
Volga
Samara
Reservoir
Samara
Orenburg
Gulf of Finland
Kirieshma
Tver
Vladimir.
Murom
Nizhniy
Novgorod
Saransk
ESTONIA
Pskov
Zagorsk
Volga
Kolomna
Sol Iletsk
G. of
Riga
Riga
LATVIA
Velikije Luki
Moscow
Podolsk.
Serpuchovo
Tula
Penza
Volga Heights
Samara
lm
ce Sea
Vitebsk
Kaluga
Lipetzk
Tambov
Saratov
Pokrovsk
Ural'sk
Ural
Makat
iipeda
LITHUANIA
Orsha.
Smolensk
Mordovo
Novo
Uzensk
Kaunas
Vilnius
Minsk
Bryansk
Orel
Yelets
Voronezh
Borisoglebsk
Volgograd
Caspian
Lowlands
RUSSIA
Kaliningrad
BELARUS
Bobruysk
Kursk
Don
Gur'yev
oszcz
orun
Białystok
Gomel'
Chernigov
Sumy
Volga
Vistula
Warsaw
Brest
Kiev
Khar'kov
Astrakhan
Caspian
Sea
Lodz
AND
Rovno
Zhitomir
Dniepr
Poltava
Kramatorsk
Donets
Lugansk
Sal'sk
Divnoye
Katowice
Kraków
UKRAINE
Cherkassy
Dnepropetrovsk
Shakhty
Rostov
Kuban
Stavropol'
OVAKIA
Chernovtsy
Vinnitsa
Yelizavetgrad
Bug
Krivoy
Rog
Donetsk
Mariupol
Sosyco
Armavir
Grozny
Machačkala
va
Miskolc
Debrecen
Dniestr
Kishinev
Nikolayev
Melitopol
Maykop
Nal'čik
Vladikavkaz
Budapest
MOLDOVA
Iaşi
Kherson.
Sea of
Azov
Kerch'
Novorossiysk
C a u c a s u s   Mts
Batumi
GEORGIA
Tbilisi
Gandsya
GARY
Cluj
Odessa
Simferopol'
Soči
zeged
otica
Sad.
Timişoara
Braşov.
Galati
Braila
Sevastopol
Black Sea
ARMENIA
AZER.
ROMANIA
Ploiesti
Yerevan
lgrade
Craiova
Bucharest
Constanţa
Danube
Batumi
arajevo
Varna.
Sinop
Ezurum
L. Van
YUGOSLAVIA
BULGARIA
Pontic Mts.
Samsun
Trabzon
L. Urmia
ALBANIA
Sofia
Plovdiv
Karabük
Kizilirmak
Siva's
ana
Skopje
F.Y.R.
MACEDONIA
İstanbul
Izmit
Adapazari
Elaziğ
Diyarbakir
Mahabad
o
Thessalonica
Bursa
Ankara
Kayseri
Gaziantep
Nusaybin
Mosul
Arbil
Eskişehir
TURKEY
Urfa
Kirkuk
GREECE
Aegean
Dardanelles
Lake
Tuz
Konya
Adana
Aleppo
Euphrates
Tigris
Patrai
Sea
Izmir
Denizli
Taurus Mts.
Mersin
ian
Piraeus
Athens
Bodrum
Antalya
SYRIA
Abu
Kamal
Baghdad
a
Crete
Khania
Iraklion
Rhodes
CYPRUS
Nicosia
Latakia
Homs.
Karbala
Limassol
Tripoli
Damascus
IRAQ
Beirut
Syrian
Desert
Ar Rutbah
LEBANON
Haifa
©Oxford Cartographers

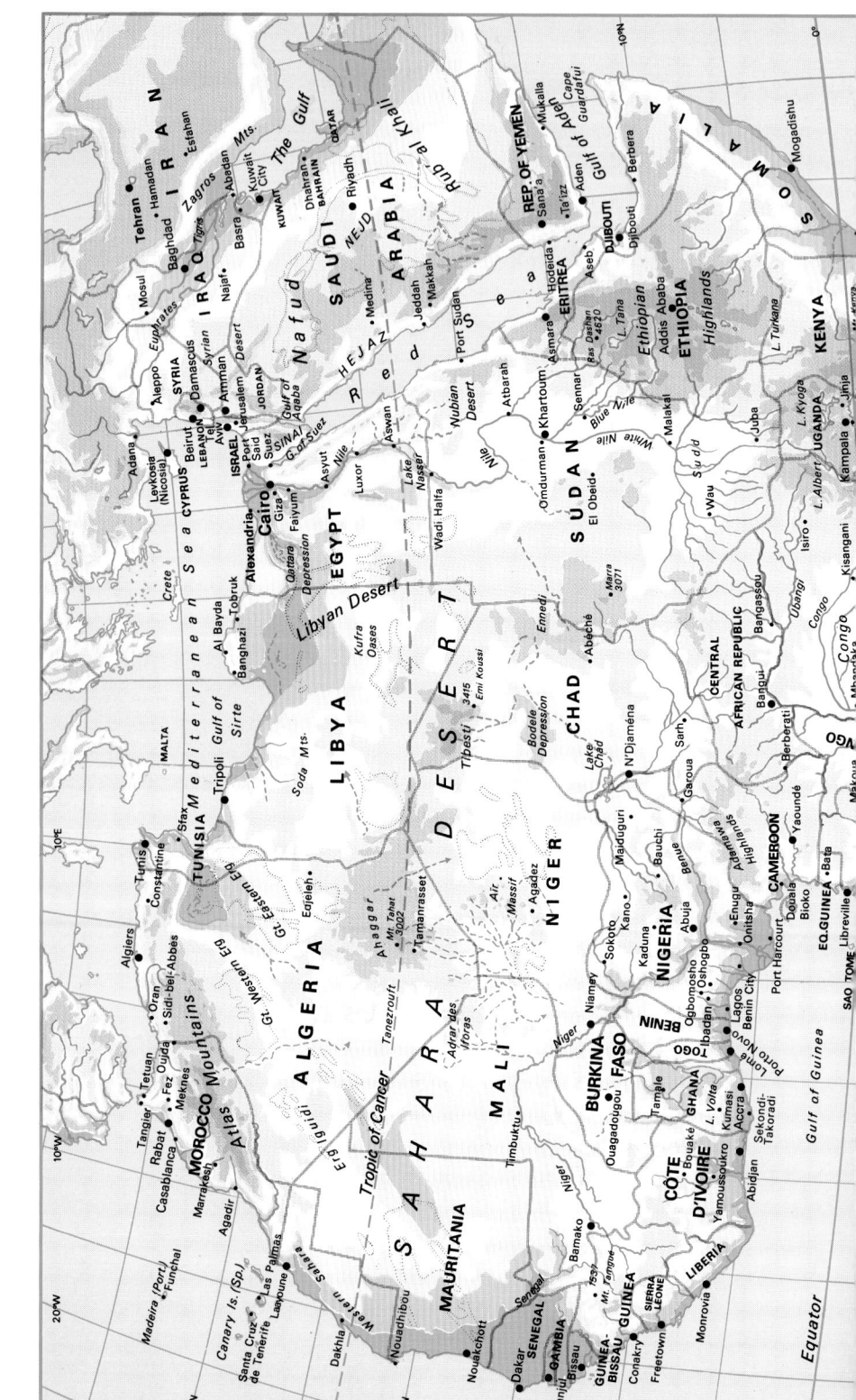

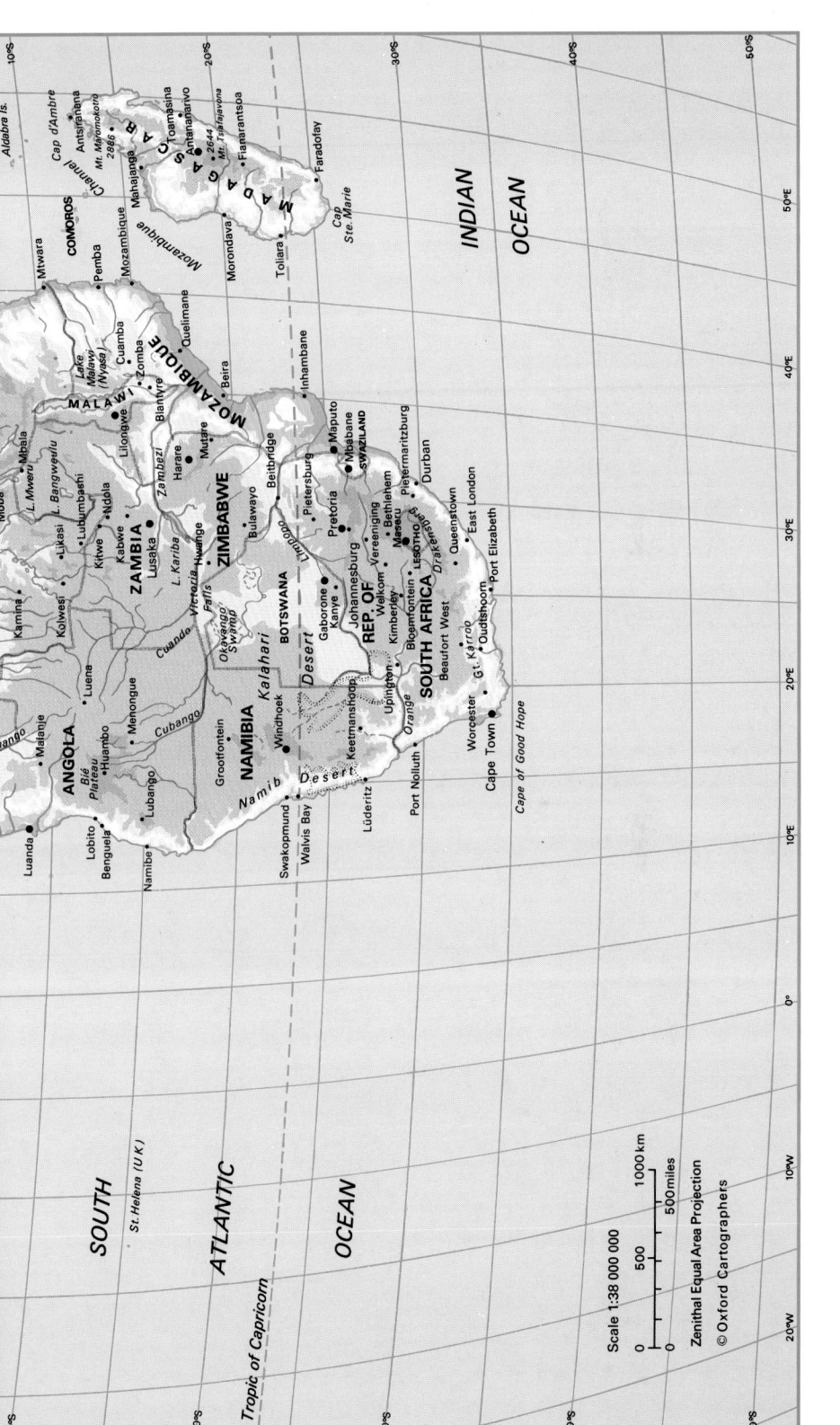

SOUTH

ATLANTIC

OCEAN

St.Helena (UK)

Tropic of Capricorn

Scale 1:38 000 000

0   500   1000 km
0   500miles

Zenithal Equal Area Projection

© Oxford Cartographers

Luanda
Lobito
Benguela
Namibe
ANGOLA
Bié
Plateau
Huambo
Lubango
Cuango
Malanje
Luena
Menongue
Cubango

Kamina
Kolwezi
Likasi
Ludumbashi
Kitwe
Ndola
ZAMBIA
Lusaka
Kabwe
L. Bangweulu
Moba
L. Mweru Mbala
L. Tanganyika

Swakopmund
Walvis Bay
Lüderitz
Namib Desert
Grootfontein
Windhoek
NAMIBIA
Keetmanshoop
Port Nolluth
Orange

Groofontein
Okavango Swamp
BOTSWANA
Gaborone
Kanye
Kalahari Desert

Victoria Falls
L. Kariba
ZIMBABWE
Bulawayo
Beitbridge
Limpopo

Cuanda
Zambezi

Upington
Beaufort West
Gt. Karroo
Worcester
Cape Town
Cape of Good Hope
Oudtshoorn
Port Elizabeth
East London
Queenstown
Port Nolluth

REP. OF
SOUTH AFRICA
Johannesburg
Welkom
Vereeniging
Kimberley
Bloemfontein
Bethlehem
Pretoria
Petersburg
Maseru
LESOTHO
Drakens
Durban
Pietermaritzburg
SWAZILAND
Mbabane
Maputo

Mwara
COMOROS
Pemba
Mozambique
MOZAMBIQUE
Quelimane
Beira
Inhambane
Nampula
Cuamba
Zomba
Blantyre
Mutare
Harare
Lilongwe
MALAWI
Lake Malawi (Nyasa)

Mozambique Channel

SEYCHELLES
Aldabra Is.
Cap d'Ambre
Antsiranana
Mahajanga
Toamasina
MADAGASCAR
Mt. Maromokotro
2886
Antananarivo
Fianarantsoa
Morondava
Toliara
Cap Ste. Marie
Mt. Tsiafajavona
2644
Faradofay

INDIAN

OCEAN

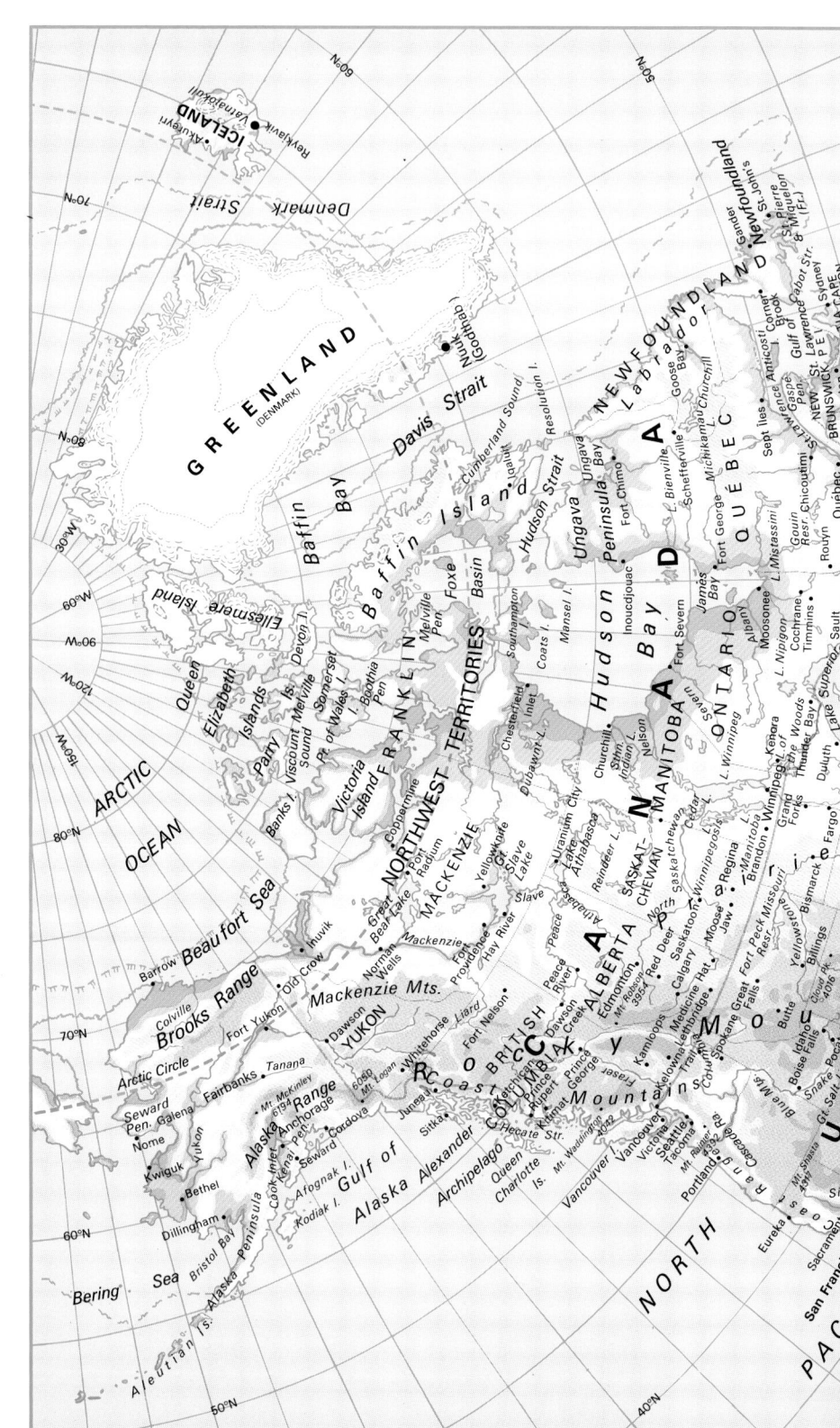

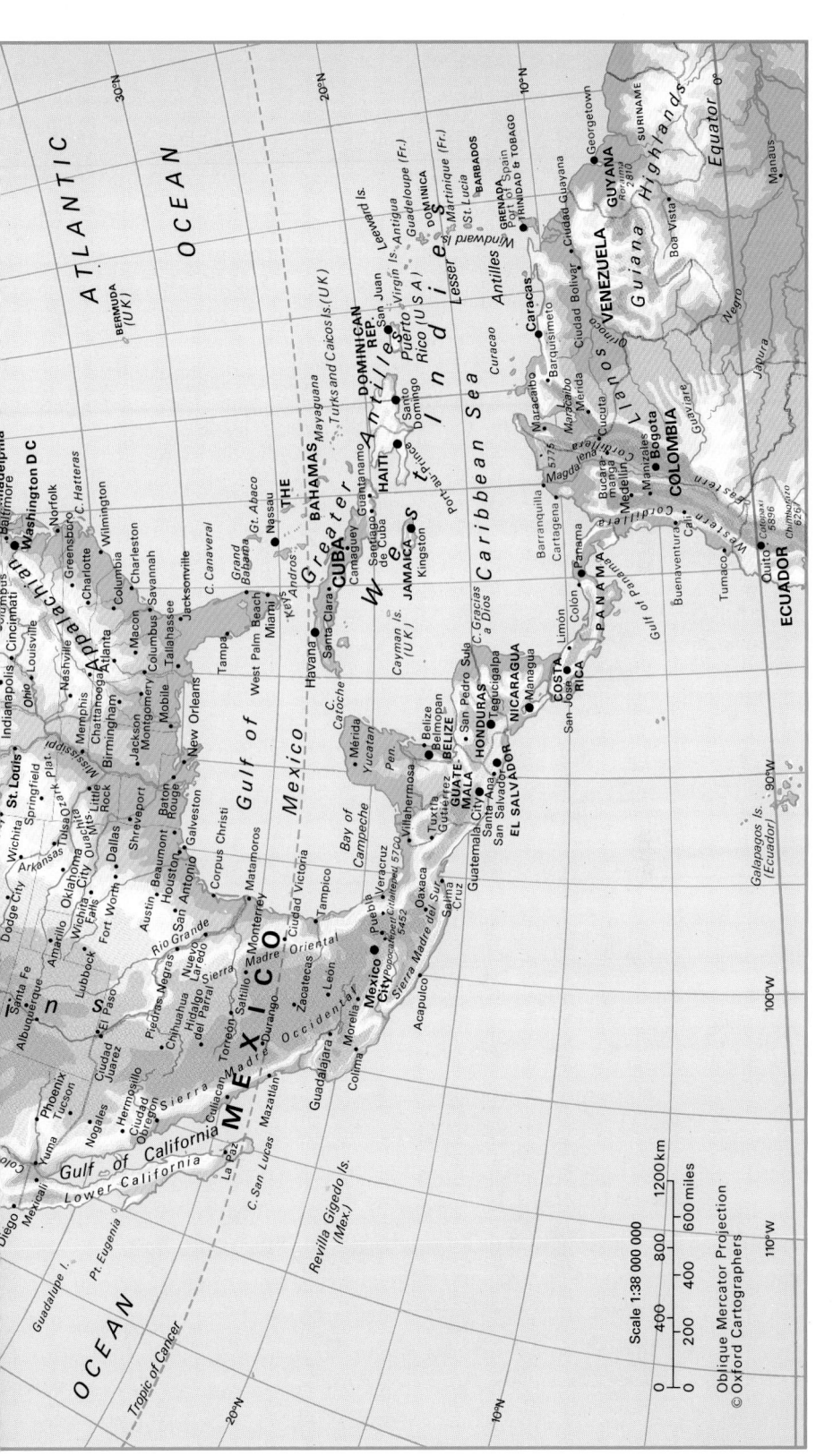

ATLANTIC OCEAN

OCEAN

BERMUDA (UK)

Baltimore
Washington D C
Philadelphia
Norfolk
C. Hatteras
Greensboro
Wilmington
Charlotte
Charleston
Columbia
Savannah
Jacksonville
C. Canaveral

Indianapolis
Columbus
Cincinnati
Louisville
Ohio
St. Louis
Springfield
Nashville
Memphis
Chattanooga
Atlanta
Macon
Columbus
Montgomery
Birmingham
Jackson
Mobile
Tallahassee

Appalachian

Wichita
Dodge City
Ozark Plat.
Little Rock
Mississippi
Wichita Falls
Tulsa
Oklahoma City
Arkansas
Red
Baton Rouge
Shreveport
New Orleans

Tampa
West Palm Beach
Miami
Key West
Keys

Grand Bahama
Gt. Abaco
Nassau
THE BAHAMAS
Andros
Mayaguana
Turks and Caicos Is.(UK)

DOMINICAN REP.
San Juan
Virgin Is.
Puerto Rico (USA)
Leeward Is.
Antigua
Guadeloupe (Fr.)
DOMINICA
Martinique (Fr.)
St. Lucia
BARBADOS
Windward Is.
GRENADA
TRINIDAD & TOBAGO
Port of Spain

Georgetown
GUYANA
SURINAME
Guiana Highlands

Equator

Manaus
Negro
Japura

VENEZUELA
Caracas
Barquisimeto
Ciudad Bolívar
Ciudad Guayana
Barcelona
Maracaibo
Maracaibo
Mérida
Cúcuta
Bucaramanga
Medellín
COLOMBIA
Bogotá
Cali
Manizales
Buenaventura
Tumaco
Quito
ECUADOR
Chimborazo 6896
Cordillera Oriental
Cordillera Occidental
Western Cordillera
Eastern Cordillera
Llanos
Orinoco
Magdalena
Guaviare
Guaviare

Greater Antilles
West Indies
Lesser Antilles
Caribbean Sea
Curaçao

CUBA
Havana
Santa Clara
Camagüey
Santiago de Cuba
Guantánamo
HAITI
Port-au-Prince
Santo Domingo
JAMAICA
Kingston
Cayman Is. (UK)

C. Catoche
C. San Antonio
Santa Cruz
Mérida
Yucatán Pen.
Belize
Belmopan
BELIZE
GUATEMALA
Guatemala City
San Pedro Sula
HONDURAS
Tegucigalpa
San Salvador
Santa Ana
EL SALVADOR
Managua
NICARAGUA
C. Gracias a Dios
Limón
San José
COSTA RICA
Colón
PANAMA
Panama
Gulf of Panama
Gulf of Darién

San Diego
Mexicali
Mexicali
Yuma
Phoenix
Tucson
Nogales
Hermosillo
Ciudad Obregón
Culiacán
La Paz
C. San Lucas
Mazatlán
Lower California
Gulf of California
Sierra Madre
Guadalupe I.
Pt. Eugenia
Revilla Gigedo Is. (Mex.)

Santa Fe
Albuquerque
Amarillo
Lubbock
El Paso
Ciudad Juárez
Chihuahua
Hidalgo del Parral
Piedras Negras
Nuevo Laredo
Torreón
Saltillo
Durango
Zacatecas
León
Guadalajara
Colima
Morelia
MEXICO
Mexico City
Popocatépetl 5452
Citlaltépetl 5700
Acapulco
Oaxaca
Sierra Madre del Sur
Sierra Madre Oriental
Sierra Madre Occidental
Veracruz
Puebla
Tuxtla Gutiérrez
Villahermosa
Bay of Campeche
Tampico
Ciudad Victoria
Matamoros
Corpus Christi
Galveston
Houston
Beaumont
Austin
San Antonio
Rio Grande
Monterrey
Dallas
Fort Worth
Wichita

Gulf of Mexico

Galápagos Is. (Ecuador)

30°N
20°N
10°N
20°N
10°N

110°W
100°W
90°W
80°W

Tropic of Cancer

Scale 1:38 000 000

0   400   800   1200 km
0   200   400   600 miles

Oblique Mercator Projection
© Oxford Cartographers

Santa Clara • **CUBA**
Camagüey
Santiago • Guantanamo
de Cuba **HAITI** DOMINICAN REP.
Turks and Caicos Is. (U K)
JAMAICA Santo San Juan Leeward Is.
Kingston Port-au-Prince Domingo *Puerto* Virgin Is. Antigua (U K)
Rico (U S A) Guadeloupe (Fr.)
Lesser DOMINICA
Martinique (Fr.)
St. Lucia
BARBADOS
Caribbean Sea Curaçao Antilles GRENADA
Port of Spain
Barranquilla Maracaibo TRINIDAD & TOBAGO
Limón Cartagena 5775 **Caracas**
Colón Panama Barquisimeto
PANAMA Maracaibo Mérida Ciudad Bolívar Ciudad Guayana
Bucara- Cúcuta Georgetown
manga **VENEZUELA** **GUYANA** Paramaribo
Medellín *Llanos* Roraima FR
Manizales 2810 **SURINAME** **GUIANA**
Buenaventura **Bogotá** Cayenne
Cali **COLOMBIA** *Guiana* Boa Vista
Tumaco Guaviare *Highlands*
Japurá *Negro*
0° **Quito** Cotopaxi
ECUADOR 5896 Marajó
Guayaquil Chimborazo Amazon I. Belém Equator
6267 Cuenca Manaus Santarém São Luís
Sullana Iquitos• •Leticia
Marañón Bacabal•
Chiclayo• S e l v a s Teresina Fortaleza
Jurua *Tapajós* C. São
Cajamarca Ucayali Purus Natal
Trujillo• **PERU** Madeira *Teles Pires* B R A Z I L Juazeiro do Norte Mossoró
Chimbote Pucallpa Cruzeiro do Sol Campina João
Huánuco Pôrto Velho *Xingu* Grande
10°S Río Branco Caruaru• Recife
La Oroya Juazeiro Paulo Alfonso• •Maceió
Callao Huancayo Serra dos Parecis *Tocantins* Aracaju•
Lima Cuzco• Barreiras• Feira de Santana
Santa Ana Trinidad Mato São Francisco •Salvador
Puno• L. Titicaca Mato Goiás• Brasília B r a z i l i a n •Ilhéus
Arequipa •La Paz Grosso Grosso •Brasília
Mollendo **BOLIVIA** Cuiabá Goiânia• *Highlands* Montes Claros
Arica Oruro Sucre Plateau Piraporaa Diamantina
Iquique Salt •Potosí Corumbá Uberlândia Belo •Governador
Flat Campo Uberaba Horizonte Valadares
20°S Tarija Grande Ribeirão Vitória
Tropic of Capricorn Antofagasta San Salvador Chaco Marília Preto Caratinga
Taltal de Jujuy Pilcomayo **PARAGUAY** Campinas Juiz Campos
San Félix I. San Salta Concepción S a São de Fora Niterói
Ambrosio I. Formosa m Paulo Volta **Rio de Janeiro**
(Chile) Tucumán Asunción p Londrina Redonda
Copiapó Catamarca Santiago del Estero Resistencia Villarrica o Santos Curitiba S O U T H
La Rioja Salinas Corrientes Paraná Passo •Florianopolis
La Serena Grandes Santa Posadas Fundo
Córdoba •Santa Fé Maria Livramento •Pôrto Alegre A T L A N T I C
Aconcagua San Juan Paraná Tacuarembo
Valparaíso 6960 •Mendoza Rosario **URUGUAY** Paysandu Pelotas
Santiago Rancagua San Luis Durazno
Juan Fernández Is. Curicó Santa **Buenos** Montevideo O C E A N
(Chile) Talca Rosa **Aires** Rocha
Chillán Bolívar La Mar del Plata
Concepción Neuquén Azul Plata
Valdivia •Colorado •Bahía Blanca
Osorno Negro Carmen de
Puerto Montt Patagones
Chiloé Chubut Viedma
Valdés
40°S Comodoro Rivadavia Peninsula
Taitao Gulf of Rawson
Pen. S. Jorge
Buenos Aires
•Deseado
L. Viedma
L. Argentino Falkland Is. (U K)
Río Gallegos •Port Stanley
Puerto Natales Strait of Magellan
50°S Punta Arenas Tierra del Fuego South Georgia
Ushuaia (U K)
Cape Horn
Scale 1:44 000 000

0   400   800   1200   1600 km

0   500   1000 miles

Oblique Mercator Projection
© Oxford Cartographers

INDONESIA

Sumatera
Sumbawa
Flores
Timor
Timor Sea

INDIAN

OCEAN

Arafura Sea

Gulf of
Carpentaria

NORTHERN
TERRITORY
KIMBERLEY
ARNHEM LAND
Darwin
Katherine
Barkly Tableland
Tennant Creek
Tanami
Desert
Alice Springs
MacDonnell Ranges
Ayers Rock
(Uluru)
Musgrave Ra.

Great
Sandy Desert

Gibson Desert

WESTERN

AUSTRALIA

Great
Victoria Desert

Nullarbor Plain

Great
Australian Bight

C. Leveque
Broome
80 Mile Beach
Mt. Bruce 1227
Hamersley Ra.
Port Hedland
N.W. Cape
Carnarvon
Meekatharra
Laverton
Geraldton
Kalgoorlie
Fremantle
Perth
Bunbury
Albany

SOUTH

AUSTRALIA

Lake Eyre
Simpson Desert
Flinders Ra.
Woomera
Oodnadatta
Whyalla
Spencer Gulf
Kangaroo I.
Mount Gambier
Adelaide

QUEENSLAND

Mt. Isa
Cloncurry
Selwyn Ra.
Sturt Desert
Grey Range
Charleville
Bourke
Darling
Broken Hill
Mildura
Murray
Bendigo
Ballarat

Cairns
Townsville
Mackay
Rockhampton
Bundaberg
Gt. Sandy I.
Brisbane
Gold Coast
Toowoomba

Great Dividing Range

New England Ra.

NEW
SOUTH
WALES
Armidale
Dubbo
Orange
Albury
Wagga Wagga
AUSTRALIAN CAPITAL TERRITORY
Canberra
Mt. Kosciusko 2230
Newcastle
Sydney
Wollongong

VICTORIA
Melbourne
Yallourn
C. Howe

King I.
Flinders I.
Bass Str.
Mt. Ossa 1617
Launceston
TASMANIA
Hobart

C. York
Gulf of Papua
Port Moresby
Torres Strait
Merauke
Tanimbar Is.
Melville I.
Wyndham
927 Mt. Broome

Coral Sea

Great Barrier Reef

PACIFIC

OCEAN

Solomon Sea
D'Entrecasteaux Is.
Louisiade Arch.

SOLOMON
ISLANDS
Santa Isabel
New Georgia
Guadalcanal
Honiara
Malaita
San Cristobal
Rennell I.
Santa Cruz Is.
Banks Is.

VANUATU
Malekula
Port-Vila

New Caledonia
(Fr.)
Chesterfield Is.
(Fr.)
Loyalty Is.
(Fr.)
Nouméa

FIJI

Tropic of Capricorn

Norfolk I.
(Aust.)

Lord Howe I.
(N.S.W.)

Tasman
Sea

NEW
ZEALAND
North Cape
Whangarei
Auckland
NORTH
ISLAND
Gisborne
Napier
Mt. Ruapehu 2797
Wellington
Nelson
Cook Strait
SOUTH Mt. Aoraki 3754
ISLAND Mt. Cook
Greymouth
Southern Alps
Christchurch
Timaru
Oamaru
Dunedin
Invercargill

10°S
20°S
30°S
40°S

100°E
110°E
120°E
130°E
140°E
150°E
160°E
170°E
180°

Scale 1:40 000 000

0   500   1000km

0   500miles

Modified Zenithal Equidistant Projection

©Oxford Cartographers

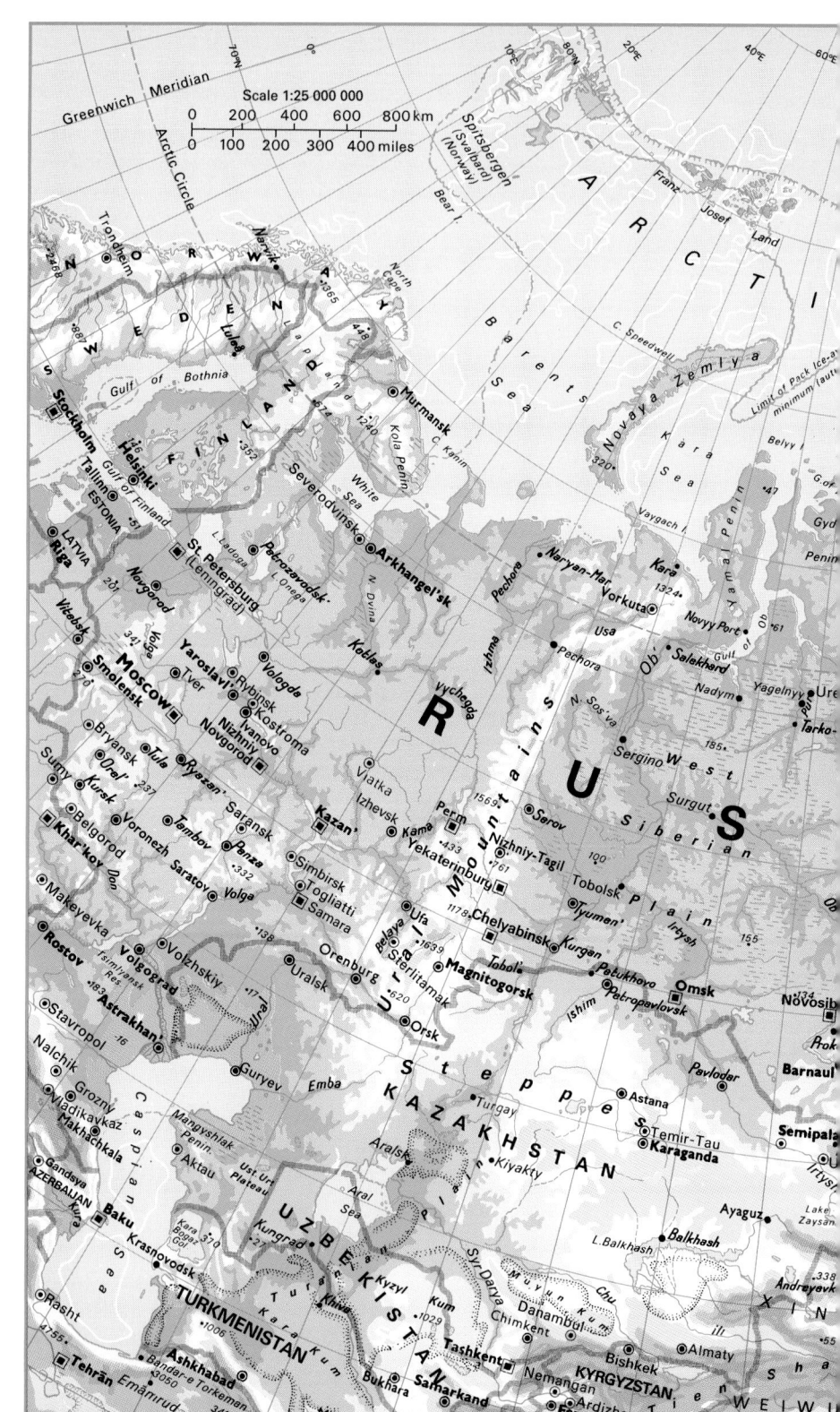

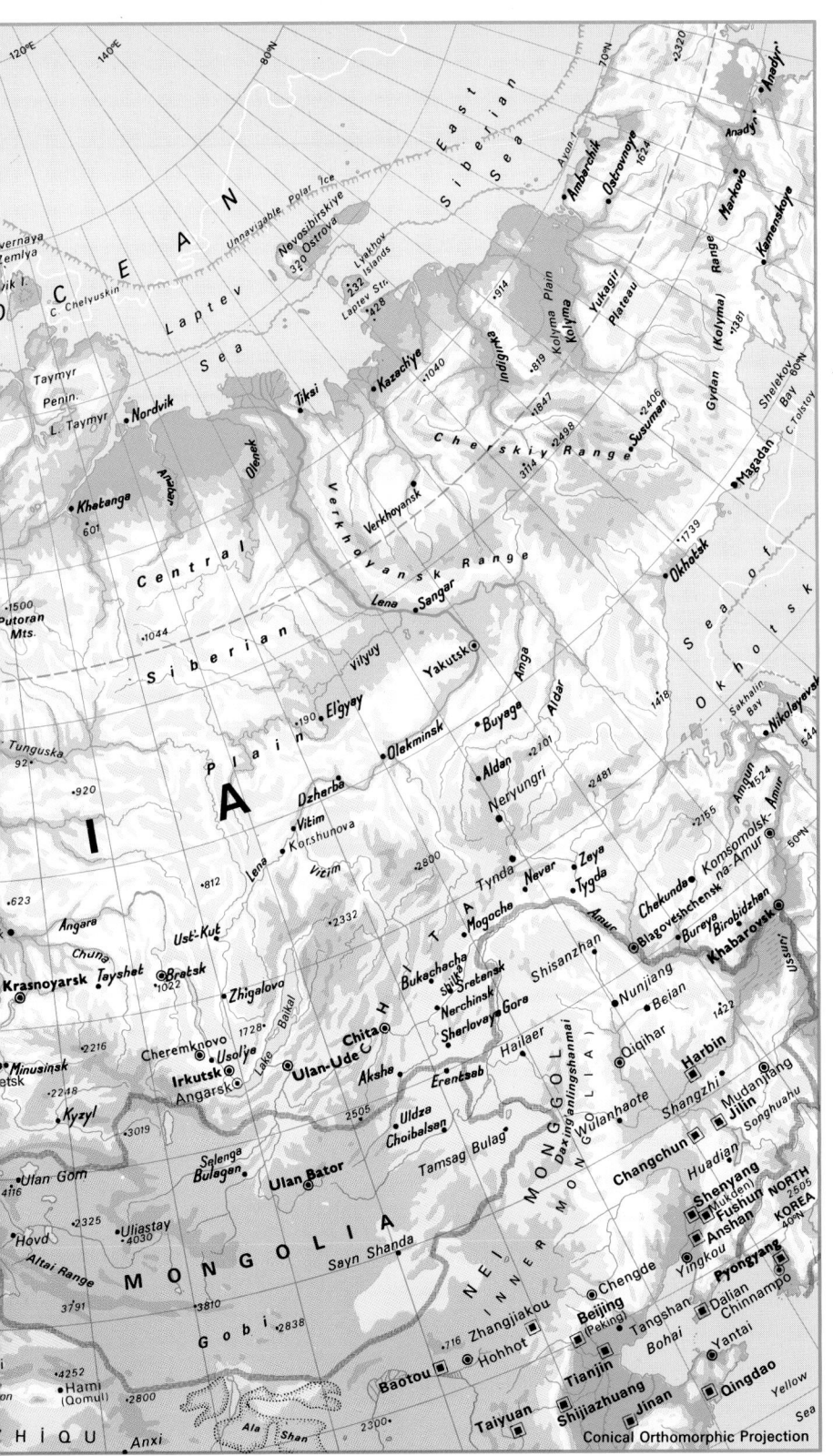

120°E
140°E
80°N
70°N

O C E A N

vernaya
emlya

vik I.

C. Chelyuskin

Taymyr
Penin.

L. Taymyr

Nordvik

•Khatanga
601

C e n t r a l

•1500
utoran
Mts.

S i b e r i a n

•1044

Tunguska
92•

•920

•623

Angara

Chuna

Krasnoyarsk   Tayshet

•Minusinsk
etsk

•2216

•2248

•Kyzyl

•3019

Unnavigable Polar Ice

Nevosibirskiye
320 Ostrova

Lyakhov
Islands

•232

Laptev Str.

•428

Laptev

Sea

Anabar

Olenek

Verkhoyansk
•

Lena Sangar

Vilyuy

•190 Elgeyay

Dzharba
•Vitim
•Korshunova

Lena

•812

Vitim

•2800

•2332

East
S i b e r i a n
Sea

Ayon I.

Ambarchik

•914
Indigirka

•Kazachye

•1040

Kolyma Plain
•819
Kolyma

•1847

Chekskiy Range
2498•
3114

Anadyr•

Anadyr

Ostrovnoye
1624

Yukagir
Plateau

2406•

Susuman

•1739

Markovo

Kamenskoye

Gydan (Kolyma)
Range
•1381

Shelekov
Bay

60°N

C. Tolstoy

Magadan

Okhotsk

S
e
a

o
f

Tiksi

Yakutsk⊙

Plain

I   A

Anga

Buyaga

Aldan

•Olekminsk

Aldan

•Alden

Neryungri

2170•

2481•

Tynda

Never

•Mogoche

Zeya
•Tygda

•2165

1418•

O
k
h
o
t
s
k

Sakhalin
Bay

Amgun
1624

Nikolayevsk

544

50°N

Komsomolsk-
na-Amur⊙

Ust-Kut

Zhigalova

•1022
Bratsk

1728•

Cheremknovo   Usolye
Irkutsk⊙
Angarsk⊙

Lake Baikal

Ulan-Ude⊙

Chita⊙

Bukachacha
Shilka
Nerchinsk
Sherlovaya Gora

Aksha

Sretensk

Mogoche

Shisanzhan

Hailaer

Amur

•Bukachacha

Blagoveshchensk⊙

Bureya

Nunjiang

Beian

Chekunda

Birobidzhan

Khabarovsk⊙

1422•

Harbin

Ussuri

Erentsab

2505•

Uldze
Choibalsan

Tamsag Bulag

Qiqihar⊙

Wulanhaote

Daxinganlingshanmai

Mudanjiang

Shangzhi•
Jilin

Songhuahu

Changchun

Huadian

Shenyang
(Mukden)
Fushun
Anshan

NORTH

2505

KOREA

40°N

Ulan Bator

Selenga
Bulagan•

Ulan Gom
4116

•2325

Uliastay
•4030

•Hovd

Altai Range

3791

3810•

M O N G O L I A

G o b i

•2838

•4252

•Hami
(Qomul)

•2800

H I Q U

Anxi

Ala Shan

N E I   M O N G O L   (I N N E R   M O N G O L I A)

Yingkou

Chengde

•716 Zhangjiakou

Hohhot

Baotou⊙

Sayn Shanda

2300•

Pyongyang

Dalian
Chinnampo

Beijing
(Peking)

Tangshan

Bohai

Yantai

Tianjin

Taiyuan

Shijiazhuang

Jinan

Qingdao

Yellow

Sea

Conical Orthomorphic Projection

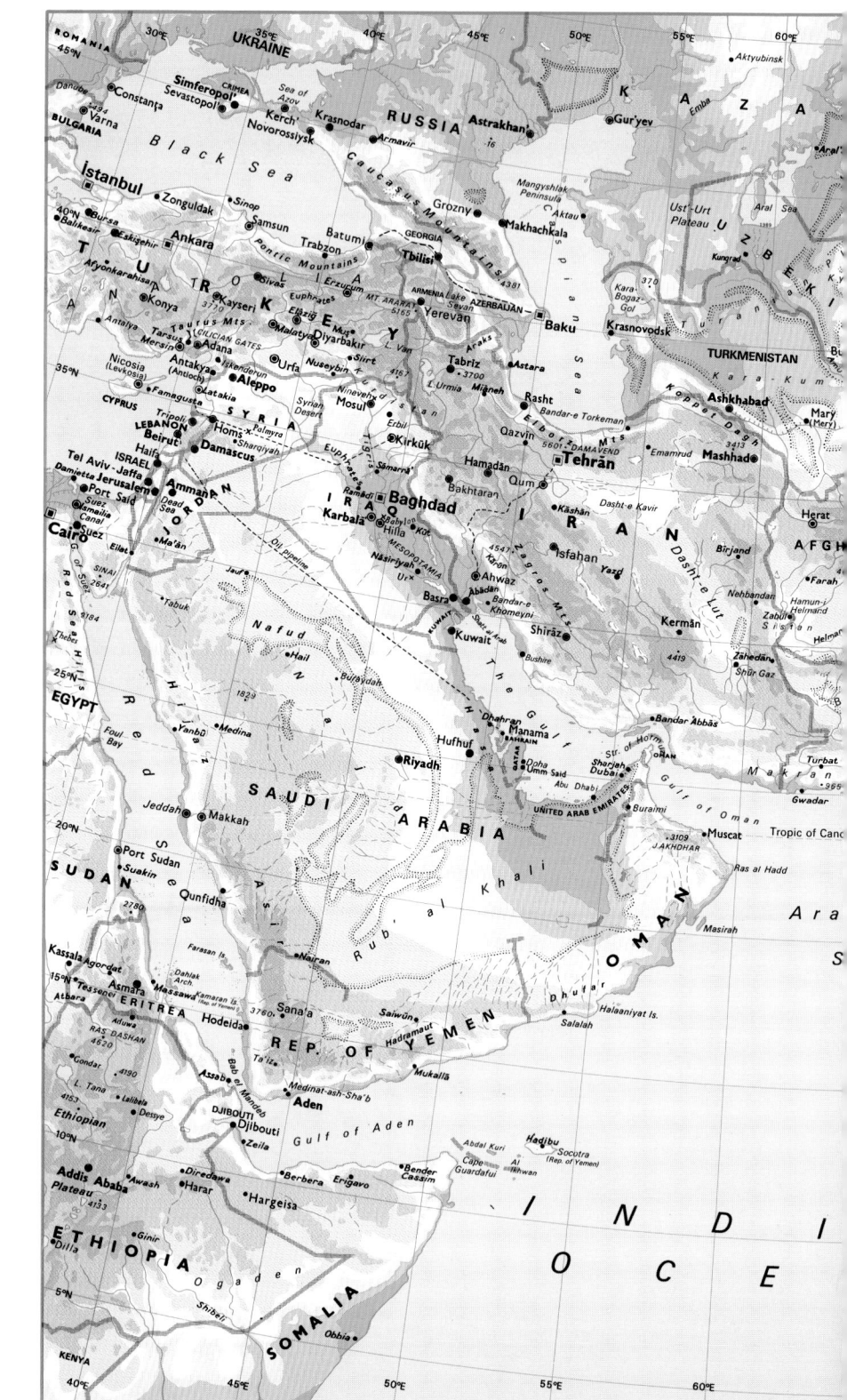

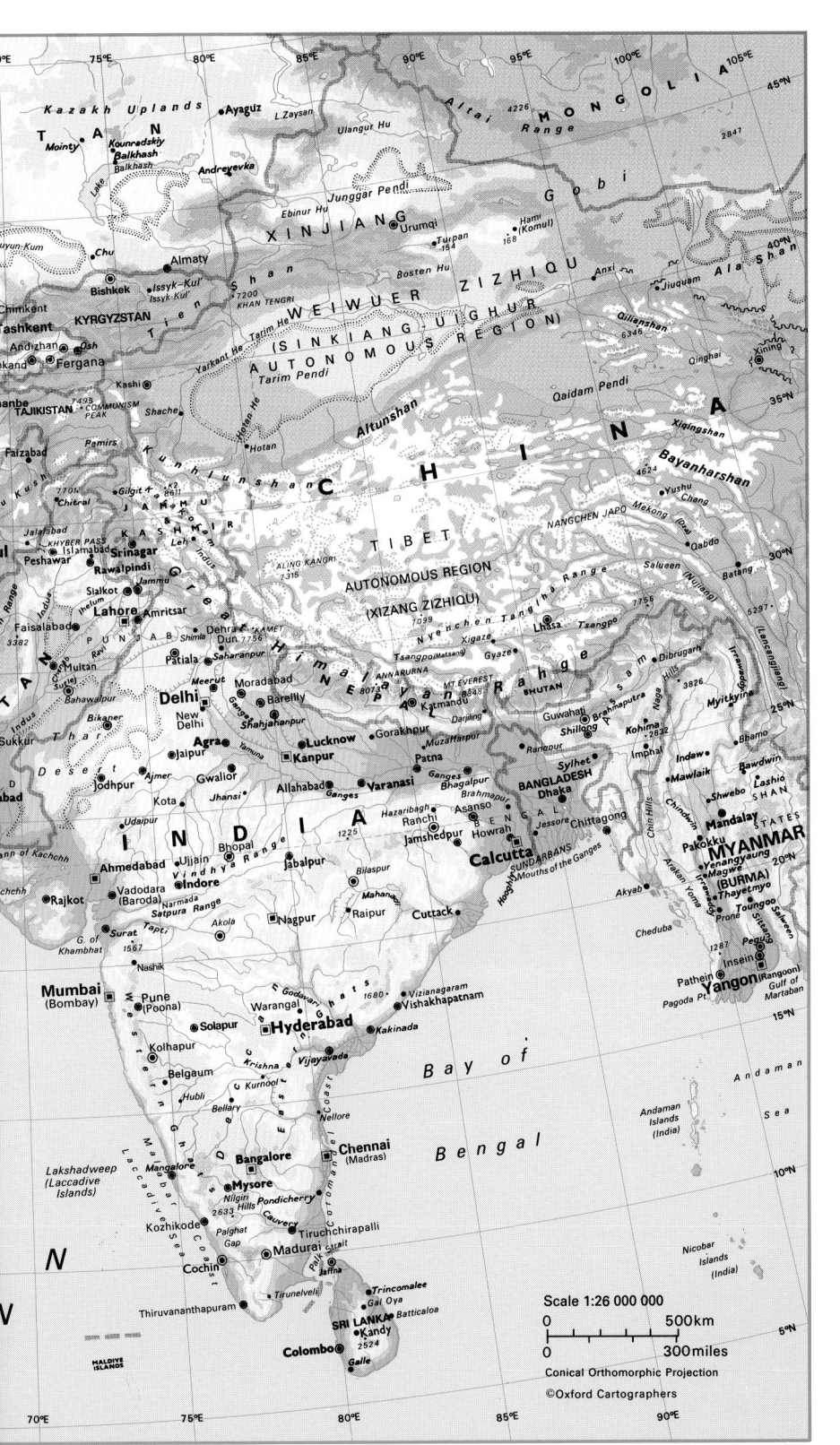

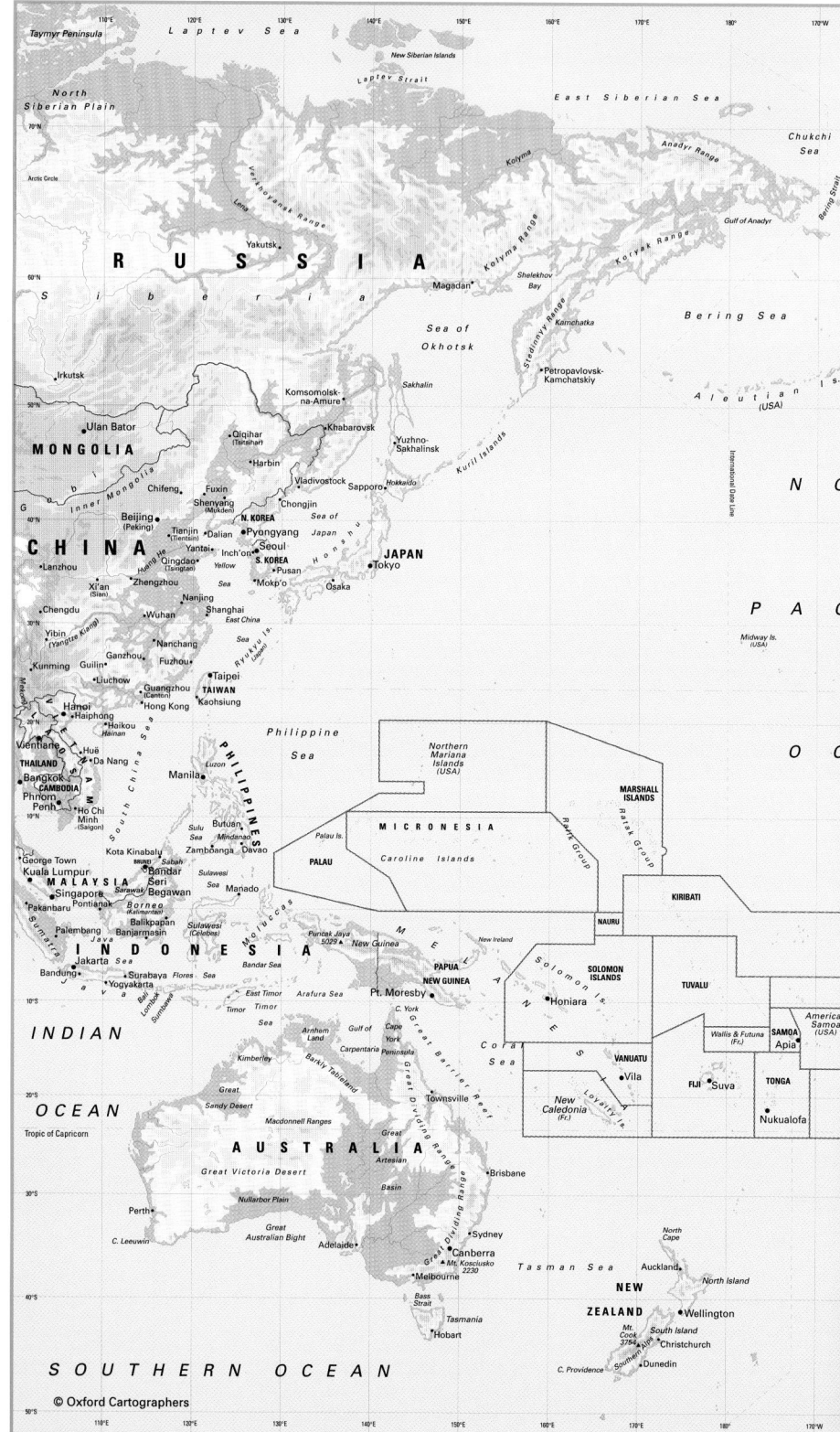

110°E   120°E   130°E   140°E   150°E   160°E   170°E   180°   170°W

Taymyr Peninsula   L a p t e v   S e a

New Siberian Islands

North
Siberian Plain

70°N

Arctic Circle

Laptev Strait

East Siberian Sea

Chukchi
Sea

Anadyr Range

Kolyma

Verkhoyansk Range

Lena

Yakutsk

R   U   S   S   I   A

60°N

S   i   b   e   r   i   a

Irkutsk

50°N

Ulan Bator

MONGOLIA

Komsomolsk-
na-Amure

Qiqihar
(Tsitsihar)

Harbin

I
n
n
e
r

M
o
n
g
o
l
i
a

Chifeng

Fuxin

Shenyang
(Mukden)

Beijing
(Peking)

C H I N A

Lanzhou

Tianjin
(Tientsin)

Dalian

Yantei

Qingdao
(Tsingtao)

Xi'an
(Sian)

Zhengzhou

Nanjing

Chengdu

Wuhan

Shanghai

Yibin
(Yangtze Kiang)

Nanchang

Kunming

Ganzhou

Guilin

Fuzhou

Liuchow

Guangzhou
(Canton)

Hong Kong

Taipei

TAIWAN

Kaohsiung

Hanoi

Haiphong

Hoikou

Hainan

Vientiane

Huë

THAILAND

Bangkok

CAMBODIA

Phnom
Penh

Da Nang

Manila

Kolyma Range

Magadan

Shelekhov
Bay

Sea of
Okhotsk

Sakhalin

Khabarovsk

Yuzhno-
Sakhalinsk

Vladivostock

Sapporo

Chongjin

N. KOREA

Pyongyang

Inch'on

Seoul

S. KOREA

Pusan

Mokp'o

Hokkaido

Kuril Islands

Sredinnyy Range

Kamchatka

Koryak Range

Petropavlovsk-
Kamchatskiy

Bering Sea

Gulf of Anadyr

Bering Strait

A l e u t i a n   Is.
(USA)

International Date Line

N   C

Sea of
Japan

J a p a n

H o n s h u

Yellow
Sea

Zhengzhou

Osaka

Tokyo

JAPAN

East China
Sea

Ryukyu Is.
(Nansei)

Philippine
Sea

Northern
Mariana
Islands
(USA)

P A C

P

Midway Is.
(USA)

O   C

Luzon

Ho Chi
Minh
(Saigon)

George Town

Kuala Lumpur

MALAYSIA

Singapore

Pekanbaru

Pontianak

Palembang

S
u
m
a
t
r
a

Jakarta

Bandung

Butuan

Sulu
Sea

Kota Kinabalu

Sabah

Zamboanga

Davao

Mindanao

BRUNEI

Bandar
Seri
Begawan

Sarawak

Sulawesi
Sea

Manado

Borneo
(Kalimantan)

Balikpapan

Banjarmasin

Sulawesi
(Celebes)

I N D O N E S I A

Java
Sea

Surabaya

Yogyakarta

Bali

Lombok

Sumbawa

J   a   v   a

Flores

Flores   Sea

Bandar Sea

East Timor

Timor

Timor
Sea

Arafura Sea

PALAU

Palau Is.

Caroline   Islands

M I C R O N E S I A

MARSHALL
ISLANDS

Ralik Group

Ratak Group

KIRIBATI

NAURU

M
o
l
u
c
c
a
s

Puncak Jaya
5029

New Guinea

PAPUA
NEW GUINEA

Pt. Moresby

New Ireland

M
E
L
A
N
E
S
I
A

Honiara

S
o
l
o
m
o
n
   Is.

Solomon Is.

SOLOMON
ISLANDS

TUVALU

Wallis & Futuna
(Fr.)

VANUATU

Vila

New
Caledonia
(Fr.)

FIJI

Suva

L
o
y
a
l
t
y
   Is.

America
Samoa
(USA)

SAMOA

Apia

TONGA

Nukualofa

INDIAN

OCEAN

Tropic of Capricorn

C. York

Cape
York

Gulf of
Carpentaria

York
Peninsula

G
r
e
a
t
   B
a
r
r
i
e
r
   R
e
e
f

Coral
Sea

Townsville

S
o
u
t
h
   C
h
i
n
a
   S
e
a

P
H
I
L
I
P
P
I
N
E
S

Arnhem
Land

Kimberley

Barkly Tableland

Great
Sandy Desert

Macdonnell Ranges

A U S T R A L I A

Great Victoria Desert

Perth

Nullarbor Plain

C. Leeuwin

Great
Australian Bight

Adelaide

Great Artesian
Basin

G
r
e
a
t
   D
i
v
i
d
i
n
g
   R
a
n
g
e

Brisbane

Sydney

Canberra

Mt. Kosciusko
2230

Melbourne

Bass
Strait

Tasmania

Hobart

Tasman   Sea

Auckland

North Island

North
Cape

NEW

ZEALAND

Wellington

Mt.
Cook
3754

South Island

Christchurch

Southern Alps

C. Providence

Dunedin

S O U T H E R N   O C E A N

© Oxford Cartographers

50°S

110°E   120°E   130°E   140°E   150°E   160°E   170°E   180°   170°W

40°N

30°N

20°N

10°N

10°S

20°S

30°S

40°S

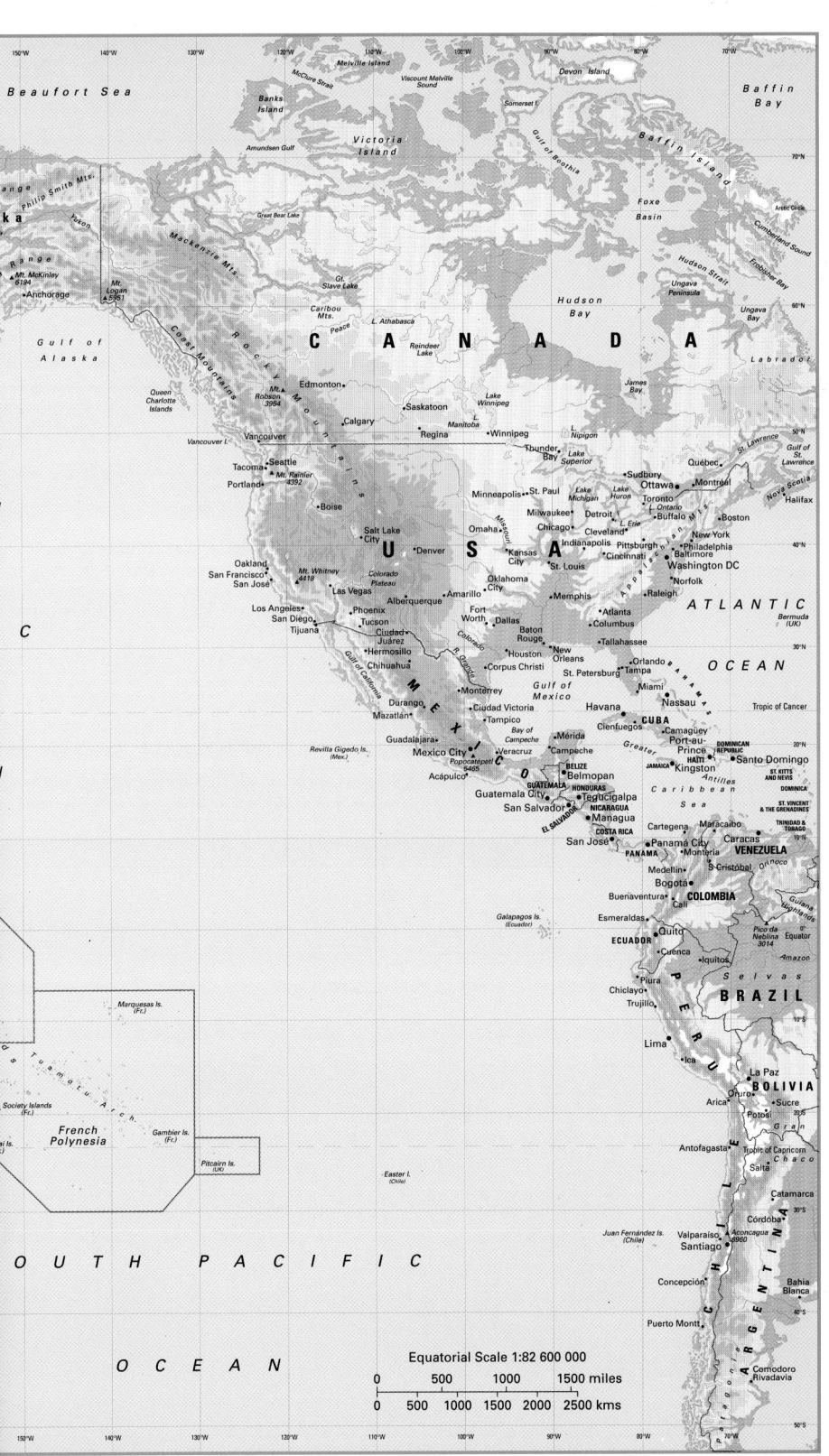

Beaufort Sea

Baffin Bay

Melville Island

McClure Strait

Viscount Melville Sound

Banks Island

Devon Island

Somerset I.

Gulf of Boothia

Baffin Island

Amundsen Gulf

Victoria Island

70°N

Arctic Circle

ange

Philip Smith Mts.

ka

Yukon

Great Bear Lake

Foxe Basin

Cumberland Sound

Frobisher Bay

Range

Mt. McKinley 6194

Mackenzie Mts.

Gt. Slave Lake

Hudson Strait

Ungava Peninsula

Mt. Logan 5951

Anchorage

Caribou Mts.

L. Athabasca

Peace

Hudson Bay

Ungava Bay

60°N

Gulf of Alaska

Rocky Mountains

Reindeer Lake

C A N A D A

Labrador

Queen Charlotte Islands

Edmonton

Mt. Robson 3954

Coast Mountains

Saskatoon

Calgary

Lake Winnipeg

Manitoba

James Bay

50°N

Vancouver I.

Vancouver

Regina

Winnipeg

L. Nipigon

St. Lawrence

Gulf of St. Lawrence

Seattle

Tacoma

Mt. Rainier 4392

Portland

Boise

Thunder Bay

Lake Superior

Sudbury

Québec

Montréal

Nova Scotia

Minneapolis

St. Paul

Lake Michigan

Lake Huron

Toronto

L. Ontario

Ottawa

Halifax

Milwaukee

Detroit

Buffalo

Boston

Salt Lake City

Omaha

Missouri

Chicago

Cleveland

L. Erie

New York

U

Denver

S

Kansas City

Indianapolis

Pittsburgh

Cincinnati

A

Philadelphia

Baltimore

Oakland

San Francisco

Mt. Whitney 4418

Colorado Plateau

St. Louis

Washington DC

San José

Las Vegas

Oklahoma City

Norfolk

Los Angeles

Phoenix

Alberquerque

Amarillo

Memphis

Appalachian

Raleigh

ATLANTIC

San Diego

Tijuana

Tucson

Fort Worth

Dallas

Atlanta

Bermuda (UK)

Ciudad Juárez

Baton Rouge

Columbus

Hermosillo

Houston

New Orleans

Tallahassee

30°N

Gulf of California

Chihuahua

R. Grande

Corpus Christi

Orlando

St. Petersburg

Tampa

OCEAN

Monterrey

Gulf of Mexico

Miami

Durango

Ciudad Victoria

Havana

Nassau

Tropic of Cancer

Mazatlán

Tampico

Bay of Campeche

CUBA

Revilla Gigedo Is. (Mex.)

Guadalajara

Mérida

Cienfuegos

Camagüey

Port-au-

DOMINICAN REPUBLIC

20°N

Mexico City

Veracruz

Campeche

Greater

Prince

Santo Domingo

Popocatepetl 5465

BELIZE

Antilles

HAITI

ST. KITTS AND NEVIS

Acápulco

C

Belmopan

JAMAICA

Kingston

DOMINICA

GUATEMALA

HONDURAS

O

Guatemala City

Tegucigalpa

Caribbean

ST. VINCENT & THE GRENADINES

San Salvador

NICARAGUA

Sea

TRINIDAD & TOBAGO

EL SALVADOR

Managua

Cartagena

Maracaibo

10°N

COSTA RICA

San José

PANAMA

Panamá City

Montería

Caracas

VENEZUELA

Medellín

S. Cristóbal

Orinoco

Bogotá

Guiana Highlands

Buenaventura

Cali

COLOMBIA

Galapagos Is. (Ecuador)

Esmeraldas

Quito

Pico da Neblina 3014

Equator

0°

ECUADOR

Cuenca

Iquitos

Amazon

Marquesas Is. (Fr.)

Piura

Selvas

Chiclayo

Trujillo

B R A Z I L

10°S

Tuamotu Arch.

P

Lima

E

Society Islands

Gambier Is. (Fr.)

Ica

R

La Paz

French Polynesia

Pitcairn Is. (UK)

Oruro

BOLIVIA

U

Sucre

ai Is. (Fr.)

Easter I. (Chile)

Arica

Potosí

Gran

Antofagasta

Tropic of Capricorn

Chaco

Salta

Catamarca

Juan Fernández Is. (Chile)

Valparaíso

Aconcagua 6960

30°S

Córdoba

O U T H   P A C I F I C

Santiago

C

A R G E N T I N A

Concepción

Bahía Blanca

H

O C E A N

Puerto Montt

I

L

40°S

Equatorial Scale 1:82 600 000

Comodoro Rivadavia

0   500   1000   1500 miles

0   500   1000   1500   2000   2500 kms

50°S

World Political

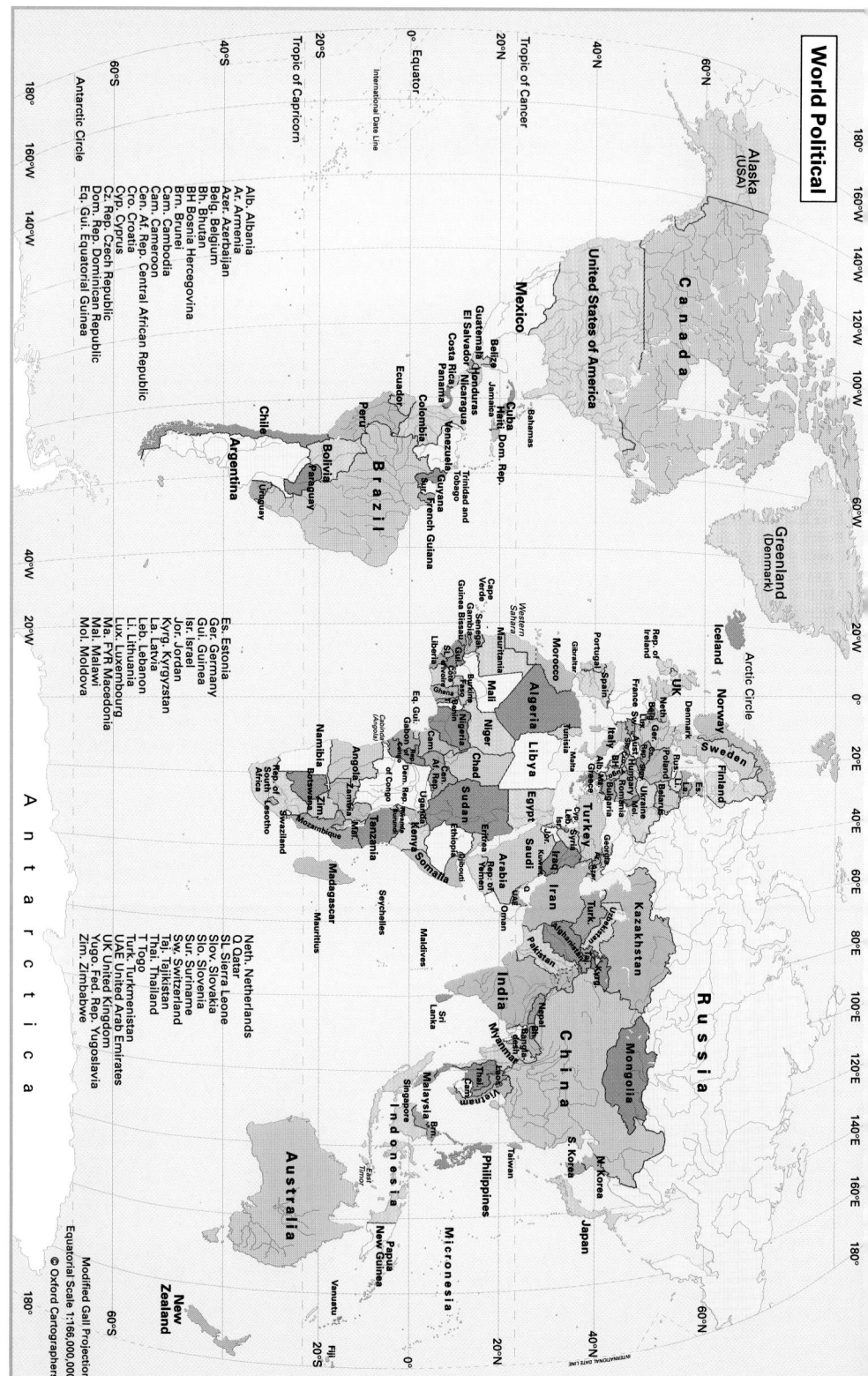

Alaska (USA)

Canada

United States of America

Mexico

Greenland (Denmark)

Bahamas
Cuba
Jamaica
Haiti Dom. Rep.
Belize
Guatemala Honduras
El Salvador Nicaragua
Costa Rica Panama
Venezuela
Colombia Guyana
Ecuador Trinidad and Tobago
Peru French Guiana

B r a z i l

Bolivia
Paraguay
Chile
Argentina
Uruguay

Iceland
Ireland
Rep. of Ireland
UK
Norway
Sweden
Finland
Denmark
Neth.
Belg. Ger.
France Swi. Aus. Hungary
Portugal Spain Italy
Gibraltar Malta
Greece
Tunisia

Western Sahara
Morocco
Mauritania
Cape Verde
Senegal
Gambia
Guinea Bissau Guinea
Sierra Leone
Liberia
Côte d'Ivoire
Ghana Togo Benin
Nigeria
Cameroon
Eq. Gui.
Gabon
Rep. of Congo
Dem. Rep. of Congo
Angola
Namibia
Botswana
Rep. of South Africa
Lesotho
Swaziland
Zim.
Mozambique
Madagascar
Mauritius
Seychelles

Algeria
Libya
Niger
Mali
Chad
Sudan
Egypt
Eritrea
Djibouti
Ethiopia
Uganda
Kenya
Somalia
Tanzania
Zambia
Mal.

Turkey
Cyprus Syria
Leb. Iraq
Jor.
Saudi Arabia
Yemen
Oman
UAE
Qatar
Kuwait
Iran
Afghanistan
Pakistan
Kazakhstan
Turk.
Uzbekistan
Kyr.
Tajik.
Georgia
Armenia Azer.

R u s s i a

Mongolia

C h i n a

Nepal
Bhutan
Bangladesh
India
Myanmar
Laos
Thailand
Vietnam
Cambodia
Malaysia Bru.
Singapore
I n d o n e s i a
Sri Lanka
Maldives
Papua New Guinea
Philippines
Taiwan
Japan
S. Korea
N. Korea
East Timor

M i c r o n e s i a

Vanuatu
Fiji

Australia

New Zealand

A n t a r c t i c a

Alb. Albania
Ar. Armenia
Azer. Azerbaijan
Beig. Belgium
BH. Bhutan
BH Bosnia Hercegovina
Brn. Brunei
Cam. Cambodia
Cam. Cameroon
Cen. Af. Rep. Central African Republic
Cro. Croatia
Cyp. Cyprus
Cz. Czech Republic
Dom. Rep. Dominican Republic
Eq. Gui. Equatorial Guinea
Es. Estonia
Ger. Germany
Gui. Guinea
Isr. Israel
Jor. Jordan
Kyrg. Kyrgyzstan
La. Latvia
Leb. Lebanon
Li. Lithuania
Lux. Luxembourg
Ma. FYR Macedonia
Mal. Malawi
Mol. Moldova

Neth. Netherlands
Qatar
Sl. Sierra Leone
Slov. Slovakia
Slo. Slovenia
Sur. Suriname
Sw. Switzerland
Taj. Tajikistan
Thai. Thailand
T. Togo
Turk. Turkmenistan
UAE United Arab Emirates
UK United Kingdom
Yugo. Fed. Rep. Yugoslavia
Zim. Zimbabwe

180° 160°W 140°W 120°W 100°W 80°W 60°W 40°W 20°W 0° 20°E 40°E 60°E 80°E 100°E 120°E 140°E 160°E 180°

60°N
40°N
Tropic of Cancer
20°N
0° Equator
International Date Line
20°S
Tropic of Capricorn
40°S
60°S
Antarctic Circle
180°
160°W
140°W

Arctic Circle
60°N
40°N
20°N
0°
20°S
40°S
60°S
20°W

INTERNATIONAL DATE LINE

Modified Gall Projection
Equatorial Scale 1:166,000,000
© Oxford Cartographers

NAMIBIA
The Republic of Namibia

AREA – 318,261 sq. miles (824,292 sq. km). Neighbours: Angola (north), South Africa (south), Botswana (east), Zambia and Zimbabwe (north-east)

POPULATION – 1,540,000 (1994 UN estimate). The main population groups are: Ovambo (587,000), Kavango (110,000), Damara (89,000), Herero (89,000), whites (78,000), Nama (57,000), coloured (48,000), Caprivians (44,000), Bushmen (34,000), Rehoboth Baster (29,000), Tswana (7,000). English is the official language, with Afrikaans, German and local languages also in use

CAPITAL – Windhoek (population 169,000, 1995)

MAJOR TOWNS – Ondangwa (33,000); Oshakati (37,000); Rehoboth (21,500); Swakopmund (18,000); Walvis Bay (50,000), 1995

CURRENCY – Namibian dollar of 100 cents at parity to South African rand

NATIONAL DAY – 21 March (Independence Day)

NATIONAL FLAG – Divided diagonally blue, red and green with the red fimbriated in white; a gold twelve-rayed sun in the upper hoist

LIFE EXPECTANCY (years) – male 57.50; female 60.00

POPULATION GROWTH RATE – 2.6 per cent (1995)

POPULATION DENSITY – 2 per sq. km (1995)

URBAN POPULATION – 27.1 per cent (1991)

MILITARY EXPENDITURE – 2.6 per cent of GDP (1996)

MILITARY PERSONNEL – 5,800: Army 5,700, Coast Guard 100

ENROLMENT (percentage of age group) – primary 92 per cent (1995); secondary 36 per cent (1995); tertiary 8.1 per cent (1995)

HISTORY AND POLITICS

The German protectorate of South West Africa from 1880 to 1915, Namibia was administered until the end of 1920 by the Union of South Africa. Under the terms of the Treaty of Versailles, the territory was entrusted to South Africa with full powers of administration and legislation over the territory. After the dissolution of the League of Nations and in the absence of a trusteeship agreement, South Africa informed the UN that it would continue to administer South West Africa.

In 1971 the International Court of Justice at The Hague delivered a majority opinion that the continued presence of South Africa was illegal. The South African government rejected this opinion, but accepted the principle that the territory should attain independence. Elections for 72 seats in Namibia's first nationally elected body took place under UN supervision on 7–11 November 1989. The South West Africa People's Organization (SWAPO) won 41 seats. Independence was declared on 21 March 1990. Namibia joined the Commonwealth on independence.

Previously a British and South African colony separate from German South West Africa/Namibia, Walvis Bay was governed from August 1992 by the joint South African-Namibian Walvis Bay Administrative Body until 28 February 1994, when South Africa renounced its claim to sovereignty over the enclave and it became part of Namibia.

Presidential and legislative elections were held on 7–8 December 1994 and won by the incumbent, Sam Nujoma, and by SWAPO respectively. In the 72-seat National Assembly SWAPO has 53 seats, the Democratic Turnhalle Alliance 15 seats, and other parties four seats.

POLITICAL SYSTEM

Namibia has an executive president as head of state who exercises the functions of government with the assistance of a Cabinet headed by a prime minister. The president is directly elected for a maximum of two five-year terms. There is a bicameral legislature consisting of the 72-member National Assembly, elected for a five-year term, and the National Council, whose 26 members are indirectly elected by the regional councils from among their own members. The National Council is elected for a six-year term, and its main function is to review and consider legislation from the National Assembly. The constitution can only be changed by a two-thirds majority in the National Assembly.

HEAD OF STATE
President, Dr Sam Nujoma, *elected* 16 February 1990, *re-elected* 8 December 1994

CABINET *as at July 1998*
Prime Minister, Hage Geingob
Deputy PM, Revd Hendrik Witbooi
Agriculture, Water and Rural Development, Helmut Angula
Attorney-General, Vekui Rukoro
Basic Education and Culture, John Mutorwa
Defence, Erikki Nghimtina
Environment and Tourism, Philemon Malima
Finance, Nangolo Mbumba
Fisheries and Marine Resources, Abraham Iyambo
Foreign Affairs, Theo-Ben Gurirab
Health and Social Services, Dr Libertine Amathila
Home Affairs, Jerry Ekandjo
Information and Broadcasting, Ben Amathila
Justice, Ngarikutuke Tjiriange
Labour and Manpower Development, vacant
Lands, Resettlement, Rehabilitation, Pendukeni Ithana
Mines and Energy, Andimba Toivo ja Toivo
National Planning Council, Saara Kuugongelwa
Prisons and Correctional Services, Marco Hausiku
Regional and Local Government and Housing, Dr Nickey Iyambo
Special Advisers, Gert Hanekom (*Economics*); Kanana Hishoono (*Political Matters*); Peter Tsheehama (*Security*)
Tertiary Education and Vocational Training, Nahas Angula
Trade and Industry, Hidipo Hamutenya
Without Portfolio, Hifikepunye Pohamba
Women's Affairs, Netumbo Ndaitwah
Works, Transport and Communication, Hampie Plichta
Youth and Sport, Richard Kapelwa-Kabajani

HIGH COMMISSION OF THE REPUBLIC OF NAMIBIA
6 Chandos Street, London WIM OLQ
Tel 0171-636 6244
High Commissioner, HE Benjamin Ulenga, apptd 1996

BRITISH HIGH COMMISSION
116 Robert Mugabe Avenue, Windhoek 9000
Tel: Windhoek 223022
High Commissioner, HE Robert H. G. Davies, apptd 1996

BRITISH COUNCIL REPRESENTATIVE, D. Crowe, PO Box 24224, 74 Bülowstrasse, Windhoek 9000

ECONOMY

Most of the labour force is employed in the agricultural sector. Deposits of diamonds along the coast and offshore along the sea bed are estimated at between 1,500 and 3,000 million carats; Namibia accounts for roughly 8 per cent of world diamond production. Walvis Bay and Lüderitz are the main ports.

In 1995 there was a trade deficit of US$98 million and a current account surplus of US$50 million. In 1994 imports totalled US$1,196 million and exports US$1,321 million.
GNP – US$3,569 million (1996); US$2,250 per capita (1996)
GDP – US$2,773 million (1994); US$1,924 per capita (1994)
ANNUAL AVERAGE GROWTH OF GDP – 2.6 per cent (1995)
INFLATION RATE – 10.0 per cent (1995)

TRADE WITH UK	1996	1997
Imports from UK	£6,892,000	£4,045,000
Exports to UK	25,280,000	17,916,000

NAURU
The Republic of Nauru

AREA – 8 sq. miles (21 sq. km)
POPULATION – 11,000 (1994 UN estimate); 8,042 (1983 census): Nauruans 4,964; other Pacific Islanders 2,134; Asians 682; Caucasians 262. About 43 per cent of Nauruans are adherents of the Nauruan Protestant Church and there is a Roman Catholic mission on the island. The main languages are English and Nauruan
CAPITAL – ΨNauru
CURRENCY – Australian dollar ($A) of 100 cents
NATIONAL DAY – 31 January (Independence Day)
NATIONAL FLAG – Twelve-point star (representing the 12 original Nauruan tribes) below a gold bar (representing the Equator), all on a blue ground
POPULATION GROWTH RATE – 1.5 per cent (1995)
POPULATION DENSITY – 514 per sq. km (1995)

HISTORY AND POLITICS

From 1888 until the First World War Nauru was administered by Germany. In 1920 it became a British Empire-mandated territory under the League of Nations, administered by Australia. A trusteeship superseding the mandate was approved in 1947 by the UN and Nauru continued to be administered by Australia until it became independent on 31 January 1968. It was announced in November 1968 that a special form of membership of the Commonwealth had been devised for Nauru at the request of its government. Bernard Dowiyogo was elected president in June 1998 after his predecessor, Kinza Clodumar, lost a vote of confidence.

POLITICAL SYSTEM

Parliament has 18 members including the Cabinet and Speaker. Voting is compulsory for all Nauruans over 20 years of age, except in certain specified instances. Elections are held every three years. The Cabinet is chosen by the president, who is elected by the parliament from amongst its members, and comprises not fewer than five nor more than six members including the president.
A Supreme Court of Nauru is presided over by the Chief Justice. The District Court, which is subordinate to the Supreme Court, is presided over by a Resident Magistrate. Both the Supreme Court and the District Court are courts of record. The Supreme Court exercises both original and appellate jurisdiction.

HEAD OF STATE
President, External Affairs, Finance, Public Service, Education, Island Development and Industry, Civil Aviation, Bernard Dowiyogo, *elected by parliament* 17 June 1998

CABINET *as at July 1998*
Health and Youth Affairs, Ludwig Scotty

Internal Affairs, Sports, Assistance to the President, Vinson Detenamo
Justice, Vassal Gadoengin
Speaker of Parliament, Kennan Adeang
Works and Community Services, Derog Gioura

BRITISH HIGH COMMISSIONER, HE Michael Peart, CMG, LVO, resident at Suva, Fiji

ECONOMY

The only fertile areas are in the narrow coastal belt and local requirements of fruit and vegetables are mostly met by imports. The economy is heavily dependent on the extraction of phosphate, of which the island has one of the world's richest deposits. In 1995, 178,415 tonnes of phosphate rock was exported. Considerable investments have been made abroad with the royalties on phosphate exports to provide for a time when production declines. In 1993 an agreement was signed with Australia for compensation to cover damage caused by phosphate mining during the Australian mandate and trusteeship periods. The compensation package is worth some £50 million (a portion of which will be paid by the UK and New Zealand governments), composed of a £33 million payment and a 20-year package of health and education programmes.
Air Nauru operates air services throughout the Pacific region and to Australia, New Zealand, Japan, Singapore and the Philippines.
GDP – US$213 million (1994); US$25,094 per capita (1994)

TRADE WITH UK	1996	1997
Imports from UK	£912,000	£1,132,000
Exports to UK	116,000	29,000

SOCIAL WELFARE

Nauru has a hospital service and other medical and dental services. There is also a maternity and child welfare service.
Education is compulsory between the ages of six and 17. There are nine primary and two secondary schools on the island with a total enrolment of about 1,600 pupils receiving primary education and 500 secondary education.

NEPAL

AREA – 56,827 sq. miles (147,181 sq. km). Neighbours: China (north), India (south, west and east)
POPULATION – 21,918,000 (1994 UN estimate). The inhabitants are of mixed stock, with Mongolian characteristics prevailing in the north and Indian in the south. The official religion is Hinduism; 87 per cent of the population are Hindus, 8 per cent Buddhist and 3 per cent Muslim. Gautama Buddha was born in Nepal. The official language is Nepali
CAPITAL – Kathmandu (population, 419,073, 1991)
MAJOR CITIES – Bhadgaon (61,122); Biratnagar (130,129); Patan (117,023), 1991
CURRENCY – Nepalese rupee of 100 paisa
NATIONAL ANTHEM – May Glory Crown Our Illustrious Sovereign
NATIONAL DAYS – 18 February (National Democracy Day); 28 December (The King's Birthday)
NATIONAL FLAG – Double pennant of crimson with blue border on peaks; white moon with rays in centre of top peak; white quarter sun, recumbent in centre of bottom peak
LIFE EXPECTANCY (years) – male 50.88; female 48.10

POPULATION GROWTH RATE – 3.8 per cent (1995)
POPULATION DENSITY – 149 per sq. km (1995)
MILITARY EXPENDITURE – 0.9 per cent of GDP (1996)
MILITARY PERSONNEL – 46,215: Army 46,000, Air Force 215
ILLITERACY RATE – 72.5 per cent
ENROLMENT (percentage of age group) – tertiary 5.2 per cent (1993)

Nepal lies between India and the Tibet Autonomous Region of China on the slopes of the Himalayas, and includes Mount Everest (29,028 ft).

The southern region, the Terai, was covered with jungle but has been more widely cultivated recently. It forms about 23 per cent of the total land area and nearly 44 per cent of the population live there. The central belt is hilly, but with many fertile valleys, leading up to the snowline at about 16,000 feet. The hills account for 42 per cent of the area and about 48 per cent of the population. The remainder of the country, the Himalayan region, consists of high mountains which are sparsely inhabited. The country is drained by three great river systems rising within and beyond the Himalayan mountain ranges and eventually flowing into the Ganges in India.

HISTORY AND POLITICS

Nepal was originally divided into numerous hill clans and petty principalities but emerged as a nation in the middle of the 18th century when it was unified by the warrior Raja of Gorkha, Prithvi Narayan Shah, who founded the present Nepalese dynasty. In 1846 power was seized by Jung Bahadur Rana after a massacre of nobles, and he was the first of a line of hereditary Rana prime ministers who ruled Nepal for 104 years. During this time the role of the monarchs was mainly ceremonial.

In 1950–1 a revolutionary movement broke the hereditary power of the Ranas and restored the monarchy to its former position. After ten years, during which various parties and individuals tried their hand at government, King Mahendra proscribed all political parties and assumed direct powers in 1960, with the object of leading a united country to democracy. In 1962 he introduced a new constitution embodying a tiered, partyless system of panchyat (council) democracy.

Mass agitation for political reform led in April 1990 to the lifting of the ban on political parties and the abolition of the panchyat system. A new constitution was promulgated in November 1990 establishing a multiparty, parliamentary system of government and a constitutional monarchy. Elections in May 1991 were won by the Nepali Congress Party.

In October 1997 the government was brought down by a vote of no confidence and replaced by a coalition government comprising the Rashtriya Prajatantra Party (RPP), the Nepal Sabdhavana Party (NSP) and the Nepali Congress Party (NCP). On 10 April 1998, Prime Minister Surya Bahadur Thapa resigned after the King refused to grant fresh elections. He was replaced as prime minister by Girija Prasad Koirala of the NCP.

POLITICAL SYSTEM

The King retains joint executive power with the Council of Ministers. The bicameral legislature consists of a 205-member House of Representatives and a 60-member National Council, including ten royal nominees.

HEAD OF STATE

HM The King of Nepal, King Birendra Bir Bikram Shah Dev, *born* 28 December 1945; *succeeded* 31 January 1972; *crowned* 24 February 1975; *married* February 1970, HM Queen Aishwatya Rajya Laxmi Devi Shah

Heir, HRH Crown Prince Dipendra Bir Bikram Shah Dev, *born* 27 June 1971

CABINET *as at July 1998*
Prime Minister, Royal Palace Affairs, Defence, Foreign Affairs, Girija Prasad Koirala
Deputy P.M, Water Resources, Sailaja Acharya
Agriculture, Chakra Prasad Banstola
Education, Housing, Physical Planning, Arjun Narsingh
Finance, Ram Sharan Mahat
Forestry, Soil Erosion, Supply, Khum Bahadur Khadka
General Administration, Bimalendra Nidhi
Home Affairs, Govinda Raj Joshi
Industry and Labour, Dhundi Raj Shastri
Information and Communications, Mahanta Thakur
Land Reform, Management and Commerce, Chirinjibi Wagle
Law and Justice, Siddhi Raj Ojha
Local Development, Prakash Man Singh
Parliamentary Affairs, Science and Technology, Om Kar Shrestha
Public Health, Krishna Bahadur Gurung
Public Works and Transport, Yijaya Kumar Gachchhadar
Tourism and Civil Aviation, Ananda Raj Dhungana
Youth, Sports, Culture and Population, Purna Bahadur Khadka

ROYAL NEPALESE EMBASSY
12A Kensington Palace Gardens, London W8 4QU
Tel 0171– 229 1594/6231
Ambassador Extraordinary and Plenipotentiary, HE Dr Singha B. Basnyat, apptd 1997

BRITISH EMBASSY
Lainchaur Kathmandu, PO Box 106
Tel: Kathmandu 410583
Ambassador Extraordinary and Plenipotentiary, HE Lloyd B. Smith, CMG, apptd 1995

BRITISH COUNCIL REPRESENTATIVE, S. Ewans, (PO Box 640), Kantipath, Kathmandu

ECONOMY

Nepal exports jute, handicrafts, carpets, hides and skins, medicinal herbs, cardamom, potatoes, tea, etc., and imports textiles, machinery and parts, transport equipment, medicine, petroleum products etc. Tourism is the single largest commercial earner of foreign exchange. Nepal's main trading partners are India, Germany and the USA.

In 1995 Nepal had a trade deficit of US$961 million and a current account deficit of US$356 million. Imports totalled US$1,374 million and exports US$348 million.
GNP – US$4,710 million (1996); US$210 per capita (1996)
GDP – US$3,637 million (1994); US$158 per capita (1994)
ANNUAL AVERAGE GROWTH OF GDP – 6.1 per cent (1996)
INFLATION RATE – 9.2 per cent (1996)
TOTAL EXTERNAL DEBT – US$2,413 million (1996)

Trade with UK	1996	1997
Imports from UK	£10,438,000	£8,676,000
Exports to UK	8,123,000	5,127,000

COMMUNICATIONS

The total length of roads is 9,534 km. Most of the major roads have been built since the 1960s, often with aid from India and China. Kathmandu is connected by road with India and Tibet. Internally, the road network links Kathmandu to Kodari and Pokhara, and Pokhara to Sunauli.

Royal Nepal Airlines operates an extensive network of domestic flights, and there are international flights to Europe, the Middle East and throughout Asia. There is an international airport at Kathmandu.

Telecommunication services, both domestic and international, are available. Television was introduced in 1984.

THE NETHERLANDS
Koninkrijk der Nederlanden

AREA – 15,770 sq. miles (40,844 sq. km). Neighbours: Belgium (south), Germany (east)
POPULATION – 15,451,000 (1996): 36 per cent Catholic, 27 per cent Reformed Church, 8 per cent Muslim. The language is Dutch, a West Germanic language of Saxon origin closely akin to Old English and Low German. It is spoken in the Netherlands and the northern part of Belgium (Flanders). It is also used in the Netherlands Antilles
CAPITAL – ΨAmsterdam (population, 1,100,764, 1994 estimate)
SEAT OF GOVERNMENT – The Hague (Den Haag or, in full, 's-Gravenhage), population 694,733, 1994 estimate
MAJOR CITIES – Eindhoven (394,469); Groningen (210,489); Haarlem (213,392); ΨRotterdam (1,076,442); Tilburg (237,398); Utrecht (546,433), 1994 estimates
CURRENCY – Gulden (guilder) or florin of 100 cents
NATIONAL ANTHEM – Wilhelmus
NATIONAL FLAG – Three horizontal bands of red, white and blue
LIFE EXPECTANCY (years) – male 74.21; female 80.20
POPULATION GROWTH RATE – 0.7 per cent (1995)
POPULATION DENSITY – 378 per sq. km (1995)
URBAN POPULATION – 60.6 per cent (1994)

The Kingdom of the Netherlands is a maritime country of western Europe, situated on the North Sea, consisting of 12 provinces (Eastern and Southern Flevoland being amalgamated to form the twelfth province). The land is generally flat and low, intersected by numerous canals and connecting rivers. The principal rivers are the Rhine, Maas, Yssel and Scheldt.

HISTORY AND POLITICS

The country was fragmented until the 16th century when, led by William (the Silent) of Orange, the Low Countries fought the Eighty Years' War (1568–1648) against Spanish rule. The Union of Utrecht (1579) united the northern provinces and in 1581 independence was declared. Dutch economic and military power flourished in the 17th and 18th centuries but the country also came into conflict with Britain and France.

In 1688 William III of Orange acceded to the English throne, reigning jointly with his wife Mary, following the abdication and flight of James II, Mary's father. The Netherlands was overrun by French Revolutionary troops in the late 18th century, becoming part of the French Empire until 1814. In 1830 the southern provinces seceded to form Belgium. The Duchy of Luxembourg was made an independent state in 1867.

The Netherlands remained neutral during the First World War but was invaded by Germany during the Second World War and occupied until the war ended. The Netherlands joined the Benelux economic union with Belgium and Luxembourg in 1948 and became a member of NATO in 1949. Most of the former Dutch colonies gained independence as Indonesia in 1949.

The most recent election to the Second Chamber was held on 6 May 1998 and resulted in a centre-left coalition of the Labour Party, People's Party and Democrats 66. The state of the parties as at May 1998 was: Labour Party (PvdA) 45; People's Party for Freedom and Democracy (VVD) 38; Christian Democratic Appeal (CDA) 29; Democrats 66 (D66) 14; Green Left 11; others 13.

POLITICAL SYSTEM
The States-General consists of the *Eerste Kamer* (First Chamber) of 75 members, elected for four years by the Provincial Council; and the *Tweede Kamer* (Second Chamber) of 150 members, elected for four years by voters of 18 years and upwards. Members of the *Tweede Kamer* are paid.

HEAD OF STATE
HM The Queen of the Netherlands, Queen Beatrix Wilhelmina Armgard, KG, GCVO, *born* 31 January 1938; *succeeded* 30 April 1980, upon the abdication of her mother Queen Juliana; *married* 10 March 1966, HRH Prince Claus George Willem Otto Frederik Geert of the Netherlands, Jonkheer van Amsberg; and has *issue*, Prince Willem (*see* below); Prince Johan Friso, *b*. 25 September 1968; Prince Constantijn Christof, *b*. 11 October 1969

Heir, HRH Prince Willem Alexander, *b*. 27 April 1967

CABINET *as at July 1998*
Prime Minister, Wim Kok (PvdA)
Deputy PM, Home Affairs, Hans Dijkstal (VVD)
Deputy PM, Foreign Affairs, Hans van Mierlo (D66)
Agriculture, Nature Management and Fisheries, Josias van Aartsen (VVD)
Defence, Netherlands Antilles and Aruba Affairs, Joris Voorhoeve (VVD)
Development Co-operation, Jan Pronk (PvdA)
Economic Affairs, vacant
Education, Culture and Science, Dr Jo Ritzen (PvdA)
Finance, Gerrit Zalm (VVD)
Housing, Planning and Environment, Margreeth de Boer (PvdA)
Justice, Winnie Sorgdrager (D66)
Ministers Plenipotentiary, C. A. S. D. Wever (*Aruba*); E. A. V. Jesurun (*Netherlands Antilles*)
Social Affairs and Employment, Ad Melkert (PvdA)
Transport and Public Works, Annemarie Jorritsma-Lebbink (VVD)
Welfare, Health and Sport, Dr Els Borst-Eilers (D66)

VVD People's Party for Freedom and Democracy;
D66 Democrats 66; PvdA Labour Party

ROYAL NETHERLANDS EMBASSY
38 Hyde Park Gate, London SW7 5DP
Tel 0171–590 3200
Ambassador Extraordinary and Plenipotentiary, HE Jan
Herman van Roijen, apptd 1995
Ministers Plenipotentiary, G. C. M. van Pallandt; R. Brouwer
(*Economic*)
Consul-General, P. W. A. Bas Backer
Defence, Naval and Air Attaché, Capt. J. J. Blok

BRITISH EMBASSY
Lange Voorhout 10, The Hague, 2514 ED
Tel: The Hague 427 0427
Ambassador Extraordinary and Plenipotentiary, HE Rosemary
Spencer, CMG, apptd 1996
Counsellors, T. C. Holmes (*Deputy Head of Mission*);
C. Bradley (*Commercial and Consul-General*)
Defence and Naval Attaché, Capt. R. St J. S. Bishop, RN

CONSULATE-GENERAL – Amsterdam
CONSULATE – Willemstad (Curaçao); Vice-Consulate –
Philipsburg (St Maarten) (both Netherlands Antilles)

BRITISH COUNCIL DIRECTOR, T. Butchard, Keizersgracht
269, 1016 ED Amsterdam

NETHERLANDS-BRITISH CHAMBER OF COMMERCE, The
Dutch House, 307–308 High Holborn, London WC1V 7LS

UK OFFICE IN THE HAGUE, Holland Trade House,
Bezuidenhoutseweg 181, 2594 AH The Hague

DEFENCE

The Army has 600 main battle tanks, 717 armoured
infantry fighting vehicles and armoured personnel
carriers, and 439 artillery pieces. The Navy has four submarines, four destroyers, 12 frigates, 13 combat aircraft and
22 armed helicopters. The Air Force has 171 combat
aircraft and 12 armed helicopters.
MILITARY EXPENDITURE – 2.1 per cent of GDP (1996)
MILITARY PERSONNEL – 56,380: Army 27,000, Navy
13,800, Air Force 11,980, Paramilitaries 3,600
CONSCRIPTION DURATION – abolished in August 1996

ECONOMY

The chief agricultural products are potatoes, wheat, rye,
barley, sugar beet, cattle, poultry, pigs, dairy products,
vegetables, fruit, flower bulbs, plants and cut flowers and
there is an important fishing industry.
    Among the principal industries are engineering, elec-
tronics, nuclear energy, petrochemicals and plastics, road
vehicles, aircraft and defence equipment, shipbuilding
repair, steel, textiles of all types, electrical appliances,
metal ware, furniture, paper, cigars, sugar, liqueurs, beer,
clothing etc.
GNP – US$402,565 million (1996); US$25,940 per capita
(1996)
GDP – US$302,313 million (1994); US$21,536 per capita
(1994)
ANNUAL AVERAGE GROWTH OF GDP – 3.5 per cent (1996)
INFLATION RATE – 2.1 per cent (1996)
UNEMPLOYMENT – 7.1 per cent (1995)

TRADE

The Dutch are traditionally a trading nation. Trade,
banking and shipping are of particular importance to the
economy. The geographical position of the Netherlands, at
the mouths of the Rhine, Meuse and Scheldt, brings a large
volume of transit trade to and from the interior of Europe
to Dutch ports. Principal trading partners are Germany,
Belgium/Luxembourg, the UK and France.

In 1996 the Netherlands had a trade surplus of
US$19,269 million and a current account surplus of
US$19,417 million. Imports totalled US$180,639 million
and exports US$197,242 million.

Trade with UK	1996	1997
Imports from UK	£12,709,300,000	£13,157,000,000
Exports to UK	11,680,900,000	11,794,600,000

COMMUNICATIONS

The total extent of navigable rivers including canals is
5,052 km. The total length of the railway system is
2,757 km, of which 1,991 km are electrified. The mercantile marine in 1995 consisted of 385 ships of total 2,903,000
gross registered tons.
    There are six national papers, four of which are morning
papers, and there are many regional daily papers.

EDUCATION

Primary and secondary education is given in both denom-
inational and state schools and is compulsory.
    The principal universities are at Leiden, Utrecht,
Groningen, Amsterdam (two), Nijmegen, Maastricht and
Rotterdam, and there are technical universities at Delft,
Eindhoven, Enschede and Wageningen (agriculture).
ENROLMENT (percentage of age group) – primary 99 per
cent (1993); secondary 84 per cent (1990); tertiary 48.9
per cent (1993)

OVERSEAS TERRITORIES

ARUBA

AREA – 75 sq. miles (193 sq. km)
POPULATION – 87,000 (1996)
CAPITAL – ΨOranjestad (population 25,000); and Sint
Nicolaas (17,000)
CURRENCY – Aruban florin

The island of Aruba was from 1828 part of the Dutch West
Indies and from 1845 part of the Netherlands Antilles. On 1
January 1986 it became a separate territory within the
Kingdom of the Netherlands. The 1983 Constitutional
Conference agreed that Aruba's separate status would last
for ten years from 1986, after which the island would
become fully independent. In 1994 this decision was
changed and it was decided that Aruba will retain its
separate status within the Kingdom of the Netherlands.

Governor, Olindo Koolman
Prime Minister, J. H. A. Eman

TRADE WITH UK	1996	1997
Imports from UK	£50,684,000	£59,094,000
Exports to UK	3,675,000	306,000

NETHERLANDS ANTILLES

AREA – 309 sq. miles (800 sq. km)
POPULATION – 207,333 (1995), Curaçao 151,448, Bonaire
14,218, St Martin 38,567, St Eustatius 1,900, Saba 1,200
CAPITAL – ΨWillemstad (on Curaçao) (pop. 50,000)
CURRENCY – Netherlands Antilles guilder of 100 cents

The Netherlands Antilles comprise the islands of Curaçao,
Bonaire, part of St Martin, St Eustatius, and Saba in the
West Indies. The Netherlands Antilles, which have a 22-
member federal parliament, are largely self-governing
under the terms of the Realm Statute which took effect in
1954.

Governor, Dr Jaime Saleh
Prime Minister, Miguel Pourier

TRADE WITH UK	1996*	1997*
Imports from UK	£33,513,000	£19,579,000
Exports to UK	6,535,000	4,557,000
*Curaçao		

NEW ZEALAND

AREA – 104,454 sq. miles (270,534 sq. km)
POPULATION – 3,681,546 (1996): 79 per cent European
stock, 13 per cent Maori, 5 per cent other Pacific
Islanders. The main religion is Christianity. In 1991 the
principal denominations were Anglican 22.1 per cent,
Presbyterian 16.3 per cent, Roman Catholic 15 per cent,
Methodist 4.2 per cent, Baptist 2.1 per cent. The official
languages are English and Maori

Islands	Area (sq. miles)	Population (census 1996)
North Island	44,281	2,749,788
South Island	58,093	930,824
Other islands	1,362	934
Total	103,736	3,681,546
Territories		
Tokelau	5	1,487
Niue	100	1,708 (a)
Cook Islands	93	18,008
Ross Dependency	175,000	

(a) 1997 estimate
CAPITAL – ΨWellington (population, 326,900, 1992
estimate)
MAJOR CITIES – ΨAuckland (929,300); ΨChristchurch
(318,100); ΨDunedin (112,400); Hamilton (153,800); Ψ
Napier-Hastings (110,200)
CURRENCY – New Zealand dollar (NZ$) of 100 cents
NATIONAL ANTHEM – God Save The Queen/God Defend
New Zealand
NATIONAL DAY – 6 February (Waitangi Day)
NATIONAL FLAG – Blue ground, with Union Flag in top
left quarter, four five-pointed red stars with white
borders on the fly
LIFE EXPECTANCY (years) – male 72.86; female 78.74
POPULATION GROWTH RATE – 1.0 per cent (1995)
POPULATION DENSITY – 13 per sq. km (1995)
URBAN POPULATION – 84.9 per cent (1991)

New Zealand consists of a number of islands in the South
Pacific Ocean, and also has administrative responsibility
for the Ross Dependency in Antarctica. The two larger
islands, North Island and South Island, are separated by a
relatively narrow strait. The remaining islands are much
smaller and widely dispersed.
    Much of the North and South Islands is mountainous.
The principal range is the Southern Alps, extending the
entire length of the South Island and having its culminating point in Mount Cook/Mount Aoraki (12,349 ft).
The North Island mountains include several volcanoes,
two of which are active. Of the numerous glaciers in the
South Island, the Tasman (18 miles long by 1¼ wide), the
Franz Josef and the Fox are the best known. The more
important rivers include the Waikato (270 miles in length),
Wanganui (180), and Clutha (210) and lakes include
Taupo, 234 sq. miles in area; Wakatipu, 113; and Te Anau,
133.
    New Zealand includes, in addition to North and South
Islands: Chatham Islands (Chatham, Pitt, South East
Islands and some rocky islets, combined area, 965 sq. km

(373 sq. miles), largely uninhabited); Stewart Island (area
1,746 sq. km (674 sq. miles), largely uninhabited); the
Kermadec Group (Raoul or Sunday, Macaulay, Curtis
Islands, L'Esperance, and some islets; population 9–10, all
government employees at a meteorological station);
Campbell Island, used as a weather station; the Three
Kings (discovered by Tasman on the Feast of the Epi-
phany); Auckland Islands; Antipodes Group; Bounty
Islands; Snares Islands and Solander.
    New Zealand has a temperate marine climate, but with
abundant sunshine. The mean temperature ranges from
15°C in the north to about 9°C in the south. Rainfall in the
North Island ranges from 35 to 70 inches and in the South
Island from 25 to 45 inches.

HISTORY AND POLITICS

The discoverers and first colonists of New Zealand were
Polynesian people, ancestors of the modern-day Maori.
The ninth century is generally considered to be the date of
the first settlement; by the 13th or 14th century there were
well-established settlements. The first European to dis-
cover New Zealand was a Dutch navigator, Abel Tasman,
who sighted the coast in 1642 but did not land. It was the
British explorer James Cook who circumnavigated New
Zealand and landed in 1769. Largely as a result of increased
British emigration, the country was annexed by the British
government in 1840. The British Lieutenant-Governor,
William Hobson, proclaimed sovereignty over the North
Island by virtue of the Treaty of Waitangi, signed by him
and many Maori chiefs, and over the South Island and
Stewart Island by right of discovery.
    In 1841 New Zealand was created a separate colony
distinct from New South Wales. In 1907 the designation
was changed to 'The Dominion of New Zealand'. The
constitution rests upon the Constitution Act 1852 and
other imperial statutes. A 1986 Constitution Act brought a
number of statutory constitutional provisions. The Statute
of Westminster was formally adopted by New Zealand in
1947.
    Following the general election of 12 October 1996, the
state of the parties in the House of Representatives was:
National Party (NP) 44 seats, Labour 37, New Zealand
First (NZF) 17, The Alliance 13, Association of Consumers and Tax Payers (ACT) 8, United Party 1. The
National Party and New Zealand First formed a coalition
government. Jim Bolger stepped down as prime minister
on 8 December 1997 and was replaced by Jenny Shipley,
who became New Zealand's first female prime minister.

POLITICAL SYSTEM

The executive authority is entrusted to a Governor-
General appointed by the Crown and aided by an Executive Council, within a unicameral legislature, the House of
Representatives. The House of Representatives consists of
120 members elected for three-year terms. 55 members are
elected by the first-past-the-post system and 60 by
proportional representation on a party list basis. There
are five Maori electorates.
    The judicial system comprises a High Court, a Court of
Appeal and district courts having both civil and criminal
jurisdiction.

GOVERNOR-GENERAL
Governor-General and Commander-in-Chief, HE Sir Michael
    Hardie Boys, KCMG, *sworn in* March 1996

THE EXECUTIVE COUNCIL *as at July 1998*
The Governor-General
*Prime Minister, Women's Affairs, New Zealand Security
    Intelligence Service,* Jenny Shipley (NP)

Deputy PM, Treasurer, Winston Peters (NZF)
Agriculture, Forestry, International Trade, Contact Energy Ltd, Lockwood Smith (NP)
Attorney-General, Justice, Waitangi Negotiations, Douglas Graham (NP)
Commerce, Fisheries, Lands, Biosecurity, Industry, Associate Minister for Agriculture, John Luxton (NP)
Conservation, Corrections, Associate Minister of Social Welfare, Associate Minister of Immigration, Nick Smith (NP)
Courts, Education, Ministerial Services, Leader of the House, Wyatt Creech (NP)
Customs, Valuation Department, Public Trust Office, Associate Treasurer, Associate Minister of Health, Tuariki John Delamere (NZF)
Education Review Office, Associate Minister of Education, Associate Minister for Pacific Island Affairs, Brian Donelly (NZF)
Employment, Peter McCardle (NZF)
Finance, Revenue, Bill Birch (NP)
Foreign Affairs, Trade, Pacific Island Affairs, Disarmament, Arms Control, Don McKinnon (NP)
Health, Associate Minister of Revenue, Bill English (NP)
Housing, Tourism, Accident Rehabilitation and Compensation Insurance, Sport, Fitness and Leisure, Murray McCully (NP)
Labour, Defence, Immigration, Energy, Business Development, Max Bradford (NP)
Maori Affairs, Racing, Associate Minister for Sport, Fitness and Leisure, Tau Henare (NZF)
Minister of State, Associate Minister of Foreign Affairs and Trade, APEC Affairs, Jim Bolger (NP)
Police, Internal Affairs, Civil Defence, Jack Elder (NZF)
Senior Citizens, Consumer Affairs, Robyn McDonald (NZF)
Social Welfare, War Pensions, Associate Minister of Health, Roger Sowry (NP)
State-owned Enterprises, Audit Department, Radio New Zealand, Associate Minister of Justice, Tony Ryall (NP)
State Services, Environment, Cultural Affairs, Crown Research Institutes, Associate Minister for Foreign Relations and Trade, Simon Upton (NP)
Transport, Research, Science and Technology, Communications, Local Government, Information Technology and Statistics, Maurice Williamson (NP)
Youth Affairs, Associate Minister of Women's Affairs, Associate Minister for Accident Rehabilitation and Compensation Insurance, Deborah Morris (NZF)

NEW ZEALAND HIGH COMMISSION
New Zealand House, Haymarket, London SW1Y 4TQ
Tel 0171-930 8422
High Commissioner, HE Rob Moore-Jones, apptd 1998
Deputy High Commissioner, C. J. Seed
Minister, J. Waugh (*Commercial*)
Head, Defence Staff, Brig. I. Duthie

BRITISH HIGH COMMISSION
44 Hill Street (PO Box 1812), Wellington 1
Tel: Wellington 472 6049
High Commissioner, HE Martin Williams, CVO, OBE, apptd 1998
Deputy High Commissioner, C. H. Salvesen
Defence Adviser, Col. P. R. Barry, CBE
First Secretary, M. A. Capes (*Commercial*)
Consul-General and Director of Trade Promotion, J. Smith-Laittan, CMG (*resident at Auckland*)

CONSULATE-GENERAL – Auckland
CONSULATE – Christchurch

BRITISH COUNCIL DIRECTOR, P. Smith

BRITISH CHAMBER OF COMMERCE FOR AUSTRALIA AND NEW ZEALAND, PO Box 141, Manuka, ACT 2603, Australia; UK OFFICE, Suite 615, 6th Floor, The Linen Hall, 162–168 Regent Street, London WIR 5TB

DEFENCE

The Army has 78 armoured personnel carriers and 43 artillery pieces. The Navy has four frigates, four patrol and coastal vessels and four armed helicopters. The Air Force has 42 combat aircraft.

MILITARY EXPENDITURE – 1.2 per cent of GDP (1996)
MILITARY PERSONNEL – 9,550: Army 4,400, Navy 2,100, Air Force 3,050

ECONOMY

Since 1984 economic reforms have changed the economy from a highly regulated, nationalized and protected economy with a large welfare state to an economy at the forefront of market economics. Finance market and labour market deregulation, privatization, VAT reform, the introduction of private sector principles in the civil service, health service and education, the ending of agricultural subsidies and the near elimination of import tariffs have all occurred. The Reserve Bank has been made independent, with a contract to keep inflation below 2 per cent. Centralized wage-bargaining has ended and widespread means-testing has been introduced throughout the welfare state, so that only the very poor receive free or subsidized healthcare and other benefits.

Agricultural production is dominated by cattle- and sheep-rearing, for meat, wool, dairy products and other by-products, such as skins, leather, etc.

Non-metallic minerals such as coal, clay, limestone and dolomite are more important than metallic ones. Coal output in 1995 was 3,300,000 tonnes. Of the metals, the most important are gold and ironsand. Natural gas deposits in the offshore Taranaki Maui field and onshore fields are increasingly being exploited and used for electricity generation and as a premium fuel. Hydroelectric power is used to generate 96 per cent of the country's electricity.

Manufacturing is based on food processing, machinery production, motor vehicle assembly, chemicals, electrical and electronic goods, and paper and printing. Tourism is the fastest growing sector of the economy, with 1,385,907 visitors in 1994–5.

In 1996 New Zealand had a trade surplus of US$487 million and a current account deficit of US$4,048 million. Imports totalled US$14,725 million and exports US$14,454 million.

GNP – US$57,135 million (1996); US$15,720 per capita (1996)
GDP – US$48,132 million (1994); US$14,649 per capita (1994)
ANNUAL AVERAGE GROWTH OF GDP – 4.3 per cent (1995)
INFLATION RATE – 2.3 per cent (1996)
UNEMPLOYMENT – 6.3 per cent (1995)

TRADE

New Zealand's largest trading partners are Australia, Japan, USA and the UK. Main exports include dairy products, meat, timber and metal and metal products. Imports include machinery, petroleum and petroleum products, plastics and motor vehicles.

Trade with UK	1996*	1997*
Imports from UK	£471,820,000	£407,550,000
Exports to UK	631,973,000	577,803,000

*Includes Niue, Tokelau and Cook Islands

COMMUNICATIONS

The national railway system is owned and operated by the privately-owned Tranz Rail Ltd. In June 1995, there were 4,439 route km of railway in operation.

During 1991–2 the vessels entered from overseas ports numbered 3,282 (gross tonnage 27,983,000) and those cleared for overseas 3,298 (gross tonnage 27,508,000). In December 1995 there were 2,977 ships registered in New Zealand (gross tonnage 482,180).

There are international airports at Auckland, Christchurch and Wellington. Air New Zealand is the national carrier.

In June 1995 there were 91,875 km of maintained roads.

EDUCATION

Schools are free and attendance is compulsory between the ages of six and 15. There are 2,240 state and 61 private primary schools and 320 state secondary schools. There are seven universities and 25 polytechnics.

ENROLMENT (percentage of age group) – primary 100 per cent (1995); secondary 93 per cent (1995); tertiary 58.2 per cent (1995)

TERRITORIES

TOKELAU (OR UNION ISLANDS)

AREA – 5 sq. miles (12 sq. km)
POPULATION – 1,487 (1996)

Tokelau is a group of atolls, Fakaofo, Nukunonu and Atafu. It was proclaimed part of New Zealand as from 1 January 1949. A Council of Faipule, composed of one elected representative from each atoll, was established in August 1992 to govern Tokelau when the council of elders (General Fono) was not in session. The position of *Ulu-o-Tokelau* (leader) was also established in 1992 and is rotated among the three Faipule members annually. Administrative responsibility for Tokelau lies with the Administrator but in January 1994 his powers were delegated to the General Fono and Council of Faipule. The Tokelau Amendment Act, passed by the New Zealand Parliament in 1996, conferred legislative power on the General Fono. New Zealand provides substantial aid (NZ$5.0 million in year ended 30 June 1994).

Administrator, Lindsay Watt
Ulu-o-Tokelau (1998), Kuresa Nasau

THE ROSS DEPENDENCY

The Ross Dependency, placed under the jurisdiction of New Zealand in 1923, is defined as all the Antarctic islands and territories between 160° E. and 150° W. longitude which are situated south of the 60° S. parallel, including Edward VII Land and portions of Victoria Land. Since 1957 a number of research stations have been established in the Dependency.

ASSOCIATED STATES

COOK ISLANDS

POPULATION – 18,008 (1996)

Included in the realm of New Zealand since June 1901, the Cook Islands group consists of the islands of Rarotonga, Aitutaki, Mangaia, Atiu, Mauke, Mitiaro, Manuae, Takutea, Palmerston, Penrhyn or Tongareva, Manihiki, Rakahanga, Suwarrow, Pukapuka or Danger, and Nassau.

Queen Elizabeth II has a representative on the islands, as does the New Zealand government. Since 1965 the islands have been in free association with New Zealand and

enjoyed complete internal self-government, executive power being in the hands of a Cabinet consisting of a prime minister and eight other ministers. There is a 25-member Legislative Assembly. New Zealand has an obligation to assist with foreign affairs and defence if requested. The New Zealand citizenship of the Cook Islanders is embodied in the constitution.

HM Representative, Apenera Short, OBE
Prime Minister, Sir Geoffrey Henry, KBE
New Zealand High Commissioner, James Kember

NIUE

POPULATION – 1,708 (1997 estimate)

A New Zealand High Commissioner is stationed at Niue, which since 1974 has been self-governing in free association with New Zealand. New Zealand is responsible for external affairs and defence, and continues to give financial aid. Executive power is in the hands of a premier and a Cabinet of three drawn from the Assembly of 20 members. The Assembly is the supreme legislative body.

New Zealand High Commissioner, W. Searell

NICARAGUA
República de Nicaragua

AREA – 50,193 sq. miles (130,000 sq. km). Neighbours: Honduras (north), Costa Rica (south)
POPULATION – 4,539,000 (1994 UN estimate): three-quarters are of mixed blood, another 15 per cent are white, mostly of pure Spanish descent, and the remaining 10 per cent are West Indians or Indians. The latter group includes the Misquitos, who live on the Atlantic coast. The official language is Spanish and the majority are Roman Catholic, although the English language and the Moravian Church are widespread on the Atlantic coast
CAPITAL – Managua (population, 608,020, 1979 estimate)
MAJOR CITIES – Chinandega (144,291); Granada (72,640); León (158,577); Masaya (78,308)
CURRENCY – Córdoba (C$) of 100 centavos
NATIONAL ANTHEM – Salve A Tí Nicaragua (Hail, Nicaragua)
NATIONAL DAY – 15 September
NATIONAL FLAG – Horizontal stripes of blue, white and blue, with the Nicaraguan coat of arms in the centre of the white stripe
LIFE EXPECTANCY (years) – male 64.80; female 67.71
POPULATION GROWTH RATE – 3.2 per cent (1995)
POPULATION DENSITY – 35 per sq. km (1995)
URBAN POPULATION – 63.3 per cent (1995)
ILLITERACY RATE – 34.3 per cent
ENROLMENT (percentage of age group) – primary 83 per cent (1995); secondary 27 per cent (1993); tertiary 9.4 per cent (1993)

HISTORY AND POLITICS

The eastern coast of Nicaragua was touched by Columbus in 1502, and was overrun by Spanish forces in 1518. It formed part of the Spanish Captaincy-General of Guatemala until 1821, when its independence was secured. In 1927 Augusto Cesar Sandino began a guerrilla war against the occupation of Nicaragua by US Marines, which continued until they were expelled in 1933. Sandino was assassinated by Anastasio Somoza, director of the National Guard, and in 1936 Somoza assumed the presidency. He was succeeded by his sons Luis and Anastasio Somoza, until 1979 when the family and the National Guard were overthrown by guerrillas of the Sandinista National Liberation Front (FSLN).

After ten years in power and a ten-year civil war against US-backed Contra guerrillas, the Sandinistas lost their parliamentary majority in elections held in February 1990. A coalition of former opposition parties, the Unión Nacional de Opositora (UNO), gained 51 seats to the Sandinistas' 39 seats in the 92-seat National Assembly and formed a government, with UNO leader Violeta Chamorro as president. With the defeat of the Sandinistas, the civil war came to an end.

President Chamorro and the UNO were forced to compromise with the Sandinistas, who controlled the trade unions, and to leave the armed forces and police under Sandinista control. Resentment among the UNO coalition members came to a head in December 1992 when UNO deputies tried to oust Chamorro from power. Chamorro ordered the police to seize the National Assembly and negotiated a new governing majority in the National Assembly of 39 Sandinistas and nine loyal UNO deputies, forcing the remaining 42 UNO deputies and Vice-President Godoy into opposition. A further 19 UNO deputies formed the Democratic Christian Union (UDC) in January 1994, which joined the governing coalition. A deadlock over constitutional reforms was broken in July 1995 when President Chamorro conceded the curbing of presidential powers. Power over taxation and international treaties has been transferred to the National Assembly. The Liberal Alliance won the legislative election in October 1996 although the Nationalist Liberal Party left the Alliance in May 1997.

On 26 December 1997, following negotiations with the government, the Andrés Castro United Front (FUAC), the last recognized active terrorist group in Nicaragua, gave up their weapons.

POLITICAL SYSTEM

The head of government is the president, elected for a five-year term, not immediately renewable. The president appoints the Cabinet. There is a unicameral legislature, the National Assembly, with 90 members elected for a six-year term.

HEAD OF STATE

President, Arnoldo Alemán Lacayo *sworn in* 10 January 1997

Vice-President, Enrique Bolanos

CABINET *as at July 1998*

Agriculture and Livestock, Mario de Franco
Attorney-General, Julio Centeno Gómez
Construction and Transport, Edgard Quintana
Defence, Jaime Cuadra Somarriba
Economy and Development, Martín Aguado
Education, Humberto Belli Pereira
Environment and Natural Resources, Roberto Stadthagen
Finance, Esteban Duque-Estrada
Foreign Affairs, Emilio Alvárez-Montalbán
Foreign Co-operation, David Robleto Lang
Health, Lombardo Martínez Cabezas
Interior, José Antonio Alvarado
Labour, Wilfredo Navarro Moreira
Presidency, Eduardo Montealegre
Social Action, Jamilet Bonilla
Tourism, Pedro Joaquín Chamorro Barrios

NICARAGUAN DIPLOMATIC REPRESENTATION
The Embassy of Nicaragua closed in May 1997.
Consulate-General: Suite 12, Vicarage House, 58-60 Kensington Church Street, London w8 4D. Tel: 0171-937 4600

BRITISH EMBASSY
PO Box A-169, Plaza Churchill, Reparto 'Los Robles', Managua
Tel: Managua 780014
Ambassador and Consul-General, HE Roy Osbourne, apptd 1997

DEFENCE

The Army has 127 main battle tanks, 166 armoured personnel carriers and 142 artillery pieces. The Navy has 15 patrol and coastal vessels at three bases. The Air Force has 16 armed helicopters. Under the Sandinista government, Nicaragua maintained armed forces of over 120,000 personnel. Since 1990, active armed forces personnel has fallen to 17,000 and service is now voluntary.
MILITARY EXPENDITURE – 1.4 per cent of GDP (1996)
MILITARY PERSONNEL – 17,000: Army 15,000, Navy 800, Air Force 1,200

ECONOMY

After the civil war the UNO government began to transform the Sandinistas' socialist economy into a free-market one. An agreement was reached with the IMF in April 1994 which provided US$662 million in credits; the Paris club pledged US$1.5 billion in June 1995.

The country is mainly agricultural. The major crops are coffee, peanuts, cotton, sugar cane, tobacco, sesame and bananas. Beans, rice, maize and ipecacuanha, livestock and timber production are also important. Nicaragua possesses deposits of gold and silver.

In 1995 there was a trade deficit of US$324 million and a current account deficit of US$706 million. In 1996 imports totalled US$1,120 million and exports US$635 million.
GNP – US$1,705 million (1996); US$380 per capita (1996)
GDP – US$2,285 million (1994); US$433 per capita (1994)
ANNUAL AVERAGE GROWTH OF GDP – 5.8 per cent (1996)
INFLATION RATE – 11.6 per cent (1996)
UNEMPLOYMENT – 14.0 per cent (1991)
TOTAL EXTERNAL DEBT – US$5,929 million (1996)

TRADE

Considerable quantities of foodstuffs are imported as well as cotton goods, jute, iron and steel, machinery and petroleum products. The chief exports are peanuts, sesame seed, cotton, coffee, beef, gold, sugar and chemicals.

Trade with UK	1996	1997
Imports from UK	£5,924,000	£3,834,000
Exports to UK	3,433,000	12,688,000

COMMUNICATIONS

Transport, except on the Pacific slope, is still difficult but many new roads have been opened. The Inter-American Highway runs between the Honduras and the Costa Rican borders; the inter-oceanic highway runs from Corinto on the Pacific coast via Managua to Rama, where there is a natural waterway to Bluefields on the Atlantic. The main airport is at Managua. The chief port is Corinto on the Pacific. There are 252 miles of railway, all on the Pacific side of the country. There are 51 radio stations and seven television stations in Managua. An automatic telephone system has been installed in major cities.

There are four daily newspapers published at Managua, apart from the official Gazette (*La Gaceta*). There are universities at León and Managua.

NIGER
République du Niger

AREA – 489,191 sq. miles (1,267,000 sq. km). Neighbours: Algeria and Libya (north), Chad (east), Nigeria and Benin (south), Mali and Burkina Faso (west). Apart from a small region along the Niger Valley in the south-west near the capital, the country is entirely savannah or desert

POPULATION – 9,151,000 (1994 UN estimate): Hausa (54 per cent) in the south, Songhai and Djerma in the south-west, Fulani, Beriberi–Manga, and nomadic Tuareg in the north. 95 per cent of the population are Muslims, with Christian and Animist minorities. The official language is French. Hausa, Djerma and Fulani are also spoken

CAPITAL – Niamey (population, 392,169, 1988 census)

CURRENCY – Franc CFA of 100 centimes

NATIONAL DAY – 18 December

NATIONAL FLAG – Three horizontal stripes, orange, white and green with an orange disc in the middle of the white stripe

LIFE EXPECTANCY (years) – male 44.90; female 48.14

POPULATION GROWTH RATE – 3.4 per cent (1995)

POPULATION DENSITY – 7 per sq. km (1995)

URBAN POPULATION – 15.3 per cent (1988)

MILITARY EXPENDITURE – 1.1 per cent of GDP (1996)

MILITARY PERSONNEL – 10,700: Army 5,200, Air Force 100, Paramilitaries 5,400

CONSCRIPTION DURATION – Two years

ILLITERACY RATE – 86.4 per cent

ENROLMENT (percentage of age group) – primary 25 per cent (1990); secondary 6 per cent (1990); tertiary 0.3 per cent (1980)

HISTORY AND POLITICS

The first French expedition arrived in 1891 and the country was fully occupied by 1914. It decided on 18 December 1958 to remain an autonomous republic within the French Community; full independence outside the Community was proclaimed on 3 August 1960.

In 1974 Lt.-Col. Seyni Kountché seized power, suspended the constitution, dissolved the National Assembly and suppressed all political organizations. He set up a Supreme Military Council with himself as president. President Kountché died in 1987 and was succeeded by his cousin, Col. Ali Saibou.

In August 1991, a national conference of all groups voted to suspend the constitution and stripped President Saibou of all powers. A transitional government held office until legislative elections in February 1993. The former ruling party, the National Movement for a Development Society (MNSD), emerged as the largest party, although the Alliance of Forces for Change (AFC) formed the government. Mahamane Ousmane of the AFC won the presidential election in March.

The defection of one of the main AFC parties from the government in late 1994 led to a parliamentary election in January 1995 which was won by the MNSD and allied parties. The president and government were overthrown in a military coup led by Col. Ibrahim Barre Mainassara on 27 January 1996. Power was assumed by a National Salvation Council, which suspended the constitution,

appointed a civilian Cabinet and created a transitional legislature until presidential and parliamentary elections could be held. A new constitution was promulgated on 12 May 1996 and the ban on political parties was lifted. Brig.-Gen. Mainassara was elected president on 8 July 1996. The pro-Mainassara National Union of Independents for Democratic Renewal won the largest number of seats in legislative elections in November 1996, though these were boycotted by main opposition groups. On 24 November 1997, President Mainassara dismissed the government led by Prime Minister Amadou Boubacar Cisse on grounds of incompetence, and appointed a new government under Ibrahim Hassane Mayaki.

INSURGENCY

An ethnic Tuareg-based insurgency began in the north of Niger in November 1991, leading the government to impose a state of emergency in April 1992. The insurgency by the Front for the Liberation of Aïr and Azawad (FLAA) aimed to gain greater local autonomy for the Tuaregs, a change to regional boundaries, the demilitarization of the north and the teaching of the Tuareg language, Tamashek. In 1993 two groups, the Front for the Liberation of Tamoust (FLT) and the Revolutionary Army of Northern Niger (RANN) split from the FLAA in protest at its entry into negotiations with the government. An interim peace agreement was signed between the government and all Tuareg groups in Ouagadougou in October 1994, and a peace accord ending the conflict and providing for a peace process was signed on 24 April 1995. On 29 November 1997, the remaining active Tuareg groups agreed a cease-fire, and in March 1998, the National Assembly voted unanimously to grant an amnesty to all rebel groups representing the Tuareg and Toubou peoples.

HEAD OF STATE
President, Brig.-Gen. Ibrahim Barre Mainassara, *sworn in* 7 August 1996

CABINET *as at July 1998*
Prime Minister, Ibrahim Hassane Mayaki
Ministers of State, Idi Ango Omar (*Agriculture and Livestock*); Oumarou Boube (*Higher Education, Research and Technology*); Aïssata Moumouni (*National Education*); Lt.-Col. Abdourahamane Seydou (*Youth, Sport and National Solidarity; Government Spokesman*)
Civil Service, Labour, Employment, Moussa Oumarou
Commerce and Industry, Ibrahim Koussou
Communication and Culture, Issa Moussa
Equipment and Infrastructure, Cherif Chako
Finance, Economic Reform, Privatization, Ide Niandou
Foreign Affairs and African Integration, Mambo Sambo Sidikou
Interior, Territorial Development, Abdoulaye Souley
Justice, Human Rights, Keeper of the Seals, Issoufou Aba Moussa
Mines and Energy, Mai Manga Boukar
Minister Delegate, Tourism, Rissa ag Boula
National Defence, Dr Yahya Tounkara
Planning, Yacouba Nabassoua
Public Health, Lt.-Col. Illo al Moustapha
Social Development, Population, Promotion of Women and Children, Mariama Sambo Abdoulaye
Tourism and Handicrafts, Aïssa Abdoulaye Diallo
Transport, Oubandawaki Issoufou Ousmane
Water Supply and Environment, Harouna Niandou

EMBASSY OF THE REPUBLIC OF NIGER
154 rue de Longchamp, 75116, Paris
Tel: Paris 4504 8060
Chargé d'Affaires, Manou Toudou

British Ambassador, HE Haydon Warren-Gash, resident at Abidjan, Côte d'Ivoire

ECONOMY

The cultivation of groundnuts and the production of livestock are the main industries and provide two of the main exports. Other agricultural products include millet, cassava and sugar cane. There are large uranium deposits at Arlit and Akouta, and this is the main export. Gold deposits exist north-west of Niamey. France and Nigeria are the main trading partners.

In 1994 Niger had a trade deficit of US$44 million and a current account deficit of US$126 million. In 1996 imports totalled US$244 million and exports US$188 million.
GNP – US$1,879 million (1996); US$200 per capita (1996)
GDP – US$2,769 million (1994); US$211 per capita (1994)
Annual Average Growth of GDP – – 6.3 per cent (1981)
Inflation Rate – 5.3 per cent (1996)
Total External Debt – US$1,557 million (1996)

Trade with UK	1996	1997
Imports from UK	£3,785,000	£2,957,000
Exports to UK	113,000	11,445,000

NIGERIA
Federal Republic of Nigeria

Area – 356,669 sq. miles (923,768 sq. km). Neighbours: Benin (west), Niger (north), Chad (north-east), Cameroon (east)
Population – 111,721,000 (1994 UN estimate); 88,514,501 (1991 census). The main ethnic groups are Hausa/Fulani, Yoruba and Ibo, and the principal languages are English, Hausa, Yoruba and Ibo. Over half the population are Muslim, these being concentrated in the north and west. In the southern areas in particular there are many Christians
Capital – Abuja, (population, 378,671), declared the federal capital in 1991
Major Cities – Ibadan (1,295,000); Kaduna (309,600); Kano (699,900); Lagos, the former capital (1,347,000); Ogbomosho (660,600); ΨPort Harcourt (371,000)
Currency – Naira (N) of 100 kobo
National Anthem – Arise, O Compatriots
National Day – 1 October (Independence Day)
National Flag – Three equal vertical bands, green, white and green
Life Expectancy (years) – male 48.81; female 52.01
Population Growth Rate – 3.0 per cent (1995)
Population Density – 121 per sq. km (1995)
Urban Population – 16.1 per cent (1988)
Illiteracy Rate – 42.9 per cent
Enrolment (percentage of age group) – tertiary 4.1 per cent (1993)

A belt of mangrove swamp forest lies along the entire coastline. North of this there is a zone of tropical rain forest and oil-palms. North of the rain forest, the country rises and the vegetation changes to open woodland and savannah. In the extreme north the country is semi-desert. The Niger, Benue, and Cross are the main rivers. The climate is tropical. The rainy season is from about April to October. During the dry season the cool *harmattan* wind blows from the desert.

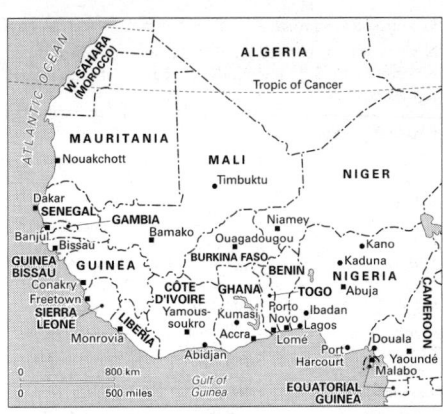

HISTORY AND POLITICS

The Federation of Nigeria attained independence as a member of the Commonwealth on 1 October 1960 and became a republic in 1963. Originally regional in structure, the Federation is now divided into 36 states and the Federal Capital Territory.

In 1966 the military took power; in 1979 civil rule was restored after elections at national and state level. After similar elections in 1983 the new administration was overthrown by the military on 31 December, this regime itself being overthrown in August 1985. A 28-member Armed Forces Ruling Council (AFRC) was sworn in and governed in conjunction with a Council of Ministers until January 1993, when they were replaced by a National Defence and Security Council (NDSC) and a civilian Transitional Council respectively to govern the country until a handover to civilian government. A presidential election on 11 June is generally believed to have been won by Chief Moshood Abiola of the Social Democratic Party but the military government declared the election invalid. The military government resigned on 26 August, handing power to the Transitional Council.

Continued instability led Defence Minister Gen. Sanni Abacha to launch a military coup on 17 November 1993 and install himself as head of state. A (military) Provisional Ruling Council and (civilian) Federal Executive Council were established to govern the country until a new constitution is passed. Strikes and pro-democracy demonstrations continued in support of Chief Moshood Abiola, who returned from exile in June 1994 to establish a rival government, for which he was imprisoned.

The National Constitutional Conference (NCC) convened by Gen. Abacha in June 1994 announced in January 1995 that Gen. Abacha should have an open-ended term of office. An attempted coup was defeated in March 1995 and political activity was restored in June, when the NCC presented the draft of a new constitution to Gen. Abacha. The military regime vowed to hand over power to an elected government in October 1998. In June 1998 Gen. Abacha died of a heart attack and was replaced by Gen. Abdulsalami Abubakar, who promised to continue with the handover to civilian rule and began the release of political prisoners. It was expected that Chief Abiola would be released, but in July he died of a heart attack while still in prison. News of his death prompted widespread rioting across the country. Gen. Abubakar announced that all elections held under Gen. Abacha's rule would be considered invalid and that fresh general elections would be held in February 1999.

FOREIGN RELATIONS

Nigeria was suspended from the Commonwealth on 11 November 1995, following the execution of nine human rights activists.

FEDERAL STRUCTURE

State	Population (1991)	Capital
Sokoto ⎫ *Zamfara ⎭	4,392,391	Sokoto Gusau
Kebbi	2,062,226	Birnin-Kebbi
Niger	2,482,367	Minna
Kwara	1,566,469	Ilorin
Kogi	2,099,046	Lokoja
Benue	2,780,398	Makurdi
Plateau ⎫ *Nassarawa ⎭	3,283,704	Jos Lafia
Taraba	1,480,590	Jalingo
Adamawa	2,124,049	Yola
Borno	2,596,589	Maiduguri
Yobe	1,411,481	Damaturu
Bauchi ⎫ *Gombe ⎭	4,294,413	Bauchi Gombe
Jigawa	2,829,929	Dutse
Kano	5,632,040	Kano
Katsina	3,878,344	Katsina
Kaduna	3,969,252	Kaduna
Federal Capital Territory	378,671	Abuja
Oyo	3,488,789	Ibadan
Osun	2,203,016	Oshogbo
Ogun	2,338,570	Abeokuta
Lagos	5,685,781	Ikeja
Ondo ⎫ *Ekiti ⎭	3,884,485	Akure Ado Ekiti
Edo	2,159,848	Benin City
Delta	2,570,181	Asaba
Rivers ⎫ *Bayelsa ⎭	3,983,857	Port-Harcourt Yenagoa
Abia	2,297,978	Umuahia
Imo ⎫ *Ebonyi ⎭	2,485,499	Owerri Abakaliki
Anambra	2,767,903	Awka
Enugu	3,161,295	Enugu
Cross River	1,865,604	Calabar
Akwa Ibom	2,359,736	Uyo

*New state, created on 1 October 1996 by dividing state immediately preceding it in list

HEAD OF STATE

Chairman of the Provisional Ruling Council and Federal Executive Council, Commander-in-Chief of the Armed Forces, Gen. Abdulsalami Abubakar, *sworn in* 9 June 1998

FEDERAL EXECUTIVE COUNCIL *as at July 1998*

Chairman, Gen. Abdulsalami Abubakar
Ministers of State, Frank Adejuwon (*Agriculture*); Rose Adunine (*Education*); Idris Alhassan Kpaki (*Federal Capital Territory*); Abu Gidado (*Finance*); Buhari Bala (*Foreign Affairs*); A. Hagher (*Health*); Umaru Dembo (*Petroleum Resources*); Kunle Oluwasemi (*Power and Steel*); Chief E. C. Okete (*Works and Housing*)
Agriculture, Malami Buwal
Aviation, Air Cdre Udo Imeh
Commerce and Tourism, Emmanuel Odogu
Communications, Maj.-Gen. P. N. Aziza
Education, Dauda Birma
Federal Capital Territory, Lt.-Gen. Jerry Useni
Finance, Chief Anthony Asuquo Ani
Foreign Affairs, Chief Tom Ikimi
Health, Rear-Adm. J. O. Ayinla
Industries, O. Akande
Information and Culture, Chief I. K. Mokelu
Internal Affairs, Bashir Dalhatu
Justice, Abdulahi Ibrahim
Labour, Uba Ahmed
Petroleum Resources, Chief Dan Etete
Planning, Ayo Ogunlade
Power and Steel, Baba Gana Kingibe
Science and Technology, Maj.-Gen. Samuel Momah
Solid Mineral Resources, Kaloma Ali
Transport, Maj.-Gen. Ibrahim Gumel
Water Resources, Hamza Sakwa
Women's Affairs, Hajo Sani
Works and Housing, Brig.-Gen. Garba Ali Mohammed
Youth and Sports, Air Cdre Samson Omeruah

NIGERIA HIGH COMMISSION

9 Northumberland Avenue, London WC2N 5BX
Tel 0171-839 1244
Acting High Commissioner, U. O. Okeke
Minister, A. A. Ella

BRITISH HIGH COMMISSION

Shehu Shangari Way (North), Maitama, Abuja
Tel: Abuja 523 2010
11 Louis Farrakhan Crescent, Victoria Island, Lagos
Tel: Lagos 261 9531
High Commissioner, HE Graham Burton, CMG, apptd 1997
Deputy High Commissioner and Counsellor (Political), R. A. Pullen
Counsellor (Economic and Commercial), D. D. Pearey
LIAISON OFFICES – Ibadan, Kaduna, Kano, Port Harcourt

BRITISH COUNCIL DIRECTOR, C. Bruton, 11 Kingsway Road, Ikoyi (PO Box 3702), Lagos. Branch offices at Enugu, Ibadan, Kaduna and Kano City

DEFENCE

The Army has 200 main battle tanks, 380 armoured personnel carriers and 431 artillery pieces. The Navy has one frigate, 51 patrol and coastal vessels and two helicopters at six bases. The Air Force has 92 combat aircraft and 15 armed helicopters.

MILITARY EXPENDITURE – 2.8 per cent of GDP (1996)
MILITARY PERSONNEL – 77,000: Army 62,000, Navy 5,500, Air Force 9,500

ECONOMY

Nigeria was a predominantly agricultural country until the early 1970s when oil became the principal source of export revenue (over 90 per cent). Since 1981 oil revenues have fallen to half their peak level and austerity measures were introduced in 1982. Recent governments have attempted to stimulate greater self-reliance by encouraging non-oil exports and the use of local rather than imported raw materials.

The government introduced economic reforms in January 1995, including lifting exchange controls and ending foreign investment controls in Nigerian or jointly-owned firms. Economic recovery has been hampered by the suspension of aid and development programmes following the execution of nine human rights activists in November 1995.

Three oil refineries are in operation at Port Harcourt, Warri and Kaduna, and steel plants at Warri and Ajaokuta. Other projects include natural gas liquefaction, petro-chemicals, fertilizers, power stations and irrigation schemes. Tin and calumbite mining on the Jos plateau, textiles and coal mining are also important.

GNP – US$27,599 million (1996); US$240 per capita (1996)
GDP – US$36,269 million (1994); US$376 per capita (1994)
ANNUAL AVERAGE GROWTH OF GDP – 1.3 per cent (1994)
INFLATION RATE – 29.3 per cent (1996)
TOTAL EXTERNAL DEBT – US$31,407 million (1996)

TRADE

The principal exports are oil, groundnuts, tin, cocoa, rubber, fish and timber. In 1994 there was a trade surplus of US$2,948 million and a current account deficit of US$2,128 million. In 1995 imports totalled US$9,332 million and exports US$10,636 million.

Trade with UK	1996	1997
Imports from UK	£432,972,000	£426,212,000
Exports to UK	293,749,000	122,395,000

COMMUNICATIONS

The Nigerian railway system, which is controlled by the Nigerian Railway Corporation, has 2,178 route miles of lines. The principal international airlines operate from Lagos, Kano and Port Harcourt. A network of internal air services connects the main centres. The principal seaports are served by a number of shipping lines, including the Nigerian National Line. A nationwide television and radio network is being developed, and ten states have their own television and radio stations.

NORWAY
Kongeriket Norge

AREA – 125,050 sq. miles (323,877 sq. km) of which Svalbard and Jan Mayen have a combined area of 24,355 sq. miles (63,080 sq. km). Neighbours: Sweden, Finland, Russia (east)
POPULATION – 4,360,000 (1996). The language is Norwegian and has two forms: Bokmål and Nynorsk. The Sami population in the north of the country speak Lappish
CAPITAL – ΨOslo (population, 758,949, 1993 estimate)
MAJOR CITIES – ΨBergen (221,717); ΨKristiansand (68,609); ΨStavanger (103,590); ΨTrondheim (142,927)
CURRENCY – Krone of 100 øre
NATIONAL ANTHEM – Ja, vi elsker dette landet (Yes, we love this country)
NATIONAL DAY – 17 May (Constitution Day)
NATIONAL FLAG – Red, with white-bordered blue cross
LIFE EXPECTANCY (years) – male 74.24; female 80.25
POPULATION GROWTH RATE – 0.6 per cent (1995)
POPULATION DENSITY – 13 per sq. km (1995)
URBAN POPULATION – 72.0 per cent (1990)

The coastline is deeply indented with numerous fjords and fringed with rocky islands. The surface is mountainous, consisting of elevated and barren tablelands separated by deep and narrow valleys. At the North Cape the sun does not appear to set from the second week in May to the last week in July, causing the phenomenon known as the Midnight Sun; conversely, there is no apparent sunrise from about 18 November to 23 January. During the long winter nights are seen the Northern Lights or Aurora Borealis.

HISTORY AND POLITICS

Norway was unified under Harald I Fairhair c. AD 900 and participated in the Viking expansion from the ninth to the 11th centuries. The accession of Magnus VII (1319)

unified the Norwegian and Swedish crowns until his son became King Haakon VI of Norway in 1343. The Norwegian and Danish crowns were united in 1380 and confirmed by the Union of Kalmar (1397) which also brought Sweden under the rule of Queen Margrethe of Denmark. Norway remained a Danish province until transferred to Sweden under the Treaty of Kiel (1814). The union with Sweden was dissolved on 7 June 1905 when Norway regained complete independence.

Norway remained neutral during the First World War and on the outbreak of the Second World War but was invaded by Germany in 1940. Neutrality was abandoned when Norway joined NATO in 1949. The Labour Party governed from 1945 to 1965 when the extensive welfare state system was built. A referendum in 1972 rejected membership of the EC.

The ruling centre-right coalition collapsed in October 1990 over the question of EC membership and was replaced by a minority Labour government. This was returned to power in the general election held on 13 September 1993. A general election was held on 15 September 1997, in which no party won an outright majority. The Labour Party has the largest number of seats (65) but the government is a minority coalition of the Christian Democratic People's Party, the Centre Party and the Liberal Party.

FOREIGN RELATIONS

The Storting voted in November 1992 to apply to join the European Community. Negotiations with the EU concluded on 1 March 1994 with a proposed accession date of 1 January 1995, subject to parliamentary and national referendum ratifications. However, in a national referendum on 28 November 1994 the electorate voted against joining the EU by 52.4 per cent to 47.6 per cent.

POLITICAL SYSTEM

Under the 1814 constitution, the 165-member *Storting* elects one-quarter of its members to constitute the *Lagting* (Upper Chamber), the other three-quarters forming the *Odelsting* (Lower Chamber).

HEAD OF STATE

HM The King of Norway, King Harald V, GCVO, *born* 21 February 1937; *succeeded* 17 January 1991, on the death of his father King Olav V; *married* 29 August 1968, Sonja Haraldsen, and has *issue*, Prince Haakon Magnus (*see* below), and Princess Martha Louise, *born* 22 September 1971
Heir, HRH Crown Prince Haakon Magnus, *born* 20 July 1973

CABINET *as at July 1998*
Prime Minister, Kjell Magne Bondevik (KrF)
Agriculture, Kåre Gjoennes (KrF)
Cultural Affairs, Anne Enger Lahnstein (SP)
Defence, Dag Jostein Fjaervoll (KrF)
Development Co-operation and Human Rights, Hilde Frafjord Johnson (KrF)
Education, Research and Church Affairs, Jon Lilletun (KrF)
Environment, Guro Fjellanger (V)
Family and Children's Affairs, Valgerd Svarstad Haugland (KrF)
Finance, Gudmund Restad (SP)
Fisheries, Peter Angelsen (SP)
Foreign Affairs, Knut Vollebak (KrF)
Health, Dagfinn Hoeybraten (KrF)
Industry and Trade, Lars Sponheim (V)
Justice and Police, Aud Inge Aure (KrF)
Local Government and Labour, Ragnhild Queseth (SP)
National Planning and Co-ordination, Eldbjoerg Loewer (V)
Petroleum and Energy, Marit Arnstad (SP)

Social Affairs, Magnhild Melteveit Kleppa (SP)
Transport, Communications, Odd Einar Doerum (V)

KrF Christian Democratic People's Party; SP Centre Party; V Liberal Party

ROYAL NORWEGIAN EMBASSY
25 Belgrave Square, London SWIX 8QD
Tel 0171-591 5500
Ambassador Extraordinary and Plenipotentiary, HE Kjell Colding, CMG, apptd 1996
Defence Attaché, Capt. T. Seim
First Secretary, I. Brusell (*Consular*)
Counsellor, S. Lindtvedt (*Commercial*)

BRITISH EMBASSY
Thomas Heftyesgate 8, 0244 Oslo
Tel: Oslo 2313 2700
Ambassador Extraordinary and Plenipotentiary, HE Richard Dales, CMG, apptd 1998
Counsellor, D. G. Blunt, LVO (*Deputy Head of Mission and Consul-General*)
First Secretary, Dr C. M. Sweeney (*Economic and Commercial*)
Defence and Naval Attaché, Lt.-Col. P. D. T. Irvine, OBE

BRITISH CONSULAR OFFICES – Oslo; Honorary Consulates at Aalesund, Bergen, Harstad, Kristiansand (South), Kristiansund (North), Stavanger, Tromsø, Trondheim

BRITISH COUNCIL REPRESENTATIVE , R. Olsen, Fridtjof Nansens Plass 5, 0160, Oslo 1

DEFENCE

Norway is a member of NATO and the headquarters of Allied Forces Northern Europe is situated near Oslo. The Army has 170 main battle tanks, 269 armoured infantry fighting vehicles and armoured personnel carriers, and 252 artillery pieces. The Navy has 12 submarines, four frigates and 24 patrol and coastal vessels at three bases. The Air Force has 79 combat aircraft.

MILITARY EXPENDITURE – 2.4 per cent of GDP (1996)
MILITARY PERSONNEL – 32,700: Army 15,800, Navy 9,000, Air Force 7,900
CONSCRIPTION DURATION – 12 months

ECONOMY

The cultivated area is about 10,826 sq. km, 3.5 per cent of the total surface area. Forests cover nearly 23 per cent; the rest consists of highland pastures or uninhabitable mountains. The chief agricultural products are grain, vegetables, milk, furs and timber.

The Gulf Stream causes the sea temperature to be higher than the average for the latitude, which brings shoals of herring and cod into the fishing grounds. In 1996 the catch totalled more than 2.6 million tonnes.

The chief industries are oil production and transport, construction, electricity supply, manufactures, agriculture and forestry, fisheries, mining, metal and ferro-alloy production and shipping. Industries providing both manufactured products and services for the development of North Sea energy resources have become increasingly important. In 1996 156,788,000 tonnes of crude oil were produced. Norway produces large amounts of hydro-electric power.

GNP – US$151,198 million (1996); US$34,510 per capita (1996)
GDP – US$120,358 million (1994); US$25,378 per capita (1994)
ANNUAL AVERAGE GROWTH OF GDP – 5.3 per cent (1996)

INFLATION RATE – 1.3 per cent (1996)
UNEMPLOYMENT – 4.9 per cent (1995)

TRADE

The chief imports are raw materials, motor vehicles, ships and machinery, clothing, foods and textiles. Exports consist chiefly of crude oil and gas, manufactured goods, fish and fish products (as canned fish, whale oils), pulp, paper, iron ore and pyrites, nitrate of lime, stone, calcium carbide, aluminium, ferro-alloys, nickel, cyanamides, etc.

In 1994 Norway had a trade surplus of US$8,321 million and a current account surplus of US$3,645 million. In 1996 imports totalled US$35,615 million and exports US$49,645 million.

Trade with UK	1996	1997
Imports from UK	£2,066,273,000	£2,655,938,000
Exports to UK	4,984,405,000	4,927,331,000

COMMUNICATIONS

The total length of railways open at the end of 1995 was 4,023 km, excluding private lines. There are 90,262 km of public roads in Norway (including urban streets). Scheduled internal air services are operated by Scandinavian Airlines System (SAS) on behalf of Det Norske Luftfartselskap (DNL), by Braathens South American and Far East Airtransport (SAFE), and by Widerøes Flyveselskap AS. There are international airports at Oslo, Bergen and Stavanger. In 1996 there were 64 daily newspapers.

CULTURE AND EDUCATION

The Norwegian language in both its present forms is closely related to other Scandinavian languages. Independence from Denmark (1814) and resurgent nationalism led to the development of 'new Norwegian' based on dialects, which now has equal official standing with 'bokmål', in which Danish influence is more obvious. Ludvig Holberg (1684–1754) is regarded as the father of Norwegian literature, though the modern period begins with the writings of Henrik Wergeland (1808–45). Some of the famous names are Henrik Ibsen (1828–1906), Bjørnstjerne Bjørnson (1832–1910), Nobel Prizewinner in 1903, and the novelists Jonas Lie (1833–1908), Alexander Kielland (1849–1906), Knut Hamsun (1859–1952) and Sigrid Undset (1882–1949), the latter two also Nobel Prizewinners. Old Norse literature is among the most ancient and richest in Europe.

Education from six to 16 is free and compulsory in the 'basic schools', and free from 16 to 19 years. The majority of the pupils receive post-compulsory schooling at 'upper secondary' schools, regional colleges akin to polytechnics, universities (four) and ten other university-level specialist colleges.

ENROLMENT (percentage of age group) – primary 99 per cent (1994); secondary 94 per cent (1994); tertiary 54.5 per cent (1994)

TERRITORIES

SVALBARD, area 24,295 sq. miles (62,923 sq. km); population 3,700; inhabitants mainly engaged in coal-mining. The Svalbard archipelago consists of the main island, Spitsbergen (15,200 sq. miles), North East Land, the Wiche Islands, Barents and Edge Islands, Prince Charles Foreland, Hope Island, Bear Island and many islands in the neighbourhood of the main group. Glaciers cover 60 per cent of the land area. The sovereignty of Norway over the archipelago was recognized by other nations in 1920 and in 1925 Norway assumed sovereignty

Jan Mayen Island was joined to Norway by law in 1930

NORWEGIAN ANTARCTIC TERRITORIES

Bouvet Island was declared a dependency of Norway in 1930

Peter the First Island was declared a dependency of Norway in 1931

Princess Ragnhild Land has been claimed as Norwegian since 1931

Queen Maud Land was declared Norwegian territory by the Norwegian government in 1939

OMAN
The Sultanate of Oman

Area – 119,498 sq. miles (309,500 sq. km). Neighbours: Yemen, Saudi Arabia and the UAE (west)

Population – 2,020,000 (1998 estimate). The inhabitants of the north are mostly Arab, though there are large communities of Hindus, Khojas and Baluch, in addition to Omanis of Zanzibari origin, especially around Salalah. However, in the mountains the inhabitants are either of pure Arab descent or belong to tribes of pre-Arab origin, the Qarra and Mahra, who speak their own dialects of Semitic origin. The official language is Arabic

Capital – ΨMuscat (population, 400,000)

Major Cities – ΨBarka; ΨMutrah and Ruwi (the commercial centres); ΨSalalah (the main town of Dhofar); ΨSohar; ΨSur

Currency – Rial Omani (OR) of 1,000 baiza

National Day – 18 November

National Flag – Red with a white panel in the upper fly and a green one in the lower fly; in the canton the national emblem in white

Life Expectancy (years) – male 67.70; female 71.80

Population Growth Rate – 1.6 per cent (1995)

Population Density – 10 per sq. km (1995)

Oman lies at the eastern corner of the Arabian peninsula. Sharjah and Fujairah (UAE) separate the main part of Oman from the northernmost part of the state, a peninsula extending into the Strait of Hormuz.

The north and the south of Oman are divided by nearly 400 miles of desert. The Batinah, the coastal plain, is fertile. The Hajjar is a mountain spine running from north-west to south-east and for the most part barren, but valleys penetrate the central massif which are irrigated by wells or a system of underground canals called *falajs* which tap the water table. The two plateaus leading from the western slopes of the mountains descend to the Empty Quarter of the Arabian Desert. Dhofar, the southern province, is the only part of the Arabian peninsula to be touched by the south-west monsoon. Temperatures are more moderate than in the north.

HISTORY AND POLITICS

Oman became part of the Islamic empire in the seventh century. From the ninth to 16th centuries the area was governed by a succession of religious leaders, or imams of the Ibadi schism of Islam. The Portuguese established trading posts on the coast in 1507 but were expelled in 1650.

In 1744 Ahmad bin Said Al bu Said established the current ruling dynasty of sultans. The country was divided between the sultan's stronghold in the coastal Muscat-Matrah region and the imam in the interior. The sultan cultivated close relations with Britain and the Sultanate of

Muscat and Oman became a British protectorate in 1798. In the late 19th century Dhofar was annexed.

In the 1950s the imam proclaimed an independent state in a revolt which was put down with British assistance. A seven-year-long Marxist uprising was crushed in 1975. The current sultan ousted his father in a palace coup in 1970 and changed the state's name to the Sultanate of Oman. Dhofar is still governed as a separate province and Muscat has special status.

Political System

A State Consultative Council established in 1981 was replaced by Sultanic decree in 1991 by a *Majlis A' shura*, or State Advisory Council. This body, meeting twice a year, consists of a representative from each of the 59 wilayats, or governorates, of the Sultanate. The Council has the right to review legislation, question ministers and make policy proposals. Effective political power remains with the sultan, who rules by decree and is advised by the Cabinet, which he appoints.

In November 1996 the sultan decreed Oman to be a hereditary absolute monarchy. On 16 October 1997, elections were held to choose 164 people for a shortlist to the State Advisory Council; the sultan chose the 82 members of the Council from them. On 16 December 1997 the sultan appointed 41 members to the new *Majlis al-dawlah* (Council of State).

Head of State

HM The Sultan of Oman, Sultan HM Qaboos bin Said al-Said, *succeeded* on deposition of Sultan Said bin Taimur, 23 July 1970

Council of Ministers *as at July 1998*

Prime Minister, Foreign Affairs, Defence and Finance, The Sultan

Personal Representative of HM The Sultan, HH Sayyid Thuwaini bin Shihab al Said

Deputy PM, HH Sayyid Fahd bin Mahmoud al Said

Minister of State and Governor of Dhofar, Sayyid Musallam bin Ali al Busaidi

Minister of State and Governor of Muscat, HE Sayyid al Mutassim bin Hamoud al Busaidi

Agriculture and Fisheries, Dr Ahmed bin Khalfan bin Mohammed al Rowahi

Awqaf and Religious Affairs, Shaikh Abdullah bin Mohammed bin Abdullah al Salimi

Civil Service, Shaikh Abdulaziz bin Matar al Azizi

Commerce and Industry, Maqbool bin Ali bin Nasir al Sultan

Communications, Salim bin Abdullah al Ghazali

Defence, HE Sayyid Badr bin Soud bin Hareb al Busaidi

Diwan of Royal Court, HE Sayyid Saif bin Hamed bin Soud

Education, Sayyid Soud bin Ibrahim al Busaidi

Electricity and Water, Shaikh Mohammed bin Ali al Qatabi

Foreign Affairs, Yusuf bin Alawi bin Abdullah

Health, Dr Ali bin Mohammed bin Moosa

Higher Education, Yahya bin Mahfoudh al Mantheri

Housing, Malik bin Suleiman al Ma'amari

Information, Abdulaziz bin Mohammed al Rowas

Interior, HE Sayyid Ali bin Hamoud al Busaidi

Justice, Shaikh Mohammed bin Abdullah bin Zaher al Hinai

Legal Affairs, Mohammed bin Ali bin Nasir al Alawi

National Economy, Ministry of Finance, Ahmed bin Abdul-Nabi Macki

National Heritage and Culture, HH Sayyid Faisal bin Ali al Said

Oil and Gas, Dr Mohammed bin Hamad bin Saif Al Romhi

Palace Office, Gen. Ali bin Majid al Ma'amari

Posts, Telegraphs and Telephones, Ahmed bin Suwaidan al Balushi
Regional Municipalities and Environment, Dr Khamis bin Mubarak bin Isa al Alawi
Social Affairs, Labour, Vocational Training, Shaikh Amer bin Shuwain al Hosni
Water Resources, Hamid bin Said al Aufi

EMBASSY OF THE SULTANATE OF OMAN
167 Queen's Gate, London SW7 5HE
Tel 0171-225 0001
Ambassador Extraordinary and Plenipotentiary, HE Hussain Ali Abdullatif, apptd 1995
Minister Plenipotentiary, Ghassan Ibrahim Shaker
Military Attaché, Gp Capt. Said Hassan Al-Shedad

BRITISH EMBASSY
PO Box 300, Muscat
Tel: Muscat 693077
Ambassador Extraordinary and Plenipotentiary, HE Richard John Muir, CMG, apptd 1994
Counsellor, N. G. F. Baird (*Deputy Head of Mission*)
Defence and Military Attaché, Brig. M. I. Keun
First Secretary (Commercial), P. Williams
Consul, G. Brown

BRITISH COUNCIL DIRECTOR, C. Hepburn, PO Box 73, Muscat. There are also offices at Salalah and Seeb

DEFENCE

The Army has 121 main battle tanks, 73 armoured personnel carriers and 91 artillery pieces. The Navy has two corvettes and 13 patrol and coastal vessels at five bases. The Air Force has 47 combat aircraft.
MILITARY EXPENDITURE – 15.7 per cent of GDP (1996)
MILITARY PERSONNEL – 44,200: Army 25,000, Navy 4,200, Air Force 4,100, Royal Household 6,500, Paramilitaries 4,400

ECONOMY

Although there is considerable cultivation in the fertile areas and cattle are raised on the mountains, the backbone of the economy is the oil industry. Petroleum Development (Oman) Ltd (owned 60 per cent by Oman Government and 34 per cent by Shell) began exporting oil in 1967. Concessions (off and on shore) are held by several major international companies. The current level of oil production is about 850,000 barrels per day.

A gas turbine power station operates at Rusail, where there is also a 200-plot industrial estate. There is a power station and a desalination plant near Muscat and flour, animal feed, cement and copper production facilities.

In 1995 there was a trade surplus of US$2,015 million and a current account deficit of US$979 million.
GNP – US$10,578 million (1995); US$4,820 per capita (1995)
GDP – US$12,646 million (1994); US$5,698 per capita (1994)
ANNUAL AVERAGE GROWTH OF GDP – 3.5 per cent (1994)
TOTAL EXTERNAL DEBT – US$3,415 million (1996)

TRADE

Trade is mainly with the UAE, UK, Japan, South Korea and China. Chief imports are machinery, cars, building materials, food and telecommunications equipment.
In 1996 imports totalled US$4,578 million.

Trade with UK	1996	1997
Imports from UK	£415,750,000	£370,422,000
Exports to UK	86,993,000	105,089,000

COMMUNICATIONS

Port Qaboos at Matrah has eight deep-water berths which have been constructed as part of the harbour facilities. A modern telecommunications service to the main population centres and an international service are operated by the General Telecommunications Organization. There are some 6,000 km of tarmac roads linking most main population centres of the country with the coast and with the towns of the UAE, though only a trunk road links the north and south of Oman. There are airports at Seeb, Salalah, Sur, Masirah, Khasab and Diba.

SOCIAL WELFARE AND EDUCATION

For many years the Sultanate was a poor country but the advent of oil revenues and the change of regime in 1970 led to the initiation of a wide-ranging development programme, especially concerned with health, education and communications. There are now over 50 hospitals with around 4,400 beds; 967 schools, with 503,529 pupils, were in operation in 1997.
ENROLMENT (percentage of age group) – primary 71 per cent (1995); secondary 56 per cent (1995); tertiary 4.7 per cent (1993)

PAKISTAN
Islami Jamhuriya-e-Pakistan

AREA – 307,374 sq. miles (796,095 sq. km). Neighbours: Iran (west), Afghanistan (north and north-west), China (north-east), the disputed territory of Kashmir, India (east)
POPULATION – 129,808,000 (1994 UN estimate); 83,780,000 (1981 census): 95 per cent Muslim, 3.5 per cent Christian, about 1 per cent Hindu, and 0.5 per cent Buddhist. Urdu is the national language, but is only spoken by a small minority of the population. The most widely used language is Punjabi, followed by Sindi and Pushto. English is used in business, government and higher education
CAPITAL – Islamabad (population, 350,000)
MAJOR CITIES – ΨKarachi (7,183,000); Lahore (4,072,000)
CURRENCY – Pakistan rupee of 100 paisa
NATIONAL ANTHEM – Quami Tarana
NATIONAL DAYS – 23 March (Pakistan Day), 14 August (Independence Day)
NATIONAL FLAG – Green with a white crescent and star, and a white vertical strip in the hoist
LIFE EXPECTANCY (years) – male 59.04; female 59.20
POPULATION GROWTH RATE – 2.9 per cent (1995)
POPULATION DENSITY – 163 per sq. km (1995)
URBAN POPULATION – 28.2 per cent (1991)

Running through Pakistan are five great rivers, the Indus, Jhelum, Chenab, Ravi and Sutlej. The upper reaches of these rivers are in Kashmir, and their sources in the Himalayas.

HISTORY AND POLITICS

Pakistan was constituted as a Dominion under the Indian Independence Act 1947, becoming a republic on 23 March 1956. Until 1972 Pakistan consisted of two geographical units, West and East Pakistan, separated by about 1,100 miles of Indian territory. East Pakistan's insistence on complete autonomy led to civil war, which broke out on 25 March 1971 and continued until December 1971 when a cease-fire was arranged. The independence of East Pakistan as Bangladesh was proclaimed in April 1972. Under the 1972 Simla Agreement with India, a line of control was established in Kashmir; Pakistan controls an area of 33,653 sq. miles (87,159 sq. km) to the north and west of the line.

The armed forces under Gen. Zia-ul-Haq assumed power in 1977 and martial law was in force from July 1977 to March 1985. Gen. Zia declared himself president in September 1978, but was killed in a plane crash in August 1988. The Pakistan People's Party (PPP) won the election to the National Assembly and Benazir Bhutto became prime minister. In August 1990 the president dissolved the National Assembly and dismissed the Bhutto Cabinet. Elections were held in October 1990 and won by the Islamic Democratic Alliance, led by Mohammed Nawaz Sharif.

In July 1993, the Army intervened to end a power struggle between President Ishaq Khan and Prime Minister Sharif by replacing them with a caretaker administration until new elections were held in October. These were won by the PPP and Benazir Bhutto resumed the premiership. The PPP candidate Farooq Leghari was elected president by an electoral college of the National and provincial assemblies.

The Bhutto government was dismissed by the president in November 1996 for alleged corruption and economic mismanagement. Elections held in February 1997 were won by the Pakistan Muslim League with 134 seats; the PPP won only 18 seats. President Farooq Leghari resigned on 2 December 1997 following a dispute with Prime Minster Sharwaz. Muhammad Rafiq Tarar was subsequently elected president.

INSURGENCY

Since early 1994 there has been civil disorder in Sind province, especially in Karachi, in two conflicts: armed militants of the Mohajir Qaumi Movement (MQM) Party, which represents Urdu-speaking Indian Muslims who fled from India at partition and their descendants, are fighting for an autonomous Karachi province; and there is an armed conflict between Shia and Sunni fundamentalists.

POLITICAL SYSTEM

The legislature is bicameral. The *Majlis as-Shoora* (National Assembly) has a five-year term and comprises 237 members, of whom 207 are directly elected, 10 represent religious minorities and 20 are co-opted women. The Senate has 87 members, with a six-year term; half of the seats are renewed every three years. In January 1997 the interim government set up a Council for Defence and National Security including members of the Cabinet and armed forces to advise on foreign, defence and economic policies. The four provinces each have a provincial assembly and are represented in both legislative chambers.

The National Assembly amended the constitution in April 1997 to remove from the president the power to dismiss the government and dissolve parliament.

FEDERAL STRUCTURE

Province	Area (sq. km)	Population (1981)	Capital
Baluchistan	347,190	4,332,000	Quetta
Federal Capital Territory Islamabad	907	340,000	—
Federally Administered Tribal Areas	27,219	2,199,000	—
North-West Frontier Province	74,521	11,061,000	Peshawar
Punjab	205,344	47,292,000	Lahore
Sind	140,914	19,029	Karachi

HEAD OF STATE

President, Muhammad Rafiq Tarar, *sworn in* 1 January 1998

FEDERAL CABINET *as at July 1998*

Prime Minister, Mohammed Nawaz Sharif

Ministers of State, Ahmad Mahmood (*Environment, Local Government and Rural Development*); Mohammad Siddique Khan Kanju (*Foreign Affairs*); Azgar Ali Shah (*Housing and Construction*); Halim Siddiqui (*Water and Power*); Tahmina Daultana (*Women's Development, Social Welfare and Special Education*)

Attorney-General, Chaudary Farooq

Commerce, Investment, Mohammad Ishaq Dar

Communications, Mohammad Azam Hoti

Culture, Sports, Tourism, Youth Affairs, Labour, Manpower and Overseas Pakistanis, Sheikh Rashid Ahmed

Education, Ghous Ali Shah

Finance, Economic Affairs, Statistics, Planning and Development, Sartaj Aziz

Food and Agriculture, Abdul Sattar Laleka

Foreign Affairs, Gohar Ayub Khan

Health, Javed Hashemi

Implementation and Inspection Commission, Lt.-Gen. Malik Abdul Majeed

Industries, Maqbool Siddiqui

Information and Mass Media Development, Mushahid Hussain

Interior, Narcotics Control, Chaudary Shujat Hussain

Kashmir Affairs, Northern Areas, States and Frontier Regions, Abdul Majid Malik

Parliamentary Affairs, Mohammad Yasin Wattoo

Population Welfare, Social Welfare, Special Education, Environment, Local Government, Rural Development, Abida Hussain

Railways, Yaqub Khan Nasser

Religious Affairs, Minorities, Raja Zafarul Haq

Water, Power, Raja Nadir Pervez

Water, Power, Petroleum and Natural Resources, Chaudary Nissar Ali Khan

HIGH COMMISSION FOR PAKISTAN

35–36 Lowndes Square, London SW1X 9JN
Tel 0171-664 9200
High Commissioner, Mian Riaz Samee
Consul-General, Sajid Hussain Chattha
Defence and Naval Adviser, Cdre A. U. Khan

BRITISH HIGH COMMISSION

Diplomatic Enclave, Ramna 5, PO Box 1122, Islamabad
Tel: Islamabad 822131/5
High Commissioner, HE David Dain, CMG, apptd 1994
Deputy High Commissioners, J. W. Watt *(Islamabad)*; D. B. Merry *(Karachi)*
Counsellor (Economic and Commercial), G. J. Dorey, CVO
Counsellor, A. J. C. Boyd, OBE
Defence and Military Adviser, Brig. B. D. Wheelwright
DEPUTY HIGH COMMISSION – Karachi
CONSULATE – Lahore

BRITISH COUNCIL REPRESENTATIVE, P. Elwood, PO Box 1135, Islamabad. There are offices at Karachi, Lahore and Peshawar

DEFENCE

On 28 and 30 May 1998, Pakistan carried out six underground nuclear tests, less than a month after India had carried out its own nuclear tests. In doing so, it became the world's seventh declared nuclear power.

The Army has 2,120 main battle tanks, 850 armoured personnel carriers, 1,830 artillery pieces and 20 attack helicopters. The Navy has nine submarines, three destroyers, eight frigates, 13 patrol and coastal vessels, seven

combat aircraft and 12 armed helicopters based at Karachi. The Air Force has 429 combat aircraft.
MILITARY EXPENDITURE – 5.8 per cent of GDP (1996)
MILITARY PERSONNEL – 834,000: Army 520,000, Navy 22,000, Air Force 45,000, Paramilitaries 247,000

ECONOMY

Agriculture employs half the workforce and contributes a quarter of GDP. The principal crops are cotton, rice, wheat and sugar cane. Pakistan has one of the longest irrigation systems in the world, irrigating 42.5 million acres. There are large deposits of rock salt.

Pakistan also produces hides and skins, leather, wool, fertilizers, paints and varnishes, soda ash, paper, cement, fish, carpets, sports goods, surgical appliances and engineering goods, including switchgear, transformers, cables and wires.

In 1996 foreign exchange reserves fell below the US$1,000 million floor decreed by the IMF and the economy went into a severe recession. Attempts to impose taxes resulted in industrial action and capital flight. The Sharif government announced an economic revival programme in March 1997 including tax and tariff reductions. In October 1997, the government devalued the rupee by 8.5 per cent, citing the strong US dollar and the currency crisis in south-east Asia. The IMF agreed a loan of more than US$1.5 billion to help finance economic reforms.

Following condemnation of Pakistan's nuclear tests in May 1998, the international community imposed economic sanctions. The government immediately announced a series of spending cuts and severe austerity measures to counteract the sanctions and protect the economy.

In 1994 there was a trade deficit of US$2,228 million and a current account deficit of US$1,804 million.
GNP – US$63,567 million (1996); US$480 per capita (1996)
GDP – US$55,535 million (1994); US$434 per capita (1994)
ANNUAL AVERAGE GROWTH OF GDP – 5.9 per cent (1996)
INFLATION RATE – 10.4 per cent (1996)
UNEMPLOYMENT – 4.8 per cent (1994)
TOTAL EXTERNAL DEBT – US$29,901 million (1996)

TRADE

Principal imports are petroleum products, machinery, fertilizers, transport equipment, edible oils, chemicals and ferrous metals. Principal exports are cotton yarn and cloth, carpets, rice, petroleum products, textiles, leather and fish.

In 1996 imports totalled US$12,131 million and exports US$9,321 million.

Trade with UK	1996	1997
Imports from UK	£344,507,000	£267,899,000
Exports to UK	390,923,000	379,162,000

COMMUNICATIONS

There are major seaports at Karachi and Port Qasim. The main airports are at Karachi, Islamabad, Lahore, Peshawar and Quetta. Pakistan International Airlines operates air services between the principal cities as well as abroad. There are 179,752 km of roads and 8,163 km of rail track.

EDUCATION

Education consists of five years of primary education (five to nine years), three years of middle or lower secondary (general or vocational), two years of upper secondary, two years of higher secondary (intermediate) and two to five years of higher education in colleges and universities. Education is free to upper secondary level.
ILLITERACY RATE – 62.2 per cent
ENROLMENT (percentage of age group) – tertiary 3.0 per cent (1991)

PALAU
Republic of Palau

AREA – 177 sq. miles (459 sq. km)
POPULATION – 17,000 (1994 UN estimate); 15,122 (1990 census); 13,900 live on Koror and Babelthaup. The population is Micronesian, and predominantly Roman Catholic with a Protestant minority. Palauan and English are official languages
CAPITAL – Koror (population, 10,493, 1994)
CURRENCY – Currency is that of the USA
NATIONAL FLAG – Light blue with a yellow disc set near the hoist
POPULATION GROWTH RATE – 2.5 per cent (1995)
POPULATION DENSITY – 37 per sq. km (1995)

The Republic of Palau consists of 340 islands and islets in the western Pacific Ocean, of which eight are inhabited. Part of the Caroline Islands group, the Palau archipelago stretches over 400 miles (644 km) between 2° and 8°N., and 131° and 138°E. Koror island is about 810 miles (1,300 km) south-west of Guam and about 530 miles (852 km) south-east of Manila.

The islands vary in terrain from the highly mountainous to low coral atolls. The climate is tropical with a rainy season lasting from June to October; the average temperature is 27°C (80°F).

HISTORY AND POLITICS

Spain acquired sovereignty over the Caroline Islands, of which the Palau archipelago is part, in 1886. After defeat in the Spanish-American war of 1898, Spain sold its remaining Pacific possessions, including Palau, to Germany in 1899. On the outbreak of the First World War in 1914, Japan took control of Palau on behalf of the Allied powers, and Japanese administration was confirmed in a League of Nations mandate in 1921. During the Second World War Allied forces gained control of the archipelago after intense fighting. In 1947 the USA entered into agreement with the UN Security Council to administer the Micronesia area, including Palau, as the UN Trust Territory of the Pacific Islands.

In July 1978, the Palau electorate voted in a referendum not to join the new Federated States of Micronesia and instead became a separate part of the UN Trust Territory. A Compact of Free Association was signed with the USA in 1982, giving Palau internal sovereignty whilst leaving foreign policy to be decided by the USA. The compact only came into effect in November 1993, however, as successive referendums refused to allow US nuclear waste and weapons into Palau. The Compact was finally implemented on 1 October 1994. Under this agreement the USA recognized the Republic of Palau as a fully sovereign and independent state and assumed responsibility for its defence for 50 years; the UN Trust Territory of the Pacific Islands was terminated. Palau was admitted to UN membership in December 1994.

The last presidential and legislative elections were held in November 1996.

POLITICAL SYSTEM

Executive power is vested in the president and vice-president, who are elected for four-year terms; the president appoints the Cabinet. There is a bicameral legislature (*Olbiil era Kelulau*) composed of the 16-member House of Delegates (one member elected from each of the 16 constituent states) and the 14-member Senate. There is also a Council of Chiefs to advise the president on matters concerning traditional law and customs. Each of the 16 component states have their own elected governors and legislatures.

HEAD OF STATE

President, Kuniwo Nakamura, *elected* 4 November 1992
Vice-President, Administration, Tommy Remengesau

CABINET *as at July 1998*

Commerce and Trade, George Ngirarsaol
Community and Cultural Affairs, Riosang Salvador
Education, Billy Kuartei
Health, Masao Ueda
Justice, Salvador Ingereklii
Minister of State, Sabias Anastacio
Resources and Development, Marcelino Melairei
BRITISH AMBASSADOR, HE Vernon Scarborough, resident at Suva, Fiji

ECONOMY

The economy remains heavily dependent on US financial support, which the USA is committed to giving under the Compact. Fisheries, tourism, subsistence agriculture and government service are the main areas of employment. Agricultural products include coconuts and copra, and Palau earns significant revenue from the sale of fishing licences to foreign fleets fishing for tuna. Tourism is being developed; there are 40,000 visitors annually. On 17 December 1997, Palau joined the International Monetary Fund, becoming its 182nd member. Its initial quota was set at 2.25 million special drawing rights.

The USA carried out an infrastructure improvement programme in the 1970s and 1980s. There are now three airports on Koror, Peleliu and Angaur which have daily flights from Guam operated by Continental Air Micronesia. Ocean freight services to Palau are provided by two shipping lines to the port at Koror. A communications centre on Arakabesang Island handles international telephone, telex, cable and facsimile communications. There is a privately owned television station and a government-operated radio station.
GDP – US$85 million (1994); US$5,833 per capita (1994)

EDUCATION AND SOCIAL WELFARE

There is a free public school system which, together with independent missionary schools, provides primary and secondary education. A tertiary technical school has been established on Koror since 1969. General medical and dental care is provided by a public hospital and a medical clinic.

PANAMA
República de Panama

AREA – 29,157 sq. miles (75,517 sq. km). Neighbours: Colombia (east), Costa Rica (west)
POPULATION – 2,631,000 (1995 estimate). Spanish is the official language

CAPITAL – ΨPanama City (population, 658,000, 1995 estimate)
CURRENCY – Balboa of 100 centésimos (US notes are also in circulation)
NATIONAL ANTHEM – Alcanzamos Por Fin La Victoria (Victory is ours at last)
NATIONAL DAY – 3 November
NATIONAL FLAG – Four quarters; white with blue star (top, next staff), red (in fly), blue (below, next staff) and white with red star
LIFE EXPECTANCY (years) – male 70.85; female 75.00
POPULATION GROWTH RATE – 1.9 per cent (1995)
POPULATION DENSITY – 35 per sq. km (1995)
URBAN POPULATION – 54.9 per cent (1995)
MILITARY EXPENDITURE – 1.4 per cent of GDP (1996)
ILLITERACY RATE – 9.2 per cent
ENROLMENT (percentage of age group) – primary 91 per cent (1990); secondary 51 per cent (1990); tertiary 30.0 per cent (1995)

HISTORY AND POLITICS

After a revolt in 1903, Panama declared its independence from Colombia and established a separate government. After 1968, control of Panama was increasingly taken over by Gen. Omar Torrijos, commander of the National Guard, following a military coup. In 1978 Gen. Torrijos withdrew from the government, and Dr Aristides Royo was elected president by the Assembly of Representatives.

An attempt in February 1988 by President Delvalle to remove Gen. Noriega as Commander of the Defence Forces failed. Noriega ousted Delvalle and replaced him with Manuel Solis Palma. Presidential elections were held in May 1989 but Noriega annulled the results and on 15 December he assumed power formally as head of state. On 20 December US troops invaded Panama to oust Noriega. Guillermo Endara, believed to have won the May elections, was installed as president. In December 1991 the Legislative Assembly approved a change to the constitution which abolished the armed forces.

The most recent presidential election, on 8 May 1994, was won by Ernesto Pérez Balladares of the Democratic Revolutionary Party (PRD).

POLITICAL SYSTEM

Legislative power is vested in a unicameral Legislative Assembly of 72 members; executive power is held by the president, assisted by two elected vice-presidents and an appointed Cabinet. Elections are held every five years under a system of universal and compulsory adult suffrage.

HEAD OF STATE

President, Ernesto Pérez Balladares, *elected* 8 May 1994, *sworn in* 1 September 1994
First Vice-President, Gabriel Altamirano Duque
Second Vice-President, Felipe Alejandro Virzi

CABINET *as at July 1998*
Agricultural Development, Carlos Sousa Lennox (ex-PA)
Canal Affairs, Jorge Ritter
Commerce and Industry, Raúl Hernández López (PLN)
Education, Pablo Thalassinos (Ind.)
Finance and Treasury, Miguel Heras Castro (Ind.)
Foreign Relations, Ricardo Alberto Arias (Ind.)
Health, Aida de Rivera (Ind.)
Housing, Dr Francisco Sánchez Cárdenas (PRD)
Interior and Justice, Raúl Montenegro (PRD)
Labour and Social Welfare, Mitchel Doens (PRD)
Planning, Guillermo Chapman (ex-PDC)
Presidency, Olmedo Miranda (PRD)

Public Works, Luis Blanco (PRD)
Women, Youth and Family, Leonor Calderón
PA Arnulfist Party; PLN National Liberal Party; Ind.
Independent; PRD Democratic Revolutionary Party;
PDC Christian Democrat Party

EMBASSY OF THE REPUBLIC OF PANAMA
48 Park Street, London WIY 3PD
Tel 0171-493 4646
Chargé d'Affaires, Alberto Watson Fabrega

BRITISH EMBASSY
Torre Swiss Bank, Calle 53 (Apartado 889) Zona 1, Panama
City
Tel: Panama City 269 0866
Ambassador Extraordinary and Plenipotentiary, HE William B.
  Sinton, apptd 1996

ECONOMY

The soil is moderately fertile, but nearly one-half of the
land is uncultivated. The chief crops are bananas, sugar,
coconuts, coffee and cereals. The shrimping industry plays
an important role in the economy. Tourism is the principal
foreign currency earner. A railway joins the Atlantic and
Pacific oceans.
GNP – US$8,249 million (1996); US$3,080 per capita
  (1996)
GDP – US$6,571 million (1994); US$2,550 per capita
  (1994)
ANNUAL AVERAGE GROWTH OF GDP – 2.5 per cent (1996)
INFLATION RATE – 1.3 per cent (1996)
UNEMPLOYMENT – 13.7 per cent (1995)
TOTAL EXTERNAL DEBT – US$6,990 million (1996)

TRADE

Imports are mostly manufactured goods, machinery,
lubricants, chemicals and foodstuffs. Exports are bananas,
petroleum products, shrimps, sugar, meat, coffee and
fishmeal.

In 1995 Panama had a trade deficit of US$575 million
and a current account deficit of US$343 million. Imports
totalled US$2,511 million and exports US$625 million.

Trade with UK †	1996	1997
Imports from UK	£66,942,000	£79,453,000
Exports to UK	11,186,000	7,783,000

†Including Colon Free Zone

THE PANAMA CANAL ZONE

With effect from 1 October 1979 the Canal Zone (647 sq.
miles) was disestablished, with all areas of land and water
within the Zone reverting to Panama. By the 1977 treaty
with the USA, the USA is allowed the use of operating
bases for the Panama Canal, together with several military
bases, but the Republic of Panama is sovereign in all such
areas. Control of the Canal will revert to Panama at noon
on 31 December 1999.

DEPENDENCIES

Taboga Island (area 4 sq. miles) is a popular tourist resort
some 12 miles from the Pacific entrance to the Panama
Canal.

Tourist facilities have also been developed in the Las
Perlas Archipelago in the Gulf of Panama, particularly on
the island of Contadora, as well as on the San Blas Islands in
the Atlantic.

There is a penal settlement at Guardia on the island of
Coiba (area 19 sq. miles) in the Gulf of Chiriqui.

PAPUA NEW GUINEA

AREA – 178,704 sq. miles (462,840 sq. km). Neighbour: Indonesia (west, on New Guinea)
POPULATION – 4,074,000 (1994 UN estimate). English is the official language; Hiri Motu and Neo-Melanesian are widely used
CAPITAL – ΨPort Moresby (population, 173,500, 1990)
MAJOR CITIES – Goroka; Lae; Madang; Mount Hagen; Rabaul; Wewak
CURRENCY – Kina (K) of 100 toea
NATIONAL ANTHEM – Arise All You Sons
NATIONAL DAY – 16 September (Independence Day)
NATIONAL FLAG – Divided diagonally red (fly) and black (hoist); on the red a soaring Bird of Paradise in yellow and on the black five white stars of the Southern Cross
LIFE EXPECTANCY (years) – male 55.16; female 56.68
POPULATION GROWTH RATE – 1.9 per cent (1995)
POPULATION DENSITY – 9 per sq. km (1995)
MILITARY EXPENDITURE – 1.4 per cent of GDP (1996)
MILITARY PERSONNEL – 4,300: Army 3,800, Navy 400, Air Force 100
ILLITERACY RATE – 27.8 per cent
ENROLMENT (percentage of age group) – tertiary 3.2 per cent (1995)

The country has many island groups, principally the Bismarck Archipelago, a portion of the Solomon Islands, the Trobriands, the D'Entrecasteaux Islands and the Louisade Archipelago. The main islands of the Bismarck Archipelago are New Britain, New Ireland and Manus. Bougainville is the largest of the Solomon Islands within Papua New Guinea.

Papua New Guinea lies within the tropics and has a typically monsoonal climate. Temperature and humidity are uniformly high throughout the year.

HISTORY AND POLITICS

New Guinea was sighted by Portuguese and Spanish navigators in the early 16th century, but remained largely isolated from the rest of the world. In 1884 a British protectorate, British New Guinea, was proclaimed over the southern coast of New Guinea (Papua) and the adjacent islands, which were annexed outright in 1888. In 1906 the Territory of British New Guinea was placed under the authority of Australia.

In 1884 Germany had formally taken possession of certain northern areas, later known as the Trust Territory of New Guinea. In 1914 the German areas were occupied by Australian troops and remained under military administration until 1921, when they became a League of Nations mandate administered by Australia. New Guinea was administered under the mandate and Papua under the Papua Act until the invasion by the Japanese in 1942 when the civil administration was suspended until the Japanese surrendered in 1945.

From 1970 there was a gradual assumption of powers by the Papua New Guinea government, culminating in formal self-government in December 1973. Papua New Guinea achieved full independence within the Commonwealth on 16 September 1975.

Following elections in June 1997, a coalition government was formed by Pangu, the People's Progress Party and the People's National Congress, under Prime Minister Bill Skate.

During 1997, the country was affected by a severe drought attributed to the El Niño weather system. By September 1997, 700,000 people were affected, with the cost of the relief effort estimated at US$500,000 per day. In July 1998, the north coast of Papua New Guinea was devastated by a tidal wave that killed more than 1,600 people and washed away entire villages, leaving more than 6,000 people homeless.

INSURGENCIES

Separatist aspirations, dormant since independence, re-emerged in 1989 when the Bougainville Revolutionary Army (BRA) mounted a successful insurrection. Government security forces withdrew from the island, enabling the BRA to declare an independent republic in May 1990. A peace accord was signed in January 1991, although the question of Bougainville's status was left unresolved. Fighting resumed and government forces returned to the island in October 1992, subsequently capturing 90 per cent of rebel-held territory. The government launched a new offensive in June 1996 after peace talks failed to produce a breakthrough. At least 7,000 people, mostly civilians, have died as a result of the insurrection.

A permanent cease-fire came into effect on 30 April 1998, bringing to an end the nine-year civil war. A small group of rebels led by Francis Ona vowed to continue the armed campaign for an independent Bougainville.

POLITICAL SYSTEM

Elections are held every five years. The National Parliament comprises 109 elected members, 20 from regional electorates, the remainder from open electorates. The Governor-General is appointed by parliament for a six-year term. Provincial governments were abolished in August 1995, and replaced with councils combining local and national politicians and headed by an appointed governor.

Governor-General, HE Silas Atopare, GCMG, appointed 14 November 1997

NATIONAL EXECUTIVE COUNCIL *as at July 1998*
Prime Minister, Information, Bill Skate (PNC)
Deputy P.M., Trade and Industry, Michael Nali (PPP)
Agriculture and Livestock, Tukape Masani
Bougainville Affairs, Sam Akoitai (Ind.)
Civil Aviation, Kala Swokin (Ind.)
Correctional Services, Peter Arul
Defence, Peter Waieng (PPP)
Education, Culture and Science, Muki Taranupi
Environment and Conservation, Herowa Agiwa
Family and Church Affairs, Titus Philemon
Finance, Dibara Yagbo (PNC)
Fisheries and Marine Resources, Sir Mekere Morauta
Foreign Affairs, Roy Yaki
Forests and Public Enterprises, Fabian Pok (Ind.)
Health, Ludger Mondo (PPP)
Housing, Mao Zeming (PDM)
Industrial Relations, Samson Napo
Justice, Jacob Wama (Ind.)
Lands, Viviso Seravo (PDM)
Mining and Energy, Philemon Embel (PPP)
Petroleum and Gas, Masket Iangalio
Police, Thomas Palika (LNA)
Provincial and Local Government, Simon Kaumi (PNC)
Public Service, Ian Ling-Stuckey (PNC)
Senior Minister of State, Sir Rabbie Namaliu
Transport, Vincent Auali
Treasury and Corporate Affairs, Iairo Lasaro (PDM)
Works, Yauwe Riyong
Youth and Employment, Mathias Karani

PPP People's Progress Party; PDM People's Democratic Movement; PNC People's National Congress; PAP

People's Action Party; LNA League for National Advancement; Ind. Independent

PAPUA NEW GUINEA HIGH COMMISSION
3rd Floor, 14 Waterloo Place, London SWIR 4AR
Tel 0171-930 0922/7
High Commissioner, HE Sir Kina Bona, KBE, apptd 1995

BRITISH HIGH COMMISSION
PO Box 212, Waigani NCD 131, Port Moresby
Tel: Port Moresby 325 1643
High Commissioner, HE Charles Drace-Francis, CMG, apptd 1997

ECONOMY

Until the 1970s the economy was based almost entirely on agriculture, principally copra, cocoa, tea, coffee, palm oil, rubber, groundnuts, spices and timber. A variety of commercial agricultural developments co-exist with the traditional rural economy. In 1995, the government initiated an austerity programme intended to reduce the budget deficit, privatize state assets and eliminate trade tariffs. Following prolonged drought and the financial crisis in south-east Asia, the country is facing its worst financial crisis since independence, with debt servicing amounting to a quarter of government spending.

There are extensive mineral deposits throughout Papua New Guinea, including copper, gold, silver, nickel, bauxite and commercial deposits of oil. The Bougainville copper mine closed indefinitely in 1989 because of the unrest on the island. It had provided more than 15 per cent of the country's annual revenue.

Industry includes processing of primary products, and brewing, packaging, paint, plywood, and metal manufacturing and the construction industries.

In 1995 there was a trade surplus of US$1,408 million and a current account surplus of US$674 million. In 1996 imports totalled US$1,730 million and exports US$2,501 million.

GNP – US$5,049 million (1996); US$1,150 per capita (1996)

GDP – US$4,804 million (1994); US$1,267 per capita (1994)

ANNUAL AVERAGE GROWTH OF GDP – 13.3 per cent (1993)

INFLATION RATE – 11.6 per cent (1996)

TOTAL EXTERNAL DEBT – US$2,359 million (1996)

TRADE WITH UK	1996	1997
Imports from UK	£7,976,000	£11,476,000
Exports to UK	107,149,000	93,201,000

COMMUNICATIONS

Air Niugini operates regular air services to other countries in the region, as well as internal air services. Several shipping companies operate cargo services to Australia, Europe, the Far East and USA. There are very limited cargo and passenger services between Papua New Guinea main ports, outports, plantations and missions. Road communications are very limited, the most important road being that linking Lae with the populous highlands. Papua New Guinea is linked by international cable to Australia, Guam, Hong Kong, Kota Kinabalu, the Far East and USA. Telecommunications are widely available.

PARAGUAY
República del Paraguay

AREA – 157,048 sq. miles (406,752 sq. km). Neighbours: Bolivia (north-west), Brazil (north-east and east), Argentina (south)

POPULATION – 5,085,325 (1994 UN estimate). Spanish is the official language of the country but outside the larger towns Guaraní, the language of the largest single group of original Indian inhabitants, is widely spoken, and is also an official language

CAPITAL – Asunción (population, 718,690)

MAJOR CITIES – Ciudad del Este (133,881); San Lorenzo (133,395)

CURRENCY – Guaraní (Gs) of 100 céntimos

NATIONAL ANTHEM – Paraguayos, República O Muerte (Paraguayans, republic or death)

NATIONAL DAY – 15 May

NATIONAL FLAG – Three horizontal bands, red, white, blue with the National seal on the obverse white band and the Treasury seal on the reverse white band

LIFE EXPECTANCY (years) – male 66.30; female 70.83

POPULATION GROWTH RATE – 2.7 per cent (1995)

POPULATION DENSITY – 12 per sq. km (1995)

URBAN POPULATION – 50.3 per cent (1992)

MILITARY EXPENDITURE – 1.2 per cent of GDP (1996)

MILITARY PERSONNEL – 35,000: Army 14,900, Navy 3,600, Air Force 1,700, Paramilitaries 14,800

CONSCRIPTION DURATION – One to two years

Paraguay is an inland subtropical state of South America, situated between Argentina, Bolivia and Brazil. It is a country of grassy plains and forested hills. In the angle formed by the Paraná-Paraguay confluence are extensive marshes, one of which, known as Neembucú (or endless) is drained by Lake Ypoa, a large lagoon south-east of the capital. The Chaco, lying between the rivers Paraguay and Pilcomayo and bounded on the north by Bolivia, is a flat plain, rising uniformly towards its western boundary to a height of 1,140 feet; it suffers much from floods and still more from drought, but the building of dams and reservoirs has converted part of it into good pasture for cattle.

HISTORY AND POLITICS

In 1535 Paraguay was settled as a Spanish possession. In 1811 it declared its independence from Spain.

Gen. Alfredo Stroessner, dictator from 1954, was overthrown in February 1989 by Gen. Andrés Rodríguez, who was elected president in May 1989. In May 1991, the first free municipal elections were held, and elections to the parliament were held in December 1991. Amendments to the constitution came into effect in June 1992. The last presidential and legislative elections were held on 10 May 1998. The presidential election was won by Raúl Cubas Grau of the Colorado Party, after its original candidate Gen. Lino Oviedo was banned from standing in elections for his part in a failed coup in 1996. In the legislative election, the distribution of seats in the Senate was: Colorado Party (CP) 24; Democratic Alliance (DA) 20; Blanco Party 1. In the Chamber of Deputies, the CP won 45 seats and the DA 35.

POLITICAL SYSTEM

The constitution provides for a two-chamber legislature consisting of a 45-member Senate and an 80-member Chamber of Deputies, both elected for five-year terms. Deputies are elected on a regional basis, the number of seats allocated to each regional department being directly proportional to the department's population. Voting is compulsory for all citizens over 18. The president is elected for a five-year term and may not be re-elected. The vice-president may only contest the presidency if he resigns his post six months before the election. The president appoints the Cabinet, which exercises all the functions of government.

HEAD OF STATE
President, Raúl Cubas Grau, *elected* 10 May 1998, *sworn in* 15 August 1998
Vice-President, Luis María Argaña

CABINET *as at August 1998*
Agriculture and Cattle Raising, Hipólito Pereira
Defence, José Segovia Boltes
Education and Worship, Celsa Bareiro de Soto
Finance, Gerardo Doll
Foreign Affairs, Dido Florentín Bogado
Health, Carmen Frutos de Almada
Industry and Commerce, Carlos Cubas
Interior, José Rubén Arias Mendoza
Justice and Labour, Angel Campos
Public Works, Communications, Victor Segovia Rios
Social and Economic Planning, Gustavo Leite
Women, Haide Carmagnola de Aquino

EMBASSY OF PARAGUAY
Braemar Lodge, Cornwall Gardens, London SW7 4AQ
Tel 0171-937 1253
Ambassador Extraordinary and Plenipotentiary, Raúl Dos Santos, apptd 1998

BRITISH EMBASSY
Calle Presidente Franco 706 (PO Box 404), Asunción
Tel: Asunción 444472
Ambassador Extraordinary and Plenipotentiary and Consul-General, HE Andrew George, apptd 1998

ECONOMY

President Rodríguez introduced an economic liberalization programme which has been continued by subsequent governments. This has reduced foreign debt and attracted foreign investment, notably from Brazil. About half of the population are engaged in agriculture and cattle raising. Cassava, sugar cane, soya, cotton and wheat are the main agricultural products. The forests contain many varieties of timber which find a good market abroad.

Paraguay's rivers are of considerable hydroelectric capacity. There is a hydroelectric power station at Acaray which exports surplus power to Argentina and Brazil. Joint projects have been undertaken with Brazil, on a hydroelectric dam at Itaipú (the largest in the world), and with Argentina, at Yacyretá.

GNP – US$9,179 million (1996); US$1,850 per capita (1996)
GDP – US$6,098 million (1994); US$1,593 per capita (1994)
ANNUAL AVERAGE GROWTH OF GDP – 1.3 per cent (1996)
INFLATION RATE – 9.8 per cent (1996)
UNEMPLOYMENT – 4.4 per cent (1994)
TOTAL EXTERNAL DEBT – US$2,141 million (1996)

TRADE

The chief imports are machinery, fuels and lubricants, vehicles, drinks and tobacco. The chief exports are soya, cotton fibres, meat, timber and coffee. The main trading partners are Brazil, Argentina and the USA.

In 1994 Paraguay had a trade deficit of US$1,277 million and a current account deficit of US$749 million. In 1995 imports totalled US$3,144 million and exports US$919 million.

Trade with UK	1996	1997
Imports from UK	£55,019,000	£64,147,000
Exports to UK	15,802,000	4,785,000

COMMUNICATIONS

There are direct shipping services from Asunción to Europe and the USA, and river steamer services for internal transport. Eight airlines operate services from Asunción. There are 27,741 km (1990) of asphalted roads in Paraguay, connecting Asunción with São Paulo (26 hours) via the Bridge of Friendship and Foz de Yguazú, and with Buenos Aires (24 hours) via Puerto Pilcomayo. There are about 4,050 miles of earth roads liable to be closed or to become impassable in wet weather. Rail services, with train ferries, provide internal and international links. Five daily and six weekly newspapers are published in Asunción.

EDUCATION

Education is free and compulsory. There is a National University in Asunción and a Catholic University.
ILLITERACY RATE – 7.9 per cent
ENROLMENT (percentage of age group) – primary 89 per cent (1994); secondary 33 per cent (1994); tertiary 10.3 per cent (1993)

PERU
República del Peru

AREA – 496,225 sq. miles (1,285,216 sq. km). Neighbours: Ecuador and Colombia (north), Brazil and Bolivia (east), Chile (south)
POPULATION – 23,532,000 (1994 UN estimate). Spanish, the language of the original Spanish stock from which the governing and professional classes are mainly recruited, is an official language, together with Quechua and Aymará. Quechua and Aymará are spoken by more than half the population
CAPITAL – Lima (including ΨCallao, population, 6,483,901, 1993 census)
MAJOR CITIES – Arequipa (624,500); Chiclayo (448,400); Chimbote (314,700); Trujillo (521,200)
CURRENCY – New Sol of 100 cénts
NATIONAL ANTHEM – Somos Libres, Seámoslo Siempre (We are free, let us remain so forever)
NATIONAL DAY – 28 July (Anniversary of Independence)
NATIONAL FLAG – Three vertical stripes of red, white, red
LIFE EXPECTANCY (years) – male 62.74; female 66.55
POPULATION GROWTH RATE – 1.7 per cent (1995)
POPULATION DENSITY – 18 per sq. km (1995)
URBAN POPULATION – 71.2 per cent (1995)

The country is traversed throughout its length by the Andes, running parallel to the Pacific coast. There are three main regions, the Costa, west of the Andes, the Sierra or mountain ranges of the Andes, which include the Punas or mountainous wastes below the region of perpetual snow, and the Montaña or Selva, which is the vast area of jungle stretching from the eastern foothills of the Andes to the eastern frontiers of Peru. The coastal area, lying upon and near the Pacific, is not tropical though close to the Equator, being cooled by the Humboldt Current.

HISTORY AND POLITICS

Peru was conquered in the early 16th century by Francisco Pizarro (1478–1541). He subjugated the Incas (the ruling caste of the Quechua Indians), who had started their rise to power some 500 years earlier, and for nearly three centuries Peru remained under Spanish rule. A revolutionary war of 1821–4 established its independence, declared on 28 July 1821. A military junta ruled Peru from 1968 until 1980 when civilian government was restored.

In April 1992 President Fujimori, faced with increasing terrorist violence, suspended the constitution, dissolved Congress and began to govern by decree. A programme of market-orientated economic reform, new anti-terrorist measures, and a streamlining of the executive, legislative and judicial institutions was undertaken. In November 1992 a legislative election was held to an 80-seat Democratic Constituent Congress (CCD) which was installed as an interim legislature and constituent assembly to write a new constitution. Parties supporting Fujimori's suspension of the constitution gained a majority in the CCD. In January 1993, the 1979 constitution was re-established and the CCD declared Fujimori constitutional head of state. The CCD produced a new constitution which was endorsed in a national referendum in October 1993.

Parliamentary and presidential elections were held on 9 April 1995, with President Fujimori winning the first round of the presidential election outright and his Cambio 90-Nueva Mayoría Party winning 67 out of 120 seats in the new Congress.

FOREIGN RELATIONS

A 50-mile stretch of the border with Ecuador has been in dispute since 1960. In 1995 an inconclusive border war was fought between the two countries, and in July 1995 a demilitarized zone was established around the disputed area. Talks are continuing to try to resolve the issue.

INSURGENCIES

Since the late 1970s the government has faced violence from drug organizations and insurgencies from two leftist guerrilla movements, the Maoist Sendero Luminoso (Shining Path) and the Movimiento Revolucionario Tupac Amaru (MRTA). Some areas of the country remain under states of emergency, but the capture of the leaders of both groups in 1992 and the anti-terrorist clampdown from 1992 to 1994 has reduced violence considerably. The Shining Path continues to launch attacks on security forces and infrastructure and has engaged in mass intimidation and execution campaigns in rural areas, with fighting having left 30,000 dead.

In 1996–7 the MRTA re-emerged, overrunning the residence of the Japanese ambassador and seizing hostages. The 126-day siege ended when Peruvian commandos stormed the building, killing all 14 terrorists. One hostage was wounded in the assault and later died.

POLITICAL SYSTEM

The constitution, promulgated in December 1993, provides for the president to be able to serve two terms rather than one, as previously; the introduction of the death penalty for terrorists; and the formation of a new 120-member unicameral Congress. A constitutional panel approved a Bill in August 1996, allowing President Fujimori to stand for a third term in office, though it is likely that a third term would have to be approved by a national referendum.

HEAD OF STATE

President of the Republic, Alberto Fujimori, *assumed office* 28 July 1990, *re-elected* 9 April 1995, *sworn in* 28 July 1995
First Vice-President, Ricardo Márquez Flores
Second Vice-President, César Paredes Canto

CABINET *as at July 1998*

Prime Minister, Alberto Pandolfi
Advancement of Women and Human Development, Miriam Schenone
Agriculture, Rodolfo Muñante Sanguinetti
Attorney-General, Blanca Nelida Colán
Central Reserve Bank, German Suárez Chávez
Defence, Julio Salazar
Economy and Finance, vacant
Education, Domingo Palermo Cabrejos
Energy and Mines, Daniel Hokama Tokashiki
Fisheries, Ludwig Meier Cornejo
Foreign Affairs, Eduardo Ferrero Costa
Health, Marino Costa Bauer
Industry, Tourism, Integration and International Trade, Alberto Cailloux
Interior, Gen. José Villanueva Ruesta
Justice, Alfredo Quispe Correa
Labour and Social Promotion, Jorge González Izquierdo
Transport, Communications, Housing and Construction, Antonio Paúcar

EMBASSY OF PERU
52 Sloane Street, London SW1X 9SP
Tel 0171-235 1917/2545/3802
Ambassador Extraordinary and Plenipotentiary, HE Eduardo Ponce-Vivanco, apptd 1995

BRITISH EMBASSY
Edificio El Pacifico Washington, Piso 12, Plaza Washington (PO Box 854), Lima 100
Tel: Lima 334738
Ambassador Extraordinary and Plenipotentiary, HE John Illman, apptd 1995

CONSULAR OFFICE – Lima
HONORARY CONSULATES – Arequipa, Cusco, Iquitos, Piura, Trujillo

BRITISH COUNCIL DIRECTOR, C. Brown, Calle Alberto Lynch 110, San Isidro, Lima 27

DEFENCE

The Army has 300 main battle tanks, 276 armoured personnel carriers, 276 artillery pieces, 25 aircraft and 59 helicopters. The Navy has eight submarines, two cruisers, one destroyer, four frigates, seven patrol and coastal vessels, seven combat aircraft and 13 armed helicopters at eight bases. The Air Force has 101 combat aircraft and 23 armed helicopters.

MILITARY EXPENDITURE – 1.7 per cent of GDP (1996)
MILITARY PERSONNEL – 203,000: Army 85,000, Navy 25,000, Air Force 15,000, Paramilitaries 78,000
CONSCRIPTION DURATION – Two years

ECONOMY

The chief products of the coastal belt are cotton, sugar and petroleum. There are large tracts of land suitable for cultivation and stock-raising (cattle, sheep, llamas, alpacas and vicuñas) on the eastern slopes of the Andes, and in the mountain valleys maize, potatoes and wheat are grown. The jungle area is a source of timber and petroleum. Other major crops are fruit, vegetables, rice, barley, grapes and coffee. The mountains contain rich mineral deposits and mineral exports include lead, zinc, copper, iron ore and silver. Peru is normally the world's largest exporter of fishmeal.

Since 1990 the government has launched a radical free-market restructuring programme which has rebuilt the foreign exchange reserves from virtually zero, reduced inflation from 7,600 per cent a year in 1990 to 11.5 per cent in 1996, cut subsidies and import tariffs, freed interest rates and privatized most state firms. Foreign investment has been encouraged and has grown dramatically. The economic recovery has increased the gap between rich and poor.

GNP – US$58,671 million (1996); US$2,420 per capita (1996)
GDP – US$42,436 million (1994); US$2,128 per capita (1994)
ANNUAL AVERAGE GROWTH OF GDP – 2.6 per cent (1996)
INFLATION RATE – 11.5 per cent (1996)
UNEMPLOYMENT – 7.1 per cent (1995)
TOTAL EXTERNAL DEBT – US$29,176 million (1996)

TRADE

The principal imports are machinery, chemicals and pharmaceutical products. The chief exports are minerals and metals, fishmeal, sugar, cotton and coffee.

In 1996 Peru had a trade deficit of US$2,000 million and a current account deficit of US$3,607 million. Imports totalled US$9,472 million and exports US$5,897 million.

Trade with UK	1996	1997
Imports from UK	£62,876,000	£85,700,000
Exports to UK	130,434,000	147,561,000

COMMUNICATIONS

In recent years the coastal and sierra zones have been opened up by means of roads and air routes. There is air communication, as well as communication by protracted land routes, with the tropical and eastern zones which lie east of the Andes towards the borders of Brazil. The Andean Highway forms a link between the Pacific, the Amazon and the Atlantic. The Pan-American Highway runs along the Peruvian coast connecting it with Ecuador and Chile.

The railway is administered by the government. There is also steam navigation on the Ucayali and Huallaga, and in the south on Lake Titicaca. Air services are maintained throughout Peru, and there is an international airport at Lima.

EDUCATION

Education is compulsory and free between seven and 16. There are 51 universities.

ILLITERACY RATE – 11.3 per cent
ENROLMENT (percentage of age group) – primary 91 per cent (1994); secondary 53 per cent (1994); tertiary 31.1 per cent (1994)

THE PHILIPPINES
Repúblika ng Pilipinas

AREA – 115,831 sq. miles (300,000 sq. km)
POPULATION – 70,267,000 (1994 UN estimate). The inhabitants are of Malay stock, with admixtures of Spanish and Chinese blood in many localities. The Chinese minority is estimated at 500,000, with smaller numbers of Spanish, American and Indian. About 90 per cent are Christian, predominantly Roman Catholics. Most of the remainder are Muslims or indigenous animists. The official languages are Filipino and English. Filipino is based on Tagalog, one of the Malay–Polynesian languages. English, the language of government, is spoken by at least 44 per cent of the population. Spanish is now spoken by a very small minority

CAPITAL – ΨManila (population, 8,594,150, 1994)
MAJOR CITIES – Bacolod (343,048); ΨCebu (699,196); ΨDavao (960,910); ΨIloilo (302,200); ΨZamboanga (464,466), 1994 estimates
CURRENCY – Philippine peso (P) of 100 centavos
NATIONAL ANTHEM – Bayang Magiliw
NATIONAL DAY – 12 June (Independence Day 1898)
NATIONAL FLAG – Equal horizontal bands of blue (above) and red; gold sun with three stars on a white triangle next staff
LIFE EXPECTANCY (years) – male 63.10; female 66.70
POPULATION GROWTH RATE – 2.7 per cent (1995)
POPULATION DENSITY – 234 per sq. km (1995)
URBAN POPULATION – 42.7 per cent (1990)

There are eleven larger islands and 7,079 other islands. The principal islands (area in sq. miles) are: Luzon (40,422); Mindoro (3,759); Mindanao (36,538); Leyte (2,786); Samar (5,050); Cebu (1,703); Negros (4,906); Bohol (1,492); Palawan (4,550); Masbate (1,262); Panay (4,446). Other groups are the Sulu islands (capital, Jolo), Babuyanes and Batanes; the Calamian islands; and Kalayaan Islands.

HISTORY AND POLITICS

The Portuguese navigator Magellan came to the Philippines in 1521 and was killed by the natives of Mactan, a small island near Cebu. In 1565 Spain undertook the conquest of the country, which was named Filipinas after Philip II of Spain. In 1896 the Filipinos revolted against Spanish rule and declared their independence on 12 June 1898. In the Spanish–American War of 1898, Manila was captured by American troops with the help of Filipinos, and the islands were ceded to the USA by the Treaty of Paris in 1898. Despite a rebellion against US rule between 1899 and 1902, the Americans remained in control of the country until 1946. The Republic of the Philippines came into existence on 4 July 1946.

Ferdinand Marcos was president from 1965 to 1986. Although he gained a majority of votes in the official count of a presidential election in February 1986, the election was marred by widespread electoral abuse and his rival, Mrs Corazón Aquino, launched a campaign of non-violent civil disturbance which gained wide support. On 25 February Marcos fled to Hawaii. Mrs Aquino took over as president and survived seven coup attempts.

Fidel Ramos was elected president in May 1992 and managed to overcome the attempted coups and legislative obstructiveness that had plagued President Aquino. The presidential election in May 1998 was won by the former vice-president, Joseph Estrada.

Legislative elections were held on 11 May 1998. The coalition of the Lakas ng EDSA/National Union of Christian Democrats won a majority in the House of Representatives.

INSURGENCIES

On 2 September 1996, the government signed an agreement with the Moro National Liberation Front (MNLF) on the creation of an autonomous Muslim region in Mindanao, Palawan, Sulu and Basilan, ending a 24-year rebellion which had left more than 120,000 people dead. The Moro Islamic Liberation Front (MILF), a radical breakaway group, threatened an upsurge in violence to disrupt the agreement. The Communist New People's Army (NPA) maintains a presence in eastern Mindanao, Negros, Samar, Bicol, the mountains of northern Luzon and Bataan. The NPA signed a cease-fire agreement with the government in December 1993; peace talks are continuing. In January 1998 there was renewed fighting as the government and MILF accused each other of breaking the cease-fire of July 1997.

POLITICAL SYSTEM

A new constitution came into force in July 1987. Legislative authority is vested in a bicameral Congress. The House of Representatives has 250 members, of whom 204 are directly elected and 46 appointed by the president for a three-year term. The Senate has 24 members, of whom 12 are re-elected every three years.

The Autonomous Region of Mindanao consists of four provinces: Sulu, Tawitawi, Lanao del Sur and Maguinadanao. There is a 24-member regional assembly and a Governor.

HEAD OF STATE
President, Minister of the Interior, Joseph Estrada, *assumed office* 30 June 1998
Vice-President, Social Welfare, Gloria Arroyo

CABINET *as at July 1998*
Agrarian Reform, Horacio Morales
Agriculture, William Dollente Dar
Budget, Benjamin Diokno
Defence, Orlando Mercado
Economic Planning, Felipe Medalla
Education, Andrew Gonzales
Energy, Mario Tiaoqui
Environment and Natural Resources, Antonio Cerilles
Executive Secretary, Ronaldo Zamora
Finance, Edgardo Espiritu
Foreign Affairs, Domingo Siazon
Health, Felipe Estrella
Justice, Serafin Cuevas
Labour, Bienvenido Laguesma
National Security Adviser, Alexander Aguirre
Presidential Legal Counsel, Henrietta Demetriou
Presidential Press Secretary, Rodolfo Reyes
Public Works and Highways, Gregorio Vigilar
Science and Technology, William Padolina
Tourism, Gemma Cruz Araneta
Trade and Industry, Jose Pardo
Transportation and Communication, Vicente Rivera

EMBASSY OF THE PHILIPPINES
9A Palace Green, London W8 4QE
Tel 0171-937 1600
Chargé d'Affaires, Maria Rowena Mendoza Sanchez
Defence Attaché, Col. P. Inserto
Commercial Counsellor, P. Sales

BRITISH EMBASSY
Locsin Building, 6752 Ayala Avenue, Corner Makati Avenue, 1226 Makati, Metro Manila (PO Box 2927 MCPO)
Tel: Manila 816 7116
Ambassador Extraordinary and Plenipotentiary, HE Adrian Thorpe, CMG, apptd 1995
Deputy Head of Mission, M. Reilly
Defence Attaché, Capt. C. C. Peach
First Secretary, E. McEvoy *(Commercial)*

BRITISH COUNCIL DIRECTOR, R. Bell, 10F Taipan Place, Emerald Avenue, Ortigas Business Centre, Pasig City 1605, Manila

DEFENCE

The Army has 460 armoured infantry fighting vehicles and armoured personnel carriers, and 242 artillery pieces. The Navy has one frigate, 63 patrol and coastal vessels and eight combat aircraft at three bases. The Air Force has 39 combat aircraft and 103 armed helicopters.

MILITARY EXPENDITURE – 1.8 per cent of GDP (1996)
MILITARY PERSONNEL – 153,000: Army 70,000, Navy 24,000, Air Force 16,500, Paramilitaries 42,500

ECONOMY

The Philippines is predominantly agricultural, the chief products being rice, coconuts, maize, coffee, sugar cane, abaca, fruits, tobacco and lumber. There is an increasing number of manufacturing industries and it is the policy of the government to diversify the economy. There are also deposits of iron, copper, gold and silver.

The Philippines has been bypassed by the economic growth of most of the rest of south-east Asia since the 1960s, mainly because of the incompetence and corruption of the Marcos regime. Recently, however, an economic reform programme of liberalization, privatization and deregulation has been put in place and has led to increased exports, increased foreign investment, and a reduction in inflation. In July 1998, the Bank of the Philippines effectively devalued the peso following attacks from speculators, prompted by the devaluation of the Thai baht. In December 1997, the government unveiled an austerity plan cutting spending by 25 per cent. Prompt and firm measures from the government are credited with limiting the damage caused by the regional economic crisis.

GNP – US$83,298 million (1996); US$1,160 per capita (1996)
GDP – US$47,082 million (1994); US$965 per capita (1994)
ANNUAL AVERAGE GROWTH OF GDP – 5.5 per cent (1996)
INFLATION RATE – 8.4 per cent (1996)
UNEMPLOYMENT – 8.4 per cent (1995)
TOTAL EXTERNAL DEBT – US$41,214 million (1996)

TRADE

Principal exports are electronic products, sugar, coconut oil, clothing, copper concentrate, lumber and copra. Principal imports are electronic components, fuels, machinery and transport equipment. The major trading partners are the USA, Japan, Singapore and Hong Kong.

In 1995 the Philippines had a trade deficit of US$8,944 million and a current account deficit of US$1,980 million. In 1996 imports totalled US$34,122 million and exports US$20,417 million.

Trade with UK	1996	1997
Imports from UK	£395,311,000	£600,112,000
Exports to UK	895,486,000	761,177,000

COMMUNICATIONS

The highway system covers about 187,000 kilometres. The Philippine National Railway used to operate 1,282 km of track, but a greater part of this is being rebuilt. There are 94 ports of entry and 164,404 vessels of various types totalling 50,467,000 tons are engaged in inter-island traffic. There are 82 national airports and 137 privately operated airports. Philippine Air Lines has regular flights throughout the Far East, to the USA and Europe, in addition to inter-island services.

EDUCATION

Secondary and higher education is extensive and there are 49 private universities recognized by the government, including the Dominican University of Santo Tomas (founded in 1611). There are also 296 state-supported colleges and universities, including the University of the Philippines, founded in 1908.

ILLITERACY RATE – 5.4 per cent

ENROLMENT (percentage of age group) – primary 100 per cent (1995); secondary 60 per cent (1995); tertiary 27.4 per cent (1994)

POLAND
Rzeczpospolita Polska

AREA – 124,808 sq. miles (323,250 sq. km). Neighbours: the Russian Federation (Kaliningrad) (north), Germany (west), the Czech Republic and Slovakia (south), Belarus, Ukraine and Lithuania (east)
POPULATION – 38,588,000 (1995). Roman Catholicism is the religion of 95 per cent of the inhabitants. The language is Polish
CAPITAL – Warsaw (population, 1,643,203, 1993), on the Vistula
MAJOR CITIES – Bydgoszcz (384,101); Gdansk (462,239); Katowice (359,776); Kraków (744,203); Lódź (835,807); Poznan (582,839); Szczecin (417,115); Wroclaw (641,386)
CURRENCY – Złoty of 100 groszy
NATIONAL ANTHEM – Jeszcze Polska Nie Zginela (Poland has not yet been destroyed)
NATIONAL DAY – 3 May
NATIONAL FLAG – Equal horizontal stripes of white (above) and red
LIFE EXPECTANCY (years) – male 67.37; female 76.00
POPULATION GROWTH RATE – 0.2 per cent (1995)
POPULATION DENSITY – 119 per sq. km (1995)
URBAN POPULATION – 61.9 per cent (1995)

HISTORY AND POLITICS

The Polish Commonwealth ceased to exist in 1795 after three successive partitions in 1772, 1793 and 1795 in which Prussia, Russia and Austria shared. The Republic of Poland, reconstituted within the limits of the old Polish Commonwealth, was proclaimed at Warsaw in November 1918, and its independence guaranteed by the signatories of the Treaty of Versailles.

German forces invaded Poland on 1 September 1939; on 17 September, Russian forces invaded eastern Poland, and on 21 September 1939 Poland was declared by Germany and Russia to have ceased to exist. At the end of the war a coalition government was formed in which the Polish Workers' Party played a large part. In December 1948, the Polish Workers' Party and the Polish Socialist Party merged to form the Polish United Workers' Party (PUWP). A new constitution modelled on the Soviet constitution was adopted in 1952, and was modified in 1976.

Steep price rises in 1980 prompted strikes which forced the government to allow independent trade unions, including 'Solidarity' led by Lech Walesa. The unions agitated for further reforms although their activities were suspended when martial law was in force from December 1981 until July 1983.

A wave of strikes resulted in talks between Walesa and the PUWP early in 1989. Multiparty parliamentary elections were held in the summer of 1989, following which the PUWP ceased to be the ruling party. The post-Communist governments have introduced a market economy but economic difficulties and a fragmented parliament have led to a succession of short-lived governments.

Elections held on 21 September 1997 were won by the right-wing Solidarity Electoral Alliance (AWS), a group of 36 parties, which formed a government with Freedom Union (UW). The AWS won 201 seats in the *Sejm* and 51 in the Senate; the UW won 60 seats in the *Sejm* and 8 in the Senate.

FOREIGN RELATIONS
In July 1997, Poland was invited to join NATO. It has also been approved by the European Commission for membership of the EU, and formal accession talks began in March 1998.

POLITICAL SYSTEM
A new constitution came into effect on 16 October 1997. The president, directly elected for a maximum of two five-year terms, appoints the prime minister and has the right to be consulted over the appointment of the foreign, defence and interior ministers. The National Assembly is the bicameral legislature, comprising a 460-member *Sejm* (Diet) and a Senate of 100 members. Both houses have a four-year term. The Senate is elected on a provincial basis.

HEAD OF STATE
President, Aleksander Kwaśniewski, *elected* 19 November 1995, *sworn in* 23 December 1995

COUNCIL OF MINISTERS *as at July 1998*
Prime Minister, Jerzy Buzek (AWS)
Deputy PM, Finance, Leszek Balcerowicz (UW)
Deputy PM, Internal Affairs and Administration, Janusz Tomaszewski (AWS)
Agriculture, Jacek Janiszewski (AWS)
Culture and Arts, Joanna Wnuk-Nazarowa (UW)
Defence, Janusz Onyszkiewicz (UW)
Economy, Janusz Steinhoff (AWS)
Education, Miroslaw Handke (AWS)
Environmental Protection, Natural Resources and Forestry, Jan Szyszko (AWS)
European Integration Committee, Ryszard Czarnecki (AWS)
Foreign Affairs, Bronislaw Geremek (UW)
Health, Wieslaw Maksymowicz (AWS)
Justice, Hanna Suchocka (UW)
Labour and Social Policy, Longin Komolowski (AWS)
Scientific Research Committee, Andrzej Wiszniewski (AWS)
Telecommunications, Marek Zdrojewski (AWS)
Transport and Maritime Economy, Eugeniusz Morawski (UW)
Treasury, Emil Wasacz (AWS)
Without Portfolio, Kazimierz Kapera *(Family Affairs)*; Jerzy Widzyk *(Floods)*; Jerzy Kropiwnicki *(Government Centre for Strategic Studies)*; Teresa Kaminska *(Social Reforms)*; Wieslaw Walendziak *(Council of Ministers)*; Janusz Palubicki *(Security Services)*
AWS Solidarity Electoral Alliance; UW Freedom Union

EMBASSY OF THE REPUBLIC OF POLAND
47 Portland Place, London WIN 3AG
Tel 0171-580 4324/9
Ambassador Extraordinary and Plenipotentiary, HE Ryszard Stemplowski, apptd 1994
Defence Attaché, Capt. I. Goreczny

BRITISH EMBASSY
No. 1 Aleja Róz, 00-556 Warsaw
Tel: Warsaw 628 1001/5
Ambassador Extraordinary and Plenipotentiary, HE Christopher Hum, CMG, apptd 1996
Counsellor, R. A. Barnett *(Deputy Head of Mission)*
Defence and Air Attaché, Gp Capt. M. Mitchell
Counsellor (Commercial and Consul-General), S. D. Pattison
HONORARY CONSULATES – Gdansk, Katowice, Poznan, Szczecin, Wroclaw

BRITISH COUNCIL DIRECTOR, J. Eyres, Al. Jerozolimskie 59, 00–697 Warsaw

DEFENCE

The Army has 1,729 main battle tanks, 1,442 armoured infantry fighting vehicles and armoured personnel carriers, and 1,581 artillery pieces. The Navy has three submarines, one destroyer, one frigate, 33 patrol and coastal vessels, 28 combat aircraft and ten helicopters at five bases. The Air Force has 356 combat aircraft and 17 attack helicopters.

MILITARY EXPENDITURE – 2.3 per cent of GDP (1996)
MILITARY PERSONNEL – 265,150: Army 168,650, Navy 17,000, Air Force 56,100, Paramilitaries 23,400
CONSCRIPTION DURATION – 18 months

ECONOMY

Poland is well endowed with mineral resources; there are large reserves of brown coal in central and south-western Poland and hard coal in Upper Silesia and the Walbrzych and Lublin regions; sulphur, copper, zinc, lead, natural gas and salt are also produced.

In 1990, the government embarked upon a series of measures designed to introduce a free-market economy. However, growth did not resume until 1992 and the public backlash against rising food prices and unemployment prompted the government to overstep the budgetary limits agreed with international creditors. The IMF prescribed a 'shock therapy' of allowing bankruptcy and ending of state subsidies to reduce the deficit. Further IMF credits followed the passing of an austerity budget and the introduction of a mass privatization bill for 600 state-owned firms in 1993.

The transition to a market economy has been painful, with unemployment doubling between 1990 and 1995. Industrial output has improved and the rate of growth of GDP has increased although inflation remains high.

Poland's major imports are petroleum, chemicals, textiles, and industrial and electrical equipment. Its major exports are fruits and vegetables, clothing, coal, non-ferrous metals, iron, steel, furniture and transport equipment. Germany is Poland's main trading partner.

In 1995 there was a trade deficit of US$3,224 million and a current account deficit of US$4,245 million. In 1996 imports totalled US$37,137 million and exports US$24,440 million.

GNP – US$124,682 million (1996); US$3,230 per capita (1996)
GDP – US$61,360 million (1994); US$2,503 per capita (1994)
ANNUAL AVERAGE GROWTH OF GDP – estimated to be 5.7 per cent in 1996
INFLATION RATE – 20.2 per cent (1996)
UNEMPLOYMENT – 13.1 per cent (1995)
TOTAL EXTERNAL DEBT – US$40,895 million (1996)

	1996	1997
TRADE WITH UK		
Imports from UK	£1,350,985,000	£1,354,407,000
Exports to UK	599,862,000	621,175,000

EDUCATION

Elementary education (ages seven to 15) is compulsory and free. Secondary education is optional and free. There are universities at Kraków, Warsaw, Poznan, Lódź, Wroclaw, Lublin and Toruń and a number of other towns.

ENROLMENT (percentage of age group) – primary 97 per cent (1994); secondary 83 per cent (1994); tertiary 27.4 per cent (1993)

CULTURE

Polish is a western Slavonic tongue, the Latin alphabet being used. Major writers include Henryk Sienkiewicz (1846–1916), Nobel Prizewinner for Literature in 1905; Boleslaw Prus (1847–1912); Stanislaw Reymont (1868–1925), Nobel Prizewinner in 1924; Czeslaw Milosz, Nobel Prizewinner in 1980; and Wislawa Szymborska, Nobel Prizewinner in 1996.

PORTUGAL
República Portuguesa

AREA – 35,514 sq. miles (91,982 sq. km). Neighbour: Spain (north and east)
POPULATION – 9,920,760 (1995); 9,833,014 (excluding the Azores and Madeira). 94 per cent of the population are Catholic. The language is a Romance language with admixtures of Arabic and other idioms
CAPITAL – ΨLisbon (population, 2,561,225, 1991)
MAJOR CITIES – ΨOporto (1,683,000)
CURRENCY – Escudo (Esc) of 100 centavos
NATIONAL ANTHEM – A Portuguesa
NATIONAL DAY – 10 June
NATIONAL FLAG – Divided vertically into unequal parts of green and red with the national emblem over all on the line of division
LIFE EXPECTANCY (years) – male 71.18; female 78.23
POPULATION GROWTH RATE – 1.7 per cent (1995)
POPULATION DENSITY – 117 per sq. km (1995)
URBAN POPULATION – 48.2 per cent (1991)

HISTORY AND POLITICS

Portugal was a monarchy from the 12th century until 1910, when an armed rising in Lisbon drove King Manuel II into exile and a republic was set up. A period of political instability ensued until the military stepped in and abolished political parties in 1926. The constitution of 1933 gave formal expression to the corporative 'Estado Novo' (New State) which was personified by Dr Antonio Salazar, prime minister 1932–68. Dr Caetano succeeded Salazar as prime minister in 1968 but his failure to liberalize the regime or to conclude the wars in the African colonies resulted in his government's overthrow by a military coup on 25 April 1974. There was great political turmoil between April 1974 and July 1976 but with the failure of an attempted coup by the extreme left in November 1975 the situation stabilized.

In the general election held on 1 October 1995, the Socialist Party (PS) won 112 seats, the Social Democrats (PSD) 88 seats, the Christian Democrats (CDS/PP) 15 seats, and the Communist Coalition (CDU) 15 seats. The Socialist candidate, Jorge Sampaio, won the January 1996 presidential election.

POLITICAL SYSTEM

Under the 1976 constitution, amended in 1982 and 1989, the president is elected for a five-year term by universal adult suffrage. The prime minister is designated by the largest party in the legislature. Legislative authority is vested in the 230-member Assembly of the Republic, elected by a system of proportional representation every four years. The president retains certain limited powers to dismiss the government, dissolve the Assembly or veto laws.

HEAD OF STATE
President of the Republic, Jorge Sampaio, *elected* 1996,
   inaugurated 9 March 1996

COUNCIL OF MINISTERS *as at July 1998*
Prime Minister, António Guterres
Deputy PM, Foreign Affairs, Jaime Gama
Agriculture, Food and Fisheries, Fernando Gomes da Silva
Culture, Manuel Maria Carrilho
Defence, José Veiga Simão
Economy, Joaquim Pina Moura
Education, Eduardo Marçal Grilo
Environment, Elisa Ferreira
Finance, António Sousa Franco
Health, Maria de Belém Roseira
Interior, Jorge Coelho
Justice, José Vera Jardim
Parliamentary Affairs, Antonio Costa
Planning, Public Works and Territorial Administration, João
   Cravinho
Science and Technology, José Mariano Gago
Solidarity, Social Security, Employment, Eduardo Ferro
   Rodrigues
Youth, Sport and Drug Addiction, José Socrates

PORTUGUESE EMBASSY
11 Belgrave Square, London SW1X 8PP
Tel 0171-235 5331
Ambassador Extraordinary and Plenipotentiary, José Gregório
   Faria, apptd 1997
Minister-Counsellor and Consul-General, A. de Almeida
   Ribeiro
Minister-Counsellor, J. Ramos Pinto
Defence Attaché, Capt. J. de Mendonca

BRITISH EMBASSY
Rua de S. Bernardo 33, 1200 Lisbon
Tel: Lisbon 392 4000
Ambassador Extraordinary and Plenipotentiary, HE Roger
   Westbrook, CMG, LVO, apptd 1995
Counsellor, A. F. Smith (*Deputy Head of Mission*)
Defence Attaché, Cdr. R. Goddard
First Secretary, P. Sinkinson (*Commercial*)

CONSULATES – Oporto, Portimão, Funchal (Madeira),
   Ribeira Grande (Azores), Macao

BRITISH COUNCIL DIRECTOR, W. Jefferson, OBE, Rua de
   Sao Marçal 174, 1294 Lisbon. There are also offices at
   Cascais, Coimbra, Oporto and Parede
BRITISH PORTUGUESE CHAMBER OF COMMERCE, Rua da
   Estrela 8, 1200 Lisbon and Rua Sa de Bandeira 784–20E,
   Frente, 4000 Oporto

DEFENCE

The Army has 186 main battle tanks, 356 armoured
personnel carriers and 284 artillery pieces. The Navy has
three submarines, ten frigates and 29 patrol and coastal
vessels at four bases. The Air Force has 96 combat aircraft.

Lisbon is the base of the NATO Iberian Atlantic
Command and the USA maintains 1,050 personnel in
mainland Portugal and on the Azores.

MILITARY EXPENDITURE – 2.8 per cent of GDP (1996)
MILITARY PERSONNEL – 95,500: Army 32,100, Navy
   14,800, Air Force 7,700, Paramilitaries 40,900
CONSCRIPTION DURATION – Four to 18 months

ECONOMY

The chief agricultural products are wines, cork, tomatoes,
potatoes, maize, wheat, rice, vegetables, olives, figs, citrus
fruits, almonds and timber. There are extensive forests of
pine, cork, eucalyptus and chestnut covering about 38 per
cent of the country. The principal mineral products are
pyrites, wolfram, uranium, iron ores, copper and sodium
and calcium minerals.

The country is moderately industrialized. The principal manufactures are motor vehicle components, clothing
and footwear, textiles, machinery, pulp and paper, pharmaceuticals, foodstuffs, chemicals, fertilizers, wood, cork,
furniture, cement, glassware and pottery. There are a
modern steelworks and large shipbuilding and repair yards
at Lisbon and Setúbal, working mainly for foreign shipowners. There are several hydroelectric power stations
and two thermal power stations.

Since joining the EC (EU) in 1986 Portugal has been
adjusting its economy to the European single market, and
to the economic and monetary union criteria laid down in
the Maastricht Treaty. The escudo joined the ERM in
April 1992; having satisfied the convergence criteria,
Portugal will be one of 11 states to adopt the European
single currency from 1 January 1999.

GNP – US$100,934 million (1996); US$10,160 per capita
   (1996)
GDP – US$69,276 million (1994); US$8,822 per capita
   (1994)
ANNUAL AVERAGE GROWTH OF GDP – 1.9 per cent (1995)
INFLATION RATE – 3.1 per cent (1996)
UNEMPLOYMENT – 5.5 per cent (1993)

TRADE

The principal imports are machinery, vehicles, agricultural products, chemicals, oil, metals and textiles. The
principal exports are automobile parts, vehicles, clothing,
minerals, pulp and paper, cork and timber, and foodstuffs
and beverages.

In 1995 Portugal had a trade deficit of US$8,484 million
and a current account deficit of US$229 million. In 1996
imports totalled US$34,094 million and exports
US$23,796 million.

Trade with UK	1996	1997
Imports from UK	£1,598,900,000	£1,661,700,000
Exports to UK	1,564,800,000	1,690,600,000

COMMUNICATIONS

There are international airports at Lisbon and Oporto, and
at Faro in the Algarve. Four morning and one evening daily
newspapers are published in Lisbon and four morning
newspapers in Oporto. There are six main weekly newspapers.

EDUCATION

Education is free and compulsory for nine years from the
age of six. Secondary education is mainly conducted in
state lyceums, commercial and industrial schools, but there
are also private schools. There are also military, naval,
technical, polytechnic and other special schools. There are
universities at Coimbra (founded in 1290), Oporto, Lisbon,
Braga, Aveiro, Vila Real, Faro, Evora and in the Azores.

ILLITERACY RATE – 10.4 per cent
ENROLMENT (percentage of age group) – primary 100 per
   cent (1993); secondary 78 per cent (1993); tertiary 34.0
   per cent (1993)

AUTONOMOUS REGIONS

Madeira and The Azores are two administratively autonomous regions of Portugal, having locally elected assemblies and governments.

Madeira is a group of islands in the Atlantic Ocean about 520 miles south-west of Lisbon, and consists of Madeira, Porto, Santo and three uninhabited islands (Desertas). Total area is 300 sq. miles (779 sq. km); population, 257,290 (1995). ΨFunchal in Madeira, the largest island (270 sq. miles), is the capital (population 44,111)

THE AZORES are a group of nine islands (Flores, Corvo, Terceira, São Jorge, Pico, Faial, Graciosa, São Miguel and Santa Maria) in the Atlantic Ocean; area 895 sq. miles (2,330 sq. km); population, 241,490 (1995). ΨPonta Delgada, on São Miguel, is the capital (population, 137,700). Other ports are ΨAngra, in Terceira (55,900) and ΨHorta (16,300)

OVERSEAS TERRITORY

MACAO

AREA – 6 sq. miles (15.5 sq. km)
POPULATION – 415,850 (1997)

Macao, situated at the mouth of the Pearl River, comprises a peninsula and the islands of Coloane and Taipa.

Macao became a Portuguese colony in 1557; in a Sino-Portuguese treaty of 1887 China recognized Portugal's sovereignty over Macao. An agreement to transfer the administration of Macao to the Chinese authorities was signed on 13 April 1987. Macao will become a 'special administrative region' (SAR) of China when transferred on 20 December 1999. The final session of the Macao SAR Basic Law Drafting Committee was held in Beijing in January 1993 and approved the Basic Law which will serve as Macao's constitution after 1999.

Macao is subject to Portuguese constitutional law but otherwise enjoys autonomy. The Governor is appointed by the Portuguese president and there is a 23-member legislative assembly, which has a three-year term. The assembly comprises seven members appointed by the Governor; eight directly elected, and eight indirectly elected by business associations.

Governor, Gen. Vasco Rocha Vieira

TRADE WITH UK	1996	1997
Imports from UK	£14,097,000	£21,163,000
Exports to UK	54,656,000	70,809,000

QATAR
Dawlat Qatar

AREA – 4,247 sq. miles (11,000 sq. km). Neighbours: United Arab Emirates (south), Saudi Arabia (south-west)
POPULATION – 551,000 (1994 UN estimate). Most of the population is concentrated in the urban district of Doha. Only a small minority still pursue the traditional life of the semi-nomadic tribesmen and fisherfolk. Arabic is the official language
CAPITAL – ΨDoha (population, 217,294, 1986)
MAJOR CITIES – Dukhan; Khor; ΨUmm Said; Wakra
CURRENCY – Qatar riyal of 100 dirhams
NATIONAL DAY – 3 September
NATIONAL FLAG – White and maroon; white portion nearer the mast; vertical indented line comprising 17 angles divides the colours
LIFE EXPECTANCY (years) – male 68.75; female 74.20
POPULATION GROWTH RATE – 2.5 per cent (1995)
POPULATION DENSITY – 50 per sq. km (1995)
MILITARY EXPENDITURE – 10.4 per cent of GDP (1996)
MILITARY PERSONNEL – 11,800: Army 8,500, Navy 1,800, Air Force 1,500
ILLITERACY RATE – 20.6 per cent

ENROLMENT (percentage of age group) – primary 80 per cent (1993); secondary 70 per cent (1993); tertiary 27.4 per cent (1994)

The state of Qatar covers the peninsula of Qatar in the Gulf from approximately the northern shore of Khor al Odaid to the eastern shore of Khor al Salwa.

HISTORY AND POLITICS

Qatar was one of nine independent emirates in the Gulf in special treaty relations with the UK until 1971. On 2 April 1970, a provisional constitution for Qatar was proclaimed, providing for the establishment of a Council of Ministers and for the formation of a Consultative Council to assist the Council of Ministers in running the affairs of the state. There are no political parties or legislature. The Amir, who had ruled since 22 February 1972, was overthrown on 27 June 1995 by his son and heir, who assumed power as Amir the same day. A coup attempt was thwarted in February 1996.

HEAD OF STATE
HH Amir of Qatar, Minister of Defence and Commander-in-Chief of Armed Forces, Shaikh Hamad bin Khalifa al-Thani, KCMG, *assumed power* 27 June 1995
Crown Prince, HH Shaikh Jassim bin Hamad al-Thani

COUNCIL OF MINISTERS *as at July 1998*
Prime Minister, Interior, HH Shaikh Abdulla bin Khalifa al-Thani
Deputy PM, HE Shaikh Mohammed bin Khalifa al-Thani
Awqaf (Religious Endowments) and Islamic Affairs, Ahmed Abdulla al-Marri
Civil Service Affairs and Housing, HE Shaikh Falah bin Jassim al-Thani
Communications and Transport, HE Shaikh Ahmed bin Nasser al-Thani
Education, Higher Education and Culture, HE Mohammed Abdulrahim Kafoud
Electricity and Water, Justice (acting), HE Ahmed Mohammed Ali al-Subaie
Energy and Industry, HE Abdulla bin Hamad al-Attayah
Finance, Economy and Trade, Yousef Hussein Kamal
Foreign Affairs, HE Shaikh Hamad bin Jassem bin Jabr al-Thani
Minister of State, Cabinet Affairs, Ali Mohamed al-Khater
Minister of State, Foreign Affairs, HE Ahmed Abdulla al-Mahmoud
Minister of State, Internal Affairs, HE Shaikh Abdulla bin Khalid al-Thani
Ministers of State, HE Shaikh Mohammad bin Khalid al-Thani; HE Shaikh Hamad bin Suhaim al-Thani; HE Shaikh Ahmed bin Saif al-Thani; HE Shaikh Hamad bin Abdulla al-Thani; HE Shaikh Hasan bin Abdulla al-Thani
Municipal Affairs, Agriculture, HE Ali Saeed al-Khayarin
Public Health, HE Abdulrahman Salem al-Kawari

EMBASSY OF THE STATE OF QATAR
1 South Audley Street, London W1Y 5DQ
Tel 0171-493 2200
Ambassador Extraordinary and Plenipotentiary, HE Ali M. Jaidah, apptd 1993

BRITISH EMBASSY
PO Box 3, Doha
Tel: Doha 421991
Ambassador Extraordinary and Plenipotentiary, HE D. Wright, OBE, apptd 1997

BRITISH COUNCIL DIRECTOR, J. Gildea, 93 Al Sadd Street, (PO Box 2992), Doha

ECONOMY

Although Qatar is a desert country, there are gardens and smallholdings near Doha and to the north, and agriculture is being developed, with self-sufficiency an aim.

The Qatar General Petroleum Corporation is the state-owned company controlling Qatar's interests in oil, gas and petrochemicals. The corporation is responsible for Qatar's oil production onshore and offshore. The large reserves of natural gas in the North Field came into production in September 1991.

Current industries include a steel mill, a fertilizer plant, a cement factory, a petrochemical complex and two natural gas liquids plants. With the exception of the cement works at Umm Bab, all these industries are at Umm Said, about 30 miles south of Doha. Qatar is also expanding its infrastructure, including electrical generation and water distillation, roads, houses, and government buildings. The recent drop in demand for crude oil has slowed the economy considerably.

In 1994 imports totalled US$1,927 million.

GNP – US$7,448 million (1995); US$11,600 per capita (1995)

GDP – US$8,074 million (1994); US$13,020 per capita (1994)

INFLATION RATE – 4.4 per cent (1991)

TRADE WITH UK	1996	1997
Imports from UK	£191,848,000	£584,335,000
Exports to UK	10,502,000	15,747,000

COMMUNICATIONS

Regular air services provided by Gulf Air and Qatar Airways connect Qatar with the other Gulf states, the Middle East, the Indian sub-continent, Africa and Europe. The Qatar Broadcasting Service transmits on medium wave, shortwave and VHF.

ROMANIA
România

AREA – 92,043 sq. miles (238,391 sq. km). Neighbours: Ukraine (north and east), Moldova (east), Bulgaria (south), Yugoslavia (south-west) and Hungary (north-west)

POPULATION – 22,680,000 (1997 estimate); 22,810,035 (1992 census): 89.4 per cent Romanian, 7.1 per cent Hungarian, 1.7 per cent gypsy, 0.5 per cent German, 0.3 per cent Ukrainian, 0.04 per cent Jews and others.

Religious affiliation: Orthodox 86.8 per cent, Roman Catholic 5 per cent, Reformed 3.5 per cent, Greek Catholic 1 per cent. Romanian is a Romance language with many archaic forms and with admixtures of Slavonic, Turkish, Magyar and French words

CAPITAL – Bucharest (population, 2,060,551, 1996), on the Dimbovita

MAJOR CITIES – ΨBräila (235,243); Braşov (319,908); Constanţa (346,830); Cluj-Napoca (332,297); Craiova (310,838); ΨGalati (327,975); Iasi (346,613); Ploiesti (253,623); Timisoara (332,277)

CURRENCY – Leu (Lei) of 100 bani

NATIONAL ANTHEM – Desteapta-te, romane (Awake ye, Romanian)

NATIONAL DAY – 1 December

NATIONAL FLAG – Three vertical bands, blue, yellow, red

LIFE EXPECTANCY (years) – male 65.88; female 73.32

POPULATION GROWTH RATE – –0.5 per cent (1995)

POPULATION DENSITY – 95 per sq. km (1995)

URBAN POPULATION – 54.7 per cent (1994)

HISTORY AND POLITICS

Romania has its origin in the union of the Danubian principalities of Wallachia and Moldavia in 1859. Although under nominal Turkish suzerainty, Alexandru Ioan Cuza was elected ruler of both territories effectively unifying them. The name Romania was adopted in 1862. Full independence was proclaimed on 9 May 1877 and was formally recognized under the Treaty of Berlin (1878) which awarded part of the territory of Dobrogea to Romania and allowed the Russians to reannex Southern Bessarabia. In 1881 Romania was recognized as a kingdom.

In 1918 the populations of Bessarabia, Bukovina, Transylvania and Banat voted in favour of union with Romania, these additions being confirmed by the Versailles Treaty (1919). In 1940 the Soviet government compelled Romania to cede Bessarabia and Northern Bukovina and the Herta Land. In the same year north-western Transylvania was ceded to Hungary and southern Dobrogea to Bulgaria.

In 1947 King Michael was forced to abdicate and Romania became 'The Romanian People's Republic'. The leading political force from the Second World War until 1989 was the Romanian Communist Party. A revolution in December 1989 led to the overthrow of Nicolae Ceauşescu, president since 1965. A provisional government abolished the leading role of the Communist Party and held free elections in May 1990.

In the elections held in November 1996 the Romanian Democratic Convention (CDR) candidate, Prof. Emil Constantinescu, was elected president and three coalitions (the CDR, the Social Democratic Union (USD), and the Democratic Union of the Romanian Magyars (UDMR)) combined to form a government. Following disagreements in the ruling coalition over the speed of economic reforms, Victor Ciorbea of the Christian Democratic National Peasants' Party (PNTCD) resigned as prime minister on 30 March 1998 and was replaced by Radu Vasile, also of the PNTCD.

POLITICAL SYSTEM

The constitution of 1991 formally makes Romania a multiparty democracy and endorses human rights and a market economy. The parliament comprises the Chamber of Deputies with 343 seats, of which 15 are reserved for ethnic minorities other than Hungarians, and the Senate with 143 seats. Both houses are elected for four-year terms.

HEAD OF STATE

President of the Republic, Prof. Emil Constantinescu, *elected* 17 November 1996

CABINET *as at July 1998*

Prime Minister, Radu Vasile (PNTCD)
Agriculture, Dinu Gavrilescu (PNTCD)
Communications, Sorin Pantis (PNL)
Culture, Ion Caramitru (PNTCD)
Education, Andrei Marga (PNTCD)
Finance, Daniel Daianu (Ind.)
Foreign Affairs, Andrei Plesu (Ind.)
Industry and Trade, Radu Berceanu (PD)
Interior, Gavril Dejeu (PNTCD)
Labour, Social Protection, Alexandru Athanasiu (PSDR)
Local Public Administration, Vlad Rosca (PNTCD)
Minister-Delegate, European Integration, attached to the Prime Minister, Alexandru Ion Herlea (PNTCD)
Minister of State, Health (acting), Justice, Valeriu Stoica (PNL)
Minister of State, National Defence, Victor Babiuc (PD)
National Minorities, Gyorgy Tokay (DUEH)
Privatization, Sorin Dimitriu (PNTCD)
Public Works and Physical Planning, Nicolae Noica (PNTCD)

Reform, Ioan Muresan (PNTCD)
Relations with Parliament, Alexandru Sassu (PD)
Research and Technology, Horia Ene (PAR)
Secretary-General of the Government, Radu Stroe (PNL)
Secretary of State, Ministry of Defence, Constantin Dudu-
    Ionescu (PNTCD)
Tourism, Sorin Frunzaverde (PD)
Transport, Traian Basescu (PD)
Water, Forestry and Environmental Protection, Romica
    Tomescu (PNTCD)
Youth and Sport, Crin Antonescu (PNL)
PNTCD Christian Democratic National Peasants' Party;
PNL National Liberal Party; PD Democratic Party; PSDR
Romanian Social Democratic Party; DUEH Democratic
Union of Ethnic Hungarians in Romania; PAR Romania's
Alternative Party; Ind. Independent

EMBASSY OF ROMANIA
Arundel House, 4 Palace Green, London w8 4QD
Tel 0171-937 9666
Ambassador Extraordinary and Plenipotentiary, HE Radu
    Onofrei, apptd 1997
Defence Attaché, Col. Vasile Huicá
Counsellor, C. Soare (*Economic*)

BRITISH EMBASSY
24 Strada Jules Michelet, 70154 Bucharest
Tel: Bucharest 312 0303
Ambassador Extraordinary and Plenipotentiary, HE
    Christopher Crabbie, CMG, apptd 1996
Counsellor, Deputy Head of Mission, E. A. Galvez
Defence Attaché, Lt.-Col. R. D. Shaw-Brown
First Secretary (Commercial), N. Sheppard

BRITISH COUNCIL DIRECTOR, H. Meixner, Calea
    Dorobantilor 14, Bucharest

DEFENCE

The Army has 1,255 main battle tanks, 1,882 armoured
personnel carriers and armoured infantry fighting vehicles, and 1,359 artillery pieces. The Navy has one
submarine, one destroyer, six frigates, 100 patrol and
coastal vessels, seven helicopters, 120 main battle tanks and
120 artillery pieces at six bases. The Air Force has 315
combat aircraft and 16 attack helicopters.
MILITARY EXPENDITURE – 2.3 per cent of GDP (1996)
MILITARY PERSONNEL – 273,550: Army 129,350, Navy
    17,500, Air Force 47,600, Paramilitaries 79,100
CONSCRIPTION DURATION – 12–18 months

ECONOMY

Romania is among the most fertile areas in Europe.
Agriculture employs 30 per cent of the workforce and
contributes 22 per cent of GDP. The principal crops are
cereals, vegetables, flax and hemp. Vines and fruits are also
grown. The forests of the mountainous regions are
extensive, and the timber industry is important.
    There are plentiful supplies of natural gas, together with
various mineral deposits including coal, iron ore, bauxite,
chromium and uranium in quantities which allow a
substantial part of the requirements of industry to be met
from local resources. Production of crude oil was 6,712,000
tonnes in 1995.
    The economy inherited from the totalitarian regime
was characterized in 1990 by state-owned and co-operative ownership, excessive centralization, rigid planning
and low efficiency. After the revolution the government
opted for a slow pace of reform with subsidized production
resulting in budget and trade deficits, high inflation and
currency depreciation. In 1994, after inflation had surpas-

sed 300 per cent annually and unemployment 10 per cent,
Romania agreed to implement an IMF austerity package in
return for loans of US$700 million.
    The government elected in 1996 vowed to institute a
programme of reform including the acceleration of re-
structuring and privatization of state-owned companies,
reduction of subsidies, full liberalization of prices and
monetary stability.
GNP – US$36,191 million (1996); US$1,600 per capita
    (1996)
GDP – US$30,023 million (1994); US$1,274 per capita
    (1994)
ANNUAL AVERAGE GROWTH OF GDP – 4.0 per cent (1994)
INFLATION RATE – 32.2 per cent (1995)
UNEMPLOYMENT – 8.0 per cent (1995)
TOTAL EXTERNAL DEBT – US$8,291 million (1996)

TRADE
The main imports are machines and equipment, mineral
fuels, textiles, chemicals and plastics. The main exports are
textiles, clothing, metallurgical products, minerals and
food products. Germany, Italy, Russia and France are
Romania's most important trading partners.
    In 1995 Romania had a trade deficit of US$1,231 million
and a current account deficit of US$1,342 million. In 1996
imports totalled US$11,435 million and exports US$8,085
million.

Trade with UK	1996	1997
Imports from UK	£210,284,000	£212,127,000
Exports to UK	182,024,000	205,360,000

COMMUNICATIONS

In 1995 there were 11,376 km of railway track, 34 per cent
of which was electrified, and 72,859 km of public roads.
The main national roads largely follow the railway lines
and almost all lead to the capital. The principal ports are
Constanta (on the Black Sea), Sulina (on the Danube
Estuary), Galati, Braila, Giurgiu and Turnu Severin. The
Danube and the Black Sea are linked by a canal completed
in 1984.

EDUCATION

Education is free and primary and secondary education are
compulsory. There are state universities in 21 cities, 45
private universities, six polytechnics, two commercial
academies, and five agricultural colleges.
ILLITERACY RATE – 2.1 per cent
ENROLMENT (percentage of age group) – primary 92 per
    cent (1995); secondary 73 per cent (1995); tertiary 18.3
    per cent (1995)

RUSSIA
Rossiiskaya Federatsiya – Russian Federation

AREA – 6,592,850 sq. miles (17,075,400 sq. km).
    Neighbours: Norway, Finland, Estonia, Latvia, Belarus
    and Ukraine (west),Georgia, Azerbaijan, Kazakhstan,
    China, Mongolia and North Korea (south). The
    Kaliningrad enclave borders Lithuania and Poland
POPULATION – 147,500,000 (1998 estimate): 87.5 per cent
    Russian, 3.5 per cent Tatar, 2.7 per cent Ukrainian, 1.3
    per cent ethnic German, 1.1 per cent Chavash, 0.9 per
    cent Bashkir, 0.7 per cent Belarusian and 0.7 per cent
    Mordovian. There are another six minorities with
    populations of over half a million and more than 130
    nationalities in total. The Russian Orthodox Church is

the predominant religion, though the Tatars are Muslims and there are Jewish communities in Moscow and St Petersburg. The language is Russian

CAPITAL – Moscow (population, 8,600,000, 1998 estimate), founded about 1147, became the centre of the rising Moscow principality and in the 15th century the capital of the whole of Russia (Muscovy). In 1325 it became the seat of the Metropolitan of Russia. In 1703 Peter the Great transferred the capital to St Petersburg, but on 14 March 1918 Moscow was again designated as the capital

MAJOR CITIES – ΨSt Petersburg (4,778,900, 1998), from 1914 to 1924 Petrograd and from 1924 to 1991 Leningrad. Other cities: Chelyabinsk (1,143,000); Kazan (1,094,000); Nizhny-Novgorod/Gorky (1,438,000); Novosibirsk/Novonikolayevsk (1,436,000); Omsk (1,148,000); Perm/Molotov (1,091,000); Rostov-on-Don (1,020,000); Samara/Kuibyshev (1,257,000); Ufa (1,083,000); Yekaterinburg/Sverdlovsk (1,367,000), 1990

CURRENCY – New Rouble of 100 kopeks
NATIONAL ANTHEM – The Patriotic Song
NATIONAL DAY – 12 June (Independence Day)
NATIONAL FLAG – Three horizontal stripes of white, blue, red

LIFE EXPECTANCY (years) – male 57.59; female 71.18
POPULATION GROWTH RATE – –0.0 per cent (1995)
POPULATION DENSITY – 9 per sq. km (1995)
URBAN POPULATION – 72.9 per cent (1995)
ILLITERACY RATE – 0.5 per cent
ENROLMENT (percentage of age group) – primary 100 per cent (1994); tertiary 42.9 per cent (1994)

Russia occupies three-quarters of the land area of the former Soviet Union.

The Russian Federation comprises 89 members: 49 regions (*oblast*) – Amur, Arkhangelsk, Astrakhan, Belgorod, Bryansk, Chelyabinsk, Chita, Irkutsk, Ivanovo, Kaliningrad, Kaluga, Kamchatka, Kemerovo, Kirov, Kostroma, Kurgan, Kursk, Leningrad, Lipetsk, Magadan, Moscow, Murmansk, Nizhny-Novgorod, Novgorod, Novosibirsk, Omsk, Orel, Orenburg, Penza, Perm, Pskov, Rostov, Ryazan, Sakhalin, Samara, Saratov, Smolensk, Sverdlovsk, Tambov, Tomsk, Tula, Tver, Tyumen, Ulyanovsk, Vladimir, Volgograd, Vologda, Voronezh, Yaroslavl; six autonomous territories (*krai*) – Altai, Khabarovsk, Krasnodar,

Krasnoyarsk, Primorye, Stavropol; 21 republics – Adygeia, Altai, Bashkortostan, Buryatia, Chechenia, Chuvash, Daghestan, Ingush, Kabardino-Balkar, Kalmykia, Karachai-Circassian, Karelia, Khakassia, Komi, Mari-El, Mordovia, North Ossetia (Alania), Sakha, Tatarstan, Tyva, Udmurt; ten autonomous areas – Aga-Buryat, Chuckchi, Evenki, Khanty-Mansi, Komi-Permyak, Koryak, Nenets, Taimyr, Ust-Orda-Buryat, Yamal-Nenets; two cities of federal status – Moscow, St Petersburg; and one autonomous Jewish region, Birobijan.

There are three principal geographic areas: a low-lying flat western area stretching eastwards up to the Yenisei and divided in two by the Ural ridge; the eastern area between the Yenisei and the Pacific, consisting of a number of tablelands and ridges; and a southern mountainous area. Russia has a very long coastline, including the longest Arctic coastline in the world (about 17,000 miles).

The most important rivers are the Volga, the Northern Dvina and the Pechora, the Neva, the Don and the Kuban in the European part, and in the Asiatic part, the Ob, the Irtysh, the Yenisei, the Lena and the Amur, and, further north, Khatanga, Olenek, Yana, Indigirka, Kolyma and Anadyr. Lake Baikal in eastern Siberia is the deepest lake in the world.

HISTORY AND POLITICS

The Gregorian calendar was not introduced until 14 February 1918. For the events surrounding the 1917 revolutions the dates given here are the Gregorian calendar dates in use in the rest of the world at the time, with the dates in the Julian calendar (os) in parenthesis.

Russia was formally created from the principality of Muscovy and its territories by Tsar Peter I (The Great) (1682–1725), who initiated its territorial expansion, introduced Western ideas of government and founded St Petersburg. By the end of Peter the Great's reign, the Baltic territories (modern-day Estonia and Latvia) had been annexed from Sweden, and Russia had become the dominant military power of north-eastern Europe. In the 18th century the partitions of Poland and wars with Turkey brought the territories of modern-day Lithuania, Belarus, Ukraine and the Crimea under Russian control, and the colonization of Siberia east of the Urals began in earnest. Russia overran the Caucasus region (modern-day Armenia, Azerbaijan and Georgia) in the early 19th century, seized Finland from Sweden in 1809 and Bessarabia from Turkey in 1812. Throughout the remainder of the 19th century Russia subdued and annexed the independent Muslim states which later formed the five Central Asian republics.

Discontent caused by autocratic rule, the poor conduct of the military in the First World War and wartime privation led to a revolution which broke out on 12 March (27 February os) 1917. Tsar Nicholas II abdicated three days later and a provisional government was formed; a republic was proclaimed on 14 September (1 September os) 1917. A power struggle ensued between the provisional government and the Bolshevik Party which controlled the Soviets (councils) set up by workers, soldiers and peasants. This led to a second revolution on 7 November (25 October os) 1917 in which the Bolsheviks, led by Lenin, seized power.

The Bolshevik (Communist) Party withdrew from the First World War under the Treaty of Brest-Litovsk (March 1918), surrendering large areas of territory. Armed resistance to Communist rule developed into an all-out civil war between 'red' Bolshevik forces and 'white' monarchist and anti-Communist forces which lasted until the end of 1922. During the civil war, Russia had been declared a Soviet Republic and other Soviet republics had been formed in Ukraine, Byelorussia and Transcaucasia. These four republics merged to form the Union of Soviet Socialist Republics (USSR) on 30 December 1922.

The Nazi–Soviet pact of August 1939 and the Second World War resulted in further territorial expansion, regaining much of the territory lost in or after 1918, as well as extending Soviet influence to the countries of eastern Europe liberated by Soviet troops. The USSR lost 26 million combatants and civilians in the war.

Joseph Stalin emerged as the undisputed party leader in 1928. He introduced a policy of rapid industrialization under a series of five-year plans, brought all sectors of industry under government control, abolished private ownership and enforced the collectivization of agriculture. He eliminated potential political opponents through purges and show trials, and total political repression lasted until his death in 1953.

Repression lessened under Khrushchev and Brezhnev, but the Communist Party remained dominant in all walks of life. This was the state of affairs when Mikhail Gorbachev became Soviet leader in March 1985. Gorbachev introduced the policies of *perestroika* (complete restructuring) and *glasnost* (openness) in order to revamp the economy, which had stagnated since the 1970s, to root out corruption and inefficiency, and to end the Cold War and its attendant arms race. The retreat from total control by the Communist Party unleashed ethnic and nationalist tensions.

On 19 August 1991 a coup was attempted by hardline elements of the Communist Party, the armed forces and the state security service (KGB) in an attempt to reimpose Communist control on the USSR. The coup was defeated by reformist and democratic political groups under the leadership of Russian President Yeltsin. Mikhail Gorbachev returned to Moscow although it became clear that effective political power was in the hands of the republican leaders, especially Russian President Yeltsin, and the Soviet Union began to break up as the constituent republics declared their independence. Gorbachev resigned as Soviet President on 25 December 1991 and on 26 December 1991 the USSR formally ceased to exist.

Russia was recognized as an independent state by the EC and USA in January 1992; it took over the Soviet Union's seat at the UN in December 1991.

A new Russian Federal Treaty was signed on 13 March 1992 between the central government and the autonomous republics. Tatarstan refused to sign the Treaty and in April 1992 declared its 'independence'. In February 1994 Tatarstan signed its own agreement with the federal government on the basis of being a 'state united with Russia'. Similarly, after declaring its 'independence' in March 1992, Bashkortostan signed a treaty with the Federation in August 1994 giving it considerable legislative and economic autonomy.

Elections to the Federal Assembly were held on 12 December 1993 and resulted in the pro-reform Russia's Democractic Choice bloc emerging as the largest party in the State Duma. The state of the parties in the State Duma following the January 1996 election was: Communist Party 157 seats; Our Home is Russia 55; Liberal Democratic Party 51; Yabloko 45; Agrarian Party 20; Russia's Democratic Choice 9; Power to the People 9; Congress of Russian Communities 5; Independents 77; others 22. Boris Yeltsin was elected president on the second ballot on 3 July 1996, ahead of Communist Party candidate Gennadi Zyuganov.

A brief period of economic growth was followed by instability in the financial markets in early 1998. President Yeltsin dismissed the cabinet in March 1998, and appointed Sergei Kiriyenko, a little-known banker, to replace Viktor Chernomyrdin as prime minister. This did little to restore confidence in the economy and following a major collapse on the Russian stock exchange, Yeltsin once more dismissed the cabinet in August 1998. He nominated Chernomyrdin as prime minister but the Duma twice rejected the appointment. To avert a constitutional crisis, Yeltsin then nominated Foreign Minister Yevgeni Primakov, seen as a compromise candidate whose appointment as prime minister would appease all factions in the Duma.

POLITICAL SYSTEM

The 1993 constitution enshrines the right to private ownership and the freedoms of press, speech, association, worship and travel, and states that Russia is a multiparty democracy. The president is head of state and of government, head of the Security Council and commander-in-chief of the armed forces and may declare war or declare a state of emergency or martial law, subject to confirmation by the Federation Council. He may chair Cabinet meetings, determine basic government policy, veto legislation, issue decrees and directives, call referendums, dismiss the government, and nominate senior judges, the prosecutor-general and the Central Bank Governor. The president nominates the prime minister and deputy prime ministers, who must be approved by the State Duma.

The president is directly elected for a maximum of two four-year terms, and may only be impeached on the grounds of treason or serious crime after rulings in both the Supreme and Constitutional Courts and two-thirds majorities in both houses of parliament. The prime minister takes over from the president in the event that he is unable to fulfil his duties.

Legislative power is vested in the Federal Assembly, comprising the Federation Council (upper house) of 178 members, two elected by each of the 89 members of the Russian Federation; the State Duma (lower house) of 450 members, of which 225 are elected by constituencies on a first-past-the-post basis and 225 by proportional representation, with a 5 per cent threshold for representation. State Duma deputies may not serve as ministers. The Council is composed of two representatives from each constituent territory of the Federation: the head of the legislative and the head of the executive body.

The State Duma, elected for four-year terms, oversees government appointments, has the power to reject the government's fiscal and monetary policies, may pass votes of no confidence in the government (which the president may ignore on the first vote), and cannot be dissolved less than one year after its election.

The judicial system consists of a Constitutional Court of 19 members appointed for a 12-year term which protects and interprets the constitution and decides if laws are compatible with it. The Supreme Court adjudicates in criminal and civil laws cases. The Arbitration Court deals with commercial disputes between companies. The new code of civil law came into force in January 1995.

INSURGENCIES

The Chechen republic declared its 'independence' in November 1991 after a nationalist coup in the republic which brought former Soviet Air Force General Dudayev to power as republican president. Chechenia refused to sign the Russian Federal Treaty in March 1992 and a constitutional stalemate ensued. Civil war began in early 1994 between Gen. Dudayev's forces and armed opposition forces of the 'Provisional Chechen Council', tacitly supported by the Russian government. On 9 December 1994 President Yeltsin ordered the Russian military to retake the republic. Chechen forces were finally forced out of Grozny in early February 1995.

A peace accord was signed on 30 July 1995 which provided for the disarming of rebels and the withdrawal of Russian troops. The agreement collapsed in October 1995, however, and a state of emergency was declared by the Russian government. The Russian-approved candidate was elected head of state of Chechenia on 17 December 1995 and concluded an autonomy accord with Russia giving the region autonomous status within the Federation. The rebels rejected the accord, and attacked Grozny in March 1996. President Yeltsin's new National Security Adviser, Gen. Lebed, resumed negotiations with the rebels in August 1996, reaching an agreement to end hostilities and to delay a decision on Chechenia's final status until 2001. The last Russian troops were withdrawn in January 1997 when presidential and legislative elections were also held in Chechenia. A treaty renouncing the use of force to resolve Chechenia's status was signed between Presidents Maskhadov and Yeltsin in May 1997. In September 1997, Chechenia introduced Sharia law, leading to public executions which were strongly criticized by Russia. A state of emergency was declared and a curfew imposed in June 1998 following an increase in serious criminal activity.

In November 1992 President Yeltsin imposed direct rule in the autonomous republics of Ingush and North Ossetia after Ingush forces attacked North Ossetia; a state of emergency was declared in the two autonomous republics in March 1993; it remains in place.

FOREIGN RELATIONS

A union treaty was signed by the presidents of Russia and Belarus in April 1997. Both countries will retain sovereignty and territorial integrity although citizens of the two countries will also be citizens of the Union.

A Founding Act was signed by Russia and NATO in May 1997 which lays down the principles of post-Cold War co-operation. A joint permanent council is to be set up.

HEAD OF STATE

President, Boris Yeltsin, elected 12 June 1991, re-elected 3 July 1996, inaugurated 9 August 1996

GOVERNMENT as at 24 September 1998
Prime Minister, Yevgeni Primakov
First Deputy PM, Yuri Maslyukov
Deputy PMs, Alexander Shokhin; Vladimir Bulgak; Valentina Matviyenko
Civil Defence, Sergei Shoigu
Defence, Igor Sergeyev
Economics, Andrei Shapovalyants
Foreign Affairs, Igor Ivanov
Fuel and Energy, Sergei Generalov
Interior, Sergei Stepashin
Justice, Pavel Krashenikov
National Policy, Ramazan Abdulatipov
Railways, Nikolai Aksenko
Transport, Sergei Frank
Chairman of the Central Bank, Viktor Geraschenko
This list includes only those ministers who had been nominated and approved at the time of going to press

EMBASSY OF THE RUSSIAN FEDERATION
13 Kensington Palace Gardens, London w8 4QX
Tel 0171-229 2666
Ambassador Extraordinary and Plenipotentiary, HE Yuri Fokine, apptd 1997
Minister-Counsellor, G. Gventsadze
Defence and Air Attaché, Maj.-Gen. V. E. Glagolev
Trade Representative, N. B. Telyatnikov

BRITISH EMBASSY
Sofiyskaya Naberezhnaya 14, Moscow 109072
Tel: Moscow 956 7200
Ambassador Extraordinary and Plenipotentiary, HE Sir Andrew Wood, KCMG, apptd 1995
Minister and Deputy Head of Mission, A. Longrigg, CMG
Defence and Air Attaché, Air Cdre M. L. Feenan, CBE
Counsellor (Commercial), S. Smith
Consuls-General: P. McDermott (Moscow); J. W. Guy, OBE (St Petersburg); I. A. Worthington (Yekaterinburg)
CONSULATE-GENERAL – St Petersburg

BRITISH COUNCIL DIRECTOR, T. Andrews, VGBIL, Ulitsa Nikoloyamskaya 1, Moscow 109189. There are also offices at St Petersburg and Yekaterinburg

DEFENCE (see also CIS entry, pages 751)

Since the demise of the Soviet Union the Russian armed forces have been considerably reduced but remain among the most powerful in the world. In July 1998 it was announced that the armed forces would be reduced to 1.2 million personnel.

The Strategic Nuclear Forces have 34 nuclear-powered ballistic missile submarines with 540 missiles, 800 intercontinental ballistic missiles, 1,820 armoured personnel carriers, 750 helicopters, 66 long-range bomber aircraft and 100 anti-ballistic missiles.

The Army has 15,500 main battle tanks, 10,193 armoured personnel carriers and armoured infantry fighting vehicles, 15,700 artillery pieces and 2,565 helicopters. The Navy has 128 submarines, one aircraft carrier, 22 cruisers, 19 destroyers, two anti-submarine vessels, 18 frigates, 182 patrol and coastal vessels, 329 combat aircraft and 387 armed helicopters. The Air Force has 1,855 combat aircraft.

Russia maintains a joint air defence force with the five Central Asian republics, maintains joint armed forces of 11,000 personnel with Turkmenistan, and was due to establish a joint armed forces with Kazakhstan by the end of 1995. It also deploys forces in Armenia (4,300), Georgia (8,500), Moldova (2,500) and Tajikistan (6,000). Russia is the world's third largest contributor to peacekeeping operations. An agreement with Ukraine on the division of the Black Sea Fleet was signed in May 1997.

MILITARY EXPENDITURE – 6.5 per cent of GDP (1996)

MILITARY PERSONNEL – 1,672,000: Missile Forces 149,000, Army 420,000, Navy 220,000, Air Force 130,000, Air Defence Troops 170,000, Paramilitaries 583,000

CONSCRIPTION DURATION – 18–24 months. Due to be ended by 2000

ECONOMY

Under the Soviet regime, an essentially agrarian economy in 1917 was transformed by the early 1960s into the second strongest industrial power in the world. However, by the early 1970s the concentration of resources on the military-industrial complex was causing the civilian economy to stagnate. This was exacerbated by the bureaucratic inefficiency of the centrally planned economic system and the poor distribution system. It was in an attempt to solve these problems that Gorbachev introduced economic restructuring (*perestroika*). Free market reforms were introduced, including the legalization of small private businesses, the reduction of state control over the economy, and de-nationalization and privatization. In May 1992 most state subsidies were abolished and price liberalization was introduced. The first stage of mass privatization of state industries began in October 1992 and the central distribution system was abolished with effect from 1 January 1993.

However, the abolition of central planning before a fully free market system was in place resulted in economic confusion. By the end of the first stage of mass privatization in June 1994 an estimated 35–40 per cent of enterprises had been privatized. On 27 October 1993 President Yeltsin issued a decree allowing the unrestricted buying and selling of land for the first time since 1917. The second stage of mass privatization was launched on 1 July 1994 and consists of the sale of residual government shares in most companies. By February 1996, 80 per cent of the economy had been privatized.

The restructuring of state enterprises has not been successful. In January 1992 economic 'shock therapy' was introduced to end hyperinflation and restore government reserves by liberalizing prices and restructuring firms to end their reliance on state subsidies. The policy was only partially implemented in 1992–4 due to parliamentary resistance. As a result industrial production declined (15.5 per cent in 1993), hyperinflation continued (900 per cent in 1993) and the rouble tumbled.

From 1994 to 1996, the economy began to stabilize with economic reforms judged to have become irreversible. Industrial output and GDP fell by 3 per cent and 4 per cent respectively in 1995, compared with 21 per cent and 18.6 per cent in 1994, a result of the government having finally gained control of the money supply. Agricultural production declined by more than 10 per cent in 1995, whereas arms sales grew by 62 per cent, rising to US$6,000 million from US$3,700 million in 1994.

Russia has received considerable international aid since 1993. In April 1993 a rescheduling of Russia's US$80 billion foreign debt was announced, which saved US$15 billion in repayments. A further US$39.5 billion was rescheduled in 1994–5. The G7 summit in Tokyo in April

1994 pledged aid of US$43 billion for structural reform and rouble stabilization, conditional on political and economic reforms. In 1995 the IMF provided US$6,800 million in stand-by credit to cover part of the budget deficit. A further three-year credit of US$10,087 million, granted in February 1996, was made conditional on the government maintaining spending limits.

In 1997, for the first time since economic reforms were introduced, Russian GDP grew by 0.4 per cent. The central bank also announced that from 1998 the redenominated rouble (1 new rouble equalling 1,000 old roubles) would be pegged to the US dollar, being allowed to fluctuate within 15 per cent of US$ = 6.1 roubles. The economic improvement was countered by speculative currency attacks following the economic crisis in south-east Asia, which forced the central bank to spend US$5 billion supporting the rouble between November 1997 and June 1998.

In May 1998 the Russian stock market went into steep decline, and interest rates were tripled to 150 per cent to avoid a devaluation of the currency. The IMF pledged US$13.7 billion to support the rouble, but in August, trading on the Russian stock exchange was suspended twice in a week after shares lost 15 per cent of their value. On 17 August, the central bank announced it was relaxing control of the rouble, in effect a *de facto* devaluation of 50 per cent, triggering panic selling of roubles, and prompting widespread fears that Russia would default on its loans. Western governments and financial institutions refused to pledge any more money to support the rouble, raising fears of hyperinflation and economic collapse.

Russia has some of the richest mineral deposits in the world. Coal is mined in the Kuznetsk area, in the Urals, south of Moscow, in the Donets basin and in the Pechora area in the north. Oil is produced in the northern Caucasus, between the Volga and the Urals, and in western Siberia, which also has large deposits of natural gas. A pipeline to bring Caspian oil into Russia via Dagestan and North Ossetia is under construction. Coal and gas deposits in Siberia and the far east (especially Yakutia) are being developed. The Ural mountains contain high-quality iron ore, manganese, copper, aluminium, platinum, precious stones, salt, asbestos, pyrites, coal, oil, etc. Iron ore is also mined near Kursk, Tula, Lipetsk, in several areas in Siberia and in the Kola Peninsula. Non-ferrous metals are found in the Altai, in eastern Siberia, in the northern Caucasus, in the Kuznetsk basin, in the far east and in the far north. 106 tonnes of gold were produced in 1997.

The vast area and the great variety in climatic conditions are reflected in the structure of agriculture. In the far north reindeer breeding, hunting and fishing are predominant. Further south, timber industry is combined with grain growing. In the southern half of the forest zone and in the adjacent forest-steppe zone, the acreage under grain crops is larger and the structure of agriculture more complex. Between the Volga and the Urals cericulture is predominant (particularly summer wheat), followed by cattle breeding. Beyond the Urals is another important grain-growing and stock-breeding area in the southern part of the western Siberian plain. The southern steppe zone is the main wheat granary of Russia, containing also large acreages under barley, maize and sunflowers. In the extreme south cotton is cultivated. Vine, tobacco and other southern crops are grown on the Black Sea shore of the Caucasus.

Moscow and St Petersburg are still the two largest industrial centres in the country, but new industrial areas have been developed in the Urals, the Kuznetsk basin, in Siberia and the far east. Most of the oil produced in the former USSR came from Russia; half the annual output comes from Tyumen Oblast in western Siberia. All industries are represented in Russia, including iron and steel and engineering.

GNP – US$356,030 million (1996); US$2,410 per capita (1996)
GDP – US$626,929 million (1994); US$1,951 per capita (1994)
INFLATION RATE – 47.6 per cent (1996)
UNEMPLOYMENT – 8.3 per cent (1995)
TOTAL EXTERNAL DEBT – US$124,785 million (1996)

TRADE

Russia's main trading partners are Germany, the USA, Italy, China and the former Soviet states. In 1996 there was a trade surplus of US$20,887 million and a current account surplus of US$9,331 million. Imports totalled US$61,147 million and exports US$88,703 million.

Trade with UK	1996	1997
Imports from UK	£1,009,250,000	£1,232,581,000
Exports to UK	1,274,785,000	1,476,772,000

COMMUNICATIONS

The European area of Russia is well served by railways, St Petersburg and Moscow being the two main focal points of rail routes. The centre and south have a good system of north-south and east-west lines, but the eastern part (the Volga lands), traversed by trunk lines between Europe and Asia, lacks north-south routes. In Asia, there are still large areas, notably in the far north and Siberia, with few or no railways. In the northern part of European Russia, the North Pechora Railway has been completed, while in the far east a second Trans-Siberian line (the Baikal-Amur Railway) is partially in use; it follows a more northerly alignment than the earlier Trans-Siberian and terminates in the Pacific port of Sovetskaya Gavan.

The most important ports (Taganrog, Rostov and Novorossiisk) lie around the Black Sea and the Sea of Azov. The northern ports (St Petersburg, Murmansk and Arkhangelsk) are, with the exception of Murmansk, ice-bound during winter. Several ports have been built along the Arctic Sea route between Murmansk and Vladivostok and are in regular use every summer. The far eastern port of Vladivostok, the Pacific naval base of Russia, is kept open by icebreakers all the year round.

Inland waterways, both natural and artificial, are of great importance in the country, although some of them are icebound in winter (from two and a half months in the south to six months in the north). The great rivers of European Russia flow outwards from the centre, linking all parts of the plain with the chief ports, an immense system of navigable waterways which carried about 690 million tons of freight in 1988. They are supplemented by a system of canals which provide a through traffic between the White, Baltic, Black and Caspian Seas. The most notable are the White Sea-Baltic Canal, the Moscow-Volga Canal and the Volga-Don Canal linking the Baltic and the White Seas in the north to the Caspian Sea, the Black Sea and the Sea of Azov in the south.

CULTURE

Russian is a branch of the Slavonic family of languages and is written in the Cyrillic script.

Before the westernization of Russia under Peter the Great (1682–1725), Russian literature consisted mainly of folk ballads (*byliny*), epic songs, chronicles and works of moral theology. The 18th and 19th centuries saw the development of poetry and fiction. Poetry reached its zenith with Alexander Pushkin (1799–1837), Mikhail Lermontov (1814–41), Alexander Blok (1880–1921), the 1958 Nobel Prize laureate Boris Pasternak (1890–1960),

Vladimir Mayakovsky (1893–1930) and Anna Akhmatova (1888–1966). Fiction is associated with the names of Nikolai Gogol (1809–52), Ivan Turgenev (1818–83), Fyodor Dostoevsky (1821–81), Leo Tolstoy (1828–1910), Anton Chekhov (1860–1904), Maxim Gorky (1868–1936), Ivan Bunin (1870–1953), Mikhail Bulgakov (1891–1940), Mikhail Sholokhov (1905–84) and Alexander Solzhenitsyn (b. 1918).

Great names in music include Glinka (1804–57), Borodin (1833–87), Mussorgsky (1839–81), Rimsky-Korsakov (1844–1908), Rubinstein (1829–94), Tchaikovsky (1840–93), Rachmaninov (1873–1943), Skriabin (1872–1915), Prokofiev (1891–1953), Stravinsky (1882–1971), Shostakovich (1906–75) and Alfred Schnittke (b. 1934).

RWANDA
Republika y'u Rwanda

AREA – 10,169 sq. miles (26,338 sq. km). Neighbours: Burundi (south), Democratic Republic of Congo (west), Uganda (north), Tanzania (east)
POPULATION – 7,952,000 (1994 UN estimate): Hutus 90 per cent, Tutsis 9 per cent, Twa (pygmy) 1 per cent. Kinyarwanda, French and English are the official languages. Swahili is also spoken
CAPITAL – Kigali (population, 156,000)
CURRENCY – Rwanda franc of 100 centimes
NATIONAL DAY – 1 July
NATIONAL FLAG – Three vertical bands, red, yellow and green with letter R on yellow band
LIFE EXPECTANCY (years) – male 45.10; female 47.70
POPULATION GROWTH RATE – 2.0 per cent (1995)
POPULATION DENSITY – 302 per sq. km (1995)
URBAN POPULATION – 5.4 per cent (1991)
MILITARY EXPENDITURE – 6.3 per cent of GDP (1996)
MILITARY PERSONNEL – 62,000: Army 55,000, Paramilitaries 7,000
ILLITERACY RATE – 39.5 per cent
ENROLMENT (percentage of age group) – primary 76 per cent (1991); secondary 8 per cent (1991); tertiary 0.6 per cent (1990)

HISTORY AND POLITICS

The majority Hutu population rebelled against Tutsi feudal rule (under the Belgian colonial authority) in 1959–61, leading to the massacre of thousands of Tutsis. Large numbers fled into exile in Uganda. In October 1961, the monarchy was abolished following a referendum. Rwanda became an independent republic on 1 July 1962, with Grégoire Kayibanda as head of state. He was deposed in 1973 and replaced by a military government under Maj.-Gen. Juvénal Habyarimana, who established a one-party state.

Armed Tutsi exiles repeatedly attempted to invade Rwanda in the 1960s and 1970s but were defeated by the predominantly Hutu army. Continued Hutu-Tutsi conflict left thousands dead over a period of 30 years. In October 1990 Rwanda was invaded by the Rwandan Patriotic Front (RPF) of exiled Tutsis and moderate Hutus, who forced the one-party MRND (National Revolutionary Movement for Development) government to introduce a multiparty constitution in 1991. After the government reneged on a 1992 peace agreement, the RPF advanced on Kigali and forced the government to restart negotiations, which led to the August 1993 Arusha peace accord. The accord provided for a transitional period under a broad-based government including the RPF until the 1995 elections, with UN forces in the country throughout the period.

During the transitional period, President Habyarimana, who had retained the interim presidency, died on 6 April 1994 in a plane crash widely believed to have been caused by a rocket attack by extremist sections of the Hutu army. The Hutu army and armed militia, the *interahamwe*, then carried out a preplanned act of genocide against the Tutsi minority and moderate Hutus; 500,000 people were massacred in three months. The civil war restarted and the RPF gradually re-established its control over the country, forcing the defeated government forces and two million Hutu refugees into exile, while another 1.2 million Hutus fled to the French 'safe zone' in the south-west. On 18 July 1994 the RPF declared victory and established a broad-based government of national unity in which moderate Hutus were given the presidency and premiership and the RPF took eight of the 22 seats.

Some 50,000–60,000 Hutu refugees died of disease in refugee camps in eastern Zaïre (now the Democratic Republic of Congo) in August–September 1994. French troops withdrew from their 'safe zone' in the south-west of Rwanda in September 1994 and were replaced by RPF forces who gradually returned most refugees in the zone to their homes. UN forces (UNAMIR II) were deployed to deter revenge attacks by Tutsis on Hutus.

In April 1995, 200,000 Hutu refugees remained in camps in the south-west controlled by armed Hutu militia members. RPF forces attacked the camps and broke the militia control in fighting which killed hundreds of people before the return of refugees was completed. In August the Zaïrean government began the forcible repatriation of some of the over one million Hutu refugees who, it felt, were destabilizing eastern Zaïre. However, after thousands had fled to the countryside rather than return to Rwanda, international pressure forced the Zaïrean government to agree to a voluntary repatriation programme organized by the UN High Commissioner for Refugees (UNHCR). In November 1994 the UN Security Council established the International Criminal Tribunal for Rwanda (ICTR) to prosecute those responsible for genocide and other international humanitarian law violations between 1 January and 31 December 1994. An estimated 200,000 Tutsi refugees who fled to Uganda in the 1960s and 1970s have returned to Rwanda. By December 1995, 500,000 refugees remained in Tanzania, and one million in Zaïre.

The 70-member Transitional National Assembly provided for by the Arusha agreement began operation on 12 December 1994 with the extremist Hutu MRND excluded. However, tensions between Tutsis and moderate Hutus in the government remain, with Prime Minister Twagiramungu and four other ministers being dismissed in August 1995 after criticizing the lack of power-sharing by the RPF and the security situation in the country.

UN forces left the country in March 1996. Killings by both Hutu militia and government forces continued, and Hutu attacks in central and western Rwanda were frequent in the first half of 1998.

At the ICTR in May 1998, former Prime Minister Jean Kambanda pleaded guilty to charges of genocide, the first admission by a senior Hutu official that genocide had taken place. His admission may be used to implicate other officials who had denied that genocide was taking place.

HEAD OF STATE
President, Pasteur Bizimungu, *sworn in* 19 July 1994
Vice-President, Defence, Maj-Gen. Paul Kagame

GOVERNMENT *as at July 1998*
The President (FPR)
The Vice-President (FPR)

Prime Minister, Pierre-Célestin Rwigyema (MDR)
Agriculture, Livestock, Environment and Rural Development, Augustin Iyamuremye (PSD)
Commerce, Industry and Co-operatives, Bonaventure Niyibizi
Communication, Charles Ntakirutinka (PSD)
Education, Col. Joseph Karemera (FPR)
Foreign Affairs and Co-operation, Anastase Gasana (MDR)
Gender, Family and Social Affairs, Aloysia Inyunba (FPR)
Handicrafts, Mining and Tourism, Marc Rugenera (PSD)
Health, Vincent Biruta
Information, Jean-Nepomunce Nayinzira (PDC)
Internal Affairs, Communal Development and Resettlement, Sheikh Abdul Karim Harerimana (FPR)
Justice, Faustin Nteziryayo (Ind.)
Ministers of State, Gérard Zirimwabagabo *(Agriculture, Livestock, Environment and Rural Development)*; Jean-Pierre Bizimana (MDR) *(Education)*; Donat Kaberuka *(Finance and Economic Planning)*; Béatrice Sebatware Panda *(Internal Affairs, Communal Development and Resettlement)*; Anastase Nderabeza *(Secretary-General in Prime Minister's Office)*
President's Office, Patrick Mazimpaka (FPR)
Public Service and Labour, Joseph Nsengimana (PL)
Public Works, Laurien Ngirabanzi (MDR)
Youth, Sports and Vocational Training, Jacques Bihozagara (FPR)

FPR Rwandan Patriotic Front; MDR Republican Democratic Movement; PSD Social Democratic Party; PDC Christian Democratic Party; Ind. Independent; PL Liberal Party

EMBASSY OF THE REPUBLIC OF RWANDA
Uganda House, 58-59 Trafalgar Square, London WC2N 5DX
Tel: 0171-930 2570
Ambassador Extraordinary and Plenipotentiary, Dr Zac Nsenga, apptd 1996

BRITISH EMBASSY
Parcelle No. 1071, Kimihurura, Kigali
Tel: Kigali 84098
Ambassador Extraordinary and Plenipotentiary, HE Graeme Loten, apptd 1998

ECONOMY

Coffee, tea and sugar are grown. Tin, hides, bark of quinine and extract of pyrethrum flowers are also exported.

In 1993 there was a trade deficit of US$200 million and a current account deficit of US$129 million. In 1996 imports totalled US$259 million and exports US$60 million.
GNP – US$1,268 million (1996); US$190 per capita (1996)
GDP – US$995 million (1994); US$65 per capita (1994)
ANNUAL AVERAGE GROWTH OF GDP – –15.9 per cent (1993)
INFLATION RATE – 7.4 per cent (1996)
TOTAL EXTERNAL DEBT – US$1,034 million (1996)

Trade with UK	1996	1997
Imports from UK	£4,170,000	£4,944,000
Exports to UK	2,478,000	1,212,000

ST CHRISTOPHER AND NEVIS
The Federation of St Christopher and Nevis

AREA – 101 sq. miles (261 sq. km)
POPULATION – 41,000 (1994 UN estimate). The language is English
CAPITAL – ΨBasseterre (population, 14,161, 1980)
MAJOR TOWNS – ΨCharlestown (1,200), the chief town of Nevis
CURRENCY – East Caribbean dollar (EC$) of 100 cents

NATIONAL ANTHEM – Oh Land of Beauty
NATIONAL DAY – 19 September (Independence Day)
NATIONAL FLAG – Three diagonal bands, green, black and red; each colour separated by a stripe of yellow. Two white stars on the black band
LIFE EXPECTANCY (years) – male 65.10; female 70.08
POPULATION GROWTH RATE – –0.5 per cent (1995)
POPULATION DENSITY – 157 per sq. km (1995)

The state of St Christopher and Nevis is located at the northern end of the eastern Caribbean. It comprises the islands of St Christopher (St Kitts) (68 sq. miles) and Nevis (36 sq. miles). The central area of St Christopher is forest-clad and mountainous, rising to the 3,792 ft Mount Liamuiga. Nevis is separated from the southern tip of St Christopher by a strait two miles wide and is dominated by Nevis Peak, 3,232 ft.

HISTORY AND POLITICS

St Christopher was the first island in the British West Indies to be colonized (1623). The Territory of St Christopher and Nevis became a State in Association with Britain in 1967. The State of St Christopher and Nevis became an independent nation on 19 September 1983.

In the July 1995 election to the National Assembly, the Labour Party won seven seats, and the People's Action Movement won one seat. Of the three seats reserved for Nevis, the Concerned Citizens' Movement won two seats and the Nevis Reformation Party won one seat. On 10 August 1998 a referendum was held in Nevis on the question of independence from St Christopher; although 61 per cent voted in favour of secession, it fell short of the two-thirds majority needed for independence.

POLITICAL SYSTEM

Under the constitution, Queen Elizabeth II is head of state, represented in the islands by the Governor-General. There is a central government with a ministerial system, the head of which is the prime minister of St Christopher and Nevis, and a National Assembly located on St Christopher. The National Assembly is composed of the Speaker, three senators (nominated by the prime minister and the Leader of the Opposition) and 11 elected representatives. On Nevis there is a Nevis Island Administration, the head being styled Premier of Nevis, and a Nevis Island Assembly of five elected and three nominated members.

Governor-General, HE Sir Cuthbert Montraville Sebastian, GCMG, OBE, apptd 1996

CABINET as at July 1998

Prime Minister, Finance, National Security, Planning, Information, Foreign Affairs, Dr Denzil Douglas
Deputy PM, Trade, Industry and Caricom Affairs, Youth, Sports and Community Affairs, Sam Condor
Agriculture, Lands and Housing, Timothy Harris
Attorney-General, Delano Bart
Communications, Works, Utilities and Ports, Cedric Liburd
Culture, Environment and Tourism, Dwyer Astaphan
Education, Labour and Social Security, Rupert Herbert
Health and Women's Affairs, Dr Earl Asim Martin

HIGH COMMISSION FOR ST CHRISTOPHER AND NEVIS
10 Kensington Court, London W8 5DL
Tel 0171-937 9522
High Commissioner for the Eastern Caribbean States, HE Aubrey Hart, apptd 1994

BRITISH HIGH COMMISSIONER, HE R. Thomas, CMG, resident at Bridgetown, Barbados

ECONOMY

The economy of the islands has been based on sugar for over three centuries. Tourism (214,000 visitors in 1995) and light industry, concentrating on brewing, food processing, clothing and electronics, are now being developed. The economy of Nevis centres on small peasant farmers, but a sea-island cotton industry is being developed for export.

The main exports are sugar, lobsters, beverages and electrical equipment. Foodstuffs, energy, machinery and transport equipment are the main imports.

In 1994 St Christopher and Nevis had a trade deficit of US$69 million and a current account deficit of US$26 million.

GNP – US$240 million (1996); US$5,870 per capita (1996)
GDP – US$146 million (1994); US$4,217 per capita (1994)
ANNUAL AVERAGE GROWTH OF GDP – 4.0 per cent (1993)
INFLATION RATE – 2.5 per cent (1996)
TOTAL EXTERNAL DEBT – US$58 million (1996)

TRADE WITH UK	1996	1997
Imports from UK	£9,387,000	£9,976,000
Exports to UK	2,929,000	9,049,000

COMMUNICATIONS

Basseterre is a port of registry and has deep water harbour facilities. Golden Rock airport, on St Kitts, can take most large jet aircraft; Newcastle airstrip on Nevis can take small aircraft and has night landing facilities. The sea ferry route from Basseterre to Charlestown is 11 miles.

ST LUCIA

AREA – 240 sq. miles (622 sq. km)
POPULATION – 145,000 (1994 UN estimate). The official language is English. A French creole is spoken by most of the population
CAPITAL – ΨCastries (population, 56,000, 1989)
CURRENCY – East Caribbean dollar (EC$) of 100 cents
NATIONAL ANTHEM – Sons and Daughters of Saint Lucia
NATIONAL DAY – 22 February (Independence Day)
NATIONAL FLAG – Blue, bearing in centre a device of yellow over black over white triangles having a common base
LIFE EXPECTANCY (years) – male 68.00; female 74.80
POPULATION GROWTH RATE – 1.8 per cent (1995)
POPULATION DENSITY – 234 per sq. km (1995)

St Lucia, the second largest of the Windward group, is 27 miles in length, with an extreme breadth of 14 miles. It is mountainous, its highest point being Mt Gimie (3,145 ft) and for the most part it is covered with forest and tropical vegetation.

HISTORY AND POLITICS

Possession of St Lucia was fiercely disputed and it constantly changed hands between the British and the French until 1814 when it was ceded to Britain by the Treaty of Paris. It became independent within the Commonwealth on 22 February 1979.

The St Lucia Labour Party defeated the ruling United Workers' Party in a general election on 23 May 1997, winning all but one of the seats in the House of Assembly.

POLITICAL SYSTEM

The head of state is Queen Elizabeth II, represented in the island by a St Lucian Governor-General, and there is a

1000   Countries of the World

bicameral legislature. The Senate has 11 members, six appointed by the ruling party, three by the Opposition and two by the Governor-General. The House of Assembly, which has a life of five years, has 17 elected members and a Speaker, who may be elected from outside the House.

Governor-General, HE Perlette Louisy, apptd 1997

CABINET *as at July 1998*
Prime Minister, Finance, Planning, Information, Public Service, Kenny Anthony
Agriculture, Fisheries, the Environment, Cassius Elias
Commerce, Industry, Consumer Affairs, Walter François
Communications, Works, Transport and Public Utilities, Calixte George
Community Development, Culture, Local Government and Co-operatives, Damian Greaves
Education, Human Resources Development, Youth and Sport, Mario Michel
Foreign Affairs, International Trade, George Odlum
Health, Human Services, Family Affairs, Women, Sarah Flood
Legal Affairs, Labour, Home Affairs, Velon John
Parliamentary Secretaries, Petrus Compton *(Attorney-General);* Menissa Rambally *(Civil Aviation, Financial Services);* Cyprian Lansiquot *(Communications, Works, Transport and Public Utilities);* Kenneth John *(Education, Human Resources Development, Youth and Sport)*
Tourism, Civil Aviation, Phillip Pierre

HIGH COMMISSION FOR ST LUCIA
10 Kensington Court, London W8 5DL
Tel 0171-937 9522
High Commissioner for the Eastern Caribbean States, HE Aubrey Hart, apptd 1994

OFFICE OF THE BRITISH HIGH COMMISSION
PO Box 227, Castries
Tel: Castries 452 2484
Acting High Commissioner, P. J. Hughes

ECONOMY

The economy is mainly agrarian, with manufacturing based on the processing of agricultural products. Principal crops are bananas, coconuts, cocoa, mangoes, breadfruit, yams and citrus fruit. Attempts are being made to increase industrialization. There were 394,000 visitors to the island in 1994.

GNP – US$553 million (1996); US$3,500 per capita (1996)
GDP – US$381 million (1994); US$3,014 per capita (1994)
ANNUAL AVERAGE GROWTH OF GDP – 6.6 per cent (1992)
INFLATION RATE – 2.7 per cent (1995)
TOTAL EXTERNAL DEBT – US$142 million (1996)

TRADE

The principal exports are bananas, coconut products (copra, edible oils, soap), cardboard boxes, beer, and textile manufactures. The chief imports are flour, meat, machinery, building materials, motor vehicles, manufactured goods, petroleum and fertilizers.

In 1994 St Lucia had a trade deficit of US$166 million and a current account deficit of US$65 million.

Trade with UK	1996	1997
Imports from UK	£18,156,000	£15,134,000
Exports to UK	52,186,000	34,029,000

ST VINCENT AND THE GRENADINES

AREA – 150 sq. miles (388 sq. km)
POPULATION – 111,000 (1994 UN estimate). The language is English
CAPITAL – ΨKingstown (population, 33,694)
CURRENCY – East Caribbean dollar (EC$) of 100 cents
NATIONAL ANTHEM – St Vincent, Land So Beautiful
NATIONAL DAY – 27 October (Independence Day)
NATIONAL FLAG – Three vertical bands, of blue, yellow and green, with three green diamonds in the shape of a 'V' mounted on the yellow band
POPULATION GROWTH RATE – 0.7 per cent (1995)
POPULATION DENSITY – 285 per sq. km (1995)

The territory of St Vincent includes certain of the Grenadines, a chain of small islands stretching 40 miles across the Caribbean Sea between Grenada and St Vincent, some of the larger of which are Bequia, Canouan, Mayreau, Mustique, Union Island, Petit St Vincent and Prune Island.

HISTORY AND POLITICS

St Vincent was discovered by Christopher Columbus in 1498. It was granted by Charles I to the Earl of Carlisle in 1627 and after subsequent grants and a series of occupations alternately by the French and English, it was finally restored to Britain in 1783. St Vincent achieved full independence within the Commonwealth as St Vincent and the Grenadines on 27 October 1979.

The governing New Democratic Party won eight seats and the United Labour Party seven seats at the election held on 15 June 1998.

POLITICAL SYSTEM

Queen Elizabeth II is head of state, represented by a Governor-General. The House of Assembly consists of 15 elected members and four Senators appointed by the government and two by the Opposition. It is presided over by a Speaker elected by the House from within or without it.

Governor-General, HE Sir Charles Antrobus, GCMG, OBE, *sworn in* 15 October 1996

CABINET *as at July 1998*
Prime Minister, National Security and Home Affairs, Sir James Mitchell, KCMG
Agriculture, Lands and Surveys, Jeremiah Scott
Attorney-General, Justice, Carl Joseph
Communications and Works, Glenford Stewart
Education, Alpian Allen
Finance, Public Service, Arnhim Eustace
Foreign Affairs, Tourism, Allan Cruickshank
Health, St Clair Thomas
Housing, Community Development, Youth and Sports, Monty Roberts
Trade, Industry and Consumer Affairs, John Horne

HIGH COMMISSION FOR ST VINCENT AND THE GRENADINES
10 Kensington Court, London W8 5DL
Tel 0171-937 9522
High Commissioner for the Eastern Caribbean States, HE Aubrey Hart, apptd 1994

BRITISH HIGH COMMISSION
Granby Street (PO Box 132), Kingstown
Tel: St Vincent 457 1701/2

High Commissioner, HE Richard Thomas, CMG, resident at Bridgetown, Barbados
Acting High Commissioner, B. Robertson

ECONOMY

This is based mainly on agriculture but tourism (218,000 visitors in 1995) and manufacturing industries have been expanding. The main products are bananas, arrowroot, coconuts, cocoa, spices and various kinds of food crops. The main imports are foodstuffs, textiles, lumber, chemicals, motor vehicles and fuel.

In 1995 St Vincent and the Grenadines had a trade deficit of US$63 million and a current account deficit of US$36 million. In 1996 imports totalled US$132 million and exports US$46 million.

GNP – US$264 million (1996); US$2,370 per capita (1996)
GDP – US$217 million (1994); US$2,248 per capita (1994)
ANNUAL AVERAGE GROWTH OF GDP – 7.4 per cent (1995)
INFLATION RATE – 4.4 per cent (1996)
TOTAL EXTERNAL DEBT – US$213 million (1996)

TRADE WITH UK	1996	1997
Imports from UK	£7,719,000	£7,992,000
Exports to UK	21,091,000	15,346,000

EL SALVADOR
República de El Salvador

AREA – 8,124 sq. miles (21,041 sq. km). Neighbours: Guatemala (north-west), Honduras (north-east and east)
POPULATION – 5,768,000 (1994 UN estimate). The language is Spanish
CAPITAL – San Salvador (population, 422,570, 1992)
MAJOR CITIES – San Miguel (182,817); Santa Ana (202,307)
CURRENCY – El Salvador colón (₡) of 100 centavos
NATIONAL ANTHEM – Saludemos La Patria Orgullosos (Let us proudly hail the Fatherland)
NATIONAL DAY – 15 September
NATIONAL FLAG – Three horizontal bands, sky blue, white, sky blue; coat of arms on white band
LIFE EXPECTANCY (years) – male 50.74; female 63.89
POPULATION GROWTH RATE – 2.2 per cent (1995)
POPULATION DENSITY – 274 per sq. km (1995)
URBAN POPULATION – 50.4 per cent (1992)
MILITARY EXPENDITURE – 1.4 per cent of GDP (1996)
MILITARY PERSONNEL – 40,400: Army 25,700, Navy 1,100, Air Force 1,600, Paramilitaries 12,000
CONSCRIPTION DURATION – 12 months

El Salvador extends along the Pacific coast of Central America for 160 miles. The surface of the country is very mountainous, many of the peaks being extinct volcanoes. Much of the interior has an average altitude of 2,000 feet. The climate varies from tropical to temperate. There is a wet season from May to October, and a dry season from November to April. Earthquakes are frequent, the most recent being in October 1986.

HISTORY AND POLITICS

El Salvador was conquered in 1526 by Pedro de Alvarado, and formed part of the Spanish viceroyalty of Guatemala until 1821. It is divided into 14 Departments.

Decades of military rule ended in March 1982 when a Constituent Assembly was elected. Subsequent presidential and parliamentary elections were boycotted by the

FMLN (Farabundo Martí National Liberation Front) guerrilla movement. Conflict between the guerrillas and the government continued throughout the 1980s until negotiations culminated in a peace plan signed in January 1992. A cease-fire took effect on 1 February and began a nine-month transition period which ended in December 1992 when the FMLN finished its disarmament and became a political party. A 'Truth Commission', established under UN auspices to investigate human rights abuses in the 1980–91 period, reported in March 1993. The report caused a political crisis when it declared that 15 senior army commanders should be removed. The government was reluctant to do so but came under economic pressure from the USA, which withheld aid for reconstruction until the officers were dismissed on 1 July 1993.

The UN Observer Mission in El Salvador (ONUSAL) monitored the 1992–4 transition process, overseeing the final destruction of FMLN arms in August 1993 and the presidential, parliamentary and local elections held in March and April 1994. Armando Calderón Sol of the ruling right-wing ARENA party won the presidential election. ARENA won 39 of the Legislative Assembly's 84 seats and formed a government with other right-wing parties; the FMLN won 21 seats.

ARENA won marginally more seats than the FMLN in legislative elections in March 1997. A presidential election is due to be held in 1999.

HEAD OF STATE
President, Armando Calderón Sol, *assumed office* 1 June 1994
Vice-President, Minister of the Presidency, Enrique Borgo Bustamante

COUNCIL OF STATE *as at July 1998*
Agriculture, Ricardo Quiñónez Avila
Defence, Gen. Jaime Guzmán Morales
Economy, Eduardo Zablah Touche
Education, María Cecilia Gallardo de Cano
Environment, Miguel Araujo
Foreign Affairs, Ramón González Giner
Interior, Mario Acosta Oertel
Justice, Dr Rubén Antonio Mejía Peña
Labour and Social Security, Eduardo Tomasino
President of the Legislative Assembly, Francisco Guillermo Flores
Public Health and Social Welfare, Dr Eduardo Interiano
Public Security, Hugo Barrera
Public Works, Roberto Bara Osegueda
Treasury, Manuel Enrique Hinds

EMBASSY OF EL SALVADOR
Tennyson House, 159 Great Portland Street, London WIN 5FD
Tel 0171-436 8282
Ambassador Extraordinary and Plenipotentiary, new appointment awaited
Chargé d'Affaires, Ramiro Recinos Trejo

BRITISH EMBASSY
PO Box 1591, San Salvador
Tel: San Salvador 263 6527
Ambassador Extraordinary and Plenipotentiary, HE Ian Gerken, LVO, apptd 1995

ECONOMY

The principal agricultural products are coffee, cotton, sugar cane, maize, shrimps and balsam, though cotton and sugar production have decreased as a result of the civil war. In the lower altitudes towards the east, sisal is produced and used in the manufacture of coffee and cereal bags. The

Salvadorean Coffee Company and the banking system are being privatized.

Existing factories make textiles, clothing, constructional steel, furniture, cement and household items.

GNP – US$9,868 million (1996); US$1,700 per capita (1996)

GDP – US$6,335 million (1994); US$1,584 per capita (1994)

ANNUAL AVERAGE GROWTH OF GDP – 25.4 per cent (1996)

INFLATION RATE – 9.8 per cent (1996)

UNEMPLOYMENT – 7.7 per cent (1995)

TOTAL EXTERNAL DEBT – US$2,894 million (1996)

TRADE

Chief exports are coffee, cotton, sugar, shrimps, sisal, balsam, meat, towels, hides and skins. The chief imports are chemicals, petroleum, manufactured goods, industrial and electronic machinery, pharmaceutical goods, vehicles and consumer goods.

In 1996 imports totalled US$2,671 million and exports US$1,024 million. In 1995 there was a trade deficit of US$1,523 million and a current account deficit of US$322 million.

Trade with UK	1996	1997
Imports from UK	£18,900,000	£22,399,000
Exports to UK	5,724,000	13,236,000

COMMUNICATIONS

The principal ports are Cutuco, La Unión and Acajutla. There are more than 12,000 km of roads and 600 km of railways. The Pan-American Highway from the Guatemalan frontier passes through San Salvador and Santa Ana, and continues to the Honduran frontier. Comalapa international airport can receive jet aircraft with daily flights to other Central American capitals, Mexico and the USA. There are 100 broadcasting stations and six television stations. Five daily newspapers are published in San Salvador.

EDUCATION

Primary education is nominally compulsory, but the number of schools and teachers available is too small to enable education to be given to all children of school age.

ILLITERACY RATE – 28.5 per cent

ENROLMENT (percentage of age group) – primary 79 per cent (1995); secondary 21 per cent (1995); tertiary 17.7 per cent (1995)

SAMOA
Ole Malo Tutoatasi o Samoa – Independent State of Samoa

AREA – 1,093 sq. miles (2,831 sq. km)

POPULATION – 171,000 (1994 UN estimate); 162,000 (1989 census), the largest numbers being on Upolu (114,980) and Savai'i (43,150). The Samoans are a Polynesian people, though the population also includes other Pacific Islanders, Euronesians, Chinese and Europeans. The main languages are Samoan and English. The islanders are Christians of different denominations

CAPITAL – ΨApia (population, 36,000, 1989), on Upolu. Robert Louis Stevenson died and was buried at Apia in 1894

CURRENCY – Tala (S$) of 100 sene

NATIONAL ANTHEM – The Banner of Freedom

NATIONAL DAY – 1 June (Independence Day)

NATIONAL FLAG – Red with a blue canton bearing five white stars of the Southern Cross

LIFE EXPECTANCY (years) – male 61.00; female 64.30

POPULATION GROWTH RATE – 0.9 per cent (1995)

POPULATION DENSITY – 60 per sq. km (1995)

Samoa consists of the islands of Savai'i, Upolu, Apolima, Manono, Fanuatapu, Namua, Nuutele, Nuulua and Nuusafee. All the islands are mountainous. Upolu, the most fertile, contains the harbours of Apia and Mulifanua, and Savai'i the harbour of Salelologa.

HISTORY AND POLITICS

Formerly administered by New Zealand (latterly with internal self-government), Western Samoa became fully independent on 1 January 1962. The state was treated as a member country of the Commonwealth until its formal admission on 28 August 1970. A constitutional amendment came into effect on 4 July 1997 changing the state's name to the Independent State of Samoa.

Suffrage was made universal following a referendum held in 1990. After elections held on 26 April 1996, the seats in the *Fono* were: Human Rights Protection Party 26; Samoan National Development Party 13; Independents 10.

POLITICAL SYSTEM

The 1962 constitution provides for a head of state to be elected by the 49-member legislative assembly, the *Fono*, for a five-year term. Initially two of the four Paramount chiefs jointly held the office of head of state for life. When one of the chiefs died in April 1963, Susuga Malietoa Tanumafili II became head of state for life. The head of state's functions are analogous to those of a constitutional monarch. Executive government is carried out by a Cabinet of Ministers.

HEAD OF STATE

Head of State for Life, HH Susuga Malietoa Tanumafili II, GCMG, CBE, *since* 15 April 1963

Deputy Head of State, Hon. Mataafa Faasuamaleaui Puela

CABINET *as at July 1998*

Prime Minister, Foreign Affairs, Broadcasting, Police and Prisons, Internal Affairs, Tofilau Eti Alesana

Deputy PM, Finance, Tourism, Trade, Commerce and Industry, Customs, Audit, Tuilaepa Sailele Malielegaoi

Agriculture, Forestry, Fisheries and Meteorological Services, Molioo Teofilo

Education, Fiame Naomi Mata'afa

Health, Misa Telefoni

Justice, Solia Papu Vaai *Labour*, Polataivao Fosi

Lands Survey and Environment, Tuala Sale Tagaloa

Posts and Telecommunications, Electric Power Corporation, Leafa Vitale

Public Works, Luagalau Levaula Kamu

Transport and Shipping, Hans Joachim Kell

Women's Affairs, Statistics, Leniu Tofaeono Avamagalo

Youth, Sports and Culture, Leota Lu II

SAMOA HIGH COMMISSION

Avenue Franklin D. Roosevelt 123, 1050 Brussels

Tel: Brussels 660 8454

Ambassador Extraordinary and Plenipotentiary, HE Tau'ili'ili U'ili Meredith, apptd 1997

BRITISH HIGH COMMISSIONER, HE Martin Williams, CVO, OBE, resident at Wellington, New Zealand

HONORARY CONSULATE – PO Box 2029, Apia

ECONOMY

Agriculture is the basis of the economy, the principal cash crops (and exports) being coconuts (copra), cocoa and bananas. Efforts are being made to develop fishing on a commercial scale. Manufacturing is very small in scope and concerned largely with processing agricultural products, but is being encouraged by the government. There were over 60,000 visitors in 1995.

In 1995 Samoa had a trade deficit of US$71 million and a current account surplus of US$10 million. In 1996 imports totalled US$100 million and exports US$10 million.

GNP – US$200 million (1996); US$1,170 per capita (1996)
GDP – US$101 million (1994); US$700 per capita (1994)
ANNUAL AVERAGE GROWTH OF GDP – 0.5 per cent (1983)
INFLATION RATE – 7.6 per cent (1996)
TOTAL EXTERNAL DEBT – US$167 million (1996)

TRADE WITH UK	1996	1997
Imports from UK	£1,264,000	£890,000
Exports to UK	12,000	8,000

SAN MARINO
Repubblica di San Marino

AREA – 24 sq. miles (61 sq. km). Neighbour: Italy
POPULATION – 25,000 (1996). The official language is Italian and the religion is Roman Catholic
CAPITAL – San Marino (population, 4,251, 1994), on the slope of Monte Titano
CURRENCY – San Marino and Italian currencies are in circulation
NATIONAL DAY – 3 September
NATIONAL FLAG – Two horizontal bands, white, blue (with coat of arms of the republic in centre)
LIFE EXPECTANCY (years) – male 73.16; female 79.12
POPULATION GROWTH RATE – 1.5 per cent (1995)
POPULATION DENSITY – 410 per sq. km (1995)
URBAN POPULATION – 90.4 per cent (1994)
GDP – US$471 million (1994); US$17,213 per capita (1994)
UNEMPLOYMENT – 39 per cent (1995)

HISTORY AND POLITICS

San Marino is a small republic in the hills near Rimini, on the Adriatic, founded, it is said, by a pious stonecutter of Dalmatia in the fourth century. The republic resisted Papal claims and those of neighbouring dukedoms during the 15th to 18th centuries, and its integrity and sovereignty is recognized and respected by Italy.

A coalition government of the Christian Democratic Party and the Socialist Party was returned in the general elections of May 1998.

The principal products are wine, cereals and fruits, and the main industries are tourism, metals, machinery, textiles and food.

POLITICAL SYSTEM

Executive power is vested in the Congress of State composed of ten ministries under the presidency of the two heads of state, who are elected at six-monthly intervals (every April and October). Legislative power is exercised by the 60-member Great and General Council which is elected for a term of five years. A Council of Twelve forms in certain cases a Supreme Court of Justice.

HEADS OF STATE
Regents, Two 'Capitani Reggenti'

CONGRESS OF STATE *as at July 1998*
Commerce and Relations with Castles Councils, Ottaviano Rossi (PDCS)
Communications, Transport, Tourism and Sport, Augusto Casali (PS)
Education, Justice and Culture, Pier Marino Menicucci (PDCS)
Finance, Budget, Planning and Information, Clelio Galassi (PDCS)
Foreign and Political Affairs, Gabriele Gatti (PDCS)
Health and Social Security, Sante Canducci (PDCS)
Industry, Handicrafts and Economic Co-operation, Fiorenzo Stolfi (PS)
Internal Affairs, Antonio Lazzaro Volpinari (PS)
Labour and Co-operation, Claudio Podeschi (PDCS)
Territory, Environment and Agriculture, Luciano Ciavatta (PS)
PDCS Christian Democratic Party; PS Socialist Party
BRITISH CONSUL-GENERAL, R. J. Griffiths, OBE, resident at Florence, Italy

TRADE

Trade with UK	1996	1997
Imports from UK	£8,557,000	£15,037,000
Exports to UK	4,140,000	6,560,000

SÃO TOMÉ AND PRÍNCIPE
República Democrática de São Tomé e Príncipe

AREA – 372 sq. miles (964 sq. km)
POPULATION – 127,000 (1994 UN estimate). The official language is Portuguese
CAPITAL – ΨSão Tomé (population, 43,420, 1991)
CURRENCY – Dobra of 100 centavos
NATIONAL DAY – 12 July (Independence Day)
NATIONAL FLAG – Horizontal stripes of green, yellow, green, the yellow of double width and bearing two black stars; and a red triangle in the hoist
POPULATION GROWTH RATE – 2.0 per cent (1995)
POPULATION DENSITY – 132 per sq. km (1995)

The islands of São Tomé and Príncipe are situated in the Gulf of Guinea, off the west coast of Africa.

HISTORY AND POLITICS

The islands were first settled by the Portuguese in 1493. In 1951 they became an overseas province of Portugal, and gained full independence on 12 July 1975. A multiparty constitution was approved by referendum in August 1990. The Movement for the Liberation of São Tomé and Príncipe-Social Democratic Party (MLSTP-PSD), which had been the sole legal party since independence, was defeated by the opposition Democratic Convergence Party (PCD) in legislative elections held on 20 January 1991. Miguel Trovoada, an independent, was elected president on 3 March 1991. The president dismissed governments in 1992 and 1994 because of mounting criticism of economic reforms. A legislative election on 2 October 1994 was won by the MLSTP-PSD with 27 seats in the 55-seat National Assembly to the PCD's 14 seats. On 15 August 1995 five junior army officers launched a bloodless military coup, arrested the president and suspended parliament and the constitution. Following Angolan mediation and an EU threat to suspend all aid, the officers relinquished power on 21 August. The president, government, parliament and constitution were restored and the officers were granted an amnesty.

A government of national unity incorporating opposition party members was appointed on 5 January 1996. Prime Minister Almeida tendered his resignation on 29 March 1996, but agreed to continue until a presidential election could be held. President Trovoada was re-elected in July 1996. In September 1996 the government lost a vote of confidence in the National Assembly and a coalition government was installed. Elections are due to be held in October 1998.

HEAD OF STATE
President and Commander-in-Chief of the Armed Forces, Miguel Trovoada, *elected* 3 March 1991, *re-elected* July 1996, *inaugurated* 3 September 1996

CABINET *as at July 1998*

Prime Minister, Raul Bragança Neto
Agriculture and Fishing, Hermengildo de Assounção Sousa e Santos
Commerce, Industry and Tourism, Cosme Bonfim Afonso Rita
Defence and Internal Security, Maj. João Quaresma Viegas Bexigas
Education, Culture, Sports, Albertino Homen dos Santos Sequeira Bragança
Foreign Relations and Communications, Homero Jerónimo Salvaterra
Health, Eduardo do Carmo Ferreira de Matos
Justice, Employment and Public Administration, Amaro Pereira de Couto
Planning, Finance, Acácio Elba Bonfim
Social Equipment and Amenities, Arlindo Afonso de Carvalho

EMBASSY OF THE DEMOCRATIC REPUBLIC OF SÃO TOMÉ AND PRÍNCIPE
Square Montgomery, 174 avenue de Tervuren, 1150 Brussels
Tel: Brussels 734 8966
Chargé d'Affaires, Antonio de Lima Viegas

BRITISH CONSULATE
Residencial Avenida, Av. Da Independencia CP 257
British Ambassador, HE Roger D. Hart, resident at Luanda, Angola
Honorary Consul, J. Gomes

ECONOMY

The economy is heavily dependent on tourism and agriculture, with cacao being the main product.
In 1995 imports totalled US$31 million and exports US$6 million.
GNP – US$45 million (1996); US$330 per capita (1996)
GDP – US$60 million (1994); US$120 per capita (1994)
TOTAL EXTERNAL DEBT – US$261 million (1996)

TRADE WITH UK	1996	1997
Imports from UK	£2,185,000	£2,706,000
Exports to UK	260,000	38,000

SAUDI ARABIA
Al Mamlaka al Arabiya as-Sa'udiyya

AREA – 830,000 sq. miles (2,149,690 sq. km). Neighbours: UAE and Qatar (east), Jordan, Iraq and Kuwait (north), Yemen and Oman (south)
POPULATION – 17,880,000 (1994 UN estimate); 16,929,294 (1992 census). Islam is the only permitted religion. The language is Arabic
CAPITAL – Riyadh (population, 1,800,000, 1991)
MAJOR CITIES – Jeddah (1.5 million); Buraydah; Dammam; Hofuf; Mecca; Medina; Tabuk

CURRENCY – Saudi riyal (SR) of 20 qursh or 100 halala
NATIONAL ANTHEM – Long live our beloved King
NATIONAL DAY – 23 September (proclamation and unification of the Kingdom, 1932)
NATIONAL FLAG – Green oblong, white Arabic device in centre: 'There is no God but God and Muhammad is the Prophet of God', and a white scimitar beneath the lettering
LIFE EXPECTANCY (years) – male 68.39; female 71.41
POPULATION GROWTH RATE – 3.7 per cent (1995)
POPULATION DENSITY – 8 per sq. km (1995)

Saudi Arabia comprises almost the whole of the Arabian peninsula, with the exception of Yemen, Oman, the UAE and Qatar. The Nejd ('plateau') extends over the centre of the peninsula, including the Nafud and Dahna deserts. The Hejaz ('the boundary') extends along the Red Sea coast to Asir and contains the holy towns of Mecca (Makkah) and Medina (Madinah). Asir ('inaccessible') is so named for its mountainous terrain, and, with the coastal plain of the Tihama, lies along the southern Red Sea coast from the Hejaz to the border with Yemen. It is the only region to enjoy substantial rainfall. The east and south-east of the country are lower-lying and largely desert.

Mecca (Al-Makkah), about 60 km east of Jeddah, is the birthplace of the Prophet Muhammad, and contains the Great Mosque, within which is the Kaaba (*Ka'abah*) or sacred shrine of the Muslim religion. This is the focus of the annual Hajj ('pilgrimage'). Medina (Al-Madinah) Al Munawwarah ('The City of Light'), some 300 km north of Mecca, is celebrated as the first city to embrace Islam and as the Prophet Muhammad's burial place.

HISTORY AND POLITICS

In the 18th century Nejd was an independent state governed from Diriya, and the stronghold of the Wahhabis, a puritanical Islamic sect. It subsequently fell under Turkish rule; in 1913 Abdul Aziz ibn Saud threw off Turkish rule and captured the Turkish province of Al Hasa. In 1920 he captured the Asir and in 1921 the Jebel Shammar territory of the Rashid family. In 1925 he completed the conquest of the Hejaz. Great Britain recognized Abdul Aziz ibn Saud as an independent ruler, King of the Hejaz and of Nejd and its Dependencies, in 1927. The name was changed to the Kingdom of Saudi Arabia in September 1932.

INSURGENCIES
Opposition to the al Saud regime has been growing, fuelled by the economic downturn. Attacks on government and US military targets, including a bomb which killed 19 people at a US Air Force base in June 1996, have been blamed on Islamic militants.

POLITICAL SYSTEM
Saudi Arabia is a hereditary monarchy, ruled by the sons and grandsons of Abdul Aziz ibn Saud, in accordance with the Sharia law of Wahhabi Islam. The line of succession passes from brother to brother according to age, although several sons of Ibn Saud renounced their right to the throne. All sons and grandsons of Ibn Saud must be consulted before a new king accedes the throne.
In 1992 King Fahd announced a new Basic Law for the system of government based on Sharia law and including rules to protect personal freedoms. The constitution is defined as the Holy Koran (*Qur'an*) and the *Sunnah* (the teachings and sayings of the Prophet Muhammad). The King and the Council of Ministers (established in 1953) retain executive power. A consultative council (*Majlis-ash-Shora*) of a chairman and 90 members appointed by the King was set up to share power with, and question, the

government and to make recommendations to the King. The Majlis-ash-Shora began meeting in December 1993 and debates government policy in the areas of the budget, defence, foreign and social affairs. Members of the ruling al Saud family are excluded from membership of the Council, which has a four-year term and takes decisions by majority vote. Cabinet ministers have terms of four years, with the possibility of a two-year extension.

In 1993 the country was reorganized into 13 provinces: Riyadh; Mecca (Makkah); Medina (Madinah); Al Qasim; Eastern; Asir; Tabuk; Hail; Northern Border; Jizan; Najran; Baha; Jouf. Each province has a governor appointed by the King and a council of prominent local citizens to advise the governor on local government, budgetary and planning issues.

The judicial system is based on Sharia law, administered by the Justice Ministry through the Sharia courts: general courts, courts of first instance, the High Sharia Court and the Appeals Court. The highest court of appeal is the Council of Ministers whose decision, signed by the King, is final and absolute.

HEAD OF STATE

Custodian of the Two Holy Mosques and HM The King of Saudi Arabia, King Fahd ibn Abdul Aziz al Saud, *born* 1923, *ascended the throne* 1 June 1982
HRH Crown Prince, Prince Abdullah ibn Abdul Aziz al Saud

COUNCIL OF MINISTERS *as at July 1998*

Prime Minister, HM The King
First Deputy PM, Commander of the National Guard, HRH The Crown Prince
Second Deputy PM, Defence and Civil Aviation, HRH Prince Sultan ibn Abdul Aziz al Saud
Agriculture and Water Resources, Abdullah ibn Abdul Aziz ibn Muammar
Commerce, Osama ibn Jaafar ibn Ibrahim al-Faqih
Consultative Council, Muhammad ibn Ibrahim ibn Jubair *(Chairman)*; Shaikh Abdullah Omar Naseef *(Vice-Chairman)*
Education, Mohammad ibn Ahmad al-Rashid
Finance and National Economy, Ibrahim ibn Abdel Aziz al-Assaf
Foreign Affairs, HRH Prince Saud al-Faisal ibn Abdul Aziz al Saud
Health, Osama ibn Abdul-Majid Shobokshi
Higher Education, Khalid ibn Muhammad al-Anqari
Industry and Electricity, Hashem ibn Abdullah ibn Hashem Yamani
Information, Fouad ibn Abdul-Salam Mohammad Farisi
Intelligence Services, HRH Prince Saud ibn Fahd *(Deputy Director)*
Interior, HRH Prince Nayef ibn Abdul Aziz al Saud
Islamic Affairs, Abdullah ibn Abdulmohsen al-Turki
Justice, Abdallah ibn Muhammed al-Shaikh
Labour and Social Affairs, Mousaed ibn Mohammad al-Sulaymi
Municipal and Rural Affairs, Mohammad ibn Ibrahim al-Jarallah
Oil and Mineral Resources, Ali Ibrahim al-Naimi
Pilgrimage, Mahmoud ibn Mohammad al-Safar
Planning, Abdul al-Wahhab Abdul Salam Attar
Public Works and Housing, HRH Prince Miteb ibn Abdul Aziz al Saud
Supreme Judicial Council Chairman, Shaikh Salih ibn Muhammad al-Lihaydan
Telegraphs, Ali ibn Talal al-Jehani
Transport, Nasir ibn Muhammad al-Sallum
Without Portfolio, HRH Prince Abdel Aziz ibn Fahd

ROYAL EMBASSY OF SAUDI ARABIA

30 Charles Street, London WIX 7PM
Tel 0171-917 3000
Ambassador Extraordinary and Plenipotentiary, HE Dr Ghazi Algosaibi, apptd 1992
Minister Plenipotentiary, Dr Mohammed Raja al-Hussainy
Defence Attaché, Brig.-Gen. B. F. al-Othman
Cultural Attaché, A. M. al-Nasser
Commercial Attaché, M. A. al-Sheddi

BRITISH EMBASSY

PO Box 94351, Riyadh 11693
Tel: Riyadh 488 0077
Ambassador Extraordinary and Plenipotentiary, HE Andrew F. Green, CMG, apptd 1996
Counsellors, W. C. Patey *(Deputy Head of Mission and Consul-General)*; R. Northern, MBE *(Commercial)*
Defence and Military Attaché, Brig. R. I. Talbot
First Secretary and Consul, S. J. Lovett
CONSULATE-GENERAL – PO Box 393, Jeddah 21411.
Consul-General, W. I. Rae, OBE
TRADE OFFICE – Dhahran/Al Khobar, PO Box 88, Dhahran Airport 31932

BRITISH COUNCIL DIRECTOR, A. Lewis, Al Mousa Centre, Tower B (PO Box 58012), Olaya Street, Riyadh 11594. There are also offices in Jeddah, Dammam and Jubail

DEFENCE

The Army has 1,055 main battle tanks, 2,820 armoured personnel carriers and armoured infantry fighting vehicles, 448 artillery pieces and 55 helicopters. The Navy has eight frigates, 29 patrol and coastal vessels and 23 armed helicopters at eight bases. The Air Force has 336 combat aircraft and 12 armed helicopters.

Saudi Arabia is base to the Gulf Co-operational Council Peninsula Shield Force of 7,000 troops. The USA, UK and France station aircraft and support units in the country to patrol the air exclusion zone in southern Iraq.
MILITARY EXPENDITURE – 12.7 per cent of GDP (1996)
MILITARY PERSONNEL – 198,000: Army 70,000, Navy 13,500, Air Force 18,000, Air Defence Force 4,000, National Guard 77,000, Paramilitaries 15,500

ECONOMY

Saudi Arabia's revenue has been lower since the drop in world oil prices from the mid-1980s onwards, and in the 1990s financial reserves have been used up to meet budget deficits. In addition the country has had the cost of the 1990–1 Gulf War, estimated at US$60,000 million. Spending cuts of 20 per cent and increases in petrol and utilities prices have been imposed in recent years in an attempt to achieve a balanced budget.

Outside the manufacturing centres which have grown up around many towns, most of the population are engaged in agriculture. The productivity of traditional dryland farming is supplemented by extensive irrigation, desalination and use of aquifers, so that agricultural production has increased greatly over the past 20 years.

The principal industry is oil extraction and processing, which produced 33 per cent of GDP in 1992. Oil was first found in commercial quantities in 1938. About 97 per cent of the total is extracted by Saudi Aramco, formerly the Arabian–American Oil Company. Aramco's 66-year lease will terminate in 1999 but the company was effectively nationalized in 1980. Proven oil reserves of 260,100 million barrels account for about one-quarter of the world's proven reserves. The country is the world's largest oil exporter and supplied 12 per cent of world demand in 1993. Recoverable gas reserves of 190 trillion cubic feet, in fields associated with crude oil and those separate from it, are beginning to be exploited. Mineral exploitation of gold, silver, copper and other minerals is also beginning, with gold production of 5.1 tonnes in 1995.

The government, in a series of five-year development plans begun in 1970, has actively encouraged the establishment of manufacturing industry. Industries have developed in the fields of construction materials, metal fabrication, simple machinery and electrical equipment, food and beverages, textiles, chemicals and plastics. Investment in industrial gases, intermediate petrochemicals, light engineering and machinery is encouraged.

Eight industrial centres have been established, the principal ones at Jubail and Yanbu, financed by the state agency Saudi Arabian Basic Industries Corporation. Linked by gas and oil pipelines, both have petrochemical complexes producing ethylene and methanol; six of the seven plants on-stream are joint ventures with American and Japanese companies.

The state agency Petromin operates nine refineries with a capacity of 1,800,000 b.p.d., producing petrol, fuel and diesel oil, liquefied petroleum gas, jet fuel, kerosene and asphalt.

GNP – US$133,540 million (1995); US$7,040 per capita (1995)
GDP – US$108,923 million (1994); US$6,977 per capita (1994)
ANNUAL AVERAGE GROWTH OF GDP – 0.5 per cent (1995)
INFLATION RATE – 1.2 per cent (1996)

TRADE

Oil remains the main source of receipts in the balance of payments. The leading suppliers of imports are the USA, the UK, Germany and Japan, and the chief customers for exports are Japan, the USA, South Korea and Singapore. There is a total ban on the importation of alcohol, pork products, firearms, and items regarded as non-Islamic or pornographic.

In 1995 there was a trade surplus of US$24,390 million and a current account deficit of US$5,324 million. In 1995 imports totalled US$28,091 million. Exports totalled US$42,614 in 1994.

Trade with UK	1996	1997
Imports from UK	£2,482,981,000	£3,800,465,000
Exports to UK	£752,605,000	£996,907,000

COMMUNICATIONS

There is one railway line from Dammam to Riyadh, which was opened in 1951 and is operated by the Saudi Government Railway Organization. It carries around 450,000 passengers and 1.9 million tons of goods per year. The line is being extended to the port of Jubail on the Gulf. A network of 80,000 miles of roads, including an expressway system, connects all the cities and main towns. There are 21 ports, of which the major ones are Dammam and Jubail (Gulf) and Jeddah, Yanbu and Jizan (Red Sea). The 15.5 mile-long King Fahd Causeway completed in 1986 connects the Eastern Province to the state of Bahrain and is the world's second longest causeway.

The government-owned Saudi Arabian Airlines (Saudia) operates scheduled services to 22 domestic airports. There are international airports at Dhahran (King Fahd), Jeddah (King Abdul Aziz), and Riyadh (King Khalid). Saudia has an extensive overseas operation, and a large number of international airlines operate into the country.

Telecommunications are being rapidly expanded with 1.78 million telephone lines in 1995 and seven earth stations linked to the Intelsat system, allowing direct dialling to 185 countries.

EDUCATION

With the exception of a few schools for expatriate children, all schools are government-supervised and are segregated for boys and girls. There are universities in Jeddah, Mecca, Riyadh (branches in Abha and Qassim), Dammam (branch at Hofuf) and Dhahran, and there are Islamic universities in Medina and Riyadh together with 83 tertiary colleges. There is great emphasis on vocational training, provided at literacy and artisan skill training centres and more advanced industrial, commercial and agricultural education institutes. Education from kindergarten to university is free, with more than 22,000 schools in 1996.
ILLITERACY RATE – 37.2 per cent
ENROLMENT (percentage of age group) – primary 62 per cent (1995); secondary 48 per cent (1995); tertiary 15.3 per cent (1994)

SENEGAL
République du Sénégal

AREA – 75,955 sq. miles (196,722 sq. km). Neighbours: Mauritania (north), Mali (east), Guinea-Bissau and Guinea (south), the Gambia
POPULATION – 8,312,000 (1994 UN estimate). The official language is French; the principal local language is Wolof
CAPITAL – ΨDakar (population, 1,641,358, 1994)
MAJOR CITIES – Kaolack (193,115), ΨSaint-Louis (132,499), Thies (216,381), ΨZinqunichor (161,680)
CURRENCY – Franc CFA of 100 centimes
NATIONAL DAY – 4 April
NATIONAL FLAG – Three vertical bands, green, yellow and red; a green star on the yellow band
LIFE EXPECTANCY (years) – male 48.30; female 50.30
POPULATION GROWTH RATE – 2.0 per cent (1995)
POPULATION DENSITY – 42 per sq. km (1995)
URBAN POPULATION – 42.9 per cent (1993)
MILITARY EXPENDITURE – 1.5 per cent of GDP (1996)
MILITARY PERSONNEL – 17,350: Army 12,000, Navy 700, Air Force 650, Paramilitaries 4,000
CONSCRIPTION DURATION – Two years
ILLITERACY RATE – 66.9 per cent
ENROLMENT (percentage of age group) – primary 54 per cent (1995); tertiary 3.4 per cent (1995)

HISTORY AND POLITICS

Formerly a French colony, Senegal elected in 1958 to remain within the French Community as an autonomous republic. It became independent as part of the Federation of Mali in June 1960 and seceded to form the Republic of Senegal in September 1960.

President Diouf was re-elected in the first round of presidential elections in February 1993 with 58.4 per cent of the vote. The legislative election in May 1998 was won by the ruling Parti Socialiste (PS), which secured 93 seats, with the Parti Démocratique Sénégalais (PDS) winning 23 seats, and the Union for Democratic Renewal 11 seats.

INSURGENCY

There is an insurgent separatist movement (Movement of Democratic Forces of Casamance (MFDC)) in the southern Casamance region. A cease-fire between the government and MFDC was signed in July 1993 but a political agreement has still to be reached and clashes continue. In January 1998, the MFDC came under attack from the army of Guinea-Bissau, which had deployed along the border with Casamance, thereby closing MFDC supply lines and preventing the use of bases in Guinea-Bissau.

POLITICAL SYSTEM
In 1963 a new constitution was approved giving executive powers to the president. Under the most recent amendments to the constitution, the president may serve a maximum of two seven-year terms. A general election for the National Assembly of 140 seats is held every five years.

HEAD OF STATE
President, Abdou Diouf, installed 1981, re-elected 1988, 21 February 1993

COUNCIL OF MINISTERS as at July 1998
Prime Minister, Habib Thiam (PS)
Ministers of State, Robert Sagna (PS) (Agriculture);
  Moustapha Niasse (PS) (Foreign Affairs and Senegalese
  Abroad); Ousmane Tanor Dieng (PS) (Presidential
  Services and Affairs)
Armed Forces, Cheikh Hamidou (PS)
Cities, Daour Cisse (PS)
Commerce, Cottage Industry and Industrialization, vacant
Communications, Serigne Diop (PS)
Culture, Abdoulaye Elimane Kane (PS)
Economy, Finance and Planning, Mamadou Lamine Loum
  (PS)
Energy, Mines and Industry, Magued Diouf (PS)
Environment and Protection of Nature, Abdoulaye Bathily
  (LD/MPT)
Equipment and Land Transport, Landing Sané (PS)
Fisheries and Maritime Transport, Alassane Dialy N'diaye
  (PS)
Interior, Gen. Lamine Cisse
Justice, Keeper of the Seals, Jacques Baudin (PS)
Labour and Employment, Assane Diop (PS)
Modernization of the State, Néné Babacar Mbaye (PS)
National Education, André Sonko (PS)
Public Health and Social Action, vacant
Scientific Research and Technology, Marie-Louise Corea (PS)
Tourism and Air Transport, Tidiane Sylla (PS)
Urban Planning and Housing, Abdourahmane Sow (PS)
Water Resources, Mamadou Faye (PS)
Women, Children and Family Welfare, Aminata Mbengue
  Ndiaye (PS)
Youth and Sports, Ousmane Paye (PS)

PS Socialist Party; LD/MPT Democratic League/Movement for the Labour Party

EMBASSY OF THE REPUBLIC OF SENEGAL
39 Marloes Road, London w8 6LA
Tel 0171-930 7237
Ambassador Extraordinary and Plenipotentiary, HE Gabriel
  Alexandre Sar, apptd 1993

BRITISH EMBASSY
20 rue du Docteur Guillet (BP 6025), Dakar
Tel: Dakar 823 7392
Ambassador Extraordinary and Plenipotentiary, HE David
  Snoxell, apptd 1997

BRITISH COUNCIL REPRESENTATIVE, S. McNulty, 34–36
Blvd. de la République, Immeuble Sonatel, BP 6232,
Dakar

ECONOMY

Senegal's principal exports are fish, groundnuts (raw and processed) and phosphates. Tourism is also of growing importance as a revenue earner.

In 1994 there was a trade deficit of US$203 million and a current account surplus of US$3 million. In 1996 imports totalled US$1,383 million and exports US$870 million.
GNP – US$4,856 million (1996); US$570 per capita (1996)
GDP – US$5,955 million (1994); US$493 per capita (1994)
ANNUAL AVERAGE GROWTH OF GDP – – 1.5 per cent
  (1989)
INFLATION RATE – 2.8 per cent (1996)
TOTAL EXTERNAL DEBT – US$3,663 million (1996)

Trade with UK	1996	1997
Imports from UK	£34,882,000	£24,950,000
Exports to UK	13,350,000	10,969,000

SEYCHELLES
The Republic of Seychelles

AREA – 176 sq. miles (455 sq. km)
POPULATION – 75,000 (1994 UN estimate). The languages
  are English, French and Creole
CAPITAL – ΨVictoria (population, 24,324, 1987), on Mahé
CURRENCY – Seychelles rupee of 100 cents
NATIONAL ANTHEM – Koste Seselwa (Seychellois Unite)
NATIONAL DAY – 18 June
NATIONAL FLAG – Five rays extending from the lower
  hoist over the whole field, coloured blue, yellow, green,
  white and red
LIFE EXPECTANCY (years) – male 65.26; female 74.05
POPULATION GROWTH RATE – 1.6 per cent (1995)
POPULATION DENSITY – 165 per sq. km (1995)
MILITARY EXPENDITURE – 2.1 per cent of GDP (1996)
MILITARY PERSONNEL – 450: Army 200, Paramilitaries
  250

Seychelles, in the Indian Ocean, consists of 115 islands spread over 400,000 sq. miles of ocean. There is a relatively compact granitic group, 32 islands in all, with high hills and mountains (highest point about 2,972 ft), of which Mahé is the largest and most populated (90 per cent of the population live on Mahé); and the outlying coralline group, for the most part only a little above sea-level. Although only 4° S. of the Equator, the climate is pleasant though tropical.

HISTORY AND POLITICS

Proclaimed French territory in 1756, the Mahé group was settled as a dependency of Mauritius from 1770, was captured by a British ship in 1794, and changed hands several times between 1803 and 1814, when it was finally assigned to Great Britain. In 1903 these islands, together with the coralline group, were formed into a separate colony. On 29 June 1976, the islands became an independent republic within the Commonwealth. A coup d'état took place in 1977. Seychelles was a one-party state from 1979 until 1991, when a multiparty democratic system was proposed by President René.
  In presidential and legislative elections held in March 1998, President René was re-elected with 67 per cent of the vote, and the Seychelles People's Progressive Front formed a government after winning 30 seats in the National Assembly.

POLITICAL SYSTEM

Under the constitution adopted in 1993, multiparty politics was institutionalized, a National Assembly of 33 members (22 elected by constituencies, 11 by proportional representation) was established and the presidential mandate was set at five years, renewable three times.

HEAD OF STATE
President, Commander-in-Chief of the Armed Forces, Defence, Interior, France-Albert René, *assumed office* 5 June 1977; *elected* 1979; *re-elected* 1984, 1989, 1993, 22 March 1998
Vice-President, Finance, Economic Planning, Communications, Environment, Transport, James Michel

COUNCIL OF MINISTERS *as at May 1998*
Administration, Noellie Alexander
Agriculture and Marine Resources, Ronny Jumeau
Education, Danny Faure
Foreign Affairs, Jeremie Bonnelame
Health, Jacquelin Dugasse
Industries and International Business, Joseph Belmont
Land Use and Habitat, Dolor Ernesta
Local Government and Sports, Sylvette Pool
Social Affairs and Manpower Development, William Herminie
Tourism and Civil Aviation, Simone de Comarmond
Youth and Culture, Patrick Pillay

SEYCHELLES HIGH COMMISSION
Box No. 4PE, 2nd Floor, Eros House, 111 Baker Street, London WIM IFE
Tel 0171-224 1660
High Commissioner, Callixte d'Offay, apptd 1998

BRITISH HIGH COMMISSION
Victoria House, PO Box 161 Victoria, Mahé
Tel: Victoria 225225
High Commissioner, HE John Yapp, apptd 1997

ECONOMY

The economy is based on tourism, fishing, small-scale agriculture and manufacturing, and the re-export of fuel for aircraft and ships. Deep sea tuna fishing by foreign fleets under licence, improved port facilities at Victoria and exports from a tuna canning factory attract growing revenues. The government is attempting to reduce the reliance on tourism, which generates 70 per cent of foreign exchange earnings, by promoting the country as an off-shore haven for financial services.
GNP – US$526 million (1996); US$6,850 per capita (1996)
GDP – US$425 million (1994); US$6,798 per capita (1994)
ANNUAL AVERAGE GROWTH OF GDP – 2.2 per cent (1991)
INFLATION RATE – – 1.2 per cent (1996)
TOTAL EXTERNAL DEBT – US$148 million (1996)

TRADE

Principal exports include fish, coconuts and cinnamon. The principal imports are foodstuffs, beverages, tobacco, mineral fuels, manufactured items, building materials, machinery and transport equipment.
In 1995 there was a trade deficit of US$163 million and a current account deficit of US$33 million. Imports totalled US$233 million and exports US$53 million.

Trade with UK	1996	1997
Imports from UK	£16,975,000	£21,415,000
Exports to UK	9,249,000	4,256,000

SIERRA LEONE
The Republic of Sierra Leone

AREA – 27,699 sq. miles (71,740 sq. km). Neighbours: Guinea (north, north-east), Liberia (south-east)
POPULATION – 4,509,000 (1994 UN estimate). The south is inhabited by peoples whose languages fall into the Mende group; the north by the Temne and smaller groups such as the Limba, Loko, Koranko and Susu

CAPITAL – ΨFreetown (population, 469,776, 1985)
CURRENCY – Leone (Le) of 100 cents
NATIONAL ANTHEM – High We Exalt Thee, Realm of the Free
NATIONAL DAY – 27 April (Independence Day)
NATIONAL FLAG – Three horizontal stripes of leaf green, white and cobalt blue
LIFE EXPECTANCY (years) – male 37.47; female 40.58
POPULATION GROWTH RATE – 2.4 per cent (1995)
POPULATION DENSITY – 63 per sq. km (1995)
MILITARY EXPENDITURE – 4.9 per cent of GDP (1996)
MILITARY PERSONNEL – 13,200: Army 13,000, Navy 200

HISTORY AND POLITICS

In the late 18th century a project was begun to settle destitute Africans from England on Freetown peninsula. In 1808 the settlement was declared a Crown colony and became the main base in West Africa for enforcing the 1807 Act outlawing the slave trade. The colony was also used as a settlement for Africans from North America and the West Indies, and Africans rescued from slave ships also settled there. In 1896 a Protectorate was declared over the hinterland.
In 1951 a new constitution was set up that united the colony of Freetown and the Protectorate and on 27 April 1961 Sierra Leone became a fully independent state within the Commonwealth. In 1971 a republican constitution was adopted and Dr Siaka Stevens became the first executive president. In 1978 Sierra Leone became a one-party state, following approval by Parliament and a referendum.
In September 1991 a new multiparty constitution was adopted and an interim government formed until a general election could be held. This government was overthrown by a coup on 29 April 1992. Captain Valentine Strasser became head of state, the House of Representatives was dissolved and all political activity was suspended. In July 1992 Strasser appointed a Council of State Secretaries to co-ordinate the day-to-day running of government, but on 16 January 1996 he was ousted in a bloodless coup by his deputy, Brig.-Gen. Julius Maada Bio. The military government surrendered power to a civilian government on 29 March 1996, following legislative elections on 26–27 February and a run-off election for the presidency on 15 March.
The Sierra Leone People's Party (SLPP) won 27 seats in the 68-member National Assembly and formed a government with the support of the People's Democratic Party and the Democratic Centre Party. The SLPP's candidate, Ahmad Tejan Kabbah, won the presidential contest, attracting 59.4 per cent of the vote.
In May 1997 army officers led by Major Johnny Koroma seized power. President Kabbah fled and a 20-member Armed Forces Revolutionary Council was set up with Koroma as chairman and Revolutionary United Front (RUF) leader Foday Sankoh as vice-chairman. In July 1997, a Nigerian-led ECOMOG force was sent to oust Koroma and restore the legitimate government. On 24 October 1997, a peace agreement was reached which provided for Kabbah to return to power within six months and granted immunity from prosecution to Koroma. There was renewed fighting in February 1998 with both sides accusing the other of breaking the cease-fire. ECOMOG troops gained control of Freetown on 12 February 1998, and ousted the Koroma regime. President Kabbah returned to Freetown on 10 March 1998.

INSURGENCY

Since May 1991 government forces have been fighting the RUF whose aim is to force all foreigners out of the country and to nationalize the mining sector. Talks between the

RUF and the civilian government produced an interim cease-fire on 23 April 1996, and a 'final cease-fire' in May. The civil war has claimed more than 10,000 lives and displaced more than half the population.

HEAD OF STATE
President, Minister of Defence, Ahmad Tejan Kabbah, *elected* 15 March 1996

CABINET *as at July 1998*
Agriculture and Environment, Harry Will
Attorney-General, Justice, Solomon Berewa
Deputy Minister of Defence, Hinga Norman
Education, Alpha Wurie
Energy, Power and Works, Thaimu Bangura
Finance, Development and Economic Planning, James Jonah
Foreign Affairs, Sama Banya
Government Spokesman, Septimus Kaikai
Health, Sulaiman Tejan Jalloh
Information, Julius Spencer
Information, Broadcasting, Tourism, Charles Spencer
Internal Affairs, Local Government, Charles Magai
Labour, Social Welfare and Sports, Abass Collier
Lands, Housing and Gender Affairs, Shirley Gbujama
Mineral Resources, Alhaji Mohamed Deen
Presidential Affairs, Momodu Koroma
Trade, Industry and State Enterprises, Allieu Bangura

SIERRA LEONE HIGH COMMISSION
33 Portland Place, London WIN 3AG
Tel 0171-636 6483/4/5/6
High Commissioner, HE Prof. Cyril Foray, apptd 1996

BRITISH HIGH COMMISSION
Spur Road, Freetown
Tel: Freetown 232563/4/5
High Commissioner, HE Peter Penfold, CMG, apptd 1997

BRITISH COUNCIL DIRECTOR, A. Thomas, PO Box 124, Tower Hill, Freetown

ECONOMY

The 1996 military government cracked down on corruption, liberalized the foreign exchange system and reduced inflation from 120 per cent to 23 per cent.

On the Freetown peninsula, farming is largely confined to the production of cassava and crops such as maize and vegetables for local consumption. In the hinterland the principal agricultural product is rice, which is the staple food of the country, and cash crops such as cocoa, coffee, palm kernels and ginger. Cattle production is also important.

The economy depends largely on mineral exports, mainly diamonds, gold and bauxite, although mineral production has been disrupted by the insurgency.

In 1994 there was a trade deficit of US$73 million and a current account deficit of US$89 million. In 1996 imports totalled US$211 million and exports US$47 million.
GNP – US$925 million (1996); US$200 per capita (1996)
GDP – US$598 million (1994); US$184 per capita (1994)
ANNUAL AVERAGE GROWTH OF GDP – – 2.8 per cent (1995)
INFLATION RATE – 23.2 per cent (1996)
TOTAL EXTERNAL DEBT – US$1,167 million (1996)

TRADE WITH UK	1996	1997
Imports from UK	£32,624,000	£30,135,000
Exports to UK	5,709,000	4,528,000

COMMUNICATIONS

Since the phasing out of the railway system in 1974 the road network has been developed considerably; there are now 7,000 miles of roads in the country, 2,000 miles being surfaced. A bridge has been constructed over the Mano River linking Sierra Leone and Liberia.

The Freetown international airport is situated at Lungi. The main port is Freetown, which has one of the largest natural harbours in the world. There are smaller ports at Pepel, Bonthe and Niti.

Radio is operated by the government. Broadcasts are made in several of the indigenous languages, in addition to English and French.

EDUCATION

Technical education is provided in the two government technical institutes, situated in Freetown and Kenema, in two trade centres and in the technical training establishments of the mining companies. Teacher training is carried out at the University of Sierra Leone, six colleges in the provinces and in the Milton Margai Training College near Freetown.
ILLITERACY RATE – 68.6 per cent
ENROLMENT (percentage of age group) – tertiary 1.3 per cent (1990)

SINGAPORE

AREA – 239 sq. miles (618 sq. km)
POPULATION – 2,987,000 (1996): Chinese 77.3 per cent, Malays 14.1 per cent, Indians (including those of Pakistani, Bangladeshi and Sri Lankan origin) 7.3 per cent and 1.3 per cent from other ethnic groups. Malay, Mandarin, Tamil and English are the official languages. At least eight Chinese dialects are used. Malay is the national language and English is the language of administration. The religions are Buddhism 31.9 per cent, Taosim 21.9 per cent, Islam 14.9 per cent, Hinduism 3.3 per cent
CURRENCY – Singapore dollar (S$) of 100 cents
NATIONAL ANTHEM – Majulah Singapura
NATIONAL DAY – 9 August
NATIONAL FLAG – Horizontal bands of red over white; crescent with five five-point stars on red band near staff
LIFE EXPECTANCY (years) – male 74.20; female 78.50
POPULATION GROWTH RATE – 2.0 per cent (1995)
POPULATION DENSITY – 4,833 per sq. km (1995)
MILITARY EXPENDITURE – 4.4 per cent of GDP (1996)
MILITARY PERSONNEL – 178,000: Army 55,000, Navy 9,000, Air Force 6,000, Paramilitaries 108,000
CONSCRIPTION DURATION – 24–30 months
ILLITERACY RATE – 8.9 per cent
ENROLMENT (percentage of age group) – primary 99 per cent (1980); tertiary 33.7 per cent (1995)

Singapore consists of the island of Singapore and 59 islets. Singapore island is 26 miles long and 14 miles in breadth and is situated just north of the Equator off the southern extremity of the Malay peninsula, from which it is separated by the Straits of Johore. A causeway crosses the three-quarters of a mile to the mainland. The climate is hot and humid. Rainfall averages 240 cm a year and temperature ranges from 24° to 32° C (76°–89° F).

HISTORY AND POLITICS

Singapore, where Sir Stamford Raffles first established a trading post under the East India Company in 1819, was incorporated with Penang and Malacca to form the Straits Settlements in 1826. The Straits Settlements became a Crown colony in 1867. Singapore fell into Japanese hands in 1942 and civil government was not restored until 1946, when it became a separate colony. Internal self-government was introduced in 1959. Singapore became a state of Malaysia in September 1963, but left Malaysia and became an independent sovereign state within the Commonwealth on 9 August 1965. Singapore adopted a republican constitution from that date.

After the general election of 2 January 1997 the People's Action Party (PAP) had 81 seats in Parliament.

POLITICAL SYSTEM

The president is directly elected for a six-year term, and can veto government decisions relating to internal security, the budget, financial reserves and the appointment of senior civil servants. The president appoints the prime minister and, on his advice, the members of the Cabinet. There is a Parliament of 83 directly elected members, with up to three further members appointed by the president.

HEAD OF STATE
President, Ong Teng Cheong, *elected* 28 August 1993, *took office* 2 September 1993

CABINET *as at July 1998*
Prime Minister, Goh Chok Tong
Senior Minister, PM's Office, Lee Kuan Yew
Deputy PM, Defence, Dr Tony Tan Keng Yam
Deputy PM, PM's Office, Brig.-Gen. Lee Hsien Loong
Communications, Mah Bow Tan
Community Development, Muslim Affairs, Abdullah Tarmugi
Education, Defence, Rear-Adm. Teo Chee Hean
Finance, Dr Richard Hu Tsu Tau
Foreign Affairs and Law, Shanmugam Jayakumar
Health and Environment, Yeo Cheow Tong
Home Affairs, Wong Kan Seng
Information and the Arts, Trade and Industry, Brig.-Gen. George Yong-Boon Yeo
Labour, Dr Lee Boon Yang
National Development, Foreign Affairs, Lim Hng Kiang
Trade and Industry, Lee Yock Suan
Without Portfolio, PM's Office, Lim Boon Heng

HIGH COMMISSION FOR THE REPUBLIC OF SINGAPORE
9 Wilton Crescent, London SW1X 8RW
Tel 0171-235 8315
High Commissioner, HE J. Y. Pillay, apptd 1996
Counsellor, Jimmy Tin Chew Chua
First Secretary, Kheng Hian Philip Ho (*Commercial*)

BRITISH HIGH COMMISSION
Tanglin Road, Singapore 247919
Tel: Singapore 473 9333
High Commissioner, HE Alan Hunt, CMG, apptd 1997
Deputy High Commissioner, A. Gooch
Defence Adviser, Gp Capt C. B. LeBas

BRITISH COUNCIL DIRECTOR, Dr J. Grote, OBE, 30 Napier Road, Singapore 258509

ECONOMY

Historically Singapore's economy was based on the sale and distribution of raw materials from surrounding countries and on entrepôt trade in finished products. An industrialization programme launched in 1968 has established manufacturing industries, including shipbuilding, iron and steel, transport equipment, textiles, footwear, wood products, micro-electronics, electrical goods, telecommunications equipment, office machinery, scientific instruments, pharmaceuticals, petroleum products, etc. Singapore has also become an important financial services centre with significant insurance and foreign exchange markets, a stock exchange, 132 commercial banks and 75 merchant banks and an oil-refining centre. In February

1998 the government announced substantial liberalizing reforms of the financial sector, aimed at allowing the country to compete more competitively with other financial sectors in the region. Singapore's major trading partners are the USA, Malaysia, the EU, Hong Kong and Japan.

In 1995 Singapore had a trade surplus of US$1,625 million and a current account surplus of US$15,093 million. In 1996 imports totalled US$131,338 million and exports US$125,014 million. Singapore has not been as badly affected as its neighbours by the economic crisis in south-east Asia, due in part to currency reserves estimated at US$118 billion.
GNP – US$92,987 million (1996); US$30,550 per capita (1996)
GDP – US$49,979 million (1994); US$23,556 per capita (1994)
ANNUAL AVERAGE GROWTH OF GDP – 7.3 per cent (1996)
INFLATION RATE – 1.4 per cent (1996)
UNEMPLOYMENT – 2.7 per cent (1995)

Trade with UK	1996	1997
Imports from UK	£2,144,680,000	£2,042,966,000
Exports to UK	2,572,600,000	2,713,666,000

COMMUNICATIONS

Singapore is one of the largest and busiest seaports in the world, with six terminals, deep water wharves and ship repairing facilities. Ships also anchor in the roads, unloading into lighters. In 1994, the total volume of cargo handled was 290,100,000 tonnes. There were 127,242 ship arrivals in 1996.

The international airport is at Changi, in the east of the island, with Singapore Airlines operating flights to 43 countries and 24,500,000 passengers using the airport in 1996. There are 67 km of railway connected to the Malaysian rail system by the causeway across the Straits of Johore, and 3,027 km of roads.

There are 19 radio and four television channels operated by the Singapore Broadcasting Corporation in the four official languages, and three private broadcasting stations.

SLOVAKIA
Slovenská Republika – The Republic of Slovakia

AREA – 18,924 sq. miles (49,012 sq. km). Neighbours: Poland (north), Ukraine (east), Hungary (south), Austria (west), the Czech Republic (north-west)
POPULATION – 5,364,000 (1994 UN estimate): 85.7 per cent are ethnic Slovaks, 10.8 per cent ethnic Hungarians, 1.4 per cent gypsy, 1.1 per cent Czech, with smaller numbers of Ruthenians, Ukrainians and Germans. The population is mainly Christian, some 60 per cent Roman Catholic and 6 per cent Protestant. The main languages are Slovak, Hungarian and Czech
CAPITAL – Bratislava (population, 451,272, 1993), on the Danube
MAJOR CITIES – Košice (238,454); Žilina (86,373); Prešov (92,013); Banská Bystrica (78,321)
CURRENCY – Koruna (Sk) of 100 haliers
NATIONAL ANTHEM – Nad Tatrou sa blýska (Storm over the Tatras)
NATIONAL DAYS – 1 January (Establishment of Slovak Republic); 5 July (Day of the Slav Missionaries); 29 August (Slovak National Uprising); 1 September (Constitution Day)

NATIONAL FLAG – Three horizontal stripes of white, blue, red with the arms all over near the hoist
LIFE EXPECTANCY (years) – male 68.34; female 76.48
POPULATION GROWTH RATE – 0.2 per cent (1995)
POPULATION DENSITY – 109 per sq. km (1995)
URBAN POPULATION – 57.0 per cent (1994)
ENROLMENT (percentage of age group) – tertiary 20.2 per cent (1995)

The Tatry (Tatras) mountains in the centre and north of Slovakia reach heights of 2,600 m (8,530 ft). The major river is the Váh which flows from the Tatry mountains to join the Danube at the Hungarian border. The climate is continental.

HISTORY AND POLITICS (*see also* Czech Republic)

At the end of the 11th century Slovakia became part of the Hungarian state when the Magyars gained control of the area. After the Hungarians were defeated in 1526, most of Hungary (including part of Slovakia) was occupied by the Turks, with the remainder of Hungary and Slovakia being incorporated into the Austrian Empire. With the establishment of the Austro-Hungarian monarchy in 1867, Slovakia again came under Hungarian control. The attempted Magyarization of Slovakia gave impetus to the national revival which had begun in 1848–9, and when the First World War came many Slovaks fought with the allies. Amalgamated into the republic of Czechoslovakia on 28 October 1918, Slovakia became independent in March 1939 as a Nazi puppet state when Germany invaded the Czech lands. Slovakia was liberated by Soviet forces in 1945 and returned to Czechoslovakia. The formation of a federal republic between the Czech lands and Slovakia was the only Prague Spring reform to survive the Soviet invasion of 1968. Following the collapse of Communist rule in 1989, the Czech and Slovak republics began to negotiate the dissolution of the federation into two sovereign states in 1992. Dissolution took effect on 1 January 1993.

A coalition government of the Movement for a Democratic Slovakia (HZDS) and Slovak National Party (SNS) was sworn in on 12 January 1993 but lost its majority in the National Council when the SNS left the government. Increasing criticism of the economic policy and authoritarian style of the government led ten HZDS members to form a new party which, in alliance with three other parties, brought down the government by a no-confidence vote in March 1994. The coalition then formed a government which was approved by President Kováč on 16 March 1994.

Legislative elections on 30 September and 1 October 1994 returned the HZDS to power at the head of a three-party coalition with the Association of Slovak Workers (ZRS) and the Slovak National Party (SNS) which took office on 13 December 1994. Antagonism between President Kováč and Prime Minister Mečiar resulted in transferral of the role of Commander-in-Chief of the Armed Forces from the president to the government in June 1995.

The state of the parties in the National Council following the 1994 election was: HZDS 61; Democratic Left Party (SDL) 18; Christian Democratic Movement (KDH) 17; Hungarian Coalition 17; Democratic Union (DU) 15; ZRS 13; SNS 9. As of July 1998, no candidate had gained the 60 per cent of the vote in the National Assembly needed to replace President Kováč, whose term ended in March 1998. The presidential elections were not contested by the ruling HZDS, who were accused by opposition parties of trying to create a constitutional vacuum; since no

president was elected by the end of Kováč's term, certain presidential powers were transferred to the prime minister. Legislative elections are scheduled for September 1998.

POLITICAL SYSTEM

The constitution vests legislative power in the National Council of 150 members elected for a four-year term by proportional representation with a five per cent threshold for parliamentary representation. The president is elected for a five-year term by the National Council; executive power is held by the prime minister and Cabinet.

Referenda on NATO membership and a directly-elected presidency were held in May 1997 but were ruled invalid due to low turnout.

HEAD OF STATE
President, vacant

CABINET *as at July 1998*
Prime Minister, Acting President of the Republic, Vladimír Mečiar (HZDS)
Deputy PMs, Sergej Kozlík (HZDS) *(Economy and Finance)*; Katarína Tóthová (HZDS) *(Legislature and Media)*; Jozef Kalman (ZRS) *(Social, Industrial and Trade Union Relations)*
Agriculture, Peter Baco (HZDS)
Construction and Public Works, Ján Mráz (ZRS)
Culture, Ivan Hudec (HZDS)
Defence, Ján Sitek (SNS)
Economy, Milan Cagala (Ind.)
Education and Science, Eva Slavkovská (SNS)
Environment, Jozef Zlocha (HZDS)
Finance, Miroslav Maxon (NAS)
Foreign Affairs, Zdenka Kramplová (Ind.)
Health, Ľubomír Javorský (HZDS)
Interior, Gustáv Krajči (HZDS)
Justice, Jozef Liščák (ZRS)
Labour, Social Affairs and the Family, Vojtech Tkáč (HZDS)
Privatization, Peter Bisák (ZRS)
Transport, Post and Telecommunications, Ján Jasovský

HZDS Movement for a Democratic Slovakia; ZRS Association of Slovak Workers; SNS Slovak National Party; NAS New Agrarian Party; Ind. Independent

EMBASSY OF THE SLOVAK REPUBLIC
25 Kensington Palace Gardens, London W8 4QY
Tel 0171-243 0803
Ambassador Extraordinary and Plenipotentiary, Igor Slobodnik, apptd 1997

BRITISH EMBASSY
Panska 16, 81101 Bratislava
Tel: Bratislava 531 9632
Ambassador Extraordinary and Plenipotentiary, HE David Lyscom, apptd 1998
BRITISH COUNCIL DIRECTOR, S. Wallace-Shaddad, PO Box 68, Panská 17, 81499 Bratislava

DEFENCE

The Army has 478 main battle tanks, 683 armoured personnel carriers and armoured infantry fighting vehicles, and 383 artillery pieces. The Air Force has 114 combat aircraft and 19 attack helicopters.
MILITARY EXPENDITURE – 2.3 per cent of GDP (1996)
MILITARY PERSONNEL – 39,750: Army 23,800, Air Force 12,000, Paramilitaries 3,950
CONSCRIPTION DURATION – 12 months

ECONOMY

From independence until mid-1994 Slovakia faced economic difficulties because of the structure of its centrally-planned and inefficiently managed economy, reliant on state-subsidized heavy industries with low productivity, and because of the ambivalent attitude to reform of the HZDS government. Problems increased in 1993 as output, exports and foreign currency reserves fell, and unemployment and inflation increased. In July 1993 the Slovak Koruna was devalued by 10 per cent in return for an IMF loan of US$89 million. Economic reform policies, including macro-economic stabilization, price liberalization, currency convertibility and extensive privatization were continued, though at a slower rate than in the Czech Republic. In mid-1994 the economic situation stabilized as the Moravčik government implemented a second round of privatization. The election of an HZDS-led government in October 1994 slowed the pace of reform.

Natural resources include brown coal, natural gas, iron ore, antimony, lead, zinc and magnesite.

In 1996 Slovakia had a trade deficit of US$2,099 million and a current account deficit of US$1,905 million. Imports totalled US$11,445 million and exports US$8,828.

GNP – US$18,206 million (1996); US$3,410 per capita (1996)

GDP – US$11,190 million (1994); US$2,331 per capita (1994)

ANNUAL AVERAGE GROWTH OF GDP – 6.9 per cent (1996)
INFLATION RATE – 5.8 per cent (1996)
UNEMPLOYMENT – 13.1 per cent (1995)
TOTAL EXTERNAL DEBT – US$7,704 million (1996)

TRADE WITH UK	1996	1997
Imports from UK	£103,549,000	£132,250,000
Exports to UK	65,491,000	73,317,000

SLOVENIA
Republika Slovenija

AREA – 7,821 sq. miles (20,256 sq. km). Neighbours: Austria (north), Hungary (north-east), Croatia (east and south), Italy (west)
POPULATION – 1,984,000 (1994 UN estimate). The population is mostly Slovenian. There are small Hungarian (0.5 per cent) and Italian (0.1 per cent) minorities, together with a Romany population. The main religion is Roman Catholicism. Slovene is the official language, together with Hungarian and Italian in ethnically mixed regions
CAPITAL – Ljubljana (population, 330,000)
MAJOR CITIES – Maribor (103,113); Celje (39,782); Kranj (36,770); ΨKoper (24,495), the only port, 1994
CURRENCY – Tolar (SIT) of 100 stotin
NATIONAL ANTHEM – Zdravljica (A Toast)
NATIONAL DAY – 25 June (Statehood Day)
NATIONAL FLAG – Three horizontal stripes of white, blue, red, with the arms in the upper hoist
LIFE EXPECTANCY (years) – male 69.58; female 77.38
POPULATION GROWTH RATE – –0.1 per cent (1995)
POPULATION DENSITY – 98 per sq. km (1995)
URBAN POPULATION – 50.0 per cent (1995)
MILITARY EXPENDITURE – 1.4 per cent of GDP (1996)
MILITARY PERSONNEL – 14,050: Army 9,550, Paramilitaries 4,500
CONSCRIPTION DURATION – Seven months

Slovenia is a small mountainous state which is the most northerly of the former Yugoslav republics. The two major rivers are the Sava and the Drava. There is a short coastline in the south-west 29 miles (46 km) in length on the Adriatic. The climate is a mixture of Mediterranean, continental and alpine.

HISTORY AND POLITICS

The area that is now Slovenia came under the control of the Habsburg Empire in the 15th century and remained so until the defeat of the Austro-Hungarian Empire in 1918. On 27 October 1918 Slovenia became part of the state of Slovenes, Croats and Serbs (later Yugoslavia) and this was confirmed by the Versailles Treaty (1919). Slovenia was reduced in size by the Italian annexation of the western third of the country and the Austrian annexation of parts of the north. In 1941 German forces invaded Yugoslavia and Slovenia was divided between Germany, Italy and Hungary. Slovenia was reformed as a constituent republic of the federal Yugoslav state in May 1945. After a dispute with Italy and nine years of international administration, the Adriatic coast and hinterland were returned to Slovenia in 1954 and Italy retained Trieste.

Slovenian fears of Serbian dominance led the Slovene Assembly in 1989 to amend the republican constitution to lay the basis of a sovereign state. The first democratic elections, held in April 1990, were won by the pro-independence 'Demos' coalition. In a referendum in December 1990, 88 per cent of the electorate voted for independence, which was declared on 25 June 1991. A ten-day war with the Yugoslav National Army followed before the Army called off hostilities and withdrew.

Legislative elections were held on 10 November 1996. Liberal Democracy of Slovenia won the most seats and formed a coalition government. President Kučan was re-elected on 23 November 1997.

FOREIGN RELATIONS

Slovenia signed an association agreement and applied for membership of the EU in June 1996. Formal accession discussions are under way. Slovenia has a temporary seat on the UN Security Council.

POLITICAL SYSTEM

The head of state is the president, elected for a five-year term. Executive power is vested in the prime minister and Cabinet of Ministers. The lower house of the legislature, the National Assembly, has 90 members directly elected for a four-year term. The upper house, the 40-member National Council, has an advisory role. The National Assembly is elected on a proportional representation basis, with one seat each reserved for the Italian and Hungarian minorities.

HEAD OF STATE

President, Milan Kučan, *elected* April 1990, *re-elected* December 1992, 23 November 1997

CABINET *as at July 1998*

Prime Minister, Janez Drnovšek (LDS)
Deputy P.M, Co-ordination, Marjan Podobnik (SLS)
Agriculture and Forestry, Ciril Smrkolj (SLS)
Co-ordination of Social Activities, Janko Kušar (DeSUS)
Culture, Josef Školjc (LDS)
Defence, Alojz Krapez
Economic Affairs, Metod Dragonja (LDS)
Economic Relations and Development, Marjan Senjur (SLS)
Education and Sports, Slavko Gaber (LDS)
Environment and Physical Planning, Dr Pavel Gantar (LDS)
European Affairs, Igor Bavcar (LDS)
Finance, Mitja Gaspari (Ind.)
Foreign Affairs, Boris Frlec (LDS)

Health, Marjan Jereb (SLS)
Internal Affairs, Mirko Bandelj (LDS)
Justice, Tomaž Marušič (SLS)
Labour, Family and Social Affairs, Tone Rop (LDS)
Local Government, Božo Grafenauer (SLS)
Science, Technology, Alojzij Marinček (SLS)
Small Enterprises, Tourism, Janko Razgoršek (LDS)
Transport and Communications, Anton Bergauer (SLS)

LDS Liberal Democracy of Slovenia; SLS Slovene People's Party; DeSUS Democratic Party of Pensioners of Slovenia; Ind. Independent

EMBASSY OF SLOVENIA
11–15 Wigmore Street, London WIH 9LA
Tel 0171-495 7775
Ambassador Extraordinary and Plenipotentiary, HE Marjan Setinc, apptd 1998

BRITISH EMBASSY
4th Floor, Trg Republike 3, 61-000 Ljubljana
Tel: Ljubljana 125 7191
Ambassador Extraordinary and Plenipotentiary, HE David Lloyd, OBE, apptd 1997

BRITISH COUNCIL DIRECTOR, F. King, Cankarjevo nabrezje 27, 1000 Ljubljana

ECONOMY

Slovenia's economy has emerged as the most stable of the former Yugoslav economies and the least affected by the end of central planning. Although it has lost its captive export market and cheap supplies of raw materials from Serbia, Slovenia is one of the richest former Communist countries. It has successfully re-orientated its exports towards Western markets, its main trading partners being Germany, Italy and France. By mid-1996, 91 per cent of companies were in the private sector.

In 1996 agriculture contributed 5 per cent to the total value of GDP, industry 33 per cent and services 61 per cent. The main agricultural products are potatoes, wheat, corn, sugar beet and wine. The major manufacturing sectors are metalworking, electronics, textiles, automotive parts, chemicals, glass products and food-processing. Tourism and transport are major export earners, with 1,400,000 tourists visiting in 1991.

In 1996 Slovenia had a trade deficit of US$853 million and a current account surplus of US$47 million. Imports totalled US$9,399 and exports US$8,305 million.
GNP – US$18,390 million (1996); US$9,240 per capita (1996)
GDP – US$15,789 million (1994); US$7,206 per capita (1994); estimated to be US$18,580 and US$9,348 per capita in 1995
ANNUAL AVERAGE GROWTH OF GDP – 4.9 per cent (1995); forecast to be 4 per cent in 1997
INFLATION RATE – 9.7 per cent (1996)
UNEMPLOYMENT – 7.4 per cent (1995)
TOTAL EXTERNAL DEBT – US$4,031 million (1996)

TRADE WITH UK	1996	1997
Imports from UK	£131,714,000	£149,494,000
Exports to UK	109,111,000	98,204,000

COMMUNICATIONS

Important road and rail communications cross the country from west to east (Milan–Ljubljana–Budapest), and north to south (Munich–Ljubljana–Zagreb–Belgrade–Athens). There are international airports at Ljubljana, Maribor and Portoroz (Adriatic Coast). Koper is an important shipment point for goods from Austria, Hungary, the Czech Republic and Slovakia.

EDUCATION

Education is compulsory and free between the ages of seven and 14. There are 823 primary schools (age seven–14), 151 secondary or middle schools (age 14–19), 30 colleges and two universities (Ljubljana and Maribor).
ENROLMENT (percentage of age group) – primary 100 per cent (1995); tertiary 31.9 per cent (1995)

SOLOMON ISLANDS

AREA – 11,157 sq. miles (28,896 sq. km)
POPULATION – 378,000 (1995 estimate); 328,723 (1991 census). English is the official language; there are over 80 local languages
CAPITAL – ΨHoniara (population, 40,000, 1991)
CURRENCY – Solomon Islands dollar (SI$) of 100 cents
NATIONAL ANTHEM – God Bless our Solomon Islands
NATIONAL DAY – 7 July (Independence Day)
NATIONAL FLAG – Blue over green divided by a diagonal yellow band, with five white stars in the top left quarter
LIFE EXPECTANCY (years) – male 59.90; female 61.40
POPULATION GROWTH RATE – 3.3 per cent (1995)
POPULATION DENSITY – 13 per sq. km (1995)

Forming a scattered archipelago of mountainous islands and low-lying coral atolls, the Solomon Islands stretches about 900 miles in a south-easterly direction from the Shortland Islands to the Santa Cruz islands. The six biggest islands are Choiseul, New Georgia, Santa Isabel, Guadalcanal, Malaita and Makira. They are characterized by thickly-forested mountain ranges intersected by deep, narrow valleys.

HISTORY AND POLITICS

The origin of the present Melanesian inhabitants is uncertain. European interest in the islands began in the mid-16th century and continued intermittently for about 300 years, when the inauguration of sugar plantations in Queensland and Fiji (which created a need for labour) and the arrival of missionaries and traders led to increased European interest in the region. Great Britain declared a Protectorate in 1893 over the Southern Solomons, adding the Santa Cruz group in 1898 and 1899. The islands of the Shortland groups were transferred from Germany to Great Britain by treaty in 1900. The Solomon Islands achieved internal self-government in 1976, and became independent in July 1978.

Following legislative elections held on 6 August 1997, the National Unity group was the largest party in the National Parliament, winning 21 seats. Bartholomew Ulufa'alu was elected prime minister.

POLITICAL SYSTEM

The Solomon Islands is a constitutional monarchy. Queen Elizabeth II is represented locally by the Governor-General. Executive authority is exercised by the Cabinet. Legislative power is vested in a unicameral National Parliament of 50 members, elected for a four-year term.

Governor-General, HE Sir Moses Pitakaka, GCMG, apptd 1994

CABINET *as at July 1998*

Prime Minister, Bartholomew Ulufa'alu
Deputy P.M., Minister of Works, Sir Baddeley Devesi
Agriculture and Fisheries, Steve Auman
Commerce and Tourism, Enele Kwainirara
Development Planning, Fred Fono

1014   Countries of the World

Education, Roni Mani
Finance, Manasseh Sogavare
Foreign Affairs, Patteson Oti
Forests, Environment and Conservation, Hilda Kari
Health and Medical Services, Dick Warakohla
Home Affairs, Revd Leslie Boseto
Lands and Housing, Jackson Piesi
Mines and Energy, Walter Naezon
Police and National Security, Lester Huckle Saomasi
Provincial Government, Japhet Waipora
Women, Youth and Sports, Roben Mesapilu

HIGH COMMISSION OF THE SOLOMON ISLANDS
Boulevard Saint Michel 28, Box 23, 1040 Brussels
Tel: Brussels 2732 7085
High Commissioner, HE Robert Sisilo, apptd 1996

HONORARY CONSULATE
19 Springfield Road, London SW19 7AL
Tel 0181-296 0232
Honorary Consul, Edward Nielsen, OBE

BRITISH HIGH COMMISSION
Telekom House, Mendana Avenue (PO Box 676), Honiara
Tel: Honiara 21705/6
High Commissioner, HE Alan Waters, apptd 1998

ECONOMY

The main imports are foodstuffs, consumer goods, machinery and transport materials. Principal exports are timber, fish, palm oil, copra and cocoa. In 1994 imports totalled US$142 and in 1995 exports totalled US$168 million.
GNP – US$349 million (1996); US$900 per capita (1996)
GDP – US$216 million (1994); US$669 per capita (1994)
ANNUAL AVERAGE GROWTH OF GDP – – 5.1 per cent (1987)
INFLATION RATE – 11.8 per cent (1996)
TOTAL EXTERNAL DEBT – US$145 million (1996)

Trade with UK	1996	1997
Imports from UK	£2,111,000	£776,000
Exports to UK	6,573,000	9,101,000

COMMUNICATIONS

Solomon Airlines operates international services to other Pacific states and Australia. Air Niugini flies from Port Moresby to Honiara. There are about 1,300 miles of road, including those in private plantations, forestry areas and roads built and maintained by councils. Telekom, a company jointly owned by Cable and Wireless and the Solomon Islands government, operates the international and domestic telephone circuits from a ground station in Honiara via the Intelsat Pacific Ocean communication satellite.

SOMALIA
Jamhuuriyadda Diimoqraadiga ee Soomaaliya

AREA – 246,201 sq. miles (637,657 sq. km). Neighbours: Djibouti, Ethiopia and Kenya (west)
POPULATION – 9,250,000 (1994 UN estimate). Somali and Arabic are the official languages. English and Italian are also spoken
CAPITAL – ΨMogadishu (population, 1,000,000, 1987 estimate)
MAJOR CITIES – ΨBerbera (15,000); Boroma (65,000); Burao (15,000); Hargeisa (20,000); ΨKisimayu (60,000)

CURRENCY – Somali shilling of 100 cents
NATIONAL DAY – under review
NATIONAL FLAG – Five-pointed white star on blue ground
LIFE EXPECTANCY (years) – male 45.41; female 48.60
POPULATION GROWTH RATE – 1.3 per cent (1995)
POPULATION DENSITY – 15 per sq. km (1995)
URBAN POPULATION – 23.5 per cent (1987)
ENROLMENT (percentage of age group) – primary 8 per cent (1985); secondary 3 per cent (1985); tertiary 2.1 per cent (1985)

HISTORY AND POLITICS

British rule in Somaliland lasted from 1887 until 1960, except for a short period in 1940–1 when the Protectorate was occupied by Italian forces. Somalia, formerly an Italian colony, was occupied by British forces in 1941. In 1950 the UN placed it under Italian administration; this trusteeship lasted until the British protectorate and the trust territory became independent as the Somali Democratic Republic on 1 July 1960. In 1969, the armed forces seized power and established a ruling Revolutionary Council under Siad Barre's leadership.

Siad Barre was overthrown by rebels in January 1991, sparking civil war between rival clan-based movements. The United Somali Congress (USC) seized control in Mogadishu and formed an interim administration under Ali Mahdi Mohammed, which was contested by the Somali Salvation Democratic Front (SSDF), the Somali Patriotic Movement (SPM) and the Somali Democratic Movement (SDM). In the north, the Somali National Movement formed a rival administration under its leader, Abourahman Ahmed Ali. Fighting between the USC and supporters of the Somali National Alliance (SNA) of Gen. Mohammed Aideed devastated Mogadishu and large parts of the south, exacerbating famine conditions. The UN Operation in Somalia (UNOSOM) proved ineffective in securing aid distribution routes and was replaced on 9 December 1992 by a UN-approved, US-led, United Task Force (UNITAF) which, having secured distribution routes, attempted to confiscate weapons, provoking retaliatory attacks from the factions.

On 4 May 1993, UNITAF handed over to a 28,000-strong UN force (UNOSOM). Clashes between the UN force, attempting to broker a settlement, and the SNA left 90 UN troops and 2,000 Somalis dead between June and November 1993. Western troops withdrew from the UN operation in March 1994, leaving UN troops from India, Pakistan and Egypt, which were easily overrun by the Somali factions.

The UN withdrew its troops in March 1995, enabling Gen. Aideed's militia to take control of the city's port and airport. On 12 June 1995, Gen. Aideed was ousted as SNA leader by a joint USC-SNA congress which nominated Osman Ali Ato as its leader. Gen. Aideed responded by declaring himself president on 15 June 1995. Gen. Aideed died of gunshot wounds in July 1996 and was replaced by his son, Hussein Aideed. Fighting between the factions continued in 1996–7 despite a brief cease-fire in October 1996.

On 22 December 1997, 26 out of the 28 factions signed the Cairo Declaration, an agreement aimed at establishing a cross-factional 13-member Presidential Council and a 189-member Council of Deputies in preparation for full elections to be held no later than 2003. The declaration was approved by both Aideed and Ali Mahdi Mohammed, although the conference to organize the composition of the new bodies has been repeatedly postponed. Since the signing of the declaration, fighting has continued.

SOL – SOU 1015

INSURGENCIES

Civil war broke out in May 1988 between the government and the opposition Somali National Movement (SNM) in the north of the country. With the downfall of Siad Barre, the SNM took control of the north-west (the former British Somaliland Protectorate) and in May 1991 declared unilateral independence as the 'Somaliland Republic'. A government and legislature was formed which elected Mohammed Ibrahim Egal as president in May 1993.

SOMALI DIPLOMATIC REPRESENTATION

The Embassy closed in January 1992.

BRITISH DIPLOMATIC REPRESENTATION

The British Embassy in Mogadishu closed in January 1991.

ECONOMY

Livestock raising is the main occupation and there is a modest export trade in livestock, skins and hides. Italy, the Gulf States and Saudi Arabia import the bulk of the banana crop, the second biggest export. Due to UN aid and pacification of the countryside, the harvest improved from 10 per cent of normal in 1992 to 50 per cent in 1993.
GDP – US$731 million (1994); US$124 per capita (1994)
ANNUAL AVERAGE GROWTH OF GDP – 10.1 per cent (1987)
INFLATION RATE – 81.9 per cent (1988)
TOTAL EXTERNAL DEBT – US$2,643 million (1996)

TRADE WITH UK	1996	1997
Imports from UK	£4,614,000	£1,682,000
Exports to UK	10,000	36,000

SOUTH AFRICA
Republiek van Suid-Afrika – Republic of South Africa

AREA – 471,445 sq. miles (1,221,037 sq. km). Neighbours: Namibia (north-west), Botswana and Zimbabwe (north), Mozambique and Swaziland (north-east), Lesotho, which is completely surrounded by South Africa
POPULATION – 41,244,000 (1994 UN estimate); 37,900,000 (1996 census): 78.9 per cent African, 11 per cent White, 7.9 per cent Coloured, 2.2 per cent Asian. The interim constitution designates 11 official languages: Afrikaans; English; Ndebele; Sesotho sa Leboa; Sesotho; Si Swati (Swazi); Tsonga; Tswana; Venda; Xhosa; Zulu. Afrikaans and English are to remain the languages of record although any citizen may correspond official business in his own language. Afrikaans is descended from old Dutch and is the language of the Afrikaner and Coloured populations
CAPITAL –The seat of the government is Pretoria (population 525,583, 1991); the seat of the legislature is Cape Town (population, 1,911,521, 1991)
MAJOR CITIES – ΨDurban (982,075); ΨEast London (167,992); Johannesburg (1,609,408); Pietermaritzburg (192,417); ΨPort Elizabeth (651,993), 1985
CURRENCY – Rand (R) of 100 cents
NATIONAL ANTHEMS – Die Stem Van Suid-Afrika (The Call of South Africa); Nkosi Sikele'i Afrika (God Bless Africa)
NATIONAL DAY – 27 April (Freedom Day)
NATIONAL FLAG – Divided red over blue by a horizontal white-fimbriated green Y; in the hoist a black triangle fimbriated in yellow
LIFE EXPECTANCY (years) – male 60.01; female 66.00
POPULATION GROWTH RATE – 2.1 per cent (1995)

POPULATION DENSITY – 34 per sq. km (1995)
URBAN POPULATION – 56.6 per cent (1991)
ILLITERACY RATE – 18.2 per cent
ENROLMENT (percentage of age group) – primary 96 per cent (1994); secondary 52 per cent (1994); tertiary 17.3 per cent (1995)

South Africa occupies the southernmost part of the African continent from the courses of the Limpopo, Marico, Molopo, Nosop and Orange Rivers to the Cape of Good Hope, with the exception of Lesotho, Swaziland and the extreme south of Mozambique. To the west, east and south lie the south Atlantic and southern Indian Oceans. Some 1,192 miles (1,920 km) to the south-east of Capetown lie Prince Edward and Marion Islands, part of South Africa since 1947.

The Orange, with its tributary the Vaal, is the principal river, rising in the Drakensberg and flowing into the Atlantic near the border with Namibia. The Limpopo, or Crocodile River, in the north, rises in the Transvaal and flows into the Indian Ocean through Mozambique.

The climate is subtropical, dry and sunny, moderated by the temperate winds from the Atlantic and Indian Oceans. Moist hot air masses from the Indian Ocean are the chief source of rainfall for most of the country.

HISTORY AND POLITICS

Hunter-gatherers, the San (Bushmen) and Khoikhoi (Hottentots) inhabited southern Africa from c.8,000 BC. Their descendants, and those of Bantu-speaking peoples who had migrated south, occupied the area when the Portuguese navigator Bartolomeu Dias charted the coast in 1488.

The colony of the Cape of Good Hope was founded by the Dutch at Cape Town in 1652 and remained a Dutch colony until Britain took possession of it in 1795. Restored to Dutch rule in 1803, it was again taken by Britain in 1806 and this was confirmed by the London Convention of 1814. A rejection of British liberalism and the desire to keep slaves led to the movement of large numbers of Boers (the descendants of Dutch settlers) north-eastwards in the years following 1834. This 'Great Trek' led to the foundation of the Orange Free State and Transvaal republics by the Boers, which were recognized by Britain in 1853–4. Natal was annexed to Cape Colony by the British in 1844 and then formed as a separate colony in 1856, to which Zululand was added in 1897 after the British victory in the Zulu wars. Transvaal and the Orange Free State (renamed the Orange River Colony) became British colonies after the Boer defeat in the Second Boer War 1899–1902. The self-governing colonies of the Cape of Good Hope, Natal, the Transvaal and the Orange River Colony became united in 1910 under the name of the Union of South Africa. Independence within the Commonwealth was gained in 1931 under the Statute of Westminster. South Africa left the Commonwealth and became a republic on 31 May 1961, largely as a result of international condemnation of apartheid and of the Sharpeville massacre.

From 1948, when the Afrikaner National Party came to power, South Africa's social and political structure was based on apartheid, a policy of racial segregation. Opposition protests culminated in the Sharpeville massacre in 1960; the African National Congress (ANC) and other opposition groups were subsequently banned. A new wave of opposition climaxed in 1976 with uprisings in Soweto, in which hundreds were shot dead. In 1984 renewed rioting in the black townships and continuing unrest led to the declaration of a state of emergency in July 1985 in 36 districts, and nationwide from 12 June 1986; it was renewed annually until 1990.

As part of its policy of apartheid, the government established a number of black 'homelands'. Six areas (Gazankulu, Lebowa, KwaNdbele, KaNgwane, Qwaqwa and KwaZulu) were designated as self-governing states. A further four (Bophuthatswana, Ciskei, Transkei and Venda) were regarded as independent republics by the South African government but never recognized as such by the UN.

MOVES TO DEMOCRACY

The first moves to reform apartheid came into effect in 1984, when a new constitution extended the franchise to the Coloured and Indian populations. Coloureds and Indians elected members to a three-house parliament, Coloured and Indian houses being added to the existing white chamber. However, whites retained effective political power and blacks remained excluded.

In 1989, F. W. de Klerk became president of South Africa and accelerated the process of reform. In 1990, the ban on the ANC and restrictions on other anti-apartheid groups were lifted; Nelson Mandela, the main ANC political detainee, was released. In 1991 the laws implementing apartheid were effectively abolished. In 1992 a referendum amongst the white electorate on continued political reform and a new constitution reached by negotiation was approved by 69 per cent to 31 per cent.

On 20 December 1991, the Convention on a Democratic South Africa (CODESA) talks between the government, ANC, Inkatha Freedom Party and other political, business and church groups, opened. CODESA reached agreement on the establishment of an inter-racial administration and the formation of a five-year coalition government following a multiracial election. On 7 September 1993, the delegates agreed to form a multiparty Transitional Executive Council (TEC), which became effective in December 1993. An interim constitution was agreed on 17 November 1993 and adopted by parliament on 22 December.

In the country's first multiracial general election held on 26–29 April 1994 the results in the National Assembly were (seats): African National Congress (ANC) 62.7 per cent (252), National Party (NP) 20.4 per cent (82), Inkatha Freedom Party (IFP) 10.5 per cent (43), Freedom Front (FF) 2.2 per cent (nine), Democratic Party (DP) 1.7 per cent (seven), Pan Africanist Congress (PAC) 1.3 per cent (five), African Christian Democratic Party 0.4 per cent (two). In the Senate the ANC gained 60 seats, the NP 17, IFP five, FF five, DP three.

The new parliament has passed two significant pieces of legislation to settle the legacy of the apartheid era. In November 1994 the Restitution of Land Rights Act was passed which established a Land Claims Commission and a Land Claims Court to restore the rights of those dispossessed of their land since the 1913 Land Act. In June 1995 the Promotion of National Unity and Reconciliation Act was passed which established a Truth Commission covering the apartheid era, with a remit to assess confessions, grant amnesties for political crimes and set compensation for victims. The first hearing opened on 15 April 1996.

POLITICAL SYSTEM

The interim constitution establishes a democratic, multiparty state, and will remain in force until 1999, when the final constitution will take effect. The final constitution, agreed by the Constituent Assembly (composed of the National Assembly and Senate) on 8 May 1996, retains the existing political structure but replaces the Senate with a National Council of Provinces, rejects the representation of minority parties in the Cabinet and incorporates a Bill of Rights.

Under the interim constitution the ten homelands have been reincorporated in South Africa. Executive power is vested in a president and Cabinet, with the president elected by parliament; two deputy presidents appointed by parties with over 20 per cent of the vote; and a Cabinet and government of national unity to last five years composed of all parties gaining over 5 per cent of the vote. Legislative power is vested in a bicameral parliament, a directly elected 400-member National Assembly elected by proportional representation, and an indirectly elected 90-member Senate composed of ten members elected by each of the nine regional legislatures.

The interim constitution also established an 11-member constitutional court to adjudicate in disputes between the three tiers of government, to interpret and certify constitutional amendments, to ensure that all executive, legislative and judicial actions conform to the Bill of Rights, to decide on the validity of the final constitution, and to protect all rights and freedoms.

The four former provinces (Cape Province, Natal, Orange Free State, Transvaal) have been replaced by nine new regions (Western Cape, Northern Cape, Eastern Cape, Free State, North-West, KwaZulu/Natal, Gauteng, Northern Province, Mpumalanga). Each region has its own prime minister, a legislature of between 30 and 100 seats elected by proportional representation, and its own constitution. At local government level, new multiracial municipal councils have their seats allocated on a 30 per cent white, 30 per cent non-white and 40 per cent non-racial basis.

HEAD OF STATE

President, Commander-in-Chief of the Armed Forces, Nelson Rolihlahla Mandela, OM, *elected by parliament* 9 May 1994, *sworn in* 10 May 1994
Deputy President, Thabo Mbeki (ANC)

CABINET *as at July 1998*

Agriculture and Land Affairs, Derek Hanekom (ANC)
Arts, Culture, Science and Technology, Lionel Mtshali (IFP)
Correctional Services, Dr Sipo Mzimela (IFP)
Defence, Joe Modise (ANC)
Education, Dr Sibusiso Bengu (ANC)
Environmental Affairs and Tourism, Dr Pallo Jordan (ANC)
Finance, Trevor Manuel (ANC)
Foreign Affairs, Alfred Nzo (ANC)
Health, Dr Nkosazana Dlamini-Zuma (ANC)
Home Affairs, Prince Mangosuthu Buthelezi (IFP)
Housing, Sankie Mthembi-Mahanyele (ANC)
Justice and Intelligence Services, Dullah Omar (ANC)
Labour, Tito Mboweni (ANC)
Mineral and Energy Affairs, Penuell Maduna (ANC)
Posts, Telecommunications and Broadcasting, Jay Naidoo (ANC)
Provincial Affairs and Constitutional Development, Mohammed Valli Moosa (ANC)
Public Enterprises, Stella Sigcau (ANC)
Public Service and Administration, Dr Zola Skweyiya (ANC)
Public Works, Jeff Radebe (ANC)
Safety and Security, Sidney Mufamadi (ANC)
Sports and Recreation, Steve Tshwete (ANC)
Trade and Industry, Alec Erwin (ANC)
Transport, Mac Maharaj (ANC)
Water Affairs and Forestry, Prof. Kader Asmal (ANC)
Welfare and Population Development, Geraldine Fraser-Moleketi (ANC)

HIGH COMMISSION FOR THE REPUBLIC OF SOUTH AFRICA
South Africa House, Trafalgar Square, London WC2N 5DP
Tel 0171-451 7299

High Commissioner, HE Cheryl Carolus, apptd 1998
Deputy High Commissioner, H. Mahlangu
Minister (Economic), S. Pretorius
Counsellors, D. Seals; S. van Heerden; G. Johannes
Air Adviser, Col. M. Venter
Army Adviser, Col. A. Leijenaar
Naval Adviser, Cdre J. Vorster

BRITISH HIGH COMMISSION
255 Hill Street, Pretoria 0002
Tel: Pretoria 483 1200
91 Parliament Street, Cape Town 8001
Tel: Cape Town 461 7220
High Commissioner, HE Maeve Fort, CMG, apptd 1996
Counsellor, Deputy High Commissioner, M. J. Lyall-Grant
Counsellor (Political), D. Woods
Defence and Military Adviser, Brig. M. Wildman
Consul-General and Director of Trade Promotion
(Johannesburg), N. McInnes
CONSULATES-GENERAL – Cape Town and Johannesburg
CONSULATE – Durban
HONORARY CONSULS – Port Elizabeth, East London

Cultural Attaché and British Council Representative, P. Brazier,
76 Juta Street, (PO Box 30637), Braamfontein 2017,
Johannesburg. There are also offices in Cape Town and
Durban

DEFENCE

The new South African National Defence Force (SANDF)
was created from the merger of the South African Defence
Forces (SADF), the Umkhonto we Sizwe (MK) armed
wing of the ANC, the Azanian People's Liberation Army
(APLA) of the PAC, and the defence forces of the four
former independent homelands. White conscription is
being phased out.

The Army has 224 main battle tanks, 4,473 armoured
personnel carriers and armoured infantry fighting vehicles, and 393 artillery pieces. The Navy has three
submarines and nine patrol and coastal vessels at two bases.
The Air Force has 114 combat aircraft and 14 armed
helicopters.
MILITARY EXPENDITURE – 2.0 per cent of GDP (1996)
MILITARY PERSONNEL – 211,440; Army 54,300, Navy
8,000, Air Force 11,140, Paramilitaries 138,000
CONSCRIPTION DURATION – Three categories (full
career; up to ten years; up to six years)

ECONOMY

Mining is of great importance, employing more than half a
million people in 1996. It is the largest source of foreign
exchange. The principal minerals produced are gold, coal,
diamonds, copper, iron ore, manganese, lime and limestone, uranium, platinum, fluorspar, andalusite, zinc,
zirconium, vanadium, titanium and chrome. South Africa
is the world's largest producer of gold, platinum, diamonds,
manganese, chrome and vanadium, and has the world's
largest reserves of chrome ore, manganese, vanadium and
andalusite.

Agriculture, forestry and fishing accounted for 4.5 per
cent of GDP in 1995. Over 50 per cent of land is pasture so
livestock farming is widespread and meat and wool
important products. Principal crops are maize, sugar cane,
fruits and vegetables, wheat, sorghum, sunflower seeds and
groundnuts. Cotton is widely grown, and viticulture is also
widespread.

Industries, concentrated most heavily around Johannesburg, Pretoria and the major ports, process foodstuffs,
metals and non-metallic mineral products, produce oil

from coal, and also produce beverages and tobacco, motor
vehicles, chemicals and chemical products, machinery,
textiles and clothing, and paper and paper products.
Manufacturing industry contributed 24 per cent of GDP
in 1996.

Energy production is based upon coal and natural gas
and the production of synthetic liquid fuel from coal. One
nuclear power station is in operation and others are
planned. South Africa exports electricity through its
electric grid connections to all states in southern Africa.
The economy has suffered from the falling price of gold as
well as recession, industrial unrest, drought and foreign
disinvestment. In September 1993 the government announced it would repay its US$5,000 million foreign debt
over an eight-year period.

Argument over the cost of the ANC's reconstruction
and development programme (RDP), including increased
spending on education, health care, new homes and
electrification, led to a run on the rand and a crisis in
foreign exchange and gold reserves, necessitating a scal-
ing-down of expenditure.

In 1995 there was a trade surplus of US$1,610 million
and a current account deficit of US$2,820 million. In 1996
imports totalled US$30,126 million and exports
US$29,330 million.
GNP – US$132,455 million (1996); US$3,520 per capita
(1996)
GDP – US$102,812 million (1994); US$2,835 per capita
(1994)
ANNUAL AVERAGE GROWTH OF GDP – 3.1 per cent (1996)
INFLATION RATE – 7.4 per cent (1996)
UNEMPLOYMENT – 4.5 per cent (1995)
TOTAL EXTERNAL DEBT – US$23,590 million (1996)

TRADE

Principal exports are gold, base metals and metal products,
coal, diamonds, food (especially fruit) and wool. Principal
imports are machinery, chemicals, motor vehicles, metals
and metal products, food, inedible raw materials and
textiles.

American and EU sanctions, in place since 1986, were
lifted in July 1991 and January 1992 respectively. The
longer-standing UN finance, oil and arms embargoes were
lifted in October 1993, December 1993 and April 1994
respectively.

South Africa's main trading partners are Germany, the
USA, the UK, Italy and Japan.

Trade with UK	1996	1997
Imports from UK	£1,880,800,000	£1,633,911,000
Exports to UK	1,220,706,000	1,389,338,000

COMMUNICATIONS

There are international airports at Johannesburg, Durban
and Cape Town. South African Airways operates international services to Europe, South America, the Far East,
Africa, Australia and the USA, and it is the principal
operator of domestic flights. Durban is the largest seaport.
Other major ports are Cape Town, Port Elizabeth, East
London, Saldanha Bay, Mossel Bay and Richards Bay. The
national railway system, and most long-distance passenger
and freight road transport are run by independent companies. The six landlocked states of Botswana, Lesotho,
Swaziland, Zimbabwe, Zambia and Malawi make extensive use of South African Railways for foreign trade.

SPAIN
España

AREA – 195,365 sq. miles (505,992 sq. km). Neighbours: Portugal (west), France (north)
POPULATION – 39,210,000 (1996 census): 96 per cent Catholic, 1 per cent Muslim. Castilian Spanish is the official language, although Basque, Catalan and Galician are spoken and have official status in the autonomous regions where they are spoken
CAPITAL – Madrid (population, 3,084,673, 1996)
MAJOR CITIES – ΨBarcelona (1,614,571); ΨMálaga (532,425); Sevilla (719,588); Valencia (763,299); Zaragoza (607,899), 1991
CURRENCY – Peseta of 100 céntimos
NATIONAL ANTHEM – Marcha Real Española
NATIONAL DAY – 12 October
NATIONAL FLAG – Three horizontal stripes of red, yellow, red, with the yellow of double width
LIFE EXPECTANCY (years) – male 73.40; female 80.49
POPULATION GROWTH RATE – 0.1 per cent (1995)
POPULATION DENSITY – 77 per sq. km (1995)
URBAN POPULATION – 64.1 per cent (1991)

The interior of the Iberian peninsula consists of an elevated tableland surrounded and traversed by mountain ranges: the Pyrenees, the Cantabrian Mountains, the Sierra de Guadarrama, Sierra Morena, Sierra Nevada, Montes de Toledo, etc. The principal rivers are the Duero, the Tajo, the Guadiana, the Guadalquivir, the Ebro and the Miño.

HISTORY AND POLITICS

Spain was a monarchy until 1931, when King Alfonso XIII left the country and a republic was proclaimed. A provisional government, drawn from the various republican and socialist parties, was formed. In July 1936 a counter-revolution broke out in military garrisons in Spanish Morocco and spread throughout Spain. The principal leader was Gen. Franco, leader of the Military-Fascist fusion, or *Falange*. Civil war ensued until March 1939, when the Popular Front governments in Madrid and Barcelona surrendered to the Nationalists (as Gen. Franco's followers were then named). Gen. Franco became president and ruled the country until his death in 1975, when, according to his wishes, he was succeeded as head of state by Prince Juan Carlos of Bourbon (grandson of Alfonso XIII) and Spain again became a monarchy. The first free election was held on 15 June 1977.

The general election of June 1993 was won by the PSOE (Spanish Socialist Workers' Party), which formed a minority government with the support of the Catalan and Basque nationalists. The withdrawal of nationalist support following the government's embroilment in the anti-terrorist GAL scandal forced Prime Minister González to call an early general election, on 3 March 1996. The Popular Party (PP) won 156 seats in the Congress of Deputies, defeating the PSOE which won 141 seats. The PP formed a minority government with the support of the Catalan nationalists.

INSURGENCIES

The Basque separatist terrorist organization ETA (*Euzkadi ta Azkatasuna* – Basque Nation and Liberty) has since its formation in 1959 carried out a terrorist campaign of bombings, shootings and kidnappings against the Spanish state and its security forces in an attempt to gain independence for the Basque country. ETA rejected regional autonomy for the Basque country in 1979 as insufficient and continued its campaign, but increased co-operation

between French and Spanish security forces and an alleged illegal anti-terrorist campaign organized by the Spanish state under the acronym GAL (*Grupos Antiterroristas de Liberación*) had greatly weakened ETA by the early 1990s. Most of its leaders were caught and jailed in 1992; the conflict has left 700–800 dead and 600 ETA members in jail.

POLITICAL SYSTEM

Under the 1978 constitution there is a bicameral *Cortes Generales* comprising a 350-member Congress of Deputies elected for a maximum term of four years, which elects the prime minister; and a Senate consisting of 208 directly elected representatives of the provinces, islands, and Ceuta and Melilla, and 48 representatives appointed by the assemblies of the autonomous regions.

Since the promulgation of the 1978 constitution, 19 autonomous regions have been established, with their own parliaments and governments. These are Andalucia, Aragon, Asturias, Balearics, the Basque country, Canaries, Castilla-La Mancha, Castilla-Leon, Cantabria, Cataluña, Ceuta, Extremadura, Galicia, Madrid, Melilla, Murcia, Navarre, La Rioja and Valencia. The Basque country, incorporating the three provinces of Álava, Guipúzcoa and Vizcaya, has the authority to raise taxes and is responsible for social services, culture and the Basque language within the region.

HEAD OF STATE

HM The King of Spain, King Juan Carlos I de Borbón y Borbón, KG, GCVO, *born* 5 January 1938, *acceded to the throne* 22 November 1975, *married* 14 May 1962, Princess Sophie of Greece *and has issue* Infante Felipe (*see* below); Infanta Elena Maria Isabel Dominga, *born* 20 December 1963; and Infanta Cristina Federica Victoria Antonia, *born* 13 June 1965
Heir, HRH The Prince of the Asturias (Infante Felipe Juan Pablo Alfonso y Todos los Santos), *born* 30 January 1968

CABINET *as at July 1998*

Prime Minister, José María Aznar López
Deputy PMs, Rodrigo de Rato y Figaredo *(Economy and Finance)*; Francisco Alvárez-Cascos Fernández *(Presidency)*
Agriculture, Food and Fisheries, Loyola de Palacio del Valle-Lersundi
Defence, Eduardo Serra Rexach
Development, Rafael Arias-Salgado y Montalvo
Education and Culture, Esperanza Aguirre y Gil de Biedma
Environment, Isabel Tocino Biscarolasaga
Foreign Affairs, Abel Matutes Juan
Health and Consumer Affairs, José Manuel Romay Beccaría
Industry and Energy, Josep Piqué i Camps
Interior, Jaime Mayor Oreja
Justice, Margarita Mariscal de Gante
Labour and Social Affairs, Javier Arenas Bocanegra
Public Administration, Mariano Rajoy Brey

SPANISH EMBASSY
39 Chesham Place, London SW1X 8SB
Tel 0171-235 5555
Ambassador Extraordinary and Plenipotentiary, HE Don Alberto Aza Arias, apptd 1993
Minister Counsellor, Don Pablo Barrios
Defence and Naval Attaché, Capt. Don Angel Cabrera
Ministers, Don L. E. Valera (*Consul*); Dr D. de Lario (*Cultural*)
Counsellor, Don Juan Sebastián de Erice (*Commercial*)

BRITISH EMBASSY
Calle de Fernando el Santo 16, 28010 Madrid
Tel: Madrid 319 0200

Ambassador Extraordinary and Plenipotentiary, HE Peter
Torry, apptd 1998
Minister, Deputy Head of Mission, J. A. Dew
Counsellors, M. H. Conner (*Commercial*); C. J. Ingham
(*Economic and Community Affairs*); M. Ramscar
Defence and Naval Attaché, Capt. P. Pacey
Consuls-General, D. G. Alexander, MBE (*Madrid*);
J. R. Cowling (*Barcelona*); M. McLoughlin (*Bilbao*)
CONSULATES-GENERAL – Madrid, Barcelona, Bilbao
CONSULATES – Alicante, Málaga, Palma de Mallorca, Las
Palmas, Seville, Tenerife
VICE-CONSULATES – Ibiza, Menorca
HONORARY CONSULATES – Santander, Vigo

BRITISH COUNCIL DIRECTOR, P. Taylor, OBE, Paseo del
General Martínez, Campos 31, 28010 Madrid. There are
offices in Barcelona, Bilbao, Las Palmas, Murcia, Palma,
Seville and Valencia

BRITISH CHAMBER OF COMMERCE, Plaza de Santa Barbara
10, 1st Floor, 28004 Madrid; Paseo de Gracia 11,
Barcelona 7; Alameda de Mazarredo 5, Bilbao 1

DEFENCE

The Army has 776 main battle tanks, 1,995 armoured
personnel carriers, 1,252 artillery pieces and 28 attack
helicopters. The Navy has eight submarines, one aircraft
carrier, 17 frigates, 32 patrol and coastal vessels, 18 combat
aircraft and 25 armed helicopters at seven bases. The Air
Force has 199 combat aircraft.
The USA maintains 2,200 naval and 230 air force
personnel in Spain.
MILITARY EXPENDITURE – 1.5 per cent of GDP (1996)
MILITARY PERSONNEL – 273,250: Army 128,500, Navy
39,000, Air Force 30,000, Paramilitaries 75,750
CONSCRIPTION DURATION – Nine months

ECONOMY

The expansion of the economy and accession to the EU
have led to changes in Spanish agriculture. It accounted for
5 per cent of GDP in 1994 and employs over 10 per cent of
the working population. The country is generally fertile,
and olives, oranges, lemons, almonds, pomegranates,
bananas, apricots, tomatoes, peppers, cucumbers and
grapes are cultivated. Other agricultural products include
wheat, barley, oats, rice, hemp and flax. The vine is
cultivated widely; in the south-west, around Jerez, sherry
and tent wines are produced. Spain has one of Europe's
largest fishing industries.
Spain's mineral resources of coal, iron, wolfram, copper,
zinc, lead and iron ores are exploited. The principal
industrial goods are cars, steel, ships, manufactured goods,
textiles, chemical products, footwear and other leather
goods. Tourism is a major industry with 62 million tourists
visiting Spain in 1996.
Spain has successfully met the convergence criteria laid
down for EU economic and monetary union and will
participate in the next stage of EMU starting on 1 January
1999. A privatization programme was begun in 1996 which
will be completed by 2000.
In 1996 Spain had a trade deficit of US$14,912 million
and a current account surplus of US$1,756 million. Imports
totalled US$121,784 million and exports US$101,993
million.
GNP – US$563,249 million (1996); US$14,350 per capita
(1996)
GDP – US$510,763 million (1994); US$12,201 per capita
(1994)
ANNUAL AVERAGE GROWTH OF GDP – 2.2 per cent (1996)

INFLATION RATE – 3.6 per cent (1996)
UNEMPLOYMENT – 22.9 per cent (1995)

TRADE

The principal imports are cotton, tobacco, timber, coffee
and cocoa, food products, fertilizers, dyes, machinery,
motor vehicles and agricultural tractors, wool and petroleum products. The principal exports include cars, petroleum products, iron ore, cork, salt, vegetables, fruits, wines,
olive oil, potash, mercury, pyrites, tinned fruit and fish,
tomatoes and footwear.

Trade with UK	1996	1997
Imports from UK	£6,371,600,000	£6,385,200,000
Exports to UK	4,730,700,000	4,879,500,000

EDUCATION

Education is free for those aged six to 18, and compulsory
up to the age of 15. Private schools (30 per cent of primary
and 60 per cent of secondary schools) have to fulfil certain
criteria to receive government maintenance grants. There
are 33 public sector universities, the oldest of which,
Salamanca, was founded in 1218. Other ancient foundations are Valladolid (1346), Barcelona (1430), Zaragoza
(1474), Santiago (1495), Valencia (1500), Seville (1505),
Madrid (1508), Granada (1531), Oviedo (1604). Private
universities are Deusto in Bilbao, Navarra in Pamplona,
Carlos III in Madrid and one in Salamanca.
ILLITERACY RATE – 2.9 per cent
ENROLMENT (percentage of age group) – primary 100 per
cent (1994); secondary 94 per cent (1994); tertiary 46.1
per cent (1994)

CULTURE

Castilian is the language of more than three-quarters of the
population of Spain. Basque, said to have been the original
language of Iberia, is spoken in Vizcaya, Guipúzcoa and
Álava. Catalan is spoken in Provençal Spain, and Galician,
spoken in the north-western provinces, is akin to Portuguese. The governments of these regions actively encourage use of their local languages.
The literature of Spain is one of the oldest and richest in
the world, the *Poem of the Cid*, the earliest of the heroic songs
of Spain, having been written about 1140. The outstanding
writings of its golden age are those of Miguel de Cervantes
Saavedra (1547–1616), Lope Felix de Vega Carpio
(1562–1635) and Pedro Calderón de la Barca (1600–81).
The Nobel Prize for Literature has five times been
awarded to Spanish authors: J. Echegaray (1904), J.
Benavente (1922), Juan Ramón Jiménez (1956), Vicente
Aleixandre (1977) and Camilo José Cela (1989).

ISLANDS AND ENCLAVES

THE BALEARIC ISLES form an archipelago off the east coast
of Spain. There are four large islands (Majorca, Minorca,
Ibiza and Formentera), and seven smaller (Aire,
Aucanada, Botafoch, Cabrera, Dragonera, Pinto and El
Rey). Area 1,935 sq. miles (5,011 sq. km); population
685,088. The archipelago forms a province of Spain, the
capital is ΨPalma in Majorca, population 323,138
THE CANARY ISLANDS are an archipelago in the Atlantic,
off the African coast, consisting of seven islands and six
islets. Area 2,807 sq. miles (7,270 sq. km); population
1,444,626. The Canary Islands form two provinces of
Spain: Las Palmas, comprising Gran Canaria, Lanzarote
(38,500), Fuerteventura (19,500) and the islets of
Alegranza, Roque del Este, Roque del Oeste, Graciosa,
Montaña Clara and Lobos, with seat of administration at
ΨLas Palmas (373,772) in Gran Canaria; and Santa Cruz

de Tenerife, comprising Tenerife, La Palma (76,000), Gomera (31,829), and Hierro (10,000), with seat of administration at ΨSanta Cruz in Tenerife, population estimate 204,948
ISLA DE FAISANES is an uninhabited Franco-Spanish condominium, at the mouth of the Bidassoa in La Higuera bay
ΨCEUTA is a fortified post on the Moroccan coast, opposite Gibraltar. Area 5 sq. miles (13 sq. km); population 70,864. ΨMelilla is a town on a rocky promontory at the Rif coast, connected with the mainland by a narrow isthmus. Population 58,449. Ceuta and Melilla are autonomous regions of Spain

OVERSEAS TERRITORIES

The following territories are Spanish settlements on the Moroccan seaboard.
PEÑÓN DE ALHUCEMAS is a bay including six islands; population 366
PEÑÓN DE LA GOMERA (or Peñón de Velez) is a fortified rocky islet; population 450
THE CHAFFARINAS (or Zaffarines) is a group of three islands near the Algerian frontier; population 610

SRI LANKA
Sri Lanka Prajatantrika Samajawadi Janarajaya

AREA – 25,332 sq. miles (65,610 sq. km)
POPULATION – 18,354,000 (1994 UN estimate): 74 per cent Sinhalese, 12.6 per cent Sri Lankan Tamils, 5.6 per cent Indian Tamils, 7.1 per cent Sri Lankan Moors, 0.7 per cent Burghers, Malays and others. The religion of the majority is Buddhism (69.3 per cent), then Hinduism (15.5 per cent), Islam (7.6 per cent), and Christianity (7.5 per cent). The national languages are Sinhala and Tamil
CAPITAL – ΨColombo (population, 615,000, 1993)
MAJOR CITIES – ΨGalle (971,000); ΨJaffna (879,000); Kandy (1,269,000); ΨTrincomalee (323,000)
CURRENCY – Sri Lankan rupee of 100 cents
NATIONAL ANTHEM – Namo Namo Matha (We all stand together)
NATIONAL DAY – 4 February (Independence Day)
NATIONAL FLAG – On a dark red field, within a golden border, a golden lion passant holding a sword in its right paw, and a representation of a *bo*-leaf, issuing from each corner; and to its right, two vertical stripes of saffron and green also placed within a golden border, to represent the minorities of the country
LIFE EXPECTANCY (years) – male 67.78; female 71.66
POPULATION GROWTH RATE – 1.5 per cent (1995)
POPULATION DENSITY – 280 per sq. km (1995)
ILLITERACY RATE – 9.8 per cent
ENROLMENT (percentage of age group) – tertiary 5.1 per cent (1995)

Sri Lanka (formerly Ceylon) is an island in the Indian Ocean, off the southern tip of India and separated from it by the narrow Palk Strait. Forests, jungle and scrub cover the greater part of the island. In areas over 2,000 ft above sea level grasslands (*patanas* or *talawas*) are found. One of the highest peaks in the central massif is Adam's Peak (7,360 ft), a place of pilgrimage for Buddhists, Hindus and Muslims.
The climate is warm throughout the year, with a high relative humidity. The two main monsoon seasons are mid-May to September (south-west) and November to March (north-east).

HISTORY AND POLITICS

The Portuguese landed in Ceylon in the early 16th century and founded settlements, eventually conquering much of the country. Portuguese rule lasted 150 years; in 1658 it gave way to that of the Dutch East India Company until 1796. The maritime provinces of Ceylon were ceded by the Dutch to the British in 1798, becoming a British Crown Colony in 1802. With the annexation of the Kingdom of Kandy in 1815, all Ceylon came under British rule. Ceylon became a self-governing state and a member of the British Commonwealth on 4 February 1948. A republican constitution was adopted in 1972 and the country was renamed Sri Lanka (meaning 'Resplendent Island').
Eight provincial councils were set up in 1988 under the Indo-Sri Lankan peace accord in an attempt to diffuse ethnic tension. Since then, except for the temporarily merged North-East province, all provinces have had elected provincial councils.
In the general election of 16 August 1994 the ruling United National Party (UNP) was defeated by the People's Alliance led by Chandrika Bandaranaike Kumaratunga. The People's Alliance, a coalition of seven parties, won 105 seats; the UNP 94 seats; and other parties, mainly Muslim and moderate Tamils, 26 seats. The People's Alliance formed a government with the support of the Sri Lankan Muslim Congress and moderate Tamil parties. Prime Minister Kumaratunga won the presidential election on 9 November 1994 with 62 per cent of the vote after the UNP candidate Gamini Dissanayake was assassinated by Tamil Tiger terrorists. President Kumaratunga handed over the premiership to her mother, the former Prime Minister Sirimavo Bandaranaike.
In August 1995 the government proposed constitutional changes intended to form a federal state with eight autonomous regions (one covering the Tamil north-east). Each region would have its own elected legislature, executive and judicial branch of government, a police force, and powers devolved from the central government. The package must be passed by a two-thirds parliamentary majority and a national referendum.

INSURGENCIES

The Liberation Tigers of Tamil Eelam (LTTE) guerrilla group has been fighting Sri Lankan forces for control of the Tamil majority areas in the north and east of the country since 1983.
The People's Alliance government came to power on a platform of negotiating a peaceful settlement, to include full autonomy for the Tamil-majority areas. Peace negotiations opened in September 1994, leading to a formal cease-fire with the LTTE which began on 8 January 1995. Fighting resumed in April 1995 after the LTTE had unilaterally broken the cease-fire and negotiations had broken down. A government offensive in April 1996 gained control over almost the entire northern Jaffna peninsula, although the rebels counter-attacked, briefly seizing a government military base in July 1996. A second government offensive in May 1997 to take control of a strategic highway on the Jaffna peninsula resulted in losses for the LTTE, though fighting continues in the area. In May 1998, pro-LTTE gunmen assassinated Sarojini Yogeswaran, the moderate Tamil mayor of Jaffna. The LTTE has up to 10,000 members.

POLITICAL SYSTEM

The 1978 constitution introduced a system of proportional representation. Legislative power is vested in the parliament, whose 225 members are directly elected for a six-year term. Executive power is exercised by the president, elected for six years, and the Cabinet.

HEAD OF STATE
President, Buddha Sasana, Defence, Finance, Chandrika Bandaranaike Kumaratunga, *elected* 9 November 1994, *sworn in* 12 November 1994

CABINET *as at July 1998*
The President
Prime Minister, Sirimavo Bandaranaike (SLFP)
Agriculture and Land, D. M. Jayaratna (SLFP)
Co-operative Development, D. P. Wickremasinghe (SLFP)
Cultural and Religious Affairs, Lakshman Jayakody (SLFP)
Education and Higher Education, Richard Pathirana (SLFP)
External Trade, Kingsley Wickremaratne (SLFP)
Foreign Affairs, Laksham Kadirgamar (SLFP)
Forestry and Environment, Nandimitra Ekanayake (SLFP)
Health and Indigenous Medicine, Nimal Siripala De Silva (SLFP)
Housing and Urban Development, Indika Gunawardena (CPSL)
Industrial Development, C. V. Gunaratna (SLFP)
Justice and Constitutional Affairs, G. L. Peiris (SLFP)
Labour, John Seneviratne (SLFP)
Livestock Development and Estates Infrastructure, S. Thondaman (SLWC)
Mahaweli Development, Maithripala Sirisena (SLFP)
Media, Posts and Telecommunications, Mangala Samaraweera (SLFP)
Planning, Implementation and Parliamentary Affairs, Jeyaraj Fernandopulle (SLFP)
Power, Irrigation, Gen. Anuruddha Ratwatte (SLFP)
Provincial Councils and Local Government, Alavi Maulana (SLFP)
Public Administration, Home Affairs, Plantation Industries, Ratnasiri Wickremanayake (SLFP)
Science and Technology, Bernard Soysa (LSSP)
Shipping, Ports, Rehabilitation of Eastern Provinces, M. H. M. Ashraff (SLMC)
Social Services, Berty Premanand Dissanayake (SLFP)
Tourism and Aviation, Dharmasiri Senanayake (SLFP)
Transport and Highways, A. H. M. Fowzie (SLFP)
Vocational Training and Rural Industries, Amarasiri Dodangoda (SLFP)
Welfare, Youth and Sport, S. B. Dissanayake (SLFP)
Women's Affairs, Hema Ratnayake (SLFP)
SLFP Sri Lanka Freedom Party; CPSL Communist Party of Sri Lanka; SLWC Sri Lanka Workers' Congress; LSSP Lanka Sama Samaja Party; SLMC Sri Lanka Muslim Congress

HIGH COMMISSION FOR THE DEMOCRATIC SOCIALIST REPUBLIC OF SRI LANKA
13 Hyde Park Gardens, London W2 2LU
Tel 0171-262 1841
High Commissioner, HE Sarath Wickremesinghe, apptd 1995
Deputy High Commissioner, C. Wagiswara
Ministers, A. Karunaratne *(Consular);* T. Ariyaratne *(Commercial)*
First Secretary, C. Obeyesekera

BRITISH HIGH COMMISSION
190 Galle Road, Kollupitiya, PO Box 1433, Colombo 3
Tel: Colombo 437336
High Commissioner, HE David Tatham, CMG, apptd 1996
Deputy High Commissioner, M. H. P. Hill
Defence Adviser, Lt.-Col. R. N. Kendell, MBE
First Secretary (Commercial and Economic), C. Haslam

BRITISH COUNCIL DIRECTOR, S. Maingay, 49 Alfred House Gardens, PO Box 753, Colombo 3

DEFENCE

The Army has 25 main battle tanks, 169 armoured personnel carriers and armoured infantry fighting vehicles, and 50 artillery pieces. The Navy has 39 patrol and coastal vessels at seven bases. The Air Force has 22 combat aircraft and 17 armed helicopters.
MILITARY EXPENDITURE – 6.5 per cent of GDP (1996)
MILITARY PERSONNEL – 227,200: Army 95,000, Navy 12,000, Air Force 10,000, Paramilitaries 110,200

ECONOMY

The staple products are tea, rubber, copra, spices and gems. There is increasing emphasis on local production of food, especially rice, and plans for the large-scale production of sugar cane, cotton and citrus fruits.

The manufacturing sector has grown considerably over the past few years and in addition to processing agricultural products, it produces ceramics, paper, leather goods, plywood, cement, chemicals, textiles, garments, ilmenite, hardware, fertilizers, jewellery and tyres. There is a petroleum refinery. By the end of 1996 1,953 foreign investment projects had been approved. Tourism attracts roughly 400,000 visitors annually.

Since regaining control of Jaffna, the government has requested £178 million in foreign aid to fund a three-year programme of reconstruction.

In 1995 there was a trade deficit of US$880 million and a current account deficit of US$546 million. In 1996 imports totalled US$5,416 million and exports US$4,095 million.
GNP – US$13,475 million (1996); US$740 per capita (1996)
GDP – US$9,811 million (1994); US$649 per capita (1994)
ANNUAL AVERAGE GROWTH OF GDP – 4.8 per cent (1991)
INFLATION RATE – 15.9 per cent (1996)
UNEMPLOYMENT – 12.5 per cent (1995)
TOTAL EXTERNAL DEBT – US$7,995 million (1996)

TRADE WITH UK	1996	1997
Imports from UK	£148,339,000	£210,624,000
Exports to UK	232,088,000	274,795,000

COMMUNICATIONS

There are over 61,200 miles of roads in Sri Lanka and a government-run railway system with 1,230 miles of lines. A satellite earth station at Padukka provides telecommunication links world-wide. The principal airport is at Katunayake, 19 miles north of Colombo. Air Lanka operates 69 flights weekly to the Gulf States, the Maldives, western Europe and the Far East.

SUDAN
Al-Jamhuryat es-Sudan Al-Democratia

AREA – 967,500 sq. miles (2,505,813 sq. km). Neighbours: Egypt (north), Eritrea and Ethiopia (east), Kenya, Uganda and the Democratic Republic of Congo (south), Central African Republic, Chad, and Libya (west)
POPULATION – 28,098,000 (1994 UN estimate). Arab and Nubian peoples populate the north and centre, Nilotic and Negro peoples the south. Arabic is the official language and Islam the state religion, although the Nilotics of the Bahr el Ghazal and Upper Nile valleys are generally Animists or Christians
CAPITAL – Khartoum (population, 924,505, 1994). The combined population of Khartoum, Khartoum North

and Omdurman (excluding refugees and displaced people) is estimated at 3,000,000

MAJOR CITIES – El Obeid (228,096); Nyala (1,267,077); ΨPort Sudan (305,385); Sharg el nil (879,105), 1993 estimate

CURRENCY – Sudanese dinar (SD) of 10 pounds

NATIONAL ANTHEM – Nahnu Djundullah (We are the army of God)

NATIONAL DAY – 1 January (Independence Day)

NATIONAL FLAG – Three horizontal stripes of red, white and black with a green triangle next to the hoist

LIFE EXPECTANCY (years) – male 51.58; female 54.37

POPULATION GROWTH RATE – 1.7 per cent (1995)

POPULATION DENSITY – 11 per sq. km (1995)

URBAN POPULATION – 27.1 per cent (1994)

MILITARY EXPENDITURE – 4.2 per cent of GDP (1996)

MILITARY PERSONNEL – 94,700: Army 75,000, Navy 1,700, Air Force 3,000, Paramilitaries 15,000

CONSCRIPTION DURATION – Three years

The White Nile, as the Bahr el Jebel, flows through Sudan from Nimule to Wadi Halfa. The Blue Nile flows from Lake Tana on the Ethiopian plateau through Sudan to join the White Nile at Khartoum. The next confluence of importance is at Atbara where the main Nile is joined by the River Atbara. Between Khartoum and Wadi Halfa lie five of the six cataracts.

HISTORY AND POLITICS

The Anglo-Egyptian Condominium over Sudan was established in 1899 and ended when the Sudan House of Representatives, on 19 December 1955, declared Sudan a fully independent sovereign state. A republic was proclaimed on 1 January 1956, and was recognized by Great Britain and Egypt. Sudan was under military rule from 1958 to 1964; under the rule of a revolutionary council headed by Col. Gaafar Mohamed El Nimeri from 1969 until April 1985 when the army command deposed Nimeri; and experienced a third military coup in June 1989 when the civilian government, in power since 1986, was overthrown by Brig.-Gen. Omar Hassan Ahmad al-Bashir. The constitution was suspended and parliament was replaced by a 15-member ruling junta (Revolutionary Command Council) who exercised control over a Cabinet. The ruling junta appointed Gen. al-Bashir as head of state on 16 October 1993 and then dissolved itself. Presidential and legislative elections were held in March 1996. President al-Bashir was elected with 75.7 per cent of the vote having faced no serious contender. Hassan al-Tourabi of the fundamentalist National Islamic Front (NIF) was elected president of the 400-member National Assembly, although political parties had officially been banned from contesting the elections.

INSURGENCIES

Nearly 17 years of insurrection in the southern provinces ended in 1972 with the signing of an agreement recognizing southern regional autonomy within the Sudanese state. However, insurrection resumed in 1983 and since then there has been civil war in the regions of Eastern and Western Equatoria in the south of the country between government forces and the Christian and Animist majority in the area, organized into the Sudan People's Liberation Army (SPLA). Although the Islamic government has officially stated that it is not attempting to introduce Sharia law in the south, the Sharia affects the two million Christians in northern areas.

Between 1991 and 1994 the SPLA was split into four factions based on tribal groups. The two principal factions were SPLA-Torit led by the original SPLA leader John Garang, and SPLA-United led by Riek Machar. By early 1994 government forces controlled most of the towns and roads in the region and launched the largest offensive since 1983, forcing the SPLA factions to resort to guerrilla tactics. Garang's SPLA-Torit faction made considerable advances against government forces in late 1995 and early 1996. In April 1996, the government signed a peace treaty with the South Sudan Independence Movement and SPLA-United who agreed to relinquish any hope of independence. SPLA-Torit rejected the agreement. In 1997 five rebel factions signed peace deals with the government; SPLA-Torit made advances in the south having been strengthened by its alliance with the National Democratic Alliance. Fighting continued into 1998. In May 1998, the government and SPLA agreed to hold a referendum on self-determination for the south, though no date for this was set.

The warfare has left an estimated 1.4 million dead, including 300,000 who died in the war-induced famine in 1988 and thousands in a similar situation in 1994. Some three million refugees have fled the fighting, either to the north, to neighbouring states or to the far south near the Ugandan border. The fighting has left large areas of the south desolate and uninhabitable. In April 1998, aid workers estimated that 500,000 people faced starvation in a new war-induced famine.

FOREIGN RELATIONS

The government has developed close relations with Iran and is believed by Western states to support international terrorism and have Iranian Revolutionary Guards' bases on its territory. Supported and dominated by the NIF, the government has since 1989 turned Sudan into an Islamic state. In August 1993 the USA placed Sudan on a list of countries it saw as sponsoring terrorism and suspended all trade apart from humanitarian goods. In 1995 Sudan's relations with its neighbours, notably Egypt, Eritrea and Uganda, deteriorated as they consider that Sudan is arming Islamic and insurgent groups in their states. In April 1996 the UN imposed sanctions on Sudan for failing to extradite three people suspected of attempting to assassinate President Mubarak of Egypt in Ethiopia in June 1996. In August 1998 the US military bombed a Sudanese factory suspected of making chemical weapons, in retaliation for alleged Sudanese collusion in terrorist attacks on US embassies in Africa.

HEAD OF STATE

President, Prime Minister, Lt.-Gen. Omar Hassan Ahmad al-Bashir, *appointed* 16 October 1993, *elected* 17 March 1996

First Vice-President, Maj.-Gen. Ali Osman Mohamad Taha

Vice-President, Gen. George Kongor

CABINET *as at July 1998*

Agriculture and Forestry, Nafi Ali Nafi
Aviation, Hamid Mohammed Ali Tourain
Cabinet Affairs, Muhammad al-Amin Khalifah
Defence, Ibrahim Suleiman Hassan
Energy and Mining, Awad Ahmad al-Jaz
Environment and Tourism, Muhammad Tahir Ila
External Relations, Mustapha Osman Ismail
External Trade, Uthman al-Hadi Ibrahim
Federal Relations, Ahmed Ibrahim al-Tahir
Finance, National Economy, Abd al-Wahhab Uthman
Health, Gen. (retd) Mahdi Babu Nimir
Higher Education and Scientific Research, Ibrahim Ahmed Omer
Information and Culture, Ghazi Salah al-Din
Internal Affairs, Brig.-Gen. Abd al-Rahim Muhammad Husayn

International Co-operation and Investment, Abdalla Hassan Ahmed
Irrigation and Water Resources, Sharif al-Tuhami
Justice, Ali Mohammad Uthman Yassin
Khartoum State Governor, Majzoub al-Khalifa
Livestock, Joseph Malwal
National Industry, Badr al-Din Sulayman
Presidential Adviser on Legal Affairs, Abd al-Basit Salih Sabdarat
Presidential Affairs, Brig. Bakri Hasan Salih
Public Service, Agnes Lukudo
Relations in the National Assembly, Abul al-Qasim Muhammad Ibrahim
Roads, Communications, Maj.-Gen. (retd) Hadi Bushra
Social Planning, Brig. Tayyib Ibrahim Muhammad Khayr
State Minister for National Defence, Ibrahim Shamseddin
Transport, Lam Akol

EMBASSY OF THE REPUBLIC OF THE SUDAN
3 Cleveland Row, London SW1A 1DD
Tel 0171-839 8080
Ambassador Extraordinary and Plenipotentiary, HE Omer Yousif Bireedo, apptd 1995

BRITISH EMBASSY
PO Box 801, Khartoum
Tel: Khartoum 777105
Ambassador Extraordinary and Plenipotentiary, HE Alan Goulty, apptd 1995

BRITISH COUNCIL DIRECTOR, D. Sloan, 14 Abu Sin Street (PO Box 1253), Khartoum.

ECONOMY

Agriculture provides employment for over half the labour force and contributes about one-third of GDP. It is based on large and medium-sized public sector irrigation projects. Mechanized and traditional agriculture is practised in areas of sufficient rainfall. The principal grain crops are *dura* (great millet) and wheat, the staple food of the population. Sesame and groundnuts are other important food crops, which also yield an exportable surplus, and a promising start has been made with castor seed. The principal export crops are cotton and sugar, and Sudan also produces the bulk of the world's supply of gum arabic. Sudan still has to achieve self-sufficiency in its production.

Livestock is the mainstay of the nomadic Arab tribes of the desert and the Negro tribes of the swamp and wooded grassland country in the south. Production has been affected by drought, famine and civil war.

The manufacturing sector contributes 9 per cent of GDP. The main manufacturing enterprises are food processing, textiles, shoes, cigarettes and batteries.

In 1995 Sudan had a trade deficit of US$510 million and a current account deficit of US$500 million. Imports totalled US$1,185 million and exports US$556 million.
GDP – US$26,328 million (1994); US$62 per capita (1994)
INFLATION RATE – 101.4 per cent (1993)
TOTAL EXTERNAL DEBT – US$16,972 million (1996)

TRADE

The principal exports are cotton, livestock, gum arabic, sugar and other agricultural produce. The chief imports are petroleum goods and other raw materials, machinery and equipment, medicines and chemicals.

Trade with UK	1996	1997
Imports from UK	£57,818,000	£50,722,000
Exports to UK	8,814,000	7,961,000

COMMUNICATIONS

The railway system, adversely affected by the civil war, has a route length of about 3,200 miles. Nile river services between Khartoum and Juba have been interrupted by the southern insurrection. Port Sudan is the country's main seaport. Sudan Airways flies services from Khartoum to other parts of Sudan and to other African states, Europe and the Middle East.

EDUCATION

School education is free for most children but not compulsory, beginning with six years of primary education, followed by three years of secondary education at general secondary schools, the more academic higher secondary schools or vocational schools. The medium of instruction is Arabic. English has not been taught in schools since new Arabization legislation came into effect in 1991.

Khartoum University has ten faculties. There is a branch of Cairo University in Khartoum, an Islamic University at Omdurman and universities at Wad Medani and Juba. In addition to the universities there are various technical post-secondary institutes as well as professional and vocational training establishments.
ILLITERACY RATE – 53.9 per cent
ENROLMENT (percentage of age group) – tertiary 3.0 per cent (1990)

SURINAME
Republiek Suriname

AREA – 63,037 sq. miles (163,265 sq. km). Neighbours: French Guiana (east), Brazil (south), Guyana (west)
POPULATION – 423,000 (1994 UN estimate). The official language is Dutch, the native language is Sranang Tongo, and other widely-used languages are Hindustani and Javanese
CAPITAL – ΨParamaribo (population, 200,970, 1993)
CURRENCY – Suriname guilder of 100 cents
NATIONAL DAY – 25 November
NATIONAL FLAG – Horizontal stripes of green, white, red, white, green, with a five-pointed yellow star in the centre
LIFE EXPECTANCY (years) – male 67.80; female 72.78
POPULATION GROWTH RATE – 0.9 per cent (1995)
POPULATION DENSITY – 3 per sq. km (1995)
MILITARY EXPENDITURE – 3.5 per cent of GDP (1996)
MILITARY PERSONNEL – 1,800: Army 1,400, Navy 240, Air Force 160
ILLITERACY RATE – 7.0 per cent

HISTORY AND POLITICS

Formerly known as Dutch Guiana, Suriname remained part of the Netherlands West Indies until 25 November 1975, when it achieved complete independence. The civilian government was ousted in 1980 by the military who appointed a predominantly civilian government in 1982.

President Shankar was overthrown in a military coup, instigated by Lt.-Col. Desi Bouterse, in December 1990; Johan Kraag, a supporter of Bouterse, was installed as president. Elections to the National Assembly were held in May 1991. The New Front for Democracy and Development, a coalition comprising opposition groups, won 30 of the 51 seats, but failed to gain the necessary two-thirds majority to appoint the president. In September 1991 a special sitting of a United People's Assembly elected New Front leader Ronald Venetiaan as president and he formed a government which amended the constitution to limit the power of the military.

The New Front won the most seats in the elections to the National Assembly on 23 May 1996 but failed to win a majority sufficient to appoint the president, and a coalition government headed by the National Democratic Party was formed.

POLITICAL SYSTEM

The unicameral legislature, the National Assembly, has 51 members, directly elected for a five-year term. The president is elected by a two-thirds majority in the National Assembly, for a five-year term of office.

HEAD OF STATE

President, Jules Wijdenbosch, *inaugurated* 14 September 1996

Vice-President, Pretaapnarain Radhakishun

CABINET *as at July 1998*

Agriculture, Animal Husbandry and Fisheries, Saimin Redjosentono (KTPI)
Defence, Ramon Dwarka Panday (KTPI)
Education, Kries Mahadewsing (BVD)
Finance, Tjan Gobardhan (BVD)
Foreign Affairs, Errol Snijders (NDP)
Internal Affairs, Sonny Kertowidjojo (KTPI)
Justice and Police, Paul Sjak-Shie (NDP)
Labour, Faried Pierkhan (BVD)
Natural Resources, Errol Alibux (NDP)
Planning and International Co-operation, Waldi Nain (Pendawalima)
Public Health, Theo Vishnudath (HPP)
Public Works, Rudolf Mangal (BVD)
Regional Development, Yvonne Raveles-Resida (NDP)
Social Affairs and Housing, Soewarto Moestadja (KTPI)
Trade and Industry, Robby Dragman (KTPI)
Transportation, Communications and Tourism, Dick de Bie (NDP)

KTPI Party for Unity and Harmony; BVD Movement for Renewal and Change; NDP National Democratic Party; HPP Hindustani Progressive Party

EMBASSY OF THE REPUBLIC OF SURINAME
2 Alexander Gogelweg, The Hague, The Netherlands
Tel: The Hague 365 0844
Ambassador Extraordinary and Plenipotentiary, HE Evert Guillaume Azimullah, apptd 1994

BRITISH AMBASSADOR, HE David Johnson, CMG, CVO, resident at Georgetown, Guyana
BRITISH CONSULATE, c/o VSH United Buildings, Van't Hogerhuystraat, PO Box 1300, Paramaribo. *Honorary Consul,* J. J. Healy, MBE

ECONOMY

Suriname has large timber resources. Rice and sugar cane are the main crops. Bauxite is mined, and is the principal export. Principal trading partners are the Netherlands, the USA and Norway.

In 1994 Suriname had a trade surplus of US$99 million and a current account surplus of US$59 million.

GNP – US$433 million (1996); US$1,000 per capita (1996)
GDP – US$1,811 million (1994); US$858 per capita (1994)
ANNUAL AVERAGE GROWTH OF GDP – −4.5 per cent (1993)
INFLATION RATE – −0.7 per cent (1996)
UNEMPLOYMENT – 12.7 per cent (1994)

TRADE WITH UK	1996	1997
Imports from UK	£12,168,000	£12,514,000
Exports to UK	14,764,000	17,015,000

SWAZILAND
Umbuso we Swatini

AREA – 6,704 sq. miles (17,364 sq. km). Neighbours: South Africa (north, west and south), Mozambique (east)
POPULATION – 908,000 (1994 UN estimate). The languages are English and Swazi
CAPITAL – Mbabane (population, 38,290, 1986)
MAJOR TOWNS – Manzini (30,000); Big Bend; Mhlume; Nhlangano; Pigg's Peak
CURRENCY – Lilangeni (E) of 100 cents (South African currency is also in circulation). Swaziland is a member of the Common Monetary Area and its unit of currency *Emalangeni* (singular *Lilangeni*) has a par value with the South African rand
NATIONAL ANTHEM – Ingoma Yesive
NATIONAL DAY – 6 September (Independence Day)
NATIONAL FLAG – Blue with a wide crimson horizontal band bordered in yellow across the centre, bearing a shield and two spears horizontally
LIFE EXPECTANCY (years) – male 42.90; female 49.50
POPULATION GROWTH RATE – 3.3 per cent (1995)
POPULATION DENSITY – 52 per sq. km (1995)
URBAN POPULATION – 24.8 per cent (1995)
ILLITERACY RATE – 23.3 per cent
ENROLMENT (percentage of age group) – primary 95 per cent (1994); secondary 37 per cent (1994); tertiary 5.1 per cent (1993)

The broken mountainous Highveld along the western border, with an average altitude of 4,000 ft, is densely forested, mainly with conifers and eucalyptus; the Middleveld, averaging about 2,000 ft, is a mixed farming area including cotton and pineapples; and the Lowveld in the east was mainly scrubland until the introduction of large sugar-cane plantations. Four rivers, the Komati, Usutu, Mbuluzi and Ngwavuma, flow from west to east.

HISTORY AND POLITICS

The Kingdom of Swaziland came into being on 25 April 1967 under a self-government constitution and became an independent kingdom, headed by HM Sobhuza II, in membership of the Commonwealth on 6 September 1968.

POLITICAL SYSTEM

The King, assisted by his appointed Cabinet, holds considerable executive, legislative and judicial authority. There is a bicameral legislative body comprising a Senate and a House of Assembly. Each of the 55 traditional *Tinkhundla* (chieftaincies) are directly elected and become members of the House of Assembly. The King appoints ten members to the House of Assembly, making 65 in all, who then elect ten members of their own number to the Senate. To these are added 20 senators appointed by the King, bringing the full membership of the Senate to 30. All political parties are banned.

Pro-democracy protests in 1996 drew concessions from King Mswati III, who promised to review the ban on political parties and to establish a People's Parliament and a National Council, although their functions were not defined. Legislative elections are due in October 1998.

HEAD OF STATE
King of Swaziland, HM King Mswati III, *inaugurated* 25 April
1986

CABINET *as at July 1998*
Prime Minister, Dr Barnabas Sibusiso Dlamini
Deputy PM, Arthur Khoza
Agriculture, Co-operatives, Chief Dambuza Lukhele
Economic Planning and Development, Absalom Dlamini
Education, Solomon Dlamini
Enterprise and Employment, Majahenkaba Dlamini
Finance, Themba Masuku
Foreign Affairs and Trade, Albert Shabangu
Health and Social Welfare, Phetsile Dlamini
Home Affairs, Prince Guduza
Housing and Urban Development, John Carmichael
Justice and Constitutional Development, Chief Maweni
  Simelane
Natural Resources and Energy, Prince Sobandla
Public Service and Information, Muntu Mswane
Public Works and Transport, Dumsane Masango
Tourism and Communications, Musa Nkambule

KINGDOM OF SWAZILAND HIGH COMMISSION
20 Buckingham Gate, London SWIE 6LB
Tel 0171-630 6611
High Commissioner, HE Revd Percy Mngomezulu, apptd
1994

BRITISH HIGH COMMISSION
Allister Miller Street, Mbabane
Tel: Mbabane 42581/4
High Commissioner, HE John F. Doble, OBE, apptd 1996

BRITISH COUNCIL DIRECTOR, B. Gallagher

ECONOMY

Manufacturing was announced to have replaced agriculture as the dominant sector in 1988, with timber, textiles
and footwear the main products. Agricultural products
include sugar cane and fruit.

In 1995 Swaziland had a trade deficit of US$100 million
and a current account deficit of US$51 million. In 1996
imports totalled US$1,079 million and exports US$893
million.
GNP – US$1,122 million (1996); US$1,210 per capita
  (1996)
GDP – US$949 million (1994); US$1,311 per capita (1994)
ANNUAL AVERAGE GROWTH OF GDP – 2.5 per cent (1995)
INFLATION RATE – 12.5 per cent (1996)
TOTAL EXTERNAL DEBT – US$220 million (1996)

TRADE WITH UK	1996	1997
Imports from UK	£2,104,000	£3,679,000
Exports to UK	40,322,000	43,069,000

COMMUNICATIONS

Swaziland's railway is about 150 miles long and connects
with the Mozambique port of Maputo and the South
African railway network to Richards Bay. A rail line to the
north-west border provides a link to Komatipoort. Most
passenger and goods traffic is carried by privately-owned
motor transport services. There is an international airport
at Manzini. Royal Swazi National Airways provides
scheduled air services to southern and eastern Africa.
International telecommunications and television services
are provided through a satellite earth station, and there is
also a national telephone network.

SWEDEN
Konungariket Sverige

AREA – 173,732 sq. miles (449,964 sq. km). Neighbours:
  Norway (west), Finland (east)
POPULATION – 8,831,000 (1994 UN estimate); 8,745,109
  (1993 census). The state religion is Lutheran Protestant,
  to which over 95 per cent officially adhere. The language
  is Swedish; in the north there are both Finnish- and
  Lapp-speaking communities
CAPITAL – ΨStockholm (population, 1,532,803, 1993)
MAJOR CITIES – ΨGothenburg (Göteborg) (444,553);
  ΨMalmö (242,706); Uppsala (181,191)
CURRENCY – Swedish krona of 100 öre
NATIONAL ANTHEM – Du Gamla, Du Fria (Thou ancient,
  thou freeborn)
NATIONAL DAY – 6 June (Day of the Swedish Flag)
NATIONAL FLAG – Yellow cross on a blue ground
LIFE EXPECTANCY (years) – male 76.08; female 81.38
POPULATION GROWTH RATE – 0.6 per cent (1995)
POPULATION DENSITY – 20 per sq. km (1995)
URBAN POPULATION – 83.4 per cent (1990)

HISTORY AND POLITICS

Sweden takes its name from the Svear people who
inhabited the region during the seventh century AD. The
Swedes participated in the Viking expansion during the
ninth to 11th centuries but thereafter focused on the east;
sovereignty over Finland was established in the 13th
century. The Union of Kalmar (1397) brought Sweden and
Norway under the rule of Queen Margrethe of Denmark.
Northern Sweden regained its independence following a
rebellion by noblemen in 1521 which resulted in the
election to the Swedish throne of Gustav I of the house of
Vasa.

Swedish influence burgeoned under the Vasa kings
despite frequent wars with Denmark. Control over Estonia
was achieved in 1561 and marriage brought Poland briefly
into the Swedish sphere of influence. Sweden's power
climaxed in the 17th century under Gustavus II Adolf. The
Danes were driven out of southern Sweden, the Baltic
coast of Russia was seized and the Swedish army pushed
into Germany after vanquishing the Catholic League. The
Treaty of Westphalia (1648) confirmed Sweden's great
power status. Swedish power waned in the 17th and 18th
centuries. Finland was lost to Russia in 1809; Norway was
ceded to Sweden under the Congress of Vienna (1814–5)
but seceded in 1905.

Sweden remained neutral during both World Wars.
Post-war party politics was dominated by Social Democrat-led coalitions which established a mixed economy and
a generous welfare state. Right-wing and centrist parties
held power from 1976–82 and 1991–4.

In the general election held on 18 September 1994 the
four-party centre-right coalition of the Moderate, Liberal,
Centre and Christian Democratic Parties was defeated by
the Social Democrats, who formed a minority government.
Elections are scheduled for September 1998.

FOREIGN RELATIONS
Sweden applied for EU membership in July 1991 and
negotiations on entry were successfully concluded on 1
March 1994. The Accession Treaty was ratified in a
national referendum on 13 November 1994 by 52.3 per
cent to 46.8 per cent and by a parliamentary vote on 15
December, enabling Sweden to accede to the EU on 1
January 1995.

POLITICAL SYSTEM

Sweden is a constitutional monarchy, with the monarch retaining purely ceremonial functions as head of state. Under the Act of Succession 1810 (with amendments) the throne is hereditary in the House of Bernadotte. The constitution is based upon the Instrument of Government 1974, which amended the 1810 Act and removed from the monarch the roles of appointing the prime minister and signing parliamentary bills into law. A 1979 amendment vested the succession in the monarch's eldest child irrespective of sex.

Executive power is vested in the prime minister and Council of Ministers. There is a unicameral legislature (*Riksdag*) of 349 members elected by universal suffrage on a proportional representation basis (with a 4 per cent threshold for representation) for four years. The Council of Ministers (*Statsråd*) is responsible to the *Riksdag*.

Sweden is divided into 24 counties (*län*) and 288 municipalities (*kommun*).

HEAD OF STATE

HM The King of Sweden, Carl XVI Gustaf, KG, *born* 30 April 1946, *succeeded* 15 September 1973, *married* 19 June 1976 Fräulein Silvia Renate Sommerlath and has *issue*, Crown Princess Victoria (*see* below); Prince Carl Philip Edmund Bertil, Duke of Värmland, *born* 13 May 1979; Princess Madeleine Thérèse Amelie Josephine, Duchess of Hälsingland and Gästrikland, *born* 10 June 1982

Heir, HRH Crown Princess Victoria Ingrid Alice Désirée, Duchess of Västergötland, *born* 14 July 1977

CABINET *as at July 1998*

Prime Minister, Göran Persson
PM's Office, Thage Peterson
Agriculture, Food and Fisheries, Annika Åhnberg
Culture, Marita Ulvskog
Defence, Björn von Sydow
Education and Science, Carl Tham
Environment, Anna Lindh
Equality Affairs, Ulrica Messing
Finance, Erik Åsbrink
Foreign Affairs, Lena Hjelm-Wallén
Health and Social Affairs, Margot Wallström
Immigration and Integration, Lars Engqvist
Industry and Trade, Anders Sundström
Interior, Jörgen Andersson
International Development Co-operation, Deputy Minister for Foreign Affairs, Pierre Schori
Justice, Laila Freivalds
Labour, Margareta Winberg
Schools and Adult Education, Ylva Johansson
Social Security, Maj-Inger Klingvall
Taxation, Thomas Östros
Trade, Leif Pagrotsky
Transport and Communications, Ines Uusmann

EMBASSY OF SWEDEN

11 Montagu Place, London WIH 2AL
Tel 0171-917 6400
Ambassador Extraordinary and Plenipotentiary, HE Mats Bergquist, apptd 1997
Minister (Economic), Mårten Grunditz
Naval and Air Attaché, Col. N. Eklund
Consul-General, G. Dannerljung

BRITISH EMBASSY

Skarpögatan 6–8, S115 93 Stockholm
Tel: Stockholm 671 9000
Ambassador Extraordinary and Plenipotentiary, HE Robert Bone, CMG, apptd 1995
Counsellor, Consul-General and Deputy Head of Mission, M. Raven

Counsellor (Economic and Commercial), G. M. Johnson, OBE
Naval and Military Attaché, Cmdr. G. Bateman
CONSULAR OFFICES – Stockholm, Gothenburg
HONORARY CONSULATES – Gothenburg, Malmö, Sundsvall

BRITISH COUNCIL REPRESENTATIVE, Dr P. Spaven, PO Box 27819, S-115 93 Stockholm
BRITISH-SWEDISH CHAMBER OF COMMERCE, Grevgatan 34, 11453 Stockholm

DEFENCE

The Army has 539 main battle tanks, 1,131 armoured personnel carriers and armoured infantry fighting vehicles, 956 artillery pieces and 107 helicopters. The Navy has ten submarines, 31 patrol and coastal vessels and one combat aircraft at four bases. The Air Force has 387 combat aircraft.

Sweden has a policy of non-alignment in peace and neutrality in war, and it maintains a 'total defence' which includes peacetime organizations for civil, economic and psychological defence.

MILITARY EXPENDITURE – 2.5 per cent of GDP (1996)
MILITARY PERSONNEL – 53,950: Army 35,100, Navy 9,500, Air Force 8,750, Paramilitaries 600
CONSCRIPTION DURATION – Seven to 15 months

ECONOMY

Less than 10 per cent of the land area is farmland and less than 3 per cent of the labour force is employed in farming, although Sweden is more than 80 per cent self-sufficient in food.

Industrial prosperity is based on natural resources: forests, mineral deposits and water power. The forests cover about half the total land surface and sustain timber, finished wood products, pulp and paper milling industries. The mineral resources include iron ore, lead, zinc, sulphur, granite, marble, precious and heavy metals (the latter not exploited) and extensive deposits of low-grade uranium ore. Industries based on mining are important but it is the general engineering industry that provides 80 per cent of Sweden's exports, especially specialized machinery and systems, motor vehicles, aircraft, electrical and electronic equipment, pharmaceuticals, plastics and chemical industries.

Hydroelectricity supplies 15 per cent of energy needs. Sweden has no significant indigenous resources of conventional hydrocarbon fuels and relies for 50 per cent of its energy needs upon imported oil and coal. Around half of Sweden's electricity is generated by nuclear power but as a result of a referendum in 1980 the nuclear programme is to be phased out by 2010. Small supplies of natural gas are imported from Denmark into southern Sweden, with the pipeline being extended to Gothenburg.

Sweden experienced a deep recession between 1990 and 1993. The centre-right government, elected in 1991, introduced austerity measures and free market economic policies of privatization, deregulation, the ending of state subsidies, trade union legislation, a floating exchange rate, central bank independence and tax reform. Further budget cuts and reductions in the public sector, local government, and the welfare state, together with tax increases, have been implemented by the Social Democratic government. In October 1997 Sweden decided not to join European economic and monetary union (EMU) at the first stage.

In 1996 there was a trade surplus of US$18,211 million and a current account surplus of US$5,723 million. Imports totalled US$66,613 million and exports US$84,509 million.

GNP – US$227,315 million (1996); US$25,710 per capita (1996)

GDP – US$222,951 million (1994); US$22,499 per capita (1994)
ANNUAL AVERAGE GROWTH OF GDP – 3.0 per cent (1995); expected to be 2 per cent in 1997
INFLATION RATE – 0.5 per cent (1996)
UNEMPLOYMENT – 7.7 per cent (1995)

TRADE
About 45 per cent of industrial output is exported, mainly in the form of cars, trucks, machinery, and electrical and communications equipment. Sweden conducts 70 per cent of its trade with EFTA and the rest of the EU.

Trade with UK	1996	1997
Imports from UK	£4,212,100,000	£4,201,800,000
Exports to UK	4,509,200,000	4,569,700,000

COMMUNICATIONS
The total length of railroads is 11,745 km. The road network is over 400,000 km in length. The mercantile marine amounted in 1996 to 2,950,000 gross tonnage. Regular domestic air traffic is maintained by the Scandinavian Airlines System and by Linjeflyg. Regular European and intercontinental air traffic is maintained by the Scandinavian Airlines System.

EDUCATION
The state system provides nine years' free and compulsory schooling from the age of seven to 16 in the comprehensive elementary schools. 95 per cent continue into further education of two to four years' duration in the upper secondary schools and a unified higher education system administered in six regional areas containing one of the universities: Uppsala (founded 1477); Lund (1668); Stockholm (1878); Gothenburg (1887); Umeå (1963) and Linköping (1967). There are 40 institutions of higher education including three technical universities in Stockholm, Gothenburg and Luleå.
ENROLMENT (percentage of age group) – primary 100 per cent (1994); secondary 96 per cent (1994); tertiary 42.5 per cent (1994)

CULTURE
Swedish belongs, with Danish and Norwegian, to the North Germanic language group. Swedish literature dates back to King Magnus Eriksson, who codified the old Swedish provincial laws in 1350. With his translation of the Bible, Olaus Petri (1493–1552) formed the basis for the modern Swedish language. Literature flourished during the reign of Gustavus III, who founded the Swedish Academy in 1786. Notable Swedish writers include Almquist (1795–1866), Strindberg (1849–1912) and Lagerlöf (1858–1940), Nobel Prizewinner in 1909. Contemporary authors include Lagerquist (1891–1974), Nobel Laureate in 1951, Martinson (1904–78) and Johnson (1900–76), Nobel Laureates jointly in 1974. Swedish scientist Alfred Nobel (1833–96) founded the Nobel Prizes for literature, science and peace.

SWITZERLAND
Schweizerische Eidgenossenschaft – Confédération Suisse – Confederazione Svizzera

---

AREA – 15,940 sq. miles (41,284 sq. km). Neighbours: France (west and north-west), Germany (north), Austria and Liechtenstein (east), Italy (south)
POPULATION – 7,040,000 (1994 UN estimate): 46.1 per cent Roman Catholic, 40 per cent Protestant, 5 per cent

other religions and 8.9 per cent without religion. The official languages are German (the first language of 63.7 per cent), French (19.2 per cent), Italian (7.6 per cent) and Romansch (0.6 per cent). German is the dominant language in 19 of the 26 cantons; French in Fribourg, Jura, Geneva, Neuchâtel, Valais and Vaud; Italian in Ticino; and Romansch in parts of the Grisons
CAPITAL – Berne (population, 321,932, 1994)
MAJOR CITIES – Geneva (438,819); Lausanne (283,631); Lucerne (180,050); Winterthur (115,994); Zürich (921,446), 1994
CURRENCY – Swiss franc of 100 rappen (or centimes)
NATIONAL ANTHEM – Trittst im Morgenrot Daher (Radiant in the morning sky)
NATIONAL DAY – 1 August
NATIONAL FLAG – Square and red, bearing a couped white cross
LIFE EXPECTANCY (years) – male 75.10; female 81.60
POPULATION GROWTH RATE – 1.0 per cent (1995)
POPULATION DENSITY – 171 per sq. km (1995)
URBAN POPULATION – 67.8 per cent (1994)

Switzerland is the most mountainous country in Europe. The Alps, from 5,000 to 15,217 ft in height, occupy its southern and eastern frontiers and the chief part of its interior; the Jura mountains rise in the north-west. The Alps occupy 61 per cent, and the Jura mountains 12 per cent of the country. The highest peak, Mont Blanc, Pennine Alps (15,782 ft) is partly in France and partly in Italy; Monte Rosa (15,217 ft) and Matterhorn (14,780 ft) are partly in Switzerland and partly in Italy. The highest wholly Swiss peaks are Dufourspitze (15,203 ft), Finsteraarhorn (14,026), Aletschhorn (13,711), Jungfrau (13,671), Mönch (13,456), Eiger (13,040), Schreckhorn (13,385), and Wetterhorn (12,150) in the Bernese Alps, and Dom (14,918), Weisshorn (14,803) and Breithorn (13,685). The Swiss lakes include Lakes Maggiore, Zürich, Lucerne, Neuchâtel, Geneva, Constance, Thun, Zug, Lugano, Brienz and the Walensee.

HISTORY AND POLITICS
The Romans invaded the area populated by Helvetii tribes in the first century BC and named the region Helvetia. The Roman Empire was overrun in the fifth century AD by Germanic tribes who are the ancestors of the modern Swiss.
The Swiss confederation achieved full independence under the Peace of Westphalia (1648), having been a province of the Holy Roman Empire since 1033. French Revolutionary forces seized Switzerland in 1789 and named it the Helvetic Republic. Independence was not restored until the Congress of Vienna (1815), which also joined Geneva and Valais to the confederation and instituted perpetual neutrality in foreign affairs. In 1847 a war broke out between the Protestant and Roman Catholic cantons, the latter being defeated. A new constitution was adopted in 1848 which enhanced the powers of the central government.
Proportional representation was introduced in 1919 and has ensured coalition governments throughout the 20th century. Women were given the vote in 1971.
On 22 October 1995, the ruling coalition, comprising the Social Democrats, the Swiss People's Party, the Radical Democratic Party and the Christian Democrats, in power since 1959, was re-elected with 162 of the 200 seats in the National Council.

FOREIGN RELATIONS
The Federal Council voted in 1992 to apply for European Community membership. The European Economic Area (EEA) Treaty between the EC and EFTA, which extends

the provisions of the EC single internal market to EFTA states, was rejected in a national referendum on 6 December 1992. Switzerland is consequently the only EFTA state outside the EEA. Switzerland has observer status at the UN.

POLITICAL SYSTEM

The federal government consists of the Federal Assembly of two chambers, a National Council (*Nationalrat*) of 200 members, and a States Council (*Ständerat*) of 46 members (two from each canton and one from each demi-canton). Members of the National Council are elected for four years, elections taking place in October. The executive power is in the hands of a Federal Council (*Bundesrat*) of seven members, elected for four years by the Federal Assembly and presided over by the president of the Confederation. Each year the Federal Assembly elects from the Federal Council the president and the vice-president. Not more than one of the same canton may be elected a member of the Federal Council; however, there is a tradition that Italian- and French-speaking areas should between them be represented on the Federal Council by at least two members.

CONFEDERAL STRUCTURE

There are 23 cantons, three of which are subdivided, making 26 in all. Each canton has its own government. The main language in 19 of the cantons is German; in the others it is French (*) or Italian (†).

Canton	Area (sq. km)	Population (1994)
Aargau (Argovie)	1,404	524,100
Appenzell-Inner Rhoden	173	14,700
Appenzell-Outer Rhoden	243	54,400
Basel-Country (Bâle-Campagne)	428	251,400
Basel-Town (Bâle-Ville)	37	197,700
Berne	6,050	943,600
*Fribourg (Freiburg)	1,671	222,100
*Geneva	282	391,100
Glarus (Glaris)	685	39,300
Graubünden (Grisons)	7,105	184,300
*Jura	836	69,000
Lucerne	1,493	337,700
*Neuchâtel (Neuenburg)	803	164,500
Nidwalden	276	36,000
Obwalden	490	31,100
St Gallen (St Gall)	2,026	440,700
Schaffhausen (Schaffhouse)	299	74,000
Schwyz	908	120,600
Solothurn (Soleure)	791	237,100
Thurgau (Thurgovie)	991	220,400
†Ticino (Tessin)	2,812	302,400
Uri	1,077	35,900
*Valais (Wallis)	5,225	269,600
*Vaud (Waadt)	3,212	601,600
Zurich	1,729	1,167,600
Zug	239	90,300

FEDERAL COUNCIL *as at July 1998*

President of the Swiss Confederation (1998), *Foreign Affairs*, Flavio Cotti (CVP)
Vice-President (1998), *Interior*, Ruth Dreifuss (SPS)
Federal Chancellor, François Couchepin
Finance, Kaspar Villiger (FDP)
Justice and Police, Arnold Koller (CVP)
Military, Adolf Ogi (SVP)
Public Economy, Pascal Couchepin (FDP)
Transport, Communications and Energy, Moritz Leuenberger (SPS)

CVP Christian Democratic People's Party; SPS Social Democratic Party; FDP Radical Democratic Party; SVP Swiss People's Party

EMBASSY OF SWITZERLAND
16–18 Montagu Place, London W1H 2BQ
Tel 0171-616 6000
Ambassador Extraordinary and Plenipotentiary, HE François Nordmann, apptd 1994
Minister, R. Reich
Defence Attaché, Col. W. Knüsli
Consul-General, R. Müller
Counsellor, D. Furgler (*Economic and Financial*)
CONSULATE-GENERAL – Manchester

BRITISH EMBASSY
Thunstrasse 50, 3005 Berne
Tel: Berne 359 7700
Ambassador Extraordinary and Plenipotentiary, HE Christopher Hulse, CMG, OBE, apptd 1997
Counsellor, Deputy Head of Mission and Director of Trade Promotion, J. Nichols
Commercial Attachés, B. Hässig, S. Valdettaro, H. Kuepfer
Defence Attaché, Lt.-Col. E. J. Gould

CONSULATE – Geneva
CONSULAR OFFICES – Berne (at Embassy), Lugano, Montreux, Valais, Zürich
DIRECTORATE OF BRITISH EXPORT PROMOTION – Consulate-General Office, Dufourstrasse 56, 8008 Zürich

BRITISH COUNCIL DIRECTOR, C. Morrissey, Sennweg 2, PO Box 532, 3000 Berne 9

BRITISH-SWISS CHAMBER OF COMMERCE, Freiestrasse 155, 8032 Zürich
SWISS-BRITISH SOCIETIES: Berne, *President*, Dr H. Beriger; Zürich, *President*, J.-P. Müller; Basle, *President*, Dr C. Grey

DEFENCE

The Army has 769 main battle tanks, 1,349 armoured personnel carriers and armoured infantry fighting vehicles, 796 artillery pieces and 60 helicopters. The Air Corps, which is part of the Army, has 161 combat aircraft.
MILITARY EXPENDITURE – 1.6 per cent of GDP (1996)
MILITARY PERSONNEL – 3,300 active (390,060 to be mobilized: Army 357,460, Air Force 32,600)
CONSCRIPTION DURATION – 15 weeks, then ten refresher courses

ECONOMY

Agriculture is followed chiefly in the valleys and the central plateau, where cereals, flax, hemp, wine and tobacco are produced, and fruits and vegetables are grown. Dairying and stock-raising are the principal industries, about 3,000,000 acres being under grass for hay and 2,000,000 acres pasturage. The forests cover about 28 per cent of the whole surface.

The chief manufacturing industries comprise engineering and electrical engineering, metalworking, chemicals and pharmaceuticals, textiles, watchmaking, woodworking, foodstuffs, publishing and footwear. Banking, insurance and tourism are major industries. 4 per cent of the workforce is employed in agriculture, 48 per cent in industry and 48 per cent in services.

In December 1997 the Swiss Bank Corporation and the Union Bank of Switzerland merged to become the United Bank of Switzerland, the largest fund manager in the world, controlling assets worth 1,300 billion Swiss francs. It was announced in August 1998 that Swiss banks will pay US$1.25 billion to survivors of the Holocaust in reparation for the banks' dealings with Nazi Germany during World War II.

GNP – US$313,729 million (1996); US$44,350 per capita (1996)

GDP – US$226,007 million (1994); US$36,096 per capita (1994)

ANNUAL AVERAGE GROWTH OF GDP – −0.7 per cent (1996)

INFLATION RATE – 0.8 per cent (1996)

UNEMPLOYMENT – 3.3 per cent (1995)

TRADE

The principal imports are machinery, electrical and electronic equipment, textiles, motor vehicles, non-ferrous metals, clothing, food and pharmaceutical products. The principal exports are machinery, chemical elements, non-ferrous metals, watches, electrical and electronic equipment and textiles.

In 1995 Switzerland had a trade surplus of US$3,237 million and a current account surplus of US$21,622 million. In 1996 imports totalled US$74,462 million and exports US$76,196 million.

Trade with UK	1996	1997
Imports from UK	£3,205,206,000	£3,008,297,000
Exports to UK	5,417,807,000	4,894,966,000

COMMUNICATIONS

There were in 1993, 5,029 km of railway tracks (Swiss Federal Railways, 2,990 km; privately owned railways 2,039 km). At the end of 1993 the total length of motorways was 1,530 km. The merchant marine consisted in 1995 of 174 vessels with a total gross tonnage of 4.36 million tonnes. Goods handled at Basel Rhine ports amounted to 13 million tonnes. Swiss airlines have a network covering 348,762 km (1990) and in 1990 carried 17,100,000 passengers. Swissair, the national airline, flies to and from the airports at Zürich, Geneva and Basel.

The Swiss electorate voted in a February 1994 referendum for a ban on foreign lorries using alpine roads, which will be phased in over ten years. From 2005 onwards foreign lorries will have to use two new north-south road-rail tunnels.

EDUCATION

Education is controlled by cantonal and communal authorities. Primary education is free and compulsory. School age varies, generally seven to 14, with secondary education from age 12 to 15. Special schools make a feature of commercial and technical instruction. Universities are Basel (founded 1460), Berne (1834), Fribourg (1889), Geneva (1873), Lausanne (1890), Zürich (1832), and Neuchâtel (1909), the technical universities of Lausanne and Zürich and the economics university of St Gall.

ENROLMENT (percentage of age group) – primary 100 per cent (1993); secondary 79 per cent (1990); tertiary 31.8 per cent (1994)

CULTURE

Modern authors who have achieved international fame include Karl Spitteler (1845–1924) and Hermann Hesse (1877–1962), awarded the Nobel Prize for Literature in 1919 and 1946 respectively.

In 1993 there were 96 daily newspapers published (76 German, 16 French, four Italian).

SYRIA
Al-Jamhouriya Al-Arabia as-Souriya

AREA – 71,498 sq. miles (185,180 sq. km). Neighbours: Lebanon (west), Israel and Jordan (south-west), Iraq (east), Turkey (north)

POPULATION – 14,315,000 (1994 UN estimate): mostly Muslim. Arabic is the principal language, but Kurdish, Turkish and Armenian are spoken among significant minorities and a few villages still speak Aramaic, the language spoken by Christ and the Apostles. English has taken over from French as the main foreign language

CAPITAL – Damascus (population, 1,549,000, 1994)

MAJOR CITIES – Aleppo (1,542,000); Hama (273,000); Homs (558,000); ΨLatakia, the principal port (303,000), 1994 estimates

CURRENCY – Syrian pound (S$) of 100 piastres

NATIONAL DAY – 17 April

NATIONAL FLAG – Red over white over black horizontal bands, with two green stars on central white band

LIFE EXPECTANCY (years) – male 64.42; female 68.05

POPULATION GROWTH RATE – 3.3 per cent (1995)

POPULATION DENSITY – 77 per sq. km (1995)

URBAN POPULATION – 51.7 per cent (1995)

The Orontes flows northwards from the Lebanon range across the northern boundary to Antakya (Antioch, Turkey). The Euphrates crosses the northern boundary near Jerablus and flows through north-eastern Syria to the boundary of Iraq.

The region is rich in historical remains. Damascus (Dimishq ash-Sham) is said to be the oldest continuously inhabited city in the world (although Aleppo disputes this claim), having existed as a city for over 4,000 years. The city contains the Omayed Mosque, the Tomb of Saladin, and the 'street which is called Straight' (Acts 9:11), while to the north-east is the Roman outpost of Dmeir and further east is Palmyra. On the Mediterranean coast at Amrit are ruins of the Phoenician town of Marath, and also ruins of Crusaders' fortresses at Markab, Sahyoun, and Krak des Chevaliers. At Tartous the cathedral of Our Lady of Syria, built by the Knights Templars in the 12th and 13th centuries, has been restored as a museum. One of the oldest alphabets in the world has been discovered at Ugarit (Ras Shamra), a Phoenician village near the port of Latakia. Hittite cities dating from 2000 to 1500 BC, have been explored on the west bank of the Euphrates at Jerablus and Kadesh.

HISTORY AND POLITICS

Once part of the Ottoman Empire, Syria came under French mandate after the First World War. Syria became an independent republic during the Second World War; the first independently elected parliament met in August 1943, but foreign troops were in occupation until April 1946. Syria remained an independent republic until 1958, when it became part, with Egypt, of the United Arab Republic. It seceded from the United Arab Republic in September 1961.

Elections to the 250-seat People's Council in August 1994 resulted in a large majority for the National Progressive Front which won 167 seats and is dominated by the Ba'ath Party, its allies being the Arab Socialist Union, Socialist Unionist Movement, Arab Socialist Party and Syrian Communist Party. Independents won 83 seats.

POLITICAL SYSTEM

The constitution promulgated in 1973 declares that Syria is a democratic, popular socialist state, and that the Arab Socialist Renaissance (Ba'ath) Party, which has been the ruling party since 1963, is the leading party in the state and society. The president is head of state and is directly elected for a four-year term. The legislature, the *Majlis al-Chaab* (People's Council) has 250 members directly elected for a four-year term.

HEAD OF STATE

President, Lt.-Gen. Hafez Al-Assad, *assumed office* 14 March 1971, *re-elected* 1978, 1985, 3 December 1991
Vice-Presidents, Abdel Halim Khaddam, Zuhair Masharqa

CABINET *as at July 1998*

Prime Minister, Mahmoud Zubi
Deputy PM, Defence, 1st Lt.-Gen. Mustafa Tlass
Deputy PM, Economic Affairs, Salim Yassin
Deputy PM, Service Affairs, Rashid Akhtarini
Agriculture and Agrarian Reform, Asad Mustafa
Assistant Secretary-General, Abdullah al-Ahmar
Awqaf (Religious Endowments), Mohammed Abd al-Rauf Ziyadah
Communications, Radwan Martini
Construction and Building, Majid Izzu Ruhaybani
Culture, Najah al-Attar
Economy and Foreign Trade, Mohammad al-Imadi
Education, Ghassan Halabi
Electricity, Mounib Saaem Aldaher
Finance, Khaled al-Mahayni
Foreign Affairs, Farouk al-Shara
Health, Iyad al-Shatti
Higher Education, Salihah Sanqar
Housing and Utilities, Husam al-Safadi
Industry, Ahmad Nizam al-Din
Information, Mohammad Salman
Interior, Mohammad Harbah
Irrigation, Abd ar-Rahman Madani
Justice, Husayn Hassun
Local Administration, Yahya Abu Asaleh
Ministers of State, Musallam Mohammed Hawwa *(Cabinet Affairs)*; Abd al-Hamid Munajjid *(Environment Affairs)*; Nasser Qaddur *(Foreign Affairs)*; Abd al-Rahim Subayi *(Planning Affairs)*; Nabil Mallah; Hanna Murad; Yusuf al-Ahmad; Abdullah Tulbah
Oil and Mineral Resources, Mohamed Maher Jamal
Presidential Affairs, Wahib Fadel
Social Affairs and Labour, Ali Khalil
Supply and Internal Trade, Nadim Akkash
Tourism, Danhu Dawud
Transport, Mufid Abd al-Karim

EMBASSY OF THE SYRIAN ARAB REPUBLIC
8 Belgrave Square, London SW1X 8PH
Tel 0171-245 9012
Chargé d'Affaires, Abdul Hassib Istwani

BRITISH EMBASSY
Kotob Building, 11 rue Mohammad Kurd Ali, Malki, Damascus (PO Box 37)
Tel: Damascus 371 2561
Ambassador Extraordinary and Plenipotentiary, HE Basil Eastwood, CMG, apptd 1996
CONSULATE – Aleppo

BRITISH COUNCIL DIRECTOR, D. Baldwin, Al Jala'a, Abu Rumaneh, PO Box 33105, Damascus

DEFENCE

The Army has 4,600 main battle tanks, 3,810 armoured personnel carriers and armoured infantry fighting vehicles, and 2,080 artillery pieces. The Navy has three submarines, four frigates, 27 patrol and coastal vessels and 24 armed helicopters at three bases. The Air Force has 579 combat aircraft and 100 armed helicopters.

Syria maintains a force of some 30,000 men in Lebanon; 1,053 UN troops are deployed on the Golan Heights.
MILITARY EXPENDITURE – 5.8 per cent of GDP (1996)
MILITARY PERSONNEL – 328,000: Army 215,000, Navy 5,000, Air Force 40,000, Air Defence Command 60,000, Paramilitaries 8,000
CONSCRIPTION DURATION – 30 months

ECONOMY

Agriculture is the principal source of production; wheat and barley are the main cereal crops, but the cotton crop is the highest in value. Tobacco is grown in the maritime plain in Sahel, the Sahyoun and the Djebleh district of Latakia. Large areas are coming under cultivation in the north-east of the country as a result of irrigation from the Thawra dam. There are an increasing number of light assembly plants as Syria's industrialization programme develops. Leather goods, wool and silk, textiles, vegetable oil, soap, sugar, plastics and metal utensils are produced. Oil has been found in the north-eastern corner of the country and production of high quality reserves is proceeding in the region of Deir ez Zor. A pipeline has been built to the Mediterranean port of Banias, via Homs. Two oil refineries are in production at Homs and Banias. Syria also has gas reserves, deposits of phosphate and rock salt, and produces asphalt.
GNP – US$16,808 million (1996); US$1,160 per capita (1996)
GDP – US$30,408 million (1994); US$2,827 per capita (1994)
ANNUAL AVERAGE GROWTH OF GDP – 3.6 per cent (1995)
INFLATION RATE – 8.2 per cent (1996)
UNEMPLOYMENT – 6.8 per cent (1991)
TOTAL EXTERNAL DEBT – US$21,420 million (1996)

TRADE

The principal imports are foodstuffs (fruit, vegetables, cereals, tea, coffee), mineral and petroleum products, textiles, iron and steel manufactures, pharmaceuticals, machinery, chemicals and timber. Exports include raw cotton, oil, cereals, fruit, phosphates, cement, livestock, other foodstuffs, textiles and raw wool.

In 1995 Syria had a trade deficit of US$143 million and a current account surplus of US$440 million. In 1996 imports totalled US$5,244 million and exports US$3,999 million.

Trade with UK	1996	1997
Imports from UK	£100,085,000	£84,382,000
Exports to UK	88,924,000	39,079,000

COMMUNICATIONS

Although railway lines run from Damascus to both Beirut and Amman, train services go only to Amman as much of the Lebanese line has been dismantled. A track has been opened connecting Homs with Damascus. A track links Homs, Hamah, Aleppo, Deir ez Zor and Qamishliye to the Iraq frontier. All the principal towns in the country are connected by roads which vary from modern dual carriageways to narrow country lanes. An internal air service operates between all major towns. The main international airport is at Damascus and there are also flights from Aleppo.

There are three daily newspapers and several periodicals in Arabic published in Damascus, and also a daily newspaper in English.

EDUCATION

Education is under state control and although a few of the schools are privately owned, they all follow a common syllabus. Elementary education is free at state schools and is compulsory from the age of seven. Secondary education is not compulsory and is free only at the state schools. There are universitites at Damascus, Aleppo, Tishrin, Latakia and the Ba'ath University, Homs.

ILLITERACY RATE – 29.2 per cent

ENROLMENT (percentage of age group) – primary 91 per cent (1995); secondary 39 per cent (1995); tertiary 17.9 per cent (1993)

TAIWAN
Chung-hua Min-kuo – Republic of China

AREA – 13,800 sq. miles (35,742 sq. km)

POPULATION – 21,450,183 (1996). Mandarin Chinese has been the official language since 1949. Now Taiwanese, spoken by 85 per cent of the population, is growing in importance

CAPITAL – Taipei (population, 2,607,010, 1996)

MAJOR CITIES – ΨKaohsiung (1,432,289); ΨKeelung (373,863), Taichung (873,514); Tainan (710,658), 1996

CURRENCY – New Taiwan dollar (NT$) of 100 cents

NATIONAL DAY – 10 October

NATIONAL FLAG – Red, with blue quarter at top next staff, bearing a 12-point white sun

An island in the China Sea, Taiwan, formerly Formosa, lies 90 miles east of the Chinese mainland. The eastern part of the main island is mountainous and forested. Mt Morrison (Yu Shan) (13,035 ft) and Mt Sylvia (Tz'ukaoshan) (12,972 ft) are the highest peaks. The western plains are watered by many rivers.

Territories include the Pescadores Islands (50 sq. miles), some 35 miles west of Taiwan, as well as Quemoy (68 sq. miles) and Matsu (11 sq. miles) which are only a few miles from mainland China.

HISTORY AND POLITICS

Settled for centuries by the Chinese, the island was ceded by China to Japan in 1895 and remained part of the Japanese empire until Japan's defeat in 1945. Nationalist Kuomintang (KMT) leader Gen. Chiang Kai-shek withdrew to Taiwan in 1949, towards the end of the war against the Communist regime in mainland China, after which the territory continued under his presidency until his death in 1975. He was succeeded as president by his son Gen. Chiang Ching-kuo who ruled until his death in 1988, when Vice-President Lee Teng-hui was appointed president. Martial law was lifted in 1987 after 38 years.

In 1991, President Lee announced that the 'period of Communist rebellion' on the Chinese mainland was over, recognizing *de facto* the People's Republic of China. The announcement also ended emergency measures which had frozen political life on Taiwan since 1949. In 1991–2 power shifted away from mainlanders to native Taiwanese with the forcible retirement of the 'Senior Parliamentarians' who had retained their seats since being elected on the mainland in 1948. The new parliament, the Legislative

Yuan, gained control of the budget, of law-making and of the appointment of the prime minister. A general election to the Legislative Yuan in December 1995 was won by the KMT with 85 of the 164 seats; the pro-independence Democratic Progressive Party won 54 seats; the pro-reunification New Party won 21 seats; independents and minor parties won four seats.

The incumbent, President Lee, won the first democratic presidential election in March 1996, with 54 per cent of the vote. On 1 September 1997, following a reshuffle of the Executive Yuan, Vincent Siew was named as prime minister.

FOREIGN RELATIONS

Taiwan (Nationalist China) held China's seat on the UN Security Council until 25 October 1971 when it was replaced by the People's Republic of China. The Republic of China is recognized by less than 40 states.

POLITICAL SYSTEM

The legislature is bicameral. The National Assembly has 334 members (106 delegates and 228 regional representatives) elected for a four-year term. The Legislative Yuan has 163 members, and serves a three-year term. Constitutional reforms passed by the Legislative Yuan in 1994 provide for the president and vice-president to be directly elected for four-year terms (previously the president was elected by parliament).

HEAD OF STATE

President, Lee Teng-hui, *appointed* 13 January 1988, *elected by parliament* 21 March 1990, *elected* 23 March 1996

Vice-President, Lien Chan

EXECUTIVE YUAN *as at July 1998*

Prime Minister, Vincent Siew

Vice-PM, Liu Chao-shiuan

Chair, Central Election Commission, Lin Feng-cheng

Chair, Fair Trade Commission, Chao Yang-ching

Chair, Mongolian and Tibetan Affairs Commission, Kao Koong-lian

Chair, National Youth Commission, Lee Chi-chu

Chair, Overseas Chinese Affairs Commission, Chiao Jen-ho

Chair, Public Construction Commission, Ou Chin-der

Chair, Research, Development and Evaluation Commission, Yang Chao-shin

Chair, Vocational Assistance for Retired Servicemen Commission, Yang Ting-yun

Director, National Palace Museum, Chin Hsiao-yi

Director-General of Budget, Accounting and Statistics, Wei Duan

Director-General, Central Personnel Administration, Clement Wea

Director-General, Government Information Office; Government Spokesman, Chen Chien-jen

Director-General, Health, Chan Chi-sheah

Economic Affairs, Wang Chih-kang

Education, Lin Ching-chiang

Environmental Protection Administration, Tsai Hsung-hsiung

Finance, Paul Chiu

Foreign Affairs, Jason Hu

Interior, Huang Chu-wen

Justice, Liao Cheng-hao

National Defence, Gen. Chiang Chung-ling

Transport and Communications, Lin Feng-cheng

Without Portfolio, Chao Shou-po; Shirley Kuo Wan-jung; Huang Ta-chou; Yang Shih-chien; Chen Chien-min

Chairs of Councils:

Agriculture, Peng Tso-kuei

Atomic Energy, Hu Ching-piao

Cultural Planning and Development, Lin Cheng-chi
Economic Planning and Development, Chiang Ping-kung
Labour Affairs, Chan Huo-sheng
Mainland Affairs, Chang King-yuh
Science, Huang Chen-tai

TAIPEI REPRESENTATIVE OFFICE, 50 Grosvenor Gardens, London, SWIW OEB

BRITISH COUNCIL REPRESENTATIVE, Dr Patrick Hart, 7th Floor, British Trade and Cultural Office, 99 Jen Ai Road, Section 2, Taipei 10625

DEFENCE

The Army has 719 main battle tanks, 1,175 armoured personnel carriers and armoured infantry fighting vehicles, 1,375 artillery pieces, 20 aircraft and 205 helicopters. The Navy has four submarines, 18 destroyers, 18 frigates, 101 patrol and coastal vessels, 31 combat aircraft and 21 armed helicopters at four bases. The Air Force has 402 combat aircraft.
MILITARY EXPENDITURE – 4.7 per cent of GDP (1996)
MILITARY PERSONNEL – 402,650: Army 240,000, Navy 68,000, Air Force 68,000, Paramilitaries 26,650
CONSCRIPTION DURATION – Two years

ECONOMY

Over the past 30 years Taiwan has transformed itself from a mainly agricultural country to a highly developed industrial economy. The industrial base has expanded to include steel, shipbuilding, chemicals, cement, machinery, electrical equipment and textiles. In 1997 agriculture contributed 3.5 per cent of GDP, manufacturing 36.3 per cent and services 60.2 per cent. Continued trade surpluses have led to one of the largest foreign exchange reserves of any country in the world. Direct shipping between Taiwan and China, which had been suspended in 1949, resumed in April 1997.

The soil is very fertile, producing sugar, rice, sweet potatoes, tea, fruit and tobacco. Livestock provided a third of the value of Taiwan's agricultural producé in 1996. Mineral resources are meagre. Taiwan produces one-tenth of its coal needs and some natural gas. There are important fisheries. The principal seaports are ψKeelung and ψKaohsiung situated in the north and south of the island respectively.

TRADE

The principal exports are electronic goods, machinery, metal goods, textiles, plastic products, and toys and games. The main imports are oil, chemicals, machinery and natural resources. The main trading partners are the USA, Japan, Hong Kong and Germany.

In 1996 imports totalled US$101,287 million and exports US$115,726 million.

Trade with UK	1996	1997
Imports from UK	£941,241,000	£1,033,670,000
Exports to UK	2,088,483,000	2,341,812,000

TAJIKISTAN
Respublika i Tojikiston

AREA – 55,251 sq. miles (143,100 sq. km). Neighbours: Uzbekistan (north-west), Kyrgyzstan (north-east), China (east), Afghanistan (south)
POPULATION – 5,513,400 (1998): 62 per cent Tajik, 23 per cent Uzbek and 8 per cent Russian, with smaller numbers of Tatars, Kirghiz, Germans and Ukrainians. The people are predominantly Sunni Muslim. The main languages are Tajik (62 per cent), Uzbek (23 per cent), Russian (8 per cent). Tajik is close to the Farsi spoken in Iran
CAPITAL – Dushanbe (population, 602,000, 1990)
CURRENCY – Tajik rouble (TJR) of 100 tanga
NATIONAL DAY – 9 September (Independence Day)
NATIONAL FLAG – Three horizontal stripes of red, white and green with the white of double width and charged with a crown and seven stars, all in gold
LIFE EXPECTANCY (years) – male 65.40; female 71.10
POPULATION GROWTH RATE – 1.9 per cent (1995)
POPULATION DENSITY – 41 per sq. km (1995)
URBAN POPULATION – 29.1 per cent (1993)
MILITARY EXPENDITURE – 10.5 per cent of GDP (1996)
MILITARY PERSONNEL – 8,200: Army 7,000, Paramilitaries 1,200
CONSCRIPTION DURATION – Two years
ILLITERACY RATE – 0.3 per cent
ENROLMENT (percentage of age group) – tertiary 20.3 per cent (1994)

The republic includes the Gorno-Badakhstan Autonomous Province and the Kulyab, Kurgan-Tyubinsk and Khodzhent Provinces. The country is mountainous with the Pamir highlands in the east and the high ridges of the Pamir-Altai system in the centre. Plains are formed by wide stretches of the Syr-Darya valley in the north and of the Amu-Darya in the south. The country has areas prone to earthquakes, and a continental climate.

HISTORY AND POLITICS

The area that is now Tajikistan was conquered by Alexander the Great in the fourth century BC and remained under Greek and Greco-Persian rule for 200 years, until the Kingdom of Kusha was established, based on Bacharia (Bukhara). Tajikistan was invaded by both the Arabs and the Samanid Persians between the seventh and ninth centuries AD. The cities of Bukhara and Samarkand were two of the most important cultural and educational centres in the Islamic world.

The Tajiks lived under the control of various feudal emirates until the area was subsumed within the Russian Empire in 1868. At the time of the Russian revolution in 1917 the central Asian emirates attempted to re-establish their independence. Soviet power was re-established in northern Tajikistan by 1 April 1918, when the Turkestan Soviet Socialist Republic was formed, and the Bukhara emirate was overthrown by Soviet forces in 1920. In 1924 the Tajikistan Autonomous Soviet Socialist Republic was formed as part of the Uzbek Republic before Tajikistan was given full republican status within the Soviet Union in 1929. Stalin deprived the Tajiks of Bukhara and Samarkand, which remained in Uzbekistan, and during Soviet rule 1,000,000 Uzbeks and 800,000 Russians were settled in Tajikistan.

Tajikistan declared independence from the Soviet Union on 9 September 1991 and became a UN member on 2 March 1992. Tension between President Nabiev's supporters and the opposition Islamic and democratic groups led to armed clashes in 1992 and Nabiev was forced to resign on 7 September 1992. The Islamic-Democratic alliance formed a government in September but civil war broke out as forces loyal to the former Communist regime rebelled against the new government. By early November, pro-Communist forces controlled virtually all the country and the Supreme Soviet installed Imamali Rakhmonov as its Speaker and head of state. Fighting continued but by

March 1993 the Islamic-Democratic forces had been defeated by government and Russian Army units and driven across the border into Afghanistan.

Fighting resumed in July between Russian and Tajik government forces and the Afghan-based rebels, leading to the establishment of a CIS peacekeeping force on the Tajik-Afghan border to contain the rebel attacks. Negotiations between the government and opposition brought about a cease-fire in October 1994 to allow for presidential and parliamentary elections. The elections were won by acting head of state Imamali Rakhmonov and the ruling (former Communist) People's Party of Tajikistan, although the elections were boycotted by most opposition groups and were condemned as undemocratic by the OSCE monitoring team. Fighting restarted along the Afghan border in early 1995. A peace agreement was signed in December 1996 which provided for the formation of a national reconciliation commission, a general amnesty and an exchange of prisoners. The agreement has held, although there have been sporadic outbreaks of violence since it was signed. Under an agreement of June 1997, Haji Akbar Turajonzoda, the opposition leader (of the United Tajik Opposition party) joined the government on 10 March 1998.

A new democratic constitution which re-established the presidency was approved in a referendum in November 1994. The legislature is the 181-seat Supreme Council (*Majlisi Oli*) which serves a five-year term. Administratively Tajikistan is divided into two regions and one autonomous region.

HEAD OF STATE
President, Imamali Rakhmonov, *elected by Supreme Soviet* 19 November 1992, *elected* 6 November 1994

COUNCIL OF MINISTERS *as at July 1998*
Prime Minister, Yahya Azimov
First Deputy PMs, Mahmadsaid Ubaydulloyev; Abdumalik Abdullojanov
Deputy PMs, Jamoliddin Mansurov; Haji Akbar Turajonzoda *(CIS Relations)*; Inoyatova Munira Abdulloyevna *(Education)*; Rustam Mirzoyev; Abdurrahmon Nazimov *(Security and the Interior)*
Administrator to the Council of Ministers, Ramazan Mirzoyev
Agriculture, Habibullo Tabarov
Chair of State Committee for Construction and Architecture, Bahavaddin Zuhuruddinov
Chair of State Property Committee, Davlatov Matlubkhon
Chair of the Supreme Council, Safarali Radzhabov
Construction, Odil Ochilov
Culture and Information, Bobokohon Mahmadov
Defence, Lt.-Gen. Sherali Khayrulloyev
Economics, Tukhtaboy Gafarov
Environmental Protection and Water Resources, Saydullo Khayrulloyev
Finance, Anvarsho Muzaffurov
Foreign Affairs, Talbak Nazarov
Foreign Economic Affairs, Izzatullo Hayoyev
Grain, Bekmurod Urokov
Health, Alamkhon Ahmedov
Industry, Shavkat Umarov
Interior, Homiddin Sharipov
Justice, Shavkat Ishmoilov
Labour, Shukurjon Zuhurov
Security, Maj.-Gen. Saidamin Zuhurov
Social Security, Abdusattor Jabborov
Trade and Material Resources, Hakim Soliyev
Transport, Fariddun Muhiddinov

HONORARY CONSULATE
33 Ovington Square, London SW3 1LJ
Honorary Consul, Benjamin Brahms

BRITISH AMBASSADOR, HE Alexander Bergne, OBE, apptd 1997, resident at Tashkent, Uzbekistan

ECONOMY
In January 1994 Tajikistan entered into a monetary union with Russia, effectively handing over monetary control to Russia in exchange for a US$100 million loan needed to prevent an economic collapse following the civil war. The Tajik rouble replaced the Russian rouble in May 1995. The economy is being reformed and privatization undertaken in order to attract foreign investment. In 1997 GDP grew by 1.7 per cent and industry grew by 9 per cent.

Agriculture is the major sector of the economy, concentrating on cotton-growing and cattle-breeding. Tajikistan also has rich mineral deposits of mercury, lead, zinc, oil, gold and uranium. Industry specializes in the production of clothing and textiles. In November 1997 and May 1998, donor conferences pledged loans totalling US$340 million to help stabilize the economic and political situation in Tajikistan.
GNP – US$1,964million (1996); US$340 per capita (1996)
GDP – US$5,074 million (1994); US$131 per capita (1994)
TOTAL EXTERNAL DEBT – US$707 million (1996)

TRADE WITH UK	1996	1997
Imports from UK	£1,598,000	£1,425,000
Exports to UK	64,000	1,501,000

TANZANIA
Jamhuri ya Muungano wa Tanzania – United Republic of Tanzania

AREA – 362,162 sq. miles (938,000 sq. km). Neighbours: Kenya and Uganda (north), Mozambique (south), Malawi and Zambia (south-west), Rwanda, Burundi and the Democratic Republic of Congo (west)
POPULATION – 30,337,000 (1994 UN estimate). Africans form a large majority, with European, Asian, and other non-African minorities. The African population consists mostly of tribes of mixed Bantu race. The official languages are Swahili and English
CAPITAL – Dodoma (population, 88,474, 1988)
MAJOR CITIES – ΨDar es Salaam (1,096,000), the economic and administrative centre; Mbeya (194,000); Mwanza (252,000); ΨTanga (172,000), 1985 estimates
CURRENCY – Tanzanian shilling of 100 cents
NATIONAL ANTHEM – Mungu Ibariki Afrika (God Bless Africa)
NATIONAL DAY – 26 April (Union Day)
NATIONAL FLAG – Green (above) and blue; divided by diagonal black stripe bordered by gold, running from bottom (next staff) to top (in fly)
LIFE EXPECTANCY (years) – male 47.00; female 50.00
POPULATION GROWTH RATE – 3.4 per cent (1995)
POPULATION DENSITY – 34 per sq. km (1995)
URBAN POPULATION – 20.8 per cent (1990)
MILITARY EXPENDITURE – 1.8 per cent of GDP (1996)
MILITARY PERSONNEL – 36,000: Army 30,000, Navy 1,000, Air Force 3,600, Paramilitaries 1,400
CONSCRIPTION DURATION – Two years

Tanzania comprises Tanganyika, on the mainland of east Africa, and the island of Zanzibar. The greater part of the country is occupied by the central African plateau from which rise, among others, Mt Kilimanjaro (19,340 ft), the highest point on the continent of Africa, and Mt Meru (14,974 ft). The Serengeti National Park covers an area of 6,000 sq. miles in the Arusha, Mwanza and Mara Regions.

HISTORY AND POLITICS

Tanganyika became an independent state and a member of the British Commonwealth on 9 December 1961, and a republic within the Commonwealth on 9 December 1962. Zanzibar, comprising the islands of Zanzibar, Pemba and Mafia, was formerly ruled by the Sultan of Zanzibar and was a British Protectorate until 10 December 1963 when it became an independent state within the Commonwealth. On 26 April 1964 Tanganyika united with Zanzibar to form the United Republic of Tanzania.

The sole legal political party from 1977 to 1992 was the Chama Cha Mapinduzi (CCM). The constitution was amended in 1992 to allow multiparty politics, with the stipulation that all parties must be active in both the mainland and in Zanzibar and that parties must not be formed on regional, religious, tribal or racial grounds.

The first multiparty presidential and parliamentary elections were held in October and November 1995. The CCM's candidate, Salmin Amour, was elected president of Zanzibar and his party won 26 seats in the Zanzibar House of Representatives. The Civic United Front gained 24 seats. Benjamin Mkapa of the CCM was elected Union president. The CCM won 186 of the 232 elected seats in the National Assembly.

POLITICAL SYSTEM

The president is directly elected and may serve two terms. The National Assembly contains 275 members, of whom 182 are elected from mainland constituencies and 50 from Zanzibar, 37 seats are reserved for women and are distributed to parties in ratio to their share of seats, five are nominated by the Zanzibar government and one is reserved for the Attorney-General. Constituency members are elected at a general election held at a maximum of five-yearly intervals.

Although Zanzibar has its own president, government and 60-member House of Representatives, Tanganyika is governed by the government of the Union. The president of Zanzibar is also a member of the Union Cabinet.

HEAD OF STATE
President of the United Republic, Benjamin Mkapa, *elected* 29 October 1995
Vice-President, Dr Omar Ali Juma

CABINET *as at July 1998*
The President
The Vice-President
President of Zanzibar, Salmin Amour
Prime Minister, Frederick Sumaye
Agriculture and Co-operatives, Paul Kimiti
Communications and Transport, William Kusila
Community Development, Women's Affairs and Children, Mary Nagu
Defence, Edgar Maokola Majogo
Education, Prof. Juma Athumani Kapuya
Energy and Mineral Resources, Dr Abdalla Kigoda
Foreign Affairs and International Co-operation, Jakaya Kikwete
Health, Dr Aaron Chiduo
Home Affairs, Ali Amer Mohammed
Industries and Trade, Dr William Shija
Justice and Constitutional Affairs, Bakari Mwapachu
Labour and Youth Development, Mohamed Seif Khatib *(acting)*
Land, Housing and Urban Development, Gideon Cheyo
Ministers of State in the President's Office, Mateo Karesi; Daniel Yona *(Finance)*; Bakari Mbonde; Juma Mkangaa; Kigunga Mgombale Mwiru; Nasoro Maloche
Ministers of State in the Vice-President's Office, Mohammed Seif Khatib
Natural Resources and Tourism, Zakia Meghji

Science, Technology and Higher Education, Jackson Makweta
Water and Livestock Development, Pius Ng'wandu
Works, Anna Abdallah

HIGH COMMISSION FOR THE UNITED REPUBLIC OF TANZANIA
43 Hertford Street, London W1Y 8DB
Tel 0171-499 8951/4
High Commissioner, HE Dr Abdul-kader Shareef, apptd 1995

BRITISH HIGH COMMISSION
Hifadhi House, Samora Avenue (PO Box 9200), Dar es Salaam
Tel: Dar es Salaam 117659/64
High Commissioner, HE Bruce Dinwiddy, apptd 1998

BRITISH COUNCIL DIRECTOR, R. Hilhorst, Samora Avenue (PO Box 9100), Dar es Salaam

ECONOMY

90 per cent of the workforce are employed in agriculture. The islands of Zanzibar and Pemba produce a large part of the world's supply of cloves and clove oil; coconuts, coconut oil and copra are also produced. The mainland's chief export crops are coffee, cotton, sugar cane, tobacco, cashew nuts, gold and diamonds. Industry is largely concerned with the processing of raw material for export or local consumption; secondary manufacturing industries include factories for the manufacture of leather and rubber footwear, knitwear, razor blades, cigarettes and textiles, and a wheat flour mill.

In September 1997, the president officially declared a state of famine in the country. As a result of poor rains, the country faced a shortfall of nearly one million tonnes of food.

In 1995 Tanzania had a trade deficit of US$658 million and a current account deficit of US$629 million. In 1996 imports totalled US$1,394 million and exports US$760 million.
GNP – US$5,174 million (1996); US$170 per capita (1996)
GDP – US$2,737 million (1994); US$119 per capita (1994)
ANNUAL AVERAGE GROWTH OF GDP – 3.0 per cent (1994)
INFLATION RATE – 19.7 per cent (1996)
TOTAL EXTERNAL DEBT – US$7,412 million (1996)

TRADE WITH UK	1996	1997
Imports from UK	£81,851,000	£77,008,000
Exports to UK	28,983,000	33,148,000

COMMUNICATIONS

The main ports are Dar es Salaam, Tanga, Mtwara, Zanzibar, Mkoani and Wete, in addition to Mwanza, Musoma and Bukoba on Lake Victoria and Kigoma on Lake Tanganyika. Coastal shipping services connect the mainland to Zanzibar, and lake services are operated on Lake Tanganyika and Lake Malawi with neighbouring countries. The principal international airports are Dar es Salaam, Kilimanjaro and Zanzibar. There are two railway systems; one connecting Dar es Salaam to Zambia, and the second having two main lines running from Dar es Salaam, one to northern Tanzania and Kenya and the other to Lakes Tanganyika and Victoria.

EDUCATION

The school system is administered in Swahili but the government is making efforts to improve English standards for the purposes of secondary and higher education. All Tanzanian secondary schools are expected to include practical subjects in the basic course. There are two institutes of higher education: the University of Dar es

Salaam, and Sokoine University of Agriculture in Morogoro.

ILLITERACY RATE – 32.2 per cent
ENROLMENT (percentage of age group) – primary 48 per cent (1995); tertiary 0.5 per cent (1995)

THAILAND
Prathes Thai – Kingdom of Thailand

AREA – 198,115 sq. miles (513,115 sq. km). Neighbours: Malaysia (south), Myanmar (west), Laos and Cambodia (east)
POPULATION – 60,206,000 (1997 census). The principal language is Thai, a monosyllabic, tonal language of the Indo-Chinese linguistic family, with a vocabulary strongly influenced by Sanskrit and Pali. It is written in an alphabetic script derived from ancient Indian scripts. Significant minorities speak Chinese (in urban areas), Lao (in the north-east), Khmer (in the east) and Malay (in the far south). The principal religion is Buddhism (94.37 per cent), with Muslim and Christian minorities
CAPITAL – ΨBangkok (population, 5,876,000, 1993)
MAJOR CITIES – Chiang Mai (167,000); Chon Buri (187,000); Muang Khon Kaen (206,000); Nakhon Ratchasima (278,000); Songkhla (243,000)
CURRENCY – Baht of 100 satang
NATIONAL ANTHEM – Pleng Chart
NATIONAL DAY – 5 December (The King's Birthday)
NATIONAL FLAG – Five horizontal bands, red, white, dark blue, white, red (the blue band twice the width of the others)
LIFE EXPECTANCY (years) – male 63.82; female 68.85
POPULATION GROWTH RATE – 1.4 per cent (1995)
POPULATION DENSITY – 117 per sq. km (1995)
URBAN POPULATION – 18.7 per cent (1990)

Thailand, formerly known as Siam, is divided geographically into four: the centre is a plain; to the north-east there is a plateau area and to the north-west mountains. The south of Thailand consists of a narrow mountainous peninsula. The principal rivers are the Chao Phraya in the central plains, and the Mekong on the northern and north-eastern borders.

HISTORY AND POLITICS

The Thai nation was founded in the 13th century. Although occupied by Burma in the 18th century, Thailand is the only country in the region not to have been colonized by a European power.

Following a revolution in 1932, Thailand became a constitutional monarchy. After a military coup in February 1991, a new constitution was approved under which the military would have significant political power. Parties aligned with the military won the general election in March 1992, but opposition to the government grew and mass demonstrations held in Bangkok, with the help of the King, forced the government from power. Military power was curbed, the 1978 constitution was restored and the interim government sacked military chiefs.

Parliamentary elections in September 1992 resulted in a majority for those parties not allied with the military. Chuan Leekpai became prime minister at the head of a coalition which implemented a number of reforms. Some 600,000 families were granted land title rights, the voting age was reduced to 18, the appointed Senate was reduced to a maximum of two-thirds of the number of House of Representatives' seats and anti-corruption laws were

introduced. In a general election on 17 November 1996, New Aspiration became the largest party in the House of Representatives and formed a six-party coalition government. As a result of the economic crisis in Asia, the government resigned in November 1997, and a new eight-party coalition government was formed under Chuan Leekpai.

POLITICAL SYSTEM

The amended 1978 constitution provides for a National Assembly consisting of a 260-member Senate appointed by the King and a 393-member House of Representatives elected by universal adult suffrage for a term of four years.

In September 1997, the House of Representatives approved a number of constitutional reforms, including making the Senate a directly-elected body instead of one appointed by the King, and changing the House of Representatives to comprise 400 MPs from single constituencies and 100 from party lists.

HEAD OF STATE
HM The King of Thailand, King Bhumibol Adulyadej, *born* 1927; *succeeded his brother* 9 June 1946; *married* 28 April 1950 Princess Sirikit Kitiyakara; *crowned* 5 May 1950; and has *issue*, Princess Ubolratana, *born* 6 April 1951; Crown Prince Vajiralongkorn (*see* below); Princess Maha Chaki Sirindhorn, *born* 2 April 1955; Princess Chulabhorn, *born* 4 July 1957
Heir, HRH Crown Prince Vajiralongkorn, *born* 28 July 1952; *married* 3 January 1977 Soamsawali Kitiyakra

CABINET *as at July 1998*
Prime Minister, Defence, Chuan Leekpai (DP)
Deputy PMs, Phichai Rattakun (DP); Suwit Khunkitti (SAP); Pancha Kesonthong (CT); Suphachai Phanitchaphak (DP) *(Commerce)*
Ministers to the Prime Minister's Office, Suphattra Matsadit (DP); Sawit Phothiwihok (DP); Churin Laksanawisit (DP); Aphisit Wetchachiwa (DP); Air Chief Marshal Sombun Rahong (PT); Chaiyot Somsap (DP)
Agriculture and Co-operatives, Pongphon Adireksan (CT)
Communications, Suthep Thuaksuban (DP)
Education, Chumphon Sinlapa-acha (CT)
Finance, Tharin Nimmanhemin (DP)
Foreign Affairs, Surin Phitsuwan (DP)
Industry, Somsak Thepsuthin (SAP)
Interior, Maj.-Gen. Sanan Kachonprat (DP)
Justice, Suthat Ngoenmun (DP)
Labour and Social Welfare, Trairong Suwannakhiri (DP)
Public Health, Rakkiat Sukthana (SAP)
Science, Technology and Environment, Yingphan Manasikan (PT)
University Affairs, Navy, Commander Decha Sukharom (CT)

DP Democrat Party; SAP Social Action Party; CT Chart Thai; PT Prachakorn Thai

ROYAL THAI EMBASSY
29–30 Queen's Gate, London SW7 5JB
Tel 0171-589 0173
Ambassador Extraordinary and Plenipotentiary, HE Sir Vidhya Rayananonda, KCVO, apptd 1994
Minister and Deputy Head of Mission, A. Chabchitrchaidol
Defence Attaché, Capt. S. Pruksa
Minister Counsellor, S. Jaovisidha (*Commercial*)

BRITISH EMBASSY
Wireless Road, Bangkok 10330
Tel: Bangkok 2530 1919
Ambassador Extraordinary and Plenipotentiary, HE Sir James Hodge, KCVO, CMG, apptd 1996

Deputy Ambassador and Counsellor, P. Sizeland
Defence Attaché, Col. J. H. Thoyts
Counsellor (Commercial), M. J. Greenstreet
Consul, B. P. Kelly
CONSULATE – Chang Mai

BRITISH COUNCIL DIRECTOR, Dr J. Richards, OBE, 254
Chulalongkorn Soi 64, Siam Square, Phayathai Road,
Pathumwan, Bangkok 10330. There is also an office in
Chiang Mai

BRITISH CHAMBER OF COMMERCE, BP Building 18th
Floor, Unit 1810, 54 Asoke Road (Sukhumvit 21),
Bangkok 10110

DEFENCE

The Army has 277 main battle tanks, 970 armoured
personnel carriers, 453 artillery pieces and four attack
helicopters. The Navy has one aircraft carrier, 14 frigates,
75 patrol and coastal vessels, 56 combat aircraft and six
armed helicopters at five bases. The Air Force has 210
combat aircraft.
MILITARY EXPENDITURE – 2.5 per cent of GDP (1996)
MILITARY PERSONNEL – 266,000: Army 150,000, Navy
73,000, Air Force 43,000
CONSCRIPTION DURATION – Two years (ended October
1997)

ECONOMY

Thailand was one of the countries worst affected by the
economic crisis in south-east Asia. Many Thai banks had
borrowed heavily to finance the booming property market,
and had suffered when the market collapsed. In March
1997, Thailand's largest finance company, Finance One,
was only saved from collapse by a Central Bank-backed
takeover. In May 1997 it was announced that, despite
emergency budget cuts, Thailand was heading for its first
fiscal deficit in over a decade, and as a result the stock
market fell to an eight-year low. Having spent US$10
billion defending the baht from speculators, in July 1997
the government allowed the currency to float freely,
resulting in a *de facto* devaluation of 20 per cent and
triggering a currency crisis throughout south-east Asia. On
5 August 1997, an IMF loan of US$16.7 billion was
announced, in return for emergency financial reforms.
However, these reforms were only implemented after a
delay and were seen by the markets as inadequate, further
damaging economic confidence. The government resigned on 3 November 1997, and was replaced by an
eight-party coalition. The new government managed to
slow the decline slightly, but the baht continued to slide,
and revised economic forecasts have predicted a contraction in the economy of 5.5 per cent. In January 1998 the
prime minister approved a move to repatriate foreign
workers, in order to provide more jobs for native Thais.
  The agricultural sector employs around half of the
labour force. In 1997 it contributed 11 per cent of GDP.
Rice remains the most important crop; other main crops
are sugar, maize, sorghum, cassava, rubber, tobacco, kenaf
and jute. In recent years fishing and livestock production
have gained importance. There are reserves of oil,
natural gas and lignite; mineral resources include tin,
tungsten, lead and iron.
  Important industrial sectors include textiles, transportation vehicles and equipment, construction materials,
brewing, petroleum refining, electrical appliances, plastics, computers and parts, and integrated circuits. In 1995,
manufacturing contributed 29.1 per cent of GDP. Since
1982 tourism has been the main foreign exchange earner.
In 1995, there were 6,951,600 foreign visitors.

GNP – US$177,476 million (1996); US$2,960 per capita
(1996)
GDP – US$117,649 million (1994); US$2,454 per capita
(1994)
ANNUAL AVERAGE GROWTH OF GDP – 8.6 per cent (1995)
INFLATION RATE – 5.8 per cent (1996)
UNEMPLOYMENT – 1.5 per cent (1993)
TOTAL EXTERNAL DEBT – US$90,824 million (1996)

TRADE

Thailand's main exports are computers and parts, cars,
integrated circuit boards, precious stones, rice, maize,
canned sea food, fabrics, sugar and tin. Main imports are
crude oil, chemicals, electrical goods, industrial machinery, iron, steel and transport equipment.
  In 1995 Thailand had a trade deficit of US$7,968 million
and a current account deficit of US$13,554 million. In 1996
imports totalled US$73,484 million and exports
US$55,721 million.

Trade with UK	1996	1997
Imports from UK	£974,064,000	£861,736,000
Exports to UK	1,187,872,000	1,222,138,000

COMMUNICATIONS

The road network, totalling 56,903 km in 1993, reaches all
parts of the country. Navigable waterways have a length of
about 1,100 km in the dry season and 1,600 km in the wet
season. There are 4,600 km of state-owned railways. Main
lines run from Bangkok to the Cambodian border, the ferry
terminal on the River Mekong opposite Vientiane, Chiang
Mai and to Hat Yai, whence lines run down both sides of the
Malay peninsula to Singapore. A new line to Sattahip on
the east coast is being constructed. Bangkok is the international airport, though airports at Chiang Mai, Phuket and
Hat Yai also receive international flights. Most major
provincial towns have airports. A mass transit system has
been planned for Bangkok.
  There are two important ports in the country. Bangkok,
which is a river port, can serve vessels up to 27 ft draught.
The deep-sea port at Sattahip caters for larger vessels.
Phuket and Songkhla deep-water ports have already been
completed and are the first to be managed privately under a
ten-year concession.

EDUCATION

Primary education is compulsory and free, and secondary
education in government schools is free. Private universities and colleges are playing an increasing role in higher
education. Out of 43 universities and other similar higher
institutes of learning, 21 are private.
ILLITERACY RATE – 6.2 per cent
ENROLMENT (percentage of age group) – tertiary 20.1 per
cent (1995)

TOGO
République Togolaise

AREA – 21,925 sq. miles (56,785 sq. km). Neighbours:
  Ghana (west), Burkina Faso (north), Benin (east)
POPULATION – 4,138,000 (1994 UN estimate). The official
  language is French; Ewe, Watchi and Kabiyé are the
  main indigenous languages
CAPITAL – ΨLomé (population, 366,476, 1983)
CURRENCY – Franc CFA of 100 centimes
NATIONAL DAY – 13 January (National Liberation Day)
NATIONAL FLAG – Five alternating green and yellow

horizontal stripes; a quarter in red at top next staff bearing a white star
LIFE EXPECTANCY (years) – male 53.23; female 56.82
POPULATION GROWTH RATE – 3.2 per cent (1995)
POPULATION DENSITY – 73 per sq. km (1995)
MILITARY EXPENDITURE – 2.1 per cent of GDP (1996)
MILITARY PERSONNEL – 7,700: Army 6,500, Navy 200, Air Force 250, Paramilitaries 750
CONSCRIPTION DURATION – Two years
ILLITERACY RATE – 48.3 per cent
ENROLMENT (percentage of age group) – primary 85 per cent (1995); secondary 18 per cent (1990); tertiary 3.2 per cent (1994)

HISTORY AND POLITICS

The first president of Togo, Sylvanus Olympio, was assassinated in 1963. His successor was overthrown by an army coup d'état in 1967 and the army commander Lt.-Col. (later Gen.) Eyadéma named himself president. President Eyadéma came under increasing popular pressure to introduce reforms in 1990 and in October the *Rassemblement du peuple togolais* (RPT), the sole legal party, approved plans for a new constitutional conference after pro-democracy riots. Riots broke out again in March 1991 in protest at the slow pace of reform, and in April the government was forced to concede a political amnesty, the introduction of a multiparty constitution and a national conference. In August 1991 the national conference stripped President Eyadéma of all powers, banned the RPT and elected Kokou Koffigoh as prime minister of an interim government. The national conference set a date of 9 February 1992 for a referendum on a new constitution.

From the second half of 1991 onwards the political situation became progressively more unstable. Troops loyal to President Eyadéma three times attempted to overthrow Koffigoh (in October, November and December 1991) but were frustrated by pro-democracy supporters. Continued violence in 1992 between the army and pro-democracy groups and among rival opposition parties forced the postponement of the referendum until September 1992, when a new multiparty constitution was agreed. In November, Eyadéma, who had regained the position of head of state in August 1992, ordered the Army to crush civil unrest and a general strike against his rule. In February 1993, as violence continued, Koffigoh and Eyadéma agreed on the formation of a crisis government, which the national conference and the Collective Democratic Opposition-2 (COD-2) declared illegal.

President Eyadéma won a presidential election in August 1993 that was boycotted by opposition parties and declared rigged by international monitors. Legislative elections to the 81-seat National Assembly were held in February 1994 and won by the opposition alliance of the Action Committee for Renewal (CAR) (36 seats) and the Togolese Union for Democracy (UTD) (7 seats), while the RPT and allied parties won 38 seats. However, Eyadéma persuaded UTD leader Edem Kodjo to form a coalition UTD-RPT government in April 1994, the RPT retaining a majority of Cabinet seats. The CAR returned to the National Assembly in August 1995, following a nine-month boycott prompted by a Supreme Court decision invalidating the election of some CAR candidates.

The presidential election of 21 June 1998 was won by Gen. Eyadéma. Opposition politicians and EU observers expressed serious doubts over the conduct of the election, and the EU announced that because of this it is considering suspending Togo from the Lomé Convention.

HEAD OF STATE
President, Gen. Gnassingbé Eyadéma, *assumed office* 14 April 1967; *re-elected* 1986, 1993, 21 June 1998

GOVERNMENT *as at July 1998*
Prime Minister, Planning and Economic Development, Kwasi Klutse
Agriculture, Livestock and Fisheries, Kokou Dake Dogbe
Civil Service, Labour, Social Security, Tchangai Kissem Walla
Communication and Civic Education, Esso Solitoki
Decentralization, Koffiui Victor Ayassou
Defence, Yaginim Bitokotipou
Environment and Forest Resources, Koffi Adade
Foreign Affairs and Co-operation, Koffi Panou
Health, Koffi Sama
Industry and Commerce, Elome Kouami Dadzie
Interior and Security, Gen. Seyi Memene
Justice and Keeper of the Seals, Solomou Baba Stanislas Temele
Mines, Equipment, Transport, Housing, Tchamdja Andjo
Minister Delegate at the Prime Minister's Office, Economic Reforms and Modernization of Administration, Florence Djokpe Essivi
Minister of State, Companies and Free Trade Zone Development, Payadowa Boukpessi
Minister of State, Finance and Privatization, Barry Moussa Barque
National Education and Research, Kodjo Edo Maurille Agbobli
Relations with Parliament and Institutions, Komi Dotse Amoudokpo
Secretary of State to the Minister of State for Economy, Finance and Budget, Amoussa Assiba Guénou
Secretary of State to the Prime Minister, Planning and Territorial Development, Tcha Gouni Ati-Atcha
Technical Education, Professional Training and Cottage Industry, Comlan Kadje
Tourism and Leisure, Tankpadja Lalle
Youth, Culture and Sports, Kouami Agbogboli Ihou

EMBASSY OF TOGO
8 rue Alfred-Roll, 75017 Paris, France
Ambassador Extraordinary and Plenipotentiary, HE Kondi Charles

BRITISH AMBASSADOR, HE Ian Mackley, CMG, resident at Accra, Ghana
There is a Consulate (BP 20050) and a Commercial Office (BP 60958 BE) in Lomé.

ECONOMY

Although the economy remains largely agricultural, exports of phosphates have superseded agricultural products as the main source of export earnings. Other exports include palm kernels, copra and manioc.

In 1994 Togo had a trade deficit of US$37 million and a current account deficit of US$57 million. In 1996 imports totalled US$404 million and exports US$196 million.
GNP – US$1,278 million (1996); US$300 per capita (1996)
GDP – US$2,023 million (1994); US$419 per capita (1994)
ANNUAL AVERAGE GROWTH OF GDP – 0.1 per cent (1990)
INFLATION RATE – 15.7 per cent (1995)
TOTAL EXTERNAL DEBT – US$1,463 million (1996)

TRADE WITH UK	1996	1997
Imports from UK	£20,039,000	£13,046,000
Exports to UK	4,459,000	2,302,000

TONGA
Kingdom of Tonga

AREA – 288 sq. miles (747 sq. km)
POPULATION – 98,000 (1994 UN estimate). The languages
are Tongan and English
CAPITAL – ΨNuku'alofa (population, 29,018, 1986), on
Tongatapu
CURRENCY – Pa'anga (T$) of 100 seniti
NATIONAL ANTHEM – E, 'Otua Mafimafi (Oh, Almighty
God Above)
NATIONAL DAY – 4 June (Emancipation Day)
NATIONAL FLAG – Red with a white canton containing a
couped red cross
POPULATION GROWTH RATE – 0.3 per cent (1995)
POPULATION DENSITY – 131 per sq. km (1995)
URBAN POPULATION – 30.7 per cent (1986)

Tonga, or the Friendly Islands, comprises a group of
islands situated in the southern Pacific some 450 miles
east-south-east of Fiji. The largest island, Tongatapu, was
discovered by Tasman in 1643. Most of the islands are of
coral formation, but some are volcanic (Tofua, Kao and
Niuafoou or 'Tin Can' Island).

HISTORY AND POLITICS

The Kingdom of Tonga is an independent constitutional
monarchy within the Commonwealth. Prior to 4 June 1970
it had been a British-protected state for 70 years. The
constitution provides for a government consisting of the
Sovereign, an appointed privy council which functions as a
Cabinet, a legislative assembly and a judiciary. The 30-
member legislative assembly comprises the King, the 11-
member privy council, nine hereditary nobles elected by
their peers, and nine popularly elected representatives
who hold office for three years. The most recent election
took place in January 1996.

HEAD OF STATE
King of Tonga, HM King Taufa'ahau Tupou IV, GCMG,
GCVO, KBE, *born* 4 July 1918, *acceded* 16 December 1965
Heir, HRH Crown Prince Tupouto'a

CABINET *as at July 1998*
Prime Minister, Agriculture, Fisheries, Marine Affairs, Baron
Vaea of Houma
Deputy PM, Education and Civil Aviation, Dr S. Langi
Kavaliku
Finance, Tutoatosi Fakafanua
Foreign Affairs and Defence, HRH Crown Prince Tupouto'a
Governor of Vava'u, Tu'i'afitu
Health, Tllitili Puloka *(acting)*
Justice, Tevita Tupou
Labour, Commerce and Industries, Masaso Paunga
Lands, Survey, and Natural Resources, Governor of Ha'apai,
Fakafanua
Police, Prisons and Fire Services, Clive Edwards
Without Portfolio, Ma'afu Tuku'i'aulahi
Works and Disaster Relief, Cecil Cocker

TONGA HIGH COMMISSION
36 Molyneux Street, London WIH 6AB
Tel 0171-724 5828
High Commissioner, HE 'Akosita Fineanganofo, apptd 1996

BRITISH HIGH COMMISSION
PO Box 56, Nuku'alofa
Tel: Nuku'alofa 21020
High Commissioner, HE Andrew Morris, apptd 1994

ECONOMY

The economy is primarily agricultural; the main crops are
coconuts, vanilla, yams, taro, cassava, groundnuts, squash
pumpkins and other fruits. Fish is an important staple food,
though recent shortfalls have led to canned fish being
imported. Industry is based on the processing of agricultural produce, and the manufacture of foodstuffs, clothing
and sports equipment.
GNP – US$175 million (1996); US$1,790 per capita (1996)
GDP – US$134 million (1994); US$1,482 per capita (1994)
ANNUAL AVERAGE GROWTH OF GDP – 4.8 per cent (1994)
INFLATION RATE – 3.0 per cent (1996)
TOTAL EXTERNAL DEBT – US$70 million (1996)

TRADE

The principal exports are copra, other coconut products,
fruit and vegetables, knitwear, leather goods and fibreglass
boats.
    In 1995 imports totalled US$77 million and exports
US$14 million.

Trade with UK	1996	1997
Imports from UK	£3,727,000	£4,892,000
Exports to UK	30,000	193,000

TRINIDAD AND TOBAGO
The Republic of Trinidad and Tobago

AREA – 1,981 sq. miles (5,130 sq. km)
POPULATION – 1,306,000 (1994 UN estimate). The
language is English. Roman Catholicism, Protestantism,
Hinduism and Islam are all practised
CAPITAL – ΨPort of Spain (population, 46,222, 1994)
MAJOR CITIES – San Fernando (55,784); ΨScarborough,
the main town of Tobago
CURRENCY – Trinidad and Tobago dollar (TT$) of 100
cents
NATIONAL DAYS – 31 August (Independence Day)
NATIONAL FLAG – Black diagonal stripe bordered with
white stripes, running from top by staff, all on a red field
LIFE EXPECTANCY (years) – male 68.39; female 73.20
POPULATION GROWTH RATE – 1.4 per cent (1995)
POPULATION DENSITY – 255 per sq. km (1995)
MILITARY EXPENDITURE – 1.0 per cent of GDP (1996)
MILITARY PERSONNEL – 6,900: Army 1,400, Coast Guard
700, Paramilitaries 4,800

Trinidad, the most southerly of the West Indian islands,
lies seven miles off the north coast of Venezuela. The
island is about 50 miles in length by 37 miles in width. Two
mountain systems, the Northern and Southern Ranges,
stretch across almost its entire width and a third, the
Central Range, lies diagonally across its middle portion;
otherwise the island is mostly flat.
    Tobago lies 19 miles north-east of Trinidad. The island
is 32 miles long at its widest point, and 11 miles wide.
    Corozal Point and Icacos Point, the north-west and
south-west extremities of Trinidad, enclose the Gulf of
Paria. West of Corozal Point lie several islands, of which
Chacachacare, Huevos, Monos and Gaspar Grande are the
most important.
    The climate is tropical. There is a dry season from
December to May, and a wet season from June to
November broken by a short dry season (the *Petite Careme*)
in September and October.

HISTORY AND POLITICS

Trinidad was discovered by Columbus in 1498, was colonized in 1532 by the Spaniards, capitulated to the British in 1797, and was ceded to Britain under the Treaty of Amiens (1802). Tobago was discovered by Columbus in 1498. Dutch colonists arrived in 1632; Tobago subsequently changed hands numerous times until it was ceded to Britain by France in 1814 and amalgamated with Trinidad in 1888. The Territory of Trinidad and Tobago became an independent state and a member of the British Commonwealth on 31 August 1962, and a republic in 1976.

The most recent general election on 6 November 1995 produced 17 seats each for the ruling People's National Movement (PNM) and the United National Congress (UNC). The UNC formed a coalition government with the National Alliance for Reconstruction (NAR) which held the remaining two seats.

POLITICAL SYSTEM

The president is elected for five years by all members of the Senate and the House of Representatives. The House of Representatives has 36 members, directly elected for a five-year term, and the Senate has 31, of whom 16 are appointed on the advice of the prime minister, six on the advice of the Leader of the Opposition and nine at the discretion of the president. Legislation was passed in September 1980 which afforded Tobago a degree of self-administration through the 15-member Tobago House of Assembly.

HEAD OF STATE
President, HE Arthur N. Robinson, *elected* 14 February 1997

CABINET *as at July 1998*

Prime Minister, Basdeo Panday
Agriculture, Lands and Marine Resources, Dr Reeza Mohammed
Attorney-General, Ramesh Lawrence Maharaj
Community Development, Culture and Women's Affairs, Daphne Phillips
Education, Dr Adesh Nanan
Energy and Energy Industries, Finbar Ganga
Finance and Tourism, Brian Kuei Tung
Foreign Affairs, Ralph Maraj
Health, Dr Hamza Rafeeq
Housing and Settlements, John Humphrey
Labour and Co-operatives, Harry Partrap
Legal Affairs, Kamla Persad-Bissessar
Local Government, Dhanraj Singh
National Security, Joseph Theodore
Planning and Development, Trevor Sudama
Public Administration and Information, Wade Mark
Public Utilities, Ganga Singh
Social Development, Manohar Ramsaran
Sport and Youth Affairs, Pamela Nicholson
Tobago Affairs, Morgan Job
Trade, Industry and Consumer Affairs, Mervyn Assam
Works and Transport, Sadeeq Baksh

HIGH COMMISSION OF THE REPUBLIC OF TRINIDAD AND TOBAGO
42 Belgrave Square, London SW1X 8NT
Tel 0171-245 9351
High Commissioner, HE Sheelagh de Osuna, apptd 1996

BRITISH HIGH COMMISSION
19 St Clair Ave, St Clair, Port of Spain
Tel: Port of Spain 622 2748
High Commissioner, HE Leo G. Faulkner, apptd 1996

ECONOMY

Trinidad and Tobago's main source of revenue is from oil. Production of domestic crude was 47 million barrels in 1996. Trinidad has large reserves of natural gas, and reserves are estimated to be in the region of 45 years at the current rates of production. An integrated steel plant, two anhydrous ammonia plants, four methanol plants, one urea plant and one iron carbide plant have been constructed at Point Lisas. An industrial complex, including an iron and steel production plant, is developing around San Fernando.

Fertilizers, tyres, clothing, soap, furniture and foodstuffs are manufactured locally while motor vehicles, radios, TV sets, and electro-domestic equipment are assembled from parts, mainly from Japan. The main agricultural products are sugar, cocoa, coffee, horticultural products and teak. There were more than 250,000 tourists in 1996.

In 1995 Trinidad and Tobago had a trade surplus of US$588 million and a current account surplus of US$294 million. In 1996 imports totalled US$2,144 million and exports US$2,500 million.
GNP – US$5,017 million (1996); US$3,870 per capita (1996)
GDP – US$5,356 million (1994); US$3,709 per capita (1994)
ANNUAL AVERAGE GROWTH OF GDP – 2.3 per cent (1995)
INFLATION RATE – 3.4 per cent (1996)
UNEMPLOYMENT – 17.2 per cent (1995)
TOTAL EXTERNAL DEBT – US$2,242 million (1996)

Trade with UK	1996	1997
Imports from UK	£83,792,000	£94,311,000
Exports to UK	53,139,000	63,328,000

COMMUNICATIONS

There are some 6,436 km of all-weather roads in Trinidad and Tobago. The only general cargo port is Port of Spain but there are specialized port facilities elsewhere for crude oil, refinery products, sugar, bauxite and cement. Regular shipping services call and many inter-island craft use the port. Another rapidly growing port is at Point Lisas where new industries powered by local natural gas are located. The national airline is Trinidad and Tobago Airways (BWIA), and the international airport, Piarco, is at Port of Spain. Caribbean Airways flies between Trinidad and Tobago.

EDUCATION

Education is free at all state-owned and government-assisted denominational schools and certain faculties at the University of the West Indies. Attendance is compulsory for children aged six to 12 years, after which attendance at free secondary schools is determined by success in the common entrance examination at 11 years. There are three technical institutes, two teachers' training colleges, and one of the three branches of the University of the West Indies is located in Trinidad. A medical teaching complex at Mt Hope operates in collaboration with the University of the West Indies.
ILLITERACY RATE – 2.1 per cent
ENROLMENT (percentage of age group) – primary 88 per cent (1995); secondary 64 per cent (1992); tertiary 7.7 per cent (1995)

TUNISIA
Al-Djoumhouria Attunusia

AREA – 62,592 sq. miles (162,155 sq. km). Neighbours: Algeria (west), Libya (south)
POPULATION – 8,896,000 (1994 UN estimate). Arabic is the official language
CAPITAL – ΨTunis (population, 1,830,634, 1994)
MAJOR CITIES – ΨBizerte (484,250); ΨSfax (732,865); ΨSousse (435,075), 1996
CURRENCY – Tunisian dinar of 1,000 millimes
NATIONAL ANTHEM – Himat Al Hima
NATIONAL DAY – 20 March
NATIONAL FLAG – Red with a white disc containing a red crescent and star
LIFE EXPECTANCY (years) – male 66.85; female 68.68
POPULATION GROWTH RATE – 1.9 per cent (1995)
POPULATION DENSITY – 54 per sq. km (1995)
URBAN POPULATION – 58.0 per cent (1990)
MILITARY EXPENDITURE – 2.0 per cent of GDP (1996)
MILITARY PERSONNEL – 47,000: Army 27,000, Navy 4,500, Air Force 3,500, Paramilitaries 12,000
CONSCRIPTION DURATION – 12 months
ILLITERACY RATE – 33.3 per cent
ENROLMENT (percentage of age group) – primary 97 per cent (1995); secondary 23 per cent (1980); tertiary 12.9 per cent (1995)

HISTORY AND POLITICS

A French Protectorate from 1881 to 1956, Tunisia became an independent sovereign state on 20 March 1956. In 1957 the Constituent Assembly abolished the monarchy and elected M. Bourguiba president of the Republic. In March 1975 the National Assembly proclaimed M. Bourguiba as president for life. He was deposed on 7 November 1987 and succeeded by President Zine el-Abidine Ben Ali. Presidential and legislative elections were held in April 1989. The Rassemblement constitutionnel démocratique (RCD) won all 141 seats in the National Assembly and President Ben Ali was elected with 99 per cent of the vote, although the elections were boycotted by the main opposition parties.

Electoral changes enacted in September 1993 provide for opposition parties to be represented in the National Assembly; the Assembly has been expanded to 163 seats, 19 of which are reserved, on a proportional basis, for those parties not winning any of the 144 first-past-the-post seats. Presidential and legislative elections held in March 1994 were won by President Ben Ali, the only candidate, and the RCD, which won all 144 constituency seats.

The country is divided into 23 regions (*gouvernorats*) each administered by a governor.

HEAD OF STATE
President, Gen. Zine el-Abidine Ben Ali, *took office* 7 November 1987, *elected* 2 April 1989, *re-elected* 20 March 1994

CABINET *as at July 1998*
Prime Minister, Hamed Karoui
Agriculture, Sadok Rabah
Communications, Ahmed Friaa
Culture, Abdelbaki Hermassi
Defence, Habib Ben Yahia
Economic Development, Taoufik Baccar
Education, Ridha Ferchiou
Environment, Town and Country Planning, Mohammed Mehdi M'lika

Finance, Mohammed Jeri
Foreign Affairs, Said Ben Mustapha
Higher Education, Dali Jazi
Industry, Moncef Ben Abdallah
Interior, Ali Chaouch
International Co-operation and Foreign Investment, Mohammed Ghannouchi
Justice, Abdallah Kallel
Minister-Delegate to the Prime Minister in charge of Women and the Family, Neziha Zarrouk
Minister-Director of the Presidential Office, Mohammed Jegham
Minister of State, Special Adviser to the President, Abdullah Kallel
Public Health, Hedi Mhenni
Public Works and Housing, Slaheddine Belaid
Religious Affairs, Ali Chebbi
Secretary-General of the Government, Ridha Grira
Social Affairs, Chedli Neffati
State Property, Real Estate Affairs, Mustapha Bouaziz
Tourism and Handicrafts, Slaheddine Maaouia
Trade, Mondher Zenaidi
Transport, Hassine Chouk
Vocational Training and Employment, Moncer Rouissi
Youth and Childhood, Raouf Najar

TUNISIAN EMBASSY
29 Prince's Gate, London SW7 1QG
Tel 0171-584 8117
Ambassador Extraordinary and Plenipotentiary, HE Prof. Mohamed Ben Ahmed, apptd 1997

BRITISH EMBASSY
5 Place de la Victoire, Tunis 1015 RP
Tel: Tunis 134 1444
Ambassador Extraordinary and Plenipotentiary and Consul-General, HE Richard Edis, CMG, apptd 1995
First Secretary, B. Bennett (*Deputy Head of Mission*)
HONORARY CONSULATE – Sfax

BRITISH COUNCIL DIRECTOR, J. McKenzie (*Cultural Attaché*)

ECONOMY

The valleys of the northern region support large flocks and herds and contain rich agricultural areas in which wheat, barley, and oats are grown. Vines and olives are extensively cultivated. Some oil has been discovered and crude oil production in 1994 was 4.5 million tons. Gas has also been discovered off the east coast but is only exploited in small quantities. Tourism is the main foreign exchange earner and there were more than 3.5 million visitors in 1994.

In 1995 Tunisia had a trade deficit of US$1,989 million and a current account deficit of US$737 million. In 1996 imports totalled US$7,745 million and exports US$5,517 million.

GNP – US$17,581 million (1996); US$1,930 per capita (1996)
GDP – US$14,069 million (1994); US$1,541 per capita (1994)
ANNUAL AVERAGE GROWTH OF GDP – 6.9 per cent (1996)
INFLATION RATE – 3.7 per cent (1996)
TOTAL EXTERNAL DEBT – US$9,887 million (1996)

TRADE

The chief exports are crude oil, phosphates, olive oil, textiles and fruit. The chief imports are machinery and equipment, foodstuffs and petroleum products. France remains the main trading partner.

Tunisia became an associate of the EC in 1969. In July 1995 a new EU-Tunisian partnership agreement was signed which aims to modernize Tunisia's economy and improve its competitiveness with a view to creating a future free trade zone with the EU.

Trade with UK	1996	1997
Imports from UK	£83,257,000	£108,303,000
Exports to UK	65,829,000	59,496,000

TURKEY
Türkiye Cumhuriyeti

AREA – 299,158 sq. miles (774,815 sq. km). Neighbours: Greece (west), Bulgaria (north), Georgia, Armenia and Iran (east), Syria and Iraq (south)
POPULATION – 61,644,000 (1994 UN estimate); 56,473,035 (1990 census). Islam ceased to be the state religion in 1928 but 98.99 per cent of the population are Muslim. The main religious minorities, which are concentrated in Istanbul and on the Syrian frontier, are Greek Orthodox, Armenian, Syrian Christian, and Jewish. The language is Turkish
CAPITAL – Ankara (Angora), in Asia (population, 3,103,000, 1994). Ankara (or Ancyra) was the capital of the Roman Province of *Galatia Prima*, and a marble temple (now in ruins), dedicated to Augustus, contains the *Monumentum (Marmor) Ancyranum*, inscribed with a record of the reign of Augustus Caesar
MAJOR CITIES – Adana (1,519,800); Bursa (1,381,300); Gaziantep (973,800); ΨIstanbul (7,784,100); ΨIzmir (2,411,500); Konya (1,069,400), 1994 estimates. Istanbul, in Europe, is the former capital. The Roman city of Byzantium, it was selected by Constantine the Great as the capital of the Roman Empire about AD 328 and renamed Constantinople. Istanbul contains the celebrated church of St Sophia, which, after becoming a mosque, was made a museum in 1934. It also contains Topkapi, former palace of the Ottoman Sultans, which is also a museum
CURRENCY – Turkish lira (TL) of 100 kurus
NATIONAL ANTHEM – Istiklal Marşi (The Independence March)
NATIONAL DAY – 29 October (Republic Day)
NATIONAL FLAG – Red, with white crescent and star
LIFE EXPECTANCY (years) – male 63.26; female 66.01
POPULATION GROWTH RATE – 1.9 per cent (1995)
POPULATION DENSITY – 80 per sq. km (1995)
URBAN POPULATION – 62.6 per cent (1995)

Turkey lies partly in Europe and partly in Asia. Turkey in Europe consists of Eastern Thrace, including the cities of Istanbul and Edirne, and is separated from Asia by the Bosporus at Istanbul and by the Dardanelles (about 40 miles in length with a width varying from one to four miles). Turkey in Asia comprises the whole of Asia Minor or Anatolia.

HISTORY AND POLITICS

On 29 October 1923 the National Assembly declared Turkey a republic and elected Gazi Mustafa Kemal (later known as Kemal Ataturk) president. In 1945 a multiparty system was introduced but in 1960 the government was overthrown by the armed forces. A new constitution was adopted in 1961 and a civilian government took office. Civilian governments remained in power until September 1980 when mounting problems with the economy and terrorism led to a military takeover.

Following the general election in November 1983 the military leadership handed over power to a civilian government. President Özal died on 17 April 1993 leading to the election by parliament of Süleyman Demirel as president. Following elections on 24 December 1995, the Islamist Welfare Party (Refah Partisi (RP)) won the most seats but was unable to form a government, enabling the True Path Party and the Motherland Party to form a coalition. The administration lasted until May 1996 when True Path withdrew following corruption allegations against Tansu Çiller, its leader. The RP and True Path formed a coalition government in June 1996, but resigned under pressure from the military. In June 1997 a secularist coalition government was formed, led by Mesut Yilmaz of the Motherland Party.

On 16 January 1998 Turkey's Constitutional Court declared the Welfare Party to be illegal, on the grounds that its Islamist policies undermined Turkey's secular constitution. Many of its members immediately joined the newly formed Virtue Party (FP) which became the largest party in the legislature with 140 members, one more than the Motherland Party.

In June 1998, Yilmaz announced that he would retire at the end of 1998, and an early election would be held in April 1999.

INSURGENCIES

Since 1984 Turkey has been fighting armed guerrillas of the Marxist Kurdish Workers Party (PKK) in the southeast of the country where Kurds are the majority population. The PKK has an estimated strength of 10,000 operating from bases in Lebanon, northern Iraq and Syria, with the latter giving tacit support and finance. The south-east remains under martial law. Since May 1993 the Turkish army has attempted to destroy the PKK by launching land and air raids against PKK bases in Syria and northern Iraq.

POLITICAL SYSTEM

A new constitution, extending the powers of the president, was approved in 1982. It provided for the separation of powers between the legislature, executive and judiciary, and the holding of free elections to the unicameral Grand National Assembly, which now has 550 members elected every five years.

Turkey is divided for administrative purposes into 76 *il* with subdivisions into *ilçe* and *nahiye*. Each *il* has a governor (*vali*) and elective council.

HEAD OF STATE

President, Süleyman Demirel, *elected by parliament for a seven-year term* 16 May 1993

CABINET *as at July 1998*

Prime Minister, Mesut Yilmaz (ANAP)
Deputy PM, Minister of State, Bülent Ecevit (DSP)
Deputy PM, National Defence, Ismet Sezgin (DTP)
Ministers of State, Güneş Taner (ANAP); Yücel Seçkiner (ANAP); Işilay Saygin (ANAP); Hikmet Sami Türk (DSP); Mehmet Salih Yildirim (ANAP); Rifat Serdaroğlu (DTP); Metin Gürdere (ANAP); Şükrü Sina Gürel (DSP); Ahat Andican (ANAP); Işin Çelebi (ANAP); Mustafa Yilmaz (DSP); Refaiddin Şahin (DTP); Burhan Kara (ANAP); Cavit Kavak (ANAP); Eyüp Aşik (ANAP); Rüstü Kazim Yücelen (ANAP); Hasan Gemici (DSP); Mehmet Batalli (DTP)
Agriculture and Rural Affairs, Mustafa Rustu Taşar (ANAP)
Culture, Istemihan Talay (DSP)
Education, Hikmet Uluğbay (DSP)
Energy and Natural Resources, Mustafa Cumhur Ersümer (ANAP)
Environment, Imren Aykut (ANAP)
Finance and Customs, Zekeriya Temizel (DSP)
Foreign Affairs, Ismail Cem (DSP)
Forestry, Ersin Taranoğlu (ANAP)
Health, Halil Ibrahim Özsoy (ANAP)
Interior, Murat Başeşkioglu (ANAP)
Justice, Oltan Sungurlu (ANAP)
Labour and Social Security, Nami Çağan (DSP)
Public Works and Housing, Yaşar Topçu (ANAP)
Tourism, Ibrahim Gürdal (ANAP)
Trade and Industry, Yalim Erez (Ind.)
Transport and Communications, Necdet Menzir (DTP)

ANAP Motherland Party; DSP Democratic Left Party; DTP Democratic Turkey Party; Ind. Independent

TURKISH EMBASSY
43 Belgrave Square, London SW1X 8PA
Tel 0171-393 0202
Ambassador Extraordinary and Plenipotentiary, HE Özdem Sanberk, apptd 1995
Minister Counsellor, Meli Mehmet Akat

BRITISH EMBASSY
Sehit Ersan Caddesi 46/A, Cankaya, Ankara
Tel: Ankara 468 6230/42
Ambassador Extraordinary and Plenipotentiary, HE David Logan, CMG, apptd 1997
Counsellor, Deputy Head of Mission, H. Mortimer
First Secretary, A. T. MacDermott *(Commercial)*
Defence and Military Attaché, Brig. A. V. Twiss
Consul-General (Istanbul), P. Hunt
CONSULATE-GENERAL – Istanbul
VICE-CONSULATE – Izmir
HONORARY CONSULATES – Antalya, Bodrum, Bursa, Iskenderun, Marmaris, Mersin

BRITISH COUNCIL DIRECTOR, C. Gobby, Esat Caddesi No:41, Kucukesat, Ankara 06660

BRITISH CHAMBER OF COMMERCE OF TURKEY INC., Mesrutiyet Caddessi No. 34, Tepebasi Beyoğlu, Istanbul (*postal address*, PO Box 190 Karaköy, Istanbul)

DEFENCE

The Army has 4,205 main battle tanks, 3,649 armoured personnel carriers and armoured infantry fighting vehicles, 4,274 artillery pieces and 38 attack helicopters. The Navy has 15 submarines, five destroyers, 16 frigates, 50 patrol and coastal vessels and 13 armed helicopters at eight bases. The Air Force has 501 combat aircraft.

Between 150,000 and 200,000 troops are stationed in the south-east of the country fighting Kurdish guerrillas.

Since its invasion of Cyprus in 1974, Turkey has maintained forces in the north of the island and at present has 30,000 men stationed there.

As a member of NATO, Turkey is host to the Headquarters Allied Land Forces South-Eastern Europe and the Sixth Allied Tactical Air Force Headquarters. US (3,034 personnel) and UK (230 personnel) air force detachments are based at Incirlik air base in southern Turkey to patrol the air exclusion zone over northern Iraq.

MILITARY EXPENDITURE – 3.9 per cent of GDP (1996)
MILITARY PERSONNEL – 821,200: Army 525,000, Navy 51,000, Air Force 63,000, Paramilitaries 182,200
CONSCRIPTION DURATION – 18 months

ECONOMY

Agricultural production accounts for some 15 per cent of GDP. About 50 per cent of the working population are in the rural sector. The principal crops are wheat, barley, rice, tobacco, sugar beet, tea, olives, grapes, figs and hazelnuts. Most of the crops are grown on the fertile littoral. Tobacco, sultana and fig cultivation is centred around Izmir, where substantial quantities of cotton are also grown. The main cotton area is in the Cukurova plain around Adana. The forests which lie between the littoral plain and the Anatolian plateau contain beech, pine, oak, elm, chestnut, lime, plane, alder, box, poplar and maple.

After agriculture, Turkey's most important industry is based on the considerable mineral wealth which is, however, relatively unexploited. The main export minerals are chromite and boron.

The bulk of the country's requirements in sugar, cotton, woollen and silk textiles, and cement, is produced locally. Other industries include vehicle assembly, paper, glass and glassware, iron and steel, leather and leather goods, sulphur refining, canning and rubber goods, soaps and cosmetics, pharmaceutical products, and prepared foodstuffs.

A customs union with the EU came into force on 1 January 1996 which was expected to boost the economy, although Greece has managed to suspend EU aid packages. A gas deal worth £14,800 million was signed with Iran in August 1996 which provided for a 20-year supply of Iranian gas.

GNP – US$177,530 million (1996); US$2,830 per capita (1996)
GDP – US$163,441 million (1994); US$2,227 per capita (1994)
ANNUAL AVERAGE GROWTH OF GDP – –3.0 per cent (1994)
INFLATION RATE – 80.3 per cent (1996)
UNEMPLOYMENT – 6.6 per cent (1995)
TOTAL EXTERNAL DEBT – US$79,789 million (1996)

TRADE

The main imports are machinery, crude oil and petroleum products, iron and steel, vehicles, medicines, chemicals and electrical appliances. Agricultural commodities (cotton, tobacco, fruits, nuts, livestock) represent 47 per cent of total exports. Other exports are minerals, textiles, glass and cement. Germany and the USA are the main trading partners.

In 1995 Turkey had a trade deficit of US$13,212 million and a current account deficit of US$2,339 million. In 1996 imports totalled US$42,465 million and exports US$23,083 million.

Trade with UK	1996	1997
Imports from UK	£1,565,938,000	£1,766,992,000
Exports to UK	932,876,000	1,043,429,000

COMMUNICATIONS

The rail network is run by the State Railways Administration. The total length of lines in operation (1993) is 10,386 km. In 1993, there were 59,770 km of roads. The Bosporus is spanned by two bridges; plans are being drawn up for a third fixed link between the two continents. The state airline (THY) operates all internal services and has services to Europe, the Far East, Africa, North America and the Middle East. Most of the leading European airlines operate services to Istanbul and some also to Ankara.

EDUCATION

Education is free and secular, and since August 1997, compulsory from the ages of six to 14. There are elementary, secondary and vocational schools. There are 27 universities in Turkey, including six in Istanbul, five in Ankara, two in Izmir, and one each in Erzurum and Trabzon.
ILLITERACY RATE – 17.7 per cent
ENROLMENT (percentage of age group) – primary 96 per cent (1994); secondary 50 per cent (1994); tertiary 18.2 per cent (1994)

CULTURE

Turkish was written in Arabic script until 1926 when a version of the Roman alphabet reflecting Turkish phonetics was substituted for use in official correspondence and in 1928 for universal use, with Arabic numerals as used throughout Europe. The revolution of 1908 led to the introduction of native literature free from foreign influences and adapted to the understanding of the people.

TURKMENISTAN
Turkmenostan Respublikasy

AREA – 188,456 sq. miles (488,100 sq. km). Neighbours: Iran, Afghanistan (south), Uzbekistan (east and north), Kazakhstan (north-west)
POPULATION – 3,808,900 (1998 estimate); 4,483,000 (1996 census): 77 per cent Turkoman, 9.2 per cent Uzbek, 6.7 per cent Russian, together with smaller numbers of Kazakhs, Tatars, Ukrainians and Armenians. Most of the population are Sunni Muslims. The main languages are Turkmenian (72 per cent), Russian (9 per cent), Uzbek (9 per cent). Turkmenian is one of the Turkic languages
CAPITAL – Ashkhabad (population, 407,000, 1990)
MAJOR CITIES – Chardzhou (164,000), Tashauz (114,000)
CURRENCY – Manat of 100 tenesi
NATIONAL DAY – 27–28 October (Independence Day)
NATIONAL FLAG – Green with a vertical carpet pattern near the hoist in black, white and wine-red; and in the lower part of the carpet design two laurel branches; in the upper hoist a crescent and five stars, all in white
LIFE EXPECTANCY (years) – male 61.80; female 68.40
POPULATION GROWTH RATE – 2.2 per cent (1995)
POPULATION DENSITY – 8 per sq. km (1995)
URBAN POPULATION – 45.2 per cent (1989)
MILITARY EXPENDITURE – 2.8 per cent of GDP (1996)
MILITARY PERSONNEL – 21,000: Army 18,000, Air Force 3,000
CONSCRIPTION DURATION – 24 months
ILLITERACY RATE – 0.3 per cent
ENROLMENT (percentage of age group) – tertiary 21.8 per cent (1990)

The republic comprises five regions: Ashkhabad; Chardjou; Krasnovodsk; Mary; and Tashauz. The country is a low-lying plain fringed by hills in the south. Ninety per cent of the plain is taken up by the Obe Kara-Kum (Black Sands) desert. The climate is hot and dry.

HISTORY AND POLITICS

Situated at the crossroads of Central Asia, the area that is now Turkmenistan has been invaded and occupied by many empires: Persian; Greek under Alexander the Great; Parthian; Mongol. A Turkmenian nation was established in the 15th century but remained riven with dissent and divided between warring emirates. From the early 19th century until 1886 Turkmenistan was gradually incorporated into the Russian Empire. Soviet control over Turkmenistan was established on 30 April 1918 when it became an Autonomous Soviet Socialist Republic. The banks, cotton refineries and oil and gas fields were nationalized before a civil war broke out in July 1918, sparked by the intervention of British troops from Iran and India. The war ended in 1920 with the withdrawal of the interventionist forces; Turkmenistan became a full republic of the Soviet Union in February 1925.

Turkmenistan declared its independence from the Soviet Union on 27 October 1991 and gained UN membership on 2 March 1992.

The autocratic government of President Niyazov has prevented any effective political opposition or free press through harassment and the continuation of authoritarianism. The political leadership has rejected political pluralism and instead a cult of personality has developed around President Niyazov. The Supreme Soviet voted on 30 December 1993 to extend the term of President Niyazov to 2002 and this was confirmed by a 99.99 per cent vote in a referendum on 15 January 1994. The Communist Party, renamed the Democratic Party, remains in power. Legislative elections to the *Khalk Maslakhaty* were won by the Democratic Party.

FOREIGN RELATIONS
In 1992 joint Turkmen–Russian armed forces of 34,000 army and air force personnel were established and remain in operation. In late 1993 Turkmen–Russian agreements were signed allowing Russian troops to protect the borders with Iran and Afghanistan; Russian citizens to undergo military training in Turkmenistan; Turkmen officers to train in Russia; and Turkmenistan to bear the cost of Russian forces in the country. Agreement on dual citizenship for ethnic Russians in Turkmenistan was also reached. In December 1993 Turkmenistan signed the CIS charter to become a full CIS member and in January 1994 became a member of the CIS economic union.

POLITICAL SYSTEM
The 1992 constitution declares the president head of state and government. The legislature is the 50-member *Majlis* (formerly the Supreme Soviet). The *Khalk Maslakhaty* (People's Council) is a supervisory body with no legislative powers.

HEAD OF STATE
President, Saparmurad Niyazov, *elected* 27 October 1990, *re-elected* 21 June 1992, *appointed head of government* 18 May 1992, *elected by referendum for an eight-year term* 15 January 1994

COUNCIL OF MINISTERS *as at July 1998*
Prime Minister, The President
Deputy PM, Agriculture and Food Processing, Pirkuly Odeyev
Deputy PM, Culture, Orazgeldi Aydogdiyev

Deputy PM, Education, Muhamed Abalakhov
Deputy PM, Energy and Industry, Saparmurat Nuryev
Deputy PM, Foreign Affairs, Boris Shikhmuradov
Deputy PM, Foreign Investment, Elly Gurbanmuradov
Deputy PM, Land Reclamation and Water Resources, Aleksandr
    Dodonov
Deputy PM, Social Security, Eylaman Shihiev
Deputy PMs, Rejep Saparov; Hudaykul Halykov
Agriculture, Ata Nobadov
Chairman, Committee for National Security, Muhamed
    Nazarov
Communications, Rovshan Kerkabov
Consumer Goods, Djamal Geklenova
Defence, Lt.-Gen. Danatar Kopekov
Economy, Matkarim Rajapov
Education, Ashyr Orazov
Foreign Economic Relations, Toily Kurbanov
Health and the Pharmaceutical Industry, Gurbanguli
    Berdymuhamedov
Interior, Gurban Kasimov
Justice, Tagandurdy Halliev
Motor Transport, Senakula Rakhmonov
Natural Resources and Environmental Protection, Pirdjan
    Kurbanov
Oil and Mineral Resources, Rejap Arazov
Trade and Resources, Khalnazar Agakhanov

EMBASSY OF TURKMENISTAN
2nd Floor South, St George's House, 14/17 Wells Street,
London WIP 3FP
Tel 0171-255 1071
Ambassador Extraordinary and Plenipotentiary, HE Murad
    Chariev, apptd 1997

BRITISH EMBASSY
3rd Floor, Office Building, Ak Altin Plaza Hotel, Ashkhabad
Ambassador Extraordinary and Plenipotentiary, HE Fraser
    Wilson, MBE, apptd 1998

ECONOMY

The large reserves of natural gas and the foreign revenue
that they earn make the country economically viable and
have enabled the government to maintain low stable prices
for basic commodities and utilities.

The principal industries are cotton cultivation, stock-
raising and mineral extraction, together with natural gas
production and the long-established silk industry. Some
fisheries exist along the Caspian Sea coast. Arable land is
irrigated by the Niyazov canal, which cuts through the
Kara Kum desert. There are estimated reserves of some
700 million tonnes of oil and 8,000,000 million cubic
metres of natural gas. Natural gas is exported by pipeline to
Ukraine and western Europe, although exports were
suspended between March 1997 and February 1998
following a dispute with Russia, which controls the pipeline. A pipeline through Iran and Turkey was opened in
December 1997, and a further pipeline to Pakistan is under
construction. There have been disagreements between
Azerbaijan and Turkmenistan over rights to Caspian oil
deposits.

In 1997 GDP fell by 15 per cent, and monthly inflation
was at 6.5 per cent in the first quarter of 1998.

GNP – US$4,319 million (1996); US$940 per capita (1996)
GDP – US$7,415 million (1994); US$2,023 per capita
    (1994)
TOTAL EXTERNAL DEBT – US$825 million (1996)

TRADE WITH UK	1996	1997
Imports from UK	£6, 265,000	£10,679,000
Exports to UK	619,000	1,912,000

TUVALU

AREA – 10 sq. miles (26 sq. km)
POPULATION – 10,000 (1994 UN estimate). About 1,500
Tuvaluans work overseas, mostly in Nauru, or as
seamen. The people are almost entirely Polynesian. The
principal languages are Tuvaluan and English. The
entire population is Christian, predominantly
Protestant
CAPITAL – ΨFunafuti (population, 2,856)
CURRENCY – The Australian dollar ($A) of 100 cents is
legal tender. In addition there are Tuvalu dollar and cent
coins in circulation
NATIONAL ANTHEM – Tuvalu Mo Te Atua (Tuvalu for
the Almighty)
NATIONAL DAY – 1 October (Independence Day)
NATIONAL FLAG – Light blue ground with Union flag in
top left quarter and nine five-pointed gold stars in the fly
POPULATION GROWTH RATE – 2.1 per cent (1995)
POPULATION DENSITY – 385 per sq. km (1995)

Tuvalu comprises nine coral atolls situated in the south-
west Pacific around the point at which the International
Date Line cuts the Equator. Few of the atolls are more than
12 ft above sea level or more than half a mile in width. The
vegetation consists mainly of coconut palms.

HISTORY AND POLITICS

Tuvalu, formerly the Ellice Islands, formed part of the
Gilbert and Ellice Islands Colony until 1 October 1975,
when separate constitutions came into force. Separation
from the Gilbert Islands was implemented on 1 January
1976. On 1 October 1978 Tuvalu became a fully independent state within the Commonwealth.

In April 1998, Prime Minister Bikenibeu Paeniu was
sworn in for a second term of office.

POLITICAL SYSTEM

The constitution provides for a prime minister and four
other ministers, who must be members of the 12-member
parliament. The prime minister presides at meetings of the
Cabinet, which consists of the five Ministers and is
attended by the Attorney-General. Local government
services are provided by elected Island Councils.

Governor-General, Sir Tulaga Manuella

CABINET *as at July 1998*
Prime Minister, Foreign Affairs, Bikenibeu Paeniu
*Deputy PM, Natural Resources, Environment, Home Affairs, Rural
    Development,* Kokeiya Malua
Health, Women's and Community Affairs, Education and Culture,
    Ionatana Ionatana
Tourism, Trade, Commerce and Finance, Alesana Kleis Seluka
Works, Energy and Communications, Otinielu Tauteleimalae
    Tausi

BRITISH HIGH COMMISSIONER, HE Michael Peart, CMG,
    LVO, resident at Suva, Fiji

ECONOMY

Most people still practise a subsistence economy, the main
staples of the diet being coconuts and fish. The main
imports are foodstuffs, consumer goods and building
materials. The only export is copra, though philatelic sales
provide a major source of revenue and handicraft sales are
increasing. However, Tuvalu is almost entirely dependent
on foreign aid. In August 1998, Tuvalu signed a deal worth
several million US dollars with a Canadian media com-

pany, granting rights to use the country's internet suffix of ".tv".

Funafuti has a grass strip airfield from which a service operates regularly to Fiji and Kiribati, and is also the only port.

GDP – US$7 million (1994); US$924 per capita (1994)

TRADE WITH UK	1996	1997
Imports from UK	£306,000	£210,000
Exports to UK	584,000	3,000

SOCIAL WELFARE

All islands are served by a dispensary and a primary school. A maritime training school caters for 60 boys a year. There is a 30-bed hospital at Funafuti.

UGANDA
Republic of Uganda

AREA – 93,065 sq. miles (241,038 sq. km). Neighbours: Democratic Republic of Congo (west), Sudan (north), Kenya (east), Tanzania and Rwanda (south)

POPULATION – 21,297,000 (1994 UN estimate). The official language is English. The main local vernaculars are of Bantu, Nilotic and Hamitic origins. Ki-Swahili is generally understood

CAPITAL – Kampala (population, 750,000, 1990)

MAJOR CITIES – Jinja (45,000); Masaka (29,000); Mbale (28,000)

CURRENCY – Uganda shilling of 100 cents

NATIONAL ANTHEM – Oh Uganda

NATIONAL DAY – 9 October (Independence Day)

NATIONAL FLAG – Six horizontal stripes of black, yellow, red, with a white disc in the centre containing the badge of a crested crane

LIFE EXPECTANCY (years) – male 43.57; female 46.19

POPULATION GROWTH RATE – 3.4 per cent (1995)

POPULATION DENSITY – 88 per sq. km (1995)

URBAN POPULATION – 11.3 per cent (1991)

MILITARY EXPENDITURE – 2.1 per cent of GDP (1996)

MILITARY PERSONNEL – 50,600: Ugandan Peoples' Defence Force 50,000, Paramilitaries 600

Large parts of Lakes Victoria, Edward and Albert (Mobuto) are within Uganda's boundaries, as are Lakes Kyoga, Kwania, George and Bisina (formerly Salisbury) and the course of the River Nile from its outlet from Lake Victoria to the Sudan border at Nimule.

Despite its tropical location, the climate is tempered by its situation some 3,000 ft above sea level, and well over that altitude in the highlands of the Western and Eastern Regions. Uganda has three National Parks and a fourth (Lake Mburo) has been designated.

HISTORY AND POLITICS

Uganda became an independent state within the Commonwealth on 9 October 1962, after some 70 years of British rule. A republic was instituted in 1967, under an executive president assisted by a Cabinet of Ministers.

Early in 1971 an army coup took place and Maj.-Gen. Idi Amin, the army commander, proclaimed himself head of state. In 1979, following uprisings and military intervention by Tanzania, President Amin was overthrown. Dr Milton Obote became president in 1980 but was ousted by a military coup in 1985. A military council was installed but the National Resistance Movement led by Yoweri Museveni captured Kampala in January 1986, securing

control of the rest of the country in the following few months. Yoweri Museveni was sworn in as president in January 1986.

President Museveni won the first direct presidential election on 9 May 1996. Supporters of the president won a majority of seats in legislative elections on 27 June. The ban on political party activity will continue until 2000.

POLITICAL SYSTEM

A Constituent Assembly was elected in March 1994 to draft a new constitution. The constitution, promulgated on 8 October 1995, endorsed the existing non-party political system. The legislature, the 276-seat National Assembly, is elected for a four-year term.

HEAD OF STATE
President, Yoweri Museveni, *sworn in* 29 January 1986, *elected* 9 May 1996
Vice-President, Agriculture, Animal Husbandry and Fisheries, Speciosa Wandira Kazibwe

CABINET *as at July 1998*
The President
The Vice-President
Prime Minister, Kintu Musoke
First Deputy PM, Foreign Affairs, Eriya Kategaya
Second Deputy PM, Tourism, Trade and Industry, Brig. Moses Ali
Attorney-General, Bart Katureebe
Education and Sports, Apollo Nsibambi
Energy and Minerals, Richard Kaijuka
Finance, Planning and Economic Development, Gerald Sendawula
Gender, Labour and Social Development, Janet B. Mukwaya
Health, Dr Crispus W. C. B. Kiyonga
Internal Affairs, Maj. Tom Butiime
Justice and Constitutional Affairs, Joash Mayanja-Nkangi
Local Government, Jaberi Bidandi-Ssali
Public Service, Amanya Mushega
Water, Lands and Environment, Henry Muganwa Kajura
Works, Housing and Communications, John Nassasira

UGANDA HIGH COMMISSION
Uganda House, 58–59 Trafalgar Square, London WC2N 5DX
Tel 0171–839 5783
High Commissioner, HE Prof. George Kirya, apptd 1990
Deputy High Commissioner, D. Ssozi
Minister Counsellor, E. Byaruhanga
Financial Attaché, A. Bamweyana

BRITISH HIGH COMMISSION
10–12 Parliament Avenue, PO Box 7070, Kampala
Tel: Kampala 257054/9
High Commissioner, HE Michael Cook, apptd 1997
Deputy High Commissioner, P. Rouse, MBE
Defence Adviser, Lt.-Col. C. Thom, OBE

BRITISH COUNCIL DIRECTOR, R. Wilkins (*Cultural Attaché*)

ECONOMY

Since 1988 the government has been successful in implementing an IMF recovery programme that has reduced the army and civil service, encouraged foreign investment, and returned property to Asians expelled by Idi Amin. A World Bank debt relief programme was implemented in April 1998 and will reduce Uganda's foreign debt by US$388 million. In November 1997, the IMF approved a US$138 million loan, and in April 1998 the IMF and the World Bank agreed to grant Uganda debt relief totalling some US$360 million.

The principal export earners are coffee, tobacco, cocoa, cotton and tea. Hydroelectricity is produced from the Owen Falls power station, some of which is exported to Kenya. The principal food crops are plantains, sugar cane, bananas, cassava, maize and sorghum; livestock raising and inshore fishing are also important.

In 1995 Uganda had a trade deficit of US$318 million and a current account deficit of US$276 million. In 1996 imports totalled US$1,188 million and exports US$604 million.

GNP – US$5,826 million (1996); US$300 per capita (1996)
GDP – US$4,930 million (1994); US$255 per capita (1994)
ANNUAL AVERAGE GROWTH OF GDP – 10.0 per cent (1995)
INFLATION RATE – 7.2 per cent (1996)
TOTAL EXTERNAL DEBT – US$3,674 million (1996)

TRADE WITH UK	1996	1997
Imports from UK	£50,751,000	£52,121,000
Exports to UK	14,867,000	20,147,000

COMMUNICATIONS

There is an international airport at Entebbe, and eight other airfields around the country. Having no sea coast, Uganda is dependent upon rail and road links to Mombasa and Dar es Salaam for its trade. There are more than 27,000 km of roads. A railway network joins the capital to the western, eastern and northern centres.

EDUCATION

Education is a joint undertaking by the government, local authorities and voluntary agencies. In 1995 Uganda had an estimated 7,905 primary schools, 774 secondary schools, and various technical training institutions and universities.
ILLITERACY RATE – 38.2 per cent
ENROLMENT (percentage of age group) – tertiary 1.5 per cent (1994)

UKRAINE
Ukraina

AREA – 233,090 sq. miles (603,700 sq. km). Neighbours: Belarus (north), Russia (north and east), Romania and Moldova (south-west), Hungary, Slovakia and Poland (west)
POPULATION – 50,500,000 (1998 estimate); 51,471,000 (1989 census): 73 per cent Ukrainian, 22 per cent Russian, with smaller numbers of Jews, Belarusians, Moldovans, Tatars, Poles, Hungarians and Greeks. The two main religions are Roman Catholicism and Orthodox. The Orthodox rite is divided between the Russian Orthodox Church with its Patriarch in Moscow and the Autocephalous Orthodox Church of the Ukraine with its own Patriarch in Kiev. There are also large numbers of Reformed Protestants in the Transcarpathian region and a sizeable Jewish community in Kiev. The main languages are Ukrainian (73 per cent) and Russian (22 per cent). Ukrainian is an Eastern Slavonic language related to Russian and Belarusian
CAPITAL – Kiev (population, 2,646,100, 1993)
MAJOR CITIES – Dnepropetrovsk (1,185,500); Donetsk (1,121,200); Kharkov (1,615,000); ΨOdessa (1,086,700), 1993 estimates
CURRENCY – Hryvna of 100 kopiykas
NATIONAL DAY – 24 August (Independence Day)

NATIONAL FLAG – Two horizontal stripes of blue over yellow
LIFE EXPECTANCY (years) – male 63.50; female 73.70
POPULATION GROWTH RATE – −0.1 per cent (1995)
POPULATION DENSITY – 86 per sq. km (1995)
URBAN POPULATION – 67.9 per cent (1993)
ILLITERACY RATE – 1.2 per cent
ENROLMENT (percentage of age group) – tertiary 40.6 per cent (1993)

The area of the present Ukraine is larger than that of the Ukrainian Soviet Republic formed in 1917–19 because of the westward territorial expansion of the former Soviet Union in the 1939–45 period and the addition of the Crimea from Russia in 1954. Ukraine now consists of 25 regions: Cherkassy, Chernigov, Chernovtsy, Crimea, Dnepropetrovsk, Donetsk, Ivano-Frankovsk, Kharkov, Kherson, Khmelnitsky, Kiev, Kirovograd, Lugansk, Lvov, Nikolayev, Odessa, Poltava, Rovno, Sumy, Ternopol, Transcarpathia, Vinnitsa, Volhynia, Zaporozhye and Zhitomir.

Most of Ukraine forms a plain with small elevations. The Carpathian mountains lie in the south-western part of the republic. The main rivers are the Dnieper with its tributaries, the Southern Bug and the Northern Donets (a tributary of the Don). The climate is moderate with relatively mild winters (particularly in the south-west) and hot summers.

HISTORY AND POLITICS

The earliest Russian state was formed in the middle reaches of the Dnieper River with its capital at Kiev in the ninth century AD. The state united the two large Slav states of Kiev and Novgorod and established the first common Russian language and nationality. The state lasted until Kiev fell to the Mongols in 1240. For the next four centuries Ukraine was invaded and ruled by Tatars, Turks, Poles, Hungarians and Lithuanians. In 1648 the Ukrainians threw off Polish rule to become independent and increasingly allied with Russia (formerly Muscovy). During the reign of Catherine the Great of Russia (1763–96) Ukraine and the Crimea came under Russian control.

By the time of the Treaty of Brest-Litovsk in March 1918, most of Ukraine had been occupied by German and Austrian forces. The Treaty forced the Soviet government in Moscow to cede parts of western Ukraine to Germany and Austria-Hungary and accept the independence of the remainder. After the defeat of Germany in 1918, Ukraine became a battleground in the Russian civil war before the imposition of Soviet rule in 1922. Ukraine became a constituent republic of the USSR on 30 December 1922.

Ukraine declared itself independent of the Soviet Union, subject to a referendum, after the failed Moscow coup in August 1991. The referendum was held on 1 December 1991 and 90 per cent of the electorate voted for independence.

Political power in Ukraine in 1991–4 rested with the former Communists, led by President Leonid Kravchuk, in loose alliance with the Rukh nationalist party. This limited political and economic change, although Leonid Kuchma, prime minister 1992–3, began to introduce economic reforms. Kuchma resigned in September 1993 after the Supreme Council obstructed his reform programme and Kravchuk effectively took over the government.

In the June 1994 presidential election Kuchma defeated President Kravchuk. A power struggle soon developed between President Kuchma and the Supreme Council. Kuchma's reformist government lost a no confidence vote in the Supreme Council but the president refused to dismiss it, and in June 1995 secured the passing of a 'constitutional treaty' by the Supreme Council. This gives the president the power to appoint the government without reference to the Supreme Council and allows greater presidential power to rule by decree. These changes were incorporated into a new constitution adopted in June 1996. The constitution also provides for the Supreme Council to be renamed the People's Council (*Narodna Rada*) and for the creation of a Constitutional Court. Following a constitutional amendment in September 1997, half of the 450 Supreme Council seats are to be elected from single-seat constituencies by a simple majority, and the other 225 are to be filled by proportional representation from party lists, with a 4 per cent barrier for representation.

In legislative elections held in March 1998, the Communist Party of Ukraine won 119 seats, well short of an overall majority, but making it the largest party in the legislature. The Popular Democratic Party won 84 seats, and the People's Movement of Ukraine 46. OSCE observers noted serious shortcomings in the electoral process, including violence and discrimination against certain candidates that 'raise[d] questions about the neutrality of the state apparatus in the election'.

INSURGENCIES

The Crimean parliament voted to make Crimea an autonomous republic in September 1991, which was accepted by Kiev, but then voted for independence in May 1992, which was not accepted, and was suspended. A Russian nationalist, Yuri Meshkov, was elected President of Crimea in January 1994 and the Crimean parliament in May 1994 restored the suspended 1992 constitution declaring sovereignty. A constitutional and political crisis in Crimea caused by a power struggle between President Meshkov and the Crimean parliament from September 1994 onwards was resolved by Ukrainian intervention in March 1995. Direct presidential rule over Crimea was imposed in April 1995, to be lifted in August following elections to the Crimean parliament which saw a dramatic drop in support for pro-Russian parties. Arkady Demydenko was appointed Prime Minister of Crimea on 26 February 1996.

A referendum in June 1994 in the Donbass region of eastern Ukraine in favour of closer economic ties with Russia and making Russian an official language was overwhelmingly passed, as was one in the Crimea in favour of dual Russian–Ukrainian citizenship.

FOREIGN RELATIONS

Since the demise of the Soviet Union, Russia and Ukraine have clashed over defence issues. All strategic nuclear weapons were placed under a central CIS command in December 1991, but on the abolition of the central command in July 1993 the government claimed possession of all nuclear weapons on its territory. Despite international pressure, the Supreme Council only ratified the START I Treaty in February 1994 and the Nuclear Non-Proliferation Treaty in November 1994.

Under a January 1994 USA–Russia–Ukraine Treaty, Ukraine agreed to transfer its nuclear arsenal to Russia for dismantling over a seven-year period. This was completed in May 1996. In return Ukraine has received a territorial guarantee from Russia, a cancellation of a large part of its debt to Russia, and nuclear security guarantees from Russia and the USA. Ukraine will also receive low-grade uranium from Russia for use in its power stations; and economic and technical aid from the USA.

In May 1997, a treaty of friendship and co-operation was signed with Russia. Agreement was also reached over the division of the former Soviet Black Sea Fleet. Russia is to gain four-fifths of the fleet and will rent most of the port of Sevastopol. The rent will be used to pay off part of Ukraine's debt to Russia.

In February 1998, a treaty on economic co-operation was signed between Ukraine and Russia which will increase trade between them by up to US$2 billion. It was announced in September 1997 that there would be annual summits for EU-Ukraine relations.

HEAD OF STATE

President, Leonid Kuchma, *elected* 10 July 1994, *sworn in* 19 July 1994

CABINET *as at July 1998*

Prime Minister, Valery Pustovoitenko
First Deputy PM, Anatoly Holubchenko
Deputy PMs, Serhiy Tyhypko (*Economy*); Valery Smoly (*Humanitarian Issues*); Mykola Bilobotskyy (*Social Policy*)
Agro-Industrial Complex, Borys Supikhanov
Chairman, Supreme Soviet, Alexander Moroz
Coal Industry, Stanislav Yanko
Culture and Art, Dmytro Ostapenko
Defence, Gen. Oleksandr Kuzmuk
Economy, Vasyl Rohovy
Education, Mykhailo Zgurovsky
Emergency Situations and Protection of the Population Against the Consequences of the Chernobyl Accident, Valery Kalchenko
Energy, Oleksiy Sheberstov
Environmental Protection, vacant
Family and Youth Affairs, Valentyna Dovzhenko
Finance, Ihor Mityukov
Foreign Affairs, Boris Tarasyuk
Health, Andriy Serdiuk
Industrial Policy, Vasyl Hureyev
Information, Zynovy Kulyk
Interior, Yurii Kravchenko
Justice, Syuzanna Stanik
Labour and Social Policy, Ivan Sakhan
Power Engineering, Alexei Shebevstov
Transport, Valery Cherep
Without Portfolio, Anatoly Tolstoukhov

There are also 20 heads of state committees.

UKRAINIAN EMBASSY
78 Kensington Park Road, London WII 2PL
Tel 0171-727 6312
Ambassador Extraordinary and Plenipotentiary, HE Volodimir Vassylenko, apptd 1998
Minister Plenipotentiary, Y. Kyrylenko

BRITISH EMBASSY
252025 Kiev Desyatinna 9
Tel: Kiev 462 0011
Ambassador Extraordinary and Plenipotentiary, HE Roy Reeve, apptd 1995
Consul-General and Deputy Head of Mission, S. Butt
Defence Attaché, Capt. L. Merrick
First Secretary (Commercial), T. Abbott-Watt

BRITISH COUNCIL DIRECTOR – M. Bird, 9/1 Bessarabska Ploshcha, Flat 9, Kiev 252004

DEFENCE

The Army has 4,063 main battle tanks, 4,842 armoured personnel carriers and armoured infantry fighting vehicles, 3,764 artillery pieces and 270 attack helicopters. The Navy has three submarines, four principal surface combat vessels and nine patrol and coastal vessels at six bases. The Air Force has 790 combat aircraft and 24 attack helicopters.
MILITARY EXPENDITURE – 3.0 per cent of GDP (1996)

MILITARY PERSONNEL – 337,900: Army 161,500, Navy 16,000, Air Force 124,400, Paramilitaries 36,000
CONSCRIPTION DURATION – 18 months to two years

ECONOMY

The Communist-led government of 1991–4 was characterized by economic mismanagement and opposition to economic reforms. The economy came close to collapse because of hyperinflation caused by the printing of money to support uneconomic enterprises, industrial output and GDP fell dramatically, and Russia threatened to cut all oil and gas supplies as Ukraine could not pay in hard currency. Ukraine has joined the CIS economic union as an associate member and is likely to seek full membership for access to better trading relations with Russia.

President Kuchma has introduced a wide-ranging economic reform programme. Ukraine has received large amounts of foreign aid in support of this programme and for the closure of the Chernobyl nuclear plant which suffered a partial meltdown in 1986. An aid package worth US$3 billion was approved by international donors in October 1996 and in August 1997 the IMF approved a stand-by credit of more than US$500 million, subject to the implementation of economic austerity measures.

Ukraine is still in disagreement with Russia over the division of assets and debts of the former Soviet Union. A large proportion of Ukraine's debt to Russia has been paid by granting Russian enterprises shares in Ukrainian firms which are to be privatized; the remainder of the debt has been rescheduled. Russia accounts for 40 per cent of Ukraine's trade turnover and supplies all its oil needs and more than half of its industrial raw materials and components. Agreement was reached with Turkey in June 1997 to build an oil pipeline which will reduce Ukraine's dependence on Russia. In May 1998 Ukraine signed an agreement with the USA allowing it to import the technology necessary to modernize its nuclear power industry.

The southern part of the country contains a coal-mining and iron and steel industrial area which was the largest in the former Soviet Union. Ukraine also contains engineering and chemical industries and ship-building yards on the Black Sea coast. Ukrainian agricultural production is good with large areas under cultivation with wheat, cotton, flax and sugar beet; stock-raising is very important. There are large deposits of coal and salt in the Donets Basin, of iron ore in Krivoy Rog and near Kerch in the Crimea, of manganese in Nikopol, and of quicksilver in Nikitovka.

The major ports are Odessa, Nikolayev, Kerch and Sevastopol.

In 1995 there was a trade deficit of US$2,702 million and a current account deficit of US$1,152 million. Imports totalled US$11,379 million and exports US$11,567 million.

GNP – US$60,904 million (1996); US$1,200 per capita (1996)
GDP – US$131,195 million (1994); US$339 per capita (1994)
INFLATION RATE – 80.3 per cent (1996)
TOTAL EXTERNAL DEBT – US$9,335 million (1996)

TRADE WITH UK	1996	1997
Imports from UK	£141,896,000	£164,777,000
Exports to UK	23,875,000	38,777,000

UNITED ARAB EMIRATES
Al-Imarat Al-Arabiya Al-Muttahida

AREA – 32,278 sq. miles (83,600 sq. km) approximately.
   Neighbours: Oman (north-east and east), Saudi Arabia (south and west), Qatar (north-west)
POPULATION – 2,377,453 (1995), of which 75 per cent are expatriates. The official language is Arabic, and English is widely spoken. The established religion is Islam
CAPITAL – Abu Dhabi (population, 450,000)
CURRENCY – UAE dirham (Dh) of 100 fils
NATIONAL DAY – 2 December
NATIONAL FLAG – Horizontal stripes of green over white over black with vertical red stripe in the hoist
LIFE EXPECTANCY (years) – male 72.95; female 75.27
POPULATION GROWTH RATE – 6.5 per cent (1995)
POPULATION DENSITY – 28 per sq. km (1995)

The United Arab Emirates is situated in the south-east of the Arabian peninsula. Six of the emirates lie on the shore of the Gulf between the Musandam peninsula in the east and the Qatar peninsula in the west while the seventh, Fujairah, lies on the Gulf of Oman. The climate varies between hot and humid in May to September and mild with erratic rainfall in October to April.

HISTORY AND POLITICS

The United Arab Emirates (formerly the Trucial States) is composed of seven emirates (Abu Dhabi, Ajman, Dubai, Fujairah, Ras al-Khaimah, Sharjah and Umm al-Qaiwain) which came together as an independent state on 2 December 1971 when they ended their individual special treaty relationships with the British government (Ras al-Khaimah joined the other six on 10 February 1972). On independence, the Union Government assumed full responsibility for all internal and external affairs apart from some internal matters that remained the prerogative of the individual emirates.

FOREIGN RELATIONS

Relations with Iran remain strained over Iran's illegal occupation of three UAE islands in the Gulf (Abu Musa and the Two Tunbs).

POLITICAL SYSTEM

Overall authority lies with the Supreme Council of the seven emirate rulers, each of whom also governs in his own territory. The president and vice-president are elected every five years by the Supreme Council from among its members. The Supreme Council appoints the Council of Ministers. A 40-member Federal National Council, drawn proportionally from each emirate and composed of appointees of the rulers, studies draft laws referred to it by the Council of Ministers.

The legal system consists of both secular and religious courts guided by the Islamic philosophy of justice. Individual emirates retain their own penal codes and courts alongside a federal court system and penal code.

FEDERAL STRUCTURE

Each emirate has its separate government, with Abu Dhabi having an executive council chaired by the Crown Prince.

Emirate	Area (sq. km)	Population (1995)
Abu Dhabi	80,000	928,360
Ajman	259	118,812
Dubai	3,900	674,101
Fujairah	1,300	76,254
Ras al-Khaimah	1,700	144,430
Sharjah	2,600	400,339
Umm al-Qaiwain	777	35,157

HEAD OF STATE

President, HH Sheikh Zayed bin Sultan al-Nahyan (*Abu Dhabi*), *elected* 1971, *re-elected* 1976, 1981, 1986, 1991, October 1996

Vice-President, Prime Minister, HH Sheikh Maktoum bin Rashid al-Maktoum (*Dubai*)

SUPREME COUNCIL

The President
The Vice-President
HH Sheikh Sultan bin Mohammed al-Qassimi (*Sharjah*)
HH Sheikh Saqr bin Mohammed al-Qassimi (*Ras Al-Khaimah*)
HH Sheikh Hamad bin Mohammed al-Sharqi (*Fujairah*)
HH Sheikh Humaid bin Rashid al-Nuaimi (*Ajman*)
HH Sheikh Rashid bin Ahmad al-Mualla (*Umm al-Qaiwain*)

COUNCIL OF MINISTERS *as at July 1998*

The Vice-President
Deputy PM, Sheikh Sultan bin Zayed al-Nahyan
Agriculture and Fisheries, Saeed Mohammed al-Raqabani
Communications, Ahmed Humaid al-Tayir
Defence, HH Gen. Sheikh Mohammed bin Rashid al-Maktoum
Economy and Commerce, HH Sheikh Fahim bin Sultan al-Qassimi
Education and Youth, Ali Abd al-Aziz al-Sharhan
Electricity and Water, Humaid bin Nasir al-Uways
Finance and Industry, HE Sheikh Hamdan bin Rashid al-Maktoum
Foreign Affairs, Rashid Abdullah al-Nuaimi
Health, Hamad Abdul Rahman al-Madfa
Higher Education and Scientific Research, HH Sheikh Nahyan bin Mubarak al-Nahyan
Information and Culture, HH Sheikh Abdullah bin Zayed al-Nahyan
Interior, Lt.-Gen. Mohammed Saeed al-Badi
Justice, Islamic Affairs and Awqaf (Religious Endowments), Mohammed Nakhira al-Dhahiri
Labour and Social Affairs, Matar Humaid al-Tayir
Minister of State for Cabinet Affairs, Saeed Khalfan al-Ghaith
Minister of State for Finance and Industrial Affairs, Dr Mohammed Khalfan bin Kharbash
Minister of State for Foreign Affairs, Sheikh Hamdan bin Zayed al-Nahyan
Minister of State for Supreme Council Affairs, Sheikh Majid bin Saeed al-Nuaimi
Petroleum and Mineral Resources, Ubayd bin Sayf al-Nasiri
Planning, Sheikh Humaid bin Ahmed al-Mualla
Public Works and Housing, Rakadh bin Salem al-Rakadh

EMBASSY OF THE UNITED ARAB EMIRATES

30 Princes Gate, London SW7 1PT
Tel 0171-581 1281
Ambassador Extraordinary and Plenipotentiary, HE Easa Saleh Al-Gurg, CBE, apptd 1991
Military Attaché, Col. B. S. B. Al-Noaimi
Cultural Attaché, A. Al-Marri

BRITISH EMBASSIES

PO Box 248, Abu Dhabi
Tel: Abu Dhabi 326600
Ambassador Extraordinary and Plenipotentiary, HE Anthony Harris, CMG, LVO, apptd 1994
Counsellor and Deputy Head of Mission, G. Pirnie
Defence and Military Attaché, Col. T. Dumas, OBE

PO Box 65, Dubai
Tel: Dubai 521070
Counsellor and Consul-General, N. Armour
Deputy Head of Post, H. Dunnachie, MBE

BRITISH COUNCIL REPRESENTATIVES

Abu Dhabi – R. Sykes, PO Box 46523, Abu Dhabi
Dubai – G. McCulloch (*Cultural Attaché*)

DEFENCE

The Army has 231 main battle tanks, 1,003 armoured personnel carriers and armoured infantry fighting vehicles, and 257 artillery pieces. The Navy has 19 patrol and coastal vessels. The Air Force has 108 combat aircraft and 42 armed helicopters.

MILITARY EXPENDITURE – 4.8 per cent of GDP (1996)
MILITARY PERSONNEL – 64,500: Army 59,000, Navy 1,500, Air Force 4,000

ECONOMY

The UAE is the Gulf's third largest oil producer after Saudi Arabia and Iran, with oil reserves of 200,000 million barrels and gas reserves of 200,000,000 million cubic feet. Oil production in 1995 accounted for 33 per cent of GDP. Other important sectors of the economy are government, re-exporting, construction, manufacturing (aluminium, cement, chemicals, fertilizers, ship repair), finance and insurance services, and transport and communications. Tourism is growing in importance, with 1,919,000 visitors in 1994. Agricultural production (vegetables, dates, fruit, eggs, flowers, olives, animal husbandry) has increased due to large-scale water desalination and irrigation projects, with 250,000 hectares of agricultural land in 1996. There is no personal or corporate taxation apart from on oil companies and foreign banks.

Fifteen major ports, of which nine are modern container terminals, handled 35 million tonnes of cargo in 1993. Six international airports (Dubai, Abu Dhabi, Sharjah, Ras al-Khaimah, Fujairah, Al Ain) are in operation.

Oil revenues over the past 30 years have enabled the government to invest heavily in education, health and social services, housing, transport and communications infrastructure, and agriculture, and enabled the UAE's citizens to have one of the highest GDPs per capita in the world.

GNP – US$42,806 million (1995); US$17,400 per capita (1995)
GDP – US$34,461 million (1994); US$20,654 per capita (1994)
ANNUAL AVERAGE GROWTH OF GDP – 2.7 per cent (1992)

Trade with UK	1996	1997
Imports from UK	£1,394,106,000	£1,546,747,000
Exports to UK	380,903,000	515,698,000

EDUCATION AND SOCIAL WELFARE

In 1995–6 there were 615 government schools, where education is free; and 390 private schools. The Emirates University is based at Al Ain (Abu Dhabi); there are also three Colleges of Technology (Abu Dhabi, Dubai, Al Ain). There were 36 government and 14 private hospitals in 1996.

ILLITERACY RATE – 15.4 per cent
ENROLMENT (percentage of age group) – primary 83 per
cent (1994); secondary 71 per cent (1994); tertiary 8.8 per
cent (1993)

UNITED STATES OF AMERICA

AREA – 3,540,321 sq. miles (9,169,389 sq. km). Neighbours:
Canada (north), Mexico (south)
POPULATION – 263,034,000 (1996 estimate). The language
is English. There is a significant Spanish-speaking
minority
CAPITAL – Washington DC (population, 7,051,495, 1992).
The area of the District of Columbia (with which the
City of Washington is considered co-extensive) is 61 sq.
miles, with a resident population (1992 estimate) of
585,221. The District of Columbia is governed by an
elected mayor and City Council
MAJOR CITIES –ΨChicago (2,721,547); Dallas (1,053,292);
ΨDetroit (1,000,272); ΨHouston (1,744,058); ΨLos
Angeles (3,553,638); ΨNew York (7,380,906);
ΨPhiladelphia (1,478,002); Phoenix (1,159,014); San
Antonio (1,067,816); ΨSan Diego (1,171,121), 1996
estimates
CURRENCY – US dollar (US$) of 100 cents
NATIONAL ANTHEM – The Star-Spangled Banner
NATIONAL DAY – 4 July (Independence Day)
NATIONAL FLAG – Thirteen horizontal stripes,
alternately red and white, with blue canton in the fly
showing 50 white stars in nine horizontal rows of six and
five alternately (known as the Star-Spangled Banner)
LIFE EXPECTANCY (years) – male 72.20; female 78.80
POPULATION GROWTH RATE – 1.0 per cent (1995)
POPULATION DENSITY – 28 per sq. km (1995)
URBAN POPULATION – 75.2 per cent (1990)

The coastline has a length of about 2,069 miles on the
Atlantic, 7,623 miles on the Pacific, 1,060 miles on the
Arctic, and 1,631 miles on the Gulf of Mexico.
   The principal river is the Mississippi-Missouri-Red
(3,710 miles long), traversing the whole country to its
mouth in the Gulf of Mexico; its main affluents are the
Yellowstone, Platte, Arkansas, and Ohio rivers. The chain
of the Rocky Mountains separates the western portion of
the country from the remainder. West of these, bordering
the Pacific coast, the Cascade Mountains and Sierra
Nevada form the outer edge of a high tableland, consisting
in part of stony and sandy desert and partly of grazing land
and forested mountains, and including the Great Salt Lake,
which extends to the Rocky Mountains. In the eastern
states large forests still exist, the remnants of the forests
which formerly extended over all the Atlantic slope. The
highest point is Mount McKinley (20,320 ft) in Alaska, and
the lowest point of dry land is in Death Valley (Inyo,
California), 282 ft below sea level.

AREA AND POPULATION

	Total land area 1990 (sq. miles)	Population census 1990
The United States (a)	3,536,278	248,709,873
Outlying areas under US jurisdiction	4,043	3,847,309
Territories	4,027	3,847,116
Puerto Rico	3,427	3,522,037
Guam	210	133,152
US Virgin Islands	134	101,809
American Samoa	77	46,773
Northern Mariana Is.	179	43,345
Other US possessions	16	193
Population abroad (b)	–	925,845
TOTAL	3,540,321	253,483,027

(a) the 50 states and the Federal District of Columbia
(b) excludes US citizens temporarily abroad on business

RESIDENT POPULATION BY RACE 1990 (Thousands)

White	199,686.1
Black	29,986.1
*American Indian	1,959.2
Chinese	1,645.5
Filipino	1,406.8
Japanese	847.6
Asian Indian	815.4
Korean	798.8
Vietnamese	614.5
Other Asian	780.0
Pacific Islander	365.0
All other races	9,804.8
†Hispanic origin	22,354.1
Cuban	1,043.9
Mexican	13,495.9
Puerto Rican	2,727.8
Other Hispanic	5,086.4
TOTAL	248,709.9

*Includes Eskimo and Aleut
†Persons of Hispanic origin may be of any race

IMMIGRATION

From 1820 to 1996, 63,140,227 immigrants were admitted
to the United States. Total number of immigrants in 1996
was 915,900, of which 402,309 came from North and South
America (163,572 from Mexico), 307,807 from Asia and
141,581 from Europe.

HISTORY AND POLITICS

The area which is now the USA was first inhabited by
nomadic hunters who probably arrived from Asia c.30,000
BC. The first (failed) European colony was founded by Sir
Walter Raleigh in 1585. By 1733 there were 13 British
colonies, composed largely of religious non-conformists
who had left Britain to escape persecution; the French and
Spanish had also founded colonies. Relations between the
colonies reflected tensions and conflicts between the
European powers in the 17th and 18th centuries; from
1689 to 1763 the French, with native Indians, frequently
attacked British settlements. In accordance with the Peace
of Paris (1763) Britain returned Cuba and the Philippines
to Spain and received Florida in return and France ceded
New Orleans and (until 1800) Louisiana to Spain.
   The War of Independence broke out in 1775 largely
because of the colonists' objection to being taxed by, but
having no representation in, the British Parliament. The
forces of the British government were defeated with
French, Spanish and Dutch assistance. The Declaration of

Independence which inaugurated the United States of America was signed on 4 July 1776; Britain recognized American sovereignty in 1783. The first federal constitution was drawn up in 1787; ten amendments, termed the Bill of Rights, were added in 1791. The 13 original states of the Union ratified the constitution between 1787 and 1790. Vermont, Kentucky and Tennessee were admitted in the 1790s but most of the states acceded in the 19th century as the opening up of the centre and west led to the creation of new states and European or neighbouring countries ceded or sold their territories to the USA.

The Civil War (1861–5) was fought over the issue of slavery, which was integral to the economy of the southern states but was opposed by the northern states. The northern states defeated the Confederacy of southern states (South Carolina, Georgia, Alabama, Florida, Mississippi, Louisiana), all of which had seceded from the Union between 1860 and 1861; they all re-entered the Union by 1870. From 1866 Negroes were given full rights as citizens.

The USA emerged as a world economic and military superpower in the 20th century and played a decisive role in the two world wars, in which it was engaged between 1917 and 1918, and between 1941 and 1945. Its economic and military (including nuclear) supremacy gave the USA a key role in shaping the post-war world. The USA facilitated the rebuilding of Europe through the Marshall Plan, oversaw the creation of the United Nations, International Monetary Fund and International Bank for Reconstruction and Development, and underpinned the new liberal world economy. The USA contended for global supremacy with the USSR and the two superpowers engaged in a costly arms race and 'cold war' fought by proxy in the Third World. The USA's opposition to communism led it into wars in Korea (1950–3) and Vietnam (1964–73). President Richard Nixon initiated détente with Russia and China in the early 1970s but was forced to resign in 1974 over corruption allegations (Watergate).

POLITICAL SYSTEM

By the constitution of 17 September 1787 (to which amendments were added in 1791, 1798, 1804, 1865, 1868,

1870, 1913, 1920, 1933, 1951, 1961, 1964, 1967, 1971 and 1992), the government of the United States is entrusted to three separate authorities: the executive (the president and Cabinet), the legislature (Congress) and the judicature.

The president is indirectly elected by an electoral college every four years. There is also a vice-president, who, should the president die, becomes president for the remainder of the term. The tenure of the presidency is limited to two terms.

The president, with the consent of the Senate, appoints the Cabinet officers and all the chief officials. He makes recommendations of a general nature to Congress, and when laws are passed by Congress he may return them to Congress with a veto. But if a measure so vetoed is again passed by both Houses of Congress by two-thirds majority in each House, it becomes law, notwithstanding the objection of the president. The president must be at least 35 years of age and a native citizen of the United States.

Presidential elections

Each state elects (on the first Tuesday after the first Monday in November of the year preceding the year in which the presidential term expires) a number of electors (members of the electoral college), equal to the whole number of Senators and Representatives to which the state may be entitled in the Congress. The electors for each state meet in their respective states on the first Monday after the second Wednesday in December following, and vote for a president by ballot. The ballots are then sent to Washington, and opened on 6 January by the President of the Senate in the presence of Congress. The candidate who has received a majority of the whole number of electoral votes cast is declared president for the ensuing term. If no one has a majority, then from the highest on the list (not exceeding three) the House of Representatives elects a president, the votes being taken by states, the representation from each state having one vote. A presidential term begins at noon on 20 January.

HEAD OF STATE

President of the United States, William Jefferson Blythe IV Clinton, *born* 19 August 1946, *elected* 1992, *re-elected* 5 November 1996, *sworn in* 20 January 1997. Democrat

THE STATES OF THE UNION

The United States of America is a federal republic consisting of 50 states and the federal District of Columbia and of organized territories. Of the present 50 states, 13 are original states, seven were admitted without previous organization as territories, and 30 were admitted after such organization.

STATE (with date and *order* of admission)	LAND AREA sq. m.	POPULATION (1990 census)	CAPITAL	GOVERNOR (end of term in office)	
Alabama (Ala.) (1819) *(22)*	50,750	4,040,587	Montgomery	Fob James *(R)*	(1998)
Alaska (1959) *(49)*	570,374	550,043	Juneau	Tony Knowles *(D)*	(1998)
Arizona (Ariz.) (1912) *(48)*	113,642	3,665,228	Phoenix	Jane Dee Hull *(R)*	(2000)
Arkansas (Ark.) (1836) *(25)*	52,075	2,350,725	Little Rock	Mike Huckabee *(R)*	(1998)
California (Calif.) (1850) *(31)*	155,973	29,760,021	Sacramento	Pete Wilson *(R)*	(1998)
Colorado (Colo.) (1876) *(38)*	103,729	3,294,394	Denver	Roy Romer *(D)*	(1998)
Connecticut (Conn.) § (1788) *(5)*	4,845	3,287,116	Hartford	John Rowland *(R)*	(1998)
Delaware (Del.) § (1787) *(1)*	1,955	666,168	Dover	Tom Carper *(D)*	(2000)
Florida (Fla.) (1845) *(27)*	53,937	12,937,926	Tallahassee	Lawton Chiles *(D)*	(1998)
Georgia (Ga.) § (1788) *(4)*	57,919	6,478,216	Atlanta	Zell Miller *(D)*	(1998)
Hawaii (1959) *(50)*	6,423	1,108,229	Honolulu	Ben Cayetano *(D)*	(1998)
Idaho (1890) *(43)*	82,751	1,006,749	Boise	Phil Batt *(R)*	(1998)
Illinois (Ill.) (1818) *(21)*	55,593	11,430,602	Springfield	Jim Edgar *(R)*	(1998)
Indiana (Ind.) (1816) *(19)*	35,870	5,544,159	Indianapolis	Frank O'Bannon *(D)*	(2000)
Iowa (1846) *(29)*	55,875	2,776,755	Des Moines	Terry Branstad *(R)*	(1998)
Kansas (Kan.) (1861) *(34)*	81,823	2,477,574	Topeka	Bill Graves *(R)*	(1998)
Kentucky (Ky.) (1792) *(15)*	39,732	3,685,296	Frankfort	Paul Patton *(D)*	(1999)
Louisiana (La.) (1812) *(18)*	43,566	4,219,973	Baton Rouge	Murphy Foster *(R)*	(1999)
Maine (Me.) (1820) *(23)*	30,865	1,227,928	Augusta	Angus King *(I)*	(1998)
Maryland (Md.) § (1788) *(7)*	9,775	4,781,468	Annapolis	Parris Glendening *(D)*	(1998)
Massachusetts (Mass.) § (1788) *(6)*	7,838	6,016,425	Boston	William Weld *(R)*	(1998)
Michigan (Mich.) (1837) *(26)*	56,809	9,295,297	Lansing	John Engler *(R)*	(1998)
Minnesota (Minn.) (1858) *(32)*	79,617	4,375,099	St Paul	Arne Carlson *(R)*	(1998)
Mississippi (Miss.) (1817) *(20)*	46,914	2,573,216	Jackson	Kirk Fordice *(R)*	(1999)
Missouri (Mo.) (1821) *(24)*	68,898	5,117,073	Jefferson City	Mel Carnahan *(D)*	(2000)
Montana (Mont.) (1889) *(41)*	145,556	799,065	Helena	Marc Racicot *(R)*	(2000)
Nebraska (Neb.) (1867) *(37)*	76,878	1,578,385	Lincoln	Ben Nelson *(D)*	(1998)
Nevada (Nev.) (1864) *(36)*	109,806	1,201,833	Carson City	Robert J. Miller *(D)*	(1998)
New Hampshire (NH) § (1788) *(9)*	8,969	1,109,252	Concord	Jeanne Shaheen *(D)*	(1998)
New Jersey (NJ) § (1787) *(3)*	7,419	7,730,188	Trenton	Christine Whitman *(R)*	(1998)
New Mexico (NM) (1912) *(47)*	121,365	1,515,069	Santa Fé	Gary Johnson *(R)*	(1998)
New York (NY) § (1788) *(11)*	47,224	17,990,455	Albany	George Pataki *(R)*	(1998)
North Carolina (NC) § (1789) *(12)*	48,718	6,628,637	Raleigh	James B. Hunt, jun. *(D)*	(2000)
North Dakota (ND) (1889) *(39)*	68,994	638,800	Bismarck	Edward Schafer *(R)*	(2000)
Ohio (1803) *(17)*	40,953	10,847,115	Columbus	George Voinovich *(R)*	(1998)
Oklahoma (Okla.) (1907) *(46)*	68,679	3,145,585	Oklahoma City	Frank Keating *(R)*	(1998)
Oregon (Ore.) (1859) *(33)*	96,003	2,842,321	Salem	John Kitzhaber *(D)*	(1998)
Pennsylvania (Pa.) § (1787) *(2)*	44,820	11,881,643	Harrisburg	Tom Ridge *(R)*	(1998)
Rhode Island (RI) § (1790) *(13)*	1,045	1,003,464	Providence	Lincoln Almond *(R)*	(1998)
South Carolina (SC) § (1788) *(8)*	30,111	3,486,703	Columbia	David Beasley *(R)*	(1998)
South Dakota (SD) (1889) *(40)*	75,896	696,004	Pierre	William Janklow *(R)*	(1998)
Tennessee (Tenn.) (1796) *(16)*	41,220	4,877,185	Nashville	Don Sundquist *(R)*	(1998)
Texas (1845) *(28)*	261,914	16,986,510	Austin	George W. Bush *(R)*	(1998)
Utah (1896) *(45)*	82,168	1,722,850	Salt Lake City	Mike Leavitt *(R)*	(2000)
Vermont (Vt.) (1791) *(14)*	9,249	562,758	Montpelier	Howard Dean *(D)*	(1998)
Virginia (Va.) § (1788) *(10)*	39,598	6,187,358	Richmond	James Gillmore *(R)*	(2000)
Washington (Wash.) (1889) *(42)*	66,581	4,866,692	Olympia	Gary Locke *(D)*	(2000)
West Virginia (W. Va.) (1863) *(35)*	24,087	1,793,477	Charleston	Cecil Underwood *(D)*	(2000)
Wisconsin (Wis.) (1848) *(30)*	54,314	4,891,769	Madison	Tommy Thompson *(R)*	(1998)
Wyoming (Wyo.) (1890) *(44)*	97,105	453,588	Cheyenne	Jim Geringer *(R)*	(1998)
Dist. of Columbia (DC) (1791)	61	606,900	—	Marion Barry *(D)* *(Mayor)*	

OUTLYING TERRITORIES AND POSSESSIONS

American Samoa	77	46,773	Pago Pago	Tauese Pita Sunia *(D)*	(2000)
Guam	210	133,152	Hagatna	Carl Gutierrez *(D)*	(1998)
Northern Mariana Islands	179	43,345	Saipan	Pedro P. Tenorio *(R)*	(1998)
Puerto Rico	3,427	3,522,037	San Juan	Dr Pedro J. Rossello *(D)*	(2000)
US Virgin Islands	134	101,809	Charlotte Amalie	Roy Schneider *(R)*	(1998)

§The 13 original states
D Democratic Party; *I* Independent; *R* Republican Party

Vice-President, Albert Gore, jun., *born* 31 March 1948

THE CABINET *as at July 1998*
Agriculture, Daniel Glickman
Attorney-General, Janet Reno
Commerce, William Daley
Defence, William Cohen
Education, Richard Riley
Energy, Bill Richardson *(to be confirmed)*
Health and Human Services, Donna Shalala
Housing and Urban Development, Andrew Cuomo
Interior, Bruce Babbitt
Labour, Alexis Herman
Secretary of State, Madeleine Albright
Transportation, Rodney Slater
Treasury, Robert Rubin
Veterans' Affairs, Jesse Brown

Other senior positions:
Ambassador to the UN, Richard Holbrooke *(to be confirmed)*
Chair, Council of Economic Advisers, Janet Yellin
White House Chief of Staff, Erskine Bowles
National Security Adviser, Samuel Berger
Environmental Protection Agency, Carol Browner
Director, National Economic Council, Gene Sperling
Director, Office of Management and Budget, Franklin Raines
Director, Small Business Administration, Aida Alvarez
Director, US Information Agency, Joseph Duffey
Trade Representative, Charlene Barshefsky
Director of CIA, George Tenet
Director of FBI, Louis Freeh
Chairman, Federal Reserve Board of Governors, Alan Greenspan

UNITED STATES EMBASSY
24 Grosvenor Square, London WIA IAE
Tel 0171-499 9000
Ambassador Extraordinary and Plenipotentiary, HE Philip
  Lader, apptd 1997
Deputy Chief of Mission, R. Bradtke
Defence and Naval Attaché, Capt. J. Mader
Minister-Counsellors, L. A. Lohman (*Administrative*);
  C. A. Ford (*Commercial*); W. G. Griffith (*Consular*)

BRITISH EMBASSY
3100 Massachusetts Avenue NW, Washington DC 20008
Tel: Washington DC 462 1340
Ambassador Extraordinary and Plenipotentiary, HE
  Christopher Meyer, KCMG, apptd 1997
Ministers, S. Wright; H. P. Evans (*Economic*); J. Taylor
  (*Defence Material*)
Head of British Defence Staff and Defence Attaché, Maj.-Gen. C.
  Vyvyan, CBE
Counsellor, R. French (*Management and Consul-General*)
Consul-General (*New York*) *and Director-General of Trade and
  Investment*, J. Ling, CMG
Cultural Attaché and British Council Director, D. Evans

BRITISH CONSULATES-GENERAL – Atlanta, Boston,
  Chicago, Houston, Los Angeles, New York and San
  Francisco
BRITISH CONSULATES – Anchorage, Charlotte, Cleveland,
  Dallas, Denver, Kansas City, Miami, Minneapolis,
  Nashville, New Orleans, Philadelphia, Phoenix,
  Pittsburgh, Portland, St Louis, Salt Lake City, San
  Diego, Seattle and Puerto Rico

BRITISH-AMERICAN CHAMBER OF COMMERCE, 275
  Madison Avenue, New York 10016; UK OFFICE, Suite
  201, High Holborn, London WCIV 6RR

THE CONGRESS

Legislative power is vested in two houses, the Senate and
the House of Representatives. The Senate has 100
members, two Senators from each state, elected for the
term of six years, and each Senator has one vote.
Representatives are chosen in each state, by popular vote,
for two years.

The House of Representatives consists of 435 Representatives, a resident commissioner from Puerto Rico and
a delegate each from American Samoa, the District of
Columbia, Guam and the Virgin Islands.

Members of the 105th Congress were elected on 5
November 1996. The 105th Congress is constituted as
follows:

Senate – Republicans 55; Democrats 45; total 100
House of Representatives – Republicans 228; Democrats 206;
  Independent 1; total 435

President of the Senate, The Vice-President
Senate Majority Leader, Trent Lott (*R*), *Mississippi*
Speaker of the House of Representatives, Newton Gingrich (*R*),
  Georgia
Secretary of the Senate, Gary Sisco
Clerk of the House of Representatives, Robin H. Carle

THE JUDICATURE

The federal judiciary consists of three sets of federal courts:
the Supreme Court at Washington DC, consisting of a
Chief Justice and eight Associate Justices, with original
jurisdiction in cases where a state is a party to the suit, and
with appellate jurisdiction from inferior federal courts and
from the judgments of the highest courts of the states; the
United States Courts of Appeals, dealing with appeals from
district courts and from certain federal administrative
agencies, and consisting of 168 circuit judges within 13
circuits; the 94 United States district courts served by 575
district court judges.

THE SUPREME COURT
US Supreme Court Building, Washington DC 20543

Chief Justice, William H. Rehnquist, *Arizona*, apptd 1986

Associate Justices
John Paul Stevens, Illinois, apptd 1975
Sandra Day O'Connor, Arizona, apptd 1981
Antonin Scalia, Virginia, apptd 1986
Anthony M. Kennedy, California, apptd 1988
David H. Souter, New Hampshire, apptd 1990
Clarence Thomas, Georgia, apptd 1991
Ruth Bader Ginsburg, New York, apptd 1993
Stephen Breyer, Massachusetts, apptd 1994

Clerk of the Supreme Court, William K. Suter

In 1996 there were 13,473,580 recorded offences: murder
and non-negligent manslaughter 19,650; forcible rape
95,770; robbery 537,050; aggravated assault 1,029,810;
burglary 2,501,500; larceny-theft 7,894,600; motor vehicle
theft 1,395,200.

DEFENCE

Each military department is separately organized and
functions under the direction, authority and control of the
Secretary of Defence. The Air Force has primary responsibility for the Department of Defence space development
programmes and projects.

Under strategic command the USA has 432 submarine-
launched ballistic missiles, 530 inter-continental ballistic
missiles, 128 heavy nuclear-capable bombers and 90
strategic defence interceptor aircraft together with multiple intelligence satellites, radars and early warning systems
throughout the world.

The Army has 7,836 main battle tanks, 24,920 armoured
infantry fighting vehicles and armoured personnel carri-

ers, 7,428 artillery pieces, 264 aircraft and 1,460 armed helicopters.

The Navy has 18 strategic submarines, 75 tactical submarines, 12 aircraft carriers, 30 cruisers, 57 destroyers, 44 frigates, 20 patrol and coastal vessels, 345 amphibious and support ships, 1,728 combat aircraft and 487 armed helicopters.

The Marine Corps has 403 main battle tanks, 1,258 amphibious armoured vehicles and 847 artillery pieces.

The Air Force has 178 long-range strike aircraft, 2,626 tactical combat aircraft and 218 helicopters.

The major deployments of US personnel overseas are: Germany (60,500); South Korea (35,920); Japan (36,930); Italy (11,300); UK (11,496); Panama (6,050); Turkey (3,029).

MILITARY EXPENDITURE – 3.5 per cent of GDP (1996)

MILITARY PERSONNEL – 1,447,600: Army 495,000, Navy 395,500, Marine Corps 174,900, Air Force 382,200

Secretary of Defence (in the Cabinet), William Cohen
Chairman, Joint Chiefs of Staff, Gen. Henry Shelton

ECONOMY AND FINANCE

In 1997 central government budget receipts totalled US$1,579.0 billion and outlays US$1,601.6 billion. The largest items of expenditure were: defence US$292.2 billion; social security US$393.3 billion, income security US$339.4 billion, debt interest US$355.8 billion. Social welfare expenditure was US$1,363,884 million in 1993 including US$657,328 million (US$2,515 per capita) spent on social insurance, US$331,910 million (US$1,274 per capita) spent on education and US$74,503 million (US$286 per capita) spent on health.

At the end of September 1992 the total gross federal debt stood at US$4,002,062 million.

GNP – US$7,433,517 million (1996); US$28,020 per capita (1996)

GDP – US$6,027,216 million (1994); US$25,514 per capita (1994)

ANNUAL AVERAGE GROWTH OF GDP – 2.4 per cent (1996)

INFLATION RATE – 2.9 per cent (1996)

UNEMPLOYMENT – 5.6 per cent (1995)

GROSS DOMESTIC PRODUCT BY INDUSTRY 1996

	US$ millions
Private industries	6,639,766
Agriculture, forestry, fisheries	129,842
Mining	113,631
Construction	306,052
Manufacturing	1,332,093
Transportation and public utilities	645,294
Wholesale trade	516,777
Retail trade	667,903
Finance, insurance, and real estate	1,448,521
Services	1,539,525
Government and government enterprises	996,270
Statistical discrepancy	−59,872
TOTAL	14,275,802

AGRICULTURE

The total number of farms in 1997 was 2,058,910, with a total area of land in farms of 968,338,000 acres, and an average acreage per farm of 470 acres. Principal crops are corn for grain, soybeans, wheat, hay, cotton, tobacco, grain sorghums, potatoes, oranges and barley. Gross income from farming in 1996 was US$233 billion. Cash income from all crops in 1996 was US$109 billion and from livestock and livestock products US$92.9 billion.

MINERALS

The value of non-fuel raw mineral production in 1997 totalled an estimated US$39 billion. Mineral exports in 1997 were valued at US$37 billion, and imports at US$58 billion. In 1997 the following quantities of minerals were produced: iron ore 62,750,000 tons; marketable phosphate rock 45,100,000 tons; copper 1,910,000 tons; zinc 573,000 tons; lead 415,000 tons.

ENERGY

Production in 1996 was 72.32 quadrillion BTU, principally coal, natural gas and crude oil. Coal accounted for almost half of energy exports of 4.71 quadrillion BTU. Imports were 23.97 quadrillion BTU, of which crude oil was 17.64 quadrillion BTU, to meet consumption of 93.87 quadrillion BTU (quadrillion=10^{15}).

TRADE

In 1996 the USA had a trade deficit of US$186,260 million and a current account deficit of US$165,590 million. Imports totalled US$822,025 million and exports US$625,073 million.

Trade with UK	1996	1997
Imports from UK	£19,833,631,000	£20,967,631,000
Exports to UK	23,011,494,000	25,028,913,000

COMMUNICATIONS

In 1996 there were 3.9 million miles of public roads and streets, of which 3.1 million miles were in rural areas and 833,623 miles were in urban areas. Surfaced roads and streets account for 60.5 per cent of the total. An estimated total of US$98,158 million was spent in 1996 on roads and streets in the United States.

The ocean-going merchant marine on 1 April 1998 consisted of 473 vessels of 1,000 gross tons and over, of which 281 were privately-owned and 192 were government-owned ships. There were 182 ships in the National Defense Reserve Fleet of inactive government-owned vessels.

According to preliminary figures, US domestic and international scheduled airlines in 1997 carried 598,941,869 passengers over 605,477,722 revenue passenger miles. Operating revenues of all US scheduled airlines were US$109,310,795,755 in 1997. Total operating expenses rose to US$100,650,209,107 in 1997. Scheduled operations showed a net operating profit of US$8,660,586,648 in 1997.

EDUCATION

All the states and the District of Columbia have compulsory school attendance laws. In general, children are obliged to attend school from seven to 16 years of age.

Most of the revenue for public elementary and secondary school purposes comes from federal, state, and local governments. Less than three per cent comes from gifts and from tuition and transportation fees.

Among the better-known universities are: Harvard, founded at Cambridge, Mass. in 1636, and named after John Harvard of Emmanuel College, Cambridge, England, who bequeathed to it his library and a sum of money in 1638; Yale, founded at New Haven, Connecticut, in 1701; Princeton, NJ, founded 1746.

ILLITERACY RATE – 0.5 per cent

ENROLMENT (percentage of age group) – primary 98 per cent (1993); secondary 95 per cent (1993); tertiary 36 per cent (1996)

US TERRITORIES, ETC

Responsibility within the federal government for the United States insular areas other than Puerto Rico and Kingman Reef lies with the United States Department of the Interior, either the Office of Insular Affairs (for American Samoa, Guam, the Northern Mariana Islands, the United States Virgin Islands, Navassa Island (3 sq. miles), Palmyra Atoll (1.56 sq. miles) and Wake Atoll (2.5 sq. miles) (shared with the United States Army Space and Missile Defense Command)) or the United States Fish and Wildlife Service (for Baker Island (0.59 sq. miles), Howland Island (1 sq. mile) and Jarvis Island (1.66 sq. miles), Midway Atoll (2 sq. miles) and Johnston Atoll (0.98 sq. miles) (shared with the Defense Special Weapons Agency)). Four of the eight populated insular areas are represented in the United States House of Representatives, Puerto Rico by a resident commissioner and American Samoa, Guam and the United States Virgin Islands each by a delegate. Although represented in the United States House of Representatives by a delegate, the District of Columbia was an incorporated territory for only three years, from 21 February 1871 to 20 June 1874.

THE COMMONWEALTH OF PUERTO RICO

AREA – 3,427 sq. miles (8,875 sq. km)
POPULATION – 3,805,766 (1997 estimate); 3,522,037 (1990 census). The majority of the inhabitants are of Spanish descent, and Spanish and English are the official languages
CAPITAL – ΨSan Juan, population of the municipality (1997 estimate), 436,331. Other major towns are: Bayamón (233,249); Carolina (189,568); ΨPonce (191,138)

Puerto Rico (Rich Port) is an island of the Greater Antilles group in the West Indies.

Puerto Rico was discovered in 1493 by Columbus and explored by Ponce de León in 1508. It was a Spanish possession until 1898, when the USA took formal possession as a result of the Spanish-American War.

The 1952 constitution establishes the Commonwealth of Puerto Rico with full powers of local government. The Legislative Assembly consists of two elected houses: the Senate of 27 members and the House of Representatives of 51 members. The term of the Legislative Assembly is four years. The Governor is popularly elected for a term of four years. Residents of Puerto Rico are US citizens. Puerto Rico is represented in Congress by a resident commissioner, elected for a term of four years, who has a seat in the House of Representatives but not a vote, although he has a right to vote on those committees of which he is a member. A plebiscite on the future constitutional status of Puerto Rico was held on 14 November 1993 in which 48 per cent voted to maintain the existing Commonwealth status, 46 per cent voted for full US statehood and 4 per cent for independence.

Principal crops are sugar cane, coffee, vegetables, fruits and tobacco. Most valuable areas of manufacturing are chemicals and allied products, metal products and machinery, and food processing.

Governor, Dr Pedro J. Rosselló

TRADE WITH UK	1996	1997
Imports from UK	£307,035,000	£392,732,000
Exports to UK	104,799,000	93,106,000

GUAM

AREA – 212 sq. miles (549 sq. km)
POPULATION – 145,780 (1997 estimate): 43 per cent Chamorro stock mingled with Filipino and Spanish blood. The Chamorro language belongs to the Malayo-Polynesian family, but with considerable admixture of Spanish. Chamorro and English are the official languages; most Chamorro residents are bilingual
CAPITAL – Hagatna. Port of entry, ΨApra

Guam is the largest of the Mariana Islands, in the north Pacific Ocean.

Guam was occupied by the Japanese in December 1941 but was recaptured by US forces in 1944. Under the Organic Act of Guam 1950, Guam has statutory powers of self-government, and any person born in Guam is a US citizen. A 21-member unicameral legislature is elected biennially. The Governor and Lieutenant-Governor are popularly elected. There is also a District Court of Guam, with original jurisdiction in cases under federal law.

Guam's two main sources of revenue are tourism and US military spending.

Governor, Carl Gutierrez
Lt.-Governor, Frank Blas

AMERICAN SAMOA

AREA – 77 sq. miles (199 sq. km)
POPULATION – 60,383 (1997 estimate)
CAPITAL – ΨPago Pago (population, 3,519)

American Samoa consists of the islands of Tutuila, Aunu'u, Ofu, Olesega, Ta'u, Rose and Swains Islands. Tutuila, the largest of the group, has an area of 52 sq. miles and a magnificent harbour at Pago Pago. The remaining islands have an area of about 24 sq. miles. Tuna and copra are the chief exports.

Those born in American Samoa are US non-citizen nationals, but some have acquired citizenship through service in the United States armed forces or other naturalization procedure. The 1960 constitution grants American Samoa a measure of self-government, with certain powers reserved to the US Secretary of the Interior. There is a bicameral legislature with popularly elected representatives and traditionally elected senators, and a popularly elected Governor.

Governor, Tauese Pita Sunia
Lt.-Governor, Togiola Tulafo

THE UNITED STATES VIRGIN ISLANDS

AREA – 134 sq. miles (347 sq. km)
POPULATION – 114,483 (1997 estimate)
CAPITAL – ΨCharlotte Amalie (population, 12,331, 1990), on St Thomas

The US Virgin Islands were purchased from Denmark and came under US sovereignty in 1917. There are three main islands, St Thomas (28 sq. miles), St Croix (84 sq. miles), St John (20 sq. miles) and about 50 small islets or cays, mostly uninhabited.

Under the provisions of the Revised Organic Act of the Virgin Islands 1954, legislative power is vested in the Legislature, a unicameral body composed of 15 senators popularly elected for two-year terms. The Governor is popularly elected. Those born in the US Virgin Islands are US citizen nationals. A referendum is to take place at a future date to determine the future political status of the islands.

Governor, Roy Schneider
Lt.-Governor, Kenneth E. Mapp

TRADE WITH UK	1996	1997
Imports from UK	£4,739,000	£11,184,000
Exports to UK	164,000	1,078,000

NORTHERN MARIANA ISLANDS

AREA – 179 sq. miles (464 sq. km)
POPULATION – 63,763 (1997 estimate)
SEAT OF GOVERNMENT – Saipan (population, 52,706, 1995 census)
The USA administered the Northern Mariana Islands as part of a UN Trusteeship until the trusteeship agreement was terminated in 1986, bringing fully into effect a 1976 congressional law establishing the Northern Mariana Islands as a Commonwealth under US sovereignty. Most of the then residents became US citizens. Those born subsequently in the Northern Mariana Islands are US citizen nationals. There is a popularly elected bicameral legislature and a popularly elected Governor.

Governor, Pedro P. Tenorio
Lt.-Governor, Jesus Sablan

THE PANAMA CANAL

As a result of the Panama Canal Treaty 1977, the Canal Zone was disestablished, with all jurisdiction over the former Canal Zone reverting to Panama with effect from 1 October 1979. Under the treaty, the United States is allowed the use of operating areas for the Panama Canal, together with several military bases, although the Republic of Panama is sovereign in all such areas. The Panama Canal Commission, an arm of the US Government, will continue to operate the canal until noon on 31 December 1999. The Panama Canal Authority, a Panama government agency, will then assume administration of the waterway.

In the fiscal year 1997, the total number of transits by ocean-going commercial traffic was 13,043; canal net tons totalled 216,874,961; cargo tons totalled 189,777,856.

URUGUAY
República Oriental del Uruguay

AREA – 68,500 sq. miles (177,414 sq. km). Neighbours: Argentina (west), Brazil (north and east)
POPULATION – 3,186,000 (1994 UN estimate): predominantly of Spanish and Italian descent. Spanish is the official language. Many Uruguayans are Roman Catholics. There is no established church
CAPITAL – ΨMontevideo (population, 1,383,660, 1992)
MAJOR CITIES – Melo; Mercedes; Minas; ΨPaysandú; Punta del Este; Rivera; Salto
CURRENCY – Uruguayan peso of 100 centésimos
NATIONAL ANTHEM – Orientales, La Patria O La Tumba (Uruguayans, the fatherland or death)
NATIONAL DAY – 25 August (Declaration of Independence, 1825)
NATIONAL FLAG – Four blue and five white horizontal stripes surcharged with sun on a white ground in the top corner, next flagstaff
LIFE EXPECTANCY (years) – male 68.43; female 74.88
POPULATION GROWTH RATE – 0.6 per cent (1995)
POPULATION DENSITY – 18 per sq. km (1995)
URBAN POPULATION – 90.1 per cent (1995)
MILITARY EXPENDITURE – 1.5 per cent of GDP (1996)

MILITARY PERSONNEL – 26,520: Army 17,600, Navy 5,000, Air Force 3,000, Paramilitaries 920
The country consists mainly of undulating grassy plains. The principal river is the Rio Negro (with its tributary the Yi), flowing from north-east to south-west into the Rio Uruguay. The climate is temperate.

HISTORY AND POLITICS

Uruguay (or the *Banda Oriental*, as the territory lying on the eastern bank of the Uruguay River was then called) resisted all attempted invasions of the Portuguese and Spanish until the early 17th century; 100 years later the Portuguese settlements were captured by the Spanish. From 1726 to 1814 the country formed part of Spanish South America. In 1814 the armies of the Argentine Confederation captured the capital and annexed the province; afterwards it was annexed by Portugal and became a province of Brazil. In 1825, the country threw off Brazilian rule. This action led to war between Argentina and Brazil which was settled by the mediation of the UK, Uruguay being declared an independent state in 1828. In 1830 a republic was inaugurated.

General elections held in 1984 marked the return to civilian rule after 11 years of presidential rule with military support. The first fully free presidential and legislative elections since 1971 were held in 1989, and were won by the *Partido Nacional Blanco*. After the 1994 elections a coalition government of the Colorado Party and Partido Nacional Blanco was appointed by President Sanguinetti (Colorado Party).

POLITICAL SYSTEM

Under the constitution the president (who may serve only a single term of five years) appoints a council of 11 ministers and a Secretary (Planning and Budget Office), and the vice-president presides over Congress. The Congress consists of a Chamber of 99 deputies and a Senate of 30 members (plus the vice-president), elected for five years by proportional representation.

The republic is divided into 19 Departments, each with an elected governor and legislature.

HEAD OF STATE
President, Dr Julio María Sanguinetti, *elected* 27 November 1994, *took office* 1 March 1995
Vice-President, Dr Hugo Batalla

COUNCIL OF MINISTERS *as at July 1998*
Economy and Finance, Luis Mosca
Education and Culture, Samuel Lichtensztein
Foreign Relations, Didier Opertti
Health, José Raúl Busto
Housing and Environment, Juan Chiruchi
Industry, Energy and Mines, Dr Julio Herrera
Interior, Luis Hierro López
Labour and Social Security, Ana Lía Piñeyrúa
Livestock, Agriculture and Fisheries, Sergio Chiesa
National Defence, Dr Raúl Iturria
Planning and Budget, Ariel Davrieux
Tourism, Benito Stern
Transport and Works, Lucio Caceres

EMBASSY OF THE ORIENTAL REPUBLIC OF URUGUAY
2nd Floor, 140 Brompton Road, London SW3 1HY
Tel 0171-584 8192
Ambassador Extraordinary and Plenipotentiary, HE Dr Agustín Espinosa Lloveras, apptd 1998

BRITISH EMBASSY
Calle Marco Bruto 1073, Montevideo 11300 (PO Box 16024)
Tel: Montevideo 622 3650
Ambassador Extraordinary and Plenipotentiary, HE Andrew Murray, apptd 1998

BRITISH-URUGUAYAN CHAMBER OF COMMERCE, Avenida Labertador Brig. Gen., Lavalleja 1641, P2-OF 201, Montevideo

ECONOMY

The economy is based on agriculture, primarily livestock. There are 10 million cattle and 25 million sheep. Rice, wheat, barley, linseed and sunflower seed are cultivated. Other foodstuffs (citrus, wine, beer), fishing and textile industries are also of importance.

Industrial development continues and, in addition to the greatly augmented textile industry, includes tyres, sheet-glass, three-ply wood, cement, leather-curing, beet-sugar, plastics, household consumer goods, edible oils and the refining of petroleum and petroleum products. There are some ferrous minerals, not extracted at present. Non-ferrous exploited minerals include clinker, dolomite, marble and granite.
GNP – US$18,464 million (1996); US$5,760 per capita (1996)
GDP – US$8,496 million (1994); US$4,199 per capita (1994)
ANNUAL AVERAGE GROWTH OF GDP – 4.9 per cent (1996)
INFLATION RATE – 28.3 per cent (1996)
UNEMPLOYMENT – 10.2 per cent (1995)
TOTAL EXTERNAL DEBT – US$5,899 million (1996)

TRADE

The major exports are meat and by-products, textiles, hides and bristle and agricultural products. The principal imports are raw materials, construction materials, oils and lubricants, automotive vehicles and machinery. Principal trading partners are Brazil, Argentina, the USA and Canada.

In 1995 Uruguay had a trade deficit of US$576 million and a current account deficit of US$358 million. In 1996 imports totalled US$3,323 million and exports US$2,397 million.

Trade with UK	1996	1997
Imports from UK	£66,251,000	£77,446,000
Exports to UK	78,357,000	74,582,000

COMMUNICATIONS

There are about 12,000 km of national highways, and 2,993 km of standard gauge railway in use. A state-owned airline, PLUNA, provides international services, and internal passenger and limited freight services are provided by TAMU, a branch of the Uruguayan Air Force. The international airport of Carrasco lies 12 miles outside Montevideo. The River Uruguay is navigable from its estuary to Salto, 200 miles north, and the Negro is also navigable as far as Mercedes.

EDUCATION

Primary and secondary education is compulsory and free, and technical and trade schools and evening courses for adult education are state controlled. The university at Montevideo (founded in 1849) has ten faculties and a new university has been built at Salto.
ILLITERACY RATE – 2.7 per cent
ENROLMENT (percentage of age group) – primary 95 per cent (1995); tertiary 27.3 per cent (1993)

UZBEKISTAN
Ozbekiston Respublikasy

AREA – 172,742 sq. miles (447,400 sq. km). Neighbours: Kazakhstan (north and west), Kyrgyzstan and Tajikistan (east), Afghanistan and Turkmenistan (south)
POPULATION – 21,206,800 (1998 estimate): 71 per cent Uzbek, 8 per cent Russian, 5 per cent Tajik and 4 per cent Kazakh, with smaller numbers of Tatars, Kara-Kalpaks, Koreans, Ukrainians and Kirghiz. The predominant religion is Sunni Muslim. Islam is tolerated within strict bounds; it is allowed to play no part in politics. The principal language is Uzbek (71 per cent) with Russian (8 per cent), Tajik (5 per cent) and Kazakh (4 per cent). Uzbek is one of the Turkic group of languages. In 1994 the government approved a six-year programme for the transfer of the Uzbek language to a Latin script
CAPITAL – Tashkent (population, 2,094,000, 1990)
MAJOR CITY – Samarkand (370,000), which contains the Gur-Emir (Tamerlane's Mausoleum), completed in 1400 by Ulugbek, Tamerlane's astronomer grandson
CURRENCY – Sum of 100 tiyin
NATIONAL DAY – 1 September (Independence Day)
NATIONAL FLAG – Three horizontal stripes of blue, white, green, with the white fimbriated in red; on the blue near the hoist a crescent and twelve stars, all in white
LIFE EXPECTANCY (years) – male 66.00; female 72.10
POPULATION GROWTH RATE – 2.1 per cent (1995)
POPULATION DENSITY – 51 per sq. km (1995)
URBAN POPULATION – 40.6 per cent (1989)
MILITARY EXPENDITURE – 3.8 per cent of GDP (1996)
MILITARY PERSONNEL – 65,000: Army 45,000, Air Force 4,000, Paramilitaries 16,000
CONSCRIPTION DURATION – 18 months
ILLITERACY RATE – 0.3 per cent
ENROLMENT (percentage of age group) – tertiary 31.7 per cent (1992)

Uzbekistan occupies the south-central part of former Soviet Central Asia, lying between the high Tienshan Mountains and the Pamir highlands in the east and south-east and sandy lowlands in the west and north-west. Uzbekistan consists of the Kara-Kalpak Autonomous Republic and 12 regions: Andizhan, Bokhara, Dzhizak, Ferghana, Kashkadar, Khorezm, Namangan, Navoi, Samarkand, Surkhan-Darya, Syr-Darya and Tashkent. Most of the country is a plain with huge waterless deserts, and several large oases which form the main centres of population and economic life. The climate is continental and dry.

HISTORY AND POLITICS

Between the sixth and fourth centuries BC the area that is now Uzbekistan was under the control of the Persians and then Alexander the Great. In the 14th century the area became the centre of a great Muslim empire under Tamerlane and then his grandson Ulugbek, following whose murder the state disintegrated. By the beginning of the 19th century three independent Khanates, Khiva, Kokand and Bukhara, existed in what is now Uzbekistan. These were gradually annexed to the Russian Empire by the middle of the 19th century. In November 1917 a Communist revolution broke out in Tashkent and parts of Uzbekistan were included in the Turkestan Soviet Republic at its formation in 1918. The remainder of Uzbekistan was under the rule of the independent states of Khiva and Bukhara, which had re-emerged in 1918, until they were

1058   Countries of the World

defeated by the Red Army and Soviet rule was established throughout the area in 1921. Under Soviet rule a massive land irrigation programme was implemented to allow the cultivation of cotton.

Uzbekistan declared its independence from the Soviet Union on 1 September 1991. Its independence was confirmed in a referendum on 29 December and recognized internationally. Elections to the new *Oliy Majlis* were held on 25 December 1994 and won by the ruling People's Democratic Party and its allies with a total of 205 seats.

The government of President Karimov is formed by the former Communist Party, which has renamed itself the People's Democratic Party. Despite the constitutionally guaranteed freedom of religion and thought, and respect for human rights and multiparty democracy, censorship is still widely used and little political opposition is tolerated. The main opposition parties, Erk (Freedom) and Birlik (Unity) nationalist parties, have been continually banned since the introduction of the multiparty constitution in December 1992. In March 1995 President Karimov's hold on power was confirmed when his term of office was extended to 2000 by a national referendum.

INSURGENCIES

Uzbek nationalism has caused violent clashes with Tajiks in the Ferghana valley in recent years. The ability to speak Uzbek is now a condition of appointment to government posts. This has severely disrupted the civil service and public sector, mostly staffed by ethnic Russians.

FOREIGN RELATIONS

President Karimov is attempting to form close ties with Turkey in the cultural and business spheres, and in 1994 began to strengthen economic ties with Russia again. Uzbek forces have been deployed in Tajikistan since late 1992 to help maintain the government and defeat the Islamic forces. In January 1998, relations with Tajikistan improved as the two countries signed a number of bilateral agreements, including an 'understanding' regarding the peace process in Tajikistan.

POLITICAL SYSTEM

Under the constitution of December 1992, the president and government hold executive power. The president may serve a maximum of two five-year terms and has the power to dissolve the 250-member Supreme Assembly (*Oliy Majlis*), which may not remove or impeach the president.

HEAD OF STATE

President, Islam Karimov, *elected* 29 December 1991, *elected by referendum for a five-year term* 26 March 1995

CABINET *as at July 1998*

Chairman of the Cabinet, The President
Prime Minister, Utkur Sultanov
First Deputy PM, Ismail Jurabekov
Deputy PMs, Bakhtier Khamidov; Alisher Azizhodjaev; Viktor Chjen; Dilbar Ghulomova; Rustam Junusov; Kayim Khakkulov; Kamildjan Rakhimov; Mirabror Usmanov; Lerik Ahmetov
Chairman, National Parliament, Erkin Khalilov
Communications, Abduwahid Djurabaev
Cultural Affairs, Khairulla Djurabaev
Defence, Maj.-Gen. Rustam Akhmedov
Education, Djura Yuldashev
Finance, Jamshed Saifiddinov
Foreign Affairs, Abdulaziz Kamilov
Foreign Economic Relations, Alyar Majidovich Ganiev
Health, Shavkat Karimov
Higher and Secondary Specialized Education, Akil Salimov
Interior, Zokirzhan Almatov

Justice, Sirodjiddin Mirsafaev
Labour, Akildjon Abidov
Municipal Economy, Victor Mikhailov
Power and Electrification, Valeriy Ataev
Social Security, Bakhodir Umursakov
Water Resources and Land Improvement, Marks Djumaniasov

EMBASSY OF THE REPUBLIC OF UZBEKISTAN
41 Holland Park, London WII 2RP
Tel: 0171-229 7679
Ambassador Extraordinary and Plenipotentiary, HE Fatih Teshabaev, apptd 1997

BRITISH EMBASSY
Ul. Gogolya 67, Tashkent 700000
Tel: Tashkent 406288
Ambassador Extraordinary and Plenipotentiary, HE Barbara Hay, MBE, apptd 1995

ECONOMY

Uzbekistan is attempting to integrate its economy with that of Kazakhstan, with which it signed an economic agreement in January 1994 to allow the free circulation of goods, services and capital and the co-ordination of credit and finance policies, budgets, taxation and customs duties. Uzbekistan is also a member of the CIS economic union and in 1994 signed an economic treaty with Russia to provide for mutually convertible currencies and to enhance private business links. In 1994–5 the government embarked on an economic reform programme under which subsidies on foodstuffs and transport were abolished and those on public utilities reduced. Peasant farmers have been granted private plots of land and inflation has been reduced.

Uzbekistan's economy is based on intensive agricultural production, and especially cotton production, made possible by extensive irrigation schemes. In 1997 agricultural output increased by 4 per cent. In addition there are some agricultural and textile machinery plants and several chemical combines. Mineral resources have begun to be exploited: in 1997 oil output was 7.9 million tonnes, and gas production was 50 billion cubic metres. The Muruntao mine is the largest open-cast gold mine in the world; in 1997, 85 tonnes of gold were produced.

Foreign direct investment exceeds US$6.2 billion. South Korea, the USA, Japan, Turkey and the UK are the main investors.

GNP – US$23,490 million (1996); US$1,010 per capita (1996)
GDP – US$38,532 million (1994); US$187 per capita (1994)
UNEMPLOYMENT – 0.4 per cent (1995)
TOTAL EXTERNAL DEBT – US$2,319 million (1996)

TRADE WITH UK	1996	1997
Imports from UK	£38,188,000	£91,001,000
Exports to UK	2,587,000	17,377,000

VANUATU
Ripablik Blong Vanuatu

AREA – 4,706 sq. miles (12,189 sq. km)
POPULATION – 165,000 (1994 UN estimate). About 95 per cent are Melanesian, the rest being mostly Micronesian, Polynesian and European. The national language is Bislama, but English and French are also official languages
CAPITAL – ΨPort Vila (population, 26,100, 1993), on Efate

MAJOR TOWN – Luganville (8,800, 1993), on Espiritu Santo
CURRENCY – Vatu of 100 centimes
NATIONAL ANTHEM – Nasonal sing sing blong Vanuatu
NATIONAL DAY – 30 July (Independence Day)
NATIONAL FLAG – Red over green with a black triangle in the hoist, the three parts being divided by fimbriations of black and yellow, and in the centre of the black triangle a boar's tusk overlaid by two crossed fern leaves
LIFE EXPECTANCY (years) – male 63.48; female 67.34
POPULATION GROWTH RATE – 2.7 per cent (1995)
POPULATION DENSITY – 14 per sq. km (1995)
URBAN POPULATION – 18.4 per cent (1989)
ENROLMENT (percentage of age group) – primary 74 per cent (1989); secondary 17 per cent (1991)

Vanuatu is situated in the South Pacific Ocean. It includes 13 large and some 70 small islands, of coral and volcanic origin, including the Banks and Torres Islands in the north. The principal islands are Vanua Lava, Espiritu Santo, Maewo, Pentecost, Ambae, Malekula, Ambrym, Epi, Efate, Erromango, Tanna and Aneityum. Most islands are mountainous and there are active volcanoes on several. The climate is oceanic tropical, moderated by the south-east trade winds which blow between May and October. At other times winds are variable and cyclones may occur.

HISTORY AND POLITICS

Vanuatu, the former Anglo-French Condominium of the New Hebrides, became an independent republic within the Commonwealth on 30 July 1980. Parliament consists of 50 members elected for a term of four years. A Council of Chiefs advises on matters of custom. Executive power is held by the prime minister (elected from and by parliament) and a Council of Ministers who are responsible to parliament. The president is elected for a five-year term by the presidents of the six provincial governments and the members of parliament.

HEAD OF STATE
President, HE Jean-Marie Leye Lenelgau, elected 2 March 1994

COUNCIL OF MINISTERS as at July 1998
Prime Minister, Donald Kalpokas (VP)
Deputy PM, Internal Affairs, Police, Labour, Immigration, Judiciary, Fr Walter Lini (NUP)
Agriculture, Forestry and Fisheries, John Morrison Willy (VP)
Education, Youth and Sports, Joe Natuman (VP)
Finance, Sela Molisa (VP)
Health, John Robert Alick (NUP)
Infrastructure, Public Utilities, Stanley Reginald (NUP)
Lands, Geology and Mines, Silas Hakwa (VP)
Ministerial Assistants, Steven Iatika (Ind.) (Economic Development); Daniel Bangtor (VP) (Economic Reforms); Willie Ollie Varasmaite (VP) (Education); Clement Leo (VP) (Foreign Affairs)
Trade, Business, Development, James Bule (NUP)
VP Vanuaaku Pati; NUP National United Party; Ind. Independent

HIGH COMMISSIONER TO GREAT BRITAIN, vacant, resident at Port Vila, Vanuatu

BRITISH HIGH COMMISSION
PO Box 567, Port Vila
Tel: Vila 23100
High Commissioner, HE Malcolm Hilson, apptd 1997

ECONOMY

Most of the population is employed on plantations or in subsistence agriculture. Subsistence crops include yams,

taro, manioc, sweet potato and breadfruit; principal cash crops are copra, cocoa and coffee. Cattle are kept on the plantations and beef is the second largest export. Principal exports are copra, meat (frozen, tinned and chilled), timber and cocoa.

There were 46,000 tourists in 1996. The absence of direct taxation has led to growth in the finance and associated industries.

In 1995 Vanuatu had a trade deficit of US$51 million and a current account deficit of US$18 million. In 1996 imports totalled US$97 million and exports totalled US$30 million.
GNP – US$224 million (1996); US$1,290 per capita (1996)
GDP – US$159 million (1994); US$1,117 per capita (1994)
ANNUAL AVERAGE GROWTH OF GDP – 3.2 per cent (1995)
INFLATION RATE – 0.9 per cent (1996)
TOTAL EXTERNAL DEBT – US$47 million (1996)

TRADE WITH UK	1996	1997
Imports from UK	£271,000	£158,000
Exports to UK	1,176,000	677,000

VATICAN CITY STATE
Stato della Città del Vaticano

AREA – 0.2 sq. miles (0.44 sq. km). Neighbour: Italy
POPULATION – 1,000 (1994 UN estimate). The language is Italian
CAPITAL – Vatican City (population, 766, 1988)
CURRENCY – Italian currency is legal tender
NATIONAL DAY – 22 October (Inauguration of present Pontiff)
NATIONAL FLAG – Square flag; equal vertical bands of yellow (next staff), and white; crossed keys and triple crown device on white band
POPULATION GROWTH RATE – 0.0 per cent (1995)
POPULATION DENSITY – 2,273 per sq. km (1995)
GDP – US$20 million (1994); US$17,930 per capita (1994)

The office of the ecclesiastical head of the Roman Catholic Church (Holy See) is vested in the Pope, the Sovereign Pontiff. For many centuries the Sovereign Pontiff exercised temporal power but by 1870 the Papal States had become part of unified Italy. The temporal power of the Pope was in suspense until the treaty of 1929 which recognized the full and independent sovereignty of the Holy See in the City of the Vatican.

Sovereign Pontiff, His Holiness Pope John Paul II (Karol Wojtyla), born at Wadowice (Krakow, Poland), 18 May 1920, elected Pope in succession to Pope John Paul I, 16 October 1978
Secretary of State, Cardinal Angelo Sodano, apptd December 1990

APOSTOLIC NUNCIATURE
54 Parkside, London SW19 5NF
Tel 0181-946 1410
Apostolic Nuncio, HE Archbishop Pablo Puente, apptd 1997

BRITISH EMBASSY TO THE HOLY SEE
91 Via Condotti, I–00187 Rome
Tel: Rome 6992 3561
Ambassador Extraordinary and Plenipotentiary, HE Mark Pellew, LVO, apptd 1997

TRADE WITH UK	1996	1997
Imports from UK	£2,160,000	£1,497,000
Exports to UK	8,000	139,000

VENEZUELA
República de Venezuela

AREA – 352,145 sq. miles (912,050 sq. km). Neighbours: Colombia (west), Guyana (east), Brazil (south)
POPULATION – 21,644,000 (1994 UN estimate): 67 per cent Mestizo, 21 per cent white, 10 per cent black and 2 per cent Indian. The language is Spanish. 96 per cent of the population is Roman Catholic
CAPITAL – Caracas (population, 2,784,042, 1990)
MAJOR CITIES – Barquisimeto (793,565); ΨMaracaibo (1,660,233); Maracay (449,180); Valencia (1,225,342), 1997 estimates
CURRENCY – Bolívar (Bs) of 100 céntimos
NATIONAL ANTHEM – Gloria Al Bravo Pueblo (Glory to the brave people)
NATIONAL DAY – 5 July
NATIONAL FLAG – Three horizontal stripes of yellow, blue, red with an arc of seven white stars on the blue stripe
LIFE EXPECTANCY (years) – male 66.68; female 72.80
POPULATION GROWTH RATE – 2.3 per cent (1995)
POPULATION DENSITY – 24 per sq. km (1995)
URBAN POPULATION – 84.1 per cent (1990)
ILLITERACY RATE – 8.9 per cent
ENROLMENT (percentage of age group) – primary 88 per cent (1992); secondary 20 per cent (1992); tertiary 28.5 per cent (1991)

Included in the area of the South American republic of Venezuela are 72 islands off the coast, with a total area of about 14,650 sq. miles, the largest being Margarita (area, about 400 sq. miles), which is politically associated with Tortuga, Cubagua and Coche to form the state of Nueva Esparta.

The mountains are the Eastern Andes and Maritime Andes, running south-west to north-east. The main range is known as the Sierra Nevada de Mérida, and contains Pico Bolivar (16,411 ft) and Picacho de la Sierra (15,420 ft). The principal river is the Orinoco, with innumerable affluents, the main river exceeding 1,600 miles in length. The upper waters of the Orinoco are united with those of the Rio Negro (a Brazilian tributary of the Amazon) by a natural river or canal, known as the Casiquiare. The coastal regions contain many lagoons and lakes, of which Maracaibo (area 8,296 sq. miles) is the largest lake in South America.

The climate is tropical, except where modified by altitude or tempered by sea breezes.

HISTORY AND POLITICS

The first Spanish settlement was established at Cumaná in 1520. During the 18th century there were a number of uprisings against Spanish rule, and troops led by Simón Bolívar finally defeated the Spanish in 1823. Venezuela became an independent republic in 1830.

Carlos Andrés Pérez and the (Social Democratic) Democratic Action (AD) party came to power in December 1988. They successfully introduced a series of free market economic reforms which led to impressive economic growth but increasing social problems. Two military coup attempts in 1992 were defeated but President Pérez resigned in May 1993 after the Supreme Court indicted him on corruption charges. Former President Rafael Caldera won the ensuing presidential election in December 1993 but his National Convergence coalition of 17 parties failed to gain majorities in either house of Congress, where the traditional AD and COPEI (Social

Christian) parties remained strong. Elections are due in November and December 1998.

POLITICAL SYSTEM
Under the 1961 constitution, executive power is held by the president, who also appoints the Council of Ministers. Legislative power is exercised by a bicameral National Congress, comprising a 201-member Chamber of Deputies and a Senate of 46 elected members plus the former presidents of constitutional governments as life members. The president and National Congress are directly elected for concurrent five-year terms.

FEDERAL STRUCTURE
Venezuela is divided into 22 states and two federal districts.

State	Area (sq. km)	Population (1990)	Capital
Amazonas	175,750	55,717	Puerto Ayacucho
Anzoátegui	43,300	859,758	Barcelona
Apure	76,500	285,412	San Fernando
Aragua	7,014	1,120,132	Maracay
Barinas	35,200	424,491	Barinas
Bolívar	238,000	900,310	Ciudad Bolívar
Carabobo	4,650	1,453,232	Valencia
Cojedes	14,800	182,066	San Carlos
Delta Amacuro	40,200	84,564	Tucupita
Falcón	24,800	599,185	Coro
Federal District	1,930	2,103,661	Caracas
Federal Dependencies	120	2,245	—
Guárico	64,986	488,623	San Juan
Lara	19,800	1,193,161	Barquisimeto
Mérida	11,300	570,215	Mérida
Miranda	7,950	1,871,093	Los Teques
Monagas	28,900	470,157	Maturín
Nueva Esparta	1,150	263,748	La Asunción
Portuguesa	15,200	576,435	Guanare
Sucre	11,800	679,595	Cumaná
Táchira	11,100	807,712	San Cristóbal
Trujillo	7,400	493,912	Trujillo
Yaracuy	7,100	384,536	San Felipe
Zulia	63,100	2,235,305	Maracaibo

HEAD OF STATE
President, Rafael Caldera Rodríguez, *elected* 5 December 1993, *sworn in* 2 February 1994

COUNCIL OF MINISTERS *as at July 1998*
Agriculture and Livestock, Ramón Ramírez López
Defence, Vice-Adm. Tito Manglio Rincón Bravo
Education, Antonio Luis Cárdenas
Energy and Mines, Erwin José Arrieta
Environment, Rafael Martínez Monro
Family Affairs, Carlos Altimari Gásperi
Federal District Governor, Abdón Vivas Terán
Finance, Freddy Rojas Parra
Foreign Relations, Miguel Angel Burelli Rivas
Health and Social Security, José Felix Oletta
Home Affairs, José Guillermo Andueza
Justice, Hilarión Cardoso
Labour, María Bernardoni de Govea
Ministers of State, Fernando Egaña *(Central Information Office)*; Guido Arnal Arroyo *(Science and Technology)*;
Presidents; Ricardo Combellas *(Commission for State Reform)*; Teodoro Petkoff *(General Planning Office)*; Oscar Sambrano *(National Council for Culture)*; Alberto Poletto *(Venezuelan Investment Fund)*; Hermmán Luis Soriano *(Venezuelan Tourism Corporation)*
Secretary of the Presidency, Asdrúbal Aguiar Aranguren

Trade and Industry, Iván Sanoja
Transport and Communications, Gen. Moíses Orozco
    Graterol
Urban Development, Francisco Gonzales

VENEZUELAN EMBASSY
1 Cromwell Road, London SW7 2HW
Tel 0171-584 4206/7
Ambassador Extraordinary and Plenipotentiary, HE Roy
    Chaderton-Matos, apptd 1996
Defence Attaché, Capt. L. E. Vargas-Lander

BRITISH EMBASSY
Apartado 1246, Caracas 1010–A
Tel: Caracas 993 4111
Ambassador Extraordinary and Plenipotentiary, HE Richard
    Wilkinson, CVO, apptd 1997
Deputy Head of Mission, Donald Maclaren of Maclaren
Defence Attaché, Col. P. A. Reynolds
First Secretary (Commercial), A. Goodworth

CONSULAR OFFICES – Caracas, Maracaibo, Margarita,
    Mérida, Puerto la Cruz

BRITISH COUNCIL DIRECTOR, P. de Quincey, Apartado
    65131, Caracas 1065

BRITISH-VENEZUELAN CHAMBER OF COMMERCE, Apartado
    5713, Caracas 1010. Torre Británica, Piso 10, Letra E,
    Av. José Félix Sosa, Altamira Sur, Caracas 1060

DEFENCE

The Army has 70 main battle tanks, 290 armoured
personnel carriers, 107 artillery pieces and five attack
helicopters. The Navy has two submarines, six frigates, six
patrol and coastal vessels, four combat aircraft and eight
armed helicopters at nine bases. The Air Force has 114
combat aircraft and 27 armed helicopters.
MILITARY EXPENDITURE – 1.2 per cent of GDP (1996)
MILITARY PERSONNEL – 79,000: Army 34,000, Navy
    15,000, Air Force 7,000, National Guard 23,000
CONSCRIPTION DURATION – 30 months

ECONOMY

Following a recession in 1993–4, the government announced a two-year economic stabilization programme in
September 1994, raising taxes, attracting foreign investment, reactivating the privatization programme and reducing government spending. In April 1996, foreign exchange controls were dismantled, supported by an IMF
stand-by credit of US$1,000 million. In March 1998 the
Inter-American Development Bank approved a US$350
million loan.
    Products of the tropical forest region include orchids,
wild rubber, timber, mangrove bark, balata gum and tonka
beans. Agricultural products include corn, bananas, cocoa
beans, coffee, cotton, rice, maize, sugar, sesame, groundnuts, potatoes, tomatoes, other vegetables, sisal and tobacco. There is an extensive beef and dairy farming industry.
Despite substantial improvements in agriculture, Venezuela is heavily reliant upon food imports, which constitute about 60 per cent of total consumption.
    The principal industry is that of petroleum, although
daily production in the oilfields (nationalized 1976) has
steadily declined since 1973 in line with Venezuela's
conservation policies. There are eight refineries. The
Orinoco heavy oil belt is being developed; estimates put
recoverable resources at 70,000 million barrels in the
Orinoco region.
    Aluminium is the second highest source of foreign
exchange after petroleum. Rich iron ore deposits in eastern

Venezuela have been developed. The government-owned
steel mill at Matanzas uses local iron ore and obtains its
electric power from hydroelectric installations on the
Caroni River. A mill at Ciudad Guayana produces
centrifugally-cast iron pipe. Other industry includes a
wide variety of manufacturing and component assembly,
principally petrochemicals, gold, diamonds and foodstuffs.
GNP – US$67,333 million; US$3,020 per capita (1996)
GDP – US$54,488 million (1994); US$2,618 per capita
    (1994)
ANNUAL AVERAGE GROWTH OF GDP – –1.6 per cent
    (1996)
INFLATION RATE – 99.9 per cent (1996)
UNEMPLOYMENT – 10.3 per cent (1995)
TOTAL EXTERNAL DEBT – US$35,344 million (1996)

TRADE

Apart from oil, the main exports are bauxite, iron ore,
agricultural products and basic manufactures. The main
imports are machinery and transport equipment, chemicals and foodstuffs. Some 50 per cent of trade is conducted
with the USA.
    In 1995 Venezuela had a trade surplus of US$7,290
million and a current account surplus of US$2,255 million.
In 1996 imports totalled US$10,532 million and exports
US$20,787 million.

Trade with UK	1996	1997
Imports from UK	£180,255,000	£203,825,000
Exports to UK	189,104,000	157,025,000

COMMUNICATIONS

There are about 93,471 km of roads, 29,954 km of them
paved. Road and river communications have made railways of negligible importance in Venezuela except for
carrying iron ore in the south-east, though the government
is expanding the network, and there are now some 363 km
of railway lines.
    The Orinoco is navigable for ocean-going ships (up to
40 ft draught) for 150 miles upstream, by large steamers for
700 miles, and by smaller vessels some 900 miles upstream.
There are seven Venezuelan airlines which between them
have a comprehensive network of internal and international flights. There is an international airport at Caracas.

VIETNAM
Công Hòa Xã Hôi Chu Nghĩa Viêt Nam

AREA – 128,066 sq. miles (331,689 sq. km). Neighbours:
    China (north), Laos and Cambodia (west)
POPULATION – 74,545,000 (1994 UN estimate). The
    language is Vietnamese
CAPITAL – Hanoi (population, 3,056,146, 1989)
MAJOR CITIES – Hai Phong (1,447,523); Ho Chi Minh
    City (3,924,435)
CURRENCY – Dông of 10 hào or 100 xu
NATIONAL ANTHEM – Tien Quan Ca (The troops are
    advancing)
NATIONAL DAY – 2 September
NATIONAL FLAG – Red, with yellow five-point star in
    centre
LIFE EXPECTANCY (years) – male 63.66; female 67.89
POPULATION GROWTH RATE – 2.4 per cent (1995)
POPULATION DENSITY – 225 per sq. km (1995)
URBAN POPULATION – 19.5 per cent (1994)
ILLITERACY RATE – 6.3 per cent

ENROLMENT (percentage of age group) – primary 95 per cent (1980); tertiary 4.1 per cent (1995)

HISTORY AND POLITICS

Following the end of the war in Vietnam in 1975, North and South Vietnam were reunified in 1976 under the name of the Socialist Republic of Vietnam. The national flag, anthem and capital of North Vietnam were adopted, and Saigon was renamed Ho Chi Minh City.

A new National Assembly of 450 members was elected in July 1997.

POLITICAL SYSTEM

Effective power lies with the Vietnamese Communist Party (VCP), its highest executive body being the Central Committee, elected by a Party Congress on a national basis. The Politburo and the Secretariat of the Central Committee exercise the real power.

The constitution of 1992 reaffirmed Communist Party rule but also formalized free market economic reforms. Presidential powers increased and the Council of Ministers was replaced by a prime minister and Cabinet. In January 1998 a Politburo Standing Board was created, comprising five high-ranking members of the Communist Party.

HEAD OF STATE
President, Tran Duc Luong
Vice-President, Nguyen Thi Binh

POLITBURO STANDING BOARD
Gen. Le Kha Phieu; Tran Duc Luong; Phan Van Khai; Nong Duc Manh; Pham The Duyet

COUNCIL OF MINISTERS *as at July 1998*
Prime Minister, Phan Van Khai
Deputy PMs, Pham Gia Khiem *(Culture, Education and the Environment)*; Nguyen Manh Cam *(Foreign Affairs)*; Nguyen Tan Dzung *(Governor of the State Bank)*; Ngo Xuan Loc *(Industry, Transportation and Construction)*; Nguyen Cong Tan *(Rural Development, Agriculture and Waterworks)*
Agriculture and Rural Development, Le Huy Ngo
Aquatic Resources, Ta Quang Ngoc
Child Protection and Care, Tran Thi Thanh Thanh
Construction, Nguyen Manh Kiem
Culture and Information, Nguyen Khoa Diem
Education and Training, Nguyen Minh Hien
Ethnic Minorities and Mountain Regions, Hoang Duc Nghi
Finance, Nguyen Sinh Hung
Government Personnel and Organization, Do Quang Trung
Government Secretariat, Lai Van Cu
Industry, Dang Vu Chu
Interior, Le Minh Huong
Justice, Nguyen Dinh Loc
Labour, War Invalids and Social Affairs, Tran Dinh Hoan
National Defence, Gen. Pham Van Tra
Physical Training and Sports, Ha Quang Du
Planning and Investment, Tran Xuan Gia
Population Activities and Family Planning, Tran Thi Trung Chien
Public Health, Do Nguyen Phuong
Science, Technology and Environment, Chu Tuan Nha
State Inspectorate, Ta Huu Thanh
Trade, Truong Dinh Tuyen
Transport, Le Ngoc Hoan

EMBASSY OF THE SOCIALIST REPUBLIC OF VIETNAM
12–14 Victoria Road, London W8 5RD
Tel 0171-937 1912/8564

Ambassador Extraordinary and Plenipotentiary, HE Huynh Ngoc An, apptd 1994

BRITISH EMBASSY
Central Building, 31 Hai Ba Trung, Hanoi
Tel: Hanoi 825 2510
Ambassador Extraordinary and Plenipotentiary, HE David Fall, apptd 1997
CONSULATE-GENERAL – Ho Chi Minh City
BRITISH COUNCIL DIRECTOR, I. Simm (*Cultural Attaché*)

DEFENCE

The Army has 1,315 main battle tanks, 1,400 armoured personnel carriers and armoured infantry fighting vehicles, and 2,330 artillery pieces. The Navy has seven frigates and 55 patrol and coastal vessels at seven principal bases. The Air Force has 201 combat aircraft and 32 armed helicopters.

MILITARY EXPENDITURE – 9.2 per cent of GDP (1996)
MILITARY PERSONNEL – 557,000: Army 420,000, Navy 42,000, Air Force 15,000, Air Defence Force 15,000, Paramilitaries 65,000
CONSCRIPTION DURATION – Two to three years

ECONOMY

Vietnam experienced economic difficulties following the imposition of socialist reforms in the south after 1975. However, economic reforms, known as 'Doi Moi' liberalization, were instituted in 1986 and have had significant success. The state's share of control has been greatly reduced in most sectors, leading to significant improvement in agricultural production, with Vietnam becoming a major rice exporter. Industry has grown and now contributes 30 per cent of GDP. Building materials, chemicals, machinery and foodstuffs are the main products.

Foreign investment has been actively encouraged. Investment was further boosted by the US decision in 1995 to establish full diplomatic and economic relations and by Vietnam's accession to ASEAN in August 1995. Oil production has increased and large natural gas reserves have been found offshore, though these are also claimed by China.

In response to the regional financial crisis, in October 1997 the government widened the dông's trading band from five to ten per cent, a *de facto* devaluation. In February 1998 the dông was officially devalued from 11,175 to the US dollar to 11,800 to the US dollar. International donors have pledged US$2.4 billion of development aid to Vietnam for 1998.

In 1994 imports totalled US$5,000 million and exports US$3,600 million.

GNP – US$21,915 million (1996); US$290 per capita (1996)
GDP – US$8,764 million (1994); US$213 per capita (1994)
TOTAL EXTERNAL DEBT – US$26,764 million (1996)

TRADE WITH UK	1996	1997
Imports from UK	£49,557,000	£94,746,000
Exports to UK	160,008,000	194,425,000

YEMEN
Al-Jamhuriya Al-Yamaniya

AREA – 203,850 sq. miles (527,968 sq. km). Neighbours: Saudi Arabia (north), Oman (east)
POPULATION – 14,501,000 (1995 census). The language is Arabic

CAPITAL – Sana'a (population, 926,595, 1995)
MAJOR CITIES – ΨAden (400,783), the former capital of
South Yemen; Hodeidah (246,068); Taiz (290,107), 1993
estimates
CURRENCY – Riyal of 100 fils
NATIONAL DAY – 22 May
NATIONAL FLAG – Horizontal bands of red, white and
black
LIFE EXPECTANCY (years) – male 49.90; female 50.40
POPULATION GROWTH RATE – 2.9 per cent (1994)
POPULATION DENSITY – 27 per sq. km (1995)
URBAN POPULATION – 26.4 per cent (1994)
ENROLMENT (percentage of age group) – tertiary 4.3 per
cent (1991)

Included in the state of Yemen are the offshore islands of
Perim and Kamaran in the Red Sea, and Socotra in the Gulf
of Aden. The border with Saudi Arabia is unclear and
remains in dispute; only the north-west corner of it is
delineated, by the 1934 Taif Accord. The highlands and
central plateau, and the highest portions of the maritime
range in the south, form the most fertile part of Arabia, with
abundant but irregular rainfall. The north is largely
composed of mountains and desert, and rainfall is generally
scarce.

HISTORY AND POLITICS

Turkish occupation of North Yemen (1872–1918) was
followed by the rule of the Hamid al-Din dynasty until a
revolution in 1962 overthrew the monarchy and the
Yemen Arab Republic was declared. The People's Republic of South Yemen was set up in 1967 when the British
government ceded power to the National Liberation
Front, bringing to an end 129 years of British rule in Aden
and some years of protectorate status in the hinterland.
Negotiations towards merging the two states began in 1979
and unification was proclaimed on 22 May 1990. The
constitution was approved by referendum in May 1991,
and a five-member Presidential Council comprising
former senior government figures of the separate states
was formed for the period of transition.

Following the general election in April 1993, the
General People's Congress (GPC, former ruling party in
the North), the Islamic Islah (Alliance for Reform) party
and the Yemeni Socialist Party (YSP, former ruling party
in the South) formed a coalition government and the
House of Representatives asked the Presidential Council
to remain in office.

Continued political tensions and a power struggle
between the former Northern and Southern Yemen elites
in mid-1993 led YSP leaders to withdraw to Aden in
August 1993. A reconciliation pact signed in February
1994 by President Saleh and Vice-President al-Beedh was
never implemented and, after sporadic clashes, a civil war
broke out on 5 May 1994 between the unmerged Northern
and Southern forces. The Southern leadership declared
secession on 20 May but fled when Aden was captured by
victorious Northern forces on 7 July, ending the civil war.

After the war a coalition government of the General
People's Congress and the Islamic Islah was formed, an
amnesty for the secessionists declared (with the exception
of key YSP leaders) and the constitution amended. The
Presidential Council was abolished and will be replaced
from 1999 with a directly elected president. Gen. Saleh was
elected president by the House of Representatives for a
five-year term. Multiparty democracy, a free market
economy and Sharia law are enshrined in the constitution.

A general election in April 1997 was won by the ruling
General People's Congress. In December 1997, the House
of Representatives endorsed the promotion of President
Saleh to the rank of Field Marshal.

HEAD OF STATE
President, Field Marshal Ali Abdullah Saleh, *took office*
22 May 1990, *elected* 1 October 1994
Vice-President, Maj.-Gen. Abd Rabbah Mansour Hadi

COUNCIL OF MINISTERS *as at July 1998*
Prime Minister, Abd al-Karim al-Iryani
Deputy P.M, Foreign Affairs, Abd al-Qadir Abd al-Rahman
Bajammal
Agriculture and Irrigation, Ahmad Salim al-Jabali
Awqaf (Religious Endowments) and Guidance, Ahmad al-
Shami
Civil Service and Administrative Reform, Muhammad Ahmad
al-Junayd
Construction, Housing and Urban Planning, Abdullah Husayn
al-Daf'i
Culture and Tourism, Abd al-Malik Mansur
Defence, Maj.-Gen. Muhammad Dayfallah Muhammad
Education, Yahya Muhammad Abdullah al-Shu'aybi
Finance, Alawi Salih al-Salami
Fisheries, Ahmad Musa'id Husayn
Industry, Abd al-Rahman Muhammad Ali Uthman
Information, Abd al-Rahman Muhammad al-Akwa
Interior, Maj.-Gen. Husayn Muhammad Arab
Justice, Ismael Ahmed Al-Wazir
Labour and Vocational Training, Muhammad Muhammad al-
Tayyib
Legal and Parliamentary Affairs, Abdullah Ahmad Ghanim
Local Administration, Sadiq Amin Aburas
Ministers of State, Mutahhar al-Sa'idi (*Affairs of the Council of
Ministers*); Faysal Mahmud Hasan Ali; Ahmad Ali al-
Bishari (*Expatriate Affairs*)
Oil and Mineral Resources, Muhammad al-Khadim al-Wajih
Planning and Development, Ahmad Muhammad Sufan
Power and Water, Ali Hamid Sharaf
Public Health, Abdullah Abd al-Wali Nashir
Social Security and Social Affairs, Muhammad Abdullah al-
Batani
Telecommunications, Ahmad Muhammad al-Ansi
Trade and Supply, Abd al-Aziz al-Kumaym
Transport, Brig.-Gen. Abd al-Malik Sayyani
Youth and Sport, Abd al-Wahhab Rawih

EMBASSY OF THE REPUBLIC OF YEMEN
57 Cromwell Road, London SW7 2ED
Tel 0171-584 6607
Ambassador Extraordinary and Plenipotentiary, HE Dr
Hussein Abdullah Al-Amri, apptd 1995

BRITISH EMBASSY
PO Box 1287, Sana'a
Tel: Sana'a 264 081
Ambassador Extraordinary and Plenipotentiary, HE Victor
Henderson, apptd 1997

BRITISH COUNCIL DIRECTOR, B. McSharry, MBE, As-
Sabain Street No. 7 (PO Box 2157), Sana'a

DEFENCE

The Army has 1,125 main battle tanks, 830 armoured
personnel carriers and armoured infantry fighting vehicles, and 512 artillery pieces. The Navy has 14 patrol and
coastal vessels at two bases. The Air Force has 61 combat
aircraft and six attack helicopters.
MILITARY EXPENDITURE – 3.7 per cent of GDP (1996)
MILITARY PERSONNEL – 146,300: Army 61,000, Navy
1,800, Air Force 3,500, Paramilitaries 80,000
CONSCRIPTION DURATION – Three years

ECONOMY

The economy has been seriously damaged by the civil war. However, the war had little effect on oil production, which averages roughly 400,000 barrels per day (bpd). The refinery at Aden was damaged in the civil war and is working at reduced capacity. An agreement was signed with the French oil company Total in September 1995 for the exploitation of liquefied natural gas over a 25-year period and the construction of a gas liquefication plant by 2000. Despite the production of oil Yemen remains one of the poorest states in the world. The critical economic situation obliged the government in 1995 to begin implementing a series of IMF and World Bank-prescribed reforms. In June 1997 international donors pledged US$1,800 million to assist the government's economic reform programme. In October 1997 the IMF approved loans of more than US$500 million, and in November 1997 the Paris Club agreed to reduce Yemen's external debt by 67 per cent, by writing off most of its debt to Russia.

Agriculture is the main occupation of the inhabitants. This is largely of a subsistence nature, sorghum, sesame, millet, wheat and barley being the chief crops. Exports include cotton, coffee, fruit, vegetables and hides. Imports include food and animals. In May 1998, Saudi Arabia lifted its ban on Yemeni nationals working in Saudi Arabia, originally imposed due to Yemen's perceived support for Iraq in the Gulf War.

In 1995 Yemen had a trade deficit of US$11 million and current account surplus of US$183 million.

GNP – US$6,016 million (1996); US$380 per capita (1996)
GDP – US$9,183 million (1994); US$1,049 per capita (1994)
TOTAL EXTERNAL DEBT – US$6,356 million (1996)

TRADE WITH UK	1996	1997
Imports from UK	£74,152,000	£72,053,000
Exports to UK	8,418,000	5,067,000

YUGOSLAVIA

Federativna Republika Jugoslavije – Federal Republic of Yugoslavia

AREA – 39,449 sq. miles (102,173 sq. km). Neighbours: Hungary (north), Romania and Bulgaria (east), the Former Yugoslav Republic of Macedonia and Albania (south), Bosnia-Hercegovina and Croatia (west)
POPULATION – 10,544,000 (1994 UN estimate): 66 per cent Serb and Montenegrin, 18 per cent Albanian, 8 per cent Muslim, 4 per cent Hungarian, with smaller numbers of Yugoslavs (no ethnic group), Croats and Bulgarians. The majority religion is Serbian Orthodox, with significant Muslim and small Roman Catholic minorities. The main language is Serbian (Serbo-Croat) (74 per cent), with Albanian and Hungarian minorities. Serbo-Croat is a South Slav language written in the Cyrillic script
CAPITAL – Belgrade (population, 1,136,786, 1991)
MAJOR CITIES – Kragujevac (146,607); Niš (175,555); Novi Sad (178,896); Podgorica (117,875), the capital of Montenegro; Priština (108,083); Subotica (100,219), 1991
CURRENCY – New dinar of 100 paras
NATIONAL ANTHEM – Hej, Slaveni, Jošte Živi Reč Naših Dedova (Oh! Slavs, our ancestors' words still live)
NATIONAL DAY – 27 April
NATIONAL FLAG – Three horizontal stripes of blue, white, red
LIFE EXPECTANCY (years) – male 69.50; female 74.49

POPULATION GROWTH RATE – 0.0 per cent (1995)
POPULATION DENSITY – 103 per sq. km (1995)
ILLITERACY RATE – 2.1 per cent
ENROLMENT (percentage of age group) – primary 69 per cent (1990); secondary 62 per cent (1990); tertiary 21.1 per cent (1995)

The climate is continental. Montenegro and southern Serbia are extremely mountainous, while the north is dominated by the low-lying plains of the Danube. The major rivers are: the Danube, which flows through the north of Serbia to Romania and Bulgaria; the Sava, which flows eastwards from Bosnia to join the Danube at Belgrade; the Drina, which flows along most of the Serbian–Bosnian border to join the Sava; and the Morava, which flows from the extreme south to join the Danube in the north.

HISTORY AND POLITICS

Serbia emerged from the rule of the Byzantine Empire in the 13th century to form a large and prosperous state in the Balkans. Defeat by the Turks in 1389 led to almost 500 years of Turkish rule. After gaining autonomy within the Ottoman Empire in 1815, Serbia became fully independent in 1878 and a kingdom in 1881. Montenegro was part of the Serbian state before it was conquered by the Turks in 1355; it became independent in 1851. At the end of the First World War Serbia and Montenegro joined with the former Austro-Hungarian provinces of Slovenia, Croatia and Bosnia-Hercegovina to form the 'Kingdom of Serbs, Croats and Slovenes' which was proclaimed on 1 December 1918 under the rule of the Serbian royal house. The state was renamed Yugoslavia in 1929. In 1941–5 Yugoslavia was occupied by Axis forces which were fought by Communist and royalist Chetnik partisans supplied by Allied forces. In 1945 with the defeat of Nazi Germany, Yugoslavia was reformed as a Communist federal republic under the presidency of partisan leader Josip Tito.

Tito died in 1980 and the delicate political balance of a rotating federal presidency was unable to contain the growing nationalist movements after his death. Efforts by the six republican presidents to negotiate a new federal or confederal structure for the country failed in 1991. On 25 June 1991 Slovenia and Croatia declared their independence from Yugoslavia. Intervention by the Federal Yugoslav Army (JNA) against local defence forces failed to prevent the disintegration of the federation and within two months the ethnically homogeneous Slovenia had negotiated its independence.

In Croatia the ethnic Serb minority refused to accept Croatia's independence and fighting began in July 1991 between Croat Defence Forces and Serbian guerrillas backed by the JNA. By September 1991 this had escalated into war between Croatia and Serbia. The war in Croatia continued until January 1992 when the EU and the UN were able to bring about a cease-fire (*see* Croatia).

Bosnia-Hercegovina adopted a memorandum on state sovereignty on 15 October 1991 and independence was affirmed in a referendum on 1 March 1992. Independence was supported by the Bosniacs (Muslims) and Croats but rejected by the ethnic Serbs and fighting between Bosniacs and Serbs broke out in March 1992. The JNA intervened against the Bosniacs but in May 1992 withdrew to Serbia and Montenegro.

On 27 April 1992 the two remaining republics of the former Socialist Federal Republic of Yugoslavia, Serbia and Montenegro, announced the formation of a new Yugoslav federation, which they invited Serbs in Croatia and Bosnia-Hercegovina to join. The new federation remains unrecognized internationally.

Federal legislative elections were held in November 1996. The Serbian Socialist Party emerged as the largest party in the federal legislature and formed a coalition government with Yugoslav United Left and New Democracy. Legislative elections were held in Montenegro in May 1998 and were won by reformists led by President Djukanovic.

INSURGENCY

The province of Kosovo in the south of Serbia is more than 90 per cent ethnically Albanian. In defiance of the Serbian authorities, presidential and parliamentary elections were held in Kosovo in May 1992, and were won by the Democratic League of Kosovo and its leader Ibrahim Rugova. Following clashes between ethnic Albanians and Serbian police in February and March 1998, the Serbian military attacked civilians in the province on the pretext of eliminating support for the Kosovo Liberation Army (KLA), an ethnic Albanian organization fighting for independence for the province. The international community condemned the brutality of the Serbian forces and a UN arms embargo was imposed on Yugoslavia, but the situation deteriorated in the following months with clashes between the KLA and security forces becoming commonplace. The civil unrest deteriorated into a state of open war. Following early gains by the KLA, Serbian forces fought back, sending tanks and artillery to engage in the systematic destruction of entire villages in the region in order to drive out KLA troops. More than 200,000 people have been left homeless by the conflict. The apparent lack of a formal leadership structure in the KLA, coupled with the intransigence of the Serbian leadership, has made finding a diplomatic resolution to the conflict difficult.

POLITICAL SYSTEM

The Federal Republic has a bicameral parliament with a directly elected 138-seat (108 Serbian, 30 Montenegrin) lower house, the Chamber of Citizens, and an indirectly elected 40-seat (20 Serbian, 20 Montenegrin) upper house, the Chamber of Republics. Both houses serve four-year terms. Executive power is vested in a federal president and government.

HEAD OF STATE

Federal President, Slobodan Milosevic, *elected by parliament* 15 July 1997

FEDERAL GOVERNMENT *as at July 1998*

Prime Minister, Momir Bulatovic
Deputy PMs, Jovan Zebic; Danilo Vuksanovic; Nikola Sainovic; Zoran Lilic; Vladan Kutlesic

Agriculture, Nedeljko Sipovac
Defence, Pavle Bulatovic
Development, Science and the Environment, Jagos Zelenovic
Economy, Rade Filipovic
External Trade, Borislav Vukovic
Finance, Dragisa Pesic
Financial Aid, Nenad Djokic
Foreign Affairs, Zivadin Jovanovic
Internal Affairs, Zoran Sokolovic
Internal Trade, Milorad Miskovic
Justice, Zoran Knezevic
Labour, Miodrag Kovac
Sports, Zoran Bingulac
Telecommunications, Dojcilo Radojevic
Transport, Dejan Drobnjakovic
Without Portfolio, Jugoslav Kostic

EMBASSY OF THE FEDERAL REPUBLIC OF YUGOSLAVIA
5 Lexham Gardens, London w8 5JJ
Tel 0171-370 6105
Ambassador Extraordinary and Plenipotentiary, HE Dr Milos Radulovic, apptd 1996
Minister-Counsellor, M. Paic
Defence Attaché, Col. Z. Djordjevic

BRITISH EMBASSY
Generala Ždanova 46, 11000 Belgrade
Tel: Belgrade 645055
Ambassador Extraordinary and Plenipotentiary, HE Brian Donelly, CMG, apptd 1998
Deputy Head of Mission and First Secretary (Political), Dr D. Landsman
Defence Attaché, Col. J. H. Crosland
First Secretary (Commercial), D. A. Slinn

BRITISH COUNCIL REPRESENTATIVE, J. McGrath, Generala Ždanova 34-Mezanin (Post Fah 248), 11001 Belgrade

MONTENEGRO

AREA – 5,331 sq. miles (13,812 sq. km)
POPULATION – 615,000: 62 per cent Montenegrin, 14.5 per cent Bosniac, 6.5 per cent Albanian and 3 per cent Serb
CAPITAL – Podgorica (population, 117,875, 1991)

The Montenegrin Social Democrat Party (former Communists) won multiparty elections in November 1996 for the 85-seat republican assembly and formed a government. The most recent presidential election was won by Milo Djukanovic, a reformist candidate favouring greater independence for the province.

President, Milo Djukanovic, *elected* 19 October 1997
Prime Minister, Filip Vujanovic

SERBIA

AREA – 34,175 sq. miles (88,538 sq. km)
POPULATION – 9,300,000, of whom 66 per cent are Serbs
CAPITAL – Belgrade (population, 1,136,786, 1991)

Serbia includes the provinces of Kosovo (population 1.6 million), of great historic importance to Serbs, and Vojvodina (population 2 million); the autonomy of both was ended in September 1990. Vojvodina, with its capital at Novi Sad, has a large Hungarian minority (21 per cent). Kosovo, with its capital at Priština, is predominantly Albanian (90 per cent). Following the conflict in Kosovo, more than 200,000 people have been left homeless and entire villages have been destroyed.

The Socialist Party of Serbia (SPS) (formerly the Communists) emerged as the largest party in multiparty elections for the 250-seat National Assembly, held in

November 1996, although the results of the election were disputed.

President, Milan Milutinovic
Prime Minister, Mirko Marjanovic

DEFENCE

The Army has 1,270 main battle tanks, 805 armoured personnel carriers and armoured infantry fighting vehicles, and 1,315 artillery pieces. The Navy has four submarines, four frigates and 34 patrol and coastal vessels at four bases. The Air Force has 241 combat aircraft and 56 armed helicopters.

MILITARY EXPENDITURE – 12.9 per cent of GDP (1996)
MILITARY PERSONNEL – 114,200: Army 90,000, Navy 7,500, Air Force 16,700
CONSCRIPTION DURATION – 12–15 months

ECONOMY

Since 1991 the economy has been devastated by the wars in Croatia and Bosnia-Hercegovina, by the UN economic sanctions and trade embargo, and because of the lack of free-market reforms. Most factories have closed. Only the evasion of UN sanctions and the country's agricultural self-sufficiency have kept it afloat. By 1993 inflation had reached 21,000 per cent a month, following continued over-printing of currency to finance war and subsidize industries. The tax system collapsed, output was one-third of pre-war levels, industry was working at one-quarter of capacity and the dinar had been devalued ten times. In January 1994 an economic stabilization package was introduced with a new superdinar pegged at one-to-one parity with the Deutsche Mark.

The UN voted to lift economic sanctions on 22 November 1995 following the conclusion of the Dayton Peace Accord. Industrial production remains extremely low. In April 1998 the dinar was devalued by 45 per cent against the Deutsche Mark. Following the conflict in Kosovo, the USA and EU froze all Yugoslav assets within their jurisdiction and banned all investment in the country.

GDP – US$16,654 million (1994); US$1,171 per capita (1994)
ANNUAL AVERAGE GROWTH OF GDP – – 2.0 per cent (1988)
INFLATION RATE – 117.4 per cent (1991)
TOTAL EXTERNAL DEBT – US$13,439 million (1996)

	1996	1997
TRADE WITH UK		
Imports from UK	£32,518,000	£37,777,000
Exports to UK	13,855,000	31,147,000

ZAMBIA
Republic of Zambia

AREA – 290,587 sq. miles (752,618 sq. km). Neighbours: Democratic Republic of Congo and Tanzania (north), Malawi (east), Mozambique, Zimbabwe and Namibia (south), Angola (west)
POPULATION – 9,373,000 (1994 UN estimate)
CAPITAL – Lusaka (population, 982,362, 1990)
MAJOR CITIES – Chingola (162,954); Kabwe (166,519); Kitwe (338,207); Luanshya (146,275); Mufulira (152,944); Ndola (376,311)
CURRENCY – Kwacha (K) of 100 ngwee
NATIONAL ANTHEM – Stand and Sing of Zambia, Proud and Free
NATIONAL DAY – 24 October (Independence Day)

NATIONAL FLAG – Green with three small vertical stripes, red, black and orange (next fly); eagle device on green above stripes
LIFE EXPECTANCY (years) – male 50.70; female 53.00
POPULATION GROWTH RATE – 3.0 per cent (1995)
POPULATION DENSITY – 12 per sq. km (1995)
URBAN POPULATION – 39.4 per cent (1990)
MILITARY EXPENDITURE – 1.1 per cent of GDP (1996)
MILITARY PERSONNEL – 23,000: Army 20,000, Air Force 1,600, Paramilitaries 1,400
ILLITERACY RATE – 21.8 per cent
ENROLMENT (percentage of age group) – primary 75 per cent (1995); secondary 16 per cent (1994); tertiary 2.5 per cent (1994)

Zambia lies on the plateau of Central Africa. With the exception of the valleys of the Zambezi, the Luapula, the Kafue and the Luangwa rivers, and the Luano valley, elevations vary from 3,000 to 5,000 feet above sea level, but in the north-east the plateau rises to occasional altitudes of over 6,000 feet. Although Zambia lies within the tropics, and fairly centrally in the African land mass, its elevation relieves it from extremely high temperatures and humidity.

HISTORY AND POLITICS

Northern Rhodesia came under British rule in 1889. It achieved internal self-government when the Federation of Rhodesia and Nyasaland was dissolved in 1963 and became an independent republic within the Commonwealth on 24 October 1964 under the name of Zambia.

Zambia was a one-party state (the United National Independence Party) from 1973 until 1990, when pressure from opposition groups led to a new constitution (August 1991) and multiparty legislative and presidential elections in October 1991. The Movement for Multiparty Democracy (MMD) won 125 of the 150 seats in parliament, and the MMD candidate Frederick Chiluba defeated Kenneth Kaunda, who had ruled since independence, in the presidential election.

Following an abortive coup attempt in October 1997, the president declared a state of emergency. 90 people were subsequently arrested in connection with the coup, including former President Kaunda. The state of emergency was lifted in March 1998.

HEAD OF STATE
President, Frederick J. Chiluba, *elected* October 1991, *re-elected* 18 November 1996
Vice-President, Lt.-Gen. (retd) Christon Tembo

CABINET *as at July 1998*

Agriculture, Food and Fisheries, Amusaa Mwanamwambwa
Commerce, Trade and Industry, Enock Kavindele
Communications and Transport, Dawson Lupunga
Community Development and Social Services, Samuel Miyanda
Defence, Chitalu Sampa
Education, Brig.-Gen. Godfrey Miyanda
Energy and Water Development, Benjamin Yoram Mwila
Environment and Natural Resources, Alfeyo Hambayi
Finance and Economic Development, Edith Nawakwi
Foreign Affairs, Keli Walubita
Health, Nkandu Luo
Home Affairs, Peter Machungwa
Information and Broadcasting, David Mpamba
Labour and Social Security, Newstead Zimba
Lands, Anoshi Chipawa
Legal Affairs, Vincent Malambo
Local Government and Housing, Ben Mwiinga

Mines and Mineral Development, Syamujaye
Syamukayumbu
Science, Technology and Vocational Training, Lawrence
Shimba
State House, Eric Silwamba
Tourism, Katele Kalumba
Without Portfolio, Michael Sata
Works and Supply, Suresh Desai
Youth, Sport and Child Development, William Harrington

HIGH COMMISSION FOR THE REPUBLIC OF ZAMBIA
2 Palace Gate, London W8 5NG
Tel 0171-589 6655
High Commissioner, HE Prof. Moses Musonda, apptd 1998
Defence Adviser, Brig.-Gen. M. G. Lisita

BRITISH HIGH COMMISSION
Independence Avenue (PO Box 50050), 15101, Lusaka
Tel: Lusaka 251133
High Commissioner, HE Thomas Young, apptd 1997
Deputy High Commissioner, P. W. D. Nessling
First Secretary (Commercial/Consular), R. Clark

BRITISH COUNCIL DIRECTOR, M. Fryars, Heroes Place,
Cairo Road (PO Box 34571), Lusaka

ECONOMY

In 1991, the MMD government began the transition from a
state-controlled economy to a free market system. Privatization has been encouraged, foreign exchange controls
have been removed and the Kwacha has been floated. Price
subsidies and tariffs have been lowered or abolished, but
high inflation and interest rates have caused widespread
hardship, and increased imports have affected manufacturing. Principal agricultural products are maize, sugar,
groundnuts, cotton, livestock, vegetables and tobacco.
Following the reforms initiated by the government, the
US government wrote off K59,000 million of debt in 1993.
The IMF lifted its suspension of Zambia, in place since
September 1987; loans worth US$1,800 million were
subsequently approved.
In 1995 imports totalled US$1,499 million and exports
US$1,196 million.
GNP – US$3,363 million (1996); US$360 per capita (1996)
GDP – US$4,114 million (1994); US$367 per capita (1994)
ANNUAL AVERAGE GROWTH OF GDP – 6.4 per cent (1996)
INFLATION RATE – 43.9 per cent (1996)
TOTAL EXTERNAL DEBT – US$7,113 million (1996)

TRADE WITH UK	1996	1997
Imports from UK	£51,544,000	£45,620,000
Exports to UK	17,726,000	32,067,000

ZIMBABWE
Republic of Zimbabwe

AREA – 150,872 sq. miles (390,757 sq. km). Neighbours:
Zambia (north), Mozambique (east), South Africa
(south), Botswana and Namibia (west)
POPULATION – 11,526,000 (1994 UN estimate);
10,400,000 (1992 census). The official language is
English, with Shona the largest indigenous language
group
CAPITAL – Harare (population, 1,189,103, 1992)
MAJOR CITIES – Bulawayo (621,742), the largest town in
Matabeleland; Chitungwiza (274,912)
CURRENCY – Zimbabwe dollar (Z$) of 100 cents
NATIONAL ANTHEM – Ngaikomberarwe Nyika Ye
Zimbabwe (Blessed be the country of Zimbabwe)

NATIONAL DAY – 18 April (Independence Day)
NATIONAL FLAG – Seven horizontal stripes of green,
yellow, red, black, red, yellow, green; a white, black-
bordered, triangle based on the hoist containing the
national emblem
LIFE EXPECTANCY (years) – male 58.00; female 62.00
POPULATION GROWTH RATE – 4.1 per cent (1995)
POPULATION DENSITY – 29 per sq. km (1995)
MILITARY EXPENDITURE – 3.8 per cent of GDP (1996)
MILITARY PERSONNEL – 60,800: Army 35,000, Air Force
4,000, Paramilitaries 21,800

HISTORY AND POLITICS

Southern Rhodesia was granted responsible government
in 1923. An illegal declaration of independence on 11
November 1965 was finally terminated on 12 December
1979. Following elections in February 1980 the country
became independent on 18 April 1980 as the Republic of
Zimbabwe, a member of the British Commonwealth.
The independence constitution was amended in 1987,
making the presidency an executive post. The president is
popularly elected for a six-year term, appoints the Cabinet
and can veto parliamentary bills. The House of Assembly
has 150 members: 120 elected, eight provincial governors,
ten traditional chiefs and 12 others appointed by the
president. A merger agreement between the ZANU (PF)
and ZAPU parties was signed in 1987 with a view to the
eventual creation of a one-party state. The new party is
known as ZANU-PF. The most recent general election
was held in April 1995 and ZANU-PF won 118 of the 120
elective seats, although it lost a by-election in November
1995. President Mugabe was re-elected for a six-year term
in March 1996, following the withdrawal of the other two
contenders.
The country is divided into eight provinces: Manica-
land, Masvingo, Matabeleland North, Matabeleland
South, Midlands, Mashonaland West, Mashonaland Central and Mashonaland East.

HEAD OF STATE
Executive President, C.-in-C. of the Defence Forces, Robert
Gabriel Mugabe, *elected* 30 December 1987, *re-elected*
March 1990, March 1996
Vice-Presidents, Simon Vengesai Muzenda; Dr Joshua
Nkomo

CABINET *as at July 1998*
Defence, Moven Mahachi
Education, Sports and Culture, Gabriel Machinga
Finance, Dr Herbert Murerwa
Foreign Affairs, Dr Stanislaus Mudenge
Health and Child Welfare, Dr Timothy Stamps
Higher Education and Technology, Ignatius Chombo
Home Affairs, Dumiso Dabengwa
Industry and Commerce, Dr Nathan Shamuyarira
Information, Posts and Telecommunications, Chenhamo
Chimulengwende
Justice, Legal and Parliamentary Affairs, Emmerson
Mnangagwa
Lands and Agriculture, Kumbirai Kangai
Local Government and National Housing, John Nkomo
Mines, Environment and Tourism, Simon Moyo
National Affairs, Employment Creation and Co-operatives,
Virginia Lesabe
National Security, Dr Sidney Sekeramayi
Planning, Richard Hove
President's Office, Cephas Msipa
Public Service, Labour and Social Welfare, Florence Chitauro
Rural Resources and Water Development, Joyce Mujuru
Transport and Energy, Enos Chikowore

Without Portfolio, Dr Eddison Zvobgo; Joseph Msika; Jess Connors

HIGH COMMISSION OF THE REPUBLIC OF ZIMBABWE
Zimbabwe House, 429 Strand, London WC2R 0SA
Tel 0171-836 7755
High Commissioner, HE Dr Ngoni Togarepi Chideya, apptd 1993
Minister-Counsellor, J. Mupamhanga
Defence Adviser, Lt.-Col. E. Zabanyana
First Secretary, B. Mutoti (*Commercial*)

BRITISH HIGH COMMISSION
Corner House, Samora Machel Avenue (PO Box 4490), Harare
Tel: Harare 772990
High Commissioner, HE Peter Longworth, apptd 1998
Deputy High Commissioner, T. Hay-Campbell
Defence Adviser, Col. A. Reed Screen, OBE
First Secretaries, A. R. Ashcroft (*Commercial*); G. M. Johnson (*Consular*)

BRITISH COUNCIL DIRECTOR, Dr J. Taylor, 23 Jason Moyo Avenue (PO Box 664), Harare

ECONOMY

Ten years of socialism and central planning in 1980–90, coupled with a period of drought, brought the economy to crisis point before free-market economic reforms were introduced with the assistance of the World Bank in 1990. Reforms have included the floating of the currency, opening the market to imports, and a reduction in subsidies. The programme has been partially implemented but the economy remains highly regulated and weak. Inflation remains high and in January 1998 there were riots following the announcement of a 21 per cent increase in the price of maize, a dietary staple. Between October 1997 and January 1998, food prices rose by 140 per cent. A general strike was held on 3–4 March 1998 in protest at the price rises. In May 1998, the United Merchant Bank was declared insolvent, prompting fears of a financial crisis across the sector.

The Supreme Court approved government plans to seize 12 million acres of predominantly white-owned farmland in June 1996, though controversy over the repossession and the question of compensation payments, mean that the future of the plan is unclear.

The country is endowed with minerals, water, forests, wildlife and other resources. The agricultural sector is well-developed and employs 68 per cent of the workforce. Tobacco remains the most important crop in terms of export (Zimbabwe is the largest exporter in the world), and maize the most important for domestic consumption. Other crops include wheat, cotton, sugar, horticultural products, fruit and vegetables. Beef is exported to the EU.

The manufacturing sector is very dependent on the agricultural sector for raw materials. Industry is also dependent on imports e.g. fuel oil, steel products and chemicals, as well as heavy machinery and items of transport. The mining sector, although contributing a relatively small portion to GDP, is important to the economy as a foreign exchange earner. Almost all mineral production is exported. Gold is the most important mineral; others are asbestos, diamonds, silver, nickel, copper, platinum, chrome ore, tin, iron ore and cobalt. There is a successful ferro-chrome industry and a substantial steel works which has been heavily subsidized by government.

Tourism is of growing importance, with more than 1,000,000 visitors in 1995.

In 1994 Zimbabwe had a trade surplus of US$158 million and a current account deficit of US$425 million. Imports totalled US$2,241 million. In 1995 exports totalled US$2,119 million.
GNP – US$6,815 million (1996); US$610 per capita (1996)
GDP – US$7,033 million (1994); US$568 per capita (1994)
ANNUAL AVERAGE GROWTH OF GDP – −2.8 per cent (1991)
INFLATION RATE – 21.4 per cent (1996)
TOTAL EXTERNAL DEBT – US$5,005 million (1996)

TRADE WITH UK	1996	1997
Imports from UK	£103,819,000	£97,531,000
Exports to UK	136,516,000	128,361,000

EDUCATION

Education is compulsory, and the language of instruction is English. Over 80 per cent of schools are government-aided. There are four universities; the University of Zimbabwe was founded in 1955.
ILLITERACY RATE – 14.9 per cent
ENROLMENT (percentage of age group) – tertiary 6.9 per cent (1995)

UK Overseas Territories

ANGUILLA

TRADE WITH UK	1996	1997
Imports from UK	£2,688,000	£5,137,000
Exports to UK	46,000	13,000

AREA – 37 sq. miles (96 sq. km)
POPULATION – 8,000 (1994 UN estimate)
CAPITAL – The Valley (population, 1,400, 1994)
CURRENCY – East Caribbean dollar (EC$) of 100 cents
FLAG – British blue ensign with the coat of arms and three dolphins in the fly
POPULATION GROWTH RATE – 2.7 per cent (1995)
POPULATION DENSITY – 83 per sq. km (1995)
GDP – US$67 million (1994); US$9,933 per capita (1994)

Anguilla is a flat coralline island in the Caribbean, about 16 miles in length, three and a half miles in breadth at its widest point and its area is about 35 sq. miles (91 sq. km). The island is covered with low scrub and fringed with white coral-sand beaches. The climate is pleasant, with temperatures in the range of 24-30° C throughout the year.

HISTORY AND POLITICS

Anguilla has been a British colony since 1650. For much of its history it was linked administratively with St Christopher, but three months after the Associated State of Saint Christopher (St Kitts)-Nevis-Anguilla came into being in 1967, the Anguillans repudiated government from St Kitts. A Commissioner was installed in 1969 and in 1976 Anguilla was given a new status and separate constitution. Final separation from St Kitts and Nevis was effected on 19 December 1980 and Anguilla reverted to a British dependency. A new constitution was introduced in 1982, providing for a Governor, an Executive Council comprising four elected Ministers and two ex-officio members (the Attorney-General and Permanent Secretary, Finance), and an 11-member legislative House of Assembly presided over by a Speaker.

The 1982 Constitution (Amendment) Order 1990 came into operation on 30 May 1990. Among the new constitutional provisions are a Deputy Governor (who replaces the Permanent Secretary (Finance) in the Executive Council and the Legislature), a Parliamentary Secretary, Leader of Opposition and Deputy Speaker.

Governor, HE Robert Harris, *apptd* 1997
Deputy Governor, Roger Cousins

EXECUTIVE COUNCIL *as at June 1998*
Chairman, The Governor
Chief Minister, Hubert Hughes
Attorney-General, Ronald Scipio
Finance and Economic Development, Victor Banks
Infrastructure, Communications and Utilities, Albert Hughes
Social Services, Edison Baird
Member, The Deputy Governor

ECONOMY

Low rainfall limits agricultural output and export earnings are mainly from sales of fish and lobsters. Tourism has developed rapidly in recent years and accounts for most of the island's economic activity. In 1996 there were 37,498 tourists and a further 48,741 day visitors.

ASCENSION

— *see* St Helena

BERMUDA

AREA – 20 sq. miles (53 sq. km)
POPULATION – 63,000 (1994 UN estimate)
CAPITAL – ΨHamilton (population, 2,277, 1994)
CURRENCY – Bermuda dollar of 100 cents
FLAG – British red ensign with the shield of arms in the fly
LIFE EXPECTANCY (years) – male 70.23; female 78.01
POPULATION GROWTH RATE – 0.8 per cent (1995)
POPULATION DENSITY – 1,189 per sq. km (1995)
GDP – US$1,684 million (1994); US$29,859 per capita (1994)

The Bermudas, or Somers Islands, are a cluster of about 100 small islands (about 20 of which are inhabited) situated in the west of the Atlantic Ocean, the nearest point of the mainland being Cape Hatteras in North Carolina, about 570 miles distant.

HISTORY AND POLITICS

The colony derives its name from Juan Bermudez, a Spaniard, who sighted it before 1515. No settlement was made until 1609 when Sir George Somers, who was shipwrecked there on his way to Virginia, colonized the islands.

Internal self-government was introduced in 1968. There is a Senate of 11 members and an elected House of Assembly of 40 members. The Governor retains responsibility for external affairs, defence, internal security and the police, although administrative matters for the police service have been delegated to the Minister of Labour, Home Affairs and Public Safety. Independence from the UK was rejected in a referendum in August 1995.

The last general election was held on 5 October 1993. The United Bermuda Party holds 22 seats, and the Progressive Labour Party 18 seats.

Governor and Commander-in-Chief, HE Thorold Masefield, CMG, *apptd* 1997
Deputy Governor, Peter Willis

CABINET *as at June 1998*
Premier, Pamela Gordon
Deputy Premier, Development and Opportunity, Jerome Dill
Education, Timothy Smith
Environment, Harry Soares
Finance, Grant Gibbons
Government and Community Services, Sen. Yvette Swan
Health and Family Services, Wayne Furbert
Labour, Home Affairs and Public Safety, Maxwell Burgess
Minister without Portfolio, Margaret Young
Telecommunications, Sen. Edward Trenton Richards
Tourism, David Dodwell
Transport, Irwin Adderley

1070 UK Overseas Territories

Works and Engineering, Jim Woolridge
Youth, Sport, Parks and Recreation, John Barritt
President of the Senate, A. S. Jackson, CBE
Speaker of the House of Assembly, Ernest DeCouto
Chief Justice, Austin Ward, QC

ECONOMY

The islands' economic structure is based on tourism, the major industry, and international company business, attracted by the low level of taxation and sophisticated telecommunications system. In 1996 a total of 576,628 visitors arrived by air and cruise ship.

Locally manufactured concentrates, perfumes, cut flowers and pharmaceuticals are the islands' leading exports. Little food is produced except vegetables and fish, other foodstuffs being imported.

In November 1995, the US, UK and Canadian governments handed over 1,500 acres of land (roughly 10 per cent of the colony), to the government. The land, which had been used for military bases, included an airport on St David's Island.

TRADE WITH UK	1996	1997
Imports from UK	£19,032,000	£55,366,000
Exports to UK	7,150,000	54,203,000

COMMUNICATIONS

One daily and two weekly newspapers are published in Bermuda. Three commercial companies operate radio and television services, including a cable-television system. The Bermuda Telephone Company and Cable and Wireless provide telecommunications links to more than 140 countries.

EDUCATION

Free elementary education was introduced in 1949. Free secondary education was introduced in 1965 for those children in the aided and maintained schools who were below the upper limit of the statutory school age of 18 (from 1969 onwards).

THE BRITISH ANTARCTIC TERRITORY

AREA – 660,000 sq. miles (1,709,340 sq. km)
POPULATION – No permanent population
FLAG – British white ensign, without the cross of St George, with the coat of arms of the Territory in the fly

The British Antarctic Territory was designated in 1962 and consists of the areas south of 60°S. latitude and bounded by longitudes 20°W. and 80°W. The territory includes the South Orkney Islands, the South Shetland Islands, the mountainous Antarctic Peninsula (highest point Mount Jackson, 10,443 ft above sea level) and all adjacent islands, and the land mass extending to the South Pole. The territory has no indigenous inhabitants and the British population consists of the scientists and technicians at the British Antarctic Survey stations. These numbered 42 during the 1997–8 winter, but this number increases considerably in the southern hemisphere's summer months with the arrival of field scientists. Argentina, Brazil, Chile, China, Korea (South), Poland, USA, Russia, Spain, Ukraine and Uruguay also have scientific stations in the territory.

The first two British Antarctic Survey stations were established in the South Shetland Islands in 1944, and by 1956 the number of stations had risen to 12. Due to the completion of field work in some areas and increased mobility, this number has now been reduced to four: Rothera (Adelaide Island), Halley (Caird Coast) and, in summer only, Fossil Bluff (George VI Sound) and Signy Island (South Orkney Islands). Fifteen other stations have been established but are at present unoccupied.

The territory is administered by a Commissioner, resident in London.

Commissioner (non-resident), Charles John Branford White, *apptd* 1997

THE BRITISH INDIAN OCEAN TERRITORY

AREA – 23 sq. miles (59 sq. km)
POPULATION – No permanent population
FLAG – Divided horizontally into blue and white wavy stripes, with the Union Flag in the canton and a crowned palm-tree over all in the fly

The British Indian Ocean Territory was established by an Order in Council in 1965 and included islands formerly administered from Mauritius and the Seychelles. The islands of Farquhar, Desroches and Aldabra became part of the Seychelles when it became independent in 1976; since then the Territory has consisted of the Chagos Archipelago only.

The Chagos Archipelago consists of six main groups of islands situated on the Great Chagos Bank and covering some 21,000 sq. miles (54,389 sq. km). The largest and most southerly of the Chagos Islands is Diego Garcia, a sand cay with a land area of about 17 sq. miles approximately 1,100 miles east of Mahé, used as a joint naval support facility by Britain and the USA.

The other main island groups of the archipelago, Peros Banhos (29 islands with a total land area of 4 sq. miles) and Salomon (11 islands with a total land area of 2 sq. miles) are uninhabited. The islands have a tropical maritime climate, with average temperatures between 25° C and 29° C in Diego Garcia, and rainfall in the whole archipelago of 90–100 inches a year.

Commissioner, Christopher Wilton, *apptd* 1998
Administrator, Louise Savill, *apptd* 1996

TRADE WITH UK	1996	1997
Imports from UK	£1,869,000	£1,406,000
Exports to UK	30,000	2,000

BRITISH VIRGIN ISLANDS

AREA – 58 sq. miles (151 sq. km)
POPULATION – 19,107 (1997 estimate; by island: Tortola 15,687; Virgin Gorda 2,885; Anegada 191; Jost Van Dyke 170; other islands 172)
CAPITAL – ΨRoad Town (population, 3,983, 1994)
CURRENCY – US dollar (US$) (£ sterling and EC$ also circulate)
FLAG – British blue ensign with the shield of arms in the fly
POPULATION GROWTH RATE – 3.4 per cent (1995)
POPULATION DENSITY – 126 per sq. km (1995)
GDP – US$171 million (1994); US$10,730 per capita (1994)

The Virgin Islands, divided between the UK and the USA, are situated at the eastern extremity of the Greater Antilles. Those of the group which are British number 46, of which 11 are inhabited, and have a total area of about 59 sq. miles (153 sq. km). The principal islands are Tortola, the largest (area, 21 sq. miles), Virgin Gorda (8¼ sq. miles), Anegada (15 sq. miles) and Jost Van Dyke (3½ sq. miles).

Apart from Anegada, which is a flat coral island, the British Virgin Islands are hilly, being an extension of the Puerto Rico and the US Virgin Islands archipelago. The highest point is Sage Mountain on Tortola which rises to a height of 1,780 feet.

The islands lie within the trade winds belt and possess a sub-tropical climate. The average temperature varies from 22°–28° C in winter to 26°–31° C in summer. Average annual rainfall is 53 inches.

HISTORY AND POLITICS

Under the 1977 constitution the Governor, appointed by the Crown, remains responsible for defence and internal security, external affairs and the civil service but in other matters acts in accordance with the advice of the Executive Council. The Executive Council consists of the Governor as Chairman, one ex-officio member (the Attorney-General), the Chief Minister and three other ministers. The Legislative Council consists of a Speaker chosen from outside the Council, one ex-officio member (the Attorney-General), and 13 elected members returned from ten electoral districts.

Governor, HE Frank Savage, CMG, OBE, LVO, apptd 1998
Deputy Governor, Elton Georges, OBE

EXECUTIVE COUNCIL *as at June 1998*
Chairman, The Governor
Chief Minister and Minister of Finance, Ralph O'Neal, OBE
Attorney-General, Dancia Penn
Communications and Works, Alvin Christopher
Health, Education and Welfare, Eileene L. Parsons
Natural Resources and Labour, Oliver Cills

Puisne Judge (resident), Justice Stanley Moore

ECONOMY

Tourism is the main industry but the financial centre is growing steadily in importance. Other industries include a rum distillery, three stone-crushing plants and factories manufacturing concrete blocks and paint. The major export items are fresh fish, gravel, sand, fruit and vegetables; exports are largely confined to the US Virgin Islands. Chief imports are building materials, machinery, cars and beverages.

TRADE WITH UK	1996	1997
Imports from UK	£5,048,000	£4,906,000
Exports to UK	12,935,000	2,953,000

COMMUNICATIONS

The principal airport is on Beef Island, linked by bridge to Tortola, and an extended runway of 3,600 ft enables larger aircraft to call. There is a second airfield on Virgin Gorda and a third on Anegada. There are direct shipping services to the UK and the USA and fast passenger services connect the main islands by ferry.

CAYMAN ISLANDS

AREA – 102 sq. miles (264 sq. km)
POPULATION – 35,000 (1994 UN estimate)
CAPITAL – ΨGeorge Town (population, 20,000, 1994)
CURRENCY – Cayman Islands dollar (CI$) of 100 cents
FLAG – British blue ensign with the arms on a white disc in the fly
POPULATION GROWTH RATE – 3.3 per cent (1995)
POPULATION DENSITY – 117 per sq. km (1995)
GDP – US$536 million (1994); US$19,351 per capita (1994)

The Cayman Islands consist of three islands, Grand Cayman, Cayman Brac, and Little Cayman. About 150 miles south of Cuba, the islands are divided from Jamaica, 180 miles to the south-east, by the Cayman Trench, the deepest part of the Caribbean. The nearest point on the US mainland is Miami in Florida, 450 miles to the north. Cooled by trade winds, the annual average temperature and rainfall are 27.2° C and 50.7 inches respectively.

HISTORY AND POLITICS

The colony derives its name from the Carib word for the crocodile, 'caymanas', which appeared in the log of the first English visitor to the islands, Sir Francis Drake. Although tradition has it that the first settlers arrived in 1658, the first recorded settlers arrived in 1666–71. The first recorded permanent settlers followed the first land grant by Britain in 1734. The islands were placed under direct control of Jamaica in 1863. When Jamaica became independent in 1962, the islands opted to remain under the British Crown.

The constitution provides for a Governor, a Legislative Assembly and an Executive Council, and effectively allows a large measure of self-government. Unless there are exceptional reasons, the Governor accepts the advice of the Executive Council, which comprises three official members and five ministers elected from the 15 elected members of the Assembly. The official members also sit in the Assembly. The Governor has responsibility for the police, civil service, defence and external affairs. The Governor handed over the presidency of the Legislative Assembly to the Speaker in 1991. The normal life of the Assembly is four years, with a general election next due in November 2000.

Governor, HE John W. Owen, MBE, apptd 1995

EXECUTIVE COUNCIL *as at June 1998*
President, The Governor
Chief Secretary, James Ryan, MBE
Agriculture, Environment, Communications and Works, John McLean, OBE
Attorney-General, Richard Coles
Community Development, Sports, Women's Affairs, Youth and Culture, Julianna O'Connor-Connolly
Education, Aviation and Planning, Truman Bodden, OBE
Financial Secretary, George McCarthy, OBE
Health, Drug Abuse Prevention and Rehabilitation, Anthony Eden
Tourism, Commerce and Transport, Thomas Jefferson, OBE
Speaker of Legislative Assembly, Capt. M. Kirkconnell, MBE

CAYMAN ISLANDS GOVERNMENT OFFICE, 6 Arlington Street, London SW1A 1RE. Tel: 0171-491 7772.
Government Representative, T. Russell, CMG, CBE

ECONOMY

With a complete absence of direct taxation, the Cayman Islands has become successful over the past 25 years as an offshore financial centre. With representation from 62 countries, there were, at the end of 1996, 648 banks and trust companies, of which local offices were maintained by 107. In addition, there were 498 licensed insurance companies and 34,000 registered companies. The Cayman Islands stock exchange opened in January 1997. Tourism, with an emphasis on scuba diving, has also been developed successfully. There were 373,200 visitors by air and 771,068 cruise ship callers in 1996.

The two industries support a heavy imbalance in trade resulting from the need to import most of what is consumed and used on the islands, and have created a thriving local economy. Import duty and fees from financial centre operations have provided revenue enabling the government to undertake heavy investment in education (which is provided free to all four- to 16-year olds), health and other social programmes.

TRADE WITH UK	1996	1997
Imports from UK	£17,284,000	£11,407,000
Exports to UK	1,372,000	35,860,000

FALKLAND ISLANDS

AREA – 4,700 sq. miles (12,173 sq. km)
POPULATION – 2,000 (1994 UN estimate)
CAPITAL – ΨStanley (population, 1,636, 1994)
CURRENCY – Falkland pound of 100 pence
FLAG – British blue ensign with the arms on a white disc in the fly
POPULATION GROWTH RATE – 0 per cent (1995)
URBAN POPULATION – 76.0 per cent (1991)

The Falkland Islands, the only considerable group in the South Atlantic, lie about 300 miles east of the Straits of Magellan. They consist of East Falkland (area 2,610 sq. miles; 6,759 sq. km), West Falkland (2,090 sq. miles; 5,413 sq. km) and over 100 small islands. Mount Usborne (E. Falkland), the loftiest peak, rises 2,312 feet above sea level. The islands are chiefly moorland.

The climate is cool. At Stanley the mean monthly temperature varies between 19° C in January and 2° C in July.

HISTORY AND POLITICS

The Falklands were sighted first by Davis in 1592, and then by Hawkins in 1594; the first known landing was by Strong in 1690. A settlement was made by France in 1764; this was subsequently sold to Spain, but the latter country recognized Great Britain's title to a part at least of the group in 1771. The first British settlement was established in 1766. After Argentina declared independence from Spain, the Argentine government in 1820 proclaimed its sovereignty over the Falklands and a settlement was founded in 1826. The settlement was destroyed by the Americans in 1831. In 1833 occupation was resumed by the British for the protection of the seal-fisheries, and the islands were permanently colonized. Argentina continued to claim sovereignty over the islands (known to them as *las Islas Malvinas*), and in pursuance of this claim invaded the islands on 2 April 1982 and also occupied South Georgia. A naval and military force dispatched from Great Britain recaptured South Georgia on 25 April and after landing at San Carlos Bay on 21 May, recaptured the islands from the

Argentines, who surrendered on 14 June 1982. A British naval and military garrison of 1,700 personnel remains in the area. A military zone of 55 miles (previously 80) remains around the islands within which Argentinian naval and air forces may not intrude.

Under the 1985 constitution, the Governor is advised by an Executive Council consisting of three elected members of the Legislative Council and two ex-officio members, the Chief Executive and the Financial Secretary. The Legislative Council consists of eight elected members and the same two ex-officio members.

Governor and Chairman of the Executive Council, HE Richard Peter Ralph, CMG, CVO, *apptd* 1996
Chief Executive, A. M. Gurr
Attorney-General, D. G. Lang, CBE, QC
Commander, British Forces, Falkland Islands, Air Cdre R. L. Dixon
Financial Secretary, D. F. Howatt
FALKLAND ISLANDS GOVERNMENT OFFICE, Falkland House, 14 Broadway, London SW1H 0BH. Tel: 0171-222 2542. *Government Representative*, Miss S. Cameron

ECONOMY

The economy was formerly based solely on agriculture, principally sheep farming with a little dairy farming for domestic requirements and crops for winter fodder. Since the establishment of an interim conservation and management fishing zone around the islands in 1987 and the consequent introduction of a licensing regime for vessels fishing within the 200-mile zone, the economy has diversified. Income from the associated fishing activities, mainly for illex squid, is now the largest source of revenue. The increase in government revenue from fishing licences has led to the establishment of a substantial health, education and welfare system. The islands are now self-financing except for defence. Chief imports are provisions, alcoholic beverages, timber, clothing and hardware. Tourism is a small but expanding industry.

In 1993 the Falkland Islands government announced a 200-mile oil exploration zone around the islands. In September 1995 the UK and Argentina signed an agreement which provided for a joint commission to co-ordinate exploration of the oil field. Exploration licences were issued in October 1996, and exploratory drilling began in April 1998. In 1995–6 the government had a budget deficit of £5 million.

TRADE WITH UK	1996	1997
Imports from UK	£19,932,000	£18,082,000
Exports to UK	5,568,000	9,949,000

GIBRALTAR

AREA – 2½ sq. miles (6.5 sq. km)
POPULATION – 27,086 (1997 estimate)
CAPITAL – ΨGibraltar
CURRENCY – Gibraltar pound of 100 pence
FLAG – White with a red stripe along the lower edge; over all a red castle with a key hanging from its gateway
POPULATION GROWTH RATE – 1.9 per cent (1995)
POPULATION DENSITY – 4,667 per sq. km (1995)

Gibraltar is a rocky promontory which juts southwards from the south-east coast of Spain, with which it is connected by a low isthmus. It is about 20 miles (32 km) from the opposite coast of Africa. The town stands at the foot of the promontory on the west side.

HISTORY AND POLITICS

Gibraltar was captured in 1704, during the War of the Spanish Succession, by a combined Dutch and English force, and was ceded to Great Britain by the Treaty of Utrecht (1713). Several attempts have been made to retake it, the most celebrated being the great siege of 1779 to 1783, when General Eliott held it for three years and seven months against a combined French and Spanish force. The Treaty of Utrecht stipulates that if Britain ever relinquishes its colonial rights over Gibraltar the colony would return to Spain. In a 1967 referendum on the colony's status, 12,138 people voted to remain a British Dependent Territory and 44 voted to join Spain. Spain closed the border with Gibraltar from 1969 to 1985 and refused to engage in any trade.

The 1969 constitution makes provision for certain domestic matters to devolve on a local government of ministers appointed from among elected members of the House of Assembly. The House of Assembly consists of an independent Speaker, 15 elected members, the Attorney-General and the Financial and Development Secretary.

The Governor retains responsibility for external affairs, defence, internal security and financial security, while the local government is responsible for other domestic matters. The Gibraltar government has recently been pressing for more local autonomy especially in its relations with the EU, and this has led to tension with the UK and Spanish governments. Gibraltar is part of the EU (with the UK government responsible for enforcing EU directives affecting Gibraltar) but is not a fully-fledged member. The Gibraltar Social Democrats won the last election in May 1996.

Governor and Commander-in-Chief, HE the Rt. Hon. Sir Richard Luce
Commander British Forces, HM Naval Base, Gibraltar, Cdre A. J. S. Taylor
Deputy Governor, M. Robinson, CMG
Attorney-General, R. Rhoda
Chief Justice, Derek Schofield
Chief Minister, Peter Caruana
Deputy Chief Minister, Trade and Industry, Peter Montegriffo
Education, the Disabled, Youth and Consumer Affairs, Dr Bernard Linares
Employment and Training, Building and Works, Jaime Netto
Environment and Health, Keith Azzopardi
Government Services and Sport, Ernest Britto
Social Affairs, Hubert Corby
Speaker, John Alcantara
Tourism, Commercial Affairs and the Port, Joe Holliday

ECONOMY

Gibraltar has an extensive shipping trade and is a popular shopping centre and tourist resort. The chief sources of revenue are the port dues, the rent of the Crown estate in the town, and duties on consumer items. The free port tradition of Gibraltar is still reflected in the low rates of import duty. A financial services industry is expanding, based on Gibraltar's status as an offshore financial centre. However, many jobs have been lost as a result of reductions in the British naval and military presence.

A total of 4,445 merchant ships (84.4 million gross registered tons aggregate) entered the port during 1997. There are 53 km of roads.

TRADE WITH UK	1996	1997
Imports from UK	£87,110,000	£82,351,000
Exports to UK	4,225,000	5,680,000

EDUCATION

Education is compulsory and free for children between the ages of five and 15 whose parents are ordinarily resident in Gibraltar. Scholarships are available for higher education in Britain. The total enrolment in government schools was 4,638 in December 1996.

MONTSERRAT

AREA – 39 sq. miles (102 sq. km)
POPULATION – 3,500 (1997 estimate)
CAPITAL – ΨPlymouth (largely destroyed by volcanic activity)
CURRENCY – East Caribbean dollar (EC$) of 100 cents
FLAG – British blue ensign with the shield of arms in the fly
POPULATION GROWTH RATE – 0 per cent (1995)
POPULATION DENSITY – 108 per sq. km (1995)
GDP – US$68 million (1994); US$6,795 per capita (1994)

Montserrat is about 11 miles long and seven miles wide. It is volcanic with several hot springs. About two-thirds of the island is mountainous, the rest capable of cultivation but volcanic activity has covered two-thirds of the island with ash and lava, destroying the economy.

HISTORY AND POLITICS

Discovered by Columbus in 1493, Montserrat became a British colony in 1632. The first settlers were predominantly Irish indentured servants from St Christopher. Montserrat was captured by the French in 1664, 1667 and 1782 but the island reverted to Britain within a few years on each occasion and was finally assigned to Great Britain in 1783.

A ministerial system was introduced in Montserrat in 1960. The Executive Council is presided over by the Governor and is composed of four elected members (the Chief and three other Ministers) and two ex-officio members (the Attorney-General and the Financial Secretary). The four Ministers are appointed from the members of the political party or coalition holding the majority in the Legislative Council. The Legislative Council consists of the Speaker, two ex-officio members (the Attorney-General and the Financial Secretary), two nominated members and seven elected members. Following elections in November 1996 the elected element of the legislature comprised the following parties: Movement for National Reconstruction (MNR) 2; People's Progressive Alliance (PPA) 2; National Progressive Party 1; Independents 2.

Governor, HE Anthony Abbott, OBE, *apptd* 1997

EXECUTIVE COUNCIL *as at June 1998*
President, The Governor
Chief Minister and Minister of Finance and Economic Development, David Brandt
Agriculture, Trade and the Environment, P. Austin Bramble
Attorney-General, Charles Eakins
Communications and Works, Rupert Weckes
Education, Health, Community Services and Labour, Adelina Tuitt
Financial Secretary, C. T. John, OBE

Speaker of the Legislative Council, Dr H. A. Fergus, CBE

ECONOMY

The economy, which consists of tourism, related construction activities, offshore business services and agriculture, has been seriously affected by relocation to the north of the island due to volcanic activity.

TRADE WITH UK	1996	1997
Imports from UK	£3,106,000	£3,109,000
Exports to UK	7,944,000	1,167,000

PITCAIRN ISLANDS

AREA – 1.9 sq. miles (5 sq. km)
POPULATION – 42 (1994 UN estimate). Since 1887 the islanders have all been adherents of the Seventh-day Adventist Church
CURRENCY – Currency is that of New Zealand
FLAG – British blue ensign with the arms in the fly.

Pitcairn is the chief of a group of islands situated about midway between New Zealand and Panama in the South Pacific Ocean. The island rises in cliffs to a height of 1,100 feet and access from the sea is possible only at Bounty Bay, a small rocky cove, and then only by surf boats. The other three islands of the group (Henderson, lying 105 miles east-north-east of Pitcairn, Oeno, lying 75 miles north-west, and Ducie, lying 293 miles east) are all uninhabited.

Mean monthly temperatures vary between 66° F (19° C) in August and 75° F (24° C) in February and the average annual rainfall is 80 inches. With an equable climate, the island is very fertile and produces both tropical and sub-tropical trees and crops.

HISTORY AND POLITICS

First settled in 1790 by the Bounty mutineers and their Tahitian companions, Pitcairn was left uninhabited in 1856 when the entire population was resettled on Norfolk Island. The present community are descendants of two parties who, not wishing to remain on Norfolk, returned to Pitcairn in 1859 and 1864 respectively.

Pitcairn became a British settlement under the British Settlement Act 1887, and was administered by the Governor of Fiji from 1952 until 1970, when the administration was transferred to the British High Commission in New Zealand and the British High Commissioner was appointed Governor. The local Government Ordinance of 1964 provides for a Council of ten members of whom six are elected.

Governor of Pitcairn, Henderson, Ducie and Oeno Islands, HE Robert J. Alston, CMG (*British High Commissioner to New Zealand*)
Island Magistrate and Chairman of Island Council, J. Warren

ECONOMY

The islanders live by subsistence gardening and fishing. Wood carvings and other handicrafts are sold to passing ships and to a few overseas customers. Other than small fees charged for gun and driving licences there are no taxes and government revenue is derived almost solely from the sale of postage stamps and income from investments. Communication with the outside world is maintained by cargo vessels travelling between New Zealand and Panama which call at irregular intervals, and by means of a satellite service providing telephone, telex and fax facilities.

TRADE WITH UK	1997
Imports from UK	£909,000
Exports to UK	228,000

EDUCATION

Education is compulsory between the ages of five and 15. Secondary education in New Zealand is encouraged by the administration, which provides scholarships and bursaries. Medical care is provided by a registered nurse when a doctor is not present.

ST HELENA

AREA – 47 sq. miles (122 sq. km)
POPULATION – 7,000 (1994 UN estimate)
CAPITAL – ΨJamestown (population, 1,332, 1994)
CURRENCY – St Helena pound (£) of 100 pence
FLAG – British blue ensign with the shield of arms in the fly
POPULATION GROWTH RATE – 0.6 per cent (1995)
POPULATION DENSITY – 54 per sq. km (1995)
URBAN POPULATION – 42.8 per cent (1987)
ILLITERACY RATE – 2.7 per cent

St Helena is situated in the South Atlantic Ocean, 955 miles south of the Equator, 702 miles south-east of Ascension, 1,140 miles from the nearest point of the African continent, 1,800 miles from the coast of South America, 1,694 miles from Cape Town. It is 10½ miles long and 6¾ broad.

St Helena is of volcanic origin, and consists of numerous rugged mountains, the highest rising to 2,700 feet (820 m), interspersed with picturesque ravines. Although within the tropics, the south-east trade winds keep the temperature mild and equable.

HISTORY AND POLITICS

St Helena was probably discovered by the Portuguese navigator, João da Nova in 1502. It was used as a port of call for vessels of all nations trading to the East until it was annexed by the Dutch in 1633. It was never occupied by them, however, and the English East India Company seized it in 1659. From 1815 to 1821 the island was lent to the British government as a place of exile for the Emperor Napoleon Bonaparte who died in St Helena on 5 May 1821, and in 1834 it was annexed to the British Crown.

The government of St Helena is administered by a Governor, with the aid of a Legislative Council, consisting of a Speaker, three ex-officio members (Chief Secretary, Financial Secretary and Attorney-General) and 12 elected members. Five committees of the Legislative Council are responsible for general oversight of the activities of government departments and have in addition a wide range of statutory and administrative functions. The Governor is also assisted by an Executive Council of the three ex-officio members and the chairmen of the Council committees.

Governor, HE David L. Smallman, LVO, *apptd* 1995
Attorney-General, K. de Freitas, OBE
Chief Administrative Health Officer, R. Essex
Chief Agriculture and Forestry Officer, R. J. Steele
Chief Auditor, R. Bladon
Chief Development Officer, K. M. Thomas
Chief Education Officer, J. Price
Chief Employment and Social Services Officer, J. MacDonald
Chief Engineer, J. Jacobson
Chief Finance Officer, D. H. Wade
Chief Justice, G. W. Martin, OBE
Chief Personnel Officer, S. I. Ellick
Chief Secretary, M. J. Clancy

Deputy Secretary, Ms E. C. Yon
Financial Secretary, M. J. Young
Postmistress, Ms I. Henry

ECONOMY

St Helena receives an annual grant from the UK which amounted to £3.3 million in 1998. The only significant export is canned and frozen fish. The other exports are a small amount of high quality coffee and cottage industry products (including lace, decorative woodwork and beadwork). James's Bay, on the north-west of the island, possesses a good anchorage. There is as yet no airport or airstrip.

TRADE WITH UK	1996	1997
Imports from UK	£7,698,000	£8,879,000
Exports to UK	386,000	594,000

ASCENSION ISLAND

AREA – 34 sq. miles (88 sq. km)
POPULATION – 1, 051 (1998 census)
CAPITAL – ΨGeorgetown
CURRENCY – Currency is that of St Helena

The small island of Ascension lies in the South Atlantic some 750 miles north-west of the island of St Helena. It is a rocky peak of purely volcanic origin. The highest point (Green Mountain), some 2,817 ft, is covered with lush vegetation and has a farm of some ten acres, producing vegetables and livestock. The island is a breeding area for green turtles and for the sooty tern, or wideawake. Other wildlife includes feral donkeys and cats, and francolin partridge.

Ascension Island's residents consist of the employees and families of the British organizations, of the contractors of the US Air Force and RAF and of the St Helena government.

British forces returned to the island in April 1982 in support of operations in the Falkland Islands. At present there are about 25 RAF personnel on the island supporting the air link to the Falklands.

HISTORY AND POLITICS

Ascension is said to have been discovered by João da Nova in 1501 and two years later was visited on Ascension Day by Alphonse d'Albuquerque, who gave the island its present name. It was uninhabited until the arrival of Napoleon in St Helena in 1815 when a small British naval garrison was stationed on the island. As HMS *Ascension* it remained under the supervision of the Board of Admiralty until 1922, when it was made a dependency of St Helena.

The British Foreign Secretary appoints the Administrator who is responsible to the Governor resident in St Helena. There is a small police force, bank and post office. The British organizations through Ascension Island Services (AIS) provide and operate various common services for the island (school, hospital, public works etc).

Administrator, Roger Huxley, *apptd* 1995

COMMUNICATIONS

Cable and Wireless PLC operates the international telephone and cable services and maintains an internal telephone service. The BBC opened its Atlantic relay station broadcasting to Africa and South America in 1967. There is a monthly shipping service and two flights a week by RAF Tristars which transit Ascension en route to the Falkland Islands. US aircraft and ships service the American base.

TRISTAN DA CUNHA

AREA – 38 sq. miles (98 sq. km)
POPULATION – 288 (1994 UN estimate)
CAPITAL – ΨEdinburgh of the Seven Seas
CURRENCY – Currency is that of the UK

Tristan da Cunha is the chief island of a group of islands in the South Atlantic which lies some 1,260 nautical miles (2,333 km) south-south-west of St Helena. Inaccessible Island lies 20 nautical miles south-west and has an area of 4 sq. miles (10 sq. km), and the three Nightingale Islands lie 20 nautical miles south of Tristan da Cunha and have an area of three-quarters of a sq. mile (2 sq. km). Gough Island lies some 230 nautical miles south-south-east of Tristan da Cunha and has an area of 35 sq. miles (91 sq. km).

All the islands are volcanic and steep-sided with cliffs or narrow beaches. Tristan itself has a single volcanic cone rising to 6,760 feet (2,060 m) and a narrow north-western coastal plain on which the settlement of Edinburgh is situated.

Inaccessible Island is a lofty mass of rock with sides two miles in length; the island is the resort of penguins and sea-birds. Cultivation was started in 1937 but has been abandoned.

The Nightingale Islands are three in number, of which the largest is one mile long and three-quarters of a mile wide, and rises in two peaks, 960 and 1,105 feet above sea level respectively. The smaller islands, Stoltenhoff and Middle Isle, are little more than huge rocks. Seals, penguins, and sea-birds visit these islands.

Gough Island is about eight miles long and four miles broad. It is a World Heritage Site, qualifying because of its unique temperate oceanic flora and fauna. It is the resort of penguins, sea-elephants, fur seals and sea-birds and has valuable guano deposits.

Gough and Inaccessible islands are nature reserves and access is strictly limited.

The islands have a warm-temperate oceanic climate which is damp and windy. Rainfall averages 66 inches a year on the coast of Tristan da Cunha.

Population is centred in the settlement of Edinburgh on Tristan da Cunha. In addition, there is a meteorological station maintained on Gough Island by the South African government. Inaccessible Island and the Nightingale Islands are uninhabited.

HISTORY AND POLITICS

Tristan da Cunha was discovered in 1506 by a Portuguese admiral (Tristão da Cunha) after whom it was named. In 1760 a British naval officer visited the islands and gave his name to Nightingale Island. In 1816 the group was annexed to the British Crown and a garrison was placed on Tristan da Cunha, but this force was withdrawn in 1817. Corporal William Glass remained at his own request with his wife and two children. This party, with two others, formed a settlement. In 1827 five women from St Helena, and afterwards others from Cape Colony, joined the party.

Due to its position on a main sailing route the colony thrived, with an economy based on trading with whalers, sealers and other passing ships. However, the replacement of sail by steam and the opening of the Suez Canal in the late 19th century led to decline.

In October 1961 a volcano, believed to have been extinct for thousands of years, erupted and the danger of further volcanic activity led to the evacuation of inhabitants to the UK. An advance party returned to Tristan da Cunha in 1963 and subsequently the main body of the islanders returned to the island.

GOVERNMENT

In 1938 Tristan da Cunha and the neighbouring islands of Inaccessible, Nightingale and Gough were made dependencies of St Helena. They are administered by the Governor of St Helena through a resident Administrator, with headquarters at Edinburgh. Under a constitution introduced in 1985, the Administrator is advised by an Island Council of eight elected members, of whom one must be a woman, and three appointed members. There is universal suffrage at 18. Elections are held every three years.

Administrator, Brian Baldwin, *apptd* 1998

ECONOMY

The island is financially self-sufficient. The main industries are crayfish fishing, fish-processing and agriculture, with the shore-based fishing industry having been developed with the construction of the boat harbour in 1967 and the re-establishment of the lobster factory in 1966. There are no taxes, income being derived from the royalties from the rock lobster fishery around the islands, interest from the reserve fund, and the sales of stamps and handicrafts, as well as vegetables, to passing ships. Tourism is increasing, the island being on the itinerary of several environmental tours. Apart from the fishing industry, the other main employer is the administration itself. There is one hospital with a resident medical officer, and a school catering for children up to age 15. Healthcare and education are free for the islanders.

COMMUNICATIONS

Scheduled visits to the island are restricted to about six calls a year by fishing vessels from Cape Town and annual calls of the RMS *St Helena* and the *SA Agulhas*, also from Cape Town. A wireless station on the island is in daily contact with Cape Town and a radio-telephone service was established in 1969, the same year that electricity was introduced to all the islanders' homes. A marine satellite system providing direct dialling telephone, telex and fax facilities was installed in 1992. Since 1998 the island has had internet and e-mail facilities, as well as a public telephone.

SOUTH GEORGIA AND THE SOUTH SANDWICH ISLANDS

AREA – 1,580 sq. miles (4,092 sq. km)
POPULATION – No permanent population

South Georgia is an island 800 miles east-south-east of the Falkland group. The population comprises a small military garrison and a civilian harbour master at King Edward Point, and staff of the British Antarctic Survey at Bird Island, to the north-west of South Georgia.

The South Sandwich Islands lie some 470 miles south-east of South Georgia. The group is a chain of uninhabited, actively volcanic islands about 150 miles long, with a wholly Antarctic climate.

The present constitution came into effect in 1985. It provides for a Commissioner who, for the time being, is the officer administering the government of the Falkland Islands.

In 1993 the UK government decreed an extension of Crown sovereignty and jurisdiction from 12 miles around South Georgia and the South Sandwich Islands to 200 miles around each in order to preserve marine stocks.

Commissioner for South Georgia and the South Sandwich Islands, Richard Ralph, CMG, CVO, *apptd* 1996

TURKS AND CAICOS ISLANDS

AREA – 166 sq. miles (430 sq. km)
POPULATION – 19,000 (1994 UN estimate)
CAPITAL – ΨGrand Turk (population, 3,691, 1994)
CURRENCY – US dollar (US$)
FLAG – British blue ensign with the shield of arms in the fly
POPULATION GROWTH RATE – 3.1 per cent (1995)
POPULATION DENSITY – 33 per sq. km (1995)

The Turks and Caicos Islands are about 50 miles southeast of the Bahamas of which they are geographically an extension. There are over 30 islands, of which eight are inhabited, covering an estimated area of 166 sq. miles (430 sq. km). The principal island and seat of government is Grand Turk.

The islands lie in the trade wind belt. The average temperature varies from 24°–27° C in the winter to 29°–32° C in the summer and humidity is generally low. Average rainfall is 21 inches a year.

HISTORY AND POLITICS

A constitution was introduced in 1988, and amended in 1993, which provides for an Executive Council and a Legislative Council. The Executive Council is presided over by the Governor and comprises the Chief Minister and five elected Ministers, together with the ex-officio Chief Secretary and Attorney-General.

At the general election of 31 January 1995, the People's Democratic Movement won eight seats and the Progressive National Party five seats in the Legislative Council.

Governor, HE John P. Kelly, LVO, MBE, *apptd* 1996

EXECUTIVE COUNCIL *as at May* 1998
President, The Governor
Attorney-General, D. Jeremiah
Chief Minister, D. H. Taylor
Chief Secretary, Ms C. Astwood, MBE
Ministers, S. Harvey; O. Skippings; H. Ewing; C. Selver; S. Rigby

ECONOMY

The most important industries are fishing, tourism and offshore finance. The islands were visited by 79,000 tourists in 1995.

TRADE WITH UK	1996	1997
Imports from UK	£924,000	£2,192,000
Exports to UK	660,000	727,000

COMMUNICATIONS

The principal airports are on the islands of Grand Turk, Providenciales and South Caicos. Air services link Providenciales and Grand Turk with Miami, the Bahamas, Haiti and the Dominican Republic. An internal air service provides a regular service between the principal islands. There are direct shipping services to the USA (Miami). A comprehensive telephone and telex service is provided by Cable and Wireless (WI) Ltd.

Events of the Year

1 September 1997 to 31 August 1998

SEPTEMBER 1997

2. In Paris, seven *paparazzi* present at the scene of the car crash that killed Diana, Princess of Wales were charged with involuntary manslaughter and failing to assist at the scene of an accident. An official memorial fund was set up for donations to the Princess's favourite charities. **4.** The royal family returned to London from Balmoral and The Queen broadcast to the nation from Buckingham Palace. **5.** The Princess's coffin was taken from the Chapel Royal at St James's Palace to Kensington Palace. **6.** The funeral of Diana, Princess of Wales took place at Westminster Abbey at 11 a.m. After the service a minute's silence was observed throughout the UK. The Princess was buried in a private ceremony on an island in a lake in the grounds of the Spencer family estate at Althorp, Northants. **8.** The TUC conference opened in Brighton. **11.** A referendum was held in Scotland on whether a Scottish Parliament should be set up and whether it should have the power to adjust tax rates; the turnout was about 62 per cent, of which 74.3 per cent voted in favour of a parliament and 63.5 per cent in favour of it having the power to adjust tax rates. **13.** The Duchess of Kent and the Deputy Prime Minister (John Prescott) attended the funeral of Mother Teresa in Calcutta, India. **14.** The leader of the Conservative Party (William Hague) was criticized for accusing the Prime Minister (Tony Blair) of making political capital out of the death of the Princess of Wales by leaking reports to the press of his dealings with the royal family in the week before the funeral. **15.** Buckingham Palace issued a statement denying that there had been disputes between the royal family and the Spencer family over arrangements for the funeral of the Princess of Wales, and saying that press reports that The Queen had opposed aspects of the arrangements were 'the direct opposite of the truth'. **17.** A referendum was held in Wales on whether an assembly should be set up; the turnout was 50 per cent, of which 50.3 per cent voted in favour of an assembly. **22.** The Liberal Democrat conference opened in Eastbourne. **24.** The Labour Party suspended nine councillors in Glasgow, including the Lord Provost, over allegations that they had accepted overseas trips in return for their support in important votes. **25.** The Home Secretary (Jack Straw) announced measures intended to cut youth crime and force parents to take responsi-bility for the behaviour of their children. **29.** The Labour Party conference opened in Brighton.

OCTOBER 1997

5. The Prime Minister arrived in Moscow for a two-day visit. **7.** The Queen and the Duke of Edinburgh arrived in Islamabad at the beginning of a state visit to Pakistan and India to mark the 50th anniversary of the two countries' independence. The Queen's arrival in India was marred by a diplomatic row over British foreign policy on Kashmir. The Conservative Party conference opened in Blackpool. The results of a ballot of the party's membership were announced: 80.78 per cent of those who voted endorsed William Hague as leader of the party and his principles for reforming the party. **10.** The Defence Secretary (George Robertson) announced that the royal yacht *Britannia* would not be replaced after being decommissioned in November 1997. **14.** The Conservative MP Piers Merchant resigned, denying newspaper allegations that he had had an affair with an 18-year-old woman; he later admitted that the affair had occurred. **17–20.** About two hundred gypsies from the Czech Republic and Slovakia arrived in Dover claiming political asylum; they were granted temporary leave to remain in Britain. **24.** The biennial Commonwealth Heads of Government meeting opened in Edinburgh. **26.** A silent march led by Cardinal Basil Hume was held in London to mark the 30th anniversary of the passing of the Abortion Act. **29.** The Prince of Wales arrived in Swaziland at the start of an eight-day tour of southern Africa. Ian Taylor resigned as a junior Opposition spokesman on Northern Ireland because of the Shadow Cabinet's decision to oppose European monetary union (EMU) at the next general election. The Government published a bill proposing that the next elections for the European Parliament should be held under a system of proportional representation.

NOVEMBER 1997

1. David Curry resigned from the Shadow Cabinet because of its decision to oppose EMU at the next general election. **4.** The Government said that Formula One motor racing would be exempt from its proposed ban on sponsorship of sporting events by tobacco companies. On 10 November after taking advice from Sir Patrick Neill, the incoming chairman of the Committee on Standards in Public Life, the Labour Party said that it would return a £1 million donation to party funds which had been made before the general election by Bernie Eccles-tone, vice-president of the Formula One Association. After conflicting reports as to whether Mr Ecclestone had offered the party a further donation and allegations that the Government's policy had been changed because of his financial support, the Prime Minister gave a television interview on 16 November in which he apologized for the Government's handling of the affair and denied that there had been any impropriety in its dealings with Mr Ecclestone. **5.** The Government published the first White Paper on overseas aid since 1975 (*see* page 1168). **6.** Labour won the Paisley South by-election with a reduced majority (*see* page 233). **7.** The Prime Minister held talks with President Chirac and the French Prime Minister, Lionel Jospin, at the Canary Wharf tower in London's docklands. **13.** The aircraft carrier *Invincible* was ordered to sail to the Mediterranean because of increased tension in the Middle East over Iraq's expulsion of six American weapons inspectors. **17.** Six Britons, including a five-year-old girl, were among 68 people killed when Islamic militants disguised as policemen shot and stabbed tourists at the Pharaonic temples in Luxor, Egypt. **19.** A report by a former Chief Social Services Inspector, Sir William Utting, was published; it disclosed high levels of child abuse in residential and foster homes, and recommended a wider choice of care places, better staff recruitment procedures and a new code of practice for choosing foster carers. **20.** A service of thanksgiving was held at Westminster Abbey to mark the 50th wedding anniversary of The Queen and the Duke of Edinburgh; it was followed by a lunch in their honour at the Banqueting House. In the evening a private ball was held at Windsor Castle following the completion of restoration work after the fire in November 1992. The Conservatives won the Beckenham by-election with a reduced majority (*see* page 233). The Liberal Democrats won the Winchester by-election with a majority of 21,556 (*see* page 233). Sixty-year-old Elizabeth Buttle became the oldest British woman to have a child when she gave birth to a son; it was later alleged that she had received fertility treatment after lying about her age. **21.** The Conservative whip was withdrawn from Peter Temple-Morris, the MP for Leominster, who had threatened to resign the party whip unless Mr Hague changed his stance on EMU; Mr Temple-Morris resigned from the Conservative Party. **22.** The royal yacht *Britannia* entered Portsmouth harbour after her final voyage before being decommissioned. **25.** The Chancellor of the Exchequer (Gordon Brown) delivered a pre-Budget statement in the House of Commons. **28.** MPs voted by a majority of 260 in favour of a private member's bill to ban hunting with dogs.

DECEMBER 1997

1. The Prime Minister appointed Lord Jenkins of Hillhead to lead a commission with the remit of recommending a 'broadly proportional' alternative to the first-past-the-post system for parliamentary elections. **2–10.** Farmers blockaded Holyhead,

Stranraer, Dover and other ports in protest against the import of cheap beef from Ireland. **3.** The Government said that the sale of beef on the bone would be banned because of the 'very small risk' that it could cause Creutzfeldt-Jakob disease (CJD). The Prime Minister announced a moratorium on the building of gas-fired power stations in order to protect the deep-mined coal industry. **4.** The Government announced the establishment of a Royal Commission to examine the funding of long-term care of the elderly. **9.** The Government published a White Paper on the NHS (*see* pages 1168–9). The oldest person in Britain, Lucy Askew, died at the age of 114. **10.** A junior Scottish Office minister, Malcolm Chisholm, and three parliamentary private secretaries, Gordon Prentice, Mick Clapham and Neil Gerrard, resigned in order to oppose government plans to cut single-parent benefit. In the House of Commons, 47 Labour back-benchers voted in favour of an amendment opposing the plans. Another parliamentary private secretary, Alice Mahon, was sacked for voting for the amendment. **11.** The royal yacht *Britannia* was decommissioned at a ceremony in Portsmouth. **14.** The Opposition called for the resignation of the Paymaster-General, Geoffrey Robinson, after revelations concerning his involvement with an offshore trust. On 20 January 1998 the Parliamentary Commissioner for Standards (Sir Gordon Downey) said that Mr Robinson had not breached House of Commons rules by not registering his interest in the trust, but that it would have been better if he had done so. **15.** The Agriculture Minister (Jack Cunningham) said that Britain would ban EU meat imports that were not subject to the same hygiene standards as British meat. **19.** William Hague married Ffion Jenkins in a ceremony in the chapel of the crypt of the House of Commons. **22.** The Government announced an £85 million aid package for beef farmers, and said that an independent inquiry would be held into the handling of the bovine spongiform encephalopathy (BSE)/CJD crisis. **24–26.** At least six people were killed when strong winds hit many parts of Britain.

JANUARY 1998

3–5. Violent storms hit many parts of Britain. **8.** At least 1,000 homes were damaged when a tornado hit Selsey, W. Sussex. **9.** The Prime Minister arrived in Japan for a five-day visit. Two independent primary schools became the first Muslim schools in Britain to qualify for state funding when their application for grant-maintained status was approved. Stephen Bayley resigned as creative director of the Millennium Dome in Greenwich, London. **12.** The Japanese government apologized for the suffering of British prisoners during the Second World War. **13.** The Education and Employment Secretary (David Blunkett) announced far-ranging reforms to the national curriculum in primary schools. **14.** The Government published proposals to establish an independent Food Standards Agency (see page 1169). Conservative MPs voted to introduce a one member, one vote system for electing party leaders. **15.** The House of Commons Home Affairs select committee recommended radical changes to the procedures for investigating complaints against police officers. **16.** The aircraft carrier *Invincible* was ordered to sail to the Gulf because of increased tension in the area over Iraq's placing of restrictions on UN weapons inspection. **19.** Twelve-year-old Sean Stewart became the youngest father in Britain when his 16-year-old girlfriend gave birth to a boy in Sharnbrook, Beds. **25.** Queen Elizabeth the Queen Mother broke her left hip in a fall at Sandringham and underwent a hip replacement operation in London the following day. **26.** Liverpool dockers reached a settlement with the Mersey Docks and Harbour Company to bring to an end a dispute which had lasted since September 1995.

FEBRUARY 1998

3. After a meeting with the Culture, Media and Sport Secretary (Chris Smith), Peter Davis resigned as director-general of the Office of the National Lottery in the light of a libel action involving Richard Branson (see page 1088). The Health Secretary (Frank Dobson) said that St Bartholomew's Hospital, London, which the previous Government had earmarked for closure, would remain open. The Prime Minister arrived in Washington DC for a three-day official visit. The Prince of Wales arrived in Sri Lanka for a four-day visit coinciding with celebrations to mark the 50th anniversary of the island's independence; he then visited Nepal and Bhutan. **9.** At the Brit Awards in London a member of the anarchist band Chumbawumba emptied an icebucket over the Deputy Prime Minister (John Prescott). **12.** The Cabinet agreed to the use of force against Iraq if diplomatic efforts failed to secure a resolution in the crisis over UN weapons inspections; on 17 February MPs voted by 493 votes to 25 in favour of the use of force against Iraq if diplomatic efforts failed. **13.** About 1,100 people were evacuated from their homes after a 1,000 lb German Second World War bomb was found in a field outside Chippenham, Wilts; on 15 February army bomb experts carried out a controlled explosion. **16.** The Leader of the Opposition (William Hague) announced a set of proposals, *Fresh Future*, for reforming the internal workings of the Conservative Party; the proposals were approved by party members on 28 March. **17.** The Home Secretary said that future judges, magistrates, police officers, Crown prosecutors, prison staff and probation officers would be required to declare if they were freemasons; a voluntary register would also be set up for current employees to declare membership. **24.** Princess Margaret suffered a mild stroke while on holiday on the Caribbean island of Mustique. **26.** More than 5,000 beacons were lit in the evening throughout Britain in protest at the Government's policies on rural issues.

MARCH 1998

1. At least 250,000 people marched through central London to protest against a bill before Parliament intended to ban hunting with dogs, and to highlight concerns about the Government's policies on the countryside in general. On 13 March the bill was 'talked out' in the House of Commons. **6.** In a change to existing protocol, Buckingham Palace announced that the Union flag would fly over the palace, and other royal palaces, unless The Queen was in residence. **9.** The Prince of Wales underwent surgery on his right knee. **17.** The Israeli prime minister (Binyamin Netanyahu) cancelled a dinner with the Foreign Secretary (Robin Cook) in Jerusalem after Mr Cook visited the controversial Har Homa settlement in east Jerusalem. **31.** All the RAF's nuclear bombs were withdrawn from service, leaving submarine-launched Trident missiles as Britain's only nuclear weapons.

APRIL 1998

2. The Prime Minister held talks with the Chinese prime minister (Zhu Rongji) at Downing Street. **9–12.** At least five people died in severe flooding in central England. **17.** A British teacher, David Mitchell, and his wife and son were kidnapped in Yemen; they were released unharmed on 4 May. **20.** The Scottish Secretary (Donald Dewar) called on the Chief Constable of Grampian (Ian Oliver) to resign after the publication of a report highly critical of the investigation by Grampian police of the abduction and murder of a nine-year-old boy by a known paedophile in July 1997. On 21 April the Grampian Police Board called for Mr Oliver's immediate resignation; on 24 April he resigned. **27.** The Government published a White Paper outlining a ten-year national anti-drugs strategy (see page 1170). **28.** *The Times* began serialization of a controversial book about Mary Bell, who was convicted of the manslaughter of two children in 1968 when she was ten years old and who had been paid for her contribution to the book; on 29 April Mary Bell and her daughter were taken into protective custody after being tracked down by tabloid newspaper reporters. On 30 April the Home Secretary (Jack Straw) launched an inquiry into the affair.

MAY 1998

4. The Prime Minister held talks with the Israeli prime minister and the Palestinian president (Yasser Arafat) in separate sessions at Downing Street. **6.** The Foreign Secretary (Robin Cook) said that an independent inquiry would be held into allegations that Britain had exported arms to Sierra Leone in contravention of the UN ban on the sale of weapons to the state. **7.** A referendum was held in London on whether a strategic authority for London with a directly-elected mayor should be established; the turnout was 34 per cent, of which 72 per cent supported the proposal. Local elections were also held in London, the metropolitan authorities, and some shire districts and unitary authorities in England. **8.** Sandline International, the company involved in supplying arms to Sierra Leone as part of a covert operation to restore the country's exiled civilian government, said that it had acted with the full prior knowledge and approval of the British government. **10.** The Foreign Secretary said that Sandline International had acted without ministerial approval. **11.** The Prime Minister said that although it would be wrong for officials to have deliberately breached the UN arms embargo, both the UN and the UK had been trying to help restore the democratic government of Sierra Leone. **12.** The Foreign Secretary said that civil servants at the Foreign Office had not been involved in a 'conspiracy' to supply arms to Sierra Leone. **14.** The permanent secretary at the Foreign Office (Sir John Kerr) withdrew an earlier statement that ministers had been told in early March about an imminent Customs and Excise inquiry into Sandline's activities. **18.** Customs and Excise said that Sandline may have breached the UN arms embargo, but that it could not press charges because of clear evidence of meetings between the company and Foreign Office officials. **24.** It was reported that Christopher Howes, a British mine clearance expert kidnapped by the Khmer Rouge in Cambodia in March 1996, had been murdered three days after the abduction. **25.** The Emperor and Empress of Japan arrived in London at the beginning of a six-day state visit. On 26 May hundreds of veterans turned their backs as the royal carriage moved down the Mall, in protest at Japan's refusal to make a formal apology for the treatment of prisoners of war during the Second World War. At a state banquet at Buckingham Palace, Emperor Akihito made a speech in which he expressed the 'deep pain' he felt because of the suffering caused by the war. **29.** Two heart surgeons and the chief executive at the Bristol Royal Infirmary, where 29 babies died during heart operations between 1988 and 1995, were found by a General Medical Council committee to have failed to pay sufficient regard to the safety and best interests of patients. On 18 June the three men were found guilty of serious professional misconduct; two of them were struck off and the third was ordered not to operate on children for three years. The Government announced a public inquiry into the case.

JUNE 1998

1. The Leader of the Opposition (William Hague) reshuffled the Shadow Cabinet. **3.** The Secretary of State for the Environment, Transport and the Regions (John Prescott) announced a 'public-private partnership' rescue package for the Channel Tunnel rail link. **5.** The Government announced that the nuclear reprocessing plant at Dounreay, Caithness, would close. **18.** The President of the Board of Trade (Margaret Beckett) announced that a national minimum wage of £3.60 per hour would be introduced in April 1999, with workers aged

18–21 receiving a minimum of £3 per hour. **22.** MPs voted to lower the age of consent for homosexuals to 16; on 22 July the House of Lords voted to keep the age of consent at 18, and the relevant clause was subsequently dropped from the legislation.

JULY 1998

5. The *Observer* published allegations that certain lobbyists had privileged access to senior ministers. On 6 July Derek Draper, a director of GPC Market Access, was suspended pending an inquiry into his activities; on 8 July he resigned. **8.** In the House of Commons, the Leader of the Opposition attacked the Government for being surrounded by 'money-grabbing cronies'. The Government published the results of its strategic defence review (*see* pages 1070–1). **19.** The Lambeth Conference opened in Canterbury. **20.** The Government published a White Paper on transport (*see* page 1071). **27.** The Prime Minister reshuffled the Cabinet; Harriet Harman, Lord Richard, Gavin Strang and David Clark were sacked, and Peter Mandelson, Alistair Darling, Baroness Jay of Paddington and Stephen Byers entered the Cabinet for the first time. The report of an inquiry conducted by Sir Thomas Legg into the 'arms to Sierra Leone' affair was published; it cleared ministers of having had prior knowledge of Sandline's plans to ship arms to the country, but criticized the judgement of the British High Commissioner, Peter Penfold, and the internal communications systems at the Foreign Office. **28.** A range of middle-ranking and junior ministerial appointments was announced. **31.** The Government announced a ban on the use of anti-personnel landmines by British troops.

AUGUST 1998

3. Gus Macdonald, the chairman of the Scottish Media Group, was appointed Minister for Business and Industry at the Scottish Office; he will receive a life peerage to enable him to sit in the House of Lords. **24.** Sudan recalled its ambassador in London and requested the withdrawal of the British ambassador in Khartoum because of Britain's support for the USA's missile attack on a chemical factory in Khartoum on 20 August. On 27 August Britain temporarily withdrew its diplomats from Khartoum.

NORTHERN IRELAND AFFAIRS

SEPTEMBER 1997

9. Sinn Fein leaders agreed during cross-party talks at Stormont to abide by the Mitchell principles of democracy and non-violence. Five Unionist parties left the talks in protest at the presence of Sinn Fein members. **11.** The IRA said that it would have problems with some of the Mitchell principles; it ruled out any disarmament during the talks process and rejected the principle that constitutional change should have the consent of the majority of the population of Northern Ireland. **15.** Substantive talks opened at Stormont. The Unionist and loyalist parties boycotted the talks; the Ulster Unionist Party (UUP) said that before it would join the negotiations it required assurances that the IRA would hand over weapons during the talks process. **16.** A 400 lb bomb believed to have been planted by a republican splinter group exploded outside an RUC base in Co. Armagh; the UUP later called for Sinn Fein's expulsion from the talks. **17.** The UUP, the Progressive Unionist Party and the Ulster Democratic Party re-entered the negotiations. **23.** In an historic meeting, Unionist, loyalist, nationalist and republican leaders met for face-to-face negotiations at Stormont; the Unionists argued unsuccessfully that Sinn Fein should be expelled from the talks. **24.** It was agreed at the talks that the issue of decommissioning terrorist weapons would be dealt with by a new independent commission and that the substantive talks would concentrate on constitutional issues. **30.** The Northern Ireland Secretary (Mo Mowlam) said that the Government would give up its power to intern suspected terrorists without trial.

OCTOBER 1997

7. Full-scale peace negotiations opened at Stormont. **13.** The Prime Minister met the participants in the peace negotiations; he shook hands with Gerry Adams during the first meeting between a British prime minister and Sinn Fein leaders since 1921. The Prime Minister was later jostled by a hostile loyalist crowd during a walk-about in east Belfast. **25.** A man was killed by a car bomb in Bangor, Co. Down. **30.** The Home Secretary (Jack Straw) announced a comprehensive review of anti-terrorist legislation. A bomb planted by the Continuity IRA, a republican splinter group, exploded in Londonderry.

NOVEMBER 1997

6–7. Several leading IRA members were reported to have resigned in protest at the restoration of the cease-fire and Sinn Fein's adoption of the Mitchell principles of democracy and non-violence. **8.** Gerry Adams said that he was 'deeply sorry' about the IRA bombing at Enniskillen in 1987. **25.** The Chief Constable of the RUC (Ronnie Flanagan) announced the end of army foot patrols in west Belfast.

DECEMBER 1997

10. An IRA prisoner escaped from the Maze prison, Co. Antrim. **11.** Gerry Adams and Martin McGuinness led the first Sinn Fein delegation to be received at Downing Street since 1921. **13–14.** Rioting broke out in Londonderry after an Apprentice Boys' parade. **27.** Billy Wright, the leader of the Loyalist Volunteer Force (LVF) who was serving an eight-year sentence at the Maze prison, Co. Antrim, was shot dead by INLA prisoners. A former IRA prisoner was shot dead and three other people were shot and wounded by the LVF in Dungannon, Co.

Tyrone, and there were disturbances in Portadown, Co. Armagh, and Ballymena, Co. Antrim. **31.** A man was killed and five people were wounded when two loyalist gunmen opened fire in a Roman Catholic bar in Cliftonville, north Belfast.

JANUARY 1998

4. UDA prisoners in the Maze prison voted to withhold their support for the peace process. **9.** The Northern Ireland Secretary met UDA, UVF and IRA prisoners in the Maze prison; the UDA prisoners subsequently restored their support for the peace process. **11.** A Roman Catholic man related by marriage to the Sinn Fein president Gerry Adams was shot dead by the LVF outside a nightclub in Belfast. **12.** The British and Irish governments issued a joint document, *Propositions on Heads of Agreement*, to be debated at the Stormont talks. Its main proposals were an elected Northern Ireland Assembly; a Council of the Isles, to be attended by the British and Irish governments and representatives of the new Scottish, Welsh and Northern Ireland assemblies; a North-South Council to promote co-operation between Northern Ireland and the Irish Republic; and balanced constitutional change. **14.** During an undercover operation in Belfast a policeman was shot and critically injured by a woman soldier who had mistaken him for a terrorist. **18.** A Roman Catholic man was shot dead in Maghera, Co. Londonderry. **19.** A prominent UDA member was shot dead by the INLA in Dunmurry, Co. Antrim. A Roman Catholic man was shot dead in south Belfast. The Prime Minister met a Sinn Fein delegation led by Gerry Adams at Downing Street. **21.** A Roman Catholic man was shot dead in central Belfast and two other men were injured in shootings in the city. **22.** A Roman Catholic man was shot and injured in north Belfast. **23.** A Roman Catholic man was shot dead in north Belfast. **24.** A Roman Catholic man was shot dead in west Belfast. A car bomb believed to have been planted by the Continuity IRA exploded outside an entertainment complex in Enniskillen, Co. Fermanagh. **25.** A Roman Catholic man was shot and injured in Lurgan, Co. Armagh. **26.** The Ulster Democratic Party (UDP) withdrew from the multi-party talks when it became clear that it was about to be excluded because of the sectarian murders perpetrated by its paramilitary associates, the UFF; the Northern Ireland Secretary said that the UDP could be reinstated at the talks if an unconditional cease-fire were restored. **27.** The British and Irish governments presented to the talks further proposals on cross-border bodies. **29.** Tony Blair announced that a judicial tribunal would be set up to establish the truth about 'Bloody Sunday', when 14 people were shot dead by soldiers in Londonderry in 1972.

FEBRUARY 1998

9. A Roman Catholic man was shot dead in Belfast by republican gunmen acting under the name

Direct Action Against Drugs. **10.** A member of the UDA was shot dead in south Belfast. **17.** Sinn Fein sought a temporary injunction at the High Court in Dublin to suspend proceedings to expel it from the multi-party talks as a result of the murders in Belfast in the preceding week; the talks were adjourned until 23 February. **18.** A Roman Catholic man was shot dead in Aghalee, Co. Antrim. **20.** Sinn Fein delegates were suspended from the multi-party talks for two weeks; Mo Mowlam said that any further IRA activity would lead to Sinn Fein's permanent exclusion. About eight people were injured when a 500 lb car bomb exploded outside a police station in Moira, Co. Down. **23.** A 300 lb bomb exploded in Portadown, Co. Armagh. The UDP were re-admitted to the multi-party talks.

MARCH 1998

3. Two men, one a Protestant and one a Roman Catholic, were shot dead in a bar in Poyntzpass, Co. Armagh. **9.** The Government halted the extradition to Germany of Roisin McAliskey on the grounds of her ill health; she was wanted in connection with an IRA bomb attack on a British army base at Osnabrück in June 1996. **10.** A mortar attack was launched on the RUC station in Armagh. **15.** David Keys, one of four men charged in connection with the Poyntzpass murders on 3 March, was found murdered at the Maze prison. **24.** Four mortar bombs were fired at the RUC base in Forkhill, South Armagh. **27.** A former RUC officer was shot dead by the INLA in Armagh.

APRIL 1998

1. The Irish Taoiseach, Bertie Ahern, said before talks with Tony Blair at Downing Street that there were 'large disagreements' between the two governments over the powers of proposed cross-border bodies. **2.** A 980 lb bomb was seized by police at Dun Laoghaire, near Dublin, from a car being driven onto a ferry bound for Anglesey. **6.** The chairman of the Northern Ireland cross-party talks, Sen. George Mitchell, issued a draft document outlining proposals for a peace settlement. **7.** The Ulster Unionists rejected the draft agreement; Tony Blair flew to Belfast to further attempts to reach a settlement. **8.** A man with links to the LVF was shot dead by the INLA in Londonderry. **10.** The British and Irish governments and the Northern Ireland politicians involved in the cross-party talks signed an agreement on achieving a political settlement in Northern Ireland. The main points of the agreement, to be put to the people of the Republic of Ireland and Northern Ireland in a referendum, were:

- a Northern Ireland assembly of 108 members, six elected by proportional representation from each existing parliamentary constituency
- a 12-member executive drawn from the assembly's membership and headed by a First Minister and a Deputy First Minister
- a North-South ministerial council, established by the assembly within a year, to direct co-operation

between Northern Ireland and the Republic of Ireland on a range of issues

- the Republic of Ireland to give up its constitutional claim to Northern Ireland and Britain to repeal the Government of Ireland Act 1920
- a British-Irish Council, with members drawn from the British and Irish governments and the assemblies in Scotland, Wales and Northern Ireland
- a smaller British police and army presence in Northern Ireland, and the removal of security installations as early as possible
- a commitment by all participants to the decommissioning of weapons and to working with an independent international commission on decommissioning, with the aim of achieving decommissioning of all paramilitary weapons within two years
- paramilitary prisoners to be released within two or three years, as long as their organization maintains the cease-fire
- an independent commission on the future of policing in Northern Ireland, to report no later than summer 1999
- human rights commissions in Northern Ireland and the Republic of Ireland

14. The Irish government released nine IRA prisoners from Portlaoise prison, near Dublin, as a 'confidence-building measure'. **17.** A Roman Catholic taxi driver was shot dead in west Belfast in what was believed to be a feud within the INLA. **21.** A Roman Catholic man was shot dead in Portadown, Co. Armagh. **25.** A Roman Catholic man was shot dead in Crumlin, Co. Antrim. **30.** The IRA said that it would not decommission any arms. A 700 lb car bomb was defused in Lisburn, Co. Antrim.

MAY 1998

1. A man believed to be a republican dissident was shot dead and five men were arrested during an attempted raid on a security van near Ashford, Co. Wicklow. **10.** At its conference in Dublin, Sinn Fein delegates voted in favour of the Belfast Agreement and supported changing the party's constitution in order to allow its members take seats in a Northern Ireland assembly; 27 IRA prisoners were allowed to leave prison temporarily in order to attend the conference. **13.** Sir Kenneth Bloomfield, the former head of the Northern Ireland Civil Service, published a report, *We Will Remember Them,* about the treatment of people bereaved or injured during the Troubles. **14.** The Prime Minister visited Northern Ireland and said that four tests would be written into forthcoming legislation to ascertain whether parties with paramilitary links had genuinely renounced violence; any party failing the tests would not be entitled to early release of prisoners or places on the proposed power-sharing executive. The loyalist terrorist Michael Stone was temporarily released from prison and attended a UDP rally in Belfast in support of the peace agreement. **15.** The LVF declared an unequivocal cease-fire. **19.** The pop group U2 gave a concert in Belfast in support of the Belfast Agreement. **20.** On a visit to Belfast, the Prime Minister drew up a handwritten pledge to the people of Northern Ireland, to encourage Unionists to support the Belfast Agreement. **22.** Referendums on the Belfast Agreement were held in Northern Ireland and the Republic of Ireland; voters in the Republic were also asked if they supported a change in the country's constitution to give up its claim to Northern Ireland. In Northern Ireland, the turn-out was about 81 per cent, of which 71.12 per cent voted in favour of the agreement. In the Republic of Ireland, the turn-out was about 55 per cent, of which 94.4 per cent voted in favour of both the agreement and the change to the constitution. **30.** Rioting broke out in Portadown, Co. Armagh, in protest at a junior Orange Order march.

JUNE 1998

24. A 200 lb car bomb believed to have been planted by republicans exploded in the centre of New-townhamilton, Co. Armagh, injuring a 13-year-old boy and causing widespread damage. **25.** Elections were held to the new Northern Ireland Assembly under a system of proportional representation; the SDLP received 22 per cent of first preference votes, the UUP 21.3 per cent, the DUP 18.1 per cent and Sinn Fein 17.6 per cent. The final distribution of seats in the Assembly was: UUP 28, SDLP 24, DUP 20, Sinn Fein 18, Alliance Party 6, UK Unionist Party 5, Progressive Unionist Party 2, Northern Ireland Women's Coalition 2, others 3. **29.** Lord Alderdice resigned as leader of the Alliance Party and was appointed interim Presiding Officer (Speaker) of the Northern Ireland Assembly.

JULY 1998

1. Members of the Northern Ireland Assembly met for the first time at Stormont; David Trimble was elected First Minister and Seamus Mallon was elected Deputy First Minister. **2.** Ten Roman Catholic churches in Northern Ireland were badly damaged in arson attacks believed to have been instigated by the LVF. **5.** Members of the Orange Order were barred by security forces from marching along the Garvaghy Road in Drumcree, Co. Armagh; the marchers had been refused permission to pass down the road by the Parades Commission. A stand-off ensued and violence broke out in loyalist areas of Northern Ireland. **6–9.** Violent protests continued in many areas of Northern Ireland and sectarian attacks were carried out on Roman Catholic properties. On 9 July the Prime Minister met four Orangemen, but the stand-off continued and there were clashes overnight between members of the security forces and loyalists attempting to breach the barricades barring them from the Garvaghy Road. **10.** Three men believed to belong to republican splinter groups were arrested in central London and several explosive devices were made safe after a surveillance operation by MI5 and anti-terrorist police. **12.** Three young brothers whose

mother was a Roman Catholic were burned to death in a sectarian arson attack on their home in Ballymoney, Co. Antrim. The stand-off at Drum-cree continued, although some Orangemen called for it to be abandoned. By late July few marchers remained at the site.

AUGUST 1998

1. A car bomb believed to have been planted by republican dissidents exploded in the centre of Banbridge, Co. Down. **6.** Thomas McMahon, who planted the IRA bomb that killed Lord Mountbatten and three other people in 1979, was released from Mountjoy prison under the terms of the Belfast Agreement. **8.** The LVF said that it had given up its campaign of violence for good. **15.** Twenty-eight people were killed and more than 200 injured when a car bomb exploded in the centre of Omagh, Co. Tyrone. On 18 August the dissident republican group the Real IRA claimed responsibility for the bombing but said that it had not intended to kill civilians; it said that its campaign of violence had been suspended. **22.** The INLA announced a cease-fire. **25.** The Prime Minister visited Omagh, and announced that Parliament would be recalled to debate new anti-terrorism measures.

ACCIDENTS AND DISASTERS

SEPTEMBER 1997

3. Sixty-five people were killed when a jet crashed outside Phnom Penh airport. **8.** More than 500 people were reported to have drowned when a ferry sank off the coast of Haiti. **19.** Six people were killed and more than 160 injured when an InterCity 125 Swansea–London train crashed into a freight train in Southall, west London; a seventh person died on 25 September. **26.** All 234 people on board were killed when an airliner crashed in smog near Medan, Sumatra. At least ten people were killed, hundreds were left homeless, and the Basilica of St Francis was badly damaged when an earthquake registering 5.5 on the Richter scale hit Assisi, Italy. **27.** At least 30 people were feared drowned when two cargo vessels collided in smog in the Straits of Malacca.

OCTOBER 1997

1. Four fishermen were missing presumed drowned after their boat sank in rough seas off north-east Scotland. **4.** All passengers and crew were rescued after fire broke out on the Cypriot-owned *Romantica* cruise ship off Cyprus. **9.** At least 400 people died when Hurricane Pauline hit the Pacific coast of Mexico. **October–December.** At least 1,500 people died when torrential rain caused flooding in Somalia.

NOVEMBER 1997

4. At least 265 people were killed and up to 2,800 were missing after Typhoon Linda hit the southern coast of Vietnam. **5.** Eight people were injured when a Virgin Atlantic Airbus was forced to crash-land at Heathrow after its undercarriage jammed. **6.** At least 31 people drowned when violent storms hit western Spain and southern Portugal. **18.** Thirty children were killed and 67 were injured when a school bus crashed off a bridge in Delhi, India. **19.** A helicopter winchman drowned off Shetland after rescuing ten crew from a wrecked cargo ship in 70-m.p.h. gales.

DECEMBER 1997

6. At least 66 people were killed when a military cargo plane crashed into a block of flats in Irkutsk, Siberia. **12.** More than 300 flights were cancelled when fire broke out in Terminal One at Heathrow airport. **15.** Eighty-five people were killed when a plane crashed on its approach to Sharjah airport, UAE. **17.** Up to 70 people were feared dead when a Ukrainian plane crashed as it approached Salonika, Greece. **19.** A Boeing 737 crashed on the island of Sumatra, Indonesia, killing 104 people.

JANUARY 1998

10. At least 50 people were killed and 10,000 injured when an earthquake registering 6.2 on the Richter scale hit northern China.

FEBRUARY 1998

2. All 104 people on board a DC9 plane were feared dead after it crashed into a mountain in the Philippines. **3.** Twenty people were killed when an American military aircraft sliced through the wire supporting a cable car at a ski resort near Cavalese in the Dolomites, Italy. **4.** At least 4,000 people were killed when an earthquake registering 6.1 on the Richter scale hit north-east Afghanistan; a further 250 people died in an aftershock on 8 February. **14.** About 100 people were killed when two trains carrying oil were derailed in Yaoundé, Cameroon. **16.** A Taiwanese airliner crashed at Taipei airport, killing all 197 people on board and seven people on the ground. **23.** At least 38 people were killed and hundreds of homes destroyed when dozens of tornadoes hit central Florida, USA.

MARCH 1998

18. Sixty-two passengers and crew were evacuated safely after the nose wheel of an aircraft collapsed on landing at Manchester airport. **21.** At least 13 people were killed when tornadoes hit the southern USA. **31.** A light aircraft carrying the Leeds United football team crash-landed at Stansted airport after an engine caught fire on take-off; there were no serious injuries.

APRIL 1998

5. Sixty-three people died in a mining accident near Donetsk, Ukraine. **9.** At least 118 Muslims were killed in a stampede near Mena, Saudi Arabia. At least 38 people were killed when a tornado hit central Alabama, USA. **21.** Fifty-three people were

killed when a Boeing 727 crashed after taking off from Bogotá, Colombia.

MAY 1998

6. At least 135 people died and more than 100 were missing after heavy rain caused severe flooding and mud slides in the hills around Naples, southern Italy. **22.** A series of earthquakes registering up to 6.8 on the Richter scale hit central Bolivia, killing at least 60 people. **22–26.** At least 111 people died in a heatwave in India. **31.** At least 4,000 people were killed when an earthquake registering 7.1 on the Richter scale hit north-east Afghanistan.

JUNE 1998

3. At least 96 people were killed when a high-speed train was derailed and crashed into a road bridge in Eschede, Germany. **14.** Five Scottish fishermen were drowned when their trawler, the *Silvery Sea*, was struck by a German coaster in the North Sea. **27.** At least 119 people were killed when an earthquake registering 6.3 on the Richter scale hit southern Turkey.

JULY 1998

16. Floods caused by heavy summer rains were reported to have killed 760 people in southern China. **17.** An earthquake registering 7.1 on the Richter scale hit the northern coast of Papua New Guinea, causing a tidal wave that swept away whole villages and killed at least 1,600 people. **27.** The Mayor of Southampton, Michael Andrews, and another man were killed when a 1940s flying boat crashed into the Solent; 16 people were rescued.

AUGUST 1998

18. At least 178 people were killed when a landslide destroyed the village of Malpa in Uttar Pradesh, northern India. **27.** The government of Bangladesh appealed for international help to cope with flooding that had killed at least 390 people since early July and left 25 million people homeless. **29.** At least 82 people were killed when a Cuban aircraft crashed during take-off at Quito airport, Ecuador.

ARTS, SCIENCE AND THE MEDIA

SEPTEMBER 1997

1. After receiving an ultimatum from the Scottish Arts Council, the board of Scottish Ballet agreed to stand down in order to secure funding for the company for the following season. **16.** The BBC announced plans to merge its television and radio news operations; after strong protests from senior journalists and editors, a compromise plan was agreed. **18.** A portrait of the child murderer Myra Hindley, part of an exhibition of work by young British artists at the Royal Academy, was damaged when protesters threw paint and eggs at it. The Academy's exhibitions secretary had defended the portrait and the exhibition, saying that 'there is no such thing as art that is immoral'. **25.** A British team led by Richard Noble set a new world land speed record of 714.144 m.p.h. in a ThrustSSC car driven by Andy Green in the Black Rock Desert, Nevada. The chairman of the Press Complaints Commission (Lord Wakeham) put forward proposals for a revised code of practice for newspapers to protect the privacy of individuals, particularly children, and preventing intrusive photography. The new code was published on 18 December and came into force on 1 January 1998. **29.** Gary Hume won the Jerwood prize for painting.

OCTOBER 1997

6. The British-born astronaut Michael Foale returned to earth after 4½ months aboard the space station *Mir*. **8.** Astronomers at the University of California, Los Angeles, said that the Hubble telescope had revealed the Pistol Star, a star in the Milky Way ten million times brighter than the Sun. **13.** Andy Green became the first person to break the sound barrier on land when he drove at 764.168 m.p.h. in ThrustSSC in the Black Rock Desert; he failed, however, to set a new world land-speed record because he did not complete a second run within an hour of the first. On the 15th Andy Green set a new world land-speed record of 763.035 m.p.h., the first supersonic record, in ThrustSSC. **15.** A rocket was launched from Cape Canaveral, Florida, carrying the Cassini-Huygens space probe on a seven-year mission to explore Saturn. **21.** Elton John's single *Candle in the Wind 1997* was named best-selling record ever, having sold 31.8 million copies since the funeral of Diana, Princess of Wales. **22.** At the British Fashion Awards, John Galliano and Alexander McQueen shared the award for Designer of the Year. **25.** The British Library Reading Room at the British Museum closed. **30.** The chief executive of the Royal Opera House (Mary Allen) told a House of Commons select committee that the theatre was facing a financial crisis. A special parliamentary commission ruled that Glasgow City Council could lend some of the Burrell Collection's works to overseas galleries in spite of the fact that this had been expressly forbidden in Sir William Burrell's bequest.

NOVEMBER 1997

3. The Secretary of State for Culture, Media and Sport (Chris Smith) said that London could not afford two opera houses and proposed that English National Opera should move out of the London Coliseum and share the Royal Opera House with the Royal Opera and the Royal Ballet. National Libraries Week began. **4.** The Broadcasting Standards Commission warned that children's television was becoming dominated by cartoons. **5.** The chairman of the Royal Opera House (Lord Chadlington) announced that a private-sector rescue package had saved the theatre from bankruptcy. **10.** Archaeologists announced that they had discovered a huge neolithic temple at Stanton Drew, near Bristol. **17.** The Royal Shakespeare Company announced a trading loss of £1.8 million for 1996–7. **19.** The first

septuplets to be delivered alive were born in Iowa, USA. **24.** The Humanities Reading Room at the new British Library at St Pancras opened. The Broadcasting Standards Commission published a new code of practice, to take effect from 1 January 1998, including the guideline that an individual's privacy should be infringed only when there is an overriding public interest in disclosure of the information.

DECEMBER 1997

2. The video artist Gillian Wearing won the Turner Prize for modern art. **3.** A report calling for the resignation of the board and the chief executive of the Royal Opera House was published by a House of Commons select committee; Chris Smith said in response that substantial changes were necessary in the management of the theatre but that precipitate change could worsen the crisis. On 4 December Lord Chadlington resigned as chairman of the board; the other members of the board offered to resign but agreed to stay until a new board could be appointed. The chief executive offered her resignation but it was refused. **8.** The DJ Chris Evans bought Virgin Radio.

JANUARY 1998

15. Sir Colin Southgate was appointed chairman of the Royal Opera House. **17.** *The Times* began to publish extracts from *Birthday Letters,* a book of poems by the poet laureate Ted Hughes about his relationship with his wife, Sylvia Plath, who committed suicide in 1963. **20.** The BBC, the ITC, the Radio Authority and S4C proposed that party political broadcasts be allowed only at election times.

FEBRUARY 1998

1. A £1 million trust fund to encourage new playwrights was launched by a theatre-loving multi-millionaire, Peter Wolff. **2.** The director of the Royal Opera, Nicholas Payne, was appointed general director of English National Opera. **4.** The Lord Chancellor (Lord Irvine of Lairg) proposed that the Press Complaints Commission should use the principle of 'prior restraint' in regulating press reporting of people's private lives; the idea was widely opposed. **5.** At the British Book Awards, *Bridget Jones's Diary* by Helen Fielding was named Book of the Year. The Hallé Orchestra was saved from immediate bankruptcy by reaching a deal with its endowment appeal fund. **9.** In a vote on the Competition Bill in the House of Lords, peers supported an amendment to prevent national newspapers from running price-cutting campaigns in order to eliminate rivals. At the Brit Awards in London, All Saints won the award for best single for *Never Ever* and The Verve were named best British group. **15.** A third symphony by Elgar, completed from the composer's sketches by Anthony Payne, was premièred at the Royal Festival Hall, London. **15–19.** A 65 ft sculpture by Antony Gormley, *The Angel of the North,* was erected at Gateshead. **20–27.** An auction of 40,000 items belonging to the late

Duke and Duchess of Windsor raised £14.5 million at Sotheby's in New York. **28.** Senior authors threatened to leave HarperCollins, the publishing company owned by Rupert Murdoch's News Corporation, after it cancelled plans, on the instructions of Mr Murdoch, to publish a book by the former governor of Hong Kong, Chris Patten, which criticised China. On 6 March HarperCollins apologized to Mr Patten for having suggested that the book had been rejected because it was not up to standard.

MARCH 1998

5. Nasa announced that a space probe had found large amounts of frozen water on the moon. **11.** The Irish businessman Tony O'Reilly bought out the Mirror Group in order to take full ownership of the *Independent* and the *Independent on Sunday*. **19.** The 22-member board of the Arts Council resigned at the request of the new secretary-general, Gerry Robinson; it was later replaced by a new ten-member board. **24.** At the Academy Awards ceremony in Los Angeles, *Titanic* won 11 Oscars, including best picture and best director. **25.** The chief executive of the Royal Opera House, Mary Allen, resigned. **29.** The percussionist Adrian Spillett was named BBC Young Musician of the Year.

APRIL 1998

20. Richard Jarman, the former general director of Scottish Opera, was appointed caretaker artistic director of the Royal Opera House. **27.** Scientists in Scotland said that they had isolated a gene believed to play an important role in the susceptibility of smokers to lung cancer. **28.** The British explorer David Hempleman-Adams reached the geographic North Pole, becoming the first person to complete the adventurers' grand slam of 11 mountaineering and polar exploration tasks.

MAY 1998

12. The European Parliament approved the controversial Life Patents Directive, allowing the patenting of biotechnological inventions. **13.** The chairman of the Press Complaints Commission (Lord Wakeham) warned newspapers not to incite violence or xenophobia in their coverage of the football world cup in summer 1998. **19.** English Heritage published the first national register of listed buildings at risk. **20.** All the members of the Arts Council's drama advisory panel resigned in protest at a reorganization of the Council's operations under its new chairman Gerry Robinson. **28.** Nasa announced that the Hubble telescope had photographed TMR-1C, the first planet ever to be seen outside the solar system. **31.** Geri Halliwell, known as 'Ginger Spice', announced that she had left the pop group the Spice Girls.

JUNE 1998

3. English Heritage published the first national survey of monuments at risk. **6.** Dame Ninette de Valois, the founder of the Royal Ballet, celebrated her 100th birthday. **17.** The Culture Secretary announced that ten people, including the sculptor Antony Gormley and the ballerina Deborah Bull, had been appointed to the newly-constituted Arts Council of England. **24.** Thomas Watson won the 1998 National Portrait Gallery BP Portrait Award. **25.** The Queen formally opened the new British Library at St Pancras, London. **30.** A report on the Royal Opera House by Sir Richard Eyre, which had been commissioned by the Culture Secretary, was published; it condemned the House for arrogance and presumption in its handling of public funds, but said that its funding should be increased and its management reformed.

JULY 1998

1. A museum dedicated to the life of Diana, Princess of Wales, opened at Althorp. *Water-lily Pond and Path by the Water* by Claude Monet was sold at Sotheby's in London for £19.8 million, a world record price for a painting by the artist. **2.** The Old Vic theatre was sold to the newly-formed Old Vic Theatre Trust for £3.5 million. **8.** A first edition of Chaucer's *Canterbury Tales* was sold at Christie's in London for £4.6 million, a record price for a printed book. Tina Brown resigned as editor of the *New Yorker*. **9.** Statues of ten Christian martyrs of the 20th century were unveiled at Westminster Abbey. **24.** The Government guaranteed free entry to national museums and galleries by 2001.

AUGUST 1998

12. The New Oxford Dictionary of English was published. **30.** Sir Simon Rattle conducted his last concert as director of the City of Birmingham Symphony Orchestra.

CRIMES AND LEGAL AFFAIRS

SEPTEMBER 1997

6. Eighteen-year-old Rachel Barraclough was found stabbed to death in Wakefield, W. Yorks. **9.** Sixteen-year-old Nathan Brown was ordered to be detained at Her Majesty's pleasure for murdering 14-year-old Carl Rickard with a machete outside a school in London in January 1997. **10.** Dennis Leckey, a senior education welfare officer, was sentenced at Manchester Crown Court to 18 years' imprisonment for sexually abusing boys in his care over a period of more than 20 years. **23.** A British nurse, Lucille McLauchlan, was sentenced in Saudi Arabia to 500 lashes and eight years' imprisonment for being an accessory to the murder of a colleague in December 1996. On 16 November the victim's brother officially accepted a cash settlement to spare the life of a second British nurse, Deborah Parry, if she were convicted of the murder.

OCTOBER 1997

2. A coroner called for an urgent review of the use by police of CS gas after an inquest jury returned a verdict of unlawful killing on a man who died in police custody in May 1996 after being sprayed with the gas. **6.** The High Court ruled that the result of the parliamentary election in Winchester on 1 May 1997, which was won by the Liberal Democrats by two votes, was void because 55 unstamped ballot papers which had been rejected could have changed the result. Two people were killed when their car was rammed from behind and crashed into oncoming traffic in Hanworth, London; Jason Humble was convicted of manslaughter and sentenced to 12 years' imprisonment on 2 April 1998. The Lord Chancellor announced plans to reform the civil justice system and to abolish legal aid in most civil cases (*see* page 1168). **22.** Duncan Bermingham was sentenced in Manchester to life imprisonment for murdering 21-year-old Rachel Thacker in August 1996. **23.** Heather Hallett was elected the first woman chairman of the Bar Council from January 1998. **24.** A woman police officer, Nina Mackay, was stabbed to death in Stratford, London. The Government published a White Paper proposing to incorporate the European Convention on Human Rights into British law (*see* page 1168). The Provincial Court of the Church in Wales found a rector, Clifford Williams, guilty of having had a six-year adulterous affair with a parishioner. **27.** Terence Storey was sentenced in Preston to life imprisonment for the murder of Revd Christopher Gray in Liverpool in August 1996. John Barr, the butcher who supplied meat linked to the outbreak of E. coli-0157 food poisoning in which 20 people died in Scotland in 1996–7, was cleared in Hamilton of recklessly supplying cooked meat for a birthday party in November 1996. **31.** A British au pair, Louise Woodward, was sentenced in Cambridge, Massachusetts, to life imprisonment for the murder of Matthew Eappen, an eight-month-old baby in her care, in February 1996. On 4 November the judge heard applications from her defence lawyers that the verdict be overturned or the conviction be reduced to manslaughter. On 10 November the judge reduced the conviction to manslaughter and sentenced her to 279 days' imprisonment; since she had already served this time on remand she was released immediately.

November 1997

3. Mohan Singh Kular was sentenced in Bristol to life imprisonment for the murder of his wife in the Punjab, India, in 1987. **5.** Six Iraqi men were sentenced at the Central Criminal Court to terms of up to nine years' imprisonment for hijacking a passenger jet to seek asylum in Britain in August 1996. **10.** Stephen Leisk was sentenced in Aberdeen to life imprisonment for the abduction and murder of nine-year-old Scott Simpson. **12.** A court in Brazil ruled that Ronnie Biggs, who escaped from Wandsworth prison in 1965, 15 months into a 30-year sentence for his part in the Great Train Robbery of 1963, would not be extradited to Britain to serve the remainder of his sentence. **14.** Alvin

Black was sentenced at the Central Criminal Court to life imprisonment for the murder of Johanna Czardebon, a German tourist, in Bedford in May 1996. **15.** Fourteen-year-old Kate Bushell was found stabbed to death near her home in Exeter. Small incendiary devices believed to have been planted by the self-styled 'Mardi Gra' blackmailer exploded outside two Sainsbury's stores in west London. **19.** Peter Smith was sentenced in Manchester to life imprisonment for torturing and murdering his girlfriend, Kelly-Anne Bates, in April 1997. **27.** The Government published a White Paper proposing reforms to the youth justice system (*see* page 1168).

December 1997

1. Detective Superintendent Raymond Mallon, the head of Middlesbrough CID and the leading exponent in Britain of 'zero tolerance' policing, was suspended over allegations that he had leaked confidential information and may have been involved in criminal activity. **2.** Derek Christian was sentenced in Leeds to life imprisonment for murdering Margaret Wilson in Burton Fleming, E. Yorks, in 1995. **3.** Andrew Evans, who was sentenced in 1972 to life imprisonment for the murder of 14-year-old Judith Roberts, was released from prison after the Court of Appeal quashed the conviction. **5.** John O'Shaughnessy was sentenced in Mold to life imprisonment for the rape and murder of nine-year-old Kayleigh Ward in December 1996. Squadron Leader Nicholas Tucker was sentenced in Norwich to life imprisonment for murdering his wife in 1995 after becoming infatuated with a Serbian interpreter while serving in Bosnia. A three-hour-old baby, Karli Hawthorne, was stolen from the maternity ward at Basildon General Hospital, Essex; she was found at an address in Basildon 14 hours later and a woman was charged with the kidnap. Barry Horne, an animal rights activist, was sentenced in Bristol to 18 years' imprisonment for carrying out arson attacks on shops in the south of England in 1994–6. **15.** Robert and Marius Maczka were sentenced in London to life imprisonment for murdering an elderly Polish couple, Josef and Kornela Ploch, in Fulham in June 1996. **16.** Brian McHugh, Patrick Kelly and James Murphy were sentenced at the Central Criminal Court to 25, 20 and 17 years' imprisonment respectively for plotting IRA bombing campaigns in mainland Britain. **17.** The Labour MP for Glasgow Govan, Mohammed Sarwar, appeared in court charged with fraud relating to his victory in the general election in May 1997. **22.** The 17-year-old son of the Home Secretary (Jack Straw) was arrested and questioned over allegations that he had sold cannabis to an undercover reporter from the *Mirror*; he was later cautioned.

January 1998

6. A murder charge against the former husband of Carol Park, who went missing in 1976 and whose body was found in Coniston Water in August 1997, was dropped because of lack of evidence. **14.** The former England football coach Terry Venables was banned for seven years by the DTI from holding company directorships after he was found to have acted dishonestly and failed to keep proper accounts. **15.** An unarmed man was shot dead by police at his home in Hastings, E. Sussex, during an investigation into drug trafficking and attempted murder. **16.** The Revd Michael Golightly was sentenced in Newcastle to five years' imprisonment for hitting his wife with a hammer in an apparently motiveless attack. **19.** George Lewis, who spent five years in prison after being framed by members of the former West Midlands serious crime squad for robberies he did not commit, was awarded £200,000 compensation in the High Court. **20.** Michael Steele and Jack Whomes were sentenced at the Central Criminal Court to life imprisonment for murdering three men in Rettendon, Essex, in 1995; all five men had been drug dealers. John M. Barr and Son, the butcher's shop implicated in the outbreak of E. coli-0157 food poisoning which killed 20 people in Scotland in 1996–7, was fined £2,250 for breaching food hygiene and safety laws. **22.** A woman and her four children died in a suspected arson attack at their home in Braunstone, Leicester. **23.** The High Court allowed compensation claims from six miners after ruling that British Coal had failed to take reasonable steps to minimize the harmful effects of coal dust, particularly in 1949–70. **27.** Detectives raided the homes of 19 serving or former CID officers as part of a major anti-corruption operation; 12 officers were suspended from duty. **29.** Victor Farrant was sentenced in Winchester to life imprisonment for the murder of Glenda Hoskins, an accountant, in 1996, and the attempted murder of Ann Fidler, a prostitute, in 1995.

FEBRUARY 1998

2. The American businessman Guy Snowden resigned from the board of the National Lottery operator Camelot after losing a High Court action against Richard Branson, who had alleged that he had been offered a bribe to abandon his bid for the franchise in 1993; Mr Snowden was ordered to pay £100,000 libel damages to Mr Branson. **3.** Carla Faye Tucker, who murdered two people in 1983, became the first woman to be executed in Texas, USA, since the Civil War. **5.** Sheila Bowler, who spent more than four years in prison after being convicted of the murder of her elderly aunt near Rye in 1992, was cleared of murder after a retrial at the Central Criminal Court. Two ten-year-old boys and an 11-year-old were cleared at the Central Criminal Court of raping a nine-year-old girl at their school in west London in 1997. **9.** David Frost was sentenced in Bristol to life imprisonment for the rape and murder of Louise Smith in 1995. **12.** Fr John Lloyd, a Roman Catholic priest, was convicted in Cardiff of indecently assaulting a 13-year-old girl in the mid 1970s; he was later sentenced to 21

months' imprisonment. **13.** A High Court judge, Mr Justice Harman, resigned after the Court of Appeal criticized him for an 'intolerable' delay of 20 months in delivering a judgment. **24.** The conviction of Mahmood Hussein Mattan, who was hanged in 1952 in Cardiff for the murder of Lily Volpert, a shopkeeper, was quashed by the Court of Appeal. Michael Gallagher, an IRA 'sleeper', was sentenced at Woolwich Crown Court to 20 years' imprisonment for conspiring to cause explosions on the mainland. **26.** Paul Longworth was sentenced in Liverpool to life imprisonment for murdering his wife Tina in January 1997 and attempting to make it look like suicide. The racehorse trainer Lynda Ramsden, her husband Jack and the champion jockey Kieren Fallon, were awarded £195,000 damages in the High Court over allegations in the *Sporting Life* that they had conspired to cheat the racing public. **27.** The Northern Ireland Court of Appeal quashed the conviction of Lee Clegg, the paratrooper who served two years of a life sentence for murdering Karen Reilly in Belfast in 1990; a retrial was ordered. Tony Neary, the former England rugby union player, was sentenced in Liverpool to five years' imprisonment for stealing £288,000 in the early 1990s.

MARCH 1998

2. Grant Harris, a consultant gynaecologist, was sentenced at the Central Criminal Court to six years' imprisonment for murdering his wife in June 1997 after she had begun divorce proceedings. **5.** A student was injured when a small incendiary device believed to have been planted by the self-styled 'Mardi Gra' blackmailer exploded near a Sainsbury's store in Forest Hill, London. **9.** Peter Humphrey was sentenced in Exeter to 12 years' imprisonment for arranging an acid attack on his estranged wife in July 1996; a babysitter at his home was badly injured instead of his wife. **19.** The conviction of John Roberts for the murder of a farmer in 1982, based solely on his confession, was quashed by the Court of Appeal on the basis of new psychiatric evidence. **24.** In a landmark civil ruling, a High Court judge ruled that Tony Diedrick, against whom no criminal charges had been brought, had murdered a doctor, Joan Francisco, in London in 1994. Four children and a teacher were shot dead when two boys opened fire at their school in Jonesboro, Arkansas. **28.** A Fulham football fan died from head injuries sustained in fighting after a match at Gillingham, Kent. **30.** The pop star Gary Glitter was charged with holding indecent images of children on his home computer.

APRIL 1998

2. Miles Evans was sentenced in Bristol to life imprisonment for the murder of his stepdaughter Zoe in January 1997. Maurice Papon was sentenced in Bordeaux to ten years' imprisonment for crimes against humanity in relation to his role in deporting Jews from the German-occupied city between 1942 and 1944. **3.** Anthony-Noel Kelly, an artist, was sentenced in London to nine months' imprisonment for stealing body parts from the Royal College of Surgeons to cast sculptures; the sentence was reduced to three months on appeal. **6.** Jong Rhee was sentenced in Chester to life imprisonment for murdering his wife Natalie by burning down the guesthouse in which they were staying in April 1997, in order to claim on insurance policies. **7.** Nicholas Burton was sentenced in Liverpool to life imprisonment for the murder of Rachel McGrath in Manchester in April 1997. **8.** The body of Kirsty Carver, a police computer operator who went missing on 5 March 1998, was found at Spurn Point, E. Yorks; on 9 April a man was charged with her murder. Patricia Bass, who was twice convicted of the murder of her mother in 1992, was released after the Court of Appeal quashed her conviction for a second time. **9.** A taxi driver who was beaten up by policemen in Liverpool in 1989 was awarded record damages of nearly £450,000 against Merseyside Police. **17.** Magdi Elgizouli, a paranoid schizophrenic, was ordered at the Central Criminal Court to be sent to a mental hospital indefinitely after he admitted murdering WPC Nina Mackay in London in October 1997. **30.** Eric Taylor, a Roman Catholic priest, was sentenced in Warwick to seven years' imprisonment for sexually abusing boys in his care in the 1950s and 1960s.

MAY 1998

4. The newly-appointed head of the Swiss Guards, Col. Alois Estermann, and his wife were shot dead in the Vatican City by another member of the Guards, who then shot himself. Theodore Kaczynski, known as the 'Unabomber', was sentenced in Sacramento, USA, to four terms of life imprisonment for an 18-year bombing campaign in which three people were killed and 29 injured. **5.** The pop star Gary Glitter was charged on five counts of indecently assaulting two young girls in the 1970s and 1980s. **7.** A nurse, Vicky Fletcher, was shot dead outside a pub in Castleford, W. Yorks; her lover, Dr Thomas Shanks, was charged with the murder. The Court of Appeal ruled that social workers and doctors had acted unlawfully in sectioning a woman under the Mental Health Act and performing a Caesarean section on her against her will, even though her life and that of the unborn baby were in danger. James Fraser Darling, a British teacher, was sentenced in Phuket, Thailand, to 33 years' imprisonment for indecent assaults on young boys. **14.** A woman, her two children and a 16-year-old babysitter were killed when an arsonist set fire to a house in Newcastle upon Tyne. **15.** Thomas 'Slab' Murphy lost a libel action in the High Court in Dublin against the *Sunday Times,* which had published an article in 1985 naming him as an IRA leader. **18.** The US Attorney-General (Janet Reno) launched an anti-trust lawsuit against Microsoft, alleging that the company's chairman, Bill Gates, had participated in an illegal conspiracy to eliminate competition from the Internet browser market. **19.** King Fahd of Saudi Arabia commuted the sentences of Lucille McLauchlan and Deborah Parry, two British nurses imprisoned in 1996 over the murder of an Australian nurse, Yvonne Gilford. The nurses arrived in Britain on 21 May and said that they were not guilty of the murder and had been coerced into signing confessions. **20.** Two Van Goghs and a Cézanne were stolen from the Museum of Modern Art in Rome; they were recovered on 6 July and eight people were arrested. **21.** A 15-year-old boy who had been expelled from school in Oregon, USA, shot his parents dead and then fired indiscriminately at people in the school, killing one pupil and seriously injuring eight others.

JUNE 1998

A report critical of the efficiency and effectiveness of the Crown Prosecution Service (CPS) was published; the Government accepted the thrust of its recommendations, including the appointment of 42 Chief Crown Prosecutors and a chief executive to administer the CPS. **9.** PC Andrew Taylor, who sprayed CS gas in the face of an elderly motorist who had parked on double yellow lines, was cleared in Luton of causing actual him bodily harm. **12.** The conviction of Patrick Nicholls, who was sentenced in 1975 to life imprisonment for the murder of 74-year-old Gladys Heath, was quashed by the Court of Appeal. **13.** In Texas, USA, James Byrd, a partially disabled black man, was tied to a van and dragged several miles to his death by three white men allegedly linked to the Ku Klux Klan. **14.** About 50 English football fans were arrested during rioting in Marseilles, France; trouble continued in the city the following day, before and during England's opening world cup match against Tunisia. **16.** The British au pair Louise Woodward, who was sentenced in November 1997 in Cambridge, Massachusetts, to 279 days' imprisonment for the manslaughter of a baby in her care, was given permission to return to Britain after the Massachusetts supreme court upheld both the verdict and the sentence. **17.** An assistant commissioner of the Metropolitan Police, Ian Johnston, publicly apologized to the family of the black teenager Stephen Lawrence, who was murdered in south London in 1993, for the handling of the police investigation into the case. **24.** James McArdle was convicted in London of planting the bomb that exploded in London's Docklands in February 1996; he was sentenced to 25 years' imprisonment. **29.** A public inquiry in London into the handling of the investigation of the murder of Stephen Lawrence was temporarily suspended after 20 members of the militant black group the Nation of Islam stormed the tribunal chamber.

JULY 1998

2. Sion Jenkins was sentenced in Lewes, E. Sussex, to life imprisonment for the murder of his 13-year-old foster daughter Billie-Jo in Hastings in February 1997. **3.** The former champion sprinter Linford Christie won a libel action in the High Court against the journalist John McVicar, who had written an article in a satirical magazine in 1995 in which he said that there was evidence that the athlete may have taken performance-enhancing drugs. **6.** Albert Walker was sentenced in Exeter to life imprisonment for the murder of Roland Platt, whose identity he had stolen in 1991 after leaving Canada to escape charges of theft and money laundering. **20.** Helen Stacey, a registered childminder, was sentenced in Norwich to life imprisonment for shaking to death a five-month-old baby in her care in May 1997. A senior warden at the Masai Mara game reserve in Kenya was charged with the murder of the British tourist Julie Ward in 1988. **24.** Two policemen were killed and a woman tourist was injured when a gunman opened fire in the Congress building in Washington DC, USA. **28.** Ryan James, a veterinary surgeon sentenced to life imprisonment in 1995 for the murder of his wife, was released after the Court of Appeal quashed his conviction because a suicide note written by his wife had been found. **30.** The Court of Appeal quashed the murder conviction of Derek Bentley, a 19-year-old epileptic with a mental age of 11, who was hanged in 1953 for the murder of a policeman in spite of the fact that his accomplice had fired the fatal shot.

AUGUST 1998

1. A former MI5 officer, David Shayler, was arrested in Paris; proceedings were instigated to extradite him to face charges under the Official Secrets Act. **29.** Kenneth Noye was arrested in southern Spain and an application was made to extradite him to Britain for questioning about the murder of Stephen Cameron in May 1996.

ECONOMIC AND BUSINESS AFFAIRS

SEPTEMBER 1997

5. Transco, the pipeline business of British Gas plc, announced 2,500 redundancies. **18.** Price Waterhouse and Coopers and Lybrand announced plans to merge, creating the largest accountancy practice in the world. **26.** The FT-SE 100 index closed at a record high of 5,226.3 and sterling fell to DM 2.8324 following speculation that the Government was adopting a more positive approach to EMU.

OCTOBER 1997

1. The American telecommunications group WorldCom made a $30 billion all-stock bid for MCI to rival an earlier bid by BT; on 15 October GTE Corporation offered $28 billion in cash, the largest cash offer ever for a company. On 10 November MCI accepted the bid from WorldCom. The FT-SE 100 index closed at a record high of 5,317.1. **2.** Bill Harrison resigned as chief executive of BZW, the investment arm of Barclays Bank. On 3

October Barclays Bank announced that it would sell the equities and advisory business of BZW; on 12 November it was bought by Crédit Suisse First Boston for £100 million. **10.** Brent Walker agreed to sell the betting chain William Hill to the Japanese investment bank Nomura for £700 million, leaving the company without an on-going business and with a debt of about £500 million; it was reported that the company would be wound up after the sale. **17.** The Chancellor of the Exchequer (Gordon Brown) said that it was extremely unlikely that the UK would join the first wave of EMU in 1999; confusion arose about his stance when an aide, Charlie Whelan, briefed journalists to the effect that the Chancellor would rule out membership of EMU during the lifetime of the current Parliament. On 27 October Gordon Brown said in the House of Commons that the UK would not achieve economic convergence with the rest of Europe, and therefore would not join EMU before the end of the current Parliament, but that there were no constitutional objections to joining and if EMU were successful the Government would want to join early in the next Parliament. Richard Branson launched a new Virgin bank account designed to cover banking, mortgage and loan requirements in one account. **20.** A new automated share dealing system (SETS) was introduced at the London Stock Exchange. **22.** The Hang Seng index in Hong Kong lost 6 per cent of its value. **23.** The Hang Seng index lost a further 10 per cent of its value. The Dow Jones index in New York closed 186.88 points down. The FT-SE 100 index closed 157.3 points down at 4,991.5, the biggest one-day fall for five years. **27.** The Hang Seng index fell a further 5.8 per cent, triggering the biggest-ever one-day fall on Wall Street where the Dow Jones index fell 554.26 points to 7,161.15. Vickers put the Rolls-Royce luxury car business up for sale. **28.** The Hang Seng index fell a further 13.7 per cent. The Dow Jones index closed 337.17 points up at 7,498.32, its largest-ever one-day rise. The FT-SE 100 index closed 85 points down at 4,755.4, having fallen at one stage by 457 points. **29.** The FT-SE 100 index closed 116.4 points up at 4,871.8. **30.** The Hang Seng index fell a further 4 per cent. The Dow Jones index closed 125 points down at 7,381.67. The FT-SE 100 index closed 69.9 points down at 4,801.9.

NOVEMBER 1997

3. The Hang Seng index rose nearly 6 per cent. The Dow Jones index closed 232.31 points up at 7,674.39. The FT-SE 100 index closed 64.1 points up at 4,906.4. **4.** Marks and Spencer announced a £2 billion expansion programme. **5.** Indonesia agreed to implement an IMF rescue package worth up to $43 billion. **6.** The Bank of England raised bank base rates by 0.25 per cent to 7.25 per cent. **7.** The Nikkei-225 index in Tokyo fell more than 4 per cent, causing big falls in the stock markets in Hong Kong, New York and London; the FT-SE 100 index closed 99.5 points down at 4,764.3. **10.** At the CBI conference in London, the Chancellor outlined proposed legislation to pave the way for the introduction of a single European currency. 13. The Industry Minister (John Battle) said that Rolls-Royce would receive £200 million of state funding in a commercial deal for an aircraft engine development project. 17. Ann Iverson was ousted as chief executive of Laura Ashley; she was replaced by David Hoare. 18. The President of the Board of Trade (Margaret Beckett) blocked the planned acquisition by Littlewoods of the home shopping catalogue business Freeman's on the grounds that it would reduce competition in the mail order sector. 19. Merrill Lynch announced an agreed £3.1 billion cash offer for Mercury Asset Management. 20. Simon Hughes was ousted as managing director of Mothercare; he was replaced by Greg Tufnell. 23. Yamaichi Securities, a leading Japanese stockbroking firm, collapsed with debts of $14.6 billion. 25. The Chancellor delivered a pre-Budget statement in the House of Commons, including the announcement that advance corporation tax would be abolished and corporation tax reduced from April 1999. The Nikkei-225 index in Tokyo closed 854.05 points down at 15,867.53. 30. South Korea signed an IMF rescue package worth up to $55 billion.

DECEMBER 1997

2. The Government announced the introduction of individual savings accounts (ISAs) to replace personal equity plans (PEPs) and tax-exempt special savings accounts (TESSAs) from April 1999. 8. Swiss Bank Corporation and Union Bank of Switzerland announced a merger. 11. Stock markets in Asia, Europe and the USA fell sharply because of the financial crisis in South Korea. 16. The Financial Services Authority published a report critical of the management and operations of Prudential Assurance. 22. The Nikkei-225 index in Tokyo fell 3.4 per cent after the sovereign debts of South Korea, Indonesia and Thailand were downgraded to junk bond status by the international credit rating agency Moody's.

JANUARY 1998

1. Ladbroke Group bought the Coral betting shop chain from Bass; on 31 March the sale was referred to the Monopolies and Mergers Commission. 5. IPC Magazines was sold by Reed Elsevier to a management group backed by the venture capitalist Cinven. 8. The Indonesian rupiah lost 20 per cent of its value against the dollar. 9. The Hang Seng index closed 360 points down at 8,894.6; the Nikkei-225, the Dow Jones and the FT-SE 100 indices also suffered heavy falls. 12. After a meeting with the IMF, President Suharto of Indonesia promised to implement reforms which had been a condition of the rescue package agreed in November 1997. The Hang Seng index closed 773.58 points down at 8,121.06 after Peregrine Investment Holdings, the largest independent stock broker in Hong Kong, went into liquidation. 21. The Indonesian rupiah lost more than 15 per cent of its value against the

dollar. 22. The newsagent and newspaper distribution chain John Menzies announced that it would withdraw from retailing and concentrate on distribution. 26. Compaq Computer Corporation agreed to buy Digital Equipment Corporation for $9.6 billion. 28. John Prescott said in the House of Commons that a request from London and Continental Railways, the Eurostar operator, for a further £1.2 billion of public money to build the high-speed rail link to the Channel Tunnel had been refused and that the company could not fulfil its obligation to build the link. The FT-SE 100 index closed at a record high of 5,372.6. 30. The pharmaceutical companies Glaxo-Wellcome and SmithKline Beecham announced plans for a merger; on 23 February the merger talks were broken off.

FEBRUARY 1998

2. The FT-SE 100 index closed at a record high of 5,590.0. 3. The FT-SE 100 index closed at a record high of 5,612.8; the companies constituting the index were valued at more than £1,000 billion for the first time. Great Universal Stores launched a hostile £1.68 billion bid for the catalogue retailer Argos. 6. Figures were published showing that the output of the UK's manufacturing industry fell by 0.5 per cent in December 1997, the fifth successive monthly fall. 13. Lloyds TSB disclosed a 26 per cent rise in pre-tax profits for 1997 to £3.16 billion. 19. The supermarket groups Kwik Save and Somerfield announced a £1.4 billion merger. 25. The insurance companies Commercial Union and General Accident announced a £15 billion merger. 27. The FT-SE 100 index closed at a record high of 5,767.3.

MARCH 1998

4. The National Audit Office published a report stating that Britain's rail leasing companies were sold into the private sector in 1996 for £700 million less than they were worth. 6. The sale of Great Western Trains to FirstGroup for £140 million was approved by the rail franchise director. The last working tin min in Europe, at South Crofty, Cornwall, closed. 9. Halifax launched a £780 million take-over bid for the Birmingham Midshires building society. W. H. Smith bought John Menzies for £68 million. Reed Elsevier and Wolters Kluwer abandoned plans to merge. 13. Sterling closed at $1.6705, its highest level for nine years. 17. The Chancellor of the Exchequer (Gordon Brown) presented the Budget to the House of Commons. 23. National Parking Corporation announced an agreed £801 million take-over by Cendant Corporation. The publishing company Random House was bought by the German company Bertelsmann for an estimated £655 million. 30. Vickers announced that a £340 million bid for Rolls-Royce from BMW had been accepted. The sterling index rose to 108.9, its highest level for ten years.

APRIL 1998

6. The FT-SE 100 index closed at a record high of 6,105.8. Citicorp and Travelers Group announced a $140 billion merger. **7.** The Savoy Group agreed to a £520 million take-over by an American consortium led by Blackstone Group. **13.** Nationsbank and Bank of America announced a $130 billion merger. **22.** Bank of New York launched a hostile $24 billion take-over bid for Mellon Bank. **24.** Great Universal Stores won control of the catalogue retailer Argos. **27.** The FT-SE 100 index closed 2.4 per cent down at 5,722.4 after heavy falls on Wall Street prompted by rumours of an interest rate rise in the USA. **28.** Trade figures for February 1998 showed a deficit of £1.74 billion, the biggest since March 1990.

MAY 1998

2. The European single currency, the Euro, was officially launched at a summit meeting in Brussels. **6.** Daimler-Benz and Chrysler announced plans for a $35 billion merger. Lord Sainsbury announced his retirement as chairman of the Sainsbury's supermarket chain. **7.** Sterling fell to DM2.9032. Vickers said that Volkswagen had submitted a bid for Rolls-Royce higher than the offer from BMW agreed in March 1998; on 5 June shareholders accepted the Volkswagen offer. On 28 July BMW and Volkswagen reached a deal under which BMW would take over the Rolls-Royce name in 2003, leaving Volkswagen with only the Bentley marque. On 30 July the chief executive of Roll-Royce Motors, Graham Morris, resigned. **11.** Shares in Thomson Travel began conditional dealings on the Stock Exchange. **18.** The fine art auction house Christie's agreed to a £721 million take-over by the French entrepreneur Francois Pinault. **19.** Dr Keith McCullagh said that he would resign as chief executive of the troubled drug development company British Biotech in September 1998. **25.** The 18 biggest banks in Japan wrote off about £45 billion in bad loans as the yen fell to its lowest level against the dollar since 1991. **27.** Share prices fell in Europe and the USA after the Russian Central Bank tripled its main interest rate to 150 per cent and the financial crisis in Asia deepened.

JUNE 1998

4. The Bank of England raised bank base rates by 0.25 per cent to 7.5 per cent. **9.** Members of the London Financial Futures and Options Exchange voted to reform the exchange and end open-outcry trading. **11.** The Chancellor of the Exchequer announced that the annual spending round would be abolished and that in future government departments would be set fixed three-year budgets. He also announced the partial privatization of National Air Traffic Services, the Commonwealth Development Corporation, the Horserace Totalisator Board and the Royal Mint. **12.** Japan released figures showing that the economy was technically in recession for the first time since 1975. **13.** The world's leading investment bank Goldman Sachs

voted to become a public company. **15.** The yen fell to 146.55 against the dollar, its lowest level for eight years. **16.** Figures were published showing that the headline inflation rate for May 1998 was 4.2 per cent, the highest level for six years. **17.** The US Federal Reserve and the Bank of Japan spent an estimated $2 billion buying the yen, which rose to 137.60 against the dollar. **19.** Members of the RAC voted in favour of the demutualization of the club's rescue service. **22.** Plans were announced for Stagecoach to buy a 49 per cent stake in Virgin Rail for £158 million. **23.** Britain's balance of payments figures for January to March 1998 showed a deficit of £3.2 billion. **24.** The leading jewellers Asprey and Garrard announced a merger. **29.** PowerGen agreed to buy East Midlands Electricity in a deal worth £1.9 billion.

JULY 1998

7. The London Stock Exchange and the Deutsche Börse in Frankfurt announced an alliance designed to allow investors access to leading quoted companies in both markets. **13.** The IMF agreed a £13.8 billion aid package for Russia. **14.** The Chancellor of the Exchequer announced the Government's spending plans until 2001, and said that an extra £40 billion would be spent on health and education (*see* page 1171). **15.** The FT-SE 100 index closed at a record high of 6,151.5. **24.** Wessex Water agreed to a £1.4 billion take-over by the American group Enron. **26.** BT announced a £6 billion joint venture with the American company AT and T. **31.** Siemens announced the closure of a semi-conductor plant on Tyneside with the loss of at least 1,100 jobs.

AUGUST 1998

11. BP announced a take-over of the American oil group Amoco in a £67.4 billion deal. **13.** Trading in Russian shares was temporarily suspended and prices on other stock markets fell sharply after the financier George Soros said that the rouble should be devalued by up to 25 per cent. **17.** The Russian Central Bank said that it would allow the rouble to float on the currency markets within a band of between six and 9.5 roubles to the dollar until the end of 1998. **21.** The FT-SE 100 index fell 190.4 points to close at 5,477.0. **26.** The rouble collapsed and the Russian Central Bank suspended trading in the currency; stock markets across Europe fell sharply. The perfume and cosmetics firm Yardley went into receivership. **27.** Trading in the rouble was again suspended and share prices fell on world stock markets. **28.** Share prices fell as the economic and political crisis in Russia continued. **31.** The Dow Jones industrial average fell 512 points, the second-biggest fall in its history.

ENVIRONMENT

SEPTEMBER 1997

2. The Government ended its opt-out of the international ban on dumping radioactive waste at sea and said that it supported proposals that discharges of hazardous and radioactive substances into the sea should be reduced to as close to zero as possible by 2020. **11.** National Power abandoned plans to burn orimulsion at Pembroke power station.

OCTOBER 1997

2. The National Trust upheld its ban on deer-hunting on its land. **13.** The UK ratified an amendment to the Basle Convention which banned the export of hazardous waste from developed countries. **29.** The Secretary of State for the Environment, Transport and the Regions (John Prescott) said that Britain would cut its carbon dioxide emissions by 20 per cent by 2010.

NOVEMBER 1997

7. As the damming of the Yangtze River in China was completed, environmentalists voiced concerns that the project would further threaten endangered animals, fish, birds and plants. **12.** The Planning Minister (Richard Caborn) said that the Government intended half of the 4.4 million new homes to be built by 2016 to be sited on farmland and in the green belt.

DECEMBER 1997

1. The UN Convention on Climate Change opened in Kyoto, Japan; on 11 December a treaty was agreed reducing emissions of 'greenhouse' gases by an average of 5.2 per cent between 2008 and 2012. **22.** The Energy and Science Minister (John Battle) announced that British Nuclear Fuels Ltd (BNFL) and Magnox Electric would merge.

JANUARY 1998

14. A 50-year ban on mining and mineral extraction in Antarctica, agreed under a protocol to the Antarctica Treaty in April 1991, came into force. **15.** The Government launched a review of planning regulations. **16.** John Prescott approved the building of up to 10,000 houses on green-belt land west of Stevenage, Herts. **25.** John Prescott said that more than half of new houses required should be built on 'brownfield' sites and that the 'predict and provide' policy, according to which councils have to identify land for new houses many years before they are to be built, should be abandoned.

FEBRUARY 1998

13. A temperature of 19.6° C was recorded at Barbourne, Worcs, making it the hottest February day ever recorded in Britain. **23.** John Prescott said that 60 per cent of new houses required should be

built on 'recycled' land and that developers would have to prove that no urban site existed before building in the countryside.

MARCH 1998

3. At least 300 tons of fish died after the waters of the River Dun, Berks, were contaminated by an unknown pollutant. **27.** The Government announced that the Countryside Commission and the Rural Development Commission would be merged.

APRIL 1998

17. Scientists at the University of Colorado, USA, said that a 25-mile long section of an ice shelf had broken away from Antarctica. **29.** John Prescott signed the Kyoto protocol, which set targets for the UK and other industrialized countries to cut their emissions of the gases responsible for global warming. The World Bank, the World Wide Fund for Nature and the government of Brazil announced a deal under which 62 million acres of rainforest would be declared a protected area.

JUNE 1998

17. The Government announced that Britain would reduce its emissions of greenhouse gases by at least 12.5 per cent of the 1990 level by 2010.

JULY 1998

23. Britain and 14 other countries signed an agreement in Sintra, Portugal, under which the remaining Magnox nuclear power stations in Britain would close by 2010 and discharges from Sellafield would be reduced to 'close to zero' by 2020. **31.** The Government cancelled more than 100 road-widening and bypass schemes; 37 schemes, including a cut-and-cover tunnel at Stonehenge, were given the go-ahead.

AUGUST 1998

5. Members of the agriculture select committee of the House of Commons said that parts of the coastline of south-east England and East Anglia should be sacrificed to the sea as part of a 'peaceful accommodation' with nature. **8.** Up to 6,000 mink were released from a farm in Ringwood, Hants, by the Animal Liberation Front, threatening 80 square miles of countryside including the New Forest. **10.** Average world-wide temperatures showed that July 1998 was the hottest month ever recorded.

SPORT

SEPTEMBER 1997

2. The West Ham defender Rio Ferdinand was dropped from the England football squad for a world cup qualifier against Moldova on 10 September because he had been convicted on 1 September of drinking and driving. **6.** Greg Rusedski became the first British tennis player to reach the final of the US

Open since 1936 when he beat Jonas Bjorkman; on 7 September he lost in the final to Patrick Rafter. **6–7.** At the world rowing championships in Aïguebelette, France, British rowers won two gold medals, two silvers and four bronzes. **15.** The first-class cricket counties voted 19–12 not to divide the county championship into two divisions. Sir John Hall announced his retirement as chairman of Newcastle United FC. After a bad-tempered match in Brive, France, a brawl broke out in a bar between members of Pontypridd and Brive rugby union clubs; both clubs were fined £30,000 by the European Rugby Cup Ltd for bringing the tournament into disrepute by their conduct during the match. **17.** Clive Woodward was appointed England rugby union coach. **19.** The Football Association (FA) said that it was investigating possible charges following breaches of its rules in the light of a Premier League report into illegal payments surrounding transfer deals.

OCTOBER 1997

8. The British yachtsman and Olympic silver medallist John Merricks was killed in a car crash in Italy. **11.** The England football team qualified for the world cup finals for the first time for eight years after drawing 0–0 with Italy in Rome; violence broke out between England fans and the Italian police during the match. On 24 October the FA published a report that blamed the Italian police for the violence. **14.** The British Athletic Federation called in administrators after declaring itself insolvent. **23.** Bryan Hamilton was sacked as manager of the Northern Ireland football team. **26.** Jacques Villeneuve won the Formula One world motor racing championship for the first time after finishing third in the European grand prix at Jerez, Spain; his main rival, Michael Schumacher, span off the track after hitting the side of Villeneuve's car. On 11 November Schumacher was stripped of his second place in the championship because he was found to have deliberately rammed Villeneuve's car. **29.** Lawrence Dallaglio was appointed England rugby union captain. **30.** An FA inquiry revealed widespread betting on football matches by players and officials in contravention of the FA's rules.

NOVEMBER 1997

7. A charge of manslaughter brought against Frank Williams, the head of the Williams-Renault Formula One motor racing team, over the death of Ayrton Senna in the San Marino grand prix in 1994, was dropped at a court in Italy. On 16 December the remaining members of the team and track officials charged with manslaughter were acquitted. **19.** Gerry Francis resigned as manager of Tottenham Hotspur FC; he was replaced by Christian Gross. **29.** Sir Peter O'Sullevan retired after 50 years of commentating on horse-racing for the BBC.

DECEMBER 1997

11. The Football League put forward five proposals for reforming its operations. The chairman of the management board of the Rugby Football Union (RFU), Cliff Brittle, put forward a blueprint for reforming rugby union in England. **12.** John Searson set a new world record of 59 days for rowing single-handedly across the Atlantic. The footballers Bruce Grobbelaar and Hans Segers were each given a six-month ban and a £10,000 fine, both suspended for two years, by the FA for assisting a Far East syndicate to forecast the results of matches. The Wales rugby union captain, Gwyn Jones, suffered a serious spinal injury while playing for Cardiff against Swansea; he subsequently announced his retirement from the sport. **14.** Greg Rusedski was voted BBC Sports Personality of the Year. **16.** The Government announced that the UK Sports Institute would be based in Sheffield. **22.** The German striker Jurgen Klinsmann, who played for Tottenham Hotspur in 1994–5, rejoined the club on loan from Sampdoria.

JANUARY 1998

7. The 12 rugby union Premiership first division clubs voted to pull out of European competition in 1998. **8.** Phials of synthetic human growth hormone were found in the luggage of a member of the Chinese team arriving for the world swimming championships in Perth, Australia; she was subsequently ordered to return to China. On 14 January four Chinese swimmers at the championships tested positive for drugs. Maurice Lindsay resigned as chief executive of the Rugby Football League to become managing director of Super League Europe. **9.** The former England rugby union captain Will Carling announced his retirement from the first-class game. **11.** The London Scottish rugby union player Simon Fenn lost part of his ear lobe in an alleged biting incident during a match at the Recreation Ground; on 13 January the Bath prop Kevin Yates was suspended pending a disciplinary hearing. On 10 February Yates was banned for six months by the RFU. **13.** Lord Wakeham resigned as chairman of the British Horseracing Board over a financial plan for racing, produced by an industry study group, which called for a 1.75 per cent cut in general betting duty. **25.** Non-league Stevenage Borough held Newcastle United to a 1–1 draw in an FA Cup fourth-round tie at Broadhall Way; Newcastle United later won the replay. **27.** Three jockeys (Jamie Osborne, Dean Gallagher and Leighton Aspell) and another man were arrested and questioned by police over allegations of horse-doping and race-fixing; they were released on bail without charge. On 28 January the three jockeys were suspended for a week by the Jockey Club. **29.** The first Test between the West Indies and England in Kingston, Jamaica, was abandoned after only 62 balls because the pitch was deemed to be dangerously uneven. The vice-chairman of the RFU, Fran Cotton, put forward radical plans for reforming the game in England, including the proposal that top players should be contracted to the RFU.

FEBRUARY 1998

7. The Winter Olympics opened in Nagano, Japan. 9. Lawrie McMenemy was appointed manager of the Northern Ireland football team. 11. The 18-year-old Liverpool striker Michael Owen became the youngest footballer to play for England since the 1880s in a match against Chile at Wembley. The first Olympic giant slalom snowboarding champion, Ross Rebagliati, was disqualified by the International Olympic Committee (IOC) after testing positive for marijuana; on 12 February he was reinstated after the Court of Arbitration for Sport ruled that the IOC had acted improperly. Snooker, pool and billiards were granted Olympic status. 12. Ruud Gullit was sacked as player-manager of Chelsea FC and replaced by Gianluca Vialli. 20. The RFU announced that Italy would be admitted to the Five Nations' Championship in 2000. Fifteen-year-old Tara Lipinski became the youngest-ever individual Winter Olympic gold medallist when she won the figure skating title at the games in Nagano. 21. England achieved the highest-ever score in the Five Nations' Championship, beating Wales 60–26 at Twickenham. 24. Brian Ashton resigned as coach of the Ireland rugby union team. 28. At the European indoor athletics championships, Ashia Hansen set a new world record of 15.16 metres for the women's triple jump.

MARCH 1998

8. At the Australian grand prix in Melbourne, David Coulthard controversially pulled aside when in the lead in order to allow his McLaren team-mate, Mika Hakkinen, to win the race because of a pre-race pact. 15. The *News of the World* published allegations that the chairman and vice-chairman of Newcastle United FC had insulted the club's fans and been abusive about local women; the two men resigned on 23 March. 24. Mike Atherton resigned as captain of the England cricket team after England lost the final Test to the West Indies by an innings and 52 runs; Adam Hollioake took over as captain for the rest of the Caribbean tour. Paul Gascoigne joined Middlesbrough FC from Rangers for £3.45 million. 28. Cambridge won the University Boat Race in a record time of 16 minutes, 19 seconds. The referee was forced to leave the pitch for several minutes during a match between Barnsley and Liverpool after being threatened by a fan who ran onto the pitch after a Barnsley player had been sent off; two more Barnsley players were sent off during the match. 29. The Women's Cricket Association voted to merge with the England and Wales Cricket Board. 30. The Football Task Force published a report on tackling racism in football.

APRIL 1998

3. The popular grey steeplechaser One Man was put down after breaking a leg during a race at Aintree. 4. The Grand National at Aintree was won by Earth Summit, which became the first horse to win the Scottish, Welsh and English Grand Nationals; only six out of 37 starters finished the race, during which one horse died and two were put down. England won the Five Nations' Championship grand slam for the fourth successive year after beating Ireland at Twickenham. Fran Cotton resigned as vice-chairman of the RFU's management board. 5. France achieved the highest-ever points total in a Five Nations match when they beat Wales 51–0 at Wembley. 7. The shot putter Paul Edwards was banned for life by the British Athletic Federation after testing positive for drugs for a second time; he lodged an appeal against the ruling. 22. Pat Whelan resigned as manager of the Ireland rugby union team. 29. The Irish Olympic swimming champion Michelle de Bruin denied that she had taken performance-enhancing drugs after the sport's international governing body, FINA, said that a urine sample taken from her in January had shown signs of adulteration. On 6 August de Bruin was banned for four years for manipulating the sample; she accused FINA of conspiring to destroy her career.

MAY 1998

1. Dennis Bergkamp was named Footballer of the Year. 2. The British boxer Spencer Oliver was taken to hospital in a coma after being knocked out during a European title fight at the Albert Hall, London; on 3 May he underwent an operation to remove a blood clot on his brain. 4. John Higgins became the world no. 1 snooker player, a position held by Stephen Hendry since 1990, when he won the world championship in Sheffield. 5. Alec Stewart was named England cricket captain for the summer Test matches. 6. Alan Shearer, the England football captain, was charged by the FA with misconduct for appearing to kick Neil Lennon in the face during a match against Leicester City on 29 April; on 12 May he was cleared of deliberately kicking the player. 7. Ray Wilkins was sacked as manager of Fulham FC and replaced by the club's chief operating officer, Kevin Keegan. 8. The RFU and English rugby union clubs reached agreement over arrangements for the future running of the sport. Kevin Bowring resigned as coach of the Wales rugby union team. 9. Celtic won the Scottish football championship for the first time in ten years; on 11 May the club's manager, Wim Jansen, resigned. Saracens equalled the highest-ever score in the rugby union Cup final when they beat Wasps 48–18 at Twickenham. 11. The swimming commentator Hamilton Bland was sacked after a report found that he taken secret payments from manufacturers while acting as a supposedly impartial adviser to local councils on the construction of swimming pools. 13. Chelsea FC won a European cup for the first time since 1971 when they beat Stuttgart 1–0 to win the European Cup Winners' Cup in Stockholm. 16. Arsenal became the second team to achieve the

League and FA Cup double twice when they beat Newcastle United 2–0 at Wembley to win the FA Cup. **27.** Eighteen-year-old Michael Owen became the youngest player to score for England when he scored the winning goal in a match against Morocco in Casablanca. The Scotland goalkeeper Andy Goram left the world cup squad after newspaper reports about his private life. **31.** Paul Gascoigne was controversially left out of the England world cup squad by the coach, Glen Hoddle.

JUNE 1998

8. Sepp Blatter was elected president of FIFA. **10.** The football world cup opened in Paris. **13.** The French yachtsman Eric Tabarly was drowned after falling from his yacht off the Welsh coast. **20.** Danny Grewcock became only the second England player to be sent off during a Test match when he was dismissed during England's defeat by New Zealand at Dunedin. **27.** Wales suffered their worst-ever rugby union defeat when they were beaten 96–13 by South Africa in Pretoria. Sam Smith became the first British woman since 1985 to reach the fourth round of the women's singles at Wimbledon when she beat the former champion Conchita Martinez in three sets. **30.** England were knocked out of the football world cup by Argentina in St Etienne in a penalty shoot-out after the match had ended in a 2–2 draw; David Beckham was sent off during the match.

JULY 1998

1. Tim Henman became the first Briton for 25 years to reach the semi-finals of the men's singles at Wimbledon when he beat Petr Korda in straight sets. **3.** A British boat, *Adventurer,* set a new world record of 74 days, 20 hours and 58 minutes for the circumnavigation of the globe by powered vessel. **4.** Jana Novotna won the ladies' singles title at Wimbledon at the third attempt, beating Nathalie Tauziat in straight sets. **5.** Pete Sampras became the third player to win five men's singles titles at Wimbledon when he beat Goran Ivanisevic in five sets. **12.** France won the football world cup for the first time when they beat Brazil 3–0 in the final in Paris. **17.** The Festina cycling team was expelled from the Tour de France after its director admitted that the team's cyclists had been provided with performance-enhancing drugs. On 24 July the 12th stage of the race was delayed by a strike by riders in protest at their treatment by the press and the police. On 29 July three teams withdrew from the race and the riders staged a go-slow, causing the 17th stage to be annulled. On 30 July two more teams withdrew from the race. **19.** A 17-year-old British amateur golfer, Justin Rose, finished joint fourth in The Open championship at Royal Birkdale; he immediately turned professional. **21.** A Briton, Brian Milton, became the first person to circumnavigate the globe in a microlight aircraft when he landed his plane at Brooklands airfield, Surrey. **27.** Two American athletes, the sprinter Dennis Mitchell and the shot-putter Randy Barnes, were suspended

after failing drugs tests. **28.** The rugby union club Coventry went into receivership.

AUGUST 1998

2. The former Olympic 400 metres silver medallist Roger Black retired from athletics after failing to be selected for the European championships in Budapest. **10.** England won a five-Test cricket series for the first time since 1986 when they beat South Africa in the fifth Test at Headingley. **23.** Great Britain finished top of the medal table at the European athletics championships in Budapest, with nine gold medals. **27.** Kenny Dalglish was sacked as manager of Newcastle United FC; he was replaced by Ruud Gullit. **27–31.** The Sri Lankan bowler Muttiah Muralitharan took 16 wickets for 220 runs in a match against England at the Oval.

APPOINTMENTS AND RESIGNATIONS

In addition to those mentioned above, the following appointments and resignations were announced:

1997

1 September: Peter Salmon was appointed controller of BBC1

9 September: Colette Bowe resigned as director of the Personal Investment Authority

12 September: Bob Phillis was appointed chief executive of Guardian Media Group

19 September: Dennis Marks resigned as general director of English National Opera; Richard Handover was appointed chief executive of W. H. Smith

25 September: Kevin Keegan was appointed chief operating officer of Fulham FC; Anthony Whitworth-Jones resigned as general manager of Glyndebourne opera house

1 October: Lord Gowrie resigned as chairman of the Arts Council of England from spring 1998; Sir Alistair Grant was appointed governor of the Bank of Scotland from May 1998

2 October: Sir Patrick Neill was appointed chairman of the Committee on Standards in Public Life

14 October: Keith Hellawell, chief constable of West Yorkshire, was appointed the first co-ordinator of government strategy against drug abuse

23 October: Ian Harley was appointed chief executive of Abbey National from February 1998

28 October: Bob Ingram was appointed chief executive-designate of Glaxo Wellcome

2 December: Richard Gamble resigned as chief executive of Royal and Sun Alliance; he was replaced by Bob Mendelsohn

18 December: Andreas Whittam Smith was appointed president of the British Board of Film Classification

1998

14 January: Gerry Robinson was appointed chairman of the Arts Council of England from April 1998

16 January: Kelvin MacKenzie was appointed deputy chief executive of Mirror Group Newspapers

21 January: Bridget Rowe resigned as editor of the *Sunday Mirror* and was replaced by Brendan Parsons, who was replaced as editor of the *People* by Neil Wallis; Derek Morris was appointed chairman of the Monopolies and Mergers Commission

30 January: Andrew Marr was replaced as editor of the *Independent* by Rosie Boycott, the editor of the *Independent on Sunday*, who took over responsibility for both titles; Mr Marr returned as editor-in-chief after the purchase of the two titles by Tony O'Reilly in March 1998

6 April: Nicholas Snowman, the head of the South Bank Centre in London, was appointed general director of Glyndebourne from September 1998

24 April: Rosie Boycott was appointed editor of the *Express*

1 May: Simon Kelner was appointed editor of the *Independent;* Andrew Marr resigned as editor-in-chief of the newspaper

12 May: Anita Roddick resigned as chief executive of the Body Shop, and became co-chairman; she was replaced as chief executive by Patrick Gournay

4 June: Stuart Higgins resigned as editor of the *Sun;* he was replaced by David Yelland

8 June: Kelvin MacKenzie resigned as deputy chief executive of the Mirror Group

21 July: Brian Williamson was appointed chairman of the London International Financial Futures and Options Exchange; Daniel Hodson resigned as its chief executive

28 July: Roger Alton was appointed editor of the *Observer* in succession to Will Hutton, who was appointed editor-in-chief

---

AFRICA

SEPTEMBER 1997

3. Troops from Great Comoro landed on the island of Anjouan in an unsuccessful attempt to quell a separatist movement. 7. Islamic militants murdered 87 people in a suburb of Algiers. 9. Algerian troops killed at least 127 members of the militant Armed Islamic Group. 16. The Moroccan government and Polisario guerrillas agreed to hold a referendum to determine whether Western Sahara should remain part of Morocco. 22. Islamic militants were suspected of killing at least 85 civilians in Algiers. 24. The Islamic Salvation Army (AIS), the military wing of the Islamic Salvation Front party in Algeria, declared a cease-fire on military activities to begin on 1 October.

OCTOBER 1997

13. Islamic militants killed 43 people in Algeria. 14. Angolan troops from the enclave of Cabinda joined Congolese rebels fighting government troops in the Republic of Congo. On 15 October the rebels took control of Brazzaville, the capital of the Republic of Congo. 26. Angola agreed to withdraw its troops from the Republic of Congo. 28. An attempted coup was put down in Zambia. 31. The UN Security Council imposed sanctions on the Angolan guerrilla movement UNITA for failing to implement the Lusaka Protocol, a 1994 UN-mediated peace agreement.

NOVEMBER 1997

17–19. More than 300 people died in Rwanda when Hutu extremists attacked a prison in an attempt to free prisoners charged with genocide. 28. The Zimbabwean government published a list of 1,503 farms to be confiscated.

DECEMBER 1997

11. At least 1,000 people were killed in north-west Rwanda in an attack by Hutus on a camp for Tutsi refugees from the Democratic Republic of Congo. 16. Nelson Mandela resigned as president of the African National Congress. 21. A group of army officers failed in an attempt to overthrow the Nigerian government. 25. Kenneth Kaunda, the former president of Zambia, was arrested in connection with the coup attempt in October 1997; he was released on 31 December. 29–30. Daniel arap Moi was re-elected president of Kenya. 31. Muslim extremists in Algeria killed 412 people.

JANUARY 1998

1. At least 284 civilians were killed in Burundi by Hutu rebels who were retreating after attacking a government military camp. 14. The government of Equatorial Guinea resigned; a new government was appointed nine days later. 16. The government of Zimbabwe agreed to delay plans to appropriate large, mainly white-owned farms, as a precondition for obtaining EU and World Bank loans. 19–21. Government troops attempted to quell unrest in Harare, Zimbabwe, which had begun in response to rises in basic food prices. 23. The former president of South Africa, P. W. Botha, was charged with contempt of the Truth and Reconciliation Commission, having ignored three subpoenas to appear before it.

FEBRUARY 1998

9. Hutu rebels were reported to have killed 58 people in a village in north-west Rwanda. Nigerian troops launched an air and artillery offensive against Sierra Leone's military junta. 12. Nigerian troops were reported to have taken control of Freetown, the capital of Sierra Leone. Four Sudanese government officials, including the Vice-President, died when the aircraft they were travelling in crashed on landing in southern Sudan. 15. Islamic

militants were suspected of killing 36 people on the outskirts of Algiers. **15–17.** Government troops killed 88 Islamic militants in Algeria. **18.** Islamic militants killed 23 people in western Algeria. **24.** Eighteen people died when a bomb exploded on a train south of Algiers.

MARCH 1998

7. About 100 people were killed in tribal clashes in western Sudan. **10.** Ahmad Tejan Kabbah, the exiled president of Sierra Leone, returned to Freetown after the military junta which had ousted him was ejected by Nigerian peacekeepers. **11.** The rebel group UNITA was declared a legal political party by the Angolan government. **23.** Albert René was elected for a second term as president of the Seychelles.

APRIL 1998

20. In Algeria, 120 policemen were arrested on charges of human rights abuses. Two Roman Catholic priests were convicted in Rwanda of the murders of over 2,000 Tutsis. **21.** At the close of nominations for the Nigerian presidential elections, President Abacha was the only candidate put forward by any of the five government-sanctioned parties. **24.** In Rwanda, thousands of people attended the executions of 22 people found guilty of genocide. **27.** Forty people were killed in a massacre in Chouardia, Algeria.

MAY 1998

1. Jean Kambanda, Rwanda's former prime minister, pleaded guilty to six charges of genocide. **7.** Peace talks in Kenya between the Sudanese government and rebels from the south ended with the announcement of a referendum on self-determination for the south of the country. **13.** Ethiopia called on Eritrea to withdraw immediately from a border area it had occupied.

JUNE 1998

2. The chief of the Armed Islamic Groups (GIA) in Algiers, Mohamed Kebaili, was killed by troops in a suburb of the city. **3.** Fighting flared up on the border between Ethiopia and Eritrea, each side accusing the other of initiating hostilities. **8.** President Abacha of Nigeria died of a heart attack. Ugandan rebels killed more than 60 people in an attack on a school in Fort Portal. **9.** Gen. Abdulsalami Abubakar was sworn in as Nigeria's new president. **15.** Hundreds of people died in Guinea-Bissau in fighting between mutinous troops led by the sacked army chief Ansumane Mane and forces loyal to President Vieira. Nigeria's new military government ordered the release of nine political prisoners. **24.** President Eyadema of Togo was re-elected. **27.** The UN mediator Alioune Blondin Beye, who played a key role in negotiations in Angola, was killed in a plane crash in Côte d'Ivoire. **31.** The UN Secretary-General Kofi Annan held talks with Chief Moshood Abiola, the jailed Nigerian pro-democracy leader, in an attempt to secure the chief's release.

JULY 1998

3. Talks aimed at ending the conflict in Guinea-Bissau broke down. **7.** In Nigeria, Chief Abiola died of a heart attack during a meeting with US officials. **8.** There was rioting throughout Nigeria following Chief Abiola's death; 45 people died. **9.** Athmane Khelifi, the leader of the GIA in Algiers, was shot dead outside the city. **15.** The Sudan People's Liberation Army announced a three-month cease-fire in the south of the country to allow aid to reach the 1.2 million people affected by famine. **18.** President Nelson Mandela of South Africa married Gracia Machel, the widow of President Machel of Mozambique. **20.** Fighting resumed in Angola after UNITA seized a number of towns across the country. President Abubakar of Nigeria announced that he would hand over control to a civilian government in early 1999 and announced the release of all political prisoners. **23.** At least 150 people died in Angola following an attack by UNITA troops.

AUGUST 1998

2. In Rwanda, 102 people died in an attack by Hutu rebels. **3.** A rebel movement in the Democratic Republic of Congo announced that it had set up an autonomous zone in the east of the country and intended to oust President Kabila. Sudan announced a unilateral cease-fire in the famine-affected south of the country. **6.** Rebel troops in the Democratic Republic of Congo, allegedly backed by Rwandan troops, reached the west of the country. **7.** Bomb attacks on the US embassies in Nairobi, Kenya, and Dar-es-Salaam, Tanzania, left 240 people dead and 5,000 injured. **9.** Ugandan troops entered the Democratic Republic of Congo to support President Kabila's government. **17.** Two people were killed after police opened fire on pro-democracy demonstrators in Maseru, Lesotho. **20.** The USA carried out a cruise missile attack on a site in Sudan linked to terrorists it believed to be responsible for the bombing of its embassies on 7 August. **21.** Zimbabwe sent troops to the Democratic Republic of Congo to support President Kabila's government. Former South African President P. W. Botha was sentenced to 12 months in jail or a fine of 10,000 rands (£1,000) after being found guilty of contempt by the Truth and Reconciliation Committee. **23.** Rebel troops advancing on Kinshasa were attacked by Angolan forces, who successfully cut off the rebel's supply lines. **25.** It was announced that democratic elections in Nigeria will be held on 20 and 27 February 1999. A bomb exploded in a restaurant in Cape Town, killing two people and injuring 24, in a suspected revenge attack following the US cruise missile strikes in Sudan and Afghanistan on 20 August. **26.** Fighting in the Democratic Republic of Congo reached Kinshasa. **31.** UNITA forces were reported to have joined the anti-government troops in the Democratic Republic of Congo.

THE AMERICAS

SEPTEMBER 1997

2. Costa Rica, Guatemala, Honduras, Nicaragua and El Salvador signed the Managua Declaration, which will create a European Union-style organization. **13–14.** The leaders of Canada's provinces and territories agreed to recognize Quebec's 'unique character'; the premier of Quebec boycotted the meeting. **17.** President Clinton rescinded a commitment to support an international ban on land-mines.

OCTOBER 1997

14. The Nevis Island Assembly voted to end Nevis's federation with St Christopher. **26.** Congressional elections were held in Argentina.

NOVEMBER 1997

5. Rudolph Giuliani was re-elected mayor of New York, USA.

DECEMBER 1997

15. Janet Jagan was elected president of Guyana. **19.** The ruling People's National Party won a general election in Jamaica.

JANUARY 1998

17. President Clinton was questioned by lawyers over allegations that he had sexually harassed Paula Jones when he was governor of Arkansas. **19.** The People's Progressive Party reached agreement with the opposition People's National Congress in Guyana to initiate a constitutional review, thereby ending protests about the election result in December. **21.** An investigation began into an alleged affair between a White House assistant, Monica Lewinsky, and President Clinton, who was accused of persuading her to lie under oath.

FEBRUARY 1998

24. Fidel Castro was reappointed president of Cuba.

MARCH 1998

7. Eighty government soldiers were killed by Marxist guerrillas in Colombia. **10.** The former Chilean dictator Gen. Augusto Pinochet retired as commander-in-chief of the armed forces and took a seat in the Senate which he will hold for life. **20.** The USA eased sanctions against Cuba.

APRIL 1998

1. The sexual harrassment case bought by Paula Jones against President Clinton was dismissed by the judge, who said that there were no 'genuine issues' worthy of a trial. **20.** Colombia's top human rights lawyer was found murdered in Bogotá. **27.**

Bishop Conedera, a leading defender of human rights in Guatemala, was found murdered at his home two days after publishing a damning report on human rights violations by the Guatemalan army during the country's 36-year civil war.

MAY 1998

11. The right-wing Colorado Party claimed victory in the Paraguayan general elections, amid widespread allegations of electoral fraud. **20.** Congress initiated an investigation of President Clinton's campaign funding in response to allegations that he had received a donation from a Chinese army officer. **21.** Marion Barry resigned as mayor of Washington DC. **24.** Thirty people were injured when a bomb went off in a church in Danville, Illinois.

JUNE 1998

21. Andres Pastrana, the Conservative candidate, won the Colombian presidential election.

JULY 1998

4. There were mass evacuations in Florida as forest fires burned out of control along the state's Atlantic coast. **20.** Jamil Mahaud was elected president of Ecuador. **24.** A gunman shot and killed two security staff in the Capitol building, Washington DC. **26.** President Clinton was subpoenaed by the grand jury investigating his alleged affair with Monica Lewinsky; on the 28th, Miss Lewinsky was granted immunity from prosecution in return for her testimony concerning her alleged sexual relations with the president.

AUGUST 1998

4. Wall Street suffered the third-biggest fall in its history; it was blamed on the Asian economic crisis. **6.** Monica Lewinsky gave evidence to a grand jury about her relationship with President Clinton and contradicted his sworn statement that they did not have sexual relations. **7.** The US embassies in Kenya and Tanzania were bombed; 240 people were killed and 5,000 injured. **10.** On Nevis, 61 per cent of the islanders voted for independence from St Christopher, but this fell short of the two-thirds majority needed for constitutional change. **17.** President Clinton testified before the grand jury regarding his relationship with Monica Lewinsky, and in a televised address admitted to an 'an inappropriate physical relationship' with her. **20.** The USA launched cruise missile attacks on targets in Afghanistan and Sudan linked to the terrorists believed to be responsible for the bombing of the US embassies in Kenya and Tanzania on 7 August. Canada's Supreme Court ruled that the province of Quebec does not have the right to separate from the rest of the country under either Canadian or international law. **31.** The general election in Belize was won by the opposition People's United Party, its leader Said Musa becoming the new Prime Minister. The Dow Jones index suffered the second largest fall in its history in the aftermath of the Russian economic crisis.

ASIA

SEPTEMBER 1997

12–18. The 15th congress of the Chinese Communist Party (CCP) was held in Beijing; on 19 September a new Politburo standing committee was selected. **25.** In Indonesia, forest fires started by landowners attempting to clear land worsened, causing widespread pollution across the region. **31.** Indian and Pakistani troops exchanged fire across their disputed border in Kashmir, killing 25 people.

OCTOBER 1997

6–7. More than 400 people died in fighting between Sri Lankan troops and Tamil Tiger rebels. **7.** Surya Bahadur Thapa was sworn in as prime minister of Nepal. **8.** Kim Jong-il was elected general secretary of North Korea's ruling Worker's Party. **15.** A bomb explosion in Colombo, Sri Lanka, killed at least 18 people.

NOVEMBER 1997

7. The Thai government resigned following criticism of its handling of the country's economic crisis; a new coalition government was formed two days later. **10.** China and Russia signed an agreement delineating their mutual border. **16.** The Chinese pro-democracy activist Wei Jingsheng was released from prison and flown to the USA. **28.** The Indian prime minister Inder Kumar Gujral resigned following the withdrawal of the Congress (I) Party from the coalition government.

DECEMBER 1997

2. President Farooq Leghari of Pakistan resigned. **9.** Peace talks opened between North and South Korea, the USA and China, seeking a formal ending to the Korean War. **10.** The capital of Kazakhstan was moved from Alma-Ata to Akmola. **18.** Kim Dae-jung was elected president of South Korea.

JANUARY 1998

11. Gunmen shot dead 24 Shia Muslims in a sectarian attack in Lahore, Pakistan. **15.** Indonesia agreed to implement an economic reform package in exchange for a US$43 billion loan from the IMF. **25.** Tamil Tiger suicide bombers detonated a bomb in Kandy, Sri Lanka, killing 11 people.

FEBRUARY 1998

4. Sri Lanka celebrated the 50th anniversary of its independence. **6.** At least nine people died when a suicide bomber detonated a bomb in Columbo, Sri Lanka. **14.** Islamic fundamentalist suicide bombers killed 43 people in Coimbatore, India. **16.** Twenty-six people died during violence on the first day of voting in India's general election. **22.** At least 66 people died when Tamil Tiger rebels launched an

attack on two navy vessels off northern Sri Lanka. Ten people died during violence in the second round of voting in India's general election. **25.** Kim Dae-jung was sworn in as president of South Korea. **27.** Both factions in Cambodia's civil war declared a cease-fire.

MARCH 1998

5. Thirty-two people were killed in a Tamil Tiger suicide bomb attack in Colombo, Sri Lanka. **15.** The Bharatiya Janata Party (BJP) was invited to form a coalition government following the general election in India, in which no party won an overall majority. **16.** At least 100 people died during fighting between the forces of Gen. Rashid Dostum and Hezb-i-Wahdat in Mazar-i-Sharif, northern Afghanistan. Further peace talks between North and South Korea, also attended by representatives from the USA and China, opened in Geneva, Switzerland. **17.** Zhu Rongji was elected prime minister of China by the National People's Congress. **19.** Atal Behari Vajpayee of the BJP was sworn in as prime minister of India. **26.** The Cambodian government claimed that the Khmer Rouge headquarters in Cambodia had been captured by defectors in a mutiny. **30.** Prince Norodom Ranariddh returned to Cambodia for the first time since being ousted in a coup in July 1997.

APRIL 1998

6. Pakistan conducted a test flight of a nuclear missile capable of hitting Delhi, India. **15.** Pol Pot, the 73-year old former dictator of Cambodia responsible for the deaths of an estimated 1.7 million people, died of a heart attack. **20.** In India's Jammu and Kashmir state, 29 people, mostly Hindus, were shot dead by militants. Wang Dan, the Chinese dissident and a student leader during the Tiananmen Square demonstrations, was released from prison and allowed to leave China. Khmer Rouge guerrillas killed 21 people in an attack on a Cambodian fishing village. **22.** The French government, separatists and French settlers agreed to hold a referendum in December to determine the constitutional future of New Caledonia. **25.** Talks between the Taleban and Afghans from the country's non-Taleban northern enclave took place in Islamabad under US mediation.

MAY 1998

11. India carried out three nuclear tests, raising fears of an arms race with Pakistan; the tests drew widespread international condemnation. **16.** Indonesia's President Suharto cancelled the unpopular austerity measures required under the IMF deal in January; 500 people had died in three months of protests. On 21 May President Suharto resigned and was replaced by Vice-President Habibie. **24.** Hong Kong's pro-democracy candidates won more than 50 per cent of the vote in legislative elections. **27.** Workers in South Korea began a nationwide strike, protesting against a wave of redundancies. **28.**

Pakistan carried out five nuclear tests, and announced that because of the severe economic sanctions applied by the international community, it would cut spending in all areas by 50 per cent. **29.** Joseph Estrada won the presidential election in the Philippines.

JUNE 1998

4. In Hong Kong 25,000 people attended a commemoration of the Tiananmen Square massacre, the first such commemoration since Hong Kong reverted to Chinese rule. **25.** President Clinton began an official visit to China. **27.** President Clinton criticized China over human rights issues at a press conference which was televised live across China.

JULY 1998

8. The Taleban banned television sets in Afghanistan. **12.** The Japanese Prime Minister Ryutaro Hashimoto resigned after his Liberal Democratic party lost 17 seats in the elections to the upper house. The Taleban captured Maimana, an opposition stronghold in the north of Afghanistan. **24.** Keizo Obuchi was elected leader of Japan's Liberal Democratic Party. **26.** The Cambodian elections were marred by violence and accusations of voter intimidation by the ruling Cambodian People's Party, although UN observers declared that in general, 'the polling achieved democratic standards'. **27.** The former Pakistani prime minister Benazir Bhutto appeared in court in Lahore to face charges of corruption. **28.** Indonesia began withdrawing its troops from East Timor. **31.** Aung San Suu Kyi, the Burmese opposition leader, was prevented from meeting colleagues and held in her car at a roadblock outside Yangon for six days before being forcibly returned home. The Diet elected Keizo Obuchi prime minister of Japan.

AUGUST 1998

3. More than 100 people were killed in heavy fighting in Kashmir. Flooding along the Yangtze river in China left millions homeless. **5.** The Cambodian People's Party won the largest share of the vote in the recent elections, but was short of the two-thirds majority needed to form a government. **8.** Prince Ranariddh rejected the Cambodian election results and refused to join a coalition government led by Hun Sen. **10.** Prince Billah of Brunei was formally invested as heir to the throne. Taleban forces took control of Mazar-i-Sharif, the last major opposition stronghold in Afghanistan. **12.** Aung San Suu Kyi was once more halted at a police roadblock after attempting to visit her supporters outside the Myanmar capital Yangon. **20.** The USA carried out a cruise missile attack on a site in Afghanistan linked to terrorists it believed to be responsible for the bombing of its embassies in Kenya and Tanzania on 7 August. **24.** Aung San Suu Kyi returned to Yangon after government officials agreed to meet members of her National League for Democracy for talks. **31.** North Korea successfully tested a new ballistic missile capable of hitting Japan.

AUSTRALASIA AND THE PACIFIC

OCTOBER 1997

10. The Papua New Guinea government and rebels from the island of Bougainville signed a truce.

NOVEMBER 1997

3. Jim Bolger announced that he would resign as prime minister of New Zealand from the end of the month; following his resignation, Jenny Shipley became prime minister.

FEBRUARY 1998

2. A ten-day constitutional convention on whether Australia should become a republic opened in Canberra; on 13 February the convention voted in favour of a republic, with a head of state elected by a two-thirds majority of parliament.

MARCH 1998

12. A four-week state of emergency was imposed in Vanuatu after riots broke out in the capital, Port Vila, as investors tried to withdraw their bank savings following rumours of a financial scandal.

APRIL 1998

20. Riot police clashed with dockers on strike in Melbourne, Australia, in protest against mass redundancies. **22.** The Australian Federal Court ordered the reinstatement of all the sacked dock workers, who had been replaced with non-union workers. **31.** In Papua New Guinea rebels gave up their weapons and signed a peace treaty formally ending a decade of civil war on the island of Bougainville.

JULY 1998

8. The New Zealand government was ordered to return land confiscated from the Maoris 30 years ago. The Australian Senate passed a bill declaring farmers' land rights more important than traditional Aborigine claims. **18.** More than 1,600 people were killed when a tidal wave swept away entire villages on the northern coast of Papua New Guinea.

AUGUST 1998

18. New Zealand's ruling coalition was formally dissolved after ministers from the New Zealand First party walked out of a Cabinet meeting. **31.** In Australia, a general election was called for 3 October 1998.

EUROPE

SEPTEMBER 1997

16. The Labour government in Norway promised to resign after receiving less than 37 per cent of the vote in the general election on 15 September. **21.** In Poland, the Solidarity Electoral Alliance defeated the ruling former communists in a legislative election; on 17 October it formed a coalition government with the Freedom Unity party. Presidential and legislative elections in Serbia produced no outright winners.

OCTOBER 1997

1. NATO-led Stabilization Force (SFOR) troops in Bosnia took control of four radio and television transmitters controlled by the Bosnian Serb leader Radovan Karadzic. 5. Less than 50 per cent of the electorate voted in a run-off for the presidential election in Serbia which was therefore ruled invalid. 6. Ten Bosnian Croats charged with war crimes were taken into detention by the International Court in the Hague after giving themselves up for trial. 9. The Italian prime minister Romano Prodi resigned after failing to gain support from within the ruling coalition for his finance bill; he was asked to remain as caretaker prime minister. 19. Milo Djukanovic was elected president of Montenegro. 31. Mary McAleese was elected president of Ireland.

NOVEMBER 1997

2–7. French lorry drivers blockaded roads across France in a strike over pay. 16. In a referendum, Hungarians voted in favour of joining NATO. 22–23. Elections were held to the People's Assembly in Bosnia. 23. Milan Kučan was re-elected president of Slovenia. 29. The Czech government resigned following a scandal over funding of the ruling party.

DECEMBER 1997

2–4. A conference on the disposal of gold confiscated by the Nazis was held in London. 7. A presidential election in Serbia produced no outright winner. 16. Josef Tosovsky, an independent, was appointed as interim prime minister of the Czech Republic. 18. Two Bosnian Croats charged with war crimes were arrested by SFOR troops in Vitez, Bosnia. 19. The International Criminal Tribunal for the Former Yugoslavia released three war crimes suspects after charges were withdrawn because of lack of evidence. 22. Milan Milutinovic, the Socialist Party candidate, was elected president of Serbia.

JANUARY 1998

5. Valdas Adamkus was elected president of Lithuania. 15. The UN Transitional Administration for Eastern Slavonia withdrew, leaving the area under Croatian control. 16. The constitutional court of Turkey banned the pro-Islamic Welfare Party. 18. Milorad Dodik was elected by the legislature as prime minister of Republika Srpska, the Serb part of federal Bosnia. 20. Vaclav Havel was re-elected president of the Czech Republic. 22. NATO troops arrested Goran Jelisic, a Bosnian Serb war crimes suspect, in Bijeljina, Bosnia.

FEBRUARY 1998

3. Levon Ter-Petrosyan resigned as president of Armenia. 9. Troops were ordered on to the streets of Tbilisi, Georgia, following an unsuccessful attempt to assassinate President Shevardnadze. 12. Glafcos Clerides was re-elected president of Cyprus. 14. Two suspected Bosnian Serb war criminals, Milan Simic and Miroslav Tadic, surrendered to SFOR. 23. Government troops quelled riots led by rebel police units in Shkodër, Albania. 24. Simo Zaric, suspected of war crimes in Bosnia, surrendered to SFOR.

MARCH 1998

1–2. At least 20 people died during clashes between Serb police and ethnic Albanians in Pristina, the capital of Kosovo province, Serbia. 4. Dragoljub Kunarac, suspected of war crimes in Bosnia, surrendered to SFOR. 5. Serb forces killed at least 20 ethnic Albanians in Kosovo during attacks on villages suspected of harbouring separatist guerrillas. 7. A military court in Rome, Italy, sentenced Erich Priebke to life imprisonment for his part in the massacre of 335 people in 1944. 11. The Danish general elections were won by the governing centre-left social democratic coalition of prime minister Poul Nyrop Rasmussen. 23. President Yeltsin of Russia sacked his entire Cabinet, including Prime Minister Chernomyrdin. The Communist Party won legislative elections in Moldova. 29. Legislative elections were held in Ukraine. 31. Victor Ciorbea resigned as prime minister of Romania. Robert Kocharyan was elected president of Armenia. 31. The UN Security Council imposed an arms embargo on the Federal Republic of Yugoslavia in an attempt to force the government to negotiate with Kosovo nationalists.

APRIL 1998

2. Radu Vasile was appointed prime minister of Romania. 15. The Czech legislature approved membership of NATO. 20. Thomas Klestil was re-elected president of Austria. 23. Twenty-two people were killed in fighting between Serbian forces and ethnic Albanians. Two Belgian cabinet ministers resigned after Marc Dutroux, the main suspect in the country's child murder scandal, escaped from police custody for three hours; the escape was seen as a further example of incompetence in the police and at all levels of the state. 24. Sergei Kiriyenko's nomination as prime minister of Russia was accepted by the Duma at the third round of voting, after his nomination had twice been vetoed. 25. The Christian Democratic party suffered a heavy defeat in regional elections in Saxony-Anhalt, Germany. 27. Serb tanks entered Kosovo in an attempt to quell ethnic unrest in the area, as fighting continued between Serb forces and ethnic Albanians. Half a million workers in Denmark began a general strike in a dispute over paid leave.

MAY 1998

4. The newly appointed commander of the Vatican's Swiss Guard and his wife were shot dead by a junior officer. **6.** The Labour Party won 40 per cent of the vote in the Dutch general election, gaining a second term in office as the largest single party in the governing coalition. **7.** The Danish parliament agreed a new pay deal to end the general strike. **10.** A coalition government was formed in the Faröe Islands by parties that seek independence from Denmark over foreign and legal affairs. **24.** Serb forces burned whole villages in Albanian areas of Kosovo, as the conflict between the Serbs and the Kosovo Liberation Army escalated. Hungary's right-wing opposition won the election. Georgia and the breakaway region of Abkhazia agreed on a cease-fire, troop withdrawals and the return of refugees in exchange for the region's autonomy within a federation. **31.** A reformist coalition led by President Djukanovic won the Montenegrin parliamentary elections.

JUNE 1998

1. An international aid package to rescue Russia from its worst financial crisis since economic reforms began was announced, halting the losses on the Moscow stock market. **2.** Violence in Kosovo escalated, with thousands of refugees leaving for Albania after reports of massacres of entire villages by the Serb forces. **8.** The USA banned investment in Yugoslavia and froze all Yugoslav assets within American jurisdiction in response to what it called 'indiscriminate violence' against ethnic Albanians in Kosovo. **20.** All EU ambassadors were withdrawn from Belarus following a dispute in which President Lukashenka of Belarus attempted to evict them from the diplomatic complex adjacent to his residence. **21.** The Social Democrats won the largest share of the vote in the Czech general election, and became the major partners in a centre-left coalition government.

JULY 1998

6. Russia and Turkmenistan signed an accord dividing up oil resources in the Caspian Sea. **7.** The Italian opposition leader Silvio Berlusconi was sentenced to two years and nine months in prison for bribing tax officials. **8.** Viktor Orban was sworn in as Hungary's prime minister. **9.** Seven people died and 87 were injured in an explosion at the Egyptian bazaar in Istanbul. **13.** The IMF and Russia agreed a US$13.7 billion package to bolster the rouble against speculation. **17.** The remains of Nicholas II, the last Tsar of Russia, were buried in the Peter and Paul Fortress in St Petersburg. **23.** President Maskhadov of Chechenia survived an assassination attempt when his armoured car was destroyed by a bomb. **26.** Serb tanks and heavy artillery attacked rebel Albanian positions in Kosovo in the most widespread and co-ordinated Serb military effort since April. **28.** The Kosovo Libera-

tion Army's stronghold of Malisevo was overrun by Serb forces.

AUGUST 1998

13. Trading on the Moscow stock exchange was suspended for the second time in a week after shares fell by 15 per cent. **14.** The Kosovo Liberation Army announced that Adem Demaci would negotiate on its behalf in peace talks over the future of Kosovo. **17.** Russia's central bank loosened its control on the rouble's exchange rate, effectively devaluing the currency by 50 per cent. **23.** President Yeltsin sacked his entire Cabinet for the second time in five months, replacing Prime Minister Kiriyenko with Victor Chernomyrdin. **26.** The rouble lost 40 per cent of its value against the Deutsche Mark after trading in dollars was suspended.

EUROPEAN UNION

OCTOBER 1997

2. The Treaty of Amsterdam was signed by the member states' foreign ministers. **25.** Italy became part of the Schengen Agreement. **25–26.** The foreign ministers of the EU member states, meeting in Mondorf, Luxembourg, failed to agree on which countries should be invited to attend accession talks in December.

NOVEMBER 1997

20–21. The EU heads of government attended a special summit in Luxembourg at which an agreement to combat unemployment was signed.

DECEMBER 1997

1. The UK was refused permission to attend meetings of the planned council for co-ordinating monetary union (Euro-X). **12–13.** The European Council, meeting in Luxembourg, agreed to consider two waves of potential new members, comprising ten eastern European countries and Cyprus. **17.** Turkey threatened to withdraw its application to join the EU unless it was included on a list of prospective candidates by June 1998.

JANUARY 1998

1. The UK assumed the presidency of the EU Council of Ministers. The constitutional council in France ruled that the constitution would have to be revised before France could ratify the Treaty of Amsterdam. **27.** The EU's statistical arm, Eurostat, said that Italy could not use capital gains tax from a gold transfer to the Bank of Italy to reduce the government's budget deficit.

MARCH 1998

12. The EU heads of state and government and those of 11 aspiring member states attended a conference in London to discuss EU enlargement.

Turkey, which had been refused accession negotiations, turned down an invitation to attend. **15.** The Greek drachma was admitted to the European Exchange Rate Mechanism (ERM). **25.** The EU Commission proclaimed that 11 member states had met the requirements for economic and monetary union. **31.** The Schengen Agreement came into force, ending routine checks at the borders of participating countries.

APRIL 1998

1. Italy became a full member of the Schengen Agreement. **27.** Greece vetoed £240 million of EU aid to Turkey, saying that the EU should not 'reward an uncivilized regime'. **31.** Staff at the European Commission staged a one-day strike in protest at reforms that threaten to end the job security of thousands of civil servants.

MAY 1998

1. EU finance ministers at the Brussels summit announced that 11 countries of the EU would go ahead with the European single currency to be launched on 1 January 1999: Austria, Belgium, Finland, France, Germany, Ireland, Italy, Luxembourg, the Netherlands, Portugal and Spain. Wim Duisenberg was appointed president of the European Central Bank. **12.** The European Parliament approved a biotechnology law that will allow patents to be taken out on the genes of humans, plants and animals, although human cloning and genetic manipulation was outlawed. **13.** The European Parliament approved a Europe-wide ban on tobacco advertising, to be introduced over the next four years. In a speech in Berlin President Clinton announced his support for Turkish membership of the EU. **18.** EU countries won exemption from US trade sanctions against companies that trade with Cuba, Iran and Libya. **25.** A meeting between Turkey and EU officials to improve the strained relations between the two was called off when the Turkish delegation failed to turn up.

JUNE 1998

1. The European Central Bank governing council held its inaugural meeting in Frankfurt. **8.** The EU froze Yugoslavia's assets and banned investment in the country in response to the violence in Kosovo. **9.** The members of the European Central Bank held their first meeting. **10.** The European Commission declared meat from younger animals to be safe from BSE, and called on the EU to allow sales of British beef to resume. **16.** At the EU summit in Cardiff, Chancellor Kohl threatened to withhold Germany's payments to the EU unless the German contribution was reduced. **17.** EU states agreed on an environmental package to cut greenhouse gas emissions by 8 per cent. **29.** The EU announced that it would hold annual summits with China in recognition of the country's growing economic and political importance.

JULY 1998

1. Austria assumed the EU presidency. **13.** President Lukashenka of Belarus and his entire government were banned from setting foot on EU soil following a row over ambassadorial residences in Belarus. **16.** The European Court of Justice ruled that trademark owners can prevent products bearing their mark from being brought into the EU without consent, which prevents supermarkets from selling branded goods at reduced prices. **20.** The EU suspended all humanitarian aid to the Taleban regime in Afghanistan in protest at its denial of equal treatment to women. **31.** The EU approved sanctions against the Angolan opposition group UNITA for failing to implement the 1994 peace accords.

THE MIDDLE EAST

SEPTEMBER 1997

4. Three bombs exploded in Jerusalem, killing at least eight people. **5.** Twelve Israeli commandos died in an ambush in southern Lebanon. **10.** The US Secretary of State Madeleine Albright arrived in Israel for talks with Israeli and Palestinian leaders. **18.** Ten people were killed in a gun and bomb attack on a bus in Cairo, Egypt. **23.** Turkish troops launched an attack on Kurdish positions in northern Iraq. **25.** The Israeli government approved the building of 300 new houses for Jews on the West Bank.

OCTOBER 1997

1. Sheikh Ahmed Yassin, the spiritual founder of the Palestinian fundamentalist movement Hamas, was released from detention in Israel. **7.** Turkey announced that its forces had killed 538 Kurdish separatists in northern Iraq. **8.** Israeli and Palestinian leaders held their first summit for eight months. **13.** Israel released nine Arab prisoners as part of a deal to secure the return of two secret agents arrested in Jordan. **29.** Iraq ordered ten US members of the UN Special Commission on Iraq to leave the country.

NOVEMBER 1997

4. Candidates loyal to King Hussein won the majority of seats in a parliamentary election in Jordan which was boycotted by the Islamist opposition. **12.** The UN Security Council imposed a travel ban on Iraqi officials responsible for blocking UN weapons inspections. **13.** Six American UN weapons inspectors were expelled from Iraq; the UN withdrew all but 19 of its 78-member inspection team. **17.** Islamic militants opened fire on tourists at Luxor, Egypt, killing more than 60 people. **21.** Iraq agreed to allow Americans to return as part of a team of UN weapons inspectors. **31.** The Israeli Cabinet approved a further, conditional withdrawal from the West Bank.

DECEMBER 1997

1. The Israeli government granted permission for the building of 900 more houses for Jews on the West Bank.

JANUARY 1998

12. Iraq banned a team of UN weapons inspectors from a suspected arms site.

FEBRUARY 1998

9. Turkey sent thousands of troops into northern Iraq to prevent Kurdish refugees from fleeing across the border in the event of American and British attacks on Iraq. 11. Turkish air attacks were reported to have killed at least 20 members of the Kurdistan Workers' Party (PKK) in northern Iraq. The UK and USA rejected an Iraqi offer to open eight sites for inspection for 60 days. 23. The UN Secretary-General signed an agreement with Iraq allowing UN weapons inspectors unlimited access to sites. 25. Iraq said it would not allow weapons inspectors unlimited access.

MARCH 1998

1. Israeli troops seized a weapons shipment allegedly destined for the Palestinian National Authority. 4. Ezer Weisman was re-elected president of Israel. 10. Three Palestinians were shot dead by Israeli soldiers near Hebron, prompting three days of rioting on the West Bank. 12. Mordechai Vanunu, who was imprisoned in Israel in 1986 for exposing Israel's nuclear weapons programme, was released from solitary confinement.

APRIL 1998

22. The Israeli prime minister Binyamin Netanyahu made a pact with the extreme right-wing Molodet party to strengthen his government's position in parliament. 27. Five Israeli soldiers were injured when their vehicle was blown up by Hizbollah guerrillas in southern Lebanon. The UN Security Council extended the oil embargo against Iraq after it failed to comply fully with the UN weapons inspection team. 31. Israel celebrated the 50th anniversary of the founding of the state of Israel.

MAY 1998

1. The US Secretary of State had separate meetings with Binyamin Netanyahu and Yasser Arafat, the Palestinian president, for discussions on the Middle East peace process. 10. Binyamin Netanyahu rejected an invitation to further peace talks on the Middle East peace process, citing unreasonable diplomatic pressure from the USA. 14. Eight Palestinians were killed and 200 wounded by Israeli forces during protests in the Palestinian territories to mark the anniversary of the creation of Israel.

JUNE 1998

17. The US Secretary of State called on Iran to join the USA in drawing a 'road map leading to normal relations', a move seen as a first step towards rapprochement with Iran and its moderate president Mohammed Khatami. 23. UN weapons inspectors found traces of VX nerve gas in Iraqi missiles, contradicting Iraq's claims that it had never developed chemical warheads. 22. Abdollah Nouri, the Iranian interior minister and a key ally of President Khatami, was impeached by hardliners in the Iranian parliament.

JULY 1998

8. The Palestinian Authority had its special observer status at the UN upgraded to a higher level. 24. The reformist mayor of Tehran was found guilty of corruption in a trial seen by many as a political battle between hardline Iranians and moderate supporters of President Khatami.

AUGUST 1998

5. Iraq's Deputy Prime Minister Tariq Aziz announced that Iraq was to end immediately all cooperation with the UN weapons inspection teams. 21. The Israeli government approved the largest expansion in settlements on the Golan Heights since the territory was occupied in 1967. 25. The terrorist Abu Nidal was arrested in Egypt. 26. Scott Ritter, a senior member of the UN weapons inspection team, resigned and accused the UN Security Council of giving in to Saddam Hussein.

INTERNATIONAL RELATIONS

OCTOBER 1997

4. Togo was admitted as the 55th member of the Organization of the Islamic Conference. 20–21. Members of the South Pacific Commission agreed in Canberra, Australia, to rename the organization the Pacific Community; the UK announced that it would rejoin in 1998. 23. The heads of state of 11 of the 12 members of the CIS met in Kishinev, Moldova. 24–27. The Commonwealth heads of government meeting was held in Edinburgh; an economic agreement, the Edinburgh Declaration, was signed.

NOVEMBER 1997

16. The Democratic Republic of Congo withdrew from the Francophone group of countries. 24–25. The heads of state and government of the member states of the Asia–Pacific Economic Co-operation (APEC) forum met in Vancouver, Canada.

DECEMBER 1997

9–11. Muslim leaders met at an Islamic summit in Tehran, Iran.

18. NATO approved the formation of a Dissuasion Force (DFOR) to replace SFOR in Bosnia. **21.** The G7 group of industrial nations met in London; an employment summit involving Russia was held the following day. **23.** The UN Secretary-General signed an agreement with the Iraqi government allowing UN weapons inspectors unlimited access to sites; the USA agreed to the deal but said that it would maintain its forces in the Gulf on alert for six months. **25.** The Iraqi government said that it would not allow weapons inspectors unlimited access to sites.

2. Austria rejected an invitation to join NATO. The UN Security Council adopted a resolution which threatened 'the severest consequences' if Iraq were to block access to suspected weapons sites.

6. The UK and France ratified the Comprehensive Test Ban Treaty, the first nuclear powers to do so. **22.** The UN Human Rights Commission adopted a resolution criticizing Nigeria and urging the junta 'to restore democratic government without delay'. **29.** The government of Gibraltar accepted a Spanish proposal for direct talks on the future of the colony, but rejected the idea of Spain 'sharing' sovereignty with Britain.

1. The US Senate ratified NATO enlargement, opening the possibility of membership to the Czech Republic, Hungary and Poland. **15.** The G8 met in Birmingham, with the issues of high-technology crime, debt in developing countries and the nuclear crisis in India and Pakistan on the agenda.

17. The USA launched a $2 billion rescue package to help the plummeting Japanese yen, following fears that China would devalue its currency and exacerbate the region's economic crisis.

10. The US Senate voted to resume agricultural exports to India and Pakistan, reducing the sanctions imposed on the countries following their nuclear tests two months previously. **17.** An international conference in Rome attended by delegates from 156 countries agreed to establish a permanent international court for crimes against humanity. **21.** The British and American governments discussed holding the trial of two suspects in the Lockerbie bombing in the Netherlands, under Scottish law.

13. Swiss banks agreed to pay US$1.25 billion to survivors of the Holocaust. **20.** The UN Security Council announced that Iraq had not met the conditions for sanctions to be lifted.

Obituaries

Abacha, Gen. Sani, president of Nigeria since 1993, aged 54 – 8 June 1998

Abiola, Chief Moshood, Nigerian opposition leader, political prisoner since 1994 after winning annulled presidential election in 1993, aged 60 – 7 July 1998

Albert, Harold, royal biographer under the pseudonym Helen Cathcart, aged 88 – 20 October 1997

Bairstow, David, England and Yorkshire cricketer, aged 46 – found dead 5 January 1998

Banda, Dr Hastings, prime minister of Malawi 1964 – 6, president 1966–71, life president 1971–94, aged 99 – 25 November 1997

Barton, Sir Derek, FRS, FRSE, chemist, Nobel laureate in 1969, aged 79 – March 1998

Beningfield, Gordon, wildlife and landscape artist, aged 61 – May 1998

Berlin, Sir Isaiah, OM, CBE, FBA, philosopher and first President of Wolfson College, Oxford, aged 88 – 6 November 1997

Bernard, Jeffrey, journalist and bon viveur, aged 65 – 4 September 1997

Berni, Aldo, co-founder of the Berni Inns restaurant chain, aged 88 – 12 October 1997

Biggs, Kenneth, GC, wartime ordnance officer, led containment of Savernake ammunition explosion in January 1946, aged 86 – 11 January 1998

Bing, Sir Rudolf, KBE, general manager of the Metropolitan Opera, New York, 1950–72, aged 95 – 2 September 1997

Bono, Sonny, American pop singer, actor and US Congressman, aged 62 – in an accident, 5 January 1998

Boyd-Carpenter, Lord (John), Conservative MP for Kingston-upon-Thames 1945–72, Chief Secretary to the Treasury 1962–4, aged 90 – 11 July 1998

Bremner, Billy, Leeds United and Scotland footballer, aged 54 – 7 December 1997

Bridges, Lloyd, American actor, aged 85 – 10 March 1998

Brook, Lady (Helen), founder of the Brook Advisory Centres, aged 89 – 3 October 1997

Burgess, Alan, writer and BBC radio producer, aged 83 – 10 April 1998

Cartwright, Dame Mary, DBE, FRS, mathematician, Mistress of Girton College 1949–68, aged 97 – 3 April 1998

Chisholm, George, OBE, jazz trombonist, aged 82 – 6 December 1997

Clark, Roger, MBE, international rally driver, aged 58 – 12 January 1998

Conan Doyle, Air Commandant Dame Jean, DBE, director of the Women's Royal Air Force 1963–6 and administrator of the literary estate of Sir Arthur Conan Doyle since 1971, aged 84 – 18 November 1997

Cookson, Dame Catherine, DBE, writer, aged 91 – 11 June 1998

Cormack, Alan, American physicist and co-winner of the Nobel prize for medicine in 1979 for work leading to the development of the CAT scan, aged 74 – May 1998

Coulson, Francis, MBE, co-proprietor and chef of the Sharrow Bay Hotel, reviver of post-war British gastronomy, aged 78 – 20 February 1998

Crabtree, Shirley (Big Daddy), wrestler, aged 67 – 2 December 1997

Craigmyle, 3rd Baron, aged 74 – 30 April 1998

Crawshaw, 4th Baron, landowner, aged 64 – 7 November 1997

Cross, Beverley, playwright, librettist and screenwriter, aged 66 – 20 March 1998

Crouch, Sir David, Conservative MP for Canterbury 1966–87, aged 78 – 18 February 1998

Cudlipp, Lord, OBE, newspaperman, chairman of the International Publishing Corporation 1963–73, aged 84 – 17 May 1998

Cummings, Michael, OBE, cartoonist, aged 78 – 9 October 1997

Curran, Sir Samuel, FRS, FRSE, FEng, physicist involved in the development of radar and of Britain's hydrogen bomb, first Principal of Strathclyde University and founder of the country's first science park, co-founder of the Enable charity, aged 85 – 25 February 1998

Dainton, Lord, PH.D., SC.D., FRS, chemist, chairman of the University Grants Committee 1973–8, chairman of the British Library board 1978–85, chancellor of Sheffield University since 1979, aged 83 – 5 December 1997

Dartmouth, 9th Earl, aged 73 – 14 December 1997

Davis, Fred, OBE, snooker player, eight times world champion, aged 84 – 15 April 1998

Denington, Baroness, DBE, chairman of the Greater London Council 1975–6, aged 91 – 22 August 1998

Denison, Michael, CBE, actor, aged 82 – 22 July 1998

Denver, John, American folk singer, aged 53 – 12 October 1997

Diamand, Peter, director of the Holland Festival 1948–65 and of the Edinburgh Festival 1965–78, aged 84 – 16 January 1998

Diemer, Walter, American inventor of bubble gum, aged 93 – January 1998

Donaldson of Kingsbridge, Lord, OBE, Labour and subsequently SDP politician, Arts minister 1976–9, aged 90 – 8 March 1998

Dufferin and Ava, Maureen, Marchioness of, socialite, aged 91 – 3 May 1998

Dunnachie, James, Labour MP for Glasgow Pollok 1987–97, aged 66 – 7 September 1997

Durbridge, Francis, crime writer, aged 85 – 11 April 1998

Edwards, Monica, children's author, aged 85 – 18 January 1998

Empson, Adm. Sir Derek, GBE, KCB, aged 78 – 20 September 1997

English, Sir David, editor of the *Daily Mail* 1971–92, aged 67 – 10 June 1998

English, Revd Donald, CBE, chairman of the World Methodist Council 1991–6, aged 68 – 28 August 1998

Eysenck, Prof. Hans, psychologist and writer, aged 81 – 4 September 1997

Fairfax, Frederick, GC, aged 80 – 23 February 1998

Farr, Sir John, Conservative MP for Harborough 1959–92, aged 75 – 26 October 1997

Fashanu, Justin, footballer, aged 37 – committed suicide, 2 May 1998

Fell, Sir Anthony, Conservative MP for Yarmouth 1951–66 and 1970–83, aged 83 – 20 March 1998

Fleming, George, international cyclist, British champion and record holder, aged 80 – 28 December 1997

Francis, Fred, inventor of Scalextric, aged 79 – January 1998

Frank, Sir Charles, OBE, FRS, physicist, aged 87 – 5 April 1998

Frankl, Viktor, psychiatrist and psychotherapist, aged 92 – 3 September 1997

Freeman, Joan, nuclear physicist, aged 80 – 18 March 1998

French, Harold, actor and theatre director, aged 97 – 19 October 1997

Gellhorn, Martha, American journalist and novelist, first female war correspondent, aged 89 – 15 February 1998

George, Frank, cybernetics pioneer, aged 76 – 10 September 1997

Gibbons, Vic, all-round time trial cycling champion 1953 and 1954, 50-miles time trial record-breaker 1955, aged 75 – 21 January 1998

Gibbs, J. C., former England rugby international, aged 95 – 11 January 1998

Gilbey, Monsignor Alfred, Roman Catholic chaplain to Cambridge University 1932–65, aged 96 – 26 March 1998

Glyn, Sir Alan, Conservative MP for Clapham 1959–64 and for Windsor (later Windsor and Maidenhead) 1970–92, aged 79 – 4 May 1998

Goizueta, Roberto, chief executive of Coca-Cola, aged 65 – 18 October 1997

Goldwater, Senator Barry, American politician, Republican presidential candidate 1964, aged 89 – 29 May 1998

Graham, Gordon, CBE, architect, aged 77 – 21 September 1997

Granville of Eye, Lord, Gallipoli veteran, Liberal/Liberal National MP for Eye 1929–51 (Independent 1943–5), aged 100 – 14 February 1998

Grappelli, Stephane, jazz violinist, aged 89 – 1 December 1997

Gray, Milner, CBE, graphic designer, aged 97 – 29 September 1997

Green, Benny, jazz saxophonist, writer and broadcaster, aged 70 – 22 June 1998

Grieve, Mary, OBE, editor of *Woman* 1940–63, aged 91 – 19 February 1998

Grieve, Percy, QC, Conservative MP for Solihull, 1964–83, aged 83 – 22 August 1998

Hackett, Gen. Sir John, GCB, CBE, DSO and BAR, MC, commander-in-chief, British Army of the Rhine 1966–8, principal of King's College London 1968–75, author, aged 86 – 9 September 1997

Hambling, Harry, banker and artist, aged 95 – 22 January 1998

Hertford, 8th Marquess, aged 67 – 22 December 1997

Hicks, David, interior decorator and designer, aged 69 – 29 March 1998

Hinsley, Prof. Sir Harry, OBE, FBA, historian and Master of St John's College 1979–89, aged 79 – 16 February 1998

Hives, 2nd Baron, CBE, aged 83 – November 1997

Hollis, Prof. Martin, FBA, philosopher, aged 59 – 27 February 1998

Howell, Lord (Denis), PC, Labour MP for Birmingham All Saints 1955–9, for Birmingham Small Heath 1961–92, minister for sport in various ministries 1964–70 and 1974–9, and minister responsible for water resources 1974–9, aged 74 – 19 April 1998

Huddleston, Rt. Revd Trevor, KCMG, Anglican monk, anti-apartheid campaigner from the 1950s, Bishop of Masasi 1960–3, suffragan Bishop of Stepney 1968–78, Bishop of Mauritius and first Archbishop of the Church of the Province of the Indian Ocean 1978–83, aged 84 – 20 April 1998

Hughes, Alex (Judge Dread), reggae singer, aged 53 – 13 March 1998

Hunt, Sir David, KCMG, private secretary to Churchill and Attlee, diplomat and *Mastermind* champion, aged 84 – 30 July 1998

Hunt, Sir Peter, FRICS, chairman from 1987 and managing director from 1978 of Land Securities property company, aged 64 – 8 December 1997

Hutchence, Michael, Australian rock star, aged 37 – 22 November 1997

Ibuka, Masaru, co-founder of the Sony Corporation of Japan, aged 89 – 19 December 1997

Ingham, Bryan, painter and sculptor, aged 61 – 22 September 1997

Innes, Hammond, CBE, writer, aged 84 – 10 June 1998

Jersey, 9th Earl, aged 88 – 9 August 1998

Jones, Prof. R. V., CH, CB, CBE, FRS, wartime intelligence scientist, professor of natural philosophy at the University of Aberdeen 1946–81, aged 86 – 17 December 1997

Jones, Sir John, KCB, CMG, director-general of MI5 1981–5, aged 75 – 9 March 1998

Josephs, Wilfred, composer, aged 70 – 18 November 1997

Karamanlis, Constantine, prime minister of Greece 1955–63 and 1974–80, and president 1980–5 and 1990–5, aged 91 – 23 April 1998

Kaye, Stubby, American actor and singer, aged 79 – 15 December 1997

Kendal, Geoffrey, actor-manager, aged 88 – 14 May 1998

Khaldei, Yevgeni, Ukrainian war photographer, aged 80 – 7 October 1997

King, Gen. Sir Frank, GCB, MBE, aged 79 – 30 March 1998

Kings Norton, Lord (Harold Roxbee Cox), PH.D., FENG, aeronautical engineer, industrialist, chancellor of Cranfield University 1969–97, aged 95 – 21 December 1997

Kissin, Lord, financier, aged 85 – 22 November 1997

Lascelles, Hon. Gerald, president of the British Racing Drivers' Club 1964–91, aged 73 – 27 February 1998

Lawrence, Syd, bandleader, aged 74 – 5 May 1998

Laxness, Halldor, Icelandic writer, Nobel laureate 1955, aged 95 – 8 February 1998

Lees-Milne, James, FRSL, FSA, conservationist, architectural historian and diarist, aged 89 – 28 December 1997

Lestor of Eccles, Baroness (Joan), Labour MP for Eton and Slough 1966–83 and for Eccles 1987–97, junior minister 1969–70 and 1974–6, chairman of the Labour Party 1977–8, aged 66 – 27 March 1998

Lewis, Shari, American puppeteer and ventriloquist, aged 65 – 2 August 1998

Lichtenstein, Roy, American artist, aged 73 – 29 September 1997

Lippert, Albert, co-founder of Weight Watchers, aged 72 – 28 February 1998

Lisle, 7th Baron, aged 94 – 29 December 1997

Llewelyn-Davies of Hastoe, Baroness, PC, Labour politician, government chief whip in the House of Lords (first woman to hold the post) 1974–9 and opposition chief whip 1973–4 and 1979–82, aged 82 – 6 November 1997

Lorant, Stefan, Hungarian-born photojournalist, first editor of *Picture Post*, aged 96 – 14 November 1997

Macartney, Allan, PH.D., deputy leader of the Scottish National Party since 1992, MEP for North-East Scotland since 1994, rector of Aberdeen University since 1986, aged 57 – 25 August 1998

McCartney, Lady (Linda), photographer, animal rights campaigner and founder of a vegetarian food business, aged 56 – 17 April 1998

MacGregor, Sir Ian, chairman of British Leyland 1977–80, British Steel 1980–3 and the National Coal Board 1983–6, aged 85 – 13 April 1998

McGregor of Durris, Lord, social historian, chairman of the Press Complaints Commission 1991–4, aged 76 – 10 November 1997

McIntyre, Dr Robert, first SNP MP (for Motherwell April–July 1945), first SNP member of Stirling council and its first SNP provost, party chairman 1948–56 and president 1958–80, aged 84 – 2 February 1998

Mankowitz, Wolf, author, playwright and scriptwriter, aged 73 – 20 May 1998

Mann, Rt. Hon. Sir Michael, a Lord Justice of Appeal 1988–95, aged 67 – 14 June 1998

Marchais, Georges, secretary-general of the French Communist Party 1972–94, aged 77 – 16 November 1997

Marsden, Betty, actress, aged 79 – 18 July 1998

Marx, Enid, artist and designer, aged 95 – 18 May 1998

Massey, Daniel, actor, aged 64 – 25 March 1998

Maynard, Joan, Labour MP for Sheffield Brightside 1974–87, aged 76 – 27 March 1998

Megaw, Rt. Hon. Sir John, CBE, a Lord Justice of Appeal 1969–80, aged 88 – 27 December 1997

Mellish, Lord (Robert), PC, Labour MP for Rotherhithe (later Bermondsey) 1946–82, Chief Whip 1969–70, 1974–6, aged 85 – 9 May 1998

Meredith, Burgess, American actor, aged 89 – 9 September 1997

Merricks, John, yachtsman and Olympic silver medallist, aged 26 – 8 October 1997

Michener, James, American novelist, aged 90 – 16 October 1997

Milburn, Rod, American hurdler, Olympic champion and world record holder in the 110 metres hurdles, aged 47 – 12 November 1997

Millar, Sir Ronald, playwright and political speechwriter, aged 78 – 16 April 1998

Mobutu Sese Seko, president of Zaïre 1965–97, aged 66 – 7 September 1997

Morgan, Dermot, Irish actor, comedian and writer, aged 45 – 1 March 1998

Morrison, 2nd Baron, aged 83 – 29 October 1997

Morroco, Alberto, OBE, RSA, artist, aged 80 – 10 March 1998

Mother Teresa, HON. OM, missionary, founder of the Missionaries of Charity, Nobel peace prize winner 1979, aged 87 – 5 September 1997

Muir, Frank, CBE, writer and broadcaster, aged 77 – 2 January 1998

Newton, Sir Gordon, editor of the *Financial Times* 1950–72, aged 90 – 31 August 1998

Nunburnholme, 4th Lord, aged 70 – August 1998

O'Sullivan, Maureen, Irish-American actress, aged 87 – 21 June 1998

Orkney, 8th Earl, aged 78 – 5 February 1998

Ormonde, 7th Marquess, MBE, aged 98 – 25 October 1997

Passmore, Victor, CH, CBE, RA, artist, aged 89 – 23 January 1998

Percival, Rt. Hon. Sir Ian, QC, Conservative MP for Southport 1959–87 and Solicitor-General 1979–83, aged 76 – 4 April 1998

Philpott, Trevor, journalist, aged 74 – 29 July 1998

Pinkerton, John, computer pioneer who designed the world's first business computer in 1951, aged 78 – 22 December 1997

Pol Pot, leader of the Khmer Rouge and dictator of Cambodia 1975–8, aged in his 70s – 15 April 1998

Porsche, Ferdinand, Austrian car designer, aged 88 – 27 March 1998

Powell, Rt. Hon. Enoch, MBE, Conservative MP for Wolverhampton South West 1950–74, Unionist MP for South Down 1974–87, Cabinet and Shadow Cabinet minister 1960–8, scholar, aged 85 – 8 February 1998

Ray, James Earl, assassin of Martin Luther King, aged 70 – 23 April 1998

Rayner, Lord, chairman of Marks and Spencer 1984–91, aged 72 – 26 June 1998

Riverdale, 2nd Baron, industrialist, aged 96 – 26 June 1998

Robbins, Harold, American novelist, aged 81 – 14 October 1997

Robbins, Jerome, American choreographer, aged 79 – 29 July 1998

Roberts, Sir Frank, GCMG, GCVO, diplomat, aged 90 – 7 January 1998

Rogers, Roy, American actor, aged 86 – 6 July 1998

Rollo, 13th Lord, aged 81 – 25 September 1997

Rowland, R. W. 'Tiny', entrepreneur, aged 80 – 24 July 1998

Rowse, A. L. (Alfred), CH, historian, aged 93 – 3 October 1997

Schnittke, Alfred, Russian composer, aged 63 – 3 August 1998

Schumann, Maurice, French foreign minister 1969–73, playing a leading role in the development of the European Common Market, aged 86 – 10 February 1998

Scoular, Jimmy, Scottish football player and manager, aged 73 – 19 March 1998

Shepard, Alan, astronaut, the first American in space and the fifth man to walk on the Moon, aged 74 – 21 July 1998

Sinatra, Frank, American singer and actor, aged 82 – 14 May 1998

Skelton, Red, American comic actor, aged 84 – 17 September 1997

Smith, Lord (Rodney), KBE, president of the Royal College of Surgeons 1973–7, aged 84 – 1 July 1998

Smythe, Capt. Quentin, VC, aged 81 – 21 October 1997

Smythe, Reg, cartoonist, creator of Andy Capp, aged 80 – 13 June 1998

Solti, Sir Georg, KBE, Hungarian-born conductor, aged 84 – 5 September 1997

Speight, Johnny, television scriptwriter and playwright, aged 78 – 5 July 1998

Spock, Dr Benjamin, American paediatrician and child psychologist, aged 94 – 15 March 1998

Squires, Dorothy, popular singer, aged 83 – 14 April 1998

Staveley, Admiral of the Fleet Sir William, GCB, First Lord of the Admiralty 1985–9, aged 68 – 13 October 1997

Swaythling, 4th Baron, merchant banker, aged 69 – 1 July 1998

Tabarly, Eric, yachtsman, aged 66 – 13 June 1998

Tait, Sir James, electrical engineer, creator and first Vice-Chancellor of the City University, London, aged 85 – 18 February 1998

Taylor, Lady (Charity), Assistant Director and Inspector of Prisons (Women) 1959–66, aged 83 – 4 January 1998

Tennstedt, Klaus, German conductor, aged 71 – 11 January 1998

Terrington, 4th Baron, aged 82 – May 1998

Tippett, Sir Michael, OM, CH, CBE, composer, aged 93 – 8 January 1998

Tonypandy, 1st Viscount, PC, Labour MP for Cardiff Central 1945–50, Cardiff West 1950–83, Speaker of the House of Commons 1976–83, aged 88 – 22 September 1997

Trease, Geoffrey, FRSL, novelist, playwright, historian and biographer, aged 88 – January 1998

Tryon, Lady (Dale), society hostess and dress designer, aged 49 – 15 November 1997

Tuzo, Gen. Sir Harry, GCB, OBE, MC, Director of Operations Northern Ireland 1971–3, Deputy Supreme Allied Commander Europe 1976–8, aged 80 – 7 August 1998

Ulanova, Galina, Russian ballerina, aged 88 – 21 March 1998

Urban, George, director of Radio Free Europe 1983–6 and director of the Centre for Policy Studies, aged 76 – 3 October 1997

Vernon, Richard, actor, aged 72 – 4 December 1997

Villiers, James, actor, aged 64 – 18 January 1998

Wall, Maj. Sir Patrick, MC, Conservative MP for Haltemprice 1954–83, Beverley 1983–7, aged 81 – 15 May 1998

Wallace of Campsie, Lord, aged 82 – 23 December 1997

Wells, John, writer, actor and director, aged 61 – 11 January 1998

Wills Moody, Helen, American tennis player, winner of eight Wimbledon, seven US and four French singles titles, aged 92 – 1 January 1998

Wilson, Carl, singer with the Beach Boys, aged 51 – 6 February 1998

Wilson of Langside, Lord (Harry), PC, QC, Solicitor-General for Scotland 1965–7, Lord Advocate 1967–70, aged 81 – 23 November 1997

Wingfield Digby, Simon, Conservative MP for West Dorset 1941–74, aged 88 – 22 March 1998

Wood, Kenneth, inventor of the Kenwood Chef electric food mixer, aged 81 – 19 October 1997

Wootton, Frank, OBE, aviation artist, aged 83 – 21 April 1998

Wyatt of Weeford, Lord, Labour MP for Birmingham Aston 1945–55 and for Leicester Bosworth 1959–70, junior minister 1951, newspaper columnist, chairman of the Horserace Totalisator Board 1976–97, aged 79 – 7 December 1997

Wynette, Tammy, American country singer, aged 55 – 7 April 1998

Yates, Philip, GC, aged 85 – 14 February 1998

Young, Robert, American actor, aged 91 – 21 July 1998

Zhivkov, Todor, president of Bulgaria 1971–89, aged 86 – 5 August 1998

Archaeology

On 24 September 1997 the new Treasure Act 1996 came into force with its attendant code of practice. Responsibility for implementing the new Act, which replaces the common law of treasure trove, lies with the Department for Culture, Media and Sport. Treasure is now defined as any object, other than a coin, which contains at least 10 per cent gold or silver and is at least 300 years old when found. Treasure also embraces all coins found together so long as they are at least 300 years old when found; if the coins contain less than 10 per cent gold or silver, there must be at least ten of them. In an important change from previous practice, any associated object, irrespective of its composition, is now included with the treasure. The definition of 'treasure' also embraces any other object that previously would have been treasure trove.

Guidance is given on the procedures to be followed on finding, or suspecting that one has found, treasure; one of the most welcome aspects of this is the formal involvement for each coroner's district in England and Wales of the local museum or archaeological body. Inquests may still be held, although now usually without a jury, and finders will still be rewarded; failure to report treasure without a good reason can result in a three-months' prison sentence or a substantial fine or both. The Treasure Act implements important improvements on the previous situation; however, there are complexities in its interpretation and a careful reading of both the Act and the code of practice will be essential, especially by metal detector users, who are more likely than most to come across treasure as now defined.

BRITISH MUSEUM REVAMP

A new permanent gallery in a museum is one of the main ways in which the public can share in the excitement of archaeological discovery, so the opening of the British Museum's Late Bronze Age, Iron Age and Roman Britain galleries in July 1997 was a major event. Although reorganized in 1967 and 1983, the new displays include a substantially increased number of exhibits. While familiar objects such as the tombstone of the procurator Julius Classicianus remain on display, the opportunity has been taken to exhibit items from some of the most important of recent excavations, including the Water Newton treasure, the Snettisham hoard and some of the Vindolanda writing-tablets. While it is satisfying to see again the large bronze head of the Emperor Hadrian and the bronze cavalry parade helmet from Ribchester, of particular interest is part of the gable end of a fourth-century AD building excavated in 1989 at Meonstoke, Hants, which is able to tell us much about Roman building techniques. These splendid collections should find new audiences now that Roman Britain is a topic in the national curriculum and the British Museum has succeeded in retaining free admission for all.

MONUMENTS AT RISK

In June 1998 English Heritage published the first Monuments At Risk Survey (MARS). The authors of the report, a team led by Professor Timothy Darvill of Bournemouth University, found that some 4,500 monuments were at high risk of substantial damage or destruction, not least from arable farming; ironically, ancient field systems were especially prominent in this high-risk category. While historic buildings at risk surveys are well-established, this is the first time that ancient monuments have been treated in the same way and the situation revealed is indeed serious; Professor Darvill is quoted as suggesting that some 44 per cent of the archaeological remains known to have existed have disappeared, the loss being especially high in south-east England, where a quarter of all monuments have gone. Damage from agriculture remains a particular threat, with farmers in some cases being able to receive more in agricultural subsidies for damaging a site than can be obtained under agreements to protect the remains in question. Other reasons for destruction include natural erosion, road construction and property development, forestry and mineral working.

STONEHENGE

One consequence of the government's spending review in July 1998 was the announcement that the road-building programme would be scaled down substantially. One road scheme to be retained is the proposal to construct a tunnel at Stonehenge to bury the A303 London to Exeter Road. The scheme involves building a two-kilometre tunnel to carry the main road away from the site and take it underground, with the intention of relieving congestion and improving the environment, especially visually, around such an important site. In addition to criticism by Parliament of the existing situation, there is little doubt that the designation of Stonehenge as a World Heritage Site has helped promote a solution. The scheme will cost about £125 million, funded, it is understood, by the Department for Culture, Media and Sport and the Department of the Environment, Transport and the Regions paying one-third each of the cost, and the rest coming from a number of sources, including the National Lottery. It will be necessary for the proposals to go through the normal planning processes and the archaeological implications of the tunnel will have to be addressed; it is unlikely that construction will begin for some five to seven years.

STANTON DREW STONE CIRCLES

According to a report in *Minerva* (March/April 1998) by Dr Andrew David of the Ancient Monuments Laboratory, in the autumn of 1997, 'there was great excitement when scientists from English Heritage found the traces of a giant prehistoric temple in Somerset, England, exceeding Stonehenge in size, and believed to be of about the same date (3200–1700 BC)'. The scientists were near the village of Stanton Drew, undertaking a geophysical survey of an area including stone circles which had been known for some 300 years. The so-called 'Great Circle' 'is the largest stone circle in Britain after Avebury in Wiltshire. Nearby are two smaller circles as well as several outlying standing stones. Together, these megaliths clearly form a united complex of monuments which, with the other stone circles and monoliths peculiar to Britain, Ireland and Brittany, are believed to be the tangible remains of a formidable tradition of Neolithic and Bronze Age religious belief. The crucial point about the results of the survey was the relationship of wooden structures to the stone circles; as Dr David puts it: 'There are nearly a hundred or so such "henges" in Britain, dating to about 3200 BC. However, at Stanton Drew there had been no previous hint that here was one of the rare sites where the feature is combined with a stone circle'. After emphasizing the size, complexity and longevity of the site, Dr David reflects: 'at this time Britain was populated by farming communities or tribes who evidently set great store in the ability of ritual activity to coerce nature into assuring a fertile and wholesome life and afterlife. The many henges and megalithic settings distributed from Orkney to Cornwall are assumed to represent such activity which, in southern England at least, reached its apogee in the creation of giant ceremonial centres such as those at Avebury, Stonehenge, Durrington Walls and, now, Stanton Drew. The creation of such technically demanding monuments, apart from seeming to express an exceptional religious imperative, also demonstrates the development of social and economic structures capable of mobilizing, marshalling, feeding and defining the native populations.'

BRONZE AGE LONG-BOAT

In June 1998 the media carried a story about the discovery of a Bronze Age long-boat found in a gravel quarry at Shardlow, Derbyshire. Initially mistaken for the trunk of a tree, the true nature of the object was realized as floodwater from the River Trent washed away silt to reveal distinguishing features. About 35 feet long and constructed out of a single oak log with a raised prow, this Bronze Age long-boat was carrying a cargo of building stone which may have been intended for use in building a causeway. The bow was broken off and it is suggested that the boat might have sunk by

accident. Jonathan Humble, the Inspector of Ancient Monuments for Derbyshire for English Heritage, remarked that, of the remains of 400 other long-boats already found, only some 24 have been sufficiently well-preserved to allow researchers to reconstruct shape, form and size. English Heritage considers the Shardlow long-boat to be one of the best-preserved and most complete examples to be discovered in Britain.

ISLE OF WIGHT COINS

The Guildhall Museum at Newport, Isle of Wight, has acquired an important group of objects found by a metal detector user; among these are 557 Roman and Iron Age coins as well as 131 personal items, including some 33 enamelled brooches. According to press reports in May 1998, the most significant objects were eight silver Iron Age coins bearing the letters CRAB, possibly an abbreviated form of a chieftain's name. The coins have an eagle on the reverse, suggesting a pro-Roman disposition, but date to before the Roman invasion of Britain. It is suggested that the coins are the first evidence that the Isle of Wight might have had a separate chieftain in the Iron Age independent of the mainland tribes and maintaining a trading relationship with the Romans in Gaul in the years before the Roman invasion of Britain.

THE CERNE GIANT

The understandable attractions of archaeological excavation have tended to draw attention away from the equally useful activity of field archaeology, which usually has the benefit of being non-destructive. A good example of the results of painstaking fieldwork is the reinvestigation of the Cerne Giant, a huge figure cut into the chalk hillside near Cerne Abbas, Dorset. Known from literary references since the 17th century, it had been suggested that the figure may be post-medieval in date. In order to assess the various theories concerning the age of this huge figure, Rodney Castleden undertook several years of fieldwork and surveys which he describes in *Current Archaeology* (March 1998). As he explains, it was necessary 'to know whether the Cerne Giant is a post-medieval joke, a prehistoric icon, or a palimpsest rendered meaningless by continual alteration'. Castleden did not think that the huge figure was either the Roman Hercules (who is never shown with an erection) or the Celtic Cernunnos (who was invariably depicted with horns). As the work proceeded, Castleden suggested that the resistivity survey might be showing a cloak wrapped over the left arm and possibly a human head held in the left hand. When considering the giant's erection, he agreed with previous suggestions 'that the phallus was originally shorter, and that the top was a separate ring representing the navel. The survey showed two lines of resistivity lows 1.25 and 2.25 metres down from the present tip of the phallus, thus corroborating that it was originally shorter and, significantly, in correct (unexaggerated) proportion to the rest of the figure'. Stressing that further work needs, and is intended, to be done to secure firmer archaeological evidence for the giant's date, Castleden concludes that 'If this survey is accepted, then each attribute of the hill figure is a clue to the giant's ethnic group. Comparable images can be found in the Iron Age, in a belt extending right across Europe from Britain to Romania. The Hirschlanden statue (Germany, 500 BC) shows a naked warrior wearing only helmet and belt: the belt has a dagger tucked into it, showing the likely function of the giant's belt – another little-noticed feature. The Hirschlanden statue has an erection. Two Gaulish bronze figurines show variations on the giant's cloak. Both are naked and, like the giant, brandish weapons in their raised right hands. One has a cloak draped over his left arm and the two ends are hanging down, like the giant's cloak; the other has his cloak wrapped more tightly around his left arm to make a ball of padding'.

ARBEIA ROMAN FORT

The investigation of the remains of the Roman fort of Arbeia, South Shields, is now one of the longest archaeological excavations in the country. In the 1997 season efforts were concentrated on one of the burnt third-century barracks. During the third century AD, Arbeia was a supply base with a garrison of the auxiliary unit *Cohors V Gallorum* (fifth Cohort of Gauls); these troops were accommodated in barracks in the south part of the fort, which burnt down in the late third or early fourth century. The excavators removed a 10 cm layer of burnt daub in which they discovered a complete iron ring-mail suit. Alexandra Croom in *Minerva* (March/April 1998) comments that 'It is thought to be the first Roman example of a whole suit found in this country.' She goes on to observe that 'There was daub below, as well as above, the ring-mail, which proves that the Roman suit must have fallen to the floor while the building burnt, and it still lay in the same untidy heap of ridges and folds that formed when it first fell.' The conditions induced by the fire, especially the dry hot daub acting as a coating, helped in the preservation of this ring-mail suit and research is revealing information about its method of construction as well as other technical details. Naturally there is speculation as to what caused the fire; Ms Croom says: 'The cause of the fire has not been identified, but there are three suggestions: deliberate demolition to clear the site for the new buildings, an accidental fire, or enemy action. However, this discovery tends to suggest that it was not deliberate demolition, since no soldier would leave behind an expensive ring-mail suit. As yet there is no evidence to help ascribe it to either of the other suggestions'.

TIME TEAM

Archaeology has a long history on television, stretching back to programmes by Sir Mortimer Wheeler. The latest television programme, *Time*

Team, is presented by Tony Robinson and broadcast on Channel 4. The format, which involves the investigation of archaeological sites within a tight time-frame, is designed to convey the excitement of archaeology. It also shows how modern scientific developments may be applied to archaeological research in the field.

Over the August bank holiday weekend in 1997, the *Time Team* undertook the first live programme, excavating the site of a Roman villa at Turkdean in the Cotswolds, an area of affluence during the Roman period when Corinium (Cirencester) was the second largest Roman settlement in Britain. The archaeological significance of the site was unknown although suspected by the landowner. The result of the live excavation was the discovery of a substantial Roman villa, although the absence of any mosaics suggests that it may not have been the home of a rich family. However, the recovery of painted plaster-work and waterproof Roman concrete indicate that one of the buildings was possibly a bath-house. The discovery of the building and a range of small finds live on television helps to increase popular interest in archaeology and encourage participation by a new generation.

TREE-RING DATING IN LONDON

In his science diary in *Current Archaeology* (July 1998) John Musty reflects upon the usefulness of tree-ring dating over the last 25 years, noting that 'Thanks to the Thames, London's Roman, Saxon and medieval riverside wharves and quays contain vast amounts of waterlogged oak timber.' Attitudes have changed from wondering whether dendrochronology works to accepting that it now frequently provides the time-scale for archaeological sites. Musty then asks: 'What has all this work achieved? In the last 25 years about 4,000 of the 20,000 excavated timbers from more than 400 sites, the majority of which are Roman and medieval, have been studied by dendrochronologists. Currently, the earliest Roman structure with precise felling dates (bark present) is the AD 52 revetment at Regis House, whilst the latest Roman structure with a precise date is the AD 293–294 pile foundations from the palatial complex in the south-west corner of the Roman city ... Excavations at No. 1 Poultry have revealed a structure (not yet completely analysed) that appears to date from AD 294–299. One of the most surprising results has been the dating of the Roman quay at Regis House to A 63–64, some ten years earlier than expected, proving that there was a very rapid rebuilding of London after the Boudican destruction of AD 60–61. Dendrochronological results have also been used to prove that timber buildings at both Cheapside and No. 1 Poultry were replaced soon after the Boudican fire. For the Saxo-Norman period one of the highlights has been the dating of a series of timber bridge abutments in Southwark. This work has shown that by *circa* AD 987–1032 the Thames was spanned by a timber "London Bridge"'.

THE REAL KING ARTHUR?

Tintagel Castle in Cornwall has long been associated with the legend of King Arthur; indeed, it is
thought that the real person called Arthur around
whom the myths grew was a war-lord from the
south-west who in the fifth or sixth centuries AD
fought peoples from across the North Sea, especially the Angles and Saxons, who were advancing
westward across England after the end of the Roman
occupation of Britain. It is not surprising, therefore,
that the media made much of the discovery at
Tintagel in August 1998 of a piece of slate bearing
the name *Artognov*, an early form of Arthur. The
discovery is hailed as the first evidence of a
connection between the historical person and the
Arthurian legend. Dr Geoffrey Wainwright, chief
archaeologist with English Heritage, said that 'This
is where myth meets history. Tintagel has provided
us with evidence of a court of the Arthurian period,
with all the buildings, the high status archaeological
finds and the name of a person'. Although archaeologists are reluctant to say that the new inscription
proves the existence of King Arthur, the leader
writer of the *Daily Telegraph* would have no truck
with such caution, stating: 'It's there, on this broken
lump of stone, deciphered beyond peradventure of a
doubt by Prof. Charles Thomas, the greatest expert
on Cornish history. "Artognou father of a descen-
dant of Coll had this made". Artognou is the old
spelling of Arthur. He was clearly important enough
to have things made, even if they are now not
particularly impressive. He was our King Arthur,
and we now have proof that he lived at Tintagel –
exactly as the legend says. What more evidence could
one possibly want? English Heritage should return
to this site without delay, and finance further
excavations. We confidently predict that Dr Wainwright's trowel will turn up the following sensational items: one stone with a curious sword-sized
aperture; one Round Table; assorted chastity belts
(picked)... Somewhere, too, is the Holy Grail, from
which Our Lord drank at the Last Supper. The
stakes are high. This is no time for dry as dust
historical reservations. Dig, dig, dig, Dr Wainwright'.

ANGLO-SAXON HORSE BURIAL

Construction works for the US Air Force at RAF
Lakenheath, near Newmarket, Suffolk, led the
Ministry of Defence to fund an archaeological
excavation there in September 1997, the results of
which are described in *Minerva* (January/February
1998) in a report by Angela Care Evans. The site
excavated was an Anglo-Saxon cemetery
investigated in the 1950s and a known contemporary settlement. The excavation revealed a cemetery
with particularly interesting finds: 'The cemetery is
made up of a discrete group of about two hundred
inhumations dating from the sixth and early seventh
centuries AD. The graves contain the men, women,
and children of a prosperous community whose
possessions reflect their status, and, in the case of the

weapon graves, something of their role within it.
Amongst the warrior graves, that of a horse and rider
suggests a position high in the contemporary
community'. The horse, which had been deliberately killed, was buried wearing its bridle and
saddle, together with a wooden bucket which may
have contained the horse's food for the afterlife.

Having described the warrior and horse burial in
some detail Ms Care Evans goes on to reflect upon
the significance of the burial: 'The Lakenheath
bridle is the third set of early Anglo-Saxon horse-
gear to be found in the last six years, and its
discovery has focused attention on the use of the
horse in Anglo-Saxon England. This was a neglected subject until the excavation in 1991 of a
complex and ornately decorated set of horse-gear
from mound 17 at Sutton Hoo, in Suffolk, and a
bridle sharing an identical set of strap links from the
Snape cemetery, a few kilometres from Sutton Hoo.
All three graves display different rituals surrounding horse burial. At Sutton Hoo, the horse and rider
were buried in separate graves beneath a common
mound and the horse's saddle and bridle were piled
in the north-west corner of the man's grave. At
Snape, only the horse's head wearing an undeco-
rated bridle, was buried. It lay outside and above a
small boat-shaped coffin and the reins, shown only
by their metal links, trailed down into the grave
almost as if held in the dead man's hands ... The
Lakenheath example of a horse and rider sharing a
common grave provides a third, and extremely rare,
variation on this style of burial. Research on the
grave is only in its initial stages, but the three sets of
horse-gear make it clear that the Anglo-Saxons took
the presentation of their horses as seriously as they
took their own – even in the arena of death'.

DEAD MEN TELL TALES

English Heritage is funding research on the large
assemblages of human remains excavated from
religious sites in London as part of the London
monasteries publication programme. Considerable
publicity was given in July 1998 to the review of the
skeletal remains of monks from Stratford Lang-
thorne in east London and Merton Priory in south
London. At Stratford, some 679 skeletons buried
during the two centuries after the Abbey's foundation in 1135 have been recovered. It was reported
that there was not much evidence of the diseases
indicating dietary deficiencies that are so often
found on medieval sites. On the contrary, the
skeletal condition known as diffuse idiopathic
skeletal hyperostosis (DISH) was noted as being
prevalent; this is associated with obesity and may
therefore reflect a rich diet or the opportunity to
overeat. It may be, as the press were quick to point
out, that the fat 'Friar Tuck' stereotype contains
more than a grain of truth.

Similar investigations are possible following the
discovery of remains in North Yorkshire. The Battle
of Towton, near Tadcaster, was one of the most
ferocious battles of the Wars of the Roses; of the

120,000 men who fought on 29 March 1461, some 28,000 died. It was, perhaps, not surprising that workmen constructing a garage in the area of the battlefield should find a mass grave containing the remains of 29 soldiers who were casualties in the battle. Archaeologists from Bradford University who examined the remains discovered that many of the soldiers had been repeatedly beaten about the head and face even after death. Many of the blows were to the top and back of the head, suggesting that the victims had been kneeling, lying down or running away. Reported as the first major find of skeletons from a battle of the Wars of the Roses, it is particularly important for specialists to have the opportunity to study these remains, which could reveal not only how the men died but also how they lived, since the condition of the bones would provide clues to health and diet.

ISLAMIC GOLD

In November 1997 the press reported that amateur divers had found Islamic gold from a wreck site off the south Devon coast. Although there was no trace of the ship itself, it was suggested that the vessel had been plying between England and Morocco and sank some time in the 1630s or 1640s. The finds were recovered less than a mile off Salcombe and included pewter, ceramics, ten cannon, four civil guns, three anchors, 400 gold coins, as well as earrings, brooches, ingots and nuggets. The gold coins and jewellery comprising the better part of the treasure have been identified as Moroccan, and the coins are thought to be the largest group of Islamic coins found together in England.

BENJAMIN FRANKLIN

In February 1998, during the restoration of 36 Craven Street, London, the house in which Benjamin Franklin lived from 1757 until 1772, before becoming one of the founding fathers of American independence, the bones of four adults and at least six children were discovered. Although the bones were under examination at the time the discovery was reported, it is suspected that they relate to Franklin's friend Dr William Hewson, a pioneer of modern surgery, who was married to the daughter of Franklin's landlady and lived at 36 Craven Street after Benjamin Franklin moved further down the street. Before the passing of the Anatomy Act of 1832, the dissection of human bodies on private premises was illegal and doctors were forced to buy their specimens from the criminal fraternity including grave-robbers; while Hewson may have acquired the bodies or bones, it is a matter of interesting speculation as to whether Franklin, much interested himself in scientific developments, would have known about these illegal experiments conducted by his friend.

UNIQUE COOMBE HAY CANAL LOCK

In autumn 1997, archaeologists investigated a unique canal lock at Coombe Hay on the Somerset Coal Canal. In order to avoid the slowness and therefore costliness of conventional locks, in 1798 Robert Weldon constructed a caisson hydrostatic lock which worked raising and lowering the barge inside a sealed box, or caisson, which could take the barge from the upper canal to the lower canal in some seven minutes. The vertical descent of 46 feet was made by the barge inside the caisson which, after air was pumped out, sank, guided by parallel motion guide bars. On reaching the bottom, a set of air- and watertight doors at the other end of the caisson matched up with the watertight door in the cistern and the boatmen who had been sealed inside then sailed the vessel through a short tunnel into the lower canal.

Disaster struck when the parallel motion bars failed and one end of the caisson plummeted straight down to the bottom, almost killing the bargees. Although it is thought that this accident may have been caused by geological problems, the caisson lock was not tried again and in due course the site was filled in and forgotten until the 1997 investigation. Conventional locks were installed in 1806 but the success of the railways saw the end of the canal as well as its unique lock.

RESURGAM

The discovery off the coast of north Wales of Britain's first mechanical submarine, which sank in 1880, was described in the media in February 1998. Called *Resurgam*, Latin for 'I shall rise', this submarine was the invention of the Revd George Garrett, a Victorian amateur engineer who had produced the world's first underwater breathing apparatus at the age of 20. With his plans on the back of an envelope and money raised through parish fetes, Garrett sufficiently impressed the Royal Navy that it offered him £60,000 if the prototype were successful. Unfortunately, after construction at Birkenhead, when the *Resurgam* put into Rhyl harbour on its way to the Solent, a hawser broke and the submarine sank. This mechanical submarine, complete with its candle-lit interior, is a crucial piece of technology in the development of Royal Navy submarines, but there is doubt at present that the funds will be available for raising the submarine, and its conservation and public display.

THE BEATLES

In summer 1998 the National Trust opened 20 Forthlin Road, Liverpool, which was the home of Paul McCartney between 1955 and 1963. The place where the Beatles wrote songs such as *She Loves You* and *Please Please Me*, the National Trust acquired the property as, in the words of Robert Woodside, 'an important landmark in the development of popular culture'. In an article entitled 'The Archaeology of the Beatles' in *Current Archaeology* (September 1997), Robert Woodside describes how the house is 'also important as an example of the works of Sir Lancelot Keay, Liverpool's city architect and director of housing 1925–1948, who was responsible for so much of the housing development in the city in the inter-war years. Despite some initial scepticism, an archaeological survey was carried out in 1996 to discover more about this unusual property.' After describing the location and construction of the house, Robert Woodside concludes: 'When people think of archaeology, they usually think of holes in the ground, grassy humps and bumps and, increasingly, historic buildings. The study of a 1950s council house may be unusual, but if we as archaeologists insist that archaeology is "the understanding of human activity through the study of the material culture of the past, then we must accept that history has no boundaries and no cut-off point. This does not mean we all have to rush off to look at modern housing, but it does mean that we should be aware that everything has a history, from prehistoric mounds to pill-boxes. Archaeology, therefore, can inform on all aspects of the past, even those events in recent memory. An understanding of that history can only help to bring more resonance and meaning to the world about us." '

Architecture

THE BRITISH LIBRARY
St Pancras, London
Architect: Colin St John Wilson and Partners

Some 23 years after its inception, the new British Library finally admitted readers through its portals in November 1997. The need for an extension had been recognized for decades, and in the 1960s this gave rise to early designs for a new building on a site opposite the British Museum in Bloomsbury. Growing awareness of conservation issues in the 1970s, however, led to the search for a new location, which culminated in the selection of the railway goods yard immediately to the west of George Gilbert Scott's famous St Pancras hotel and terminus station building. Initial design work commenced in 1975–6 and construction started in 1982, so any critique of this building must recognize that its completion nearly a quarter of a century later puts the organizational concept, design response, and technical and aesthetic characteristics in an unnatural time-frame.

Perhaps the most striking aspect of the new building – and, as a major public institution central to the intellectual life of Britain, one that gave rise to much of the early criticism – is its undemonstrative and reserved external appearance. Eschewing the bold, confident regularity and symmetrical discipline of the classical tradition, its forms are irregular and asymmetric, receding away from the public domain of Euston Road, sometimes stepped, sometimes angled, under layers of sloping roofs. Seen from the south-west corner, with few windows punctuating the expanses of solid red brickwork, the long, low-slung building forms a sympathetic foil to the towering and frothy fantasies of Scott's Gothic red-brick masterpiece across the road. This blending of colour, which extends to the slate roofs and even to the colour of painted metalwork, allied to the articulation of form, allows these strange bedfellows to work well together.

While the building steps forward to address the street frontage directly on the corner of Midland Road and Euston Road, on the western side it is set back a considerable distance from the main road, thus creating a large open square which functions as the public space from which the building is entered. The square is screened from Euston Road with an arrangement of walls, railings and planters accommodating semi-mature trees. It is entered through a substantial gateway, built up in tiered volumes of brickwork, with a heavy lintol panel announcing the name of the building, and doors cut out of metal fretwork screening composed solely of the words 'British Library' repeated line after line.

On entering the courtyard one is immediately presented with Eduardo Paolozzi's dramatic sculpture of Isaac Newton (inspired by Blake's famous illustration) raised on a brick plinth. The courtyard is paved in red brick, set into square panels by bands of white Portland stone, and the careful planning of features, steps, planting and flagpoles creates the diagonal route that leads to the main entrance, positioned between the east and west wings of the library below the central roof planes that tumble down towards the ground almost to door height.

Once past the low eaves-line and the almost domestic scale of the entrance, the sloping roofs are revealed as the defining planes of an enormous public concourse and entrance hall some five storeys in height. It is a three-dimensional tour-de-force, with open galleries criss-crossing at the rear, and flights of stairs leading away to the reading rooms on either side. Light pours in from above through clerestories set into slots in the sloping roof planes, drawing one onwards and upwards through a series of ascending levels towards the heart of the building. A shop and exhibition galleries which are open to the public are located at ground level to the left; the readers' ticket office is to the right.

From the foyer, stairs descend to the basement cloakrooms and lavatory facilities, while readers can pass on up another wide flight of stairs, overlooked by a huge and colourful tapestry by R. B. Kitaj on literary themes, towards the entrance stiles. Set within a low stone balustrade, these control access to the main reading rooms via further flights of stairs that peel off on each side at various levels.

Materials and workmanship speak forcefully of quality and durability. Red brickwork and white Travertine marble line the walls. The red brick and stone banding of the courtyard carries through on the floors, which then progress into polished stone, while leather-covered bronze hand-rails adorn the stairs and reinforce the message of quality.

In a central position, set back behind the screen of galleried walkways, lies the inner sanctum of this great complex – a 17-metre-high bronze and glass 'treasure chest' housing the King's Library, the collection of some 60,000 leather-bound volumes assembled by George III and donated to the nation by George IV. Stored on moveable shelves, they sit as a glowing testament to the history and civic importance of the British Library as a vital part of the national heritage. The whole construction is placed on a shiny black marble floor, whose reflections seem to suggest that the treasure trove continues down into the earth, a symbol, perhaps, of the immense catalogue of books stored in the depths below the public domain.

Central to the Library's organization is the design and disposition of the various reading rooms, which are structured according to the characteristics of their particular subject matter – humanities or science. The Humanities wing ranges to the west along Ossulston Street, where readers typically spend long periods researching a few selected texts, ordered and delivered from the miles of shelving hidden below ground, rather than taken from open shelving. Here the two major reading rooms are square on plan and three storeys in height, with each successive tier stepping back to reveal more of the enormous volume at each level and provide a choice of seating environments, some enclosed in intimate spaces, others exposed to the full height of the space. Natural daylight floods in from the tall ranges of clerestory windows overhead, and shafts of sunlight pick out the sloping white plastered ceiling surfaces around the perimeter, where the cruciform columns sweep up and out linking walls and ceilings together. The feeling of spaciousness and light is maximized by the predominant whiteness of the surfaces, columns, walls, ceilings and balcony fronts, all brought together in an interplay of space, form and structure. Furniture and fittings are comfortable and well-crafted. The leather-topped reading surfaces are generously proportioned, and provided with individual overhead lights and power points for laptop computers, mounted into the oak framing of the ranges of interlinked desks.

The Science wing is to the east and follows the angled line of Midland Road. Those with a scientific leaning depend more on a wide range of current periodicals and recent papers, which need to be accessible on open stacks. Here the reading rooms are long, tall, linear spaces, created by cutting a narrow void along the western edge of the wing as it projects beyond the linking central spaces to north and south. With daylight again flooding in through high-level clerestory windows, this permits the same level of grandeur and inter-floor visibility as can be enjoyed in the more open humanities spaces, and enables the three levels of book stacks to read as a unified entity. Pairs of readers' desks are set out along the perimeter of each level overlooking the space below, all with direct access to the material on the shelves.

At the southern end of the Science wing on the corner of Midland Road and Euston Road there is a spacious conference suite with a variety of meeting-rooms and a tiered lecture theatre set out round a terraced foyer, with seating alcoves for informal gatherings. A large porthole window to one side provides views out into the entrance courtyard, and back towards the figure of Newton hunched over his dividers.

The British Library has so far cost £511 million. At 108,000 square metres, it is the largest library in Britain, and its 340 kilometres of shelving can accommodate some 12 million volumes – not enough, of course, to handle the ever-growing volume of published work. Other archives will still be needed for less popular material, but these are linked to a rapid retrieval system capable of sourcing practically any stored book in half an hour.

The building is, inevitably, underpinned by all the highly developed servicing technologies that are available today, yet these are never allowed to intrude for their own sake, but are handled in a manner consistent with the building's design philosophy. In this, individual spaces acquire their own architectural characteristics through an expression of their functional requirements, while the constituent elements are related to each other via an understandable and logical pattern of circulation and access in which all the elements, as in a good book, are easily readable and form a coherent whole. As befits a great public institution, the fabric is built to last and will therefore age with dignity. The spaces are unique and inspirational, and they will engender respect and admiration. Even the forth-right rearguard among the former British Library's readers have now taken to their new home and are generous in their praise for what has been achieved.

CLYDE AUDITORIUM, SCOTTISH EXHIBITION AND CONFERENCE CENTRE
Glasgow
Architect: Foster and Partners

Poised on a prominent but desolate site on the edge of the River Clyde, this new 3,000-seater auditorium is so distinctive that it has already been nicknamed the 'Armadillo'. Forty metres tall at its highest point and 140 metres in length, the external envelope is a series of eight interlocking cylindrical shell vaults, covered in shiny aluminium standing seam roofing, and linked by a series of glazed, panelled and louvred slots.

The simplicity of the concept hides the complex geometry required to work out the volumes and surfaces, and during the design stages much use was made of three-dimensional computer programming and graphic presentation. The inherent stiffness of standing seam roofing-sheets was a determining factor in the design of the curving faces as the material has a maximum natural 'droop' of about 38 metres radius, the tightest curve achievable without special curving processes. The cylindrical segments each rise to a ridge line, and the leading edge of each successive segment arches forward at progressively greater angles away from the highest central section to form a dramatic pointed overhanging prow at each end, where the main public access points are located. The arched segments are supported at their edges by tubular steel trusses filling the slots between successive steps, while the stability of the overall structure is achieved by bracing the largest central shell and hanging each of the progressively smaller shells from this central stiffened bay.

This shiny, aggressive yet brittle skin forms the enclosure for what the architects refer to as an 'industrial theatre', a large multi-purpose conference hall with three major tiered seating areas facing a proscenium arch, behind which a concrete and steel fly-tower extends 25 metres above the stage. This allows scenery flats to be raised and lowered, and the hall is therefore capable of accommodating operatic and musical performances as well as business conferences, exhibitions and product launches, which increasingly exploit a multitude of theatrical effects. Ultimately, the range of activities to be expected here may be limited to the more commercial end of the event spectrum as tight budgetary constraints have resulted in less than generous backstage facilities likely to discriminate against grand opera finding a home here.

The auditorium itself is a grand and comfortable space, with first-class acoustics and excellent sightlines. It is technically sophisticated, with a complex arrangement of lighting rigs spanning the main space, interspersed with the exposed downstand air ducts that are also used to help control the acoustic characteristics of the space.

The auditorium space is contained within parallel pairs of concrete walls which curve away from the proscenium arch around the main body of the hall and back to define a pointed junction at the rear, though here the walls are in fact cut back to accommodate the main public entrance and foyer spaces sheltered under the prow of the easternmost cladding segment. The essential plan shape is, therefore, very simple, like a pointed light bulb – the stage area being the cap, the hall the glass. The concrete diaphragm walls contain the principal access and exit stairs, connecting the three levels of the auditorium with the various circulation areas and foyers and eventually to the exits at ground-floor level.

The main circulation spaces are somewhat arbitrary in plan and rather constricted, being defined by the smooth, grey-painted concrete walls of the hall on the one side and the stepped vaults of the external cladding on the other. The elimination of substantial amounts of glazing within the slots, that would otherwise have provided penetrating shafts of sunlight and dramatic views out, is an unfortunate loss to the constraints of economy. The principal perimeter circulation route is located at first-floor level, and is approached by a bifurcated symmetrical arrangement of lifts, escalators and stairs from the ground-floor entrance at the east end. The building's axial symmetry is pursued rigorously throughout, with great concentration on neat and careful detailing, and no relaxation into free-form shapes or dynamic asymmetry.

The disjointed nature of the immediate urban context made it all the more important to create a strong architectural statement, robust and concentrated enough to focus the attention in the remnants of Glasgow's industrial heartland. Given the remarkably short time period available – 28 months from commission to practical completion – and the extremely tight budget of £26 million to build the largest auditorium in Britain and the fourth-largest in Europe, the architects have produced a memorable and innovative structure that will be a popular and dramatic alternative to the existing 2,500-seat

Royal Concert Hall in Glasgow. The first of many live events commenced in September 1997, and the building has already hosted a wide range of performances, from rock concerts to dance shows, as well as a range of business functions.

THE RUSKIN LIBRARY
University of Lancaster
Architect: MacCormac Jamieson Prichard

John Ruskin (1819–1900), author of many influential treatises on art, architecture, nature and the mysteries of life, has long exerted a strong hold on the imagination of artists and academics alike. His personal collection of books, manuscripts and paintings was for many years split between the Whitehouse Ruskin Collection, at Bembridge School on the Isle of Wight, and a similar collection housed at Ruskin's Lake District home at Brantwood on Lake Coniston. They were brought together with the help of National Lottery funding at the University of Lancaster by Professor Michael Wheeler as part of 'the Ruskin programme'. Completed in November 1997 at a cost of £1.9 million, the Ruskin Library is a dramatic, memorable and romantic jewel of a building.

The design brief required storage facilities for the archive, including an additional 25 per cent allowance for future acquisitions, a gallery for exhibiting items from the collection, a secure reading room accommodating up to eight readers, and back-up facilities such as office space, catalogue room, workshop, lavatory and servicing facilities.

The site places the building in a prominent position on the western boundary of the university campus, an outpost standing guard alongside both a major road and a principal pedestrian pathway leading to the heart of the campus. Yet though seen first, the Ruskin Library forms the final destination of a winding approach route which leads from the entrance to the old library on the central campus spine, onwards to the new extension of the old library on the west side (carried out by the same firm of architects), and finally over a terrace and out along a path.

The design incorporates many references to Ruskin's major preoccupations and interests; allusions to Venice and Italian church architecture, for example, are numerous. The solid bronze panelled doors of the Ruskin Library are housed in a dark, box-like frame projecting out of a recessed, full-height, glazed screen, in turn framed by the angled, prow-like ends of curved walls. When seen from the wide terrace at the rear of the library extension, it appears to float within a lagoon of waving grass, the strongly curving side walls appearing like a boat floating in water, an effect which is enhanced by the bridge-like pathway linking the terrace to the main entrance. The exterior treatment is strongly reminiscent of the cathedral at Siena; narrow horizontal stripes of precast concrete bands coloured with grey-green granite aggregate contrast with the main panels of white concrete blocks, shot-blasted with a reflective marble aggregate to provide sparkle, laid in alternating stretcher and soldier courses. The individual stones in the band courses are separated by square 'bosses' of stainless steel that add an extra degree of complexity to the massive masonry walls, whose opposing curves, separated by a clear gap at each 'prow', suggest the symbolic form of cupped hands protecting something fragile, vulnerable and valuable.

The themes of protecting enclosure and concealed treasure are carried through into the planning and three-dimensional organization of the interior, in which a central, free-standing volume contains the archival material. This is surrounded on both sides by a tall, narrow space that reinterprets the moat concept with glass panels inserted into the floor giving glimpses of the archive structure plunging into the basement below – as though seen through water. A spiral stair winds up through the central block connecting the various archive levels with a meeting-room at the top. At the opposite end to the tall reception foyer is the main reading room, again a dramatic two-storey construction with its glazed window screen giving glimpses out over the surrounding roads and landscape and on into the distance to Morecambe Bay, some five miles distant.

Where the external walls curve out around the central archive, the space is given over to back-up offices on the ground floor and to two gallery spaces on the first, south and north sides symmetrically opposed. Each is approached via a curving staircase from the foyer and is bounded on the inner side by a series of secure display cabinets. These are built into the upper part of the battered walls enclosing the offices below. One cabinet position on each side is converted into an opening which gives access to a glass bridge forming a cross-passage leading through the archive and past the meeting-room to the other gallery, thus enabling one to complete a circuit. The arrangement provides another symbolic reference to the elements of Gothic church architecture, structured around the basic spatial components of nave, crossing, narthex and sanctuary.

In contrast to the stark and dramatic simplicity of the exterior, the interior is rich in colour and texture and intimate in scale, though with a seriousness and dignity befitting the almost religious intensity of the formal concept. The central archive space is treated as though it were a huge ark, or treasure chest. Framed in pale oak, the panels of this 'casket' are treated in waxed and polished plaster in a rich red ochre colour. The framing members themselves are detailed, with the intersection points highlighted and expressed by means of elongated polished bronze cruciform inserts. Guarding the casket, the severe and rather sinister-looking battered walls to the offices on either side are finished with a black pigmented render sealed with linseed oil. Internal rendered walls maintain the natural red ochre theme and also introduce a brighter, light-reflecting yellow, while overhead, the timber

beams exposed within the roof structure have been grit-blasted to accentuate their surface texture. Overlooking the entrance and set within an opening in the end of the central archive is positioned an etched glass window by the artist Alexander Beleschenko. This re-emphasizes Ruskin's preoccupation with Venice, being etched with an image from a daguerrotype by Ruskin of the north-west portal of St Mark's cathedral.

OFFICE BUILDING
No. 1 Poultry, City of London
Architect: Stirling Wilford and Partners

In the heart of the City of London, this monumental new building strikes a vibrant discord with the finely detailed Classical architecture of its neighbours. No. 1 Poultry, like the British Library, has had a long and strife-torn gestation. The triangular site was formerly occupied by some eight listed buildings, the most notable of these being the Mappin and Webb building, a Gothic landmark dating from 1870 and occupied by the famous jewellers. With its ornate window detailing and dramatic spired tower, it had become a potent reminder of Victorian London, and conservationists fought long and hard to defend it in the many public inquiries which preceded the construction of No. 1 Poultry.

The story of the new building starts in the 1960s when property developer Lord Palumbo invited the early-modernist architect Mies van der Rohe to design an American-style metal and glass tower block fronting onto an open plaza. Following a famous and protracted public inquiry held in the early 1980s, the scheme was rejected, so in 1985 Palumbo commissioned James Stirling to design a quite different building, following the lines of the original block and respecting the medieval street pattern. The design was finalized three years later and, following its submission for planning permission, was drawn into yet another hard-fought planning inquiry and legal battle. Attitudes to conservation had by then developed considerably, but this time the scheme was approved, and detailed design work could proceed. Tragedy struck in 1992, however, before construction work had started, when Stirling suddenly died. The burden of completing the work fell to his surviving partner, Michael Wilford, who carried through the design principles and the stylistic approach that had already been established.

Designed as a speculative office block, commercial considerations demanded that the maximum amount of usable floor space be created, together with an acceptable degree of architectural articulation on the outside. The external envelope is, in fact, much more dramatic and sculpted than the average speculative office block, and betrays Stirling's fascination with the handling and interplay of simple but monumental geometric forms. Here, the idea of a central circular courtyard linking the opposing street frontages is expressed as a gigantic drum, rising up through the heart of the building to the skyline, and acting as a counterpoint to the triangular plan shape of the building on its site. Indeed, the basic idea of juxtaposing triangles and circles informs the entire building, not only in three-dimensional elements but in flooring patterns, ceilings and fittings.

The external skin is characterized by bold banding of two-colour stone cladding, alternating in layers of pink and buff. At the apex of the site a tower rises out of the angled side walls which frame a huge arched window screen cut into the prow of the building. This opening can also function as an entrance to the building and gives access to a long, arched, stone staircase leading up to the first floor.

A grey stone string course arches over the glazed screen and forms a base plinth for another tall glazed section, this time projecting forward, with angled sides coming to a point as the stone front of the tower is set back. From here, the side walls continue up in plain buff stonework to terminate in gigantic outward curving Egyptian cornices, while on the central face a striped cylindrical stone tower, housing a huge, simplistic clock face with red hands, emerges from the glazed prow below and punctuates the skyline at the corner, to be terminated by a tall flagpole.

Moving down the street elevations, the façades curve in and out, large panels of curtain walling interspersed with more solid stretches where individual window openings are set into the stripey stonework. Here, the geometric interplay continues, the curtain wall panels progressing to a pointed apex, and the stonework sections following a large radial curve. On either side of the entrance arch, halfway down each long elevation, the angled glazed section sits on top of the radiused stonework, which in turn rests on a series of giant, striped pilasters capped with a huge bull-nosed roll moulding. In the central bay, a two-storey Egyptian-style opening is cut into the stonework base where the main pedestrian cross route provides access into the heart of the building. Above it the stonework and glass relationship is reversed, thus reinforcing the notion that, for all its apparent mass, the stonework is just as thin a cladding as the glazing.

The central drum forms the circulation focus of the building, and it is now also possible to arrive directly from the Underground, passing shops and cafés en route before emerging into the central space. Here, the interplay between circular and triangular forms becomes most pronounced, with light-well openings creating a triangular shape – part inside, part outside the stone-clad inner cylinder of space. The pink and buff banded stonework is carried into the central drum, where the flat, projecting façade elements are clad in brightly coloured glazed tiles punctuated by pink and yellow window frames.

Unlike most speculative office buildings, most of the servicing plant has been located at basement level to allow for a superb roof garden, set out in three different sections. Running around the top of the central drum is a large timber pergola, set with trailing plants, projecting forward from the striped stone perimeter wall. From here, a gate provides access to a private garden with a geometric lawn and low box hedges, which leads towards the apex of the building and onwards to the two flanking decks of the 'bridge' on either side of the clock tower facing the Bank road junction. It is proposed to use part of this roof garden as overspill space for a new restaurant, to be called Le Coq d'Argent (references to the address and the architect, among others).

Despite criticism during the inquiry and while the design and construction proceeded, the building is an idiosyncratic yet powerful statement from one of Britain's most internationally recognized architects. It is big, brash, positive and distinctive, and because of the absence of fine detail, monumental in scale. To many it remains a disturbing intrusion into a distinguished architectural context.

However, attitudes will no doubt mellow as this post-modern period piece becomes a familiar part of the City.

AMERICAN AIR MUSEUM
Duxford, Cambridgeshire
Architect: Foster and Partners

Situated just a few miles south of Cambridge, Duxford Airfield was first used as an airbase by the RAF in 1918, when British pilots, training for the First World War, were joined by an American squadron. In the Second World War it became a Battle of Britain fighter base, and from 1943 to 1945 was occupied by the US Eighth Air Force. There have therefore been long-standing American connections with this particular stretch of Cambridgeshire countryside. After its closure in 1961, the airfield was taken over by the Imperial War Museum and subsequently opened to the public. Hangars, some dating from the First World War, were utilized as exhibition halls for the museum's collections.

Those aeroplanes which were displayed out in the open, however, soon fell victim to the damp English climate, and the onset of serious corrosion heralded the need for some form of protective shelter in which to display and preserve the collection of historic aircraft. The project was initiated over a decade ago, but financial difficulties caused by recession meant that its realization was delayed until fundraising efforts in the USA and Saudi Arabia were bolstered by the recent award of a Heritage Lottery Fund grant.

The brief was to design a building capable of accommodating and displaying a number of different aircraft. Most importantly, however, it needed to be big enough to house a B-52 Stratofortress, the huge, long-range bomber employed in Vietnam and in the Gulf War, which has a 61-metre wingspan and stands 16 metres high to the top of its tailfin. It was hoped that other, smaller aircraft could be suspended above the floor. The building also needed to be economical to build, with low running and maintenance costs, as income is limited to money taken in admission charges. Heating was therefore felt to be unjustifiable economically so thermal capacity and humidity control needed consideration. Early design studies indicated that a concrete structure could be designed to keep the internal temperature above the dew point, thus eliminating condensation and allowing the dehumidifying plant to be an economic size. The large mass of the concrete structure also provides a considerable degree of thermal capacity and inertia, delaying temperature changes caused by heat transmission and smoothing out the highs and lows during the day–night cycle.

Sited at one end of the airfield, the museum building is essentially a large, single-span, vault-like structure, based on a geometric form known as a torus, which resembles a ring doughnut in shape. The arched roof profile is produced by slicing through the perimeter of this form. Elliptical on plan, the shallow dome is then sliced in half through its centre point to generate the final shape of the building. The vaulted roof emerges from a sloping, grassy embankment around its circumference. Where the shell-like structure is cut through, fronting the airfield, the resulting shallow arched profile is filled with an enormous glazed screen, 90 metres long and 18.5 metres high at the centre, and stiffened by paired vertical steel-plate mullions that have a curved profile to the interior. A ribbon of glazing separates the solid roof structure from the landscaping, permitting a flood of daylight to enter which lights the rear walls and the curving ramped promenade that follows the elliptical plan shape. The grassy berm varies in height, starting at runway level at each end of the glazed front wall and sweeping up to a point higher up the vault at the rear. The glazed window slot follows this line, and helps to articulate the internal plan and circulation route from the outside.

The concrete roof is constructed from two separate shells, inner and outer, each 100 mm thick, built up from pre-cast concrete panels fitted together to form a vault. The use of the torus form simplified the design (the torus is defined by only two constant radii), minimizing the number of panel varieties to only six for the entire roof and thus being economical to construct. The inner shell is constructed from panels shaped like an inverted T in cross-section, the verticals of the Ts acting to separate the inner and outer shells and forming a series of vertical ribs to which the panels of the outer shell are fixed. Two sockets are provided in each of the inner panels for the suspension of loads, each having a capacity of 12 tonnes, which is more than sufficient to handle the weight of the smaller suspended aircraft.

Forces exerted on the double-skin roof construction are transferred into an in-situ concrete ring beam set inside the line of the rear wall, and are thence transferred across the glazed crescent slot via short steel struts into a second lower in-situ concrete ring beam. From this member the loads are transferred into the raking abutment walls, and massive concrete foundations provide the necessary horizontal resistance to keep the arched shape from collapse.

Visitors approach the museum from the northwest – that is, from the rear – through a tunnel cut into the highest point of the surrounding earthworks. A glass memorial sculpture by Renato Niemis, etched with the outlines of American aircraft missing in action during the Second World War, flanks the entrance. The entrance resembles a bomb shelter, but once through the linking passage a startling view is presented as the visitor emerges onto a first-floor balcony looking straight at the nose of the B-52 bomber. A surprising variety of war planes are arranged cheek by jowl around the massive hangar floor while others float above, patrolling the 'concrete sky'. The clear glass panelled balcony front curves away, and the promenade ramps downwards to right and left, reaching ground-level at the opposing ends of the glazed front screen. The rear walls are set at a steep angle and divided into sloping panels between the structural buttress-shaped columns, brightly lit by the crescent-shaped rooflight immediately overhead. Concealed behind the rear wall, and under the grassy slopes, are a number of exhibition rooms, lavatory facilities, services and plant.

Many of the planes held in the collection are still operational, and the glass façade has been designed to be demountable (the massive steel mullions are hinged at their base) so that aircraft can be taken in and out. Many historic aircraft are still flown from Duxford, and the vantage point provided by this new museum gives an excellent view of an airfield that is still very much alive with the buzz and roar of aeroplanes. The museum's designers have sought to create a landmark building of classic simplicity, in which the strength and grandeur of the concrete hangar vault provide a perfect foil to the delicately wrought and finely detailed metalwork of these historic flying-machines. Their clarity of vision and the aptness of the form and detailing have been publicly recognized by the museum being declared joint winner of the Royal Fine Art Commission's Building of the Year Award 1998.

Bequests to Charity

The list below represents some of the principal charitable bequests from wills published since the last edition. The exact values of residues of estates cannot be accurately assessed, since prior bequests and inheritance tax on any personal bequests have to be deducted from the net figures given; no inheritance tax is ever payable on a charitable bequest.

Although she left no bequests to charity, the publication of the will of Diana, Princess of Wales on 2 March 1998 was of considerable public interest. The Princess's estate was valued at £21,711,485 gross (£21,468,352 net); after inheritance tax, this was £12,966,020. In December 1997 a variation order was obtained by representatives of Prince William and Prince Harry to set aside £100,000 to establish a fund for income from intellectual property rights. The Princess left £50,000 to her butler, Paul Burrell, and mementos to her 17 godchildren. The remainder of her estate is divided equally between Prince William and Prince Harry, who will receive an income until they are 30 years old, when they will inherit the capital.

The list is headed by the largest charitable bequest for some years, from the estate of Ronald Diggens, who left just over £77 million. He left his freehold land at Fowey, Cornwall, to the National Trust and the residue to the Lankelly Foundation, which he established in 1968. One of the largest specific gifts was left by William Macdonald, who left a bequest of £8 million upon trust for his daughter Thelma for life and then to St Dunstan's absolutely. Two bequests of £1 million were also left to Jewish charities; Hyman Fine left this sum to Jewish Care, and Martha Mindelsohn left a similar sum to the Keith and Joan Mindelsohn Charitable Trust.

Other large gifts to charity this year were left by Edward Shorto, who left the residue of his estate of just over £5 million equally between a local church and hospital and seven other charities, including the Stephenson Locomotive Society. Leslie Brasnett left the residue of his estate between three charities, Lavender Willoughby-Hancock left the residue of her estate equally between the Guide Dogs for the Blind Association and the Sussex Police Welfare Board, and Olive Bedford left the residue of her estate to the Joseph Rowntree Housing Trust in York. They all left estates of over £3 million.

There was an unusually large number of bequests left to specific charitable trusts. These included the residues of the estates of Patrick Heagerty, to the Heagerty Charitable Trust, Kenneth Purchas, to the Richard and Christine Purchas Charitable Trust, Jonathan Vickers, to the Jonathan Vickers Settlement, Doris Phillips, to the Phillips Trust, Asher Hyman, to the Fanny Rose and Asher Hyman Charitable Trust, Richard Williamson, to the Williamson Benevolent Trust, and Ruth Drummond-Jackson, to the J. G. Graves Charitable Trust, Sheffield.

There was also a greater number than usual of large bequests left to charities at the discretion of executors or trustees. Wilhelmina Minet left seven large bequests to specific charities in her will and the residue of her estate for such charitable objects as her trustees in their absolute discretion selected. Richard Wilcox left the residue of his estate in a similar fashion, but specifying that the charities selected should have among their objects 'the provision of medical research and/or treatment and/or care and/or animal welfare'. Margaret-Helene Markus directed that her trustees should distribute at least half the residue of her estate to animal charities, and at least one-fifth to cancer charities and one-fifth to those caring for the elderly, including the hospice movement. James Dawson instructed his trustees to select charities dealing with the relief of human suffering, including institutions for the care of incurable terminal illness, cancer and old age. Robert Davidson, Richard Radcliffe, Violet Tillyer, Margaret Thomson, Vincent Spencer and Millicent Smith made no specific qualification and left the decision entirely in the hands of their executors.

Irene Mauchline left all her estate to charity, including two churches, two Masonic lodges and the rest to the Royal Masonic Benevolent Institution. Among others who left their entire estate to charity were Ronald Wesson, to the British Heart Foundation, Alan Lefevre, to the National Trust, Albert Green to St Ann's Hospice, Manchester, Dorothy Whittington, to the Spastics Society (now Scope), and Lily Dutfield to the Children's Hospital in her home city of Sheffield.

Lady Heathcoat Amory left the residue of her estate to the Knighthayes Garden Trust, where she lived, and another famous political name, Elizabeth Balfour, left the residue of her estate to the Balfour Historic Museum Trust in Winchester. Antoinette Powell-Cotton left the residue of her estate to the Powell-Cotton Museum in nearby Birchington. Two Cambridge colleges feature in the list; Corpus Christi shared the residue of the £3.2 million estate of Helen Stuart with the Friends of the Clergy Corporation, and St John's College shared the residue of the estate of one of its Fellows, Henry Pelling, with the Save the Children Fund. Marjorie Durose left the residue of her estate between the British Heart Foundation and Great St Mary's Church, Cambridge, the latter to be used for charitable purposes in connection with the elderly and infirm, for religious purposes in connection with University students, and for such other charitable purposes as the vicar and churchwardens selected. Finally, mention must be made of a will not listed: that of comedian Charlie Chester included a bequest of £10,000 to the Grand Order of Water Rats, with the wish that this would 'assist in placing a permanent Poet Laureate's Chair for the current Poet Laureate and to perpetuate the idea of one in the Grand Order of Water Rats'.

Philippa Louisa Adams, of London W12, £3,058,028 (the residue to the PDSA)

Joyce, Lady Heathcoat Amory, of Knightshayes Court, Tiverton, Devon, £889,773 (the residue to the Knightshayes Garden Trust)

Florence Macbride Anderson, of London SW7, £5,390,996 (the residue equally between the Cancer Research Campaign, Wood Green Animal Shelter, Spastics Society, Salvation Army, St Dunstan's, British Red Cross Society, National Trust and Guide Dogs for the Blind Association)

Margaret Grace Backhouse, of Ashington, W. Sussex, £2,887,207 (£200,000 each to the British Heart Foundation, National Trust and PDSA, £100,000 each to the Cancer Relief Macmillan Fund, and St Barnabas Hospice, Worthing, and the residue equally between the RNLI and Guide Dogs for the Blind Association)

Allan Baines, of Bridlington, E. Yorks, £1,410,650 (the residue equally between the Royal Star and Garter Home, Richmond, Marie Curie Cancer Care and RNLI)

Elizabeth Marian Maxwell Balfour, of Headbourne Worthy, Hants, £951,413 (the residue to the Balfour Historic Museum Trust, Winchester)

Vera May Barton, of Winsford, Cheshire, £2,331,051 (the residue equally between the NSPCC, Children's Society, PDSA, and St Luke's Hospital for the Clergy, London)

Olive Marjorie Bedford, of Gildersome, Leeds, £3,910,232 (the residue to the Joseph Rowntree Housing Trust, York, for the provision of a residential care home)

Philip Beynon, of Newton, Swansea, £1,756,144 (the residue equally between the Gower Society, Swansea, and the Glamorgan Wildlife Trust)

Leslie Stanley Brasnett, of Exmouth, Devon, £3,570,551 (the residue equally between the USPG, Children's Society and Church of England Pensions Board)

Robert Davidson Buchanan, of Farnham Royal, Bucks, £2,760,782 (the residue for such charity or charities as his trustees think fit)

Lady Pauline Frances Chapman, of London EC2, £1,348,593 (the residue equally between the National Trust and National Art Collections Fund)

Charles John Cocks, of Wallasey, Merseyside, £980,554 (three-quarters of the residue to the Shrewsbury School Foundation, and one-quarter to the Salvation Army)

Antoinette Powell-Cotton, of Margate, Kent, £1,713,122 (the residue to the Powell-Cotton Museum, Birchington)

James Archibald Dawson, of Derby, £831,388 (the residue for such charitable objects or purposes for the relief of human suffering as his trustees select)

Jeanne Clementine Dickinson, of Bath, £1,088,580 (the residue equally between the RSPCA and Imperial Cancer Research Fund)

Ronald William Diggens, of Moor Park, Middx, £77,340,831 (his freehold land at Fowey, Cornwall, to the National Trust, and the residue to the Lankelly Foundation, established by him in 1968)

Margaret Dobson, of Scarborough, N. Yorks, £3,705,809 (the residue equally between St Catherine's Hospice,

Scarborough, the Motor Neurone Disease Association, Save the Children Fund, NSPCC, Children's Society, Barnardo's, and the Calvert Trust (Challenge for the Disabled), Cumbria)

Marjorie Eileen Durose, of Barnet, Herts, £906,466 (the residue equally between the British Heart Foundation and Great St Mary's Church, Cambridge, for charitable purposes in connection with the elderly and infirm, for religious purposes in connection with University students and for such other purposes as the vicar and churchwardens select)

Lily Dutfield, of Beighton, Sheffield, £507,991 (all her estate to the Children's Hospital, Sheffield)

Joyce Lilian Dudley Marno-Edwards, of Clare, Suffolk, £1,159,372 (the residue to the Joyce Marno-Edwards Fund at West Suffolk Hospital, Bury St Edmunds, for the treatment of cancer and orthopaedics)

Sylvia Rose Ellis, of Canford Cliffs, Dorset, £1,018,215 (the residue to Tenovus, for their research laboratory at Southampton)

Joan Farrow, of Farnham Common, Bucks, £2,296,439 (the residue equally between the Salvation Army, National Trust, Barnardo's, RNLI and Canterbury Cathedral restoration fund)

Pamela Joyce Lois Diana Faulkner, of Farnham, Surrey, £1,911,693 (£3,000 and seven-tenths of the residue to the Farnham Maltings Association, and three-tenths of the residue to Marie Curie Cancer Care)

Winifred Joan Fearnside, of Shurlock Row, Berks, £1,080,892 (four-fifths of the residue to the Fearnside Foundation, for the promotion of education and physical development of children and young persons, and the public at large to improve their condition of life, in equestrian sports)

Hyman Fine, of London N2, £7,849,661 (£1,000,000 to Jewish Care)

James Gilchrist Fyfe, of Taunton, Somerset, £1,728,170 (£10,000 and one-seventh of the residue each to the Salvation Army, Glasgow, and the Princess Louise Scottish Hospital for Limbless Sailors and Soldiers, £5,000 and one-seventh of the residue each to the Royal Society for the Relief of Indigent Gentlewomen of Scotland, the Imperial Cancer Research Fund, the Muscular Dystrophy Group, Glasgow, and the Scottish National Institution for War Blinded, and one-seventh of the residue to the RNLI, Edinburgh)

Fredericke Gampell, of London N6, £2,312,118 (the residue equally between the British Council of the Shaare Zedek Medical Centre, London, the AJR Charitable Trust, Jewish Care, Mencap and Jewish Deaf Association)

Elsie Gibson, of Shrewsbury, £858,850 (the residue equally between Marie Curie Cancer Care and the Macmillan Nurses Appeal)

Roy Broadstock Gould, of Maidstone, Kent, £823,309 (the residue equally between the Animal Health Trust, Newmarket, and the PDSA)

Albert Eric Green, of Chadderton, Lancs, £509,206 (all his estate to St Ann's Hospice, Manchester, for the general purposes of the hospices at Heald Green and Little Hulton)

Winifred Gregory, of Blackboys, E. Sussex, £872,788 (the residue to the Catholic Church of Our Lady Immaculate and St Philip Neri, Uckfield)

Stanley John Charles Griggs, of Banstead, Surrey, £837,337 (the residue equally between Fegans Child and Family Care, Tunbridge Wells, and the Salvation Army)

Lavender Mary Willoughby-Hancock, of Hove, E. Sussex, £3,225,925 (the residue equally between the Guide

Dogs for the Blind Association and Sussex Police
Welfare Board)

Alice Maud Harding, of Broadbridge Heath, W. Sussex,
£1,669,152 (the residue equally between the Children's
Society, NSPCC, and the RNIB, for the Sunshine House
Nursery, East Grinstead)

Hilda May Hayward, of Hastings, E. Sussex, £1,235,202
(the residue to the Sunshine Fund for Blind Babies and
Young People)

Patrick John Heagerty, of Hassocks, W. Sussex, £2,210,504
(the residue to the Heagerty Charitable Trust)

Phyllis May Herdman, of Worthing, W. Sussex, £899,887
(the residue to the RNLI)

George Jack Hartridge Horne, of Worthing, W. Sussex,
£2,722,000 (30 per cent of the residue each to the
Scripture Gift Mission and Overseas Missionary
Fellowship and the remainder of his estate variously to
17 other charities)

Asher Hyman, of Edgware, Middx, £1,476,428 (the residue
to the Fanny Rose and Asher Hyman Charitable Trust)

Arthur Mortimer Jackson, of Sale, Cheshire, £1,313,305
(the residue equally between the British Heart
Foundation and Arthritis and Rheumatism Council)

Mayo Jackson, of Leeds, £1,043,325 (the residue to the
Leeds Home for Aged Jews)

Ruth Julia Drummond-Jackson, of Sheffield, £1,033,761
(the residue to the J. G. Graves Charitable Trust,
Sheffield)

Mary Mali Kramer, of London w5, £1,560,231 (the residue
equally between the RNIB, Royal British Legion Haig
Fund and Cancer Research Campaign)

Margaret Evelyn Tatham Lamb, of Worthing, W. Sussex,
£4,167,211 (one-twelfth of the residue each to Christian
Aid, NSPCC, RNIB, Cancer Research Campaign,
Spastics Society, Age Concern, RNLI, National Trust
and St Joseph's Hospice, London, and one-24th of the
residue each to Barnardo's, Guide Dogs for the Blind
Association, Donkey Sanctuary, Sidmouth, RSPCA,
Gifford House for Disabled Men, Worthing, and St John
Divine Church, West Worthing)

Joan Margaret Lander, of Wellington, Salop, £1,396,070
(the residue to the National Trust)

Katharine Margaret Law, of Sandwich, Kent, £1,725,485
(the residue equally between the RSPCA, and the
Pilgrim's Hospice, Canterbury)

Violet Marjorie Lee, of Stoke Bishop, Bristol, £822,838
(the residue to the Blue Cross)

Alan Lionel Lefevre, of East Molesey, Surrey, £620,497
(all his estate to the National Trust)

John Kennedy Lindsay, of Newtownabbey, Co. Antrim,
£769,690 (the residue to the Presbyterian Church in
Ireland, for charitable purposes in connection with
Africans studying in the UK)

William Hector Macdonald, of Arkley, Herts, £22,588,705
(£8,000,000 to a daughter for life and then to St
Dunstan's)

James Frederick Maddocks, of Wincanton, Somerset,
£2,887,232 (the residue equally between Ridley House
League of Friends at Wincanton Memorial Hospital, the
Friends of Verrington Hospital, Wincanton, the League
of Friends of Yeovil District Hospital, Wincanton
Memorial Hall Foundation, Wincanton Recreational
Trust, the Wincanton Branch of the Red Cross, and the
National Trust, for the improvement of the gardens at
Stourhead, Wilts, especially disabled facilities)

Margaret-Helene Markus, of London sw1, £4,461,976 (the
residue for such charitable bodies and purposes as her
trustees decide, provided that at least 50 per cent be used
for animal welfare and health, at least 20 per cent for

research and relief of cancer, and at least 20 per cent for
the care of the elderly and the hospice movement)

Leslie Gerald Matthews, of London ec4, £978,851 (the
residue to the Methodist Homes for the Aged)

Violet Jane Matton, of Seaford, E. Sussex, £1,696,269 (the
residue to the RNLI)

Irene Mauchline, of Bridge of Earn, Perth, £1,496,874
(£100,000 each to the Southern Cross Masonic Lodge,
and the Kelvin Partick Lodge, Glasgow, £60,000 to the
Church of St John, Greatham, Cleveland, £40,000 to the
Church of All Saints, Shirley, Surrey, and the whole of
the remainder of her estate to the Royal Masonic
Benevolent Institution)

Elizabeth Marjorie Milne, of Prestwich, Manchester,
£1,602,735 (the residue equally between the Church of
England Pensions Board, and 'Chethams Hospital
School of Music', Princess Christian College and the
Family Welfare Association, all in Manchester, and St
Mary the Virgin Parish Church, Prestwich)

Martha Joan Mindelsohn, of Edgbaston, Birmingham,
£4,695,364 (£1,000,000 to the Keith and Joan
Mindelsohn Charitable Trust, and the residue equally
between Birmingham Jewish Welfare Board, RNLI,
Warwickshire Masonic Benevolent Fund, and the
Friends of Queen Elizabeth Hospital, Birmingham)

Wilhelmina Crapo Wheeler Minet, of London w8,
£5,641,833 (£250,000 each to St Mary Abbots Church,
Kensington, National Trust, the American Museum in
Britain, the Huguenot Society, and the Weald and
Downland Open Air Museum, Sussex, £100,000 each to
the Attingham Summer School Trust, London, and the
English Speaking Union, both for scholarships and
awards, and the residue for such charitable institutions
or objects as her trustees select)

Thomas Mitchell, of Bowdon, Cheshire, £938,895 (the
residue to the Imperial Cancer Research Fund)

Joan Henderson Monks, of Pulborough, W. Sussex,
£1,174,476 (£50,000 to Barnardo's, and the residue to
the Woodland Trust)

Lilian Morris, of Reading, £878,378 (the residue equally
between the Imperial Cancer Research Fund and
Arthritis and Rheumatism Council)

Albert William James Mursell, of Canford Cliffs, Dorset,
£2,250,841 (one-fifth of the residue each to the RAF
Association and Multiple Sclerosis Society, and three-
20ths of the residue each to King Edward VII Hospital
for Officers, London, Help the Aged, British Heart
Foundation and Imperial Cancer Research Fund)

Hannah Maud Nicholas, of Paignton, Devon, £3,658,698
(10 per cent of the residue each to the National
Osteoporosis Society, Imperial Cancer Research Fund,
Marie Curie Cancer Care, Arthritis and Rheumatism
Council and Action for Dysphasic Adults, 9 per cent to
the National Children's Home, 8 per cent to the
Multiple Sclerosis Society, and 5 per cent each to the
Royal London Society for the Blind, National
Schizophrenia Fellowship, Animal Health Trust,
Newmarket, Animal Welfare Trust, Watford, and
National Asthma Campaign)

Myrtle Maud Campbell-Orde, of Cranleigh, Surrey,
£1,227,572 (three-quarters of the residue to the RNLI,
for the Criccieth Station, towards a lifeboat to be called
the Myrtle Maud, and one-quarter of the residue to the
World Wide Fund for Nature)

Rita Mary Paske, of Whitestone, Herefordshire,
£2,086,501 (£50,000 to Westhide Parish Church and
£25,000 to Hampton Bishop Parish Church, both for the
upkeep of the churches and churchyards, and the residue
equally between the International League for the
Protection of Horses, Animal Health Trust,

Newmarket, Guide Dogs for the Blind Association, Brooke Hospital for Animals, London, Home of Rest for Horses, Aylesbury, Injured Jockeys Fund, Imperial Cancer Research Fund, and the Freda Pearce Foundation at St Michael's Hospice, Bartestree, Hereford)

Daphne Marjorie Helen Nash-Peake, of Tewkesbury, Glos, £815,104 (the residue to the Distressed Gentlefolk's Aid Association)

Henry Mathison Pelling, of St John's College, Cambridge, £1,857,975 (the residue equally between St John's College, Cambridge, and the Save the Children Fund)

Doris Gertrude Phillips, of Northampton, £1,636,169 (the residue to the Phillips Trust, for such charitable purposes as she directed her trustees to support)

Neil Thomas Pitts, of Pedmore, Stourbridge, £817,949 (the residue equally between the National Trust and the Inland Waterways Association)

Kenneth Alfred Purchas, of London w1, £2,202,589 (the residue to the Richard and Christine Purchas Charitable Trust)

Richard Thomas Radcliffe, of Nilgiris, India, £1,156,022 (the residue for such charitable institutions or objects in England as his trustees select)

Marion Hope Rattey, of Honiton, Devon, £2,866,342 (a large number of small charitable bequests, and £20,000 and one-third of the residue each to Great Ormond Street Hospital for Sick Children, London, and the National Trust, and one-third of the residue to the Children's Hospice South West, Barnstaple)

Doreen Joan Ricketts, of Braintree, Essex, £702,604 (all her estate equally between Bristol Municipal Charities, for Bristol Grammar School, and Bristol University, for post-graduate study in the arts and humanities)

Sir Frank Kenyon Roberts, of London w8, £2,875,298 (the residue equally between Barnardo's, Save the Children Fund and Institute of Cancer Research)

Norbert Augustine Shann, of Hove, E. Sussex, £801,800 (the residue to the Little Sisters of the Poor of St Augustine's Home, Liverpool)

Edward Herbert Charles Shorto, of East Budleigh, Devon, £5,088,697 (the residue for such charitable institutions and objects in Great Britain as his trustees select, desiring they include the RNLI, Exmouth Branch, PDSA, All Saints Church, East Budleigh, Friends of Budleigh Salterton Cottage Hospital, the Institution of Mechanical Engineers Benevolent Fund, Rugby School, St Loyes College, Exeter, Guide Dogs for the Blind Association, Exeter, and the Stephenson Locomotive Society)

Esther Simpson, of London NW3, £587,287 (the residue to the Society for the Protection of Science and Learning)

Millicent Edna Smith, of Welford-on-Avon, Warwickshire, £589,662 (the residue for such charitable institutions or objects as her trustees think proper)

Vernon Russell-Smith, of Petworth, W. Sussex, £1,334,484 (the residue equally between Alzheimer's Disease Society, Cancer Relief Macmillan Fund and Save the Children Fund)

Frank Speak, of Clitheroe, Lancs, £2,826,376 (one-fifth of the residue to St Mary's Church, Clitheroe, for any improvement to the Church or surrounds, and two-25ths of the residue each to the Salvation Army, RNID, Children's Society, Spastics Society, Barnardo's, RNIB, Marie Curie Cancer Care, NSPCC, the Blackburn Orphanage and the North Lancashire Cheshire Home, Garstang)

Vincent Leslie Spencer, of Chorlton cum Hardy, Manchester, £789,122 (the residue for such charitable purposes as his trustee thinks fit)

Eric Spivey, of Sidmouth, Devon, £832,963 (£150,000 each to Sidmouth Victoria Hospital Comforts Fund and Cancer Research Campaign, £80,000 to Sidmouth Hospiscare, £20,000 to Salcombe Regis Church, £10,000 to the Sid Vale Association Trust, and the residue to the National Trust)

Helen Winifred Stuart, of Yateley, Hants, £3,250,309 (the residue equally between the Friends of the Clergy Corporation and Corpus Christi College, Cambridge)

Winifred Clare Taunton, of London w8, £2,282,063 (the residue equally between the Salvation Army and Guide Dogs for the Blind Association)

Margaret Louise Fulton Thomson, of Rutherglen, Glasgow, £792,393 (the residue for such charitable institutions or societies as her trustees decide)

Violet Beatrice Tillyer, of Tiverton, Devon, £831,492 (the residue for such charitable objects or purposes in England as her trustee selects)

Eileen Dorothy Tweddle, of Southport, Merseyside, £850,957 (the residue to the Northwest Cancer Research Fund, Southport Committee Branch)

Rose Vaci, of London NW2, £1,223,089 (half the residue to the Jewish Blind Society)

Jonathan Vickers, of West Malling, Kent, £1,714,463 (the residue to the Jonathan Vickers Charitable Settlement)

Winifred May Walbridge, of Bridport, Dorset, £1,236,034 (certain land at Bridport and half the residue to the Imperial Cancer Research Fund, and half the residue to the parish of Symondsbury, Bridport, for the benefit of its inhabitants)

Ronald William France Wesson, of Stratford-upon-Avon, Warwickshire, £798,397 (all his estate to the British Heart Foundation)

Dorothy Emily Whittington, of Moreton-in-Marsh, Glos, £509,144 (all her estate to the Spastics Society [now Scope])

Richard Charles Wilcox, of Gerrards Cross, Bucks, £5,466,267 (the residue for such charity or charities having among their objects medical research and/or treatment and/or care and/or animal welfare as his trustees select)

Richard Hunt Williamson, of Retford, Notts, £1,383,823 (the residue to the Williamson Benevolent Trust)

Doris Marguerite Withers, of Eastbourne, E. Sussex, £2,081,949 (the residue equally between the Antiquarian Booksellers Association Benevolent Fund, Marie Curie Cancer Care, Royal Commonwealth Society for the Blind, National Trust, Salvation Army and International Fund for Animal Welfare)

Raymond Lamprey Witney, of Whitstable, Kent, £756,656 (the residue to Canterbury Diocesan Board of Finance, for the promotion of the Christian faith)

William Wood, of Melbourne, Derbys, £988,606 (the residue to the Imperial Cancer Research Fund)

Doreen Mary Worthington, of Budleigh Salterton, Devon, £709,586 (the residue to Sheffield University, for a research scholarship or fellowship)

Mary Ingle Wright, of Swinton, Manchester, £920,828 (the residue to the Insight Trust Fund)

Broadcasting

TELEVISION

As audiences sat down in their millions to watch two very different events during 1997–8, the age of digital television seemed as remote as Tudor England. Coverage of the funeral of Diana, Princess of Wales and of England's glorious defeat against Argentina in the World Cup generated huge audiences. France '98 was a victory for the most popular terrestrial networks, ITV and BBC1, as BSkyB's supporters rejected the company's ever-expanding channel offerings and instead tuned in to the free-to-air channels. The Argentina match was watched by a record-breaking 26 million people on ITV while 19.1 million people witnessed Diana, Princess of Wales' funeral on BBC1; proof that, New Britain or not, when the nation experiences an emotional trauma it still turns to the national broadcaster and that terrestrial television's role as a genuinely mass communicator has yet to be seriously eroded by non-terrestrial networks.

Yet many commentators believe the genuinely collective viewing experience will shortly become a folk memory, as anachronistic as the inter-war heyday of radio when families listened in silence to their favourite programmes on the wireless. They forget that a similar theory was expressed more than a decade ago with cable's arrival in the UK. In the digital future, runs the argument, viewers will select their entertainment via an electronic programme guide enabling them to steer through 200 or so channel choices.

For the majority of viewers in 1997–8 this seemed a distant, even daunting prospect. The delayed launch of both satellite and terrestrial digital services created further confusion. Nevertheless the BBC and several leading commercial broadcasters committed huge sums to developing digital services. It emerged that over the next five years the corporation plans to invest a billion pounds in digital services. In the year under review these new services began to gradually emerge, although for most viewers they were an irrelevance. Critics, however, suggested that one reason why programme quality was erratic, to say the least, was because too much money and effort were being invested in unproven technology and in services for which there was little, if any, consumer demand. Some argued that new digital channels should be left to genuinely commercial players.

In November 1997 the BBC's ambitions to launch a domestic round-the-clock television news station were finally realized with the launch of News 24, a service prompted by the advent of digital television. In its opening weeks the channel was ridiculed by critics for its lack of professionalism. In one notorious incident, News 24 flashed the words 'Government advert' over the Foreign Secretary, Robin Cook, during live coverage of him speaking at an international conference. This was particularly galling for the corporation since Sky News, BSkyB's rolling news station, was now widely and belatedly acknowledged as a valuable addition to the television mix. Its coverage of Diana's death, one of the biggest television news stories ever, proved beyond doubt that it could rise to the challenges offered by an event that caught the public's imagination.

Also in the autumn the BBC launched three new commercial channels in partnership with the US-backed cable programmer, Flextech, under the umbrella title UKTV. These were UK Horizons, specializing in factual material, UK Arena, an arts service, and UK Style, offering lifestyle programming. However, despite these initiatives, which brought a new sense of urgency to the debate over growing commercialism at the BBC, most viewers continued to judge the corporation by its offerings on BBC1, BBC2 and its five national radio networks.

THE DOCU-SOAP COMES OF AGE

For television, 1997–8 was the year when the popular documentary series, the so-called documentary soap, came into its own. With a chronic shortage of new drama and sitcom hits, the documentary soap, often scheduled before the 9 p.m. family viewing watershed on BBC1, helped the corporation to compete effectively against ITV. However, after several years in decline the commercial network was beginning to show signs of a revival towards the end of the year, helped by a strong performance from the veteran *Coronation Street*, successfully revamped by producer Brian Park. The campaign to free Deirdre Rachid became a national talking point, with even the Prime Minister, Tony Blair, taking a personal interest in her case.

The documentary soap was neither greatly original nor much liked by the critics, but many viewers responded strongly to these vignettes of ordinary people going about their daily lives, provided the subject matter was dramatic enough and the characters had charisma. It is no exaggeration to say that the success of the docu-soap led to the emergence of a new kind of TV star. The BBC's docu-soap hits during 1997–8 included *Driving School*, *The Cruise* and *Hotel*. Each featured a strong female lead; more than 12 million people tuned in to watch Maureen Rees in *Driving School* battle to pass her test on her seventh attempt; *Hotel*, filmed at Liverpool's Adelphi Hotel, turned combative manager Eileen Downey into a minor celebrity. But perhaps the biggest docu-soap star of all was Jane McDonald, who emerged as the love interest in *The Cruise*. There was even a follow-up featuring her wedding and a number one record. However, not every docu-soap succeeded – one conspicuous failure was *Pleasure Beach*, a portrait of the Blackpool holiday Mecca – but the genre looks set to remain a mainstay of the schedules until viewers become satiated.

Some commentators feared that as far as documentaries were concerned the networks were gradually abandoning the high ground. In January 1998, the lobby group Campaign for Quality Television accused ITV of failing to commit adequate time or money to serious documentary. Subsequently David Liddiment, ITV's new programme head, said he would put factual shows back 'into the heart of the schedule'. It will be 1998–9 before we see the full fruits of his endeavours.

ITV jumped on the docu-soap bandwagon somewhat belatedly, and with mixed results. Their biggest hit was *Airline*, a portrait of Britannia Airways and its passengers, watched by more than 12 million viewers in the spring. The company's charismatic steward, BJ, became a popular figure. Another hit was *Neighbours from Hell*, examining the conflicts between neighbouring households. Less successful was *Babewatch*, a series depicting the careers of fledgling models.

This spate of factual programming led to several controversies, the most high-profile surrounding Carlton Television's award-winning *The Connection*, although the show had in fact been broadcast in 1996. In May the *Guardian* published allegations that large parts of the film, which purported to show a Colombian drug runner smuggling heroin into London, were faked. The subsequent furore raised questions over how far programme makers will go to 'stunt up' scenes in order to win high audiences. The row, which was the subject of an investigation by the Independent Television Commission (ITC), renewed criticism of Carlton's apparent lack of commitment to quality shows. Ironically Carlton was just beginning to live down its reputation for poor programming when the story was published; the company's adaptation of Wilkie Collins' *The Woman in White*, part of the BBC's Christmas line-up, was generally welcomed by critics.

FACTUAL FURORE

It was not only Carlton which had a tough time establishing the credibility of its factual shows. Channel 4, under the management of new chief executive Michael Jackson, faced embarrassment when it emerged that a Cutting Edge film, *Rogue Males*, contained made-up sequences. Inevitably the BBC did not escape the critics' gaze, but attempts to undermine the credibility of the corporation's docu-soap, *The Clampers*, failed. However, another BBC factual series, *Cumbrian Tales*, was axed overnight following press reports that its producer was also the owner of the pub depicted in the series.

Despite widespread concern over falling standards in documentaries, there were a number of highlights during 1997–8. In autumn 1997, BBC2's *The Nazis: A Warning from History*, featuring unseen footage and recollections of survivors, including unrepentant Nazis, was praised by all. Critics also welcomed the latest series from Brian Lapping, *The Fifty Years War – The Arabs and Israelis*, in which participants in one of the world's most intractable conflicts gave first-hand and sometimes contradictory accounts of high political drama. In spring 1998, another BBC2 series documenting recent history, *Windrush*, which chronicled the story of Britain's post-war immigrants, was widely praised. In July 1998, *42 Up*, the latest instalment of Michael Apted's endlessly fascinating documentary about 14 people growing up in contemporary Britain, was another reminder that the traditional documentary could still win a decent time slot (9.30 p.m.) on a mainstream network. (The programme was, as usual, made by Granada Television; ITV had declined to show it so the BBC stepped in.)

Princess Diana's death inevitably led to a spate of documentaries. Two of the most watched were ITV's sensation-seeking *Diana: Secrets Behind the Crash*, shown in spring 1998 and examining the various conspiracy theories surrounding her death, and *Diana: My Sister the Princess* featuring Sally Magnusson interviewing Earl Spencer. Some suggested the programme was timed to boost attendance at the newly opened Diana Museum at Althorp, the Earl's British home. On a more upbeat note the ubiquitous Michael Palin scored again with his latest travelogue, *Full Circle*. BBC2's *Great Composers*, a series of director-led films portraying the giants of serious music, also had its high points; the programme devoted to Bach was outstanding. Generally the year was not a great one for arts programmes, a shortcoming admitted by John Birt, the BBC's director-general, in his annual review published in July. The problem was not restricted to the BBC. TV critics hope that Mr Jackson's new regime at Channel 4 will improve all aspects of arts coverage on his station.

The BBC's natural history unit, celebrating its 40th anniversary, won widespread praise for its autumn series of six special programmes, each highlighting a particular species, presented by Sir David Attenborough. It was no surprise that the *Wildlife Special* on the polar bear, containing extraordinary pictures of a mother bear giving birth and swimming underwater, won the best factual photography BAFTA award. Another highlight was BBC2's *Land of the Tiger*.

In a related field, the BBC enjoyed several successes with its science programming. Arguably the most notable achievement in this genre was BBC2's *Evolution Weekend*, featuring several high-quality films and a high-powered round-table discussion chaired by Melvyn Bragg, proof that intelligent talk had not completely vanished from the small screen. Of more dubious quality was the much-publicized BBC1 series, *The Human Body*, presented by fertility guru Professor Robert Winston. Using state-of-the-art technology audiences were given remarkable, close-up views of the human anatomy. Several commentators thought the series was far too populist. Nevertheless, by ending the run with film of a man (literally) drawing his last breath, it showed that after the thousands of glamorized fictional deaths fed to viewers on an almost daily basis, it was possible to see someone dying with dignity on the small screen.

Drama Dips

The year 1997–8 was more uneven than usual in terms of the major networks' drama offerings, the backbone of the schedules. There were some undoubted high points, but as BBC1 and ITV once again struggled to find a new, long-running series to replace such ageing warhorses as *Casualty* and *London's Burning*, the genuine successes tended to be one-off series or single dramas such as Jack Rosenthal's bittersweet follow-up to *Eskimo Day*, *Cold Enough for Snow*, starring Maureen Lipman and Tom Wilkinson, shown by BBC1 over the New Year. An undoubted triumph was Tony Marchant's eight-part *Holding On*, an ambitious and often harrowing account of personal and corporate corruption in contemporary London. At the centre of this multi-plotted saga was the apparently whiter-than-white tax inspector Shaun, played by David Morrissey.

The Lakes, Jimmy McGovern's latest teleplay, was another contemporary series demonstrating that however bland and predictable parts of the viewing menu become, there are still writers who are prepared to take risks. *The Lakes*, it must be said, was not in the same class as *Cracker*, McGovern's most successful work to date, yet this story of divided loyalties within a Lake District community offered a refreshing take on this much-romanticized part of the British Isles and John Simm's performance as Danny was widely admired. In typical McGovern style, the sex scenes left little to the imagination. Overshadowing both Marchant and McGovern as a writer who over the decades has provided inspiration for generations of television dramatists, Charles Dickens. BBC2's adaptation of *Our Mutual Friend*, the novelist's last completed work, was, critics agreed, brilliantly realized by writer Sandy Welch and a cast that included familiar TV faces Paul McGann, Anna Friel, Pam Ferris, Timothy Spall and (again) David Morrissey.

Another impressive period adaptation, BBC1's version of Fielding's *Tom Jones*, starring Max Beesley as the 18th-century rake, also impressed reviewers. Nevertheless in March 1998, Chris Smith, the Culture and Media Secretary, accused the corporation of over-subscribing to costume dramas. 'Formulaic historical drama without any real bite isn't going to work with the viewers', he complained. Smith wanted to see more contemporary fare on the small screen. This was easier said

than done. Well-crafted period drama is expensive, but it does sell overseas. This is one reason why ITV tackled numerous costume classics throughout 1997–8. The results were erratic. One of the surprise successes was a version of Hardy's *Far from the Madding Crowd*, hailed by critics, including the *Financial Times*' Chris Dunkley, who said it was of such a high calibre it could have been produced by the BBC. For once, there was no gimmicky star casting and the serial stayed faithful to the book. Newcomer Paloma Baeza was a highly convincing Bathsheba. Unfortunately the programme was screened in July 1998, a time when viewing dips. Less successful were adaptations of *Wuthering Heights* and another Hardy novel, *Tess of the D'Urbervilles*.

During the year both main stations invested heavily in dramas dominated by female casts. One of the most hyped was Deborah Moggach's sexually explicit *Close Relations*, starring Amanda Redman, Sheila Hancock and Kate Buffrey, shown on BBC1. It was entertaining enough, but hardly broke new ground. Of more interest was Kay Mellor's *Playing the Field*, a gritty six-parter about a group of working-class women who either played for or supported Castlefield Blues, an all-women football team. The *Sunday Times*' A. A. Gill regarded the trend as a politically-correct plot by women to take over television. A more plausible explanation was the voracious search for high ratings and both networks' copycat tactics.

More imaginative was *Invasion: Earth*, BBC1's belated attempt to cash in on *The X Files*' success. Created by *Cardiac Arrest* writer Jed Mercurio, this sci-fi thriller promised more than it delivered and failed to achieve high ratings, but the special effects were unusually good for a TV series. Another attempt at reinventing a familiar format was *City Central*, a new BBC1 Saturday night police saga, premièred in the spring and starring ex-*EastEnders* heart-throb Paul Nicholls. Hailed as a *Z Cars* for the 1990s, the programme was intended as a possible successor to *Casualty* but many critics were underwhelmed. Another disappointment was BBC2's *In the Red*, a satire revolving around the BBC, a centre-ground political party and a succession of bank managers being murdered. Despite the contribution of adaptor Malcolm Bradbury and a star-packed cast including Stephen Fry as the controller of Radio 2 and Richard Wilson as the BBC chairman, the overall effect was too incredible for its own good.

The Bill Gets Caught

Not long ago, drama series depicting men and women in uniform could guarantee a satisfactory level of success. Not any more, it seems; contemporary viewers have more choice and are more discerning. Despite its police setting, *City Central* demonstrated how hard it is to succeed in popular drama. *The Bill*, ITV's long-running, thrice-weekly cop soap, amplified the point. In January 1998 the series was revamped following a big dip in ratings. New, younger characters were introduced; the storylines were extended beyond a single episode to encourage audiences to watch more than one episode, and the protagonists' private lives came to the fore. But the results were mixed. Following the relaunch *The Bill* was dealt another blow with the death of actor Kevin Lloyd, famous to millions as Sun Hill's 'Tosh' Lines. On BBC1 *EastEnders* also had a difficult year, despite some strong storylines including the return of superbitch Cindy Beale, Grant and Tiffany's separation, and Kathy's farewell to Albert Square.

If popular drama was proving a headache for the main networks, finding new sitcom hits was a nightmare. Newcomers *Spark* (BBC1) and *Holding the Baby* (ITV) struggled with audiences below seven million; the jury is still out on BBC1's *Kiss Me Kate*, starring Caroline Quentin as a thirtysomething counsellor; *Get Real*, yet another ITV flatshare comedy, was relegated to the margins of the schedule during the summer, and even the high-profile *Babes in the Wood*, starring Samantha Janus, Denise Van Outen and Natalie Walter, failed to impress critics. The return of Steve Coogan on BBC2 in *I'm Alan Partridge* did please reviewers. Even so, it was minority TV and unlikely to evolve into a mass audience show. Another BBC2 entertainment hit was the Asian sketch show, *Goodness Gracious Me*, originally a cult hit for Radio 4. The show cut across cultural barriers and is due to return in 1999.

One of the year's biggest programme controversies involving the BBC emerged in March with the *National Lottery Big Ticket Show*. Critics claimed the series compromised the corporation's standing as a public service broadcaster and encouraged gambling. In Parliament, BBC basher Gerald Kaufman rubbished the programme, describing it as 'seedy'. More successful was the return during the winter of veteran chat show host Michael Parkinson in a late-night Friday slot. The doyen of television talk was in sparkling form. One of many highlights was Sir David Attenborough's elegant and hugely funny performance; for once Billy Connolly, a fellow guest, was lost for words. As *Parkinson* returned, another BBC institution, film critic Barry Norman, bowed out, leaving the corporation to join Sky.

THE TRASHING OF TRASH TV

A different sort of talk show, if that is the right description, was provided by the *Jerry Springer Show*, part of ITV's rejuvenated day-time line-up launched in March. But Springer's outrageous stunts were criticized by the regulators. Lady Howe, chair of the Broadcasting Standards Commission, claimed the show was 'at the edge of acceptability' for its time slot (1.30 p.m.). She suggested this style of 'victim entertainment' was a contemporary equivalent of the medieval stocks. In one infamous encounter, fists flew when a man was humiliated after his girlfriend of two years revealed on air that

she was in fact a he. In August 1998 the ITC said that the programme, denounced by critics as 'trash television', had attracted a spate of complaints from viewers and was in breach of family viewing requirements.

Surprisingly, perhaps, there was still room for innocence on the main networks. However, the cynical view was that the BBC's day-glo dolls, the Teletubbies, had been created as much to please the accountants as the under-fives. Certainly, Tinky Winky, Dipsy, Laa-Laa and Po provided the corporation with its most successful merchandising ploy ever, generating a cool £23 million.

CHANNEL 4 FALTERS

The year 1997–8 was a period of transition for Channel 4, with the full impact of new chief executive Michael Jackson still to make itself felt on the screen. It was not a vintage year for the station, and in May 1998 the ITC reflected the views of many reviewers when it accused the network of not being innovative enough. During 1997–8 most of its dramas disappointed critics, notably what should have been the flagship winter show, *Mosley*, the first non-comic series from *Birds of a Feather* creators Laurence Marks and Maurice Gran. Jonathan Cake played the British fascist, with a strong supporting cast featuring Jemma Redgrave and Emma Davies. The consensus was that the politician's serial adultery was given too much space in the story, leaving too little room for the politics. The programme broke television's last verbal taboo by using the word c∗∗∗ in the final episode; very Channel 4. Other under-achievers were the eagerly-awaited adaptation of Anthony Powell's *A Dance to the Music of Time* and Lynda La Plante's *Killer Net*. The station's biggest recent sitcom hit, *Father Ted*, returned for a third series and was again in strong form. Alas, it was the programme's swan song owing to the sudden death of Dermot Morgan, the actor who played the eponymous priest.

In the spring Channel 5 celebrated its first year on air. By August the station was well on its way to achieving commercial success and there were even signs of its somewhat lacklustre programming improving. To date its successes have included live and exclusive football internationals, several Hollywood movies, *The Real Monty* (a documentary about male strippers), and *Swindon Superbabes*; confirmation, perhaps, that its values have more in common with Sky than with the UK's traditional terrestrial networks. It has also begun to show an increasing number of adult feature films, so-called 'soft porn'.

RADIO

The 75th anniversary of the BBC was celebrated across both radio and television during the autumn, but it was radio where audiences got by far the greater sense of history. This is hardly surprising since the corporation started broadcasting in November 1922, a good three decades before television emerged as a mass medium. The special programmes included a commemorative *Any Questions* and an edition of *Loose Ends* broadcast live from the Savoy Hotel. But as far as the British middle classes were concerned, the most significant radio event of the year was the much-heralded radical overhaul of Radio 4. The station's new schedule, featuring 53 new programmes, was finally launched in April following 18 months of extensive audience research overseen by controller James Boyle. The sheer scale of Boyle's changes was unprecedented. As Paul Donovan wrote in the *Sunday Times*: 'Previous bosses tinkered with specific parts of the output … (but) Boyle is the first to have looked at the whole schedule, seven days a week, from the inshore waters at 5.50 a.m. to the national anthem at 12.45 a.m.'

Aware that the network was in 'gentle decline', having lost 500,000 listeners in the past five years, Boyle's strategy hoped to reposition Radio 4 and enable it to attract new, younger listeners without alienating the faithful. Another aim was to encourage more people to sample the network's non-news and current affairs offerings. It was a high-risk policy and it is still too early to tell whether Boyle will succeed in an ever-more competitive radio market. Figures published in August 1998 suggest the changes have led to more people tuning in to Radio 4 but listening for shorter periods. Moreover Boyle's objective of persuading greater numbers to tune in when *Today* finishes at 9 a.m. was not being fulfilled.

No 'Dumbing Down'

Replacing such familiar Radio 4 fare as *Kaleidoscope, Week Ending* and *Breakaway*, and shunting *Yesterday in Parliament* from FM to long wave, was bound to anger traditionalists. Yet even those critics who were determined to regard Boyle's changes as another symptom of the BBC reneging on its public service commitments had to accept that his revamped schedule contained some gems. John Peel's sideways look at family life, *Home Truths*, broadcast in the former Saturday morning *Breakaway* slot, was praised by critics. *Front Row*, the new weekday arts programme, may not be up to the high standards of *Kaleidoscope*, but it demonstrated a confidence often lacking in BBC television arts coverage.

Moreover, there was no discernible 'dumbing down' in the overall Radio 4 programme mix; the 1998 Reith Lectures, given by the *Daily Telegraph*'s distinguished military writer, John Keegan, received a higher profile than ever before. The former BBC1 quiz, *Mastermind*, axed by television, re-emerged on Radio 4, presented by the donnish Peter Snow. Some critics detected a politically correct attitude in the changes, in line with many of Mr Birt's policies. But many listeners welcomed what they saw as a wider range of individual voices, and a less 'stuffy' texture, with more effort to genuinely

reflect Britain's cultural and ethnic diversity rather than concentrating too heavily on the perceived concerns of 'Middle England'. In any case the broadcasters given more airtime under the new look were generally veterans; Melvyn Bragg, Jonathan Dimbleby, Michael Buerk, Libby Purves and Sue Lawley all benefited from the changes. However, the newly ennobled Bragg was subsequently forced to vacate the presenter's chair on *Start the Week* because the BBC feared there might be a clash of interests between his new status as a Labour peer and his position as a broadcaster discussing policy issues.

Swinging Radio 2

Meanwhile the pace of modernization at Radio 2, the BBC's most popular radio network, continued to gather speed. Fortysomethings, raised on the rock greats of the sixties, found increasingly more to listen to on a station once synonymous with swinging sounds from the 1940s and 1950s. The BBC claimed with some justification that Radio 2's programming encompasses a wider range of musical styles than any of its competitors. To prove that it was determined to bridge the generation gap, network controller James Moir announced in March that his new presenters included Mark Lamarr, famous for appearing on BBC2's spoof quiz show *Shooting Stars*, and the effortlessly hip musical maverick Jools Holland. There was also a new series on soul music and a documentary featuring reggae legend Bob Marley. It was appropriate that in July 1998 station veteran John Dunn announced his retirement, handing over his slot to Johnnie Walker, one of the most musically well-informed ex-Radio 1 DJs. Another new signing to Radio 2 was Des Lynam, hot from his triumph hosting the World Cup on BBC Television.

Throughout 1997–8 Radio 1's performance continued to attract controversy. With Chris Evans having long vacated the breakfast show and now the proud new owner of Virgin Radio, where he continued to host the early morning programme, Radio 1's problems at the start of the day failed to disappear. In October 1997 station chief Matthew Bannister relaunched the *Breakfast Show* with co-presenters Kevin Greening and Zoe Ball replacing Mark Radcliffe and Marc 'Lard' Riley. Initially the audience responded well to the new programme but by the summer there were signs that Evans had begun to win back listeners.

During the year Radio 1 strove to strengthen its coverage of live and specialist music. There was extensive programming devoted to the major festivals – Glastonbury, Phoenix and Tribal Gathering. One of the station's latest recruits, DJ Judge Jules, helped increase its credibility with the dance music fraternity. The network was praised for broadcasting *Blue Jam*, the latest programme from satirist Chris Morris, arguably the most dangerous man in broadcasting. The show was aired in the early hours of the morning and quickly developed a cult following. Despite a new controller, Andy Parfitt, taking over from Mr Bannister in February, no further policy shifts were anticipated.

At the other end of the musical spectrum, Nicholas Kenyon's drive to increase Radio 3's popularity continued to arouse the suspicion of station diehards. However, there were signs that his strategy of attempting to make the station more accessible to a wider range of listeners was beginning to pay dividends. Audience figures were up – by around 250,000 a week – and the station's profile was higher than it had been for a long time. When Kenyon announced in the summer that he would be standing down, the BBC made it clear that there would be no return to the network's old elitist ways.

FIVE LIVE TRIUMPHS

Radio Five Live had another strong year; audiences were up and in May judges at the Sony awards voted the network station of the year. Radio 5 dominated the ceremony, winning five gold medals, including one for its coverage of the death of the Princess of Wales. The main concern for Radio 5 is how it might be affected by a resurgent Talk Radio, following the successful take-over bid led by ex-*Sun* editor Kelvin MacKenzie and backed by Rupert Murdoch's News International. MacKenzie is due to launch his first Talk schedule in October. Some commentators think that if he is successful Radio 5 will be hardest hit. One potential problem is Radio 5's dependence on sports rights, particularly Premier League soccer which accounts for its biggest audiences on Saturdays and weekday evenings. The BBC has the rights until the summer of 2001, but MacKenzie can be an extremely canny operator.

Audience figures published in August showed Talk achieving its best-ever figures, with 2.6 million people tuning in weekly, an annual increase of 413,000. Several new signings during the year including Kirsty Young, the Channel 5 news presenter, had helped improve the station's fortunes. Overall the BBC continued to lose audience share to commercial stations; figures published in August 1998 showed that independent broadcasters were achieving a record 51.1 per cent of listeners, against the corporation's 46.8 per cent. London stations performing well included Capital FM and new-comer Xfm.

Classic FM, under the new management of chief executive Ralph Bernard, fared better in 1997–8 than during the previous year. Audiences were up, a result of a shift away from non-music based programmes. In early 1998 *Gardeners' Question Time* was axed. New shows included what some regarded as a long overdue feature, a listener request show, broadcast at lunchtime. New signings included David Mellor, who presented his programmes, *Across the Threshold*, from his home in Docklands, and Simon Bates. Classic FM also scored with a 'World Cup-free zone' during the summer.

Meanwhile digital radio seemed an even more uncertain prospect than digital television because of the economic uncertainty facing it. Only one group,

Digital One, bid for the digital national radio licence in June 1998. Sets are initially likely to cost between £400 and £500.

TELEVISION AWARD WINNERS

BAFTA AWARDS 1997

Best single drama – *No Child of Mine*
Best drama series – *Jonathan Creek*
Best drama serial – *Holding On*
Best light entertainment – *The Fast Show*
Best comedy – *I'm Alan Partridge*
Best actor – Simon Russell Beale, *A Dance to the Music of Time*
Best actress – Daniela Nardini, *This Life*
Best comedy performance – Steve Coogan, *I'm Alan Partridge*
Best light entertainment performance – Paul Whitehouse, *The Fast Show*
Best factual series – *The Nazis: A Warning from History*
Best arts programme (Huw Wheldon award) – *The South Bank Show: Gilbert and George*
Flaherty documentary award – *True Stories: The Grave*
Best news and current affairs journalism – *Panorama: Valentina's Story*
Best sports/events coverage – Sky: *Rugby Union*
BAFTA Fellowship – Bill Cotton
Alan Clarke award (for outstanding creative contribution to television) – Ted Childs
Richard Dimbleby award (for most important personal contribution on screen in factual television) – David Dimbleby
Lew Grade award (for a significant and popular programme) – *A Touch of Frost*
Dennis Potter award – Kay Mellor
International Television Programme award – *Friends*
Special Award – Roger Cook

RADIO AWARD WINNERS

SONY RADIO AWARDS 1998

Best event – BBC network, *The Funeral of Diana, Princess of Wales*
Best comedy – *Blue Jam* (BBC Radio 1)
Best sports – BBC Radio 5 Live, *Wimbledon; The British Lions Test*
Best drama – *The Trick is to Keep Breathing* (BBC Radio 4)
Best arts – *Designs for Living: Falling Water* (BBC Radio 3)
Best news – BBC Radio 4, BBC Radio 5 Live, *The Death of the Princess of Wales*
Best short form – *GRF Christmas Story* (Clyde 1 FM)
Best feature: music – *The Club that Scott Built* (BBC Radio 2)
Best feature: talk/news – *The Coroner* (BBC Radio 4)
Best special interest music – *Songs of the Sufi Mystics* (BBC World Service)
Best talk/news broadcaster – Anna Raeburn (Talk Radio)
Best DJ – Jo Whiley (BBC Radio 1)
Gold award (contribution to British radio 1997–8) – Chris Evans (Virgin Radio)
Station of the Year (up to 1 m listeners) – Moray Firth Radio
Station of the Year (1–12 m listeners) – BBC Radio WM
UK Station of the Year (broadcasting primarily to the UK) – BBC Radio 5 Live

Conservation and Heritage

THE NATURAL ENVIRONMENT

WILDLIFE CHARTER

In November 1997, 22 wildlife conservation bodies signed a charter proposing better protection for Sites of Special Scientific Interest (SSSIs) and other protected sites. Figures published by English Nature, the statutory nature conservation body in England, show that nearly half of England's 4,000 SSSIs have 'an unfavourable conservation status', i.e. they are suffering some form of damage or neglect. An annual average of 208 cases of damage to SSSIs has been reported in recent years. In Northern Ireland, every site sampled by the RSPB had suffered damage. Some of this damage is perfectly legal. For example, the tenant farmer who ploughed up part of a natural grassland SSSI in the Conwy valley of Wales in 1997 could justly claim that his landlord, the Severn-Trent water company, had failed to inform him about the designation; nor was the company bound to tell him.

The measures proposed in the charter consist mainly of legal technicalities to close such loopholes: better access to SSSIs, more powers to stop damage and restore sites, and the availability of by-laws to all SSSIs. There is also an appeal for better incentives for farmers who want to use land in more environmentally friendly ways. Some of these measures would require legislation, which the Government has committed itself to in the form of a new Wildlife and Countryside Act. But, more fundamentally, it will require a significant shift of agricultural subsidies from production to conservation to make any real difference.

PEAT PROBLEMS

Much of Thorne Moor and Hatfield Chase, Humberside, the two largest lowland peat bogs left in England, have been stripped away by commercial peat companies. Permission to extract peat dates back 50 years, and so predates any conservation designation. It was granted at a time when peat was still cut by hand, and the much more destructive potential of modern milling machines was unknown. In 1992 English Nature made a controversial compromise deal to preserve the less damaged parts of Thorne Moor and Hatfield Chase as nature reserves in return for allowing peat stripping to continue on the rest.

However, most of the site is notified as an SSSI, since even the worked areas retain biological and archaeological interest, and there is some potential for restoration. In 1997 English Nature decided to denotify the parts of Thorne Moore and Hatfield Chase which it considered least interesting. Vir-

tually all environmental bodies involved with peatland protested, and were given considerable public support. The Environment Minister (Michael Meacher) invited English Nature to reconsider its proposal, and it duly did so. In the meantime, peat milling goes on. Campaigners have proposed a levy on the sale of UK peat to reduce the demand and supply, and to generate funds for conservation. The alternative of compensating companies for loss of profit would be unrealistically expensive.

WATER AND HOMES

Concerns about the damage to wildlife sites through water abstraction continue. In 1998 English Nature identified 79 SSSIs that urgently need protection. They include rivers and wetland sites damaged by low flows, leaking silage clamps and yard run-off, by effluent from sewage works and septic tanks, or by boreholes which are causing some sites to dry out in summer. English Nature's report was issued at the same time as the Government embarked on a review of water prices in England and Wales for 2000–5. Wildlife campaigners want water charges to include a levy to protect or restore wildlife sites, for example by building more phosphate-stripping works. In an opinion poll, householders indicated their willingness to pay more for water in return for a cleaner environment, and the public have been encouraged to write to OFWAT and their local water company about their concerns.

The problem will become more acute when the forecast 4–5 million additional homes are built in England. Kent, where 116,000 homes are to be built by 2011, is already experiencing drought problems; for example, the headwaters of the River Darent dried up in 1997. The Government was advised that in West Sussex 38,000 was the maximum number of new houses the county could absorb without serious environmental damage, not least to the water supply. The Government, however, set the target at 51,000 homes. Unfortunately, the planning process does not at present include an assurance of sufficient local water supplies to fulfil needs and protect the environment. Many abstraction licences were granted 30 years ago, and carry no time limit or restrictions on volume. Although the Environment Agency can prosecute when pollution standards are breached, it has no powers to prevent over-abstraction, nor can it normally revoke licences, since it has no funds to compensate water companies. These issues are now under review.

ENGLISH NATURE

Baroness Young of Old Scone, the former chief executive of the RSPB, was appointed chairman of English Nature in spring 1998. The quango had a difficult year, with voluntary wildlife bodies accus-

ing it of ineffectiveness in protecting SSSIs, such as
Offham Down, Sussex, where the owner ploughed
up virgin downland in order to attract a flax subsidy,
and Thorne Moor (*see* above). The organization's
budget has been cut in the last two years, with the
loss of some 70 staff, and there have been reports of
stress and low morale among its normally highly
committed workforce.

In June 1998 a parliamentary committee heard
evidence from farming, landowning and conservation bodies on English Nature's performance. The
committee criticized the organization for undue
secrecy and subservience, but concluded that its
annual grant should be raised in line with its
increasing responsibilities. Its budget for 1999–
2000 has therefore been increased by an extra
£6 million. It is to be hoped that this, combined
with Baroness Young's energetic, hands-on style,
will encourage English Nature to champion wildlife
more effectively. At the RSPB, Baroness Young is
replaced by Graham Wynne, the Society's former
conservation director.

Toxic Chemicals

New regulations came into force in 1998 giving the
Environment Agency greater authority to enforce
the proper disposal of dangerous chemicals on
farmland. A new generation of sheep-dip chemicals
based on synthetic pyrethroids has had deadly
consequences for wildlife when used or stored
carelessly. The new dips replaced organo-phos-
phate ones because they were less dangerous to
human beings; unfortunately, they are much more
dangerous to invertebrates. A teaspoonful entering a
river can kill aquatic invertebrates for hundreds of
metres downstream.

The year 1997 was the worst on record for sheep-
dip pollution. The Environment Agency cited 30
cases of widespread damage, including much of the
River Eden, Cumbria. Farmers are advised to use
dips in dry weather and to dispose of it on level
ground well away from water courses; but these
conditions are likely to be hard to meet in the
uplands where most sheep are reared. Rare species
like the pearl mussel are at risk, and naturalists are
worried about toxins being passed on through the
food-chain and poisoning animals like the otter,
which is only just starting to recover from the effects
of DDT spraying 30 years ago.

Protected Species

In March 1998 legal protection was extended to 33
rare or threatened species, among them the water
vole, the basking shark and the marsh fritillary
butterfly. It also became an offence to trade in wild
bluebells. Britain holds about one-fifth of the
world's bluebells and many of the finest bluebell
woods. Until now it has been legal to harvest and sell
bluebell bulbs with the permission of the landowner, and they supported an export trade estimated to be worth £1 million a year. Those convicted
of selling wild bluebell bulbs will face fines of up to

£2,500. The stag beetle can also no longer be sold.
There are reports of a trade in specimens, mainly to
continental collectors, which might jeopardize an
already declining species. Other species protected
under the latest five-yearly review are four species
of fungus and several kinds of mosses. A species of
moth, the viper's bugloss, was taken off the protected list; despite legal protection it has become
extinct.

Millennium Seed Bank

The Royal Botanic Garden at Kew has unique
facilities for cold-storing seeds in low-humidity
rooms where they can remain viable for decades, if
not centuries. A grant from the Heritage Lottery
Fund has enabled Kew to expand its facilities at
Wakehurst Place, Sussex, where the aim is to store
seed from some 10 per cent of the world's flowering
plants by 2010.

At present the Seed Bank is concentrating on
British flora, aiming to store seed of every native
species (though there are problems with storing the
fleshier seeds like the acorn). The initial programme runs from 1999 to 2000, when some 800
native flowers, trees and ferns should enter the
bank. The programme relies mainly on volunteers
to collect the seed and to clean and dry them at
Wakehurst Place prior to storage. In the process, we
are finding out more about the seeding rates of wild
plants. Some hardly seed at all, at least in poor years,
or are grazed before the seeds can ripen.

In the longer term, Kew intends to increase the
genetic diversity of banked seed by collecting from
different sites across Britain. Seed is already being
used in reintroduction schemes, but the purpose of a
seed bank is essentially an insurance against un-
predictable events in the wild. If, in future, a species
becomes extinct, its genetic material, at least,
should survive.

Badgers

An independent review body of scientists appointed
to investigate the problem of bovine tuberculosis
has recommended an experiment to assess the
effects of badger culling on farms. Since 1971 the
Ministry of Agriculture has selectively gassed or
trapped badgers on farmland because they are
believed to transmit tuberculosis to cattle. Surprisingly, we are not much better informed about it now
than we were then, though badgers have become
commoner in the meantime – there may be as many
as 400,000 of them, producing 100,000 cubs a year.
The experiment will involve killing every badger
within ten different randomly chosen square kilometres, and comparing the results with sites where
no culling has taken place. For the time being, all
official culling outside the experimental areas will
cease. A second experiment will compare the
effectiveness of methods of animal husbandry as a
means of minimizing contact between cattle and
badgers. The review body's proposals were accepted by the Government in August 1998.

BIRD MONITORING

Concern has been expressed about declining numbers of skylarks. A study by the RSPB showed that in the far north of Scotland nesting larks had declined by 81 per cent between 1995 and 1998. The cause is more likely to be found on their wintering grounds on farmland than on their nesting sites on the moors, though many of these have been afforested since the 1980s. Overall, skylarks have declined by 61 per cent over the past 25 years. Other birds showing a comparable level of decline include the lapwing, grey partridge, turtle dove, songthrush and tree sparrow. The year 1998 was a particularly poor one for house martins. Most rare birds, on the other hand, are doing comparatively well, partly because their special needs are often met on nature reserves.

Such trends are discovered by long-term monitoring, most notably by the nests records scheme and bird-ringing organized by the British Trust for Ornithology (BTO). However, the work has been undermined by budget cuts from the BTO's main grant body, the Joint Nature Conservation Committee (JNCC), which has had its own funding cut by the statutory conservation quangos.

DEVELOPMENT

Rainham Marshes, in the London Borough of Havering, is the last remaining tract of undeveloped marshland near London. It supports a wide range of plants, birds and insects, some of them nationally rare, including breeding lapwing and redshank, with hen harriers and short-eared owls in winter. Although it is an SSSI, developers have had their eye on the area since the 1980s. English Partnerships, the statutory urban regeneration agency, has now applied for planning permission to develop up to 60 per cent of the SSSI, partly using public funds. The development would include a business park, a 'drive-through restaurant', a petrol station and an hotel. Friends of the Earth are challenging the application on a legal technicality, claiming that English Partnerships requires the Secretary of State's approval and that it is breaking its own guidelines on wildlife protection. Given its location, there are only two options open for Rainham Marshes – development, or total protection as a nature reserve.

An SSSI and two rivers were threatened by ball-clay mining in Devon. English China Clay International wanted to dig up and move natural habitat at Brock's Farm SSSI and dump waste on the cleared land. After a public inquiry, the inspector rejected the plan, partly on the grounds that a previous attempt to 'translocate' wildlife habitats there had failed. As an expert witness put it, 'if you move it, you lose it'.

Watts Blake Bearne, a multinational mining company, received permission to expand its clay pit by diverting the nearby Teign and Bovey rivers. The plan was opposed by the Environment Agency on the grounds that it would have an irreversible impact on the wildlife and landscape of the valley.

The Environment Secretary (John Prescott) has issued a stop notice and ordered a public inquiry.

An award of £2.7 million from EU funds to build a funicular railway to the summit of Cairn Gorm was delayed, pending the outcome of legal action from objectors.

SEA EMPRESS

The findings of the Sea Empress inquiry, set up in 1996, were announced in February 1998. Some 72,000 tonnes of light crude oil were spilled from the wreck off the Pembrokeshire coast. About 40 per cent evaporated, about 6 per cent came ashore, and the rest was assumed to have dispersed in the water to be degraded naturally by micro-organisms.

The known environmental impact was surprisingly light, thanks to the time of year – February, when most birds were absent – and a change in wind direction away from the coast. The most visible impact was the spread of seaweed on shores after the population of limpets had been wiped out. Although 7,000 common scoters, guillemots and razorbills were oiled, it is thought that even more birds die from minor but frequent tank-flushing incidents. Few of the oiled birds recovered alive are expected to have survived for more than a year. Fish and commercial shellfish were not seriously affected. Rock-pool life was damaged along some 200 km of coast, including the near-total destruction of a rare starfish, *Asterina phylactica*. Lichens in the splash zone at Milford Haven have not yet recovered. It is likely that more damage was done to marine invertebrates by dispersant-spraying than from the oil itself. The total value of damage caused by the spill is estimated at £150 million.

Among the inquiry's recommendations were further research on the ecological impacts of dispersal-spraying and the extension of the 'polluter pays' principle to 'post-spill' operations.

EXMOOR PONIES

Genetic fingerprinting at Leicester University, using DNA samples taken from thoroughbred Exmoor ponies, indicate that the pony is closely related to prehistoric wild horses known only from fossil remains. Unlike most breeds of horse, the Exmoor pony has evolved largely naturally, as adaptations to a cold, wet climate and meagre rations. The scientists concluded that although the pony has been absorbed into the hill-farming system and its distribution and breeding are under human control, it has changed little in appearance since prehistory. The pony came close to extinction during the Second World War, when its numbers fell to only 50; there are now about 700 world-wide. Conservationists have identified it as the ideal grazing animal for heathland and scrubby moors because of its hardiness.

SNOWDON

The National Trust has launched a public appeal for £3 million to buy a 4,000-acre estate including the southern flank of Snowdon. Sir Antony Hopkins, the actor, has pledged £1 million. Despite being part of a National Park (and a National Nature Reserve), Snowdon has its share of problems; there are too many sheep, paths are eroding, and there is a dilapidated building at the summit which apparently no one can afford to replace. Some feel that there should not be any kind of building on a mountain summit. Purchase of the estate may enable the Trust and the Park to have another attempt at finding a solution that balances visitor needs with the environmentally sensitive character of the area.

THE BUILT ENVIRONMENT

Conservation activity in 1997-8 was again dominated by the Heritage Lottery Fund (HLF). Although the Heritage Memorial Fund, the HLF's sister organization under the aegis of the National Heritage Memorial Fund, has suffered progressive reductions in its grant-in-aid from central government (from £8 million in 1996-7 to £2 million in 1998-9), the HLF had, by May 1998, awarded £1,010,000,000 to a total of 1,862 projects.

Although the grants awarded in each year since the HLF was set up in January 1995 have been affected by programmes concentrating on particular areas, for example, capital projects for museums and galleries, the 1998-9 budget envisages £50-£70 million each year going towards historic buildings in the UK. Some £10 million of that goes towards places of worship in England, matching the £10 million already allocated through English Heritage. Historic buildings benefited too from grants to museums which were housed in listed structures, and from the Urban Parks Programme, announced in January 1996. By May 1998, £104,409,239 had been awarded to 174 historic parks, including £4.3 million to Lister Park, Bradford, £6.7 million to the Botanical Gardens at Sheffield, £4.5 million to the central parks at Southampton, £5.1 million to Mount Wise Park, Plymouth, £3 million to the churchyard of the Cathedral at Birmingham, and £1.8 million to Russell Square, central London.

RESTRICTIONS LIFTED

From March 1998 the National Heritage Act 1997 removes any restriction on the nature of the applicant to the HLF, which can henceforth include private individuals and commercial companies. It also increases trustees' powers beyond the conservation or enhancement of what had hitherto been called heritage 'things'; eligibility is extended to schemes that deal solely with improved access, education or interpretation. These new powers make it easier for trustees to underwrite, as they have done since May 1997, the conservation area partnership schemes of English Heritage. Subse-

quently renamed the Townscape Initiative, HLF allocated £8 million towards the repair and enhancement of historic buildings and public spaces within conservation areas in each of the years from 1998-9 to 2000-1.

The range of projects grant-aided by the HLF has demonstrated the wide interpretation the Trustees have put on the word 'heritage'. Museums and galleries have been unsurprising beneficiaries; grants have included £11.9 million to the National Portrait Gallery, £7.3 million to the Wallace Collection, £18.75 million to the Tate Gallery to create a Gallery of British Art by 2001, and £15 million to Manchester City Art Gallery. However, other projects receiving assistance have included: Stoneleigh Abbey, Warks (£7.37 million), 36 Craven Street, near Charing Cross station, London, the home of Benjamin Franklin (£528,000), a new education centre for Canterbury Cathedral (£2.25 million), Hadlow Tower at West Malling, Kent, one of the most extraordinary of all Georgian follies(£963,000), Chatham Historic Dockyard (£10 million), the former *Glasgow Herald* building, Glasgow (£3.5 million, to allow the refurbishment of one of the first buildings to be designed by Charles Rennie Mackintosh), the National Historic Ships database, Scotland (£152,000), the Cornwall Industrial Heritage Centre, Camborne (£1.173 million), Somerset House, London (£10 million), and St Paul's Church, Deptford (£1.435 million, to restore one of the greatest Baroque churches of London).

ENGLISH HERITAGE

The HLF and other Lottery distributors allocate funds from what has been called a system of voluntary taxation. The distributors of funds from official or involuntary taxation are by no means as rich. The budget of English Heritage was £129.7 million in 1996-7, but the Government's grant-in-aid to the body has fallen from £109.7 million in 1995-6 to £102.2 million in 1998-9. The shortfall has been partly made up by a substantial rise in income from other sources, including admissions to properties, retail and catering, membership subscriptions and Lottery grants. Grants paid by English Heritage for the maintenance and repair of historic buildings and scheduled monuments totalled £35.5 million in 1996-7 - £10.3 million to churches, £4 million to cathedrals, £10.2 million to secular buildings and monuments of outstanding interest, and £9.2 million for conservation area and town schemes.

The largest single grant was £523,000 to the National Trust's Ightham Mote in Kent, followed by £500,000 to Liverpool's Roman Catholic cathedral. Money directed to other areas in 1996-7 included £5.4 million towards rescue archaeology and £1.35 million towards ancient monuments; the separate schemes for grants to historic buildings and ancient monuments have now been combined. The repair and maintenance of its own 409 monuments (of which 127 are now managed locally) consumed £21.3 million in 1996–7.

A major new English Heritage attraction in 1998 was Down House in Kent, the home of Charles Darwin, which was one of several repaired with substantial grant aid from the HLF. Particular initiatives in the year directed attention towards the protection of stone roofing and barrack buildings, but by far the largest was the Buildings at Risk campaign launched in May 1998, the first ever national audit of England's outstanding historic buildings at risk through neglect and decay. It highlighted 1,500 Grade I and Grade II* buildings in varying degrees of disrepair, and set aside some £5 million towards the cost of tackling the problem. A similar Monuments at Risk campaign launched a few weeks later, to assess the condition of archaeological remains, estimated that some 4,000 were at high risk of serious damage or destruction, and that 22,000 known archaeological sites had been destroyed since 1945.

CADW

The equivalent of English Heritage in Wales is Cadw, which is advised by the Historic Buildings Council for Wales. By March 1996 the number of listed buildings in Wales stood at 18,395, with Cadw grants in the year 1995–6 totalling £3,788,000, a reduction of some 9.5 per cent on the previous year. Grant recipients included a prisoner of war camp near Bridgend, built in the late 1930s; the only surviving salt warehouse in Wales, at Newbridge, Powys; and 39 town schemes dealing with areas including Harlech, Tremadog and the Lower Dock Street area of Newport.

In 1997 the Welsh affairs select committee of the House of Commons urged the establishment of at least one building preservation trust and the employment of suitably qualified conservation staff within each local authority. Its criticism of the comparative lack of measures to protect the quintessential Welsh building type, the Nonconformist chapel of the 18th and 19th centuries, led to the listing programme by Cadw being accelerated and money being allocated by the organization to launch a Welsh Chapels Conservation Trust, expected to be fully operational by 2000.

HISTORIC SCOTLAND

North of the border the relevant quango is Historic Scotland, grants from which support some 44,000 listed buildings. It is also responsible for an enterprising publishing programme, which resulted in books in 1997 on fire protection, international conservation charters and stone cleaning. In 1997–8 Historic Scotland awarded £12 million to 135 projects, introduced a building conservation register of suitably qualified professionals and commenced a pilot project for the control of external alterations to listed churches. Private enterprise included further expansion in the work

of the Scottish Lime Centre, with courses offered in Edinburgh.

LISTING

The bedrock of any conservation policy is the identification and protection of historic buildings through statutory lists. At December 1997 the number of listed buildings in England, on a new counting principle which enumerates terraces as single rather than multiple entries, stood at 451,287. In 1997 a total of 327 properties were removed from the lists as a result of re-assessments provoked by error, new facts or licensed and unlicensed alterations. In the year to March 1998, 58 other listed buildings were given consent to demolish. Additions to the lists in 1997–8 included the pottery (1921) built by Bernard Leach at St Ives, Cornwall; a house in Bedfordshire which was found to contain the remains of decoration by Whistler in 1880; the oldest Ashkenazi synagogue still in use in the English-speaking world, in Plymouth; and Waterloo Bridge in London, dated 1939–45.

The number of conservation areas, which protect the external appearance of streets as opposed to individual buildings, stood at 8,724 at the end of 1997. However, the degree of protection which local authorities could exercise was severely compromised by a judgment in the House of Lords in February 1997, which limited the control of demolition to all or substantially all of the building in question.

At the end of 1997 the number of scheduled ancient monuments stood at 17,351. Newcomers to the list included a smugglers' cache on Tresco, Isles of Scilly; a medieval hermit's cave at Plumpton, Yorkshire; and two sections of a Roman road on Otmoor, Oxfordshire. By June 1997 the number of registered historic parks and gardens in England had risen to 1,280.

CHURCHES CONSERVATION

Protection of places of worship in England has always been complicated by the existence of the ecclesiastical exemption enjoyed by the Anglicans, the Roman Catholics, the Methodists, the Baptists and the United Reformed Church. This was the subject of a government-commissioned review, carried out by John Newman, which reported in early 1998 and which suggested certain reforms. The launch of the Sacred Land Project redirected attention towards holy buildings and land, whilst expansion in the work of the Open Churches Trust, paid for by Lord Lloyd-Webber, provided increased grants towards the cost of keeping such buildings open to the public.

One of the greatest Victorian buildings in Manchester, St Francis Gorton Church was adopted as a building at risk by the World Monuments Fund, which went some way towards assuaging the loss through demolition of the same city's St Alban's Church, Cheetham, a noble work of 1857. In the course of the year the Friends of Friendless

Churches was formally recognized as the body sponsored by Church and state to take on redundant Anglican places of worship within Wales. Its equivalent in England, the Churches Conservation Trust, had 311 churches in its care by December 1997. The Historic Chapels Trust, established in 1992 to do the same for non-Anglican properties, had a portfolio of six buildings at the same date.

UNDER THREAT

Listing creates a presumption in favour of retention, but it does not insist upon preservation in perpetuity. Important buildings threatened in 1997 with demolition included Sandown Hall, Liverpool; the medieval tithe barn at Crowle, Worcestershire; the imposing former hospital built in the 1850s at Powick, Hereford and Worcester; and the school at Durnford, Greater Manchester, designed by the architect Edgar Wood. Major conservation battles centred on the Royal William Yard at Plymouth, a remarkable assemblage of late-Georgian buildings earmarked for conversion to a retailing outlet, and the Grade II* listed Free Trade Hall at Manchester, which the local authority proposed to gut and replace, with the exception of two main elevations, with a 20-storey tower block. A major victory in the year was the decision of the Bishop of London to rebuild in traditional form the medieval church of St Ethelburga's, in the City of London, which was destroyed by the IRA bombs of 1992 and 1993.

New institutions launched during the year included the Mausolea and Monuments Trust, set up to care for these often neglected structures; a Cathedrals Research Unit, based in York; the Ancient Farm Buildings Trust, based in Herefordshire, the Phoenix Trust, the largest of all building preservation trusts, geared to take on conservation and conversion projects costing up to £5 million each; and, perhaps most significantly of all, the Institute of Historic Building Conservation (IHBC). The IHBC succeeded the Association of Conservation Officers, and for the first time created a professional institute to which those involved in the management, protection and repair of listed buildings could belong and by whom they could be vetted.

Major research projects funded by the HLF were launched on the Jewish built heritage, 20th century military structures, and public monuments and statuary. The Royal Commission on the Historical Monuments of England marked the year by publishing research on Georgian and Victorian farmsteads and historic hospitals.

The nurturing of talent was encouraged by the launch of an award for the conservation of historic bridges through the Institution of Civil Engineers, and acceptance by the Royal Institute of British Architects of the need for a specialist register of conservation architects.

NEW ATTRACTIONS

The year also saw new attractions, with the opening to the public for the first time of historic houses like Compton Verney, Warwickshire, which now houses the British Folk Art collection, and a new centre for the study of Scottish bagpipes in Glasgow, housed in a formerly derelict church. Uppark, the National Trust property in Sussex, and Windsor Castle both reopened after the repair of devastating fire damage.

The National Trust enjoyed a net increase in its membership of 100,000 in 1996–7, to become easily the largest conservation organization in the world, with 2,390,000 members. The Trust broadened the normal definition of 'heritage property' by opening to the public in 1998 the house in Liverpool where Paul McCartney grew up and wrote many of the Beatles' most famous songs. In 1997 it also announced plans to create a museum within a former workhouse of 1837 at Thurgarton, Nottinghamshire, if a grant application to the HLF is successful.

The period under review ended in July 1998 with the publication by the Government of a consultation paper proposing the amalgamation of the Royal Commission on Historical Monuments for England and English Heritage, the continuation of 'heritage' as a Lottery 'good cause' beyond 2001 and the restoration of the budget of the National Heritage Memorial Fund.

Dance

The year began as the last had ended – with rows and recriminations over the Royal Opera House. The Royal Ballet embarked on its life away from the House inauspiciously, with a misguided season at the Labatt's Apollo, Hammersmith, that reportedly lost £750,000. A House of Commons select committee accused the House of being 'a shambles' in October 1997. The Culture Secretary, Chris Smith, then instigated a review of lyric theatre in London, to be conducted by Sir Richard Eyre, but appeared to prejudge the outcome of the review by favouring the idea that the Royal Opera House should accommodate not only the Royal Opera and the Royal Ballet, but also English National Opera, thereby saving ENO's costs at the London Coliseum. By November the House was said to be within a week of declaring itself bankrupt and was saved only by the intervention of anonymous wealthy benefactors. Midland Bank rather unhelpfully chose this moment to withdraw its long-standing sponsorship of both the Royal Opera and Birmingham Royal Ballet, on the grounds that opera and ballet were too elitist, and the Paul Hamlyn Foundation withdrew its subsidy of cut-price opera tickets for young people.

In early December, the chairman of the Commons select committee, Gerald Kaufman, swung his axe. The committee called for the resignation of the Royal Opera House board with immediate effect, saying that it 'would prefer to see the House run by a philistine with the requisite financial acumen than by the succession of opera and ballet lovers who have brought a great and valuable institution to its knees'. The chairman also recommended that the House should lose its Arts Council grant if the board did not go. While the report made many valid criticisms, it failed to address the House's fundamental problem: because it receives inadequate public subsidy, it is forced to rely on wealthy and well-connected people who may or may not have the appropriate skills and competence. The House has therefore been run in an atmosphere of formal and informal patronage that militates against clear lines of responsibility and accountability. An institution in a permanent state of financial crisis is also liable to react with either despair or defiance, both of which have been evident in the House's management in recent years, and neither of which are likely to produce a stable, well-run organization. Nevertheless, the board bowed its collective head and resigned; the chairman, Lord Chadlington, later denounced the committee's report as 'insulting and hysterical'. In January 1998 Sir Colin Southgate, the chairman of EMI, was appointed chairman of the House, and a largely new board was gradually assembled.

In February 1998 the Royal Opera's director, Nicholas Payne, was appointed general director of ENO. In March the House's chief executive, Mary Allen, the former secretary-general of the Arts Council who had been in place for less than a year, resigned in the face of the new chairman's decision to appoint an artistic general director for the House. In April the former general director of Scottish Opera, Richard Jarman, was appointed to the position as a stop-gap solution. In May, a 'secret' letter from the Royal Opera House to Chris Smith found its way into the newspapers; it stated that Covent Garden could be forced to remain closed unless it received an extra £15 million of public subsidy with which to run the new theatre and make it accessible to a wider audience. This provoked renewed calls for the House to be 'privatized' (i.e. have all its subsidy withdrawn). When the Eyre report was finally published in June 1998, it attacked the House for snobbery, complacency and mismanagement, but rejected the idea of moving ENO into the organization and recommended that, when the House had put its affairs in order, it should in fact receive increased public subsidy. This unexpected and perhaps unwelcome conclusion has left Chris Smith in something of a dilemma; at the time of going to press, the dilemma was unresolved.

Arts Council Reforms

The Arts Council itself underwent a transformation in 1998. The chairman of Granada Group, Gerry Robinson, replaced Lord Gowrie as chairman of the Council and instigated a reorganization of the Council that provoked widespread resignations. In June, the new chairman forced the entire Council to resign, and replaced it with a smaller Council of mainly younger members, including the ballerina Deborah Bull; the importance of the specialist advisory panels was simultaneously downgraded. The Council's annual grant for 1997–8 was pegged at the previous year's level (£186.1 million), causing its funding of the Royal Opera House, Birmingham Royal Ballet and English National Ballet among others to be cut. Further reforms of the Arts Council's role are planned. The Chancellor of the Exchequer's spending review, announced in summer 1998, will produce extra money for the arts over a three-year period, but it seems unlikely that ballet, not deemed an essential element in New Labour's 'Cool Britannia', will be a major beneficiary.

It is to be hoped that Deborah Bull's duties on the Arts Council will not herald the end of her dancing career. She is one of the major talents at the Royal Ballet, which had a year of distinctly mixed fortunes and relied largely on the classics to bring in audiences at its new venues. However, the dancers seemed determined to prove the worth of their company and their art by dancing with real vigour and confidence. They were hampered as usual by an unimaginative choice of repertoire and, this year, by the quality of several of the venues in which they performed. Ashley Page provided a bold new work, *Cheating, Lying, Stealing*, beautifully danced in particular by Viviana Durante, who returned to the company from a year's leave of absence, and Irek Mukhamedov, whose dramatic power and expressiveness remain undimmed. The company finally appointed a new music director, Andrea Quinn, in early 1998.

The biggest cause for celebration in the year was the 100th birthday of the company's founder, Dame Ninette de Valois, on 6 June 1998. This was marked by a gala at the Barbican Theatre which revived extracts from some of de Valois's own works, long unseen, and produced many affectionate tributes from past and present members of the Royal Ballet companies. The year ended on a high note with a successful season at the London Coliseum. The company has invited the Cuban star Carlos Acosta to join them from autumn 1998, and the repertoire planned for 1998–9 promises more interest and variety than the year under review. It will also include performances at the new Sadler's Wells Theatre, which is nearing completion and should provide an appropriate and exciting new venue for this company and many others.

Birmingham Royal Ballet, which must be thanking its lucky stars that it is no longer part of the Royal Opera House organization, also staged a tribute to de Valois: it revived her 1940 work *The Prospect Before Us*, which had not been seen for nearly 50 years. The work is inspired by the drawings of Thomas Rowlandson, and concerns two rival theatre managers in London in the 1780s. Jean Bedells, who had danced in the original production, reconstructed much of the choreography, and the company's director, David Bintley, created steps to fill in remaining gaps. The result was an entertaining and enjoyable work, described by one critic as 'a perfect English comic ballet'. It was only one element in a very successful season for the company. Bintley's full-length dramatic ballet, *Edward II*, was brought into the company's repertoire, having been created for the Stuttgart Ballet. It was as well-received in Britain as it had been in Germany, and produced excellent performances from its large cast. The company also gave the first performances by a British company of Balanchine's *Orpheus*, on a triple bill devoted entirely to Balanchine works.

MEMORIAL FUNDING

English National Ballet also had a highly successful season. It mounted a new production of *The Nutcracker*, imaginatively conceived by the company's director Derek Deane, and with stylish designs by Sue Blane. It was dedicated to the company's former patron, Diana, Princess of Wales. Later in the year the company received a donation of nearly £1 million from the Princess's memorial fund, which it will use to mount new productions, develop new audiences and look after the health and welfare of young dancers. The other big new production of the year was *Romeo and Juliet*, staged by Derek Deane in the round at the Royal Albert Hall. It was interesting to compare this with last year's in-the-round *Swan Lake*. In many ways *Romeo and Juliet* was the more successful production, since it was conceived from scratch for the Hall and could make full use of the arena's entrances and exits and the dramatic possibilities of the Verona townsfolk milling around the huge floor space. However, the need to keep audiences on all sides involved produced almost incessant turning steps in the choreography; even then crucial moments of the drama were lost to some viewers. Happily, Deane did not feel it necessary to substitute a happy ending for the more usual tragic one, as he had with *Swan Lake*. The company ended the season deficit-free, in spite of reduced funding from the Arts Council.

Scottish Ballet's season threatened to be over before it had begun. The dance committee of the Scottish Arts Council recommended that funding to the company be withdrawn, after a row about a proposed merger of the orchestras of Scottish Ballet and Scottish Opera and criticisms over the company's reduced level of performing activity. The committee was also rumoured to favour contemporary dance over classical ballet. In the event, funding was continued, but on the condition that the board and the artistic director, Galina Samsova, resign, and a new artistic director be found to overhaul the company's repertoire. At the time of going to press, no appointment had been made. Nevertheless, the company found plenty of support from within the ballet world, and staged Ashton's *La fille mal gardée*, with sets and costumes loaned from Birmingham Royal Ballet and guest appearances by Wayne Sleep as Alain, as its Christmas show. It also, and less successfully, revived Peter Darrell's *Tales of Hoffmann* – the performance of Adam Cooper in the leading role won more praise than the production. Cooper also created a new ballet for the company, an enjoyable jazz piece entitled *Just Scratchin' the Surface*, while Sheridan Nicol's *Faerie Feet* was less well-received.

Aside from his work with Scottish Ballet, Adam Cooper starred with Sarah Wildor of the Royal Ballet and Lynn Seymour in the new production of *Cinderella* by Matthew Bourne for Adventures in Motion Pictures in autumn 1997. This was set during the Blitz, and followed the now well-established AMP formula of transposing a familiar classic work to a more modern setting and treating it with cheerful disrespect. In fact, Bourne obviously has a clear understanding of why the classics have endured, and his work is witty, enjoyable and sometimes moving. However, although he has a very strong sense of theatre, most of his choreography is unmemorable and fails to make acceptable use of the music, which makes for an ultimately unsatisfying dance experience. The production was superbly designed by Lez Brotherston, who won the Laurence Olivier award for outstanding achievement in dance for his work on *Cinderella*.

Brotherston's designs were also the most successful element of Northern Ballet Theatre's two new productions during the season: *Giselle*, staged by the company's director Christopher Gable in a war-torn urban ghetto, in which Giselle is a member of a community living under martial law and Albrecht a soldier with whom she falls in love; and *The Hunchback of Nôtre Dame*, choreographed by Michael Pink with a new score by Philip Feeney, which was full of action and produced a fine performance from Luc Jacobs as Quasimodo, but was ultimately confusing and uninspiring. City Ballet of London (formerly London City Ballet) also mounted a new production of a classic – this time *The Sleeping Beauty*, choreographed by Michael Rolnick – but it did little credit to the company's ambitions. The season ended, however, with the company's funding secured for at least a year thanks to sponsorship from the Rothermere Foundation.

RAMBERT THREE-YEAR PLAN

Rambert Dance Company continued to win plaudits, both for its dancers and for its repertoire. Christopher Bruce, the company's director, was awarded a CBE in the Queen's Birthday Honours for his services to dance. In September 1997 Christopher Nourse was appointed executive director of the company, and in April 1998 Bruce and Nourse announced the launch of a three-year plan to take the company through to its 75th anniversary in 2001. They reaffirmed their commitment to new work and to reviving works from Rambert's distinguished past, confirmed their relationship with their regular orchestra, London Musici, and pledged themselves to develop audiences, increase educational work and strengthen the company's financial position. Two successful new works were performed during the season, *Greymatter* by Didy Veldman and Jeremy James's *Gaps, Lapse and Relapse*, and Jiří Kylián's powerful *No More Play* entered the repertoire. The most exciting performances, however, were of the dance-drama *Cruel Garden*, created in 1977 by Bruce and Lindsay Kemp. This is based on the life of Federico García Lorca, who was killed by Spanish fascists in 1936; the work was revived to mark the centenary of Lorca's birth. With effective designs by Ralph Koltai and a dramatic score by Carlos Miranda, *Cruel Garden* has lost none of its power and was superbly danced, especially by Conor O'Brien as the central Lorca figure.

The two towering figures of British contemporary dance, Richard Alston and Siobhan Davies, continued to impress. Alston marked 30 years as a choreographer and created four new works for his company, set up in 1994 after the demise of London Contemporary Dance Theatre. The Siobhan Davies Dance Company celebrated its tenth anniversary in 1998, although Davies herself has been choreographing since 1972. Her company has been augmented to ten dancers for this anniversary year; it performed *The Art of Touch* and a new work, *Bank* (with a score performed on cardboard boxes), in autumn 1997, and opened its spring tour with a revival of the award-winning *Winnsboro' Cotton Mill Blues* together with another superb new work, *Eighty-Eight*, set to Conlon Nancarrow's fractured piano pieces and with designs by David Buckland and Peter Mumford.

Dance Umbrella 1997 paid the price for bringing the Mark Morris Company to London the previous summer. Its investment in this season, though highly worthwhile, meant that the festival was noticeably smaller than usual and used only three venues over a four-week period. It still managed to produce some highlights, especially Javier de Frutos (with his flamboyant, full-blooded work *Grass*, set to Puccini's *Madam Butterfly*), Maguy Marin, Stephen Petronio, Rosemary Butcher and Siobhan Davies. Interesting works during the year also came from Darshan Singh Bhuller (whose *Planted Seeds* was set in Bosnia and produced fine performances from the dancers), Lea Anderson (with *The Featherstonehaughs Draw on the Sketch Books of Egon Schiele*, a 70-minute work inspired by the emotions of the tormented artist), Nigel Charnock (who created two new pieces of dance-theatre, *Heroine* and *Human Being*), Russell Maliphant (who performed *Shift* and *Critical Mass* at the Spring Loaded festival at The Place), Mark Murphy (who created the highly enjoyable, sophisticated murder-mystery *Nothing But the Truth* for his company V-Tol) and Charles Linehan (who won the Jerwood prize for young choreographers and created *Rialto* for the Spring Loaded festival). Jonathan Burrows was appointed resident choreographer at the South Bank Centre for a year, and presented his 'choice' – an evening showcasing work by his favourite dance-makers (Michael Clark, William Forsythe, Dan Caspersen, Meg Stuart, Amanda Miller and Paul Selwyn Norton).

LOTTERY FUNDING

Contemporary dancers (both professional and students) will soon have a bigger, better London venue in which to rehearse and perform. In autumn 1997 The Place was awarded £5.081 million of National Lottery funding to redevelop the centre, build new studios and improve the stage. Lottery funding is also enabling the Northern School of Contemporary Dance in Leeds to undertake a massive building project, including the complete refurbishment of the Riley Theatre, a disused synagogue used as a theatre by the school since 1987.

The most interesting visitors to the UK in the year under review were American. Merce Cunningham performed his monumental show, *Ocean*, in Belfast in November 1997; Twyla Tharp brought several works to the Barbican in July 1998;

and a small group of 'stars of New York City Ballet' performed works by Balanchine, Ulysses Dove, Christopher Wheeldon and Christopher D'Amboise at the Queen Elizabeth Hall in July–August 1998. Their first performance was dedicated to Jerome Robbins, the great American choreographer and creator of *West Side Story*, who had died the previous day at the age of 79. The other major loss during the year was the great Russian ballerina Galina Ulanova, who died in March 1998 at the age of 88. She created a sensation with her performances in London in 1956 in Lavrovsky's production of Prokofiev's *Romeo and Juliet* with the Bolshoi Ballet; for many, this has remained the pinnacle of balletic achievement against which other performances will forever be judged.

PRODUCTIONS

ROYAL BALLET
Founded 1931 as the Vic-Wells Ballet
Royal Opera House, Covent Garden, London WC2E 9DD
World première:
Cheating, Lying, Stealing (Ashley Page), 16 June 1998. A one-act ballet. Cast led by Viviana Durante, Irek Mukhamedov, Mara Galeazzi and William Trevitt
Company première:
A Royal Ballet (Christopher Wheeldon), 24 July 1998. A one-act ballet. Music, Beethoven; design, Christopher Wheeldon. Dancers, Gillian Revie, Belinda Hatley, Bruce Sansom, William Trevitt
Full-length ballets from the repertoire: *Romeo and Juliet* (MacMillan, 1965), *Giselle* (Coralli/Perrot, prod. Wright 1985), *The Sleeping Beauty* (Petipa, prod. Dowell 1994), *Cinderella* (Ashton, 1948), *La Bayadère* (Makarova after Petipa, 1980), *Swan Lake* (Petipa/Ivanov, prod. Dowell 1987), *Manon* (MacMillan, 1974).
   One-act ballets and *pas de deux* from the repertoire: *Les Patineurs* (Ashton, 1937), *Tales of Beatrix Potter* (Ashton, adapted for the stage by Dowell, 1992), *Peter and the Wolf* (Hart, 1995), *The Rake's Progress* (de Valois, 1935), *Birthday Offering* (Ashton, 1956), *Concerto* (MacMillan, 1966), *Don Quixote pas de deux* (Petipa, 1869), *Talisman pas de deux* (Petipa, 1889), *Raymonda Act III* (Nureyev after Petipa, 1964).
   Due to the closure of the Royal Opera House, the company gave seasons in London at the Labatt's Apollo, Hammersmith, the Royal Festival Hall, the Barbican Theatre and the London Coliseum. The company toured to Madrid for the first time, performing *The Sleeping Beauty* in November–December 1997, and toured *Cinderella* to Turin in March 1998 and *Cinderella* and *The Sleeping Beauty* to Frankfurt in March–April 1998.
   Two groups of Royal Ballet dancers performed in Sheffield, Blackpool, Bath, High Wycombe, Dartford, Woking, Darlington and Northampton in February–March 1998 (the 'Dance Bites' tour), giving new works by William Tuckett (*Puirt-A-Beul* and *Dream of Angels*), Christopher Wheeldon (*A Royal Ballet*), Ashley Page (*When We Stop Talking*), Cathy Marston (*Words Apart*), Tom Sapsford (*Horseplay*) and Matthew Hart (*Highly Strung*), and works by MacMillan (*Las Hermanas*, 1963) and Forsythe (*In the middle, somewhat elevated*, 1988).
   On 15 June 1998 the company gave a gala performance at

the Barbican Theatre to mark the 100th birthday of Dame Ninette de Valois. It included *The Rake's Progress*, a selection of extracts from other works created by de Valois (including *The Gods Go A-Begging, Job, Orpheus and Eurydice, The Prospect Before Us* (performed by dancers from Birmingham Royal Ballet), *The Haunted Ballroom, Checkmate*, and *Every Goose Can*), a *pas de quatre* created by David Bintley, the finale of *Soirée Musicale* (created by MacMillan in honour of de Valois's 90th birthday and danced by students of the Royal Ballet School) and *Birthday Offering*. Dancers from the Royal Ballet led the Royal Ballet School performance of *La Bayadère* at the London Coliseum on 18 July 1998.

BIRMINGHAM ROYAL BALLET
Founded 1946 as the Sadler's Wells Opera Ballet
Birmingham Hippodrome, Thorp Street, Birmingham B5 4AU
World première:
The Protecting Veil (David Bintley), 3 June 1998. A one-act ballet. Music, John Tavener; design, Ruari Murchison. Dancers, Ambra Vallo, Dorcas Walters, Monica Zamora, Isabel McMeekan, Victoria Marr, Robert Parker, David Justin, Joseph Cipolla, Ander Zabala, Andrew Murphy
Company premières:
Edward II (David Bintley), 9 October 1997. Music, John McCabe; costumes, Jasper Conran; sets, Peter Davison. Cast led by Wolfgang Stollwitzer, Sabrina Lenzi, Andrew Murphy and Joseph Cipolla
   Orpheus (Balanchine), 16 October 1997. Music, Stravinsky; design, Isamu Noguchi. Cast led by Joseph Cipolla, Andrew Murphy, Catherine Batcheller and Chi Cao
   Grosse Fuge (Hans van Manen), 25 February 1998. Music, Beethoven; sets, Jean-Paul Vroom. Cast led by Wolfgang Stollwitzer, Andrew Murphy, Joseph Cipolla and Kevin O'Hare
   The Prospect Before Us (de Valois), 3 June 1998. Music, William Boyce, arr. Constant Lambert; design, Roger Furse after Thomas Rowlandson. Cast led by Michael O'Hare, Joseph Cipolla and David Justin
Full length ballets from the repertoire: *The Nutcracker* (Ivanov, prod. Wright, additional choreography by Vincent Redmon, 1990), *Far from the Madding Crowd* (Bintley, 1996).
   One-act ballets from the repertoire: *Serenade* (Balanchine, 1934), *The Four Temperaments* (Balanchine, 1946), *Symphony in Three Movements* (Balanchine, 1972), *Elite Syncopations* (MacMillan, 1974), *Symphonic Variations* (Ashton, 1946).
   On 20–21 February 1998 a choreographic project was presented in Birmingham. It involved a collaboration between choreographers from within the company, who staged Saint-Saëns' *Carnival of the Animals* and Vivaldi's *The Four Seasons*. Students from the theatre design course at the University of Central England provided sets and costumes.
   In addition to four seasons at the Birmingham Hippodrome, the company toured to Sunderland, Bradford (two seasons), Bristol (two seasons), Plymouth, Liverpool and Manchester. It also toured to South Africa (Johannesburg, Pretoria and Cape Town) in June–July 1998, with *Far from the Madding Crowd, Agon* (Balanchine, 1957) and *Carmina Burana* (Bintley, 1995).

ENGLISH NATIONAL BALLET
Founded 1950 as London Festival Ballet
Markova House, 39 Jay Mews, London SW7 2ES
World premières:
The Nutcracker (Derek Deane), 13 November 1997. Music, Tchaikovsky; design, Sue Blane. Cast led by Tamara Rojo, Greg Horsman, Robert Tewsley and Lucia Lacarra
Romeo and Juliet (Derek Deane), 18 June 1998. A production

staged in the round at the Albert Hall, London. Music, Prokofiev; design, Roberta Guidi di Bagno. Cast led by Tamara Rojo and Roberto Bolle

Full-length ballets from the repertoire: *Swan Lake* (Petipa/ Ivanov, prod. Struchkova 1993), *The Sleeping Beauty* (Petipa, prod. Hynd 1993).

The full company toured to Oxford, Manchester (three seasons), Southampton (two seasons), Liverpool, London (the London Coliseum and the Royal Albert Hall) and Oxford.

In April–May 1998 the company split into two groups and went on two small-scale tours (called *Tour de Force*). One group toured *Square Dance* (Balanchine, 1957), *X N Tricities* (Bigonzetti, 1994) and *Perpetuum Mobile* (Hampson, 1997) to Crawley, Dartford, Poole, Swindon and Reading. The other toured a new work by Christopher Hampson (*Country Garden*), *Sphinx* (Tetley, 1977) and *Who Cares?* (Balanchine, 1970) to Truro, Bexhill-on-Sea, Barnstaple, Scunthorpe and Barrow-in-Furness.

RAMBERT DANCE COMPANY
Founded 1926 as the Marie Rambert Dancers
94 Chiswick High Road, London W4 1SH

World premières:
Greymatter (Didy Veldman), 19 September 1997. Music, Philip Feeney; design, Lez Brotherston
Gaps, Lapse and Relapse (Jeremy James), 20 February 1998. Music, Peter Morris; costumes, John Richmond

Company premières:
No More Play (Jiří Kylián), 29 August 1997. Music, Webern; design, Jiří Kylián and Joke Visser
August Pace (Merce Cunningham), 27 May 1998. Music, Michael Pugliese; design, Afrika (Sergei Bugaev)

Works from the repertoire: *Stream* (Bruce, 1996), *Moonshine* (Bruce, 1993), *Rooster* (Bruce, 1991), *Swansong* (Bruce, 1987), *Petite Mort* (Kylián, 1991), *Port for Angels* (Jonsson, 1997), *Airs* (Taylor, 1978), *Axioma 7* (Naharin, 1991), *Cruel Garden* (Bruce and Kemp, 1977).

The company performed in Manchester, Woking, Bournemouth, Leeds, High Wycombe, Swansea, Cardiff, Nottingham, Plymouth, Truro, Newcastle upon Tyne, Oxford, Edinburgh, Northampton and Norwich. It also toured to Hungary, Germany and Luxembourg in January 1998, and to the USA and Mexico in March 1998.

RICHARD ALSTON DANCE COMPANY
Founded 1994
The Place, 17 Duke's Road, London WC1H 9AB

All works danced by the company are choreographed by Richard Alston.

World premières:
Brisk Singing, 22 October 1997. Music, Jean-Philippe Rameau; design, Jeanne Spaziani
Light Flooding into Darkened Rooms, 22 October 1997. Music, Denis Gaultier and Jo Kondo; costumes, Fotini Dimou
Red Run, 12 February 1998 (commissioned by the Holland Dance Festival and premièred in The Hague). Music, Heiner Goebbels; costumes, Elizabeth Baker
Triple X, 21 February 1998. A solo danced by Jason Piper. Music, Purcell

Works from the repertoire: *Rumours, Visions* (1994), *Orpheus Singing and Dreaming* (1996), *Okho* (1996).

The company performed in Brighton, Cambridge, Huddersfield, Manchester, Horsham, Nottingham, Stevenage, Woking, Birmingham and London (Queen Elizabeth Hall). It also performed in the Netherlands (The Hague) in February 1998 (*see* above) and returned to the Netherlands (Middleburg) in June 1998 to perform *Okho*.

SCOTTISH BALLET
Founded 1956 as the Western Theatre Ballet
261 West Princes Street, Glasgow G4 9EE

World premières:
Just Scratchin' the Surface (Adam Cooper), 4 June 1998. Music, classic jazz recordings including Duke Ellington and Oscar Peterson; design, Lez Brotherston. Cast led by Vladislav Bubnov, Catherine Evers, Preston Clare, Keith Prested, Lorna Scott, Campbell McKenzie and Oliver Rydout
Faerie Feet (Sheridan Nicol), 4 June 1998. Music, the Peat Bog Faeries; cast, ten dancers including Campbell McKenzie

Company première:
La fille mal gardée (Ashton), 20 November 1997. Music, Herold; design, Osbert Lancaster. Cast led by Yurie Shinohara, Campbell McKenzie, Kenn Burke and Wayne Sleep

Full-length ballet from the repertoire: *Tales of Hoffmann* (Darrell, 1972).

One-act ballet from the repertoire: *Five Rückert Songs* (Darrell, 1978).

The company performed in Glasgow (four seasons), Aberdeen, Edinburgh (three seasons) and Newcastle upon Tyne.

Film

'I'm the king of the world!' announced writer-director-producer James Cameron, collecting the Academy Award for best picture 1997, the eleventh Oscar bestowed on his film *Titanic*. Cameron's triumphalism met with widespread derision – especially after he compounded this impression of hubris by writing a letter to the *LA Times* a few days later calling for the 'impeachment' of the newspaper's film critic, Kenneth Turan. Turan's crime? He felt *Titanic* was an unworthy winner, a sentimental melodrama which sinks under trite, anachronistic dialogue and leaden performances.

While many critics echoed Turan's reservations, about the script in particular, the American media gave *Titanic* a rapturous reception on its unveiling in the autumn of 1997. 'It is this generation's *Gone with the Wind*', proclaimed Janet Maslin in the *New York Times*. In Britain, the *Sun* called it 'the movie of the century'. The public appeared to endorse such sentiments. In the States, *Titanic* topped the box-office charts for months, and was still going strong after 32 weeks, with cumulative gross takings of $593 million – and counting. In Britain it was the same story; its record-breaking £68.6 million take ($114 million) represented 25 per cent of the total UK box-office revenue in the first six months of 1998. And world-wide, *Titanic* became the first film to exceed $1 billion. (To keep the numbers in perspective, however, it is worth noting that *Titanic* is only 23rd in the popularity stakes in terms of admissions, having been seen by only half as many people as *Gone with the Wind*.)

Major Disaster

Such success seemed a distant prospect in the summer of 1997, when the film failed to meet its original release date. After five years of planning, James Cameron had got the backing of two major studios, Twentieth Century Fox and Paramount, to secure a budget estimated at $100 million. It wasn't enough. A stickler for detail whose *Terminator* credentials allowed him what amounted to complete autonomy, Cameron had a new production facility built in California to house a 775-foot replica of the famous liner, as well as a 17-million gallon tank in which to sink it. The shooting schedule doubled to six months, rumours circulated about tensions on the set, and the budget came in at a staggering $200 million – another record-breaking figure. Given that the film's fledgling stars Leonardo DiCaprio and Kate Winslet didn't have a box-office hit between them, *Titanic* had all the hallmarks of a studio-bankrupting flop – more like *Heaven's Gate* than *Gone with the Wind*. It reached the point where Cameron forwent his own directing fees in order to get the film finished.

In the event, he was richly rewarded for his faith; Fox and Paramount voluntarily recompensed him to the tune of $75 million when the film's success became clear. And the film itself? At 195 minutes, it takes its time to get going, but there is no mistaking the sense of scale and spectacle. Cameron exploits state-of-the-art digital special effects to create a genuine awe. It is true that his story is melodrama at its most contrived and simplistic: penniless young artist and adventurer Jack (DiCaprio) steals the aristocratic Rose (Winslet) from her rich, arrogant fiancé (played as a sneering villain by Billy Zane). But aside from the obvious points about class and women's role in society – Rose is a rebel spirit, and indeed takes the most active role in subsequent events – this framework does provide an irresistible point of emotional entry for the disaster that strikes some two hours into the picture. And it is as a disaster movie that *Titanic* most impresses. It captures not just the initial terror of the collision, but sustains and embellishes this mood, as the ship lists, breaks up, and finally goes down. This horribly prolonged 'sinking feeling' is no less apocalyptic a vision than the nuclear nightmares of Cameron's *Terminator* films, and might justifiably be seen as Hollywood's darkest hour: sixty minutes of panic, corruption, murder and chaos, culminating in the terrible sight of hundreds of ghostly pale shadows freezing in the icy black waters.

Deep and Meaningful?

Regardless of its fiercely debated merit (and it could not hold a candle to Curtis Hanson's superb film noir *LA Confidential*, which had to content itself with four Academy Awards, including best adapted screenplay and best supporting actress), *Titanic*'s significance will be profound in industry terms. If the film had sunk without trace, it might conceivably have spelled the end of the blockbuster era. Hollywood had already shown signs of concern after the high-profile disappointments of *Speed 2*, *Batman and Robin*, and *The Lost World*. In a ratio of cost-to-profit, these big budget spectaculars were outclassed by the likes of *Bean* and *The Full Monty*. While *Titanic* represented a huge commercial gamble, the fact that it hit the jackpot will probably have an inflationary effect on American film-making as a whole. Certainly, Leonardo DiCaprio's fee has gone up more than tenfold to about $20 million a film.

'Does this mean size does matter?' asked Cameron, rhetorically, in another acceptance speech (this time for the Golden Globes). The point was echoed in the advertising tag line for the second most-hyped movie of the year, *Godzilla*: 'Size does matter'. This American remake of the popular Japanese movie monster was supposed to emulate the success of *Independence Day*, also from the director-writer team Roland Emmerich and Dean Devlin. The budget this time was about $120 million, although Sony spent another $50 million on promotion in the USA. These kinds of sums only add up in a global marketplace, which is why *Godzilla*, like so many contemporary American films, aims for simplicity, spectacle and noise over sophistication and wit – qualities which do not necessarily translate internationally. The pitfalls are amply demonstrated in the sloppily over-extended *Godzilla*, which stumbled to a domestic box-office total of $134 million.

While *Godzilla* confined itself to destroying New York landmarks, *Deep Impact* and *Armageddon* progressed from the Big Apple to flood the entire US eastern seaboard (*Deep Impact*), decimate Paris (*Armageddon*), and threaten the entire world (both). Sharing identical plots about a meteor on collision course with Earth, the films were distinguishable along gender lines. Mimi Leder's *Deep Impact* adopted a passive, feminine, spiritual approach, and starred Téa Leoni as a TV reporter coming to terms with her own demise; Michael Bay's *Armageddon* opted for a gung-ho machismo with Bruce Willis committing hara-kiri in outer space to save the world. Whether these four films (the most commercially successful in the first six months of 1998) represent some kind of millennial *Zeitgeist* at work, or simply a new phase in the development of digital effects, is anyone's guess.

ODDLY INTELLIGENT

Mercifully, against all the odds, strains of intelligence persist in American film-making. These can be divided into two schools: the raw recruits and the veterans, as exemplified in the nominees for the 1997 best actor Oscar: Jack Nicholson (*As Good As It Gets*), his old *Easy Rider* comrade Peter Fonda (*Ulee's Gold*), Robert Duvall (*The Apostle*), Dustin Hoffman (*Wag the Dog*), and Matt Damon (*Good Will Hunting*). The 27-year-old Damon was the only one aged under 55. He co-wrote *Good Will Hunting* with his equally youthful friend and co-star Ben Affleck in frustration at the roles they were being offered, and though this tale of a brilliant mind trapped in working-class neuroses was a little too pat, it was sensitively handled by director Gus van Sant, and full of charming touches. Another of van Sant's protegés, 23-year-old Harmony Korine, followed up his script for the controversial *Kids* with a breathtakingly audacious directorial début, *Gummo*. This semi-documentary portrait of an imaginary Ohio town, and especially its delinquent youth, incorporated techniques from cinéma-vérité, surrealism and absurdism to produce a shocking, provocative, but ultimately liberating assault on middle-class pieties.

More conventional, but still very fresh, was Paul Thomas Anderson's *Boogie Nights*, a bravura second film which borrowed from *GoodFellas* and *Nashville* to make what must stand as the definitive chronicle of the 1970s' and 1980s' porn scene. A mite exhibitionist, perhaps, but then Anderson has plenty to boast about, and after his slinkily subtle first film, *Hard Eight*, was ignored, who can blame him for wanting to make a bit of a stir? Impressed by his flair and cine-literacy, critics inevitably dubbed Anderson the 'new Tarantino', but the old one proved he should not be underestimated with his long-awaited *Jackie Brown*, a mature, intelligent adaptation of Elmore Leonard's novel *Rum Punch*. Although Robert De Niro and Samuel L. Jackson did sterling work in supporting roles, the central love story fell on the unlikely shoulders of 1970s' cult icons Pam Grier and Robert Forster, both of whom turned in career-revitalizing performances. Tarantino, clearly, had done a lot of growing up in the four years since *Pulp Fiction*.

Veterans like De Niro can use their clout to get 'difficult' films made, and, when they're made, get them noticed. Hoffman's participation in the topical White House satire *Wag the Dog* is a case in point. Scripted by David Mamet and Hillary Henkin over a matter of days, and shot in less than a month, *Wag the Dog* was an unruly comedy in which a US president mounts a virtual war with Albania in order to deflect attention from a brewing sex scandal. It made up in topicality what it lost in finesse – but it would never have seen the light of day if it had gone through the conventional studio development system.

CRIME OF PASSION

Duvall's *The Apostle* is another telling example. Long established as one of the best actors in the business, Duvall is nevertheless not deemed a sufficient box-office draw to get the go-ahead for his own projects. He therefore spent $5 million of his own money to finance his second feature film as writer and director, a subtle, moving tale of a Southern evangelist who murders his ex-wife's lover in a fit of passion and moves to a backwater town to seek his redemption in the eyes of God. Duvall does not turn a blind eye to his preacher's faults, nor to his virtues. It is a warm, heartfelt film with a marvellous performance from Duvall at its centre.

The results are not always so effective, but other examples of ageing stars flexing their creative muscles include Clint Eastwood directing the languorous, eccentric character piece *Midnight in the Garden of Good and Evil*, Robert Redford's *The Horse Whisperer*, Woody Allen's *Deconstructing Harry*, and, most bizarrely, Warren Beatty's *Bulworth*, a political fable in which Beatty's suicidal US senator suddenly decides to speak the truth about racial and social discrimination. But there are few directors with this kind of power. Both Robert Altman and Francis Coppola were reduced to adapting John Grisham legal thrillers in search of elusive commercial success. Coppola earned his best reviews for a long time with *John Grisham's The Rainmaker*, to give it its full title, but despite the presence of Matt Damon in the lead, and an excellent ensemble cast, the film never caught the public's imagination. In

Altman's case, the plan backfired completely, with *The Gingerbread Man* failing to satisfy his fans or Grisham's after painful wrangling with PolyGram over the final cut. PolyGram were more indulgent towards the Coen brothers, whose *The Big Lebowski* was a wild and woolly but often wonderfully entertaining comic homage to Raymond Chandler and to Altman's film of *The Long Goodbye*.

Martin Scorsese was allowed to make *Kundun*, a mesmeric, visionary film about the early life of the 14th Dalai Lama, up to and including his flight from the Chinese, but the picture proved too exotic to withstand mixed reviews and a half-hearted publicity campaign by Buena Vista (who were involved in delicate negotiations with the Chinese at the time). *Kundun* was the most artistically arresting and adventurous movie to come out of a Hollywood studio this year, but it was treated as an aberration – which, in a way, it was.

SPIELBERG AT WAR

Steven Spielberg, of course, writes his own ticket. While his Dreamworks SKG studio has yet to find an identity of its own, Spielberg himself is going through a productive spell. The disappointingly didactic *Amistad* was eclipsed within six months by the appearance of *Saving Private Ryan*, a Second World War platoon story of ground-breaking power and honesty starring a restrained Tom Hanks and the ubiquitous Matt Damon. From the opening 30-minute salvo of the D-Day landings, it is clear this is virtuoso film-making. Spielberg restates his reputation as the most technically accomplished director of his generation, but he allies that here with a fine script and a profound compassion. 'What is a man's life worth in war?', the film asks, crucially holding us to account.

Despite its graphic violence, *Saving Private Ryan* opened to excellent box-office in the USA and will doubtless figure prominently in next year's Academy Awards, where its main competition is likely to come from Peter Weir's *The Truman Show*. This Jim Carrey vehicle exploits an ingenious post-modern conceit; Truman Burbank grows up in the island town of Sea Haven, entirely oblivious to the fact that everyone around him is an actor in a reality soap opera. Andrew Niccol's script works both as a satire on a society reaching media saturation point, and as an existential parable, with Truman as Everyman, pleading with the unseen 'eye-in-the-sky', his director, Christoff (played with beady authority by Ed Harris). The most memorable comedy since *Groundhog Day*, *The Truman Show* was the best surprise of what turned out to be a better-than-average year.

Although Britain could point to a number of notable film successes, the biggest stories happened behind the scenes. A round of musical chairs saw many of the powerful figures in the industry moving offices. David Aukin, head of Film Four, was lured away to form a new production company, HAL, along with Trea Hoving and Colin Levanthal, as a

British adjunct to the American company Miramax. Aukin was succeeded at Film Four by Paul Webster, himself an old Miramax man. At the British Film Institute (BFI), Alan Parker succeeded Jeremy Thomas as president, and John Woodward left the producers' organization, PACT, to replace Wilf Stevenson as director. Andreas Whittam Smith was appointed president of the British Board of Film Classification in time to usher through Adrian Lyne's *Lolita* uncut, and James Ferman announced that he would retire at the end of 1998 after two decades as the public face of the board. PolyGram, the Dutch entertainment conglomerate, was sold and immediately put its predominantly British-led film division on the market. The first-ever Minister for Film, Tom Clarke, lost his job in the Cabinet reshuffle in July 1998, and even Barry Norman made a move – he switched to Sky, 26 years after he launched BBC1's *Film '72*.

LACKING INSPIRATION

While the Lottery franchise scheme that had been announced with much fanfare at Cannes 1997 proved a slow-starter (six films in production, none yet released), the Arts Council's own independent Lottery-backed productions tended to fall into a middle-brow no-man's-land; *Keep the Aspidistra Flying*, *The Woodlanders*, *Shooting Fish* and *Love and Death on Long Island* had their supporters, but lacked that spark of inspiration which might have silenced those critics carping about the misuse of public funds.

The film policy review group set up by the Government reported in March 1998. Chaired by PolyGram's Stewart Till, the review called for an All-Industry Fund, a voluntary levy on film and video exhibitors and distributors to support British film development and distribution to the tune of £15 million. While the industry remained sceptical about this plan, tax breaks for film production announced by the Chancellor, Gordon Brown, were universally welcomed as a further stimulant to a film-making scene now reaching critical mass – begging the question, what is to become of all those British films shot opportunistically with insufficient development and little prospect of finding an audience? (In 1996, 40 per cent of the 128 films shot in Britain went unreleased.)

In July 1998 the Secretary of State for Culture, Chris Smith, announced a radical overhaul of the support network for the arts, including film. He outlined a process of streamlining and rationalization leading to the merger of all public film institutions in a new body, provisionally known as the Film Council. While the plans call for a three-month consultation period, there seems little doubt that the BFI, British Screen Finance and the British Film Commission will be brought together. The new Film Council will probably have a dual role, a cultural remit on the one hand and an industrial one on the other, and will probably take over the disbursement of Lottery film funds from the Arts

Councils. On the same day as Smith's announcement, the BFI announced its own restructuring programme, giving priority to education and national accessibility over feature film production, and effectively preparing the 66-year-old institute for its own demise. The one gaping hole in the Government's vision is its failure to support avant-garde independent experimental film-making, the sector traditionally backed by the BFI and which has given us such celebrated directors as Derek Jarman, Peter Greenaway, Bill Douglas and Terence Davies. Ironically, in what may prove its last year, BFI production came up with two acclaimed features, *Under the Skin* and *Love is the Devil*, which rather put the Lottery-funded films to shame.

ACADEMIC SUCCESS

On screen, it was the usual mixed bag of hits and misses. Notable among the former was the continuing popularity of *The Full Monty* (which garnered four Oscar nominations and picked up the statuette for best score), an impressive four Academy Award nominations in the best actress category – though Judi Dench (*Mrs Brown*), Kate Winslet (*Titanic*), Julie Christie (*Afterglow*) and Helena Bonham Carter (*The Wings of the Dove*) all lost out to Helen Hunt for *As Good As It Gets* – and a significant home-grown hit in *Sliding Doors*, a clever romantic comedy with Gwyneth Paltrow, John Hannah and John Lynch. Ironically, like *The Full Monty*, this took an injection of American support – in the form of producer Sydney Pollack – to get made, and owed a lot of its appeal to the American star Paltrow (sporting an impeccable London accent).

Sadly, while the cinema-going habit continues to grow throughout Britain (spurred on by the continued proliferation of multiplex cinemas), Hollywood still dominates our screens. Foreign language titles are playing to smaller and smaller audiences, and the repertory circuit is crumbling. In 1998, the only foreign films to attract much attention were Almódovar's *Live Flesh* – his best film in a decade – and Abbas Kiarostami's Cannes 1997 winner *The Taste of Cherry*. Neither played more than a handful of screens outside London. The rule for British films is not much more encouraging. Twenty-five-year-old Shane Meadows made an auspicious feature-length début with the chirpy drama *TwentyFour Seven*, but despite a wide release and an expensive advertising campaign it proved a box-office flop. It was the same story with John Boorman's *The General* and Neil Jordan's *The Butcher Boy* – examples of a spirited revival in Irish film-making which met with apathy on the British mainland.

But the best British film of the year was undoubtedly Gary Oldman's first film as writer-director, *Nil by Mouth*. With its hand-held camera-work, brutal honesty and searing performances from Ray Winstone and Kathy Burke, this overwhelming autobiographical account of domestic strife, drug abuse and alcoholism in south-east London recalled the immediacy and impact of John Cassavetes and Alan

Clarke. Typically, it took the French Hollywood director Luc Besson to secure financial backing, but here at least was an authentically British film that cried out to be seen.

FILM AWARD WINNERS

ACADEMY AWARDS 1997
Best picture – *Titanic*
Best director – James Cameron, *Titanic*
Best actor – Jack Nicholson, *As Good as it Gets*
Best actress – Helen Hunt, *As Good as it Gets*
Best supporting actor – Robin Williams, *Good Will Hunting*
Best supporting actress – Kim Basinger, *LA Confidential*
Best original screenplay – *Good Will Hunting*
Best adapted screenplay – *LA Confidential*
Best foreign language film – *Character* (Netherlands)
Best original musical or comedy score – *The Full Monty*
Best original dramatic score – *Titanic*
Best original song – 'My Heart Will Go On', *Titanic*
Best cinematography – *Titanic*
Best art direction – *Titanic*
Best film editing – *Titanic*
Best costume design – *Titanic*
Best sound – *Titanic*
Best sound effects editing – *Titanic*
Best visual effects – *Titanic*
Best make-up – *Men in Black*
Best animated short – *Geri's Game*
Best documentary feature – *The Long Way Home*
Best short documentary – *A Story of Healing*
Best live action short – *Visas and Virtue*
Lifetime achievement – Stanley Donen

BAFTA AWARDS 1997
Best film – *The Full Monty*
David Lean award (best achievement in direction) – Baz
    Luhrmann, *William Shakespeare's Romeo and Juliet*
Best actor – Robert Carlyle, *The Full Monty*
Best actress – Judi Dench, *Mrs Brown*
Best supporting actor – Tom Wilkinson, *The Full Monty*
Best supporting actress – Sigourney Weaver, *The Ice
    Maiden*
Alexander Korda award (British film of the year) – *Nil By
    Mouth*
Best foreign language film – *L'Appartement*
Best original screenplay – Gary Oldman, *Nil By Mouth*
Best adapted screenplay – Craig Pearce and Baz
    Luhrmann, *William Shakespeare's Romeo and Juliet*
Academy Fellowship – Sean Connery

CANNES FESTIVAL 1998
Palme d'Or – *Mia Eoniotita Ke Mia Mera (Eternity and a Day)*
Best director – John Boorman, *The General*
Best actor – Peter Mullan, *My Name is Joe*
Best actress (joint) – Elodie Bouchez, Natacha Regnier, *La
    Vie Revée des Anges*
Grand Jury prize – *La Vita e Bella*

BERLIN FESTIVAL 1998
Best film (Golden Bear) – *Central Station*
Special Jury prize (Silver Bear) – *Wag the Dog*
Best director – Neil Jordan, *The Butcher Boy*
Best actor – Samuel L. Jackson, *Jackie Brown*
Best actress – Fernanda Montenegro, *Central Station*

Literature

The death of Diana, Princess of Wales in August 1997 led to a tide of books about her; 15 were announced within a fortnight of her death. The most controversial was the revised edition of Andrew Morton's *Diana: Her True Story* (Michael O'Mara), which was published in October 1997 and went straight to the top of the bestseller lists. It sold nearly 76,000 copies in the first four weeks, boosted by Morton's 'revelation' that the Princess had indeed been the source of the information it contained. At the same time there was a strong backlash against Morton who was perceived to be profiting from the Princess's death; there was no significant change in the content of the book from the original 1992 text. Morton's companion volume *Diana: Her New Life* was also reprinted and reached the bestseller lists; and the same publisher's picture book *Diana: Her Life in Pictures* sold well. Together these titles boosted Michael O'Mara to the status of third most profitable publisher in the UK by the end of the year.

Distaste about the speed at which publishers leapt on the Diana bandwagon led to pledges from many in the book trade to make contributions to the Princess's favourite charities, or to her memorial fund, among them a percentage of profits from Quadrillion's *Diana: A Tribute to the People's Princess* by Peter Donnelly (which had a print run of over a million copies) and from photographer Tim Graham's *Diana, Princess of Wales: A Tribute* (Weidenfeld). And the full cover price of *Flowers in the Park* (Martin Miller), a collection of photographs of the floral tributes, was donated.

Julie Burchill wrote an angry, idiosyncratic and much derided song of praise, *Diana* (Weidenfeld), in the same year as she published her own defiantly titled and variously received memoir *I Knew I Was Right*. Beatrix Campbell's *Diana, Princess of Wales: How Sexual Politics Shook the Monarchy* (Women's Press) expressed a republican, feminist view of Diana as the victim of an outdated institution. There were psychological and theological interpretations of the reactions to her death, such as *When a Princess Dies: Reflections from Jungian Analysts* (Harvest) edited by Jane Haynes and Ann Shearer, and Ted Harrison's *Diana: Icon and Sacrifice* (Lion). There were other picture books, for example the bestselling *Diana: Portrait of a Princess* by Jayne Fincher (Taschen Callaway) and recyclings of Morton's revelations, as in *Diana: The Untold Story* (Boxtree) by Richard Kay and Geoffrey Levy. In *Diana: Her Life in Fashion* (Pavilion), Georgina Howell argued that Diana's choice of clothes was symbolic. A New Jersey mother, Mary Robertson, who briefly employed Diana as a nanny, wrote *The Diana I Knew* (Piatkus), offering such aperçus as the fact that her appetite was still healthy at the age of 18. And there were children's books, including Nicholas Allan's simplistic cartoon *The Happy Princess* (Red Fox), Ladybird's *Diana: Princess of Wales: A Tribute to Our Princess*, and a photographic record of the tributes of children by Ruth Corney with text by Diana's cousin Robert Spencer, *To Diana with Love from the Children* (Piccadilly Press).

MATTERS OF PRINCIPLE

In February and March 1998 the publishing house HarperCollins took a beating from the press after Stuart Proffitt, publisher of its trade division, resigned. He claimed he was leaving on principle because Rupert Murdoch, chairman and chief executive of HarperCollins, opposed the publication of *East and West*, by Chris Patten, the last governor of Hong Kong. The book, about Patten's time as governor and about the future of Far Eastern economies, had been signed up in July 1997, but Murdoch was allegedly concerned that Patten's criticisms of China's communist regime would damage his NewsCorp business interests in southeast Asia.

An outcry ensued about editorial interference by the proprietor of a conglomerate, and about cowardice in the face of Chinese totalitarianism. The resignation of one individual – which was complicated by the fact that Proffitt was said to be unhappy about a recent restructuring within the company, and rumoured to have had 'uneasy relationships with other staff' – turned into a national row about commercial interests and freedom of speech. HarperCollins authors, including Simon Heffer, Jonathan Power and Timothy Garton Ash, deserted their publisher in protest, returning advances. Eight others, including Fay Weldon, Penelope Fitzgerald, Doris Lessing and Sir Frank Kermode, spoke out against the decision not to publish Patten's book. Jung Chang, whose book about three generations of her Chinese family, *Wild Swans*, had been a huge bestseller for HarperCollins, took her next book elsewhere. Chris Patten's agent, Michael Sissons of Peters, Fraser and Dunlop, refused for a while to submit any new material to the publisher. Meanwhile Rupert Murdoch accused the senior managers at HarperCollins of 'screwing up' because they had 'invented' reasons why they did not want to publish, fobbing Patten off with the suggestion that it was the disappointing quality of the book that had prompted them to withdraw from the contract.

There was a general feeling that, aside from the issue of censorship, Patten had not been dealt with honestly. Proffitt sued the company for constructive dismissal, and Patten sued it for breach of contract. Patten's book was resold to Macmillan, which had originally matched the £125,000 that HarperCollins had bid for the book at auction.

Proffitt edited the book as a freelance. He then also found a new job as publishing director at Penguin Press. HarperCollins sustained what was felt to be a 'serious self-inflicted wound', but even so the company and its managers were not without their sympathisers. Some authors, including John Major and novelist Frank Delaney, remained loyal.

QUESTIONS OVER CENSORSHIP

In May Macmillan published a book by Gitta Sereny that had been announced in its catalogue without any descriptive blurb. It turned out to be *Cries Unheard*, about Mary Bell who, as a child herself, had smothered two other children. Sereny had previously written about this subject in *The Case of Mary Bell* (1972) but *Cries Unheard* was written with the co-operation of Bell, now in her forties and living under a new identity. It caused outrage because part of the advance was paid to Bell for her contribution. Questions were asked in the House of Commons about whether this was proper and the Prime Minister declared that it was not. The tabloids tracked down Bell, who was living with her daughter, and revealed her history. Bookshops in Newcastle upon Tyne, where Bell committed the murders, refused to display the book, as did the Waterstone's branch in Harrods. Nonetheless it sold 2,500 copies in the first week of publication, after serialization in the press, taking it to the top of the non-fiction bestseller lists. Sereny, whose previous book was the award-winning *Albert Speer: His Battle with Truth*, and who has become something of a specialist in investigating and explaining 'evil' behaviour, gave a sympathetic account of the life of Bell, who was herself the victim of abuse as a child. Hostility to the book concentrated on the payment made to Bell, but there were also those who went so far as to say that it should never have been published at all. This reopened the debate about censorship, as well as raising questions about whether there are limits to what a biographer may do.

Other instances of censorship occurred during the year. In October 1997, a student copied pictures from a book of photographs by Robert Mapplethorpe, which had been published in 1992. The West Midlands police were called in to investigate, and seized copies of the book from the library at the University of Central England. The Crown Prosecution Service advised in March 1998 that *Mapplethorpe: Photographs* could be breaking the obscenity laws. The publisher, Cape, refused to withdraw the book from sale. If the police mount a successful prosecution, all copies of a book by a respected artist, which was published more than five years ago, will have to be destroyed.

Police officers also took action over promotional posters in a Southampton bookshop which reproduced the cover of Irvine Welsh's novel *Filth*, showing the image of a pig in a policeman's helmet. Two passing policemen took offence and confiscated the posters. These were eventually returned, and put back in the window, with a sign explaining what they were about. Meanwhile at Muswell Hill in London, a local community police officer asked for the posters to be removed from a bookshop window. There were those who felt this censorship was petty and ridiculous, and others who believed the posters were an incitement to abuse and should not be displayed out of courtesy to the police.

PRIZE CARPING

In 1997 there was much carping, as usual, over the Booker Prize, which unusually went to a first novel, Arundhati Roy's *The God of Small Things*. The grumblers complained that the shortlist included relative unknowns, notably Madeleine St John (*The Essence of the Thing*) and Mick Jackson (*The Underground Man*), and overlooked such expected contenders as John Banville (*The Untouchable*), Ian McEwan (*Enduring Love*) and Carol Shields, whose *Larry's Party* went on to win the Orange Prize for Fiction.

The Orange Prize was itself controversial; the shortlist included only one work by a British author, Pauline Melville's *The Ventriloquist's Tale*, set in Guyana. The press was stirred up by the implication that British novels were inferior. The list also included what would generally be regarded as genre titles, notably Deirdre Purcell's romance *Love, Like, Hate, Adore*.

In October 1997 the Orange Prize launched an initiative that tapped into a trend in British reading habits; the spread of reading groups, informal gatherings in people's homes at which the members, principally but not exclusively women, recommend to each other and discuss books. The prize organizers invited groups to register, and offered discounts on books on the Orange shortlist; they also produced a pack that suggested how to set up and run a reading group. Celebrities who were already reading group members backed Orange's initiative, and the features pages of the press observed the trend at length.

Such grass-roots groups have now established themselves firmly in British culture. Not only do they stimulate the nation's literary life, helping to make reading fashionable, sociable and fun, but they also nurture word-of-mouth bestsellers: books whose sales escalate long after the initial promotion. In 1998 the bestseller lists consistently featured *Bridget Jones's Diary* by Helen Fielding (Picador, first published in July 1997) and Louis de Bernières's *Captain Corelli's Mandolin* (Minerva, first published in May 1995), prime examples of word-of-mouth sellers. Both were acknowledged in the British Book Awards, where they took the Author of the Year and the Book of the Year awards respectively.

Another phenomenon much remarked upon during the year was the continuing success of 'The Little Books', small volumes of aphorisms and tips for living, priced at £1.99 and published by Penguin. *The Little Book of Calm* by Paul Wilson was the most successful of these, originally published in October

1996 and still lingering around the top of the bestseller lists some two years later. *The Little Book of Hugs* was close behind and others sold in quantity, including *The Little Book of Dreams* by Joan Hanger. Inevitably, two spoofs came out, and also became bestsellers: Craig Brown's *The Little Book of Chaos* (Warner) and Rohan Candappa's *The Little Book of Stress* (Ebury), somewhat undermining conclusions that the success of the original had to do with a change in the national psyche, and a (possibly post-Diana) surge in the desire for inner peace.

John Gray's *Men Are From Mars, Women Are From Venus* (Thorsons) continued to dominate sales of popular psychology books. It had originally been published in May 1993 and pigeonholed differences between the sexes in a seductive if spurious way. Bill Bryson's travel books journeyed up and down the paperback lists, without wandering beyond them – *Notes from a Small Island* (first published in August 1996) and *Neither Here Nor There* (out in July 1998). Sebastian Junger's *The Perfect Storm*, about a tragic accident at sea in freak conditions, was an unusual and consistent bestseller for Fourth Estate. And a particularly popular fiction début was comic actor Ardal O'Hanlon's black and alienated comedy *The Talk of the Town* (Sceptre).

Significant new fiction published during the year included Don de Lillo's much lauded epic of American life, *Underworld* (Picador), William Boyd's enjoyably farcical *Armadillo* (Hamish Hamilton), Nadine Gordimer's *The House Gun* (Bloomsbury) about a middle-class South African on trial for murder, John Updike's novel of historical reflections from 2020, *Toward the End of Time* (Hamish Hamilton), Toni Morrison's disturbing and much praised *Paradise* (Chatto), Anne Tyler's fine black comedy *A Patchwork Planet* (Chatto), and Jane Smiley's *The All True Travels of Lidie Newton*, set during the Civil War, and bought for a six-figure sum by the publisher, Flamingo. Sebastian Faulks, whose last novel, *Birdsong*, was a literary bestseller, had a new book, about the adventures of a young woman in occupied France in 1942, *Charlotte Gray* (Hutchinson), and Nick Hornby followed *High Fidelity* with *About a Boy* (Gollancz), which explored the social value of a knowledge of popular culture through the relationship between a vacuous bachelor and a nerdy schoolboy; it sold film rights before publication.

A novel that attracted an unusual amount of opprobrium was Hanif Kureishi's *Intimacy*, the narrative of a man who leaves his wife, as Kureishi had just done. Many saw it as a justification for his own actions, and attacked it for the smugness and callousness of its protagonist. Others, such as Craig Raine, damned it for pretentiousness of style. However, the personal and critical hostility it aroused failed to keep it out of the bestseller lists.

Writers revealed in more depth during the year included Truman Capote, whose life was conscientiously researched by George Plimpton, editor of the *Paris Review*, Alexander Solzhenitsyn, whose biography by D. M. Thomas was well received, William Hazlitt, whose life and work were reassessed by Tom Paulin, and Gore Vidal, who was dissected by Fred Kaplan. The reclusive J. D. Salinger fell from his pedestal with the publication of a memoir, *At Home in the World* by Joyce Maynard, who had been seduced by him at the age of 16, and lived with him for two years before being coldly dismissed. She recorded, among other peculiarities and defects of his behaviour, his obsessive fastidiousness about food, claiming her book was not an act of revenge but an autobiography in which he happened to have a bit part.

BOOK DAY TAKES OFF

1998 was remarkable for the success, on 23 April (Shakespeare's birthday), of the second World Book Day. The first had been orchestrated at only three months' notice in 1997, and, though useful groundwork was done, it was not until 1998 that the one-day bookfest came into its own. Twelve million £1 vouchers, funded by the book trade (and not, as was misconstrued, by the Government) were distributed to schoolchildren across the country, thanks to sponsorship from Securicor and the support of the Department for Education and Employment. Schools, bookshops and libraries around Britain staged special book-related events: readathons, book quizzes, competitions, readings, storytellers, author visits, performances and (in the shops) daylong discounts; institutions produced their own collections of favourite reads, and bookshop customers were invited to write their own reviews; book events went into the streets, shopping centres and hospitals; and children and celebrities assembled for a partially televised event at the Globe Theatre in London. The BBC also joined in with daily short films during the preceding fortnight in which celebrities enthused about their favourite books – Tony Blair chose *Ivanhoe* – as well as a book quiz, a documentary about world literature on the day, and many references in its children's programmes. A specially commissioned book was published at £1, for those who could spend no more than their voucher: *The Children's Book of Books*, a compilation of choices by celebrities of their favourite children's books, with extracts – this time Tony Blair chose Tolkien. The day did not go off entirely without a hitch. The voucher scheme depended on the goodwill of booksellers to honour it, and *The Children's Book of Books*, which was supplied free to bookshops, was intended to offset losses. But, while 12 million vouchers were distributed, only one million copies were produced of *The Children's Book of Books*. These tended to be snapped up by the big chains, and some smaller independent bookshops were unable to get them. A few opted out of the scheme in protest. On the whole, though, the British book trade was very pleased with the impact on business, and there is enthusiasm for a repeat of the voucher scheme next year. Book sales were substantially up in the weeks around 23 April.

There is an international aspect to World Book Day. The idea originated in Spain, where in Barcelona on St George's Day friends have exchanged books and roses since 1926. Last year 38 other countries celebrated World Book Day too. This year the Internet enabled a good many school and library projects to network internationally, allowing reviews and recommendations to be exchanged. Hammicks bookshops also teamed up with Oxfam shops so that customers could bring unwanted books for resale in aid of world-wide literacy schemes. Many of the fund-raising activities tied in with the day donated proceeds to Book Aid International, which supplies books to countries in need.

1999, will, however, see more than one day's celebration of reading in Britain. The National Year of Reading begins in September 1998, with different themes for events around the country each month: stories in September, poetry in October, pre-school books in November, plays in December and so on. Liz Attenborough, former director of Penguin Children's Books, has been appointed director of the promotional year. And a London Festival of Literature, to be held in March 1999, received £200,000 from the National Lottery Arts for Everyone.

AMERICAN INVASION

The experience of book buying took a dramatic turn this year, when a giant American bookselling chain entered the British market. In September 1997 Borders bought the London-based Books Etc. chain for £40 million, and in August 1998 the first Borders Bookstore opened on Oxford Street in London. Stores are also planned to open in 1999 in Brighton, Leeds, Glasgow and on London's Charing Cross Road. This development is both a symptom and a catalyst of a change in the nature of British bookshops, which will be vying with each other to offer the public a more sophisticated book buying experience. The chains now compete to be not merely shops but 'leisure environments' to which we go 'destination shopping', in order not just to buy books but to listen to music, read a newspaper, have a coffee or even a pint – Borders is the first British bookshop to have a licensed bar. (Since its opening Borders had a bit of trouble with members of the public sitting down at the centrally located grand piano that was intended for special events, and playing it.) The new Waterstone's in Glasgow is another example of the 'category killer' as retailing jargon would have it, already offering an environment along American lines even before the arrival of Borders. It boasts a coffee shop, Internet café, sofas and listening posts. Now the British chain is set to put up a fight for custom with the new Borders wherever branches appear; an Oxford Street Waterstone's, for instance, is to open in the year 2000 slightly closer to the Underground than the Borders bookstore. Book buyers will be well served on the nation's high streets, unless there are casualties in the battle between the giants. Meanwhile there are rumours that another US bookselling chain, Barnes and Noble, is looking for a foothold in the UK. London's Charing Cross Road, the traditional heartland of British bookselling, came under threat during the year from high rents that could close down some of its specialist independent bookshops; it is hoped that negotiations with the landlord, the Soho Housing Association, will save them.

For those who do not want to go out to buy books in the new leisure environment, it is increasingly possible to buy them in the incomparably leisurely environment of their own home. Internet bookselling has arrived. Amazon.com, the Internet bookseller and one of the fastest-growing companies in the USA, bought a UK Web retailer called Bookpages; and not to be outdone W. H. Smith bought the Internet Bookshop, the largest retailer of its kind in Europe. Many publishers and leading UK booksellers now trade through the Net – arguably, bookshops have to have the sofas, pianos and coffee shops to make going out worthwhile.

It was a good year for 20-year-old Oxford undergraduate Richard Mason, who sold his first novel, *The Drowning People*, along with a follow-up novel, to Michael Joseph and Penguin for just over £100,000 (though the idea gained currency in the media that he had been paid over £200,000). Mainly written when he was 19, the novel is a murder mystery narrated by a 60-year-old man who has just killed his wife; his story goes back 40 years to a betrayal by his wife's identical cousin, the narrator's 'first grand passion'. Despite the author's youth, the publisher praised his 'old-fashioned, formal style', but the press seemed even more excited about his Hugh Grantish good looks. *The Drowning People* also commanded a six-figure advance from a German publisher, and film rights were sold for over $1 million. Publication is planned for spring 1999.

Richard Mason was not the only young author to strike a deal with a publisher during the year. Erica Jong's daughter, Molly Jong-Fast, was signed up by Hodder on the basis of two chapters. The book-to-be, *Girl*, optimistically compared to *The Beautiful and the Damned*, also found publishers in Germany and the USA, but will not appear until the year 2000, when the author will have reached the ripe old age of 21.

BIG HIT WITH WIZARDS

In the world of children's books, one of the great commercial and critical successes was J. K. Rowling's *Harry Potter and the Philosopher's Stone* (Bloomsbury), which won the Smarties Prize, the British Book Awards Children's Book of the Year and the Children's Book Award, and was shortlisted for the Carnegie Medal and the *Guardian* Fiction Prize (surprisingly, it did not appear on the Whitbread children's novel shortlist). It tells the story of a boy who goes to a boarding school for wizards, and has been a huge hit with children. *Harry Potter and The Chamber of Secrets*, the second of a planned seven-book series (all of which were worked out by the author before the first was published), immediately topped both adult and children's hardback bestseller lists on publication in August.

For the first time, the Royal Mail sponsored the Library Association's prestigious Carnegie Medal. It was won by a relative unknown, Tim Bowler, for his lyrical exploration of bereavement, *River Boy*. A set of stamps celebrating children's literature was launched at the Carnegie award ceremony. Among the books commemorated by the stamps were *The Lion, The Witch and the Wardrobe* in honour of the

centenary of the birth of C. S. Lewis (1898–1963). The year also saw the centenary of the death of Lewis Carroll (1832–1898), and the 40th birthday of Michael Bond's Paddington Bear, both of which were marked by publishing ventures and exhibitions at London museums. Meanwhile BBC Radio 4's children's book programme, *Treasure Islands*, invited listeners to vote for their favourite children's authors; perennial favourite Roald Dahl came out on top.

LITERARY PRIZEWINNERS

Nobel Prize 1998 – Dario Fo

Commonwealth Writers Prize 1998 – Peter Carey, *Jack Maggs*

First work – Tim Wynveen, *Angel Falls*

Prix Goncourt 1998 – Patrick Rambaud, *La Bataille (The Battle)*

Booker Prize 1997 – Arundhati Roy, *The God of Small Things*

Whitbread Prize 1997: overall winner – Ted Hughes, *Tales From Ovid*

Novel – Jim Crace, *Quarantine*

First novel – Pauline Melville, *The Ventriloquist's Tale*

Biography – Graham Robb, *Victor Hugo*

Poetry – Ted Hughes, *Tales From Ovid*

Children's novel – Andrew Norriss, *Aquila*

David Higham Prize 1997 – Ronald Wright, *A Scientific Romance*

Forward Prize 1997 (poetry) – Jamie McKendrick, *The Marble Fly*

First collection – Robin Robertson, *A Painted Field*

William Hill Sports Book of the Year 1997 – Simon Hughes, *A Lot of Hard Yakka*

Smarties Prize 1997 (children's books):

Age 0–5 – Charlotte Voake, *Ginger*

Age 6–8 – Jenny Nimmo, Anthony Lewis, *The Owl Tree*

Age 9–11 – J. K. Rowling, *Harry Potter and the Philosopher's Stone*

Crime Writers Association 1997:

Gold Dagger (fiction) – Ian Rankin, *Black and Blue*

Gold Dagger (non-fiction) – Paul Britton, *The Jigsaw Man*

Silver Dagger (fiction) – Janet Evanovich, *Three to Get Deadly*

John Creasey Memorial Dagger – Paul Johnston

British Book Awards 1997 – Helen Fielding, *Bridget Jones' Diary*

Illustrated – Tim Smit, *The Lost Gardens of Heligan*

Children's – J. K. Rowling, *Harry Potter and the Philosopher's Stone*

Encore Prize 1997 (second novel) – joint winners Timothy O'Grady, *I Could Read the Sky* and Alan Warner, *These Demented Lands*

Orange Award 1998 (women writers) – Carol Shields, *Larry's Party*

Somerset Maugham Awards 1998 – Rachel Cusk, *Country Life*; Jonathan Rendall, *This Bloody Mary*; Kate Summerscale, *The Queen of Whale Cay*; Robert Twigger, *Angry White Pyjamas*

Betty Trask Prize 1998 (authors under 35) – Kiran Desai, *Hullabaloo in the Guava Orchard*

McKitterick Prize 1998 (first novel by a writer over 40) – Eli Gottlieb, *The Boy Who Went Away*

W. H. Smith Prize 1998 – Ted Hughes, *Tales From Ovid*

Mail on Sunday/John Llewellyn Rhys Prize 1998 – Phil Whitaker, *Eclipse of the Sun*

Cholmondeley Awards 1998 (poetry) – Roger McGough, Robert Minhinnick, Anne Ridler, Ken Smith

T. S. Eliot Prize (poetry) – Don Paterson, *God's Gift to Women*

Romantic Novel of the Year 1998 – Angela Lambert, *Kiss and Kin*

Carnegie Prize 1998 (children's) – Tim Bowler, *River Boy*

Kate Greenaway 1998 (children's illustrated) – P. J. Lynch, *When Jessie Came Across the Sea*

Opera

At the Royal Opera House, Covent Garden, the builders moved in the day after the 1996–7 season closed. In September 1997, Mary Allen, selected by the chairman of the board, Lord Chadlington, after the resignation of Genista McIntosh, took up the post of chief executive. Meanwhile the House of Commons culture select committee, chaired by Gerald Kaufman, investigated the financial affairs of the House, saved from bankruptcy only by large donations from two members of the board, Mrs Vivien Duffield and Lord Sainsbury. The select committee's report was damning in the extreme, condemning the Opera House for its style of management and accusing it of gross incompetence in its financial affairs. As a solution, Culture Secretary Chris Smith proposed that the Royal Opera, the Royal Ballet and English National Opera should be housed under one roof after the reopening of Covent Garden. This idea was greeted with howls of protest, not merely from the companies themselves, but from many eminent figures in the artistic world, and Sir Richard Eyre, former director of the Royal National Theatre, was asked to draw up a report on the subject.

At the beginning of December 1997 Lord Chadlington and the entire board resigned. Sir Colin Southgate, previously chairman of the EMI music group, was appointed chairman of the Royal Opera House in January 1998, and a new board was appointed. Advisory boards were also set up for the opera and ballet companies, that for opera being chaired by Michael Berkeley, the composer and artistic director of the Cheltenham Festival. In March, Mary Allen resigned as chief executive, opening the way for a new general director of appropriate artistic merit to be found for the Royal Opera House when it reopens. Meanwhile, Richard Jarman, former general director of Scottish Opera, was appointed interim artistic director on a two-year fixed contract. Jarman also assumed the responsibilities of Nicholas Payne, whose contract as director of the Royal Opera had expired at the end of the season.

The Eyre report, published at the end of June 1998, brought few surprises and little consolation. To general relief it condemned the idea of three companies sharing the rebuilt Covent Garden. While making many detailed recommendations for the management structure and day-to-day running of the Royal Opera House, some of them already proposed by the new board, the report recognized that additional government support was necessary. It also praised the high quality of the Royal Opera's performances during the 1997–8 season, despite the unsuitability of some of the theatres and halls in which the company was forced to perform.

Several Royal Opera productions were awarded prizes: the Royal Philharmonic Society's 1997 Award for Opera was given to Richard Hickox for his conducting of a semi-staged performance of Vaughan Williams' The Pilgrim's Progress, which brought a long-neglected masterpiece to vivid life. Hickox also conducted the much praised production of Britten's The Turn of the Screw, which received the Evening Standard 1997 Award for Opera. The playing of the orchestra of the Royal Opera House was considered to be of a very high standard throughout the season, particularly in two concert performances: the first, Wagner's Parsifal, with Placido Domingo in the title role, should have been conducted by Bernard Haitink, the musical director, but he was in hospital and Heinz Fricke took over; the second, Richard Strauss's Die Ägyptische Helena, which has never been staged in London, was conducted by Christian Thielemann.

After the closure of the London season, the Royal Opera went on tour, visiting foreign festivals at Baden Baden and Savonlinna and winning golden opinions from press and public alike. The company then appeared for the second year running at the Edinburgh Festival, where a new production by Elijah Moshinsky of the Verdi opera originally written for London, I masnadieri, was unveiled; the Royal Opera also contributed a revival of Don Carlos and two concert performances of Luisa Miller. Other operas at the 1998 Edinburgh Festival were Scottish Opera's new production of Bedřich Smetana's Dalibor, conducted by Richard Armstrong and directed by David Pountney, and a concert performance of Smetana's Libuše, conducted by Oliver von Dohnanyi, with an entirely Czech and Slovak cast, headed by Eva Urbanova in the title role.

UPSETS AT ENO

English National Opera had its own troubles during the year, mainly caused by the state of the London Coliseum and the necessity of finding a large sum of money to restore the building. In September 1997 Dennis Marks, general director of ENO, resigned, because, it was presumed, his plan to move the company from the Coliseum into a newly built theatre was turned down. Paul Daniel, having assumed the post of music director on 1 August 1997, took over temporarily as artistic director, and fought tooth and nail against the idea of ENO joining the Royal Opera and Royal Ballet at Covent Garden. That plan was dropped, and Daniel was further supported by the appointment as general director of ENO of Nicholas Payne, with whom he had previously worked at Opera North. Payne took up the appointment when his contract with the Royal Opera expired at the end of the 1997–8 season.

Despite these troubles, Daniel's first season was an artistic triumph, beginning with a new production of *The Flying Dutchman* which he conducted in September 1997, when the orchestra brought the raging wind and sea right into the Coliseum.

Daniel also conducted new productions of Janáček's *From the House of the Dead* (preceded by Mark-Anthony Turnage's *Twice Through the Heart*, a mono-drama that received its première at the 1997 Aldeburgh Festival), Offenbach's *The Tales of Hoffmann*, and Massenet's *Manon*. Other interesting new productions included *Il trittico*, Puccini's three one-act operas, and the world première (postponed from the previous year) of *Doctor Ox's Experiment*, an opera by Gavin Bryars, with libretto by Blake Morrison based on a story by Jules Verne. *Dr Ox* played to 85 per cent capacity over its run of five performances, a record for a modern opera.

Other operatic premières included *And the Snake Shed Its Skin*, based on the *Epic of Gilgamesh*, with music by Habib Faye and text by David Freeman, which was performed in April 1998 by Opera Factory at the Drill Hall followed by a short tour to Oxford, Birmingham, Cambridge and Reading. Then Opera Factory, having lost its Arts Council grant, was disbanded, depriving Britain of its one genuinely original opera company. During the 16 years of its existence, the company, directed by David Freeman, produced a string of highly provocative productions. Based first at the Drill Hall, then the Queen Elizabeth Hall, Opera Factory performed works ranging from Mozart's *Così fan tutte* to Tippett's *The Knot Garden*, from *The Beggar's Opera* to Harrison Birtwistle's *Punch and Judy* and *Yan tan tethera*. It will be sorely missed.

Hey Persephone! by Deirdre Gribbin, with text by Sharman Macdonald, was premièred at the Cheltenham International Festival in June 1998, and then repeated in London by Almeida Opera in July. *Hey Persephone!* transferred the Greek myth of Persephone and Demeter to present-day Glasgow. Almeida Opera, which won the Prudential Award for Opera in 1997, also offered a double bill of operas by Guo Wenjing, *Night Banquet* (première) and *Wolf Cub Village* (first British performance) during July.

A NIGHT IN THE TERMINAL

Glyndebourne Touring Opera opened its 1998 season in September with the première of *Flight* by Jonathan Dove, prior to the work's introduction to the Glyndebourne Festival in 1999. *Flight* is set in an airport, where the characters, whose flight has been delayed, spend the night in the terminal. The Touring Opera's other two productions were Handel's *Rodelinda* and Mozart's *Così fan tutte*, both newly staged at the 1998 Festival, when *Rodelinda*, conducted by William Christie, was highly praised.

Così fan tutte, directed by Graham Vick, and the Festival's other new production, Verdi's *Simon Boccanegra*, were found controversial by the critics, though capacity audiences loved them. *Boccanegra* saw the return of Sir Peter Hall, absent from

Glyndebourne since he resigned as director of productions in 1990, to the Sussex opera house to stage Verdi's opera there for the second time. Among the revivals, John Cox's 25-year-old production of *Capriccio* was brought out to mark the 25th anniversary of Dame Kiri te Kanawa's first appearance at Glyndebourne, when she sang the Countess in *Le nozze di Figaro*. Te Kanawa sang the first six performances of Countess Madeleine in Strauss's 'conversation piece', and Dame Felicity Lott, who first sang Countess Madeleine with GTO in 1976, the second six, providing an evening of total enchantment. At the end of August, Anthony Whitworth-Jones, the general director, retired and was succeeded by Nicholas Snowman, formerly chief executive of the South Bank Centre.

Despite chronic shortages of funds, the regional companies also managed to offer interesting repertories. Opera North began the season with a new production of Bohuslav Martinů's *Julietta*, directed by David Pountney, and ended it with Verdi's *Joan of Arc*, directed by Philip Prowse, both works of considerable rarity. Opera North also presented Stephen Sondheim's *Sweeney Todd* to great acclaim. Scottish Opera had co-operated with Nottingham Playhouse at the 1997 Edinburgh Festival to present the original, 1912 version of the Strauss/Hofmannsthal *Ariadne auf Naxos*, in which the opera is preceded by Molière's *Le bourgeois gentilhomme*. However this version is strictly festival fare, and when *Ariadne* was introduced into Scottish Opera's general repertory in March 1998, the more usual 1916 version, with the opera preceded by a Prologue, was given instead.

Two of Welsh National Opera's new productions, Mozart's *La clemenza di Tito* and Monteverdi's *L'incoronazione di Poppea*, were brought to the Shaftesbury Theatre in London, thanks to the company's long-time sponsor AMOCO. Monteverdi's opera, directed by David Alden, was particularly popular, as were new productions of the original, seven-scene version of Mussorgsky's *Boris Godunov*, and of Britten's *Billy Budd* later in the season. Meanwhile Music Theatre Wales, the recipient of the 1997 Prudential Award and renowned for its clever productions and out-of-the-way repertory, performed Harrison Birtwistle's *Punch and Judy* at the Cheltenham International Festival in July 1998, and the Queen Elizabeth Hall in London later in the month.

The 1998 Promenade Concerts at the Royal Albert Hall opened on 17 July with a performance of Berlioz's *La damnation de Faust* conducted by Andrew Davis. Other operatic Proms included Rameau's *Zoroastre*, given by Les Arts Florissants, conducted by William Christie; *King Roger* by Karol Szymanowski, with the City of Birmingham Symphony Orchestra conducted by Simon Rattle; Verdi's *Falstaff*, conducted by John Eliot Gardiner and semi-staged by Ian Judge; *Porgy and Bess*, in celebration of the centenary of George Gershwin's birth, with Willard White and Cynthia Haymon in the title roles; and the new Glyndebourne production of *Simon Boccanegra*. In addition, John Harle's *Angel Magick* received its first London performance, conducted by the composer and staged by David Pountney.

DISTINGUISHED PERFORMERS

Sir Georg Solti, born in Hungary but a naturalized British subject, died in September 1997, aged 85. He was music director of the Royal Opera from 1971 to 1981, a decade during which the company's reputation was exceptionally high. Solti conducted notable performances at Covent Garden of operas by Mozart, Verdi, Wagner, Richard Strauss and Benjamin Britten, as well as the British stage première of Arnold Schönberg's *Moses und Aron* in 1965. In the 1980s and 1990s he returned to Covent Garden many times as conductor, and was appointed music director laureate after a performance of *Otello* in 1992. His last appearance there was at the farewell gala on 14 July 1997, the night before the bulldozers moved in, when he conducted the fugue from the final scene of Verdi's *Falstaff*. Solti conducted the first complete cycle of Wagner's *Der Ring des Nibelungen* on record, and made many other notable operatic recordings. He was appointed KBE in 1971.

Sir Rudolf Bing, also a naturalized British subject, died in September 1997 aged 95. Born in Vienna, he became general manager of Glyndebourne Opera in 1936. He was instrumental in founding the Edinburgh Festival, of which he was director from 1947 to 1949. In 1951 he became general manager of the Metropolitan Opera in New York, a position he held until 1972. Peter Diamond, who died in January 1998 aged 86, was also director of the Edinburgh Festival, from 1965 to 1978. Alan Kitching, opera director and translator, died in September 1997, aged 90. In the years between 1959 and 1975 he presented 15 operas by Handel at the Unicorn Theatre in Abingdon, with his wife Frances as conductor.

Beverley Cross, who died in March 1998 aged 66, wrote the libretti for three of the most successful new British operas during the 1960s and 1970s: *The Mines of Sulphur* by Richard Rodney Bennett, produced at Sadler's Wells Theatre in 1965; *Victory*, by the same composer, based on the novel by Joseph Conrad, produced at Covent Garden in 1970; and *The Rising of the Moon* by Nicholas Maw, first performed at Glyndebourne in 1970 and revived at the 1990 Wexford Festival. George Lloyd, the Cornish composer who died in June 1998 aged 85, wrote several operas; *Iernin*, a Celtic opera, was produced in 1934 in Penzance, and repeated in London at the Lyceum Theatre the following year; *The Serf* was premièred at Covent Garden during the English Opera Society season in October 1938; *John Socman*, his most ambitious opera, was commissioned by the Carl Rosa Company for the Festival of Britain and first performed at the Bristol Hippodrome in 1951.

Kenneth Neate, the Australian tenor, died in June 1997, aged 82. He was a member of the Covent Garden Company from its inception in 1946 until 1950. His roles included Don José in *Carmen*, Tamino in *The Magic Flute*, the Duke in *Rigoletto*, Rudolfo in *La bohème*, Alfredo in *La traviata* and Pinkerton in *Madama Butterfly*. In 1959 he returned to Covent Garden to sing Edgardo in *Lucia di Lammermoor* with Joan Sutherland in the title role. Oreste Kirkop, a tenor born in Malta, died in May 1998, aged 74. After appearing with the Carl Rosa, he joined Sadler's Wells in 1952, where his roles included Turiddu in *Cavalleria rusticana*, Cavaradossi in *Tosca* and Rodolfo in *Luisa Miller*. He also sang the Duke in *Rigoletto* at Covent Garden with great success in 1954.

Anne Wood, who died in June 1998 aged 90, began her career as a singer. After the Second World War she became a director and general manager of the English Opera Group. In 1949, together with the soprano Joan Cross, she founded the Opera Studio, which developed first into the London Opera School and later into the National School of Opera. When this was superseded by the London Opera Centre, under the auspices of the Royal Opera, both Wood and Cross resigned. In 1965 Anne Wood founded Phoenix Opera, a touring company which staged many notable productions, including Mozart's *Così fan tutte* conducted by Yehudi Menuhin, Rossini's *Barber of Seville* directed by Tyrone Guthrie, Britten's *Albert Herring* directed by Joan Cross and Friedrich von Flotow's *Martha*. In 1975 the Arts Council withdrew its grant, and Phoenix Opera foundered, apart from a few isolated performances. Anne Wood continued to teach at the Guildhall School of Music.

In the New Year honours lists, the composer Richard Rodney Bennett, whose operas include *The Ledge* (1961) and *Penny for a Song* (1968) as well as *The Mines of Sulphur* and *Victory* with texts by Cross (mentioned above), received a knighthood. The bass Gwynne Howell became a CBE; he has sung for many years with both the Royal Opera and English National Opera, in a very wide repertory, ranging from Mozart and Rossini to Wagner and Verdi. The Queen's Birthday honours lists awarded the conductor John Eliot Gardiner a knighthood. Gardiner, founder of the Monteverdi Choir and Orchestra, started his career as a conductor of early music, and of operas by Gluck, Handel, Mozart and other 18th-century composers. Latterly he has widened his repertory to include many operas of the 19th and 20th centuries.

On the same occasion, Peter Brook was made a Companion of Honour. In his early twenties, between 1948 and 1950, the theatre, opera and film director staged some highly controversial productions at Covent Garden. These included *Boris Godunov*, designed by George Wahkevich, the world première of *The Olympians* by Sir Arthur Bliss, and, most sensational of all, Strauss's *Salome* with designs by Salvador Dali, which was abandoned after six performances. His staging of Gounod's *Faust* at the Metropolitan Opera, New York also caused a scandal. Later he founded the International Centre for Theatre Research in Paris. *La tragédie de Carmen*, his version of Bizet's opera, toured in Europe and the USA.

PRODUCTIONS

In the summaries of company activities shown below, the dates in brackets indicate the year that the current production entered the company's repertory.

ROYAL OPERA
Founded 1946
Royal Opera House, Covent Garden, London WC2E 9DD
Productions from the repertory: at Royal Albert Hall *Otello* (1987), *La traviata* (1994); at Shaftesbury Theatre *Così fan tutte* (1995); at Edinburgh Festival Theatre *Don Carlos* (1996).
New productions at the Barbican Theatre:
Giulio Cesare (Handel), 13 September 1997. Conductor, Ivor Bolton; director, Lindsay Posner; designer, Joanna Packer. Amanda Roocroft (Cleopatra), Ann Murray (Cesare), Catherine Wyn-Rogers (Cornelia), David Daniels (Sesto), Brian Asawa (Tolomeo), Gerald Finley (Achilla), Jonathan Peter Kemp (Nireno)
Platée (Rameau), 22 September 1997. Conductor, Nicholas McGeegan; director, Mark Morris; designers, Adrianna Lobel (sets), Isaac Mizrahi (costumes). Jean-Paul Fouchécourt (Platée), Diana Montague (Junon), Nicole Tibbela (La Folie/L'Amour), Mark Padmore (Mercure/Thespis), François Le Roux (Jupiter/Momus)
The Turn of the Screw (Britten), 2 October 1997. Conductor, Colin Davis; director, Dorothy Warner; designers, Jean Kalman and Tom Pye (sets), John Bright (costumes). Joan Rodgers (Governess), Vivian Tierney (Miss Jessel), Jane Henschel (Mrs Grose), Ian Bostridge (Peter Quint), Pippa Woodrow (Flora), Edward Burrowes (Miles)
The Merry Widow (Léhar), 23 October 1997. Conductor, Dietfried Bernet; director, Graham Vick; designer, Richard Hudson. Felicity Lott (Hanna), Juliette Galstian (Valencienne), Luca Canonici (Camille), Thomas Allen (Danilo), Claudio Desderi (Baron Zeta)
Il barbiere di Siviglia (Rossini), 24 November 1997. Conductor, Antonello Allemandi; director/designer, Nigel Lowery. Carmen Oprisanu (Rosina), Yvonne Howard (Berta), Paul Austin Kelly (Count Almaviva), Roberto Frontali (Figaro), Donald Maxwell (Bartolo), Sergei Aleksashkin (Basilio)
Le nozze di Figaro (Mozart), 19 January 1998. Conductor, Steven Sloane; director, Patrick Young; designer, Roger Butlin. Nuccio Focile (Susanna), Gillian Webster (Countess Almaviva), Dagmar Peckova (Cherubino), Yvonne Howard (Marcellina), Natale de Carolis (Figaro), Dmitri Hvorostovsky (Count Almaviva), Gwynne Howell (Dr Bartolo), Robin Leggate (Don Basilio)
Other new productions:
Paul Bunyan (Britten), 5 December 1997, at Snape Maltings. Conductor, Richard Hickox; director, Francesca Zambello; designer, Hildegard Bechtler. Susan Gritton (Tiny), Thomas Randle (Inkslinger), Mark Padmore (Slim), Jeremy White (Helson), Peter Coleman Wright (Narrator)

I masnadieri (Verdi), 17 August 1998, at Edinburgh Festival Theatre. Conductor, Edward Downes; director, Elijah Moshinsky. Paula Delligatti (Amalia), Franco Farina (Carlo), Dmitri Hvorostovsky (Francesco), Carlo Columbara (Massimiliano), Julian Konstantinov (Moser)
Concert performances:
The Pilgrim's Progress (Vaughan Williams), 3 November 1997 at Barbican Hall. Conductor, Richard Hickox. Gerald Finley (Pilgrim), Gwynne Howell (John Bunyan), Jeremy White (Evangelist)
Elisabetta (Donizetti), 16 December 1997 at Royal Festival Hall. Conductor, Carlo Rizzi. Andrea Rost (Elisabetta), Leah-Marian Jones (Fedora), Giuseppe Sabbatini (Potoski), Robin Leggate (Czar), Alessandro Corbelli (Michele)
The Enchantress (Tchaikovsky), 31 January 1998 at Royal Festival Hall. Conductor, Valery Gergiev. Galina Gorchakova (Nastasya), Larissa Diadkova (Princess Yevpraxia), Gegam Grigorian (Prince Yury), Nikolai Putilin (Prince Nikita), Paul Whelan (Potap)
Andrea Chénier (Giordano), 23 February 1998 at Royal Festival Hall. Conductor, Richard Armstrong. Jose Curia (Chénier), Maria Guleghina (Maddalena), Anthony Michaels Moore (Gérard)
Der Freischütz (Weber), 3 March 1998 at Barbican Hall. Conductor, Bernard Haitink. Melanie Diener (Agathe), Christiane Oelze (Annchen), Thomas Moser (Max), Thomas Allen (Ottokar), Kurt Rydl (Kaspar)
Mefistofele (Boito), 14 March 1998 at Barbican Hall. Conductor, Bernard Haitink. Elena Prokina (Margherita/Elena), Patricia Bardon (Martha/Pantalis), Richard Margison (Faust), Samuel Ramey (Mefistofele)
Parsifal (Wagner), 23 April 1998 at Royal Festival Hall. Conductor, Heinz Fricke. Deborah Voigt (Kundry), Placido Domingo (Parsifal), Jukka Rasilainen (Amfortas), Sergei Leiferkus (Klingsor), John Tomlinson (Gurnemanz)
La rondine (Puccini), 18 May 1998 at Royal Albert Hall. Conductor, Gianluigi Gelmetti. Angela Gheorghiu (Magda), Rosemary Joshua (Lisette), Roberto Alagna (Ruggero), Francesco Piccoli (Prunier)
Die Ägyptische Helena (R. Strauss), 22 May 1998 at Royal Festival Hall. Conductor, Christian Thielemann. Deborah Voigt (Helena), Lyuba Kazarnovskaya (Aithra), Nancy Maltsby (Omniscient Sea-Shell), John Horton Murray (Menelaus), Alan Titus (Althair)

ENGLISH NATIONAL OPERA
Founded 1931
London Coliseum, St Martin's Lane, London WC2N 4BS
Productions from the repertory: *Tosca* (1994), *The Mikado* (1986), *Così fan tutte* (1994), *The Magic Flute* (1988), *Eugene Onegin* (1994), *Xerxes* (1985), *La bohème* (1993), *The Fairy Queen* (1995), *Carmen* (1995).
New productions:
The Flying Dutchman (Wagner), 15 September 1997. Conductor, Paul Daniel; director, Stein Winge; designer, Timian Alsaker. Willard White (The Dutchman), Rita Cullis (Senta), David Rendall (Erik), Stephen Richardson (Daland)
From the House of the Dead (Janáček), 20 October 1997. Conductor, Paul Daniel; director, Tim Albery; designer, Stewart Laing. Andrew Shore (Shishkov), Robert Brubaker (Luka), John Daszak (Skuratov), John Graham Hall (Shapkin), Roberto Salvatori (Chekunov), Malcolm Rivers (The Commandant), Gale Pearson (Aleya)
Twice Through the Heart (Mark-Anthony Turnage), 20 October 1997. Conductor, Nicholas Kok; directors, Patti Powell and Tim Albery. Susan Bickley (woman)

Falstaff (Verdi), 15 November 1997. Conductor, Oliver von Dohnanyi; director, Marcus Warchus; designer, Laura Hopkins. Alan Opie (Falstaff), Rita Cullis (Alice Ford), Keith Latham (Ford), Mary Plazas (Nannetta), Charles Workman (Fenton), Catherine Wyn-Rogers (Mistress Quickly), Susan Connolly (Meg Page), Anthony Mee (Bardolph), Mark Beesley (Pistol), Andrew Forbes-Lane (Dr Caius)

The Elixir of Love (Donizetti), 26 January 1998. Conductor, Michael Lloyd; director, Jude Kelly; designer, Robert Jones. Mary Plazas (Adina), Barry Banks (Nemorino), Ashley Holland (Belcore), Andrew Shore (Dulcamara)

The Tales of Hoffmann (Offenbach), 24 February 1998. Conductor, Paul Daniel; director, Graham Vick; designer, Tobias Hoheisel. Julian Gavin (Hoffmann), Rosa Mannion (Olympia/Antonia/ Giulietta/Stella), John Tomlinson (Lindorf/Coppelius/Dr Miracle/ Dapertutto), Susan Parry (Nicklausse/Muse), Jean Rigby (Antonia's Mother), Andrew Forbes-Lane (Andrès/ Cochenille/Frantz/Pittichinaccio), David Marsh (Luther/Crespel), Riccardo Simonetti (Hermann/ Schlemil)

Il trittico (Puccini), 8 April 1998. Conductor, Shao-Chia-Lu; director, Patrick Mason; designer, Joe Vanek. *The Cloak*, Rosalind Plowright (Giorgetta), David Rendall (Luigi), Philip Joll (Michele). *Sister Angelica*, Anne Williams-King (Angelica), Elizabeth Vaughan (The Princess). *Gianni Schicchi*, Andrew Shore (Schicchi), Margaret Richardson (Lauretta), Gwyn Hughes Jones (Rinuccio)

Manon (Massenet), 13 May 1998. Conductor, Paul Daniel; director, David McVicar; designer, Tanya McCallin. Rosa Mannion (Manon), John Hudson (Chevalier des Grieux), Ashley Holland (Lescaut), Anthony Mee (Guillot de Morfontaine), Christopher Booth-Jones (de Brétigny), John Connell (Count des Grieux)

Doctor Ox's Experiment (Gavin Bryars), 15 June 1998 (world première). Conductor, James Holmes; director, Atom Egoyan; designers, Michael Levine (set), Sandy Powell (costumes). Bonaventura Bottone (Doctor Ox), Riccardo Simonetti (Ygène), Nicholas Folwell (Van Tricasse), Mark Richardson (Nicklausse), Valdine Anderson (Suzel), David James (Frantz), Della Jones (Aunt Hermance)

OPERA NORTH
Founded 1978
Grand Theatre, 40 New Briggate, Leeds LS1 6NU
Productions from the repertory: *Aida* (1988), *Così fan tutte* (1997), *The Barber of Seville* (1987).

New productions:
Julietta (Martinů), 3 October 1997. Conductor, Steuart Bedford; director, David Pountney; designers, Stefan Lazaridis (set), Marie Jeanne Lecca (costumes). Rebecca Caine (Julietta), Paul Nilon (Michel), Alan Oke (Commissar/Clerk/Postman/Forest Warden)

The Magic Flute (Mozart), 17 December 1997. Conductor, Brad Cohen; director, Annabel Arden; designers, Rae Smith (set), Paula Constable (costumes). Margaret Richardson (Pamina), Cara O'Sullivan (Queen of Night), Jamie MacDougall (Tamino), Eric Roberts (Papageno), Clive Bayley (Sarastro)

Sweeney Todd (Sondheim), 17 January 1998. Conductor, James Holmes; director, David McVicar; designers, Michael Vale (set), Kevin Knight (costumes). Steven Page (Sweeney Todd), Beverley Klein (Mrs Lovett), Karl Daymond (Anthony Hope), Christopher Saunders

(Tobias), Lucy Schaufer (Johanna), Malcolm Rivers (Judge Turpin)

Eugene Onegin (Tchaikovsky), 9 May 1998. Conductor, Steven Sloane; director, Dalia Ibelhauptaite; designers, Giles Cadle (set), Sue Wilmington (costumes). Alwyn Mellor (Tatyana), Emer McGilloway (Olga), Eiddwen Harrhy (Larina), Frances McCafferty (Filipievna), Paul Nilon (Lensky), Peter Savidge (Onegin), Norman Bailey (Prince Gremin)

Joan of Arc (Verdi), 22 May 1998. Conductor, Richard Farnes; director/designer, Philip Prowse. Susannah Glanville (Joan), Julian Gavin (Charles VII), Keith Latham (Giacomo)

Performances were given at the Grand Theatre, Leeds, and on tour at Nottingham, Manchester, Newcastle upon Tyne, Hull and Sunderland.

SCOTTISH OPERA
Founded 1962
39 Elmbank Crescent, Glasgow G2 4PT
Productions from the repertory: *Norma* (1982), *Peter Grimes* (1994), *Tosca* (1980), *La traviata* (1989).

New productions:
Rigoletto (Verdi), 4 September 1997. Conductor, Richard Armstrong; director, Kenny Ireland; designer, Richard Aylwin. Boris Trajaner (Rigoletto), Claire Rutter (Gilda), Paul Charles Clark (Duke of Mantua)

Ariadne auf Naxos (R. Strauss), 18 March 1998. Conductor, Richard Armstrong; director, Martin Duncan; designer, Tim Hatley. Diana Montague (Composer), Nigel Douglas (Major Domo), Anne Evans (Ariadne), Lisa Saffer (Zerbinetta), John Horton Murray (Bacchus)

The Queen of Spades (Tchaikovsky), 5 May 1998. Conductor, Richard Armstrong; director/designer, Yannis Kokkos. Elmira Magomedova (Lisa), Jadwiga Rappe (Countess), Vladimir Kuzmenko (Herman), Alexander Poliakov (Tomsky), Boris Trajanov (Yeletsky)

Dalibor (Bedřich Smetana), 3 September 1998 at Edinburgh Festival Theatre. Conductor, Richard Armstrong; director, David Pountney; designers, Ralph Koltai (set), Sue Willmington (costumes). Leo Marian Vodicka (Dalibor), Vivien Tierney (Jitka), Kathleen Broderick (Milada), Stephen Allen (Vitek), Christopher Purves (Budivoj), Jiri Kalendovsky (Benes)

Performances were given in the Theatre Royal, Glasgow, and on tour at Edinburgh, Sunderland, Aberdeen and Inverness.

WELSH NATIONAL OPERA
Founded 1946
John Street, Cardiff CF1 4SP
Productions from the repertory: *Carmen* (1997), *Tosca* (1994), *La traviata* (1988).

New productions:
Fidelio (Beethoven), 12 September 1997. Conductor, Carlo Rizzi; directors, Patrice Caurier, Moshe Leiser; designers, Christian Fenouillat (set), Agostino Cavalca (costumes). Suzanne Murphy (Leonore), Rebecca Evans (Marzelline), Adrian Thompson (Florestan), Gidon Saks (Pizarro), Donald McIntyre (Rocco), Peter Hoare (Jaquino), Andrew Greenan (Don Fernando)

La clemenza di Tito (Mozart). 12 October 1997. Conductor, Charles Mackerras; director/designer, Yannis Kokkos. Glen Winslade (Tito), Isabelle Vernet (Vitellia), Katarina Karnéus (Sesto), Paula Hoffman (Annio), Lisa Milne (Servilia), Umberto Chiummo (Publius)

L'incoronazione di Poppea (Monteverdi), 11 December 1997. Conductor, Rinaldo Alessandrini; director, David Alden; designers Paul Steinberg (set), Buki Shiff (costumes). Catrin Wyn Davies (Poppea), Paul Nilon

(Nero), Sally Burgess (Ottavia), Michael Chance (Ottone), Linda Kitchen (Drusilla/Pallade), Neil Jenkins (Arnalta), Linda Ormiston (Nutrice/Venus), Gwynne Howell (Seneca), Linda Tuvås (Amor)

Billy Budd (Britten), 14 February 1998. Conductor, Andrew Litton; director, Neil Armfield; designer, Brian Thompson. Christopher Maltman (Billy Budd), Nigel Robson (Captain Vere), Philip Ens (Claggart), Ivan Sharpe (Novice), David Barrell (Redburn), Stephen Richardson (Flint), Grant Dickson (Dansker)

Boris Godunov (Mussorgsky), 16 May 1998. Conductor, Carlo Rizzi; director, David Pountney; designer, Huntley/Muir. Willard White (Boris), Neil Jenkins (Shuisky), John Daszak (Grigori/ Dmitri), Gwynne Howell (Pimen), Jonathan Veira (Varlaam), Peter Hoare (Simpleton), Joanna Campion (Feodor)

Performances were given in the New Theatre, Cardiff, and on tour at Oxford, Plymouth, Southampton, Birmingham, Liverpool, Bristol, Swansea, Llandudno and the Shaftesbury Theatre, London.

GLYNDEBOURNE FESTIVAL OPERA
Founded 1934
Glyndebourne, Lewes, East Sussex BN8 5UU

The Festival ran from 21 May to 28 August 1998. *Kát'a Kabanová* (1988), *Capriccio* (1973) and *Le Comte Ory* (1997) were revived.

New productions:
Così fan tutte (Mozart), 21 May 1998. Conductor, Andrew Davis; director, Graham Vick; designer, Richard Hudson. Barbara Frittoli (Fiordiligi), Katarina Karnéus (Dorabella), Daniela Mazzucato (Despina), Roberto Sacca (Ferrando), Natale de Carolis (Guglielmo), Alan Opie (Don Alfonso)

Rodelinda (Handel), 13 June 1998. Conductor, William Christie; director, Jean-Marie Villégier; designers, Nicolas de Lajatre, Pascale Cazales (set), Patrice Cauchetier (costumes). Anna Caterina Antonacci (Rodelinda), Louise Winter (Edwige), Andreas Scholl (Bertarido), Kurt Streit (Grimoaldo), Umberto Chiumme (Garibaldo), Artur Stefanowicz (Unulfo)

Simon Boccanegra (Verdi), 4 July 1998. Conductor, Mark Elder; director, Peter Hall; designer, John Gunter. Giancarlo Pasquetto (Boccanegra), Elena Prokina (Amelia), Terje Andersen (Adorno), Alastair Miles (Fiesco), Peter Sidhom (Paolo)

GLYNDEBOURNE TOURING OPERA
Flight (Jonathan Dove), 24 September 1998 (world première). Conductor, David Parry; director, Richard Jones; designers, Giles Cadie (set), Nicki Gillibrand (costumes). Anne Mason (Minsk Woman), Ciaron McFadden (Controller), Mary Plazas (Tina), Ann Taylor (Stewardess), Nuala Willis (Older Woman), Richard Coxon (Bill), Steven Page (Minsk Man), Garry Magee (Steward), Richard Van Allen (Immigration Officer).
Flight, Rodelinda and *Così fan tutte* were performed at Glyndebourne, Oxford, Woking, Norwich, Southampton, Manchester, Plymouth and Northampton, from 24 September to 10 December 1998.

GARSINGTON OPERA
Founded 1989
Garsington Manor, Garsington, Oxford OX44 9DH

The season ran from 8 June to 5 July 1998.

New productions:
La pietrà del paragone (Rossini), 8 June 1998. Conductor, Charles Peebles; director, Stefano Vizioli; designer, Susanna Rossi Jost. Patricia Bardon (Clarice), Steven

Page (Asdrubale), Charles Workman (Giocondo), Paolo Rumetz (Pacuvio), Riccardo Novaro (Macrobio)

Lucio Silla (Mozart), 9 June 1998. Conductor, Steuart Bedford; director, Aidan Lang; designer, Anthony Baker. Thomas Randle (Lucio Silla), Maria Fortuna (Giunia), Anne Dawson (Cecilio), Linda Kitchen (Celia), Elena Ferrari (Cinna)

Falstaff (Verdi), 18 June 1998. Conductor, Stephen Barlow; director, Stephen Unwin; designer, Pamela Howard. Elizabeth Gale (Alice Ford), Kate Ladner (Nannetta), Mary King (Meg Page), Fiona Kimm (Mistress Quickly), Aled Hall (Fenton), Robert Poulton (Falstaff), Roderick Earle (Ford), Richard Angas (Pistol)

ENGLISH TOURING OPERA
Founded 1980 as Opera 80

La cenerentola and *The Marriage of Figaro* were toured to Richmond, High Wycombe, Dartford, Crewe, Bath, Buxton, Basingstoke, Wolverhampton and Weston-super-Mare, between 15 October and 28 November 1997.

Fidelio and *La cenerentola* were toured to Cambridge, Poole, Reading, Brighton, London (Peacock Theatre), Ipswich, Darlington, Yeovil, Exeter, Truro, Crawley, Lincoln, Preston, Ulverston, Cheltenham and Warwick, between 24 February and 29 May 1998.

OPERA NORTHERN IRELAND
Founded 1982
35 Talbot Street, Belfast BT1 2LD

Autumn season at the Grand Opera House, Belfast:
Aida (Verdi), 19 September 1997. Conductor, Martin André; director, Jamie Hayes; designer, Nick Barnes. Jean Glennon (Aida), Hyacinth Nicholls (Amneris), Badri Maissouradze (Radames), Jonathan Veira (Amonasro)

Idomeneo (Mozart), 20 September 1997. Conductor, Stephen Barlow; director, Harry Silverstein; designer, Linda Buchanan. Louise Walsh (Ilya), Emma Selway (Idamante), Virginia Kerr (Elettra), Mark le Brocq (Idomeneo)

Spring season at the Grand Opera House, Belfast:
Hansel and Gretel (Humperdinck), 1 March 1998. Conductor, Graham Jackson; director, Aidan Lang; designer, Lez Brotherston. Diana Gilchrist (Gretel), Fiona Campbell (Hansel), Elizabeth Hetherington (Mother), Patricia Boylan (Witch), Robert Poulton (Peter)

Parliament

In its manifesto *Because Britain Deserves Better* the Labour Party said that it recognized a 'national crisis of confidence in our political system to which Labour will respond in a measured and sensible way' and promised it would be 'committed to the democratic renewal of our country through decentralization and the elimination of government secrecy'. It went on to promise that if elected it 'would meet the demand for decentralization of power to Scotland and Wales ... subsidiarity is as sound a principle in Britain as it is in Europe. Our proposal is for devolution not federation. A sovereign Westminster Parliament will devolve power to Scotland and Wales. The Union will be strengthened and the threat of separatism removed'. For English local government it promised a new partnership based on promoting economic, social and environmental well-being, and for London in particular it offered 'a new deal ... with a strategic authority and a mayor, each directly elected'. It also promised to continue the work of the previous Government on proposals for a new devolved legislative body for Northern Ireland. Proposals were also put forward for the reform of the House of Lords, for the development of more open government, the reform of the funding of political parties and action on freedom of information and guaranteed human rights.

Once in power Labour moved quickly; one of its first acts was to introduce the Referendums (Scotland and Wales) Bill 1997 to allow the people of Scotland and Wales to vote in separate referendums on the devolution proposals, set out in White Papers published in July 1997 as the bill went through Parliament. There was a 60.4 per cent turnout for the two-question referendum held in Scotland on 11 September 1997; 74.3 per cent voted in favour of a Scottish parliament and 63.5 per cent in favour of the parliament having tax-raising powers. With this mandate the Government introduced the Scotland Bill in the House of Commons on 18 December 1997, when the Scottish Secretary (Donald Dewar) said that the bill was 'a genuinely historic document in which the whole nation can take pride ... enshrining a far-reaching settlement and providing the basis for new politics in Scotland'. Legislative powers would be passed to the Scottish parliament over all areas except those that should remain at Westminster to maintain the unity of the UK. The new parliament would have law-making powers over the health service, the criminal justice system, education, housing, transport, the environment and agriculture so that 'the Scottish Parliament will take decisions which affect the everyday lives of the Scottish people'. There would be a fixed four-year parliamentary term with provision for elections within that period in exceptional circumstances and

electors would be asked to vote twice in the elections to the parliament: once for a constituency member and once for regional members drawn from lists submitted by registered political parties or individuals standing in their own right. The parliament would have the power to vary the basic rate of income tax for Scottish taxpayers by up to 3 pence. Donald Dewar warned the Conservative opposition in the House of Lords that the bill 'had the backing of the clear manifesto commitments and the decisive referendum outcome as well as the endorsement of the House of Commons'.

The second reading of the bill in the Commons was on 12 and 13 January 1998 when Donald Dewar, who had announced that he would resign from the Government and Parliament in 1999 to stand for the post of First Minister in the Scottish government, called it 'a catalyst for change ... bringing back popular legitimacy, while creating the basis to reinvigorate Scottish life ... creating an institution that can speak for the people of Scotland, is closer to their needs and concerns, and is ultimately accountable to them'. The Conservative constitutional affairs spokesman (Michael Ancram) moved a motion accepting and respecting the views of the Scottish people for a devolved parliament but believing that the bill was not an acceptable measure as it failed to create a constitutional settlement which was stable and enduring within the UK, undermined Scotland's role both in Europe and the UK and, because of its lack of clarity on taxes and resources, threatened the interests of Scottish businesses, people and jobs. He felt that the bill contained 'seeds that will loosen the bonds that hold together the United Kingdom and could well lead to its break up' and that 'the haphazard and curiously arrogant way in which the Government have approached the legislation has at times bordered on the irresponsible'. He was particularly concerned by the West Lothian question, which he described as the English dimension: 'Surely it is quite clear that within the Union we cannot have a parliament where some members can vote on matters affecting the constituents of others but where they can no longer vote on them on behalf of their own constituents.' The Liberal Democrat Scottish affairs spokesman (Jim Wallace) welcomed and substantially supported the bill as it 'provides for a modern, democratic parliament for a modern democratic nation'. He did warn that they would scrutinize the bill carefully in committee, seeking especially the Government's justification of why some powers were to be reserved. The leader of the Scottish National Party (Alex Salmond) was more cautious in his welcome. But he said that 'as a step in the right direction, it is good for Scotland. Also a Scottish parliament has been validated by the people of Scotland – the ultimate sovereignty ... And the issue of independence will be determined by that ultimate constitutional authority, the people of Scotland, at the ballot box ... We regard this not as an event – a once-and-for-all transfer – but as part of the process of democratic awakening in the nation of Scotland.' Some Labour back-benchers did voice concern about the bill, notably Tam Dalyell (Linlithgow), who had originally raised the so-called West Lothian question. Dalyell felt also that there had been 'a lack of understanding of how significant are the special advantages that Scotland has enjoyed within the United Kingdom under the existing dispensation – the extra Members of Parliament, the extra financial allocation and the powerful position of the Secretary of State for Scotland'. He was also concerned that 'the deal must not be seen by the English majority as giving Scotland unacceptable, one-sided privileges and advantages. If that happens the settlement cannot endure.' The Conservative motion was defeated by 411 votes to 148, a government majority of 263, and the second reading was passed by a similar margin.

After some discussion about whether all stages of constitutional bills should be taken on the floor of the House, the committee stage of the bill was held on a timetable over eight days on the floor of the House of Commons during January, February and March. With a majority of 179 the Government was never likely to be defeated on any amendments but the Opposition ensured that the clause by clause analysis was very thorough. On 4 March former prime minister John Major made a rare speech in the Commons to discuss the clauses relating to Scottish representation at Westminster: 'Scotland cannot have extra privileges; it cannot have more public expenditure; it cannot have excessive representation in the House; it cannot have constitutional advantages over the rest of the United Kingdom – if that United Kingdom is to remain united, as I wish it to ... this is a divisive bill.'

On the first day of the report stage in the Commons (6 May 1998), the Conservatives attempted to pass a new clause dealing with the role of Scottish members of the House of Commons, which Michael Ancram claimed was 'about how to retain fairness and balance within the United Kingdom Parliament, which we believe this bill threatens to undermine'. Tam Dalyell, although he abstained in the vote, spoke of what he called 'a latent constitutional crisis ... the situation cannot be ignored any longer. The English dimension is now on the political agenda.' Donald Dewar dismissed these fears, saying, 'I do not believe it will turn out to be that problem but, if it does, it can be coped with on the basis of tolerance and common sense that have always been the hallmark of United Kingdom politics' and he accused the Conservatives of trying to turn a difficulty into 'a crisis that will destroy and promote turmoil in the country'. In a division the new clause was rejected by 277 votes to 136. The third reading was on 19 May; Michael Ancram felt

that the bill 'creates an unacceptable constitutional imbalance within the United Kingdom'. Alex Salmond strongly supported the bill 'despite its failings because I believe that this is a process, not an event; a beginning, not an end'. Tam Dalyell thought that the bill had fanned the 'slow candle of English nationalism ... sooner or later Hon. Members will find that the structure cannot last in anything recognizably like its current form'. Jim Wallace said Liberal Democrats would have much pleasure in giving the bill a third reading on the 100th anniversary of the death of Gladstone (the great campaigner for home rule for Scotland) as it would allow 'change for the better in the government of Scotland'. The bill received a third reading without division.

When the bill moved to the House of Lords, similar arguments were advanced. The second reading on 17 and 18 June was, as is usual, unopposed; given that it was a manifesto commitment endorsed by a referendum, the Upper House would be unlikely to amend the bill without the approval of the Government. As Parliament rose for the summer recess at the end of July 1998, the bill had been in committee in the Lords for eight days, with the Lords returning in October to continue committee stage discussion.

WELSH ASSEMBLY

In Wales on 18 September 1997 the result of the one-question referendum saw 559,419 agree with the Government's proposals for a Welsh assembly and 552,698 disagree, a majority of just over 6,700 in a turnout of 50.3 per cent. Conservative back-bench MP Richard Shepherd (Aldridge-Brownhills) pointed out that this majority was probably less than the 'many Welsh residents in constituencies such as mine and others throughout the West Midlands and the rest of the country' who were denied a vote. The Government of Wales Bill was introduced in the House of Commons on 27 November 1997. The assembly would have 60 members, 40 elected by the first-past-the-post system from existing parliamentary constituencies and 20 from electoral regions under the additional member system of proportional representation. Virtually all the functions of the Secretary of State for Wales would be transferred to the assembly. The assembly would have the power to reform Welsh quangos and the Welsh health authorities. The Welsh Secretary (Ron Davies) said, 'the National Assembly for Wales will be a new and effective form of government, based on modern working and political parties for the good of the whole of Wales. I hope to see political parties working together in a positive way and the development of structures which will allow individuals as well as other groups to get their voice heard'.

The second reading in the Commons was on 8 and 9 February 1998 and Ron Davies called it 'an historic moment for Wales ... seeking agreement to the principle that there should be a national assembly for Wales – a new institution that will both herald a new style of more inclusive politics that better fits the needs and the character of Wales, and open to public scrutiny and accountability the machinery of government of Wales.' The Conservative spokesman Michael Ancram moved an amendment deploring the Government's failure to respond to and allay the legitimate fears of the Welsh people and the omission from the bill of any statutory assurances in relation to the supremacy of the Westminster Parliament, to the protection of geographic and cultural minorities, and to safeguarding the position of Wales within the UK and its voice within Europe. He said that 'we are being asked to go where three out of every four Welsh electors feared to tread'. Like the Scotland bill, he felt 'the bill signals the start of a legislative process that will loosen the bonds that hold together the United Kingdom; it will create new tensions and animosities between component parts of the United Kingdom, which, unattended, could break the United Kingdom apart ... Conservative Members still believe in the Union and in the value of the United Kingdom – this unique amalgam of nations, cultures and traditions, which has proved and can continue to prove, a significant force for good, both at home and beyond.' The Liberal Democrat spokesman on Welsh affairs (Richard Livsey) welcomed the bill as a 'great opportunity to get it right for Wales ... I make no apology for making remarks that may be slightly critical of certain aspects but they are made in the spirit of co-operation and to achieve an assembly that is fair, democratic, just, free and united ... we believe that it is our duty to create an assembly of which we in Wales can all be proud ... we shall leave for the next generation something worthwhile, which they can get their teeth into in the 21st century'. The leader of Plaid Cymru (Dafydd Wigley) supported and accepted the bill 'for what it is – although it falls well short of the ideal that we envisaged'. He pledged to address in committee concerns, especially over the role of regional committees, but wished the bill 'a speedy passage, albeit – I hope – in a strengthened form ... It is our duty to create a national assembly for Wales that is worthy of the support of the ordinary people of Wales'. Voices of concern, if not dissent, from the Labour back benches came from Tam Dalyell, for the same reasons that he had expressed over the Scottish legislation, Denzil Davies and Allan Rogers, and from Llew Smith, who had campaigned for a No vote in the referendum. The Conservative amendment was defeated by 375 votes to 144, and the second reading was passed by 374 votes to 143.

Although originally the Government had agreed to only certain clauses being taken on the floor of the House, in the event it introduced a motion on 15 January to take the committee stage on the floor of the House and the bill had seven days in committee on a timetable during January, February and March. Although again the Government was in no danger of suffering a defeat, on 18 March, in response to points made by the Opposition, the Government did introduce amendments to allow the assembly to operate through a 'Cabinet style' administration, giving the First Secretary the power to appoint a Cabinet, allowing the assembly to delegate any of its functions to the First Secretary or to any committee, and requiring the standing orders to provide for oral and written answers on the Westminster parliamentary model.

On the first day of the report stage on 25 March, the Opposition forced divisions on a new clause concerning the power to enter into concordat (not to allow any such concordat unless the Westminster Parliament had approved it first), which it lost by 309 votes to 129, and on two of the clauses relating to the system of additional member voting, which it also lost heavily. On third reading on 26 March, Michael Ancram felt that one of the bill's fundamental flaws was 'that it fails to provide assurance to those who fear divisions within Wales and gives no assurances on financial security or the provision of finance ... the bill asks Wales to rely on unenforceable and valueless concordats, which can be breached unilaterally.' He concluded, 'the assembly in its present form does no service to Wales ... it is a ship without a mast, without a compass, without an engine and without a rudder. It is also full of leaks.' Dafydd Wigley thought it was 'an historic day for Wales, although the assembly offers significantly less than my party wanted. That does not make it an assembly not worth having; it is worth having for what it is ... we have every intention of making the assembly work for Wales, not withstanding the fact that it will not have all the powers we believe are necessary to get the best possible deal for Wales.' Richard Livsey said the aim was 'to build a new Wales of which we can all be proud. We believe that this legislation gives us a really good chance to do just that.' The bill received a third reading without division.

The bill moved to the House of Lords for an unopposed second reading on 21 April. As with the Scotland bill, the Lords was unlikely to amend the bill against the Government's wishes and the committee stage lasted for five days during May and June with report and third reading completed during July. The bill received royal assent on 31 July 1998.

NORTHERN IRELAND AGREEMENT

In Northern Ireland, the new Labour Government picked up the progress made by its predecessors with the Anglo-Irish Agreement, the Downing Street Declaration and the Framework Document, all of which it had supported in opposition. This work continued until the historic Good Friday agreement was signed on 10 April 1998, an event that was welcomed by all the major parties in the Commons.

The Northern Ireland (Elections) Bill was introduced in the House of Commons on 21 April and rushed through all its stages to receive royal assent on 7 May, thus enabling elections to an assembly if the Good Friday agreement was approved. In the referendum on the Good Friday agreement held in Northern Ireland on 22 May 1998, an 80.98 per cent turnout registered a 71.12 per cent vote in favour of the agreement. The elections to the assembly were held on 25 June and a clear majority was gained by pro-agreement candidates, endorsing the outcome of the referendum. On 1 July the leader of the Ulster Unionist Party, David Trimble, was elected as First Minister and the deputy leader of the SDLP, Seamus Mallon, was elected as his deputy. Following this, the Northern Ireland Bill was presented in the House of Commons on 15 July. The bill would give the assembly responsibility for shaping policies on matters such as health, education, industrial development and the environment, ending the use of Orders-in-Council by the Westminster Parliament. The Secretary of State for Northern Ireland (Mo Mowlam) said that the bill was 'one of the most important of the present Parliament ... we have drafted a bill to give effect faithfully to the whole agreement, so far as legislation is needed, adding to the machinery only where necessary to make it work. We have moved heaven and earth to consult parties and to draft and introduce a bill as swiftly as possible so that the assembly can be up and running very early in the New Year.'

The second reading was in the Commons on 20 July, somewhat overshadowed by events at Drumcree where Orangemen were trying to assert their right to hold a march. Mo Mowlam admitted that the bill had been prepared in record time and that because of this government amendments would need to be introduced and she promised that, as with other Northern Ireland legislation, the Government would be flexible and sympathetic to other amendments intended to improve the way in which the bill reflected the agreement. She said, 'the people of Northern Ireland have begun an historic journey towards a new future. The bill is another crucial milestone on the way. It is Parliament's opportunity to show solidarity and support for the people of Northern Ireland and to take forward their democratic wish.' The Conservative Northern Ireland spokesman (Andrew Mackay) welcomed the measure in general terms and agreed that nothing 'undermines the sovereignty of the United Kingdom or implies some slippery slope towards a united Ireland – there are clear lines of accountability back to the assembly.' He mentioned, however, concerns over two issues – the release of political prisoners and the entry into Government of political representatives of those organizations yet to establish a commitment to exclusively democratic and peaceful methods. David Trimble welcomed the bill as giving 'government closer to the people and more responsive to their needs'. He hoped that the provisions of the bill would be accompanied by an end to violence but felt that the present situation 'gives much cause for concern'. The Liberal Democrat spokesman on Northern Ireland (Lembit Opik) called it 'a magnificent day

for Northern Irish affairs in this Parliament'. Opposition to the bill was headed by the leader of the Democratic Unionist Party, Revd Ian Paisley, who claimed that 'the bill fails utterly to live up to the Prime Minister's pledges and promises'. The second reading was passed by 322 votes to nine, with five Ulster MPs and four Conservative MPs voting against. The committee stage of the bill was taken on the floor of the House in the penultimate week before the summer recess and the remaining stages in the last week. The third reading was passed by 215 votes to eight (six Ulster MPs and two Conservatives). The bill will be taken in the House of Lords as soon as the Lords return in the autumn and should become law before the end of the year.

LONDON ASSEMBLY

Fulfilling its manifesto commitment to a referendum in London and following the White Paper *New Leadership for London* published in July 1997, the Government introduced in the House of Commons on 29 October 1997 the Greater London Authority (Referendum) Bill, which would pave the way for a referendum on the proposals for an elected mayor and separately elected assembly for London. The Deputy Prime Minster (John Prescott) called this 'the next step towards giving Londoners a choice on how their city is run'. He was proposing a one-question referendum, as 'the Government sees the question of the mayor and the assembly as part of a balanced package providing clear accountability ... there is no sound case for a mayor without an assembly or an assembly without a mayor. Both mayor and assembly would have an important, complementary role to play.'

The bill had its second reading in the House of Commons on 10 November. Introducing the debate, the Minister for London and Construction (Nick Raynsford) said, 'the referendum will be an historic opportunity for Londoners to take control of their destiny, to right the wrongs of the past and to erase the insult done to the people of London by a Government who cared little for the capital, disregarded the wishes of its people and left it for 11 long years without leadership and without a voice'. The Conservative home affairs spokesman (Sir Norman Fowler) moved an amendment declining a second reading on the grounds that the measure failed to provide for separate consultation on the assembly and the mayor. He said that the Conservatives could support the principle of a directly elected mayor acting as a voice for London but he was worried that 'Londoners can express an opinion about the need for a mayor but cannot express a separate opinion about the need for an assembly ... the Government are not prepared to allow the public to express a view on any question where the public might disagree with their opinion.' He also expressed concern that Londoners were being asked to vote on what they think of the idea of a mayor and a directly elected assembly, 'but they will not know what powers either will have' as not even a White

Paper had been published. The Liberal Democrat spokesman on London (Simon Hughes) outlined his party's policy: ' we are strong advocates of constitutional reform. We support devolution in Wales, Scotland and Northern Ireland and we believe strongly in regional government for England. As part of that policy, we are committed in our manifesto to an elected strategic authority for London', but he too was concerned that 'we should not ask people to give the Government an unsigned cheque and agree to a referendum on an incomplete proposal'. He concluded, 'we want two questions … The first is whether there should be a directly elected regional government for London. The second is whether, in addition, there should be a directly elected mayor.' The amendment was defeated by 342 votes to 167, and the second reading similarly passed.

The committee stage of the bill was taken on the floor of the House on 19 and 24 November. An amendment calling for the referendum not to be held until two months had elapsed after the publication of the detailed proposals was defeated by 339 votes to 118, and an amendment on having two separate questions was defeated by 311 votes to 157. An attempt to stop the third reading on 26 November was defeated by 324 votes to 176.

In committee stage in the House of Lords on 13 January 1998, the Government was defeated when a Conservative amendment to clause 1, calling for the publication of the bill on the establishment of the assembly and the election of the mayor to be eight weeks before the holding of any referendum, was passed by 128 votes to 122. In report on 29 January, the Government was again defeated when a Liberal Democrat amendment on clause 1, allowing for a separate vote on the two elements of the package (assembly and mayor), was passed by 111 votes to 104. A related amendment on the form that the ballot paper would have to take to accommodate this change was similarly passed. These defeats were overturned in the Commons on 11 February. The Lords accepted these on 19 February and the bill received royal assent on 23 February. The White Paper *A Mayor and Assembly for London* was finally published on 25 March.

The referendum held on 7 May 1998 had a disappointingly low turnout of just 34 per cent, of whom some 72 per cent voted in favour of the proposals. The Government is committed to introducing a bill defining the powers of the assembly and the mayor in the next Queen's Speech to allow for elections to be held as early as autumn 1999.

LORDS OPPOSITION

The defeats for the Government in the House of Lords on the London authority bill highlighted one problem faced by the new Labour Government: how to deal with the unelected Upper House, with its Opposition majority. In the course of the 1997–8 parliamentary session the Lords defeated the Government some 30 times on diverse issues. These included passing amendments to such major bills as the Firearms (Amendment) Bill, when Lord Howell (Lab.) successfully moved an amendment to exempt disabled persons from the blanket ban and Lord Stoddart of Swindon (Lab.) successfully moved an amendment to allow international competition shooting to continue in secure centres; to the Human Rights Bill, when Baroness Cox (C.) successfully moved an amendment exempting religious schools, colleges and charities from the scope of the bill; to the Competition Bill, when Lord McNally (LD) succeeded in introducing a new clause on the abuse of dominant position by national newspapers; and other amendments to the Bank of England Bill, the Data Protection Bill, the National Minimum Wage Bill, the Social Security Bill and the School Standards and Framework Bill (four times). All of these had to be overturned in the Commons.

It was not only over key government bills that the Lords proved a thorn in the Government's side. On 27 January 1998, following a furore about the decision to ban the sale of beef on the bone, two Conservative peers (Lord Kimball and Lord Willoughby de Broke) moved a motion to annul the regulations banning the sale which was passed by 207 votes to 97. This was little more than a symbolic gesture as the Order was already in force and could not be withdrawn and an attempt by the Liberal Democrats to pass the same motion in the Commons failed by 312 votes to 196 on 10 February.

The most high-profile defeats in the Lords were on the Teaching and Higher Education Bill and the Crime and Disorder Bill. On the third day of report stage on the Teaching and Higher Education Bill on 2 March, the House of Lords amended clause 16 by passing an amendment moved by the Conservative Scottish affairs spokesman (Lord Mackay of Ardbrecknish) to ensure that English and Welsh students going to Scottish universities were not charged £4,000 for attending what would be four-year courses at the Scottish institutions, when Scottish students and students from other European Union countries would only be charged £3,000. This defeat was overturned in committee in the House of Commons, but when asked to accept this on 23 June, instead of the Commons version, the House of Lords passed an amendment moved by Lord Mackay of Ardbrecknish which would in effect reinstate the Lords' original amendment. On 1 July the Government was able to comfortably overturn this defeat in the Commons by 325 votes to 185, but one Labour MP (Denis Canavan) voted against the Government and some 30 others abstained. When this latest Commons version returned to the Lords for approval on 7 July, the Lords did not insist on their original amendment but instead passed a different version designed to achieve the same end, moved by Lord Steel of Aikwood (LD). The former Labour minister Lord Shore of Stepney expressed his 'feeling of repugnance' at the Government's stance and voted for this new amendment. With time running out before the summer recess and the possibility of the bill being lost if the situation continued, this amendment was rejected by the Commons on 13 July by 300 votes to 128, when the Education and Employment Secretary (David Blunkett) offered a review of the situation after one year. On 14 July the Lords passed a compromise amendment without a division after a 40-minute suspension of the House to allow discussion, when it was agreed that the findings of the review would be binding, which was in turn approved by the Commons on 15 July. The bill received royal assent on 16 July.

On the third reading of this bill on 10 March, an amendment was moved by Baroness Young (C.) to strengthen the role of the General Teaching Council by giving it responsibility for standards of teaching, standards of conduct and medical fitness to teach; when this was passed by 137 votes to 112, the government whip Lord Whitty accused the opponents of the bill of a hypocritical attitude and of 'posing' as the friends of students, and then refused to withdraw the remark. This led to Earl Russell (LD) moving a very rarely used vote on 'asperity of speech' (a form of motion of censure), which was passed by 168 votes to 99.

The other bill where the Lords caused the Government to amend its plans for fear of losing the bill was the Crime and Disorder Bill. Although this measure had started in the Lords, a new clause moved by Ann Keen (Lab.) at the Commons report stage on 22 June to lower the age of consent for homosexuals to 16 years was added to the bill by 336 votes to 129 on a free vote. When the Lords were asked to approve the Commons amendments on 22 July, an objection to this amendment moved by Baroness Young (C.) was passed by 289 votes to 122. When the bill returned to the Commons on 28 July, the Government did not press to reinstate the clause but promised to bring in a separate bill on the issue 'at the earliest opportunity'. This allowed the rest of the bill to progress and gain royal assent on 31 July.

There had also been fears that the House of Lords would hold up the progress on the Wild Mammals (Hunting with Dogs) Bill, a Private Member's Bill introduced by Labour back-bencher Michael Foster (Worcester) to outlaw fox-hunting. In the event the bill was killed off in the Commons when, despite receiving a second reading on 28 November by 411 votes to 151, opponents tabled so many amendments for discussion at report stage that the debate ran out of parliamentary time in this session.

Although there was some tinkering with reform of the Upper House, for instance with the passing of a report reforming the ceremony of introduction in the House of Lords, no concrete proposals were put forward by the Government. Calls from the Labour benches to introduce a bill to reform the House of Lords grew stronger as the session continued. Asked on 10 June by Labour back-bencher Don Touhig to 'assure the House that the Government are determined to end the right of hereditary peers to sit in Parliament', the Prime Minster (Tony Blair) replied, 'I confirm that. It is not just the injustice of hereditary peers sitting in the other place and making laws; there is an in-built majority of three to

one in perpetuity for the Conservative party in the House of Lords, irrespective of who wins the general election.' In reply to Labour back-bencher David Hanson a week earlier Tony Blair had said, 'We are committed to the reform of the hereditary element of the House of Lords, for two reasons. First, it cannot possibly be right that people sit as legislators in Houses of Parliament on the basis that their birth makes them hereditary peers. Secondly, it is an absolute democratic scandal that hereditary Conservative peers outnumber the peers of the elected Government of the day by three to one ... it is our job, as New Labour to remove that and make our Houses of Parliament democratic.' The removal of the chief whip in the Lords (Lord Richard) in Tony Blair's first reshuffle at the end of July 1998 and his replacement with Baroness Jay of Paddington, someone felt to be more combative and ready to fight for reform, was seen as a sign that legislation to reform the Upper House would be introduced in the 1998–9 session of Parliament.

ROWS AND REBELS

In the House of Commons the new Government was able to maintain a tighter grip on party discipline throughout the year, with dissenting voices limited to a handful of occasions. The most notable was in December 1997 when Malcolm Chisholm (an Under-Secretary at the Scottish Office) and three Parliamentary Private Secretaries resigned their posts because they could not support the Government over the withdrawal of benefit payments to lone parents. This had come to a head on 10 December in the remaining stages of the Social Security Bill when the Government won the vote on the lone parents clause by 457 votes to 107; the Conservatives voted with the Government but some 47 Labour back-benchers voted against a three-line whip and a similar number abstained. Other occasions included Denis Canavan moving an amendment to the Teaching and Higher Education Bill (Lords) on 8 June covering financial support to students which was defeated by 313 votes to 176 but which saw some 33 Labour back-benchers voting for the amendment and a similar number abstaining; and during the remaining stages of the Competition Bill on 8 July, the Labour chairman of the Treasury select committee (Giles Radice) and other senior Labour chairmen of select committees moved a new clause relating to the dominant position of national newspapers, which was defeated by 301 votes to 68; in all some 23 Labour back-benchers voted against the Government, with a similar number abstaining. Otherwise, so successful was the control of the back-benchers that there were accusations of 'toadying' during set piece events such as Prime Minister's question time.

More worrying for the Government was the fact that dissent appeared to be growing as Parliament moved towards the summer recess. The Sandline/ Arms for Africa affair had seen an unseemly row between the foreign affairs select committee, chaired by a senior Labour MP (Donald Anderson) and with a majority of Labour members, and the

Foreign Secretary (Robin Cook) over access to official Foreign Office documents, though the publication of the Legg report into the whole affair on 27 July seemed to defuse the situation somewhat. The so-called 'cash for access' row saw several back-benchers criticizing the relationship of some lobbying firms with certain areas of government and provoked Opposition accusations of 'cronyism'. This led the Prime Minster to ask the Cabinet Secretary to issue revised guidelines for ministers, special advisers and civil servants on contact with lobbyists.

Lack of progress on freedom of information legislation after the publication of the White Paper *Your Right to Know* on 11 December led to an Early Day Motion tabled on 22 July by former Labour chief whip Derek Foster and signed by 185 back-benchers (nearly all Labour) expressing 'concern at the prospect of any delay in bringing the measure forward' and calling for the publication of a draft bill 'before the end of the current session'. Concern was also expressed over the dropping in the reshuffle of the Chancellor of the Duchy of Lancaster (David Clark), who had been in charge of the freedom of information legislation. Carried out just before the summer recess, the reshuffle caused further strain. On 29 July Labour back-bencher Paul Flynn asked whether the Prime Minister was aware that 'the Welsh group of Labour members is bewildered and unhappy about the decision to sack' junior Welsh Office minister Win Griffiths, and following his resignation from the Government, the former Minister for Welfare Reform, Frank Field, made a personal statement in the Commons on 29 July

which suggested that there were tensions and power struggles going on within the Government.

At the end of its first full session the Government can look back on several major constitutional manifesto commitments fulfilled. Whilst the Opposition has attempted to influence the legislation, it has proved fairly powerless to do so. Its argument that new assemblies would 'create strains which could well pull apart the Union … and risk rivalry and conflict' has fallen on deaf ears. It has encountered more success with sustained attacks on issues such as 'cronyism' and it is generally agreed by Westminster pundits that the Leader of the Opposition, William Hague, usually has the better of the Prime Minister at question time. But this is to little avail outside the rarified atmosphere of Parliament. Nationally the Government's standing remains high in the opinion polls, except in Scotland, where, ironically, support for the Scottish National Party appears to be growing at the expense of the Labour Party as the elections for the Scottish parliament approach.

The House of Commons was recalled from recess on 2 September 1998 to debate the Criminal Justice (Terrorism and Conspiracy) Bill, introduced following the Omagh bombing on 15 August. There were protests from both Labour and Opposition members that the bill was flawed, having been drafted hastily, and that it was being railroaded through Parliament with inadquate time for debate. All stages were taken in the Commons on 2 September and in the Lords on 3 September, and the Act received royal assent on 4 September.

PUBLIC ACTS OF PARLIAMENT

This list commences with five Public Acts which received the royal assent before September 1997. Those Public Acts which follow received the royal assent after August 1997. The date stated after each Act is the date on which it came into operation; c. indicates the chapter number of each Act.

Appropriation (No. 2) Act 1997 c.57, 31 July 1997
Grants certain sums out of the Consolidated Fund for the service of the year ending 31 March 1997 and appropriates the supplies granted in this session of Parliament

Finance (No. 2) Act 1997 c.58, 31 July 1997
Amends the law relating to taxation, *inter alia*, it introduces a new scheme of allowances for films and alters the tax credit system for dividends and distributions

Education (Schools) Act 1997 c.59, various dates, some to be appointed
Provides for the abolition of the assisted places scheme

Law Officers Act 1997 c.60, 30 September 1997
Enables the Solicitor-General to exercise the functions of the Attorney-General and the Attorney-General for Northern Ireland

Referendums (Scotland and Wales) 1997 c.61, 31 July 1997
Makes provision for referendums to be held in Scotland and Wales in relation to the creation of a parliament (with tax-varying powers) or assembly respectively; and for connected purposes

Ministerial and other Salaries Act 1997 c.62, 6 November 1997
Amends the 1975 Act by introducing a formula which will increase salaries by the average percentage by which the mid-points of the senior civil service bands are increased from 1 April 1998; and provides for connected purposes

Local Government Finance (Supplementary Credit Approvals) Act 1997 c.63, 6 November 1997
Amends the law relating to supplementary credit approvals which are issued to local authorities in England and Wales by Ministers to authorize certain specific capital expenditure

Firearms (Amendment) (No. 2) Act 1997 c.64, various dates
Extends the class of prohibited weapons to include small-calibre pistols

Local Government (Contracts) Act 1997 c.65, various dates, some to be appointed
Makes provision as to the powers of local authorities to enter into contracts and to enable the expenditure of local authorities making administrative arrangements for magistrates' courts to be treated otherwise than as capital expenditure

Plant Varieties Act 1997 c.66, various dates, some to be appointed
Makes provision regarding rights in relation to plant varieties, for the Plant Varieties and Seeds Tribunal and extends the time limit for institution of proceedings for contravention of seeds regulations

Consolidated Fund (No. 2) Act 1997 c.67, 17 December 1997
Applies certain sums out of the Consolidated Fund to the service of the years ending 31 March 1998 and 1999

Special Immigration Appeals Commission Act 1997 c.68, various dates, some to be appointed
Establishes the Special Immigration Appeals Commission and makes provision for its jurisdiction

Supreme Court (Offices) Act 1997 c.69, 17 December 1997
Makes provision with respect to the qualification for appointment as and tenure of office of Permanent Secretary to the Lord Chancellor and Clerk of the Crown in Chancery

Education (Student Loans) Act 1998 c.1, various dates, some to be appointed
Makes provision with respect to public sector student loans

Public Processions (Northern Ireland) Act 1998 c.2, part on 16 February 1998 and the remainder on 2 March 1998
Amends the law relating to public processions in Northern Ireland and provides for the establishment and functions of the Parades Commission for Northern Ireland

Greater London Authority (Referendum) Act 1998 c.3, 23 February 1997
Makes provision for the holding of a referendum on the establishment of a Greater London authority and for expenditure in preparation for such an authority as well as conferring additional functions on the Local Government Commission for England in connection with the establishment of such an authority

Consolidated Fund Act 1998 c.4, 18 March 1998
Applies certain sums out of the Consolidated Fund to the service of the years ending 31 March 1997 and 1998

Fossil Fuel Levy Act 1998 c.5, 1 April 1998
Amends the Electricity Act 1989 s. 33

Wireless Telegraphy Act 1998 c.6, 18 June 1998
Makes provision for the grant of licences, other than television licences, under the 1949 Act and promotes the efficient use and management of the electro-magnetic spectrum for wireless telegraphy

Nuclear Explosions (Prohibition and Inspections) Act 1998 c.7, day to be appointed
Gives effect to certain provisions of the Comprehensive Nuclear Test Ban Treaty adopted in New York on 10 September 1996

Employment Rights (Dispute Resolution) Act 1998 c.8, various dates, some to be appointed
Makes provision for the renaming of industrial tribunals, methods of resolving employment disputes, the adjustments of awards of compensation for unfair dismissal; and for connected purposes

Northern Ireland (Emergency Provisions) Act 1998 c.9, 8 April 1998
Postpones the expiry and otherwise makes amendments to the 1996 Act

Criminal Procedure (Intermediate Diets) (Scotland) Act 1998 c.10, 8 April 1998
Amends the law retrospectively in relation to intermediate diets in summary criminal proceedings

Bank of England Act 1998 c.11, day to be appointed
Makes provision in relation to the constitution, regulation, financial arrangements and functions of the Bank of England and makes various amendments to the Banking Act 1987, the Financial Services Act 1986 and the Companies Act 1989

Northern Ireland (Elections) Act 1998 c.12, part on 7 May 1998 the remainder on 28 May 1998
Makes provision for the establishment of an assembly for Northern Ireland and for the election of its members

Animal Health (Amendment) Act 1998 c.13, 21 July 1998
Makes provision for the improvement of the welfare of animals in quarantine

Social Security Act 1998 c.14, various dates, some to be appointed
Makes provision as to the making of decisions and the determination of appeals under enactments relating to social security, child support, vaccine damage payments and war pensions

Magistrates' Courts (Procedure) Act 1998 c.15, various dates, some to be appointed
Amends the Magistrates' Courts Act 1980 to make provision in relation to certain criminal proceedings in magistrates' courts and about proof of previous convictions and orders

Tax Credits (Initial Expenditure) Act 1998 c.16, 21 May 1998
Authorizes the incurring of expenditure in connection with the replacement of certain social security benefits with income tax credits

Petroleum Act 1998 c.17, various dates, some to be appointed
Consolidates certain enactments about petroleum offshore installations and submarine pipelines

Audit Commission Act 1998 c.18, 18 September 1998
Consolidates Part II of the Local Government Finance Act 1982 and other enactments relating to

the Audit Commission for Local Authorities and the NHS in England and Wales

Community Care (Residential Accommodation) Act 1998 c.19, 11 August 1998
Restricts the amount of the personal capital which may be taken into account by a local authority in determining whether a person should be provided with residential accommodation that would be, or be treated as, provided under the National Assistance Act 1948 Part III

Late Payment of Commercial Debts (Interest) Act 1998 c.20, various dates, some to be appointed

European Communities (Amendment) Act 1998 c.21, 11 June 1998
Makes provision consequential on the Treaty signed at Amsterdam on 2 October 1997 which amended the EU treaty

National Lottery Act 1998 c.22, various dates, some to be appointed
Makes further provision in relation to the National Lottery by, *inter alia*, providing for the establishment of the National Endowment for Science, Technology and the Arts, and for connected purposes

Public Interest Disclosure Act 1998 c.23, various dates, some to be appointed
Protects individuals who make certain disclosures of information in the public interest (e.g. that a criminal offence has been committed); allows such persons to bring victimization actions; and for connected purposes

Road Traffic Reduction (National Targets) Act 1998 c.24, 2 July 1998
Makes further provision for road traffic reduction targets

Registered Establishments (Scotland) Act 1998 c.25, 9 July 1998
Adds to the classes of establishment which require to be registered under section 61 of the Social Work (Scotland) Act 1968; and for connected purposes

Pesticides Act 1998 c.26, 9 September 1998
Amends the Food and Environment Protection Act 1985 in respect of the powers concerning pesticides and the enforcement of provisions relating to pesticide control

Criminal Justice (International Co-operation) (Amendment) Act 1998 c.27, 9 September 1998
Amends Section 12 of the 1990 Act by allowing a person to manufacture or supply certain substances (which manufacture or supply would otherwise be a criminal offence) with the express consent of a constable

Appropriation Act 1998 c.28, 16 July 1998
Applies a sum out of the Consolidated Fund to the service of the year ending 31 March 1999; appropriates the supplies granted in this session of Parliament and repeals certain Consolidated Fund and Appropriation Acts

Data Protection Act 1998 c.29, various dates, some to be appointed
Makes provision for regulation of the processing of information relating to individuals, including the obtaining, holding, use or disclosure thereof, e.g. by giving rights of access to personal data held by any data controller on written request and receipt of a fee

Teaching and Higher Education Act 1998 c.30, various dates, some to be appointed
Makes provision for the establishment of General Teaching Councils for England and Wales and for the registration, qualification and training of teachers and inspection thereof; for grants and loans to and fees payable by students in higher or further education; to enable the higher and further education councils in Scotland to discharge certain functions jointly; to enable young people to have time off work for training or study; and for purposes connected with education

School Standards and Framework Act 1998 c.31, various dates, some to be appointed
Makes new provision with respect to school education and provision of nursery education otherwise than at school, and for other purposes connected with schooling and education

Police (Northern Ireland) Act 1998 c.32, day or days to be appointed
Makes provision about policing in Northern Ireland, and for connected purposes

Landmines Act 1998 c.33, day to be appointed
Promotes the control of anti-personnel land-mines; and for connected purposes

Private Hire Vehicles (London) Act 1998 c.34, day or days to be appointed
Provides for the licensing and regulation of private hire vehicles (one constructed or adapted to seat fewer than nine passengers other than a licensed taxi or public service vehicle) and their drivers and operators within the Metropolitan Police division and the City of London

Northern Ireland (Sentences) Act 1998 c.35, day to be appointed
Makes provision about the release on licence of certain persons serving sentences of imprisonment in Northern Ireland

Finance Act 1998 c.36, 31 July 1998
Amends the law relating to taxation, *inter alia*, in relation to self-assessment for companies, changes in the structure and reliefs for capital gains tax, transfer pricing, and the removal of the cash basis of accounting for most traders

Crime and Disorder Act 1998 c.37
Government of Wales Act 1998 c.38
National Minimum Wage Act 1998 c.39
Criminal Justice (Terrorism and Conspiracy) Act 1998 c.40

WHITE PAPERS, REPORTS, ETC.

On 18 October 1997 the Lord Chancellor (Lord Irvine of Lairg) announced proposals to reform the civil justice system. These included:
– the Legal Aid Board to enter into contracts with solicitors for their services at a fixed price for undertaking a certain number of cases each year
– legal aid to be abolished for most civil damages cases and other money claims
– the 'merit test' to be tightened so that only the most deserving cases are pursued
– the 'no win, no fee' principle for the payment of lawyers to be extended to all civil proceedings except family cases, with plaintiffs taking out insurance to cover the defendant's costs should they lose the case
– the high earnings of defence lawyers in complex or lengthy trials to be curbed
– a community legal service to be established to encourage mediation
– the implementation of Lord Woolf's proposals for reforming civil justice procedures put forward in July 1996

Rights Brought Home was presented to Parliament on 24 October 1997 by the Home Secretary (Jack Straw). The main proposals were:
– the European Convention on Human Rights to be incorporated into UK law through a Human Rights Bill (introduced in the House of Lords on 23 October 1997)
– all future legislation to be interpreted as far as possible in a way which is compatible with the Convention; if this is not possible, the legislation to be amended, using a fast-track procedure, to bring it into line

Eliminating World Poverty: a Challenge for the 21st Century was presented to Parliament by the Secretary of State for International Development (Clare Short) on 5 November 1997. The main points were:
– a reaffirmed commitment to meeting the internationally-agreed target of halving world poverty by 2015
– a reinstated target of 7 per cent of GNP to be spent on development assistance
– new partnerships to be formed with developing countries, other development agencies, the private sector and voluntary organizations
– a consistency of approach to be adopted in wider policies affecting development, including trade, investment, agriculture and the environment
– the Aid and Trade provision to be ended and replaced by stronger partnerships with the private sector
– stronger emphasis to be placed on public awareness and an annual development policy forum to be held
– the Government to work for world-wide aid effectiveness, the elimination of tied aid, the

acceptance of core labour standards and a renegotiation of the Lomé Convention

No More Excuses: A New Approach to Tackling Youth Crime in England and Wales was presented to Parliament by the Home Secretary (Jack Straw) on 27 November 1997. The main elements were:
– a statutory statement of the principal aim of the youth justice system, i.e. to prevent offending by young people, and of the duty on youth justice practitioners to have regard to this aim
– faster and more efficient procedures from arrest to sentence to be introduced
– a new sentence, a detention and training order, to be introduced, comprising 50 per cent custody and 50 per cent community supervision
– long-term reform of the youth courts, including youth panels to deal with first time offenders

Building Partnerships for Prosperity: Sustainable Growth, Competitiveness and Employment in the English Regions was presented to Parliament by the Deputy Prime Minister (John Prescott) on 3 December 1997. The main proposals were:
– English Partnerships and the Commission for the New Towns to be merged by 1 April 2000
– the Rural Development Commission to be wound up
– nine regional development agencies to be set up

The New NHS: Modern, Dependable was presented to Parliament by the Health Secretary (Frank Dobson) on 9 December 1997. It included the following proposals for reforming the NHS in England:
– the internal market to be abolished, with a saving of £1 billion of 'red tape' costs over the lifetime of the current Parliament
– teams of GPs and community nurses to work together in primary care groups serving about 100,000 patients, and to take one of four options of levels of responsibility, including managing a single unified budget for health care in their area
– long-term service agreements to replace annual contracts between health authorities, primary care groups and NHS trusts, and to include explicit quality standards
– NHS trusts to have new statutory duties of quality and partnership and to be required to publish details of their performance
– health authorities in due course to relinquish direct commissioning responsibility but to draw up three-year health improvement programmes and allocate funds to primary care groups; fewer health authorities covering larger areas to result from the changes
– a new NHS charter to be drawn up
– an annual survey of patients and carers to be conducted
– management costs to be capped and a national schedule of reference costs to be drawn up

- evidence-based national service frameworks to be established
- a national institute for clinical excellence to be set up
- a new system of clinical governance to be established
- a commission for health improvement to be set up to oversee the quality of clinical services locally
- incentives and sanctions to be put in place to enhance performance and efficiency
- a national performance framework to be used to measure the performance of the NHS
- all GP surgeries and hospitals to be connected to NHSnet, a computerized information system
- suspected cancer sufferers to see a specialist within two weeks of a request from their GP

Designed to Care was presented to Parliament by the Secretary of State for Scotland (Donald Dewar) on 9 December 1997. It included the following proposals for reforming the NHS in Scotland:
- the internal market to be abolished
- the number of trusts to be reduced and management costs to be cut, resulting in savings of £100 million
- GP fundholding to be replaced by primary care trusts and networks of GPs in local health care co-operatives
- a single stream of funds to cover both hospital services and drugs
- health improvement programmes to be developed
- one-stop clinics to provide tests, results and diagnosis on the same day
- electronic links to all GP surgeries
- a Scottish health technology assessment centre to be established
- a process of quality assurance for clinical services to be established
- an acute services review to be conducted

Your Right to Know: Freedom of Information was presented to Parliament by the Chancellor of the Duchy of Lancaster (David Clark) on 11 December 1997. The main proposals were:
- people to be given the right to see almost all official information across the whole public sector, unless it would clearly harm one or more of seven specified interests or be against the public interest
- an independent Information Commissioner to be appointed, answerable to the courts and with the power to order the release of information
- a new criminal offence to be created for wilfully destroying, altering or withholding records or hampering an investigation by the Information Commissioner

The Food Standards Agency: A Force for Change was presented to Parliament by the Agriculture Minister (Jack Cunningham) on 14 January 1998. The main proposals were:
- an independent Food Standards Agency to be established, reporting to the Department of Health

- the agency to cover the whole of the UK, with separate executives for Scotland, Wales and Northern Ireland
- the agency's annual costs to be funded mainly by a charge on the food industry
- the agency's functions to include monitoring the safety and standards of all food for human consumption; commissioning research and developing new policies; co-ordinating and monitoring the standards of food law enforcement; and advising and informing the public, ministers and the food industry

Putting Patients First, a White Paper on the NHS in Wales, was presented to Parliament by Welsh Office Health Minister (Win Griffiths) on 15 January 1998. The main proposals were:
- the internal market and GP fundholding to be abolished
- local health groups to be established, comprising health professionals, health authorities, local authorities and other local interests
- a statutory requirement for NHS organizations to co-operate with each other to be introduced
- health authorities to take the lead in drawing up five-year health improvement programmes
- a national institute for clinical excellence to be established to offer guidance on best practice
- a commission for health improvement to be established to monitor quality standards
- the Welsh Office to develop national service frameworks for major diseases
- an NHS charter for Wales to be produced
- a national survey of patients to be conducted
- a corporate plan for the NHS in Wales to be drawn up in advance of the creation of the Welsh Assembly
- cost savings to be made over five years and redirected to patient services

A White Paper on fair employment was presented to Parliament by the Northern Ireland Secretary (Mo Mowlam) on 11 March 1998. Its main proposals were:
- a new statutory obligation on the public sector in Northern Ireland to promote equality of opportunity in a variety of areas
- a new Equality Commission to police the implementation of the statutory obligation
- a 'targeting social need' initiative, linked to a 'promoting social inclusion' drive
- the extension of fair employment law to cover the provision of goods, facilities and services
- a range of measures to combat unemployment and the community unemployment differential
- other changes to fair employment legislation

A Mayor and Assembly for London was presented to Parliament by the Deputy Prime Minister (John Prescott) on 25 March 1998. The main proposals were:
- a Greater London authority to be established, comprising a mayor elected by the 'supplementary vote' system of proportional representation,

and a 25-member assembly elected by the 'additional member' system; elections to be held every four years

– the authority to have responsibility for transport, planning, economic development and regeneration, the environment, policing, fire and emergency planning, culture and sport, and health, with an annual budget of about £3.3 billion
– the authority to cost about £20 million to set up and £20 million a year to run; 80 per cent of the running costs to be met by central government and 20 per cent from the council tax
– a new 23-member Metropolitan Police authority to be established, with 11 members coming from the assembly and the rest appointed by the Home Secretary
– a new fire and emergency planning authority to be established
– two new executive bodies, Transport for London and the London Development Agency, to be established and to be directly accountable to the mayor
– the assembly to be responsible for scrutinizing the mayor's activities and the performance of the new authorities and executive bodies
– a monthly public question-time to be held, and an annual state of London debate
– a referendum on the proposals to be held on 7 May 1998
– if approved, the first elections to be held in 1999 or 2000

Tackling Drugs to Build a Better Britain was presented to Parliament by the Leader of the House of Commons (Ann Taylor) on 27 April 1998. It presented a ten-year plan for reducing drugs misuse, including the following objectives and proposals:

– the proportion of people under 25 using illegal drugs to be reduced
– the level of reoffending among drugs misusers to be reduced
– the participation of drugs misusers in treatment programmes to be increased
– the access to drugs among 5–16-year-olds to be reduced
– expenditure on drugs-related policies to be better targeted on preventive policies
– children to be taught about the dangers of drugs from the age of five, both within and outside formal education settings
– police resources to be targeted on the detection of drugs-related crime, and community anti-drugs networks to be encouraged
– the number of drugs misusers denied immediate access to appropriate treatment to be reduced
– diplomatic efforts to be increased to achieve a reduction in drug trafficking
– a proportion of the assets seized from drugs traffickers to be used for anti-drugs programmes

Fairness at Work was presented to Parliament by the President of the Board of Trade (Margaret Beckett) on 21 May 1998. The main proposals were:

– union recognition to be granted if 40 per cent of the eligible workforce votes in favour of it, and to be automatic where more than 50 per cent of the workforce are union members; firms with fewer than 20 employees to be exempt
– every employee to be entitled to be represented by a union official over any grievance or disciplinary matter
– anyone dismissed for taking part in lawful industrial action to be entitled to appeal to an unfair dismissal tribunal
– the qualifying period for claiming unfair dismissal to be reduced to one year
– the £12,000 limit on compensation for unfair dismissal to be removed
– an entitlement to three months' parental leave after one year's service, including for adoptive parents
– the qualifying period for extended maternity absence to be reduced to one year
– maternity leave to be extended to 18 weeks
– the right to reasonable time off for family emergencies regardless of length of service

A White Paper on strategic export controls was presented to Parliament by the President of the Board of Trade (Margaret Beckett) on 1 July 1998. Its main proposals were:

– parliamentary scrutiny of secondary legislation on strategic export controls
– the purposes for which export controls can be imposed to be set out in secondary legislation
– stronger powers for the Government to take action against the proliferation of weapons of mass destruction
– controls on the transfer of technology by intangible means, e.g. via fax or e-mail
– additional controls on the trafficking of, and brokering of deals in, certain goods between overseas countries
– exporters to be required to report the necessary information to enable the UK to meet its reporting obligations to international bodies

Modern Forces for the Modern World: The Strategic Defence Review was presented to Parliament by the Defence Secretary (George Robertson) on 8 July 1998. It included the following main proposals:

– the creation of joint rapid reaction forces, a joint RN/RAF fixed wing force (Joint Force 2000), a joint battlefield helicopter command, a joint Army/RAF ground-based air defence organization, a rapidly deployable joint force headquarters, and a joint defence centre; the Chief of Joint Operations at the Permanent Joint Headquarters to have enhanced powers
– four more roll-on roll-off container ships to be acquired

- improved defence medical services, logistic enhancements and improved nuclear, biological and chemical defences
- two large aircraft carriers to be procured for the Royal Navy
- the Royal Naval Reserve to be increased by 350
- reductions to be made in the numbers of attack submarine, surface escort and mine countermeasure forces
- the Army front line to be restructured to provide six deployable armoured or mechanized brigades
- an air manoeuvre brigade and an additional armoured reconnaissance regiment to be created
- the Army's strength to be increased by 3,300, the tank regiments to be restructured, and the Territorial Army to be modernized and have its strength cut to 40,000
- a range of new missiles to be procured for the RAF
- the Tornado GR4 bomber and the Nimrod-R to be improved, and the air transport fleet to be modernized
- the Reserve Air Forces to be increased by 270
- the front line to be reduced by 36 fast jet combat aircraft and two squadrons to be disbanded
- defence diplomacy to be one of the missions of the UK armed forces, and more readily-available forces to be declared as potentially available to the UN
- the nuclear deterrent capability to be reduced to the minimum required, with only one submarine on patrol at any time
- improvements to be made in the recruitment, training and welfare of personnel
- new procurement processes to be introduced (the 'Smart Procurement' initiative) and the Procurement Executive to be turned into a defence agency
- a 4-star Chief of Defence Logistics to be appointed, and a single Defence Transport and Movements organization to be created
- the Army Technical Support Agency to be absorbed into an integrated army equipment support organization
- the Naval Aircraft Repair Organization and most of the RAF Maintenance Group Defence Agency to be merged
- a joint Defence Storage and Distribution Agency to be created by April 1999
- excess estate holdings to be disposed of

A comprehensive spending review, *Modern Public Services for Britain: Investing in Reform* was presented to Parliament by the Chancellor of the Exchequer (Gordon Brown) on 14 July 1998. The White Paper outlined the Government's spending plans for 1999–2002, and included the following:
- an increase in spending on education of on average over 5 per cent a year above the rate of inflation between 1998–9 and 2001–2
- an increase in spending on the NHS of on average nearly 4.75 per cent a year above the rate of inflation between 1998–9 and 2001–2

- an extra £1,700 million to improve public transport and modernize the road and rail network
- an extra £4,400 million on spending to regenerate cities and housing
- child benefit for over-16s to be replaced by a means-tested educational maintenance allowance for those who stay on at school
- a new criminal justice strategy to ensure fast-track justice for persistent young offenders and reduce crime
- £1,100 million to be invested in science
- the international development budget to be increased by £1.6 billion
- new quality standards for government departments and efficiency targets for key public services
- public sector pay to be 'fair and affordable'
- eye-test charges for pensioners to be abolished and a minimum income to be guaranteed
- better social services for the elderly and disabled
- the Ministry of Agriculture, Fisheries and Food and the Child Support Agency to be reformed
- extra resources to be provided for the implementation of devolution in Scotland, Wales and Northern Ireland
- access to the arts and museums to be widened
- over £100 million to be provided for reducing by two-thirds the number of people sleeping rough
- surplus government assets to be disposed of

A New Deal for Transport: Better for Everyone was presented to Parliament by the Deputy Prime Minister (John Prescott) and the Secretaries of State for Wales, Scotland and Northern Ireland (Ron Davies, Donald Dewar and Mo Mowlam) on 20 July 1998. The main proposals were:
- a Strategic Rail Authority to manage passenger railway franchising and with the power to impose stiffer penalties on rail companies that fail to meet targets for punctuality and reliability
- charges for workplace parking and for driving into town centres; trial schemes for motorway charges at traffic bottlenecks and road tolls in rural beauty spots
- local transport plans to be developed by local authorities
- measures to improve the safety of children who walk or cycle to school
- higher expenditure on buses and half-price tickets for pensioners
- additional resources to be allocated for better road maintenance and traffic information and management
- regional ports and airports to be developed
- a national public transport information system to be in place by 2000
- a new commission for integrated transport to advise the Government and monitor the implementation of policy

Promoting Disabled People's Rights was presented to Parliament by the Minister for Disabled People (Alan Howarth) on 21 July 1998. The main proposal was the establishment of a Disability Rights Commission to work towards the elimination of discrimination against disabled people

Travel Choices for Scotland was presented to Parliament by the Secretary of State for Scotland (Donald Dewar) on 22 July 1998. The main points were:
– the recognition of the particular transport needs of rural Scotland
– air and ferry services to the islands to be improved
– road charges and charges for workplace parking
– local authorities to have greater powers to ensure better bus services
– a £90 million public transport fund to support local authority transport strategies

Fairer, Faster and Firmer: A Modern Approach to Immigration and Asylum was presented to Parliament by the Home Secretary (Jack Straw) on 27 July 1998. The main proposals were:
– a new national body to plan and co-ordinate welfare support for asylum seekers
– the budget for such support to be separated from the social security budget
– accommodation to be provided where necessary on a no-choice basis, anywhere in the UK
– a voucher scheme to be used and cash payments to be minimized
– 10,000 people waiting since before 1993 for their applications to be heard normally to be allowed to stay
– bail hearings to be introduced after the first seven days of detention of immigrants or asylum-seekers
– a single, more streamlined appeal procedure
– regulation of non-qualified immigration advisers
– registrars to be given statutory powers to prevent bogus marriages
– the right of appeal for visitors refused entry to the UK to be restored
– domestic staff to be allowed to enter the UK with their employers only if they have specialized skills

Modern Local Government: In Touch with the People was presented to Parliament by the Deputy Prime Minister (John Prescott) on 30 July 1998. The main proposals were:
– directly-elected mayors with executive powers to be allowed in every town and city in England, subject to support in a local referendum
– about 100 'beacon' councils to be designated, to act as centres of excellence upon which other councils should model themselves
– councils to be required to adopt a code of conduct, overseen by a national independent standards board
– voting in local elections to be made easier
– referendums to be obligatory over controversial plans
– one-third of councillors to be elected annually
– compulsory competitive tendering to be replaced by a 'best value' procedure, with new national performance indicators for efficiency, cost and quality

– councils to be allowed to raise local business rates, to a maximum of 1 per cent of the national business rate in any one year and with the backing of local businesses

Science and Discovery

New Moons for Uranus

Brett Gladman and his team from the Canadian Institute for Theoretical Astrophysics at the University of Toronto, used the 5-metre Hale telescope to study the planet Uranus and to try to detect any faint moons round the planet. Photographs were taken on two consecutive nights.

On comparing the images, the team found two objects travelling with the planet. At magnitudes +20 and +22, the objects are the faintest satellites ever picked up by an earth-based telescope. These observations were confirmed a month later by other observatories. This increases the number of known satellites around Uranus to 17.

The brighter of the two objects, S/1997U2, is estimated to be about 150 km in diameter and the other, S/1997U1, about 60 km. Brian Marsden and Gareth Williams of the Harvard-Smithsonian Center for Astrophysics confirmed that the objects are genuine satellites, although they were unsure at first about the fainter one. Both satellites have inclined, highly eccentric retrograde orbits. The smaller one orbits at a mean distance of 7.2 million km from Uranus and takes 1.6 years to complete a revolution; the larger takes 3.5 years to orbit the planet, at a mean distance of 12.2 million km. Both moons have a reddish colour, due possibly to the action of cosmic and ultraviolet radiation on an organic-rich icy surface. It is thought that they were once members of the Kuiper Belt but were captured by Uranus at a later stage. The suggested names for the moons are Sycorax for the larger moon and Caliban for the smaller.

Jupiter and its Moons

The Hubble Space Telescope's Near Infra-red Camera and Multi-Object Spectrometer (NIC-MOS) has identified clouds above the normal visible cloud layers on Jupiter. A band of methane gas, located between two cloud layers of ammonia, has been shown to absorb reflected sunlight at a wavelength of 2 microns (in the infra-red region of the spectrum). More details have also been published on the planet's complex wind system. David Atkinson and colleagues at the University of Idaho have shown that the wind speed increases as the lower regions of the atmosphere are penetrated. At the tops of clouds seen on normal photographs of the planet, the speeds are in the region of 80 to 100 metres per second; 35 km lower down, the wind speed increases to 170 metres per second and remains at this value for the next 65 km. The composition of the atmosphere also varies with location on the planet. The atmospheric probe released by NASA's Galileo spacecraft in 1995 found much less water than scientists had expected, but subsequent information has shown that the area investigated was one of a series of dry regions; the surrounding areas contain as much as 100 times more water. The dry regions cover less than 1 per cent of the total surface area and appear to be areas where winds converge and create huge down-draughts.

Photographs taken by Galileo have shown that over a five-month period, a dark spot some 400 km in diameter has appeared on Jupiter's moon Io. The spot is centred on the volcanic crater named Pillan Patera. The crater is certainly active; in June 1998 both Galileo and the Hubble Space Telescope observed a plume of gas about 120 km high over Pillan.

In December 1997 a close fly-by of another of Jupiter's moons, Europa, revealed that the moon may have a global sub-surface ocean; from the data, scientists are of the opinion that ice has been warmed to a slushy consistency. Some of the craters on the surface have filled with slushy ice. There are also fractures filled by smooth ribbons of fresh ice, and features similar to jumbled iceberg debris have also been identified.

The Face on Mars

When the Viking spacecraft landed on Mars in 1976, its orbiting component took photographs of the surface of the planet in more detail than had previously been possible. Of particular interest was an area called Cydonia, a region of tablelands and steep, flat-topped hills situated along an escarpment separating the heavily cratered highlands from the lower-lying plains situated to the north. One of the photographs issued with a Jet Propulsion Laboratory press release contained a feature described as a mountain resembling a human face. The feature was 3 km across and the photograph was taken from a range of 1,873 km.

Unfortunately, the description was taken literally by some members of the public, who claimed that the feature was an artificial structure built by an extinct race of Martians. They felt their case was strengthened when, in 1993, cameras on board the Mars Observer spacecraft failed to operate just as they were about to photograph the area. It was claimed that the authorities did not want the face on Mars to be photographed again.

The mystery, if there ever was one, has been cleared up by photographs taken by the Mars Orbital camera on the Mars Global Surveyor. The area was photographed when the spacecraft was near to its closest approach to the planet on 5 April 1998. Atmospheric conditions were ideal and the angle of solar illumination was favourable. The critical photograph covered an area 41.5 km long and 4.4 km wide, giving a resolution of 4.3 metres per pixel, some ten times better than the earlier photographs. And the photograph showed that the 'face' was nothing more than a pile of rocks!

MARTIAN METEORITE QUERIES

In August 1996, scientists announced that research on a meteorite, ALH 84001, found in the Allan Hills in Antarctica seemed to indicate that the meteorite had come from Mars. This belief was based on the composition of the carbonate deposits found in the meteorite. Within these carbonate deposits were found fossil structures shaped like miniature bacteria and from a detailed study of these, scientists at NASA reported that the rock had originated on Mars and possibly carried evidence of the remnants of life which had existed there in the distant past.

There is now some doubt that this explanation is the correct one, following research on the carbonate structure found in a meteorite which fell in Tunisia in 1931. A team led by Phillipe Gillet of the École Normale Supérieure in Lyon has suggested that the carbonate deposits on samples of the Tunisian meteorite collected in 1994 look uncannily like those found in ALH 84001. However, no such structures have been found in the samples which were collected on the day that the meteorite fell in 1931. This suggests that the bacterial structures in the carbonate deposits are terrestrial contamination, and that the bacteria have infiltered the meteorite during the last 63 years. Consequently, the explanation put forward by NASA for the AHL 84001 meteorite is in doubt; research continues.

WATER ON THE MOON

During its radar surveillance of the Moon in 1994 the US military satellite *Clementine* detected what was thought to be water ice in the south polar region. Ice cannot survive in areas which are exposed to direct sunlight, so the only regions where it could exist are areas where sunlight cannot penetrate, such as at the bottom of craters. To follow up these discoveries, another probe, *Lunar Prospector*, was launched in January 1998. On reaching the Moon, the probe was initially placed in an 11.8 hour elliptical orbit, which was later adjusted to a circular orbit about 100 km above the lunar surface. The probe contained equipment to perform four tasks: to look for signs of lunar ice; to determine the composition of the lunar crust; to make a more detailed map of the lunar gravitational field; and to look for evidence of a lunar magnetic field.

The probe confirmed the presence of water ice in both the north and south polar regions in quantities far greater than expected. It is thought that each cubic metre of polar soil contains up to 19 litres of water. The icy regions cover between 10,000 to 50,000 square km in the north and 5,000 to 20,000 square km around the south pole. The source of the water is thought to be comets and meteoritic impacts. The water is thought to have collected in the very cold regions and could remain for millions of years.

The remaining tasks are continuing satisfactorily; scientists are learning about the composition and structure of the Moon. After a year in orbit the probe will be lowered to just 10 km above the surface for more detailed mapping.

SOLAR RESEARCH

The Solar and Heliospheric Observatory (SOHO), a satellite designed to monitor solar behaviour, has enabled the rotation of the Sun to be tracked at levels below the visible surface. Scientists have found that solar flares produce seismic waves in the Sun's interior. A solar quake produces ripples similar to those caused by a stone being thrown into water, but the disturbance travels about 80,000 km in an hour before fading. The solar waves accelerate from 35,000 km per hour initially to 400,000 km per hour before fading.

SOHO has also discovered at least a dozen tornadoes located in the polar regions of the Sun, with diameters about the size of the Earth. Superimposed on the steady wind speed of 15 km per second are gusts with speeds of up to 140 km per second. The hot gases in these tornadoes spiral away from the Sun, gathering speed as they go. Research is currently being carried out to determine how these gases react with the solar wind further out in space.

Another discovery has been the identification of near-polar jet streams that lie completely below the Sun's surface and have rotational speeds much higher than that of the surroundings. It was previously thought there was a smooth fall-off of rotational speed as the polar regions were reached. Near the equator, in sunspot latitudes, bands of gas lying parallel to the solar equator produce shear zones, which could be linked to sunspot activity. These can penetrate as much as 20,000 km below the surface.

SOHO has recorded many instances of the Sun throwing out huge clouds of gas, called Coronal Mass Ejections (CMEs). When these hit the Earth, they can cause power cuts, communication failures and auroral displays. The CMEs seem to explode in a kind of chain reaction; disturbances in the magnetic field lead to one explosion, followed by another anywhere on the Sun's surface. It is thought that magnetic loops connect areas in opposite hemispheres.

CLOSE CALL IN SPACE

On the night of 6 December 1997, James V. Scotti was using the Spacewatch Telescope on Kitt Peak, Arizona, an instrument specially designed to detect objects which will pass close to the Earth on their journey around the Sun. He had already recorded nine asteroids when another appeared on the monitor screen which, on closer examination, proved to be a Near Earth Asteroid (NEA). The Minor Planet Center was alerted and all interested observatories were requested to make observations but adverse weather conditions meant that only the

Japanese were successful. On 23 December, a Minor Planet electronic circular was issued announcing the discovery of 1997 XF_{11}. The object was classed as an Apollo asteroid, with a diameter of 1.2×2.4 km.

The size of the object, and the fact that it would approach as near to the Earth as 0.00031 astronomical units (or 28,830 miles; 1 AU = 93 million miles) classed the object as a Potentially Hazardous Asteroid (PHA). Gareth V. Williams and Brian Marsden of the Minor Planet Center appealed for more observations, but, since a nominal orbit published five days earlier indicated an extraordinarily close approach, Marsden put out circular 6837, announcing a miss of only 45,000 km (28,125 miles) on 26 October 2028. Calculations showed that the chances of an actual impact with the Earth could be as high as 1 in 1,000. This was picked up by the media, creating widespread panic.

Meanwhile, astronomers at the Jet Propulsion Laboratory had recorded observations of 1997 XF_{11} during its last close approach to the Earth. When Williams and Marsden used this data and other data calculated independently at JPL, a new estimate for the close approach was given as 950,000 km, and the incident quickly reverted to a non-event as far as the media were concerned.

FUTURE OF THE UNIVERSE

Although it is known that the Universe is expanding, cosmologists have not yet found evidence to show whether this expansion will go on for ever (the open Universe theory), or whether it will gradually slow down and the Universe will contract on itself, causing a 'Big Crunch' (the closed Universe theory). A significant factor in determining the future of the Universe is the presence or absence of dark matter. Although there are many indications to suggest that it exists, dark matter has not yet been detected. Since stars and gas at present account for only about 10 per cent of the mass required for contraction to happen scientists are keen to identify the form of dark matter. The gravitational force of all the matter in the Universe should slow down the expansion, but if the galaxies are moving fast enough, their speed will never fall to zero. The speeds of recession will gradually decrease towards certain values, and the Universe will expand for ever.

Recent work at Princeton University supports the open Universe theory. Neta Bahcall and Xiaohui Fan paid particular attention to the massive galaxy clusters lying billions of light-years from the Earth. According to current theories, a low density universe will form most of its massive clusters during the early days of the Universe, but in a higher density universe, clusters can continue to form later and could be forming at the present time. If our Universe is such a high-density universe, it would contain a far greater number of clusters today than it did hundreds of millions of years ago. Given that light from distant galaxies originally left those galaxies hundreds of millions of years ago, a greater number of observed 'nearby', and hence later, clusters, compared to those seen at greater distances, would indicate that this is such a universe. However, this has not been found to be the case.

STELLAR PLANETARY SYSTEMS

Reports announcing the discovery of a star orbited by a planet, or at least a brown dwarf, are frequent. Many of these reports are not substantiated by subsequent research; others require further study. The stars themselves seem to range over virtually the whole of the stellar spectrum. Some are quite likely candidates; others, if the reports are shown to be correct, would necessitate rethinking the explanations of stellar planetary systems.

The problems of locating planets are considerable. Initially, an accurate study of the motion of the star may reveal cyclical motions suggestive of the presence of a planet, but rapid stellar rotation, magnetic activity or pulsations within the star could also be explanations for these variations. These causes have to be eliminated before a claim for the existence of a planet can be made.

The red giant Aldebaran, in the constellation of Taurus, seems to have passed the tests eliminating internal causes for fluctuations in its behaviour. The motion of Aldebaran seems to indicate an orbit of eccentricity 0.18 with a period of 650 days. If this motion can be explained as orbital, it means that a planet or brown dwarf with a mass 11 times that of Jupiter is in orbit around the star. Observations using increasingly powerful telescopes continue.

GREATER RED SHIFTS

Red shift is a measure of the distance and speed of recession of a galaxy with respect to the Earth. A value for the red shift of a galaxy is found by measuring the shift in the spectral lines of the starlight towards the red end of the spectrum, when the galaxy is travelling away from the Earth. As the latest telescopes come on-line, astronomers are penetrating further into space. Until recently, the furthest object recorded had a red shift of just under 5, but during the last year red shift values of over 5 have been found.

A galaxy identified as 0140+326RDI was discovered by American astronomers from Johns Hopkins University, using the 10-metre Keck II telescope in Hawaii. During an analysis of the light from a very faint galaxy in the constellation of Triangulum, they noticed another even fainter object of magnitude +26, never before recorded on photographs. The photograph showed an emission line in the far end of the visible spectrum. More detailed observations revealed that the object was further away and had a red shift of 5.34, the first ever recorded over 5. The American team believe that the light from the galaxy started out as ultraviolet light from hydrogen atoms and has been travelling towards the Earth for the last 10,000 million years.

This new red shift record was short-lived. Esther Hu and Lennox Cowrie from the University of

Hawaii, and Richard McMahon of Cambridge University analysed the extremely faint Lyman-alpha emission (in the ultraviolet region of the spectrum). This revealed a new galaxy with a red shift of 5.64 which is thought to have been formed when the Universe was only 500 million years old, roughly 5 per cent of its present age. They also identified several others which are nearly as distant, suggesting that there may be many more galaxies at these and at even greater distances. McMahon believes that with the telescopes currently available, it may be possible to identify galaxies with red shifts up to 6.5.

MINI-QUASAR MYSTERY

Observations made at the Hartebeesthoek Radio Astronomy Observatory in South Africa and the Australia Telescope Compact Array in New South Wales have identified an exceptionally small quasar which is ejecting material at 99.9994 per cent of the speed of light. Of particular interest is that the object, known as PKS 0405–385, brightened and then faded in less than an hour; from this one can deduce that the source is less than a light-hour across, i.e. about the size of Jupiter's orbit around the Sun.

Quasars are normally not much bigger than the solar system but their output in energy is enormous, a typical one emitting more energy than a hundred giant galaxies. At present, it is believed that quasars contain energetic charged particles that whirl around in a strong magnetic field, generating powerful radio-waves (synchrotron radiation). However, it would not be possible for an object as small as this new source to generate the observed radio energy by a synchrotron process. An alternative explanation is that the cause of the fluctuations may be due to something outside the quasar, such as turbulence in the gas of the interstellar medium. This, however, would limit the size of the quasar to 0.5 microarc seconds and when the distance is taken into account, make the diameter of the quasar about a light-month. This is still too small to account for the observed radio fluctuations.

David Jauncey of the Australia Telescope National Facility has offered a third explanation. The fast flickering might be due to the radio-emitting region approaching us at close to the speed of light. It is known that a quasar can eject jets of material at exceptionally high speed from its centre, thought to be a massive black hole.

However, a month after the fluctuations were recorded in June 1996, they stopped. It has been suggested that the source has grown too large to twinkle due to turbulence. The quasar continues to be monitored in case the fluctuations recommence.

FRAME-DRAGGING

One of the ramifications of Einstein's General Theory of Relativity is that any spinning object will exert a dragging force on nearby space and time. This effect, known as frame-dragging, would only be measurable near intense gravitational fields such as those existing around neutron stars and black holes.

If a black hole has a nearby star orbiting it, material is torn from the star to form an accretion disc around the black hole. As this disc spirals down into the black hole, it heats up and emits x-rays which can be detected. Under normal circumstances, the plane of the accretion disc would be expected to remain orientated in a constant direction, but if frame-dragging were taking place, the accretion disc would gyrate round the spin axis of the black hole.

Teams at the Massachusetts Institute of Technology and at the Astronomical Observatory of Rome independently studied the x-ray brightness of the accretion discs around several black holes. Both teams observed that the discs were wobbling by amounts in agreement with predictions. These results were presented at a meeting of the American Astronomical Society.

Francis Everitt, a physicist at Stanford University, claims that the data did not constitute a quantitative result. He believes that the *Gravity Probe B* satellite, designed expressly for detecting frame-dragging, will gather sufficiently accurate data to provide better answers. However, it may not be necessary to wait for this launch if recent work by a team from the National Research Council of Italy and Rome University is confirmed. These scientists believe they have detected the effect of frame-dragging caused by the rotation of the Earth, using laser measurements for determining the positions of two satellites LAGEOS and LAGEOS II. It is claimed that the positions of these satellites can be fixed to within one centimetre; results show that the satellite orbits have drifted two metres due to the frame-dragging effect of the Earth's rotation.

RECORD GAMMA-RAY BURST

For some time astronomers have been puzzled by the arrival of random bursts of gamma rays which last for only a few seconds. The cause of these bursts is unknown but it is generally thought that they are generated when two neutron stars collide. Neutron stars are extremely dense stars; a spoonful of matter from one would weigh 100 million tons. Neutron stars are not quite large enough to condense down to black holes which are points of infinite density from which not even light can escape.

All gamma-ray bursts are extremely powerful and, according to Ralph Wijers of Cambridge University who has made a study of these events, bursts are thought to occur once in 100 million years. If one did occur in the neighbourhood of the Sun, it would wipe out life on the Earth. There is speculation about whether mass extinctions have been caused by nearby supernovae but there is no doubt about the outcome of a nearby gamma-ray burst.

A gamma-ray burst recorded in December 1997 seems to have been the most powerful explosion ever witnessed. Designated GRB 971214, it originated in a galaxy 12 billion light years distant. The burst, which lasted for only a few seconds, was as bright as the whole universe and released as much energy in that time as our Milky Way galaxy does in 200 years. It is considered to be the most powerful explosion since the Big Bang, and the light from the explosion started on its journey when the Universe, thought to be about 14 billion years old, was in its infancy.

The event was monitored by scientists at the Californian Institute of Technology in Pasadena; as the glow from the burst faded, they identified an extremely faint galaxy in the same position as the gamma-ray source. Analysis of the event continues.

ANTARCTIC OZONE HOLE

Holes in the ozone layer of the atmosphere develop over the Arctic and Antarctic regions in each hemisphere's spring, and shrink in autumn and winter.

The British Antarctic Survey (BAS) has played a prominent role in recording the behaviour of the ozone hole in the Antarctic. During 1997 members discovered that the hole covered a much larger area and started to grow much earlier each spring than previous findings had suggested.

New equipment, involving a French-designed instrument capable of recording the thickness of the ozone layer during the southern hemisphere's winter, was set up at the northernmost point of the Antarctic continent, at what was once the BAS Faraday base but is now owned by Ukraine. The equipment recorded the first signs of the ozone hole in the middle of the southern winter, in June; previously monitoring of the hole only became possible later in the year, when the Sun rose higher in the sky.

Jonathan Shanklin of the BAS has commented that the theory of the mechanism by which the hole develops has had to be revised. It was previously thought that the hole developed in the middle and worked its way outwards, but it has now been found that the hole starts at the edges two months earlier and works its way inwards with increasing speed. The fact that the hole is larger and starts to develop earlier raises the possibility that the amount of ultraviolet radiation received by the inhabitants of southern South America could be much higher than previously believed.

EL NIÑO LENGTHENS THE DAY

The El Niño weather system has produced many sensational and devastating effects on the world's weather, and also, surprisingly, a recordable effect on the Earth's rotation and hence on the length of the day.

El Niño causes a reversal in the direction of the ocean currents across the Pacific Ocean, causing havoc to established weather patterns. Near the Equator, the winds which normally blow from east to west are slowed down and the westerly winds are speeded up. The overall effect is to speed up the rotation of the atmosphere in the direction of the Earth's rotation. As the atmosphere speeds up it gains momentum at the expense of the Earth itself, resulting in the Earth being slowed down, thus making the day longer. The magnitude of this effect has been measured using the Very Long Baseline Interferometer (VLBI), a coupled array of more than 100 radio telescopes situated in different parts of the world.

The arrival times of signals from distant quasars are monitored by the VLBI as the Earth rotates. The Goddard Space Flight Center recorded variations in the arrival times of these quasar signals and so was able to detect variations in the length of the day by amounts as small as five millionths of a second. Analysis of these variations since the start of the latest El Niño in summer 1997 has shown that the day has lengthened by 0.4 milliseconds.

THE EARTH'S CORE

It was once thought that the Earth's core was metallic, consisting mainly of iron or a combination of nickel-iron. The core's density, when corrected for the effects of temperature and pressure, however, proved to be far too low for pure iron or mixtures of iron and nickel, and it was then believed that the core must contain large quantities of lighter elements. There have been many suggestions as to what this material might be, e.g. sulphides, carbides and silicon, but none have satisfactorily explained the obervations. The matter forming the Earth is thought to have separated about 4,500 million years ago into various layers, with silicates in the upper layers and iron in the central region or core. This does not, however, explain the overall distribution of the iron and silicates.

Work at the Tokyo Institute of Technology has thrown new light on the problem. Scientists heated and compressed a mixture of iron and silica to create the conditions thought to exist in the core and then exposed them to water. The hydrogen was rapidly absorbed by the iron whilst the oxygen combined with the silica. Very quickly, 25 per cent of the atoms in the iron complex were trapped hydrogen atoms. The possibility of large quantities of hydrogen in the core had previously been dismissed as hydrogen was thought to be too volatile to be trapped in this way. The high proportion of hydrogen in the iron may have prevented other elements from sinking into the core. This would explain the abundance of iron-loving elements in the mantle, and why the core is so light.

A DRY AUSTRALIA

Some 70 million years ago, the level of the sea was about 250 metres higher than it is today. A problem that has long puzzled geologists is why Australia managed to remain a dry continent whilst most of the rest of the world lay under water.

Michael Gurnis of the California Institute of Technology has developed a computer model which provides a possible answer. It involves the movement of the tectonic plates and also the heat flow in the underlying mantle of the Earth. The model commences about 130 million years ago, at a time when a slab of heavy oceanic crust was dipping down underneath eastern Australia. It shows that when the subduction stopped, the landmass moved over the cold sinking slab, resulting in over half the continent being flooded; this took place about 120 million years ago. Then Australia bent back upwards, rising to a maximum height at the time when global sea-level peaked.

Australia then moved northwards and gradually sank to its present level, the surface remaining above the existing sea-level the entire time. Gurnis believes that the slab which kept Australia dry now lies in the lower mantle just below a mid-oceanic ridge lying to the south of Australia. It is known that this area has a rather unusual composition for an ocean floor, and that the contours of the sea floor have regions that are unusually deep. It is thought that material rising to form the new sea floor may contain sections of the subducted slab, with a composition contrasting strongly with the surrounding oceanic crust. This situation is believed to be unique amongst mid-oceanic ridges.

MEDITERRANEAN LANDSLIDE

Evidence has recently been published of a major submarine landslide in the western Mediterranean Sea which could have produced a drastic climatic change at the end of the last Ice Age.

Guy Rothwell of the Southampton Oceanography Centre has revealed that seismic studies of the Balearic abyssal plain lying to the west of Sardinia indicate the existence of an unusual sedimentary layer of mud some 8 to 10 metres thick lying about 10 metres below the current sea floor. The layer is reported to be transparent to acoustic waves. Radio-carbon dating of sediments above and below the layer indicates that it was formed about 22,000 years ago . The layer is thought to have been caused by a huge landslide which covered an area about three time the size of Wales. At the time of the landslide the ice-cover was at its greatest extent and the sea-level at its lowest for some 120,000 years. The sea-level had dropped 50 metres over the previous several thousand years and started to rise again about 22,000 years ago.

It is not known for certain what caused the landslide, but Euan Nisbet of Royal Holloway College, University of London, thinks that methane hydrates in the sea floor may have been responsible. The sedimentary layer beneath the mud layer was rich in organic material, which produces methane as it decays. This would have been trapped as icy hydrates by the high pressure and low temperature of the ocean. As the sea-level fell the pressure would have dropped, making the methane hydrate unstable. It is not clear what caused the slide, but once the sea floor started to slip, the escaping methane would have behaved as a lubricant, fuelling the landslide. The result was a slump of 500 cubic km of mud over the sea floor. This would have produced gigantic tsunamis all around the Mediterranean coast. It is estimated that the slide could have released 500 million tons of methane, and this would also have had a pronounced effect upon the composition of the atmosphere, which contained only about a billion tons of the gas at the time.

HISTORY RECORDED BY PEAT

The moss growing in a peat bog relies on the atmosphere for its nutrients and so absorbs any changes in the atmosphere brought about by pollution; it is then buried by subsequent layers of peat. The various layers in a peat bog provide a record of the changes in climatic conditions and the amount of pollution over the last few thousand years. William Shotyk and colleagues of the University of Bern in Switzerland studied the changes in the composition of the peat layers of the 6-metre thick Étang de la Gruyère peat bog in the Jura Mountains to produce such a record.

Their work shows that after the end of the last Ice Age, there was a constant concentration of lead in the atmosphere of about 0.28 parts per million, except for the period when the climate was cooled by extensive volcanic activity in France. Another anomaly was noticed at the time when farmers in Europe first started tilling the land about 5,000 years ago. A third surge came 3,000 years ago, when the Phoenicians started trading in Spanish lead. The lead content in the atmosphere continued to increase in line with the increasing Greek and Roman metallurgical industries. The concentration fell during the Middle Ages, only to increase spectacularly with the onset of the Industrial Revolution. The peat deposit also recorded the increase in lead smelting in 1905 and again in 1967 when the use of lead in the petrol industry reached a maximum. At this point, a value of 85 parts per million of lead was registered.

CAUSES OF MASS EXTINCTIONS

In recent years there has been much interest in uncovering the reasons behind the mass extinctions on Earth in the past and determining the chances of similar events occurring in the future. Most theories involve collisions in one form or another between the Earth and an extraterrestrial object, but a completely new theory also seems to explain many of the features associated with such events.

Erik M. Leitch of the California Institute of Technology and Gautam Visisht of NASA's Jet Propulsion Laboratory have highlighted a compelling correlation between mass extinctions and the position of the solar system relative to the spiral arms of the Milky Way galaxy. They traced the Milky Way's spiral arms by charting the locations of large clouds of ionized hydrogen. These are identified by the presence of hot, short-lived stars that are formed when spiral density waves pass though the galaxy's gaseous disc. The speed at which these waves are propagated is then estimated. With information on the known motion of the solar system, it has been possible to estimate when the solar system passed through the various arms of the spiral. It was found that the solar system was either in or very near to a spiral arm at times when the major extinctions took place on the Earth.

It is known that supernovae are more likely to explode in the vicinity of the solar system when the Sun is in a spiral arm. In addition, the spiral arms also contain giant molecular clouds, which, if the conditions are right, will disturb the orbits of the solar system's outlying comets and asteroids and send them on a path towards the Earth. All these events could indicate a high probability of a correlation between the solar system's position in a spiral arm and the extinctions recorded during the last 500 million years of the Earth's history. It is comforting to know that it will be another 140 million years before the solar system next enters a spiral arm!

Although the extinction of the dinosaurs 65 million years ago is now widely accepted to be linked to a meteoroid impact, the case for a link between other mass extinctions and impacts is less well documented. Hungarian scientists have suggested that the Permian extinction some 250 million years ago, which is thought to have wiped out some 90 per cent of all life on the Earth, might be linked to a nearby supernova explosion. This possibility was first proposed 20 years ago by American physicists, but Csaba Detre, of the Geological Institute of Hungary, and Imre Toth, of the Konkoly Observatory in Budapest, have carried the investigation further, studying the effects of a nearby supernova on terrestrial rocks.

A supernova explosion at a distance of a few tens of light-years from the Earth would remove the ozone layer, resulting in ultraviolet light from the Sun and the supernova penetrating the atmosphere and killing surface plants and animals. Hot gas and plasma from the explosion would disrupt the Earth's magnetosphere, allowing cosmic rays to reach the ground and cause more devastation. The Hungarians say that they have identified what could be the remnants of the supernova in the rocks from the period in many areas around the world. They have found metal-rich globules 3 to 20 micrometres in diameter which are thought to have originated outside our solar system. Detre is currently carrying out studies of the isotopes and trace elements in the globules.

Rise of the Dinosaurs

Palaeontologists believe that during a mass extinction about 200 million years ago at the end of the Triassic period and the beginning of the Jurassic period, most of the large reptiles that dominated the Triassic period died out quickly and were replaced by a greater number of dinosaurs. Because fossils for the Triassic-Jurassic periods are relatively rare, it has not been possible to determine the rate at which this transition took place. The late Triassic is the

period during which many of the present-day land vertebrates first evolved; these included many mammals and the dinosaurs.

Work by Paul Olsen of the Lamont-Doherty Earth Observatory, part of Columbia University in Palisades, New York, has identified fossil footprints from the period in question, which are far more numerous than fossil skeletons. Along the shores of the numerous lakes in eastern North America, fossil footprints of some dinosaurs have been identified, but more numerous were the tracks of a wide range of non-dinosaur reptiles. These include rhynchosaurs (pig-sized herbivores), aetosaurs (armadillo-like creatures) and phytosaurs (crocodiles), as well as small plant-eating reptiles. However, the dominant predators were the rauisuchians, short-snouted distant relatives of today's crocodiles. Olsen found that although the dinosaurs survived the end of the Triassic, these other reptiles suddenly vanished from the fossil record. It is thought that with the removal of the rauisuchians, the dinosaurs quickly came to dominate. Thus, Olsen's findings concur with the previous theory that a sudden extinction of reptiles was followed by an increase in the population of dinosaurs.

Faeces from T. rex

Much is known about the anatomy and habits of dinosaurs, but little is known about how and what they ate. An insight into the diet of *Tyrannosaurus rex* has recently been provided by detailed study of a giant fossilized turd. Nearly 3 litres in volume, it was unearthed in 1995 in south-western Saskatchewan, Canada, by Karen Chin of the US Geological Survey. Timothy Tokaryk, a palaeontologist from the Royal Saskatchewan Museum in Regina said that the fossil, which is called a coprolite, was the largest known from a dinosaur and the first from a meat-eating dinosaur.

T. rex lacked grinding teeth so it could not chew its food. The animal pulverized each mouthful into tiny pieces by means of its huge peg-like teeth. The victim in this case was probably a young herbivore about the size of a cow. This suggests the dinosaur was an active predator of healthy prey rather than a scavenger of old and sick animals. Most of the crushed bones in the coprolite escaped damage, suggesting that the digestive juices of the dinosaur were very weak and completely different from those of crocodiles, which dissolve bones. The bone fragments make up nearly half the contents of the coprolite, suggesting that rather than tearing the meat off the bone or even swallowing its prey whole in a manner similar to many reptiles, *T. rex* ground up the whole animal before swallowing. Peter Andrew of the Natural History Museum in London, a specialist in coprolites, is of the opinion that the bones are still in sufficiently good condition to allow molecular analysis of their DNA.

DINOSAURS ON THE ISLE OF WIGHT

The Isle of Wight is the premier site in Europe for dinosaur fossils. One reason for this is that the cliffs in which the fossils are found are rapidly falling away, revealing numerous examples of creatures, some of which were previously unknown. A prospector recently unearthed a black claw which could not be associated with any known creature, so it is assumed that it must have belonged to a previously unknown species of predator. Steve Hutt, curator of the island's museum of geology, was excited about the find, but said that such finds were only to be expected. Two years ago, another previously unknown species of dinosaur was found in the same stretch of cliffs. Over the last 150 years, 12 whole skeletons have been found, two of which were of previously unknown species.

The reason for the presence of so many dinosaur finds in so small an area is that the fossils have been preserved in the Wealden clay. Much of north-west Europe was, at the time, a forested, sub-tropical basin, with abundant vegetation ideal for herbivorous dinosaurs, which also made the area ideal for the carnivores to feed on the herbivores. Changes in the local climatic conditions made the region covering the Isle of Wight an area into which the remains of animals were washed down by rivers and floods and then encased in the clay, where they have remained for millions of years. At the present time the Isle of Wight is gradually rising, with the clay deposits now forming crumbling cliffs. Erosion of these cliffs, mainly due to winter storms, can be as much as 1 metre per year. Exposed fossils are either swept into the sea or fall onto the beach where they are collected by geologists and other enthusiasts.

THE DEVELOPMENT OF FLIGHT

There is no consensus among scientists about how animals first took to the skies. An original approach to the problem has been taken by Robert Dudley, a zoologist at the University of Texas in Austin, who thinks the solution lies in the composition of the atmosphere. He claims that animals of various kinds were able to take to the skies as a result of a surge in the amount of oxygen in the atmosphere.

Although our present-day atmosphere is just 21 per cent oxygen, this has not always been the case. About 250 to 370 million years ago, during the late Palaeozoic era, the proportion of oxygen rose to 35 per cent following the appearance of plants on the Earth. Dudley commented that at above 35 per cent oxygen, the air mixture could spontaneously combust. Nevertheless, this high oxygen content helped to create giant insects. Dragonflies with wing-spans of over 70 cm have been identified from the fossil record. Bodies of this size could only have existed in such a plentiful supply of oxygen. Records show that as the percentage of oxygen dropped, these huge creatures faded from the scene.

A second peak in the oxygen level, identified by data from marine sediments and climate models, occurred about 100 million years later, in the mid-Jurassic period. The oxygen content peaked at 26 per cent and then remained high throughout the Cretaceous and much of the Tertiary period. Dudley believes that it was during this period that vertebrates began to fly. He thinks that the first birds appeared in the late Jurassic, the pterosaurs (flying dinosaurs) in the Triassic, and bats possibly in the Cretaceous period.

The extra oxygen in the atmosphere would have helped the vertebrates to produce the extra energy needed for flight. In addition, the oxygen would have made the atmosphere more dense and this would also have made flight easier. This new approach has opened up new possibilities for understanding the evolution of flight.

HUMANS OUT OF AFRICA

During the last few decades much research has been carried out and many new theories advanced to explain how humans colonized the world. Most theories support the claim that early humans emerged from Africa and spread world-wide some 120,000 years ago, with argument concentrated on the process by which this took place.

This widely accepted theory was cast into doubt by claims that modern humans were living in Australia at a time before it was thought that they had emerged from Africa. Stone tools at the Jinmium site in the Northern Territory were found to have a date suggesting that the area was occupied some 176,000 years ago, nearly 60,000 years before the accepted emergence from Africa. In addition, engravings at the site were dated at 75,000 years old, establishing them as the oldest known rock art in the world.

However, a team headed by Richard Roberts of La Trobe University in Melbourne has challenged these findings. Using a technique called optically stimulated luminescence to date the time of burial of individual grains of sand, the team found that the site was only 6,000 to 10,000 years old. This overturns the claim that Australia had been colonized by humans before early humans emerged from Africa but does not advance understanding of the emergence or the colonization.

THE OLDEST FOOTPRINTS

The problems surrounding the preservation of the oldest known footprints made by modern humans have now been resolved. It was originally decided to keep them *in situ* but pressure from scientists, conservationists, etc., has prevailed and they are now to be preserved in a museum.

The footprints are thought to be those of a woman and child, and were made in soft sandstone some 117,000 years ago. David Roberts of the South African Council for Geoscience in Cape Town discovered the prints in 1995 at a site on the shores of Langebaan Lagoon in South Africa's West Coast National Park. It was decided to leave the prints where they were found, but Roberts warned that the wind and waves that cracked open the sandstone to reveal the prints would soon destroy them. He noticed visible erosion in the prints over a period as short as six weeks. He was also concerned that the prints might be destroyed by waves undercutting the cliff face. The original intention was to cover the prints with a thin layer of an opaque removable material to protect them from the sea, while the shoreline would be protected by rock-filled iron baskets and a viewing platform to prevent damage and erosion by visitors.

However, damage caused by people visiting the area led to the change of plan and now the sandstone blocks containing the prints will be transferred to a museum, although this move will also present problems. Keith Taylor, a stone conserver with Taylor Pearce Restoration in London, is one of a team of advisors; he has warned that the sandstone is very fragile. It is proposed to impregnate the footprints with a hardening material and to cut out the blocks of sandstone with a high-pressure water-jet. The holes made in the cliffs will be filled with a cast resembling the original prints.

SEEING IN THE DEEP

Most fish living in the deepest regions of the oceans rely for sight on bioluminescence. This is produced in living organisms by photophores, which generally emit blue light with wavelengths between 470 and 490 nanometres. Most fish-eyes are tuned specifically to these wavelengths. However, two genera of stomiid fish (*Aristostomias* and *Pachystomias*) have two types of photophores, one emitting blue light and the other red light with a wavelength of about 700 nanometres, which is invisible to other fish. For the stomiid fish to use this facility for locating prey, they would need to have a pigment in the eyes that would enable them to detect the red light in addition to the two known pigments that detect the shorter wavelengths. Ronald Douglas of City University, London, and Julian Partridge of the University of Bristol have identified this pigment and have also thrown light on the mechanism used by the stomiids in hunting for food.

Douglas and Partridge have found a third species of fish, a dragon fish (*Malecosteus niger*), which uses red light for hunting prey but does not have a red-sensitive pigment in its retina. In this case, the retina contains a derivative of chlorophyll which absorbs red light and then stimulates the pigment for seeing blue light. The source of the chlorophyll is unknown. It had been thought that chlorophyll functions only in plants and bacteria; there is no animal known that can synthesize chlorophyll. It is therefore assumed that the fish must gain the chlorophyll from its food, but the mechanism by which it does so remains unknown.

MENDING BROKEN BONES

A new technique for mending broken bones is being developed by Japanese scientists. It has proved successful in mending the bones of an injured rabbit and research is now being carried out with larger sheep bones; if this is successful, the technique will be tried on human fractures.

Research carried out at Kyoto University has shown that a fractured tibia (shin bone) mended more quickly and was stronger when small slivers of coated titanium were inserted into the fracture. The procedure usually used by British surgeons is to allow the break to heal naturally.

It has been known for some time that pieces of metal can be used as an anchor to help synostosis, the process whereby bones grow and join together after a fracture. Titanium is ideal for this purpose because it is light, tough and non-corrosive, but unfortunately bone will not graft to titanium. Calcium phosphate in the form of apatite, a naturally occurring mineral, has the excellent property that bone will readily grow round it, but it is too fragile to be used in loadbearing bones.

A technique has been developed using titanium covered with a mixture of titanium oxide and apatite. This allows a bone to graft onto the outside of the coating while the inner core provides the strength and durability of the titanium metal. The process involves heating titanium to 600° C in an alkaline solution and then applying the coating. The coating graduates from 100 per cent apatite on the outside to 100 per cent titanium oxide on the surface in contact with the metal, combining the bonding properties of apatite and the strength of titanium to produce an ideal joint.

RADON AND LUNG CANCER

Most of the information published about the effects of the radioactive gas radon on the health of the population is based on data relating to people who work or have worked in an environment where the risk of exposure to radiation is high, such as workers in nuclear plants or in mines where the uranium content is high. The results of these studies have then been extrapolated to conditions where the overall radioactivity is quite low, such as the granite masses of Devon and Cornwall. In these areas the uranium content is generally low, but buildings built on or out of the local granite have in some cases shown quite high levels of radon.

The health risk to people living in these areas was not clear, but a recent study by one of the country's leading epidemiologists has provided a better picture of the link between exposure to radon in the home and lung cancer.

Sarah Darby, principal scientist with the Imperial Cancer Research Fund Cancer Epidemiology Unit at Oxford, compared radon concentrations in the homes of 982 lung cancer victims in Devon and Cornwall with those of 3,185 controls. After allowing for variations due to smoking and social background, she found that people exposed to more than 200 becquerels per cubic metre were 20 per cent more likely to develop lung cancer, compared to those exposed to 20 becquerels per cubic metre, the average for Britain as a whole; 200 becquerels per cubic metre is the level above which the British government recommends remedial treatment. With every 100 becquerels above this level, the risk of developing lung cancer rises by 10 per cent.

The National Radiological Protection Board (NRPB) fully supports this work. A recent survey carried out by NRPB found 15,237 houses in Cornwall and 5,674 in Devon where the radon concentration was above 200 becquerels per cubic metre. The Board believes that 1 in 20 lung cancer deaths in Britain may be due to radon.

THE BOSE-EINSTEIN CONDENSATE

One of the most spectacular advances in scientific discovery during the last few years has been the study of matter at a temperature of less than a millionth of a degree above absolute zero ($-273°$ C). In June 1995 Eric Cornell and Carl Wieman of the Joint Institute for Laboratory Astrophysics in Boulder, Colorado, succeeded in cooling 2,000 rubidium atoms to a temperature of less than 100 billionths of a degree above absolute zero. For ten seconds the identity of the individual atoms was lost and the atoms behaved as though they were a single 'superatom'. All the physical properties of the original atoms, such as their motion, became identical; their motion had previously been random.

This new state of matter, called a Bose-Einstein condensate (BEC), was predicted by Albert Einstein in 1925 from calculations made by the Indian physicist Satyendra Nath Bose. A few months after Cornell and Wieman's success, two other establishments succeeded in creating BECs; Randall Hulet at Rice University in Houston, Texas, used lithium atoms, and Wolfgang Ketterle at Massachusetts Institute of Technology used sodium atoms. Ketterle subsequently succeeded in creating a condensate with 10 million atoms and more recently has successfully made two separate BECs and brought them together. When they overlapped the result was an interference pattern showing constructive and destructive bands. This showed that a BEC acts not like a group of particles but like a wave. A BEC can therefore be thought of as the matter counterpart of a laser, except that in the condensate it is atoms rather than photons that move in perfect unison.

Of great interest is the macroscopic window that a BEC provides into the strange world of quantum mechanics, which is based on the belief that elementary particles such as electrons have wave properties and which uses these properties to describe the structure and interactions of matter. These effects cannot be observed due to the incoherent behaviour of the individual atoms, but in a BEC the wave nature of each atom is exactly in phase with all the other atoms, with the result that the quantum mechanical waves can be seen with the naked eye. Ongoing work in this field should help to clarify, or modify, theories about the basic laws of quantum mechanics.

EXTENSION OF RADIO-CARBON DATING

Stable carbon and its radioactive isotope are absorbed from the atmosphere by plants and animals during their lifetime and remain within their cells after they die. Unlike the stable isotope of carbon, however, the radioactive isotope decays at a known rate. Thus, by measuring the ratio of the concentrations of the two isotopes in a given body, an estimate for the age of the body can be made. Although in theory the method is simple, there are practical difficulties which introduce uncertainties into the values obtained by this method.

The atmospheric levels of radioactive carbon are constantly changing, so carbon dating has to be calibrated by an independent method, such as variations in the widths of tree-rings (dendrochronology). Using very old tree-rings, such as those from the bristlecone pine, in conjunction with those of living trees, it has been possible to estimate ages up to about 10,000 years ago. For greater ages other techniques have had to be used.

Hiroyuki Kitagawa, of the International Research Centre for Japanese Studies in Kyoto, has made a study of the well-preserved sedimentary layers in the bed of the nearby Lake Suigetsu. The bed consists of layers coloured black and white, similar in appearance to a bar code. By measuring the carbon content in the various layers, Kitagawa has been able to extend the radio-carbon dating calibration by a further 35,000 years, making it possible to use this technique for objects as old as 45,000 years.

This extension should permit a fuller understanding of the migratory pattern of early European cave painters. It should also throw light on the question of when people crossed the Bering Strait from Asia to America on a land bridge. Current estimates place this between 12,000 and 47,000 years ago.

Theatre

There can be no doubt about which theatre dominated the agenda this year. Down a side-street in Islington, north London, the Almeida, once a warehouse and seating less than 400 people, has generated easily the most interest and excitement. Star power has for a long time fuelled the West End, where it is well-established that the presence of certain performers will guarantee an audience no matter what they appear in. Subsidized theatre has never been able to compete on wages, and has in any case feared that a big name will unbalance a production and detract from the work (the use of television names in the West End has often been decidedly tacky). The achievement of the Almeida has been to attract a succession of actors who have been chosen for the play and not vice versa.

It says much for the persuasive powers of artistic directors Jonathan Kent and Ian McDiarmid that the French actress Juliette Binoche, the American actor Kevin Spacey and the Irish actor Liam Neeson agreed to come to the Almeida, in spite of the fact that it pays only £250 a week. This is hardly a tempting carrot; and certainly not what persuaded Binoche to play in *Naked*, a little-known drama by Pirandello; Spacey, already well-known here for the film *LA Confidential*, to cross the Atlantic to be in Eugene O'Neill's *An Iceman Cometh*; or Liam Neeson to play Oscar Wilde in David Hare's play *The Judas Kiss*. This last production was the first sign that Kent and McDiarmid were keen to spread their wings beyond Islington. It opened in the Playhouse in the West End and, ironically, was the least successful of the three shows. This was not because of Richard Eyre's direction but because of Hare's inert script, and because Neeson, rusty after a long absence from the stage, only skimmed the surface of the role and never looked as though he was consumed by passion for Tom Hollander's high-pitched Bosie.

Star Performances

Riding high on her Oscar-winning performance in *The English Patient*, Binoche played Ersilia, the nanny whose charge dies in mysterious circumstances. Binoche's great beauty and obvious difference from the rest of the English cast heightened the enigma of Ersilia, a woman who struggles to find out who she is as four men try to foist their version of her identity upon her. It is a disturbing, elusive play and certainly not easy to understand. Nevertheless, the production moved into the Playhouse in the West End for a limited run. It made way for Howard Davies' production of *The Iceman Cometh* at the Almeida. In O'Neill's four-and-a-half-hour epic, Kevin Spacey surpassed even the most hyped-up expectations as Hickey, once a genial good-timer who is eagerly awaited by the drunken down-and-outs who live in the rooming house above Harry Hope's dive. What made Spacey's performance so remarkable was his relaxed energy and his ability to surprise, continually revealing new aspects of the much-altered, fanatical Hickey who had the demented air of a born-again Christian who comes knocking at the door in the middle of supper. Demand for seats was so great that the production was moved to the Old Vic (which was empty at the time as the owners Ed and David Mirvish were trying to find a new buyer; it was later bought by a consortium and is now run by a trust).

In the summer the Almeida demonstrated even greater ambition with the announcement that it planned to open four new productions at the Malvern Festival: Racine's *Phèdre*, in a new translation by Ted Hughes, and *Britannicus* with Diana Rigg and Toby Stephens, both later to move into the West End; Brecht's *Puntila and his Man Matti* with leading physical theatre performers from The Right Size; and Shaw's *A Doctor's Dilemma*, which had already been seen in London. It was an enormous gamble for the tiny theatre. *Puntila* moved to Edinburgh after Malvern and became the hit of the festival, with Hamish McColl as Puntila, who is generous and sentimental when drunk and coldly calculating when sober. The production, one of the few to celebrate the German playwright's centenary, proved enormously entertaining as well as instructive – a rare achievement, according to those who normally find Brecht's preachiness unbearable.

Greenwich Theatre

The new Labour government was expected to give increased support to the arts, but at first it proved a disappointment. References by members of the Government to 'Cool Britannia' and to British creativity appeared to include fashion, film and music but not theatre. Lottery proceeds for the arts were substantially reduced when the Government announced that it was creating a new cause to which funds would be directed. The London Arts Board stated that it could no longer fund all its clients and that it was necessary to cut some theatres in order to keep others going. The surprise was that it chose to cut Greenwich Theatre, as well as the King's Head and several black theatre companies. Sir Cameron Mackintosh stepped in to help the King's Head, but the Greenwich Theatre closed its doors; ironically, just a mile down the road from the theatre millions of pounds are being spent on the Millennium Dome.

In July 1998 the Wyndham report pointed out that the reputation and vitality of the West End not only produces far more in government tax revenue than is received by subsidized companies such as the National and the RSC, but that it also generates a vast amount of wealth and employment among subsidiary services. The report was careful to point out that none of this would be possible without the existence of the subsidized sector, on which the West End leans heavily. Coinciding with this report was the vastly better news that the Chancellor was adding £290 million to the arts budget over three years. Most of this money will be swallowed up in making national museums and galleries free again, but it should still mean that some theatres will be able to make up the losses of the last five years.

TREVOR NUNN AT THE NATIONAL

Trevor Nunn took over as artistic director of the Royal National Theatre in October 1997, as Sir Richard Eyre, the previous artistic director, opened his final production – Tom Stoppard's new play, *The Invention of Love*. This is about the poet A. E. Housman, best known for *A Shropshire Lad*, and weaves themes of love, scholarship and memory around the meeting of the old poet and his younger self. It is a tender examination of a life in which homosexual love had been suppressed, unlike the catastrophic and impulsive life of Housman's contemporary Oscar Wilde, with whom Housman is compared. The play is dense, rich with classical allusions that can be daunting for those without a classical education, and provided the opportunity for many theatre baiters to leap into the attack when it won the Evening Standard award for best new play. But there was no denying the depth of emotion as John Wood's quixotic, desiccated older Housman met Paul Rhys as his younger self enslaved by his love for his athletic heterosexual friend Jackson.

Trevor Nunn chose to open his account at the National with a classic, albeit one that is rarely performed: Ibsen's *Enemy of the People* in a new version by Christopher Hampton, with Ian McKellen as the awkward and vain Dr Stockmann who refuses to submit to the 'unthinking majority'. Ibsen wrote the play in a rage after many of his liberal supporters came out against his controversial *Ghosts* for, as he saw it, self-serving political reasons. McKellen personified both the scientist who discovers that the water in the spa is contaminated and the naive politician who cannot understand why the town turns against him when they realize that the closure of the baths will deter tourists and destroy the town's lucrative trade. Nunn showed that the Olivier stage held no fears for him with a design by John Napier that encompassed the whole town rather than just Stockmann's house.

As the year progressed it became clear that Nunn's scheme for financial survival is to mount a selection of what he believes to be sure-fire winners in order to be able to take risks elsewhere; some of the 'risks' proved to be very popular as well. Thus *Peter Pan, The Prime of Miss Jean Brodie* and *Oklahoma!* subsidized more ambitious productions of Bulgakov's *Flight*, Frank McGuinness' *Mutabilitie* and Michael Frayn's *Copenhagen*. There was great interest when Nunn announced that he would be directing a previously unperformed play by

Tennessee Williams, discovered by Vanessa Redgrave, in a joint production with the Alley Theatre in Houston and the Moving Theatre. Entitled *Not about Nightingales*, a reference to Keats' ode to beauty which the play rejects in favour of more radical, political causes, it was inspired by a real-life case and dedicated to the memory of four prisoners who, as punishment for refusing to eat the prison food, were locked in an airless hole heated to 200 degrees; all four men died. Corin Redgrave played the prison governor who refuses to brook any opposition and the American actor Butch O'Fallon played the prison leader who leads the men into the fatal revolt. A sprawling young man's play that is too long, too melodramatic and too corny in places, nevertheless it has some pertinent comments to make about institutions that are cut off from the rest of the world.

OKLAHOMA!

Nunn also directed the musical *Oklahoma!* himself. The choice was criticized by some as unsuitable for the National, but popular consensus was that this was an irresistible production generating an atmosphere of sheer joy and confirming Nunn's assertion that *Oklahoma!* is great theatre as well as a great musical. Two unknowns in the cast were much praised, Hugh Jackman as Curly and Josefina Gabrielle as Laurey, as was Nunn for allowing the musical's savage undertone to be heard through the boisterous hoe-downs.

A major Christmas production, likely to return for many years to come, was *Peter Pan* in the version originally seen at the RSC, with Alec McCowen as the narrator, the voice of J. M. Barrie himself. Peter was played by Daniel Evans, not, as is traditionally the case, by a woman. A wonderfully nostalgic nursery set was created by John Napier, and Ian McKellen shed the grand roles to play both the vain, weak Mr Darling and the silky, stammering, sartorially elegant Captain Hook. The flying was particularly spectacular as the children, following Peter to the Never-Never Land, threatened to soar over the audience.

Another major production at the National was *The Prime of Miss Jean Brodie* with Fiona Shaw as the inspiring but deluded Edinburgh teacher marking her favourites out for particular attention until one of them is driven to betray her and destroys them both. Phyllida Lloyd's production courageously introduced Christian imagery to illustrate the rise and fall of Miss Brodie, who encourages her 'gals' to reach for a life of heady romanticism rather than settling for marriage and a job in a bank. Shaw created her own eccentric bohemian, eradicating memories of Maggie Smith in the role and proving once again what a fine comedian she can be.

WEST END

The West End continued to thrive and to attract a much younger audience than in previous years. As always, it lent heavily on the subsidized sector, including the productions of *An Iceman Cometh* and *Naked* mentioned above. *Closer*, a major success at the National last year, with its lethal dissection of sexual relationships, moved into Shaftesbury Avenue for a lengthy run. David Hare's *Amy's View* also transferred from the National, in this case to the Aldwych, a venue much better suited to its portrayal of an actress from an era in which the West End reigned supreme. Its limited, sold-out run coincided with speculation over whether its star, Dame Judi Dench, would win an Oscar for her portrayal of Queen Victoria in the film *Mrs Brown*. In the event she did not, but the press coverage contributed to a rousing reception for her performance every evening.

Do You Come Here Often?, written and performed by The Right Size, was a definite sign that the West End was changing. Hamish McColl and Sean Foley are normally seen at the Battersea Arts Club or the Lyric Hammersmith but this show, in which they are imprisoned as hostages in a bathroom with ever-lengthening fake beards, was another sign of the growing popularity of physical theatre. Cheek by Jowl, the touring group that has been taking classics all over the world since the beginning of the 1980s, brought its last-ever production into the Playhouse. *Much Ado About Nothing* had all the trademark qualities of Cheek by Jowl: a simple, eloquent design by Nick Ormerod, a fresh, engaging approach to the text by director Declan Donnellan, and a young talented cast who clearly will go far. Saskia Reeves returned to the company to play a warm, spirited Beatrice not above getting drunk at the festivities for the Duke. Regrets that Cheek by Jowl was breaking up were slightly mollified by the knowledge that Donnellan and Ormerod will remain a team.

One of the reasons that the West End is attracting younger audiences must surely be the continuing presence of the Royal Court in the Duke of York's and the Ambassadors. Ian Rickson took over as the Royal Court's artistic director from Stephen Daldry, who retains a watching brief over the building programme at the company's home in Sloane Square. Last year's hit *The Weir* was moved from the Ambassadors into the Duke of York's and continued to amaze audiences with the truthfulness of the acting and the lyricism of the writing. Caryl Churchill's *Blue Heart*, a collaboration with Out of Joint, was a genuinely experimental piece of work consisting of two short pieces. In the first, *Heart's Desire*, a married couple await the return of their daughter from Australia. Each time the action starts, it is halted and then replayed with increasingly wild variations evoking a whole range of tensions and terrors lurking within suburbia. In the second, *Blue Kettle*, a middle-aged man cons old women into believing he is the long-lost son they gave up for adoption. As chaos spreads, the words 'blue' and 'kettle' creep into the dialogue until finally they engulf it. Max Stafford-Clark handled the brittle text with a mesmerizing brilliance.

IONESCO'S CHAIRS

In another collaboration, this time with Théâtre de Complicité and the French Theatre season, the Royal Court revived Ionesco's *The Chairs* in a brilliant translation by Martin Crimp, directed by Simon McBurney and with Geraldine McEwan and Richard Briers in the cast. McEwan and Briers, in superlative comic form, played a nonagenarian married couple filling the stage with chairs as they greet a host of invisible guests to hear a last message for humanity. When the spokesman finally arrives all he does is scribble gibberish on the wall. Ionesco called the play 'a tragic farce' and this production perfectly captured that paradox.

David Mamet's *The Old Neighbourhood*, also a Royal Court production, was full of Chekhovian yearning for dreams that were never realized. Unusually, Mamet explores his Jewish roots and his own unhappy childhood in three short plays. Most memorable was Zoë Wanamaker as Jolly, who angrily and compulsively trawls through a past in which she and her brother Bobby were coldly treated by their mother, their non-Jewish step-father and his children. Hopes for the future lie with Rebecca Prichard, whose *Yard Gal* was co-commissioned by the Royal Court and Clean Break and who was first discovered through the Royal Court's Young Writers' Festival.

More traditional West End fare included a classy revival of Edward Albee's *A Delicate Balance* with Eileen Atkins, Maggie Smith and John Standing as the hosts who are alarmed when their best friends unexpectedly move in. On the surface this is a conventional family drama with frequent sallies to the drinks cabinet; underneath, it is a bleak satirical account of an isolation that increases with age, and of the demands and obligations of family and friendship. Atkins was outstanding as the frighteningly reasonable Agnes, who uses words to keep her feelings at bay. Alan Ayckbourn's *Things We Do for Love* moved down to London from Scarborough, acquiring Jane Asher along the way. She played Barbara, the career woman who deep-froze all her emotions when she was a prefect at school. In a play about the connection between love, pain and humiliation, Ayckbourn was up to his old tricks with a set which is divided into three tiers so that the different floors of the house that Barbara owns can all be seen, but only one in full. In the basement there is only a glimpse of the ceiling, on which the postman who rents the room is painting a massive nude picture of Barbara, and in the top flat all one can see is the occupants' feet; only in the middle flat, Barbara's own, is it possible to take in the view from floor to ceiling.

An unexpected hit was *A Letter of Resignation*, a quiet, old-fashioned drama by Hugh Whitemore with Edward Fox as the Conservative Prime Minister Harold Macmillan, who during the Profumo scandal had to deal with another man's marital infidelity while painfully aware that his own marriage was hardly an example of traditional family values. The much-admired Peter Hall company was forced to vacate the Old Vic when the Mirvishes announced their decision to sell. At the Piccadilly, Sir Peter opened Molière's *Le Misanthrope* in a new translation by Ranjit Bolt with Elaine Paige as Célimène and Michael Pennington as the acerbic Alceste. Later it was joined in repertoire with *Major Barbara*, Shaw's play on ethics and the arms trade with Jemma Redgrave as the zealous Barbara and Peter Bowles as Undershaft.

At the Comedy a double bill of *The Real Inspector Hound* and *Black Comedy*, celebrating London in the 1960s, proved enormously popular and a great launching pad for the new company Warehouse Productions. In *The Real Inspector Hound* Stoppard creates the world of an Agatha Christie thriller and then imagines what would happen if a pair of critics became involved in the plot. Nichola McAuliffe excelled as Mrs Drudge, the housekeeper who is convinced that 'something is up'. In *Black Comedy* Peter Shaffer famously borrows from an eastern tradition in which two warriors fight each other in broad daylight as though they were in the dark. The comic possibilities were endlessly explored in Greg Doran's skilfully cast production.

MUSICALS

Musicals were as prolific as ever, and as crucial to the vitality of the West End. It was a year in which the American musical dominated; the only major English musical was Andrew Lloyd Webber's *Whistle Down the Wind*, rewritten and redirected after a brief showing in Washington last year. It is based on the book by Mary Hayley Bell which was turned into a film in the 1950s, and is set in Lancashire where a group of children mistake a runaway convict for Jesus Christ. Lloyd Webber and Patricia Knop, who are responsible for the book of the musical, have transposed the location to the bible belt of America in the belief that such a move makes the story more probable. Like *The Phantom of the Opera*, it includes an outsider – the criminal who hides in a barn and is looked after by hordes of winsome children, led by Lottie Mayor's Swallow. Lloyd Webber has enlisted Jim Steinman from Meatloaf as his lyricist, and one of the musical's problems is that it tries to appeal to everyone, from the hard driving numbers between the local villain and his black girlfriend to the schmaltz of the children. It is too early to say whether Lloyd Webber will triumph once more.

Chicago came to London trailing clouds of hype from New York. First produced without much success here in the 1970s, it is set in the 1930s but its story of murder and fickle fame, showbiz and justice strikes home in the 1990s, particularly as real-life American courtroom dramas have recently been hitting the headlines. Far removed from the sentimentality of most musicals, *Chicago* is brassy, cynical and outrageous with leading roles for a shyster lawyer and two murderesses who hope to capitalize on their new-found fame. Director Walter

Bobbie has a minimal set, just the band rising behind the action, while the actors themselves use no more than a few chairs on which to twist and turn. From the opening number, *All that Jazz* with its dazzling combination of pelvic thrusts, angled titfers and sinuous bodies wrapping themselves round the scaffolding on the side of the stage, it was clear that this was going to be a big hit – and so it has proved.

The other two long-awaited musicals from America were *Rent* and *Showboat*. Jonathan Larson, the 35-year-old who wrote the book, music and lyrics of *Rent*, based on Puccini's *La bohème*, died of a brain tumour before the show opened off-Broadway. Unusually the show has a contemporary setting, and is about trying to hold it together with talent and not much money on the streets of New York today. Like the 1960s musical *Hair*, *Rent* is a tribal affair, in which anybody over the age of 25 is restricted to guest appearances on the answerphone. In the same way that the kids in *Hair* were bound together against the draft and the Vietnam war, so the kids in *Rent* are united against AIDS and a rapacious landlord. If Larson had lived he would surely have done more work on the sometimes tortuous story. *Rent* is unlikely to become a classic, but there are some terrific songs and great performances from the American stars.

AMERICAN CLASSIC

Showboat, a definite classic, was directed by Harold Prince with a mammoth American cast. Often credited as the first musical, it was written by Jerome Kern and Oscar Hammerstein in 1927. It was revolutionary because the songs were integrated into the story, which starts in the 1880s and ends in the late 1920s, and because it was brave enough to tackle such contentious themes as mixed marriages, racism, and illegitimacy. For all its ground-breaking attributes, however, and in spite of stirring songs that range from *Ol' Man River* to *Can't Help Lovin' Dat Man*, the characters are extremely flimsy. Prince tried to create unity out of the sprawling story, especially in a second half that moves away from the Mississippi, the real heart of the show. In spite of excellent reviews, the production did not do well enough in London to be recast when the Americans had to return home.

An unlikely success was *Kat and the Kings* which first opened at the Tricycle in Kilburn. The musical told the story of District Six, a mixed race area in Cape Town which defied the segregation laws until the authorities tore it down. Sailors travelling round the Cape in the 1950s used to bring in American records featuring such black stars as the Platters, the Coasters and Nat King Cole. *Kat and the Kings* is loosely based on the life of Salie Daniels, who appeared in the show as the older Kat, looking back on his glory days when he and his friends were in a band playing the American hits. There was some disappointment that the music was so derivative, but the amiability and talent of the performers won the day, and the musical received an unexpected visit from Nelson Mandela when the show moved to the West End.

ROYAL SHAKESPEARE COMPANY

The RSC was as prolific as ever, but also struggled to find a new role for itself following the decision to leave the Barbican in London for half the year. The autumn openings in Stratford proved difficult and unpopular and there were reports of very small audiences after Christmas. Once again the company announced that it was reducing the length of its contracts in order to try and attract more actors. A mediocre season meant that the company once more acquired a large deficit and some of its ambitious touring plans had to be cancelled. Although the company appeared to be developing a new role for itself outside London, providing Shakespearean productions in the rest of the country, critics wondered how it was going to remain a company of international standing if it did not play a major role in London and attract the best actors.

Later in the year the company's artistic director, Adrian Noble, announced that the RSC was putting in a bid for Lottery funding to rebuild the main house at Stratford. Although few would deny that the 1930s building lacks intimacy and defeats many of today's young directors, the application has come in just as a ceiling on Lottery bids has been introduced. The RSC may have to wait a long time before there is any possibility of raising the money. As if to prove that a new main house is needed, the most exciting productions were in the smaller spaces. Michael Attenborough's Romeo and Juliet, which opened in the Pit, was set in the poor south; the Montagues and Capulets were transformed into Sicilian clans struggling to survive at the turn of the century. The wedding became a street party at which the guests were fed on hotpot. Zoë Waites as Juliet was consumed by her own sexuality and Ray Fearon as Romeo was totally at the mercy of his hormonal overdrive. The joy of Attenborough's production was its confident creation of a world in which the audience became completely involved.

Another small-scale production, Tim Supple's The Comedy of Errors, introduced some of the qualities of the Arabian Nights into the play, underscored with live, Middle-Eastern music. Greg Doran's production of Cyrano de Bergerac was a huge hit in the Swan with Antony Sher giving a bravura performance as the wordsmith with the unfortunate conk and Alexandra Gilbreath as a more than usually feisty Roxane. The production later transferred to the West End. Adrian Noble's own production of The Tempest was by far the most memorable of the season on the main stage at Stratford. Once again he used a ramp jutting out into the audience, on which David Calder's vehement Prospero was able to observe others unobserved. Visually beautiful (designed by Anthony Ward), there were breathtaking images of sky and storm and of a huge horned shell in which Caliban resides.

The extravagant design of a production like The Tempest is in complete contrast to productions at Shakespeare's Globe in London, which becomes more and more popular with audiences. Productions there, however, continue to excite controversy for the way in which audiences are encouraged to boo and hiss, turning the plays into melodramas and ironing out all Shakespeare's ambiguities. Critics squirmed at The Merchant of Venice as Norbert Kentrup's Shylock was hissed by noisy audiences; Marcello Magni's Lancelot Gobbo unusually proved the highlight of the show. There is still much to be learned about playing the space, and about finding ways of both provoking and controlling audiences' reactions so that the more rowdy scenes can be enjoyed and attention still reigned in for those that require more concentration.

REGIONS

At Chichester the highlight of the year was David Leveaux's production of Electra for which Zoë Wanamaker as the grieving daughter won an Olivier award when the production moved to the Donmar. Shelagh Stephenson's An Experiment with an Air-Pump was inspired by Joseph Wright's famous painting which depicts an experiment to show that life cannot exist in a vacuum. The play switches between 1799 and 1999 as it explores the moral duty of a scientist and was produced by the Royal Exchange Manchester in Upper Campfield Market. Another lively Manchester production was Animal Crackers, a re-creation of the Marx Brothers film, revived by popular demand with Ben Keaton as Groucho, Joseph Alessi as Chico and Toby Sedgwick as Harpo, directed by Gregory Hersov and Emil Wolk. It was seen at the Barbican later in the year. The West Yorkshire Playhouse was the home for The Good Woman of Sharkville, an exhilarating version of Brecht's The Good Woman of Sezchuan, adapted by Gcina Mhlope and Janet Suzman and directed by Suzman. The setting is transferred to modern South Africa, where the end of apartheid has not brought an end to unemployment, deprivation, corruption or drug abuse. Less happy was You'll Have Had Your Hole by the cult author Irvine Welsh, also in Yorkshire, which received the most abusive reviews for a long time. Nottingham saw the revival of the National Theatre of Brent after a nine-year gap. Having intended to perform Love upon the Throne, on the subject of the marriage and divorce of Charles and Diana, the death of Diana forced Patrick Barlow and John Ramm to come up with another show in two weeks. The result was The Mysteries of Sex with tantric warm-ups and a skim through the history of Henry VIII and his wives.

Finally, the Crucible in Sheffield capitalized on the success of the films The Full Monty and Brassed Off, both set in South Yorkshire, and produced Paul Allen's adaptation of the latter, breaking box-office records. It is not often that adaptations of films work on stage, but this one benefited from the presence of a live band onstage throughout and proved a stirring experience for audiences.

PRODUCTIONS
September 1997 to August 1998

LONDON PRODUCTIONS

ADELPHI, WC2 (18 November 1997) *Chicago* (John Kander, Fred Ebb) with Ruthie Henshall, Ute Lemper, Henry Goodman, Nigel Planer; director, Walter Bobbie

ALBERY, WC2 (7 October 1997) *Stepping Out – The New Musical* (Denis King, Mary Stewart David) with Liz Robertson, Felicity Goodson; director, Julia McKenzie. (3 March 1998) *An Ideal Husband*, transferred from the Gielgud

ALDWYCH, WC2 (29 October 1997) *The Boys in the Band* (Mart Crowley) with Robert Hart, Luke Williams, Paul Venables, Norman Cooley; director, Kenneth Elliott. (5 January 1998) *Amy's View*, transferred from the Royal National. (1 July) *Whistle Down the Wind* (Mary Hayley Bell, adapt. Andrew Lloyd Webber, Jim Steinman) with Lottie Mayor, Marcus Lovett; director, Gale Edwards

ALMEIDA, N1 (4 November 1997) *Tongue of a Bird* (Ellen McLaughlin) with Deborah Findlay, Miriam Karlin; director, Peter Gill. (December) *The Government Inspector* (Gogol, adapt. John Byrne) with Ian McDiarmid, Tom Hollander; director, Jonathan Kent. (18 February 1998) *Naked* (Pirandello, adapt. Nicholas Wright) with Juliette Binoche, Oliver Ford Davies; director, Jonathan Kent. (2 April) *The Iceman Cometh* (Eugene O'Neill) with Kevin Spacey, Rupert Graves, Clarke Peters, James Hazeldine, Mark Strong; director, Howard Davies. (3 June) *The Doctor's Dilemma* (Shaw) with James Callis, Victoria Hamilton, Tony Britton and Ian McDiarmid; director, Michael Grandage

AMBASSADORS, WC2 (8 September 1997) *The Censor,* transferred from the Duke of York's. (9 October) *Faith* (Meredith Oakes) with Jimmy Gallagher, Callum Dixon; director, John Burgess. (19 November) *One More Wasted Year* (Christophe Pellet) with Paul Bettany, Mathew Rhys; director, Mary Peate. (25 November) *Bazaar* (David Planell) with Adrian Edmondson, Nitzan Sharron, Nicholas Woodeson; director, Roxana Silbert. (December) *Stranger's House* (Dea Loher, trans. David Tushingham) with Mathew Rhys, Christopher Ettridge, Gillian Hanna. (January 1998) *Never Land* (Phyllis Nagy) with Michelle Fairley, Sheila Gish, Anthony Calf, Pip Donaghy; director, Steven Pimlott. (20 February) *I Am Yours* (Judith Thompson) with Lynda Baron, Geraldine Somerville, Kerry Fox; director, Nancy Meckler. (April) *Been So Long* (Che Walker) with Mark Letherton, Michele Austin, Gary McDonald, Sophie Okonedo; director, Roxana Silbert. (7 May) *Yard Gal* (Rebecca Prichard) with Amelia Lowdell, Sharon Duncan-Brewster; director, Gemma Bodinetz. (3 June) *Gas Station Angel* (Ed Thomas) with Richard Lynch, Siwan Morris; director, Ed Thomas

APOLLO, W1. *Popcorn,* since March 1997

APOLLO VICTORIA, SW1. *Starlight Express,* since 1984

ARTS, WC2 (29 September 1997) *Dorian* (Wilde, adapt. David Reeve) with Mark Huggins, Nicholas Pound, Marcello Walton; director, Mehmet Ergen. (5 November) *The Popular Mechanicals* (Keith Robinson, Tony Taylor) with Simon Walter, Cal McCrystal; director, Geoffrey Rush. (June 1998) *Disco Pigs* (Enda Walsh) with Cillian Murphy, Eileen Walsh; director, Pat Kiernan. (3 August) *No Way to Treat a Lady* (William Goldman, adapt. Douglas J. Cohen) with Donna McKechnie, Joanna Riding, Paul Bown, Tim Flavin; director, Neil Marcus. (28 August)

Biloxi Blues (Neil Simon), a National Youth Theatre production; director, Edward Wilson

BARBICAN, EC2 (14 October 1997) *Shintoku-maru* (Shuji Terayama), a Ninagawa Company production; director, Yukio Ninagawa. (4 November) *Henry V*, transferred from Stratford. (4 December) *Hamlet*, transferred from Stratford. (17 December) *The Merry Wives of Windsor,* transferred from Stratford. (20 January 1998) *Cymbeline,* transferred from Stratford. (12 February) *Much Ado About Nothing,* transferred from Stratford. (25 May) *Measure for Measure* (Shakespeare), co-production with Nottingham Playhouse, first produced at Edinburgh Festival 1997, with John Ramm, Lisé Stevenson, Oscar Pearce, Sean Baker. (June) *The Possessed* (Dostoevsky, adapt. Lev Dodin), a Maly Drama Theatre production; director, Lev Dodin. (16 July) *The Man Who Came for Dinner* (Kaufman and Hart), a Steppenwolf Company production; director, James Burrows. (28 August) *Hamlet* (Shakespeare), a Ninagawa Company production; director, Yukio Ninagawa

THE PIT (29 October 1997) *Romeo and Juliet* (Shakespeare) with Zoe Waites, Chook Sibtain; director, Michael Attenborough. (3 December) *The Spanish Tragedy,* transferred from Stratford. (15 December) *Little Eyolf,* transferred from Stratford. (21 January 1998) *The Mysteries: The Creation* and *The Passion,* transferred from Stratford. (11 February) *Everyman,* transferred from Stratford. (March) *Krapp's Last Tape* (Beckett) with Edward Petherbridge; directors, Edward Petherbridge, David Hunt. (15 April) *The Unexpected Man* (Yasmina Reza, trans. Christopher Hampton) with Michael Gambon, Eileen Atkins; director, Matthew Warchus. (20 May) *Love's Fire* (various, including Tony Kushner, John Guare, Wendy Wasserstein, Eric Bogosian, Marsha Norman, Ntozake Shange and William Finn), an Acting Company production; director, Mark Lamos. (June) *The Gift* (Angela de Castro) with Angela de Castro. (21 July) *2.5 Minute Ride* with Lisa Kron

BUSH, W12 (September 1997) *Disco Pigs* (Enda Walsh) with Cillian Murphy, Eileen Walsh; director, Pat Kiernan. (13 October) *Mackeral Sky* (Hilary Fannin) with Ruth Hegarty, Gillian Raine, Emma McIvor; director, Mike Bradwell. (14 November) *Caravan* (Helen Blakeman) with Elizabeth Estensen, Emma Cunliffe, Pip Donaghy; director, Gemma Bodinetz. (7 January 1998) *Martin and John* (Dale Peck, adapt. Sean O'Neil) with Sean O'Neil; director, Eileen Vorbach. (5 February) *Sabina* (Snoo Wilson) with Suzanne Vidler, Paul McGann, David Gant, Mark Long; director, Andy Wilson. (18 March) *Deep Space* (Alex Johnston) with Patrick Leech, Alex Johnston; director, Jimmy Fay. (22 April) *A Question of Mercy* (David Rabe) with Seth Gilliam, Richard Bekins, David Chandler; director, Doug Hughes. (June) *Love You, Too* (Doug Lucie) with Susannah Doyle, Miranda Foster, Reece Dinsdale, Sam Graham; director, Mike Bradwell. (10 July) *Sugar Sugar* (Simon Bent) with Nicolas Tennant, Deborah McAndrew; director, Paul Miller

CAMBRIDGE, WC2. *Grease,* since 1996

COMEDY, WC2 (16 October 1997) *A Letter of Resignation* (Hugh Whitemore) with Edward Fox, Clare Higgins, Julian Wadham; director, Christopher Morahan. (16 April 1998) *The Real Inspector Hound* (Tom Stoppard) and *Black Comedy* (Peter Shaffer) with Desmond Barrit, Nichola McAuliffe, Anna Chancellor, David Tennant, Gary Waldhorn; director, Gregory Doran

CRITERION, W1. *The Complete Works of William Shakespeare (Abridged)* and *The Complete History of America (Abridged),* since 1996

DOMINION, WCI. *Beauty and the Beast,* since May 1997

DONMAR WAREHOUSE, WC2 (17 September 1997) *Enter the Guardsmen* (Ferenc Molnar, adapt. Craig Bohmler, Marion Adler) with Janie Dee, Alexander Hanson, Nicky Henson, Angela Richards; director, Jeremy Sams. (October) *Electra,* transferred from Chichester. (10 December) *The Front Page* (Ben Hecht, Charles MacArthur) with Griff Rhys Jones, Alun Armstrong; director, Sam Mendes. (March 1998) *In a Little World of our Own* (Gary Mitchell), a Foundry Company production; director, Robert Delamere. (March) *Tell Me* (Matthew Dunster), a Northern Stage production; director, Richard Gregory. (March) *Timeless* (David Greig) with Keith Macpherson, Paul Thomas Hickey, Molly Innes, Kate Dickie; director, Graham Eatough. (24 March) *Sleeping Around* (Hilary Fanin, Stephen Greenhorn, Abi Morgan, Mark Ravenhill), a Paines Plough production; director, Vicky Featherstone. (8 April) *The Bullet* (Joe Penhall) with Miles Anderson, Barbara Flynn, Andrew Tiernan, Neil Stuke, Emily Woof; director, Dominic Cooke. (13 May) *3 by Harold Pinter: A Kind of Alaska, The Collection* and *The Lover* (Pinter) with Douglas Hodge, Lia Williams, Colin McFarlane, Penelope Wilton, Bill Nighy, Brid Brennan, Harold Pinter; directors, Karel Reisz, Joe Harmston. (24 June) *How I Learned to Drive* (Paula Vogel) with Helen McCrory and Kevin Whately; director, John Crowley

DRURY LANE THEATRE ROYAL, WC2. *Miss Saigon,* since 1989

DUCHESS, WC2 (9 October 1997) *Scissor Happy* (Bruce Jordan, Marilyn Abrahams, adapt. Neil Mullarkey, Lee Simpson, Jim Sweeney) with Gaye Brown, Lee Simpson, Jim Sweeney; director, Neil Mullarkey. (March 1998) *Brief Lives* (John Aubrey, adapt. Patrick Garland) with Michael Williams; director, Patrick Garland. (10 June) *The Unexpected Man* (Yasmina Reza, trans. Christopher Hampton), transferred from the Barbican Pit. (26 August) *Things We Do For Love* (Ayckbourn), transferred from the Gielgud

DUKE OF YORK'S, WC2 (17 September 1997) *Blue Heart: Heart's Desire* and *Blue Kettle* (Caryl Churchill), an Out of Joint production; director, Max Stafford-Clark. (24 October) *Fair Game* (Edna Mazya's *Games in the Backyard,* adapt. Rebecca Prichard) with T. J. Sorrell, Simeilia Hodge-Dalloway, Dean Ensor; director, Roxana Silbert. (19 November) *The Chairs* (Eugène Ionesco, trans. Martin Crimp) with Richard Briers, Geraldine McEwan; director, Simon McBurney. (18 February 1998) *The Weir* (Conor McPherson), a 1997 Theatre Upstairs production; director, Ian Rickson. (30 April) *Cleansed* (Sarah Kane) with Stuart McQuarrie, Suzan Sylvester; director, James Macdonald. (17 June) *The Old Neighborhood* (David Mamet) with Colin Stinton, Zoë Wanamaker, Diana Quick; director, Patrick Marber

FORTUNE, WC2. *The Woman in Black,* since 1989. (Sunday matinees) *Marie,* since 1995

GARRICK, WC2. *An Inspector Calls,* the 1992 National Theatre production, since 1995

GATE, WII (25 September 1997) *Danton's Death* (Georg Büchner); director, David Farr. (October) *Woyzeck* (Büchner, adapt. William Fiennes) with Michael Shannon, Kate Ashfield; director, Sarah Kane. (November) *Leonce and Lena* (Büchner) with Christopher Staines, Sarah Belcher; director, David Farr. (2 January 1998) *Klaxons, Trumpets and Raspberries* (Dario Fo, trans. Jonathan Dryden Taylor), a Juggling Fiends Theatre production. (5 February) *The Child* (Jon Fosse) with Peter Sproule, Sophie Thursfield, Andrew Whipp. (5 February)

Leatherface (Helmut Krausser) with Paul Viragh, Katy Carmichael. (March) *Epitaph for the Whales* (Yoji Sakate, trans. Mark Sparrow) with Lilo Baur, Clive Mendus, Matt Abley; director, Kazuyoshi Kushido. (March) *The Measle* (15 April) *The Caracal/Dossier* (Ronald Akkerman). (May) *Franziska* (Frank Wedekind, trans. Philip Ward, adapt. Eleanor Brown) with Christopher Bowen, Lydzia Englert; director, Georgina Van Welie. (June) *Outside on the Streets* (Wolfgang Borchert, trans. Tom Fisher) with Sean Gallagher; director, Gordon Anderson. (July) *Herakles* (Euripides, trans. Kenneth McLeish) with Alistair Petrie, Tanya Ronder; director, Nick Philippou. (7 August) *The Clowness* (Gerlind Reinshagen) with Paula Wilcox

GIELGUD, WI (October 1997) *An Ideal Husband,* transferred from the Old Vic. (3 March 1998) *Things We do For Love* (Alan Ayckbourn) with Jane Asher, Steven Pacey, Serena Evans; director, Alan Ayckbourn

GLOBE, SEI (23 May 1998) *The Merchant of Venice* (Shakespeare) with Kathryn Pogson, Mark Rylance, Norbert Kentrup, Lila Baur, Jack Shepherd and Marcello Magni; director, Richard Olivier. (28 May) *As You Like It* (Shakespeare) with Anastasia Hille, Leader Hawkins, Paul Hilton, Marcello Magni; director, Lucy Bailey. (21 July) *Otra Tempestad* (*Another Tempest,* adapt. from *The Tempest* (Shakespeare)), a Teatro Buendia production; director, Flora Lauten. (13 August) *The Honest Whore* (Thomas Dekker) with Mark Rylance, Lilo Baur; director, Jack Shepherd. (13 August) *A Mad World, My Masters* (Middleton) with Jonathan Cecil, Belinda Davison, John McEnery; director, Sue Lefton

GREENWICH, SE10 (October 1997) *A View from a Bridge* (Arthur Miller) with Desmond Barrit, Robert Hands, Eleanor Tremain; director, Rachel Kavanaugh. (December) *David Copperfield* (Dickens, adapt. Matthew Francis) with Paul Bailey, Damien Matthews, Peter Hugo-Daly, Susan Porrett; director, Matthew Francis. (February 1998) *Romeo and Juliet* (Shakespeare) with Kate Fleetwood, Nicholas Irons; director, Rupert Goold

HAMPSTEAD, NW3 (9 September 1997) *The Prince of West End Avenue* (Alan Isler) with Kerry Shale; director, Sonya Fraser. (October) *My Boy Jack* (David Haig) with David Haig, Belinda Lang, Sarah Howe; director, John Dove. (27 November) *Heritage* (Stephen Churchett) with George Cole, Tim Pigott-Smith, Gwen Taylor; director, Mark Rayment. (January 1998) *Terms of Abuse* (Jessica Townsend) with Suzan Sylvester, Emma Bird; director, Julie-Anne Robinson. (4 February) *Fairytaleheart* (Philip Ridley) with Victoria Shalet, Zoot Lynham; director, Philip Ridley. (13 February) *Featuring Loretta* (George F. Walker) with Matilda Ziegler, Con O'Neill, Neil Stuke; director, Robin Lefevre. (March) *English Journeys* (Steve Waters) with Lizzy McInnerny, Lloyd Hutchinson, Gem Durham; director, Gemma Bodinetz. (March) *Apocalyptica* (Philip Ridley) with Peter Copley, Ian Gelder, Julie Legrand; director, Matthew Lloyd. (30 March) *Give Me Your Answer Do!* (Brian Friel) with Niall Buggy, Sorcha Cusack, Gawn Grainger, Geraldine James; director, Robin Lefevre. (May) *Nabokov's Gloves* (Peter Moffat) with Greg Wise, Niamh Cusack, Ruth Gemmell; director, Ian Brown. (13 July) *After Darwin* (Timberlake Wertenbaker) with Jason Watkins, Ingeborga Dapkunaite, Michael Feast; director, Lindsay Posner

HAYMARKET THEATRE ROYAL, SWI (21 October 1997) *A Delicate Balance* (Edward Albee) with Maggie Smith, Eileen Atkins, Annette Crosbie, John Standing; director, Anthony Page. (21 April 1998) *New Edna – The Spectacle!* with Barry Humphries; director, Alan Strachan. (25 August) *An Ideal Husband,* transferred from the Albery

HER MAJESTY'S, SW1. *The Phantom of the Opera*, since 1986

LONDON (formerly LABATTS) APOLLO, W6 (14 July 1998) *Doctor Dolittle* (Leslie Bricusse) with Philip Schofield, Jane Hassell, Julie Andrews; director, Stephen Pimlott

LONDON PALLADIUM, WC1 (5 May 1998) *Saturday Night Fever*, with Adam Garcia, Tara Wilkinson, Anita Louise Combe, Simon Greiff; director, Arlene Phillips

LYCEUM, WC2. *Jesus Christ Superstar*, since 1996

LYRIC, W1 (29 September 1997) *Maddie* (Stephen Keeling, Shaun McKenna, Steven Dexter) with Summer Rognlie, Graham Bickley, Lynda Baron; director, Martin Connor. (25 November) *Cyrano de Bergerac*, transferred from Stratford. (April) *Closer* (Patrick Marber), transferred from the Royal National

LYRIC, W6 (September 1997) *The Wasp Factory*, transferred from Leeds. (23 October) *The Milk Train Doesn't Stop Here Anymore* (Tennessee Williams) with Rupert Everett, David Foxxe; director, Philip Prowse. (6 December) *Treasure Island* (Stevenson) with Tom Georgeson; director, Neil Bartlett. (5 February 1998) *Cause Célèbre* (Terence Rattigan) with Diane Fletcher, Amanda Harris, Laurence Mitchell; director, Neil Bartlett. (18 May) *Kindertotenlieder* (Rückert, with music by Mahler) with Harriet Innes, Rebecca Blankenship; director, Robert Lepage. (10 July) *What You Get and What You Expect* (Jean-Marie Bisset, trans. Jeremy Sams), an Ideal Theatre Company production; director, Thierry Harcourt. (August) *Juicy Bits* (Kay Adshead) with Kay Adshead, Anthony Sergeant, Victoria Worsley; director, Sarah Davey

LYRIC STUDIO (October 1997) *The Reckless are Dying Out* (Handke), a 606 Theatre production; director, Gordon Andersen. (19 November) *Orpheus* (Kenneth McLeish) with Ann Firbank, Shelley King, Gary Turner; director, Nick Philippou. (January 1998) *Fossil Woman* (Louise Warren) with Alison Edgar; director, Helena Uren. (3 February) *Lakeboat* (David Mamet) with Juim Dunk, Simon Harris, Jon Welch, Joe May; director, Aaron Mullen. (March) *The Barbers of Surreal* (Rossini), a Folkbeard Fantasy production. (April) *The Criminals* (Jose Triana) with Joanna Foster, Miranda Foster, Peter Sullivan; director, Ian Brown. (21 April) *Briefs* (various), from Shaker Productions; director, Alison Edgar. (19 May) *Take Away* (Stephen Clark), a Mu-Lan Theatre Company production; director, Stephen Knight. (14 July) *Richard III* (Shakespeare), an Oddbodies production; director, John Mowat. (5 August) *Happy Savages* (Ryan Craig), a Pluto Productions production; director, David Evans

MERMAID, EC4. *The Hop-Pickers*

NEW LONDON, WC2. *Cats*, since 1981

OLD VIC, SE1 (14 September 1997) *Playhouse Creatures* (April de Angelis) with Saskia Reeves, Sheila Gish, Jo McInnes; director, Lynne Parker. (October) *Snake in the Grass* (Roy MacGregor) with John Normington, Kevin Whatley; director, Dominic Dromgoole. (November) *Shining Souls* (Chris Hannan) with Shirley Henderson, Alison Peebles, Conleth Hill, Tom Mannion; director, Chris Hannan. (11 May 1998) *The Pantomimes of Bip* and *The Bowler Hat* (Marcel Marceau), a New Mimodrama Company production with Marcel Marceau. (19 June) *The Iceman Cometh*, transferred from the Almeida.

OPEN AIR. (May 1998) *A Midsummer Night's Dream* (Shakespeare) with Michael Elwyn, Debby Bishop, Nicola Duffett, Daniel Flynn; director, Rachel Kavanaugh. (June) *Troilus and Cressida* (Shakespeare), by The New Shakespeare Company; director, Alan Strachan.

(23 July) *Gentlemen Prefer Blondes* (Anita Loos, Joseph Fields, adapt. Jule Styne, Leo Robin) with Sara Crowe, Debby Bishop; director, Ian Talbot. (August) *The Jungle Book* (Kipling), a New Shakespeare Company Youth Theatre production; director, Antony Tuckey

PALACE, WC2. *Les Miserables*, since 1985

PHOENIX, WC1. *Blood Brothers*, since 1991

PICCADILLY, W1 (March 1998) *Waiting for Godot*, 1997 Old Vic production; director, Peter Hall. (13 March) *The Misanthrope* (Molière, trans. Ranjit Bolt) with Michael Pennington, Elaine Paige, Peter Bowles, Anna Cartaret, David Yelland; director, Peter Hall. (1 May) *Major Barbara* (Shaw) with Jemma Redgrave, Peter Bowles, Anna Cartaret, Michael Pennington, David Yelland; director, Peter Hall

PLAYHOUSE, WC2 (10 October 1997) *HRH* (Snoo Wilson) with Corin Redgrave, Amanda Donohoe; director, Simon Callow. (19 March 1998) *Judas Kiss* (David Hare) with Liam Neeson, Tom Hollander; director, Richard Eyre. (23 April) *Naked*, transferred from the Almeida. (3 June) *Much Ado About Nothing* (Shakespeare), a Cheek By Jowl production; director, Declan Donnellan

PRINCE EDWARD, W1 (28 April 1998) *Show Boat* (Hammerstein, Kern) with Michel Bell, George Grizzard, Carole Shelley Terry Burrell, Teri Hansen; director, Harold Prince

PRINCE OF WALES, W1. *Smokey Joe's Café*, since 1996

QUEENS, W1 (15 November 1997) *Bugsy Malone* (Alan Parker, Paul Williams), a National Youth Music Theatre production; director, Edward Snipes. (25 March 1998) *Saucy Jack and the Space Vixens*, transferred from Southampton. (10 June) *Elton John's Glasses* (David Farr) with Brian Conley, Will Keen, Gabrielle Glaister; director, Terry Johnson

ROYAL COURT and THEATRE UPSTAIRS, SW1. Closed for refurbishment 1996–8; performances at the Ambassadors and Duke of York's theatres

ROYAL NATIONAL THEATRE, SE1, COTTESLOE (25 September 1997) *The Invention of Love* (Tom Stoppard) with John Wood, Paul Rhys, Michael Bryant, Michael Fitzgerald; director, Richard Eyre. (24 October) *Othello* (Shakespeare) with David Harewood, Claire Skinner, Simon Russell Beale; director, Sam Mendes. (14 November) *Mutabilitie* (Frank McGuinness) with Patrick Malahide, Anton Lesser, Aisling O'Sullivan; director, Trevor Nunn. (January 1998) *The Day I Stood Still* (Kevin Elyot) with Adrian Scarborough, Oliver Milburn; director, Ian Rickson. (27 February) *Not About Nightingales* (Tennessee Williams) with Finbar Lynch, Corin Redgrave, James Black; director, Trevor Nunn. (16 April) *Our Lady of Sligo* (Sebastian Barry) with Sinéad Cusack, Nigel Terry, Catherine Cusack; director, Max Stafford-Clark. (22 April) *Oh What a Lovely War* (Joan Littlewood) (in a mobile Big Top at Bernie Spain Gardens) with Clive Hayward, Joanna Riding, Elizabeth Renihan, Sonia Swaby; director, Fiona Laird. (28 May) *Copenhagen* (Michael Frayn) with Matthew Marsh, David Burke, Sara Kestelman; director, Michael Blakemore. (24 July) Pidgin Macbeth (Shakespeare, adapt. Ken Campbell), a Pidgin Players production; directors, Ken Campbell, Toby Sedgwick

LYTTELTON (4 September 1997) *Chips with Everything* (Arnold Wesker) with Rupert Penry-Jones, Julian Glover, Eddie Marsan; director, Howard Davies. (30 September) *Les Fausses Confidences* (Marivaux), a Comédie-Française production; director, Jean-Pierre Miquel. (16 October) *Closer*, transferred from the

Cottesloe. (March 1998) *The London Cuckolds* (Edward Ravenscroft, adapt. Terry Johnson) with Ben Miles, Anthony O'Donnell, Caroline Quentin, Robin Soans; director, Terry Johnson. (2 May) *Othello* (Shakespeare) with David Harewood, Claire Skinner, Simon Russell Beale; director, Sam Mendes. (2 June) *The Day I Stood Still* (Kevin Elyot); director, Ian Rickson. (20 June) *The Prime of Miss Jean Brodie* (Muriel Spark, adapt. Jay Presson Allen) with Fiona Shaw, Susannah Wise, Nicholas Le Provost, Adam Kotz; director, Phillida Lloyd. (20 August) *Tarry Flynn* (Patrick Kavanagh, adapt. Conall Morrison), a Dublin Abbey Theatre production; director, Conall Morrison

OLIVIER (12 September 1997) *An Enemy of the People* (Ibsen) with Ian McKellen, Stephen Moore, Alan Cox, John Woodvine; director, Trevor Nunn. (8 December) *Peter Pan (The Boy Who Would Not Grow Up)* (J. M. Barrie, adapt. Trevor Nunn, John Caird) with Jenny Agutter, Alec McCowen, Daniel Evans, Ian McKellen; directors, John Caird, Fiona Laird. (February 1998) *Flight* (Mikhail Bulgakov) with Alan Howard, Kenneth Cranham, Michael Mueller; director, Ron Hutchinson. (28 May) *Flight* (Mikhail Bulgakov, adapt. Ron Hutchinson) with Abigail Cruttenden, Alan Howard, Kenneth Cranham, Michael Mueller; director, Howard Davies. (6 June) *Brassed Off* (Mark Herman), transferred from the Crucible, Sheffield. (July) *Oklahoma!* with Josefina Gabrielle, Hugh Jackman, Maureen Lipman; director, Trevor Nunn

ST MARTINS, WC2. *The Mousetrap*, since 1974

SAVOY, WC2 (9 December 1997) *The Magistrate*, transferred from Chichester. (20 April 1998) *A Letter of Resignation*, transferred from the Comedy

SHAFTESBURY THEATRE, WC2 (12 May 1998) *Rent* (Jonathan Larson) with Adam Pascall, Anthony Rapp, Krysten Cummings, Bonny Lockhart, Jessica Tezier; director, Michael Greif

STRAND, WC2. *Buddy*, since 1995

THEATRE ROYAL, E15 (September 1997) *When Love and Desire Become a Sin* (Prabjot Dolly Dhingra), a Moti Roti production; director, Keith Khan

TRICYCLE, NW6 (September 1997) *A Tainted Dawn*, a Tamash Theatre Company production; directors, Sudha Bhuchar, Kristine Landon-Smith. (October) *Kat and the Kings* (David Kramer, Taliep Petersen) with Salie Daniels, Jody Abrahams, Loukmaan Adams; director, David Kramer. (10 November) *Angels and Demons*, a Besht Tellers production; director, Rebbecca Wolman. (December) *Sive* (John B. Keane) with Marion O'Dwyer, Aine Ni Mhuirí, Catherine Walker; director, Ben Barnes. (January 1998) *Iced* (Ray Shell), a Black Theatre Co-operative production; director, Felix Cross. (19 February) *Kat and the Kings*, October production. (19 March) *Dance of Death* (Strindberg, adapt. Carlo Gébler) with Marion Bailey, Michael Cochrane, Tim Woodward; director, Nicholas Kent. (30 April) *Sitting in Limbo*, a Carib Theatre production; director, Anton Phillips. (18 May) *Europeans Only* (Pieter-Dirk Uy) with Pieter-Dirk Uy. (June) *The Little Violin* (Dickens' *Dr Marigold's Prescriptions*, adapt. Jean-Claude Grumberg, Adrian Mitchell) with Peter Nicholas, Clive Llewellyn and Grace Mattaka; director, Erica Whyman. (16 June) *The Basset Table* (Susanna Centlivre), a Bristol Old Vic production; director, Polly Irvin

VAUDEVILLE, WC2 (20 October 1997) *She Knows, You Know* (Jean Fergusson) with Jean Fergusson. (6 January 1998) *Do You Come Here Often?* with Hamish McColl, Sean Foley. (March) *Kat and the Kings*, transferred from the Tricycle. (12 August) *Loot* (Orton), transferred from Chichester

VICTORIA PALACE, SW1 (10 November 1997) *Fame: the Musical*, transferred from the Cambridge after tour. (25 February 1998) *Girls' Night Out* (Dave Simpson), also touring. (19 May) *Sweet Charity* (Neil Simon, adapt. Cy Coleman, Dorothy Fields) with Bonnie Langford, Mark Wynter, Johanne Murdock, Cornell John; director, Carol Metcalfe

WHITEHALL (5 November 1997) *The Slow Drag* (Carson Kreitzer) with Liza Sadovy, Kim Criswell, Christopher Colquhoun; director, Lisa Forrell

WYNDHAM'S, WC2. *Art*, since 1996

YOUNG VIC, SE1 (1 September 1997) *The Comedy of Errors* (Shakespeare), 1996 RSC production; director, Tim Supple. (October) *Jane Eyre* (Charlotte Brontë, adapt. Polly Teale), a Shared Experience production; director, Polly Teale. (4 November) *The Opium Eaters*, a Brouhaha company production. (24 November) *More Grimm Tales* (adapt. Carol Ann Duffy); director, Tim Supple. (December) *Change of Heart*, a Stratcona company production; directors, Ann Cleary, Ian McCurrach. (11 February 1998) *Henry VIII*, transferred from Stratford. (26 February) *Camino Real*, transferred from Stratford. (25 March) *Uncle Vanya* (Chekhov, trans. David Lan) with Stephen Dillane, Anastasia Hille, Linus Roache, Jo McInnes; director, Katie Mitchell. (5 May) *People Show Number 105*, a People Show Company production. (14 May) *Twelfth Night* (Shakespeare), a Young Vic production; director Tim Supple. (16 May) *Mirror Lore*, a Jackie Chan production; director, Tim Supple. (19 May) *The Lost and Moated Land*, a Theatre Rights production; director, Penny Bernand. (22 May) *As I Lay Dying* (Faulkner, adapt. Edward Kemp), a Young Vic production; director, Tim Supple

OUTSIDE LONDON

BIRMINGHAM: REPERTORY (September 1997) *Keep on Running* (Bizet's *Carmen*, adapt. Bob Carlton) with Kate O'Sullivan, Ben Fox, Kevin Pallister; director, Bob Carlton. (24 October) *Julius Caesar* (Shakespeare) with Michael Cashman, Timothy Walker, David Bark-Jones, James Dreyfus; director, Anthony Clark. (5 December) *The Snowman* (Raymond Briggs, adapt. Bill Alexander, Howard Blake) with Kasper Cornish; director, Bill Alexander. (February 1998) *Home Truths* (David Lodge) with Brian Protheroe, Cliff Howells, Rachel Pickup; director, Anthony Clark. (March) *The Rocky Horror Show* with Jason Donovan, Ross O'Hennessy, Michael Cashman, Simma Morecroft; director, Christopher Malcolm. (23 April) *Ursula* (Howard Barker) with Sarah Theresa Belcher, Caroline Hetherington, Belinda Kelly, Jules Melvin; director, Howard Baker. (5 May) *Frozen* (Bryony Lavery) with Anita Dobson, Tom Georgeson, Josie Lawrence; director, Bill Alexander

BRISTOL: OLD VIC (11 September 1997) *With Love From Nicolae* (Lin Coghlan) with Nicola Redmond, Aneta Christ, Jonah Russell; director, Philip Osment. (October) *Macbeth* (Shakespeare) with Pete Postlethwaite, Nick Brimble, Richard Howard; director, George Costigan. (November) *The Man with Green Hair* (Nick Darke) with Emma Brown; director, Andy Hay. (April 1998) *The Bassett Table* (Susannah Centlivre) with Harriet Thorpe, Tom McGovern, Patti Love, Clare McCarron; director, Polly Irvin

CHICHESTER: FESTIVAL (29 September 1997) *The Magistrate* (Arthur Wing Pinero) with Ian Richardson, Graham Crowden, Abigail McKern; director, Nicholas Broadhurst. (20 April 1998) *Joseph and the Amazing Technicolour Dreamcoat* (Lloyd Webber, Rice), a Bill

Kenwright production. (20 May) *Saturday, Sunday... and Monday* (Eduardo de Filippo) with David Suchet, Dearbhla Molloy; director, Jude Kelly. (3 July) *Racing Demon* (David Hare) with Denis Quilley, Dinsdale Landen, Paul Venables; director, Christopher Morahan. (July) *Loot* (Orton) with Fred Ridgeway, Gary Richards, Tracy-Ann Oberman; director, David Grindley. (11 August) *Chimes at Midnight* (Orson Welles) with Simon Callow, Keith Baxter, Tam Williams, Sarah Badel; director, Patrick Garland

MINERVA (10 September 1997) *Electra* (Sophocles, adapt. David Leveaux, trans. Frank McGuiness) with Zoë Wanamaker, Andrew Howard, Marjorie Yates; director, David Leveaux

EDINBURGH: ROYAL LYCEUM (October 1997) *Dead Funny* with Andy Gray, Jennifer Black, Robert Carr; director, David Robb. (November) *Much Ado About Nothing* (Shakespeare) with Elaine C. Smith, Forbes Masson, Tom McGovern; director, Kenny Ireland. (February 1998) *Juno and the Paycock* (Sean O'Casey) with Roy Hanlon, Conleth Hill; director, Mark Lambert. (March) *Mother Courage and her Children* (Brecht) with Deirdre Molloy, Maggie Steed, David Shaw-Parker; director, Kenny Ireland. (5 July) *Whisky Galore* (Compton Mackenzie, adapt. Paul Godfrey), a Mull Theatre production; director, Alasdair McCrone. (August) *Life is a Dream* (Calderón), a Royal Lyceum Theatre Company production; director, Calixto Bieito

GLASGOW: CITIZENS (January 1998) *The Relapse* (Vanbrugh) with Greg Hicks, Trevyn McDowell; director, Philip Prowse. (February) *Macbeth* (Shakespeare) with Gerard Murphy, Anne Myatt; director, David MacDonald. (March) *The Millionairess* (Bernard Shaw) with Anne Myatt, Stuart Bowman; director, Giles Havergal

LEEDS: WEST YORKSHIRE PLAYHOUSE (4 September 1997) *Of Mice and Men* (Steinbeck), director, Ian Brown. (10 October) *The Good Woman of Sharkville* (Brecht's *The Good Person of Sezchuan*, adapt. Geina Mhlophe, Janet Suzman), a Market Theatre of Johannesburg production; director, Janet Suzman. (24 October) *The Importance of Being Earnest* (Wilde) with Una Stubbs, James Wallace, Ruth Grey; director, Lynne Parker. (29 November) *The Pirates of Penzance* (Gilbert and Sullivan, adapt. Joseph Papp); director, Ian Talbot. (19 February 1998) *You'll Have Had Your Hole* (Irvine Welsh) with Malcolm Shields, Tam Dean Burn, Billy McElhany; director, Ian Brown. (April) *Blast From the Past* (Ben Elton) with Imogen Stubbs, Oliver Cotton. (June) *Spend Spend Spend!* (Steve Brown, Justin Greene) with Rosemary Ashe, Sophie-Louise Dann, Nigel Richards; director, Justin Greene. (June) *Rita, Sue and Bob Too* (Andrea Dunbar) with Thomas Craig, Michelle Abrahams, Hannah Storey; director, Natasha Betteridge. (July) *Proposals* (Neil Simon) with Damien Goodwin, Paul Shelley, Geraldine Fitzgerald; director, Ian Brown

COURTYARD (18 September 1997) *Odysseus Thump* (Richard Hope) with David Threlfall; director, Jude Kelly. (6 November) *Jar the Floor* (Cheryl L. West) with Jennifer Calvert, Marilyn Coleman, Ginny Holder; director, Topher Campbell. (14 January 1998) *Weekend Breaks* (John Godber) with Dicken Ashworth, Adrian Hood, Judi Jones; director, John Godber

LEICESTER: HAYMARKET (17 April 1998) *There are Crimes and There are Crimes* (Strindberg) with Timothy Walker, Sara Stewart; director, Linda Marlowe

MANCHESTER: ROYAL EXCHANGE (October 1997) *Much Ado About Nothing* (Shakespeare) with Josie Lawrence,

John McAndrew, Michael Mueller; director, Helena Kaut-Howson. (November) *The Deep Blue Sea* (Rattigan) with Susan Wooldridge, David Fielder; director, Marianne Elliott. (February 1998) *An Experiment with an Air-Pump* (Shelagh Stephenson) with David Horovitch, Derbhla Molloy

MOLD: THEATR CLWYD, EMLYN WILLIAMS (31 October 1997) *Abigail's Party* (Mike Leigh) with Elaine Caxton, Judith McSpadden, Vivien Parry, Steffan Rhodri, Llion Williams; director, Fiona Buffini. (6 November) *Entertaining Mr Sloane* (Orton) with Robert Blythe, Jimmy Gardner, Joseph McFadden, Lynne Verrall; director, Dominic Cooke. (21 January 1998) *The Journey of Mary Kelly* (Siân Evans) with Rachel Sanders

ANTHONY HOPKINS (31 October 1997) *Equus* (Peter Shaffer) with Frank Grimes, Oliver Ryan, Lynne Verrall, Robert Blythe; director, Terry Hands. (20 November) *Rape of the Fair Country* (Alexander Cordell, adapt. Manon Eames); director, Tim Baker. (5 December) *A Christmas Carol* (Dickens); director, Terry Hands. (22 January 1998) *Afore Night Come* (David Rudkin); director, Dominic Cooke

NOTTINGHAM: PLAYHOUSE (March 1998) *Angels Rave On* (Michael Eaton) with Sean Harris, Caroline Trowbridge, Treva Etienne; director, Jonathan Church. (23 April) *A Fool and His Money* (Molière, trans. Jeremy Sams) with James Bolam; director, Martin Duncan. (June) *Suddenly Last Summer* (Tennessee Williams) with Jaime Robertson, Louise Delamere, Linda Marlowe; director, Ralph Koltai

PLYMOUTH: THEATRE ROYAL (15 September 1997) *The Country Wife* (William Wycherley); director, Laurence Boswell

SCARBOROUGH: STEPHEN JOSEPH (June 1998) *Comic Potential* (Ayckbourn) with Janie Dee, Nicholas Haverson, Jacqueline King, John Branwell. (7 July) *Perfect Pitch* (John Godber) with John Branwell, Jennifer Luckraft, Jacqueline King, James Hornsby; director, John Godber. (August) *Love Songs for Shopkeepers* (Tim Firth) with Bill Champion, Janie Dee; director, Alan Ayckbourn

SHEFFIELD: CRUCIBLE (26 September 1997) *What the Butler Saw* (Orton) with Cheryl Campbell; director, Michael Grandage. (31 October) *King Lear* (Shakespeare) with Tim Barlow; director, Deborah Paige. (12 December) *My Fair Lady* (Lerner, Loewe) with Clive Carter, Sarah-Jane Hassell; director, David Sulkin. (March 1998) *Brassed Off* (Mark Herman, adapt. Paul Allen) with Shaun Dooley, James Thornton, Freya Copeland; director, Deborah Page. (16 June) *The Tempest* (Shakespeare), a Compass Theatre production

SOUTHAMPTON: NUFFIELD (29 September 1997) *Mail Order Bride* (James Robson); director, Patrick Sandford. (24 October) *Saucy Jack and the Space Vixens* (Charlotte Mann), a co-production with Counterpoint Theatre; director, Keith Strachan. (14 November) *A Taste of Honey* (Shelagh Delaney); director, Daniel Buckroyd. (9 December) *The Wizard of Oz* (Harold Arlen, E. Y. Harburg); director, Patrick Sandford. (3 February) *The Brothers of the Brush* (Jimmy Murphy), a Nuffield Theatre Company production; director, Patrick Sandford. (20 March) *Waiting for Godot* (Beckett). (23 April) *The Seduction of Anne Boleyn* (Claire Luckham) with Simon Robson, Jessica Lloyd; director, Patrick Sandford. (21 May) *Abigail's Party* (Mike Leigh) with Isobel Black, Damian Myerscough, Claire Fisher, Clive Flint, Louise Plowright; director, Patrick Sandford

STRATFORD: ROYAL SHAKESPEARE THEATRE (5 September 1997) *Henry V* (Shakespeare) with Michael Sheen; director, Ron Daniels. (25 November) *Twelfth*

Night (Shakespeare) with Scott Handy, David Calder, Clare Holman, Helen Schlesinger; director, Adrian Noble. (10 December) *The Merchant of Venice* (Shakespeare) with Phillip Voss, Julian Curry, Helen Schlesinger; director, Gregory Doran. (19 February 1998) *The Tempest* (Shakespeare) with David Calder, Scott Handy, Penny Layden; director, Adrian Noble. (30 April) *Measure for Measure* (Shakespeare) with Clare Holman, Stephen Boxer, Robert Glenister, Adrian Schiller; director, Michael Boyd

SWAN (3 September 1997) *Cyrano de Bergerac* (Rostand, trans/adapt. Anthony Burgess) with Antony Sher, Alexandra Gilbreath; director, Gregory Doran. (18 November) *Romeo and Juliet*, transferred from The Pit. (9 December) *Bartholomew Fair* (Jonson) with Stephen Boxer, Poppy Miller; director, Laurence Boswell. (18 February 1998) *The Two Gentlemen of Verona* (Shakespeare) with John Dougall, Tom Goodman-Hill, Dominic Rowan; director, Edward Hall. (29 April) *Talk of the City* (Stephen Poliakoff) with David Westhead, Angus Wright, Kelly Hunter; director, Stephen Poliakoff

THE OTHER PLACE (22 October 1997) *Beckett Shorts: Out of the Dark (Footfalls, Rockaby, Not I)* and *Over the Years (Embers, A Piece of Monologue, That Time)* (Beckett) with Juliet Stevenson, Nigel Cooke, Debra Gillett; director, Katie Mitchell. (26 November) *Roberto Zucco* (Bernard-Marie Koltès, trans. Martin Crimp) with Zubin Varla, Penny Layden, Jimmy Chisholm; director, James Macdonald. (11 December) *Goodnight Children Everywhere* (Richard Nelson) with Cathryn Bradshaw, Simon Scardifield; director, Ian Brown. (18 February 1998) *Shadows: Riders to the Sea* and *In the Shadow of the Glen* (Synge) and *Purgatory* (Yeats) with Stephen Kennedy, Stella McCusker, Mairead McKinley; director, John Crowley. (7 May) *Bad Weather* (Robert Holman) with Susan Brown, Susan Engel, Emma Handy, Ryan Pope, Paul Popplewell; director, Stephen Pimlott

Best actress – Janet McTeer, *A Doll's House* (tour)
Best director – Janet Suzman, *The Cherry Orchard* (Birmingham Repertory Theatre and Market Theatre, Johannesburg)
Best actor in a supporting role – Andrew Schofield, *Scouse: A Comedy of Terrors* (Everyman Theatre, Liverpool)
Best actress in a supporting role – Pauline Flanagan, *The Desert Lullaby* (Lyric Theatre, Belfast)
Most outstanding contribution – Peter Cheeseman, director of the rep in Stoke-on-Trent and Newcastle-under-Lyme

EVENING STANDARD AWARDS 1997

Best play – *The Invention of Love* (Sir Tom Stoppard)
Best comedy – *Closer* (Patrick Marber)
Best musical – *Lady in the Dark* (Kurt Weill, Ira Gershwin)
Best actor – Ian Holm, *King Lear*
Best actress – Eileen Atkins, *A Delicate Balance*
Best director – Sir Richard Eyre, *King Lear; The Invention of Love*
Most promising playwright – Conor McPherson, *The Weir*
Special award – Sir Richard Eyre for his directorship of the Royal National Theatre 1988–97

CRITICS' CIRCLE AWARDS (DRAMA SECTION) 1997

Best new play – *Closer* (Patrick Marber)
Best musical – *Chicago*
Best actor – Ian Holm, *King Lear*
Best actress – Judi Dench, *Amy's View*
Best director – Sir Richard Eyre, *King Lear; The Invention of Love*
Most promising playwright – Conor McPherson, *The Weir*
Jack Tinker award (most promising newcomer) – Liza Walker, *Closer*
Critics' Circle annual award (distinguished service to the arts) – Dame Judi Dench

THEATRE AWARD WINNERS

LAURENCE OLIVIER AWARDS 1998

Best new play – *Closer* (Patrick Marber)
Best new musical – *Beauty and the Beast* (Howard Ashman, Tim Rice, Alan Menken)
Best actor – Ian Holm, *King Lear*
Best actress – Zoë Wanamaker, *Electra*
Best director – Sir Richard Eyre, *King Lear*
Best performance in a supporting role – Sarah Woodward, *Tom and Clem*
Best actor in a musical – Philip Quast, *The Fix*
Best actress in a musical – Ute Lemper, *Chicago*
Best supporting performance in a musical – James Dreyfus, *Lady in the Dark*
Special award – Ed Mirvish, David Mirvish for outstanding contribution to restoring and operating the Old Vic

REGIONAL THEATRE AWARDS 1997

Best new play – *Popcorn* (Ben Elton) (Nottingham Playhouse and West Yorkshire Playhouse)
Best musical – *Divorce Me, Darling* (Sandy Wilson) (Chichester Festival Theatre)
Best touring production – *A Midsummer Night's Dream* (English Shakespeare Company International)
Best show for children/young people – *Beauty and the Beast* (Laurence Boswell) (Young Vic Theatre)
Best actor – Bill Nighy, *Skylight* (Royal National Theatre tour)

Weather

JULY 1997

Rainfall totals were generally below normal. The 1st was a very wet day in Scotland when 90.2 mm (3.62 in) of rain fell at Relugas (Highland). The 2nd was wet over England and Wales and flooding occurred in northern Scotland; hundreds of people were evacuated as Elgin was cut off. Rain fell over south-east England on the 4th and the 8th brought thunderstorms to London, Surrey, Hertfordshire and the east Midlands, with violent rainfall causing flooding in many places. At Leatherhead (Surrey) 51.8 mm (2.04 in) of rain fell, 23 mm (0.91 in) of it in just five minutes. London rail services were severely disrupted and floods 5 ft (1.6 m) deep were reported in South Norwood. The 10th brought thunderstorms to Northern Ireland when 48.4 mm (1.91 in) of rain fell at Corgary (Co. Fermanagh). Rain fell in western areas on the 12th and more generally on the 13th. Some heavy rain fell over England and Wales on the 17th. The 19th was a dry day everywhere. On the 22nd rain fell over northern areas, spreading further south on the 23rd. The 24th brought rain to most areas. Rain was confined to northern areas on the 27th and 28th, becoming more general on the 29th and 30th. Rain fell almost everywhere on the 31st.

Monthly mean temperatures were near normal everywhere. The highest temperature recorded was 28.8°C (83.84°F) at London Weather Centre on the 23rd and the lowest was −3.1°C (26.42°F) at Altnaharra (Highland) on the 9th.

Sunshine totals were generally above normal. The highest daily total was 15.8 hours at Cape Wrath (Highland) and at Wattisham (Suffolk) on the 9th and at Bastreet (Cornwall) on the 21st.

AUGUST 1997

Rainfall totals were generally well above normal, except in north-west areas of England and Wales. West Cornwall received over 259 per cent of its normal amount. Heavy rain fell over scattered areas on the 3rd, when 131.8 mm (5.19 in) fell at Stithians (Cornwall) and 124.5 mm (4.9 in) fell at Wendron (Cornwall). Thunderstorms and heavy rain occurred over southern England on the 4th and 5th; 74.0 mm (2.91 in) fell at Longburton (Dorset) on the 5th and flooding occurred in southern Wales, the West Country and the south-west Midlands. Road surfaces were swept away by floods, a landslide blocked the M25 near Reigate, and air and rail traffic was badly delayed. In Gloucester the Bristol Hotel wine cellar was flooded and the landlord had to pour £20,000-worth of wine and beer down the drain. Heavy rain fell over southern England on the 6th when 85.9 mm (3.39 in) fell at Epsom College (Surrey). On the 7th, 77 mm (3 in) of rain fell in east Devon in 45 minutes, closing the A30 and flooding many homes. The 8th brought rain to Scotland. On the 12th showers of sand fell over parts of Cambridgeshire and a mini tornado accompanied by hail the size of golf balls damaged a garden and furniture at Eastington Park (Glos). An earthquake measuring 1.8 on the Richter scale affected Oxton (Notts). Thunderstorms were widespread on the 13th and 92.0 mm (3.62 in) of rain fell at Balmain (Highland). Widespread thunderstorms occurred on the 17th when 33.0 mm (1.30 in) of rain fell in 15 minutes at Lingfield Park (Surrey). A whirlwind uprooted a tree in the grounds of Hereford Cathedral on the 20th. Rain fell generally on the 21st and mainly over western areas on the 23rd, becoming widespread again over England and Wales on the 24th and 25th. On the 25th flooding occurred in parts of East Anglia, the West Country and Wiltshire and on sections of the M25 and M40. Two people were killed on the A3 in Surrey. Heavy rain fell over Cornwall on the 26th when 34.5 mm (1.36 in) fell at Davidstow Moor. Rain and thunderstorms were widespread on the 27th and 38.9 mm (1.53 in) of rain fell over the Isle of Wight. Rain was again widespread on the 28th and heavy in southern areas on the 29th, when 38.2 mm (1.51 in) fell in Cardiff. Rain and thunderstorms were again widespread on the 31st.

Monthly mean temperatures were generally well above normal and it was the second hottest August since 1659. The heat expanded the metal of Blackpool Tower, causing it to grow one inch in height. The highest temperature recorded was 32.1°C (89.78°F) at Norwich (Norfolk) on the 12th and the lowest was 1.7°C (35.06°F) at Altnaharra (Highland) on the 24th.

Sunshine totals were around normal. The highest daily total was 15.5 hours at Fair Isle (Shetland) on the 4th.

SEPTEMBER 1997

Rainfall totals were generally below normal. It was the driest September since 1986. Rain affected all western areas on the 2nd. A tornado struck a farm at Sutton-on-Trent (Notts) and huts containing 40 pigs were swept 30.5 m (100 ft) into the air and thrown almost half a mile, killing the pigs. A girl was hurled across a room when lightning struck a computer she was using; she was not seriously hurt. At Upper Black Laggan logger station (Dumfries and Galloway) 112.0 mm (4.41 in) of rain fell. The 3rd was a wet day everywhere and the 6th brought heavy rain or showers to Scotland and Northern Ireland with thunderstorms in the Western Isles. The 11th brought rain or drizzle to most areas. Showers turned to heavy rain over Scotland on the 14th and 15th; 75 mm (2.95 in) of rain fell at

Edinbane (Isle of Skye) on the 14th and 106 mm (4.18 in) fell at Blaenau Ffestiniog (Gwynedd) on the 15th. The heavy rain continued on the 16th. At Greenock (Strathclyde) 54 mm (2.13 in) of rain fell. The 18th was foggy over England and Wales and the 24th brought fog to many places. On the 28th heavy rain fell over Scotland and northern England with gales in exposed places.

Monthly mean temperatures were generally near or above normal. The highest temperature recorded was 28.9°C (84.02°F) at Jersey (Channel Islands) on the 19th and the lowest was −3°C 26.6°F) at Altnaharra (Highland) on the 20th.

Sunshine totals were generally above normal. The highest daily total was 12.7 hours at Eastbourne (E. Sussex) on the 2nd.

OCTOBER 1997

Rainfall totals were generally below normal, although the second week of the month was very wet. The 6th brought rain to most areas with thunderstorms over East Anglia. Rain was heavy in places on the 7th with thunderstorms across England and Wales. Heavy rain fell over southern areas on the 8th when 54.3 mm (2.14 in) fell at Leverton (Lincs). The 9th was wet almost everywhere and 40.5 mm (1.59 in) of rain fell at Culzean Castle (Devon). The 11th was wet over England and Wales. The 14th was another generally wet day and 31.3 mm (1.23 in) of rain fell at Eskdalemuir (Dumfries and Galloway) on the 16th. The 18th was a foggy day in all areas except Scotland. The 19th was another foggy day. Rain or showers affected the far north of Scotland between the 24th and the 29th.

Monthly mean temperatures were generally around normal. The highest temperature recorded was 26°C (78.80°F) at Shoeburyness (Essex) on the 1st and at Nantmor (Gwynedd) on the 18th, the latest date that such a high temperature has been recorded anywhere in the UK. The lowest temperature was −8.1°C (17.42°F) at Redesdale (Northumberland) on the 29th.

Sunshine totals were generally above normal and it was the sunniest October since 1959. The highest daily total was 10.9 hours on the Isle of Wight on the 10th.

NOVEMBER 1998

Rainfall totals were above normal in most areas and it was the third wettest November since 1970. There were frequent thunderstorms. On the 1st and 2nd there was fog in the south. Rain fell over England and Wales on the 4th, and the 5th was a generally wet day with thunderstorms in central and southern England; 37.4 mm (1.49 in) of rain fell at Duncannan (Dumfries and Galloway) and 37 mm (1.46 in) fell at Boscombe Down (Wilts). Heavy rain fell over south-east England on the 6th, when 40.4 mm (1.7 in) fell at Weybourne (Norfolk). The 7th brought heavy rain to Wales and central and southern England, when 53.6 mm (2.11 in) fell at Penzance (Cornwall). The rain spread north on the 8th, and on

the 9th, 38.2 mm (1.51 in) of rain fell at Herstmonceux (E. Sussex). On the 12th freezing fog formed in southern areas. Fog was also a feature of the 13th. Rain or drizzle fell almost everywhere on the 14th and 15th and rain was widespread on the 16th, with fog on eastern coastal areas of England. Heavy rain fell in the west on the 17th, when 101.9 mm (4.0 in) fell at Lochearnhead (Central) and at Davidstow Moor (Cornwall). Rain was again widespread on the 18th and 19th with thunderstorms across southern England on the 19th, which was a windy day with gales around coastal areas of Scotland. The 20th was another generally wet day and on the 22nd fog was persistent in many areas. After morning fog on the 23rd it became a fairly wet day except in Scotland. Rain became heavy in places on the 26th, when 53.3 mm (1.39 in) fell at Dyce (Grampian). The 27th was another generally wet day, as was the 28th when 57.5 mm (2.26 in) of rain fell at Amlwch (Anglesey).

Monthly mean temperatures were 1.9°C (3.4°F) above normal over central England and it was the second warmest November since 1978 and the seventh warmest this century. The highest temperature recorded was 17.7°C (63.9°F) at Kinloss (Grampian) and at Altnaharra (Highland) on the 16th. The lowest temperature was −5.3°C (22.5°F) at Benson (Oxon) on the 1st.

Sunshine totals were near or below normal. The highest daily total was 9.2 hours at Bognor Regis (W. Sussex) on the 1st.

DECEMBER 1997

Rainfall totals were around normal in spite of some very heavy falls of rain. The 1st was wet over southern England, with wintry showers in the north and East Anglia. On the 2nd early rain turned to snow over London, Kent, Essex, Surrey and Sussex with 6–10 cm (2–4 in) lying in places. Patchy rain, sleet or snow fell over central areas on the 3rd. There was heavy rain in the north on the 5th, when 102.5 mm (4.04 in) fell at Glen Etive (Highland). The 6th was windy in the north. Rain fell mainly in the west on the 7th and 8th. The 9th was wet over south-west England; 34.4 mm (1.36 in) of rain fell at Davidstow Moor (Cornwall). Rain fell in all areas on the 10th and 11th. The 17th brought snow to northern, central and southern England; 15 cm (6 in) fell over the Mendips, Dartmoor and Plymouth. The 18th was a generally wet day everywhere followed by fog in the south overnight; 35.3 mm (1.39 in) of rain fell at Folkestone (Kent). The 19th was wet in the north and east with fog elsewhere; 31.2 mm (1.23 in) of rain fell at Dyce (Grampian). Fog persisted all day in some places on the 20th and 21st but rain became widespread again on the 22nd and 23rd. Heavy rain fell over all areas on the 24th when 33.5 mm (1.32 in) fell at Knockareven (Co. Fermanagh). A gust of 97 knots (111.7 mph) was recorded on the Lleyn Peninsula (Gwynedd). Rain and thundery showers driven by gales fell almost everywhere on the 25th and five fishermen were drowned in the Irish Sea. Winds gusted over 61

knots (70 mph) over London and southern England.
Gusts of 96 knots (111 mph) were recorded at
Aberdaron (N. Wales) and a gust of 78 knots (90
mph) blew away a section of Blackpool's north pier
and jetty. A woman was killed by a falling tree in
Bromborough (Merseyside) and two people were
killed in car accidents in Liverpool and Caernafon.
Parts of the coast road in Co. Down were flooded by
high tides and a stable block in Scarborough was
blown down; the very frightened horses had to be
rescued at the height of the storm. This was the
worst storm since that of December 1993. Strong
winds swept the country again on the 26th and three
people were killed when a falling tree crushed their
car at Pengam (Gwent). Rain fell across central and
northern areas of England, Wales and Northern
Ireland on the 28th. The 29th had rain or drizzle
mainly in the south and west but rain spread across
the whole of the UK on the 30th.

Monthly mean temperatures were 1°C (1.8°F)
above normal. The highest temperature recorded
was 15.2°C (59.36°F) at London, Southampton and
Gatwick on the 10th and the lowest was −8.3°C
(17.06°F) at Shap (Cumbria) on the 2nd and at
Trawscoed (Dyfed) on the 3rd.

Sunshine totals were around normal and the
highest daily total was 8.3 hours at Swanage (Dorset)
on the 13th.

THE YEAR 1997

Rainfall totals were near normal for most areas. The
year 1997 was the third warmest since 1659, only
1949 and 1990 being slightly warmer. The last 100
years have been the warmest century of this
millennium. The year was also sunnier than
normal. January was the driest since 1779, with
below normal temperatures and above normal
sunshine. Gusts of 110 knots (126.7 mph) were
recorded at Cairngorm (Highland) on the 13th.
February was a wet and windy month. On the 17th
116.1 mm (4.6 in) of rain fell at Burn Banks
(Cumbria), and Cairngorm recorded gusts of 133
knots (153.2 mph) on the 22nd. Temperatures were
mainly above normal and sunshine totals near
normal. March was the seventh driest this century,
but was another windy month; Cairngorm recorded
a gust of 135 knots (155 mph) on the 6th. Temperatures and sunshine totals were above normal. April
was a very dry month. Temperature and sunshine
were both generally above normal. In May rainfall
was near or slightly above normal but there were
some heavy falls and widespread thunderstorms;
166 mm (6.5 in) of rain fell at Avon (Hants) on the
31st and gusts of 102 knots (117 mph) were recorded
at Rhyl (Clwyd) on the 29th. Temperature and
sunshine were both above normal. June was the
wettest since 1860 with widespread thunderstorms
and a gust of 97 knots (112 mph) was recorded at
Cairngorm on the 7th. Temperatures were mostly
around normal but sunshine totals were below
normal. July was the fourth successive July to be
drier than normal though flooding occurred in

Scotland on the 8th. Temperature and sunshine
were both mostly above normal. August was a very
wet month with frequent thunderstorms. It was the
second hottest August since 1659. Sunshine totals
were around normal. The summer (June to August)
as a whole was the warmest since 1958, with
temperatures 1°C (1.8°F) above normal. September
was a generally dry month but some very heavy falls
of rain did occur. October was another generally dry
month with near normal temperatures. It was the
sunniest October since 1959. November was the
third wettest since 1970 with frequent thunderstorms and it was the second warmest since 1978 and
the seventh warmest this century. December was a
windy month and a storm on the 25th was the worst
since the storm of December 1993. It was the second
warmest December since 1988.

JANUARY 1998

Rainfall totals were generally above average. Heavy
rain fell over most areas on the 1st when 114.2 mm
(4.49 in) fell at Drumnatarran (Highland). Winds
reached gale force in western areas and a gust of 83
knots (95.6 mph) was recorded. A tanker went
aground near Torquay (Devon) and a man was
killed at Nettlebed (Oxon) in a car crash caused by
the bad weather. The 2nd was another stormy day
with heavy rain in the south and west; 34.8 mm (1.37
in) of rain fell at Davidstow Moor (Cornwall).
Heavy rain and gales with sleet, hail and thunder
affected most areas on the 3rd when 47.6 mm (1.87
in) of rain fell at Tulloch Bridge (Highland). Traffic
was disrupted in many areas as gusts reached 90
mph over Wales, south-west England, Scotland and
Northern Ireland. A motorcyclist was killed when
blown into another vehicle near Aberdeen. The old
Severn Bridge was closed and flood alerts were
issued on 32 rivers in Devon and Cornwall. On the
4th gales affected southern Britain with a gust of 91
knots (102 mph) recorded at Portland Bill (Dorset)
and a gust of 100 knots (115 mph) recorded at
Mumbles (W. Glam). Many thousands of homes
were without power and all forms of transport were
severely disrupted. A trawler sank off Lands End
and 50 cars were damaged when a ferry was hit by a
freak wave ripping off the bow panels in the English
Channel. A man was killed when a tree hit his car at
Wombourne (Staffs). This was the worst weather
since the gale of 1987 and the structural repair bill is
estimated at £500 million. The 5th brought snow to
East Anglia and thunderstorms to southern England; 105.5 mm (4.16 in) of rain fell at Nant-y-Maen
(Dyfed). Rain fell mainly in the west and south on
the 6th, over most of England, Wales and Northern
Ireland on the 8th and Scotland on the 9th, when
49.1 mm (1.93 in) fell at Tiree (Hebrides). A tornado
left a £2 million trail of damage in Selsey (W.
Sussex). Heavy rain fell almost everywhere on the
13th when 32.8 mm (1.29 in) fell at Point of Ayre
(Isle of Man). The 14th and 15th brought rain or
drizzle to many areas. Snow fell over Scotland on
the 18th, with 19 cm (7.48 in) lying at Aviemore.

Rain affected all other areas. The 19th saw snow showers in the north and east with rain in the south. Rain fell over western Scotland on the 20th Rain fell mainly over the western half of the UK on the 21st and mostly over the northern half on the 22nd and 23rd. Rain fell in the far north of Scotland on the 27th.

Monthly mean temperatures were generally above normal. The highest temperature recorded was 17.3°C (63.14°F) at Prestatyn (Clwyd) on the 10th and the lowest was −11.5°C (11.3°F) at Altnaharra (Highland) on the 20th.

Sunshine totals were generally above normal. The highest daily total was 8.6 hours at Saunton Sands (Devon) on the 27th.

FEBRUARY 1998

Rainfall totals were generally well below normal. It was the seventh driest February this century. Snow fell over Scotland on the 2nd. Rain was widespread on the 6th except in East Anglia and south-east England. The 7th brought rain to south-east England and rain fell from northern Wales to northern Scotland on the 8th. Most rain fell over Northern Ireland and southern Scotland on the 9th, spreading to Wales on the 10th; 54.3 mm (2.14 in) of rain fell at Greenock (Strathclyde) on the 10th. On the 11th 178.8 mm (7.04 in) of rain fell at Keil (Tayside). Heavy rain fell in the far north of Scotland on the 12th when 131.7 mm (5.19 in) fell at Broadford (Isle of Skye). Rain fell from northern Wales to northern Scotland on the 14th, with fog over southern areas. Rain or drizzle fell mainly in the west on the 15th. The 17th was foggy in many southern areas. Fog was slow to clear in many parts of England on the 18th and rain returned to Scotland on the 19th and to western areas on the 20th. Rain or showers were widespread on the 21st with thunder over Lincolnshire and Oxfordshire. Rain fell mainly in western areas on the 26th and more generally on the 27th. Gales across western and northern Scotland on the 26th extended to northern Wales on the 27th. Snow fell over Scotland, Northern Ireland and northern England on the 28th, with some isolated snow showers further south.

Monthly mean temperatures were well above normal generally and it was the second mildest February since 1869. A temperature of 19.6°C (67.28°F) at Barbourne (Worcs) on the 13th set a new UK record for February. The lowest temperature during the month was −7.3°C (18.86°F) at Hurn Airport (Dorset) on the 4th.

Sunshine totals were generally above normal. The highest daily total was 9.7 hours at Guernsey (Channel Islands) on the 17th, Swanage (Dorset) on the 23rd and Cleethorpes (Lincs) on the 28th. The winter months (December to February) was the fifth mildest this century. Rainfall was slightly below normal.

MARCH 1998

Rainfall totals were mostly near or above normal, with most of the rain falling early in the month. On the 1st there was snow in the north, when 12 cm (4.7 in) lay at Lybster (Highland). There were gales over the Hebrides in the evening. The 2nd was a generally wet day when 81.5 mm (3.21 in) of rain fell at Nant-y-Maen (Dyfed). The 3rd was another wet day and 44.4 mm (1.75 in) of rain fell at Capel Curig (Gwynedd). It was windy, especially in the south. The 4th was another windy day with gales along the English Channel. Snow showers fell over Scotland with rain further south. Heavy rain fell over England and Wales on the 5th and 39.4 mm (1.56 in) fell at Nantmor (Gwynedd). The 6th was another very wet day generally and 60.7 mm (2.39 in) of rain fell at Aberhosan (Powys). On the 7th 122 mm (4.37 in) of rain fell at Strachan (Grampian). The 10th was another generally wet day with gales over the Hebrides and the Isle of Man. Rain or drizzle fell over Scotland on the 15th and 16th and in the evening of the 19th. The 23rd saw rain return to Scotland. Heavy rain fell over many areas on the 24th, when 61.6 mm (2.24 in) fell at Nantmor (Gwynedd). Heavy rain was widespread on the 25th, when 57.6 mm (2.26 in) fell at Nantmor. Some rain fell over southern counties on the 28th and more generally on the 29th. On the 31st there was morning fog over England and Wales.

Monthly mean temperatures were generally above normal and it was the seventh warmest March this century. The highest temperature recorded was 20°C (68°F) at Warcop (Cumbria) on the 28th and the lowest was −17°C (1.4°F) at Altnaharra (Highland) on the 1st.

Sunshine totals were near or below normal. The highest daily total was 11.0 hours at Camborne and St. Mawgan (Cornwall) on the 20th.

APRIL 1998

Rainfall totals were well above normal everywhere and it was the wettest April since 1818 and the third wettest since 1766. Rain or drizzle affected most areas on the 1st, with fog over southern England; 101.2 mm (3.99 in) of rain fell at Great Dun Fell (Cumbria). The 2nd was a similar day but rain fell over the Midlands and northern England; 40.6 mm (1.59 in) fell at Long Framlington (Northumberland). The heavy rain moved into Scotland on the 3rd, when 69.7 mm (2.75 in) of rain fell at Strachan (Grampian). Rain or showers fell almost everywhere on the 4th, when 62 mm (2.44 in) fell at Glen Tanner House (Highland). On the 5th the 76.9 mm (3.03 in) of rain fell at Blairgowrie (Tayside). On the 6th there were thunderstorms over south-east England and East Anglia. The 7th brought numerous thunderstorms with hail to central and southern England and tornadoes were reported from Wincanton (Somerset) and Taunton (Somerset). Heavy rain fell in many areas on the 8th and thunderstorms with hail affected southern England. A tornado caused damage in Milton Keynes (Bucks) and 91.5

mm (3.60 in) of rain fell at Staplow (Herefordshire). On the 9th thunderstorms in the south formed a band from East Anglia across the Midlands to Wales. Rainfall was very heavy at times and caused local flooding; 63.7 mm (2.51 in) of rain fell at Marholm (Cambs) and 75.5 mm (2.97 in) fell at Lutton (Northants). The 10th brought rain, sleet, snow and thunder to England and Wales, with the snow in the west and the thunder in the east; 67.1 mm (2.64 in) of rain fell at Sylnflect Reservoir (Norfolk). A tornado was reported on the Isle of Sheppey. The 11th brought snow and sleet north of a line from Cardigan to the Humber, with rain further south; 30 cm (11.81 in) of snow accumulated at Cynwyd (Gwynedd). On the 12th 74.7 mm (2.94 in) of rain fell at Gosmore (Cambs) Rain and snow fell almost everywhere on the 14th, with thunder over Kent and east London; 49 mm (1.93 in) of rain fell at Moel-y-Crio (Clwyd). Rain and snow affected northern Wales, the Midlands and southern England on the 15th, and northern and southern England on the 16th when 38 mm (1.5 in) fell at Long Framlington (Northumberland). Rain spread to most of England, Wales and Northern Ireland on the 19th. Persistent heavy rain fell generally on the 21st and 22nd. Rain fell over many areas on the 23rd, with thunderstorms again in the east. Thunderstorms were widespread on the 27th and 28th, with hail in many places. Rain was mostly confined to the south-west on the 29th and 30th; 92.5 mm (3.75 in) of rain fell at Venford Reservoir (Devon) on the 29th.

Monthly mean temperatures were around normal. The highest temperature recorded was 22.4°C (72.32°F) at Northolt and London Weather Centre (Gtr London) on the 22nd and the lowest was −9°C (15.8°F) at Altnaharra (Highland) on the 10th.

Sunshine totals were around normal and the highest daily total was 13.7 hours at Kirkwall (Orkney) on the 18th.

MAY 1998

Rainfall totals were below normal everywhere. Heavy rain fell over northern Wales and northern England on the 5th. Rain or drizzle fell over most areas on the 6th, becoming confined to Scotland on the 7th. Thunderstorms were frequent and widespread over south-west England, northern Wales and the Midlands. The 12th became foggy over much of England and Wales. The 13th was a generally foggy day. Thunderstorms were widespread throughout the UK on the 14th, with fog mainly in the west. The 16th to 18th were foggy in coastal areas. The 19th and 20th brought rain to Scotland. Rain or showers became widespread on the 26th, with thunderstorms in south-east England; 53.4 mm (2.11 in) of rain fell at Lasham (Hants) and 50.5 mm (1.99 in) fell at Swindon (Wilts). On the 27th 49.3 mm (1.94 in) of rain fell at Margate (Kent). Some heavy rain fell in northern England on the 28th, when 56.9 mm (2.23 in) of rain fell at High Westwood, Ebchester (Durham). Heavy rain fell over northern England, southern Scotland and Northern Ireland on the 29th, when 37 mm (1.46 in) fell at Lochranza (Isle of Arran). Some heavy rain fell in south and south-west England on the 30th and over northern England and southern Scotland on the 31st.

Monthly mean temperatures were generally near or above normal. The highest temperature recorded was 28.6°C (83.48°F) at Southampton (Hants) on the 13th and the lowest was −2.7°C (27.14°F) at Altnaharra (Highland) on the 1st.

Sunshine totals were near or above normal. The highest daily total was 15.4 hours at Stornoway (Outer Hebrides) on the 29th.

JUNE 1998

Rainfall totals were well above normal everywhere and it was the fourth wettest June this century. The 1st produced heavy rain from East Anglia to south-west England, with thundery showers further north and rain over Scotland; 35.9 mm (1.41 in) of rain fell at Elmdon (W. Midlands). Heavy rain fell over England and Wales on the 2nd, when 52.0 mm (2.05 in) fell at Emley Moor (W. Yorks). Heavy rain fell over northern areas on the 6th, when 39.9 mm (1.57 in) fell at Kirkwall (Orkney). There were thunderstorms over Scotland and northern England on the 7th, when 38.6 mm (1.52 in) of rain fell at Aviemore (Highland). The 8th was a very wet day everywhere and 75.3 mm (2.96 in) of rain fell at Nantmor (Gwynedd). On the 9th 37.6 mm (1.48 in) of rain fell at Rackwick (Orkney). Rain or showers fell everywhere on the 10th, when 31.5 mm (1.24 in) fell at Moel-y-Crio (Clwyd). The 11th was wet over England and Wales and snow was reported in the Highlands of Scotland. Rain fell over most of England and Wales on the 13th and 14th and everywhere on the 15th. On the 17th heavy rain fell over England and Wales, when 44.7 mm (1.76 in) fell at Nantmor (Gwynedd). The 18th was another wet day over England, Wales and Northern Ireland. The 19th was mainly dry except in Scotland. There was more rain over England, Wales and Northern Ireland on the 20th, and heavy rain in northern areas on the 22nd. Rain was more widespread on the 23rd, when 48.1 mm (1.89 in) fell at Nantmor (Gwynedd). Rain fell almost everywhere on the 24th. The 26th and 27th were mostly wet with widespread thunderstorms. The 29th brought heavy rain to southern England and on the 30th 186.9 mm (7.36 in) of rain fell at Parracombe (Devon).

Monthly mean temperatures were around normal. The highest temperature recorded was 31.6°C (88.88°F) at Jersey (Channel Islands) on the 20th and the lowest was −4.6°C (23.72°F) at Altnaharra (Highland) on the 4th.

Sunshine totals were mostly below normal. The highest daily total was 17.3 hours at Lerwick (Shetland) on the 15th.

AVERAGE AND GENERAL VALUES 1996–8 (June)

	Rainfall (mm)				Temperature (°C)				Bright Sunshine (hrs per day)			
	Average 1961–90	1996	1997	1998	Average 1961–90	1996	1997	1998	Average 1961–90	1996	1997	1998
England and Wales												
January	77	63	14	117*	3.8	4.4	2.4	5.3*	1.6	0.8	1.7	1.7*
February	55	83	120	23*	3.8	2.7	6.5	7.4*	2.4	3.1	2.5	3.3*
March	63	43	32	97*	5.6	4.4	8.3	8.1*	3.5	2.1	4.2	2.5*
April	53	51	25	125*	7.7	8.3	8.8	7.9*	4.9	4.6	5.6	4.3*
May	56	57	75	33*	10.9	9.1	11.5	12.9*	6.2	6.0	7.8	6.8*
June	58	30	128	124*	13.9	14.1	14.0	14.2*	6.4	8.1	4.7	5.0*
July	56	41	48	–	15.7	16.2	16.4	–	6.0	7.2	7.4	–
August	68	80	95	–	15.6	16.4	18.7	–	6.0	6.7	6.5	–
September	70	34	35	–	13.6	13.6	14.3	–	4.5	4.8	5.4	–
October	77	91	68	–	10.7	11.7	10.4	–	3.2	3.6	4.3	–
November	81	128*	117	–	6.6	6.0	8.6	–	2.2	2.8*	1.5	–
December	82	54*	108	–	4.7	3.1	6.0	–	1.5	1.7*	1.3	–
Year	796	755*	865	–	9.4	9.2	10.5	–	4.0	4.3*	4.4	–
Scotland												
January	117	89	56	166*	3.1	4.7	3.1	4.3*	1.3	0.9	1.3	1.2*
February	78	141	268	199*	3.1	2.5	4.8	7.4*	2.4	2.7	2.3	1.3*
March	94	60	138	123*	3.9	3.9	6.8	5.9*	3.2	2.2	3.2	2.3*
April	60	108	76	123*	6.5	7.4	7.8	6.1*	4.8	3.5	3.6	4.9*
May	67	78	113	57*	9.3	7.7	9.3	10.5*	5.6	6.1	5.8	5.4*
June	67	65	104	113*	12.1	12.3	12.0	11.3*	5.6	6.3	4.9	5.7*
July	74	78	90	–	13.6	13.6	14.9	–	4.9	5.0	5.3	–
August	92	68	65	–	13.5	14.7	16.1	–	4.9	4.6	6.3	–
September	111	64	114	–	11.5	12.5	11.9	–	3.5	5.1	4.7	–
October	120	227	80	–	9.1	10.1	8.9	–	2.6	2.4	3.1	–
November	118	193	139	–	5.3	4.1	7.7	–	1.7	2.3	1.3	–
December	116	98	182	–	3.9	2.8	5.3	–	1.0	1.3	0.9	–
Year	1114	1269	1425	–	7.9	8.0	9.1	–	3.5	3.5	3.6	–

* Provisional figures, subject to alteration by the Met Office
Source: Data provided by the Met Office

WEATHER RECORDS

World Records

Maximum air temperature	57.8°C/136°F
San Louis, Mexico, 11 August 1933	
Minimum air temperature	−89.2°C/−128.56°F
Vostok, Antarctica, 21 July 1983	
Greatest rainfall in one day	1870 mm/73.62 in
Cilaos, Isle de Réunion, 16 March 1952	
Greatest rainfall in one calendar month	9300 mm/366.14 in
Cherrapunji, Assam, July 1861	
Greatest annual rainfall total	22,990 mm/905.12 in
Cherrapunji, Assam, 1861	
Fastest gust of wind	201 knots/231 mph
Mt Washington Observatory, USA, 12 April 1934	

United Kingdom Records

Maximum air temperature	37.1°C/98.8°F
Cheltenham, Glos, 3 August 1990	
Minimum air temperature	−27.2°C/−17°F
Braemar, Grampian, 11 February 1895 and 10 January 1982	
Greatest rainfall in one day	280 mm/11 in
Martinstown, Dorset, 18 July 1955	
Greatest annual rainfall total	6528 mm/257 in
Sprinkling Tarn, Cumbria, 1954	
Fastest gust of wind	150 knots/173 mph
Cairngorm, Highland, 20 March 1986	
Fastest low-level gust*	123 knots/141.7 mph
Fraserburgh, Grampian, 13 February 1989	
Highest mean hourly speed	92 knots/106 mph
Great Dun Fell, Cumbria, December 1974	
Highest low-level mean hourly speed*	72 knots/83 mph
Shoreham-by-Sea, Sussex, 16 October 1987	

* below 200 m/656 ft

WIND FORCE MEASURES

The *Beaufort Scale* of wind force has been accepted internationally and is used in communicating weather conditions. Devised originally by Admiral Sir Francis Beaufort in 1805, it now consists of the numbers 0–17, each representing a certain strength or velocity of wind at 10 m (33 ft) above ground in the open.

Scale no.	Wind Force	mph	knots
0	Calm	1	1
1	Light air	1–3	1–3
2	Slight breeze	4–7	4–6
3	Gentle breeze	8–12	7–10
4	Moderate breeze	13–18	11–16
5	Fresh breeze	19–24	17–21
6	Strong breeze	25–31	22–27
7	High wind	32–38	28–33
8	Gale	39–46	34–40
9	Strong gale	47–54	41–47
10	Whole gale	55–63	48–55
11	Storm	64–72	56–63
12	Hurricane	73–82	64–71
13	–	83–92	72–80
14	–	93–103	81–89
15	–	104–114	90–99
16	–	115–125	100–108
17	–	126–136	109–118

TEMPERATURE, RAINFALL AND SUNSHINE
At selected climatological reporting stations, July 1997–June 1998 and calendar year 1997

Ht	height (in metres) of station above mean sea level
°C	mean air temperature
Rain	total monthly rainfall
Sun	mean daily bright sunshine (hours)

Source: data provided by the Met Office

	Ht m	*July 1997* °C	Rain mm	Sun hrs	*August 1997* °C	Rain mm	Sun hrs	*September 1997* °C	Rain mm	Sun hrs	*October 1997* °C	Rain mm	Sun hrs
Lerwick	82	12.9	32.3	4.3	14.2	75.9	6.5	10.8	86.8	3.6	7.8	101.0	2.3
Stornoway	15	14.2	51.5	5.4	15.5	38.6	6.8	11.7	105.2	3.8	9.4	55.5	2.7
Dyce	65	15.0	63.7	5.5	16.3	52.7	5.9	12.4	25.6	5.7	9.3	32.9	3.6
Eskdalemuir	242	14.2	113.8	5.8	15.6	75.9	4.9	11.1	142.9	4.7	7.6	89.8	3.3
Aldergrove	68	15.7	71.4	7.0	16.9	53.3	6.5	13.0	37.4	4.6	10.2	77.8	2.5
Leeds	64	15.7	101.1	4.9	19.1	51.9	6.3	14.1	13.6	4.7	10.0	39.5	3.4
Valley	10	15.7	71.5	6.9	17.5	54.6	7.0	14.4	36.4	5.0	11.3	40.7	4.1
Elmdon	98	16.8	35.2	7.6	19.2	73.5	5.9	13.9	21.9	5.4	9.6	54.0	4.9
Skegness	6	16.3	43.5	6.9	18.8	75.6	6.9	14.2	11.5	5.2	10.5	59.5	4.3
Bristol	42	18.1	50.5	8.3	20.2	147.1	5.3	15.8	29.6	5.4	12.0	63.4	4.9
St. Mawgan	103	16.0	30.8	7.8	17.9	122.6	5.1	15.2	49.4	6.7	12.7	83.2	3.4
Hastings	45	17.0	19.5	9.1	19.7	100.4	7.1	15.8	3.1	7.6	12.1	107.9	6.0

	November 1997 °C	Rain mm	Sun hrs	*December 1997* °C	Rain mm	Sun hrs	*The Year 1997* °C	Rain mm	Sun hrs	*January 1998* °C	Rain mm	Sun hrs	*February 1998* °C	Rain mm	Sun hrs
Lerwick	7.2	108.4	0.4	5.7	112.9	0.9	7.8	1123.4	2.9	4.5	105.3	0.7	5.4	214.9	1.2
Stornoway	8.6	103.9	1.6	6.4	153.5	1.0	9.4	1199.5	3.6	5.5	181.5	1.1	7.2	216.4	1.0
Dyce	7.3	251.7	1.1	5.3	100.9	0.9	9.2	948.0	3.9	4.3	80.5	1.4	8.1	9.8	2.3
Eskdalemuir	6.5	139.8	1.0	3.8	229.7	0.7	8.0	1703.0	2.9	2.8	158.0	1.1	5.8	132.9	1.0
Aldergrove	8.3	113.5	1.3	6.2	96.6	1.4	80.0	818.3	3.6	5.1	76.1	1.7	7.9	22.3	2.0
Leeds	8.4	71.5	0.8	6.5	74.0	1.2	10.9	622.4	4.1	5.6	83.6	1.6	8.6	8.7	3.1
Valley	9.7	109.7	1.6	7.4	102.2	1.6	10.9	681.2	4.5	6.5	95.0	2.2	8.0	29.6	2.3
Elmdon	8.0	46.6	–	5.1	42.8	–	10.3	562.8	–	3.3	–	–	7.1	–	–
Skegness	8.8	53.7	1.6	6.0	82.0	1.1	10.4	567.7	4.4	5.3	83.3	1.9	7.4	9.7	4.3
Bristol	10.0	93.0	2.1	7.3	102.0	1.8	12.0	863.6	4.6	6.6	116.8	2.2	8.6	20.0	3.6
St. Mawgan	10.4	189.8	2.3	7.7	99.7	3.1	11.4	925.2	5.0	6.8	125.6	3.0	8.3	21.2	3.7
Hastings	10.3	148.1	2.3	7.1	98.0	1.7	11.2	789.0	5.5	6.3	99.4	2.5	7.0	7.2	3.8

	March 1998 °C	Rain mm	Sun hrs	*April 1998* °C	Rain mm	Sun hrs	*May 1998* °C	Rain mm	Sun hrs	*June 1998* °C	Rain mm	Sun hrs
Lerwick	4.2	144.8	2.4	5.3	50.8	5.7	8.5	31.4	6.4	9.3	105.0	6.7
Stornoway	6.0	143.5	2.0	6.1	62.7	6.7	9.8	30.6	5.4	10.5	72.7	6.9
Dyce	6.2	72.3	3.0	6.0	116.4	4.5	10.5	21.2	5.7	11.9	59.0	5.3
Eskdalemuir	5.4	153.3	1.9	5.5	132.1	3.9	10.6	75.2	5.4	11.0	185.3	3.6
Aldergrove	7.8	67.6	1.8	7.3	84.4	5.1	11.6	25.6	5.2	13.1	93.6	5.1
Leeds	8.5	81.7	3.1	8.0	120.4	3.9	13.2	39.0	5.9	14.5	109.2	4.7
Valley	8.6	96.1	2.5	8.0	91.8	6.4	12.3	16.0	7.3	13.4	120.9	5.7
Elmdon	7.6	–	–	7.9	–	–	12.2	13.0	–	13.8	103.0	–
Skegness	7.8	50.7	2.2	8.3	62.6	3.9	11.7	18.0	6.1	14.8	45.7	5.4
Bristol	9.3	113.4	2.7	8.9	104.7	4.4	15.0	25.8	7.9	15.3	107.6	5.1
St. Mawgan	8.9	86.0	2.7	8.2	142.4	5.6	13.4	43.8	7.5	14.1	108.8	6.3
Hastings	8.7	60.9	2.7	9.2	82.6	5.2	14.5	8.2	8.6	15.1	90.5	6.0

METEOROLOGICAL OBSERVATIONS London (Heathrow)

Temperature maxima and minima cover the 24-hour period 9–9 h; mean wind speed is 10 m above the ground; rainfall is for the 24 hours starting at 9 h on the day of entry; sunshine is for the 24 hours 0–24 h; averages are for the period 1961–90. *Source:* Data provided by the Met Office

JULY 1997

		Temperature Max. °C	Min. °C	Wind knots	Rain mm	Sun hrs
Day	1	18.5	11.8	5.3	Trace	3.9
	2	18.6	10.4	6.0	0.4	5.5
	3	17.4	10.3	7.4	8.0	1.6
	4	18.3	11.7	2.3	2.2	1.7
	5	22.4	10.8	2.9	0.0	12.2
	6	24.8	12.4	3.2	0.0	8.2
	7	26.7	14.6	2.3	0.0	9.8
	8	27.6	15.4	3.0	0.8	7.4
	9	26.3	15.7	6.0	0.0	14.7
	10	22.8	14.2	6.7	0.0	9.0
	11	23.8	13.1	2.5	0.0	6.8
	12	25.0	13.2	4.6	Trace	8.8
	13	24.2	15.9	6.8	1.8	7.6
	14	24.1	14.8	4.0	0.2	5.6
	15	25.1	15.0	6.3	0.0	5.5
	16	22.2	15.1	0.4	1.9	4.9
	17	20.4	15.0	4.8	0.4	1.1
	18	20.8	11.9	6.3	1.6	5.8
	19	24.8	14.2	4.6	0.0	11.7
	20	24.9	12.7	4.7	Trace	15.2
	21	25.4	14.3	3.7	0.0	14.3
	22	26.7	14.4	2.6	0.0	12.3
	23	27.7	15.6	3.0	Trace	8.1
	24	24.4	17.5	5.8	3.8	1.5
	25	24.0	13.7	5.3	Trace	12.1
	26	21.4	13.1	6.3	7.6	1.8
	27	25.1	16.0	5.3	0.0	10.9
	28	25.8	13.0	2.8	0.0	12.7
	29	27.3	14.8	6.2	1.2	14.1
	30	24.4	15.5	7.0	0.2	9.3
	31	18.2	15.0	5.5	6.0	0.0
Total		–	–	–	34.6	241.1
Mean		23.5	13.1	4.8	–	–
Temp °F		74.3	55.6	–	–	–
Average		22.5	13.1	7.4	46.0	194.5

AUGUST 1997

		Temperature Max. °C	Min. °C	Wind knots	Rain mm	Sun hrs
Day	1	24.2	14.3	5.5	Trace	2.2
	2	23.2	15.2	3.2	Trace	9.6
	3	21.5	14.9	5.5	2.1	0.9
	4	21.8	15.1	10.0	9.5	2.5
	5	22.8	15.7	8.5	0.0	3.2
	6	26.7	16.1	4.7	31.6	3.4
	7	26.8	17.9	5.5	0.0	6.5
	8	30.9	17.4	2.5	0.0	12.1
	9	28.5	18.5	2.5	0.0	13.4
	10	31.5	18.2	6.9	Trace	11.7
	11	29.6	21.1	3.6	Trace	3.7
	12	29.5	18.0	2.4	5.2	2.4
	13	27.0	19.7	4.6	0.0	9.1
	14	26.3	14.7	3.6	0.0	12.9
	15	28.4	15.1	3.1	0.0	12.8
	16	29.4	16.9	3.4	0.2	11.3
	17	24.8	18.8	2.3	Trace	1.6
	18	39.7	17.8	3.4	0.0	10.2
	19	31.1	18.4	5.0	0.0	10.9
	20	29.5	18.0	4.1	0.0	3.9
	21	26.9	17.7	4.5	Trace	3.2
	22	25.1	19.9	3.8	Trace	0.6
	23	27.1	19.9	6.5	Trace	4.0
	24	24.8	19.3	5.8	7.3	3.7
	25	22.3	17.6	3.1	1.6	1.7
	26	23.3	11.8	4.8	0.2	9.6
	27	19.7	13.3	6.8	9.4	2.5
	28	20.3	11.6	7.3	0.4	6.1
	29	20.9	14.2	9.6	5.4	7.2
	30	21.8	14.4	5.3	0.4	3.5
	31	24.8	13.5	9.3	Trace	5.0
Total		–	–	–	70.5	194.2
Mean		25.8	16.6	5.1	–	–
Temp °F		78.4	61.9	–	–	–
Average		22.1	12.8	7.2	51.0	186.7

SEPTEMBER 1997

		Temperature Max. °C	Min. °C	Wind knots	Rain mm	Sun hrs
Day	1	21.7	15.1	6.3	0.0	7.2
	2	21.9	11.6	5.3	Trace	11.8
	3	19.5	14.4	7.1	1.8	0.0
	4	21.8	15.3	4.2	0.0	10.3
	5	19.7	12.6	3.2	0.4	1.0
	6	20.9	9.8	5.2	Trace	10.3
	7	22.6	14.0	4.3	0.0	5.0
	8	22.5	9.1	4.3	0.0	11.8
	9	22.0	12.5	4.4	0.0	11.7
	10	21.2	9.8	2.6	0.0	11.1
	11	20.6	11.7	5.6	0.4	2.1
	12	20.1	13.0	8.1	4.0	7.6
	13	17.7	6.9	6.7	0.0	11.2
	14	19.0	6.9	3.9	0.0	7.7
	15	20.3	9.0	6.9	0.0	4.0
	16	22.0	12.0	6.7	0.0	9.7
	17	21.9	10.7	2.1	0.0	5.9
	18	25.1	10.9	2.8	0.2	8.5
	19	17.8	15.8	7.9	Trace	0.0
	20	18.8	14.7	10.2	0.0	3.6
	21	19.1	9.3	5.6	0.0	10.4
	22	21.4	8.6	5.3	0.0	10.5
	23	21.2	9.9	6.7	0.0	10.4
	24	20.4	10.0	5.6	0.0	3.0
	25	19.8	15.4	5.5	0.0	2.1
	26	22.1	13.2	6.1	0.0	6.6
	27	19.4	13.6	5.1	0.0	0.1
	28	19.9	10.1	2.8	Trace	2.8
	29	23.5	12.1	2.2	Trace	3.7
	30	21.6	15.2	2.9	0.0	0.2
	31					
Total		–	–	–	6.8	190.3
Mean		20.8	11.8	5.2	–	–
Temp °F		69.4	53.2	–	–	–
Average		19.3	10.8	7.1	51.0	144.7

OCTOBER 1997

		Temperature Max. °C	Min. °C	Wind knots	Rain mm	Sun hrs
Day	1	25.5	16.0	4.9	0.0	7.5
	2	19.7	12.5	2.5	0.0	10.2
	3	18.8	11.4	1.8	0.0	4.0
	4	20.4	10.4	3.8	0.0	6.6
	5	17.8	9.8	3.3	0.0	0.5
	6	21.6	10.5	4.0	7.8	5.0
	7	17.3	11.5	7.2	4.0	5.0
	8	18.5	12.1	6.0	4.4	0.0
	9	19.4	13.8	11.6	5.6	0.9
	10	17.7	10.5	8.9	Trace	8.9
	11	11.9	9.4	4.8	12.8	0.0
	12	12.6	9.2	6.0	0.0	7.9
	13	12.1	6.3	5.3	0.4	4.2
	14	13.3	2.6	2.9	9.6	0.1
	15	13.9	5.4	2.2	Trace	0.0
	16	17.3	10.2	3.8	0.2	0.0
	17	19.5	12.8	5.9	0.0	5.9
	18	22.5	11.6	3.0	0.1	9.7
	19	22.8	10.0	2.5	Trace	7.2
	20	13.6	11.4	9.5	Trace	0.0
	21	13.0	8.6	9.6	0.0	9.4
	22	13.9	3.2	3.9	0.0	9.0
	23	13.8	5.2	3.5	Trace	7.6
	24	12.0	7.1	3.5	0.0	6.2
	25	12.1	1.2	1.4	0.0	9.2
	26	12.7	0.1	0.8	0.0	6.9
	27	13.3	3.6	4.3	0.0	2.2
	28	9.8	2.2	7.9	0.0	9.5
	29	11.8	-1.5	1.8	0.0	9.1
	30	10.6	-2.5	0.3	0.0	4.6
	31	13.3	-1.4	0.8	0.0	8.7
Total		–	–	–	44.9	166.0
Mean		15.9	7.5	4.4	–	–
Temp °F		60.6	45.5	–	–	–
Average		15.4	8.0	7.2	58.0	107.2

NOVEMBER 1997

		Temperature Max. °C	Min. °C	Wind knots	Rain mm	Sun hrs
Day	1	12.6	−1.0	–	0.2	8.5
	2	9.2	0.0	0.1	0.2	2.9
	3	11.6	1.7	8.5	0.0	1.8
	4	14.2	5.9	7.8	1.0	3.1
	5	15.9	7.2	7.8	3.7	4.7
	6	14.5	10.7	2.3	Trace	0.0
	7	13.8	7.8	4.2	3.6	2.6
	8	13.9	9.3	10.9	1.2	4.7
	9	10.4	7.4	6.6	0.2	2.1
	10	11.4	7.2	4.8	0.6	5.4
	11	12.5	3.6	0.8	0.0	4.3
	12	11.3	−0.4	0.2	0.0	6.4
	13	10.0	0.2	0.6	0.4	1.4
	14	13.6	0.2	2.5	0.7	0.3
	15	15.3	3.4	2.6	2.6	0.0
	16	16.4	13.5	4.6	Trace	0.0
	17	15.4	12.6	6.9	Trace	0.0
	18	13.6	10.5	7.8	2.6	0.0
	19	13.3	10.0	6.5	8.0	0.3
	20	12.2	10.0	5.8	2.8	1.3
	21	10.9	4.8	3.5	0.8	2.5
	22	12.7	3.0	2.8	4.2	4.2
	23	11.7	4.9	5.2	0.2	4.1
	24	9.0	6.9	8.6	0.2	0.0
	25	10.1	5.3	5.1	Trace	0.0
	26	11.9	6.6	–	4.6	0.0
	27	11.1	9.1	2.1	7.4	0.0
	28	14.1	8.0	8.2	0.2	3.0
	29	12.1	8.5	7.2	1.6	3.7
	30	8.9	8.4	5.3	0.0	0.0
	31					
Total		–	–	–	47.1	67.3
Mean		12.5	6.2	5.0	–	–
Temp °F		54.5	43.2	–	–	–
Average		10.4	4.1	8.0	55.0	68.1

DECEMBER 1997

		Temperature Max. °C	Min. °C	Wind knots	Rain mm	Sun hrs
Day	1	6.4	0.0	1.2	6.0	0.2
	2	4.0	0.7	4.8	Trace	0.3
	3	4.9	0.6	2.5	0.0	0.0
	4	6.9	1.7	2.5	0.0	4.2
	5	9.1	−1.7	1.1	0.0	2.1
	6	11.2	−0.2	5.8	Trace	1.4
	7	11.5	6.9	7.9	1.0	0.2
	8	13.3	8.2	8.1	0.2	3.5
	9	14.0	8.0	7.5	5.0	0.6
	10	15.0	9.6	10.7	0.6	2.8
	11	14.5	11.4	8.9	0.2	2.2
	12	9.1	5.3	4.8	0.0	6.5
	13	8.3	0.2	1.4	0.0	3.4
	14	9.9	2.4	1.5	Trace	6.6
	15	6.3	3.7	7.1	Trace	0.2
	16	3.2	3.0	12.8	0.2	0.0
	17	7.8	−0.9	12.0	6.8	0.0
	18	10.3	−0.2	5.3	4.4	0.0
	19	8.8	7.8	1.5	Trace	0.0
	20	9.9	6.9	1.6	0.0	0.0
	21	6.6	6.0	1.0	Trace	0.0
	22	8.4	4.1	5.1	5.2	0.0
	23	13.3	6.5	5.2	1.4	0.2
	24	13.9	8.4	10.8	4.0	0.0
	25	12.6	8.3	11.5	4.8	0.1
	26	9.6	7.6	7.7	3.2	2.1
	27	8.4	3.4	3.7	Trace	2.2
	28	7.7	0.2	3.6	0.2	0.2
	29	9.1	2.3	2.2	1.0	0.9
	30	12.3	3.5	7.3	3.0	2.1
	31	9.4	6.8	6.0	Trace	6.0
Total		–			47.2	48.0
Mean		9.5	4.2	5.6	–	–
Temp °F		49.1	39.6	–	–	–
Average		8.0	2.3	8.1	57.0	46.2

JANUARY 1998

		Temperature Max. °C	Min. °C	Wind knots	Rain mm	Sun hrs
Day	1	10.0	2.3	8.6	12.4	3.5
	2	12.7	4.3	8.5	7.0	0.9
	3	11.5	6.4	12.6	5.8	2.3
	4	9.3	3.2	13.9	12.0	0.1
	5	7.6	2.3	7.2	6.6	2.6
	6	12.3	1.0	4.8	4.4	0.5
	7	11.3	2.2	8.4	2.2	4.2
	8	13.4	4.8	11.1	0.8	0.2
	9	15.0	10.6	7.4	0.0	4.7
	10	13.1	7.1	1.7	0.2	6.3
	11	11.8	4.4	3.6	Trace	0.6
	12	12.0	7.1	3.5	Trace	0.0
	13	12.6	7.6	7.8	7.2	2.4
	14	10.8	7.5	7.0	1.0	4.2
	15	11.7	5.3	6.6	Trace	2.9
	16	9.4	6.4	4.9	0.0	3.8
	17	10.4	1.4	4.4	2.2	2.2
	18	9.7	6.3	10.8	6.4	0.1
	19	6.5	6.2	8.0	0.0	0.1
	20	5.4	0.9	4.1	0.0	4.6
	21	7.3	−1.6	0.8	0.0	0.3
	22	6.1	1.8	3.0	0.0	0.0
	23	4.9	−1.6	4.0	Trace	0.1
	24	7.4	−0.7	5.4	0.0	5.1
	25	4.8	2.2	8.6	Trace	0.0
	26	5.6	2.2	5.8	0.0	5.7
	27	4.4	0.6	1.9	Trace	0.0
	28	5.1	2.1	1.8	0.2	3.6
	29	8.0	0.7	0.5	0.0	0.9
	30	7.7	1.4	0.2	0.0	3.3
	31	6.5	3.0	4.0	0.2	0.0
Total		–	–	–	68.6	65.2
Mean		9.2	3.5	5.8	–	–
Temp °F		48.6	38.3	–	–	–
Average		7.1	1.4	8.5	52.0	51.7

FEBRUARY 1998

		Temperature Max. °C	Min. °C	Wind knots	Rain mm	Sun hrs
Day	1	2.6	−2.4	1.8	0.0	5.0
	2	7.4	−3.9	2.1	0.0	6.2
	3	6.7	−1.2	0.9	Trace	6.2
	4	9.5	−2.9	1.6	Trace	7.5
	5	11.0	−0.7	1.5	0.0	3.0
	6	9.6	4.6	5.2	2.8	0.0
	7	9.0	3.0	4.8	Trace	5.9
	8	11.8	0.8	3.6	0.0	4.7
	9	10.9	3.4	5.5	0.0	2.5
	10	12.1	6.7	4.8	0.0	1.8
	11	15.3	7.7	5.7	0.0	2.9
	12	15.5	6.6	3.3	0.0	1.9
	13	18.6	7.9	2.0	0.0	8.5
	14	17.7	3.1	1.3	Trace	8.5
	15	15.9	4.1	2.3	0.0	3.6
	16	12.5	6.9	7.2	Trace	3.4
	17	13.4	4.2	1.7	0.0	8.0
	18	11.7	3.4	2.3	Trace	5.9
	19	13.3	4.2	2.8	0.0	0.0
	20	15.6	6.8	4.6	0.0	1.1
	21	11.5	8.6	6.4	0.8	0.9
	22	9.9	2.7	3.4	0.2	7.8
	23	11.6	2.0	2.2	1.0	0.0
	24	11.7	4.7	2.2	0.0	2.0
	25	12.9	3.5	1.4	0.0	8.0
	26	9.6	4.7	5.1	Trace	0.0
	27	10.3	7.2	11.1	1.8	0.1
	28	8.0	3.0	7.7	Trace	7.7
	29					
	30					
	31					
Total		–	–	–	6.6	113.1
Mean		11.6	3.5	3.7	–	–
Temp °F		52.9	38.3	–	–	–
Average		7.5	1.5	8.8	35.0	67.3

MARCH 1998

		Temperature Max. °C	Min. °C	Wind knots	Rain mm	Sun hrs
Day	1	10.7	0.7	7.3	Trace	4.7
	2	12.6	5.4	9.8	5.2	0.8
	3	15.2	8.1	15.1	6.2	0.0
	4	10.7	8.3	12.6	0.0	4.8
	5	11.5	4.5	10.0	9.4	6.8
	6	12.9	6.8	10.0	5.2	0.0
	7	13.1	9.9	11.0	5.2	5.6
	8	10.3	7.1	5.8	Trace	4.4
	9	9.5	0.1	2.7	0.0	10.3
	10	9.0	−0.1	9.1	6.7	0.0
	11	9.6	5.6	7.8	0.6	3.4
	12	8.5	2.0	3.4	2.0	3.0
	13	11.3	3.8	2.1	0.0	0.0
	14	10.8	2.8	2.0	0.0	2.9
	15	11.0	5.0	2.9	0.0	0.0
	16	10.6	7.6	2.5	0.0	0.0
	17	12.7	7.9	2.4	0.0	0.3
	18	14.6	5.0	2.4	0.0	6.9
	19	12.9	4.3	1.2	0.0	9.7
	20	13.5	2.3	2.3	0.0	6.3
	21	10.7	8.7	2.8	0.0	0.0
	22	12.5	6.8	2.7	0.0	4.9
	23	10.0	7.2	3.3	Trace	0.1
	24	9.3	1.8	4.7	2.8	2.2
	25	10.6	4.9	7.6	4.0	0.0
	26	12.9	6.4	8.0	2.4	0.0
	27	14.5	10.4	4.6	0.0	0.0
	28	16.5	8.6	2.8	0.4	2.5
	29	17.6	9.7	4.8	0.4	0.0
	30	15.8	12.9	4.6	Trace	1.2
	31	14.0	4.4	1.3	0.6	4.1
Total		–	–	–	51.1	84.9
Mean		12.1	5.7	5.5	–	–
Temp °F		53.8	42.3	–	–	–
Average		10.3	2.7	8.9	47.0	110.1

APRIL 1998

		Temperature Max. °C	Min. °C	Wind knots	Rain mm	Sun hrs
Day	1	12.4	7.5	2.3	3.5	0.0
	2	13.7	8.9	5.4	2.8	3.5
	3	14.2	9.3	10.1	6.8	7.0
	4	14.4	6.4	14.0	0.4	5.2
	5	14.4	7.9	9.7	7.0	5.0
	6	12.9	8.0	4.8	3.0	5.4
	7	14.3	5.4	2.3	0.4	4.9
	8	12.4	3.4	3.2	5.4	4.7
	9	10.8	6.3	6.3	3.8	0.7
	10	9.0	3.7	3.6	2.8	0.1
	11	7.8	4.8	5.5	0.8	0.7
	12	9.2	0.1	4.5	Trace	9.9
	13	9.1	0.6	4.3	0.8	8.2
	14	7.6	0.6	3.8	7.0	1.7
	15	6.0	1.0	3.7	6.4	0.0
	16	9.0	0.6	2.8	3.2	1.5
	17	8.0	4.3	7.7	Trace	0.0
	18	8.8	4.2	4.5	2.2	1.3
	19	12.7	5.9	4.3	8.4	1.3
	20	15.1	6.7	3.9	Trace	7.6
	21	13.8	6.2	4.8	0.8	0.1
	22	22.2	9.6	5.9	1.0	5.9
	23	14.5	11.1	6.0	1.6	1.3
	24	16.6	7.8	7.4	2.4	2.6
	25	16.7	9.9	4.7	3.6	5.0
	26	15.5	5.7	5.9	1.8	9.8
	27	14.1	5.2	1.4	4.3	6.4
	28	14.8	5.0	3.3	2.4	7.6
	29	16.2	6.0	7.5	Trace	4.5
	30	13.3	9.6	8.0	Trace	3.5
	31					
Total		–	–	–	82.6	115.4
Mean		12.6	5.7	5.4	–	–
Temp °F		54.7	42.3	–	–	–
Average		13.1	4.7	8.5	45.0	146.9

MAY 1998

		Max. °C	Min. °C	Wind knots	Rain mm	Sun hrs
Day	1	10.3	8.1	7.5	Trace	0.0
	2	15.7	7.9	6.0	Trace	10.1
	3	12.4	7.7	5.8	Trace	6.5
	4	16.7	2.3	1.8	Trace	8.2
	5	14.3	7.5	5.9	Trace	1.2
	6	17.2	10.3	9.3	0.2	3.9
	7	16.2	11.8	10.3	0.0	1.8
	8	22.6	8.5	4.6	Trace	7.4
	9	22.6	13.5	4.6	Trace	13.3
	10	23.0	12.4	5.0	0.2	8.8
	11	23.0	10.7	5.4	0.0	7.5
	12	22.1	10.7	5.3	0.0	7.9
	13	24.9	11.0	2.4	1.0	9.2
	14	24.5	14.5	3.0	6.8	1.4
	15	25.7	11.8	3.9	0.0	13.5
	16	24.2	10.7	4.2	0.0	14.4
	17	21.6	9.4	4.8	0.0	14.4
	18	23.1	8.6	3.4	0.0	10.7
	19	23.8	10.5	3.5	0.0	14.1
	20	24.5	11.9	2.3	Trace	13.4
	21	18.0	14.4	4.8	0.0	5.7
	22	18.0	8.3	2.0	0.0	7.3
	23	17.2	10.6	3.2	Trace	0.7
	24	18.1	11.8	2.4	0.0	2.7
	25	19.6	11.3	3.2	4.5	2.6
	26	17.0	11.1	2.7	10.8	1.2
	27	12.2	7.8	2.9	0.6	0.4
	28	17.2	8.3	3.1	3.8	4.3
	29	18.7	11.4	3.5	0.0	12.7
	30	22.0	8.1	6.8	4.0	14.3
	31	20.4	12.1	4.4	0.0	8.5
Total		–	–	–	31.9	228.1
Mean		19.6	10.2	4.5	–	–
Temp °F		67.3	50.4	–	–	–
Average		17.0	8.0	8.1	51.0	193.7

JUNE 1998

		Max. °C	Min. °C	Wind knots	Rain mm	Sun hrs
Day	1	21.4	8.8	4.0	7.8	8.5
	2	19.5	13.5	8.8	3.4	6.2
	3	18.9	11.9	9.5	0.6	6.9
	4	17.2	10.9	7.0	0.0	0.5
	5	18.4	10.2	9.2	Trace	3.1
	6	23.4	14.0	8.3	1.0	5.7
	7	21.3	11.2	9.3	1.0	10.2
	8	17.2	11.2	10.3	3.4	2.3
	9	19.8	14.3	12.8	3.2	3.1
	10	17.5	11.6	6.5	5.6	4.7
	11	13.0	10.1	6.6	1.8	0.3
	12	17.8	5.1	4.3	0.2	12.6
	13	15.5	10.5	7.1	11.6	0.1
	14	18.1	12.0	3.3	6.0	2.9
	15	18.3	10.9	4.5	2.8	2.8
	16	18.1	12.3	4.0	0.6	4.3
	17	17.9	9.4	3.5	6.6	3.0
	18	18.6	11.9	6.0	Trace	0.0
	19	25.2	14.4	4.3	Trace	7.2
	20	28.4	15.1	6.9	Trace	7.3
	21	25.2	17.1	6.3	Trace	12.6
	22	21.8	11.7	6.0	1.0	11.4
	23	20.5	13.4	6.5	0.4	0.3
	24	23.8	15.2	6.7	7.4	9.2
	25	20.2	13.0	5.9	1.4	6.5
	26	18.6	12.2	9.8	5.6	0.3
	27	20.3	13.4	7.8	8.8	7.0
	28	22.2	11.1	–	Trace	12.4
	29	19.0	10.9	4.9	9.4	4.9
	30	19.6	13.6	3.5	0.0	5.7
	31					
Total		–	–	–	89.6	158.4
Mean		19.9	12.0	6.7	–	–
Temp °F		67.8	53.6	–	–	–
Average		20.4	11.0	7.6	51.0	198.5

Sports Results

For 1999 sports fixtures, *see* pages 12–13
For 1997–8 sporting events, *see* pages 1093–6

ALPINE SKIING

WORLD CUP 1997–8

MEN
Downhill: Andreas Schifferer (Austria), 655 points
Slalom: Thomas Sykora (Austria), 521 points
Giant Slalom: Hermann Maier (Austria), 620 points
Super Giant Slalom: Hermann Maier (Austria), 400 points
Overall: Hermann Maier (Austria), 1,685 points

WOMEN
Downhill: Katja Seizinger (Germany), 520 points
Slalom: Ylva Nowen (Sweden), 620 points
Giant Slalom: Martina Ertl (Germany), 591 points
Super Giant Slalom: Katja Seizinger (Germany), 445 points
Overall: Katja Seizinger (Germany), 1,655 points

Nations Cup: Austria, 13,625 points

AMERICAN FOOTBALL

AFC Championship 1998: Denver Broncos beat Pittsburgh
  Steelers 24–21
NFC Championship 1998: Green Bay Packers beat San
  Francisco 49ers 23–10
XXXII American Superbowl 1998 (San Diego, 25 January):
  Denver Broncos beat Green Bay Packers 31–24
World Bowl 1998: Rhein Fire beat Frankfurt Galaxy 34–10
British League Division 1 final 1998: London Os beat Sussex
  Thunder 20–0

ANGLING

NATIONAL COARSE CHAMPIONSHIPS 1997
Division: 1
Venue: Stainforth and New Junction Canal; *no. of teams:* 84
Individual winner: A. Whiteley (Leeds and District), 9 kg
Team winners: Barnsley and District, 888 points

Division: 2
Venue: Rivers Cam and Ouse; *no. of teams:* 78
Individual winner: R. Finch (Suffolk County), 30.620 kg
Team winners: Suffolk County, 684 points

Division: 3
Venue: Shropshire Union Canal; *no. of teams:* 82
Individual winner: A. Lemon (Tyddcote AC), 5.600 kg
Team winners: Van Den Eynde Goole Avengers, 864
  points

Division: 4
Venue: Middle Trent; *no. of teams:* 79
Individual winner: L. Watkin (Negas AC), 11.500 kg
Team winners: Mansfield Piscatorials, 672 points

Division: 5
Venue: Basingstoke Canal; *no. of teams:* 75

Individual winner: R. Jagger (Stocksbridge Works), 11.530
  kg
Team winners: Image Matchman Supplies, 691 points

Ladies' Championship
Venue: Gold Valley Lakes; *no. of competitors:* 28
Winner: Linda Day (Doncaster)
Team: Shiplake and Binfield

ASSOCIATION FOOTBALL

LEAGUE COMPETITIONS 1997–8

ENGLAND AND WALES
Premiership
1. Arsenal, 78 points
2. Manchester United, 77 points
Relegated: Bolton Wanderers, 40 points; Barnsley, 35 points;
  Crystal Palace, 33 points

Division 1
1. Nottingham Forest, 94 points
2. Middlesbrough, 91 points
Third promotion place: Charlton Athletic
Relegated: Manchester City, 48 points; Stoke City, 46
  points; Reading, 42 points

Division 2
1. Watford, 88 points
2. Bristol City, 85 points
Third promotion place: Grimsby Town
Relegated: Brentford, 50 points; Plymouth Argyle, 49
  points; Carlisle United, 44 points; Southend United, 43
  points

Division 3
1. Notts County, 99 points
2. Macclesfield Town, 82 points
3. Lincoln City, 75 points
Fourth promotion place: Colchester United
Relegated: Doncaster Rovers, 20 points

Football Conference
Champions: Halifax Town, 87 points
Relegated: Telford United, 42 points (reinstated after
  Slough Town were voted out of the Conference);
  Gateshead, 35 points; Stalybridge Celtic, 29 points
League of Wales: Barry Town, 104 points
Women's Premier League: Everton

SCOTLAND
Premier Division
1. Celtic, 74 points
2. Rangers, 72 points
Relegated: Hibernian, 30 points

Division 1
1. Dundee, 70 points
2. Falkirk, 65 points
Relegated: Partick Thistle, 36 points; Stirling Albion, 34
  points

Division 2
1. Stranraer, 61 points
2. Clydebank, 60 points

Relegated: Stenhousemuir, 40 points; Brechin City, 32
points

Division 3
1. Alloa Athletic, 76 points
2. Arbroath, 68 points
Bottom: Dumbarton, 31 points

NORTHERN IRELAND
Irish League Championship: Cliftonville, 68 points

CUP COMPETITIONS

ENGLAND
FA Cup final 1998 (Wembley, 16 May): Arsenal beat
Newcastle United 2–0
Coca Cola (League) Cup final 1998: Chelsea beat
Middlesbrough 2–0 a.e.t.
Auto Windscreens Shield final 1998: Bournemouth 1,
Grimsby Town 1 a.e.t. Grimsby Town won 2–1 on
golden goal rule
FA Vase final 1998: Tiverton Town beat Tow Law Town
1–0
FA Trophy final 1998: Cheltenham Town beat Southport
1–0
Arthur Dunn Cup final 1998: Old Foresters beat Old
Brentwoods 3–1
Charity Shield 1998: Arsenal beat Manchester United 3–0
Women's FA Cup final 1998: Arsenal beat Croydon 3–2
Women's League Cup final 1998: Arsenal 2, Croydon 2 a.e.t.
Croydon won 5–4 on penalties

WALES
Welsh Cup final 1998: Bangor City 1, Connah's Quay 1 a.e.t.
Bangor City won 5–3 on penalties
League of Wales Cup final 1998: Bangor City 1, Barry Town
1 a.e.t. Barry Town won 5–4 on penalties

SCOTLAND
Scottish Cup final 1998 (Celtic Park, 16 May): Heart of
Midlothian beat Rangers 2–1
Coca Cola (League) Cup final 1997 (Ibrox, 30 November):
Celtic beat Dundee United 3–0
League Challenge Cup final 1997: Falkirk beat Queen of the
South 1–0

NORTHERN IRELAND
Irish Cup final 1998: Glentoran beat Glenavon 1–0 a.e.t.

EUROPE
European Champions' Cup final 1998 (Amsterdam): Real
Madrid beat Juventus 1–0
European Cup-Winners' Cup final 1998 (Stockholm): Chelsea
beat Stuttgart 1–0
UEFA Cup final 1998: Inter Milan beat Lazio 3–0
European Super Cup final 1998: Chelsea beat Real Madrid
1–0

INTERNATIONALS

WORLD CUP QUALIFYING MATCHES
1997
11 Oct	Rome	Italy 0, England 0
	Celtic Park	Scotland 2, Latvia 0
	Brussels	Belgium 3, Wales 2
	Lisbon	Portugal 1, N. Ireland 0

FRIENDLIES
1997
12 Nov	Brasilia	Brazil 3, Wales 0
	St Etienne	France 2, Scotland 1
15 Nov	Wembley	England 2, Cameroon 0
1998	Wembley	England 0, Chile 2
11 Feb		
25 March	Berne	Switzerland 1, England 1
	Ibrox	Scotland 0, Denmark 1
	Cardiff	Wales 0, Jamaica 0
	Windsor Park	Northern Ireland 1, Slovakia 0
22 April	Wembley	England 3, Portugal 0
	Easter Road	Scotland 1, Finland 1
	Belfast	N. Ireland 1, Switzerland 0
23 May	Wembley	England 0, Saudi Arabia 0
	New York	Colombia 2, Scotland 2
27 May	Casablanca	Morocco 0, England 1
29 May	Casablanca	England 0, Belgium 0
		Belgium won 4–3 on penalties
30 May	Washington DC	USA 0, Scotland 0
3 June	Valletta	Malta 0, Wales 3
	Santander	Spain 4, N. Ireland 1
6 June	Tunis	Tunisia 4, Wales 0

EUROPEAN CHAMPIONSHIPS QUALIFYING MATCHES
1998
5 Sept	Stockholm	Sweden 2, England 1
	Anfield	Wales 0, Italy 2
	Istanbul	Turkey 3, N. Ireland 0
	Vilnius	Lithuania 0, Scotland 0

WORLD CUP FINALS 1998

France, 10 June–12 July

FIRST ROUND
Group A: Brazil, 6 points; Norway, 5 points; Morocco, 4
points; Scotland, 1 point
Group B: Italy, 7 points; Chile, 3 points; Austria, 2 points;
Cameroon, 2 points
Group C: France, 9 points; Denmark, 4 points; South Africa,
2 points; Saudi Arabia, 1 point
Group D: Nigeria, 6 points; Paraguay, 5 points; Spain, 4
points; Bulgaria, 1 point
Group E: Holland, 5 points; Mexico, 5 points; Belgium, 3
points; South Korea, 1 point
Group F: Germany, 7 points; Yugoslavia, 7 points; Iran, 3
points; USA, 0 points
Group G: Romania, 7 points; England, 6 points; Colombia,
3 points; Tunisia, 1 point
Group H: Argentina, 9 points; Croatia, 6 points; Jamaica, 3
points; Japan, 0 points

SECOND ROUND
Brazil beat Chile 4–1; Italy beat Norway 1–0; France 0,
Paraguay 0 (France won 1–0 in golden goal extra time);
Denmark beat Nigeria 4–1; Germany beat Mexico 2–1;
Holland beat Yugoslavia 2–1; Croatia beat Romania 1–0;
Argentina 2, England 2 after golden goal extra time
(Argentina won 4–3 on penalties)

QUARTER-FINALS
Italy 0, France 0 (France won 4–3 on penalties); Brazil beat
Denmark 3–2; Croatia beat Germany 3–0; Holland beat
Argentina 2–1

SEMI-FINALS
Brazil 1, Holland 1 (Brazil won 4–2 on penalties); France
beat Croatia 2–1

THIRD PLACE PLAY-OFF
Croatia beat Holland 2–1

FINAL
Stade de France, Paris, 12 July
France beat Brazil 3–0

ATHLETICS

WORLD HALF MARATHON CHAMPIONSHIPS
Kosice, Slovakia, 4 October 1997

MEN
Individual: Shem Kororia (Kenya), 59 min. 56 sec.
Team result: Kenya, 2 hr. 59 min. 54 sec.

WOMEN
Individual: Tegla Loroupe (Kenya), 1 hr. 08 min. 14 sec.
Team result: Romania, 3 hr. 27 min. 40 sec.

EUROPEAN CROSS-COUNTRY CHAMPIONSHIPS
Lisbon, Portugal, 14 December 1997

MEN
Individual: Carsten Jorgensen (Denmark), 27 min. 19 sec.
Team: Portugal, 34 points

WOMEN
Individual: Josiane Llado (France), 15 min. 45 sec.
Team: France, 21 points

AAA INDOOR CHAMPIONSHIPS
Birmingham, 7–8 February 1998

MEN

	min.	sec.
60 *metres:* Darren Braithwaite (Haringey)		6.57
200 *metres:* Julian Golding (Blackheath)		20.46
400 *metres:* Solomon Wariso (Haringey)		45.71
800 *metres:* Wilson Kitchumba (Kenya)	1	47.85
1,500 *metres:* Joseph Mills (Blackheath)	3	50.30
3,000 *metres:* = David Taylor (Blackheath) and Rod Finch (Team Solent)	8	00.37
60 *metres hurdles:* Tony Jarrett (Haringey)		7.59
3,000 *metres walk:* Martin Bell (Cardiff)	12	08.61

	metres
High jump: Ben Challenger (Belgrave)	2.27
Pole vault: Nick Buckfield (Crawley)	5.30
Long jump: Chris Davidson (Newham)	7.43
Triple jump: Julian Golley (TVH)	16.49
Shot: Shaun Pickering (Haringey)	18.95

WOMEN

	min.	sec.
60 *metres:* Joice Maduaka (Essex Ladies)		7.34
200 *metres:* Donna Fraser (Croydon)		23.15
400 *metres:* Vikki Jamieson (Lagan Valley)		53.04
800 *metres:* Hayley Parry (Swansea)	2	02.91
1,500 *metres:* Shirley Griffiths (Wakefield)	4	23.56
*3,000 *metres:* Sarah Singleton (Liverpool)	9	35.04
60 *metres hurdles:* Denise Allahgreen (Liverpool)		8.21

* Held at Birmingham, 22 February 1998

	metres
High jump: Susan Jones (Wigan)	1.89
Pole vault: Janine Whitlock (Trafford)	4.11
Long jump: Denise Lewis (Birchfield)	6.29
Triple jump: Ashia Hansen (Shaftesbury-Barnet)	14.19
Shot: Judy Oakes (Croydon)	18.23

EUROPEAN INDOOR CHAMPIONSHIPS
Valencia, Spain, 27 February–1 March 1998

MEN

	min.	sec.
60 *metres:* Agetos Pavlakakis (Greece)		6.55
200 *metres:* Sergei Osovich (Ukraine)		20.40
400 *metres:* Ruslan Mashchenko (Russia)		45.90
800 *metres:* Nils Schumann (Germany)	1	47.02
1,500 *metres:* Rui Silva (Portugal)	3	44.57
3,000 *metres:* John Mayock (GB)	7	55.09
60 *metres hurdles:* Igor Kazanov (Latvia)		7.54

	metres
High jump: Artur Partyka (Poland)	2.31
Pole vault: Tim Lobinger (Germany)	5.80
Long jump: Alexei Lukashevich (Ukraine)	8.06
Triple jump: Jonathan Edwards (GB)	17.43
Shot: Sven-Oliver Buder (Germany)	21.47
Heptathlon: Sebastian Chmara (Poland)	6,415 points

WOMEN

	min.	sec.
60 *metres:* Melanie Paschke (Germany)		7.14
200 *metres:* Svetlana Goncharenko (Russia)		22.46
400 *metres:* Grit Breuer (Germany)		50.45
800 *metres:* Ludmila Formanova (Czech Republic)	2	02.30
1,500 *metres:* Theresia Kiesl (Austria)	4	13.62
3,000 *metres:* Gabriela Szabo (Romania)	8	49.96
60 *metres hurdles:* Patricia Girard (France)		7.85

	metres
High jump: Monica Iagar (Romania)	1.96
Pole vault: Anzhela Balakhonova (Ukraine)	4.45
Long jump: Fiona May (Italy)	6.91
Triple jump: Ashia Hansen (GB)	15.16
Shot: Irina Korzhanenko (Russia)	20.25
Pentathlon: Urszula Wlodarczyk (Poland)	4,808 points

NATIONAL CROSS-COUNTRY CHAMPIONSHIPS
Leeds, 14 March 1998

MEN (14.2 km)
Individual: Dominic Bannister (Shaftesbury-Barnet), 44 min. 45 sec.
Team: Bingley Harriers, 140 points

WOMEN (8 km)
Individual: Mara Myers (Parkside), 28 min. 59 sec.
Team: Shaftesbury-Barnet, 49 points

WORLD CROSS-COUNTRY CHAMPIONSHIPS
Marrakesh, Morocco, 21–22 March 1998

MEN (12 km)
Individual: Paul Tergat (Kenya), 34 min. 01 sec.
Team: Kenya, 12 points

MEN (4 km)
Individual: John Kibowen (Kenya), 10 min. 43 sec.
Team: Kenya, 10 points

WOMEN (8 km)
Individual: Sonia O'Sullivan (Ireland), 25 min. 39 sec.
Team: Kenya, 30 points

WOMEN (4 km)
Individual: Sonia O'Sullivan (Ireland), 12 min. 20 sec.
Team: Morocco, 57 points

LONDON MARATHON
26 April 1998

Men: Abel Anton (Spain), 2 hr. 07 min. 56 sec.
Women: Catherina McKiernan (Ireland), 2 hr. 26 min. 25 sec.

EUROPEAN CUP SUPER LEAGUE
St Petersburg, Russia, 27–27 June 1998

MEN

	min.	sec.
100 *metres:* Stephane Cali (France)		10.32
200 *metres:* Doug Walker (GB)		20.42
400 *metres:* Mark Richardson (GB)		45.81
800 *metres:* Andrea Longo (Italy)	1	45.40
1,500 *metres:* Giuseppe D'Urso (Italy)	3	44.58
3,000 *metres:* Dieter Baumann (Germany)	7	41.92
5,000 *metres:* Alberto Garcia (Spain)	13	37.45
3,000 *metres steeplechase:* Alessandro Lambruschini (Italy)	8	32.96
110 *metres hurdles:* Colin Jackson (GB)		13.17
400 *metres hurdles:* Ruslan Mashchenko (Russia)		48.49
4 × 100 *metres relay:* Great Britain		38.56
4 × 400 *metres relay:* Great Britain	3	00.95

	metres
High jump: Sergei Klyugin (Russia)	2.28
Pole vault: Yevgeni Smiryagin (Russia)	5.60
Long jump: Kiril Sosunov (Russia)	8.38
Triple jump: Jonathan Edwards (GB)	17.29
Shot: Mika Halvari (Finland)	20.79
Discus: Dimitri Shevchenko (Russia)	65.14
Hammer: Heinz Weis (Germany)	79.68
Javelin: Boris Henry (Germany)	84.77

Team points: Great Britain 111, Germany 108½, Russia 102, Italy 101, France 89½, Czech Republic 87, Spain 67½, Finland 52½

WOMEN

	min.	sec.
100 *metres:* Irina Privalova (Russia)		11.04
200 *metres:* Erika Suchovska (Czech Republic)		22.96
400 *metres:* Helena Fuchsova (Czech Republic)		51.33
800 *metres:* Larisa Mikhailova (Russia)	1	58.01
1,500 *metres:* Olga Komyagina (Russia)	4	05.88
3,000 *metres:* Olga Yegorova (Russia)	9	04.03
5,000 *metres:* Paula Radcliffe (GB)	15	06.87
100 *metres hurdles:* Brigita Bukovec (Slovenia)		12.89
400 *metres hurdles:* Tatyana Tereschuk (Ukraine)		54.15
4 × 100 *metres relay:* Russia		42.49
4 × 400 *metres relay:* Russia	3	25.52

	metres
High jump: Zuzana Kovacikova (Czech Republic)	1.98
Pole vault: Daniela Bartova (Czech Republic)	4.35
Long jump: Fiona May (Italy)	7.08
Triple jump: Fiona May (Italy)	14.65
Shot: Irina Korzhanenko (Russia)	20.65
Discus: Natalya Sadova (Russia)	64.18
Hammer: Olga Kuzenkova (Russia)	65.89
Javelin: Tanja Damaske (Germany)	62.30

Team points: Russia 124, Germany 108, France 93, Czech Republic 89, Great Britain 81, Italy 78, Ukraine 64, Slovenia 45

EUROPEAN COMBINED EVENTS CUP – SUPER LEAGUE
Tallinn, Estonia, 4–5 July 1998

MEN
Individual: Erki Nool (Estonia), 8,628 points
Team: Czech Republic, 23,974 points

WOMEN
Individual: Marie Collonville (France), 6,215 points
Team: Russia, 18,331 points

AAA CHAMPIONSHIPS
Birmingham, 24–26 July 1998

MEN

	min.	sec.
100 *metres:* Darren Campbell (Belgrave)		10.22
200 *metres:* Doug Walker (Newham EB)		20.35
400 *metres:* Iwan Thomas (Newham EB)		44.50
800 *metres:* Jason Lobo (Blackburn)	1	49.68
1,500 *metres:* John Mayock (Cannock)	3	39.38
5,000 *metres:* Karl Keska (Birchfield)	13	41.61
*10,000 *metres:* Dermot Donnelly (Annadale)	28	43.17
3,000 *metres steeplechase:* Christiam Stephenson (Cardiff)	8	32.76
110 *metres hurdles:* Colin Jackson (Brecon)		13.37
400 *metres hurdles:* Paul Gray (Cardiff)		49.81
10,000 *metres walk:* Martin Bell (Cardiff)	41	48.81

	metres
High jump: Dalton Grant (Haringey)	2.20
Pole vault: Kevin Hughes (Haringey)	5.40
Long jump: Nathan Morgan (Birchfield)	8.11
Triple jump: Jonathan Edwards (Gateshead)	17.12
Shot: Mark Proctor (RAF)	19.50
Discus: Rob Weir (Birchfield)	62.82
Hammer: Michael Jones (Belgrave)	72.13
Javelin: Steve Backley (Cambridge Harriers)	84.78
†*Decathlon:* Rafer Joseph (Dacorum)	7,126 points

WOMEN

	min.	sec.
100 *metres:* Joice Maduaka (Essex Ladies)		11.40
200 *metres:* Katharine Merry (Birchfield)		23.46
400 *metres:* Allison Curbishley (Edinburgh)		50.92
800 *metres:* Diane Modahl (Sale)	2	02.73
1,500 *metres:* Lynn Gibson (Oxford City)	4	12.72
5,000 *metres:* Andrea Whitcombe (Parkside)	15	43.03
*10,000 *metres:* Tara Krzywicki (Charnwood)	34	37.04
100 *metres hurdles:* Keri Maddox (Sale)		13.20
400 *metres hurdles:* Natasha Danvers (Croydon)		56.27
5,000 *metres walk:* Gillian O'Sullivan (Ireland)	21	52.68

	metres
High jump: Jo Jennings (Essex Ladies)	1.88
Pole vault: Janine Whitlock (Trafford)	4.10
Long jump: Denise Lewis (Birchfield)	6.44
Triple jump: Connie Henry (Shaftesbury)	13.90
Shot: Judy Oakes (Croydon)	17.82
Discus: Shelley Drew (Sutton)	60.82
Hammer: Lorraine Shaw (Sale)	60.71
Javelin: Lorna Jackson (Edinburgh)	57.89
†*Heptathlon:* Clova Court (Birchfield)	5,639 points

* Held at Bedford, 4 July 1998
† Held at Derby, 30–31 May 1998

EUROPEAN CHAMPIONSHIPS
Budapest, Hungary, 18–23 August 1998

MEN

	hr.	min.	sec.
100 *metres:* Darren Campbell (GB)			10.04
200 *metres:* Doug Walker (GB)			20.53
400 *metres:* Iwan Thomas (GB)			44.52
800 *metres:* Nils Schumann (Germany)		1	44.89
1,500 *metres:* Reyes Estevez (Spain)		3	41.31
5,000 *metres:* Isaac Viciosa (Spain)		13	37.46
10,000 *metres:* Antonio Pinto (Portugal)		27	48.62
Marathon: Stefano Baldini (Italy)	2	12	01
3,000 *metres steeplechase:* Damian Kallabis (Germany)		8	13.10
110 *metres hurdles:* Colin Jackson (GB)			13.02
400 *metres hurdles:* Pawel Januszewski (Poland)			48.17
4 × 100 *metres relay:* Great Britain			38.52
4 × 400 *metres relay:* Great Britain		2	58.68
20,000 *metres walk:* Ilya Markov (Russia)	1	21	10
50,000 *metres walk:* Robert Korzeniowski (Poland)	3	43	51

	metres
High jump: Artur Partyka (Poland)	2.34
Pole vault: Maksim Tarasov (Russia)	5.81
Long jump: Kiril Sosunov (Russia)	8.28
Triple jump: Jonathan Edwards (GB)	17.99
Shot: Oleksandr Bagach (Ukraine)	21.17
Discus: Lars Riedel (Germany)	67.07
Hammer: Tibor Gecsek (Hungary)	82.87
Javelin: Steve Backley (GB)	89.72
Decathlon: Erki Nool (Estonia) points	8,667

WOMEN

	hr.	min.	sec.
100 *metres:* Christine Arron (France)			10.73
200 *metres:* Irina Privalova (Russia)			22.62
400 *metres:* Grit Breuer (Germany)			49.93
800 *metres:* Yelena Afanasyeva (Russia)		1	58.50
1,500 *metres:* Svetlana Masterkova (Russia)		4	11.91
5,000 *metres:* Sonia O'Sullivan (Ireland)		15	06.50
10,000 *metres:* Sonia O'Sullivan (Ireland)		31	29.33
Marathon: Manuela Machado (Portugal)	2	27	10
100 *metres hurdles:* Svetla Dimitrova (Bulgaria)			12.56
400 *metres hurdles:* Ionela Tirlea (Romania)			53.37
4 × 100 *metres relay:* France			42.59
4 × 400 *metres relay:* Germany		3	23.03
10,000 *metres walk:* Annarita Sidoti (Italy)		42	49

	metres
High jump: Monica Iagar-Dinesco (Romania)	1.97
Pole vault: Anzhela Balakhonova (Ukraine)	4.31
Long jump: Heike Drechsler (Germany)	7.16
Triple jump: Olga Vasdeki (Greece)	14.55
Shot: Vita Pavlysh (Ukraine)	21.69
Discus: Franka Dietzsch (Germany)	67.49
Hammer: Mihaela Melinte (Romania)	71.17
Javelin: Tanja Damaske (Germany)	69.10
Heptathlon: Denise Lewis (GB)	6,559 points

GRAND PRIX 1998 FINAL
Moscow, Russia, 5 September 1998

MEN

	min.	sec.
100 *metres:* Frankie Fredericks (Namibia)		10.11
400 *metres:* Mark Richardson (GB)		44.88
1,500 *metres:* Hicham El Guerrouj (Morocco)	3	32.03
3,000 *metres:* Haile Gebrselassie (Ethiopia)	7	50.00
400 *metres hurdles:* Stephane Diagana (France)		48.30

	metres
High jump: Javier Sotomayor (Cuba)	2.31
Pole vault: Maksim Tarasov (Russia)	5.95
Triple jump: Charles Friedek (Germany)	17.33
Shot: John Godina (USA)	21.21
Hammer: Tibor Gecsek (Hungary)	81.21
Overall winner: Hicham El Guerrouj (Morocco)	

WOMEN

	min.	sec.
100 *metres:* Marion Jones (USA)		10.83
400 *metres:* Falilat Ogunkoya (Nigeria)		49.73
1,500 *metres:* Svetlana Masterkova (Russia)	4	03.79
3,000 *metres:* Gete Wami (Ethiopia)	8	40.11
100 *metres hurdles:* Michelle Freeman (Jamaica)		12.56

	metres
Long jump: Marion Jones (USA)	7.13
Discus: Natalya Sadova (Russia)	68.50
Javelin: Tanja Damaske (Germany)	68.40
Overall winner: Marion Jones (USA)	

WORLD CUP
Johannesburg, South Africa, 11–13 September 1998

MEN

	min.	sec.
100 *metres:* Obadele Thompson (Americas/Barbados)		9.87
200 *metres:* Frankie Fredericks (Africa/Namibia)		19.97
400 *metres:* Iwan Thomas (GB)		45.33
800 *metres:* Nils Schumann (Germany)	1	48.66
1,500 *metres:* Laban Rotich (Africa/Kenya)	3	40.87
3,000 *metres:* Dieter Baumann (Germany)	7	56.24
5,000 *metres:* Daniel Komen (Africa/Kenya)	13	46.57
3,000 *metres steeplechase:* Damian Kallabis (Germany)	8	31.25
110 *metres hurdles:* Falk Balzer (Germany)		13.10
400 *metres hurdles:* Samuel Matete (Africa/Zambia)		48.08
4 × 100 *metres relay:* Great Britain		38.09
4 × 400 *metres relay:* USA	2	59.28

	metres
High jump: Charles Austin (USA)	2.31
Pole vault: Maksim Tarasov (Europe/Russia)	5.85
Long jump: Ivan Pedroso (Americas/Cuba)	8.37
Triple jump: Charles Friedek (Germany)	17.42
Shot: John Godina (USA)	21.48
Discus: Virgilijus Alekna (Europe/Lithuania)	69.66
Hammer: Tibor Gecsek (Europe/Hungary)	82.68
Javelin: Steve Backley (GB)	88.71

Team points: Africa 110, Europe 109, Germany 102, Americas 97, USA 94, Great Britain 89, Asia 64, Oceania 53

WOMEN

	min.	sec.
100 *metres:* Marion Jones (USA)		10.65
200 *metres:* Marion Jones (USA)		21.62
400 *metres:* Falilat Ogunkoya (Africa/ Nigeria)		49.52
800 *metres:* Maria Mutola (Africa/ Mozambique)	1	59.88
1,500 *metres:* Svetlana Masterkova (Russia)	4	09.41
3,000 *metres:* Gabriela Szabo (Europe/ Romania)	9	00.54
5,000 *metres:* Sonia O'Sullivan (Europe/ Ireland)	16	24.52
100 *metres hurdles:* Glory Alozie (Africa/ Nigeria)		12.58
400 *metres hurdles:* Nezha Bidouane (Africa/ Morocco)		52.96
4 × 100 *metres relay:* USA		42.00
4 × 400 *metres relay:* Germany	3	24.2

	metres
High jump: Monica Iagar-Dinescu (Europe/ Romania)	1.98
Long jump: Heike Drechsler (Germany)	7.07
Triple jump: Olga Vasdeki (Europe/Greece)	14.64
Shot: Vita Pavlysh (Europe/Ukraine)	20.59
Discus: Franka Dietzsch (Germany)	67.07
Javelin: Joanna Stone (Oceania/Australia)	69.85

Team points: USA 96, Europe 94, Africa 88, Russia 87, Americas 81, Germany 75, Asia 45, Oceania 42

BADMINTON

Thomas Cup final 1998 (Men's World Team Championship): Indonesia beat Malaysia 3–2
Über Cup final 1998 (Women's World Team Championship): China beat Indonesia 4–1

ENGLISH NATIONAL CHAMPIONSHIPS 1998
Haywards Heath, January–February

Men's Singles: Darren Hall beat Colin Haughton 15–12, 15–5
Ladies' Singles: Julia Mann beat Rebecca Pantaney 11-5, 11-1
Men's Doubles: Simon Archer and Chris Hunt beat Julian Robertson and Nathan Robertson 15–7, 15–10
Ladies' Doubles: Joanne Goode and Donna Kellogg beat Nicola Beck and Joanne Davies 13–15, 15–8, 17–15

Mixed Doubles: Joanne Goode and Simon Archer beat Donna Kellogg and Chris Hunt 18–13, 15–7

SCOTTISH NATIONAL CHAMPIONSHIPS 1998
Edinburgh, February

Men's Singles: Bruce Flockhart beat Jim Mailer 15-8, 15–3
Ladies' Singles: Anne Gibson beat Gillian Martin 11–8, 11–6
Men's Doubles: Russell Hogg and Kenny Middlemiss beat Alastair Gatt and David Gilmour 15–6, 7–15, 15–8
Ladies' Doubles: Elinor Middlemiss and Sandra Watt beat Kirsteen McEwan and Pam Whiteford 15–6, 15–7
Mixed Doubles: Elinor Middlemiss and Kenny Middlemiss beat Jillian Haldane and Russell Hogg 15–5, 15–7

WELSH NATIONAL CHAMPIONSHIPS 1998
Porthmadog, January–February

Men's Singles: John Leung beat Geraint Lewis 15–11, 15–11
Ladies' Singles: Kelly Morgan beat Gail Osbourne 11–2, 11–1

Men's Doubles: Andrew Groves-Burke and Geraint Lewis beat Neil Cottrill and Roger Pierce 15–12, 15–8
Ladies' Doubles: Gail Osbourne and Katy Howell beat Sarah Williams and Natasha Groves-Burke 15–12, 8–15, 17–15
Mixed Doubles: Kelly Morgan and John Leung beat Sarah Williams and Andrew Groves-Burke 15–6, 15–6

ALL-ENGLAND CHAMPIONSHIPS 1998
Birmingham, March

Men's Singles: Sun Jun (China) beat Ong Ewe Hock (Malaysia) 15–1, 15–7
Ladies' Singles: Ye Zhaoying (China) beat Zang Ning (China) 11-5, 11-8
Men's Doubles: Lee Dong-soo and Yoo Yong-sung (S. Korea) beat Candra Wijaya and Tony Gunawan (Indonesia) 15–10, 15–10
Ladies' Doubles: Ge Fei and Gu Jun (China) beat Jang Hye-ock and Ra Kyung-min (S. Korea) 15–7, 15–7
Mixed Doubles: Ra Kyung-min and Kim Dong-moon (S. Korea) beat Rikke Olsen and Michael Sogaard (Denmark) 15–2, 11–15, 15–5

BASEBALL

World Series Winners 1997: Florida Marlins
American League Championship Series winners 1997: Cleveland Indians
National League Championship Series winners 1997: Florida Marlins

---

BASKETBALL

MEN
World Championship final 1998: Yugoslavia beat Russia 64–62
Championship play-off final 1998: Birmingham Bullets beat Thames Valley Tigers 78–75
League Trophy final 1998: Sheffield Sharks beat London Towers 82–79
National Cup final 1998: Thames Valley Tigers beat Leicester Riders 82–78
National League Championship 1998: Greater London Leopards

WOMEN
World Championship final 1998: USA beat Russia 71–65
Championship play-off final 1998: Sheffield Hatters beat Thames Valley 66–63
National Cup final 1998: Thames Valley beat Sheffield Hatters 68–46
National League Championship 1998: Sheffield Hatters

BILLIARDS

World Matchplay Championship 1998: Mike Russell (England) beat Peter Gilchrist (England) 8–5
UK Professional Championship 1997: Geet Sethi (India) beat Roxton Chapman (GB) 698–293
British Open 1998: Peter Gilchrist (England) beat Geet Sethi (India) 1,328–903

BOWLS – INDOOR

MEN

World Championships 1998
Preston, January–February

Singles: Paul Foster (Scotland) beat Mervyn King
(England) 7–1, 5–7, 7–5, 7–4
Pairs: Graham Robertson and Richard Corsie (Scotland)
beat Gary Smith and Andy Thomson (England) 7–4,
4–7, 6–7, 7–1, 7–0

National Championships 1998
Melton Mowbray, April

Singles: Jamie Mills (South Forest) beat Clive Benham
(Ilminster) 21–18
Pairs: Handy Cross beat Exonia 21–13
Triples: Teignbridge beat Dorchester 20–7
Fours: Nottingham beat Stanley 21–16

British Isles Championships 1998
Swansea, March

Singles: Robert Newman (England) beat Sandy Syme
(Scotland) 21–11
Pairs: Scotland beat Wales 19–18
Triples: Scotland beat Wales 24–14
Fours: Ireland beat Scotland 22–18

Hilton Trophy (Home International Championship) 1998:
Scotland
Liberty Trophy (Inter-County Championship) final 1998:
Durham beat Hampshire 128–127

WOMEN

World Championships 1998
Llanelli, April

Singles: Caroline McAllister (Scotland) beat Carol Ashby
(England) 3–1

National Championships 1998
Hopton-on-Sea, February–March

Singles: Carol Ashby (Eastbourne) beat Liz Shorter
(Norwich) 21–15
Pairs: Eldon, Newcastle beat Diss 23–17
Triples (two wood): Handy Cross, High Wycombe beat
Preston, Brighton 13–11
Triples (four wood): March, Cambs beat Sutton, Surrey
15–13
Fours: Cherwell, Oxfordshire beat Blackpool Borough
26–9

British Isles Championships 1998
Perth, March

Singles: Caroline McAllister (Scotland) beat Margaret
Johnston (Ireland) 21–11
Pairs: Scotland beat Ireland 27–17
Triples: England beat Wales 21–20
Fours: Wales beat England 18–12

Home International Championship 1998: Scotland
Atherley Trophy (Inter-County Championship) final 1998:
Nottinghamshire beat Gloucestershire 134–96

BOWLS – OUTDOOR

MEN

National Championships 1998
Worthing, August

Singles: Grant Burgess (Gilt Edge) beat Les Gillett
(Banbury Borough) 21–20
Pairs: Stoke Coventry beat Lincoln St Giles 24–12
Triples: Bolton beat Sandwich, Kent 23–17
Fours: Banbury Borough beat Summerhill 20–13

British Isles Championships 1998
Ayr Northfield, July

Singles: Richard Brittan (England) beat Steve Jackson
(Wales) 21–18
Pairs: Channel Islands beat Scotland 17–15
Triples: England beat Channel Islands 17–8
Fours: Scotland beat England 24–15

Home International Championship 1998: Scotland
Middleton Cup (Inter-County Championship) final 1998:
Lancashire beat Warwickshire 117–109

WOMEN

National Championships 1998
Royal Leamington Spa, August

Singles (four woods): Norma Shaw (Norton, Durham) beat
Gill Mitchell (Kettering Lodge) 21–11
Singles (two woods): Maureen Christmas (Cambridge
Chesterton) beat Cindy Edmondson (Skelton,
Cumbria) 15–11
Pairs: Yeovil beat Shepherd's Bush 19–14
Triples: Colchester beat Yeovil 18–17
Fours: Atherley, Southampton beat Western Park, Leics
23–7

British Isles Championships 1998
Llandrindod Wells, June

Singles: Betty Morgan (Wales) beat Joyce Lindores
(Scotland) 25–18
Pairs: England beat Wales 25–16
Triples: England beat Wales 19–12
Fours: Wales beat England 20–19

Home International Championship 1998: Wales
Johns Trophy (Inter-County Championship) final 1998: Surrey
beat Leicestershire 139–76

BOXING

PROFESSIONAL BOXING
as at 1 September 1998

World Boxing Council (WBC) Champions

Heavy: Lennox Lewis (GB)
Cruiser: Juan Carlos Gomez (Cuba)
Light-heavy: Roy Jones (USA)
Super-middle: Richie Woodhall (GB)
Middle: Hacine Cherifi (France)
Super-welter: Keith Mullings (USA)
Welter: Oscar De La Hoya (USA)
Super-light: vacant
Light: Cesar Bazan (Mexico)
Super-feather: Genaro Hernandez (Mexico)
Feather: Luisito Espinosa (Philippines)
Super-bantam: Erik Morales (Mexico)

Bantam: Joichiro Tatsuyoshi (Japan)
Super-fly: Cho In-Joo (S. Korea)
Fly: Chatchai Sasakul (Thailand)
Light-fly: Saman Sorjaturong (Thailand)
Straw: Ricardo Lopez (Mexico)

WORLD BOXING ASSOCIATION (WBA) CHAMPIONS

Heavy: Evander Holyfield (USA)
Cruiser: Fabrice Tiozzo (France)
Light-heavy: Roy Jones (USA)
Super-middle: Frank Liles (USA)
Middle: William Joppy (USA)
Junior-middle: Laurent Bouduani (France)
Welter: Ike Quartey (Ghana)
Super-light: Khalid Rahilou (France)
Light: Jean-Baptiste Mendy (France)
Super-feather: Yongsoo Choi (S. Korea)
Feather: Fred Norwood (USA)
Super-bantam: Enrique Sanchez (Mexico)
Bantam: Nana Konadu (Ghana)
Super-fly: Satoshi Iida (Japan)
Fly: Hugo Soto (Argentina)
Light-fly: Pitchinoi Siriwat (Thailand)
Straw: Rosendo Alvarez (Nicaragua)

INTERNATIONAL BOXING FEDERATION (IBF) CHAMPIONS

Heavy: Evander Holyfield (USA)
Cruiser: Imamu Mayfield (USA)
Light-heavy: Reggie Johnson (USA)
Super-middle: Charles Brewer (USA)
Middle: Bernard Hopkins (USA)
Junior-middle: Yory Boy Campas (Mexico)
Welter: Felix Trinidad (Puerto Rico)
Junior-welter: Vince Phillips (USA)
Light: Shane Mosley (USA)
Junior-light: Roberto Garcia (USA)
Feather: Manuel Medina (Mexico)
Junior-feather: Vuyani Bungu (S. Africa)
Bantam: Tim Austin (USA)
Junior-bantam: Johnny Tapia (USA)
Fly: Mark Johnson (USA)
Junior-fly: vacant
Mini-fly: Zolani Petelo (S. Africa)

BRITISH CHAMPIONS

Heavy: Julius Francis
Cruiser: Johnny Nelson
Light-heavy: Crawford Ashley
Super-middle: vacant
Middle: Glenn Catley
Light-middle: Ensley Bingham
Welter: Geoff McCreesh
Light-welter: Jason Rowland
Light: Wayne Rigby
Super-feather: Charles Shepherd
Feather: Jon Jo Irwin
Super-bantam: Michael Brodie
Bantam: Paul Lloyd
Fly: vacant

EUROPEAN CHAMPIONS

Heavy: vacant
Cruiser: vacant
Light-heavy: vacant
Super-middle: Dean Francis (GB)
Middle: Agostino Cardamone (Italy)
Light-middle: Javier Castillejo (Spain)
Welter: vacant
Light-welter: Soren Sondergaard (Denmark)

Light: Billy Schwer (GB)
Junior-light: Anatoly Alexandrov (Russia)
Feather: Billy Hardy (GB)
Super-bantam: Sergei Devakov (Ukraine)
Bantam: Johnny Bredahl (Denmark)
Fly: David Guerault (France)

COMMONWEALTH CHAMPIONS

Heavy: Julius Francis (GB)
Cruiser: Darren Corbett (GB)
Light-heavy: Crawford Ashley (GB)
Super-middle: David Starie (GB)
Middle: Paul Jones (GB)
Light-middle: Kevin Kelly (Australia)
Welter: Kofi Jantuah (Ghana)
Light-welter: vacant
Light: David Odoi Tetteh (Ghana)
Super-feather: vacant
Feather: Paul Ingle (GB)
Super-bantam: Michael Brodie (GB)
Bantam: Paul Lloyd (GB)
Fly: Alfonso Zvenyika (Zimbabwe)

AMATEUR BOXING

AMATEUR BOXING ASSOCIATION (ABA)
CHAMPIONSHIP WINNERS 1998

Super-heavy (91+ kg): Audley Harrison
Heavy (91 kg): Neil Hosking
Cruiser (86 kg): Tony Oakey
Light-heavy (81 kg): Courtney Fry
Middle (75 kg): John Pearce
Light-middle (71 kg): Chris Bessey
Welter (67 kg): David Walker
Light-welter (63.5 kg): Nigel Wright
Light (60 kg): Andrew McLean
Feather (57 kg): Darren Williams
Bantam (54 kg): Levi Pattison
Fly (51 kg): James Hegney
Light-fly (48 kg): Jamie Evans

CHESS

PCA World Champion: Garry Kasparov (Russia)
FIDE World Championship 1998: Anatoly Karpov (Russia)
  beat Vishy Anand (India) after a speed chess play-off
British Champion 1998: Nigel Short
Women's World Champion: Zsuzsa Polgar (Hungary)
British Women's Champion 1998: Susan Lalic

CRICKET

TEST SERIES

WEST INDIES V. ENGLAND

Kingston (29 January–2 February 1998): Match drawn
  (abandoned because of dangerous pitch)
Port of Spain (5–9 February 1998): West Indies won by 3
  wickets. England 214 and 258; West Indies 191 and
  282–7
Port of Spain (13–17 February 1998): England won by 3
  wickets. West Indies 159 and 210; England 145 and
  225–7
Georgetown (27 February–2 March 1998): West Indies won
  by 242 runs. West Indies 352 and 197; England 170 and
  137

Bridgetown (12–16 March 1998): Match drawn. England 403 and 233–3 dec.; West Indies 262 and 112–2
St John's (20–24 March 1998): West Indies won by an innings and 52 runs. England 127 and 321; West Indies 500–7 dec.

ENGLAND v. SOUTH AFRICA

Edgbaston (4–8 June 1998): Match drawn. England 462 and 170–8; South Africa 343
Lord's (18–21 June 1998): South Africa won by 10 wickets. South Africa 360 and 15–0; England 110 and 264
Old Trafford (2–6 July 1998): Match drawn. South Africa 552–5 dec.; England 183 and 369–9
Trent Bridge (23–27 July 1998): England won by 8 wickets. South Africa 374 and 208; England 336 and 247–2
Headingley (6–10 August 1998): England won by 23 runs. England 230 and 240; South Africa 252 and 195

ENGLAND v. SRI LANKA

The Oval (27–31 August 1998): Sri Lanka won by 10 wickets. England 445 and 181; Sri Lanka 591 and 37–0

OTHER TEST SERIES

Pakistan v. South Africa (October 1997): South Africa won 1–0; two matches drawn
Australia v. New Zealand (November–December 1997): Australia won 2–0; one match drawn
Pakistan v. West Indies (November–December 1997): Pakistan won 3–0
India v. Sri Lanka (November–December 1997): 3 matches, all drawn
Australia v. South Africa (December 1997–February 1998): Australia won 1–0; two matches drawn
Sri Lanka v. Zimbabwe (January 1998): Sri Lanka won 2–0
New Zealand v. Zimbabwe (February 1998): New Zealand won 2–0
South Africa v. Pakistan (February–March 1998): South Africa 1, Pakistan 1; one match drawn
Zimbabwe v. Pakistan (March 1998): Pakistan won 1–0; one match drawn
India v. Australia (March 1998): India won 2–1
South Africa v. Sri Lanka (March 1998): South Africa won 2–0
Sri Lanka v. New Zealand (May–June 1998): Sri Lanka won 2–1

ONE-DAY INTERNATIONALS

WEST INDIES v. ENGLAND

Bridgetown (29 March 1998): England won by 16 runs. England 293–5; West Indies 277
Bridgetown (1 April 1998): West Indies won by 1 wicket. England 266; West Indies 267–9
St Vincent (4 April 1998): West Indies won by 5 wickets. England 209–8; West Indies 213–5
St Vincent (5 April 1998): West Indies won by 4 wickets. England 149; West Indies 150–6
Port of Spain (8 April 1998): West Indies won by 57 runs. West Indies 302–5; England 245

ENGLAND v. SOUTH AFRICA

The Oval (21 May 1998): South Africa won by 3 wickets. England 223–9; South Africa 224–7
Old Trafford (23 May 1998): South Africa won by 32 runs. South Africa 226–9; England 194
Headingley (24 May 1998): England won by 7 wickets. South Africa 205–8; England 206–3

INTERNATIONAL CUPS

Sharjah Champions Trophy final 1997: England beat West Indies by 3 wickets. West Indies 235–7; England 239–7
World Series Cup final 1998: Australia beat South Africa 2–1
Sharjah Cup final 1998: India beat Australia by 6 wickets. Australia 272–9; India 275–4
Emirates Cup final 1998: Sri Lanka beat England by 5 wickets. England 256–8; Sri Lanka 260–5
Women's World Cup final 1997: Australia beat New Zealand by 5 wickets. New Zealand 164; Australia 165–5

WEST INDIES v. ENGLAND 1997–8
(Test Averages)

WEST INDIES BATTING

	I	NO	R	HS	Av.
P. A. Wallace	3	0	198	92	66.00
C. B. Lambert	3	0	188	104	62.66
B. C. Lara	9	1	417	93	52.12
C. L. Hooper	8	2	295	108*	49.16
S. Chanderpaul	9	1	272	118	34.00
I. R. Bishop	3	1	62	44*	31.00
R. I. C. Holder	2	0	55	45	27.50
S. C. Williams	6	0	141	62	23.50
J. C. Adams	6	0	113	53	18.83
D. Williams	7	0	98	65	14.00
S. L. Campbell	6	0	79	28	13.16
C. E. L. Ambrose	8	1	83	31	11.85
D. Ramnarine	2	0	19	19	9.50
C. A. Walsh	6	4	15	6	7.50
N. A. M. McLean	4	1	22	11	7.33
K. C. G. Benjamin	4	1	7	6*	2.33

Played in one match: J. R. Murray, 4; F. A. Rose, 2
*Not out

WEST INDIES BOWLING

	O	M	R	W	Av.
C. E. L. Ambrose	205.5	62	428	30	14.26
D. Ramnarine	91	37	148	9	16.44
J. C. Adams	15	7	19	1	19.00
C. L. Hooper	190.5	61	355	15	23.66
C. A. Walsh	261.2	63	564	22	25.63
N. A. M. McLean	78	15	203	5	40.60
F. A. Rose	20	6	53	1	53.00
I. R. Bishop	50	7	163	3	54.33
K. C. G. Benjamin	63	14	166	3	55.33

Also bowled: C. B. Lambert, 1–0–1–0; S. Chanderpaul, 10–3–35–0

ENGLAND BATTING

	I	NO	R	HS	Av.
M. R. Ramprakash	5	1	266	154	66.50
A. J. Stewart	11	1	452	83	45.20
G. P. Thorpe	11	3	339	103	42.37
N. Hussain	11	2	295	106	32.77
M. A. Atherton	11	0	199	64	18.09
M. A. Butcher	9	1	125	28	15.62
R. C. Russell	9	1	90	32	11.25
J. P. Crawley	4	0	45	22	11.25
D. W. Headley	9	2	69	31	9.85
A. J. Hollioake	2	0	14	12	7.00
A. R. C. Fraser	8	0	44	17	5.50
A. R Caddick	7	0	19	8	2.71
P. C. R. Tufnell	8	3	11	6	2.20

Played in one match: R. D. B. Croft, 26,14

ENGLAND BOWLING

	O	M	R	W	Av.
A. R. C. Fraser	187.2	50	492	27	18.22
R. D. B. Croft	58.1	18	139	6	23.16
D. W. Headley	171.3	28	546	19	28.73
A. R. Caddick	120	31	388	13	29.84
M. R. Ramprakash	41	9	118	3	39.33
P. C. R. Tufnell	212.5	67	438	7	62.57

Also bowled: A. J. Hollioake, 5–0–12–0; M. A. Butcher, 5–1–16–0

ENGLAND v. SOUTH AFRICA 1998
(Test Averages)

ENGLAND BATTING

	I	NO	R	HS	Av.
M. A. Butcher	6	0	338	116	56.33
M. A. Atherton	10	1	493	103	54.77
A. J. Stewart	10	1	465	164	51.66
R. D. B. Croft	6	4	90	37*	45.00
N. Hussain	10	0	347	105	34.70
M. R. Ramprakash	9	1	249	67*	31.12
D. G. Cork	9	1	99	36	12.37
G. P. Thorpe	6	0	63	43	10.50
I. D. K. Salisbury	3	0	27	23	9.00
D. Gough	6	1	43	16*	8.60
A. R. C. Fraser	8	2	39	17	6.50
M. A. Ealham	4	0	24	8	6.00
A. Flintoff	3	0	17	17	5.66
G. A. Hick	3	0	9	6	3.00

Played in one match: A. F. Giles, 16*,1; N. V. Knight, 11,1; S. P. James, 10,0; D. W. Headley, 2,1
*Not out

ENGLAND BOWLING

	O	M	R	W	Av.
A. R. C. Fraser	203.3	55	492	24	20.50
D. Gough	130.5	26	388	17	22.82
D. G. Cork	174.4	29	573	18	31.83
D. W. Headley	22	2	69	2	34.50
M. A. Ealham	38	10	105	2	52.50
A. F. Giles	36	7	106	1	106.00
A. Flintoff	35	4	112	1	112.00

Also bowled: M. R. Ramprakash, 5–0–17–0; M. A. Butcher, 14–5–37–0; I. D. K. Salisbury, 25–3–106–0; R. D. B. Croft, 87–20–211–0

SOUTH AFRICA BATTING

	I	NO	R	HS	Av.
W. J. Cronje	7	1	401	126	66.83
L. Klusener	3	1	108	57	54.00
J. N. Rhodes	7	0	367	117	52.42
J. H. Kallis	7	0	294	132	42.00
D. J. Cullinan	8	1	287	78	41.00
G. Kirsten	8	1	257	210	36.71
S. M. Pollock	6	1	146	50	29.20
M. V. Boucher	6	0	84	35	14.00
G. F. J. Liebenberg	6	0	59	21	9.83
A. A. Donald	6	3	29	7*	9.66
M. Ntini	2	1	4	4*	4.00
P. R. Adams	4	1	10	6*	3.33

Played in one match: B. M. McMillan, 54,7; S. Elworthy, 48,10; A. M. Bacher, 22
*Not out

SOUTH AFRICA BOWLING

	O	M	R	W	Av.
A. A. Donald	243.2	69	653	33	19.78
S. M. Pollock	219.5	72	464	18	25.77
J. H. Kallis	158.1	65	306	11	27.81
P. R. Adams	180.1	58	388	13	29.84
M. Ntini	81	27	210	6	35.00
L. Klusener	90	25	217	6	36.16
S. Elworthy	31	9	79	1	79.00

Also bowled: D. J. Cullinan, 2–0–2–0; B. M. McMillan, 20–0–46–0; W. J. Cronje, 29–10–65–0

COUNTY CHAMPIONSHIP TABLE 1998

Order for 1997 in brackets	P	W	L	D	Bt	Bl	Pts
Leicestershire (10)	17	11	0	6	47	51	292
Lancashire (11)	17	11	1	5	30	56	277
Yorkshire (6)	17	9	3	5	47	63	269
Gloucestershire (7)	17	11	5	1	23	65	267
Surrey (8)	17	10	5	2	38	57	261
Hampshire (14)	17	6	5	6	27	61	202
Sussex (18)	17	6	7	4	30	63	201
Warwickshire (4)	17	6	8	3	35	60	200
Somerset (12)	17	6	7	4	30	54	192
Derbyshire (16)	17	6	7	4	28	55	191
Kent (2)	17	5	5	7	18	59	178
Glamorgan (1)	17	4	6	7	36	55	176
Worcestershire (3)	17	4	6	7	32	59	176
Durham (17)	17	3	9	5	30	65	158
*Northamptonshire (15)	17	4	5	8	31	52	146
Nottinghamshire (13)	17	3	10	4	20	60	140
Middlesex (4)	17	2	9	6	28	52	130
Essex (8)	17	2	11	4	16	58	118

* 25 points deducted for an unfit pitch

FIRST CLASS BATTING AVERAGES 1998

Qualifying requirement: 6 completed innings

	I	NO	R	HS	Av.
J. P. Crawley	28	3	1,851	239	74.04
W. J. Cronje	12	2	704	195	70.40
D. J. Cullinan	17	4	900	200*	69.23
G. Kirsten	19	5	892	210	63.71
J. L. Langer	28	5	1,448	233*	62.95
B. F. Smith	24	4	1,240	204	62.00
D. S. Lehmann	16	0	969	200	60.56
M. B. Loye	22	2	1,198	322*	59.90
A. Habib	22	5	952	198	56.00
J. H. Kallis	14	3	612	132	55.63
M. G. Bevan	19	2	935	149*	55.00
M. S. Atapattu	7	1	316	114	52.66
N. H. Fairbrother	17	2	759	138	50.60
S. P. James	28	1	1,339	227	49.59
A. D. Brown	22	1	1,036	155	49.33
D. J. Millns	10	4	289	99	48.16
S. T. Jayasuriya	9	1	382	213	47.75
K. J. Barnett	32	6	1,229	162	47.26
M. J. Wood	29	6	1,080	200*	46.95
G. F. J. Liebenberg	17	3	642	104*	45.85

*Not out

FIRST CLASS BOWLING AVERAGES 1998

Qualifying requirement: 20 wickets taken

	O	M	R	W	Av.
M. Muralitharan	226.3	77	463	34	13.61
V. J. Wells	199.1	66	514	36	14.27
C. White	147.1	36	391	25	15.64
C. A. Walsh	633	164	1,835	106	17.31
Saqlain Mushtaq	475	136	1,119	63	17.76
A. D. Mullally	448.4	156	1,128	60	18.80
M. P. L. Bulbeck	154.4	28	609	32	19.03
T. A. Munton	278.5	71	708	37	19.13
D. A. Leatherdale	111.4	22	416	21	19.80
A. R. Caddick	687.2	156	2,082	105	19.82
R. S. C. Martin-Jenkins	141.5	43	437	22	19.86
A. R. C. Fraser	480.3	122	1,224	61	20.06
A. A. Donald	302.2	89	785	39	20.12
A. C. Morris	314	65	1,012	50	20.24
G. M. Hamilton	415	100	1,212	59	20.54
M. P. Bicknell	494.1	141	1,340	65	20.61
A. M. Smith	522.3	139	1,440	68	21.17
K. J. Dean	465.3	96	1,572	74	21.24
P. V. Simmons	170.5	44	491	23	21.34
Wasim Akram	335.5	75	1,025	48	21.35

Source for averages and county championship table: ECB/PA Cricket Record

OTHER RESULTS 1998

Benson and Hedges Cup final: Essex beat Leicestershire by 192 runs. Essex 268–7; Leicestershire 76

NatWest Trophy final: Lancashire beat Derbyshire by 9 wickets. Derbyshire 108; Lancashire 109–1

Sunday League Champions: Lancashire

MCC Trophy (Minor Counties knockout final): Devon beat Shropshire by 8 wickets. Shropshire 201–9; Devon 204–2

Minor Counties Championship final: Staffordshire beat Dorset by a higher run rate. Staffordshire 177–6 and 170–9; Dorset 92

National Club Championship final: Doncaster Town beat Bath by 6 wickets. Bath 229–5; Doncaster Town 233–4

National Village Championship final: Methley beat Apperley by 61 runs. Methley 238–3; Apperley 177

Varsity Match (one-day): Cambridge beat Oxford by 134 runs. Cambridge 257–8; Oxford 123

Varsity Match (three-day): Cambridge beat Oxford by 91 runs. Cambridge 249–9 dec. and 176; Oxford 180–3 dec. and 199

CYCLING

World Cup series overall winner 1997: Michele Bartoli (Italy), 280 points

Tour of Britain 1998: Stuart O'Grady (Australia)

Tour of Italy 1998: Marco Pantani (Italy)

Tour de France 1998: Marco Pantani (Italy)

Tour of Spain 1998: Abraham Olano (Spain)

World Open Road Race Championship 1997: Laurent Brochard (France)

World Open Cyclo-Cross Championship 1998: Mario de Clercq (Belgium)

World Cyclo-Cross Cup series overall winner 1998: Richard Groenendaal (Netherlands), 260 points

British Open Road Race Championship 1998: Matt Stephens (Harrods-Giant)

British Open Cyclo-Cross Championship 1998: Nick Craig (Diamond Back)

Women's World Road Race Championship 1997: Alessandria Cappellotto (Italy)

Women's National Road Race Championship 1998: Megan Hughes (Adidas-SciCon)

Women's British Open Cyclo-Cross Championship 1998: Caroline Alexander (Team Ritchey)

DARTS

Skol World Championship 1998: Phil Taylor (England) beat Dennis Priestley (England) 6–0

Embassy World Championship 1998: Ray Barneveld (Holland) beat Richie Burnett (Wales) 6–5

EQUESTRIANISM

Show Jumping

World Cup final 1998: Rodrigo Pessoa (Brazil) on Baloubet du Rouet

British Jumping Derby 1998 (Hickstead): John Whitaker (GB) on Gammon

Three-Day Eventing

Badminton Horse Trials 1998: Christopher Bartle (GB) on Word Perfect II

British Open Horse Trials 1998 (Gatcombe Park): Blyth Tait (New Zealand) on Ready Teddy

Burghley Horse Trials 1998: Blyth Tait (New Zealand) on Chesterfield

ETON FIVES

County Championship final 1998: Warwickshire beat Berkshire 2–1

Amateur Championship (Kinnaird Cup) 1998: Robin Mason and Jonathan Mole beat E. Taylor and R. Tyler 3–0

Holmwoods Schools' Championship 1998: St Olave's I beat Harrow I 3–1

Barber Cup final 1998: Old Cholmeleians beat Old Salopians 2–1

League Championship (Douglas Keeble Cup) 1998: Old Olavians I

FENCING

MEN

BRITISH CHAMPIONS 1998

Foil: Sam Johnson (Sussex House)

Epée: Quentin Berriman (Haverstock)

Sabre: Ian Williams

International Epée 1998: Mathieu Denis (France)

Corble Cup 1998 (international sabre tournament): Stanislaw Pozdniakov (Russia)

WOMEN

BRITISH CHAMPIONS 1998

Foil: Linda Strachan (Boston)

Epée: Georgina Usher (London Thames)

Sabre: Caroline Stevenson

Ipswich Cup 1998 (international epée world cup series): Tamara Estery (Cuba)

GOLF (MEN)

THE MAJOR CHAMPIONSHIPS 1998

US Masters (Augusta, Georgia, 9–12 April): Mark O'Meara (USA), 279

US Open (Olympic Club, San Francisco, 18–21 June): Lee Janzen (USA), 280

The Open (Royal Birkdale, 16–19 July): Mark O'Meara (USA), 280*

US PGA Championship (Sahalee Country Club, Seattle, 13–16 August): Vijay Singh (Fiji), 271

PGA EUROPEAN TOUR 1997

German Masters (Motzener See): Bernhard Langer (Germany), 267

World Matchplay Championship (Wentworth): Vijay Singh (Fiji) beat Ernie Els (S. Africa) by 1 hole

Pairs Tournament (Bordeaux): Michal Jonzon and Anders Forsbrand (Sweden), 343*

Oki Pro-am (Madrid): Paul McGinley (Ireland), 266

Volvo Masters (Jerez): Lee Westwood (GB), 200

European Tour Order of Merit 1997: 1. Colin Montgomerie (GB); 2. Bernhard Langer (Germany); 3. Lee Westwood (GB)

World Cup 1997 (Kiawah Island, S. Carolina): Colin Montgomerie (GB), 266

World Open Championship 1997 (Atlanta, Georgia): Mark Calcavecchia (USA), 271

PGA EUROPEAN TOUR 1998

World Championship of Golf 1998 (Scottsdale, Arizona): Colin Montomerie (GB) beat Davis Love III (USA) by 2 holes

Johnnie Walker Classic (Phuket, Thailand): Tiger Woods (USA), 279

Heineken Classic (Perth, Australia): Thomas Björn (Denmark), 280

South African Open (Durban): Ernie Els (S. Africa), 273

South African PGA (Johannesburg): Tony Johnstone (Zimbabwe), 271

Dubai Desert Classic: José-Maria Olazábal (Spain), 269

Qatar Masters (Doha): Andrew Coltart (GB), 270

Moroccan Open (Agadir): Stephen Leaney (Australia), 271

Portuguese Open (Penina): Peter Mitchell (GB), 274

Cannes Open: Thomas Levet (France), 278

Spanish Open (Barcelona): Thomas Björn (Denmark), 267

Italian Open (Castelconturbia): Patrik Sjöland (Sweden), 195

Turespana Masters/Balearic Open (Santa Ponsa): Miguel-Angel Jiménez (Spain), 279

International Open (The Oxfordshire): Darren Clarke (N. Ireland), 273

PGA Championship (Wentworth): Colin Montgomerie (GB), 274

European Tournament Players' Championship (Hamburg): Lee Westwood (GB), 265

English Open (Hanbury Manor): Lee Westwood (GB), 271

European Grand Prix (Slaley Hall): abandoned due to rain

Madeira Island Open: Mats Lanner (Sweden), 277

French Open (Paris): Sam Torrance (GB), 276

Irish Open (Druid's Glen): David Carter (GB), 278*

Loch Lomond World Invitational: Lee Westwood (GB), 276

Dutch Open (Hilversum): Stephen Leaney (Australia), 266

Scandinavian Masters (Kungsängen): Jesper Parnevik (Sweden), 273

German Open (Berlin): Stephen Allan (Australia), 280

European Open (K Club, Co. Kildare): Mathias Grönberg (Sweden), 275

International Open (Munich): Russell Claydon (GB), 270

European Masters (Crans-sur-Sierre): Sven Strüver (Germany), 263*

British Masters (Forest of Arden): Colin Montgomerie (GB), 281

Lancôme Trophy (St-Nom-La-Bretêche, France): Miguel-Angel Jiménez (Spain), 273

German Masters (Cologne): Colin Montgomerie (GB), 266

MAJOR TEAM EVENTS

Alfred Dunhill Cup final 1997 (St Andrews, 16–19 October): South Africa beat Sweden 2–1

World Cup 1997 (Kiawah Island, S. Carolina): Ireland, 545

AMATEUR CHAMPIONSHIPS

British Amateur Championship 1998 (Muirfield): Sergio Garcia (Spain)

English Amateur Championship 1998 (Woodhall Spa): Mark Sanders (Bristol and Clifton)

Welsh Amateur Championship 1998 (Prestatyn): Mark Pilkington (Pwllheli)

Scottish Amateur Championship 1998 (Prestwick): Graham Rankin (Palacerigg)

Brabazon Trophy (English Open Strokeplay) 1998 (Formby): Peter Hansson (Sweden), 287

Welsh Open Strokeplay 1998 (Southerndown): David Patrick (Mortonhall), 279

Scottish Open Strokeplay 1998 (Moray and Elgin): Lorne Kelly (Cowal), 275

Lytham Trophy 1998 (Royal Lytham and St Anne's): Lorne Kelly (Cowal), 288*

Berkshire Trophy 1998 (The Berkshire): Mark Hilton (E. Sussex National), 284

International Match 1998 (Orléans): France beat England 12½–11½

Home International Championship 1998 (Royal Porthcawl): England

European Amateur Championship 1998 (Bordeaux, France): Paddy Gribben (N. Ireland), 274

President's Putter 1998 (Rye): Neil Pabari (Oxford) beat Jamie Warman (Cambridge) 2 and 1

Halford Hewitt Cup 1998 (for public schools' old boys) (Deal): Charterhouse beat Tonbridge 3–2

Varsity Match 1998 (Rye): Cambridge beat Oxford 9–6

* After a play-off

GOLF (WOMEN)

US Women's Open 1998 (Kohler, Wisconsin): Se Ri Pak (S. Korea), 290*

Women's World Championship 1997 (Seoul): J Inkster (USA), 280

WPG EUROPEAN TOUR 1997

Italian Open (Il Picciola, Sicily): Valerie Van Ryckeghem (Belgium), 288*

Air France Open (Deauville): Loraine Lambert (Australia), 213

European Cup (Praia d'El Rey, Portugal): Men's Senior Tour beat Women's European Tour 13–7

European Tour Order of Merit 1997: 1. Alison Nicholas (GB); 2. Helen Alfredsson (Sweden); 3. Marie-Laure de Lorenzi (France)

EUROPEAN LPGA TOUR 1998

Evian Masters: Helen Alfredsson (Sweden), 277

Austrian Open (Graz): Lynette Brooky (New Zealand), 203

Chrysler Open (Sjögärde Club, Sweden): Laura Davies (GB), 284

German Open (Treudelberg): Lora Fairclough (GB), 282
Championship of Europe (Gleneagles): Catriona Matthew (GB), 276
British Open (Royal Lytham and St Anne's): Sherri Steinhauer (USA), 292
Compaq Open (Malmö, Sweden): Annika Sorenstam (Sweden), 279
Irish Open (Ballyliffin): Sophie Gustafson (Sweden), 214*

MAJOR TEAM EVENTS

Solheim Cup 1998 (Dublin, Ohio, USA): USA beat Europe 16–12
Curtis Cup 1998 (amateur) (Minneapolis): USA beat GB and Ireland 10–8

AMATEUR CHAMPIONSHIPS

British Open Championship 1998 (Little Aston): Kim Rostron (Clitheroe)
English Amateur Championship 1998 (Walton Heath): Elaine Ratcliffe (Sandiway)
Welsh Amateur Championship 1998 (Ashburnham): Louise Davis (Conwy)
Scottish Amateur Championship 1998 (North Berwick): Elaine Moffat (St Regulus)
British Strokeplay 1998 (Stirling): Nienke Nijenhuis (Holland), 297
English Strokeplay 1998 (Broadstone): Emma Duggleby (Malton and Norton), 306
Welsh Strokeplay 1998 (Rolls of Monmouth): Georgina Simpson (Cleckheaton and District), 150
Scottish Strokeplay 1998 (Portland and Royal Troon): Karen-Margethe Juul (Denmark), 225
Home International Championship 1998 (Burnham and Berrow): England
European Amateur Championship 1998 (Noordwijkse, Holland): Giulia Sergas (Italy), 295
* After a play-off

GREYHOUND RACING

Cesarewitch 1997 (Catford): Tralee Crazy
St Leger 1997 (Wembley): Tralee Crazy
Oaks 1997 (Wimbledon): Flashy Get
Grand Prix 1997 (Walthamstow): El Grand Señor
Television Trophy 1997 (Hall Green): Moanrue Slippy
Grand National 1998 (Hall Green): El Tenor
Derby 1998 (Wimbledon): Tom's the Best
Scurry Gold Cup 1998 (Catford): I'm Frankie
The Masters 1998 (Reading): You Wil Call
The Regency 1998 (Brighton): Million Percent
Gold Collar 1998 (Catford): Lenson Billy

GYMNASTICS

World Rhythmics Champion 1997: Elena Vitrischenko (Ukraine)

BRITISH MEN'S CHAMPIONSHIPS 1997
Nottingham, November

British Champion: Kevin Atherton (Telford)
Individual Apparatus Champions:
Floor: Ross Brewer (Woking)
Pommel Horse: Kanukai Jackson (Harrow)
Rings: Craig Heap (North Tyne)
Vault: Kanukai Jackson (Harrow)
Parallel Bars: Andrew Atherton (Telford)

High Bar: Andrew Atherton (Telford)
British Men's Team Champions 1998 (Adam Shield): Woking
British Women's Team Champions 1998: South Essex
British Rhythmics Champion 1998: Laura Mackie (Scotland)

HOCKEY

MEN
National League 1998: Cannock
Hockey Association Cup final 1998: Cannock beat Beeston 4–1
National Indoor Club Championship final 1998: Reading beat East Grinstead 9–8
County Championship final 1998: Surrey beat Cheshire 1–0
Champions Trophy final 1997: Germany beat Australia 3–2
World Cup final 1998: Holland beat Spain 3–2 after sudden death overtime
European Club Championship final 1998: Athletic Terrassa (Spain) beat Amsterdam (Holland) 2–1
European Indoor Club Championship final 1998: Harvestehuder Hamburg (Germany) beat Durkheimer (Germany) 6–3
European Cup Winners' Cup final 1998: Den Bosch (Holland) beat SKA Ekaterinburg (Russia) 4–0
Varsity Match 1998: Oxford beat Cambridge 4–0

WOMEN
National League 1998: Slough
AEWHA Cup final 1998: Clifton 1, Slough 1. Clifton won 5–4 on penalties
National Indoor League 1998: Slough
County Championship final 1998: Dorset 0, Surrey 0. Dorset won 3–0 on penalties
World Cup final 1998: Australia beat Holland 3–2
European Nations Indoor Cup final 1998: Germany beat England 8–0
European Club Championship final 1998: Russelsheim (Germany) 1, Slough (England) 1. Russelsheim won 3–2 on penalties
European Indoor Club Championship final 1998: Russelsheim (Germany) beat Eintracht Frankfurt (Germany) 7–4
European Cup Winners' Cup final 1998: Amsterdam (Holland) beat Dinamo Suny (Ukraine) 6–0

HORSE-RACING

RESULTS

CAMBRIDGESHIRE HANDICAP
(1839) Newmarket, 1 mile

1994   Halling (3y), (8st 8lb), F. Dettori
1995   Cap Juluca (3y), (9st 10lb), R. Hughes
1996   Clifton Fox (4y), (8st 2lb), N. Day
1997   Pasternak (4y), (9st 1lb), G. Duffield

PRIX DE L'ARC DE TRIOMPHE
(1920) Longchamp, 1½ miles

1994   Carnegie (3y), (8st 11lb), T. Jarnet
1995   Lammtarra (3y), (8st 11lb), F. Dettori
1996   Helissio (3y), (8st 11lb), O. Peslier
1997   Peintre Célèbre (3y), (8st 11lb), O. Peslier

CESAREWITCH
(1839) Newmarket, 2 miles and about 2 f

1994   Captain's Guest (4y), (9st 9lb), A. Clark
1995   Old Red (5y), (7st 11lb), L. Charnock
1996   Inchcailloch (7y), (7st 10lb), R. Ffrench
1997   Turnpole (6y), (7st 10lb), L. Charnock

THE CLASSICS
ONE THOUSAND GUINEAS
(1814) Rowley Mile, Newmarket, for three-year-old fillies

Year	Winner	Betting	Owner	Jockey	Trainer	No. of Runners
1995	Harayir	5–1	H. Al-Maktoum	R. Hills	R. Hern	14
1996	Bosra Sham	10–11	Wafic Said	P. Eddery	H. Cecil	13
1997	Sleepytime	5–1	C. Wacker III	K. Fallon	H. Cecil	15
1998	Cape Verdi	100–30	Godolphin	F. Dettori	Saeed bin Suroor	16

Record time: 1 minute 36.71 seconds by Las Meninas in 1994

TWO THOUSAND GUINEAS
(1809) Rowley Mile, Newmarket, for three-year-olds

Year	Winner	Betting	Owner	Jockey	Trainer	No. of Runners
1995	Pennekamp	9–2	Sheikh Mohammed	T. Jarnet	A. Fabre	11
1996	Mark of Esteem	8–1	Godolphin	F. Dettori	Saeed bin Suroor	13
1997	Entrepreneur	11–2	M. Tabor	M. Kinane	M. Stoute	16
1998	King of Kings	7–2	Mrs J. Magnier/M. Tabor	M. Kinane	A. O'Brien	18

Record time: 1 minute 35.08 seconds by Mister Baileys in 1994

THE DERBY
(1780) Epsom, 1 mile and about 4 f, for three-year-olds

The first winner was Sir Charles Bunbury's Diomed in 1780. The owners with the record number of winners are Lord Egremont, who won in 1782, 1804, 1805, 1807, 1826 (also won five Oaks); and the late Aga Khan, who won in 1930, 1935, 1936, 1948, 1952. Other winning owners are: Duke of Grafton (1802, 1809, 1810, 1815); Mr J. Bowes (1835, 1843, 1852, 1853); Sir J. Hawley (1851, 1858, 1859, 1868); the 1st Duke of Westminster (1880, 1882, 1886, 1899); and Sir Victor Sassoon (1953, 1957, 1958, 1960).

Record times are: 2 min. 32.31 sec. by Lammtarra in 1995; 2 min. 33.80 sec. by Mahmoud in 1936; 2 min. 33.84 sec. by Kahyasi in 1988; 2 min. 33.88 by High-Rise in 1998; 2 min. 33.9 sec. by Reference Point in 1987.

The Derby was run at Newmarket in 1915–18 and 1940–5.

Year	Winner	Betting	Owner	Jockey	Trainer	No. of Runners
1995	Lammtarra	14–1	S. M. Al-Maktoum	W. Swinburn	Saeed bin Suroor	15
1996	Shaamit	12–1	Khalifa Dasmal	M. Hills	W. Haggas	20
1997	Benny The Dip	11–1	L. Knight	W. Ryan	J. Gosden	13
1998	High-Rise	20–1	Sheikh Mohammed Obaidh Al Maktoum	O. Peslier	L. Cumani	15

THE OAKS
(1779) Epsom, 1 mile and about 4 f, for three-year-old fillies

Year	Winner	Betting	Owner	Jockey	Trainer	No. of Runners
1995	Moonshell	3–1	M. Al-Maktoum/Godolphin	F. Dettori	Saeed bin Suroor	10
1996	Lady Carla	100–30	Wafic Said	P. Eddery	H. Cecil	11
1997	Reams of Verse	5–6	Prince K. Abdulla	K. Fallon	H. Cecil	12
1998	Shahtoush	12–1	Mrs D. Nagle/Mrs J. Magnier	M. Kinane	A. O'Brien	8

ST LEGER
(1776) Doncaster, 1 mile and about 6 f, for three-year-olds

Year	Winner	Betting	Owner	Jockey	Trainer	No. of Runners
1995	Classic Cliché	100–30	Godolphin	F. Dettori	Saeed bin Suroor	10
1996	Shantou	8–1	Sheikh Mohammed	F. Dettori	J. Gosden	11
1997	Silver Patriarch	5–4	P. Winfield	P. Eddery	J. Dunlop	10
1998	Nedawi	5–2	Godolphin	J. Reid	Saeed bin Suroor	9

Record time: 3 minutes 1.60 seconds by Coronach in 1926 and Windsor Lad in 1934

CHAMPION STAKES
(1877) Newmarket, 1 mile, 2 f

1994   Dernier Empereur (4y), (9st 4lb), S. Guillot
1995   Spectrum (3y), (8st 10lb), J. Reid
1996   Bosra Sham (3y), (8st 8lb), P. Eddery
1997   Pilsudski (5y), (9st 2lb), M. Kinane

*HENNESSY GOLD CUP
(1957) Newbury, 3 miles and about 2½ f

1994   One Man (6y), (10st), A. Dobbin
1995   Couldn't Be Better (8y), (10st 8lb), D. Gallagher
1996   Coome Hill (7y), (10st), J. Osborne
1997   Suny Bay (8y), (11st 8lb), G. Bradley

*KING GEORGE VI CHASE
(1937) Kempton, about 3 miles

1994   Algan (6y), (11st 10lb), P. Chevalier
†1995   One Man (8y), (11st 10lb), R. Dunwoody
1996   One Man (8y), (11st 10lb), R. Dunwoody
1997   See More Business (7y), (11st 10lb), A. Thornton

*CHAMPION HURDLE
(1927) Cheltenham, 2 miles and about ½ f

1995   Alderbrook (6y), (12st), N. Williamson
1996   Collier Bay (6y), (12st), G. Bradley
1997   Make A Stand (6y), (12st), A. McCoy
1998   Istabraq (6y), (12st), C. Swan

*QUEEN MOTHER CHAMPION CHASE
(1959) Cheltenham, about 2 miles

1995   Viking Flagship (8y), (12st), C. Swan
1996   Klairon Davis (7y), (12st), F. Woods
1997   Martha's Son (10y), (12st), R. Farrant
1998   One Man (10y), (12st), B. Harding

*CHELTENHAM GOLD CUP
(1924) 3 miles and about 2½ f

1995   Master Oats (9y), (12st), N. Williamson
1996   Imperial Call (7y), (12st), C. O'Dwyer
1997   Mr Mulligan (9y), (12st), A. McCoy
1998   Cool Dawn (10y), (12st), A. Thornton

LINCOLN HANDICAP
(1965) Doncaster, 1 mile

1995   Roving Minstrel (4y), (8st 3lb), K. Darley
1996   Stone Ridge (4y), (8st 12lb), D. O'Neill
1997   Kuala Lipis (4y), (8st 6lb), T. Quinn
1998   Hunters Of Brora (8y), (9st), J. Weaver

*GRAND NATIONAL
(1837) Liverpool, 4 miles and about 4 f

1995   Royal Athlete (9y), (11st 10lb), J. Titley
1996   Rough Quest (10y), (10st 7lb), M. Fitzgerald
1997   Lord Gyllene (9y), (10st), A. Dobbin
1998   Earth Summit (10y), (10st 5lb), C. Llewellyn

Record times: 8 minutes 47.8 seconds by Mr Frisk in 1990;
9 minutes 1.9 seconds by Red Rum in 1973

*WHITBREAD GOLD CUP
(1957) Sandown, 3 miles and about 5 f

1995   Cache Fleur (9y), (9st 10lb), R. Dunwoody
1996   Life Of A Lord (10y), (11st 10lb), C. Swan
1997   Harwell Lad (8y), (10st), Mr R. Nuttall
1998   Call It A Day (8y), (10st 10lb), A. Maguire

JOCKEY CLUB STAKES
(1894) Newmarket, 1½ miles

1995   Only Royale (6y), (8st 11lb), F. Dettori
1996   Riyadian (4y), (8st 9lb), T. Quinn
1997   Time Allowed (4y), (8st 6lb), J. Reid
1998   Romanov (4y), (8st 9lb), J. Reid

KENTUCKY DERBY
(1875) Louisville, Kentucky, 1¼ miles

1995   Thunder Gulch, G. Stevens
1996   Grindstone, J. Bailey
1997   Silver Charm, G. Stevens
1998   Real Quiet, K. Desormeaux

PRIX DU JOCKEY CLUB
(1836) Chantilly, 1½ miles

1995   Celtic Swing (9st 2lb), K. Darley
1996   Ragmar (9st 2lb), G. Mossé
1997   Peintre Célèbre (9st 2lb), O. Peslier
1998   Dream Well (9st 2lb), C. Asmussen

ASCOT GOLD CUP
(1807) Ascot, 2 miles and about 4 f

1995   Double Trigger (4y), (9st), J. Weaver
1996   Classic Cliché (4y), (9st), M. Kinane
1997   Celeric (5y), (9st 2lb), P. Eddery
1998   Kayf Tara (4y), (9st), F. Dettori

IRISH SWEEPS DERBY
(1866) Curragh, 1½ miles, for three-year-olds

1995   Winged Love (9st), O. Peslier
1996   Zagreb (9st), P. Shanahan
1997   Desert King (9st), C. Roche
1998   Dream Well (9st), C. Asmussen

ECLIPSE STAKES
(1886) Sandown, 1 mile and about 2 f

1995   Halling (4y), (9st 7lb), W. Swinburn
1996   Halling (5y), (9st 7lb), J. Reid
1997   Pilsudski (5y), (9st 7lb), M. Kinane
1998   Daylami (4y), (9st 7lb), F. Dettori

KING GEORGE VI AND QUEEN ELIZABETH DIAMOND
STAKES
(1952) Ascot, 1 mile and about 4 f

1995   Lammtarra (3y), (8st 9lb), F. Dettori
1996   Pentire (4y), (9st 7lb), M. Hills
1997   Swain (5y), (9st 7lb), J. Reid
1998   Swain (6y), (9st 7lb), F. Dettori

GOODWOOD CUP
(1812) Goodwood, about 2 miles

1995   Double Trigger (4y), (9st 5lb), J. Weaver
1996   Grey Shot (4y), (9st), P. Eddery
1997   Double Trigger (6y), (9st), M. Roberts
1998   Double Trigger (7y), (9st 5lb), D. Holland

*National Hunt
†Run on 6 January 1996 because of bad weather

STATISTICS

WINNING FLAT OWNERS 1997

Sheikh Mohammed   £1,460,279
Hamdan Al-Maktoum   1,323,595
Khalid Abdulla   1,176,545
Godolphin   1,149,906
Maktoum Al-Maktoum   899,976
Landon Knight   743,842
Michael Tabor/Mrs John Magnier 703,145
Lord Weinstock   652,927
Robert Sangster   630,504
Peter Winfield   494,650

WINNING FLAT TRAINERS 1997

Michael Stoute	£2,131,543
John Gosden	1,799,154
Henry Cecil	1,612,865
John Dunlop	1,431,803
Saeed bin Suroor	1,162,334
Barry Hills	1,014,233
Luca Cumani	1,006,963
Mark Johnston	913,015
David Loder	761,498
Paul Cole	758,623

LEADING FLAT BREEDERS 1997

	Value
Sheikh Mohammed	£1,439,522
Shadwell Farm	901,088
Juddmonte Farms	891,792
Landon Knight	674,440
Gainsborough Stud Management	647,138
Cheveley Park Stud	453,024
Ballymacoll Stud	430,701
Hesmonds Stud	330,651
Newgate Stud	318,470
Hascombe and Valiant Studs	257,906

WINNING FLAT SIRES 1997

	Horses	Races won	Total value
Silver Hawk (1979) by Roberto	11	15	£899,249
Polish Precedent (1986) by Danzig	13	21	695,355
Sadler's Wells (1981) by Northern Dancer	34	44	688,359
Efisio (1982) by Formidable	36	71	582,323
Danehill (1986) by Danzig	37	48	573,216
Nashwan (1986) by Blushing Groom	19	30	551,686
In The Wings (1986) by Sadler's Wells	14	20	542,374
Soviet Star (1984) by Nureyev	12	20	522,185
Fairy King (1982) by Northern Dancer	27	37	520,670
Machiavellian (1987) by Mr Prospector	19	26	516,909

WINNING FLAT JOCKEYS 1997

	1st	2nd	3rd	Unpl.	Total mts
Kieren Fallon	202	147	119	479	947
Frankie Dettori	176	115	94	395	780
Kevin Darley	128	108	96	510	842
Pat Eddery	116	87	65	363	631
John Reid	110	105	97	510	822
Seb Sanders	105	127	113	601	946
Darryll Holland	104	96	77	443	720
Jason Weaver	100	89	70	392	651
Richard Hills	85	73	86	280	524
Tim Sprake	84	71	87	503	745
Michael Hills	84	64	72	341	561

WINNING NATIONAL HUNT JOCKEYS 1997–8

	1st	2nd	3rd	Unpl.	Total mts
Tony McCoy	253	163	92	323	831
Richard Johnson	120	137	105	398	760
Richard Dunwoody	103	76	64	274	517
Mick Fitzgerald	102	86	71	326	585
Adrian Maguire	93	65	53	187	398
Carl Llewellyn	82	77	84	318	561
Andrew Thornton	80	72	83	359	594
Norman Williamson	77	69	72	290	508
Peter Niven	73	43	54	192	362
*Robert Thornton	71	73	75	328	547

* Conditional (apprentice) jockey
The above statistics are the copyright of *The Sporting Life*

ICE HOCKEY

World Championship final 1998: Sweden beat Finland 1–0
Super League Championship play-off final 1998: Ayr Scottish Eagles beat Cardiff Devils 3–2
Super League Championship 1998: Ayr Scottish Eagles
Benson and Hedges Cup final 1997: Ayr Scottish Eagles beat Cardiff Devils 2–1
Stanley Cup final 1998: Detroit beat Washington 4–0

ICE SKATING

BRITISH CHAMPIONSHIPS 1997
Hull, December

Men: Steven Cousins
Women: Jenna Arrowsmith
Pairs: Marsha Poluliaschenko and Andrew Seabrook
Ice Dance: Charlotte Clements and Gary Shortland

EUROPEAN CHAMPIONSHIPS 1998
Milan, January

Men: Alexei Yagudin (Russia)
Women: Maria Butyrskaya (Russia)
Pairs: Elena Berezhnaya and Anton Sikharulidze (Russia)
Ice Dance: Pasha Grishuk and Evgeny Platov (Russia)

WORLD CHAMPIONSHIPS 1998
Minneapolis, March–April

Men: Alexei Yagudin (Russia)
Women: Michelle Kwan (USA)
Pairs: Elena Berezhnaya and Anton Sikharulidze (Russia)
Ice Dance: Anjelika Krylova and Oleg Ovsyannikov (Russia)

JUDO

WORLD CHAMPIONSHIPS 1997
Paris, October

MEN

Heavyweight (over 95 kg): David Douillet (France)
Light-heavyweight (95 kg): Pavel Nastula (Poland)
Middleweight (86 kg): Jeon Ki-young (S. Korea)
Welter (78 kg): Cho In-chol (S. Korea)
Lightweight (71 kg): Kenzo Nakamura (Japan)
Junior lightweight (65 kg): Kim Hyuk (S. Korea)
Bantamweight (60 kg): Tadahiro Nomura (Japan)
Openweight: Rajal Kubacki (Poland)

WOMEN

Heavyweight (over 72 kg): Christine Cicot (France)
Light-heavyweight (72 kg): Noriko Anno (Japan)
Middleweight (66 kg): Kate Howey (GB)
Welter (61 kg): Severine Vandenhende (France)
Lightweight (56 kg): Isabel Fernandez (Spain)
Junior lightweight (52 kg): Marie-Claire Restoux (France)
Bantamweight (48 kg): Tamua Ryoko (Japan)
Openweight: Daina Beltran (Cuba)

BRITISH NATIONAL CHAMPIONSHIPS 1997
Cannock, December

MEN

Heavyweight (over 95 kg): Richard Blanes
Light-heavyweight (95 kg): Daley Lasebikin
Middleweight (86 kg): Sam Delahay
Light-middleweight (78 kg): Luke Preston
Lightweight (71 kg): Anthony Johnson

Featherweight (65 kg): Simon Moss
Bantamweight (60 kg): James Johnson

WOMEN
Heavyweight (over 72 kg): Simone Callender
Light-heavyweight (72 kg): Rowena Birch
Middleweight (66 kg): Karen Powell
Light-middleweight (61 kg): Rosie Felton
Lightweight (56 kg): Nicola Fairbrother
Featherweight (52 kg): Elise Summers
Bantamweight (48 kg): Vicki Dunn

LAWN TENNIS

MAJOR CHAMPIONSHIPS 1998

AUSTRALIAN OPEN CHAMPIONSHIPS
Melbourne, 19 January–1 February

Men's Singles: Petr Korda (Czech Republic) beat Marcelo
   Rios (Chile) 6–2, 6–2, 6–2
Women's Singles: Martina Hingis (Switzerland) beat
   Conchita Martinez (Spain) 6–3, 6–3
Men's Doubles: Jonas Bjorkman (Sweden) and Jacco Eltingh
   (Holland) beat Todd Woodbridge and Mark
   Woodforde (Australia) 6–2, 5–7, 2–6, 6–4, 6–3
Women's Doubles: Martina Hingis (Switzerland) and
   Mirjana Lucic (Croatia) beat Lindsay Davenport (USA)
   and Natasha Zvereva (Belarus) 6–4, 2–6, 6–3
Mixed Doubles: Venus Williams and Justin Gimelstob
   (USA) beat Helena Sukova and Cyril Suk (Czech
   Republic) 6–2, 6–1

FRENCH OPEN CHAMPIONSHIPS
Paris, 25 May–7 June

Men's Singles: Carlos Moyà (Spain) beat Alex Corretja
   (Spain) 6–3, 7–5, 6–3
Women's Singles: Arantxa Sànchez Vicario (Spain) beat
   Monica Seles (USA) 7–6, 0–6, 6–2
Men's Doubles: Jacco Eltingh and Paul Haarhuis (Holland)
   beat Mark Knowles (Bahamas) and Daniel Nestor
   (Canada) 6–3, 3–6, 6–3
Women's Doubles: Martina Hingis (Switzerland) and Jana
   Novotna (Czech Republic) beat Lindsay Davenport
   (USA) and Natasha Zvereva (Belarus) 6–1, 7–6
Mixed Doubles: Venus Williams and Justin Gimelstob
   (USA) beat Serena Williams (USA) and Luis Lobo
   (Argentina) 6–4, 6–4

ALL-ENGLAND CHAMPIONSHIPS
Wimbledon, 22 June–5 July

Men's Singles: Pete Sampras (USA) beat Goran Ivanisevic
   (Croatia) 6–7, 7–6, 6–4, 3–6, 6–2
Women's Singles: Jana Novotna (Czech Republic) beat
   Nathalie Tauziat (France) 6–4, 7–6
Men's Doubles: Jacco Eltingh and Paul Haarhuis (Holland)
   beat Todd Woodbridge and Mark Woodforde
   (Australia) 2–6, 6–4, 7–6, 5–7, 10–8
Women's Doubles: Martina Hingis (Switzerland) and Jana
   Novotna (Czech Republic) beat Natasha Zvereva
   (Belarus) and Lindsay Davenport (USA) 6–3, 3–6, 8–6
Mixed Doubles: Serena Williams (USA) and Max Mirnyi
   (Belarus) beat Mirjana Lucic (Croatia) and Mahesh
   Bhupathi (India) 6–4, 6–4

US OPEN CHAMPIONSHIPS
New York, 31 August–13 September

Men's Singles: Patrick Rafter (Australia) beat Mark
   Philippoussis (Australia) 6–3, 3–6, 6–2, 6–0
Women's Singles: Lindsay Davenport (USA) beat Martina
   Hingis (Switzerland) 6–3, 7–5

Men's Doubles: Sandon Stolle (Australia) and Cyril Suk
   (Czech Republic) beat Mark Knowles (Bahamas) and
   Daniel Nestor (Canada) 4–6, 7–6, 6–2
Women's Doubles: Martina Hingis (Switzerland) and Jana
   Novotna (Czech Republic) beat Lindsay Davenport
   (USA) and Natasha Zvereva (Belarus) 6–3, 6–3
Mixed Doubles: Serena Williams (USA) and Max Mirnyi
   (Belarus) beat Lisa Raymond (USA) and Patrick
   Galbraith (USA) 6–2, 6–2

TEAM CHAMPIONSHIPS

Davis Cup final 1997: Sweden beat USA 5–0
Fed Cup final 1997: France beat Holland 4–1
Fed Cup final 1998: Spain beat Switzerland 3–2
LTA County Cup 1998:
   Men: Hampshire and Isle of Wight
   Women: Surrey

NATIONAL CHAMPIONSHIPS 1997
Telford, November

Men's Singles: Tim Henman (Oxon) beat Chris Wilkinson
   (Hants) 6–1, 6–4
Women's Singles: Sam Smith (Essex) beat Louise Latimer
   (Warks) 6–4, 6–1
Men's Doubles: Danny Sapsford (Surrey) and Tom Spinks
   (Norfolk) beat Andrew Foster (Staffs) and Paul
   Robinson (Yorks) 6–3, 1–0 ret.
Women's Doubles: Lucie Ahl (Devon) and Mandy
   Wainwright (Essex) beat Julie Pullin (Sussex) and
   Lorna Woodroffe (Surrey) 4–6, 7–5, 7–6

MOTOR CYCLING

---

500 CC GRAND PRIX 1997

Australian (Phillip Island): Alex Criville (Spain), Honda
Riders' Championship 1997: 1. Michael Doohan (Australia),
   Honda, 340 points; 2. Tadayuki Okada (Japan), Honda,
   197 points; 3. Nobuatsu Aoki (Japan), Honda, 179
   points

500 CC GRAND PRIX 1998

Japanese (Suzuka): Max Biaggi (Italy), Honda
Malaysian (Pasir Gudang): Michael Doohan (Australia),
   Honda
Spanish (Jerez): Alex Criville (Spain), Honda
Italian (Mugello): Michael Doohan (Australia), Honda
French (Toulon): Alex Criville (Spain), Honda
Madrid (Jarama): Carlos Checa (Spain), Honda
Dutch (Assen): Michael Doohan (Australia), Honda
British (Donington Park): Simon Crafar (New Zealand),
   Yamaha
German (Sachsenring): Michael Doohan (Australia),
   Honda
Czech (Brno): Max Biaggi (Italy), Honda
San Marino (Imola): Michael Doohan (Australia), Honda
Catalonian (Barcelona): Michael Doohan (Australia),
   Honda

Senior Manx Grand Prix 1998: Gordon Blackley (Honda)
Senior TT 1998, Isle of Man: Ian Simpson (Honda)
Junior TT 1998, Isle of Man: Michael Rutter (Honda)

British Superbike Champion 1998: Niall Mackenzie (Yamaha)
500cc World Motocross Champion 1998: Joel Smets (Belgium),
   Husaberg

MOTOR RACING

FORMULA ONE GRAND PRIX 1997

Japanese (Suzuka): Michael Schumacher (Germany), Ferrari

European (Jerez): Mika Hakkinen (Finland), McLaren-Mercedes

Drivers' World Championship 1997: 1. Jacques Villeneuve (Canada), Williams-Renault, 81 points; 2. Heinz-Harald Frentzen (Germany), Williams-Renault, 42 points; 3. Jean Alesi (France), Benetton-Renault, 36 points

Constructors' World Championship 1997: 1. Williams-Renault, 123 points; 2. Ferrari, 102 points; 3. Benetton-Renault, 67 points

FORMULA ONE GRAND PRIX 1998

Australian (Melbourne): Mika Hakkinen (Finland), McLaren-Mercedes

Brazilian (São Paulo): Mika Hakkinen (Finland), McLaren-Mercedes

Argentine (Buenos Aires): Michael Schumacher (Germany), Ferrari

San Marino (Imola): David Coulthard (GB), McLaren-Mercedes

Spanish (Barcelona): Mika Hakkinen (Finland), McLaren-Mercedes

Monaco (Monte Carlo): Mika Hakkinen (Finland), McLaren-Mercedes

Canadian (Montreal): Michael Schumacher (Germany), Ferrari

French (Magny-Cours): Michael Schumacher (Germany), Ferrari

British (Silverstone): Michael Schumacher (Germany), Ferrari

Austrian (Zeltweg): Mika Hakkinen (Finland), McLaren-Mercedes

German (Hockenheim): Mika Hakkinen (Finland), McLaren-Mercedes

Hungarian (Budapest): Michael Schumacher (Germany), Ferrari

Belgian (Spa-Francorchamps): Damon Hill (GB), Jordan-Honda

Italian (Monza): Michael Schumacher (Germany), Ferrari

Luxembourg: Mika Hakkinen (Finland), McLaren-Mercedes

Indianapolis 500 1998: Eddie Cheever (USA), Dallara Aurora

Le Mans 24-hour Race 1998: A. McNish (GB), L. Aiello (France) and S. Ortelli (France), Porsche

MOTOR RALLYING

1997

San Remo Rally: Colin McRae (GB), Subaru Impreza

Rally Australia: Colin McRae (GB), Subaru Impreza

RAC Rally: Colin McRae (GB), Subaru Impreza

Drivers' World Championship 1997: Tommi Makinen (Finland), Mitsubishi Lancer, 63 points

Manufacturers' World Championship 1997: Subaru, 114 points

1998

Paris-Dakar Rally: Jean-Pierre Fontenay (France), Mitsubishi

China Rally 1998: Colin McRae (GB), Subaru Impreza

Monte Carlo Rally 1998: Carlos Sainz (Spain), Toyota Corolla

Swedish Rally: Tommi Makinen (Finland), Mitsubishi Lancer

Safari Rally: Richard Burns (GB), Mitsubishi Lancer

Rally of Portugal: Colin McRae (GB), Subaru Impreza

Catalunya Rally: Didier Auriol (France), Toyota Corolla

Corsica Rally: Colin McRae (GB), Subaru Impreza

Argentine Rally: Tommi Makinen (Finland), Mitsubishi Lancer

Acropolis Rally: Colin McRae (GB), Subaru Impreza

New Zealand Rally: Carlos Sainz (Spain), Toyota Corolla

Rally of Finland (Jyvaskyla, Finland): Tommi Makinen (Finland), Mitsubishi Lancer

Rally of Wales 1998: Martin Rowe, Renault Megane

Scottish Rally 1998: Alister McRae, Volkswagen Golf Gti

Ulster Rally 1998: Gwyndaf Evans, Seat Ibiza

British Champion 1998: Martin Rowe, Renault Megane

NETBALL

TESTS AND INTERNATIONALS

1997		
6 Dec	Brighton	England 35, New Zealand 47
8 Dec	Cardiff	Wales 39, New Zealand 77
10 Dec	Birmingham	England 41, New Zealand 53
13 Dec	Newcastle	England 45, New Zealand 75
1998		
24 Jan	Belfast	N. Ireland 26, Wales 67
8 Feb	Cardiff	Wales 39, England 48
5 April	Sydney	Australia 72, England 32
6 April	Sydney	Australia 62, England 27
17–19 April	Cardiff	England 84, N. Ireland 19
		England 62, Scotland 18
		England 96, Malta 11
		England 54, Wales 37
		Scotland 51, N. Ireland 46
		Scotland 51, Malta 37
		N. Ireland 67, Malta 51
		Wales, 72, N. Ireland 34
		Wales 87, Malta 16
		Wales 60, Scotland 35
9 July	Hemel Hempstead	England 56, West Indies 48
11 July	Birmingham	England 50, West Indies 51
15 July	Sheffield	England 55, West Indies 56
17 July	Cardiff	Wales 42, West Indies 47

Inter-County Championship final 1998: Middlesex beat Essex Metropolitan 15–14

National Clubs Championship final 1998: Grasshoppers beat Response Electrical 43–41

English Counties League Championship 1998: Essex Metropolitan

National Clubs League Championship 1998: Linden

POLO

Prince of Wales's Trophy final 1998: Jerudong Park beat Ellerston 9–8

Queen's Cup final 1998: Ellerston beat Labegorce 13–3

Warwickshire Cup final 1998: Lovelocks beat Black Bears 10–9

Gold Cup (British Open) final 1998: Ellerston beat C. S. Brooks 13–6

Coronation Cup 1998: Chile beat England 8–7
Prince Philip Trophy 1998: Ellerston beat Lovelocks 12–8
Arena Gold Cup 1998: Ashfronts beat Clubhouse 19–14
Arena European Nations 1998: Young England beat England 15–14
Varsity Match 1998: Cambridge beat Oxford 13–1

RACKETS

World Singles Champion: James Male (GB)
World Doubles Challenge 1998: Neil Smith and Shannon Hazell (GB) beat Willie Boone and Peter Brake (GB) 7–6
Professional Singles Championship final 1998: Neil Smith beat Peter Brake 3–2
British Open Singles Championship final 1998: Willie Boone (GB) beat Toby Sawrey-Cookson (GB) 4–0
British Open Doubles Championship final 1998: James Male and Mark Hue Williams (GB) beat Neil Smith and Shannon Hazell (GB) 4–1
Amateur Singles Championship final 1997: James Male beat Guy Barker 3–0
Amateur Doubles Championship final 1998: Willie Boone and James Male beat Mark Hue Williams and Matthew Windows 4–0
National League 1998: Old Wellingtonians
Noel Bruce Cup final 1997 (public schools' old boys' doubles championship): Eton I (Willie Boone and Guy Smith-Bingham) beat Wellington I (Toby Sawrey-Cookson and Tim Cockroft) 4–3
Varsity Match 1998: Oxford beat Cambridge 3–0

REAL TENNIS

World Singles Challenge 1998: Robert Fahey (Australia) beat Julian Snow (GB) 7–4
Professional Singles Championship final 1998: Chris Bray (GB) beat Paul Tabley (Australia) 3–2
Professional Doubles Championship final 1998: Chris Bray and Mike Gooding (GB) beat James Male and Ruaraidh Gunn (GB) 3–0
British Open Singles Championship final 1997: Chris Bray (GB) beat Robert Fahey (Australia) 3–0
British Open Doubles Championship final 1997: Julian Snow and James Male (GB) beat Robert Fahey (Australia) and Mike Gooding (GB) 3–0
Amateur Singles Championship final 1998: Julian Snow (GB) beat Nigel Pendrigh (GB) 3–0
Amateur Doubles Championship final 1998: Julian Snow and James Acheson-Gray (GB) beat Nigel Pendrigh (GB) and Tim Goodale (USA) 3–1
Henry Leaf Cup final 1998 (public schools' old boys' doubles championship): Canford I beat Winchester I 2–0
Varsity Match 1998: Oxford beat Cambridge 5–1
Women's British Open Singles Championship final 1998: Penny Lumley (GB) beat Sue Haswell (GB) 2–0
Women's British Open Doubles Championship final 1998: Sally Jones and Alex Garside (GB) beat Fiona Deuchar (Australia) and Charlotte Cornwallis (GB) 2–1

ROAD WALKING

RWA Men's National 20 km Walk
Leicester, 21 March 1998
Individual: Martin Bell (Cardiff), 1 hr. 27 min. 22 sec.
Team: Leicester, 46 points

RWA Women's National 10 km Walk
Leicester, 21 March 1998
Individual: Lisa Langford-Kehler (Wolverhampton), 47 min. 10 sec.
Team: Sheffield, 16 points

European Road Walking Cup
Dudince, Czech Republic, 25 April 1998
Men's 20 km: Francisco Fernandez (Spain), 1 hr. 20 min. 31 sec.
Men's 50 km: Tomasz Lipiec (Poland), 3 hr. 42 min. 57 sec.
Men's overall team: Spain, 45 points
Women's 10 km: Nadyezda Ryashkina (Russia), 43 min. 06 sec.
Women's overall team: Russia, 15 points

RWA Men's 10 Miles Walk
Leicester, 16 May 1998
Individual: Andi Drake (Coventry), 1 hr. 11 min. 14 sec.
Team: Road Hoggs, 34 points

RWA Women's 10 Miles Walk
Leicester, 16 May 1998
Individual: Vicky Lupton (Sheffield), 1 hr. 21 min. 15 sec.
Team: Sheffield, 11 points

RWA Men's 20 Miles Walk
Brighton, 6 June 1998
Individual: Les Morton (Sheffield), 2 hr. 43 min. 01 sec.
Team: Coventry, 23 points

RWA Women's 5,000 m Walk
Brighton, 6 June 1998
Individual: Kim Braznell (Dudley), 24 min. 35 sec.
Team: Birchfield, 15 points

Men's National 50 km Walk
Chesterfield, 29 August 1998
Individual: Tim Watt (Steyning), 4 hr. 32 min. 00 sec.
Team: Leicester, 14 points

Women's National 20 km Walk
Chesterfield, 29 August 1998
Individual: Vicky Lupton (Sheffield), 1 hr. 44 min. 35 sec.
Team: Steyning, 15 points

ROWING

WORLD CHAMPIONSHIPS 1998
Cologne, Germany, 6–13 September

MEN
Coxed pairs: Australia
Coxless pairs: Germany
Coxed fours: Australia
Coxless fours: Great Britain
Single sculls: Rob Waddell (New Zealand)
Double sculls: Germany
Quad sculls: Italy
Eights: USA

WOMEN
Coxless pairs: Canada
Coxless fours: Ukraine
Single sculls: Irina Fedotova (Russia)
Double sculls: Great Britain
Quad sculls: Germany
Eights: Romania

NATIONAL CHAMPIONSHIPS 1998
Strathclyde Country Park, July

MEN
Coxed pairs: Upper Thames
Coxless pairs: Leander

Coxed fours: Notts County RA
Coxless fours: Notts County RA
Single sculls: Greg Searle (Molesey)
Double sculls: Castle Semple/Glasgow
Quad sculls: Isis/London/Rob Roy/Queen's Tower
Eights: Scullers Molesey Comp

WOMEN
Coxless pairs: Upper Thames
Coxed fours: Kingston/Imperial College/Thames/Marlow
Coxless fours: Lady Eleanor Holles/St Peter's School
Single sculls: Katherine Grainger (St Andrew)
Double sculls: King's School Canterbury/Tideway Scullers
Quad sculls: King's School Canterbury/Tideway Scullers/
   Kingston/Headington School
Eights: Thames A

THE 144th UNIVERSITY BOAT RACE
Putney–Mortlake, 4 miles 1 f, 180 yd, 28 March 1998

Cambridge beat Oxford by 3 lengths; 16 min. 19 sec.
Cambridge have won 75 times, Oxford 68 and there has
been one dead heat. The record time is 16 min. 19 sec.,
rowed by Cambridge in 1998

Women's Boat Race 1998 (Henley): Cambridge beat
   Oxford by 1¼ lengths; 6 min. 25 sec.

HENLEY ROYAL REGATTA 1998

Grand Challenge Cup: Ruder Club Hansa von 1898 e.V.
   Dortmund and Berliner Ruder Club (Germany) beat
   Société d'Encouragement du Sport Nautique and
   Emulation Nautique de Bordeaux (France) by 2½
   lengths
Ladies' Challenge Plate: Harvard University (USA) beat
   Cambridge University and Star Club by 1½ lengths
Thames Challenge Cup: London A beat Bowbridge by ⅔
   length
Temple Challenge Cup: Imperial College, London beat
   University of Wales College, Cardiff by 1 length
Princess Elizabeth Challenge Cup: Radley College A beat St
   Mary's Preparatory School (USA) by ½ length
Stewards' Challenge Cup: Leander beat Danmarks Rocenter
   (Denmark) by ¾ length
Prince Philip Challenge Cup: Hrvatski Veslacki Klub 'Gusar'
   Split (Croatia) beat Emulation Nautique de Boulogne
   and Aviron Valentinois (France) by ¾ length
Queen Mother Challenge Cup: Augusta (USA) beat
   Commercial (Ireland) by 1 length
Visitors' Challenge Cup: Isis beat Imperial College, London
   by 1¾ lengths
Wyfold Challenge Cup: Bowbridge beat Worcester by 1
   length
Britannia Challenge Cup: Oxford Brookes University beat
   Neptune (Ireland) by ¾ length
Fawley Challenge Cup: Windsor Boys' School and Claire's
   Court School beat Wycliffe College by 3 lengths
Silver Goblets and Nickalls' Challenge Cup: L. Beghin and A.
   Beghin (France) beat O. Martinov and N. Saraga
   (Croatia) easily
Double Sculls Challenge Cup: Y. Deslavière and F. Kowal
   (France) beat G. Rackman and R. Tucker (USA) by 3
   lengths
Diamond Challenge Sculls: J. Koven (USA) beat G. Searle
   (Molesey) by 2¼ lengths
Princess Royal Challenge Cup: M. Brandin (Sweden) beat G.
   Douglas (Australia) by 1¾ lengths
Women's Invitation Eights: San Diego (USA) beat Marlow
   and Thames by ⅓ length

OTHER ROWING EVENTS

Cambridge Lents 1998: Men, Trinity; *Women,* Emmanuel

Oxford Torpids 1998: Men, Oriel; *Women,* Osler-Green
Oxford Summer Eights 1998: Men, Oriel; *Women,* Osler-
   Green
Cambridge Mays 1998: Men, Caius; *Women,* Pembroke
Head of the River 1998: Men, Leander I; *Women,* Marlow A
Scullers Head of the River 1998: Greg Searle (Molesey)
Doggett's Coat and Badge 1998: David Bushnell (Upper
   Thames)
Wingfield Sculls 1998: Greg Searle (Molesey)
London Cup 1998: Ian Watson (London)
Thames World Sculling Challenge 1997: Men, Greg Searle
   (GB); *Women,* Guin Batten (GB)

RUGBY FIVES

National Singles Championship final 1997: Ian Fuller beat
   Neil Roberts 15–5, 15–10
National Doubles Championship final 1998: Wayne Enstone
   and Neil Roberts beat Ian Fuller and David Hebden
   15–10, 15–8
National Club Championship 1998: Alleyn Old Boys
National Schools' Singles Championship final 1998: Ben Lovett
   (Christ's Hospital) beat Giles Corner (St Paul's) 9–11,
   11–4, 11–2
National Schools' Doubles Championship final 1998: St Paul's I
   beat St Paul's II 11–1, 11–5
Varsity Match 1998: Oxford beat Cambridge 243–190

RUGBY LEAGUE

TESTS

1997		
1 Nov	Wembley	Great Britain 14, Australia 38
8 Nov	Old Trafford	Great Britain 20, Australia 12
16 Nov	Elland Road	Great Britain 20, Australia 37

COMPETITIONS

Challenge Cup final 1998 (Wembley, 2 May): Sheffield
   Eagles beat Wigan Warriors 17–8
Division 1 Grand final 1998: Wakefield Trinity beat
   Featherstone Rovers 24–22
World Club Championship final 1997: Brisbane Broncos beat
   Hunter Mariners 36–12
Varsity Match 1998: Cambridge beat Oxford 24–10

AMATEUR RUGBY LEAGUE 1997–8

County Championship: Yorkshire
National Inter-League Open Age Shield Competition: Bradford
National Cup Open Age Competition: Redhill
National League Premier Division Champions: Blackbrook

RUGBY UNION

FIVE NATIONS' CHAMPIONSHIP 1998

7 Feb	Paris	France 24, England 17
	Dublin	Ireland 16, Scotland 17
21 Feb	Twickenham	England 60, Wales 26
	Murrayfield	Scotland 16, France 51
7 March	Wembley	Wales 19, Scotland 13
	Paris	France 18, Ireland 16
21 March	Dublin	Ireland 21, Wales 30
22 March	Murrayfield	Scotland 20, England 34
4 April	Twickenham	England 35, Ireland 17
5 April	Wembley	Wales 0, France 51

	P	W	D	L	Points		Total
					F	A	
France	4	4	0	0	144	49	8
England	4	3	0	1	146	87	6
Wales	4	2	0	2	75	145	4
Scotland	4	1	0	3	66	120	2
Ireland	4	0	0	4	70	100	0

OTHER INTERNATIONAL MATCHES

1997
15 Nov	Twickenham	England 15, Australia 15
	Dublin	Ireland 15, New Zealand 63
16 Nov	Swansea	Wales 46, Tonga 12
22 Nov	Old Trafford	England 8, New Zealand 25
	Murrayfield	Scotland 8, Australia 37
29 Nov	Twickenham	England 11, S. Africa 29
	Wembley	Wales 7, New Zealand 42
30 Nov	Dublin	Ireland 33, Canada 11
6 Dec	Twickenham	England 26, New Zealand 26
	Murrayfield	Scotland 10, South Africa 68
20 Dec	Bologna	Italy 37, Ireland 22

1998
24 Jan	Treviso	Italy 25, Scotland 21
7 Feb	Llanelli	Wales 23, Italy 20
26 May	Suva	Fiji 51, Scotland 26
6 June	Brisbane	Australia 76, England 0
	Harare	Zimbabwe 11, Wales 49
13 June	Sydney	Australia 45, Scotland 3
	Bloemfontein	South Africa 37, Ireland 13
20 June	Dunedin	New Zealand 64, England 22
	Brisbane	Australia 33, Scotland 11
	Pretoria	South Africa 33, Ireland 0
27 June	Auckland	New Zealand 40, England 10
	Pretoria	South Africa 96, Wales 13
4 July	Cape Town	South Africa 18, England 0

European Club Cup final 1998 (Bordeaux, 31 January): Bath beat Brive 19–18

Women's World Cup final 1998 (Amsterdam, 16 May): New Zealand beat USA 44–12

DOMESTIC COMPETITIONS

Premiership: League 1, Newcastle Falcons, 38 points; *League 2,* Bedford, 38 points

National League: Division 1, Worcester, 48 points; *Division 2 (north),* Birmingham/Solihull, 46 points; *Division 2 (south),* Camberley, 47 points

County Championship final 1998: Cheshire beat Cornwall 21–14

Tetley's Bitter Cup final 1998: Saracens beat Wasps 48–18

Scottish Premiership: Division 1, Watsonians, 44 points; *Division 2,* Glasgow Hawks, 58 points; *Division 3,* Selkirk, 48 points

Scottish Cup final 1998: Glasgow Hawks beat Kelso 36–14

Welsh National League: Premier Division, Swansea, 35 points; *Division 1,* Caerphilly, 81 points; *Division 2,* Tredegar, 54 points; *Division 3,* Llantrinsant, 55 points; *Division 4,* Vardre, 54 points

Welsh Challenge (Swalec) Cup final 1998: Llanelli beat Ebbw Vale 19–12

Irish League: Division 1, Shannon, 24 points; *Division 2,* Galwegians, 26 points; *Division 3,* Portadown, 20 points; *Division 4,* County Carlow, 16 points

Ulster Cup final 1998: Dungannon beat Malone 19–16

Services Championship 1998: Army beat Royal Navy 36–22; Royal Navy beat Royal Air Force 11–8; Army beat Royal Air Force 23–7

Varsity Match 1997: Cambridge beat Oxford 29–17

Middlesex Sevens final 1998: Barbarians beat Leicester 38–28

SHOOTING

129TH NATIONAL RIFLE ASSOCIATION IMPERIAL MEETING
Bisley, July 1998

Queen's Prize: Philip Bennison, 300.40 v-bulls
Grand Aggregate: Jane Messer, 648.80 v-bulls
Prince of Wales Prize: A. McCullough, 75.13 v-bulls
St George's Vase: Stuart Collings, 150.21 v-bulls
Allcomers Aggregate: Jane Messer, 372.42 v-bulls
National Trophy: England, 2,048.225 v-bulls
Kolapore Cup: Great Britain, 1,176.140 v-bulls
Chancellor's Trophy: Cambridge University, 1,150.106 v-bulls
Musketeers Cup: Nottingham University, 581.55 v-bulls
Vizianagram Trophy: House of Lords, 622.24 v-bulls
County Long-Range Championship: Norfolk, 567.45 v-bulls
Mackinnon Challenge Cup: England, 1,163.138 v-bulls
The Ashburton: Epsom, 474 points
The Elcho: Scotland, 1,677.142 v-bulls
The Albert: Stuart Collings, 212.19 v-bulls
Hopton Challenge Cup: Stuart Collings, 947.70 v-bulls

CLAY PIGEON SHOOTING

World Sporting Championship 1998: George Digweed (England), 191 + 17
International Down-the-Line Cup 1998: England, 5,840/6,000
International Skeet Cup 1998: Scotland
International Sporting Cup 1998: England, 897/1,000
British Open Down-the-Line Championship 1998: Michael Milne (Scotland), 297/300
British Open Skeet Championship 1998: Rob Hibbert (England), 100/100
British Open Sporting Championship 1998: Richard Faulds (England), 74 + 23
Mackintosh Trophy 1998: Canada, 5,935/6,000
Coronation Cup 1998: John Winn (England), 379/400

SNOOKER

1997
Regal Masters: Nigel Bond (England) beat Alan McManus (Scotland) 9–8
Grand Prix: Dominic Dale (Wales) beat John Higgins (Scotland) 9–6
Benson and Hedges Championship: Andy Hicks (England) beat Paul Davies (Wales) 9–6
UK Professional Championship: Ronnie O'Sullivan (England) beat Stephen Hendry (Scotland) 10–6
German Open: John Higgins (Scotland) beat John Parrott (England) 9–4

1998
Regal Welsh: Paul Hunter (England) beat John Higgins (Scotland) 9–5
Benson and Hedges Masters: Mark Williams (Wales) beat Stephen Hendry (Scotland) 10–9
Regal Scottish Open: Ronnie O'Sullivan (England) beat John Higgins (Scotland) 9–5
Thailand Masters: Stephen Hendry (Scotland) beat John Parrott (England) 9–6
Irish Masters: Ronnie O'Sullivan (England) beat Ken Doherty (Rep. of Ireland) 9–3; Doherty was awarded the title after O'Sullivan failed a drugs test
British Open: John Higgins (Scotland) beat Stephen Hendry (Scotland) 9–8

World Championship: John Higgins (Scotland) beat Ken Doherty (Ireland) 18−12

Women's National Championship 1997: Karen Corr (Bourne) beat Kelly Fisher (Pontefract) 4−2
Women's UK Championship 1997: Karen Corr (Bourne) beat Lynette Horsburgh (Blackpool) 4−3
Women's Scottish Regal Masters 1998: Karen Corr (Bourne) beat Kelly Fisher (Pontefract) 4−1
Women's Welsh Regal Masters 1998: Karen Corr (Bourne) beat Tessa Davidson (Bicester) 4−0
Women's British Open 1998: Karen Corr (Bourne) beat Kelly Fisher (Pontefract) 4−0

SPEEDWAY

Elite League Champions 1997: Bradford
Elite League Riders' Championship 1997: Greg Hancock (USA)

GRAND PRIX 1998

Czech (Prague): Tony Rickardsson (Sweden)
German (Pocking): Tony Rickardsson (Sweden)
Danish (Vojens): Hans Nielsen (Denmark)
British (Coventry): Jason Crump (Australia)
Swedish (Linkoping): Tony Rickardsson (Sweden)
Polish (Bydgoszcz): Tomasz Gollob (Poland)

World Champion 1998: Tony Rickardsson (Sweden)
World Team Cup final 1998: USA
World Championship, Overseas final 1998: Jason Lyons (Australia)
World Championship, British final 1998: Chris Louis (Ipswich)
World Championship, Intercontinental final 1998: Brian Karger (Denmark)

SQUASH RACKETS

MEN
World Open Championship final 1997: Rodney Eyles (Australia) beat Peter Nicol (GB) 3−0
World Team Championship final 1997: England beat Canada 3−0
European Team Championship final 1998: England beat Finland 3−1
European Club Championship 1998: Pontefract (GB)
British Open Championship final 1998: Peter Nicol (GB) beat Jansher Khan (Pakistan) 3−0
National Championship final 1998: Simon Parke (Yorks) beat Mark Chaloner (Lincs) 3−0

WOMEN
World Open Championship final 1997: Sarah Fitz-Gerald (Australia) beat Michelle Martin (Australia) 3−2
European Team Championship final 1998: England beat Germany 3−0
European Club Championship 1998: Lee-on-Solent (GB)
British Open Championship final 1998: Michelle Martin (Australia) beat Sarah Fitz-Gerald (Australia) 3−0
National Championship final 1998: Sue Wright (Kent) beat Cassie Jackman (Norfolk) 3−1

SWIMMING

WORLD CHAMPIONSHIPS 1998
Perth, January

MEN
50 metres freestyle: Bill Pilczuk (USA)
100 metres freestyle: Alexander Popov (Russia)
200 metres freestyle: Michael Klim (Australia)
400 metres freestyle: Ian Thorpe (Australia)
1,500 metres freestyle: Grant Hackett (Australia)
100 metres backstroke: Lenny Krayzelburg (USA)
200 metres backstroke: Lenny Krayzelburg (USA)
100 metres breaststroke: Frederik Deburghgraeve (Belgium)
200 metres breaststroke: Kurt Grote (USA)
100 metres butterfly: Michael Klim (Australia)
200 metres butterfly: Denis Silantiev (Ukraine)
200 metres medley: Marcel Wouda (Holland)
400 metres medley: Tom Dolan (USA)
4 × 100 metres freestyle relay: USA
4 × 200 metres freestyle relay: Australia
4 × 100 metres medley relay: Australia

WOMEN
50 metres freestyle: Amy Van Dyken (USA)
100 metres freestyle: Jenny Thompson (Australia)
200 metres freestyle: Claudia Poll (Costa Rica)
400 metres freestyle: Chen Yan (China)
800 metres freestyle: Brooke Bennett (USA)
100 metres backstroke: Lea Maurer (USA)
200 metres backstroke: Roxana Maracineanu (France)
100 metres breaststroke: Kirsty Kowal (USA)
200 metres breaststroke: Agnes Kovacs (Hungary)
100 metres butterfly: Jenny Thompson (Australia)
200 metres butterfly: Susie O'Neill (Australia)
200 metres medley: Wu Yanyan (China)
400 metres medley: Chen Yan (China)
4 × 100 metres freestyle relay: USA
4 × 200 metres freestyle relay: Germany
4 × 100 metres medley relay: USA

NATIONAL CHAMPIONSHIPS 1998
Sheffield, July

MEN
50 metres freestyle: Mark Foster (University of Bath)
100 metres freestyle: Sion Brinn (University of Bath)
200 metres freestyle: Paul Palmer (University of Bath)
400 metres freestyle: Paul Palmer (University of Bath)
1,500 metres freestyle: Graeme Smith (Stockport Metro)
50 metres backstroke: Martin Harris (Tower Hamlet)
100 metres backstroke: Adam Ruckwood (City of Birmingham)
200 metres backstroke: Adam Ruckwood (City of Birmingham)
50 metres breaststroke: Darren Mew (University of Bath)
100 metres breaststroke: Darren Mew (University of Bath)
200 metres breaststroke: Adam Whitehead (City of Coventry)
50 metres butterfly: Mark Foster (University of Bath)
100 metres butterfly: James Hickman (City of Leeds)
200 metres butterfly: James Hickman (City of Leeds)
200 metres medley: James Hickman (City of Leeds)
400 metres medley: James Hickman (City of Leeds)
4 × 100 metres freestyle relay: City of Leeds
4 × 200 metres freestyle relay: University of Bath
4 × 100 metres medley relay: University of Bath

WOMEN
50 metres freestyle: Susan Rolph (City of Newcastle)
100 metres freestyle: Susan Rolph (City of Newcastle)

200 metres freestyle: Claire Huddart (City of Leeds)
400 metres freestyle: Vicki Horner (Stockport Metro)
800 metres freestyle: Sarah Collings (University of Bath)
50 metres backstroke: Melanie Marshall (S. Lincs)
100 metres backstroke: Sarah Price (University of Bath)
200 metres backstroke: Helen Don-Duncan (Ashton Central)
50 metres breaststroke: Jaime King (University of Bath)
100 metres breaststroke: Jaime King (University of Bath)
200 metres breaststroke: Linda Hindmarsh (City of Leeds)
50 metres butterfly: Yvetta Hlavacova (Czech Republic)
100 metres butterfly: Caroline Foot (York City Baths)
200 metres butterfly: Margaretha Pedder (Portsmouth Northsea)
200 metres medley: Susan Rolph (City of Newcastle)
400 metres medley: Samantha Nesbit (Portsmouth Northsea)
4 × 100 metres freestyle relay: City of Leeds
4 × 200 metres freestyle relay: City of Leeds
4 × 100 metres medley relay: University of Bath

TABLE TENNIS

European Nations Cup final 1998: Germany beat Sweden 3–2

ENGLISH NATIONAL CHAMPIONSHIPS 1998
Bath, March

Men's Singles: Matthew Syed (Berks) beat Desmond Douglas (Warks) 3–2
Women's Singles: Lisa Lomas (Berks) beat Nicola Deaton (Derbys) 3–1

Men's Doubles: Alan Cooke (Derbys) and Desmond Douglas (Warks) beat Gareth Herbert (Berks) and Terry Young (Berks) 2–0
Women's Doubles: Andrea Holt (Lancs) and Lisa Lomas (Berks) beat Nicola Deaton (Derbys) and Gemma Schwartz (Berks) 2–0
Mixed Doubles: Nicola Deaton (Derbys) and Alan Cooke (Derbys) beat Andrew Eden (Lancs) and Andrea Holt (Lancs) 2–1

VOLLEYBALL

MEN
World League 1998: Cuba
National League Championship 1998: Tooting Aquila
National Cup final 1998: Tooting Aquila beat Sheffield 3–1

WOMEN
Grand Prix final 1998: Brazil beat Russia 3–0
National League Championship 1998: London Malory
National Cup final 1998: London Malory beat Ashcombe Guildford 3–0

YACHTING

Whitbread Round-the-World Race (set off from Southampton, 21 September 1997; arrived Southampton 24 May 1998): Paul Cayard (Sweden) in EF Language, 836 points

Winter Olympic Games 1998

Nagano, Japan, 7–22 February 1998

ALPINE SKIING (MEN)
Downhill: Jean Luc Cretier (France)
Slalom: Hans Petter Buraas (Norway)
Giant Slalom: Hermann Maier (Austria)
Super Giant Slalom: Hermann Maier (Austria)
Combined: Mario Reiter (Austria)

ALPINE SKIING (WOMEN)
Downhill: Katja Seizinger (Germany)
Slalom: Hilde Gerg (Germany)
Giant Slalom: Deborah Compagnoni (Italy)
Super Giant Slalom: Picabo Street (USA)
Combined: Katja Seizinger (Germany)

BIATHLON (MEN)
10 kilometre: Ole Björndalen (Norway)
20 kilometre: Halvard Hanevold (Norway)
4 × 7.5 kilometre relay: Germany

BIATHLON (WOMEN)
7.5 kilometre: Galina Kukleva (Russia)
15 kilometre: Ekaterina Dafovska (Bulgaria)
4 × 7.5 kilometre relay: Germany

BOBSLEIGH
2-man: = Italy I and Canada I
*4-Man: Germany II
* only three runs

CROSS-COUNTRY SKIING (MEN)
10 kilometre classical: Bjorn Daehlie (Norway)
15 kilometre pursuit: Thomas Alsgaard (Norway)

30 kilometre classical: Mika Myllylae (Finland)
50 kilometre free: Bjorn Daehlie (Norway)
4 × 10 kilometre relay: Norway

CROSS-COUNTRY SKIING (WOMEN)
5 kilometre classical: Larissa Lazutina (Russia)
10 kilometre pursuit: Larissa Lazutina (Russia)
15 kilometre classical: Olga Danilova (Russia)
30 kilometre free: Yulia Chepalova (Russia)
4 × 5 kilometre relay: Russia

CURLING (MEN)
Winners: Switzerland

CURLING (WOMEN)
Winners: Canada

FIGURE SKATING
Men: Illya Kulik (Russia)
Women: Tara Lipinski (USA)
Pairs: Oksana Kazakova and Artur Dmitriev (Russia)
Ice Dance: Pasha Grishuk and Evgeny Platov (Russia)

FREESTYLE SKIING (MEN)
Moguls: Jonny Moseley (USA)
Aerials: Eric Bergoust (USA)

FREESTYLE SKIING (WOMEN)
Moguls: Tae Satoya (Japan)
Aerials: Nikki Stone (USA)

ICE HOCKEY (MEN)
Winners: Czech Republic

ICE HOCKEY (WOMEN)
Winners: USA

LUGE (MEN)
Singles: Georg Hackl (Germany)
Doubles: Germany (Stefan Krausse and Jan Behrendt)

LUGE (WOMEN)
Singles: Silke Kraushaar (Germany)

NORDIC COMBINED
Individual: Bjarte Engen Vik (Norway)
4 × 5 kilometre relay: Norway

SHORT TRACK SPEED SKATING (MEN)
500 metres: Takafumi Nishitani (Japan)
1,000 metres: Kim Dong-Sung (S. Korea)
5,000 metre relay: Canada

SHORT TRACK SPEED SKATING (WOMEN)
500 metres: Annie Perreault (Canada)
1,000 metres: Lee Kyung-Chun (S. Korea)
3,000 metre relay: South Korea

SKI-JUMPING
90 metre: Jani Soininen (Finland)
120 metre: Kazuyoshi Funaki (Japan)
Team: Japan

SNOWBOARDING (MEN)
Halfpipe: Gian Simmen (Switzerland)
Giant Slalom: Ross Rebagliati (Canada)

SNOWBOARDING (WOMEN)
Halfpipe: Nicola Thost (Germany)
Giant Slalom: Karine Ruby (France)

SPEED SKATING (MEN)
500 metres: Hiroyasu Shimizu (Japan)
1,000 metres: Ids Postma (Netherlands)
1,500 metres: Adne Sondral (Norway)
5,000 metres: Gianni Romme (Netherlands)
10,000 metres: Gianni Romme (Netherlands)

SPEED SKATING (WOMEN)
500 metres: Catriona LeMay Doan (Canada)
1,000 metres: Marianne Timmer (Netherlands)
1,500 metres: Marianne Timmer (Netherlands)
3,000 metres: Gunda Niemann-Stirnemann (Germany)
5,000 metres: Claudia Pechstein (Germany)

MEDAL TABLE

	Gold	*Silver*	*Bronze*	*Total*
Germany	12	9	8	29
Norway	10	10	5	25
Russia	9	6	3	18
Austria	3	5	9	17
Canada	6	5	4	15
USA	6	3	4	13
Finland	2	4	6	12
Netherlands	5	4	2	11
Japan	5	1	4	10
Italy	2	6	2	10
France	2	1	5	8
China	0	6	2	8
Switzerland	2	2	3	7
South Korea	3	1	2	6
Czech Republic	1	1	1	3
Sweden	0	2	1	3
Belarus	0	0	2	2
Kazakhstan	0	0	2	2
Bulgaria	1	0	0	1
Denmark	0	1	0	1
Ukraine	0	1	0	1
Australia	0	0	1	1
Belgium	0	0	1	1
Great Britain	0	0	1	1
	69	68	68	205

Commonwealth Games 1998

Kuala Lumpur, Malaysia, 11– 21 September 1998

ATHLETICS (MEN)

	hr.	min.	sec.
100 *metres:* Ato Boldon (Trinidad and Tobago)			9.88
200 *metres:* Julian Golding (England)			20.18
400 *metres:* Iwan Thomas (Wales)			44.52
800 *metres:* Japhet Kimutai (Kenya)		1	43.82
1,500 *metres:* Laban Rotich (Kenya)		3	39.49
5,000 *metres:* Daniel Komen (Kenya)		13	22.57
10,000 *metres:* Simon Maina (Kenya)		28	10.02
Marathon: Thabiso Moqhali (Lesotho)	2	19	15
3,000 *metres steeplechase:* John Kosgei (Kenya)		8	15.34
110 *metres hurdles:* Tony Jarrett (England)			13.47
400 *metres hurdles:* Dinsdale Morgan (Jamaica)			48.28
4 × 100 *metres relay:* England			38.20
4 × 400 *metres relay:* Jamaica		2	59.03
20,000 *metres walk:* Nick A'Hern (Australia)	1	25	59
50,000 *metres walk:* Govindasamy Saravanan (Malaysia)	4	10	05

	metres
High jump: Dalton Grant (England)	2.31
Pole vault: Riaan Botha (S. Africa)	5.60
Long jump: Peter Burge (Australia)	8.22
Triple jump: Larry Achike (England)	17.10
Shot: Burger Lambrechts (S. Africa)	20.01
Discus: Robert Weir (England)	64.42
Hammer: Stuart Rendell (Australia)	74.71
Javelin: Marius Corbett (S. Africa)	88.75
Decathlon: Jagan Hames (Australia)	8,490 points

ATHLETICS (WOMEN)

	hr.	min.	sec.
100 *metres:* Chandra Sturrup (Bahamas)			11.06
200 *metres:* Nova Peris-Kneebone (Australia)			22.77
400 *metres:* Sandie Richards (Jamaica)			50.18
800 *metres:* Maria Mutola (Mozambique)		1	57.60
1,500 *metres:* Jackie Maranga (Kenya)		4	05.27
5,000 *metres:* Kate Anderson (Australia)		15	52.74
10,000 *metres:* Esther Wanjiru (Kenya)		33	40.13
Marathon: Heather Turland (Australia)	2	41	24
100 *metres hurdles:* Gillian Russell (Jamaica)			12.70
400 *metres hurdles:* Andrea Blackett (Barbados)			53.91
4 × 100 *metres relay:* Australia			43.39
4 × 400 *metres relay:* Australia		3	27.30
10,000 *metres walk:* Jane Saville (Australia)		43	57

	metres
High jump: Hestrie Storbeck (S. Africa)	1.91
Pole vault: Emma George (Australia)	4.20
Long jump: Joanne Wise (England)	6.63
Triple jump: Ashia Hansen (England)	14.32
Shot: Judith Oakes (England)	18.83
Discus: Beatrice Faumuina (New Zealand)	65.92
Hammer: Debbie Sosimenko (Australia)	66.56
Javelin: Louise McPaul (Australia)	65.90
Heptathlon: Denise Lewis (England)	6,513 points

BADMINTON

Men's Singles: Wong Choon Hann (Malaysia)
Men's Doubles: Malaysia
Women's Singles: Kelly Morgan (Wales)
Women's Doubles: England
Mixed Doubles: England
Men's Team: India
Women's Team: England

BOWLS (LAWN)

Men's Singles: Roy Garden (Zimbabwe)
Men's Pairs: Australia
Men's Fours: Northern Ireland
Women's Singles: Lesley Hartwell (S. Africa)
Women's Pairs: Scotland
Women's Fours: South Africa

BOXING

Light-fly: Sapok Biki (Malaysia)
Fly: Richard Sunee (Mauritius)
Bantam: Michael Yomba (Tanzania)
Feather: Alex Arthur (Scotland)
Light: Raymond Nahr (Ghana)
Light-welter: Michael Strange (Canada)
Welter: Jeremy Molitor (Canada)
Light-middle: Chris Bessey (England)
Middle: John Pierce (England)
Light-heavy: Courtney Fry (England)
Heavy: Mark Simmons (Canada)
Super-heavy: Audley Harrison (England)

CRICKET

Winners: South Africa

CYCLING (MEN)

Sprint: Darryn Hill (Australia)
1,000 *metres Time Trial:* Shane Kelly (Australia)
Individual Pursuit: Bradley McGee (Australia)
Team Pursuit: Australia
20 *kilometres Scratch Race:* Michael Rogers (Australia)
Points Race: Glenn Thompson (New Zealand)
42 *kilometres Road Individual Time Trial:* Eric Wohlberg (Canada)
184 *kilometres Road Race:* Jay Sweet (Australia)

CYCLING (WOMEN)

Sprint: Tanya Dubnicoff (Canada)
Individual Pursuit: Sarah Ullmer (New Zealand)
Points Race: Allana Burns (Australia)
28 *kilometres Road Individual Time Trial:* Anna Wilson (Australia)
92 *kilometres Road Race:* Lyne Bessette (Canada)

DIVING (MEN)

1 *metre springboard:* Evan Stewart (Zimbabwe)
3 *metres springboard:* Shannon Roy (Australia)
Platform: Alexander Despatie (Canada)

DIVING (WOMEN)

1 *metre springboard:* Chantelle Michell (Australia)
3 *metres springboard:* Eryn Bulmer (Canada)
Platform: Vyninka Arlow (Australia)
Synchronized, Solo: Valerie Hould-Marchand (Canada)
Synchronized, Duet: Canada

GYMNASTICS (MEN)
Individual: Andrei Kravtsov (Australia)
Floor: Andrei Kravtsov (Australia)
Pommel Horse: Andrei Kravtsov (Australia)
Rings: Pavel Mamine (Australia)
Vault: Simon Hutcheon (S. Africa)
Parallel Bars: Andrei Kravtsov (Australia)
Horizontal Bar: Alexander Jeltkov (Canada)
Team: England

GYMNASTICS (WOMEN)
Individual: Zeena McLaughlin (Australia)
Floor: Annika Reeder (England)
Beam: Trudy McIntosh (Australia)
Vault: Lisa Mason (England)
Assymetric Bars: Lisa Skinner (Australia)
Team: Australia

GYMNASTICS (RHYTHMIC)
Individual: Erika Stirton (Canada)
Hoop: Erika Stirton (Canada)
Rope: Erika Stirton (Canada)
Clubs: Erika Stirton (Canada)
Ribbon: Erika Stirton (Canada)
Team: Malaysia

HOCKEY
Men: Australia
Women: Australia

NETBALL
Winners: Australia

RUGBY (SEVEN-A-SIDE)
Winners: New Zealand

SHOOTING (MEN)
Air Pistol, Individual: Michael Gault (England)
Air Pistol, Pairs: England
Air Rifle, Individual: Chris Hector (England)
Air Rifle, Pairs: England
Free Pistol, Individual: Michael Gault (England)
Free Pistol, Pairs: England
Centre-Fire Pistol, Individual: Jaspal Rana (India)
Centre-Fire Pistol, Pairs: India
Rapid-Fire Pistol, Individual: Metodi Igorov (Canada)
Rapid-Fire Pistol, Pairs: Australia
Small-Bore Rifle (Prone), Individual: John Paton (Canada)
Small-Bore Rifle (Prone), Pairs: South Africa
Small-Bore Rifle (3 Positions), Individual: Timothy Lowndes (Australia)
Small-Bore Rifle (3 Positions), Pairs: Canada
Trap, Individual: Michael Diamond (Australia)
Trap, Pairs: India
Skeet, Individual: Desmond Davies (Wales)
Skeet, Pairs: Cyprus

SHOOTING (WOMEN)
Air Pistol, Individual: Annemarie Forder (Australia)
Air Pistol, Pairs: Australia
Air Rifle, Individual: Nurul Baharin (Malaysia)
Air Rifle, Pairs: Canada
Sport Pistol, Individual: Christine Trefry (Australia)
Sport Pistol, Pairs: Australia
Sport Rifle (Prone), Individual: Roopa Unikrishnan (India)
Sport Rifle (Prone), Pairs: Australia
Sport Rifle (3 Positions), Individual: Susan McCready (Australia)
Sport Rifle (3 Positions), Pairs: Canada

SHOOTING (OPEN)
Full-Bore Rifle, Individual: Desmond Davies (Wales)
Full-Bore Rifle, Pairs: Northern Ireland

SQUASH
Men's Singles: Peter Nicol (Scotland)
Men's Doubles: England
Women's Singles: Michelle Martin (Australia)
Women's Doubles: England
Mixed Doubles: Australia

SWIMMING (MEN)
50 metres freestyle: Mark Foster (England)
100 metres freestyle: Michael Klim (Australia)
200 metres freestyle: Ian Thorpe (Australia)
400 metres freestyle: Ian Thorpe (Australia)
1,500 metres freestyle: Grant Hackett (Australia)
100 metres backstroke: Mark Versfeld (Canada)
200 metres backstroke: Mark Versfeld (Canada)
100 metres breaststroke: Simon Cowley (Australia)
200 metres breaststroke: Simon Cowley (Australia)
100 metres butterfly: Geoff Huegill (Australia)
200 metres butterfly: James Hickman (England)
200 metres medley: Matthew Dunn (Australia)
400 metres medley: Trent Steed (Australia)
4 × 100 metres freestyle relay: Australia
4 × 200 metres freestyle relay: Australia
4 × 100 metres medley relay: Australia

SWIMMING (WOMEN)
50 metres freestyle: Susan Rolph (England)
100 metres freestyle: Susan Rolph (England)
200 metres freestyle: Susan O'Neill (Australia)
400 metres freestyle: Susan O'Neill (Australia)
800 metres freestyle: Rachel Harris (Australia)
100 metres backstroke: Giaan Rooney (Australia)
200 metres backstroke: Katy Sexton (England)
100 metres breaststroke: Helen Denman (Australia)
200 metres breaststroke: Samantha Riley (Australia)
100 metres butterfly: Petria Thomas (Australia)
200 metres butterfly: Susan O'Neill (Australia)
200 metres medley: Marianne Limpert (Australia)
400 metres medley: Joanne Malar (Canada)
4 × 100 metres freestyle relay: Australia
4 × 200 metres freestyle relay: Australia
4 × 100 metres medley relay: Australia

TEN-PIN BOWLING
Men's Singles: Kenny Ang (Malaysia)
Men's Doubles: Malaysia
Women's Singles: Cara Honeychurch (Australia)
Women's Doubles: Australia
Mixed Doubles: Australia

WEIGHTLIFTING
Up to 56 kg
Snatch: Mehmet Yagci (Australia)
Clean and Jerk: D. Wilson (India)
Combined: Arumugum Pandian (India)
Up to 62 kg
Snatch: Marcus Stephen (Nauru)
Clean and Jerk: Marcus Stephen (Nauru)
Combined: Marcus Stephen (Nauru)
Up to 69 kg
Snatch: Sebastien Grouix (Canada)
Clean and Jerk: Muhamad Hamidon (Malaysia)
Combined: Sebastien Grouix (Canada)
Up to 77 kg
Snatch: Satheesha Rai (India)
Clean and Jerk: Damian Brown (Australia)
Combined: Damian Brown (Australia)
Up to 85 kg
Snatch: Stephen Ward (England)
Clean and Jerk: Leon Griffin (England)
Combined: Leon Griffin (England)

Up to 94 kg
Snatch: Kiril Kounev (Australia)
Clean and Jerk: Kiril Kounev (Australia)
Combined: Kiril Kounev (Australia)
Up to 105 kg
Snatch: Akos Sandor (Canada)
Clean and Jerk: Akos Sandor (Canada)
Combined: Akos Sandor (Canada)
Over 105 kg
Snatch: Darren Liddel (New Zealand)
Clean and Jerk: Darren Liddel (New Zealand)
Combined: Darren Liddel (New Zealand)

MEDAL TABLE

	Gold	Silver	Bronze	Total
Australia	80	60	58	198
England	36	47	53	136
Canada	30	31	38	99
Malaysia	10	14	12	36
South Africa	9	11	15	35
New Zealand	8	7	19	34
India	7	10	8	25
Kenya	7	5	4	16
Jamaica	4	2	0	6
Wales	3	4	8	15
Scotland	3	2	7	12
Nauru	3	0	0	3
Northern Ireland	2	1	2	5
Zimbabwe	2	0	3	5
Ghana	1	1	3	5
Cyprus	1	1	1	3
Mauritius	1	1	1	3
Tanzania	1	1	1	3
Trinidad and Tobago	1	1	1	3
Bahamas	1	1	0	2
Mozambique	1	1	0	2
Barbados	1	0	2	3
Lesotho	1	0	0	1
Cameroon	0	3	3	6
Namibia	0	2	1	3
Seychelles	0	2	0	2
Sri Lanka	0	1	1	2
Bermuda	0	1	0	1
Fiji	0	1	0	1
Isle of Man	0	1	0	1
Pakistan	0	1	0	1
Papua New Guinea	0	0	1	1
Uganda	0	0	1	1
Zambia	0	0	1	1

Sports Records

ATHLETICS WORLD RECORDS
AS AT 5 SEPTEMBER 1998

All the world records given below have been accepted by the International Amateur Athletic Federation except those marked with an asterisk* which are awaiting homologation. Fully automatic timing to 1/100th second is mandatory up to and including 400 metres. For distances up to and including 10,000 metres, records will be accepted to 1/100th second if timed automatically, and to 1/10th if hand timing is used.

MEN'S EVENTS

TRACK EVENTS	hr.	min.	sec.
100 metres			9.84
Donovan Bailey, Canada, 1996			
200 metres			19.32
Michael Johnson, USA, 1996			
400 metres			43.29
Butch Reynolds, USA, 1988			
800 metres		1	41.11
Wilson Kipketer, Denmark, 1997			
1,000 metres		2	12.18
Sebastian Coe, GB, 1981			
1,500 metres		3	26.00
Hicham El Guerrouj, Morocco, 1998			
1 mile		3	44.39
Noureddine Morceli, Algeria, 1993			
2,000 metres		4	47.88
Noureddine Morceli, Algeria, 1995			
3,000 metres		7	20.67
Daniel Komen, Kenya, 1996			
5,000 metres		12	39.36*
Haile Gebrselassie, Ethiopia, 1998			
10,000 metres		26	22.75*
Haile Gebrselassie, Ethiopia, 1998			
20,000 metres		56	55.6
Arturo Barrios, Mexico, 1991			
21,101 metres (13 miles 196 yards 1 foot)	1	00	00.0
Arturo Barrios, Mexico, 1991			
25,000 metres	1	13	55.8
Toshihiko Seko, Japan, 1981			
30,000 metres	1	29	18.8
Toshihiko Seko, Japan, 1981			
110 metres hurdles (3 ft 6 in)			12.91
Colin Jackson, GB, 1993			
400 metres hurdles (3 ft 0 in)			46.78
Kevin Young, USA, 1992			
3,000 metres steeplechase		7	55.72
Bernard Barmasai, Kenya, 1997			

RELAYS		min.	sec.
4×100 metres			37.40
USA, 1992, 1993			
4×200 metres		1	19.11
Santa Monica TC, 1992			
4×400 metres		2	54.20
USA, 1998			
4×800 metres		7	03.89
GB, 1982			

		min.	sec.
4×1,500 metres		14	38.8
Federal Republic of Germany, 1977			

FIELD EVENTS	metres	ft	in
High jump	2.45	8	0½
Javier Sotomayor, Cuba, 1993			
Pole vault	6.14	20	1¾
Sergei Bubka, Ukraine, 1994			
Long jump	8.95	29	4½
Mike Powell, USA, 1991			
Triple jump	18.29	60	0¼
Jonathan Edwards, GB, 1995			
Shot	23.12	75	10¼
Randy Barnes, USA, 1990			
Discus	74.08	243	0
Jürgen Schult, GDR, 1986			
Hammer	86.74	284	7
Yuriy Sedykh, USSR, 1986			
Javelin	98.48	323	1
Jan Zelezny, Czech Rep., 1996			
Decathlon†		8,891 points	
Dan O'Brien, USA, 1992			

† Ten events comprising 100 m, long jump, shot, high jump, 400 m, 110 m hurdles, discus, pole vault, javelin, 1500 m

WALKING (TRACK)	hr.	min.	sec.
20,000 metres	1	17	25.6
Bernard Segura, Mexico, 1994			
29,572 metres (18 miles 660 yards)	2	00	00.0
Maurizio Damilano, Italy, 1992			
30,000 metres	2	01	44.1
Maurizio Damilano, Italy, 1992			
50,000 metres	3	40	57.9
Thierry Toutain, France, 1996			

WOMEN'S EVENTS

TRACK EVENTS		min.	sec.
100 metres			10.49
Florence Griffith-Joyner, USA, 1988			
200 metres			21.34
Florence Griffith-Joyner, USA, 1988			
400 metres			47.60
Marita Koch, GDR, 1985			
800 metres		1	53.28
Jarmila Kratochvilova, Czechoslovakia, 1983			
1,500 metres		3	50.46
Qu Yunxia, China, 1993			
1 mile		4	12.56
Svetlana Masterkova, Russia, 1996			
3,000 metres		8	06.11
Wang Junxia, China, 1993			
5,000 metres		14	28.09
Jiang Bo, China, 1997			
10,000 metres		29	31.78
Wang Junxia, China, 1993			
100 metres hurdles (2 ft 9 in)			12.21
Yordanka Donkova, Bulgaria, 1988			
400 metres hurdles (2 ft 6 in)			52.61
Kim Batten, USA, 1995			

RELAYS	min.	sec.
4×100 metres		41.37
GDR, 1985		
4×200 metres	1	28.15
GDR, 1980		
4×400 metres	3	15.17
USSR, 1988		
4×800 metres	7	50.17
USSR, 1984		

FIELD EVENTS	metres	ft	in
High jump	2.09	6	10¼
Stefka Kostadinova, Bulgaria, 1987			
Pole vault	4.59	15	0¾
Emma George, Australia, 1998			
Long jump	7.52	24	8¼
Galina Chistiakova, USSR, 1988			
Triple jump	15.50	50	10
Inessa Kravets, Ukraine, 1995			
Shot	22.63	74	3
Natalya Lisovskaya, USSR, 1987			
Discus	76.80	252	0
Gabriele Reinsch, GDR, 1988			
Hammer	73.14*	239	11
Mihaela Melinte, Romania, 1998			
Javelin	80.00	262	5
Petra Felke, GDR, 1988			
Heptathlon†			7,291 points
Jackie Joyner-Kersee, USA, 1988			

†Seven events comprising 100 m hurdles, shot, high jump, 200 m, long jump, javelin, 800 m

ATHLETICS NATIONAL (UK) RECORDS
as at 5 September 1998

Records set anywhere by athletes eligible to represent Great Britain and Northern Ireland

MEN

TRACK EVENTS	hr.	min.	sec.
100 metres			9.87
Linford Christie, 1993			
200 metres			19.87
John Regis, 1994			
400 metres			44.36
Iwan Thomas, 1997			
800 metres		1	41.73
Sebastian Coe, 1981			
1,000 metres		2	12.18
Sebastian Coe, 1981			
1,500 metres		3	29.67
Sebastian Coe, 1985			
1 mile		3	46.32
Steve Cram, 1985			
2,000 metres		4	51.39
Steve Cram, 1985			
3,000 metres		7	32.79
David Moorcroft, 1982			
5,000 metres		13	00.41
David Moorcroft, 1982			
10,000 metres		27	18.14*
Jon Brown, 1998			
20,000 metres		57	28.7
Carl Thackery, 1990			
20,855 metres	1	00	00.0
Carl Thackery, 1990			
25,000 metres	1	15	22.6
Ron Hill, 1965			
30,000 metres	1	31	30.4
Jim Alder, 1970			
3,000 metres steeplechase		8	07.96
Mark Rowland, 1988			
110 metres hurdles			12.91
Colin Jackson, 1993			
400 metres hurdles			47.82
Kriss Akabusi, 1992			

RELAYS	min.	sec.
4×100 metres		37.77
GB team, 1993		
4×200 metres	1	21.29
GB team, 1989		
4×400 metres	2	56.60
GB team, 1996		
4×800 metres	7	03.89
GB team, 1982		

FIELD EVENTS	metres	ft	in
High jump	2.37	7	9¼
Steve Smith, 1992, 1993			
Pole vault	5.80*	19	0¼
Nick Buckfield, 1998			
Long jump	8.23	27	0
Lynn Davies, 1968			
Triple jump	18.29	60	0¼
Jonathan Edwards, 1995			
Shot	21.68	71	1½
Geoff Capes, 1980			
Discus	66.64*	218	8
Perris Wilkins, 1998			
Hammer	77.54	254	5
Martin Girvan, 1984			
Javelin	91.46	300	1
Steve Backley, 1992			
Decathlon			8,847 points
Daley Thompson, 1984			

WALKING (TRACK)	hr.	min.	sec.
20,000 metres	1	23	26.5
Ian McCombie, 1990			
30,000 metres	2	19	18
Christopher Maddocks, 1984			
50,000 metres	4	05	44.6
Paul Blagg, 1990			
26,037 metres (16 miles 315 yards)	2	00	00.0
Ron Wallwork, 1971			

WOMEN

TRACK EVENTS	min.	sec.
100 metres		11.10
Kathy Cook, 1981		
200 metres		22.10
Kathy Cook, 1984		
400 metres		49.43
Kathy Cook, 1984		
800 metres	1	56.21
Kelly Holmes, 1995		
1,500 metres	3	58.07
Kelly Holmes, 1997		
1 mile	4	17.57
Zola Budd, 1985		
3,000 metres	8	28.83
Zola Budd, 1985		
5,000 metres	14	45.51
Paula Radcliffe, 1997		
10,000 metres	30	48.58*
Paula Radcliffe, 1998		

100 metres hurdles			12.80
Angela Thorp, 1996			
400 metres hurdles			52.74
Sally Gunnell, 1993			

RELAYS		min.	sec.
4×100 metres			42.43
GB team, 1980			
4×200 metres		1	31.57
GB team, 1977			
4×400 metres		3	22.01
GB team, 1991			
4×800 metres		8	23.8
GB team, 1971			

FIELD EVENTS	metres	ft	in
High jump	1.95	6	4¾
Diana Elliott, 1982			
Pole vault	4.31*	14	1¾
Janine Whitlock, 1998			
Long jump	6.90	22	7¾
Beverley Kinch, 1983			
Triple jump	15.15	49	8½
Ashia Hansen, 1997			
Shot	19.36	63	6¼
Judy Oakes, 1988			
Discus	67.48	221	5
Margaret Ritchie, 1981			
Hammer	64.90	212	11
Lorraine Shaw, 1995			
Javelin	77.44	254	1
Fatima Whitbread, 1986			
Heptathlon		6,736 points	
Denise Lewis, 1997			

*Awaiting ratification

SWIMMING WORLD RECORDS
AS AT 5 SEPTEMBER 1998

MEN		min.	sec.
50 metres freestyle			21.81
Tom Jager, USA			
100 metres freestyle			48.21
Alexander Popov, Russia			
200 metres freestyle		1	46.69
Giorgio Lamberti, Italy			
400 metres freestyle		3	43.80
Kieren Perkins, Australia			
800 metres freestyle		7	46.00
Kieren Perkins, Australia			
1,500 metres freestyle		14	41.66
Kieren Perkins, Australia			
100 metres breaststroke		1	00.60
Fred Deburghgraeve, Belgium			
200 metres breaststroke		2	10.16
Mike Barrowman, USA			
100 metres butterfly			52.15
Michael Klim, Australia			
200 metres butterfly		1	55.22
Denis Pankratov, Russia			
100 metres backstroke			53.86
Jeff Rouse, USA			
200 metres backstroke		1	56.57
Martin Lopez-Zubero, Spain			
200 metres medley		1	58.16
Jani Sievinen, Finland			
400 metres medley		4	12.30
Tom Dolan, USA			

4×100 metres freestyle relay		3	15.11
USA			
4×200 metres freestyle relay		7	11.95
CIS			
4×100 metres medley relay		3	34.84
USA			

WOMEN		min.	sec.
50 metres freestyle			24.51
Jingyi Le, China			
100 metres freestyle			54.01
Jingyi Le, China			
200 metres freestyle		1	56.78
Franziska van Almsick, Germany			
400 metres freestyle		4	03.85
Janet Evans, USA			
800 metres freestyle		8	16.22
Janet Evans, USA			
1,500 metres freestyle		15	52.10
Janet Evans, USA			
100 metres breaststroke		1	07.02
Penny Heyns, South Africa			
200 metres breaststroke		2	24.76
Rebecca Brown, Australia			
100 metres butterfly			57.93
Mary Meagher, USA			
200 metres butterfly		2	05.96
Mary Meagher, USA			
100 metres backstroke		1	00.16
Cihong He, China			
200 metres backstroke		2	06.62
Krisztina Egerszegi, Hungary			
200 metres medley		2	09.72
Wu Yanyan, China			
400 metres medley		4	34.79
Chen Yan, China			
4×100 metres freestyle relay		3	37.91
USA			
4×200 metres freestyle relay		7	55.47
GDR			
4×100 metres medley relay		4	01.67
China			

Weights and Measures

SI UNITS

The Système International d'Unités (SI) is an international and coherent system of units devised to meet all known needs for measurement in science and technology. The system was adopted by the eleventh Conférence Générale des Poids et Mesures (CGPM) in 1960. A comprehensive description of the system is given in *SI The International System of Units* (HMSO). The British Standards describing the essential features of the International System of Units are *Specifications for SI units and recommendations for the use of their multiples and certain other units* (BS 5555:1993) and *Conversion Factors and Tables* (BS 350, Part 1:1974).

The system consists of seven base units and the derived units formed as products or quotients of various powers of the base units. Together the base units and the derived units make up the coherent system of units. In the UK the SI base units, and almost all important derived units, are realized at the National Physical Laboratory and disseminated through the National Measurement System.

Base Units

metre (m) = unit of length
kilogram (kg) = unit of mass
second (s) = unit of time
ampere (A) = unit of electric current
kelvin (K) = unit of thermodynamic temperature
mole (mol) = unit of amount of substance
candela (cd) = unit of luminous intensity

Derived Units

For some of the derived SI units, special names and symbols exist; those approved by the CGPM are as follows:

hertz (Hz) = unit of frequency
newton (N) = unit of force
pascal (Pa) = unit of pressure, stress
joule (J) = unit of energy, work, quantity of heat
watt (W) = unit of power, radiant flux
coulomb (C) = unit of electric charge, quantity of electricity
volt (V) = unit of electric potential, potential difference, electromotive force
farad (F) = unit of electric capacitance
ohm (Ω) = unit of electric resistance
siemens (S) = unit of electric conductance
weber (Wb) = unit of magnetic flux
tesla (T) = unit of magnetic flux density
henry (H) = unit of inductance
degree Celsius (°C) = unit of Celsius temperature
lumen (lm) = unit of luminous flux
lux (lx) = unit of illuminance
becquerel (Bq) = unit of activity (of a radionuclide)
gray (Gy) = unit of absorbed dose, specific energy imparted, kerma, absorbed dose index
sievert (Sv) = unit of dose equivalent, dose equivalent index
radian (rad) = unit of plane angle
steradian (sr) = unit of solid angle

Other derived units are expressed in terms of base units. Some of the more commonly-used derived units are the following:

Unit of area = square metre (m^2)
Unit of volume = cubic metre (m^3)
Unit of velocity = metre per second ($m\,s^{-1}$)
Unit of acceleration = metre per second squared ($m\,s^{-2}$)
Unit of density = kilogram per cubic metre ($kg\,m^{-3}$)
Unit of momentum = kilogram metre per second ($kg\,m\,s^{-1}$)
Unit of magnetic field strength = ampere per metre ($A\,m^{-1}$)
Unit of surface tension = newton per metre ($N\,m^{-1}$)
Unit of dynamic viscosity = pascal second (Pa s)
Unit of heat capacity = joule per kelvin ($J\,K^{-1}$)
Unit of specific heat capacity = joule per kilogram kelvin ($J\,kg^{-1}\,K^{-1}$)
Unit of heat flux density, irradiance = watt per square metre ($W\,m^{-2}$)
Unit of thermal conductivity = watt per metre kelvin ($W\,m^{-1}\,K^{-1}$)
Unit of electric field strength = volt per metre ($V\,m^{-1}$)
Unit of luminance = candela per square metre ($cd\,m^{-2}$)

SI Prefixes

Decimal multiples and submultiples of the SI units are indicated by SI prefixes. These are as follows:

multiples	submultiples
yotta (Y) $\times 10^{24}$	deci (d) $\times 10^{-1}$
zetta (Z) $\times 10^{21}$	centi (c) $\times 10^{-2}$
exa (E) $\times 10^{18}$	milli (m) $\times 10^{-3}$
peta (P) $\times 10^{15}$	micro (μ) $\times 10^{-6}$
tera (T) $\times 10^{12}$	nano (n) $\times 10^{-9}$
giga (G) $\times 10^{9}$	pico (p) $\times 10^{-12}$
mega (M) $\times 10^{6}$	femto (f) $\times 10^{-15}$
kilo (k) $\times 10^{3}$	atto (a) $\times 10^{-18}$
hecto (h) $\times 10^{2}$	zepto (z) $\times 10^{-21}$
deca (da) $\times 10$	yocto (y) $\times 10^{-24}$

METRIC UNITS

The metric primary standards are the metre as the unit of measurement of length, and the kilogram as the unit of measurement of mass. Other units of measurement are defined by reference to the primary standards.

Measurement of Length

Kilometre (km) = 1000 metres
Metre (m) is the length of the path travelled by light in vacuum during a time interval of 1/299 792 458 of a second
Decimetre (dm) = 1/10 metre
Centimetre (cm) = 1/100 metre
Millimetre (mm) = 1/1000 metre

Measurement of Area

Hectare (ha) = 100 ares
Decare = 10 ares
Are (a) = 100 square metres
Square metre = a superficial area equal to that of a square each side of which measures one metre

Square decimetre = 1/100 square metre
Square centimetre = 1/100 square decimetre
Square millimetre = 1/100 square centimetre

MEASUREMENT OF VOLUME

Cubic metre (m^3) = a volume equal to that of a cube each
 edge of which measures one metre
Cubic decimetre = 1/1000 cubic metre
Cubic centimetre (cc) = 1/1000 cubic decimetre
Hectolitre = 100 litres
Litre = a cubic decimetre
Decilitre = 1/10 litre
Centilitre = 1/100 litre
Millilitre = 1/1000 litre

MEASUREMENT OF CAPACITY

Hectolitre (hl) = 100 litres
Litre (l or L) = a cubic decimetre
Decilitre (dl) = 1/10 litre
Centilitre (cl) = 1/100 litre
Millilitre (ml) = 1/1000 litre

MEASUREMENT OF MASS OR WEIGHT

Tonne (t) = 1000 kilograms
Kilogram (kg) is equal to the mass of the international
 prototype of the kilogram
Hectogram (hg) = 1/10 kilogram
Gram (g) = 1/1000 kilogram
*Carat (metric) = 1/5 gram
Milligram (mg) = 1/1000 gram

*Used only for transactions in precious stones or pearls

METRICATION IN THE UK

The European Council Directive 80/181/EEC, as
amended by Council Directive 89/617/EEC, relates to
the use of units of measurement for economic, public
health, public safety or administrative purposes in the
member states of the European Union. The provisions of
the directives were incorporated into British law by the
Weights and Measures Act 1985 (Metrication) (Amendment) Order 1994 and the Units of Measurement Regulations 1994; these instruments amended the Weights and
Measures Act 1985. Parallel statutory rules amending
Northern Ireland weights and measures legislation were
made in May 1995.

The general effect of the 1994 and 1995 legislation is to
end the use of imperial units of measurement for trade,
replacing them with metric units – *see* below for timetable
for UK metrication. Imperial units can, however, be used in
addition to metric units, as supplementary indications.

IMPERIAL UNITS

The imperial primary standards are the yard as the unit of
measurement of length and the pound as the unit of
measurement of mass. Other units of measurement are
defined by reference to the primary standards. Most of
these units are no longer authorized for use in trade in the
UK – *see* below.

MEASUREMENT OF LENGTH

Mile = 1760 yards
Furlong = 220 yards
Chain = 22 yards

Yard (yd) = 0.9144 metre
Foot (ft) = 1/3 yard
Inch (in) = 1/36 yard

MEASUREMENT OF AREA

Square mile = 640 acres
Acre = 4840 square yards
Rood = 1210 square yards
Square yard (sq. yd) = a superficial area equal to that of a
 square each side of which measures one yard
Square foot (sq. ft) = 1/9 square yard
Square inch (sq. in) = 1/144 square foot

MEASUREMENT OF VOLUME

Cubic yard = a volume equal to that of a cube each edge of
 which measures one yard
Cubic foot = 1/27 cubic yard
Cubic inch = 1/1728 cubic foot

MEASUREMENT OF CAPACITY

Bushel = 8 gallons
Peck = 2 gallons
Gallon (gal) = 4.546 09 cubic decimetres
Quart (qt) = 1/4 gallon
*Pint (pt) = 1/2 quart
Gill = 1/4 pint
*Fluid ounce (fl oz) = 1/20 pint
Fluid drachm = 1/8 fluid ounce
Minim (min) = 1/60 fluid drachm

MEASUREMENT OF MASS OR WEIGHT

Ton = 2240 pounds
Hundredweight (cwt) = 112 pounds
Cental = 100 pounds
Quarter = 28 pounds
Stone = 14 pounds
*Pound (lb) = 0.453 592 37 kilogram
*Ounce (oz) = 1/16 pound
*†Ounce troy (oz tr) = 12/175 pound
 Dram (dr) = 1/16 ounce
 Grain (gr) = 1/7000 pound
 Pennyweight (dwt) = 24 grains
 Ounce apothecaries = 480 grains
 Drachm (ʒ) = 1/8 ounce apothecaries
 Scruple (℈) = 1/3 drachm

*Units of measurement still authorized for use for trade in the UK
†Used only for transactions in gold, silver or other precious metals, and
articles made therefrom

PHASING-OUT OF IMPERIAL UNITS IN THE UK

The Weights and Measures Act 1985 enacted the legal
units for the United Kingdom. It was amended to
implement the provisions of European Council Directive
80/181/EEC, as amended by Directive 89/617/EEC, by
the Weights and Measures Act 1985 (Metrication)
(Amendment) Order 1994 and the Units of Measurement
Regulations 1994, and by parallel statutory rules in
Northern Ireland in May 1995.

The effect of the amended legislation is to phase out the
use of imperial units for trade, replacing them with metric
units. With effect from 30 September 1995 imperial units
ceased to be authorized for use in the UK for economic,
public health, public safety and administrative purposes,
with the following exceptions:

Units of measurement authorized for use in specialized fields between 1 October 1995 and 31 December 1999

Unit	Field of application
fathom	Marine navigation
fluid ounce ⎫ pint ⎭	Beer, cider, water, lemonade, fruit juice in returnable containers
ounce ⎫ pound ⎭	Goods for sale loose from bulk
therm	Gas supply

Units of measurement authorized for use in specialized fields from 1 October 1995, without time limit

Unit	Field of application
inch ⎫ foot ⎪ yard ⎬ mile ⎭	Road traffic signs, distance and speed measurement
pint ⎰ ⎱	Dispense of draught beer or cider Milk in returnable containers
acre	Land registration
troy ounce	Transactions in precious metals

MEASUREMENT OF ELECTRICITY

Units of measurement of electricity are defined by the Weights and Measures Act 1985 as follows:

ampere (A) = that constant current which, if maintained in two straight parallel conductors of infinite length, of negligible circular cross-section and placed 1 metre apart in vacuum, would produce between these conductors a force equal to 2×10^{-7} newton per metre of length

ohm (Ω) = the electric resistance between two points of a conductor when a constant potential difference of 1 volt, applied between the two points, produces in the conductor a current of 1 ampere, the conductor not being the seat of any electromotive force

volt (V) = the difference of electric potential between two points of a conducting wire carrying a constant current of 1 ampere when the power dissipated between these points is equal to 1 watt

watt (W) = the power which in one second gives rise to energy of 1 joule

kilowatt (kW) = 1000 watts

megawatt (MW) = one million watts

WATER AND LIQUOR MEASURES

1 cubic foot = 62.32 lb
1 gallon = 10 lb
1 cubic cm = 1 gram
1000 cubic cm = 1 litre; 1 kilogram
1 cubic metre = 1000 litres; 1000 kg; 1 tonne
An inch of rain on the surface of an acre (43560 sq. ft) = 3630 cubic ft = 100.992 tons
Cisterns: A cistern 4 × 2½ feet and 3 feet deep will hold brimful 186.963 gallons, weighing 1869.63 lb in addition to its own weight

WATER FOR SHIPS
Kilderkin = 18 gallons
Barrel = 36 gallons
Puncheon = 72 gallons
Butt = 110 gallons
Tun = 210 gallons

BOTTLES OF WINE
Traditional equivalents in standard champagne bottles:
Magnum = 2 bottles
Jeroboam = 4 bottles
Rehoboam = 6 bottles
Methuselah = 8 bottles
Salmanazar = 12 bottles
Balthazar = 16 bottles
Nebuchadnezzar = 20 bottles

A quarter of a bottle is known as a *nip*
An eighth of a bottle is known as a *baby*

ANGULAR AND CIRCULAR MEASURES

60 seconds (″) = 1 minute (′)
60 minutes = 1 degree (°)
90 degrees = 1 right angle or quadrant
Diameter of circle × 3.141 6 = circumference
Diameter squared × 0.7854 = area of circle
Diameter squared × 3.141 6 = surface of sphere
Diameter cubed × 0.523 = solidity of sphere
One degree of circumference × 57.3 = radius*
Diameter of cylinder × 3.141 6; product by length or height, gives the surface
Diameter squared × 0.7854; product by length or height, gives solid content

*Or, one radian (the angle subtended at the centre of a circle by an arc of the circumference equal in length to the radius) = 57.3 degrees

MILLION, BILLION, ETC.

Value in the UK

Million	thousand × thousand	10^{6}
*Billion	million × million	10^{12}
Trillion	million × billion	10^{18}
Quadrillion	million × trillion	10^{24}

Value in USA

Million	thousand × thousand	10^{6}
*Billion	thousand × million	10^{9}
Trillion	million × million	10^{12}
Quadrillion	million × billion US	10^{15}

*The American usage of billion (i.e. 10^{9}) is increasingly common, and is now universally used by statisticians

NAUTICAL MEASURES

DISTANCE

Distance at sea is measured in nautical miles. The British standard nautical mile was 6080 feet but this measure has been obsolete since 1970 when the international nautical mile of 1852 metres was adopted by the Hydrographic Department of the Ministry of Defence. The cable (600 feet or 100 fathoms) was a measure approximately one-tenth of a nautical mile. Such distances are now expressed in decimal parts of a sea mile or in metres.

Soundings at sea were recorded in fathoms (6 feet). Depths are now expressed in metres on Admiralty charts.

SPEED

Speed is measured in nautical miles per hour, called knots. A ship moving at the rate of 30 nautical miles per hour is said to be doing 30 knots.

knots	m.p.h.	knots	m.p.h.
1	1.1515	9	10.3636
2	2.3030	10	11.5151
3	3.4545	15	17.2727
4	4.6060	20	23.0303
5	5.7575	25	28.7878
6	6.9090	30	34.5454
7	8.0606	35	40.3030
8	9.2121	40	46.0606

TONNAGE

Under the Merchant Shipping Act 1854, the tonnage of UK-registered vessels was measured in tons of 100 cubic feet. The need for a universal method of measurement led to the adoption of the International Convention on Tonnage Measurements of Ships 1969, which measures, in cubic metres, all the internal spaces of a vessel for the gross tonnage and those of the cargo compartments for the net tonnage. The convention has applied since July 1982 to new ships, ships which needed to be remeasured because of substantial alterations, and ships whose owners requested remeasurement. On 18 July 1994 the convention became mandatory and all vessels should have been remeasured by that date; however, there is a backlog and some vessels have not yet been remeasured.

DISTANCE OF THE HORIZON

The limit of distance to which one can see varies with the height of the spectator. The greatest distance at which an object on the surface of the sea, or of a level plain, can be seen by a person whose eyes are at a height of five feet from the same level is nearly three miles. At a height of 20 feet the range is increased to nearly six miles, and an approximate rule for finding the range of vision for small heights is to increase the square root of the number of feet that the eye is above the level surface by a third of itself. The result is the distance of the horizon in miles, but is slightly in excess of that in the table below, which is computed by a more precise formula. The table may be used conversely to show the distance of an object of given height that is just visible from a point on the surface of the earth or sea. Refraction is taken into account both in the approximate rule and in the table.

Height in feet	range in miles
5	2.9
20	5.9
50	9.3
100	13.2
500	29.5
1,000	41.6
2,000	58.9
3,000	72.1
4,000	83.3
5,000	93.1
20,000	186.2

TEMPERATURE SCALES

The SI (International System) unit of temperature is the kelvin, which is defined as the fraction $1/273.16$ of the temperature of the triple point of water (i.e. where ice, water and water vapour are in equilibrium). The zero of the Kelvin scale is the absolute zero of temperature. The freezing point of water is 273.15 K and the boiling point (as adopted in the International Temperature Scale of 1990) is 373.124 K.

The Celsius scale (formerly centigrade) is defined by subtracting 273.15 from the Kelvin temperature. The Fahrenheit scale is related to the Celsius scale by the relationships:

temperature $°F = ($temperature $°C \times 1.8) + 32$
temperature $°C = ($temperature $°F - 32) \div 1.8$

It follows from these definitions that the freezing point of water is 0°C and 32°F. The boiling point is 99.974°C and 211.953°F.

The temperature of the human body varies from person to person and in the same person can be affected by a variety of factors. In most people body temperature varies between 36.5°C and 37.2°C (97.7–98.9°F).

Conversion between scales

°C	°F	°C	°F	°C	°F
100	212	60	140	20	68
99	210.2	59	138.2	19	66.2
98	208.4	58	136.4	18	64.4
97	206.6	57	134.6	17	62.6
96	204.8	56	132.8	16	60.8
95	203	55	131	15	59
94	201.2	54	129.2	14	57.2
93	199.4	53	127.4	13	55.4
92	197.6	52	125.6	12	53.6
91	195.8	51	123.8	11	51.8
90	194	50	122	10	50
89	192.2	49	120.2	9	48.2
88	190.4	48	118.4	8	46.4
87	188.6	47	116.6	7	44.6
86	186.8	46	114.8	6	42.8
85	185	45	113	5	41
84	183.2	44	111.2	4	39.2
83	181.4	43	109.4	3	37.4
82	179.6	42	107.6	2	35.6
81	177.8	41	105.8	1	33.8
80	176	40	104	zero	32
79	174.2	39	102.2	− 1	30.2
78	172.4	38	100.4	− 2	28.4
77	170.6	37	98.6	− 3	26.6
76	168.8	36	96.8	− 4	24.8
75	167	35	95	− 5	23
74	165.2	34	93.2	− 6	21.2
73	163.4	33	91.4	− 7	19.4
72	161.6	32	89.6	− 8	17.6
71	159.8	31	87.8	− 9	15.8
70	158	30	86	−10	14
69	156.2	29	84.2	−11	12.2
68	154.4	28	82.4	−12	10.4
67	152.6	27	80.6	−13	8.6
66	150.8	26	78.8	−14	6.8
65	149	25	77	−15	5
64	147.2	24	75.2	−16	3.2
63	145.4	23	73.4	−17	1.4
62	143.6	22	71.6	−18	0.4
61	141.8	21	69.8	−19	− 2.2

PAPER MEASURES

Printing Paper		*Writing Paper*	
516 sheets	= 1 ream	480 sheets	= 1 ream
2 reams	= 1 bundle	20 quires	= 1 ream
5 bundles	= 1 bale	24 sheets	= 1 quire

Brown Papers

	inches		*inches*
Casing	46 × 36	Imperial Cap	29 × 22
Double Imperial	45 × 29	Haven Cap	26 × 21
Elephant	34 × 24	Bag Cap	24 × 19½
Double Four Pound	31 × 21	Kent Cap	21 × 18

Printing Papers

	inches		*inches*
Foolscap	17 × 13½	Double Large Post	33 × 21
Double Foolscap	27 × 17	Demy	22½ × 17½
Quad Foolscap	34 × 27	Double Demy	35 × 22½
Crown	20 × 15	Quad Demy	45 × 35
Double Crown	30 × 20	Music Demy	20 × 15½
Quad Crown	40 × 30	Medium	23 × 18
Double Quad Crown	60 × 40	Royal	25 × 20
Post	19¼ × 15½	Super Royal	27½ × 20½
Double Post	31½ × 19½	Elephant	28 × 23
		Imperial	30 × 22

Writing and Drawing Papers

	inches		*inches*
Emperor	72 × 48	Copy or Draft	20 × 16
Antiquarian	53 × 31	Demy	20 × 15½
Double Elephant	40 × 27	Post	19 × 15¼
Grand Eagle	42 × 28¾	Pinched Post	18½ × 14¾
Atlas	34 × 26	Foolscap	17 × 13½
Colombier	34½ × 23½	Double Foolscap	26½ × 16½
Imperial	30 × 22	Double Post	30½ × 19
Elephant	28 × 23	Double Large Post	33 × 21
Cartridge	26 × 21	Double Demy	31 × 20
Super Royal	27 × 19	Brief	16½ × 13¼
Royal	24 × 19	Pott	15 × 12½
Medium	22 × 17½		
Large Post	21 × 16½		

INTERNATIONAL PAPER SIZES

The basis of the international series of paper sizes is a rectangle having an area of one square metre, the sides of which are in the proportion of $1:\sqrt{2}$. The proportions $1:\sqrt{2}$ have a geometrical relationship, the side and diagonal of any square being in this proportion. The effect of this arrangement is that if the area of the sheet of paper is doubled or halved, the shorter side and the longer side of the new sheet are still in the same proportion $1:\sqrt{2}$. This feature is useful where photographic enlargement or reduction is used, as the proportions remain the same.

Description of the A series is by capital A followed by a figure. The basic size has the description A0 and the higher the figure following the letter, the greater is the number of sub-divisions and therefore the smaller the sheet. Half A0 is A1 and half A1 is A2. Where larger dimensions are required the A is preceded by a figure. Thus 2A means twice the size A0; 4A is four times the size of A0.

Subsidiary Series

B sizes are sizes intermediate between any two adjacent sizes of the A series. There is a series of C sizes which is used much less. A is for magazines and books, B for posters, wall charts and other large items, C for envelopes particularly where it is necessary for an envelope (in C series) to fit into another envelope. The size recommended for business correspondence is A4.

Long sizes (DL) are obtainable by dividing any appropriate sizes from the two series above into three, four or eight equal parts parallel with the shorter side in such a manner that the proportion of $1:\sqrt{2}$ is not maintained, the ratio between the longer and the shorter sides being greater than $\sqrt{2}:1$. In practice long sizes should be produced from the A series only.

It is an essential feature of these series that the dimensions are of the trimmed or finished size.

A Series

	mm		*mm*
A0	841 × 1189	A6	105 × 148
A1	594 × 841	A7	74 × 105
A2	420 × 594	A8	52 × 74
A3	297 × 420	A9	37 × 52
A4	210 × 297	A10	26 × 37
A5	148 × 210		

B Series

	mm		*mm*
B0	1000 × 1414	B6	125 × 176
B1	707 × 1000	B7	88 × 125
B2	500 × 707	B8	62 × 88
B3	353 × 500	B9	44 × 62
B4	250 × 353	B10	31 × 44
B5	176 × 250		

C Series / DL

C Series	*mm*	DL	*mm*
C4	324 × 229	DL	110 × 220
C5	229 × 162		
C6	114 × 162		

BOUND BOOKS

The book sizes most commonly used are listed below. Approximate centimetre equivalents are also shown. International sizes are converted to their nearest imperial size, e.g. A4 = D4; A5 = D8.

		inches	*cm*
Crown 32mo	C32	2½ × 3¾	6 × 9
Crown 16mo	C16	3¾ × 5	9 × 13
Foolscap 8vo	F8	4¼ × 6¾	11 × 17
Demy 16mo	D16	4⅜ × 5⅝	11 × 14
Crown 8vo	C8	5 × 7½	13 × 19
Demy 8vo	D8	5⅝ × 8¾	14 × 22
Medium 8vo	M8	5¾ × 9	15 × 23
Royal 8vo	R8	6¼ × 10	16 × 25
Super Royal 8vo	suR8	6¾ × 10	17 × 25
Foolscap 4to	F4	6¾ × 8½	17 × 22
Crown 4to	C4	7½ × 10	19 × 25
Imperial 8vo	Imp8	7½ × 11	19 × 28
Demy 4to	D4	8¾ × 11¼	22 × 29
Royal 4to	R4	10 × 12½	25 × 31
Super Royal 4to	suR4	10 × 13½	25 × 34
Crown Folio	Cfol	10 × 15	25 × 38
Imperial Folio	Impfol	11 × 15	28 × 38

Folio = a sheet folded in half
Quarto (4to) = a sheet folded into four
Octavo (8vo) = a sheet folded into eight
Books are usually bound up in sheets of 16, 32 or 64 pages. Octavo books are generally printed 64 pages at a time, 32 pages on each side of a sheet of quad.

CONVERSION TABLES FOR WEIGHTS AND MEASURES

Bold figures equal units of either of the columns beside them; thus: 1 cm = 0.394 inches and 1 inch = 2.540 cm

LENGTH			AREA			VOLUME			WEIGHT (MASS)		
Centimetres		Inches	Square cm		Square in	Cubic cm		Cubic in	Kilograms		Pounds
2.540	1	0.394	6.452	1	0.155	16.387	1	0.061	0.454	1	2.205
5.080	2	0.787	12.903	2	0.310	32.774	2	0.122	0.907	2	4.409
7.620	3	1.181	19.355	3	0.465	49.161	3	0.183	1.361	3	6.614
10.160	4	1.575	25.806	4	0.620	65.548	4	0.244	1.814	4	8.819
12.700	5	1.969	32.258	5	0.775	81.936	5	0.305	2.268	5	11.023
15.240	6	2.362	38.710	6	0.930	98.323	6	0.366	2.722	6	13.228
17.780	7	2.756	45.161	7	1.085	114.710	7	0.427	3.175	7	15.432
20.320	8	3.150	51.613	8	1.240	131.097	8	0.488	3.629	8	17.637
22.860	9	3.543	58.064	9	1.395	147.484	9	0.549	4.082	9	19.842
25.400	10	3.937	64.516	10	1.550	163.871	10	0.610	4.536	10	22.046
50.800	20	7.874	129.032	20	3.100	327.742	20	1.220	9.072	20	44.092
76.200	30	11.811	193.548	30	4.650	491.613	30	1.831	13.608	30	66.139
101.600	40	15.748	258.064	40	6.200	655.484	40	2.441	18.144	40	88.185
127.000	50	19.685	322.580	50	7.750	819.355	50	3.051	22.680	50	110.231
152.400	60	23.622	387.096	60	9.300	983.226	60	3.661	27.216	60	132.277
177.800	70	27.559	451.612	70	10.850	1147.097	70	4.272	31.752	70	154.324
203.200	80	31.496	516.128	80	12.400	1310.968	80	4.882	36.287	80	176.370
228.600	90	35.433	580.644	90	13.950	1474.839	90	5.492	40.823	90	198.416
254.000	100	39.370	645.160	100	15.500	1638.710	100	6.102	45.359	100	220.464
Metres		Yards	Square m		Square yd	Cubic m		Cubic yd	Metric tonnes		Tons (UK)
0.914	1	1.094	0.836	1	1.196	0.765	1	1.308	1.016	1	0.984
1.829	2	2.187	1.672	2	2.392	1.529	2	2.616	2.032	2	1.968
2.743	3	3.281	2.508	3	3.588	2.294	3	3.924	3.048	3	2.953
3.658	4	4.374	3.345	4	4.784	3.058	4	5.232	4.064	4	3.937
4.572	5	5.468	4.181	5	5.980	3.823	5	6.540	5.080	5	4.921
5.486	6	6.562	5.017	6	7.176	4.587	6	7.848	6.096	6	5.905
6.401	7	7.655	5.853	7	8.372	5.352	7	9.156	7.112	7	6.889
7.315	8	8.749	6.689	8	9.568	6.116	8	10.464	8.128	8	7.874
8.230	9	9.843	7.525	9	10.764	6.881	9	11.772	9.144	9	8.858
9.144	10	10.936	8.361	10	11.960	7.646	10	13.080	10.161	10	9.842
18.288	20	21.872	16.723	20	23.920	15.291	20	26.159	20.321	20	19.684
27.432	30	32.808	25.084	30	35.880	22.937	30	39.239	30.481	30	29.526
36.576	40	43.745	33.445	40	47.840	30.582	40	52.318	40.642	40	39.368
45.720	50	54.681	41.806	50	59.799	38.228	50	65.398	50.802	50	49.210
54.864	60	65.617	50.168	60	71.759	45.873	60	78.477	60.963	60	59.052
64.008	70	76.553	58.529	70	83.719	53.519	70	91.557	71.123	70	68.894
73.152	80	87.489	66.890	80	95.679	61.164	80	104.636	81.284	80	78.737
82.296	90	98.425	75.251	90	107.639	68.810	90	117.716	91.444	90	88.579
91.440	100	109.361	83.613	100	119.599	76.455	100	130.795	101.605	100	98.421
Kilometres		Miles	Hectares		Acres	Litres		Gallons	Metric tonnes		Tons (US)
1.609	1	0.621	0.405	1	2.471	4.546	1	0.220	0.907	1	1.102
3.219	2	1.243	0.809	2	4.942	9.092	2	0.440	1.814	2	2.205
4.828	3	1.864	1.214	3	7.413	13.638	3	0.660	2.722	3	3.305
6.437	4	2.485	1.619	4	9.844	18.184	4	0.880	3.629	4	4.409
8.047	5	3.107	2.023	5	12.355	22.730	5	1.100	4.536	5	5.521
9.656	6	3.728	2.428	6	14.826	27.276	6	1.320	5.443	6	6.614
11.265	7	4.350	2.833	7	17.297	31.822	7	1.540	6.350	7	7.716
12.875	8	4.971	3.327	8	19.769	36.368	8	1.760	7.257	8	8.818
14.484	9	5.592	3.642	9	22.240	40.914	9	1.980	8.165	9	9.921
16.093	10	6.214	4.047	10	24.711	45.460	10	2.200	9.072	10	11.023
32.187	20	12.427	8.094	20	49.421	90.919	20	4.400	18.144	20	22.046
48.280	30	18.641	12.140	30	74.132	136.379	30	6.599	27.216	30	33.069
64.374	40	24.855	16.187	40	98.842	181.839	40	8.799	36.287	40	44.092
80.467	50	31.069	20.234	50	123.555	227.298	50	10.999	45.359	50	55.116
96.561	60	37.282	24.281	60	148.263	272.758	60	13.199	54.431	60	66.139
112.654	70	43.496	28.328	70	172.974	318.217	70	15.398	63.503	70	77.162
128.748	80	49.710	32.375	80	197.684	363.677	80	17.598	72.575	80	88.185
144.841	90	55.923	36.422	90	222.395	409.137	90	19.798	81.647	90	99.208
160.934	100	62.137	40.469	100	247.105	454.596	100	21.998	90.719	100	110.231

Abbreviations

A	Associate of
AA	Alcoholics Anonymous
	Automobile Association
AAA	Amateur Athletic Association
AB	Able-bodied seaman
ABA	Amateur Boxing Association
abbr(ev)	abbreviation
ABM	Anti-ballistic missile
abr	abridged
ac	alternating current
a/c	account
AC	Aircraftman
	(*Ante Christum*) Before Christ
	Companion, Order of Australia
ACAS	Advisory, Conciliation and Arbitration Service
ACT	Australian Capital Territory
AD	(*Anno Domini*) In the year of our Lord
ADC	Aide-de-Camp
ADC (P)	Personal ADC to The Queen
adj	adjective
Adj	Adjutant
ad lib	(*ad libitum*) at pleasure
Adm	Admiral
	Admission
adv	adverb
AE	Air Efficiency Award
AEEU	Amalgamated Engineering and Electrical Union
AEM	Air Efficiency Medal
AFC	Air Force Cross
AFM	Air Force Medal
AG	Adjutant-General
	Attorney-General
AGM	air-to-ground missile
	annual general meeting
AH	(*Anno Hegirae*) In the year of the Hegira
AI	Artificial intelligence
AIDS	Acquired immune deficiency syndrome
AIM	Alternative Investment Market
alt	altitude
am	(*ante meridiem*) before noon
AM	(*Anno mundi*) In the year of the world
	amplitude modulation
amp	ampere
	amplifier
ANC	African National Congress
anon	anonymous
ANZAC	Australian and New Zealand Army Corps
AO	Air Officer
	Officer, Order of Australia
AOC	Air Officer Commanding
AONB	Area of Outstanding Natural Beauty
AS	Anglo-Saxon
ASA	Advertising Standards Authority
	Amateur Swimming Association
asap	as soon as possible
ASB	Alternative Service Book
ASEAN	Association of South East Asian Nations
ASH	Action on Smoking and Health
ASLEF	Associated Society of Locomotive Engineers and Firemen
ASLIB	Association for Information Management

ATC	Air Training Corps
AUC	(*ab urbe condita*) In the year from the foundation of Rome
	(*anno urbis conditae*) In the year of the founding of the city
AUT	Association of University Teachers
AV	Audio-visual
	Authorized Version (*of Bible*)
AVR	Army Volunteer Reserve
AWOL	Absent without leave
b	born
	bowled
BA	Bachelor of Arts
BAA	British Airports Authority
	British Astronomical Association
BAF	British Athletics Federation
BAFTA	British Academy of Film and Television Arts
Bart	Baronet
BAS	Bachelor in Agricultural Science
	British Antarctic Survey
BBC	British Broadcasting Corporation
BBSRC	Biotechnology and Biological Sciences Research Council
BC	Before Christ
	British Columbia
B Ch (D)	Bachelor of (Dental) Surgery
BCL	Bachelor of Civil Law
B Com	Bachelor of Commerce
BD	Bachelor of Divinity
BDA	British Dental Association
BDS	Bachelor of Dental Surgery
B Ed	Bachelor of Education
BEM	British Empire Medal
B Eng	Bachelor of Engineering
BFI	British Film Institute
BFPO	British Forces Post Office
BL	British Library
B Litt	Bachelor of Letters *or* of Literature
BM	Bachelor of Medicine
	British Museum
BMA	British Medical Association
B Mus	Bachelor of Music
BOTB	British Overseas Trade Board
Bp	Bishop
B Pharm	Bachelor of Pharmacy
B Phil	Bachelor of Philosophy
Br(it)	Britain
	British
BR	British Rail
Brig	Brigadier
BSc	Bachelor of Science
BSE	Bovine spongiform encephalopathy
BSI	British Standards Institution
BST	British Summer Time
Bt	Baronet
BTEC	Business and Technology Education Council
B Th	Bachelor of Theology
Btu	British thermal unit
BVM	(*Beata Virgo Maria*) Blessed Virgin Mary
BVMS	Bachelor of Veterinary Medicine and Surgery
c	(*circa*) about

C	Celsius
	Centigrade
	Conservative
CA	Chartered Accountant (*Scotland*)
CAA	Civil Aviation Authority
CAB	Citizens' Advice Bureau
Cantab	(of) Cambridge
Cantuar:	of Canterbury (*Archbishop*)
CAP	Common Agricultural Policy
Capt	Captain
Caricom	Caribbean Community and Common Market
Carliol:	of Carlisle (*Bishop*)
CB	Companion, Order of the Bath
CBE	Commander, Order of the British Empire
CBI	Confederation of British Industry
CC	Chamber of Commerce
	Companion, Order of Canada
	City Council
	County Council
	County Court
CCC	County Cricket Club
CCF	Combined Cadet Force
C Chem	Chartered Chemist
CD	Civil Defence
	compact disc
	Corps Diplomatique
Cdr	Commander
Cdre	Commodore
CDS	Chief of the Defence Staff
CE	Christian Era
	Civil Engineer
C Eng	Chartered Engineer
Cestr:	of Chester (*Bishop*)
CET	Central European Time
	Common External Tariff
cf	(*confer*) compare
CF	Chaplain to the Forces
CFC	Chlorofluorocarbon
CFS	Chronic Fatigue Syndrome
CGC	Conspicuous Gallantry Cross
CGM	Conspicuous Gallantry Medal
CGS	Centimetre-gramme-second (*system*)
	Chief of General Staff
CH	Companion of Honour
ChB/M	Bachelor/Master of Surgery
CI	Channel Islands
	The Imperial Order of the Crown of India
CIA	Central Intelligence Agency
Cicestr:	of Chichester (*Bishop*)
CID	Criminal Investigation Department
CIE	Companion, Order of the Indian Empire
cif	cost, insurance and freight
C-in-C	Commander-in-Chief
CIPFA	Chartered Institute of Public Finance and Accountancy
CIS	Commonwealth of Independent States
CJD	Creutzfeld-Jakob disease
C Lit	Companion of Literature
CLJ	Commander, Order of St Lazarus of Jerusalem
CM	(*Chirurgiae Magister*) Master of Surgery
CMG	Companion, Order of St Michael and St George

CND	Campaign for Nuclear Disarmament	
c/o	care of	
CO	Commanding Officer	
	conscientious objector	
COD	Cash on delivery	
C of E	Church of England	
COI	Central Office of Information	
Col	Colonel	
Con	Conservative	
cons	consecrated	
Cpl	Corporal	
CPM	Colonial Police Medal	
CPRE	Council for the Protection of Rural England	
CPS	Crown Prosecution Service	
CPVE	Certificate of Pre-Vocational Education	
CRE	Commission for Racial Equality	
CSA	Child Support Agency	
CSE	Certificate of Secondary Education	
CSI	Companion, Order of the Star of India	
CVO	Commander, Royal Victorian Order	
d	(denarius) penny	
DA	District Attorney (USA)	
DBE	Dame Commander, Order of the British Empire	
dc	direct current	
DC	District Council	
	District of Columbia	
DCB	Dame Commander, Order of the Bath	
D Ch	(Doctor Chirurgiae) Doctor of Surgery	
DCL	Doctor of Civil Law	
DCM	Distinguished Conduct Medal	
DCMG	Dame Commander, Order of St Michael and St George	
DCMS	Department for Culture, Media and Sport	
DCVO	Dame Commander, Royal Victorian Order	
DD	Doctor of Divinity	
DDS	Doctor of Dental Surgery	
DDT	dichlorodiphenyl-trichloroethane	
del	(delineavit) he/she drew it	
DETR	Department of the Environment, Transport and the Regions	
DFC	Distinguished Flying Cross	
DfEE	Department for Education and Employment	
DFID	Department for International Development	
DFM	Distinguished Flying Medal	
DG	(Dei gratia) By the grace of God	
	Director-General	
DH	Department of Health	
DHA	District Health Authority	
Dip Ed	Diploma in Education	
Dip HE	Diploma in Higher Education	
Dip Tech	Diploma in Technology	
DJ	Disc jockey	
DL	Deputy Lieutenant	
D Litt	Doctor of Letters or of Literature	
DM	Deutsche Mark	
D Mus	Doctor of Music	
DNA	deoxyribonucleic acid	
DNB	Dictionary of National Biography	
do	(ditto) the same	
DoE	Department of the Environment	

DOS	Disk operating system (computer)	
DP	Data processing	
D Ph or		
D Phil	Doctor of Philosophy	
DPP	Director of Public Prosecutions	
Dr	Doctor	
D Sc	Doctor of Science	
DSC	Distinguished Service Cross	
DSM	Distinguished Service Medal	
DSO	Companion, Distinguished Service Order	
DSS	Department of Social Security	
DTI	Department of Trade and Industry	
DTP	Desk-top publishing	
Dunelm:	of Durham (Bishop)	
DV	(Deo volente) God willing	
E	East	
Ebor:	of York (Archbishop)	
EBRD	European Bank for Reconstruction and Development	
EC	European Community	
ECG	Electrocardiogram	
ECGD	Export Credits Guarantee Department	
ECSC	European Coal and Steel Community	
ECU	European Currency Unit	
ED	Efficiency Decoration	
EEC	European Economic Community	
EEG	Electroencephalogram	
EFA	European Fighter Aircraft	
EFTA	European Free Trade Association	
eg	(exempli gratia) for the sake of example	
EIB	European Investment Bank	
EMS	European Monetary System	
EMU	European Monetary Union	
EOC	Equal Opportunities Commission	
EPSRC	Engineering and Physical Sciences Research Council	
ER	(Elizabetha Regina) Queen Elizabeth	
ERD	Emergency Reserve Decoration	
ERM	Exchange Rate Mechanism	
ERNIE	Electronic random number indicator equipment	
ESA	European Space Agency	
ESP	Extra-sensory perception	
ESRC	Economic and Social Research Council	
ETA	Euzkadi ta Askatasuna (Basque separatist organization)	
et al	(et alibi) and elsewhere	
	(et alii) and others	
etc	(et cetera) and the other things/ and so forth	
et seq	(et sequentia) and the following	
EU	European Union	
Euratom	European Atomic Energy Commission	
Exon:	of Exeter (Bishop)	
f	(forte) loud	
F	Fahrenheit	
	Fellow of	
FA	Football Association	
FANY	First Aid Nursing Yeomanry	
FAO	Food and Agriculture Organization (UN)	

FBA	Fellow, British Academy	
FBAA	Fellow, British Association of Accountants and Auditors	
FBI	Federal Bureau of Investigation	
FBIM	Fellow, British Institute of Management	
FBS	Fellow, Botanical Society	
FC	Football Club	
FCA	Fellow, Institute of Chartered Accountants in England and Wales	
FCCA	Fellow, Chartered Association of Certified Accountants	
FCGI	Fellow, City and Guilds of London Institute	
FCIA	Fellow, Corporation of Insurance Agents	
FCIArb	Fellow, Chartered Institute of Arbitrators	
FCIB	Fellow, Chartered Institute of Bankers	
	Fellow, Corporation of Insurance Brokers	
FCIBSE	Fellow, Chartered Institution of Building Services Engineers	
FCII	Fellow, Chartered Insurance Institute	
FCIPS	Fellow, Chartered Institute of Purchasing and Supply	
FCIS	Fellow, Institute of Chartered Secretaries and Administrators	
FCIT	Fellow, Chartered Institute of Transport	
FCMA	Fellow, Chartered Institute of Management Accountants	
FCO	Foreign and Commonwealth Office	
FCP	Fellow, College of Preceptors	
FD	(Fidei Defensor) Defender of the Faith	
FE	Further Education	
fec	(fecit) made this	
FEng	Fellow, Royal Academy of Engineering	
ff	(fecerunt) made this (pl)	
	folios following	
ff	(fortissimo) very loud	
FFA	Fellow, Faculty of Actuaries (Scotland)	
	Fellow, Institute of Financial Accountants	
FFAS	Fellow, Faculty of Architects and Surveyors	
FFCM	Fellow, Faculty of Community Medicine	
FFPHM	Fellow, Faculty of Public Health Medicine	
FGS	Fellow, Geological Society	
FHS	Fellow, Heraldry Society	
FHSM	Fellow, Institute of Health Service Management	
FIA	Fellow, Institute of Actuaries	
FIBiol	Fellow, Institute of Biology	
FICE	Fellow, Institution of Civil Engineers	
FICS	Fellow, Institution of Chartered Shipbrokers	
FIEE	Fellow, Institution of Electrical Engineers	
FIERE	Fellow, Institution of Electronic and Radio Engineers	
FIFA	International Association Football Federation	
FIM	Fellow, Institute of Metals	
FIMM	Fellow, Institution of Mining and Metallurgy	
FInstF	Fellow, Institute of Fuel	
FInstP	Fellow, Institute of Physics	

FIQS	Fellow, Institute of Quantity Surveyors
FIS	Fellow, Institute of Statisticians
FJI	Fellow, Institute of Journalists
fl	(*floruit*) flourished
FLA	Fellow, Library Association
FLS	Fellow, Linnaean Society
FM	Field Marshal
	frequency modulation
fo	folio
FO	Flying Officer
fob	free on board
FPhS	Fellow, Philosophical Society
FRAD	Fellow, Royal Academy of Dancing
FRAeS	Fellow, Royal Aeronautical Society
FRAI	Fellow, Royal Anthropological Institute
FRAM	Fellow, Royal Academy of Music
FRAS	Fellow, Royal Asiatic Society
	Fellow, Royal Astronomical Society
FRBS	Fellow, Royal Botanic Society
	Fellow, Royal Society of British Sculptors
FRCA	Fellow, Royal College of Anaesthetists
FRCGP	Fellow, Royal College of General Practitioners
FRCM	Fellow, Royal College of Music
FRCO	Fellow, Royal College of Organists
FRCOG	Fellow, Royal College of Obstetricians and Gynaecologists
FRCP	Fellow, Royal College of Physicians, London
FRCPath	Fellow, Royal College of Pathologists
FRCPE *or* FRCPEd	Fellow, Royal College of Physicians, Edinburgh
FRCPI	Fellow, Royal College of Physicians, Ireland
FRCPsych	Fellow, Royal College of Psychiatrists
FRCR	Fellow, Royal College of Radiologists
FRCS	Fellow, Royal College of Surgeons of England
FRCSE *or* FRCSEd	Fellow, Royal College of Surgeons of Edinburgh
FRCSGlas	Fellow, Royal College of Physicians and Surgeons of Glasgow
FRCSI	Fellow, Royal College of Surgeons in Ireland
FRCVS	Fellow, Royal College of Veterinary Surgeons
FREconS	Fellow, Royal Economic Society
FRGS	Fellow, Royal Geographical Society
FRHistS	Fellow, Royal Historical Society
FRHS	Fellow, Royal Horticultural Society
FRIBA	Fellow, Royal Institute of British Architects
FRICS	Fellow, Royal Institution of Chartered Surveyors
FRMetS	Fellow, Royal Meteorological Society
FRMS	Fellow, Royal Microscopical Society
FRNS	Fellow, Royal Numismatic Society
FRPharmS	Fellow, Royal Pharmaceutical Society

FRPS	Fellow, Royal Photographic Society
FRS	Fellow, Royal Society
FRSA	Fellow, Royal Society of Arts
FRSC	Fellow, Royal Society of Chemistry
FRSE	Fellow, Royal Society of Edinburgh
FRSH	Fellow, Royal Society of Health
FRSL	Fellow, Royal Society of Literature
FRTPI	Fellow, Royal Town Planning Institute
FSA	Fellow, Society of Antiquaries
FSS	Fellow, Royal Statistical Society
FSVA	Fellow, Incorporated Society of Valuers and Auctioneers
FT	*Financial Times*
FTI	Fellow, Textile Institute
FTII	Fellow, Chartered Institute of Taxation
FZS	Fellow, Zoological Society
GATT	General Agreement on Tariffs and Trade
GBE	Dame/Knight Grand Cross, Order of the British Empire
GC	George Cross
GCB	Dame/Knight Grand Cross, Order of the Bath
GCE	General Certificate of Education
GCHQ	Government Communications Headquarters
GCIE	Knight Grand Commander, Order of the Indian Empire
GCLJ	Knight Grand Cross, Order of St Lazarus of Jerusalem
GCMG	Dame/Knight Grand Cross, Order of St Michael and St George
GCSE	General Certificate of Secondary Education
GCSI	Knight Grand Commander, Order of the Star of India
GCVO	Dame/Knight Grand Cross, Royal Victorian Order
GDP	Gross domestic product
Gen	General
GHQ	General Headquarters
GM	George Medal
GMB	General, Municipal, Boilermakers and Allied Trades Union
GMT	Greenwich Mean Time
GNP	Gross national product
GNVQ	General National Vocational Qualification
GOC	General Officer Commanding
GP	General Practitioner
Gp Capt	Group Captain
GSA	Girls' Schools Association
HAC	Honourable Artillery Company
HB	His Beatitude
HBM	Her/His Britannic Majesty('s)
HCF	Highest common factor
	Honorary Chaplain to the Forces
HE	Her/His Excellency
	Higher Education
	His Eminence
HGV	Heavy Goods Vehicle
HH	Her/His Highness
	Her/His Honour
	His Holiness
HIM	Her/His Imperial Majesty

HIV	Human immunodeficiency virus
HJS	(*hic jacet sepultus*) here lies buried
HM	Her/His Majesty('s)
HMAS	Her/His Majesty's Australian Ship
HMC	Headmasters' Conference
HMI	Her/His Majesty's Inspector
HML	Her/His Majesty's Lieutenant
HMS	Her/His Majesty's Ship
HMSO	Her/His Majesty's Stationery Office
HNC	Higher National Certificate
HND	Higher National Diploma
HOLMES	Home Office Large Major Enquiry System
Hon	Honorary
	Honourable
hp	horse power
HP	Hire purchase
HQ	Headquarters
HR	Human resources
HRH	Her/His Royal Highness
HSE	Health and Safety Executive
	(*hic sepultus est*) here lies buried
HSH	Her/His Serene Highness
HWM	High water mark
I	Island
IAAS	Incorporated Association of Architects and Surveyors
IAEA	International Atomic Energy Agency
IATA	International Air Transport Association
ibid	(*ibidem*) in the same place
IBRD	International Bank for Reconstruction and Development
ICAO	International Civil Aviation Organization
ICBM	Inter-continental ballistic missile
ICFTU	International Confederation of Free Trade Unions
ICJ	International Court of Justice
ICRC	International Committee of the Red Cross
id	(*idem*) the same
IDA	International Development Association
IDD	International direct dialling
ie	(*id est*) that is
IEA	International Energy Agency
IFAD	International Fund for Agricultural Development
IFC	International Finance Corporation
IHS	(*Iesus Hominum Salvator*) Jesus the Saviour of Mankind
ILO	International Labour Office/ Organization
ILR	Independent local radio
IMF	International Monetary Fund
IMO	International Maritime Organization
Inc	Incorporated
incog	(*incognito*) unknown, unrecognized
INLA	Irish National Liberation Army
in loc	(*in loco*) in its place
Inmarsat	International Maritime Satellite Organization
INRI	(*Iesus Nazarenus Rex Iudaeorum*) Jesus of Nazareth, King of the Jews
inst	(*instant*) current month

Intelsat   International Telecommunications Satellite Organization
Interpol   International Criminal Police Commission
IOC   International Olympic Committee
IOM   Isle of Man
IOU   I owe you
IOW   Isle of Wight
IQ   Intelligence quotient
IRA   Irish Republican Army
IRC   International Red Cross
Is   Islands
ISBN   International Standard Book Number
ISO   Imperial Service Order
    International Standards Organization
ISSN   International Standard Serial Number
ITC   Independent Television Commission
ITN   Independent Television News
ITU   International Telecommunication Union
ITV   Independent Television

JP   Justice of the Peace

K   Köchel numeration (*of Mozart's works*)
KBE   Knight Commander, Order of the British Empire
KCB   Knight Commander, Order of the Bath
KCIE   Knight Commander, Order of the Indian Empire
KCLJ   Knight Commander, Order of St Lazarus of Jerusalem
KCMG   Knight Commander, Order of St Michael and St George
KCSI   Knight Commander, Order of the Star of India
KCVO   Knight Commander, Royal Victorian Order
KG   Knight of the Garter
KGB   (*Komitet Gosudarstvennoi Besopasnosti*) Committee of State Security (*USSR*)
kHz   kiloHertz
KKK   Ku Klux Klan
KLJ   Knight, Order of St Lazarus of Jerusalem
ko   knock out (*boxing*)
KP   Knight, Order of St Patrick
KStJ   Knight, Order of St John of Jerusalem
Kt   Knight
KT   Knight of the Thistle
kV   Kilovolt
kW   Kilowatt
kWh   Kilowatt hour

L   Liberal
Lab   Labour
Lat   Latitude
lbw   leg before wicket
lc   lower case (*printing*)
LCJ   Lord Chief Justice
LCM   Least/lowest common multiple
LD   Liberal Democrat
LDS   Licentiate in Dental Surgery
LEA   Local Education Authority
LHD   (*Literarum Humaniorum Doctor*) Doctor of Humane Letters/Literature
Lib   Liberal

Lic   (*Licenciado*) lawyer (*Spanish*)
Lic Med   Licentiate in Medicine
Lit   Literary
Lit Hum   (*Literae Humaniores*) Faculty of classics and philosophy, Oxford
Litt D   Doctor of Letters
LJ   Lord Justice
LLB   Bachelor of Laws
LLD   Doctor of Laws
LLM   Master of Laws
LM   Licentiate in Midwifery
LMS   Local management in schools
LMSSA   Licentiate in Medicine and Surgery, Society of Apothecaries
loc cit   (*loco citato*) in the place cited
log   logarithm
Londin: of London (*Bishop*)
Long   Longitude
LS   (*loco sigilli*) place of the seal
LSA   Licentiate of Society of Apothecaries
Lsd   (*Librae, solidi, denarii*) £, shillings and pence
LSE   London School of Economics and Political Science
Lt   Lieutenant
LTA   Lawn Tennis Association
Ltd   Limited (liability)
LTh or L Theol   Licentiate in Theology
LVO   Lieutenant, Royal Victorian Order
LW   long wave
LWM   Low water mark

M   Member of
    Monsieur
MA   Master of Arts
MAFF   Ministry of Agriculture, Fisheries and Food
Maj   Major
max   maximum
MB   Bachelor of Medicine
MBA   Master of Business Administration
MBE   Member, Order of the British Empire
MC   Master of Ceremonies
    Military Cross
MCC   Marylebone Cricket Club
MCh(D)   Master of (Dental) Surgery
MD   Managing Director
    Doctor of Medicine
MDS   Master of Dental Surgery
ME   Middle English
    Myalgic Encephalomyelitis
MEC   Member of Executive Council
MEd   Master of Education
mega   one million times
MEP   Member of the European Parliament
MFH   Master of Foxhounds
Mgr   Monsignor
MI   Military Intelligence
micro   one-millionth part
milli   one-thousandth part
min   minimum
MIRAS   Mortgage Interest Relief at Source
MLA   Member of Legislative Assembly
MLC   Member of Legislative Council
MLitt   Master of Letters
Mlle   Mademoiselle
MLR   Minimum lending rate
MM   Military Medal
Mme   Madame
MN   Merchant Navy
MO   Medical Officer/Orderly

MoD   Ministry of Defence
MoT   Ministry of Transport
MP   Member of Parliament
    Military Police
mph   miles per hour
M Phil   Master of Philosophy
MR   Master of the Rolls
MRC   Medical Research Council
MS   Master of Surgery
    Manuscript (*pl* MSS)
    Multiple Sclerosis
MSc   Master of Science
MSF   Manufacturing, Science and Finance Union
MTh   Master of Theology
Mus B/D   Bachelor/Doctor of Music
MV   Merchant Vessel
    Motor Vessel
MVO   Member, Royal Victorian Order
MW   medium wave

N   North
n/a   not applicable
    not available
NAAFI   Navy, Army and Air Force Institutes
NASA   National Aeronautics and Space Administration
NAS/UWT   National Association of Schoolmasters/Union of Women Teachers
NATO   North Atlantic Treaty Organization
NB   New Brunswick
    (*nota bene*) note well
NCIS   National Criminal Intelligence Service
NCO   Non-commissioned officer
NDPB   Non-departmental public body
NEB   New English Bible
nem con   (*nemine contradicente*) no one contradicting
NERC   Natural Environment Research Council
nes   not elsewhere specified
NFT   National Film Theatre
NFU   National Farmers' Union
NHS   National Health Service
NI   National Insurance
    Northern Ireland
NIV   New International Version (*of Bible*)
No   (*numero*) number
non seq   (*non sequitur*) it does not follow
Norvic: of Norwich (*Bishop*)
NP   Notary Public
NRA   National Rifle Association
NS   New Style (*calendar*)
    Nova Scotia
NSPCC   National Society for the Prevention of Cruelty to Children
NSW   New South Wales
NT   National Theatre
    National Trust
    New Testament
NUJ   National Union of Journalists
NUM   National Union of Mineworkers
NUS   National Union of Students
NUT   National Union of Teachers
NVQ   National Vocational Qualification
NWT   Northwest Territory
NY   New York
NZ   New Zealand

OAPEC	Organization of Arab Petroleum Exporting Countries	PGA	Professional Golfers Association	RADA	Royal Academy of Dramatic Art
OAS	Organization of American States	PGCE	Postgraduate Certificate of Education	RADC	Royal Army Dental Corps
OAU	Organization of African Unity	PhD	Doctor of Philosophy	RAE	Royal Aerospace Establishment
Ob *or* obit	died	pinx(it)	he/she painted it	RAEC	Royal Army Educational Corps
OBE	Officer, Order of the British Empire	pl	plural	RAeS	Royal Aeronautical Society
OC	Officer Commanding	PLA	Port of London Authority	RAF	Royal Air Force
ODA	Overseas Development Administration	PLC	Public Limited Company	RAM	Random-access memory (*computer*)
		PLO	Palestine Liberation Organization		Royal Academy of Music
OE	Old English omissions excepted	pm	(*post meridiem*) after noon	RAMC	Royal Army Medical Corps
OECD	Organization for Economic Co-operation and Development	PM	Prime Minister	RAN	Royal Australian Navy
		PMRAFNS	Princess Mary's Royal Air Force Nursing Service	RAOC	Royal Army Ordnance Corps
OED	*Oxford English Dictionary*	PO	Petty Officer	RAPC	Royal Army Pay Corps
Offer	Office of Electricity Regulation		Pilot Officer	RAVC	Royal Army Veterinary Corps
			Post Office	RBG	Royal Botanic Garden
Ofgas	Office of Gas Supply		postal order	RBS	Royal Society of British Sculptors
OFM	Order of Friars Minor (*Franciscans*)	POW	Prisoner of War	RC	Red Cross
		pp	pages		Roman Catholic
Ofsted	Office for Standards in Education		(*per procurationem*) by proxy	RCM	Royal College of Music
		PPARC	Particle Physics and Astronomy Research Council	RCN	Royal Canadian Navy
OFT	Office of Fair Trading	PPS	Parliamentary Private Secretary	RCT	Royal Corps of Transport
Oftel	Office of Telecommunications			RD	Refer to drawer (*banking*)
Ofwat	Office of Water Services	PR	Proportional representation		Royal Naval and Royal Marine Forces Reserve Decoration
OHMS	On Her/His Majesty's Service		Public relations		Rural Dean
OM	Order of Merit	PRA	President of the Royal Academy		
OND	Ordinary National Diploma			RDI	Royal Designer for Industry
ONO	or near offer	Pro tem	(*pro tempore*) for the time being	RE	Religious Education
ONS	Office for National Statistics	Prox	(*proximo*) next month		Royal Engineers
op	(*opus*) work	PRS	President of the Royal Society	REME	Royal Electrical and Mechanical Engineers
OP	Opposite prompt side (*of theatre*)	PRSE	President of the Royal Society of Edinburgh	Rep	Representative
		Ps	Psalm		Republican
	Order of Preachers (*Dominicans*)	PS	(*postscriptum*) postscript	Rev(d)	Reverend
	out of print (*books*)	PSBR	Public sector borrowing requirement	RFU	Rugby Football Union
op cit	(*opere citato*) in the work cited			RGN	Registered General Nurse
OPCS	Office of Population Censuses and Surveys	psc	passed Staff College	RGS	Royal Geographical Society
		PSV	Public Service Vehicle	RHA	Regional Health Authority
OPEC	Organization of Petroleum Exporting Countries	PTA	Parent-Teacher Association	RHS	Royal Horticultural Society
		Pte	Private		Royal Humane Society
OPRAF	Office of Passenger Rail Franchising	PTO	Please turn over	RI	Rhode Island
		PVC	Polyvinyl chloride		Royal Institute of Painters in Watercolours
OPS	Office of Public Service				Royal Institution
ORR	Office of the Rail Regulator	QARANC	Queen Alexandra's Royal Army Nursing Corps	RIBA	Royal Institute of British Architects
OS	Old Style (*calendar*)			RIP	(*Requiescat in pace*) May he/she rest in peace
	Ordnance Survey	QARNNS	Queen Alexandra's Royal Naval Nursing Service		
OSA	Order of St Augustine	QB(D)	Queen's Bench (Division)	RIR	Royal Irish Regiment
OSB	Order of St Benedict	QC	Queen's Counsel	RL	Rugby League
OSCE	Organization for Security and Co-operation in Europe	QED	(*quod erat demonstrandum*) which was to be proved	RM	Registered Midwife
					Royal Marines
O St J	Officer, Order of St John of Jerusalem	QGM	Queen's Gallantry Medal	RMA	Royal Military Academy
		QHC	Queen's Honorary Chaplain	RMN	Registered Mental Nurse
OT	Old Testament	QHDS	Queen's Honorary Dental Surgeon	RMT	National Union of Rail, Maritime and Transport Workers
OTC	Officers' Training Corps				
Oxon	(of) Oxford Oxfordshire	QHNS	Queen's Honorary Nursing Sister	RN	Royal Navy
		QHP	Queen's Honorary Physician	RNIB	Royal National Institute for the Blind
		QHS	Queen's Honorary Surgeon		
p	page	QMG	Quartermaster General	RNID	Royal National Institute for the Deaf
p	(*piano*) softly	QPM	Queen's Police Medal		
PA	Personal Assistant	QS	Quarter Sessions	RNLI	Royal National Lifeboat Institution
	Press Association	QSO	Quasi-stellar object (quasar)		
PAYE	Pay as You Earn		Queen's Service Order	RNMH	Registered Nurse for the Mentally Handicapped
pc	(*per centum*) in the hundred	quango	quasi-autonomous non-governmental organization		
PC	personal computer			RNR	Royal Naval Reserve
	Police Constable	qv	(*quod vide*) which see	RNVR	Royal Naval Volunteer Reserve
	politically correct				
	Privy Counsellor			RNXS	Royal Naval Auxiliary Service
PCC	Press Complaints Commission	R	(*Regina*) Queen	RNZN	Royal New Zealand Navy
PDSA	People's Dispensary for Sick Animals		(*Rex*) King	Ro	(*Recto*) on the right-hand page
PE	Physical Education	RA	Royal Academy/Academician	ROC	Royal Observer Corps
PEP	Personal equity plan		Royal Artillery	Roffen:	of Rochester (*Bishop*)
Petriburg:	of Peterborough (*Bishop*)	RAC	Royal Armoured Corps	ROI	Royal Institute of Oil Painters
PFI	Private Finance Initiative		Royal Automobile Club	ROM	Read-only memory (*computer*)

RoSPA	Royal Society for the Prevention of Accidents
RP	Royal Society of Portrait Painters
rpm	revolutions per minute
RRC	Lady of Royal Red Cross
RSA	Republic of South Africa
	Royal Scottish Academician
	Royal Society of Arts
RSC	Royal Shakespeare Company
RSCN	Registered Sick Children's Nurse
RSE	Royal Society of Edinburgh
RSM	Regimental Sergeant Major
RSPB	Royal Society for the Protection of Birds
RSPCA	Royal Society for the Prevention of Cruelty to Animals
RSV	Revised Standard Version (of Bible)
RSVP	(Répondez, s'il vous plaît) Please reply
RSW	Royal Scottish Society of Painters in Watercolours
RTPI	Royal Town Planning Institute
RU	Rugby Union
RUC	Royal Ulster Constabulary
RV	Revised Version (of Bible)
RVM	Royal Victorian Medal
RWS	Royal Water Colour Society
RYS	Royal Yacht Squadron
s	second
	(solidus) shilling
S	South
SA	Salvation Army
	South Africa
	South America
	South Australia
SAE	stamped addressed envelope
Salop	Shropshire
Sarum:	of Salisbury (Bishop)
SAS	Special Air Service Regiment
SBN	Standard Book Number
SBS	Special Boat Squadron
ScD	Doctor of Science
SCM	State Certified Midwife
SDLP	Social Democratic and Labour Party
SEAQ	Stock Exchange Automated Quotations system
SEN	State Enrolled Nurse
SERPS	State Earnings Related Pension Scheme
SFO	Serious Fraud Office
SHMIS	Society of Headmasters and Headmistresses of Independent Schools
SI	(Système International d'Unités) International System of Units
	Statutory Instrument
sic	so written
Sig	Signature
	Signor
SJ	Society of Jesus (Jesuits)
SLD	Social and Liberal Democrats
SMP	Statutory Maternity Pay
SNP	Scottish National Party
SOE	Special Operations Executive
SOS	Save Our Souls (distress signal)
sp	(sine prole) without issue
spgr	specific gravity
SPQR	(Senatus Populusque Romanus) The Senate and People of Rome
SRN	State Registered Nurse
SRO	Self Regulating Organizations

SS	Saints
	Schutzstaffel (Nazi paramilitary organization)
	Steamship
SSC	Solicitor before Supreme Court (Scotland)
SSF	Society of St Francis
SSN	Standard Serial Number
SSP	Statutory Sick Pay
SSSI	Site of special scientific interest
STD	(Sacrae Theologiae Doctor) Doctor of Sacred Theology
	Subscriber trunk dialling
stet	let it stand (printing)
stp	Standard temperature and pressure
STP	(Sacrae Theologiae Professor) Professor of Sacred Theology
Sub Lt	Sub-Lieutenant
SVQ	Scottish Vocational Qualification
TA	Territorial Army
TB	Tuberculosis
TCCB	Test and County Cricket Board
TD	Territorial Efficiency Decoration
TEC	Training and Enterprise Council
TEFL	Teaching English as a foreign language
temp	temperature
	temporary employee
TES	Times Educational Supplement
TGWU	Transport and General Workers' Union
THES	Times Higher Education Supplement
TLS	Times Literary Supplement
TNT	trinitrotoluene (explosive)
trans	translated
trs	transpose (printing)
TRH	Their Royal Highnesses
TT	Teetotal
	Tourist Trophy (motorcycle races)
	Tuberculin tested
TUC	Trades Union Congress
TVEI	Technical and Vocational Education Initiative
U	Unionist
UAE	United Arab Emirates
uc	upper case (printing)
UCAS	Universities and Colleges Admissions Service
UCATT	Union of Construction, Allied Trades and Technicians
UCL	University College London
UDA	Ulster Defence Association
UDI	Unilateral Declaration of Independence
UDM	Union of Democratic Mineworkers
UDR	Ulster Defence Regiment
UEFA	Union of European Football Associations
UFF	Ulster Freedom Fighters
UFO	Unidentified flying object
UHF	ultra-high frequency
UK	United Kingdom
UKAEA	UK Atomic Energy Authority
UN	United Nations
UNESCO	United Nations Educational, Scientific and Cultural Organization

UNHCR	United Nations High Commissioner for Refugees
UNICEF	United Nations Children's Fund
UNIDO	United Nations Industrial Development Organization
Unita	National Union for the Total Independence of Angola
UPU	Universal Postal Union
URC	United Reformed Church
US(A)	United States (of America)
USDAW	Union of Shop, Distributive and Allied Workers
USM	Unlisted Securities Market
USSR	Union of Soviet Socialist Republics
UTC	Co-ordinated Universal Time system
UVF	Ulster Volunteer Force
v	(versus) against
VA	Vicar Apostolic
	Victoria and Albert Order
VAD	Voluntary Aid Detachment
V and A	Victoria and Albert Museum
VAT	Value added tax
VC	Victoria Cross
VCR	video cassette recorder
VD	Venereal disease
	Volunteer Officers' Decoration
VDU	Visual display unit
Ven	Venerable
VHF	very high frequency
VIP	Very important person
Vo	(Verso) on the left-hand page
VRD	Royal Naval Volunteer Reserve Officers' Decoration
VSO	Voluntary Service Overseas
VTOL	Vertical take-off and landing (aircraft)
W	West
WCC	World Council of Churches
WEA	Workers' Educational Association
WEU	Western European Union
WFTU	World Federation of Trade Unions
WHO	World Health Organization
WI	West Indies
	Women's Institute
Winton:	of Winchester (Bishop)
WIPO	World Intellectual Property Organization
WMO	World Meteorological Organization
WO	Warrant Officer
WRAC	Women's Royal Army Corps
WRAF	Women's Royal Air Force
WRNS	Women's Royal Naval Service
WRVS	Women's Royal Voluntary Service
WS	Writer to the Signet
WTO	World Trade Organization
YMCA	Young Men's Christian Association
YWCA	Young Women's Christian Association
Ψ = seaport	

Index

Lambeth 532, 557
  Archdeacon 409
  Education Authority 441
Lammas (term day) 9
Lampeter University College 452
Lanarkshire:
  Education Authorities 442
  Lord Lieutenant 564
  North 533, 565
  South 533, 565
Lancashire 529, 543, 544
  Central, University of 446
  Education Authority 439
  MEPs 271–2, 272
  Police Authority 374
Lancashire, West 532, 550
  MP 249
Lancaster 531, 548
  Archdeacon 403
  Bishop (RC) 414
  Bishop (Suffragan) 403
  Duchy of 295
  University 447
Lancaster and Wyre, MP 249
Land Authority for Wales 352
Land Court, Scottish 365
Land Registers:
  of Northern Ireland 330
  of Scotland 316–17
Land Registry, HM 316–17
  regional offices 316
Lands Tribunal 370
  Scotland 370
Language colleges 426
Laos 783, 928
  map 831
La Paz 783, 820
Larne 568
Las Palmas 1019
Latvia 784, 928–30
  map 869
Lauderdale, Tweeddale, Ettrick and,
  MP 267
Laurence, Captain Timothy 117
Law:
  adoption 651
  births 651–2
  citizenship 652–3
  consumer 653–5
  custody of children 657
  death 652, 655–6
  divorce 656–9
  domestic violence 658
  education and training 458–9
  employment 659–60
  franchise 666–7
  intestacy 669
  jury service 660–1
  leases 661–2
  legal aid 662–4
  legitimacy 660
  marriage 652, 664–6
  proceedings against Crown 655
  separation 657
  tenancies 661–2
  town and country planning 666
  voters' qualifications 666–7
  wills 667–9
Law Commission 317
  Scottish 317
Law courts:
  England and Wales 354–64
  Northern Ireland 367–8
  Scotland 364–7
  tribunals 359–72
Law lords 136, 157, 354
Lawn tennis 1220
Law Officers 276, 317, 320
  departments 317, 320–1
Law Societies 458–9

Law terms 9
Lay magistrates 354
Leader of the Opposition 221, 224
League of Arab States 758
Leamington, Warwick and, MP 259
Leap year 81
Leases, legal notes 661–2
Lebanon 783, 930–2
Leeds 529, 538, 545
  airport 504
  Archdeacon 408
  Bishop (RC) 414
  Education Authority 440
  MEP 272
  MPs 249
  universities 447, 448
Legal advice and assistance scheme 663
Legal affairs (1997–8) 1086–90
Legal aid 662–4
Legal Aid Board 317
  Scottish 317
Legal education and training 458–9
Legal Services Ombudsmen 317–18
Legal tender 611, 612
Legal year 86–7
Legitimacy, legal notes 660
Leicester 529, 538, 545
  Archdeacon 406
  Bishop 164, 406
  Education Authority 440
  MEP 272
  MPs 249
  universities 448
Leicestershire 529, 543, 544
  Education Authority 439
  Police Authority 374
Leicestershire North West 531, 548
  MP 249
  Nottingham and, MEP 273
Leigh, MP 249
Leighlin, Kildare and, Bishop (RC) 415
Leith and Edinburgh North, MP 265
Lelu 952
Length, measurement 1234, 1236–7
Lent 82
Leominster, MP 249
Lesotho 782, 932–3
Lewes 531, 548
  Bishop (Suffragan) 404
  MP 249
Lewes and Hastings, Archdeacon 404
Lewisham 532, 557
  Archdeacon 409
  Education Authority 441
  MPs 249
Lewis with Harris 562
Leyton and Wanstead, MP 249
Liberal Democrats 225
  development 224
  financial support 224
  local government
    representation 529–33
  MEPs 269–70
  MPs 226–33
  spokesmen 225
  whips 225
Liberal Party 224, 732
  development 224
Liberia 782, 933–4
  map 971
Libra, first point of 69
Librarianship training 459
Libraries, national 318–19
Library and Information Commission 318
Libreville 781, 877
Libya 782, 934–5
Licences:
  driving 509
  fishing 583
  marriage 664, 665

Licences *continued*
  television 673
  vehicle 509
Licensing corporations, medical 459–60
Lichfield 531, 548
  Archdeacon 406
  Bishop 164, 406
  MP 250
Liechtenstein 784, 935–6
Life expectancy tables 114
Life insurance:
  business 629
  companies 630–2
Life peers 136, 157–63
  forms of address 135
Lifetime Learning Directorate,
  Employment and 296
Lighthouse authorities 319, 510
Lighthouses 510
Lighting-up time 71
Lihou 570
Lilongwe 782, 941
Lima 783, 983
Limavady 568
Limerick, Bishop (RC) 416
Limerick and Killaloe, Bishop 412
Lincoln 531, 538–9, 548
  Archdeacon 406
  Bishop 164, 406
  MP 250
Lincolnshire 529, 543, 544
  Education Authority 439
  North 529, 545
  North East 529, 545
  Police Authority 375
Lincolnshire and Humberside:
  South, MEP 272
  University 448
Lincoln's Inn 459, 598
Lindisfarne, Archdeacon 407
Lindsey:
  Archdeacon 406
  East 530, 547
  West 532, 550
Linlithgow, MP 266
Lisbon 784, 988
Lisburn 568
Lismore, Waterford and, Bishop (RC) 416
Literature:
  (1997–8) 1148–52
  awards 1149–50, 1152
  Booker prize 1149, 1152
  Nobel prize 423
Lithuania 784, 936–7
  map 869
Littlehampton, Bognor Regis and,
  MP 238
Liverpool 529, 539, 545
  airport 504
  Archbishop (RC) 414
  Archdeacon 407
  Bishop 164, 406
  Education Authority 440
  MPs 250
  universities 448
Livery companies, London 554–6
Livingston 496
  MP 266
Ljubljana 785, 1012
Llandaff, Bishop 411
Llanelli, MP 262
Lloyd's of London 598, 627–8
Local administration, commissions
  for 320
Local Agenda 21, 572
Local authorities:
  changes 523, 527
  England 529–32, 543–51
  government support for 605
  London 532, 557

Queen Elizabeth the Queen Mother
  continued
  office 121
  Orders of Chivalry 170, 171, 172
Queen Maud Land 975
Queens:
  British 131–2
  of England 129–31
  of Scots 132–3
Queen's Awards 670–2
Queen's Bench Division 354, 356
  Lord Chief Justice 356
Queen's Coroner and Attorney 357
Queen's Gallery 593
Queensland 804
Queen's Messengers, Corps of 303
Queen's Proctor 350
Queen's Remembrancer 357
Queen's University of Belfast 451
Queen Victoria 127, 131
  descendants 127–9
Quito 783, 863

Rabat 782, 956
Racial Equality, Commission for 335
Racing:
  athletics 1206–9
  greyhound 1216
  horse 13, 1216–18
  motor 1221
Rackets 1222
Radio:
  (1997–8) 1131–2
  audience share 673
  awards 1132
  BBC 675–6
  digital 675
  independent stations 676–81
  time-signals 74–5
Radio Authority 335–6, 673
Radiocommunications Agency 349
Radiography training 460
Radiological Protection Board,
  National 328
Radiotherapy training 460
Radnorshire, Brecon and, MP 262
Rail Regulator, Office of the 336, 505
Railtrack 505–6
Railways 505–6
  enquiries 505
  National Museum 324, 595
  operating companies 505
  privatization 505
  safety 506
  White Paper 505, 1171
Railways Board, British 287
Rainfall:
  averages 1199
  records 1200–3
Rallying, motor 1221
Ramadan 9, 86
Rambert Dance Company 1141, 1143
Rampton Hospital 307
Ramsar Convention 579
Ramsbury, Bishop (Suffragan) 409
Rangoon 959
Raphoe, Bishop (RC) 416
Raphoe, Derry and, Bishop 412
Rarotonga 785, 968
Ras al Khaimah 1049
Rate Collection Agency (Northern
  Ireland) 330
Rates 524
  Northern Ireland 528
Rayleigh, MP 253
Reading 529, 545
  Bishop (Area) 407
  Education Authority 440
  MPs 253
  University 451

Real tennis 1222
Recognized clearing houses 635
Recognized investment exchanges 635
Reconstruction and Development,
  International Bank for, UN 769
Recorders 360–2
  Northern Ireland 367
Record offices:
  Corporation of London 337
  House of Lords 336
  Public Record Office 336
  Scottish 337
Redbridge 532, 557
  Education Authority 441
Redcar and Cleveland 529, 545
  Education Authority 440
Redcar, MP 253
Red Cross and Red Crescent Movement,
  International 757–8
Red Deer Commission, *see* Deer
  Commission for Scotland
Reddish, Denton and, MP 242
Redditch 496, 531, 549
  MP 253
Red-letter days 87
Refraction, Mean 75
Regent's Park 599
Regent's Park and Kensington North,
  MP 253
Regina 834
Regional Advisory Councils, further
  education 443
Regional arts boards 283
Regional councils, Scotland 527
Regional Development Agencies 522
Regional offices:
  government 304–5
  NHS Executive 479
Register Office, General 342, 652
Registers of Scotland 316–17
Registrar-General, Scotland 342
Regnal year 87
Reigate:
  Archdeacon 409
  MP 253
Reigate and Banstead 531, 549
Relief and Works Agency for Palestine
  Refugees in the Near East 764
Religion in UK 396–9
  statistics 396
Religious festivals 9, 82–6
Religious Society of Friends 420
Remembrance Sunday 9
Removal days, Scotland 9
Renfrewshire 533, 565
  East 533, 565
  Education Authorities 442
  Lord Lieutenant 564
Renfrew West, MP 267
Repton, Bishop (Suffragan) 404
Research associations, industrial 708–10
Research Councils:
  Biotechnology and Biological
    Sciences 704
  Council for the Central Laboratory
    of 705
  Economic and Social 705
  Engineering and Physical Sciences 706
  Medical 706
  Natural Environment 707
  Particle Physics and Astronomy 707
Research Institutes, Scottish Agricultural
  and Biological 705
Resignations (1997–8) 1096–7
Restormel 531, 549
Restrictive Practices Court
  Clerk 357
  members 357
Retail Price Index 609
Retirement pensions, *see* Pensions
Réunion 782, 876

Revenue support grant 525
Review bodies, pay 337–8
Reykjavik 784, 895
Rhineland Palatinate 882
Rhode Island 1052
Rhondda, MP 263
Rhondda, Cynon, Taff 532, 560
  Education Authority 442
Rhymney, Merthyr Tydfil and,
  MP 262–3
Ribble:
  MPs 253–4
  South 531, 549
Ribble Valley 531, 549
Richard Alston Dance Company 1143
Richborough, Bishop (Suffragan) 401
Richmond (Yorkshire):
  Archdeacon 408
  Cleveland and, MEP 271
  MP 254
Richmond Park, MP 254
Richmondshire 531, 549
Richmond upon Thames 532, 557
  Education Authority 441
Riga 784, 929
Right ascension 69, 71, 72
Rio Earth Summit 571
Ripon:
  Bishop 164, 408
  Skipton and, MP 255
Rivers, longest 108
Riverside (Liverpool), MP 250
Riyadh 784, 1004
Road passenger services 508
Roads 506–10
  building programme 507
  private finance 507
  review 507
  usage 509
  White Paper 507, 1171
Road safety 508
Roads Service (Northern Ireland) 330
Road Town 783, 1070
Road walking 1222
Robert Gordon University 451
Rochdale 529, 545
  Archdeacon 407
  Education Authority 440
  MP 254
Rochester:
  Archdeacon 408
  Bishop 164, 408
Rochford 531, 549
  and Southend East, MP 254
Rodrigues Island 950
Rogation days 83
Rogation Sunday 9, 83
Roman calendar 89
Roman Catholic Church 413–16
  apostolic nuncios 414, 415
  Great Britain 414–15
  Holy See 413, 1059
  Ireland 415–16
  overseas 416
  patriarchs in communion with 416
Romania 785, 991–2
Roman indiction 9, 87
Rome 784, 911
  Treaty of 772
Romford, MP 254
Romsey, MP 254
Ronaldsway (Isle of Man) 504
Roseau 782, 861
Ross, Cork and, Bishop (RC) 415
Ross, Cork, Cloyne and, Bishop 412
Ross, Moray and Caithness, Bishop 411
Ross, Skye, and Inverness West MP 267
Ross and Cromarty, Lord Lieutenant 564
Ross Dependency 785, 966, 968
Rossendale 531, 549
  and Darwen, MP 254

Stop-press

ROYAL HOUSEHOLDS

Master of the Horse – The Lord Vestey replaces The Lord Somerleyton

PEERAGE

Baron Coleraine married

Died: 3rd Viscount Rothermere; 2nd Baron Marks of Broughton

BARONETAGE AND KNIGHTAGE

Died: Sir Geoffrey Bateman; Rt. Hon. Sir Denys Buckley; Sir Eric Callard; Sir Frank Ereaut; Vice-Adm. Sir John Hayes; Sir Horace Heyman; Sir Francis Renoug; Air Chief Marshal Sir Frederick Rosier; Sir Guy Sauzier; Sir Rupert Speir; Sir Michael Straker; Sir Arthur Vick

PRIVY COUNCIL

Sir Denys Buckley died

PARLIAMENT

Political parties – David McLetchie elected leader of the Scottish Conservatives; Allan Macartney, MEP, senior vice-convenor of the SNP, died

MPs – Tommy Graham, *Lab.* Renfrewshire West, expelled from Labour Party and will sit as an independent

MEPs – Allan Macartney, MEP, died

GOVERNMENT DEPARTMENTS AND PUBLIC OFFICES

Arts Council of Northern Ireland – Miss M. O'Neill appointed vice-chairman

Bank of England – Ms M. Lowther appointed Chief Cashier

BBC – Matthew Banister appointed chief executive, BBC Productions; Sam Younger replaced by Mark Byford as head of the World Service

ECGD – A. Brown appointed to Export Guarantees Advisory Council

Offer – Prof. Littlechild to be replaced as Director-General of Electricity Supply by Callum McCarthy

Equal Opportunities Commission – chairwoman Ms K. Bahl relinquishes post Nov. 1998

Ofgas – C. Spottiswood to be replaced as Director-General of Gas Supply by Callum McCarthy

Victoria and Albert Museum – J. Scott is acting chairman of board of trustees until new chairman appointed

Museum of London – R. Hambro replaces P. Revell-Smith as chairman of board of governors

National Investment and Loans Board – D. W. Midgley to be a commissioner of Public Works Loan Board

Rail Regulator – J. Swift to relinquish post in Nov. 1998

DTI – Dr J. Taylor replaces Sir John Cadogan as director-general of Research Councils from Jan. 1999

LAW COURTS AND OFFICES

Lord Justice of Appeal – Sir Simon Tuckey; Sir Anthony Clarke appointed

High Court appointments – C. A. St J. Gray, QC; R. C. Klevan, QC (Queen's Bench Division)

Circuit judges – D. B. D. Lowe; D. A. Paiba (SE circuit) retired

Sheriffs – Sheriff J. D. Lowe (Glasgow and Strathkelvin) died

Sheriff-clerks – D. Nicoll appointed to Dundee; R. Cockburn appointed to Glasgow

DEFENCE

Navy – J. M. de Halpert promoted Rear Admiral; replaces Rear Adm. Malbon as Naval Secretary/Chief Executive of Naval Manning Agency in Dec. 1998

RAF – Air Vice-Marshal P. Norriss promoted Air Marshal; replaced Lt.-Gen. Sir Robert Hayman-Joyce as Deputy Chief of Defence Procurement (Operations); Norriss replaced as Director-General Air Systems 1 by Air Vice-Marshal A. Nicholson

CHURCH OF ENGLAND

London – Brian Masters, Area Bishop of Edmonton, died

ENERGY

Director-Generals of Electricity Supply and of Gas Supply to be replaced by Callum McCarthy, who will become Energy Regulator

TRANSPORT

Rail Regulator – J. Swift to relinquish post in Nov. 1998

LOCAL GOVERNMENT

Lord Mayor of London 1998–9 – The Lord Levene of Portsoken, elected 29 September

TRADE UNIONS

President of the TUC 1998–9 – Hector MacKenzie (UNISON)

Union for Bradford and Bingley Staff affiliated to TUC

SOCIETIES AND INSTITUTIONS

RNLI – B. Miles replaced as director by A. Freemantle

COUNTRIES OF THE WORLD

Albania – British Ambassador now Stephen Nash

Belize – Said Musa (People's United Party) became prime minister on 1 September

Bosnia-Hercegovina – Elections on 12 September won in Republika Srpska by ultra-nationalist Nikola Poplasen, and in Bosniac-Croat federation by Ante Jelevic and Alija Izetbegovic; overall federation president will be Zivko Radisic

Brunei – British High Commissioner now Stuart Laing

Germany – general election on 27 September lost by ruling Christian Democratic Union party; Kohl resigned as Chancellor and CDU party leader

Malta – Nationalist Party won legislative elections on 5 September; Eddie Fenech-Adami became prime minister

Russian Federation – Alexander Shokhin resigned as Russian deputy prime minister on 25 September

Sweden – Social Democratic Party lost support in the general election on 20 September, but will probably stay in power in a coalition

SPORTS RECORDS
Swimming – men's 4 × 200 freestyle relay: Australia,
  7 min. 11.86 sec.

OBITUARIES

August 1998
26 Frederick Reines, American physicist and Nobel
  laureate in 1995, aged 80

September 1998
 2 Roy Bradford, MP at Stormont 1965–73, aged 77
  3rd Viscount Rothermere, newspaper proprietor,
  aged 73
 6 Akira Kurosawa, Japanese film director, aged 88
11 Frank Haynes, Labour MP for Ashfield 1979–92,
  aged 72
13 George Wallace, former governor of Alabama, aged
  79
14 Yang Shangkun, president of China 1988–92, aged
  91
19 Patricia Hayes, actress, aged 88
21 Florence Griffith-Joyner, athlete, aged 38

EVENTS – SEPTEMBER 1998

2. The British and Irish parliaments were recalled to
debate and pass anti-terrorist legislation drawn up after
the bombing at Omagh on 15 August. Thousands of
students in Myanmar demonstrated against the country's military rulers. **3.** President Clinton visited
Northern Ireland. The Russian rouble reached a new
low of 17.5 to the US$. **6.** Iran moved troops to its
border with Afghanistan after Iranian diplomats and
journalists in Afghanistan were killed by Taleban
soldiers. **7.** The seven states involved in fighting in the
Democratic Republic of Congo held talks on the
conflict and the future of the country. The satellite
television group BSkyB announced a £625 million
agreement to buy Manchester United FC. **8.** There
were anti-government demonstrations in Jakarta, Indonesia and Phnom Penh, Cambodia. The Commonwealth
Games opened in Malaysia. **9.** The Royal Opera House
announced plans to shut down the Royal Opera
company for 11 months in 1999 in order to save money.
11. The report of independent prosecutor Kenneth
Starr was published on the Internet and alleged 11
offences that might constitute grounds for the impeachment of President Clinton. **13.** The death toll as a result
of the flooding in Bangladesh rose to 950. President
Zeroual of Algeria called early presidential elections for
February 1999 and announced he would not be standing for re-election. **14.** The Northern Ireland Assembly
met for the first time at Stormont. **16.** Turkish forces
killed 53 Kurdish rebels near the border with Iraq. **17.**
The Queen and the Duke of Edinburgh arrived in
Brunei for a three-day state visit; on 20 September they
arrived in Malaysia for a four-day state visit, during
which The Queen closed the Commonwealth Games in
Kuala Lumpur. **20.** Camilla Carr and Jon James, British
aid workers who were kidnapped by rebels in Chechenia in July 1997, were released from captivity. Anwar
Ibrahim, the former deputy prime minister of Malaysia,
was arrested for demonstrating against the government.
21. President Clinton's videotaped testimony to the
grand jury investigating his alleged misconduct was
broadcast unedited on television. **21–25.** Hurricane
Georges hit the Caribbean. **24.** Diplomatic relations
between the UK and Iran were upgraded after the
Iranian government withdrew its support for the *fatwa*
against Salman Rushdie.